D1194094

· THE ·

# CONTINUUM *Complete*
# *International*
# ENCYCLOPEDIA
# OF SEXUALITY

*Edited by*:

ROBERT T. FRANCOEUR, Ph.D., A.C.S.

*and*

RAYMOND J. NOONAN, Ph.D.

———⟫•0•⟪———

*Associate Editors*:

*Africa*: Beldina Opiyo-Omolo, B.Sc.
*Europe*: Jakob Pastoetter, Ph.D.
*South America*: Luciane Raibin, M.S.
*Information Resources*: Timothy Perper, Ph.D. &
Martha Cornog, M.A., M.S.

———⟫•0•⟪———

*Foreword by*:

ROBERT T. FRANCOEUR, Ph.D., A.C.S.

———⟫•0•⟪———

*Preface by*:

TIMOTHY PERPER, Ph.D.

———⟫•0•⟪———

*Introduction by:*

IRA L. REISS, Ph.D.

· THE ·

# CONTINUUM *Complete*

# *International*

# ENCYCLOPEDIA

# OF SEXUALITY

*Updated, with More Countries*

**continuum**
NEW YORK · LONDON

2004

The Continuum International Publishing Group Inc
15 East 26 Street, New York, NY 10010

The Continuum International Publishing Group Ltd
The Tower Building, 11 York Road, London SE1 7NX

Typography, Graphic Design, and Computer Graphics by
Ray Noonan, ParaGraphic Artists, NYC http://www.paragraphics.com/

Printed in the United States of America

Library of Congress Cataloging-in-Publication Data

The Continuum complete international encyclopedia of sexuality / edited
by Robert T. Francoeur ; Raymond J. Noonan ; associate editors, Martha
Cornog . . . [et al.].
    p.   cm.
A completely updated one-volume edition of the 4-volume International
encyclopedia of sexuality (published 1997-2001), covering more than 60
countries and places, 15 not previously included.
Includes bibliographical references.
ISBN 0-8264-1488-5 (hardcover : alk. paper)
1. Sex—Encyclopedias.   2. Sex customs—Encyclopedias.   I. Title:
Complete international encyclopedia of sexuality.   II. Francoeur, Robert
T.   III. Noonan, Raymond J.   IV. Cornog, Martha.   V. International
encyclopedia of sexuality.
HQ21.I68   2003
306.7′03—dc21                                                    2003006391

# Contents

For updates, corrections, and links to many of the sites referenced in these chapters, visit *The Continuum Complete International Encyclopedia of Sexuality on the Web* at http://www.SexQuest.com/ccies/.

Readers of *CCIES* are invited to submit important news items or reports of findings of new sex research being done in any of the countries covered here, or any other country in the world. We will try to keep the SexQuest *CCIES* website updated with your help. Send items in English if possible, with appropriate citations, to Raymond J. Noonan, Ph.D., CCIES Editor, Health and Physical Education Department, Fashion Institute of Technology, 27th Street and 7th Avenue, New York, NY 10001 USA, or by email to rjnoonan@SexQuest.com.

# How to Use This Encyclopedia

### The Editors

This encyclopedia contains virtually all of the information presented in the first four volumes of the *International Encyclopedia of Sexuality* published in 1997 and 2001, with fifteen additional countries and places. The original entries have been updated, typically by the original authors or by new authors or commentators; all have had some copyediting refinements. Some entries have been completely rewritten, as noted at the beginning of those chapters. We have endeavored to clearly notate updated material by enclosing the section, paragraph, or sentence in square brackets, starting with *Update* or *Comment* followed by the year it was written, and ending with the appropriate author. In some cases, it serves to modify the existing material when we have kept the original information in context for historical comparison; at other times, it expands the information. In most chapters, some sections were written by specific authors (or one of the editors), whose name or names appear at the beginning of the section.

The information on each country in this encyclopedia is organized mostly according to the standard outline below. The thirteen major headings are also listed on the first page of each chapter with the appropriate page numbers for that country. The reader interested in drawing comparisons on specific issues between different countries will find page references for specific topics and refinements, beyond the major headings, in the index at the end of this volume. Checking this index under a specific topic—premarital sex, teenage pregnancy, puberty rites, or sexual harassment, for example—the reader will find page references that facilitate comparisons among the five-dozen countries included in this volume.

Demographics and a Brief Historical Perspective
  A. Demographics
  B. A brief historical perspective

1. Basic Sexological Premises
  A. Character of gender roles
  B. Sociolegal status of males and females
  C. General concepts of sexuality and love

2. Religious, Ethnic, and Gender Factors Affecting Sexuality
  A. Source and character of religious values
  B. Character of ethnic values

3. Knowledge and Education about Sexuality
  A. Government policies and programs
  B. Informal sources of sexual knowledge

4. Autoerotic Behaviors and Patterns
  A. Children and adolescents
  B. Adults

5. Interpersonal Heterosexual Behaviors
  A. Children
  B. Adolescents
  C. Adults
    Premarital relations, courtship, and dating
    Sexual behavior and relationships of single adults
    Marriage and family
    Cohabitation and monogamy
    Divorce, remarriage, and serial monogamy
    Extramarital sex
    Sexuality and the physically disabled and aged
    Incidence of oral and anal sex

6. Homoerotic, Homosexual, and Bisexual Behaviors
  A. Children and adolescents
  B. Adults

7. Gender Diversity and Transgender Issues

8. Significant Unconventional Sexual Behaviors*
  A. Coercive sex
    Child sexual abuse, incest, and pedophilia
    Sexual harassment
    Rape
  B. Prostitution
  C. Pornography and erotica
  D. Paraphilias

9. Contraception, Abortion, and Population Planning
  A. Contraception
  B. Teenage (unmarried) pregnancies
  C. Abortion
  D. Population programs

10. Sexually Transmitted Diseases and HIV/AIDS

11. Sexual Dysfunctions, Counseling, and Therapies

12. Sex Research and Advanced Professional Education
  A. Graduate programs and sexological research
  B. Sexological organizations and publications

13. Important Ethnic, Racial, and/or Religious Minorities

References and Suggested Readings

---

*In Section 8, Significant Unconventional Sexual Behaviors, we consider coercive sexual behaviors (rape, sexual harassment, and child sexual abuse), prostitution, pornography, paraphilias, and fetishes. As a general rule, sexologists and the general public tend to view heterosexual relations between consenting adults in an ongoing relationship, such as marriage, as the norm. It is true that such sexual relations are the modal pattern or norm in every culture. However, the earlier reviews of premarital sex, extramarital sex, alternative patterns of marriage, homosexuality, and bisexuality in Sections 5 and 6 serve to illustrate that, in any country, variable percentages of people engage in sexual behaviors which depart from this assumed "conventional" norm. Sexologists have struggled for some time to develop acceptable terminology to describe these "other" sexual practices. "Unconventional behaviors" appears to be the least judgmental and restrictive label for "other behaviors," and definitely preferable to other labels such as "sexual deviance" or "sexual variance," which convey a sense of pathology, dysfunction, or abnormality to such behaviors.

The social meaning of a specific "unconventional behavior" is defined by its situation and social context. Exhibitionism, for example, has one meaning when engaged in by a couple in private, a different meaning when engaged in on the stage of a "go-go" bar for patrons of that bar, and a third meaning when engaged in on a public street. Second, some of these behaviors are, in fact, quite common. Serious estimates cited in the United States chapter suggest that 10% of adult Americans engage in sadomasochist or bondage sex play, 15% of Americans have a foot or related fetish and three million Americans engage in "swinging." Although the number of individuals who engage in any particular form of "unconventional behavior" may be small, it seems clear that in most countries, taken together and added to the forms of nonmarital sexual expression, that rather large percentages of people do participate in some "other" "unconventional" form of sexual practice.

# Foreword

Robert T. Francoeur, Ph.D., A.C.S.

S omeone said, "Never tackle anything that is not a challenge."

In 1991, a publisher invited me to edit a 350-page single-volume *International Encyclopedia of Sexuality* (*IES*). The plan was to invite 20 sexologists in 20 countries to prepare 20-page chapters on sex and love, marriage and family in their countries. It seemed like an easy project to tackle after editing the 766-page *Complete Dictionary of Sexology*. Having attended national and international meetings of sexologists for 30 years, I could easily recruit 20 colleagues to write 20 chapters on their countries. The problem came when my recruits fell so in love with describing sex and love, marriage and family-and much more-in their countries, that they completely ignored my "15,000- to 18,000-word limit." As the word spread, other sexologists offered to write about sex in their countries. After five years work, we published three volumes covering 32 countries. With even more countries already in the works, we published a fourth volume, with 17 additional countries, in 2001.

At that point, despite very enthusiastic and glowing reviews, despite international acclaim and the endorsement of *Library Journal*, *Choice*, and the World Association for Sexology, we decided not to publish a fifth volume of *IES* with even more countries. Libraries cannot afford the shelf space or the cost of a five-volume *IES*. Instead, we thought it best to update all 49 countries in the original four volumes and add a dozen new countries, all in a single, large-format volume.

Now, after 11 years of work by 270 authorities on six continents, we have a truly unique up-to-date *Continuum Complete International Encyclopedia of Sexuality* (*CCIES*) with in-depth studies of sexual attitudes and behavior in five-dozen countries. It is a far richer resource and reference work than we could have imagined when we started this project 11 years ago.

Looking back on this adventure, I would like to share some thoughts and ruminations with the reader. Creating this *Encyclopedia* has been a long and complex process. If it is a monument of sexual knowledge, its importance and usefulness are solely because of the magnificent contributions of 230 experts from five-dozen nations around the world. Their work, far more than mine, makes this *Complete Encyclopedia* an unequaled repository of scientific and scholarly information about human sexuality.

To be sure, many works of undeniable importance have claimed to speak about *human* sexuality, but in the *CCIES* we hear the voices of many nations and cultures. With voices from more than a quarter of the nations of the world, I believe we can speak of this volume as a true encyclopedia of *human* sexuality. Ultimately, the subjects who have provided the data are not college students, as has been so commonly the case in academic studies of sexuality in, for example, the United States. Don't get me wrong. The sexual attitudes and behavior of college students are interesting, and their sexuality should not be ignored. But in this volume, we are hearing from a far wider and richer sample of human beings than college-aged students. Our authorities come from almost every discipline and worldview imaginable.

Without in the least minimizing the other essays in our *CCIES*, let me single out first the contributions about sexuality in China and in India. Together, these two nations comprise some 40% of humanity. When, next, we consider the contributions about other Asian nations, the Muslin nations, Africa, South America, and Europe, we begin to see a truly international picture of *human sexuality*. And it has been the immense patience and skill of the contributors to the *Encyclopedia* that have created such a worldwide scope. It has been a collaborative, and incredibly challenging adventure. Among my inspiring experiences, I include the following:

- One day I had a question about some data in the Botswana chapter. Five minutes after I emailed Dr. Ian Taylor, he emailed me back with the clarification I needed. A question to Alain Giame at INSERM in Paris brought a return cellular communication from Dr. Giame on some rain-forest tributary of the Amazon River.
- In 1995, while touring France, a fellow American I had just met quizzed me about the books I write. My rather-vague mention of *IES* prompted Julanne McCarthy to ask if I would like a chapter on Bahrain. Without knowing where Bahrain was, I said, "Of course," never thinking anything would come from a casual, "Of course." Months later, a FedEx package appeared in my mailbox, sent the day Julanne and her museum-director husband returned to the U.S. "The information in this chapter was gathered and written by Julanne McCarthy *and 28 Bahraini professionals and expatriates who are not to be identified in any way.*"
- While trying to recruit Radhouan Mhiri, M.D., president of the Arab Institute of Sexology and Somatotherapy, to write a chapter on Tunisia, he mentioned Abderrazak Moussaïd, founder of the Moroccan Society of Sexology and a physician at the University of Casablanca. Several emails and a month later, on my first night of vacation in Morocco, Dr. Moussaïd whisked me out of a hotel lobby, assuring my wife he would bring me back safe and sound. At dinner, a vehement discussion erupted as Moussaïd cajoled four colleagues—in Arabic and French, of course—to join him to write a chapter on Morocco. Very little English was spoken, but I received their chapter a few months later.

Along the way, I have learned about many different customs, and more importantly, about the social context that surrounds these customs. To name a few customs that are very foreign to my Western mind: widow inheritance, "adultery hoots" in Ghana, *Hijra* in India, living apart together (LAT) in Germany and Sweden, transgendered *kaneeths* in Bahrain and *kathoey* in Thailand, temporary marriage (*mut'a*) in Iran, the Virgin Mary's influence in Ireland, very different constructs of male homosexuality in the Islamic cultures, hymen reconstruction in South Korea and Greek Cyprus, *fazendo tudo* ("try everything") advice given to both Brazilian boys and girls, taboos on sexual communications between males and females, even husbands and wives, in many cultures, and the subordinate role of women in many cultures, where female orgasm is either unknown or feared as a prelude to insanity.

Despite my pride in initiating and editing the four volumes of *IES*, and now the comprehensive updated *CCIES*, I have to admit that this *Encyclopedia* is only a beginning. As we read through the essays, we learn how very little we really know about *human* sexuality. We have only begun to touch the surface of this hugely complex and ancient phenomenon. Much work remains to be done. Yet, I feel that the contributors to these volumes have eased the way for future scholars. Our contributors have blazed new pathways. In the process, I have learned some lessons I would like to share:

- Whenever we talk about any sexual attitude, value, or behavior, we are talking about a cultural snapshot. Think of a tour bus stopping at a scenic lookout. Camera-toting tourists rush off the bus, flip off their lens caps, squint through the viewfinder, scan the site, and take a snapshot or two. Unlike the casual tourist, our *CCIES* authors are very familiar with their own landscapes. As professional researchers and sexologists, their snapshots are more skillfully composed, more perceptive, and more alive to the cultural context and meaning of the observations than any casual observer could present.
- The snapshots created by the 270 contributors to *CCIES* are as true to reality as possible. But we should never forget that each snapshot is also flavored by the gender, education, and professional training of the sexologist presenting it.
- Likewise, we should not forget the social/economic/political/religious/historical context in which each sexual pattern, value, behavior, or attitude developed and is now supported.
- Although we can observe many commonalities in the values, attitudes, behaviors, and trends reported in this volume, idiosyncratic variations exist within each more-general variation within any culture, and between cultures. The richness and diverse flavors of human sexualities can be fascinating.
- The English language is rich in its nuances, but often in these chapters, the reader will find descriptions of sexual concepts and constructs, such as homosexual identity versus men having sex with men, transgendered, paraphilias, and sexual satisfaction, harassment, and dysfunction, which do not translate into Western patterns of thought. Does premarital virginity and sexual abstinence, for instance, simply require no vaginal intercourse? Or does it include no oral or anal sex? No kissing before marriage? No holding hands? Or all of these, plus no visual contact before marriage?

While editing, I also became aware of some worldwide problems we face:

- How can we deal with sexual health issues—not just the obvious issue of HIV/AIDS, but also access to affordable contraception and STD diagnosis and treatment, as well as general medical care?
- How can we promote the reality of gender equality and equal legal rights for all, regardless of sexual identity, role, and orientation?
- How can we provide basic comprehensive sexuality education for all, even in countries where the traditional taboos, the government, or religious tenets restrict or prohibit comprehensive and timely education?
- How can we promote recognition of the sexual rights and needs of all humans—children, adolescents, adults, the elderly and those disabled, whether male or female?
- What strategies do we need to address issues of population growth and decline?
- And finally, what steps do the nations of the world need to take to help immigrants adjust when they find themselves living in a very different and foreign culture, with very different traditions, values, and attitudes?

I happily end this Preface by repeating my sincere thanks to everyone who has given so generously of their knowledge, time, and energy to produce what my good friend and long-time editor/adviser, Jack Heidenry, described as a "Herculean effort." This *Complete Encyclopedia* and the four earlier volumes of *IES* are the product of a wonderful team of colleagues, my fellow editor and skillful designer/typographer, Ray Noonan, our associate editors, and many new and old friends, with whom I have had the truly exciting and great pleasure of working. They join me, I am sure, in the hope that scholars around the world will find *CCIES* a rich and useful resource and reference.

# Preface

Timothy Perper, Ph.D.

What can a modern reader make of a book calling itself *Continuum Complete International Encyclopedia of Sexuality*? In the past, it could have been a *Baedeker's*—a *Guide Michelin*—to the sexual hotspots of the world, or a swinger's and sophisticate's tourguide to the super-sexy clubs of the international sex scene. It might well have contained addresses and ratings of brothels in far-flung places. Or perhaps it was a seriocomic autobiographical tale of a young person turned loose on the world of sex.

There was also a time that an *International Encyclopedia of Sexuality* would have recounted "the curious erotic customs" of people native to Borneo, Upper Nepal, and the tributaries of the Amazon, with a chapter (once obligatory in such works) about footbinding among the Chinese, crammed between strange stories about marriage rites among Polish villagers, African pastoralists, or Paraguayan landholders. And the illustrations—old-style black-and-white photographs—would have shown a peasant wedding in the Tyrol, a bride in Hindustan, the groom's party in Southern Russia, or anywhere else older times believed dwelt "primitive" or "simple" people.

Each of these has been a genre in sexual writing, as are dry-as-dust treatises of solemn university professors awash in jargon, incomprehensible tables of statistics, and deadly dull theorizing. Any and all could fill a book called *Continuum Complete International Encyclopedia of Sexuality*.

One value of the book you now hold is to reveal how much Western sexological writing has changed over two or so centuries. The essays here were each written by a person or persons native to the land and culture described or familiar with it through years of life and study there. Each of the authors is trained in one or another academic discipline, from cultural anthropology to medical sexology. The language is international scientific English, stylistically straightforward and uncomplicated. And thanks to the Editors' foresight, the chapters all follow a common outline, covering similar topics in similar orders—which ought to facilitate comparisons among cultures. After a brief introduction, each chapter deals with a single society, discussing religious and ethnic sexual values, gender roles and the sociology of men and women, relationships between sexuality and love, sex education formal and informal, autoeroticism, heterosexuality and marriage and the family, homoeroticism, gender conflicts, and "unconventional" sexual behavior—including rape, prostitution, pornography, and erotica—followed by material on contraception, abortion, and population planning, and ending with a discussion of sexually transmitted diseases and sex counseling/therapy. It is quite a palate of topics.

And you will notice that it is a serious list of topics. Perhaps nothing else so well illustrates how Western and Westernized writing on sexuality has refocused over two centuries. Today, we "moderns"—which means only that we Westernized intellectuals proudly call ourselves modern and, by implication, think others primitive—disdain older modes of sexological writing and publication. For many years, a primary form of "sexological" writing was the illustrated book—please, to be sold only to medical professionals!—with titles like *Femina Libido Sexualis*, and containing a mish-mash (to our modern eyes) of "medico-scientific" material on female anatomy, circumcision practices, phallic worship, all ostensibly published for "the advancement of knowledge," but actually printed as erotica and hidden from the censor's vigil by their Latinisms and their faux-science. But the mainstay of such works—definitions, discussions, and depictions of "female sexual beauty"—is absent in modern sexological writing, and is equally absent from this *International Encyclopedia of Sexuality*. Gone are the black-and-white photographs of nude women, steel engravings of Arab weddings, and suggestively titled but oh-so-innocent tales of life in the Turkish *seraglio*.

Today, sexuality has become the focus of intense concern, often outright anxiety. Topics that we today consider "sexologically appropriate" border more and more closely on psychological, medical, and social pathology. We are concerned with the criminality of sexual acts, their morality, their capacity to index—if not to stir up—social destruction and vehement conflict. Furious debates over pornography and deep concern about child sexual abuse illustrate how much, for us, sexuality no longer focuses on sexual beauty, be it male or female, but on sexual ugliness, disease, and crime.

To a large extent—though it varies by author—this focus on sexological pathology and problems is shared by all the chapters in the *International Encyclopedia*. No wonder, either we live in a world of sexual change and rearrangement, where politics, more than nudity, seems the proper companion of the goddess of love, Aphrodite herself. For us, sexuality represents the body in flux: not a Heraclitean flow of all things growing and waning, but embodied future shock and upheaval. Books celebrating "sexual beauty" or regaling the reader with "odd and curious marriage customs" of foreign people could be written only in days that themselves had firm and clear sexual guidelines—a sexual culture—to shape readers' behavior and assure them that they were culturally normal by the standards of their own Western societies. But—*rota fortuna*—things change.

There is a story told—apocryphally, I am afraid—of an Indian tourguide at the temples of Khajuraho, famed for what Westerners perceive as highly erotic sculptures. A woman ethnologist, primarily interested in these sculpted images of the most variegated forms of copulation imaginable, continued to ask to be shown those portions of the temple grounds. The guide steadfastly refused, saying only, "But they aren't interesting, miss."

The point is not the tourguide's recalcitrance. Instead, let us wonder where he obtained the phrase he used to defend his efforts at censorship: "They aren't interesting." Partly, to be sure, he expressed a personal emotion, but we can readily imagine British tourists in the days of the Indian Raj expressing dismay and anxiety by saying precisely the same—"These statues are not interesting." In those days—that is, for many years indeed—sexuality was not interesting to the normal Westerner outside the bedroom and those all-male soirees with which folklore bedecks the 1890s and similar eras of "sexual excess."

So *Continuum Complete International Encyclopedia of Sexuality* reveals a fascinating aspect of how our own—Western or Westernized—visions of sexuality have shifted. Today, we find sexuality much more openly important, even if public and media attention often focuses on its less-pleasant sides, e.g., exploitation of women in pornography. Unlike our recent ancestors, we find sexuality interesting to extents that would have deeply shocked and troubled both the British visitors to Khajuraho and its Indian tourguide.

Over the intervening century, sexuality has slipped loose from its originally tight moorings in Western and Westernized societies. Today, it touches all aspects of life: certainly, it seems to touch everything in the media! One can plausibly argue that these are not deep social or psychological changes, but merely that previously dominating masks and disguises have fallen away to reveal what probably was always there—widespread interest in sexuality among many people indeed.

In this newly unmasked interest, we all need good, solid information—not rumor, hearsay, travelers' tales, and secret books celebrating female pulchritude across the globe—but good data, compiled with serious intent and presented with serious purpose. Such intentions and purposes *Continuum Complete International Encyclopedia of Sexuality* achieves. I do not perceive its seriousness of outline or topic as antisexual so much as I see it as antifrivolous. We do not trivialize sexuality nowadays and we live in an era of "serious works about sex."

We cannot escape the solemnification of sexuality, not because solemnity is foisted upon us by prudes, but because we understand that sexuality is dangerous as well as pleasurable. Yet we also carry within ourselves a desire to worry about sexuality—an echo from older days when sexuality was taboo for polite discussion and a matter only of whispered gossip, something to worry about. In our modern world, sexuality is legitimated partly by surrounding it by a veil of worried concern, e.g., about pornography, child sexual abuse, sexual Satanism, and the like. Knowledge has been bought at the price of thinking that sexuality ought to be studied and worked at. Whatever instincts exist (modern sexological scholarship denies them), they do not operate easily or comfortably today. If sexuality no longer wears the obscuring masks of the past—the opaque black garb that once clothed the body—then instead it wears translucent gauze, not erotic so much as disinfectant. In modern sexology, sexuality inhabits the forums of research, and *Continuum Complete International Encyclopedia of Sexuality* is quite modern.

Its importance—considerable, I think—exhibits another change in sexological discourse, to use a revealing and portentous word made popular by academic sexologists. In older days, only one officially sanctioned form of discourse existed about sex: the language and meanings of moralists, churchmen typically, that upheld certain visions of how we should write about sex. Though he had predecessors, Kinsey changed all that permanently, in effect substituting technicalisms for a dying moralism in sexual language. A curious consequence is that sexology no longer speaks to the masses about matters they understand and know. As modern life fractalizes, sexology has sprouted many officially sanctioned discourses, such as postmodernist criticism, feminism, conservative rhetoric, biomedicalese, all antipopulist, all above the heads of the man and woman in the street (or bedroom). Indeed, it sometimes takes an expert to understand that the topic is sex. Nonetheless, adherents of these different discourses spend much time examining each other's prose with the officiousness of churchmen hunting out sinful thoughts. Sex remains a charged, powerful topic, and its significance will not diminish soon. Its powers radiate outwards from an embodied center to touch arenas of disagreement, like politics, that nonetheless remain more comfortable than open sexuality, at least for many people.

And so this *International Encyclopedia* raises a curious question: Will there come a time when sexuality can display itself nude? Or is nude sexuality still "not interesting"? Judging from public worry over Madonna's *Sex*, with her deliberate evocation of nudity, we still share a great deal with the Indian tourguide. However, the authors of the chapters in this book are closer kin to the woman ethnologist who wished to examine those statues. For her and her modern scholarly descendants, sexuality is interesting, even if still garmented in sociological, psychological, and biomedical gauze. Whereas we Westernized intellects still feel that Aphrodite must be partly covered, nonetheless many layers of wrapping and disguise have been removed. To the prude, it is all to the bad (even if "not interesting"). To the scholar, it is an important step towards understanding sexuality itself. To the modern reader, *Continuum Complete International Encyclopedia of Sexuality* will be more interesting than a *Baedeker* to the world's sex clubs or an autobiography of a reprobate or even a lusciously colored edition of the once banned *Thousand and One Nights*: It provides a thoroughly scholarly examination of what is still not fully exposed even in an enlightened modern world—or, judging from the temples at Khajuraho itself, the partly enlightened and partly interested modern world.

# An Introduction to the Many Meanings of Sexological Knowledge

Ira L. Reiss, Ph.D.

Welcome to this treasure chest of sexological knowledge and understanding. You will find in this volume a wealth of information concerning sexuality in a very wide range of human societies. To introduce this extremely rare and valuable *Continuum Complete International Encyclopedia of Sexuality*, I will not review the fascinating reports of these authors. Instead, what I shall do is to try to afford the reader some perspective on the many ways that this knowledge can be understood and used. I will focus on three controversial aspects of cross-cultural work where scientific fads and fashions have tended to limit how that knowledge is presented. Having a broader view of these three aspects of cross-cultural studies should help the reader to utilize the accounts of sexuality in this *Encyclopedia* more completely.

I will first deal with the question of how our personal values and other assumptions about the world enter into the way we do our scientific work on sexuality, and what we can do about it. Secondly, I will deal with the current emphasis upon stressing the uniqueness of each society and the criticism of the search for cultural universals. And thirdly, I will deal with the important question of taking the "insider" and the "outsider" perspective when studying a society's sexual customs. By discussing these three controversial areas and suggesting possible resolutions, the reader should be better prepared to make his or her own judgments on what is valuable in sexological knowledge.

## Issue One: Science, Values, and Assumptions

There are those who still perceive of science and society as properly separated by an impenetrable wall. In this "positivist" view, the scientist is protected from "bias" by his or her withdrawal from taking sides on any of the basic value disputes in a society. As a result, we supposedly get a "value-free" and "pure" form of knowledge rather than a "biased" or "value-laden" point of view. That is still a popular view concerning science and society. Nevertheless, I contend that that sort of sharp separation of science and society is based upon an erroneous view of the way science really operates in society.

In my view, science cannot be separated from society, for it is an institution existing in a human society and conducted by human beings. Science, and its practitioners, can no more avoid the influences of the broader society than can the mass media, corporate business, government, religion, education, or the family. Further, the very support of science by a society depends on people's believing that science is useful to the solution of the problems of that society. The high value placed upon physical science emanates from the advances it has produced in valued areas such as health, industry, and warfare. Denying this connection to society does not produce a lack of bias in science. Instead, it may produce an inability to be explicit about one's values to others, and perhaps even to oneself.

Most obviously in the social sciences and in sexual science, where we seek to understand the way humans behave and think, there can be no meaningful separation of science from society and its values. But this does not mean that we cannot avoid bias in our scientific methods. Rather, if science is to maintain its claim to being fair, reasonable, logical, precise, and cautious, then it must acknowledge the possible values of the scientist and learn how to prevent them from overwhelming our scientific methods. Scientists cannot prevent bias in their work by simply claiming to be value-free. Rather, as I shall seek to illustrate, scientists must do it by demonstrating that they are value-aware. Let me illustrate my meaning with a research project I was involved in not long ago.

In 1988, a colleague, Robert Leik, and I set out to develop a probability model that would compare two strategies for reducing the risk of an HIV infection (Reiss & Leik 1989). The two strategies to be compared were: (1) to reduce the number of sexual partners or (2) to use condoms with all partners. Although utilizing both strategies simultaneously is clearly the safest way to reduce the risk of HIV, a great many people seem to choose to do one or the other. The model we built compared the risk in these two strategies using a very wide range of estimates of several key factors: (a) the prevalence of HIV, that is, the likelihood of picking an infected partner; (b) the infectivity of the HIV virus, that is, the likelihood of becoming infected with HIV if one picked an infected partner and had unprotected sex with that person; (c) the failure rate of condoms, ranging from a low of 10% to a high of 75%; and (d) the number of partners ranging from one to 20.

What we found was virtually unqualified support for the greater probability of avoiding HIV infection by using condoms rather than by reducing partners. In almost all cases, even if one had only one or two partners over a five-year period, if one did not use condoms with them, one had a higher risk of HIV infection than someone with 20 partners who did use condoms. This was true even if condoms were assumed to have a failure rate between 10 to 25%. Our conclusion was that those giving advice and counsel should recommend condom usage as the more effective tactic.

Now this project with its probability model was surely a scientific project, and the results of testing our models seemed unequivocal. Nevertheless, although the great majority of the scientific community fully endorsed and used our findings and suggestions, a few scientists did not accept our interpretation of our results. We received criticism from scientists who said that people will not use condoms to prevent HIV infection and so our findings were meaningless in the real world. There were others who said that publishing our results would encourage people to increase the number of partners and that would lead to more HIV infections. Some other critics raised the question whether having more than one partner and using condoms was worth even the very small increased risk that we described.

This difference of interpretation of our findings is not a result of the poor scientific judgment of our critics, as much as we might have liked to think that. Rather it was basically a consequence of some scientists' not sharing our values and assumptions about the world in which we live. Specifically, our critics did not accept our view that people will use condoms to protect themselves. Instead, our critics believed in a more emotional than rational view of human sexual choices. They held this view despite the evidence that gays have greatly increased their condom usage and even teenagers indicated similar dramatic increases in the late 1980s (Reiss 1990). Other critics rejected our assumption that motivations for having more sexual partners have very little to do with the publication of an article like ours. Finally, unlike some of our critics, we made no assumptions about whether condom-protected sex with several partners was worth the increased risk involved.

Our critics and we clearly had different assumptions and values regarding sexuality, and that was the reason why they questioned our evaluation of the evidence from our model. They did not disagree with the results of the model, but they disagreed with our assumptions about sexuality. The reader should note that the assumptions we make about sexuality are not only factual assumptions, but they embody value judgments. For example, we valued people who learn how to protect themselves, and supported the moral right of people to make their own personal choices regarding the number of partners that they have.

We might not have become so fully aware of our assumptions if our critics had not spoken out, revealing that they made different assumptions and had different values about sexual behavior. The critics would never have undertaken our study because, lacking the belief that condoms will be used to prevent HIV infection, why should one study that strategy? Also, as one scientific journal editor wrote to us, his values would stop him from publishing an article that seemed indifferent to the norms of sexual monogamy. These differences in values and assumptions do not just enter into the choice of research projects, but as is apparent here, they enter into the very interpretation of the meaning and worth of that research.

The important point here is that no scientist can undertake a research project without making some set of assumptions regarding human behavior. And those assumptions also influence how to interpret the validity and worth of the findings. As our critics demonstrate, our interpretation that recommending condoms is the safest path to take is not one that inevitably follows from our probability model's evidence. Our recommendation of condom use follows only if you also share our assumptions about human behavior. The great majority of sexual scientists do share our view and so they agreed with our interpretation. Where all scientists share the same assumptions, we are the most likely to be blind to the fact that we are even making any assumptions. Without the critical response, we would not have become so aware of our own assumptions, and of those of our critics.

To believe that science operates in a vacuum devoid of values and assumptions about human behavior is to delude ourselves as scientists. Further, unless we realize the assumptions we are making, and put them forth explicitly, we will be unable to comprehend fully one basis upon which we are judging the worth of our scientific work. Only by becoming more value- and assumption-aware will we be able to be more even handed and fair in evaluating and understanding the basis of our scientific judgments. Such awareness makes the scientist more thoughtful about what assumptions will be accepted, and more conscious of the possibility that we must be sure not to allow these assumptions to bias our gathering of evidence.

The recent findings concerning causes of homosexuality offer another illustration of the point I am making here. The 1993 work of Dean Hamer published in *Science* created a public storm of interest. Hamer and his collaborators reported that they found on the long arm of the X-chromosome a possible location of a special set of genes that were present in 33 out of 40 families with two gay brothers. The support this finding found depended in part on the background assumptions of the particular scientists. Those who, like biologist Simon LeVay (1990), stress biological factors as determinant of human behavior, are more willing to conclude that biological factors are key pieces in the homosexual puzzle. Other scientists in social science fields where nurture is stressed more than nature, make assumptions about humans that lead them to be hesitant to accept Hamer's work as anything more than mostly speculative at this point.

There are also values associated with any position on nature and nurture. Whether we are a biologist or a sociologist, if we oppose the status quo in society, we are more likely to want to emphasize the plasticity of human inheritance. In addition, those scientists who feel that seeing homosexuality as strongly biologically determined would lessen societal prejudice, may also be more likely to accept biology as definitive. Conversely, those who, like myself, oppose prejudice, but who note that prejudice continues against groups with known biological differences such as blacks and women, do not feel pressure to endorse biological etiology.

One very important conclusion from these and other examples is that our assumptions and values can easily have an impact on our interpretation of research findings. But that does not mean that we should conclude that all sexologists are "biased" or all research on sex is "unfairly" interpreted. Rather, what it says to me is that all members of a society, including scientists, have values and make assumptions about human sexual behavior. Better than pretending that we can be neutral and value-free, we should openly assert our assumptions and values so we can check each other's scientific work and promote a clearer, and more balanced and fairminded evaluation of the worth of our research results.

Bias or distortion of evidence is unacceptable in scientific work. We seek to use the most reliable and valid measures, to publish our results for criticism by others, and to follow rules of careful reasoning and fair gathering of evidence. Making our scientists more "value-assumption aware" will help us minimize the times when these unstated assumptions overwhelm our science. We cannot eliminate assumptions, but we can demand that they be made explicit, and require scientific rigor regardless of what assumptions are made. Then we can, as scientists, reach consensus on which explicit assumptions we are willing to accept, and thereby decide what will be accepted as knowledge in our science of sexuality. When you read the accounts in this book, try to discern the author's assumptions. Finding assumptions is not by itself an indication of a flawed account. Rather, it is a way of giving you deeper insight into the meaning of that author's account.

### Issue Two: Scientific Fads about Cultural Universals

There is little question that during the past several decades, the anthropological and sociological work on different societies has stressed the uniqueness of cultures and criticized attempts to find cultural universals (Suggs & Miracle 1993). If we apply our awareness of the place of assumptions in scientific work, we may surmise that this emphasis is a result of assuming that people and societies are basically different and do not universally share any significant characteristics. Further, that assumption may be based on the value judgment that stressing how different we are builds tolerance, whereas emphasizing universal traits among different societies encourages people to criticize the society that is not like their own.

All our views are but partial views of whatever reality is out there. If we all share the exact same assumptions about the world, we will never become aware of what these assumptions are, and we will not be alert to the possible biasing of our scientific evaluations. It is in this sense that accepting but one narrow view of what is worth pursuing, and making that a compulsory position, is dangerous to the growth of sound scientific methods and to the careful evaluation of evidence.

In opposition to the current scientific fad of stressing differences, David Suggs and Andrew Miracle, in their overview on cross-cultural sex research, point to the need to find commonalities in societies around the world. They say: "We need more work on sexuality from those research strategies that are specifically oriented toward seeking an explanation of 'Culture'—as opposed to 'cultures'" (1993, 490).

They cite my 1986 book, *Journey into Sexuality: An Exploratory Voyage*, as one of the few attempts to find such commonalities while not denying the importance of cultural differences. In that book, I set out to try to locate the key areas of our social life that, in any society, most directly shape our sexuality. I started with the assumption that, unless the evidence indicated otherwise, we can assume that, "with careful attention to the social context, intercultural comparisons can be made" (Reiss 1986, 7). After examining a large number of cultures, I developed my Linkage Theory, which asserted that sexual customs in all societies were most crucially linked to the *power, ideology,* and *kinship* segments of that society. This I called the (PIK) Linkage Theory.

I did not ignore differences in the way individual societies create such linkages. To be sure, a class system in America may be very different from a class system in Kenya. But that does not prevent us from saying they both have a class system and examining how that class system relates to existing sexual customs. So I would say to the reader, look for the important differences among the cultures described, but also compare societies and see if you can detect some commonalities among the cultures, such as I suggest in sexuality being linked to power, ideology, and kinship systems in every society (Reiss 1989). I believe that finding commonalities in our sexual lives can enhance our tolerance for the cultural differences that exist. We can better identify and have empathy for a people with whom we believe we share some important similarities.

## Issue Three: The Insider and the Outsider Perspective

In the last few decades, the emphasis in cross-cultural work has been on what Kenneth Pike has called the Emic or "insider" approach and less on the Etic or "outsider" approach. The concepts of Emic and Etic were first put into print by Kenneth Pike in 1954 and have since become common jargon in anthropology. Some anthropologists, like Marvin Harris, have made modifications in Pike's concepts but still utilize them (Headland, Pike, & Harris 1990). Let me try to clarify these very important terms and relate them to a third and final issue concerning how we view other societies.

The originator of the concepts of Emic and Etic, Kenneth Pike, indicated his current meaning in a 1990 book, when he said:

I view the emic knowledge of a person's local culture somewhat as Polanyi views bicycle riding. A person knows how to act without necessarily knowing how to analyze his action. When I act, I act as an insider; but to know, in detail, how I act (e.g., the muscle movements), I must secure help from an outside disciplinary system. To use the emics of nonverbal (or verbal) behavior I must act like an insider, to analyze my own acts, I must look at (or listen to) material as an outsider. But just as the outsider can learn to act like an insider, so the insider can learn to analyze like an outsider. (Headland, Pike, & Harris 1990, 33-34)

Although it is a bit of a simplification, Emic can be seen as the insider view constructed by people in a culture, and Etic the outsider view constructed by science seeking to understand that culture. The recent fad in social science, as I have noted in my discussion of the emphasis placed on cultural uniqueness, is to emphasize the Emic view. The possibility of an Etic view that can conceptually compare and find commonalities in different cultures is too often overlooked and/or criticized today.

I support the essential worth of both Emic and Etic approaches and I reject the notion that we must give priority to an Emic or an Etic view. Some of the support for promoting the Emic view comes from those who feel that we should not make invidious comparisons of cultures and should rather just accept them. I, of course, share the tolerance values behind such an approach. But as a social scientist, I must be allowed to compare and contrast and to develop understandings that go beyond just saying all cultures are unique. I must also add that there are societies, like the Nazi society under Hitler and many other totalitarian reigns of terror that exist today in our world, that I do not want to tolerate. I want more than the insider view of a people on which to base my understanding of a society.

Another point to be aware of in this debate is the fact that there is much that people in any society do not understand about their own culture. How many people in Western society understand enough to be able to suggest workable solutions to the many social problems they see in their society? One of the major values of any science is to afford a broader perspective on a social problem area. It is true that the outsider view that scientific explanation can provide will be based on some assumptions about human beings, but the attempt will still be to evaluate carefully and fairly the evidence relevant to that perspective. This is precisely what Robert Leik and I were trying to do when we compared the two strategies for reducing HIV infection. Our assumptions were clear, and we attempted to evaluate fairly the choices in light of those assumptions.

If we opt only for the insider's views and deny the possibility of an outside scientific explanation that goes beyond the insider's views, then we are reducing ourselves to the role of stenographers writing down what people believe, and stopping there. I think an Etic science perspective is far too valuable to toss away that easily. True, science has limitations in its assumptions and in its fads and fashions. But science presents us with the opportunity to arrive at a consensus as to how to understand most effectively, and perhaps change, a particular sexual problem. Such a scientific consensus will never be the total picture of reality, but it will be valuable in our search for solutions. It offers something beyond what the partisan person can offer in his or her Emic viewpoint, and I would therefore reject any postmodern, relativist attempts to play down the value of an Etic perspective in sexology or in any science.

Readers of this *International Encyclopedia* should keep in mind the Emic and Etic distinction, the relative advantages and limitations of these vantage points, and watch for efforts by the authors to balance these views. Some authors are native to the country they are writing about. Others are not native and write from an outsider's perspective, even though they may have lived in the country for many years. Being aware of the vantage point from which the individual contributors to this *Encyclopedia* speak will help the reader make the most advantageous use of the information presented.

## Quo Vadis, Cross-Cultural Sexology?

Let me try to sum up the implications of my approach to cross-cultural sexual knowledge and its value to you in reading this *Encyclopedia*. First, I would suggest that seeing how science and value assumptions interact should make us more likely to want our science of sexuality to do more than present abstract knowledge. We will want science to deal with the problem areas that mean the most to us. This sort of post-positivist view of sexual science makes science a major helper in reconstructing or reinventing ways of living that can promote the resolution of the many sexual problems that confront us.

True, there may well be conflicting solutions proposed by scientists with different value assumptions, such as I encountered with my probability model on HIV infection. But we can still examine scientifically what will best help to resolve problems from the viewpoint of the set of assumptions most of us in a community will endorse. Further, people with different assumptions can put forth different tactics to resolve social problems. We can examine the reasoning and evidence relevant to competing assumptions. We can choose based on what type of world we want to create.

The scientific search for evidence to examine our solutions can still be rigorous and will be scrutinized, particularly by those who do not fully accept our assumptions. I see the future as favoring this movement towards a sexual science that helps us create the type of world we consensually agree we want. I see the problem-resolution aspect of sexology as very important, because it will promote the value of sexual science in the minds of the public, and that will help fund the important research and theory work we want to do.

On the second issue of commonalities: If you accept my position on the legitimacy of searching for cultural universals as well as for cultural variability, then we in sexology can search for common elements in our sexual lives in societies around the world. In the over 200 societies I examined in my 1986 book, I found universal condemnation of what that society judged to be "excessive" sexual force and to what that society saw as "undue" sexual manipulation (Reiss 1986, 1990). So we have at least a minimal cross-cultural area of ethical agreement on what sexual acts ought to be prohibited: sexual force and sexual manipulation. Of course, within this area of agreement there are quite different definitions of what is "excessive" sexual force and what is "undue" sexual manipulation. But within any society, we can, as sexual scientists, seek to find what changes in custom would best avoid that culture's conception of "unacceptable" force and manipulation.

In Western cultures, I believe we would agree that avoiding force and manipulation is best accomplished by promoting preparation for sexuality that emphasizes honesty, equality, and responsibility between the sexual actors. I have developed the evidence and reasoning on this in a recent book (Reiss 1990). Western cultures are moving towards an ethical standard that accepts a wide range of sexual acts, providing they are honestly, equally, and responsibly negotiated. As the accounts in this *Encyclopedia* will reveal, there surely are significant differences even within Western societies as to how to define unacceptable force and manipulation, and also on defining what is meant by honesty, equality, and responsibility in sexual relationships and how to achieve that. But at least there is some common ground for such a dialogue to take place, and I believe sexologists should take the lead in examining and researching this vast area of possible ethical agreement.

Although non-Western societies are pursuing the same goal of reducing unacceptable force and manipulation, there are many significant differences in the ways that these societies may seek to control these outcomes. Promoting honesty, equality, and responsibility in sexuality may not be so popular in some of these societies. So clearly individual attention to particular societies is needed. But I stress that it is in the search for universals here that we are led to explore cultural differences. These are not opposing goals.

Finally, in line with my position on the insider and outsider approaches, I encourage taking both an Emic and an Etic approach so as to gain more complete answers to the sexological questions that interest us. The insider view is essential for any successful resolution, because it is people that must put into action any resolution to a social problem. But we must also go beyond individual viewpoints, for it may well be that in unintended ways we promote the very outcomes that we then condemn as problems. Our conflicted and negative view of sexuality in America is a cause of the very problems that our conflicted and sex-negative people then condemn (Reiss 1990).

If we who have devoted our career to the study of sexuality cannot state what our assumptions are and offer useful resolutions to our shared sexual problems, then who can? A famous American sociologist, Robert S. Lynd (1939, 186) many years ago made this very point about social science in general:

> Either the social sciences know more than do the 'hard headed' businessman, the 'practical' politician and administrator, and the other de facto leaders of the culture as to what the findings of research mean, as to the options the institutional system presents, as to what human personalities want, why they want them, and how desirable changes can be effected, or the vast current industry of social science is an empty facade.

The cross-cultural analysis of sexual customs in this encyclopedia should help us to understand and to cope better with the dramatic changes occurring in sexual customs in so many societies today. I have discussed elsewhere other reasons why we need to make our assumptions explicit and thereby make our sexology more problem-resolution centered (Reiss 1993). All I need add here is that the more society feels that sexology can aid in resolving our sexual problems, the more our field will be valued and will flourish. I hope we who are sexologists will resolve our internal disputes on issues like those discussed in this chapter by taking the broader and more eclectic view of science and its role in society that I have presented. While doing this, we must hold to the great value of scientific method—we must reject the nihilistic and relativistic conclusions that some who would dismiss science altogether promote today. I hope that as you read the fascinating chapters in this book, the key issues and ideas I have put forth will help you to obtain a deeper insight into human sexuality. I wish you all: Bon Voyage to the many societies described herein!

## *References*

Hammer, D. H., S. Hu, V. L. Magnuson, N. Hu, & A. M. L. Pattatucci. 1993 (July 16). A linkage between DNA markers on the X chromosome and male sexual orientation. *Science,* *261*:321-327.

Headland, T. N., K. L. Pike, & Marvin Harris, eds. 1990. *Emics and etics: The insider/outsider debate.* Newbury Park, CA: Sage Publishers.

LeVay, S. 1993. *The sexual brain.* Cambridge, MA: MIT Press.

Lynd, R. S. 1939. *Knowledge for what? The place of social science in American culture.* New York: Grove Press.

Reiss, I. L. 1986. *Journey into sexuality: An exploratory voyage.* Englewood Cliffs, NJ: Prentice-Hall.

Reiss, I. L. 1989. Society and sexuality: A sociological theory. In: K. McKinney & S. Sprecher, eds., *Human sexuality: The societal and interpersonal context.* Norwood, NJ: Ablex Publishing Corp.

Reiss, I. L. 1990. *An end to shame: Shaping our next sexual revolution.* Buffalo, NY: Prometheus Books.

Reiss, I. L. 1993 (February). The future of sex research and the meaning of science. *Journal of Sex Research, 30*:3-11.

Reiss, I. L., & R. K. Leik. 1989 (November). Evaluating strategies to avoid AIDS: Number of partners vs. use of condoms. *Journal of Sex Research, 26*:411-433.

Suggs, D. N., & A. W. Miracle, eds. 1993. *Culture and human sexuality: A reader.* Pacific Grove, CA: Books/Cole Publishing Co.

# Argentina

## (*República Argentina*)

Sofia Kamenetzky, M.D.
*Updates by S. Kamenetzky*

## Contents

> This miraculous indigenous America
> Made everything at a fantastic scale
> Wanting to look at the sky,
> she raised herself on the Andean Mountains
> And her cross, instead of wood,
> is made of stars.[1]

## *Demographics and a Brief Historical Perspective*

ROBERT T. FRANCOEUR

### A. Demographics

Argentina, the second-largest country in South America with 1,073,518 square miles (2,780,399 km²), occupies most of the southern tip of the American continent. It extends from slightly above the Tropic of Capricorn to Antarctica, on which it keeps a constant military and research presence. Hence, it has a variety of climates and the different natural resources associated with them, although it is best known for its fertile pampas of the temperate region. The Patagonia plateau in the south is flat or rolling. The rugged Andes Mountains mark Argentina's western border with Chile on the west. Bolivia and Paraguay are Argentina's northern neighbors, while Brazil and Uruguay lie to the northeast.

In July 2002, Argentina had an estimated population of 37.8 million. (All data are from *The World Factbook 2002* (CIA 2002) unless otherwise stated.)

**Age Distribution and Sex Ratios**: *0-14 years*: 26.3% with 1.05 male(s) per female (sex ratio); *15-64 years*: 63.2% with 1.0 male(s) per female; *65 years and over*: 10.5% with 0.7 male(s) per female; *Total population sex ratio*: 0.98 male(s) to 1 female

**Life Expectancy at Birth**: *Total Population*: 75.48 years; *male*: 72.1 years; *female*: 79.03 years

**Urban/Rural Distribution**: 90% to 10%

**Ethnic Distribution**: Caucasian: 97%; Mestizo, Indian, or otherwise nonwhite groups: 3%

(CIA 2002)

**Religious Distribution**: Nominally Roman Catholic: 92%, with less than 20% practicing; Protestant: 2%; Jewish: 2%; other: 4%

**Birth Rate**: 18.23 births per 1,000 population

**Death Rate**: 7.57 per 1,000 population

**Infant Mortality Rate**: 17.2 deaths per 1,000 live births

**Net Migration Rate**: 0.63 migrant(s) per 1,000 population

**Total Fertility Rate**: 2.41 children born per woman

**Population Growth Rate**: 1.13%

**HIV/AIDS** (1999 est.): *Adult prevalence*: 0.69%; *Persons living with HIV/AIDS*: 130,000; *Deaths*: 1,800. (For additional details from www.UNAIDS.org, see end of Section 10B.)

**Literacy Rate** (*defined as those age 15 and over who can read and write*): 96.2% (1995 est.); attendance in school is compulsory to age 14

**Per Capita Gross Domestic Product** (*purchasing power parity*): $12,000 (1997 est.); *Inflation*: 4%; *Unemployment*: 25% (end of 2001); *Living below the poverty*

*Communications*: Sofia Kamenetzky, M.D., Postal Box 352530, Palm Coast, FL 32135-9727 USA; mkamen@aol.com.

*line*: 37% (2001 est.). By the end of 2002, half of Argentina's population was living below the poverty line. In 2001 and 2002, the economy of Argentina went into a tailspin and the nation came close to bankruptcy (see update at the end of Section 1B, A Brief Historical Perspective, below).

### B. A Brief Historical Perspective

Nomadic indigenous tribes roamed the pampas when the Spaniards arrived in 1515 and 1516. The land quickly became a part of the Spanish empire. By the late 19th century, nearly all the native peoples had been killed.

The long period of disorder that followed the colonists' declaration of independence in 1816 ended only when a strong centralized government developed. Large-scale Italian, German, and Spanish immigration after 1880 spurred modernization, and major social reforms were instituted in the 1920s. Military coups were common from 1930 to the 1946 election of General Juan Perón as president. Perón and his wife, Eva Duarte (died 1952), effected labor reforms, but suppressed freedom of speech and the press, closed religious schools, and ran the country into serious debt. A series of military and civilian regimes followed Perón's ouster in 1955. After an 18-year exile, Perón returned in 1973 and was elected president. When he died ten months later, his second wife, Isabel, who had been elected vice president, succeeded him, becoming the first woman head of state in the Western Hemisphere. Mrs. Perón was ousted in 1976, amid charges of corruption.

The military junta that followed existed in a state of siege with guerrillas and leftists. An estimated 5,000 people were killed and thousands jailed and tortured. Democratic rule returned in 1983 after Great Britain successfully defended the Falkland Islands in 1982. In 1985, five former junta members were found guity of murder and human rights violations. By 1989, the nation suffered, as severe hyperinflation and political problems sparked looting and rioting in several large cities. Perónist President Carlos Saúl Menem, elected in 1989 and again in 1995, has introduced harsh but necessary economic measures to curtail hyperinflation, control government spending, and restructure the foreign debt.

[*Update 2003*: The presidency of Carlos Menem that started in 1989 with hopes of a long period of stabilization and prosperity ended with the deepest economic crisis known since Argentina organized itself as a modern nation by the end of the 19th century. Neither the International Monetary Fund, nor the World Bank or the Interamerican Development Bank, explained clearly to the world how such a profound economic deterioration took place.

[Just a few years ago, Argentina was largely a middleclass nation with the highest per-capita income in Latin America. The Gross National Product (GNP) per capita that was $9,950 in 1997 is estimated to have fallen in 2002 to less than $4,700, which is the threshold above which the country becomes a contributor to international organizations rather than being just a borrower (World Bank Development Report 1999; Executive Board UN Development Program 2002).

[Foreign public debt started mounting and reached $132 billion by the end of 2001. At the same time, unemployment is estimated as being as high as 25%.

[The absence of political leaders with a clear vision of the future, and the cynicism and greediness of those in power who dispose of government revenues as their private property, led to disastrous policies. Bank assets were stripped, leaving the average citizen without access to their deposits, while rich Argentines and foreign enterprises timely sent their money to foreign accounts. The Argentine peso that remained pegged to the dollar since the early 1990s was devaluated, and is above three pesos to a dollar at the time of writing this update. As *The New York Times* reports, the situation of most Argentines has dramatically changed:

> According to the most recent statistics, issued in January 2003, at least 60 percent of the country's 37 million people now lives in poverty, defined as an income of less than $220 a month for a family of four. Even more alarming, more than a quarter the population is classified as 'indigent,' or living on less than $100 a month for a family of four (Rohter 2003).

[Every day children and old people die of hunger. People in the affluent neighborhoods of Buenos Aires put leftovers from their meals in separate garbage bags to provide a concentration-camp ration for the survival of night scavengers.

[Survival, a powerful human force, is originating other, more-positive initiatives as a response to the economic and social chaos. One creative scheme is the organization of bartering networks where people can exchange goods and services. Professionals, farmers, health service workers, homemakers, teachers, and people from all occupations participate in these exchanges. (*End of update by S. Kamenetzky*)]

## 1. Basic Sexological Premises

### A/B. Gender Roles and Sociolegal Status of Males and Females

In Latin American societies, the sexual behavior of women is always much more conditioned by norms, rules, regulations, and taboos than the sexual behavior of men. Argentina is no exception. Women were supposed to reach marriage in a virginal state, and then take care of the home, go to church, bear and educate children, and support their men in political, professional, and economic activities.

For a long time, this double standard was accepted without open criticism. But since the late 1940s, women have taken steps towards equal rights and independence from parents, spouses, and lovers. Of course, the first steps were taken by women with college degrees and businesswomen. They started painfully opening spaces in Argentina's political, economic, legal, and educational arenas. The governments have also opened opportunities for them in political and administrative positions. Today, we see women in university chairs, legal benches, large corporations, research laboratories, journalism, medicine, and all fields of art. However, it is still possible to observe discrimination against women and privileges given to men, not because of their excelling in a job or profession, but simply because they are males.

### C. General Concepts of Love and Sexuality

Virginity is no longer a condition for marriage. On the contrary, before deciding to engage in a permanent relationship, most women want to know their future spouse in bed. Argentine women are exercising their new roles in markets and societies with a flexible mental attitude that tries to integrate all aspects of their complex new situation. They know that it is not easy to balance their responsibility as mothers and lovers with their workplace obligations; they need to walk a tightrope and compromise, giving, when needed, more visibility to their men. They do not want to renounce breastfeeding their babies, because they know its importance for healthy development; hence, they are fighting to increase the availability of daycare facilities close to their workplace. Accepting now their share of responsibility in maintaining a healthy sexual life, they take the initiative in foreplay and learn techniques to introduce variety in sexual intercourse, while at the same time, they try to increase both depth and scope in the emotional and intellectual communications within the couple.

For males, it is sometimes difficult to internalize these changes in the patterns of family life. However, most are starting to perceive that they enrich the relationship and are beneficial for both partners. The advantages of sharing two incomes, and participating in the rearing and education of the children, awakens emotions and provides a joy never felt before. Men are also learning to relax when making love, enjoying alternate passive and active roles, and accepting the fact that they can also be seduced and excited.

Women's liberation from submission to parents, brothers, and spouses is slowly harmonizing male and female energies and leading to a win-win situation for both, although the way to this end is not yet free of obstacles that will take pain to remove. Most of the population still believes in a double standard, but increased dissatisfaction with their sexual lives shows that their rigid positions of the past are cracking.

## 2. Religious, Ethnic, and Gender Factors Affecting Sexuality

### A. Source and Character of Religious Values

The influence of the Catholic Church was and is hegemonic. Ninety percent of Argentina's population identify themselves as Roman Catholic, although the percentage of active churchgoers is much less.

A very conservative interpretation of Catholic dogma shaped life during colonial times. The powerful grip of the Church in Argentina's life was not relaxed after independence from Spain in 1810, nor when the country was finally organized as a modern state towards the end of the 19th century. Throughout the history of Argentina, secular powers have had to battle against a Church determined to maintain its hold on the institutions of civil life, like education, the availability of contraception and abortion, and even the registration of major events in the lives of the people, like births, marriages, and deaths.

The values and beliefs of Catholic doctrine have been inscribed in the minds of the Argentine people in a way that has proven difficult to delete. Outstanding among these are the Church's views on the social roles of males and females, its insistence on seeing the body as a root of evil, the need to free the spirit from the urges of the flesh, and sexual intercourse viewed as a curse brought upon humans with no other objective or justification than the preservation of the human species.

The influence of this dogma has led, as one might expect, to a dichotomous, often-schizophrenic pattern of behavior. Recently, three Catholic women in Uruguay, Argentina's neighboring country, investigated Catholic women's ideas on and practices of sexuality and maternity. Their sample included hundreds of women from Argentina, Uruguay, and Paraguay, countries which share a similar historical and cultural evolution. The women commonly expressed dissatisfaction with their sexual lives, and had developed the strategy of "not feeling" or "getting used to putting up with it." Others were oppressed by the idea that sex is sinful and felt bad after each sexual encounter. While many of the women interviewed felt God as a close friend, they viewed the Church as distant, disciplinary, and controlling.[2]

### B. Source and Character of Ethnic Values

Before the arrival of the Spaniards in 1516, Argentina was inhabited by fierce, indomitable tribes that valued their freedom and had learned to survive by adapting to the climate and resources of the different regions of the country. Except for the Northwest, which was conquered by the Peruvian Incas, the indigenous populations of Argentina did not develop the complex, and, in some aspects, advanced civilizations whose remains can still been seen in Mexico and Peru. The indigenous people who inhabited the pampas were mercilessly condemned to extinction by the thirst for land of the Spanish conquerors first, and the new South American nation later on. A few still survive in small reserves, especially in the Northeast, where the Jesuits had organized them in productive communities that were destroyed after the expulsion of the order in 1767 from Spain and all her colonies.

This, and the fact that Argentina never had a very active slave trade, explains the predominance of a population of European origin. Between 1850 and 1940, some 6.6 million Europeans joined the 1.1 million people already living in the country in 1850.[3] In 1991, Argentina's population was 32.7 million, having grown in the previous decade at the rate of 1.3% per year.[4]

From 1810, when the links with Spain were severed, to 1853, when a unified nation started its organizational development, Argentina was a field of constant quarrels among feudal provincial warlords and between these *caudillos* and the two aristocracies of money and of culture based in the port city of Buenos Aires. The two aristocracies were trying to control the chaos, often for their own benefit, and neglecting the needs of the rural population.

From 1853 on, Argentina moved solidly on the roads of social and economic development until it ranked in the early decades of the 20th century among the ten most-developed countries of the world. In his study of Argentine history, David Rock comments:

> By the outbreak of World War I, per capita income equaled that in Germany and the Low Countries, and was higher than in Spain, Italy, Sweden, and Switzerland. Having grown at an average annual rate of 6.5% since 1869, Buenos Aires had become the second largest city of the Atlantic seaboard, after New York, and by far the largest city in Latin America.... By 1911, Argentina's foreign trade was larger than Canada's and a quarter of that of the United States. Argentina was the world's largest producer of corn and linseed, second in wool, and third in live cattle and horses. Though it ranked only sixth as a wheat producer, it was third, and in some years the second, largest exporter. Despite the competition for land from cattle and forage crops, the expansion of wheat farming after 1900 outpaced Canada's.... By and large, working-class conditions in Buenos Aires were much the same as in Western European cities.... By comparison with American [U.S.A.] cities in this period, Buenos Aires was relatively free of ethnic ghettoes, and its highly mobile labor force made it also a city with little permanent unemployment.[5]

However, the brightness of these figures hides the shadows and contradictions of the Argentine society and economy of that time. As the same historian points out:

> By 1914 Argentina had . . . evolved into an extremely mixed and diverse society. Across the regions extreme modernity and immutable backwardness coexisted. Expectations remained high that the imbalances would steadily recede as the present wave of growth continued, for there was still much to accomplish.[6]

In 1930, with the global economic crises and the first local military coup, the development trend stopped and reversed. Instead of being included among the high-income economies in the World Bank tables, Argentina is now among the upper-middle-income countries, where it shares positions with Brazil, Uruguay, Mexico, and Venezuela from the American continent, Gabon and Botswana from Africa, and Latvia, Lithuania, Portugal, and Greece from Europe.[7]

The economic and cultural mismanagement of the country could not, however, destroy one of the main achievements of the organizational period of the country: the establishment of a gratuitous, compulsory, tax-sustained, and public education. Although the quality of education suffered from all those years of regressive, and sometimes fascist attacks, quantitatively it still is reaching the whole of the country, allowing everybody at least to read and write, and with these instruments, giving the vast majority of Argentines access to information offered by a large market of diverse publications. In 1990, the pupil-teacher ratio in the primary schools was 19 students per teacher; 1970 data put the ratio in secondary schools at 44:1, and for colleges at 22:1.[8]

Argentina can be seen as a large tapestry woven with different threads, each thread representing the diverse nationalities and cultures that came to the country from different regions of the world, among them Spaniards, Italians, British, French, Germans, Polish, as well as Jews and Muslims of different ethnic origins. The basic canvas on which this tapestry is woven is the native Argentines themselves, descendants of the early *conquistadors* and the populations that inhabited the land when the *conquistadors* arrived in the 15th century. While a few represent a pure white or native lineage, most are products of hybridization. The result is a tapestry without a clear-cut design, a tapestry whose lines twist and appear as a *sfumato*.

Because the plantation economy never was important in Argentina, the introduction of African slaves never reached large proportions. The few slaves that were in the country at the time of its independence from Spain (in 1810) were freed immediately after in 1813. They gathered in the suburbs of Buenos Aires, mixed quickly with the remaining population, and gave birth to a cultural group, the *mulattos*, who have produced their own artistic expressions. From their music evolved the tango of which I will say more later.

Jorge Luis Borges, a great Argentine poet and writer, saw Argentina seesawing between the search for progress through mimicking foreign cultures, especially the European and North American cultures, and a deep-seated provincialism that refused to change inherited colonial patterns. Borges sought to transcend these trends by developing an ability to understand and talk with both the universal and the local.[9]

The period of accelerated economic development and social transformation (1860-1930) was a period of mimetism promoted in the school system and marketplace. During this period, provincialism found refuge among limited social groups at both ends of the economic spectrum. At the bottom level, it translated into the crude behavior of the persecuted *gauchos*, the *mestizo* cowboys of the Argentine pampas, and of the *compadritos* of the suburbs of the large cities, whom Richard Powers, a dance historian at Stanford University, defines as "a folk antihero somewhere between a bully, a thief and a pimp."[10] At the upper economic scale, some large land owners and church members remained nostalgic of bygone days when they were masters of the country and kept the mind of the people restrained by dogmas and myths.

Paradoxically, the provincialism of the lumpen-proletariat engendered a form of music, the tango, that would acquire universal acceptance and soon invade the salons of the sophisticated outer-oriented aristocracy. The tango expresses the sadness of displacement: from rural fields to crowded suburbs for the natives and for the immigrants from their many diverse landscapes of Europe. It also mixes instruments from the natives—the guitar—and the immigrants—the fiddle and the *bandoneùn*, a concertina-like German instrument. The words often speak of crude, brothel-oriented sex, and of betrayal and revenge, but there is also tender romance and the longing for stable relationships. Some tangos shift from individual feelings to social criticism and become vitriolic pictures of a face that Argentina hides under its economic and cultural exploits.[11] A few examples in Table 1 illustrate this. Somehow, the chronology of these examples reflects a parallel slow zigzagging movement of Argentine society towards more gentleness.

The tango was created by males for males. It reflected well the traits of the social structures among the poor urban population and those immigrants who decided to join them. The tango muses about the hybridization, the resentment, the sadness, and the longing for women that were scarce, because most of the immigrants who stayed in the city were single, while those who came with families looked for a piece of land in the countryside. The hybridization in the poor neighborhoods of Buenos Aires produced insecure males who resorted to macho postures when observed or ridiculed by their peers.[14]

[*Comment 1997*: In addition to the value of *machismo* mentioned above, Argentine sexual attitudes and behaviors are strongly influenced by three other values—*marianismo*, *ediquetta*, and *pronatalism*—which are commonly shared with some minor variations across the Latino world of South and Central America. To avoid duplication in several chapters, these four basic values are described in detail in Section 1A, Basic Sexological Premises, in the chapter on Puerto Rico in this *Encyclopedia*. (*End of comment by R. T. Francoeur*)]

Since 1953, provincialism has made repeated attempts to regain the dominant position it held before 1853, but it was often infiltrated by foreign fascist and Nazi influences. These attempts, beside damaging the country's cultural and economic development, succeeded in drastically changing the image of Argentina in the rest of the world. David Rock's seminal book on Argentina summarizes this change in two beautiful paragraphs.[15] Before 1930:

> Indeed, for many decades many Europeans believed that Argentina offered an opportunity equal to, if not greater than, North America. The *pampas estancieros* enjoyed the reputation that Texas or Arab oil magnates have today, and the expression *riche comme un Argentin* remained a commonplace among the French until the 1930s. In 1907, George Clemenceau perceived the genesis of a great new national community originating from a spirit he equated with Manifest Destiny in the United States. "The real Argentino [sic]," he commented, "seems to me convinced there is a magic elixir of youth which springs from his soil and makes of him a new man, descendant of none, but ancestor of endless generations to come." The Spanish philosopher José Ortega y Gasset issued a similar pronouncement in 1929. The Argentine people, he declared, "do not content themselves with being one nation among others: they hunger for an overarching destiny, they demand of themselves a proud future. They would not know a history without triumph."

In his second paragraph, David Rock reflects on the Argentina of 1987:

> Such copious expectations and laudatory reflections form a stark and bitter contrast with more recent judgments. For at least the past two decades economists have classified Argentina in the underdeveloped or "third" world, and by the 1960s Argentina was becoming a byword for political instability, inflation, and labor unrest. During the 1970s a

**Table 1**

**Sexual Implications of Tango Music**

| Tango | Spanish Text | Translation |
|---|---|---|
| (1905) *La Morocha* Words: Angel Villoldo Music: Enrique Saborido Subject: feelings of a woman from Buenos Aires (as seen and written by a man, of course!) | Soy la morocha argentina, la que no siente pesares y alegre pasa la vida con sus cantares, Soy la gentil compañera del noble gaucho porteño, la que conserva el cariño para su dueño. | I am the dark Argentine, who never has sorrows and happily goes through life singing her songs. I am the gentle companion of the noble "gaucho porteño," who keeps her love for her master. |
| (1924) *Griseta* Words: José González Castillo Music: Enrique Delfino Subject: prostitution | Mezcla rara de Museta y de Mimí con caricias de Rodolfo y de Schaunard, era la flor de París que un sueño de novela trajo al arrabal. Y en el loco divagar del cabaret, al arrullo de algún tango compadrón, alentaba una ilusión: soñaba con Des Grieux, quería ser Manon. | Strange mixture of Museta and Mimí with strokes from Rodolfo and Schaunard,[12] she was the flower of Paris that a romantic dream brought to the suburb [of Buenos Aires]. In the crazy rambling of the cabaret, with bully tangos for lullabies, she was cherishing an illusion: she was dreaming with Des Grieux, wanting to be Manon.[13] |
| (1926) *Íntimas* Words: Ricardo Luis Vignolo Music: Alfonso Lacueva Subject: romantic | Hace tiempo que te noto que estás triste, mujercita juguetona pizpireta Que te pasa? Desengaños que has sufrido? Hay recuerdos de amor inolvidables . . . Y hay vacíos imposibles de llenar! | Since long I see you sad, little playful and lively woman. What happens? Disappointments that hurt? There are memories of love that are unforgettable . . . And there are voids impossible to fill! |
| (1928) *Silbando* Words: José Gonzalez Castillo Music: Sebastián Piana y Cátulo Castillo Subject: betrayal and punishment. | Una calle . . . Un farol . . . Ella y él . . . y, llegando sigilosa, la sombra del hombre aquel a quien lo traicionó una vez la ingrata moza . . . Un quejido y un grito mortal y, brillando entre la sombra, el relumbrón con que un facón da su tajo fatal. | A street . . . A street light . . . She and he . . . and, silently approaching, the shadow of the man that she once unmindfully betrayed . . . A whine, a deathly scream, and shining from under the shadows, the flash of bright light of a knife piercing its fatal stab. |
| (1933) *Si Volviera Jesús* Words: Dante A. Linyera Music: Joaquín M. Mora Subject: cultural criticism | Veinte siglos hace, pálido Jesús, que miras al mundo clavado en tu cruz; veinte siglos hace que en tu triste tierra los locos mortales juegan a la guerra. Sangre de odio y hambre vierte el egoismo. | For twenty centuries, pale Jesus, you are looking at the world nailed to your cross; for twenty centuries in your sad land crazy mortals play war. Egoism is shedding blood of hatred and hunger. |
| (1968) *Balada para un Loco* Words: Horacio Ferrer Music: Astor Piazzolla Subject: modern, pure poetry. | Quereme así, piantao, piantao, piantao . . . Abrite a los amores que vamos a intentar la mágica locura total de revivir . . . Vení, volá, vení! | Love me as I am, wild, wild, wild . . . Open up to love, we will attempt the magic insanity of a total renovation . . . Come, fly with me, come! |

sudden procession of horror stories emanated from Argentina—unbridled popular riots, guerrilla warfare, assassinations, abductions, imprisonment of dissidents, institutionalized torture, and eventually mass murder. For a time Argentina elicited a single association: *los desaparecidos*, the thousands of students, workers, writers, lawyers, architects, and journalists, men and women alike, who had "disappeared," simply vanished without trace. At this time too, Rio de Janeiro, Mexico City, Los Angeles, Paris, New York, London, and Rome became refuges for a vast Diaspora of political and economic exiles from Argentina.

David Rock asks: What went wrong? My response, based on my own and my husband's studies of the socioeconomic evolution of Argentina, and our existential experience there, is that the 1930 regressive coup stopped the process by which Argentina, inspired by Jeffersonian philosophy, was con-

stantly redesigning her coat of laws and regulations in order to adjust to changes in her growing physical and economic body, these changes being in turn induced by changes in the global economy and by the scientific and technological advances that humankind was achieving. That coup pushed Argentine society into the seesawing mentioned above, and from 1930 to 1983, with successive coups, the regressive forces became increasingly powerful.

Since 1983, Argentina is slowly and painfully regaining its democratic structures and its ideals of constant progress of both economies and minds. Will she be able to go beyond mimetism and provincialism and realize the synthesis that Borges and many others were longing for?

This summary of Argentine evolution as an independent nation should help readers to see Argentine sexual mores as the result of a complex mix of influences from the regressive and progressive periods of Argentine history. More details on Argentine history and sociology will be given in the following sections of this chapter when required for a better understanding of a particular subject.

## 3. Knowledge and Education about Sexuality

### A. Historical Perspectives

Argentina really started its life as a modern country in 1853, when a generation of progressive politicians organized the country, promoted public education, and produced a radical transformation in the economy and society.

A census in 1869 reveals that:

> four-fifths of the population was illiterate and housed in mud and straw shacks. Twenty years later, although conditions varied greatly among the regions, in some areas education, housing, and consumption standards bore comparison with the most advanced parts of the world. By the late 1880s, the nation's population was increasing by threefold every 30 years.[16]

Outstanding among those new politicians is Sarmiento, an Argentine educator who was president of the republic between 1868 and 1874. In his inaugural address he said: "We need to transform the poor 'gauchos' into people useful to society. For this purpose, the whole country should become a school."[17]

In 1847, Sarmiento had traveled through Europe to learn of the successes and failures of educational systems. Nothing of what he saw satisfied him. He wanted to know of a school system capable of developing reasoning power in the magical and mythical minds of poor peasants.

Then, one of his friends suggested that he visit the United States and get acquainted with the work that Horace Mann was doing in the school system of Massachusetts. He crossed the Atlantic and visited not only with Horace Mann, but also with other brilliant Bostonian Unitarians who were meeting at the Divinity School of Harvard, among others, Henry W. Longfellow and Ralph W. Emerson.

The friendships he established then were further cultivated during his second sojourn as Argentine Ambassador to the United States, from 1864 through 1868. When Sarmiento assumed the presidency of Argentina, Mary Mann, the widow of Horace Mann, was instrumental in sending to Argentina a group of 65 American schoolteachers, with whom Sarmiento and his Ministry of Education, Nicolás Avellaneda, who succeeded Sarmiento as president of Argentina, began to organize the country's educational system. Primary schooling was free and compulsory for all. The number of well-furnished schools constantly increased, and teachers, who were quickly formed by their American counterparts in normal schools, were conferred high social status and adequate monetary rewards.

Prior to this, the monopoly of the Catholic Church over education kept the common people ignorant of the advances in science, technology, and political organizations that were taking place in the world. The education of people of certain rank and fortune was a little better, but ineffective for the development of the country. Only a small number of young men, and even fewer young women, managed to break the fences that an education based on theology created in their minds. However, these few opened the doors to the outside world, other cultures, and great foreign thinkers. Even if they were studying in a Church-managed university, they would smuggle in, often with the help of prominent and open-minded priests, books from Jefferson and the great philosophers of the French Revolution, which they secretly read and discussed with friendly priests.

All this changed when Sarmiento and Avellaneda decided to organize the new school system to provide an education for life in the here and now. It is for this reason that Sarmiento and Mrs. Mann agreed that all the schoolteachers sent from the United States would be females, so as to serve as role models for Argentine households. Sarmiento and Mrs. Mann wanted them to bring new knowledge through words, and a new vision of life through the example of their lives. Since then, the children of poor and uneducated native peasants, and of equally poor and uneducated immigrants, had access to scientific knowledge and learned about their own nature, about what it meant to be human. They would learn how babies are born, how to cut their umbilical cords, how to change and clean their diapers, and how to take care of babies and their own bodies.

In the years of political freedom, social progress, and economic growth that followed, issues on sexuality and the status of women began to be discussed. They were introduced mainly by female politicians of the Socialist Party, and by the youth who by 1918 had achieved success in their fight to change the university system that resisted Sarmiento's reform and, although no longer managed by the Catholic Church, had remained scholastic. It is interesting to observe that while the socialists were bringing a message of sexual liberation, the communists, when they split from the democratic socialists, adopted a moral code based on strict monogamy.

Sarmiento's progressive work on the schools affected many other aspects of Argentine life. One of these aspects was a surge in bookstores that would offer writings of the most-varied orientation, writings to which youth had access and which often supplemented and amplified the information they were given at school.

The 1930 military coup started a slow process of reversing Sarmiento's ideas on education. The purpose of education now focused on keeping pace with the advances in the natural sciences and technology, while preventing students from acquiring a vision of life that would contradict the obsolete moral codes of a narrow theology. However, the alliance of the most-reactionary members of the Catholic hierarchy with the military never managed to take the schools completely backwards. Argentina's life had irreversibly changed, and what was not taught in the classrooms, the students would learn in their households and in the streets, although sometimes the information would reach them distorted or incomplete. For quite a while after the first military coup, books on sexuality could still be freely obtained in the bookstores. Later on, more-reactionary military coups would censor even this source of information.

### B. The Situation Today

Currently there are no sexual education programs at the primary-school level. It is left to the teachers to give some information as part of the classes on biology. In the few cases in which a teacher decides to do so, it is no more than a description of the reproductive organs in plants and animals, and some references to the role of ovaries and testes in human reproduction, with no explicit mention, or even less, showing of pictures of the genitals.

It would be easy, however, to introduce full courses on sexual education in all Argentine public schools. All that is needed is an order of the National Educational Council, which by law decides on the nature and extension of primary-school programs. The members of the council are appointed by the president of the country following advice of the ministry of education. Once decided at the level of the central government, there are no elective local educational boards where parents could either oppose or suggest the idea of providing sexual education to the students. The provincial educational councils have jurisdiction only over provincial schools, not on those established by the national government. Although a few sophisticated private schools have developed advanced programs of sexual education, these schools reach only a tiny minority of children of rich urban households.

The same possibilities of organizing national programs of sex education are open for secondary schools (high schools), because they too report to the authority of the central government. But here again, the situation changes from one school to the other, depending on its director (principal), and is, in general, well behind the demands of the present. Neither primary nor secondary schools have recovered yet from the regressive trend imposed on them by decades of regressive military coups and brief civilian intervals.

For further information about sex education, see Section 5, Interpersonal Heterosexual Behaviors, below.

## 4. Autoerotic Behaviors and Patterns

In Argentine society, despite official Catholic negative views of sex outside the marital union, it is usually seen as normal for preteenage boys to play exploratory games with other boys, and girls with other girls. These games are seen by most parents as part of the process of growing up. It allows the child to reassure him- or herself of the normality of his or her body by comparing it with the body of a friend, relative, or schoolmate, although sometimes, instead of being a reassurance, it could generate anxieties, as when girls compare the size of their breasts and boys the size of their penises. It is also a source of anxiety when a boy feels sexually excited by another boy and fears he is becoming gay.

Freedom for these kinds of exploratory games was greater in bygone days when Argentine society had less violence, and drugs were not as common. In the past, boys would gather in parks and compete to see who threw their semen further while masturbating. Parks were also a place where couples would meet for sexual encounters, and teenagers would peep on their activities without disturbing the partners.

## 5. Interpersonal Heterosexual Behaviors

### A. Children

See Section 4 immediately above.

### B. Adolescents

What is known about the sexuality of Argentine adolescents is limited to anecdotal reports, most of which deal with middle- and upper-class urban teenagers, rather than with rural poor and urban street children. In this limited context, my personal experience in the 1970s in developing a sexual education program for students, ages 13 through 17, of middle-class households may be informative. This program was for a prestigious coed secondary school of suburban Buenos Aires, the Colegio Nacional San Isidro. After a dialogue with the parents aimed at interesting them in the sexual education of their sons and daughters, an integrated approach led the students to discuss biological and social aspects of sexual behavior in relation to their personal development and the establishment of interpersonal relations.

Although the students were offered the possibility of presenting their questions anonymously in writing, they preferred to come out openly with their questions. Their greater concerns were with the emotional and spiritual aspects involved in a sexual relationship. One vividly remembered example is typical of the concerns and perspective these youth had. A 15-year-old male student asked: "Can you know when your partner is pregnant without perform-

ing a lab test?" I left the student to share first his own views, and his answer was: "I think that when one is deep in love, one can detect subtle changes in mood and behavior of his lover that indicate a potential pregnancy."

Among the biological issues, girls were more interested in knowing more about the physiology of menstruation, pregnancy, and delivery, while boys wanted to reassure themselves that masturbation and nocturnal involuntary ejaculations were normal and could be enjoyed free of guilt and shame. Both sexes converged in expressing that they were facing the awakening of their sexual potential with anguish and feelings of being all alone in this experience. They all needed to be reassured that there was nothing abnormal in their bodily sensations, and in the fantasies and feelings these sensations often evoked.

In 1931, when Argentina's freedom to experiment with and discuss these subjects was not yet fully eroded, an Argentine scholar, Anibal Ponce, studied the problems of growing up in Argentine society in a book titled *Ambition and Anguish among Adolescents*. Regarding the common feelings of being isolated and alone, he said:

> With a personality not yet formed, and while trying to awkwardly build the structures of his ego, the adolescent suffers more than anybody else, the anguish of solitude, because he or she needs more than anybody else the support of the others.[18]

Unfortunately, since my experience in 1970, the situation has deteriorated for Argentine adolescents, who find in their society less and less support for their existential anguish. In 1993, while researching this paper, this deterioration was obvious in my talks with adolescents. In a meeting with a group of them, ages 15 to 17, they told me about the typical pattern of a course on sexual education in a school that chooses to implement it. The teacher does not allow questions from the students during the presentations. At the end, he agrees to receive a few. Sensing that the instructor is insecure and unable to facilitate a dialogue in depth, the students then prefer to end the class quickly, declaring they have nothing to ask.

The teenagers confessed that it is attitudes like this, repeated in their homes, that make them view society and family cynically. Surrounded by injustice and hypocrisy, they feel they can do little to get the adults to change. They were, for instance, very disturbed by the expulsion of two students from their schools when they became pregnant.

The situation is no better at the college level. There are no courses of sexual education in Argentine universities, except, and this only since the 1960s, at their schools of medicine (see Sections 11, Sexual Dysfunctions, Counseling, and Therapies, and 12, Sex Research and Advanced Professional Education, below).

### Premarital Sexual Activities

Sexual behavior differs from one group of Argentine youth to another depending on their social class and place of residence. Social belonging and location determine different levels of knowledge, repressions, and attitudes towards life in general, and sex in particular.

In the larger cities, like Buenos Aires, Cordoba, Mendoza, Rosario, and Santa Fe, youth are exposed to a cosmopolitan vision of life and receive more information on sex and sexuality. They are also freer to experiment with this vision and information than youth living in smaller towns, where family control is strong and where cultural patterns are rather narrow.

For rural youth, it is quite different. On the one hand, they receive information on sex and sexual behavior just from observing nature in which they are totally immersed, and from the relation between genders in the family where members enjoy little privacy, if any. On the other hand, the prevailing Catholic Church writes deep into the unconscious of every boy and girl, but especially of the latter, ideas of guilt and sin that trouble the pleasure that the early awakening of the senses in the rural milieu can bring. Neither boys nor girls are taught about the relational and recreational aspects of sex, and the possibilities offered by modern technology for keeping under control the reproductive aspects. Hence, the purely instinctive sex leads to pregnancy, confronting the boy with the responsibility of an early marriage that he is not yet ready to assume, and the girl with the responsibility of an unwanted motherhood for which she also is not prepared.

Youngsters in the big cities have easy access to magazines where sexuality is soberly analyzed, even if their parents and the Church hide such information from the youngsters. They know about contraceptive techniques and can acquire contraceptives in the pharmacies without problem. However, the guilt and shame associated with sex are also present here and, as usual, instead of promoting either safe sex or abstinence, these only lead to quick sexual contacts. Under the uncontrollable pressure of a hormonal flood released in a hurry and in the most unromantic places, boys and girls neglect prevention of pregnancy and disease. For youth in the poverty belts around the big cities, the situation is compounded by the lack of money. Even if they would prefer to use contraceptives, they cannot buy them and there are no places where they can get these free. Only the army distributes free condoms to the soldiers when they leave the barracks on their weekly leave days. Knowing the limited budget for healthcare within the army, the Church has not complained to the military, with which they keep good relations, pretending instead to ignore a practice that otherwise they could not openly accept.

### First Sexual Experiences

In late 1993, the author had long conversations with different groups of young people in Buenos Aires. These mainly middle-class youths, ages 18 to 24, were encouraged to bring to the meetings problems related to their sexual life and development.

One subject recurrent in these meetings was their difficulty in establishing a fruitful dialog with their parents. Repeatedly, they expressed regret that aspects of their lives that engender so many anguishes and fears could not be explicitly discussed in the intimacy of their households.

Contrasting the information gathered in these meetings with my previous experience in medical private practice in Argentina, it became clear that sexual activities are initiated at increasingly earlier ages. Most of the interviewed youths defined their first experiences as disappointing. Asked why, they always responded that it was so because of a lack of romance. Most boys had been initiated in whorehouses, under the pressure of fathers who would arrange the visit, and this happened without a previous intimate talk that could soothe the anxiety of the teenager by discussing what he may expect to happen and how to protect himself from diseases, mainly AIDS, about which the teenager had already heard at school. Such experiences, they said, left bitter memories, which for some disappeared when they fell in love and discovered the ingredient they were longing for: romance. The boys all agreed that the experience at the whorehouse was felt as an obligation to fulfill in order to affirm their virility.

Among girls, the memories of their being deflowered were somewhat different from the boys. Some did not bother to get prior information about the meaning and the possible consequences of their first sexual encounter. They perceived their first intercourse as the fulfillment of a strongly felt de-

sire that, at the same time, would transgress a social taboo. Hence, they reached the situation with many expectations, and as much anxiety as boys said they did. For other, more-entrepreneurial-type female students, it was a calculated action to get rid of their virginity, which they perceived as an obstacle to enter into a more mature and fulfilling sexual life. These girls sought information from doctors in private gynecological practice and acquired the necessary contraceptive technology to protect themselves.

### Reflections about Sex Policies and Politics from Meetings with Youth

The young's perception is that society is not providing appropriate responses to their needs of knowing more about sexuality and sensuality. The information they get at home, school, and church is incomplete and biased by the prejudices of the adults. Although short articles dispersed in different magazines are useful, they cannot fully fill the gap. They would prefer an honest, open, uninhibited dialogue with parents, teachers, and priests.[19] They see the AIDS epidemic slowly changing the situation, although they consider that their survival is in danger, because society is reacting too slowly and is still not assuming full responsibility, preferring to stick to old patterns of thought and behavior rather than save lives.

The more-enlightened youth perceive many deficiencies in the information process, deficiencies that they say may risk the future of a stable relationship. For instance, they are not told that, although syphilis and gonorrhea can still be easily cured, these diseases may make it easier for the AIDS virus to invade the immune system. Girls are not told that chronic or repeated inflammation of the genital tissues may lead to infertility and ectopic pregnancies.

A generalized opinion among youth is that it is necessary to invest in improving and updating education and information to secure the future of the country. The impression left on me by my meetings in Buenos Aires is that middle- and upper-class youth are slowly evolving from a macho behavior, which still is deeply programmed into their minds by their acculturation, to an attitude of better understanding of their own and the opposite sex's sexuality. They are learning to integrate male and female traits in their own personality, and to harmonize the roles of males and females in the marketplace, households, and political arenas. They are also starting to understand and respect those who show preferences for intimate relationships with persons of their own sex.

However, the majority of the Argentine population is unchanged. It is unclear at this time whether the elite youth of the urban middle and upper class, as they mature, will influence the democratic process that reopened in 1983 to introduce changes in the educational and legal systems that could usher larger groups into a new vision of their sexual life.

[*Update 2003*: Argentine teenagers face serious risks in their sexual life, especially concerning sexually transmitted diseases and premature maternity. Those risks arise from the lack of information, of deficient health services, and of disregarding responsibilities towards oneself and one's partners.

[The health and sanitary authorities are not lending sufficient attention to these risks, despite statistics indicating that the number of cases of AIDS among Argentine children is the highest in Latin America. Their mothers, who often are less than 20 years old, infected about 90% of those HIV-positive children (CRLP 2000).

[Around 86% of women between 15 and 19 years of age use contraceptives in the City of Buenos Aires, while the percentage is much smaller in the rest of the country—between 31% and 45%. However, these figures do not indicate the degree of responsibility and of knowledge with which those contraceptives are being used. Independently of their diverse lifestyles, most youngsters, when interviewed, express needs for emotional support and for a complete sexual education that should include knowledge on contraceptive technologies, but not be limited to this subject alone. Public health services do not satisfy these needs.

[During the interviews sustained while writing the original chapter for this encyclopedia, youngsters expressed different approximations to sexual activity. But all of them—those who had begun to exercise their sexuality at a very early age as well as those who were not yet active, those who had multiple partners as well as those in more-stable and long-term relationships—confessed not to know much about their own bodies and about the sexually transmitted diseases. They were ashamed to seek preventive information or early treatment from medical services. The economic crisis that the country has suffered, since the 1997 publication of this chapter, adds poverty to ignorance in increasing the emotional and physical damages that Argentine youth is suffering.

[Argentina should take immediate measures to establish programs of sexual education in all the country, teaching youngsters how to protect themselves, resist pressures when sexual activity is not yet desired, and diminish the risk of their sexual encounters by negotiating with their partners. The provinces of Rio Negro, Neuquén, and Mendoza have assumed leadership in this direction by establishing services in the area of sexual and reproductive health for adolescents by law.

[Those who oppose these programs argue that discussing human sexuality at an early age awakes prematurely the curiosity of the youngsters and advances their initiation in sexual activity. After evaluating 1,000 sexual programs of education in diverse countries of the world, the World Health Organization has arrived at the contrary conclusion. Courses in sexual education do not advance the age at which sexual activity usually starts in the respective culture. Moreover, in some cases, the major and better knowledge defers the experimentation (Population Information Program 1995).

[Because young Argentines are making decisions with neither knowledge nor responsibility, they compromise their health and the economy of their homes. Because the Argentine State ignores its role in the sexual education of its youth, it compromises the future of the country with a long-term social and economic overload of sexually transmitted diseases and unwanted pregnancies. (*End of update by S. Kamenetzky*)]

## C. Adults

### Marriage and the Family

Mature people, who married before the recent shift in sexual behavior towards more openness and gender equity acquired the intensity and spread they now have, are being bombarded by the mass media and performing arts with messages that carry a heavy sexual and sensual content, telling about new techniques for lovemaking, new roles within the couple, new risks in extramarital relationships, and so on. These issues are also conversation matter among friends and families, and at business meetings and almost any social gatherings.

Inevitably, mature couples start imitating the open and direct language of their younger counterparts. This, and the perceived risks of extramarital affairs since the AIDS epidemic, is leading them to recreate their sexual life and expand their erotic horizon. They are discovering that fantasy and playfulness within the couple are the best antidotes of boredom. Men are learning to ask their spouses to use new forms of stimulation with them; they are learning that it is more important for them and their partners to be mutually tender and understanding than it is to count their performance points. Oral sex and anal intercourse are losing their status, especially among younger Argentines, as techniques practiced only with prostitutes. Masturbation is increasingly viewed not only as a form of self-satisfaction, but also as a means of sharing sensual and orgasmic experiences without penetration.

### Extramarital Sex

We still find married men who maintain a longstanding relationship with a second woman, sometimes with the knowledge and approval from his spouse, and even of his grownup children. For some couples, it is a solution that keeps their marriage alive: The man is free to express sexual needs that he does not dare to reveal to his wife, and the woman is relieved from pressures to change her sexual behavior, a task that for her heavily structured personality may be so painful that she prefers to share her partner with another woman. These are generally women with limited horizons in their lives and a very low sexual appetite.

Fewer are the number of couples where the man and woman both have temporary extramarital relationships under mutual knowledge and agreement. This is the most risky modality in today's Argentina, because many of the men resist the use of condoms and ignore whether their occasional partners may be HIV-positive.

### Older Adults

The new ways of thinking and making love are also resounding among couples over age 55. Often it is their own children and grandchildren who awaken them to the new sexual behavioral patterns. In Argentina, there is still strong interaction among the generations, and the oldest easily perceive the freedom that the new generations have won. Nowadays, a granddaughter moving from home to the apartment of her boyfriend is not grounds for scandal. And grandparents do not stay away from a wedding where the bride in a long white gown shows signs of pregnancy.

Indeed, these are open-minded elderly who keep their own sensuality and vitality alive; they are not ashamed to show tenderness between them through hugging and kissing. These are people who consult the urologist at the first signs of impotence in the man, or the gynecologist when the woman's sex drive declines. Most elderly couples, however, have not reached this openness. They let their sexual drive disappear without seeking remedies. Many drift into depression and develop hypochondriac behavior.

### Incidence of Oral and Anal Sex

In Argentine society, both oral and anal sex carry a negative connotation, especially for older persons and among the traditional middle- and upper-class families. Argentine youth, however, seems to be taking a new look at these sexual expressions, according to what they said at the meetings.

Girls were divided in their responses. One group accepts and practices oral sex as a way of avoiding the risk of pregnancy and maintaining their virginity until marriage. For another group, it was a more-intimate form of sexual relationship, somehow more romantic than intercourse. Youth holding this latter view believed that oral sex should only be engaged in with a stable partner, and not in the first exploratory encounters. Some other girls joined some boys in rejecting this way of expressing love to a partner, and thought that only prostitutes could practice fellatio on boys. The older the boys are, the more easily they accept oral sex as a normal part of dating and within marriage.

Prejudices against anal sex are even stronger among older adults, and even the younger set. A minority of the youths in the groups I spoke with accepted anal sex, and then only for fully committed couples and not as part of dating. The boys agree that: "A woman will never ask for it." The old injunction against sodomy is still well alive in their subconscious.

## 6. Homoerotic, Homosexual, and Bisexual Behaviors

Argentina still is, to a large extent, a macho society, and machos detest gays, whom they see as effeminate. For a majority of the population, including physicians and psychologists, homosexuality is felt to be a perversion and a disease. Teenagers who feel a strong attraction to members of their same sex experience, first, extreme confusion about their feelings. When the picture becomes clear in their mind, they awake to the unpleasant reality of belonging to a group that society marginalizes.

Gayness, however, is increasingly being tolerated, and a gay movement is gaining increased strength and fighting for its rights, which ten years ago was impossible even to think of. The scorn for gays is higher among lower- and middle-class men than among members of the upper class. There always were artists and writers whose homosexuality was known among the elites, but carefully kept out of scrutiny from the media and the masses.

Lesbians are still not too visible in Argentine society, in keeping with the Victorian tradition, which never wanted to think about sexual activities in a relationship between two females.

Contrasting the social attitude that openly scorns gays, although sheltering them when they belong to special groups, we see Argentines as quite uninhibited in publicly expressing tenderness and affection among people of the same or different sex. Men of all ages will embrace and kiss each other when meeting, and there are also exchanges of kisses among men and women who are relatives or friends, and, of course, among women themselves. The increased publicity about the spread of AIDS has not acted as a deterrent of these affectionate expressions.[20] (See the discussion of same-sex sex rehearsal play in Section 4, Autoerotic Behaviors and Patterns.)

To be gay or lesbian in a repressive environment whose stereotypes are the macho man and the submissive reproductive woman is not an easy task indeed. Anyone who deviates from a strict heterosexual behavior is ridiculed: A gay is not a man, a lesbian is a degenerate woman. However, to be bisexual is not so annoying, as long as one's same-sex behavior is kept very private.

The young gay faces the hostility of society by withdrawing from his heterosexual circles to a subculture where he can find both lovers and understanding study and sport mates. Successful professionals have solved their problems by choosing to retreat into more-accepting cultures where they can be openly gay without jeopardizing their future. In private discussions, young gays report that their most traumatizing experience is when they decide to open up to their families and are rejected.

With a population of 12 million in Buenos Aires, one would expect a larger number of gay and lesbians than the numbers one can estimate from the few who have left the closet. These few, however, are very active in promoting the rights of the whole community. They speak for the visible and the invisible, helping the latter to openly assume their identities. They have formed organizations that have been given legal status, they have an official meeting and business place, and they publish and distribute documents to the press and public. In these documents, they tell of their suffering, explain their lifestyles, and ask support for their fight for more legal freedom to be themselves and for equal rights with people of other sexual orientations. There is a whole gay and lesbian culture that is emerging, with gay masseurs who announce their services in the most-important papers and gay bars and discos. (I have not heard of any lesbian bar.)

I also did not find neighborhoods exclusively or predominantly homosexual. Most mix with the mainstream population of their own social class. Those who have a well-defined and highly visible economic or political role are still in the closet. The same is true for members of the armed forces and the Church. To confess their lifestyle and orientation would be suicidal. On the other hand, among artists, writers, moviemakers, actors, dancers, and university professors, to admit openly they are gay may bring rejection from the most conservative members of society, but they end up being accepted, and sometimes even see their popularity increase.

Who are those conservative members of the Argentine society? First, of course, are the orthodox Catholics who still believe that sexuality and sensuality ought to be repressed to achieve spiritual development. If all sexual and sensual manifestations are sinful except in marriage, homosexuality is particularly so. It is unnatural, a perversion of nature. Second, the orthodox Jews who still follow the Torah's abomination of this kind of relationship that in the past deserved capital punishment.

Third, in the domain of medical science, many have not yet evolved to a humanist, integrative, harmonizing approach. Orthodox psychoanalysts still consider consistency in the male or female physical and mental development as essential to a normal personality. They believe homosexuality originates in conflicts and traumas that therapy can face and resolve. In the chairs of sexuality of the schools of medicine, complex biological schemes are used to disguise the view among traditional physicians that homosexuality violates the laws of nature.

The irrational fear of physical love between partners of the same sex still pervades Argentine society. The overall situation can be described with the same words that Erwin J. Haeberle used to describe the prevalent attitude of society in the United States 20 years ago:

> Typically, they do not know any homosexuals, do not want to meet them, but would like them to be controlled, contained, put away, locked up or eliminated.[21]

Argentine society still is far from taking seriously the role of sexuality in the physical, emotional, and spiritual life of men and women. It still has to reflect on other words of Haeberle:

> The ultimate liberation of both homosexuals and heterosexuals can lie only in the abandonment of all labels and in everyone's freedom to explore his own sexual potential, whatever it may be.[22]

## 7. Gender Diversity and Transgender Issues

Argentina was always a male-dominated society where those who do not behave in the macho way were scorned by men and women alike. However, with the return to democratic freedom, and TV messages from foreign countries penetrating into the intimacy of households, attitudes are slowly changing. Thus, the erotic minorities have had a chance to come out of the closet and express themselves.

For the moment, the masses react to them with neither violence nor acceptance, rather with curiosity. In the world of the performing arts, cases are well known of transvestism, and because these persons are celebrities, the public accepts them with smiles and gentle jokes.

If things are not easy for noneffeminate gays or nonmasculine lesbians, they are even more difficult for those who identify themselves with the opposite sex in manners and clothing, and even more so for those who want to see their bodies change towards the features of the other sex.

Some heterosexual transvestites have acceptance from their mates, and sometimes from their children, to cross-dress in the intimacy of their homes. In this way, men, who seem to outnumber women in practicing this sexual behavior, can safely express the feminine part of their personalities. In their work and social environment, these men usually return to macho stereotypes.

Those who desire to change their sex physically and be socially recognized as a member of the other sex should seek legal authorization for both procedures, the surgical acts and biochemical treatments needed, and the right to change names and status. Usually the authorization is denied on the basis of Article 91 of the Criminal Code that considers them as mutilations that would affect the capacity of women to engender children, which is considered as their primary social role. The law punishes with jail the patient who has changed sex and the doctor who performed the operation; the medical license of the latter is also revoked.

Change of sex in Argentina has a tragic history. In 1958, a prestigious physician, Dr. Defacio, went into self-imposed exile after suffering several years in prison because he had changed the sex of a man, Mauro Fernandez Vega, who, in turn, was never able to get new identity documents. Now another man, Javier Alberto Urbina, who claims to feel uncomfortable with his sexual identity and desires to be transformed into a woman, has started a public campaign for the right of any person to own his or her body. For this purpose, he has challenged government and society alike, standing before the doors of the Argentine Congress with billboards asking the abolition of Article 91. The Permanent Assembly for Human Rights is supporting his actions, according to a letter he proudly exhibits. In the letter, the President of the Assembly acknowledges Mr. Urbina's contributions to the cause of civil rights and individual freedom. The letter says that Mr. Urbina's actions may result in the legal recognition of the right to decide freely on matters that concern one's own body. However, legislators seem insensitive to this claim.

## 8. Significant Unconventional Sexual Behaviors

### A. Coercive Sexual Behaviors

*Sexual Abuse and Incest*

There are no statistics on incest. Professionals in the medical and legal fields who deal with family violence and abuse encounter cases at all social levels, but they seem to be more frequent in rural areas and among poor people.

Adolescent girls are often raped by the older males of the family, and fathers often use them as sexual objects after the death of the mother, or when the spouse's work keeps her for long periods outside the home. Abusive males are usually unemployed people with a past of family violence, high consumption of alcohol, social inadequacy, and impulsive behavior. However, although less frequent, cases are also known in which the male is the head of a well-to-do household and respected by his community.

Lawyers at the Office for the Protection of Minors who mainly deal with cases of incest among the lower classes are surprised at how often they find that the abuser has no perception of having committed a crime. This office is now working with a multidisciplinary team of professionals. This, and the recent institution of oral court hearings, is increasing knowledge about the extent and motivations of this unconventional sexual behavior.[23]

It is in private medical practice that cases of incest within middle- and upper-class families surface. Young females acknowledge the trauma of an early unwanted incestuous relationship when coming for treatment of sexual dysfunction in their marriages.

*Sexual Harassment*

On December 19, 1993, a decree of Argentina's federal government introduced the legal concept of sexual harassment in its administrative procedures and Criminal Code. The decree was prepared by the Secretariat of the Civil Service with the help of the Women's National Council.

The decree punishes sexual harassment independently of the hierarchical levels occupied by aggressor and assaulted, and regardless of their respective sex. Sexual harassment is defined as:

> Any reiterative activity, whether this be a behavior, a purpose, a gesture, or a bodily contact, that is not accepted and reciprocated by the person to whom it is aimed, that humiliates her or him, and that involves a threat against the stability of employment or the opportunities for advancement.

This action by the administration was promoted by the Secretariat for Women of the civil servants' labor union (Uniùn del Personal Civil de la Naciùn) that provided information on the increase of this type of behavior in different government organizations: the Ministry of Public Health and Social Action, the Secretariat of Tourism, the National Atomic Energy Commission, the National Institute of Technology, the Ministry of Economy, Customs, National Parks Service, and many others. After the decree was issued, more than 700 cases were initiated in the city of Buenos Aires alone.

Sexual harassment is punished through an administrative indictment that may end with a dismissal from public service. The administrative procedure, however, does not preclude legal action by the offended person, because the same decree introduces in the Criminal Code, Article 124B that reads as follows:

> Those who use their hierarchical position or any other situation of employment to induce another to satisfy his or her sexual requirements, be this or not carnal intercourse, will be punished with two to four years of prison.

This decree is important because it shows that Argentine women are expanding their political presence and are winning the collaboration of men who know, from well inside the system, the injustices perpetrated against women. Men and women both hope that the new legal situation will not be spuriously used to either accomplish personal vengeance or obtain undue economic gains.

*Rape and Family Violence*

Despite these aspects of sexual violence in Argentine society, such behaviors have been affected by the educational reforms instituted at the end of the 19th century, producing a more genteel society. However, violence within the household is still considerable, especially from husband to wife. Abuses of this kind are seldom reported to police, because women know that the members of the latter usually behave in the same manner in their homes.

Among the poorest households, since their early infancy, girls observe the violent behavior of their fathers, particularly when they return home intoxicated with alcohol. The mother is beaten and bruised, and a sexual encounter may follow that amounts to a rape. Faced with a society that, until recently, did not recognize female rights, the woman capitulates, represses her feelings, closes herself within her taciturn dreams, and continues laboring for the survival of her family, especially her offspring. Even then, if she does not manage to hide at least some of her earnings, the male may spend them with another woman and with friends imbibing alcohol.

Once more the tango draws on this popular behavior. A male songwriter puts on the lips of a female protagonist who falls in love with a hoodlum the following words:

> Now, even if he beats me
> my boy from the shanties
> knows that I love him
> with all my passion
> that I am all his
> that for him is my fond attention
> and that it will be ours the child
> product of this love sickness.[24]

The lawyers at the judicial branch that deals with family violence estimate that there has been recently an increase of some 40% in the cases of women beaten and practically raped. However, rape in public places of the large cities or by intruders in private homes is not as frequent as in other countries, although with an increase in unemployment, especially among youth, this violent behavior is also starting to increase.

Lawyers admit that, when a girl or young woman is raped, the experience of going through the legal procedures and crude and insensitive examinations by forensic doctors could be more traumatic than the rape itself. The Argentine Criminal Code punishes with four years of prison the culprit of an incest with or rape of a minor.

A new brand of young lawyers, judges, psychologists, and sociologists are trying to uncover the economic and social roots of this violent behavior. As Martha Mercader, an Argentine writer of whom I will write more later, says, "Rape is not an animal act. Because it is a denial of human rights, it is an aberrant product of human culture."[25]

[*Update 2003*: In Argentina's daily life, whether in the households, in society, or even in cultural circles, it is easy to perceive what in the popular language is called "machismo." It is a male attitude of superiority that disregards the human dignity, intellectual merits, and economic worth of females.

[The situations in which women are victims of violence and criminal attacks have recently multiplied because of the deep political and economic crisis the country is undergoing. Corporal punishments that may end with death, forced sexual engagements that hurt the women physically and mentally, rapes, and child abuse, are all common features in Argentine society. Most of these events are not reported. There are fears of reprisals, concerns for how they may affect the offspring, worries about being left without means of subsistence, and lack of support from parental families. Women do not trust the police, because they know that the same *machista* mentality pervades its members.

[Argentine legislators have tried to modernize the laws related to acts of sexual violence against women, children, and teenagers. In 1999, laws were passed on crimes against sexual integrity. The new laws have changed most of the problems of sexual violence from the category of crimes to

that of conflicts, which authorizes the judges to arbitrate or seek conciliation.

[Rape goes well beyond conflict. Raping is a criminal attack that involves many physical and mental consequences. The attacked person may contract AIDS or other sexually transmitted diseases, could subsequently suffer depression, even suicidal thoughts, and could have difficulties in reassuming a pleasant, satisfying sexual behavior. Legal protection and social equity for both genres of all ages require more than just changes in the laws. True protection and equity will be achieved through a profound educational reform aimed at structuring people's consciousness in the appreciation of the physical, mental, emotional, and spiritual benefits of a sexuality exercised with mutual respect and responsible freedom. (*End of update by S. Kamenetzky*)]

## B. Prostitution

### The Past

The *gauchos*, the native inhabitants of the country, themselves products of the heavy breeding between the early *conquistadors* and the indigenous population, and of the lower-class Spaniards who arrived in the wake of those *conquistadors*, seldom commercialized the sexual favors of women. A *gaucho* would take a woman as his sexual partner and could abandon her after some time without remorse. His mind was not programmed into thinking marriage, nor seeking stability, but neither did it contain programs that would make it acceptable, even less desirable, to make profits by exploiting his or any other woman. The *gauchos* were fearless, quarrelsome, but honest *machos*, skilled in the use of knives and *boleadoras*,[26] who wandered on their horses through the vast expanses of flat land that are the Argentine pampas.

After the efforts by Sarmiento and Avellaneda to build more rational structures on the magical and mythic mind of the Argentine population (see Section 3A, Knowledge and Education about Sexuality, Historical Perspectives), the situation changed for both the *gauchos* and their women. In 1880, the image of a country that would develop following European models was well set in the minds of the country's leaders. The *gauchos* had to transform themselves from vagrant free hunters who lived with women practicing subsistence gardening and husbandry into a rural labor force for the large ranches that the wealthy started to organize, or find a place in the smaller agricultural undertakings of the immigrants that started to flock to the Argentine pampas. The new generations were prepared by Sarmiento's schools to assume the new role, but they were betrayed by the large landowners, who did not treat them as salaried labor within a capitalist system, but rather as peasants attached to the lord's land who rendered services to the lord in exchange for a place where they could build their shacks and where their wives could tender a garden and raise some chickens, in addition to work as maids or cooks in the landlord's house. The older *gauchos*, not enough acculturated into the new system or economic and social relationships, would often rebel. The police would then seize them and send them to the armies that were battling the remaining southern indigenous populations and expanding the agricultural frontiers for the "civilized" land-based entrepreneurs. In brief, the displaced *gauchos* were making room for the *estancias* of the old native oligarchy and the settlements of the newly arrived middle-class Europeans.

The women of the older *gauchos* sent to the frontiers as cannon fodder were left without support and would often join the wives of the settled laborers as servants and sexual objects of the landowner families. They also became prostitutes in the small villages of the rural areas with their population of single rural laborers and traveling salesmen. An Argentine writer, José Hernandez, who knew well the mindsets and lifestyles of the *gauchos*, wrote an epic poem about their suffering because of their inability to adjust to the transformational process, and the often rough way in which this process took place. It was a process that sacrificed the human dignity of the lower classes to the purpose of building a modern, productive nation. And the women suffered the most from this process.[27]

Most of the immigrants came seeking possibilities for earning their livelihood through hard work, risky but honest investments, and the use of the best available technologies. However, as in any migratory inflow, some elements came with the idea of making money quickly by exploiting native people and land. A few used prostitution as the means to accumulate wealth and wield power.

Argentina would soon become one of the most active centers of the so-called white slave traffic. In Buenos Aires, Rosario, Mendoza, and other cities of the country, powerful entrepreneurial organizations, affiliated with even more-powerful European organizations, enslaved an unbelievable number of young women lured or forced to leave their European villages to become the merchandise of a very profitable trade in a wide variety of brothels.[28]

Just one of the organizations, known as the Zwi Migdal, owned 2,000 brothels where 30,000 women were each producing monthly an average of 3,000 Argentine pesos for their pimps.[29] To put this amount in due perspective, I should remind the reader that at that time the peso had the same value as the dollar, and that a sales clerk in a department store would earn less than 100 pesos per month. This gave the exploiters a tremendous financial power, and they used it to buy cooperation and loyalty from police, city and immigration officers, judges, ministers, medical doctors, and congressmen.

Who sustained such a large demand? Although for different reasons, all social classes made their contributions. The rich were looking for the merriment and diversity of sexual practices that they would never dare to ask from their wives, the respectable matrons whose aim was only to bear and raise children, manage households, and organize social activities. The poor came to brothels because either they had to prove to themselves everyday by using many women that they were *machos*, or because they were feeling lonely. Loneliness was particularly harsh on the immigrants to the large cities, who initially were without family or social groups with which to relate. But the poor native *porteûo machos*[30] also often felt lonely, frustrated, and sad. They put these feelings into music and created the tango. One of the tangos declares: "In my life I had many, many chicks, but never a loving woman."[31]

Bully *porteûos* would mix in the brothels with long-shoremen, sailors, farmers seeking city fun, employees of government offices, banks, and large stores, small businessmen taking a break from their shops, and youths having their first experiences. Brothels varied in size and amenities according to the class they were catering to. Most were just a succession of small rooms that barely accommodated a double-size bed. In the remaining space, a chair would provide a place for the customer's clothes, and a washbowl would be the only available means for the customer's and prostitute's hygiene. A typical construction would be two rows of ten rooms, each with a latrine at the end of each row. In the more-expensive brothels, there would be a grand receiving hall with sofas, vases, and paintings on the walls. There, rooms were more spacious and some would have mirrors on walls and ceilings. They were the places for the rich who could afford to pay from 5 to 15 pesos.[32]

The white-slave traffic to Argentina continued growing during the last two decades of the 19th century and the first three decades of the 20th century. Already in 1892, a German magazine, *Das Echos*, commented on a trial that took place in Lemberg, Austria, where 22 persons were condemned for sending young women to different parts of the world under the pretext that they would be employed as maids, cooks, and nursemaids. Because the defendants were Jews, the magazine, in addition to denouncing an abominable trade, used the case to encourage anti-Semitic undercurrents of German politics that would open up in the German political arena some decades later.[33]

Between 1920 and 1930, Albert Londres, an officer of the French Sureté Genérale investigating the ramifications of the international white-slave traffic, decided to mix himself in the life of the small Polish villages where many of the women were bought or seduced. He finally published a book, *Le Chemin de Buenos Aires* (*The Way to Buenos Aires*), whose influence among Argentines who were fighting to stop the traffic proved to be decisive.[34]

Meanwhile, homosexuals, outcasts of Argentine society until recently, were, on the one hand, persecuted by the police, and, on the other hand, using some prostitutes and their madams for their own purposes. In Buenos Aires, for instance, a group of wealthy and influential, but closeted homosexuals organized young prostitutes to lure handsome young men into luxurious orgies in specially arranged places. They would be unwittingly photographed, and the pictures would be used to blackmail them into providing sexual favors to the hosts of the orgies.[35]

Finally the empire built by the traffickers, which was facilitated by the regulation of the exercise of prostitution, was destroyed when the government moved to the opposite behavior and made organized prostitution illegal. Never was the Argentine market really a free market for sexual services, meaning by this, a market where the suppliers chose the profession out of their own free will, exercised it on their own and for their own benefit, and could enter and exit the market freely. Only very recently is it possible to see a type of prostitution that can be assimilated to small businesses.

## From Regulation to Prohibition

The Argentine empire of whoredom was born and grew up sheltered by the regulated status of the brothels under laws and decrees whose declared purpose was to protect both suppliers and consumers of sexual services. In fact, it protected neither and only served to replace risky capitalistic forms of exploitation of sexual services with a capitalism of political patronage that benefited bureaucrats and scoundrels.

Regulation of prostitution is always based on the premise that prostitution is an inevitable evil, hence, it should be regulated in order to minimize the damages to society from its practice. Some of the regulatory decrees dictated by city councils in Argentina were quite detailed in their requirements. One included the following rules:[36]

- To establish a brothel, it was necessary to file an application with the municipality indicating the location. A tax was required.
- The buildings had to be placed in a given zone, and not display any particular sign that would identify it as a brothel. They also had to have a bedroom for each woman working in the brothel. Prostitutes could not reside anywhere other than at the brothel, which was her official domicile. The women could not show themselves at the balconies or through the windows of the building, nor could they solicit in the streets.

- To work in a given brothel, each woman had to be registered with the sanitary authorities, who during the registration process, had to establish when the woman arrived to the city, from where she came and how, who was with her during the trip, and how she decided to join the brothel. If, from the interrogatory, it was established that the woman was a victim of deceit or coercion, she had to be advised that she could sue the offender and be offered assistance to do so.
- Each prostitute was then given a "sanitary notebook" with her picture, personal data, registration number, and the main articles of the decree that concerned her rights as provider of a service, among which were the following:
  - Whatever commitments she might undertake, she was free to stay or quit the brothel in which she lived and worked.
  - The woman who managed the brothel could not compel them to buy given clothes or other objects.
  - Debts were no reason to compel them to stay in a given brothel.
  - Nobody could exert violence of any kind on them, or submit them to abuse and punishments.

Later on, at the request of the Argentine Association Against White Slave Traffic, a page was added to the "sanitary notebook," stating in Spanish, German, French, Yiddish, English, and Italian:

> This is a free country. Nobody can be compelled to work as a prostitute. Whoever wants to exit from the profession can contact [here the name and address of the organization was given] that will see to her defense and help her.

In this notebook, the City Sanitary Services recorded the results of the mandatory periodical medical examinations. If the woman was found to be infected with a disease, she was to be taken to a hospital and remain there until dismissal. The sanitary notebook had to be shown to any customer that would request it to attest to her health condition.

The madam managing a brothel could not leave the brothel for more than 24 hours without notifying the sanitary authorities, who had to authorize leaves in writing and never for more than 15 days. She also could not accept any prostitute in the brothel who had not first registered and passed a medical examination. She had to take her pupils personally to the periodical medical examination at a hospital or have them ready if the examination was done at the site, in which case the brothel had to have a special room equipped with all the furniture and instruments the sanitary authorities requested. The madam also had to report immediately to the sanitary authorities whenever a prostitute felt ill, whether it be from a sexually transmitted or any other type of disease. If the woman could not be taken to the sanitary authority, a doctor would examine her at the brothel and decide whether to send her to a hospital.

It is easy to imagine the gigantic corruption that this naive attempt to protect customers and suppliers generated. The big trade organizations mentioned above bought the protection of the police, who were in charge of enforcing the regulations, and bribed justices and politicians, who all ignored the transgressions in favor of concentrating on the humanitarian provisions aimed at avoiding deceit and violence, and at protecting, at least partially, the free exercise of the profession. In reality, this approach did little to protect the health of the women and their clients, as elementary mathematics show.

With an average of ten daily services per woman and two examinations per week, and accepting that the exami-

nations were thoroughly performed, which often was not the case, only the first client after the examination could be considered free from contracting a venereal disease. The women had no protection from customers already infected. Hence the chances of safe sex for the other 30 or 40 clients that would visit the same woman before she went to the next examination were constantly decreasing. We should remember that the customers were not subject to compulsory medical control, and that many might not have shown any symptom for some time, while others would suffer in silence and continue practicing sex with prostitutes, lovers, and wives.

Although there are no official statistics from that period, we know from studies made by some concerned physicians, and from the clamor in the press, that the number of cases of gonorrhea and syphilis kept increasing. From a study by the director of the sanitary services of Rosario, Dr. José M. Fernandez, we learn that the examinations practiced during one year—October 1, 1930, through September 30, 1931—revealed that 73% of the prostitutes had a positive serological reaction to syphilis and close to 100% of them were carriers of gonococcus.[37]

Finally, a law was promulgated by the federal government on December 30, 1935, ordering the closure of all brothels throughout the nation. It even criminalized the provision of sexual services by a single person in her own home.

Anticipating this abrupt policy change, several measures were taken by public institutions and grassroots organizations to protect the women that the law would leave without job and home.

### *The Situation Today*

The 1935 law ended the corrupting empire of large organizations involved in the white-slave traffic, but it could not end the exercise of individual prostitution. The application of the law to individual prostitution was even declared unconstitutional, because Article 19 of the Argentine Constitution says: "Private activities that do not affect public order and morality and do not harm other people are reserved to the judgment of God and off-limits to the authority of magistrates."

Hence, an adult person who by spontaneous decision engages in sex with other consenting adults, for money or otherwise, cannot be penalized unless the practice takes place in such a way that it offends or harms third parties.

On the other hand, the change in mores that took place in the world after World War II was strongly felt in Argentina. Internally, the Perónist movement drastically elevated the status of the working class, including rural labor, and Eva Perón's actions sped the recognition of women's political, economic, and social rights. The large masses of single immigrants, to whom the brothel provided a recreational and physiological outlet, are pictures from a distant past. The *machos* of the suburbs of Buenos Aires and other big cities are drowned by a wave of proud blue-collar workers who may have consenting lovers in addition to their official spouses, but would never exploit one or the other. Contraceptives and information about them reach women and men of all social classes. For quite a while, penicillin brought control over venereal diseases. All this allowed women to consent to premarital and extramarital sexual relations.

However, prostitution has not disappeared. Teenagers, sometimes by their own initiative, but more often under the pressure of peers or their fathers, seek prostitutes for their sexual initiation. Then there are the handicapped and those who do not dare to share with lovers and spouses their need for special sexual practices. And as always, sailors and other single travelers from the countryside and abroad. Single women and married men with hidden homosexual or bisexual tendencies are also asking for sexual services. Hence, male prostitutes have made their appearance in the market.

The modern Argentine male and female prostitutes advertise their services through newspapers. A typical announcement reads: FIRST NAME; Your place or mine from Monday to Sunday; Telephone number. Some include the price. In one single issue of a popular newspaper, I found eight advertisements with prices ranging from 15 pesos to 40 pesos, which equaled the same amount of dollars in 1993 exchange.

Another form of advertising is the use of taxi drivers and hotel bell captains as intermediaries. These agents receive part of the price in exchange for referring clients. In the large hotels, the bell captains may have an album with pictures of different prostitutes from which the guest may choose.

Sex titillation by phone is also making its inroads. It is being introduced by representatives of foreign organizations. Romance through the line, as one of the announcements reads, is offered by calling a number in the United States, Hong Kong, or Mexico.

The spread of AIDS has further reduced direct trade of services and has made room for these telephone and other electronic alternatives. They are used for those who do not find a way to create romance and introduce fantasy in their relationships. Most of the well-informed youth are now seeking to satisfy all their sexual needs through a committed relationship that may or may not end in marriage. Usually, they contract marriage when they decide to have children. Among homosexuals, who are now more accepted by society, there is also a trend toward less promiscuity and more-stable monogamous relations.

Prostitution is still a topic of discussion in the news media and for journalists. It is becoming clear that prostitution is a cultural as well as an economic problem. A morality that denies and represses bodily needs will never solve the problem. It can only increase the demand for commercial providers of sexual services. And a society where greed on one side creates poverty on the other will inevitably create greedy profiteers and needy prostitutes.

## C. Sex in Argentine Mass Media: Erotica and Pornography

*Literature*

A review of the Argentine literature of the last few decades shows that Argentine writers often describe in detail heterosexual, gay, and lesbian sexual encounters in their novels. The practice of sprinkling some sexual spices to add flavor to the narration is not limited to romantic novels; it occurs also in historical novels, and indeed in psychological novels that delve deep into the feelings of their characters.

This literature has led middle-class urban readers to rethink their own attitude towards sexuality and sensuality. It helps in lifting the last traces of *machismo*, of seeing love and sex as two separate things that are practiced with different women, and of perceiving homosexuality as a perversity. In a historical novel set between 1851 and 1862, for instance, Martha Mercader, a famous novelist, defines in just one sentence the most common mindset among young military men in the first armies of the equally young Republic: "He [the protagonist of the novel, an adjutant in the recently organized National Guard] must always be on top; on top of Indians, of the blacks, of the *gauchos*, of the peasants, and of the females."[38]

This same novelist dared to reveal her own sensual and sexual life in an autobiography in which she describes her puberty within a family and a society hampered by a multitude of taboos, the fantasies of her adolescence fueled by the movies that Hollywood sent to Argentina in the 1940s, the difficulties women had to choose freely and assume responsibilities, her conflicts with the rigid mindset of an intellectual husband that was progressive in his ideology and conservative in his social and sexual behavior, and conflicts that ended in a sour divorce. Her personal history illustrates the limitations to which women were, and, to some extent, are still often subjected. For some, the limitations amounted to a veritable enslavement.[39]

When we compare the historical novels published in the 1980s by this writer with the books of the same genre published in the 1970s by another famous Argentine writer, Beatriz Guido, we perceive the advances made in language openness and in acknowledging women's feelings, their desires, their erotic fantasies, and their voluptuous carnality.

For instance, in one of her books,[40] Beatriz Guido describes the initiation of two young men with prostitutes. It is a description almost devoid of emotions: The two adolescents do not even ask one another about how they performed. They leave the brothel in silence and walk through the streets talking economics. The scene reflects what was then acceptable in Argentine society.

By contrast, Martha Mercader, in another of her novels,[41] talking through a heroine of the time of the war among provincial *caudillos*, recounts the sufferings of innumerable Argentine women of the past and reveals things that today's Argentine women are still longing for. The main character questions, already in the 1830s, the role of reproductive machines that the Church has assigned to women. She is a woman that is consumed by passion for life and yearns for opportunities to share with her husband both her sensual desires and her intellectual potential, her abilities to perceive the social, political, and even military situation in which they live. By insisting on doing so, she destroys her relationship that cannot survive a destabilization of the macho role of her husband. Through Juana Manuela, her character, Martha is calling for further changes in a society that still is repressive and castrating.

It is worth mentioning a rare book discovered while browsing in an old bookstore of a provincial city. Its title is *Textos Eróticos del Rio de la Plata (Erotic Texts from the River Plate)* by Robert Lehmann Nitsche, a German anthropologist.[42] It was published originally in Leipzig, Germany, in 1923, under the pen name of Victor Borde, and includes an exhaustive collection of popular songs, poems, proverbs, riddles, sentences, and remarks with a high sexual, sensual, and erotic content. In 1956, after Julian Caceres Freyre, an Argentine scholar, obtained a copy of the German original from a bibliophile friend, a group of entrepreneurial editors undertook the task of translating it into Spanish. The 1981 Spanish edition contains the full original text, plus an article anonymously published by Lehmann in the journal *Kryptadia* in 1901.[43]

Lehmann arrived in Buenos Aires in 1897 to work at the Anthropological Museum of La Plata, the capital of the province of Buenos Aires, when he was only 25 years old, and resided there until 1930. Compelled by his curiosity and animated by a truly scientific passion for honest and forthright research, Lehmann did not hesitate to survey all sources, from ordinary rural folks to prostitutes and pimps. He questioned his students at the University of La Plata and gathered graffiti from public latrines, restrooms, and from prison walls. His work has rescued from oblivion popular customs and traditions that progress would consign to burial without a trace, because Argentine scholars considered them too vulgar and embarrassing to be scientifically studied.

Lehmann used the material he compiled to compare popular myths, prejudices, and stereotypes, some of which are still part of the collective Argentine subconscious. He dared to undertake this task at a point in the evolution of humankind when sexuality was still a bad word even in Europe, where he had to publish the result of his work either anonymously or under a false name.

After 1933, the Nazis tried to use Lehmann in their intelligence network about Argentina, given the deep knowledge the scientist had of the country, but he refused and was ostracized from the scientific community until his death in 1938.

To give the readers a flavor of this collector's work, I provide translations of one each of its riddles, sayings, and limericks. Riddles are usually innocent, but the solution is sexually charged (see Table 2).

*Popular Magazines*

It is through popular magazines that we can see more clearly the changes taking place in Argentine society. The numerous, so-called magazines for women are found everywhere: homes, hairdressers, doctor's offices, almost any place there is a waiting room. And in almost every issue, there are articles about sex and eroticism, some signed by respected local and foreign professionals. Articles cover a variety of subjects, such as contraception, the influence of a healthy sexual life on the physical and mental well-being of women, or how to improve marital relationships. Three other types of magazines deal with sexuality and eroticism:

- Magazines that deal with sexual issues avoiding pornographic images, shying away from even full frontal nudity. They are rather expensive, exhibit a good quality of printing, and aim at informing a public that accepts a scientific, although popular, rather than academic language. One such magazine claims the collaboration of professionals from the Masters and Johnson Institute and the American Association of Sex Educators, Counselors, and Therapists to produce illustrative videos that are distributed together with some of the issues. One such issue included the following subjects: best techniques to enjoy an intense sexuality; the skin: an ally of eroticism; how to make of your bedroom the most erotic place; your way of kissing reveals how you make love; techniques to renew sexual passion without changing partners; initiation to anal sex without traumas; the art of

undressing to seduce your partner; the importance of oral sex during pregnancy; safe sex: condoms, a way of taking care of yourself without handicapping your pleasure.
- Magazines of sexual humor with pornographic texts and cartoons, but no pictures.
- Clearly pornographic magazines, devoid of any artistic quality, some with scatological content.

Foreign magazines like *Playboy* and *Penthouse* can also be bought in some newsstands.

*Television and the Video Industry*

With the return of democracy in 1983, it became possible to openly discuss and present sexual issues on television. Well-known physicians, psychiatrists, psychologists, sexologists, and writers are invited by popular anchorpersons and questioned on all kind of sexual matters.

This situation contrasts with an experience I had in the early 1970s. As medical advisor to an Argentine enterprise, I was helping to design a strategy to introduce the first tampon manufactured in Argentina, a task of which I felt very proud, because it would allow Argentine professional and working-class women to feel more comfortable at their workplace. However, I soon discovered that the word "menstruation" could not be used in advertising the product on television or in newspapers and magazines.

Argentine television programs are now following on the line of pioneer shows in the United States and Europe that favor participation of the public and encourage them to share in a discussion of intimate problems. Argentines who know the languages can now receive these American programs, and also European programs, directly on their screens through satellite and cable.

The videotape industry is partially handicapped by the fact that Argentine television uses the so-called PAL system that cannot play either VHS or Betamax recorded cassettes. The market is composed mainly of foreign video pornography converted to the PAL system and subtitled in Spanish. It is a new market where a fast-growing demand is allowing businesses to make good profits. X-rated material is displayed in a separate room limited to adults who pay the store fees and deposit.

However, legislative revisions have not kept pace with changing public attitudes, and the old laws are used from time to time to crack down on the video-pornography business. In 1994, for instance, more than 300 titles were sequestered from one establishment and the store closed on the grounds that Article 128 of the Criminal Code considers obscene exhibitions as assaults against public morality. Some politicians and judges seem to still be under the grip of a repressive mentality, but many of them, and certainly the public in the large cities, are reacting and fighting for their freedom to see and read what pleases them. Despite obstructions from conservative forces, the public's preferences are being respected. The higher courts are also reversing conservative decisions from lower courts, although desperately slowly.

---

**Table 2**

**Riddles Are Usually Innocent, But the Solution Is Sexually Charged**

| Type of Erotic Text | Original Text | English Free Translation | Comments |
|---|---|---|---|
| Riddle | En un campo monterano<br>Hay un pájaro francés,<br>Tiene huevos y no pone,<br>Tiene un ojo y no ve. | In a hunting field<br>There is a French bird,<br>It has eggs, but doesn't lay<br>It has an eye, but doesn't see. | The solution is the penis. Popularly, the testicles are called eggs. |
| Saying | A toro viejo<br>le gusta el<br>pasto tierno. | Old bulls like<br>tender pastures. | |
| Limerick | ¡Puta que soy<br>desgraciada!,<br>Dice la parda Loreta;<br>¡Todos me meten por el culo<br>Y ninguno por la cajeta! | Shit! I am so depressed,<br>says the mulatto Loreta;<br>It is always my ass that is holed,<br>never my cunt. | |

*Movies, Theater, and the Arts*

Most of the erotic films shown in Argentina, films that would be rated R or X in the U.S.A., come from European countries, particularly France, Italy, Sweden, and lately Spain. Picaresque films, many based on classics of literature, such as Boccacio's *Decameron* or Chaucer's *Canterbury Tales*, are shown without censoring their most realistic details, which may include frontal nudity. The United States is the source of all the violent pornography and thrillers imported.

After the return of democracy, the Argentine cinema industry has itself produced many risqué films. One describes a famous historical case of a young Argentine priest and a young lady of the Argentine aristocracy who fell desperately in love in the years just before the organization of the Republic. They leave family and Church to escape from Buenos Aires to the countryside. However, the combined powers of Church, money, and state persecute them implacably until they are detained and executed without trial. Because she is pregnant, the executioners gave her to drink a liter of holy water before facing the squad, so as to make sure that her child would die baptized. The film describes the tragedy in beautiful and poignant images, without sparing the torrid love scenes of the distressed lovers when they find themselves for the first time alone and far from their asphyxiating social environment.

There is also a mild censorship in the theater. A play called *La Lección de Anatomía* (*The Anatomy Lesson*), in which the actors play their role in the nude, was playing for a long time in Buenos Aires, night after night, for nearly ten years.

In galleries of art, nudes are shown without hesitation or shyness. However, in the contradictory society that Argentina is, with regressive forces battling for survival and power, isolated episodes of censorship still happen, although a slowly operating judicial system repairs the damages in the end. For instance, in 1986, three photographic artists who were exhibiting their work at a cultural center found their pictures of nude people sequestered. The judge who issued the order resisted pressure from colleagues and public opinion, and the appeal of the lawyers of the defendants, for almost a year before returning the material to their owners.

Finally, the popular tango, whether danced in private salons or presented as part of a theatrical show, is often a display of eroticism at its purest macho style, the male proudly exhibiting his skills, his strength, and his power over women.

## 9. Contraception, Abortion, and Population Planning

### A/B. Contraception and Population Planning

It is estimated that the population of what is today Latin America was around 50 million at the start of its conquest by Spain and Portugal.[44] Wars, brutal exploitation in mines and fields, and new diseases acquired from the conquerors because a lack of antibodies among the indigenous populations soon depopulated the continent. The conquerors then resorted to two policies: In some colonies, they started importing Africans as slave labor, and in all colonies, they promoted maximum use of women's fertility, whether they be Spanish, native, or African. Every child, whether from wedlock or not, was welcomed.

Pronatalist policies were maintained after independence. The new countries needed people, first to sustain the wars of independence, then feed the armies of local warring lords, and later to develop the empty lands. More recently, it was believed that a large population would keep salaries low, neglecting the fact that impoverished masses do not make good consumer markets for the products and services that enterprises generate. Despite the influence of Catholicism, the concept of family has remained very lax. This explains why the number of illegitimate children has continued to run high. In some countries, it averages, even recently, 70% of all newborns.[45]

Argentina has not been an exception to these pronatalist policies and the use of women as reproductive machines. However, its population did not grow as fast as in other Latin American countries. This is because of the formation of a well-informed large middle class that could not support families of the size that was usual among the upper class, and at the same time, did not share the loose idea about family ties expressed by the lower class. Middle-class couples quickly learned to use contraceptives acquired through private channels. In Argentina, contraceptives never were distributed or subsidized by the government, except for the army draftees who were given condoms for prophylactic reasons rather than population concerns.

During a relatively recent period, 1975-1983, during which the country was governed by repressive military juntas, there was an attempt to encourage larger families by giving monetary awards for each newborn, and by paralyzing the activity of the clinics privately supported by the Argentine Association for the Protection of the Family. Besides the fact that the amount of money was ridiculously small, the military ignored the real feelings of the women of the urban working class. They had a different program in mind than to have a lot of children. From my own work as a gynecologist at a union-supported hospital, I know their reasoning. They wanted to save from their salaries and buy a sewing machine or other equipment that would allow them to do some market work at home, postponing maternity until the couple's joint income would allow them to raise one or two children decently.

In the year 1972, the Argentine Association for the Protection of the Family managed 58 clinics around the country. That year, the number of new users of contraceptives was 23,000. Of these, 66% preferred the pill and 33% chose an IUD. The clinics were also offering services for the early detection of genital cancer and the treatment of infertility.

Nowadays, in the large cities, contraceptives of all kinds—pills, condoms, diaphragms, IUDs, and vaginal spermicides—are available. Condoms, pills, and vaginal spermicides can be freely bought in pharmacies. Women who can afford to pay, can use the services of private physicians to help them acquire the right diaphragm or to insert an IUD. Hospitals and clinics supported by the labor unions provide similar services to working women and spouses of workers.

The situation is more difficult for women who live in scarcely populated distant rural areas. There, both birthrates and infant mortality are still high when compared with urban figures or those in the more-developed rural areas close to the large cities. In the less-developed areas, the government is now trying to organize family planning services as part of its program of mother-child care.

[*Update 2003*: There are no programs related to reproductive health at the national level. At the provincial level, the situation varies from one province to the other, depending on two fundamental factors. One is the magnitude of resources assigned to public health in general, and to reproductive health in particular, in each provincial budget. The other factor hinges on the predominant political influence in the respective province. This last factor refers to the longstanding conflict in Argentina's policymaking between, on the one hand, liberal leaders with a modern consciousness and concerns for the needs of the population, and, on the other hand, conservative leaders associated with an obsolete Catholic Church that still adamantly represses the modern expressions of sexuality, love, and life.

[Until 1998, the federal government was assigning some 4% of the GDP to public health, and close to 90% of the population had access to sanitation (World Bank Development Report 1999). That year, it was decided to transfer to the provinces the responsibility to cover 87% of the cost of their respective health systems. The majority of the provinces have neither sufficient funds, nor the appropriate leadership to articulate those programs.

[The country is now calling for a very different approach: a comprehensive national health program that includes reproductive health and links to educational reforms that introduce those subjects in all curricula. It was expected that educational establishments at all levels would teach their students how to take care of their health and to enjoy the physical, emotional, and spiritual manifestations of their sexuality with responsibility towards themselves, their partners, and the economy of their households and the nation, avoiding unwanted pregnancies and sexually transmitted diseases. The undersecretariat for population that was created in 1993 at the federal level, which included a federal counsel on population, was dedicated mainly to demographic studies and regulation of migration. It did not assume any initiative to promote policies or educational programs for a responsible procreation.

[We will mention only a few examples of the diverse provincial efforts that attempt to organize programs of reproductive health overcoming precariousness of financial resources and ideological conflicts.

1. City of Buenos Aires

   The city's constitution declares that the reproductive and sexual rights are part of the basic human rights, and proclaims nondiscrimination in the exercise of those rights for neither ethnic, racial, or gender reasons, nor for the sexual orientation of the citizens.

2. Mendoza, Rio Negro and Neuquén

   These provinces have similar laws on reproductive health and sexuality. They aim at providing information and organizing counseling services.

3. Jujuy

   In spite of the governor's opposition, who vetoed an initial project, the legislature unanimously insisted on approving a law creating a provincial program for maternity and the prevention of sexually transmitted diseases.

4. Santa Fe

   The municipality of Rosario, the most important city of this province, enforced two decrees: one creating a program for the early detection of cervical cancer, and another organizing a comprehensive program on women's health.

5. Entre Rios

   The legislature voted a law whose objective was to provide information and advice for a healthy and responsible exercise of sexuality. The governor vetoed it.

6. San Luis

   One of the most interesting experiments is taking place in this province. Working together with private organizations, the government has presented a project for a law of reproductive health that was accepted by the legislature, and is expected to soon be regulated and implemented. The activity of Gaia, a private group headed by Laura Lerner Emmer—who is joined in participation by local professionals and educators—deserves to be emphasized. They organized a Latin American encounter, "Being Born in 2002," to discuss themes centered on love, family relations, procreation, and birth. Among the subjects explored at the encounter, we find: love and sexuality, methods for dealing with fertility and childlessness and the ethical problems raised by those methods, relations between parents and children, problems faced by single mothers and fathers, and new ways of looking after pregnant women and of delivering babies. The encounter is also a good example of efforts to transform the old unfortunate antinomies among ideologies, beliefs, and interests into constructive participatory polarities. "Being Born in 2002" was sponsored by UNICEF, the government of the province of San Luis, the municipality of the city of San Luis, the National University of San Luis, the Catholic University of Cuyo, and various foundations and private professional groups (Gaiasanluis).

7. Tucumán

   In the past, this was a rich province, known as "the garden of the republic" for the fertility of its land and the beauty of its subtropical vegetation and breathtaking panoramas. Now, it offers a deplorable picture of misery and neglect. The chaotic state of the finances of the province has reached such extremes as not to be able to provide gauze and alcohol for surgery in the public hospitals. Children die of hunger or survive in a state of cachexia. "Problems that we used to see in photographs from Africa, now we are facing them here," said Dr. Teresa Acuña, a pediatrician in one of the hospitals (Rohter 2003). Indigent women in despair seek abortions, which, because of the way they are performed, often end in deaths, which are hidden in the statistics under other gynecological categories. There are no programs for reproductive healthcare. At the initiative of some doctors, and with the support of pharmaceutical companies, oral contraceptives are now be given free to poor women, who, in some cases, sell them to buy bread. There are no programs to give advice on contraceptive technologies and monitor their use. (*End of update by S. Kamenetzky*)]

## C. Abortion

Everybody who practices gynecology in Argentina knows that abortion is widely used by women of all social classes to end unwanted pregnancies. This happens despite the injunction against abortion in the Argentine Criminal Code that penalizes with prison women who have abortions and the professionals who perform this service, with the sole exception of a pregnant woman who is mentally deranged. Abortions are common despite the strong influence on personal lives and politics of the dominant Catholic Church.

Abortion is a practice that everybody knows of and practices when needed, but nobody talks about. Argentina is a society that, instead of fighting against the powerful forces that arrogate to themselves control over women's bodies, prefers to tolerate the officially condemned practice with a mischievous twinkle of tacit agreement among professionals and citizens. Criminal processes and denunciation of abortion practices are rare, and the police only intervene when a woman dies as a consequence of an abortion practiced by a nonprofessional.

Given these conditions, there are no figures for abortion in Argentina, but it is believed that its practice is widespread in all Latin America. In 1974, the International Planned Parenthood Federation estimated that some five million abortions were performed each year in the region. This corresponds to a rate of 65 abortions for each 1,000 women of reproductive age, and to 500 abortions for each 1,000 live births.[46]

In the cities, women who typically seek medical help for abortions are either married, mature women who already have several children, or very young single women, high school and college students. That women resort to abortion mainly to put a stop to the increase of family size was confirmed by surveys organized by the Centro Latinoamericano de Demografia (CELADE).[47] In Buenos Aires, women with two children reported 39.6 abortions per 1,000 women in their lifetimes, while women with three children reported 93.5 per 1,000.

Studies on the relationship between abortion and socioeconomic position suggested that middle-class women resorted to abortion more frequently than upper- or lower-class women. More-recent studies, in Buenos Aires during the 1960s and 1970s, revealed that the highest rate of abortion was among women with college educations. These studies tells us two things: one, that women of the upper classes can afford to raise more children than they would really want, hence avoiding inner conflicts with their deep-seated religious programming, as well as outer conflicts with their social Catholic environment; second, that abortions among the lower classes leave no written or oral record, because they are not performed by professionals, and the women deny having them to avoid problems for themselves and for those who helped them in the procedure.

When abortion is performed by obstetricians in clinics or their offices following state-of-the-art procedures, with instruments duly sterilized, use of anesthesia, and post-operation care to avoid hemorrhages and infections, it seldom leads to complications. It is quite different when abortion is practiced by folk healers and unregistered midwives, with neither asepsis nor anesthesia and using primitive instruments. It is even worse when rural women in despair resort to pouring chemicals inside their vaginas, ingest toxic substances they have heard induce abortion, or use wires and the like to destroy the fetus. The end results are hemorrhages that lead to death if the woman cannot reach a hospital for a transfusion, or infections that may also lead to death if untreated. Other frequent ailments produced by these crude abortion procedures are the destruction of the vaginal walls, and the production of adhesions on the uterine endometrium.

In the end, many of these women who provoke an abortion by themselves or with inexperienced help end up in obstetric and gynecological wards of national and provincial hospitals, overloading an already tight supply of beds, blood, drugs, and medical time. Again, there are no statistics for Argentina, but it is estimated that one of every five beds in those wards are occupied by women suffering complications from self-induced or poorly performed abortions, and statistics for Latin America disclose that up to 41% of all blood used in hospitals is consumed by those cases.[48]

This picture of individual suffering and high social costs indicates a need to change policies. Abortion rates and morbidity and mortality from their complications can only be reduced by:

- providing appropriate sexual education and stimulating the use of contraceptives;
- legalizing abortion to take the procedure out of inexperienced or desperate hands, making it, instead, easily available from well-trained professionals; and
- increasing accessibility to well-equipped medical centers in case of complications.

[*Update 2003*: Abortion continues to be illegal, with two exceptions: for the pregnant woman's life or health. These two exceptions are very seldom used, because, although the law does not require authorization from the judi-

cial system for such an abortion, health professions are reluctant to go ahead on their own, and equally reluctant to seek court approval. Inexperienced people, in sordid environments and with no asepsis, perform most abortions. This should cause alarm among the public health institutions. The total number of abortions is overwhelming. The Center for Reproductive Law and Policy (CRLP) estimates that the incidence of abortion in Argentina is somewhere between 350,000 and 400,000 abortions annually. Although it is estimated that one third of all maternal deaths are caused by abortion, the real number may be higher, because some may be hidden under other gynecological or obstetric areas (CRLP 2000).

[Rather than focusing on the costs to the economy and to the health of the Argentine family, the public discussion continues to center around ideological issues. Sexual education from an early age, and easy access to contraceptives when the age of reproduction is reached, could save money and lives, not only by avoiding abortions, but also by preventing the spread of sexually transmitted diseases. While under the present legislation, women are chastised and the medical profession is handcuffed, a wider understanding of human nature, with its need of a healthy sexuality, could make both women and men more free, and family life more happy. (*End of update by S. Kamenetzky*)]

## 10. Sexually Transmitted Diseases and HIV/AIDS

### A. Sexually Transmitted Diseases

In Argentina, the most frequently reported sexually transmitted diseases (STDs) are trichomoniasis, genital chlamydia, gonorrhea, genital herpes, syphilis, genital papilloma virus, chancroid, and indeed AIDS. There is a worrisome increase in the number of cases of the traditional STDs, particularly syphilis, gonorrhea, and human papilloma virus. Risky as they are on their own, they also increase the susceptibility to acquire genital cancer and HIV infections.

In the field of STDs, Argentina is a prime example of a global trend that took the total number of cases in the world to 250 million in 1990, at a rate of 685,000 new cases each day.[49] From 1987 through 1991, the number of cases of gonorrhea decreased in 15 Latin American countries, but not those of primary or secondary syphilis. Twelve of these countries also saw an increase in congenital syphilis. Although most of these figures are only approximate, they tell us that there is an urgent need to mobilize all the available technologies to check the spread of these diseases,

The real numbers are difficult to obtain. Some diseases that present undramatic symptoms are initially ignored. A case in point is chlamydia, which is only detected in 70% of the cases when women come for other reasons for a gynecological examination. Once detected, the cases are only reported to the healthcare authorities if the examination took place in a public hospital; private medical offices are not required to report this disease.

The lack of an appropriate sexual education among all social classes, an attitude of indifference and/or shame in relation to prophylactic measures, and a medical system that is not well prepared for early detection and treatment, all combine to increase the rate at which STDs are growing. Exceptions are the detection and treatment of syphilis and gonorrhea. The pronatalist policies of Argentina since the organization of the country has meant that doctors were trained and medical services organized to take special care of the health of pregnant mothers and newborns.

This occurs in three different medical environments. The most advanced environment is provided by private medical practices in doctors' offices and *sanatorios*.[50] In this privileged environment, only prejudice or ignorance can prevent doctors from providing timely prophylactic advice, early diagnosis, and appropriate treatment of STDs.

Another environment is made up of the *sanatorios* organized and supported by the labor unions. The number and size of medical institutions of this type increased steadily from 1946 through 1955 during the populist administration of Juan Domingo Perón and his activist wife, Evita. Some, like the one owned by the Association of Metal Workers in Buenos Aires, were well-equipped and responded to the needs of the working class, supplying information on STDs and providing early detection and advanced treatment services. In others, equipment and services had to adjust to lesser resources. Neither individual labor unions nor their confederation ever issued policies related to the kind of services to be provided in their *sanatorios* for STDs. It all depended on the caliber and convictions of the medical personnel who were hired as management and staff. However, the wards of dermatology, urology, gynecology, and obstetrics of these union-supported medical services have helped large numbers of workers and their families to become aware of the risks of STDs and have induced them to seek early detection and treatment.

The last environment is provided by the hospitals supported by the federal and provincial governments and the municipalities. They are entrusted with two missions: One is to provide medical services to the poorest sectors of the population, those who do not have access to either private nor union-supported medical services; the other is to serve as training grounds for the students of medicine from the public universities, which in Argentina are the most prestigious. Initially, services provided at hospitals were totally free, but the disastrous management of Argentina's economy for more than 50 years slowly eroded their physical and human assets. Recently, these facilities have been charging a small fee as a contribution to the huge recurrent and investment costs involved in their maintenance.

This small fee may further discourage the population from the shantytowns in the poverty belts around the large cities from seeking early diagnosis and treatment for STDs. Although public transportation is relatively cheap and efficient, they are already discouraged by having to make more than one trip to the hospital before being given their diagnosis, and by being unable to obtain the necessary medications once the diagnosis is made.

Prostitutes form another segment of the population of the large cities that requires special consideration. In Buenos Aires, children of both sexes from the shantytowns pour into the city and become prey of drug traffickers and pimps. Through shared needles and sexual intercourse, they are infected with all kinds of STDs, further contributing to their spread in their original milieus and the city at large.

The picture of three levels of medical services describes properly the situation in Buenos Aires, the other large cities, such as Rosario and Bahia Blanca, and most of the provincial capitals. In the rural areas, we may only find small infirmaries where doctors struggle to help the poor people without having at their disposal either laboratory services or appropriate equipment, such as colposcopes and stocks of drugs for early diagnosis and treatment of STDs. To make things even worse, poor rural people are more easily programmed than their urban counterparts to feel shame and guilt when affected with an STD. This prevents them from asking for medical help even from those elementary healthcare facilities, even at the cost of suffering crucial pain and loss of income, and of spreading STDs to other members of their impoverished societies.

The conditions in which the very poor rural and urban people live may require a different medical approach when dealing with STDs than the now standard scientific approach of first investigating the etiology of the disease and then establishing the appropriate treatment. If the physician tells a poor sick person that he should come again to find out the results of clinical tests, and only then get the prescription and go to the nearest pharmacy for the medication, this person may never return. Meanwhile, the disease may be spread to others. Hence, a syndrome approach has been developed in which the physician examines the person and immediately gives the patient the appropriate medication during the first office visit and at no cost.

It may sound nonsensical to propose this approach, which is widely used in the poorest countries of the world, for use in a country like Argentina that has 2.99 doctors per 1,000 population compared with only 0.03 in Tanzania and 2.38 in the United States, 5 hospital beds per 1,000 population compared again with only 0.9 in Tanzania and 5.3 in United States, but we should realize that there are poverty spots where medical services are well below the average for the country, and that the inhabitants of these poverty spots contribute greatly to the incidence and fast-growing rate of STDs.[51] In poverty-stricken areas, the dilemma for the physician is whether to act quickly on the basis of what he or she sees without waiting for accurate tests, or to wait and, in the process, turn the untreated STD carrier into an uncontrolled spreader.

I could not obtain precise information on the incidence of STDs at the different social levels of Argentine society, but my own experience, from the mid-1950s to the mid-1970s, and the experience of physicians I interviewed while preparing this report, show that a large number of women that come to a medical office or the outpatient services of a hospital for gynecological problems, pregnancy controls, or advice on family planning are infected with STDs.

Consider just one of these diseases, the genital human papilloma virus, which, with 30 million new cases worldwide in 1992, ranks third among STDs.[52] The corresponding increase in the number of cases in Argentina has led to research work and the organization of seminars on the subject. Prominent among these is the work in three hospitals of Buenos Aires under the direction of Dr. Angélica Teyssie, who also acted as vice president of the Third Argentine Congress of Virology. In one of the hospitals, the work centers around the influence of hormones on the development of the disease in pregnant women with lesions in the uterine cervix. A team at another hospital works instead with young men with penile and urethral warts, while the third hospital concentrates on young women with vulvar lesions. The latter are followed to confirm the suspicion that the papilloma virus may be responsible for the onset of cervical cancer as late as five to 30 years after the primary infection.[53]

STDs are having a very negative impact on the Argentine economy. This impact cannot be measured solely in terms of the number of deaths caused by STDs, because many nonfatal conditions are responsible for a great loss of healthy life and significant demands on the healthcare system. A better indicator is the one jointly developed by the World Bank and the World Health Organization, which is the number of disability-adjusted life years (DALYs) lost because of a particular disease or group of diseases in a given time period.

The DALY indicator is obtained through a rather complex statistical process. First, for each death, the number of years of life lost is calculated as the difference between the actual age of death and the expectation of life at that age in a low-mortality population. Then the disability losses are calculated by multiplying the expected duration of a disease (to remission or to death) by a weight factor that measures the severity of the disability in comparison with loss of life—for example a weight factor of 0.22 was assigned to pelvic inflammatory disease, while dementia carries a weight factor of 0.6. Then the combined death and disability losses are further corrected by discounting them at a rate of 3%, so that future years of healthy life are valued at progressively lower levels, and by an age weight, so that years of life lost at different ages are given different relative values. By multiplying these indicators by the total number of deaths for each age and disease and summing up across all ages and conditions, it is possible to figure out the global burden of disease for a given demographic area in millions of DALYs lost in a given year. From these, two other indicators can be derived: the equivalent number of infant deaths that would produce the same effect, and the number of DALYs lost per 1,000 population.

The World Bank and the World Health Organization have estimated that in 1990, Latin America and the Caribbean area was burdened with a loss of 103 million DALYs, which is equivalent to the death of 3.2 million infants and represents an incidence of 233 DALYs per 1,000 population. STDs and HIV accounted for 6.6% of the total, ranking third, after perinatal causes (9.1%) and neuropsychiatric diseases (8%), among the different diseases included in the study. STDs and HIV contribute more to the burden of disease than cancer (5.2%), and cerebrovascular or ischemic heart disease (2.6% and 2.7%, respectively), but less than injuries, which amount to 15% of the total.[54]

Unfortunately, I could not find specific statistics for Argentina, but what I have heard and observed leads me to estimate that the relative contributions of STDs and HIV to the burden of disease is not too different from that for the whole of Latin America. The high burden calls for active intervention by the governments, but a solution is hampered by a lack of information about STDs across all sectors of the population, and by a lack of resources for preventing and curing the disease among the poorest sectors. The latter problem could be solved if the government reallocated its expenditures to provide financial support for essential clinical services. However, government should limit its direct involvement in the provision of the services because it generates an expensive and inefficient bureaucracy; the government should instead promote the participation of grassroots nongovernmental organizations (NGOs) in the task.

Although government and NGOs should also work together in the delivery of information, the government's role in this should be more prominent than in the delivery of services, because the structure of the Argentine educational system makes it easy and cost effective for the government to include sexual education at all levels of the system. Most of the schools are under the authority of either the federal or the provincial governments. There are no local city or county educational boards to interfere with the decisions of what should be taught, and the largest part of Argentine households send their children to the state-supported public schools. Certainly, this is the case for the poorest sectors in both rural and urban areas.

Schools should find the language that is most appropriate for conveying information on STDs to each population group and each geographical area. It should be language able to overcome deep-rooted and long-established feelings of shame and guilt. Schools can be used to teach these subjects not only to children, but also to their parents and the public at large, including the elderly whose sexuality should not be discounted, and who, by becoming better informed, could play a more positive role in reinforcing appropriate behavioral patterns among the younger members of the households to which they belong.

Information useful to counteract the spread of STDs should not be limited to the causes of the disease, its symptoms, and ways of preventing and curing them. Information provided at schools, by social workers, and by NGOs should go well beyond this to develop a positive attitude towards the body, a shame- and guilt-free recognition of instinctive drive, and an ability to establish tradeoffs between the instinctual urges and the constraints imposed to the satisfaction of these urges by the need to build healthy households and societies. Poor peasants and sophisticated urbanites can both understand a well-phrased and well-delivered message that these tradeoffs do not mean a repression of one's erotic life, but rather its enhancement by seeking to make it free of disease.

In the schools of medicine, which are all state-supported, doctors, nurses, and other paramedicals should be enabled to discuss STDs openly and clearly with their clients, avoiding scientific jargon and making them feel at ease when uncovering their bodies and their feelings. Young doctors, nurses, and paramedicals so trained could, in turn, facilitate in-service seminars for older physicians, nurses, and paramedicals who have not received any information on human sexuality.

The task of fighting STDs does not, however, stop with the schools, physician offices, clinics, hospitals, and rural first-aid rooms. It is a task that should involve all social organizations. Private businesses can also play an important role. The traditional Sunday soccer games that attract huge crowds could be used to distribute witty messages on the use of prophylactic measures and the high personal and social costs that result from neglecting them.

Argentina is a society that has to come to terms with the spread of STDs and the factors that contribute to this spread, such as the existence of poverty spots, male and female prostitution, and the consignment of persons with sexual preferences that do not conform with what is considered traditional behavior to a closeted sexual life that becomes much more healthy when it is integrated into all walks of a country's life. Argentina should learn that open discussion is more cost effective than denial when facing problems.

## B. HIV/AIDS

In Latin America, Argentina ranks fourth, after Brazil, Mexico, and Colombia, in the number of people affected with HIV. In December 1993, the Argentine government approved a new plan to fight against the disease that had already afflicted 2,897 persons, while there was an estimated 100,000 other people infected with the virus but not yet showing signs of disease. In the first nine months of 1993, 411 cases were recorded by the Ministry of Public Health and Social Action. It was expected that the total number of cases for that year would reach the 1,000 mark.[55]

Marcelo del Castillo, a physician at the Hospital de Clinicas of Buenos Aires, believes that 30 to 50% of the people infected with HIV or suffering from AIDS are not recorded in the official statistics.[56]

A study by three pediatric hospitals of Buenos Aires—Garrahan, Pedro Elizalde, and Ricardo Gutierrez—found 400 children infected with HIV who were being treated. Of these, 63% lived in suburban areas, 30% within the city limits, and 7% came from other parts of the nation.[57]

Eduardo Lopez, the chief of the department of infectious diseases at the Hospital Gutierrez, told a journalist that most of the treated children die before their third year, and that the earlier the symptoms appear, the worse is the prognosis. Lopez, who received a prize from the National Academy of Medicine for his studies on AIDS, pointed out that 90% of the children are infected by their mothers during pregnancy and delivery.[58]

According to Lopez's studies, 20% of the HIV-positive mothers are 15 to 19 years old, and those below 24 years of age amount to 70% of the total number. Most of them, 59.4%, are addicted to intravenous drugs, while the remaining 35.9% have partners who are HIV-positive and 90% are drug addicts.[59]

These statistics show that the fight against AIDS should be integrated with the fight against the ravages of drug addiction, and that both fights require improved education and delivery of information to the youngest segments of the population. This has been recognized in the governmental plan that proposes to introduce information on these subjects in the high schools and universities starting with the school year 1994.[60] The plan will evaluate the possibility of extending its action to the primary level, and the Ministries of Education, Labor, and Interior will work together with the Youth Institute in forming community leaders who are prepared to deal with the subjects of AIDS and drugs. The plan is quite ambitious. In addition to the already mentioned educational and community work, it includes medical action aimed at providing medical care and medicines to those who do not have any coverage, a better knowledge of the situation through improved statistics on the epidemics, and increased controls on the blood banks.

While the government expects these to accomplish their objectives with an investment of only $10 million for the year 1994, the private sector is experimenting with interesting initiatives. One such private-sector experiment was designed and undertaken by the Foundation for Quality and Participation, in the small town of Rojas in the Province of Buenos Aires, where children ages 10 to 13 attending a primary school are being led by a volunteer medical doctor with full support of the principal and teachers of the school.[61] Students in this project focus on the following tasks:

- Search in the library and study material about AIDS to learn how the disease is contracted, its symptoms, the work of HIV in the human body, and social aspects of the AIDS epidemics.
- Discuss the subject among themselves, with their families, the teachers, and the principal.
- Visit the local hospital, get acquainted with people hospitalized with AIDS, and talk with the physicians in charge of them and with the hospital's director.
- Poll people in the street about their level of information on AIDS, the measures they were taking for their own protection, and their attitude towards people already suffering from the disease.

At the point I learned about this initiative, the children had drawn a declaration defining their own feelings and the results of their learning process. Their declaration exposed their understanding of the complexity of this problem, the difficulties doctors face in treating the disease, the high cost to individuals, families, and our community resulting from dealing with the disease and trying to prevent its dissemination, and the complications that educational authorities face in bringing appropriate information to the schools. Recognizing these key aspects of AIDS, the children then said they were willing to assume their role in the fight against the AIDS epidemic with responsibility, "engaging ourselves in contributing our grain of sand."

This experiment shows that every segment of the population can respond creatively to a well-organized stimulus to promote their participation in solving social problems. The success of the Foundation for Quality and Participa-

tion project in getting young children to assume their responsibility in dealing with AIDS raises a serious question about what is not being done in a similar way to engage the adults.

Many male heterosexual adults still believe that AIDS is a disease of homosexuals. Many married women think they will be spared until they get the disease from a bisexual or drug-addicted spouse. It is true that in Buenos Aires, three fourths of the all AIDS cases are either homosexuals or heterosexuals who got the disease through sharing needles, but the other one in four cases involves nonaddicted married women, some of whose partners are neither bisexuals nor drug addicts.

It is clear that any plan to decrease the social and economic impact of AIDS in Argentina, as in any society, requires an emotional engagement that facilitates an important paradigmatic change of beliefs and behavior. This paradigmatic change is essential to increasing the use of condoms, decreasing promiscuity, promoting the use of disposable needles among drug addicts, understanding and respecting those who suffer, and helping individuals everywhere to enjoy sex while minimizing the risks for oneself and society. In addition to emotional engagement, such changes in individual attitudes require the support of the social groups to which the individuals belong, namely, families, schools, private businesses, and churches.

[*Update 2002*: UNAIDS Epidemiological Assessment: As of December 31, 2001, 21,117 AIDS cases had been reported in Argentina. The incidence rate for 2000 was 48.9 per million population. The ratio of male/female is currently 3:1. The epidemic has been concentrated in the large urban areas where 87.5% of cases reported occurred, principally in the suburbs of the province of Buenos Aires. The most common mode of HIV transmission is sexual contact (37.9%), mainly heterosexual (25.3%); followed by intravenous drug users, which accounts for 37.9% of the reported cases; and, finally, perinatal transmission (6.8%).

[Information on HIV infection comes from sentinel sites, which have been systematically collecting data across the country since the beginning of 1998. All jurisdictions gather data on a semiannual basis. The National Registry of HIV-infected people was started on June 1, 2001. The number of reporting sentinel sites increased 400% between 1998 and the first semester of 2001. However, only data from pregnant women and blood donors are sent by all jurisdictions. In other selected populations, the number of reporting sites varies from one period to another. HIV prevalence among pregnant women tested has decreased from 0.75% in the first semester of 1998 to 0.46% in the first semester of 2001. Prevalence among blood donors has also diminished during the same period, from 0.23% to 0.13%. Data on the prevalence of HIV among sex workers from four jurisdictions of the country, including the city of Buenos Aires, show a reduction from 6% to 2.39% in the 1998-to-2001 period. On the other hand, HIV prevalence among inmates in penitentiary units has increased, rising from 17.91% to 23.10% during the same time period. Among STD patients, HIV prevalence has risen from 0% to 3.99% in the first semester of 2001, based on data reported from seven jurisdictions. Finally, data from two provinces (Buenos Aires and Cordoba) show that the prevalence among injecting drug users went from 18.31% to 19.44% in the semester of 2000.

[The estimated number of adults and children living with HIV/AIDS on January 1, 2002, were:

| | | |
|---|---|---|
| Adults ages 15-49: | 130,000 | (rate: 0.7%) |
| Women ages 15-49: | 30,000 | |
| Children ages 0-15: | 3,000 | |

[An estimated 1,800 adults and children died of AIDS during 2001.

[At the end of 2001, an estimated 25,000 Argentine children under age 15 were living without one or both parents who had died of AIDS. (*End of update by the Editors*)]

## *11. Sexual Dysfunctions, Counseling, and Therapies*

### A. Concepts of Sexual Dysfunction and Treatment

Until the 1960s, physicians had no better knowledge of human sexuality than the average Argentine citizen. And even after some education was introduced into the medical training, the information they received was prejudiced, biased, and antiscientific. In an interview with a physician and psychoanalyst, I was told that in the year 1963, the chair of hygiene at the School of Medicine of the University of Buenos Aires was still telling the students that "Women experience sexual needs after reaching 25 years of age and only during their ovulatory period," and "During infancy, adolescence, and first years of youth, women have no sexual needs."

The chairs of gynecology, genitourinary diseases, and hygiene studied and taught the pathogenic aspects of the sexual organs and reproductive mechanisms, but refused to consider with the same objective scientific approach the sexual behavior of healthy females and males. In my interviews with medical doctors during 1993, I perceived they still do not feel comfortable in discussing these issues, especially in relation with the erotic minorities, the group that Erwin Haeberle calls "the sexually oppressed," which include the aging, the homosexuals, the handicapped and disabled, people with specialized sexual interests, and persons committed to mental hospitals or imprisoned.

Young and old physicians know that prestigious institutions, such as the American Psychiatric Association, have made clear that they do not consider homosexuality, whether masculine or feminine, a disease. However, they still feel that it is a perversion, a degeneration. I know of one male teenager who was subjected to electroshock treatment when his parents discovered his gay tendencies and put him under treatment with a psychologist. However, even in those cases in which counseling seeks to soothe the patient rather than to cure him or her, the prejudices of the therapists are perceived by their customers, making it difficult for them to assert their sexual preferences and seek a healthy insertion in a hostile society.

This is true not only for homosexuality, but also for many aspects in the sexual life of heterosexual people. When people come for advice on sexual problems—like frigidity, impotence, fast ejaculation or difficulties in ejaculating, painful sex, sex during pregnancy and after delivery, consequences on sexual life of drugs and surgical procedures, sex among the aging, etc.—gynecologists, obstetricians, urologists, and the general practitioner find that they all are confused. Although their scientific formation in the field of sexuality is incomplete, from the little they know, they perceive that science and common sense run against their ideologies and beliefs. The internal battles between these two opposing patterns of thinking and behaving only adds confusion and distress to ignorance.

Every time I talked with people suffering from sexual problems, they told me how much they would benefit from sound advice and support. They think that medical schools should not only give their students advanced training in human sexuality, but also should organize courses on human sexuality open to the population at large. My experience with a seminar on sexuality that I facilitated for aging people confirms this need. The group of elder women and men unanimously expressed their gratitude for having been allowed, at least for a few hours, to open up their feelings and show that they still are sexual beings with their own particular needs and desires.

For the moment, this seems rather difficult to accomplish. When a program in a school of medicine goes beyond the biological subjects of sexual differentiation and human reproduction, it is to cover technological subjects like contraception and abortion, or mainstream approaches to sexuality in infancy and adolescence, masturbation, and sexual inadequacy. The move beyond conventional teaching never reaches the subject of the sexually oppressed. Argentina, however, is changing fast, and the day may be not too far away in which these subjects, and the broader implications of sexuality for our personal lives, our societies, and our economics, will be freely, honestly, and humanly discussed in all classrooms, and in all walks of Argentine life.

### B. Impact of the Psychoanalytic School

Escaping from persecution and war, some professionals and scholars in the field of psychoanalysis left Europe and found refuge in Argentina. Here, they organized the first college-level studies on psychoanalysis in all Latin America. They planted these seeds in fertile ground. The terrain was already fertilized by brilliant psychiatrists, such as José Maria Ramos Mejia and José Ingenieros, and a self-taught psychologist, Anibal Ponce. They reflected the state-of-the-art of a science that was trying to apply to its domain the same positivistic, mechanistic approach that was yielding dramatic results in the hard sciences. Their problem was—and still is for many scientists who have not yet evolved from those stages of development of our rational mind—that instead of creating new theories around newly observed facts, they tried to bend facts into accommodating existing theories and classifications. Some of the statements of these forerunners in the field of sexuality now make us smile. Seeking a cause-effect relationship between biology and sexual behavior, they thought that all gay men were hairless, and all lesbians were bearded women.[62]

However, they deserve recognition for having brought the subject to academic circles and college teachings from which they were previously excluded. They also deserve recognition for their open-mindedness; they never thought that their teachings were cast in stone or steel forever. With Renan, one of their French masters, they thought that "the greatest progress brought about by modern rationality was its replacing the condition of being with the condition of becoming, replacing the concept of the absolute with the concept of the relative, and immovability with movement."[63]

The disciples of the pioneers became the first disciples of the European psychoanalysts, and the work of both found their ideas and their practice spreading quickly among the upper and middle classes of Argentina, who were suffering the stress of fast-changing social mores, an unstable economy, and cycles of stifling and fostering political freedom. The country has now one of the largest per-capita ratios of psychoanalysts and psychologists, and the highest number of people who have been psychoanalyzed.

The influence of Freudian psychology reaches even those who cannot afford to pay the high price of psychoanalytic treatment. Psychologists and psychiatrists are writing informative, easy-to-read, popular books and articles that propagate the main ideas and findings of modern psychology on sexuality and sexual behavior among a literate population. At all levels, they are helping Argentines to come to grips with their ambivalent heritage of an officially repressed sexuality, a society where the male is the active performer and the women the passive comptroller, both hiding their deepest feelings, and an intrinsically hedonistic way of life.

To take this movement one step further, Argentina will need to promote formal and informal sexual education that:

> goes beyond the narrow subject of reproduction to include a discussion of sexual feelings and fantasies, pleasures, beliefs, superstitions, and dysfunctions. It must further discuss sexual attitudes in different societies and historic periods, erotic art, sex legislation, and indeed "sexual politics." Finally it can't be restricted to children, but must address itself to the whole population.[64]

## *12. Sex Research and Advanced Professional Education*

Some limited research is being currently conducted on aspects of human sexuality in Argentina. These include:

- Contraception, focusing on investigations of the effectiveness of different contraceptive methods, their side effects, and the number of users, as well as surgical procedures for sterilization.
- Sexually transmitted diseases.
- Sexual behavior. Schools of psychology are currently supporting dissertation research on male, female, and child prostitution, sexual violence (rape, incest, and spousal abuse), and homosexuality. Because the results of these studies seldom reach large masses and have little impact on the population's attitudes toward diverse sexual behaviors, popular magazines and journals regularly support surveys of their own.
- Sexual dysfunctions, such as impotence, premature ejaculation, lack of orgasmic response, and aversion to sexual intercourse. Such studies usually follow the approach proposed by William Masters, Virginia Johnson, and Helen Singer Kaplan. Unfortunately, few urologists and gynecologists are informed or prepared to assist in these types of problems.

As mentioned in the section on education, very little is being done in Argentina at the university level to meet the needs of an increasingly sophisticated population with an advanced formation of professionals and technicians. Medical and paramedical personnel, along with judges, lawyers, and teachers, are increasingly aware of their need for advanced education on sexual issues and topics. They frequently feel at a loss when asked to render a judgment or verdict, or to provide guidance or information on sexual issues.

Professionals interested in advancing their own sexological knowledge, as well as contributing to sexological research, can now voice their interests and convey their suggestions to the public and to government officials and agencies through the Sociedad Argentina de Sexualidad Humana. Address: Dr. León Guimdim, Director, Darragueira 2247, P.B. "B," 1425 Buenos Aires, Argentina.

## *Epilogue*

Argentina is a society in transition. The rigid and hypocritical sexual mores of her past have created a double standard for males and females in Argentine society, and a double standard for women themselves that separated the virgin vestals of the households from the pleasure providers. Slowly, women and youngsters are creating more equitable, honest, and open relationships between and within the two genres. They are also seeking a difficult balance between the need to give free expression to their sexual drive and keep it alive during the whole life span, and the need to

build responsible, stable, and healthy households. Men are slowly joining the efforts and starting to perceive the benefits that the changes are bringing to them too.

Will these changes end all traces of a repressive, unjust, and often violent past? Will they finally bring integration and harmony to the sexual field, and contribute to pacifying and developing the entire Argentine society? Only the future will tell.

## *Acknowledgments*

There are a good many friends, colleagues, and young people who, in one way or another, have contributed to this work. I am beholden to all of them. In particular, I would like to express my heartfelt gratitude to the following:

Dra. Bacigalupo, a university lawyer who specializes in family violence, for sharing his views on the situation of males and females in Argentine households.

Licentiate Isabel Garcia, from the Argentine Council of Women, for information on sexual harassment.

Licentiate Mariana Iurcovich, from the Argentine Center for Prevention of AIDS and the International Society for AIDS Education, for orienting me to sources of data on this disease.

Dr. Alberto Woscoff, Chair of Dermatology, National University of Buenos Aires, for information on herpes.

Dr. Enrique Copolillo, the Chair of Gynecology at the National University of Buenos Aires and a dear friend, for supplying information on STDs.

Dr. Carlos Martinez Vidal, Professor Emeritus of the National University of Buenos Aires, an old friend, an early dreamer of social justice, and a proficient tango dancer, for sharing sexual memories of his youth.

Hernán Federico, a young friend, for organizing my encounters with teenagers and youth.

Dr. Kutznezoff, sexologist and sexual educator, for his observations on sexual education at the university level.

Martha Mercader, writer and Congresswoman, for the many talks in which she conveyed her views of the situation of Argentine women that she feels from the depth of her heart and the breadth of a rich experience.

Last but not least, I must express my beholdeness to my husband, Mario, a learned scholar in the field of human consciousness, with whom I share dreams and realities, and who translated and typed this report from my Spanish manuscript. Without his help, his love, and unflinching support, this work would have never been accomplished.

## *References and Endnotes*

CIA. 2002 (January). *The world factbook 2002*. Washington, DC: Central Intelligence Agency. Available: http://www .cia.gov/cia/publications/factbook/index.html.

CRLP. The Center for Reproductive Law and Policy. 2000. *Women of the world: Laws and policies affecting their reproductive lives. Latin America and the Caribbean. Progress Report 2000*. Chapter on Argentina begins on p. 13. See: http://crlp.org/pdf/wowlac_pr00_argentina.pdf.

Executive Board United Nations Development Program. See: http://www.undp.org/execbrd/word/DP2002CRP9.doc.

Gaiasanluis. See: http://www.gaiasanluis.org/.

Population Information Program. 1995 (October). *Population report: Meeting the needs of young adults, Series J, Number 41*. Johns Hopkins School of Public Health, Center for Communication Programs.

Rohter, L. 2002 (March 2). Once secure, Argentines now lack food and hope. *The New York Times*. Available: http://www .nytimes.com.

UNAIDS. 2002. *Epidemiological fact sheets by country*. Geneva, Switzerland: Joint United Nations Programme on HIV/

AIDS (UNAIDS/WHO). Available: http://www.unaids.org/
hivaidsinfo/statistics/fact_sheets/index_en.htm.

*World Bank development report 1998-99*. 1999. New York: Oxford University Press, pp. 190, 202.

1. A reference to the constellation, the Southern Cross, that can be seen from under Southern hemisphere skies. The verses on a free translation and arrangement by the translator are from a long poem by an Argentine poet, Horacio G. Rava, *The son of America*, Tucuman (Argentina): Sociedad Sarmiento, 1961.

2. Mariella Mazzotti, Graciela Pujol, and Carmen Terra, *Una realidad silenciada. Sexualidad y maternidad en mujeres catolicas*. Montevideo: Editorial Trilice, 1944.

3. Data on immigrants taken from the article on Argentina in *Funk & Wagnalls's new encyclopedia*, vol. 2 (Funk & Wagnalls's, New York, 1979), p. 234. Data on population by 1850 is from David Rock, *Argentina 1516-1987: From Spanish colonization to Alfonsin*. Berkeley and Los Angeles: University of California Press, 1987, p. 132.

4. World Bank. *World development report 1993*. New York: Oxford University Press, 1993, p. 289.

5. Rock, *Argentina 1516-1987*. p. 172. Note between brackets by the author.

6. *Ibid.*, p. 182.

7. World Bank, *World development report 1993*, p. 239.

8. Data is from the World Bank, *World development report 1993*, p. 295. Figures for primary education are expressed as the ratio of pupils to the population of school-age children. The gross enrollment ratio exceeds 100% because some pupils are younger or older than the country's standard primary school age. The data on secondary-school enrollment are calculated in the same manner. For Argentina, the secondary-school age is considered to be 12 to 17 years. The tertiary enrollment ratio is calculated by dividing the number of pupils enrolled in all postsecondary schools and universities by the population in the 20-to-24 age group.

9. See Jorge Luis Borges. *El tamaño de Mi Esperanza*. Buenos Aires: Seix Barral, 1993.

10. As quoted in Chiori Santiago, The tango is more than a dance—It is a moment of truth. *Smithsonian*. November 1993, p. 152.

11. All the examples are taken from Jose Gobello and Jorge A. Bossio, eds. *Tangos, letras y letristas*. Buenos Aires: Plus Ultra, 1979.

12. Museta, Mimi, Rodolfo, and Schaunard are characters in the novel, *Scénes la vie de Boheme*, written in 1851 by Henry Murger.

13. Des Grieux and Manon are characters in the novel, *Manon Lescaut*, written in 1733 by Antoine François Prévost D'Exiles. This reference and the previous show the strong influence of French culture in Argentina, a culture that spilled over from the upper class to the middle classes and reached the suburbs through the tango.

14. Carlos A. Floria and César A. Garcia Belsunce. *Historia de los Argentinos*, vol. 2. Buenos Aires: Editorial Larousse, 1992, p. 271.

15. Rock, *Argentina 1516-1987*, p. xxi.

16. *Ibid.*, p. 118.

17. Floria and Garcia Belsunce, *Historia de los Argentinos*, p. 140.

18. Anibal Ponce, *Ambición y Angustia de los adolescentes*. vol. II, p. 537, in Hector P. Agosti, ed., *Obras-completas de Anibal Ponce*. Buenos Aires: Editorial Cartago, 1974.

19. Teenagers from Jewish families trust a little more their rabbis than teenagers of Catholic families trust their priests. The main reason they give is that priests are not married and have more trouble with their own sexuality than they do.

20. It is even more surprising to see that the tradition of the *mate* is kept in this time of AIDS. *Mate* is a traditional beverage prepared with the herb *Yerba mate* (*Ibex paraguarensis*), which is native to the Southeast part of South America, a region that includes the northeast of Argentina, Paraguay, and the south of Brazil. The herb is staffed in a dried and hollowed gourd, covered with water just at its boiling point, and sipped through a metallic straw. The *mate* circulates among people who are socializing, each taking a full gourd of the beverage by turns. Many diseases of the mouth and teeth have been blamed on this custom, which some fear could also transmit AIDS from a person who ignores his or her being a carrier of the virus. *Mate* can indeed be taken also as a tea, but the traditional way in Argentina, Paraguay, and Brazil is as described.

21. Erwin J. Haeberle, *The sex atlas*. New York: Seabury Press, 1978, p. 452.

22. *Ibid.*, p. 453.

23. In trying cases in which the sexual rights of a minor have been violated, some legal districts have decided to hold actual court proceedings with oral testimony. Prior to this, all legal proceedings were transacted through written reports and depositions to the judge, a procedure that placed serious limits and a heavy burden on the judge and the judge's staff. Oral testimony in court allows for elaborations, explanations, and cross-examinations that are not possible with written depositions. Oral testimony can also provide a better understanding of the nature of the crime, its motivations, and its consequences in the life of the minor.

24. From the tango *Arrabalero*, words by Eduardo Calvo and music by Osvaldo Fresedo, as quoted in Gobello and Bossio, *Tangos, letras y letristas*, p. 24.

25. Martha Mercader, *Para ser una mujer*. Buenos Aires: Planeta, 1992, p. 286.

26. A weapon consisting of two or more heavy balls secured to the end of one or more strong cords, hurled to entangle the legs of cattle and other animals.

27. Hernandez has his *gaucho* hero Martin Fierro condoning the attitude of a woman who became prostitute. Knowing the desperate situation she went through when her partner was sent to the southern armies, he says about her commerce: "What else could the poor woman do to avoid starving to death!"

28. There is no doubt that the women were considered slaves of the brothel owners, part of their chattel. I will cite just one of the innumerable stories recorded in the literature. This has been taken from Ramón Cortés Conde and E. H. Cortés Conde, *Historia negra de la prostitución*. Buenos Aires: Editorial Plus Ultra, 1978, pp. 135-136. A prostitute in a brothel of Tucumán is sold to another pimp by the pimp who was exploiting her since she was 13. During the transfer, she manages to circumvent the vigilance of her new owner and escapes hidden in a freight train to Buenos Aires where she finds work at a factory. Four years after her flight, the two old pimps find out where she is, wait for her one early morning when she is walking to the factory, beat her savagely, and permanently disfigure her face with a knife.

29. Rafael Ielpi and Hector Zinni, *Prostitución y Rufianismo*. Buenos Aires: Editorial de la Bandera, 1986, p. 191.

30. The inhabitants of Buenos Aires are also known as *porteños*, which means those who live at the port. *Machismo* is a Spanish expression for male chauvinism and *macho* means a male with exalted physical and cultural manhood attributes.

31. Words from the tango, *El patotero sentimental* (*The sentimental brawler*), written by Manuel Romero (1891-1954) and taken from José Gobello & Jorge Bossio, *Tangos, letras y letristas*, p. 168). The words in Spanish are: *En mi vida tuve muchas, muchas minas, pero nunca una mujer*. The word *Nina*, which is a slang expression, could mean a lover or a prostitute; it is a woman with whom one dates or lives, who is part of one's possessions, and whom one may even exploit.

32. The description of the brothels and the prices paid are taken from Ielpi and Zinni, *Prostitución y Rufianismo*.

33. The article is reproduced in *La Nación*, December 30, 1982, which still is one of Buenos Aires' largest newspapers. During all the decades of the infamous traffic, responsible Argentine newspapers kept denouncing the situation and the corruption of Argentine politicians and bureaucrats who were benefiting from it.

34. Ielpi and Zinni (*Prostitución y Rufianismo*, p. 18) reproduce a typical story included in Londres's book. It describes how traffickers sitting around the family table were discussing with the parents a contract that would guarantee their daughter a job (nature not disclosed) and the family a monthly stipend for three years. The young woman solemnly promises not to shame the family by breaking the contract!

35. Ramón Cortés Conde and E. H. Cortés Conde, *Historia negra de la prostitución*. Buenos Aires: Editorial Plus Ultra, 1978, pp. 145-46.

36. This is a summary of the rules that Ielpi and Zinni, (*Prostitución y Rufianismo*, pp. 29-32), quote from the ordinance Number 27 approved by the city council of Rosario on November 16, 1900.

37. From a report written in 1932 by Dr. Juan Carlos Alvarez for the City Council of Rosario that was considering a shift from regulatory policies that made of Rosario a hotbed of organized prostitution to a policy that would end by closing all the brothels.

38. Martha Mercader, *Belisario en son de guerra*. Buenos Aires: Editorial Planeta, 1984.

39. Martha Mercader, *Para ser una mujer*. Buenos Aires: Editorial Planeta, 1992.

40. Beatriz Guido, *Escandalos y soledades*. Buenos Aires: Editorial Losada, 1970, pp. 63-65.

41. Martha Mercader, *Juana Manuela, mucha mujer*. Buenos Aires: Editorial Planeta, 1983.

42. Robert Lehmann-Nitsche (Victor Borde), *Textos eróticos del Rio de la Plata*. Buenos Aires: Libreria Clásica, 1981.

43. Anónimo. *Chistes y desvergüenzas del Rio de la Plata*, from *Kryptádia, recueil de documents pour servir a étude des traditions populaires*, vol. 7. Paris: H. Wolter, Éditeur, 4 rue Bernard Palissy, pp. 394-399.

44. Benjamin Viel and Sofia Kamenetzky, La crisis poblacional en América Latina. *Population Reports, Serie J. Nu-*

mero 18. Washington, DC: The George Washington University Medical Center, 1978, p. J-1.

45. *Ibid.*, p. J-4.

46. Population Information Program, Complications of abortion in developing countries. *Population Reports, Series F. Number 7*. Baltimore: The John Hopkins University, July 1980, p. F-144.

47. *Ibid.*, p. F-148.

48. *Ibid.*, p. F-118.

49. World Bank, *Investing in health, world development. Report 1993*. New York: Oxford University Press, p. 115.

50. In Argentina, an institution where sick people or injured persons are given medical or surgical treatment is called a hospital when it is organized and sustained by the state; it is called a *sanatorio* when it is a private undertaking.

51. The statistics have been taken from World Bank, *Investing in health*, pp. 208-209.

52. *Issues in world health, Population reports. Series L; Number 9*. Baltimore: John Hopkins School of Hygiene and Public Health, June 1993, p. 3.

53. *Ibid.*

54. For more details on calculations and statistics that use DALYs, see World Bank, *Investing in health*, pp. 26-27, 213-225.

55. Lucio A. Mansilla. Rige el nuevo plan de lucha contra el SIDA. *La Nación* [Buenos Aires], December 1, 1993, p. 1.

56. James Brooke, In deception and denial, an epidemic looms: AIDS in Latin America. *The New York Times*, January 24, 1993, p. Al.

57. Lucio A. Mansilla, Crece el numero de niûos con SIDA. *La Nación* [Buenos Aires], November 25, 1993, p. 18.

58. *Ibid.*

59. *Ibid.*

60. In Argentina, the school year goes from March to November.

61. Fundación por la Calidad y la Participación. Buenos Aires, Argentina: Ciudad de la Paz 2944, 1429. Tel. 544-3535.

62. José Ingenieros, *La psicopatologia en el arte*. Buenos Aires: Ramon J. Roggero y Cia, 1950, p. 152.

63. José Ingenieros, *Las fuerzas morales*. Buenos Aires: Or Editorial Futuro, 1947, p. 11.

64. Haeberle, E. *The sex atlas*, p. 478.

# Australia
## (The Commonwealth of Australia)

Rosemary Coates, Ph.D.
*Updates by R. Coates and Anthony Willmett, Ph.D.*

## Contents

> Always there, blood hanging above the clans of
> the barramundi:
> Always there, people with moving buttocks.
> *Song 16: Ross River Cycle* (trans. Berndt 1976)

## Demographics and a Brief Historical Perspective

ROBERT T. FRANCOEUR

### A. Demographics

Australia occupies an island continent of 2,966,200 square miles (7,682,400 km²), almost as large as the continental United States, southeast of Asia. Australia is the world's sixth-largest nation. It is surrounded on the west and south by the Indian Ocean, the Pacific Ocean on the east, and the Timor Sea and Arafura Seas on the north. The nearest land neighbors are New Guinea and Indonesia on the north, the islands of New Caldonia, Vanuatu, and Solomon across the Coral Sea in the northeast, New Zealand and Fiji across the Tasman Sea in the southeast, and Tasmania 150 miles (240 km) to the south. Along the coast, east of the Great Dividing Range, the rainfall is heavy with jungles in the Cape York Peninsula reaching north toward New Guinea. The interior lands and western plateau are arid desert; the northwest and northern territories arid and hot.

The indigenous people of Australia, known collectively as Australian Aborigines, constitute 1.95% of the population; about 50,000 are full-blooded and 150,000 part-Aboriginal. The majority, mostly of mixed descent, live in urban

*Communications*: Rosemary Coates, Ph.D., Curtin University, Shelby Street, Shenton Park, Western Australia 6008, Australia; icoatesr@info.curtin.edu.au. *Updates*: Anthony Willmett, Ph.D., Australian Catholic University National, Prospect Road, Mitchelton, Queensland 4053, Australia; t.willmett@mcauley.acu.edu.au.

(CIA 2002)

areas. Most full-blooded Aborigines live in rural and remote areas of the interior and the north of the continent and maintain important aspects of their traditional cultures. Because there are significant regional variations, generalizations cannot be made. There is a wide range of living conditions and adaptation to Western pressures; however, most Aborigines remain socioeconomically disadvantaged despite compensatory legislation.

Of the nonindigenous people, the longest family history of residence in Australia can be traced back eight generations. This population comprises people from all over the world, although the majority are European in origin.

Australia's population grew from 3.8 million at the turn of the 19th century to 19.2 million in 2000. Natural increase has been the main source of growth since the turn of the century, contributing two thirds of the total increase between 1901 and 2000. Net overseas migration, while a significant source of growth, is more volatile, fluctuating under the influence of government policy, as well as political, economic, and social conditions in Australia and the rest of the world. In 1999-2000, there was a 16% increase in net overseas migration over the previous year, from 85,000 to 99,100 persons. Since 1962, falling fertility has led to a fall in the rate of natural increase. ABS (Australian Bureau of Statistics 2002) population projections indicate that continued low fertility, combined with the increase in deaths from an aging population, will result in the natural increase falling below zero sometime in the mid 2030s.

Despite the concentration of people in the larger cities, Australia is not a homogeneous society, having an indigenous population, a history of European settlement, and, more recently, immigration from Asia and Africa. (All data are from *The World Factbook 2002* (CIA 2002) unless otherwise stated.)

**Age Distribution and Sex Ratios**: *0-14 years*: 22% with 1.05 male(s) per female (sex ratio); *15-64 years*: 67% with 1.03 male(s) per female; *65 years and over*: 11% with 0.84 male(s) per female; *Total population sex ratio*: 0.76 male(s) to 1 female

**Life Expectancy at Birth**: *Total Population*: 77.78 years; *male*: 74.67 years; *female*: 81.04 years

**Urban/Rural Distribution**: 85% to 15%, with the cities scattered along the widely separated coastlines

**Ethnic Distribution**: Caucasian: 94%; Asian: 4%; Aboriginal: 1.9%

**Religious Distribution**: Anglican: 27%; Roman Catholic: 27%; other Christian denominations 22%; non-Christian religions: 3% (more recently, immigration from Southeast Asia and the Middle East has expanded Buddhist and Muslim numbers considerably, and increased the ethnic diversity of existing Christian denominations). Approximately one quarter of all Australians either stated that they had no religion or did not adequately respond to the census question (Australian Bureau of Statistics 2002).

**Birth Rate**: 14.13 births per 1,000 population

**Death Rate**: 7.37 per 1,000 population

**Infant Mortality Rate**: 7.1 deaths per 1,000 live births

**Net Migration Rate**: 6.33 migrant(s) per 1,000 population

**Total Fertility Rate**: 1.82 children born per woman

**Population Growth Rate**: 1.31%

**HIV/AIDS** (1999 est.): *Adult prevalence*: 0.1%; *Persons living with HIV/AIDS*: 12,940; *Deaths*: < 100. (For additional details from www.UNAIDS.org, see end of Section 10B.)

**Literacy Rate** (*defined as those age 15 and over who can read and write*): 100% (1980 est.); portion of youths attending 15 years of compulsory schooling: 95%

**Per Capita Gross Domestic Product** (*purchasing power parity*): $23,200 (2000 est.); *Inflation*: 1.4%; *Unemployment*: 6.4%

## B. A Brief Historical Perspective

When the British Captain James Cook explored the eastern coast of the Australian continent in 1770, it was inhabited by a variety of different tribal peoples. The first settlers, mostly convicts, soldiers, and British government officials, began arriving in 1788. By 1830, when Britain claimed the whole continent, the immigration of free settlers began to accelerate. Australia was proclaimed as a Commonwealth of the British Empire in 1901.

Racially discriminatory policies were abandoned in 1973, after three million Europeans, half of them British, had entered the country since 1945. In 1993, the Prime Minister announced a plan to make Australia a republic, independent of the British Commonwealth by the year 2001. [*Update 2003*: With a change in the political climate, this has not come to fruition. (*End of update by R. Coates*)]

## NON-ABORIGINAL AUSTRALIA

## 1. Basic Sexological Premises

### A. Gender Roles

In common with many other countries, Australia is struggling with changing gender roles. Although one of the first countries in the Western world to introduce women's suffrage, other aspects of gender equality have been slower to develop. It was not until the early 1970s, through the activities of well-organized women's groups, that successive legislation has been introduced in support of women's rights. These include laws governing equal opportunity, antidiscrimination, and family law issues.

It has been claimed that, although Australia is one of the most advanced industrial democracies in the world, it is, nevertheless, a sexist society, where women are valued only in terms of being a commodity (Dixson 1976; Mercer 1975). This legacy from the original white settlement is gradually changing, although manifestations continue to be expressed in the phenomena of "mail-order brides" and "sex tours." Both of these customs tend to exploit neighboring Asian countries where poverty forces young women (and some young boys) into bargaining with their bodies.

From the time of initial white settlement up to the early 1960s, women have been "brought" to the country to fulfill the needs of men. The transportation of British convicts to the colonies of Australia is well documented. Female convicts were transported to become servants for the administrators and to meet the sexual needs of both free men and convicts. The first governor of the early colony was instructed by the British government "to keep the female convicts separate till they can be properly distributed among the inhabitants" (Clark 1950, 117). These women were used to serving the needs of men, but were not deemed suitable as wives for the free settlers. As the number of single, free male settlers increased, the British government began to offer young, single, healthy women free passage to Australia. A not dissimilar attitude persisted through to the early 1960s, where successive Australian governments gave a high priority to the immigration of young, single, healthy women.

The history of white, female settlement in Australia is one of the antecedents of the nature of male-female roles and relationships in contemporary Australia. Another significant antecedent was the nature of the pioneering activities undertaken by men in the early decades of white settlement. The concept of "mateship" is a legend of male-to-male relationships, to the extent that it has a place as a literary genre in its own right. The "typical" Australian male has been, until very recently, portrayed as a "good bloke," and a real "mate." In the early years of settlement, the harshness of the country and the nature of pioneering, gold exploration, and farming led men to work in pairs or small groups, often isolated for months at a time from other people. There was an unspoken pact of mutual protection and reliance. Folklore is rich with stories of self-sacrificing "mates." Historical accounts have continued to emphasize masculine activities and associations, and ignored the role of women in pioneering the country, thus helping to reinforce the image of an Australian man who relates to other men, with women being generally ignored. Australian participation in World Wars I and II re-emphasized masculine bonding, and the stories, fact or fiction, of "mateship" and sacrifice continue to be celebrated annually with the commemoration of Anzac Day on April 25. In the view of some, it is on this day that the divide between the white men and women of Australia is most emphasized. The emphasis on male sporting activities and the associated icons are current manifestations of traditional "mateship."

Social conventions, however, are undergoing change, albeit too slowly for supporters of the women's movement. Experiences in Australia are similar to those reported from America, Britain, and some of the European countries, in that the majority of women are in paid employment, but continue to take the major responsibility for home management (Baxter 1992; Chisholm & Burbank 1991). The concept of the "glass ceiling" is well documented, and the proportion of women in senior executive positions in all areas is very low. For example, of the 35 universities in Australia, only two have women as their vice chancellors, less than 13% of federal politicians are women, and a similar percentage of senior positions in the federal public service are held by women, with one woman judge of the high court. There is evidence to suggest that younger men do not have the same expectations of clearly defined gender roles as their fathers, although this does not translate into equal sharing of domestic duties (Edgar & Glezer 1992).

### B. Sociolegal Status of Men and Women

In adulthood, men and women are treated equally under the law. Anomalies exist in the status of male children vis-à-vis female children. For example, the age of consent for sexual acts is 16 years; however, the age of consent for males to have sex with other males is 21 years. There is no recognition in the law for female-to-female sexual acts. [*Update 2003*: In 2002, changes have been made to some State laws bringing a greater level of equality to the laws. For example, in Western Australia, various laws have been amended to ensure equal status under the law for those in same-sex or *de facto* heterosexual relationships. (*End of update by R. Coates*)] Women's social status, while being protected by various laws, remains, nevertheless, inhibited by misogyny and more-subtle cultural factors.

## C. General Concepts of Sexuality and Love

Sex is generally viewed as a recreational activity, serving purposes that go beyond procreative ones. It is customary for individuals to couple for reasons of love, with conventional concepts being promoted in European romantic terms. The media, including films, books, television, popular music, and advertising, promotes physical and emotional attraction and idealistic pairing.

Arranged marriage is not an acknowledged practice; however, it does occur in those ethnic groups that follow a particular cultural tradition.

## 2. Religious, Ethnic, and Gender Factors Affecting Sexuality

The dominant culture from the early days of European settlement was Anglo-Saxon and Gaelic, with strong Catholic and Anglican religious influences. Later large-scale migration attracted significant numbers of Italian and Greek people, thus enriching the culture and strengthening the Catholic religious traditions. More-recent migration has increased the ethnic diversity, with people from many of the African countries, the Middle East, Southeast Asia, and India. This has resulted in an increase in the number of people who follow non-Christian traditions such as Islam and Buddhism.

Recent data from the Commonwealth Bureau of Statistics show that 26.1% of the population describe themselves as Roman Catholic, 23.9% Anglican, and 23% follow other Christian movements. Twenty-five percent declare themselves as having no religion. Two percent of the population are classified as non-Christian, with 0.7% being Muslim, 0.5% Buddhist, and 0.4% Jewish (Castles 1992; Australian Bureau of Statistics 2002). Public sexual mores are influenced by traditional Judeo-Christian teachings, although there is an active, fundamentalist minority.

The legal system is unequivocally British in origin and practice. The criminal and other pertinent legislative codes in all states and territories have as their foundation British law. Modifications have occurred over the ensuing period, resulting in variations between different states and territories. [*Update 2003*: The decriminalization of prostitution and the establishment of procedures to conduct a brothel have occurred in some States. Contesting views, which include possible legal action and a court challenge, exist between the Catholic Church and the Queensland State government about antidiscrimination legislation, when such legislation includes shoring up the legal rights of gay and lesbian couples (*Courier Mail* 2002). (*End of update by A. Willmett*)]

## [A. Religious Influences and Changes

ANTHONY WILLMETT (*Update 2003*)

[At the turn of the 21st century, two major pillars of society—education systems and the churches—appear to be enmeshed in confusion over their roles in enhancing or controlling the sexuality of young people in their care. While educators promote the importance of education for life in all the meanings of that term, the media reveal ever more incidents of inappropriate behaviors by teachers and clergy. While all agree that children must be protected from inappropriate behaviors, there is currently little agreement on how this should be achieved. Societal responses to these revelations have polarized so, that, while some wish to enforce a return to "the Bible as literal truth" or to "a morality of control," others believe that ever more open discussion will assist young people to regain control of their own emerging sexuality.

[Australian newspapers report incidents of sexually inappropriate behavior in religiously affiliated schools, while at the same time, the list of clergy or members of religious orders of nearly all denominations who are accused and/or convicted of sexual misdemeanors with young people increases in length. For some commentators, the answer is for a "return to the old morality," whereby sexuality is kept firmly within its place, defined strictly as within marriage and for the purposes of procreation. For others, it is precisely this "controlling morality" that has led to the current situation, whereby children appear to be most greatly at risk in precisely those institutions where they might expect to be safest.

[Auxiliary Bishop Francis Patrick Power of the Catholic Diocese of Canberra and Goulburn broke ranks by calling for a study of priestly celibacy. In a widely reported interview on ABC Radio in September 2002, he suggested that priests who have left the ministry to marry should be allowed to exercise their priestly ministry. He called for a rethinking of the Church's teaching on sexuality, and proposed that gays and lesbians should be recognized as human beings with needs and desires. He said that the Church's current teaching on the morality of homosexuality implies a "double moral standard, since a significant percentage of Australian priests are known to be gay" (*National Catholic Reporter* [U.S.] 2002). He also warned that the exclusion of women from positions of authority fosters "a feeling of disenchantment" among Catholics.

[The issue of how the Church might respond to lesbian and gay people who wish to have their commitment to a lifelong faithful relationship affirmed by the Church was vigorously debated at the Eighth Assembly of the Uniting Church in Australia. The Assembly was divided on the issue. (*End of update by A. Willmett*)]

## 3. Knowledge and Education about Sexuality

### A. Sexual Education in Public Schools

Each state and territory, through their respective education authority, has a curriculum that provides for personal development and education in sexuality. These have been developed by experienced educators and offer well-rounded, age-related programs for both primary and secondary education. The implementation of such programs, however, is variable, and no child in Australia is guaranteed a consistent and continuing sexuality education. Curricula packages are available, through the educational authorities, to both public and private schools. To date there is no education authority that has made sexuality and relationship education a required subject. Teachers and parents have the option of deciding what, if anything, is presented to children.

Today's young parents are more prepared to provide their children with sexual information and are offering a wider range of information than their own parents did. The result of this form of education is also variable and young people report that they would prefer to receive a comprehensive and consistent formal education by properly trained teachers (Coates 1992). No education department offers preservice or in-service training to meet this need.

Typically, the curriculum packages often deal with a variety of health and personal development issues and integrate the sexuality elements at appropriate stages. For example, concept of self and one's position within a family structure are included in the syllabus designed for the early years of primary school, as is nutrition and personal hygiene. Biology and reproductive sexuality is generally offered before the emotional aspects of human sexuality, although personal safety and the concept of invasion of private "space" is suggested for the 6- and 7-year-olds. Information on gender identity and sexual orientation is suggested for secondary school students at about 15 and 16 years of age.

Thus, the deficiencies within the system are the facts that the curriculum is optional and that teachers are not trained specifically to teach human sexuality, and in some areas, teachers are instructed not to answer questions posed by students on certain topics.

## [B. Sexual Education in Catholic Schools

ANTHONY WILLMETT (*Update 2003*)

[An examination of teaching about sexuality in Catholic schools (Willmett 2002) reveals that there is little agreement on how best to prepare young people for a sexually healthy life through their formal educational experiences. In fact, two polarized positions have emerged. At one extreme is the suggestion that traditional moral orthodoxy should be reaffirmed fundamentally by controlling and suppressing acknowledgment of the developing sexuality of young people. At the other end is the suggestion that it is precisely because of this suppression and lack of knowledge and understanding of the role of sexuality among students and their teachers, as well as parents and the clergy, that the current situation has developed.

[The Roman Catholic Education system in Australia is the largest unified denominational system in the country. There are links between religious education and sexuality education in these schools, and when the topic is sexuality, educators register a range of reactions that have an impact on their confidence and comfort in presenting material. These dilemmas and concerns can be described in pedagogical, professional, and personal terms.

### [*Pedagogical Challenges*

[Pedagogical problems in sexuality education in Catholic schools are often associated with: curriculum rationale, design, and implementation; curriculum content; teaching and learning strategies; students' classroom questions—particularly unpredictable questions; resources; and, assessment and evaluation (Bruess & Greenberg 1994; Hedgpeth & Helmich 1996; Sears 1992; Willmett 2002). Problems connected with curriculum rationale, design, and implementation, often stem from an understanding of and rationale for sexuality education in a school setting. Different outcomes will determine if sexuality education is viewed as a theological, a therapeutic, or an educational endeavor. If the program is seen in theological terms, the religious educator may seek to inculcate in students the values and beliefs of the sponsoring Church community; if the program is seen in therapeutic terms, the religious educator may seek to heal or soothe students' feelings and behaviors to conform to some desirable standard; if the religious educator sees the program in educational terms, the aim will be to enhance students' understanding and appreciation of human sexuality.

[School communities are confronted with the issue of who is responsible for the explicit sexuality education curriculum. Specific outcomes will be seen to be appropriate to schools if educators acknowledge explicitly that learning about sexuality is an ongoing process that continues throughout life (Coates 1997; G. Moran 2001). Different outcomes will also be established when a curriculum is designed solely on the basis of syllabus requirements, rather than as a whole school approach. A whole school approach that employs a collaborative and consultative process involving students, parents, and community representatives, has the potential to link the school appropriately to lifelong learning (Willmett, 2001).

[Problems connected with curriculum content include: identifying developmentally appropriate content material; catering for any overlap and/or repetition of material; and, determining how material that is sometimes described as "sensitive" will be handled. The relevance of the explicit program is a particular challenge to students and parents. Making education and sexuality education relevant to needs and interests is an essential element in learner empowerment (Hedgepeth & Helmich 1996). Parents, teachers, and the local community need to ask learners what they need and want to learn.

[Problems connected with teaching and learning strategies include a hesitancy to adopt teaching and learning strategies that are applied successfully in other curriculum areas. Teaching and learning strategies that invite personal responses in other curriculum areas become problematic in sexuality education, because of the perceived "private and personal" nature of the topics. This is highlighted when it comes to answering students' questions in the classroom. Cries of "What do I say?," "What am I allowed to say?," or "How far can I go?" are heard more often regarding sexuality education than other curriculum areas (Willmett 1998).

[Problems associated with resources include their availability and appropriateness. While there has been some improvement, Australian-produced resources are relatively sparse. Students may not find in the available overseas resources a context that matches their own. In addition, Church and school leaders may deem some materials unacceptable if they raise themes or issues that contradict the expressed values of their community. Resources may be inappropriate if they omit specific religious references, or if they appear to be aggressively religious or seek to preach rather than teach.

[Assessment and evaluation also pose problems, not only because they are connected with and inform the rationale, design, and implementation of sexuality education, but also because they may not exist. Teachers may be comfortable and skilled when it comes to assessing knowledge and skills, but anxious if there is a perception or expectation to assess behavior.

### [*Professional Dilemmas and Problems*

[Teachers are aware of sexuality education as providing information for educated choices. They are also aware of sexuality education as an arena of professional insecurity (Willmett 2002). Teachers have a sense of the contesting views about sexuality and sexuality education—both within and outside the Catholic tradition (Chater 2001; Francoeur & Perper 1998; Hogan 1993; Lebacqz 1999; Whitehead & Whitehead 1994, 2001). Heterosexist assumptions underlying course content is one example (Bosacki 2001; Epstein & Johnson 1998; Harrison, Hillier, & Walsh 1996; Selling 2001). Other professional dilemmas and problems involve perceived or real relationships. Relationships between the classroom teacher and the parents or the employing authority, for example, the school board, diocesan authority, parish priest, or minister, can present the religious educator with difficulties, particularly if there are philosophical and educational differences about sexuality education in the school or Church setting. In addition to problems associated with employing authorities, concern about lobby groups or the media also has an impact on teachers' professional confidence.

[Professional problems in sexuality education can be found in relation to expectations placed on classroom teachers. While they do not want to be judgmental and wish to explore contesting views about sexuality with students in the classroom, teachers do not know how to do so (Went 1985; Willmett 2002; Ziebertz 1992). The extent to which teacher preservice and in-service programs offer method, as well as content courses on sexuality, is a problem for the profession. The absence of professional associations for teachers in this field might be linked to this situation.

[One important professional problem that confronts the classroom teacher is how to narrow the gap between the rhetoric and the reality of an understanding about, and an approach to, sexuality and sexuality education in the school setting—including the classroom program (Sears 1992; Willmett 2002). How well, for example, does the explicit curriculum match the lived experience of people in the school or Church community? How do the policies, practices, programs, procedures, places, and people reinforce and complement what is presented in the explicit curriculum?

[*Personal Concerns*

[Teachers experience sexuality education as a focal point for discrepancy (Willmett 2002). Discrepancies appear in relation to the lived experience of the members of the Catholic community and the official teachings of the institutional Church (Dominian 2001; Grey & Selling 2001; Whitehead & Whitehead 1994, 2001). They also appear in relation to the role of the teacher in the classroom, for example, as a substitute parent, and in relation to the philosophy and educational approach that underpins the sexuality education program in the classroom (Hedgepeth & Helmich 1996; J. Moran 2000; Willmett 2002). A background question for each parent, educational leader, and classroom teacher is: Do I believe sexuality is a private matter, best left to family to educate, or are there public and communal dimensions, which require intelligent conversation in other educational settings beyond family? The response to this issue will help to determine their comfort and confidence in presenting material.

[Teachers also experience sexuality education as personal anxiety. Fear, uncertainty, and concern for their well-being are different ways teachers experience sexuality education. Fear and uncertainty about loss of employment or about being reported to relevant authorities is experienced by teachers (Willmett 2002). Any unease or discomfort with issues of sexuality felt by Catholic educational leadership, and by classroom teachers, will be readily conveyed to students. Their uneasiness will reinforce students' suspicions that the topic of sexuality is somehow off-limits or embarrassing. At their most basic, these personal concerns confront Catholic educational leaders and classroom teachers with their own history, education, and experiences of sexuality. All adults have to confront and respond to their unique childhood experiences and formation in sexuality; this task is immediate and consequential for those responsible for presenting sexuality material in classrooms. Any sexuality educator reflects upon his or her own inventory of attitudes to a range of issues concerning the human body, sexual feelings, behavior and orientations, and the plurality of community sexual standards (Coll 1994; Francoeur & Perper 1998). Catholic educational leaders and classroom teachers may experience the need to gain certainty by resolving all the issues and questions before venturing into the classroom.

[As with any area of teaching and learning, classroom teachers may feel constrained by their own lack of knowledge; they may lack familiarity with some basic knowledge. They may have difficulty resolving the dilemma between sexuality being viewed as an act and as law, or as a relationship and as Gospel within the Catholic tradition (Francoeur & Perper 1998; Dominian 2001; Hogan 1993). The resolution to this dilemma will influence the selection and presentation of material. All the factors described above will contribute to a sense of the relative comfort or relative discomfort on the part of Catholic educational leadership and the classroom teacher when presenting topics on sexuality. (*End of update by A. Willmett*)]

## 4. Autoerotic Behaviors and Patterns

Large-scale sexological surveys have not been conducted in Australia. As a consequence, much information offered here is based on small surveys and anecdotal evidence. Research undertaken by Coates over a period of seven years and confined to Western Australia (Coates 1987) indicates that, among a population of 678 young adults, 87% of females and 93% of males reported having engaged in self-pleasuring at least once in the preceding six months. More recent research undertaken by Ferroni (1993), who reviewed 658 women, classified into three groups—namely, women with gynecological problems, women who had had a hysterectomy, and healthy women, respectively—found that 70% of her respondents reported autoerotic behavior.

Current mores about autoerotic behavior reflect the Judeo-Christian influence coupled with a more relaxed Australian attitude toward most aspects of sexual behavior. Self-pleasuring as a topic of conversation has, to a certain extent, lost its taboo status. Likewise, the use of pornographic material as a stimulus, either alone or with a partner, is a subject of discussion for some young people.

## 5. Interpersonal Heterosexual Behaviors

### A. Children

There is little information available about types of sexual behavior and whether patterns of sexual experimentation have changed. However, anecdotal reporting indicates that Australian children are no different from children in other countries and engage in sexual rehearsal play. This is conventionally curbed by witnessing adults, although enlightened parents will take the opportunity to educate their children about private and public, acceptable and unacceptable, behavior. Many parents will tell their children that it is acceptable to engage in self-pleasuring as long as they confine it to the privacy of the bedroom. It is not customary for children to witness adult sexual interactions nor for children to be initiated into sexual activity by an adult. There are no pubertal initiation ceremonies in the nonindigenous population.

### B. Adolescents

Results of a survey of 2,000 respondents aged 16 to 25 years suggest that adolescents are probably more sexually experienced than their parents were at the same age (McCabe & Collins 1990). Intercourse is occurring at an earlier age than ten years ago and in greater numbers. The mean age of first intercourse is about 16 years, and by the age of 18, nearly 60% of young people report that they are sexually active. There is also a reported increase in the number of sexual partners at a given age.

Casual sex is still an important part of adolescent sexual activity, although most sexual experience in adolescence probably occurs in the context of a steady relationship. Explanations for the initiation of sexual intercourse include curiosity, peer pressure, and the need to be loved. The rates of sexual experience are greater in males than in females (Dunne et al. 1993; Cubis 1992). Peer pressure from boys is strong, and many young women report that their first experience of intercourse was not a positive one.

Sexual activity and socioeconomic status have not been shown to be related, but pregnancy and carrying to term are associated with lower socioeconomic status. Pregnancy is no longer a reason to precipitate marriage, with less than 20% of detected adolescent pregnancies resulting in marriage prior to the birth of the baby.

Not surprisingly, data from the Family Planning Association and other sources indicate that adolescents are among the poorest users of contraceptives. Age, a reluctance to acknowledge to others that they are sexually active, and distrust of authorities are possible reasons for the low utilization of the services offered.

Research by Moore and Rosenthal (1991) indicate that young people continue to resist the use of condoms even in the context of safer sex practices and HIV/AIDS. Males are more likely to place the responsibility on their partners and females express a distaste for condoms. It has been suggested that heterosexuals do not believe that they are at risk, that AIDS has been seen as a disease of the sexually deviant or other stigmatized groups (e.g., drug users), and that HIV transmission has been identified with groups, not sexual practices (Kippax 1991).

## C. Adults

*[Single Lifestyle Increasing*

*[Update 2001*: Recent demographic studies at the Australian National University indicate that about a quarter of young Australians will never get married, and those who do will take longer than their parents to marry. Projections in early 2001 suggested that 27% of men and 23% of women ages 15 to 20 will not be married by age 50. At that age, their chances of getting married would be slim. The trend to delay marriage is affecting all age groups and both sexes in Australia. For example, in 1999, 18% of 35-year-old women were unmarried. By 2015, that percentage will nearly double to 33%. Even allowing for *de facto* cohabiting relationships, which were not counted as marriage, "coupledom" will be even rarer than in past decades. A new avenue for easier divorce through the Federal Magistrates Service, and the growing tendency for women to attend universities and undertake a career are the two driving forces behind the decline of "coupledom." Marital trends in Australia have swung wildly in the past century. In 1921, 17% of Australian women never married; in 1981, only 4% never married. In 1999, it was about 9%. Corresponding figures for men are slightly higher. (*End of update by R. T. Francoeur*)]

### Cohabitation, Marriage, and Family: Structure and Patterns

Cohabitation is a common practice in Australia, to the extent that it is officially recognized for property distribution on dissolution. The term *de facto* has been in common usage for at least 30 years and is applied to couples who live together without undergoing a formal marriage ceremony. A high proportion of young people live together for a considerable period prior to marriage. Over 60% of adults believe that living together before marriage is acceptable, and about 50% of all people under the age of 30 do live together prior to marriage. Thirty percent of these say that they do not believe in marriage. One third state that they would

leave the relationship if they were not growing in it (Glazer 1993).

Since the 1970s, the age at first marriage has risen, with a resultant rise in the age of the primiparous mother. The average family size is around 2.4 children and there is a greater focus on women's having a career outside of the home.

[*Update 2003*: Like many of the developed countries, Australia has had a significant drop in its birthrate over the past ten years. Concern about the declining rate is being expressed through the development of support schemes to encourage women to take time out from work to have babies. There is now a greater recognition that the majority of women work, and that many of them would like to continue their career after childbirth. There is a greater level of awareness that the business environment must become both child- and woman-friendly. (*End of update by R. Coates*)]

### Divorce and Remarriage

When Australians do marry, monogamy is the conventional custom. Divorce and remarriage have become increasingly accepted in the past 20 years, and it is estimated that one in four marriages will end in divorce, with the current rate being 11 per 1,000 marriages. Close to 60% of previously married men and 25% of previously married women remarry (Castles 1992, 169, 172).

### Nonmonogamous Relationships

Recently, in at least one capital city, a group in support of nonmonogamous relationships has been established. It is distinctly different from the "swinging" groups of the 1970s. The group advertises under the rubric "Beyond Monogamy" and advocates responsible and mutual polyfidelity.

### Sexuality and the Physically Disabled

Since the United Nations International Year of the Disabled in 1979, Australia has been making a concerted effort to make provision for, as well as change the attitudes toward, people with disabilities. Recognition has been given to emotional relationships and sexual rights and the needs of both the intellectually and physically disabled. However, once again, the provision of education, counseling, and other services is variable. Predominantly dependent upon local expertise, interest, and influence, programs may or may not be offered. In Western Australia, a comprehensive education program has been developed for the intellectually disabled, whereas very little of a formal nature is provided for the physically disabled. In other states, there have been some exceptionally enlightened programs for adults with acquired disabilities.

Legislation, governing such things as antidiscrimination and equal opportunity, provides protection for the rights of the disabled. Community housing, as opposed to institutional dwellings, enhances possibilities for the disabled to exercise their sexual options.

### Incidence of Anal and Oral Sex

There is no reliable data on the incidence of oral and anal sexual activities in Australia. Coates' Western Australia survey (1992) indicates that at least 73% of her sample had experience at least once with both fellatio and cunnilingus; 32% had experimented with anal sex. Both oral and anal sexual practices are included in information about safer sex practices with precautions to be taken to avoid HIV transmission. The general acceptance of such messages (with few notable, and predictable, objections) may indicate an assumption that these practices are within the norms of acceptable sexual relationships.

## 6. Homoerotic, Homosexual, and Bisexual Behaviors

### A. Legal and Social Status of Gays and Lesbians

Homosexuality has been subjected to both legal and social sanctions. However, there has been a gradual reduction of hostility toward homosexuality and a concomitant change in legislation in the past 20 years. Under the equal-rights legislation, same-sex couples are generally afforded similar rights to opposite-sex couples. This recognition has been extended to residency status in this country for the partner of a gay or lesbian person. Despite official acceptance and a generally sanguine attitude, there is still a prominent homophobic element within this society. Predominantly this is expressed against gay men through so-called poofter-bashing, where gangs of youths go to public gay venues for the express purpose of assaulting (presumed) gay men. Certain fundamentalist religions actively campaign for the reintroduction of legislation against homosexuality.

All states have repealed laws against same-sex activities between consenting adults in private. In Western Australia, the legislation may be unique in the English-speaking world, where the document is prefaced with a disclaimer to the effect that the Parliament does not condone the behavior.

There is a strong and active network of gay men and lesbian women, with all the major cities and many rural areas having constituted organizations. A number of these organizations are at least 30 years old and have been at the vanguard of political activism and in the provision of counseling and education services. These organizations were also crucial to the early and positive response to HIV/AIDS policy development, education, counseling, and treatment. In addition, there are support groups throughout the country for the parents and friends of gay people.

There are a number of domestic gay publications, the most notable quality magazines being *Outrage* and *The Advocate*. Typically, women are less well catered for, although there is a national networking newsletter called *Grapevine*, which provides a contact service. Most of the cities have dedicated bookshops, and all dealers of sexually explicit material stock magazines aimed at gay men.

The Sydney Gay and Lesbian Mardi Gras, held in March each year, is reported to be the largest in the world and attracts thousands, including many international visitors. The Mardi Gras parade is conducted through the streets of Sydney and is a popular event for families to attend on what is, normally, a warm summer evening. The Sydney City Council supports the Mardi Gras as an important income-generating event. A fundamentalist Christian group prays for rain to mitigate the success of the event.

[*Update 2003*: In November 2002, the Gay Olympics were staged in Sydney, with 18,000 competitors and 25,000 visitors. The Governor of the State of New South Wales opened the Games after a welcoming speech from one of the country's most prominent High Court Justices. The support afforded to the Games was a clear indication that the economic value of the "pink dollar" is recognized and that there is a greater level of acceptance of people who are same-sex oriented. (*End of update by R. Coates*)]

### B. Sexual Outlets and Relationship Patterns

*Gay Men*

The largest gay population is in the city of Sydney, with Oxford Street being the best-known area for at least a particular subgroup to congregate. An area on this street known as "The Wall" is the place male sex workers congregate. Sydney, Melbourne, Brisbane, Perth, Adelaide, Canberra, and the Gold Coast all have a number of acknowledged gay and lesbian venues, including bars, restaurants, nightclubs, and theaters. These venues are recorded in the publication *Gay Guide*. Smaller towns have similar venues, but tend to have a lower profile.

It is easy to stereotype the patterns of behavior for gay men; however, it would be more accurate to say that there is as much diversity in relationship and sexual patterns among the gay population as there is among the nongay population. The spectrum—from long-term monogamous relationships, serial monogamy, triads, groups, to frequent, anonymous sex, and sexual abstinence—would all be represented within the gay community.

One representative pattern of gay male behavior has most recently been documented by researchers from Macquarie University in New South Wales. The study revealed that urban gay men had high levels of knowledge about HIV transmission and had substantially changed their sexual behavior. Attachment to the gay community, defined as sexual, social, or cultural/political, was found to increase the likelihood of behavior change. Isolation and nonattachment decreased the chance of sustained behavior changes (Crawford et al. 1991).

In contrast, results of a study of men who use the beats in western Sydney differ somewhat from the Macquarie study. Wherrett and Talbot (1991) found that 40% of men reported they practiced unprotected anal intercourse with casual partners, 10% with regular partners, and 95% of the sample reported having experience of anal/genital intercourse without condoms at some time in their lives. Forty-eight percent of men stated that they had had unprotected intercourse within the last six months. The authors suggest that the findings from these and other similar studies reveal that there are large numbers of men who have sex with men who are not attached to the gay community and are the least likely to adopt safer sex practices.

*Lesbian Women*

Lesbian women have had a much lower profile until relatively recently and would appear to be less well catered for in terms of venues. Some years ago, the women shared the male venues, often having a "women only" night. Today, at least in the larger cities, there are venues just for women.

Again the relationship patterns would cover the entire spectrum. A comparison between gay men and lesbian women in terms of fidelity and number of partners would probably show similarities with matched, so-called heterosexual groups.

*Gay Parents*

A number of both gay men and lesbian women have exercised their option to become parents. The methods used have ranged from selecting a sexual partner for the specific purpose of conceiving, to artificial insemination and IVF.

There have been examples of a parent's gaining custody of children on the grounds of the homosexual orientation of the other parent. However, homosexuality, per se, would not necessarily ensure loss of child custody.

*Bisexuality*

People who actively engage in sexual relationships with both men and women may be considered the invisible group. There is frequently a lack of recognition and acceptance by the gay and lesbian community, many of whom claim that those who identify themselves as "bisexual," in fact have not come to terms with their "homosexuality." Further, the concept of bisexuality is ignored by the general community.

Personal experience as a counselor and educator leads one to believe that there is a degree of covert bisexuality among males. One common mode of expression for married men in making regular visits to anonymous sex venues, such as "T-Rooms" and Saunas. Prior to the recognition of HIV/AIDS, the author was aware of a number of bisexual groupings, mainly triadic relationships. Whether the number of self-identified bisexuals has declined, or simply gone underground because of prevailing attitudes, is unknown.

Data collected from 1986 to 1991 by a telephone counseling service for bisexual men and their female partners revealed that 59% of the male callers were married. Over that period, there was a consistent decline in the number of bisexual men who reported participation in unprotected male-to-male anal sex, paralleled by a small, steady increase in safer-sex knowledge levels. There were, however, a number of misconceptions about safer-sex behavior, with the role of oral sex in HIV transmission the least well understood. Younger men were more likely to participate in high-risk behaviors (Palmer 1991).

## 7. Gender Diversity and Transgender Issues

### A. Transsexualism

Transsexualism is recognized as a medical condition in Australia and provision is made for sex reassignment. The program follows the model developed by John Money at Johns Hopkins University Hospital (Baltimore) in the United States. Because of the need to maintain surgical skills, there are only two designated venues for surgery to be conducted: one in South Australia, the other in New South Wales. The preparatory program, however, is offered in a number of cities.

The standard approach, after assessment and definitive diagnosis, is to provide a program of hormone therapy, social training, and counseling for a minimum period of two years prior to undergoing surgery. For some individuals, the program is too lengthy. Because of the close proximity of a number of Asian countries where relatively inexpensive surgery is offered, a number will opt out of the program and elect early surgery, not always with positive results.

All states and territories, except South Australia, have yet to make provision for changing the birth certificate and/or providing individuals with documentation that would allow recognition of their reassigned gender.

On the occasions where a transsexual has been confined to prison, there have been instances where the authorities have placed the person in a prison appropriate to her/his reassigned gender. There have also been instances where the contrary has occurred.

### B. Transvestism

Self-reporting and anecdotal information indicates that a high proportion of people who cross-dress are professional men who are heterosexually oriented, in heterosexual relationships, and have children. It has also been estimated that one in ten men cross-dress.

Support groups for both transvestites and transsexuals exist in four of the states; however, there is no national body.

## 8. Significant Unconventional Sexual Behaviors

### A. Coercive Sex

*Child Sexual Abuse and Incest*

The incidence of incest and child sexual abuse may be much greater than reported figures. In a survey of 1,000 university students in the State of Victoria, Goldman and Goldman (1988) asked about childhood sexual experi-

ences, and found that 28% of females and 9% of males reported some form of sexual abuse from adults; 76% of the perpetrators were known to the child. It is estimated that girls under the age of 18 face odds of between one in ten and one in four chances of sexual abuse within the family, generally by a father or stepfather (Allen 1990).

Child abuse and incest in the Aboriginal population has been noted as a major concern, anecdotal evidence suggesting that incidence may be substantial (Hunter 1992).

Legislation provides for an "age of consent," generally 16 years, and any "indecent dealings" are liable to a penalty of four years imprisonment with hard labor and "with or without a whipping."

There is legislation against "incest by an adult female," which states that any woman "who permits her father or son or other lineal ancestor or descendant, or her brother or half-brother, to have carnal knowledge of her . . . is guilty of a misdemeanor, and is liable to three years imprisonment with hard labor for three years" (Western Australia Criminal Code, 118).

Throughout the country, various crisis centers, refuges, support groups, and treatment centers provide facilities for both child and adult victims. Like most community organizations, funding is limited, volunteer support is a major factor, and there are never enough resources.

It is important to note that all facilities mentioned in this chapter pertain to the major population centers; rural Australia itself is very poorly served in all areas of sexuality.

*Sexual Harassment and Coercion*

It is estimated that sexual harassment in the workplace occurs for young women about 50% of the time in a first paid job, and is a significant risk for women throughout their working lives. Some years ago, the Federal Labour Government introduced legislation and promoted education in the area. Throughout Australia, government instrumentalities, nongovernment organizations, and many private companies now have provision for reviewing complaints. As understanding of what constitutes harassment improves and the mechanisms for lodging a complaint tested, the number of cases reported has increased. A number of men have lodged successful claims, although the majority of complainants are women.

*Sexual Assault and Rape*

Allen (1992) states that the so-called developed countries have comparable patterns of sexually abusive behaviors, and that although rates may vary between countries and regions, certain probabilities remain. It is estimated that occasional or habitual violence perpetrated by men against women occurs in at least a quarter (some research suggests a third) of all sexual relationships. It is estimated by workers in the area that one in five women will be a victim of sexual assault by the age of 18 years.

Most cities and large towns have counseling and other services for the victims of sexual assault. Many cases go unreported, however, a number of victims will seek the services of agencies such as a Sexual Assault Referral Center and may or may not be referred on to the police. Not all victims who report directly to the police are referred to an independent agency. Thus, it is difficult to quantify the number of cases. As an example, however, the Sexual Assault Referral Center in Perth, Western Australia, servicing a total population of a little over a million, has approximately 800 new cases reported each year.

The incidence of reported male rape seems to be increasing. Generally men are most at risk when placed in all-male environments, such as prison.

## B. Sex Workers (Prostitution)

The act of prostitution has never been illegal in Australia. But during the last decade of the 19th century and the first decade of the 20th century, a range of legislative measures were enacted that made most prostitution-related activities illegal.

In the state of Victoria and the Australian Capital Territory, prostitution-related activities have been decriminalized and legislation enacted to provide for the lawful conduct of business. In all other states and territories, "living off the earnings or keeping premises for the purposes of prostitution" are illegal. [*Update 2002*: A change in legislation in Western Australia is currently passing through the Parliament, and it is anticipated that by 2003, sex workers will be able to operate legally under certain restrictions. These restrictions deal mainly with the placement and operation of brothels and health issues. (*End of update by R. Coates*)] In most states, a policy of "control and containment" is operated through the local police (generally the vice squad). Through this policy, the number of brothels are limited, independent operators are closed down, and the workers in the brothels are required to undergo monthly medical checks. All workers must have a current health statement saying they are disease-free. Any worker who has an infective disease is not permitted to work. There is a very high level of condom usage, with most workers charging substantially more if a client insists on sex without a condom. Many workers, however, have a technique for rolling on a condom, using their mouths and without the client's being aware.

Workers have their own magazine and newsletter that is aimed at being both informative and entertaining. There are also community organizations that provide support and information for people in the sex industry.

## C. Pornography and Erotica

Since the 1970s, the dominant trend has been toward liberalization, facilitating the availability of sexually explicit material. Since 1971, principles applying to the classification and censorship of films, videos, and printed material have been generally agreed on by federal and state governments, thus abandoning the attempt to prohibit pornography. These principles relate to age, public offensiveness, consumer protection, and sexual violence against nonconsenting persons. Material classified as "restricted" may only be sold in designated areas of news agents and specialist shops, or be sealed if on open display. Films with a "restricted" category may not admit minors under the age of 18 years. One state does not permit "restricted" films to be shown on a Sunday—a rather anachronistic situation.

Much of the material is imported, although Australia also has an active production industry. It is claimed that the Australian Capital Territory has the most liberal attitude and, hence, is the source of the majority of locally produced material. This claim has not been substantiated.

Recently, in at least one state, consideration has been given to the need for, or indeed the feasibility of, monitoring pornographic material obtained through computer sources.

## 9. Contraception, Abortion, and Population Planning

### A. Contraception

According to Siedlecky and Wyndham (1990), there have been six successive waves of contraceptive innovation in Australia; the main methods used in the early part of the century were condoms, douching, withdrawal, and abortion. Later, quinine pessaries and other spermicides were the most-used methods. By the late 1940s, the diaphragm, first introduced in the 1920s, became popular, and the intrauterine device during the 1950s and early 1960s. The introduction of the oral contraceptive in 1961 dramatically increased the number of women using contraceptives.

Oral contraception is still the most frequently used method for Australian women under the age of 30. Older women tend to return to more traditional methods (especially the diaphragm, following adverse reports about IUDs and the pill). However, couples are increasingly choosing sterilization, with more than 50,000 men and women undergoing sterilization per annum (Siedlecky & Wyndham 1990).

Depo-Provera has not been approved by the Australian Drug Evaluation Committee (ADEC) and is, therefore, still officially on trial, although it has been used for 20 years for the treatment of cancers of the breast, uterine lining, and kidney. As the drug is commercially available, the ADEC has indicated that if physicians have strong reasons for prescribing its use as a contraceptive, then they may do so. Its use in this manner has been controversial and is opposed by feminist groups. The short- and long-term side effects are not known, and indiscriminate prescription without adequate information, documentation, and follow-up for clients—particularly its disproportionate use among disadvantaged women (institutionalized, blacks, migrants, and intellectually disabled)—has given rise to controversy.

Currently, a variety of contraceptives is readily available to most Australians. The most accessible are condoms, which are sold in supermarkets as well as pharmacies and "sex shops." Oral contraceptives have been available, on prescription, in Australia since the early 1960s, and an upward trend in the age of marriage has been attributed to its widespread use (Siedlecky & Wyndham 1990). [*Update 2002*: In 2002, there have been more positive moves for the acceptance of "the morning after" pill. (*End of update by R. Coates*)] The Family Planning Association provides accessible contraceptive advice and prescriptions. School-based education programs generally offer contraceptive information as part of the curriculum.

### B. Teenage Pregnancy and Abortion

With regard to adolescent contraceptive behavior, Condon (1992) notes that approximately 25% of 15- to 19-year-olds become pregnant. Forty percent of these choose to terminate the pregnancy, which indicates that the pregnancy was unplanned and that contraceptive measures were either not used or failed.

### C. Abortion

It is estimated that, despite restrictive laws, approximately 60,000 abortions are performed annually in Australia (Siedlecky & Wyndham 1990). Regulation of abortion is a matter of state legislation. During the 1960s, abortion-law reform groups were established in all states. This was often associated with the establishment of Family Planning Clinics and pro-choice, women's health services. The struggle to liberalize the laws has been ongoing and not very successful. In 1969, South Australia was the first state to make abortion legal. The Northern Territory adopted similar legislation. In other states, wider interpretation of the laws has made abortion easier to obtain and lawful under certain circumstances. The reason is that the Australian judiciary has supported principles established by common-law decisions—for example, the Bourne case in England in 1938, in which the judge stated that abortion was lawful if performed in good faith and for the purpose of preserving the life of the mother, which is interpreted to mean not only her physical existence, but also her physical and mental health. However, in some states there have been no test cases and no precedent set, and the situation is far from satisfactory for all concerned.

Surveys of public opinion indicate that most people think that abortion should be legally available for a range of indications (Graycar & Morgan 1990; Anderson 1986). The Royal Commission on Human Relationships (1977) provided the most comprehensive account of all aspects of sexual and family behavior in Australia in the 1970s, and recommended abortion-law reform. The antiabortion lobby, represented mainly by the Right to Life Group, became organized in the early 1970s to defend the status quo against the push for legislative change from abortion-law reform groups. During the 1980s, attacks began with renewed vigor following activities in the United States and the introduction of more restrictive legislation. Activities have continued with picketing of abortion clinics and attempts at legislative change—for example, a campaign to withdraw rebates for termination procedures from the national health insurance.

In summary, it may be said that Australian women have sought abortion as a solution to unplanned pregnancy for at least the past 100 years, in spite of the legal restrictions and prevailing moral attitudes. Restrictive abortion legislation does not save more babies but rather loses more mothers. The decline in morbidity and mortality arising from abortion has been a result of better techniques, use of blood transfusion and antibiotics, but also from changes in attitudes that have brought abortion into the open and allowed women to obtain earlier operations. There is still reluctance to allow women to decide for themselves, and abortion is likely to remain a contentious issue (Siedlecky & Wyndham 1990, 101).

### D. Population Planning Programs

The documented history of population planning in Australia began with white settlement. It commenced with attempts to control Aboriginal populations through murder, the removal of children from their parents, and deliberate attempts to "breed out." At the same time, campaigns for increasing the white population through active immigration programs and aggressively promoting the role of wife and mother were adopted. Political, legal, medical, and religious institutions conspired to reduce women's options and to prevent access to contraception. Despite this, Family Planning Organizations have an honorable and effective history throughout Australia.

## 10. Sexually Transmitted Diseases and HIV/AIDS

### A. Sexually Transmitted Diseases

Australian figures on the rate of sexually transmissible diseases are similar to the rates in other developed countries. The age groups most affected are those between 15 and 30. The most common infections are chlamydia, gonorrhea, genital herpes, HIV, genital warts, syphilis, and hepatitis B. Penicillin-resistant gonococcal infection is on the increase.

Health and education services are generally good in the major cities and towns, however, many rural areas are dependent on local general practitioners. Practitioners, especially in the designated STD (Sexually Transmitted Disease) clinics, are cognizant of the need to establish patient rapport and trust. Counseling is provided in government clinics, as well as education.

Control of infection is mediated through preventative measures, the provision of expert services, and through expeditious contact tracing. Most STDs are reportable and a national register is maintained for epidemiological purposes. The data is published through the federal health agency in the *Community Disease Intelligence*.

The rate of infection among the indigenous population is higher than in the nonindigenous population for a number of reasons, including reduced access to education, poor living conditions, and generally lower standards of healthcare.

### B. HIV/AIDS

Australia was one of the first countries to recognize the serious public health risk posed by HIV/AIDS, and instituted health promotion strategies very early. In addition, resources were allocated to both private and public organizations to cater for those who were already infected and to target those who were considered to be most at risk. Despite pockets of resistance and some cases of extreme bigotry, the overall strategy has proved to be relatively successful. The predicted rates of infection for the end of the 1980s suggested a doubling of newly diagnosed cases, when in fact there has been a slight decline.

As of December 1992, the cumulative number of diagnoses of HIV infection in Australia was 16,788, with 82% being classified as acquired through homosexual/bisexual contact, 4.9% through intravenous drug use, and 2.8% through homosexual/bisexual contact and intravenous drug use. Six percent of infections were acquired through heterosexual sex and 3.4% were infected through blood transfusion. The cumulative total of women diagnosed was 408 and the number of children was 92. The current rate of new diagnosis is approximately 96 per 100,000 (*Australian HIV Surveillance Report*, April 1993).

Although HIV infection is recognized as a serious risk, knowledge and education does not always translate into changed behavior and attitudes. High-risk groups that need particular attention are those homeless young people who are associated with prostitution and drug use.

[*Update 2002*: UNAIDS Epidemiological Assessment: Australia was among the first countries in the world to report AIDS cases. Retrospective analyses of epidemiological data indicate that HIV incidence peaked in 1984, followed by a rapid decline. This trend has continued in the 1990s, with a decrease in reported AIDS cases from 955 in 1994 to 212 in 2000. This decline in incidence is projected to continue. The decline in AIDS diagnoses since 1996 has been much more rapid than originally predicted in the mid 1990s. It is now clear since around 1996, that the additional decrease in the number of AIDS diagnoses is because of the use of effective combinations of antiretroviral therapy for the treatment of HIV infection. Annual reported diagnoses of HIV infection have also declined steadily, from more than 2,308 in 1987 to about 723 in 2000. An estimated 12,000 people were living with HIV/AIDS in Australia at the end of 2001. The proportion of women among reported cases has been gradually increasing, from 0% in 1983 to 10% in 2000. HIV infection in children remains rare.

[Overall rates for other STDs have declined since the mid-1980s, with particular reduction among high-risk groups, such as male homosexuals and female sex workers. However, rates of STD among indigenous populations continue to be substantially higher than in the nonindigenous population by a factor of 10 to 100 times.

[The estimated number of adults and children living with HIV/AIDS on January 1, 2002, were:

| | | |
|---|---|---|
| Adults ages 15-49: | 12,000 | (rate: 0.1%) |
| Women ages 15-49: | 800 | |
| Children ages 0-15: | 140 | |

[Less than 100 adults and children are estimated to have died of AIDS during 2001.

[No estimate is available for the number of Australian children who had lost one or both parents to AIDS and were under age 15 at the end of 2001. (*End of update by the Editors*)]

## 11. Sexual Dysfunctions, Counseling, and Therapies

The incidence of sexual dysfunction in the community is unknown. There are, however, a number of dysfunction services, both private and public. Community-based resources include organizations such as Rape Crisis Centers, Incest Survivor's Association, Women's Health Centers, Migrant Health Centers, Gay and Lesbian Counseling Services, various AIDS organizations, Marriage Guidance, and the Family Planning Associations. These all provide both crisis assistance and counseling services to varying degrees. All of these organizations are restricted by lack of satisfactory funding, since they are dependent upon government grants and fund-raising activities.

It is difficult to quantify the number of practitioners who specialize in sexual counseling and therapy. There are two major organizations that attempt to bring these practitioners together: the Australian Society of Sex Educators, Researchers, and Therapists and the Western Australian Sexology Society. In population terms, the state of Western Australia is much smaller than the Eastern states; however, it appears to be the trailblazer in sexology and has a well-coordinated network of practitioners and resources.

## 12. Sex Research and Advanced Professional Education

### A. Advanced Education

There is only one university-accredited postgraduate program in sexology in Australia; This is offered through the Division of Health Sciences at Curtin University of Technology in Western Australia. The program was established in 1979 by this author. [*Update 2002*: Students have the option of taking a master's-level program focusing on sexual counseling and therapy or on forensic sexology. The latter is believed to be a world first. The unit also offers supervision for research students at the master's and Ph.D. levels. The duration of the coursework for the master's programs is three semesters, for the research master's, four semesters, and for the doctorate, a minimum of four semesters. (*End of update by R. Coates*)]

Throughout the Australian university system, various professional programs, such as social work, medicine, nursing, and psychology, provide some elements of sexology in their courses. However, other than the options offered through Curtin University, there is no systematic and comprehensive program for students in the health and helping professions, nor in education.

In 1992, the Australian College of Veneriologists, in collaboration with the Australian Society of Sex Educators, Researchers, and Therapists, offered a program in sexual health counseling. These two organizations provide participants with a diploma on completion.

The Family Planning Association of Australia offers regular training programs for medical practitioners and nurses. In addition, ad hoc programs are offered for professionals and nonprofessionals. The Family Planning programs are nationally accredited and various professional organizations recognize these for continuing education credits. Address: Family Planning Australia, Inc. Lua Building, Suite 3, First Floor, 39. Geils C, P.O. Box 9026, Deakin, ACT 2600 Australia (Phone: 61-6/282-5298. Fax: 61-6/285-1244). The address for Family Planning Victoria is: 266-272 Church Street, Richmond 3121 Australia (Phone: 61-3/429-1868).

The address for the Australian Association of Sex Educators, Counselors, and Therapists is: P.O. Box 346, Lane Cove NSW, 2066 Australia (Phone: 61-2/427-1292).

### B. Research

Most of the research dollars and interest have tended to be in the areas of fertility (control and enhancement) and in the area of HIV/AIDS. In-vitro fertilization programs have had a prominent profile and work is undertaken in several states.

Of the research that has been undertaken to examine behaviors or attitudes, few have been based on random samples. Most studies have been limited to small, targeted, and often self-selected samples, and frequently relatively unsophisticated survey instruments have been used.

Several areas of current research suggest new political agendas. For example, funded surveys that have used whole population samples have looked at practices and attitudes surrounding HIV/AIDS, STDs, fertility, and reproductive technology.

The address for the Australian Society of Sex Educators, Researchers, and Therapists is: 21 Carr Street, Coogee, New South Wales 2034 Australia.

The address for the Western Australian Sexology Society is: c/FPA, 70 Roe Street, Northbridge, Western Australia 6000 Australia.

*The Journal of Sex and Marriage and the Family*, published by the Family Life Movement of Australia, recently changed its name to the *Australian Journal of Marriage and Family*.

Four other Australian journals publish articles of interest to sexologists: *Australian Forum*, published bimonthly by Gordon and Gotch; *Healthright*, published quarterly by Family Planning Australia, New South Wales; *Australian and New Zealand Journal of Family Therapy*, published quarterly by the Family Therapy Association, South Australia; and *Venerology*, published quarterly by the National Venerology Council of Australia.

## Conclusion

The nonindigenous people of Australia reflect the cultural attitudes and behaviors of their predominately European origins. There are variations because of the cultural mix; however, the dominant religions, legislation, and education are essentially Western, and public sexual morality reflects the values of these institutions.

## ABORIGINAL AUSTRALIA

Aboriginal traditions are complex and varied. There are elements of the culture that are the exclusive province of certain individuals or groups and are not permitted to be revealed to others. Sensitivity on sexual matters has precluded any extensive anthropological study. The major, detailed work is that of Ronald and Catherine Berndt, who spent more than 30 years observing, participating, and documenting Aboriginal cultures in the northern regions of Australia.

It is impossible for a non-Aboriginal person to present cultural traditions accurately, and it would be impertinent to try. Through the assistance of Dr. Robert Tonkinson, Professor of Anthropology at the University of Western Australia, I present below some examples of traditional Aboriginal practices. There is no attempt to be inclusive nor comprehensive, and the material should not be viewed as generalizable, nor necessarily current.

The concept of the Dreaming is of fundamental importance to Aboriginal culture and embraces the creative past—where ancestral beings instituted the society—the present, and the future. The Aboriginal worldview integrates human, spiritual, and natural elements as parts of the whole and is expressed through rituals (Tonkinson 1991).

While the basic social unit is the family, there is a complex system of classificatory kinship that dictates marriage rules. Kinship status imposes responsibilities and behaviors toward other kin. A basic feature of the kinship system is that the siblings of the same sex are classed as equivalent, so that, for example, the sisters of a child's mother would all be classed as "mother." The children of one's parents' siblings would, therefore, be classed as "brothers" and "sisters." Through this system, kinship may be extended to include people who do not have a blood relationship.

The moiety system of social classification provides correct intermarrying categories, although it does not determine marriage partners. Within moieties, there are groupings which, for want of a better word, have been classified as "clans," although a more accurate translation of the words used by the people themselves might be "crowd" or "lot." A clan is usually identified by an association with a natural species, for example, the barramundi clans (named after a species of fish), or Eaglehawk. Each clan has a dialect and each person is a member of one linked dialect-clan pair, which is that of her or his father. This categorization has significance in all aspects of social activity and includes specific mythic and ritual knowledge and beliefs. The clan indicates territorial possession as well as belief system. Membership of the dialect-clan group defines a person's social position, as well as their belief system (Berndt 1976).

A traditional Aboriginal view of sexuality is that it is a natural urge to be satisfied. It has symbolism beyond the individual, being linked to fertility in all its manifestations. Representations of sex, through songs, dances, and paintings, relate to the human activity and to seasonal change, to the growth and decay of plants, and to the regeneration of nature. Reproduction of humans and of the natural world is vitally important, and obedience to ancestrally ordained laws is the responsibility of adult humans. The correct performance of rituals guarantees continuity of life-giving power and fertility from the spiritual realm (Tonkinson 1991).

## 1. Gender Relationships

In traditional Aboriginal societies, there was a pervasive egalitarian ethos that placed every adult as the equal of others of the same sex. The operation of the kinship system exerted an overall balance in male-female relationships (Tonkinson 1991). Earlier ethnographers have tended to present Aboriginal culture as a traditional male-dominant, female-subordinate, hunting and gathering society (Warner 1937; Parsons 1964). It has been argued, however, that this view is a narrow one generated through the androcentricity, and possibly the ethnocentricity, of the authors (Merlan 1988). Other authors have emphasized the complementary nature of gender roles, without conflict (Berndt 1980). The complexity of the Aboriginal worldview and the concept of the Dreaming may have contributed to the differing perspectives of the ethnographers. The Dreaming, which contains the lore of creation and the permanence of the interrelationship of all things, is maintained through the different contributions to it made by women and men. Women's narrative of the Dreaming deals with the rhythms of family life, while men's narrative deals with the rhythms of the life of the whole group. Thus, there are male and female domains that are connected and complementary.

Gender difference is a significant aspect of Aboriginal symbolism, and consequently, there are gender-specific rituals. Many rituals relate to productive activities and utilize parallel symbols, for example, the *woomera* (throwing stick used by males when hunting) and the digging stick (used by females when gathering insects). Certainly, men and women

share a sense that both "men's business" and "women's business" are indispensable (Merlan 1988).

Specific areas are designated for men's rituals and women's rituals, and women and men are excluded from each other's sites. Physical punishment would be incurred if there was intrusion into the domain of the opposite gender; however, the depth of meaning associated with the rituals ensures that the power of suggestion preserves sanctity. Because both men and women have ritual domains, there is a strong sense of propriety, and self-esteem is derived from this (Merlan 1988). While much ritual activity involves both sexes, mature men control both the ritual proceedings and the scheduling of activities.

## 2. Sexual Ceremonies and Rituals

### A. Puberty Rituals

Initiation ceremonies assisted the transition from childhood to adulthood with highly elaborated rituals for boys. Modeled on death (of the boy) and birth (of the man) they dramatized separation from women, in particular from the mother. Rules of kinship dictated the allocation of roles and responsibilities in initiation as in all social behavior. Guidance, reassurance, and support were guaranteed, as was chastisement if rules were broken.

For females, puberty rites were simple. The transition to adulthood was based on sexual maturation and included sexual activity. However, menarche, marriage, and childbirth have not been ritualized or publicly celebrated in Aboriginal societies.

### B. Defloration

Ritualistic defloration was practiced in some parts of Australia, but no longer occurs. Ceremonies varied; however, one example dating back to the 1940s has been described by Berndt, and related to people from the northeastern region of Arnhem Land. Girls who were to undergo the ritual were called "sacred" and deemed to have a particularly attractive quality. The men made boomerangs with flattened ends, to be used as the instrument of defloration prior to ritualistic coitus. Men, girls, and boomerangs were smeared with red ocher, symbolizing blood. A special windbreak or screen was prepared for the girls, the entrance of which was called the sacred vagina. The screen was intended to prevent men from seeing "women's business."

Prior to her defloration, a girl may have lived in seclusion for a period of time with certain older women, observing food taboos. The older women taught the girls songs, dances, and sacred myths. At the end of the seclusion period, there was a ritual bathing at dawn.

In some areas, a girl may have lived in her intended husband's camp for a period of time. After the seclusion period, she would be formally handed over to her husband and his kin, and the marriage consummated.

In other areas, a girl may have been unaware that her marriage was impending and be seized by her intended husband and his "brothers" while she was out collecting food with the older women. Her husband's "brothers" had sexual rights to the girl until she had settled down in his camp (Berndt & Berndt 1988).

Earlier anthropological reports (Roth 1897, cited in Berndt 1988) described rituals that have involved the forced enlargement of the vagina by groups of men using their fingers, with possum twine wound round them or with a stick shaped like a penis. Several men would have intercourse with the girl and later would ritually drink the semen. Mitigating this was the second part of the ritual which allowed dancing women to hit men against whom they had a grudge with fighting poles without fear of retaliation.

## C. Circumcision

Circumcision was a common, though not universal, practice. In many areas, Aboriginal men believed that the uncircumcised penis would cause damage to a woman, which was one reason why sexual activity of an uncircumcised boy was viewed negatively. Rituals associated with circumcision were secret and sacred and were considered "men's business." Full details have not been disclosed to outsiders and what is offered here are those aspects that are permitted.

Women danced close to the circumcision ground but were not permitted to watch. During totemic rituals, the boy who was about to be circumcised was present, but often could not see what was going on. It was at that time that he was told the meaning of the songs. Just before dawn, he would be led to a group of older men who used their bodies to form a "table" upon which the young boy was placed. After the circumcision, the boy returned to his seclusion camp and the rest of the group moved to another campsite, as happened after a death. In some areas, the foreskin was eaten by older men, in others the boy wore it in a small bag around his neck; in others it might have been buried.

There were a number of postcircumcision rites that included the young man's being taken on a journey around his totemic country.

At a later stage, subincision may have taken place. Again, the initiate was taken into seclusion and, later, the procedure conducted using the human "table." The partially erect penis was held up and the incision made on the underside. Subincision of the penis was regarded as the complementary right to defloration. Stone blades were prepared while thinking of coitus, and it was believed that semen flowed more rapidly after subincision (Berndt & Berndt 1988). Subincision had religious validation, proved in many areas through reference to the penile groove of the emu or the bifid penis of the kangaroo. Subincision was not for contraceptive purposes, as was commonly believed by nonindigenous people. In fact, in many areas, semen was not credited with having a role in procreation. In all areas of Australia, spiritual forces were believed to be central to procreation. Physiological maternity, as well as paternity, was denied, with the belief that a plant, animal, or mineral form, known as the conception totem, was assumed by the spirit-child, who then entered its human mother (Tonkinson 1991).

## D. Courtship and Marriage

Rules of kinship restricted sexual freedom and set the parameters for selection of spouses; however, premarital and extramarital sex was appropriate. It is expected that everyone marries. Marriage rules may give the impression that there was no room for the concept of "romantic love" in Aboriginal traditions. However, an insight into the nature of male-female sexual relationships may be obtained through some of the traditional myths, often expressed in song cycles. These include reference to affection, as well as physical satisfaction and mutual responsibility. The songs make explicit reference to circumcision rituals, to menstruation, semen, and to defloration.

One ritualistic means of courtship is reported through the Golbourn Island song cycles (Berndt 1976). In the songs, young girls engage in making figures out of string, the activity causing their breasts to undulate: This and the figures they make are designed to attract men. Undulation of the buttocks was also used, along with facial gestures, that indicate a girl was willing to meet a boy in a designated area. These activities usually occurred around the time of menarche. Menstrual blood had an erotic appeal for men and some sacred myths allude to that theme. Menstrual blood was also seen as sacred, and, by extension, women were sacred during their menstrual period.

In song and dance, intercourse and erotic play is celebrated as joyful and beautiful. Intercourse has significance as it maintains populations, both human and nonhuman, and therefore produces food. It is through intercourse that the seasons come and go, and it is only through the changing of the seasons that plants can grow.

Infant betrothal was an important aspect of Aboriginal cultures and was often associated with men's ritual activities, especially circumcision. In the Western desert region, for example, the main circumciser had to promise one of his daughters to the novice in compensation for having ritually "killed" him.

Girls were often given to their husbands while still prepubertal, but coitus did not usually commence until her breasts had grown. In this context, girls may have had their first sexual experience by the age of 9 and boys by the age of 12.

Standards of beauty or attractiveness varied; however, obvious physical disabilities were seen to be a disadvantage and, similar to Western culture, youth is most highly valued.

## E. Love Magic

The use of songs, dances, and other rituals were used to attract a prospective lover or to rekindle passion in an existing relationship. Members of either sex employed love magic, which was thought to cause the person who was the object of it to become filled with desire. On occasions, a large-scale ritual dance of an erotic nature was used as a general enhancement of sexuality. Both sexes were involved, although the pairs of dancers who simulated intercourse were of the same sex. The intention, however, was aimed at arousing heterosexual desires (Tonkinson 1991).

## 3. Contraception and Abortion

Traditionally, the Australian Aborigine, like other hunting and gathering societies, had low levels of fertility. Ethnographers have found little evidence of plant contraceptives or abortifacients. There is no evidence of infanticide ever being used.

Current fertility rates among the indigenous population is lower than in the nonindigenous population. This, in part, may be because of the generally lower levels of healthcare and standards of hygiene, and the higher levels of STD infections, all because of a serious neglect on the part of successive governments.

## 4. Homosexuality, Bisexuality, and Gender Diversity

The Berndts (1988) have commented that the traditional way of life placed so much emphasis on heterosexual relationships that there has been little evidence (to ethnographers) of other modes of sexual expression. They do, however, mention that "homosexual experimentation and masturbation" are reported among boys and young men when temporarily segregated from the women. Berndt goes on to say that examples of female homosexuality is even more rare and that "the close physical contacts which Aborigines indulge in are deceptive in this respect" (Berndt & Berndt 1988, 195).

Contemporary urban life has demonstrated that homosexuality is known among the Aboriginal community, with gay and lesbian Aboriginals participating in the local gay culture.

There is no evidence in the literature of gender dissonance in traditional Aboriginal cultures.

## 5. Incest

The kin relationship, rather than a biological one, dictates the incest taboo (Tonkinson 1991). In traditional societies, the incest taboo extends to all the members of one's own moiety, with certain exceptions during sacred rituals. For example, during the defloration ceremony, a man inserts the defloration boomerang into a woman whose formal relationship to him is roughly the equivalent of his wife's mother; he then has coitus with her as a sacred ritual considered important from the point of view of fertility.

As mentioned previously, there is current concern that the incidence of child sexual abuse is increasing among the Aboriginal population. This may well be as a consequence of dislocation from traditional structures.

## 6. Education

Apart from the services available to all, there are a number of services specifically for Aboriginal populations. These include infant and maternal health and welfare services, fertility counseling, and STD and HIV/AIDS education programs. Nevertheless, there is a greater need for services to be extended, relevant, and accessible.

## Summary

Some aspects of Australian Aboriginal cultures have been presented within the context of traditional societies. The majority of Aborigines living in Australia today have had their cultural heritage eroded by the dominant migrant culture and the urbanization of certain regions. Current attitudes and sexual behaviors are influenced by Western religions and Western law. The attitude of earlier generations of migrants has left Australian Aborigines with a shorter lifespan, lower fertility rates, and higher rates of infant mortality and sexually transmitted diseases than non-Aboriginal Australians. Various governments and other agencies are attempting to ameliorate this situation; however, there is still a long way to go to achieve equity and to dismantle prejudice.

## References and Suggested Readings

Allen, J. A. 1990. *Sex and secrets: Crimes involving Australian women since 1880.* Melbourne: Oxford University Press.

Australian Bureau of Statistics. 2002. Available: http://www.abs.gov.au.

*Australian Public Service Staffing Statistics Report,* 1993.

Baxter, J. Summer 1992. Power attitudes and time: The domestic division of labour. *Journal Comparative Family Studies,* 23(2):165-82.

Berndt, R. M. 1976 *Three faces of love: Traditional Aboriginal song-poetry.* Melbourne: Thomas Nelson Ltd.

Berndt, C. H. 1980 Aboriginal women and the notion of the 'marginal man.' In: R. M. & C. H. Berndt, eds., *Aborigines of the west: Their past and present.* Perth: University Western Australia Press.

Berndt, R. M., & C. H. Berndt. 1988. *The world of the first Australians.* Canberra: Aboriginal Studies Press.

Berndt, R. M., & R. Tonkinson, eds. 1988. *Social anthropology and Aboriginal studies: A contemporary overview.* Canberra: Aboriginal Studies Press.

Bosacki, S. L. 2001. Spirituality, gendered subjectivities, and education in preadolescents: Canadian preadolescents' reflections on gender-roles and their sense of self. *International Journal of Children's Spirituality,* 6(2): 207-221.

Bruess, C. E., & J. S. Greenberg. 1994. *Sexuality education: Theory and practice* (3rd ed.). Madison, WI: Brown & Benchmark.

Castles, I. 1992. *Year book Australia 1992.* Canberra: Australian Bureau of Statistics.

Chater, A. 2001. Another country: An exploration of the subversive in sexuality and spirituality. *International Journal of Children's Spirituality,* 6(2):176-184.

Chisholm, J. S., & V. K. Burbank. 1991 Monogamy and polygyny in southeast Arnhem Land. *Ethology & Sociobiology,* 12(4):291-313.

CIA. 2002 (January). *The world factbook 2002.* Washington, DC: Central Intelligence Agency. Available: http://www.cia.gov/cia/publications/factbook/index.html.

Clark, M. 1950. *Selected documents in Australian history 1788-1850.* Sydney: Angus & Robertson.

Coates, R. 1997. Australia. In: R. T. Francoeur, ed., *The international encyclopedia of sexuality: Volume 1, Argentina to Greece* pp. 87-115). New York: Continuum.

Coates, R. 1992. *Parent's prerogative versus school based sexuality education.* Occasional Paper 8. Perth: Edpak.

Coates, R. 1987. *Reports from the ATASKA Study. Occasional Paper 3.* Perth: Edpak.

Coll, R. A. 1994. What it means to be human. In: *Christianity and feminism in conversation* (pp. 69-88). Mystic, CT: Twenty-Third Publications.

Condon, J. T. 1992. Adolescent pregnancy: Abortion, relinquishment for adoption and parenting. In: R. Kosky, H. S. Eshkevari, & G. Kneebone, eds., *Breaking out: New challenges in adolescent mental health* (pp. 36-50). Canberra: National Health and Medical Research Council.

Connell, R. W., et al. 1988. *Social aspects of the prevention of AIDS: Study A–Report No. 1: Method and sample.* Sydney: Macquarie University.

*Courier Mail* [Brisbane]. 2002 (November 13).

Crawford, J., et al. 1991. *Social aspects of the Prevention of AIDS Project.* New South Wales: Macquarie University.

Cubis, J. 1992. Contemporary trends in adolescent sexual behaviour in Australia. In: R. Kosky, H. S. Eshkevari, & G. Kneebone, eds., *Breaking out: New challenges in adolescent mental health.* Canberra: National Health and Medical Research Council.

Dixson, M. 1976. *The real Matilda: Woman and identity in Australia 1788 to 1975.* Sydney: Penguin Books.

Dominian, J. 2001. Sexuality and interpersonal relationships. In: J. A. Selling, ed., 2001). *Embracing sexuality: Authority and experience in the Catholic Church* (pp. 3-21). Aldershot: Ashgate Publishing.

Dowsett, G. 1991. Social research on AIDS: Examples from Macquarie University, Sydney. *Venereology,* 4(1):38-42.

Dunne, M. et al. 1992-1993. *HIV Risk & Sexual Behaviour Survey in Australian secondary schools.* Canberra: Australian Government Publishing Service.

Edgar, D., & H. Glazer. April 1992. A man's place? Reconstructing family realities. *Family Matters,* 31:36-39.

Epstein, D., & R. Johnson. 1998. *Schooling sexualities.* Buckingham: Open University Press.

Ferroni, P. A. 1993. *The effects of hysterectomy and gynaecological conditions on women's sexuality and self-esteem* (Unpublished doctoral thesis). Canberra: ANU.

Francoeur, R. T., & T. Perper. 1998. Religious, ethnic, and gender factors affecting sexuality. In: R. T. Francoeur, P. B. Koch, & D. L. Weis, eds., *Sexuality in America: Understanding our sexual values and behavior* (pp.18-29). New York: Continuum.

Glazer, H. 1993. *Lifematters.* Sydney: ABC Radio.

Goldman, J. D. G. 1992. Children's sexual cognition and its implications for children's court testimony in child sexual abuse cases. *Australian Journal Marriage & Family,* 13(2): 78-96.

Goldman, R., & D. G. Goldman. 1988. The prevalence and nature of child sexual abuse in Australia. *Australian Journal Sex, Marriage & Family,* 9:49-106.

Grbich, C. 1992. Societal response to familial change in Australia: Marginalisation. *Journal Comparative Family Studies,* 23(1):79-94.

Grey, M., & J. Selling. 2001. Marriage and sexuality in the Catholic Church. In: J. A. Selling, ed., *Embracing sexuality: Authority and experience in the Catholic Church* (pp. 179-196). Aldershot: Ashgate Publishing.

Harrison, L., L. Hillier, & J. Walsh. 1996. Teaching for a positive sexuality: Sounds good, but what about fear, embarrassment, risk and the "forbidden" discourse of desire. In: L. Laskey & C. Beavis, eds., *Schooling & sexualities* (pp. 69-82). Geelong, Victoria: Deakin Centre for Education and Change, Faculty of Education.

Hedgepeth, E., & J. Helmich. 1996. *Teaching about sexuality and HIV: Principles and methods for effective education.* New York: New York University Press.

Hill, J. 1991. *Contraception and fertility regulation: The law and sexuality in western Australia.* Perth: Family Planning Association of Western Australia.

Hogan, A. 1993. Morality, ethics, Catholic ethics. In: *On being Catholic today: What kind of person should I be?* (pp. 1-22). North Blackburn, Victoria: Harper Collins.

Hunter, E. 1992. Aboriginal adolescents in remote Australia. In: R. Kosky, H. S. Eshkevari, & G. Kneebone, eds., *Breaking out: New challenges in adolescent mental health.* Canberra: National Health & Medical Research Council.

Keene, I. 1988. Twenty-five years of Aboriginal kinship studies. In: R. M. Berndt & R. Tonkinson, eds., *Social anthropology and Aboriginal studies: A contemporary overview.* Canberra: Aboriginal Studies Press.

Lebacqz, K., ed. 1999. *Sexuality: A reader.* Cleveland, OH: The Pilgrim Press.

Loach, L. 1992. Bad girls: Women who use pornography. In: L. Segal & M. McIntosh, eds., *Sex exposed: Sexuality and the pornography debate.* London: Virago.

McCabe, M. P., & J. K. Collins. 1990. *Dating, relating and sex.* Sydney: Horwitz Grahame.

Mercer, J. 1977. *The other half: Women in Australian society.* Sydney: Penguin Books.

Merlan, F. 1988. Gender in Aboriginal social life: A review. In: R. M. Berndt & R. Tonkinson, eds., *Social anthropology and Aboriginal studies: A contemporary overview.* Canberra: Aboriginal Studies Press.

Moore, S. M., & D. A. Rosenthal. 1991. Condoms and coitus: Adolescents' attitudes to AIDS and safe sex behaviour. *Journal Adolescence, 14*(3):211-227.

Moran, G. 2001. Partners: Religious and moral education. In: M. Ryan, ed., *Echo and silence: Contemporary issues for Australian religious education* (pp. 231-247). Katoomba, NSW: Social Science Press.

Moran, J. P. 2000. *Teaching sex: The shaping of adolescence in the 20th century.* Cambridge, MA: Harvard University Press.

*National Catholic Reporter* [U.S.] 2002.

National Health and Medical Research Council. 1990. *Handbook on sexually transmitted diseases.* Canberra: Australian Government Publishing Services.

Palmer, W. A. 1991. *Men who have sex with men in Australia: A report of the Gammaline Telephone Counselling Service.* Melbourne: Health Department Victoria.

Parsons, T. 1964. *Social structure and personality.* New York: Free Press of Glencoe.

Pinto, S., A. Scandia, & P. Wilson. 1990. *Prostitution laws in Australia.* Canberra: Australian Institute Criminology.

Rollins, B. 1989. *Sexual attitudes and behaviours: A review of the literature.* Melbourne: Australian Institute of Family Studies.

Sears, J. T., ed. 1992. *Sexuality and the curriculum: The policies and practices of sexuality education.* New York: Teachers College Press.

Selling, J. A., ed. 2001a. *Embracing sexuality: Authority and experience in the Catholic Church.* Aldershot:Ashgate Publishing.

Selling, J. A. 2001b. The development of Catholic tradition and sexual morality. In: J. A. Selling, ed., *Embracing sexuality: Authority and experience in the Catholic Church* (pp. 149-162). Aldershot: Ashgate Publishing.

Siedlecky, S., & D. Wyndham. 1990. *Populate and perish: Australian women's fight for birth control.* Sydney: Allen and Unwin.

Simon Rosser, B. R. 1992. *Gay Catholics down under: The journeys in sexuality and spirituality of gay men in Australia and New Zealand.* Westport, CT: Praeger.

Sullivan, B. 1990. The business of sex: Australian government and the sex industry. *Australian and New Zealand Journal of Sociology, 27*(1):3-18.

Tonkinson, R. 1991. *The Mardu Aborigines: Living the dream in Australia's desert* (2/e). New York: Holt, Rinehart & Winston.

Uniting Church in Australia Assembly Task Group on Sexuality. 1997. *Uniting sexuality and faith.* Collingwood: The Joint Board of Christian Education.

UNAIDS. 2002. *Epidemiological fact sheets by country.* Geneva, Switzerland: Joint United Nations Programme on HIV/AIDS (UNAIDS/WHO). Available: http://www.unaids.org/hivaidsinfo/statistics/fact_sheets/index_en.htm.

Warner, W. L. 1937. *A black civilization.* New York: Harper.

Went, D. 1985. *Sex education—Some guidelines for teachers.* London: Bell & Hyman.

Western, J. S. 1992. Human sexuality in Australia: The quest for information. In: *Rethinking sex: Social theory and sexuality research.* Victoria: Melbourne University Press.

Wherrett, L., & W. Talbot. 1991. *HIV/AIDS prevention, homosexuality and the law.* Canberra: Department of Community Services and Health.

Whitehead, E. W., & D. Whitehead. *A sense of sexuality: Christian love and intimacy.* New York: Crossroad.

Whitehead, E. W., & J. D. Whitehead 2001. *The wisdom of the body: Making sense of our sexuality.* New York: Crossroad.

Willmett, T. 2002. *Conceptions of sexuality education held by a group of primary school teachers in the Catholic Archdiocese of Brisbane.* Unpublished doctoral dissertation, Queensland University of Technology, Brisbane, Australia.

Willmett, T. 2000. *Personal development education: A model for developing PDE in a school community.* Brisbane: Interpersonal Dynamics.

Ziebertz, H. 1992. Sex, love and marriage, the view of religious education teachers in Germany. *British Journal of Religious Education, 14*(3):151-156.

# Austria

## (*Republik Österreich*)

Dr. Rotraud A. Perner, L.L.D.*

*Translated and Redacted by*
Linda Kneucker

*Updates by Linda Kneucker, Raoul Kneucker, and
Martin Voracek, Ph.D., M.Sc.*

## Contents

## *Demographics and a Brief Historical Perspective*

ROBERT T. FRANCOEUR

### A. Demographics

Located in south central Europe, Austria is a land-locked nation strategically located at the crossroads of central Europe. With a landmass of 32,378 square miles (83,858 km²), Austria is slightly smaller than the state of Maine. Austria's neighbors include Switzerland and Liechtenstein on the west, Germany and the Czech Republic on the north, Slovakia and Hungary on the east, and Slovenia and Italy on the south. Austria is very mountainous, with the Alps and their foothills covering the western and southern parts of the nation. The northern margin and eastern provinces, including the capital of Vienna, are in the Danube River basin.

Since the collapse of the Habsburg (often spelled Hapsburg in English) Empire in 1918 after World War I, Austria comprises only nine states (or provinces). Clockwise, they are: Lower Austria, Vienna, Burgenland, Styria, Carinthia, Upper Austria, Salzburg, Tyrol, and Vorarlberg. In Burgenland, the smallest and farthest east, Hungarian and Croatian influences are noticeable, whereas Vorarlberg, lying farthest west, tends strongly towards Switzerland.

In July 2002, Austria had an estimated population of 8.17 million, with 20% (1.7 million) living in Vienna. (All data are from *The World Factbook 2002* (CIA 2002) unless otherwise stated.)

*Communications*: Main author: Mag. Dr. Rotraud A. Perner, Postfach 23 A-1013, Vienna, Austria; rotraud.a.perner@chello.at. *Updates*: Linda and Raoul Kneucker, Neustiftgasse 73-75/St. 2/14, A-1070 Vienna, Austria; kneucker@magnet.at. *Additional comments*: Martin Voracek, Ph.D., M.Sc., Univ.-Klinik für Tiefenpsychologie und Psychotherapie AKH / Währinger Gürtel 18-20 A-1090, Wien, Austria; martin.voracek@chello.at.

(CIA 2002)

**Age Distribution and Sex Ratios**: *0-14 years*: 16.4% with 1.05 male(s) per female (sex ratio); *15-64 years*: 68.2% with 1.02 male(s) per female; *65 years and over*: 15.4% with 0.62 male(s) per female; *Total population sex ratio*: 0.95 male(s) to 1 female

**Life Expectancy at Birth**: *Total Population*: 78 years; *male*: 74.85 years; *female*: 81.31 years

**Urban/Rural Distribution**: 53% to 47%

**Ethnic Distribution**: German: 88%; non-nationals, including Croatians, Slovenes, Hungarians, Czechs, Slovaks, Roma (Gypsies): 9.3%; naturalized: 2%

**Religious Distribution**: Roman Catholic: 78%; Protestant: 5%; Muslim and other: 17%

**Birth Rate**: 9.58 births per 1,000 population

**Death Rate**: 9.73 per 1,000 population

**Infant Mortality Rate**: 4.39 deaths per 1,000 live births

**Net Migration Rate**: 2.45 migrant(s) per 1,000 population

**Total Fertility Rate**: 1.4 children born per woman

**Population Growth Rate**: 0.23%

**HIV/AIDS** (2001 est.): *Adult prevalence*: 0.1%; *Persons living with HIV/AIDS*: 843; *Deaths*: < 100. (For additional details from www.UNAIDS.org, see end of Section 10B.)

**Literacy Rate** (*defined as those age 15 and over who can read and write*): 98; attendance rate for nine years of compulsory school: 95% (education is free and compulsory from age 6 to 15)

**Per Capita Gross Domestic Product** (*purchasing power parity*): $27,000 (2001 est.); *Inflation*: 2.6%; *Unemployment*: 4.8%; *Living below the poverty line*: NA

### B. A Brief Historical Perspective

The Romans conquered Austrian lands from Celtic tribes around 15 B.C.E. In 788 of the Common Era, the territory was incorporated into Charlemagne's Holy Roman Empire. By 1300, the House of Habsburg had gained control of the land. In the next few hundred years, they added to their realm vast territories in all parts of Europe.

Austria's dominance of Germany was undermined in the 18th century and ended with the rise of Prussia in 1866. However, the 1815 Congress of Vienna confirmed Austria's control of a large empire in southeast Europe, consisting of Germans, Hungarians, Slavs, Italians, and others. The Austro-Hungarian dual monarchy was established in 1867, when Hungary was given some autonomy. Fifty years of peace followed.

The 1914 assassination of Archduke Franz Ferdinand, the Habsburg heir, by a Serbian nationalist, led to World War I and dissolution of the Habsburg Empire when Austria, Germany, and the Ottoman Empire were defeated. Austria was then reduced to a small republic with the borders it has today. Nazi Germany invaded Austria in 1938; the republic was reestablished in 1945 under Allied occupation. Full independence and neutrality were restored in 1955.

[*Update 2003*: Politically, Austria is a democratic federal republic, with a proportional voting system. After the grand coalition between the moderately conservative People's Party and the moderate Social Democrats as a result of the 1995 elections, the political scene changed radically in 2000, when the nationalistic right-of-center Freedom Party received 26% of the votes, more than doubling the number from the earlier election, and was invited by the People's Party to form a coalition government. European Union sanctions, and weekly demonstrations that continued for the entire two years of the coalition government, followed. The European Court of Human Rights sent a commission, known as "The Three Wise Men," to investigate whether or not democracy was in danger, and the sanctions were lifted in September 2000. Jörg Haider, who had been the leader and loudest voice of the right-wing party, eventually lost his effectiveness. New elections were held in November 2002, and the Freedom Party lost two thirds of its support. The Greens gained in the last election, and it is not yet clear whether or not the grand coalition will again be entered into, or if there will be new political constellations. (*End of update by L. Kneucker*)]

There had been a radical change in Austria's political situation since October 3, 1999. The Parliamentary mandates in early 2000 were: 65 for the Social Democrats, and 52 for both the People's Party and the Freedom Party (with clear self-acknowledged fascist tendencies). The environmentalist Greens held 14 seats, and the Liberal Forum was no longer represented. There was, thus, a coalition government between the conservatives and the Freedom Party. Observers expected this alliance to bring a distinct increase of conservative, restrictive, and xenophobic ideas. The first sign of this conservative swing was seen in the abolishment of the Federal Ministry for Women's Affairs, which had, in its ten-year existence, been strongly engaged in combating violence against women and enacting harsher punishment for sexual offenses.

## 1. Basic Sexological Premises

### A. Character of Gender Roles

At the end of the 1960s, a kind of "velvet" cultural revolution began. Austria's women became conscious of the discrimination they experienced as women, their reduced roles as reproducers, and discrimination in the labor market. Social politics, activated by women in the new feminist movement, brought considerable social change, especially in the first years of the Socialist Government, between 1970 and 1983. Two signals of this revolution were the appointment of a State Secretary for Women's Rights in 1979 and, in 1990, establishment of a Ministry for Women's Affairs.

Women benefited most from the educational reforms of the 1960s and 1970s, even if there is still a difference in educational levels between men and women. The employment of women increased at the beginning of the 1970s and, in 1992, 62% of all women between the ages of 15 and 59 were gainfully employed. Improved training and the more skilled qualifications of women had, however, little influence on their salaries and positions. The average gross income of men was 43% higher than that earned by women.

In the course of the Family Law Reform of 1978, the marriage laws were changed from the legally incapacitating discriminatory laws against women to an emphasis on marriages based on partnership. Before this reform, the man was the "head of the family," and the woman had to take on his name. The man decided the place of residence. He could forbid his wife to work and could make all decisions concerning the children. His wife had to obey his "orders."

The practically unchanged sole responsibility of women for the care of children, the lack of institutions, such as day-care centers and kindergartens, a shortage of qualified part-time jobs, as well as potential motherhood, still greatly lessen the possibilities for women in the labor market. Women are subject to certain work prohibitions that are supposed to protect them, e.g., night shifts, but actually make entering certain occupations more difficult. Women who want both children and careers, something that is a matter of course for men, can often fulfill this only with double or triple burdens. Although it has been legally possible since January 1, 1990, for fathers to take leaves of absence from work for childcare (*Karenzurlaub*) until the child's second birthday, few men take such leaves. Many men also have difficulties with the legally established partnership in running a household, dividing the responsibilities of earnings, running the household, and raising children.

### B. Sociolegal Status of Males and Females

According to the equality principles of the Austrian constitution, all citizens (written in masculine form) are equal before the law (Article VII). Nevertheless, there are gender-specific differences in some laws that cannot be biologically justified, such as the legal protection for pregnant women and mothers.

Women and men are considered sexually mature when they are 14 years of age, i.e., they are seen as adult enough to be able to accept desired sexual contacts and refuse those they do not want (Perner 1994). In the case of homosexual contacts, however, the lawmakers believe that young men are not able to decide independently for or against them until they are 18. Women and men who are 19 are both considered to be of full legal age, but the marriageable age for women is 16, and for men 19 years. Women can retire with pension at age 60, five years earlier than men, but, as of 2019, the age will be successively raised for women who were born after 1962 and, eventually, the pension age for men and women will be the same—65 years. There is no military conscription for women.

### C. General Concepts of Sexuality and Love

The general sexual concept of love is within a heterosexual relationship. It is based on love and should be realized, preferably, in a life-long marriage, or at least as a partnership for life or a stable partnership. As a result of this attitude, practically all young Austrian women were married in the early 1960s. Since the 1970s, there has been a change to more pluralism: The age for marriage and for bearing the first child has risen; the number of those who marry and have children has fallen. The number of extramarital births has risen, as well as the possibility of divorce and remarriage of those who have divorced. Still, the wish to marry is prevalent among 70 to 80% of youth.

Norms and attitudes relating to sexuality have also changed since the end of the 1960s. The availability of different methods of birth control and the possibility for legal abortion within the first three months (trimester) have given many women their first feelings of freedom regarding sexuality. Considering the frequent occurrence of sexual violence against women, it is, however, only possible in a limited way to talk about the sexual liberation of women.

Except in a few ethnic groups and religious minorities, virginity is not given any special value at the time of marriage. Although "wild" marriages and unmarried mothers and their children were stigmatized and legally discriminated against in the 1960s, life partnerships, "illegitimate" children, and single mothers are increasingly accepted in society. Likewise, relationships before marriage that include sexual intercourse and a series of monogamous relationships are accepted, and not only the ideal of "one great love." Despite the Church's opposition (e.g., by forbidding the use of most birth control methods), sexual desire and procreation are seen as separate from one another; as proven by the low fertility rate of 1.5 children per woman.

The norm for sexual intercourse is still the "complete" face-to-face heterosexual coitus with ejaculation. The attitude towards homosexuality is still negative, socially excluding, and, in traditional Catholic circles, openly hostile. Its impact can be seen in attempts to maintain legal discrimination against homosexual lovers. However, in recent years in Austria, the discussion in favor of recognition of homosexual partners is no longer taboo, and is in fact increasing.

## 2. Religious, Ethnic, and Gender Factors Affecting Sexuality

### A. Source and Character of Religious Values

To be religious in Austria is a sort of "social-cultural matter of course" accompanied by a certain amount of social pressure. The majority of Austrians are members of the Roman Catholic Church, which exerts a traditionally dominant role in comparison to other religious communities. Especially during the time of Austrian Fascism, 1934-1938, the cultural and political life was determined by the Catholic Church. Austria was organized as a so-called corporate country that met the Catholic concept of a corporate system (Encyclical, *Quadragesimo Anno* of Pius XI: 15.5.1931). It was seen as the responsibility of the State to guard moral life. In this model, according to the Constitution of 1934, women were only considered equal to men if laws did not determine otherwise. In 1929 and in 1930, Pope Pius XI had confirmed the subordinate role of the woman in marriage in two encyclicals.

Since 1970, the number of withdrawals from the Catholic Church has increased dramatically, especially because of the sexual morals of the Church that are no longer accepted by many of its believers (above all, because of the prohibition of the pill in the encyclical, *Humanae Vitae*, by Pope Paul VI in 1968). These teachings define the Catholic view regarding the rigid regulations of the sexes: Mary, the Mother of God, as childbearing without sexuality (on the basis of the virgin birth) as a model for women was emphasized. Virginity was given the highest value, and a motherhood of sacrifice was propagated as the essential duty of women. During the period of National Socialism, the veneration of Mary and the ideal of chastity were mixed with ideas of "racial purity" and therefore fit into the National Socialist regime.

Sexuality in Catholicism is only permitted in the insoluble state of marriage, since for hundreds of years biological reproduction was considered the one purpose of marriage. The encyclicals of Pope Pius XI (1930) dealing with marriage underlined the value of love in marriage that was especially confirmed later by the Second Vatican Council (1962-1965): The value of this love exists, even without reference to procreation. It is bound to marriage, with sexual intercourse, as a permanent unity. The moral system, according to the teachings of the Church, requires that heterosexual coitus must not interfere with the possibility of procreation. However, intercourse is also permitted when procreation is not possible (during the woman's monthly infertile period) or no longer possible (after menopause).

Marriage in Catholic teaching is the replica of the love of God for human beings: Christ is the bridegroom, the Church is the bride, and the Catholic family is the smallest church community, the "home church." The love relationship of the responsible couple, according to this concept, includes "natural birth control" (measurement of the infertile days of the woman).

According to the encyclical *Humanae Vitae* (1968), every form of active birth control is forbidden by the Church. However, this opinion does not require absolute obedience, as it is not a question of infallible dogma, but a writing of the pope. Because of the acceptance of the theological concept of "immediate animation," the presence of the soul at the moment of conception, abortion was (and is) considered murder. In 1991, one third of all Austrians and 40% of the female population stated that religion was meaningful for conducting their life. Forty percent of those who were religious thought that sex education in schools was damaging. A third of the religious wished that homosexuality would be again legally punishable (of the non-believers, one fourth wanted this).

The 1995 encyclical *Evangelium Vitae* (John Paul II) condemned abortion, as well as birth control, as generally being enemies of "life." Masturbation was seen as a terrible sin, or, at least, as against the rules. In the same way, practiced homosexuality was condemned as immoral.

Mostly it is the rural and farming population that lives according to Catholic norms. However, the majority of Austrians do not think highly of the ever-increasingly authoritarian path the Vatican has been taking. The comments of the official Church regarding sexual themes are reacted to with resistance.

In 1995, a Church referendum was initiated, calling for a "sisterly church," i.e., demanding that women be admitted to Church offices. It opposed the compulsory celibacy of priests, protested against the equating of birth control with abortion, and pleaded that questions of sexual morals be the responsibility of the individual's personal conscience.

In the minority Protestant churches, heterosexuality and one life-long marriage are seen as values that in a specific way correspond to the will of God. Marriage is, however, a worldly concern and therefore does not have a sacramental character as in the Catholic Church. For unborn life, the same rights of protection are given as for persons; but abortion is not categorically considered murder.

Discussion of homosexuality is still controversial in the Protestant church. In 1992, the theological commission published a statement declaring:

- the right of people to determine their own lifestyles;
- homosexuals must be respected and accepted in Christian communities;
- an ethical judgment on homosexuality in today's humanistic understanding cannot be found in the Bible; and
- a homosexual identity cannot be "turned around" or cured.

In Austria's Protestant churches today, those who identify themselves as homosexuals can be employees as well as pastors. The blessing of homosexual couples is not yet officially possible in the Protestant churches. However, an agenda for a concept for blessings is being worked out and will probably be accepted at the next synod.

In contrast, the "Invocavit" declaration of 1995, which was signed by 150 Protestant theologians and church employees as a reaction to the General Synod, rejected homosexuality, considering it contradictory to the will of God, the creator. It was considered a "destructive aberration of emotional life." In the view of the authors, homosexuals may not be employees in the church, and church blessings for homosexual couples are rejected as well.

The synod of the Neo-Catholic Church of Austria resolved that homosexuals are to be respected in their personalities, beliefs, and their cooperation in their communities. For homosexual life companions who intend their relationships to be permanent, church blessings were made possible at the synod of October 18, 1997.

## 3. Knowledge and Education about Sexuality

### A. Government Policies and Programs

In the 19th century and earlier, sex education was part of the Catholic educational instructions. The emphasis was on what was forbidden, and on remaining chaste and faithful before and in marriage. Masturbation was forbidden as a sin. Sexual intercourse before marriage, with or without force, was taboo and therefore not talked about. Nevertheless, the first sexual intercourse of aristocratic young men was often arranged by their fathers, when it was clear they had completed puberty. They were taken to a brothel for their first sexual experiences. In the upper-middle class or among prosperous farmers, sexual availability was expected from the female servants. If one became pregnant, she was sent away.

After the establishment of the Republic in 1918 and the election of the first female representatives, the female pioneers of the Social Democratic Party continually demanded institutions for sex education and counseling, and their priority was to increase help with questions about birth control. The first attempts were made when the Social Democrats took over the government in the capital, Vienna, through the work of the legendary City Councilman Julius Tandler. At the same time, Wilhelm Reich, a student of Freud, established the first outpatient sex clinics. With the growing strength of National Socialism and the emigration of the leading Jewish doctors, the initiative came to a standstill. After the end of World War II, it took about 25 years until the women's movement could push for a new abortion law and address questions of sex education. At practically the same time, at the suggestion of the parents' council of the Education Ministry, a seminar conducted by experts in September 1969 provided the push, making possible the decree, *Sex Education in the Schools* (November 24, 1970), in which sex education was introduced as an interdisciplinary principle of instruction.

A *Media Package* was prepared by the Federal Ministry of Education and the Federal Ministry for Family Affairs (now known as the Federal Ministry for the Environment, Youth, and Family) as the main teaching tool from 1984 to 1989. This production produced a vehement argument between the Marxist-oriented progressive psychoanalysts and Christian-conservative repressive-oriented sex educators. In the final edition that came out with the title, *Love with Responsibility*, basic sexology was emphasized, and, in the didactic part, a wealth of suggestions for exercises and games for the classroom was given.

The Catholic-oriented Institute for Marriage and Family, with the support of the Education and Family Ministries, developed a program, *Working Group: Parents, Stu-*

*dents and Teachers—Partners in Sex Education.* For this, specially trained moderators in the schools offered general help in establishing communication between the groups and in working out concrete sex education projects for specific schools. This was done at no cost to the schools. (For additional information on sexuality education in the schools and at home, see Section 5B below).

In addition, both ministries offered special booklets. *Gynnie*, cosponsored by the Austrian Medical Association, provided answers to relevant gynecological questions, as well as questions about relationships. Brochures were also published for non-students; for example, the Family Ministry offered *So That Love Can Grow*, along with accompanying group discussions and help in seminars concerning topics of sexuality. Austrians seeking counseling and advice can turn to 220 family and partner counseling centers that have been established all over Austria and are financially supported by the Family Ministry. Four of these centers are explicitly declared as counseling centers for sex and sexuality. The Austrian Society for Planned Parenthood, founded in 1966, has established six counseling centers with an emphasis on birth control. These centers are in hospitals, and one is especially for young people. There, examinations can be carried out and contraception prescribed and distributed. Another initiative of this group is Herzklopfen (Heart Throbbing), which offers confidential telephone counseling especially for young people, and is therefore available on Saturday afternoons.

[*Update 2003*: During the Conservative Party and Freedom Party coalition, the name of the Ministry of Social Affairs and Health was changed to the Ministry of Social Affairs and Generations (BMSG). Radical social changes were not made, but the renamed ministry issued a brochure for young people, *Love, Sex and So*, in 2002, which replaced all earlier educational materials (http://www.bmsg .gv.at/bmsg/relaunch/jugend/welcome.htm). The new brochure has been criticized by the Catholic Church as being "too liberal." HOSI (2003) has a comparative chart of all European countries up-to-date concerning "punishable" acts by gays and lesbians (Graupner 2003). (*End of update by L. Kneucker*)]

### B. Informal Sources of Sexual Knowledge

*Bravo*, a German magazine for young people, is widely read in Austria, mainly, however, by less educated youngsters. In the late 1980s and early 1990s, *Rennbahn Express* (*Racetrack Express*) was quite popular and widely read by educated young people. Although it offers sexual information on two full pages 11 times a year, answers letters to the editor about sex, carries regular columns on health relating to sexuality, and has an Internet Web page offering counseling, the magazine is now decidedly out-of-fashion among young people, leaving the field open for new magazines to move in.

The media offers popular, if not always serious sexual information. The *Kronen Zeitung*, a daily newspaper in small format published in Vienna, offers "the man in the street" flowery-formulated but simply expressed answers to questions related to sex, and every Tuesday publishes letters from readers. Some newspapers in the provinces copy these letters. The original radio program, *Sex Hotline*, appreciated by many older listeners, was offered by ORF, the Austrian Radio, every two weeks on Fridays for two hours beginning at midnight. After 5 years, the program was given a new name, *Love Line*, and a year later was taken off the air, because the public was no longer as interested as in earlier years. *Zick Zack*, a program for youth that also offered young people the opportunity to call up and ask for advice, was a success, but was no longer aired after January

1995. Until 1997, there was a radio talk show that was replaced by *Joe's Nachtclub* (*Joe's Nightclub*) every Saturday from midnight until 2 a.m. While these informal sources of sexuality information come and go, Austrian media consistently provides some popular sources of information on sexuality.

## 4. Autoerotic Behaviors and Patterns

### A. Children and Adolescents

Austria is a country without any tradition in sex education and pedagogy. To a large extent, moral values are stamped, "Repress the bodily functions" by the Catholic Church, as well as by the Puritanism of the *petite bourgeoisie*. Masturbation may be still tainted as sinful and forbidden for many older Austrians, who view it as "tainting your soul" ("*schwarze Pädagogic*") or still believe the myth that the number of ejaculations in their lives will be limited to 1,000—"*1,000 Schuß, dann ist Schluß*" ("1,000 shots poured and then there is nothing more").

Nevertheless, masturbation is widespread among young people, and aside from traumatic sexual experiences, autoeroticism is among their very first conscious sexual experiences. Among boys, 60% of the 13-year-olds and 80% of the 14-year-olds have experience in masturbation, and 100% of the 16-year-olds. According to Nöstlinger and Wimmer-Puchinger (1994), girls have less experience with masturbation than boys: 25% of the 13-year-olds and 50% of the 17-year-olds. European studies indicate that masturbation is experienced earlier than it was in the 1960s, especially for girls. There are no comparative figures for Austria, but it can be assumed that the tendency is similar.

### B. Adults

In Austrian studies, questions about masturbation are either not asked or are peripheral questions. Langbein and Fritsch (1991) remarked that masturbation was not thematically included in the basic Institut für Empirische Sozialforschung (IFES, Institute for Empirical Social Research) study, since international studies would in any case show that around 90% of all adults practice masturbation. A study by Senger and Hoffmann (1993) reported that about three quarters of all men and less than two thirds of all women masturbate, whereas the frequency of men, 1.6 times weekly, is twice that of women. Single people masturbate above the average, 2.2 times each week, and persons under the age of 40 masturbate more often than older people.

Adult heterosexuals who consult clinicians on the issue of masturbation usually do so because they view masturbation as taboo and something that is done in secret with a bad conscience. Many ask if it is "normal" to have the need to masturbate parallel to sexual intercourse.

The problem hardly affects homosexual men, because they view mutual masturbation as a favored sexual outlet. When AIDS emerged, "jack-off parties" became just as popular in Austria's gay communities as in other countries. These parties were held in private circles where community masturbation as a safer-sex method was practiced. Verified information from lesbians is not available, although the tendency is probably rising, as it is for women in general. Stronger self-determination in sexuality and more confident attitudes about their own bodies—"My body belongs to me!"—have probably contributed positively to the frequency of masturbation for both heterosexual and lesbian women.

Altogether, the viewpoint that masturbation is by all means an enrichment, and not only a substitute for one's sex life in a partnership, is gaining recognition, even if slowly and still unmentionable in public.

Masturbation does not cease when Austrians get older. Although there are no statistics available for Austria, the experiences in supervised residential situations reveal that, just as seen in international studies, masturbation in old-age homes or nursing homes is part of daily life.

## 5. Interpersonal Heterosexual Behaviors

### A. Children

The uncontested right of children to their individual forms of sexuality, as recognized by sexual researchers, is acknowledged only hesitantly by the general public. The only context in which children's sexuality is usually mentioned or discussed is in the context of sexual abuse.

When observed, any form of children's sexual activities—masturbation, "playing doctor," father-mother games—are often repressed and denied, because "what is not permitted, does not exist." A still-restrictive sex education concept tries to condemn children's sexual behavior with "black pedagogical" sanctions, or to keep it a secret. Rethinking these questions began slowly in the early 1990s.

### B. Adolescents

Young people enter puberty earlier than they did a few generations ago. The first menstruation also takes place earlier. Eleven-year-olds who have their first periods are now the rule rather than the exception.

Based on law, a decree known as the "Sex Education Decree" was issued by the Ministry for Education about 15 years ago. Sex education was to be given at schools as an interdisciplinary subject, with the strong participation of parents. In the middle of the 1980s, the Austrian Institute for Family Research undertook a study to find out how far the program had actually been put into practice. The first finding of this study was that when sex education is taught, it was in two subject areas: in biology classes, where information is emphasized, and in religion classes, where values are emphasized. Thereupon, the Institute developed a model that is called *Love Talks* to coordinate the two. It is the only model for sex education in Austrian schools, and has been adopted for use in South Tyrol, Germany, and the Czech Republic. The second finding showed that sex education is not a question of knowledge, but rather a communication problem. This information was incorporated into *Love Talks*. A moderator, who comes from outside the school, works to bring parents, teachers, and students together at one table to discuss pertinent topics. In addition, a sex education program for the school (workshops, field trips, etc.) is planned for different levels and classes. How this is concretely carried out depends on the individual interests of the school. The cost of the moderator is covered by the Ministry for Education, and therefore, the model can be offered to the schools at no additional cost.

Meanwhile, time and again, there are discussions about including sex education as a regular school subject in the curriculum. Up to the present, however, sex education as an educational means to support the capability of entering and experiencing relationships in all of their complexity is only available through *Love Talks*.

Sex education is not necessarily keeping pace with the personal experiences of youth. Although sex education in schools has been established as an educational principle for more than two generations, only half of the young people are actually given sex education in schools. At home the situation is the same. In a large-scale study about the sexuality of youth in 1994, 1,108 young people between the ages of 15 and 18 were questioned. The responses were: 94% of all young people had been in love once—on average, at 12.9 years old the first time, with 14 years old most often reported as the age. By age 14, 91% had had a date, and 89% had already "put their first kiss behind them" (with the average age for their first kiss at about 13). For male students, the percentages were clearly lower.

Young people reported their first romantic friendships, on average, at the age of 14, when 72% of the 1,108 students sampled had already had a steady partner. On average, at age 15, the first petting took place for 62% of those surveyed. The least experienced with petting were male students who lived in the country, 44%; the most experienced were female apprentices living in the cities, 91%. Forty-three percent of the young people reported that they already had had their first heterosexual experiences other than petting at age 15. The highest percentage was among male apprentices in cities, where 85% reported having had their first heterosexual [oral sex] experience, clearly above the average. The average young person was 15.5 years old the "first time," with the first sexual intercourse taking place at the age of 16: girls 33% and boys 36%. Among the girls, 4% were less than 13 years old; 3% of the boys were under age 13. In the 14-to-15 age group, more girls have had sexual intercourse than boys.

The sexually experienced young people reported having had sexual intercourse a number of times. The most frequent sexual intercourse took place with a steady partner (40%); and 39% reported that they had had two or three partners. Only 4.5% of the girls and 11% of the boys had had sexual experience with more than five partners. At the time of the study, 72% had a steady boy- or girlfriend. The average duration of a friendship for young people was 11 months; the response most often given was 60 days.

Kissing and cuddling are the sexual activities most often indulged in, reported by 98.5%. Eighty-five percent reported "petting" and 66% sexual intercourse. Their emotional level and sense of sexual faithfulness play an important role for young people. Only 6% reported that they had been "unfaithful" to their partners.

A lasting relationship is an ideal for 79% of young people. Almost two thirds emphasized the wish to marry, and three fourths expressed the desire to have children. There was no significant difference between boys and girls. The figures from the study coincide with information from counseling and work with young people, where the expectation of traditional values, such as partnership, faithfulness, family, and so on, are clearly articulated.

## C. Adults

The legal regulations on the protection of minors generally set the "age of consent" at 14 years for consensual sexual relationships. This applies to both heterosexual and lesbian relationships. For male homosexual relationships, the age of consent is 18. Sexual relationships between adults and minors over 15, with the exception of gay male relationships, are legally permitted, as long as force or coercion is not used, and there is no exploitation of a dependent relationship.

About 18% of the adult Austrians between the ages of 17 and 70 live as "singles." The trend towards living alone is quickly rising. In 1993, about 900,000 people lived on their own; two years later, the figure was 1.2 million, an increase of 33%..

"Typical" singles are women over 50 years of age. Twenty-five percent of this age group lives alone, although whether they are divorced, widowed, or simply without partners is not known. Other singles include young men— 38% of all those under the age of 30—as well as young women in school, about 40%, and farmers, 20%. Females in colleges and universities are more likely to live alone than their non-academic peers.

The incidence of sexual intercourse among singles is low. More than half have no sexual partner, and only one in ten have intercourse once a week (Langbein & Fritsch 1991). Only 5% live as "swinging singles," i.e., have several sex partners at the same time. Of these, 42% want a steady relationship.

Another trend is a steady relationship without a common household, currently about 16%. A third of the young couples under the age of 30, and practically half of all divorced persons, have such relationships. Of those, 68% said that they have sexual intercourse at least once a week. Only 6% do without sexual activities completely. Of those couples who live separately, two thirds stated that they had happy and intensive love relationships, whereas of those pairs living together, only 56% expressed this view. Altogether, sex is more important to those who do not live together than it is to those who do live together. Nineteen percent had the opinion that sex was the strongest bond to their partners, and 59% are satisfied with their sex lives. Of those who live together, 8% felt that sex was the strongest bond, and 49% are satisfied with their sex lives.

About one third of all Austrian women between the ages of 16 and 70 live in a common household with their partners. The reference to the age limit of 70 is important, because in the study cited here, people over 70 were not included. If they are added to the figures, then the number of single households rises, and the number of pairs sharing a household becomes smaller. Higher life expectancy and lower birthrates lead to a constantly rising proportion of single older women. Senger and Hoffmann (1993) point out in their study that 22% live alone, 22% live in a partnership without children, and 56% live in a traditional family with children. The trend points clearly to families with one child.

Every third marriage does not last. In large cities, every second marriage ends in divorce. In the country, where traditional values and social controls have a stronger influence, the rate of divorce is clearly lower.

The average number of acts of sexual intercourse among adult Austrians is 2.4 times a week. The modal value is, however, once a week (21.1%). Twenty percent have intercourse up to twice a week, and just as high is the share of those who have intercourse less than once a month or never. This tendency is sinking. In 1980, only 11% of those asked answered that they had less sexual intercourse than once a month or never, and at least 63% responded with at least once a week, and in 1991 it was only 53%. Men are somewhat more active than women—2.6 times a week for men, and 2.1 times a week for women. This indicates that women are "more faithful" than men.

As varying as the survey data is for "faithfulness," the proportion has stayed the same. For every unfaithful woman there are two unfaithful men (12% to 20.7% in contrast to 29% to 40.1%, respectively). Compared to these figures, nine out of ten Austrians responded that faithfulness in a relationship is especially important.

The satisfaction with the extent and quality of one's sex life is relatively high. Sixty-seven percent (men 63%, women 71%) indicated that they did not wish for more sex. Only 16% (24% men, 8% women) were not satisfied. The sexually most active is the group of 30- to 49-year-olds (at least once a week—60%), and satisfaction is here somewhat higher than the average (men 65%; women 8%). The majority of Austrians are satisfied with the length of intercourse: 28% said that the average sexual act lasted more than half an hour, and around half spend ten to 30 minutes. There is a significant difference between housewives and working women: 70% of the housewives are content with their sexual lives, as opposed to 53% of working women.

That women are, in general, more sexually contented than men is certainly linked with the still prevailing Catholic image of the woman who is to remain passive and take the place to which she is directed. The growing employment of women appears to allow a slow but certain emancipation process to develop.

For unconventional sexual practices, there are no legal restrictions, as long as they are carried out with mutual consent and injuries do not result. There are practically no statistics about the societal acceptance of fetishes, sadomasochism, or other unconventional sex games. What pleases both is permitted, as long as this is not spoken about too publicly. Advertisements are permitted.

About 60% of Austrians practice oral sex (men 70%; women 52%). Heterosexual anal intercourse is acknowledged as a possibility by about one third (40% of the men, but less than 20% of the women).

The wish for group sex is felt by a third of Austrians. Around 1,000 persons actually look for appropriate saunas and clubs so that they can practice group sex and partner exchange, and this is done by, above all, the educated, independently employed, and freelancers. Interest is highest among young men between the ages of 16 and 29. Seven percent of the men enjoy this, but only 1% of the women.

The sexuality of the aging is an area that has undergone very little research, because the issue is largely suppressed in public. "Love," as the most important element in a relationship with a partner, is mentioned by only one quarter of the women and one third of the men, and only 4% mention sexuality as the element that binds one partner to the other. That does not mean that sexuality no longer plays a role: 45% of the men and 21% of the women between the ages of 50 and 60 stated that they had sexual intercourse at least once a week. International studies reveal regular sexual contact also by those who are over 70. In Austria, there are no figures available. Observations and experience working with aging people show, however, that sexuality in old age is not passé, only the quality changes. As with young people, manual practices have an important place, although they are often discriminated against as "senile disinhibition." A serious consideration of sex in old age has only begun, and this, slowly. Those studying this question are usually people who work in health professions.

Similarly not discussed is the sexuality of handicapped persons. The legal regulations of protection against encroachment, abuse, and exploitation of dependency are also supposed to apply to the mentally handicapped. Within these regulations is the controversy about the sterilization of mentally handicapped persons. Until 1974, compulsory sterilization was carried out on mentally handicapped persons. The basis for this was the *Reichsüberleitungsgesetze* of the National Socialist legal system. Such regulations did not exist in the Austrian penal code before 1938. Still today, the sterilization of mentally handicapped persons can be carried out against the will of the affected person, if the parents or the guardian and the responsible court give their permissions for the operation. The question does arise whether or not a mentally retarded individual has the possibility to understand the operation. According to reliable reports, this permission is given less and less in recent years, partly because of strong protests from human rights activists.

Until recently, the sexual needs and rights of handicapped persons are often ignored or denied in public discussion. Now at least, thanks to the initiative of the handicapped themselves and organizations for the handicapped, a serious discussion has begun, albeit slowly. One of the major reasons, and goals, of the discussion is so that institutions, such as homes or nursing hospitals, can create the necessary basic conditions that permit and safeguard intimacy, as well as allow physical contact between those who live and work there.

## 6. Homoerotic, Homosexual, and Bisexual Behaviors

Data that would allow reliable conclusions about how many Austrian women and men are homosexual are scanty, and until now were only available as a "by-product" of two empirical studies about the sexual behavior of Austrians. Langbein and Fritsch reported in 1991 that 200,000 Austrians identified themselves as homosexual or bisexual, i.e., about 3% according to a representative study by Weiss and Perner in 1991 for Institut für Empirische Sozialforschung. In a study done by Senger and Hoffmann (1993) based on a questionnaire distributed by the popular newspaper, *Neue Kronenzeitung*, 6.2% of the men and 9.6% of the women who answered declared themselves homosexual. Seven percent of the women responded as bisexual. [*Comment 2000*: It was not clear from the newspaper report whether the 7% of the women who responded as bisexual were part of the 9.6% or in addition to it. (*End of comment by R. T. Francoeur*)] However, the author assumes that the differences between these Austrian data and data from other countries are not significant.

Studies concerning how many young people have homosexual experiences during adolescence, or about a "coming-out" phase do not exist. The comparison of data from other countries with testimony from those affected lead to the conclusion that the coming out of homosexual Austrians does not differ from other white Europeans or North Americans: Most of them define themselves as definitely homosexual by the ages of 19 to 21. The length of time for the coming out of girls is increasingly similar to that of boys. The differences between city dwellers and those who live in the country play a large role for both sexes. Comparatively, however, few young Austrians are without prejudices. And few have access to positive information about homosexuality. Those who do have this information are mostly homosexuals and lesbians, and most of these are in Vienna.

Gay male adolescents seeking to establish personal contact with peer or older homosexuals, or wrestling with the decision of whether or not to come out face two obstacles. Gay males over age 19 face the risk of legal charges if they develop a personal relationship with another gay under age 18. In addition, the societal reaction to AIDS resulting in negative attitudes toward homosexuals has also made coming out more difficult. In comparison, young women have an easier time coming out, since the silence about lesbians and a lesbian way of life has been broken, and consequently models of behavior have become socially visible.

However, the societal, legal, social, and political situation is, as mentioned above, typified by numerous discriminations. Basically, it has been observed and established that brutal forms of discrimination are employed against male homosexuals (in the penal code and in working situations), while lesbians are more likely to encounter silence, ridicule, or put-downs in the popular media and in the health-care community. Anti-pornography laws are seldom if ever invoked to restrict portrayals of lesbian sexuality used by the pornography industry for their erotic appeal to heterosexual men, but erotic videos made by lesbians for lesbians are very often confiscated and forbidden.

With respect to the legal situation of homosexuality, prior to the "small reform" of Austrian criminal laws in 1975, sexual acts between members of the same sex were punishable. This was a tradition that goes back to the Empress Maria

Theresia in Article 74 of the "*Constitutio Criminalis Theresiana*" (1768), a criminal code issued for the Habsburg countries, where the death penalty was permitted. In 1852, Article 129 of the Austrian Penal Code stipulated hard prison sentences between one and five years for "unnatural fornication" for both sexes. The resistance of Catholic organizations prevented removing female homosexuality from the realm of the criminal in 1930.

During the time of the National Socialist occupation, Article 129 still applied and Austrian laws concerning homosexuality remained in effect. From 1938 until 1945, an unknown number of homosexual Austrians, who were identified with a pink triangle that they were forced to sew on their clothing, were sent to concentration camps and murdered. Lesbians were persecuted as "anti-social" and sent to work and penal camps. The number of trials involving homosexuals of both sexes and the number of those condemned to prison multiplied. However, basic historiographic research has not yet been done.

Unlike other groups who have been officially recognized as victims and, as such, have received some indemnity and some compensation from the Republic of Austria, homosexuals have not been compensated, not only because of the objections of the interest groups of survivors of the concentration camps, but also because the responsible federal ministers for social affairs have refused to recognize homosexuals as political victims.

Until the "small reform" of the criminal code removed "simple homosexuality" from the criminal code in 1975, about 13,000 Austrians were convicted of "unnatural fornication" between 1950 and 1971, of which 5% were women. After 1971, because of special pressure from the Catholic Church, conservative circles, and government advisors, four articles discriminatory against homosexuals were introduced into the Austrian Criminal Code:

- Article 209 states that a sexual relationship between someone over the age of 19 with someone who is younger than 18—the "age of consent"—is a criminal act. (See Update 2003 at the end of this section.)
- Article 210, which made prostitution between men punishable and, therefore, forced it into the underground, was removed in 1989, based on arguments pertaining to AIDS prevention.
- Article 220 forbids both sexes to advertise fornication with animals or persons of the same sex.
- Article 221 forbids both sexes to establish associations with the same goals.

On November 26, 1996, Article 220 forbidding advertising and Article 221 forbidding the establishment of associations were eliminated from the criminal code. However, the age of consent for boys (Article 209) remained in effect. In Austria, the age of consent for male homosexuals was 18; for female homosexuals and heterosexuals, however, it was 14 years of age.

Other forms of discrimination can also be found in civil law, especially in rental laws, vis-à-vis life partnerships of homosexuals, and even stronger regarding laws regarding marriage, employment, and social insurance. Central to this discrimination is the definition of "relatives," which includes marriage partners, parents, children, and in certain instances heterosexual partners. Only those mentioned, for example, have the right to be party to contracts. In 1998, the definition of "relationships" was extended to include homosexual partnerships.

Because of its important social and political position and as a regular advisor in questions of legal reforms, the Catholic Church, with its strong discriminatory policy against homosexuals, has the possibility to act in far more cases than in those involving only religious questions. In comparison, the Protestant and Neo-Catholic churches in Austria play an insignificant political role.

In the fields of medicine, psychiatry, psychology, psychotherapy, and health institutions, there are at least no official attempts to force people to be heterosexual. In Vienna, lesbians and gay men can turn to a few homosexual or unprejudiced doctors and psychotherapists.

Although in the pedagogical professions there are no official prohibitions against the employment of homosexual educators, in practically all occupations unconventional sexual preferences are kept secret. Individual cases of firing are known. Information about homosexuality is not made available in the teacher training. However, in the last few years, students in Vienna's Academy for Social Professions have been permitted to do internships at homosexual associations.

In scientific research, only one study of lesbians and gay men has been financially supported by the government. At Austrian universities, the personal initiative of a few dedicated scholars has introduced some lectures on lesbian and gay studies in the areas of sociology, psychology, and political science. Notice was given to self-acknowledged lesbians at the University of Vienna at the beginning in the early 1990s that lesbian and other homosexual research is not considered among the mainstream disciplines. Supporters of this research are always under pressure to scientifically prove the legitimacy of their studies.

The possibility for an undisguised and self-determined homosexual way of life depends strongly on geographical and social conditions. By and large, Austria is a country with small-town structures, and social and sociosexual control mechanisms, which have remained intact despite tourism. Hence, homosexuals avoid the cultural difficulties of living in the country and towns and move to the larger cities, especially Vienna, where there is a certain protection, on the one hand, and on the other, better opportunities for contacts. The question of "How do I tell my parents?" is much more difficult in rural villages, not only because of the possible ostracism of the person affected, but also for the family from which he or she comes.

In the past few years, the trend among homosexual men to establish permanent relationships has become apparent, on the one hand, because of the influence of AIDS, but, on the other hand, because of increasing socialization opportunities. How many lesbians or gays live in partnership is unknown. How far these structures differ from those in heterosexual partnerships is now (in late 2000) being studied for a dissertation at the Department of Psychology at the University of Vienna.

Sexual practices made a striking shift in the 1980s because of AIDS. Austria was the first country in Europe with a sex education brochure about AIDS. The brochure was done through an initiative of the gay movement. The social pressure to use protection in anal and oral intercourse is very strong, especially in towns where activist groups exist. According to Senger and Hoffmann, oral intercourse is the most frequent practice among homosexuals, followed by anal intercourse. (However, since the study is based on responses to a questionnaire in a popular newspaper to which Senger has contributed a popularly written column for years, the representativeness and lack of bias in the sample is certainly questionable). There are no researched statistics on the sexual practices of lesbians. Based on the work of Shere Hite and the Kinsey Institute, one can assume that in Austria, as elsewhere in Europe and North America, oral intercourse and digital stimulation are the most frequent sexual lesbian practices.

Lesbians and gay men have organized themselves, although rather late, because of rigorous criminal laws as well as everyday persecution, even though Vienna, at the time of the First Republic (1918-1934) was one of the European centers of homosexual subculture and a very differentiated homosexual movement existed. These early traditions were completely destroyed by Austrian fascism (1934-1938) and National Socialism (1938-1945), both in substance, in organization, and in persons.

The first modern organizations for lesbians grew out of the autonomous feminist movement in the 1970s. Today, independent lesbian separatist feminist groups exist in Vienna as well as in some other provincial capitals. Their members are usually active in various areas of the independent feminist movement. Gays began to organize themselves only at the end of the 1970s. The first institution was the Homosexual Initiative (HOSI) Vienna, which is also active in various international homosexual associations (ILGA—International Lesbian and Gay Association, ILIS—the International Lesbian Information Service, and IGLYO—International Gay and Lesbian Youth Organization). In Church circles, Homosexuality and Church, an ecumenical working group, is significant, as well as the Ecumenical Platform of Homosexual Clergymen (ÖPSSÖ). At present, there are a number of lesbian and gay pressure groups that are also active in international homosexual associations. The high point on the lesbian–gay calendar is the Gay Pride Day at the end of June that usually includes a demonstration. For lesbians, March 8, the International Women's Day is a "must." In 1984 and 1989, Vienna was the venue for the Annual Conference of the International Lesbian and Gay Association (ILGA), and was organized by HOSI, Vienna.

[*Update 2003*: Each year, a different European city is chosen to organize the events for "Europride," a month-long festival of activities and a parade with participants from all over Europe. Vienna was the site chosen for 2001. Over 100,000 participants took part in the parade and other events, bringing gays and lesbians into an even clearer self-confidence. It also marked a major development in the visibility of the homosexual men and women in Austrian culture.

[Another important development was the repeal of Article 209, one of four articles introduced into the Austrian Criminal Code in the 1970s under strong pressure from religious conservatives, the Catholic Church, and government advisors. Article 209 stated that a sexual relationship between a man over the age of 19 with someone who is younger than 18—the "age of consent"—is a criminal act. The age of consent for female partners was already 14. In June 2002, the Federal Constitutional Court declared Article 209 PC unconstitutional. On July 10, Article 209 was repealed by Parliament; the general age of consent was set at age 14 for both gay and heterosexual relationships, and the law went into effect one month later. However, at the same time, new criminal code provisions were enacted:

[Under the provisions of 207b, it is now a criminal offense to engage in sexual activities if the older partner takes advantage of the immaturity of his partner, or takes advantage of his partner because he is more mature. The penalty for this is up to a year in jail or a fine. Sexual acts with a boy or girl under the age of 16 are illegal if the offender takes advantage of his or her situation as a drug addict, an illegal immigrant, or homeless. Here, too, the penalty is up to a year in jail or a fine. Finally, sexual acts are illegal if a remuneration of any kind is rendered to anyone under the age of 18 years. Therefore, sexual contact with child prostitutes is punishable for those who pay. The penalty can be up to three years in jail.

[Experts wonder, however, why politicians have not seen the need for such provisions before. The heterosexual age of consent in Austria has been 14 since 1803, and for two centuries, heterosexual youth has been completely unprotected against such offenses. LGBT activists, therefore, view the new provisions with great skepticism and will closely monitor whether they are applied only or mainly against gays and lesbians.

[Despite the repeal of the old provisions, cases have been heard in court under the old, discriminatory laws. The European Court of Human Rights made known, in January 2003, that Austria was being fined for applying the paragraphs that are no longer legal. The Homosexual Initiative Vienna, at its General Assembly in 2002, demanded compensation for all those penalized under the old laws. (*End of update by R. A. Perner and L. Kneucker*)]

[*Update 2003*: Austria has an estimated 300,000 to 700,000 Austrian gay and bisexual males, many of whom are represented by a variety of smaller activist and support associations organized around special-interest agendas and purposes. One such subgroup, Austrian Gay Professionals (AGPRO), was organized in 1998 to represent a large number of Austrian managers. AGPRO is affiliated with the European Gay Managers Association (EGMA). In 2003, membership included more than 1,000 professional managers. Among the projects sponsored by the AGPRO with its European partners is a "Diversity Label," given as an award to firms that offer a work environment that is free from discrimination.

[In early 2003, according to a local Viennese newspaper, the Association sent a formal request to the manager of the most famous European ball held during Carnival, the Viennese Opera Ball. The formal request was that homosexual couples, one partner in a white tuxedo, the other in black, be included in the traditional opening presentation of young debutantes and their partners. In the article, the president of AGPRO reported that the woman who is in charge of the ball turned pale for a few minutes, and then turned down the request. The AGPRO president added the comment that his organization is patient—and will ask politely again in the coming year.

[AGPRO's request to be part of the Opera Ball may seem insignificant to those not familiar with Viennese and European social tradition. But in the European context, Vienna's Opera Ball is one of "the most important" events of the Carnival season. People come from all over the world to attend—diplomats and politicians, the leaders of European social life. The Ball is featured on prime-time television, with careful attention to which prominent people are in which box and with whom. Being part of the opening of the ball is one of those events many upper-class young people aspire to. If gay couples were part of the opening, it would draw the world's attention to the situation. I'm not sure that is why AGPRO wants to have gay couples there. It is more likely a question of "equal rights." But either way, it would be a spectacular change if gay couples were part of the opening. In terms of social recognition and awareness, for "social persons," parents who attend balls, whose families aspire to have a daughter or son "open the ball"—the girls all in white for the formal opening, and the proclamation "alles Walzer" ("Everyone waltz, the ball can begin"), it would be revolutionary to have gay couples be a part of the Opera Ball with all its media coverage. (*End of update by L. Kneucker*)]

## 7. Gender Diversity and Transgender Issues

Estimates put the number of transgendered persons in Austria between 1,000 and 2,000, but the figure might be closer to 5,000.

Austria at present has no laws dealing with transsexuality. In 1983, the Federal Ministry of Internal Affairs ascertained that there were too few cases for such laws. Nevertheless, the Federal Ministry for Work, Health, and Social Matters has published recommendations for the treatment of transsexuals. Before medical treatment, there must be an ongoing psychotherapeutic accompaniment that lasts at least one year, i.e., a minimum of 50 hours. After the psychotherapeutic findings have been established, hormone treatment and the so-called "everyday test" can be carried out.

When transsexuality is established, a doctor's verification can be demanded, in which the diagnostic assignment to the opposite sex, as well as the correlation between the treatment and the outward appearance is presented, with the maximum validity of two years. The high costs for the treatment are only partly covered by public health insurance.

In Austria, relatively few doctors perform sex change operations (in Vienna, Salzburg, and Innsbruck) and they are considered comparatively less experienced than their foreign colleagues.

After the operation, it is possible to change the first name in the personal status in all documents, although the authorities may show resistance. Before, transsexuals could only choose a gender-neutral name. In this connection, the transgender movement advocates not having the gender recorded in the birth registry as well as all other documents. The position expressed in the movement is that many operations would be superfluous if society did not demand a strictly known identification with one of the two sexes.

Marriages of those who have undergone an operation are considered dissolved with the change of sex. Here, apparently, in the course of the acceptance of such marriages lies the fear that, as a consequence, homosexual marriages may no longer be forbidden. There is official pressure for divorce. Government officials can also make contact with the person's own children difficult. As for employers, the pressure for agreed-upon severance is the normal practice. Many transsexual (transgendered) persons do not find new employment after they have changed their names and legal status. Prostitution is sometimes their only means of supporting themselves.

In June 1995, a four-day international human rights tribunal took place in Vienna that dealt with the discrimination against lesbians, gays, and transgendered persons. The indictment ascertained that lesbians, gays, and transsexual persons are discriminated against in various ways and that there is in no way legal protection. Accordingly, the government and Parliament were asked to initiate activities to counteract the situation. In February 1999, the first Austrian interdisciplinary symposium on transsexuality was held. As of early 2000, there were two self-help groups for transgendered persons, both in Vienna.

## 8. Significant Unconventional Sexual Behaviors

### A. Coercive Sex

*Child Sexual Abuse, Incest, and Pedophilia*

[*Update 2003*: In 1992, as the scandal of clergy sexual abuse and pedophilia spread around the world, from Canada to Australia, South Africa to Hong Kong, and across Europe from Ireland to Pope John Paul II's native Poland, Vienna's Cardinal Hans Hermann Groer, Austria's ranking Catholic clergyman, was accused of repeatedly sexually molesting young boys, priests, and monks, creating a state of "spiritual dependency" among the young clergy, in which the cardinal demanded sexual favors in return for advancement in the Church's hierarchy. For three years, the Austrian Church's

governing body refused to investigate the case and, at the same time, defamed the accusing victims in the media, making it clear that a fundamental taboo had been touched upon. Finally, in 1995, as the Pope prepared to visit predominantly Catholic Austria, Vatican investigators confirmed that the cardinal had taken advantage of his position as father-confessor to intimidate young boys and clergy. The Pope then requested, received, and accepted the cardinal's resignation. The cardinal retired to a monastery.

[Ten years after the scandal broke, the Austrian Bishops Conference still had not issued general guidelines for dealing with the problem, preferring instead to allow each of Austria's nine dioceses to set up their own ombudsman, who is responsible for seeing to it that the problem is taken seriously, the dangers eliminated, and the victims are aided. As of early 2003, five dioceses had taken this action. Some Church functionaries have been removed from their posts. In Linz, basic principles have been formulated; in Vienna, such actions are being considered. Vienna's ombudsman, who is also the student chaplain for thousands of university students, but has no authority, has stated that the situation reflects society's ills in general. There is, both in Austria and elsewhere, still not enough consciousness and recognition of the problems, sufficient information, administrative transparency, and openness, plus too much secrecy and even cover-up. In Austria and the many other countries where this scandal has erupted, there is an obvious and urgent need for enactment of clear government and Church policies to protect the young from abuse. (*End of update by L. Kneucker*)]

The Austrian criminal code states that the sexual abuse of children—defined as sleeping with or fornication with minors—will be punished with up to ten years in prison.

About 500 cases of sexual abuse a year are reported to the authorities, but the actual frequency is estimated at from ten to 25,000. In 1997, 848 cases were reported, involving 231 male and 617 female victims (Federal Ministry of the Interior, Statistics on Victims 1997). The unusually high level of unreported cases that do not appear in statistics (*graue Zone*) can be understood because the perpetrator is usually closely associated with the close social circles of the victim—24% occur within the family, and the probability of bringing charges against someone in such a close relationship diminishes.

Eighty to 90% of the victims are girls, mostly between the ages of 6 and 11 years of age. The perpetrators are up to 80% men from all social levels. According to the Federal Ministry for Environment, Youth, and Family, every third to fourth girl and every eighth to ninth boy will be sexually abused.

To fight the sexual abuse of children, literature on the subject asks for an emancipating education and a change from gender-specific power structures. To this end, various institutions and places for maltreated and abused children have been established, including emergency telephone hotlines for children and child protection centers.

Austria has no pedophilia movement in favor of the legalization of sex with minors such as exists, for example, in the United States.

*Sexual Violence Against Women*

The women's movement removed the taboo from the subject of sexual violence against women in the 1970s. It was pointed out that forced sex has less to do with sexuality than with power, conditioned by the differences between the social positions of men and women.

The first "women's house" in Austria was built in 1978. In a short time, it was overfilled. Today, in Vienna there are three such houses, and in the other provinces another 15, where women threatened with domestic or marital violence can seek refuge. In 1982, women set up the first emergency telephone for raped women and girls. At present, there are seven emergency telephone services in the larger towns. These refuges have been initiated for the most part by autonomous women's groups, and they experience great financial difficulties, because there is very little financial support from government agencies.

### Sexual Harassment

The public debate about sexual harassment at the workplace began in the late 1980s. In a study conducted in 1981, 81% of the women surveyed indicated that once, or more than once, they had experienced sexual advances by men against their will at work (Federal Ministry for Work, Health, and Social Affairs). Those affected are more often single women, frequently in insecure positions, and relatively often in typical occupations for females, especially secretaries. The perpetrators are frequently substantially older than their victims and, over-proportionally, their supervisor or manager (Federal Ministry for Work, Health, and Social Affairs 1993).

A law was enacted in 1993 that not only declared sexual harassment itself punishable, but also addressed negligence on the part of the employer in dealing effectively with the complaint. In the same way, the creation of a hostile and humiliating work environment at the workplace is forbidden. The person discriminated against has the right to demand reasonable damages, at least a minimum of ATS 50,000.

Since then, it is possible to start a legal procedure, but all women who, up to now, have sought legal process, were forced to leave their jobs while pursuing legal remedy. The official responsible for equal treatment questions has demanded protection against dismissal for victims.

### Rape

The crime of rape is treated in the criminal code as "punishable acts against morals." On the contrary, it would be more appropriate, at the present time, not to choose an abstract morality as a basis for protection, but rather the violation of sexual self-determination, i.e., the sexual integrity of the person. With the reform of the penal laws in 1989, rape within marriage or common-law marriage became punishable, but only upon application of the woman. In the past, the woman's inability to resist determined possible conviction as well as the extent of punishment. Today, the extent of the violence by the aggressor is decisive. Punishment for graver cases of rape is between one and ten years, for less violent assaults between six months and five years. The provisions of the law are formulated in gender-neutral language; men as rape victims are acknowledged. Still needed are improved counseling and support for women by the police and courts, help during the investigations, as well as increased claims for damages and psychological injuries suffered.

In connection with rape, old prejudices are still commonly held, such as the overpowering sexual drive of men or the alleged yearning of women for brutal sexual intercourse. The guilt is often assigned to the woman or shared guilt is assumed, as she is accused of having sexually provoked the perpetrator. Because she agreed to a meeting, the American notion of "date rape" is played down even in legal proceedings, since the woman's agreement is assumed. Rape within marriage is still represented by the notion that the husband has sexual control over his wife. It is therefore not surprising that affected women, whether out of a sense of resignation or shame, seldom report marital rapes.

According to police statistics, 507 rapes were known in 1997, of which 35 took place within marriages. Trials often end in acquittals. In 1990, one third of the accused were found "not guilty."

## B. Prostitution

Provincial governments regulate prostitution in Austria and only one of the nine states outlaws it. Pimping is forbidden and punishable, but it obviously exists. Until 1989, male prostitution was a criminal offense. Prohibition was lifted especially in the interest of AIDS prevention. Officially recognized prostitutes are registered with the police, and must undergo examinations for sexually transmitted illnesses once a week. Since 1984, prostitutes must pay income tax. However, tax estimates are often too high and arbitrary to be paid, forcing many prostitutes into the underground. Although prostitution was put on an equal footing with other occupations, social and pension rights are not included. Prostitutes can voluntarily pay for health insurance, but have no rights to a pension or to the same protection as pregnant women—they fall through the loopholes of the social system.

There are hardly any studies concerning prostitution and the social situation of prostitutes. According to the Health Office of the City of Vienna, there are 630 female and 5 male prostitutes officially registered. Illegal prostitution is many times higher; many women who are registered as bartenders and hostesses work as prostitutes. In Vienna, about 5,000 prostitutes work each day. There are no figures for the whole of Austria.

The appearance of AIDS and the opening of Eastern European borders had a far-reaching influence on prostitution. HIV tests are required on a regular basis for prostitutes. As a result of the opening of the borders to the former Eastern countries (Czech Republic and Slovakia) in 1989, there was a rise in competition, and an increase of "secret" prostitution. It is known that international organizations are involved in the traffic of women. In Austria, many prostitutes come from Eastern Europe, Brazil, the Dominican Republic, Thailand, and the Philippines.

## C. Pornography and Erotica

Pornography is regulated through a federal law passed in 1990, "The Federal Act Against Obscene Publications and for the Protection of Youth Morally Endangered." Because this law is considered completely out-of-date in progressive circles, its total reform was begun in 1992, two years after its enactment. The reform is still being worked on in the Federal Ministry of Justice. A new version of the law has already failed to pass, because of pressure by conservatives and church groups.

The immediate cause for seeking a reform was a study initiated by the Federal Ministry of Environmental, Youth, and Family Issues about the existence and distribution of video films showing violent acts against children. The goal was to stop the production and dissemination of such films. A broad discussion began about whether punishment should be limited to trade in such videos, or extended to include ownership or possession as well. In addition, punishment was aimed at the presentation of violence; however, pornography without violence and presentations of sexual acts between members of the same sex were to be liberalized. But since no agreement could be reached with the People's Party coalition partner, the Social Democrats, who had been working for this reform, they could not carry it through. In 1994, punishment for producing, selling, and possessing child pornography was written into law.

[*Comment 2000*: A trichotomy of pornographic material is widely accepted in Austria, namely soft pornography or erotica with limited or no explicit sex acts (e.g., *Playboy* magazine and the like), hardcore pornography with explicit sex acts, and hardcore pornography with legally prohibited "violent" content. The minimum age for a person buying soft porn/erotica, a *Playboy* magazine for instance, is 16 years. The minimum age for buying porn or entering an adult video store where hardcore pornography is available for rental or sale is 18 years. Violent content, including bestiality, sexual acts involving minors, and violent sexual acts is, of course, legally forbidden in Austria.

[Gay pornography is not forbidden in Austria, and almost every adult shop has a section featuring gay porn. Furthermore, in recent years a few gay adult stores have opened in Vienna. (*End of comment by M. Voracek*)]

Punishment is limited to those who produce or distribute obscene texts, pictures, or films or other obscene objects for profit (Paragraph 1, Pornography Law). Possession or non-commercial exchanges of violent pornography is still permitted.

## 9. Contraception, Abortion, and Population Planning

### A. Contraception

The attitude of the Austrian population to questions of family planning is influenced by the Catholic sexual dogma, based on the "Pill Encyclical" (*Humanae Vitae*) of 1968, in which contraception and abortion were equally condemned.

Results from surveys show contradictory attitudes. The belief of most women in the effectiveness of family planning is confronted by the reality of unwanted pregnancies. Being relatively well informed about contraception is not borne out by the use of contraceptives. Thirty-nine percent of first live births and far more pregnancies were generated despite the use of contraceptives. Women with higher educational achievements, fewer religious bonds, and who live in cities have more faith in the planning of pregnancies. The higher the job qualifications, the fewer unwanted pregnancies occur. The same is true in cities, as compared to rural areas. In all of Austria, there are more than 200 publicly supported family and partnership counseling centers, whose responsibilities include counseling about pregnancy and informing clients about birth control methods.

Contraceptive preference and use changed drastically in the 1970s. After the rapid spread of the use of hormonal contraceptives, there followed, at the end of the decade, again a gradual turning away from the pill and turning to the coil IUD and sterilization, as well as to natural methods of contraception. The pill, however, remained the most-used contraceptive, being used by one third of all women at risk for pregnancy. Seen internationally, Austria is a "pill stronghold." Those who use the pill, but are anxious that it may be detrimental to their health, have two more reasons for using it anyway: reliability and convenience. Birth control is still something left to women, although, since the appearance of AIDS, contraceptives are advertised by public authorities.

Forty-two percent of all sexually active and fertile women between the ages of 15 and 44 take the pill. This rate declines as women get older. Students and religious women take the pill less often. Women who use no contraceptive constitute the next largest group, at 18%. Twelve percent use unreliable contraceptive methods, mainly withdrawal or coitus interruptus. In fourth place on the frequency scale is the condom, followed by the coil IUD, and then spermicides. The diaphragm is only marginally used.

The choice of contraceptive method depends on the level of education, the importance of religion, the size of the hometown, and the age of the woman. In groups with lower incomes, unreliable methods are often used. The higher the education, the more the pill is taken and the less coitus interruptus is employed.

In terms of convenient availability, the pill is made more difficult, because a doctor must prescribe it, whereas condoms are readily available in apothecaries, drugstores, and in machines in men's toilets of almost all bars, restaurants, cafes, clubs, discos, and the like.

### B. Teenage (Unmarried) Pregnancies

Among nations for which out-of-wedlock pregnancy statistics are available, Austria has one of the highest rates of out-of-wedlock births. Since the 1960s, the number of illegitimate births has been rising while the rate of children born to married couples has declined. In 1998, the number of births was 80,321, of which 23,588 were born out-of-wedlock. Currently, one quarter of all live births are out-of-wedlock, double or triple the rates in the neighboring countries. This appears to be a continuing trend. Within Austria, however, there are large regional differences, with the large cities having especially high rates. [*Comment 2000*: With regard to these regional-level differentials, apart from the urban-rural differential, it is also noteworthy that some areas within Austria, independently from the urban-rural differential, consistently experience high out-of-wedlock birthrates. The most prominent case for this observation is Carinthia, the southernmost of Austria's nine states, which traditionally, for centuries, has had the highest out-of-wedlock birthrates within Austria. (*End of comment by M. Voracek*)]

Still higher than the rate of illegitimate births altogether is the rate of out-of-wedlock first-born children. At the end of the 1980s, about every third first-born was born to unwed parents; 60% of all women did not have their first babies conceived within marriages. From this it follows that in many regions of Austria, the out-of-wedlock birth of the first child is the rule, rather than the exception.

Since 1989, single mothers are automatically given guardianship over their children; prior to 1989, the mother had to apply for custody.

### C. Abortion

In 1787, as a result of the Enlightenment, the death penalty for abortions was removed from the "*Josephinisches Strafgesetzbuch*" (Penal Code of Emperor Joseph II), and replaced with a long prison sentence. This law is the basis for the current abortion paragraphs, which, with the exception of the era of National Socialism, was in effect until 1974. Under this law, abortion, in every case, even those carried out for medical indications, was punishable. Since 1869, according to the Roman Catholic Church, every abortion from the time of fertilization incurs an automatic penalty of excommunication.

In the 1960s, only a small percentage of abortions were actually punished by law. It was also clear that only those persons who were poor where prosecuted. Estimates from that time assume from 30,000 to 100,000 abortions per year. In addition to the illegal abortions carried out within Austria, "abortion tourism" began to countries with more liberal laws, above all, to Great Britain and Holland.

With the votes of the Social Democrats, the abortion articles were abolished as part of the amendments of the Criminal Code in 1975. Instead, time-limited permission (*Fristenlösung*) went into effect. According to the law, which is still binding, abortion is basically punishable, but will not be punished when the abortion is carried out within the first three months after implantation (nidation) or after the fourth month if a medical or eugenic indication is presented, or the person is still a minor. In order not to be punishable, the following prerequisites must be met:

- permission of the pregnant person;
- strict adherence to the three-month limit;
- counseling beforehand by a doctor; and
- neither doctors nor other medical personnel can be forced to participate.

The operation must take place in a public hospital, clinic, or private practice, normally under anesthesia by aspiration. The costs are only carried by the national health system if there is a medical necessity. In Austria, no records of abortions are kept.

If the pregnant woman is below the age of consent (i.e., has not yet completed her 14th year of age), abortions are not punishable even after the fourth month, but they require the permission of her legal representatives, usually her parents. There is no unanimous opinion in the legal literature on this question if the pregnant woman is still a minor and has not yet completed her 19th year of age.

In recent years the discussion about abortion has again flamed up. Kindled mainly by the leading members of the Catholic Church, the discussion ostensibly circles around the emphasis on the "right to life" based on the European Convention on Human Rights and Fundamental Freedoms, 1958, and the connected question: When does human life begin? In addition, the function of required counseling has become an important issue, because those who demand that abortion be punished also oppose sex education for the purpose of avoiding unwanted pregnancies. It appears obvious that opposition to the right of women to self-determination about their own bodies is the real motivation of those who oppose abortion. The opposition of these political factions delayed the government's efforts to allow distribution of Mifegyne (RU-486, the abortion pill) in Austria.

As in some other Western industrial nations, Austria has liberal abortion laws accompanied by a high degree of tabooing and insufficient infrastructure to carry out the operations. Even today, hospitals in the provinces dominated by the conservative People's Party refuse to perform abortions.

[*Abortion and Embryonic Stem Cell Research*
RAOUL KNEUCKER (*Update 2003*)
[In 2001, a major controversy surfaced in Europe and North America involving abortion, the definition of person, cloning, and research on the therapeutic use of embryonic stem cells. The official Austrian position regarding the use of human embryonic stem cells in scientific research is negative, without exception. The constitutional freedom of research would, of course, prevent state interference with biomedical research, but funding by state authorities can be withheld. This policy question became part of the Austrian political discourse in 2001-2002, as it has become in the U.S. The debate also erupted in all the other European Union (EU) member states, when the final decision on the European research program and grants for health research had to be made in the Council of Ministers in mid 2002.

[The European research program was adopted with Austria, Germany, Ireland, and Italy voting "no," because they did not support the funding of human embryonic stem cell research. The motives of these countries were as different as their respective national regulations. In voting together, however, they formed a "qualitative minority." In the voting regime of the EU, a qualitative minority can block any decision. Austria and all the other member states of the EU accepted a clause that, in all research activities, fundamental ethical principles must be adhered to. Stem cell research is restricted to research for improving human health, and to countries where national legislation permits such research activities. No funds will be given to research activities aiming at human cloning for reproductive purposes, intending to modify the genetic heritage of humans, or intending to create human embryos solely for the purpose of research or procurement, including by means of cell nuclear transfer.

[In later procedures, only Austria and Italy kept to their rigorous negative positions; but instead of simply applying the majority rule, the Council decided to ask the European Commission for a status report on European stem cell research and for a comparative legal study to be completed in the Autumn of 2003, in all practical terms setting a funding moratorium (Matthies 2002). The Council made it clear that: (a) a final decision will be taken by the end of 2003, but (b) no member state should be prejudiced by the EU if they decide to reconsider their positions or rewrite their laws.

[The Austrian position (which is unlikely to change when a new government is formed during 2003) was declared by the Federal Chancellor and the Federal Minister of Education, Science, and Culture (the coordinating authority in EU matters of research and technology). The position is political and ethical in nature. Within the public discourse in Austria, it is the most rigorous view, congruent only with the position of the Roman Catholic bishops' conference in Austria. It deviates from the majority opinion of the Bioethics Commission of the Federal Chancellor rendered in January 2002 (Gmeiner & Koertner 2002). Legal regulations in Austria would permit a different position: National legislation (*Fortpflanzungsmedizingesetz*) allows in-vitro fertilization, but bars the creation of supernumerous embryos, and using embryos for research and industrial purposes. Unused embryos must be destroyed after one year. Furthermore, Austria has not ratified any of the international biomedicine conventions (e.g., Council of Europe, and United Nations). The Bioethics Commission of the Chancellery recommended ratification of the Council of Europe Convention on Human Rights and Biomedicine; however, no steps have yet been taken. As of early 2003, the Bioethics Commission was debating a recommendation to add legislation in order to protect human embryos. (*End of update by R. Kneucker*)]

## D. Populations Programs

By international comparison, Austria is distinguished by noticeably low birthrates. In the 1980s, Austria had the third-lowest birthrate in the world after Italy and Germany; in the 1930s, it was the lowest in the world.

Despite continually pessimistic voices from the press since the 1970s that speak about a threatening situation, Austrians have very reserved attitudes towards the intervention of the state. There is no openly declared policy for a planned population. The influence of the State on reproductive behavior occurs indirectly, through establishment of financial and institutional incentives.

The population policies of the National Socialist dictatorship, the goal of which was to eliminate life that was unworthy of reproduction and to increase the "German race," led to an economic boom and a temporary increase in births, beginning in 1938. After the war, a family support policy was developed that provided both tax relief and other social support. These have been in effect since the 1950s as a permanent part of Austrian social policies.

In 1954 and 1955, a Family Support Fund was established to effect the distribution of money for family support as well as to influence pronatalist attitudes. And, indeed, there was a temporary baby boom at the end of the 1950s and beginning of the 1960s.

The decrease of births in the late 1960s and 1970s brought about a discussion about population-policy measures, in which the Social Democratic Party and the labor unions participated, in order to achieve more financial support for births, and so on. The People's Party and the Catholic Family Organization wanted to introduce more tax incentives for families with children. Altogether, Austria is one of the countries with the highest rates of family support.

In the 1980s, a program was initiated to combat sterility among women that included the possibility for artificial insemination. The "Medical Reproduction Law" of 1992 permitted in-vitro fertilization (IVF) for heterosexual infertile couples who lived together. Surrogate motherhood and ovum donation, however, are forbidden. The first Austrian test-tube baby was born in 1982. Every year, about 2,000 IVF attempts are made. The success quota is very small, among other reasons, because the majority of women give up before the completion of the very burdensome program required.

## 10. Sexually Transmitted Diseases and HIV/AIDS

### A. Sexually Transmitted Diseases

Since the 1920s, it has been compulsory to report diseases transmitted through sexual intercourse. The current law, the AIDS Act of 1986, requires reporting of: syphilis, gonorrhea, ulcus molle (soft ulcer, soft chancre), lymphogranuloma venerum (pudendal ulcer), granuloma inguinale (groin ulcer or ulcerating granuloma of the pudendum), as well as full-blown cases of AIDS. Registered prostitutes are also legally required to be examined at regular intervals (weekly) for venereal diseases. These statistics are maintained by the Health Office of the City of Vienna. The available statistics published in medical journals are still not reliable, because it can be presumed that only an estimated 20% of the actual cases are reported to the health authorities. Nevertheless, it is possible to understand the trend from these figures: Reported cases of syphilis and gonorrhea are diminishing, while non-reportable diseases, such as chlamydia and Trichomonas infections, are clearly increasing.

In Vienna, a little under 1,000 cases of syphilis and gonorrhea were reported in both 1993 and 1994, the last year for which data has been published. A slight rise in cases of syphilis can be explained by the registration of persons from former Yugoslavia, for whom genital scarring was reported but treatment could not be ascertained. In the Health Office of Vienna, from which about one fifth of all the figures in Vienna come, a tendency towards a decrease in cases of gonorrhea became apparent after the high point had been reached right after the borders to the Czech Republic and Slovakia were opened at the beginning of the 1990s.

The treatment of STDs, as well as counseling, takes place in clinics with the appropriate professional departments and with established doctors, mainly dermatologists, and less frequently, urologists and gynecologists. Vienna has a special outpatient clinic where poor people can receive counseling, examinations, and treatment at no cost.

Programs in education and prevention practically do not exist. With the exception of AIDS, sexually transmitted disease is not a topic spoken about in public. The public campaigns, such as the one carried out by the company that produces Acyclovir, are the exceptions. The manufacturing firm advertised its product, and at the same time promoted the use of condoms as protection against the contagious contraction of herpes.

### B. HIV/AIDS
*Government Regulations*

As early as 1986, Austria had its own AIDS law, since it could not be sensibly included either in the laws concerning epidemics nor venereal diseases. As a result, clear cases of AIDS, according to the American CDC classification, as well as cases of death, must reported to the Federal Ministry for Health; reports include the sex, date of birth, and the initials of the person, but not his or her name. HIV infections are not reported, to guarantee the anonymity of persons infected with HIV and to prevent possible discrimination in schools, at the workplace, and so on.

Commercial sexual activities are forbidden to those infected with HIV, and this is anchored in law. Registered prostitutes are, in addition, required every three months to undergo an HIV-antibody test. Also regulated by law is the right of an HIV-infected person to attend school, as long as the affected person is able to physically meet the demands. The same is true, *de jure*, for the carrying on of other occupations. An HIV infection is a reason for ineligibility for military service.

While HIV tests are not carried out in the standard procedure when blood tests are made, the law does not prohibit testing for HIV without the permission of the person involved. In hospitals, especially in Vienna, mass screenings were made without the permission of the patients. This doubtful procedure, which caused vehement discussion, was made legitimate in a directive issued at the beginning of the 1990s by the City Council member responsible for such matters.

Austria's health insurance regulates that those who are infected with HIV, and people ill with AIDS, may use the national insurance the same as anyone else. Private insurance companies, (e.g., organizations offering life insurance, are increasingly demanding HIV-antibody tests and/or excluding those with HIV infections and those with AIDS.

*Statistics for HIV Infections and AIDS*

Since the beginning of the AIDS pandemic in the early 1980s through 1997, the registered (cumulative) numbers for Austria were:

- 7,609 people currently infected with HIV;
- 2,036 people currently living with AIDS; and
- 1,243 Austrians who have died of AIDS.

The number of new infections in 1998 was 92 and 18 in 1999. Between January 1 and October 30, 2000, 366 new HIV-infections were registered. Although these statistics from the Department of Virology of the University of Vienna Medical School, as of October 30, 2000, and published December 1, 2000, are highly reliable, the CIA *World Factbook* (1999 estimate) gives the adult prevalence of HIV/AIDS as 0.23%, with 9,000 Austrians living with HIV/AIDS and less than 100 deaths attributed to the infection. Note the difference between 1,243 deaths and less that 100 due to HIV/AIDS. At the same time, the AIDS-Help organization in Vienna claims that the realistic number is 15,000 to 18,000 infections. [*Comment 2000*: Based on my experience at the University of Vienna General Hospital Department of Documentation and Research, I believe this estimate from AIDS-Help is exaggerated. Where are these additional cumulative 7,000 to 9,000 people? Certainly, they are not under medical treatment. Sooner or later, these unreported persons infected with HIV or AIDS will die. Then, because Austria has a very high autopsy rate and, therefore, one of the most accurate mortality statistics worldwide, such cases would be detected at least postmortem. But the autopsy and causes-of-death statistics give no evidence for the alleged unreported cases of HIV infections and AIDS cases (*End of comment by M. Voracek*)]

Homosexual and bisexual men were the main affected group, but recently, the number of new infections in this group has declined steadily. This can most likely be attributed to a change in behavior, based on the increased information available to the public. In the case of intravenous drug users, the number of new infections is stable. However, the number of cases of new infections by way of heterosexual sexual intercourse is rising drastically. In this trend, women are especially affected.

At the end of May 1999, the number of AIDS illnesses recorded cumulatively since 1983 was 1,905. Of this number, 1,198 had already died; 738 were homosexual or bisexual persons, 476 were drug users, 258 became ill through heterosexual contact, 281 persons became ill for other or not-known reasons: 74 hemophiliacs, 38 as a result of blood transfusions, 25 maternal transmission to children, and 15 homosexual or bisexual persons plus IV-drug users. The overall gender ratio was: men 1,547 (994 died), and women 358 (204 died).

[*Update 2002*: UNAIDS Epidemiological Assessment: Testing is mandatory in all blood/plasma organ donors, as well as for prostitutes. Data on HIV are available through those screening programs. There is no national register for HIV cases.

[Several surveys have been conducted among injection drug users and prisoners. HIV prevalence among injection drug users increased from 13% in 1986 to 27% in 1990 in Vienna. In Innsbruck, prevalence reached 44% in the time period of 1985-1990. Prevalence in prisons is estimated around 0.5% to 1.3%, 5 times higher than in the general population. UAT is not legal in Austria. Incidence of syphilis has decreased in the late 1980s to reach a stable level of 1 to 2.9 cases per 100,000.

[The estimated number of adults and children living with HIV/AIDS on January 1, 2002, were:

| | | |
|---|---|---|
| Adults ages 15-49: | 9,900 | (rate: 0.2%) |
| Women ages 15-49: | 2,200 | |
| Children ages 0-15: | < 100 | |

[Less than 100 adults and children are estimated to have died of AIDS during 2001.

[No estimate is available for the number of Austrian children who had lost one or both parents to AIDS and were under age 15 at the end of 2001. (*End of update by the Editors*)]

### Treatment and Research

HIV tests can be administered in hospitals, clinics, and numerous doctors' offices. Anonymous and free-of-charge tests can only be given at privately supported AIDS-help organizations. Treatment is possible at all university clinics and some larger hospitals. In Vienna, two wards for AIDS patients were set up, where stationary as well as day-care medical attention is possible. Extramural care causes personnel and financial problems and is largely limited to private nursing activities. However, people ill with AIDS can have the same social services, help at home, home food delivery, and so on, as others who are either ill or need care.

Since Austria has a very strict drug law, the treatment of AIDS is limited to traditional orthodox medicine and proven methods. The medical profession is generally skeptical about alternative ways of treatment; they are not financially supported and are exclusively available only through private initiative and payments.

In research, Immuno, a pharmaceutical company with laboratories in Austria, leads worldwide in the development of vaccines. The use of gene technology is followed by the public with skepticism. Militants active in animal protec-

tion are leading a vehement discussion about the experimentation with animals.

### Prevention

Despite legal requirements, there is no national policy regarding AIDS in Austria.

Homosexual and bisexual men were those most affected by AIDS at the beginning of the 1980s. Information and explanations were offered first by lesbian and gay organizations exclusively. In 1985, HOSI Vienna (Homosexual Initiative Vienna) played a decisive role in the founding of the Austrian AIDS Help organization, a private organization, but financed with help from the Federal Ministry for Health. Information, availability of tests, and the support of social workers lay mainly in the hands of this nongovernmental organization. In 1991, the Austria-wide organization was split into several regional AIDS Help organizations that are subsidized by the government.

In recent years, a number of other nongovernmental organizations have been established: the "Buddy" association, the Names Project, and other groups providing information. These groups have taken on different tasks, especially in prevention, education, and support services, but receive absolutely no governmental or public subsidy.

Information and educational campaigns are only offered sporadically by the health authorities. HIV/AIDS as a theme appears about every two years for a few weeks on billboards and in TV-spot announcements. Such campaigns are usually directed to the whole population ("AIDS Affects Us All") or to young people. Only in recent years has it been possible to talk about condoms publicly. Certain areas, for example, the theme of lesbians and AIDS, do not even appear in public discussions. Recommendations do exist that an educational campaign regarding information about AIDS be held at schools, but the means to carry out this campaign either do not exist, or the funding is inadequate.

With respect to behavior among young people, although less than 10% of sexually active girls and boys see a real danger of HIV infection, 28%—in rural areas as high as 40%—thought about AIDS at the time of their first sexual intercourse. For 31% of the young people, AIDS is a subject that they have never thought about; 13% are very concerned, and 39% reported that they never restricted their sexual lives because of AIDS; but, after all, more than half used a condom most of the time.

The amount of information known to homosexuals is especially high. In one study, 74% of the gays interviewed said that they had changed their sexual habits when AIDS appeared. Forty-one percent reduced the number of partners they had; 87% practiced "safer sex" from then on; 74% used condoms; 64% avoided ejaculation in the mouth of their partners; 22% gave up anal intercourse; 21% said that they now live in a monogamous partnership, and 36% are in a lasting relationship.

## 11. Sexual Dysfunctions, Counseling, and Therapies

Traditionally, in "silent Catholic Austria," sexual dysfunctions are only treated, if at all, in the offices of urologists, gynecologists, or in the four specialized sexual counseling centers. [*Comment 2000*: Andrology is emerging in Austria, as it is in other European countries, as a medical specialization dealing with male health and sexual problems. (*End of comment by M. Vorachek*)]

People who do not "function" sexually, or who suffer from failure anxieties, usually define themselves as ill. They are often treated as fools or insulted, and are often accused of deliberately refusing to have sex. There have been cases of men murdering their sexual partners because they were laughed at or belittled by them.

There are hardly any statistical records on the incidence of various sexual dysfunctions. In a survey carried out in a newspaper by Senger and Hoffmann (1993), 5% of the women identified failure to experience orgasm, 8% had pain during sexual intercourse, and 15% had cessation of sexual arousal. Of the men who replied, the researchers found that 10.4% had erection disorders, 27.3% had premature ejaculation, and 4.7% stated that they did not achieve erection. The investigators ascertained that 36.2% of the men, but only 22.3% of the women who responded, said they had problems with sex.

In June 1991, a study was made by an institute that carries out empirical research (IFES, Institut für Empirische Sozialforschung) of various areas of sexuality. Altogether, 1,667 persons (800 men, 867 women) between the ages of 16 and 69 were surveyed. Of these, 591 (35%) answered that religion was of great importance to them, and 276 (17%) found absolutely no influence from religion. In response to the question of whether or not discussions about sexuality had taken place at home, 913 (55%) said "no," 427 (26%) said "yes," and 84 (5%) answered "yes, often." Sixty-seven percent of those asked lived together with their partners in one household, and 17% lived alone without partners. Questions about partners received the following answers: 68% of those who lived in separate households had sex with their partners at least once a week, compared to 56% of those who lived together; 4% had no sex (6% of those living together); 19% felt that sex was the strongest binding element to their partners (8% of those living together); 29% had already experienced "extramarital" affairs (18% of those living together); 78% were able to talk to their partners about sexual problems (69% of those living together); and 59% were very satisfied with the sex in their partnership (49% of those living together).

Since sexual dysfunctions are still primarily looked at as organic illnesses, patients go to their family doctors or specialists and are usually sent, only if the doctors are younger and informed, to specialized counseling centers, i.e., psychologists or therapists, after unsuccessful treatment with orthodox medicine. Full payment by the public health plan is only made, however, if the therapist is a doctor; if not, partial subsidy is available. In cases where clinical psychologists have contracts with the public health insurance authorities, the psychological diagnosis is financially covered.

[*Comment 2000*: The Vienna General Hospital, where the Medical Faculty of the University of Vienna is located, is the largest hospital facility in Middle Europe, with 40-some departments, institutes, and divisions, including psychoanalysis and psychotherapy. Sexual research, counseling, and treatment occur in these divisions even though there is not a distinct sex clinic as such. (*End of comment by M. Voracek*)]

## 12. Sex Research and Advanced Professional Education

### A. Graduate Programs and Sexological Research

Only one working group exists in all of Austria for reproductive biology and sexual medicine, and that is located in the Department of Medical Biology and Human Genetics at the University of Innsbruck. There is no university chair (professorship) for sexology, sexual psychology, or sex education in Austria. The only postgraduate training for physicians is offered at the Vienna International Academy for Holistic Medicine (Wiener Internationale Akademie für Ganzheitsmedizin), with educational programs in sexual pedagogy, counseling, and therapy.

Continuing education in various sexual therapy aspects are offered by some psychotherapeutic organizations. For this, the Austrian Professional Association of Psychotherapists has set up its own working group

Because there is no university professorship in sexology, there is no openly declared research on questions of sexuality. But, indeed, in the context of psychological, sociological, and medical institutes, sexual themes are researched. In addition, research on sexual topics is carried out in some of the 128 state-sponsored and non-university research institutes and facilities. Until now, individual research projects have been generously supported by certain government ministries, above all, the Federal Ministry for Women's Affairs, Family, and for Education.

The Austrian Society for Research in Sexology (Österreichische Gesellschaft für Sexualforschung, ÖGS, (Postfach 23, A-1013 Wien, Austria), founded in 1979 in Vienna, has been especially active since 1996, and wrote into its statutes the responsibility for the compilation and dissemination of research findings. The organization also reviews relevant drafts of laws and is politically active.

Up to now, private research work in sexology has been financed by daily or weekly publications. Sexual researchers have financed their studies partly through grants from the pharmaceutical industry, their own resources, and partly from their sponsoring media.

Since 1991, the main author of this chapter and chairperson of the Austrian Society for Research in Sexology, Dr. Rotraud A. Perner, has been conducting a three-year training program in sexual counseling and sexual pedagogy at the Vienna Academy for Holistic Medicine. This advanced education program has also been offered since 1999 at the Association for Prophylactic Health Work in Linz. The Austrian Institute for Family Research (Österreichisches Institut für Familienforschung, ÖIF) trains moderators for *Love Talks* that are given in the elementary and secondary schools. Within the framework of the Austrian Professional Association of Psychotherapists, continuing educational courses are offered for some branches of sexual phenomena, for example, sexual abuse of children and sexual dysfunctions.

### B. Sexological Organization and Publications

*Sexus*, the quarterly magazine of the Austrian Society for Research in Sexology (Österreichische Gesellschaft für Sexualforschung, ÖGS), was first published in 1989, and began to appear with regularity in 1996.

The main sexological organizations in Austria are:

Austrian Planned Parenthood Society (Österreichisches Gesellschaft für Familienplanung, ÖGF), Bastiengasse 36-38, A-1180 Vienna, Austria.

Austrian Society for Research in Sexology (Österreichische Gesellschaft für Sexualforschung, ÖGS), Postfach 23, A-1013 Vienna, Austria.

Austrian Institute for Family Research (Österreichisches Institut für Familienforschung, ÖIF), Gonzagagasse 19, A-1010 Vienna, Austria.

## 13. Important Ethnic and Religious Minorities

In Austria, Croatians, Slovenes, Sinti, and Roma ("Gypsies") are considered minority groups. The majority of the guest workers, those who came to Austria for jobs, the second generation of whom live here, are citizens of former Yugoslavia and Turkey. Those who work without permits are mostly from Eastern Europe. Africans and African-Americans are mostly students or United Nations employees. The largest non-Christian religious group is Islamic. Data about the sexual attitudes and behavior of these ethnic groups have not been gathered.

However, it is known that family members in the second generation of Muslim guest workers live in a cultural conflict that affects girls more than boys, although the fundamentalist movement has not been noticed in public until recently. The sexuality of girls is more intensely controlled than that of boys in Islamic families that defend themselves against assimilation. A double moral standard is evident. Female virginity plays a large role and homosexuality is a great taboo. According to social workers, the reconstruction of the hymen is carried out in operations in Viennese hospitals. Whether, and how often, female circumcision is carried out cannot be determined.

[*Comment 2000*: The Department of Gynecology and Obstetrics at the Vienna General Hospital/Medical Faculty, University of Vienna, has all patient information forms, including information on sexuality, family planning, birth control, AIDS, and homosexuality, in German, Turkish, and Serbo-Croatian. Most likely, other hospital facilities and counseling centers have similar patient information materials. (*End of comment by M. Vorachek*)]

## Conclusion

As the new millennium begins in Austria, several trends become clear. Religious and cultural minorities who have settled here lose their specific identities as the children are integrated into general Austrian cultural traditions, but parents within these minorities try to enforce their sexual norms as long as their influence is possible.

Sexual violence in the home is receiving more and more attention and is increasingly discussed in public. The activities connected to the Internet and child pornography do not go unnoticed here, and both the private associations of the Internet providers in Austria and the Federal Ministry of the Interior have provided "hotlines" so that people can report what they find or receive. Organizations have set up emergency telephone numbers for battered women and children subject to abuse, as well as for young people who have questions about sex or fear that they are pregnant. The first seminar to train professionals in crisis intervention for children, especially in cases of sexual abuse, was held on the campus of the University of Vienna in the summer of 1999, set up by a private association that works to combat abuse, and financially supported by the European Union. Even though basic sexual "morals" have not changed, the public is better informed, and much work is being done to give women and victims empowerment and the feeling of confidence so that they can speak up about problems that were, not so long ago, kept secret as if they did not exist.

## References and Suggested Readings

Gmeiner, R., & U. Koertner. 2002 (September). Die bioethik-kommission beim bundeskanzleramt. A report published in: *Das Recht der Medizin*, 6:164-173.

Graupner, H. 2003. *Sexuality, youth protection & human rights: A European priority area.* Available in English at: www.graupner.com/englisch/index.asp; or http://members.aon.at/graupner (Helmut Graupner is one of the founding members of the Austrian Society for Sexology (ÖGS).

CIA. 2002 (January). *The world factbook 2002.* Washington, DC: Central Intelligence Agency. Available: http://www.cia.gov/cia/publications/factbook/index.html.

Hite, S. 1976. *The Hite report on female sexuality.* New York: Macmillan.

Hite, S. 1978. *The Hite report on male sexuality.* New York: Alfred A. Knopf.

HOSI. 2003. *Sexuality, youth protection & human rights: A European priority area.* Available in German at: http://www.hosiwien.at; in English at: www.graupner.com/englisch/index.asp; or http://members.aon.at/graupner.

Institut für Empirische Sozialforschung (IFES, Institute for Empirical Social Research). 1991. *A representative study by Weiss and Perner.* Vienna: Österreichische Gesellschaft für Familien Plannung (Planned Parenthood Association of Austria).

Kinsey, A. C., et al. 1948. *Sexual behavior in the human male.* Philadelphia: Saunders.

Kinsey, A. C., et al. 1953. *Sexual behavior in the human female.* Philadelphia: Saunders.

Langbein, K., & S. Fritsch. 1991. *Land der sinne [Land of senses].* Vienna: ORAC Publishers.

Matthies, L., ed. 2002 (June). *Survey on opinions from national ethics committees or similar bodies, public debate and national legislation in relation to human embryonic stem cell research and use* (vols. I & II).

Nöestlinger, C., & B. Wimmer-Puchinger. 1994. *Geschuetze liebe—Jugendsexualitaet und AIDS [Protected love: The sexuality of youth and AIDS].* Vienna: Jugend & Völk Verlag.

Perner, R. 1998. *Scham macht krank [Shame leads to sickness].* Vienna: Aaptos Verlag.

Perner, R. 1994. *Ungeduld des leibes—Die zeitrhythmen der liebe [The impatience of the body—Love's time rhythm].* Vienna/Munich: ORAC Publishers.

Senger, G., & W. Hoffmann. 1993. *Oesterreichische intim [Intimate Austria].* Vienna/Munich: Amalthea Verlag.

UNAIDS. 2002. *Epidemiological fact sheets by country.* Geneva, Switzerland: Joint United Nations Programme on HIV/AIDS (UNAIDS/WHO). Available: http://www.unaids.org/hivaidsinfo/statistics/fact_sheets/index_en.htm.

Weiss, F., & R. Perner. 1991. *A representative study for IFES, the Institut für Empirische Sozialforschung (Institute for Empirical Social Research).* Vienna: Österreichische Gesellschaft für Familien Plannung (Planned Parenthood Association of Austria).

# Bahrain
## (*Al-Bahrayn*)

Julanne McCarthy, M.A., M.S.N.*
*Updates by the Editors*

## Contents

## Demographics and a Brief Historical Perspective

ROBERT T. FRANCOEUR

### A. Demographics

The State of Bahrain is an archipelago of some 33 islands, totaling 268 square miles (694 km²), located in the middle of the southern shore of the Arabian Gulf, almost halfway between Shatt Al-Arab in the north and Muscat to the south. The islands lie approximately 20 miles (32 km) from the eastern province of Saudi Arabia and 2 to 18 miles (3 to 29 km) from Qatar. Bahrain's neighbors are Saudi Arabia on the west and Qatar on the east. Bahrain has been joined by a causeway to Saudi Arabia since late 1986. This causeway has had a profound effect, and has greatly influenced certain aspects of Bahrain society. Bahrain Island, the largest in the group, is the location of the current capital city, Manama. It is approximately 30 miles (48 km) long and 10 miles (16 km) wide and is linked by causeways to the islands of Muharraq on the northeast and Sitra on the east coast. Outside the capital, the landscape is covered by fertile gardens and palm trees in the northern third, and there is the desert with the oil and gas reserves in the remainder. Most of the population lives in the northern portion, while the central desert area contains the remains of the 100,000 or more *tumuli* (ancient burial mounds) and a few towns and villages. The southern third of Bahrain Island is mainly a noninhabited restricted area. Most of the islands are now joined by causeways to the main island, except the Hawar Island group, which lies offshore.

In July 2002, Bahrain had an estimated population of 656,397, including 228,424 non-nationals. (All data are from *The World Factbook 2002* (CIA 2002) unless otherwise stated.)

**Age Distribution and Sex Ratios**: *0-14 years*: 29.2% with 1.03 male(s) per female (sex ratio); 50.9% of the Bahraini people are under age 20; *15-64 years*: 15-64 years: 67.7% with 1.43 male(s) per female; *65 years and over*:

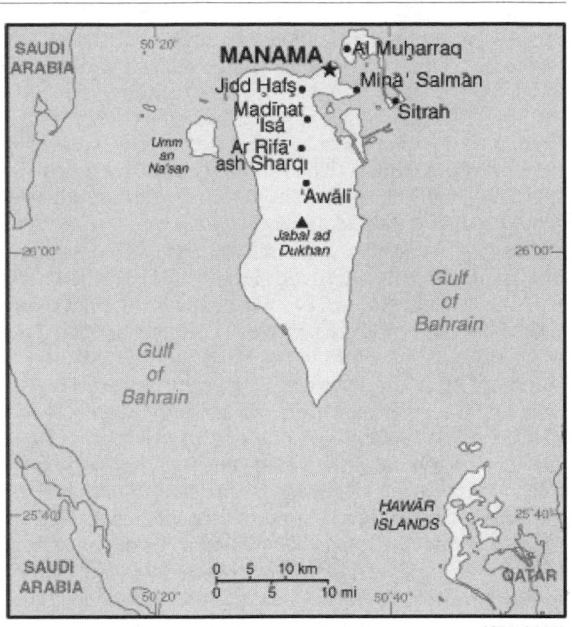

(CIA 2002)

3.1% with 1.03 male(s) per female; *Total population sex ratio*: 1.29 male(s) per 1 female

**Life Expectancy at Birth**: *Total Population*: 73.47 years; *male*: 71.05 years; *female*: 75.96 years

**Urban/Rural Distribution**: 82% to 18%

**Ethnic Distribution**: Bahraini: 63%; Asian: 19%; other Arab: 10%; Iranian: 8%

**Religious Distribution**: Shi'a Muslim: 70%; Sunni Muslim: 30%

**Birth Rate**: 19.53 births per 1,000 population

**Death Rate**: 3.95 per 1,000 population

**Infant Mortality Rate**: 19.18 deaths per 1,000 live births

**Net Migration Rate**: 1.09 migrant(s) per 1,000 population

**Total Fertility Rate**: 2.75 children born per woman (1995 est.)

**Population Growth Rate**: 1.67%

**HIV/AIDS**: *Adult prevalence*: NA; *Persons living with HIV/AIDS*: NA; *Deaths*: NA (For additional details from www.UNAIDS.org, see end of Section 10B.)

**Literacy Rate** (*defined as those age 15 and over who can read and write*): 88.5% (*male*: 91.6%, *female*: 84.2%) (1995 est.); *attendance for nine years of compulsory school*: 95% (education is free and compulsory from age 6 to 15)

**Per Capita Gross Domestic Product** (*purchasing power parity*): $13,000 (2001 est.); *Inflation*: 1.5%; *Unemployment*: 15% (1998 est.); *Living below the poverty line*: NA

### B. A Brief Historical Perspective

Bahrain has long been a port of call—for more than 6,000 years—and cuneiform tablets describe in ancient times the fresh water springs, the dates, and the marketplace in Bahrain, which attracted Gulf trading ships to the offshore harbor. These ancient travelers were shuttling between Mesopotamia, Bahrain, and the Indus Valley. Archeological finds have identified Bahrain as "Dilmun, the land of the living," mentioned in the Sumerian epic, *Gilgamesh*. Other archeologists have suggested that Bahrain was the Garden of Eden. Traditionally, people were farmers, fishermen, and merchants. There were no Bedouins or semi-Bedouins living in Bahrain (Taki 1974). Since the late 19th century, the form of

---

*The information in this chapter was gathered by the author and 28 Bahraini and expatriate professional colleagues. The original organization and presentation of this material was done by Julanne McCarthy.

government has been a traditional monarchy with succession passed from father to son (unlike other Gulf and Middle East countries where succession is brother to brother). Between 1861 and 1971, Bahrain was a British protectorate. There were three social classes in Bahrain until 1932—royalty, merchants, and farmers (Khuri 1980). The discovery of oil in 1932 led to many changes in traditional customs and initiated the beginning of a middle class in the society.

Bahrain saw a resurgence in its trading and commercial sector, and particularly growth in banking, during the 1970s because of the Lebanese civil war. Many institutions, with their expatriate workforce, moved to Bahrain, attracted by its tolerable social environment. There are now expatriates from over 60 countries living in Bahrain and working in various government agencies, private businesses, service institutions, and family homes. There are also tourists from the Gulf and around the world visiting Bahrain. These current commercial activities, and the past contact with traders and people from different cultures for centuries, has given Bahrain a unique cultural pattern and a cosmopolitan air. The latter has not been seen in other Gulf cities, like Dubai, until recently. The people of Bahrain and their respect for, and tolerance of, different cultural values makes Bahrain unique in many ways from its neighbors.

## 1. Basic Sexological Premises

There is a dearth of documented data regarding the nature of human sexuality in Bahrain. The data presented here are based on the few documented studies which are available. A thorough search was conducted of all the national bibliographies which have been compiled, government records, and the local print media, including newspapers, and local and regional journals in English. No one until recently conducted research in the realm of human sexuality in Bahrain; however, studies have been carried out on related areas by anthropologists, economists, doctors, nurses, psychologists, and social workers. All these data were pulled together, and with structured interview data, were used to write this basic document regarding the status of knowledge on, or related to, human sexuality in Bahrain according to the outline provided by the *Encyclopedia*'s general editor. It is hoped that researchers will be stimulated to study this topic in Bahrain and to present supplementary data from Arabic sources.

There may be a logical explanation why there is a dearth of literature regarding human sexuality, as the local culture, predominantly based on Islam, holds as a core value the suppression of external manifestations of sexuality in public, i.e., one should not present oneself in a sexually provocative manner. Believers are extolled not to draw attention to the body form, therefore the men's *thobe* (long, loose shirt-like garment) and the women's *jellabiya* (long, loose dress) are the preferred clothing style for many, at home and at work (unless there are uniform or safety restrictions). However, expatriates of all nationalities comment on the sheerness of some of the men's' summer white *thobes* and how a person's underwear is sometimes visible, which appears in contradiction to the stated norm. Personal preference in dress is allowed, so expatriates and Bahrainis are seen wearing a variety of clothing styles. Suppression of sexuality is also seen in the practice of women covering their hair partially (*Muhtashima*) or fully (*Muhajiba*), and even their face partially (*Burga*) or fully (*Mutanaqiba*). The practice of veiling in public has increased during the last ten years and can be seen among young as well as elderly women. Use of makeup, nail polish, and perfumes intending to draw attention are discouraged in public. Modesty in dress extends into the home. If a woman has chosen to veil, then even in the home she must veil in the presence of unrelated male relatives, but not in the presence of women, children, or her immediate male relatives. Covering of the body is also observed among siblings where even sisters, according to the Koran, are not to be uncovered among themselves. Among married couples, dress expectations vary and can cause some dissension. Some men state that in their own home they would like to wear shorts when it is hot, but their wives do not approve. The Koran's injunction is for the man, the middle area from the waist to the knees not be naked. It is acceptable for men engaged in athletics to wear shorts, and for fisherman or men in certain other occupations. There is an ingrained belief in some communities, however, that older males can lose their dignity and respect if they run or jog "half naked" in the streets or public parks (Fakhro 1991, 48).

Unrelated males and females are not to touch. The strict conservative definition is that touching is a sin. Great effort is made by everyone not to touch accidentally. As a local sign of respect and to purify oneself, people may spit to the side first before potential contact. This is a local custom and not dictated in Islam. Then, in case of an accidental contact, e.g., while handing over change, the person is considered clean. Bahraini informants explained this is a traditional practice, and Catholic nuns reported being the recipients. Most expatriates have never seen or heard of this practice.

Other traditional social controls practiced include animadversion against eye contact between men and women, especially strangers. Lack of eye contact by a man to a woman is a traditional sign of respect. Likewise, a woman who is unveiled is strongly advised not to smile at strangers (men outside her own family), and men and women should keep their eyes down when walking in public. Today, these practices may or may not be followed in the workplace by people who see each other frequently, and also depending on the work situation (e.g., serving the public). However, in public places, many people follow these injunctions. More recently, Westernized good manners such as courtesy, politeness, and cordial relations with customers and coworkers have been promoted in the private schools and service-industry sector. Bahraini business leaders, through the public media and through in-house newsletters, are promoting good manners as being good for business. Total quality management concepts are being incorporated into the local businesses and society; however, some resistance is met because of traditional values, e.g., women should not smile at an unrelated man.

The general aversion of speaking about sexual matters, or even the urogenital system, extends to doctor-patient relationships. Patients are reluctant to discuss their genitalia, and doctors are reluctant to ask about the genitalia, and even omit these from a physical exam. This has resulted in junior doctors missing the correct diagnosis, and consultants later correcting the situation. As a result, there is suspected underreporting for various diagnoses, e.g., priapism in children with sickle cell disease (Al-Dabbous 1991). This same reluctance has influenced studies regarding menopause in women that concentrate on osteoporosis and rarely mention psychosexual symptoms (Sadat-Ali et al. 1993).

### A. The Character of Gender Roles

Gender roles in Bahrain show a variety of manifestations and reflect the person's educational level, socioeconomic level, religious sect, urban or village background, and the degree of contact with local expatriates, as well as travel, study, or work abroad. In Islam, women have the freedom to be a traditional mother or to work (Kahtanie 1992, 6). Women have had opportunities to expand their roles from their traditional roles in Bahrain during the last 30 years. Great strides have been made by many women in the fields of education, medicine, nursing, other health-related professions, finance, clerical work, computers, light manufacturing, banking, and veterinary science, for example. These women in successful jobs are having an effect on the characteristics of gender roles in Bahrain. A comparison between the past and today reveals the significant changes which have occurred, and some of the driving forces which have helped women to achieve higher economic status in Bahrain.

The traditional lifestyle of a Bahraini Shi'a village woman in 1960 was described by Hansen (1967). The Bahraini village lifestyle was similar to that described in Oman in 1974-1976 (Wikan 1982), however, with a few differences, i.e., the wives of Bahraini fisherman and farmers worked outside the home. The fisherman's wife helped to clean and sell fish, while the latter helped their husbands in the fields and in marketing (Rumaihi 1976, 153). In contrast, women living in the towns and cities were exposed to very different circumstances as they were restricted to running their household and to childrearing. As a result, they developed very different lifestyles and gender roles. Among the wealthy, the epitome of status was to have nothing to do all day and to have all work done by servants (Waly 1992).

During the latter part of the 1890s, an agent of change in the status of women was the arrival of the American missionaries sponsored by the Dutch Reformed Church of New Brunswick, New Jersey. The group established, in stages, informal classes in Arabic for boys and girls, then separate classes, and later formal classes, all held in Arabic. Families of various ethnic and religious groups in Manama sent their children to classes for free, and later for a fee. There were complaints from conservative men regarding education for women; however, some girls had been taught in Koran schools (*al mutawa*) prior to this time. The American Mission School, now Al Rajah School, had its first university graduate, a licensed teacher, as school mistress for girls in 1919 (Anthony 1984, 231). The first secular boys school, Al-Hadaya Al-Khalifiya, was opened in 1919. The first secular girls school, Al-Khadija Al-Kubra, was established in 1928, and again there were complaints from conservative males (Belgrave 1956, 94). The Government, in spite of such protests, allowed female education to continue. The Government schools have always been separate but equal for the sexes, and reportedly they follow the same curriculum and use the same textbooks. The complete history of women's secular education has been reported by Duwaigher (1964).

The early expatriate female teachers, Americans, Egyptians, and Lebanese, became role models for women in terms of possible educational achievements and different clothing fashions. As girls' schools became more prevalent, women were needed as teachers, and in the 1950s, the first Bahraini women traveled to Cairo and Beirut to study. Opportunities in the field of education working as teachers and principals were the first professional roles for women. The Government did not promote women studying abroad, but neither did it prohibit them.

A hospital-based nursing school was established in 1959, and in 1961, two male nurses were sent to London for further study. In 1976, the College of Health Science was opened and there were opportunities for women and men in nursing, and later, in other health-related fields. Women continued to travel abroad for their medical studies to Jordan, Beirut, and Egypt, and they now hold positions as heads of departments, deans, and professors. There were never any Bahrain Government restrictions prohibiting women from traveling abroad for study, even when alone. In other Gulf countries, there are now restrictions on women traveling abroad alone.

Of course, family restrictions and concerns determined, then and now, if a woman could travel abroad alone or accompanied. Women who are professionals now, when interviewed, said they knew of Bahraini women who had college degrees (their teachers or relatives), and some who had traveled abroad (doctors, teachers, or relatives), and they were their role models. When they were young, these women hoped that if they had good grades in school, then they also would have these opportunities. Of course, men always had these opportunities and were sponsored by their families or the Government.

Another important force for change was the discovery of oil in Bahrain and the operation of the Bahrain Petroleum Company (BAPCO) refinery under the auspices of Standard Oil of California and Texaco (Caltex). An influx of expatriate workers from the UK, New Zealand, U.S.A., and elsewhere moved to Bahrain and lived in the oil town of Awali. Many Bahraini men obtained training and jobs at the refinery. Some Bahraini women worked in the homes of these expatriates, while men obtained jobs as drivers. Women for the first time now had their own money and became more active in the economic system (Taki 1974). There had always been merchants in the cities in Manama and Muharraq, but now more of the economy was based on cash wages, and the refinery as a major employer contributed to the development of a new middle class (Khuri 1980). By 1995, 18.4% of Bahraini women and 55.2% of expatriate women were working.

Today many females are attending school, which is still noncompulsory. In the past, there was a gender gap; however, now, a higher percentage of girls than boys attend (Baby 1996b). Some girls still receive schooling only at home because of strict family values. Government standardized exam results show that females receive a disproportionate share of the high and excellent grades over their male counterparts. This trend has been seen for the last 40 years (Belgrave 1960, 96). These educational trends have implications for women in terms of admission and access to scholarships to Bahrain University, where in the summer semester of 1996, 52% of the new students were women (Ahmed 1996). Women have long been the majority at the university. Women with high grades are also meeting the criteria for admission to the Arabian Gulf Medical College and the College of Health Science. According to local bank managers who give applicants exams, women score higher than men, and many clerical and teller jobs have been given to women, some of whom have worked up to the position of bank branch managers and executive officers (Moore 1996). These women who have done well and obtained good jobs now have assumed some different roles in society, i.e., they may be supporting their elderly parents partially or fully; they may be making more money than their husbands who may have their *Tawyehi* (high school diploma) or less. Also, they may be more desirable to some men who want or need a partner who can help support the family and make possible extras, such as travel and private schooling for their children.

Anyone watching the Bahrain Government television channels sees what appears to be a male-dominated culture; and in the political sphere, this view reflects reality, as there are no women in the Government at the level of Undersecretary or above. There are, however, 11 Director (head of Directorate) positions now held by women (Noor 1996). Since the recent 1996 government changes, women holding government positions are less frequently seen on television as keynote speakers. This is the public "persona" of the culture. There is a wide divergence among intellectuals regarding how much power and opportunity are available to Bahraini women in reality.

One school of thought suggests that throughout a history of 6,000 years, women have held more power, authority, and responsibility in Bahrain than in other Gulf countries. Ebtihage Al-A'Ali (1991) states that since Dilmun times, men and women in Bahrain have held complementary positions, not competing positions. There was a Dilmun god of the sea, and a goddess of the land. When pearling was a major source of income, men went off in their boats for months at a time while their wives held their families together on shore (Noor 1996). Some wives even worked outside the home to supplement their husband's income. The author states that there is nothing in the Koran prohibiting women from working, only local traditions that have developed. Ms. Al-A'Ali suggests that when Western companies became active in Bahrain after 1930, the reason they did not employ women was because of their cultural values and notions of men being dominating versus complementary. She posits that these formal organizations in Bahrain are based on imported models and thought. She concluded her report stating that one of the unique attributes of Bahraini society is that its island traditions do not restrict the employment of women in top management positions. Her thesis is supported by recent newspaper articles highlighting women who have achieved top positions in private banks and government sector businesses, such as petroleum engineering, and even as Directors in the Government (Moore 1996; Noor 1996).

A completely contrasting view regarding gender roles in Bahrain is presented by Farouq Amin (1982). He notes Bahrain was the first Gulf state to have education for women (1928), and female social organizations, e.g., Bahrain Young Ladies Association (1965). However, Farouq Amin also cites values hurting working women. Employers are reluctant to hire women because of their high fertility rates (the average family size in 1983 was 7.9). Many husbands are not in favor of their wives working, so women quit after marriage. Women are responsible for child care. Twenty percent of rural women are not allowed to study in school. Women have the right to refuse a mate suggested by their family, but not the right to choose. The opening of Bahrain University meant it was no longer necessary to send women abroad for study. The Government is not actively helping women through its policy on sex segregation in the schools, and by its policy of providing women study opportunities mainly in socially acceptable jobs, such as teaching, nursing, and secretarial work. In the 1980s, neither government job bonuses nor housing benefits were given to women. In conclusion, Amin (1982) notes that a value on masculinity, based on religious and traditional values, precludes a large number of women from continuing their study, working outside the home, and even choosing their own spouse.

A second pessimistic view of gender roles is presented by Al-Sharyan who states that the division of labor in Bahrain is not just an economic division, but also reflects lifestyle, prestige, and social honor. Also he states that the labor market is made up predominantly of culturally disadvantaged categories, i.e., nondominant women and immigrants (1987, 353). Exploitation and sexual inequality have neither been reduced nor eliminated. Women did not demand more rights or could not, so, in order to establish wider access to resources, they tended to act so as to reinforce traditional social norms and values (1987, 344). Women concentrated in particular specialties and are thus confined to a fairly narrow range of jobs within the occupational structure. As a result, there is a rigid differentiation in the labor market along sexual lines based on the patriarchal characteristics of the society which are now consolidated (1987, 350). This is reflected in women being the leaders of organizations for the blind, deaf, handicapped, and nursing.

Gender roles in Bahrain probably fall in between the two extremes presented by the above studies. A Bahraini economist listed the five social ills which he felt most confined women to an inferior status in Arab society, i.e., the chastity requirement, early marriage, the dowry, polygamy, and divorce (Taki 1974, 11). Changes are slowly being seen in two of these practices, e.g., early marriage and the dowry. Another practice which prohibited women's development is veiling, which excludes women from many fields of activity (Boserup 1970, 127). Some women have made it to top positions in spite of these "social ills," and 18.4% of Bahraini women are working and 55.2% of non-Bahraini women are working. No studies have been done on working women regarding marital status and number of children; what sacrifices were made by them; and, if they are married, whether there is any correlation with their husbands' education level. Is there a "glass ceiling" in the Government, withholding jobs from women above the level of Director? What role does a girl's self-confidence play in pursuit of education, type of spouse, work opportunity after marriage, and family planning? What are the long-term implications of higher school grades of women, and their academic achievements at the college level in terms of their choices of marital partners, marital relations, the stability of their marriage, and the effect of their education on the educational success of their children? Who is the breadwinner and who is the boss? Further studies in these areas would be very informative for government planners and policymakers.

## B. Sociolegal Status of Males and Females, Children and Adults

The sociological status of males and females as children, adolescents, and adults are clearly defined in the Koran and interpreted by the Bahrain legal system, which is based on a combination of Sharia law and British jurisprudence which are expressed through codes (Ziskind 1990, 41). All births are recorded and rights are granted according to the nationality of the father. Everyone in the country has access to free medical care after their birth, including expatriates. Bahraini women can sign their own operation permits in hospitals or use their thumb prints; however, because of local tradition, the husband, or even other relatives, tend to sign permits. This practice is perpetuated by medical staff who ignore or who are unfamiliar with patients' rights. This practice has also been witnessed in Saudi Arabia (Abu-Aisha 1985). Hospitals in Bahrain do not have statements regarding patients' rights and responsibilities.

All local children can have a place in the Government schools. Education is free for all Bahrainis, and a place in the Government schools is provided for all who register. Girls have access to all areas, including religious studies and technical education. Expatriate parents send their children to various private schools, which are based on various preferences: ethnic (French School, Indian, Pakistani, Japanese, or Filipino), religious (St. Christopher's School–Anglican and Sacred Heart–Roman Catholic), or socioeconomic (Bahrain School, Al Hekma). Bahrainis who pass the entrance exam are entitled to attend Bahrain University and scholarships are available. The majority of students to date have been women, and more are of the Shi'ite sect.

Previously, during the 1960s, the Government made efforts to promote full employment for qualified male adults in companies such as BAPCO, the Defense Force, and other government ministries, and companies. However, now this is not economically feasible, so there is much competition for government and nongovernment jobs. Also the World Bank and other financial organizations are stressing the need for less government control and more free-market economic activity in the country. As a result, unemployment is becoming a national concern. How this will affect women's work opportunities is not known. All workers are protected by various work laws, and due-process rules for firing workers are enforced.

Men and women can own property inherited from their parents based on the rules of Islam for the distribution of property; however, this differs according to Sunni or Shi'ite affiliation. Women keep their family name after marriage and all their property remains in their names, without becoming joint property or being held in their husband's name (Badawi 1980, 23). Women in Bahrain own many small businesses, shops, boutiques, and compounds of rental villas. All marriages and divorces are registered in the Court to ensure people are legally protected. Family disputes over property can be brought to the Courts for adjudication.

Bahrain had a "Special Treaty Relationship" with the United Kingdom until 1971. Now the political system of the country is a traditional monarchy under an Amir. All officials are appointed and there has been no suffrage for anyone since 1975 when the parliament was dissolved (Curtis 1977). Formerly, there were elections for municipal councils and women and men both had the right to vote. The one Constituent Assembly election held in 1972 allowed only men to vote and there have been no subsequent elections.

Individuals, who violate the laws of the State or strictures regarding certain behaviors, are brought before the various Courts, and fined or confined. Even expatriates appear before the Bahrain Courts, which are held in Arabic, for traffic violations, medical negligence lawsuits, drug trafficking, theft, and visa violations. Other minor violations, including being seen eating during the daylight hours of Ramadan, may result in fines for expatriates and tourists. During Ramadan, the media informs residents and visitors of all restrictions.

There are certain individuals whose legal rights are not clearly defined because of their unclear birth status. These are the foundlings (*laqeet*) who have been abandoned, and whose family and nationality is unknown. They are basically homeless and have no papers. Between the early 1920s and the 1950s, the American Mission Hospital had an affiliated orphanage and school for these children. Later, during the 1950s and 1960s, the Government hospital was their legal residence until a job was found for them. Since the 1970s, they have been cared for in the Children's Home in Gudhaibia, which provides for these children with the help of volunteers.

Life is not easy for these individuals. The foundlings are taken care of and have access to free healthcare and education; however, they have no documents and this prohibits them from obtaining any passport, owning property, procuring government employment, and other social benefits. The female foundlings are easily placed in permanent foster homes of Muslim Bahrainis, as under Islam they are not considered adoptable in the full Western sense. The females fare better and generally marry, and can inherit special gifts if any are willed to them. The males are not placeable in foster homes as they are not related to the women in the family, so rules of seclusion and veiling restrict placement. The males spend their lives in government institutions. They cannot be raised by non-Muslim Bahrainis.

*Voting Rights for Islamic Women*

[*Update 2002*: In February 2002, in a pioneering move for the Islamic nations, Bahrain's King Hamad bin Isa al-Khalifa announced a new constitution that gave women the right to vote and run for office. In May, Bahraini women participated both as voters and candidates for office for the first time in a national election. Although many voters judged the women candidates more qualified than some male candidates, women voters, especially among the poor, tended to follow their husband's view and vote for male candidates. The results were overwhelmingly in favor of traditional religious parties, with all 31 women running in a field of more than 300 candidates losing their bid for office. One woman candidate sought a *fatwa*, a religious ruling, from Sheik Yusuf al-Qaradawi, an influential Muslim scholar who appears on *Al Jazeera*, the Arab satellite television network. Women could run for office, he said, especially after they were past their childrearing years and their wisdom could be applied outside the home, just as long as everybody avoided looking at each other unnecessarily at council meetings. The Koran only forbade a woman from running an entire nation.

[Political analysts in Bahrain, both male and female, agreed that the failure of the women to win any seats was due more to the lack of organization in their campaigns than to cultural reasons. Also, the Islamic religious parties ran a single candidate in each district while two or more women ended up splitting the vote in some districts. Women candidates quickly discovered not only the opposition of the conservative religious leaders, but also the difficulty of meeting voters and presenting their case in a society that segregates men and women in most aspects of daily life. Some women candidates were quite creative in meeting the new challenges of running for office. One woman carried a Koran and a Bible with her in all her campaign stops. When a woman promised to vote for her, she made her swear on the appropriate holy text. Later, when the voter's husband tried to make the wife vote for a male candidate, she could say she had made a holy oath and had to keep it (MacFarquhar 2002). (*End of update by the R. T. Francoeur*)]

## C. General Concepts and Constructs of Sexuality and Love

Sexual suppression, except in a heterosexual marriage, is the expected norm in Bahraini culture. Within a legal marriage, the sexual relationship of the couple is between the husband and wife, and based on their religious beliefs and personal preferences.

Cleanliness is associated with sexuality. A person should be clean and attractive before and after engaging in sexual activity. Cleanliness may include removal of part or all body hair for women, and some or all hair for men also. Activities before sex include at least partial bathing, if not full bathing; use of attractive incense or perfumes; makeup for women depending on the couple's choice; and attractive lingerie, depending on personal choice and economic status. Some women attend exercise classes to tone up their bodies, however this is not the norm, and obesity among men and women is a problem in the Gulf (Bin Hamad et al. 1991). Some couples may disrobe while others remain covered or partially covered during sexual activities. There have been no studies on practices related to sexuality in the home or bedroom. After sexual intercourse, all Muslims are expected to wash, and for the woman to wash completely, including her hair. If a woman arrives at a party with wet hair, then jokes may be made about her possibly preceding sexual activities.

Women who smoke are considered to be sexy by young men according to informants. Traditionally, some Bahraini women smoked the hubbly-bubbly (*Al-gadow*) at home, at the village springs, and at parties when offered (Hansen 1967, 89). Bahraini women do not smoke cigarettes openly at work (unlike some expatriates), and are only occasionally seen smoking in their cars or at restaurants. Recently, security guards have noted that a few teenage girls and younger women have been noted to have cigarettes in their purses. The prevalence of smoking among working women in Bahrain is estimated to be 20% based on the one study published (Al-Khateeb 1986). Women have a meeting house in Adliya where they can go to socialize and smoke. Middle Eastern women in countries other than the Gulf area, such as Jordan, Egypt, and Turkey smoke openly; however, this is not a local custom. There have been no studies published in Bahrain regarding why women smoke; however, a study in Saudi Arabia (AlFaris et al. 1995) stated that relief of stress was the most commonly admitted reason for smoking (48.9%), followed by no reason (28.5%), and imitation (12.2%).

Children are important in an Arab family. The traditional wedding wish says "from the woman children, from the man money." All men desire a boy to retain their name, and a woman will continue getting pregnant until she has a son to please her husband, and herself. After the birth of the first child, the father and mother relinquish their name to that child, until there is a male child. They are called the "father of" *Abu . . .* and the "mother of" *Um . . .* (Curtis 1977, 55). This practice reinforces the importance of children in the society and is not meant to denigrate or detract from a woman or man's status. If a couple has difficulty conceiving, there are two in-vitro fertilization (IVF) units in the country.

The Western concept of love is used by few members of Bahraini society to describe their feelings for their spouse. Parents will clearly state they love their children and their parents and have a duty towards them. An individual's relationship, in certain cases, may be closer with their parents, siblings, and children than with their spouse; this depends on the type of marriage they entered into.

The nature of family relationships has been reported in a thesis by Kahtanie (1992) who asked married Bahraini couples about their coping strategies when facing life strains in marital and parental roles. Twenty-five married couples attending a Health Center participated. The researcher noted that marriages in Bahrain are based on mutual understanding, but conflicts and frustration can occur when confronting stress. Participants described the parental role as one of the most important roles in Bahrain (Kahtanie 1992, 1). The participants, however, were not eager to share their coping mechanisms. Eighty percent said they would rely on God. Traditionally, a couple's support system included parents, grandparents, and/or a neighbor; however, now only 84% said they would ask these people for assistance. The remainder said they would handle the problems themselves. Twenty percent said the doctor was of no help. The chief causes of marital stress included nonacceptance by spouse, non-reciprocity and lack of give-and-take in the relationship, and role frustration (Kahtanie 1992, 23). Forty percent of the men said their wife was not a good sexual partner. Most of the couples adjusted to their lives by doing things to avoid differences, solving differences between them by yelling, shouting, and keeping out of the other's way. Their coping responses included not telling anyone of their problems, because Bahrain is small and information can spread. Other coping mechanisms included controlled reflection versus emotional disharmony; comparison to other marriages; passive forbearance versus self-assertion, and selective ignoring. Sixty percent of the participants said they keep most of their feelings to themselves (Kahtanie 1992, 46).

The implications of this forbearance, ignoring, and internalization are mentioned by Kahtanie in conjunction with Chaleby's 1987 study on how unhappy marriages are reflected in various psychosomatic disorders seen, especially among women in Saudi Arabia. These women reported that incompatibility in intimacy and socializing, not meeting their husband before marriage, and polygamy lead

to stress, which was expressed as complaints of backache, headache, pain syndromes, or other symptoms suggesting underlying anxiety (Chaleby 1987).

An interesting trend detected by Kahtanie was that the higher the education of the woman, the less she was able to cope with problems in the marriage (1992, 36). Avoidance coping mechanisms elicited by Kahtanie are reflected in other aspects of family life or work, e.g., people say "it's not like we were prevented, we just did not ask or raise this issue." Personal adjustment and avoidance of confrontation is a core value in Bahraini society. This value is seen in other island cultures around the world (Hall 1996) and has implications for how change is introduced or not introduced into a society.

## 2. Religious, Ethnic, and Gender Factors Affecting Sexuality

### A. Religious Values (*Din*)

The predominant religion in Bahrain is Islam, which is also the state religion. This has implications on all aspects of daily life and sexuality, as there is no separation of church and state, religion and daily life. Religious affiliation is the most important single attribute determining an individual's social status in Bahrain society (Al-Sharyan 1987, 345). Religion continues as an all-encompassing pervasive guide which directs and divides up the hours of each day. Bahrainis are members of either the Sunni or Shi'ite sects of Islam, 30% and 70%, respectively. The ruling family belongs to the Sunni sect. Many expatriates living in Bahrain are non-Muslim and are free to practice their respective religions openly and at their own places of worship, such as churches (Anglican, Roman Catholic), chapels (Interdenominational, Dutch Reformed–USA), and other places of public worship (e.g., Hindu temple). Other groups meet in homes or apartments (Mormons, a few local Jewish families) for prayer. Expatriate groups retain their own cultural values and language and generally socialize among themselves. There are many ethnic, cultural, and social clubs that advertise their activities which anyone can attend. The interaction of all these expatriates among their own groups and with Bahrainis will be developed further in this report with regard to aspects of human sexuality.

During the Friday noontime service in the mosque, the imams teach their congregation the religious point of view regarding all aspects of their life. At the time of the night prayer, special lecture activities are scheduled. There are special religious booklets, e.g.: *Al-moamalat Al-islamiyah* (about banking, charity, selling, and buying) and *Al-Ebadat* (praying, social conduct, *Haj*, and fasting), available to guide people in their lives according to the Prophet's teachings. Non-Muslim expatriates are expected to respect the religion and customs of the country. There are three major illicit acts in Islam: fornication, alcohol consumption, and eating pork. According to Islam, sexual matters are private matters and sexual behaviors are appropriate only between married heterosexuals.

Islamic law requires people to be modest in their dress and the body must be covered in public. For a man, this includes the part from his hips to his knees, while for a woman this comprises all her body from the top of the head to the ankles, excluding the face, hands, and feet. Expatriate women are not required to be covered completely in Bahrain, unlike Saudi Arabia; however, they are expected to dress modestly in public.

While the practice of veiling exists in Bahrain, the percentage of women wearing a veil has varied through the years, depending on rural or urban habitation and social class. Veiling practices posed a difficulty to the early American Mission doctors who were all men, and it was not until the 1930s that there was a female doctor, and then only for two weeks a year. In spite of this, one quarter of the operations at that time were on women, and in increasing numbers, Bahraini women gradually attended the mission hospital and were seen by male doctors (The American Mission Hospital 1933-1934, 7). In the early days, a hole was made in the veil and the specific area of the mouth, face, or body was exposed. Today, some women or their husbands still request that the woman be seen only by a female doctor; however, this is not always possible. Now more and more families choose to pay and attend the clinic of the "best" doctor in their speciality regardless of gender.

The superego, according to psychoanalytic theory, is the portion of the personality associated with ethics, self-criticism, and the moral standard of the community. Two psychiatrists in Saudi Arabia describe Arab culture, particularly in the [Arab] peninsula, as characterized by a deeply rooted set of moral codes, social values, customs, and rituals of behavior. The collective attitude toward such conventions is rather strict and inflexible (Al-Khani & Arafa 1990).

The traditional extended family (*atilab*), which has an authoritarian and hierarchical structure, has the main role in transmitting values and securing conformity, and is the basic and most influential social system. Al-Khani and Arafa state that this practice leads to the development of a superego developmental system that is characterized by the cultivation of shame (*Ayeb*) rather than guilt, and the enhancement of conformity and fear of other's criticism rather than individualism and self-criticism. A consequence in Saudi Arabia is seen in the number of patients, markedly males, who comprise 97.2% of clients who see a psychiatrist for the treatment of social phobias. These statistics reflect a cultural attitude that discourages females from seeking psychiatric care.

The study of superego development in Saudi Arabia and the concept of shame (*Ayeb*) needs to be considered as a possible explanation for some of the differences seen among Bahrainis in the practice of their stated religious beliefs. Followers of any religion vary from true and fervent believers who practice all aspects of their faith to those who follow certain aspects and disregard others. Situational ethics is a term used in the West to describe why the degree of compliance to religious rules is not always 100%, and how people justify their daily practice based on the situations encountered and what is/was the higher right. This term is not commonly used in relation to Islam; however, this report will show that men and women and/or their families decide what religious practices relating to human sexuality they will follow in their personal lives all the time, or some of the time, or which rules they will ignore completely depending on the social situation. Traditional cultural values, such as shame (*Ayeb*), at times, may supersede the higher religious ideals. Also according to Al-Sharyan, Eastern loyalty remains fixed and strong toward familial and tribal values whatever the influence of modernization (1987, 342).

Bahrainis respond to differences in people's adherence to religious values in a mature way, i.e., people know when they should pray—Shi'ite three times a day and Sunni five times a day. The call to prayer from numerous minarets announces prayer time. People are not forced out of stores and restaurants during the "exact" prayer time. Although the Government television channels announce prayer times, programs are not discontinued for 15 to 20 minutes as in Saudi Arabia. The attitude in Bahrain is that mature people and true believers know what they should do without coercion.

Islam condones sexual activity in marital heterosexual relationships (Fakhro 1991). Homosexuality is forbidden (*haraam*). There is no enforced Bahrain state law prohibiting this practice which does exist. Anal sex is *haraam* ("the sky shakes when doing it"); however, it is practiced between men and women, and men and men. Although prostitution is discouraged in the Koran, it is legal in Bahrain. There were early attempts to regulate it by Court decree (1937). Child abuse, including sexual abuse and incest cases, are seen by healthcare workers in Bahrain. Divorce is looked upon with strong disfavor by the Prophet; however, divorce rates are increasing to the detriment of children and the elderly. Islam is vehemently against drinking alcohol, and prohibits the use for pleasure of any drug that can harm the intellect or the body, including tobacco (Fakhro 1991). However, all the above practices are prevalent in Bahrain society to the detriment of health promotion programs in the society. As mentioned, while religious teachings expound ideal values, humans cannot always reach the ideal. This report will present some of the ideals and rules regarding aspects of human sexuality, and the current gaps seen between the ideal and reality.

## B. Ethnic Values

There are more than 60 nationalities represented among expatriates living in Bahrain, and they comprise about one third of the total population. Most of these individuals do not have the option of ever becoming a Bahraini citizen, unless they marry a Bahraini, perform in a special job category, or meet other stringent qualifications, such as religious or five-year residency status. As a result, most expatriates make no effort to become assimilated into the local culture. Some learn Arabic out of necessity because of their job; however, most join social organizations and clubs where they can meet their own compatriots. All these expatriate groups have brought their various religious, moral, and social values with them, and these are reflected in the variety of dress styles seen (sari, sleeveless blouses, tight pants, no bras, miniskirts, and jogging shorts) which are seen on the local streets and in shops. Likewise, attitudes towards alcohol use, pornography, prostitution, and unmarried and extramarital relationships vary from group to group and individual to individual. Concepts regarding degrees of nudity vary greatly, and differences among expatriates are reflected where they take their children swimming. There is one private beach attended only by expatriates wearing bikinis and bikini briefs (women and men). Also at this beach, women are seen topless at times when they are changing their clothes. Because of the nudity, some Westerners do not take their children to this beach and limit their outings only to clubs or their residential compound pools.

The age distributions in the Bahraini and expatriate populations are significantly different, with 52.9% of the expatriates being between age 20 and 49 while only 43.6% of the locals are in that age group. Most expatriates are between the ages of 20 and 49 because they are brought in to supplement the local workforce. Expatriates comprise a significant proportion of the workforce, approximately 33%, and, it should be noted, they are living in Bahrain during their most sexually active years. The largest group of expatriates is from South Asia, with approximately 120,000 from India, Pakistan, Bangladesh, and Sri Lanka. Another large group are the Filipinos, comprising more than 16,000 workers.

Bahrainis are very tolerant of the expatriates and their different lifestyles. No restrictive dress codes have been passed; no religious police (*Muttawa*) censure people verbally or physically. People are arrested only for blatant, public violations of the Ramadan fast during daylight hours. Bahrainis must be credited for their highly hospitable culture and tolerance of people from different cultures and religions. Occasionally, situations arise because of the dichotomy of values, particularly regarding dress codes, which are a very obvious difference. Personal or public conflicts sometimes result which require resolution. Bahraini children are taught from a very young age that modesty and covering of the body is proper. Occasionally, a child may experience confusion when their first teacher is wearing a sari and the abdomen and arms are exposed, as well as her hair. Children report feeling uncomfortable at school during their first days because of the "embarrassment" that they feel seeing the teacher's abdomen. Parents explain about differences in national dress and these issues are resolved. More-public conflicts occur, but rarely, such as that seen in 1994 when mainly male and female expatriate runners in a competition jogged though some conservative villages wearing tank tops and jogging shorts. The local media later reported some stones were thrown at the runners. Such events subsequently have been routed through mainly desert areas away from the villages.

Ethnic attitudes towards other aspects of sexuality, such as prostitution, vary widely. In some cultures, such as Thailand, women know and accept that their husbands frequent prostitutes, while the Filipinos are mainly Catholic and such activity is considered a mortal sin. In spite of this prohibition, the Filipinos in Bahrain are attracted to the money available through prostitution and have the reputation of being one of the ethnic groups active in this practice.

## 3. Knowledge and Education about Sexuality

### A. Government Policies and Programs for Sex Education

There is a national curriculum which is taught in the boys and girls schools using the same textbook. The course content offered to intermediate school students is not labeled as sex education. An introduction to human anatomy and physiology is taught to students around the ages of 10 to 12, depending on a student's school entry age. This basic course is purely an anatomy and physiology approach to sexuality, and male and female informants said they learned about eggs, sperm, menstruation, etc. Family planning is now also covered in this course. There is no discussion of personal relationships or human sexuality, as this is considered *haraam*. There is little discussion of sexually transmitted diseases (STDs) as the emphasis is on normal anatomy and physiology. Some informants report that they did understand what their teacher said, so that when they started menarche, they already understood what was happening to their bodies; however, one woman reported that when she started menstruating, she was afraid she had hurt herself and cried, then told her mother. Another informant mentioned that the intermediate-level course was not enough. "She did not know how babies got out of the body, maybe through the rectum?" In her case, she did not understand about the birth process until she took another course in college. At the Tawyehi level (grades 10 to 12), further anatomy and physiology courses are taught only to those in the science stream or curriculum. Students in the arts or commercial streams have no further courses. There have been no studies reported on the effectiveness of these general intermediate-level courses, or senior school science courses, or the extent of knowledge or accuracy of knowledge among students or Tawyehi graduates.

Graduates from the College of Health Science reported that there were classes where students had to present topics and discuss material relating to the genitourinary system. The females said they were very embarrassed in the coed class, and were sweating; however, the subject was taught as scheduled. Everyone felt more comfortable with the other subjects in the curriculum.

An expatriate physician in 1987 wrote the only article regarding the sexual responsibilities of physicians seen to date in the national medical journals (Gravesen 1987). Other physicians have written on related topics, such as reproductive fertility (Rajab 1984), and urogenital problems of the elderly (E. Amin 1984). In general, the term human sexuality is simply not used.

There have been no studies published in Bahrain regarding the knowledge of women about the climacteric (menopause), and the physical changes they can expect, nor its effect on their libido. Two hospitals have started menopausal clinics to meet the needs of older women, and there have been a number of articles in the general press about the advances made in hormone replacement therapy. There are also no data available regarding women's knowledge regarding mammogram screening, pelvic screening for cancer, osteoporosis, or other preventive measures which are needed and available. Only recently have physicians in Gulf countries reported psychosocial symptoms related to menopause, in Kuwait (Al-Quttan & Omu 1996) and in Saudi Arabia (Sadat-Ali 1993). Reportedly, there is a reluctance among physicians to study osteoporosis in this age group, which showed a high incidence of the disease in the pilot study (Sadat-Ali 1993), or other related topics. The general opinion expressed by female informants is that a lot of older women "suffer at home when going through the change."

Regarding human sexuality courses for the general public, there are lectures offered at the Primary Health Centers regarding pregnancy care and delivery; however, there are no lectures addressing issues associated with "human sexuality." The Bahrain Family Planning Association (B.F.P.A.) also offers lectures; videos and booklets about family planning are available from their library.

### B. Informal Sex Education

Informants mentioned a variety of informal sources for their early sex education, as most said parental instruction was rare and consisted of "don't touch it" or "don't let anyone touch." Regarding parental instruction, the range of responses included those who said, "I could never talk to my mother/father about that," "She/he did not encourage us to ask," "Mother didn't tell," and "We didn't ask mother," to those whose parents were supportive and "explained when asked," to parents who approached them first and "gave them books to read," and/or "explained everything to them." Some girls were told riding bikes and horses could be harmful, so they should be careful. All informants, men and women, said they discussed sex-related topics with their friends; some did or did not discuss such sex-related matters with their older or younger siblings. All informants likewise said that the media had an influence on their knowledge, including movies (Indian, Arabic, Western), music (Arabic, Western), and books and magazines. Some mentioned how their friends or coworkers, at the time of their engagement, gave them graphic information on "what to do" and "how to do it."

Human sexuality teaching to hospital patients can only be confirmed for cardiac patients attending the Shaikh Mohammed Bin Khalifa Bin Salman Al Khalifa Cardiac Center, as their patient-teaching booklet (in Arabic and English) covers all aspects of sexual behavior after heart attacks and surgery. Urologists and obstetric/gynecology staff discuss human sexuality topics with their patients; however, they have no teaching booklets for them.

## 4. Autoerotic Behaviors and Patterns

### A. Children and Adolescents

Infibulation, clitoridectomies, and other forms of female genital mutilation have never been performed on Bahraini females. The practice is not seen in the entire Gulf region and Hicks (1993) clearly mentions this distinction. It was practiced in the Saudi Arabian peninsula in Yemen (Muhsen & Crofts 1991). Some expatriate Muslim children and women born elsewhere, e.g., in the Sudan or Egypt, who have been circumcised, are seen in Bahrain's medical facilities. It was only in July 1996 that Egypt banned circumcision of girls in all state medical facilities ("Girl Circumcision Ban," 1996); however barbers and doctors are still performing the procedure and girls are hemorrhaging to death in Egypt.

Informants report that Bahraini children around the ages of 2.5 and 3 begin to touch themselves in the genital region like children around the world. As soon as relatives see this activity beginning, the child is taught this is not socially acceptable, and every time the behavior is seen, the child is admonished verbally not to do it (physical punishment is not used). Bahraini children do not walk around naked and always have clothes on.

All the female informants report that their mothers from a very early age taught them how to sit with their legs together, to sit carefully and to ensure they are covered properly, and how not to sit (not to squat, and "not to let anything show"). Some report that they were taught how to wash their genitals in a proper way, and now they are teaching or taught it to their female children, e.g., with a closed finger and thumb position, and not with their fingers reaching and feeling. The prevalence of this particular washing method is not known. When girls reach the age of 10 to 12, their general play activities become restricted, and all reported their mothers told them their bodies would be changing and that they needed to behave in a careful manner. The concept of virginity and being careful with sharp objects was instilled in them. The incidence or types of autoerotic behaviors in this age group have not been studied.

## B. Adults

Adult autoerotic behaviors have not been studied in Bahrain. A study was conducted in a conservative region of Saudi Arabia regarding women and breast self-exams (BSE). Half of the women attending a clinic had information about BSE; however, 12.1% said they did not think they should touch their breast, and 9.0% said it was embarrassing for them to do BSE (Akter et al. 1995). No studies have reported on whether men conduct regular self-exams for testicular cancer or have annual prostate exams. Annual prostate screening is not promoted, and rectal exams are done only upon patient request in many cases. These exams may be deleted because of the sexual overtones and the staff feeling uncomfortable conducting them. Further research on preventive health screening and cultural prohibitions would be informative.

Pornography is prohibited by law; however, its definition is not clear. Magazines are seen in the country (e.g., *Playboy*) which are illegal, while *The Sun*, the United Kingdom newspaper typically featuring a topless woman on page three, is not. Men bring these magazines into the country and some keep them at their mothers' houses when their wives do not approve of them.

There are X-rated movies or blue movies available in Bahrain, as well as what may be called provocative movies which include a few seconds of partial nudity, belly dancing, or heavy petting. There have been cases reported of couples making X-rated movies or blue movies for themselves, and later these somehow got into others' hands which caused great embarrassment to those involved. Other blue movies have been smuggled in from distribution centers in Saudi Arabia or abroad. Expatriates have been arrested at the Saudi Causeway transporting such tapes in their cars. Another video source of stimulation to men are

the wedding party videos from Bahrain, Saudi Arabia, or Qatar which are copied and distributed unknown to the sister, relative, or sister's friend who held the original. Informants report that some of their brothers have seen and even sold copies of these videos, which include Gulf women with their hair uncovered, dressed in miniskirts, with tight clothes, or low-cut necklines. The adolescent boys and young men watch these movies when available.

Sexual devices are not sold in the country; however, they are brought in by people who travel abroad. Informants said that some people keep them for their own use, while others are sold. Sexual devices are not defined as illegal by law. One incident was reported of a Saudi Arabian woman returning to Saudi Arabia who had bought a sexual device elsewhere. Saudi Arabian Customs could not take it from her, because such items are not mentioned in customs laws, and the woman retained her device.

Aphrodisiacs from various sources are used, but their prevalence has not been studied. Some compounds from local or imported herbs are thought to have beneficial powers for improving male potency, female fertility, or for curing venereal diseases. Such herbs are available from traditional herbalists (*Al Ashab*) in the various *suqs*, or from traditional midwives. References on this topic are limited in content (Bushiri & Davis 1996; Abdul & Saheb 1990; Abu-Zaid, 1966). The latter source in Arabic describes the herbs used in the Gulf and methods of treatment which were brought in from India, Syria, Sudan, and Egypt. Some individuals also request hormone shots from their physicians. Testosterone therapy should be avoided as much as possible; if used, then monitoring of the prostate is needed (E. Amin 1984, 30).

Alcoholic beverages are freely available in Bahrain through retail liquor outlets, hotel bars, and restaurants unlike other Gulf countries. Liquor is served openly to Bahrainis, expatriates, and tourists. Liquor has not always been so available. Traditionally, Arak, the local liquor made from dates, was confiscated by the police (British and local). Then foreigners were allowed to purchase liquor if they held a special permit. At this time, a black market in imported spirits flourished (Belgrave 1960), and Arak was made by hidden stills. Then retail liquor outlets were licensed and sales flourished. Islam's prohibition of alcohol is based on its intoxicating effect on the brain (*khumr*). Modern scholars in the Tufseer advise people, "Don't put your hand in a dangerous thing." Hotel bars, restaurants, and clubs frequented by locals and tourists are also frequented by prostitutes.

Some individuals experiencing difficulties of any psychological or organic nature, including sexual, traditionally would go to the *mutta wa* (religious man or woman) and ask for assistance. The *mutta wa* would say words from the Koran to cure the person (Al-Maki 1996, 16). These psychosomatic cures were reportedly effective in some cases.

Fracture of the penis is a urological emergency situation which requires immediate identification and surgery in order to prevent morbidity to the patient. Prior to 1988, there were fewer than 100 cases reported in the medical literature (Sandozi et al. 1988). Urologists in the Gulf during the last ten years have reported dozens of such cases. Fracture of the penis may occur during coitus, or by a direct blow, by abnormal bending of an erect penis, or through other sexual aberrations. Men report hearing a crack, then feel a sharp pain with subsequent loss of erection, deformity, discoloration, and swelling, but no micturation (painful urination) difficulties. If surgical treatment is not provided quickly, the condition results in serious morbidity, including deformation of the erect penis, weak erections, and reduced sexual performance. The surgical procedure is described by Taha et al. (1988).

Various reports have been published in the Gulf regarding penile fracture, including eight cases in Kuwait involving seven expatriates living without their wives. Their injury was self-inflicted in four patients and because of accidental trauma in three cases. In one case, a Sudanese male was trying to negotiate a hymen and vagina which had strictures from the ritual practice of female circumcision and clitoridectomy (Sandozi et al. 1988). Numerous other cases have been reported in Abu Dhabi (Al-Saleh et al. 1985) and Qatar (El-Sherif et al. 1991), with nine cases in four years in the United Arab Emirates (Hamarnah 1993), Bahrain (E. Amin 1994), and Iran (Asgari et al. 1996). As mentioned, the incidence of this urological injury is generally low, but review of the literature shows the incidence of this injury is higher in the Arabian Gulf region (Hamarnah et al. 1993). Some authors suggest the various etiological factors include relatively large numbers of single male expatriates, and married men living away from their spouses, in a Muslim country which contributes to the genesis of this injury. Sandozi et al. suggest that excessive libido and sexual urges which cannot be relieved may play a part in the causation of penile fracture (1988). Expatriate workers in Saudi Arabia do not usually socialize with Saudi women, and nightlife activities are rare because of segregation of the sexes, (Abbas & Satwekar 1989). In Bahrain there are many opportunities to socialize, including discos (Belgrave 1968).

Priapism is a painful, persistent, penile erection without sexual excitement and is a result of engorgement of the corpora cavernosa. Priapism can be self-induced with various drugs, and occasionally cases are seen at medical facilities. Priapism is also a known complication secondary to sickle cell disease (SSD). Reports from the U.S.A. show that 50% of boys/men with SSD can be affected, i.e., report having one occurrence or more of priapism. Studies in the Gulf show that priapism is a common complication of SSD, e.g., in Saudi Arabia with 18.4% of SSD patients reporting at least one experience (Al-Dabbous & Al-Jama 1993). In Bahrain, the incidence of priapism prevalence is low at 2.0% (Rasromani et al. 1990, 114), and the incidence of SSD is 2.0%, while the sickle cell trait is 11.2%.

Informants were asked about an incongruous aspect of culture seen in Bahrain. For example, American wrestling programs are seen on local television and in other Gulf countries. These programs are very popular and individual wrestlers are known by names. The wrestlers generally have extravagant makeups, hairstyles, and outfits. Some of these outfits are only tight bathing suits and this is shown on local TV. Informants state that wrestlers themselves are not seen as provocative, as wrestling is a traditional sport from the days of the Ottomans, and it is seen as exercise or family entertainment. However, it was noted that if a girl had tapes of wrestling matches and watched wrestling in an "entranced" manner, then that was another issue. Surprisingly, bodybuilding competitions are held annually in Bahrain, and participants are Bahraini men.

While public autoerotic behaviors are infrequently seen in Bahrain, they are occasionally reported. An elderly Western expatriate visitor attending church was horrified as an expatriate male sitting next to her masturbated during the service. She reported she was afraid, but could not get up because the church was so crowded. Female Asian expatriates report situations where taxi drivers have begun masturbating while they were in the taxi. The reputation of this Asian group is rather low morally, which may be why they are exposed to more encounters of this nature. Expatriate women all note that, in Bahrain, these incidents are very rare, unlike the frequency of similar incidents they were exposed to in Saudi Arabia, i.e., you could not look men in their eyes or below their chests.

## 5. Interpersonal Heterosexual Behaviors

### A. Children

*Sexual Exploration, Sex Rehearsal Play,*
*and Rites of Passage*

Children seen touching other children in any suggestive manner are firmly instructed that this behavior is not appropriate. All sexual exploration and sexual rehearsal play, if noted by the parents or relatives, is strongly extolled as forbidden.

All Bahraini boys are circumcised according to the requirement in the Koran. The procedure is usually performed in the first 40 days after birth in a hospital or Health Center Day Case Unit. Traditionally, up until about ten to 15 years ago, boys of 6 of 7 years of age were circumcised by a doctor or a traditional barber. This latter practice has been stopped in Bahrain, although it continues in Saudi Arabia and is thought to be a source of hepatitis C infections in that country (Arya 1996, 229). Traditionally, after the circumcision, money and sweets were distributed to other children in the family and to the boy's friends and neighborhood children (Curtis 1977, 55). This practice has now almost died out.

There are no ceremonies marking adolescence or adulthood. Children, upon reaching age 7, begin to attend the mosque regularly in order to learn more about their religion, and this is their rite of passage to full membership in the community.

### B. Adolescents

There are no female puberty rituals in Bahrain. Women mention that when they reached the age of menarche, they informed their mothers, and the girls in return were told, "they were now a woman," "they needed to behave like a woman," "to be careful of covering," that "they could no longer play outside with children," and "to be especially protective of their virginity." Their mothers usually told other female relatives or friends that their daughter was now a woman, but there was no party or ceremony. Women reported gossiping to their sisters and how they were happy that they were normal.

A few studies have been done regarding the experience of menstrual cycle symptoms among Bahraini women (Al-Gaseer 1990), Saudi women (Atallah et al. 1990), and Kuwaiti women (Ibrahim et al. 1979). The age of onset of menarche in the region varies from 10 to 17 years of age with an average of 13 years. Women in the younger age groups, 17 to 24 years, report more menstrual symptoms, while educated women report more menstrual and premenstrual symptoms than single women (Al-Gaseer 1990; Ibrahim et al. 1979). Some women report they called their period "my auntie"; other euphemisms include "Hajiya came," and "I gave birth."

Many Arab women reportedly do not use tampons because of the sexual connotation of placing something in the vagina; also, they fear tampons will make their vagina wide. A third belief is that "washing out is cleaner" than keeping it inside. Some Westernized married women report using tampons, but they said unmarried girls and teenagers would never use them.

The traditional notion that a menstruating women is unclean (*Najis*) still pervades the belief system, although Al-Malki states this notion was rejected by the Prophet (1996, 19, 27). Menstruating women are not to fast on the affected days during Ramadan or on other religious days, but must make up these days later. A woman should not be divorced by her husband when she is menstruating; likewise, sexual relations are prohibited during menstruation (Al-Faruqi 1988, 72).

Once a women's menstrual cycle has started, there is only one occasion when it needs to be strictly regulated and that is when a women plans to go on *Umrah* or the *Haj*. A woman cannot go to Mecca and perform the prayers in the Kaabah or other rituals if she is menstruating. Girls or women with regular periods or irregular periods are given primolat N tablets for 21 days for suppression of the period, or sometimes birth control pills to regulate them, so they can plan on when to make *Umrah* or *Haj*, and they are ensured of being "clean."

The relationships between adolescent unmarried males and females, aside from family relationships, are strictly controlled by families. The majority of boys and girls attend segregated government schools until their graduation from Tawjehi (high school). There have been coeducational expatriate schools for decades in Bahrain, such as St. Christopher's, Sacred Heart, the Bahrain School (American), and the Indian School, which a percentage of Bahrainis have attended. During the last ten years, expensive coeducational private schools have opened specially catering to Arabic-speaking Bahraini and expatriate Arab students, e.g., Al Bayan, Ibn Khaldoon, and Al Hekma. In all the coeducational schools, boys and girls study together, take school trips with their parents' permission, and sometimes socialize. Dating in the Western sense is not the norm. This is the only opportunity for some students to meet members of the opposite sex. Students in mixed groups may also socialize in the shopping malls and hamburger and pizza places. Male teenagers are freer to spend time out of the house with friends, expatriate students, and workers.

## C. Adults

### Premarital Relations, Courtship, and Dating

Bahraini parents strictly control, or at least monitor, their daughter's meetings with men, and discourage anything more than necessary, talking relationships. As mentioned earlier, dating in the Western sense is not the norm. There are instances known where Bahraini women dated expatriate men, including those in the American military during the time of the Gulf Crisis and Gulf War (1990-1991), and these women actively sought out these relationships. These situations are very rare as most families are very strict. One informant reported recently seeing two Persian Bahraini women trying to pick up two American military men in Manama. The two men quickly declined and kept walking, as these relationships are strongly discouraged by the U.S. military because of security and other reasons.

### Sexual Behavior and Relationships of Single Adults

Single men have premarital sexual relationships, while single Bahraini women ideally do not. Single adults are expected to be chaste in their relations, and the girls are expected to be virgins at the time of marriage. A man may have an expatriate girlfriend or girlfriends, or a boyfriend in Bahrain or abroad. The prevalence of these patterns have not been studied among men, nor their prevalence in relationship to venereal disease in Bahrain.

Some Bahraini single women do have affairs. Reportedly, this behavior is very rare, and the meetings are conducted in hotels or elsewhere in Bahrain, and preferably where there are "no eyes," or when they are both abroad. A single women who is not a virgin will face difficulty finding a husband if she is known to have lost her virginity "not by a normal condition," meaning not through marriage. An affair places her in an abnormal or doubtful situation. The

women who are known not to be chaste will find it difficult to ever get married (Taki 1974, 11). A few rare marriages do occur, informants reported, but this is not common, as the man's family will be against the marriage if they have any knowledge that the girl is not a virgin. There have been no reports about Bahraini women traveling abroad for hymen repair surgery.

When expatriate women are seen with a man, it is generally assumed that they are "friends," or lovers until it is clarified that they are married. This attitude extends to Western or Asian women, all of whom are generally considered to have loose morals until their actions prove otherwise. The Government does not get involved in the affairs of expatriates unless a man files a claim of adultery against his wife. In these cases, the residence permits of the woman and her lover are usually revoked and they are deported. This is done quietly, unlike the 1990s case in the United Arab Emirates which received worldwide press coverage.

Conservative Bahraini men and families, if they know someone is having an affair, will enforce certain rules of social behavior in order to protect their wives or families from this person's influence. They will not allow their wives to invite into their house a married or unmarried woman who is living with a man or who has a male "friend," even if the woman is the wife's coworker, compatriot, or friend. These same women are not allowed to sit in the wife's car seat, i.e., the front right passenger seat so they have to sit in the back seat. In most cases, the husband or extended family (*Allah*) even ask the woman not to see such a friend at all socially, because being together could affect the wife's name and they should not be friends. In some cases, an association is allowed to continue with conditions, and in some cases, it is continued in defiance of family wishes when the undesirable person is brought into the house.

Social sanction extends to men who bring their lovers or socially unacceptable partners to a party. One such situation occurred at an Embassy party, when an elderly man arrived with his much younger, diamond bedecked, Filipina guest. Suddenly there was a collective inhaling of breath and staring by the Bahraini dignitaries, and the frosty censure could be felt in the air immediately. The man was greeted as per custom, while the woman was totally ignored and spent her time among the women at the party.

### Marriage and Family

Bahrain has the reputation among all the Gulf countries of being a place "where people can marry who they want." All informants, males and females, agree this is true to a large extent. Women clearly state that the "woman has the right to say no" to any man who is recommended by her family. Farouq Amin amends this and states women have the right to refuse, but not the right to choose (1986). Men stated that, based on their subjective knowledge, perhaps 50% of marriages in Bahrain are arranged. In reality, this figure is 75% (Kahtanie 1992, 41). This incidence is much lower than in Oman or the United Arab Emirates. In the latter country, a law was passed in 1996 stating the man should see the woman before their marriage. Regardless of the stereotype in the Gulf that Bahrainis can marry who they want, there are still six different types of marriages seen in Bahrain, according to Kahtanie (1992). They include arranged marriage, cousin marriage, couples who have not met before, couples who met, forced marriages, and educated-later marriages. Both women and men reported that some men are now showing a preference for, and are choosing, educated working women, even those years older, who can be a partner and who can help in providing financial extras for the family (Taki 1974; Kahtanie 1992, 39).

Marriage selection and choice of mates ideally follows the Islamic pattern, i.e., religion is the first selection factor, while the second factor is the monetary status or potential monetary status of the male and beauty in the female. According to the Koran, individuals cannot marry those who suckled at the same breast and are a milk brother, *Akh Bil Radha'a*. For all types of marriage, the permission of the father or brother is required, and in addition, for soldiers, military approval is needed. For members of the royal family, Amiri Court approval is required.

Marriage brokers (*al khatba*) are still used to arrange meetings in spite of telephones and automobiles, and even though 39% of marriages are consanguineous marriages (Al-Naser 1993; S. Al-Arrayed 1995). Many marriages are still arranged between families. The Islamic associations also play a role in helping individuals find a partner. Men and women can complete a questionnaire at their local association, providing information on education, age, background, and preferences. Association staff match applicants, and they and their families can arrange to meet.

Arranged marriages can succeed or fail. Men stated that the couple may "fall in love" or find they are compatible. A lot of these mainly younger couples also divorce during the first or second year; couples in these arranged marriages stay married, especially after they have a family. In some cases, one of the spouses (either man or woman) falls in love with the other, but this feeling may never be returned, e.g., the wife may say, "our marriage was arranged and he is a good father," and the man, meanwhile, has much stronger feelings for his wife or vice versa.

The reasons given for women agreeing so easily with their parents regarding arranged marriages include the following: Girls are afraid to say no to their parents for any reason because of the way they were raised; the girl may not know any other man or does not have any feeling of attachment to anyone in particular; it is better to be married than unmarried (Taki 1974); or a girl does not want to wait too long and to be told "the train has left." For all these reasons, a girl may acquiesce to her parents' wishes. A man, likewise, may easily follow his family's choice of wife for his first marriage, but if widowed, or if he marries a second time, the woman will be of his choosing.

Consanguineous marriages now comprise 39% of marriages, down from 45.5% in previous generations (Al-Arrayed 1995). This trend for preferential first cousin marriage has serious health implications, including effects on sexual development for the children produced by these couples. The coefficient for inbreeding in Bahrain is 0.0145 (Al-Naser 1993). The child mortality rate in Bahrain is three times that of Japan, even though Bahrain is ranked as an otherwise low-mortality population. The Bahrain Child Health Survey of 1989 showed that one quarter of births occurred between first cousins. The mortality rate for these offspring during their first month and first 23 months is two times higher than children of unrelated parents. The study showed that women who marry relatives, especially their first cousin, tend to marry younger, are illiterate, their parents were illiterate, and they live in rural areas. Other practices contributing to higher mortality include polygynous marriage, remarriage after divorce, short intervals between births, employment of women only in the home, breastfeeding for an average of 10.6 months, malnutrition, and lower socioeconomic status. The author of the study suggested that the government needs to discourage first cousin marriage, to raise the marriage age to 18, to teach the illiterate about birth spacing which is part of Islamic teaching, and to allow polygamy only if the man can afford it (Al-Naser 1993). Sheikha Al-Arrayed disagrees with the contraindi-cations for consanguineous marriage and cites its traditional history and social benefits, even though 42.8% of her sample reported familial genetic diseases (1995).

Some Bahraini men marry expatriate women who are Muslims or non-Muslims. They meet while studying at European, American, or Asian universities, while working in hospitals, or while traveling. The man's family may accept or reject the woman, depending on her religion, country of origin, or other factors. Bahrainis may marry other Gulf Cooperation Council (GCC) nationals with family approval, and occasionally Indian or Pakistani Muslims, but rarely Westerners who have converted to Islam. In these cross-cultural marriages, it is the woman's choice what passport she wishes to maintain. Holders of non-Bahraini passports cannot own property in Bahrain.

Once the agreement of the two individuals has been given to marry, regardless of the type of marriage, then the families decide upon the monetary arrangements for the dowry (*mahr*), which is a gift symbolizing love and affection (Badawi 1980, 17). According to Islamic law, there is a marriage contract (*Al-Rayd*) for all Muslim marriages. This contract specifies the money the man and/or his family will pay at the time of the official engagement in the mosque, any "seconds" if all the money is not available at once, and the "last" money to be paid at the end of the marriage upon divorce or death. The first and second money can be paid to the woman or to her father for holding. Any "second" money, in case of the early death of the man, is paid before the money in the estate is apportioned to other heirs; or any other money he may have borrowed or was holding for his wife is paid first, as the money was hers, *fit ajulain*, in life or death. The contract once signed is a legal document and is blessed in the mosque and then registered with the Courts.

The amount of the dowry paid in 1994 at the time of the engagement varied from BD400 to more than BD2,000 according to the *Statistical Abstract 1994*. Distribution of dowries paid by non-Bahrainis are shown and also tracked in terms of amount and geographical distribution in the country (*Statistical Abstract 1994*: Table 3.53).

The current generation may use the woman's dowry to buy furnishings for the home, rather than having it held by the father or put into her separate bank account. This arrangement depends upon the couple and their relationship. The man's family may also be required to pay for an expensive hotel wedding reception. This depends on the families involved and the contract arrangements. Women report that they were told by their mothers from the time they were young, "never give your money to your husband." If their money is loaned to the husband, it is generally done legally with a contract.

The financial straits of some young men and their families make it difficult for these men to marry. During the last few years, several benevolent social organizations, including the various Islamic Associations, have arranged group weddings once a year, so some or all of the costs of the dowry and weddings are alleviated. These costs can be prohibitive for the young men and prevent them from marrying ("Mass Wedding" 1996). A description of a traditional Sunni wedding ceremony is given by Al-Khalfan (1993), and a Shi'ite ceremony is described by Hansen (1967).

After the engagement, which is equivalent legally to a Western marriage, the woman may move into the man's father's house. Ideally, women do not become pregnant during this engagement time and should wait until after the public wedding ceremony. The engagement is usually less than one year, and longer engagements are discouraged. If the woman does become pregnant, the family then decides if a family or public wedding will take place.

During the "engagement" period, some couples decide unilaterally or mutually that they are not compatible and they will divorce. According to the *Statistical Abstract 1994*, 28% of the Bahraini divorces were before there was any sexual union, 16.5% for non-Bahraini divorces (*Statistical Abstract 1994*: Table 3.74). In the 1994 report, 19% of the marriages lasted longer than one year (*Statistical Abstract 1994*: Table 3.77). Once the Court grants a divorce, a delay of three months is required (*Al' Idda*) to ensure the women is not pregnant, then the divorce is finalized. Islam discourages divorce and teaches reconciliation is better.

A man can say the word *talaq* three times in his home to divorce his wife, then the couple has two options. They can see a religious man, a sheik, for his opinion, or attend a court. In both situations, the conditions surrounding the statement will be assessed, i.e., was *talaq* said in a calm manner or was the man under stress? Was the woman in a state of purity (*tuhr*)? If under stress, then the courts will consider *talaq* as said once. If said in a calm manner, then the legal divorce proceeding will go forward with review of the provisions in the marriage contract. The specific laws pertaining to divorce and inheritance are governed by Sharia law. The Shi'ite follow the *Ja'afari*, and the Sunni the *Maliki* rite.

Women can obtain a divorce for certain prescribed reasons: The man disappears or is absent; the man is impotent; if the marriage causes the wife mental or physical illness, e.g., man is a homosexual, wife battering, or adultery; nonsupport by the man; or if a special condition clause was included in the contract as a condition for marriage (Ramzani 1985). In July 1996, a landmark divorce case was publicized in Bahrain's newspapers. A women was able to divorce her husband who had AIDS, as she said she was at risk for contracting it through sexual contact.

Marriage and divorce rates are tracked by the Central Statistics Organization. The general divorce rate is 1.7/100 population, and the general marriage rate is 7.5 (*Statistical Abstract 1994*: Table 3.45). The trend is one divorce for approximately every 4 to 4.5 marriages. Eighty percent of the marriages and 85% of the divorces were among Bahraini couples (*Statistical Abstract 1994*: Table 3.44). Bahrainis in 1994 also married Asians, other Arabs, other Gulf Arabs, Europeans, and Americans. The divorces followed the same general distribution (*Statistical Abstract 1994*: Table 3.44). Among Bahraini couples, 91% were married for the first time, while among expatriate couples, only 56% of the men were married for the first time. The age range of women marrying showed 1.6% were 19 years or younger, however, this age range accounted for 8.9% of the divorces in 1994 (*Statistical Abstract 1994*: Table 3.43). Trends show young divorced men and women frequently remarry (*Statistical Abstract 1994*: Table 3.56).

If a woman was proven barren before the divorce, or if she wishes to keep her children and not have to give them to her mother or her ex-husband, then the woman may choose not to remarry, in which case, she will continue to live in her parent's house. Her family will continue to protect her and, now that she is divorced, she needs more protection from men who may assume she is "more easy" in her ways.

Ideally, a man informs his wife if he wishes to take another wife. However this is not always practiced. The woman may be told afterwards. She may discover the other marriage or marriages in a sudden way, e.g., during the Government census when the Government census taker is trying to determine which wife he is talking to; some find the other wife and husband in a new house she paid for, or in some cases, the wife may never know. There are Bahraini men who have families in Egypt, India, Philippines, or elsewhere, of which their Bahraini families are unaware. In some cases, the family only finds out when the man dies and the various wives make inheritance claims on the estate.

A man's marriage of another wife is generally not a valid claim for divorce, as a man may legally have up to four wives at one time. Most women do not want to share their husband and their family usually supports them (Taki 1974). The possibility of polygamy makes wives anxious, especially if they are barren or fail to produce male children. Women voice their feelings of insecurity in a serious or joking manner, as they do not know if their husband already has another wife or if he plans to do so. He can also say to them, "if you do not do this, I will look for another." There is a greater risk for older women, as there is always the threat that the husband could take a younger wife. The latter is one concern which reportedly makes women keep menopause a secret, as they do not want their spouses to know of it out of fear that he may take a younger wife.

Women make great efforts to keep their husbands satisfied and, traditionally, this included placing packs of rock salt in their vagina after delivery (A. Mohammed 1978; Rajab 1978). The purpose of the salt crystals was to reduce the size of the vagina after delivery to normal or less than normal size so the man will feel more pleasure (Dickson 1915; Hansen 1967, 108). The use of rock salt and its effects has been documented since the early 20th century by the doctors at the American Mission Hospital in their annual reports, and in Kuwait and Saudi Arabia (Dickson 1915) and Oman (Doorenbos 1976). The main result was rock salt atresia of the cervix, so that in subsequent deliveries the cervix was so tough, it had to be cut to allow delivery. Another effect of the salt packs was unexplained elevation of the patients' temperature after delivery and suspected sepsis. Records show in 1938 that the first MRCOG consultant attended delivery of 84 patients and 79 had rock salt atresia. The Ministry of Health took a proactive approach to this problem and registered, trained, and supervised all the traditional midwives. By the late 1970s, this practice "was nearly died out" (Rajab 1979, 7). However cases are still seen, even as recently as 1996 in the Maternity Hospitals. In the latter case, an elevated temperature was noted and, upon examination, it was found the woman had inserted a vaginal pack of rock salt. Herbal passaries known as *mamool* were also used to tighten the vagina, drain lochia, and promote involution of the uterus (Al-Darazi 1984, 37-38). Some women used a combination of salt crystals, herbal passaries, and antiseptic solutions. Vaginal douches of datol, a strong disinfectant, are still commonly used after childbirth. Regarding resumption of sexual relations after delivery, the wife usually stays with her mother for the first 40 days after delivery and may have also stayed with her mother for one month prior to delivery (Curtis 1977, 47).

Serial monogamy is seen in Bahrain, and some women are divorced and remarried three or more times during their lifetime, and men marry more often. As women become older, their chances for remarriage lessen. There are no reports outlining the common causes of divorce, although in the one study conducted on coping mechanisms of Bahraini couples, marital sexual satisfaction was an issue raised by 25% of the husbands (Kahtanie 1992). The Islamic rules of inheritance work against remarrying or polygamy, and the sons generally oppose remarriage which might engender other children, thereby affecting other inheritors (Taki 1974).

### Extramarital Relationships

There is a type of marriage referred to in the Koran as *al Mut'a*, or temporary marriage. At the time of the Prophet, this practice was allowed for the soldiers who spent many years away from their homes. If the woman the soldier kept became pregnant, then she was to become a full legal wife. The Prophet himself later stopped this practice, and Umar bin Khatab, shortly after the Prophet's time, again instructed men to stop these type of alliances, as women should be taken as legal wives only.

This practice of temporary marriage has continued only among the Shi'ite. One example is described as seen in Sar Village by Hansen (1967, 127). In this particular marriage, the girl did not leave her village to live with her husband in A A'li. Currently, the term *Al Mut'a* has taken on a new meaning. Men who are having an affair may use this term to describe their current relationship; however, there is no legal basis for this type of relationship today (Al-Faruq 1988, 6).

The extent to which Bahraini and expatriates are involved in extramarital affairs is not known. Anecdotal stories are passed around when an incident occurs, e.g., a Bahraini store owner was called to testify to the police about the good behavior of his Bahraini worker. The worker had severely beaten an Indian neighbor who was found to have been sleeping with the man's wife. Incidentally, this woman was "covered" whenever she appeared in public.

### The Changing Nature of Bahraini Marriage and Household

Three major changes have occurred in Bahrain which are driving forces for change in Bahraini families and family relationships. Household structures have changed from mainly extended families (*Allah*) of 20 to 30 members living under one roof, to variable forms, including traditional extended households with several generations of family members to nuclear family households (no Arabic word to describe this) located in one of the new cities, e.g., Isa Town, Hamad Town, or a flat. Another major change in all types of households since the 1970s has been the introduction of Asian maids. These maids clean the house, cook, and, depending on the family, assume a little or a lot of influence in childrearing practices. However, these maids are economically, and in terms of power, "the lowest of the low" (Al-Sharyan 1987, 350). Their presence has helped the wife to go out and work outside the home, as childrearing is done with the help of the maid. Formerly, the presence of a grandmother would have been the only means allowing a woman to work outside. A third change was the introduction of private automobiles in the 1950s. The automobiles allowed family members to take tours together, and men took their families to beaches and oases. More activities could be planned together as a family (Taki 1974). These three factors have contributed to the breakdown of the extended family and increased prevalence of conjugal families.

Some women reportedly are very frustrated in their marriages. They are working at a job, running the house, may be making more than their husbands, and are not shown any interest or appreciation by their husbands. Some state that the husband's attitude is "I take your money and you do what I tell you." The men may be out every night visiting traditional coffeehouses smoking *shisha*, playing chess or dominoes. They may be out drinking in hotel bars or restaurants. The men receive many invitations for lunch and the tendency is for them to take every opportunity to be out of the house. The men spend little time with the children and some have the attitude, "have them and wait until they grow up." Women get frustrated if their husbands are lazy. Traditionally, men and women lived separate lives in Bahrain and their social networks were segregated (Taki 1974). The frustrations expressed by some women reflect the continuing trend of separate lives maintained by some husbands while their wives are expecting more from a marriage. Information on these divergent lifestyles and expectations would be helpful to increase public awareness, and to teach couples how to resolve these different expectations from a marriage in order to control the number of divorces.

Children and the elderly are suffering the consequences of divorce. The woman returns to her family with the children, depending on their age, or the children go to the father and most likely a stepmother for their upbringing. If the woman remarries, her parents or the husband definitely have custody of the children. After marital breakups, society suffers a greater burden in terms of juvenile delinquency because of unsupervised children (Al-Falaij 1991), an increase of malnutrition and infant mortality (Al-Naser 1993), and abandonments of the elderly in Government hospitals.

### Sexuality and the Physically Disabled and Older Persons

The physically disabled can marry in Bahrain and whether they do depends on their family and the extent of their problems. There are institutes for the blind (Noor Institute for the Blind), deaf (AlFarisi Rehabilitation Center for the Deaf), and handicapped (National Bank of Bahrain Rehabilitation Home for Handicapped Children) in Bahrain where they receive special training. Bahrain has long been the recognized leader in the Gulf for the training of those who are handicapped, and for providing them with education and employment opportunities.

If the man is affected with a handicap, the family may find him a bride locally, or more likely abroad, in India. The chance of a handicapped woman marrying depends on the effort made by the family on her behalf, and the presence of a maid to help her. Male informants stated that a handicapped woman would have difficulty marrying because of her limitations in organizing the house. People with mobility handicaps from polio, birth injuries, or later trauma injuries do marry, but this depends on the injury. Again, if there is difficulty finding a spouse, families will find a wife for their son in India, while the daughter may remain at home her entire life.

Those who are mentally retarded generally do not marry, but there is no law prohibiting marriage. A case was cited where a family employed the son in the business and found him a wife. Male informants queried why anyone would want to marry a retarded woman, as she could not organize the home.

The elderly in Bahrain comprised 5.5% of the population according to the 1991 census. The elderly are defined as older than 60 years of age. The elderly remarry, but it is more likely the men will remarry. Marriage statistics for 1994 show that the oldest age for marriages was 40 to 44 for women and 50-plus for men. However, it should be noted that age is a relative matter. All births were not recorded in the past, so many 40- to 80-year-olds do not know their exact age. Also, people adjust their birth dates, i.e., men have reported that they added years at the beginning of their working life so they could get Government employment at an earlier age. Others drop years, especially when in their 40s, by changing all their legal documents after saying a mistake was made earlier. Also when people are asked their age, many just underestimate it, e.g., one man said he was 45 when asked by a hospital surveyor. The surveyor reported she looked at him and thought to herself 60 to 65 minimum. The man saw her pausing and said, "50 to 55, whatever you like." The official Government retirement age is 55 for women and 60 for men. There has been no study on the relationship of changing of birth data in the official records and work benefits and entitlements. The life expectancy at birth in 1995 in Bahrain is 74.2 years for women and 69.9 years for men (76 and 71 respectively according to the *1996 World Almanac*), both figures being higher than the average for other Arab states, 64.1 and 61.5 years respectively (Baby 1996b).

Regardless of the recorded age, the physical condition of the middle-aged or elderly affects their sexual ability. Among the elderly in Bahrain, long-term complications of diabetes, hypertension, and cardiovascular diseases can result in male impotence. Since the 1980s, penile prostheses have been available to treat men who are known to have organic causes of their impotence (E. Amin 1984). This procedure is available in public hospitals and with greater confidentiality in private hospitals.

### Incidence of Anal Sex, Fellatio, and Cunnilingus

There are no enforced legal restrictions in Bahrain regarding the practice of oral sex or anal sex. Informants reported that according to Islam, oral sex is allowed. The rationale is mutually satisfying sexual positions including oral sex are considered normal. Some women say they are reluctant to participate in oral sex, although Bahraini and Western women participate to keep their husbands satisfied.

Anal sex is considered abnormal activity and associated more with homosexual activity, of which it is considered a possible precursor, so it is forbidden (*haraam*). Reportedly, if a man even asks his wife to perform anal sex, she has the right to file for divorce. Anal sex is practiced, however, and while the woman may not agree, the husband in some cases is threatening by saying "if you don't, I will go elsewhere." Also women do not file for divorce.

Occasionally, women discuss this activity with friends or doctors because of the discomfort they experience and the need for creams or suppositories to soothe small rectal tears. Some women find out about their brother's anal sex activities indirectly when they complain about discomfort and an inability to sit down. One informant reported that a friend's brother, who was engaging in anal sex for money, told his sister that he had no money and the man paid him BD50.

## 6. Homoerotic, Homosexual, and Bisexual Behaviors

### A. Children and adolescents

There have been no studies or even articles published in English regarding these topics. In a few rare publicized cases involving a rape and/or a murder, it was revealed, for example, that an adolescent male was involved in a long-term homosexual relationship with an older expatriate male, or that a young boy was a victim of a homosexual rape by one man or a gang of boys. There are no statistics available on these topics since 1956.

### B. Adults

Objective data are not available regarding adult behaviors relating to homoerotic, homosexual, or bisexual behaviors. Very few male homosexuals openly admit their homosexuality and most get married to keep up appearances. Since homosexuality is *haraam* and abhorred according to Islam, most relationships are discrete in order to protect the family name or a spouse. Male informants report that there are now some Bahraini gay men who openly reveal that they are gay, and who state they have no intention of marrying, but this may be fewer than 5% of the gay men in the population. Anecdotal stories are related by informants; however, no one could contribute any information on specific behaviors, such as roles or courtship patterns. Islam prohibits homosexual or lesbian relationships, so most couples do not openly admit their relationships, and there is no way to legalize these relationships in Bahrain.

There is a homosexual community comprised of expatriates who are more open about their sexual orientation,

e.g., Filipinos and Thais, who are unlike the Bahrainis who are very careful to hide their sexual proclivities. There was an incident in the early 1990s when 20 to 30 Filipino homosexuals were deported by the Government. Despite this, the Filipino gay community now flourishes as before.

Patterns in sexual outlets for homosexual men have not been studied. Filipinos report male drivers (Arabs or Asians) put their hands on the knee of the passenger, and the Filipino has to indicate his preference. Filipino men and others working in barbershops approach their customers by offering to massage them. Such approaches are reported by many men including Bahrainis and expatriates. Men report having to shop around for a barbershop where they feel comfortable and "don't have any problems." Women report friends and families warn other families where they should take their sons to have their hair cut and where not to leave their sons alone. Some parties in the desert reportedly are another venue which men use to meet potential contacts.

Women, as they are kept under more careful watch of their parents, meet other women in school, at friends' houses, weddings, or parties. Women are free to meet at any time, as they are always encouraged to socialize with other women. Only one informant personally knew a lesbian who had told him that she and her friends meet at school or the university, and that lesbians usually marry and have children while continuing their female relationships. This woman said there were a large number of Bahraini lesbians in the community.

The prevalence of lesbian relationships in Bahrain is not known. Male and female informants all mentioned they knew about Bahraini lesbians. Female relationships are considered "safe" by parents, so the women meet easily and often. Like the gay men, lesbians are frequently married and have children. Expatriate lesbians are more open about their sexual proclivities and these women dress in a style that is immediately identifiable by their countrymen, e.g., Filipina "T-birds," or Scandinavian lesbians among others. The incidence of female-to-female STD or HIV infections has not been reported.

Bisexual adults usually marry in Bahrain and each spouse may have a lover on the side (lesbian, gay, or heterosexual). Only anecdotal stories are available regarding this topic, and there are no data on the prevalence of hidden bisexuality in Bahrain.

A question is frequently raised by expatriates regarding homosexual activity in the country. Are the men truly homosexuals, bisexuals, or heterosexuals? What role does opportunity for sexual release play in their behavior? A story was related about an incident in a hotel. Several Saudis gave money to the male Asian hotel clerk and told the clerk to find them some women. The clerk took the money. The men called down to the desk several times to find out where the women were. During the last call when the clerk said no women were available, the men said, "You come up then."

## 7. Gender Diversity and Transgender Issues

### A. Transvestites, Transgenderists, and Transsexuals

Male transvestites or *benaty* (males dressing as females) are seen occasionally in public, e.g., attending a public festival, while in the hospital, or shopping. Informants report that this is "much more common in Kuwait." People are tolerant, mainly ignore them, and do not talk about them. A few comment on the behaviors seen, e.g., "high voice," "makeup," or "using a fan," but do not relate to the nature of the person. Bahraini men dressed as women have been reported as providing the entertainment at exclusive parties where expatriates are rarely invited. One female British author reported attending such a party as her introduction to the country a few years ago. It is not known what proportion of these male transvestites are homosexuals, bisexuals, or heterosexuals.

In some situations, men have been known to dress as women for other reasons, mainly in order to breach security, e.g., to get into a dormitory to visit a friend, to get into a female prison to visit someone, and to hide from the police. The latter practice has caused some problems, and now female security guards are being used in Government agencies, as only a woman can touch or search a woman. One Filipino passed as a female maid for a couple of years before being caught by his employer.

Cross-dressing by males is not considered an act of juvenile delinquency in other parts of the world; however, in Bahrain, Saudi Arabia, and the rest of the Gulf region, which has strict religious-based norms, cross-dressing is seen as a clear instance of alienation from traditional values (Al-Falaij 1991). One study showed 4% of Saudi male juvenile delinquents were cross-dressing (Al-Ghamdi 1986). While there are no published data for Bahrain on cross-dressing, 12.4% of male juvenile delinquents and 16% of female delinquents in one study in Bahrain were accused of moral delinquency (Buzaboon 1986, 151).

Women in the Gulf have a long practice of wearing the *sirwal* chemise—long full pants with long loose overshirts seen among all Pakistanis (males and females) and some Indians. This fashionable 'Punjabi-style' outfit is worn by men and women alike in Bahrain by many nationalities and is also fashionable in the West. The only differences between men's and women's styles are the type of material, style of buttons, and decoration. Loose pantsuits are another preferred style of dress for women to preserve modesty. Women are frequently seen wearing loose pants in the whole Gulf region. There is no association between a woman wearing slacks and being lesbian among Gulf countries. There are lesbian Filipinas known as "T-birds" who dress like a man and who flatten their breasts. They purposely are trying to look like a man. There have been Scandinavians who have pointed out lesbians from their own country. They report, "See how they wear a shirt and pants like that. Only lesbians dress like this at home, so we can identity them easily."

The incidence of transgenderists has not been studied at all. None of the informants reported knowing any Bahraini who said, "I am this gender but trapped in this body." Westerners and Filipinos report knowing of people making such comments in their home countries.

Voluntary sex-change operations for completely gendered adults to the opposite sex are not done in Bahrain and they are illegal. This view is supported by the Koran and the Prophet's teachings (Al Herbish et al. 1996). If there is confusion regarding the sex organs of a child at birth, then investigations will be conducted to determine sex assignment of the person. Sex-change protocols followed for newborns are similar to those published in Saudi Arabia (Taha & Magbol 1995). If the sex organs are predominantly those of a male, the male sex will be assigned; likewise if those of a female, the female sex is assigned. Unfortunately, some problems are not apparent until the time of puberty (Abdul Jabbar 1980; Farsi et al. 1990). A study in Saudi Arabia on intersex disorders detected in puberty or later reported that all genetic males, known as females, accepted sex reassignment as males. Females incorrectly known as males did not readily accept sex reassignment, as culturally the male sex is preferred (Taha & Magbol 1995; Al-Herbish et al. 1996). The nature and incidence of some cases in Bahrain have been reported by S. Al-Arrayed (1996).

The man's chances for remarriage are limited mainly by his financial resources and his ability to pay the marriage contract divorce settlement, and if he can afford the dowry for a new wife. Poor men unable to provide well for their families have been known to marry four wives, as there are currently no regulations regarding minimal income; however, this is now being recommended (Ahdeya Ahmed 1996). In other Gulf countries, men are being encouraged to take a second wife in order to reduce the numbers of unmarried local women. The U.A.E. Government extends soft loans to finance taking a second wife, and men already having foreign wives are now eligible.

## B. Specially Gendered Persons

The *kaneeth* (xanith) is a specially gendered person reported historically in the Gulf (Wikan 1982) and still seen today. The prevalence of these male transvestites/homosexuals is not known. None of our informants have personally known such individuals; however, many reported they have heard others talk about this topic. Some informants described people they have known and/or their families. One Bahraini informant reported that "the person they knew like this was Omani and he lived in our neighborhood and he was the best cook." Another reported, "There is a man who is married, and he has children, but he is also like this." Others said, "This was more common in the past." Following up on this comment, a long-time expatriate resident mentioned "that soon after independence and after the British left, all the Omani men were sent back home in dhows from Manama. People went to the sea front to see the dhows cast off. These men had worked as maids, (there were no female maids then), as singers in bands at women's parties, and were eunuchs." These Omani men sound like the description of the third gender *kaneeth* described by Wikan in Oman in the 1970s (Wikan 1982).

When asked about the term *kaneeth*, Bahrani informants did not agree that the *kaneeth* is a third gender. The term in Arabic means a male or female homosexual. Bahrainis said some marry and have children, so are bisexuals according to the English definition. *Kaneeths* in Bahrain would not necessarily show feminine manners, or dress in a more feminine style, unlike those reported in Oman, but would wear a *thobe* or Western-style men's clothing.

## 8. Significant Unconventional Sexual Behaviors

### A. Coercive Behaviors and Neglect

#### Child Physical Abuse and Neglect

The incidence of child abuse has not been studied or reported in the medical literature in Bahrain. Articles published in Bahrain have alerted physicians to note and report suspected cases (Al-Ansari 1992; Molloy et al. 1993). Two hospital informants noted knowing of only two cases of child abuse in the past 11 years in Bahrain, and in one case the mother was mentally disturbed, while in the second case the child was handicapped. Similar abuse of handicapped children is also mentioned in Saudi Arabia (Al-Eissa et al. 1991). Two articles on childhood trauma in the Gulf (Bahrain and Saudi Arabia) did not mention if any of the cases were because of child abuse (E. Amin 1979; Al-Otham & Sadat Ali 1994). Nonaccidental burning of children is another type of abuse which may exist in Bahrain and which requires a team approach to detection and treatment (Saeed 1992). Child abuse does exist in Kuwait, and is reported in increasing frequency (Al-Rashied 1988), and in Saudi Arabia (Al-Essa et al. 1991; Qureshi 1992). A case of Munchausen Syndrome by proxy has been reported in Saudi Arabia (Al-Mugeiren et al. 1990) and doctors in Bahrain have been alerted to note such cases (Molloy et al. 1993).

School teachers have also been educated regarding child abuse and are to report suspected cases of child abuse to the social worker. One study was conducted regarding teacher awareness of symptoms (Ali 1996). Since schooling is not compulsory, or may be conducted at home with home study, teachers cannot know of the full extent of this problem. According to the Koran, children are to be treasured, and strict discipline and physical means of discipline are not commonly used. From ages 1 to 7, parents are exhorted to love and care for their children, and from 7 years onward to be as a friend to guide their child.

The extent of abuse to which children are subjected from the many maids employed in the country likewise is not known. However, Al-Rashied in 1988 noted in Kuwait that child abuse has been noted more often after increased reliance on babysitters. Individuals report knowing of suspected abuse cases in Bahrain, and when they were confirmed, the maids were deported. In one example, a Filipina brought to work for a family was found using physical means to control the children and scaring them so much their personalities changed, which is how the parents first became aware of the problem. Another South Asian maid absconded, and was later caught working as a prostitute. The parents then wondered if she had been entertaining men in the home, as the children had reported previously that the maid used to lock them in their rooms when the parents were away.

Many of the cases of child abuse are not physical abuse or battered child syndrome, but neglect, or cases of failure to thrive. Bahraini doctors have been alerted to note these cases (Al-Ansari & Al-Ansari 1983). One expatriate, for example, reported thefts from her vegetable garden. The culprit was eventually caught and it was a young boy who was hungry. Investigation of the case showed there were four wives and 40 children in the family and an unemployed head of the family. The expatriate dropped all charges. Social workers have reported finding neglected handicapped children who were being kept in boxes in the home so these children had severe contractures. In these cases, the mothers had many other children to care for. Side effects of medical procedures are sometimes not noted by parents among their large number of children until the damage is irreversible. Young children are sometimes left in cars overnight and they die in the extreme heat as their absence in the house was not noted. A study on the impact of family size on morbidity showed crowding, poor sanitation practices, low education, and poor personal hygiene resulted in more family visits to health centers (Nasib et al. 1983).

The Bahrain Government has an effective means of helping abused children once identified. All reported cases of abuse and neglect are investigated and social workers and community healthcare nurses follow up each case, even daily, if it is felt this is needed. Even though all government healthcare services are free to all residents, utilization of psychiatric services for children by parents is low. In 1981 and 1982, the last published data, only .016% of children were referred for psychiatric help, while it is estimated 5 to 20% of children could benefit from the services. Boys outnumbered girls in conduct disorders, while girls had more reactive and neurotic disorders (Al-Ansari & Al-Ansari 1980). The possible underlying causes of childhood psychiatric problems were not discussed in the article.

Charity from the Government, the Red Crescent, or other family members may not be meeting all the physical needs of some families. Other agencies and social organizations provide needy families family aid (Jameyat Al-Islah, Jameyat Al-Islamiya, Jamiyat Al-Tarbiat Al-Islamiya, Sunduq Al-

Infaq Al-Khairi, and Al-Eslah Society's Welfare Committee). Only official begging is sanctioned in the country, i.e., women mainly are licensed and have a permit to visit shop owners to solicit charity and usually only during the month of Ramadan. However, beggars (men and women) can be seen in many parts of the capital city on a regular basis.

## Child Sexual Abuse

The worldwide current awareness of family sexual abuse started in the 1980s (Patten 1991). The incidence of child sexual abuse in Bahrain has not been documented in any published reference. Hospitals keep their own statistics which are not officially reported. In contrast to rarely seen cases of battered child syndrome, several cases of sexual abuse are seen every week by hospital medical personnel, nurses, and social workers, according to informants. The number of children seen by private doctors and in private hospitals is also not reported. A team of doctors and a psychologist are now addressing this issue, and perhaps data on prevalence and trends will be available in the future. The lasting impact on the children involved and their families, and the relationship of sexual abuse to dysfunctional families to broken homes because of other social factors, such as high unemployment, have not been studied or reported.

Sexual abuse is detected in various ways, including the wife catching the father and daughter. In some cases, bleeding in the genital or rectal area may be the first sign seen by parents or reported by the child; a skin rash or symptom of a sexually transmitted disease (STD) may be the first sign. Babies of 6 to 8 months, toddlers, preadolescent, and adolescent children are the victims. In some cases, the abuse is from a male relative (father, uncle, or brother), or outsider, or gang of boys who may be sexually abusing the male or female child in question. Cases are reported of maids playing with and sexually abusing male or female children. None of the reported cases are as extreme as the male mutilation seen in Saudi Arabia by a mentally disturbed mother (Hegazi 1990). Incest and sexual abuse cases reportedly occur among Bahraini and non-Bahrainis, including South Asian expatriates. Healthcare personnel state Pakistanis are more frequently involved; however, there are no clear data on trends.

The extent and frequency of police involvement in sexual abuse cases varies. If an outsider or group of boys is involved, and a male child was abused, then the police may be called. If a female child was abused and a male relative was involved, e.g., the father, then the police are not called. In these latter cases, the female child may more often be taken to a private doctor, or to no doctor. In the last ten years, there have been two publicized cases of young girls raped by expatriate men. One was a 5-year-old child playing outside her house. Neighbors and family members caught the expatriate Asian man and severely beat him. The second case involved an Asian school guard who raped a young preadolescent female student.

## Pedophilia

Pedophilia has not been studied; however, pedophilia regarding young boys is talked about and is not a new practice. During the late 1980s, there was a man reportedly raping young boys in the Muharraq area. The case was discussed opening by worried parents, but the outcome of this situation was not publicized. Bahraini pedophiles paying boys for sex both in Bahrain and abroad are known, and such cases are discussed openly by older members of the local community. Groups of older boys are sometimes involved in rapes of young boys, however, these data are not reported. Pedophilia in Saudi Arabia, in contrast, is considered a major crime, and

those caught are sometimes beheaded, depending on the extenuating circumstances such as alcohol use and kidnapping.

### Acquaintance, Date, Marital, and Stranger Rape

The prevalence of rape is not reported. Isolated cases are known to occur, and a few have been reported in the print media, usually no more than one case in a year. Those reported in the media generally involved expatriates and sometimes Bahrainis. One case of homosexual rape of a young village boy by an older village boy resulted in the child's murder. Stranger rape does occur, e.g., one Asian woman (a maid), took a taxi ride late at night and was raped by the driver. She also contracted a severe case of genital herpes from this incident. The frequency of rape in Bahrain, in comparison to cities of 500,000 to 600,000 people, would provide valuable comparative data. Many Bahraini families possibly do not reports rapes because of the shame involved, and Asian women are reluctant to report also, so accurate figures are difficult to obtain; but underreporting of rape is the situation in all countries around the world. Marital rape has not been studied.

### B. Sexual Harassment

Sexual harassment has not been studied in Bahrain in the workplace, nor in social situations. According to the Sura Al Noor, unrelated men and women ideally should talk about essential things only. Women government workers have been known to call and harass a male coworker over the telephone while at work, but this is very rare. Likewise, the occasional male coworker has been known to harass a female coworker at work or in social situations. These incidents are reported as very rare; however, the real prevalence is not known, as Asian females in particular are reluctant to report any problems or to cause trouble for fear of losing their jobs. Bahraini females are also reluctant to report such cases because of the lack of witnesses and the shame of making the problem publicly known. There was one publicized case of telephone harassment, which continued after a Bahraini woman married. The harassment resulted in a murder plot, after which the man's body was discovered in the desert. The husband was jailed for life and the woman for a shorter term.

Women report that off-color jokes may be told in their presence when they are a member of a group. The men will "look out of the corner of their eye" to see if they were overheard. The women say they have been schooled not to respond in any way, or to indicate that they heard what was said.

Touching between men and women in public, such as holding hands, is seen occasionally; however, at work it is limited to an occasional handshake. An unrelated man should not touch a woman, according to Islam. Some women refuse to shake hands even in professional situations, or some wear gloves, or a glove on the right hand. This practice can be seen on the television during graduations and other public ceremonies when an official shakes everyone's hand.

Body language has been studied among the Arabs for many years, and social distance is reportedly closer than seen in some Western countries. Men talking to men, and women talking to women may be standing within 6 to 10 inches (15 to 25 cm) of each other. In Bahrain, however, this social distance appears to be extended between members of the same sex to 12 to 18 inches (30 to 45 cm) so expatriates do not have the same "close" feelings as when talking to some Mediterranean nationalities. Among males and females, this talking distance is usually further apart at two to three feet (60 to 90 cm). Very rare exceptions to this rule occur when someone is agitated and they may poke with a finger at an expatriate person's arm while making a point and usually without realizing what they are doing. Occasionally, a powerful man may put their hand on a woman's back, but this is rare, and the expatriates say they feel uncomfortable. Among the various expatriate groups in Bahrain, this social distance varies depending on the age (hand holding seen among male or female teenagers) or the nationality. Hugging when meeting a person is more common among the Filipinos, while casual kissing is seen among all groups, including Bahrainis, at the airport upon departure or arrival. Hand holding among men is a common sight amongst grown men. Bahrainis, South Asians, and Filipinos are seen holding hands on the streets. The practice is also seen among some women, but it is less common.

Kissing between men is a common practice and is seen in the media, in public, and at work. Kissing on the cheek, forehead, and shoulder is a sign of respect, and among friends a sign of welcome. Kissing between women is also seen frequently in public and at work as a sign of respect, and of greeting, especially if the women have not seen each other recently or some one is returning from a trip.

### C. Prostitution

Prostitution has existed in Bahrain for many years and the *British Agency Annual Reports* include data on this topic. There was an increase in prostitution reported between 1926 and 1937 in the British reports. A number of foreigners earning good pay came to Bahrain from Persia, Iraq, and India without their families, and this caused an increase in prostitution, which is a matter of supply and demand.

The history of prostitution in Bahrain since World War I has been discussed in various sources. Designated brothel areas were established (Rumaihi 1976, 193). There was formerly a section of west Manama, between Naim and the Police Fort, known as "Gubla," and an area in Muharraq known as "Al Grandol." There were brothels in these areas with female prostitutes, and the male prostitutes were almost as numerous as women. A February 8, 1937, court decree ordered that prostitutes should live and work only in these two designated places. Prostitutes living or working elsewhere would be deported. The court ruling also ordered the deportation of those "highly professional" prostitutes. The female prostitutes were predominantly from Persia, Iraq, and Oman, with Persians commanding the highest prices, then Iraqis and Omanis, respectively. The female prostitutes were all known as "Daughters of the Wind" according to Belgrave (1960); Bahraini informants report they were known as "Daughters of Love."

The male prostitutes were chiefly Omani boys (Belgrave 1960). All the Omani men did not live in this area, as some also lived with families who could afford their services. Later, there were Bahraini women who were the children of former slaves also working in these areas, while Belgrave (1960) notes the presence of foreign women "who had become Bahrain subjects by the simple expedient of marrying Bahrainis." Among these various groups of women, some were divorced, more commonly they were poor, and a few married women did it for the money or even pleasure. The brothels themselves were attended by men of all socioeconomic classes and ethnic groups.

Bahrainis now in their early 40s or older all reported a range of knowledge regarding this topic and the location of the districts. Some knew of such a former "Red Light" district, but they were not sure where it was exactly. Some said they used to visit it with their parents while on business trips, for example, to collect rent. Others reported they visited the area because it was where "all the action was." One informant said he collected bottles and cans for recycling and used the money to visit the ladies. Another informant reported she was very young, but she remembered seeing a man with a young boy. When she asked her mother why the man had the young boy, her mother answered "he is married to him."

The term *Grandal* is still used in another context by elderly people to describe or comment on an individual whose behavior is "loose" according to preferred standards. Such a woman is called a *Grandal*, or it is said she is acting like a *Grandal*. Older people listening understand the connotations of the term. The areas designated for prostitutes started to decline in the early 1970s, and prostitution activities became more dispersed throughout the country with the opening of hotels. Still, women reportedly can be seen standing in doorways in the old Gubla area in Manama.

Various reasons are given for the decline of this area in town and the recent changes seen in prostitution patterns. First, in the early 1970s, there were major political and economic changes seen in Oman. The current Sultan deposed his father and began investing millions of riyals in major infrastructure improvements in the country. There was an improvement in job opportunities, so many Omanis returned home. Second, the local, economic development of the 1970s because of the boom in oil prices resulted in the building of many new apartment blocks so there were flats (apartments) available in many parts of the city. Also the British military wanted flats and villas in which to live, so there was a building boom, and then Bahrainis moved into these dwellings also (Taki 1974). People could have more privacy away from their families. Third, the economic boom of the 1970s also meant people had more disposable income and could afford extras like paying for a small flat or small villa. Fourth, the economic boom of the 1970s resulted in an increase of expatriate laborers between 20 and 50 years of age, including those from the Philippines and Sri Lanka. These two groups, all informants state, are highly involved in prostitution in Bahrain. Some Filipinas are paid a monthly salary or given gifts of sometimes up to BD400 (US$1,000) or more by their male friend. Because of the low opinion of Filipinas in general, women with families, and even elderly women over 60, report being approached directly or indirectly for prostitution (money is brushed on their arm or flashed so they can see it). Finally, after Bahrain gained full independence from the United Kingdom in 1971, U.K. residents were granted special visa privileges, i.e., no visa was required for the first three months of entry. Many U.K. residents came to Bahrain and the United Arab Emirates in the Gulf looking for jobs and employment opportunities. Some of the British women found jobs, others sponsors, and others travel between Bahrain and the United Arab Emirates and are seen frequenting the hotels working as prostitutes. This visa law was changed in 1996, and a visa is now required for U.K. residents as a result of reciprocal changes instituted by the European Union.

After the opening of the Saudi Causeway in late 1986, local women experienced many problems while they were walking on the streets, in shopping malls, or attending parties in hotels. The Causeway also led to an increase in the number of incidents reported by women who said they or their friends were approached by Saudis. Western women with their children reported being approached in shopping malls by Saudi men and being offered money for their services. Bahraini women, because of the problems, began avoiding hotels even for wedding parties on Wednesdays, Thursdays, and Fridays to prevent such situations from occurring. Women working in public areas in Government buildings are given hotel phone numbers by Saudis, and many have requested job changes to less public areas as a consequence. These situations were predicted by Wilsher in 1982, and reflect an expansion of the prostitution activities described by Faroughy (1951, 20) who stated that "prostitu-

tion forbidden in Saudi Arabia has greatly increased under the complacent eyes of the authorities and Bahrein has become a kind of 'pleasure island.'"

Solicitation for prostitution is quite open. Expatriate men report being approached by women in hotels and shopping malls. One first-time consultant visitor from the U.S.A. in 1989 was invited to look at a photo album of women by a taxi driver taking him from the airport to his business appointment. The visitor reported being absolutely amazed to see this in a strict religious country. A Filipino man attending a hotel disco with a group of friends approached a Western woman and asked her for a dance and was told "you cannot afford me."

The nationality of female prostitutes has changed through the 1980s and 1990s. During the 1980s, Filipinas could be seen going off with men they picked up, even while in family pizza restaurants. Sri Lankans were available on certain streets in various areas of Manama. Also, there continues to be a main street in Adliya commonly referred to as the "meat market," where Filipinas walk about at night. New nationalities of prostitutes have been seen during the 1990s. Since the breakdown of Communism, Russians began traveling freely to the Gulf. Many came to Bahrain and the United Arab Emirates for shopping, and there was a billion dollars in Russian trade for the United Arab Emirates during 1995 alone. Some of the women also came to sell small items, while others came as prostitutes. Russian women were available in some of the expensive hotel restaurants frequented by Saudis, and outside two- and three-star hotels and other restaurants frequented by other tourists. Many of them advertised their services for BD20 ($53) by holding up two fingers. One informant asked to see the C.P.R. (Central Population Registry) residence cards of Russian women outside an expensive restaurant. They had current C.P.R. cards and their profession was listed as "business." By the summer of 1996, Bosnian female prostitutes were reportedly working out of one of the mid-size hotels. These women usually asked for the equivalent of BD25-50 or a gift, such as a watch, if money was not available. Adolescent Ethiopian prostitutes have been seen on the Exhibition Road area with pagers.

Prostitution is not illegal in Bahrain, and it must be mentioned that solicitation for prostitution is not as blatant in Bahrain as that seen in Abu Dhabi, where women constantly walk up to men standing alone on the street, or while waiting for transport.

## D. Pornography and Erotica

All pornographic materials are strictly prohibited by law and are confiscated by customs officials if detected. Most, if not all, expatriates coming to Bahrain are told that three items are strictly prohibited, i.e., pornography, items on the Israeli boycott list or made in Israel, and cultured pearls. The latter two classes of items are seen, however. Cultured pearls are not to be sold in Bahrain, but are worn, and the boycott list has changed since the Gulf War.

Pornography is available in Bahrain, e.g., magazines, as they are not picked up by security upon arrival as easily as metal items (by the metal detector), or drugs (by drug-sniffing dogs), or computer diskettes containing pornography. All videos are viewed by customs agents at the airport upon arrival; others are retained and can be picked up later in Manama at the censorship office. Blue videos are still smuggled in, as well as items on the Israeli boycott list; these reportedly are "not that difficult to find." Arrests of individuals holding blue movies or computer diskettes containing pornography, and those caught selling them are sometimes publicized in the newspapers as a deterrent. Relatives and roommates may turn in the sellers or users to the police. Names of the culprits may be publicized in the press or withheld.

## E. Sex-Related Murders, Suicide, Self-Mutilation, and Sex with Animals

Murders in Bahrain have been very rare for the first nine decades of the 20th century. The British advisor reported in the *Bahrain Government Annual Reports Volume II 1937-1941* that "usually about one or two murders are dealt with by police during the year." This general trend continued until the 1990s.

The early reports also mentioned that "occasional murders may take place which are not detected, especially women and newly born children." These women were put to death by their relations because "they had dishonored the family. Killing a woman for this reason was considered by many Arabs to be justified" (Belgrave 1960, 100). Belgrave notes that he knew of cases where an unmarried girl was "put away" because she was pregnant, but he knew of no cases of a wife being killed because she was unfaithful. One case was related in the late 1980s of an expatriate Arab man and his brothers who managed to forcibly take the man's wife to their home country. They informed the wife's Western doctor they were going to have the woman and the child killed for bringing shame on the family. No action could be taken as there was no crime in Bahrain. This practice has been stopped in Bahrain for decades.

Currently, it is reported that the majority of pregnant, unmarried Bahraini women are sent abroad for abortions or practice self-induced abortion to avoid bringing shame on themselves and their family. Others may check into a maternity hospital, sometimes under a false name, and leave the child behind in the hospital.

Prostitutes in the former brothel areas were sometimes murdered by jealous lovers, according to Belgrave (1960, 103). More recently, during the last ten years, there were two sex-related murders involving Filipinas. The media reported one was murdered at work, reportedly by a Pakistani lover, while the other body was found in a dumpster near a hotel.

Sex-related murders between individuals who are or were lovers have been reported, but they are very rare. During the last ten years, there were several publicized heterosexual cases in the media, e.g., a Filipino couple (the man murdered the woman, and then killed himself), and a South Asian woman was killed by her lover. There have been a couple of homosexual-related murders, for example, one village man killed his lover and buried him in the yard. And in another case, a younger Bahraini male (late teens) killed his elderly British lover.

Suicide because of shame about sexual matters is rare, but does occur. An Indian woman whose child was found to be HIV-positive confessed that she was involved with a Pakistani male. After an investigation, it was determined he had slept with a Filipina, who had been involved with a Saudi. The Indian woman committed suicide soon after the investigation, and her family (husband and son) were deported, as they were HIV-positive.

Successful suicides versus parasuicides appear to be more common among Asians in Bahrain, particularly Indian males and females. Firearms, except for antiques, cannot be legally held by the general public in Bahrain, so serious suicide attempts are made by means of hanging, electrocution, drinking of kerosene or self-immolation, slitting of wrists to cause arterial bleeding, and drug overdose. Investigations published in the press show that the men are usually depressed over their financial situation or illegal residency status, while the women are having work difficulties (termination or warning letters) or family difficulties in India or locally. Some Indian women are trapped in abusive marriages to Bahrainis and have no place to seek assistance. Other precipitating factors may include sexual abuse by the husband's male relatives and other family situations.

One research study on suicide has been published to date (Metery et al. 1986). In 1981, the police suicide register showed 150 people attempted suicide mainly by ingesting drugs for a rate of 0.04%. Religious values (suicide is a mortal sin in Islam) and social stigma possibly contributed to the low rate (Metery et al. 1986). This study showed more women, generally unmarried in their 20s, attempted suicide, and 60% had attended their local health centers within the previous six months complaining of somatic symptoms such as headache and body aches. This study did not indicate the number of Bahrainis or non-Bahrainis listed in the suicide register. A growing pattern of self-induced drug overdoses is reported among Saudi women (Malik et al. 1996), Kuwaiti (Emura et al. 1988), and Qatari women (El-Islam 1974). The precipitating event(s) leading to suicide need to be studied.

Parasuicide survivors (impulsive attempts) are brought to healthcare facilities. A six-month audit of Medical Department admissions between late 1995 and early 1996 in one general hospital showed 1.08% of the admissions were parasuicide attempts, with a ratio of 4.5 females to males, the same ratio of Bahrainis to non-Bahrainis, and the same ratio of impulsive situations versus psychiatric histories. Causes of impulsive attempts included exam failures, problems at work, a fight with a family member, recent divorce, recent parental death in the family, and marital arrangements.

One case of self-mutilation by a Thai male who became depressed, reportedly when his girlfriend left, was reported in the press. Urological surgeons in the large government hospital performed successful surgery in this case. Attempts of this nature are extremely rare (one case in ten years).

Another deliberate self-harm (DSH) practice known as "jumping syndrome" appears to be common in the Gulf States, and is seen increasing in prevalence in Qatar (El-Islam 1974), Saudi Arabia (Mahgoub 1990), and Kuwait (Suleiman et al. 1986). Predominantly Asians, and mainly females with an average age of 29 years, are jumping off buildings in an attempt to kill themselves. Studies show that many have died, while others have had extensive fractures and required long-term hospitalization for an average of 56 days, which places a cost burden on the Gulf States free health services. The proportion of unsuccessful attempts resulting in minor injuries is not known. The females jumping, in most cases, had no history of previous psychological illness. Sexual and physical abuse are the most important factors which push females to deliberate self-harm. Some of the jumping syndrome survivors alleged that this was the reason; however, sexual abuse was not proven (Sadat-Ali et al. 1995, 189). Reportedly, this is the method of choice for suicide in Kuwait because of the non-availability of drugs (Suleiman et al. 1986). Cases of jumping syndrome have not been reported in the media in Bahrain; however, medical personnel have been alerted to this trend.

There have been no studies conducted regarding Bahrainis having sex with animals, and there are no local anecdotal stories discussed regarding this topic. An archaeology text by Bushiri (1992) discusses seals found in Bahrain and Kuwait from the Dilmun period which show intercourse between a man and a bull, which the man performed from behind the bull while holding the rear of the bull.

## 9. Contraception, Abortion, and Population Planning

### A. Contraceptives

Attitudes regarding contraception vary from couples who accept all children as the will of God and who make no effort to prevent pregnancy, to those who plan, space, and limit their families. In the former situation, many women report it is the husband who feels more strongly about this issue and who refuses to use contraception. In some cases, the women want more children and the husband refuses, e.g., the woman may be the second or third wife and the husband has many children, including sons, from a previous marriage(s), so he may then have a vasectomy after only two children from the last wife. The wife may then feel cheated and expresses regrets. Other families quote the Koran's injunction to be able to provide for their children well, so they use various forms of birth control (condoms, IUDs, or pills) to space their children. Spacing varies from one to three or even 15 years. Women say, "My husband told me I can get pregnant again after three years," and men have said, "On my salary, I can only afford to have this number, so we needed to space our children." Among the college-educated, some boldly say, "Two is enough." One Government publication reported that 50% of Bahraini families are using some form of contraception and another report states that 54% of married women are using contraception (A. A. Ahmed 1995, 15). The local birthrate of 2.91% is still one of the highest in the world. There are other factors motivating high pregnancy rates, including certain segments of society who are having children simply to outnumber other segments of society for potential political gains.

A group of Bahraini intellectuals from several specialties organized the Bahraini Family Planning Association (B.F.P.A.) in 1975. Bahrain has the only F.P.A. in the Gulf and is one of 15 in the Arab region with their regional headquarters in Tunis. There are 165 country associations in the world with their main office in London. There are approximately 200 active members in Bahrain promoting the association's work. A survey was conducted by the association in 1983 to test the attitudes and knowledge of the population regarding contraception. This initial survey showed promising results, and the association has been active ever since. The association has facilitated other research by providing data, contacts, or support to researchers, and several theses have been completed (Al-Darazi 1984, 1986; Al-Gaseer 1990). The B.F.P.A. contributed US$10,000 towards the costs of the 1996 National Family Health Survey of 5,000 randomly selected Bahrain families, including 26,000 individuals. The survey was sponsored by the Gulf Cooperation Council Ministers of Health and the U.N.D.P. The questionnaire included items relating to reproduction and sexual health. The report with analysis was expected in 1997.

The funding for the B.F.P.A. organization comes in part from funds redistributed by the B.F.P.A. Central Committee to countries around the world. The local president is on the B.F.P.A. Board, the Central Committee, and the Budget Committee. Other funds come from donations by local individuals, various institutions, and the Government, i.e., Ministry of Labor and Social Affairs. Contraceptive aids are given by the B.F.P.A. to the Ministry of Health for distribution to families in the Primary Health Clinics, Salmaniya Medical Center, or the Maternity Hospitals. The B.F.P.A. also accepts gifts of clothes and other items, which are distributed to needy families. Annual reports are prepared at the local, regional, and federation levels describing activities of the association.

The activities of the B.F.P.A. are geared toward increasing public awareness of the types of contraceptives available for family planning. There is no local opposition; however, an occasional non-Bahraini will raise opposition to their work. The association provides lectures to representatives of local groups who then go back and talk with members of their respective group. The B.F.P.A. has videos, cassette tapes, and pamphlets, as well as a library, at their association headquarters in Gafool. The current five-year plan has four main goals which the group is trying to reach, i.e., youth awareness, promotion of counseling and family planning, empowerment, and development of volunteerism and fundraising.

Family planning nurses working in Maternal-Child Health indicate that there has been a trend toward increasing use of tubal ligations and vasectomies for birth control, even among village residents. B.F.P.A. and the staff nurses state that people are better educated about their options for birth control, have the desire to space children, and many want to limit children out of economic necessity, e.g., because of the recession and no jobs. Nurses praise the support of the Bahrain Family Planning Association and their assistance in providing free contraceptives, and, at times, clothing or goods to needy families.

Free contraceptive aids are available from the Government at all the Primary Health Centers and at the Government hospitals for all Bahrain's residents. Free tubal ligations and vasectomies are likewise available and are being used increasingly by older couples as a means of birth control. Health education courses regarding contraception are presented at the Government Primary Health Care Centers, and videotapes are also available. The *1993 Annual Report for Primary Health Care in Bahrain* notes that "due to religious beliefs and traditional attitudes," a total of 4,573 visits were made during 1992 for family planning services. Out of these visits, 2,917 women initiated a contraception method, and 263 received IUDs. A total of 8,660 women received family planning counseling sessions, which was 7.8% of females in the child-bearing age (Fouzi Amin 1993). A study conducted in one Health Center in the United Arab Emirates included 908 women between 15 to 44, and 50% of them were using some means of contraception (Blankensee et al. 1995).

Many doctors discuss birth control options, including sterilization, with grand multigravida (more than eight to ten children) and high-risk patients (those with repeated Cesarean sections and other complications) at the time of delivery. Doctors document when the patient refuses to have a procedure, or has signed a sterilization permit. After delivery, the doctors indicate if the patient has requested some form of birth control and what choice was made. The doctors' personal beliefs play a factor in whether birth control options, such as a tubal ligation, are even mentioned. Some couples, after making their own choice, may be told by a doctor that their choice to have a tubal ligation is *haraam* (forbidden). More assertive and more educated couples will find another doctor, while others may be ashamed or afraid to discuss this matter with another doctor. There are no institutional ethical standards to guide physicians regarding this matter, or to suggest that they refer couples to another doctor who is willing to discuss such matters. If a woman is declared unfit, e.g., mentally retarded or unfit to be a mother, the family can request she be sterilized.

Condoms are sold openly in grocery stores and pharmacies. There are many private clinics in Bahrain, and three private hospitals, where birth control information and supplies are available for a fee.

Data on birth control practices of the various expatriate populations are not reported. Misconceptions regarding pregnancy abound, and some Indian girls are prohibited by teachers and parents from swimming in coed pools for fear they will get pregnant. The knowledge of Syrian, Jordanian, Palestinian, and Beluchi women has not been studied, and they are the expatriates having the largest families.

## B. Teenage Pregnancies (Unmarried)

Although unmarried pregnancies occur, their incidence and prevalence among Bahrainis and non-Bahrainis, and teenagers specifically, are not known. A Bahraini girl/woman and her family will try to cover up such a scandalous incident. Male informants all knew of women "in trouble," while female informants rarely knew of anyone.

Teenage pregnancies are not a major problem as seen in the West, because a girl's behavior is strictly monitored by her parents. A girl, from the time she is 10 to 12, is kept close at home when not in school. Even if she attends the University, her parents know where she is and her daily schedule. Most girls are married after completion of Tawyehi or college, and some later even in their 30s; however, until she is married, a girl is expected to live at home. A Kuwaiti researcher supports this perception that "illegitimate pregnancy is a problem of small dimension in Muslim societies" (Hathout 1979). No objective data are available on this topic.

The children of unmarried women, in the early part of the 20th century, were at times murdered with the girl by family members (Belgrave 1960, 101-102). Other infants were abandoned on municipal rubbish dumps, *Samadah*, at the corners of streets, or placed outside the hospital (Belgrave 1960, 103). Some of these foundlings were looked after in the American Mission Orphanage. Others were cared for in the Government hospital, and very often foundlings were taken in by women who had no family. Another view was noted by Charles Belgrave who wrote that "for the children there was very little stigma in illegitimacy" (1960, 103). He said he knew several young men "who were proud of belonging to important families, though on the wrong side of the blanket."

Currently four to six abandoned children a year are referred to the Children's Home. The number of expatriate women and maids becoming pregnant is not known, as many return to their homes to deliver. Rare cases are reported in the media, e.g., an expatriate maid delivered a child which died and the body was buried in the garden, and later a child in the family uncovered the body while playing. In this case, the expatriate woman was deported. Other newspaper reports note court cases where, for example, a young boy found a dead baby wrapped in a cloth outside the home, and he told his mother who alerted the Police Station.

## C. Abortion

Abortions are provided in Bahrain only under strict religious regulations, i.e., a person cannot decide to have an abortion because of lack of birth control or an unwanted birth or rape. Abortions for these reasons are illegal. One study was conducted in Kuwait on "unwantedness," so it is a phenomenon seen in the Gulf. In Kuwait, the women tried to induce abortion with medicines, violent exercise, or mechanical interference (Hathout 1979). Objective data on this topic is not available for Bahrain.

A medically indicated abortion allowable by Sharia law can be obtained in a government hospital, usually before three months, if the fetus has been found to be deformed, or with a congenital defect detected through ultrasound, amniocentesis, or other tests. Early abortions can also be performed if the pregnancy poses a threat to the life of the mother, and early deliveries are done if the woman has life-threatening conditions such as PET or placenta previa. The justification for these abortions is to save the woman's life and to preserve the family, as she has other children to care for, and "she is the root of the family while the fetus is the branch which is sacrificed to save the root" (Hathout 1979). In the case of the fetus with a defect, the rationale for abortion reportedly is to prevent suffering.

The attitude to abortion, especially in the case of an unmarried pregnancy, varies from liberal, "Why didn't she have an abortion when she was outside the country?" to very conservative, "She had an abortion outside and this needs to be reported to the religious police." Some informants report that the majority of unmarried Bahraini women have abortions outside the country because of the shame (*ayeb*) of an illegitimate birth. Illegal abortions do occur in Bahrain. Informants reported, "She drank some liquid and had an abortion." Others report, "She was told to take seven to eight birth control pills for three days, but it did not work." Nurses report this latter method is seen and is effective. Some individuals try other self-induced methods which are more dangerous, including dilatation of the cervix, and insertion of items into the uterus. A Filipina abortionist was caught operating in Bahrain in 1995 after a Saudi client became septic because of the abortion and, during interrogation, revealed the abortionist to the police. All the considerable money the abortionist had in her bank account was confiscated by the Bahrain Government and she was deported.

## D. Population Policy

The population growth of Bahrain is 2.9%, which is one of the highest in the world. The effect of this high population growth, and its effect on the country's growth and development, has been discussed in many reports and in the media. There is currently no government policy to educate people regarding the need to reduce population growth. All informants stated that there is no policy that women should be encouraged to use some means of birth control or to have a tubal ligation after so many children, e.g., four.

The Government has instituted a fee of BD100 (US$265) for all expatriates who deliver in government facilities and who are non-entitled workers, or the spouses of non-entitled workers. This may be an indirect means of discouraging expatriate births, or a way of controlling their spacing. For many expatriates to pay BD100 a year out of a monthly salary of BD60-80 is a great burden. Likewise, the Government requires male workers to be making a minimal salary of BD250 before they can bring their families to Bahrain. Another means of controlling the number of expatriates and their burden on the health service is to deny residence visas for elderly relatives (over 65). Generally, work visas for government jobs are not given to expatriates over 60 to 65 years for men and 55 years for women.

Premarital counseling is encouraged by the Government and is provided free in the Primary Health Centers and government hospitals. In 1992, 545 couples received premarital counseling and among them, 89 abnormal findings were detected (Fouzi Amin 1993, 27). Premarital counseling is being encouraged, but is not yet required among Bahrainis because of the high incidence of first cousin marriage (39%) and the high frequency of genes for blood disorders in the population, including sickle cell disease, G6PD deficiency, a variety of major and minor thalassemias (Nadkarni et al. 1991), as well as other congenital anomalies (Sheikha Al-Arrayed 1996).

Other Arab countries, such as Egypt, have population control slogans such as "look around." Other Islamic countries, such as Pakistan and Iran, have developed programs to educate people to limit their families to two or three children. Bahrain has no public policy to date. Approximately

0.1% of the recent Ministry of Health budget has been spent on family planning, while 0.2% has been spent on control of illegal drugs, and 0.3% on medical exams of newly hired expatriate workers (*1991 Ministry of Health Report*).

## 10. Sexually Transmitted Diseases and HIV/AIDS

### A. Sexually Transmitted Diseases

*Incidence, Patterns, and Trends of STDs*

Venereal diseases were reported by the first American missionaries who arrived in Bahrain in the late 1890s and early 1900s (Rajab 1979). The missionary doctors were able to test for gonorrhea in the early 1900s and found it was a common disease. Venereal disease in 1914 ranked next to malaria (Patterson 1914). A high proportion of the population was suffering from the ophthalmic form of gonorrhea, which was rampant according to the *Government of Bahrain Administrative Report* for 1926-1937, and the *Bahrain Government Annual Reports 1926-1960*. Venereal infections ranked high, along with smallpox, malaria, dysentery, and trachoma.

Tracking of a second STD was started after a definite diagnosis for syphilis was possible by 1933-34 at the American Mission Hospital's Laboratory (1933-34, 9). During the 1940s, there were over a thousand cases treated annually, and by 1948, venereal infections had spread even more, and 200 patients were treated as inpatients and 1,200 as outpatients. At that time, the Government took certain stern measures against foreign women of loose character (Al-Khalifa 1982). Venereal infections started coming down after the introduction of new medicines, and Bahrain was the pioneer for the whole region in developing an infrastructure to improve healthcare. In 1952, the Public Health Department (P.H.D.) was separated out as a distinct entity, and its statistics show that after 1965, venereal infection trends are greatly reduced from the 1940s (Al-Khalifa 1982, 219). The P.H.D. laboratory is the preferred lab for testing blood samples of infectious diseases and all positive samples are sent to them for confirmation and follow-up of personal contacts.

The incidence of STDs has been studied mainly in relation to their effect on urinary tract infections and antibiotic drug resistance (Yousef et al. 1991), infertility, and impotence, rather than the epidemiology of their occurrence and relationship to various types of sexual activity.

The overall frequency of male urethritis and STDs in Bahrain is low, 108/100,000 (541/500,000) versus 1,600/100,000 in the U.S.A.; however, the isolates of *Nisseria gonorrhea* found are often highly resistant or show diminished sensitivity to penicillin (Yousef et al. 1991, 94). The number of gonorrhea cases peaked in 1980 to over 600 cases per year. The 1994 figures were the same as 1990 (379 to 380 cases/year). Gonococcal infections in 1994 ranked third after influenza and chicken pox. In contrast to Bahrain's statistics, the first case of *Nisseria gonorrhea* in a pregnant Saudi woman was only reported in 1988 (Abdul Khaliq & Smith 1988).

Syphilis cases reported to the P.H.D. in Bahrain have been increasing since 1990 from 37 to 104 cases in 1994 (*Statistical Abstracts 1994*). These rates (0.019%) are low in comparison to other parts of the Middle East and may reflect reporting inconsistencies or treatment outside Bahrain. A seven-year study conducted in Saudi Arabia on 90% of hospital births (Saudis and non-Saudis) showed an increase from 0.2% to 1.5% overall incidence of syphilis in 1986 (Abbas & Satwekar 1989). This rate is high in comparison to European statistics, but lower than other Middle East and African data. Endemic syphilis is prevalent in the Middle East, and all

cases of syphilis are treated as infectious until proven otherwise. Up to 20% of adult Bedouins in Saudi Arabia have been exposed to endemic syphilis *bejel* (Abbas & Satwekar 1989). Secondary syphilis symptoms may be the first noted and treated. In Saudi Arabia, this has been reported by Basri and Smith (1991). In one case, the husband was being treated in a VD clinic but did not tell either of his wives, and one wife was never brought for treatment. In another case, a Somali bisexual had many sexual contacts, and in the third case, the patient denied any extramarital contacts. A problem in Saudi Arabia, which is difficult to overcome, is tracking of contacts. The first case of congenital syphilis was reported in Kuwait in 1987 (Hariri & Helin 1987).

The seroprevalence of chlamydial infections was shown to be 44% of 100 pregnant women randomly screened in Bahrain. This suggests a high prevalence of chlamydial disease in the population, although some of the antibody-positive cases may be from old ocular infections (Rajab et al. 1995). The U.S.A. average is 3 to 5%, and 15 to 20% in an STD clinic. In Saudi Arabia, the rates ranged from 10% of women seen in a gynecology clinic to 30.6% of men attending an STD clinic. Chlamydia, overall, accounted for 11% of all gynecological infections seen in one Saudi Arabian hospital (Qadri et al. 1993). Another study in a Saudi Arabian STD clinic showed 46% of males and 36% of female were affected, while 2% of men and none of the women attending a Primary Health Care clinic were affected (Qadri et al. 1993). Genital forms in Saudi Arabia were estimated at 38.4% and ocular forms at 61.6%. Chlamydial infections can be a cause of blindness, and is a familiar disease, especially where there is overcrowding, large numbers of children, lack of water, and poor hygiene. The prevalence of people with and without overt genital disease is higher in Saudi Arabia than in developed countries, but similar to rates seen in Bahrain. The role of chlamydia in female infertility because of blocked tubes was reported by Babag and Al-Mesbar (1993), who state that chlamydia is high in the Saudi Arabian population, but significantly higher in infertile women.

Hepatitis B is now classified as a sexually transmitted disease. The percentage of the Bahrain population affected is 2% (Mahnon & Fernandez 1972). This incidence is higher in Saudi Arabia (14%) and 9% in Oman (Al-Dhahry et al. 1994). Saudi Arabia and Oman have high endemicity of hepatitis B, while Bahrain has more hepatitis C (4.7%) versus Saudi Arabia (0.2 to 5.0%) (Bakir 1992). Currently, hepatitis C is not classified as an STD. A study on the risk of transmission of hepatitis B infection among family members in Bahrain showed a transmission rate of 26% (Parida & Effendi 1994).

Human papiloma virus (HPV) is a sexually transmitted agent which has been shown to have a strong relationship with neoplasms of the female genitalia. One study showed the rate of infection among 25- to 35-year-old women in Bahrain to be 63% (Sunderaj 1990).

*Treatment for STDs*

Treatment for STDs is provided free to all Bahrainis; however, because of the nature of the disease and its social implications, people generally attend private clinics, see consultants in the private hospitals, or even attend clinics outside Bahrain for treatment. There is a specialized private venereal disease clinic in the Gudaibiya area.

Prevention of spread of STDs through tracking of sexual contacts is a problem in the Middle East (Basri & Smith 1991). Affliction with VD is seen as a sign of low morality, so patients vehemently deny any extramarital affairs. The men may not tell even their wives they are being treated. The men may have had casual sex (as seen in Saudi studies) while overseas, so their contacts are unknown and are lost. The Bahrain Public Health Department tries to determine all contacts. Other forms of prevention include vaccinating all newborns in Bahrain for hepatitis B according to WHO guidelines to prevent a burden later in the healthcare system. Other prevention efforts include public education lectures, programs in the media, and other methods. These programs do not include the incidence of these diseases in Bahrain nor their prevalence in the various ethnic groups, but mainly stress the need to make a general concerted effort to prevent them by good moral behavior.

One direct method for prevention of STDs has been tried in Bahrain, as in other Arab countries. During the late 1980s, the Jordanian Government started handing all single male travelers a card warning about the dangers of AIDS. Likewise in Kuwait, information pamphlets are distributed at the airport warning travelers about the dangers of sexual diseases outside the country. As many Arab men take single or male-only group vacations to the Far East and Europe, such prevention problems were instituted by several Arab countries. Traveling Bahrainis state that at the Bahraini Airport, pamphlets on STDs are likewise distributed, but men report this is not on a consistent or daily basis as in other countries. Another direct way of prevention, by prohibiting sex vacations, was in effect for awhile. Visas were required to travel to certain countries, e.g., Thailand. These restrictions have since been lifted.

There are Bahraini men who regularly travel to Thailand, Philippines, Hong Kong, or elsewhere for sex vacations. Some are unmarried, others married. Informants have reported that one single man was asked, "Aren't you afraid of contracting some disease?" he responded by saying, "God's will." He could not be convinced of the unsafe nature of his activities. Another married man makes two trips a year. When he was asked about safe sex, he shrugged his shoulders. Another man, a well educated and highly paid professional, would make Asian trips and repeatedly return with ophthalmic infections and expected his doctor to cure him again. The incidence of these trips is not known, nor how many use "safe sex" during these encounters. There are Bahraini women having affairs in Bahrain, usually in hotels or flats, as well as abroad. The number who have contracted STDs because of an affair has not been studied or reported. The annual number of venereal cases published by the Government does not distinguish among Bahrainis and non-Bahrainis, nor do they make any distinction among those who contracted the STD from their husband or wife, through a local affair, or an affair abroad. There are no statistics regarding how many are divorced or unmarried and living on their own versus individuals living in parental homes. All this information is needed to detect trends and to plan effective prevention programs.

## B. HIV/AIDS

### Incidence, Patterns, and Trends

Doctors in Bahrain were first alerted in 1985 to the new disease called AIDS (*flocks al mana'ah al mukta sabah*), and lectures were given in 1989 and 1990. The first public reports on the occurrence of HIV in the population appeared in 1990. At that time, 95% of the HIV carriers reportedly were drug users, and 5% had received organs or blood outside the country (Fulafel 1990). The latter group going to India have a risk of 1:12 of HIV seroconversion following transplantation in Bombay, based on figures from other Gulf countries (Al-Dhahry 1994, 314).

HIV testing is done in government facilities. No consent is obtained from individuals before testing. Now all conscripts into the Bahrain military and civilian employees of the military are tested for HIV, HBV, HCV, sickle cell disease, G6PD deficiency, and other relevant factors, depending on family history and country of origin. Staff are tested upon employment and during retroactive screening regimens. Patients attending the Shaikh Khalifa Bin Mohammed Al Khalifa Cardiac Center for any invasive procedure are all routinely checked for blood-borne viral diseases. Expatriates positive for HIV will not be treated at the Cardiac Center unless they have an emergency condition, and like all positive expatriates, will be sent to their home country immediately under Public Health Laws. Other hospital and clinic patients, excluding dialysis patients, are not routinely tested, and are checked based on the nature of their current signs and symptoms. If an HIV-positive result is returned, generally elective surgical procedures are canceled.

Expatriate workers recruited for all government healthcare facilities are tested, as well as maids, cooks, and beauticians who are processed through recruitment agencies and hired to work in Bahrain. Bahrain does not require an "AIDS-free certificate" for all expatriates, including wives and children, taking up residence before their arrival in the country, unlike Kuwait and Saudi Arabia, which require all expatriates taking up residence in the country to be HIV-free. The United Arab Emirates Health Department screens everyone in the country for HIV on a periodic basis, as their expatriate workforce comprises 70% of the population. Over 1,600 HIV-positive cases have been detected to date in the U.A.E., with the majority of cases detected among Asian expatriates, who were deported.

*HIV Incidence among Newborns, Children, and Adults.* HIV-positive status is seen among newborns in Bahrain. The incidence is not known, as women and babies are not being screened as done in 37 states in the U.S.A. and elsewhere. The suspected rate of infection at the time of birth, or later from breastfeeding, is not known, nor the number of newborns who later revert to HIV-negative status.

Children of various ages have been detected positive for HIV and have died from AIDS. The first AIDS death in Bahrain in the 1980s was a child infected through a blood transfusion given abroad. The known routes of HIV transmission have been vertical, mother to child, and from blood transfusions received abroad. Infections from sexual abuse have not been revealed to date, if such data are known. The rate of horizontal transmission among family members is also not known. A few adolescent HIV and AIDS cases have been seen in healthcare facilities.

The incidence of HIV infections among adults has been reported by the Government. More men than women have tested HIV-positive. The proportion of Bahrainis versus expatriates is not clearly indicated in the Government data. In 1991, according to Ministry of Health figures, 0.09% out of 7,374 blood donors were positive as were 0.01% of 8,173 reporting for their preemployment physical exam. The trends show an increasing number of reported cases each year for men and women. All expatriates who test positive for HIV are deported according to the Government's Public Health rules (as are those with hepatitis B and C, tuberculosis, and leprosy). The potential drain of these expatriate individuals on healthcare funds, and the possibility of cross infection to others, are the rationale of the Government enforcement of deportation rules.

There are three main patterns of HIV infection seen among men. Intravenous drug users comprise the largest number. During the late 1980s, government media releases indicated IV-drug use was the primary known source of HIV infection among men (Fulafel 1990). Heterosexual, bisexual, or homosexual activities, including multiple sex partners in Bahrain or abroad, e.g., India, Thailand, Philippines, and Western countries, are the second source. Blood transfusions abroad, in countries where blood is not routinely tested, e.g., India and the Philippines, remains a third route of infection.

There is a long history of hard drug use among men in Bahrain. Iranian opium was marketed between Iran, London, and Hong Kong by the British trading ships of the East India Company during the late 19th century and into the early 20th century. Some opium was shipped to Bahrain via dhows. Opium was sold in herb shops in Manama called *Abdareen* shops. These sales continued during the 1920s and 1930s. There was widespread use among those of Persian descent, Beluchis, and Indians. People usually smoked opium, but as their tolerance developed, they began taking it orally. One man used to see his relative putting three to four pieces of opium in his mouth and drinking it with tea. Unlike the other groups, the Arabs only used opium for medicinal purposes to treat headache or stomachache, and it was given in small quantities diluted in milk to put a child to sleep.

The use of opium later declined in the early 1940s when it was outlawed and became a controlled substance. Then new types of drugs, including IV drugs became prevalent. A study from 1980 to 1984 showed an annual increase in cases of drug involvement and narcotics dependence (Mattar 1985). In 1991, the Bahrain courts heard 197 drug-related cases involving 433 drug users or traffickers of several nationalities.

Currently, drug use is strictly controlled and there are frequent arrests at the airport, mainly of expatriates who try to bring in heroin, opium, and hashish (marijuana). Other drug caches of heroin have been found at sea hanging on buoys. Occasionally, someone is caught, usually an expatriate trying to bring in drugs via the Saudi Causeway. In spite of controls at all ports of entry, supplies of drugs are readily available on the Island. School principals have openly told students what places to avoid, as they are known for drug sales. People report having relatives who are IV users of hard drugs. Money is given to them by family members to purchase drugs. Others may rob to support this habit. The Government newspapers every week contain information about court hearings for drug use, drugs confiscated at the airport, drug sales, or drug-related deaths—all among men. The incidence of these drug hauls is reported by the Ministry of the Interior. The incidence and prevalence of IV-drug use among the population is not reported, but it is a major factor in HIV transmission in the country. Narcotics Anonymous has a local chapter, and reformed addicts attend, speak at local seminars, and give public lectures upon request. They talk about the 12-step rehabilitation program and how it helped them, once they admitted they were addicted to drugs.

The extent of bisexual activities and the danger of HIV transmission because of these unsafe sex contacts has implications on the future health of the women to whom these men are married and their offspring. The frequency of interaction among homosexual and bisexual men is not known; however, anecdotal stories show that Bahraini men have been known to have Western expatriate lovers in Saudi Arabia and elsewhere, unknown to their Bahraini wives. Also, naive young women sometimes discuss their personal relations with coworkers, including their husbands' practices during intercourse, e.g., "needing a cucumber in his rectum."

The patterns of HIV infection among women in Bahrain differ from men. Their numbers are very low. The early cases in the 1980s were seen among women who contracted the virus during operations abroad, or from blood transfusions, e.g., from India. Their positive status many times was discovered when the patient attended a hospital for another procedure. More recently, women are being infected during heterosexual activities with their husbands or a lover; fortunately, these cases are rare to date. Transmission of HIV infection from a wife to her husband has occurred, but these cases are also rare.

Among healthcare workers, there have been no documented cases of HIV contracted through blood contact or sharp injuries. However, several cases and deaths from hepatitis B and hepatitis C infections from patients are known in the community. The practice of deporting HIV-positive expatriates, and deaths of some Bahraini patients from AIDS, have kept the known number of HIV cases in Bahrain below 200 for the last ten years. The published cases of AIDS are listed as 20 (Wahdan 1995).

If there are data kept on the incidence of HIV among homosexuals, lesbians, and bisexual persons, they are not published, nor are they in the public domain.

### Availability of Treatment, Prevention, and Government Policy

The Government of Bahrain provides free healthcare for all Bahrainis who are HIV carriers. Government workers must provide care for these individuals, and doctors are aware of all current treatments available abroad. All experimental medications are not available in the country; prophylactic antibiotics to prevent *Pneumocystis carrini* are available.

Regarding expatriates, the Government policy regarding HIV/AIDS includes the following:

1. Recruiting agencies need to test workers in certain service areas in their home countries, including maids, beauticians, cooks, and healthcare workers. In Saudi Arabia and Kuwait, all seeking residence, not just workers, are tested prior to arrival.
2. The above categories of workers are retested after arrival.
3. All expatriates found positive for HIV, HBV, or HCV are deported.
4. All expatriates who are later tested and found positive are deported.
5. There is no scheduled testing for all the inhabitants of the country. (Countrywide testing has been conducted in the UAE and Kuwait.)
6. Local drug users who test positive are incarcerated if their behavior shows they are a risk to others, or upon the request of concerned family members.

Research regarding the topic of HIV is scanty. The Government conducted one study in the late 1980s regarding the population's knowledge about AIDS. The majority reported it was "an expatriate problem." Another study was conducted among military conscripts, and it showed the men knew about the disease, but some were unclear about transmission routes and prevention measures (Parida 1992). A study conducted by medical students showed that only 5.9% of Bahrainis understood the modes of transmission for AIDS, and 32.2% believed it could be cured (Chand n.d.). Obviously, more public health education is needed regarding the topic. A 1995 study on nurses' knowledge about AIDS has not been reported to date. In 1995, the Government announced appointments to a National AIDS Committee.

The United Nations resident coordinator and UN Development Program (UNDP) resident representative, Dr. Faysal Abdul Gadir, has been outspoken regarding shying away from the AIDS threat:

> Once again there is the problem of people not acknowledging that in fact it is a problem. . . . Forget for a minute the sociocultural view that it is impossible to contract it

due to religious and social regulations. The reality is people are contracting the disease and we can't close our eyes and say it is the problem of industrial and non-Muslim countries. We cannot say it is irrelevant to us. It will mean a drain on the budget as the State will have to take care of each patient until he dies. (Gadir 1996)

Lectures are provided occasionally to the public on HIV and AIDS in the Government Health Centers and videos are also shown. The Ministry of Health has distributed booklets in Arabic about AIDS. Indirectly, the Government provides knowledge about AIDS though the choice of movies shown on government-controlled television channels (Arabic and English). The WHO sponsored an AIDS-awareness day in 1995. Discoveries of the latest AIDS advances are sometimes published in the local government-controlled newspapers (Arabic and English). During the 1996 Ninth International AIDS Conference, daily updated information was printed in the local English-language newspaper.

Public education about the dangers of AIDS is not provided on a continuing basis. There are no active government media programs, such as the public service advertisements seen on the television in the U.K., U.S.A., or other countries. There are no large posters shown on hoardings (signboards), or at bus stops or public malls as seen in India, Hong Kong, and Botswana. There are no notices about safe sex, or clean needles on the doors of pubic toilet stalls, or at the airport like you see in Australia or Hong Kong. The overall health education budget for the Ministry of Health in 1991 was 0.1% of the total budget or US$120,000 (BD56,229,000) for education regarding all areas.

[*Update 2002*: UNAIDS Epidemiological Assessment: Bahrain has established a regular reporting system for AIDS and HIV testing and results. Injecting drug use accounts for 67% of all AIDS cases until 2000. Although the registered prevalence of HIV among injecting drug users was in 1989 and 1990 around 8% and 3%, respectively, a steady decrease was noted from 1991 onward to reach less than 1% in 2000. HIV cases among pregnant women are sporadic and no particular HIV trends are noted among this group. Premarital testing was introduced in 1999 and seroprevalence in this group is less than 0.1%.

[Blood safety measures are strictly observed in Bahrain, and HIV screening data cannot be used to describe HIV trends nationally. Screening of TB and STD patients is reported yearly and the results are not significant. During the period 1995-2000, the seroprevalence of syphilis among blood donors and pregnant women in Bahrain was around 0.22%. During 1998-2000, the prevalence among STD patients was five times higher and exceeded 1% during 1998-2000.

[The estimated number of adults and children living with HIV/AIDS on January 1, 2002, were:

| | |
|---|---|
| Adults ages 15-49: | < 1,000  (rate: 0.3%) |
| Women ages 15-49: | 150 |
| Children ages 0-15: | NA |

[No estimate is available for the number of adults and children who died of AIDS during 2001.

[No estimate is available for the number of Bahraini children who had lost one or both parents to AIDS and were under age 15 at the end of 2001. (*End of update by the Editors*)]

## 11. Sexual Dysfunctions, Counseling, and Therapies

### A. Definition of Sexual Dysfunction

The definition of sexual dysfunction can be based on the patient's perception and/or on underlying organic and psychological causes. There have been no reports published in the Bahrain medical journals on this topic, although various lectures on related topics have been presented.

### B. Availability of Diagnosis and Treatment

The patient's perception of sexual dysfunction needs to be assessed accurately by urologists and other healthcare professionals. In some cases, the individual who is normal may be comparing himself to what others say they are capable of performing, e.g., intercourse once a week versus three times a day (E. Amin 1994). Many patients are reluctant to describe sexuality and sexual aspects of their marriage, as seen in the study among primary healthcare patients conducted by Kahtanie (1992). Once a psychological basis for sexual dysfunction is diagnosed, the patients are referred to the psychiatrist if they agree. Many patients in Bahrain and the Gulf do not seek psychiatric help until their difficulties become more prominent and continuous and interfere with their marital or social life (Al-Khani & Arafa 1990). Acceptance of psychiatric referrals has increased dramatically during the last ten years, although education level and perception of any shame associated with psychiatry still inhibit individuals getting the help they may need. Bahrain provides free psychiatric service for anyone in the country, and the Psychiatric Hospital and outpatient clinics are well staffed with highly trained Arabic- and English-speaking Bahraini and expatriate male and female doctors.

Individuals with addictions whose behavior is erratic, including their sexual activities, can receive free psychiatric treatment and can attend addiction clinics or drug detoxification programs. There are also longstanding, self-help groups, such as Alcoholics Anonymous (held at American Mission Hospital), and a new local chapter of Narcotics Anonymous (founded in 1996). There are known cases where addicted individuals having HIV continued to be irresponsible in their sexual behavior, and their families asked to have them placed in jail to control them in the interest of the public welfare and prevention of cross infection.

Organic causes of sexual dysfunction are varied and their incidence is rising. The incidence of congenital anomalies in Bahrain is 20%. This figure is based on the 80% of deliveries which are conducted in the Ministry of Health facilities (excluding the military and private hospitals, and home births). Anomalies of the genitourinary system rank second at 2.5/1,000 after musculoskeletal at 2.8/1,000 (Al-Arrayed 1987). This rate is lower than 21.6/1,000 in Al-Ain and 12.9/1,000 in Abu Dhabi, and 6.6-8.5/1,000 in Saudi Arabia (Topley & Dowda 1995). The author notes that all malformations, based on international studies, may not be noted at birth (only 43%), or during the first six months (82%). Other problems are noted later, especially those of a sexual nature, which may be detected only during adolescence, or later after marriage.

Organic causes of sexual problems seen in Bahrain and the Gulf area include undescended testes, hypospadias (Al-Arrayed 1987), webbed penis (Husa & Al-Samarrai 1990), intersex disorders requiring gender reassignment, such as Turner's Syndrome, Kleinfelter's Syndrome, and XX genotype females/phenotype males, and XY women (Al-Arrayed 1996). Expert surgical help is available, as well as penile prosthesis implants. Endocrinologists can provide adjuvant hormonal therapy, as needed. Clinical psychologists or psychiatrists can provide counseling for individuals and/or their families on gender identification and possible social outcomes. In order to prevent the continual rise in occurrence of organic causes of sexual dysfunction among the young, doctors are recommending genetic counseling for individuals before marriage and after the birth of an affected child. A genetic counseling group clinic has been established; however, participation is voluntary. Screening on 515 couples in a Health Center showed that among them, 89 had abnormal findings detected (F. Amin 1993). A similar recommendation for genetic counseling was made in Kuwait (Telbi 1988).

## 12. Sex Research and Advanced Professional Education

There are no institutes or programs for sexological research in the State of Bahrain. Nor are there any post-college or graduate-level programs for the advanced study of human sexuality, or any sexological journals or periodicals. Occasionally, a related article will be published in the two national medical journals:

*Bahrain Medical Bulletin.* Editorial Officer, Box 32159, State of Bahrain. Tel: 0973-265 258; Fax: 0973-277 036.

*Journal of the Bahrain Medical Society.* Editorial Office, Box 26136, Manama, State of Bahrain. Tel: 0973-742 666 (5-10 p.m. local time); Fax: 0973-715 559.

There are also no national or regional sexological organizations among the six Gulf Cooperation Council member states (Bahrain, Saudi Arabia, Kuwait, Qatar, United Arab Emirates, and Oman). There is a Bahrain Sociologists Society, which has published a series of monographs in Arabic. Bibliographies available on Bahrain include:

Ailan, R. M. 1996. *Bibliography for Women in the State of Bahrain* (in Arabic). Bahrain: Information Center for Women and Children.

Badu, B., & M. Awad. 1995. *Arab Women Bibliography: A Study Conducted in Eight Arab Countries.* Tunisia: Center for Arab Women Training and Research. (Includes French and English titles for Bahrain, Egypt, Jordan, Kuwait, Lebanon, Morocco, Palestine, Yemen; database to be updated annually.)

Davis, G. A. 1993. *Catalog of the Bahrain Historical and Archaeological Society Library* (English titles). Bahrain: Historical and Archaeological Society, P.O. Box 5087, Juffair, Bahrain.

Manzer, B. 1996. *BMED: An Index to Gulf Medical Journal Holdings in the Al Farsi Library (1979-1995).* Bahrain: Ministry of Health, Al-Farsi Library, College of Health Science, P.O. Box 12, Sulmaniya, Bahrain.

Sarhan, M. M. 1995. *National Bibliography, Vol. 1.* Fakhrawi Book Shop Printing & Publishing, Translation, Bahrain: P.O. Box 1643, Manama, Bahrain.

*Statistical Abstracts 1994.* 1995. State of Bahrain, Central Statistics Organization, Directorate of Statistics.

Information is available in English and Arabic on related topics in the following libraries:

Bahrain Family Planning Association Headquarters, Al-Qufool, Bahrain Tel: 0973-232233, 256622 Fax: 0973-276408.

Al-Farsi Library, College of Health Sciences, P.O. Box 12, Ministry of Health, Al Sulmaniya, Bahrain. Tel: 0973 255555 ext. 5202 Fax: 0973 252569 Telex: 8511 HEALTH BN.

## References and Suggested Readings

Abbas, S. M. A., & S. R. Satwekar. 1989. Positive treponematosis in Saudi antenatals and their perinatal outcome over a 7-year period. *Saudi Medical Journal, 10*(4):301-304.

Abdul, F. 1995. Penile prosthesis: A revolution in treatment of erectile dysfunction. *The Journal of the Kuwait Medical Association, 27*(4):303-307.

Abdul, H. H., & H. Saheb. 1990. *The complete book of home remedies.* New Delhi: Orient Paperbacks.

Abdul Jabbar, F. A., M. A. Al-Meshari, M. A. Hafeez, & M. O. Malik. 1980. Male intersex XX: A case report. *Saudi Medical Journal, 1*(2):149-151.

Adbul Khaliq, S. A., & E. L. Smith. 1988. Gonoccaemia in pregnancy: First report of a case in Saudi Arabia. *Saudi Medical Journal, 9*(1):86:88.

Abu Aisha, H. 1985. Women in Saudi Arabia: Do they not have the right to give their own consent for medical procedures? *Saudi Medical Journal, 6*(2):74-77.

Abu-Zaid, A. A. U. 1996 (April). Trade and folk medicine in old Jeddah (in Arabic). *Al-Ma'thurat Al Sha'biyyah: A Specialized Quarterly Review of Folklore* (Qatar), *42*:82-96.

Ahmed, A. 1996 (April 2). Strict conditions guide polygamy. *Gulf Daily News* (Eng. ed., Bahrain), p. 2.

Ahmed, A. A. 1995. *An overview of health services in Bahrain.* Bahrain: Ministry of Health Report.

Ahmed, A. 1996 (August 12). Jobs to receive priority. *Gulf Daily News* (Eng. ed., Bahrain), p. 2.

AIDS: 1985. *Bahrain Medical Bulletin, 7*(2):64.

Akhter, S. S., T. Filani, M. Gadella, & A. Al-Amir. 1995. Beliefs and attitudes about breast self exam in Al-Qassim Region of Saudi Arabia: A study of women attending primary health care clinics. *Saudi Medical Journal, 16*(6):493-497.

Al-A'Ali, E. 1991. *The phenomenon of women in management: An alternative perspective and implication in the case of Bahrain.* Doctoral dissertation, University of Lancaster, UK.

Al-Ansari, A., & B. Shubar. 1982. The child and adolescent psychiatric population of Bahrain: Comparative data. *Bahrain Medical Bulletin, 4*(3):83-87.

Al-Ansari, A., & H. Al-Ansari. 1983. Failure to thrive. *Bahrain Medical Bulletin, 5*(1):23-26.

Al-Ansari, A. M. 1992. Treatment issues in child abuse and neglect. *Journal of the Bahrain Medical Society, 4*(3):89.

Al-Arrayed, A. S., & S. Chandra. 1996. Prevalence of antibodies to hepatitis C virus. *Journal of the Bahrain Medical Society, 8*(1):13-16.

Al-Arrayed, S. 1987. Congenital anomalies in Bahrain. *Bahrain Medical Bulletin, 9*(2):70-73.

Al-Arrayed, S. S. 1995. The frequency of consanguineous marriages in the State of Bahrain. *Bahrain Medical Bulletin, 17*(3):63-67.

Al-Arrayed, S. S. 1996. Chromosomal abnormalities in 500 referred cases in Bahrain. *Bahrain Medical Bulletin, 18*(1):2-4.

Al-Dabbous, I. A. 1991. Priapism in two children with sickle cell disease at Qateef Central Hospital. *Bahrain Medical Bulletin, 13*(3):104-106.

Al-Dabbous, I. A., & A. H. Al-Juma. 1993. Priapism in sickle cell disease in Qateef Central Hospital. *Saudi Medical Journal, 14*(5):440-442.

Al-Darazi, F. A. 1984. *Assessment of Bahraini women's health and illness cognitions and practices.* Master's thesis, University of Illinois, Chicago.

Al-Darazi, F. A. 1986. *Health and illness cognition among Bahraini women.* Doctoral dissertation, University of Illinois, Chicago.

Al-Dhahry, S., P. Aghanashiniker, H. Al-Marhuby, M. Buhl, A. Daar, & M. Al-Husani. 1994. Hepatitis B, delta and human immunodeficiency virus infections among Omani patients with renal diseases: A seroprevalence study. *Annals of Saudi Medicine, 14*(4):312-315.

Al-Eissa, Y. A., et al. 1991. The battered child syndrome: Does it exist in Saudi Arabia? *Saudi Medical Journal, 12*(2):129-133.

Al-Falaij, A. A. 1991. *Family conditions, ego development and sociomoral development in juvenile delinquency: A study of Bahrain adolescents.* Doctoral dissertation, University of Pittsburgh.

Al-Falaij, A. A. 1993. Family conditions, ego development and sociomoral development in juvenile delinquency: A study of Bahrain adolescents. *Journal of Bahrain Medical Society, 5*(3):168.

Al-Faris, E., M. Al-Rajhi, & M. Al-Nour. 1995. Smoking among females attending a health center in Riyadh, Saudi Arabia. *Annals of Saudi Medicine, 15*(5):525-527.

Al-Faruqi, L. 1988. Women. *Muslim society and Islam.* Plainfield, IN: American Trust Publications.

Al-Gaseer, N. 1990. *The experience of menstrual symptoms of Bahraini women*. Doctoral dissertation, University of Illinois, Chicago.

Al-Ghamdi, H. 1986. The dynamic forces in the personalities of juvenile delinquency in the Saudi Arabian environment. *Transcultural Psychological Research Review, 23*:248-250.

Al-Hariri, S., & I. Helin. 1987. Congenital syphilis. *The Journal of the Kuwait Medical Association, 21*(4):335-338.

Al-Herbish, A. S., N. A. M. Al-Jurayyan, A. M. Abo Bakr Mohammed, A. Abdulla, M. Al-Husain, A. A. Al-Rabeah, P. J. Patel, A. Jawad, & A. I. Al-Samarrai. 1996. Sex reassignment: A challenging problem. Current Medical and Islamic Guidelines. *Annals of Saudi Medicine, 16*(1):12-15.

Al-Jishi, A. 1982. *Bahrain Ministry of Interior working paper on juvenile delinquency*. Bahrain: Ministry of Interior Press.

Al-Khalifa, A. bin K. 1982 (January). The inception and development of health services in Bahrain. *Al-Watheeka (Journal of the Historical Documents Centre, State of Bahrain), 8*: 241-229.

Al-Khani, M., & M. M. Arafa. 1990. Social phobia in Saudi Patients. *Annals of Saudi Medicine, 10*(6):615-619.

Al-Khateeb. 1986. Trends of tobacco smoking among physicians, journalists and teachers in Bahrain. *Bahrain Medical Bulletin, 8*(1):19-23.

Al-Malki, N. 1996 (April). The superstitions of the Qatari people. *Al-Ma'thurat Al-Sha'biyyah: A Specialized Quarterly Review of Folklore* (Qatar), *42*:82-96.

Al-Naser, Y. E. 1993. *Inequalities in child survival in Bahrain: The role of marriage patterns in a low mortality population.* Ph.D. dissertation, University of London.

Al-Mugeiren, M., & R. S. Genelin. 1990. A suspected case of Munchausen's syndrome by proxy in a Saudi Child. *Annals of Saudi Medicine. 10*(6):662-665.

Al-Othman, A., & M. Sadat-Ali. 1994. Pattern of pediatric trauma seen in a teaching hospital. *Bahrain Medical Bulletin, 16*(3):87-89.

Al-Quttan, N., & A. A. E. Omu. 1996. The pattern of menopause in Kuwait and the need for hormone replacement therapy. *The Journal of the Kuwait Medical Association, 28*(2):152-157.

Al-Rashied, A. A. 1988. Introduction to the 'battered baby syndrome.' *The Journal of the Kuwait Medical Association, 22*(3):193-194.

Al-Saleh, B. M. S., E. R. Ansari, I. H. Al-Ali, J. Y. Tell, & A. Saheb. 1985. Fracture of the penis seen in Abu Dhabi. *Journal of Urology, 134*:274-275.

Al-Sharyan, A. A. 1987. *The cultural division of labour in less developed countries: The case of Bahrain*. Ph.D. dissertation, University of Exeter, UK.

Ali, N. 1996. *Child abuse*. Master's thesis: University of Texas, Austin.

Amin, E. 1979. Statistics for child trauma. *Bahrain Medical Bulletin, 5*(2):19.

Amin, E. 1984. Urological problems of the elderly. *Bahrain Medical Bulletin, 6*(1):29-30.

Amin, E. 1994. Male impotence. Monday morning doctors' lecture series. Bahrain Defence Force Hospital, April 11, 1994.

Amin, F. 1982. *A study of Bahrain's family*. Bahrain: Government Press.

Amin, F. 1993. *Annual report: Primary health care*. Bahrain Ministry of Health, Primary Health Care.

Anthony, T. A. 1984 (January). Documentation of the modern history of Bahrain from American sources 1900-38: Historical records of the American Mission, New Brunswick, New Jersey. *Al-Watheeka (Journal of the Historical Documents Centre, State of Bahrain), 4*:243-229.

Arya, S. C. 1996. Risk factors in acquiring hepatitis C infection in Saudi Arabia. *Annals of Saudi Medicine, 16*(2):229.

Asgari, M. A., et al. 1996. Penile fracture. *Journal of Urology, 155*:148-149.

Atallah, N. L., N. J. Sharkawi, & J. J. Campbell. 1990. Age at menarche of school girls in the Asir Region of Saudi Arabia with a note on adult heights and weights. *Saudi Medical Journal, 11*(1):59-63.

Babag, Z. A., & A. Al-Mesbar. 1993. The role of chlamydia trachomatis infection in infertility. *Annals of Saudi Medicine, 13*(5):423-428).

Baby, S. 1996a (August 18). UN praises Bahrain's health care. *Gulf Daily News* (Eng. ed., Bahrain), p. 1.

Baby, S. 1996b (August 18). Quality of life in Bahrain ranking among the best. *Gulf Daily News* (Eng. ed., Bahrain), p. 2.

Badawi, J. A. 1980. *The status of women in Islam*. Plainfield, IN: MSA of US and Canada.

Bakir, T. M. F. 1992. Age-specific prevalence of antibody to hepatitis C virus (HCV) among the Saudi population. *Saudi Medical Journal, 13*(4):321-324.

Basri, N. A., & E. L. Smith. 1991. Three cases of secondary syphilis presenting in different departments. *Saudi Medical Journal, 12*(6):461-463.

Belgrave, C. H. 1960. *Personal column*. London: Hutchinson and Co., Ltd.

Belgrave, C. H. 1968 (May-June). Bahrain from Dhow to discoteque. *Mid East, 8*:32-37.

Belgrave, J. H. 1975. *Welcome to Bahrain*. London: The Augustan Press.

Bin Hamad, T., E. B. Larbi, & J. Absool. 1991. Obesity in a primary health centre: A retrospective study. *Annals of Saudi Medicine, 11*(2):163-166.

Blanckensee, D. J., A. M. Montague, J. M. O'Keefe, M. Steinback, & J. H. Ahsood. 1995. Contraceptive usage in UAE national women. *Emirates Medical Journal, 13*:197-202.

Boserup, E. 1970. *Woman's role in economic development*. London: George Allen and Unvin.

Bushiri, A. A. 1985-1986. Dilmun culture. *Dilmun (Journal of the Bahrain Historical and Archeological Society), 13*: 7-16.

Bushiri, A. A. 1992. *Dilmun culture*. Bahrain: Ministry of Information, National Council for Culture, Arts and Literature.

Bushiri, A. A., & G. A. Davis. 1996. Local herbs reputed to have aphrodisiac powers. Unpublished manuscript.

Buzaboon, B. Y. 1986. *A study of psychological and environmental factors associated with delinquency*. Doctoral dissertation, University of Wales.

Chaleby, K. 1982. Traditional Arabian marriage and mental health in a group of outpatients in Saudi Arabia. *Acta Psychiatry Scandinavia, 77*:139-142.

Chaleby, K. 1987. Social phobia in Saudi. *Social Psychiatry, 22*:167-170.

Chand, I. n.d. New AIDS awareness campaign urged. *Gulf Daily News* (Eng. ed., Bahrain).

CIA. 2002 (January). *The world factbook 2002*. Washington, DC: Central Intelligence Agency. Available: http://www.cia.gov/cia/publications/factbook/index.html.

Curtis, J. L. 1977. *Bahrain: Language, customs and people*. Singapore: Tun Wah Press.

Dickson, H. R. P. 1915. *The Arab of the desert: A glimpse into Badawin life in Kuwait and Sau'di Arabia*. London: n.p.

Doorenbos, H. 1976. Postpartum salt packing and other medical practices: Oman, South Arabia, In: F. X. Grollig & H. R. Halley, eds., *Medical Anthropology* (pp. 109-111). Paris: Mouton Publishers.

Duwaigher, S. M. 1964. *Development of women's education in Bahrain*. Master's thesis, American University, Beirut.

El-Islam, M. F. 1974. Hospital referred parasuicide in Qatar. *Egyptian Journal of Mental Health, 15*:101-112.

El-Islam, M. F. 1982. Arabic cultural psychiatry. *Transcultural Psychiatry Research Review, 19*:5-21.

El-Islam, M. F. 1984. Cultural change and intergenerational relationships in Arab families. *International Journal of Family Psychiatry, 4*:55-63.

El-Rufaie, O. E., A. A. Al-Quorain, F. A. Azzoni, & S. S. Al-Khalifa. 1991. Emotional aspects of functional abdominal pain. *Saudi Medical Journal, 11*(6):450-452.

El-Sherif, A. E., W. Dauleh, N. Allowneh, & P. V. Jayan. 1991. Management of fracture of the penis in Qatar. *British Journal of Urology*, 68:622-625.

Emura, M. K., N. Abdulla, A. Saudah, A. R. Al-Asfoor, & M. E. El-Islam. 1988. Attempted suicide by drug overdose in Kuwait. *Saudi Medical Journal*, 9:182-187.

Fakhro, A. M. 1991. Health promotion policies. *Bahrain Medical Bulletin*, 13(2):47-48.

Falafel, R. A. 1990. AIDS: A moral issue or public hazard. *Journal of the Bahrain Medical Society*, 2(2):53-55.

Faroughy, A. 1951. *The Bahrein Islands (750-1951): A contribution to the study of power politics in the Persian Gulf.* New York: Verry, Fisher and Company, Inc.

Farsi, H. M. A., H. A. Mosli, M. M. Rawas, T. N. Rehamy, & S. A. Hemdi. 1990. Persistent Mullerian duct syndrome in an adult: A case report. *Annuals of Saudi Medicine*, 10(3): 330-332.

Felimban, F. M. 1993. The smoking practices and attitudes towards smoking of female university students in Riyadh. *Saudi Medical Journal*, 14(3):220-224.

Gadir, F. A. 1996 (July 19). Gulf cannot afford to ignore AIDS threat. *Gulf Daily News* (Eng. ed., Bahrain), p. 1.

Girl circumcision ban. 1996 (July 19). *Gulf Daily News* (Eng. ed., Bahrain), p. 5.

Goode, W. J. 1962. *World revolution and family patterns.* Glencoe, IL: The Free Press, Collier MacMillan, Ltd.

Gravesen, R. G. 1987. Sexual responsibilities of physicians. *Bahrain Medical Bulletin*, 9(2):82-86.

Hall, E. T. 1959. *The silent language.* New York: Doubleday & Co.

Hall, E. T. 1966. *The hidden dimension.* New York: Doubleday & Co.

Hamarnah, S. A., Z. H. Safiki, & A. J. M. Saleh. 1993. Fracture of the penis. *Emirates Medical Journal*, 11:25-27.

Hansen, H. 1967. *Investigations in a Shi'a village in Bahrain.* Copenhagen: National Museum of Denmark–Publications of the Ethnographical Series, Vol. 12.

Harrison, P. 1904 (January-March). Our medical work. *Quarterly Letters of the Arabian Mission (New Brunswick, New Jersey)*, 88. Also in: Anthony, T. A. 1984 (January). Documentation of the modern history of Bahrain from American sources 1900-1938: Historical records of the American Mission, New Brunswick, New Jersey. *Al Watheeka* (Journal of the Historical Documents Centre, State of Bahrain), 4:243-229.

Hathout, H. 1979 (June). Unwantedness as an indication for abortion. *The Journal of the Kuwait Medical Association*, 13:89-92.

Health check law for expats clear. 1996 (14 June). *Gulf Daily News* (Eng. ed., Bahrain), p. 4.

Hegazi, M., H. Fadaak, A. Saharty, & A. Wafiq. 1990. One stage penile and urethral reconstruction–A new extension of inferiorly based rectus abdominus myocutaneous flap. *Annals of Saudi Medicine*, 10(5):564-566.

Hicks, E. K. 1993. *Infibulation: Female mutilation in Islamic northeastern Africa.* New Brunswick and London: Transaction Publishers.

Husain, M. T., & A. Y. Al-Samarrai. 1990. Webbed penis in Arab children. *Annals of Saudi Medicine*, 10(5):531-534.

Ibrahim, M. E., H. M. Hathout, M. A. A. Moussa, & M. A. Razaq. 1979. Gynecological and obstetric survey of the Ministry of Public Health Nurses in Kuwait. *The Journal of the Kuwait Medical Association*, 13(1):27-37.

Ismail, M. A. 1990. The role of the primary health center in the early management of infertility and impotence. *Journal of the Bahrain Medical Society*, 2(2):134-136.

Johnson, P. 1958. *Journey into chaos.* London: MacGibbon and Kees.

Kahtanie, K. 1992. *A study of coping strategies experienced by Bahraini married couples when faced with life strains in marital and parental roles.* Master's thesis, University of Texas, Medical Branch, Galveston.

Khalfan, M. A. 1973. How they lived 2–The dying customs of Bahrain, Series 1–The marriage ceremony. *Dilmun (The Journal of the Bahrain Archaeological and Historical Society)*, 5:14.

Khuri, F. I. 1980. *Tribe and state in Bahrain.* New York: The University of Chicago Press.

Kutub, M. 1982. *Islam: The misunderstood religion*, Malaysia: Polygraphic Press Sdn. Bhd.

MacFarquhar, N. 2002 (May 22) In Bahrain. Women run, women vote, women lose. *The New York Times*, p. A3.

Mahgoub, O. M., et al. 1990. Deliberate self-harm in the migrant populations in the Eastern Province of Saudi Arabia, *Saudi Medical Journal*, 11:473-477.

Mahgoub, O. M., H. B. Adbel-Hafeiz, A. Al-Quorain, H. Al-Idrissu, G. Al-Ghassab, & I. Absood. 1991. Life events stress in Saudi peptic ulcer patients of the Eastern Province. *Annals of Saudi Medicine*, 11(6):669-673.

Mahmon, E. F. 1992. Experience of hepatitis B in Bahrain. *Journal of the Bahrain Medical Society*, 4(1):64-66.

Malik, M., A. Belal, T. E. Mekter, & H. Al-Kinary. 1996. Drug overdose in the Asir region of Saudi Arabia, *Annuals of Saudi Medicine*, 16(1):33-36.

Mass wedding job. 1996 (July 11). *Gulf Daily News* (Eng. ed., Bahrain).

Mattar, A. M. 1985. Drug abuse. *Bahrain Medical Bulletin*, 7(2):5355.

McDermott, A. 1973 (May 2). Women in Saudi Arabia. *The Guardian* (London).

Metery, G. E., A. M. Matar, & R. R. Hamadeh. 1986. Early recognition and prevention of attempted suicide in primary health care. *Bahrain Medical Bulletin*, 9(1):12-16.

Mohammed, A. A. 1978. *Traditional health practices of the post-partum Bahraini women.* Master's thesis, University of Illinois, Chicago.

Mohammed, F. A. 1986. *Women and social change in Bahrain.* Master's thesis, University of Essex, UK.

Molloy, J., D. Al-Hashimi, & F. T. Al-Mahroos. 1993. Children in jeopardy: Munchausen syndrome by proxy. *Journal of the Bahrain Medical Society*, 5(3):154-159.

Moore, R. 1996 (August 5). Sky is the limit for a career in banking. *Gulf Daily News* (Eng. ed., Bahrain), p. 2.

Moore, R. 1996 (August 8). Keeping ALBA a step ahead, *Gulf Daily News* (Eng. ed., Bahrain), p. 3.

Muhsen, Z., & A. Crofts. 1991. *Sold.* London: Warner Books/Little, Brown and Company, UK.

Nadkarni, K. V., S. S. Al-Arrayed, & J. P. Bapat. 1991. Incidence of genetic disorders of haemoglobins in the hospital population of Bahrain. *Bahrain Medical Bulletin*, 13(1):1924.

Nasib, T. A., R. R. Hamadah, & H. K. Armenian. 1983. The impact of family size on morbidity at a primary health care centre in Bahrain. *Bahrain Medical Bulletin*, 5(2):65-72.

Noor, E. 1996 (August 8). Bahraini women forging ahead. *Gulf Daily News* (Eng. ed., Bahrain), p. 5.

Parida, S. K. 1992. Knowledge, attitude and behavior of army personnel towards HIV infection. Ninth International Conference on AIDS, Berlin.

Parida, S. K., & K. Effendi. 1994. Viral infection among family members of carriers of HbsAg in Bahrain. *Journal of the Bahrain Medical Society*, 6(2):61-63.

Patterson, L. M. 1904 (April-June). Two weeks at the hospital. *Quarterly Letters of the Arabian Mission (New Brunswick, New Jersey)*, 50. Also in: Anthony, T. A. 1984 (January). Documentation of the modern history of Bahrain from American sources 1900-1938: Historical records of the American Mission, New Brunswick, New Jersey. *Al-Watheeka (Journal of the Historical Documents Centre, State of Bahrain)*, 4:243-229.

Patton, M. Q., ed. 1991. *Family sexual abuse: Frontline research and evaluation.* Newbury Park, CA: Sage Publications, Inc.

Qadri, S. M. H., J. Akhter, & K. Ignacio. 1993. Incidence of chlamydia infections in a large metropolitan hospital in Saudi Arabia. *Saudi Medical Journal*, 14(2):152-155.

Qureshi, N. A. 1992. The battered child syndrome: Does it exist in Saudi Arabia? (letter to editor) *Saudi Medical Journal*, *13*(4):369-370.

Rajab, K. E. 1979. Milestones in the medical history of Bahrain with special reference to maternity and child welfare. *Bahrain Medical Bulletin*, *1*(1):6-9.

Rajab, K. E. 1984. Getting around infertility. *Bahrain Medical Bulletin*, *9*(2):58-60.

Rajab, K. E., A. A. Yousef, & S. Rustan. 1995. Prevalence of chlamydial infection among pregnant women in Bahrain. *Journal of the Bahrain Medical Society*, *7*(1):17-19.

Ramzani, N. 1985. Arab women in the Gulf. *The Middle East Journal*, *39*:258-276.

Rasromani, K., A. M. Mohammed, S. Al Mahroos, & I. Mannan Khan. 1990. Priapism in sickle cell disease. *Bahrain Medical Bulletin*, *12*(3):113-115.

Rumaihi, M. G. 1976. *Bahrain: Social and political changes since the First World War.* London and New York: Bowker (in association with the Centre for Middle Eastern and Islamic Studies of the University of Durham, NC, USA).

Sadat-Ali, M., A. Y. El-Hassan, E. M. Ibrahim, H. Al-Frehi, & F. Al-Muhanna. 1993. Osteoporosis in Saudi women: A postmenopausal pilot screening. *Annals of Saudi Medicine*, *13*(3):272-274.

Sadat-Ali, M., I. Al-Habdan, & S. Marwah. 1995. The dilemma of jumping syndrome. *Journal of the Bahrain Medical Society*, *7*(3):187-190.

Saeed, T. 1992. Non-accidental burning in children. *Journal of the Bahrain Medical Society*, *4*(3):90.

Sandozi, S., N. Z. Al-Awadhi, & S. Ghazali. 1988. Fracture of the penis: Experience of 8 cases. *The Journal of the Kuwait Medical Association*, *22*(3):274-276.

Sarhan, M. M. 1995. *Bahrain National Bibliography, Vol. I* (Eng. ver.). Bahrain: Fakhrawi Book Shop Printing & Publishing.

*Statistical abstract 1994.* State of Bahrain, Central Statistics Organization, Directorate of Statistics.

Suleiman, M. A., A. A. Nashef, M. A. A. Moussa, & M. H. El-Islam. 1980. Psychological profile of the parasuicide patients in Kuwait. *International Journal of Psychiatry*, *32*: 16-22.

Sunderaj, S. 1989. Human papiloma virus and cervical neoplasia in Bahrain. *Journal of the Bahrain Medical Society*, *1*(1):8-11.

Taha, S., A. Sharayah, B. A. Kamal, et al. 1988. Fracture of the penis: Surgical management. *Internal Surgery*, *73*:63-64.

Taha, S. A., & G. M. Magbol. 1995. The pattern of intersex disorders and gender reassignment in the Eastern Province of Saudi Arabia. *Saudi Medical Journal*, *16*(1):17-22.

Taki, A. H. 1974. *The changing status of the Bahraini woman.* Bahrain: Oriental Press.

Telbi, A. S. 1988. Neonatal screening: The need for introducing a new service in Kuwait. *The Journal of the Kuwait Medical Association*, *22*(3):195-196.

The American Mission Hospitals Bahrain. *Persian Gulf: Report for 1933-34.* New Brunswick, NJ: Dutch Reformed Church Archives.

Topley, J., & A. Dewda. 1995. Pattern of congenital anomalies among UAE nationals. *Saudi Medical Journal*, *16*(5):425-428.

UNAIDS. 2002. *Epidemiological fact sheets by country.* Geneva, Switzerland: Joint United Nations Programme on HIV/AIDS (UNAIDS/WHO). Available: http://www.unaids.org/hivaidsinfo/statistics/fact_sheets/index_en.htm.

Wahdan, M. H. 1995. AIDS–The Past, present and future in the Eastern Mediterranean region. *Eastern Mediterranean Health Journal*, *1*(1):17-26.

Waly, T. 1992. *Private skies: The courtyard pattern in the architecture of the House Bahrain.* Bahrain: Al Handasah Center Publication.

Wikan, U. 1982. *Behind the veil in Arabia: Women in Oman.* Chicago: The University of Chicago Press.

Wilsher, P. 1982 (November 21). Leading the Saudi into temptation. *Sunday Times* (London), p. 18.

*World almanac and book of facts 1993.* New York: World Almanac/Scripps Howard Company, p. 732.

Yousef, A. A., M. R. Wallace, & K. M. Bendayna. 1991. Male urethritis in Bahrain: The increasing incidence of resistant gonorrhea. *Bahrain Medical Bulletin*, *13*(3):94-96.

Yousef, A. A., M. R. Wallace, B. H. Baig, & K. E. Rajab. 1991. Prenatal serologic screening in Bahrain. *Scandinavian Journal of Infectious Diseases*, *23*:781-783.

Yousef, A. 1994. Prenatal screening of syphilis toxoplasmosis and hepatitis B in patients infected with HIV in Bahrain. *Transactions of the Royal Society of Tropical Medicine and Hygiene*, *88*:60.

Ziskind, D. 1990. *Labor laws in the Middle East.* Los Angeles, CA: Litlaw Foundation.

# Botswana

Godisang Mookodi, Oleosi Ntshebe, and Ian Taylor, Ph.D.*

## Contents

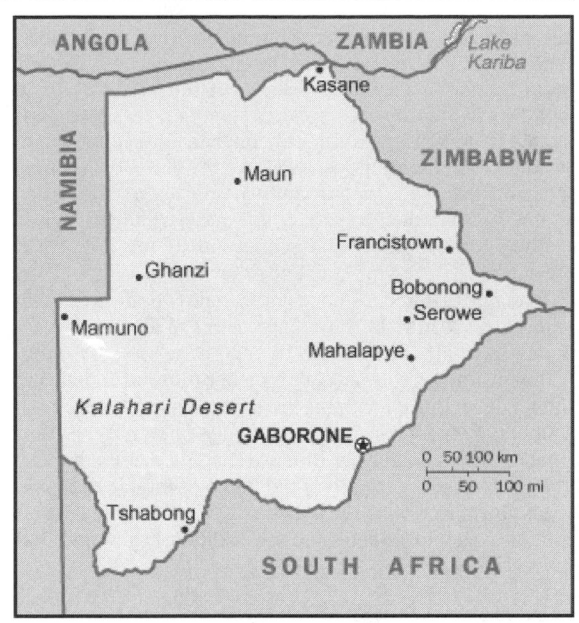

(CIA 2002)

## Demographics and a Brief Historical Perspective

ROBERT T. FRANCOEUR

### A. Demographics

Botswana is located in southern Africa, just north of South Africa, with Angola to the northwest, Zambia to the northeast, Zimbabwe to the east, and Namibia to the west. With a total area of 231,800 square miles (600,370 km²), Botswana is slightly smaller than the state of Texas. In the southwest, the Kalahari Desert supports nomadic San Bushmen and wildlife. In the north, farming is carried on amid salt lakes and swamplands. Livestock graze on the rolling plains in the east. The climate is semiarid, with warm winters and hot summers.

In July 2002, Botswana had an estimated population of 1.59 million. These estimates take into account the effects of excess mortality because of AIDS. This can result in lower life expectancy, higher infant mortality and death rates, lower population and growth rates, and changes in the distribution of the population by age and sex than would otherwise be expected. (All data are from *The World Factbook 2002* (CIA 2002) unless otherwise stated.)

**Age Distribution and Sex Ratios**: *0-14 years*: 40% with 1.01 male(s) per female (sex ratio); *15-64 years*: 55.8% with 0.93 male(s) per female; *65 years and over*: 4.2% with 0.68 male(s) per female; *Total population sex ratio*: 0.95 male(s) to 1 female

**Life Expectancy at Birth**: *Total Population*: 35.29 years; *male*: 35.15 years; *female*: 35.43 years

**Urban/Rural Distribution**: 63% to 37%

**Ethnic Distribution**: Tswana: 79%; Kalanga: 11%; Basarwa: 3%; others, including Kgalagadi and white: 7%. Note that these are mere estimates, as the government does not carry out ethnic censuses.

**Religious Distribution**: Indigenous religions: 85%; Christian: 15%

**Birth Rate**: 28.04 births per 1,000 population

**Death Rate**: 26.26 per 1,000 population

**Infant Mortality Rate**: 64.72 deaths per 1,000 live births

**Net Migration Rate**: –0.24 migrant(s) per 1,000 population

**Total Fertility Rate**: 3.6 children born per woman

**Population Growth Rate**: 0.18%

**HIV/AIDS** (1999 est.): *Adult prevalence*: 35.8%; *Persons living with HIV/AIDS*: 290,000; *Deaths*: 24,000. (For additional details from www.UNAIDS.org, see end of Section 10B.)

**Literacy Rate** (*defined as those age 15 and over who can read and write*): 70%

**Per Capita Gross Domestic Product** (*purchasing power parity*): $7,800; *Inflation*: 6.6%; *Unemployment*: 40% (the official rate is 21%); *Living below the poverty line*: 47% (2001 est.)

### B. A Brief Historical Perspective

The earliest known inhabitants of the region were the San, who were followed by the Tswana. Today, over three quarters of the population are ethnic Tswana. The terms for the country's people, Motswana (*sing.*) and Botswana (*pl.*), refer to their national rather than ethnic identities. Encroachment by the Zulus in the 1820s, and by the Boers from Transvaal in the 1870s and 1880s, threatened the peace in the region. In 1885, Britain established a protectorate, known as Bechuanaland. In 1961, Britain granted a constitution to the country. Self-government began in 1965 and the country became independent the next year. Botswana is Africa's oldest democracy.

In its early years, Botswana maintained good relations with its white-ruled neighbors, but that changed in later decades as the government harbored rebel groups from Rhodesia and South Africa. Although Botswana is rich in diamonds, it has a high unemployment rate and stratified socioeconomic classes. In 1999, the nation suffered its first budget deficit in 16 years, because of a slump in the international diamond market. Nevertheless, the nation remains one of Africa's wealthiest and most stable countries.

## 1. Basic Sexological Premises

### A. Character of Gender Roles

In Botswana, patriarchal sex/gender systems relegate males to positions of power and women to subordinate po-

*Communications*: Dr. Ian Taylor, Department of Political and Administrative Studies, University of Botswana, Private Bag 00705, Gaborone, Botswana; tayloric@mopipi.ub.bw.

sitions within the context of cultural beliefs and practices. Patriarchal beliefs are based in cultural beliefs. Tswana culture makes a clear division between the public-political and the private-domestic spheres—women are largely relegated to domestic activities of childcare, and home maintenance. Men continue to dominate the arena of political decision-making within traditional political forums, such as the 'kgotla,' the house of chiefs and parliament. While women form a significant proportion of the electorate, they hold very few political positions.

Gender differences occur in the education of females and males. While there are equal enrollment rates for females and males in the first nine years of schooling, the enrollment figures for males outnumber those of females in higher levels of education, including vocational training schools. Enrollment rates at the only university in Botswana, the University of Botswana, show that the highest gender discrepancies are in the fields of engineering and technology, as well as the Faculty of Science, where the ratios of males to females are approximately 8:1 and 3:1, respectively.

## B. Sociolegal Status of Males and Females

Botswana operates a dual legal system that consists of two 'legal' systems that are expected to operate side by side. On the one hand, there is what is known as Customary Law—which basically consists of laws based on the different customs and traditions of various ethnic groups. The second system is that of the General Law that is an adaptation of Roman and Dutch Law that was imposed during the colonial period from 1889 to 1966.

While the constitution of Botswana stipulates that there shall be no discrimination on the basis of sex, both legal systems reflect the strong influence of patriarchy. There are no clear distinctions between female and male children according to the laws. The distinctions begin at adolescence, largely in the area of punishment. In the context of customary law, corporal punishment is used within the context of 'minor' crimes, such as petty theft, and in minor civil offenses, such as indecent exposure and the use of insulting language. While both sexes may be sentenced to corporal punishment, it is largely practiced on male adolescents and adults.

There are certain aspects of the employment act that discriminate against women. The employment act prohibits the employment of women as soldiers in the army, as well as miners working underground.

## C. General Concepts and Constructs of Sexuality, Love, Marriage, and Family

It is difficult to generalize concepts and constructs of sexuality and love, as there have been very few context-based studies on these concepts and constructs from which one can draw conclusions. Worth noting, however, is the influential work of anthropologist Isaac Schapera, who documented the customs and practices of Tswana groups in present-day Botswana and South Africa during the early part of the 20th century.

Tswana groups had gender-specific rites of passage that served to prepare young persons for adulthood and to control premarital fertility. Young adolescent males would undergo *bogwera*, which included circumcision and seclusion in the wild, during which time they would be taught survival tactics, as well as tribal laws and customs. Pubescent girls would undergo *bojale* in the village, through which they received formal instruction preparing them for the assumption of domestic and agricultural chores, as well as appropriate sexual behavior upon marriage.

Marriage in traditional pre-colonial Tswana groups was a lengthy multistage affair arranged through families, rather than by individuals. Individuals typically married soon after undergoing initiation rites. Marriage negotiations were initiated by a group comprised of the groom's 'key' male relatives: his paternal uncles and male representatives from his mother's family. These representatives of the groom's family initiated the process by meeting with representatives from the prospective bride's kinship group. After a period of time, the groom's family would offer a formal betrothal. The formal betrothal (*patlo*) included the provision of gifts to the woman's family, such as a cow, and a blanket for the paternal aunt of the woman (Schapera 1966).

The effects of socioeconomic changes and cultural diffusion are evident in present-day Botswana popular culture.

## 2. Religious, Ethnic, and Gender Factors Affecting Sexuality

### A. Source and Character of Religious Values

According to *The World Factbook 2002* (CIA 2002) about 85% of the people of Botswana hold to indigenous religions and only 15% are affiliated with Christian denominations. However, in our view, the predominant religious beliefs in Botswana can best be described as "modified Christian." For the larger part of the 20th century, the religious institutions that were given legitimacy in Botswana were those from Western countries. These included: the Roman Catholic Church, the Anglican Church, the London Missionary Society, the Dutch Reformed Church, and others.

While traditional indigenous religious rites, such as ancestor rituals, were largely outlawed during the colonial era, many of these indigenous beliefs have been integrated with Christian doctrine in the new "spiritual" churches. Many of the "new" churches follow a Christian dogma that integrates aspects of traditional cultural practices—some of which have been outlawed. One example is the practice of polygamy, which was outlawed before independence. Polygamy is practiced under customary traditions among the Mazezuru; however, it is practiced "informally" within the context of some religious movements.

### B. Source and Character of Ethnic Values

Botswana is a country that is characterized by ethno-cultural heterogeneity. The nation is essentially composed of a number of ethnic groups, each of which has their own languages—some of which are variations of dialects. These ethnic groups have their own peculiar customs and beliefs.

The ethnic groups can generally be divided into two main categories: Setswana-speaking and non-Setswana-speaking groups. The main Setswana-speaking groups include the Bakwena, Bangwaketse, Bangwato, Bakgatla, Barolong, Bamalete, Batawana, and Batlokwa. The common feature among these groups is that they all share Setswana as a common language. They do, however, use different dialects of Setswana. The non-Setswana-speaking groups include the Basarwa (San or Bushmen), Bakalanga, Baherero, Bayei, Bambukushu, Basubia, as well as people of European, Asian, and African origin.

It must be noted that Setswana is the official language. This is justified on the basis that most of the citizens of Botswana are Setswana-speaking groups. This integration of other ethnic groups has many implications for the interpretation of culture and tradition, and perhaps explains why there is a scarcity of information on sexuality within the context of cultural diversity.

## 3. Knowledge and Education about Sexuality

### A. Government Policies and Programs

Botswana has no policy on sex education. Issues of sexuality are highlighted in the National Population Policy, and are discussed under Reproductive Health. The school curricula offer adolescent and sexual reproductive health through Guidance and Counseling. Other school subjects, such as science, also subscribe to the idea of Sexual and Reproductive Health. This is reflected by the topics that are integrated into the school curricula: personal guidance, social guidance, sexuality and HIV/AIDS, family life education, teenage pregnancy and HIV/AIDS, sexually transmissible infections and HIV/AIDS, as well as HIV/AIDS care and support. Topics are more comprehensive and detailed for secondary-school level than they are for primary-school level.

### B. Informal Sources of Sexual Knowledge

There exists among the Tswana the tradition of reticence on sexual matters between parents and young people. Young people are more comfortable discussing sexuality with their friends and other members of the extended family than they are with their parents. Studies done in the country show that parents are uncomfortable talking about sexuality with their children, but for others, it may be just lack of access to sexual health information and services.

It is also evident that sexual norms have changed over time in Botswana, and parents feel they can no longer exercise control over their children as compared to the past, where relationships between young people were governed by strong societal norms that protected them. These norms also encouraged their respect for elders. However, in spite of little contribution by parents as a source of sex education, there seems to be a considerable amount of information about AIDS and increasing condom use among the youths. The sexual attitudes of youth are positive about condom use, and they are more likely to be engaged in safer sexual practices now than in the 1990s, even though their sexual behaviors are still risky.

## 4. Autoerotic Behaviors and Patterns

Most people in Botswana do not feel very comfortable talking about their own sexuality, and autoeroticism is no exception. However, negative attitudes towards such behavior appear prevalent in Botswana. As one sex education magazine put it, "masturbation has always been associated with trashy magazines and males especially 'bo-sacmen.' Society has come to define it in an extremely narrow minded manner" (University of Botswana 2001, 10).

## 5. Interpersonal Heterosexual Behaviors

### A. Adolescents

*Puberty Rituals and Premarital Sexual Relationships*

Anthropologist Isaac Schapera (1970) documented the customs and practices of Tswana groups in Botswana and South Africa during the early part of the 20th century.

Tswana groups had gender-specific rites of passage that served to prepare young persons for adulthood and to control premarital fertility. Young adolescent males would undergo *bogwera*, which included circumcision and seclusion, during which time they would be taught survival tactics as well as tribal laws and customs. Pubescent girls would undergo *bojale* in the village, through which they received formal instruction that prepared them for the assumption of domestic and agricultural chores, as well as what was deemed as appropriate sexual behavior upon marriage. Current indications are that these rites of passage are no longer being practiced among different ethnic groups. These processes are now mostly left to individual parents and educational institutions.

Over the years, much debate (within civil society and in certain government sectors) has focused on adolescent sexual activities. One of the key concerns has been the relatively high rate of teenage pregnancy in Botswana. Botswana Health Surveys consistently indicate that the average age at first birth for women in Botswana is 18 years. Data from the United Nations Development Programme rates teenage pregnancy at 19%. Teenage pregnancies are cited as a problem because they contribute to girls dropping out of school. Studies conducted on sexual behavior among adolescents point to the high rates at which young persons are engaging in sexual activities. While most of the sexual relationships are between young persons in the same age cohorts, indications are that many young women are engaging in sexual relationships with older men, who are often referred to as "sugar daddies" for financial reasons.

The discussion of teenage sexual relationships has been largely limited to 'problem' areas, such as teenage pregnancy and the spread of HIV/AIDS. This is partly because of the ambivalence in larger society about being seen to 'legitimate' premarital sexual relations. The HIV/AIDS prevalence rates point to the fact that up to 15% of all HIV-infected persons are in the age cohort 15 to 19 years. As a result, more attention is turning to understanding the challenges faced by young people, both females and males, in a rapidly changing environment. Within that context, the National AIDS Coordinating Agency (NACA) and the government AIDS/STD Unit are working with various nongovernmental organizations to assess youth sexuality, as well as developing appropriate measures to raise awareness and empower young people to negotiate safe sex or abstain.

### C. Adults

*Premarital Relations, Courtship, and Dating*

See Section 1C, Basic Sexological Premises, General Concepts and Constructs of Sexuality, Love, Marriage, and Family.

*Sexual Behavior and Relationships of Single Adults*

When Botswana attained her independence from Britain in 1966, more than 80% of the population resided in the rural areas, depending on family-based subsistence agriculture for survival. In some instances, family incomes were supplemented with remittances from migrant workers in South Africa. Statistics from the 1991 census indicate that 45% of the population of Botswana currently resides in towns or 'urban villages.' The urban villages are primarily those in which the majority of the population does not rely on agriculture as their main source of livelihood. The rate of rural-urban migration is high, with both women and men leaving the rural areas in search of a 'better life.' These changes have had profound impact on individuals as well as family forms in Botswana. While gaining their independence from parents and extended family influences on the one hand, the lives of young adults in Botswana are embedded in a juxtaposition of traditional culture and the trappings of modernity.

Sexual behavior and relationships of single adults should be seen within the context of rapid socioeconomic change, gender identities, and unequal power relations between women and men. Men are traditionally expected to initiate and control sexual activity. This places women in a subordinate position with regard to the negotiation of safe sex, particularly with regard to the use of condoms.

*Marriage and Family: Structures and Patterns*

Table 1 presents data on marital status by sex for the three census periods 1971, 1981, and 1991. The figures on marital status reveal a significant decline in the proportion married (by over 14%) between 1971 and 1991. While the mean age at marriage for men used to be significantly higher than that for women, the gap has been closing steadily over the years. There are significant gender differences in the categories separated/divorced and widowed, with more than 50% of the female population over 65 years being widowed compared to only 10% of men. This gender difference can be attributed to the tendency for men to remarry, or establish new co-residential consensual relationships following the deaths of their spouses, while women remain single.

A study conducted by the Women and Law in Southern Africa Research Trust (WLSA) in 1996 reflected a range of family forms that reflect the rapidly changing nature of social relations. While the conventional, male-headed family-form based on marriage remains common, there is evidence that a large proportion of families consist of mother-child dyads, as well as cohabitants, both forms of which are on the increase. The study observed that while the interests of the collective remained paramount, individuals who are part of the societal collective articulate their interests and needs through a constant negotiation of cultural practices and individual autonomy. While families vary in form and content, the pursuit of material and emotional support continue to be of paramount importance in determining family membership.

## 6. Homoerotic, Homosexual, and Bisexual Behaviors

Homosexuality is a taboo subject in Botswana, and this is generally reflected in the attitudes of the officials and the society at large. People very rarely come out publicly to declare that they are homosexuals. The homosexual community as a whole is rejected, victimized, and sometimes blackmailed. This is because of societal myths, and because homosexuality is a forbidden subject in Batswana culture. Homosexuals face stigmatization and prejudice from family members, friends, and society in general. Indeed, same-sex activity between males and females is illegal in Botswana. The Botswana Penal Code makes those found guilty of 'carnal knowledge of any person against the order of nature'; 'carnal knowledge of an animal'; or 'permits a male person to have carnal knowledge of him or her against the order of nature,' is liable to imprisonment for a term not exceeding seven years (Republic of Botswana 1986).

Thus, the social status of homosexual, lesbian, and bisexual couples is legally illicit and there are no legal provisions providing for equality with heterosexual couples. The Lesbians, Gays and Bisexuals of Botswana (LEGABIBO) Charter was drafted in response to those amendments to the Botswana Penal Code, which came into effect on April 30, 1998, and extended the seven-year maximum penalty for men caught engaging in same-sex sexual relations to women as well. The Charter emerged at a workshop on Lesbian and Gay Rights on May 2-3, 1998, hosted by Ditshwanelo–The Botswana Centre for Human Rights. The government has so far refused to register LEGABIBO as an nongovernmental organization. Because homosexuality itself is illegal in Botswana, LEGABIBO is in an awkward position. A spokesman from the organization claimed that "the government has stated that it will refuse to register our organization because to do so would be tantamount to registering an organization of criminals. Thus we can't raise funds to do our work" (*Sunday Independent* [Johannesburg], September 26, 1999). Homosexuals have no social or legal protection available for these experiencing prejudice or discrimination, and LEGABIBO has urged its constituency to choose very carefully those to whom they tell about their sexuality.

Prosecutions for homosexual activity are, however, rare. The last known case was the high-profile example in 2001 where a Botswana resident, who was accused of engaging in sexual relations with another man, filed an application in the country's High Court challenging the state's "unnatural sexual liaisons" laws. The fact remains though that homosexual liaisons are conducted furtively and there is no "out" community of any note.

In fact, the depth of opposition to homosexual behavior in Botswana runs deep. For instance, in 1999, the Botswana Christian Council called for a relaxation of social and legal prohibitions against homosexuality and organized a seminar at the University of Botswana. However, the overwhelmingly youthful student audience rejected such calls out of hand, with one youth leader quoted as saying the majority of Botswana's people are "traumatized by homosexuality" and "other ideas from overseas and (European and American) donors." It is very common for homosexuality to be dismissed as a "Western" disease and "unAfrican," even though there are numerous indigenous societies in Africa where same-sex relations are common.

## 7. Gender Diversity and Transgender Issues

The status of transvestites, transgenderists, and transsexuals in Botswana is not a topic of discussion in Botswana, simply because such behavior would be seen as being extremely strange and unusual. There are reports, however, that a handful of transvestites (less than ten) meet occasionally in a bar in central Gaborone. With regard to transgenderists or transsexuals in Botswana, there is no information on such people, and it is so far unheard of.

**Table 1**

**Percentage of Population by Marital Status and Gender of Persons Aged 15 and Older in 1971, 1981, and 1991**

| Marital Status (%) | 1971 | | 1981 | | 1991 | |
| --- | --- | --- | --- | --- | --- | --- |
| | Male | Female | Male | Female | Male | Female |
| Never Married | 44 | 37 | 51.7 | 44.5 | 54.8 | 49.5 |
| Married | 47.1 | 42.9 | 44.4 | 41.5 | 29 | 27.2 |
| Cohabiting | n/a | n/a | n/a | n/a | 12.2 | 12 |
| Separated/Divorced | 5 | 6.6 | 2.1 | 3.3 | 1.7 | 2 |
| Widowed | 2.1 | 11.9 | 1.8 | 11 | 1.5 | 8.5 |
| Mean Age at Marriage | 29.4 | 24 | 30.8 | 26 | 30.8 | 28 |

(*Source*: Mukamaambo 1995, 58)
n/a: not covered by the census

## 8. Significant Unconventional Sexual Behaviors

### A. Coercive Sexual Behaviors

*Child Sexual Abuse, Incest, and Pedophilia*

Child sexual abuse in Botswana occurs against the background of age and gender-based hierarchies that subordinate the status of children, particularly girl-children to adult authority. Much of the child sexual abuse takes place within homes and is perpetrated by male family members.

*Sexual Harassment*

The Botswana legal system is silent on the issue of sexual harassment. The University of Botswana is one of the few organizations that have a policy on sexual harassment. The policy defines sexual harassment as: any unwanted, unsolicited, and/or repeated sexually discriminatory remarks made which are offensive and objectionable to the recipient, or which cause the recipient discomfort and humiliation, or which the recipient believes interfere with the performance of his or her job or study, undermine job security or prospects, or create a threatening or intimidating work or study environment. Sexual harassment continues to be shrouded in secrecy in Botswana, and the absence of legislation contributes to the reluctance of victims to report it.

*Rape*

Police statistics in Botswana point to a recent increase in the frequency of rape. In a study conducted among 25 police stations comparing, among other things, the number of reported cases of rape and defilement of girls under 16 years between the years of 1995 and 1998 rose by 18.3% between 1996 and 1998, while reported cases of defilement rose by an alarming 65%. During those years, almost 58% of the victims were in the age category 16 to 30 years; those under 16 years constituted 27%. The majority of the suspects/perpetrators were between the age of 18 and 32 years. The Police Study on Rape, as well as the Study on Violence on Women, indicated that more than two-thirds of all rapes are committed by men known to their victims.

*"Dry Sex" or "Wet Sex"*

[*Comment 2003*: As noted in Section 8D, Significant Unconventional Sexual Behaviors, Female Genital Mutilation and Other Harmful Practices, of the Nigerian chapter, sexual relations in subequatorial Africa are male-dominated, with the male initiating coitus and dictating its style and pace. Female response and satisfaction are not considered important. Coitus usually takes place with no foreplay. The male-above position is standard, and marital coitus is for procreation, not for pleasure. Women in many African cultures do not even know what female orgasm is, and may have never experienced it. In describing mating customs in the chapter on Ghana, Augustine Ankoma reports that penile-vaginal penetrative sex with little foreplay is the normal sexual style. Although among the well-educated youth some forms of foreplay are gaining a foothold, fellatio and cunnilingus are abhorrent. Genital manipulation is hardly accepted, and, traditionally, women feel shy to touch the penis, and most men are not interested in having their genitals manipulated.

[These male-oriented cultural values underlie what is appropriately termed "dry sex," a common practice throughout sub-Saharan Africa. The "dry sex" mating behavior fits comfortably with the male distaste for vaginal secretions and foreplay, and disinterest in female sexual arousal and orgasm. In this setting, males quickly reach orgasm and satisfaction. Women are left with painful intercourse, no arousal, and no orgasm.

[In many African cultures, women prepare themselves to pleasure their husbands with a dry vagina by mixing the powdered stem and leaf of the Mugugudhu tree with water, wrapped in a bit of nylon stocking and inserted in vagina for 10 to 15 minutes before intercourse. Other women use Mutendo wegudo, soil mixed with baboon urine, which they obtain from traditional healers. Still others use detergents, salt, cotton, or shredded newspaper. These swell the vaginal tissue, make it hot, and dry it out. The women admit that sexual intercourse is "very painful, but our African husbands enjoy sex with a dry vagina" (Schoofs 2000).

[The inevitable results of "dry sex" include increased friction, vaginal lacerations, suppression of the vagina's natural bacteria, and torn condoms (when these are used). All these consequences increase a woman's risk of STD and HIV infections. Fortunately, the tradition of "dry sex" is waning among the educated urban young, but any change in this traditional mating behavior is also resisted because of rejection of Western gender roles (Stellwaggon 2001).

["Dry sex" is a well-established and more-or-less widespread practice in various subequatorial African cultures. It is very common in Southern Africa, particularly in Zimbabwe, Zambia, Malawi, some parts of Nigeria, some parts of Uganda, Southern Sudan, and even in Kenya and Botswana. The only difference is in what these women use for drying up their vaginas.

[In the northwest part of Tanzania and neighboring regions, "wet sex" is widely known and practiced. "Wet sex" consists of foreplay where there is intense stimulation by the male partner on the woman's labia and clitoral regions. This stimulation results in copious production of secretions (thought to come from Bartholin's glands). People talk about it openly, sometimes mixed with a sense of humor and intertribe jokes. Some researchers have blamed this practice for the high incidence and prevalence of HIV and STDs. The implications of this kind of information for action plans (resource inputs and sociocultural issues) are enormous. Now that these behaviors have been brought into public attention, a well-thought-out survey that is representative of different segments of the populations becomes essential for an effective public health policy (Tanzania, personal communication 2003). In March 2003, when the editor of this encyclopedia inquired whether "dry sex" was observed in Botswana, Dr. Ian Taylor replied: "'Dry sex' is common in Botswana as well and leads to vaginal tears and lesions which help spread HIV/AIDS, it is true." (*End of comment by B. Opiyo-Omolo*)]

### B. Prostitution

While prostitution is outlawed by the Penal Code, it is widely practiced in Botswana, predominantly by women. The different types of prostitution include 'streetwalkers' and individuals who frequent establishments where alcohol is sold. In addition, there are an increasing number of prostitutes who focus specifically on long-distance drivers. While little is known about the incidence of child prostitution, girls and young women may engage in sex for financial and material gains from older men.

## 9. Contraception, Abortion, and Population Planning

Botswana has made remarkable progress in the provision and delivery of health facilities and services, but in spite of these improvements, aspects of reproductive health relating to abortion, teenage pregnancies, and HIV/AIDS remain issues of concern. The increase in HIV/AIDS and sexually transmitted diseases has emphasized the demands for distribution of condoms in the country.

## A. Contraception

The current use of contraception in Botswana has been reported by 44% of women aged 15 to 49 years (Central Statistics Office 2001). Majelantle and Letamo (1999) further show that 61% of women attending antenatal clinics in the country have used contraceptive methods.

The most popular method used by women is the pill, followed by condom, injection, intrauterine device, and female sterilization. Condom use is, however, low among women aged 35 years and above, despite its widespread distribution as a strategy to curb the spread of HIV/AIDS. Traditional practices of breastfeeding and postpartum abstinence continue to be important among rural women and are less favorable among urban women.

Teenagers are far less likely to use contraception than older women; however, virtually all of the sexually active youths aged 15 to 24 years had used a condom at least once. There is also high awareness of condoms, high condom use, and consistency, as well as delayed onset of sexual activity among the youth. Condom knowledge and its role in STD/AIDS prevention have been reported at 100% among urban adolescents (10 to 19 years). Attitudes towards condom use are also positive among the young people in Botswana, but the problem is still with embarrassment and the purchasing of condoms.

Women's education level has been found to correspond positively with contraceptive prevalence, and male partners still play a role in the decision of a woman to use contraceptives.

## B. Teenage (Unmarried) Pregnancies

There is a high incidence of teenage pregnancy in Botswana, and this is indicative of unprotected sex and, therefore, has serious implications for the spread of HIV infection as well as other STDs. The rate of teenage pregnancy is one in every three women aged 15 to 49 who attend antenatal clinics. The majority of these teenage women are single and their pregnancies take place outside marriage.

Teenage childbearing also poses social, economic, and reproductive health risks to the young women. These include social and economic problems, such as dropping out of school, rejection by their families and community, and unemployment, and health risks, such as low birth weight, unsafe abortions, incidence of still births, and implications for the spread of STDs, specifically HIV.

The mean age at first sexual intercourse for teenagers is 17.5 years and the mean age at first birth is 18.6 years.

## C. Abortion

There is very little information available in Botswana on abortion. This could be because of the fact that abortion is treated as a sensitive topic and is highly stigmatized in Tswana society.

Abortion is illegal in Botswana. It is only permitted within the first 16 weeks of pregnancy under the following conditions: when the pregnancy is a result of rape, defilement, or incest; when the pregnancy poses a physical or mental health risk to the pregnant woman, and, finally, when the unborn child would suffer from or later develop serious physical or mental abnormalities or disease. These conditions are observed only when a medical doctor from a government or registered private hospital or clinic approved by the Director of Health Services confirms in writing that the continuation of the pregnancy would risk the life of either the mother or child.

Even though abortion is illegal, it is apparent that a substantial number of women in Botswana resort to illegally induced abortion (Majelantle & Letamo 1999). These induced abortions are done under unhygienic conditions and are performed by untrained persons, who use dangerous instruments and abortifacients.

With abortion being illegal, educated and wealthy women are reported to obtain their abortion services from South Africa, because in Botswana, induced abortions are only provided for certain medical conditions. Majelantle and Letamo (1999) show that women aged 35 years and above have had multiple abortions.

In its attempts to reduce maternal mortality, the Government of Botswana is aiming to reduce the mortality rate, estimated between 200 and 300 deaths per 100,000 live births in 1991, by at least 50% in 2011. Government hospitals and clinics also provide post-abortion counseling.

## D. Population Control Efforts

Botswana has one of the highest population-growth rates in Africa, at 3.5% per year between 1981 and 1991. If, however, the population continues to grow at this rate, it will make it difficult for the economy to support gains achieved over a long period of time. Thus, the challenge is is to reduce the growth rate of the population and increase the growth rate of the economy.

The young age structure of the population will persist for several years into the future as young women enter the reproductive age. The rapid population growth also places a burden on national and international efforts aimed at reducing poverty and improving the well-being of the population.

Efforts made to control the population growth include the provision of reproductive health and family planning services, counseling, and promoting modern methods of contraception, especially the condom, at all government hospitals and clinics.

The main emphasis is on human development and welfare dimensions in order to enhance the quality of population and improve the living standards, and as a result, the National Population Policy contains explicit and comprehensive strategies to influence population trends in a manner conducive to the attainment of sustainable human development. The Ministry of Finance and Development Planning is responsible for ensuring the integration of population factors in national plans and strategies for sustainable development at all levels.

## 10. Sexually Transmitted Diseases and HIV/AIDS

### A. Sexually Transmitted Diseases

Sexually transmitted diseases found in Botswana include genital warts, herpes simplex type 2, gonorrhea, and syphilis. These STDs may be the major determinants of the HIV epidemic in Botswana, as a relationship has been established between STDs and HIV transmission in the country. STDs present the third most common cause of attendance at public health facilities (NACA 2002, 30).

According to the National AIDS Coordinating Agency (2002), the prevalence of STDs in the country appears to be declining among women using family planning methods for the years 1993, 1997, and 2002. This pattern is the same for syphilis, gonorrhea, and *Trichomonas vaginalis*, *but* it is accelerating for *Chlamydia trachomatis* and herpes simplex type 2. The incidence of STDs among adolescents is higher as compared to women aged 35 and above. This is attributed to the low attendance of teenagers at antenatal clinics, and has worsened with the spread of the HIV/AIDS epidemic. Since STDs facilitate the transmission of HIV, and HIV prolongs the duration of symptoms, the prevention and management of STDs and HIV/AIDS has been made the highest priority in the National Sexual

Reproductive Health Programme. In addition to the prevention strategies in Botswana, data on STDs are routinely collected through the epidemiological reporting system.

However, there is still little data in the country on STD surveillance, making it difficult to give an exact picture of the magnitude of STDs in Botswana. Certain factors have been identified to influence this inability to accurately estimate STDs in the country, and include the asymptomatic nature of STDs among women, and the fact that some people with symptomatic STDs do not seek treatment from public health facilities or seek treatment at all.

Control of STDS in Botswana is considered as one of the main prevention strategies for HIV transmission, and according to the Ministry of Health (1998), STD control in Botswana encompasses a comprehensive program based on effective case management of symptomatic STDs in healthcare facilities. This strategy calls for sound diagnosis, effective antibiotic treatment, preventive efforts that entail patient education on risk reduction, condom use, and the referral of sexual partners.

## B. HIV/AIDS

Botswana's 1.7 million population has the highest HIV/AIDS infection rate in the world, and HIV/AIDS affects both urban and rural areas with the same intensity. In the early stages of the epidemic, prevalence was higher in urban areas than rural, but the clear distinction does not exist anymore.

AIDS in Botswana is spreading mainly by the heterosexual route (Macdonald 1996, 1325), and several factors may have contributed to the rapid spread of HIV/AIDS in the country, among these are social/sexual factors:

- Relative gender inequality: the position of women in the society, particularly their lack of power in negotiating sexual relationships.
- High levels of STDs: The presence of STDs has been shown to facilitate transmission and acquiring of HIV infection.
- Social migration patterns: Botswana has one of the most mobile populations in the world, and for years, Batswana have had to be mobile and live regularly in two to four different abodes, on a cattle post, in farmlands, a village, and towns). Circulating often between these areas for extended periods, especially during long weekends, has proved to be one of the driving forces of the epidemic in Botswana.
- Disintegration of traditional family patterns: Most of the pregnant women in Botswana are single, and sentinel surveys done in the country show a high HIV prevalence among single mothers who attend antenatal clinics as compared to married mothers. This is also an indication that many Batswana engage in short-term relationships and have other sexual partners subsequently.
- Lack of recreation facilities in the country and lenient law enforcement on the sale of alcohol to minors also make it easy for the youth to engage in risky sexual behaviors.

Given the current infection rates, the infant-mortality rate is expected to increase from 57 to 60 per 1,000 live births by the year 2005 (National AIDS Coordinating Agency 2002, ii). The population of orphans is predicted to increase from 139,000 to 214,000 by the year 2010. As the figures indicate, many children have been orphaned, and before the introduction of the prevention of mother-to-child HIV-transmission program, many babies were born infected with the HIV virus. Other age groups are not spared. It is estimated that in 2002, about 258,000 persons aged 15 to 49 years

were infected with HIV. However, the HIV prevalence in age groups 15 to 19 and 20 to 24 years has remained fairly stable in the last three years, indicating that the rate of new infections is not increasing as it was in the last ten years. This pattern could be attributed to high condom use, a relatively high awareness level, reduced numbers of sexual partners, declining STD incidence, and delayed onset of sexual activity among the youth (Ministry of Health 2001, 3; NACA 2002, 44).

A sentinel survey done in 2002 showed the HIV infection rate to be nine times higher in females aged 15 to 19 years than in males. Higher rates in females in young age groups are attributed to behavioral data. It has been shown that condom use is higher among males than females; girls engage in sexual relationships earlier than boys. Girls also engage in sexual relationships with older men for economic reasons. The prevalence of HIV in pregnant women aged 15 to 49 and women aged 15 to 19 years is outlined in Table 2 for the years indicated.

With the first tentative HIV/AIDS case reported in 1985, there is still no preventive vaccine or cure against HIV. However, the government of Botswana has various initiatives to address the HIV/AIDS epidemic. This is evidenced by the huge political commitment, the increase in resource mobilization and utilization, and the multisectoral collaboration and cooperation at all levels. The president of Botswana, H. E. Festus Mogae, has recognized HIV/AIDS as "the greatest challenge Botswana has faced" and has warned his nation that HIV/AIDS "threatens the country with annihilation." The president even chairs the National AIDS Council, the government structure that coordinates all HIV/AIDS-related activities in the country.

The Government of Botswana pays for at least 80% of all HIV/AIDS activities in the country. Other achievements made in the combat against HIV/AIDS in Botswana include the provision of highly active antiretroviral therapy (HAART) to the public at no cost, vaccine development, the Voluntary Counselling and Testing Programmes, the Community Home Based Care, the orphan and vulnerable children program, as well as the nationwide Prevention of Mother to Child Transmission (PMTCT) program to all public health facilities. Prevention and treatment of opportunistic infections is also provided at all public health facilities in the country.

Despite the achievements, there is still no provision made in terms of the distribution of condoms or safer sex education to the homosexual community. Consensual same-sex sexual intercourse remains illegal in Botswana. [*Comment 2003*: The practice of "dry sex," as noted earlier, is also a factor in HIV transmission. (*End of comment by R. T. Francoeur*)]

[*Update 2002*: UNAIDS Epidemiological Assessment: HIV sentinel surveillance among antenatal clinic attendees began in Botswana in 1990. In 2001, median HIV prevalence among antenatal clinic attendees tested in Botswana

### Table 2

### Percentage Distribution of HIV Prevalence among Women by Age and Year

| Year | 15-19 years | 15-49 years |
|------|-------------|-------------|
| 1992 | 16.4 | 18.1 |
| 1998 | 28.6 | 35.7 |
| 2000 | — | 38.5 |
| 2001 | 24.1 | 36.2 |
| 2002 | — | 35.4 |

(*Source*: The National AIDS Coordinating Agency, 2002, 20)

in 22 health districts (190 sites) was 36.3% with a range of 25.8 to 55.8%; 12 districts had rates between 30% and 40% and 7 districts had rates above 40%. HIV prevalence among antenatal clinic attendees in Botswana increased rapidly from 18.1% in 1992 to 32.4% in 1995, 38.5% in 2000, and 36.3% in 2001.

[Major urban areas in Botswana include Gabarone, Francistown, and Selebi-Phikwe. In Gabarone, HIV prevalence increased from 14.9% in 1992 to 39.1% in 2001, while in Francistown, the increase was from 23.7% in 1992 to 44.9% in 2001. In Selebi-Phikwe, HIV prevalence doubled from 27% in 1994 to 55.6% in 2001. Sites outside the major urban areas are also experiencing increasing HIV infection trends. In 2001, median HIV prevalence in areas outside the major urban areas was 38.6%, with rates ranging from 26.4% to 50.9%. The 15-to-19 and 20-to-24 age groups exhibit high and increasing HIV infection trends. HIV prevalence among the 15-to-19 year olds at all sites increased from 16.4% in 1992 to 24.1% in 2001. Among the 20-to-24 year olds, the increase was from 20.5% in 1992 to 39.5% in 2001. Peak HIV prevalence rates were observed among the 25-to-29-year-old antenatal clinic attendees; rates in this age group were 50.4% and 48.4% in 2000 and 2001, respectively.

[There is no information available on HIV prevalence among sex workers in Botswana. HIV prevalence among STD patients shows an upward trend. In Gabarone, HIV prevalence among male STD clinic attendees increased from 22% in 1992 to 44.1% in 1996, and then to 48.2% in 2000. Similarly in Francistown, HIV prevalence among male STD clinic patients increased from 29.7% in 1994 to 60% in 1997 and has remained around that figure since then. Outside Gaborone and Francistown, HIV prevalence among male STD clinic patients tested in six sites increased from no evidence of HIV infection in 1985 to 1987 to a median of 53% in 1998; in 1999, HIV prevalence among male STD clinic patients tested at these sites ranged from 44.2% to 62%.

[The estimated number of adults and children living with HIV/AIDS on January 1, 2002, were:

| | | |
|---|---|---|
| Adults ages 15-49: | 300,000 | (rate: 38.8%) |
| Women ages 15-49: | 170,000 | |
| Children ages 0-15: | 28,000 | |

[An estimated 26,000 adults and children died of AIDS during 2001.

[At the end of 2001, an estimated 69,000 Batswana children under age 15 were living without one or both parents who had died of AIDS. (*End of update by the Editors*)]

## 11. Sexual Dysfunctions, Counseling, and Therapies

There is no information or data available.

## 12. Sex Research and Advanced Professional Education

The Directorate of Research and Development at the University of Botswana is the first point of contact for all stakeholders interested in conducting or sponsoring research and development in Botswana. This office works with all University of Botswana faculties, departments, schools, centers, associated institutes, affiliated institutes, and together with the Government of Botswana and nongovernmental organizations (NGOs) to facilitate and coordinate quality research in the country. This office also advises the Office of the President on applications made by researchers. Research on sexual and reproductive health matters is done through the Ministry of Health, Family Health Division. The National AIDS Coordinating Agency is responsible for coordinating all research on HIV/AIDS in Botswana.

There are, however, no programs or NGOs which specifically deal with issues of human sexuality; instead, issues of human sexuality are often incorporated into mandates of the different NGOs. There is also no association for sexologists or journals on sexuality in Botswana.

Information on sexual and reproductive health can be obtained from the Ministry of Health, Family Health Division. The University of Botswana, Department of Nursing Education offers courses, some at the undergraduate and postgraduate levels.

## 13. Significant Ethnic Minorities

### Sexual Attitudes and Behaviors among the Basarwa/San

The Basarwa (or San) are hunters and gatherers who live in Southern Africa below the Congo–Zambezi watershed. The Republic of Botswana is home to over half (approximately 42,000) of all the San in the region. This indigenous group is distinct culturally, and their way of life is different, from other ethnic groups in Botswana. Basarwa are mostly found in the remote areas, and the population has high illiteracy levels. The Basarwa's way of life has adapted over the generations as they lived in contact with other ethnic groups; as a result, their way of life today can take the form of a sedentary villager, part- or full-time unskilled laborer, and squatters in freehold farms as herders and hunters. All these socioeconomic and cultural changes have had an impact on their sexual lifestyles. However, some of their cultural practices still hold to this day.

Basarwa culture is permissive to sexual activity at very early ages, often prior to puberty. This is because of the relative openness and acceptance of adult sexuality. Prepuberty marriages also exist. Traditional initiation customs encourage safer sex practices among the youths, and prohibit sexual intercourse outside marriage. Thus, in the Basarwa tradition, one sex partner is preferred. However, with modernization and urbanization, the traditional controls over sexuality have lapsed and the youth are now having multiple sexual partners.

Marriage relations among the Basarwa have no legal procedures, apart from gaining the mutual agreement of the spouses involved and their respective families (Guenther 1986). The majority of the marriages are monogamous, but this trait is slowly eroding as the Basarwa now live and mix with other ethnic tribes in Botswana. Marriages are within the same age group, as compared with other tribes in the country where intergenerational relationships and marriages are permissible.

Early marriages are, however, often sought for young people if they are maturing quickly to prevent the possibility of premarital pregnancies, and this contributes to nearly all children knowing their parents. Failure to marry is rare among the Basarwa, and this is in contrast to other tribes in Botswana where a lot of families are female-headed.

The use of modern contraceptives among the Basarwa is very low. This is because they live in rural areas, and their access to health facilities and services are limited in terms of distance, affordability, and acceptability. Attitudes towards condom use are positive among school-going adolescents, even though their parents do not favor modern contraceptives. Most Basarwa adults rely on traditional medicine, and this is because it is part of their culture and their primary accessible choice.

Most Basarwa children in the school-going-age group live in a boarding school, away from their parents for extended periods of time, and they miss out on their parental guidance, chaperoning on matters of sexuality, as well as on traditional education and initiation that is conducted at puberty.

Incidence of HIV/AIDS is still quite low among the Basarwa, between 3 and 6% as compared with national averages of 20 to 35% (Lee & Susser 2002). This incidence is, however, enviable in this era, because they are found in the heart of the world region worst hit by the epidemic. Basarwa girls and women now engage in materially motivated sexual relationships with "rich" men from other ethnic groups. This, however, makes them vulnerable to reproductive health problems related to sexual debut and teenage childbearing.

## References and Suggested Readings

Botswana Police Service. 1999. *Report of a study on rape in Botswana*. Gaborne: Government Printer.

Central Statistics Office. 2001. *Botswana multiple indicator survey–2000*. Gaborone, Botswana.

CIA. 2002 (January). *The world factbook 2002*. Washington, DC: Central Intelligence Agency. Available: http://www .cia.gov/cia/publications/factbook/index.html.

Guether, M. 1986. *The Nharo Bushmen of Botswana–Tradition and change*. Helmut Buske Verlag.

Lee, R. B., & I. Susser. 2002. *Quarterly*. Available: http:// www.cs.org/publications/CSQ/261/leesusser.htm.

Lesetedi, G. N., & N. L. Ngcongco. 1995 (May). A demographic and socio-economic profile of women and men in Botswana: A review of summary indicators of population composition and distribution, mortality, marriage, migration and economic activity. In: *1991 population and housing census dissemination seminar, 1-4* (pp. 51-61). Gaborone: Government Printer.

Majelantle, R., & G. Letamo. 1999.The reproductive health problems of teenage childbearing in Botswana. In: H. M. Yousif, ed., *Research paper no. 1.*

Ministry of Health, Botswana, & World Health Organisation. 1999 (September). Observational health facility survey for the evaluation of STD case management in primary health care facilities in Botswana.

Ministry of Health, Government of Botswana. 2001. The sexual behavior of young people.

Mukamaambo, E. 1995. Demographic and socio-economic situation in Botswana. In: Government of Botswana, *1991 population and housing census dissemination seminar, 1-4, May, 1995* (pp. 51-61). Gaborone: Government Printer.

National AIDS Coordinating Agency (NACA), Botswana. 2002. Second generation HIV/AIDS surveillance. *A Technical Report.*

Republic of Botswana. 1986. *Penal code*. Gaborone: Government Printer.

Schapera, I. 1970. *A handbook of Tswana laws and customs*. London: Frank Cass and Company.

Schoofs, M. 2000. AIDS: The agony of Africa. *The Village Voice* [New York, NY, USA] (A Pulitzer Prize-winning 8-part series). Available: http://www.villagevoice.com/specials/africa/.

Tanzania, 2003. Personal communications between Yusuf Hemed and the editor, R. T. Francoeur.

UNAIDS. 2002. *Epidemiological fact sheets by country*. Geneva, Switzerland: Joint United Nations Programme on HIV/ AIDS (UNAIDS/WHO). Available: http://www.unaids.org/ hivaidsinfo/statistics/fact_sheets/index_en.htm.

University of Botswana. 2001. *AIDucation brochure*. Gaborone: AIDS Information Booklet.

Women and Law in Southern Africa Trust. 1992. *Maintenance laws and practices in Botswana*. Gaborone: Printing and Publishing.

Women and Law in Southern Africa Trust. 1997. *Botswana families and women's rights in a changing environment*. Gaborone: Printing and Publishing.

Women's Affairs Department. 1999. *Report on the study on the socio-economic implications of violence against women in Botswana*. Gaborone: Government Printer.

# Brazil

## (*República Federativa do Brasil*)

Sérgio Luiz Gonçalves de Freitas, M.D.,* with
Elí Fernandes de Oliveira and Lourenço Stélio Rega, M.Th.
*Updates and comments by Raymond J. Noonan, Ph.D.,
and Dra. Sandra Almeida, and Luciane Raibin, M.S.*

## Contents

## *Demographics and a Brief Historical Perspective*

ROBERT T. FRANCOEUR

### A. Demographics

Brazil occupies the eastern half of South America; with 3.28 million square miles (8.5 million km²), Brazil is larger than mainland United States. Its neighbors include French Guiana, Surinam, Guyana, and Venezuela on the north, Columbia, Peru, Bolivia, Paraguay, and Argentina on the west, Uruguay in the south, and the Atlantic Ocean on the east. In the north, a heavily wooded Amazon basin and tropical rain forest covers half the country. All 15,814 miles (25,450 km) of the Amazon River are navigable. The northeast is semiarid scrubland, heavily settled, and poor. With more resources and a favorable climate, the south central region has almost half the county's population, and produces three quarters of the farm goods and four fifths of the industrial output. Most of the major cities are on the 4,600 miles (7,400 km) of tropical and subtropical coastlines.

In July 2002, Brazil had an estimated population of 176.03 million. Estimates for this country explicitly take into account the effects of excess mortality because of AIDS, which can result in lower life expectancies, higher infant mortality and death rates, lower population and growth rates, and changes in the distribution of population by age and sex than would otherwise be expected. (All data are from *The World Factbook 2002* (CIA 2002) unless otherwise stated.)

**Age Distribution and Sex Ratios**: *0-14 years*: 28% with 1.04 male(s) per female (sex ratio); *15-64 years*: 66.4% with

*Communications: Main author*: Sérgio Luiz Gonçalves de Freitas, M.D., Associação Brasileira de Sexologia, Rua Tamandaré 693-Conj 77, 01525-001 São Paulo–SP–Brasil. *Updates*: Raymond J. Noonan, Ph.D., Health and Physical Education Department, Fashion Institute of Technology of the State University of New York, 27th Street and 7th Avenue, New York, NY 10001 USA; 212-217-7460; rjnoonan@ SexQuest.com. Luciane Raibin, M.S., 315 South Avenue, Garwood, NJ 07027 USA; L.Raibin@hotmail.com.

(CIA 2002)

0.97 male(s) per female; *65 years and over*: 5.6% with 0.68 male(s) per female; *Total population sex ratio*: 0.97 male(s) to 1 female

**Life Expectancy at Birth**: *Total Population*: 63.55 years; *male*: 59.4 years; *female*: 67.91 years

**Urban/Rural Distribution**: 77% to 23%

**Ethnic Distribution**: Caucasian (including Portuguese, German, Italian, Spanish, and Polish): 55%; Mixed Caucasian and African: 38%; African: 6%; others, including Japanese, Arab, and Amerindian: 1%

**Religious Distribution**: Nominally Roman Catholic: 70%; Protestant: 5%; Muslim and other: 17%

**Birth Rate**: 18.08 births per 1,000 population

**Death Rate**: 9.32 per 1,000 population

**Infant Mortality Rate**: 35.87 deaths per 1,000 live births

**Net Migration Rate**: –0.03 migrant(s) per 1,000 population

**Total Fertility Rate**: 2.05 children born per woman

**Population Growth Rate**: 0.87%

**HIV/AIDS** (1999 est.): *Adult prevalence*: 0.57%; *Persons living with HIV/AIDS*: 540,000; *Deaths*: 18,000. (For additional details from www.UNAIDS.org, see end of Section 10B.)

**Literacy Rate** (*defined as those age 15 and over who can read and write*): 83.3% for both males and females

**Per Capita Gross Domestic Product** (*purchasing power parity*): $7,400 (2000 est.); *Inflation*: 7.7%; *Unemployment*: 6.4%; *Living below the poverty line*: 22%; socioeconomically, 80% of Brazil's population are classified as low income

### B. A Brief Historical Perspective

The first European to reach the land that is now Brazil is generally believed to have been the Portuguese navigator Pedro Álvares Cabral in 1500. At that time, the country was sparsely settled by various indigenous tribes, whose decimated descendants survive today mostly in the Amazon basin. In the following centuries, Portuguese colonists gradually pushed inland, bringing along with them a large number of African slaves. Slavery was not abolished until 1888.

In 1808, the King of Portugal moved the seat of his government to Brazil when threatened by Napoleon's army, and Brazil became a kingdom under Dom João VI. When

Dom João returned to Portugal, his son Pedro proclaimed the independence of Brazil in 1822 and he was acclaimed emperor. In 1889, when the second emperor, Dom Pedro II, was deposed, the United States of Brazil was proclaimed as a republic. The country was renamed the Federative Republic of Brazil in 1967.

A military junta controlled the government between 1930 and 1945. A democratic government prevailed from 1945 to 1964 when the institution of new economic policies aggravated inflation and triggered a military revolt. The next five presidents were military leaders. Strict censorship was imposed and political opposition suppressed amid charges of torture and other human rights violations. In the 1974 elections, when the official opposition party made significant gains, some relaxation in the censorship occurred.

Brazil's agricultural production soared between 1930 and the 1970s. In the same years, vast mineral resources and a huge labor force enabled Brazil to make major industrial advances. However, soaring inflation and an unbalanced, two-tiered society with a very wealthy few and a majority of people barely managing to survive, led to a severe economic recession. Brazil's foreign debt, one of the largest in the world, required restructuring in 1982. Announcement of a comprehensive environmental plan to develop the Amazon basin brought an international outcry from environmentalists deeply concerned about the growing destruction of the Amazon ecosystem that is so vital to the world environment.

## 1. Basic Sexological Premises

### [The New Civil Code: *Update 2001-2003*

RAYMOND J. NOONAN and SANDRA ALMEIDA

[On January 10, 2003, a new civil code with 2,046 articles took effect, which included significant changes affecting the private and family lives of Brazilians. In August 2001, after 26 years of debate, Brazil's Congress, the House of Deputies, voted to replace the 1916 Civil Code. It was signed into law in January 2002 by Brazil's then-President Cardoso, and now makes women and men equal under the law (Rohter 2001; Galanternick 2002). In fact, the law places equality in the Code itself with gender-neutral terminology, referring to "person" in its second article, rather than to *woman* or *man* generally; in the old code, it used to be just *man*. In the same article, it reaffirmed the rights of the unborn from conception, while specifying that legal personhood began with a live birth, although this was apparently not related to the debate on abortion, which remains illegal under the penal code. The Code also changed the age of majority, always the same for both women and men, from 21 to 18, which is now equal in both the civil and penal codes. The age of emancipation was changed from 18 to 16, and can be effected by either the mother or the father; before, only the father had that legal power.

[Among the provisions, the new code revised the concepts of marriage and family, and established equality between the sexes in a relationship. A marriage is any planned union where a man and woman share their life together as spouses, and religious marriages became legally equal to civil marriages. Now, the *sociedade conjugal* ("conjugal society" or as-married association) rests with the couple as a whole; before, it was the sole responsibility of the male, thus ending the father's unilateral legal power. The new understanding of marriage is a planned life communion, based on the equality of rights and obligations of the spouses. The direction of the conjugal society is exercised as a collaboration by the husband and wife, always in the interests of the couple and children. This is in contrast to the past, in which, under the influence of the Roman Catholic Church, the in-

terests of the family as a symbol beyond the core individuals were paramount. The family was reconceived as a group formed through a civil or religious ceremony, a stable relationship between a man and a woman (cohabitation), or a community directed by a man or a woman, i.e., a single-parent-headed household. With respect to proving the stability of a nonmarried relationship, it is no longer necessary to wait a minimum period of two years to demonstrate it; it is enough that the union be public, continuous, and enduring.

[Under the new code, several provisions further make partners in a marriage equal, changing marriage contracts and inheritance rights. Under the old code, separate, partial, or community property was declared at the inception of a marriage; now, it can be changed during its course, facilitating access to a property change. Also, the dowry given by the father of the bride to her future husband was eliminated (it is interesting to note that only in 1962 was a law passed that allowed a wife to work without the permission of her husband). The husband now has the option of using his wife's last name, which before was only available to the wife. In inheritance, the proportions of property received by parents, children, and the spouse have changed and are now shared equally; before, the children received the greater amount, and then the parents and spouse, in that order. Adopted and "illegitimate" children also gained a right to inheritance and share equally with the others, as well as children conceived through assisted reproduction.

[Divorce and separation practices changed with the following provisions in the new code: There is no longer a minimum of two years required being married before a divorce is allowed; now a couple may divorce after one year. (It is also interesting to note that divorce in Brazil was legalized only in 1978.) After separation, if an agreement is not reached, the courts will give custody of the children to the parent who has the better living conditions (taking into account the emotional and financial stability, and the level of education of the parents) and the ability to raise them. Now, also, the desires of the children are taken into account. Before, even if the woman had guardianship of the children, the father had final patrial authority; now, both have familial authority over major decisions related to the children. However, if a parent punishes the children too harshly, abandons the children, or practices acts against public morals and good conduct, he or she loses family authority, including guardianship, under the new code. A man is now also able to ask for alimony from his divorced spouse. Although adultery is still a reason to end a marriage, under the new code, a spouse who commits adultery can remarry without limitation; before, marrying the person with whom one had an adulterous affair was prohibited by law. The "end of love" is now a valid reason for separation, which was not allowed before (incompatibility was starting to be used by some judges, but it was not in the law).

[Some other changes might be considered curiosities by many of the world's standards. For example, the new code eliminates the annulment of a marriage by the husband if he finds out that his wife lost her virginity before marriage. It also eliminates the expressions "legitimate" and "illegitimate" from being specified on birth certificates, which used to be done, because the legal circumstance of a child's birth inside marriage versus outside marriage affected inheritance rights; if a child was not legal, the inheritance was less. Also, the state cannot require or establish rules for family planning, e.g., sterilization. Relatives by blood have also been redefined to consist of those persons only four levels away; before, six levels were included as blood relations. Still, despite these significant changes, the law is considered already outmoded in some subjects, because of the 26-year time lag from when it was written to when it was passed. For example, nothing is said of subsequent sex-related developments, such as transsexualism, bioethics, or assisted reproduction (except with respect to the presumption of paternity for purposes of inheritance, as noted above), although some more-recent efforts to include marriages between two gay individuals failed. The following sections thus serve as a backdrop to the ideals embodied in the new code (*O Globo* 2001; *Código Civil* 2002; *Folha de S. Paulo* 2003). (*End of update by R. J. Noonan and S. Almeida*)]

## A. Character of Gender Roles

Brazil being a typically Latin and machismo society, males enjoy a superior, almost demigod status. This is reinforced by the economic dependence of women. Only about 18% of the women are employed outside the home; the majority devote their time to caring for their house and children. Nevertheless, women do possess some privileges that protect them in the workplace. For example, they may retire five years earlier than men and maternal leave is available during illness of a child. A special pregnancy leave permits them to be away from work for 120 days after childbirth. However, all these apparent privileges significantly reduce the chances and competitiveness for women seeking to enter the workforce.

[*Editor's Note 1997*: In addition to the value of *machismo* mentioned above, Brazilian sexual attitudes and behaviors are strongly influenced by three other values—*marianismo*, *ediquetta*, and *pronatalism*—which are commonly shared, with some minor variations, across the Latino world of South and Central America. To avoid duplication in several chapters, these four basic values are described in detail in Section 1A, Basic Sexological Premises, in the chapter on Puerto Rico in this volume. (*End of note by R. T. Francoeur*)]

[*Comment 1997*: The structure of sexual life in Brazil has traditionally been conceived in terms of a model focused on the relationship between sexual practices and gender roles—on the distinction between masculine activity (*atividade*) and feminine (*passividade*) as central to the order of the sexual universe. *Comer* (to eat) describes the act of penetration during sexual intercourse, while *dar* (to give) describes those who passively offer themselves to be penetrated and possessed by their active partners. In some respects, these role distinctions are more fundamental than is sexual anatomy. For details on the implications of these premises, see Sections 5, Interpersonal Heterosexual Behaviors, and 6, Homoerotic, Homosexual, and Bisexual Behaviors, below. (*End of comment by R. T. Francoeur*)]

[*Update 1997*: In 1986, the Delegacia da Mulher, The Women's Advocacy group, was formed to protect women against sexual and physical violence. All the employees of this agency are women, because women feel more secure filing complaints when they are speaking to other women. Only 3% of the members of Parliament are women. Feminist organizations are small, not very popular, and have little influence in society.

[Nevertheless, over 20% of Brazilian families are supported exclusively by women. Moreover, the results of a national survey (representing 35% of the economically active women in the country) by *Veja/Feedback* has described the average Brazilian woman over 25 as follows:

She's married, has two children, entered the work market in the 1980s and wants to earn more. Contrary to her mother and grandmother, she recognizes that eternal marriage does not exist. All-providing husbands do not exist. She prepares herself almost by intuition to keep going alone in life.

In everyday family life, she does everything for the children but gives less to the husband—a husband who still

identifies the woman as the support of the home and the happiness. The two become estranged. For this woman busy with her own life, criminal violence and the preservation of health are preoccupations more important than sexual pleasure or the fear of getting older. For that woman who does not work outside of the house, the model of the ideal woman is exactly of one who sweats her body and the double shift [inside and outside the home]. (*Veja* 1994, 11)

[This same 1994 survey (p. 15) reported the following primary concerns of women: violence against women, 98%; sexual abuse, 96%; daycare for children, 94%; equal salaries, 79%; free choice of contraceptives, 73%; more political participation, 73%; division of duties at home, 70%; and legalization of abortion, 56%. (*End of update by R. J. Noonan and S. Almeida*)]

[*Update 2002*: Even though Brazil is still a very male-dominated country, we are seeing slight but significant changes. Every day women are moving into strictly male-dominated professions. Kátia Alves Santos, for example, is the first Secretary of Safety in Brazil. In Bahia, a very conservative state, she is responsible for 46,000 officers and 3,000 inmates. In Bahia, women occupy 49% of all police chief positions in the state. More and more women are entering politics. Marta Suplicy, at one time a leading Brazilian sexologist, became mayor of the city of São Paulo in January of 2001, and there were rumors that she might run for president in the then-upcoming elections. The latest census shows that 26% of women are considered to be head of household. Even with these advances, women are still paid less then men for the same job. In 1999, women were paid 60.7% of what males received for comparable work. This was, however, a significant increase from 53.2% in 1992. A direct relationship between more women working and the birthrates can be drawn. In 1960, the birthrate was 6.3 children per woman. As more women entered the workforce, that number has been decreasing, 3.5 in 1985, 2.6 in 1992, and 2.3 in 1999.

[Men in Brazil have also started to change their attitudes about male and female roles. Over half of Brazilian working-men, 51.2%, now help in house chores; this might not seem like a large number, but it was only 35.8% in the early 1990s. Those numbers indicate a change in the overall culture, clearly suggesting cultural changes toward more equality of males and females and away from the machismo culture found in South America. (*End of update by L. Raibin*)]

## B. Sociolegal Status of Males and Females

From the legal viewpoint, Brazilian males and females have equal legal rights as children, adolescents, and adults. Adults, those over 18 years of age, both men and women, have the right and obligation to vote. Voting is mandatory. Each voter receives a receipt documenting his or her fulfillment of this obligation. Wages of a worker who does not have this receipt will be attached by the state in the month following the elections. Adolescents between 16 and 18 years of age have the right to choose to vote or not to vote.

[*Comment 1997*: The traditional role of Brazilian women as housewife, derived from the 19th-century European ideal, was that of the "unproductive queen of the house," who was responsible for the respectability and harmony of the household and envied by the working woman. When one achieved the status of housewife, she gained dignity and a higher social status. However, growing numbers of Brazilian women have finally come to recognize their own power and the possibility of being an agent of change. In the last 20 years, the number of economically active women in Brazil grew by 70% to 23 million—39% of Brazil's population of women—a figure almost equal to the populations of Holland and Denmark combined (*Veja* 1994). (*End of comment by R. J. Noonan and S. Almeida*)]

A law restricting abortion has produced some discussion about women's rights that developed into a sort of political campaign. Recently, the List of the Rights of Children has been promoted with considerable publicity. The intention is to provide minors with greater protection against the violence they are victims of in the large cities.

[*Comment 1997*: Poverty and the inability of Brazil's majority poor to limit the number of offspring they have drives many youth to abandon their families and make their own lives on the street. Typical of Brazil's urban scene is the city of Salvador. In 1993, Salvador's 2.5 million inhabitants included a floating population of some 16,000 youths, working, playing, begging, stealing, and sleeping on the street. This was up 33% from an estimated 12,000 in 1990. About 100 Salvadorian street children are murdered each year by right-wing extremists. Social recognition of this problem and efforts to remedy it are vital to Brazil's future. (*End of comment by R. T. Francoeur*)]

## C. General Concepts of Sexuality and Love

The development of the communication media, especially television, has greatly influenced the concept of love and sexual behavior of the population. Every day, viewers of soap operas may witness episodes in which the sexual behavior of the protagonists is very permissive. This has definitely transformed Brazilian sexual relations in two ways. Such programs decrease sexual taboos and endorse sexual permissiveness, especially in the areas of the sexually uncommon and "deviant" sexual behaviors.

Overall, the sexual attitudes of Brazilians depend on gender, age, region of residence, and religious influences. The rural population and the migrant rural workers living in large cities suffer profound influences from Catholicism's religious teachings and ceremonies. This group is also characterized by a low level of education and culture. In this group, premarital and extramarital sexual contact is condemned. The Catholic Church approves only the natural means of family planning and condemns abortion. Ignoring Church doctrine, many in this group favor the contraceptive hormonal pill and surgical sterilization; the incidence of condom use is much lower. The Evangelical churches accept the use of the contraceptive pill as well as other methods, but are also vehemently opposed to abortion. Claims that the IUD is an abortifacient rather than a contraceptive method have caused its usage to be proscribed by Evangelicals. However, some government programs support use of the IUD in women of low income with numerous children.

Among Brazilians with a higher level of education, especially in the large cities, various forms of petting are acceptable, as well as premarital sex and extramarital sex, the latter being less frequent than the former. A variety of contraceptives are accepted as normal, with a preference for the contraceptive pill, surgical sterilization, condom, and abortion, in that order. Brazil is the world champion of cesarean births, 35% of all births. The majority of cesarean section deliveries are accompanied by sterilization of the woman through tubal ligation.

In comparing attitudes toward sexuality and love among Brazilians of different socioeconomic levels and different regions of the country, it seems to us that two different societies exist. One culture maintains the traditional attitudes of the Third World; the other culture has been influenced by the modernization trends commonly seen around the world and has gradually adopted more permissive attitudes.

[*Comment 1997*: Popular women's magazines have the purpose of transmitting the cultural norms, such as monog-

amy, similar to those in the U.S. and other countries. The August 1994 Portuguese edition of *Cosmopolitan*, called *Nova*, for example, highlights such issues for women as "A guide to self-confidence," "Attracting the right man," and "Monogamy: Is it possible to keep the fires hot?" (*End of comment by R. J. Noonan and S. Almeida*)]

## 2. Religious, Ethnic, and Gender Factors Affecting Sexuality

### A. Source and Character of Religious Values

The predominant religion in Brazil is Roman Catholicism, primarily because the Roman Catholic Church has determined that newborns must be baptized and officially registered as Roman Catholic at birth. In 1992, it was estimated that of the country's 148 million people, 70% are Catholics, 20% are Protestants (Baptists, Presbyterians, Pentecostals, Evangelicals, etc.), and 10% are Spiritualists (Mystics, Umbandists, Voodooists, etc.). The predominance of Christian religions has set the stage for the war against abortion, which is officially condemned as a crime. However, in most cities, abortion occurs underground. For similar reasons, sexual education in the public schools is generally nonexistent.

[*Update 2002*: The religious debate over recognition and acceptance of homosexual persons in the Christian churches was accented in October 2002, when the Dean and the 3,500-member congregation of the Holy Trinity Cathedral in Recife, in the northeast of Brazil, decided to withdraw themselves from the Episcopal Church of Brazil. Holy Trinity is the largest Anglican Church in Latin America. At first, the Dean and congregation claimed the reason for the schism was the bishop's support for development of alternative rites to bless divorcées (at the end of a divorce process), and alternative rites to bless couples who are already living together or do not want to marry according to the civil law because of the economic implications. But these are issues Brazilian society has long ago debated and accepted. Holy Trinity Cathedral is a conservative evangelical church, within the mostly evangelical and conservative diocese of Brazil.

Later comments by the Dean indicated that the real issue for the schism was the "exaggerated liberty homosexual people have in the Church," even though the Recife diocesan canons clearly state that no one from a homosexual orientation, or even those who accept this orientation as normal, could be ordained within that diocese. (Ribas, Personal communication October 2, 2002) (*End of update by R. T. Francoeur*)]

### B. Source and Character of Ethnic Values

Brazil has four distinct races of people: Caucasians 54%; Mestizo (mixed race) 34%; Negroes 10%; and Asians 2%. There are also about 200,000 indigenous Indians. Portuguese, Africans, and mulattos make up the vast majority of the population, with Italian, German, Japanese, Indian, Jewish, and Arab minorities.

Brazil was colonized in 1500 by the Portuguese, making it the only Portuguese-speaking country in all of Latin America. Youth is highly valued in this nation where 51% of the population is under the age of 27. This is obvious in many aspects of Brazilian life. For instance, kissing and petting by couples in the streets, theaters, and public places are generally tolerated in liberal Brazilian society, despite conservative religious influences.

[*Comment 1997*: In this respect, Brazilians tend to allow expressions of sexuality and eroticism that are quite unacceptable in other areas of the Latino world, especially in public. This disparity can be traced to a unique blend of Roman Catholic and native Indian values with a strong African influence. Like other Latinos, Brazilians have taboos and restrictions on public sexual behavior. However, Brazilians draw an important distinction between public and private behaviors that preserves traditional Indian and African values. "Within four walls, beneath the sheets, and behind the mask of *carnaval*, everything can happen!" "Everything," or *tudo*, refers to the world of erotic experiences and pleasure. The phrase *fazendo tudo*, "doing everything," means Brazilian men and women have an obligation to experience and enjoy every form of sexual pleasure and excitement, or more precisely those practices that the public world most strictly prohibits. This, however, must all be done in private, behind the mask, between four walls, or under the sheets.

[The concept of *tudo* is the key element in the domain Brazilians call *sacanagem* (DaMatta 1983). *Sacanagem* is an extremely complex cultural category, with no suitable English translation, except perhaps "the world of erotic experience" or the "erotic universe." Within this erotic world, erotic pleasure is an end in itself, and the classifications of active/passive, the sex of the partner, and the acts engaged in are secondary. A Brazilian most clearly embodies the erotic ideal of *sacanagem* by doing everything, particularly those practices that the public world most condemns and prohibits. The transgression of public norms called for by *sacanagem* brings the playfulness of *carnaval* into everyday life (Parker 1987; Moitoza 1982; Francoeur 1991, 43-47). (*End of comment by R. T. Francoeur*)]

[*Comment 1997*: The African influence on Brazilian life and sexuality takes many forms. For instance, at all levels of Brazilian society, it is customary to offer a guest *cafézinho*, a small cup of espresso made by pouring water over powdered coffee through a cloth strainer. One way this custom is practiced illustrates the influence of how black magic brought to Brazil by slaves from Africa is still strong in some parts of the country. This custom can give the *casadoiras*, young women looking to get married, an opportunity to enhance their prospects of getting married. The young women believe that if they pour the coffee through their own panties and give the drink to their unsuspecting boyfriends, the men will be attached to them forever and will not be able to escape marriage. In *The Scent of Eros: Mysteries of Odor in Human Sexuality* (New York: Continuum Press, 1995, 83-84), Kohl and Francoeur have suggested a possible scientific basis of this folk custom, which occurs in some African cultures, among African Americans in the southern United States, as well as in Brazil. The soiled undergarment used as a filter may contain pheromones, which have been found in primate and human vaginal secretions. Released into the coffee, these may serve as a natural sex attractant or aphrodisiac. However logical it is in terms of what we know about vaginal pheromones, this suggestion is speculation and untested by experimental research. (*End of comment by R. J. Noonan and S. Almeida*)]

Racial prejudices exist, but they are concealed, and racial conflict and skirmishes/clashes are rare, except when economic interests lead to attacks on indigenous peoples in the Amazon basin. Couples with clearly different ethnic origins are very commonly seen in any public gathering. There exists a great mingling of the races that gives Brazil a preeminently Mestizo population, especially in the north and northeast. In the south, those of European Caucasian descent, i.e., German, Italian, Spanish, and Portuguese, predominate.

[*Comment 1997*: The expression *pé na cozinha* ("foot in the kitchen") illustrates the intermixing of the white and non-white races common in Brazil. The phrase goes back to the Brazilian colonial era when the slaves brought from Africa worked in the kitchens and the white masters would have sexual relations with them. Some of the offspring resulting from these illicit liaisons had very light traces of the African influence in their appearance and were considered to be white with their "foot in the kitchen," meaning they had some African features. *Pé na cozinha* is still used today to describe a person who has a vestige of African characteristics. (*End of comment by R. J. Noonan and S. Almeida*)]

## 3. Knowledge and Education about Sexuality

### A/B. Government Policies, Sex Education Programs, and Informal Sources

It is necessary to emphasize that sexual education has been somewhat taboo in Brazil. Since the late 1980s, however, some sexual education programs have surfaced in the private schools. In São Paulo (in 1987), an experimental study of sexual education in five public schools revealed that sex education helped improve student scores in all their subjects, as well as improved the relationships between parents, students, and teachers.

Truthfully, in Brazil, there is no government program for the sexual education of its youth. Recently, in the principal cities of the country, a Program of Adolescent Support surfaced that informs, orients, and teaches adolescents about their sexuality through educational interviews and seminars.

One study revealed that 72% of the men and 45% of the women received their first information about sex from friends and schoolmates. It also showed that in the large cities, youth learned about sex mainly from movies and magazines. It seems that Brazilian families generally prefer that their offspring obtain their sexual information through the school system and published material, such as adult and pornographic magazines. This frees the parents, who feel insecure speaking about sex, from ever mentioning such a "delicate subject" in the family circle and to their children.

One consequence of this lack of sexual education was uncovered in an unusual study of 150 women treated for anorgasmia. They were very poor and worked hard in the fields. They lived in rural areas without radio or television before they married, and had no time to watch television even when it was available. None of these women ever received any sexual education from family members or school. Over a third of them did not know that the sexual act was a normal part of marriage, although they knew that prostitutes and other bad men and women engaged in *sacanagem* ("the world of erotic experience"). For these women, sexual intercourse was not a moral behavior, but immoral and indecent. When they found out what sex was and that it was a part of marriage, they thought that their husbands were crazy and felt as if they had been raped. For these women, the lack of sexual knowledge was the major cause of anorgasmia. In addition, 20% of the wives abandoned the therapy because their marriages were destroyed by violence. For 80 of the women in this study, other factors were responsible for the anorgasmia. These poor rural women are not typical of the real universe of most Brazilian women (de Freitas 1990).

These women had access to sexual therapy only because AB-SEX, headed by the main author, introduced this therapy as a free part of Public Health in 1986 in São Paulo. At present, many of these patients are living in a big city and have been married more than ten years.

[*Comment 1997*: On the television program, "Fantástico," in late 1994 on TV Globo, a national Brazilian network, reporters interviewed two researchers, Emídio Brasileiro and Marislei Espíndola from the city of Goiânia, who had conducted a sex survey over the preceding five years. The researchers, whose book, *Sexo: Problemas e Soluções*, was to be published by the end of the year, reported that children wanted to know what sex was for; adolescents wanted to know what sex was like; young adults at about 20 years old wanted to know how to avoid the consequences of sex; adults from about 30 wanted to know how to educate their children about sex; those over 40 think they know everything about sex; and those around 60 think it's too late. A few of the questions that these researchers said they were most often asked included: 1. Can a pregnant woman have sex? 2. When is a young person ready for his first sexual intercourse? 3. Sexually, is it easier to be a man or a woman? and 4. If I have sex before or during a sports competition, will I decrease my physical performance? (*End of comment by R. J. Noonan and S. Almeida*)]

## 4. Autoerotic Behaviors and Patterns

A 1983 questionnaire survey indicated that boys and girls in an urban group of 3- to 5-year-olds played together in such a way as to touch or see each others' sexual organs, especially when no adults were present. When this type of behavior was observed in a school setting by some teachers at Colégio Batista Brasileiro in São Paulo, the main author was invited to provide some orientation for the teachers. As we know, this type of behavior in infancy is practically universal and independent of social class or ethnic origins.

As mentioned earlier, it is uncommon for parents to speak about sex to their children at home. When childhood sexual curiosities are not satisfied by the parents, the child naturally seeks answers on their own from other sources. Usually such persons or sources they turn to are not prepared or adequate to guide them efficaciously. In terms of self-pleasuring, the child is likely to encounter one of two attitudes or value judgments. One opinion, and probably the less frequently encountered, is that self-pleasuring is a normal component in the psychosexual development of children. The other opinion views masturbation as a negative road to human development.

Regardless of the value message encountered and the lack of external support, 92% of adolescent boys and 45% of girls engage in self-pleasuring. However, the fear of being found out by parents or other kin is a common accompaniment. In our research, 66% of the boys and 36% of the girls began self-pleasuring between 10 and 15 years of age.

While the Evangelical Protestants express a great preoccupation with, and a negative view of, self-pleasuring, Roman Catholic doctrine also condemns this behavior as disordered and seriously sinful, but seldom if ever mentions it. There are no significant statistics about childhood and adolescent autoeroticism.

## 5. Interpersonal Heterosexual Behaviors

### A. Children

In a retrospective research project about child and adolescent sexual behavior, 57% of all adults played sex games as children (de Freitas 1991). The children, in general, do not receive any sort of sexual guidance or information from their parents, yet their sexual behavior seems generally adequate and appropriate for their developmental ages as psychologists understand this.

Going through the phases of sexual self-discovery and autoeroticism characteristic of infancy, the children imitate their parents and are influenced by peers and the mass media, movies, and television.

Recent research has uncovered that 60% of those interviewed admitted to having played doctor and other games that included the mutual touching of their bodies and the sexual parts when they were children. The majority engaged in this kind of play with children of both sexes. However, there was a tendency for girls to play more with girls, while boys played mostly with children of the opposite sex.

We must call attention to the fact that only 60% of the subjects interviewed revealed having practiced this type of play in childhood, when it is well known that the frequency of this activity is much higher all over the world. From this we understand that many respondents omitted the truth from their information about their infancy. To speak of childhood sexuality is an intolerable outrage for many Brazilians. Even today in our culture, childhood sexuality is a taboo theme that cannot be mentioned with total tranquillity because of the intense anxiety it awakens in adults. Most adults want to forget the sexual experiences of their childhood because they were punished for demonstrating an interest in those activities. This perhaps explains the fact that many people, especially women over 45 years of age, did not answer the questions about sexual play in childhood.

While our observations and data are limited, two general forms of childhood sexual behavior have been observed. Children, 2 to 4 years old, generally limit themselves to speaking words of sex, showing their penises or buttocks, or even lifting the little girls' skirts and making drawings of nude girls or urinating boys. Children, 5 to 7 years old, seek closer contact with the opposite sex. Meanwhile, attitudes of punishment by the older family members for erotic play reinforce fear and redirect behavior towards self-pleasuring in private.

[*Comment 1997*: In contrast with Euro-American sexual values that frown on sexual rehearsal play among children and adolescents, Brazilian culture expects young boys and girls to experiment with sexual pleasure and prepare for marriage within certain limits and in private.

[In the game *troca-troca*—literally "exchange-exchange"— pubescent and adolescent boys take turns, each inserting his penis in the other's anus. In addition, the early sexual interactions of adolescent boys and girls draw on a wide range of nonvaginal sexual practices, in particular on anal intercourse, in order to avoid both unwanted pregnancy and rupture of the hymen, still an important sign of a young woman's sexual purity (Parker 1987). (*End of comment by R. T. Francoeur*)]

Clitorectomy does not exist in Brazil. Male circumcision exists only in the Jewish community. However, postectomy to shorten the prepuce is performed for uncircumcised boys with a long prepuce.

### B. Adolescents

*Puberty Rituals*

Some social celebrations are observed when girls celebrate their 15th birthday. In some rural cities, this involves a "Big Party" with the fathers presenting their daughters to society and the girls dancing their first waltz. In upper-class urban families, these girls are then allowed to court and have a boyfriend. [*Editor's Note 1997*: See also the discussion of *quinceañera* in Section 2, Latino Perspectives, of the U.S.A. chapter. (*End of note by R. T. Francoeur*)]

*Premarital Sexual Activities and Relationships*

The period of puberty involves biological, psychological, and sociological transformations. In Brazilian girls, menarche occurs between the ages of 10 and 13, having already had the partial growth of the breasts and the hips. Research shows that 62% of Brazilian mothers try to teach their daughters about their first menstruation before it occurs. Meanwhile, 38% of the young women confess not having any knowledge of the phenomenon before it happened.

Research indicates that the first menstruation in girls causes a strong emotional reaction that prompts the girls to inform their mothers. It is rare that girls hide their menarche from their mothers, although 15% of the subjects interviewed reported that as their response. The reaction of the boys to the signs of sexual maturation and their first nocturnal emission depends on the level of information they have received from their older friends. Unlike girls' reaction to menarche, boys almost always hide their first nocturnal emission from their parents, preferring to tell their older friends. The sexual maturation of puberty brings interest in the opposite sex, but the majority only start dating about age 15.

Sexual intercourse is generally initiated between the ages of 12 and 17 for men and 17 to 20 for women, again confirming a more permissive standard for men than for women. About the age of 16, dating becomes more intimate with noncoital sexual contact more evident. By age 16, 17% of the men and 8% of the women have had sexual intercourse. Only 40% of the women and 52% of the men revealed that their first sexual experience was positive and pleasant.

Research on adolescents in Botucatu, a rural area of the São Paulo district, and in the capital of São Paulo district revealed sharp differences in the sexual behavior of adolescents. In the rural cohort of 290 adolescents, we found that 65 youngsters or 22.4% had already had heterosexual contact between ages 13 and 19 years. Nineteen of these adolescents had experienced coitus, while 46 had only played sex games without having penile-vaginal intercourse. Of this group, 60% had a pleasant sexual experience and 40% felt guilt, mental anguish, and remorse. By comparison, in a parallel group of 290 youths in the city of São Paulo, a similar number and percentage of adolescents had already had heterosexual contact. However, the breakdown was reversed, with 41 youths or 13.8% having experienced coitus, and 24 engaging in noncoital sex play, or outercourse. In the urban cohort, sexual contact was pleasurable for 69.3%. This demonstrates that the urban Brazilians are more liberal and more venturesome in their sexual behavior.

## C. Adults

### Premarital Courtship, Dating, and Relationships

In research conducted by AB-SEX (1991), 81% of adult men reported having had premarital relations, while 53% of women reported the same behavior. Again, this was more commonly reported in the large cities. The preoccupation of women with virginity is more evident in the rural zones in the interior of the country, and less so in the state capitals. Among college students in the larger cities who are politically active and quite influential, there is often a shame attached to being a virgin.

Recent data indicate that single adults suffer from pressure to be married, but about 7% of Brazilian women between the ages of 35 and 45 years of age have children without being married, only 2% of whom marry after the birth of their first child. Single men between the ages of 37 and 46 prefer to remain single, even if their partners have children. There are many couples in the lower economic class who start a family and have many children without being married. About one quarter of all women are pregnant when they get married.

### Marriage and the Family

The majority of marriages occur between the ages of 20 and 25, about 65% of all marriages. As in the developed nations, the small family model has become the standard. An accentuated fall in fertility has been noticed, since we have gone from the average of 6.3 children per woman in the 1960s to a current average of 2.8 children. This has come as a result of a series of transformations to which we generally refer as the process of modernization of Brazilian society.

In Brazil, monogamy is the fundamental pattern; bigamy and polygamy are illegal. Research in 1991, reported by IPPM (Institute of Market Research of São Paulo), found that in São Paulo, 54% of the people are opposed to female adultery while an equal number are against male adultery. Extramarital sex is acceptable under "certain circumstances" to 25% of the men and 23% of the women. People in smaller cities and economically lower are more rigorous in their opposition to extramarital sexual relations.

The average frequency of marital intercourse ranges between twice a week and three times per month. However, more and more of those interviewed say that they might feel happier if they had sex more often; they often added that they would feel less anxiety (*E acrescentam que seriam menos nervosos*).

[*Comment 1997*: Based on the University of Chicago's report on sexuality in America, which had recently been released, TV Globo, a national network, in the last quarter of 1994 conducted a mini-survey of the frequency with which Brazilians have sexual relations. On the television program "Fantástico," they reported that 17.6% of Brazilians have sexual relations once a week, 35.9% have none, and 46.5% do so two or more times per week. They also interviewed two researchers, Emídio Brasileiro and Marislei Espíndola, who had conducted a sex survey over the preceding five years. These researchers reported finding that men appeared to be more liberal about sex, but actually were more conservative, in comparison to women, who were apparently more conservative, but actually were more liberal. (*End of comment by R. J. Noonan and S. Almeida*)]

In 1978, divorce was legally recognized after 25 years of Parliamentary discussion. The most frequent cause of divorce is extramarital sex, 33%, followed by excessive use of alcohol, physical violence, personality incompatibility, and irreconcilable differences. Usually it takes from two to four months to obtain a divorce. Divorced persons are not allowed to remarry for at least three years. Bigamy is considered a felony and a guilty verdict is accompanied by a jail term to be determined by a judge. The majority of divorces occurs between three to seven years after marriage. Frequently the divorcing couple has no children, 41%, or only one child. Divorce after 20 to 30 years of marriage is rare, and seems to be connected with andropause (the Brazilian term for male menopause) or menopause.

In one out of every five divorces, the mother retains custody of the child, while the male must pay alimony usually equal to 30% of his salary. In cases where the male refuses or stops paying alimony to the ex-wife, he is immediately arrested by order of the courts.

### Sexuality and Older Persons

[*Update 1997*: Lucia Helena de Freitas, a Brazilian psychologist and gerontologist, studied the sexuality of a group of retired commercial workers who participated in the cultural activities of a social club. She found that 73.8% of them still had sexual relations, with 35.7% doing so two or three times a week, 21.4% once a week, and 16.7% less often. Almost all the interviewees (90.5%) felt the necessity of having sexual relations; 95.2% believed that sexual desire does not end with age, with 40% saying that it increased with age and 59% thinking the opposite. However, 33.3% believed that pleasure during the sexual act increased with age, as opposed to 66.7% who said the pleasure decreased. Regarding orgasm, 28.6% said they were able to reach it quickly against 40.5% who said they needed more time. Only 13.5% of women said they experienced a change in their sexual life as a result of menopause; some said they reached orgasm more quickly once they stopped menstruating. In the case of men, 4.8% acknowledged problems of impotency. Freitas concluded that with the advance of age, typically the frequency of sex decreases, but the quality does not. (*Manchete* 1992, 40). (*End of update by R. J. Noonan and S. Almeida*)]

### Incidence of Anal and Oral Sex

IPPM's (Institute of Market Research of São Paulo) survey revealed that at least 23.5% of São Paulo residents (Paulistanos), 12.6% of Rio de Janeiro residents (Cariocas), and 18.8% of those in other Brazilian cities reject oral sex because they consider it abnormal. Also, 53% of the Paulistanos, 38.6% of the Cariocas and 45.7% of those in other cities consider anal sex abnormal; 10% refused to answer.

The belief that oral and anal sex are abnormal sexual practices has its origin in many sources. One of these is the moral order, based in the Catholic tradition. This tradition believes sex in itself to be a mortal sin if it does not involve vaginal intercourse for the purpose of procreation within matrimony, and condemns all other erotic practices. Thus all sexual activities without a procreative end are considered taboos and sexual perversions that should be avoided.

In spite of this prohibition, many people go against the conventional sexual standards, since the primary message of Brazilian folk culture—*fazendo tudo*—prompts a freedom of sexual expression in private where anything can happen and everything is possible, encouraging everyone to broaden one's repertoire of sexual practices even when they violate public sexual norms in private.

The IPPM survey, for example, showed that, at least occasionally, 52.9% of Cariocas, 37.8% of Paulistanos, and 42.1% of other Brazilians have practiced anal intercourse. Statistical analysis revealed that men 30 to 45 years of age were three times more likely to solicit anal sex than women. These results confirm that among married couples, as elsewhere, it is generally the male that initiates new sexual practices, while the female frequently is limited to accepting passively her partner's solicitation. This presents a "delicate situation" for the female who is pressured to accept anal or oral sex, because there are no legal restrictions in Brazil.

The emphasis on *fazendo tudo*, *tesão* (excitement), and *prazer* (enjoyment) promotes "rather elaborate and varied forms of sexual foreplay, a strong emphasis on oral sex, and especially a focus on anal sex" (Parker 1987, 164). Interviews of 5,000 men and women throughout Brazil revealed that over 50% of those surveyed in Rio de Janeiro, and over 40% of those in the rest of Brazil, reported practicing anal sex at least occasionally (Santa Inêz 1983, 41).

### Carnaval

In Brazilian sexual culture, the annual celebration and unrestrained exuberance of Carnaval is typical of

> an erotic universe focused on the transgression of public norms through a playfulness reminiscent of . . . one's adolescent sexual experience and the excitations they produced play[ing] themselves out again repeatedly throughout adult life. They undercut the effects of sexual prohibitions and make polymorphous pleasures such as oral and anal intercourse, an important part even of married, heterosexual relationships. Such acts [whether engaged in with same or other gendered persons, with a nonspouse or stranger], along with the *tesão* or excitement which is thought to underlie them and the *prazer* or enjoyment which is understood to be their aim, are essential to the Brazilian sexual culture, with its context of 'no shame,'

'within four walls,' 'beneath the sheets,' or 'behind the mask.' (Parker 1987, 165)

## 6. Homoerotic, Homosexual, and Bisexual Behaviors

[*Comment 1997*: The categories of homosexuality (*homossexualidade*), heterosexuality (*heterossexualidade*), bisexuality (*bissexualidade*), and a distinct homosexual identity (*identidade homossexual*) were introduced into Brazilian culture in the mid-20th century by social hygienists, medical doctors, and psychoanalysts.

[Despite their current prevalence in the media, these concepts of sexual classification remain, in large measure, part of an elite discourse. As mentioned in Sections 1B, A Brief Historical Perspective, and 2A, Religious, Ethnic, and Gender Factors Affecting Sexuality, Source and Character of Religious Values, Brazilian sexual culture is centered on the distinction between masculine activity—eating (*comer*), conquering and vanquishing (*vencer*), and owning and possessing (*possuir*)—and feminine passivity (giving, being penetrated, dominated, subjugated, and submissive). In keeping with the overriding importance of every male considering himself macho, the Brazilian male considers himself heterosexual man (*homem*), as long as his dominant mode of sexual expression involves active phallic penetration, regardless of the gender of the partner being possessed and penetrated.

[If the category of "men" or *homens* seems clear, its counterpart is less so. Those who *dão* (give or submit) include biological women or *mulheres*, and others, the biologically male *viado* (deer), *bica* (worm, intestinal parasite), and the feminine form of *bicha* (best translated as queer or faggot). Though endowed with male anatomy, the *viado* or *bicha* is linked with the fundamentally passive social role of *mulher*, not *homem*. Within these categories, a male can have sexual relations with *mulheres*, *viado*, and *bicha* and maintain his masculine (heterosexual) identity, provided he exercises phallic dominance. In any discussion of sexual behaviors, gender orientation, and AIDS education, it is essential to keep in mind this Brazilian folk model.

[The interplay between traditional and modern medical models of sexual behavior is evident within the open, shifting, and flexible subculture of *entendidos* and *entendidas* ("those who know") in Brazil's larger cities. Organized around same-sex practices and desires, this subculture is found in certain bars, beaches, saunas, discos, and the like. *Entendidos* (studs) are sometimes contrasted with *homens*, and the traditional *bicha* as the passive partner of the active *bofe*. Both the *entendidos* and *bofe* are considered masculine *homens* despite their participation in same-sex activity.

[The same dichotomy structures the increasingly open presence of the once almost-invisible "lesbian" subculture, where *sapatão* (big shoe, dyke, or butch) contrasts with *sapatilhão* (slipper or femme dyke) (Parker 1987). (*End of comment by R. T. Francoeur*)]

In Brazil, homosexuals communicate among themselves with their own subcultural language, including the signal of an earring in the left ear for gay men and a left ankle bracelet for lesbians. This combination of in-group verbal and nonverbal communication allows homosexual persons to function in a generally hostile environment.

The recent IPPM (Institute of Market Research of São Paulo) survey made it clear that homosexuality is one of the areas of human sexuality most marked by prejudice. Over half, 51.5%, of Paulistanos, 57.1% of Cariocas, and 56.3% of those in other cities oppose homosexuality. On the other hand, a small number of those interviewed, only 13.5%,

8.7%, and 9.4%, respectively, in these same areas, consider homosexuality normal conduct. We do not have data concerning the number of homosexuals in the country, but it is probable that it is similar to that of other Latin American countries.

The social status of homosexuals is favorable only among those who have achieved fame in the arts, music, theater, movies, television, and haute couture. A homosexual orientation and lifestyle seem to facilitate self-promotion and professional success in these fields. In other areas of professional life, homosexuality is not a positive factor. In recent research in São Paulo, it was found that homosexuals, especially those with an exaggerated behavior, were usually rejected for employment following interviews with the company psychologists, although these same psychologists deny being prejudiced against homosexuals. In some areas, such as sales, there are minimal chances for an overt homosexual to find employment. Discrimination is also strong against overt lesbians. But, since they are generally more discreet and less overt in their behavior, they are not as easily identified. They only call attention to themselves when they are on a date with a younger (fem) lover, or when they cause a scene triggered by jealousy when the (fem) lover speaks to men.

Legal problems arise only when homosexuals become physically violent or when they wish to marry legally. Brazil's laws do not permit homosexuals or lesbians to marry.

Homosexual prostitution, especially when transvestites are involved, is the object of frequent police raids. However, this repression does not appear to have much effect on this, considering the open activity at night on the streets in the large cities.

Religious restrictions on these sexual practices are stronger among the Catholics, 68% of whom condemn homosexual behavior, even though there are cases involving homosexual priests who continue to practice their duties. The Catholic Church officially teaches that homosexual activities are contrary to the procreative purpose of sex.

The Protestants do not persecute homosexuals, but instead seek to help them recuperate through faith in God. There are many cases where homosexuals who were passive (bottoms) and prostituted themselves, have been regenerated or cured, becoming heterosexual to the extent of marrying and having children. They even lost their effeminate behaviors. (*Os protestantes não perseguem os homossexuais, mas procuram ajudá–los na recuperação, em que homossexuais passivos e que ate se prostituíam na noite, tornaram–se heterossexuais, casando–se, tendo filhos e perdendo os trejeitos efeminados.*)

## 7. Gender Diversity and Transgender Issues

There are no legal restrictions on transvestites in Brazil. However, in Brazil, transvestism is a marginal phenomenon (*um fenômeno marginal*, implying "practiced by a criminal element of society"). Transvestites are often men who work during the day, and at night apply makeup, dress as women, and work the street or nightclubs to prostitute themselves with men or bisexual couples. Legally, they are considered prostitutes and are treated as such by the police.

In Brazil, sex-change surgery for transsexuals is considered to be mutilation surgery, and legislation prohibits surgical treatment of a transsexual. Participation in such medical treatment is considered a felony for both the patient and surgeon.

Some transsexuals have gone to Europe to be operated on and change their sexual identity. However, these are isolated cases, because the majority of the transsexuals are content to dress as women at night and prostitute themselves.

Surgical techniques are well developed in Brazil so that many cases of congenital ambiguous or anomalous genitals are regularly corrected with surgery. These operations try to preserve the sexual (gender) identity adequate to the patient.

## 8. Significant Unconventional Sexual Behaviors

### A. Coercive Sex

Sexual violence is a crime for which there are provisions in the Brazilian Penal Code. The law protects citizens against sexual assaults in four categories: *estupro* or rape; *tentativa violenta ao pudor*, a violent attempt against *pudor* (meaning chastity, decency, modesty, virtue, purity, and more), or sexual molestation involving violence; *posse sexual através de fraude*, sexual possession through fraud; and *atentado ao pudor mediante fraude sem violência*, or an attempted violation of *pudor* involving fraud.

The first two categories of sexual assaults involve violence, and if grave physical harm results, the crime is viewed as aggravated and the convicted offender subject to a heavier sentence. In some cases, even if the victim consented to or invited the sexual partner, the law considers violence to have been part of the sexual act. These are usually cases where the victim is under 14 years of age, mentally incompetent, or unable to offer physical resistance.

### Sexual Abuse, Incest, and Pedophilia

Sexual relations involving an adult or older adolescent with a child is legally termed sexual victimization (*victimização sexual*). When sexual victimization involves a relative of the victim, it is classified as incest.

Since 1982, there have been more reports of this type of behavior because of the feminist movement and the fact that females are the most common victims. The frequency of such acts is very difficult to establish because only the gravest and most brutal cases become known to the authorities. Research conducted in São Paulo by Azevedo between December 1982 and December 1984 showed that only a small percentage, about one in 25 cases, of incest and pedophilia are reported to the authorities.

Research in greater São Paulo found that 87% of the cases of pregnancy in girls up to the 14 years of age resulted from incest perpetrated by the father, uncle, or stepfather of the victim. About 6% of the victims surveyed by Azevedo were males. In 70% of the cases of incest, the biological father was the perpetrator. The majority of such aggressors were 30 to 39 years old and blue-collar workers.

### Rape and Sexual Harassment

Rape is punishable by a minimum sentence of three years solitary confinement (*reclusão*) in prison. The sexual violence documented in police and court records is deceptive, because most cases of sexual violence are not reported to crime detection units and because the requirements of the law to gain a conviction of either sexual violence or seduction are excessive. A man can only be found guilty of a crime of seduction if the women is under the age of 18, and even then, a guilty verdict is rare. Only a male who seduces an underage, minor virgin and continues having coitus with her is at risk of being convicted of seduction. If convicted, he may be sentenced to two to four years in prison. If the woman seduced is under the age of 14, then the crime becomes one of rape and the minimum sentence is three years in jail. If the woman seduced is over 18 years of age, there is no crime unless there is a serious threat, violence, or suspected violence.

*Domestic Violence*

[*Update 1997*: Being beaten by a husband is no longer just crying at home, suffering in silence, and ashamed to say anything. It is now judged as a crime and taken seriously by society. With the opening of the doors on August 6, 1985, of the 150 women's precincts (Delegacias da Mulher), police stations directed by women who specialize in domestic violence against women, Brazilian women made a great gain. These police stations became the arm of the judiciary most trusted and least feared to be used by the people. For many years, the beating of women was not seen by policemen as a crime, but rather a minor domestic affair that did not involve them. This picture has now changed significantly. Initially, 80% of the cases involved women who had been beaten two or three times by their husband; today, the majority file a report at the first strike. An average of 300 women are seen each day (*U.S. News & World Report* 1994, 40-41; *Veja* 1994, 20).

[In 1991, Brazil's highest appeals court threw out the "honor defense" in adultery cases that allowed men who were accused of murdering their wives and/or their wives' lovers to escape punishment by arguing that they were defending their honor (*U.S. News & World Report* 1994, 41). (*End of update by R. J. Noonan and S. Almeida*)]

## B. Prostitution

Prostitution, whether heterosexual or homosexual, is not a criminal offense in Brazil unless it involves public solicitation or *pudor em público* (a public violation of *pudor*, meaning chastity, decency, modesty, virtue, purity, and more). In 1970, the liberation of the press, which strongly influenced sexual liberty, accentuated the reduction in female prostitution in the larger cities. Meanwhile, the increase in libertinism (*o aumento da libertinagem*, meaning debauchery, hedonism, immorality, and more) has facilitated the appearance of male prostitution in public places, for both heterosexual and homosexual contacts. The presence of houses of prostitution (*casas noturnas*) has decreased, being replaced by massage parlors, telephone callgirls, and street soliciting. A large number of motels have appeared throughout the larger cities, often catering only to couples seeking private encounters or to prostitutes and their clients.

Statistics on the total number of prostitutes in Brazil do not exist, but the police estimate their number at about one million for the whole country.

There is a Prostitutes Association or union (Associação de Prostitutas) founded in 1986, with its main purpose to obtain recognition of prostitution as a legal profession. So far, this effort has produced no results.

## C. Pornography and Erotica

The military regime that dominated Brazil from 1964 to 1985 repressed the publication of erotica and sexually explicit films. Since 1985, there has been a great surge in the number of pornography shops and erotic films, videos, and publications. Presently both hard- and soft-core pornography is easily accessible in Brazil. Both television and cinema theaters exhibit erotic films. Scenes showing sex with children or animals are strictly avoided, as is any depiction of sadomasochism, although sexual cruelty and violence may sometimes be shown.

[*Update 1997*: In 1995, a growing concern about the spread of AIDS, confusion over sexual values among the young, and the competition among television's prime-time soap operas to stage the steamiest love scenes, provoked a social backlash against Brazil's fabled comfort with sensuality. In July 1995, the weekly news magazine, *Veja*, identified 95 nude shots, 74 sex acts, and 90 scenes with smutty dia-

logue in a week's worth of programming on the five major networks. Complaints from individuals, local governments, and church groups have prompted the federal government to investigate the prevalence of sex on prime-time television and recommend steps to control this (Schrieberg 1995). (*End of update by R. T. Francoeur*)]

## D. Paraphilias

Some specialists deal with paraphilic clients, but there are no statistics on the incidence or types of paraphilias encountered in clinical practice, or among the general population.

Bestiality or zoophilia is a widely distributed sexual practice, both geographically and historically. Its frequency is greater among adolescents in the rural areas, generally constituting a temporary sexual outlet or experimentation rather than a long-term behavior. Our surveys found that 12% of Paulistanos and Cariocas and 17% of other, non-urban respondents reported erotic contact with animals in their childhood or adolescence. This behavior is much rarer among Brazilian women.

# 9. Contraception, Abortion, and Population Planning

## A. Contraception

Forty years ago in the rural areas of Brazil, families not infrequently had between ten and 20 children. In recent years, that number has decreased, especially in the large cities. The average number of children in a family has gone from 6.3 in 1960 to 2.8 in 1993.

Some progress has been made by the federal government in contraception and sexual education. Since 1986, the government has directed its efforts to educate young women in the use of contraceptives in order to reduce the number of teenage unmarried pregnancies. The programs are run by nurses and social workers who also teach the use of the contraceptive pill and condom use for STD prevention. These programs operate mostly in the large cities, such as São Paulo, Rio de Janeiro, Brasília, Belo Horizonte, and Recife.

Some branches of the federal government, such as SUS (Sistema Único de Saúde) offer free distribution of contraceptive pills as an IUD replacement for women who do not want to become pregnant. Research undertaken by the IPPM (Institute of Market Research of São Paulo) showed that 73% of those interviewed favor family planning in Brazil. In Rio de Janeiro, the number reached 83% of the women and 78.9% of the men. Only 8.5% of those interviewed in Rio de Janeiro and 6.8% of those in other cities declared themselves totally and radically opposed to birth control.

[*Update 1997*: Although 75% of Brazil's 154 million people are Roman Catholic, the world's largest Roman Catholic population, every relevant statistic shows that most people ignore the Church's teachings on contraception and abortion. In a June 1994 survey of 2,076 Brazilian adults, 88% of the respondents said they did not follow the Church's teachings; for women 25 to 44, this figure was 90%. On a national scale, Brazil has experienced one the the most radical reductions in family size recorded in modern history. With 40% of adult Brazilian women working outside the home, the fertility rate in the developed south is below the replacement level of 2.1 children per woman; in the impoverished northeast, it is 4.0, but this is well below the 5.8 recorded in the region in 1980 (Brooke 1994).

[About two thirds of the married women practice some form of contraception; 43% use oral contraceptives and 42% have been sterilized. The government, pressed by the Catholic bishops, has maintained laws against abortion and sterilization and blocked legislative efforts to provide free contraceptives through Brazil's national health service. Virtually all clinics that dispense contraceptives and information are maintained by private groups. Although opinion polls show that Brazilian women want universal access to modern contraceptives, they have little power to press this in the political establishment. Brazil has no women as state governors or Supreme Court justices; women hold only 4.7% of the seats in the 580-member Congress; and no women in the Brazilian Bar Association are directors, although 52% of the Association's members are women (Brooke 1994). (*End of update by R. T. Francoeur*)]

[*Update 1997*: The Brazilian woman is having fewer children than in the past. The average number of children for Brazilian women has been steadily decreasing over the last four decades. The 1991 Census reported an average of 2.7 children as compared to 6.28 children in 1960, 5.76 children in 1970, and 4.35 children in 1980 (*Anuário Estatístico Brasileiro 1992*, cited in *Veja* 1994, 75). The decrease may be attributed to several factors, including the use of contraceptives, sterilization, and abortion, as opposed to the worldwide economic and social reasons for the decline.

[In contrast with the 1994 report by Brooke cited above, the Instituto Brasileiro de Geografia e Estatística—Anticoncepção (Institute of Geography and Statistics, IBGE, Contraception), 1988, cited in *Veja* (1994, 75), reported that the majority of women, 23 million women or 62%, do not use a contraceptive method. As a result 1.4 million unwanted pregnancies result in abortion (Alan Guttmacher Institute, cited in *Veja* 1994, 75). Of the methods of contraception that are most used, the oral contraceptive pill is used by 43% of the women, sterilization is used by 42%, 7% use the calendar method, 2% use condoms, 1% use the IUD, and 5% use other methods (Instituto Brasileiro de Geografia e Estatística—Anticoncepção 1988, cited in *Veja* 1994, 75). The pill, sterilization, and the IUD account for 86% of the contraceptive use in Brazil, as compared to their combined use of 38% in other "developed" countries (Instituto Brasileiro de Geografia e Estatística—Anticoncepção 1988, World Health Organization—Reproductive Health 1990, cited in *Veja* 1994, 75).

[Among the live births, 32% are done by cesarean section, the highest rate in the world, as compared to 29% in Puerto Rico, 24% in the United States, 10% in England, and 7% in Japan (World Health Organization 1991, cited in *Veja* 1994, 75). One reason for the high incidence of cesarean deliveries in Brazil can be traced to the high number of women who choose to have a tubal ligation done at the same time to limit future births. United Nations statistics show that maternal mortality is also high, with 150 deaths per 100,000 births, as compared to 3 deaths, 12 deaths, and 1,000 deaths per 100,000 births for Japan, the United States, and Guinea, respectively. In the rural areas, 35.6% of the births are done at home versus 7% in the urban areas.

[Of those people who use condoms, women at every age level buy fewer condoms than men. A Brazilian company reports that, on average, 12% of the condoms bought are bought by women and 88% are bought by men. The breakdown by age level is as follows: Among those 15 to 19, 5% are bought by women and 95% by men; of ages 20 to 24, 18% by women and 82% by men; of ages 25 to 29, 19% by women and 81% by men; of ages 30 to 39, 23% by women and 77% by men; and of ages 40 or older, 28% by women and 72% by men (Dispomed Comercial Ltda., cited in *Veja* 1994, 75). (*End of update by R. J. Noonan and S. Almeida*)].

## B. Teenage Unmarried Pregnancies

There are no reliable statistics on the number of unwed teenage pregnancies in Brazil.

In recent research among adolescents, we found that 16% of the subjects approved of the IUD as a contraceptive method while 48% disapproved. Meanwhile, the lack of information about sexuality and contraception has caused many single adolescent females to become pregnant. In São Paulo, 54% of the adolescent males interviewed considered women's preoccupation with pregnancy a female problem for which the female is solely responsible. Even with the risk of AIDS infection, 35% of the adolescents refused to use condoms because they believe it takes away from their pleasure. All these factors contribute to an increasing number of unwed teenage pregnancies. SUS (Sistema Único de Saúde) has an unwanted pregnancy education and prevention program for female adolescents in several regions of São Paulo, and similar programs exist in other capital cities. Practically nothing is available in the rural areas.

Many young women faced with an unwanted pregnancy resort to clandestine abortion clinics to hide the pregnancy from family. When the unwanted pregnancy does not end in a clandestine abortion, it is more frequent for the unwed adolescent mother to remain single than to marry the father. In the majority of cases, 51.8%, the young fathers shirk their responsibility as a parent.

## C. Abortion

With the increase in sexual activity, the number of abortions in Brazil is slowly growing. Article 128 of the Penal Code of 1940 allows only two reasons for legal abortion: when the pregnancy is the result of rape or when there is no other way to save the woman's life.

Abortion statistics are not reliable or consistent. In 1989, the World Health Organization reported nearly 5 million abortions a year in Brazil, about 10% of the number of abortions performed worldwide. A research study in São Paulo, 1993, revealed 4.5 million induced abortions per year in Brazil. The incidence is highest among women ages 15 to 19, with 136 abortions per every 1,000 women in this age bracket. Nationally, there are 8.3 illegal abortions for every 100 pregnancies. Brazil records about 400,000 hospitalizations for medical complications of abortions annually; in the United States only 10,000 women experience complications requiring hospitalization.

In 1989, a National Research of Health and Nutrition study conducted by the Institute of Geography and Statistics (IBGE), found the index of abortions greater among women of the southeast, 16.4%, than among women of the northeast, 14.4%. These two regions accounted for 75% of all the pregnant women in Brazil. These statistics are informative when one recalls that the southeast region has a higher standard of living than the northeast. In the poorer northeast, there were 45 pregnant women per 1,000 women; in the more economically developed southeast, the rate was 33 per 1,000 women. This is in keeping with the hypothesis that a higher standard of economic development and better standard of living leads to a lower number of pregnancies. A second factor in the incidence of clandestine abortions is the number of previous pregnancies a woman has had. Of 13,862,844 women who were pregnant in the past five years, 14.9% terminated a pregnancy at least once. Among women who had had four previous pregnancies, 47.1% terminated the fifth pregnancy. Among women who had had five previous pregnancies, 77.1% terminated a subsequent pregnancy.

Several reasons are commonly cited to justify the legalization of abortion in Brazil: (1) a woman's right to control her own body, (2) socioeconomic factors, such as the lack of support and sustenance for children resulting from unwanted pregnancies, (3) "if so many people are doing it, why not legalize it?" (4) fetal malformations, (5) therapeutic abortions are already legal to save a mother's life, and (6) abortion is already allowed in cases of rape. Other factors supporting the legalization of abortion include the increase in sexual promiscuity, which increases the number of illegal abortions, and the chaos in the official system of public health, which reduces the distribution of contraceptives that could reduce the incidence of illegal abortions.

Presently, a task force of the Federal Council of Medicine is proposing the legalization of abortion for cases where the fetus will be born with serious or irreversible physical or mental problems. If this proposal is approved by The National Congress, then abortions will become legal in private or public hospitals, up to the 24th week of gestation, with the consent of the pregnant woman and the affidavit of two doctors. However, abortion continues to be a crime in Brazil today.

### D. Population Control Efforts

There are numerous efforts to promote a reduction in the population growth in Brazil. It is worrisome to find that São Paulo has 16.4 million inhabitants, being the second largest city in the world, second only to Tokyo, Japan, with 20 million inhabitants. Government campaigns carried on television and in newspapers inform people on the need to prevent an excessive growth of the population that does not have the necessary infrastructures, especially work and food supplies, to support it. Haphazard, uncontrolled population growth has led to the appearance of abandoned children, beggars, and would-be criminals (*marginais desocupados*) with nothing to do, all of whom are a heavy burden to a society without sufficient support structure.

The small family model has been in place in the large Brazilian cities since 1960, when the average of 6.3 children per family started to drop to the current 2.8 children per family. In rural areas, which comprises the largest area of the country, the average number of children in a family is still high at 5.7. However, we can assume that an accentuated drop in fertility in Brazil has resulted from the family planning campaigns. Reports tell us that 65% of the Brazilian couples of reproductive age use some type of contraceptive, with female surgical sterilization predominating. For example, in the United Kingdom female sterilization accounts for 8% of all contraception, in Belgium 5%, and in Italy 1%. In Brazil, female surgical sterilization accounts for 27% of the contraceptive usage. Hormonal therapies account for 25%, IUDs 1.3%, and vasectomies 0.7%. Other less-effective methods account for 11% of all contraception used.

## 10. Sexually Transmitted Diseases and HIV/AIDS

### A. Sexually Transmitted Diseases
*Incidence, Patterns, and Trends*

The incidence of gonorrhea, which had diminished considerably until 1960, increased greatly with the sexual liberty that developed in the 1970s. Syphilis also increased during that period of greater sexual promiscuity. With the advent of AIDS, the condom that had been used solely by prostitutes to avoid disease or pregnancy became the principal method of protection against the transmission of the HIV virus, and in the process benefited the campaigns against other STDs in our country.

In Brazil, STDs have increased significantly in the younger population, 15 to 20 years old. Based on statistics from several states, we estimate that 15% of the youth has already contracted a venereal disease. This amounts to about 2.2 million youths.

The Ministry of Health wants to encourage the war against the incidence of STDs through educational campaigns. They believe that any serious effort to control STDs must begin in the schools. According to Dr. Belda, venereal diseases are symptomatic of what he called a "social sickness," because their basic causes are connected to the behavior of individuals and communities. Among the factors cited as responsible for the changes in sexual conduct are the increase in promiscuity, variation in sexual customs, the migration of populations, and greater ease in transportation. We also admit that the increasing use of contraceptives also serves to increase promiscuity. Along with increased promiscuity, there is increased risk of contracting venereal diseases such as syphilis, gonorrhea, venereal lymphogranuloma, chancroids, inguinal granuloma, genital herpes, condyloma acuminatum, and HIV.

The most frequent STDs are syphilis and gonorrhea. The other STDs are not very common and escape the Health Ministry's statistical control. Syphilis is found in men in its primary phase, mostly because of its obvious clinical signs. However, it goes unnoticed in women, being confused with other vulvar inflammations. When it is diagnosed in women, it is most often in the secondary phase as a part of prenuptial exams. That is why the campaigns must especially reach groups such as prostitutes, homosexuals, and unwed youth.

Despite the lack of credible data, there is much evidence to indicate a new surge in gonorrhea in Brazil. In Rio de Janeiro, the incidence of gonorrhea grew by 120% between 1968 and 1972 while the population grew only 6%.

### B. HIV/AIDS
*Incidence and Transmission*

At the end of 1992, The Ministry of Health reported a total of 31,466 cases of AIDS in Brazil. An estimated 450,000 Brazilians are infected with the HIV virus but present no clinical signs characteristic of the disease. São Paulo has the largest number of cases, 18,755 patients, followed by Rio de Janeiro with 4,933 cases and Rio Grande do Sul with 1,468 cases. Out of a total of 31,466 AIDS patients, 13,874 have already died, according to a report from the AIDS Division.

The known cases of AIDS in newborns are few and rare. Recent reports indicate only 634 perinatal cases. Of all the occurrences, 3.6% or 1,143 were found in people under 15 years of age. Among adolescents, ages 15 to 20, the incidence of AIDS associated with IV-drug use has risen from 3% in 1980 to 24% in 1993. While there has been a reduction in the number of infections transmitted by sexual contact, authorities are increasingly concerned about this rising transmission of the virus among IV-drug users. According to the latest report (1993), 19,060 of the 31,466 total AIDS cases were victims of heterosexual, bisexual, or homosexual transmission. Another 8,508 have contracted the disease through contact with infected blood. In adults, the ratio is seven infected males for every one female infected with the virus.

In a research project in Rio de Janeiro involving 1,350 men and women between 15 and 59 years of age, the authors found that 100% of homosexual and bisexual respondents were informed about AIDS. However, only 38.8% of the men and 18.3% of the women had changed their sexual practices to avoid AIDS. The government campaigns stress the importance of using the condom as a means to avoid AIDS. Many homosexuals and bisexuals do not use condoms because it "inhibits sexual pleasure." They say the use of the condom is not well accepted because a man may be offended if a woman insists he use one or a woman may become suspicious if a man uses one. Weighing the risks of losing a partner who already loves you against the risk of contracting AIDS, many people choose to take the risk of contracting the disease.

In the Brazilian cultural tradition, the notion of homosexuality is more related to a passive (receptive) versus an active (penetrative) role. As Parker noted:

> The medical/scientific model has often been reinterpreted in traditional folk concepts, with their emphasis not on sexual object choice, as in the categories *homossexualidade* or *heterossexualidade*, but rather on *atividade* and *passividade*. In popular thought, the category of *homossexuais* or 'homosexuals' has generally been reserved for 'passive' partners, while the classification of 'active' partners in same-sex interactions has remained rather unclear and ambiguous. (Parker 1987, 162)

This causes some men to classify themselves as heterosexual, when in reality they are homosexual or bisexual. The result is that many AIDS prevention programs adopted from the United States to reach males engaging in anal intercourse do not reach their target audience. The disease is spreading among homosexuals and heterosexuals alike as a consequence of poor sexual knowledge and a lack of care. There has not been any research among lesbians, but it seems to us that there has not been an increase in disease among these women except among those who use IV drugs (Paiva 1995).

### Availability of Treatment and Prevention Programs

Prevention programs for AIDS using the slogans "Use a Condom" or "Practice Safe Sex" copy the North American models and do not take into account the particularities of sexuality in Brazil (Parker 1987). The practice of anal sex, as noted in Section 5C, Interpersonal Heterosexual Behaviors, Adults, is much more common between men and women in Brazil than in the United States, where it is a more frequent behavior among homosexuals.

There is a great mobilization of the community in a program of AIDS prevention through the development of several societies, the organization of lectures (*palestras*), the showing of films, professional health courses, the distribution of pamphlets, and information on radio and television programs. Meanwhile, religious groups protest and critique the campaigns because they seem to support solely the use of the condom and the disposable syringe. They believe it would be more educational and formative to discourage homosexuality, promiscuous sex, and drug use.

There has been no lack of the drug AZT. Even though it is a very expensive drug and not very efficacious in the treatment of AIDS, it has been distributed freely to patients with HIV who report to the Health Centers. Presently, Brazil is fourth worldwide in the number of AIDS cases, according to the World Health Organization. The United States has the most cases, followed by Uganda and Tanzania. France is fifth and Zaire is sixth (1992 data). Several years ago, Parker noted that:

> it is clear that a careful examination of the cultural context in Brazil inevitably leads to the conclusion that the health problem posed by AIDS and facing Brazilian society is potentially far more widespread and serious that has thus far been acknowledged. . . . Brazil is facing an epidemic disease that is potentially as devastating as the other serious public health problems that already exist there, and a combination of prejudice, short-sighted planning, and economic instability has left Brazilian society almost entirely unprepared to confront it. (Parker 1987, 169)

Presently, much attention has been given to the protection of those who work in the health industry and have contact with the high-risk groups in the general population, especially adolescents. The voluntary testing for HIV has been encouraged, and there is a campaign to protect those who test positive against discrimination.

### Government Policy

[*Update 2001*: In 1997, Brazil introduced a controversial policy to manufacture its own generic AIDS medicines and distribute them free to patients. By 2001, this controversial program had turned Brazil into a global leader in fighting the AIDS pandemic. In the 1980s, Brazil was one of the hardest-hit countries. By early 2001, while 20% of South African adults and 5% of Haitians were HIV-positive, only 0.6% of Brazilians were HIV-infected. The AIDS death rate in Brazil was cut in half between 1996 and 1999. Despite opposition from the Roman Catholic Church, some 10 million condoms were distributed during Carnaval celebrations in 2001. Frank prevention talk, and free medicine and treatment have put Brazil in the position of being a role model for the world (Rosenberg 2001).

[In March 2001, the first batches of the AIDS vaccines, Alavac vCP1452 (France) and MN rGP120 (United States), arrived in Brazil to be tested for human side effects by 40 volunteers. This study is part of a larger study sponsored by the United States government to study the vaccines in several developing countries. Researchers for O Projecto Praça XL, the AIDS research group of the Federal University of Rio de Janeiro (UFRJ), hope to study the side effects and immunobiological responses of the human body to the new AIDS vaccines, starting in June 2001. (*End of comment by L. Raibin*)]

[*Update 2002*: UNAIDS Epidemiological Assessment: The HIV/AIDS epidemic in Brazil is showing clear signs of stabilization. The incidence of AIDS has remained stable over the last five years at around 20,000 new cases per year, or 14 new cases per 100,000 population, and HIV prevalence also appears to be stabilizing across all sentinel surveillance studies conducted in the last four years.

[In 2000, 16,477 samples collected at 140 antenatal clinic sites were analyzed as part of sentinel surveillance of pregnant women. The national HIV prevalence in antenatal clinic settings was found to be 0.61%. When disaggregated by size of urban population, the prevalence in cities with more than one million inhabitants was found to be 1.25%. In cities with populations between 500,000 and 1,000,000, the prevalence was 0.34%; cities with populations between 200,000 and 500,000 had a prevalence of 0.46%, municipalities with populations 50,000 and 200,000, prevalence of 0.50%, and among cities with fewer than 50,000 inhabitants, 0.22%.

[Based on this study, it was estimated that in 2000 there were 597,443 individuals of both sexes between the ages of 15 and 49 years with HIV infection in Brazil, corresponding to a prevalence of 0.65%. UNAIDS estimates for the end of 2001 place the figure at 610,000 individuals living with HIV/AIDS, a prevalence of 0.65%.

[A 2001 study on 869 intravenous drug users in five urban areas found a median prevalence of 36.9%. A study of sex workers conducted in 2000 with 2,712 women in eight cities found median HIV prevalence to be 6.1%. Between March 1997 and October 2001 seven rounds of surveillance were conducted to establish the prevalence of HIV among STD patients. In total, 41,229 patients were tested, averaging 5,890 patients across 32 clinics per round. Median HIV prevalence for the period was 2.9%, with a decreasing trend from 4.2% in March 1997 to 2.7% in October 2001.

[In 2001, estimates of incidence and prevalence were developed for other STDs. Of the STDs examined, HPV prevalence was highest, at 15.17%, followed by HSV2 (0.76%), l. vaginalis (3.4%), syphilis (2.06%), trichomoniasis (1.92%), and gonorrhea (0.71%). Incidence was highest for l. vaginalis (5.1%), followed by trichomoniasis (2.32%), gonorrhea (1.82%), l. pallidum (1.10%), HPV (0.81%) and HSV-2 (0.76%).

[The estimated number of adults and children living with HIV/AIDS on January 1, 2002, were:

| | | |
|---|---|---|
| Adults ages 15-49: | 600,000 | (rate: 0.7%) |
| Women ages 15-49: | 220,000 | |
| Children ages 0-15: | 13,000 | |

[An estimated 8,400 adults and children died of AIDS during 2001.

[At the end of 2001, an estimated 130,000 Brazilian children under age 15 were living without one or both parents who had died of AIDS.

[*Adults in this UNAIDS Fact Sheet are defined as women and men aged 15 to 49. This age range covers people in their most sexually active years. While the risk of HIV infection obviously continues beyond the age of 50, the vast majority of those who engage in substantial risk behaviors are in the latter group. (*End of update by the Editors*)]

## 11. Sexual Dysfunctions, Counseling, and Therapies

### A/B. Concepts of Sexual Dysfunction and Treatment

Sexology has been a medical specialty in Brazil since September 30, 1980. But, the majority of the physicians and the public are not aware of this. Brazilian culture exalts the virile man, and erectile dysfunction is considered a great shame. This leads men to depression and the common practice of not admitting they are impotent and blaming the woman when forced to admit it. Various sexual therapy clinics have emerged in the large cities, some of them without any modern scientific basis. There are a few legitimate groups that deal mostly with male sexual dysfunctions; a breakdown of such clinical treatment includes lack of erection 52%, ejaculatory problems 26%, and reduced libido 22%.

The use of vascular surgery is very common for male erectile dysfunction, followed by the insertion of a prosthesis to improve erection, for problems of an organic origin. Psychotherapy and hormone therapy are used in psychogenic problems.

Since 1986, the Department of Sexology of the ARE–Várzea do Carmo in São Paulo has been exclusively dedicated to the treatment of female sexual dysfunctions. Their case distribution is: inhibited sexual desire/arousal 37%, anorgasmia 61%, and vaginismus 2%. In a study of 150 clients at this clinic, Sergio L. Freitas found that 80% of the treated women were cured of their symptoms, while 20% dropped out of therapy for several reasons. Half of the women treated did so without their husband's knowledge. The husband's machismo jealousy and pride will not permit them to seek help openly. It was necessary to combine psychoanalytical and gynecological methods, and the techniques of Helen Singer Kaplan's *New Sex Therapy*, with a reconditioning and remedial sexual education. The main causes of sexual disturbances were related to sexual disinformation, negative early sexual experiences, and a poorquality sex life. The average age was 32 years old. Treatment lasted from three to ten weeks. We found that 27% of the women were married without knowing that the sexual act was normal conduct in matrimony. Sixty percent were virgins when they married; 87.7% found their first sexual relation to be somewhere between bad and awful; 13.3%

found it to be acceptable; while none rated their early sexual experiences as either good or great.

The training of professionals for diagnosis and treatment takes place at the institutes mentioned in Section 12A, below. Certificates are awarded at a postgraduate level, following both theoretical and practical training through the observation of cases in active therapy.

Recent economic conditions have taken their toll on Brazilian sexuality. In a tropical land soaked with sensuality, economic anxieties are tarnishing a point of Brazilian national pride: bedroom performance. Harried by an annual inflation of 2,500%, two thirds of the adults surveyed in 1994 complained that the economic crisis was dampening their libido. Brazil's sex crisis is manifest at the dilapidated motels that line the roads into Rio de Janeiro. These establishments, featuring ceiling mirrors and suggestive names like "Lipstick," "Pussycat," and "L'Amour," offer hourly rates. Opened in the economic go-go years of the 1970s, many of these 225 motels in Rio are now deteriorating for lack of maintenance. Once discreet, they now fight to survive by advertising on television and offering promotions like discount lottery tickets or free lunches. Even so, Rio's motel industry trade association estimates that motels are renting their rooms at discounts averaging 40%. Respondents in a Brasmarket poll listed the following reasons in descending importance for the flagging sex drive: insecurity, lack of money for a date, street crime that keeps people at home, and lack of money for a motel.

## 12. Sex Research and Advanced Professional Education

### A. Institutes and Programs for Sexological Research

Sexology was recognized as a medical specialty in Brazil in 1980. Some postgraduate courses are offered at the Institute Saedes Sapietiae and at the Institute Havelock Ellis. These courses have been run by the Department of Sexology–ARE–Várzea do Carmo since 1986 by Dr. Sérgio Freitas. They offer practical training in sexology to professionals in the areas of psychology, nursing, social work, and medicine. The text, *Becoming a Sexual Person* (R. T. Francoeur, 2nd ed., New York: Macmillan, 1991), has been utilized as the basis for graduate courses in sexology, along with research in the area of sexuality and behavior of the Brazilian woman since 1992. Interest for this clinical specialty has had a recent impulse because of the XI World Congress of Sexology, held in June 1993 in Rio de Janeiro.

Among the organizations carrying on research, promoting courses, and running conventions on human sexuality in Brazil are the following:

Brazilian Association of Sexology (AB-SEX) (Associação Brasileira de Sexologia). Dr. Sérgio Luiz G. de Freitas, M.D., President. Address: Rua Tamandaré, 693 - Conj. 77, 01525-001 São Paulo, SP, Brazil.

Brazilian Sexual Impotency Research Society. Sociedade Brasileira de Pesquisa sobre Impotência Sexual. Roberto Tullii, M.D., Director. Address: Alameda Gabriel Monteiro da Silva, 1719, 01441-000 São Paulo, SP, Brazil.

Brazilian Sexual Education Association. Associação Brasileira de Educação Sexual. Address: Alameda Itú, 859, Apto 61, 01421-000 São Paulo, SP, Brazil.

Brazilian Society of Sexology. Isaac Charam, M.D., President. Address: Praça Serzedelo Correia, 15, Apto 703, 22040-000 Rio de Janeiro, RJ, Brazil.

Brazilian Society of Human Sexuality. Sociedade Brasileira de Sexualidade Humana. Address: Av. N.S. Copacabana, 1072, s. 703, 22020-001 Rio de Janeiro, RJ, Brazil.

Sexology Nucleus of Rio de Janeiro. Núcleo de Sexo-logia do Rio de Janeiro (NUDES). Address: Av Copacabana, 1018, Grupo 1109, 22060-000 Rio de Janeiro, RJ, Brazil.

National Sexology Commission of the Brazilian Federation of the Societies of Gynecology and Obstetrics. Comissão Nacional de Sexologia da Federação Brasileira das Sociedades de Ginecologia e Obstetrícia (FEBRASGO). Address: Edf. Venancio 2000, Bloco 50, Sala 137, 70302-000 Brasília, DF, Brazil.

Paranaense Commission of Sexology. Comissal Paranaense de Sexologia. Address: Rua General Carneiro, 181 - 4º andar. Maternidade do Hosp. de Clínicas, 80060-000 Curitiba, PR, Brazil.

Department of Sexology–ARE–Várzea do Carmo. Departamento de Sexologia–ARE–Várzca dc Carmo. Address: Rua Leopoldo Miguez, 257, 01518-000 São Paulo, SP, Brazil.

### B. Sexological Publications and Journals

The only sexological journal published in Brazil is *Jornal da AB-SEX*, published since 1986 by the Brazilian Association of Sexology (AB-SEX) (Associação Brasileira de Sexologia). Address: Rua Tamandaré, 693, Conj. 77, 01525-001 São Paulo, SP, Brazil.

Some newspapers, magazines, and other popular periodicals publish columns dealing with sexual interests that provide an insight into Brazilian sexual cultures and behaviors. These include *Notícias Populares* (SP), *Claúdia*, *Nova*, and *Carícia* (Editora Abril).

## 13. Sexual Behaviors of Aboriginal Indians

### A. Puberty Rituals and Premarital Activities

The behavior of several indigenous tribes of Brazil is similar, except for some variations particular to each native culture. The indigenous groups, such as the Kapalo, Xavantes, Tupinambas, and the Alpinages, have developed similar rituals for children and adolescents.

A girl is promised as a future bride while she is still very young, usually about 5 years of age. The future groom is a male adolescent, about 16 years old, who will marry her when she enters puberty and has her first menstruation. After her first menstruation, the girl is taken to the women's house (*Oca*). There she will remain for an entire year without being permitted to see sunlight or trim her hair. After a year's time, she is removed from the house and prepared for the nuptial party. She will be married to that same young man, who is now about 26 years of age.

Among the Kapalo, rituals of preparation for the male adolescent begin when he completes his 16th birthday. He must pass tests of courage, physical endurance, and resistance to pain. The boy must run through the forest for several kilometers while carrying a tree trunk. He must climb a tree and insert his arm into a bee or wasp hive, descending only after he has been stung several times. He must not hurry his descent nor run from the tree. He must also not scream or cry in pain. The boy must also demonstrate his skill in hunting and fishing with arrows (nets and hooks are not permitted for fishing). After passing all these tests, he is considered to be an adult. He will no longer live in the boys' house and must now reside in the unmarried men's house (*Oca*). He will then begin to take part in the adult fights and competitions.

At this point, he begins his sexual initiation. He may have sexual relations with any widow, older single women, and his older brother's wife. Sexual intercourse occurs mostly between people of different generations: the older generation teaches the younger generation.

Virginity is of secondary value. Girls usually lose their virginity before their wedding. The explanation is simple. The young women and men are not knowledgeable of the ways of the world. They marry old people of the opposite sex so they can learn from them.

### B. Sexual Behaviors of Single Adults

Because girls are married about age 5, there is a lack of young single women. Young men thus must be content with much older women. Although most are postmenopausal and sterile, there is the advantage of having a wife who knows how to cook, tend the fire, and keep the house. Thus, single young men will take any old woman for a bride, even if they do not find her attractive. As soon as it becomes possible, she will be traded for a younger wife. Men can only have sexual relations with fertile women after they have executed at least one enemy in a ritual killing.

Sometimes, the parents of the groom offer him an enemy to execute. However, if he wishes to marry a young woman, he must capture and kill an enemy himself. Because of this ritual, a single young man very seldom marries a fertile young woman before he is at least 30 years old. Men may only take part in war expeditions between the ages of 26 and 40 years of age. A man that has never imprisoned any slaves is labeled a "bad apple," or weak, timid, and cowardly (*Mebek*). He will never marry.

### C. Cohabitation, Marriage, and Monogamy

There is cohabitation without marriage, but once married, a woman's fidelity is demanded. Older men may reserve for themselves a high number of women, especially if they have gained power or prestige as warriors, medicine men, or Great Chiefs (*Caciques*). Old men are privileged; they can even reserve prepubescent (premenarche) girls for themselves. When a *Cacique* receives a young girl from her parents, he will wait for the first menstruation before having sexual intercourse with her. It is taboo to have sexual relations before menarche. There are frequent cases where there is reciprocal affection between a couple, and they remain united until the death of one of the consorts.

Dissolution of a marriage occurs with ease and frequency. Any incident as simple as a domestic disturbance or indisposition can lead to separation. The major cause of breach is the wife's adultery. In these cases, the mildest punishment is for the wife to be returned to her parents. A man may also repudiate, or even kill an adulterous woman, according to the tribe's natural laws. However, a man's adultery is received with approval by the community, which is amused by it. When a pregnant woman, widowed, divorced, or with a traveling husband, has sexual relations with another man, there is the difficulty in determining the father of the child. Such children, known as *Maraca*, "fruit of two seeds," are buried alive immediately following their birth.

This procedure also occurs any time twins are born. They believe twin children are generated by antagonistic spirits and must therefore be sacrificed.

After a birth there are some sexual prohibitions. The husband must abstain from sexual relations from the beginning of the pregnancy until the child can walk by itself or is at least a year old. This is the reason why men may have several wives (polygyny). In this manner, a man only has sexual relations with the same wife two years after the beginning of pregnancy.

## References and Suggested Readings

Abortos ilegais chegam a 6 milhões por ano. 1990 (November 9). *O Estrado de São Paulo*, p. 12.

Azevedo, M. A. 1985. *Mulheres espancadas: Violência denunciada*. São Paulo: Editora Soma.

Brasil realiza 10% dos abortos no *mundo*. 1989 (January 1). *Folha de São Paulo*.

Brooke, J. 1994 (September 2). With Church preaching in vain, Brazilians embrace birth control. *The New York Times*, pp. A1, A3.

CIA. 2002 (January). *The world factbook 2002*. Washington, DC: Central Intelligence Agency. Available: http://www.cia.gov/cia/publications/factbook/index.html.

Cirurgias clandestinas chegam a 5 milhões. 1987 (July 2). *Folha de São Paulo*. Caderno C, p. 7.

Código Civil, Lei Nº 10.406 [Civil Code, Law No. 10.406], Presidência da República, Casa Civil, Subchefia para Assuntos Jurídicos, signed January 10, 2002. Available: http://www.presidencia.gov.br/ccivil_03/LEIS/2002/L10406.htm.

Da Matta, R. 1978. *Carnavais malandros e heróis: Para uma sociologia do dilema brasileiro*. Rio de Janeiro: Zahar Editores.

Da Matta, R. 1983. Para uma teoria de sacanagem: Uma reflexão sobre a obra de Carlos Zefiro. In: J. Marinho, ed., *A Arte Sacana de Carlos Zefiro* (pp. 22-39). Rio de Janeiro: Editora Marco Zero.

Fernandes, F. 1989. *Organização social dos tupinambas*. São Paulo: Editora Hucitec.

*Folha de S. Paulo*. 2003 (January 10). Código Civil: Veja o que muda [Civil Code: Look at what's changed]. *Folha Online–Especial*. Available: http://www1.folha.uol.com.br/folha/especial/2003/codigocivil/veja_o_que_muda.shtml.

Freitas, S. L. G. 1989. *Sexologia ao alcance de todos*. São Paulo: Editora Comunidade (out of print).

Freitas, S. L. G. 1993. *Relatório freitas—Comportamento sexual da mulher brasileira*. São Paulo: Editora Soma.

Galanternick, M. 2002 (January 12). World briefing: Americas: Brazil: Equality for women. *The New York Times*, p. A5.

IPPM. 1983. *Hábitos e atitudes sexuais dos brasileiros*. Cultrix e Lab. Syntex do Brasil.

Loyola, M. A., ed. 1994. *AIDS e sexualidade: O ponto de vista das ciências humanas* [*AIDS and sexuality: The point of view of the social sciences*]. Rio de Janeiro, RJ, Brasil: Relume Dumará/Universidade do Estado do Rio de Janeiro.

*Manchete*. 1992 (October 10). Sexo depois dos 60 [Sex After 60], p. 40.

Maybury-Lewis, D. 1983. *Sociedade xavante*. São Paulo.

Muraro, R. M. 1983. *Sexualidade da mulher brasileira: Corpo e classe social no Brasil* [*Sexuality of the Brazilian woman: Body and social class in Brazil*]. Petrópolis, RJ, Brasil: Vozes.

O Brasil tem 10% dos abortos feitos no mundo. 1990 (November 9). *Folha de São Paulo*, Caderno C, p. 4.

*O Globo*. 2001 (August 16-18). O novo código. . . . *O Globo* [Rio de Janeiro], p. 1 (multiple articles). Available: http://www.oglobo.com.

Paiva, V. 1995. Sexuality, AIDS and gender norms among Brazilian teenagers. In: H. ten Brummelhuis & G. Herdt, eds., *Culture and sexual risk: Anthropological perspectives on AIDS*. Amsterdam: Gordon and Breach Science Publishers.

Parker, R. G. 1984. The body and self: Aspects of male sexual ideology in Brazil. Paper presented at the 83rd Annual Meeting of the American Anthropological Association, Denver, Colorado.

Parker, R. G. 1985. Masculinity, feminity, and homosexuality: On the anthropological interpretation of sexual meanings in Brazil. *Journal of Homosexuality*, *11*(3/4):155-63.

Parker, R. G. 1987. Acquired immunodeficiency syndrome in urban Brazil. *Medical Anthropology Quarterly*. n.s., *1*(2): 155-75.

Parker, R. G. 1991. *Corpos, prazeres e paixões: A cultura sexual no Brasil contemporâneo* [*Bodies, pleasures and passions: Sexual culture in contemporary Brazil*] (Trans. M. T. M. Cavallari). São Paulo, SP, Brasil: Editora Best Seller. English translation published as *Pleasures and passions: Sexual cultures in contemporary Brazil*. Boston: Beacon Press.

Parker, R., C. Bastos, J. Galvão, & J. S. Pedrosa, eds. 1994. *A AIDS no Brasil* [*AIDS in Brazil*]. Rio de Janeiro, RJ, Brasil: Relume Dumará/Associação Brasileira Interdisciplinar de AIDS/Instituto de Medicina Social, Universidade do Estado do Rio de Janeiro.

Rega, L. S. 1989. *Aspectos éticos do abortamento*. A monograph.

Ribas, Reverend Mario. Personal communication. mribas@iron.com.br (All Saints' Rectory, Praca Washington 93, 11065-600 Santos, São Paolo, Brazil.)

Rohter, L. 2001 (August 19). Slow to yield, Brazil passes equal rights for its women. *The New York Times*, section 1, p. 4.

Rosenberg. 2001 (January 28). Look at Brazil: How to solve the world's AIDS crisis. *The New York Times Magazine*, pp. 26ff.

Saffioti, H. I. B., & M. Muñoz-Vargas, eds. 1994. *Mulher brasileira é assim* [*The Brazilian woman is like this*]. Rio de Janeiro, RJ, Brasil: Editora Rosa Dos Tempos Ltda.

Santa Inêz, A. L. de. 1983. *Hábitos e atitudes sexuals dos brasilieros*. São Paulo: Editora Cultrix.

Schrierberg, D. 1995 (October 9). Samba warnings: Porn and promiscuity provoke a backlash. *Newsweek*, p. 52.

Suplicy, M. 1983. *Conversa sobre sexo*. Petrópolis: Editora Vozes.

Suplicy, M. 1985. *De Mariazinha a Maria*. Petrópolis: Editora Vozes.

Suplicy, M. 1994. Sexuality education in Brazil. *SIECUS Report, 22*(2):1-6.

UNAIDS. 2002. *Epidemiological fact sheets by country*. Geneva, Switzerland: Joint United Nations Programme on HIV/AIDS (UNAIDS/WHO). Available: http://www.unaids.org/hivaidsinfo/statistics/fact_sheets/index_en.htm.

*U.S. News & World Report*. 1994 (April). Battered by the myth of machismo: Violence against women is endemic in Brazil, p. 41.

*Veja especial: Mulher: A grande mudança no Brasil* [*Veja especial: Woman: The big change in Brazil*], August/September 1994.

# Bulgaria

Michail Alexandrov Okoliyski, Ph.D.,
and Petko Velichkov, M.D.*

## Contents

## Demographics and a Brief Historical Perspective

ROBERT T. FRANCOEUR

### A. Demographics

Bulgaria is located in southern Europe, with Romania and the Danube River on its northern border, the Black Sea on the east, Turkey and Greece on the south, and Macedonia and Yugoslavia on its western border. With a total landmass of 42,823 square miles (110,910 km²), Bulgaria is slightly larger than the state of Pennsylvania. The terrain is mostly mountainous, with lowlands and rolling hills in the north and southeast. The Balkan Mountains cross the center of the country, east to west. The Rila, Pirin, and Rhodope Mountains are in the west and south. The climate is temperate, with cold damp winters and hot dry summers. Nearly two fifths of Bulgaria's land is arable, and a fourth of this is irrigated, mostly in the southeast during the dry summer season. About a fifth of the country is pastureland and one third forested. Over the centuries, the strategic position of Bulgaria and Turkey in the Balkan Peninsula enabled the two nations to control a key trade and migration route between Europe and the Middle East.

According to the latest national survey (National Institute of Statistics (NIS), March 1, 2001), Bulgaria had a population of 7.98 million. Since the previous census in 1992, the population has declined by 6.6%. (All data are from *The World Factbook 2002* (CIA 2002) unless otherwise stated.)

**Age Distribution and Sex Ratios**: *0-14 years*: 14.6% with 1.06 male(s) per female (sex ratio); *15-64 years*: 68.5% with 0.97 male(s) per female; *65 years and over*: 16.9% with 0.72 male(s) per female; *Total population sex ratio*: 0. 94 male(s) to 1 female

**Life Expectancy at Birth**: *Total Population*: 71.5 years; *male*: 67.98 years; *female*: 75.22 years

**Urban/Rural Distribution**: 69% to 31%

---

*\*Communications*: Michail Alexandrov Okoliyski, Ph.D., National Center of Public Health, Sofia, Bulgaria; mental@mbox .cit.bg; Petko Velichkov, M.D., Human Sexuality Research Foundation, Sofia, Bulgaria; sexology@acad.bg; http://www.sexology .bol.bg.

(CIA 2002)

**Ethnic Distribution**: Bulgarian: 83.6%; Turk: 9.5%; Roma (Gypsy): 4.6%; Macedonian, Armenian, Tatar, Gagauz, Circassian, and others: 2.3% (NIS 2001; CIA 2002)

**Religious Distribution**: Bulgarian Orthodox: 83.8%; Muslim: 12.1%; Roman Catholic: 1.7%; Jewish 0.8%; Uniate Catholic: 0.2%; Protestant, Gregorian-Armenian, and other: 1.6% (1998 est.)

**Birth Rate**: 8.05 births per 1,000 population

**Death Rate**: 14.42 per 1,000 population

**Infant Mortality Rate**: 14.18 deaths per 1,000 live births

**Net Migration Rate**: –4.74 migrant(s) per 1,000 population

**Total Fertility Rate**: 1.13 children born per woman

**Population Growth Rate**: –1.11% (2002 est.); –1.14% (NIS 2001 est.)

**HIV/AIDS** (1999 est.): *Adult prevalence*: 0.01%; *Persons living with HIV/AIDS*: 346; *Deaths*: < 100. (For additional details from www.UNAIDS.org, see end of Section 10B.)

**Literacy Rate** (*defined as those age 15 and over who can read and write*): 98%; attendance for nine years of compulsory school; education is free and compulsory from age 6 to 16

**Per Capita Gross Domestic Product** (2001 est.) (*purchasing power parity*): $6,200; $5,720 (NIS est.); *Inflation*: 7.5%; *Unemployment*: 17.5%; 21.7% (NIS est.); *Living below the poverty line*: 35%; 21% (NIS est.)

### B. A Brief Historical Perspective

About 3500 B.C.E., the Thracians established the first civilization in what is now known as Bulgaria. In the fourth decade C.E., this region became part of the Roman Empire. As the Roman Empire declined, the Goths, Huns, and Avars moved in. In the 6th century, Slavs from what are now northwest Ukraine and southeastern Poland settled the region. In 679 C.E., the nomadic Bulgars from central Asia crossed the Danube River from the north and took control of the region, blending with the Slavs. The first Bulgarian kingdom was established in 681 and gradually became the most powerful state in the Balkans. Under Simeon I, who ruled from 893 to 927, Bulgaria experienced a golden age, as Macedonia, Albania, Serbia, and other parts of the

Byzantine Empire came under its influence. In 865, Boris I adopted Orthodox Christianity. Between 893 and 1280, the Bulgars twice conquered most of the Balkan Peninsula. In 1396, the Ottoman Turks invaded the land and made it a Turkish province until 1878. Bulgaria's position on the northern border of Turkey made its occupation by the Ottomans particularly harsh and inescapable.

In 1878, after winning the Russo-Turkish War (1877-1878), Russia forced Turkey to give Bulgaria its independence. Fearing the growing influence of Russia and Bulgaria in the Balkans, European powers intervened at the 1878 Congress of Berlin and fashioned Bulgaria's territory into a small principality ruled by Alexander, a nephew of the Russian Czar.

Prince Ferdinand of Saxe-Colburg-Gotha succeeded Alexander and declared Bulgaria a kingdom independent of Russia in 1908. After losing the Second Balkan War (June to August 1913) and all the territory it had gained in the First Balkan War (1912-1913), Bulgaria joined Germany in World War I. After being defeated in World War I, Ferdinand abdicated in favor of his son in 1934-1935. After joining the Germans in World War II, Bulgaria switched sides when Russia declared war on Bulgaria in September 1944. In three days, Russia took control of the country and installed a communist regime. The People's Republic of Bulgaria was officially established in 1946. Communist domination ended in 1990 with multiparty elections and movement toward political democracy and a free-market economy. High inflation, unemployment, corruption, and crime have been problems in recent years. In 2000, Bulgaria started on the path to eventual integration into the North Atlantic Treaty Organization (NATO) and the European Union (EU).

## 1. Basic Sexological Premises

### A. Character of Gender Roles  PETKO VELICHKOV

The social stereotypes concerning gender roles in Bulgaria are highly influenced by the long-lasting patriarchal tradition. Nevertheless, there are some considerable variations according to ethnic groups. In the present day, one can find some remnants of a patriarchal (men rule) model among the Turks, Armenians, Jews, and Gypsies. In general, Bulgarians did not subscribe to a macho style of social functioning. Ethnopsychological research has shown that the male domination was quite limited mostly in its outer expressions. Usually, Bulgarian men never made any major decision concerning the family's well-being without asking the opinion of their wives. In most families, women were (and often still are) the treasurers of the family's wealth. This kind of relationship was idiosyncratic for Bulgaria, but was not specific for the rest of the Balkan Peninsula (Panov 1914).

### B. Sociolegal Status of Males and Females

The United Nations Convention on the Rights of the Child is the fundamental principle of the Child's Protection Law. To monitor and enhance the implementation of this law, a State Agency for Child Protection has been in operation since October 2002.

During the totalitarian regime (1944-1989), great emphasis was put on the women's emancipation. However, Bulgarian women were already accustomed to such a model, as by the end of the 19th and the beginning of the 20th century, during three successive wars, when men were permanently absent for years, the country's economic output retained a peacetime level. Women successfully substituted for men as manpower in all kinds of labor.

In the present day, the concept of equal rights between the sexes is guaranteed by the Constitution. Article 6, paragraph 2 reads: "All persons shall be equal before the law. There shall be no privileges or restriction of rights on the grounds of race, nationality, ethnic self-identity, sex, origin, religion, education, opinion, political affiliation, personal or social status or property status." This principle is further elaborated in the legislation and is valid for the entire legal system of Bulgaria. The age of consent in Bulgaria is 18 years.

The Constitution also regulates the protection of motherhood, the recognition of its social function, and the joint responsibility of men and women in parenthood. According to article 14, "the family, motherhood, and childhood shall enjoy the protection of the State and society." Article 47, paragraph 2 reads: "Mothers shall be the object of special protection on the part of the State and shall be guaranteed prenatal and postnatal leave, free obstetric care, alleviated working conditions, and other social assistance." Either spouse can benefit from postnatal leave.

The Republic of Bulgaria is a party to most international instruments on human rights, as well as to international conventions on the rights of women such as the Convention on the Elimination of All Forms of Discrimination against Women, the Convention on the Political Rights of Women, the Convention on the Nationality of the Married Women, the Slavery Convention, the Convention for the Suppression of the Traffic in Persons and the Exploitation of the Prostitution of Others, as well as to most of the ILO Conventions regarding the labor conditions of women.

Many women's nongovernmental organizations (NGOs) have been registered in this country and, especially, during the last decade. Their aims include promoting the accomplishments of women in social life and the observance of their rights, elaborating and implementing programs and projects on the problems of women, their development, and progress, engaging in cultural, educational, charity, and international activities, and assisting women in business, scientific, and research work. Finally, they provide legal and psychological assistance to victims of violence, and so on.

The Penal Code contains a number of provisions related to violence against women. The relevant chapters titled "Crimes Against the Person" and "Crimes Against Marriage, Family and Youth" contain provisions directly concerning women, like abduction of a female person for the purpose of forcing her to enter into marriage (article 177, paragraph 2) or a parent or other relative receiving a consideration to permit his or her daughter or relative to conclude a marriage (article 178, paragraph 1); violating an obligation to a spouse or relative in an ascending or descending line, who is incapable of caring for him- or herself, and thereby placing him or her in a position of serious embarrassment (article 181); entering into marital relations with a female person under the age of 16 (articles 190, 191, and 192); persuading a female person to practice prostitution or abducting a female person for the purpose of her being placed at the disposal of others for acts of lewdness (articles 155 and 156), and so on. Legislation is envisaged to protect women from sexual harassment and exploitation of their economic dependence or low status in the workplace (Boskova 1998).

A recent public poll has demonstrated that Bulgarian men show strong approval for the existing egalitarian model. Only 6.7% of men expressed a negative attitude toward women's emancipation. The same research demonstrated equal representation of both sexes in the structure of the workforce: 46.7% women and 53.3% men. There were no significant differences in the educational level according to sex, although women's pay is nearly 30% less than men's. One possible explanation is that most women are employed in agriculture, textiles, and sewing manufacturing, education, healthcare, and other highly underpaid areas (Sociology Agency "Pleades 2002").

## C. General Concepts of Sexuality and Love

The socioeconomic and moral values in Bulgaria tend to vary, and hence, the growing variety of sexuality concepts and constructs, as well as the ways they are expressed.

Since ancient times, women's ideal was to raise children and maintain coziness in the family's home. Men were expected to ensure material comfort and protection. At that time, the tribal tradition of marriage was quite liberal (Draqganov 1984). The pairbonding process was based on mutual attraction and love. If pregnancy occurred, then marital rituals were performed (Kaloyanov 1995). In the pagan tradition, both male and female sexuality was highly prized, which is demonstrated by an unusually affluent erotic folklore (Sheytanov 1932).

In 865 C.E., Bulgarians adopted Christianity and the society switched to the Judeo-Christian patriarchal model. This transition was rather slow and was disrupted by the forced conversion to Islam of a significant portion of the population during the 14th to 19th centuries.

With the industrialization of the country in the 19th and 20th centuries, the patriarchal family model gave way to the nuclear family. Actually, the serial monogamy model is on the rise. A plausible reason behind this phenomenon might be the very high—and mostly unrealistic—expectations of modern Bulgarians toward partnership, marriage, parenthood, and children. Love, friendship, and material comfort are the key factors to a marital relationship. In 66% of families, both spouses rank love first as a reason for their marriage, 23% rank friendship first, and only 9% rank material comfort first "Pleades 2002").

## 2. Religious, Ethnic, and Gender Factors Affecting Sexuality

PETKO VELICHKOV

### A. Source and Character of Religious Values

The strongest religious values among Bulgarians are rooted in Orthodox Christianity, although some vague reminiscences of the ancient pagan tradition are adding some nuances. The common Bulgarian folk have not been famous for their religiousness. As a rule, the religious doctrine is subject to rather down-to-earth interpretations, and fanaticism or fundamentalism is not prized at all. The restrictive attitude toward sexuality has vanished with the patriarchal morality.

### B. Source and Character of Ethnic Values

The contemporary Bulgarian nation is a highly rich ethnic blend. Various cultures with their specific ethics have met and blended in this land, which has always been at a crossroad between the Western world and the East, as well as between the North and the South. Hence, the diversity in attitudes, ranging from pronounced openness and tolerance to moderation in sexual matters.

## 3. Knowledge and Education about Sexuality

MICHAIL OKOLIYSKI

*A Caution*: The short and deep political and economic changes of recent years in Eastern Europe have created a difficult situation regarding sexual behavior and AIDS prevention in Bulgaria. On the one hand, rapid modernization and the opening to the West have created an overabundance of new sexual options (pornography, commercial sex work, the self-identification of sexual minorities, etc.). On the other hand, there is no public education on the dangers of the new sexual freedom, no sex counseling, no educational literature, no outreach to persons at risk, or no concerted prevention ef-

fort. According to this situation of poverty and crime, there are some cynical voices in Bulgaria that would claim it is unnecessary to spend effort and money on empirical scientific and prognostic studies about social risks. But when we search for answers to these problems only in the "here and now" perspective without trying to learn about people's attitudes and behaviors, it is clear that the results of the health prevention programs will be negative. Under these circumstances, it is very difficult to run scientific studies. Given this reality, the picture of sexuality in Bulgaria provided in this chapter is based on the few studies and surveys available, namely:

- 2002: *Overview of HIV/AIDS in South Eastern Europe.* International Organization for Migration (I.O.M.) and UNICEF.
- 2000: A.S.A. *A representative high school students survey of Sofia and the country.* United Nations Development Program/Mental Health (UNDP/MH), conducted by A.S.A.; Sofia sample—761 students; national sample—1666 students; 9-12 grade. Comparative data for Sofia are for a comparable age (16-year-olds).
- 1999. *Conditions of AIDS prevention in Bulgaria.* Michail Okoliyski, Humboldt University (Dissertation), Berlin, http://edoc.hu-berlin.de/abstract.php3/ dissertationen/phil/okoliyski-michail-alexandrov.
- 1996: *Reproductive Behavior Family Planning. Contraceptives Use.* (An empirical sociological survey directed by Mihail Mirchev). A.S.A.-MH, Ministry of Health, The Phare Programme, Sofia (Mirchev, Jachkova, Kasakova, Velikova).
- 1995: National Health Center. *A NHC Representative Survey of Sofia* (1044 respondents, 9-11 grade).
- 1995: *AIDS and Sexuality*; a study based on a representative sample for Sofia on 15- to 17-year-olds. The Agency for Socioeconomic Analyses—A.S.A., June-July, 1995.
- 1992: Argirova, R., D. Beschkov, O. Troschev, E. Bodscheva, V. Georgieva, *The AIDS Experience*, AIDS-Centre, Sofia.
- 1988: *Medical Academy Representative Survey of Sofia* (1100 respondents, 9-11 grade).

### A/B. Formal and Informal Sources of Sexual Knowledge

There is very little sex education for Bulgaria's youth in the schools and at home.

For effective AIDS prevention among Bulgaria's youth and others target groups, health professionals need insights into the behavior patterns and motives that hide behind epidemiological data. In order to gain a better understanding of sexual knowledge, attitudes, and practices in Bulgaria, Michail Okoliyski (1999) undertook a survey using face-to-face interviews on the "Conditions of AIDS prevention in Bulgaria" during his doctoral studies at the Humboldt-University in Berlin under the scientific guidelines of Prof. Erwin. J. Haeberle. The resulting dissertation is the result of the analysis of an initial survey of IV-drug users, persons with homosexual, bisexual, and heterosexual behavior, and people who are selling sexual services. Although the survey respondents were not a representative sample, their responses can provide, with caution, some insights into the sexual attitudes, knowledge, and behaviors of Bulgarians in general. The study was conducted in the period 1997-1998 in the capital city of Bulgaria, Sofia.

Of those answering Okoliyski's questionnaire, 84.7% received their sexual knowledge from friends, with 20.3% through the media. Only 15.3% received sex education from their parents. This confirms the claim of many Bulgarian educators that sex is still a taboo subject in most Bulgarian families. The fact that only 13.6% learned anything about sex from their teachers reflects the general absence of sex education in Bulgarian schools, where students are taught a total of only two hours about the biological differences between the sexes. There is a total lack of formal education with regard to the psychological and social aspects of sex. As a result, Bulgarian adolescents feel abandoned by their elders as far as their own sexual problems are concerned. They still get their sexual knowledge "in the streets" (see Table 1).

Knowledge about HIV/AIDS is obtained in a quite different way. Most Bulgarians learn about it from the media, since friends and peer groups are largely uninformed because of a lack of any intensive government campaigns. Again, parents and schools play a very modest role, illustrating once again the inadequacy of formal sex education. There is one relative difference between our target groups, however. Persons with bisexual and homosexual behavior receive more AIDS information from their friends and peer groups (see Table 2).

The ideas of sexuality and sexual behavior in the youth population in Bulgaria are becoming more and more pragmatic. In 2000, 15.2% of 16-year-old students in Sofia *do not agree* that sex without love is useless (A.S.A. UNDP/ MH 2000). Five years ago, they were 12.2% (NHC 1995), and in 1988, just 8.2% (Med. Academy Represent. Survey Sofia 1988). There are changing attitudes towards using commercial sex services. A third of the students (from the national sample) support a possible legalization of prostitution, and 6.7% state they have used commercial sex.

According to the same survey, 11.2% of students who have an active sexual life have a positive attitude to accidental sexual contacts, and the attitude to this is that 7.8% are neutral. In other words, 19% of the sexually active teenagers consider accidental sexual contacts permissible. Even more informative is the fact that 33.4% of surveyed students who have a sexual life would under certain circumstances take part in group sex.

There is an abrupt rise in positive attitudes towards condom use, but it is not accompanied by actual behavior. At the same time, the share of respondents who would not insist with their partner on condom use remains at the 1995 level and even increases by 2% (see Table 3). In 2000, the attitude that *condoms reduce sexual pleasure* is still the greatest obstacle to their use. The share of students who do

not share the opinion rises in comparison with 1995 by only 4%. Factors such as feeling embarrassed to buy a condom are no longer valid—over 60% of students would not feel embarrassed to buy a condom (see Table 4).

HIV/AIDS awareness among Sofia students in 2000 is almost the same as in 1995. Indicators of awareness such as the understanding that *the disease is incurable* and that *a week after sexual intercourse, transmitted virus cannot be identified* are rising. The basic knowledge that *the virus is transmitted through sperm, blood, and vaginal secretions* remains at the same level for all samples (76% to 78%).

At the same time, there are indications that anal sex risk-awareness is decreasing. In 1995, 39.8% of 15- to 16-year-old students in Sofia were aware that anal intercourse is the riskiest one, while only 32.9% of same-age students know that today. At the national level, this knowledge is common for 36.8% of high school students. Additional analyses failed to confirm the hypothesis that lowered awareness of anal sex risk is connected to the higher tolerance to homosexuals in the last few years.

HIV/AIDS awareness, as with prevention attitudes, depends on the type of school, size of settlement, and ethnic background. Thus, for instance, the knowledge of the long latent period of HIV is common for 35.7% of vocational school students, 51.1% of secondary school students, and 70.0% of high school students. Other indices do not show such substantial differences among students in vocational and secondary schools. The basic line of division is between vocational and secondary schools, on the one hand, and high schools, on the other.

Understanding of the subjective HIV-infection risk is an important indicator of awareness of the problem. Available data show little development in the understanding of the subjective HIV-infection risk. The majority (50%) of students do not *worry* that they personally can be infected. On the national level, only 19% perceive HIV as a big danger and are

**Table 3**

**Would You Refuse Sexual Contact If Your Partner Would Not Use a Condom?**

|  | 1988 | 1995 | 2000 (16-year-olds) |
|---|---|---|---|
| Definitely yes | 13.1% | 16.8% | 22.9% |
| I think yes | 14.3 | 22.6 | 19.9 |
| I cannot say | 38.8 | 26.8 | 26.3 |
| I think I would not insist | 19.9 | 20.2 | 15.3 |
| I would definitely not insist | 13.9 | 13.6 | 15.7 |

*Source*: Medical Academy, 1988; NHC/ASA, 1995; UNDP/MH/ ASA, 2000; Comparable Sofia Samples.

**Table 4**

**Do You Think That Condom Use Makes Sexual Intercourse Unpleasant?**

|  | 1988 | 1995 | 2000 (16-year-olds) |
|---|---|---|---|
| Definitely yes | 14.2% | 14.0% | 12.3% |
| I think yes | 13.9 | 17.2 | 10.2 |
| I cannot say | 52.5 | 35.9 | 38.1 |
| Probably not | 10.6 | 16.4 | 18.6 |
| Definitely not | 8.7 | 16.4 | 20.8 |

*Source*: Medical Academy, 1988; NHC/ASA, 1995; UNDP/MH/ ASA, 2000; Comparable Sofia Samples.

**Table 1**

**Sources of Sexual Knowledge**

|  | Parents | School | Friends | Media |
|---|---|---|---|---|
| Bisexual behavior | 6.7% | 20 % | 80 % | 6.7% |
| Homosexual behavior | 15 | 5 | 85 | 25 |
| Heterosexual behavior | 15.4 | 15.4 | 92.3 | 23.1 |
| IV-drug use | 27.3 | 18.2 | 81.8 | 27.3 |

**Table 2**

**Sources of Information about HIV and AIDS**

|  | Parents | School | Friends | Media |
|---|---|---|---|---|
| Bisexual behavior | 6.7% | 6.7% | 73.3% | 40 % |
| Homosexual behavior | 5 | 30 | 50 | 75 |
| Heterosexual behavior | 14.3 | 14.3 | 21.4 | 71.4 |
| IV-drug use | 16.7 | 8.3 | 16.7 | 66.7 |

thinking about that. An important fact is that this attitude is higher in smaller settlements and teenagers of families of lower social and economic status. Additional analyses show an important connection between HIV/AIDS unawareness and subjective risk perception. Thus, for instance, teenagers, who are not aware that the HIV virus is transmitted through blood, sperm, and vaginal secretions, perceive this risk as higher. Therefore, we are not talking so much about awareness of the problem, but rather about the higher level of concern, which is always connected to less awareness.

Be it so, this concern has changed only a fraction in the last five years. And this is only natural from the point of view of insignificant changes in HIV/AIDS awareness. Nevertheless, there is a slight increase in subjective risk perception in the last 12 years (see Table 5).

However, this is just one side of the gradation that shows how often students received information from one source or another. It must be mentioned that such data are to a large degree conditional. Respondents tend to point to sources that *should inform* and not the ones they *actually used*. A significant fact is that the influence of information sources in Sofia is different from that for the country as a whole.

Despite this conditional status of the data, it is evident that the influence the same channel (information source) exerts in Sofia and in the countryside is different. Obviously, the influence potential of Sofia schools is higher than that of the countryside. On the other hand, friendships in the province are probably closer and more influential.

## 4. Autoerotic Behaviors and Patterns
MICHAIL OKOLIYSKI

Only a minority of the respondents of the Okoliyski survey made between 1998 and 1999 reported not engaging in this sexual practice (see Table 6). Also, the intensity and the

### Table 5

**How Big Is the Possibility That You Will Become AIDS Infected?**

|  | 1988 | 1995 | 2000 (16-year-olds) |
|---|---|---|---|
| No risk exists | 26.1% | 27.7% | 21.4% |
| The risk is small (I am not worried) | 46.5 | 42.0 | 40.3 |
| There is some possibility | 15.5 | 21.0 | 22.2 |
| The risk is considerable, I often think about it | 9.1 | 5.7 | 10.7 |
| There is very big possibility |  | 3.6 | 5.3 |

*Source*: Medical Academy, 1988; NHC/ASA, 1995; UNDP/MH/ASA, 2000; Comparable Sofia Samples.

### Table 6

**How Often in the Week Do You Practice Masturbation?**

|  | Never | More than once | Every day | Several times daily |
|---|---|---|---|---|
| Bisexual behavior | 20 % | 73.3% | 0% | 6.7% |
| Homosexual behavior | 10 | 75 | 15 | 0 |
| Heterosexual behavior | 35.7 | 64.3 | 0 | 0 |
| Drug users | 33.3 | 66.7 | 0 | 0 |

frequency of the masturbation were high: About two thirds of the respondents practice sexual self-sufficiency (self-stimulation) more than once a week. The survey data show that the sexual self-sufficiency and the mutual partner masturbation (hand and body massage) are an important part of the sexual lives of these people. Although these sexual practices are used mainly in connection with other sexual variations, they are an important part of the sexual lives of these people.

[*Comment 2003*: Sex therapists have noticed a bullish tendency of acceptance towards sexual self-gratification, especially among single males. In married couples, male as well as female masturbation is perceived as some kind of deviation rater than a sign of the couple's malfunctioning (Archives of Human Sexuality Research Foundation (H.S.R.F.) unpublished data). (*End of comment by P. Velichkov*)]

## 5. Interpersonal Heterosexual Behaviors
### A. Children
[*Comment 2003*: Very little is known about children's sexuality in Bulgaria, and no research has been carried out on this topic. [*End of comment by P. Velichkov*)]

### B. Adolescents                    PETKO VELICHKOV
Some ethnic differences have been perceived concerning menarche and the age of first sexual intercourse for females (see Table 7). The average age at which male adolescents start their sex life is 16.1 years (Tzekov 2003).

### C. Adults
*Marriage, Affairs, and Divorce*   PETKO VELICHKOV
The institution of marriage, in Bulgaria, is in a transition as more than one fifth of the households are in fact couples in a steady relationship without official marriage. Thus, in 2002, about 40% of the children are born of some kind of nonmarital relationship. As the marital index, currently at 4 per 1,000—half the rate of 20 years ago—is plunging down, it is only natural for the divorce index to be affected at a lower rate. Thus, when the number of officially registered marriages decreases, implicitly the probability for divorce also decreases, but not at the same pace of 1.3 per 1,000 (Belcheva 2002).

*Sexual Satisfaction*            PETKO VELICHKOV
It has been established that 63% of women in the age range of 20 to 31 years, cohabiting with a male partner, had sexual intercourse two or three times weekly. Among married women in the same age range, less than 20% attained such a frequency. In the tenth year of marriage, 38% of husbands are not happy with their marital sex; of them, 43% of men rank as a first cause the diminished interest of their wife toward sex; 67% of wives declared that they had been solicited for sex more frequently than they would have wished to be "Pleades 2002").

*Sexual Relationships*           MICHAIL OKOLIYSKI
A significant majority of people were in a committed (*unpromisk* "non-promiscuous") sexual relationship: 65.6%

### Table 7

**Estimated Age of Menarche and Sexarche (2003 Estimates)**

|  | Age at Menarche | Age at First Sex Contact |
|---|---|---|
| Roma girls | 12.2 | 14.6 |
| Turk | 12.8 | 15.4 |
| Bulgarian | 13.5 | 16.8 |

were with a partner-relationship; 26.2% were without a partner-relationship; and only 29% of the respondents have more than one partner at the same time (Okoliyski 1999) (see Table 8). There are also some changes in the quantitative parameter of the partner relationships in recent years, with a decrease in the number of sexual partners.

*Incidence of Oral and Anal Sex* PETKO VELICHKOV

Anal sex, fellatio, and cunnilingus are not subject to any restrictions, provided they are practiced between consenting adults. According to therapists, anal sex in heterosexual relationships is almost exclusively initiated by the male. Nowadays, fellatio and cunnilingus are willingly accepted by most couples as an element of their loveplay. Cunnilingus is regarded as a must by most men with premature ejaculation (H.S.R.F.).

## 6. Homoerotic, Homosexual, and Bisexual Behaviors

MICHAIL OKOLIYSKI

Respondents in the Okoliyski 1999 survey engaging in same-sex and bisexual behavior were very ambivalent toward their own sexuality: 46.7% of the sample with bisexual behavior and 75% of the respondents with homosexual behavior were negative about their own sexuality (see Table 9). In our opinion, this statistic shows that they did not consider their sexuality as a common part of human sexual behavior. Since the late 1960s and early 1970s, homosexual activity between consenting adults is no longer prosecuted. This decriminalization was an official step toward emancipation of the sexual minorities made under the totalitarian regime. As we know from other researchers, two types of commercial sex workers do appear to be at risk of HIV transmission. In the first place, those without a self-identity, and in the second place, those resulting from isolation and stigmatization; the absence of social support and control may discourage condom use. Anyway, unsafe sex practices may result from this lower degree of institutionalization in prostitution, which may result in unsafe sex practices.

## Table 8

### Adult Sexual Relationship Partner Situation*

|  | Bisexual behavior | Homo-sexual behavior | Hetero-sexual behavior | Drug Use | Total |
|---|---|---|---|---|---|
| I live in a partner-relationship | 73.3% | 50% | 78.6% | 66.7% | 65.6% |
| I live without a partner-relationship | 0 | 45 | 21.4 | 33.3 | 26.2 |
| I have more than one partner at the same time | 26.7 | 5 | 0 | 8.3 | 8.2 |

*confirmative answers.

## Table 9

### Is Your Sexual Behavior Acceptable to Society?

|  | Bisexual behavior | Homosexual behavior | Heterosexual behavior | Drug Use |
|---|---|---|---|---|
| Yes | 40 % | 20% | 71.4% | 50 % |
| No | 46.7 | 75 | 7.1 | 33.3 |
| I don't know | 3.3 | 5 | 21.4 | 6.7 |

## 7. Gender Diversity and Transgender Issues

PETKO VELICHKOV

A search into the archive of the former sexology outpatient clinics has shown that, for a 35-year period, gender-conflicted clients composed only a tiny share of the patient population, only 0.1%. A total number of 47 persons were transsexuals looking for sex reassignment. Among them, as many as 38 were female-to-male patients and only 9 were diagnosed as male-to-female transsexuals. (The fact that more than half of the biologically male transsexuals emerged during the first seven years following the abolishment of the dictatorship may suggest some socioeconomic explanation to the striking discrepancy of the male/female ratio.)

Twenty-three persons, 15 female and 8 male, obtained a legal sex reassignment procedure. After at least one year of "adaptation" period, 21 patients (14 female and 7 male) proceeded with a sex-reassignment surgery. (The first operation in Bulgaria on a female-to-male transsexual after a legal sex reassignment was performed in 1988 by an andrologist and plastic surgeon team.

Two of the transsexuals decided not to undertake surgery. They felt comfortable and satisfied with the legal change of their sex alone and have not pursued surgery. The follow-up on the operated patients demonstrated a beneficial effect mostly on the quality of their lives.

Actually, there are no special legal regulations concerning transsexuals. Sex-reassignment procedures are performed on transsexuals within the existing legal framework that is being routinely applied to intersexual cases. The court presumes that sex assignment at birth, exclusively based on the appearance of the external genitalia, may be inaccurate (H.S.R.F. unpublished data).

## 8. Significant Unconventional Sexual Behaviors

**A. Coercive Sexual Behaviors** PETKO VELICHKOV

One of the most acute social problems to emerge during the political transition period is the increase in the national crime rate, which in the late 1990s reached unprecedented levels. For example, in 1989, the number of annually registered crimes was only 663 per 100,000 persons, while over the next 10 years this figure annually approximated 3,000 per 100,000. Crime is among the major sources of distress and concern of the population (see Table 10). Women in particular have become affected increasingly. Since the mid-1990s, the

## Table 10

### 2001 Crime Statistics

|  | Crimes reported | Persons Convicted* |
|---|---|---|
| Totals | 24,291 | 28,729 |
| These totals included: |  |  |
| Crimes against the person, comprising: | 1,735 | 1,819 |
| Debauchery | 328 | 325 |
| Rape | 139 | 164 |
| Crimes against marriage, family, and youth | 969 | 952 |

*The number of Crimes and Convicted persons do not match because sentences are pronounced on crimes committed during previous years.

number of women who have been victims of crime has risen by over 60% (United Nations 2001).

## B. Prostitution
MICHAIL OKOLIYSKI

*Sexual Behavior of Commercial Sex Workers (CSW)*

Under the Bulgarian penal legislation, persons who organize or distribute sex services are subject to penalty. Women introduced to this activity are not subject to penalty. Article 156, paragraph 1 of the Bulgarian Penal Code provides a penalty of 10 years in prison and a fine of up to BGN100 for anyone convicted of kidnapping a person of the female sex to commit her to obscene activities.

The legal status of prostitution determines to a large degree the non-transparency of researching and understanding thereof. The Epidemiological Control and Surveillance System does not record the professional status of infected people. It is even less possible to do that with regard to female prostitutes. However, a number of subgroups of women can be separated according to the different types of prostitution:

*Street and Highway Prostitution.*

These are girls who work on the outside, in central and peripheral city and town areas—railways and bus stations, streets, highways, border and roadside motels, and TIR parking lots. They are known as "crew girls." The majority are of Roma (Gypsy) or Turkish descent, young, low-educated, with no health or sexual education. Characteristic behavior models include parental violence, selling the girl into the business, or total exploitation of her income by the procurer or the whole family. The factor that makes this group one of the highest risk groups is "regular customers." With the flow of time, the girls start to regard them as reliable partners and, therefore, lower safety measures when serving them. Another factor is different cultural and religious attitudes to safe sex and condoms that some of the multinational customers have. A specific subgroup is notable—the group of "transit girls," who travel with one customer from border to border, and then either return with their next customer or go to a third border. This extremely high mobility, as well as supposedly low typical level of working conditions and safety, turns it into one of the highest risk groups with regard to both HIV/STD risk and physical safety.

*Hotel Prostitution.* Hotels have a constant contingent of attending girls with set prices and working hours. In the summer, some of them are sent to the seaside "on business trips."

*Companion Clubs.* This business is under tight control. The tariffs of all clubs offering sex services are strictly uniform. The girls are aged 18 to 22. They come from all social strata—schoolgirls and college-girls, as well as married working girls who work as call-girls. Beside Bulgarians, the clubs employ many foreigners, mainly Russian and Ukrainian. Characteristics of the clubs are unconditional safety measures and condom use; medical examinations and testing are obligatory, according to certain information.

Unofficially, there exists another subgroup of elite prostitutes. Closely related to the high levels of the business organization, they and their work gain no publicity. They are called "escort" girls.

Sociological data regarding CSWs were gathered by the Health and Social Environment Foundation for the years 1997 to 1999. These data were collected in face-to-face interviews with "highway" CSWs using standardized questionnaires. The 1997 survey covered 167 girls working in Lom, Russe, and Sofia. The 1998 and 1999 follow-up surveys covered 63 and 66 CSWs, respectively, in the same places. The surveys were held within the framework of this project and the AIDS on Wheels project. The results were:

- *Age*: More than 10% of the girls were below age 16. Thirty to 50% were 16 to 18 years old. The other two age groups, 18 to 22 and over 22 comprise 40% of the women.
- *Education*: Elementary education was the prevailing level of education—with 40.1% of the group members. Girls who have primary and secondary education form equal proportions of the commercial sex workers—24% each.
- *Ethnic Background*: Bulgarians form the largest ethnic community within the group—46.7% of the interviewees described themselves as Bulgarians. Of ethnic minorities, girls of Roma background form a 33.5% share, Bulgarian Muslims 6.6%, and 5.4% are Turkish. A not-so-small share of Roma girls describes themselves as Bulgarians.
- *Marital Status*: 23.4% of the interviewees were divorced, 7.8% were single, 6% were married, and 5.4% stated they were living with a friend/constant partner.
- *Social Background and Material Status*: most of the group representatives are of lower social and economic status—unemployed or low-paid or unskilled workers. Most of the village girls come from families of farmers. These data apply mostly to women working on the outside.
- *Health Care Related Behavior*: No stable habits of going for prophylactic examinations were observed. For over a third of the women, the reason to seek healthcare was health disorders. On the other hand, more than 85% of the women admitted that no one had ever prevented them from seeing the doctor, regardless of whether they had had a health problem or wanted to have a prophylactic examination. Attitudes toward the quality of services offered by the respective health facilities should also be accounted for. The general attitude toward healthcare is positive. Confidence in the preservation of personal secrets, however, is low.

## C. Pornography and Erotica
PETKO VELICHKOV

Pornography was prohibited in Bulgaria until 1989. That means there was no such business or market. But interested individuals could obtain some imported materials at their personal risk.

After the last political changes in the early 1990s, the pendulum switched to the other side and pornography flooded the market, although it could still be prosecuted. The trick is that the law does not specify what exactly pornography is, and so the business and the merchants are offering only "erotica." In 13 years, the interest in pornography and its market has visibly shrunk.

## 9. Contraception, Abortion, and Population Planning
PETKO VELICHKOV

### A. Contraception

As soon as abortion on request was legalized in the mid 1950s, it became the most common form of birth control in this country.

Nowadays, 76% of the women admit to using some kind of contraception. However, there are a great variety of methods according to socioeconomic status. A small portion of the well-to-do women (middle class included) has access to modern contraception. The rest benefits predominantly from the calendar method, withdrawal, and condoms (in order of frequent use). (Data supplied by V. Tzekov, expert in gynecology at the Human Sexuality Research Foundation).

There are very few NGOs that provide contraceptive means for the needy, and when they do, this is on a rather irregular basis.

See data on condom use in Section 10, Sexually Transmitted Diseases and HIV/AIDS.

### B. Teenage (Unmarried) Pregnancies

Each year, about 5% of Bulgarian women in their fertile age give birth between ages 15 and 19.

### C. Abortion

First-trimester abortion on request is legal, provided it takes place in a state medical institution, and post-abortion contraceptive counseling is legally required. In 2002, an estimated 41.2% of pregnancies were terminated by an abortion (V. Tzekov, expert in gynecology at Human Sexuality Research Foundation, unpublished data).

### D. Population Programs

Studies show that economic hardships have encouraged negative tendencies in reproductive and sexual behavior, hence, a negative population growth. The two-children model is still present among Bulgarians, but only as an unattainable ideal. So far, no effective pronatalistic policy has been elaborated and implemented in this country (Belcheva 2002).

## 10. Sexually Transmitted Diseases and HIV/AIDS

MICHAIL OKOLIYSKI

### A. Sexually Transmitted Diseases

*STD Trends*

The rate of sexually transmitted non-HIV/AIDS infections, which is an indicator of HIV infection, has increased over the last ten years. Since 1990, there has been an alarming trend in the number of syphilis cases. Whereas, in 1990, the number of newly recorded syphilis cases was 378 (4.5 out of 100,000), in 1999, there were 2,509 new cases (30 out of 100,000). According to the World Health Organization (WHO) criteria, some regions of the country are on the verge of an epidemic outbreak. The hepatitis B and C infection rates in Bulgaria are several times higher than that in some European countries. The large number of chronic cases resulting in disability and death, combined with the considerable expenditures for their treatment, make them socially and economically important.

*Condoms and Safe and Unsafe Sexual Practices*

Detailed data were collected by the first author from respondents concerning the types and safety of their sexual contacts. Respondents were asked about their specific sexual acts. The vast majority of the people with heterosexual, bisexual, and homosexual behavior, in general, often used condoms; only the group of the intravenous drug users used condoms very inconsequently—66.7% of them performed unsafe coitus and cunnilingus. Half of the drug users were willing to perform fellatio without the protection in order to secure money for drugs. This group of drug users represents diverse segments of the population, who, in turn, are characterized by inconsequent and low frequencies of condom use, a high prevalence of STDs, and inadequate knowledge of the basic concepts of HIV transmission and prevention (see Table 11). About 50% of the respondents indicated changes in their sexual behavior because of AIDS (see Table 12), but there is the potential danger of infection with HIV for about half of the respondents who do not use condoms regularly (see Table 13).

*Evaluation of Condoms.* A series of questions were asked to elicit beliefs and attitudes about condoms. In fact, the opinion of the respondents on condoms was predominantly negative.

Frighteningly, nearly half the respondents report that they do not use condoms regularly, 27.3% report that when they use alcohol or drugs, they do not care about AIDS, and 41% said they usually do not use condoms (see Table 14).

### Table 11

**Sexual Practices of Intravenous Drug Users, With and Without Condoms During the Last Sexual Relations***

| | Not practiced | With condom | Without condom |
|---|---|---|---|
| Vaginal intercourse (Coitus) | 0% | 33.3% | 66.7% |
| Masturbation/Body massage | 0 | 0 | 100 |
| Cunnilingus | 33.3 | 0 | 66.7 |
| Petting | 20 | 0 | 80 |
| Fellatio | 50 | 0 | 50 |
| Anal sex | 90.9 | 0 | 9.1 |
| Group sex | 100 | — | — |
| Sadomasochistic sex | 100 | — | — |

*confirmative answers

### Table 12

**Changes of Sexual Behavior**

| | Bisexual behavior | Homo-sexual behavior | Hetero-sexual behavior | Drug users | Total |
|---|---|---|---|---|---|
| Yes | 60% | 50% | 64.3% | 59% | 49.2% |
| No | 40 | 50 | 35.7 | 50 | 50.8 |

### Table 13

**How Often Do You Have Condoms When You Are Going Out?**

| | Bisexual behavior | Homosexual behavior | Heterosexual behavior | Drug users |
|---|---|---|---|---|
| Always | 73.3% | 40% | 28.6% | 16.7% |
| Sometimes | 20 | 35 | 35.7 | 25 |
| Never | 6.7 | 25 | 35.7 | 58.3 |

### Table 14

**Attitudes to Condoms***

| | Bisexual behavior | Homo-sexual behavior | Hetero-sexual behavior | Drug users | Total |
|---|---|---|---|---|---|
| I use condoms because of AIDS/STDs | 66.7% | 50 % | 50 % | 16.7% | 47.5% |
| I don't use condoms | 33.3 | 40 | 42.9 | 50 | 41 |
| When I use alcohol/drugs, I don't care about AIDS | 21.4 | 15 | 33.3 | 50 | 27.3 |

*confirmative answers

Condoms were not only inconsequential in use, but they also are not always available for the commercial sex workers. The respondents did not seem to consider accessibility or cost to be important obstacles to condom use, but nearly 21% reported that they never have condoms when going out and 29% said condoms were sometimes unavailable when needed; 50% always have condoms.

## B. HIV/AIDS

*HIV/AIDS History and Current Status*

The first HIV-positive case in Bulgaria was diagnosed 18 years ago, in 1989. At the start of the epidemic in the country (1985-1986), in most of the cases the virus was imported from Africa, and the infection sources were sailors who had had sexual intercourse in the ports of Zaire, South Africa, and other African countries.

In 1986-1987, all hemophiliacs living in the country were subjected to obligatory testing, and 11 HIV-positives were found among them. They were probably infected before 1985 (i.e., before testing of each donated blood unit was introduced).

A few years later, after 1991, the picture was totally changed. At present, in over 70% of the time, transmission is from an infected Bulgarian citizen to another person within the country.

Bulgaria is still considered a low HIV/AIDS-prevalence country. By May 15, 2000, there had been registered a total of 287 HIV-positive people—75 of whom have AIDS—and 73 AIDS deaths. The statistical index for the spread of the disease among adult men and women used in AIDS-related reports is 2.2—a number comparable to the figures for Africa. Analysis of the distribution of the registered HIV-positive cases by sex shows that 70% of the infected are men and 30% are women. In 2000 (May 15), the number of newly registered HIV-positives was 17, 14 of whom were men (82.3%) and 3 were women (17.7%).

Analysis of age distribution shows the majority are men aged 20 to 40, and, in particular, 21 to 30 year olds. Another worrying fact is that about 7% of HIV-positives are aged 15 to 19.

Among people living with AIDS in the period from 1977 to 1999, most affected were people in the active age—15 to 49 year olds (93%), with 7% over 50 years old; 67% of the people living with AIDS are men. There are no people living with AIDS aged 0 to 14.

The main mode of transmission in our country is sexual transmission—83%, mostly heterosexual—about 70% of the HIV-positive cases. Infected blood transfusions account for 14%, and mother-to-child transmission for 1%. So far, there have been registered 8 HIV-positive injecting drug users. Until 1993, there were no HIV-positive injecting drug users.

A comparison of these data with published data about the mode of transmission in developed countries shows considerable differences (WHO, *Weekly Epidemiological Record*, 74:409-420). The main mode of transmission in industrialized countries is homosexual/bisexual (37%), followed by heterosexual (32%), transmission through injecting drug use (26%), transmission through blood transfusion (25%), perinatal infection (1%), and other (1%).

Regarding the geographical distribution of HIV-positive cases in the country, it is notable that the biggest concentration of infected people is found in the following cities: Sofia 65, and Burgas 59 (mainly sailors working on fishing ships, who have stayed for a long time in African ports and had heterosexual relationships there). The number of HIV-positive cases in the city of Burgas continues to rise also through intracity transmission. There are 19 HIV-positive cases in

Varna. The number of HIV-positives in Gabrovo is 18 and has remained constant since 1993, although, since 1997, there have been registered 2 or 3 connected cases. Then come the cities of Plovdiv with 16, Stara Zagora with 13, and others. The Ministry of Health states that the distribution by regions of the newly registered cases by May 15, 2000, was as follows: the city of Sofia: 5, Haskovo: 2, Lovech: 2, and 1 HIV-positive person in each of the regions of Sofia, Blagoevgrad, Dobrich, Pleven, Gabrovo, Silistra, and Plovdiv. The HIV virus has spread among almost all social groups and professions, though, regretfully, not all registered HIV-positive people declare their profession. A large number of them have been transferred to less physically demanding jobs following recommendation by the state.

The WHO record ranks Bulgaria seventh of the ten countries most at risk of infection over the next 10 years. Based on the prognosis, if effective measures are taken now, the HIV epidemic could be contained in Bulgaria.

The health experts revealed the main determinants in the rapid growth of HIV/AIDS infection in Bulgaria. The following factors directly affect the infection rate: risky sexual behavior (unprotected sex); high incidence of sexually transmitted infections; and risky injecting drug use practices (shared needles and syringes). Some of the indirect factors are: poverty (economic insolvency); prostitution; drug and alcohol abuse; low health awareness; low general education of some vulnerable groups; and high (labor) mobility. The lack of an overall policy addressing high-risk behavior and HIV/AIDS prevention, as well as the ineffectiveness of the relevant institutions, agencies, and services, and the transition are other indirect factors.

In medical practice, blood products and invasive procedures pose the highest risk. Among the indirect factors are: lack of standards and good practices, and insufficient skills for diagnosis, consultation, and treatment of HIV/AIDS.

## C. Most Vulnerable Groups

Several groups have been identified by UNICEF and the International Organization for Migration (I.O.M.) (2002) as the most vulnerable to HIV/AIDS and STDs.

*Adolescents and Young People*

The analysis indicated that young people have not developed sufficient social and life skills necessary for making responsible decisions about their sexual activities. Statistics show a marked increase in the number of ever-younger individuals engaging in risky behavior—not attending or dropping out of school, being unemployed, engaging in juvenile crime, prostituting themselves (especially those aged 16 to 24), abusing drugs (particularly injecting drugs), abusing alcohol and smoking, and engaging in risky sexual practices. The number of young girls who are pregnant for the first time (mostly unwanted and/or unplanned) and the abortion rate in Bulgaria are significantly higher than in other countries in Europe. Registered STD cases, including syphilis, are rapidly increasing. In fact, people under the age of 24 account for most of the registered HIV cases.

*Injecting Drug Users*

Over the past few years, the number of injecting drug users has increased consistently. Currently, the number of the HIV-positive cases among injecting drug users in Bulgaria is comparatively small. However, experts indicate that there is an enormous risk of a dramatic increase of HIV among this population in the near future. One indicator is the high rate of hepatitis B and C among them. In addition, many injecting drug users engage in risky sexual behavior. Methods for early detection of the virus among injecting drug users are necessary to prevent the rapid spread of the virus through unsafe injecting practices.

## Prostituting Women and Men

This is a non-homogeneous and difficult-to-access group, which is highly vulnerable to HIV/AIDS and other STDs. The risk factors include: the criminal element of the commercial sex business, violence and trafficking, marginalized social status, risky sexual practices, and social stigma.

## Men Who Have Sex with Men

There are three main subgroups within the gay community: the elite, which is highly restrictive; the middle, which is mobile and versatile with a high rate of mixing; and the lowest subgroup, composed mainly of outsiders and Roma. This subgroup is especially vulnerable. It is mobile with the lowest level of information, which makes intervention difficult. They engage in very risky sexual practices, they seldom use condoms, and many of them prostitute. The men-who-have-sex-with-men community as a whole is vulnerable to HIV/AIDS and other STDs because of several risk factors: inconsistent condom use, multiple casual sex partners, and relatively short permanent relationships.

## Roma Community (Gypsies)

Available information indicates that the Roma community is the most vulnerable among the ethnic minorities. This is because of a number of interrelated factors: a rapidly disintegrating patriarchal system, which is not being replaced by a new, sustainable social structure; ever increasing social isolation accentuated by a 90% unemployment rate; a poor economic culture; absence of social skills and motivation for socialization; increasing rates of prostitution, drug abuse, crime, and mobility; and other practices increasing the risk of HIV/AIDS and other STDs. In addition, health experts suggest that most Roma women have banal STDs, which increases the risk of more serious infections, such as HIV and hepatitis B.

The available data regarding the level of risk in Roma sexual behavior are limited and, to some extent, contradictory. There was a sociological survey conducted by Mirchev and ASSA-M in 1996, according to which 58% of Roma populations begin their sexual life before reaching the age of 16. But ASA data for the year 2000 show the average age of first sexual intercourse for Bulgarians in general is also 15 to 16.

The generalizations below are based most of all on experts' observations and on impressions from the work of nongovernmental organizations that have as their priority the Roma community. These organizations include SEGA, Georgi Bogdanov and IGA, Dimitar Russenov, and the Napredak Romany Foundation (in Pazardjik). According to these organizations, Roma women begin their sexual lives at 12 and Roma men at 14 to 15. These observations were made on the Roma communities in the vicinity of Pazardjik, Plovdiv, Stara Zagora, and Sliven. At the same time, Roma NGOs consider that early entrance into sexual life is connected with early marriage. If that is true, then the early beginning of sexual life should not be interpreted as risk behavior, since it is begun with a permanent partner.

Roma NGOs emphasize that one of the important HIV-related determinants is the repressive attitude to premarital sexual behavior and sexual behavior before living together. The belief is that the value of the unstained wife provokes premarital bisexual behavior and oral and anal sex practices. The question remains whether such premarital risk behavior exists when marriage is contracted at age 12 to 14.

Impressions of the liberalization of sexual behavior are voiced, which, by the way, is characteristic for Bulgarians too (A.S.A.–UNDP/MH 2000). What is of importance is that with low awareness, the liberalization of sexual values can bring about an increase in the risk of sexual behavior. According to quoted NGOs, repressive attitudes towards sexual relations with members of other ethnic groups decline. The opinion is that this is more valid for men than for women. Anthropological observations by Haralan Alexandrov show that Roma values impose repressive attitudes towards the sexual behavior of women and permissive ones towards that of men. This places Roma women in a status of double minority, which makes them an especially at-risk group.

NGOs have confirmed the conclusion made earlier in discussing prostitution, about the prevalence of highway and street prostitution among Roma girls. It is considered that Roma prostitutes come from the lowest social and economic strata of the community, quite often from broken families or disintegrated clans. These girls are usually brought from another settlement—at great distance from their place of work. Roma NGOs emphasize that there exist no restrictive values suppressing the business of procurers. The community is inclined to blame the *guilt* of prostitution on the *alien* girl (that comes from another settlement) rather than on the procurer—the man who brings income into the quarter. These observations have been confirmed by police officials from Pazardjik to the IGA Foundation.

## Pilots and Aircraft Crews

According to a Ministry of Transport and Communication official, the sexual behavior of the mobile group of pilots and stewards/stewardesses is at highest risk with respect to the transmission of HIV or other sexually transmitted infections. Representatives of this group are in the employment of Balkan Airways, Hemus Air, Air Via, and Heli Air, the latter offering mainly tourist services in the Indian Ocean (the Maldives and Thailand). These pilots are away from their families almost throughout the year.

Statistical data about aircraft crews are available in the Ministry of Transport and Communication and the Aviopolyclinics with the Medical Transport Institute, where crews are serviced, and where certificates of professional and health fitness are issued. Experts estimate the number of pilots and stewards working for all Bulgarian airways at a little over 1,000, including people who work exclusively abroad. These estimates exclude Bulgarian pilots working for foreign airways.

Pilots' stays abroad range from some hours to some days. The mobility of aircraft crews is increased by the fact that every member of the airways' staff is entitled to a so-called service ticket. It is usually used with the family. It entitles them to free travel to any destination. On the other hand, in the last 6 or 7 years, the stay of aircraft crews is very limited—up to several days, depending on the routes.

According to a Balkan Airways official, risky sexual behavior is due *more to curiosity than to length of stay*. Balkan Airways considers this group well controlled from a medical point of view. All employees pass medical examinations on an annual or semiannual basis; this makes possible determining the level of professional fitness. Before every flight, aircraft crews pass a medical examination in a special medical room at the Sofia Airport. This is a routine medical examination, but it includes an alcohol test. Pilots are highly motivated to control their health themselves, as their job is well-paid and highly profiled: *if they lose their job, they cannot find work anywhere else, all the more so now that there have been reductions lately*.

The pilots and stewardesses are in good financial standing, which makes possible commercial sex contacts. In the opinion of a Balkan Airways official, many of them travel together with their lovers. On the other hand, pilots and stewardesses form an extremely closed group and maintain contacts mainly among themselves. Second-family practices do occur, but unlike sailors' relationships, these are most often within the crew.

### Isolated Groups and Imprisoned Individuals

Very often, the lack of opportunities for heterosexual intercourse, stress, altered values, violence within the group, and the lack of contact with the outside world result in risky homosexual behavior and prostitution, which increases the risk of HIV and STDs.

### D. Education of Target Groups

Confusing messages about AIDS have repeatedly irritated the general public in Bulgaria. Modest government efforts have been undermined by contradictory reports in the mass media and by various journalistic horror scenarios that failed to become true. It seems that, in actual fact, the majority is hardly as well informed as it believes (Okoliyski 1999). Thus, it is striking to note that few actually change their risky behavior. For example, 66.7% of the IV-drug users believe themselves to be well informed, but only a few practice "safe sex" or "safe use." Moreover, fewer persons with exclusively heterosexual behavior consider themselves well informed (50%), in comparison with the other target groups (drug use: 66.7%, homosexual behavior: 60%, or bisexual behavior: 60%). This can only mean that the latter groups get their information not from public campaigns, which are still mostly directed at the heterosexual majority, but from friends and peers. Finally, although a majority feels sufficiently informed, 66.5% maintain, nevertheless, that there is not enough AIDS information and AIDS counseling in Bulgaria.

The contradiction between feeling well informed on the one hand and, on the other, believing the information to be inadequate, suggests that Bulgarians, inside or outside of any particular target group, have a different concept of AIDS prevention, and expect future prevention campaigns to be different from what has been offered so far. In particular, it seems that AIDS prevention in Bulgaria should be more specifically tailored to specific groups.

[*Update 2002*: UNAIDS Epidemiological Assessment: As of mid 2001, Bulgaria has reported a cumulative total of 340 cases of HIV infection acquired primarily through heterosexual transmission. HIV testing is mandatory among blood donations and systematic among many subgroups of the population. Since 1992, HIV testing is voluntary for pregnant women, STD patients, and injecting drug users in treatment centers. Diagnosed HIV-infected cases are recorded in a national HIV database. Prevalence data come mostly from ongoing testing programs. The number of pregnant women tested has dropped considerably between 1991 and 1992. It is unclear whether women having abortions continued to be tested after 1991. In addition to the change in testing policy, the economic crisis in 1991-1992 resulted in a 25% drop in birthrates. The incidence of syphilis has been in the range of 20 to 30 per 100,000 over the last few years.

[The estimated number of adults and children living with HIV/AIDS on January 1, 2002, were:

| | |
|---|---|
| Adults ages 15-49: | 400 (rate: 0.1%) |
| Women ages 15-49: | NA |
| Children ages 0-15: | NA |

[No estimate is available for the number of adults and children who died of AIDS during 2001.

[No estimate is available for the number of Bulgarian children who had lost one or both parents to AIDS and were under age 15 at the end of 2001. (*End of update by the Editors*)]

## 11. Sexual Dysfunctions, Counseling, and Therapies

PETKO VELICHKOV

A study based on the records of the former sexology clinics has shown that the sex ratio of the clients is 8 males to one female. Clinic visitations initiated by both of the sexual partners together represent only 7% of all visits. Men are complaining of premature ejaculation in 48% of the cases and in 41% of some kind of erectile failure. The 11% left seek consultations for diminished sexual interest, delayed or lack of ejaculation, some orgasmic trouble, paraphilias, and so on.

Women are mostly concerned with difficult or the lack of orgasm (with or without diminished desire) in 72% of the cases, 13% with lack of sexual desire, 12% with vaginismus, and the remaining 3% are experiencing dyspareunia (coital pain), paraphilias, and so on.

The proposed treatment ranges from medicaments to some kind of psychotherapy (mostly behavioral). In the majority of cases, a combination of both is suggested.

The society is not exempt from some pejorative attitude toward sexually dysfunctional persons. However, this disposition has been on a downward trend over the past 20 years.

During the course of the healthcare reforms in Bulgaria, sexology consultations previously offered for free by the public sector were discontinued altogether. Private clinics are offering services, but their competence and level of expertise is not subject to control or certification in any way (H.S.R.F archives).

## 12. Sex Research and Advanced Professional Education

PETKO VELICHKOV

As in the rest of the Eastern Block countries, the healthcare service in Bulgaria was highly centralized and exclusively state-owned and operated. Nonetheless, for more than 35 years, a few sexology clinics and a research unit were in operation. Because of a reform in the national healthcare service, since 1999, all sexology services were closed down and no alternative has been introduced.

In an effort to alleviate this adverse situation, the Human Sexuality Research Foundation was established. Unfortunately, this NGO is surviving practically with no external financial support and exclusively on voluntary principle. Postal address: 16, Kosta Lulchev Str., bl. 244. app. 36, Sofia 1113, Bulgaria; email address: sexology@acad.bg.

## Conclusion

PETKO VELICHKOV

Up until now, there has been no large-scale, systematic, and reliable research on sexuality in Bulgaria. Even if such research is carried out, it is very unlikely to demonstrate the existence of some striking peculiarity linked to the sex, sexual concepts, and practices of Bulgarian people. Because of its geographical position, the country was constantly exposed to intensive external influences by various cultures. Bearing in mind that conservatism is not a strong feature of the local mentality, one can imagine how difficult it is to keep one's own style in sexuality unaltered.

## References and Suggested Readings

Argirova, R., D. Beschkov, O. Troschev, E. Bodscheva, & V. Georgieva. 1992. *The AIDS experience*. Sofia: AIDS-Centre.

A.S.A.–UNDP/MH. 2000. *A representative high school student survey of Sofia and the country*. Agency for Socioeconomic Analyses (ASA) & United Nations Development Program/Mental Health (UNDP/MH), conducted by ASA.

A.S.A. 1995 (June-July). AIDS and sexuality: A study based on a representative sample for Sofia on 15-17 year olds. The Agency for Socioeconomic Analyses (ASA).

Belcheva, M. 2002. *Fertility and reproductive behavior.* Sofia: Dunav Press.

Boshkova, L. 1998. *The rights of women in Bulgaria in human rights in Bulgaria.* United Nations Development Programme, Sofia; Friedrich Ebert Foundation, Sofia, Information and Documentation Centre of the Council of Europe, Sofia.

CIA. 2002 (January). *The world factbook 2002.* Washington, DC: Central Intelligence Agency. Available: http://www.cia.gov/cia/publications/factbook/index.html.

Draqganov, M., et al. 1984. *Ethno-psychology of the Bulgarians.* Sofia.

H.S.R.F. Unpublished data in the Archives of the Human Sexuality Research Foundation.

I.O.M. 2002. *Overview of HIV/AIDS in South Eastern Europe.* I.O.M. (International Organization for Migration) and UNICEF.

Kaloyanov, A. 1995. *The Bulgarian shamanship.* Sofia.

Mirchev, M. 1996. *Reproductive behavior family planning. Contraceptives use* (An empirical sociological survey directed by Mihail Mirchev). ASSA–M, Ministry of Health, The Phare Programme, Sofia. (Mirchev, Jachkova, Kasakova, & Velikova).

*National Statistics Institute, Bulletin.* 2002. Sofia.

National Health Center (N.H.C.). 1995. *(National) representative survey of Sofia (1,044 respondents, grades 9-11).*

Okoliyski, M. 1999. *Conditions of AIDS prevention in Bulgaria.* Humboldt University (Dissertation), Berlin. Available: http://edoc.hu-berlin.de/abstract.php3/dissertationen/phil/okoliyski-michail-alexandrov.

Panov, T. 1914. *A psychology profile of the Bulgarian people.* Sofia.

"Pleades 2002." Sexes at labor and home. Sofia: Sociology Agency (In press).

Sheytanov, N. 1932. The sexual philosophy of the Bulgarian (An introduction to our unofficial folklore). *Philosophical Review* [Sofia], *3*:241-256.

Tzekov, V. 2003. Expert in gynecology at Human Sexuality Research Foundation (Unpublished data).

UNAIDS. 2002. *Epidemiological fact sheets by country.* Geneva, Switzerland: Joint United Nations Programme on HIV/AIDS (UNAIDS/WHO). Available: http://www.unaids.org/hivaidsinfo/statistics/fact_sheets/index_en.htm.

*United Nations Development Program, Country's profile.* 2001. Sofia: Author.

(CIA 2002)

# Canada

Michael Barrett, Ph.D, Alan King, Ed.D.,
Joseph Lévy, Ph.D., Eleanor Maticka-Tyndale, Ph.D.,
Alexander McKay, Ph.D., and Julie Fraser, Ph.D.
*Rewritten and updated by the Authors*

## Contents

## *Preamble*

This chapter, updated to January 2003, retains much of
the content of the 1996-97 version, which we use, where
possible, as a basis for comparison with current data and as
a reference point, where necessary, for new or revised interpretations. Given Canada's ethnocultural, linguistic, religious, and urban/rural diversity (see Section A, Demographics, below), and its sociological and gender diversity
(Sections 1, Basic Sexological Premises, and 2, Religious,
Ethnic, and Gender Factors Affecting Sexuality), we continue to wonder whether it is possible to present an over-

view of the sexuality of Canadians. The risk in attempting to
do so is that one will "homogenize" the rich diversity by
taking the "average" opinion or the median frequency of
specific behaviors as a reflection of what Canadians are like
sexually. On the other hand, a focus on different subgroups
within the population may beg the question of whether Canada has a national identity pertaining to sexual customs, beliefs, and practices. At the national ("macro") level, there
are quantitative data about some aspects of behavior—although there have been no large-scale studies of adult sexual behavior in Canada—but it is often difficult to interpret
such information in ways that would further our understanding about the particularities of "Canadian" sexuality.
On the other hand, studies on selected populations in specific settings, the "micro" approach, are often designed to
describe or explain the behavior of that group, but they are
seldom done in ways that would permit comparisons across
Canada or over time. While sexological research in Canada
has grown significantly over the last 20 years, it is still a
new field and these limitations on our national database are
neither surprising nor insurmountable. Our compromise,
therefore, has been to incorporate elements of both the
macro and micro approaches, to provide quantitative information where possible, and to make cautious inferences
where empirical evidence is lacking.

## *Demographics and a Brief
Historical Perspective*

### A. Demographics

Canada occupies the northern half of the North American
continent with the United States on its southern border, the
North Atlantic Ocean on the east, and the North Pacific
Ocean and Alaska on its western coast. Although geographically Canada is the largest country in the Western Hemisphere with 3.852 million square miles (9.976 million km²),
including the Yukon, Nunavut, and Northwest Territories,
only about 10% of its landmass is suitable for permanent
large-scale settlement, and only slightly more than that for
permanent agriculture. The population of about 31.4 million
(2002 Census data) is distributed unevenly among the ten
provinces and two territories, with Ontario, Quebec, British
Columbia, and Alberta accounting for 85% of the total (see
Table 1). About 80% of Canadians live in cities, primarily in

*Communications*: F. Michael Barrett, Ph.D., University of Toronto, Zoology Department, 25 Harboard Street, Toronto, ON, M5S
3G5, Canada; barrett@zoo.utoronto.ca.

the southern regions of the country. In 2001, 51% of Canada's population were concentrated in four broad regions: the extended Golden Horseshoe in Southwestern Ontario; Montréal and nearby areas; the Lower Mainland of British Columbia and Southern Vancouver Island; and the Calgary-Edmonton corridor. A 3,300-mile (5,300-km) shared border with the United States, a free-trade agreement, and extensive consumption of U.S. media, expose Canadians to strong economic and cultural influences from a country with ten times its population. However, the history, composition (e.g., religious and ethnoracial mix, socioeconomic diversity), and structure (e.g., legal, medical) of the two neighbors differ in ways that have an important influence on sexuality in the two countries.

Canada's ten provinces, plus the Yukon, Nunavut, and Northwest Territories, are linked through a central federal government, but the various levels of federal, provincial, regional, and municipal government have differing levels of responsibility for health, education, social welfare, legislation, and other areas that have an impact upon sexuality and sexual health.

In July 2002, Canada had an estimated population of 31.4 million. (All data are from Statistics Canada or from *The World Factbook 2002* (CIA 2002) unless otherwise stated.)

**Age Distribution and Sex Ratios**: *0-14 years*: 18.7% with 1.05 male(s) per female (sex ratio); *15-64 years*: 68.4% with 1.01 male(s) per female; *65 years and over*: 12.9% with 0.74 male(s) per female; *Total population sex ratio*: 0.98 male(s) to 1 female

The proportion of Canadians over age 65 increased from 12% to 12.6% from 1995 to 2001, while the proportion under 15 dropped from 21% to 18.8% over the same period. In 1991, Beaujot predicted by 2010 a rise in the proportion over 65 to 16% and a drop in the proportion under 15 to 16%. This projection was based on continuation of what was then an unprecedentedly low fertility rate in Canada (1.67 in the early 1990s). In fact, the fertility rate continued to decline to 1.52 by 2001, suggesting that the shift toward more older and fewer younger Canadians may proceed more quickly than previously projected. The large segment of the population now in the middle years, i.e., the "baby boom" generation born between the late 1940s and the early 1960s, has exerted considerable influence on social and cultural patterns in Canada, from the "sexual revolution" of the late 1960s to the economic expansion of the 1980s. This generation currently holds many of the positions in government, business, healthcare, and the media, and might therefore be expected to influence public policy in relation to sexuality (i.e., in areas such as education, law, healthcare, etc.).

**Life Expectancy at Birth**: *Total Population*: 76.8 years; *male*: 76.3 years; *female*: 83.3 years

**Urban/Rural Distribution**: 80% to 20%

**Ethnic Distribution**: British Isles origin: 28%; French origin: 23%; other Europeans: 15%; Amerindian: 2%; other (mostly Asian, African, and Arab 6%; mixed backgrounds: 26%

**Religious Distribution**: (1991 census) Roman Catholic: 46%; Protestant: 36%; Muslim and Other: 18%. The changing age structure of the population, coupled with high life expectancy and a declining rate of natural population increase (0.6% in 1995), are all characteristic of the demographic transition seen in other industrialized northern countries (see basic demographic data for Canada in Table 2).

**Birth Rate**: 11.1 births per 1,000 population

**Death Rate**: 7.5 per 1,000 population

**Infant Mortality Rate**: 4.95 deaths per 1,000 live births

**Net Migration Rate**: 6.07 migrant(s) per 1,000 population

**Total Fertility Rate**: 1.52 children born per woman

**Population Growth Rate**: 0.96%

**HIV/AIDS** (1999 est.): *Adult prevalence*: 0.3%; *Persons living with HIV/AIDS*: 49,000; *Deaths*: 400. (For additional details from www.UNAIDS.org, see end of Section 10B.)

**Literacy Rate** (*defined as those age 15 and over who can read and write*): 97%

**Per Capita Gross Domestic Product** (*purchasing power parity*): $27,700 (2001 est.); *Inflation*: 2.8%; *Unemployment*: 7.2%; *Living below the poverty line*: 19.7% (1995; using Low Income Cut-Off)

Although the total fertility rate has been below replacement level for about 30 years (about 1.52 children per woman in 2001), a natural population increase of 0.33% per

## Table 1

### Population Distribution in Canada (Estimated 2002)

| Province/Territory | Population (in Thousands) | Percentage of Total |
|---|---|---|
| CANADA (January 2002, est.) | 31,414 | |
| Newfoundland | 531.6 | 1.7 |
| Prince Edward Island | 139.9 | 0.4 |
| Nova Scotia | 944.8 | 3.0 |
| New Brunswick | 756.7 | 2.4 |
| Quebec | 7,455.2 | 23.7 |
| Ontario | 12,068.3 | 38.4 |
| Manitoba | 1,150.8 | 3.7 |
| Saskatchewan | 1,011.8 | 3.3 |
| Alberta | 3,113.6 | 9.9 |
| British Columbia | 4,141.3 | 13.3 |
| Yukon | 29.9 | 0.1 |
| Northwest Territories | 41.4 | 0.1 |
| Nunavut | 28.7 | 0.1 |

*Source*: *Quarterly Demographic Statistics*, Statistics Canada, Catalogue No. 91-002, 2002.

## Table 2

### Basic Demographic Data for Canada (2001)

| | |
|---|---|
| Total population: | 31,081,900 (July 1, 2001) |
| Total population: | 30,769,900 (July 1, 2000) |
| Births: | 329,791 |
| Deaths: | 227,076 |
| Natural increase: | 102,715 |
| Birth rate: | 10.7/1,000 population |
| Death rate: | 7.4/1,000 population |
| Rate of natural increase: | 3.3/1,000 population (0.33%) |
| Immigration: | 250,346 |
| Net immigration: | 199,605 |
| Net immigration rate: | 6.5/1,000 population (0.65%) |
| Total population increase: | 302,320 |
| Annual population growth rate: | 0.98% |
| % population growth from natural increase: | 34.0% |
| % population growth from net immigration: | 66.0% |
| Population doubling time: | 71.4 years |
| Total fertility rate (est.): | 1.52 births/woman aged 15-49 |
| Life expectancy at birth: | male 76 years; female 82 years |

*Data from*: *Annual Demographic Statistics*, 2001. Statistics Canada, Catalogue No. 91-213-XPB, 2001. See also *Report on the Demographic Situation in Canada* 2002. Statistics Canada, Catalogue No.91-209-XPE.

year, coupled with a net immigration rate of 0.65%, gave Canada a growth rate of 0.98% in 2001 (see Table 2), one of the highest among the world's industrialized countries. Net immigration contributed about 66% of Canada's population increase in 2001, and projections for the future suggest that immigration will continue to have a significant impact on Canada's demography.

By law the federal government is required to state in advance of any year the intended total number of immigrants, refugees, etc., that will be admitted to Canada in that year. As a result of new legislation passed in 2002 (the Immigration and Refugee Protection Act), the most recent of these ongoing Annual Reports to Parliament on Immigration was the first to be submitted under the new Act. The plan for 2003 calls for 220,000-245,000 new permanent residents, of whom 60% are categorized as economic class, 26% as family class, and 13% as refugees. Family class refers to a foreign national who is the spouse, common-law partner, conjugal partner, child, or parent of a Canadian citizen or permanent resident. This category reflects a governmental commitment to family reunification. Economic class refers to those immigrants who are skilled workers. Unlike the earlier emphasis on occupation-based criteria, the 2003 plan looks to flexible/transferable skills in the trades, and in the technical and professional domains, as well as proficiency in English and/or French. While the government has maintained a commitment to those individuals entering Canada as Refugee class, economic and social factors (e.g., the presence of relatives in Canada) will also be taken into account. By 2011, immigration is expected to account for all of Canada's net labor force growth, and by 2031, for all net population growth.

Immigration patterns in the recent past and in the future will thus continue to alter the already varied ethnocultural composition of the Canadian population, particularly in the larger urban centers to which a high proportion of immigrants have been drawn. For example, in 2000, 90% of immigrants went to three provinces (Ontario, British Columbia, and Quebec) and 75% of these went to the largest urban centers in these provinces (Toronto, Vancouver, Montreal), with Toronto receiving well over half of this group. Canada's changing ethnocultural composition is worth considering here because the continuing trend to ethnocultural diversity means that a wide range of attitudes, traditions, and practices surrounding marriage, sexuality, sex-role expectations, and sexual taboos are now present as a source of both variety and potential challenge in Canadian society. For example, in contrast to the current national ethnic distribution data from the 1991 census, the top five sources of immigrants to Canada in 2000 were the People's Republic of China (16.2%), India (11.5%), Pakistan (6.2%), Philippines (4.4%), and Korea (3.4%). The United States and United Kingdom were seventh and tenth respectively, together representing 4.6% of immigrants in 2002.

## B. A Brief Historical Perspective

ROBERT T. FRANCOEUR

The French explorer, Jacques Cartier, who reached the Gulf of St. Lawrence in 1534, is generally regarded as the founder of Canada, although John Cabot, an English seaman had sighted Newfoundland 37 years earlier, and Vikings are believed to have reached the same area centuries before either Cartier or Cabot. The French pioneered settlement by establishing Quebec City in 1606, Montreal in 1642, and declaring Canada a colony in 1663. The British acquired Acadia (Nova Scotia) in 1717 and captured Quebec in 1759. By 1763, Britain had gained control of the rest of New France. The Quebec Act of 1774 gave the French in

Upper Canada the right to their own language, religion, and civil law. The English presence in Canada increased during the American Revolution, when many American colonists loyal to the crown moved north to Canada. Fur traders and explorers pioneered paths to the west, with Sir Alexander Mackenzie reaching the Pacific in 1793.

Upper and Lower Canada, later known as Quebec and Ontario, and the Maritime Provinces developed their own local legislative assemblies in the 1700s, and reformers called for a more responsible government. The War of 1812 between Britain and the United States delayed the move toward a more democratic government, but by 1837 political agitation had led to rebellions in both Upper and Lower Canada. Lord Durham's report recommended union of the two parts into one colony, to be called Canada. This union continued until 1867 when the Dominion of Canada was established with Ontario, Quebec, Nova Scotia, and New Brunswick. A federal system of government was developed, modeled on the British parliament and cabinet structure under the Crown. In 1982, Canada ended its last formal legislative link with Britain by assuming control over its constitution. In 1987, the so-called Meech Lake Agreement would have assured constitutional protection for Quebec's efforts to protect its French language and culture. Its failure in 1990 sparked a separatist revival which remains a major issue for the country. In 1992, the Northwest Territories approved creation of a self-governing homeland for the 17,500 Inuit living in the Territories, to be known as Nunavut, "Our Land." In June of 1993 the Canadian Parliament passed the "Nunavut Land Claims Agreement Act" and the "Nunavut Act." Finally, on April 1, 1999, the territory of Nunavut officially joined the federation of Canada.

## C. Ethnocultural Composition: Ethnic Origins and Recent Immigration

The face of Canada, as is true for the United States and Australia, has been shaped by immigrants. European settlers from the United Kingdom (U.K.) and France are considered the two founding nations of Canada (and the current ethnic composition of the population still reflects that background). However, many First Nations groups were already inhabiting the region when these settlers arrived, including Cree, Dakota, Dene, Gitksan, Gwich'in, Huron, Innu, Inuit, Mohawk, Micmac, Naskapi, Ojibway, Saulteaux, and Salish. In the 1996 census, 1.1 million people (3.9% of the population) identified either single or mixed aboriginal ancestry. Overall, 28 percent of Canada's population in 1996 reported ethnic origins other than British, French, or Canadian. Data cited above on source countries for immigration in 2000 suggest that this percentage has probably shifted upward in the last 10 years.

Canada's 1996 census (the most recent data available at writing) provides the most accurate and current profile of the the ethnic origins of people living in Canada. A review of 1991 census data by Renaud and Badets (1993) and selected observations from a major study on families in Canada (Vanier Institute of the Family 1994) are also used below to summarize the increasingly diverse ethnocultural composition of Canadian society.

Ethnic origin is taken to mean the cultural or ethnic group to which one's distant relatives belonged. In the 1996 census, respondents were asked to indicate whether their ancestry was a single ethnic group (e.g., French) or multiple (two or more groups, e.g., British and French). Unlike the previous census, respondents were also given the option "Canadian" as a potential ethnic origin. It should be noted that the addition of the "Canadian" category changed the relative distribution of ethnic origins significantly, particularly for the British and French categories, as well as rendering a direct comparison of 1991 and 1996 census data more difficult. Rounded percentages for the largest groupings for the 1996 census were:

Canadian (19%), British Isles only (17%), combination British, French, or Canadian and other (16%), combination British and French or Canadian (10%), European single origin (13%), French only, i.e., French and Acadian (9%), single East and South East Asian origin (5%), aboriginal (4%), and South Asian (2%).

A report by Badets and Chui (1994) documents the changing pattern of immigration to Canada that has produced such ethnocultural diversity. While early immigrants to Canada came predominantly from the United Kingdom and Europe, that trend has shifted, particularly during the 1980s, 1990s, and into the 21st century. Between 1981 and 1991, 48% of immigrants to Canada were born in Asian countries, 25% in Europe and the United Kingdom, 10% in Central and South America, 6% each in the Caribbean and Africa, and 4% in the United States. In 1991, about 16% of Canada's population was born outside the country, which is not much different from the 15% figure reported 30 years earlier. Of these, 54% were from Europe and the United Kingdom and 25% from Asian countries. Most of the 4.3 million people in Canada in 1991 who were born outside the country either had become or were expected to become Canadian citizens.

About 94% of them live in four provinces (Ontario, British Columbia, Quebec, and Alberta), predominantly in one of the three largest metropolitan areas (Toronto, Montreal, and Vancouver). For example, 38% of Toronto's population in 1991 was not born in Canada. This rich ethnocultural diversity in some areas of the country provides a variety of sociosexual customs and gender-role expectations that must be considered in education, healthcare, and public policy related to sexuality. These issues include: developing effective ways to prevent HIV infection among communities of First Nations people and other ethnocultural groups; differing attitudes and beliefs toward sexuality between first-generation immigrant parents and their children or between recent immigrants and the "predominant" culture; cross-cultural differences in gender-role expectations, deference to authority, emphasis on reproduction and childrearing as the rationale for marriage; arranged marriages; attitudes and policies toward women who experienced genital mutilation(female circumcision) and wish it for their children; willingness of some groups to use sex selection to provide a child of the preferred sex, usually male; and varied traditions concerning public discussion about sexuality, sex education, and discussion between the sexes about sexual problems and dysfunctions.

## D. Linguistic Diversity

As expected from the ethnic origins of the population, 59% of Canadians reported English as their only first language (i.e., the one they learned at home in childhood and still understand), 23% French, and 18% one of the "nonofficial" languages (2001 census). In examining the ten-year trend from 1991 to 2001, the percentage of individuals claiming English as their first language changed only slightly from 61% to 59%. Similarly, the percentage claiming French as their first language dropped only slightly from 24 to 23%. The largest change, however, was noted in the percentage of individuals claiming a non-official language. This percentage rose from 13% to 17% from 1991 to 1996, and then from 17% to 18% from 1996 to 2001. The rise from 1991 to 1996 represents a 15% increase in people who claim a mother tongue other than French or English. Furthermore, this growth is 2.5 times faster than the overall growth rate of the Canadian population. Most French-speaking Canadians live in Quebec (in 1996, 86% of Canada's French-speaking population lived in Quebec), but there are groups of Acadians in New Brunswick and French-speaking communities in other parts of Canada. Immigrants (those not born in Canada) accounted for about two thirds of those whose first language was neither English nor French and for about three quarters of those who spoke a language other than English or French at home.

## 1. Basic Sexological Premises

### A. Character of Gender Roles

At present, over half of Canadian women who are raising children also work outside the home. As of 1998, for individuals between 25 and 54 years of age, 81% of never-married women and 85% of never-married men were working. Among married individuals age 25 to 54, 77% of women and 94% of men were working. Compared to the fewer than 50% of married women working in 1976, this represents a sizeable increase in the number of married women employed outside the home (Vanier Institute 2000). Although single (never married) women and men are equally likely to be employed (59 to 60% for both sexes in 1981 and 1991), the proportion of married women employed increased from 47% in 1981 to 56% in 1991. This represents a major change in the employment experience of women and is a reflection of changed economic circumstances, more single-parent families, and the altered gender-role expectations and opportunities for women over the last 30 years. However, the majority of women continue to work in occupations where women are traditionally concentrated. In 2001, 70% of all employed women were found in the areas of teaching, nursing and related health occupations, clerical or other administrative positions, or sales and service occupations. This is compared with 30% of employed men. Thus, although the population of women in traditional female occupations has slowly declined from 1987 to 2001 (from 74% to 70%), and men and women are approaching equality in labor force participation, the labor force remains sex segregated with men and women concentrated in different areas.

In her book, *Gender Relations in Canada*, Marlene Mackie (1991) identified the evolution of feminism and of the feminist movement in Canada as a major influence on gender-role expectations, on women's social and economic status, on their perceptions of themselves as agents for change, and, hence, on the social and interpersonal aspects of relationships within and between the sexes. The most recent wave of that movement, beginning in the late 1960s, has gradually altered the legislative landscape regarding equal employment, pay equity, access to legal abortion and contraception, sexual harassment, maternity leave, daycare, and a range of other issues that affect women's social and economic well-being. Mackie (1991) suggests that the "official" beginning of the feminist movement in Canada occurred in the period that preceded the federal government's decision, in 1967, to establish the Royal Commission on the Status of Women. The commission's mandate was to assess the prevailing situation regarding the position of women in Canada, and then to "recommend what steps might be taken by the Federal Government to ensure for women equal opportunities in all aspects of Canadian society" (Mackie 1991, 255). Three years later, after hearings across Canada, the commission issued its report which contained 167 recommendations (Mackie 1991).

Mackie suggests that three dimensions of feminism—liberal, socialist, and radical—have each had an impact on different spheres of life in Canada. Liberal feminism mobilized action to establish the Royal Commission and guided the emergence and agenda of large national organizations, such as the National Action Committee on the Status of Women, the Canadian Advisory Council on the Status of Women, and the provincial liaison groups. These groups have acted to achieve equity in the workplace, fair property rights when marriages end in divorce, and a host of other changes that reformed the existing social system. Socialist feminists challenged the oppression of women within the economic system and within the family and approached some of the same agenda items as liberal feminism but from a different perspective. Their focus on both class and gender issues aligned this branch of feminism with the concerns of lesbians, immigrant women, and women of color (Adamson et al. 1988, as cited in Mackie 1991). Radical feminists and socialist feminists, says Mackie, share the premise "that the dominant male culture promulgates a picture of reality that buttresses patriarchy and denigrates women." (Mackie 1991, 260). Citing Adamson et al. (1988), Mackie views radical feminism as instrumental in the establishment of rape crisis centers, in campaigns against pornography, and in founding shelters for battered women. The lesbian/gay liberation movement has taken place almost concurrently with the women's movement and embodies and is informed by many of the same concepts of gender equality, personal freedom, and human rights.

From an institutional and legislative perspective, it would appear that liberal feminism has influenced contemporary government policy and corporate practice. These changes have been the source of some conflict. For example, the Toronto-based group R.E.A.L. Women of Canada (Realistic, Equal, Active, for Life), founded in 1983, now has chapters in all provinces and is the most prominent of the organizations opposing at least some of the legislative and social trends encouraged by the feminist movement. This group opposes policies that it believes either undermine the family or promote homosexuality as an acceptable alternative to heterosexual marriage. It advocates programs that would allow women to choose to stay at home with their children (e.g., through tax credits that would permit this option in lieu of universal daycare). The organization is on the right politically and in terms of social policy and gender relations, and it espouses a more traditional and restrictive sexual philosophy than that of most Canadians. The growth of the political and religious right in Canada, although it has occurred to a lesser extent than in the U.S., suggests strong dissatisfaction, in this group, with some aspects of the trend to more egalitarian gender relations. Men's rights groups in Canada, e.g., In Search of Justice, also believe that some of the legislative changes influenced by the feminist movement have unfairly disadvantaged men. Most of their efforts have centered on issues of child custody and support following divorce.

The nascent men's movement in Canada—not to be confused with men's rights groups—has at least two "branches." One emphasizes the consequences for men of traditional, socially imposed male roles and seeks new ways to be male. The other, represented by groups such as Men Against Sexism, considers patriarchy and men's violence to be the major threats to women and seeks to change the structures and forms of social organization that perpetuate domination of one group by another at the interpersonal, social, or international level (see Kaufman 1987). The latter group has an annual white ribbon campaign to highlight men's opposition to violence against women.

## B. Sociolegal Status of Males and Females

In the formation and enforcement of laws and policies, Canada is a federation of provinces and territories. Some areas of jurisdiction—e.g., the criminal code that governs sexual assault, sex work, divorce, and censorship—are federal and require the passage and modification of laws by the Canadian Parliament. The enforcement of most laws, through policing and the courts, however, as well as jurisdiction over matters of education, civil conduct (e.g., allowable conduct in various locations, property offenses, alcohol, and tobacco laws), family law (e.g., division of property in divorce, parental rights, and responsibilities), and delivery of healthcare, are within provincial or local jurisdiction. Consequently, it is difficult to draw conclusions that apply across the country. In some locations, most notably Quebec and British Columbia, federal and local laws have been applied in a manner that supports greater equality between men and women and protection of various segments of society from discrimination. In others, e.g., Alberta and Saskatchewan, there has been a more limited interpretation and application of related federal legislation and passage of fewer provincial laws providing protection of groups and guarantees of equal treatment.

Equality before the law, regardless of gender and sexual orientation, is a relatively modern development in Canada. Legislation and court rulings that established such equality, though generally considered to have begun in the late 1800s with the "Person's" case, in which women were included in all legal documents under the status of "person" (prior to this, only men were included), are primarily a phenomenon of the past 35 years. Several landmark changes, which will be referred to throughout this chapter, include:

- 1969—Sweeping legislative changes, referred to as "getting the government out of the bedrooms of the nation," were initiated by Parliament. These struck down a variety of laws restricting sexual activities, including the dissemination of information on birth control, and enshrined in law the principle that any activities between two consenting adults, conducted in private, were beyond the jurisdiction of law.
- 1970s—Universal provision of medical care without direct payment was instituted in each province. With this change, medical diagnostic and treatment procedures associated with sexuality, such as treatment for gender dysphoria, difficulties in sexual functioning, birth control, abortion, and infertility, became available to all Canadians without direct cost.
- 1968-1985—A series of changes in the laws governing divorce. Prior to this period, divorce required a parliamentary decree and could be granted only for reasons of adultery. The criteria for granting divorce were broadened and their application transferred to the courts. This change saw an immediate and sharp increase in the number of divorces granted across the country. It is noteworthy that property settlements and child custody matters are within provincial jurisdiction, and so vary across the country.
- 1980s—A series of changes in Quebec family law took Quebec from the position of having the most conservative to having the most progressive set of provincial statutes. Under the new laws, women were guaranteed an economic and legal status independent of that of their husbands. This was symbolized in women's retaining their name in marriage, and included equal sharing of family property, decision making, and of roles and rights as parents. Prior to this, for example, wives were under their husbands' control in determination of residence, property was owned wholly by men unless special contracts were arranged prior to marriage, decisions about children (e.g., with respect to medical care, education, and residence) were exclusively under the control of fa-

thers (at least in law), and the line of inheritance was primarily from father to son, with considerably less to wives and daughters.

- 1982—The Canadian Charter of Rights and Freedoms was declared law. This has been the basis for court challenges of other legislation, policies, and actions that have restricted or dictated rights and access, primarily of women, people with various disabilities, and homosexuals to areas and services in Canadian society (e.g., jobs, housing, insurance, particular medical services, spousal benefits, and parental rights).
- 1985—"Rape" was removed from the Criminal Code and replaced by several categories of assault that involve sexual contact, and laws addressing sexual contact with children were revised. Of note is the fact that the new law removed the onus of proof of lack of consent from women, and allowed women to file charges of sexual assault against their husbands. More recent changes and court rulings have further modified legal proceedings in this area. These are discussed in Section 8A, Significant Unconventional Sexual Behaviors, Coercive Sex.
- 1988—A Supreme Court of Canada decision overturned the laws restricting women's access to abortion. This continues to be a contentious issue among Canadians; but 15 years after this ruling, abortion still remains outside the jurisdiction of the Criminal Code.
- 1996—Sexual orientation was formally added to the Canadian Human Rights Act on June 20, 1996. Section 3(1) of the Canadian Human Rights Act was amended to prohibit discrimination based on sexual orientation.

While many other legislative changes and court rulings have influenced the sociolegal status of various groups of Canadians, these are generally considered among the landmarks that have established the contemporary position of men and women, adults and children, and people of different sexual orientations.

Today, men and women are equal before the law in Canada, and the Canadian Charter of Rights and Freedoms enshrines this principle. Both the public and private sector have adopted policies to increase the proportion of women in those work settings in which they have been traditionally underrepresented, and employment equity legislation has been implemented in the public sector in some provinces to rationalize pay scales according to job requirements. Men continue, however, to predominate in positions of power and leadership (e.g., government and major corporations).

Equal treatment of lesbian and gay individuals in law and in areas of employment, housing, and so on, is increasing, to a sizable degree because of court challenges and threatened challenges (which have used the Charter of Rights and Freedoms) to eliminate discriminatory practices. Equal treatment does not exist, however, with respect to parental rights, spousal relationships, employee benefits, and other such issues, although court decisions continue to set precedents in the absence of legislated change (see Section 6, Homoerotic, Homosexual, and Bisexual Behaviors). It is increasingly common for large corporations to extend such benefits even though they are not yet required in law to do so.

Current legislation regarding nonconsensual sexual behavior does not discriminate on the basis of sex (e.g., sexual assault law applies to both sexes). Children under the age of 14 cannot consent to sexual activity with an adult (i.e., anyone 18 or over), and an adult engaging in such activity with a child could be charged with "sexual interference," or "sexual assault" (because consent, even if given, is not legally recognized) (MacDonald 1994). An "invitation to sexual touching" would also be illegal if the invitee was un-

der 14. In the foregoing offense categories, a person of 12 or 13 would be deemed able to give consent if the other person was not more than two years older and was not in a position of authority over the complainant.

The acts associated with sexual interference and invitation to sexual touching are also proscribed when done toward a person 14 to 17 by someone in a position of trust, authority, or dependency. The legislated age of consent for anal intercourse is 18, in contrast to 14 for other sexual activities. Specifically, individuals under the age of 18 cannot consent to anal intercourse unless legally married. However, this has been debated in the courts. In 1995, the Ontario Court of Appeal struck down the relevant section of the criminal code, with two judges finding it discriminatory with respect to age and one with respect to sexual orientation. A similar outcome was noted in a Quebec Court of Appeal in 1998.

There is also a statute on "corrupting children" (i.e., anyone under 18) by exposing them to adultery, sexual immorality, habitual drunkenness, and the like, but this provision is rarely prosecuted (MacDonald 1994). In general, the contentious nature of consent laws is also reflected in the frequent demands by various professional groups (e.g., Canadian Association of Chiefs of Police) and family and children's rights activists to raise the age of consent to 16. However, such amendments have yet to be considered.

Although Canadian law defines adults as those 18 or over, there are provincial variations affecting such things as tobacco, alcohol use, and age of consent to medical treatment. For example, it is illegal to sell tobacco products to someone under 18 in Canada, but that age was raised to 19 in Ontario. The ages at which it is legal to sell alcohol to someone vary across the provinces, ranging between 18 and 21 years. Consent to treatment provisions also vary by province. For example, for several years Quebec has set 14 as the general age of consent, including for birth control, abortion, and STD treatment. Ontario's Consent to Treatment Act, which became law in 1995, was designed primarily to regulate treatment, particularly of those incapacitated or vulnerable in some way, when existing law is unclear. It also applies to treatment of children. For example, physicians, nurses, and clinic staff working outside hospital settings may treat children of 12 or even 11 without parental notification based on the practitioner's judgment of the child's capacity to give informed consent. Contentious areas in this regard might include prescribing birth control pills, pregnancy counseling, or diagnosis, counseling, and treatment for STDs. Notification of parents when the child does not wish to be informed is left to the prudent judgment of the practitioner, and confidentiality of records would be handled in a similar manner. However, if the treatment is given in a hospital setting, parental consent to treatment would be needed for children under 16. Some other provinces set age of consent to treatment closer to the age of 16. These issues reflect the current attempts to balance children's rights and parents' rights when the two appear to be in conflict. A similar balancing in relation to acceptance of children's testimony in court is also taking place in Canada (see Section 8A, Significant Unconventional Sexual Behaviors, Coercive Sex, on sexual abuse).

Canada is in a stage of change with respect to matters of law and policy regarding the status of men, women, children, the variously abled and disabled, and individuals of differing sexual orientations. If the trends of recent years continue, the change will be in the direction of provision of greater guarantees of equal treatment, increased access to a variety of sexual health services, protection of individual rights, and protection against discrimination. However, there are segments of Canadian society that challenge these changes and have mounted various campaigns to limit their scope. The future picture with respect to legal matters cannot be predicted.

## C. General Concepts and Constructs of Sexuality

There have been no systematic, large-scale national studies on the sexual attitudes or conduct of Canadian adults. In November 1993, a major Canadian polling agency (Decima Research) conducted a national telephone survey of 1,610 Canadian residents randomly selected from the ten provinces (*Maclean's*/CTV Poll 1994), in which a variety of questions involving sexual attitudes were included. [*Note*: Neither the Northwest Territories nor the Yukon were included because of their sparse population; sample sizes in the less-populated provinces were increased to reduce province-by-province errors.] The following sampling of the survey findings provides some background for subsequent speculation on Canadians' perspectives on sexuality and public policy. Given the small sample size and the methodological limitations of such a study, the results are at best indicative.

Most survey respondents felt that in the last 10 to 20 years, Canadian attitudes on sexual matters had become far more permissive (43%) or more permissive (30%), with a higher percentage of those over 55 years old viewing the change as far more permissive (e.g., 59% of 55- to 64-year-olds vs. 32% of 25- to 34-year-olds). One reflection of the change in permissiveness is Canadian attitudes toward pre-marital sex (i.e., premarital intercourse). In a 1990 national survey of adults, Bibby and Posterski (1992) found that 80% agreed or strongly agreed that premarital sex was acceptable. This compares to 68% in agreement in 1975. Approval ranged from 92% among 18- to 34-year-olds (vs. 90% in 1975) to 59% of those 55 and over (vs. 42% in 1975). Slightly more people disagreed than agreed that a person should have more than one sexual partner before marriage (50% disagreed, 39% agreed, and 11% had no opinion). In a 1995 study with a similarly representative sample of Canadian adults, Bibby (1995) found continued high levels of acceptance of sex outside of marriage (this includes "premarital" and "intermarital" activity) among the young (89% of 18- to 34-year-olds approved) and an ongoing increase in acceptance among older Canadians (62% of those over 55 approved vs. 42% in 1975). Bibby (1995) attributed the latter shift to aging of the baby boom generation that came of age in the 1960s, and suggested that by 2010, about 85% of Canadians would approve, with 15% remaining opposed.

With respect to having an extramarital affair, 80% of respondents to the *Maclean's*/CTV poll said it was never OK, 10% not usually OK, and 6% sometimes or always OK. This response did not differ according to gender, but respondents from Quebec, and French-speaking respondents in general, were less likely to say "never OK" (about 65 to 67% vs. 79 to 91% in the other provinces). Respondents were somewhat less likely to condemn extramarital affairs under all circumstances (e.g., "it is totally unacceptable for a married person to have an affair"). In this case, 70% agreed or strongly agreed, whereas 22% disagreed and 7% strongly disagreed. Men were slightly more likely to be accepting than women. There was no difference based on age, but respondents from Quebec were much less likely to agree strongly that it was always unacceptable (19%) and more likely to disagree or strongly disagree (45%). Bibby (1995) also found low levels of approval, in that 85% in 1995 said that extramarital sex was always or almost always wrong (compared to 78% in 1975). Although, responses differed by age (78% for 35- to 54-year-olds vs. 90% for those 18 to 34 and 55 and over), Bibby noted that overall, Canadians' attitudes toward extramarital sex have become less approving over the last 20 years. This does not seem to be a simple reflection of aging of the population, because young people are among the most disapproving.

When asked if they considered masturbation to be a healthy part of one's sex life, 8% strongly agreed, 57% agreed, 30% disagreed, and 5% strongly disagreed. There were no sex differences in agreement, older respondents were less likely to agree (although 52% of those 65 and older agreed), and Quebec again had the highest agreement, with 78% overall considering masturbation to be a healthy part of one's sex life.

When asked if they would feel uncomfortable talking with their children about sex, few indicated that they would be uncomfortable (about 17%). This indirect declaration of comfort was evident for both sexes and for the age groups most likely to be involved in rearing young children or teens. It is unlikely that this perceived comfort always translates into actual discussion, particularly in the area of sexual decision-making. For example, Bibby and Posterski (1992) found that while a sizable percentage of teens identified parents as the first source they would consult when making decisions about what is "right and wrong" (45%), or about school (45%) or a major problem (31%), fewer chose parents first for decisions about "sex" (8%) or relationships (7%); friends were most likely to be chosen in both of the latter categories (55% and 75%, respectively).

Legislation prohibiting discrimination on the basis of sexual orientation is now common in most provinces, and this trend, although actively opposed by some individuals and groups, reflects a shift in Canadian attitudes (Section 6 discusses gay/lesbian issues in more detail). Two of the *Maclean's*/CTV survey questions assessed attitudes toward homosexuality. When asked if "it would be fine if one of my kids turned out to be gay," 11% of respondents strongly agreed, 45% agreed, 29% disagreed, and 14% strongly disagreed. Women were more accepting than men in this regard (64% of men agreed vs. 49% of women), younger were more accepting than older respondents, and those in Quebec were more likely to agree (85%) than in the rest of Canada (46%). On the statement "It would bother me if openly gay and lesbian people were teaching in the schools," the responses generally paralleled those above (56% would not be bothered, 44% agreed that they would be bothered; women were slightly more accepting than men). Bibby (1995) also found evidence of increasingly accepting attitudes toward homosexuality (32% said it was not at all wrong and 16 % sometimes wrong in 1995), up from 38% acceptance in 1990 and 28% in 1975. This still leaves half the population considering homosexuality always or almost always wrong. Interestingly, Bibby (1995) also found that between 1990 and 1995, during a period of active debate about inclusion of gay rights in the Human Rights Code (which occurred in 1996), approval of the idea that gays and lesbian should have the same rights as other Canadians dropped from 80% in 1990 to 67% in 1995. Bibby saw it as somewhat paradoxical that "just when Canadians are exhibiting both an increasing acceptance of homosexuality and greater social comfort with lesbians and gays, they now are also exhibiting increasing discomfort with the idea of extending them equal rights" (Bibby 1995, 74). One might argue that this is a temporary shift based on a tendency of some Canadians to be displeased with both sides in periods of acrimonious and politicized debate.

Television, the print media, and film provide Canadians with regular reminders of social policy issues related to sexuality (pornography, prostitution, sexual abuse, etc.). While these themes will be examined in later sections, survey respondents' attitudes on selected examples give an indication of the prevailing dynamic on such matters. For example, 52% agreed that prostitution should be legalized, with a slightly higher proportion of males than females and of Québécois versus non-Québécois agreeing. Interestingly, agreement was lowest among 18- to 24-year-olds (33% agreed but 57% disagreed, including 26% who strongly disagreed). In contrast, 60 to 64% of 35- to 54-year-olds agreed. Concerning the acceptability of people watching sexually explicit movies, 60% of males versus 34% of females said it was sometimes or always OK and 25% of males versus 48% of females said it was never OK. The statement "pornography is always degrading to women" yielded agreement from 69% of respondents (58% of men and 80% of women). Since respondents gave higher levels of agreement to the idea that "erotic magazines and movies can help make your sex life more interesting" (50% of males and 38% of females agreed) it would appear that Canadians make some distinction between the term "erotica" (which they associate with pleasure) and pornography (which they associate with harm). As we show in Section 8C, Significant Unconventional Sexual Behaviors, Pornography and Erotica, it is the latter distinction that forms the basis for current obscenity law in Canada.

Taken collectively, the foregoing observations support the conclusion that more Canadians in the 1990s than in prior years accept, or are at least tolerant of, a wider diversity of forms of sexual conduct, expression, and communication. This is particularly the case in areas outside the domain of marriage, as seen in the continued lack of acceptance of extramarital sex by the vast majority of Canadians, and by increased acceptance of an unmarried couple living together (in 1995, 78% of Canadians approved, Bibby 1995). However, as Bibby and Posterski (1992) observed, these changes are more a result of population change than of individual change.

> The sexual revolution changed the way Canadians viewed sex outside of marriage. But, having succeeded in transforming attitudes and behavior about sex, the revolution has long been over. What we have witnessed in the past decade or so is the transmission of the new sexual values from first-generation revolutionists to their offspring. The reason the national figures of acceptance have risen over the past 20 years is not because young people are becoming more permissive than their parents. Rather, the protests of grandparents troubled by the changes have—with their passing—been relegated to history. (Bibby & Posterski 1992, 40)

Of note is the consistently greater acceptance and tolerance of diverse forms of sexual expression on the part of French-speaking (primarily resident in the province of Quebec) as compared to other Canadians. This theme, repeated in other sections of our review, is considered by sociologists to be related to a general decline in the influence of the Roman Catholic Church in Quebec, coupled with the rapid move of women into the labor force in this province; again, this is reflective not so much of a change in individual attitude, but of population and demographic changes over the years.

## 2. Religious, Ethnic, and Gender Factors Affecting Sexuality

### A. Religion and Religious Observance

In a report based on the 1996 *General Social Survey*, Clark (1998) examined the reported religious affiliations of Canadians 15 and over and found 45% to be Romans Catholic, 20% mainline Protestant (United, Anglican, Presbyterian, Lutheran), 6% conservative Protestant, and 3% claimed

affiliation with one of the Eastern non-Christian religions (Islam, Hinduism, Buddhism, or others). In general, this reflects a drop in the number of individuals claiming mainline Protestant affiliation and an increase in those with Eastern non-Christian traditions. These figures reflect the British and French origins of the country and the historical predominance of British and European immigration. Other non-Christian religious affiliations, beginning with the First Nations peoples and extending to subsequent immigration by different groups, include: Judaism, Buddhism, Islam, Hindu, and Sikh. The Christian "fundamentalist" religious presence that has challenged sex education and secular sexual laws and attitudes in some parts of the U.S. is less prevalent in Canada, although "conservative" religious groups are among the only ones that have increased in numbers in recent years. The number of individuals 15 and over claiming no religious affiliation has also risen from 1% in 1961, to 13% in 1991, and finally, to 14% by 1996.

Attendance at religious services has generally been declining since the mid-1940s. In 1990, 24% attended at least once a week, 12% once a month, and 27% once a year. By 1996, only 20% of the adult Canadian population reported attending religious services every week, and 10% said they attended only once or twice a year. A further 32% who claimed religious affiliation did not attend religious services at all. This decline has also been noted across all age groups. Those 65 and over were more likely to be weekly attenders in 1990 (42%) than those of younger ages (15 to 24 years: 15%; 25 to 44 years: 18%; 45 to 64 years: 32%). By 1996, these rates has dropped to 34% for those age 65 and over and to 12% for 15- to 24-year-olds. Nevertheless, a telephone survey of 4,510 adults conducted in 1993 by the Angus Reid Group (a major polling agency) for *Maclean's* (a national news magazine with wide distribution) (April 12, 1993) reported that 78% affiliate themselves with a Christian denomination, 74% disagree with the statement "I am not a Christian," and about 65% stated belief in traditional Christian theological doctrines. Similarly, Bibby's Project Canada survey revealed in 1995 that the vast majority of Canadians (81%) still believe in God.

The trend to secular beliefs that conflict with Church doctrine is seen in the fact that, among self-described Roman Catholics polled, 91% approve of artificial birth control, 82% condone premarital sex, 84% would allow priests to marry, 55% view homosexual behavior as morally acceptable, and only 20% support the Church's stance that abortion should be opposed in all circumstances except when the life of the woman is at risk. At the other end of the spectrum, when a church moves away from traditional patterns, as the United Church of Canada did by accepting the ordination of non-celibate, homosexual clergy, a sizable minority felt the church was becoming too liberal in its teachings. Those on the conservative end of the belief spectrum within their denominations are the most active opponents of abortion and proponents of "abstinence-only" sex education in the schools.

Among the almost 4,000 15- to 19-year-old high school students surveyed by Bibby and Posterski (1992), though 79% identified themselves with a particular organized religious denomination, only 19% of 15-year-olds and 13% of 19-year-olds attended weekly religious services, 15% said they received a high level of enjoyment from their involvement in an organized religion, and 24% viewed themselves as committed. Despite the apparently low and declining interest in organized religion (10% considered religious involvement "very important"), 24% rated "spirituality" and 46% "the quest for truth" as very important. Bibby and Posterski (1992) found that teens are highly receptive to spiritual and values-related issues. Supernatural beliefs also appeared to be more common than one might expect based on religious involvement. For example, the percentages agreeing with various supernatural beliefs were: God exists (81%), Divinity of Jesus (80%), some people have psychic powers (69%), life after death (64%), astrology (52%), extrasensory perception (52%), contact with the spirit world (44%), and 'I will be reincarnated' (32%). These percentages are similar in most respects to those for adults asked the same questions in a 1990 survey (see Bibby & Posterski 1992).

These data suggest that while most Canadians are moving away from active involvement in religious institutions, they retain a core of religious beliefs and an interest in spiritual ideas and philosophies. Given this trend, it would be expected that the specific teachings of and stands taken by religious institutions on issues of sexuality might have less influence on Canadians today than they did in the past. This is illustrated most explicitly in the attitudes of French Canadians compared to the teachings of the Roman Catholic Church. For some newer Canadians, however, results of some research suggest that affiliation with religious institutions and involvement in their activities may remain important, with churches, temples, and mosques providing a center for activities of ethnic communities (Maticka-Tyndale et al. 1996). Though to date there are no large-scale studies of the influence of religion and religious involvement in different immigrant groups, results from research by sociologists across North America suggest that the teachings of religious institutions will have more influence on individuals and communities where involvement in those institutions is higher.

## B. Ethnocultural Diversity and Sexuality

The varied ethnocultural backgrounds of Canadians described above have significant implications for sexuality and sexual health. Behavior is strongly influenced by social and cultural factors, and recent immigrants to Canada, in particular, may face complex challenges in understanding and adapting to a new culture. However, it is difficult in a brief review to encompass the ways that cultural traditions in other spheres of social life both reflect and create expectations regarding sexual behavior for Canada's varied ethnocultural groups. In most cases, national statistical data on specific aspects of sexual behavior do not exist, and it is rare to find qualitative studies focused on the broad aspects of sexual activities and beliefs within different ethnocultural communities. Concerns about AIDS and sexual abuse have generated research within selected communities. Examples include a network of studies in several ethnocultural communities. The largest of these, the federally funded *Ethnocultural Communities Facing AIDS* study, was conducted in collaboration with representatives from six communities—Chinese, South Asian, Horn of Africa, English-speaking Caribbean, North African Muslim, and Latin American—in the three cities that receive the largest proportion of immigrants to Canada (Montreal, Toronto, and Vancouver). This project used a combination of ethnographic and survey techniques and had two goals: (1) the development of a knowledge base about cultural and psychosocial factors influencing sexual behaviors that place people at risk for HIV infection; and (2) formation of recommendations for prevention programming in these communities. Overviews of results and recommendations from the qualitative phase of research were published in the six-booklet report, *Many Voices:HIV/AIDS in the Context of Culture.* Final reports based on community surveys were also prepared (see Health Canada 1994a-f, for community reports; also Adrien et al. 1995; "HIV" 1996; Maticka-Tyndale et al. 1995).

## 3. Knowledge and Education about Sexuality

### A. Government Policies and Programs

Because Canadian political structures and social life are based on a relatively nonintrusive conception of democratic society, formal sources of sex education have, for the most part, refrained from overtly imposing specific "doctrinal" sexual values on Canadians. For example, institutions such as the public schools have generally not sought to inculcate particular views on the acceptability of premarital sex. Instead, the school is more likely to offer information and guidance intended to help students make informed decisions about their sexual behavior; counseling and health facilities generally operate from the premise of providing information and care (e.g., to decrease sexually transmitted disease and unwanted pregnancy) regardless of position or status. This is not to say that sex education in the schools is free of ideology or that some Canadians would not wish stronger influence for their particular ideological position. Nevertheless, it appears that school-based sexuality education generally aspires to a non-doctrinal stance based on democratic principles (see McKay 1997).

Because education in Canada falls under provincial rather than federal jurisdiction, the Ministry of Education (or Department of Education) for each of the ten provinces and three territories usually has its own guidelines and/or curricula for sexuality education and its own procedures for implementing them. However, there are various programs through which the national government collaborates with the provinces and/or operates independently in this area, particularly within the context of the Division of Sexual Health Promotion and STD Prevention and Control. The federal government provides funding for a variety of provincial organizations and researchers concerned with education and treatment pertaining to sexual health (AIDS, STDs, sexual-abuse prevention, women's reproductive health, etc.). For example, both the AIDS Information and Education Services Unit of Health Canada, which operates within the Programs Division of the Health Promotion Directorate of the Health Programs and Services Branch, and the AIDS Care, Treatment, and Support Unit of Health Canada, which operates within the Preventive Health Services Division of the Health Services Directorate of the same Branch, provide this kind of federal-provincial linkage.

A joint venture between Health Services and Health Promotion led to production in 1994 of the *Canadian Guidelines for Sexual Health Education.* The *Guidelines*, produced by a national working group coordinated by the Sex Information and Education Council of Canada (SIECCAN) under a contract agreement with Health Canada, provide a unifying framework, a philosophy, and a set of principles to unite and guide those providing, planning, or updating sexual health education programs and/or services for people of all ages across Canada. The *Guidelines* can be used as a frame of reference for assessing both the overall network and the individual components of existing sexual health education programs and related services at the national, provincial, or local level. However, the document cautions against a single "authoritative" definition of sexual health as a static phenomenon that can be readily identified, and hence prescribed, by experts. Sexual health education is seen as "a broadly based, community-supported enterprise in which the individual's personal, family, religious, and social values are engaged in understanding and making decisions about sexual behavior and implementing those decisions" (Minister of Supply and Services 1994, 4). A revised set of guidelines is slated to be released in mid-2003.

Another joint venture that involved the federal government and the provincial ministries of health and education supported development and evaluation of "Skills for Healthy Relationships," a program about sexuality, AIDS, and other STDs for early high school students. Developed by the Social Program Evaluation Group at Queen's University, Kingston, Ontario, the program is now available to any school/school board or Ministry of Education that wishes to assume the cost of duplicating the materials (available from the National AIDS Clearinghouse of the Canadian Public Health Association). An in-service training session for teachers is an important component of the program, as was the large-scale program evaluation done independently by researchers not involved with development or implementation of the program (Warren & King 1994). Other federal and provincial/territorial government programs related to HIV/AIDS prevention and treatment (see Section 10, Sexually Transmitted Diseases and HIV/AIDS) and to other aspects of sexual health will be discussed as the relevant topics arise throughout the chapter.

## Sexuality Education in Elementary and Secondary Schools

All provinces and territories have school programs that include sexuality education, although the content and extent of implementation varies considerably between provinces and within different parts of the same province. While school-based sexuality education programs are a provincial responsibility, the federal government has a variety of programs through which it can assist sexuality education in schools or sexual health education for all ages in the community. As noted above, the Division of Sexual Health Promotion and STD Prevention and Control, the National Health Research and Development Program, the Division of HIV/AIDS Epidemiology and Surveillance (Bureau of HIV/AID, STD, and TB in the Centre for Infectious Disease Prevention and Control Canada), and other government departments may support researchers and community organizations in diverse sexuality education programs and services. Local public health units within specific municipalities of each province are also actively involved in public education about contraception, AIDS and other STDs, sexual abuse, and other aspects of sexual health, and they may do so in school settings as well.

There have been only a few national surveys of the availability of sexuality education in Canadian schools (for reviews, see Barrett 1990, 1994), and no detailed national studies of the classroom content of sexuality education that would indicate the extent to which provincial guidelines and curricula are translated into classroom programming. There is, however, enough information from individual provinces to indicate significant advances in sexuality education over the past 15 years fueled to a large extent by emerging concerns about HIV/AIDS, other STDs, and sexual abuse, and also by ongoing concerns about teen pregnancy.

Survey findings throughout the 1980s, 1990s, and into 2002, have consistently shown broad public support for some form of sexuality education in the schools (Langille et al. 1996; Lawlor & Purcell 1989; McKay & Holowaty 1997; McKay, Petrusiak, & Holowaty 1998; Ornstein 1989; Weaver et al. 2001, 2002). As in earlier studies (Verby & Herold 1992), the more recent reports also show support for HIV/AIDS education, which now appears in many curricula in grades 5 and/or 6 (ages 9 to 11). Although it is often difficult for such studies to include detailed assessment of respondents' opinions about specific content, or their views on the more subtle aspects of philosophy and attitudes that they might wish to see inculcated, Canadians appear to be strongly supportive of the the involvement of schools in sexuality education. Nevertheless, a minority perceives contemporary sex education to be skewed toward liberal, secular attitudes, particularly in the areas of abortion, homosexuality, teen sexuality, and access to contraceptive information and services, and actively promulgates a more restrictive agenda in all of these areas. Although historically this view has been expressed as an opposition to sexuality education in the schools, at present it is more likely to focus on either the specific value positions that schools should adopt, the appropriateness of particular topics (e.g., homosexuality, contraception, and abortion), or the ways in which student behavior should be influenced (e.g., abstinence-only programs).

There are few settings other than schools through which almost all young people can be reached with a planned educational program that addresses the broad range of topics subsumed under the heading of sexuality education. Sexuality education in schools is almost invariably integrated into a broader program of Health Education, Personal and Social Relationships, Family Life Education, Religious and Moral Education, and similar subjects, but this varies between provinces (or even within provinces) and there is, therefore, no standard national curriculum for sexuality education. However, most school curricula are based on a statement of principles and a guiding philosophy that emphasizes self-knowledge, acceptance of individual development, social obligations, personal values, the avoidance of problems (e.g., sexual coercion, teen pregnancy, STDs, etc.), and to a lesser and varied extent, the development of satisfying sexual relationships. Material is presented in a hierarchy based on age appropriateness, with a number of previously excluded or delayed topics now appearing at earlier ages (e.g., AIDS and avoidance of sexual exploitation).

Sex education in schools is evolving in Canada, from first-generation programs that focused primarily on knowledge about reproduction and birth control (on the assumption that students would translate this information into self-protecting behavior), to second-generation programs that included factual information plus skills in communication and relationships (on the assumption that these generic skills would translate as above) (Kirby 1992; Kirby et al. 1994; McKay 1993), to the newly emerging programs that are rooted in conceptual models of behavior change that include knowledge acquisition, development of attitudes and behavioral intentions in support of sexual health, motivational supports, and development of situation-specific skills (see, for example, McKay 2000, 2001; McKay et al. 2001). The Skills for Healthy Relationships program for grade 9 students (aged 13-14) described above is an example of this approach (Warren & King 1994). This gradual transition in Canadian sexuality education (most programs are second-generation type) reflects an increasing desire of educators and public health professionals to design interventions that affect sexual health behavior and outcomes. There is also an emerging interest in applying these concepts to elementary school education (Wackett & Evans 2000), although deciding which behaviors to assess and the willingness of schools to survey younger students on such topics remain largely unmet challenges.

One of the complaints about traditional sex education has been that it does not work, i.e., teen pregnancies and STDs remain high. The problem is that early sex education programs simply anticipated such outcomes, although they were neither designed for nor taught in ways that would achieve these specific behavioral objectives. Students did become more knowledgeable and more insightful about their own and other people's feelings and behavior—both desirable outcomes—but this type of knowledge-based sex education is not generally expected to have a major impact on behavior (for a review, see Fisher & Fisher 1992, 1998). With the continued concern about AIDS and other STDs, schools are being asked to influence behavior (postponing sexual involvement, encouraging abstinence, increasing condom use and safer sex practices, etc.) and not just to increase knowledge.

While Canada has experienced localized opposition to sex education in the schools, that opposition today, as noted above, is seldom to the school's involvement in sexuality education, per se, but to the presumed "liberal" values of such programs. Public discourse on this issue has affected curriculum development to varying degrees across Canada and it is against the competing pressures of heightened expectation, anticipated "traditional" opposition, and limited resources, that school-based sexuality education continues to develop. A detailed overview of recommended or required sexuality education content in Canadian elementary and secondary schools is beyond the scope of this chapter (for a review, see Barrett 1994).

### Outcomes of School-Based Sexuality Education

The final report on the Skills for Healthy Relationships program (Warren & King 1994) is the largest study ever undertaken in Canada on the long-range outcome of a school-based sexuality education program. As noted above, the program was developed by the Social Program Evaluation Group at Queen's University, Kingston, Ontario, with collaboration and support from provincial and territorial ministries of education and health, the Council of Ministers of Education, Canada, the National Health Research and Development Program, and the Division of HIV/AIDS Epidemiology and Surveillance (Bureau of HIV/AIDS, STD, and TB in the Centre for Infectious Disease Prevention and Control Canada). The Skills for Healthy Relationships program provides grade 9 students (ages 13-14) with a carefully structured and theoretically based educational intervention on AIDS, other STDs, and sexuality. It features cooperative learning (small groups), parent/guardian involvement (six interactive activities), active learning (role playing, behavioral rehearsal), peer leaders (in small groups, modeling skills), video instruction, and journaling and development of a personal action plan (assertiveness goal). The skills component is a major feature of the program, and outcome measures, assessed by questionnaires just after students had taken the program and one and two years later, included indicators of change related to these skills (assertiveness, communication with parents, regular condom use if sexually active, etc.). The comparison groups in each of the four provinces in which the program was tested were students who took their school's regular grade 9 AIDS/STD program.

Two years later, students who took the program said they had been changed by the program in a number of ways: more comfort talking about personal rights with a partner (72%), talking about condoms (67%), ability to refuse or negotiate something I don't want to do (58% in both cases), more assertive (53%), and always use condoms with my partner (61%) (Warren & King 1994). Compared to the nonparticipant group, participants at the two-year follow-up:

- were more likely to have gained compassion toward people with AIDS;
- had more-positive attitudes toward homosexuality;
- showed greater knowledge of HIV/AIDS;
- were more likely to express the intent to communicate with partners about condom use;
- were no more likely to have the intent to use condoms (this was initially high in both groups);

- were no more likely to report "always" using a condom (about 41% of both groups said they always did so; about half reported using a condom the last time they had intercourse); and
- females were more likely to declare that they would respond assertively if they were pressured unwillingly to have sex.

As would be expected, in the period from grade 9 to 11, the proportion of students who had experienced intercourse increased for both sexes in both groups. However, the percentage of both sexes who said they had ever had intercourse was slightly lower in the participant group two years after the program (51% comparison vs. 42% participant for males; 49% comparison vs. 46% participant for females). The students from both groups who were most likely to have unprotected intercourse were those who took risks in areas such as alcohol consumption, use of cannabis, and skipping classes. They were also more likely to be doing poorly in school (Warren & King 1994). These latter observations highlight the important behavioral influence of social and relationship factors that may well be difficult to change through school-based interventions alone.

In Canada, Orton and Rosenblatt's (1986, 1991, 1993) pioneering research on a multisectoral approach to pregnancy prevention in Ontario showed that rates of adolescent pregnancy declined more rapidly in the late 1970s and early 1980s in those localities that provided young people with both school-based sexuality education and access to clinical services. Orton (1994) points out that the usual practice of reporting only province-wide data for teen pregnancy has tended to obscure the "inequality gap" between individual localities with respect to the decline in teen pregnancies. We have, therefore, been less likely to note the successes in localities that combined prevention programs in both the educational and public health sectors, and also less able, and willing, to recognize and target resources toward those settings that needed special assistance because they were less advantaged for providing such programs (e.g., rural and northern localities). Orton (1994) argues that: "Policies and programs of sexual health have the potential to reduce social inequalities by reducing rates of adolescent pregnancy and STDs, and also by reducing the wide variation in rates between jurisdictions and groups within Canada" (p. 223).

Based on an analysis of policies and programs in education, public health, and social services in Ontario, Orton (1994) argues that "intersectoral collaboration can contribute to greater and more equitable access to sexual health education and services," but that such collaboration requires "strong policy directives at all three ministries" (p. 222). Her findings in Ontario argue for "the effectiveness of centralized policy direction (public health), and the ineffectiveness of a decentralized approach (education and social services) to achieve equitable access to effective programs" (Orton 1994, 223).

There are numerous examples of the successful implementation of programs meeting Orton's criteria. The province of Saskatchewan is attempting to strengthen sexual health education. Its planning document, *Toward Sexual and Reproductive Health in Saskatchewan*, from a province attempting to strengthen sexual health education, shows how a centralized initiative from the Ministry of Health invited multisectoral collaboration in program and policy development (Saskatchewan Health 1993) along the lines that Orton (1994) recommends. Nova Scotia also provides another example of a multiple-component intervention (Langille 2000). Carried out between 1996 and 1999, the Amherst Initiative for Healthy Adolescent Sexuality brought together community groups (including schools), parents, teenagers, healthcare professionals, and interested citizens to promote adolescent sexual health. Comparisons between 1996 and 1999 show important changes in knowledge, attitudes, and behavior among grade 9 to 12 students at Amherst Regional High School. Of particular note was a decrease of 31% in the age-adjusted pregnancy rate for Amherst women in 1998, compared to 1995 to 1997. Such a finding is encouraging, and certainly in support of a multisectoral approach.

[*Update 1999*: With a comprehensive compulsory sexuality education program in place in all of the Alberta province's schools since 1990, a recent survey found that teenagers in Alberta are postponing intercourse for longer than their counterparts in other Canadian provinces, leading some to argue that mandatory sexuality education programs play a role in encouraging teens to delay sexual activity. According to a survey of 82,000 Canadians published in the *Calgary Herald*, only 8% of females in Alberta ages 15 to 19 said they had sex before age 15, compared to the national average of 13%. Among Calgary's 15-to-19-year-olds, 7% reported having sex before age 15. Supporters of comprehensive sexuality education attribute these lower rates to a decade of comprehensive compulsory sexuality education in the schools and to easy access to family planning clinics. Calgary's teen pregnancy rate is among the lowest in Canada and the world. Critics of the program argue that an abstinence-based sexuality education program would drive the figures down even further. Critics also claim that sex education that does not specifically counsel abstinence has always increased teen pregnancy and STD rates (*Kaiser Daily Reproductive Health Report* 1999). (*End of update by R. T. Francoeur*)]

There are a number of issues facing the continued growth and improvement of sexuality education in Canadian schools. For example, the duration, content, and quality of such education varies considerably between schools and within and between provinces, but it is uncertain whether governments will continue to give sexuality education the required priority and resources. Canadian schools face increasing financial and staffing constraints and there is a growing demand to focus more on basic areas like language skills, science, computer technology, and so on, which may lead, by default or design, to either a lower priority for sexuality education or to a more limited, problem-centered focus on selected topics. Given the various sexual ideologies, religious traditions, and ethnocultural backgrounds within the Canadian population, it has been difficult to find a broad public consensus on how to deal with controversial issues in schools (teen sexuality, homosexuality, etc.). The past climate of cautiousness and conflict on such issues still continues to impede implementation of high-quality sexuality education programs in many areas. The goal identified in the *Canadian Guidelines for Sexual Health Education*, i.e., universal access to a broadly based, comprehensive, and integrated approach to sexual health education, suggests high national expectations and intentions, but uncertain resources and competing priorities are part of the reality facing attempts to fully implement such a program.

### Sexuality Education and Related Services Through Public Health Units and Other Such Agencies

Provincial and Territorial Public Health Units play a major role in sexual health education and related services in Canada, and they are often in the forefront of community sexual health education campaigns. For example, the Program Requirements and Standards section of Ontario's *Mandatory Health Programs and Services Guidelines* (Ontario Ministry of Health 1989) lists four pages of expectations and program standards for sexual health and STDs. Boards of health and public health nurses are the front-line staff involved in addressing these issues with clients of all ages and socioeconomic status. The demands on this growing bureaucracy have increased in recent years in response to changing patterns of sexual behavior among youth, increasing ethnocultural diversity and immigrant populations in cities, population aging, AIDS, concerns about sexual abuse prevention for all ages, and other such issues. In the face of growing demand and limited resources, provision of service is varied across Ontario (this is probably true for all provinces) and, for the same reasons, the additional mandate to do community needs assessments and outcome evaluations of sexual health programs is also difficult to sustain.

A variety of nongovernmental agencies are also involved in sexuality education and related services. The Sex Information and Education Council of Canada (SIECCAN), founded in 1964, maintains a resource library and information service, publishes the *Canadian Journal of Human Sexuality* and the *SIECCAN Newsletter*, provides consultation services and professional education workshops, and facilitates development of new resources, such as the *Being Sexual* series (Ludwig & Hingsburger 1993), *After You Tell* (Ludwig 1995), and the previously described *National Guidelines for Sexual Health Education*. The Planned Parenthood Federation of Canada (PPFC) has a long history of advocacy, education, and resource distribution on contraception and sexuality. PPFC administers the Sex Education and Research Clearinghouse (SEARCH), a national center for distribution and development of sexuality education resource materials. Local Planned Parenthood offices now provide sexual health education and services and some, such as The House, in Toronto, administer adolescent health centers that are equipped to address a broader range of health issues than contraception and pregnancy counseling. The Canadian AIDS Society and local AIDS committees and organizations do educational outreach that includes some aspects of sexuality education, as do other groups with particular concerns about sexuality, such as the Disabled Women's Network and the British Columbia Coalition on AIDS and Disability. The Canadian Public Health Association, the Canadian Association of School Health, the Canadian Infectious Diseases Society, the Society of Obstetricians and Gynecologists of Canada, and a number of other nongovernmental organizations contribute at the national level to public sexuality education.

### B. Informal Sources of Sexual Knowledge

Despite the growing role of schools and public health authorities in public education about such topics as contraception, STDs, and HIV/AIDS prevention, informal sources (peers, family, and the media) are probably the primary influence on sexual attitudes and knowledge. Adolescents have been the focus of most research in this area.

For example, when asked to list their main sources of AIDS information, grade 11 students ($N = 9,617$) surveyed in the *Canada Youth and AIDS Study* ranked television first, followed, respectively, by print materials, school, family, friends, and doctors/nurses (King et al. 1988). The first three rankings were the same for grade 7 ($N = 9,925$) and grade 9 ($N = 9,860$) students. Although these informal sources were identified as the main source of AIDS information for Canadian youth, a majority of the young people surveyed said they would have preferred a more formal source of information, such as doctors or nurses. A more recent study in Ontario found that school was the main and preferred source of health information (McKay & Holowaty 1997).

Ornstein's (1989) study of AIDS-related knowledge, behavior, and attitudes of Canadian adults ($N = 1,259$)

found that, similar to the students in King et al.'s study, television (39%) and newspapers (23%) led the list of respondents' self-identified "main sources of information about AIDS." Magazines were identified by 9% and health authorities (e.g., physicians, nurses, hospitals, and clinics) by only 2.5%. Although not asked to self-identify their sources of information, one study of British Columbia youth (McCreary Centre Society 1993) indicates that 84% of participants were taught about AIDS in school and 72% knew how or where to get information. This trend was seen to increase with grade level. As well, 50% had talked with their parents about AIDS.

In the survey phase of the *Ethnocultural Communities Facing AIDS* study, conducted in English-speaking Caribbean, Latin American, and South Asian communities (only men from the South Asian communities participated in the survey), the rank ordering of where respondents preferred to get information about HIV/AIDS was identical in all three communities and to both of the two earlier studies (Maticka-Tyndale et al. 1995). Ornstein's (1989) conclusion that "in the main, Canadians rely on the mass media rather than more specialized publications to learn about AIDS" (p. 52), clearly applies regardless of age and probably also regardless of ethnocultural background. Although no more recent studies have been done, this is likely still the case.

While various forms of media, particularly television, have been Canadians' main source of information about AIDS, the picture changes somewhat when sources of information on sexuality in general are examined. Again, informal sources of information predominate. However, with sexuality in general, as opposed to AIDS, peers and family become the most commonly cited sources of information. The World Wide Web and other computer-assisted information systems are having a growing impact on students' access to sexuality-related content, but the potential of this medium as a formal resource for sexuality education (see Humphreys et al. 1996) has yet to be exploited.

When King et al. (1988) asked a national sample of students about their main sources of information about sex, grade 7 (aged 11-12) and grade 9 (aged 13-14) students ranked family first out of six possible sources of sex information. Though friends were ranked fifth by grade 7 students, they rose to third for grade 9 students, and first for grade 11 students. The latter group ranked family a close second. Friends remained first for college/university students, with family dropping to third place, replaced by print materials in second. Interestingly, school dropouts ranked previous schooling first, friends second, and family third as their main sources of sex information. In a comparable study of Newfoundland students done in 1991, Cregheur et al. (1992) found that grade 11 students (aged 16-17) ranked friends first as their main source of information about sex, followed by school, television, family, and print materials. Interestingly, compared to the King et al. (1988) national sample, grade 11 students in the Cregheur et al. study (1992) were less likely to cite friends, family, television, and print materials as their main sources of information about sex, and more likely to cite school.

The role of peers and parents as important informal sources of information and support is evident from the results of three studies. King et al.'s (1988) study of Canadian teens found that, overall, teens agreed that they talked with their close friends about sex (increasing from 56% in grade 7 to 75% in grade 11), that people of the opposite sex like them (51% in grade 7, 73% in grade 11), and that they discuss their problems with their friends (62 to 71%). Among grade 9 students questioned in a 1992 evaluation of the "Skills for Healthy Relationships" program (see Warren

& King 1994), 59% of females and 38% of males agreed that "I can talk to my mother about sexual matters" (26% of females and 41% of males agreed that they could talk to their fathers about sexual matters). Finally, Herold's (1984) study of young women visiting a birth control clinic found that two thirds of the women had received birth control information from girlfriends, about half from schools or reading materials, 25% from their mothers, and 2% from their fathers. The importance of peers is highlighted in Herold's (1984) conclusion that

> peers provide teenage girls with information, legitimization and support. Girlfriends are the most important source of information about birth control, and teenage girls who are socially isolated in the sense of having few friends often delay getting birth control because they lack peer support. (p. 105)

The impact of informal sources of learning on sexual values is a much-discussed issue in Canada. In a study of values and sex education in Montreal-area English-language high schools, Lawlor and Purcell (1988) surveyed 667 grade 9 and grade 11 students about a variety of topics related to sex education. Asked where they learned their moral values related to sexuality, the students again ranked peers at the top. Friends away from school were ranked first, followed, respectively, by classmates, home, television and movies, books and magazines, in school from teachers, in school from religious teaching, and rock/pop music and lyrics. It is noteworthy that these students ranked rock/pop music and lyrics last out of a possible eight sources of sexual values, since there has been increasing speculation in the Canadian media that popular music and rock videos may have a negative impact on the sexual attitudes of young people. For the eight sources for learning sexual values, the most pronounced gender difference was for the item "in the home," which was ranked third by grade 9 girls and second for grade 11 girls, but fifth by both grade 9 and grade 11 boys.

While public policy and sex education literature generally acknowledge the important role that parents play in the sexual development of children, there has been surprisingly little research on the direct communication of sexual knowledge from parents to their children. In a study of 200 Canadian university women (Herold & Way 1983), subjects reported which sexual topics they had discussed with their parents. Eighty percent had talked about attitudes towards premarital sex with their mothers, 55% with their fathers; 70% had discussed contraception with their mothers, 29% with their fathers; 15% had discussed oral sex or masturbation with their mothers, 2% with their fathers; and 9% had talked about sexual techniques with their mothers, less than 1% with their fathers.

Several general observations can be made based on these studies. First, family, peers, and media form a triad of influence and education with respect to issues related to the sexuality of young Canadians. In general, there is a developmental shift that occurs in the relative place of family, peers, and media sources during adolescence. Between about grade 9 (13 to 15 years of age) and grade 11 (16 to 17 years of age), peer influence rises to top rank, and that of family decreases in importance, in some cases even outranked by the more impersonal media (e.g., print materials). In addition, at least for university women, mothers in particular have been a potential source of information and influence in matters of sexuality. The foregoing results support Bibby and Posterski's (1992) observation that the apparent changes in attitudes and conduct are not individual changes, but a "coming of age" of a new generation of Canadians—the children of the "sexual revolution" generation—who are forming their own reference groups of information and influence.

## 4. Autoerotic Behaviors and Patterns

In the insufficiently heated bedroom on the northwest corner of the house in Park Place, I was taken by surprise by the first intimations of a pleasure that I did not at first know how to elicit from or return to the body that gave rise to it, which was my own. It had no images connected with it, and no object but pure physical sensation. It was as if I had found a way of singing that did not come from my throat.

—A man's recollection from his boyhood in *So Long, See You Tomorrow*, William Maxwell (1980)

In the early 1900s, the first sex education classes in Ontario schools taught young boys about the dangers of masturbation. Students were told that seminal fluid contained a vital force that nourished the brain and muscles, and that wasting it through any sexual excess, but particularly through masturbation, was physically and mentally depleting to the individual. Furthermore, students were also told that a man could pass this depleted condition on to his offspring. These dual beliefs in vitalist physiology and in the inheritance of acquired characteristics provided the "secular" rationale for prohibitions that were already part of the religious teachings of the time. Canada's long-abandoned eugenic sterilization law of 1902 had its origins in the period when such teaching became popular (for review, see Bliss 1970). Sex education at that time was generally silent on female masturbation—often ignoring its very possibility—but when it was mentioned, the dire consequences for reproductive health and mental stability were strongly emphasized. Mothers were told to be watchful lest their children fall into the habit that, they were warned, was notoriously difficult to break.

Over 90 years later, masturbation has gone from being a sin to a normal part of sexual development in children and a healthy aspect of sexual expression in adults. This general impression would have to be documented from qualitative sources, since we have been unable to locate any published national data on masturbation frequency in any age group. Survey results cited in Section 1C, Basic Sexological Premises, General Concepts and Constructs of Sexuality, indicate that a majority of Canadians adults view it as a healthy expression, although a sizable minority either disagreed (30%) or strongly disagreed (5%) with this view. Sex education literature almost invariably refers to masturbation as normal, and recommendations for parents usually pertain to the importance of privacy and of not instilling guilt. Sexuality education for children and young adults with developmental disabilities places particular emphasis on teaching in this area because public masturbation, even when it arises through lack of social skills, can lead to embarrassment, restriction of social opportunities by caregivers, or exploitation by others. The Sex Information and Education Council of Canada (SIECCAN) publishes and distributes a 17-booklet sexuality education series for people with developmental disabilities—*Being Sexual: An Illustrated Series on Sexuality and Relationships*—that includes clearly illustrated, detailed, sex-positive information about female masturbation (Ludwig & Hingsburger 1993) and male masturbation (Hingsburger & Ludwig 1993). The series is designed for people who have problems with language, learning, or communication, and all books are translated into Blissymbols, making the series the only resource of its kind in the world. Blissymbolics, a symbolic language developed by C. K. Bliss and described in *Semantography*, published in 1949, was intended to be a means of communication across all language groups. It is now used by people with disabilities, and others, to facilitate expressive speech. The Canadian organization responsible for this work is Blissymbolics Communication International.

One paper on childhood masturbation written by Canadian authors relies on U.S. statistics for occurrence and incidence data to suggest that 90 to 94% of males and 50 to 60% of females have masturbated during their lifetime, that the highest incidence is among 16- to 20-year-olds (86% masturbate; the frequency is higher in males than females), and that masturbation declines with age in men but increases toward middle age in women (Leung & Robson 1993). While some religious groups consider masturbation to be sinful or an unacceptable indulgence, the common reaction in Canada appears to range from benign acceptance (and little discussion) to enthusiastic approval, reflective of the general shift toward a larger proportion of the population's acceptance and endorsement of various forms of sexual expression.

## 5. Interpersonal Heterosexual Behaviors

### A. Children

There have been no national studies on the sexual behavior or sex-role rehearsal play of Canadian children. While it seems likely that sexual curiosity and exploratory play would follow patterns similar to those described by U.S. researchers (see Martinson 1994), we do not know of any studies that would provide empirical support for this conjecture in Canada.

### B. Adolescents

It is important to place the sexual behavior of Canadian adolescents as a group within the context of prevailing social, political, and economic conditions and of other individual variables, such as their personal characteristics and relationships, their attitudes toward sexuality, and their increasing exposure to sexual images and information through television, films, and magazines. Although it is misleading to generalize about such a diverse group, the findings of two national studies with large samples described earlier offer important background insights against which to assess more-recent reports on adolescent sexual health in Canada. The *Canada Youth and AIDS Study* (Social Program Evaluation Group, Queen's University, King et al. 1988) is the only large-scale national study of both the attitudes and sexual behavior of Canadian adolescents and young adults. The sample included approximately 19,500 grade 9 and 11 students, 14 to 17 years of age. "Project Teen Canada" 1992, which replicated a national survey of 15- to 19-year-olds conducted in 1984, had a sample of 3,600 15- to 19-year-olds and investigated attitudes and beliefs (not behavior) about a range of topics, including sexuality (Bibby & Posterski 1992). More recently, national data assembled by the Canadian team for the Alan Guttmacher Institute's international comparative study of adolescent sexual health in developed countries (France, England, Sweden, Canada, United States) (Darroch, Frost, Singh, et al. 2001) have provided a 1990s overview of selected aspects of the sexual health of Canadian adolescents (Maticka-Tyndale, Barrett, & McKay 2000; Maticka-Tyndale, McKay, & Barrett 2001; Singh, Darroch, Frost, et al. 2001; Darroch, Singh, Frost, et al. 2001; Maticka-Tyndale 2001). These varied sources, and others, are used below as a starting point to examine the sexual attitudes and behavior of Canadian adolescents.

### Sexuality and Self-Esteem

Self-concept refers to the way individuals describe their abilities, personalities, and relationships, whereas self-esteem refers to the value placed on these personal characteristics (King et al. 1988). Research has repeatedly demonstrated strong associations between self-concept, self-esteem, and sexual conduct, particularly for adolescents. These are, therefore, important concepts to consider in this section on adolescent sexual conduct. In King et al.'s national study, while Canadian teens generally agreed that they had confidence in themselves (88 to 90% of grade 7, 9, and 11 males, 81 to 87% females) (King et al. 1988), ambivalence is reflected in a variety of areas, particularly for young women. Between 51% and 53% of grade 7, 9, and 11 females reported that they would "change how I look if I could" (vs. 37 to 38% for males); 37% of grade 7 females and 51% and 54% of grade 9 and 11 females agreed with the statement, "I need to lose weight" (vs. 21 to 24% for males); and 32 to 41% of females agreed that "I often feel depressed" (vs. 27 to 30% for males). At the same time, 84 to 89% said, "I have a lot of friends," 81 to 84% said "I am a happy person," and 71 to 74% said, "The future looks good to me."

Similar findings on self-esteem of Canadian 11- to 15-year-olds are reported in *The Health of Canada's Youth* (King & Coles 1992), part of an international collaborative study designed to collect comparative health-related information on young people in Austria, Belgium, Canada, Finland, Hungary, Norway, Poland, Scotland, Spain, Sweden, and Wales. In the section on social adjustment, King and Coles (1992) observe that, "compared with young people from European countries, young Canadians are experiencing more strain in their relationships with their parents and even with each other" (p. 96). Yet Canadian students were more likely than those in most other participating countries to find it easy to talk to friends of either sex about things that really bother them. This concurrence of positive self-regard on the one hand, and anxiety or dissatisfaction with specific areas of their lives on the other, has also been noted in other studies of slightly older Canadian youth as well.

For example, Bibby and Posterski (1992) also noted the generally high self-esteem of teens (e.g., 82% of females and 90% of males agreed that the statement, "I can do most things well," described them either very well or fairly well). However, these adolescents had concerns about a number of areas, including achievement in school (this was an issue for both sexes) and personal safety (a major concern for females). About three times as many females as males (56% vs. 20%) agreed that there was an area "within a mile (or kilometer) of your home where you would be afraid to walk at night." About 95% of both young women and men plan to have careers, but there appears to be a continuing gender gap in areas that may have an impact on sexual and gender relationships. For example, females were more likely than males to rate certain values as "very important" (concern for others, 75% vs. 48%; forgiveness, 71% vs. 45%, and honesty, 82% vs. 56%) (Bibby & Posterski 1992).

Though these studies support the general contention that Canadian adolescents have a relatively positive self-concept and high self-esteem, they also demonstrate clear and important gender differences. Young women express specific concerns about appearance and safety, and focus greater attention on values that relate to relationships than those of individual achievement or success. Considerably fewer young men, on the other hand, show concern for appearance or focus attention on relationship values and, by and large, they seem unconcerned about personal safety. These characteristics are of particular importance when considering their potential influence on relationships between young men and women and the ability of each to realize the expectations they have set for their futures.

### Attitudes Toward Sexuality and Relationships

Attitudes toward sexual intercourse before marriage (i.e., "premarital sex") have been widely used as an indicator of sexual permissiveness. In King et al.'s study (1988), among grade 11 students (ages 15 to 17), 13% said unmarried people should not have sex and 76% said it is all right for people to have sex before marriage if they are in love (74% female, 78% male) (agreement combines the "strongly agree" and "agree" categories on a five-point Likert scale) (King et al. 1988). More recently, *Maclean's* (2001) reported findings based on R. Bibby's book, *Canada's Teens: Today, Yesterday and Tomorrow*, that 82% of Canadian teens believe that love is an acceptable reason for sex before marriage, while 58% feel that liking someone is sufficient.

In their slightly older sample in 1992, Bibby and Posterski found that: 86% of females and 88% of males agreed with sex before marriage for people in love (the value was 93% for both sexes in Quebec); 51% of females and 77% of males agreed with sex before marriage when the people involved liked each other (81% and 91%, respectively, in Quebec); 40% of females and 73% of males agreed that sexual relations were OK within a few dates (60% and 82%, respectively, in Quebec); and 5% of females and 20% of males agreed with sexual relations on a first date if people like each other (9% and 23%, respectively, in Quebec). A study of attitudes toward use of power in sexual relations among college students in Quebec (Samson et al. 1996) found that the majority of students refused to see the expression of sexuality as a locus of power, but viewed it more in the context of shared affection and pleasure.

The tendency toward increasing permissiveness with greater levels of affection is a longstanding North American tradition among young people and adults. In fact, Widmer, Treas, and Newcomb (1998), in an international comparison of attitudes toward nonmarital sex, found that a full 69% of Canadians felt premarital sex was "not at all wrong," with an additional 15% feeling it is "only sometimes" wrong. Similar findings were reported by Bibby (1995), with respondents endorsing "not at all wrong" 57% of the time and "sometimes wrong" 23% of the time. The greater levels of approval among Quebec students may be characteristic of the more sex-accepting attitude of Quebec society in general, and particularly of the francophone segment of the population. In contrast to their attitudes toward premarital sex, only 9% of young people in Bibby and Posterski's (1992) total teen sample approved of extramarital sex (12% vs. 9% for francophone and anglophone Quebec teens), with this figure falling to less than 5% for Catholic teens who attended church two to three times per month.

Bibby and Posterski (1992) found that 87% of teens outside of Quebec approved of unmarried people living together (95% among francophone Québécois and over 80% among Catholic students in Quebec). Among teens outside of Quebec, 65% approved of people having children without being married (88% among francophone Québécois).

In the areas of homosexuality and gay rights, teens were more likely to support social justice and rights for the gay population (68% approval overall outside of Quebec, 83% in Quebec) than to approve of homosexual relations (33% approval outside of Quebec, 55% among francophone Québécois). King et al. (1988) found a sizable percentage of grade 7, 9, and 11 students agreeing that "homosexuality is wrong" (45%, 42%, 38%, respectively) and a surprisingly small percentage agreeing that they would feel comfortable talking with a homosexual person (18%, 22%, and 29%, respectively). With increasing discussion of gay rights and homosexuality in the media, we might expect these numbers to change, although there remains a dichotomy between many young people's acceptance of gay rights and their acceptance of homosexuality. Since students with the lowest tolerance for people with AIDS also had the most negative attitudes toward homosexuality, and vice versa (King et al. 1988), the widespread mandating of HIV/AIDS education in Canadian schools in recent years may well have led to greater compassion for people with AIDS and less stigmatizing of gay people because of their presumed association with AIDS. Indeed, a 1992 study (Warren & King 1994) of over 2,000 grade 9 students from four provinces who received an educational program about sexuality and AIDS ("Skills for Healthy Relationships") found that 23% considered homosexuality to be wrong (vs. 42% in the 1988 national sample) and 60% felt that "homosexuals should be allowed to be teachers" (vs. 39% in the 1988 study).

In fact, in a report on more recent work by R. Bibby, *Maclean's* (2001) revealed that while in the 1980s, only 26% of teens approved of same-sex relationships, a full 54% of young people now support same-sex relationships, with 75% believing that homosexuals should be entitled to the same rights as anyone else. In a slightly older sample, a study by Canadian Press/Leger Marketing (2001) shows that among 18- to 24-year-olds, 89% believe in equal rights for gays and lesbians, 81% support same-sex marriage, and 73% endorse adoption by same-sex parents. Taken together, these results suggest a growing tolerance among teens and young adults.

This background information on sexual attitudes and self-esteem provides a context for discussing the specific sexual behaviors of Canadian adolescents.

## Sexual Behavior of Adolescents

The 1970s and 1980s saw gradual changes in sexual behavior of Canadian young people consistent with the "sexual revolution" in attitudes that began in the 1960s. University students were the common research sample for many of the past studies on sexual behavior of youth, because parents and school boards were generally disinclined to give approval for questions on the specifics of sexual behavior in surveys of younger teens. Although similarly restricted on some topics (e.g., questions about oral sex and anal sex were asked only of college/university students, school dropouts, and "street youth"), the *Canada Youth and AIDS Study* provided evidence that "young people are more sexually active than adults may realize." For example, 31% of grade 9 males (14 to 15 years old) and 21% of females reported at least one instance of sexual intercourse. For grade 11 students (16 to 17 years old), the figures were 49% and 46% respectively. For comparison, the values for first-year college/university students (19 to 20 years old) were 77% of males and 73% of females. Hence, a sizable majority of Canadian teens have had at least one experience of vaginal intercourse by the time they are 19. In data culled from the *National Population Health Survey* in 1996-1997, Maticka-Tyndale, McKay, and Barrett (2001) state that over 70% of youth then age 20-24 had experienced first intercourse before the age of 20. These and other findings are part of a linear shift downward for both men and women in terms of age of first intercourse, a shift that has been more drastic for women who are now catching up to men.

Over half of younger teens have engaged in some form of sex play. For example, about 74% of grade 11 students (75% of the males; 73% of the females) and over half of grade 9 students (61% of the males; 53% of the females) have experienced "petting below the waist" (King et al. 1988). Among the reasons offered for their first experience of sexual intercourse, 19-year-olds in the 1988 sample reported love (48% of the females; 24% of the males), physical attraction (8% of the females; 25% of the males), curiosity (16% of the females; 12% of the males), passion (8%

of the females; 11% of the males), and drug and/or alcohol use (6% for both sexes). King, Coles, and King (1990) found that about 2% of both male and female 19-year-olds identified themselves as either homosexual or bisexual, but the details of their self-identification and behavior were not obtained.

In a late 1980s study of Quebec grade 11 high school students ($N = 1,231$, average age, 17 years), Otis et al. (1990) found that French- and English-speaking boys did not differ in the proportion who had experienced intercourse (62.4% vs. 54.1%), in number of partners among those with such experience (3.4 vs. 4.1), or in likelihood of condom use (46.9% vs. 48.8%). English-speaking male high school students were less likely than their francophone counterparts to report that a partner was using the birth control pill to prevent conception (33.7% vs. 48.8%). Among francophone versus anglophone high school girls, however, differences were apparent in terms of intercourse experience (61.5% vs. 30.1%), number of lifetime partners (2.8 vs. 1.8), use of the birth control pill (56% vs. 22%), and use of condoms (30.9% vs. 83.7%). These differences may reflect more longstanding relationships or sexual experience among francophone girls (age at first intercourse was 14.9 vs. 15.7) or a greater emphasis among francophone students on contraception and less so on STD prevention (see also Otis et al. 1994). In a recent review of research on the sexual behavior of different populations of high school students in Quebec, Otis (1996) noted that 12 to 23% of first-year and 47 to 69% of fifth-year high school students had ever had intercourse. Among those who had ever had intercourse, 1 to 8% reported same-sex sexual activity, 7 to 37% anal sex, and 1% involvement in prostitution. A sizeable minority of this group had six or more partners (12 to 22% for 15-year-olds; 27 to 47% for 18-year-olds, depending on the study).

Although peer pressure in its broadest definition undoubtedly affects teens in many ways, only a minority state that they feel pressure from their friends to be sexually active. Among grade 9 students, 16% of males and 8% of females agreed that they felt such pressure (21% and 6%, respectively for grade 11 students) (King et al. 1988). However, a sizable proportion of younger teens may have some uncertainty on this matter, since 55% of grade 9 students surveyed by Bibby and Posterski (1992) responded "don't know" to the statement, "I am not influenced by my peers" (41% agreed that they were not so influenced, 14% agreed, implying that they were). Even if peer group pressure does not usually influence the decision to be sexually active, peer group norms probably influence this and other important aspects of sexual behavior (e.g., decision to use condoms, safer sex practices, attitudes toward gender equity, etc.). Sexual health educators encourage the development of such peer norms as a positive reinforcement for "healthy" sexual behavior.

An evaluation study of the "Skills for Healthy Relationships" sexuality curriculum (Warren & King 1994), provides the most up-to-date national information available on the prevalence of vaginal, oral, and anal sex among grade 9 and 11 students in Canada (3,750 grade 9 and 3,000 grade 11 students from eight school boards in four provinces) (see Table 3). Overall, these findings indicate a large increase in experience of both vaginal and oral sex between grades 9 and 11, and considerable similarity between the sexes in both grades (particularly in grade 11) in terms of their reported experience of both behaviors. As we will note later in relation to sexual behavior of university students, similarity of acts between the sexes does not necessarily mean similarity of motivation, interpretation, or expectation with respect to these activities.

## C. Adults

### Premarital Relations, Courtship, and Dating

This material is addressed in Section 5B, Adolescents, above, and in the section below.

### Sexual Behavior and Relationships of Single Adults

Most of the research on premarital or nonmarital sexual activity of single Canadian adults has been done on university students. The *Canada Youth and AIDS Study* reported that about 77% of men and 73% of women in college/university had experienced intercourse, 68% of males and 64% of females had engaged in oral sex, and 14% of males and 16% of females had at least one experience of anal sex. Among those who had had intercourse, 23% of the females and 15% of the males said they had only ever had one partner (two partners, 9% for males, 15% for females; three to five partners, 28% for males, 35% for females; six to ten partners, 22% for males, 17% for females; and 11 or more partners, 27% for males, 11% for females) (King et al. 1988). About 7 to 8% of both sexes reported having had a sexually transmitted disease (King et al. 1988). These findings are for first-year university students and probably underestimate the average experience of students in all years.

In the most recent review of sexual behavior of college students in Quebec (1 to 2 years younger on average than university students), Samson et al. (1996) reported that 76% had ever had intercourse. Within this group, 9 to 14% reported experience of anal sex, 8% same-sex contacts, and 27 to 42% had 4 or more partners. For university students (Otis 1996), 86 to 90% had sexual intercourse, 18% had anal sexual contact, and 35% had 5 or more partners. In a study of anglophone and francophone university students (N = 1,450 men and women from four universities in Montreal), Lévy et al. (1993) found that 88% of French-speaking versus 81.5% of English-speaking men had had intercourse at least once; the values for females were 88% versus 74.5%. While the sexes did not differ within language groups, French-speaking women were significantly more likely to have had intercourse than English-speaking women. This was also true for oral sex experience (86% vs. 79.2% in French-speaking vs.

English-speaking men; 85.4% vs. 73.1% in French-speaking vs. English-speaking women).

This trend toward convergence of the overt sexual behavior of male and female university students in Canada (and elsewhere) has been noted since the early to mid-1970s (Barrett 1980). In terms of the occurrence of different sexual activities in a sample of 585 francophone university students in Quebec, one might suggest that this behavioral convergence is complete (Frigault et al. 1994; see Table 4). However, it would be incorrect to assume that similarity between the sexes in terms of sexual acts implies that similar "causal paths" influenced those activities (Maticka-Tyndale 1991). For example, Table 4 shows male/female differences in the perception of which sex has the greatest influence on the decision to engage in sexual activity. While neither sex assigned that role "mostly" to their partner (about 3% for both males and females), males were much more likely to perceive themselves as the influencer, whereas females perceived the decision to be equally shared or only slightly more influenced by the male. Females were also more likely to report that they had experienced sexual harassment or mistreatment and more likely to think often or very often about AIDS in the context of their sexual relationship. Despite the

### Table 3

**Occurrence of Vaginal, Oral, and Anal Sexual Activity in a Large Sample of Canadian Teens (1992)[1]**

| | Percentage Responding in Each Category | | | |
|---|---|---|---|---|
| | Grade 9 (N ~ 3,750) | | Grade 11 (N ~ 3,000) | |
| | Female | Male | Female | Male |
| **Vaginal sex** | | | | |
| Never | 80 | 73 | 53 | 51 |
| 1 or 2 times | 7 | 11 | 8 | 13 |
| 3 or more | 13 | 16 | 39 | 36 |
| **Oral sex** | | | | |
| Never | 79 | 73 | 53 | 52 |
| 1 or 2 times | 8 | 11 | 11 | 13 |
| 3 or more | 13 | 16 | 36 | 35 |
| **Anal sex** | | | | |
| Never | 96 | 94 | 92 | 90 |
| 1 or 2 times | 3 | 3 | 5 | 3 |
| 3 or more | 1 | 3 | 3 | 7 |

[1]Respondents were students in the experimental and comparison groups of the Skills for Healthy Relationships program evaluation (8 school boards in 4 provinces) (Warren & King 1994). Grade 9 students are generally 13-15 years old; grade 11, 16-17 years old.

### Table 4

**Sex Roles and Aspects of Sexual Experience Among Francophone University Students (1994)**

| Activity or Experience (in the past year unless otherwise indicated) | Percentage Giving the Response | |
|---|---|---|
| | Female (N = 316) | Male (N = 269) |
| Ever had sexual intercourse | 90.8 | 81.4 |
| Ever had oral-genital sex | 88.8 | 80.3 |
| Ever had anal sex | 18.7 | 18.7 |
| Have you had a steady partner in the last year? | 76.4 | 66.8 |
| Who has the greatest influence on the decision to engage in sexual relations? | | |
|    Mostly you | 8.4 | 28.1 |
|    You a little more so than partner | 9.9 | 22.7 |
|    Equal | 53.8 | 39.4 |
|    Partner a little more than you | 24.8 | 6.4 |
|    Mostly partner | 3.1 | 3.4 |
| Have you had sexual relations with someone when you definitely didn't want to? | | |
|    Never or rarely | 93.9 | 92.7 |
| Have you ever given in to a partner's pressure for sexual relations? | | |
|    Never or rarely | 78.3 | 72.4 |
| Experiences of sexual harassment | | |
|    Unwanted physical advances (touching, kissing) | 31.7 | 21.7 |
|    Physical violence of a sexual nature | 6.7 | 1.1 |
| Do you think about AIDS in the context of your sexual relationships? | | |
|    Never | 41.4 | 42.3 |
|    Rarely, seldom | 33.0 | 43.8 |
|    Often, very often | 25.6 | 13.9 |

Data from Frigault et al. (1994). Respondents average age 21 years, 95% never married, 90% raised Catholic, all university-level students in Montreal, 1.5% said they were homosexual, 0.9% bisexual.

convergence of behavior, we suspect that sex differences in the social and interpersonal contexts for sexual activity are important considerations, and that these differences may be even more common among university students in other parts of Canada.

Maticka-Tyndale's (1991) study of factors that predicted Quebec college (i.e., CEGEP) students' ($N = 866$) perception of their susceptibility to HIV/AIDS also showed clear evidence of sex differences, despite considerable similarity between the sexes in overt behavior. (*Note*: Quebec is the only province with a two-year intermediate "college" program [CEGEP] between the end of grade 11 [age 16] and the beginning of university. CEGEP students are generally 17 to 21 years old and, therefore, younger than university students.) Maticka-Tyndale's conclusion about this group of students was as follows:

> Though the actions may be converging, the causal factors associated with male and female sexuality are decidedly different. If there is concern for understanding male and female sexuality, or with devising programs which will encourage changes in sexuality to reduce risk, it is these causal factors which must be addressed, not merely the final acts. (Maticka-Tyndale 1991, 60-61)

Since there have been few Canadian studies on ethnocultural differences in sexual behavior, Maticka-Tyndale and Lévy's (1992) comparison of sexual experiences among Quebec CEGEP students is of interest. Their results demonstrate differences between students from different ethnic backgrounds, but since the sample size is small (total $N = 317$, group sizes 10 to 196), the results should be viewed with caution. In their comparison of francophone Canadian, English Canadian, Greek, Haitian, Italian, and Jewish (both English- and French-speaking) students, French Canadians ($N = 196$) indicated the broadest range of heterosexual experiences (88 to 98% reported kissing, body kissing, body caressing, and genital caressing), 80% had oral sex, and 75% had experienced intercourse. At the same age, Greek (22%), Italian (33%), and anglophone Jewish students (38%) were the least likely of all groups to have engaged in intercourse, and Greek students were less likely to have participated in oral sex (27%) than were the other nonfrancophone Canadian groups (48 to 65%), and less likely to report body kissing (44%), genital caressing (29%), and the other noncoital behaviors.

Respondents who had experienced sexual intercourse were also compared on their use of various contraceptive methods. The question asked about methods they had ever used and, therefore, more than one response was possible. Among all students, the most common methods were the pill (43 to 81% across all groups), condom (45% to 88%), and withdrawal (45 to 67%). Some students may have sequentially tried several methods. For example, withdrawal, which is often employed in early experiences, was used at some time by about one half or more of all six groups (Greek students were not included in this analysis because of the small number with intercourse experience). Haitian and French Canadian students were significantly less likely to report this method (45% and 49%) than were English Canadians. Haitians were more likely to report "none" (37%), compared to 6% for French and English Canadian and francophone Jewish students and 11 and 12% for Italian and anglophone Jewish students. Haitian students were also less likely to report condom use (45% vs. 72 to 88% for the other groups). Interestingly, the differences noted above in some aspects of behavior were not generally observed in relation to personal assessment of AIDS risk among these Quebec students. The Haitian population in Montreal warrants special mention with respect to AIDS risk because their higher incidence of AIDS at the beginning of the AIDS "epidemic" in Canada led to the early, and incorrect, assumption that Haitians had a special susceptibility within the group.

Overall, these results suggest that most Canadian young adults will experience some tension between their own attitudes, expectations, desires, and behaviors, as well as between these and the expectations set by their family and cultural milieu. The reported behaviors of young men and women suggest a move away from what was typically referred to as a "double standard" (i.e., the application of differential norms, expectations, and penalties to the sexual actions of men and women). However, if one considers both the observed differences in some aspects of self-concept, self-esteem, and relationship values and the findings from research on the situational, personal, and interpersonal factors influencing male/female sexual conduct, it is clear that certain gender differences still prevail. With respect to comparisons between ethnocultural groups, research demonstrates both differences and similarities within and between Canada's ethnic groups. These observations reinforce our introductory contention that generalizing one pattern to all Canadians is not just difficult, but probably impossible.

The ethnocultural differences in actual behavior reported in the Quebec study (Maticka-Tyndale & Lévy 1992) reflect a common phenomenon in Canada's larger cities. First- and second-generation students from different cultural backgrounds do not all adopt the behavioral pattern of the dominant culture. Agencies providing sexuality education, counseling, and related services have had to become more conscious of the impact that Canada's linguistic and ethnocultural diversity can have on gender-role behavior, attitudes toward different types of sexual activity, dating customs, and a range of other issues that can directly or indirectly affect sexual health.

The current sexual behavior of French Canadian young adults in Quebec reflects, and in many respects exceeds, the pattern of liberalization seen elsewhere in North America and in other parts of Canada. For example, a review of studies of young adults and adults in Quebec found that among 20- to 24-year-olds, 89 to 93% had intercourse, with a high proportion (over 50%) reporting four or more partners. Among adolescents and young adults who were involved with youth centers that address problems of social adaptation, 70 to 93% had intercourse, of whom 48 to 60% had more than six partners and 5 to 15% had been involved in prostitution (Otis 1996). English Canadian youth and young people from other ethnocultural backgrounds are more similar than different in many aspects of their behavior, although young adults, overall, are not as homogeneous a group as their portrayal in the media might suggest.

## Marriage and Family: Structure and Patterns

*Profiling Canadian Families*, a 1994 report by the Vanier Institute of the Family, used data from the 1991 Canadian census to provide a current profile of Canadian marriage patterns and family structure. A later update, *Profiling Canadian Families II* completed in 2000 provides more recent information. The Institute's broad and unconventional definition of family contrasts with the structural definition applied in statistical analyses. They state:

> Family is defined as any combination of two or more persons who are bound together over time by ties of mutual consent, birth and/or adoption and who, together, assume responsibilities for variant combinations of some of the following: physical maintenance and care of group members; addition of new members through procreation and adoption; socialization of children; social control of members;

production, consumption and distribution of goods and services; and affective nurturance-love. (The Vanier Institute 1994, 10)

While this definition acknowledges the continuing trend toward varied family constellations within Canadian society, it does not easily conform to that used for the purpose of statistical data gathering. Statistics Canada defines family in structural terms as

a now-married couple (with or without never-married sons and/or daughters of either or both spouses), a couple living common-law (again with or without never-married sons and/or daughters of either or both partners), or a lone parent of any marital status, with at least one never-married son or daughter living in the same dwelling. (Dumas & Peron 1992)

The latter definition applies to the marriage, family, and divorce information that follows.

The proportion of the population living in families, while declining since 1971 when it was 89%, stabilized between 1991 and 1996 at 84%. Because Canadian law does not recognize the "spousal" relationship of gay and lesbian couples, this number probably underestimates the percentage who perceive themselves as part of a family. However, as of 2001, Statistics Canada found 34,200 individuals identifying as same-sex common-law couples. This represents 0.5% of all couples. Among Canadians in families, 45% are married with children, 29% are married without children, 15% are lone-parent families (about one fifth of these are male lone-parent families), 6% are common-law without children, and 6% are common-law with children.

Several trends have been documented in the structure and form of Canadian marriages and families that have a direct impact on sexuality. These include age of first marriage, divorce rates and subsequent remarriage, number and timing of children, and spousal and parental roles. Since 1970, there has been a steady increase in the age of first marriage for both men and women. The average age of first marriage in 1970 for men was 25.1 years and 22.7 years for women. By 1990, this age had risen to 27.9 for men and 26 for women. By 1999, the age of first marriage for men was 29.8 and 27.8 for women (Vanier Institute 2000). For both men and women, this represents an increase of four years in the average age of first marriage since the mid-1970s. This trend toward later first marriage is relatively recent and reverses the earlier trend toward younger age at first marriage observed throughout the first half of the 20th century. It has accompanied the changes in attitudes and practices with respect to premarital sexual activity, the increase in formation of common-law unions, lengthening of time of education, and entry of women into the labor force in increasing numbers.

As already discussed, initiation of sexual activity occurs well before marriage for the majority of Canadians (ten years or more on average). Though there are no reliable studies of sexual activity in the early part of the 20th century, it is generally accepted that premarital sex, to the degree it is practiced today, is a phenomenon of the latter part of that century in Canada. In addition, marriage is no longer the first step for establishing a couple union. Younger Canadian women are more likely to start their conjugal life in the context of a common-law relationship, although many of these will eventually marry. According to Statistics Canada, 42% of women ranging in age from 30 to 39 in 2001 are likely to first enter a common-law relationship, yet close to 80% are estimated to get married later in their conjugal lives. However, this finding is not representative of all of Canada's provinces. Often the exception, in Quebec, first common-law unions are less

likely to end in marriage. Among women ranging in age from 30 to 39 who began their conjugal lives in a common-law relationship, only one third of these married their common-law partner, compared with 59% for women in other Canadian provinces. In general, the total number of common-law relationships in Canada has grown significantly in the past 20 years. The proportion of all couples living in common-law relationships doubled in Canada from 6% to 10% between 1981 and 1991. In 1991, 1 in 9 Canadians lived common-law, compared to 1996 when 1 in 7 lived common-law. The shift from 1991 to 1996 represents a further growth of 28%.

In the *Ethnocultural Communities Facing AIDS* study, differences in proportion of respondents currently living common-law were documented for three participating groups. Nine percent of women and 17% of men in the English-speaking Caribbean communities, 8% of women and 5% of men in the Latin American communities, and 2% of men in the South Asian communities were in common-law relationships (Maticka-Tyndale et al. 1995). Of all the provinces, Quebec has the highest percentage of common-law families (24% of all couples were living in a common-law relationship in 1996). This represents a tripling from 8% in 1981 and indicates a general trend among the young in Canada, and particularly in Quebec, to begin their cohabiting relationships prior to marriage, and for some to continue to do so in lieu of marriage. Common-law couples are also prevalent in the Yukon (23%) and Northwest Territories (27%).

A second factor influencing marriage and family structure has been the large-scale entry of women into the labor force. In 1990, for example, 70% of couples with children under 19 had both partners employed compared to 30% in 1970 (Vanier Institute 1994). To examine the broader trend, for children under 15 years of age in two-parent families, the incidence of both parents working rose from 43% to 58% to 60% from 1981 to 1991 to 1996, according to Statistics Canada. This has provided women with greater independence and is considered an important influence on the delay in age at first marriage, age of first childbirth, single-parent (mother only) families, and divorce rate. It has also produced tensions within families, as many individuals and couples find it difficult to meet their own and others' expectations with respect to spousal, parental, broader familial, and occupational responsibilities.

Canadians are having fewer children and delaying the birth of the first child to a later age. Average age at first birth was 23.3 years in 1971, 24.8 years in 1981, and 26.4 years in 1991 (Vanier Institute 1994). As of 1995, the age of first births has remained constant at 26.4 (Vanier Institute 2000). In addition, there is an increase in the number of single-parent families, both as a result of divorce and of single women (and a small number of single men) raising children without partners. About 15% of families in Canada are "lone parent" families, with approximately 80% of these involving female parents (Statistics Canada 1996). Some of the foregoing factors are addressed more comprehensively in Section 9D, Contraception, Abortion, and Population Planning, Population Planning. Here we note only that these factors have an important influence on family structure, sexuality, and couple relationships.

Before 1968, divorce was permitted only if one of the partners had committed adultery. The divorce rate throughout the 1950s and early 1960s was around 200 divorces per 100,000 married women per year. The 1968 Divorce Act expanded the grounds for divorce to include: acts such as adultery or physical or mental cruelty; permanent marriage breakdown (e.g., desertion, imprisonment, or living apart for at least three years). The divorce rate rose steadily through the 1970s to around 1,100 per 100,000 married women in 1981. A revised Divorce Act in 1985 made marriage breakdown the sole grounds for divorce; conditions included separation for one year or more (accounting for 93% of all divorces in 1986), adultery, physical cruelty, and mental cruelty (see Dumas & Peron 1992). By the time of the 1996 census, over 1.6 million reported being divorced, a 28% increase from 1991.

The number of years of marriage prior to divorce is decreasing and the incidence of divorce per marriage is increasing. Possibly 40% of couples married in the early 1990s will experience divorce. The rising divorce rate has increased the pool of people available for remarriage and, as a consequence, in 1996, one third of all marriages involved at least one previously married spouse. Nevertheless, the remarriage rate seems to be falling. In the 1990s, the rate of remarriage for men dropped from 63.2 per 1,000 population to 45.4, and for women from 22.8 to 19.4 The reason for this drop is likely because of the fact that many divorced people are choosing common-law unions over remarriage (Vanier Institute 2000). Despite the changing patterns described above, the average Canadian married in the 1960s will probably spend about 35 to 40 years of their life married to someone.

Of course, these data and trends can only be examined for those counted as "families" in various government and research documents. What must be remembered is that some Canadians also form what the Vanier Institute's definition would clearly identify as a "family," but their experiences are not represented in these data. These include gay and lesbian couples who form long-term commitments, share responsibilities and care for each other, and who may also raise children. They include the sometimes more communally shared commitments to fulfilling the responsibilities of family life found in some native communities. In the absence of research and documentation, we can only recognize that these alternative relationship and family forms exist, but cannot draw any conclusions about their prevalence or life course.

Together the changes described above portray Canadian marital and family relationships as units with flexible boundaries. Later marriages, common-law unions, divorce, and remarriage speak of the flexibility of boundaries, with an increasing number of individuals moving in and out of marriage or marriage-like relationships. Canadians remain committed to marriage, however, with most spending more than half of their adult lives in marriage or marriage-like relationships.

Children are more likely to experience the influence of several parent-like individuals in their lives and to be aware of and familiar with a variety of relationship types as an increasing number of parents move through several partnerships. Courts, however, remain relatively conservative in their custody and visitation rulings in cases of divorce, at times restricting custody and access to children on the part of a parent who is openly involved with a sexual partner who is not her spouse. This appears to reflect a dominant view of the preferred family form for childrearing as consisting of a heterosexual, married couple. This is evident, in particular, with respect to a parent who is gay or lesbian, with courts most commonly granting custody, whenever possible, to a nongay or lesbian parent and often restricting or placing limits on visitation on the part of the gay or lesbian parent.

## Sexual Behavior of Adults

In the absence of a Kinsey-type national survey of sexual behavior, Canadians have historically relied on U.S. statistics to draw inferences about the situation in Canada. Such inferences are less common today as social scientists increasingly document ways in which Canadians differ from their American neighbors in family patterns, laws, attitudes, and health. However, the only available Canadian data typically pertain to selected groups (teens, university students, gay men, etc.) rather than to the adult population as a whole, and come from studies done for a specific purpose (e.g., to assess risk behaviors related to HIV infection, to determine the occurrence and incidence of coercion in sexual relationships, etc.). This makes it difficult to obtain a global sense of the sexual behavior of adult Canadians.

The 1990 *Health Promotion Survey* from Statistics Canada asked a few questions about adult sexual behavior (e.g., number of partners, opinions about various methods of preventing STDs, age at first intercourse, etc.). Among the approximately 6,000 respondents to the question on the age at first intercourse (excluding those who refused to answer or had not had intercourse, approximately 3.3% in each case), the results were: under 15, 4.7%; 15 to 16, 16.3%; 17 to 19, 38.2%; 20 to 24, 32.9%; 25 to 29, 6.0%; over 29, 2.0%. These results were for the entire sample of adults of all ages. As previously mentioned, the National Population Health Survey in 1996-1997 revealed over 70% of youth then age 20 to 24 having experienced first intercourse before the age of 20 (Maticka-Tyndale, McKay, & Barrett 2001). On a much smaller scale, a 2002 poll conducted for *Maclean's*, Global TV, and *Southam News* consulted 1,400 Canadian adults by phone. Fifty-seven percent of these respondents reported first intercourse at under 19 years of age, while 15% were under 15 years of age.

Three recent surveys conducted by Health Canada provide some information on selected aspects of adult sexual behavior in Canada. These are the National Population Health Survey (NPHS), conducted in December 1994 and January 1995, and the Canada Health Monitors (CHM) surveys (1994 and 1995). Given the range of issues addressed in such surveys, the focus of sexuality-related questions that are included is often on selected behaviors associated with health risks, rather than on the broader psychosocial aspects of sexuality and relationships. For example, the CHM (1994) survey found that among 15- to 19-year-olds who had experienced intercourse in that year, 44% of males and 33% of females had more than one sexual partners. Comparable figures for 20- to 24-year-olds were 41% for males and 19% for females; for 25- to 29-year-olds, 20% for males and 8% for females; and for those 30 and over, 14% for males and 4% for females. These findings approximate those from the NPHS 1995 study which had a total sample size of approximately 7,200 (in comparison to CHM 1994 which had about 2,200). CHM 1994 also found that among 15- to 19-year-old males, 41% said they used a condom always or most of the time with a regular partner, whereas 85% did so with a non-regular partner. This type of survey information is of some interest for STD or HIV/AIDS prevention, but it does not provide the kind of insight into the social context and intra/interpersonal dynamics of behavior that would be afforded by a national study focused broadly on sexuality and sexual health (e.g., comparable to the study in the United States by Laumann et al. 1994).

The previously cited Decima Research poll (*Maclean's/ CTV Poll 1994*) and a comparable national telephone survey in 1995 (*Maclean's/CTV Poll 1995*) provide information on selected aspects of adult sexual activity in Canada (see Table 5). While the decline in frequency of sexual activity with age (i.e., from the mid-50s onward) is expected, it is difficult to analyze this finding in more depth because the results are uncorrected for marital status and access to partners, and also because it is unclear how respondents interpreted the term "have sex." Similarly, the fact that about one in ten said they had had an affair while married is of interest, but we do not know how men and women of different ages understood the term "affair" or how they might have responded to the question, "Have you ever had sex with someone other than your partner while married?" The fact that we have such limited national data on adult sexual behavior is an impediment to informed public discourse, policy development, and provision of sexual health education and related services.

Studies of adult sexual behavior and attitudes in Quebec reveal a significant shift away from the traditional sexual script that linked sex, marriage, and reproduction, to one that places greater emphasis on communication and pleasure. There are few Canadian studies that address the frequency of different sexual behaviors of married and cohabiting adults, let alone the more complex variables of pleasure, desire, and sexual satisfaction. The work of Samson et al. (1991, 1993) is therefore of particular interest in this respect. Their research addressed these questions in a study of married and cohabiting, heterosexual, French-speaking Montreal adult residents ($N = 212$, mean age 36.9) surveyed in the late 1980s. Based on the respondents' estimates of their annual number of intercourse experiences, they found weekly intercourse frequency rates varied with age as follows: 3.1 times per week (18- to 24-year-olds), 2 times/week (25 to 34), 1.8 times/week (35 to 44), 1.6 times/week (45 to 54), 0.8 times/week (55 to 64), and 0.9 times/week (65 or older). Overall, male and female subjects (respondents were not each others' partners) did not differ significantly in reported average frequency. Duration of relationship influenced intercourse frequency, with those in "new dyads" (less than two years) averaging four times per week, in "young dyads" (two to ten years) averaging 2.3 times per week, and those in "older dyads" (over ten years) averaging 1.4 times per week. This difference held even when age was factored out (Samson et al. 1991).

Composite sexual satisfaction scores were calculated from questions on frequency, desire, pleasure, and overall assessment of the respondent's sexual life. These scores did not correlate with either age or duration of relationship, but those with the higher satisfaction scores reported significantly more frequent intercourse. Respondents also rated their general satisfaction with their regular partner. Overall, 50% of the respondents said they were "fully satisfied" with their regular sexual partner. This was the upper response on a scale that proceeded from "fully satisfied" to "not at all satisfied"

and suggests a high level of satisfaction in this sample. The fact that general satisfaction did not correlate with age or duration of relationship, but did correlate with intercourse frequency, suggests some link between intercourse frequency and relationship satisfaction, although response bias may confound the findings (e.g., satisfied subjects may overestimate intercourse frequency).

Respondents were also asked about occurrences of active oral-genital sex in the preceding year, where "active" is defined as "stimulated with the mouth the genitals of their regular sexual partner" (Samson et al. 1993). Overall, 80% had engaged in active oral-genital sex (no difference between the sexes), but the percentages were higher for younger groups (e.g., 90% for those 18 to 34, 81% for those 35 to 54, and 38% for those over 55). Those with higher than average education (13 years or more) were more likely to engage in the behavior than those with less (88% vs. 74%). The average weekly frequency rates according to age grouping were: 1.6 times per week (18 to 34), 0.8 times per week (35 to 54) and 0.4 times per week (55 plus). There was no sex difference in average reported frequency, but, as with intercourse, oral-genital sex was more frequent in new and young dyads versus older dyads. Frequency was also greater in couples with no children and in those who had one child compared to those with two or more children. These differences remained when age and length of relationship were factored out. As with intercourse frequency, oral-genital sex frequency also correlated with both sexual satisfaction and general partner satisfaction, perhaps because these behaviors are correlated with each other and are an increasingly common part of the sexual script of many adults (Samson et al. 1993). The authors also noted that for those who engaged in oral-genital sex, neither "religiosity" nor church attendance affected annual frequency (although "religious" people were less likely to include oral sex in their sexual repertoire).

During the 1960s, a number of factors began to influence sexual values in Canada, including the introduction of the contraceptive pill, the increasing media coverage of sexuality, and the opening up of public discourse about sexuality that began in the 1960s and continued into the 1970s and 1980s. The concurrent impacts of the feminist movement, the gay rights movement, changes in legislation, and the increased freedom in the media to portray and "commercialize" sexuality, produced conflict with, and gradual change of, many traditional attitudes and behaviors. These changes have occurred across Canada, but francophone Quebec appears to have changed more, and more rapidly in some respects (see Lévy & Sansfaçon 1994). The development of sexology as an academic discipline in Quebec in the early 1970s may have had a modest or—as Gemme (1990) suggests—a major influence on these changes. What can be said with certainty is that since Canada's only university department of sexology was founded at the University of Quebec at Montreal in 1969, sexologists in Quebec have had an opportunity to document these changes in a segment of the population, francophone Québécois, in a way that has not occurred to the same extent for Canada as a whole. As is true elsewhere in Canada, the research emphasis in the 1980s and 1990s has been on youth, primarily university students, preuniversity CEGEP students, and, more recently, younger high school students.

The most recent data on sexual behavior of Canadian adults comes from a 1995 mailed survey of 1,713 respondents (return rate about 60%) who were proportionally representative of the overall population in terms of community size, gender, marital status, edu-

**Table 5**

**Selected Data on Sexual Activity of Canadian Adults**

| | Percentage Responding in Each Category | | | | | | |
|---|---|---|---|---|---|---|---|
| | Two or More Partners in Past Year[1] | | Ever Had an Affair While Married[2] | Frequency of "Having Sex" per Month | | | |
| | Male | Female | | None | 1-5 | 6-10 | 11+ |
| Male (total) | — | — | 13.9 | — | — | — | — |
| Female (total) | — | — | 7.3 | — | — | — | — |
| 18-24 | 32 | 18 | 7.3 | 15 | 38 | 17 | 30 |
| 25-34 | 30 | 5 | 7.5 | 6 | 25 | 34 | 35 |
| 35-44 | 4 | 4 | 10.1 | 9 | 30 | 33 | 28 |
| 45-54 | 18 | 1 | 17.4 | 16 | 41 | 31 | 13 |
| 55-64 | 5 | 0 | 13.2 | 23 | 52 | 17 | 8 |
| 65+ | 5 | 2 | 6.5 | 54 | 42 | 2 | 2 |

[1]*Maclean's*/CTV Poll (1994). $N = 1,610$ respondents across Canada contacted by telephone.

[2]*Maclean's*/CTV Poll (1995). $N = 1,200$ respondents across Canada. Those never married (10% women, 19% men) and not responding to this question (8% women, 3% men) are not included in the average.

cation, ethnic origins, and age. The latter included 35% aged 18 to 34, 38% aged 35 to 54, and 27% aged 55 or over (Bibby 1995). Responses to the question, "How often do you engage in sex?" yielded the following national percentages: daily (3%); several times a week (25%); once a week (25%); two-to-three times a month (14%); once a month (9%); hardly ever (13%); never (11%). Bibby noted some provincial variations (e.g., 35% of Quebec respondents said several times a week or more vs. 24% in Ontario), but gave no explanation for the differences.

Not surprisingly, people under 40 reported higher frequencies. Once a week or more was reported by 58 to 78% of men and women aged 18 to 49 (never was 2 to 7%). Although this rate was lower for 60- to 69-year-olds (men 30% with 5% never; women 25% with 41% never) and for those over 70 (22% for men with 25% never; 7% for women with 58% never), Bibby points out that about 1 in 5 men and 1 in 15 women over 70 reported this upper end of his scale of frequency of sexual activity. Bibby also found little difference in the weekly frequency of sexual activity of various religious groups, although married Roman Catholics (64%) were slightly more likely to report weekly or greater sexual activity than the conservative or mainline Protestant denominations (50 to 55%). Those with no religious affiliation reported 77%, a finding that Bibby explains as related to the younger age of this group rather than to religious affiliation. Other data on adult sexual behavior are discussed below in the context of condom use and safer sex practices (Section 10, Sexually Transmitted Diseases and HIV/AIDS).

## *Ethnocultural Variations in Sexual Behaviors of Single Heterosexually Experienced Adults*

Because the focus of the survey phase of the *Ethnocultural Communities Facing AIDS* study was on heterosexual transmission of HIV/AIDS, only certain questions were asked about sexual activity. In this study, 377 men and women from the English-speaking Caribbean communities in Toronto, 364 men from the South Asian communities in Vancouver (the survey team was advised that it was inappropriate to survey South Asian women about sexual matters), and 352 men and women from the Latin American communities in Montreal were surveyed. Participants were located through community organizations and in locations where members of each community were known to congregate. To insure a broad representation from each community, the samples were stratified by age (respondents ranged from 16 to 50 years), time since immigration to Canada, and also by gender in the Latin American and English-speaking Caribbean communities. Great care was taken in developing appropriate wording of the survey items and in translation of those items to the dominant ethnic language in the Latin American (Spanish) and South Asian (Punjabi) surveys. Table 6 summarizes responses of single adults to questions on current sexual partnerships and sexual activity during the past year. (*Note*: Given the limitations of such a study, including wide age range and small sample size in particular subgroups, the results should be interpreted with caution. However, these are the only data of their kind available for specific ethnic

communities, and given Canada's changing pattern of immigration and increasing ethnocultural diversity [see Section C in the introductory demographics and historical perspective section], they merit attention in this chapter.)

Different patterns of relationship formation are evident in each of the communities as well as for men and women (Table 6). Overall, men reported a larger number of sexual partners and a higher proportion entered sexual relationships with new partners in the previous year. However, the variations between men and women across the different groups were as great as those between men and women in any one group. These results, and others from this study, support the observation that has already been made that diverse patterns of sexuality are represented in Canada's population.

## *Sexuality and Disability*

While Canadians are aware of the social rights of people with disabilities, the issues surrounding sexuality and disability do not appear to have had a great impact on public consciousness. The concern about sexual abuse of people with disabilities may be an exception to this generalization. However, healthcare professionals and people with disabilities have raised the profile of sexual health issues (privacy, autonomy, rights to information, services, etc.) in the last 20 years, and there is a growing literature on the sexual implications of various disabling conditions and chronic illnesses.

The first major conference on sexuality and physical disability in Canada took place in Toronto in 1974. Cosponsored by the Canadian Rehabilitation Council for the Disabled and the Sex Information and Education Council of Canada (SIECCAN) and intended as a local event, it drew 150 participants from across Canada, an indication of the limited attention the topic had received prior to that time. Subsequent changes in attitudes and awareness have led to increased education on sexuality and disability among re-

### Table 6

**Sexual Behavior of Single[1] Heterosexually Experienced Respondents in the *Ethnocultural Communities Facing AIDS* Study: English-Speaking Caribbean, South Asian, and Latin American Communities**

| | Percentage Responding in Each Category | | | | |
|---|---|---|---|---|---|
| | English-Speaking Caribbean | | South Asian | Latin American | |
| | Women (*N* = 190) | Men (*N* = 187) | Men (*N* = 364) | Women (*N* = 176) | Men (*N* = 176) |
| Total number single respondents (*N*) | 119 | 106 | 123 | 91 | 95 |
| Number sexual partners in past year | | | | | |
| None | 6 | 9 | 5 | 8 | 17 |
| 1 | 46 | 34 | 17 | 74 | 38 |
| 2-5 | 39 | 46 | 49 | 11 | 35 |
| 6 or more | 9 | 10 | 29 | 8 | 11 |
| Number with any sexual partners in past year | *N* = 103 | *N* = 91 | *N* = 117 | *N* = 84 | *N* = 82 |
| New sexual partner in past year | 54 | 70 | 75 | 28 | 51 |
| In a long-term relationship | 69 | 65 | 41 | 65 | 59 |
| Number in long-term relationship | *N* = 71 | *N* = 62 | *N* = 47 | *N* = 50 | *N* = 45 |
| Monogamous | 79 | 60 | 65 | 94 | 84 |
| Partner monogamous | 36 | 54 | 52 | 68 | 93 |

*N* values in brackets = total respondents in survey sample.
Data adapted from Adrien et al. (1996).
[1]Includes never married and previously married (separated, divorced, widowed).

habilitation and healthcare professionals, either in their original training or through in-service workshops and seminars. For example, SIECCAN representatives have conducted over a hundred of the latter events in the last 20 years, and other organizations, such as the former Alberta Institute for Human Sexuality in the 1970s and 1980s, have also raised professional consciousness in this field.

In British Columbia, the Sexual Medicine Unit at the University Hospital, Shaughnessy Site, pioneered the development of assessment and treatment strategies for sex-related consequences of physical disabilities and chronic illness, including training of sexual healthcare clinicians in this specialty area (Miller et al. 1989), and research on sexuality and spinal cord injury (Szasz 1989), sperm retrieval for fertility enhancement (Rines 1992), sexual implications of multiple sclerosis in both sexes, and a variety of other such areas. Across Canada, a number of associations for people with disabilities or chronic illnesses now provide resource materials on the sex-related aspects of specific conditions, and some, such as the Multiple Sclerosis Society of Canada, have been particularly active in public education and professional training about sexuality and multiple sclerosis (Barrett 1991). Recent issues of the *Canadian Journal of Human Sexuality on Sexuality and Disability* (1992) and *Sexuality and Cancer Treatment* (1994) also reached a national audience of professionals.

The Disabled Women's Network has produced a number of publications addressing sexuality and disability issues, including a guide for healthcare professionals (DAWN 1993a) and a resource book on healthcare for women with disabilities (DAWN 1993b). Although there are no national professional or consumer groups that focus specifically on sexuality and physical disability, a variety of advocacy groups address this issue—e.g., the British Columbia Coalition for the Disabled has an AIDS and Disability program and the Coalition of Provincial Organizations of the Handicapped has also written on sexual rights of disabled persons (COPOH 1988). In 1992, Linda Crabtree began publishing *It's Okay*, which grew into a 32-page, consumer-written quarterly on sexuality, sex, self-esteem, and disability distributed across Canada and internationally (Crabtree 1994). Currently edited and published by Susan Wheeler (1996), *It's Okay* is the first and only publication of its kind in Canada that provides a forum for personalized discussion of sexual health and relationship issues for people with a variety of disabling conditions.

Sexual issues that affect people with developmental disabilities (sex education, privacy, contraception, marriage, sterilization, etc.) have been an ongoing focus of attention and policy development since the early 1970s. At the provincial level, most schools, Associations for Community Living, and residences for developmentally disabled children and adults have acknowledged the right to sexuality education and counseling, and have developed curricula and other services to meet those needs. In Ontario, a network of groups concerned with sexuality education, counseling, and related services has formed an umbrella organization, the Ontario Sexuality and Developmental Disability Network (OSDDN), to facilitate communication, professional development, resource sharing, and advocacy within the field. There is still too little training in sexuality for professionals who work with developmentally disabled clients, although in-service workshops in this area are increasingly common. These have resulted, to a great degree, in response to recognition of the frequency of occurrences of sexual abuse of people with disabilities (Roeher Institute 1992; Sobsey 1994; Sobsey et al. 1994). The Federal government's Family Violence Prevention Division has funded national and local programs to prevent abuse of people with

disabilities, and the National Clearinghouse on Family Violence assembles and distributes resource materials on this topic, including those on sexual abuse. The National Health Research and Development Program (NHRDP) of Health Canada has also funded national research on sexual abuse of people with disabilities (e.g., Mansell & Wells 1991).

Sexuality education for disabled teens and adults increasingly recognizes the positive as well as the problem-prevention aspects of sexuality, and Canadian resources reflect this trend (Ludwig 1991; Maksym 1990). The previously mentioned 17-booklet series, *Being Sexual: An Illustrated Series on Sexuality and Relationships*, published by SIECCAN in 1993, is the only resource of its kind in the world to include Blissymbol translation of key messages along with the English text. It is designed specifically for use with people who have problems with language learning and communication and includes a user's guide and explanation of all Blissymbols used in the text of each book (SIECCAN 1993).

It is generally accepted that people with developmental disabilities have the right to contraception and to other services available to any individual in society, although this theoretical right implies that support will be available to access such services, and this is not always the case. The Canadian Supreme Court in the "Eve" decision effectively prohibits sterilization of people with developmental disabilities unless they are able to give informed consent. Although it is now more common for people with developmental disabilities to marry, the right to marry is confounded by at least three different types of legislation (Endicott 1992). In some settings, e.g., Ontario and the Northwest Territories, it is against the law for any person to issue a marriage license to or to perform a service of marriage for someone who the person might reasonably know is mentally handicapped. This statute has been changed in Ontario to omit reference to mental handicap and to place the restriction on people who "lack the capacity to marry," but as Endicott (1992) points out, this provision may discourage marriage even if it does not violate the Canadian Charter of Rights and Freedoms. In other provinces, e.g., Alberta, Manitoba, and Quebec, a person who has been declared incapable in other areas, such as handling finances, is considered incapable of marrying, unless he or she provides certification from a doctor or other "official" source that he or she understands the responsibilities involved in marriage. British Columbia and Prince Edward Island prohibit marriage for people with developmental disabilities, whereas Saskatchewan, New Brunswick, Nova Scotia, Newfoundland, and Yukon have no law blocking marriage (i.e., people should have the "capacity" to marry, but there are no statutes to enforce the rule about capacity) (Endicott 1992).

## Incidence of Anal and Oral Sex

Since the 1969 change to the Criminal Code, sexual activity in private between consenting adults has generally not been a criminal concern in Canada. Previously taboo behaviors such as oral and anal sex have become increasingly common in the heterosexual population, but even with the recent research interest generated by concerns about HIV/AIDS, there have been few population studies on the incidence of these behaviors. A late-1980s study in Montreal, Quebec, reported that 75% had engaged in oral sex and 15% in anal sex in a sample of heterosexual university students (mean age 22 years); 64% of both sexes reported engaging in unprotected (without condom use) oral sex and about 6 to 7% in unprotected anal sex (Samson et al. 1990). Previous parts of this section provide other limited data on these behaviors in adults.

In the *Ethnocultural Communities Facing AIDS* study (see Table 6 and prior references), participants who had initiated new sexual partnerships in the past year were asked about anal intercourse in these relationships. In the English-speaking Caribbean communities, 20% of women and 21% of men reported anal intercourse, as did 17% of women and 41% of men in the Latin American communities, and 41% of men in the South Asian communities (Maticka-Tyndale et al. 1996). Qualitative, in-depth interview methodologies have demonstrated different meanings attached to anal intercourse. For some, for example, this is an alternative to vaginal intercourse when it is necessary to maintain virginity. Both incidence and meaning would have to be taken into consideration in creating a profile of sexuality; however, there is no research available that fully explores these issues.

Although sexual activity in private between consenting adults is not generally a concern of the Criminal Code, anal intercourse is listed as an offense punishable on summary conviction. It is not "illegal" when engaged in, "in private, by a husband and wife, or by any two persons, each of whom is 18 years of age or more, both of whom consent to the act." In law, a person under 18 cannot consent to anal intercourse; age of consent for most other sexual activities is generally 14, although a number of restrictions apply to 14- to 17-year-olds, some of which will be discussed elsewhere (for review, see MacDonald 1994). An act is considered not to have been done in private if a third person participates or is present (e.g., group sex or if someone is watching or able to observe because of the setting). This provision of the Criminal Code has been used to prosecute gay men, but it sends an indirect signal to heterosexuals about the taboo nature of anal sex, at least in the "official" sense that any law implies disapproval. This taboo may well be an impediment to safer sex practices or to disclosure of STD infections acquired in this way.

## 6. Homoerotic, Homosexual, and Bisexual Behaviors

### A. General Observations

There has been little historical analysis of same-gender sexual activity in Canada, and the record that exists in court documents, press reports, and other archival material is sometimes confounded by the various coded ways in which same-sex activity and relationships were described. In his history of the regulation of gay and lesbian sexuality in Canada, Kinsman (1987) notes that native societies had a variety of names and meanings for same-sex relations, that English and French colonists in the 19th century used labels such as "crime against nature," "secret sin," "sex perversion," "sexual immorality," "social evil," "sodomy," and "buggery" (the latter was proscribed in Canadian law until 1969), and that "homosexuality" and "lesbianism" appeared only with the emergence of the medical and social sciences in the early 1900s and "gay" only recently. He offers evidence of cross-dressing by white women in 19th-century Canada (this activity provided access to economic and social privilege and perhaps to erotic relationships with women) and of the emergence of male homosexual networks in the 1880s, which created a public consciousness and identity for this disapproved, and now publicly labeled, category of men called homosexuals. He recounts the recent emergence of gay and lesbian networks in the 1950s and 1960s and the legislative and political changes that led, in 1969, to the decriminalizing of homosexual acts between consenting adults over the age of 21. The subsequent legislative changes of the 1980s and 1990s reflect the emerging legal protection of the rights of gays and lesbians concurrent with a gradual shift in public acceptance of gay relationships.

As of June 20, 1996, section 3(1) of the Canadian Human Rights Act was amended to prohibit discrimination based on sexual orientation. While the human rights codes in a number of provincial and territorial governments also reflect a commitment to protect the rights of gays and lesbians, this has not come without a certain degree of controversy. The case of Vriend v. Alberta (1996) is particularly noteworthy, wherein the Supreme Court of Canada reversed a 1994 ruling protecting the omission of sexual orientation from Alberta's Individual Rights Protection Act. With the reversal, the Supreme Court proclaimed that the Legislature's omission was tantamount to approving ongoing discrimination of homosexuals and was in violation of section 15 of the Canadian Charter of Rights and Freedoms. This set a precedent for all other provinces and territories whose human rights codes do not explicitly protect the rights of gays and lesbians.

Federal practice has already been altered in the military after a 1992 decision in which a woman, released from the Canadian military because of her lesbian relationship, successfully challenged the ruling. The decision noted "that the military's policy prohibiting homosexuals is not valid, because it violates the constitutional guarantee of equality and freedom of association" (Bell 1991). In October 1999, the government officially ended its policy of barring homosexuals from joining the Canadian armed forces. This followed a decision to admit women to all branches of the armed forces, except submarines and combat roles.

However, a wide range of rights now extended to married and common-law heterosexual couples are not available to gay couples, and legislative change in these areas has, therefore, been one of the focuses of gay rights activity in Canada. The presence of publicly gay members in the federal Parliament, and of an increasing number of provincial and municipal gay politicians, is a reflection of changing public attitudes in this area. Nevertheless, Kinsman's (1987) identification of homosexuality as one of the "battlefields of sex" in Canada is probably still correct—the others are prostitution, abortion, women's reproductive rights, sexuality of youth, pornography, and sexual violence against women and children. Nevertheless, a number of recent court rulings have shown movement in this area.

In May 1999, the Supreme Court of Canada handed down one of the most far-reaching homosexual rights rulings anywhere, when it declared in an 8-to-1 decision that Ontario's Family Law Act was unconstitutional in denying homosexuals the right to apply for alimony from each other. In ruling that the legal benefits available to "spouses" cannot be limited to heterosexual couples to the exclusion of same-sex partners, this decision opened a challenge to a wide range of federal and provincial laws, including those governing adoption, marriage, pensions and taxes, that include reference to "spouse."

In February 2000, the Canadian government announced an overhaul of 68 federal statutes to erase most legal differences between heterosexual and homosexual couples. When the overhaul is completed, homosexual couples will enjoy the same benefits and responsibilities as heterosexual couples, whether married or cohabiting. The only remaining differences appear to be that marriage takes effect immediately and brings the ability to get divorced and change family names, while a cohabiting or same-sex couple have to wait one year for legal recognition. Government estimates suggest there are about 140,000 homosexual households in Canada, although it is not known how many of these are actually homosexual relationships and how many are simply two persons of the same sex living together for family or convenience reasons.

In addition to securing benefits for same-sex couples, other legal work has concerned itself with the definition of marriage. Appearing as a rider to the Same-Sex Recognition Bill in 2000, marriage has been defined as a union between "one man and one woman." Given such an understanding, debate continues in Canada over marriage and legal recognition of same-sex unions, revealing a country divided, with contradictory opinions and rulings among provinces, and between the courts and Parliament. In a 2002 Discussion Paper presented by the Department of Justice, the Government of Canada has suggested that Parliament is the appropriate venue for sorting out such questions. However, the courts have made rulings that have presented a direct Parliamentary challenge. Amidst this turmoil, what can be said with great certainty is that the amount of movement in this area in recent years has been without precedent.

In the fall of 2001, the British Columbia Supreme Court upheld the opposite-sex requirement of marriage, arguing that while it results in inequality for gay and lesbian couples, it was not based on a discriminatory set of beliefs. Furthermore, they argued that the inequality was justified, as the Charter does not require that marriage be made into something that it is not by definition. Nor did they feel that the federal Parliament has the constitutional authority to alter the opposite-sex meaning of marriage.

In Ontario, the Divisional Court in 1993 also upheld the opposite-sex requirement of marriage. However, in July 2002 a different panel of the Ontario Divisional Court found this requirement to be in breach of the guarantee of constitutional equality for gays and lesbians, ruling 3 to 0 that Canada's Charter of Rights and Freedoms requires the provincial government to recognize the right of gays and lesbians to marry people of their own gender. Activists hailed the ruling as a major legal victory with national consequences. The suit was brought by a lesbian couple and a gay male couple after the Ontario government refused to register their January 2001 joint wedding ceremonies performed at a Toronto church. Parliament was given two years to address this issue and, if they fail to do so, the common law in Ontario will be automatically changed to allow unions of "two persons." In September of 2002, the Quebec Superior Court made a similar finding as that of the Ontario Divisional Court. Currently the case in Ontario and the aforementioned case in British Columbia have been merged into one and are awaiting a Supreme Court decision that will have far-reaching consequences.

In examining the position of Parliament in this domain, one finds contradiction. In 1999, Parliament voted to take all reasonable steps to maintain the opposite-sex meaning of marriage. Further, in 2000, section 1.1 was added to the Modernization of Benefits and Obligations Act, which clarified the continued understanding of marriage as the "lawful union of one man and one woman." Finally, in 2001, the opposite-sex meaning of marriage was also confirmed in Quebec in section 5 of the Federal Law-Civil Law Harmonization Act, No.1. The decisions of the Ontario Divisional Court and the Quebec Superior Court are inconsistent with the Parliamentary stance, and some have expressed concern that the courts may be "over-stepping" their constitutional role and engaging in "judicial activism."

On a provincial level, four provinces have enacted or are considering laws relating to same-sex unions. In June 2002, the Quebec legislature unanimously granted same-sex couples the right to form "civil unions," which entitle gay couples to virtually the same rights and obligations as heterosexual married couples have. Nova Scotia and Manitoba have enacted similar legislation allowing gay and lesbian couples to record their relationships in a civil registry. Alberta, in its Marriage Act set out that marriage requires partners to be of the opposite sex for the purposes of solemnization, yet, in a bill before the legislature, raised the possibility of legal rec-

ognition of same-sex couples. With the exception of Alberta's Marriage Act, many lesbian and gay activists consider these provincial decisions to be highly positive.

Because the ten Canadian provinces have the power to register marriage ceremonies while the federal government regulates marriage qualifications, experts expect considerable legal wrangling before the issue is finally resolved by the Supreme Court (Krauss 2002). As for the role of Parliament, they are currently gathering national opinion about the issue in preparation for future action. [*Editor's Note*: See "Canada" in Last-Minute Updates chapter at end of volume.]

Metropolitan Community Church and other churches in Canada covenant gay relationships in a public ceremony, but this is not legally recognized as a marriage. While no law expressly prohibits marriage, a 1974 court decision on this matter ruled that the definition of marriage meant an opposite-sex couple. Since common-law couples in Canada now receive most of the employee benefits that accrue to married couples, many municipalities and some corporations are extending these benefits to gay couples (i.e., domestic partnerships based on the same conditions of relationship that apply for common-law couples). Since the gay and lesbian population in Canada includes people with a variety of relationship and lifestyle choices, there is no universal agreement in the gay community about whether couples in general should have privileges that others do not, or whether gay couples want to be governed by statutes designed primarily for heterosexual couples with children. Nevertheless, altering existing legislation and policies that discriminate against gay couples has been used as one way of achieving social equity. As with other areas of contention about sexuality and public policy, these issues are often decided in the courts rather than the legislature.

## B. Gay and Lesbian Adolescents

While men have generally self-identified as gay at an earlier age than women, it appears that young people of both sexes are now self-identifying as gay, lesbian, or bisexual at an earlier age. This may be explained by the increasing acceptance of gay people, the visible presence of a supportive gay community, and greater awareness of sexuality. However, many gay youth have strongly negative experiences in high school, either because of overt discrimination if they are open about their orientation or because fears of mistreatment keep them from disclosing. Gay bashing still occurs, and this fear, coupled with uncertainty and self-recrimination about their sexual feelings and the difficulty of finding people to confide in, can make this an intensely negative period in the lives of gay youth. Because they are often stigmatized and isolated, it is likely that gay youths have a higher risk of suicide than do teens on average. Counseling and support services for gay youths are now available in some cities, and a number of programs, such as the Sexual Orientation and Youth Project of Central Toronto Youth Services, have helped to sensitize and train teachers and health professionals about these issues. Overall, gay youths in Canada still face major challenges in their personal development, particularly if they live in smaller cities and rural areas. From its inception, an Ontario telephone hotline for gay, lesbian, and bisexual youths in Ontario (1994) was overwhelmed with calls for advice and information, and the provincial government, therefore, offered additional funding to meet the demand.

The process of self-identification and coming out has been discussed extensively in Canada, but there is little quantitative research done to document these experiences for gay and lesbian youth. In interviews with 60 gay and lesbian youth (average age 19), Schneider (1991) identified the factors frequently named as contributing to their labeling themselves gay or lesbian—most chose more than one factor. Emergence of same-sex attraction and feelings was mentioned most often by both sexes, but males were more likely to identify this as "general same sex attraction" (7% of females vs. 73% of males), whereas females associated their sexual feeling with falling in love with someone of the same sex (83% of females vs. 10% of males). Same-sex sexual experience was identified by 33% of females and 37% of males as a validation of their ability to experience pleasure with the same sex and of the sense that "it seemed right for them." Males were more likely than females to identify "casual and anonymous sex over an extended period of time" as a factor in their self-identification as gay (0% of females vs. 40% of males). Although a number of young men who listed this option said they often felt guilty about such encounters and vowed to stop them, they also noted that the experiences contributed to their recognition that their attraction was toward men.

Lack of interest in the opposite sex (10% of females vs. 33% of males) was a relevant factor in that most had dated heterosexually and were aware of their disinterest, but it was less influential as a salient clue in self-identification because many assumed early on that they would eventually be attracted to opposite-sex partners. More than half identified "contact with lesbians/gays" (67% of females vs. 50% of males) as an important influence, suggesting that positive role models reinforce self-acceptance. This seems likely since such contact was also the most common contributor to their feeling positive about their lesbian/gay identity (93% of females vs. 80% of males). First long-term relationships contributed to self-identification for 73% of females and 37% of males (Schneider 1991).

These findings are consistent with the self-identification and coming-out processes encountered in other countries with restrictive religious and social traditions surrounding homosexuality. The effect of these negative social attitudes and experiences is reflected in the high levels of thoughts of suicide or suicide attempts, periods of extreme anxiety and depression, social withdrawal, and loneliness—all of which occur in teens, but were often associated by this group with their struggles surrounding sexual orientation and acceptance by others (Schneider 1991).

Canadian schools have been slow to introduce adequate discussion of gay and lesbian sexuality into school curricula, and those that attempt to do so often encounter strong opposition from organized groups from the religious right—the larger mainstream denominations may be less restrictive and some even supportive. The only high school curriculum resource guide in Canada on homosexuality and homophobia was developed by the Toronto Board of Education in the late 1980s amidst extensive public debate. The Board approved the curriculum guide in 1992. The Toronto Board of Education's Student Support Services program also administers a Human Sexuality program in which an educator/counselor visits local high schools to talk directly about homophobia and to let gay/lesbian/bisexual students know, without singling them out, that the board has a counseling and support group designed to address their needs. At the time of writing, this was the only program of its kind in Canada and one of two such programs in North America.

## C. Service Agencies

There is an extensive network of lesbian/gay/bisexual organizations, service agencies, and interest groups in most large Canadian cities, and national organizations such as EGALE (Equality for Gays and Lesbians Everywhere), and provincial ones, such as the Coalition for Les-

bian and Gay Rights in Ontario, provide a centralized focus on particular issues.

Most of the large Protestant church denominations in Canada accept ordination of gay and lesbian clergy. Unitarian-Universalist churches were the first to ordain gay and lesbian clergy who are in sexual relationships and to have an official policy of welcoming gay and lesbian members and affirming their relationships. Of the large Protestant denominations in Canada, only the United Church of Canada, after prolonged and divisive debate, has extended acceptance into the clergy to those who are in sexual relationships. All others require, at least in terms of "official" policy, that gay and lesbian clergy be celibate. This applies also in the Roman Catholic Church, in which celibacy is required of priests (only men are permitted to be priests) regardless of sexual orientation. Most large denominations also have identified groups for gay and lesbian members (Dignity—Roman Catholic and Integrity—United Church) and some, such as the United Church of Canada, are seeking ways to find congregations prepared to accept qualified openly lesbian/gay ministers.

Canada has many gay and lesbian organizations at the provincial and local levels. Some address social justice and legislative and policy issues, others emphasize community service and education. The various AIDS Committees across Canada have drawn heavily on the gay community for expertise in all areas of their mandate and also for volunteer work and peer support. In addition, local groups, such as PFLAG (Parents and Friends of Lesbians and Gays) in Ontario, also provide information and mutual support for families of gay and lesbian youth or adults.

## D. Behavioral Patterns

There have been few large-scale studies of gay male sexual behavior in Canada and none of lesbian sexual behavior. *Men's Survey 90* surveyed the sexual practices of 1,295 men (mean age 34, 73.7% with partial or complete college education) recruited from 12 bars and three bathhouses in Toronto in 1990 (Myers et al. 1991). This is the largest number of gay and bisexual men ever surveyed in Canada, but the results may not apply to smaller cities or rural areas elsewhere in the country. The study was designed to investigate AIDS knowledge, attitudes, and behavior. The AIDS-related findings will be reported in Section 10B, Sexually Transmitted Diseases and HIV/AIDS, HIV/AIDS.

About 48% said they had had sex only with men in their lifetime, 35.3% had previously had sex with women but had only done so with men in the past year, and 13% were bisexual. The reported number of partners in the past year ranged from none (6%), one (16.8%), two to nine (37.8%), 10 to 14 (12.4%), 15 to 24 (9%), to 25-plus (18.1%). Among those who reported a current relationship with a man (35.8%), 33.9% said it was monogamous, 55.7% that it was not or presumed not to be monogamous, and 10% were uncertain; 5.4% had a regular female sex partner.

When asked about sexual activity in the past three months, 11% said none, 28.4% said no anal sexual activity, 39.9% said protected (i.e., with condom) anal sex, and 20.7% unprotected (no condom used) anal sex. In the latter group, the measure was based on even one act of unprotected anal sex and the percentage was higher for a monogamous partnership (31.4%) versus 14.1% for unpartnered men. Other sexual practices reported in the previous three months included mutual masturbation (81.7%), insertive oral-genital sex (76.2%), deep tongue kissing (75.9%), receptive oral-genital sex without seminal contact (74.1%), receptive and insertive oral-anal sex (33.9% and 27.9%), and receptive oral-genital sex with ejaculation (27%). Unprotected anal sex in the last three months was more common in men under 35, in those with high school or less versus college education (26.7% to 30.7% vs. 17.5% to 18.6%), and in men who were previously heterosexual or previously bisexual in their behavior.

Lévy et al. (1994a) have also studied sexual behavior and safer sex practices in a sample of gay men in Montreal, Quebec; see Section 10B, Sexually Transmitted Diseases and HIV/AIDS, HIV/AIDS, Table 17.

## 7. Gender Diversity and Transgender Issues

Although Canadians have become less rigid in their gender-role expectations for both sexes in recent decades, their reaction to cross-dressing and cross-gender behavior is often a mixture of discomfort and fascination. The popular media have given considerable coverage to issues of transsexualism, transvestism, gender-reassignment surgery, and cross-dressing, although to date, no studies have formally measured Canadian's awareness of these matters, nor does knowledge always equate with tolerance. In addition to prejudice, individuals seeking gender reassignment may face additional problems financing such surgery as well. For example, as of October 1, 1998 the Government of Ontario delisted coverage for sex-reassignment surgery as a benefit of the Ontario Health Insurance Plan. Other Canadian provinces that cover the costs of surgery include Manitoba, Saskatchewan, Alberta, and Newfoundland. Furthermore, accessing such surgery in Canada has become much more difficult than in previous decades.

At the time when Blanchard and Steiner (1990) published their work on the clinical treatment of gender identity disorder, Canada had four centers that did gender-reassignment surgery as part of the treatment for gender identity disorders: the Gender Identity Clinic at the Clarke Institute of Psychiatry in Toronto, Ontario (Blanchard & Steiner 1990); the Gender Dysphoria Clinic at the Vancouver General Hospital in British Columbia (Watson 1991); the Human Sexuality Unit at the Montreal General Hospital in Quebec (Wilchesky & Assalian 1991); and the joint program of the Department of Sexology, University of Quebec at Montreal and Le Comité sur le Transsexualité of Centre Hospitalier de l'Hôtel Dieu, also in Montreal.

Since that time, however, a number of recent changes have altered this state of affairs, and while these programs continue to provide consultation, there is far less surgery done in Canada. The Gender Identity Clinic at the Clarke Institute (currently and henceforth referred to as the Centre for Addiction and Mental Health, CAMH) has largely faltered because of a lack of public (i.e., government) funding for the CAMH program. As a result, few individuals seeking assistance for transgender issues use the CAMH services. In fact, there is currently no gender-reassignment surgery conducted at all in Ontario. In the last decade, all surgeries done under the auspices of Clarke/CAMH were performed in England. Similarly, the majority of surgeries previously performed in Vancouver now take place in Colorado. In Quebec, the majority of surgery is conducted by private surgeons, Drs. Brassard and Menard, who also run a private clinic for aftercare on Yale Island.

All programs employ more or less similar formats and criteria for treatment, generally adopting the "Standard of Care" advocated by the Harry Benjamin Society. This is an internationally respected protocol observed the world over with few variations. The Vancouver program is reportedly somewhat less restrictive in the circumstances under which it approves hormone treatment and surgery. The Vancouver

program uses a variety of factors to develop a "management plan." These include "intensity of cross-gender identification, degree of obsession with cross-dressing, extent of investment in versus abhorrence of sex and reproductive organs, desire for cross-gender hormone administration, need versus fantasy of sex reassignment, and nature of eroticism." "Sexual orientation is considered an independent factor not directly relevant in the evaluation of gender disorders" (Watson 1991, 4). The plan may include a combination of hormonal treatment, psychotherapy (individual, family, and group), speech therapy, and vocational rehabilitation. The decision about referral for surgery is based on "the extent of cross-gender identification and proven ability to adapt in the chosen gender role" (Watson 1991, 8), the latter evidenced by a minimum of one year living in the new role.

The program at CAMH requires a one-year "real-life test" prior to hormonal treatment and a minimum of two years living in the cross-gender role before approval is given for surgery. Specific requirements that must be met before recommendation for surgery is approved include: employment or student status in the new role (this requirement is a potential source of conflict with current or future employers); change of all documents (bank account, driver's license, health insurance, etc.) providing proof of cross-living (employer letter, statement of earnings, etc.); proof of divorce in the case of those who are legally married (a protection for the surgeon); and other such requirements (Clemmensen 1990). The rationale for these restrictions, which can generate anxiety and animosity among patients, is that postoperative regret and poor outcome are more likely if these criteria are not followed, although there is debate in the research literature as to the actual degree of postoperative regret experienced by transsexuals choosing surgery.

The Montreal General Hospital group has similar criteria and a varied program that includes a strong emphasis on group support (Wilchesky & Assalian 1991). The Department of Sexology/Hôtel Dieu program was established in the early 1970s and follows assessment criteria similar to those described above for the Clarke Institute. It is different from the others in that the Department of Sexology does the assessments, therapy, and recommendation for surgery for the hospital clinic and is also an active center for research on gender identity. Group counseling is provided, but when the department itself offers such groups, it is because the activity includes a research component, not because it is a standing service.

The legal status of postsurgical male-to-female and female-to-male transsexuals is precarious in Canada, and they have little or no protection in 8 out of 10 provinces. However, their civil rights status is becoming clearer in Ontario and British Columbia. British Columbia has enshrined "gender identity" in their Human Rights Code and position papers have been forwarded in Ontario. Although the health plans in about one half of provinces will cover surgery and it is legal to change one's birth certificate postoperatively, the law appears to define one's sex based on chromosomal composition. A more recent case in Quebec, however, presents a better indication of the complicated picture for transsexual individuals. As it currently stands, a name can be changed only in the face of complete surgical alteration. For female-to-male, this includes a double mastectomy, hysterectomy, phalloplasty, and removal of the ovaries. For male-to-female, this entails complete neovaginal surgery. Furthermore, even with such surgical interventions, sex cannot be changed on any document.

In a 1992 legal decision in Ontario, the judge annulled the marriage of a woman and a female-to-male transsexual on the grounds that the law does not permit marriage between two people of the same sex. This means that a postoperative male-to-female transsexual can legally marry another female (and this has occurred in Canada), and that postoperative transsexuals who marry (the issuing of a marriage license is based on appearance and not genetics) and later seek divorce, may have their marriage declared invalid.

At the social level, transsexuals face significant problems with education, employment, and social acceptance. Support groups are present in some large cities, and organizations such as the Metamorphosis Research Foundation have shown the importance of support and education services for people with gender conflicts. Other programs, like the 519 program in Toronto, one of the first outreach programs for transsexual and transgender youth and sex workers, also provides free counseling and food to a group of individuals who are multiply marginalized within the larger social matrix.

The problems and issues faced by intersex individuals—personal, legal and medical—are different, yet again, from those of transgendered individuals.

## 8. Significant Unconventional Sexual Behaviors

### A. Coercive Sex

*Sexual Abuse of Children*

In Canada, child abuse refers to physical, sexual, and emotional abuse or neglect. All provinces and territories, except the Yukon, require any person who knows of or suspects such abuse to report it to child welfare authorities. The Yukon identifies teachers and childcare workers as the groups with a legal duty to report. It is difficult to estimate the prevalence of child abuse because of the secrecy and privacy involved, and because jurisdictions vary in what and how they report (e.g., some record both allegations and investigations while others report only the latter [Johnson 1996a]).

Sexual contact between children and adults is strongly proscribed in Canada, and the phenomenon of child sexual abuse is now increasingly recognized as a longstanding problem that has been insufficiently addressed at all levels of society. Major reports of such abuse in the past ten years have focused public and professional attention on child abuse in general, and sexual abuse in particular. For example, the criminal conviction of Catholic brothers for physical and sexual abuse of male residents at a Roman Catholic orphanage in Newfoundland, the growing reports of sexual abuse of children in some aboriginal and First Nations communities in which poverty, alcoholism, and drug use are widespread, and the response to disclosure of similar abuses of large numbers of children in a small Ontario community have been among the most publicized of many such accounts. These incidents reinforced the concerns expressed in the *1984 Badgley Commission Report, Sexual Offenses Against Children and Youth*, which indicated that by age 16, approximately 5 to 9% of males and 15 to 20% of females had experienced some form of unwanted sexual touching, and that 1 to 3% of females under 16 had experienced forced intercourse (Lindsay & Embree 1992).

Changes in the Canadian Criminal Code in 1988 expanded the old provision that prohibited sexual intercourse with a person under 14. For example, the relevant section of the code speaks of a "young person," defined as a person 14 years of age or more but under the age of 18. Changes were also made with the inclusion of the offenses of "sexual interference" (s.151), "invitation to sexual touching" (s.152), and "sexual exploitation" (s.153). Sexual interference is explained as follows:

Every person who, for a sexual purpose, touches, directly or indirectly, with a part of the body or with an object, any part of the body of a person under the age of fourteen is guilty of an indictable offense and liable to imprisonment for a term not exceeding ten years or is guilty of an offense punishable on summary conviction. (MacDonald 1994, 16)

The addition of "invitation to sexual touching" makes it an offense

to invite, counsel, or incite a person under fourteen to touch him/herself or any other person, directly or indirectly, if the invitation is made for a sexual purpose. For example, it is a criminal offense to suggest that a young boy masturbate for the voyeuristic pleasure of the person making the suggestion. (MacDonald 1994, 16)

Finally, although including the types of acts covered under sections 151 and 152, the offense of "sexual exploitation" under the Criminal Code refers specifically to sexual acts carried out by a person

who is in a position of trust or authority towards a young person or is a person with whom the young person is in a relationship of dependency.

Section 150(2) of the Canadian Criminal Code provides further clarification of the role of consent in regard to sexual offenses with young persons. This section provides that where an accused is charged with sexual interference, invitation to sexual touching, exposure, or sexual assault with respect to a complainant at least 12 years of age but under the age of 14, it is not a defense that the complainant consented to the activity unless the accused is at least 12 years of age but under 16, is less than two years older than the complainant, and is not in a position of trust or authority towards the complainant, nor in a relationship of dependency with the claimant. In short, MacDonald (1994, 16) notes that since children under 14 are not assumed to be able to give consent, "it is not a defense that the complainant consented to the activity that forms the subject matter of the charge" (MacDonald 1994, 16). Further, MacDonald notes that the prohibition on sexual activity with a person under 14 does not apply if "the child is at least twelve years old, is consenting, and the other person involved is less than two years older than the child and is not in a position of trust, authority or support toward the child" (MacDonald 1994, 17). Sexual contact between an adult and a child would also fall under the sexual assault section of the Code (a child cannot give legal consent to the contact), thus adding to the variety of provisions in Canadian law that address sexual contact between adults and children.

*The Canadian Incidence Study of Reported Child Abuse and Neglect* (CIS) was the first nationwide study to examine child maltreatment in Canada. Conducted between October and December 1998, this study provides data on physical abuse, sexual abuse, neglect, and emotional maltreatment of children age 0 to 15 based on 7,672 investigations from 51 separate cites in all of Canada's provinces and territories. In Ontario, it is mandatory for children's aid societies to investigate all reports of abuse. These are then deemed "substantiated" (there is sufficient evidence for the investigator to conclude that abuse occurred), "suspected" (can neither substantiate nor rule out abuse), or "unsubstantiated" (there is sufficient evidence that maltreatment did not occur). Child sexual abuse occurs when an adult or youth uses a child for sexual purposes. Sexual abuse includes fondling, intercourse, incest, sodomy, exhibitionism, and commercial exploitation through prostitution or the production of pornographic materials.

In the case of sexual abuse investigations reported in the 1998 CIS study, the most common forms of substantiated sexual abuse were touching/fondling genitals (68% substantiated), attempted and completed sexual activity (35% substantiated), and exposure (12% substantiated). Sexual exploitation (6% substantiated) and sexual harassment (4% substantiated) were less common forms of child sexual abuse (Trocmé et al. 2001). An analysis of victim characteristics reveals that 69% of victims are girls and 31% are boys, with girls age 4-7 and 12-15 victimized about twice as often as those in the 0-3 and 8-11 age categories.

Among all cases of substantiated sexual abuse in the 1998 CIS, the majority of alleged perpetrators were either relatives (44%) or non-relatives (29%). Of those alleged perpetrators who were related to the victim, they were equally likely to be a biological father or stepfather and less likely to be the biological mother, foster, or adoptive parent. Those who fall under the category "other relatives" were by far the single most significant category comprising 44% of those who commit sexual abuse.

In the past decade, there has been an increasing involvement of police in situations that could lead to criminal charges, particularly where sexual and physical abuse are concerned. According to the 1998 CIS, sexual abuse was by far the most likely type of maltreatment to result in charges laid by police (70%).

On a provincial level, the 1998 *Ontario Incidence Study of Reported Child Abuse and Neglect* (OIS 1998) (Trocmé et al. 2002), conducted as part of the 1998 CIS study, was based on a sample of 3,053 child-maltreatment investigations. Figures do no include maltreated children who were not reported to a children's aid society. Findings from this study show that between 1993 and 1998, the estimated number of child-maltreatment investigations increased 44% in Ontario. The total number of substantiated cases doubled from 12,300 in 1993 to 24,400 in 1998. Over this time period, there was a 44% decrease (3,400 in 1993 to 1,900 in 1998) in substantiated investigations of sexual abuse. This is consistent with a similar decrease noted in the United States (Jones et al. 2001). Trocmé et al. (2002) suggest that while such a decrease could indicate more-effective prevention programs and criminal-charging policies, it is also possible that these same policies have caused victims and their parents to be less willing to disclose and report sexual abuse.

The *Étude sur l'Incidence et les Caractéristiques des Situations d'Abus, de Négligence, d'Abandon et de Troubles de Comportement Sérieux Signalés à la Direction de la Protection de la Jeunesse au Québec* (EIQ) [*Quebec Incidence Study of Reported Child Abuse, Neglect, Abandonment and Serious Behaviour Problems*] is also the first study of its kind ever to be carried out in Quebec. The EIQ was based on referrals reported to the Director of Youth Protection between October 1 and December 31, 1998. Sixteen of Quebec's 19 child-protection agencies took part in the study by documenting the child-maltreatment or serious behavior problem referrals reported during that period. The study found 3.0 per 1,000 cases of sexual abuse, with girls being reported for sexual abuse more commonly than boys. Situations of sexual abuse referred to touching/fondling in most cases (64%), with relatives (27%) often identified as perpetrators, as well as "another" person (28%). About 26% of child victims of sexual abuse lived with at least one parent who was him- or herself a victim of maltreatment during his or her childhood, suggesting a potential intergenerational reproduction of maltreatment. These findings are based on a 2002 summary posted by the Centre of Excellence for Child Welfare, with the permission of the Institut Universitaire dans le Domaine de la Violence chez les Jeunes, Les Centres Jeunesse de Montréal.

Although the overall incidence of substantiated child maltreatment in the Ontario study is about one half that in the U.S.A. in 1990 (21/1,000 vs 43/1,000), this difference is almost entirely because of the higher rate of child neglect in the U.S.A. (4.64/1,000 vs. 2.0/1,000). The substantiated sexual abuse rates were very similar in both countries (1.57/1,000 vs. 1.65/1,000 in the U.S.).

Such findings and the growing public concern about sexual abuse of children have led some to wonder about the possibility of fabrication of such allegations in divorce or child-custody proceedings.

In Canada, the Divorce Act governs both custody and access and requires that the courts consider the best interests of the child as the standard in such cases. Zarb's (1994) detailed analysis of the legal situation in Canada indicates that legal decisions in this area are rare because such matters are usually settled without a trial. When a trial does occur, transcripts are often kept confidential. She notes that when allegations are unfounded, the court generally awards unsupervised access, and sometimes full custody, and that unproven accusations lead to supervised or unsupervised access depending on the judge's perception of the best interests of the child. In weighing the rights of an accused parent (almost invariably the father) against the possible risk to the child, Zarb indicates that Canadian courts should and do err on the side of caution.

Zarb (1994) points out that there is a greater occurrence of allegations of sexual abuse on interim applications for custody, but she argues that this does not necessarily mean that false allegations are generally and cynically used as a "bargaining chip" in such cases. Among the possible reasons for unfounded allegations, she cites (1) the excessive influence of media reports that lead to overinterpretation of innocuous behavior as abuse, (2) the emotional fragility of newly separated parents, (3) the belief among some adults that children do not know enough about sex to be able to make up events and, therefore, that there is no reason to doubt their reports, (4) the lack of trust in separated couples, and (5) the fear that failure to report suspicions may lead to an accusation of negligence. When accusations are founded, Zarb notes that case law offers "no clear consensus in Canada with respect to how much contact a child victim of incest should have with his or her abusive parent after disclosure" (Zarb 1994, 108). She sees a consensus for continued access in such cases (in Canadian law access means, at a minimum, the right to make inquiries and to get information about the child's schooling, health, etc.) only when the child wants it, when the abusive parent has affirmed that the child's accusation was correct, and when the other parent can protect the child from the offending parent, if necessary.

This area is a source of debate in Canada, as is the growth of an "assessment industry" that some perceive as predisposed to finding sexual abuse when other explanations for alleged incidents are possible (Zarb 1994). In the absence of judicial consensus on many of these contentious issues, Zarb (1994) sees the need for much more research on the prevalence of sexual contact between adult relatives and children, and on the related issue of "the child's best interests," when such allegations are made and/or substantiated.

When child sexual abuse cases go to court, there have been a number of recent changes in Canadian law and procedure that make the experience less onerous for the child witness while respecting the right of an accused to a fair trial. Young's (1992) review of evidentiary issues in cases of child sexual abuse in Canada cites measures that include: use of screens so that the child witness need not see the accused while testifying, use of closed circuit television, use of videotaped statements, and increasing acceptance of children as reliable witnesses under appropriate circumstances. All have been challenged as contrary to the rights of the accused, but Young (1992) sees the legislative trend leaning toward a balance that recognizes the past disenfranchisement of children in the courts for reasons that some now consider invalid.

In 1997, a Parliamentary committee, the Special Joint Committee on Child Custody and Access, was asked to assess the need for a more child-centered approach to family law policies and practices, and in December 1998 released its report, *For the Sake of the Children*. The Government of Canada has taken an approach to family justice reform that is consistent with the spirit of this report, in that it removes the terms custody and access from the Divorce Act and bases parenting decisions solely on the best interests of the child. While the "best interests of the child" has been the core principle of family law in Canada for some time, this core principle was reaffirmed and strengthened by adding a list of best-interest criteria to the Divorce Act. In instances where allegations of sexual abuse are present, weighing the "best interests of the child" against the threat of false allegations of abuse are identified as serious complications associated with high-conflict cases. The lack of data pertaining to the actual incidence of false allegations in Canada was identified as an additional worry in the Government of Canada's Response to the Report of the Special Joint Committee on Child Custody and Access tabled on May 10, 1999. A serious problem, though, is that the actual incidence of false allegations of child abuse in Canada is not known, and it is an inherently difficult issue to research.

This issue, moreover, is one that crosses jurisdictions and will require the cooperation of numerous agencies and organizations if it is to be addressed properly. We therefore agree with the Committee's recommendation that the Government of Canada work with the provinces and territories to encourage child welfare agencies to track investigations of allegations of abuse in the context of parenting disputes in order to provide a statistical basis for a better understanding of this problem.

### Sexual Harassment

Sexual harassment is illegal in Canada under the Canadian Human Rights Act and also under all provincial and territorial acts respecting human rights. Aggarwal's (1992) detailed review notes that the first such documented case in Canada occurred in Ontario in 1980, when the Ontario Board of Inquiry determined that "sexual harassment amounts to sex discrimination prohibited under the Ontario Human Rights Code." This decision has become the basis for judgments by human rights tribunals in other provinces and at the national level.

In 1983, the Canadian Human Rights Commission adopted a definition of sexual harassment as including:

(1) verbal abuse or threats; (2) unwelcome jokes, remarks, innuendoes, or taunting; (3) displaying of pornographic or other offensive or derogatory pictures; (4) practical jokes which cause awkwardness or embarrassment; (5) unwelcome invitations or requests, whether indirect or explicit, or intimidation; (6) leering or other gestures; (7) unnecessary physical contact such as touching, patting, pinching or punching; (8) physical assault. (Aggarwal 1992)

There are now many different definitions of sexual harassment being applied in labor relations codes, university policies, and guidelines covering a range of agencies and work settings. Most definitions, such as that adopted at one Canadian university, indicate that sexually harassing behavior "is sexual in nature and is unwanted by the person to whom it is directed." In order for a behavior to constitute sexual harass-

ment, it "must affect the recipient's employment, instruction, or participation in university activity or interfere with the recipient's environment, performance, or evaluation" (cited in Aggarwal 1992).

Although the application of these codes has been a source of debate in some settings, there appears to be general agreement that sexual harassment is a problem, and that some form of control and/or redress is needed. A 1991 poll cited by Aggarwal (1992) indicated that 37% of women and 10% of men had experienced such harassment; other studies of selected groups have indicated larger percentages, mostly of women, frequently involving incidents in the workplace, and often unreported.

Most provincial human rights codes specifically identify sexual harassment in the workplace as a violation. Ontario's 1990 Code, for example, specifies that every person should be free from:

1. a sexual solicitation or advance made by a person in a position to confer, grant, or deny a benefit or advancement to the person where the person making the solicitation or advance knows or ought reasonably to know that it is unwelcome.
2. a reprisal or threat of reprisal for the rejection of a sexual solicitation or advance where the reprisal is made or threatened by a person in a position to confer, grant, or deny a benefit or advancement to the person. (Aggarwal 1992)

This definition implicitly notes that sexual harassment is a misuse of power and constitutes a "poisoning of the work environment" and is not simply misunderstood courtship behavior. Nevertheless, misunderstandings in this area abound and most procedures appear to incorporate the intentions of fairness to each party, confidentiality (although not anonymity of the complainant with respect to the respondent), adjudication, and the potential for remedy without formal disciplinary proceedings. It would be unwise to assume universal agreement and comfort with harassment codes, particularly on university campuses, where such policies have been cited as a threat to academic freedom and to open discourse on discomforting topics. Defenders claim that such policies, and the administrative machinery needed to adjudicate them, are not simply a way of reinforcing "political correctness," but a means of addressing a problem that disadvantages not only women but other groups such as gay/lesbian/bisexual students or employees.

Many policy and procedural guides on sexual harassment now include harassment on the basis of sexual orientation. This is consistent with the inclusion of sexual orientation as a protected category in most provincial human rights codes. The Criminal Code also has sections on "stalking," the persistent following or watching of someone. It is also illegal to watch or beset a person's residence or place of work. The popular media have reported on entertainment celebrities being "stalked," usually women stalked by men, and have thereby raised awareness of this phenomenon in the general population.

### Sexual Abuse and Sexual Assault (Rape)

Readers interested in an overview of legal and legislative aspects of sexual assault can find an excellent review of Canadian trends in the 1980s and early 1990s in *Confronting Sexual Assault: A Decade of Legal and Social Change* (Roberts & Mohr 1994). In addition, the Canadian Panel on Violence Against Women received 800 submissions and heard thousands of personal stories from individuals in 139 communities across Canada. The Panel's final report, *Changing the Landscape: Ending Violence, Achieving Equality* (Minister of Supply and Services 1993), while providing a broad sampling of personal stories and recommendations concerning women's experience of violence in Canada, is less reliable as a source of statistical data on the incidence or occurrence of such experiences. The large volume of publication and government activity in the area of sexual abuse and assault during the 1980s and into the 1990s is a reflection of the consciousness raising that has occurred in the past ten to 15 years. The report of the 1984 Committee on Sexual Offenses Against Children and Youth and the more recent revelations of sexual abuse of children in care (see Gripton & Valentich 1990) are but two examples of this burgeoning awareness.

Although forced sexual intercourse is a serious offense, the word "rape" is no longer used in the Criminal Code of Canada. The offenses of rape and indecent assault were replaced in the code in 1983 by the categories of sexual assault (level 1), sexual assault with a weapon (level II—victim threatened with a weapon or caused bodily harm), and aggravated sexual assault (level III—victim is maimed, disfigured, or has her or his life endangered during the assault).

The new laws have produced several important changes in how sexual assault is viewed and treated in the courts. First, it is now possible to charge one's spouse with sexual assault, something that could not be done under the former "rape" laws. Second, the law is nongender or sexual-orientation specific. Thus, assault of men by women, and assault by someone of the same gender are all offenses under this law (though, to date, charges have rarely been brought in the latter). Finally, it is less common for interrogations of victims about past sexual behaviors or the specific sexual acts that occurred to be permitted in court proceedings. The specific circumstances under which such interrogations may occur are now prescribed in a bill that outlines how questions of consent and mistaken belief of consent should be handled in court proceedings.

Possible maximum prison sentences for levels I to III sexual assaults are ten years, 14 years, and life respectively, although sentences are usually less, and many occurrences that would probably meet the legal definition of sexual assault, particularly level I, go unreported or do not go to trial.

The first level of these offenses, sexual assault, is not defined in the code. Sexual assault incorporates the legal definition of assault (use of force or threat of force on a person against her or his will) coupled with the idea that the assault was of a sexual nature or violated the sexual integrity of the victim. The prevalence of sexual assault, or of offenses that would have legally constituted sexual assault had they been reported, is difficult to assess, but some authors suggest that only one in ten of such occurrences is reported. Recorded sexual-assault statistics for Canada in 1995 list 28,216 incidents (10% of all violent incident reports) with 97% level I and 3% level II or level III. The national report rate of 124/100,000 population in 1992 was 10% higher than in 1991, consistent with a trend of about a 12%-per-year increase since the new assault law was introduced in 1983. This probably reflects an increase in reporting, although the incidence may also have increased. Rates varied from 64/100,000 in Quebec to about twice that in Ontario, and 895/100,000 in the Northwest Territories (Statistics Canada 1992; Roberts 1994). Non-sexual-assault rates show similar variability. The rate of level I sexual assault in Canada in 1995 (approximately 100 per 100,000) was 11.9% lower than in 1994, the second year in a row of decline after the prolonged period of increase from 1983. This rate was still 35.5% higher than in 1985 (Johnson 1996a; Hendrick 1996). At present, it is difficult to assess the relative contribution of the varied factors (law reform, better reporting, and increased incidence of of-

fenses) that led to the 1983-1993 increase and the recent 1994-95 decline in level I sexual assault incidents (Johnson 1996b). In contrast to level I sexual assaults, the less common level II and level III assaults have declined since 1985; both dropped about 35% between 1991 and 1995 (Hendrick 1996).

In 14% of level I incident reports in 1992, the police did not pursue the case beyond preliminary investigation. The "unfounded" rate (i.e., police have determined that a crime was not committed) for level I to III cases has been fairly consistent at 10 to 15% since 1983. To say that a report was "unfounded" does not necessarily imply that an intentionally false allegation was made. When there is sufficient evidence to lay a charge, the case is "cleared by charge." This happened 49% of the time for level I reports in 1992, 57% for level II, and 64% for level III, indicating that charges occur more often in cases in which the definition of the offense is clear, and therefore, more likely to lead to conviction. Clearance rates for all charges have increased since 1983 (43% in 1983-85 vs. 50% in 1990-92). In 1991-92, incarcerations occurred for 60% of level I convictions and 90% for levels II and III. An analysis of reports to selected police departments in Canada in 1992 found that 84% of assault victims were female, 98% of those charged were male, most of those charged were over 25 years of age (67%), and most assaulted were under age 18 (63%). About 20% of assailants were reported as strangers, 32% as casual acquaintances, and 28% as parents or other family members. The reported assaults usually took place in a private dwelling (63%), 61% involved threat of physical force, 1% involved firearms, and 18% other weapons.

To what extent do official reports reflect actual experience? Statistics Canada's *Violence Against Women Survey* (1993) surveyed 13,300 Canadian women 18 and over to assess their experience of physical and sexual violence. The study was reported to be the first national survey of its kind anywhere in the world (*The Daily*, Statistics Canada 1993). The specific findings on "sexual assault" are based on recent and lifetime experience of "unwanted sexual touching" ("Has a stranger or man other than a spouse or boyfriend ever touched you against your will in any sexual way, such as unwanted touching, grabbing, kissing, or fondling?") and of "sexual attacks" ("Has a stranger, date or boyfriend, spouse or other man ever forced you or attempted to force you into any sexual activity by threatening you, holding you down, or hurting you in some way?"). Using these definitions, 39% reported experiencing one of these since age 16 (24% sexual attack, 25% unwanted sexual touching, and 10% both). Overall, 58% had more than one lifetime experience of sexual touching and 42% of sexual attack; 5% reported at least one experience of either in the previous 12 months (Roberts 1994). While the experience had negative emotional impact in 85% of cases, only 6% said they had reported these incidents to police (11% in the case of sexual attacks, 4% for sexual touching), and of those reported to police, 63% of the complainants were under the age of 18. Reasons for not reporting included: the incident was too minor (44% overall; 28% for sexual attack vs. 53% for unwanted sexual touching), the expectation that police would not be able to do anything (12%), protection of privacy (12%), or it was dealt with in other ways (12%) (Roberts 1994).

When participants in the *Ethnocultural Communities Facing AIDS* study were asked whether they had ever been coerced or forced to have sex with someone against their will, 37% of women and 19% of men from the English-speaking Caribbean communities, 5% of men from the South Asian communities, and 8% of women and 1% of men in the Latin American communities reported they had.

Of particular interest is the fact that in the English-speaking Caribbean communities, percentages reporting coercion or force were higher for those who had been in Canada longer (34% of those in Canada longer than 15 years, men and women combined, vs. 20% of those in Canada less than 15 years). This was so even when age and marital status were held constant, suggesting that coercion is a more common experience here than in the Caribbean (Maticka-Tyndale et al. 1995).

In the *Violence Against Women Survey*, the lifetime reports of unwanted sexual touching and sexual attacks (collectively referred to as "sexual assault" according to the expanded legal definition) were usually linked to dates or boyfriends or someone known to them, and less often to strangers (19%). Based on reports of one or more such experiences in the previous 12 months (5% of the sample), Roberts (1994) estimates that 18% of women aged 18 to 24 years had experienced some form of sexual assault. Figures for the other age groups were: 8% (25 to 34), 5% (35 to 45) and 2% (45 to 54) (results exclude data involving marital partners). In addition, report rates among women with post-secondary education were double those for respondents with high school education or less (Roberts 1994).

### Treatment for Victims and Offenders

Treatment for children and adults who have been sexually abused is in great demand and, despite the growth in such services in recent years, the need outstrips both financial resources and the availability of adequately trained professionals. Canada has over 70 community-based, sexual-assault services staffed primarily by volunteers. These kinds of services (telephone crisis lines, accompaniment of victims in hospital, police interviews, court, counseling and support groups, etc.) are responding not only to current reports of assault, but to past abuse that is only now being dealt with as a result of publicity surrounding this issue.

Marshall (1992) recommends three areas of societal response to sexual offenses: preventing or at least reducing the incidence; assistance to victims; dealing with offenders through incarceration and specialized cognitive-behavioral treatment programs. He notes that treatment programs for sex offenders have been employed with some success in Canadian penitentiaries, hospitals, and community-based outpatient clinics. Since most offenders will eventually be released, such treatment is considered a vital part of social policy. Marshall (1992) cites recidivism rates of 10% in a five-year follow-up study of treated offenders who had a comprehensive program that addressed five target areas: cognitive factors, sexual issues, social functioning, life management, and relapse prevention; for untreated offenders, the recidivism rate was 35%. Antiandrogen treatment is used with some offenders during treatment and subsequent to release.

"Gating" (i.e., immediate rearrest upon release) of offenders who have completed their sentences, but are still considered dangerous, has been used in Canada, as has the placing of conditions on released offenders (e.g., restricting men who have committed offenses against children from going near schools, etc.). The former has been declared in violation of charter rights, and a current test case in Ontario will determine whether the latter does so as well. Both issues reflect the extensive concern that prevails in Canada around the risk of sexual assault and abuse. Growing public awareness of the long-term consequences for many victims of sexual abuse has undoubtedly contributed to the perception of dangerousness that colors public discourse about sexuality.

### Sexual Coercion and Assault—College and University Students

A large-scale study of unwanted sexual experiences conducted at the University of Alberta in 2000 (LoVerso, 2001) paints a picture of sexual assault on one university campus. This study revealed examples of sexual assault, particularly among first- and second-year students. Of the 1,297 students participating, 37% of participants' most serious unwanted sexual experiences happened while registered at the University of Alberta. Over 90% of the most serious unwanted sexual experiences were perpetrated by men, 41.8% of which were non-romantic acquaintances compared with 27.9% who were romantic acquaintances. Physical force was reported in 23.5% of the most serious cases, while the majority involved some form of coercion or pressure.

DeKeseredy and Kelly (1993) conducted a national study of sexual mistreatment and assault on university campuses using a sample of 1,307 men and 1,835 women from classes in over 40 universities and community colleges across Canada. Respondents were young (median age 20 for females, 21 for males), unmarried (about 80% for both sexes; those married were asked to respond based on their dating relationships), and primarily in their first or second year of study (66%). The results presented here are for women's reports of their experiences of abusive behavior in dating relationships and men's reports of their own abusive behavior. (For commentary on the study and the circumstances of its public release, see Gartner 1993, Fox 1993, and Kelly 1994.)

The study determined incidence rates (past year) and prevalence rates (since starting university or college) for a variety of experiences that were described in detail in the research questionnaires and that corresponded, in some cases, to legal definitions of sexual harassment or level I or II sexual assault. For example, "Have you ever given in to sex play (fondling, kissing or petting but not intercourse) when you didn't want to because you were overwhelmed by a man's continual arguments and pressure?" yielded an 18.2% incidence response (7.8% of men said they had been the source of such an outcome for a female partner in the past year) and 31.8% prevalence (14.9% of men said they had exerted such pressure on a partner since beginning university/college; see Table 7.

DeKeseredy and Kelly (1993) suggest that their reported incidence and prevalence figures for sexual abuse in dating relationships may be underestimated, that the problem is as serious in Canada as has been reported for the U.S.A., that the attempt of some males to "mirror the dynamics of patriarchal marriages" in their dating situations may contribute to mistreatment of their partners, and that men and women bring different interpretations of consent to such relationships. Kathleen Cairns (1993) at the University Calgary has identified the different self-perceptions and scripts that many men and women in university bring to these interactions (sexual entitlement on the part of males and sexual accommodation on the part of females) and suggested that attention to such scripts could provide a basis for understanding and eventually reducing the incidence of coercive behavior. She proposes that sex education for young women should focus on assertiveness and refusal skills, on "development of a sense of self as sexual subject, and on the related understanding of the nature of female sexual desire" (Cairns 1993, 211). Young men should learn how to develop a broader awareness of sensuality, feeling, and of girls and women as persons; both sexes need to recognize that it is social-derived sexual scripts and power differences, not immutable biology, that leads to sexual coercion.

Research by Sandra Byers and her students at the University of New Brunswick also adopts a sexological rather than purely legalistic and legislative approach to understanding and changing sexually coercive behavior (see Byers 1991; O'Sullivan et al. 1994; O'Sullivan & Byers 1993). For example, Byers and Lewis (1988) found that desired level of sexual activity was the same for men and women in 90% of dating for college-age couples, that women were no more likely than men to refuse a partner's sexual initiation (although men initiated more often), that when disagreements occurred in desired level of sexual activity, men did not, in the vast majority of cases, try to persuade, coerce, or force their partners, and that most stopped the unwanted activity when asked. While these and other findings suggest that Canadian college students are at various stages in the transition to more egalitarian gender and sexual relationships, the level of mistreatment experienced and perceived by college and university women remains a significant issue on many campuses.

### Sexual Assault and Coercion of People with Disabilities

There is a high prevalence of sexual assault and abuse in the lives of people with physical or developmental disabilities, and this area has generated a variety of educational, research, and prevention programs (The Roeher Institute 1992; Sobsey 1994; Sobsey et al. 1994). The Disabled Women's Network has been particularly active in raising awareness of this issue at both the local and national level through pamphlets for consumers and an educational guide for healthcare professionals. The federal government's Family Violence Prevention Division funds a variety of programs that deal with violence in general, and sexual abuse in particular, against people with disabilities.

### Physician-Patient Sexual Contact

Patient-physician sexual involvement is an important area of professional misconduct that has received increased attention in Canada in recent years. Subsequent to the report in Ontario of the Task Force on Sexual Abuse of Patients (TFSAP 1991), an act was passed (Regulated Health Professions Amendment Act, 1993, SO1993, c37) which identified "strict guidelines for reporting such activity and disciplining physicians" (Lamont & Woodward 1994). A task force of the College of Physicians and Surgeons of Ontario (CPSO) mandated to respond to the report that the CPSO had commissioned, identified three categories of impropriety that would receive different penalties. They were:

1. Sexual impropriety: any behavior such as gestures and expressions that are sexually demeaning to a patient or that demonstrate a lack of respect for the patient's privacy.
2. Sexual transgression: any inappropriate touching of a patient, short of sexual violation, that is of a sexual nature.
3. Sexual violation: sex between a physician and a patient, regardless of who initiated it, including but not limited to sexual intercourse, genital-genital contact, oral-genital contact, oral-anal contact, and genital-anal contact. (CPSO 1992, as cited in Lamont & Woodward 1994, 1434).

The Committee on Physician Sexual Misconduct established by the College of Physicians and Surgeons of British Columbia (1992) proposed 97 different recommendations for responding to the issues surrounding patient-physician sexual contact. The College also funded a mailed survey of all practicing physicians in British Columbia (4,513 responses, 72.3% response rate, 78.9% males), which found that 20.7% of the responding physicians, and 62.3% of psychiatrists, had seen a patient who reported having had sexual contact with another physician (Maurice et al. 1994a). Female physicians were more likely than male physicians (31.2% vs. 17.8%) to indicate that they had heard such a revelation from a patient. Among the physicians who were asked questions about their personal behavior, 3.5% of the 1,414 who responded (69.5% response rate) said they had had at least one sexual experience with someone who was a current patient at the time of the sexual contact (3.8% of male vs. 2.3% of female respondents). This figure was 7.4% for

### Table 7

**Incidence and Prevalence Rates for Different Aspects of Sexual Abuse Reported by a National Sample of Canadian University/College Students**

|  | Incidence[1] (%) | | Prevalence[1] (%) | |
| --- | --- | --- | --- | --- |
| Situation | Women (N = 1,835) | Men[2] (N = 1,307) | Women (N = 1,835) | Men[2] (N = 1,307) |
| Have you given in to sex play (fondling, kissing, or petting, but not intercourse) when you didn't want to because you were overwhelmed by a man's continual arguments and pressure? | 18.2 | 7.8 | 31.8 | 14.9 |
| Have you had sex play (fondling, kissing, or petting, but not intercourse) when you didn't want to because a man threatened or used some degree of physical force (twisting your arm, holding you down, etc.) to make you? | 3.3 | 1.1 | 9.4 | 2.2 |
| Has a man attempted sexual intercourse (getting on top of you, attempting to insert his penis) when you didn't want to because a man used some degree of physical force (twisting your arm, holding you down, etc.) but intercourse did not occur? | 3.9 | 0.6 | 8.5 | 1.6 |
| Have you given in to sexual intercourse when you didn't want to because you were overwhelmed by a man's continual arguments and pressure? | 11.9 | 4.8 | 20.2 | 8.3 |
| Have you ever had intercourse when you didn't want to because a man threatened or used some degree of physical force (twisting your arm, holding you down, etc.) to make you? | 2.0 | 1.7 | 6.6 | 1.5 |
| Have you had intercourse when you didn't want to because you were drunk or high? | 7.6 | 2.2 | 14.6 | 4.7 |

[1]Incidence (in the past year), prevalence (since beginning university/college).
[2]Male responses indicate percentage who said they had been the source of such experiences for a woman.
Data from DeKeseredy and Kelly (1993). Median age for females 20 years, for males 21 years.

those who said they had had sexual contact with a former patient (8.1% of male vs. 4.3% of female respondents).

Maurice et al. (1994b) have also surveyed members of the public in British Columbia to assess their opinions and experience concerning patient-physician sexual contact. Questionnaires mailed to 6,000 women and 2,000 men yielded 2,456 responses (2,079 women, 376 men). When asked whether a physician had ever touched their private body parts for what seemed to be sexual reasons, 4.7% of the women and 1.3% of the men said yes. In addition, 6% of women and 2.5% of men said a doctor had made sexual remarks that upset them and 0.3% reported sexual activity with a former physician (0.7% with a doctor who was their current physician at the time of the contact).

Ontario and British Columbia have now passed legislation that requires physicians to report to their provincial medical college (i.e., registration body) any suspicions or knowledge they may have of physicians engaging in sexual contact with patients.

A large sample of Canadian obstetricians and gynecologists (i.e., 782 members of the Society of Obstetricians and Gynecologists of Canada, response rate 78%) has also been surveyed on this issue via mailed questionnaire (Lamont & Woodward 1994). Based on the CPSO definitions of impropriety, transgression, and violation: 37% of female respondents and 19% of males said they were aware of actions by a colleague that fitted one of the categories; fewer (10% overall) knew another obstetrician-gynecologist who had done so; 3% of males and 1% of females reported such involvement themselves; and 4% and 2%, respectively, said they had been accused of such involvement; 97% said such contact was never therapeutic and 58% saw it as an abuse of power. Respondents varied in the type of penalty they felt should be applied for different levels of offense, with a hierarchy based on level and with females generally favoring stronger penalties (e.g., 39% of females vs. 21% of males favored permanent loss of license for a sexual violation, 11% vs. 3% for a transgression). Respondents differed on the amount of time they felt should elapse before it was permissible to begin a relationship with a former patient that might lead to sexual activity (never acceptable, 14%; 6 months to over one year, 53%; OK after public termination of the professional relationship, 11%). The Canadian Medical Association published a *Policy Summary* on these matters, both to guide physicians and the public and to generate discussion and ongoing review of the policies (CMA Policy Summary 1994).

### Sexual Homicide

Although sexual homicide is rare, the horror of such events and the publicity surrounding them is a source of considerable anxiety and concern in Canada. As a consequence, amendments have been proposed to the Criminal Code, the Prison Reformatories Act, and the Corrections and Conditional Release Act that would permit continued incarceration of dangerous offenders even after their court-imposed sentences for previous crimes have been completed. Using homicide statistics from 1974-86 in Canada, Roberts and Grossman (1993) found that about 4% of recorded homicides were sexual homicides (i.e., murders that occur as part of the commission of a sexual offense). Over this period, the number of such homicides did not increase nor did the proportion of homicides classified as sexual homicides. The victims were primarily female (85%) and the perpetrators were almost exclusively male (99%). Compared to the period 1961-70 when 20% of the victims were under age 21, the more recent period had 49% under the age of 21. About 30% of such crimes involved a stranger and

33% an acquaintance. Close family members were infrequently victims, in contrast to other homicides (about 12% of all murders were of spouses), and alcohol and drugs were involved in 25% of sexual homicides, slightly less than for homicides in general. The wide publicity given to sexual homicides has focused attention on all aspects of sexual assault and violence. Research and public policy initiatives address the complex problems of preventing sexual assault of all kinds, of treating victims and their families, of treating offenders, most of whom will eventually be released from prison, and of predicting dangerousness of adults after the fact and of youth before they offend.

### B. Prostitution

While prostitution among consenting adults has never been illegal in Canada per se, the practice has long been considered immoral, and the Criminal Code has been used to prosecute prostitutes and, more recently, their customers. In 1983, the Special Committee for the Study of Pornography and Prostitution (the Fraser Committee), established by the Justice Minister in 1983, was mandated to examine all aspects of prostitution in Canada and to make recommendations for changes in what was perceived, at the time, to be an unenforceable law on solicitation. In their 1985 report, the Fraser Committee made more than 100 recommendations, including one that prostitution-related activities by both prostitutes and customers be removed from the Criminal Code and another that small-scale, nonresidential commercial prostitution establishments should be allowed to operate. The federal government, however, did not act upon these two recommendations. The Committee's 15 recommendations dealing with adult prostitution included the proposal that, because it was the nuisance aspect of public solicitation by adult prostitutes that most concerned the public—teen prostitution will be addressed below—an addition to the nuisance provisions of the Criminal Code pertaining to solicitation would help to alleviate this problem (Gemme 1993).

In a review of legal, criminological, and sexological perspectives on prostitution in Canada, Gemme (1993) examined the implications of legal changes made subsequent to the Commission's report. He notes that although prostitution is not strictly illegal,

> almost all activities which permit one to practice prostitution are illegal (solicitation; to deliver service to many in the same place; to operate or to find oneself in a bawdy house; to transport toward this place; to initiate someone into prostitution or to live from the prostitution of others. (Gemme 1993, 227)

The increased visibility of street prostitution in Canadian cities throughout the 1980s may account for both the public perception that it is a "serious problem" (about 25% of Gallup poll respondents said so in 1984, 1988, and 1992) (Wolff & Geissel 1992) and for the 1985 change in the law which prohibited not only solicitation, as in the past, but also communication for the purpose of prostitution. In attempting to eliminate the nuisance effect of prostitution on nonparticipating members of the public, the law also defined automobiles as a "public place" in which such communication might occur. These changes were intended to decrease street prostitution, to make it easier to get prosecutions, and to prosecute both clients and prostitutes (Gemme 1993).

One effect of the 1985 change in the law was an increase in the recorded number of prostitution offenses from 1,225 in 1985 to 10,134 in 1992. Of the latter, about 90% were for communicating (reflecting a significant increase in client prosecutions), with the remainder split between procuring and bawdy-house convictions (Wolff & Geissel 1992). Jurisdictions may vary in the extent to which they prosecute and, although they cannot legislate in areas already covered by the Criminal Code, some have applied municipal regulations in order to facilitate prosecution (e.g., Montreal prostitutes convicted in one area were prohibited from being found in that area for one year). In assessing the law's application in Montreal, a city that accounted for 16% of Canada's reported prostitution offenses in 1992, Gemme (1993) and Gemme and Payment (1992) made the following observations:

1. Police efforts to implement the law in areas where prostitution was prevalent reduced the number of prostitutes in those areas, but shifted them to other areas, including residential ones, without reducing total numbers.
2. Arrests were easier and more frequent, since the courts had agreed that charges could be laid even though an undercover officer was "posing" either as a prostitute or client. The vast majority of communication arrests of potential clients involved a police officer posing as a prostitute.
3. Although 20 to 25% of prostitutes were male, only 11% of prostitution arrests were of males and no clients of male prostitutes were arrested (because police officers were less inclined to "pose" in that situation).
4. Although the pursuit of equity in application of the law has led to more clients being charged, the overall approach to prostitution in Canada continues to marginalize sex trade workers and often exposes them to mistreatment and abuse, experiences that preceded the entry of many into prostitution (e.g., 44% of Gemme's (1993) interviewees reported sexual abuse and 33% rape prior to entry into prostitution).

Adolescent prostitution is a significant concern in the large cities where adult prostitution is also more common (e.g., Toronto, Montreal, Vancouver, Calgary, and Edmonton accounted for about 80% of all recorded communicating offenses in 1992) (Wolff & Geissel 1994). Given the sizable number of runaway and subsequently homeless youths who gravitate to the urban core, service agencies are called upon to address the reasons for their running away from home (which may include physical or sexual abuse) and the subsequent consequences should they become involved in prostitution. While it is a criminal offense in Canada "to obtain or attempt to obtain the sexual services of a person under age 18, for consideration (i.e., any kind of payment or reward)" (MacDonald 1994, 19), Wolff and Geissel (1994) suggest that adolescent prostitution is a survival strategy arising from prior stressors and that supportive environments may be more important than legislative measures in addressing this problem.

### C. Pornography and Erotica

Canadians have a long history of debate over what legal sanctions the government could or should impose on sexually explicit books, magazines, films, and the like. As these materials became more readily available in the 1970s, it became popular to attempt to distinguish between obscenity and pornography on the one hand and erotica on the other. The growth of video sales, cable television, satellite technology, computer networks, and other communication technologies has made access to a wide range of sexual materials, particularly film and video, both more common and more likely to be used and approved at some level by women and men. For example, a 1992 Gallup Poll reported that 55% of Canadians 18 and over felt that adults should be able to buy or rent videos with explicit depictions of sexual intercourse; 37% said no and 7% had no opinion. Approval was highest in Quebec (69%), in accord with the more per-

missive and accepting attitudes of Québécois in the area of sexuality, and lowest in Atlantic Canada (49%). Approval was higher among men (64%) than women (46%) and among young versus older respondents (66% of those over 65 disapproved vs. 30% for those 18 to 29).

The current Obscenity Law—pornography is only mentioned in a new section on "child pornography"—applies to the making of a book, film, magazine, object, sex aid, recording, painting, and so on, that "corrupts public morals." "For the purposes of this Act," the law states, "any publication a dominant characteristic of which is the undue exploitation of sex, or of sex and any one of the following subjects, namely crime, horror, cruelty, and violence, shall be deemed obscene" (p. 22). MacDonald (1994) points out that obscenity is that which exceeds contemporary standards of community tolerance. The court's perception of this standard has shifted over time so that "nowadays hard-core pornography involving consensual adult sex is not considered legally obscene. However, scenes of sexual violence, degradation, and humiliation are still generally prohibited. Depictions of ejaculation upon another person, for example, are sometimes held to be degrading and therefore obscene" (MacDonald 1994, 22).

Despite a 1985 government committee report (Fraser Commission 1985) that could find no evidence for a causal link between pornography and crimes against women, Canadian public opinion and legislative sentiment has leaned toward legal control, particularly when sexuality and violence are involved. A 1992 Supreme Court decision in the Butler case adopted the notion that it was social harm, not necessarily the explicitness of the sexual content, that should be proscribed. Justice Sopinka's judgment argued that "we cannot afford to ignore the threat to equality resulting from exposure to audiences of certain types of violent and degrading material. Materials portraying women as a class as objects for sexual exploitation and abuse have a negative impact on the individual's sense of self-worth and acceptance." The decision, which now guides the way obscenity cases are charged, interpreted, and prosecuted in Canada, is based on the judge's definition of harm, i.e., that the material "predisposes persons to act in an antisocial manner as, for example, the physical or mental mistreatment of women by men, or what is debatable, the reverse." Avoidance of the presumed harm associated with pornography is, according to the judgment, "sufficiently pressing and substantial to warrant some restriction of the full exercise of the right of freedom of expression."

The guidance offered by the Butler decision does not alter the Criminal Code, which still includes the defense of serving the public good, i.e., "No person shall be convicted of an offense under this section if the public good was served by the acts that are alleged to constitute the offense and if the acts alleged did not extend beyond what served the public good." The notion of doing good while doing harm is difficult, but apparently not impossible, to reconcile.

In practice, it is the local police who lay charges and customs officials who detain books and magazines destined for entry into Canada. Rather than have the matter decided after the fact, some provinces such as Ontario have boards that view, in advance, all videos and films approved for distribution or showing. Nevertheless, it is still possible for local police to charge distributors of material approved by the board, and for subsequent prosecution under federal law. Despite official statements to the contrary, it appears that Canada Customs has been particularly restrictive on publications destined for the gay/lesbian/bisexual audience. Both Glad Day Books in Toronto, a pioneer in marketing gay and lesbian literature, and Little Sister's Book and Art Emporium in Vancouver, initiated lawsuits over books blocked by Customs. The latter is being supported by the British Columbia

Civil Liberties Association in a 1994-95 challenge to the provisions of the Customs Act that have allowed Customs to ban and detain books. The detentions usually apply to visual or verbal descriptions of sex with violent overtones (sadism and masochism, bondage, etc.), but other materials are also stopped if the title implies restricted content. Ironically, even a book by American feminist Andrea Dworkin, an opponent of pornography but not a proponent of Canada's new "harm-based" law as a way of dealing with it (Toobin 1994), has been stopped at Customs. Shortly before the Little Sister's case began, Canada Customs removed depictions of anal penetration from its guidelines for detaining or banning books, a restriction that probably contradicts provincial human rights code provisions that prohibit discrimination based on sexual orientation. In 1996, the court subsequently granted the plaintiff bookstore an interim injunction to enjoin the continued policy of systematic inspection by customs.

Human rights legislation in Canada may also be invoked in attempts to limit access to sexually explicit materials. For example, in early 1993 the Ontario Human Rights Commission established a board of inquiry to address complaints that local stores selling *Penthouse* and *Playboy* created a "poisoned environment" for women. Although the board of inquiry was halted in late 1993, the issues surrounding legislative regulation of sexual depictions is likely to continue.

Canada's "child pornography law," introduced in 1993, makes it an offense punishable by a maximum of ten years imprisonment to make, print, publish, or possess for the purpose of publication, any material classified as "child pornography." Possession is also prohibited and punishable by up to five years. In both cases, someone charged could be found not guilty "if the written material alleged to constitute child pornography has artistic merit or an educational, scientific, or medical purpose." Child pornography is defined as "a photographic, film, video, or other visual representation, whether or not it was made by electronic or mechanical means" that has one or more of the following features: (1) it "shows a person who is or is depicted as being under the age of 18 years and is engaged in or is depicted as engaging in explicit sexual activity"; (2) "the dominant characteristic of which is the depiction, for a sexual purpose, of a sexual organ or the anal region of a person under the age of 18 years"; or (3) "any written material or visual representation that advocates or counsels sexual activity with a person under the age of 18 years that would be an offense under this Act" (MacDonald 1994, 23).

However, the initial introduction of the child pornography law was considered hasty by some and in need of fine-tuning. A series of subsequent legal cases pertaining to this law are instructive in this regard. In October of 1993, Toronto artist Eli Langer was charged under this law for paintings of people engaged in sexual activity. Some of these individuals appeared to be males under the age of 18. A judge ruled the work to have "artistic merit" and the charges were dropped. Nevertheless, the Ontario government used a forfeiture application to seize the work as child porn. Langer's work was subsequently returned to him. In February of 2000, an Ottawa father of two children was arrested after a photo-lab technician flagged pictures of this man's four-year-old son playing without pajama bottoms. The charges were dropped, but the husband and wife involved were required to take a parenting course and spent the majority of their savings in legal expenses. Most recently, the Supreme Court of Canada ruled on the case of John Robin Sharpe, a 67-year Vancouver man charged with possession of child porn. Sharpe had pictures of boys as young as seven engaged in sex and a collection of his own writings titled "Kiddie Kink Classics." The Supreme Court and two lower courts in British Columbia acquitted Sharpe on the basis that the charge violated his rights under the Charter of Rights and Freedoms.

Contention surrounding the child pornography law has centred around the need to balance the protection of children from sexual exploitation with the need for freedom of thought, belief, and expression this is protected in the Charter of Rights and Freedoms. One British Columbia judge who had been involved in the Sharpe case expressed concern that the law, as currently understood, was perilously close to criminalizing merely "objectionable thoughts." That said, there was agitation to remove the offense of possession from the child pornography law. However, critics pointed out that the removal of the offense of possession as unconstitutional would make it exceedingly more difficult to investigate and prosecute more serious offenses, such as the the sale and distribution of pornographic materials. This debate was played out in the Supreme Court of Canada with a decision coming forth in January of 2002. The child pornography law that was ultimately upheld prohibits not only the possession of pornographic material involving children, but also written material depicting unlawful sexual activity with a child. The exceptions to this include material that is "for the public good" or otherwise defensible for it's artistic, educational, medical, or scientific merit. Two further exceptions were also added at that time, the first of which speaks to written materials or visual representations created and held by the accused alone, exclusively for personal use. The latter includes visual recordings created by or depicting the accused that do not depict unlawful sexual activity and are for private use only (Baer, 2002).

Court proceedings on obscenity cases have been a common occurrence in Canada, and the courts, rather than legislators, appear to be the ultimate arbiters who weigh research evidence and public opinion in such matters. The development of phone sex lines, computer sex services, and other such means for accessing sexually explicit content are also testing the Canadian penchant for legislation in such areas. Although it is subject to some legal restriction, sexually explicit material is widely available in Canada.

## 9. Contraception, Abortion, and Population Planning

### A. Contraception: Attitudes, Availability, and Usage

Although contraceptive pills, condoms, and other forms of contraception were available in Canada prior to 1969, it was only in that year that the law was changed to legalize the advertising, dissemination, and distribution of such methods for the purpose of contraception. The establishment of the Family Planning Division within the federal ministry of health in 1972 was consistent with the government's policy that adult Canadians should be able to determine voluntarily the number and spacing of their children. An important aspect of the division's work was to support development of community public health programs to reduce teen pregnancy. When the division was discontinued in 1976, due in part to opposition from quarters opposed to its mandate, the loss impaired development of services in smaller communities that needed both the resources and initiative provided by this kind of federal program (Orton & Rosenblatt 1993) Other divisions within Health Canada took up this mandate, as did the provinces, and contraceptive information and services are now generally available through public health units, Planned Parenthood centers, private physicians, pharmacies, and a variety of clinics and health centers. While knowledge about contraceptive methods is generally good, application of that knowledge, in terms of both motivation and finding a method suitable for each individual, is still a significant issue, not only for teens, but also for young adults who are increasingly postponing childbearing until their 30s and beyond.

While availability of contraceptive education and services for adults and teens has increased following legalization in 1969, a 1990 *Report on Adolescent Reproductive Health* (Health and Welfare Canada 1990) noted that teens, particularly in rural areas, still lacked adequate access to contraception and related sexual health services. To the extent that this deficiency reflected teen discomfort with the settings in which such services were provided, some high schools have established Sexuality Health centers (Campbell 1991) and some jurisdictions have introduced condom machines in the high schools (A. Barrett 1992). Neither of the above was then, or is now, a common occurrence in Canadian schools. Such programs generally arise only after an assessment of community needs and consultation with parents. When they do occur, they probably reflect an already high level of community acceptance. Indeed, the school-based sexuality education programs described in Section 3A, Knowledge and Education about Sexuality, Government Policies and Programs, and community agencies, such as public health units, Planned Parenthoods, and so on, are among the most common "official" sources through which students can get accurate information about contraception. Physicians also provide contraceptive information, as do websites sponsored by such organizations and by prominent medical groups such as the Society of Obstetricians and Gynaecologists of Canada. As a result, the 1998 Canadian contraception study found widespread familiarity with, and generally favorable opinions about, the contraceptive pill, condoms, and male and female sterilization among women aged 15-44 (Fisher, Boroditscky, & Bridges 1999). Familiarity and favorable ratings were lower for the female condom, injectable contraception, spermicides, cervical cap, and other such methods that might expand the range of options available to women as they make changes in contraception suitable for them at different times in their reproductive lives.

*Contraceptive Practices*

The 1993, 1995, and 1999 Canadian Contraception Studies (CCS) (Fisher, Boroditsky, & Bridges 2000; Fisher & Boroditsky 2000; Boroditsky, Fisher, & Sand 1995, 1996) are among the few national sources of information on trends and current practices in contraceptive use in Canada in the 1990s. The 1995 General Social Survey also asked a national sample about current contraceptive use, but because it did not ask about current sexual activity, authors who use these findings have done so with caution (see Maticka-Tyndale, Barrett, & McKay 2000). This section relies on these national sources and a sampling of provincial studies to document current contraceptive practices in Canada and trends through the 1990s and into 2003.

For a variety of reasons, including religious conviction, some Canadians choose to use natural family planning methods (symptothermal method, etc.), and a number of organizations (e.g., SERENA) and agencies (clinics in Catholic hospitals) offer education and support for users of this method. Overall, however, Canadians are most likely to use the pill, condoms, and IUD early in their sexual lives, with sterilization (tubal ligation and vasectomy) being a popular method in later years.

Based on reports of current use among all married women aged 18-44 who were having intercourse, the 1998 CCS found that 28% used oral contraception, 31% condoms, 26% male sterilization, 14% female sterilization, 8% withdrawal, and 2-4% rhythm, IUD, or barrier methods. A small percentage used multiple methods. Among unmarried women aged 15-44, the comparable values were 66% pill, 64% condom, 1-3 sterilization, 12% withdrawal, 4% barrier methods, and 2% rhythm. Because most studies throughout the 1990s in Canada have focused on contraception and condom use among teens and young adults, these latter observations provide a reference point for the findings that follow.

Although young adults who are regularly involved with a sexual partner are most likely to use birth control pills for contraception, public health officials have encouraged the additional use of condoms as added protection against STDs. Free condom distribution by public health units has been used as a means to promote "dual protection" among pill users (Ullman & Lathrop 1996). In a survey of 249 male and 237 female urban, heterosexually active (in the past year) university students, Myers and Clement (1994) found that 52.2% of males and 39.7% of females reported condom use during vaginal intercourse. All respondents indicated at least one instance during the past year in which they had not used a condom during intercourse. Table 8 gives some of their choices from a list of 15 possible reasons for not using a condom the last time they had unprotected intercourse.

In their replies to attitudinal questions about sex and condom use (strongly agree 1 to strongly disagree 5), females more strongly disagreed than males with the statements "safer sex is boring" (mean scores of 4.1 for females vs. 3.7 for males), "condoms are a turnoff" (3.4 for females vs. 3.1 for males), "it's safe for long-term lovers to have whatever sex they want with each other" (2.6 for females vs. 2.4 for males), "it's hard to have safer sex with alcohol or drugs" (3.2 for females vs. 2.6 for males), and "it's hard to have safer sex with an attractive person" (4.0 for females vs. 3.4 for males). Although both sexes agreed that "sexual enjoyment is an important part of life," females gave slightly more agreement (1.9 for females vs. 1.7 for males) (Myers & Clement 1994). Overall, female university students showed more positive attitudes toward condom use and a stronger be-

**Table 8**

**Reasons Identified by Heterosexual University Students for Not Using a Condom the Last Time They Had Unprotected Sexual Intercourse[1]**

| Reason for Not Using a Condom During Last Act of Unprotected Sexual Intercourse[2] | Percentage Citing the Reason | |
| --- | --- | --- |
| | Female | Male |
| Was with regular sex partner | 55.7 | 49.1 |
| Thought we were safe | 44.3 | 47.4 |
| Did not have a condom[3] | 24.6 | 45.6 |
| Did not want to use one | 27.0 | 35.3 |
| No sex with anyone else | 25.8 | 24.3 |
| Sex was so exciting[4] | 17.4 | 30.6 |
| Partner didn't want to use one[5] | 13.8 | 27.8 |
| Using drugs or alcohol[3] | 4.2 | 13.3 |
| Had just met partner[5] | 4.2 | 12.1 |
| Was embarrassed to buy | 3.6 | 5.2 |

[1]Results from Myers and Clement (1994, 52). Sample includes 249 male and 237 female heterosexually active university students (average age ~22 years); 83.6% of respondents had used condoms at some point in their lives, 69.4% in the last year.

[2]Percentages add up to more than 100 because some respondents picked more than one of the 15 possible reasons on a list of options.

[3]sig. diff., $p < 0.001$

[4]sig. diff., $p < 0.005$

[5]sig. diff., $p < 0.05$

lief in their ability to use condoms than did male university students. This, in turn, translated into more conscientious practices reported by women than men. Two important subtexts in negotiations about condom use are a behavioral norm of serial monogamy among Canadian university students (i.e., there is never more than one partner, but partnerships do not last for more than a few months) and the traditional cultural norm that leads women to trust and defer to their partners, and men to expect this.

In a 1991 study of young adults (aged 15 to 29) in Quebec, 14.7% of sexually active respondents said they had never used a condom (9% for ages 15 to 19, 15.2% for ages 20 to 24, 16.8% for ages 25 to 29 years old). Another 41.3% said they had stopped using them (28.5% for ages 15 to 19, 40.2% for ages 20 to 24, 48% for ages 25 to 29), and 44% said they still used them (62.5% for ages 15 to 19, 44.6% for ages 20 to 24, 35.2% for ages 25 to 29). Among those in the total sample who were respectively either currently using or had previously used condoms, the reasons for ever having used condoms (multiple choices possible) were: contraception (77%, 83%), danger of STD (65%, 45%), new partner (29%, 27%), many partners (11%, 8%), and had or have an STD (2%, 4%) (Santé Quebec 1991). The findings suggest that many young people in Quebec may use condoms for contraception early in their sexual interactions and then shift to other methods of contraception and away from condoms as they get older and perhaps more established in a relationship.

Among college students (CEGEP) in Quebec, 18% said they had not used a contraceptive method the first time they had intercourse, 14% used a condom and the pill, 11% the pill only, and 55.3% a condom only. When asked about the contraceptive method used the last time they had sexual intercourse, 4.2% said none, 18% said the condom and pill, 49.2% the pill only, 26% the condom only, and 1.7% used other methods (Samson et al. 1996). In a study of contraceptive use by 745 sexually active anglophone and francophone university students in Montreal and Ontario, Lévy et al. (1994b) found that in the previous six months (1992-93) 72.4% overall reported using the pill, either alone (35.4%) or in combination with a condom (19.1%) or with other methods (17.9%), whereas condom use with the pill or other methods was less common (41.7%). The sizable percentage using some method of contraception (97.7%) and the lower percentage incorporating condom use (41.7%) is consistent with the suggestion that pregnancy prevention still predominates over STD/HIV prevention in the decision-making of a sizable percentage of university students. Although most students had only one partner in the previous six months (85.2%), having had more than one partner was the variable that correlated most strongly with condom use. Condom use was less common among those with higher coital frequency.

Tonkin's (1992) study of 15,549 students in grades seven to 12 in public and independent schools in British Columbia provided data on a variety of social and health-related issues affecting young people. With specific reference to sexual activity and contraceptive use, he found that 33% of males and 28% of females in the sample had ever had intercourse. For those in grade 12 (ages 17 to 18), the figures were 55% for males and 52% for females. Among the British Columbia high school students who were currently "sexually active," 64% of males and 53% of females said they used a condom in their last experience of sexual intercourse. Overall, 49% of sexually active students said they used condoms, 25% birth control pills, 8% withdrawal, 2% other methods, and 13% no method; 3% said "not sure."

A convenience sample of 660 15- to 18-year-old females in Toronto (Insight Canada Research 1992) found that among the 41.8% who said they were sexually active, the contraceptive methods used were condoms (29%), condoms and the pill (24%), the pill (22%), condoms and foam (4%), other (3%), or no birth control (26%).

The 1995 Canadian Contraception Study (Boroditsky et al. 1996) used a self-administered questionnaire to assess the contraceptive attitudes and practices of a random sample of 1,428 women aged 15 to 44 (57.5% married, 42.5% unmarried) drawn from 20,000 households that had previously agreed to be subjects in market research studies. Based on all respondents in the sample, the percentages currently using various methods of birth control were as follows: the pill (30%); condom (25%); male sterilization (14%); female sterilization (12%); IUD (11%); no method (15%); none because pregnant or trying to get pregnant (7%); withdrawal (5%); hysterectomy/menopause (3%); cream/jelly/foam (3%); rhythm (3%); IUD (1%); and diaphragm (1%). Not surprisingly, sterilization (male or female) was used by 38% of all married women versus 7% of not currently married women of all ages. Since the study did not determine the proportion of young unmarried women who were sexually active, or lesbian, it is not known what proportion of the 15% of nonusers had no need of contraception. However, among teens who have ever used the pill, 35% said they started using it before their first intercourse, 22% as soon as they became sexually active, and 33% within one year.

Based on his research with university students, William Fisher (1989), from the University of Western Ontario, has described a "Contraceptive Script" that Canadians typically follow. This script outlines a common progression of contraceptive methods that are used as individuals first become sexually active and form committed relationships. When young Canadians first become sexually active they typically use either no contraception or one or a combination of condoms and withdrawal. The use of oral contraception is usually begun after a woman has been sexually active for a period of time, or when she considers her sexual partnership to have become "long-term" or "committed." When relationships are terminated, it is not uncommon for contraceptive practices to return to an earlier form (e.g., to cease using oral contraception and rely on withdrawal or condoms in new partnerships), though as women move through a larger number of partnerships, they more typically continue using oral contraceptives. Though there has been no single large-scale national study to test Fisher's script, the studies cited here, and others, consistently provide support for the conclusion that the Contraceptive Script is commonly followed.

With respect to contraception and STD prevention at first intercourse, a study of grade 10 and 12 high school students in Regina, Saskatchewan, in 2000 suggests that the stereotype of unplanned and unprotected first intercourse may be changing. Among the 539 females and 470 males who reported on their contraceptive use at first intercourse, 42.3% overall used condom only, 27.8% used condom and pill, 6.6% used pill only, and 6.8% used other methods alone or in combination (Hampton, Smith, Jeffery, & McWatters 2001). Overall, about 80% used a reliable method of contraception and 72% used a condom. Males and females did not differ in this respect, nor in the percentage who used no method (15.9% of females and 16.3% of males). Among all students who had intercourse, about half felt that their parents would strongly or somewhat disapprove of their having sex, whereas over 70% of student surveyed who had not had intercourse expected such parental disapproval. Interestingly, a high percentage of all students who anticipated parental disapproval for their having sex felt that their parents would approve of their using condoms.

Among unmarried women aged 18-29, the 1998 CCS found that well over 80% used contraception at first intercourse with their current partner, and slightly fewer used contraception at their most recent intercourse with this partner (Fisher & Boroditsky 1999). However, condom use was noticeably higher at first than most-recent intercourse, and pill use was higher at most-recent than first intercourse.

In the *Ethnocultural Communities Facing AIDS* study, respondents in long-term relationships were asked about their current contraceptive practices. Eighteen percent of women and 28% of men from the English-speaking Caribbean communities reported no contraceptive use, compared to 12% of South Asian men, and 20% of women and 24% of men from the Latin American communities. Condoms were the most common contraceptive reported in all communities (62% of English-speaking Caribbean women and 54% of men, 47% of South Asian men, and 37% of Latin American women and 44% of men), followed by oral contraceptives (49% of English-speaking Caribbean women and 33% of men, 26% of South Asian men, and 30% of Latin American women and 22% of men) (Maticka-Tyndale et al. 1995).

## B. Teen Pregnancy

Canadian statistics on teen pregnancy do not distinguish between married and unmarried teens, nor is it possible to determine the extent to which marriage may have been precipitated by unintended pregnancy (although this tendency is much less likely than 20 years ago). Given that teen marriage rates are low and that most teen pregnancies are assumed to be unplanned and unwanted, Canadians generally approach teen pregnancy as a problem (although this may not be so in some northern aboriginal or First Nations communities where teen sexuality and pregnancy are less stigmatized).

A major review of teen pregnancies in Canada from 1974-1997 (Dryburgh 2000) plus Statistics Canada data for 1998 provide background to the current situation. The pregnancy rate is established by combining data on registered live births, therapeutic abortions in hospital (and only since the 1990s, in free-standing clinics), plus registered stillbirths, hospitalized

### Table 9

**Rates of Teen Pregnancy, Abortion, Miscarriage, and Birth for Canada, the Provinces and Territories in 1998[1]**

| Province/ Territory | Rate per 1,000 15-19 Year Old Females | | | |
|---|---|---|---|---|
| | Pregnancy | Abortion | Miscarriage | Birth |
| CANADA | 41.7 | 20.9 | 1.0 | 19.8 |
| Newfoundland/ Labrador | 31.5 | 9.7 | 1.4 | 20.4 |
| Prince Edward Island | 36.4 | 5.6 | 1.0 | 29.7 |
| Nova Scotia | 39.7 | 15.3 | 0.4 | 24.0 |
| New Brunswick | 37.8 | 10.0 | 1.3 | 26.4 |
| Quebec | 40.0 | 24.4 | 0.7 | 14.9 |
| Ontario | 38.1 | 20.3 | 0.6 | 17.2 |
| Manitoba | 65.2 | 23.2 | 3.4 | 38.7 |
| Saskatchewan | 52.8 | 13.4 | 1.5 | 38.0 |
| Alberta | 50.9 | 23.3 | 2.2 | 25.4 |
| British Columbia | 38.8 | 21.7 | 0.9 | 16.1 |
| Yukon | 58.3 | 29.6 | 0.0 | 28.7 |
| Northwest Territories[2] | 117.0 | 24.9 | 1.9 | 90.3 |

[1]1998 was the fourth consecutive year of decline in Canada's teen pregnancy rate subsequent to a high of 48.8/1,000 in 1994.
[2]Includes Nunavut.
*Source*: Health Division, Statistics Canada (2002).

cases of spontaneous abortion, and so on. From 1974 to 1997, the teen pregnancy rate (births per 1,000 women aged 15 to 19) dropped from 53.7 in 1974 to 41.1/1,000 in 1987, and then, in a reversal of this downward trend, increased steadily each year to 48.8/1,000 in 1994, whereafter, it has declined each year to 41.7/1,000 in 1998. This unexplained shift upward in teen pregnancy rates in the late 1980s and early 1990s was observed in a number of developed countries (Singh & Darroch 2000). The residual effect in Canada may be a continuing public perception that teen pregnancy rates are increasing. While this is not so, the percentage decline in teen pregnancy rates in Canada from 1970-1995 was less than in some of the countries that we often use for comparison (e.g. France, Germany, Sweden, Denmark, and Australia), although comparable to others (e.g. England, New Zealand, Scotland, and Spain) (see Singh & Darroch 2000; Darroch, Singh, & Frost 2001; and Maticka-Tyndale 2001).

Teen pregracy rates vary by province and territory, with the lowest levels in 1998 in Newfoundland and Labrador (31.5/1,000) and the highest in Yukon, Manitoba, and Northwest Territories (including Nunavut) (58.3/1,000 to 90.3/1,000) (see Table 9). Because teen abortion rates also vary by province, the birthrates to 15-19-year-olds range from 14.9/1,000 in Quebec to 90.3/1,000 in the Northwest Territories (including Nunavut), with an overall national rate of 19.8/1,000 (comparable to England, lower than the United States, and double or more the rates in Sweden and France) (see Darroch, Singh, & Frost 2001).

Given the tendency of teenaged females to have somewhat older male partners, a sizable percentage of the males involved in the pregnancies of 18- to 19-year-olds may not have been "teens" themselves. An analysis of U.S. teen pregnancies and births (which occur at a significantly higher rate than in Canada) reported that 70% of the male partners were over 20 (Males 1992). A comparable national analysis has not been done in Canada, but an update on adolescent birth statistics for the City of Toronto in 1993 (Phillips 1994) revealed a similar pattern to that in the U.S. Of the 364 births to 15- to 19-year-olds in Toronto in 1993, 54% (*N* = 196) had a record of the father's age. Of these fathers, 25% were 15 to 19, 45% were 20 to 24, and 30% were over 25. Among the 18- to 19-year-old females (65% of the births in the sample), the father's age was 15 to 19 for 18%, 20 to 24 for 51%, and over 25 for 31%. Among the 15- to 17-year-old females who gave birth, fathers' ages were 15 to 19 (44%), 20 to 24 (30%), and over 25 (26%). The available data covering STD cases for 1992 also support the conclusion that a sizable percentage of STD cases in female adolescents were acquired from males over the age of 19. Although these results cannot be generalized to the entire population, they are an indication that the majority of teen pregnancies may not involve male teen partners. It is not known what proportion of the pregnancies were either planned or desired.

In 1989, 58% of pregnant 18- to 19-year-olds gave birth (66% in 1975), 36% had induced abortions (25% in 1975 when abortion was less accessible), and 6% had other recorded pregnancy terminations (9% in 1975). In 1989, the absolute number of births to 15- to 17-year-olds was 46% less than in 1975, and to 18- to 19-year-olds, 40% less. Given the personal consequences of teen pregnancy for parent and child, prevention of unwanted pregnancy remains an important sexual and reproductive health issue in Canada (Wadhera & Strachan 1991).

## C. Abortion

In 1988, the Supreme Court of Canada effectively decriminalized abortion in Canada by declaring the existing law (revised in 1969) unconstitutional. Prior to this, abortion was illegal unless done by a doctor in an approved hospital, following certification by the hospital's therapeutic abortion committee that the woman's life or health would be endangered if the pregnancy continued. The Supreme Court decision was based on a woman's right to "life, liberty and the security of the person" under Canada's Charter of Rights and Freedoms. That decision has not eliminated the continuing struggle by some antiabortion groups to discourage abortion and block legal access to it. Campaign Life Coalition, Alliance for Life, Canadian Physicians for Life, and Human Life International are among the best known of the groups supporting this view. The groups most identified with retaining and improving women's right and access to abortion and educating about these issues are, respectively, the Canadian Abortion Rights Action League (CARAL) and Childbirth by Choice. A major impetus to change in the Canadian law has been the repeated charging, conviction, and subsequent acquittal of Dr. Henry Morgentaler for providing illegal abortions, i.e., illegal because, although medically safe and performed in a clinical setting, it was not done in an accredited hospital.

Dr. Morgentaler (and others) have now established clinics in a number of Canadian cities; all have been extensively picketed and some have been directly attacked—the original Toronto clinic was destroyed by arson in 1983. Many providers of abortion in clinics and hospitals continue to experience varying levels of picketing and/or harassment by protesters. In several provinces (e.g., Alberta and Ontario), the harassment of patients, staff, nurses, and/or the physicians who perform abortions has led to injunctions to prevent protesters from demonstrating directly in front of some clinics or physicians' residences.

The impact of public attitudes and disagreements about abortion, and the continuing acrimony surrounding this issue, extends widely into debates about sexuality education in schools, availability of clinical services, public health policies, and religious beliefs. A 1989 national survey found that 27% of Canadians thought abortion should be legal under any circumstance, 59% legal under certain circumstances, 12% illegal under all circumstances, and 3% had no opinion. This pattern of response has been consistent since 1975 (Muldoon 1991). In 1989, at the time that the federal government was considering a bill to recriminalize abortion (i.e., effectively a return to the 1969 version of the law), a national opinion poll commissioned by CARAL found that 62% disagreed with this plan, 28% agreed, and 9% had no opinion or did not reply. One year later, after the bill had been passed by the House of Commons and sent to the Senate for approval, a similar poll had responses of 66%, 25%, and 9%, respectively. The Senate defeated the "recriminalization" bill in January 1991. This meant that no federal law was in place and that abortion would be dealt with, as in other medical matters, by provincial and medical regulations. That is the current situation.

At present, all provinces except Prince Edward Island (PEI) provide varying degrees of access to abortion in hospitals, and all but PEI (which pays under special circumstances) will pay some or all of the cost under health plan coverage. There are now a total of 17 free-standing clinics (i.e., separate from hospitals) in Canada that provide abortion (none in Saskatchewan, PEI, or the territories) with the host province paying full costs in two provinces, partial costs in four, and no costs in the remaining four. Access to abortion still varies considerably across Canada, and there is significant financial hardship involved for women in many settings, particularly in remote Northern areas and in PEI, Newfoundland, and Saskatchewan (the three most rural provinces). Abortion continues to be a focus and flashpoint for differing beliefs and ideologies about sexuality and social policy.

When asked to identify the circumstances of pregnancy under which they would consider legal abortion acceptable, Canadians surveyed in 1990 gave higher approval under conditions such as harm to the woman's health (82%), pregnancy from rape or incest (73%), or the strong chance of serious defect in the baby (69%), than under specific social conditions, such as low family income (38%) (Muldoon 1991). These distinctions have prevailed in such surveys for over 20 years and suggest that Canadians, although generally approving of legal access to safe abortion, also have opinions about the criteria they would like to see used when such decisions are made.

In 1998, there were 110,520 therapeutic abortions in Canada, 61.7% in hospitals, 38% in free-standing clinics, and slightly less than 0.3% in the U.S. (see Tables 10, 11, and 12). This represents 32 abortions per 100 live births and 15.4 abortions per 1,000 women aged 15 to 44. The inci-

### Table 10

#### Abortion Data for Canada (1998)

| Year | Total Abortions[1] | Abortions per 100 Live Births | Percent Abortions Reported from: | | |
|------|------|------|------|------|------|
| | | | Hospitals | Clinics | U.S.A. |
| 1998 | 110,520 | 32.2 | 61.7 | 38.0 | 0.3 |
| 1997 | 111,819 | 32.0 | 64.3 | 35.5 | 0.3 |
| 1996 | 111,757 | 30.5 | 66.7 | 33.0 | 0.3 |

[1]Abortion rate (1998): 15.7 abortions/1,000 women aged 15-44.
*Source*: Canadian Institute for Health Information and Health Division, Statistics Canada (2002).

### Table 11

#### Age-Specific Abortion Rates and Percentages for Canada (1998)

| Age Group | Age Specific Abortion Rate/1,000 in Age Group[1] | Percent Distribution of Known Hospital and Clinic Abortions According to Age Group |
|------|------|------|
| 15-19 | 20.9 | 18.9% |
| 20-24 | 32.4 | 29.3 |
| 25-29 | 21.1 | 20.1 |
| 30-34 | 13.6 | 14.8 |
| 35-39 | 8.1 | 8.8 |

[1]Abortion rate (1998): 15.7/1,000 women aged 15-44.
*Source*: Canadian Institute for Health Research and Health Division, Statistics Canada (2002).

### Table 12

#### Marital Status and Prior Abortion History of Women Receiving Abortions in Canada (1998)

| Percent Abortions in 1998 According to Marital Status[1] | | Percent Abortions in 1998 According to Prior Abortion History[1] | |
|------|------|------|------|
| Single | 57.8% | No prior abortions | 60.6% |
| Married | 17.4% | One | 25.6% |
| Separated | 2.3% | Two or more | 11.8% |
| Common Law | 6.0% | Unknown | 2.1% |
| Widowed | 0.3% | | |
| Unknown | 14.4% | | |

[1]Based on known cases in hospitals, plus clinics in Ontario and Alberta, collectively representing about two thirds of abortions in Canada in 1998.
*Source*: *Therapeutic Abortion Survey*, Canadian Institute for Health Information and Health Division, Statistics Canada (2002).

dence of unreported abortions is unknown but probably quite low. It has been suggested that the increase in the absolute number of abortions in the late 1980s and early 1990s may have been because of a prolonged economic recession, but this pattern may also reflect younger women's desire for greater financial security prior to childbearing, which fits with the continued decline in fertility rates (Wadhera & Miller 1997). In 1998, women under 20 accounted for about 21% of abortions, and about half of the women who sought abortions had one or more children. The 1998 teen abortion rate of 20.9 abortions/1,000 women aged 15 to 19 is within the range observed throughout the 1990s (19.3-22.0/1,000 15-19-year-olds) and represents about one half of all pregnancies in this age group. This rate is consistent with the national and international evidence (reviewed by Bissell 2000) that an appreciable number of teens (excluding those who are married or do not have access to abortion services) may have chosen to become pregnant or to continue an unplanned pregnancy.

One problem for Canadian women seeking access to hospital abortions has been the waiting time involved. This is an issue not only because of increased risk and anxiety, but because of the restrictions placed on late abortions in some settings. Data collected on 59,694 therapeutic abortions conducted in hospital settings in 1992 showed that almost 90% were within the first 12 weeks of pregnancy. Time since conception for all cases was: less than 9 weeks (35.5%); 9 to 12 weeks (53.5%); 13 to 16 weeks (6.7%); 17 to 20 weeks (1.7%); over 20 weeks (0.3%); and unknown (2.2%). The so-called abortion pill, RU-486, which disrupts gestation early in pregnancy, has not yet been approved for testing or release in Canada.

### D. Population Planning

To the extent that a population policy attempts to influence the size, rate of growth, distribution, age structure, or composition of a population, Canada does not have such a policy. Federal government policy ensures the right of people to regulate the number and spacing of their children, but does not directly advocate increasing population size through more births. The fertility rate has been below replacement since 1971 and a *de facto* policy favoring continued growth was in the setting of higher immigration levels at about 250,000 per year for the 1989-94 period, which was considerably higher than in previous years. The federal government's immigration plan for 2003 projects 220,000 to 245,000 immigrants and reflects a continuing blend of economic and humanitarian goals, rather than a population policy per se.

At the provincial level, Quebec, has offered a financial incentive to women who give birth in any year, presumably as a means of maintaining the francophone population (and perhaps total population as well, since Quebec's fertility rate is the lowest in Canada). Quebec also has some influence on immigration to that province (i.e., to maintain Quebec's share of total population, which was 23.7% in 2002), an agreement arising from Quebec's relationship with the rest of Canada, and an option that some other provinces also wish to exercise. In fact, the actual proportion of immigrants to Canada who settle first in Quebec has been dropping annually from 22.4% in 1991 to 12.5% in 1994 (Dumas & Belanger 1996). Overall, Canada has no stated national policy concerning distribution of the population. Immigrants settle predominantly in only a few provinces where jobs and other family members are located (e.g., over half of all immigrants come to Ontario, 25% of these to the Metropolitan Toronto area), but this is the result of circumstance and economics and not as a guided policy decision regarding population distribution.

## 10. Sexually Transmitted Diseases and HIV/AIDS

### A. Sexually Transmitted Diseases
*Incidence, Patterns, and Trends*

The final report of the Royal Commission on New Reproductive Technologies, published in 1993, argued that a countrywide strategy was needed to prevent STDs and that this "must become a priority if we are to reduce the prevalence of infertility among Canadian couples in the future" (Royal Commission on New Reproductive Technologies 1993). Research done for the commission showed that many people lacked adequate access to quality reproductive health services that could either reduce their risk of acquiring STDs or provide rapid diagnosis and treatment. This was noted particularly for isolated and rural areas, and for many adolescents, single adult women, people with disabilities, and cultural and linguistic minorities.

Despite the decreasing incidence of some STDs in the early 1990s, Gully and Peeling (1994) reported that STDs remained the most common reportable infections in Canada. This was and is an ongoing concern because about one third to one half of women who acquire an STD (usually chlamydia or gonorrhea) will develop pelvic inflammatory disease (PID), representing about 80% of all cases of PID. While it is difficult to estimate accurately the rates of PID, Health Canada data cited in the Royal Commission report gave age-specific rates of between 243/100,000 and 306/100,000 for women in the four age groups 15 to 19, 20 to 24, 25 to 29, and 30 to 34. STDs appear to play only a small role in male infertility in Canada, but the most recently available incidence data presented in Table 13 suggest that STDs continue to be an important health concern for both sexes. In the 10 years that followed publication of the Royal Commission report, we have seen both gains and reversals in STD-prevention efforts.

#### Table 13

**Number and Percentage of Selected Reportable Sexually Transmitted Disease Cases by Age and Sex in Canada (2000)***

| Categories (Age/Years) | Number of Reported Cases (Percentage of All Cases) | | | |
| --- | --- | --- | --- | --- |
| | Gonoccocal Infection | Infectious Syphilis | Chlamydia | Hepatitis B* |
| Rate | 20.2/100,000 | 0.7/100,000 | 151.1/100,000 | 10.5/100,000 |
| Total | 6,222 | 171 | 46,452 | 2,815 |
| Male | 3,850 (61.9) | 111 (64.6) | 13,557 (29.2) | 1,805 (64.1) |
| Female | 2,368 (38.1) | 60 (35.1) | 32,869 (70.8) | 984 (35.0) |
| Under 15 | 58 ( 0.9) | 0 ( 0.0) | 554 (11.9) | 77 ( 2.8) |
| 15-19 | 1,407 (22.6) | 7 ( 4.1) | 14,792 (31.8) | 176 ( 6.3) |
| 20-24 | 1,566 (25.2) | 15 ( 8.8) | 17,003 (36.6) | 360 (12.8) |
| 25-29 | 963 (15.5) | 23 (13.5) | 7,163 (15.4) | 482 (17.1) |
| 30-39 | 1,477 (23.7) | 59 (34.5) | 5,064 (10.9) | 860 (30.6) |
| 40-59 | 690 (11.1) | 56 (32.7) | 1,592 ( 3.4) | 684 (24.3) |
| 60+ | 51 ( 0.8) | 11 ( 6.4) | 74 ( 0.2) | 135 ( 4.8) |

*Note*: Numerical totals may not match since age and/or sex unspecified in a small proportion of cases.

*Hepatitis B data are for 1995.

*Data source*: Division of Sexual Health Promotion and STD Prevention and Control, Bureau of HIV/AIDS, STD & TB, Health Canada 2002.

In 1997, Health Canada published national goals for STD prevention that set cautiously optimistic targets (based on 1995 rates) for reductions by 2000 and 2010 in the rates of all major STDs and their sequelae (see Patrick 1997a in a special theme issue of the *Canadian Journal of Human Sexuality* on STDs and Sexual/Reproductive Health). For example, based on a steady 5-year decline in reported cases of chlamydia to a rate of 127/100,000 in 1995, a goal of 80/100,000 for 2000 and 50/100,000 by 2010 was reported (Patrick 1997b). Infectious syphilis was to be maintained at less than 0.5/100,000 by 2000, with endemically acquired syphilis to be eliminated by 2010 (Romanowski 1977). Similar expectations for declines in gonorrhea (Alary 1997) and PID and ectopic pregnancy (MacDonald & Brunham 1997) were reported, as were conceptual analyses of the behavioral and social changes needed to achieve these goals (Maticka-Tyndale 1997; Fisher 1997). Health Canada's routinely updated *Canadian STD Guidelines* also provide guidance for STD prevention and management.

The most recent data available show an unexpected resurgence of STDs in the late 1990s and early 2000s (Patrick, Wong, & Jordan 2000). For example, reporting rates for gonorrhea, which had declined from over 40/100,000 in 1990 to a low of 14.9/100,00 in 1997, increased in each of the three subsequent years to a rate of 20.2/100,000 in 2000 (Table 3). Similar changes have been noted for chlamydia, which had declined to 112/100,000 by 1997, but increased yearly thereafter to 151/100,000 in 2000, and for infectious syphilis, which remained below the national goal at 0.4/100,000 in 1997, but increased to 0.7/100,000 in 2000.

About 78% of reported cases of chlamydia in 2000 (58% in the case of gonorrhea) involved youth aged 15-24 (Table 13). The reported chlamydia rate among females aged 15-19 in 2000 was over 5 times that for males, and rates for both sexes were considerably higher in 2000 than in 1997 and over double the national goal set for 2000 (Patrick et al 2000). Although some slight increase in chlamydia rates had been expected in the mid-1990s as a result of more sensitive and less-invasive testing, the recent upward trend, which is also seen in gonorrhea, is unlikely to be explained solely by improved detection of existing cases. The trend is also not unique to Canada. International comparative studies of STD rates among youth in developed countries suggest that Canada has lower gonorrhea rates among teens of both sexes than the United States, comparable rates to England and Wales, and higher rates than Sweden, France, Finland, Belgium, and Denmark (Panchaud et al. 2000). In the case of chlamydia, rates in the mid-1990s were high in all but Belgium and France among these comparator countries, with Belgium and France showing the most sizeable rates of decline in chlamydia rates among teens from 1990-1996. Subsequent increases in Canada and other developed countries will require a revisiting of this analysis, along with an explanation for the recent upward trend.

STD rates vary considerably between provinces, reflecting differences in age structure, migration, and socioeconomic circumstances. For example, in 2000, the national gonorrhea rate of 20.2/100,000 included values of 0-6/100,000 in Newfoundland, PEI, and New Brunswick, 6.0-9.1/100,000 in Nova Scotia and Quebec, respectively, 16.9-24.2/100,000 in Yukon Territories, British Columbia, Alberta, and Ontario, 44.7-57.3/100,000 in Saskatchewan and Manitoba, respectively, and 318-346/100,000 in the Northwest Territories and Nunavut. Overall, the gonorrhea rate in Canada has declined by more than 50% in the last 10 years, even with the increases from 1997-2000. The national goal to eliminate endemically acquired gonorrhea by 2010 will require efforts to reverse that trend. In the case of

infectious syphilis, the national goal set in 1996-97 was to maintain rates below 0.5/100,000, which was seen at the time as the most realistic option, given the low likelihood of a global eradication plan. More recently, in response to a localized outbreak of syphilis in Vancouver, British Columbia, and several neighboring regions, Wong and Jordan (2000) renewed the call for a national strategy to eradicate endemic syphilis in Canada.

Given that the Royal Commission on New Reproductive Technologies identified STDs as the primary preventable cause of infertility among Canadians, the continuing high incidence of chlamydial infection, particularly among young women, is a major concern that might also be well served by a national elimination strategy. Both diagnosis and treatment for chlamydia are widely available in Canada, but there are significant problems with control of this disease, because many people show no symptoms, the duration of infectiousness is long, and many people do not complete their course of medication if symptoms clear up quickly (Gully & Peeling 1994). These issues are particularly significant for teenage females who have the highest rates in Canada for chlamydia (Table 14).

Among the nonreportable STDs, herpes simplex 2, and human papilloma virus (HPV) infections are the most worrisome in Canada. Although it is difficult to obtain accurate national data, the evidence suggests that HPV is becoming more common, particularly in the younger age groups. Herpes simplex 2 seroprevalence has probably also increased in Canada in the last ten years as in the U.S. There were approximately 55,000 recorded patient visits for genital herpes in Canada in 1993, a number that includes multiple visits and probably underestimates the prevalence of infection.

There have been no studies specifically addressing perception of risk for STDs, and actions taken by individuals to prevent STDs, though studies on prevention of sexual transmission of HIV/AIDS, and some on contraceptive use also address STD prevention through condom use. In the Santé Quebec study (1991), about 50% of women and 60% of men in all age categories perceived themselves to be at risk

**Table 14**

**Rates for Selected Sexually Transmitted Diseases Among Canadian Teens (15-19 Years of Age) (1997-2000)**

| | | Males | | Females | |
|---|---|---|---|---|---|
| | | Cases | Rate/ 100,000[1] | Cases | Rate/ 100,000[1] |
| Chlamydia | 1997 | 1,510 | 145.6 | 9,588 | 971.6 |
| | 1998 | 1,934 | 184.0 | 10,599 | 1,063.4 |
| | 1999 | 1,976 | 186.7 | 11,428 | 1,138.9 |
| | 2000 | 2,339 | 220.0 | 12,451 | 1,236.1 |
| Gonococcal infections | 1997 | 333 | 31.5 | 725 | 69.7 |
| | 1998 | 327 | 31.1 | 799 | 80.2 |
| | 1999 | 337 | 31.8 | 798 | 79.5 |
| | 2000 | 435 | 40.9 | 971 | 96.4 |
| Infectious syphilis | 1997 | 1 | 0.1 | 2 | 0.2 |
| | 1998 | 2 | 0.2 | 5 | 0.5 |
| | 1999 | 1 | 0.1 | 8 | 0.8 |
| | 2000 | 0 | 0.0 | 7 | 0.7 |

[1]Age specific rates.

*Data source*: Division of Sexual Health Promotion and STD Prevention and Control, Bureau of HIV/AIDS, STD & TB, Health Canada 2002.

of contracting an STD. When asked what factors they thought would increase the likelihood of their using condoms (responses were "agree," "more or less agree," "disagree"), the statement "partner requested it" was the only one that received more "agree" than "disagree" responses (66% agree, 23% disagree). Other suggested options that might have influenced condom use were: if condoms were less expensive (32% agree, 54% disagree), condoms were more accessible (38% vs. 53%), thinner condoms (26% vs. 58%), better knowledge about how to use them (24% vs. 69%), and more use of condoms by those around me (36% vs. 55%).

## B. HIV/AIDS

The tragedy of HIV/AIDS has focused public attention on a wide range of sexual, ethical, and public policy issues touching all segments of society. Its devastating impact on gay men, on people with hemophilia, and increasingly on other segments in society, has forced Canadians to address not only the pragmatic aspects of prevention and treatment, but also the core questions of homophobia, discrimination (not only toward gay men and lesbians, but also toward people who are ill or disabled), our attitudes toward different sexual practices, our comfort with explicit discussions of sexual behavior, and a broad range of issues unresolved during the "sexual revolution" of the 1960s and the "gay rights revolution" of the 1970s.

### Incidence, Patterns, and Trends

As of June 30, 2002, Health Canada's Centre for Infectious Disease Prevention and Control (CIPDC) had received reports of 18,336 cases of AIDS (90.9% in adult men, 7.8% in adult women, and 1.1% in children under 15 (see Table 15). However, estimates in the 1990s indicated that only about 85% of cases will eventually be reported (i.e., for a variety of reasons, underreporting is about 15%). Because there are also delays in reporting in any year and because the annual figures are corrected for such delays and for underreporting, Canada has probably had closer to 14,000 cases of AIDS in adults to the end of 1993. Based on these adjusted estimates, the growth in the number of cases

### Table 15

### Reported Cases of AIDS in Canada as of June 30, 2002[1]

| Adults | Total Reported Cases | Percent of Total | Reported Deaths |
|---|---|---|---|
| Male | 16,669 | 90.9 | 11,721 |
| Female | 1,437 | 7.8 | 814 |
| Subtotal | 18,124[4] | 98.7 | 12,535 |
| **Children[2]** | | | |
| Male | 111 | 0.6 | NR |
| Female | 97 | 0.5 | NR |
| Subtotal | 208 | 1.1 | 117 |
| **Total** | 18,336[5] | 100.0 | 12,652[3] |

[1]*Source*: Health Canada, HIV/AIDS in Canada. *Surveillance Report to June 30, 2002*, Division of HIV/AIDS Epidemiology and Surveillance, Centre for Infectious Disease prevention and Control, Health Canada.

[2]Children under 15 years of age.

[3]Delays for both AIDS reporting and death reporting make it inadvisable to subtract the latter from the former to calculate the number of Canadians living with AIDS.

[4]Subtotal includes 18 cases where gender was unknown.

[5]Total includes 4 cases where age was unknown.

of people with AIDS in Canada is as follows (value is total cases for the indicated time period): 1979-83 (107); 1984-88 (3,889); 1989 (1,668), 1990 (1,756); 1991 (1,906); 1992 (2,267); 1993 (2,379).

During the period between April 1991 and March 1992, Canada had an annual AIDS incidence rate of 5.7 cases per 100,000 person years. Compared to the 31 European countries, this incidence rate was higher than all but Spain, Switzerland, France, and Italy. However, for this time period, Canada's 5.7 per 100,000 incidence rate was substantially lower than the 17.7 per 100,000 rate in the United States (Remis & Sutherland 1993). Based on known cases of people with AIDS reported in Canada during 1992 ($n = 1,330$), 93.9% were male and 6.1% female, distributed according to age as follows: 0 to 14 years (1.2%); 15 to 19 (0.2%); 20 to 24 (2.3%); 25 to 29 (12.9%); 30 to 39 (46.2%); 40 to 59 (34.9%), 60 and over (2.3%).

It is estimated that over 80% of the deaths to date have been gay men. While men who have sex with men accounted for 79% of all new cases of AIDS in 1987, that percentage had dropped to 69% in 1994 (*CCDR* 1996). In contrast, injection drug use, which was the risk factor associated with 1% of new cases in 1987, accounted for 6% of cases reported in 1994. Based on the experience of AIDS in adults to 1994, the risk factors identified with transmission were: homosexual/bisexual activity (77%), injection drug use (3%), both of the above (4%), heterosexual activity (9%), receiving HIV-infected blood or clotting factor (4%), and no identified risk factor (4%) (LCDC 1994).

It is unknown how many people in Canada are currently infected with HIV. One estimate from the *Canadian Communicable Disease Report* (1992) put the number at 30,000 to 40,000. In the 1996 *CCDR*, the estimate was 45,000. Estimates cited by Remis and Sutherland (1993) state that the prevalence of HIV infection among homosexually active men is 10 to 15%. The same report cites seroprevalence estimates in intravenous drug users ranging from 1 to 2% in the city of Toronto to 15 to 20% in the city of Montreal. Seroprevalence estimates from seven separate studies on adult women indicate seroprevalence rates per 1,000 adult women of 0.1 in Alberta, Saskatchewan, Manitoba, Prince Edward Island, Yukon, and Northwest Territories, 0.2 to 0.3 in British Columbia, Ontario, New Brunswick, and Nova Scotia, 0.6 in Quebec, and 1.2 in Newfoundland. Four provinces, Ontario, British Columbia, Alberta, and Quebec, account for 95% of all cases in Canada.

Shifts in the epidemiology of the disease and the potential for further change make it difficult to predict the incidence and distribution of HIV infection among specific populations. For example, the proportion of cases of AIDS in adults resulting from male-to-male sexual transmission has been steadily decreasing from 81.5% in 1988 to 73.5% in 1992 and 1993. The proportion of adults with AIDS who are injection drug users has been increasing from 4.6% in 1988 to 10.2% in 1993 (LCDC 1994). The number of people who acquired AIDS from blood products (hemophiliacs and others) peaked in 1988 and blood testing initiated in 1985 has almost eliminated this risk factor. (A national commission is currently investigating the Canadian blood supply [Krever Commission] and may identify populations who received blood products during or prior to 1985, but have not been notified or tested.) Reported cases of AIDS in women increased in each of the three-year periods between 1982 and 1990, and the cumulative incidence of AIDS in women in Quebec is almost four times the national average (probably because of the higher number of immigrants from countries where AIDS is more common) (Remis & Sutherland 1993).

## Prevention, Treatment, Government Programs, and Policies

The development of strategies and policies to prevent the spread of HIV infection has required basic research on Canadians' knowledge about AIDS, their attitudes toward people with AIDS, their perception of the government's role in prevention and treatment, and on aspects of their behavior that might place them at risk of infection. As of the mid-1980s, there had been no large-scale national surveys available as a basis for addressing such questions. In late 1988, the Institute for Social Research at York University conducted a national telephone interview survey of a representative sample of 1,259 Canadian adults to obtain data relevant to these issues (Ornstein 1989). By the time of the survey, there had been considerable public discussion about AIDS in the media and most respondents were knowledgeable about transmission, the distinction between AIDS and HIV infection, and the effectiveness of different methods of prevention. Nevertheless, 26% believed that blood donors were at risk of infection and another 5% did not know. In addition, a sizable minority (9 to 12%) believed that HIV could be spread by food preparation, that it could be cured if treated early, and that people who were infectious would show symptoms of the disease. Another 12 to 18% did not know the answers to these questions.

Among the groups or agencies that respondents perceived as having a major responsibility for AIDS education (as opposed to "some" or "should not be involved"), parents were identified most often (82%), followed by doctors and STD clinics (about 75%), and federal and provincial governments, public health agencies, and community AIDS organizations (58 to 70%). While 45.6% said churches should have some responsibility, 35.2% said they should not be involved. It is perhaps a reflection of Canadians' deference to medical and parental authority that doctors and parents were rated so highly, since neither group has been a major source of HIV/AIDS information for most people. Indeed, television and newspapers were the most frequent sources of AIDS information identified by respondents (39% and 23%, respectively).

Ornstein (1989) summarized his findings on Canadian attitudes toward some of the sociopolitical aspects of AIDS as follows:

1. Sixty-nine percent of Canadians would permit their child to continue to attend a school class taught by a teacher who was infected with HIV, and another 8% would do so with qualifications.
2. Eighty percent of Canadians believe that HIV-infected persons should be legally protected from discrimination by landlords and employers. [*Note*: Discrimination in employment based on HIV status is generally prohibited in Canada, and people with AIDS cannot be summarily dismissed because of that status.]
3. By more than a two-to-one majority, Canadians support anonymous testing for HIV. [*Note*: Although AIDS is a reportable disease, anonymous testing for HIV infection is available in some clinics. In addition, samples may be submitted anonymously by a physician who knows the identity of the donor.]
4. There is very strong support for allowing physicians to demand a test for HIV from patients they suspect to be infected, and for compelling HIV-infected individuals to disclose the names of their sexual contacts.
5. About 60% of Canadians oppose providing needles to injection drug users. [*Note*: Needle-exchange programs are now operating successfully in a number of Canadian cities.]
6. A nearly two-to-one majority indicates support for allowing high school students to obtain condoms in their schools (Ornstein 1989, 101).

## HIV/AIDS Issues in Various Ethnocultural Communities

In late 1989 and early 1990, Health Canada (then called Health and Welfare Canada) initiated national consultations to identify the specific needs of ethnocultural communities with respect to HIV/AIDS prevention. The *Ethnocultural Communities Facing AIDS* project arose from those discussions. Epidemiological and demographic data gathered in the first phase were used to identify six participating communities (South Asian and Chinese in Vancouver, communities from the Horn of Africa and English-speaking Caribbean communities, and Latin American and Arabic-speaking communities in Montreal). Community-identified representatives for each group formed the six Regional Research Groups, which met regularly with the researchers. Each community group included community leaders, healthcare professionals, people working in the AIDS field, and others. Six in-depth reports were produced as a result of the qualitative research (focus groups in each community and interviews) (Health Canada 1994a-f; available from the National AIDS Clearinghouse). The reports illustrate "the ways in which individual life experiences in the country of origin, combined with the challenges of recent emigration, can affect sexual health." Selected observations from the reports give an indication of the type and complexity of issues involved for the different communities.

Many recent immigrants find Canada to be a country of relatively liberal sexual values compared to their country of origin. Because they often come to Canada with more conservative sexual norms and customs than found in "mainstream" Canadian culture, members of some ethnocultural groups require HIV/AIDS-prevention education programs that are designed to be culturally appropriate for their particular group. In some of these ethnocultural communities, an explicit discussion of sexuality between parents and children or between men and women is taboo. For example, in a focus group, Punjabi women discussed how "some girls do have sexual experiences before marriage, but will never talk about them because doing so would 'wreck their reputation'" (Health Canada 1994e, 11). Or as a woman from the Horn of Africa commented, "Since our childhood, sex was presented to us negatively, and there is no way we can appreciate talking about it" (Health Canada 1994b, 16).

In addition, in some of these culturally distinct Canadian communities, there is a denial of the existence of gay, lesbian, and bisexual behavior among community members. As one focus-group participant from the South Asian community suggested, "A man who has sex with men won't accept the fact that he is gay" (Health Canada 1994e, 12). Or, as told by a study participant from the Horn of Africa, "People do not want to acknowledge or believe that homosexual behavior, or gay men, lesbians, and bisexuals, exist in their community. This denial leads those men and women who want to have same sex relationships to hide their behavior 'in the closet'" (Health Canada 1994b, 14).

Negotiating condom use is particularly difficult in some of these communities. For example, in the Chinese communities, "Most people who participated in interviews and focus groups report that condoms are not being used to prevent AIDS and other STDs. Women feel they are powerless to instigate condom use with their husbands or male partners, because it raises issues of 'trust' and 'promiscuity'" (Health Canada 1994f, 13). In some ethnocultural communities, condoms are seen as preventing a male from fulfilling his role in procreation or in maintaining his family line or the racial group. A woman from the English-speaking Caribbean islands suggests that within her communities, "There's a general conception that the condom equals genocide. You commonly hear men saying, 'my seed has to flow'" (Health Canada 1994c, 12).

The findings of the qualitative phase of the *Ethnocultural Communities Facing AIDS* project illustrate that the values, norms, and customs related to the discussion of sexuality, sexual orientation, gender roles, and condom use, among other issues, are sometimes unique to particular ethnocultural communities. In the third survey phase of this project, questions were asked about various sexual experiences, risk perception, condom use, and psychosocial determinants of condom use with new sexual partners. Table 16 summarizes a selection of results in each of these communities.

Perceptions of personal risk and of the degree to which AIDS poses a problem varied between communities. For example, respondents from the Latin American communities were most likely, and those from the South Asian communities were least likely, to consider AIDS a problem in their communities. South Asian men were least likely, by far, to consider themselves at risk for HIV infection and also the least likely to have been tested for HIV. No more than four individuals from any of the communities reported that they had tested positive for HIV infection. Reports of condom use with new partners support the conclusion that a minority in each of the communities is using condoms consistently. There was no statistical association between frequency of condom use and perception of risk in any of the communities.

The survey also examined the major psychosocial determinants of planning to use condoms in future sexual relationships. Both the strength of these determinants and their specific content varied across the communities. These results, together with those from the qualitative phase, underscore the need in Canada to develop HIV/AIDS intervention strategies suitable for the target audience's ethnocultural identity.

## National, Provincial, and Local Resources for Prevention

The Canadian AIDS Society, a coalition of over 90 local AIDS Committees and other community-based organizations, is actively involved in advocacy, public education, treatment, care, and support for people with AIDS. Most community AIDS initiatives in Canada began in, and are sustained by the gay community, with support from all levels of government and the local community. The second revised edition of the Society's *Safer Sex Guidelines* (Canadian AIDS Society 1994) provides authoritative guidance for educators and counselors on assessing the risk of HIV transmission via different sexual behaviors and on reducing that risk.

## Safer Sex Practices of Selected Populations

*Gay and Bisexual Men.* In 1991-92, the first national survey in Canada to assess possible effects of different variables on HIV-test-seeking and sexual behavior of men who have sex with men was conducted in 35 cities across Canada (Myers et al. 1993). The sample of 4,803 men (20.9% over the age of 22) was recruited from gay-identified settings in seven geographical regions, and questionnaires, administered in English or French, were used for data collection. The salient measure of sexual risk-taking reported in the study was at least one instance of unprotected anal intercourse in the previous three months. Overall, 22.9% reported at least one instance of unprotected anal intercourse (15% reported having had unprotected receptive anal intercourse), 64.7% said that they had had an HIV test, and 11.8% reported that they were HIV-positive.

Comparisons based on city size (cities under 500,000, 500,000 to 1 million, and over 1 million), indicated that those from smaller cities were considerably less likely to have been tested (55.2% vs. 63.2 and 69.2%) and somewhat more likely to have engaged in unprotected anal intercourse (26.3% vs. 23.5% and 20.9%).

Lévy et al. (1994a) reported higher levels of condom use during anal sex among francophone gay men who were in occasional versus stable partnerships, and lower levels of condom use in both groups during oral sex (Table 17). The findings are consistent with other reports of increased use of safer-sex practices among multipartnered gay men.

*High School Students.* The *Canada Youth and AIDS Study* reported on the knowledge, attitudes, and behavior with respect to AIDS of over 38,000 Canadian youth aged 11 to 21 (King et al. 1988). The study, which provided a fairly comprehensive picture of the sexual behavior of Canadian high school students, found that 31% of males and 21% of females had had intercourse by grade 9. By grade 11, these percentages increased to 49% for males and 46% for females. AIDS was second to pregnancy as the outcome of sexual intercourse that high school students worried most about. Although this study did not measure condom use among high school students, 48% held negative attitudes toward condoms.

In a late-1980s study of grade 11 students ($N = 1,275$, average age 17 years) in

## Table 16

**Selected Responses to Questions Related to HIV/AIDS Risk and Perception of Risk in Communities Participating in the Ethnocultural Communities Facing AIDS Project**

| | Percentage Responding in Each Category | | | | |
| | English-Speaking Caribbean | | South Asian | Latin American | |
| | Women ($N = 190$) | Men ($N = 187$) | Men ($N = 364$) | Women ($N = 176$) | Men ($N = 176$) |
|---|---|---|---|---|---|
| AIDS is a problem in our community: | | | | | |
| Agree | 50 | 48 | 30 | 90 | 86 |
| Neither agree nor disagree | 11 | 8 | 39 | 7 | 11 |
| Disagree | 38 | 44 | 32 | 2 | 3 |
| Believe at risk for HIV infection: | | | | | |
| Yes | 32 | 30 | 11 | 29 | 40 |
| Maybe | 38 | 41 | 29 | 30 | 25 |
| No | 30 | 29 | 60 | 40 | 35 |
| Have been tested for HIV | 38 | 37 | 21 | 30 | 32 |
| Frequency of condom use with new partners: | | | | | |
| Never | 12 | 6 | 13 | 12 | 14 |
| Sometimes | 62 | 66 | 38 | 59 | 56 |
| Always | 26 | 29 | 47 | 28 | 30 |

Data adapted from Maticka-Tyndale et al. 1996.

Montreal, Quebec, Joanne Otis and her colleagues found that 53% of respondents who had had intercourse (about 60% of both sexes) said they used a condom the first time. Only 18.2% said they did so constantly thereafter; 67.2% reported using the pill for contraception (Otis et al. 1990). The best predictor of a student's stated intention to use a condom with a future new partner was whether or not the female was using oral contraception, i.e., the intention to use condoms was lowest if it was assumed that the female would be taking the pill, and greatest if she was not. Otis et al. (1990) proposed that Canadian educators should reinforce the acceptability and desirability of condom use with a new partner, even if the female partner is using oral contraception (see also Otis et al. 1994). In a recent review of studies on adolescent sexual behavior, Otis et al. (1996) made the following observations related to HIV prevention among high school students in Quebec in 1995: (1) 50 to 75% said they had used a condom at first intercourse, an increase between 1988 and 1995; (2) about 50 to 60% of all sexual contacts involved condom use and 13 to 48% used a condom in all their sexual relations; (3) 22% of 15-year-olds and 39% of 18-year-olds said they had taken an STD test and 14% of high school teens had taken an HIV test. In the population of adolescents surveyed at youth or leisure clubs and at youth centers (for young people with social or other problems), the numbers were higher in all categories. For example, at youth and leisure clubs, 65% reported condom use at first intercourse, 38% used condoms in all their sexual relations, and 41% had taken an HIV test.

Studies in the provinces of Alberta and Nova Scotia have also reported on the frequency of condom use among high school students. In the Alberta study, 41% of "sexually active" high school students indicated that they either did not or infrequently used condoms, and 59% reported that they frequently or always used condoms during sexual intercourse (Varnhagen et al. 1991). In one study of Nova Scotia high school students, 55% reported using condoms "more than just some of time"; 35% always used condoms (Langille et al. 1994). Another school-based survey in Nova Scotia (Poulin 1996) found approximately 61% of grade 12

## Table 17

### Condom Use and Sexual Behavior in Francophone Gay Men: A Comparison of Men in Stable Partnerships and Men with Occasional Partners

| Sexual Activity in Past Six Months | Percentage of the Group Reporting the Behavior | |
|---|---|---|
| | Stable Partnerships[1] (*N* = 276) | Occasional Partners[2] (*N* = 336) |
| Fellatio (active) | 92.6 | 92.8 |
| Used condom[3] | 3.8 | 9.4 |
| Fellatio (received) | 94.1 | 96.7 |
| Used condom | 3.9 | 6.4 |
| Anal sex (active) | 54.6 | 43.0 |
| Used condom | 61.3 | 90.7 |
| Anal sex (received) | 51.5 | 34.8 |
| Used condom | 59.9 | 92.9 |

[1]66% said the relationship was exclusive.
[2]29% said they had one partner in the last 6 months (Average for group = 10).
[3]Condom used means in all such activities in the previous 6 months. Data from Levy et al. (1994a).

students having had sexual intercourse during the past year, 40% indicating they had had two or more sexual partners. Of those who were sexually active, only 32% reported always using a condom.

Although the reported frequency of condom use among Canadian high school students is less than adequate for HIV/AIDS prevention, this group appears to use condoms more frequently than either college/university students (e.g., King et al. 1988; Ramsum et al. 1993) or adults (e.g., Ontario Ministry of Health 1992).

*College/University Students.* Because they are mostly young, single, highly sexually active, and accessible to researchers, college/university students have been widely used in studies of knowledge, attitudes, and behaviors related to HIV/AIDS. The *Canada Youth and AIDS* study found that among college students, 77% of males and 73% of females had at least one experience of intercourse. Sixty-eight percent of the males and 64% of the females reported having oral sex; 14% of the males and 16% of the females reported having anal sex. Numbers of partners for males and females, respectively, was: one (23%, 36%); two (12%, 17%), three to five (29%, 26%), six to ten (17%, 14%), and 11 or more (19%, 7%). Forty-four percent of males and 30% of females identified AIDS as the outcome of sex that worried them most (pregnancy was much higher at about 60%, and other STDs much lower at 4%). When those who had intercourse were asked about condom use, the responses for males and females, respectively, were: always (19%, 11%), most of the time (16%, 9%), sometimes (43%, 52%), and never (22%, 28%) (King et al. 1988).

A comparison of British Columbia university students surveyed in 1988 (in the same year as the *Canada Youth and AIDS* study), and again in 1992, indicated no change in the number who reported being sexually active within the last six months (62%), a slight decline in the proportion with multiple partners (i.e., 2 to 7 partners in the last 6 months) from 30% to 24% of those who were sexually active, and some increase in the proportion using condoms "always" (17% to 25% in 1992) or "most times" (6% to 15%). However, the number reporting never used condoms (51% vs. 40% in 1992) or sometimes used (26% vs. 20% in 1992) remained high (Ramsum et al. 1993). This study is consistent with the findings of other studies of university students that have found that, although they are highly knowledgeable about HIV/AIDS, this group's perceived risk has not been sufficient to overcome some of the barriers to consistent condom use (e.g., immediate accessibility, inconvenience, peergroup perceptions, religious beliefs, influence of alcohol, etc.) (Ramsum et al. 1993).

Another study of college students in Montreal found that perceived risk of HIV infection was correlated with having a friend who had had an HIV test and having more than one coital partner. For women, the level of trust in a relationship was also correlated with perceived risk of HIV ("I trust this person, I must be at low risk"). For men, their confidence in their ability to assess whether or not it was necessary to use condoms with a particular partner was also correlated with perceived risk of HIV infection (Maticka-Tyndale & Lévy 1993). Recent reviews on condom use among college students in Quebec (Otis et al. 1996; Samson et al. 1996) found: 47 to 67% used condoms at first intercourse, an increase from 1983-1995; condom use was less common with a regular partner (38%) than with occasional partners (66%; 34% had taken an STD test and 14% an HIV test). The comparable findings among university students (Otis et al. 1996) were: 42.5% said they used condoms at first intercourse, fewer used condoms with a regular partner (34%)

than with an occasional partner (88%), and 14% had taken an HIV test. Current prevention efforts with this group are increasingly using theoretically based approaches to behavior change (Fisher & Fisher 1992) that stress information, motivation, and behavioral skills (IMB), and identification with people known to have AIDS (i.e., influencing personal perception of risk). Because empirical research increasingly indicates that educational interventions based on an IMB approach are successful in helping people perform sexual health problem-prevention behavior, the IMB approach is recommended by Health Canada's *Canadian Guidelines for Sexual Health Education* (Minister of Supply and Services Canada 1994).

*Street Youth.* Street youth represent a particularly high-risk group for HIV infection because of the greater likelihood of involvement in prostitution, IV-drug use, unprotected homosexual or bisexual activity, and backgrounds of family disruption, abuse, and attendant low self-esteem. As part of the *Canada Youth and AIDS* study, 712 street youth aged 15 to 20 were interviewed about their sexual practices and HIV-risk behavior (Radford et al. 1990). Ninety-four percent of the sample was sexually active, 32% never used condoms, 32% used condoms sometimes or most times, and 26% always used condoms; 75% used drugs and 12% occasionally injected drugs (half using shared needles). Needle-exchange programs in several major cities have helped reduce the spread of HIV in street youth, but this selected population remains at high risk and is therefore the focus of significant outreach programs by a variety of youth-serving agencies. The First National Conference on HIV/AIDS and Youth held in Toronto in 1989 led to publication of a *National Inventory of AIDS Organizations for Youth*, listing over a hundred such organizations and agencies across Canada.

More recent studies of street youth (Frappier & Roy 1995; McCreary Centre Society 1994) indicate that 85 to 98% have had sexual intercourse. For over 60%, age of first intercourse was before 13 years. Fifty-two to 78% reported having six or more sexual partners in their lifetime, with many reporting inconsistent condom use.

*First Nations People.* Few studies have investigated the incidence of HIV infection among First Nations People in Canada. One study of a high-risk population in the city of Vancouver found an infection rate of 6% among First Nations People (Rekart et al. 1991).

The *Ontario First Nations AIDS and Healthy Lifestyle Survey* (Myers et al. 1993) is the largest Canadian study to date on the HIV/AIDS-related knowledge, attitudes, and behavior of First Nations People. At the time the study was initiated in 1989-90, there was little AIDS education for this population, but there was significant concern about the risk of infection in such close communities with a tradition of early sexual activity and ongoing experience of "social, economic, psychological, spiritual, and political concerns" and of other factors contributing to "the inequities in health that First Nations People experience" (Myers et al. 1993). Consultation with four Provincial Territorial organizations (Association of Iroquois and Allied Indians, Grand Council Treaty Number Three, Nishnawbe-Aski Nation, and the Union of Ontario Indians) resulted in interviews with 658 individuals (about an equal number of males and females) from 11 First Nations communities across Ontario.

In this sample of First Nations People, overall knowledge of HIV/AIDS was relatively low. For example, although 97.6% knew that "A person can get AIDS from having sex without a condom with someone who has AIDS," 85.3% incorrectly believed that donating blood could result in HIV infection for the donor; 18.3% gave an incorrect answer and

49.1% were uncertain in response to the item "Using Vaseline with a condom makes it weak and easier to break." Of the respondents who had heard of AIDS, 6.8% reported having been tested for HIV (7.8% of this group had tested positive) and 71.9% felt they had no risk for HIV infection. An additional 18.9% felt they had only a small chance of getting AIDS. About 40% of the men and 18% of the women had two or more sexual partners in the past year. Approximately 16% of the respondents reported having participated in anal sex at least once in their lifetime. In the 12 months prior to the survey, 29.8% of the respondents reported no sexual activity, 44.8% inconsistently used HIV-infection prevention measures when having sex, 12.1% never used condoms for vaginal or anal intercourse, and 13.3% reported engaging in only mutual masturbation or always using condoms for vaginal and anal intercourse. A recent analysis of the data on condom use from the study identifies a range of sociodemographic and behavioral factors associated with use or non-use of condoms, and discusses the findings in the context of the limited research available on safer-sex practices in First Nations populations (Burchall 1997).

The authors of the Ontario First Nations AIDS and Healthy Lifestyle Survey concluded from their findings that in order to be successful, HIV/AIDS-prevention efforts aimed at First Nations People must be culturally appropriate. They write, "The approach must be holistic and rooted in the culture, traditions, and customs of aboriginal communities, and therefore must embrace the entire community including the youth, parents, elders, and community leaders" (Myers et al. 1993, 63). For a country of considerable multicultural diversity, this principle of cultural appropriateness is an important facet of HIV/AIDS-prevention efforts aimed at Canadian audiences.

### The Direct and Indirect Costs of AIDS

Efforts to figure the costs of AIDS commonly focus on calculating the direct medical costs of treating persons with HIV and AIDS, the costs of healthcare professionals' salaries, research, hospital care, medication, and psychological support for affected families and close relatives. The direct medical costs of treating one Canadian with HIV/AIDS from the time of infection to death is estimated at between $150,000 and $215,000.

Seldom, if ever, considered are the indirect costs of the disease in lost future earnings caused by AIDS-related deaths. In a pioneering 1995 study sponsored by the British Columbia Center for Excellence in HIV/AIDS, economist Robin Hanvelt and colleagues (1994) estimated that AIDS has already cost Canada $3.3 billion in lost future earnings for all the men aged 25 to 64 years old who died from AIDS between 1987 and 1992. The average estimated loss of future earnings per death was $651,200 in 1990 figures. The total loss in future earnings attributable to HIV/AIDS in Canada was exceeded only by those for ischemic heart disease, suicide, motor-vehicle accidents, and lung cancer. Hanvelt believes his calculations, based on a six-year study of 5,038 Canadian men who died of HIV/AIDS, are conservative. While the annual future loss of income remained relatively stable or declined for other causes of death, earnings lost through HIV- and AIDS-related deaths more than doubled from $309 million in 1987 to $817 million in 1992. Hanvelt estimates that the indirect costs of AIDS-related deaths in Canada will exceed $1.5 billion in 1996.

Combining estimates of direct and indirect costs of HIV/AIDS provides a clearer and more realistic picture of the social costs in terms of lost creativity, skills, knowledge, and productivity resulting from the premature death of thousands of young people.

[*Update 2002*: UNAIDS Epidemiological Assessment: It is often instructive to examine the rates of HIV infection by subgroup. However, it should be noted that estimates of positive HIV-test results by exposure category are limited to the extent that such statistics reflect only those cases where exposure category is reported. As a result, these figures tend to underestimate total exposure rates by category and are much lower than overall totals.

[Information on HIV prevalence among pregnant women is available since 1989. HIV-prevalence studies among pregnant women indicate an overall rate for Canada of between 3 and 4 per 10,000. Large metropolitan areas generally have higher prevalence rates: for example, 5.1 per 10,000 for Vancouver versus 1.9 per 10,000 for the rest of British Columbia province (outside Vancouver) in 1989 to 1994; 13 to 20 per 10,000 for Montreal versus 0 to 3.5 per 10,000 for the rest of Quebec in 1994 to 1995. Although women in general continue to be a minority of those newly infected with HIV, it is noteworthy to examine the absolute number of new positive HIV-test results for females from 1995 to 2000. While a decline was noted from 1995 to 1996 to 1997 (528, 541, and 456 cases, respectively), this did not continue in 1998, 1999, and 2000 (493, 544, and 544 cases) (Health Canada 2001).

[For sex workers (both male and female), there are six HIV-prevalence studies that had such information. Overall, between 1985 and 1993 and in major urban centers, the prevalence rates ranged from 1.9% for sex workers only and 1 to 22% for sex workers who were also injection drug users.

[Recent prevalence data on men who have sex with men in Canada shows a decline until 1998, which leveled off in 1999 and appears to have increased in 2000. The 2000 increase is the first noted since the 1980s. Prior to this time, there had been a trend toward decline in positive HIV reports among men who have sex with men (Health Canada 2001). Studies of specific cohorts in Vancouver have also shown this trend, but not in Montreal (Martindale et al. 2001; Remis et al. 2001).

[In examining the rates of positive HIV-test reports among injection drug users in Canada, one sees a general decline from 1995 to 2000. For example, the highest rates of incidence and reporting in some of the larger cities in 1996 (about 500 new cases) appears to have dropped notably in 2000 (about 300 new cases) (Health Canada 2001; Patrick et al. 2001). Nevertheless, it is unclear whether this decline is a function of saturation of the highest risk populations as opposed to the success of public policy (Patrick, Wong, & Jordan 2000).

[Among clients at STD clinics, HIV prevalence rates in sites outside major urban areas were approximately constant at about 1% during 1985 to 1994. However, the rate in major urban areas appears to have decreased from 15.8% in early 1985 to 1988 to 1.5 to 6% in 1991 to 1995. Interpretation of the validity of this decrease is complicated by the paucity of truly comparable data.

[The gradual decline in the number of new cases of HIV infection in Canadian adults from 1995 to 1998 has not continued (Patrick, Wong & Jordan 2000). According to Health Canada (2000), the rate of decline has leveled off between 1998 and 2000.

[The estimated number of adults and children living with HIV/AIDS on January 1, 2002, were:

| | | |
|---|---|---|
| Adults ages 15-49: | 55,000 | (rate: 0.3%) |
| Women ages 15-49: | 14,000 | |
| Children ages 0-15: | < 500 | |

[An estimated less than 500 adults and children died of AIDS during 2001.

[No estimate is available for the number of Canadian children who had lost one or both parents to AIDS and were under age 15 at the end of 2001. (*End of update by the Editors*)]

## 11. Sexual Dysfunctions, Counseling, and Therapies

Dr. Stephen Neiger, the founder of the Sex Information and Education Council of Canada, was probably the first practitioner to introduce "modern" sex therapy to the Canadian scene in the early 1960s. Neiger's behavioral approach to the common sexual dysfunctions (primary or secondary anorgasmia, vaginismus, and painful intercourse in women, erectile dysfunction and premature ejaculation in men) was a contrast and challenge to the traditional belief that treatment of such problems required psychotherapy to determine their root causes. Neiger viewed many such problems as a product of inadequate education, cultural taboos, and the anxiety and negative reinforcement generated by unrealistic performance expectations. The growing North American interest in sex therapy in the early 1970s, spurred by the release of Masters and Johnson's *Human Sexual Inadequacy*, and by the prospect of rapid, symptom-oriented treatment, led to increasing demand for such help and the implicit expectation that medical professionals would be adequately trained to provide it.

While such training has indeed become more available in Canada and more accessible to Canadian therapists because of developments in the U.S., the situation at present is quite limited. Canadians do have wide access to counseling about sex-related topics, since professionals from a variety of backgrounds (physicians, social workers, psychologists, public health nurses, occupational therapists, school guidance counselors, and clergy) may be trained, to varying degrees, to assist with sexual concerns as part of their broader work requirements. They do this counseling in a variety of settings, including private practice, hospitals, community health centers, family service agencies, sexual assault centers, and so on, and are bound by the ethical standards of their professions and individual agencies. Such individuals have generally not been trained as sex therapists and would probably refer clients with problems that required such therapy. There are still few people trained as sex therapists and few opportunities for such training in Canada. The Department of Sexology at the University of Quebec at Montreal and the Department of Family Studies at the University of Guelph in Ontario are the only institutions in Canada to offer postgraduate training and degrees in sex therapy (see addresses in Section 12B, Sex Research and Advanced Professional Education, Canadian Sexological Organizations and Publications).

Since there are no official self-regulating colleges of sex therapy in the provinces or nationally as there are for other medical specialties, the question of who is a sex therapist and how they are trained is a continuing issue in Canada. Alexander's (1990) review of sexual therapy in English-speaking Canada identifies this concern about standards for training and practice as a primary reason for the formation of the Board of Examiners in Sex Therapy and Counseling in Ontario (BESTCO) in 1975. The ten founding therapists, all members of the Ontario Association for Marriage and Family Therapy (OAMFT), established criteria for training and certification of therapists that they then applied to themselves and to subsequent members. They assumed that provincial or national certification of sex therapists was imminent and that the group would be prepared for that event. That step toward regulation of sex therapists has not taken place. BESTCO remains the only group in Canada that has a formal, nonstatutory certification procedure for certifying already-accredited marriage and family therapists who wish to have their specialization in sex therapy recognized by a body of their peers.

Some sex therapists in Canada are certified by the American Association of Sex Educators, Counselors, and Therapists (AASECT), by the U.S.-based Society for Sex Therapy and Research (SSTAR), by the American Board of Sexology, and/or by other comparable international organizations specifically identified with sex therapy; others are certified for work in their field, e.g., medicine, nursing, psychology, pastoral counseling, marriage and family therapy, and related fields, which may or may not require specific advanced training before unsupervised practice in sex therapy can be done. For example, physicians can do sex therapy but do not have a formal requirement for certification of that specialty, despite the scarcity of such training in most medical schools. On the other hand, there are many physicians in Canada who are specialists in sexual medicine, but whose specialty is still not recognized by the Royal College of Physicians and Surgeons of Canada.

Only physicians and psychiatrists are permitted to bill the provincial health plans for sex therapy services, but their numbers are insufficient to meet the demand. Private sex therapy can be expensive for the average person, although some insurance plans will cover part of the cost of therapy if done by psychologists, social workers, or other health professionals covered by specific plans. Because of Canada's size and the location of therapists in large urban centers, sex therapy is simply not available to most people in smaller communities.

Canada has also had a chronic shortage of trained therapists who can work with people with paraphilias, gender disorders, psychiatric disorders, or medical conditions with sexual implications. Professionals who treat children and adults who have been sexually abused or assaulted, and those working with sex offenders, also require more training in sexuality than is currently available.

Sex therapists are expected to have accredited training in marital, family, and relationship therapy and to then acquire advanced skills and experience in sex therapy. The options for the latter in Canada include:

1. attending the week-long, Intensive Sex Therapy Training Institute offered at the University of Guelph, Ontario, prior to the annual Guelph Sexuality Conference;
2. obtaining supervision time with a therapist credentialed as a supervisor by a recognized accrediting body (AASECT, BESTCO, etc.);
3. taking the clinical training program in the Department of Sexology in the University of Quebec at Montreal (in French); or
4. becoming a member of a sexual medicine unit that trains therapists (e.g., the Sexual Medicine Unit at the University of British Columbia has had a longstanding program to train nurses and social workers as sexual healthcare clinicians, an excellent grounding for subsequent certification in sex therapy).

Continuing issues influencing the development of sex therapy in Canada include:

1. Feminist redefinition of "dysfunction" and development of new models for thinking about sexual response in the context of women's experience, rather than as a biologically mandated sequence of physiological events;
2. recent technological and pharmacological developments in the treatment of erectile dysfunction (e.g., injections and vacuum constriction devices), sexual desire disorders, and paraphilias;
3. the relationship between sex therapists and self-help movements, such as the 12-step programs for sex and love addiction (e.g., Sex and Love Addicts Anonymous);
4. the debate about the role of therapists in facilitating recovered memories of childhood sexual abuse and the therapeutic, legal, and political implications of practice in this area; and
5. dealing equitably with ethnocultural differences pertaining to sexuality. For example, the Canadian Medical Association recently banned physicians from doing the procedure referred to as ritual circumcision (Brighouse 1992) or genital mutilation (Omer-Hashi & Entwistle 1995), which is common in some parts of Africa and requested by some immigrants to Canada.

## 12. Sex Research and Advanced Professional Education

### A. Sexological Research and Postgraduate Programs

Most sexological research in Canada is done by individuals or groups linked either directly or indirectly with universities. This work almost invariably occurs within specific academic disciplines (e.g., history, sociology, psychology, women's studies, philosophy, medicine, epidemiology and public health, education, family studies, criminology, etc.) rather than in a university department of sexology. The Department of Sexology at the University of Quebec at Montreal is the only department of sexology in Canada. Founded in 1969, it offers Bachelor's and Master's programs in human sexuality taught in French by approximately 20 full-time academic staff representing many fields of specialization. The master's program, which began in 1980 and was officially recognized by the university in 1985, offers internships, projects, courses, and other practical training in counseling and sex education (Dupras 1987). Candidates for the master's program in counseling come primarily from related fields, such as medicine, psychology, criminology, and social work, while those in the education stream usually come from the Bachelor of Human Sexuality Program (Dupras 1987; Gemme 1990). The Department is the major center for research on human sexuality in Quebec and also publishes *Bibliosex, a biannual bibliography of sexuality literature in Canada and internationally.*

Some academic departments in other parts of Canada offer graduate programs in human sexuality (e.g., University of Guelph, Department of Family Studies), but it is more common for graduate research on sexuality topics to occur within master's and Ph.D. programs in specific academic disciplines. Since 1978, the Family Studies Department has sponsored an intensive week-long annual June conference and training institute on sexuality at the University of Guelph, Ontario. The Departments of Psychology at both the University of Western Ontario and the University of New Brunswick are two examples of strong graduate research training in sexuality within a particular field. The Department of Sociology and Anthropology at the University of Windsor has the largest complement of sociologists—four—in a single department who are actively conducting research in sexuality. The department offers three undergraduate courses and one graduate seminar in sexuality, and students are able to pursue an undergraduate honors or a master's degree specializing in Family and Sexuality.

A number of medical faculties also provide postgraduate training in sexology. For example, the Sexual Medicine Unit at the University of British Columbia offers a clinical and research setting through which residents in Obstetrics and Gynecology and in Psychiatry can obtain advanced training. A number of other hospitals have Sexual Medicine Units or similar specialized services (e.g., the Sexual Health Unit at Montreal General Hospital), but there have been no national reviews of postgraduate sexuality training for physicians or for any of the other health disciplines, either as it pertains to research training, the subject of this section, or sex therapy training, which was discussed in Section 11, Sexual Dysfunctions, Counseling, and Therapies.

In her report to a 1994 gathering of Chinese and North American sex educators and researchers in China, Byers (1995) noted that training in sexological research within specific disciplines is highly variable across Canada. Such training often occurs only because a faculty member hired for expertise in another academic area is also interested in sexuality. This situation makes the necessary multidisciplinary requirements of sexological training more difficult to find, and trainees, particularly in smaller centers, may not have easy access to a network of like-minded colleagues. She notes that this fragmentation has made it hard for sex research to flourish as a field in English Canada, even though individual researchers and research groups have achieved considerable recognition (Byers 1995). For example, the Gender Identity Unit at Toronto's Clarke Institute of Psychiatry is internationally known for research on transsexuality, the Social Program Evaluation Group at Queen's University in Kingston, Ontario, has published major studies on adolescent sexual behavior, the Department of Psychology program at the University of New Brunswick is well known for research on the psychology of male-female sexual interactions in dating and longer-term relationships, the Sexual Medicine Unit at the University of British Columbia is known particularly for work on sexuality, disability, and chronic illness, researchers in the Sociology and Anthropology Department at the University of Windsor have developed international reputations for their qualitative and multimethod research on homosexuality and on sexual transmission of HIV, and the research done in the Department of Psychology at the University of Western Ontario has influenced Canadian policy and practice in the prevention of teen pregnancy, STDs, and HIV infection. Despite these achievements, the discipline-based focus of much sex research has made it difficult to achieve a public profile for the sexological research community in Canada.

The Canadian Sex Research Forum, founded in 1969, is Canada's only national organization dedicated to a multidisciplinary focus on sexological research. The *Proceedings* of the CSRF meetings have been published annually by the Sex Information and Education Council of Canada, first in the *SIECCAN Newsletter* (1982-1985), then in the *SIECCAN Journal* (1986-1991), and now in the *Canadian Journal of Human Sexuality* (1992-present). In Quebec, l'Association des Sexologiques de Québec promotes various aspects of sexual science, and the biannual journal *Revue Sexologique/ Sexological Review* publishes national and international papers, the majority in French, many by Quebec researchers.

There appear to be many more people doing sexuality research in Canada than the approximately 100 Canadians who are members of CSRF and/or the Society for the Scientific Study of Sexuality (SSSS) in the United States. A systematic record of this large group would both identify, and perhaps unify, those individuals who, despite their primary identification with another academic discipline, also share a common interest in sexology. Such a record might also enhance training and supervision of sex researchers by facilitating cross-disciplinary communication. This issue is one of many that a workshop at the 1993 Canadian Sex Research Forum meeting identified as a major deficiency in

the training of many sex researchers in Canada and internationally (Aronoff, McCormick, & Byers 1994).

## B. Canadian Sexological Organizations and Publications

*Addresses of Organizations*

L'Association des Sexologues de Québec, 695 St. Denis, Suite 300, Montreal, Quebec, Canada H2S 2S3.

Sex Information and Education Council of Canada (SIECCAN), 850 Coxwell Avenue, East York, Ontario, Canada M4C 5RI.

Canadian Sex Research Forum, c/o Pierre Assalian, M.D., Executive Director, 1650 Cedar Avenue, Room B6-233, Montreal, Quebec, Canada H3G 1A4.

The Department of Sexology, University of Quebec at Montreal, 455 Boulevard Rene Levesque East, Montreal, Quebec, Canada H3C 3P8.

Planned Parenthood Federation of Canada, 1 Nicolas St., Suite 430, Ottawa, Ontario, Canada K1N 7B7.

*Sexological Publications*

Three Canadian publications provide a professional focus on sexological issues and research:

*Canadian Journal of Human Sexuality* (4 issues per year), Sex Information and Education Council of Canada (SIECCAN), 850 Coxwell Avenue, East York, Ontario, Canada M4C 5RI.

*Revue Sexologique/Sexological Review* (2 issues per year), c/o Editions I.R.I.S., 4932 rue Adam, Montreal, Quebec, Canada H1V 1W3.

*Bibliosex* (2 issues per year), c/o Professor Robert Gemme, University of Quebec at Montreal, Department of Sexology, Case Postale 8888, Canada H3C 3P8.

## Conclusions

Four themes run through this profile of sexuality in Canada. The first is of a country composed of a variety of ethnocultural groups including the oldest, aboriginal inhabitants, the dominant English and French residents, and the newer arrivals from a variety of countries. Though there has been little "group specific" research, the available evidence suggests that different groups can have quite distinctive cultural attitudes and practices in the area of sexuality. Canada's French-Canadians, about whom there has been considerable research, consistently demonstrate attitudes that are more accepting and permissive than those of other Canadians; they initiate sexual activity somewhat earlier than others and are more likely to form committed partnerships without the legal status of marriage. Quebec, the province where the majority of French-Canadians live and the location of Canada's only Department of Sexology, has demonstrated the greatest acceptance of individual choice in sexual matters and has the most egalitarian family laws of any province in the nation. Considering the historical domination of the Roman Catholic Church in Quebec, these results demonstrate the reduction of influence of religious institutions in the lives of French-Canadians, a change that is now occurring for some other groups of Canadians as well. While French-Canadians set one end of a continuum of attitudes and practices, each ethnocultural group in Canada has its own distinctive pattern of attitudes and practices, each embedded in unique communities and community institutions.

The second theme is of a country in which formal services, research, and education in sexuality are scattered and varied. In some regions, these are comprehensive and sophisticated, in others they are sparse and few. Research, graduate and postgraduate training, and therapeutic and clinical work in sexuality are not organized or provided in a coherent manner and are highly dependent on the presence of interested individuals. Sexuality as an academic discipline, and sexual health services beyond those related to reproduction and sexually transmitted diseases, are not generally recognized or supported through national associations or university departments.

The third theme is of a country that is in the process of reconceptualizing gendered and sexual relationships in its laws, culture, and policies. This is seen in the recent changes in laws, and in court challenges in areas such as sexual assault, sexual harassment, pornography and obscenity, access to medical procedures as part of sexual and reproductive health, and guarantees of equal treatment and rights for all Canadians regardless of gender, ability, or sexual orientation. It is also seen in the changing portrayals of sexuality in culture.

Finally, Canada is a country in which liberal and conservative (or permissive and restrictive) perspectives on sexuality compete for influence in the marketplace of ideas and ideology. To date, changes in legislation and policy have been in the direction of supporting individual rights, freedom of choice and expression, and recognition of diversity. Not all Canadians support these changes, however. Whether this direction will continue as part of Canada's future will be influenced, in part, by developments in all four of these themes.

## Acknowledgments

We are grateful for the diverse contributions that the following individuals made during preparation of this chapter: Diana Powell, Bill Fisher, Mary Bissell, Christine Donald, Louis-Robert Frigault, Jeanne Guillaume, Katharine Kelly, Ross Laver, Joanne Otis, Robin Rowe, Alan Mirabelli, and Dot Whitehouse. Thanks also to Robert T. Francoeur for his encouragement and support as editor of this *Encyclopedia*.

## References and Suggested Readings

Adamson, N., L. Brislan, & M. McPhail. 1988. *Feminist organizing for change: The contemporary women's movement in Canada*. Toronto: Oxford University Press.

Adrien, A., G. Godin, P. Cappon, S. Manson-Singer, E. Maticka-Tyndale, & D. Willms. 1995. *Ethnocultural communities facing AIDS*. Ottawa, Ontario: Health Canada, NHRDP final report.

Adrien, A., G. Godin, P. Cappon, S. Manson-Singer, E. Maticka-Tyndale, & D. Willms. 1996. Overview of the Canadian study on the determinants of ethnoculturally specific behaviours related to HIV/AIDS. *Canadian Journal of Public Health*, 87(Supp. 1):S4-S10.

Aggarwal, A. P. 1992. *Sexual harassment: A guide for understanding and prevention*. Toronto: Butterworths Canada Ltd.

Alary, M. 1997. Gonnorhea: Epidemiology and control strategies. *Canadian Journal of Human Sexuality*, 6:151.

Alexander, E. 1990. Sexual therapy in English-speaking Canada. *SIECCAN Journal*, 5(1):37-43.

Aronoff, D., N. McCormick, & S. Byers. 1994. Training sex researchers: Issues for supervisors and students. *Canadian Journal of Human Sexuality*, 3(1):45-51.

Badets, J., & T. W. L. Chui. 1994. Canada's changing immigrant population. *Statistics Canada, Focus on Canada Series*, Catalogue No. 96-311E.

Baer, N. 2002 (December 20). *Protecting the rights of children. The front page: Justice Canada*. Retrieved March 23, 2003 from the World Wide Web: http://canada.justice.gc.ca/en/dept/pub/jc/vol1/no2/protect.html.

Barrett, A. 1990. Condom machines in high schools: Better late than never. *SIECCAN Newsletter*, 25(1):1-5.

Barrett, F. M. 1980. Sexual experience, birth control usage and sex education of unmarried Canadian university students:

Changes between 1968 and 1978. *Archives of Sexual Behavior*, 9:367-389.

Barrett, M. 1994. Sexuality education in Canadian schools: An overview in 1994. *Canadian Journal of Human Sexuality*, 3(3):199-207.

Barrett, M. 1990. Selected observations on sex education in Canada. *SIECCAN Journal*, 5(1):21-30.

Beaujot, R. 1991. *Population change in Canada: The challenges of policy adaptation*. Toronto: McClelland and Stewart.

Bell, L. 1991. *On our own terms: A practical guide for lesbian and gay relationships*. Toronto: Coalition for Lesbian and Gay Rights in Ontario.

Bibby, R. W. 1992. *The Bibby report: Social trends Canadian style*. Toronto: Stoddart Publishing.

Bibby, R. W. 1995. *Project Canada national survey of adult Canadians*.

Bibby, R. W., & D. C. Posterski. 1995. *Teen trends: A nation in motion*. Toronto: Stoddart Publishing.

Bissell, M. 2000. Socio-economic outcomes of teen pregnancy and parenthood: A review of the literature. *Canadian Journal of Human Sexuality*, 9:191-204.

Blanchard, R., & B. Steiner, eds. 1990. *Clinical management of gender identity disorders in children and adults*. Washington: American Psychiatric Press Inc.

Bliss, M. 1970. Pure books on avoided subjects: PreFreudian sexual ideas in Canada. Canadian Historical Association, Annual Meeting, Winnipeg, pp. 89-108.

Boroditsky, R., W. Fisher, & M. Sand. 1996. The 1995 Canadian contraception study. *Supplement of the Journal of the Society of Obstetricians and Gynaecologists of Canada*, 18(12):1-31.

Brighouse, R. 1992. Ritual female circumcision and its effects on female sexual function. *Canadian Journal of Human Sexuality*, 1(1):3-10.

Burchall, A. N. 1997. Condom use among first nations people living on-reserve in Ontario. M.Sc. thesis. Graduate Department of Community Health, University of Toronto, Canada.

Byers, S. 1991. Gender differences in the traditional sexual script: Fact or fiction. *SIECCAN Journal*, 6(4):16-18.

Byers, S. 1995. Sexology in Canada: A growing field. Paper presented at the First Symposium on Sexology: East and West, in Beijing, China, October, 1993. *SIECCAN Newsletter* (in *Canadian Journal of Human Sexuality*, 4(1):79-83.

Cairns, K. 1993. Sexual entitlement and sexual accommodation: Implications for female and male experience of sexual coercion. *Canadian Journal Human Sexuality*, 2(4):203-213.

Campbell, E. R. 1991. Establishing adolescent sexuality health centres in high schools: The Ottawa Carleton experience. *SIECCAN Newsletter*, 26(2):4-7.

Canadian AIDS Society. 1994. *Safer sex guidelines: Healthy sexuality and HIV, A resource guide for educators and counsellors*. Ottawa, Ontario: Canadian AIDS Society.

*Canada communicable disease report. Syphilis trends in Canada, 1991-1992*, vols. 20-14. 1994. Ottawa: Health Canada.

*Canada communicable disease report supplement. 1996 (June). Notifiable diseases annual summary*, vol. 2252.

*Canada communicable disease report supplement. 1995. Canadian guidelines for the prevention, diagnosis, management and treatment of sexually transmitted diseases in neonates, children, adolescents and adults*. Ottawa: Health Canada.

Canadian Institute of Child Health. 1994. *The health of Canada's children*. Ottawa, Ontario: Canadian Institute of Child Health.

Chui, T. 1996 (Autumn). Canada's population: Charting into the 21st century. *Canadian Social Trends*. Catalogue. No. 11-008-XPE.

CIA. 2002 (January). *The world factbook 2002*. Washington, DC: Central Intelligence Agency. Available: http://www.cia.gov/cia/publications/factbook/index.html.

Clemmenson, L. H. 1990. The 'real-life test' for surgical candidates. In: R. Blanchard, & B. W. Steiner, eds., *Clinical management of gender identity disorders in children and adults*. Washington, DC: American Psychiatric Press, Inc.

CMA policy summary. 1994. The patient-physician relationship and the sexual abuse of patients. *Canadian Medicine Association Journal, 150*(11):184A-C.

College of Physicians and Surgeons of British Columbia. 1994. *Crossing the boundaries: The report of the Committee on Physician Sexual Misconduct*. British Columbia: College of Physicians and Surgeons of British Columbia.

Committee on Sexual Offences Against Children and Youth 1984. *Sexual offences against children (vol. 1)*. Ottawa: Canadian Government Publishing Centre.

COPOH. 1988. *Dispelling the myths: Sexuality and disabled persons*. Winnipeg, Manitoba: Coalition of Provincial Organizations of the Handicapped.

CPSO. 1992. *Report on the Task Force on the Sexual Abuse of Patients Recommendations Reviewed by Council*. Toronto, Ontario: College of Physicians and Surgeons of Ontario.

Crabtree, L. 1994. *It's okay: Adults write about living and loving with a disability*. St. Catharines, Ontario: Phoenix Counsel Inc., One Springbank Drive, St. Catharines, Ontario L2S 2K1.

Cregheur, L. A., J. M. Casey, & H. G. Banfield. 1992. *Sexuality, AIDS and decision-making: A study of Newfoundland youth*. St. John's, Newfoundland: Office of the Queen's Printer.

*The Daily*, Statistics Canada. Therapeutic Abortions. 1994. Catalogue No. 11-001E.

*The Daily*, Statistics Canada. The violence against women survey. 1993 (November 18). Catalogue No. 11-001E.

Darroch, J., J. Frost, S. Singh, & Study Team. 2001. Teenage sexual and reproductive behavior in developed countries: Can more progress be made? *Occasional Report No.3* (pp. 102ff.). New York: Alan Guttmacher Institute.

Darroch, J., S. Singh, J. Frost, & Study Team. 2001. Differences in teen pregnancy rates among five developed countries: The role of sexual activity and contraceptive use. *Family Planning Perspectives, 33*:244-250, 281.

DAWN, 1993a. *Women with disabilities: A guide for health care professionals*. Toronto: Disabled Women's Network.

DAWN, 1993b. *Staying healthy in the nineties: Women with disabilities talk about health care*. Toronto: Disabled Women's Network.

DeKeseredy, W., & K. Kelly. 1993. The incidence and prevalence of woman abuse in Canadian university and college dating relationships. *Canadian Journal of Sociology, 18*(2): 137-159.

Department of Justice Canada. (2002). *Marriage and legal recognition of same-sex unions: A discussion paper*. Ottawa: Supply and Services Canada.

Dryburgh, H. 2001. Teenage pregnancy. *Health Reports, 12*:9-19. Statistics Canada, Catalogue 82-003.

Dumas, J., & A. Belanger. 1996. *Report on the demographic situation in Canada 1995*. Ottawa: Statistics Canada, Catalogue No. 91-209E.

Dumas, J. & Y. Caron. 1992. *Marriage and conjugal life in Canada*. Statistics Canada, Catalogue No. 91-534E.

Dupras, A. 1987. The graduate program (Master's degree) in sexology at the University of Quebec at Montreal. *SIECCAN Journal, 2*(1):25-32.

*EIQ Summary (Quebec Incidence Study of Reported Child Abuse, Neglect, Abandonment and Serious Behaviour Problems)*. 2002. Posted by the Centre of Excellence for Child Welfare, with the permission of the Institut Universitaire dans le Domaine de la Violence chez les Jeunes, Les Centres Jeunesse de Montréal.

Endicott, O. 1992. Can the law tell us who is not 'The marrying kind'? *Entourage, 7*(2):9.

Fisher, W. A. 1989. Understanding and preventing teenage pregnancy and sexually transmissible disease/AIDS. *SIECCAN Journal, 4*(2):3-25.

Fisher, W. 1997. A theory-based framework for intervention and evaluation in STD/HIV prevention. *Canadian Journal of Human Sexuality, 6*:105-112.

Fisher, W., & R. Boroditsky. 2000. Sexual activity, contraceptive choice and sexual and reproductive health indicators among single Canadian women aged 15-29. *Canadian Journal of Human Sexuality, 9*:79-93.

Fisher, W., R. Boroditsky, & M. Bridges. 1999. The 1998 Canadian contraception study. *Canadian Journal of Human Sexuality, 8*:211-216.

Fisher, J., & W. A. Fisher. 1992. Understanding and promoting AIDS preventive behaviour: A conceptual model and educational tool. *Canadian Journal of Human Sexuality, 1*:99-106.

Fisher, W. & J. D. Fisher. 1998. Understanding and promoting sexual and reproductive health behavior: Theory and method. *Annual Review of Sex Research, 9*:39-76.

Fox, B. J. 1993. On violent men and female victims: A comment on DeKeseredy and Kelly. *Canadian Journal of Sociology, 18*(3):321-324.

Frank, J. 1996. 15 years of AIDS in Canada. *Canadian Social Trends*. Summer Catalogue No. 11-008-XPE.

Frappier, J. Y., & E. Roy. 1995 (July). *HIV seroprevalence and risk behaviours study among adolescents with maladaptive and social problems in Montreal*. Final report prepared for NHRDP.

Fraser Commission Report. 1985. *Pornography and prostitution in Canada: Report of the Special Committee on Pornography and Prostitution in Canada*, vols. 1, 2. Ottawa: Minister of Supply and Services Canada.

Frigault, L. R., J. Lévy, L. Labonté, & J. Otis. 1994. *La santé, la vie sociale et la sexualité des étudiantes et étudiants de l'Université de Montréal*. Montreal, Quebec: Department of Sexology, University of Quebec at Montreal.

Gartner, R. 1993. Studying woman abuse: A comment on DeKeseredy and Kelly. *Canadian Journal of Sociology, 18*(3):313-320.

Gemme, R. 1990. Sexology in Quebec. *SIECCAN Journal, 5*(1):3-10.

Gemme, R. 1993. Prostitution: A legal, criminological and sociological perspective. *Canadian Journal of Human Sexuality, 2*(4):227-237.

Gemme, R., & N. Payment. 1992. Criminalization of adult street prostitution in Montreal, Canada: Evaluation of the law in 1987 and 1991. *Canadian Journal of Human Sexuality, 1*(4):217-220.

Ghalam, N. Z. 1993 (Spring). Women in the workplace. *Canadian Social Trends, Statistics Canada*, pp. 2-6.

Godin, G., E. Maticka-Tyndale, A. Adrien, S. M. Singer, D. Willms, P. Cappon, R. Bradet, T. Daus, & G. LeMay. 1996. Understanding the use of condoms among Canadian ethnocultural communities: Methods and main findings of the survey. *Canadian Journal of Public Health, 87*(Supp. 1): 33-37.

Gripton, J., & M. Valentich. 1990. A Church in crisis: Child sexual abuse in the Catholic Church. *SIECCAN Journal, 5*(4):37-45.

Gully, P. R., & R. W. Peeling. 1994. Control of genital chlamydial infection. *Canadian Journal Infectious Disease, 5*(3):137-139.

Hampton, M. R., P. Smith, B. Jeffery, & B. McWatters. 2001. Sexual experience, contraception and STI prevention among high school students: Results from a Canadian urban centre. *The Canadian Journal of Human Sexuality, 10*:111-126.

Hanvelt, R. A., et al. Indirect costs of HIV/AIDS mortality in Canada. *AIDS, 8*(10):F8-F11.

Health and Welfare Canada. 1990. *Report on adolescent reproductive health*. Ottawa, Ontario: Health Services and Promotion, Minister of Supply and Services, H39-185/1990E.

Health Canada. 1994a. *Many voices, HIV/AIDS in the context of culture: Report for the Latin American community*. Ottawa: Health Canada.

Health Canada. 1994b. *Many voices, HIV/AIDS in the context of culture: Report for the communities from the Horn of Africa.* Ottawa: Health Canada.

Health Canada. 1994c. *Many voices, HIV/AIDS in the context of culture: Report for the English-speaking Caribbean communities.* Ottawa: Health Canada.

Health Canada. 1994d. *Many voices, HIV/AIDS in the context of culture: Report for the Arab-speaking community.* Ottawa: Health Canada.

Health Canada. 1994e. *Many voices, HIV/AIDS in the context of culture: Report for the South Asian communities.* Ottawa: Health Canada.

Health Canada. 1994f. *Many voices, HIV/AIDS in the context of culture: Report for the Chinese communities.* Ottawa: Health Canada.

Health Canada. 2001. *HIV and AIDS in Canada. Surveillance report to December 31, 2000.* Division of HIV/AIDS Epidemiology and Surveillance, Bureau of HIV/AIDS, STD & TB, Health Canada.

Health Division, Statistics Canada. 1996. *Therapeutic abortions, 1994.* Statistics Canada, Catalogue No. 82-219-XPE.

Health Reports. 1996. *Health Reports, 8*(2):49-50.

Hendrick, D. 1996. Canadian crime statistics, 1995. *Juristat, 16*(10). Canadian Centre for Justice Statistics, Statistics Canada, Catalogue No. 85-002-XPE.

Herold, E. 1984. *Sexual behaviour of Canadian young people.* Markham, Ontario: Fitzhenry and Whiteside.

Herold, E., & Way. 1983. Oral-genital behaviour in a sample of university females. *Journal of Sex Research, 19*:327-338.

Hextall, N. 1989. An evaluation of the Teen-Aid Program in Saskatchewan. *SIECCAN Newsletter, 24*(1):3-13.

Hingsburger, D., & Ludwig, S. 1993. *Male masturbation.* Book 5 in *Being sexual: An illustrated series on sexuality and relationships.* East York: Sex Information and Education Council of Canada.

HIV/AIDS in the context of culture. 1996 (May/June). The Canadian study on the determinants of ethnoculturally specific behaviours related to HIV/AIDS. [Supplement 1]. *Canadian Journal of Public Health, 87.*

Humphrey. T., L. Gibson, & K. Maki. 1996. Sex ed on the Web: Exploring solutions to traditional instructional challenges. *Canadian Journal of Human Sexuality, 5*(4).

Insight Canada Research. 1992. *The adolescent female and birth control.* Toronto, Ontario: Insight Canada Research.

Johnson, H. 1996A. Children and youths as victims of violent crimes. *Juristat, 15*(15). Canadian Centre for Justice Statistics, Statistics Canada, Catalogue No. 85-002.

Johnson, H. 1996b. Violent crime in Canada. *Juristat, 16*(6). Canadian Centre for Justice Statistics, Statistics Canada, Catalogue No. 85-002-XPE.

Jones, A. M., D. Finkelhor, & K. Kopiec. 2001. Why is sexual abuse declining? A survey of state child protection administrators. *Child Abuse & Neglect, 25*:1139-1158.

*The Kaiser Daily Reproductive Health Report.* 1999 (September 10).

Kaufman, M., ed. 1987. *Beyond patriarchy: Essays by men on pleasure, power and change.* Toronto: Oxford University Press.

Kelly, K. 1994. The politics of data. *Canadian Journal of Sociology, 19*(1):81-85.

King, A. J. C., R. P. Beazley, R. W. Warren, C. A. Hankins, A. S. Robertson, & J. L. Radford. 1988. *Canada youth and AIDS study.* Kingston, Ontario: Social Program Evaluation Group, Queen's University.

King, M. A., B. J. Coles, & A. J. C. King. 1990. *Canada youth and AIDS study technical report.* Kingston, Ontario: Queen's University, Social Program Evaluation Research Group.

King, M. A., & B. J. Coles. 1992. *The health of Canada's youth.* Ottawa, Ontario: Minister of Supply and Services Canada.

Kinsman, G. W. 1987. *The regulation of desire: Sexuality in Canada.* Montreal: Black Rose Books.

Kirby, D. 1992. School-based programs to reduce risk-taking behaviors. *Journal of School Health, 62*:280-287.

Kirby, D. et al. 1994. School-based programs to reduce sexual risk behaviours: A review of effectiveness. *Public Health Reports, 109*(3):339-360.

Krauss, C. 2002 (July 14). Court rules that Ontario must recognize same-sex marriages. *The New York Times*, International Section, p. 9.

Laboratory Centre for Disease Control. 1994. *Quarterly surveillance update: AIDS in Canada. April 1994.* Ottawa, Ontario: Bureau of Communicable Disease Epidemiology, LCDC, Health Canada.

Lamont, J., & C. A. Woodward. 1994. Patient-physician sexual involvement: A Canadian survey of obstetricians-gynecologists. *Canadian Medical Association Journal, 150*(9):1433-1439.

Langille, D. B. 2000. *Adolescent sexual health services and education: Options for Nova Scotia.* Halifax, Nova Scotia: Maritime Centre of Excellence for Women's Health.

Langille, D. B., R. Beazley, J. Shoveller, & G. Johnston. 1994. Prevalence of high risk sexual behaviour in adolescents attending school in a county in Nova Scotia. *Canadian Journal of Public Health, 85*(4):227-230.

Langille, D. B., D. J. Langille, R. Beazley, & H. Doncaster. 1996. *Amherst parents' attitudes towards school-based sexual health education.* Halifax, Nova Scotia: Dalhousie University.

Laumann, E. O., J. H. Gagnon, R. T. Michael, & G. K. M. Harding. 1994. *The social organization of sexuality: Sexual practices in the United States.* Chicago:The University of Chicago Press.

Lawlor, W., & L. Purcell. 1988. *A study of values and sex education in Montreal area English secondary schools.* Montreal, Quebec: Department of Religion and Philosophy in Education, McGill University.

Lawlor, W., & L. Purcell. 1989. Values and opinions about sex education among Montreal area English secondary school students. *SIECCAN Journal, 4*(2):26-33.

Leung, A. K. C., & W. L. M. Robson. 1994 (April). Childhood masturbation. *Clinical Pediatrics,* 238-241.

Lévy, J. J., & D. Sansfaçon. 1994. Les orientations sexuelles. In: F. Dumont, S. Langlois, & Y. Martin, eds., *Traité des problèmes sociaux* (pp. 455-471). Montreal: Institut Québécois de Recherche sur la Culture.

Lévy, J. J., A. Dupras, M. Perrault, M. Dorais, & J.-M. Samson. 1994. *Déterminants des comportements sexuels des hommes homosexuels francophones de Montréal.* Rapport de recherche, Département de Sexologie, Université du Québec à Montréal.

Lévy, J. J., L.-R. Frigault, A. Dupras, J.-M. Samson, & P. Cappon. 1994. *Déterminants des stratégies contraceptives parmi des étudiantes universitaires du Québec et de l'Ontario.* Rapport de recherche, Département de Sexologie, Université du Québec à Montréal.

Lévy, J. J., A. Dupras, J.-M. Samson, P. Cappon, L.-R. Frigault, & A. Larose. 1993. *Facteurs de risques face au SIDA et comportements sexuels des étudiants universitaires de Montréal.* Rapport de recherche non publié. Département de Sexologie, Université du Québec à Montréal.

Lindsay, D., & J. Embree. 1992. Sexually transmitted diseases: A significant complication of childhood sexual abuse. *Canadian Journal of Infectious Disease, 3*(3):122-128.

LoVerso, T. 2001. *A survey of unwanted sexual experiences among University of Alberta students.* University of Alberta: Alberta.

Ludwig, S. 1991. *Sexuality: A curriculum for individuals who have difficulty with traditional learning methods.* Newmarket, Ontario: Municipality of York Public Health.

Ludwig, S., & D. Hingsburger. 1993. *Female masturbation.* Book 6, in *Being sexual: An illustrated series on sexuality and relationships.* East York: Sex Information and Education Council of Canada.

Ludwig, S. 1995. *After you tell.* Toronto: Sex Information and Education Council of Canada. Available in English and French.

MacDonald, N. W., & R. Brunham. 1997. The effects of undetected and untreated sexually transmitted diseases: Pelvic inflammatory disease and ectopic pregnancy in Canada. *Canadian Journal of Human Sexuality,* 6:161-170.

Mackie, M. 1991. *Gender relations in Canada: Further explorations.* Markham: Butterworths Canada Ltd.

*Maclean's.* 1993. Special report: The religion poll.

*Maclean's.* April 12.

*Maclean's*/CTV Poll. 1994 (January 3). Canada under the covers. *Maclean's, 107*(1). Additional data from Decima Research, Toronto, Canada, provided by *Maclean's.*

*Maclean's*/CTV Poll. 1995 (January 2). *Maclean's.* Additional data from Decima Research, Toronto, Canada, provided by *Maclean's.*

Maksym, D. 1990. *Shared feelings: A parent guide to sexuality education for children, adolescents and adults who have a mental handicap.* Downsview, Ontario: Roeher Institute.

Males, M. 1992. Adult liaison in the 'epidemic' of 'teenage' birth, pregnancy and venereal disease. *Journal of Sex Research, 29:*525-545.

Mansell, S., & D. Wells. 1991. *Sexual abuse of children with disabilities and sexual assault of adults with disabilities: Prevention strategies.* Ottawa: Health Canada, National Clearinghouse on Family Violence.

Martindale, S., K. J. P. Craig, K. Chan, M. L. Miller, D. Cook, & R. S. Hogg. 2001. Increasing rate of new HIV infections among young gay and bisexual men in Vancouver, 1995-99 vs. 2000. *Canadian Journal of Infectious Diseases, 12*(suppl B) Abstract 929P, 62B.

Martinson, F. M. 1994. *The sexual life of children.* Westport, CT: Bergin and Garvey.

Maticka-Tyndale, E. 1991. Sexual scripts and AIDS prevention: Variations in adherence to safer sex guidelines by heterosexual adolescents. *Journal of Sex Research, 28:*45-66.

Maticka-Tyndale, E. 1997. Reducing the incidence of sexually transmitted disease through behavioural and social change. *Canadian Journal of Human Sexuality,* 6:89-104.

Maticka-Tyndale, E. 2001. Sexual health and Canadian youth: How do we measure up. *Canadian Journal of Human Sexuality,* 10:1-17.

Maticka-Tyndale, E., F. M. Barrett, & A. McKay. 2000. Adolescent sexual and reproductive health in Canada: A review of national data sources and their limitations. *Canadian Journal of Human Sexuality,* 9:41-65.

Maticka-Tyndale, E., G. Godin, G. LeMay, A. Adrien, S. Manson-Singer, D. Willms, P. Cappon, & R. Bradet. 1996. Phase III of ethnocultural communities facing AIDS: Overview of findings. *Canadian Journal of Public Health,* 87(Supp. 1): S38-S43.

Maticka-Tyndale, E., & J. J. Lévy. 1992. *Sexualité, contraception et SIDA chez les jeunes adultes: Variations ethnoculturelles.* Montréal: Editions du Méridien.

Maticka-Tyndale, E., A. McKay & F. M. Barrett. 2001 (November). Teenage sexual and reproductive behavior in developed countries: Country report for Canada. *Occasional Report No.4* (p. 52), New York: Alan Guttmacher Institute.

Maurice, W. L., S. B. Sheps, & M. T. Schecter. 1994a. *Sexual involvement with patients: A survey of all clinically active physicians in a Canadian province.* Unpublished report.

Maurice, W. L., S. B. Sheps, & M. T. Schecter. 1994b. Physician sexual misconduct: Public opinion and experience. Presented at the Canadian Sex Research Forum meeting, Elora, Ontario, September 1994. Unpublished report.

Maxwell, W. 1980. *So long, see you tomorrow.* New York: Knopf.

McKay, A. 1993. Research supports broadly-based sex education. *Canadian Journal of Human Sexuality,* 2(2):89-98.

McKay, A. 1996. Rural parents' attitudes toward school-based sexual health education. *Canadian Journal of Human Sexuality,* 5(1):15-23.

McCreary Centre Society. 1993. *Adolescent health survey: Province of British Columbia.* Prepared by Larry Peters and Aileen Murphy.

McCreary Centre Society. 1994. *Adolescent health survey: Street youth in Vancouver.* Prepared by Larry Peters and Aileen Murphy. Principal investigator: Roger Tonkin, Burnaby, B.C., Canada.

McKay, A. 1993. Research supports broadly-based sex education. *Canadian Journal of Human Sexuality,* 2(2):89-98.

McKay. A. 1997. *Sexual ideology and schooling: Toward a democratic philosophy of sexuality education* [Ph.D. thesis]. Graduate Department of Theory and Policy Studies in Education, University of Toronto, Canada.

McKay, A. 2000. Prevention of sexually transmitted infections in different populations: A review of behaviourally effective and cost-effective interventions. *Canadian Journal of Human Sexuality,* 9:95-120.

McKay, A. 2001. *Common questions about sexual health education.* Toronto, ON: The Sex Information and Education Council of Canada. Available: http://www.sieccan.org.

McKay, A., W. Fisher, E. Maticka-Tyndale, & F. M. Barrett. 2001. Commentary: Adolescent sexual health education. Does it work? Can it work better? An analysis of recent research and media reports. *Canadian Journal of Human Sexuality,* 10:127-135.

McKay, A., & P. Holowaty. 1997. Sexual health education: A study of adolescents' opinions, self-perceived needs, and current and preferred sources of information. *Canadian Journal of Human Sexuality,* 6:29-38.

McKay, A., M. Petrusiak, & P. Holowaty. 1998. Parents' opinions and attitudes toward sexuality education in the schools. *Canadian Journal of Human Sexuality,* 7:139-145.

Miller, S., G. Szasz, & L. Anderson. Sexual healthcare clinician in acute spinal cord injury unit. *Archives of Physical Medicine Rehabitation,* 62:315-320.

Minister of Public Works and Government Services Canada. 2003. *Canadian guidelines for sexual health education.* Community Acquired Infections Division, Population and Public Health Branch, Health Canada, Ottawa (revised and updated version in press).

Minister of Supply and Services Canada. 1993. *Changing the landscape: Ending violence, achieving equality. Final report, The Canadian Panel on Violence Against Women.* Ottawa: Minister of Supply and Services Canada, Catalogue No. SW45-1/1993E.

Minister of Supply and Services Canada. 1994. *Canadian guidelines for sexual health education.* Ottawa: Minister of Supply and Services, Catalogue No. H39-300/1994E.

Muldoon, M. 1991. *The abortion debate in the United States and Canada: A sourcebook.* New York: Garland Publishing.

Myers, T., & C. Clement. 1994. Condom use and attitudes among heterosexual college students. *Canadian Journal of Public Health,* 85:51-55.

Myers, T., L. M. Calzavara, R. Cockerill, V. W. Marshall, & S. L. Bullock. 1993. *Ontario First Nations AIDS and healthy lifestyle survey.* Ottawa: Canadian Public Health Association.

Myers, T., D. Lucker, K. Orr, & E. Jackson. 1991. *Men's survey '90. AIDS: Knowledge, attitudes and behaviours. A study of gay and bisexual men in Toronto.* Toronto: AIDS Committee of Toronto.

Omer-Hashi, K., & M. Entwistle. 1995. Female genital mutilation: Cultural and health issues and their implications for sexuality. *Canadian Journal of Human Sexuality,* 4(2):137-147.

Ontario Ministry of Health. 1992. *Ontario health survey 1990.* Toronto: Ontario Ministry of Health.

Ornstein, M. 1989. *AIDS in Canada: Knowledge, behaviour and attitudes of adults.* Toronto: Institute for Social Research, York University.

Orton, M. 1994. Sexual health education in Ontario: A survey of three sectors. *Canadian Journal of Human Sexuality,* 3(3):209-225.

Orton, M., & E. Rosenblatt. 1986. *Adolescent pregnancy in Ontario: Progress in prevention (Report 2)*. Hamilton, Ontario: McMaster University, School of Social Work, Ontario Adolescent Pregnancy Project.

Orton, M., & E. Rosenblatt, E. 1991. *Adolescent pregnancy in Ontario 1976-1986: Extending access to prevention reduces abortions and births to the unmarried (Report 3)*. Hamilton, Ontario: McMaster University, School of Social Work.

Orton, M. J., & E. Rosenblatt. 1993. *Sexual health for youth: Creating a three sector network in Ontario*. Toronto: Ontario Study of Adolescent Pregnancy and Sexually Transmitted Diseases, Faculty of Social Work, University of Toronto.

O'Sullivan, L. F., & E. S. Byers. 1993. Eroding stereotypes: College women's attempts to influence reluctant male partners. *Journal of Sex Research, 30*:270-282.

O'Sullivan, L. F., K. A. Lawrance, & E. S. Byers. 1994. Discrepancies in desired level of sexual intimacy in long term relationships. *Canadian Journal of Human Sexuality, 3*(4): 313-316.

Otis, J., G. Gaston, J. Lambert, & R. Pronovest. 1990. Adolescents and condom use: The difference between contraception and STD/AIDS prevention. 6th International Conference on AIDS, San Francisco, 1990. Unpublished data in text is from this study.

Otis, J., D. Longpré, B. Gomez, & R. Thomas. 1994. L'infection par le VIH et les adolescents: Profil comportemental et cognitif de jeunes de milieux communautaires différents. In: N. Chevalier, J. Otis, & M.-P. Desaulniers, eds., *Éduquier pour preventir le SIDA*. Quebec: Publications MNH.

Otis, J. 1996. Santé sexuelle et prévention des MTS et de l'infection au VIH: Bilan d'une décienee de recherche auprès des adolescent(es) et des jeunes adultes québecois(es). Ministère de la Santé et des Services Sauciaux (Québec).

Patrick, D. M. 1997a. The control of sexually transmitted diseases in Canada: A cautiously optimistic overview. *Canadian Journal of Human Sexuality, 6*:79-87.

Patrick, D. M. 1997b. Chlamydia control: Components of an effective control strategy to reduce the incidence of Chlamydia trachomatis. *Canadian Journal of Human Sexuality, 6*:143-150.

Patrick, D. M., M. Tyndall, P. G. A. Cornelisse, K. Li, C. H. Sherlock, M. L. Rekart, S. A. Strathdee, S. L. Currie, M. T. Schechter, & M. V. O'Shaughnessy. 2001. The incidence of hepatitis C virus infection among injection drug users during an outbreak of HIV infection. *Canadian Medical Association Journal*, in press.

Patrick, D. M., T. Wong, & R. A. Jordan. 2000. Sexually transmitted infections in Canada: Recent resurgence threatens national goals. *Canadian Journal of Human Sexuality, 6*: 149-165.

Phillips, J. 1994. *Adolescent births and STDs and age of male partner*. Toronto Department of Public Health, Community Health Information Section, unpublished internal update, June 30, 1994.

Poulin, C. 1996. *Nova Scotia student drug use 1996: Technical report*. Drug Dependency Services Division, Nova Scotia Department of Health and Dalhousie University.

Radford, J. L., A. King, & W. K. Warren. 1990. *Street youth and AIDS*. Kingston, Ontario: Social Program Evaluation Group.

Ramsum, D. L., S. A. Marion, & R. G. Mathias. 1993. Changes in university students' AIDS-related knowledge, attitudes and behaviours, 1988 and 1992. *Canadian Journal of Public Health, 84*(4):275-278.

Rekart, M. L., J. Barrett, C. Lawrence, & L. Manzon. 1991. HIV and North American aboriginal peoples. VII International Conference on AIDS, Florence, Italy, June 16-21.

Remis, R., M. Alary, J. Otis, E. Demers, J. Vincelette, B. Turmel, R. Lavoie, R. Leclerc, B. Masse, R. Parent, & the Omega Study Group. 2001. HIV infection in the OMEGA cohort of men who have sex with men in Montreal: Update to September 2000. *Canadian Journal of Infectious Diseases, 12*(suppl B), Abstract 326, 61B.

Remis, R. S., & W. D. Sutherland. 1993. The epidemiology of HIV and AIDS in Canada: Current and future needs. *Canadian Journal of Public Health, 84*(supp. 1):534-538.

Renard, V., & J. Badets. 1993 (Autumn). Ethnic diversity in the 1990s. *Canadian Social Trends*, 17-22.

Rines, B. 1992. Fertility enhancement for spinal cord injured men and their partners. *Canadian Journal of Human Sexuality, 1*(4):201-206.

Roberts, J. V. 1994. Criminal justice processing of sexual assault cases. *Juristat Service Bulletin* (Canadian Centre for Justice Statistics), *14*(7):1-19.

Roberts, J. V., & M. G. Grossman. 1993. Sexual homicide in Canada: A descriptive analysis. *Annals of Sex Research, 6*: 5-25.

Roberts, J. V., & R. M. Mohr. 1994. *Confronting sexual assault: A decade of legal and social change*. Toronto: University of Toronto Press.

Roeher Institute. 1992. *No more victims: Manuals to guide the police, social workers and counsellors, family members and friends, and the legal profession in addressing the sexual abuse of people with a mental handicap*, 4 vols. North York, Ontario: The Roeher Institute.

Romanowski, B. 1997. Syphilis: Epidemiology and control. *Canadian Journal of Human Sexuality, 6*:171-176.

Royal Commission on New Reproductive Technologies. 1993. *Proceed with care: Final report of the Royal Commission on New Reproductive Technologies*, Vol 1. Ottawa: Minister of Government Services Canada.

Samson, J. M., J. J. Lévy, A. Dupras, & D. Tessier. 1990. Les comportements sexuels des Montréalais francophones. *Contraception, Fertilité, Sexualité, 18*:277-284.

Samson, J. M., J. J. Lévy, A. Dupras, & D. Tessier. 1991. Coitus frequency among married or cohabiting heterosexual adults: A survey in French Canada. *Australian Journal of Marriage and Family, 12*(2):103-109.

Samson, J. M., J. J. Lévy, A. Dupras, & D. Tessier. 1993. Active oral-genital sex among married and cohabiting heterosexual adults. *Sexological Review, 1*(1):143-156.

Samson, J. M., J. Otis, & J. J. Lévy. 1996. Risques face au SIDA relations de pouvoir et styles de communication sexuelles chez les étudiantes des cégeps francophone du Québec. Rapport de recherche. Département de Sexologie, Université du Québec à Montréal.

Santé Québec. 1991. *Enquête québécoise sur les facteurs de risques associés au SIDA et autres MTS; La population des 15-29 Ans*. Québec: Ministère de la Santé et des Services Sociaux.

Saskatchewan Health. 1993. *Toward sexual and reproductive health in Saskatchewan: Report on the Advisory Committee on Family Planning to the Minister of Health*. Regina, Saskatchewan: Saskatchewan Health.

Schneider, M. 1991. Developing services for lesbian and gay adolescents. *Canadian Journal of Community Mental Health, 10*(1):133-150.

SIECCAN. 1992. Sexuality and disability. *Canadian Journal of Human Sexuality, 1*(4).

SIECCAN. 1993. *Being sexual: An illustrated series on sexuality and relationships* (17 booklets). East York, Ontario: Sex Information and Education Council of Canada.

SIECCAN. 1994. Sexuality and cancer treatment. *Canadian Journal Human Sexuality, 3*(2).

Singh, S., & J. Darroch. 2000. Adolescent pregnancy and childbearing: Levels and trends in developed countries. *Family Planning Perspectives, 32*:14-23.

Sobsey, D. 1994. *Violence and abuse in the lives of people with disabilities*. Baltimore, MD: Paul H. Brookes Publishing Co.

Sobsey, D., D. Wells, R. Lucardie, & S. Mansell. 1994. *Violence and disability: An annotated bibliography*. Baltimore, MD: Paul H. Brookes Publishing Co.

Statistics Canada. 1990. *General social survey*. Ottawa: Statistics Canada.

Statistics Canada. 1992. *Canadian crime statistics: Sexual assault*. Catalogue No. 85-205. Ottawa: Statistics Canada.

Statistics Canada's Violence against women survey. 1993. *The violence against women survey*. Ottawa: Statistics Canada.

Szasz, G. 1989. Sexuality in persons with severe physical disability: A guide to the physician. *Canadian Family Physician, 35*:345-351.

Szasz, G., & C. Carpenter. 1989. Clinical observations in vibratory stimulation of the penis of men with spinal cord injuries. *Archives of Sexual Behaviour, 18*(6):461-473.

Task Force on Sexual Abuse of Patients. 1991. *Final report of the Task Force on Sexual Abuse of Patients*. Toronto: College of Physicians and Surgeons of Ontario.

Tonkin, R. 1992. *British Columbia—The adolescent survey*. Burnaby, British Columbia: The McCreary Centre Society.

Toobin, J. 1994. (October 3). Annals of law: X-rated. *New Yorker*.

Toronto Board of Education. 1992. *Sexual orientation: Focus on homosexuality, lesbianism and homophobia. A resource guide for teachers of health education in secondary schools*. Toronto: Toronto Board of Education.

Trocmé, N., B. Fallon, B. MacLaurin, S. Bartholomew, J. Ortiz, J. Thompson, W. Helfrich, & J. Daciuk. 2002. *The 1998 Ontario incidence study of reported child abuse and neglect (OIS 1998)*. Toronto: Centre of Excellence for Child Welfare, Faculty of Social Work, University of Toronto.

Trocmé, N., D. McPhee, K. T. Kwok, & T. Hay. 1994. *Ontario incidence study of reported child abuse and neglect*. Toronto: Institute for the Prevention of Child Abuse.

Ullman, R., & L. Lathrop. 1996. Impact of free condom distribution on the use of dual protection against pregnancy and sexually transmitted disease. *Canadian Journal of Human Sexuality, 5*(1):25-29.

UNAIDS. 2002. *Epidemiological fact sheets by country*. Geneva, Switzerland: Joint United Nations Programme on HIV/AIDS (UNAIDS/WHO). Available: http://www.unaids.org/hivaidsinfo/statistics/fact_sheets/index_en.htm.

Vanier Institute of the Family. 1994. *Profiling Canada's families*. Ottawa: Vanier Institute of the Family.

Vanier Institute of the Family. 2000. *Profiling Canada's families II*. Ottawa: Vanier Institute of the Family.

Varnhagen, C. K., L. W. Svenson, A. M. Godin, L. Johnson, & T. Salmon. 1991. Sexually transmitted diseases and condoms: High school students' knowledge, attitudes and behaviours. *Canadian Journal of Public Health, 82*(2):129-131.

Verby, C., & E. Herold. 1992. Parents and AIDS education. *AIDS Education and Prevention, 4*:187-198.

Wackett, J., & L. Evans. 2000. An evaluation of the choices and changes student program: A grade 4 to seven sexual health education program based on the Canadian guidelines for sexual health education. *SIECCAN Newsletter, 35*(2), in *Canadian Journal of Human Sexuality, 9*:265-273.

Wadhera, S., & W. J. Miller. 1997 (Winter). Marital status and abortion. *Health Reports, 9*(3), Statistics Canada, Catalogue 82-003-XPB.

Wadhera, S., & J. Strachan. 1991. Teenage pregnancies, Canada, 1925-1989. *Health Reports, 3*(4):327-347.

Wadhera, S., & Millar, W. G. 1996a. Pregnancy outcomes. *Health Reports, 8*(1):7-15.

Wadhera, S., & Millar, W. G. 1996b. *Reproductive health: Pregnancies and rates*, Canada, 1974-1993.

Warren, W. K., & A. J. C. King. 1994. *Development and evaluation of an AIDS/STD/sexuality program for grade 9 students*. Kingston, Ontario: Social Program Evaluation Group, Queen's University.

Watson, D. B. 1991. Overview of Vancouver General Hospital's gender dysphoria clinic. *SIECCAN Journal, 6*(1):3-8.

Weaver, A. D., E. S Byers, H. A. Sears, N. Cohen, & H. E. Randall. 2002. Sexual health education at school and at home: Attitudes and experiences of New Brunswick parents. *Canadian Journal of Human Sexuality, 11*:19-31.

Weaver, A. D., E. S. Byers, H. A. Sears, J. N. Cohen, & H. E. Randall, H. E. 2001. *New Brunswick parents' ideas about sexual health education*. Fredericton, N.B.: Department of Psychology, University of New Brunswick, Canada.

Wheeler, S. 1996. *It's okay, 5*(1). Sureen Publications, Box 23102, 124 Welland Ave., St. Catharines, Ontario, Canada L2R 7P6.

Widmer, E., J. Treas, & R. Newcomb. 1998. Attitudes toward nonmarital sex in twenty-four countries. *Journal of Sex Research, 35*:349-358.

Wilchesky, M., & P. Assalian. 1991. Assessment and treatment of transsexuals: The Montreal General Hospital approach. *SIECCAN Journal, 6*(1):47-50.

Wolff, L., & D. Geissel. 1994. Street prostitution in Canada. *Canadian Social Trends, Summer, 1994*. Statistics Canada, Catalogue No. 11-008E.

Young, A. H. 1992. Child sexual abuse and the law of evidence: Some current Canadian issues. *Canadian Journal of Family Law, 11*:11-40.

Zarb, L. H. 1994. Allegations of childhood sexual abuse in custody and access disputes: What care is in the best interests of the child? *Canadian Journal of Family Law, 13*:91-114.

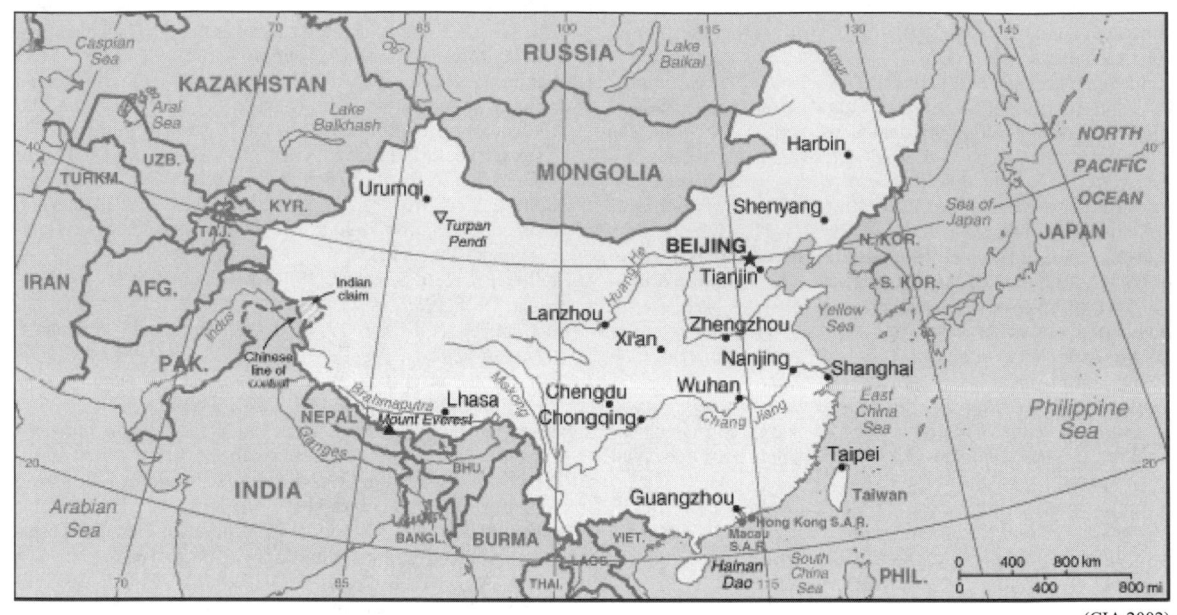

(CIA 2002)

# China

## (*Zhonghua Renmin Gonghe Guo*)
## (The People's Republic of China)

Fang-fu Ruan, M.D., Ph.D., and M. P. Lau, M.D.*
*Updates by F. Ruan and Robert T. Francoeur, Ph.D.;*
*Comments by M. P. Lau*

## Contents

*Communications: Fang-fu Ruan, M.D., Ph.D., P.O. 70571, Oak-
land, CA 94612-0571 USA; ruanff@yahoo.com; M. P. Lau, M.D.,
280 Spadina Avenue, Suite 302A, Toronto, Ontario M5T 3A5
Canada.

*Editor's Note*: In this chapter, Dr. Fang-fu Ruan's report and analysis of sexual attitudes and behavior in China follows our standard 13-topic structure. In Part 2, Dr. M. P. Lau provides a summary and analysis of the Kinsey-like 1992 *Sexual Behavior in Modern China: A Report of the Nationwide "Sex Civilization" Survey on 20,000 Subjects in China*. Readers should consult Part 2 for additional information on specific topics discussed by Fang-fu Ruan in Part 1.

## Demographics and a Brief Historical Perspective

ROBERT T. FRANCOEUR

### A. Demographics

The People's Republic of China is the largest country in Eastern Asia, embracing 3.7 million square miles (9.58 km²). China is smaller than Russia and Canada, but slightly larger than the contiguous 48 United States. China is bordered by Korea in the east, Mongolia in the north, Russia in the northeast, Kazakhstan, Kirghizstan, and Tajikistan in the northwest, Afghanistan and Pakistan in the west, India, Nepal, Sikkim, and Bhutan in the southwest, and Myanmar (formerly Burma), Laos, and Vietnam in the south, and the Pacific Ocean in the east. Only one tenth of the land is cultivated, although the eastern half of China is one of the best-watered lands in the world, with vast farmlands and three great rivers, the Yangtze or Chang, the Huang or Yellow River, and the Xi. In addition to the pressing issue of population control, China faces major environmental obstacles to its continued economic progress. China's heavy reliance on coal as a fuel produces major problems from acid rain and air pollution from greenhouse gases and sulfur dioxide. China also faces major water shortages, particularly in the north, water pollution from untreated wastes, and loss of an estimated one fifth of its agricultural land since 1949 from soil erosion, desertification, deforestation, and economic development.

In July 2002, China had an estimated population of 1.28 billion. (All data are from *The World Factbook 2002* (CIA 2002) unless otherwise stated.)

**Age Distribution and Sex Ratios**: *0-14 years*: 24.3% with 1.1 male(s) per female (sex ratio); *15-64 years*: 68.4% with 1.06 male(s) per female; *65 years and over*: 7.3% with 0.89 male(s) per female; *Total population sex ratio*: 1.06 male(s) to 1 female

**Life Expectancy at Birth**: *Total Population*: 71.86 years; *male*: 70.02 years; *female*: 73.86 years

**Urban/Rural Distribution**: 27% to 73%

**Ethnic Distribution**: The vast majority of Chinese people, 91.9%, are Hans (ethnic Chinese, or Han Chinese). The remaining 8.1%, over 91 million people, include 55 other ethnic groups. Minority nationalities with population of over one million are the Bai, Bouyei, Dai (Thai), Dong,

Hani, Hui, Kazak, Korean, Li, Manchu, Miao, Mongolian, Tibetan, Tujia, Uighur, Yao, Yi, and Zhuang (see Section 13, Ethnic Minority Resources)

**Religious Distribution**: Officially atheistic, but traditionally pragmatic and eclectic, with Daoism (Taoism) and Buddhism the most common; Muslim: 2% to 3%; Christian: 1% (est.)

**Birth Rate**: 15.85 births per 1,000 population

**Death Rate**: 6.77 per 1,000 population

**Infant Mortality Rate**: 27.25 deaths per 1,000 live births

**Net Migration Rate**: –0.38 migrant(s) per 1,000 population

**Total Fertility Rate**: 1.82 children born per woman (1995 est.)

**Population Growth Rate**: 0.87%

**HIV/AIDS** (1999 est.): *Adult prevalence*: < 0.2%; *Persons living with HIV/AIDS*: 1.25 million (January 2001); *Deaths*: 17,000 (1999 est.). The Chinese government was challenged by the United Nations Secretary General to recognize the threat of HIV/AIDS among its 1.2 billion people and face a devastating epidemic that could destroy the nation. (For additional details from www.UNAIDS.org, see end of Section 10B.)

**Literacy Rate** (*defined as those age 15 and over who can read and write*): 81.5% (*male*: 89.9%, *female*: 72.7%). The 1992 literacy rate was 78%, with nine years schooling required and 96% attendance in primary school.

**Per Capita Gross Domestic Product** (*purchasing power parity*): $4,300 (2001 est.); *Inflation*: 0.8% (2001 est.); *Unemployment*: 10% among urban Chinese. China has a substantial unemployment and underemployment problem.

[*Update 2002*: As a developing country, China has the largest population in the world, 1.28 billion in July 2001, or 22% of the world's population. The China Population and Information Network (China POPIN) estimates China's population in 2010 will be 1.380 billion people. Despite family planning programs, China's annual net population growth in recent years has still been around 13 million. China's population is also very unevenly distributed, with 94% living in the southeastern part of the country, which occupies 43% of the country's total land area. According to 1996 statistics, 71.63% of the population lives in the countryside, so the level of urbanization is very low. China's arable land is only 7% of the world's total, with a crop production that is only one quarter of the world per capita average crop. China's per capita fresh water is also one quarter of the world average. For over four decades, China has witnessed dramatic economic development, but because of rapid expansion of the population, the indices related to living standards are still very low. China's per capita grain production is less than 400 kilograms; per capita residential floor area in urban areas is 8.1 square meters; and the number of hospital beds for every 1,000 people is only 2.34. Of the country's 2,143 counties, 592 are poverty ones with an annual per capita income of less than RMB Yuan 250 (US$43). Each year, one quarter of the increase in national income is used for the new increase in population. China has at least 20 million people reaching working age every year. Insufficient employment has produced a surplus labor force of over 100 million in the countryside. The huge population base and an annual population growth of 13 million are in serious conflict with the country's socioeconomic development, utilization of natural resources, and environmental protection. It has become a major factor that restricts socioeconomic development and the improvement of people's quality of life in China. (State Family Planning Commission Of China: http://www.sfpc.gov.cn, on June 2, 1999.) (*End of update by F. Ruan*)]

## B. A Brief Historical Perspective

The remains of various humanlike creatures, who lived as early as several hundred thousand years ago, have been found in many parts of modern China. The oldest human remains found in China were those of "Peking man," who lived approximately 578,000 years ago. Neolithic agricultural settlements, dating from about 5000 B.C.E. have been found in the Huanghe basin. Imperial China lasted almost 4,000 years, from the Xia dynasty (c. 2200-1500 B.C.E.) to the Qing dynasty (1644-1911 C.E.). Bronze metallurgy reached a peak during the Shang dynasty of Northern China (c. 1500 B.C.E. to c. 1000 B.C.E.), along with Chinese pictographic writing. Imperial China was marked by a succession of dynasties and interdynastic warring kingdoms. The range of Chinese political and cultural domination waxed and waned, expanding from the north to the south and west at various times, as science, technology, and culture flourished in great sophistication. Rule by non-Hans (foreigners), the Mongols during the Yuan dynasty (1271-1368), and the Manchus in the Qing dynasty (1644-1911), did not alter the underlying Chinese character of the culture.

Cultural and political stagnation in the 19th century left China vulnerable to internal rebellions that left tens of millions dead and Russian, Japanese, British, and other foreign powers exercising control over some key parts of the country. Imperial rule ended in 1911 with the formation of the Republic of China in 1912. Between 1894 and 1945, China was involved in major conflicts with Japan. In 1895, China gave up Korea, Taiwan, and other territories. Japan seized the northeast provinces of Manchuria in 1931, and invaded China proper in 1937. Following World War II, China regained the territories it had previously lost to Japan. In 1949, the People's Republic of China was proclaimed by Chinese Communist leader Mao Zedong; the nationalist Republic of China (Kuomintang) retired to Taiwan.

The Great Leap Forward, 1958 to 1960, tried to force the pace of economic development through intensive labor on huge new rural communes and an emphasis on ideological purity. The program was abandoned when it encountered serious resistance. In 1965, the Great Proletarian Cultural Revolution was launched in an effort to reestablish the revolutionary purity of the principles of Chairman Mao Zedong, with massive purges and the forced relocation of millions of urban teenagers into the countryside. This effort gradually petered out as pragmatism regained its influence. Despite the violent repression of democratic demonstrations by over 100,000 students and workers in the 1989 Tiananmen Square outside Beijing's Great Hall of the People, China has followed a painfully slow, halting, but definite transition and adjustment to a partial free-market economy and more-democratic policies.

## PART 1.

# 1. Basic Sexological Premises

## A. Character of Gender Roles

In order to understand and evaluate the recent situation of gender roles in China, it is necessary to begin with some understanding of the roots of female oppression in the traditional Chinese society and family. In its earliest history, China was a matriarchal society, until Confucius and Mencius defined the superior-inferior relationship between men and women as heaven-ordained more than 2,000 years ago. In traditional Chinese society, women should observe the Three Obediences and the Four Virtues. Women were to be obedient to the father and elder brothers when young, to the husband when married, and to the sons when widowed.

Thus Chinese women were controlled and dominated by men from cradle to grave. The ideal of feminine behavior created a dependent being, at once inferior, passive, and obedient. Thus, for more than 2,000 years, for the vast majority of Chinese women, belonging to a home was the only means to economic survival. But they had no right to select a husband, let alone the right to divorce or to remarry if widowed. They had no right to their physical bodies. Those who defied such institutionalized oppression were persecuted, ostracized, and sometimes driven to suicide. [*Comment 1997*: This may not apply to the lower class and marginal people. (*End of comment by M. P. Lau*)]

The functional importance of all women in traditional China lay in their reproductive role: In such a patriarchal and authoritarian society, the function of women was to reproduce male descendents. Since descent was patrilineal, a woman's position within her natal family was temporary and of no great importance. The predominant patrilineal household model, in combination with early marriage, meant that a young girl often left home before she was of significant labor value to her natal family. Hence, education or development of publicly useful skills for a girl was not encouraged in any way. Marriage was arranged by the parents with the family interests of continuity by bearing male children and running an efficient household in mind. Her position and security within her husband's family remained ambiguous until she produced male heirs. [*Comment 1997*: Then she might become manipulative and exploitive. (*End of comment by M. P. Lau*)] In addition to the wife's reproductive duties, the strict sexual division of labor demanded that she undertake total responsibility for childcare, cooking, cleaning, and other domestic tasks. Women were like slaves or merchandise.

A real liberation and revolution in the female's role has occurred in the People's Republic of China (PRC). The first law enacted by the PRC government was the Marriage Law of 1950. The law is not only about marriage and divorce, but also is a legal statement on monogamy, equal rights of both sexes, and on the protection of the lawful interests of women and children. [*Comment 1997*: However, it took years for the law to become more than words on paper and move into real life. (*End of comment by M. P. Lau*)]

## B. Sociolegal Status of Males and Females

*The Changing/Unchanging Status of Women*

In 1954, the constitution of the People's Republic of China restated the 1950 principle of the equality of men and women and protection of women: "Article 96: Women in the People's Republic of China enjoy equal rights with men in all spheres of political, economic, cultural, social, and domestic life."

Under this principle, major changes happened in the social roles of women in the PRC, especially in the areas of

**Table 1**

**Sex Ratios in China (1948)**

|                        | Female | Male  |
|------------------------|--------|-------|
| Nationwide Average     | 100    | 109.6 |
| Shandong (*the lowest*)| 100    | 99.0  |
| Hubei                  | 100    | 109.1 |
| Wuhan                  | 100    | 124.1 |
| Beijing                | 100    | 125.7 |
| Zungqing               | 100    | 130.4 |
| Dalian                 | 100    | 194.0 |

*From*: Long Guanhai: *Shehui Yu Ren* [*Society and Human Beings*]. Taipei, Taiwan: Chuanji.

work and employment, education, freedom in marriage and divorce, and family management. For example, 600,000 female workers and urban employees in China in 1949 accounted for 7.5% of the total workforce; in 1988, the female workforce had increased to 50,360,000 and 37.0% of the total. [*Comment 1997*: Most women continue to be employed as cheap labor, but this is not a condition limited to China. (*End of comment by M. P. Lau*)]

A neighborhood survey in Nanjing found that 70.6% of the women who married between 1950 and 1965 had jobs. Of the women who married between 1966 and 1976, the percentage of those employed stood at 91.7%; by 1982, 99.2% of married women were breadwinners.

A Shanghai neighborhood survey reported that 25% of the wives declared themselves boss of the family, while 45% said they shared the decision-making power in their families. Similar surveys in Beijing found that 11.6% of the husbands have the final say in household matters, while 15.8% of families have wives who dominate family decision-making. The other 72.6% have the husband and wife sharing in decision-making. A survey in Nanjing revealed that 40% of the husbands go shopping in the morning. Many husbands share kitchen work. Similar surveys of 323 families in Shanghai found 71.1% of husbands and wives sharing housework. (Dalin Liu's study of *Sexual Behavior in Modern China* (1992) contains statistical data about domestic conflicts and the assignment of household chores.)

Although the situation of women has changed dramatically from what went before, in actuality, women still are not equal with men. For example, it is not unusual to find that some universities reject female graduate students, and some factories and government institutions refuse to hire women. The proportion of professional women is low. Women fill only 5.5% of the higher-level jobs such as technicians, clerks, and officials.'s In a country of 220 million illiterates, 70% are women. Women now make up only 37.4% of high school students and only 25.7% of the university-educated population. Moreover, actual discrimination against women still exists, and continues to develop. Many women have been laid off by enterprises that consider them surplus or redundant employees. Only 4.5% of the laid-off women continued to receive welfare benefits, including bonuses and stipends offered by their employers. Many enterprises have refused to employ women, contending their absences from work to have a baby or look after children are burdensome.

*Male-Preferred, Female Infanticide, and the Sex Ratio Problem*

China was, and in many ways still is, a Confucianist country. Confucianism said that: "There are three things which are unfilial, and to have no posterity is the greatest of them." In Chinese society "having posterity" means "having a male child." Therefore, not having a male offspring is regarded as the worst possible problem a family can have psychologically, economically, and sociologically.

[*Update 2003*: Even before the founding of the People's Republic of China, at a time when very little or no contraception was available, and before the advent of the one-child-per-family policy in the PRC, female infanticide was widely used, as data on sex ratios clearly show (see Table 1).

[According to a survey done by gynecology professor Gu Zusan, 80% of rural families want a boy, not a girl. Therefore, one of the side effects of the "one child" policy is the practice of female infanticide. Certainly, female infanticide has not been a critical problem nationwide yet. But, in some places it does happen; for example: The 1982 sex ratios in villages in Wuhan and Hubei were:

| Sex ratios: | in a Wuhan community | | in a Hubei village | |
| --- | --- | --- | --- | --- |
| Age | Female | Male | Female | Male |
| 0-1 | 100 | 154 | 100 | 503 |
| 0-3 | 100 | 124 | 100 | 384 |
| 0-5 | 100 | 112 | 100 | 182 |

(*End of update by F. Ruan*)]

In the 1970s, China's newborn sex ratio was 106 males for every 100 females. It was probable that in Wuhan, Hubei, and other places as well, female infanticide was being practiced. In 1986, even the government Beijing newspaper *Zhongguo Fazibao* (*China Law News*) reported this problem (September 11, 1986): "According to the survey by Zungqing Women Association, there were 2,800 cases of female infanticide in Zungqing in 1984. It was a very serious and severe problem." The newborn sex ratio in China has risen year by year: In 1986, it was 110 males for every 100 females; in 1987, 111; and in 1990, 112. In September and October 1992, a nationwide survey of 380,000 newborns showed the sex ratio was as high as 118.5:100.

[*Update 2003*: In a spring 2002 report in the journal *International Security*, demographers Valerie Hudson and Andrea Den Boer estimate that China will have between 29 million and 33 million unmarried males ages 15 to 34 by the year 2020. Other estimates put the number of young, unmarried men, of *guang guan* ("bare branches" or "barren sticks") in 2020 at 40 million. That number equals the combined female population of Taiwan and South Korea. The probable main but not sole cause, according to Chinese researcher Chu Junhong in a 2001 report in the *Population and Development Review*, is prenatal screening and selective abortion of female offspring. Despite a 1995 Maternal and Child Health Law that bans use of ultrasound scanning for selective abortion, one study found that 36% of the abortions reported in a rural Chinese county were done to weed out the girls. Chinese parents are generally willing to accept a firstborn daughter if they can have a second child. In Anhui and other provinces, the firstborn male-female ratio is 111 males to 100 females, but more than 3 to 1 for second births. To avoid adding more millions of males to this unprecedented and long-term crisis, China is urging provincial governments to pass and enforce very strong laws banning the use of ultrasound scanning and selective abortion. The male surplus is also increasing because female infants are breastfed for shorter periods than boys. Female infanticide and abandonment also contribute to the male surplus: In some areas, up to 90% of young children in orphanages are female (Wiseman 2002).

[Many Asian nations are experiencing a similar sex-ratio imbalance, although none as severe as China's. Hudson and Boer estimate the number of missing women in China at 40.6 million, India 37.1 million, Bangladesh 3.5 million, Pakistan 3.3 million, Afghanistan 0.9, Taiwan 0.6 million, and Nepal 600,000.

[Social trends exacerbate the sex-ratio imbalance. There is a decline in arranged marriages, especially in the cities where women, not men, are doing the choosing. To be chosen by a woman, a man needs to be educated and have a stable good-paying job. Among unmarried rural men, 97% never finished high school and 40% are illiterate. In the migration from farm to city, women have turned to factory jobs on the booming eastern coast while the men are drawn to public-works projects in the nation's interior. Zhang Yi, a demographer at the Chinese Academy of Social Sciences, found one factory town in the southeast province of Guandong with 200,000 migrant women and just 4,000 local men. Grossly outnumbered, the local women were very hostile to the female immigrant workers.

[Increasingly, the government and demographers are trying to anticipate the likely social consequences of this imbalance. In the mid-1800s, the Nien Rebellion broke out in the eastern city of Shandong where men outnumbered women 129 to 100. At that time, a quarter of all Chinese men could not find wives. The frustrated males turned to banditry and then to open rebellion against the Qing dynasty. At their height, 100,000 Nien rebels controlled territory with a population of 6 million. The rebels held out against the government for 17 years.

[Following historical precedents, the government may impose ever stricter authoritarian rule, thereby delaying the move to democracy. The government is already bringing poor young men into the paramilitary People's Armed Police, which is assigned to crush riots and suppress other social disturbances. Another possibility would be to stir up border wars with its neighbors that would siphon off the surplus males. Huge construction projects and public works could also help absorb the surplus males (Wiseman 2002). (*End of update by R. T. Francoeur*)]

## C. General Concepts of Sexuality and Love

In mainland China today, the only sexual behavior that is acknowledged to be legally and morally permissible is heterosexual intercourse within monogamous marriage. A wide variety of sexual behaviors are explicitly proscribed. Thus, prostitution, polygamy, premarital and extramarital sex (including cohabitation arrangements), homosexuality, and variant sexual behaviors are all illegal. Because even normal sexual expression is viewed with contempt as a less important activity of life, not only are pornography and nudity banned, but any social activity with sexual implications—such as dancing—may be subject to restrictions. Even the marriage relationship is given little consideration. For example, according to official statistics, approximately 360,000 married persons live apart from their spouses, and this figure increases at a rate of 100,000 per year. Most of these separations occur because individual citizens are not free to move from one place to another, or to change their places of employment.

Public policy and law related to sexuality seriously and severely have an impact on individual and social lives. Contemporary China is a noteworthy example of a totalitarian government's attempt to control or repress the sexual aspects of an individual's life. It exemplifies, as well, how sexually repressive policies are not actually effective in inhibiting sexual desire in private lives, nor in curbing the struggle for human sexual rights and freedom.

[*Update 2001*: As an expression of the sex-negative policies in China, many sex-related behaviors were cited and punished as "gangster activities" in the 1980 Criminal Law of the People's Republic of China. Homosexual behaviors and all kinds of paraphilias may be punished as "gangster activities." A positive change occurred in 1997 with the Revised Criminal Law of the People's Republic of China: "gangster activities" were deleted from the Criminal Law that was adopted on March 14, 1997. (*End of update by F. Ruan*)]

The major move toward democracy in mainland China after Mao was the "Democracy Wall" movement during 1978 and 1979. During this brief period, the government allowed young people to express their desire for personal freedom and democracy by placing "big character" posters on a wall that came to be known as the "Democracy Wall." The Democracy Wall was also used for advocating sexual liberation. The author vividly recalls visiting the wall on February 20, 1979, and seeing two poems about sexual rights. One was titled "The Eulogy of Sexual Desire," the other "Open Sex." In posters like these, China's youth first made a courageous stand on the importance of sexual openness to their country's modernization.

Students also carried posters advocating sexual freedom during the nationwide demonstration by university students in the winter of 1986-87. While sexual liberation was not a major explicit goal of the 1989 democracy movement, its importance was understood, and its value implicit in one of the loveliest events that occurred then: During a hunger strike in Tiananmen Square, a wedding was held for one of the demonstration leaders. The bride and groom, the maid of honor (General Commander Chai Ling, now an internationally known heroine of the struggle for democracy), and the best man (Chai's husband, Vice General Commander Feng Congde) were all fasting, as were classmates attending the wedding. Yet all the celebrants were laughing joyously. The wedding was the ideal symbol of the connection between the longing for liberty and the desire for love, romance, marriage, personal happiness, and fulfillment.

[*Update 1997*: In 1996, Suiming Pan, head of the Institute for Research in Sexuality and Gender at the Renmin University of China in Beijing, analyzed 11 social surveys on sexuality in Chinese cities between 1986 and 1995 and reinterviewed 103 men and 73 women. The ten factors listed below, which Pan (1996) identified as affecting sexological research and studies in China, also reveal some important insights into the general concepts of love and sexuality that prevail in Chinese culture.

1. For most people, the Chinese sexual vocabulary is either cryptic or considered dirty and abusive.
2. The more familiar with each other people are, the more difficult it is to talk about sex.
3. There is often a sexual undertone to the interaction between heterosexual interviewers and interviewees.
4. Many tragic or socially illegitimate sexual matters would rather be forgotten than discussed with the interviewees.
5. Female interviewers are often considered "bad women."
6. Chinese people view pornography, sex workers, and nonmarital sex as illegal.
7. Ordinary people do not understand why researchers study sexuality.
8. Most ordinary people are unable to evaluate and express their own sexual feelings, or even their behavior.
9. Most females feel like vomiting when questioned about sexual matters.
10. Ordinary people think that if you ask a question about a kind of sexual behavior or relationship, then it means that you really like it yourself.

The first nine of these ten points reflect ignorance, stigma, and inhibition, with only the last point expressing a common viewpoint frequently encountered in other countries. (*End of update by R. T. Francoeur*)]

## 2. Religious, Ethnic, and Gender Factors Affecting Sexuality

### A. Source and Character of Religious Values

China is a multi-religion country, with a vast proportion of the population professing no religion. Some worship ancestors and/or Shens ("kindly spirits"). Many subscribe to more than one of the main religions: Buddhism, Taoism, Islam, Catholicism, several major Protestant religions, and Confucianism. As a religion, Taoism is considered a genuine indigenous religion of China in the sense that Buddhism, Islam, Catholicism, and Protestantism were imported from foreign countries, while Confucianism is taken to be more secularly oriented in doctrine.

Confucianism is based on writings which are attributed to Confucius (551-479 B.C.E.), the first great educator, philosopher, and statesman of China, and his followers, including Mencius (372-289 B.C.E.), a political thinker who believed in democracy. Confucianism dominated Chinese sociopolitical life for most of Chinese history.

Confucius and Mencius themselves expressed a rather positive view of human sexuality. For example, The Master (Confucius) said, "I have not seen one who loves virtue as he loves sex" (*Confucian Analects Book IX*, chapter 17); "Food and drink and the sexual relation between men and women compose the major human desires" (*The Book of Rites*, one of the major Confucianism classics, chapter 9). In *The Works of Mencius*, one of the major Confucianism classics (book 6, part 1), we find: "Eating food and having sex are both of human nature."

It was not until much later that sexual conservatism became a feature of Neo-Confucian philosophy. The crucial change was initiated by several famous Neo-Confucianists, including Ch'eng I (1033-1107), and Chu Hsi (1130-1200). Ch'eng I summarized the Neo-Confucian viewpoint as "Discard human desires to retain the heavenly principles."

When asked whether it was justifiable for a widow to remarry when pressed by poverty and hunger, he replied, "It is a small matter to die as a result of starvation, but a serious evil to lose chastity toward one's dead husband by remarrying." Chu Hsi stressed the inferiority of women and the strict separation of the sexes, and forbade any manifestation of heterosexual love outside of wedlock. Chu Hsi laid the foundations of Neo-Confucianism as the sole state religion. It encouraged a puritanical and strictly authoritarian form of government, including the establishment of censorship and thought control. However, the government had difficulty enforcing these views on the lower class or *sciao-ren* (the non-exemplary class of people).

Taoism has both a philosophical and a religious tradition in China. Although philosophical Taoism flourished early in the 5th century B.C.E., Taoism as a religion did not develop until the 1st century of the Common Era. Next to Confucianism, it ranks as the second major belief system in traditional Chinese thought. The philosophy of Taoism outlined in Laotzu's *Tao Te Ching* offers a practical way of life. Both philosophical and religious Taoism included in their classics some positive ideas about sex. For example, from Lao-tzu's *Tao Te Ching*: "All things have their backs to the female and stand facing male. When male and female combine, all things achieve harmony" (chapter 42, translated by S. Mitchell, Harper & Row, 1988). And from *Taiping Jing* (*The Canon of Peace and Tranquility*), an early classic of religious Taoism: "Through the way of copulation between husband and wife, the Yin and Yang all obtain what they need and Heaven and Earth become peace and tranquility;" "Based on one Yin and one Yang, Heaven allows both man and woman to exist and to be sexually attractive to each other, therefore life can be continued."

Yin-Yang is a major philosophical concept developed during the Zhou dynasty (1027-221 B.C.E.). The concepts of Yin and Yang may be found in the majority of important Chinese classics, including such a major classic of Confucianism as the *I-Ching*, and such a Taoist classic as the *Tao-te-ching*. Thus, the Yin-Yang philosophy is among the most important unifying concepts of Chinese culture. According to the Yin-Yang philosophy, all objects and events are the products of two elements, forces, or principles: Yin, which is negative, passive, weak, and destructive; and Yang, which is positive, active, strong, and constructive. It was very natural for the Yin-Yang doctrine to become the basis of Chinese sexual philosophy. The Chinese have used the words Yin and

Yang to refer to sexual organs and sexual behavior for several thousand years. Thus *Yin Fu*, "the door of Yin" means vulva, *Yin Dao*, "the passageway of Yin" means vagina, and *Yang Ju*, "the organ of Yang" means penis. The combination of these words into the phrases *Huo Yin Yang* or *Yin Yang Huo He*—"the union or combination of Yin and Yang"—describes the act of sexual intercourse.

Buddhism was first introduced into China in the 1st century C.E. from India. Chinese Buddhism was of the Mahayana (Great Vehicle) school, so named to distinguish it from the earlier form of Buddhism known as Hinayana (Lesser Vehicle). Among Tibetan peoples, it is distinguished by its emphasis on the Buddhist *Tantras*. Most Buddhist schools denied sexual desire, and traditionally Buddhist monks have been celibate. But, it is not the case of the school of Mi-tsung (Mantrayana, or Tantrism). Sex was the major subject of Mi-tsung. Mi-tsung was very similar to some sects of Taoism, and stressed the sexual union.

Even Mi-tsung said that *Buddhatvam yosidyonisamasritam* ("Buddheity is in the female generative organs"). In China, "Tibetan Esoteric Sect" (Tibetan Mi-tsung) flourished in the Yuan dynasty, especially from the time of Kubilai Khan (1216-1294 C.E.).

Islam reached China in the mid-7th century through Arab and Persian merchants. Islam has a large following among ten of China's minorities: Hui, Uighur, Kazak, Tatar, Kirghiz, Tajik, Ozbek, Dongxiang, Salar, and Bonan. The number of believers is about 14 million, mostly in Xinjiang, Gansu, Ningxia, Yunnan, Qinghai, Inner Mongolia, Henan, Hubei, Shandong, Liaoning, Beijing, and Tianjin.

Catholicism was introduced into China as early as 635 C.E. By 1949, the number of Catholics in China had reached 2.7 million. Protestantism was introduced into China in 1807. After the Opium War, missionary activity increased and Christianity became a part of the Chinese culture. For example, T'ai-p'ing-T'ian-Kuo, a great peasant rebellion in the Ging dynasty, from 1851 to 1864, was conducted under the banner of God and Christianity. By 1949, China had 700,000 Christians. Generally speaking, Catholicism and Protestantism strengthened the sex-negative and repressive attitudes in China on an official level.

## B. Source and Character of Ethnic Values

There are some differences in sexual lifestyles among the different ethnic groups in China. For example, among Tibetan ethnics, plural marriages including polygyny and polyandry exist beside monogamous marriages. In some Tibetan families, brothers may share one woman as a common wife. There is also great variety in the way one religious factor has an impact on the sexual attitudes in different ethnic groups. For example, Islam takes on slightly different expressions among its many followers in ten of China's minority nationalities: Hui, Uygur, Kazak, Tatar, Kirgiz, Tajik, Dongxiang, Salar, and Bonan. [*Comment 1997*: Similar accounts of the material in this section can be found in Ng and Lau (1990) and Bullough (1976). The *Yearbooks* of the *Encyclopedia Britannica* provide the latest updates on the religious and ethnic composition of the population. (*End of comment by M. P. Lau*)]

## 3. Knowledge and Education about Sexuality

### A. Government Policies and Programs for Sex Education

In line with its general policy of suppressing any discussion of sexuality, the Chinese government neglected the development of sex education courses for the general curriculum. It was not until the early 1980s that model programs were developed, and even then, discussion was usually limited to the necessity of using contraception to limit population growth. In the 1950s, 1960s, and 1970s, not only was there a complete lack of systematic sex education, but only a few booklets on sexuality had been published. The most popular one, *Knowledge of Sex* (*Xing-di-zhi-shi*), was published in 1957. Most of these booklets are devoted to social topics, such as love and marriage, and medical topics, such as sexual dysfunctions. Only a few pages discuss aspects of sexual relationships, such as arousal, sexual responses, and frequency of intercourse. Yet, for more than 20 years, *Knowledge of Sex* was virtually the only sex booklet available to a population of 800 to 900 million people. (See also Part 2, the 1992 Survey of Sexual Behavior in Modern China, Sections B, Adolescent Sexuality, and C, College Students.)

In 1980, heartened by the end of the Cultural Revolution, a few authors and publishers began to produce new materials. The first effort was a new edition of *Knowledge of Sex* published by People's Medical Publishing House. The first printing of 2.5 million copies, released in June 1980, was sold out almost immediately, and some people resold their copies at nearly double the original price.

Between 1980 and 1984, more than ten new sex booklets were published. Two of them became bestsellers. The first, *Required Readings in Wedding Hygiene* was originally published in September 1980, and by November 1981 had already been reprinted eight times, for a total of more than 7.5 million copies. The second, *Questions and Answers about Wedding Hygiene*, was published in July 1984 with a printing of 4.2 million copies.

Finally, in the mid-1980s, four major types of pressure led national and local officials to acknowledge the need for sex education programs. First, the population growth continued to be a very serious problem. A birth control program had been instituted in January 1973, but it became unavoidably clear that to implement the program effectively, young people would have to be given sexual information essential to understanding and using contraception. Second, rates of teenage pregnancy, juvenile sex crime, and sexually transmitted diseases seemed to be increasing. It was stated that sex education offered the best hope for diminishing these problems. Third, medical professionals felt that the numbers of patients they were treating for sexual dysfunction demonstrated a need for improved education. And finally, as a result of the new "open-door" policy of receptiveness to Western cultural influence, and a simultaneous increase in personal freedoms, the Chinese people were expressing a desire to improve their lives, including their sexual lives.

The first high school sex education courses were introduced in 1981 in Shanghai. In early 1986, 40 Shanghai middle schools, about 10% of the city's total, introduced an experimental sex education course for coed classes in the 12- to 13-year age group. In addition to helping students understand the physiological and psychological changes they were undergoing, the course was designed to teach hygiene and sexual morality. By June 1986, nearly a 100 Shanghai middle schools gave sex education courses. And, by February 1988, 6,000 middle schools all over China had instituted sex education courses: Thirteen of the 28 provinces, including Shanghai, Jiangsu, Tianjin, and Helongjiang, had made sex education courses part of the standard middle school curriculum. In February 1988, the State Council announced that sex education courses would be established in middle schools nationwide.

From January to October 1985, a special series of columns titled "Essays on Sex Education" by the author of this chapter was published in *Required Readings for Parents*, the leading national monthly magazine on child and adolescent education (Ruan 1985). The series consisted of ten rather long articles on various aspects of sexuality and sex education. It was the first systematic treatment of such topics to be published since the founding of the People's Republic of China in 1949. The "First National Workshop on Sex Education" was held in Shanghai on July 22 to August 7, 1985. This was the first such conference convened in mainland China since 1949. It was an interdisciplinary workshop, attended by more than 80 professionals from 18 provinces, most them of in the fields of birth control, sociology, urology, and high school and college education. The author was the major instructor. Also in 1985, the author served as chief editor, and as a major contributor, for a large updated volume of the *Handbook of Sex Knowledge*, published by the Scientific and Technological Literature Publishing House in Beijing. Although it was intended to be the most up-to-date text of its kind, the book could not include any descriptions of sexual positions or any nude illustrations (except anatomical drawings). Despite these self-imposed restrictions, the first printing was limited to 500,000 copies by the government. After the author left China for the United States at the end of 1985, he was asked to prepare a new version to include knowledge on the prevention of AIDS. In 1988, the revised edition was jointly published by the Scientific and Technological Literature Publishing House and the People's Medical Publishing House (Ruan 1985/1988), one of the two publishers officially permitted to publish books on sex. Yet in 1988, the government allowed the showing of a film that explicitly referred to the *Handbook*. The movie, titled *Mandarin Duck Apartments* (to the Chinese, a pair of mandarin ducks symbolizes an affectionate couple), includes a scene in which an old woman counsels a young newlywed who feels that sex is dirty and shameful. The old woman shows her the *Handbook*, explaining that findings in sexual science show that women have as much right as men to enjoy sex.

After the Tiananmen Square massacre in 1989, the government fell into its old habit of including sexual restrictions in a wave of political repression. But, because of huge pressure to deal with population control, STDs, and the prevention of teenager pregnancy, the government can no longer inhibit and stop sex education. Sex education classes, exhibitions, meetings, and publications are still continuing and developing in China today. [*Comment 1997*: Pei-Kum Yao has chronicled in detail the development of adolescent sex education since 1920 in Appendix III of Dalin Liu's *Sexual Behavior in Modern China*, 1992. (*End of comment by M. P. Lau*)]

[*Update 2001*: *Ren Zhi Chu*, a nationwide monthly sexuality education journal, is the most popular and only journal of its kind in China. This journal, which was started in 1990 by the Guangdong Committee of Family Planning in Guangzhou, has had phenomenal growth. Recent annual circulation has been one million to 1.2 million copies. In 1999, its circulation was ranked 28th among social-cultural journals in the world. (Hongling Wei, an editor of *Ren Zhi Chu, personal communication). (End of update by F. Ruan)*]

[*Update 2002*: Several mid-2002 reports in the *Beijing Star Daily* and the *People's Daily* described important new developments in sex education in China.

[While it has been widely acknowledged that sex and sex education have long been a sensitive issue in China and many people are too embarrassed to talk openly about the subject, Rong Hua, vice-chairwoman of the Beijing Municipal Women's Federation, described the results of a survey of 1,500 Beijing families as "astonishing." Most parents, Rong pointed out, try to avoid answering their children's questions and do not know what to do when they find their children are making opposite-sex friends.

[Seventy-four percent of the parents surveyed admitted they did not give their children any sex education at all; about 50% admitted they were too embarrassed to do so. While 28% of parents gave their children simple explanations when they asked about sex, only 3% gave detailed explanations. Some parents offered appropriate books to their children and some take them to educational exhibitions on the topic.

[According to Rong and other experts, the survey underlined the need for parents to give truthful answers to their children's questions on sex and for more sex education to be included in family education programs.

[Meanwhile, the *Beijing Star Daily* announced publication of new sex education textbooks for middle-school students that open up discussion of sex, drugs, and contraception. The Haidian District in Beijing, home to several prestigious universities, will take the lead in introducing the textbooks, the first of their kind in Beijing, to its middle schools in September 2002. The books break new ground in teaching youngsters how to deal with sexual harassment, take emergency contraception measures, and keep away from drugs. They also cover AIDS, venereal diseases, "online love," and premarital sex.

[Publication of the pilot series was a major step forward within the educational system, but teachers and parents were playing a more crucial role in guiding teenagers towards healthy ideas on sex-related issues, experts noted. At the same time, adults are being urged to overcome their embarrassment and openly talk about sex for the healthy physical and psychological growth of the younger generation.

[In June 2002, South China's Hainan province began distribution of a television series, *Sex Education for Children in Primary and High Schools*, on video compact disc. Jointly produced by the Central China University of Science and Technology and the Hainan Yongyu Filming and Cultural Communication Limited Company, the series is China's first sex-related popular-science television program targeting young people. The 10-lecture program teaches youngsters about basic sex knowledge, self-protection, sex hygiene, and how to deal with their developing sexuality. The series comes in three versions, a primary, junior high, and senior high school edition. Initially, only the primary school edition will be available on video compact disc. Because the series is specially made for children's psychology and is easy to understand, analysts said it will spare parents and schoolteachers the awkwardness that usually accompanies sex education. (*End of update by R. T. Francoeur*)]

## B. Informal Sources of Sexual Knowledge

Given the government's authoritarian control described in the section above, it is obvious that informal sources of sexual information, such as television talk shows, radio phone-in programs, and popular magazines, commonly found in more democratic and open countries, are very limited in China because they are illegal and are severely punished. [*Comment 1997*: Underground sources continue to flourish, and official control has been relaxing as more emphasis has been shifted from ideology to economy. (*End of comment by M. P. Lau*)]

## 4. Autoerotic Behaviors and Patterns

Self-pleasuring is still condemned by most of the Chinese people, including even some sex educators and sex researchers. It is widely said that frequent self-pleasuring will cause neuroses, sexual dysfunctions, and even severe diseases. Although in 1985, the author pointed out in his popular article, "On Masturbation", and in his *Handbook of Sex Knowledge*, that self-pleasuring is normal sexual behavior, neither harmful nor sinful, it will take time for people to accept this updated viewpoint on self-pleasuring. According to *A Report of the Nationwide "Sex Civilization" Survey on 20,000 Subjects in China* (1992), only 39.0% of college and university students said that they engaged in self-pleasuring, male students (59.0%) much higher than female students (16.5%). But Dr. Lee's survey in 1989 in Shanghai showed that 93.1% of male students at colleges and universities said that they engaged in this behavior. In the *"Sex Civilization" Survey*, 15.9% of married couples said that they engaged in self-pleasuring. (See also Part 2, the 1992 Survey of Sexual Behavior in Modern China, Sections B, Adolescent Sexuality, C, College Students, and D, Married Couples, for data on masturbation in the nationwide survey by Dalin Liu.)

## 5. *Interpersonal Heterosexual Behaviors*

### A/B. Children/Adolescents

Because of the pervasive social pressures, reinforced by some messages given by some medical practitioners and the lack of sexual education, sexual expression other than heterosexual marital sex, (including sexual play and sex rehearsal play, both alone and with peers), is punished when discovered. Such behavior is seldom, if ever, reported or commented on in public. No puberty rites are observed to mark sexual maturation.

### *Premarital Sexual Activities and Relationships*

A study in a major city in Quangdong province found that of 123 young women undergoing premarital examinations, 75 (61%) had already experienced intercourse. In a 1991 survey in which questionnaires were distributed to a random sample of 1,003 unmarried university students in Beijing, including equal numbers of men and women, of 559 respondents, 106 (19%) said they had engaged in sex. Lack of private space is a major problem for young lovers. Many young people have little choice but to meet in parks. And where, five years ago, couples were likely to sit demurely together on a bench, it is now acceptable to hug and kiss, ignoring people passing by only a few feet away. Some couples disappear into the bushes. In Dalin Liu's 1992 survey, 18% of the married couples admitted to having sex with a previous partner; 86.3% of those sampled approved of such encounters. (See also Part 2, the 1992 Survey of Sexual Behavior in Modern China, Sections B, Adolescent Sexuality, and C, College Students, for data on premarital courtship and sexual attitudes and behavior among adolescent males and females and college students in the 1992 nationwide survey.)

### C. Adults

#### *Unmarried Adults*

For several thousand years, the Chinese people have tried to adhere to the simple dictum: "Get married at a marriageable age." And for centuries it would have been true to say that no Chinese would want to remain single for his or her entire life. But in recent years, China's unmarried population has been growing at a steady rate. For example, in 1982, there were 11,267,000 unmarried Chinese people aged between 28 and 49 years old, or 4.36% of the total population in the 28-to-49 age range. Of these, 10,556,000 were male (93.67%) and 714,000 female (6.33%). (See also Part 2, the 1992 Survey of Sexual Behavior in Modern China, Sections C, College Students, and D, Married Couples, for data on premarital sexual attitudes in the nationwide survey.)

Recently, the Chinese people have started to replace their old-fashioned social concepts with ones that respect the rights of the unmarried; to remain single is now as much a personal right as the right to marry. An important factor in this shift was a greater respect for the rights of freedom, which should prove a blessing both to individuals and society.

[*Update 1997*: In every public park in China, a large billboard at every entrance warns against "offence against public decency," just as there are notices in dance halls prohibiting anyone from "dancing with faces or cheeks touching the partner's." In reality, such "indecencies" are practiced by most people, and law enforcers are becoming more and more tolerant.

[An analysis of detailed observations of courtship and petting behaviors engaged in by married, unmarried, and status-unknown couples in 13 public parks in six Chinese cities, Beijing, Guangzhou, Zheng-zhou, Hohehaote, Chong-qing, and Xian, during the summers between 1985 and 1989, provides an insight into the heterosexual courtship behavior of young Chinese couples in that era: In the five years, from 1985 to 1989, petting behavior in public parks increased, forcing authorities to be more tolerant of behavior that previously was unacceptable. The decreasing social control by the authorities reflected more tolerance in the society's political direction. Attitudes toward public petting were the most diversified in Beijing. The most permissiveness was found mainly in parks used mostly by blue-collar workers, as compared to parks used mostly by white-collar workers and "cadres." Finally, in a country with a strong tradition of double standards in sexual morals for females and males, it was surprising that in Beijing, only 31 to 40% of the females were fully passive, and at least 18 to 27% initiated petting to a small degree when it came to less intimate petting behavior in more-private settings in the parks. "It could never be imagined in the old days that so many females would allow themselves to be petted in public, even if they were absolutely passive" (Pan 1993, 184).

[In 1987, there was the movement against "bourgeoisie liberalization," and in 1989, a "counterrevolutionary rebellion" in Beijing. It is uncertain whether and how these efforts could or did affect the petting limits, but it seems that the grimmer a movement is, the more timid the petting couples are, and the less permissive the nearby people are to the petting. It is also interesting to note that no amount of social control, be it by propaganda, moral condemnation, or daily administrative measures, is as effective as a large-scale political movement once every few years in reinstating the official petting limits (Pan 1993, 192; Burton 1988). (*End of update by R. T. Francoeur*)]

#### *Cohabitation*

Beginning in the late 1970s, the increased tolerance of nonmarital cohabitation in the West began to influence China's younger generation. College students and young intellectuals, in particular, were attracted to this lifestyle. Some of the younger or more open-minded sociologists also asserted the necessity of overcoming the disadvantages of traditional marriage. Actually, the act of cohabitation might be an act of defiance and courage, or simply a consequence of overcrowding and the lack of living space. These young Chinese risked being arrested.

The definition of unmarried cohabitation used in compiling official statistics makes it difficult to estimate the popularity of this behavior in the sense it is understood in the West. The official figure of 2.69 million couples in unmarried cohabitation in 1989 seems low, considering that some areas report that as many as 50% of couples living together live in unmarried cohabitation. As for couples marrying under the legal age (22 for males; 20 for females), China's State Family Planning Commission reports that 6.1 million such marriages took place in 1987 alone. According to China's 1990 census, 5.8% of 15- to 21-year-old males and 15- to 19-year-old females were "married." That means that 8.5 million Chinese "married" under the legal age. Two and a half million babies—10% of all births—were born to underage couples in that year. The same news article reports an estimate by the Marriage Administration Division of the National Department of Civil Administration that 30% of China's "married" couples are living together without having received an official marriage certificate, and that the number is growing (see Section 9D, Contraception, Abortion, and Population Planning, Population Control Efforts).

*Marriage and the Family*

Although China has a long history of polygamy, in contemporary mainland China, only monogamy is legal and morally permissible. On May 1, 1950, a new Marriage Law was promulgated. It stated that "The New-Democratic marriage system, which is based on the free choice of partners, on monogamy, on equal rights of both sexes, and on the protection of the lawful interests of women and children, shall be put into effect," and that "Bigamy, concubinage, child betrothal, interference with the remarriage of widows, and the exaction of money or gifts in connection with marriage, shall be prohibited." The revised marriage law of 1980 followed the same principles as the 1950 law.

*Marital Sex*

A surprising 91% of the 8,000 married couples interviewed by Dalin Liu (1992) in cities and rural areas expressed satisfaction with their spouse. However, when Dalin looked deeper, he found that the average Chinese couple has intercourse four to seven times a month, with peasants invariably reporting 25% more sex than city couples. However, 34.1% of the rural couples and 17.2% of city couples admit to less than one minute of foreplay or none at all. Consequently, 44.7% of urban wives and 37% of rural wives experience pain during intercourse. Only 16.8% of rural couples kiss or embrace apart from lovemaking. (See also Part 2. The 1992 Survey of Sexual Behavior in Modern China, Section D, Married Couples, for data on marital sex and satisfaction in the 1992 nationwide survey.)

Marital dissatisfaction is very common in China today. Some estimate that as many as 60% of the Chinese are unhappy with their marriages. A survey of 3,000 young people in Wuhan, the capital of Hubei province, showed that only 20% of respondents were satisfied with their marriage. In a survey of 600 couples, all residents of big cities, 70% said they were unhappy with their sex lives. A random survey of married couples in Shanghai found that 45% were unhappy with their sexual relationships. A survey of 6,000 divorce cases in five large cities, including Beijing, Shanghai, Guangzhou (Canton), Wuhan, and Xi'an, by ten newspapers showed that 72% of divorces are caused by disharmony in sexual life. [*Update 2001*: A four-year survey of "The Quality of Marriage in China" found that only 3% of the couples surveyed rated their marital sex as "fully satisfying," 75% rated it "so-so," while 22% rated it "low quality." (December 2, 2000, Shenzhen Evening News). (*End of update by F. Ruan*)]

*Divorce*

Although the divorce rate is not very high in China, it is increasing rapidly. In 1978, some 170,449 couples divorced; in 1979, 192,894 couples; in 1980, 180,378 couples; 186,891 couples in 1981; 210,930 couples in 1982, 420,000 couples in 1983, and 450,000 couples in 1984. In 1985 and 1986, the annual average was 500,000 couples. The divorce figure rose to 587,000 couples in 1987, and 630,000 couples in 1988. In 1989, nationwide official statistics showed that 9,851,000 couple applied for marriage; 9,348,000 couples, about 95%, were approved and given a marriage certificate. In the same year, 1,307,000 couples applied for divorce; 752,000, about

58%, were approved and given divorce certificates. The marriage rate was 16.8 per 1,000 persons and the divorce rate 1.35 per 1,000 persons.

[*Update 1997*: With rapid economic growth creating new hopes and expectations, and Government interference in personal lives receding steadily, the divorce rate in Beijing more than doubled from 12% in 1990 to 24.4% in 1994, according to the *Beijing Youth Daily*. This statistic compares the number of marriages and divorces in a given year. While the national divorce rate in mid-1995 was 10.4, far behind that in the United States and European nations, officials admit that the divorce rate is rising all over China, and faster in the cities than in rural areas. Among the factors contributing to the new trend are the new social and economic freedoms, the rising expectations that women bring to marriage, and a remarkable increase in extramarital affairs. More than 70% of divorces are currently initiated by women with the most common reason being an extramarital affair on the part of the husband.

[Increasingly, among urban Chinese and even among government officials who once actively opposed divorce, divorce is being viewed as a an acceptable alternative to an unhappy marriage. Many officials even recognize a positive side to divorce. When both parties agree, a divorce can be granted in three days; not long ago, the wait was years. Important as the government's attitudinal shift is, the larger factors are the growing expectations women bring to marriage today and their growing demands in an era of expanding opportunity. In the past, women were happy to settle for a stable income, a home, and children. To these expectations, women are now adding romance, sex, and affection. While women increasingly enjoy more independence and choices in career, place to live, husband, and lover, they are also more subject to unemployment. Meanwhile, the shift has also brought a resurgence of traditional male values, including the right to have an affair.

[Prior to the current surge in divorces, China experienced two other waves of rapidly rising divorce rates: The first occurred in the 1950s when returning victorious Communist soldiers abandoned their farms and rural wives to move to the city; the second came during and just after the Cultural Revolution, between 1966 and 1980 (Faison 1995). (*End of update by R. T. Francoeur*)]

[*Concubinage*

[*Update 2003*: For thousands of years, Chinese emperors and government officials surrounded themselves with concubines, while traders and businessmen maintained a wife in every port. Under British rule (1841 to 1997), concubines were legal in Hong Kong. In the past generation, enough Hong Kong men have led the double life to father an estimated 520,000 children. In 1999, a local Hong Kong court exercised its separate legal jurisdiction to grant Hong Kong residency to the half-million children born to the second wives of Hong Kong men. That decision would have added significantly to Hong Kong's 6.5 million people packed into a very limited 416 square miles (1,077 km$^2$). It also created some serious legal consequences for the "One Country, Two Systems" policy. Not surprisingly, a mainland Chinese court overturned the local decree.

[With Hong Kong and the former Portuguese colony of Macao now under mainland Chinese rule, the borders are increasingly porous, and concentrations of second wives and concubines are expanding in small cities and suburbs within commuting distance of Hong Kong and Macao and along the main rail lines from Hong Kong and Macao to Guangzhou, as well as across southeast China.

[Concerned about the negative effects of the concubine tradition on China's family-planning policies of one child per family in the cities and a tolerated two children in the rural areas, the government is now trying to eliminate or at least reduce concubinage. This will not be easy, for both economic and jurisdictional reasons.

[Mass migration and economic dislocation have made concubines a major problem across the country wherever rural poverty meets the affluence of the new free market's restrained capitalist economy. For a modest $200 monthly rent in a village of concubines, a moderately affluent married businessman can enjoy the comfort of an attractive devoted second wife. Second wives are easy to find on farms just outside cities. There is also a flourishing business of go-betweens who recruit young women happy to trade the hard life on a poor farm in some distant province for the luxury of a two-bedroom apartment with some modern conveniences in the bustling suburb of a modern city.

[The government tries to combat migration from the farms to the cities by issuing every adult a work permit allowing that person to work legally only within a certain distance of their birthplace. Permits to migrate to a city are strictly limited. In becoming a concubine, a young woman can leave her rural home without a work permit and be supported by a "husband."

[A law introduced in 2000 in Shenzhen, just outside Hong Kong's Kowloon destrict, provides a prison sentence of 10 months for "factual bigamy"; a single act of adultery is still not a crime. Under a new law in Guangdong province, which includes both Shenzhen and Dongguan, long-term cohabitation by an unmarried couple is now a crime and can bring a two-year sentence to a labor camp. However, the police face a near insurmountable obstacle proving long-term cohabitation when a monthly lease or no lease enables a man to move his second wife to a new apartment on very short notice.

[The current separate legal jurisdictions of Hong Kong, Macao, and China also make prosecution very difficult. If a Hong Kong woman wants to take her bigamist husband into a Chinese court, she must first make sure that the Chinese police can prove that the husband is living with his mistress somewhere in one of the populous mainland villages of concubines (Landler 2000; Luk 2002). (*End of update by R. T. Francoeur*)]

### Extramarital Sexual Activities

Sex between consenting adults is technically not illegal in China, but the police have broad powers to suppress activities that they consider antisocial. Elderly women who staff local "neighborhood committees," the grassroots eyes and ears of the government, also try to stop activities of which they disapprove. But discreet affairs have a good chance of escaping detection and interference. Means of birth control were not always available to unmarried youths, but women knew they could get an abortion. Extramarital affairs seem to occur much more than generally believed, although they are conducted in such secrecy that little statistical information is available. Perhaps the best evidence of these affairs is divorce rates: about one third of the divorces in Beijing from 1984 to 1985 were caused by extramarital relationships. In the Third Symposium of Family Problems in 1991, an expert said that 40% of divorces are caused by extramarital sexual relationships. If these findings are at all typical, then the increasing divorce rate must reflect an increase in the number of extramarital relationships.

A survey in Beijing found that members of at least 10% of the sample of 600 couples had had extramarital sex. Perhaps most significant is a nationwide survey that showed that 69% of the people surveyed did not think extramarital affairs are wrong. In Dalin Liu's 1992 survey, 69% condoned extramarital sexual relations.

### Incidence of Oral and Anal Sex

Several factors influence both attitudes towards and experience with oral and anal sex. In a 1989 survey with 1,279 respondents in 27 cities, nearly seven out of ten Chinese reported that they have had anal sex with heterosexual partners. Professor Pan found that only 6% of the 600 heterosexual couples he surveyed in big cities had had anal intercourse at least once.

In ancient erotic art and fiction, oral sex, including mutual "69" oral sex, is not unusual. Considering the lack of information about sexual behaviors that prevailed until recently, and Dalin Liu's finding that 34% of rural couples and 17% of urban couples engaged in less than a minute of foreplay, it is not likely that oral sex is as common as it was in ancient China. No general survey data is available. Many modern Chinese think oral sex is too "dirty." In 1988, a survey of 140 homosexual males in Shanghai revealed that only 19 persons, 13.6%, said they had had oral sex, and only four persons, 2.8%, had experienced anal sex. At a 1990 World Health Organization meeting on the spread of AIDS in China, Pan reported that 7.7 out of 10 Chinese have had anal sex with a heterosexual partner. Few data are available on anal sex among homosexuals because of the taboo character of that population as well as studies of same-sex behavior (Burton 1990). (Dalin Liu's *Sex Culture in Ancient China* provides extensive information about sexual deviance in China.)

## 6. Homoerotic, Homosexual, and Bisexual Behaviors

Male homosexuality may have been a familiar feature of Chinese life in remote ancient times. The official Chinese historical records indicate that during the Spring-Autumn and Chin-Han Era (770 B.C.E. to 24 C.E.), male same-sex behavior was not a crime or considered immoral behavior. On the contrary, it was sometimes the noble thing to do. For example, in Western Han (206 B.C.E. to 8 C.E.), ten of the 11 emperors each had at least one homosexual lover or shared some same-sex behavior. During the Western and Eastern Jin and Southern and Northern Dynasties (256 to 581 C.E.), male homosexuality seemed also acceptable in the broader upper-class society.

Considering the many and varied records of homosexuality in ancient China, one would expect to find evidence of homosexuality in modern China. However, literature regarding contemporary homosexuality is scarce at best, although it is available in Taiwan and Hong Kong. Thus it was a genuine breakthrough when, through a rather unique and unexpected set of events, the situation of homosexuality in China was openly discussed for the first time in a positive context: In 1985, Ruan, the author of this chapter, using a pen name, Jin-ma Hua, published an article in a widely circulated Chinese health magazine, *To Your Good Health*. The article pointed out that homosexuality has occurred in all nations, all social strata, and in all eras in human history, and that homosexuals deserve a reasonable social status. Many of the readers of *To Your Good Health*, most of them gay, wrote to the magazine's editor in response to the article.

By April 1986, a total of 60 letters had been received by the editor of *To Your Good Health*, and forwarded to Ruan. A striking aspect of the letters from gay men is their immense relief at having an opportunity to express their feelings. Many letters expressed the writers' pain and conflicting desires for both confidentiality and a chance to overcome their isolation. Clearly, the chief source of pain for China's gay men derives from the fear of societal punishment, including arrest, and possible sentence to labor reform camp or prison.

The mental pressure and anguish arising from the fear that their true identity might be discovered is often unbearable. The social pressure, pain, and inner conflict homosexuals suffer can be so intense that they come to consider or even attempt suicide. Of the 56 who responded to Hua's article, 15, or more than 25%, mentioned suicide attempts. Of all the hopes and dreams expressed in these moving letters, three types of aspirations were outstanding. The first concerned the human rights issue—the belief that society should accept homosexuals and their right to express their sexuality without social or legal condemnation. The second concerned the issue of freedom to interact with other homosexuals—the wish that society would provide them with means to make contacts and form relationships, just as it does for heterosexuals. The third concerned the issue of knowledge—the wish that objective and scientific studies would be conducted and publicized in order to improve societal understanding. In 20 letters, the hope that some agency would facilitate social contacts among homosexuals took the form of a request that "Dr. Hua" or his publishers do so. In Hua's article, two actual cases of gay life in Hubei and Shanghai had been described. All 20 letters requested the names and addresses of these two men in order to establish contact with them. Some men, though they did not use the word for "club," expressed the wish to create this type of organization. There were 18 letters pointing out the need for development and/or publication of more information about homosexuality.

Regarding the legal situation of homosexuals in mainland China now, although there is no specific statement concerning the status of homosexuals in the current Criminal Law of the People's Republic of China, Article 106 says, "All hooliganism should be subjected to arrest and sentence." In practice, homosexual activity has been included in "hooliganism." As noted above, even the small sample of letters Ruan received contained a report of a man who received a five-year jail term for homosexuality.

Silence, especially a silence based on repression and enforced ignorance, must not be mistaken for approval or tolerance. When public figures do speak out on homosexuality, it is usually to condemn it. For example, in the 1990s, a famous attorney even wrote that "homosexuality . . . disrupts social order, invades personal privacy and rights and leads to criminal behavior." A leading forensic psychiatrist said that "homosexuality is against social morality, interferes with social security, damages the physical and mental health of adolescents, and ought to be a crime."

Another common reaction to the suggestion that homosexuality exists in China is denial. Clear evidence of the official denial of homosexuality was provided by the internationally well-known sexologist, Dr. Richard Green, the series editor of "Perspectives in Sexuality: Behavior, Research, and Therapy." In his "Series Editor's Comment" for Ruan's book *Sex in China: Studies in Sexology in Chinese Culture*, he wrote:

Less than a year before the 1989 massacre in Tiananmen square, I lectured on human sexuality at Peking Union Medical College. I described my research on the nonsexual behaviors of young boys that predicted later homosexuality. I asked the physicians in the audience whether comparable childhood behaviors were found among Chinese boys. I was told that there were no homosexuals in China. (Ruan 1991)

But, this official attitude of denying homosexuality in China can no longer be justified. In late 1991, officials in Shanghai, the largest city in China, recognized that there are about 10,000 homosexuals in the city. Actually, the number of homosexuals may be over 200,000, according to the

*World Weekly* (September 1, 1991). Changzheng Hospital in Tianjin, the third largest city in China, reported in a medical paper that in the past four years, out of 366 STD cases, at least 61 cases of syphilis resulted from male homosexual behavior; 80% of the cases involved anal sex, 10% oral sex, and other 10% anal plus oral sex. Most of the cases (80%) involved sexual activity in public toilets. More than 80% of the homosexual partners were strangers. Their ages ranged from 16 years to 60 years, with two thirds of the group falling between 20 and 30 years of age. Most of them were workers, some were cadres, teachers, and others.

Yet another reaction is to admit that perhaps homosexuality does exist in China, but to insist that, when it occurs, it is the result of Western influence; it was referred to as "spiritual pollution," and "Western social diseases," originating in "Western ideology and thoughts."

Finally, there are those who, when faced with undeniable evidence of homosexuality, respond by seeking to eliminate it. Even many physicians still fail to recognize homosexuality as simply one possible sexual orientation. For example, in Harbin, one of the largest cities in northeastern China, physicians now use the discredited approach of "treating" homosexuality with electric shock therapy to discourage erotic thoughts.

In ancient times, Chinese culture was characterized by a very tolerant attitude toward same-sex female behavior. Lesbians in China today are even more closeted than gay males. (See also Xiaomingxiong—alias Samshasha 1984, and Lau & Ng 1989).

When Ruan received letters from homosexuals all over China in 1985 and 1986, not one was from a woman. The only women who are willing to discuss their homosexuality are the few who have already been imprisoned for this behavior and have little to lose. An exception to the usual difficulty in locating lesbians is the experience of Chinese journalists, He and Fang, who were actually more successful in contacting lesbians than gay males in their 1989 survey of homosexuality in China. They wrote six stories about lesbians compared to one about gay males.

He and Fang had to rely on interviews with women who were jailed for "sex crimes," or crimes of violence inspired by sexual jealousy. Because so many investigations of female homosexuality are based on interviews with prisoners, it has been all too easy for Chinese people to develop a stereotype of lesbians as immoral, frustrated people (Sheridan & Salaff 1984).

In early 1992, a new and more humane homosexual policy emerged. This started with two young lesbians in Wuwei County, Anhui province, whose parents opposed their homosexual relationship very much. The angry parents finally reported the affair to the local police department. After several months of investigation, the police department of Wuwei County arrested these two female lovers and restrained them 15 days on charges of "misconduct."

The Wuwei County police department then referred the case to higher institutions until the Public Security Department of Central Government in Beijing heard the case. The Public Security Department replied and instructed the county police that because, under current laws, there was no article that specifies punishment for such behavior and relationship, it could not treated as "misconduct." Therefore, the Wuwei Police Department released the two women and let them live together as "husband" and "wife." Usually the older woman takes the role of "husband," and wears male clothing, while the younger one takes the role of "wife" and prefers to stay in the home. It is a very good signal to show that, at least some police officers, especially senior ones, have started to change their attitude toward homosexuality and other sexual variations. But, recently a reversal still occurred. In May 1993, the government closed down the first gay saloon, "Men's World," located in Beijing. It had opened appeared on November 22, 1992, and came out in public on February 14, 1993.

(See also Part 2, the 1992 Survey of Sexual Behavior in Modern China, Sections B, Adolescent Sexuality, C, College Students, and D, Married Couples, for data on views of homosexuality and the incidence of same-sex behavior among adolescents, college students, and married couples in the nationwide survey.)

[*Update 2001*: Hongling Wei, editor of *Ren Zhi Chu* (sexual education journal), estimates that about 36 million to 48 million mainland Chinese men, 3 to 4% of the population, are homosexual or bisexual (Personal communication to Ruan).

[Research on homosexuality in China was pioneered in the 1990s by three noted scholars. Dr. Yinghe Li, a sociologist of sex who studied at the University of Pittsburgh (USA), Dr. Beichuan Zhang, a researcher on same-sex love, and Professor Suiming Pan, a sociologist of sex and Director of the Institute for Sociology of Sex at The People's University, Beijing. Dr. Li has interviewed and surveyed homosexuals and authored a monograph *Subculture of Homosexuality* (1998, Beijing). Dr. Zhang wrote the most comprehensive academic Chinese monograph on *Same Sex Love* (1994, Jinan: Shangdong Scientific and Technic Press). In his early investigation of homosexual behaviors in 1997 to 1998, Dr. Zhang discovered that only one third of the over 400 homosexuals he interviewed used condoms (Beichuan Zhang: "Men, sexual relationships, AIDS," *Ren Zhi Chu* 1999, 9: 36). Table 2 lists the results of a 1998 nationwide random investigation of sexual attitudes toward homosexuality among ordinary Chinese.

[In early 2001, the 8,000-member Chinese Psychiatric Association concluded that homosexuality is not a perversion and removed homosexuality from its list of mental illnesses in its new diagnostic manual. The step added to a growing tolerance of gays and lesbians in China, where an underground culture of gay bars, websites, and sports clubs flourishes. Taking advantage of loosening social restrictions over the past two decades, gay couples now live together discreetly. In major cities like Shanghai, some musicians and artists are openly gay, although many homosexuals endure harassment. The diagnostic manual retains an entry on homosexuality as a possible cause of depression, and other problems for patients who are uncomfortable with their orientation. Treatment can include therapy meant to change a patient's orientation to heterosexual, but such therapy was rare in China. (*End of update by F. Ruan*)]

## 7. Gender Diversity and Transgender Issues

Recognition of transsexualism in human society is a relatively recent phenomenon, especially in the closed society of mainland China. In January 1983, with the author's assis-

**Table 2**

**Chinese Attitudes Toward Homosexuality**

| Homosexuality ... | Completely agree | Rather agree | Rather disagree | Do not agree |
|---|---|---|---|---|
| Is an inversion | 52.2% | 30.8% | 10.0% | 3.7% |
| Is immoral | 17.2 | 22.6 | 43.3 | 13.6 |
| Is biological | 10.1 | 28.9 | 32.9 | 23.3 |
| Is normal | 5.5 | 12.4 | 26.6 | 51.6 |
| Gay marriage OK | 4.5 | 6.3 | 20.2 | 65.3 |

tance, the first male-to-female transsexual surgery was performed in the Plastic Surgery Department of the Third Hospital of Beijing Medical University.

The greatest difficulty facing transsexuals in China is that of gaining the acceptance of their families and society. It is nearly impossible to obtain permission to perform transsexual surgery. A psychiatrist told the author that he had seen two transsexual patients who, after being repeatedly denied transsexual surgery, used knives to remove the penis by themselves. The problem is not a lack of appropriate surgical techniques and facilities. In fact, both general plastic surgery and such precise surgical techniques as reimplantation of severed fingers are very advanced in China. Dr. Xia, in the Plastic Surgery Department of the Third Hospital of Beijing Medical University, has successfully operated simultaneously on a male-to-female transsexual and a female-to-male transsexual with mutual exchange and transplantation of ovaries and testicles; this surgery took 19 hours. If permission were given, transsexual surgery could be performed with little difficulty in most large hospitals. The problem is really perceptual and ideological. The absence of scientific research on the subject means that there is nothing to counteract the statements of the popular press, which describes transsexualism as not merely outlandish, but as evidence of the inroads of "decadent Western culture." This ideological tone effectively inhibits surgeons' willingness to perform transsexual surgery.

[*Comment 1997*: In early Chinese history, hundreds of males were castrated every year to become eunuchs. Some of these were transsexuals. In other words, transsexuals in the past had a legal option transsexuals do not have in China today. (*End of comment by M. P. Lau*)]

## 8. Significant Unconventional Sexual Behaviors

### A. Coercive Sex

*Rape and Pedophilia*

Rape, pedophilia, and any behavior which "subjects women to indignities or carries out other gangster activities," are all clearly illegal, according to Articles 139 and 160 of the 1980 Criminal Law of the People's Republic of China. It is very interesting to note that although China has an official policy severely repressing sex and heavily punishing sex crime, nevertheless, such crimes in mainland China continue to increase from year to year. The Chinese government does not publicize the number of sex crimes, but some figures are available from academic articles. For example, in Shanghai, the largest city in China, the number of rapes increased from 100% (as the basis for comparison) in 1979 to 377% in 1983. Nationwide, the number of reported rapes rose from a base 100% in 1979 to 340% in 1983. (See also Part 2. The 1992 Survey of Sexual Behavior in Modern China, Section E, Sex Offenders, for data in the 1992 nationwide survey.)

Teenage rapists, in particular, increased from a base of 100% in 1980, to 150% in 1981, 192% in 1982, and 311% in 1983. While there was a slight decrease in 1984, the absolute number still increased, and in 1985, it increased by 42.5% in Shanghai over the previous year.

In China, every year, a lot of people were shot by the government as the penalty for crime. Many of them were related to crimes of sex, love, and marriage. In Beijing, the capital of the People's Republic, for instance, out of 52 cases for which executions were carried out in 1984, crimes of sex, love, and marriage accounted for 67.4% of all death penalties.

The juvenile crime rate from 1979 to 1981 increased more than 25%. Statistics from three cities from 1980 to 1983 showed 13% of juvenile crimes involved sex crimes.

Most of them involved 13- to 15-year-olds. Forty percent of male delinquents charged by the Juvenile Delinquent Correction Institution were charged with "sexual crimes and mistakes"; 95% of the female delinquents, some as young as 12 years, were charged with sexual violations, which may or may not have involved rape.

### Incest and Sexual Harassment

Certainly, incest and sexual harassment exist in China. No general survey data are available. "Sexual harassment" as a new word in Chinese (*Xingsaorao*) translated from English, is now used in China. Traditionally, it was included in the concept of *liumong xingwei* or *tiaoxi funu*, both terms indicating any behavior which sexually subjects women to indignities. *Liumong xingwei* and *tiaoxi funu* are clearly illegal, according to Articles 139 and 160 of the 1980 Criminal Law of the People's Republic of China.

### [Sexual Violence and Crimes of Passion

[*Update 2001*: In early 2001, Shanghai's State Prosecutor reported that China's massive floating population of rural migrants was playing a major role in the dramatic rise in extramarital affairs, divorces, and domestic violence. In 1999, the Prosecutor reported that over one million of the eight million Chinese in the city of Shanghai proper had obtained a divorce. Domestic violence reportedly affected a third of Shanghai's families and half of the city's homicides were crimes of passion. (*End of update by F. Ruan*)]

### B. Prostitution

China's first brothels were likely established in the Spring-and-Autumn period (770 B.C.E. to 476 B.C.E.) by the famous statesman and philosopher Guan Zhong (? to 645 B.C.E.), who used them as a means of increasing the state's income. It is clear that the institution of government-run prostitution reached its peak in the Tang (618 to 905 C.E.) and Sung (960 to 1279 C.E.) Dynasties. In ancient China, where most women had no opportunity to acquire an education, and formal contact between men and women was frowned upon, it was the role of the courtesan to entertain a man and be his friend. Every prominent official, writer, artist, or merchant customarily left his wife at home when he traveled; instead, he was accompanied by women skilled in making men feel comfortable. Courtesans with literary, musical, or dancing ability were especially desirable companions, and many became famous historical figures. However, the prostitutes working in privately owned brothels mainly provided sexual services. (See also the profile of a female prostitute in Part 2. The 1992 Survey of Sexual Behavior in Modern China, Section E, Sex Offenders, for data on prostitution in the 1992 nationwide survey.)

From the Sung to the Ming Dynasties, government-run and privately owned prostitution existed side by side in China. Early in the Ging dynasty, from 1651 to 1673 C.E., the Manchu Emperors Shun-chih and Kang-hsi gradually abolished both local and imperial governmental involvement in operating prostitution. Thus, for most of the Ching dynasty, prostitution in China was a private enterprise. For most of the Republican period in mainland China (1912 to 1949), some prostitutes were registered while others plied their trade illegally.

When the Chinese Communists took power, one of the first social changes they introduced was the abolition of prostitution. Only one month after the Communist army took control of Beijing (Peking) on February 3, 1949, the new municipal government announced a policy of limiting and controlling the brothels. Less than eight weeks after the founding of the People's Republic of China, on October 1, 1949, more than 2,000 Beijing policemen raided and closed all 224 of the city's brothels, arresting 1,286 prostitutes and 424 owners, procurers, and pimps. Other cities soon followed suit. In Shanghai, China's most populous city, there were 5,333 arrests of prostitutes between 1950 and 1955.

In October 1957, in a new attempt to maintain order, the 81st Session of the Standing Committee of the First National People's Congress adopted a new law titled Rules on the Control of and Punishment Concerning Public Security of the People's Republic of China. The legislation announced the policy on banning prostitution. In 1979, at its Second Session, the Fifth National People's Congress adopted the first criminal law in the PRC, The Criminal Law of the People's Republic of China, which took effect January 1, 1980. Under this Law, the punishment for coercing prostitution was more severe: "Article 140: Whoever forces a female to engage in prostitution shall be sentenced to a fixed term of imprisonment of 3 to 10 years."

The severe repression of prostitution did not prevent its accelerated revival in the late 1970s and throughout the 1980s and 1990s. The first official report of the recurrence and development of prostitution in mainland China appeared in March 1983. It reported that

> According to the incomplete statistics from the three largest cities, Beijing, Shanghai, Tianjin, and four provinces, Guangdong, Fujian, Zhejiang and Liaoning, from January, 1982 to November, 1982, more than 11,500 persons were discovered to be involved in prostitution. More than 1,200 persons were owners and pimps of underground brothels; more than 4,200 women were prostitutes; and 1,800 persons, including 223 visitors from foreign countries, Hong Kong and Macao, were customers of prostitutes. Fifteen hundred people were fined, 790 were detained, 691 were arrested, and 662 were sent to labor camps. More than 900 underground brothels were banned and closed.

The growth of prostitution in Guangzhou (Canton) alone was amazing. In 1979, only 49 pimps, prostitutes, and customers were caught. In 1985, this number had increased to approximately 2,000. In one month of 1987, 11,946 people were arrested for involvement in prostitution, and in both the preceding and following months, the figures rose to more than 13,000.

Prostitutes and their customers appeared everywhere, in hotels, inns, hair salons, single-family homes, apartments, dormitories, underground brothels, and taxis, in every city and every province. Between January 1986 and July 1987, 18 prison camps for prostitutes were opened, and by December, the number of camps had more than tripled to 62.

Statistics collected in 1986 in the city of Guangzhou (Canton), in Guangdong province, supply some information about the men who patronize prostitutes. In 1986, of 1,580 customers who were caught, 41% were from the city, 34.5% from other parts of the province, 15.3% from other provinces, 6.1% from Hong Kong and Macao, and 3.7% from other countries. Fully two thirds of the customers were Communist Party members and county officials.

There is no doubt that economic motives fuel the current rapid growth of prostitution in mainland China. The possibility of earning as much as 10,000 Yuan new income in only two or three months, versus the average Chinese income of only about 100 Yuan per month, is a powerful incentive.

Since the late 1980s, even harsher measures were taken in the effort to curtail prostitution, including arrests of foreign citizens. In June 1988, in the Shenzhen Economic Zone, which abuts Hong Kong, there was a mass arrest of 122 prostitutes and 100 customers. In the small town of Deqing, about a 100 miles (160 km) west of Canton, a man accused of being a pimp was executed.

The opposition to prostitution also has an ideological basis. In the lexicon of China's Communist leadership, "prostitution" is a very bad word. Deng Xiaoping, the top leader in China, is particularly strong in his opposition to prostitution and advocates severe penalties, because he believes it tarnishes his country's reputation. According to a formal report, more than 200,000 prostitutes and customers were caught in 1991 alone, and more than 30,000 prostitutes were sent to forced labor camps, 80% of them streetwalkers.

Some of those arrested in the anti-prostitution movement received sentences as severe as the death penalty. In Wenzhou city, Zhenjiang province, a woman and a man were sentenced to death because they had owned several underground brothels, employing 14 prostitutes. In Beijing, a 55-year-old man was given a death sentence because in 1988 he had allowed prostitutes to use the offices in a hospital about 20 times.

[*Update 2001*: China currently has an estimated three million female commercial sex workers, according to a personal communiqué from Hongling Wei, editor of *Ren Zhi Chu*. (*End of update by F. Ruan*)]

## C. Pornography and Erotica

In China, erotic painting and erotic fiction occurred over 1,000 years ago, in the Tang dynasty. The official prohibition of erotic art and literature started as early as about 800 years ago, in the Yuan dynasty. After the founding of the People's Republic of China on October 1, 1949, a strict ban on erotic fiction and pornography of any kind was imposed nationwide. In the 1950s and 1960s, the policy of banning erotica was very effective. In the whole country, almost no erotic material was to be found. There were few difficulties implementing this policy until the mid-1970s.

Then, the legalization and wide availability of pornography in several Western countries during the late 1960s and early 1970s, coupled with China's growing openness to the outside world, increased the supply of such material available for underground circulation.

In recent years, the suppression of pornography has become a very serious political and legislative concern. The number of arrests and the severity of sentences on people involved in pornography have both increased in the attempt to suppress it entirely.

By the late 1970s, "X-rated" films and videotapes were being smuggled into China from Hong Kong and other countries. (In China, these are known as "yellow videos" and "yellow" refers to erotica). Yellow videos quickly became a fad. At first, the only people who could view these tapes were rather highly placed Party members and their families, because only they had access to videotape players, which were very rare and expensive in China at that time. Before long, however, "yellow videos," including the well-known American pornographic movie *Deep Throat*, were available to more people, although still very secretly and only through small underground circles. Some people used the tapes to make money; tickets for video shows were very expensive, usually 5-10 Yuan per person (at the time most people's monthly salary was only about 40 to 50 Yuan).

Sometimes, people who were watching these tapes engaged in sexual activity, even group sex. Because yellow videos were usually shown in small private rooms to very small audiences whose members knew each other well, a party atmosphere often prevailed. It was very easy for young people to initiate sexual activity when they were aroused by what they saw.

At about the same time, erotic photographs, reproductions of paintings, and books were also smuggled into mainland China. They, too, were sold at a great profit. One small card with a nude photo would cost as much as 5 to 10 Yuan.

There was a strong reaction at the highest levels of the Chinese Communist Party and the Government. The police were ordered to confiscate every type of pornographic material, from hand-copied books to "yellow" audiotapes and films. Severe penalties were ordered for all people involved in the showing or viewing of "yellow" videos, and, in April 1985, a new antipornography law was promulgated. The nationwide crackdown on pornography led to numerous arrests and confiscations in city after city. For example, by October 1987 in Nanchang, the capital of Jiangxi province, 44 dealers in pornography had been arrested and 80,000 erotic books and magazines confiscated. It was reported that an underground publishing house with 600 salesmen had been circulating erotic materials in 23 of China's 28 provinces, making a profit of 1,000,000 Yuan (in that period about US$300,000) in two years.

A Shanghai Railway Station employee was sentenced to death because he and four other persons organized sex parties on nine different occasions; during these, they showed pornographic videotapes and engaged in sexual activity with female viewers. The other organizers were sentenced to prison, some for life.

The climax of this wave of repression seemed to occur on January 21, 1988, when the 24th session of the Standing Committee of the Sixth National People's Congress adopted supplemental regulations imposing stiffer penalties on dealers in pornography. Under these regulations, if the total value of the pornographic materials is between 150,000 Yuan and 500,000 Yuan, the dealer shall be sentenced to life imprisonment.

In a nationwide strike against pornography beginning a few weeks after the Tiananmen Square massacre, on July 11, 1989, 65,000 policemen and other bureaucrats were mobilized to investigate publishing houses, distributors, and booksellers. By August 21, more than 11,000,000 books and magazines had been confiscated, and about 2,000 publishing and distributing centers, and 100 private booksellers were forced out of business. But then Deng Xiaoping, China's top leader, went further by declaring that some publishers of erotica deserved the death penalty. It may be at least one of the most severe political punishments against "pornography" ever suggested by a national leader anywhere in the world. After this, in July 1990, the Supreme People's Court issued a new decree stating that the death sentence is the proper penalty for traffickers in prostitution and/or pornography.

## 9. Contraception, Abortion, and Population Planning

### A. Contraception

All kinds of contraceptive measures, from condom to pill, are available and used in China's practice of family planning. In 1989, it was estimated that more than 70% of couples of child-bearing age were using contraceptives, over 8.8 million males had undergone sterilization injections or operations, including a new reversible sterility operation. For females, the most popular birth control method was the intrauterine device (IUD). Used by 60 million women in the country, the IUD accounts for 41% of the total contraceptive measures; female sterilization operations constitute 36%. Research on a variety of oral contraceptives in the country has also reached advanced levels, and these contraceptives are available to the public. Breakthroughs have recently been reported in the development of medicines for terminating early pregnancy. In 1992, a survey showed that 83.4% of married couples have adopted contraceptive practices. [*Update 2002*: Table 3 shows a comparison between 1992 and 1997 contraceptive usage. (*End of update by F. Ruan*)] (See also Part 2, the 1992 Survey of Sexual Behavior in Modern

China, Sections B, Adolescent Sexuality, C, College Students, and D, Married Couples, for additional data on contraception usage in the nationwide survey.)

## B. Unmarried Teenage Pregnancies

See Section 5, Interpersonal Heterosexual Behaviors.

## C. Abortion

In China, abortion as a secondary measure to terminate an unwanted pregnancy is not only a legal right, it is even a legal responsibility. If a woman already has a child, she will be asked to terminate her unplanned pregnancy by abortion in the first trimester, and even as late as the second trimester. Generally speaking, in mainland China, one third of pregnant women have undergone an abortion. From 1985 to 1987, 32 million abortions were done, 80% of these pregnancies being the result of failed contraception. (See the discussion of "Fewer births—the one-child policy," in Section D below).

## D. Population Control Efforts

China's population policy consists of two components: decreasing and limiting the quantity of the population, and improving the quality of the population. To reduce the numerical growth of the population, three main measures are practiced: late marriage, late childbearing, and fewer births—the "one-couple-one-child policy." The basic measure used to improve the quality of the population involves efforts to prevent birth defects. (See also Part 2, the 1992 Survey of Sexual Behavior in Modern China, Sections B, Adolescent Sexuality, C, College Students, and D, Married Couples, for data on attitudes toward government limitation of family size among adolescents, college students, and married couples in the 1992 nationwide survey.)

This dual population policy is proving to be effective: China had 200 million fewer babies born in 1988 than in 1970. The result has been a saving of 3 trillion Yuan ($802 billion). China has successfully controlled its annual population growth rate to less than 1.5%, as compared with 2.4% in underdeveloped countries and 2.2% in Asia. During the 1960s, the average Chinese woman gave birth 5.68 times (the figure includes infant deaths, stillbirths, and abortions). This dropped to 4.01 during the 1970s and to 2.47 in the 1980s. The average population growth rate dropped from 2.02% during the period from 1949 to 1973 to 1.38% from 1973 to 1988.

### Later Marriage

Generally, until the recent past, the Chinese people were controlled on the local level by *danwei*—the unit or institution one belongs to. In order to marry, a couple must have a legal registration and a permit letter from his or her *danwei*.

**Table 3**

**Contraceptive Methods in China in 1992 and 1997**

|                      | 1992  | 1997  |
|----------------------|-------|-------|
| Vasectomy            | 12.0% | 9.2%  |
| Female Sterilization | 39.0  | 40.0  |
| IUD                  | 40.0  | 43.4  |
| Implant              | 0.5   |       |
| Pill                 | 5     | 2.1   |
| Condom               | 4     | 4.0   |
| Spermicide           | 0.2   |       |
| Others               | 0.6   |       |

*From*: China Population Information and Research Center, http://www.cpirc.org.cn, on June 11, 1999.

Usually one's *danwei* leader checks one's age—while the minimum legal marriageable age is 22 for males and 20 for females, "later marriage age" policy stipulates an age of 27 to 28 for males and 24 to 25 for females in order to help in the control of population.

A 1991 survey in Nanjing, the former capital of China and the capital of Jiangsu province, showed that the average marriage age was 27.5 for males and 25.8 for females. In 1949, the average first marriage age for females was 18.57, in 1982, it increased to 22.8 years old.

[*Update 2003*: In May 1971, Seymour Topping, assistant managing editor for *The New York Times*, was the first Western journalist to meet the Communist Army as it entered Nanjing, Chiang Kai-shek's fallen capital. Late marriage was already a part of the new government's population plan, as a physician at the commune hospital at the August First Commune north of Shenyang explained to Topping:

"We are encouraging the boys and girls to marry late. There is no fixed age, and postponing marriage is entirely voluntary. We suggest twenty-five for men and twenty-three for women in the countryside. We tell them late marriage is good for the country. It is better for their health, gives them more time to study and to make a bigger contribution to socialist construction." In the urban areas even later marriage is urged, twenty-five or twenty-six for women and twenty-seven or twenty-eight for men. Under old Chinese customs it was common for families to arrange child marriages. (Topping 1972)

[*Later Births*

[Married women are urged not to have a baby before 25 to 28 years of age, but no later than 30 years of age, in order to achieve the twin goals of later childbearing and healthier birth.

[*Fewer Births, the "One-Child Policy"*

[From the late 1970s to the early 1980s, China's family planning policy evolved from "One couple, two children," to "One couple, better one child," and then to "One couple, only one child." From advocating "One couple, one child," the government moved to punishing parents who have more than one child. In 1988, the "one-child policy" became a little more flexible to allow couples in rural areas with one daughter to have a second child, hopefully male, with planned spacing.

[On May 3, 1988, Ms. Peng Peiyun, the new minister in charge of the State Family Planning Commission, restated the official birth control policy at the opening ceremony of the International Conference on Strategic Management of Population in Beijing. Included was a statement of the long-term birth policy:

The country's current family planning policy is to promote late marriage and late birth, fewer but healthier births, the practice of "one couple, one child"; to allow couples in rural areas with one daughter to have a second child with planned spacing; and to avoid second or multiple births outside their control. A certain flexibility will be given to ethnic minority peoples. (Cheng Hong: "Minister Restates Long-Term Birth Policy," *China Daily*, May 4, 1988)

Allowing the peasants to have a second child was a welcome change. Hopefully, this will reduce the resistance to the original "one child" policy, so that China's birth control policy will more effective. (*End of update by F. Ruan*)]

[*Update 1997*: By the mid-1990s, the "one-child policy" had produced an obvious but unintended and serious sex imbalance that is already producing some major improvements in the very low position women have traditionally held in this male-dominated society. Initially, the traditional preference for sons coupled with the "one-child policy" has led to ultrasound scans during pregnancy followed by selective abortion for female fetuses. In January 1994, a new family law took effect that prohibited ultrasound screening to ascertain the sex of a fetus, except when needed on medical grounds. Under the new law, physicians can lose their license if they provide sex-screening for a pregnant woman (Reuters 1994). Even after birth, "millions of Chinese girls have not survived to adulthood because of poor nutrition, inadequate medical care, desertion, and even murder at the hands of their parents" (Shenon 1994; see also Section 1B, Basic Sexological Premises, Sociolegal Status of Males and Females) (*End of comment by F. Ruan*)]

[*Update 1997*: [The 1990 census showed about 205 million Chinese over the age of 15 were single in a total population of 1.2 billion. Overall, three out of five single adults were male. However, government figures show that, while the vast majority marry before they turn 30, eight million Chinese in their 30s were still single in 1990, with men outnumbering women by nearly ten to one. Demographics suggested that by the turn of the 20th century, tens of millions of Chinese men will be unwilling or willing lifelong bachelors.

[A government-sponsored computer-dating service, the Great Wall Information Company, founded in Beijing in 1989, and others often sponsored by provincial and city governments, are swamped by eager men searching for a mate. One of the most popular television shows nationwide is "We Meet Tonight," a cross between a talent show and the "Dating Game," hosted by Ms. Yang Guang since its first showing in 1990.

[With women in short supply, the men are learning to be realistic and not set their expectations too high. In reality, the women now set the standards, making their choice of a prospective husband based on the intelligence, education, and financial status of many candidates. Another benefit for the women, prompted by the concurrent move towards a free-market economy in which scarcity equals value, is that women can no longer be treated as chattel.

[Custom has held that a man should marry a woman several years younger and with less education than he has. This left older unmarried women, especially those with more education, almost no hope of finding a husband. With the growing shortage of single women, increasing numbers of men are being forced to consider marrying an older woman. There is a saying being heard more commonly in the countryside that a man who marries a woman three or more years older has found a bar of gold and benefits from her maturity.

[On the negative side, Chinese sociologists and journalists have suggested that the drastic increase of unwilling bachelors in a society that values the family and sons above all else may well produce an increase in prostitution, rape, and male suicide. Bounty hunters have already found a lucrative market for abducting young city women and delivering them to rural farmers desperate for brides.

[To restore the balance of sexes, some observers suggest the government could be forced to offer incentives, like free higher education and tax breaks, to encourage couples to have girls. This could result in a huge change in the way women are treated throughout the society (Shenon 1994).

[India is facing a similar sex imbalance with similar factors, the value of male offspring and efforts to reduce population growth. With 900 million people, India has nearly 133 single men for every 100 single women. In the industrialized world, sex ratios are more balanced; in some cases, Japan and the United States in particular, unmarried women outnumber single men, 54 to 46 (Shenon 1994). (*End of update by R. T. Francoeur*)]

### Healthier Birth, or "Preventing Birth Defects"

Every year in China, 13 infants per 1,000 are found to suffer from physical defects. The death rate is 26.7 per 1,000 births and the deformity rate is 35.7 per 1,000. Most are the victims of inbreeding and such hereditary diseases as some mental illnesses, hemophilia, and chromosome defects. This is a big burden to society and the families that have a child with a serious birth defect.

Since 1988, Dr. Wu Ming, a famous expert in medical genetics, has joined the author of this chapter in publications, speeches, and lectures advocating the prevention of birth defects. The basic information was written by the author of this chapter in his book *New Knowledge on Prevention of Birth Defects*, published in Beijing by People's Medical Publishing House (Ming 1981). This was the first book of its kind since 1949 and the founding of the People's Republic of China.

In the early 1980s, the concept of healthier birth, or prevention of birth defects, had already become an important component of China's policy on population control. In 1986, the Ministry of Health and the Ministry of Civil Administration stipulated that a medical examination would be a national requirement for marriage approval.

Gansu province is one of the poorer provinces in China. Out of its population of 23 million, more than 260,000 are mentally retarded. This has become a very severe social burden for the province. In 1988, Gansu province adopted a law to force persons who have severe hereditary or congenital mental retardation (I.Q. 1) to be sterilized before marriage, or abort any fetuses conceived, in order to prevent severe birth defects. From January 1989 to June 1991, 6,271 mentally retarded persons were sterilized. Later, several other provinces, including Fujian, Guangdong (Canton), Henan, Liaoning, and Sichuan, adopted the same law. Premier Li Peng and Ms. Peng Peiyun, the minister in charge of the State Family Planning Commission, have spoken out in support of this local law. This indicates that sterilization of mentally retarded persons may become national law in the near future.

In January 1994, a new family law went into effect that banned sex-screening of fetuses (mentioned above) and forbade couples carrying serious genetic diseases to have children. Marriage was prohibited for persons diagnosed with diseases that "may totally or partially deprive the victim of the ability to live independently, that are highly possible to recur in generations to come, and that are medically considered inappropriate for reproduction." A list of the applicable diseases was published shortly after the law went into effect (Reuters 1994).

### [Challenges and Problems

[*Update 2002*: *China's Huge Population Base and Unbalanced Regional Development*. Despite advances in family planning, China's huge population base increases by about 21 million births every year, producing an annual net increase of 13 million. Such a growth pattern will continue for a considerable period of time and it constitutes a heavy burden on China's socioeconomic development. In addition, the regional development is unbalanced, with major differences between urban and rural areas, among cities of different sizes, among coastal, inland, and remote areas, coupled with differences in fertility levels and family planning activities that have produced inescapable difficulties.

[*Enforcing Training of Family Planning Professionals*. China's population and family planning activities started at a time when its economy, culture, and education were still not developed. Although family planning professionals have combined learning with practices through trial and error and made achievements, their ideological, educational level, limited knowledge in some relevant fields, management methods, and professional skills are still not enough to keep track of the rapid developments in the natural and social sciences and technology. At present, the proportion of professionals with a college background is still rather low (14.07%). Professionals with medium and advanced levels of expertise account for 4.52% and 0.49%, respectively. Effective measures must be taken to enforce their training.

[*Improve Family Planning Services for the Floating Population and Disadvantaged.* Services for the migrant population, the unemployed, and non-resident people are new and difficult problems that have arisen with the establishment of a market economy and a series of associated social transformations. Solutions must be sought from the management mechanism and service provisions, and so on.

[*Serving an Aging Population.* The census in 1990 and the 1% population sample survey in 1995 showed that the old-age population, those over 65 years, grew from 5.58% in 1990 to 6.69% in 1995 (80.8 million people). The census result showed that the total dependency ratio of the population has been on the rise, from 49.86% in 1990 to 50.22% in 1995. Strategies for the problems of population aging and insurance for the aged need to be further clarified.

[China has developed and improved its population and family planning programs in response to the change and evolution of domestic and international situations. Since the International Conference on Population Development (ICPD) held in Cairo in 1994, China has given much publicity to the program of action formulated at the Conference. Through a series of meetings with various state departments, NGOs, scientists, and experts, the Chinese government has been trying to work out strategies for fulfilling the program of action of ICPD in accordance with China national characteristics. Solutions include:

- Further clarify the guiding principle of coordinating population and family planning with socioeconomic development; make further efforts to control population growth; improve people's quality of life; make general and comprehensive plans for environmental and resource protection and socioeconomic development, and maintain sustainable development.
- Develop a change in the way of thinking and working: Adopt an integrated approach of closely combining the promotion of family planning with socioeconomic development, and take all measures to solve the population problems; realize a combination of social restrictions with a benefit-oriented mechanism, which is based on scientific management, including publicity and education, and the delivery of multiple services. For over a decade, Chinese family planning professionals have spared no effort to achieve the aim of controlling the population growth and improving people's life quality, and making a contribution in stabilizing the population of the world. In the face of new conditions and new problems following socioeconomic development, people have awakened to the need and possibility of change. "Quality Services," "Informed Choice," and other pilot projects have provided examples and enlightenment for change. Many new experiences and practices fitting local characteristics have been created.
- Combine family planning with reproductive healthcare, expand the scope of service, and improve the quality of service, as well as the reproductive health of all people.

- Pay attention to studies and countermeasures to new conditions and problems. Emphasis has been put on the floating-population problem in urban family planning activities. A meeting on urban family planning was held in 1996. Puberty education will continue to be an object of major importance (SFPCC 1999).

[*Male-preferred, Sex Ratio, and Birth Control.* Relevant research shows that China's high sex ratio is caused by failure to register baby girls and selective abortion. This phenomenon usually happens in rural areas where the fertility rate drops quickly, where family planning consultation and good services are scarce, and where people have a preference and need for baby boys. If left unattended, the problem will affect the health and status of women and baby girls and the stability of society in the future. Therefore, efforts should be kept on publicity and education, on implementing the relevant laws and statutes, and to ensure the correct recording of statistics (SFPCC 1999; Gao 1989; Legge 1970; Holly & Bransfield 1976).

[*Chinese Male-Preferred Tradition.* China was, and in many ways still is, a Confucianist country. Confucianism said that: "There are three things which are unfilial, and the greatest of these is to have no offspring." In Chinese society "having posterity" means having a male child. Therefore, having no son is regarded as the worst possible problem a family can have, psychologically, economically, and sociologically. In traditional Chinese society and the family, women had no real identity until they married, and no security until they contributed sons to their husband's patrilineage. A measure of the family's fortunes was the number of sons who survived to adulthood, and, because females were married into other families at least by puberty, they did not represent an investment which would eventually pay off for the family (Holly & Bransfield). (*End of update by F. Ruan*)]

## 10. Sexually Transmitted Diseases and HIV/AIDS

### A. Sexually Transmitted Diseases

Since the 1980s, sexually transmitted diseases have been spreading to every province and all the major cities in China. Statistics show that in 16 major cities, the average incidence of STDs was 21.02 per 100,000 in 1987. In some cities, the incidence was as high as 336 per 100,000, resembling that in some Western countries. In Helongjiang province alone, the incidence of STDs increased at the rate of 8.9 times per year from 1982 to 1988. By the end of 1988, when this province had the fourth-highest incidence in the country, 4,558 cases had been reported; and it was estimated that reported cases represented only 20% of the total incidence. Nationwide, the number of STD cases reported from 1980 through the end of 1988 was 140,648, with more than 56,000, over 39% of these, occurring in 1988 alone. In 1992, the figure of 45,996 new reported STDs cases was 4.86% higher than in 1991.

### B. HIV/AIDS

In the mid-1990s, China claimed to have one of the lowest incidences of AIDS in the world. The first case of AIDS discovered in China, in June 1985, was that of an American tourist. As of August 1989, only three cases of AIDS had been discovered. All three were infected abroad. Also, by July 27, 1989, only 26 cases of HIV infection had been diagnosed. In October 1989, the first AIDS case in a native Chinese citizen was identified. The patient had sought medical care using an assumed name and was found to be suffering from secondary syphilis. The hospital later tested his blood serum and found it was HIV-antibody positive. By the time the young man was identified, he had already left the country. According to the head of the National AIDS Center, this patient said he had had homosexual relationships with foreigners. By December 1, 1992, 969 cases of HIV-positives and 12 cases of AIDS patients were reported; nine of the 12 AIDS patients had already passed away as of mid-1993. Gil (1991) has provided a valuable early ethnographic and epidemiological perspective on HIV/AIDS in the People's Republic based on field visits to Beijing, Chengdu, and Kunming, the latter in Yunnan province, site of China's most severe nidus of HIV infection.)

In December 1996, the Health Ministry announced an official count of 4,305 cases of HIV infection. Privately, experts admit the real number already exceeds 100,000 cases (Wehrfritz 1996).

The accelerating spread of HIV/AIDS in China has recently been linked with the cultural aversion to giving blood. This aversion fosters a seller's market that all but guarantees an impending disaster. Most donors are poor migrants struggling to make ends meet. Some make their living as sex workers as well as from selling blood, and some are drug addicts. In addition, government clinics commonly reuse the needles used to draw blood, and only a third of the nation's blood supply is screened for HIV contamination.

The sale of blood inevitably leads to people willing to exploit and profit from the shortage. The government has recently broken up rings of blood brokers, known as "bloodheads," who have kidnapped or drafted people as donors by paying corrupt officials heading work units. The bloodheads then sell the blood to local government blood stations where directors may be willing to overlook the source and its risk just to have an adequate blood supply. In late 1996, a draft law was circulating among senior health officials that would outlaw the buying and selling of blood for clinical use. While such a law could definitely reduce the risk of HIV infection in the normal course of transfusions and surgery, it would leave China with a drastic shortage of essential blood. Officials could fall back on coercion, mandating regular blood donations for members of the military, police, and state unions. The cost of bringing the public health clinics' blood donation practices up to minimal standards for this age of AIDS will be prohibitively expensive, although this has to be done to avert disaster. Another approach already initiated by the government is to reeducate the people. Pop star Jackie Cheung has been recruited by China's Red Cross to help break the cultural aversion to donating blood with popular songs with the humanitarian appeal to "Reach out, spread some love today." This approach has worked in Hong Kong, but the change in attitude there took 40 years (Wehrfritz 1996).

[*Update 2002*: China's HIV/AIDS problem is extremely complex, and may involve four simultaneous epidemics. One is the result of transmission of contaminated blood in the Chinese blood-banking system just mentioned. A second epidemic involves the sex industry, primarily in eastern China; this is being fueled by the surplus of males and unofficial government estimates that as many as 13% of all Chinese women are involved in prostitution. Added to these two epidemics are at least two separate intravenous-drug abuse epidemics under way in the country (Garrett 2002).

[By September of 1999, official figures reported 15,088 HIV-infected persons, 477 cases of persons with AIDS, and 240 deaths because of the infection. The actual situation was much worse than these figures might indicate. One expert pointed out that before 1994 most HIV-positive persons were intravenous-drug users in Yunan province. By June 1998, HIV-positive persons were found in all 31 provinces of China. In 1993, China had an estimated 10,000 HIV-positive cases; in 1994, 30,000; in 1995, 100,000 cases; in 1998,

300,000 cases; and in 1999, over a half million cases. Nationwide, the number of infected persons is increasing at a rate of 30% each year (*China News Weekly*, September, 2000).

[The infection is spreading much faster than 30% a year. For example, in Guangdong province the current growing rate is 89.5% per year. In the four-year period between 1986 to 1989, Guangdong province reported discovering only four HIV-positives cases; by October 30, 2000, health officials reported 1,419 HIV-positives and AIDS patients, although the number of actual cases may already have reached more than 20,000 cases. Before 1996, the infections mainly were through sexual behaviors; from 1997 to the present, transmission has been mainly through intravenous-drug use and sharing needles (*Yangcheng Evening News*, December 8, 2000). In 2001, experts estimated that in the near future the annual cost of HIV/AIDS for China will be 770 billion Yuan or Chinese dollars, or about US$ 92.77 billion (*China News Weekly*, September 2000). (*End of update by F. Ruan*)]

[*Update 2001*: China has consistently issued totally unrealistic estimates of the number of STD and HIV/AIDS cases among its 1.2 billion people. That changed in early 2001 when the government raised its estimate of people with STDs by well over 800%, from 830,000 to more than eight million. That number is now estimated to be rising by almost 40% a year.

[In early 2001, China's national registry listed 20,711 HIV/AIDS patients among 1.2 billion people. About the same time, the state-run *China Daily* estimated that more than a half-million Chinese were HIV-positive or had AIDS. Government experts warned that this half million could double in 2001 unless some strong, fast action was taken. Experts outside China estimated that in early 2001, at least 1.2 million Chinese were already infected. After years of silence, health minister Yin Dakui called on Chinese society "to go to war against HIV/AIDS," stressing that "men are particularly important in this fight." Film stars and popular writers joined the crusade.

[The city of Chengdu (Sichuan province) announced new AIDS Prevention and Management Regulations. Scheduled to go into effect in May 2001, the law prohibits persons with HIV/AIDS from marrying and requires police to test prostitutes, drug users, and other high-risk persons within five days of their being arrested. Any Chinese returning to China after a year abroad must be tested for HIV. Pregnant women with HIV/AIDS should be persuaded to have an abortion. The law also bans HIV/AIDS persons from working as kindergarten teachers, surgeons, and in other professions. The United Nations AIDS program in Beijing and Chinese experts quickly criticized the Chengdu regulations. The draconian character of the law is not unusual in China, but the serious public protests by *The Chengdu Worker's Daily* and by Beijing-based government AIDS officials was a definitely new development.

[China faces several major obstacles in its effort to control STDs and HIV/AIDS. A widespread prejudice against people with the AIDS virus encourages local officials to conceal cases and block research, making an effective public health policy very difficult. Most Chinese doctors know very little about STDs and HIV/AIDS. The country's medical services cannot keep up with the spread of syphilis and gonorrhea. Added to the medical scene is an early-stage sexual revolution that began with U.S. President Richard Nixon's trip to China two decades ago and involves a rapid rise in prostitution and extramarital affairs, and continuing poor sex education. Patients are usually too shy to discuss their STD problem with any doctor, but they do frequent illegal roving clinics that advertise their quack remedies in public toilets. A final factor is the fact that the government has spent very little on programs to control STDs and HIV/AIDS. From 1996 to 1997, Thailand spent $74 million on AIDS prevention, India $7.4 million, and Vietnam $4.5 million. In the same two years, China spent only $2.75 million. (*End of update by F. Ruan*)]

[*Update 2002*: UNAIDS Epidemiological Assessment: HIV/AIDS was first reported in China in 1985. By September 2001, the cumulative *reported* number of people with HIV/AIDS reached 28,133, with a total of 1,208 AIDS cases and 641 AIDS-related deaths. An estimated 820,000 persons were living with HIV by the end of 2001. The prevalence rate among people aged 15 to 49 years is 0.11%. However, only about 5% of estimated HIV/AIDS are reported.

[HIV prevalence data indicated a focused, explosive spread of infections among injection-drug users and no significant spread in the non-injection drug-using population. Although HIV/AIDS cases have been detected in all provinces, HIV transmission is focused primarily among injection-drug users in certain provinces. For example, the HIV prevalence rate was found to range from 44% to 85% in selected communities of drug users in Yunnan and Xinjiang.

[The percentage of female prostitutes who do not use condoms decreased from 66.7% in 1999 to 49.1% in 2000 to 37.4% in 2001 (median). The percentage of injection-drug users who report sharing of equipment increased from 31.7% in 1999 to 33.7% in 2000 to 45% in 2001. Trichomoniasis and chlamydia infections are the most prevalent STDs.

[The estimated number of adults and children living with HIV/AIDS on January 1, 2002, were:

| | |
|---|---|
| Adults ages 15-49: | 850,000 (rate: 0.1%) |
| Women ages 15-49: | 220,000 |
| Children ages 0-15: | 2,000 |

[An estimated 30,000 adults and children died of AIDS during 2001.

[At the end of 2001, an estimated 76,000 Chinese children under age 15 were living without one or both parents who had died of AIDS. (*End of update by the Editors*)]

[*Update 2002*: In October 2002, United Nations Secretary-General Kofi Annan warned that "The forecast for China is 5% orphans by 2010, of which 4.5% will be due to AIDS" (Garrett 2002). (See Table 4.) (*End of update by the Editors*)]

## 11. Sexual Dysfunctions, Counseling, and Therapies

Professor Dalin Liu's survey showed that 34% of rural couples and 17% of urban couples said they engaged in less than a minute of foreplay, sometimes none at all. Not surprisingly, 37% of rural wives described intercourse as painful. While urban couples may be more adventurous sexually, they are not necessarily more satisfied. Professor

**Table 4**

**Leaders in an Expanding Pandemic: Current and Projected HIV/AIDS Infected Adults**

| (in millions) | Current Number Infected | | 2010 |
|---|---|---|---|
| | Government Data | Expert Estimates | Expert Estimates |
| India | 4.0 | 5 to 8 | 20 to 25 |
| Nigeria | 3.5 | 4 to 6 | 10 to 15 |
| Ethiopia | 2.7 | 3 to 5 | 7 to 10 |
| China | 0.80 | 1 to 2 | 10 to 15 |
| Russia | 0.18 | 1 to 2 | 5 to 8* |

*Garrett 2002

Suiming Pan's sample of 600 couples were all residents of big cities, and 70% of them said they were unhappy with their sex lives, and a random survey of married couples living in Shanghai found that 45% were unhappy with their sexual relationships. According to Professor Kang Jin, president of the Shanghai Committee of Rehabilitation of Male Dysfunctions, in 1989 at least 20% of China's adult male population was suffering from some type of sexual dysfunction. Now, clinics of sexual counseling, sex therapy, or Western and/or traditional Chinese sexual medicines have been established in most big cities (see Section 5C, Interpersonal Heterosexual Behaviors, Adults).

## 12. Sex Research and Advanced Professional Education

No sex research existed between 1949, when Mao and his Communist Party took control over mainland China, and 1979. There were some studies on the reproductive system and reproductive endocrinology, but these were in the biological and medical fields, not behavioral studies. However, since 1979, and especially after 1985, sex research has become an apparently growing, even prosperous, field. China's sex research was started and developed under the names of "sex education" and "sexual medicine," two fields that are accepted and permitted by the government and society. Before the beginning of the open-door policy in 1979, even sex education and sexual medicine were nonexistent.

The year 1982 saw a breakthrough for sexology in China. In that year, Robert Kolodny, William Masters, and Virginia Johnson's *Textbook of Sexual Medicine* (1979) was translated into Chinese under the guidance of Professor Wu Jieping, with the actual translation being done by his graduate students. The Chinese edition, titled *Xingyixue [Sexual Medicine*], was published by Scientific and Technological Literature Publishing House, Beijing. It is the first contemporary and updated Western sex book published in China since the founding of the PRC in 1949.

The year 1985 marked another turning point for sexuality education and sexology in China. In that year, Ruan's article, "Outline of the Historical Development of Modern Sexual Medicine," was published by the *Encyclopedic Knowledge*, and his series, "Essays on Sex Education: Ten Lectures," were published in *Required Readings for Parents*. From July 22 to August 7, 1985, the First National Workshop on Sex Education was held in Shanghai, with Ruan as the major instructor. In October 1985, the *Handbook of Sex Knowledge*, the first large modern book on sexuality written by Chinese and in Chinese, was published in Beijing by Scientific and Technological Literature Publishing House, with Ruan as editor-in-chief. All of these events were strong signs indicating the establishment and development of sexology in China. More and more sexual social surveys, publications on sex, and development of academic sexological journals and societies have followed.

As early as 1984, a project on survey and analysis of sex, love, marriage, family conflict, and crimes was carried out by the Beijing Society for Studies on Marriage and Family. This project was headed by Ms. Wu Cangzhen, Associate Professor of Marriage Law at China Politics and Law University in Beijing.

The most famous and important sexual social survey is the Shanghai Sex Sociological Research Center's *National Sex Civilization Survey* headed by Dalin Liu, professor at Shanghai University. Using 40 paid assistants and volunteer interviewers, between February 1989 and April 1990, the center obtained responses to 239 questions surveyed from 19,559 people in over half of China's 27 provinces. The 1992 publication in China caused a sensation all over South-East Asia. Planned and executed from beginning to end without government order or interference, this survey was supported by private Chinese sponsorship. It has already greatly contributed to a more uninhibited dialogue about sexual issues within China, strengthened the status and prestige of Chinese sexologists, and facilitated the organization of various regional and national associations and national and international conferences. An American translation of this monumental work was published in 1997 by Continuum Publishing Company, New York. The most striking trend found in this study is the deterioration of the strong tie between sex and marriage. This survey was published in December 1992 in Shanghai by Joint Publishing, Sanlian Books Company, titled *Zhongguo Dangdai Xingwenhua—Zhongguo Lianwanli "Xingwenming" Diaoza Baogao* [*Sexual Behavior in Modern China—A Report of the Nationwide "Sex Civilization" Survey on 20,000 Subjects in China*]. It is a large volume, with 866 pages and 677,000 characters. (See Part 2. The 1992 Survey of Sexual Behavior in Modern China, Addendum, for details on this nationwide survey.)

Between 1985 and 1991, sex researcher Pan Suiming, Associate Professor at the Department of Sociology at the China Renmin University in Beijing, and his assistants conducted seven social surveys on sex. "Behavioral Analysis of Heterosexual Petting in Public—Observations on Chinese Civil Parks" reported on 23,532 cases between 1985 and 1989 in 13 parks in six cities. "Dissemination of Three Kinds of Sexual Information and the Accepter's Response" involved 1,610 respondents in Shanghai, 1989; "Influence of Sex Knowledge and Attitude on Sexual Behavior—The Condition, Motive, and Orgasm" had 603 samples in Beijing, 1988-89, and "Relations Between Satisfaction of Sexual Life and the Marriage" was based on 977 samples in Beijing, 1989. Seven hundred sixty-six respondents participated in the "Chinese Readers' Answers to the Questionnaire in the Chinese Edition of The Kinsey Report Since 1989," with research still in progress. "Deep Sexual Behavior Survey—Relations of Sexual Mores, Ideas, Affection, and Behavior," with 1,279 samples in 27 cities, 1989, indicated that nearly seven out of ten Chinese have had anal sex with heterosexual partners, and that men reached orgasm about 70% of the time in contrast to 40% for women. "A Sampling Survey on Students' Sexual Behavior in Every University and College in Beijing" examined 1,026 respondents in 1991.

Between 1985 and 1992, more than 300 books on sexuality were published in mainland China, including the Chinese translations of classical works by Sigmund Freud, Havelock Ellis, Margaret Mead, Alfred C. Kinsey, and R. Van Gulik. The first professional academic journal of sexology, *Sexology of China*, was published in March 1992 by Beijing Medical University.

On May 23, 1988, the country's first college-level sexology course was introduced at China People's University in Beijing. This special two-week program, called "Training Workshop on Sex Science," consisted of workshops on 20 topics, conducted by 17 professors and experts. The program was attended by 120 people from 26 of China's 28 provinces. As of mid-1993, 26.7% of the universities and colleges in China have a course on human sexuality or sex education.

Since 1987, a series of six nationwide conferences on sexology have been held in China. For example, the "Sixth Chinese Congress of Science of Sex," was held on May 3, 1992, in Nanjing, the capital of Jiangsu province. About 500 experts attended the congress, and over 400 academic papers in the fields of sex education, sociology of sex, psychology of sex, sexual medicine, and STDs were accepted by the Congress. The "First International Conference of Sexology"

was held on September 12 to 15, 1992, in Shanghai. Over 20 participants came from 13 foreign countries, and over 300 participants from all over China. About 100 academic papers on sexual medicine, sex education, sociology of sex, and psychology of sex were accepted by the conference.

There are two important Chinese sexological periodicals: *Sexology* (formerly *Sexology of China, Journal of Chinese Sexology*) (started in 1992). Journal Address: Beijing Medical University, 38 Xue Yuan Road, Beijing 100083, The People's Republic of China. Editor's Address: The Public Health Building (Fourth Floor), Beijing Medical University, No. 83 Hua Yuan Road, Beijing 100086, China

*Apollo and Selene*. A bilingual Chinese/English magazine of sexology published in Shanghai by the Asian Federation for Sexology started in the summer of 1993. Address: Asian Federation (Society) for Sexology, 2 Lane 31, Hua Ting Road, Shanghai, People's Republic of China.

The main sexological organizations in China are:

Chinese Sex Education Research Society. Director: Dr. Jiahuo Hong. (Founded in Shanghai in 1985.). Address: The Shanghai College of Traditional Chinese Medicine, 530 Ling Ling Road, Shanghai, 200032, People's Republic of China.

Shanghai Sex Education Research Society, founded in Shanghai in 1986. Address: The Shanghai College of Traditional Chinese Medicine, 530 Ling Ling Road, Shanghai, 200032, People's Republic of China.

Sexology of China Association (founded in Beijing in 1995; preparatory committee founded in 1990). Director: Professor Guangchao Wang, M.D. Address: Beijing Medical University, 38 Xue Yuan Road, Beijing, 100083, People's Republic of China.

Institute for Research in Sexuality and Gender. Address: Professor Sui-ming Pan, Director, Post Office Box 23, Renmin University of China, 39# Hai Dian Road, Beijing 100872, People's Republic of China; fax: 01-256-6380.

Chinese Association of Sex Education. Address: Mercy Memorial Foundation, 11F, 171 Roosevelt Road, Section 3, Taipei, Taiwan, Republic of China; phone: 886-2/369-6752; fax: 886-2/365-7410.

China Family Planning Association. Address: 1 Bci Li, Shengguzhuang, He Ping Li, Beijing, People's Republic of China.

China Sexology Association. Address: Number 38, XueYuan Lu, Haidion, Beijing 100083, People's Republic of China; phone: 86-1/209-1244; fax: 86-1/209-1548.

Shanghai Family Planning Association. Address: 122 South Shan Xi ltoad, Shanghai 200040, People's Republic of China; phone: 86-21/2794968; fax: 86-21/2472262 Ext. 18.

Shanghai International Center for Population Communication China (SICPC). Address: 122 South Shan Xi Road, Shanghai 200040, People's Republic of China; phone: 86-21/247-2262; fax: 86-21/247-3049.

## PART 2. THE 1992 SURVEY OF SEXUAL BEHAVIOR IN MODERN CHINA: A REPORT OF THE NATIONWIDE "SEX CIVILIZATION" SURVEY ON 20,000 SUBJECTS IN CHINA*

M. P. LAU

### A. The Survey

This is the report of a survey of sexual behavior in the People's Republic of China, conducted from 1989 to 1990.

---

*Editor's Note*: The following section is adapted from M. P. Lau's detailed analysis of the original 1989-1990 Chinese version of the nationwide Kinsey-like survey of *Sexual Behavior in China*. This

Unprecedented in scope and scale, the survey involved 28 sites (cities, towns, and villages) in 15 of the 27 provinces or autonomous regions. A total of 21,500 questionnaires, with 239 items covering a wide range of variables were distributed, and 19,559 of the returned replies were found suitable for study. About 500 investigators were involved, including about 200 field workers, most of whom were female volunteers. There was a caucus of about 40 core leaders, with coordinating headquarters at the Shanghai Sex Sociology Research Center. The main academic leaders were Dalin Liu, Liping Chou, and Peikuan Yao of Shanghai and Minlun Wu (M. L. Ng) of Hong Kong.

This study has been compared to the *Kinsey Reports* (1948, 1953) in the popular media (Burton 1990). For the first time in history, we have extensive scientific data on the sexual behavior of the contemporary Chinese, who comprise 22% of the world population. Information is available on puberty, romantic love, mating, marriage, marital life, marital sex, premarital sex, extramarital sex, abortions, divorces, as well as data on family planning, women's issues, prostitution, pornography, sexual transgressions, and sexual variances, both as to attitudes and behavior.

In this review-essay, I provide a synopsis of some of the major findings of the survey through eight profiles of male and female adolescents and college students, urban and rural married couples, a female prostitute, and a male sex offender. I will then present a brief critique of the study methodology and suggestions for future research.

## B. Adolescent Sexuality

In this section, I present two composite profiles constructed from 91 tables of statistics compiled during the national survey of 28 secondary (or middle) schools in ten Chinese cities or suburbs. Secondary schools were not common in the countryside and the rural population was difficult to survey. In all, 6,900 questionnaires were issued and 6,092 were collected and analyzed. Each questionnaire contained 42 multiple-choice questions with some open-response categories. While the sample surveyed is not representative of all secondary schools owing to resource constraints, attempts were made to achieve as much diversity as possible. Some significant influences on sexual attitudes and practices were demonstrated, such as exposure to modernization, degree of enlightenment, and gender differences.

In 1989, there were 47.7 million secondary school students in China (4.29% of the national population of 1.112 billion), of whom 58.4% were male. Fully 97.8% of children reaching school age were sent to primary schools, and 74.6% of primary school graduates proceeded to secondary schools. There are six grades in each secondary school: Junior Middle 1, 2, and 3, and Senior Middle 1, 2, and 3, and the age range is normally 12 to 18. In the sample studied, the mean age was 15.53 ($SD = 1.78$). The features described in the profiles represent the means, modes, medians, or usual ranges, or the proportions in the sample. There is a wealth of detail in the book for further reference.

### Profile 1: An Adolescent Female

The typical female adolescent respondent is a 15.5-year-old student in an urban or suburban secondary school. She comes from a stable family of workers or cadres, and has one

sibling. She reached puberty at age 13, with menarche in the summer, and development of secondary sexual characteristics. (This is a later age compared with secondary school students in Hong Kong or Japan, but earlier than that described in China 25 years ago). At age 14.5, she began to have sexual interests, and desired to associate with boys, mostly for socialization or mutual assistance, or because of a "crush" on a boy for his good looks, but she has been too shy or "busy" to take action. (For comparison, a Japanese peer would have begun to have such interests and desires at age 12 to 13). She acquired most of her sexual knowledge from books, magazines, and movies, and would feel excited by casual physical touches and by conversation on sexual topics.

Among the secondary school girls in the survey, 7.4% wished for some bodily contact with a male, and 12.1% reported having been aroused to desire sexual intercourse. (Again, these percentages are much lower than those of Japanese peers). More than a third of secondary school girls reported having male friends since age 14, without infatuation and often in group settings. By 15.5 years of age, 11.1% were dating boys and 6% were "in love." The legal age for a female to marry in China is 20, and most girls think marrying early is not good or "would affect study."

Only 4.7% of adolescent girls reported a history of masturbation, usually since age 13.5; about 50% said they continued the practice. (In Japan, 9% of secondary schoolgirls have masturbated, and most persist in the habit). While 44.3% of female adolescents stated masturbation is "bad," almost 40% said they did not understand the question.

Less than 2% of adolescent girls have engaged in each of kissing, hugging, or sexual touching, and only 1% reported having sexual intercourse (slightly higher in southern China). These rates are far below those found among Japanese schoolgirls (up to 25.5% and 8.7%, respectively).

In well-developed urban areas, adolescent sex education has been available in classrooms, but has focused on physiology and hygiene, with little information on coitus, pregnancy, childbirth, contraception, homosexuality, paraphilias, and sexually transmitted diseases. Secondary schoolgirls would like more guidance on issues of romantic love, sexual impulses, and socialization. They discuss sexual issues with their mothers, sisters, and female peers, but not with teachers or fathers.

### Profile 2: An Adolescent Male

The typical male adolescent respondent is a 15.5-year-old secondary school boy who comes from a stable family of workers or cadres and has one sibling. He has had seminal emissions since age 14.5, and most have been spontaneous nocturnal emissions. He has started developing secondary sexual characteristics. (These maturational milestones are later than those of a similar youth in Japan, but earlier than those in China 25 years ago.) At age 14.5, he began to show sexual interests, and wished to associate with girls, mostly because of attraction to their appearance or "tender disposition," but he was too shy or "busy" to act upon his feelings. (A Japanese boy would have commenced to have such interests and desires at age 12 to 13). He obtained most of his sexual knowledge from books, magazines, and movies, and has seen pictures of female nudity and experienced some casual sexual touching.

About one third of adolescent males reported desire for bodily contact with females, and 42.9% said they had been aroused enough to crave sexual intercourse. (Again, these percentages are much lower than those of Japanese peers).

Although almost half of male adolescents said that they had had female platonic friends since age 14, often in group activities, only 12.7% were currently dating a girl, and

survey was published in Chinese in 1992; an English translation was published by Continuum (New York) in 1997. Lau's review-essay was published in *Transcultural Psychiatric Research Review* (1995, vol. 32, pp. 137-156). The *Encyclopedia*'s editor, R. T. Francoeur greatly appreciates the permission of Dr. Lau and Laurence J. Kirmayer, M.D., editor of the *Transcultural Psychiatric Research Review*, to include Lau's critique in this chapter.

7.6% reported being "in love." The legal age for a male in China to marry is 22, and most boys agree that marrying early is not good or "would affect study."

Only 12.5% of male adolescents reported a history of masturbation, usually starting at age 13.5; half reported they had continued the practice. (In Japan, 30% of junior high school students have masturbated, and fully 81.2% of those in senior high school, with most students continuing the habit). More than half of adolescent males consider masturbation "bad," but 21.2% said they did not understand the question.

Less than 5% of secondary school males have engaged in each of kissing, hugging, or sexual touching, and 0.9% have had sexual intercourse (slightly more in Southern China). (These rates are remarkably low compared to those in Japan, where up to 23.1% of high school boys have experienced sexual kissing and 11.5% coitus).

Adolescent boys tend to discuss their needs and problems with male peers, rather than with teachers, parents, or siblings.

## C. College Students

In 1989, there were about 82,000 post-secondary students in China. A study of this group is of immense importance as they are destined to become the future leaders of the country. Intellectually well endowed and highly educated, they are still young, malleable, open minded, and sensitive to new ideas and trends. In the process of maturation as scholars, they confront the various phenomena associated with modernization and accelerating change. They interact with a "campus culture," which may be a cultural melting pot and a frontier of novel concepts and ideologies. Restricted by demands for sexual abstinence and expectations of monogamy, they try their best to cope with their libido and desire. Their perceptions, perspectives, beliefs, and behavior will have profound effects on the future of nation-building, participation in the world community, and global stability.

This section presents two composite profiles condensed from 136 tables of statistics collected during the survey of 24 post-secondary colleges (including universities, teachers' colleges, academies of traditional medicine, training centers for cadres and security personnel, and an oceanography institute) in nine metropolitan areas. The institutions were selected according to practicality and diversity. Questionnaires with 63 items were distributed in classrooms and the purpose of the investigation explained. Confidentiality was assured. In addition to the group administration, some individual interviews were conducted. A total of 3,360 valid replies were analyzed. The mean age was 20.28 years (*SD* = 3.13) with 56.8% male.

### Profile 3: A Female University Student

The typical female college student in the survey is a 20-year-old student in the faculty of arts. Her father was college-educated and holds a professional, technical, or managerial job. She had menarche at age 13.5, followed by the development of secondary sexual characteristics. She was unprepared for menarche and sought advice from her mother or peers. She received little sex education and acquired most of her sexual knowledge from books, news media, novels, peers, her mother, and her sisters. She found her teachers and parents "ignorant, busy, uncaring, conservative, and rigid." She would feel excited by depictions of sexual matters, and has been exposed to nudity through pictures in the media.

She thinks romantic love should be allowed but "properly guided," that the main purpose of copulation is to have a family, and that the female can be an active partner during sexual intercourse. She believes that premarital sex may be acceptable if the partners are mutually in love and willing, but extramarital sex should be censured, even if consensual. She considers homosexuality to be a perversion or illness, and would offer comfort to a homosexual friend and advise him or her to seek psychiatric treatment. She feels that homosexuality is something to be ashamed of and pitied but not severely punished.

Fully 70% of college women were not content with their bodies, with concerns about being overweight, hirsute, or other features; 25% were not satisfied with their secondary sexual characteristics, for example, thinking that their breasts are undersized. While 15.6% did not like their own gender, 42.8% stated they would prefer to be a male if they had a choice.

Among the college women surveyed, 16.5% had a history of masturbation, starting from age 13 to 14, and 8.2% still masturbated at a frequency of about once a week. Most respondents thought masturbation is "harmless" and "normal."

While 63.4% of female college students in the sample desired a heterosexual relationship, only 6.3% of them had had a sexual partner. Sexual contacts (including kissing, embracing, genital touching, and coitus) were infrequent and covert and commonly began after age 17. Contraception involved the use of "safe periods," pills, or condoms.

While 5.8% reported an inclination towards exhibitionism and 2.8% were predisposed to transvestitism, interest in other paraphilias was uncommon. The majority (87.3%) of college women reported that on seeing a nude female in a public bathroom, they would probably feel indifferent, but 3.9% said they might "come to like it."

Homosexual contacts were infrequent: 8.4% reported having been kissed or caressed, 3.2% had experienced homosexual masturbation, and less than 3% reported genital-to-genital contacts; 0.7% reported they would engage in homosexual contact if the opportunity arose.

### Profile 4: A Male University Student

The typical male college student in the survey is a 20-year-old student in the faculty of engineering, science, or medicine. His parents had post-secondary education, and his father is a professional, technical, or managerial worker. He had his first seminal emission at age 14.5, followed soon by the appearance of pubic and then facial hair. (Compared with his secondary school counterparts, his sexual development started at a slightly later age). He received little sex education and was quite unprepared when he had his first seminal emission. He did not ask anyone for an explanation.

He acquired most of his sexual knowledge from books on hygiene and health, news media, novels and pornographic art, and from his male peers. He found his parents and teachers insensitive and outdated in knowledge and attitude. He holds liberal views about romantic love and is permissive about reading sexual material. He thinks that masturbation is harmless and normal. He believes that sexual intercourse would enhance love and give physical pleasure, as well as serving the purpose of building a family. He endorses the idea of a female being an active partner during sexual intercourse.

He thinks premarital sex would be acceptable if the partners are both willing and mutually in love, especially if they are prepared to marry each other, and extramarital sex, if consensual, may be permitted under certain circumstances. He would be quite aroused by references to sexual matters, and has seen pictures of nudes in the media, but is unlikely to have seen women in the nude.

One fourth of college males were not satisfied with some of their secondary sexual characteristics, such as sparsity of pubic hair or perception of the penis as undersized. A larger proportion (70%) were not content with other aspects of their body, such as shortness of stature, presence of pimples or freckles, and sparsity or grayness of scalp or facial hair. Gender dysphoria was uncommon, and only 8.3% of male college students surveyed wished to be female.

Almost two thirds of college males (59%) had a history of masturbation, starting at age 14 to 16, and 39.5% continued to masturbate at the rate of about once a week. Sexual contacts, including kissing, embracing, genital touching, and coitus, were reported to be infrequent and mostly covert. These activities usually began after age 17 and the male tended to take an active role. Only 12.5% of college males reported that they had had sexual partner(s), usually only one. Contraception involved "safe periods," condoms, and coitus interruptus.

While most male college students considered homosexuality a perversion or illness to be sympathized with and offered treatment, 11.9% conceived of homosexuality as normal behavior for a small group of people. Homosexual contacts were infrequent, with 7.0% reporting kissing or caressing, 8.6% homosexual masturbation, and less than 3% genital-to-genital or anal touching; 1.5% would consider seeking someone out to engage in homosexual activity.

Paraphilias were rare among male college students, with 5.6% feeling prone to exhibitionism, but hardly any reporting other paraphilic tendencies. On seeing a nude male in a public bathroom, most would feel indifferent, but 5.4% said they might come to "like it."

When asked how they would respond if they found out that their fiancée had lost her virginity to another male, 20% of male college students said they would leave her, but 60% would find it tolerable.

## D. Married Couples

This section presents composite portraits of an urban couple based on 6,210 married persons surveyed in 15 cities (nine coastal and six inland urban centers), and a rural couple typical of 1,392 married residents surveyed in three villages. A mixture of random and non-random sampling methods was used, steering a fine line between what was practical (e.g., considering the difficulties of gathering data from illiterate or unsophisticated persons), and what would be theoretically desirable (e.g., relative representativeness). A total of 396 tables of actuarial data were compiled, covering a wide range of sexual, marital, and family variables. There was a preponderance of female interviewers and interviewees. Many volunteer field workers came from women's groups, such as labor unions, family planning units, and obstetrical teams, and they were able to build good rapport with women respondents, who often appeared eager to share their intimate knowledge of family life with those whom they could trust. Overall, 68.1% of urban and 78.2% of rural interviewees were female.

### Profile 5: An Urban Couple

The spouses in the typical urban married couple in the survey were about 36 to 37 years of age and of above-average education compared with the general national population. They reported their health status as average or above average. The husband was a professional, technical, office, or managerial worker, and had received slightly more education than his wife, being twice as likely to have attended a post-secondary institute. The wife was a professional, technical, factory, or office worker. They have been married for about 11 years. They married of their own will, after an introduction by a third person and a period of courtship.

They consider mutual "love" and "understanding" more important in marriage than material comfort, political views, or evaluation by society. They believe that the purpose of marital sex is primarily to satisfy emotional and physical needs, rather than to fulfill an obligation or a "tradition" or to achieve reproduction, and there should be no prudery about it. They have sexual intercourse four to five times per month on average. The couple would like to have children because the latter "would add interest to life" and it is an aspect of "social responsibility." They would like to have a boy and a girl.

Of urban couples surveyed, 60% considered their marriage satisfactory, with greater satisfaction reported by the male partner, those with more education, those in professional, technical, or managerial positions, and those in the earlier years of marriage. Of those surveyed, 55.5% indicated good or fair (25.3%) levels of sexual satisfaction. Husbands reported greater enjoyment of coitus and gave more importance to coital frequency, styles of intercourse, and climaxes. The duration of foreplay tended to be brief, most often less than ten minutes, and gave less pleasure to the woman. In case of sexual disharmony, 44% felt there should be open discussion, 13.4% would seek medical help, and 24% would just "leave it" alone. Most couples endorsed women taking initiative in sex, such an attitude being especially common among males, the better educated, and in the southern cities. As urban married women gain more freedom, independence, and self-esteem, they feel less compelled to have sex against their will, and would ask to be excused without feeling guilty.

Most couples experienced their first sexual intercourse on their wedding night, but prenuptial sex was admitted by 24.9% of urban husbands and 15.8% of urban wives. It should be noted that premarital coitus was most often (80%) consummated with a "future spouse," and such behavior was endorsed by a majority (90%) of the urban couples polled. Sex before matrimony with someone who is not a "future spouse" tended to occur among urban youths in southern China, soldiers stationed in cities, and the less educated. (The number of abortions of premarital pregnancies has been on the rise, reaching 16% of those age 20 and over and single in a city in Jiangsu, and 90% of first abortions in a city in Zhejiang, both cities in the vicinity of Shanghai.)

Higher frequency of intercourse was associated with younger age, the earlier years in marriage, highest or lowest levels of education, being a manual or service worker, more privacy of the bedroom, temperate climate, and greater sense of obligation to perform. Sexual intercourse occurs most often just before sleep among younger and middle-aged couples, and at "no fixed time" among the young and the elderly. In terms of sexual practices, 56.5% of couples change positions during sex, and 65.2% are nude sometimes or often during sex; nudity during sex is more frequent among the young, the better educated, and in the southern cities.

Questions about orgasms were not asked, as the investigators had found it quite difficult to elicit such information, but enjoyment of "sexual pleasure" was found to depend on the techniques, experience, and relationship; sexual pleasure had a more gradual onset in women, both physiologically and psychologically. Most couples reported they experienced sexual pleasure frequently (especially males) or sometimes (especially females), with highest rates in southern China. In a sampling of 1,279 men and women in 41 cities, Suiming Pan found men reach orgasm 7.2 times out of every 10 attempts; this contrasts with 4.1 times for women. In Dalin Liu's survey, one third of the urban women and one fourth of the rural women claimed to experience a feeling of pleasure (*kuaigan*) "very often," while 58.2 and 76.8%, respectively, experienced it "sometimes."

A history of masturbation was obtained from 17.1% of respondents—much more often from husbands than from wives, and from couples in southern cities—but nearly all of the respondents claimed it happened only occasionally. While 41.7% regarded masturbation as a "bad habit" and 13.1% considered it normal, fully 30% gave no clear answer. Only 0.5% admitted homosexual experience, but considerable denial or ignorance was suspected.

Among urban husbands, 10.2% admitted to a history of extramarital sex. Extramarital sex was more common among service or manual workers, or businessmen, those less than 25 years of age or more than 56, and those espousing a liberal or hedonistic attitude towards life. Urban wives were unlikely to have risked extramarital sex, but it was more likely to occur in middle age. These rates are far below those published in the Kinsey reports (1948, 1953). Nevertheless, the impact of extramarital affairs may be considerable. During divorce proceedings in five cities in China in 1985, the occurrence of extramarital affairs was confessed in two thirds of the cases. In Shenzhen, a town bordering Hong Kong, 91.8% of divorce cases in 1987 involved a "third person." While 66.2% of married urban respondents said that they accept the national policy of having only one child per family, 28.5% think such a restriction unreasonable. If they had only a daughter, 35.5% would want to have one more child, but not if this would incur punishment from the government. Birth control measures used by urban couples included: diaphragms (42.8%), tubal ligation (9.4%), other mechanical means (18.3%), pills (5.9%), vasectomy (2.3%), other methods (e.g., "safe periods," coitus interruptus, unknown) (15.5%), and none (5.8%).

Sexual knowledge was generally quite limited and resource material not readily available, especially to women. About two thirds (62.4%) of urban couples had read one of the four popular basic manuals on sexual knowledge available at the time of the survey, such as the one written for the newly wed, which mostly consider anatomy and physiology. Additional sexual knowledge was obtained from books, movies, and radio (35.6%), through personal experience (22.7%), and from same-sex peers or those in counseling positions. Most couples (70.4%) are interested in reading or viewing media with sexual themes, but 48.9% have found opportunities lacking. Women would like to know more about child education and physical hygiene, while men are interested in sexual techniques and interpersonal skills. Although 61.8% of urban couples would explain the birth process to a child, 25.4% would evade the question, and the rest would express displeasure or indifference, or give a false answer.

*Profile 6: A Rural Couple*

The typical rural married couple surveyed were about 35 years old, of average education compared with the general national population, and reported their health status as average or above average. They were engaged in farming, herding, fishing, or forestry, and were unlikely to have received post-secondary education. They have been married for about 11 years; he at age 23 and she at 22. They married of their own will (wholly or partly), although matchmaking was prevalent until one or two generations ago, and still occurred in a few locales.

They consider "love" and "understanding" more important in their union than the opinions of society. They believe that the main aims of marital sex are to fulfill physical and emotional needs, to go along with tradition, and to accomplish reproduction, and that they need not be prudish about it. They have sexual intercourse five to six times per month on average. They would like to have children, mostly for the sake of old-age security, but also to propagate their lineage.

Of rural couples surveyed, 65% regard their marriage as satisfactory. Greater satisfaction was reported by the female partner, those better educated, and those under 25 or over 45 years of age. In case of sexual disharmony, 44% would engage in open discussion, 23.2% would seek medical help, and 21% would just "leave it" alone.

Most married rural couples experienced sexual intercourse for the first time on the wedding night, but premarital sex was admitted by 7.3% of rural husbands and 17.3% of rural wives. Premarital coitus was usually performed with a future spouse, and such behavior was endorsed by the vast majority of rural couples surveyed. Sex before marriage with someone who was not a future spouse occurred more commonly among older males and females when the feudal system allowed sexual permissiveness in certain forms of social transactions, and also among those who are younger, more educated, and liberal minded.

Higher frequency of intercourse was associated with more demand by the husband and greater compliance by the wife, having been married for a longer duration, and temperate climate. Sexual coitus occurred most often just before sleep, but also often "at no fixed time," as rural couples tended to have a less structured schedule of daily life compared with their urban counterparts.

About half (45%) of rural couples reported changing position during sex, and 57.2% said they were nude sometimes or often during sex; sexual nudity was more common among the young, the less educated, and in southern climates. In Shanxi province, some farmers traditionally sleep naked.

A history of masturbation was obtained from 10.1% of rural husbands or wives, more often from those in the South; nearly all described it as episodic. Most (73.4%) considered masturbation a "bad habit," but 9.6% deemed it "natural." Only 2.3% admitted homosexual experiences, suggesting considerable ignorance about the term.

Among rural married couples, the level of sexual satisfaction reported was good (66.6%) or fair (27.6%), with wives more easily satisfied than husbands. The duration of foreplay tended to be brief, usually five minutes or less, but neither partner had high expectations of gratification from it. Most couples endorsed women taking initiative in sex (this attitude was more common among males, the better educated, and in south China), but they would still prefer the male partner to be more active.

Among rural husbands, 9.3% admitted to a history of extramarital sex; higher rates were found among service or manual workers or businessmen, those under 25 or over 56 years of age, and those who gave evidence of a "pleasure-seeking predisposition" on several attitude measures. Rural wives were unlikely to have experienced extramarital sex.

Most rural couples would like to have a boy and a girl, but 48.5% would accept having only one child. After having a daughter, 60.3% want an additional child, and 6% still want one at the risk of sustaining some official penalty. In a 1989 survey, 68.1% of rural women wanted to have two children, 25.7% wanted one child, and 3.1% did not want children. Slightly lower percentages were found among rural men. Contraceptive methods utilized include: diaphragm (50.8%), tubal ligation (21.8%), pills (7.5%), vasectomy (1.2%), others (12.3%), and none (6.4%). On the other hand, infertility because of sexual dysfunctions was common (e.g., more than 25% of about 40,000 family planning counseling cases seen in 1984 to 1989), but most were said to be somewhat amenable to medical or herbal therapy.

Sexual knowledge was generally quite deficient, and resources not easily available, although 77.1% of rural couples had read one of the four popular basic manuals on sexual knowledge available at the time of the survey. Otherwise, the pattern was similar to that of urban couples. While 47.8% of rural couples would explain the birth process to a child, 33.8% would evade the question, and the rest would ignore or upbraid the child, or give a false answer.

*Comment*

An overview of the accounts of urban and rural married couples given in this section shows the emergence of two patterns: (1) respondents who are traditional and conservative in ideology, cautious and guarded towards novel ideas, moralistic and suppressive of self-expression, and less imbued with modern education tend to reside inland and in rural territories, are service or manual workers, and are more commonly female; and (2) respondents who are modernistic and individualistic in orientation, liberal and open in attitude, rational and objective in deliberation, and have been exposed to more contemporary and/or Western ideology tend to reside in urban areas, near seacoasts or in southern China, are professionals or technical workers, and are more often male.

Of course, there are many exceptions to these broad generalizations. Those who are not well educated may also be gullible and suggestible, and experience sexual permissiveness as a relic of feudal systems, such as variations of a master-slave relationship, indigenous forms of marital or quasi-marital arrangements or cohabitation, such as concubinage and other forms of polygamy (McGough 1981). Other situational, subcultural, idiosyncratic, or deviant variations in sexual behavior are noted throughout the book. The investigators also present detailed analyses of factors affecting sexual satisfaction and sexual pleasure, as well as data on marital cohesion, domestic conflicts, marital breakdown, and sex in old age.

We see in this section a spectrum of variations in sexual behavior corresponding to the different stages of adaptation and change, resistance, and retrenchment in response to modern and Western ideologies. There has been a general liberalization of attitudes, which is not yet matched by comparable changes in practice. Keenly aware of the dangers of an abrupt eruption of sexual instinctual drive, and deeply ingrained in a tradition of moderation and communal responsibility, the writers of the book repeatedly urge caution, restraint, and "proper socialization." While stressing the importance of being knowledgeable and educated, and of individual entitlement and gratification, heavy emphasis is also placed on family harmony, social stability, and the inculcation of moral values by advice and counseling, didactic education, and "propaganda." An analysis of sexual mores and superego and their possible practical impacts can be found in the books by Ng (1990) and by Wen and colleagues (1990) and in the paper by Ng and Lau (1990).

## E. Sex Offenders

In the 1980s, rates of crime in China rose in leaps and bounds, with alarming increases in sexual offenses in the young and relatively less increase in violent crimes. This section presents composites of a female prostitute and a male sex offender with modal characteristics abstracted from 137 tables of statistical information gathered in a survey of inmates of prisons and reformatories, supervised by security and reform officials, with guarantees of strict confidentiality. These institutions were located in nine areas, with most of the respondents from Shanghai (49%), Chengdu (22.8%), and Soochow (11%). A total of 2,136 subjects took part, with 67.5% males; 385 were female prostitutes.

Unfortunately, the various kinds of sex offenses were lumped together (except for female prostitution), and the data analyzed as a whole. Subjects included categories of "criminals," people with "infractions of the law," and those

accused of "misconducts (wrongdoings, misdemeanors)." The judicial system gives latitude to officials to grade antisocial behavior and to dispose of violators according to pragmatic and situational considerations. For details and the extent of variations, the reader must refer to the book under review and its bibliography.

*Profile 7: A Female Prostitute*

The typical incarcerated female prostitute in the survey was 20 years old and came from a rural family, financially "average" or "above average." She was discontented with her lot and inclined to seek more money, pleasure, or adventure. She left school early and may have retained some part-time manual work. She may have been betrothed or married, with an "average" or discordant relationship, but a sex life that has been mostly satisfactory. Although emphasizing feelings as an important element in human relationship, she was cynical about romantic love, and may have become bitter and vindictive after she had been cheated on or abused. She was ambivalent towards traditional feminine roles, chastity, and sexual restraint, but still viewed them as ideals and wished that she could conform.

She first ran afoul of the law after age 15. She was often seen as a victim of circumstances as well as an offender, and evoked sympathy from public officials, who would subject her to criticism, warning, "education," and "administrative discipline," before instituting legal penal measures, such as labor reform and "thought reform." While incarcerated, she would indulge in daydreaming or in artistic diversions to sublimate her libido.

The number of prostitutes, pimps, and their patrons known to the law has been increasing rapidly in China, especially in Shanghai and Guangzhou. Prostitutes make up most of the nation's female sex offenders. The survey data and clinical observation show that prostitutes tend to be young and immature, vain and "insatiable," given to pleasure-seeking rather than to toil and tedium, vulnerable to temptation, and deficient in self-restraint. Also noteworthy are the contributing social factors of inequality of gender status, lack of emotional nurturing and support for dependency needs in parental and marital homes, and the prevalence of opportunities for deviant outlets. The survey also uncovered the "low quality" or "poor civilization" of the parents and other family members, in the forms of less education, ignorance, narrow worldviews, weakness of bonding, and lack of moral guidelines. These social forces need to be considered in any plans for prevention. After release from jail, 20 to 30% of female sex offenders released in Shanghai relapse. Relapse rates depend on the intensity of rehabilitation.

*Profile 8: A Male Sex Offender*

The typical incarcerated male sex offender in the survey was about 28 years old and single. He had some secondary school education and was a manual worker or tradesman. He had his first seminal emission at age 16.5, still has nocturnal emissions once or twice a month, and masturbates about six times a month. He first witnessed sexual coitus at age 17, most likely at a peer's home or in a movie or videotape. He admits having "average" or "strong" sexual desire, and exposure to sexual scenes tends to arouse him and predispose him to errant sexual behavior.

He came from a home where his parents, especially his mother, had little education but an "average" or "comfortable" income, yet he still tended to feel deprived. He seldom talked to his parents and felt that family life was dull and meaningless. The family was generally permissive, but would express anger when a sexual offense or misconduct was committed. In a small percentage of cases, there was another family member with a history of criminal or sexually promiscuous behavior.

He emphasized the importance of sex and love, but relished instant pleasure. He would choose a partner based on appearance, feelings, and temperament, and would want a mate for sexual purposes even at an early age and outside the boundaries of wedlock. He likes movies, music, socializing, gossiping, womanizing, gambling, detective stories, and martial arts. He would be easily aroused by sexual material but may not act on it. Such material has become increasingly public and readily accessible. He probably has a few friends with a history of sexual offense or misconduct. He acquired his sexual knowledge mostly from his peers or the media, rather than from parents, siblings, or teachers, and has often found his questions unanswered.

Most offenders were convicted of their first sexual offense before age 29. The most common offenses were "hooliganism" (a vague umbrella term comprising various kinds of uncivil, indecorous, unmannerly, or licentious behavior), "promiscuity," rape, and sex with a minor. Other male sex offenses included bigamy, extramarital relations, abetting prostitution, male prostitution, incest, and enforced sex with the aged or the disabled. There has been a trend to commit crimes less by violent means, and more by deception and enticement. The survey data and clinical observation show that the male sex offenders are generally immature, chauvinistic, and emotionally needy. They are said to be of "low quality," and their families and social backgrounds are described the same way. Married male sex offenders reported fairly good marital and sexual relationships with their spouses, with frequent sexual intercourse (about ten times per month).

Upon conviction, most offenders expressed regret and cooperated with the sentence. While in prison, they try to suppress their sexual drives, but 6.3% admit to masturbation and 0.7% to homosexual activity. While some psychological or medical therapy may be provided for this sexual frustration, there has been no general policy to cope with the problem.

## F. Comments on the Research Methods

Technically, the nature and scope of this survey made the task very difficult. Sexuality is a matter of privacy and confidentiality and a topic often misunderstood and stigmatized. The peasantry was difficult to reach, in terms of both logistics and communication. There was little financial support, especially after the Tiananmen events. However, there was a groundswell of moral support from both inside and outside China, and many "comrades" from the tightly organized, stratified bureaucratic infrastructure in the nation, especially from women's groups, contributed their time, energy, and ingenuity, frequently working "to the point of exhaustion." Professor Liu and the core leaders were able to marshal the support of diverse groups at various levels in governmental, academic, educational, legal, labor, industrial, literary, media, and publishing sectors. The results have been partially presented at conferences inside and outside China, but since the book was written in Chinese, a wider dissemination of the findings awaits translation into other languages. An English translation of this full report was published in 1997 by Continuum (New York), the publisher of this *International Encyclopedia of Sexuality*.

The investigators were well aware of the limitations of the study. They experienced numerous stumbling blocks and frustrations, and encountered criticism and derision. It was not possible to obtain a completely representative sample, but a study of selected mainstream or significant groups in accessible locales is still very meaningful. Efforts were made to collect data from diverse parts of China, and a mixture of random and non-random sampling was used. The large sample sizes may allow statistical adjustments for some of the biases in further analysis.

The questionnaires were as comprehensive as circumstances permitted. In the interest of not being too intrusive, many questions were addressed only to attitudes and beliefs, as respondents would feel too hesitant to report actual behavior or practice in some areas.

Limitation of time and resources precluded the compilation of an index. Materials on some special topics are scattered throughout the book. For example, data on homosexuality have to be found laboriously from more than ten places, and information on premarital sex must be traced from some eight sources among the pages. Bibliographical notes are appended to each section, but even the names of European authors are written in Chinese.

## G. Discussion and Conclusion

This groundbreaking study is of immense value from a heuristic and theoretical point of view. No study of human sexuality can be complete without including a major human culture of the world and its most populous country. This study should provoke further questions at biological, psychological, sociocultural, and historical levels, and stimulate the emergence of new hypotheses and concepts, both in Chinese and other cultures. The methodology developed can serve as a template for future testing and improvement.

The practical import of this study cannot be overemphasized. It should equip the nation with more knowledge to meet the challenges of sexuality, both at the individual and at the societal levels. Wary of the perils of a sexual "revolution" with sudden release of pent-up drives, the authors repeatedly stress the importance of an interpersonal perspective and "sociological imperative." Despite the authors' claim to be non-authoritarian, many opinions and conclusions are judgmental and moralistic and delivered in a didactic, paternalistic tone not usually encountered in scientific writing.

As much as it is a towering accomplishment, this study should be placed in perspective by considering directions for future research. Professor Liu came up with a short list of tasks: further analysis of the data collected; more publicity and application of findings; and further study of special groups, such as homosexuals, ethnic minorities, the aged, the disabled, and servicemen. This inventory, however, is very limited and should be amplified to include the following: (1) improvement of the questionnaires and methodology; (2) extension of sampling, to include more underrepresented groups, including the overseas Chinese, and to allow further cross-cultural comparisons; (3) replication of the study and follow-up in longitudinal studies; (4) detailed case studies of individuals, subcultures, communities, families, institutions, opinion leaders, practitioners, practices, policies, and polities in this field; (5) further interpretation in cultural and historical terms and contribution to theory building; and (6) study of the impact of sociocultural changes and biological breakthroughs.

## 13. Ethnic Minority Resources

ROBERT T. FRANCOEUR

As mentioned in the introductory section on demographics, China has a population of well over a billion people. The vast majority of Chinese people, 91.9%, are Hans (ethnic Chinese, or Han Chinese). The remaining 8.1%, over 91 million people, include 55 significant other ethnic groups. Minority nationalities with population of over one million are the Bai, Bouyei, Dai (Thai), Dong, Hani, Hui,

Kazak, Korean, Li, Manchu, Miao, Mongolian, Tibetan, Tujia, Uighur, Yao, Yi, and Zhuang.

In the past decade, there has been growing interest in documenting the cultures of ethnic minority women in Yunnan province in southwest China. The provincial capital is Kunming. The Yunnan Publicity Centre for Foreign Countries has undertaken a "Women's Culture Series" on the different ethnic groups found in Yunnan province. The soft-cover 100-page booklets in this series contain both color photographs and text describing the life and customs of women. This series constitutes a small but valuable library. Among the volumes are: *Flowers, Love Songs and Girls: The Bulangs*; *Women Bathed in Holy Water: The Dais*; *Women Not to Be Bound in Waistbands: The Deangs*; *Face-Tattooed Women in Nature: The Dulongs*; *Holy Journey for Soul: The Huis*; *The Restless Female Souls: The Jinuos*; *Love Through Reed-Pipewind and Mouth String: The Lahus*; *Plateau Women in Transition: The Mongolians*; *Where the Goddesses Live: The Naxis*, and; *Nymphs of Folk Songs: The Zhuangs*.

This series is published by the Yunnan Publishing House, 100 Shulin Street, Kunming 65001 China, and distributed by the China International Book Trading Corporation, 35 Chegongzhuang Xilu, Beijing 100044 China (P.O. Box 399, Beijing, China).

## Conclusion

TIMOTHY PERPER

Because the People's Republic of China is one of the most populous nations, decisions made by its people and by its government about sexuality directly affect its population growth and therefore have global importance. Since the establishment of the People's Republic in 1949, China has undergone immense, and sometimes profoundly convulsive changes. A half-century ago, China was devastated by years of civil and external war, its people widely illiterate, and its poverty profound. No matter what one feels about the Mao dynasty—if that word is metaphorically permissible—the achievements of the Chinese people in the past 50 years have been awe-inspiring. China has become a major industrial power and its population is widely literate.

From the 1949 revolution onward, China's government has increasingly become deeply involved in the reproductive decision making of its citizens. Those who study sexuality and understand its implications for world population growth must surely hope that China's own scholars, and others who know its rich history, many languages, and varied cultures, will continue and expand their studies of sexuality in China. Because China is both a crucible and a harbinger of the future, these studies will be invaluable for documenting how decisions made by the Chinese people and government will inevitably affect the future of everyone on the earth.

## *Acknowledgment for Part 2: A Report of the Nationwide "Sex Civilization" Survey on 20,000 Subjects in China*

M. P. gratefully acknowledges the secretarial help of Christine H. K. Lau and of Lucie A. Wilk.

## *References and Suggested Readings*

Bullough, V. L. 1976. *Sexual variance in society and history* (Chap. 11: Sexual theory and attitudes in ancient China). Chicago: University of Chicago Press.

Burton, S. 1990 (May 14). China's Kinsey report. *Time Magazine*, p. 95.

Burton, S. 1988 (September 12). The sexual revolution hits China. *Time Magazine*, pp. 66-67.

CIA. 2002 (January). *The world factbook 2002*. Washington, DC: Central Intelligence Agency. Available: http://www.cia.gov/cia/publications/factbook/index.html.

Evans, H. 1997. *Women and sexuality in China: 1949 to the present*. New York: Continuum.

Gao, A. 1989 (October 5). China's population policy is proving to be effective. *China Daily*.

Garrett, L. 2002 (October 15). AIDS seen as threat to world: Experts say five big nations face devastation by 2010. *Newsday* [New York, USA].

Gil, V. E. 1991 (November). An ethnography of HIV/AIDS and sexuality in the People's Republic of China. *Journal of Sex Research, 28*(4):521-537.

Holly, A., & C. T. Bransfield. 1976. The marriage law: Basis of change for China's women. In: Iglitzin & Ross, eds., Women in the world: A comparative study (pp. 363-373). Santa Barbara, CA: Clio Press.

Kinsey, A. C., W. B. Pomeroy, & C. E. Martin. 1948. *Sexual behavior in the human male*. Philadelphia: W.B. Saunders.

Kinsey, A. C., W. B. Pomeroy, C. E. Martin, & P. H. Gebhard. 1953. *Sexual behavior in the human female*. Philadelphia: W.B. Saunders.

Kolodny, R., W. Masters, & V. Johnson. 1979. *Textbook of sexual medicine*. Boston: Little, Brown.

Landler, M. 2000 (August 14). Dongguan journal: For Hong Kong men, mistresses on the mainland. *The New York Times*.

Lau, M. P. 1995. Sex and civilization in modern China. (A review-essay on *Sexual behavior in modern China*, by Dalin Liu, M. L. Wu (Ng), and L. Chou). *Transcultural Psychiatric Research Review, 32*:137-156.

Lau, M. P., & M. L. Ng. 1989. Homosexuality in Chinese culture. *Culture, Medicine, and Psychiatry, 13*:465-488.

Legge, J., (trans.) 1970. *The Work of Mencius* (p. 313). New York: Dover Pub., Inc.

Lieh-Mak, F., K. M. O'Hoy, & S. L. Luk. 1983. Lesbianism in the Chinese of Hong Kong. *Archives of Sexual Behavior, 12*(1):21-30.

Liu, D. L. 1993. *The sex culture of ancient China* (In Chinese). Ningxia People Publishers and Xinhua Bookshops. ISBN 7-277-00935-1/I.204.

Liu, D. L., & M. L. Ng, eds. 1993 *Chinese dictionary of sexology*. Helungjian: People's Publication Co.

Liu, D., M. L. Ng, L. P. Zhou, & E. J. Haeberle. 1992/1997. *Zhongguo dangdai xingwenhua: Zhongguo lianwanli xianwenming diaozha baogao. [Sexual behavior in modern China: Report on the nationwide survey of 20,000 men and women]* (1st ed., in Chinese). 1992. Shanghai: Joint Publishing Co. English translation published by Continuum (New York), 1997.

Luk, H. 2002 (August 29). Hard times for economy and amour. Newark [New Jersey, USA] Star-Ledger, p. 2.

McGough, J. P. 1981. Deviant marriage patterns in Chinese society. In: A. Kleinman & T. Y. Lin, eds., *Normal and abnormal behaviour in Chinese culture* (pp. 171-201). Dordrecht, Holland: D. Reidel.

Ming, W. 1981. *New knowledge on prevention of birth defects*. Beijing: People's Medical Publishing House.

Needham, J. 1983. *Science and civilization in China, volume 5, part V: Spagyrical discovery and invention: Physiological alchemy* (Sexuality and the role of theories of generation). Cambridge, UK: Cambridge University Press.

Ng, M. L., ed. 1990. *Theories of sex*. Hong Kong: Commercial Press.

Ng, M. L., & L. S. Lam, eds. 1993. *Sexuality in Asia. Selected papers from the conference on sexuality in Asia*. Hong Kong College of Psychiatrists.

Ng, M. L., & M. P. Lau. 1990. Sexual attitudes in the Chinese. *Archives of Sexual Behavior, 19*(4):373-388.

Pan, S. 1996. Factors inhibiting Chinese people from answering questions on sexuality. A presentation at the combined Eastern/Midcontinent meeting of the Society for the Scientific Study of Sexuality, Pittsburgh, PA, May 3-5, 1996.

Pan, S. 1996. A sampling survey on students' sexual behavior in every university and college in Beijing. *Street. 10*:35-38. Also in *China Journal of Research in Youth, 11*.

Pan, S. 1995. Sexuality and relationship satisfaction in Mainland China. *Journal of Sex Research, 7*(4):1-17.

Pan, S. 1994. A sex revolution in current China. *Journal of Psychology and Human Sexuality* (USA), *6*(2):1-14. Full text published in Chinese, in *Research in Youth, 2*, 1994.

Pan, S. 1994. Chinese wives: Psychological and behavioral factors underlying their orgasm frequency. *China Psychology* (in Chinese), *8*.

Pan, S. 1994. Deep sexual behavior survey—Relations of sexual mores, idea, affection, and behavior (Full text in Chinese) *Chinese Psychology Health, 7*, pp. 168-171.

Pan, S. 1993/1994. Deep sex survey: Relationship among sexual ideas, orgasm, and behavior. A paper given at the Conference on Gender Issues in Chinese Society, Miami Beach, FL, USA, August 1993. Published in part in Chinese in *Chinese Psychology Health, 7*, 1994.

Pan, S. 1993 (September). Marriage and sexuality in current Beijing City *Beijing Marriage in the Late 1980s*. Beijing: Beijing Government.

Pan, S. 1993. Quantitative behavioral analysis of public heterosexual petting in Chinese civil parks. In: Ng & Lam, eds., *Sexuality in Asia* (pp. 173-184). Hong Kong: Hong Kong College of Psychiatrists.

Pan, S. 1993. China: Acceptability and effect of three kinds of sexual publication. *Archives of Sexual Behavior, 22*(1): 59-71.

Pan, S. 1991. Influence of sex knowledge and attitude on sexual behavior—The condition, motive, and orgasm. Privately published in *Textbook of socio-sexology* for use by sociology students at Remin University of China, Beijing.

Pan, S. 1990. Relations between satisfaction of sexual life and the marriage. In: The Beijing Society for Research in Marriage and Family, ed., *Research in the new development of marriage in Beijing City*. Beijing: The Office of Social Science Planning of Beijing City Government.

Pan, S. Chinese readers' answers to the questionnaire in the Chinese edition of the Kinsey report since 1989, Unpublished.

Pan, S, & P. Aggleton. 1995. Male homosexual behavior and HIV-related risk in China. In: *Bisexualities and AIDS: International perspectives*. London: Taylor and Francis Group Ltd.

Reuters News Service. 1994 (November 15). New Chinese law prohibits sex-screening of fetuses. *The New York Times*.

Ruan, F. 1985. Outline of the historical development of modern sexual medicine. *Encyclopedic knowledge*. Beijing: China Encyclopedia Press.

Ruan, F. 1985. *Essays on sex education: Ten lectures. Required readings for parents*. Beijing: Beijing Press.

Ruan, F. 1991. *Sex in China: Studies in sexology in Chinese culture*. New York: Plenum Press.

Ruan, F. [using pseudonym J. M. Huaj]. 1985. Homosexuality: An unsolved puzzle. *Zhu nin jiankang* [*To your good health*], *1985*(3):14-15.

Ruan, F., ed. 1985/1988. *Xing zhishi shouce* [*Handbook of sex knowledge*]. Beijing: Scientific and Technological Literature Publishing House. Revised 1988 edition published jointly by the Scientific and Technological Literature Publishing House and the People's Medical Publishing House. This book consists of 18 chapters as follows: (1) Science of

Sex; (2) Sex Organs; (3) Sex Hormones; (4) Sexual Development; (5) Psychology of Sex; (6) Sexual Response; (7) Sexual Behaviors; (8) Sexual Hygiene; (9) Sexual Dysfunctions; (10) Sexual Varieties; (11) Sex Crime; (12) Sex and Marriage; (13) Sex and Reproduction; (14) Sex in Illness; (15) Sex and Drugs; (16) Sex in the Aged; (17) Sex Therapy; and (18) Sex Education.

Ruan, F., & V. L. Bullough. 1988. The first case of transsexual surgery in Mainhand China. *Journal of Sex Research, 25*: 546-547.

Ruan, F., & V. L. Bullough. 1989a. Sex in China. *Medical Aspects of Human Sexuality, 23*:59-62.

Ruan, F., & V. L. Bullough. 1989b. Sex repression in contemporary China. In: P. Kurtz, ed., *Building a world community: Humanism in the 21st century* (pp. 198-201). Buffalo, NY: Prometheus Books.

Ruan, F., & K. R. Chong. 1987 (April 14). Gay life in China. *The Advocate, 470*:28-31.

Ruan, F., & Y. M. Tsai. 1987. Male homosexuality in the traditional Chinese literature. *Journal of Homosexuality, 14*: 21-33.

Ruan, F., & Y. M. Tsai. 1988. Male homosexuality in contemporary Mainland China. *Archives of Sexual Behavior, 17*: 189-199.

Ruan, F., V. L. Bullough, & Y. M. Tsai. 1989. Male transsexualism in Mainland China. *Archives of Sexual Behavior, 18*:517-522.

Sankar, A. 1984. Spinster sisterhoods. In: M. Sheridan & J. Salaff, eds., *Chinese working women*. Bloomington, IN: Indiana University Press.

SFPCC. State Family Planning Commission of China: Available: http://www.sfpc.gov.cn, 0n 06/11/1999.

Shapiro, J. 1987 (October 18). Scenes from the kalideidoscope: Chinese lives. *The New York Times Book Review*, p. 7.

Shenon, P. 1994 (August 16). A Chinese bias against girls creates surplus bachelors. *The New York Times*, pp. A1, A8.

Sheridan, M., & J. Salaff, eds. 1984. *Chinese working women*. Bloomington, IN: Indiana University Press.

Topping, S. 1972. *Journey between two Chinas* (pp. 291-293). New York: Harper & Row.

UNAIDS. 2002. *Epidemiological fact sheets by country*. Geneva, Switzerland: Joint United Nations Programme on HIV/AIDS (UNAIDS/WHO). Available: http://www.unaids.org / hivaidsinfo/statistics/fact_sheets/index_en.htm.

Van Gulik, R. H. 1961; 1974. *Sexual life in ancient China: A preliminary survey of Chinese sex and society from ca. 1500 B.C. till 1644 A.D*. Leiden: E. J. Brill.

Wehrfritz, G. 1996 (November 11). China: Blood and money: The marketplace has helped spread AIDS. *Newsweek*, p. 50.

Wen, S. H., J. D. Zeng, & M. L. Ng. 1990. *Sex and moral education*. Hong Kong: Joint Publishing.

Wiseman, P. 2002 (June 19). China thrown off balance as boys outnumber girls. *USA Today*, pp. 1-2.

Xiaomingxiong. 1984. *History of homosexuality in China* [*Zhongguo tongxingai shilu*]. Hong Kong: Samshasha and Pink Triangle Press.

Zhang, X., & S. Ye. 1986. *Chinese lives: An oral history of contemporary China* (W. J. F. Jenner & C. Lingang, eds.). New York: Pantheon Books.

Zhang, X., & S. Ye. 1986. *Chinese profiles: An oral history of contemporary China*. Beijing, China: Chinese Literature; distributed by China Book Trading Corp.

# Colombia

José Manuel Gonzáles, M.A.,* Rubén Ardila, Ph.D.,
Pedro Guerrero, M.D., Gloria Penagos, M.D., and
Bernardo Useche, Ph.D.
*Translated by*
Claudia Rockmaker, M.S.W., and Luciane Raibin, M.S.
*Updates by the Editors; Comment by Luciane Raibin, M.S.*

## Contents

## Demographics and a Brief Historical Perspective

ROBERT T. FRANCOEUR

### A. Demographics

Located in the northwest corner of South America, Colombia is bordered by the Caribbean Sea on the north, Panama on the northwest, the Pacific Ocean on the west, Ecuador and Peru on the south, and Brazil and Venezuela on the east. With a landmass of 439,735 square miles (1,138,910 km²), Colombia is larger than Texas and smaller than Alaska. Three mountain ranges, the Andes, the Western, and the Central and Eastern Cordilleras, run through the country from north to south. The eastern range is mostly high tablelands and is densely populated. The Magdalena River rises in the Andes and flows north to the Caribbean Sea through a rich alluvial plain. The sparsely settled eastern plains are drained by the Oronoco and Amazon Rivers. Colombia is the only South American country with coastlines on both the North Pacific Ocean and the Caribbean Sea. The climate is tropical along the coast and in the eastern plains, and cooler in the highlands.

In July 2002, Colombia had an estimated population of 41 million. (All data are from *The World Factbook 2002* (CIA 2002) unless otherwise stated.)

**Age Distribution and Sex Ratios**: *0-14 years*: 31.6% with 1.02 male(s) per female (sex ratio); *15-64 years*: 63.6% with 0.95 male(s) per female; *65 years and over*: 4.8% with 0.81 male(s) per female; *Total population sex ratio*: 0.97 male(s) to 1 female

**Life Expectancy at Birth**: *Total Population*: 70.85 years; *male*: 67 years; *female*: 74.83 years

**Urban/Rural Distribution**: 73% to 27%

**Ethnic Distribution**: *mestizo*: 58%; Caucasian: 20%; *mulatto*: 14%; black: 4%; mixed black-Amerindian: 3%; and Amerindian: 1%

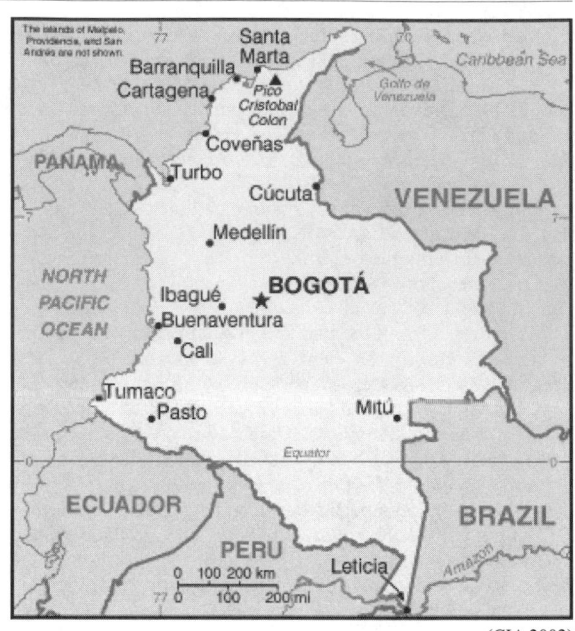

(CIA 2002)

**Religious Distribution**: Roman Catholic: 90%
**Birth Rate**: 21.99 births per 1,000 population
**Death Rate**: 5.66 per 1,000 population
**Infant Mortality Rate**: 23.21 deaths per 1,000 live births
**Net Migration Rate**: –0.32 migrant(s) per 1,000 population
**Total Fertility Rate**: 2.64 children born per woman
**Population Growth Rate**: 1.6%
**HIV/AIDS** (1999 est.): *Adult prevalence*: 0.31%; *Persons living with HIV/AIDS*: 71,000; *Deaths*: 1,700. (For additional details from www.UNAIDS.org, see end of Section 10B.)
**Literacy Rate** (*defined as those age 15 and over who can read and write*): 91.3%
**Per Capita Gross Domestic Product** (*purchasing power parity*): $6,300 (2001 est.); *Inflation*: 7.6%; *Unemployment*: 17%; *Living below the poverty line*: 55%

### B. A Brief Historical Perspective

Prior to the arrival of Europeans, the area that is now Colombia was home to various sedentary and semi-sedentary cultures, including the kingdoms of Funza and Tunja and the semi-sedentary Chibcha, who might have numbered about a million. Some of the area was part of the Inca Empire. By the 1530s, Spain had conquered the area and in 1538 established the colony of New Granada, with its capital in Bogatá, within the jurisdiction of the Viceroyalty of Peru. In 1740, a new Viceroyalty was established that included modern-day Colombia, Ecuador, Panama, and Venezuela. In 1819, forces under Simon Bolívar defeated the Spanish at the Battle of Boyacá, and the area gained its independence in 1821.

Colombia then became part of the Federation of New Granada. Venezuela and Ecuador broke away from this federation in 1829. By the 1850s, Colombia and Panama had adopted a federal system, but the system quickly deteriorated with the semi-sovereign states locked in a constant struggle with the central government for autonomy. In 1903, when the Colombian government rejected an offer by the United States for construction of a canal in Panama, the United States supported a revolt by Panama, which then declared its independence from Colombia.

*Communications*: Mtro. José Manuel González, M.A., Apartao Aereo 1190, Barranquilla, Colombia; jmgonzalez@playnet.net.co. Rubén Ardila: psycholo@latino.net.co. Bernardo Useche: busechea @aol.com.

Since the 1850s, Colombian politics have been characterized by a struggle between two groups that early on coalesced into the Liberal and Conservative parties. The ongoing Liberal-Conservative struggle has led to at least six civil wars, usually ending in interparty compromise. For most of the last century, the Roman Catholic Church played a major role in Colombia's social life and political struggles. The 1987-1988 Concordat gave the Church "official protection," while the state assumed authority over public education. The Church's central position in Colombian society was not substantially affected by the Concordat of 1942.

The worldwide depression of the 1930s seriously disrupted both the economy and the politics of Colombia. The overall economic collapse, coupled with the Conservative Party's brutal repression of the labor movement, led to a Liberal victory in 1930, followed by a new civil war between peasants loyal to the two parties. By 1934, Liberal president Alfonso López had inaugurated his "Revolution on the March" program of socioeconomic reform.

During the 1946 elections, Conservatives won the presidency with a minority of the overall vote, defeating a split Liberal Party. Armed conflict instigated by leaders of the two parties erupted to start *La Violencia*, from 1948 to 1957, during which more than 200,000 people died. In the summer of 1957, the two parties reached an agreement on constitutional reform that was designed to last 16 years and allow for regular alternation of the presidency between the two parties. This agreement lasted 11 years, until 1968, when constitutional revisions allowed official recognition of other political parties.

The 1960s and 1970s were marked by the emergence of terrorist and paramilitary groups on both the right and left, some with ties to the drug trade. This violence greatly reduced the power-sharing monopoly of the two parties. Since 1989, political violence has claimed over 35,000 lives. In March 1990, one of the most notorious left-wing groups, M-19, laid down its arms, entered the political mainstream, and won 19 of the 70 seats in a constitutional convention called to rewrite the Constitution. Other left-wing groups soon followed suit.

Colombia has also had to cope with a thriving and growing narcotics trade. Throughout the 1980s, narco-terrorists murdered and kidnapped government officials, journalists, and innocent bystanders with impunity. Despite the assassination of four presidential candidates prior to the 1990 election, the Liberal Party won with a vigorous campaign against the narcotics trade. In 1994, another Liberal president was elected on the promise to invest billions of dollars to improve Colombia's infrastructure using money from newly discovered oil fields. Between the summer of 1995 and September 1996, the government arrested the seven top members of the Cali drug cartel.

[*Comment 2003*: Like most third-world countries, Colombia's economy is unstable. The instability is exacerbated by the battle between the government, the "Drug Cartel," and paramilitary groups inside the country. In the past few years, this conflict has escalated, and human life has lost much of its value. Today, someone is kidnapped every three hours in Colombia. In 2002 alone, there were 2,986 kidnappings. Since 1996, this number has grown to 18,795. In this same period, over 800 people have died in captivity. Nine out of ten kidnapping cases last for about three months. Among the victims are politicians, businessmen, professionals, and common people, whose only reason for being kidnapped is to finance the "guerrilla" and other paramilitary groups.

[In the hopes of trying to appease the "guerrilla" and paramilitary groups, the Colombian government has even given these groups control over specific territories in the country. In these regions, cocaine plantations are common and the Revolutionary Armed Forces of Colombia (FARC) charge the growers taxes on the crops to help finance their activities. The government knows of these activities but cannot do anything to prevent it.

[The United States has partnered with the Colombian government to fight organized crime. There are close to 100,000 men involved in this effort. In 2002, the homicide rate in the country was 60 deaths per 100,000 inhabitants. In Bogotá, the capital city, the rate is a lower (31 deaths per 100,000 inhabitants).

[The victims are meticulously chosen, and it is this fact that is the most disturbing. In the past few years, four presidential candidates, two ex-ministers of justice, 10 supreme-court justices, a dozen journalists, hundreds of magistrates, and thousands of police officers have been murdered. In 2002, over 70 police officers were killed. The minister of defense, Martha Lucia Ramirez, has alerted the religious community, because the violence towards the clergy has also been escalating. In 2002, 13 clergymen were killed.

[This daily environment of unpredictable violence has, of course, widespread effects on the intimate lives, emotions, and psychology of Colombians of all classes and stations in life and society (*Estado de Sao Paulo*, March 23, 2003). (*End of comment by L. Raibin*)]

## 1. Basic Sexological Premises

BERNARDO USECHE

### A. The Cultural Legacy

Observing pieces of Pre-Colombian art and the descriptions of the historians of the Indies (when the colonists arrived), one finds strong evidence that the majority of the aboriginal tribes inhabiting the Colombian territory freely practiced the pleasurable side of sexuality. Among the art pieces of the time, one encounters representations of all possible sexual attitudes: masturbation, heterosexual activity, oral sex, homosexual activity, and bestiality. With the arrival of the Spaniards in the 16th century, the sexual interests of the conquistadors towards the Indian women made interracial marriages very popular. The evidence of interracial marriage is evident in the fact that 58% of Colombians today are *mestizo* Spanish/Amerindian and 14% *mulatto* black/Caucasian. At the same time, the Spaniards brought the Catholic religion and the repression of eroticism. The arrival of the African slaves during the 17th and 18th centuries signified a new miscegenation and the integration of new cultural elements favorable to pleasure rather than procreative sexuality. At the time of independence from Spain and the birth of the republic in the 19th century, a nation had been forged that, with respect to sexuality, was somewhere between the exalted libido of the macho population and the erotophobic restrictions of their profoundly religious culture. Toward the end of the 20th century, especially in recent decades, the progressive influences of North American culture have been added to Colombian culture. Profound transformations to the family structure and the traditional ideology have been generated by the changes in the Colombian economy at the end of the 20th century. This has opened a new sexual panorama that is much more complex than in colonial times.

Even though there are important urban, rural, and regional differences, today's sexual attitudes in Colombia are characterized by a double standard, where men are permitted all types of sexual activities while "decent" women are limited to sexual activities within the confines of marriage for reproduction purposes. There is, however, the beginning of a more permissive attitude towards a woman's sexual pleasures if she is in a serious relationship, because the impoverished situation of the majority of Colombians makes it very hard for couples to maintain stable ties.

Colombia continues to be a country where the majority of the population is Catholic, with traditions deeply rooted in the cultural values of Spain. But the few studies that have been done on this issue indicate that the sexual conduct of the people frequently does not conform with the Church's religious norms. This implies that *machismo* has played an important role in Colombian society. It has perpetuated discrimination towards women in family life, the work environment, and throughout society as a whole. *Machismo* places great value on female virginity, emphasizes the importance of the extended family, and supports the underlying concept of sin and guilt as it pertains to sexuality.

The modernization of Colombia, beginning in the 1930s and continuing well into the 1980s, changed many of these societal values. Colombia was transformed from a rural country to an urban country. No longer was religion the focal point of education. In spite of opposition from the Catholic Church, couples were having fewer children and birth control was more widely used. The status of women improved considerably. Employment of women outside the home has led to changes in the family structure. It allowed women to make choices, including how many children they bear, as well as changed their societal status. These societal changes, brought about by the modernization, industrialization, and urbanization of Colombia, continue into the start of the 21st century.

## B. Sexual Roles

*Machismo*, with its horrible discrimination against woman, is still present in Colombian family life, the work environment, and society. There are few men, even those in the lower socioeconomic bracket, who help with the housework or the raising of the children. With the impoverishment of the country, the number of single mothers who are head of the household increases constantly, but they are still not given the basics: same work, same salary, or even a job. This situation has driven many women and their daughters to prostitution. Politically, women were given equal rights under the law in the 1950s, but they are still the minority in positions of power or in government jobs. Only in the last decade has it been possible for Catholic couples to get a divorce. Abortion is still illegal in Colombia, even though there are estimates that over 300,000 illegal abortions are performed each year. A growing sexual liberation of women has been observed in the past 30 years, but the differences in the sexual conduct of young people of both sexes are still very significant, as seen in Table 1.

In the movement toward gender/sexual equality in Colombia, we find sexologists like Helí Alzate, who was one of the first to vehemently refute the assumed physical, intellectual, and emotional inferiority of women. Also, intellectuals like Maria Lay Londoño and Florence Thomas, pioneers of the feminist movement since the 1970s, have dedicated enormous efforts to the study of couples and the promotion of sexual equality. The ground won by women in respect to their sexuality has not yet had an impact on the *machismo* attitudes of men. When it does, as it likely will in the near future, one can expect a crisis in the current model of masculinity.

## 2. Religious, Ethnic, and Gender Factors Affecting Sexuality

JOSÉ MANUEL GONZÁLES

Recent studies (Bodnar et al. 1999; Gonzáles 1999a) show the presence of important religious beliefs related to sexuality. The concept of sin related to pleasure in sex, birth control, and some religious concepts that emphasize feminine resignation, are important in the sexual life and relationship of couples in Colombia. According to Paulo Romeo, Apostolic Nuncio in Colombia, the Catholic Church is losing 200 practitioners daily (*El Tiempo* 1997). According to the calculation presented at the Assembly of Bishops, only 60 of every 100 people baptized will take their first communion. According to Carlos Alzate of the Episcopal Conference of Colombia, only 15 out of 100 people who consider themselves Catholics on surveys go to Mass (*El Tiempo* 1997).

To better understand our sexuality, it is necessary to understand the influences of the three biggest ethnic groups in our heritage: the Spanish culture, the African culture, and the Indian culture (González 2000).

- The Spanish cultural influence, which is a mix between the Arab-Andaluzian influences, mixes the glorification of sensuality and eroticism in its most beautiful form with the Spanish Catholic Inquisition's very strong repressive ideas. This is a major influence in much of what is known about sexuality in Latin America.
- The African culture looked at sexuality, eroticism, and sexual vigor as natural phenomena. Much is known about this influence on contemporary Colombian culture.
- The sexuality of the local aborigines was quite varied, but there is not much information about their common features and differences. When the conquistadors arrived in Colombia, they encountered a wide variety of indigenous cultural attitudes regarding sex, a sample of which follows:
- The Panches, a Caribbean culture, practiced female infanticide and clitorectomies eight days after birth. If the child survived the sexual mutilation, its marriage was immediately arranged. If the firstborn was a female, she was immediately killed.
- Among the Lanches in the Boyacá region, if a women had five consecutive boys, the youngest would get special attention and was expected to take on the female role. They were brought up as females and were married off to a male.
- The Pamtagoros of Caldas were very puritanical and disapproved of any nudity. Their women were covered up to their ankles and were very careful, when sitting, not to show their legs. On the other hand, the Pijaos from Tolima would proudly show off their genitals.
- Both male and female Quimbayas from the western side of the central Andes were very sexually active. Among the Muiscas, from Cundinamarca and Boyacá, there was total freedom with respect to premarital sex, whereas among the Pijaos, it was common for the husband to kill his bride if she was not a virgin. The Pantagoros accepted infidelity, whereas the Pijaos pun-

### Table 1

**General Differences of Sexual Conduct**

| Sexual Activity | Men Percent | Number Responding | Women Percent | Number Responding |
|---|---|---|---|---|
| Masturbation | 92.3% | 379 | 43.2% | 604 |
| Vaginal coitus | 62.2 | 379 | 30.8 | 604 |
| Oral sex | 44.8 | 353 | 23.1 | 566 |
| Anal sex | 20.6 | 355 | 7.7 | 560 |
| Group sex | 21.6 | 310 | 1.6 | 492 |
| Same sex | 17.1 | 346 | 9.3 | 572 |
| Victim of rape or sexual abuse | 6.4 | 345 | 13.9 | 583 |

(Useche 1999)

ished infidelity very severely. An unfaithful Pijaos woman would be given to the single men of the village for their pleasure, after which she would be buried up to her waist in a public place where she would be whipped to death. The Muiscas had similar punishments for female infidelity.

- Both the Muiscas and the Quimbayas celebrated fertility festivals where they would get drunk and have sexual relations without restrictions. The Liles from the Valle would marry their sisters and nieces. The female Guane, from Santander del Sur, were very involved with the conquistadors. They were described as being the prettiest, the whitest, the cleanest, and the ones with the greatest ability to learn Spanish.
- Among the Noanamas and the Taso, from Choco, anal sex between men was very common. Sexual relations with women were only for reproductive purposes. Most female infants were drowned at birth.

## 3. Knowledge and Education about Sexuality

PEDRO GUERRERO

### A. Government Policies and Programs

We can affirm with full accuracy that from the Spanish Conquest to the passing of Resolution 03353 by the Ministry of Education in July 1993, sexuality education in Colombia has functioned according to the guidelines set forth by the Catholic Church. Accordingly, sermons originating from the scriptures and dictated from the pulpit were obligingly echoed in all educational institutions.

Our medical students receive their sexological training via lectures in gynecology, urology, and psychology. However, this coursework does not include the erotic aspects of sexuality. It only deals with biological reproduction and the pathologies found in the genital organs. Sexually transmitted diseases are generally discussed with apprehension. At the same time, therapy for sexual dysfunctions remains unknown, and the concept of the woman and the family is rooted in the old patriarchal ideology.

#### National Program on Sexual Education

The National Program on Sexual Education is best described as a set of principals and guidelines that collectively form the knowledge base, attitudes, behaviors, and values of sexuality. Its purpose is to meet the needs of Colombians in living a healthy, responsible, and gratifying sexual lifestyle, while promoting gender equality. Furthermore, it encourages the people to redefine the traditional roles of men and women, as well as the patriarchal family structure, thus attaining greater equality between marital couples and parents and their children. In addition, the National Program on Sexual Education encourages men and women, without coercion or pressure, to choose the appropriate time at which to bear children. As a result, they need to learn to adequately utilize effective birth control methods. The guidelines proposed by the National Program on Sexual Education should be viewed as a framework for the formation and pedagogical organization of sexual education programs in Colombian schools. Therefore, this proposal is optional and not mandatory.

The following items should be taken into consideration while reviewing these guidelines:

1. We must acknowledge the importance that culture plays in sexual education. Culture holds ethical values, morals, and spiritual and religious convictions. These not only determine the significance of the multiple dimensions of human existence, but also determine the people's level of acceptance of the academic proposals.

2. We must understand that sexuality is a fundamental dimension of humanity, which is ever-present in the lives of all men and women.

3. It is suggested that sexual education be integrated into the curriculum from a science and humanities context. This would then serve as an introduction to self-esteem, independence, interpersonal relationships, and health.

4. Sexual education is thought to be the responsibility of the educational community, including all educational institutes in both the public and private sectors, teachers and administrative staff, and parents and students.

5. The family is considered to be the primary source of education for children, as stated in Article 68 of the National Constitution of Colombia. In accordance with Article 68, the family reserves the right to choose the quality of education for their children. It is noted that the family unit serves as a model for the child's future perspectives on sexuality. It is in the family where children of both sexes learn their first lessons on solidarity, sensitivity, and gratitude. It is where a child learns to love and be loved, to tolerate and be tolerated, to hold a dialogue, to share, and to respect and value life. By the same token, it can also be the place where a child can experience and later repeat child abuse, sexual abuse, gender discrimination, and other types of domestic violence.

6. The importance of *etiquette* in sexual education is evident. The National Constitution of Colombia addresses the issue of the rights and responsibilities as they pertain to the concept of sexuality. Among other rights, the Constitution stipulates the rights of all to personal development, the equality of rights and responsibility of a couple, and the right to choose the number of children they are to bear, among other rights.

7. It is suggested that sexual education should be a pedagogical program that forms the basis of all fundamental studies. That being said, all educational institutions are left with the task of creating their own sexual education programs.

8. The proposed curriculum consists of developing programs that focus on basic sexual education themes, as they relate to the individual student, the couple, the family, and society as a whole. Each fundamental objective is to be modified to the age and grade level, the developmental level, and the specific needs of the target audience. The proposed programs target primary through secondary grade levels. Suggested topics include: identity, tolerance, reciprocity, life in general, affection, communication, love–sexuality, responsibility, imagination, and critical-thinking skills.

9. Workshops for educators are a suggested method of sharing information, as opposed to traditional methods like didactic lectures. In workshops, individuals can share information with the group in an open forum.

In order to test the effectiveness of the National Sexual Education Programs, two studies were initiated. The first case study, conducted by the Ministry of National Education, investigated 332 schools in 155 school districts in Colombia. Using quantitative methods, it was found that 92% of the schools utilized the sex education programs. These schools reported a marked improvement in school morale, as related to sexuality themes.

The second case study, also conducted by the Ministry of National Education, complimented the previous study in that it investigated the pedagogical process of the National Sex Education Programs in academic institutions. Utilizing qualitative methods to examine 16 subjects at different developmental stages in four different regions of Colombia, this study indicates that the sex education programs are at a critical phase of development. They have been introduced to the school system, and opened up avenues of employment and a new view on sexuality, but they have also identified four areas where further effort and development are needed:

1. Restructuring the aspects of human sexuality taught;
2. Promoting policies and other movements geared towards sexual well-being and reproduction with youth, both within and outside the educational system;
3. Increased utilization of sex education programs in academic institutions and successful replication of studies indicating their effectiveness; and
4. Participation and support from the congressional body, the judicial system, and educational institutions at both the national and international levels, for human sexuality, sex education, sexual health, and reproduction.

## B. Informal Sources of Sexual Knowledge
JOSÉ MANUEL GONZÁLES

Investigations conducted by a variety of groups that strongly support sex education have found that parents are reclaiming their roles as the primary informants of sex education. Mantilla (1993) reported that men's primary sources of information on sexuality were: friends, mother, father, and school. Women reported that their primary sources of information on sexuality were: friends, mother, school, and father. Gutierrez and Franco (1989) found that women reported that their primary sources of information on sexuality were: school, mother, friends, and the general media. Men reported that their primary sources of information were: friends, school, the general media, and father. The Institute of Social Securities (Instituto de Seguros Sociales 1994) found that adolescents posed questions regarding sexuality primarily to their mothers, 47% of females and 20% of males, whereas only 16% questioned their friends and 11% questioned their fathers.

Every day, the Colombian mass media discusses sexuality more freely. Several related programs have surfaced. Maria Ladi Londoño-Cali, was one of the first pioneers in this area. Lucia Nader and Marta Lucia Palacio joined in on two major networks, Caracol and RCN (Palacio 1999), and presented a compilation of the most frequently asked questions by her viewers. In print, the pioneering column on sexuality was "Window to Sexuality" (González 1998, 1999b). This column was originated by José Manuel Gonzáles and is presently written by Fernando Bohorquez, Ph.D. The *Herald* (Barranquilla) has published an entire page dedicated to human sexuality since 1999, titled "Love and Intimacy" (González 2000). The pioneering television program was *Sexology on Television*, hosted by Elkin Mesa (August 1979). Lucia Nader, Marta Lucia Palacio, Alonso Acuña, and Pedro Guerrero initiated another program, titled *It's Time to Live*. This program touched on all aspects of human sexuality. It was a popular program that also served as a basis for a book by the same name. Lucia Nader developed a magazine titled *In Private* (1996). Its theme was fundamentally sexuality. *Accent* was a magazine geared towards the gay community, published in 1997. Both publications have since gone off the market because of financial difficulties.

## 4. Autoerotic Behaviors and Patterns

### A. Children and Adolescents
Erotic autostimulation is rather common among children. Ardila (1986a) interviewed 700 mothers, pertaining to different Colombian subcultures, and found that three out of four mothers reported masturbatory behavior among children of 4 years of age. Acuña and associates (1986) explored the existence of this behavior and the anxiety that it causes for parents. In general, this type of autoexploratory and sexual gratification behavior is repressed by the adults.

Autoerotic behaviors are also common among adolescents. Masturbation generally starts between the ages of 13 and 15 (Alzate 1989; Domínguez et al. 1988; González 1995; Giraldo 1981; Gutiérrez & Franco 1989; Useche 1999). Among the adolescents, between 60% and 95% of men and 14% and 68% of women have masturbated at least once in their lives (Alzate 1989; Domínguez et al. 1988; González 1995; Giraldo 1981; Gutiérrez & Franco 1989; Useche 1999). In general, feelings of guilt and anxiety are reported with respect to masturbation (Domínguez et al. 1988; González 2000; Gutiérrez & Franco 1989).

### B. Adults
Sexual autostimulation is also very common among adults. About 90% of men and 70% of women report having masturbated at least once in their lives (Alzate 1989; Elijaike et al. 1987; González 1979, 1985, 1995, 2000). The majority of those studies report a greater incidence of masturbatory behavior in those who are less religious.

A relationship between the personality, as measured by Eysenck's MPI test, and masturbation has been detected by González (1979). Men with high scores in introversion have confirmed a higher frequency of masturbatory behavior. Women with high scores for neuroticism have demonstrated a lower frequency of masturbatory behavior as compared to woman with normal scores. With relation to age, it has been reported that in people over 60 years of age, single women masturbate more than men (Bardugo & Segura 1988, González & González in press).

Sexual autostimulation generates many negative feelings. There are many myths and misinformed beliefs on the subject (Giraldo 1981; González 2000). In a recent survey done in the four biggest cities of Colombia, it was found that only 32% of women and 53% of men find masturbation to be a healthy sexual behavior. The rest believe that it is a crazy conduct that should be avoided, because it is a sexual deviance and a sin (*Semana* 1999).

## 5. Interpersonal Heterosexual Behaviors
JOSÉ MANUEL GONZÁLES

### A. Children
Childhood sexual rehearsal play and sexual exploration are quite common. One out of every two mothers reported observing sexual rehearsal play in their 4-year-old children (Ardila 1986). Still, childhood sexuality is a theme that produces great anxiety in adults (Acuña et al. 1986; González 2000).

### B. Adolescents
There are no widespread rituals of initiation to puberty. In some rural areas on the Caribbean coast of Colombia, it is common for adolescents to engage in sexual acts with animals, namely mules (González 2000).

Sexual activity among adolescents occurs frequently and functions according to the traditional male-dominant cultural pattern. Forty-four percent of Colombians initiate sexual interactions between the ages of 11 and 18. By 18 years of age, 72% of males and 40% of females have had sexual intercourse, according to Ministry of Health of Colombia (Ministerio de Salud 1994). Generally, female adolescents' first sexual encounter occurs with their boyfriends. Often, sexual relations between Colombian adolescents stem from an intimate relationship and not from an encounter with a prostitute (Bonder et al. 1999; González 1995; González et al. 2000; Useche 1999).

## C. Adults

### Premarital Relations, Courtship, and Dating

Premarital sex is quite common in Colombia. In recent studies, it was found that 90.4% of males and 62.8% of females have engaged in premarital sex prior to starting college life (González et al. 2000). Love is usually on the forefront. It is a fundamental part of Colombian culture: music, magazine articles, soap operas, and movies (Bodnar et al. 1999; González 1998; Guerrero 1996a, 1996b). In recent years, initiating friendships and intimate relationships has become easier. Formal introductions are no longer required. People have become more direct in their approach.

In recent studies, González (2000) found that men experience difficulties in expressing love and affection. It is common that people have unrealistic expectations regarding love, and, as a consequence, great frustrations and clashes between fantasy and reality in relationships. Frequently, the expectation is that the lover will satisfy all of their needs, provide unconditional love, and be who they want them to be and not who they actually are. They believe that pain, suffering, and jealousy are essential parts of a relationship. Generally, the woman is expected to be responsible for the affective part of the relationship. She is often expected to prove her love by engaging in sex with her partner. It is also believed that a sure way of keeping a man, or winning him back, is through sex. All the conditions aforementioned make choosing an appropriate mate difficult. Frequently, a partner is not chosen on reality-based merits. Instead, he or she is chosen on unrealistic expectations, which inevitably will lead to a failed relationship.

### Sexual Behavior and Relationships of Single Adults

Among adults, there exists a misconception of what sexual pleasure is. Generally, they do not understand the physiological and/or psychological concepts of eroticism. As a result, there exist irrational and unhealthy beliefs (González et al. 2000). Sex is commonly seen as bad, dirty, ugly, and degrading. This sex-phobic mindset distorts and impedes a healthy sexual lifestyle (González 1981). Often egotism is perceived as a process leading towards reproduction. Anything else is seemingly considered illegal, promiscuous, and guilt-ridden (González 1999a).

According to the *machismo* ideology, males tend to initiate sexual activity earlier than females. It tends to be more intense and promiscuous (Alzate 1989; Bodnar et al. 1999; González et al. 2000; Institute of Social Securities 1993; Useche 1999). Adult males will have more sexual partners than their female counterparts: One out of every three males reported having two or more sexual partners in the last 12 months, whereas only three out of every 100 females reported multiple partners (Institute of Social Securities 1993). Generally, the male initiates sexual interactions within the relationship. Couples engage in sex frequently: 2% reported daily sexual activity, 19% reported sexual activity several times a week, 41% reported weekly sexual activity, and 16% reported monthly sexual activity (Ministerio de Salud 1994). The sexual positions most frequently practiced were the missionary man-on-top/woman-on-bottom position, the straddle where the woman sits on top of the man, and the rear-entry position with the man behind the woman (González 1994).

Eljaiek et al. (1987) found that almost 50% of the couples surveyed did not engage in sexual relations during menses, and almost 10% discontinued sexual activity during pregnancy. There also exists a great irresponsibility, for both men and women, in practicing safe sex and using some form of contraception. There is a high rate of sexual dissatisfaction for both genders (González 1998).

### Marriage and Family

Colombians place a great importance on feeling as though one is "in love." Love is the primary motivating factor for matrimony, as reported by 87% of women and 69% of men (Eljaiek et al. 1987).

The marriage rate has decreased while the rate of cohabitation has increased, especially in the younger population. Mature couples in their mid-80s reported that 84% were married through the Catholic Church, while 15% cohabitated. Married couples in their mid-30s reported that 44% were married through the Catholic Church, while 54% cohabitated (Rojas 1997). The average age for matrimony or cohabitation has decreased for males and has increased for women (Presidential Council for Youth, Women, and Their Families 1994).

Rojas (1998) found that couples feel unfulfilled in their relationships. They feel that their counterparts do not demonstrate affection both physically and verbally, that they do not support their efforts, and that they do not make them feel valued. Additionally, they feel that there is a lack of communication with regards to problems, misunderstandings, and resolutions. Rojas also noted that of the couples surveyed, 50% did not have a set time in which to communicate.

The marital union in Colombia tends to be non-democratic and lacks equality between the partners. Often women seek gender equity, only to be met with violence from their counterparts. There also exist religious beliefs that support submissiveness and perpetuate this unjust marital relationship (González 2000). Misinformation pertaining to masculinity, femininity, and their interrelatedness permeates societal expectations. Men are perceived in terms of money, power, bravery, and freedom. Women, on the other hand, are perceived as tender, submissive, tolerant, able to bear suffering, and having a need to sexually satisfy their partner at the expense of her own sexual needs. These *machismo*-based values are believed to be biological in nature, disregarding educational, physiological, and/or psychological cultural factors (González 1998, 2000).

There has been an increase in separations and multiple sequential marriages in Colombia: 35% of all couples surveyed have been separated at least once (Presidential Council for Youth, Women, and Their Families 1994). Zamudio and Rubiano (1991b) found that the primary causes for separations among Colombian couples were: infidelity, jealousy, or falling in love with another person, falling out of love or falling into a rut, and financial difficulties, in that order.

According to Gutierrez de Pineda (1975), there are four types of family structures: Andino, Santandereano, Negroide, and Antioqueno. These are characterized by the following factors:

- *Andino Family Structure* in the Cundinamarca and Boyaca regions. The dominant feature in this region is the patriarchal structure in which the father is the head of the household. The mother and children are viewed as subordinates. The male children imitate the father while the girls imitate the mother. Initially, the mother is the disciplinarian. However, as the boys grow older, the father tends to intervene more frequently.
- *Santandereano Family Structure* in the Santanderes. Here, the power of the male over the female is evident. His aggressiveness and physical dominance characterize the male. He takes great pride in his sons; however, he withholds any type of affection. Great emphasis is placed on the rift between social classes.
- *Negroide Family Structure* on the Atlantic Coast, in the regions of Chocco and Magdalena, Cauca, and the lower

region of Antioquia. The basic characteristic of this family structure is the incidence of cohabitation. For men, it is considered prestigious to have multiple partners. Much attention is focused on the male genitals. The man is determined to father a vast number of children without regard for the childrearing responsibilities. Usually, the mother raises the children with the almost complete absence of the father.

• *Antioqueno Family Structure* in the regions of Antioquia, Caldas, Risaralda, Quindio, El Valle, Tolima, and parts of El Chocco. Here, religion has a great impact on the family structure. Catholic matrimonies are a dominant feature. The traditional gender roles are practiced. The man is the head of the household, but the woman rules in the home. The mother is strict with her daughters, especially as it pertains to sexuality. She is compliant with her sons, especially the youngest one.

Although these discrepancies are no longer as rigid as they once were, the general tendency continues to follow these traditional patterns (Gutierrez de Pineda 1975).

### Extramarital Sex

Infidelity is an important element in a Colombian marriage (González 1998). Murillo (1993) found that there were three males for every one female who engaged in extramarital sexual relationships. Nadar and Palacio (1989) found the same results. Nadar and Palacio also found that 30% of separations were a result of infidelity. Findings indicate that there is a greater incidence of infidelity for men as the socioeconomic levels rise higher. For women, infidelity is more common at the upper-middle-class levels (Rojas 1997). A common misconception is that a man's infidelity is less serious because he is biologically driven, whereas women's infidelity is not.

### Sexuality and Physically Disabled and Elderly Persons

Colombian sexology has little literature regarding disabled and elderly persons. The prevailing attitude is that this population is nonsexual and has no need for sexual intimacy. In a recent study of adults over the age of 60, González and González (in press) found that 94% of the men and 24% of the women maintain sexual interactions with their mates; males engaged in sex every two weeks, whereas women engaged in sex on a monthly basis. Seventy-six percent of men and 36% of women reported that there was a decrease in gratifying sexual intercourse after the age of 60. It was reported that 88% of these older men and 30% of the women are satisfied with their sex life. Eighty-two percent of the men and 18% of the women reported that they continue to seek out their partners for sexual activity. Forty percent of the men surveyed reported having sexual relations with someone other than their regular partner. Eighty percent of men and 52% of women reported that relations with their partners are at least cordial. Forty percent of all women surveyed reported that they do not have a good relationship with their partners. Seventy-two percent of men and 50% of women reported that they continue to be affectionate with their partners. The authors believe that the predominant *machismo* values distort a couple's lifestyle, resulting in resentful women.

### Incidence of Anal and Oral Sex

Although there are no laws prohibiting anal sex and oral sex, they continue to be highly criticized in public and frequently practiced in private. Almost 80% of men and 70% of women have engaged in oral sex, now a regular part of foreplay (Eljaiek et al. 1987; González 1994, 1998).

## 6. Homoerotic, Homosexual, and Bisexual Behaviors

RUBEN ARDILA

There has long been an interest in homosexuality in Colombia. Behaviors that can be categorized as homosexual have been noted within the cultures that existed in Colombia during the arrival of the Europeans. However, the study of homosexuality is filled with methodological ambiguities. There are certain behaviors that may or may not be considered *homosexual* by today's societal standards. Even so, these behaviors existed long before the arrival of the Spaniards. As in other cultures, homosexual behaviors were found more frequently among men than women.

From the onset of studies on sexuality amongst Colombians, homosexuality was always an interest (Alzate 1978, 1982; Botero 1980; González 1985). It was found that there were differences in homosexual activity between men and women. In Bogotá, 28% of the men and 13% of the women reported having had same-sex relationships. Interestingly, there was a marked difference between the various cities in Colombia. These ratios are not limited to homosexual activities exclusively. It reflects the number of individuals who engaged in some type of sexual activity with someone of the same sex. It could have been an isolated incident and/or the regular practice of homosexual or bisexual behaviors.

### Anthropological and Social Aspects

José Fernando Serrano (1997, 1998), an anthropologist, has pointed out that the formation of the homosexual identity, as described by societal constructs, has been a long process. He reviewed sociological studies originating in Colombia and indicated which ones supported the argument of sexual orientation. He also argued the problem of collective identities at the international level.

The modernization of Colombia, which took place in the latter half of the 20th century, enabled people to look outside their immediate society and expand their provincial traditions. It enabled them to study ideas from other countries, primarily from France and other regions of Europe, and the United States. The gay and lesbian liberation movements of Germany, several other European nations, and later from the United States slowly made their way to Colombia. Nevertheless, they had a great impact on the organization of the gay and lesbian movements. Modernization gradually brought about internationalization, globalization, and societal changes that influenced people's private lives.

### Homosexual Identity

The beginnings of organized homosexual groups in Colombia began in 1970. Manuel Antonio Velandia, a sociologist and philosopher, initiated them. He associated with people who were interested in human rights, social change, and the general counterculture of the 1960s and 1970s on an international level. These gay and lesbian movements were difficult to organize, and were at times very short lived. Finally, in the late 1980s and 1990s, gay and lesbian groups succeeded in uniting and achieving their goals (Velandia 1999).

Velandia founded the Gay Liberation Group and the Homosexual Liberation Movement of Colombia in 1976. He also organized the first Gay Pride March in 1983 in Bogotá. These movements gained importance in 1998 and 1999 and included weeklong lectures on sexual diversity, collective identity, human rights, legislation, and other related topics. However, gay and lesbian communities are slow in coming. Although gay meeting places have been established since the 1970s, homosexual literature remains unseen. The first writings pertaining to the gay lifestyle—poetry, novels, theater, and soap operas—surfaced in the 1980s. This is not to discount earlier works by P. Barba Jacob. Today, soap operas and movies frequently touch on homosexuality.

The Constitution of Colombia, passed in 1991, prohibits discrimination in any form or manner. It recognizes that all people have the right to free personal development. The Constitution stipulates that homosexuals may not be discriminated against based on their sexual orientation. Sexual orientation that is not shared by the majority does not justify unequal treatment.

The rights given by the Colombian Constitution pertaining to sexual orientation during the 1990s have been favorable for homosexuals and bisexuals. For example, in April 1991, a law was passed that protects an individual's rights to free sexual identity. It affirms that homosexuality should be considered valid and legitimate. The Colombian Constitution also addressed the debate regarding homosexual educators. They determined that homosexuality has no bearing on an individual's ability to teach (in September 1998). Additionally, in July 1999, the Colombian legislature passed a law protecting homosexuals in the military. It states that individuals may reveal their status as homosexuals and continue to be held to the same norms and expectations as heterosexuals.

The Colombian legislature has defined the family as a union of a man and a woman (March 7, 1996). However, it went on to acknowledge the rights of partners, including same-sex couples, in terms of inheritance, transfer of assets, and financial support, among other things. There have been several attempts to legalize homosexual marriages, as has been done in several other areas, e.g., Denmark since 1989, Norway since 1993, Sweden since 1995, Iceland since 1996, Hungary since 1996, and Holland since 1997. In some cases, there exist legal sanctions against same-sex marriages because of the possibility of adoption. There are, however, gay activist groups who support the legalization of the *gay family* in all aspects, including adoption. The Family Pride coalition is one of the most important advocates of this movement.

One of the most recent proposals, in September 1999, sought to equalize the rights of homosexual couples with those of heterosexual couples. For instance, after two years of cohabitation, the couple may apply for Social Security benefits. Additionally, should the relationship end because of death, one partner may inherit the assets of the other. There already are companies in the private and public sectors that will allow an employee's partner of the same sex to register for benefits.

### Psychological Investigations

Psychological studies regarding homosexuality, bisexuality, and homoeroticism have been conducted by Octavio Giraldo and his team (1979, 1981, 1982) at the University of "El Valle." Similar studies have been led by Ruben Ardila (1985, 1986, 1995, 1998) at the National University of Colombia.

Ruben Ardila has focused on sexual orientation in the studies he has conducted for the past 15 years. Some of the issues he has researched have been: adaptation of homosexual males, lesbianism, sexual orientation, heterosexual attitudes towards homosexuals, stability of the homosexual couple, the lifecycle of homosexuals and lesbians, the biological aspects of homosexuality, politics as they pertain to homosexuality, and other related topics.

One such study looked at the adaptation of male homosexuals (Ardial 1998). There were 100 subjects, between the ages of 18 and 52 years of age. They all scored a five or six on the Kinsey Scale (indicating predominantly or exclusively homosexual). The following factors were studied: depression, solitude, timidity, social alienation, interrelations with heterosexuals, interrelations with homosexuals, sexual practices, traditional values, religion, morals, conformity, acceptance of homosexuality, emotional stability, guilt, concept of homosexuality as a mental illness, effeminacy, responsibility, interrelations with the opposite sex, secretiveness of homosexuality, personal adjustment, and psychosomatic symptoms.

The results indicate that Colombian homosexuals are well adapted and do not present any pathological qualities. However, 10% manifested signs of severe depression, while 44% were highly stable. Only 4% reported feeling guilty about their homosexuality. Fifty-nine percent stated that they had positive interpersonal relations, and 48% accepted their homosexuality. For further material on diverse aspects of sexual orientation for both women and men, see the References and Suggested Readings section.

### Sexual Orientation in Colombian Society

Our society, based on the Judeo-Christian faith, has a very negative attitude towards homosexuality. Homosexuality is viewed as a violation, an illness, or a deviation from the norm that threatens normal behaviors and society. This homophobic view has permeated Colombian society throughout its history, although there have been different levels of acceptance, depending on the individual's level of education, rural-versus-urban setting, age, and their affiliation with the Catholic Church. There is a deeply rooted belief that homosexuals are a threat to society, good upbringing, and family values. Similarly, homosexuality is thought to be related to child sexual abuse, AIDS, substance abuse, delinquency, and other serious social problems.

Homosexuals are discriminated against in education, in the workplace, in housing, in the mass media, and generally in daily living. This homophobia has its origins in the Latin American cultures, which practice *machismo*, emphasize the importance of the family unit, and are highly influenced by the Catholic Church. In spite of this, the situation has considerably improved in recent years, from the homosexual liberation movements in the 1970s to the legislative, medical, and psychological advances that occurred later. In the larger cities of Colombia, especially those with higher levels of education, homosexuals are accepted. They are respected and are considered equal to heterosexuals. In these areas, discrimination is hardly noticeable. It is no longer believed that male homosexuals are less masculine than heterosexual males or that lesbians are any less feminine than female heterosexuals are. Additionally, there are certain groups within the Church who have worked towards improving the quality of life for gays and lesbians. Social support has shown improvement, which will then lead to a more pluralistic, diversified, and egalitarian society.

## 7. Gender Diversity and Transgender Issues

BERNARDO USECHE

As in most of the Latin American countries, Colombia also does not have serious studies or reliable statistics on the frequency or psychological evolution of those people whose sexual identity is not well-defined or is confused. But, based on clinical exams and interviews with those people, it is possible to differentiate two large groups.

In the first group, one encounters heterosexual and homosexual transvestites and a few male-to-female transsexuals who were born and raised in lower-class environments and have socially isolated themselves in areas dedicated mostly to prostitution. Because of the almost nonexistent control over the sale of hormones in the country, it is quite easy for such people to seek physical changes through automedication with estrogen. This type of hormonal auto-medication normally starts during adolescence and has the effect of changing the body type to the feminine phenotype, even though the vast majority of this group will not seek surgical sex reassignment.

Given the context of the social problems encountered by people living in poverty, members of this first group become sexually active at a very early age and soon transition to promiscuity and prostitution. A few work as strippers in the clubs that are very common in the prostitution areas of the big cities. A few others, under the auspices of "transformists," work as singers or actresses in nightclub shows. Very seldom, and only if sex-reassignment surgery is involved, will someone from this group obtain some type of professional therapy through the almost nonexistent public health system. Members of this group also have received some help and orientation from nongovernmental agencies involved in the prevention of HIV infection.

The following quote perfectly demonstrates what happens to members of this group:

> I began to dress permanently as a woman and take hormones when I was 18, and that provoked adverse emotional reaction from my parents who kicked me out of the house. They accepted me as a homosexual but not as a transsexual. The only place that accepts me as I am is the brothel where I go to work when I need money. (Author's clinical notes)

The second group is composed of those who belong to the upper classes, many of whom have college degrees and work as professionals. This group is currently composed of transvestites, fetishist transvestites, and some transsexuals who have access to information regarding their sexual identity, especially through the Internet. Some have their own Web pages and communicate among themselves, taking advantage on the initial anonymity of cyberspace to better understand themselves. Even though this group has the means to obtain professional help and counseling through private practice, they seldom do so. This is because of the fact that many therapists have no knowledge on the subject, and some even have a negative attitude to those who approach them with these problems. In the words of one client in this group:

> In the anguish of my situation I went to a psychiatrist who referred me to the best sex therapist in this city. In our first meeting, the sexologist was very frustrating and I felt offended and attacked. I never returned. (Author's clinical notes)

In recent years, sex-reassignment surgery has been performed in large cities like Bogotá, Cali, and Medellín.

## 8. Significant Unconventional Sexual Behaviors

JOSÉ MANUEL GONZÁLES

### A. Coercive Sex

*Child Sexual Abuse and Incest*

Colombian law considers child sexual abuse a crime under Articles 303, 304, and 305 of the Penal Code. It is calculated that one Colombian child is sexually molested every six hours (Afecto Foundation 1999). In the great majority of cases, the aggressor is a person the victim knows (Florez & Consuegra 1998). These authors studied the cases of 80 girls under the age of 15 in the urban area of Barranquilla. In 53% of the cases, the aggressor was someone the victim knew but was not a family member, 41% of the perpetrators were family members, and only 6% were complete strangers. In 1.25% of the cases, pregnancy was a consequence.

Incest is also considered a crime under Article 259 of the Penal Code. Even though there are no reliable statistics, it is widely calculated that incest is a common phenomenon. In a recent survey conducted in the four largest cities, *Semana* (1999) found that 3% of males and 1% of females had had sexual relations with their father, mother, or a sibling.

In Colombia, 2 million children are victims of abuse, 850 of whom were in critical condition at the time of the Afecto Foundation survey (1999). In Colombia, an estimated 148 of every 1,000 Colombian children are abused in some way. Of these 148, 100 are verbally abused, 40 are physically abused, and 8 are sexually abused (*El Tiempo* 1999).

*Sexual Harassment*

Sexual harassment is not considered a crime in Colombia. Even though there are no reliable statistics, it is a very common phenomenon in academic and work environments. The *machismo* cultural pattern makes many men think it is their God-given right to sexually harass their female employees and coworkers.

*Rape*

Rape is considered a crime under Article 298 of the Penal Code and does happen with some frequency. Profamilia (Planned Parenthood of Colombia 1995) found that 5.3% of women in the fertile age group have been forced to have sexual relations. Before 1996, forced sexual relations within married couples were not considered a crime. With the creation of Law 294 under Article 25, forced sexual relations within married couples are now a crime.

Spousal abuse is a very common phenomenon. In 1996, of the 42,963 cases seen by the Legal Medicine group, 71% involved spousal abuse. Of those cases, 95% of the victims were women, with a ratio of 18 women for every man. The group at most risk of abuse are women between the ages of 25 and 34. In a 1998 study in several Colombian cities, 14.3% of the persons interviewed said that they had been attacked by their spouses (*El Tiempo* 1998). Further interviews showed that 60% of the women had been verbally, physically, psychologically, or sexually attacked by their husbands or partners. Twenty percent were physically attacked and 10% were forced to have sexual relations with their husbands (Profamilia 1995). Most of these women tried to solve their problems without the intervention of the police or other governmental agencies. Most of these women were completely passive regarding the attacks of their partner. Most battered women say that the main causes of the aggression are drunkenness and jealousy on the part of their partners. The most common physical abuses are punches 88%, kicks 27%, and shoves and pushes 24%. In 35% of the cases, the episode is observed by a child (Profamilia 1995).

### B. Prostitution

Prostitution is considered a crime under Articles 308, 309, 311, and 312 of the Penal Code. In 1998, the Renacer Foundation estimated 30,000 Colombian boys and girls were engaged in prostitution. At the same time, the Foundation estimated that there were 90,000 sex workers in the country. The sex trade seems to be increasing in the past five years, particularly in the tourist areas and with minors. In the most recent government administrations, there has been a greater emphasis on efforts to combat situations, such as the sex trade, that are problematic to the community.

### C. Pornography and Erotica

Pornography possession and its use among adults are not crimes. Article 312 of the Penal Code does limit and penalize the circulation of pornographic material for minors under age 18 years. Pornographic movies can be seen or rented with great ease in the cities. Pornographic magazines circulate all over the country. A 1999 survey by *Semana* shows that 48% of men and 35% of women think that pornographic movies and magazines make their sexual life more interesting. Regarding pornographic magazines, 13% of men and 3% of women reported having read one in the previous 30 days. It is also interesting to note that 16% of men and 44% of women had never read a pornographic magazine in their lives. As for pornographic movies, 21% of men and 6% of women confirmed having had seen a pornographic movie in the previous 30 days. Also, 14% of men and 39% of women stated that they had never seen a pornographic movie in their lives. In the large cities, live sexual shows are performed, but 65% of men and 85% of women claimed they had never seen one (*Semana* 1999).

The new digital media, Internet, and World Wide Web have also been affecting sexual relationships: 17% of men and 4% of women affirmed having visited a pornographic site on the Internet. Also, 14% of men and 4% of women admitted to having engaged in phone sex.

## 9. Contraception, Abortion, and Population Planning
GLORIA PENAGOS

### A. Contraception

Birth control, more commonly known as family planning, was introduced in Colombia in 1964. It was managed under the sponsorship of population and medical specialists. The objective was to improve the health of women and their children, to facilitate the growth of women in areas related to motherhood, and population control.

Although the majority of Colombians practice Catholicism, which prohibits the use of any type of artificial birth control, economic and social needs, marital instability, and constant changes in the family structure have led to the acknowledgment of the civil rights of all couples and their children. Thus, the contradiction between what is forbidden by the Catholic Church and what is practiced by the general public has led to an appreciation of the right to the enjoyment of sexuality without the burden of pregnancy. The majority of people continue to practice Catholicism without feeling the guilt put upon them by the Church regarding birth control. Close to three quarters of all women in a relationship, 72.2%, utilize some method of birth control. However, for every six women using birth control, only one man uses a contraceptive (Profamilia 1995). Table 2 shows a comparison of the use of birth control worldwide and the usage in Colombia in 1995.

The most commonly used methods of birth control are tubal ligation and vasectomy. Recently, Colombia's Social

### Table 2

**A Comparison of Birth Control Methods Used Worldwide and in Colombia (1995)**

| Contraceptive Method | Worldwide Usage | Colombian Usage |
|---|---|---|
| Tubal ligation | 13.0% | 16.9% |
| Vasectomy | 5.9 | 0.7 |
| Vaginal suppository | 1.0 | 1.0 |
| Oral contraceptives | 8.0 | 8.5 |
| Intrauterine device (IUD) | 9.0 | 7.4 |
| Injectable contraceptives | 1.0 | 1.8 |
| Coitus interruptus | 4.0 | 6.0 |
| Rhythm | 4.0 | 5.3 |
| Condom | 5.0 | 4.3 |

Security System and medical service providers, the equivalent of Medicaid in the United States, now fund these procedures. In the past, they may not have been funded by the government out of deference to religious authorities rather than for economic reasons. Nonetheless, the cost of unwanted pregnancies and abortions reinforces the current position.

Oral contraceptives are the second most frequently used contraceptive method. According to Article 100 of the Social Security act, provision of oral contraception is mandatory. However, 70% of Colombians who use oral contraceptives obtained them through the private sector, whereas 30% obtained them through the public sector. This evident lack of active participation by the state would suggest that most families prefer to incorporate the cost of oral contraceptives into the family budget rather than rely on the government.

Colombia has several laws that protect the rights of women and children; however, implementation is often lacking. Family planning is viewed as an individual's right and an obligation of the state. The Constitution of 1991, Articles 17 through 30, denounces all forms of discrimination against women: "Women have civil rights as they pertain to reproduction and the judicial system equal to men in education, nationality, employment, health, matrimony and family." Two other articles deal with pregnancy and children:

- Article 42 stipulates that a couple has the right to freely and responsibly choose the number of children they will bear. They will provide and educate them while they are minors unable to provide for themselves.
- Article 43 states that men and women have equal rights and opportunities. A woman cannot be discriminated against. The law also protects a woman while pregnant and postpartum, and the state will provide financial assistance and food supplements should she be unemployed and/or homeless. The state will assist women who are heads of households.

The aforementioned legal structure allows us to reflect on how little the state is actually doing to defend the rights of individuals, and, in failing to acknowledge the discrimination, women suffer within Colombia's poorly organized health system.

### B. Teenage (Unmarried) Pregnancies

One out of every ten adolescents has had sexual relations between the ages of 13 and 14 years. Four out of every ten adolescents have had sexual relations between the ages of 15 and 17 years. Seven out of ten have had sexual relations by the time they reach the age of 18.

One out of every three adolescents believes that abortion is unacceptable; however, 70% feel that it may be necessary in certain situations. Sixty-two percent have had some discussion on sexually transmitted diseases and 95% understand that anyone can contract AIDS. The contraceptive methods most commonly used by adolescents are: the condom (94%), oral contraceptives (77%), and contraceptive suppositories (60%). The rhythm method is the least-used method (42%), which coincides with women's lack of awareness of their menstrual cycle (Profamilia 1995).

There has been an increase in birthrates among adolescents. This may be because of several factors: earlier onset of puberty, earlier onset of sexual activities, low socioeconomic levels, low levels of education, increased age for marriage, changes in value system because of urbanization, and the increased ability of communication.

According to a study conducted by the University of Colombia (Universidad Externado de Colombia 1992), one third of all women between the ages of 15 and 19 years, of low educational level, and who had at least one child, were single, lived in an urban area, and were more fertile than their counterparts living in rural areas.

Profamilia (1995) reported that 17% of women between the ages of 15 and 19 years were mothers or were pregnant at the time of the study. At the age of 19, four out of every ten women surveyed were mothers and 9% already had at least one child. It was also reported that 33.6% did not utilize birth control because they believed that they were infertile. Ten percent of these women and 2.8% of their contemporaries are opposed to the use of birth control. Three percent were unfamiliar with birth control methods and 7.9% were afraid of the side effects. These results reflect the lack of adequate information, existing myths, unawareness, and a lack of responsibility in spite of knowing the consequences.

Pregnancy in adolescents brings with it many consequences, including compromised physical and mental health and both economic and social challenges, which affect the mother, father, and child, as well as the family and society as a whole. The education dropout rate in this population is very high, leading to limited employment opportunities. Children born of adolescents show a higher incidence of prematurity, lower birthweight, more congenital diseases, and a higher incidence of abandonment and abuse. It is estimated that about 10% of children of teenage mothers are given up for adoption (Pardo & Uriza 1991).

### C. Abortion

The actual incidence of abortion in Colombia is unknown. It is estimated that 24% of all pregnancies end in abortion and 26% result in unwanted pregnancies (Profamilia 1995). In a 1992 study, *The Incidence of Abortion in Colombia*, researchers at the Universidad Externado de Colombia found that 30% of urban women between the ages of 15 and 49 years had had at least one abortion, with the highest incidence among women between ages 20 and 29 years. In at least 78% of those cases, no birth control was utilized; the remaining 22% had used a birth control method that failed and resulted in pregnancy. There is a 22% incidence of abortion among women ages 45 to 49 years of age, and a 19.4% incidence of abortion among women ages 50 to 55. A third of the women surveyed reported that they had been pressured by their partners to abort.

Abortion is illegal in Colombia, and women go to health clinics much too late in the pregnancy when they show complications that cannot be resolved on their own. Complications are the most common reason for aborting, and abortion is the leading cause of death for Colombian women. There is an estimated 300,000 illegal abortions yearly. In other words, for every 10 births, there are four illegal abortions, and one out of every 100 women between the ages of 15 and 49 years old has had at least one abortion. The women most likely to abort are those who failed to use contraceptives.

The majority of families in Colombia are rooted in the traditional patriarchal family structure, based on economic, political, and religious power, which conditions women to utilize family planning methods. However, contraception should not be limited only to birth control. The meaning and implications of contraception should also include the significance, attitudes, and values people place on relationships, affection, and sexuality. These factors should take us beyond the stereotypes created by patriarchal gender roles, thus facilitating a better understanding of the individual, their health, and their relationships (Londoño 1996). In this extended meaning of contraception, it is necessary for women to acquire higher educational levels to attain better employment opportunities. They should be able to access better social security and health systems. The medical assistance model should not be solely based on doctors and technology, but also on the premise of caring for one's self and gaining the knowledge women need to balance, preserve, and improve their health.

### D. Population Programs

Since the introduction of contraceptives in the mid-1960s, Colombia's population growth rate has decreased steadily. Between 1980 and 1995, Profamilia estimates the population growth rate decreased by 23%. On average, there were 7 children born per family in the 1960s. In early 2001, the average Colombian family has 2.8 children per family. However, the averages vary from region to region. In the mountainous regions, the average family size is 4.3 children. Education level also plays an important role in determining the number of children per family. On average, there are 5 children per family for women with no formal education versus 1.8 children per family for women with higher levels of education (Profamilia 1995).

## 10. Sexually Transmitted Diseases and HIV/AIDS

### A. Sexually Transmitted Diseases

JOSÉ MANUEL GONZÁLEZ and GLORIA PEGANOS

*Incidence*

A true evaluation of the incidence of sexually transmitted diseases (STDs) is very difficult in any country, because the percentage of actual cases is considerably higher than the number of cases reported to health officials. In 1994, the Institute of Social Security found that 2% of Colombian males and 1.1% of females had some type of STD. The most common infections were gonorrhea, condylomas (warts), genital herpes, and syphilis. The majority of cases occurred in people between the ages of 15 and 44. Useche (1999) found that 4% of male students in high school reported some type of STD. Zuluaga and contributors (1991) found that 16.4% of male and 2.4% of female Mendellin University students had had some type of STD, the most common being gonorrhea and condylomas. Among university students from Baranquilla, González (1985) found that 13% of males and 1% of females had had some type of STD. In a follow-up study ten years later, González (1995) found that 12% of males and 2% of females had had some type of STD, with gonorrhea being the most prevalent. In the last few years, the incidence of STD cases has grown considerably. This is in part because of teenagers having sexual relations earlier that in previous times, teenagers having sex without protection, and cultural stereotypes that only sex workers can get STDs and not promiscuous men. When the increase in STDs is compared to the increase in the population, however, one can actually see a slight decrease in the overall percentage of STDs in the population.

*Papilloma and Condyloma Infections.* Although the actual incidence of STD infections is not known, there has been a large increase in the number of new diagnosed cases, in conjunction with other infections like gonorrhea, syphilis, nongonococcal urinary tract infections, trichomonas, and HIV. Ninety percent of the precancerous lesions in the uterine matrix test positive for the papilloma virus. Between 75% and 80% of the atypical cell cultures in women between the ages of 15 to 25 show infections of the human papilloma virus. Based on this, when tested, 40% of their partners are also infected by the disease.

*Gonococcal Infections.* Only 33% of acute cases of inflammatory pelvic disease (IPD or PID) test positive on the Tayler

Martin test, but this result is in direct relationship to the beginning of the infection and when the sample was taken. Half of the gonococcus-infected patients are asymptomatic and therefore can present the following complications: Asymptomatic tuboperitoneal factors result in infertility in 20 to 30% of patients, chronic pelvic inflammatory disease in 20 to 25%, chronic pelvic pain in 5 to 15%, ectopic pregnancies in 7%, and irregular menstrual cycles in 5%.

*Syphilis.* The number of congenital syphilis cases has decreased in Colombia. In 1998, the following number of cases were reported in Colombia by region. Costa Altántica, 64; Amazonia, 25; Orinoquia, 21; Oriente, 193, including Boyacá, Cundinamarca, Satanderes, Tomolina, and Bogotá; and Occidente, 347, including Caldas, Antioquia, Chocó, Quindío, and Valle. Two cities in the Occidente must be highlighted: Antioquia with 99 cases and Valle with 149 cases. The incidence of reported cases of congenital syphilis is 36.6 cases per 100,000 live newborns (Ministerio de Salud 1998, 1999).

*Treatment*

There are some formal programs available for the treatment of STDs. However, they are poorly organized and not fully developed as of early 2001.

## B. HIV/AIDS

JOSÉ MANUEL GONZÁLES and GLORIA PENAGOS

On January 5, 1983, a 23-year-old woman, a known prostitute, was hospitalized at the University Hospital of Cartagena. She died four months later. She was the first person to be officially diagnosed with AIDS in Colombia (González 2000). According to the Colombian Coalition Against AIDS, there are 200,000 people living with HIV (González et al. 2000). Every hour someone new is infected.

In 1997 and 1998, 81% of all reported cases were between the ages of 15 and 44 years (Ministerio de Salud 1998). Even though the group most at risk for contracting AIDS are adolescents, the general public continues to remain unaware of the dangers involved. Of households with children under the age of 18 years, 63.3% believe that they were not at risk of contracting HIV/AIDS. There was no discussion on AIDS prevention in 39% of households where there were minors under the age of 18 years.

According to the Colombian Ministry of Health, in 1986, there was one woman for every 47 men infected with HIV. In 1997, the ratio was one woman to four males. It was estimated that in 2001, the ratio will be 1:1. The risk among women is quite high and is believed to be related to the social inequity between men and woman. Women are kept at the subordinate level socially, by marital status, and economically, which contributes to their inability to adequately protect themselves. Consequently, religious beliefs that reject the use of condoms, anal sex at the insistence of the male, failing to acknowledge adultery for fear of being accused of infidelity, all these factors and other similar ones lead to an increase in HIV/AIDS-positive women (Penagos 1997).

Sexual contact constitutes the primary mode of transmitting HIV/AIDS (Ministerio de Salud 1998). For females, heterosexual contact accounted for 91.5% of cases of HIV infection, blood transfusions for 1.7%, and 6.8% became infected during delivery or perinatally. (No percentage was given for other modes of transmission, notably intravenous drug usage.) In men, 56.1% contracted HIV through heterosexual relations, 41.8% through homosexual/bisexual contact, perinatal transmission was 0.7%, and by transfusions were 1.4%.

One of the most important factors contributing towards the transmission of AIDS is the lack of adequate information. González (2000) conducted a study with university students, in which the following information was found:

- 95% of the students were unaware that anal penetration is the most high-risk sexual activity that may lead to the transmission of AIDS;
- 78.9% were unaware that it may take three months or more for an AIDS test to come up positive once a person is infected;
- 66.4% were unaware that it may take five to ten years to develop any AIDS-related symptoms;
- 48.1% were unaware that individuals may transmit HIV as quickly as they have acquired it; and
- 41.2% were unaware that semen is the body fluid that carries the highest concentration of HIV.

The study also found that 80.2% of men and 88.5% of women believe that there is a high risk of contracting AIDS while having unprotected sex with someone you do not know. Fifty-six percent of men and 66.9% of women believe that there is a high risk of contracting AIDS while having unprotected sex with an occasional partner; 14.8% of men and 16.1% of women believe that there is a high risk of contracting AIDS while having unprotected sex with a regular partner. As is evident, there is a popular misconception that AIDS can only be transmitted through unprotected sex with a one-time partner or an occasional partner. Consequently, people who are in new (exclusive) sexual relationships fail to practice safe sex. They do not take into account previous sexual partners nor have they taken an AIDS test (González et al. 2000).

Generally, there is minimal use of condoms. González and colleagues (2000) found that 33% of males and 53% of females have never used condoms during vaginal penetration. It was also reported that 48.4% of men and 63.2% of women never used condoms during anal sex.

The Colombian Constitution of 1991 enacted laws that protects the rights of all citizens. These laws stipulate that anyone living with HIV/AIDS, with or without financial means, can receive social security benefits. Although there exists budgeting and administrative problems that may delay the process, everyone has the fundamental right to medical care, psychological care, and pharmacological care. Generally, those individuals living with HIV/AIDS have access to antiviral medication.

On June 12, 1997, the Colombian Ministry of Health passed Decree #1543. It provides a standardized protocol for people with AIDS that indicates their rights and obligations. The protocol is as follows:

- Written consent from an individual is required in order to obtain an AIDS test.
- A healthcare provider or institution cannot deny care to someone diagnosed with HIV/AIDS.
- Comprehensive care must be provided: psychological, biological, and social.
- All records pertaining to patient care must remain confidential.
- Requesting an AIDS test to secure or maintain access in an educational facility, religious center, political group, cultural center, rehabilitation center, workplace, or health-related services, or to gain entry to a country is strictly prohibited.
- AIDS-test results may only be exchanged between patient and a qualified caregiver.
- Guaranteed job relocation when needed.

The decree also created CONASIDA (National Council on AIDS). It is comprised of the Ministry of Health, Ministry of Education, Ministry of Communication, Ministry of Employment, Colombian Institute of Family Wellness, National Institute of Health, Public Defendants, the Institute of Drug Administration and Regulations, ONUSIDA (AIDS Organization of the United Nations), representatives from nongovernmental organizations (ONGs), and advocates for AIDS victims. Generally, people who are living with AIDS are involved in political development and decision-making processes, as recommended by ONUSIDA. Presently, the ONGs are changing the image of AIDS from a "terminal disease" to a "treatable chronic disease."

AIDS prevention programs and assistance to victims of AIDS are faced with serious financial problems. There have been government budget cuts since 1998. Additionally, discrimination and rejection of AIDS victims are two problems that must be addressed in health and sexuality.

[*Update 2001*: According to the CIA *World Factbook*, the estimated adult prevalence rate for HIV/AIDS in 1999 was 0.31%, with 71,000 Colombians living with HIV/AIDS and 1,700 deaths because of the infection. (*End of update by R. T. Francoeur*)]

[*Update 2002*: UNAIDS Epidemiological Assessment: The first AIDS case in Colombia was recorded in 1983. As of December 2001, the reported cumulative number of persons living with HIV/AIDS was 19,603. Of this total, 6,437 are AIDS cases and 13,166 are HIV cases; 84.6% are males and 15.4% are females. According to the National Statistics Administrative Department (DANE), there are 12,410 registered AIDS deaths, although only 3,645 AIDS deaths have been registered at the MOH; 807 of the DANE-registered deaths are among children younger than 15 years. National estimates of the total number of people living with HIV/AIDS vary from 139,000 to 148,000.

[Sexual transmission accounts for 78.0% of reported cases, mother-to-child transmission for 1.6%, and blood transmission for 0.6%. In 19% of registries, mode of transmission has not been recorded. Among those with known sexual transmission, 47.7% were heterosexual, 34.0% homosexual, and 28.2% bisexual. The annual male-to-female ratio has changed from 18:1 in 1986 to 4:1 in 2000. Of the total number of HIV infections reported, 44% were in persons aged 15 to 35 years.

[The first case of vertical transmission in Colombia was reported in 1987. Since then, 615 cases have been registered, with a sustained increase since 1995. Analysis of the regional data collected between 1990 and 1995, in conjunction with the results of five sentinel anonymous unlinked studies conducted between 1992 and 1999, indicates that there are important geographical differences in the predominant mode of HIV transmission through sexual contact. Injection drug users who have sex with men (IVISM contact) remains predominant in Bogotá and in the central western region; in these areas, men who have sex with men accounted for more than 50% of infections registered between 1990 and 1995, with a male-to-female ratio of 28:1 and 9:1, respectively. In the Caribbean and in the northeastern regions, HIV infection has spread mostly through heterosexual contact, with a male-to-female ratio of 2:7.1. The estimated prevalence among the adult general population is 0.37%. Sentinel studies have been conducted in a varied number of cities. The largest study, conducted in 1999 in 11 cities, among pregnant women, female sex workers, and STD patients, found HIV-prevalence rates of 0.2%, 0.6%, and 0.8%, respectively. In 1999, a study conducted in Bogotá among men who have sex with men showed an 18% HIV-prevalence rate.

[The estimated number of adults and children living with HIV/AIDS on January 1, 2002, were:

| | | |
|---|---|---|
| Adults ages 15-49: | 140,000 | (rate: 0.4%) |
| Women ages 15-49: | 20,000 | |
| Children ages 0-15: | 4,000 | |

[No estimate is available for the number of adults and children who died of AIDS during 2001.

[At the end of 2001, an estimated 21,000 Colombian children under age 15 were living without one or both parents who had died of AIDS. (*End of update by the Editors*)]

## 11. Sexual Dysfunctions, Counseling, and Therapies

JOSÉ MANUEL GONZÁLES

Until the 1980s, sexual dysfunction was unknown as a health-related problem. Traditionally, treatments for sexual problems were seen as something unnecessary and even excessive. Generally, people who suffered from sexual dysfunctions failed to seek professional help because of embarrassment or guilt, even though, for more than 50 years, there have been private institutions in Colombia that provided sex therapy (González 1999c).

In the last five years, there has been an important change in the outlook on sexual dysfunction. The National Program on Sexual Education has generated a change in attitude towards sexuality and sexual health. There are now a few professionals who specialize in clinical sexology. An association of professional sex therapists has yet to be organized. In the next few years, there will be an increase in the quantity and quality of sex therapists because of the high demand for their services.

Dr. Rodriguez A. [*sic*] was the pioneer in sexual therapy in Colombia (González 1999c). He studied abroad in France, where he specialized in reflexology. In the late 1940s, he returned to Santafé de Bogotá, where he founded a clinic for sexual dysfunctions. He trained prostitutes in collaboratively assisting in his patients' treatments. This is what is now called sexual surrogates, or bodywork therapists. However, an animosity developed between Dr. Rodriguez A. and his colleagues that resulted in lawsuits and other legal problems. Consequently, Dr. Rodriguez A. closed his institute in Santafé de Bogotá (Guerrero 1997) and shortly thereafter opened a sexual therapy clinic in Fusagasuga. He died in the late 1970s.

In the late 1960s, a group of doctors and psychologists, including Heli Alzate, Cecilia Cardinal de Martin, Octavio Giraldo, and German Ortiz Umana, developed an interest in sexology and sexual therapy. In 1968, Heli Alzate offered the first formal courses in sexology to medical students attending the University of Caldas in Manizales. Octavio Giraldo offered courses in sexology to medical students at the University of El Valle. In 1971, Celcilia Cardinal de Martin and German Ortiz Umana offered coursework in sexology at the University of Rosario de Bogotá. José Manuel Gonzáles initiated the coursework in sexology in the Metropolitan University of Barranquilla in 1976. Luis Dragunsky offered coursework on sexology at the University of Santo Tomas in Bogotá in 1977. During this time, the first texts on sexology were published: *Medical Sexology in Summation* (Alzate 1978), *Lectures in Sexology* (Dragunsky & Gonzáles 1979), and *Exploration of Human Sexuality* (Giraldo 1981).

In May 1978, the Colombian Institute on the Development of Advanced Studies (ICFES) brought together a group of specialists to discuss and evaluate the state of sexology as a science: Heli Alzate, Cecilia Cardinal de Martin, Octavio Giraldo, José Manuel Gonzáles, and German Ortiz Umana. They generated an important document, which stated specific recommendations (ICFES 1978). As a result of this meeting, the participants felt a need to develop a committee that would coordinate the efforts and publicize the findings of studies that would support the development of sexology in Colombia.

One year later, the Colombian Association of Sexology was founded in June 1979. The original founders were: Heli Alzate, Maria Clara Arango, Mario Bedoya, Cecilia Cardinal de Martin, Luis Dragunsky, Mario Gartner, Octavio Giraldo, José Manuel Gonzáles, Maria Ladi Londoño, Saulo Munoz, German Ortiz Umana, Francisco Sanchez, and Jorge Villarreal Mejia. The elected president was Heli Alzate. As a consequence, sex therapy has developed its own niche in the larger cities. The group in Manizales has generated the most investigations and published internationally. The Cali group, with Octavio Giraldo, Mari Ladi Londoño, Javier Murillo, Diego Arbelaez, Nelssy Bonilla, Monica Lozada, and other colleagues, has been most active in advocating for the rights of minorities and the oppressed: women and homosexuals. Two other active groups, in Bogotá, Medellín, have pioneered in the treatment of premature ejaculation, erectile problems, patients suffering from various psychosexual dysfunctions, prolonging the pleasure phase, transsexuals, and interesting ways of dealing with infertile couples (Acuña et al. 1997).

Sex therapy in Colombia is marked by several characteristics (González 1999c):

- It is interdisciplinary, although most of the professionals in the field are also trained in the medical or psychological fields.
- It originates mostly from behavioral psychology, cognitive psychology, and human development, with little basis in psychotherapy.
- It provides advocacy for the rights of minority groups and oppressed groups, specifically homosexuals and lesbians.
- Private practice and college coursework solely dedicated to sex therapy is nonexistent. Most sex therapists have maintained their origins in psychology and/or medicine.
- There is an absence of formal training for sex therapists. In 1983, Luis Dragunsky and José Manuel Gonzáles founded the first accrediting committee, the Colombian Association of Sexology (CAS). Only five sex therapists have been accredited by CAS and very few Colombian sex therapists are accredited by the Latin American Federation of Sexological Societies and Sexual Education (FLASSES).
- There is extensive coverage by the mass media.

There has been active participation by most sex therapists in the events sponsored by the Colombian Association of Sexology.

## 12. Sex Research and Advanced Professional Education

BERNARDO USECHE

Generally, scientific studies in Colombia are very scarce and poorly funded. In 1999, the total budget earmarked by Colciencias, a government body responsible for all studies conducted in Colombia, was approximately US$6,000,000. Only recently have there been doctoral programs in the basic sciences. However, there are no doctoral programs offered in disciplines that could directly contribute towards the study of sexology, such as physiology, anthropology, psychology, or sociology. It is in this context that we must understand the limited development of the study of human sexuality in Colombia.

In recent years, Abel Martinez of the University of Pedagogy and Technology of Tunja has specialized in the study of *Colombian Sexual Archeology* (unpublished). He presents a poetic description of sexuality during the Spanish Conquest, colonization, independence, and the beginning of the Republic. The study of the mythology of the aborigines and the key role the erotic played in the blending of the races is evident throughout his work. In *Daughters, Wives and Lovers*, anthropologist Suzy Bermudez discusses the same timeframe covered by Abel Martinez, the Spanish Conquest to the Republic. However, she took a feminist perspective, dealing with native women, European women, African slave women, married women, widows, and single women. Although it was not her main objective, Bermudez attempted to clarify how social class, ethnicity, and age play an important role in understanding the history of women's sexuality in Colombia.

In the second half of the 20th century, Virginia Gutierrez de Pineda (1975) led an important anthropological investigation that set the foundation for the comprehension of human sexuality for Colombians. In her analysis and classification of the various cultural elements that correspond to the different regions of Colombia, Gutierrez explained the logic behind the different types of marriages and polygamy, and the significance of prostitution and homosexuality thought to be tolerated but tacitly encouraged by religious subcultures in hopes of preserving young women's virginity and protecting the institution of matrimony. Her description of families in the second half of the 20th century is considered to be a key reference for anyone wanting to study the changes in the sexuality of Colombians at the end of the century.

Heli Alzate, another pioneer of sexology in Latin America, developed an extensive and rigorous curriculum for the School of Medicine at the University of Caldas. He also published four books and numerous scientific articles in North American and European publications. A member of the editorial committee of the *Archives of Sexual Behavior* for a quarter century, Alzate has theorized a conceptual model of the function of erotica and completed three studies pertaining to sexuality:

1. Evaluation of a curriculum pertaining to sexuality (Alzate 1990);
2. Sexual behavior of secondary-level students and university-level students (Alzate 1989; Useche, Alzate, & Villegas 1990; Alzate & Villegas 1994); and
3. Studies pertaining to vaginal erogeneity (Alzate 1985; Alzate & Hoch 1986; Alzate, Useche, & Villegas 1989).

Alzate also evaluated the knowledge and sexual attitudes of his medical students with an adapted version of the Sexual Knowledge and Attitude Test, or SKAT, originally formulated by Harold Lief. Later results from his modified SKAT, or ACSEX, indicated that it is possible to impart scientific knowledge and achieve a positive attitude towards sexuality utilizing coursework in sexology, audiovisual media, and active class participation from medical students.

The studies of the sexual behavior of the younger generation with secondary- or university-level education in one of the most traditional and conservative areas of Colombian culture give a fair picture of the evolution of Colombian sexuality in the past quarter-century, the incidence of first sexual encounters, the motives behind sexual activity, the types of couples, and, above all, the differences in sexual behaviors between genders.

Of particular interest, in view of the significant growth of the women's liberation movement in recent years in Colombia, are several studies on the erogenous zones of the vagina. According to these studies, the majority of women, if not all, have vaginal erogenous zones, frequently located in the anterior vaginal wall, which, if stimulated appropriately, will culminate in orgasm. Colombian researchers consider this a vital factor in the context of normal sexuality of the woman and also as important in the treatment of coital dysfunctions of women. Alzate believes that the theories, that have thus far been conceptualized to explain these sexual dysfunctions, should be revised. He also believes that sex therapists who are confronted with these issues should recognize the necessity of referring clients for gynecological exams so as to locate their erogenous zones (Alzate 1997b). Alzate also introduced modifications of the human sexuality functioning model originally proposed by William Masters and Virginia Johnson and later enriched by Helen Singer Kaplan. Alzate's premise was to "seek out and responsibly enjoy pleasure." Presently, there are no other systemic studies by Colombians in the field of sexology other than those provided by Alzate.

At the international level, publications by Colombians in the area of human sexuality are very scarce, almost nonexistent. However, there have been other unpublished works that originated in Colombia. Florence Thomas's 1994 *Dissertation on Love and Communication* analyzed communications from a gender perspective, and Guillermo Carvajal (1993) completed a psychoanalytic vision of the adolescent. Pedro Guerrero (1985) led a study on the use of erotica in literature by some of the most prominent writers in Colombia, and Maria Ladi Londoño has published numerous articles dealing with sexuality and reproductive rights. In a recent study, also of note, is Ruben Ardila's 1998 study of 100 male homosexuals, which found that, generally, these individuals did not have serious adaptation problems, nor did they seem to suffer from adjustment issues.

The *Latin American Journal on Sexology of Colombia* (ISSN 0120-7458), with a base in Colombia, serves as the medium for the Latin American Federation of Sexological Societies and Sexual Education (FLASSES).

The Colombian Society of Sexology, founded in 1979, has organized ten congress meetings, several seminars, and other academic events. These have involved world-renowned researchers, among others, Eli Coleman, John Money, Ira Reiss, Eusebio Rubio, Luis Dragunsky, Joseph LoPiccolo, Andres Flores Colombino, and Ruben Hernandez.

Other sexological studies in Colombia have been conducted by students in their postgraduate studies. These are generally non-funded and usually remain unpublished. Some of these studies have originated from the University of Bogotá (Bodner et al. 1999), University Simon Bolivar of Barranquilla (González 1999b; González et al. 2000), and the University of Caldas in Manizales (Useche 1999). Since the Ministry of Education established the National Project on Sexual Education in 1993, there has been a significant increase in the need for these studies. Private universities have thus developed them.

In terms of the future, we hope that the small group of dedicated and diverse Colombian professionals interested in sexological issues will be able to continue their work with sexological organizations and individuals around the world, and thereby contribute to a more solid and in-depth understanding of human sexuality, if the economic crisis in Colombia allows.

## References and Suggested Readings

Acuña, A. 1987. *Tercera edad y sexualidad.* IV Congreso Colombiano de Sexología, Medellín, 9-12 de octubre.

Acuña, A., L. Nader, M. Palacio, & P. Guerrero. 1993. *Sexo al día: Es tiempo de vivir.* Bogotá: Unidad de Psicoterapia y Sexualidad Humana.

Acuña, A., M. Palacio, & P. Guerrero. 1986. *Sexo: En los niños.* Santafé de Bogotá: Editora Cinco.

Alzate, H. 1977. Comportamiento sexual de los estudiantes de medicina. *Acta Médica Colombiana, 22:*111-118.

Alzate, H. 1978. *Compendio de sexología medica.* Santafé de Bogotá: Temis.

Alzate, H. 1985. Vaginal eroticism. *Archives of Sexual Behavior, 14:*529-537.

Alzate, H. 1987. *Sexualidad humana* (2 edición). Bogotá: Editorial Temis.

Alzate, H. 1989. Sexual behavior of unmarried Colombian university students: A follow-up. *Archives of Sexual Behavior, 18:*239-250.

Alzate, H. 1990. Effectiveness of an independent sexology course for Colombian medical students. *Medical Teacher, 12:*69-75.

Alzate, H. 1997a. *Sexualidad humana* (Reimpresión de la 2ª edición). Bogotá: Temis.

Alzate, H. 1997b. *La sexologie a l'université de Caldas, Manizales, Colombie. Panoramiques.* Paris: Arléa-Corlet.

Alzate, H., & Z. Hoch. 1986. The 'G spot' and 'female ejaculation': A current appraisal. *Journal of Sexual & Marital Therapy, 12:*211-220.

Alzate, H., B. Useche, & M. Villegas. 1989. Heart rate change as evidence for vaginally elicited orgasm intensity. *Annual of Sex Research, 2:*345-357.

Alzate, H., & M. Villegas. 1994. Sexual behavior of unmarried Colombian university students in 1990. *Journal of Sex Education and Therapy, 20:*287-298.

Ardila, R. 1985. La homosexualidad en Colombia. *Acta Psiquiátrica y Psicológica de América Latina* [Buenos Aires], *31:*191-210.

Ardila, R. 1986a. *Psicología del hombre colombiano.* Santafé de Bogotá: Planeta.

Ardila, R. 1986b. Homosexualidad y aprendizaje. *Revista Latinoamericana de Sexología, 1:*45-54.

Ardila, R. 1995 (26 de Noviembre). Nuevos hallazgos sobre homosexualidad. ¿Fatalidad biológica o deformidad cultural? *El Tiempo Lecturas Dominicales,* pp. 2-4.

Ardila, R. 1998. *Homosexualidad y psicología.* México: El Manual Moderno.

Berdugo, E., & A. Segura. 1988. *Estudio descriptivo del comportamiento sexual de las personas mayores de 60 años en Barranquilla* (Tesis de grado). Barranquilla: Facultad de Psicología, Universidad del Norte.

Bodnar, Y., E. Tovar, R. Arias, N. Bogoya, P. Briceño, J. Murillo, & E. Rodriguez. 1999. *Cultura y sexualidad en Colombia.* Bogotá: Universidad Distrital Francisco José de Caldas.

Botero, E. 1980. *Homofobia y homofilia. Estudios sobre la homosexualidad, la bisexualidad y la represión de la conducta homosexual.* Medellín, Colombia: Editorial Laelon.

Caballero, M. C. 1996. Conocimiento y comportamiento de riesgo de infección por VIH en estudiantes universitarios. Un caso: Universidad Industrial de Santander. *Revista Latinoamericana de Sexología, 11*(1):41-56.

CIA. 2002 (January). *The world factbook 2002.* Washington, DC: Central Intelligence Agency. Available: http://www.cia.gov/cia/publications/factbook/index.html.

Colombia. Consejería Presidencial para la juventud, la mujer y la familia. 1994. *Año Internacional de la Familia. 1994, 1*(2).

Colombia. *Instituto Nacional de Medicina Legal y Ciencias Forenses. Regional Norte.* 1996. Primer semestre (Boletín informativo).

Domínguez, E., A. Mendoza, L. Merlano, M. & Navas. 1988. *Estudio descriptivo del comportamiento sexual del estudiante de Bachillerato de Barranquilla* (Tesis de grado). Barranquilla: Facultad de Psicología, Universidad del Norte.

Dragunsky, L. 1977. *El mito del sexo.* Bogotá: Editorial Pluma.

Dragunsky, L., & J. Gonzales. 1979. *Lecciones de sexología.* Santafé de Bogotá: Editorial Pluma.

*El Tiempo. El Catolicismo pierde clientela.* 1997 (13 de Julio). p. 17A.

Eljaiek, L., M. Saade, & P. Vargas. 1987. *Estudio descriptivo del comportamiento sexual de hombres y mujeres que mantienen relación de pareja* (Tesis de grado). Barranquilla: Facultad de Psicología, Universidad del Norte.

Florez, P., & E. Consuegra. 1998 (16 de Octubre). *Abuso sexual en adolescentes. IX Jornada Científica de Ginecoobstetricia.* Barranquilla: Universidad Libre.

Fuscaldo, M., R. Mercado, & M. Rolong. 1987. *Estudio descriptivo del comportamiento sexual del estudiante universitario en Barranquilla* (Tesis de grado). Barranquilla: Facultad de Psicología, Universidad del Norte.

Giraldo, O. 1979. La homosexualidad masculina: Una revisión. *Revista Latinoamericana de Psicología, 9*:81-100.

Giraldo, O. 1981. *Explorando las sexualidades humanas.* México: Trillas.

Giraldo, O. 1982. Más allá de la heterosexualidad. *Avances en Psicología Clínica Latinoamericana, 1*:79-94.

González, J. M. 1979. Masturbación: Un proyecto de investigación. *Revista Sexualidad Humana y Educación Sexual, 2*(1):11-17.

González, J. M. 1985. *El comportamiento sexual del universitario.* Santafé de Bogotá: Fundación para el Avance de la Psicología.

González, J. M. 1993. SIDA: Síndrome de inmunodeficiencia adquirida. *Serenidad. Revista del Programa de Alcoholismo y Drogadicción, 1*(3):8-10.

González, J. M. 1994. *Educación de la sexualidad.* Barranquilla: Club del Libro.

González, J. M. 1995. Diferencias genéricas en el comportamiento sexual de estudiantes universitarios solteros de Barranquilla. *Revista Latinoamericana de Sexología,* (2):161-76.

González, J. M. 1996. El aporte de la Sociedad Colombiana de Sexología. *Revista Latinoamericana de Sexología,* Separata 1, 166-192.

González, J. M. 1997. *Eyaculación precoz: Evaluación y tratamiento.* X Seminario Colombiano de Sexología, Barranquilla, 1-3 de Noviembre.

González, J. M. 1998. *Sexología y periodismo: Una columna de preguntas sobre temas sexuales en un periódico colombiano.* 8 Congreso Colombiano de Psicología, Santafé de Bogotá, Abril 30-Mayo 3.

González, J. M. 1999. Abuso sexual infantil en mujeres alcohólicas y drogadictas de Barranquilla. *Revista Terapia Sexual* [Brasil], *2*(1):37-43.

González, J. M. 1999a. Pobreza, valores humanos y sexualidad. *Revista Encuentro Bolivariano, Barranquilla, 2*(2):121-126.

González, J. M. 1999b. Sexualidad y sesarrollo. *Revista Investigación Bolivariana, Barranquilla, 2*(2):195-199.

González, J. M. 1999c. La terapia sexual en Colombia: 1948-1998. *Revista Terapia Sexual, 2*(1):33-36.

González, J. M. 1999d. Pobreza, salud sexual y desarrollo. *Revista Salud Sexual, 2*(1):25-30.

González, J. M. 2000. *Amor & intimidad en el caribe colombiano.* Barranquilla: Editorial Antillas.

González, J. M., M. Alonso, & I. Pinto. 1991. Sexualidad y farmacodependencia en pacientes de dos clínicas de Barranquilla, Colombia. *Revista Latinoamericana de Sexología, 6*(3):235-246.

González, J. M., J. Cepeda, L. Fonseca, N. Burgos, I. Pinto, & L. Sanchez. 1996. Estudio descriptivo de la sexualidad en 30 mujeres farmacodependientes de Barranquilla, Colombia. *Archivos Hispanoamericanos de Sexología, 3*(1): 79-91.

González, J. M., I. Gomez, & T. de Cortes. 1977. Comportamiento sexual: Un estudio exploratorio. *Revista Latinoamericana de Psicología, 9*(1):13-20.

González, J. M., & J. Gonzales. en prensa. *Sexualidad en el adulto mayor.*

González, J. M., J. C. Marin, D. Chala, R. Schmalbach Fruto, & N. de Albade Alba. 2000. *Juventud y VIH/SIDA: Una experiencia universitaria en el caribe colombiano.* Barranquilla: Editorial Antillas.

González, J. M., M. C. Rosado, M. Bernal, & J. C. Marin. 2000. *Pobreza, salud sexual y desarrollo.* Bogotá: Plaza & Jane.

Guerrero, P. 1985. *El miedo al sexo.* Bogotá: Antares.

Guerrero, P. 1996a. Amor, sexualidad y matrimonio en los medios de comunicación. *Revista Latinoamericana de Sexología,* Separata 1, 129-135.

Guerrero, P. 1996b. Amor, sexualidad y matrimonio en los graffiti. *Revista Latinoamericana de Sexología,* Separata 1, 136-139.

Guerrero, P. 1997. Comunicación personal.

Gutierrez de Pineda, V. 1975. *Familia y cultura en Colombia.* Santafé de Bogotá: Instituto Colombiano de Cultura.

Gutierrez, M. de, & G. Franco. 1989. Encuesta sobre sexualidad en adolescentes. *CAFAM. II Curso de atención integral al adolescente.* Santafé de Bogotá: CAFAM.

Instituto de Seguros Sociales (ISS) [Institute of Social Securities]. 1994. *Encuesta nacional sobre conocimientos, actitudes y practicas relacionadas con las enfermedades de transmisión sexual, SIDA, enfermedades cardiovasculares, cáncer y accidentes.* Santafé de Bogotá: ISS.

Londoño, M. L. 1991. *Prácticas de libertad.* Cali: Impresor Feriva.

Londoño, M. L. 1996. *Memorias Congreso Sexualidad y Género . . . Un proceso cultural.* VII Congreso Colombiano de Sexología, Medellín, Mayo 23 al 25, 1996.

Mantilla, A. 1993. El modelo Gamma de educación sexual. En: *Asociación salud con prevención. Sexualidad en la adolescencia.* Santafé de Bogotá: Editorial Presencia.

Ministerio de Salud. 1994. *Estudio nacional de salud mental y consumo de sustancias psicoactivas.* Santafé de Bogotá: Ministerio de Salud de Colombia.

Ministerio de Salud. 1995. *Boletín epidemiológico nacional, Enero-Marzo.*

Ministerio de Salud. 1997 (15 de Marzo). *Boletín epidemiológico nacional, 2*(5).

Ministerio de Salud. 1997. *Medicina legal en cifras. Enero-diciembre 1996-1997.* Bogotá: Instituto Nacional de Medicina Legal y Ciencias Forenses.

Ministerio de Salud. 1998 (30 de Noviembre). *Boletín Epidemiológico Nacional, 3*(22).

Ministerio de Salud 1998. *Lineamientos para la política de salud sexual y reproductiva.* Santafé de Bogotá: Dirección General de Promoción y Prevención.

Ministerio de Salud, Oficina de Epidemiología. Informe Quincenal Epidemiológico Nacional. (Enero 15) *Dirección general de promoción y prevención, 4*(1).

Murillo, J. 1993. Relaciones extramatrimoniales, celos y familia. *Revista Latinoamericana de Sexología, 8*(1):56-65.

Murillo, J. 1996. *Trabajadoras sexuales.* Palmira: CORPICH.

Nader, L., & M. L. Palacio. 1989. Relaciones extramaritales. En: *Es tiempo de vivir. Unidad de psicoterapia y dexualidad humana.* Santafé de Bogotá.

Nader, L., M. L. Palacio, & A. Acuña. 1997. *Modelo terapéutico en disfunciones sexuales.* X Seminario Colombiano de Sexología, Barranquilla, 1-3 de Noviembre.

OPS/OMS, Programa Regional de SIDA/ETS. *Vigilancia del SIDA en las Américas. Informe trimestral 10 de junio de 1997.* OPS/HCA/97.006.

Organización Panamericana de la Salud 1985. *La salud del adolescente y el joven en las Américas* (Publicación científica N. 489). Washington, DC.

Ortiz, G. 1993. El sexo de asignación, el de crianza y los papeles sexuales en la familia. *Revista Latinoamericana de Sexología, 8*(1):38-45.

Palacio, M. L. 1999. *Hablemos de sexo con Marta Lucía Palacio.* Bogotá: Intermedio.

Pardo, F., & G. Uriza. 1991 (Abril-Junio). Estudio de embarazo en adolescente en 11 instituciones Colombianas. *Revista Colombiana de Obstetricia y Ginecología* [Bogotá], *42*(2): 109-121.

Penagos, G. S. 1997. Mujer, género y SIDA. *Memorias Congreso Internacional de ETS, SIDA.* Medellín.

PNUD—Programa de las Naciones Unidas para el Desarrollo. 1995. *Informe sobre desarrollo humano 1995.* New York: Naciones Unidas.

Profamilia. 1995. *Encuesta nacional de demografía y salud 1995.* Santafé de Bogotá: Profamilia (Planned Parenthood of Colombia).

Riso, W. 1996. *Deshojando margaritas. Acerca del amor tradicional y otras malas costumbres.* Santafé de Bogotá: Norma.

Rojas, N. 1997. *La pareja* (7ª edición). Santafé de Bogotá: Planeta.

Rojas, N. 1998. *Qué nos une. Qué nos separa.* Santafé de Bogotá: Planeta.

Ruiz, M. 1996. Conocimientos, actitudes y comportamiento sexual de los adolescentes. *Memorias XX Congreso Colombiano de Obstetricia y Ginecología.* Medellín.

*Semana.* 1996 (9 de Enero). La gran encuesta del 96 (Edición 714).

*Semana.* 1997 (28 de Julio). Sexo: Informe especial (Edición 795).

*Semana.* 1999 (30 de Agosto). Sexo 99 (Edición 904).

Serrano, J. F. 1997. Entre negación y reconocimiento. Estudios sobre "homosexualidad" en Colombia. *Nómadas Universidad Central* [Bogotá], *6*:67-79.

Serrano, J. F. 1998. Igualdad, diferencia y equidad en la diversidad de la experiencia sexual. Una mirada a las discusiones sobre los derechos sexuales de lesbianas y gays. *Memorias del Tercer Seminario Nacional sobre Ética, Sexualidad y Derechos Reproductivos* (pp. 25-54), CERFAMI, Medellín, Colombia, agosto 13 y 14 de 1998.

Servicio Seccional de Salud de Risaralda. 1997. *Plan de información y educación sexual a la mujer y a la familia.*

UNAIDS. 2002. *Epidemiological fact sheets by country.* Geneva, Switzerland: Joint United Nations Programme on HIV/AIDS (UNAIDS/WHO). Available: http://www.unaids.org/hivaidsinfo/statistics/fact_sheets/index_en.htm.

Universidad Externado de Colombia. 1992. *La incidencia del aborto en Colombia* [*The incidence of abortion in Colombia*] Bogotá: Universidad Externado de Colombia.

Useche, B. 1999. *5 Estudios de sexología.* Manizales: ARS Ediciones.

Useche, B., M. Villegas, & H. Alzate. 1990. Sexual behavior of Colombian high school students. *Adolescence, 25*(98):291-304.

Velandia, M. A. 1999. *Y si el cuerpo grita . . .* Bogotá: Equiláteros. Proyecto de Diversidad y Minorías Sexuales de Colombia.

Zamudio, L., & N. Rubiano. 1991a. *La nupcialidad en Colombia.* Santafé de Bogotá: Universidad Externado de Colombia.

Zamudio, L., & N. Rubiano. 1991b. *Las separaciones conyugales en Colombia.* Santafé de Bogotá: Universidad Externado de Colombia.

Zuluaga, L., C. Soto, & D. Jaramillo. 1991. *Problemas de salud asociados al comportamiento sexual en estudiantes de ultimo año.* Medellín: Universidad de Antioquia.

# Costa Rica
## (Republic of Costa Rica)

Anna Arroba, M.A.*

## Contents

## *Demographics and a Brief Historical Perspective*
ROBERT T. FRANCOEUR

### A. Demographics

This Central American country lies between Nicaragua and the Lake of Nicaragua to the north and Panama to the south. Its area of 19,730 square miles (51,100 km²) slightly exceeds that of the combined states of Vermont and New Hampshire in the U.S. Its western border is the North Pacific Ocean with a narrow Pacific coastal region. About 300 miles (480 km) offshore, the 10-square-mile (26-km²) Cocos Island is under Costa Rican sovereignty. The Caribbean Sea marks Costa Rica's eastern border.

Costa Rica's climate is tropical and subtropical, with a dry season from December to April and a rainy season from May to November. A cooler climate prevails in the highlands. Costa Rica's terrain consists of narrow coastal plains separated by rugged mountains. The country has four volcanoes, two of them active, which rise near the capital of San José in the center of the country. One of the volcanoes, Irazu, had a destructive eruption in 1963-1965.

In July 2002, Costa Rica had an estimated population of 4.008 million (1,969,680 females and 2,038,585 males). (All data are from *The World Factbook 2002* (CIA 2002) unless otherwise stated.)

**Age Distribution and Sex Ratios**: *0-14 years*: 30.8% with 1.05 male(s) per female (sex ratio); *15-64 years*: 63.9% with 1.02 male(s) per female; *65 years and over*: 5.3% with 0.87 male(s) per female; *Total population sex ratio*: 1.02 male(s) to 1 female

**Life Expectancy at Birth**: *Total Population*: 77.7 years; *male*: 75.6 years; *female*: 79.9 years

**Urban/Rural Distribution**: 50% to 50%

**Ethnic Distribution**: white (including *mestizo*): 96.5%; black: 1.9%; Amerindian: 1.3%; Chinese: 0.2%

**Religious Distribution**: Roman Catholic: 76.3%, Evangelical: 13.7%; Jehovah's Witnesses 1.3%, other: 4.8%; none: 3.2%

*Communications*: Anna Arroba, M.A., Apt. 583-2050, San Pedro Montes de Oca, Costa Rica; aarroba@cariari.ucr.ac.cr. Research for this chapter was provided by Laura Fuentes Belgrave, B.A.

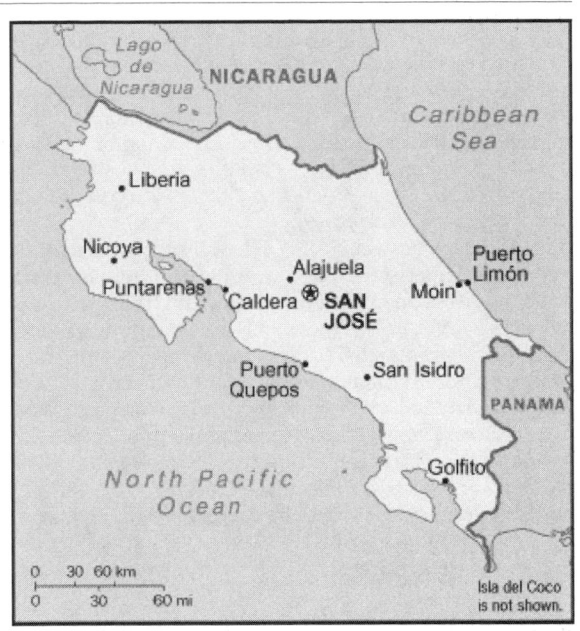

(CIA 2002)

**Birth Rate**: 21.4 births per 1,000 population
**Death Rate**: 4.1 per 1,000 population
**Infant Mortality Rate**: 10.8 deaths per 1,000 live births
**Net Migration Rate**: –0.52 migrant(s) per 1,000 population

**Total Fertility Rate**: 2.42 children born per woman
**Population Growth Rate**: 1.61%

**HIV/AIDS** (1999 est.): *Adult prevalence*: 0.54%; *Persons living with HIV/AIDS*: 12,000; *Deaths*: 750. (For additional details from www.UNAIDS.org, see end of Section 10B.)

**Literacy Rate** (*defined as those age 15 and over who can read and write*): 95.5% (education is free and compulsory from age 6 to 15

**Per Capita Gross Domestic Product** (*purchasing power parity*): $8,500 (2001 est.); *Inflation*: 12.1% (2002 est.); *Unemployment*: 5.2% (2002 est.); *Living below the poverty line*: 20.6% (1999 est.)

### B. A Brief Historical Perspective

Costa Rica was inhabited by an estimated 25,000 Guaymi Indians when Columbus explored it in 1502. Few of the indigenous people survived the Spanish conquest, which began in 1563. The region grew slowly and was administered as a Spanish province. Costa Rica achieved independence in 1821, but was absorbed for two years by Agustín de Iturbide in his Mexican empire. Costa Rica seceded from the Central American Federation in 1838 and became a republic in 1848. Except for the military dictatorship of Tomás Guardia from 1870 to 1882, Costa Rica has enjoyed one of the most democratic governments in Latin America. Since the civil war of 1948 and 1949, there has been little social conflict and free political institutions have been preserved. The presidency of Rodrígo Carazo Odio (1978-1986) was marked by a disastrous decline in the economy. Oscar Arias Sanchez, who became president in 1986, prevented the neighboring Nicaraguan Contra rebels from using Costa Rican territory as a safe haven, and played a central role in negotiating settlements in both the Nicaraguan and the Salvadoran civil wars. He was awarded the Nobel Peace Prize in 1987. During 1993, there was an unusual wave of kidnappings and hostage-taking, some of it related to the international cocaine trade. José Maria Figueres Olsen of the National Liberation Party became president in 1994. He favored greater government intervention in the economy and other measures that the International Monetary Fund was unhappy about. As a result, the World Bank withheld $100 million of financing. In 1998, Miguel Angel Rodriguez of the Social Christian Unity Party became president. A border dispute with Nicaragua has threatened Costa Rica's tourism industry in the ecologically rich San Juan River area.

Costa Rica has achieved a relatively high standard of living in comparison to the rest of the Central American countries. Its economy is based on tourism, foreign investment, and agriculture. The country is noted for its political stability, and for its relative investment in health and in education and not in maintaining an army. However, as studies show, during the last 20 years, there has developed a large gap in income between one sector of the population who live at first-world standards (levels of consumption, private bilingual education, travel, etc), and other sectors with diminishing capacities to purchase even the bare necessities.

## 1. Basic Sexological Premises

### A. Character of Gender Roles

The situation of women's sexualities in this small country reflects some unique and particular traits in the national gender social arrangements, and it also reflects larger universal trends, which affect women individually and collectively. Unlike the rest of the Central American countries that have suffered revolutions, invasions, genocide, civil war, and natural disasters, this country has had the freedom and time to develop a women's movement, with its accompanying gender studies and theories, which in varied ways have been put into practice in different areas of the law, such as women's rights, women's studies at a graduate level, and so on. This concerted effort has had positive results. Domestic and sexual violence in all its multifaceted aspects has not only been made visible, but is being fought through a national program of prevention of violence. As a result of many years of work with lawyers, judges, and doctors, nowadays, men who rape or engage in sex with their own children or other children are sent to jail for 12 years or more. In March of 2003, an Evangelical pastor was sentenced to 61 years for repeatedly abusing a 12-year-old girl. Likewise, women's sexual and reproductive health and rights, after the world congresses in Cairo and Beijing, are on the agendas of some women's organizations and some state institutions, with projects mainly directed at young adolescent women. Progress is being made, with the creation of a National Committee on Reproductive and Sexual Health and Rights and with changes in the attention women receive in health centers, to name just a few. This is not to say that there has not been opposition, mainly from doctors, lawyers, and the Church.

These significant steps, however, must be understood in the larger context. This small country, with a "democratic" and non-military tradition, during the 1980s and early 1990s served, on the one hand, as a springboard for U.S. activities (cultural and political) throughout Central America and, on the other, as an exemplary exception, which had to be kept free of the region's endemic contamination—political upheaval. The "Americanization," or more specifically, the "Miamification," with American influences arriving via the Cuban community in Miami, Florida, has seen the proliferation of U.S. education, products of all types, movies, cable television, and magazines, as well as U.S.-style gyms and diet or aesthetic centers, shopping malls, pornography, sex shops, and cosmetic surgery.

The body culture of this society has been affected by globalization and has undergone drastic changes in the last 20 years. The increasing secularization, where the control of women by fathers and husbands, as well as by social institutions, like the Church, has changed. The control of women's virginity, marriageability, and reproduction has loosened and has been supplanted by an emphasis on women's control of their bodies—their appearance and shape. Anorexia and bulimia are problems particularly among middle-class female adolescents. The fast turnover of women's images, through ads, pornography, and movies, emphasizing parts of the nearly always-white bodies, has also affected men's attitudes towards women and towards their own physicality and sexuality, and how they think about women.

The globalization process has deepened the differences between the rich and the poor. Since 1979, half a million Nicaraguans, 70% female, have fled the hunger and unemployment in their country, and have made Costa Rica their home. The thriving tourist industry, Costa Rica's principal income, has stimulated the prostitution and pornography industries; children are for sale to older men. At the same time, Costa Rica has become an international center for cosmetic surgery. White and slim are the models that surround us in the ads, medical pamphlets, and television. Many women and some men come to Costa Rica, principally from the United States and some from Europe, to undergo cosmetic surgery, because it is cheaper than at home.

As for sex, it would be erroneous to talk about a sexual culture in terms of "Costa Ricans do this or that . . ." as a national characteristic, or even to say that some women are liberated, others not. What becomes clear after working with hundreds of women from different social backgrounds are the common elements, such as ignorance, silence, and helplessness that color their experience, regardless of social class or religion. It is sad, though familiar, to hear women admit to faking orgasms; but it is painful to hear them admit to not knowing what an orgasm is, and even worse, to not knowing what a clitoris is—or to hear peasant women say, "My husband uses me twice or three times a week."

We could attribute this to poverty and a Third-World mentality, but this is a too-narrow perspective. Most women are ignorant about sex and their sexuality, and in particular, about their bodies, in all cultures that I know. Here, it is relevant to understand that we are talking about two very distinct but articulated worlds that exist in most nations: First and Third worlds, separated not by North/South, developed/undeveloped—but by gender constructions predicated on class differences, on maintaining power inequalities between women and men, and on the perpetuation of the "undevelopment" of all women. Ignorance about the body and sex, invisibility of the diversity of preferences and lifestyles, violence in its multifaceted forms, poverty, pornography, and so on, all contribute to maintaining women in an undeveloped status and mentality.

The situation of men's sexuality, compared with women's, reflects some unique and particular traits, as well as larger, universal trends. In the last eight years, research on the behavior of specific groups of men has initiated a process of deconstruction of the mythical, monolithic, universal male. Latin American masculinity has been conflated with *machismo*, something that is seen as particular to Latin men, hence the idea of the Latin lover, but also the idea that all Latin American men are *machistas*, and what is more, much more *machistas* than, let's say, North American or British men.

When we step out of the realm of stereotype and begin to decipher and interpret reality, in this case, the reality of how men live their sexuality in Costa Rica, we begin to detect a reality colored by ignorance, silence, and compulsion. Compulsion here denotes obligation, a performance pressure.

Men have the obligation to demonstrate their "masculinity" at all times, at work, in public, when courting, in bed. They have learned to push, cajole, and manipulate in order to get what they want sexually. This, in feminist terms, is one of the components of sexism, another word for *machismo*. *Machismo*, as defined by an 18-year-old Costa Rican youth is "men's fear that women will surpass them." As defined by a university professor, it is "a complex of strategies aimed at keeping male control of power resources regarding women; it is a set of beliefs and practices regarding men's superiority over women."

The cultural particularities of this type of sexism has different manifestations and clear guiding principles. The following are phrases from men of varying social backgrounds in a men's support group: men are unfaithful by nature; men are polygamous by nature; it is genetic; men have the right to every female; the penis has a life and personality of its own; men have to show women about sexuality; it is a man's job to please women sexually; and so on. Some married men have lovers. Some men have more than one, maybe two, three, or even four lovers at a time. These relationships vary in intensity and significance. Some men have additional families.

The male's need to demonstrate his manhood is done through the constant acting out of an active sexuality, where he proves that "it can work" and that he "does it very well." Women, on the other hand, according to these men, should be passive and ignorant. The reduction of male sexuality to a functioning virile organ precludes pleasure and sensuality and other erotic stimulants. Sex is about penetration, and all rituals—dining out, wine, and candles—that are a buildup for intercourse. If it does not take place, men are disappointed and feel that they have failed. When asked when they felt they had become men, many answered, when they first "penetrated" a woman. Only a few years ago, it was a custom for young men to be taken by their fathers to visit prostitutes in order to have their first experience of intercourse, and consequently, become a man.

It is not surprising that men live their sexuality with stress, pain, and anguish. Male sexuality, like that of women, is predicated on ignorance. Men are ignorant about their bodies and their genitals, and needless to say, they are ignorant about women's bodies and genitals. At the same time, they feel threatened and "feminized" by ideas that point to erotic pleasure, to communication and sensuality. And they also feel threatened when asked to take responsibility for their sexuality, when asked to use the condom, for example.

In Madrigal's 1998 study of sexual behavior of truck and trailer drivers in Central America—Guatemala, El Salvador, Honduras, Nicaragua, Costa Rica, and Panama—we find a group of men who travel from country to country, are absent from their homes and families for long periods of time, and who habitually have sexual relations with sex workers—sometimes with transvestites or with homosexuals—in the border towns of all the countries. Their truck, particularly the cabin, becomes a second home, where they keep their things, sleep, and have sexual relations. A second family is formed by becoming friends with the prostitutes. Often sex workers are picked up at one border and dropped off at the next, where they, in turn, pick up another trailer driver. Commercial sex is mobile, and they compare themselves to sailors: "To be a trailer driver is like being a sailor: The sailor has a love in every port, the trailer driver in each customs town." Infidelity by their wives or partners is not tolerated, but they justify their own infidelity by saying, "it is men's right," "men never stop having sexual relations," "it is natural in men," or "it is impossible to hold on for 15 days," and so on.

But sexual pleasure is not a bilateral event. A 1992 study found that two out of five women had never experienced orgasm. Foreplay is rare; sex is equated with intercourse, and this, says sexologist Mauro Fernandez, seldom lasts more than two or three minutes. Premature ejaculation is a problem for 70% of sexually active Costa Rican men.

A 1992 survey by *La Republica* newspaper revealed that 87% of married and cohabiting women in a sample survey said they had been unfaithful before the age of 45. Two out of every five wives or widows over age 60 reported having had extramarital affairs at some time in the past. Most of these women, however, reported only a few instances of extramarital sex, which usually occurred, they said, because they did not feel loved or valued.

## B. Current Family Patterns and Gender Roles

Until the late 1960s, the demands of farm life encouraged Costa Ricans to have large families. After living conditions improved and government health programs provided prenatal care, the birthrate reached a world high in 1960, 55.4 births per 1,000 population. Then, a phenomenon occurred that intrigued population experts: the birthrate dropped to 29.5 per 1,000 in 1975. Costa Rica is the only Latin American country—and one of very few in the world—in which the birthrate has fallen so sharply. The 25% drop between 1960 and 1968 occurred despite Church and state opposition to birth control. Since the 1970s, however, the government has promoted family planning.

The "family" in Costa Rica is a very important institution, and it is the center of people's lives. They have been close exclusive units with extended close kinship networks, where relatives gather on important events. Nowadays, although many people strive to create secure families, there have been many social changes that have affected and changed the traditional family unit. Families are smaller, many women work outside of the home, many children have migrated to other countries, and there are more divorces and many single-parent households, particularly single mothers. In an effort to recognize the reality of women's situation, in the process of the feminization of poverty, many feminist scholars began to change the concept to "families," as a way of deconstructing the monolithic, naturalizing, all-encompassing concept of nuclear families—parents and their unmarried children— that made up 53% of all Costa Rican households in 1996. In four out of five of these families, the parents were married; the rest cohabited in *unión libre*, "free union," a legally recognized relationship. Female-headed households, mostly single mothers and their unmarried children—and often their daughter's children as well—accounted for 20% of all households. Couples without children and one-person households, mostly among the elderly, accounted for about 12%. The remaining 15% were extended-family households—couples living with at least one of their children and one or more grandchildren or other relatives. Many free unions are as stable as marriages; they are sometimes called *matrimonies de hecho—de facto* marriages. Recognizing this fact, a 1995 law gives cohabiters exactly the same rights and obligations as married couples, including "divorce" after three years with accompanying provisions for child support and division of property.

Vestiges of older gender roles are reflected in the many popular songs that depict women as willing to sacrifice everything for a man's love. But women are increasingly challenging double standards, as did the Costa Rican suffragists before 1949. A revived women's movement has flourished since the 1980s, when poverty, which especially affects women and children, began to increase. By 1993, some 40 well-established feminist groups existed, with goals ranging from bank credit for women to the eradication of domestic violence and gender stereotypes in schooling—

the Law Against Domestic Violence was established in 1996. Of over 180 delegations to the Fifth International Women's Conference in Beijing in 1995, Costa Rica's was one of only ten that approved the proposed platform for action without reservations.

Males increasingly have had to accept changes in gender roles. Many more fathers play with their children. Government now expresses support for gender equality. The 1990 Law for Promotion of the Social Equality of Women applies to many areas of life, ranging from political party caucuses to images used in advertisements. Violations of antidiscrimination laws are frequent. In 2002, the Law of Paternity was created to make men economically responsible for the children they engender; their DNA is tested when they contest or deny paternity.

## 2. Religious, Ethnic, and Gender Factors Affecting Sexuality

### A. Source and Character of Religious Values

Costa Rica is one of the few nations in the world with an official religion: Roman Catholicism. Thus, the public education system includes religious instruction for all students. All Costa Ricans contribute through their taxes to the salaries of the clergymen. The Church is represented at all official government functions and there is no aspect of national life that is not influenced by it. Most Costa Ricans are baptized, married, and blessed before interment by Catholic priests. Crucifixes and saints' pictures are prominent in homes, schools, government offices, and motor vehicles. Shrines to the Virgin are common in public buildings, parks, and front yards. All this expresses, if not a religious practice, definitely, a deeply imbedded cultural practice.

Some four out of five Costa Ricans say they are Catholic. But their Catholicism has long been blended with indigenous, occult, and secular beliefs and practices. The Catholic majority is still reluctant to accept many Church doctrines. Many do not believe in an afterlife and have no qualms about practicing contraception or consulting witches and fortune-tellers. As school enrollment has grown, both the number and the percentage of children who receive the two weekly catechism lessons has also increased. Confirmation takes place around age 15. Many Costa Ricans consider classes in Catholic doctrine essential to the formation of the "Costa Rican character."

The 1949 Constitution retained the 1871 constitutional provision that "neither clergy nor laymen may make political propaganda of any sort by invoking religious motives or by taking advantage of religious belief." But clergy can exert political influence in other ways. Padre Benjamin Nuñez was active in the PLN (Partido Liberación Nacional) until his death in 1994. He had also been "married" two times and had children. However, the Church is very actively involved in the gender politics of the country, a politics that goes beyond political parties. One writer charges that the Catholic Church has become "a State within a State," the fourth power of the government. He regards its official status as a violation of the liberty of conscience supposedly guaranteed by the Constitution. Thanks to government policies since the 1940s and to the clergy's "constant reprimands, admonitions and social pressures on the members of the three powers of the Republic," its power is evident in all aspects of public life.

The Church has the power of veto in many public and private decisions. When a group of lesbians tried to organize an international conference in the country in 1990, the Church reprimanded the government for having given permission to the organizers, and public opinion was stirred up against the event. The minister of justice declared that for-

eign participants would be prohibited from entering the country, adding that lesbians are easy to recognize. The jokes in the press said that he had created a 'lesbometer.'

To date, the Costa Rican government has been unable to teach sex education in high schools. The Catholic Church has rejected the instruction manuals prepared for this purpose by the Ministry of Education, arguing that the texts contained "moral irregularities." The Church demanded changes be made, insisting on their own blueprint of sex education, which is opposed to premarital sex, non-reproductive sexual practices, abortions, most family planning methods including the condom, and respect for sexual diversity. It also includes an open and hostile rejection of feminism and gender theories.

In 1998, during the administration of President Miguel Angel Rodríguez, a project named Amor Joven (Young Love) was created by the INAMU (National Institute of Women's Affairs) and by the First Lady, Lorena Clare. This project followed the guidelines of the Cairo+5 proposals, and was aimed at working women and empowering adolescent mothers by preparing them from a human rights and gender perspective for a sexuality based on knowledge and negotiation. The Church hierarchies denounced the project, and for many months all priests were instructed to denounce and criticize it from their pulpits. The Church said that the project was immoral and that it would induce the youngsters to promiscuous behavior. As the Church was on the Board of this government project, they wielded considerable political clout. If the government insisted in executing the project as it stood, the Church would persuade the public to go against the government. The Church changed the project by eliminating words, such as, gender, sex, vagina, penis, self-determination, and autonomy. The project died from asphyxia.

In 1998, a group of women's NGOs, together with the Ombudswoman and the then-Vice Minister of Health, Dr. Xenia Carvajal, organized and managed to put enough pressure on the Doctor's Association of Costa Rica, which until then, made all decisions regarding sterilizations, abortions, and other sexual and reproductive matters. The demand was that these decisions should not be made by an exclusive group, but by an interdisciplinary and interinstitutional group. A committee was created, which includes members of NGOs, universities, and government institutions, as well as international organizations in the country. As a result, a decree was promulgated that declared it the right of every woman to be sterilized on demand. The Church's reaction was extreme, as was that of a certain conservative public, and it retaliated by going along with the decree on the condition that a Day of the Unborn be created in the country—July 27 is that day. All this reinforces the pro-life movement and Opus Dei, the extreme conservative wing of the Catholic Church.

How Catholicism is practiced varies greatly among the population. Some speak of having "blind faith"; young urbanites deny any religious belief. Most people fall somewhere in between, practicing their religion "their way," following a marked cultural pattern of individualism, a highly personal, syncretic approach to religion. Many Catholics question the authority of the clergy, particularly after the snowball effect regarding the sexual abuse of young boys and girls by priests, which became public and visible in the United States, and which also broke the silence of abuse in this culture. Many Costa Ricans insist on freedom to decide for themselves how many children they should have: "If the *padre* wants me to have more, let *him* feed them." A young, newly married *campesino* (farmer) told us, "The pope preaches that birth control is a sin, but I think he's mistaken in that," (Biesanz).

Likewise, many priests are tired of hearing bishops urge moral reform and charity, as well as more preaching of the gospels, as the only solutions to poverty and other social ills. Many of these priests are active in community projects.

Many Catholics have become disillusioned with their Church and have sought alternative practices, mainly in Protestant Evangelical churches, which abound in the country. This is a worldwide phenomenon, which has forced the Vatican to renovate their zeal and direct their attention at specific topics, such as, sexuality, birth control, abortion, feminism and gender theories, and homosexuality—all the crucial points fought for by feminists in the Cairo and Beijing Conferences. At the same time, Church authorities have directed their attention to the governments of Catholic countries, and put pressure directly there.

It is interesting and fearful to see how this works in this culture. Before the Cairo+5 meeting in The Hague in 1999, a Vatican official made personal calls to different government ministers, insisting that Costa Rica adhere to the Vatican guideline in the official presentation in The Hague. To this date, this direct pressure from the Vatican has not produced anyone with the strength to tell the Church to keep out of its business. Fear of losing power and voters has made some Protestant presidents convert to Catholicism. One Vatican tactic was to invade the Beijing+5 conference in New York in 2000, with barefooted monks in subtle colored habits, which forced many of the participants to meet clandestinely. Another Vatican tactic is to invite all the presidents in the region, including some ministers, congresspersons, and their wives, to an audience with the Pope himself. The spell of obedience is cast, the conservative wing of the Church is vindicated, and the work towards change becomes even harder.

### B. Source and Character of Ethnic Values

Costa Rican Indians have never been a homogeneous group. The 400,000 or so aborigines living in the area in 1502 belonged to many societies, distinct both politically and culturally. Today's 30,000 Indians—about 1% of Costa Rica's population—include members of the Bribri, Huetar, and Talamanca cultures. Almost all live as subsistence farmers in 75 communities within the 22 officially designated Indian reserves, which compose about 6% of the national territory.

The fertility of Indian women is higher than the rest of the female population, with an average of 4.1 children, whereas, other women in the country have an average of 2.7. The organization by age and sex shows that this population is younger than the rest of the country. The percentage of people younger than 15 years of age is 46%, and those over 65 years only 3.7%, in contrast to the rest of the country which is at 5.6%. Illiteracy is high—the average attendance at school in the reserves is 3.6 years; in some areas, it is less than one year. Three quarters of the indigenous peoples live in dispersed rural reserves. There are no investigations about the sexuality of the Indian or the black communities.

### 3. Knowledge and Education about Sexuality

As noted earlier, there is no sex education in Costa Rica, and there is no national policy for sexual education. The Ministry of Education is supposed to be in charge of sexual education, and although they have elaborated a conceptual document of what sexual education should contain, it has not materialized. The Church is the biggest opposition to sexual education, insisting that it should be the task of parents to educate, and to promote abstinence. The Ministry of Health also has a document about sexual education; the Faculty of Education in the University of Education has an Office of Sexual Education and a full-time professor in charge. All this with no evidence of sexual education.

### 4. Autoerotic Behaviors and Patterns
No information is available.

### 5. Interpersonal Heterosexual Behaviors
#### A/B. Adolescents and Adults
*Male and Female Sexuality*

The subject of human sexuality has only become evident in Costa Rica during the last ten years. This is in part because of the introduction of sexology by sexologists, to the high incidence of teen pregnancies, to the HIV/AIDs epidemic, to the introduction of gender theories and studies, and most of all, to the process of globalization and the influence of North American and European immigrants. Sexuality has been analyzed from the standpoint of the problematic consequences it has on women, and, mainly in women's magazines and journals, on how to achieve more pleasure and more orgasms. Heterosexuality as a patriarchal institution has come under scrutiny in the Woman's Studies master's program in the University of Costa Rica, and in some NGOs.

On the other hand, government projects directed at poor young women center their discourses on the sexuality of young adolescent women and on the prevention of unwanted pregnancies. Meanwhile, popular magazines dealing with sexual enhancement concentrate on male coital pleasure and ignore information that could make women the protagonists of their own sexuality. Sexual pleasure as a right is not the objective. In the case of poor women, the problem of unwanted pregnancy is frequently seen as the woman's problem only, and the men responsible disappear and are invisibilized. Women's sexuality is represented as being the cause of the problem.

*Negotiating Safe and/or Pleasurable Sex*

In one study of sexual behavior and expectations in relation to pregnancy prevention and family planning, Schifter and Madrigal (1996) compared a poor coastal community characterized by poverty, unemployment, and female-headed families with urban, middle-class, young women and men from stable two-parent homes.

In the poor coastal community studies by Schifter and Madrigal, the young daughters learn about sexuality from romantic or religious sources—pure and unblemished love, fidelity in marriage, and virginity before marriage. The sons, also influenced by these discourses, learn from gender discourses and from erotic literature, and concentrate more on pleasure. However, both sexes aspire to happiness in marriage and to saving their virginity for marriage. The young women clearly expressed themselves in terms of getting a man, of marrying, and of having a "normal" family, the romantic heterosexual script predominating. At the same time, in the face of a harsh reality, their bodies are the only means for obtaining recognition and pleasure. It is not surprising, say the authors, that these youngsters experiment with varied sexual practices from an early age, such as bestiality, group sex, sadomasochism, anal, and oral sex.

Despite defending the religious conceptions about sexuality, the consequences of their lack of alternatives are the contradictions between what they say and what they practice. Poverty makes the romantic ideal of marriage a material impossibility, and not having access to other status symbols, like professions or political power, they are limited to concentrating everything on their bodies and not in other aspects of life. The young women have a reputation to protect; the men have to prove their manhood and insist that their "girlfriends" prove their love by giving in to their sexual demands. "When one sins for love, everything can be forgiven," many of the young women alleged; in this way, love is a cleanser of sins, and a short-lived palliative. It is only when the men fall in love that they adopt a "romantic" and protective stance to their loved one, and begin to make a clear distinction between her and "other" women, and for a brief period, their idea about men's superiority diminishes.

In this community, gender roles are much more traditional, much more dichotomous than the youth community described above. Gender in the poor coastal community is determined by the physical activity that each person carries out. According to their own definition, everyone who is "active" and "aggressive" is a man. And all those who are "passive" and "dominated" are women. It is in this context that the phenomenon of the "*cachero*" and its particular symbolism emerges. In this community, similar to the marginal cultures of prisons, or in "*transvesti*" prostitution, sexuality is not defined by the sexual object, but by who dominates whom. In the case of the *cacheros*, we have heterosexual men, generally married and with children, who have sex with passive homosexuals. Nobody makes fun of these men, because they know only too well that these are very "masculine" men capable of physical aggression. For this reason, to be a *cachero* does not carry a stigma. On the contrary, a *cachero* is considered to be a *macho*, so manly in fact that he "screws" both men and women.

The other community in this study is urban and middle class, and the young women and men originate from stable two-parent homes. This group was much more informed about pregnancy, STD prevention, and AIDS. They are also very clear about the importance of both sons and daughters studying for a career, and for waiting to marry until they are established. In their case, the religious mandates to wait to have sex until married, and the prohibition of the use of contraceptives, becomes obsolete when faced with long university studies. The control of women by men, however, is done under more symbolic and mental forms. Sexuality is a restricted terrain for women, where they are prohibited from acquiring knowledge and experience, unless it is with their boyfriends. Sexual relations before marriage are permitted as long as it is under the control of a man who is their "protector." Flexibility in relation to women's virginity is contrasted with the high price that women pay when they become single mothers or are not able to marry. Single women are relegated to poverty or to taking care of their families, that is, if these forgive them their error. Working in workshops with women from this background, I have found that, despite the clarity about becoming economically solvent, many of these women live out a body culture marked by self-rejection and obsession with their size and form. Many diet constantly, some begin to have cosmetic surgery from a very early age, and some prefer to have cesarean births in order not to lose their shape. The sexuality of the women from these two communities is influenced by distinct body cultures, in the sense that there are different attitudes and expectations, and vastly different experiences. Nonetheless, the inability to negotiate safe and/or pleasurable sex marks both groups.

*Balancing Women's Conflicting Values*

In another study of adolescent women in a marginal urban community with a high incidence of early pregnancy, illiteracy, and underemployment (Preinfalk Fernandez 1988), it became clear that the young women were pressured into having sexual intercourse by the men, and also by their girlfriends. At the same time, these young women are aware that their value resides in being virgins, but also in having a man and in keeping him. The young men's preoccupation is in "scoring" the highest number of females, and sex is practiced with no protection of any kind. Unwanted pregnancies are the result, and sometimes the man stays for a while in a stable

union. Once women have lost their virginity, they develop many different strategies to negotiate their "desirability," for an experienced woman is seen as a slut. This is also an element that exists among the middle class. We could attribute these ideas about the "good" and "bad" women to the Catholic culture, and in many ways it has a profound influence on the collective mentality, but there are many other influences that persistently devalue and debase women and their bodies. Women are depicted as objects in pornography, advertisements, television, and every medium imaginable. And this is accompanied by the increase in violence against women and in what some now term "femicide," the assassination of women.

## 6. Homoerotic, Homosexual, and Bisexual Behaviors

### A. Sociolegal Status, Issues, and Lifestyles

*Sociolegal Status*

Specialists who work with homosexual populations reckon that they constitute 10% of the population in Costa Rica. Homosexuality has been and still is, though to a subtly lesser degree, a taboo subject. There are gay men and lesbian women in all walks of life, government institutions, the Church, etc., and in all social classes. Many live their lives quietly, minding their own business, and not congregating; others socialize in gay or lesbian bars; some form similar-minded groups (e.g., feminists, activists). But this country is homophobic, and until some individuals began to study gender theories, and later others began to work in preventing the AIDS epidemic from spreading, homosexuality was treated as a pathology, with many stereotypes in the public mind and media.

Homosexuality is not a crime in the Penal Code of 1971. Before these reforms were introduced, the punishment for sodomy was one to three years in prison (article 233). Since 1971, there has been no basis for the prosecution of homosexuality, as long as it occurs between two consenting adults and passive participants are more than 17 years of age. Prostitution is not considered a crime either, unless it is practiced in a "scandalous" manner. There are strict laws against pimping (owning a brothel) and inducing minors to practice prostitution. Most convictions are for these two reasons. In order to prosecute an adult prostitute, there must be some other infraction, such as moral indecency, public scandal, suspicion of drugs, or vagrancy. Unlike female prostitutes, male prostitutes are not regulated by law, nor are they required to be tested for venereal diseases.

*Gay Lifestyles*

In many ways, in recent years, the subject of homosexuality has begun to come out of the cultural closet. This is mainly because of the political work done by both groups and to the particular ability of certain individuals who took advantage of the VIH/SIDA (HIV/AIDS) pandemic to make visible the situation of gay men, and of men who have sex with men. Through the work of a now-extinct NGO, ILPES (Instituto Latinoamericano de Prevención y Educación en Salud [Latin American Institute of Prevention and Health Education]), many research projects were carried out about homophobia, stereotypes, and sexual behavior between men in prisons, among male prostitutes, and transvestite prostitutes. Through their work with support groups of gay men, and the promotion of prevention and the use of condoms in bars and places frequented by gays, the incidence of VIH was reduced in this group. Through their work with lawyers, doctors and hospital workers, policemen, prison workers, university professors and students, and many other groups, the real situation of gay men was made visible, as well as the homophobia inherent in this culture—and in every individual, including gay men themselves. One of the aims of this work was to change the discriminatory attitude to a more tolerant attitude towards gay men. Still, at present, homosexuality is a taboo subject, and gays have suffered rejection, invisibilization, violence, and even death in recurring gay-bashing episodes.

In one of the earlier publications by Jacobo Schifter, director of ILPES, he described very clearly how homophobic attitudes amongst homosexual men worked to their detriment. There existed total mistrust between them: They would never reveal their full name and even less where their family lived or their place of work, so that an ex-lover would not be tempted, in a fit of rage, to call the family or work and reveal his true identity. Neither would they reveal who their current lover is, because they would face a barrage of insults about him: "He is *una loca* (a queen)," "He has slept with half of San José," "He has AIDS," etc. The ultimate violence in this chain of events, including stealing or destroying each other's property at parties, is the murder of gays by other gays. Between 1988 and 1996, 25 gay men were tortured and then murdered by the *chulos* (pimps) that they had taken to their homes. Another violence that gays faced was with the police. These would keep vigilance on the gay bars, and at any pretext, they would charge in and beat up the gays inside and make roundups. One explanation for this could be the fact that some of the police are closet homosexuals; another could be that they share the same masculine ideology where women are not involved. They live in close physical contact with each other: They work, eat, sleep, socialize, and live together for long periods. This creates a particular erotic and dangerous dynamic within the repressive function of the police.

Another aspect of gay culture is the emphasis on youth and physical beauty. Anyone who does not fit this model is rejected without mercy. Aging is feared. In Costa Rica, to be gay is to be an adolescent, and gays are discouraged from going to gay bars and dances after they are 30. Forty is considered to be old. Relationships are short lived; even when both profess to being in love, the relationship does not transcend the passionate phase, and soon, one or other of the partners begins to look elsewhere.

During the 1950s and 1960s, gays met in distinct public places to have casual and anonymous sex: saunas, parks, cinemas, and urinals. This pattern, though still in force, has changed because of the creation of bars for gays and lesbians. This created a pattern where some gays would seek out sexual partners, but many still sought encounters in public places. Although the repression has diminished, the sexual pattern of anonymous sex continued, principally by very isolated or by closeted gays. Bisexuals and married men sporadically frequent these places. Contact is made by the individuals touching their genitals, a common practice in heterosexual men in this country, but with the particular connotation with gays of "you can have all this," or by jangling their keys, a sign that they have a car or a house where they can go to. After this, verbal contact is made. Frequently, in the less illuminated parts of parks or urinals or narrow passages between houses, men masturbate each other or practice fellatio. Penetration and group sex take place in safer locales, like cinemas. Middle-class bisexuals and gays frequent saunas more than the other public places. Public spaces are also places for sexual workers to practice their trade. Muggings and stabbings are common occurrences, as well as police roundups. This violence and danger is part of the erotic attraction for many of these men who initiated their sexual life on the street, "I like the fear . . .," "I want to participate in the danger . . .," two men told Schifter (1997).

By 1998, violence had noticeably increased in these public places, in part, because of the appearance of the *chapulines* or "locusts." Locusts are male and female juvenile gang members who mug and rob people, and are compared to swarming pests. They are very antagonistic to gays and are responsible for several murders of gays in the last few years. They, like the gays, have taken over public places to impose their own culture of sex, robbery, and death. At some vague time during the past few years, the locusts ceased to be mere delinquents and became part-time *cacheros*. Many of them stopped mugging gays and began to have anal sex with them *and* then rob them (Schifter 1999).

In the interviews carried out in the El Salon ILPES project, both *cacheros* and locusts had the common history of childhood abuse. They were all beaten by their fathers; many were sexually abused. Some lived with mothers who were prostitutes or with alcoholic fathers who abused them sexually. The locust from the smallest family had seven siblings and the one from the largest had 18. The mothers, fathers, or stepfathers are often unemployed, often alcoholic, or/and addicted to drugs, lost their patience, and vented their rage on their children. These adult men were the most sadistic and brutal and imposed their power physically. No longer able to provide food regularly for their families, they maintained their macho privileges through violence. Thus, the locusts' school of violence is closely related to gender issues; it serves to preserve gender imbalances. Most of these youngsters had been thrown out of their home and had made the streets their habitat. They make a living from robbery, the sex trade, and drugs. Inured to the penetration of their bodies by violent and inept parents or guardians, their bodies became a battlefield. The locusts are obsessed with orifices. Theirs must remain closed to the world, those belonging to others are ready to be taken, the same as open public places. To the locust, a homosexual is someone who allows his body to be invaded. Why do they, then, copy the *cachero*'s behavior? If they have *chapulinas* in their own group, why did they turn from criminals to sex workers? According to Schifter, the relationship developed through sharing the same physical spaces. But, more importantly, for the first time, someone was looking at them and finding them attractive underneath their shabby clothes. Attractive well-endowed locusts would find new benefits. Now a new class was emerging: the handsome *chapulines* with large penises and big bottoms. Those who did not satisfy the demands of the market remained as intermediaries of the "good beef." This changed the culture in the parks and public places. For a few hours each day, undocumented delinquents, drug addicts, and criminals, who were despised and feared by decent people, became public porn stars. A new Cinderella was born. The new heroes could now have sex with their victims and make good money out of them. Some of them had queues of men waiting to perform fellatio on them (Schifter 1999).

Gays and locusts might share the same spaces, but there exists a clear clash of cultures. They do not speak the same language. For gays, with their sexual model of the body and its pleasures, and locusts with their vision of the vulnerable body, communication is a tortuous road. Some gay murders have been committed by locusts. These crimes go beyond simple robbery. They are forms of torture that are impregnated with a profound degree of rage. One gay was killed by three men; they had amputated both arms, one leg, and his penis. They had cut the flesh on his arms and legs to shreds, and he had 12 stab wounds in his rectum. Ten *chapulines* were asked to explain this and other equally violent murders, some of them having been at the point of killing—or have actually killed—a gay client, or *pagador*, as they call them. Some agreed that the motive was robbery. Another said that they were premeditated, especially when there are three perpetrators and the assault takes place in a hotel or the victim's home. These crimes occur when the locusts have taken a combination of drugs: crack, marijuana, and alcohol. "The three victims discussed were stabbed in the ass, the mouth, and the dick," says one. "This means the locusts wanted to punish them for being gays, for letting themselves be fucked." However, there are triggers to this violence. If the client cheats them of money, when they touch them improperly, when they are humiliated, when they are feminized or asked to do "women's things," like kissing, allowing penetration, giving oral sex, if they are asked to wash dishes, or to help in preparing food for dinner like chopping onions.

For the locusts, clients are a source of income; unlike gays, sexual pleasure is totally irrelevant to them. The majority are heterosexual and do not enjoy sex with men. When a client establishes a relationship with a locust, the latter expects some form of compensation when the relationship is broken off. Juan killed Victor when, after three years of being his client, Victor found himself another locust. Gerardo cut off one of his client's testicles when he found out that he was paying another locust more than him.

### Transvestites

Another group studied by ILPES is the homosexual transvestite prostitute community in San José. Schifter (1997, 1999) maintains that an analysis of the Costa Rican transvestite community shows an elasticity in sexual orientation that challenges the essentialist theories. The men who practice transvestism have different sexual orientations and different degrees of femininity and masculinity. Schifter believes that the physical space, in combination with the *paqueteo* (the packaging used in order to pass as women), are very important in producing changes in sexual orientation. Many transvestites are heterosexual men, married and with children, who like to dress as women, but do not have sexual relations with men. In Costa Rica, this group is the most concealed. They do not form part of any community, nor are they prostitutes, like some homosexuals.

Most of the transvestites contacted became aware of their orientation around 12 years of age. Many of them were initiated sexually by an older man; some say they wanted that experience, although others were obviously abused. Prostitution is their only means of making a living. They are thrown out of their homes and find no other option. They spend a great deal of their earnings on their clothes, makeup, and wigs. They have clothes for work, others for shows, and more-ordinary gear for everyday activities. The padding of hips, legs, and breasts are done with foam, rolled-up toilet paper, or cloth. Others use hormones, particularly contraceptive pills, which can be bought over the counter. Some use Depo-Provera, or whatever pill is available.

They share living and workspace, often cramped apartments, or the "bunker," a heavily secured row of rooms. A minority of transvestites come from fairly affluent middle-class homes. One of these, a doctor's son, carries out his trade unbeknown to his family. One day, one of his father's colleagues, another doctor, came to buy his services and did not recognize him dressed as a woman with a blonde wig. Originally, they lived and worked in a poor red-light area of the city and attracted poorer clients. When they migrated to a lower-middle-class area, they attracted more-affluent clients.

Previously, this area was used by female prostitutes; little by little the transvestites took over, and the prostitute's clients changed from heterosexual to bisexual orientation, in a slow process that was begun by the more feminine-looking transvestites passing with their clients. Eventually, the female prostitutes left, leaving the whole area to the transvestites. It was when cocaine became easily available and was used by the clients, that they allowed themselves to be touched and fondled by the transvestites. They began to say that they "liked it more" than with the female prostitutes, and began to recommend their friends. Some of the clients are members of Parliament and professional people.

But life is hard, and every night they expose themselves to insults, stabbings, being thrown bags of urine or excrement, or stones or bottles by men who make a sport of this violence. The priests denounce them in church, together, according to them, with other "scum," like homosexuals and prostitutes. Some defend themselves by throwing stones at cars. Much of this takes place in front of the houses where people have lived for 30 or more years; some of the neighbors have organized themselves in order to change the situation, but to little avail.

In 1990, when Schifter (1998) asked transvestites the number of sexual contacts that they had had in their lives, the average was 9,371. In 1997, the average was 4,835. In the year before the survey, the average was 830.4, making that 15.9 sexual contacts per week. In the month of the interview, there were 44.8 contacts, that is, 11.2 weekly contacts. Some transvestites say they make, on average, six contacts nightly. If we calculate that there exist 100 to 150 transvestites in San José, and each one has an average of four sexual partners, we can reckon that about 600 men use their sexual services in one day (Schifter 1998).

Many clients treat the transvestites as women with a penis, unlike their own permanent lovers, who treat them as women and do not want to see their penis. The majority of these partners were heterosexuals, some with children. Some still consider themselves heterosexual, others homosexuals or bisexuals. Interestingly, the transvestites do not consider their partners to be homosexuals.

### Male Prostitution and Bisexuality

Another study by Schifter (1998) focused on a very specific sexual culture within the realm of male prostitution: the young men of a lower-middle-class brothel catering to pederasts. These youths are neither homosexual nor bisexual, in the sense of being attracted to only men or both men and women. The only characteristic that identifies them as bisexual is their sexual behavior while prostituting themselves. This places them within the culture known as *cachera*—men who have sexual relations with other men, but who are heterosexual in all other respects. Some of them are students (at school) or professionals, and some still live with their families, while others have moved into their own homes. The youths are between 13 and 27 years of age. A few live in a brothel, but the majority arrive at night to attend to clients. For some, the money is spent on crack, alcohol, and luxury extras. Some of them help out at home. The clients are bisexual in their orientation. Most of them are married men with children, who are completely "in the closet," leading a heterosexual life in public, with occasional visits to the brothel. Some clients are homosexuals. They are made up of nationals and foreigners.

### Lesbian Lifestyles

The situation of lesbians is different. Sporadically, they were included in the ILPES project. But, as in other countries where gays and lesbians have fought together for homosexual rights, lesbian women ended up supporting the men, but this was not reciprocated. There is a new NGO, CIPAC (Centro de Investigaciones para América Central—Derechos Humanos de Gays y Lesbianas [Central American Research Center—Lesbian and Gays' Human Rights]), which is changing this pattern by working shoulder to shoulder with both groups. But here, lesbians are analyzing themselves from the perspective that they have more in common with other women than with men, gay or not. If women, in general, have been invisibilized in history, even more so have lesbian women. Even in the feminist movement, made up of a high percentage of lesbians, the subject is not discussed, consequently producing much tension in the groups.

For several years in the 1980s and early 1990s, the lesbian group, Las Entendidas, published a journal called *La Boletina*, with poetry and information, and analytical articles about lesbianism, feminist theories, and about lesbian women's lives. The work of Ester Serrano, based on in-depth interviews with nine lesbian women, set out to find out how some lesbians have established groups and what this has meant for them. All these women learned in their childhood that lesbian women suffer, are problematic, are abnormal, and cannot be "good" mothers. They also learned that they should make themselves invisible. All the women interviewed had absorbed these homophobic sentiments. The first gay bars opened in the 1970s, and for the first time, gays and lesbians had a place for themselves where they could enjoy themselves, and where they could meet and be with other lesbians openly. However, these bars were populated by young people, and for many older lesbians, they were aggressive, patriarchal places. Not only this, in those early years, these bars were secret places, where gays or lesbians had access only by asking to see the owner. They were regularly raided by the police. In this context, "butch" lesbians formed into a group called "The Buffaloes," who came together as protectors of the other "weaker" women. They made a buffer between the "femme" women and the police, receiving the blows, having their noses broken. Another strategy created in the still-existing La Avispa [The Wasp] bar, was to turn a red light on as a warning of a police raid. Immediately, the same-sex couples would change partners and pretend to be heterosexual.

All the lesbian women interviewed, with some exceptions, lived in the closet in relation to their families, and all hid their identity at work. This changed as they became aware of their rights, particularly in the younger generation. The older lesbians were more circumspect because of the generalized homophobia, and to the fact that the fight for gay rights had not taken place. In the beginning of the 1990s, gays and lesbians began to celebrate Abril Saliendo del Silencio ["April Coming Out of the Silence"], which publicly celebrated the existence of gays and lesbians in Costa Rica. From this time on, they decided to carry on dancing with their same-sex partners, raid or no raid, marking a hiatus in their history. The feminist movement, the gay and lesbian movement, and the distinct lesbian congresses in Europe, North America, and Latin America have also strengthened the lesbian women in Costa Rica—although it is important to emphasize, no lesbian working in a state institution has come out openly about her identity.

## 7. Gender Diversity and Transgender Issues

Transvestites have been discriminated against and scorned. Often their own families throw them out of their home. Since the 1990s and the work of ILPES in the project of men who have sex with men that was centered on prevention of HIV/AIDS, some transvestites became activists and began to defend their rights. (See discussion of transvestites in the preceding Section 6.)

## 8. Significant Unconventional Sexual Behaviors

### A. Coercive Sexual Behaviors
*Child Sexual Abuse, Incest, and Pedophilia*

From the 1980s on, child sexual abuse and incest have been studied in Costa Rica and, as a consequence, different nongovernmental organizations specialized and grew around this subject. It is estimated that one out of three women have suffered some kind of sexual abuse before the age of 18, and one out of five men. Twenty years later, laws to prevent this abuse have been created, and a campaign organized by governmental and nongovernmental institutions and organizations have trained doctors, lawyers, social workers, teachers, and other professionals to detect this social cancer in children, and to refer the cases for investigation. Many abusers are now jailed. There are signs and information in highways, shops, and institutions, as well as television ads, that denounce sexual abuse. The effects of incest and abuse are devastating, and this is now taken into account when treating female mental patients, as well as other persons in institutions like jails.

*Sexual Harassment*

Through the work of organized feminists in government and nongovernmental organizations and universities, the Law Against Sexual Harassment in the Workplace and in Educational Centers was created in March 1995. The consequences can lead the abusers to be suspended or fired from their work. Sexual harassment was a serious problem for women in a culture that has permitted men to stare, whistle, make lewd remarks, and even touch women in the street or in public places. This was called *piropos*, or flattery, part of the *machistas* behavior permitted prior to the development of human rights and feminism.

### A. Prostitution, Child Prostitution, and Sex Tourism

The sexual exploitation of children and adolescents in Costa Rica is a social problem only recently recognized, even though it has a long history in the country and is documented in various texts dating back to the 18th century. Until 1997, the criminal code currently in force did not penalize the corruption of minors (premature and perverse sexual acts) if the victim had been "previously corrupted." Nor was there a legal statute against child prostitution. Through the dynamic work of NGOs (Casa Alianza, the Paniamor Foundation, Ser y Crecer Foundation, and the Procal Foundation), Costa Rica began to analyze the situation and to change its legislation.

The sexual exploitation of children occurs within the family (incest), or outside of it (prostitution, for example). But both cases involve a variety of diverse interrelated factors. For girls, several studies have shown that the vast majority entered into prostitution as a result of living on the street. In this sense, running away can be interpreted as being expelled from the family, as this act is often associated with abuse, abandonment, and neglect. In 1996, in the World Congress Against Commercial Sexual Exploitation of Children, held in Sweden, nongovernmental organization and the End Child Prostitution in Asian Tourism campaign (ECPAT) made a specific reference to the problem in Costa Rica, namely, that it attracted many tourists and residents from the United States and Europe who "take advantage of their stay" to participate in the local sexual exploitation of women, girls, and boys.

There are few studies of child prostitution in Costa Rica. Among these are the works of Tatiana Treguear and Carmen Carro (1994, 1997), who carried out two qualitative studies on the experiences of prostituted girls. The 1994 research was part of a Central American project with 30 prostituted adolescent girls between the ages of 13 and 17 in San José. In 1997, these same authors carried out a broader research endeavor with 50 prostituted adolescent girls between the ages of 9 and 17. This work addressed the risk factors associated with prostitution and provided an analysis of the reasons why they left home and their current living conditions. Sexual abuse as an antecedent of sexual exploitation was very common, given that 41 of the 50 girls reported that they had been sexually abused. Other factors that make Costa Rican children and adolescents vulnerable to prostitution include the extreme poverty of 10% of the population and the high percentage of adolescent girls who do not attend school. In addition, many women have their first child between the ages of 15 and 18, and 41% of all children are born to single mothers. Other factors include the consumption of drugs and alcohol.

In the last 15 years, a new phenomenon in the country has been the appearance of children in the streets. The "street phenomenon" stems from poverty, urban sprawl, and lack of alternatives, and is related to mistreatment and violence within the family. In some cases, boys and girls abandon their home for the street because they have nowhere else to go or they have been forced out. In other cases, in order to survive, these children must find the resources to do so. Once on the streets, the children forge new emotional ties in the form of couples or peer groups, bonds for affection and protection that help them to survive in an environment characterized by abuse, humiliation, and persecution. Drug consumption is often linked with life in the streets and also plays an important role in sexual exploitation, because many boys and girls continue with their addiction while they are being prostituted. Alcohol and illegal drugs, such as crack, cocaine, and marijuana, as well as paint thinner and glue, are staples in this population.

Another important aspect in analyzing drug consumption is how it relates to gender. Given that prostitution is primarily associated with the female gender, the challenge is how to interpret drug and alcohol abuse of girls and women. Studies demonstrate that the risk factors associated with substance abuse among women focus on violence, child sexual abuse, and rape. Specifically, they highlight four risk factors associated with especially difficult situations: sexual harassment and abuse, prostitution, unemployment and the prevailing need for support, and domestic violence (Claramunt 1999). These youths use their addiction as a way of numbing their pain and dealing with the situation. A second important element that contributes to high rates of sexually transmitted diseases, including HIV/AIDS, is the absence of protection measures associated with high intoxication levels and the lack of *power over prostitution customers*.

Those who sexually exploit children and adolescents are supported by many social sectors in Costa Rica that tolerate and justify the sexual marketing of children and adolescents. They come from a wide range of social groups and classes. They are white-collar workers, laborers, relatives, businessmen, political leaders, government officials, and police officers. Over the last few decades, Costa Rica experienced a rise in the sex tourism so prevalent in many Third World countries. Costa Rica's principal income comes from tourism, and the attraction for sex tourists was the low cost and young age of the boys and girls, as well as by the ease of prostitution. Thousands of pedophile tourists learn about Costa Rica through the Internet and magazines, sample guides, or catalogues that include pictures of naked girls and boys, and maps or directions that point out the location where the children are. These tourists are aided directly in the street or bars and hotels by taxi drivers and waiters, who contact the pimps

or the owners of prostitution houses. In some cases, these places are known as "cradle houses," because the children that live there are given food and clothing in exchange for prostitution. The greatest demand for girls and boys are the ports on the Pacific and Atlantic coasts where expensive boats and yachts arrive.

The organization Casa Alianza has been the most dynamic in making visible and in denouncing the sexual exploitation of children and adolescents in the country. Casa Alianza, directed by Bruce Harris, established itself in the country in 1996. It regularly receives denouncements and hate mail, which are filtered and investigated and then passed on to the Prosecutor's Office of Sexual Crimes. This office was created in 1998, but it has not been institutionalized in the Judicial Power and has no resources. Casa Alianza managed to obtain funds from the British Embassy and since then, there are about 50 people condemned, arrested, or waiting trial for sexual crimes. Two thirds are Costa Rican and one third are foreign. Casa Alianza has received more death threats in Costa Rica than in Guatemala, where it also has a program with street children and where there is more overt violence. When sexual exploitation is investigated, many powerful financial interests are touched. In 2002, there were 110 convictions, which included pimps, intermediaries, and clients.

In 2002, five members of the Costa Rican Pedophile Association were condemned, but unlike Chile, which created a Pedophile Unit, which as of April 2003 has discovered 18 pedophile networks in Costa Rica, there has not been one follow up in Costa Rica. According to Harris, there are girls brought to Costa Rica from the Dominican Republic, the Philippines, Bulgaria, Russia, Colombia, Nicaragua, and Panama. They are taken to exclusive clubs, where 60% of the clients come from the United States and the rest from Europe and other countries. These are men between 55 and 60 years of age. In San José, there are an estimated 3,000 girls, nearly all between 9 and 10 years of age. Similar estimates apply to the trade in the ports on both coasts. The average price of a virgin girl is about $400.

The pimps work in families; when one member is jailed, a daughter or son continues the activity; when they are arrested, a cousin carries on. Women are the main recruiters in the case of the girls, sometimes friends of the girl take her and receive a commission. These women are motherly; they feed and take care of the children. There are other pimps who distribute their cards in poor areas, telling the youngsters that if they want to earn some money to call them. Many do. These children do not do this because they like it; they do it to be able to eat. The Costa Rican Pedophile Association frequented the poorest areas in San José, where, for $15, these children could eat for a whole week.

Child pornography is not illegal in Costa Rica, which is a big problem, as Harris believes that there is a direct link between the use of pornography and the subsequent use and abuse of children. There was a university professor, who also worked in the prestigious Arias Foundation (created by ex-President Oscar Arias, a Nobel Peace prize winner), who had 6,000 pictures of child pornography in his computer at work, but he could not be prosecuted, and still continues as a professor. Distribution of child pornography, but not possession, can be prosecuted.

## 9. Contraception, Abortion, and Population Planning

### A. Contraception

In spite of the Catholic Church's prohibition, the attitude towards birth control is open. People can buy condoms at supermarkets and at pharmacies. The pill can be bought over the counter at pharmacies. However, for the last five years, there has not existed a national campaign for birth control, and although the Social Security System provides birth control services, women in many communities do not attend these clinics, due in part to ignorance, timidity, or lack of insurance. Adolescents generally do not attend the clinics, for similar reasons as the adult women, but also because they are often turned away and told not to have sex until they are married—clearly reflecting the attitude of healthcare workers about adolescents and their being sexually active. However, the fact that 40% of pregnancies are unwanted or unplanned in Costa Rica reflects other emotional, gender, and cultural inhibitions in relation to using contraceptives. It is known that many men do not want to use condoms, and that some do not allow their partners to use protection. There is a waiting list for women waiting to be sterilized after the 1999 Reproductive Health Decree, which allowed women to be sterilized on demand, without their husband's or the doctor's permission. The middle-class consult their private doctors about contraceptives.

## B. Teenage (Unmarried) Pregnancies

More than 800 teenage girls age 14 or younger, some as young as 12 years old or even younger, have babies every year. This has been the average number for five years. In 2000, it reached the peak number of 956. PANI (Patronato Nacional de la Infancia [National Institution for the Protection of Children]), which attends these girls, says that they are the victims of sexual abuse. And 15,000 adolescents over age 14, have children every year. The PANI is preparing a campaign to prevent sexual abuse. The CCSS (the Social Security System) initiated in April 2003 a new campaign directed at this teen population, with the aim of postponing early sexual encounters. More than 50% of teenage mothers conceive during casual sexual encounters; and when it is with "boyfriends," the relationship is fragile. Sixty percent of these pregnancies take place between 14 and 16 years. Many are high-risk pregnancies. Of all the children that die each year before they are one year old, 55% are premature, and of these, 74% are children of women who are under 20 years of age. There are hotline telephone programs for people to call in about their sexual problems—73% of calls in the year 2002 were made by adolescent women.

## C. Abortion

In January 2003, Costa Ricans were moved by a story published in the major newspaper, *La Nación*, about a 9-year-old girl who had been sexually abused and was pregnant. The newspaper article read as follows:

### Nine Year Old Girl Three Months Pregnant.
### Alarm at Child's Pregnancy

*Turrialba*. There will only be 9 years of difference between this mother and her child. This small generational gap will probably make them share children's games more than anything else. The reason being that Rosa (fictional name given in order to protect her real identity) today is 12 weeks pregnant. And she is a 9-year-old girl. This case has moved Turrialba (the town where Rosa lives). Daughter of Nicaraguan immigrants, coffee pickers, Rosa is the victim of abuse by a 20-year-old local farm worker. As a consequence, her physical and emotional state is very delicate. So much so, that the doctor's at the William Allen Hospital, have decided to keep her interned in order to observe her pregnancy. The doctor's have asked that this case be in the hands of the Ministry of Health. —Ramiro Rodríguez, reporter, *La Nación*. (Miller 2003)

This story has created a major controversy in both her homeland of Nicaragua and in Costa Rica—lawyers, physicians, Church leaders, and feminists weighing in with passion. This time, it was not because there was a proposal to amend the abortion statute in the Criminal Code, as was the case in 1993 when a Member of Congress, Nury Vargas of the PUSC (Partido Unión Social Cristiana), presented a law project in the Legislative Assembly to modify article 121 of the Penal Code. That proposal would have added a paragraph to allow abortion in the case of incest or rape. The proposal was rejected. The Catholic Church and public opinion also rejected the initiative, and Nury Vargas left the Congress under duress. This time, it was about the fact that abortion was rejected by the authorities, alleging that the consequences of an induced abortion would be more negative than her carrying the pregnancy to term and having the child. But there was another element: Rosa's parents were not informed that in the actual legislation there exists the possibility of therapeutic abortion when the "mother's health" is endangered. Rosa was moved to a hospital in the capital and kept away from her parents.

Meanwhile, feminists groups discussed this very delicate problem, and some presented a document with clear proposals in relation to Rosa's case. It was clear that there would not be an abortion for her, and it took a delegation of Nicaraguans who came and took the child to Nicaragua, where eventually, after much controversy there, an abortion was carried out in a private clinic.

This case has been positive for diverse reasons. It broke the silence on the subject of abortion in a country where it is practiced in secret, either in private clinics or by other means. Since Nury Vargas presented her proposal and was rejected, a mantle of fear, and thus, of silence, has hung over the subject. No one has wanted to bring it forward, not even feminists, except in reference to the need to do more research on the subject. Today, different women's groups, including government institutions, are discussing it, though behind closed doors. In May 2003, a forum on the subject of abortion, organized by and directed at feminists and NGOs, was held in order for this group to begin to formulate a clear standpoint.

The actual legal situation regarding abortion in the country is as follows: Induced abortion is classified as a crime in the Penal Code of 1970, included in the crimes against life. The penalties vary according to whether an abortion has been carried out with or without the woman's consent, and depending if the fetus has reached six months of gestation. Abortion is not punishable only when the woman's life is in danger, and in this case, the procedure can be carried out by a doctor or an authorized obstetric nurse. However, there are many doctors who, for reasons of religious faith, will not carry out an abortion.

The law in the country is restrictive and criminalizing, punishing women who decide to abort and those who carry out the procedure. Doctors who suspect that a woman has provoked an abortion are obliged to report this to the OIJ (Organización de Investigación Judicial [Organization of Judicial Investigation]). Years ago, operations were carried out periodically to detect and jail the doctors who practiced abortions. Very few were jailed; some left the country. Very few women were jailed also, and at the present moment in 2003, there are neither women who have aborted nor doctors in prison. However, a lay woman accused of carrying out abortions is serving a three-year sentence. She is an untrained midwife, with a lot of practical experience in her region.

This permissive attitude shows a more tolerant stance on behalf of the medical culture to a reality that affects the female population. But the subject is taboo, and abortions are still clandestine experiences affecting women's individual and collective health. At an individual level, it affects a woman physically, emotionally, and psychologically because of the complications that could present themselves, and because of the danger and loneliness a woman faces. At a collective level, the community's health is affected when the impact is not made visible by the underrecording of cases; when appropriate reproductive health services to attend the need for contraception are not met; when postabortion services are not available; and when women's sexual and reproductive needs are not recognized. These are needs that Costa Rica must address if it is to remain as a member country of the United Nations resolutions of the 1994 Conference in Cairo.

In spite of the fact that the United Nations Human Rights Committee (April 1999) recommended that Costa Rica's "legislation should be amended in order to introduce exceptions to the general prohibition of all abortions," the actual Costa Rican Legislature has the intention of increasing the penalties for abortions. This decision is backed by some articles in the Constitution, which point out that the religion of the State is Catholic, Apostolic, and Roman, and that human life is inviolable.

The Law Project under discussion in the Committee of Juridical Affairs of the Legislative Assembly has introduced the expression "the product of conception," eliminating the idea of the fetus. It preserves the image of abortion as unacceptable, but it incorporates the following modifications: a) the requisite for informed consent has been eliminated, and b) the figure of the *comadrona* (midwife) is included. In another attempt to control and restrict the right to choose, in November 2002, Article 379 of the Penal Code was modified and included all "those who advertise procedures, instruments, medicaments or substances destined to provoke abortions," would be fined.

The Gender Analysis Group of the Penal Code Project, headed by INAMU (Instituto Nacional de Asuntos de las Mujeres [National Institute of Women's Affairs]), and confirmed by government and nongovernmental participation, has developed an alternative document, which will be presented to the Committee of Juridical Affairs in 2003. It includes a norm in relation to abortion with impunity, which takes into account as not punishable the interruption of pregnancy in the following cases: when the person is under 12 years of age; in the case of rape; and when it is with informed consent and until 12 weeks of gestation. This would be an addition to the existing figure of therapeutic abortion.

Abortion in Costa Rica is a problem of public health; this is evident when studying the following data for the period 1990-1994:

- In 1990-1994, 12.4% of maternal deaths were because of abortions;
- In 1984-1991, the National Health Services—CCSS (Caja Costarricense de Seguro Social)—serviced an annual average of 8,669 hospitalizations for the consequences of illegal abortions.
- In 1984-1991, the rate of induced abortions per 1,000 women between 15 and 49 years in the same period was 10.36% (Brenes 1995).
- According to CCSS data for 2000, there were 9,710 abortions in Costa Rica's main hospitals.

However, these figures are aggregates, which does not permit us to see whether they were spontaneous abortions or complications because of illegally induced abortions. Also, abortions in private clinics are not registered.

It is important to point out that there does not exist a protocol in the health-system hospitals for practicing therapeu-tic abortions in case the woman's life is in danger. This is pointed out in the Parallel Report of the CEDAW, which will be presented as a recommendation in June 2003.

At the present time, women in Costa Rica are ignorant about the possibilities of having therapeutic abortions in case their lives are in danger. It is known that women receiving chemotherapy have not been informed of the possibility of abortion when faced with an unplanned and unwanted pregnancy. Instead, their treatment is suspended until the pregnancy is full term, putting both lives in serious risk.

### D. Population Programs

Costa Rica does not have a problem of overpopulation. In fact, during the coffee, sugar cane, and other harvests, there was always a shortage of labor until the Nicaraguan immigrants came. However, there are certain groups, adolescent women, Indian, and other poor women, who are the target of birth control programs. There are a few women who have as many as 18 children, but they are the exception.

## 10. Sexually Transmitted Diseases and HIV/AIDS

### A. Sexually Transmitted Diseases

There has been a gradual reduction in the reporting of most STDs, particularly gonorrhea, whose incidence plummeted from 433.8 per 100,000 population in 1982 to 123.7 in 1990, and 68.6 in 1995. The incidence of syphilis also decreased from 99.8 per 100,000 population in 1982 to 54.3 in 1990, and 44.7 in 1995. The persistence of congenital syphilis in noteworthy, with the number of reported cases each year somewhere between 90 and 150.

### B. HIV/AIDS

At the end of 1987, the national record of AIDs cases showed for the first time that homosexual and bisexual men were the most affected by the epidemic. During the next few years, this pattern worsened, and of the 1,000 cases recorded by 1996, 70% were homosexual and bisexual men (Schifter 1998).

In 1990, the first National Survey on AIDS was carried out with research on Costa Rican sexuality, including questions about when they first initiated their first sexual relations and with whom, the use of condoms or contraceptives, and so on. This was the first investigation in Latin America that clearly showed that knowledge and information and praxis did not have a perfect relationship. People knew certain things about AIDS, but did not put them into practice. A very small segment of society practiced safe sex, because several cultural factors prevented them from using condoms. What was discovered is that men have ten times more sexual partners than women, that the age of initiation had not varied over the last 40 years—it varied in only 15% of men and in 16% of women—but what had changed was the person with whom they had their first experience. Generations back, men had their first sexual encounter with a sex worker; nowadays, this only applied to a small minority. Drugs and alcohol were elements linked to unsafe sexual practices, as well as a great deal of sexual ignorance and prejudices in young generations. In 1991, the first survey of men who have sex with men in Latin America was carried out in a community with homosexual practices, where high numbers of unsafe practices were discovered. Forty percent of the men engaged in unsafe sex. This 40% was 10 times higher than studies in the U.S. found. Many of these men also had sex with women, leading to a considerable number of heterosexuals being infected with HIV.

In the 1990s, new NGOs appeared with the specific aim of combating the VIH/SIDA epidemic. ILPES was principally directed at the gay community and at men who have sex with men. Fundación Vida offered psychological support for HIV persons. Members of Triángulo Rosa were activists who worked with human rights. ASOVIHSIDA (Asociación de Personas VIH/SIDA [Association for Persons with HIV/AIDS]) was an association made up of HIV-infected persons, which offered legal advice and also worked in human rights. There was a prevention program in the Ministry of Health, and a national committee of governmental and nongovernmental organizations. However, by 1998, these programs had disappeared because of a lack of funds, with a couple of exceptions. In this period, gay activists won the battle for the right for persons with HIV to receive the medical cocktail to prolong their lives from the national health system. In 2003, Costa Rica received $4 million from the Global Fund to combat the epidemic.

According to the Fundación Vida, there are 2,340 cases of AIDS diagnosed by the Ministry of Health in March 2003; these are the cases being treated in the national health system. Many people are being treated privately and their cases are not being reported. Experts estimate that there could be around 25,000 HIV-infected persons in the country.

[*Update 2002*: UNAIDS Epidemiological Assessment: No epidemiological assessment is available for 2002.

[The estimated number of adults and children living with HIV/AIDS on January 1, 2002, were:

| | | |
|---|---|---|
| Adults ages 15-49: | 11,000 | (rate: 0.6%) |
| Women ages 15-49: | 2,800 | |
| Children ages 0-15: | 320 | |

[An estimated 890 adults and children died of AIDS during 2001.

[At the end of 2001, an estimated 3,000 Costa Rican children under age 15 were living without one or both parents who had died of AIDS. (*End of update by the Editors*)]

## 11. Sexual Dysfunctions, Counseling, and Therapies

Sexologists are definitely a new phenomenon in Costa Rica, and consequently, the subject of sex is treated in a more open manner on television and radio programs, in magazines, and in diverse literature. *Sexo Sentido* [*Sex Sense*], a very popular radio program aired by the University Radio (University of Costa Rica) is very open in its discussions of sexual topics and issues. Different sexologists who appear on *Sexo Sentido* have studied sexology in Mexico, California, Argentina, and other places, and have varied perspectives.

Viagra has made penile dysfunction a subject that can be discussed and treated. At the same time, articles about female sexual problems and therapy, and about the female Viagra or the clitoral pump to stimulate women's arousal appear in magazines and newspapers (*La Nacion* 2000). We could say that at last the truth is coming out about the sexual misery lived by so many people. However, the problem that I detect is that centuries of silence and ignorance cannot be breached merely by the high production of new information or by the new discourses about the right to pleasure. What is not named does not exist, and for many women, the very process of naming is the very first step of appropriating their bodies and their genitals. On the positive side, the state of men's and women's sexuality in this country is not that different from others, but the ice has been broken on the subject of sexuality, which is the beginning of breaking the silence.

It is impossible for men, and particularly women, to identify or acknowledge that they have a sexual dysfunction when their culture gives them no basis for comparison. For instance, a 1992 study found that two out of five women

had never experienced orgasm. Although sexologists and therapists are aware that the most common female dysfunctions are lack of feeling and arousal and the inability to reach orgasm, it is likely that 40% of Costa Rican women will not even be aware of their dysfunctional sexual relationships. In a culture that has a centuries-long taboo on the discussion of sexual matters, it is also likely that men will not acknowledge any problem with premature ejaculation and lack of erection. There are, however, some positive signs that Costa Ricans are becoming more aware of and willing to talk about what constitutes normal, healthy, and pleasurable sexual relations for both women and men.

## 12. Sex Research and Advanced Professional Education

### A. Institutes and Programs for Sexological Research

In 1988, Javier Ortiz, a trained sexologist, created Fundación Gaia (Gaia Foundation), a center for health, sexual therapy, nutrition, and so on. He had the first television program where people came to talk and the public phoned in. For the first time in Costa Rica, subjects such as orgasm, lack of orgasm, and premature ejaculation were discussed. He published a book, *The Hundred Questions and the Gender Rainbow*, where he details the most frequently asked one hundred questions, that take into account: sexual desire, the orgasms, female and male ejaculation, pregnancy, birth, and postpartum.

Mauro Fernandez, a gynecologist and sexologist, founded the Costa Rican Sexologist Institute in 1990. They do not train therapists, but guided by Masters and Johnson's research, they concentrate on sexual education, and also on research. They have produced *Lola and Paco: A Sexual Education Manual*, directed at children; a guide on non-hormonal contraceptives; a guide about the human papilloma virus; and *Pillow Manual*, a sexual education guide. Dr. Fernandez, in particular, gives many talks and participates on radio shows, where the public can phone in. In 2003, 22 women and 12 men work in the Costa Rican Sexologist Institute. There are about 50 staff people working on different projects. They assist between two and 300 clients each month, and up to about 150 clients are attended to each month by staff sexologists, gynecologists, psychologists, or lawyers. Other sexologists, including some women, have private practices.

## References and Suggested Readings

Biezans, M. H., R. Biesanz, & D. Z. Biesanz. 1999. *The Ticos. Culture and social change in Costa Rica.* Boulder, CO, USA: Lynne Rienner Publishers.

Brenes, I. 1994. *Actitudes y prácticas del aborto inducido en Costa Rica* [*Attitudes and practice of induced abortions in Costa Rica*] (Thesis for postgraduate degree in statistics). University of Costa Rica.

CIA. 2002 (January). *The world factbook 2002.* Washington, DC: Central Intelligence Agency. Available: http://www.cia.gov/cia/publications/factbook/index.html

Campos Guadamuz, A., & J. M. Salas Calvo, eds. 2002. *Masculinidades en Centro América* [*Masculinities in Central America*], San José, CR: WEM & FIG/ACDI.

Claramunt, M. C., 1999. *Sexual exploitation in Costa Rica: Analysis of the critical path to prostitution for boys, girls and adolescents.* UNICEF, Costa Rica.

Faerron, A. L. 2002. *La educación para la sexualidad en el contexto de la sociedad Costarricense: Análisis del proceso de diseño y gestión del Programa Amor Joven (1998-2001)* [*Sexual education in the Costa Rican context: Analysis of the design and execution of the Young Love Program (1998-*

*2001)*] (Thesis for postgraduate degree in the Women's Studies Program). University of Costa Rica.

Madrigal Pana, J. 1998. *El vaivén de un cabezal. Un estudio sobre los traileros en América Central y su relación con el Sida*. San José, CR: Editorial Ilpes.

Miller, T. C. 2003 (March 24). Raped, pregnant and only 9, her abortion divides Nicaragua. *Los Angeles Times*; *Newark* [New Jersey] *Star-Ledger*, p. 18.

Ortiz Gutiérrez, J. 1996. *Las 100 preguntas y el arco iris del género* [*100 questions and the gender rainbow*]. San Pedro, CR: Fundación Gaia.

Preinfalk Fernandez, M. L., 1998. *Vivencias y practicas sexuales de las mujeres jóvenes residentes en Rincón Grande de Pavas* [*Sexual experiences and practices of young female residents of Rincón Grande of Pavas*] (Thesis for postgraduate degree in Women's Studies). University of Costa Rica and National University, Costa Rica

Schifter, J. 1997/1998. *La casa de Lila. Un estudio de la prostitución masculina*, San José, CR: Editorial Ilpes, 1997. (Published in English: *Lila's house. Male prostitution in Latin America*. New York: Haworth Press, 1998.

Schifter, J., 1999/2000. *Caperucita Rosa y el lobo Feroz. Sexo público Latino*. San José, CR: Editorial Ilpes, 1999. (Published in English: *Public sex in a Latin society*. New York: Haworth Hispanic/Latino Press, 2000.

Schifter Sikora, J., & J. Madrigal Pana. 1996/1997. *Las gavetas sexuales del Costarricense y el riesgo de infección con el VIH* [*The sexual compartments of the Costa Ricans and the risk of HIV infection*]. San José, CR: Imediex, 1996. (Published in English: *The sexual construction of Latino youth: Implications for the spread of HIV/AIDS*. New York: Haworth Press, 1997.

Schifter Sikora, J., & J. Madrigal. 1997. *Ojos que no ven . . . Psiquiatría y homofobia*. San José, CR: Editorial Ilpes. (Published in English: *Eyes that do not see: Psychiatry and homophobia*. New York: Haworth Press.

Serrano Madrigal, E. 2002. *De la memoria individual a la historia social. Grupos de encuentro de las mujeres lesbianas Costarricenses* [*From individual to social history. Costa Rican lesbian women's groups*] (Thesis for postgraduate degree in Women's Studies), University of Costa Rica—National University, Costa Rica.

UNAIDS. 2002. *Epidemiological fact sheets by country*. Geneva, Switzerland: Joint United Nations Programme on HIV/AIDS (UNAIDS/WHO). Available: http://www.unaids.org/hivaidsinfo/statistics/fact_sheets/index_en.htm.

# Croatia
## (The Republic of Croatia)

Aleksandar Štulhofer, Ph.D., Vlasta Hiršl-Hećej, M.D., M.A.,
Željko Mrkšić, Aleksandra Korać, Ph.D., Petra Hoblaj,
Ivanka Ivkanec, Maja Mamula, M.A., Hrvoje Tiljak, M.D.,
Ph.D., Gordana Buljan-Flander, Ph.D., Sanja Sagasta,
Gordan Bosanac, Ana Karlović, and Jadranka Mimica
*Updates by the Authors*

## Contents

## *Demographics and a Brief Historical Perspective*

ROBERT T. FRANCOEUR

### A. Demographics

Croatia is a former Yugoslav republic east of the Adriatic Sea and opposite the eastern coast of Italy in southeastern Europe. With approximately 21,830 square miles (56,542 km²), Croatia is slightly smaller than the state of West Virginia in the United States. The Dinaric Mountains, which run from northwest to southeast mark a barren rocky region, while the Zagorje region in the north, around the capital Zagreb, is a land of rolling hills. The Drava, Danube, and Sava Rivers border the eastern fertile agricultural region of the Pannonian plain, Slavonia. The northern part of Croatia stretches about 270 miles (435 km) from the Istrian peninsula in the northwest on the Adriatic Sea to the Vojvodina region of Yugoslavia on the east. Croatia's neighbors are Slovenia and Hungary on the north, Yugoslavia on the east, and Bosnia and Herzegovina on the southeast. In the far south, Croatia shares a small border, south of Dubrovnik, with Montenegro. Croatia's western coastline, which includes many islands, stretches about 300 miles (483 km) from Slovenia at the northern end of the Adriatic Sea to Montenegro at the Adriatic's southern end, opposite the boot of Italy.

In July 2002, Croatia had an estimated population of 4.39 million. (All data are from *The World Factbook 2002* (CIA 2002) unless otherwise stated.)

**Age Distribution and Sex Ratios**: *0-14 years*: 18.3% with 1.05 male(s) per female (sex ratio); *15-64 years*: 66.3% with 1.01 male(s) per female; *65 years and over*: 15.4% with 0.6 male(s) per female; *Total population sex ratio*: 0.94 male(s) to 1 female

(CIA 2002)

**Life Expectancy at Birth**: *Total Population*: 74.13 years; *male*: 70.52 years; *female*: 77.06 years

**Urban/Rural Distribution**: 56% to 44%

**Ethnic Distribution**: Croat: 89.6%; Serb: 4.5%; Bosnian: 0.5%; Muslim: 0.4%; Italian: 0.4%; Hungarian: 0.4%; Slovenian: 0.3%; Albanian: 0.3%; Montenegran: 0.3%; Czech: 0.2%; Roma: 0.2%; others: 3.2% (2001 National Census)

**Religious Distribution**: Roman Catholic: 76.5%; Orthodox: 11.1%; Muslim: 1.2%; Protestant 0.4%, others and unknown: 10.8% (1991)

**Birth Rate**: 12.8 births per 1,000 population

**Death Rate**: 11.31 per 1,000 population

**Infant Mortality Rate**: 7.53 deaths per 1,000 live births

**Net Migration Rate**: 9.72 migrant(s) per 1,000 population

**Total Fertility Rate**: 1.93 children born per woman

**Population Growth Rate**: 1.12%

**HIV/AIDS** (1999 est.): *Adult prevalence*: 0.02%; *Persons living with HIV/AIDS*: 350; *Deaths*: < 100. (For additional details from www.UNAIDS.org, see end of Section 10B.)

**Literacy Rate** (*defined as those age 15 and over who can read and write*): 97%; education is free and compulsory from ages 7 to 15. In 1991, 9% of the population age 15 years and older had a college or university education.

**Per Capita Gross Domestic Product** (*purchasing power parity*): $8,300 (2001 est.), $4,566 (National Bank Croatia, 2001 cst.); *Inflation*: 5%; *Unemployment*: 23%; *Living below the poverty line*: 5% (World Bank Study 2000)

### B. A Brief Historical Perspective

Most probably, the Slavic Croats originally came from the region around the Polish city of Krakow. In several waves during the 6th century, Croatian tribes arrived in the region that is now Croatia, but was then the Roman provinces of Pannonia and Dalmatia. The Croats converted to Christianity between the 7th and 9th centuries and adopted the Roman alphabet under the rule of Charlemagne. In 879, Pope John XIII proclaimed the Croats independent from Byzantine and Frankish invaders. An independent kingdom was established, which reached its peak in the 11th century. Following a defeat in a war with the Hungarians in 1097, the

*Communications*: Dr. Aleksandar Štulhofer, University of Zagreb, Department of Sociology, Faculty of Philosophy, I. Lucica 3, 10 000 Zagreb, Croatia; fax: 385-1-615-6879; astulhof@ffzg.hr.

Croatian chiefs and Hungarian king politically united the two nations under the Hungarian king in 1102, although Croatia retained its autonomy.

When the Turks defeated the Hungarians in 1526, more than two thirds of Croatia fell under Ottoman rule until the end of the 17th century. Unlike other Balkan states whose religious affiliations shifted under Muslim Ottoman rule, Catholicism remained strong in Croatia, becoming in effect one of the defining traits of the Croatian identity. The rest of Croatia chose Ferdinand of Austria as its king, entering the Habsburg domain. With the 1867 establishment of the Austro-Hungarian kingdom, Croatia and Slavonia came under Hungarian jurisdiction and remained part of the Austro-Hungarian Empire until it was defeated in 1918 at the end of World War I. In October 1918, Croatia declared its independence, and on December 1, joined Montenegro, Vojvodina, Serbia, and Slovenia to become a part of the Kingdom of Serbs, Croats, and Slovenes. In 1929, the nation changed its name to the Kingdom of Yugoslavia.

When Germany invaded Yugoslavia in 1941, Croatia became a Nazi puppet state. Croatian Fascists, the Ustashe, launched a purge of Serbs and Jews. Already in June 1941, the first antifascist guerilla units, the Partisans, were organized. After Germany was defeated in 1945, Croatia became a republic in the new Socialist Republic of Yugoslavia. Unlike other communist countries in Europe, Yugoslavia was never a member of the Warsaw pact, but one of the founders of the Non-Alignment movement. On June 25, 1991, the Croatian Parliament declared its independence from Yugoslavia. A devastating six-month civil war followed, with great destruction and the loss of thousands of lives, before the advance of the Serb-dominated Yugoslav military was halted and a United Nations ceasefire was signed on January 2, 1992. In May and August of 1995, the Croatian army finally returned western Slavonia and the central region of Krajina to Zagreb's control. The last Serb-held enclave, East Slavonia, was peacefully returned to Croatian control on January 15, 1998, after being a United Nations' protected zone for several years.

## 1. Basic Sexological Premises

### A. Character of Gender Roles

Unlike other European communist countries, Tito's Yugoslavia (1945-1990), independent from Soviet influence, has been extremely open towards Western cultural production, both in terms of high and popular cultures. This influence was amplified by the fact that from the 1960s on, Croats traveled and worked extensively in the West. In addition, throughout the 1970s and 1980s, the Croatian coast on the Adriatic was a major European tourist destination. This influence changed attitudes and lifestyles in the Mediterranean part of Croatia considerably, affecting even the small island communities. As a result, contemporary Croatian culture is deeply marked by permissiveness and liberal attitudes regarding gender and sexuality. Premarital sex is an unquestionable rule, as well as the right to sexual pleasure. This is especially true for the younger generations, brought up on Hollywood movies and teen sequels, MTV, and, recently, a local edition of *Cosmopolitan* magazine.

The adult world represents a more complicated picture. In the context of sexuality, there are several lines of division within the general population. These divisions are: sex/gender, education, religiousness, and place of residence. As elsewhere, the more educated people are the more permissive and tolerant of diversity and variety. This was confirmed in numerous public-opinion surveys carried out in the last decade. Older people, who tend to be less educated, place more importance on their religious identity, and are, consequently, less permissive and tolerant. Their attitudes toward sexuality and gender roles follow the traditional Catholic pattern of the Central European past, emphasizing a rigid division of gender roles, the sexual double standard, and the rejection of all nonstandard sexual choices, particularly homosexuality.

It should be noted that the majority of Croatian men and women define themselves as religious. However, the nature of this identity is largely generation-specific. Younger generations express their religiousness both as a part of the national tradition, a marker of ethnonational identity, and as an individualized faith. Their religious identity is secularized and oblivious to the sexual moralities of the Church. According to the World Value Survey Croatia (1995), over 70% of the respondents in a nationally representative sample disagreed with the statement that religion offers the best guidance in sexual matters.

Whereas the rural areas in Croatia still exhibit elements of Catholic patriarchy, particularly in the older generations, urban places are generators of permissiveness and, somewhat less often, gender equality. It seems that Croatian public opinion is, at the moment, almost equally divided between nontraditional and permissive (more educated, younger, and urban) residents and religiously traditional men and women. This can be illustrated by a result from the 1996 Social Capital survey (Štulhofer, Karajić, & Meštrović 1996) carried out on a representative national sample. When asked whether women and men should have equal rights to sexual expression, 57% of respondents agreed. In general, women are less supportive of the traditional gender-role division.

### B. Sociolegal Status of Males and Females

The Titoist version of "socialist" transformation stressed the importance of gender equality. This was one of the departing points for the new society in leaving behind the decaying bourgeois society. Because of this ideological stance, women and men were granted equal rights since the end of World War II, especially in education and the labor market. Sex discrimination was officially discouraged and equal salaries were guarantied, although, in reality, little has been done to change the prevailing male-dominated culture. Because the feminist movement was regarded as liberal, middle-class, Western reformism, and therefore politically suspicious, the criticism of communist gender policy was severely limited. After 1990, the process of post-communist transition, especially the economic transformation, significantly affected certain privileges, such as long maternity leaves, and social services, such as preventive health services and free kindergartens, designed to improve women's social position.

Women composed 46% of the labor force in 1997, but their average salary was lower than men's. In addition, they were overrepresented among the unemployed in the age cohorts 25 to 34 and 35 to 44 in 1999. On the other hand, women are becoming more visible in politics. They occupy slightly more than one fifth of all parliamentary seats (7% in 1997), and have positions in higher education, the sciences, and top management. During the first half of the 1990s, a significant number of female professionals became entrepreneurs, helping in the development of the market economy and changing the old image of male-dominated industry. Still, women are far from similar representation and prominence in all the sectors mentioned.

Abortion has been legal in Croatia since the early 1970s. The secularized version of Catholicism discussed above is evident in the stability of attitudes and public perception regarding abortion. During the last decade, according to studies carried out in 1990, 1992, 1995, and 2000 by the Faculty of Political Science in Zagreb, the percentage of pro-choice respondents was constantly over 70%. This was the reason why the previous nationalist and pro-populationist government (1990-2000), which often sought and received support from the Catholic Church, refrained from changing the abortion law, in spite of frequent appeals from Church authorities.

The legal rights of children stem from the *Convention on the Rights of the Child* ratified in the early 1990s. Although real-life situations are different, especially in the rural areas, the new Family Law (of 1998) prohibits corporal punishment. Primary education, the first eight years of schooling, is compulsory. The legal age in Croatia is set at 18, but because of meager salaries, a housing shortage, and high rents, young people rarely leave the parental home before starting a professional career. Actually, a significant number of people continue to live with their parents, even after they have married.

## C. General Concepts of Sexuality and Love

Contemporary Croatia is a relatively permissive society, especially in the large urban centers. From the 1970s on, the traditional Catholic culture has been gradually replaced with sexual permissiveness, i.e., tolerance toward premarital, nonreproductive, and even extramarital sex. For most urbanites, sexuality equals love and pleasure. However, the relationship between these two dimensions, romantic love and erotic pleasure, is often perceived as confusingly inconsistent. Apart from the intimate dilemmas and/or rebellion it causes within younger generations, the still-dominant societal script of the unity of love and pleasure supports the continuation of the double standard. Based on the popular conviction that love is more important for women than for men, sexual capital (defined as the aggregate of individual sexual experience) is almost never evaluated in a gender-neutral way. Unlike male sexual capital, female sexual capital tends to be negatively correlated with social respectability. This remains true even for Croatian teenagers.

Regardless of the fact that most people agree that there should be no gender difference in the pursuit of sexual happiness, men and women often differ in their attitudes regarding the preferred path. According to a 1998-1999 study of urban sexual styles (Štulhofer 2000), 56% of female respondents and 33% of male respondents agreed that "sex is enjoyable only with the loved one," whereas 26% and 44%, respectively, disagreed. Interestingly, the gender gap was far less pronounced in the case of romantic love. Almost 50% of women and over 40% of men did not feel that "romantic love is overrated." Of the opposite opinion were 29% of women and 25% of men. The prevalence of the *relational concept* of female sexuality, in which love (emotions) provides justification for sexual pleasure, demands the perfect match between sexual and relationship needs. As one recent study pointed out (Štulhofer 1999a), it is precisely the women with the most active sexual lives who reported the most frequent guilty feelings about sex.

In general, it can be safely said that the majority of Croats, at least at one point in their lives, firmly believe in romantic or "true love." Notions of an ideal partner and long-lasting erotic happiness are still the essence of the prevailing image of intimate life. On the other hand, there seems to be a growing number of media suggestions, recently also found in women's magazines, stressing that, if or when love fails, one should go after the pleasure.

## 2. Religious, Ethnic, and Gender Factors Affecting Sexuality

Patriarchal characteristics of traditional cultural patterns in Croatian villages and small towns used to permeate all sexual habits. The inherited moralities are still influential in the less urbanized parts of the country, especially in the cultural reproduction of female gender/sexuality. During the last two decades, however, traditional moral codes have been continuously losing their grip, especially in younger rural generations, and have been partially replaced by the recognition of sexuality as an essential need.

## A. Source and Character of Religious Values

Traditionally, the Roman Catholic Church has held a central role in the culture and worldview of the majority of Croats. Throughout the centuries, Catholic faith has served as an ethnic marker and common interpretative denominator, and as such, it became an integral part of all the dimensions of individual and social life. Church institutions, with their educational, cultural, and legal impact, provided a general framework of life. Naturally, this included both legal and conceptual (discursive) power over sexual meanings and practices, which is probably most transparent in the case of "unfaithfulness" and related collective sanctions. In a historical perspective, it should be noted that the Catholic Church in Croatia combined the laws of the Bible and other religious norms with elements of local pagan beliefs and traditions, bringing its teaching as close as possible to the life reality of a poor rural population.

According to Catholic teachings, everything that deviates from the religious norms had to be publicly sanctioned. In essence, the aberrations were dealt with in a gender-specific manner. Two sets of rules were tacitly developed. The first, based on the symbols of female impurity, provided concepts and methods of punishment that were utilized to control women. The second, organized around the images of almighty father, a breadwinner and the head of the family, was instrumental in tolerating the heterosexual transgressions of men. This double standard is clearly visible in the Church practice regarding confession. In the case of female sexual transgressions (premarital or extramarital sex), the institution of confessional secrecy was annulled. That has often resulted in public "trials" led by a priest in which "deviant" women were punished both socially (being expelled from home, ostracized, or isolated) and symbolically—usually by stripping off her maiden symbols (cap, scarf, sash, or apron, depending on the region). The Church was notably less vigilant in cases of polygyny, when the second woman was brought into the house after the first one, the legal wife, was announced infertile. This Church control over everyday eroticism and sexuality can still be found in some remote and underdeveloped areas.

## B. Character of Ethnic Values

The cultural tradition of Croatia is a product of various regional and ethnic influences (Stein Erlich 1971/1966). Although predominantly formed by the Croatian ethnic group, its symbols and values were profoundly influenced by historic ties—primarily of an economic, military, and marital nature—with the Serbs, Muslims, and Bosnians, and the Slovenes, Italians, Austrians, and Hungarians. However, this diversity of ethnic cultural influences has a strong common denominator—religious control of sexuality, as described in the previous section. Occasional aberrations from religious codes can be found in magical rituals and practices specific for a certain locality and time.

Often a substitute for the socially proscribed "real thing," erotic and sexual fantasies and longings are expressed through folk songs and popular sayings, male vulgarities and female curses, geographical names, and nicknames. In some regions (e.g., Slavonia), where it is freely used at collective celebrations such as marriages, obscene language is much more than a subversion. Many festivities, especially those that take place in spring (Carnival) or summer, are rich with rituals that include sexual innuendoes. In spite of modern permissiveness and erotic saturation in the mass media, they enjoy popularity even nowadays.

Sexual codes and messages are also notable in folk dresses and their ornaments. Most often, one finds symbols or "simulations" of fertility, such as *guzalo*, a device that a woman would use to make her buttocks look fuller. Also, village women would use various techniques of deception to make their breasts look bigger, while men would use a codpiece or stuff their crotch with various objects to appear better endowed. Sometimes, the clothing ornaments would take the shape of a vulva or penis, or they would include images of sexually vigorous animals (a cock, rabbit, or horse). Pieces, like sashes, aprons, or maiden caps (and specific ornamentation or coloring) were frequently employed to signal female sexual status, i.e., virginity or marital commitment.

## 3. Knowledge and Education about Sexuality

### A. Government Policies and Programs

Croatia has never had a systematic, school-based sex education program and is still waiting for one. Although there were some efforts as early as the mid-1960s aimed at introducing some kind of educational program in primary and secondary education (Košiček 1965), they did not accomplish much. For the last 30 years, sex education in Croatian schools amounts to infrequent STD and HIV/AIDS one-hour medical lectures in secondary schools. Not even those minimal, non-comprehensive, and non-interactive interventions are formally organized. In most cases, they are left to the initiative of a local physician, teacher, or schoolmaster. As a consequence, most teenagers outside of the big cities receive only the most elementary information on human reproduction offered in biology class.

Recently, a small network of social scientists, medical doctors, and feminists started coordinating their efforts and pushing forward an introduction of a comprehensive sex education curriculum in Croatian primary and secondary schools. Adolescents seem to be fully supportive of such an initiative. Almost 90% are in favor of school-based sex education. Public opinion is similarly favorable. In a recent national poll (Štulhofer, Karajić, & Meštrović 1996), more than 70% of respondents agreed with a compulsory sex education program.

Interestingly, during the last decade, there might have been a peculiar form of (anti)sex education in Croatian schools. Namely, one quarter of students interviewed in a study claimed that the religious education class offered in primary schools had significantly influenced their sex lives (Štulhofer, Jureša, & Mamula 1999).

[*Update 2002*: In spite of the fact that Croatia still lacks a systematic and comprehensive school-based sex education program, an important advance was made in the education of mentally challenged youth. Under the auspices of the Croatian Association of Societies of Persons with Mental Handicap, a sexuality counseling office for mentally challenged youth was started in 1999. Based on this experience, an excellent handbook was prepared a year later (Bratković 2000). (*End of update by A. Štulhofer*)]

### B. Informal Sources of Sexual Knowledge

According to recent surveys (Hiršl-Hećej, Šikanić-Dugić, & Dobravc-Poljak 1998; Štulhofer, Jureša, & Mamula 1999), Croatian adolescents learn about sexuality primarily through youth magazines, television, and peers. The magazines, including the very popular Croatian edition of *Cosmopolitan*, extensively discuss sex, often sending conflicting messages. More precisely, they emphasize both sexual liberation and equality of young women, and the "naturally given" relational concept of female sexuality. In addition, media images often stress female beauty and erotic appeal as the central personal quality.

As elsewhere, peer pressure is one of the central aspects of adolescent sexual development. In Croatia, peers are important for the timing of the first intercourse, contraceptive choices, and the formation of sexual attitudes. However, peer influence is perceived by adolescents as moderate in effect. Less than 10% of surveyed freshmen acknowledge substantial influence of friends on their sexual behavior.

A recent study pointed out intergenerational differences in the mother–daughter conversation about sexuality. According to the results, younger generations of mothers are significantly more likely to discuss sex with their preteen and teenage daughters. These conversations seem to have an effect on the daughters' satisfaction with their first coital experience.

Although the effects are unexplored, pornography, especially explicit videotapes, is an additional source of sexual knowledge. According to a study (Štulhofer, Jureša, & Mamula 1999), 80% of female students and 98% of male students (all freshmen) are familiar with explicit movies. On average, they had their first exposure at the age of 13.

## 4. Autoerotic Behaviors and Patterns

### A. Children and Adolescents

In the past, the autoerotic behavior of children and adolescents had an extremely negative connotation, derived both from Catholic tradition and 19th-century medical concepts. If discovered, children were punished for masturbation. Masturbatory practice, especially in preschool children, was viewed by the parents either as their own failure in childrearing or as the child's developmental disorder. As a result, numerous adolescents grew up troubled by guilt feelings.

During the 1980s, adolescent masturbation was gradually normalized. A similar thing happened with the autoerotic behavior of children in the 1990s, at least within urban culture and educated circles. Nowadays, parents generally accept the fact that masturbation is a universal practice of children of both sexes. More and more, it is regarded as a normal expression of children's curiosity and body explorations. However, if a child masturbates excessively (seven to eight times a day), experts suggest that parents should pay close attention, because this can be a sign of urogenital infection, neglect, or child abuse.

In a survey carried out on a large sample of urban adolescents, ages 18 to 20 just starting college, 52% of female students and 7% of male students reported that they never masturbate. One-in-two males masturbate once a week or more frequently; among female students, this is the case with one in every ten (Štulhofer, Jureša, & Mamula 1999).

### B. Adults

According to a study on sexual attitudes and behavior in the five largest Croatian cities (Štulhofer 1999b), 3% of men between 18 and 48 years of age, and more than one fourth (28%) of women of the same age, have never masturbated. Interestingly, a significant number of respondents of both sexes (23% of women and 19% of men) stated that they ceased to masturbate. Among this group of respondents, the married ones are overrepresented, which might suggest certain moral tension between masturbation and marital sexual life.

In general, masturbation is regarded as a pleasurable and completely normal erotic activity. However, most people are extremely secretive about it, not the least because masturbation can be perceived as a sign of an inability to attract sexual partners.

## 5. Interpersonal Heterosexual Behaviors

### A. Children

*Sexual Exploration and Sex Rehearsal Play*

No data exist on the sexual activities of Croatian children. In the 1990s, child sex abuse erupted, both as a moral panic and as a public recognition of a grave, long-suppressed, and overlooked problem. As an unfortunate result, systematic research on childhood sexuality is currently regarded as far too controversial.

### B. Adolescents

*Puberty Rituals and Premarital Relationships*

According to the research on the sexual behavior of adolescents in Croatia carried out from 1971 to the present, the proportion of adolescents with sexual experience is increasing and the age of sexual debut has decreased somewhat. In 1971, 16% of adolescent girls and 30% of adolescent boys between 15 and 19 years of age had experienced coitus (Trenc & Beluhan 1973). Twenty years later, the proportion had increased to 22.1% of girls and 48.9% of boys (Štampar & Beluhan 1991). The latest studies point out that 24.3% of girls and 46.3% of boys, high school students between 15 and 19 years of age, have experienced coitus (Hiršl-Hećej, Šikanić-Dugić, & Dobravc-Poljak 1998). Living with both parents and attendance at grammar school, which is an indicator of family socioeconomic status, decrease the probability of sexual experience in urban adolescents.

On average, young people in Croatia have their first sexual intercourse at 17, but more than a third of sexually active adolescents have their sexual debut at the age of 15 or earlier (Štulhofer, Jureša, & Mamula 1999). Adolescent girls in Croatia report fewer sexual partners than their male peers; almost 40% of girls and 65% of boys between 15 and 19 years of age have had two or more lifetime sexual partners, and 22% of girls and 44% of boys have had three or more. The pattern of sexual relationships among adolescents is the well-known serial monogamy. They remain faithful to their partner until the relationship is over and then move to another relationship.

Adolescents have sexual intercourse sporadically and less frequently than older single people. The frequency of sexual intercourse among adolescents is related to the proportion of actual sexually active youth; 35% of sexually experienced girls and 39% of sexually experienced boys did not have any sexual relationship in the last three months. Whereas 26% of girls and 35% of boys had sporadic sexual intercourse, only 27% of girls and 14% boys have had sexual intercourse regularly every week.

Generally, young women report longer sexual relationships than young men do. Almost half of sexually experienced girls, in contrast to 17% of boys, reported that their longest sexual relationship lasted six months and longer; 27% of girls, and only 5% of boys, had a sexual relationship that lasted more than a year (Štulhofer, Jureša, & Mamula 1999).

### C. Adults

Reflecting the current state of Croatian sexology, no nationally representative sexual behavior surveys are available so far. The only empirical evidence regarding adult sexual behavior comes from two studies funded by popular newspapers. Both studies used relatively large samples of over 1,000 respondents and were exclusively urban. Data on sexual behavior, presented in this chapter, were collected in the more recent of the two studies (*Sexual Styles Survey*, 1998-1999; see also: Štulhofer 1999ab, 2000). It should be emphasized that younger, more educated, and financially better-off respondents are greatly overrepresented in the samples used for the following analyses.

*Premarital Relations*

Premarital sexual relations are a rule in contemporary Croatia. Most people start their sexual life as teenagers; the average age at first intercourse is 18 for women and 17 for men. Premarital sex is generally viewed as perfectly normal and its absence is often considered suspect. In a nationally representative survey on social attitudes and values (Štulhofer, Karajić, Meštrović 1996), only 16% of respondents, mostly older and of rural background, were disapproving of premarital sexual relations.

*Sexual Behavior and Relationships*

Heterosexual behavior in Croatia seems to be stamped by numerous gender differences. As in most international sex surveys, women have fewer lifetime sexual partners than men. On average, adult women report four sexual partners whereas men report nine partners. The difference is already present in adolescence.

The analysis of sexual pleasure points out another notable difference. Women experience orgasm every second time they have sex, whereas men climax nine times out of ten. This gap is partially responsible for the fact that almost 60% of female respondents faked orgasm at least once. However, the correlation between the frequency of orgasms and satisfaction with one's sex life is weak.

In terms of the frequency of sexual intercourse, most respondents have sex two to three times a week (39%) or once every week (32%). For an equal number of people (15%), sex happens either considerably less frequently ("once a month"), or considerably more frequently ("almost daily"). Asked whether they found the frequency of sex in their relationship "too low," "too high," or "just right," 25% of women and 40% of men answered that it was "too low." On the other hand, there are 23% of women and 13% of men who found the frequency "too high." Unexpectedly, when analyzing gender differences in accepting a partner's sexual advances for the sake of his or her pleasure, both female and male respondents rejected a traditional perception. Compared to women, men were almost twice as likely to engage in sex just because their partner wanted it (Štulhofer, Karajić, Meštrović 1996).

Because of the relational model of female sexuality and related social expectations, the ideal of romantic love has traditionally been somewhat more appealing to women. One indicator of this is the differential willingness to engage in fleeting sexual encounters or "one-night stands." More than half of women surveyed (54%) and one quarter of men claimed no such experience.

There is a popular belief in Croatia that women are more open and talkative about their sexuality. Men, it is believed, are less likely to discuss their sexual experience, either because of their "machismo" or because they lack the skills necessary to communicate emotionally charged personal matters. Empirical data provide some support for this perception. A significantly larger number of women (63%) than men (45%) "often" talk about their sex life with friends. Only 2% of women never discuss sex with their partners, in comparison to eight times as many men.

There is a notable absence of gender differences in overall sexual satisfaction, whether measured directly or indirectly. When asked directly, 59% of women and 51% of men consider their sexual lives satisfactory. On an indirect measure, the results are similar: 37% of women and 38% of men stated that "imagination is better than sexual reality" (Štulhofer, Karajić, Meštrović 1996).

As previously mentioned, romantic love is the dominant schema of heterosexual relationships in Croatia. The ideals of long-lasting love and erotic passion, open communication and understanding, emotional support, and loyalty are the very core of the contemporary concept of intimate relationship. It is widely recognized that, in reality, one usually has a hard time trying to realize these ideals, but nevertheless, most Croats, especially younger generations, firmly believe that romantic love is the highest intimate accomplishment. Potential partners are evaluated accordingly. When asked to rank the three most important qualities in an ideal partner, women state tenderness, loyalty, and charm. According to men, the top three characteristics are charm, fidelity, and tenderness. Physical beauty, financial success, intellect, and sensuality seem to be of secondary importance.

### Marriage and Family

Marriage remains a highly important social image in Croatia. Most people regard it as a *conditio sine qua non* of happiness and fulfillment in life. According to a 1995 nationally representative survey by the Faculty of Political Science in Zagreb, 87% of Croatian citizens disagreed with the statement that "marriage is an outdated institution" (World Value Survey Croatia 1995).

In another large-scale social survey (Štulhofer, Karajić, & Meštrović 1996), 70% of respondents described marriage as "extremely important." In comparison, 85% stated that children are "extremely important in life," but only 52% said the same for sex. The high status of marriage is also reflected in the fact that Croats marry at higher rates than neighboring Slovenes, Hungarians, or nearby Austrians and Italians.

In reality, marriage in Croatia is still far from the ideal picture of gender equality that most people start with nowadays. Because most married women work outside the home, a customary practice from the 1950s on, they are quite often faced with a double workload. Homemaking and raising children are still disproportionately woman's obligations, especially outside the few metropolitan centers. It should be noted, though, that among younger couples, there seem to be a lot more equality and a less-rigid division of spousal roles than was the case before. Another important trend is an increase in the number of single households. In 1991, they comprised 18% of all the households in Croatia.

### Cohabitation

Cohabitation is rare in Croatia, even in metropolitan settings; recent surveys suggest that only 2% of the population are living together "as married." The primary reasons for such a situation are the low standard of living and high apartment rents. There is a push factor for marriage, because the resolution of a young couple's housing problem requires, in principle, the pooling of two families' resources. Even when the financial situation is not a restrictive factor, cohabitation is usually perceived, by the couple, their friends, and families, as a prelude to marriage. Only 7% of the children in Croatia are born out of wedlock.

### Divorce

Divorce rates have been surprisingly stable since the 1960s. In 1966, there were 15 divorce cases per 100 new marriages; in 1998, there were 16. As a consequence, most children grow up in families with both parents present. The situation is somewhat different in the four largest cities (Zagreb, Osijek, Rijeka, and Split), where there are, on average, 31 divorces per every 100 new marriages (Statistički Ljetopis 1999).

### Sexual Satisfaction

In comparison to sexually active singles, married individuals are more satisfied with their sex lives. Among the former, 18% are dissatisfied and 55% are satisfied with their sexual lives; only 9% of married respondents are dissatisfied and 60% are satisfied. It seems that the declining frequency of marital sex may not be of central importance for sexual (dis)satisfaction, at least for married couples under the age of 50, most of whom have sex about twice a week.

### Extramarital Sex

According to the media, there is a rampant sexual infidelity among married couples in Croatia. Thus, it is no wonder that almost 50% of urban women and almost 40% of urban men are not sure if their partner is faithful. By contrast, our data suggest a much lower incidence of extramarital sex. One third of men and 16% of women admit that they had other sexual partners while in marriage.

### Sexuality and the Physically Disabled and Aged

At the moment, there are no studies on the sexual behavior of older people, and none on the sexuality of disabled persons. In addition, these topics are never even touched upon by the media and they remain completely invisible. The only information about the social perception of older people's sexuality can be found in the jokes that circulate in public. All of them, but especially those involving older female characters, reflect extremely youth-centered, prejudicial, and negative attitudes.

[*Update 2002*: As previously mentioned, the Croatian Association of Societies of Persons with Mental Handicap opened a sexuality counseling office for mentally challenged youth in 1999. In 2000, the Association published an excellent handbook based on this experience (Bratković 2000). (*End of update by A. Štulhofer*)]

### Oral and Anal Sex

There are no legal restrictions on any type of sexual contact. Oral sex, both fellatio and cunnilingus, seems to be a widespread practice, almost universal among the younger generations. Among urbanites between 18 and 48 years of age, 10% of women and 13% of men were never orally stimulated, and 11% of women and 9% of men have never orally stimulated their partner. Most people surveyed, men and women alike, placed oral sex at the very top of the list of sexual sensations they would like to experience more often. Anal sex is considerably less prevalent: 56% of metropolitan women and 61% of men have experienced it at least once. The relatively high numbers of respondents who tried anal sex undoubtedly reflect the specific character of the sample and cannot be generalized (Štulhofer, Karajić, Meštrović 1996).

The difference between the incidence of oral and anal sex can be explained, at least partially, by pointing out the powerful negative attitudes surrounding the latter sexual outlet. Anal sex is often identified with homosexuality and, therefore, regarded as deviant. Moreover, traditional body taboos and hygienic restrictions operate against anal eroticism, suppressing experimentation.

## 6. Homoerotic, Homosexual, and Bisexual Behaviors

To describe, in short, the position of homosexuals in Croatia, one can use the phrase "absorbed by silence." During the 1970s, in the period when the gay and lesbian movement in the United States and Western Europe was becoming a recognized political factor, Croatia was a part of communist Yugoslavia, a country where homosexuality was invisible and never discussed. It was mentioned only jokingly or used as an insult. The situation changed somewhat in the 1980s. As the AIDS epidemic became a global concern, prompting discussion about various aspects of human sexual behavior—and thus raising questions about differences—the Croatian Ministry of Health started an AIDS-prevention media campaign, in which homosexuality, when mentioned, was lumped together with prostitution and drug abuse. Many gays in Croatia remember the 1980s as the beginning of an awakening. The first gay organization appeared at the time, and later, when some bars started to welcome gay audiences, a rudimentary gay scene was created.

During the first half of the 1990s, the war for national independence and a conservative right-wing government fostered the "building of a strong Croatian society" based on Catholic traditions and ethnic identity. At the same time, however, the civil sector started to develop with support from the international community. New nongovernmental organizations (NGOs) focused on the protection of human rights, which provided a much-needed counterpoint to the official line. Still, the rights of sexual minorities were never openly discussed or promoted.

Homosexuality is rarely mentioned in the Croatian media. When it is covered, there is often a criminal subtext (homosexuality is presented as a cause or facilitator of crime) or in other "scandalous" contexts which serve to reinforce prejudices. No wonder that gay men are commonly defined as effeminate types unable to resist affectation. Lesbians are usually stigmatized as heterosexual, men-hating women going through a perverse phase, or are considered to be men trapped within a female body.

According to the results of two large national surveys (Štulhofer 1999b; Črpić & Rimac 2000), around 50% of respondents are extremely homophobic. In 1995, 53% of respondents stated that they would not like to have a homosexual person as a neighbor. Four years later, 46% of respondents were of the same opinion. Among women and the younger generations, especially in large urban centers, the social distance from gays and lesbians is less pronounced. Almost two thirds of the students of the University of Zagreb stated that their friend's sexual orientation is irrelevant to them.

It is important to note that there is no positive term for homosexual persons in Croatian. Aside from the neutral *homoseksualac* (homosexual), only demeaning and offensive labels exist, with *peder* (faggot) being used most frequently. Thus, as Croatian translators at the European Parliament have recently discovered, the word *gay* is impossible to translate.

Gay and lesbian issues are occasionally explored in off-theater plays, alternative exhibitions, and translated books. Most of these cultural events escape the public eye and media coverage. It is interesting to note that the first (and still the only) sexological book on homosexuality was published in 1986 by Košiček. Encouraging normalization and social acceptance of homosexuality, it met only marginal attention. Partially because homosexuality is still invisible, and because of the lack of self-organizing and activism, rare attempts to promote gay and lesbian rights and/or expose discrimination are usually perceived as "tasteless," and they are dismissed with comments such as: "Why do they have to advertise their private affairs?"

[*Update 2002*: In 2000, the first lesbian NGO in Croatia, LORI (Lesbian Organization Rijeka), was registered. In 2002, Iskorak—the Group for Promotion and Protection of Different Sexual Orientation, founded mainly by gay men, was registered, as well as the lesbian project, Kontra. The year 2002 seems to have been a turning point for lesbians, gays, and bisexual persons in Croatia: The first Gay Pride

was organized in the capital, Zagreb. This collective coming out resulted in many public debates, but most importantly, sexual minorities became socially visible.

[In Croatian bookstores, one can find only a few books on homosexuality, none of them written by Croatians. In June 2002, as an introduction to the first Croatian Gay Pride, a gay and lesbian NGO organized the first GLBT cultural week in Zagreb, promoting and presenting queer culture. In the same year, the NGO, Center for Peace Studies, organized a queer seminar for students and citizens. Another NGO, the Center for Women's Studies, has been organizing seminars concerning lesbian issues for several years. (*End of update by S. Sagasta & G. Bosanac*)]

## A. Children and Adolescents

The first sexual activities among children, often of a same-sex nature, are understood as exploratory play and, therefore, are perceived by most parents as a part of the growing-up process. For most gay men, adolescence represents the period, confusing and conflicting, in which the self-defining process and the confrontation with social expectations begin. Finding yourself different from others makes it equally hard to be accepted, as well as to accept your own difference. Bisexual feelings and activities are often a part of this self-defining phase. Unlike a couple of decades ago, first same-sex contacts and intimate relationships occur mostly among peers. Contacts between adolescents and adults, it seems, have almost disappeared.

## B. Adults

*Sexual Outlets, Relationships, and Lifestyles*

If we analyze personal ads in newspapers and on Web pages, we notice two distinct types of partner-seeking. The first is focused on sexual encounters with a more-or-less specific outlet. The second type emphasizes meeting and befriending a man, which may or may not include sex. What seems to be most interesting is the fact that both types of partner-seeking include a similar set of criteria for "Mr. Right." He has to be discrete, masculine, an outsider to the gay scene, and sexually inexperienced. He is someone whom you could introduce to your non-gay friends and parents as "my best pal" without arousing suspicion. The gay male who should be avoided at any cost is the *tetka* (aunt). He is too much of a "she," i.e., effeminate and passive, well known to the homosexual community, and indiscriminate in his choice of sex partners. As one of the most frequent remarks regarding gays who are "too sensitive" goes: "They embarrass us. Just look at them—no wonder that society doesn't like our kind."

Beyond placing a newspaper personal advertisement, the possibilities for finding Mr. Right involve cruising areas such as parks, public toilets, and, in the summer, the beaches along the coastline. Every larger city has at least one nonofficial gay place, a coffee shop or a discotheque. In 1999, the first openly gay nightclub (Bad Boy) was opened in Zagreb. For men living in smaller communities, weekend visits to the closest urban center have been a typical aspect of gay life. For many of them, these visits are the only chance to express their sexual identity. During the second half of the 1990s, the Internet has had a major role, both in finding partners and in strengthening homosexual identity. The first Croatian gay website was started in 1996. Today, there are several sites offering information on gay culture and lifestyles. They provide chat services, a virtual meeting space, and forums for discussing gay issues.

For most gay men, meeting in public is not easy. Because they are still closeted or have only partially come out, the choice of place is a difficult one. "I should avoid being seen in gay company," and "Do I want to be spotted in a bar that is considered to be a part of the scene?" are frequent dilemmas. An additional problem for coming out in Croatia is that, because of the economic situation, a large number of men in their late 20s still live with their parents. Economic independence is quite rare. Unlike others, gay men who manage to live with their partners have usually come out fully.

There is no specific type of relationship between gay men in Croatia. Some are open, others are monogamous. Sexual exclusivity is, usually, a matter of mutual agreement. Some couples adopt the heterosexual model of gender roles.

In regard to the lesbian population, long-term lesbian relationships are rather rare. Increased sustainability of such relationships is noticeable between more-experienced lesbians (women over 30). The economic situation, the high unemployment rate, and the pressure of Catholic and patriarchal morality all work against long-term relationships. Women who have moved to larger cities feel the need to gain experience and expand their circle of acquaintances, thus becoming the most visible lesbians on the scene. Women who are in serious relationships avoid the scene and larger gatherings in order to protect their exclusive relationships. The presence of a *butch*-and-*femme* dichotomy varies according to social class and the level of lesbian awareness. Copying the *macho* patterns of Croatian society, most Croatian lesbians tend to feel more *butch*. This should be partly understood as an attempt to reject the stereotype of the "real" woman. However, the *butch*-and-*femme* dichotomy is less present among younger lesbian women.

The lesbian community operates in small closed groups. They are highly stratified and do not allow for mixing of different social classes, professions, or social ranks in general. Within the current scene, most lesbian women have no interest in feminism or lesbian human rights. Political activism is not what the average young woman in the lesbian community has on her mind. Being interested primarily in sexual activity, they often absorb the sexism and machismo of the wider society.

Lesbian women living in provincial towns usually migrate to the capital. Some continue their migration and move permanently to Western countries, mostly the Netherlands, Finland, Sweden, the USA, and Germany.

Thus far, 1999 was the most fruitful year for lesbian activities. Kontra, the lesbian network, organized numerous workshops, and the Center for Women's Studies offered lectures in lesbian theory. Nevertheless, lesbian women are still inert when it comes to activism, so the basic need for a safe, women-only, gathering place has still not been met. Many lesbians are trying to find a substitute in cyberspace using the Croatian Lesbian website.

[*Update 2002*: Safe socializing of lesbians and gays is possible only within newly established gay or lesbian NGOs and in the one and only gay night bar in Croatia. The first was Bad Boy, which was opened in 1999 and closed in 2001, shortly after the opening of a second night bar, Global. However, the recent growth and development of the gay and lesbian movement now encourage young gays and lesbians to live their lives more openly. (*End of update by S. Sagasta & G. Bosanac*)]

*Legal Aspects and Social Status*

There is no legal prohibition of different sexual practices as long as they involve consenting adults. Homosexual, both gay and lesbian, couples are not allowed to register their partnership, nor are they allowed to marry. Furthermore, they cannot seek assisted procreation nor adopt a child. During recent discussions regarding the latest changes in family legislation, some NGO activists were trying to push for a more tolerant view on same-sex unions, but without success.

The Catholic Church is very influential in Croatia. Its status has been strengthened during war times because it represented ethnonational identity and tradition. Interestingly, the Church has been extremely silent in regards to homosexuality issues. Only recently has the Catholic press begun to echo Vatican statements on the World Gay Pride parade in Rome in late 2000 and the question of same-sex marriage.

The press has also recently explored homosexuality in the army. Unfortunately, the coverage was exclusively focused on a case of alleged same-sex abuse. It remains to be seen if homosexuality in the armed forces will become an issue to be publicly discussed. So far, there have been no such indications.

[*Update 2003*: In January 2001, a team of two young lawyers and a professor from the Faculty of Law at the University of Zagreb started a public discussion about their proposal of a Constitutional Law on Gender Equality. In May of 2002, gay and lesbian NGOs started a campaign to change the Family Act, demanding the rights to marry or to register their partnership and to adopt children. They also proposed amending the Constitution to include a statement on the unacceptability of discrimination based on sexual orientation. The Ministry of Social Welfare proposed to the Croatian government changes in the Family Act, including legalization of registration of the same-sex partnerships. In March 2002, the Ministry of Defense publicly proclaimed that homosexuality is not an obstacle to join the armed forces. At the request of Iskorak, the Croatian Psychiatric Association (CPA) wrote a letter explaining their official position on homosexuality, stating that homosexuality cannot be characterized as an illness or any mental disorder. The same request was sent to the Croatian Medical Chamber on two occasions. As of early 2003, the Chamber had not replied. (*End of update by S. Sagasta & G. Bosanac*)]

## C. Activism, Problems, and Perspectives

By the end of the 1980s, the development of civic initiatives in the former Yugoslavia had some impact on gay issues. The beginning of the war put an end to further organizing and the promotion of gay and lesbian rights. The initiative was renewed in 1999, prompted by the opening of the first gay nightclub. An NGO was founded and registered, but to this day, it has not had its public debut. At the end of 2000, a fragmentary discussion of same-sex marriage began, which included several lawyers and politicians. However, it received almost no publicity.

If one can judge by mailing-list discussions on gay Web pages and personal communications, there is a palpable dissatisfaction with the state of human rights among the Croatian gay population, especially in regards to marriage and child adoption. However, gay men still seem to be reluctant to voice their interests in the real social arena.

Feminist NGOs were the starting point for lesbian organization in Croatia, and they have remained the main support. Within the women's organizations, there were a couple of lesbian women whose efforts made a lesbian network possible. In the second half of the 1990s, Kontra was founded to motivate lesbian women from all over the country to establish a communication network. It was envisioned as a community that would join the strivings and activities of lesbian women from small towns, as well as the capital, and link them to similar international organizations. Kontra's main activity is a lesbian SOS hotline—"for women who love women." It was launched on November 24, 1997. In addition, Kontra activists organize gatherings, lesbian film evenings, and lesbian exhibitions, workshops, and lectures. Parallel with the founding of Kontra, a lesbian publishing project was launched. Because Press is oriented toward the improvement of lesbian culture and literature. In 1998, the first collection of Croatian lesbian poetry (Sagasta 1998) was published, as well as a lesbian fanzine, *Just a Girl*, serving as a discussion forum by lesbians for lesbians and a source of information for lesbian women in Croatia.

[*Update 2002*: The first officially registered lesbian group, LORI, was founded on October 19, 2000, in Rijeka. It is significant that the local government provided LORI with office space. In 2001 and 2002, LORI accomplished three projects: establishing an Internet center and a reference center, and initiating a research study funded by the central government to investigate media coverage of homosexuality in Croatia. The results point to a marginal position of gays and lesbians in Croatian society. Interestingly, the media covers almost twice as many stories of male homosexuality than female homosexuality (LORI 2001). In 2002, LORI started educational programs for lesbian women. LORI's activists are organizing numerous workshops dealing with the media's representation of homosexual rights, European Union and United Nations laws concerning human rights, collective action and lobbying, and so on.

[On January 12, 2002, a new GLBT NGO called Iskorak (Coming Out) was founded in Zagreb and immediately became a fact of public life because of an intensive media promotion. Within a few months after the registration, Iskorak had more than 100 members, and in August 2002, a branch was founded in Osijek, the largest town in Eastern Croatia. Together with the lesbian NGO Kontra, Iskorak launched a campaign for legislation changes designed to improve the legal status of sexual minorities. A national Internet gay portal (www.gay.hr) and a GLBT e-zine were launched; within a few months, the website was receiving more than two million visits (hits) per month. Also, in 2002, Kontra established the first Croatian lesbian library.

[In April 2002, gay and lesbian NGOs, together with other citizen initiatives for gay and lesbians rights, founded the National Coordination of LGBTT Groups. As a logical result of these developments, Kontra and Iskorak decided to organize the first Gay Pride in Croatia, called *Iskorak Kontra Predrasuda* (*Coming Out Against Prejudice*). The Croatian Gay Pride Organization Committee was elected with a task of raising homosexual visibility in Croatian society. Gay Pride was held in Zagreb on June 29, 2002, as a legitimate meeting of Croatian citizens. There were between 200 and 300 participants protected by almost an equal number of special police forces and security officers. Five Parliament members joined the Pride event, together with the Minister of Interior Affairs. A group of protesters, mostly skinheads, shouted insults and tried to stop the march. Real violence took place after the march, when about 20 persons were attacked and beaten in the streets. Shortly after the Pride event, a strongly negative reaction to the march appeared in the official (and most-influential) Catholic newspapers in Croatia, *Glas Koncila*. (*End of update by S. Sagasta & G. Bosanac*)]

### D. Bisexuality

Croatian society treats bisexuality almost the same way as it treats homosexuality. Both bisexual and homosexual men and women are "invisible." The only difference is that, whereas homosexuality occasionally finds its way into the press, this never happens with bisexuality. At the moment, there is no specific bisexual activity; bisexual men usually gravitate toward the gay community.

The relationship between the gay and bisexual populations is intriguing. Among gay men, one can often hear that bisexuals are in fact gay men who are unable or unwilling to accept their homosexuality. Although there are no reliable data on the number of bisexual men, most gay men are convinced that it must be high. One often encounters men in committed heterosexual relationships who seek male sexual partners. Some of them readily admit that "It is much easier to live a double life, than to be exposed." As mentioned before, many gay men recall their bisexual attempts as a phase in life.

## 7. Gender Diversity and Transgender Issues

It is very difficult to get insight into the prevalence of gender-conflicted persons in Croatia. No public data exist, but almost 100 hospital admissions a year have been attributed to diagnoses that can be related to transgender or transsexual health problems.

Transvestites, transgenderists, and transsexuals can be regarded as a phenomenon with marginal public concern. The country's development after the disintegration of the former Yugoslavia has turned the public interest to other more-immediate concerns of daily life, such as overall well-being, unemployment, and related problems, socioeconomic differentiation, and other pressing matters. However, gender-conflicted persons have been recognized, and the phenomenon has been presented in the media. In contrast to a decreasing ethnic tolerance in the last decade, public opinion regarding gender-conflicted persons has shown positive development. One could say that there is a public "silent approval" and acceptance of gender-conflicted persons. Their specific needs have been approved and their specific ways of living have been accepted.

On the other side, one could say there is a "silent disapproval" of transgender intervention among the medical professions. In spite of the absence of legislative obstacles to sex-change operations—since 1993, a person can request the change of sex in the state register—the procedure is very complicated because of the resistance of medical professionals to become involved in such procedures. Psychiatrists tend to demand extended psychological testing, counseling, and prolonged psychotherapy before approving sex-reversal surgery. Surgical procedures and hormonal treatments are difficult to fit within the health-insurance scheme, causing economic obstacles to sex change. There is neither a special institution nor doctors educated for transgender patients. A few sex-assignment-surgery procedures have been performed each year, but it is reasonable to believe that the hidden demand for transgender interventions might be much higher.

Legal issues related to sex changes are also complicated, but the law defines the problem, and the new gender status can be legally recognized. Gender-conflicted persons have not yet been organized either in formal organizations or in informal support groups. At the moment, it seems that the Internet is the most significant source of information and (international) support for transgendered people in Croatia.

[*Update 2002*: In 2000, *Tijelo Žene* (*Women's Body*), a novel on the phenomenon of transsexualism, interesting for both its artistic and sociocultural perspectives, was published in Zagreb (Bakarić 2000). In spite of its detailed and well-researched treatment of the subject, which included a fictional political turmoil caused by the public coming-out of a male-to-female transsexual, the novel did not gain wide attention. (*End of update by A. Štulhofer*)]

## 8. Significant Unconventional Sexual Behaviors

### A. Coercive Sex
*Child Sexual Abuse, Incest, and Pedophilia*

The child sexual abuse issue is relatively new in Croatia. It has been highlighted in the past few years because of an increase in media coverage and the efforts of professionals working in the field. This, in turn, has led to an increased public awareness that cases of sexual abuse do occur in Croatia. Greater awareness from both professionals and the public has had an effect on the process of reporting cases of child abuse. The data from the Ministry of Internal Affairs show a substantial threefold increase in the number of reported cases of sexual offenses against children (under the age of 14) during the past five years: 1995, 63 cases; 1996, 89 cases; 1997, 72 cases; 1998, 140 cases; and 1999, 207 cases.

Along with the increased awareness, there have been a few other factors contributing to this change. One has been the formation of a special department within the police force. The Department Against Juvenile Delinquency now employs specially educated and trained professionals dealing with the issue of child sexual abuse. Furthermore, in October 1997, a hotline for abused and neglected children, Brave Telephone, was established. In the last three years of its existence, the number of calls has tripled. More than 20 calls are received each week during a six-hour daily shift.

Unfortunately, there is still a serious lack of educated professionals and dedicated institutions. The problems of identification and prosecution of child sex abuse cases (in 1999, five persons were convicted of child rape), treatment of victims and families, and possible interventions remain. It is often the case that some professionals fail to report a case because of their ignorance, lack of information or courage, or simply because they resent legal obligations (court testimony, etc.). Another problem of vital importance is the slow implementation of the existing laws that protect children in cases of sexual abuse, both in court and during the investigation. There is no multidisciplinary approach during interviews, the legislative process goes on for a long period of time, and the predominant attitude is to dismiss the child's statement because of the lack of the court-admissible evidence. Recently, there have been some new developments in the court procedure that allow for the child's testimony to be taken in front of a camera. Because it is a skilled professional who is conducting this filmed interview, which has the legal power of testimony, this situation is not nearly as stressful as the one in which the child has to confront the alleged perpetrator and be cross-examined (Šuperina & Garačić 2000).

[*Update 2002*: In the last few years in Croatia, the awareness of the experts and the public about child sexual abuse has grown substantially, and more attention has been drawn to the problem. However, there has not been enough research done on this subject concerning the incidence and rate of abuse or the causes and consequences of abuse. Reasons for this lack of research include not only the fear or resistance of people when it comes to discussing such a "taboo" topic in a relatively conservative society, but also the lack of scientific knowledge and the nonexistence of the validated instruments for measurement of abuse experiences.

[Another difficulty in assessing the data on child abuse involves the ethical problems regarding children as participants. Multiple questioning may additionally traumatize the child, especially the sexually abused child. Ethical issues arise when the scientist conducts research and establishes that there are children in the sample with abuse experience and, at the same time, is not allowed to use the data to provide concrete help to the child. Also, parents may not allow their children to participate in such research, and the children's therapists may find that questioning is contrary to the current therapeutic goals. On the other hand, clinical samples are usually biased in the direction of the presence of more severe problems.

[Since the original chapter on sexuality in Croatia was written in 2000, the following research studies on the sexual abuse of children were carried out:

• [The Child Abuse Experience Inventory (Karlović, Buljan Flander, & Vranić 2001), based on The Comprehensive Child Maltreatment Scale for Adults (Higgins & McCabe), was validated on a sample of 328 students at the University of Zagreb. It is a questionnaire measuring different forms of child abuse, including sexual abuse. The students were given questionnaires, which they could take home with them and return anonymously. All together, 45% of the participants returned the questionnaires. Internal reliability of the whole inventory and of the Sexual Abuse Scale were shown to be high. The principal component analysis of the whole inventory extracted four factors: 1) emotional abuse and witnessing emotional abuse; 2) mild forms of physical abuse and witnessing physical abuse; 3) emotional neglect and witnessing neglect; and 4) severe forms of physical abuse and sexual abuse. Apart from screening purposes, the inventory can be useful as a basis for structured interviews.

• [In another retrospective study (Gabelica, Karlović, & Vranić 2002) carried out on 505 university students, some form of sexual abuse in childhood was experienced by 19% of respondents (25% of the female subjects and 11% of the male). Abusers are more often male family members (29% of the abused participants experienced sexual abuse by family members), or male strangers (for 52% of these participants). Sexual abuse by a friend or known person outside the family was experienced by 39% of these participants. Some participants experienced abuse from multiple sources, not just one person. The most-often experienced forms of sexual abuse are: sexually touching a child's body, genitals, or breasts, masturbating in front of the child, showing pornography, making a child touch or masturbate the adult, penetrating the child's genitals with a finger, oral sex, and so on.

[When it comes to the age at which the abuse was experienced, about 15% to 20% of the abused population experienced it at an age below 5, 39% between age 6 and 8, 26% between age 9 and 11, and 48% between age 12 and 14. It is obvious that some experienced abuse over a number of years. Regarding the awareness of what was happening during the abuse, 53% of those who had the experience answered that they were aware of it, 19% answered they were not aware of it, while 28% were not sure.

[Most of those with abuse experience (62%) have not told anyone about what happened. Some of the reasons were: not thinking it was necessary, not knowing where to turn for help, being ashamed, being afraid of threats, and thinking no one would believe it. Regarding their present need for professional help, 57% of those with sexual abuse experience feel they do not need professional help, 14% feel they do need it, while 29% are not sure about it.

• [In another research study, child sexual abuse experiences were assessed on a sample of 310 high-school students of Sisačko-Moslavačka County in Croatia. The analyses point out that 12% of the participants (18% of the girls and 5% of the boys) had experienced some form of sexual abuse in childhood. (As in the previous study, all forms of sexual contact with an adult before the age of 14 were coded as sexual abuse.) In our view, these numbers constitute a conservative estimate. It is possible that the method of collecting data (group testing) affected the results, since the participants could not feel completely anonymous.

[A big step towards a systematic approach and multidisciplinary work in the field of child sexual abuse will be the opening of the Abused Children Center in Zagreb, which was expected in late 2002 or early 2003. This will be an independent institution established by the local government and supported by the Ministries of Social Welfare and Health. The institution would integrate a variety of activities, including provision of direct help for abused children and their families, educating professionals, supervising their work, conducting scientific research, working on raising public awareness within the field of child abuse, and forensic evaluation. (*End of update by G. Buljan-Flander & A. Karlović*)]

### Sexual Harassment

Sexual harassment became a public topic only recently. Media coverage is sporadic and unsystematic, which reflects the lack of a commonly shared definition. Thus, raising awareness about the problem is still in its infancy. Like all other forms of sexual coercion, sexual harassment is, above all, gender related. Far more women than men are its victims, whereas the perpetrators are in most cases men.

There is no integrated approach to the problem. If anything, it is usually sexual harassment at the workplace that is discussed. So far, there have been a couple of television shows on the subject, as well as a booklet published by a nongovernmental agency. Other forms of sexual harassment—obscene phone calls, sexual suggestions whispered or yelled in the street, sexist jokes in schools and academia, etc.—are only rarely mentioned. Not surprisingly, most forms of sexual harassment remain unrecognized, i.e., they are not perceived as problematic. Women's complaints are often dismissed as hysterical, humorless, or simply malicious. It is not rare that a harassed woman refrains from voicing her protest, fearing that she will be perceived as overreacting.

Sexual harassment is not punishable by criminal law, but it can be part of an offense against an employee's duties. At the moment, there is only one big company in Croatia that has incorporated sexual-harassment prevention and sanctioning. Furthermore, its workers have participated in gender-equality training provided by a women's organization.

[*Update 2002*: At the beginning of 2002, the Croatian public was overwhelmed with the issue of sexual harassment in the Croatian Army. Two high officers were accused of the sexual harassment of 18 female office workers employed in a military complex in the city of Bjelovar. Given the fact that the Ministry of Defense and the military in general are notorious for their rigidity, conservatism, and male-dominated personnel and atmosphere, the harassed women were reluctant to complain to their officers. Instead, they wrote a letter to women Members of Parliament and a head of the Parliamentary Committee of Internal Affairs and National Security. The latter called a meeting with women from the NGOs for women's rights and from the Parliamentary Committee for Gender Equality (PCGE), which resulted in a series of public letters of protest requesting an investigation of this case of sexual harassment. Under this public pressure, the Ministry of Defense created a second investigating commission. The first investigation, by an entirely male commission, reached the conclusion that there was no inappropriate behavior in the case. A second investigation, including members of both sexes and a feminist psychologist, was still investigating as of November 2002. However, three major results have already been achieved:

1. the accused officers, while under the disciplinary procedure, are out of office and unable to scare or influence the witnesses;
2. all the plaintiffs were able to keep their posts, despite the fear and threats of the loss of employment if they went public with the problem; and
3. important legal changes were introduced into the Law on Military Service. Sexual harassment became one of the legitimate reasons for undertaking internal discipline procedures, and sexual harassment is now recognized as an act that violates the rights of employees (Article 58).

[As for sexual harassment in higher education, several research projects were conducted within Croatian universities in the last couple of years (Leinert-Novosel 2000; Leinert-Novosel & Štingl 2001; Janeković Roemer, Tadinac Babić, & Štulhofer 2002: http://www.ffzg.hr/dokumenti/suz_ff.pdf). The results of these research studies have been discussed at roundtables and public panels, and published in a number of articles and interviews in daily newspapers and magazines. This publicity may have influenced the readiness to report cases of sexual harassment in higher education, as suggested by an increase in reporting following the media attention (Mamula 2002). (*End of update by M. Mamula*)]

### Rape

Sexual violence, especially rape, is still a taboo, a topic rarely discussed. In spite of the efforts of women's organizations to sensitize public opinion, the general perception is that rape is an extremely rare crime. In addition, rape myths are occasionally evoked, resulting in a trivial framing of sexual violence. Even people who encounter victims of rape in their line of duty, such as healthcare workers, the police, and court officers sometimes express similar views. This directly influences the number of filing charges and the prosecuting of such cases. On the other hand, women's experiences and data collected by women's groups and nongovernmental organizations suggest that sexual violence in Croatia is much more frequent than presented by the police, criminal courts, or media. According to the records of the State Bureau for Statistics, there were 100 cases of rape reported to the police in 1999. The prosecution was started in only 66 cases; 55 persons were convicted for rape and 13 for attempted rape (Šuperina & Garačić 2000).

However, if we take into account the records of women's organizations, the real numbers seem to be significantly higher. According to a preliminary analysis of data collected from five women's counseling centers (called Stop the Violence Against Women), for each reported rape, there may be up to 19 unreported rapes. In a study carried out on a sample of urban women between 18 and 48 years of age, only 3% of all cases of sexual victimization were reported to the police (Štulhofer 1999b). The reasons given for not reporting rape are numerous. Usually the perpetrator is an acquaintance, friend, or lover of the woman, which makes reporting socially more complicated, not to mention the additional difficulties such relationships create in the legal case. Furthermore, women often face an embarrassing and frequently humiliating court procedure, disbelief, and even ridicule. Police and court officers do not receive any training in dealing with victims of sexual violence. Finally, many sexually assaulted women, especially those living in rural areas, are unwilling to disclose what happened to them because of shame and/or fear of stigmatization, both within and outside their families.

According to the 1997 Criminal Code, rape is defined as coercive coitus or a coital equivalent (anal or oral penetration), and penalties range from 1 to 10 years of prison. It is important to note that in present legislation, since 1997, rape is considered as a criminal offense both inside and outside of marriage. The law proscribes that if an offender and a victim live in a marital union, the offender will be prosecuted only by the victim's private lawsuit. Because the recognition of marital rape is a relatively recent legal innovation in Croatia, and also a rarely discussed one, a large number, or even the majority, of women may be unaware of it (Šuperina & Garačić 2000).

*[Trafficking in Women and Children*

[*Update 2002*: Despite many reports about the growth in the trafficking of migrants to the West from Central and Eastern Europe and the Commonwealth of Independent States (the former Soviet Union), very little research has actually been conducted on this subject. Reports are often based on journalists' investigations and police records. Main routes from the Balkan region to Western Europe seem to lead from the Federal Republic of Yugoslavia to Hungary and Austria. Alternative routes lead through Bosnia and Herzegovina and Croatia to Slovenia, or across the sea from the Croatian coast to Italy.

[Croatia seems to be a transit country for trafficking in women and children for sexual exploitation (TWCSE) en route to Western Europe. However, during the war, because of the presence of international military forces, many foreign women ended up in Croatian illegal brothels. Croatia shares its borders with Bosnia and Herzegovina and the Federal Republic of Yugoslavia, where illegal migrations and trafficking in women are very extensive. According to the Bosnia and Herzegovina report on TWCSE, most trafficked women enter Bosnia and Herzegovina illegally. From Moldavia, Romania, and Ukraine they are brought by car to Belgrade or Novi Sad. Traffickers have "collecting centers" in Serbia, where they keep these women until they arrange their travel to Bosnia and Herzegovina. Many women trafficked from Eastern Europe enter Bosnia and Herzegovina via Bijeljina. The staging area for trafficking, near Bijeljina, is a huge unregulated marketplace, known as "Arizona," with several brothels situated near the border between the two Bosnian entities, Croatia and the Federal Republic of Yugoslavia. At this marketplace, most women are eventually sold to Bosnian, Croatian, or Slovenian traffickers.

[Over the last two years, counter-trafficking activities in Croatia have been initiated by international organizations in an attempt to target all relevant partners. As a result of this work, a roundtable on trafficking in human beings was held at the Organization for Security and Co-operation in Europe (OSCE) Mission to Croatia in cooperation with the International Organization for Migration (IOM) at the end of 2000. The reason behind the meeting was the necessity to build up a partnership among governmental agencies/institutions, parliamentarians, international organizations, embassies, and international and national NGOs in order to initiate and implement better legislation, law enforcement, prevention activities, and victim assistance and protection programs. The outcomes were the initiation of the National Counter Trafficking Body (though its coordinator was not appointed until June 2001), and subsequently, the inclusion of counter-trafficking activities in the National Plan of Action drafted by the Government Commission for Gender Equality. In addition, a team of social researchers was employed to carry out an assessment study.

[The report was presented at the end of 2001, after more than five months of fieldwork, during which numerous interviews were held with police officers, clients, traffickers, bar owners, social workers, journalists, and, despite all the ef-

forts, with only a few trafficked women (Štulhofer, Raboteg-Šarić, & Marinović 2002). The research combined field interviews, content analyses of major Croatian newspapers and magazines, a public-opinion survey (regarding the perception and information on TWCSE), and an analysis of police records. In brief, the report pointed out the changing dynamics and structure of TWCSE in the post-war period, as well as numerous problems with policing—ranging from outright corruption to systematic minimization and misrepresentation of the problem. The authors suggested nine operative measures aimed at increasing the efficiency of combating smuggling-in people, increasing the efficiency of combating TWCSE, and establishing programs providing aid to the victims of TWCSE.

[Following the recommendations and responding to the ensuing media campaign, Croatian authorities intensified collaboration with international organizations. Currently, a shelter house for the victims of TWCSE has been approved and the project is underway. Important legal reforms, informative campaigns, public education, and special training for the police and border patrols still need to be introduced in Croatia. (*End of update by A. Štulhofer*)]

## B. Prostitution

The available data concerning the scope of prostitution are very partial and more often based on estimates than on real documentation. So far, there has been only two social science studies on prostitution in Croatia, both of very limited scope. The actual number of prostitutes in Croatia, therefore, remains unknown. Here, as well as in most other countries, police reports represent the only source of information regarding the scope of prostitution. In 1999, there were 365 registered prostitutes in Zagreb only. (Some recent journalistic estimates go as high as 500.) If we talk about trends, there is a clear increase in the number of prostitutes registered by the police (120 registered in 1996 versus 365 in 1999), but it has to be taken into account that the forms, or types of prostitution, are changing too (Šuperina & Garačić 2000).

Croatian law defines prostitution and sexual solicitation as a punishable offense against public order and morality. Convicted persons are fined or sentenced with up to 60 days of prison time. On the other hand, organizing prostitution (pimping) is a criminal act. The police generally focus on prostitutes who are lower in the hierarchy, that is, those who solicit on the streets, while prostitutes from hotels, massage parlors, and the like, are usually "protected," often because of their clients' social status. Because of the legislative regulations, sex workers are not only stigmatized and marginalized, but also deprived of any kind of healthcare. There are no state or NGO-sponsored programs offering medical, legal, or educational assistance to sex workers. Recently, the STD and HIV/AIDS concerns were stated as the main reason behind a low-key initiative for decriminalization of prostitution in Croatia.

The post-communist turmoil (transition) and related social costs, the war and the arrival of international military forces, the development of a market economy and booming entrepreneurship, as well as the opening of state borders have led to the increase in prostitution and the development of different forms of prostitution, previously unknown in Croatia. This mostly applies to massage parlors, escort services, call girls, and nightclubs. Contemporary prostitution in Croatia generally exists in three forms: street prostitution, the so-called cellphone prostitution, and the elite prostitution.

The majority of women who solicit on the streets are Croatian (70%), but there is also a significant number of women from Bosnia and Herzegovina. The majority of elite prostitutes, working in nightclubs, hotels, or escort agencies, come from Eastern Europe, mainly from the Ukraine (52%). Only 10% of the high-class prostitutes or call girls are local women. A comparison of the age of street and elite prostitutes reveals that street prostitutes are significantly older, generally 39 to 43 years old, than elite prostitutes (24 to 28 years of age). Another significant difference between street and elite prostitutes is their education. Whereas most street prostitutes have only an elementary-school education—none of them has any college or university education—those of higher rank have, on average, completed secondary-school education. In addition, every fifth elite prostitute has a college or university degree (Šuperina & Garačić 2000).

As has already been stated, the war, the arrival of international forces, and the social costs of transition have, both independently and combined, prompted the growth of prostitution in Croatia. There seems to be a growing number of trafficked women from Eastern Europe feeding this growth. According to police reports, most of them came illegally to Croatia in the hope of finding good paid work in nightclubs, massage parlors, and the like. Of those arrested and then deported, 47% have been working and living in nightclubs.

[*Update 2002*: In September 2002, without warning, the Minister of Internal Affairs announced his initiative to legalize prostitution. The statement immediately provoked a heated public debate. On one side, there are those who advocate decriminalization and fiercely oppose legalization, claiming that legalization will benefit the state budget, but not sex workers. On the other side are those who claim that legalization would create better conditions for control and official supervision over the activity. Interestingly, both sides agree that Croatian society is not yet ready for the legalization, having in mind the potential message this reform could send to the large contingent of the unemployed. So far, the Church has been surprisingly silent on the issue. (*End of update by P. Hoblaj*)]

## C. Pornography and Erotica

Croatian law does not prohibit the production and distribution of pornography, unless it is child pornography. However, legal sanctions penalize the broadcasting of pornography on radio and television. Although there is no explicit legal definition of "pornography," public exposure and the sale of publications with explicit sexual materials are prohibited, unless wrapped in non-transparent covers, everywhere, except in sex shops. In reality, explicit magazines are sold on every newsstand.

There are a dozen sexually explicit magazines currently sold in Croatia. Soft-core magazines include Croatian editions of *Playboy* (circulation about 45,000) and *Penthouse*. Sex shops can be found in all larger cities. Explicit videotapes are available in all video-rental stores. (According to a recent study carried out on a metropolitan sample, 26% of women and 41% of men find sexually explicit movies "considerably arousing.") The video revolution has driven all but one X-rated movie house, located in the Croatian capital, out of business. As elsewhere, the fast-growing popularity of the Internet offers wide new possibilities of pornography consumption. Although their popularity is in decline, it is interesting to note that peep-show theaters are registered as providing "cultural entertainment."

[*Update 2002*: Croatian sexually explicit Internet pages started to appear only five years ago. By the beginning of 1998, the first sex site was registering up to 10,000 daily visits. In the meantime, several commercial erotic sites were started, as well as numerous amateur ones. There is no special legal treatment of these sites, and the only requirement for starting a commercial sexually explicit website is to register a company offering online services. (*End of update by P. Hoblaj*)]

## 9. Contraception, Abortion, and Population Planning

### A. Contraception

How common is unprotected sex among Croatian youth? Recent surveys found that 53% of adolescents used condoms during their first intercourse; at the most recent intercourse, 48% of girls and 57% of boys used condoms. Ten years ago, the figures were 10% and 24%, respectively. The surveys confirmed that younger generations are more likely than older generations to practice safer sex at first intercourse. Still, 22% of sexually active adolescents use no means or methods of contraception, and 21% use unreliable methods such as coitus interruptus or natural methods. Only 6% of surveyed adolescents use hormone pills. Forty percent of adolescent girls and 43% of boys believe that the pill jeopardizes the health and looks of young women.

Although condom use has increased substantially, contraceptive use is far from consistent. Less than half (43%) of urban adolescents in Croatia use some form of protection regularly. We can only speculate about the rates of contraceptive use in rural areas, but they are most probably significantly lower. Because Croatia lacks any systematic sex education, inconsistent contraceptive use should not be surprising. According to Hiršl-Hećej, Šikanić-Dugić, and Dobravc-Poljak (1998), 67% of the surveyed secondary-school students received basic information about family planning and contraceptives in schools. Only 46% of them have talked with their parents about those issues.

In Croatia, teenage women can obtain hormonal pills from a gynecologist, but the low-dose pills appropriate for this age are not covered by medical insurance. Their high price makes them unaffordable for a large number of young women. The majority of contraceptives are not included in the national health-insurance system. Reproductive health and contraception counseling centers for teenagers are extremely rare, and there is a pronounced deficit of youth-friendly reproductive health services, birth control counseling, and distribution of contraceptives in Croatia.

Sexual behavior and reproductive health are still sensitive issues for youth, issues fraught with social taboos and personal inhibitions. The major source of information about protection from pregnancy and sexually transmissible diseases (STDs) are teen magazines and television. Knowledge about STDs is fragmentary, except for HIV/AIDS. Less than a quarter of adolescents have ever heard of chlamydia trachomatis (16%) and human papilloma viruses (23%). However, the knowledge and awareness of HIV/AIDS has significantly contributed to the increased use of condoms. Although the share of adolescents not using contraception has decreased and the number of adolescents using condoms has increased, there is still a high percentage of sexually active adolescents who use no protection. This reflects the lack of sexual and health education, accessibility and availability of counseling services, and affordability of contraceptives.

Because no representative sex-behavior study has ever been carried out, data on adult contraceptive use are fragmentary and illustrative at best. In a sample of metropolitan residents between 18 and 48 years of age (Štulhofer 2000), 30% stated that they always use some form of protection. On the other hand, almost every fifth respondent (19%) never uses contraception. Most urbanites use condoms (43%) and hormonal contraception (25%). Of other methods, 14% use the IUD, 6% use "natural methods," and 10% practice coitus interruptus (withdrawal). Among those who have one-night stands, more than a third (35%) never use condoms. A slightly lower percentage of respondents (32%) use condoms every time they have a brief sexual experience. When asked if the responsibility for contraceptive use should be placed more on women than men, 27% of respondents agreed and 49% of respondents disagreed with the statement. Among the latter, women and younger respondents were overrepresented.

### B. Teenage (Unmarried) Pregnancies

Only 5.2% of all live births in 1998 were to mothers 15 to 19 years old; slightly more than one quarter of these (25.7%) were unmarried. There has been an overall decline in adolescent birthrates in the last decade. The percentage of total live births to mothers under age 20 was 8.4% in 1989, which decreased to 5.2% in 1998. In 1991, the adolescent birthrate, live births to women under 20 years of age per 1,000 women aged 15 to 19, was almost 30; in 1998, it decreased by almost half (16.5). It is unclear whether and how much the decrease in teenage pregnancies was caused by changes in female education and living conditions during the transition period.

Aside from the decline in adolescent birthrates during the last decade, another important change has occurred. Marriage rates have declined even more quickly, and more births than before are occurring among *unmarried* teen mothers. The share of nonmarital births to mothers under the age of 20 was 17.1% in 1989, which increased to 25.7% in 1998.

### C. Abortion

Since 1978, abortion can be induced on the request of a pregnant woman until the tenth week after conception. After ten weeks, an abortion has to be approved by a professional committee, taking into account medical reasons or the fact that the conception is a consequence of a sexual crime. A 16-year-old woman can seek an induced abortion by a simple request. For younger persons, the consent of the parents or another legal representative is required. In spite of legal obligations, some hospitals refused to perform abortions during the 1990s, following the neo-conservative, pro-life ideals of the right-wing government. This refusal to perform abortions was based on an organized and coordinated conscientious objection of gynecologists "following their religious and moral feelings." As of late 2000, abortion was not included in the health-insurance system. The costs, exceeding US$200, are roughly two thirds of an average monthly salary.

In 1999, a little over 8,000 notifications of legally induced abortion were received, a continued decline in comparison to previous years. Most women who requested an abortion were between 30 and 39 years of age and already had two children. According to official statistics, the incidence of abortion remained stable for the 15 years prior to 1990, with about 40,000 to 50,000 abortions per year, or 70 to 80 abortions per 100 live births. In the last ten years, the number of legally induced abortions has declined sharply: 1990, 38,644; 1992, 26,223; 1994, 19,673; 1996, 12,339; and 1999, 8,064). However, these statistics do not include abortions carried out in private clinics, a practice that is illegal. The abortion rate (the number of legally induced abortions per 1,000 women age 15 to 49) was 34 in 1990 and 7 in 1999! The abortion rate among women under age 20 was 8 in 1991, which decreased to less than 4 in 1998. The abortion ratio, abortions per 100 live births, was 84 in 1990, which decreased to 19 in 1998.

### D. Population Programs

In the past three decades, the number of births in Croatia has decreased by more than a third, from 69,229 in 1979 to 45,179 in 1999. The falling child delivery trend in younger age groups (below age 20) and the rising child delivery trend (above the age of 35 years), characteristic of the developed countries, have also been found in Croatia. The decline in number of births that has lasted for years was accelerated by the war-related events. As a result, Croatia entered a depopulation trend (negative population growth) in 1991. The war was only one of the factors triggering negative population growth. Among others were and still are the rising unemployment rate, decreasing social and economic well-being, and other transition-related factors. During the 1990s, the government made some efforts to promote population growth. Aside from occasional nationalistic and patriarchic declarations emphasizing motherhood as the prime female contribution to the new Croatian State, there was hardly any clear and systematic policy. A limited amount of money was provided as a "child incentive," both as a bonus and tax reduction. Families with three or four children received additional benefits. None of these efforts have produced any effect.

## 10. Sexually Transmitted Diseases and HIV/AIDS

### A. Sexually Transmitted Diseases
*Incidence, Patterns, and Trends*

At present, the incidence of the "classical" sexually transmitted diseases (syphilis and gonorrhea) and HIV/AIDS is relatively low. There are no signs of an STD epidemic developing as a consequence of war-related and/or transitional conditions. The incidence of gonorrhea and syphilis steadily decreased during the 1980s and the 1990s, as shown in Table 1. Interestingly, the opposite trend is present in the adolescent population. The incidence rate of newly registered cases of syphilis and gonorrhea among individuals under the age of 20 was 8.6 in 1989, which increased to 12.9 in 1998.

Our clinical experience and STD research reveal a notable increase in the incidence and prevalence of all other sexually transmitted diseases, including chlamydia trachomatis, HPV infections, genital herpes, nonspecific urethritis, hepatitis B, pelvic inflammatory disease (PID), and dysplasiae (CIN), particularly among adolescents. Within various samples of sexually active adolescent women in Croatia, the prevalence of chlamydia was 10 to 27%, HPV infections 9 to 12%, candida infections 28%, and abnormal cervical cytological findings of PAP smears (CIN I, CIN II, CIN III) 22%.

It should be noted that the accurate number of sexually transmitted diseases is currently unknown, because the

### Table 1

#### The Incidence of Syphilis and Gonorrhea

| Incidence of Syphilis | | Incidence Rate of New Cases |
|---|---|---|
| 1985 | 129 cases | |
| 1989 | 80 cases | 1.71 per 100,000 inhabitants |
| 1995 | 50 cases | |
| 1998 | 14 cases | 0.31 per 100,000 inhabitants |
| **Incidence of Gonorrhea** | | **Incidence Rate of New Cases** |
| 1985 | 1,597 cases | |
| 1989 | 446 cases | 9.52 per 100,000 inhabitants |
| 1995 | 52 cases | |
| 1998 | 48 cases | 1.07 per 100,000 inhabitants |

health statistics are notoriously incomplete. Presumably, the incidence of the so-called "new" sexually transmitted diseases equals the rates in Western European countries. The incidence of the "classical" STDs seems to be much lower than reported in Eastern Europe.

*Availability of Treatment and Prevention Efforts*

The law requires that all new cases of the "classical" STDs must be reported to the central epidemiological service and the National Institute of Public Health. Infected persons are required to disclose information about sexual partners to health professionals. Diagnosis and treatment are easily available in all larger cities.

## B. HIV/AIDS

*Incidence, Patterns, and Trends*

Croatia is among the countries least affected by the HIV/AIDS epidemics. The incidence rate of AIDS in Croatia is less then 4 per 1,000,000 inhabitants. HIV transmission occurs through sexual activity and needle sharing. Because of the social stigmatization of homosexuality and the complete absence of relevant behavioral research, there is no systematic information about male-to-male HIV-infection routes.

The first case of AIDS in Croatia was reported in 1986. In the next 13 years, there were 151 other cases, 84% of them involving male patients. As of the end of 1999, almost two thirds of those patients had died. The number of new cases remained stable during the 1990s, with 11 cases (1989), 14 cases (1993), 15 cases (1995), 16 cases (1997), 12 cases (1998), and 15 cases (1999). The structure of all AIDS cases between 1986 and 1999 is shown in Table 2. Regarding young people, one case has been reported in the 15-to-19 age group and six in the 20-to-24 age group.

In recent years, the proportion HIV/AIDS-infected persons who are homosexual or bisexual has decreased. At the moment, the prime risk group seems to be composed of heterosexual men whose profession requires spending long periods of time abroad, such as sailors. There are no new HIV/AIDS cases among hemophiliacs, confirming that blood products are controlled and safe; HIV testing is compulsory for blood donations.

The low incidence of HIV infection in Croatia is well-demonstrated by the results of preventive and anonymous screening for HIV. In the anonymous testing of 179,919 persons in 1999, only 45 were found to be HIV-positive, a very low percentage of 0.025%. The incidence is even lower among blood donors (0.001%). Keeping in mind that a rapid assessment study of heroin use in five Croatian cities in 1998 pointed out a widespread needle-sharing practice, there is still a surprisingly low percentage of HIV-positive persons (0.6%) among drug addicts (Ajduković, Ajduković, & Prišlin 1991).

*Availability of Treatment and Prevention Programs*

Triple antiretroviral HIV/AIDS therapy, consisting of a protease inhibitor plus two nucleoside analogue reverse tran-

### Table 2

### Populations Affected by AIDS

| Population | Percentage of Total |
|---|---|
| Homosexual/bisexual individuals | 46.7% |
| Heterosexual individuals | 25.0% |
| Partners of HIV-positive individuals | 10.5% |
| IV-drug users | 9.2% |
| Hemophiliacs | 5.3% |
| Children of HIV-positive mothers | 1.3% |

scriptase inhibitors, is currently available in Croatia. Since 1999, the therapy is covered by the national health-insurance system. (The national insurance also includes the treatment following the accidental professional exposure of health workers.) Consequently, the proportion of HIV-positive individuals who developed AIDS-related symptoms has decreased substantially. The new prognostic techniques using viral-load tests have been available in Croatia since 1998.

Serological examination regarding HIV status was inaugurated in Croatia in 1986. Voluntary testing for HIV antibodies is encouraged, and counseling for HIV-positive persons is provided. According to a special instruction, health professionals are obliged to protect the anonymity of HIV-positive persons and AIDS patients.

An HIV/AIDS-prevention and control program prepared by the National Commission for HIV/AIDS Prevention in 1990 includes the implementation of a broad range of preventive measures. These include strict control of human blood products, relevant public education, staff training, and the development of diagnostic facilities. Several NGOs joined in organizing needle-exchange programs and educational campaigns that were usually focused on adolescents. In the second half of the 1990s, the Ministry of Health started a large and expensive campaign aiming at HIV/AIDS prevention among the general population. Brochures, fliers, television advertisements, and billboards promoting responsible sexual conduct were all over the country for more than six months. The main characteristic of the campaign was the way it specified the notion of sexual responsibility. It stressed the importance of sexual monogamy and alluded to condom use, although condoms were never mentioned by name nor graphically presented. The huge campaign completely refrained from providing the central piece of information regarding condoms in HIV/AIDS prevention. No evaluation study was ever carried out.

For the majority of the Croatians, the main source of information about HIV/AIDS is the mass media. Adolescents have more and more accurate information about AIDS than the rest of the population. As could be expected, attitudes toward HIV-positive individuals and AIDS patients are more negative among older generations. In the recent European Values Survey (Črpić & Rimac 2000), 46% of respondents in a nationally representative sample said that they do not want AIDS patients as neighbors.

*[Rapid Assessment and Response (RAR)*

[RAR is a means for undertaking a comprehensive assessment of public health issues, and it is particularly useful for assessing complex public health issues, such as sexual behaviors, HIV/AIDS, and other sexual and reproductive health issues. RAR is triangulating data obtained through a series of quantitative and qualitative data sources and provides insights into patterns of risk behaviors, as well as suggesting outlines required for interventions.

[RAR research in 2001 focused on the assessment of risks associated with HIV/AIDS in especially vulnerable young people in Croatia—drug users, sex workers, and out-of-school youth (Kuzman, Mimica, Mardešić, et al. 2002). The field study was carried out in the four largest cities (Zagreb, Rijeka, Osijek, and Split). The team surveyed 265 adolescents and carried out 41 in-depth interviews and 15 focus groups. In addition, a number of professional service providers and policymakers were interviewed. The findings revealed that young people do perceive recreational drugs as influencing both the frequency of sexual contacts and condom use. Even so, accidental or unplanned sexual contacts often happen under the influence of drugs, and condom use (in these episodes) is sporadic at best.

[Comparing the results of RAR with earlier research findings from school-based KABP surveys, it seems that HIV/AIDS and STD-risk perception is much lower among especially vulnerable youngsters. Only about 15% of the respondents report regular condom use. The major obstacle to condom use seems to be attitudinal, as young people of both sexes associate unprotected sex with a display of trust and confidence in the partner. There is also a widespread belief that condoms reduce sexual pleasure.

[The RAR study recommended several measures that would decrease the rate of HIV/AIDS-associated risk behaviors, particularly among people belonging to highly stigmatized groups, such as drug users, sex workers, and men having sex with men. In order to achieve a desirable impact, the issues of stigmatization and marginalization must be politically addressed. (*End of update by J. Mimica*)]

[*Update 2002*: UNAIDS Epidemiological Assessment: The reported incidence of AIDS in the last few years is between 1.5 and 4.2 per 1,000,000 population. Eighty-three percent of reported AIDS cases were acquired through sexual routes of transmission. Diagnosed HIV infections are reported to a national database. By the end of 2001, a total of 327 HIV cases were reported. The rate of reported syphilis cases remains at the range of 0.2 to 0.4 per 100,000 population.

[The estimated number of adults and children living with HIV/AIDS on January 1, 2002, were:

| Adults ages 15-49: | 200 | (rate: 0.1%) |
| Women ages 15-49: | < 100 | |
| Children ages 0-15: | < 10 | |

[An estimated less than 10 adults and children died of AIDS during 2001.

[No estimate is available for the number of Croatian children who had lost one or both parents to AIDS and were under age 15 at the end of 2001. (*End of update by the Editors*)]

## 11. Sexual Dysfunctions, Counseling, and Therapies

In contrast to the broad public and medical attention to contraception and STDs, sexual dysfunction has never been an issue of great interest for Croatian medical professionals. There is no comprehensive approach to sexual dysfunctions that makes a rather strict distinction between different types of dysfunction. At least three different types have been recognized, and each is diagnosed and treated by a different medical specialist.

Sexual dysfunctions related to an underlying chronic disease causing the dysfunction, for instance, impotence in male diabetic patients or painful intercourse in postmenopausal women with vaginal atrophy, are considered as a complication of the chronic disabling disease, and accordingly, are diagnosed and treated by an internist, a vascular surgeon, or a gynecologist. Various medicament treatment possibilities are available for these medical problems, and most of them are covered by health insurance. However, surgical procedures, such as penile prosthesis implantation, are not available and patients in need have to be surgically treated out of the country.

Sexual dysfunctions related to psychological causes are considered a psychological medical problem. Impotence or sexual aversion caused by a psychological dysfunction is usually referred to a psychiatrist or a psychologist both to confirm the diagnosis and for treatment. The treatment includes psychotropic drugs or psychotherapy, both mainly available within the health-insurance scheme.

Finally, sexual dysfunctions related to partner-relation problems are considered a relationship problem. Mostly, these conditions are confirmed by family doctors and treated by various experts: family physicians, psychologists, marital counselors, and others. If generated in the premarital relations of youngsters, these dysfunctional problems are regarded as the problems of adolescence. Treatments are based on different psychological approaches not always covered by health/social insurance.

This division in diagnostics and treatment of sexual dysfunction problems are the result of a lack of any specific education in sexual dysfunction. There are no specialists in sexology, and sexology courses in medical training are rare and insufficient. For that reason, there is no comprehensive approach to the treatment of sexual dysfunction. Moreover, because there is no medical data collection specifically on sexual health issues, it is impossible to get an insight into the incidence and prevalence of sexual dysfunction. As previously explained, these problems can be registered as complications of chronic diseases, psychological problems, or marital problems. In these circumstances, family physicians are regarded as the medical professionals who have more experience with patient complaints related to sexual dysfunction than any other specialty. However, there is no evidence to support that estimate, nor is there any evidence about how well the family physicians respond to patients' complaints.

[*Update 2002*: In 2001, the first research study on the prevalence of sexual dysfunctions was carried out on a community sample of 547 metropolitan women between 20 and 60 years of age (Štulhofer, Gregurević, Štulhofer, 2002). (A similar study of male sexual dysfunctions was in progress as of late 2002.) The results suggest that a significant proportion of women experience moderate to severe difficulties in sexual functioning: 14.5% report the lack of sexual desire, 9.2% arousal difficulties, 20.1% orgasmic problems, and 10.4% sexual pain problems. Altogether, 36% of the respondents seem to be suffering from one or more sexual dysfunctions. Noteworthy, homosexual and bisexual women report better sexual health than heterosexual women. [There has been no significant breakthrough in the diagnostic and/or therapy of sexual disorders, apart from the registration of Pfizer's Viagra. Following the registration, a series of educational seminars on erectile dysfunction was organized for medical doctors. The main agenda was to promote the new drug. Although registered, Viagra is not covered by the national health-insurance scheme. (*End of update by A. Štulhofer*)]

## 12. Sex Research and Advanced Professional Education

### A. Graduate Programs and Sexological Research

At the moment, sex research in Croatia is an exception, a strange enterprise within the social and medical sciences. There are no sexological institutes, research units, or programs educating future sexologists. Also, there is no sexological association or any related civic initiative at the moment. The reasons behind this sorry state of affairs are several. The main one seems to be the lack of any sexological tradition in Croatia before the 1970s. In addition, sex research is considered to be of marginal scientific importance, both within social and medical science circles. Consequently, very few scholars and/or practitioners have incentives to specialize in sexology, which, as mentioned, requires studying abroad. Finally, there is a funding problem. So far, sex research in Croatia has been financially supported either by international health organizations or by local popular journals.

A brief history of sex research in Croatia begins in the 1970s, when the first surveys exploring the sexual behavior and attitudes of primary and high school students were carried out by a group of gynecologists and social medicine specialists. Similar studies, mostly small-scale, continued in the next decade. Because almost all of them were marked by a lack of theoretical concept and by methodological and statistical naiveté, they have resulted in very limited advancement in scholarly understanding of the observed phenomena.

Recognition of the HIV/AIDS problem at the end of the 1980s prompted a new phase in sex research in Croatia, marked by the entry of the social sciences. As a result, the first (and still the only) large-scale sex study was carried out on a national sample of young people (Ajduković, Ajduković, & Prišlin 1991). Theoretically and methodologically well-grounded, it measured shared information on HIV/AIDS, related-risk assessment, and risk-taking behaviors. Unfortunately, societal concerns with HIV/AIDS were too brief and failed to produce more studies or engage more than a half-a-dozen psychologists. The third phase started in the mid-1990s, with a rising affinity for sexology among the younger generation of sociologists and psychologists. Stirred by a new undergraduate course, Sociology of Sexuality, which was offered at the University of Zagreb as the first course dealing exclusively with human sexuality in the history of Croatian higher education, this interest resulted in thematic issues on human sexuality in two leading Croatian social science journals. At the moment, it seems that sex research is gaining popularity among social scientists, but losing popularity within the medical sciences.

In recent years, only two semi-training programs have been offered. Both were designed and organized by medical experts. The first, Sexology for Family Medicine Practitioners, focused on providing general information on human sexuality to family-medicine practitioners. The second and more extensive program, Knowledge, Love, and Happy Family, offered comparable content to high school teachers and school psychologists. Occasionally, there are one-day seminars on child sexual abuse and STD and HIV/AIDS prevention. In the last couple of years, various nongovernmental organizations and women's groups began organizing seminars focused mainly on sexual harassment and sexual violence. A summer school in Family Planning, held once a year at the Inter University Centre (in Dubrovnik), is an interdisciplinary seminar discussing links between reproductive health issues, reproductive rights, sexuality, and sex education.

## B. Programs for Advanced Study

There are no graduate programs in human sexuality. Because there are just a few sex researchers in Croatia, with various scholarly backgrounds, future programs will necessarily have to be of interdisciplinary character. Considering the traditionally rigid divisions between disciplines, this seems to be an additional problem for the development of sexology.

There are no sexological journals in Croatia. However, in recent years, there has been a marked increase in the number of scholarly papers on human sexuality submitted to social science journals. It is promising that most of the authors are young scholars beginning their careers.

An international conference on sexuality in post-communist countries, Sexualities in Transition, was held in Dubrovnik in 2001. The conference brought together sex researchers from central, east, and southeast Europe, and the West. Focused on the impact of a macro social change (the transitional decade: 1989-1999) on various aspects of sexuality, this event may serve as a boost to Croatian sexology.

## References and Suggested Readings

Ajduković, D., M. Ajduković, & R. Prišlin. 1991. *AIDS i mladi* [*AIDS and youth*]. Zagreb: Medicinska Naklada.

Bakarić, T. 2000. *Tijelo žene* [*Women's body*]. Zagreb: Durieux.

Bratković, D. 2000. *Edukacija o spolnosti osoba s mentalnom retardacijom.* [*Sex education of mentally challenged individuals*]. Zagreb: Hrvatski Savez Udruga za Osobe s Mentalnom Retardacijom.

CIA. 2002 (January). *The world factbook 2002*. Washington, DC: Central Intelligence Agency. Available: http://www.cia.gov/cia/publications/factbook/index.html.

Črpić, G., & I. Rimac. 2000. Pregled postotaka i aritmetičkih sredina: Europsko istraživanje vrednota—EVS 1999 [Basic descriptive analysis of European values survey—Croatia 1999]. *Bogoslovska Smotra, 52*(2):191-232.

Gabelica, D., A. Karlović, & A. Vranić. 2002. Incidencija zlostavljanosti u djetinjstvu na uzorku zagrebačkih studenata [*Incidence of childhood abuse in a college sample*]. *Suvremena Psihologija* (in press for 2002).

Grujić-Koračin, J., M. Džepina, & A. Beluhan. 1993. Spolno ponašanje hrvatske mladeži i njen odnos prema kontracepciji [Sexual behavior of Croatian youth and their relation toward contraception]. *Gynecol. Perinatol., 3*:147-150.

Hiršl-Hećej, V., N. Šikanić-Dugić, & J. Dobravc-Poljak. 1998. *Survey on knowledge, attitudes and sexual behavior of adolescents—Students of secondary schools in Zagreb*. Zagreb: Children's Hospital Zagreb.

Karlović, A., G. Buljan Flander, & A. Vranić. 2001. The validation of the child abuse experience inventory. *Suvremena Psihologija, 4*(1-2):93-110.

Košiček, M. 1962. *Seksološki leksikon* [*Sexological lexicon*]. Zagreb: Privreda.

Košiček, M. 1965. *Seksualni odgoj* [*Sex education*]. Zagreb: Epoha.

Košiček, M. 1986. *U okviru vlastitog spola* [*In the realm of one's own sex*]. Zagreb: Mladost.

Kuzman, M., J. Mimica, V. Mardešić, K. Mušković, & K. Kožul. 2002. *HIV/AIDS-related risk behaviours in especially vulnerable young people in Croatia*. Zagreb: UNICEF.

Leinert Novosel, S. 2000. *Ne znači ne* [*No means no*]. Zagreb: Savez Studenata Hrvatske & TOD.

Leinert Novosel, S., & A. Štingl. 2001. *Ne znači ne* [*No means no*]. Zagreb: Demokratska Inicijativa Mladih.

LORI. 2001. *The Croatian media on homosexuality*. Rijeka: LORI (Lesbian Organisation Rijeka).

Mamula, M. 2002. *Annual report of Women's Center Against Sexual Violence*. Zagreb: Center for Women War Victims.

Sagasta, S. 1998. *Igre ljubavi i ponosa* [*Games of love and pride*]. Zagreb: Because.

Sagasta, S. 2001. Lesbians in Croatia. *European Journal of Women's Studies, 8*(3):357-372.

Štampar, D., & A. Beluhan. 1991. Spolnost adolescenata u Hrvatskoj [Sexuality of Croatian adolescents], *Arhiv ZMD, 35*:189-205.

*Statistički ljetopis* [*Statistical yearbook*]. 1999. Zagreb: Central Bureau of Statistics.

Stein Erlich, V. 1966. *Jugoslavenska porodica u transformaciji*. Zagreb: Liber. (Eng. ed., 1971: *Family in transition: A story of 300 Yugoslav villages*. Princeton, NJ: Princeton University Press.)

Štulhofer, A. 1999a. Hypnerotomachia Poliae: Seksualni stilovi urbanih žena u Hrvatskoj [Female sexual styles in urban Croatia]. *Revija za Sociologiju, 30*(1-2):1-17.

Štulhofer, A. 1999b (August 6). Seksualno stanje nacije 1999 [Sexual state of the nation 1999]. *Globus, 452*:58-63.

Štulhofer, A. 2000. Govoriti jedno, činiti drugo? Spol, stavovi o spolnosti i heteroseksualno ponašanje u urbanoj Hrvatskoj [Gender, sexual attitudes, and heterosexual behavior in urban Croatia]. *Revija za Sociologiju, 31*(1-2):63-79.

Štulhofer, A., V. Jureša, & M. Mamula. 1999. *Longitudinalno praćenje znanja o spolnosti, spolnog ponašanja i relevantnih stavova adolescenata* [*A report on adolescent sexual knowledge, attitudes, and behavior*]. Zagreb: State Office for the Protection of Family, Motherhood, and Youth.

Štulhofer, A., N. Karajić, & M. Meštrović. 1996. *Sociokulturni kapital Hrvatske—Istraživački izvještaj* [*Social capital in Croatia—Research report*]. Zagreb: Ekonomski Institut.

Štulhofer, A., M. Gregurović, & D. Štulhofer. 2002. Women's sexual health, sexual satisfaction, and sexual orientation. *Društvena istraživanja* (in print).

Štulhofer, A., Z. Raboteg-Šarić, & L. Marinović. 2002. *Trafficking in women and children for sexual exploitation.* Zagreb: IOM.

Šuperina, M., & A. Garačić. 2000. Učestalost kaznenih djela protiv spolne slobode i spolnog ćudoređa u Republici Hrvatskoj [Frequency of criminal offenses against sexual freedom and sexual morality in the Republic of Croatia]. *Hrvatski Ljetopis za Kazneno Pravo i Praksu, 7*:399-456.

Trenc, P., & A. Beluhan. 1973. Ispitivanje stavova i aktivnosti u seksualnom životu srednjoškolske omladine [Experience and attitudes of secondary school students concerning sexual life]. *Arhiv ZMD, 17*(6):269-320.

UNAIDS. 2002. *Epidemiological fact sheets by country.* Geneva, Switzerland: Joint United Nations Programme on HIV/AIDS (UNAIDS/WHO). Available: http://www.unaids.org/hivaidsinfo/statistics/fact_sheets/index_en.htm.

World Value Survey Croatia. 1995. *Research report.* Zagreb: Erasmus Guild.

(CIA 2002)

# Cuba

## (*República de Cuba*)

Mariela Castro Espín, B.Ed., M.Sc., and María Dolores
Córdova Llorca, Ph.D., main authors and coordinators,*
with Alicia Gónzalez Hernández, Ph.D.,
Beatriz Castellanos Simons, Ph.D., Natividad Guerrero
Borrego, Ph.D., Gloria Ma. A. Torres Cueto, Ph.D.,
Eddy Abreu Guerra, Ph.D., Beatriz Torres Rodríguez,
Ph.D., Caridad T. García Álvarez, M.Sc., Ada Alfonso
Rodríguez, M.D., M.Sc., Maricel Rebollar Sánchez,
M.Sc., Oscar Díaz Noriega, M.D., M.Sc., Jorge Renato
Ibarra Guitart, Ph.D., Sonia Jiménez Berrios,
Daimelis Monzón Wat, Jorge Peláez Mendoza, M.D.,
Mayra Rodríguez Lauzerique, M.Sc., Ofelia Bravo
Fernández, M.Sc., Lauren Bardisa Escurra, M.D.,
Miguel Sosa Marín, M.D., Rosaida Ochoa Soto, M.D.,
and Leonardo Chacón Asusta

## Contents

*Communications*: Mariela Castro Espín, M.Sc., Director of the
National Centre for Sexual Education (CENESEX); presidenta, XVI
Congreso Mundial de Sexologia (Havana 2003); marielac@infomed
.sld.cu. María Delores Córdova, Ph.D., Subdirectora de Investigationes, CENESEX; cenesex@infomed.sld.cu.

## Demographics and a Brief Historical Perspective

### A. Demographics

MARÍA D. CÓRDOVA

Cuba is the largest island (40,520 square miles, 104,945 km²) in the Cuban Archipelago, composed of the Isle of Youth and some 1,600 isles and cays. Located in the Caribbean Sea, at the entrance of the Gulf of Mexico, Cuba is the westernmost island of the Greater Antilles. Its north shore is washed by the Atlantic Ocean, and the east shore faces the Windward Passage. Cuba is bordered on the south by the Caribbean Sea and on the west by the Yucatan Channel. The Bahamas and United States are the nearest countries to the north, Haiti to the east, Jamaica and South America to the south, and Mexico to the west.

Since Cuba has an east-west-oriented, elongated, and narrow shape, its rivers cannot be long and plentiful. Among the largest ones are the Cauto in the eastern region and the Zaza in the central region. Some relatively low mountain ranges cross the Cuban territory. The most outstanding are: the Sierra del Rosario in the west, the Trinidad mountain range in the central region, and the Sierra Maestra in the east.

The climate is semitropical, with alternating dry and rainy seasons. June through November is the hurricane season. From 1800 to 2001, 176 hurricanes have battered the island of Cuba.

In December 2002, Cuba had an estimated population of approximately 11,217,680 inhabitants. The following demographic features are from the *Anuario Estadístico de Cuba 2001* (Oficina Nacional de Estadísticas 2002) and the *UNDP Informe del Desarrollo Humano, Anuario Estadístico de Salud* (MINSAP 2002), except where supplemented with data from *The World Factbook 2002* (CIA 2002) by the Editors (notated as [*WFB*]).

**Age Distribution and Sex Ratios**: *0-14 years*: 20.9% with 1.06 male(s) per female (sex ratio) [*WFB*: 20.6%, 1.06]; *15-59 years*: 64.5% with 1.01 male(s) per female [*WFB*: 69.3%, 1.01 (*15-64 years*)]; *60 years and over*: 14.49% with 0.86 male(s) per female [*WFB*: 10.1%, 0.86 (*65+ years*)]; *Total population sex ratio*: 1 male(s) to 1 female [*WFB*]

**Life Expectancy at Birth**: *Total Population*: 76.15 years; *male*: 74.20 years; *female*: 78.23 years [*WFB*: *Total population*: 76.6; *male*: 74.2; *female*: 79.15]

**Urban/Rural Distribution**: 75.26% to 24.71%; the capital city of Havana has 2,181,535 inhabitants.

**Ethnic Distribution**: [*WFB*: mulatto: 51%; white: 37%; black: 11%; and Chinese:1%]

**Religious Distribution**: [*WFB*: nominally 85% Roman Catholic prior to Revolution; Protestant, Jehova's Witnesses, Jews, and Santeria also represented]

**Birth Rate**: 12.4 births per 1,000 population [*WFB*: 12.08 births per 1,000]

**Death Rate**: 7.1 per 1,000 population [*WFB*: 7.35 deaths per 1,000]

**Infant Mortality Rate**: 6.2 deaths per 1,000 live births; in-hospital live births: 99.9% [*WFB*: 7.27 deaths per 1,000]

**Net Migration Rate**: –2.9 migrant(s) per 1,000 population [*WFB*: –1.21 per 1,000]

**Total Fertility Rate**: 1.6 children born per woman

**Population Growth Rate**: 0.23% (2.3 per 1,000 inhabitants in 2001) [*WFB*: 0.35%]

**HIV/AIDS** (1999 est.) [*WFB*: *Adult prevalence*: 0.03%; *Persons living with HIV/AIDS*: 2,800 (2001 est.); *Deaths*: 120.] (For additional details from www.UNAIDS.org, see end of Section 10B.)

**Literacy Rate** (*defined as those age 15 and over who can read and write*): 97%; 99.1% of primary school-age children are actually in school; education is free and compulsory from age 6 to 14 [*WFB*: *male*: 96.2%, *female*: 95.3%, *total* 95.7%]

**Per Capita Gross Domestic Product** (*purchasing power parity*): 2,618 Cuban pesos in 2001 (adjusted to the 1997 rate; official exchange rate: 1 Cuban peso = 1 USD) [*WFB*: $2,300]. The GDP increased 3.0% during 2001, thus continuing a positive trend that began in 1995. However, this accumulative increase did not make possible the recovery of the standard of living and the basic social services (health, education, and housing) that prevailed prior to 1990. The lack of foreign investment and foreign exchange are the greatest obstacles for economic growth. According to the HDI, Cuba ranked 55 among 173 countries in 2002. [*WFB*: *Inflation*: 7.1%; *Unemployment*: 4.1% (2001 est.); *Living below the poverty line*: NA]

In Cuba, the State is fully responsible for the healthcare of the population. Health is conceived as a fundamental aspect of the quality of life and is also a strategic objective in societal development. The entire population has access to free medical services. In every neighborhood, there are a family physician and a nurse per 176 persons. General family physicians provide healthcare to 99.1% of the population. The budget allocated to health amounted to 17.2% of the total budget in 2001. Per capita healthcare costs covered by the State are US$162.30.

## B. A Brief Historical Perspective

JORGE RENATO IBARRA GUITART

The indigenous population had lived in Cuba for about 10,000 years before they entered into contact with the European civilization. There were three main groups of Indians, in different developmental stages, living under the Primitive Community regime. The Guanahatabeyes survived by gathering plant foods, hunting, and fishing. They lived in caves and only used artifacts made of shells. The Ciboneyes lived along the coasts. Fishing was their main means of subsistence and they knew how to carve stone. The Taínos were the most numerous and developed group. They practiced agriculture and made polished stone and pottery artifacts.

On October 27, 1492, the great admiral, Christopher Columbus landed for the first time in Cuba, and explored some sites in the northeast of the island. In 1510, a host of 300 Spanish warriors, led by Diego Velázquez, coming from Hispaniola, began the conquest of Cuba. The *conquistadores*, sword in hand and with the Christian cross as a banner, crushed the initial resistance of the natives led by Hatuey, an Indian chief, and began the occupation of the territory. Bloodshed had become the means through which the *conquistadores* forcibly imposed their rule and founded the first seven towns throughout the island.

The intense process of land occupation during the 16th century saturated the land property. Throughout the 16th and 17th centuries, land structure consisted of large haciendas in the hinterland, and small agricultural properties. The latter were located in strips next to towns and within large plantations. In Cuba, feudal production relationships did not take hold because of the scarce population—the Indians were gradually being wiped out—and because production was mainly cattle-raising. On the other hand, Spain had imposed a taxation and monopolistic system that hampered large-scale mercantile production. A subsistence economy prevailed during those early centuries.

From 1512 on, African slaves were brought to the island, but it was not until the 17th century that the large-scale introduction of black slaves began. Changes in land exploitation brought about the partition and sale of land, thus favoring the extension of sugar cane plantations and tobacco-growing lands. The occupation of Havana by the British in 1762 encouraged both free trade and the slave trade. Spain recovered its colony and, years later, promoted reforms under the "Enlightened Despotism" policy, aimed at encouraging the arrival in Cuba of new settlers and of slave manpower, which made possible large-scale mercantile production of sugar, tobacco, and coffee. From 1790 to 1868, the Cuban-born, land-owning class favored reformism and annexation alternatively; the *petite bourgeoisie* and a few landowners showed a trend toward independence from Spain; and the slaves were for abolition.

The deepening of the contradictions between the metropolis and the colony, and the failure of several reformist proposals, brought about, on October 10, 1868, a war for national liberation and the abolition of the slavery headed by the founding father of the Cuban nation, Carlos Manuel de Céspedes. During this war, known as the Ten Years' War, the Afro-Spanish culture, which brought about Cuban nationality, began to integrate. In this liberation struggle, the insurgent forces faced many divisions and material difficulties and, at its end, the land-owning civilian leadership accepted pacification proposals when there was a relative balance of forces. Other more consistent people's leaders, such as Antonio Maceo, decided to continue the war and issued the "Protest of Baraguá," a document against the capitulations agreed on with Spain.

From 1892 on, after the failure of the first independence attempt, significant activities headed for a new uprising against the colonial power began. José Martí, political leader of the new insurrection being planned by Cuban emigrants, united patriots in exile under the Cuban Revolutionary Party. Some time later, troops were recruited for a national liberation army with the collaboration of 1868-war veterans.

On February 24, 1895, the first uprising took place and a week later, the leaders of the liberation war, José Martí, Máximo Gómez, and Antonio Maceo, landed in Cuba. Martí died in combat a few days after his arrival. The rebel army, known as *mambises*, spread the war throughout the national territory by a successful campaign brilliantly led by Gómez and Maceo. Most of the sugar wealth that was to be destroyed by the insurrectionists was in the western provinces. As a result of the revolutionary forces' advance, Spain changed its political and military tactics. In a desperate attempt to hold the island, it authorized Captain-General Valeriano Weyler to implement a concentration policy of countryside people in urban centers that brought about the starvation, destruction, and death of a large number of civilians. But this policy also failed, and the colonialists accepted a grant of autonomy to the Island. Nevertheless, Cuban troops went on fighting and controlled rural areas. Under those circumstances, the U.S. battleship Maine blew up in Havana's harbor, and the United States, which already had important economic interests in Cuba, declared war on Spain. Thus began the Spanish-Cuban-American war that ended with the defeat of Spain and the signing of the Paris Peace Treaty, authorizing the United States to militarily occupy Cuba for an indefinite period.

In 1901, a Constitutional Convention was called to set the political destiny of Cubans. The United States imposed on the members of the convention the adoption of the Platt Amendment as an appendix to the Cuban Constitution. The Platt Amendment considerably limited the sovereignty of the future Republic. Although it was initially rejected by the assembly, it was finally adopted under Washington's pressure. Thus came into being the Republic of Cuba on May 20, 1902. In 1903, the Trade Reciprocity Treaty with the U.S., an instrument of the economic penetration promoted by the United States to maintain its trade hegemony in Cuba, was signed.

From 1902 to 1933, successive administrations, subordinate to Washington's plans, fostered the large-scale introduction of U.S. capital and the consolidation of an oligarchy allied to them. In 1933, Gerardo Machado's dictatorial régime was toppled, after facing both the negative consequences of the ongoing world economic crisis and the strong opposition of the national revolutionary movement that had come into being in the 1920s. After a period of political instability because of the struggle between progressive and conservative forces, the failure of the 1935 general strike ended the 30-year revolutionary period. Taking advantage of the lack of unity of the revolutionaries, the new dictator, Fulgencio Batista, effectively repressed the resistance of the people's sectors. At this stage, the United States changed its political hegemony methods toward Latin America through the "Good Neighbor" policy that nullified the Platt Amendment in Cuba and paved the way for the signing of a new Trade Reciprocity Treaty and the Sugar Quota Law, which limited the free entry of Cuban sugar into the U.S. market.

Once consolidated in power, Batista's military régime considered several international circumstances and consented to a democratic opening whose high point was the calling of the 1940 Constitutional Convention. The Constitution of 1940 endorsed most of the social and political demands of the revolutionary and reformist sectors, but many of them could not be implemented because the required complementary laws were not adopted. After several years of struggle from the opposition, the Cuban Revolutionary Party (Auténtico) came into power in 1944, but it did not implement with enough depth its national-reformist platform. The Auténtico administrations sank the country into non-governance, political administrative crises, corruption, and political skepticism. Then, the Party of the Cuban People (Ortodoxo) was set up, headed by Eduardo Chibás, who launched a series of public campaigns that awoke the national revolutionary awareness.

When general elections were called, Fulgencio Batista began a new coup d'état on March 10, 1952, assuming all powers and suppressing the Constitution of 1940. From then on, the traditional parties were unable to organize a solid popular resistance movement; thus, new revolutionary organizations came into being resolved to carry on an armed struggle to overthrow Batista's dictatorship. This new stage of armed struggle began with the attack on the Moncada and Carlos Manuel de Céspedes garrisons on July 26, 1953, by a revolutionary movement led by Fidel Castro, who launched a platform of political and social demands in a document titled, "History Will Acquit Me." Also of importance was the struggle of Cuban students led by José Antonio Echeverría, who founded the Revolutionary Directory and organized a head-on fight against the dictatorship, which reached its highest point in the attack on the Presidential Palace in 1957. The failure of reformist alternatives, especially that of the Society of Friends of the Republic, demonstrated the impossibility of a peaceful solution to the national political crisis. Fidel Castro, after some initial setbacks, organized a strong guerrilla movement in the mountains, from where he descended, after defeating Batista, on January 1, 1959.

The recently constituted revolutionary government promoted important measures to guarantee political control and promote important social and economic changes. Among the first of these were the disbanding of the army and of the political parties committed to Batista's dictatorship, and among the latter, the first Agrarian Reform Law and the nationalization of banks and other U.S. companies, as well as the confiscation of the large domestic private companies. These changes, which took place in a relatively brief time period, were accelerated by the hostile policies of the United States toward the Cuban revolution. Although the initial measures of the Cuban government were not socialist, Washington manifested its overt opposition to the path taken by the Revolution by putting an end to the sugar quota, fuel supplies, and the sale of spare parts. Finally, when the revolutionary government radicalized its stands, the United States imposed an economic blockade banning all trade, including medicines and foodstuffs. This blockade not only affects bilateral trade, but also Cuba's trade with the rest of the world.

Those measures, aimed at paralyzing the Cuban economy, were accompanied by an intense subversive campaign fostered by the CIA. The CIA gave material and logistical support to counterrevolutionary groups with headquarters in the United States and also carried on actions on the island. Especially outstanding were their support operations for the counterrevolutionary bands in the Escambray Mountains and the Playa Girón (Bay of Pigs) invasion. But the revolutionary government, whose social change policies were backed by the great majority of the people, mobilized the people and held back the counterrevolutionary offensive. After the Bay of Pigs defeat, the CIA destabilization schemes, aimed at bringing about an invasion of U.S. regular troops, gave way to the October 1962 Missile Crisis. During that crisis, the principled resolve of the revolutionary leadership was confirmed. In this conflict with the United States, Cuba received the solidarity of the Soviet Union and the socialist camp that offered markets for sugar and supplied Cuba with oil, armaments, raw materials, and inputs. Deeply involved in the transformations that were taking place, and in view of United States harassment, the Cuban revolutionaries decided to come together in a single political party that took different names until, in 1965, it became the Communist Party of Cuba (PCC).

In the social field, the revolutionary government developed important programs for the benefit of the general population, such as a literacy campaign, free education and healthcare for all, the lowering of the unemployment rate, and the improvement of social security, among others.

In 1991, with the collapse of the socialist camp and the onset of the globalization process, Cuba started a series of reforms headed toward its inclusion in the world economy, but without relinquishing its socialist-oriented model.

## 1. Basic Sexological Premises

### A. The Cultural Perspective

MARÍA D. CÓRDOVA LLORCA

To understand the sexuality of Cubans, both male and female, nowadays, it is necessary to study the development of "Cubanness" (*la cubanidad*). "Cubanness is mainly the characteristic quality of a culture, that of Cuba" (55). Both the Cuban culture and nation developed together, the former being the source and the expression of the latter. Both are the result of the *mestizaje* of Spanish culture, which was brought from its different regions by its less-favored people, and the African culture brought by thousands of slaves uprooted by force from their various tribes.

This mixture is not exclusive of Cubans, but has unique characteristics in the island. The pre-Columbian Indians, present in all Ibero-American nations, the autochthonous basis of those peoples, were wiped out in Cuba by the colonial régime. The long slavery and Spanish-rule period, the "tutelage" of the Anglo-Saxon northern neighbors, and even the Asian presence, marked the necessary differences with the other American nations of Spanish origin.

The physical location, geography, and climate of the Cuban Archipelago have also left their hallmark on our idiosyncrasy, "The hot climate of our land influences our character ... makes our blood and mind boil, and often takes hold of our will in irrepressible hurricanes of passion. How is the Cuban soul? How is the result of the melting pot of different civilizations expressed in Cuba?" (55).

"Cuba is an 'ajiaco.' A miscegenation of cooking styles, a miscegenation of races, a miscegenation of cultures. A thick broth of civilization that bubbles in the Caribbean stove" (55). The daring Spaniards of the conquest and of the successive colonizing immigrations imported their adventurous temperament, their warrior impulsiveness, their intolerance in the fight against infidels, Andalusian grace, and Castilian chivalry. With them also came a sustained impermanence: "that constant restlessness, that fickle impulsiveness, that temporary nature of attitudes were the primary inspirations of our collective character, fond of impulse and the adventure of excitability and of luck, of the achievement and hope of chance" (56).

With the colony and slavery came the African blacks, brought with no will or ambition, uprooted by force from their country, and forced to work like beasts. This gave rise to their constant rage, their longing to flee, to be emancipated and to change. African culture especially influenced art, religion, and the collective emotional nature of Cubans. "The culture and soul of the blacks, always undergoing a transition crisis, penetrates Cubanness in the miscegenation of flesh and cultures, imbuing it with the juicy, sensual, frolicsome, tolerant, accommodating, talkative emotionality that is their gracefulness, their charm and their strongest resistance strength to survive in the constant boil of upsetting experiences that has been the history of this country" (56)

Cuban men and women, heirs of these roots who grew up in a perennial struggle, first to obtain and later to maintain their independence, always in defense of their mixed-blood culture, nowadays consider themselves satisfied for being Cuban, characterized by: joy and mockery, openness, sensibility, spontaneity, sociability, liveliness, mischievousness, and intelligence, as well as the bad manners on occasion, impulsiveness, a bit of superficiality, and not much self-criticism (39).

Sexuality, deeply rooted in the Cuban identity, is marked by the presence of eroticism in the image of both sexes, for its intentionality to seduce and win over the other, in his or her cult of sexuality. "Cuba is a country in which people constantly look at each other and are undressed by a glance, where skin suddenly appears and clothes become transparent" (71). Eroticism is markedly manifested in the all the gestures of Cubans, in all art expressions, especially in dance and in the popular dances known the world over.

Cuban men are perceived as flirtatious, frolicsome, and cunning with women, with high regard for manliness and *machista* par excellence (39)—authoritarian and womanizer. On the other hand, women are perceived as "coquettish, dressy and sexy with men," and self-denying and faithful mothers and wives.

### B. Character of Gender Roles

MARÍA D. CÓRDOVA LLORCA

In a par-excellence male-centered culture, *machismo* and sexism characterize the history of gender roles in Cuba. During colonial times and for a long time in the pseudo republic period, women were always discriminated against: nice married women were discriminated against at home, fated to reproduction and subjected to their husbands. Those considered not-nice, on the streets, were rejected as "easy" or prostitutes, but were tolerated if they kept a low profile.

"Female sexuality always occupied an important place in the system of values, as norms of virtuous behavior, mainly during the 19th century. This was very evident in the periodicals of those times" (71). The ideal woman was a dedicated mother, giving birth to all the children she conceived, modest, a faithful wife, passive, and only responsive to male sexuality.

Men were seldom mentioned in the press, and if so, it was only to reassert their masculinity. They could make use of their sexuality as they pleased. Infidelity was accepted as inherent to the male role. Their wives guaranteed their descendants, since they were only the mothers of their children. Generally, sexual fantasies and enjoyment were only fulfilled outside the home with lovers and prostitutes.

On the other hand, marriage was the cornerstone of Cuban society. Frequently, it became a business to preserve or rescue family economy. Nevertheless, if discreet, concubinage and cohabitation were allowed. Cohabitation was very frequent with actual and freed slaves and among the peasants.

Sex-related crimes like abduction, rape, pederasty, and prostitution were dealt with in a sexist manner. Women were always considered guilty, and were even criticized for accusing men.

Homosexuality was also discriminated against. Although socially rejected, it was not considered a crime in the Civil Code adopted in the 1950s. Full divorce was legalized in 1934, much earlier than in other Latin American countries.

The hallmark of the 1959 victorious revolution also left its imprint on gender roles. Equality of rights is recognized in the Constitution of the Republic, which, in Chapter 1, Article 9, states: "... all able-bodied men or women will have the opportunity to obtain employment, enabling them to contribute to the ends of society and to meet their own needs" (24).

The 1961 literacy campaign, the free access to compulsory and lay education, the sustained programs of prevention and healthcare for all, especially women, children, and youngsters, as well as the massive incorporation of women in the social and labor fields, and their resolute and demanding participation have had a gradual influence in all spheres of life: in their family, with their husband or partner, and even in the way of living their sexuality.

In Chapter IV on the family, it is recognized that: "Marriage . . . is based on the absolute equality of rights and duties of the spouses, who should undertake home-keeping and the comprehensive education of their children by common effort, in a manner compatible with the social activities of both" (24).

## C. General Concepts of Sexuality and Love

C. ALICIA GONZÁLEZ HERNÁNDES and
C. BEATRIZ CASTELLANOS SIMONS

In Cuban everyday life, sexuality is associated with the couple's erotic and love relationship, which is true, but limits or stereotypes the concept to one of its spheres, leaving out all its wealth, diversity, and complexity.

Sexual life is, in essence, a dialogue, an interaction, between persons of the same sex and of the other sex, including all kinds of relationships with the desired and/or loved person.

Sexuality is a personality dimension, built and expressed from the moment of birth and during the whole lifetime, through a set of representations, concepts, thoughts, emotions, needs, feelings, attitudes, and behaviors that make up a psychologically and physically male or female sexed being, which goes beyond the couple's relationship and is evident in all that a person is and does in his or her personal, family, and social life.

Therefore, the study and description of couple relationships will allow us to probe the feelings, and the physical and spiritual experiences that are the *raison d'être* of one the most important gifts of life: pleasure and love. But limiting sexuality only to that aspect will not cover the wide range of communication that takes place in the interactions that may occur during the lifetime of a human being.

Sexuality is developed and expressed as a manifestation of personality in several dimensions and qualities to be discussed as follows:

* Individual: Sexuality develops in the inner self that always defines itself as a human being possessing sex. It is perceived from within, and is projected without, in masculinity or femininity. This unique and unrepeatable personalized character of sexuality, as an expression of identity, makes it possible to explain the diversity of ways of living and feeling it, its flexibility and malleability, the fact that its paths are not predetermined, and that each human being can approach them in a unique manner leaving his or her imprint on them. At the same time, the individual is projected in a unique manner in the remaining dimension of his or her partner, the family, and society—thus the undeniable social content of sexuality.
* The couple represents the transcendency of sexuality to an essentially social-interaction dimension where the meeting with the other self takes place. Emotional and erotic bonds are established in physical and spiritual communication, when giving and receiving pleasure, satisfaction, love, and happiness. The human couple, as we understand it, is a dialectical dyad that differentiates itself from other persons, but each member of the couple keeps, at the same time, his or her identity, without relinquishing her or his self. When, on the contrary, there is symbiotic union, where one member of the couple absorbs the identity of the other, the couple ceases to be a space for growth, the full expression of sexuality, and self-realization of personality.
* The family is the first socialization agent of personality and sexuality. It is the most stable reference group throughout life in the formation of values, convictions, behavior patterns, conceptions, and sexual attitudes. Family bonds boost human communication and emo-

tional ties. Within the family, life is reproduced, when the couple or the individual freely decide to have a descendant. It is within this group that girls and boys, since early ages, learn the male and female behavior models, from which they build their identity and gender role, essential processes for the development of sexuality
* Society is the widest context in which the individual interacts and communicates with persons of both sexes throughout his or her life in a great diversity of activities: in games, studies, work, and participation in community life from the intellectual, political, artistic, scientific, or recreational points of view. From this dimension come culturally predominant gender models and patterns, from which the individual's sexuality is learned and evaluated. Therefore, that dimension is inherent to our total being, a human being that undoubtedly transcends biology. It isn't a mechanical exact replica of the world of social relationships. Its essence is completed and fulfilled in spirituality, in the subjective that exists as concrete reality in a unique and creative personality, capable of transforming the physical and cultural environment and itself in daily praxis.

In Cuba, from January 1959 on, objective and subjective changes of great significance have taken place in the way of life of both sexes, especially in the exercise of all the facets of women's performance, bringing about the progressive development of an ever-comprehensive male and female sexuality, on the basis of the principles of fairness and collaboration.

Although it is unquestionable that large strides have been taken towards a more responsible, pleasant, and happy sexuality, myths, taboos, and prejudices that prevent living this important sphere in all its fullness still persist. Therefore, since the 1960s, a National Sex Education Program, which will be explained further on, is being implemented with the aim of overcoming all the obstacles that still prevent many human beings from being sexually fulfilled, responsible, and authentic.

## 2. Religious, Ethnic, and Gender Factors Affecting Sexuality

MARÍA D. CÓRDOVA LLORCA

The triumphant Revolution in 1959 brought about an increase in social justice and equality patterns, among them in religious freedom. As Aurelio Alonso, a renowned Cuban researcher, states: "Up to 1959, discrimination was not a State policy, but of the religions themselves. Catholicism was the hegemonic religion, which assured its supremacy through a close relationship with the dominant classes" (69).

From that date on, the different religious beliefs that characterize Cuban syncretism, acquired equal footing in the discourse of the State. This syncretism is nurtured by the African religions brought by the slaves during the colonial period, and by the Catholicism of the Spaniards: "Catholic aspects are present in African religions and African religious aspects are present in Catholicism" (69). However, the equality in the political discourse and in the exercise of law, was not automatically assimilated in the people's minds. Therefore, various forms of discrimination took place, at certain moments, on the part of some institutions. "Having religious beliefs became a deficit, an 'ideological weakness'" (69).

At the beginning of the 1990s, religious freedom increased qualitatively after the IV Congress of the Communist Party and the 1992 constitutional reform. "The fact that believers of all religions could join the Communist Party implied a tacit change in the way of evaluating religious faith among us, that is to say, a rectification" (69). Also, during those years a significant increase in the membership of the Christian religions took place, for example in the Evangelical and Baptist churches, among others.

[*Comment 2003*: In connection with sexuality, there are certain differences within the religious mosaic of today. This is, for example, the case of Santería, as the "Regla de Ocha" is known in Cuba.

[Santería, arising from the Yoruban culture, is practiced, with different degrees of commitment to their religious beliefs, by men and women of different races, ages, educational levels, professions, and sexual orientation.

[The Yoruban religion consists of a group of deities possessing their own mythology, whose symbolic content becomes essential elements to be imitated by the initiated. Thus, a son or daughter of Shango, a deity considered "hot," because his sphere of action has to do with fire and war or burning virility, will try to make those characteristics part of his or her personality traits, in order to establish a singular relationship with Shango's nature.

[Shango, besides representing masculinity, is also considered the owner of the batá drums. The ritual dance performed for this deity is full of sensuality and eroticism, highlighting, with non-ambiguous and extremely expressive movements, the part of the body where virility and masculinity resides.

[Oshun is another deity in whose rituals, parties, and dances there is an element of sensuality, which excites the senses and provokes sexuality. She is considered the owner of the rivers and the goddess of love. Her daughters could be the archetype or, maybe, the stereotype of Cuban women disseminated throughout the world: sexy, provocative, loving, passionate, and sex symbol. (*End of comment by Sonia Jiménez Berrios*)]

[*Comment 2003*: On the other hand, the Christian churches have historically considered sexuality taboo, and therefore, that topic is not mentioned. However, in the current world, and particularly in our country, in some Christian denominations, there has been an opening in their dealing with sexuality because of its importance in the education of children and youngsters and in the adoption of healthier sexual behaviors.

[For Christians, sexuality is part of God's creation. Men and women were created as sexual, sexed beings. However, sexuality can only be fully expressed in the context of marriage. Among the purposes of sexuality in marriage, according to Christian denominations, are: satisfaction of the need for company and companionship, togetherness and stability of the couple, and mutual pleasure and enjoyment, as well as reproduction.

[All sexual practices outside of marriage, like premarital sex, adultery or conjugal infidelity, and homosexuality, are not approved by Christianity. According to Christian precepts, the persons who engage in those sexual practices run physical, psychological, and moral risks, although, at present, some denominations have assumed more flexible stands on this matter. Another non-approved practice is induced abortion. For some Christians, it is a way of putting an end to the life of a human being. (*End of comment by Daimelis Monzón*)]

### 3. Knowledge and Education about Sexuality

MARIELA CASTRO ESPÍN

Cuba has traveled a long way in research on sexuality, sex education, and counseling. The outstanding studies and medical care provided by the medical doctors, Celestino Alvarez Lajonchere, R. Bustamante, and Ángel Custodio Arce, among others, date back to the beginning of the 20th century.

From 1959 on, sex education has been a priority of the Cuban social model. Since 1962, the Federation of Cuban Women (FMC) and the Ministry of Public Health launched campaigns and national programs addressing the problems of women's sexual and reproductive health. Later on, a working group was set up, headed by the FMC. Early in 1970, the Ministry of Education and the Young Communist Union joined the working group. This group defined the main priorities of the National Sex Education Program to be implemented through public policies, mainly centered on childhood, the young, and on equality of woman's rights (34).

In 1976, as a result of the institutionalization process in which the Constitution was revised, the Standing Commission for Children, Youth, and Women was established in the National Assembly of the People's Power of the Republic of Cuba (Parliament). The National Working Group on Sex Education (GENTES), officially implemented in 1977, became part of the parliamentary commission.

In that context, the Provincial and Municipal Commissions on Sex Education were established to implement the National Program in their territories, and the same entities of GENTES were represented.

The actions of the National Sex Education Program had greater coverage and became more complex. Thus, in 1989, GENTES became the current National Center of Sexual Education (Centro Nacional de Educación Sexual, CENESEX), whose mission is to manage sex education policies in Cuba and coordinate the participation of governmental entities and civil society organizations in charge of education, counseling, therapy, social communication, and community work in the field of sexuality.

Since the early 1960s, this program, has maintained an interdisciplinary and intersectoral approach. It is aimed at the Cuban population as a whole, regardless of age, sex, sexual orientation, cultural level, and physical, sensory, and intellectual capacities. Among their objectives, the following stand out:

- Development of sex education as part of the individual's comprehensive education.
- Promotion of sexual health as a fundamental part of the quality of life in the different age groups and population segments.
- Systematic reflections at the social and community levels that modify stereotypes and prejudices and promote attitudes and behaviors favoring the development of a healthy, full, and responsible sexuality.

These are the objectives that, at present, guide educational, research, healthcare, community work, and social communication actions in the fields of education, counseling, and sexual therapy, which are carried out by different government entities, especially the Ministries of Health (MINSAP), Education (MINED), and Culture (MINCULT), as well as by civil society organizations, such as the Federation of Cuban Women and the Young Communist Union.

### A. Government Policies and Programs

GLORIA MARÍA ANTONIA TORRES CUERTO

Since the 1970s, the Ministry of Education (MINED) has been carrying out a Sex Education Program in all schools, as a prioritized objective of the Cuban educational policy. The program is based on basic educational principles, centered on the formation of values and the need for a comprehensive development of the student's personality, as part as their training for life.

"The above-mentioned Program had to overcome important resistance to its implementation on the part of the educational institution, although the teaching personnel receiving professional training were more open to reflection on these topics. At that time, work was essentially centered in the improvement of school texts with some reproductive health and gender equity topics" (13).

Sex education at schools is free and provided by the State. It is carried out on the same basis as the National Sex Education Program. It is included in the curriculum and supplemented with extracurricular activities and family education. It is based on the cross-section content system on sexuality included in the system of school subjects.

The program is developed through classes, extracurricular activities, and activities with the students' mothers and fathers. These activities are conceived and carried out following an alternative sex education approach, based on the determination of basic educational needs (SANEBAS), through participatory activities and the implementation of action research findings.

This program of the Cuban National Educational System is established at all educational centers of the country, in preschool, elementary, special, junior high school, high school, technical professional, adult education, and the teacher-training universities. In the latter, sex education is included in undergraduate and graduate subjects in order train future teachers. On-the-job training is also available to teachers.

As a result of the program, school dropouts due to pregnancy and marriage have decreased—from 1,038 in the 1997-1998 academic years to 240 in 2000-2001. On the other hand, there has been a decrease of early sexual relations from 31% to 10% in the adolescent population. At the same time, the use of birth-control methods has also increased, especially the use of condoms. Now, two thirds of the sexually active adolescents are using condoms.

On the other hand, at medical universities, sexuality and sex education topics are included in the curriculum, elective courses, and regular undergraduate courses. They are also dealt with in graduate, diploma, and master's degree courses in the continuing education of health professionals.

At the University of Havana, the Art University, and the University of Informatics, sexuality content is included in university extension activities and are widely accepted by students.

## B. Sexuality Education in the Community

ADA C. ALFONSO and MARISEL REBOLLAR

Since its inception, the revolutionary government began to carry out community education work with the aim of increasing the cultural and educational level of the population, whose great majority had been denied access to education because of economic reasons. Since the very beginning, women were the ones that benefited most, their training aimed at incorporating them into social life with resources that would allow them to join the social and labor movement.

Very soon, sexuality topics were discussed in community debates (in 1962). In the 1980s, there were specialized community sex education places and activities in the country's territories. The most outstanding are: the House for Women and Family Counseling (COMF), Adolescent and Young Men and Women Counseling Centers, health education departments, the family doctor and nurse's office, and community action undertaken by schools. They provide interdisciplinary sexual and reproductive health promotion and prevention, as well as sex education in general.

During all those years, the aims of the actions by the above-mentioned institutions have changed, according to the needs of the times and the particular conditions of the local regions. During the initial years, emphasis was given to reproductive health. The essential objectives of family planning education were to avoid the risks of abortion as a control practice and to minimize the risks of unwanted pregnancies. These objectives were accompanied by a policy of providing highly specialized abortion services at all hospitals of the country, to avoid the heath risks of clandestine abortions.

Later on, healthcare services became aware that men should also take part in sexual healthcare, and programs, geared to earlier ages and adolescents at schools, were added to the above-mentioned places and activities.

With the appearance of HIV/AIDS, topics on sexually transmitted infections (STI) were broadened. Programs aimed at educating the population in general for the prevention of sexually transmitted diseases began to be implemented. Early in the 1980s, the Operative Group for Controlling and Combating AIDS (GOPELS) was established to coordinate and implement intersector work against this epidemic. In 1998, the National Center of STI-HIV-AIDS Prevention, with provincial and municipal representation, was created. This center is in charge of implementing the National Program of HIV-AIDS Prevention and Control.

"The educational aspect of this Program has, as a general objective, been to promote healthy behaviors, attitudes and sexual practices that make possible a more adequate self-evaluation of the individual's risk to be infected with HIV-AIDS and influence in the prevention of new infections" (49). Although the programs were initially centered in not very encouraging messages associated with death, very soon the messages were aimed at educating the population to coexist with HIV-infected persons and those suffering from AIDS, to sensitize the population in general and especially the more vulnerable age groups, in the importance of using protection methods and of responsible and safe sexual practices.

Recent years have witnessed an evolution of sex education topics at the community level. Pleasure and gender-equity perspectives have been included in the programs, especially in the methodological approach, among which people's education is outstanding.

Another professional community workspace is the Methodology of Community Correction Processes (ProCC), a psychosocial intervention alternative for working in "supposed health normality" (*Normalidad Supuesta Salud*, NSS), that is to say, the discomforts of daily life that are suffered day by day, but are not questioned because they are considered normal, and professional care is not sought even though they take a high toll on the health and well-being of the population.

According to Mirtha Cucco García, Dra., director of the "Marie Langera" Community Center, Madrid, this methodology has been applied by health, education, and culture professionals to sensitive problems, such as women's mental health from a daily-life approach; ignorance and the resistance to the sex education of their children on the part of fathers and mothers; how middle-aged women experience their sexuality; being a woman and the life project as a young woman; the relationship between the roles of mother and father; professional roles and decision making; and the sexuality of third-age adults.

Following the ProCC methodology, national community-intervention programs have been carried out, for example, the Growing in Adolescence Program, financed by the Cuban government and the United Nations Population Fund with the purpose of decreasing voluntary abortion in the adolescent population.

## C. The Situation Today    MARÍA D. CÓRDOVA

According to data from *Informe de Balance Anual del CENESEX, 2001*, the actions taken by the National Program on Sex Education benefit significant sectors of the population. For example, those carried out in 2001 were:

- In social communication: the National Center of Sexual Education (CENESEX), the Young Communist Union (UJC), and the Cuban Radio and Television Institute (ICRT) made 48 shows for national TV, such as "Our Sexuality" for adolescents, "The Charms of Sexuality" and "Speaking Seriously" for youngsters, and "Sexuality and Daily Life" for all ages; "The Sixth Sense," a weekly space in *Juventud Rebelde* newspaper; in *Mujeres*, *Muchachas*, and *Somos Jóvenes* magazines; as well as publishing, since 1994, the quarterly specialized magazine, *Sexología y Sociedad*, for professionals and the general population. All these initiatives have played an important advocacy role in Cuban society.
- In community work: The Ministry of Public Health, (MINSAP), the Federation of Cuban Women (FMC), the Young Communist Union (UJC), and the National Center of Sexual Education (CENESEX) have carried out over 30 community intervention programs that address sexuality at all ages: "The Family, a Place for Human Development," "Growing During Adolescence," "Discovering Roads," "Values and Sexuality," "Comprehensive Adolescent Care," and "Responsible Motherhood and Fatherhood," among others. In addition, there are also 175 Houses for Women and Family Counseling of the FMC, where 78,734 health providers, 79,237 social workers, and 13,659 professional collaborators provide individual and group counseling and carry out various community-extension processes.
- The Education Program for a Responsible Sexual Behavior, undertaken by the Ministry of Education (MINED) in collaboration with CENESEX and the UNFPA, has benefited 12,000 educational institutions, and over 2 million people, among them, boys and girls, adolescents, youngsters, mothers, fathers, and teachers.

## 4. Autoerotic Behaviors and Patterns

MARIELA CASTRO ESPÍN

No quantitative research addressing autoerotic behavior has been reported. However, in local sex education surveys conducted by CENESEX using group methodologies and some qualitative techniques of data collecting, it has been evident that autoerotic behaviors continue to be perceived with prejudice and fear, and are more accepted and reported by males than by females. Traditional beliefs regarding their supposed negative effects were expressed, although opinions considering them a healthy behavior were also detected (63, 35, 14, 4).

In a research study conducted in the City of Havana (37) with 88 middle-aged women, 62.5% recognize masturbation with their mate as a normal practice, 20.4% consider it exclusive of men, and only 7.9% consider it immoral. In another research study conducted with 100 Havana male adolescents, only 20% experienced their first ejaculation when masturbating, which contrasts with the higher values reported in foreign studies (52).

In the educational professional context, several actions have been taken to contribute to an adequate understanding of this aspect of sexuality, for example, in the methodological guidelines for daycare-center teachers. Since the foundation of this educational institution in 1961, and later in the Childhood Institute in 1971, there were methodological guidelines for teachers for not repressing genital manipulation and/or masturbatory behaviors, as well as sexual games by the children. It is recommended to try to attract their attention to other interesting activities (45).

## 5. Interpersonal Heterosexual Behaviors

### A. Children
MARIELA CASTRO ESPÍN

In several local surveys conducted in two provinces, it was reported that the majority of boys and girls aged 2 to 6 (9.71%) do not know how to explain their gender identity. When interviews were carried out with sexed puppets, the girls (64.27%) recognized gender identity mainly through conventional attributes, such as clothes, length of hair, eyes with makeup, and ornaments, while the boys recognized the essential genital and secondary sexual characteristics differences (50.25%). The choice of toys and games by the majority of boys and girls (over 60% in all the investigations) followed traditional sexist patterns.

It also reported (73) that adults have no knowledge of children's sexuality, regardless of educational level, sex, or economic status. In many cases, mothers and fathers only recognize the existence of sexuality in their male children, as they can have erections at very early ages, which are related to the tendency to genitalize sexuality, still frequent in the social realm. The persistence of gender-role stereotypes among the fathers and mothers was also evident. Gender roles are learned since early childhood, in the choice of the color of clothes, expressions of affection, and toys and games, among others.

The main concerns of adults, in connection with the sexuality of their sons and daughters, are the possibility of contracting diseases, that they would turn out to be homosexuals or victims of sexual violence, and how they can provide their children with adequate sex education. Specific concerns, for example, include how to act regarding masturbation and timing of the first intercourse, among others.

A representative quantitative research study on the sexual behaviors of Cubans has not been conducted. Nevertheless, in reflection activities, parents and educators have shared their observations of children's sexual behavior, such as: sexual games, exploration of the genitals as part of getting to know their own body, masturbation, and questions relating to daily life experiences, such as, pregnancy, childbirth, the sexual body differences of children and adults, and fertilization, just to mention the most frequent.

### B. Adolescents
NATIVIDAD GUERRERO

Research on adolescent sexuality in Cuba has focused essentially on the following: age at the first sexual relationship, gender, and sexual and reproductive health, among others.

The age at which sexual relations take place for the first time changed from one decade to the next one. In the 1980s, according to surveys (20), the first sexual relations took place between age 17 and 18 years. At the end of the 1990s, the adolescents stated that their first sexual intercourse took place between age 14 and 15 years.

Even though the majority does not use condoms (less than 50% in that population segment), more persons are using them and recognizing their importance. Contradictorily, there is greater knowledge of birth-control methods, but not an increase in their use. The contraceptives known and used by young people are condoms, the pill, and IUD, among others.

Frequently, at this age, sexual intercourse is not preceded by feelings of love and trust. Nevertheless, it is performed out of curiosity, to project an image of maturity, to enjoy the pleasure of the moment, because the situation required it, and so on.

On many occasions, this behavior is unknown by adults because of poor adult-adolescent communication. The adolescents state their need to discuss sexuality with their parents; however, adults do not feel prepared for it.

Among Cuban adolescents, casual intimate sexual relations are beginning to be seen, that is to say, a formal courtship does not necessarily have to exist to engage in intercourse. On particular occasions, they have intercourse with partners with whom they have interpersonal relations of friendship or companionship.

Pregnancy, abortion, and menstrual regulation—used to interrupt pregnancies—as well as sexually transmitted diseases, do not reach statistically significant figures in Cuba, because of the intervention of specialized professionals, but they must be addressed by specialists to lower their occurrence, because it is fundamentally during this stage that sexually transmitted diseases are contracted for the first time, and they can be very harmful.

For the majority of adolescents, partner choice continues to be an important process in their lives, but the traits taken into consideration vary. Love and respect are aspirations of female and male adolescents, but characteristics that go against the transparency and health of couple's relations, such as interest in material things and social status, already count, and are being reported in some surveys as motives for establishing a courtship (20).

This means that sexual intercourse does not come about out of love, understanding, and trust; these concepts are changing. The influence of "more advanced" Western cultures that also globalize hedonism, prostitution, and drug addiction all over the world cannot be denied.

In recent surveys (36) with focal groups composed of female and male adolescents, the following gender differences were found:

- Since the beginning, males showed concern with STDs and the use of condoms, although they consider it necessary to use them when having vaginal intercourse with occasional partners. They consider the use of condoms unnecessary after several weeks or a few months with the same partner.
- The girls spoke of pregnancy prevention, not about STDs.
- The boys only spoke of pregnancy when their partner was pregnant.
- No boy considers protection necessary in oral or anal sex.
- There are no differences between girls and boys in the initiation of the courtship, the negotiation for the use of condoms, and the possibility of refusing caresses, although it can have a slight prevalence in males.
- Being behind in school and dropping out of school, "doing nothing" (not working or studying), are related with pregnant adolescents or early motherhood.
- Early sexual relations are associated with dysfunctional homes and parents with social problems, such as alcoholism, imprisonment, and so on.

Adolescents require constant training. In surveys conducted by the Center for Youth Studies (20), adolescents show that sexuality is one of the topics of greatest interest. Adolescence is a stage of frequent worries, doubts, curiosity, and also risks due to the psychological characteristics of adolescents. This emphasizes the need to carry out and maintain permanent action aimed at this age group.

At these ages, educational and preventive work is essential to maintain a healthy society. Thus, programs such as "Growing in Adolescence" (16), "Discovering Roads," "Values and Sexuality," "Education for a Responsible Sexual Behavior" (47), and "Comprehensive Care for Adolescents" (49) are being implemented, and new ones are being planned to decrease negative expressions of sexuality.

Cuban professionals are constantly improving the education of youth. Their effectiveness is ever-increasing. There are advances in the quality of preventive work focusing on essential problems.

## C. Young Adults NATIVIDAD GUERRERO

Sexual and interpersonal relationships of Cuban youth are a continuum regarding adolescence because, at this stage, expressions of sexuality, which initially could have been safe or non-safe and full of love or casualness are consolidated, depending on the sex education of the individual since childhood. Thus, as in the previous stage, the wide range of social behavior should be stressed.

During youth, a stage between ages 18 and 24, for some up to 30 years of age, cohabitation and marriage consolidate. There are also separations and divorces mainly as a consequence of the inconsistencies of couples in the psychological subjective domain.

The topic of living together is more frequent during this period. Family conflicts resulting from an unmarried couple's decision to cohabitate have become very frequent. Sometimes there is a lack of understanding between various generations. Three generations sharing the same home characterizes the Cuban family, especially in the City of Havana. Therefore, preventive work is foreseen in this sensitive topic.

Among young men and women, expressions of interpersonal relationships having to do with sexuality, such as jealousy, separation, and divorce, associated with lack of experience or the making of wrong decisions based on a superficial, hasty, choice of partner, or on not knowing the partner well, are similar to those reported in other countries.

It is a stage during which couples decide to have their own family. Motherhood and fatherhood become important life events, for which young men and women do not always feel prepared, but there is willingness to become good fathers and mothers (21).

Sexuality plays a very important role in the lives of young men and women, as well as professional and general cultural education and employment. These areas are simultaneously developed in daily life throughout this lifecycle period.

In this stage of searching for and consolidating a love relationship, a change of love partners is frequent. Those changes are health risks if the necessary precautions are not taken.

"Single motherhood" as an expression of the desire to have children is not very frequent in this age group, but mainly in women near 30 years of age. The struggle for gender equity was misinterpreted by some girls when considering that they could perform simultaneously both roles of mother and father. It has been made very clear that it is an erroneous belief.

Most pregnancies leading to childbirth are wanted. It is, for the young fathers and young mothers and the whole family, a happy event that requires of a great deal of collective effort.

Possibly, during this stage, unlike any other, sexuality is enjoyed in a significant manner. When the necessary precautions are not taken, sexually transmitted diseases can be contracted. For example, most of the persons who live with HIV or have AIDS in Cuba were infected at this stage or during adolescence. There are also problems from the psychological point of view. Disillusion, despair, failure, and infidelity sometimes lead young men and women to very critical situations that are surpassed with professional help.

As in the case of adolescents, less than 50% of the young women and men use condoms. Generally, they know how to use birth-control methods, but knowing does not mean using. Nevertheless, a wider receptivity for birth-control methods has been found. Those who use them generally choose IUDs, pills, and condoms (21). Sex education programs like "My Life Project" for young men and women have also been implemented (6).

During this stage, sexual dysfunctions are rare. However, if sexual dysfunctions occur, they are associated with premature ejaculation. Traditional gender-role demands play tricks on young men, generally associated with situational phenomena, stress, and so on.

### D. Adults
MARÍA D. CÓRDOVA

The sexuality of the Cuban adult male and female is not divergent from global patterns. As a result of the growing freedoms of the1960s and 1970s, and the sex education received through various means, premarital intercourse soon after meeting a partner or having been formally introduced is spontaneous, frequent, and accepted, especially in the most densely populated urban areas. There are still adults who identify sexuality with sex, essentially genital sex (17). It has also been found that occasionally adults may be knowledgeable regarding sexuality, but taboos on sexuality still endure in a couple's relations and in family sex education (35).

*Machismo* is still present in the culture of adults, but change is evident. While the social recognition of woman is increasing, change in the family is slower (14, 26, 66). Several local surveys have shown that men generally approach women with strong fantasies, while women are more emotionally motivated. That is why women are generally made responsible for the affective aspect of the couple's and the family relationship (34, 65).

One of the reasons for the above changes is the increasing incorporation of women into the workforce and into social activism in general. In 2001, 37.4% of the active workforce in the state civil sector were women, as well as 68.2% of medium- and high-level technicians; 31.2% held decision-making positions and 35.96% of the Parliament's seats were occupied by women in 2003; 63.1% of higher education students were women, as well as 62.7% of the graduates at that educational level. In Cuba, 64.3% of teachers, 54.6% of doctors, 72.9% of public health providers, and 51.95% of scientists and technicians are women (53).

Another of the reasons that conditions the changes in the Cuban social realm in gender issues is the work carried out by the Federation of Cuban Women, from 1961 on, to raise the cultural, political, and technical level of women and to increase their social participation. This was done mainly through magazines such as *Mujeres* and *Muchachas*, in important segments on national and regional radio and TV stations, as well as visible positions in the communities and the federation's congresses and scientific meetings where gender issues, in Cuban society, have been addressed at length.

Marriage is the most widespread way of constituting a family. That is why the marriage rate is 4.8 and the divorce rate is 3.3 (per 1,000 inhabitants). However, cohabitation has increased among the youth. In 1981, for every 100 married youths (between 15 and 19 years old), 189 cohabited (5).

The social policy of the Cuban government, as stated in the Constitution, has among its explicit aims: to strengthen the role of the family, to protect all family members, as well as, the attainment of family relationships based on love, mutual respect, reciprocal help, and shared responsibility. In 1975, the Family Code, which legally regulates family institutions—marriage, divorce, and parental-filial relationships—was adopted. In the Constitution of the Republic of Cuba and the Civil and Penal Codes, there are provisions on all aspects that protect the family as the fundamental cell of society.

Today's Cuban family tends to be small. A significant change occurred between 1953 and 1981 when the average number of family members dropped from 4.9 to 4.1 in 1981 (5). The general fertility rate for women 15 to 49 years old dropped from 57.3 in 1992 to 45.7 in 2001 (53). Nuclear families—families made up of the couple and their children—prevail; in 1995, they accounted for 50.9% of the total families. Extended families (40.5%) are more frequent in Havana, the capital of the country.

According to a nationwide study of 1,200 families from different social strata (60), a model of unequal distribution of domestic chores was prevalent in 59.4%. The "traditional model" prevails; therefore, the woman is solely responsible for household chores (12). Nevertheless, this fact is not homogeneously present in all the families under study; it varied in terms of social class, educational level, work activity, and occupation of the woman. In this study, a marked tendency of both parents not to assign responsibilities and housework to their sons and daughters or to allow their responsible and active participation in daily family dynamics was also reported.

Further evidence of the heavy burden borne by Cuban women was found in a survey on time use conducted in five municipalities. According to that survey, the total weekly work time of women is 20% longer than that of men. Women's household work time is equal to paid work time, and women enjoy considerably less free time than men.

In a research study conducted with 1,125 families having adolescent sons and daughters, it was observed that mothers were the ones who most frequently held conversations with their sons and daughters, expressed their love more often, were more persuasive, and had greater control of their behaviors, which indicate that women continue being mainly responsible for the education of the family (5).

In the educational process of the family, gender socialization plays an important role. An analysis of gender socialization shows a persistence of sexist behavior patterns that are transmitted within the family and also, a group of change indicators. In other words, although sons and daughters continue being educated in a differentiated manner and for a traditional family model, there is also, in many families, a more symmetrical couple model being transmitted to male and female descendants. A woman's role is not limited to being a mother and a wife. She is also a worker and a community activist, and her role includes the full exercise of the sexual and reproductive rights of the couple's members, which facilitates a greater enjoyment of sexuality and empowerment to assume fertility control.

Representative research studies on the sexual behavior of Cuban adults are few. Nevertheless, the findings of some local surveys can be discussed, for example, two surveys conducted on adult women receiving medical care for menopause at a Havana hospital. In-depth interviews showed that 69.2% identified sexuality with sex; 46.1% were anorgasmic; 76.9 had a passive attitude toward sexual relations; 61.6% had played sex games, 46.17% made love to please their husband; 61.5% felt that in middle-age their sexual desires wane; and 69.3% engaged with less frequency in sexual intercourse (37, 71). In another study conducted with 200 women receiving medical care for the same reason in other hospitals, a decrease of the libido was found in 19.5%. According to the researchers, this decrease was related to gender cultural stereotypes on menopause, not to biological causes (8).

### D. Older Adults
OSCAR DÍAZ NORIEGA

At the end of 2001, older adults over 60 years old accounted for 13.6% of the Cuban population. It is expected that in the 2025 this percentage will be 25%. According to the study, *SABE* (*Health and Well-Being of the Older Adult*), carried out by the National Statistics Office in the City of Havana, 44% of the dwellings housed at least an older man or woman, and 8% of the total dwellings housed a person 80 years old and older (54).

In our country, several investigations on the elderly (both men and women) of all provinces have been conducted to learn the sexual behavior of persons over 60 years. It was found that, generally, those who have a steady partner are sexually active until more advanced ages than those who do not. In different studies, it was found that 50% to 75% of the interviewed persons were sexually active, engaging in intercourse with penis penetration as the main form of satisfaction of their sexual desires. The prevailing coitus frequency among the persons under study was once every 15 days; although a considerable number reported weekly relations and, as a curious fact, at least one person in every province reported daily sexual intercourse (30, 62, 65). It is interesting that when sexual dysfunction of one of the couple's members prevents intercourse, they give up all sexual activity, including caresses, kisses, and so on.

When analyzing the reasons for the lower level of sexual activity of persons who lack a steady sexual partner, gender must be considered. In our research, widows were the majority of those not having a steady sexual partner. Those women stated that, on occasion, they felt sexual desires, but because of self-censorship and/or social pressures, they try to channel those desires to other activities, like reading, manual work, or other ways, with the hope of focusing attention on nonsexual activities. As rule, relatives do not approve that widows begin new relations, and those who challenge that rejection are exposed to pressures that range from psychosocial to economic.

In a survey carried out in the City of Havana with old men, it was found that the reaction of the immediate family can range from mockery to physical violence or ceasing all economic support (28). In 2001, 6.47% of all marriages involved men over 60 years old, and 2.96% women that same age. That same year, men over 60 years were involved in 6.99% of the divorces, in comparison to 4.38% of women over 60 years of age (53).

The main reason that men with no steady partner gave for stopping sexual activity is fear of "not performing adequately," this is say, that their sexual performance would disappoint their sexual partner.

A very curious fact, in the interviews carried out during the last two years, is a growing trend to stop having sexual activity with occasional partners because of fear of sexually transmitted infections.

## E. Sex Policies and Politics  MARIELA CASTRO ESPÍN

Cuban policy on sexuality, as an inalienable right of all human beings, is explicit in the priorities contained in the National Program on Sex Education, in the text of several laws of the Civil, Family, and Penal Codes, as well as in an implicit manner in the chapters on Health, Education, and Culture of the Constitution of the Republic of Cuba, currently in force.

In the Constitution of the Republic of Cuba, it is set out that: "The State guarantees the full freedom and dignity of man, the enjoyment of his rights, the exercise and fulfillment of his duties, the comprehensive development of personality" (24, Chapter I Article 9). In another article, it is specified that: "Discrimination on account of race, skin color, sex, national origin, religious beliefs and any other condition detrimental to human dignity are banned and punished by law" (Chapter VI, Article 42).

The priorities of the National Program on Sex Education (15) are:

1. The right of all persons regardless of sex, race, age, sexual orientation, sensory, intellectual, and physical abilities and skills, political and religious beliefs to receive sex education as part of their comprehensive education.

2. The right of all persons, with no exception, to receive sexual healthcare within a comprehensive conception of health.
3. The respect for human dignity, from which is derived the respect for the sexual rights of all men and women.
4. The creation of material and ideological conditions to promote the development of a full, healthy, responsible, and happy sexuality.
5. Development of local management in the communities for covering the needs of vulnerable groups of the population.

Regarding this subject, particular policies are designed and implemented by several government institutions and civil society organizations for providing care to different population groups, among which the following national programs are outstanding:

- "Toward a Responsible and Happy Sexuality," a sex education program taught at schools;
- The "Mother and Child Program," which includes several special programs, such as: "Adolescent Comprehensive Health," "Responsible Motherhood and Fatherhood," and "Infantile and Juvenile Gynecology";
- "Audiovisual Project for Children, Adolescents, and Youths";
- "Prevention and Control of STIs and HIV/AIDS"; and
- "Comprehensive Care for Older Adults," to mention a few.

The Infantile and Juvenile Gynecology Program, according to Jorge Peláez Mendoza, M.D., provides, among its services, differentiated abortion and menstrual regulation care. Among its main objectives are the lowering of abortion incidence at those early ages and, if abortion is unavoidable, offering access to a safe one, through humane and skilled care, including psychological support and education, as well as to guarantee a supply of birth-control methods in the post-abortion stage, for an free informed choice.

The necessary requirements for providing differentiated care are:

- To devote at least one day to the "sole" care of adolescents.
- All personnel working in these services should be qualified and trained in infantile and juvenile gynecology and adolescent reproductive health.
- To guarantee the active participation of a psychologist before, during, and after the procedure, and to provide emotional support to the patient and her family. Whenever possible, the family doctor accompanies his or her patient the day the procedure is performed.
- To make sure, when the patient is discharged, that she receives follow-up medical care in the infantile and juvenile consultation and control with birth-control methods.

The actions that should be carried out in the provision of medical care are:

- To give information to the adolescent and her companions about the performance of the procedure, its risks, most frequent complications, and what is done if there is evidence of complications.
- To obtain the adolescent's informed consent, as well as that of her parents or tutors.
- Performance of the procedure by a gynecology specialist, a nurse, and anesthesia personnel previously trained in infantile and juvenile gynecology.
- Give the adolescent, after being discharged, an appointment for infantile and juvenile gynecology consultation for follow-up, counseling, and monitoring of birth-con-

trol use in the infantile and juvenile gynecology consultation.

This work methodology has been implemented nationwide since at least 1998. An outstanding drop of complications has been achieved with this procedure, mainly when it is repeated. The use of birth-control methods has increased in this age bracket, and there is a non-statistically significant reduction in the overall incidence of abortion in these age groups.

## 6. Homoerotic, Homosexual, and Bisexual Behaviors

MARIELA CASTRO ESPÍN and EDDY ABREU GUERRA

For many years, in the Cuban social realm, as in almost all Western-culture countries, there is disdain and an accusatory attitude toward homosexuality. Homosexuality is still considered by some a disease, an aberration, or an immorality, preserving some features of the traditional rejection.

The historical evolution of the modern age and the deep changes made by the Cuban Revolution in its quest for social justice for all men and women brought about a gradual favorable change of opinion on homosexuality. In the 1990s, more flexibility was observed in the understanding and acceptance of homosexuality in different social and cultural environments. However, there is still prejudice, stereotypes, and moralizing ideas that demean homosexual behavior.

As far back as the 1950s, no legal regulation penalizing homosexual behavior was stipulated in the Penal Code, although nondiscrimination for sexual preferences is not explicitly stated. There is a total absence of legislation of any kind on that topic (68).

Regarding marriage, the Family Code stipulates that it "is the concerted voluntary union of a man and a woman with legal competence, with the aim of living a common life" (43). Nevertheless, in daily practice currently, it is relatively frequent that homosexual and lesbian couples live together with steady partners.

Research on homosexuality mainly deals with the psychological and social aspects, and on the characteristics of male homosexuals. In the last two years, family dynamics studies have included homosexuals and lesbians. But there is still little research.

In those surveys that have been done, it was found that homosexuals are not exempt from family and educational conflicts. "The variable—being homosexual—within the family framework, marks the whole relationship with a sense of guilt and vulnerability, both the relation of the homosexual with his family and that of his family with him" (61).

Homosexuals, mainly in large cities like Havana, have different behaviors from the rest of the population. They go to certain public places, which have become meeting places, where they plan and carry out different activities of their daily life. They do not consider themselves either sick or morally undesirable, and do not associate their sexual orientation with pathologies, but with genetic, biological causes. There are homosexuals who consider themselves in a range from healthy to excluded.

The cultural actions undertaken, in films, plays, literature, and in other media, as well as the educational actions on the radio and TV, in the press and specialized magazines, such as *Sexología y Sociedad*, promote the debate and the sensitization of the audience receiving those messages, which contributes to the understanding and respect for homosexuals and lesbians from the scientific and artistic discourse.

On the other hand, the National Center of Sexual Education promotes respect for diversity through the implementation of the sex education policy contained in its current National Program. This shows that, currently, there are conditions for deeper educational work in the promotion of respect for the different sexual orientations.

## 7. Gender Diversity and Transgender Issues

MAYRA RODRÍGUEZ LAUZERIQUE and
OFELIA BRAVO FERNÁNDEZ

In Cuba, one frequently hears certain expressions—with a strong negative moral judgment—denoting the false belief among the people, and even in professional contexts, that transsexuals and transvestites are homosexuals.

Since the 1970s, a team of specialists has been working to provide medical care for patients with this identity disorder. In June 1984, a document was drafted by the National Commission on Sexual Counseling and Therapy, as part of the working strategies of the Ministry of Public Health and of the National Sex Education Center, with the aim of establishing standard approaches among our professionals and to establish the legal bases for the treatment of this identity disorder. As of that date and until the year 2002, 59 persons—predominantly white (only one black patient)—have received medical care. Of these, 57 requested a sex change from male to female and only two from female to male.

A case study performed by specialists from the National Center of Sexual Education (63) shows some characteristics of 13 transsexual Cubans that received care in 1994. The cases studied reflect the same trend as the total of cases that received care, as 13 wanted a male-to-female transformation and only two a female-to-male. Lack of conformity with their own sex was found in the subjects studied, as a trend, starting at age 3. For most, early schooling elapsed without difficulties; however, during adolescence, they experienced the first lack of understanding and rejection by their peer group. Most have a high IQ and only three were average. Adolescence was recognized by them as a difficult period, mainly because of body-image conflicts, and especially because of the rejection of their own genitals. Their sexual desires, as perceived by them, seemed to be weak or mediated by values that led them to live alone. Those who had partners insisted that they needed company and understanding. Their personal relations were friendly and, in general, they were positively valued by the community in which they lived and, in some cases, where they worked.

## 8. Significant Unconventional Sexual Behaviors

MARIELA CASTRO ESPÍN, MARÍA D. CÓRDOVA
LLORCA, and LAUREN BARDISA ESCURRA

### A. Coercive Sexual Behaviors

*Child Sexual Abuse*

The relations that adults establish with boys and girls are socially, historically, and economically conditioned. Children need to be in contact with others for the survival of the species, for personality development, and to grow healthy in order to become self-reliant. Adults, playing different roles, lead the socialization and learning processes of boys and girls in various contexts. The Cuban social model has an essential objective: the full development of the human being; and, therefore, it has created conditions that allow our boys, girls, adolescents, and youths to be protected in various ways.

The Penal Code identifies several crimes that are characterized by sexual acts with children. In its Title 11, "Crimes against the normal development of the sexual relations and against the family, childhood and youth" expresses the fundamental elements of unlawful acts, such as rape (Art. 298), pederasty with violence (Art. 299), sexual abuse (Art. 300), and corruption of minors (Art. 310).

Various studies have been carried out on child sexual victimization. For example, between 1990 and 1991, 209 cases of children victims of sexual abuse, in criminal proceedings at the Provincial Tribunal of the City of Havana, whose perpetrators were not acquitted, were studied (57). Among these minors, 77.9%, or 163, were female compared with 46 males, 25.4%. Of the total sample, 156 (74.6%) were under 12, while 53 (25.4%) were between 12 and 15 years of age, and the youngest victim was 1 year old.

The offenses categorized by the Court, according to the effective Penal Code, were:

- Sexual abuse: 149 (71.3%)
- Rape and attempted rape: 40 (19.1%)
- Pederasty and attempted pederasty: 10 (4.8%)
- Corruption of Minors: 10 (4.8%)

Sexual crimes usually occur in places relevant to the lives and activities of the victims and during their normal activity schedules. Whether or not there is a previous relationship between the victim and the offender may determine certain peculiarities in the crime. According to statistics, when the crime was committed by a stranger, the perpetrator was under 35 years of age, the sexual abuse was characterized by rough treatment and the presence of blood, victims were usually over 10 years of age, and the crime was committed in places where the minors did not generally carry out their activities. When the offender was someone known by the minor, the characteristics of the abuse were significantly different.

In the above-mentioned study, slightly over half of the victims suffered from psychopathological disorders previous to the abuse and with no significant statistical relationship with family dysfunction or the characteristics of the perpetrator. A fourth of the victims was behind in school according to their age or had poor academic achievement before being victims of such abuse.

When physically examined, no signs were found of the traumatic marks characteristic of the classic child abuse syndrome when minors are victims of sexual crimes.

Sexual information in these victims is usually scant; it is infrequent for the sexual crime to represent a revictimization or for the victimized minor to have his or her own criminal record.

There is a significant relationship between some characteristics of the victim's family environment and the peculiarities of the crime:

- In most cases, the background of the family is dysfunctional and is characterized by habitual beatings or punishments as forms of correction, while promiscuity was not found to be predominant. The most common family attitude regarding sexual topics with the minor is far from being educational.
- As a trend, the victimization takes place in the victim's home, particularly, when the perpetrator is the stepfather. Victimization is also significantly associated to behavioral ex-post-facto changes that do not classify in the sequelae legal category, even when they represent forms of posttraumatic stress.
- There was an almost absolute prevalence of male perpetrators, significantly above 35 years of age when compared with those who victimize adult women, but with the average age near 35. Most of the abuse was accomplished single-handedly against isolated victims.
- Adults who sexually abuse girls and boys have an average high school educational level, most of them do not typically have criminal records, and much less do they relapse in such an activity.

- The prevalence of sexual victimization of girls by men, in the family or subcultural environments or both, may be linked to a gender-based male-centered education characteristic of our environment, linking the problem under study to social actions geared to correcting such deformations and their consequences.

*Family Violence and Violence Against Women*

In Cuba, despite a social project granting women equal opportunities for the exercise of power and social participation, there are myths circulating in the realm of communities, as well as traditional models of gender socialization, from which violent behaviors emerge.

The following figures (2) allow us to make progress in the in-depth study and approach of the subject matter.

- There are reports showing a total of 2,690 cases of violence and, of these, 332 cases of minors who are victims of violence. Data segregated by sex were not found in all cases, but in at least 1,639 cases of abused subjects, 63% of the total were female victims, including 217 girls.
- In studies that do not deal directly with the problem of violence, 45% of the interviewees knew persons who exercised violence on their own children, punishing them strongly or hitting them.
- Between 1990 and 1995, of all the women in the files of the Institute of Legal Medicine as a result of homicides in the City of Havana, 45% died at the hands of their spouses and 52% of those homicides took place inside the victim's home. This shows the relationship between homicide and marital violence.
- The studies indicate that 46.9% of the female victims were murdered by their spouses and that only 16.2% of the men were murdered by their wives.
- All the women who committed murder and homicide against their partners did so in response to violence against them.
- The scenario where violence is mostly exercised against women is in their home.
- A study on serious crimes committed in the City of Havana reports that, of a total of 468 cases, 28.8% of the victims were women.

In research conducted in two of the provinces with the highest rate of female victimization, case studies were made. In every case, there was a background of violence in the women's families of origin and in that of their spouses, as well as a tendency to cohabitation, common-law marriages, and teenage motherhood. All the women showed a low self-esteem and felt incapable of breaking on their own the cycle of violence in which they were immersed (59). In another province, there are reports of marital violence, more physical and more sexual on the part of the man, psychological on the part of the woman (70).

In a sexual abuse study of 150 women victims and only two men, also in 1990-1991 in City of the Havana, 70% were rapes of women between 16 and 25 years of age. They were assaulted by strangers in 60% of the cases. In 87.33% of the cases, there was shedding of blood. The perpetrators were also in the same age group; they were single and, although they did not have criminal records, there were negative opinions about their social behavior in 70% of the cases (44).

The family, and in particular women, given their educational functions with their children and daughters, play a fundamental role in the socialization of violence and nonviolence. Hence, women become the target population in any strategy geared at the prevention of violence in any of its manifestations, and especially, of violence against themselves.

The political will of the State to guarantee the protection of the family and of each citizen is expressed in various legislation: Constitution of the Republic, Family Code, Labor Code, Civil Code, and Penal Code. Nevertheless, the existence of family violence is not yet recognized, which could be related to the fact that it is not considered a social phenomenon.

Prevention and treatment of family violence in Cuba are carried out through comprehensive actions. In 1997, the Work Group for the Prevention and Treatment of Family Violence (10) was created, which is coordinated by the Federation of Cuban Women and made up permanently by the Ministry of Education, the Ministry of Public Health, the Ministry of the Interior, the Institute of Legal Medicine, the Attorney General of the Republic, the National Sex Education Center, the Center for Psychological and Sociological Research, the University of Havana, the Cuban Institute of Radio and Television, and the People's Higher Court. Their objective is to design and to implement a joint action plan to contribute to the prevention and treatment of this problem and to make proposals to other social organizations and entities when appropriate.

The composition of the group facilitates the implementation of objectives and tasks through the structures and functions of each member agency and organization, as well as through the people that represent them in the community: teachers, doctors, policemen, judges, and prosecutors, among others.

## B. Prostitution

MARIELA CASTRO ESPÍN and MARÍA D. CÓRDOVA LLORCA

In Cuba, the origins of prostitution date back to the Spanish conquest and colonization process, carried out essentially "by single men who brought harlots, fundamentally from the Canary Islands, in their ships." On the island, first aboriginal women and later black women were forced to practice prostitution. This activity was so prosperous in colonial and republican times that by the mid-1950s, Cuba was known as "The Brothel of the Caribbean." Back then, prostitution was allowed but discriminated against. Public scandal was punished, and it was said: "You can exercise prostitution, but behind closed doors. And with that they did not want to protect the prostitute; but the client" (29).

In 1959, there were around 100,000 prostitutes in Cuba in a population of six million inhabitants. The strategy to eradicate this phenomenon emerged from the certainty that the fundamental causes were associated with the conditions of exploitation and poverty to which a great number of women were subjected, contingent on the existing economic and social situation of neocolonial dependence (40).

Since its inception, the Cuban Revolutionary Government has developed social programs geared at dignifying the human condition of men, and especially of women, which allowed the elimination of the material and social supports of prostitution. Among the actions taken were the closing of all brothels and the penalizing of pimping, pimps being considered as exploiters, all of which allowed them to significantly minimize the different expressions of prostitution in Cuba for more than 20 years.

However, during the economic crisis of the 1990s, this phenomenon reemerged in the Cuban social reality. Many researchers consider the economic problems that have generated new forms of social inequality, and the subsequent damage in the ideological and moral spheres, as elements that could be conditioning the persistence of these sexual practices. Researcher Aurelio Alonso of the Center for Psychological and Sociological Research of the Ministry of Science, Technology, and the Environment, states: "Prostitution is mentioned as one of social costs of the changes, but more serious than that is the problem of the progressive inequality of the standard of living, moreover, also a fundamental cause of the increase of prostitution. It is borne out of inequality, not out of abstract shortages, not out of abstract poverty, or abstract neglect. It is true; we have lived through this collapse without having neglect. But perhaps protection is not yet enough" (69).

A survey (22) conducted on this topic has mainly involved young females aged from 20 to 24 years, of any race, mainly single, and with no children. Their experience regarding sexuality is characterized by instability and preference for foreigners, since foreigners have more possibilities of satisfying their economic needs. They rarely acknowledge themselves as prostitutes, but as *luchadoras* or *jineteras*, and they are socially known by these terms that for them mean to go out to have a good time, to get to know good places, and to widen their circles of relations.

The bonds established with the prostituting client in many cases end up being affectionate and with a communication that goes beyond the foreigner's brief stay in the country. They are not often carriers of sexually transmitted diseases, although as of late, a slight increase is observed among the groups that are devoted to the exercise of prostitution, mostly in men that have sex with men. These women have a schooling level of 9 to 12 years.

"The reason for the re-emergence of prostitution—according to the girls' own statements—is because they have found in it a quick way to meet their economic needs and those of their family. They also state that the amount of money that is obtained from this type of sexual practice is higher than the wages earned by working" (23). Current prostitution in Cuba is distinctive, because people are responsible for their situation in the sense that "they do not do it so much to cover their basic needs, but to maintain an above-the-average consumer status" (32). This choice of lifestyle is determined, as noted previously, by the social, economic, educational, and family conditions.

Behind prostitution hide some old myths that in some way the *jineteras* themselves assume in order to justify their behavior, uplift their injured self-esteem, and alleviate their guilt. Among them are those related with the "easy life," or that it is the oldest profession. In our country, when accepting the epithet of *jinetera* or *luchadora* and not of prostitute, when saying "my body is not me," these persons alienate themselves from their own actions, trying to protect themselves from self-criticism (32). Male prostitution is hushed.

Anyway, the persons who put their body on sale, alienated or not, suffer, feel guilt, and become marginal. "In the most common practice of sex-for-sale in Cuba, the truth is that most of the times the prostitute (male or female) is a victim of him/herself, but always a victim, and contempt toward the human being has never been an option for the Cuban society." At present, different social strategies are coordinated and should continue to be improved regarding this situation.

## C. Pornography and Erotica

MARIELA CASTRO ESPÍN

Currently, the excess of (non-educational) information on sexuality is a problem for many countries: For example, pornography with exclusively commercial purposes distorts the true essence of human sexual behavior.

Up to our days, in Cuba this is not a great social concern, because there is a ban on the sale or entry into the country of literature and videos classified as pornographic, with the purpose of protecting the new generations from its harmful influences.

This is possible because a legal basis exists in Article 86 of the Code on Childhood and Youth for their protection, which reads: "The mass media should contribute to the comprehensive training of children and youths. The Cuban Institute of Radio and Television, the Ministry of Culture and related organizations in charge of publishing written material guarantee the constant development of these resources and their highest quality" (40).

Literature available to our youth, in addition to the national radio and television programs, count on the advisory opinion of specialists, fundamentally psychologists and sociologists, who analyze the psychological particularities of the target audience of these spaces, in accordance with the ethical values promoted by our society.

Institutional policies prioritize educational messages both in literature and in the social media. In Cuban radio and TV, there are various permanent spaces on sexuality to offer popular scientific information for different age groups.

The participation of prestigious specialists on these topics in national programs with high ratings is frequent. At the moment, there is an audiovisual program sponsored by youth and student organizations, where the topics of sexuality have a strong and important presence in spaces for adolescents, with segments called "Our Sexuality," "The Charms of Sexuality" for the young, and for adults, "Sexuality and Our Daily life," among others.

In the Cuban Penal Code, Article No. 310, Corruption of Minors, penalizes the distribution and ownership of any form of pornography, which functions as a restraint for the negligible attempts at the production and introduction of these products in our country.

In recent years, the Cuban State has been able to verify that all these actions are not enough to protect some boys and girls, mainly adolescents who have been the victims of foreign pornography dealers, who have used them to make videos and take pictures that are later sold in the US and in some European countries. This has put the Cuban authorities on the alert in order to establish more effective mechanisms of control and protection in favor of our children.

*Cuban Eroticism*          MARIELA CASTRO ESPÍN

Eroticism and sensuality are broadly visible in the daily life of Cuban men and women, as well as in all the different cultural expressions, such as theater, cinema, literature, painting and sculpture, music and contemporary folklore, popular dance, and in the world-renowned Cuban School of Ballet.

The blending of the Spanish and the African cultures in the so-called cultural syncretism that characterizes Cubanness has a singular eroticism load that is seen in the expressiveness, the gestures, way of walking, the language, and the passion of which Cuban men and women are proud.

Carolina de la Torre, a distinguished researcher of Cuban identity, stated: "I have found that, contrary to other Latin American peoples, Cubans have a high self-esteem when compared to North Americans, and that the identity of the Cuban is strong and clearly delineated, based in very solid representations and affections, and accompanied by pride and commitment with the nation. . . . Therefore, we are humane, cheerful, extroverted" (25), and Cubans assume to be *machistas* and, occasionally, bad-mannered.

## 9. Contraception, Abortion, and Population Planning

MIGUEL SOSA MARÍN

In Cuba, after 1959, as part of the deep social transformations carried out, the Ministry of Public Health implemented its first work programs; a series of measures and actions were developed that would set down the basis for the achievements that may be shown today regarding health. Family

planning, from that time on, has been linked, mainly, with women's and children's health, and in accordance with the right of the free reproduction of the couple.

Among the most important health programs that are being implemented is the Mother and Child Program, in which care is provided during different stages of the reproductive process: prenatal, birth, and postnatal and puerperium, as well as in the follow-up and control of the healthy child. Directly linked to this program are the actions for family planning, which could be the supply of information, counseling, education, and services that have been rendered for more than 20 years, and which have improved the quality of life of the mother and child and the well-being of the family.

Although there has not been in Cuba a policy to increase or to decrease the population, there are a number of basic principles that are the right of the family, the couple, and specifically of women, to decide the number of children and birth spacing; the right to freely decide is respected, and the exercise of women's equality and actions to reduce mother and child risk are being undertaken.

Regarding the above, the Family Planning Program has been implemented since the 1980s, with the following objectives: to achieve responsible actions based on the sense of responsibility of the couple to have children, so that they may have the children they want at the favorable moment for the child, the mother, and the family, in such way that they have the appropriate conditions for their comprehensive development.

In the framework of this program, couples are offered counseling, education, and services, including couples with infertility problems. The program is based in the community and supported by the subsystem of family medicine. It is in the family physician's office (17, 217) where most of the actions are carried out to improve reproductive health and family planning. There are 444 family planning services at the community level in the entire country.

At the primary health level, in polyclinics, specialized appointments for family planning (204) are offered, with effective and modern methods for this process, geared fundamentally at caring for the cases of high reproductive risk, which cannot be solved with more traditional methods or at the family doctor's office. The specialized contraception and infertility care provided in these offices could only be offered before at a secondary care level, therefore, it has been an improvement with wider access for the users. The team of physicians who provide this medical care is made up essentially of specialists in gynecoobstetrics, family medicine, psychology, and internal medicine, as well as obstetric nurses and social workers. If necessary, specialized consultations take place. Contraceptive coverage through modern devices is 72.1%. Adding 1.2% who adopt recommended traditional methods gives a total coverage of 73.3%.

In Cuba, there has been such a decrease in fertility that the country now has similar levels to those of developed countries. According to data of the Ministry of Public Health and the National Office of Statistics, the general fertility (per 1,000 women of fertile age, 15-49 years) was around 57.3 in 1992 and 45.7 in 2001. Birthrates were around 12.7 to 12.4 (per 1,000 inhabitants) between 1996 and 2001 (53). This shows that Cuba, among the developing countries, is the country that has been able to lower the Global Fertility Rate most with a moderate effort in family planning. The fertility rate according to the mother's age in 2001 is shown in Table 1.

In the 1970s, a series of local surveys on knowledge and use of birth-control methods was conducted for the first time. In 1987, a National Fertility Survey reported a high prevalence of knowledge and use of contraceptives among the women interviewees: 84% had used them sometimes and 68% were using them at the time of the survey; 97% knew birth-control methods and classified them according to effectiveness, with first place to IUDs, oral contraceptives, and surgical sterilization.

An analysis of fertility determinants showed that the use of birth-control methods has been the most important factor in lowering the fertility rate.

Birth control usage, as well as the practice of abortion, are widespread throughout the country. Since 1965, abortions in Cuba are performed in medical institutions. Essentially, it is a reproductive right enjoyed by Cuban women and is also performed on medical grounds. An abortion is limited to the first ten weeks of gestation; at a later stage, it is only performed under extreme medical conditions. All abortions are performed by specialized personnel and under appropriate conditions in the gynecology and obstetric hospitals and other health installations. Adolescents are provided with special attention, being one of the fundamental elements of their sexual and reproductive healthcare. Since 1987, the Penal Code penalizes illegal abortions, those performed without the consent of the woman, those not performed in health institutions, and those performed by unskilled persons.

Research has shown that a considerable percentage of abortions result from the negligence of the couple and the non-use of birth-control methods. Thus, it is important to have those effective methods at hand and to use them appropriately.

## 10. Sexually Transmitted Diseases and HIV/AIDS (SIDA)

ROSAIDA OCHOA and LEONARDO CHACÓN

In our country, programs for the prevention and control of STDs and HIV/AIDS are being implemented. These programs have national coverage and are focused on three health levels. Although the spread of these diseases is not excessively alarming, actions are being multiplied to combat them. Prevention strategies are ever more specific, and emphasis is given to the most vulnerable populations. The main mode of transmission of HIV is sexual relations.

### A. Status of the HIV/AIDS Epidemic

The national HIV/AIDS epidemic spreads slowly but continuously. Up to December 2001, 3,874 people have been diagnosed with AIDS, of which 3,024 (78%) are men and 850 (22%) women (see Table 2). Of the total of those diagnosed with HIV, 1,526 developed AIDS and 955 died. The national estimate is 0.05%. The provinces with highest incidence are the City of Havana, Villa Clara, Sancti Spiritus, and Pinar del Río.

The youths between 15 and 35 years of age are the most affected age group. Men having sex with other men (MSM) have significantly the highest infection rate, accounting for 61.7% of the persons living with HIV and 79% of the men's total (see Table 3).

In 1996, antiretroviral treatments began to be used. Initially its use was scant, but by 2001, 98% of all AIDS cases received a range of five medications in antiretroviral treatments. At present, efforts are being made to give wider coverage and to increase the quantity of medications.

[*Update 2002*: UNAIDS Epidemiological Assessment: HIV seroprevalence information among antenatal clinic attendees is available since the late-1980s from Cuba. At the national level, reporting of antenatal women tested indicates there is no evidence of HIV infection in this group. There is no information available on HIV prevalence among sex workers, IV-drug users, or male STD clinic patients.

[The estimated number of adults and children living with HIV/AIDS on January 1, 2002, were:

| | |
|---|---|
| Adults ages 15-49: | 3,200 (rate: < 0.1%) |
| Women ages 15-49: | 830 |
| Children ages 0-15: | < 100 |

[An estimated 120 adults and children died of AIDS during 2001.

[At the end of 2001, an estimated 1,000 Cuban children under age 15 were living without one or both parents who had died of AIDS. (*End of update by the Editors*)]

### B. Status of STDs

The STD program considers syphilis and gonorrhea as infections that must be of compulsorily reported. Their incidence is different from HIV/AIDS. Syphilis and gonorrhea tend to annually decrease, while the spread the HIV/AIDS epidemic shows an upward trend. The reasons for that difference have not been sufficiently explained. The epidemiological data on those infections of the last decade are shown in Table 4.

At the end of 2001, the national syphilis rate was 55.5 per 100,000 inhabitants and gonorrhea was 131.7. Young-

### Table 1

**Fertility Rate by Mother's Age in 2001**

| Mother's Age | Rate* | Mother's Age | Rate* |
|---|---|---|---|
| 15-19 | 50.3 | 35-39 | 22.1 |
| 20-24 | 89.5 | 40-44 | 3.7 |
| 25-29 | 83.9 | 45-49 | 0.2 |
| 30-34 | 52.3 | Total | 45.5 |

*Per 1,000 women of that age (53).

### Table 2

**Persons with HIV by Sex and Year of Diagnosis, 1986-2001**

| | 1986 | 1987 | 1988 | 1989 | 1990 | 1991 | 1992 | 1993 | 1994 | 1995 | 1996 | 1997 | 1998 | 1999 | 2000 | 2001 |
|---|---|---|---|---|---|---|---|---|---|---|---|---|---|---|---|---|
| Total | 99 | 75 | 93 | 121 | 140 | 183 | 175 | 102 | 122 | 124 | 234 | 363 | 362 | 493 | 545 | 643 |
| Men | 76 | 61 | 58 | 87 | 101 | 125 | 119 | 73 | 90 | 88 | 181 | 295 | 284 | 413 | 450 | 523 |
| Women | 23 | 14 | 35 | 34 | 39 | 58 | 56 | 29 | 32 | 36 | 53 | 68 | 78 | 80 | 95 | 120 |

### Table 3

**Total of Men Diagnosed by Year: Comparison with Men Who Have Sex with Men (MSM), 1986-2001**

| | 1986 | 1987 | 1988 | 1989 | 1990 | 1991 | 1992 | 1993 | 1994 | 1995 | 1996 | 1997 | 1998 | 1999 | 2000 | 2001 |
|---|---|---|---|---|---|---|---|---|---|---|---|---|---|---|---|---|
| Men | 76 | 61 | 58 | 87 | 101 | 125 | 119 | 73 | 90 | 88 | 181 | 295 | 284 | 413 | 450 | 523 |
| MSM | 20 | 33 | 27 | 57 | 73 | 105 | 99 | 62 | 73 | 69 | 156 | 251 | 262 | 352 | 421 | 406 |

sters and the young adults between ages 15 and 35 years account for most of the STDs. The provinces of highest incidence of gonorrhea were the City of Havana, Camaguey, Santiago de Cuba, and Guantánamo. The highest incidence of syphilis is found the City of Havana, Santiago de Cuba, and Camaguey (see Table 5).

The achievements of the Program on STD Prevention and Control are reflected in the decrease congenital syphilis cases. The data from the last decade are shown in Table 6.

## 11. Sexual Dysfunctions, Counseling, and Therapies

### BEATRIZ TORRES RODRÍGUEZ

In studies conducted by several investigators on an apparently healthy population, it was shown that 30% to 40% of the subjects had sexual dysfunction. Erectile dysfunction had the highest incidence, followed by premature ejaculation (27, 75).

The incidence of women seeking sexual therapy is relatively low, but in recent years, the percentage of women under therapy is gradually increasing. For example, in a survey of cases that received medical care in the City of Havana, women accounted for 18% in 1991, and up to 27% in 1995 (11), while in another publication, the same authors stated that 30% of women receiving medical care were anorgasmic. In another survey of apparently healthy women, it was found that 35% of interviewees had orgasmic dysfunctions (76).

The specialty of clinical sexology is still nonexistent in Cuba. Sexual therapy, which would train future professionals for diagnosis and treatment of sexual dysfunctions, is not included in the syllabus of related specialties. Therefore, interdisciplinary groups were formed as a solution to the problem. At surgical clinical general hospitals, the interdisciplinary group is made up by psychiatry, psychology, internal medicine, urology, gynecology, endocrinology, and angi-

ology specialists, among others. This group carries out several psychological, pharmacological, and surgical strategies developed for the specific conditions and characteristics of each group.

Generally, the procedure of these work teams begins with a diagnostic consultation, where it is determined if there is a dysfunction or if the patient needs sexual counseling. Next, the possible causes of dysfunctions are explored. During this process specific assays are made and appropriate action taken.

The National Program on Sex Education offers the possibility to all the interdisciplinary groups to carry out its counseling and sex education programs, with slight variations to meet specific needs. Meetings covering aspects, such as, the physiology of the male and female genitals, human sexual response, sexual dysfunction, and the importance of a couple's communication, among others, are held. In those meetings, patients and couples receive counseling and training on the sexuality aspects unknown by them. These programs are still eminently educational and are currently being improved.

The organization of sexual therapy services is not limited to the capital; in each province of the country, there is at least an interdisciplinary group providing care to patients.

A master's degree, diploma, and basic courses and work site visits to the National Center of Sexual Education (CENESEX) contributes to the scientific updating of professionals who compose those interdisciplinary groups.

The psychological techniques mostly used in sexual therapy are the following: Couple therapy, social abilities training, rational emotive therapy (myths and irrational ideas related to sexuality), and relaxation.

For diagnosing sexual dysfunctions in Cuba, interviews and physical examinations are mostly used. More than six years ago, the journal *Sexología y Sociedad* published a proposal for sexual therapy diagnosis norms and for the use of complementary tests (74).

In treatment requiring sildenafil or a penile prosthesis, which, on many occasions, are not available because of the difficult current economic conditions, the following variants have been used: 1. for diabetic polyneuropathy: ozone therapy; 2. for alcoholic polyneuropathy: ozone therapy; 3. for arterial failure: magnetic chamber and ozone therapy or hyperbaric chamber plus magnetic chamber; 4. for vein failure: acupuncture; and 5. for priapism prevention in intracavernous injections with vasoactive drugs: acupuncture.

In persons over 60 years of age, sexual therapy follows the same pattern as for earlier ages. As a rule, in our country, women don't seek medical care for sexual dysfunctions, except if they fail to give pleasure to their male partner. Therefore, there are not many female cases to report on. For example, during 2001, at a polyclinic in the City of Havana, according to Oscar Díaz Noriega, M.D., only six older women received medical care, accounting for only 8% of all those receiving care: three with lubrication dysfunction, one for sexual desire dysfunction, and two anorgasmics.

Regarding men, the main consultation cause was erectile dysfunction. The main causes of the 65 cases who received medical care in another doctor's office in the City of Havana in 2001 were: diabetic polyneuropathy 21; arterial failure 9; a mixture of the former and the latter conditions 6; hypofunction of the smooth muscle 6; Shy Draguer's syndrome 1; hypogonadism 4; Parkinson's disease 2; and a wide range of non-organic dysfunctions, including: couple-relations dysfunctions, monotonous sexual relations, not attractive partner, over demand, or false expectations of sexual performance (65).

### Table 4

#### Cases of Gonorrhea and Syphilis, 1990-2001

|  | 1990 | 1991 | 1992 | 1993 | 1994 | 1995 |
|---|---|---|---|---|---|---|
| Gonorrhea | 35,722 | 32,109 | 26,303 | 20,781 | 34,224 | 45,200 |
| Syphilis | 9,205 | 10,036 | 11,110 | 9,956 | 11,551 | 14,339 |

|  | 1996 | 1997 | 1998 | 1999 | 2000 | 2001 |
|---|---|---|---|---|---|---|
| Gonorrhea | 40,576 | 33,948 | 29,648 | 23,225 | 19,067 | 14,792 |
| Syphilis | 15,818 | 15,814 | 13,400 | 12,285 | 9,198 | 6,233 |

### Table 5

#### Rates of Syphilis per Year and Difference in Percentage

| Year | Rate per 100,000 | Decrease in Percentage |
|---|---|---|
| 1998 | 121.1 | −15.3 |
| 1999 | 110.2 | −8.3 |
| 2000 | 82.1 | −25.2 |
| 2001 | 55.5 | −32.4 |

### Table 6

#### Cases of Congenital Syphilis, 1990-2001

|  | 1990 | 1991 | 1992 | 1993 | 1994 | 1995 |
|---|---|---|---|---|---|---|
| Congenital syphilis | 12 | 9 | 11 | 10 | 11 | 1 |

|  | 1996 | 1997 | 1998 | 1999 | 2000 | 2001 |
|---|---|---|---|---|---|---|
|  | 11 | 2 | 1 | 0 | 1 | 0 |

As an alternative to sildenafil and similar drugs, and to penile prosthesis and implantation, which are unavailable on occasion, the following have been used: hyperbaric chamber or rectally administered ozone therapy for polyneuropathies and hypofunction of the carvernous smooth muscle, and magnetic chamber and ozone therapy or hyperbaric chamber in arterial failure. Results have been favorable in 54% of the cases (including cured and improved) receiving these treatment variants.

The higher institutes or universities at each Cuban province have gone a long way in teaching, research, and counseling on sexuality. They have counseling centers for diagnosis and counseling on sexuality, couple and family relations for students, teaching and non-teaching personnel, and various community groups.

## 12. Sex Research and Advanced Professional Education

CARIDAD T. GARCÍA, ALICIA GONZÁLEZ, and MARÍA D. CÓRDOVA

Research on sexuality, in its widest sense, has been conducted by several government institutions and civil society organizations from the perspective of different professions. Sexuality has been studied by investigators in various medical specialties, psychologists, educators, and sociologists from the health, education, and culture sectors, as well as from the Center for Woman Studies of the Federation of Cuban Women and the Center for Youth Studies, among others.

There is a wide range of theoretical and methodological research approaches, quantitative or qualitative studies, action research, and, more recently, a coherent comprehensive approach with a wide understanding of sexuality as a research subject.

The most frequent research topics are: sexuality and gender, sexual health, sexuality at the different ages, education, counseling, and sex therapy, gender and family violence, contraception, and sexuality in the mass media, among others.

One of the first research studies on sex education is "The Improvement of Ways and Methods for Sex Education in Cuba." Conducted in the 1980s by the Ministry of Education and the "Enrique José Varona" Higher Teachers' Training Institute, this research focused on the sexuality of adolescents and school-age young men and women and their families, and the effectiveness of the educational influence of professors. This research paved the way for many other studies conducted at educational centers and teachers' training universities.

Since the early and mid-1970s, public health research on sexuality was conducted, such as research by Professor Celestino Álvarez Lajonchere, addressing sexuality from the gynecological-obstetric perspective. Other surveys were carried out with chronic disease patients, such as diabetes mellitus, by the psychologist, Rafael Alvisa, and the medical doctors, B. Arce and J. Mas of the Reproductive Health Group, National Institute of Endocrinology. The early studies of the Federation of Cuban Women and the Center of Sexual Education (CENESEX) must be highlighted.

It is important to point out that in 1987, a National Fertility Survey covered a wider range of topics, not just specific fertility data, thus contributing extensive nationwide information. This survey is the reference work for Cuban sexuality.

On the other hand, since 1979, studies were conducted on a wide variety of hormonal contraceptives (oral and vaginal tablets, injectables, and implants) and their relationship to women's sexual response, especially clinical manifestations and sexual desire. No negative relationship was found, except for the vaginal tablets, because of genital manipulation and when their prescription was not accompanied by specialized contraceptive advice.

Since 1975, surveys were made on men attempting to establish relationships between knowledge and use of contraceptive methods and sexuality. Among their results, myths and taboos related to the use of condoms were found. Most of the male subjects attribute the use of a condom to a decrease of sexual desire and they don't incorporate it in their foreplay.

It was also found in a group of Cuban researchers who studied sexuality during the course of diseases, such as diabetes mellitus, hyperprolactinemia, hirsutism, acromegalia, and premature menopause, among others, whose evolution is linked in the literature to such manifestations as: decrease or exacerbation of sexual desire, anorgasmia, absence of ejaculation, retrograde ejaculation, impotence, depression, and anxiety. In the Cuban findings, there is a relationship between depression and impotence, independent of the presence of diabetes mellitus, and more desire dysfunctions in hyperprolactinemic men and women, and more impotence in men suffering hyperprolactinemia. Increased desire was found in groups of women with hirsutism. In early non-surgical menopause, it was found that most of the subjects maintained sexual desire and orgasm.

Other studies on the relationship between infertility and sexuality in Cuban couples, and in connection with the "infertility crisis" and body representations and their functions, showed a higher frequency of sexual relations in infertile couples, but more difficulties in making body representations and in expressing feelings. In lower educational level groups, myths connecting fertility with sexual response were found more in men than in women.

Findings connecting aging to sexuality date back to 1990. Surveys conducted at Grandfathers' and Grandmothers' Centers on third-age subjects show clear-cut gender differences. Men reported to be still sexually active, but in a different way from previous life stages, while the majority of women do not have a partner, which is linked to the life expectancy of over 70 years for both, but which is higher in the women. Therefore, they become widows at a higher frequency.

The first work found on the sexuality of male homosexuals in Cuba is a thesis presented at the Sociology Faculty in September 1999, which showed homosexual sexual initiation at adolescence in most adult interviewees. The subjects stated that they had satisfactory sexual relations, but to a certain extent, at certain stages of their lives, because of family pressure based on social stereotypes, had to assume an unsatisfactory heterosexual sexual role.

Generally, since the early 1970s, Cuban researchers in many specialties have continued to study the inexhaustible, diverse, and magical field of the human sexuality in a sociocultural context, where fantasy, eroticism, sensuality, and affectivity mix to produce a their own local, as well as universal result.

In terms of continuous graduate education, it must be highlighted that in Cuba, there are many centers of higher learning that, in coordination with CENESEX, develop a system of studies for graduate degrees in the fields of sexology and sexuality education. In this sense, it must be emphasized that CENESEX offers free courses, two diploma courses on sexuality education and sexual counseling and sexual therapy, as well as a master's course in sexuality. At the Medical Sciences University of Havana, two diploma courses on sexuality and the medical sciences, and sexuality are offered.

On the other hand, the "Enrique José Varona" Teachers' Training University offers free courses and another master's degree course in sexual education. Both master's degree courses deal with education, counseling, and sexual therapy from an education and health perspective.

The health sector, which includes the medical sciences universities, has been implementing for more than 10 years a set of sexual health prevention and education programs. Worthy of mention, because of their social impact, are the following programs: Mother-Child, Care for Pregnant Women, Responsible Motherhood and Fatherhood, and Comprehensive Adolescent Medical Care.

## References and Suggested Readings

CIA. 2002 (January). *The world factbook 2002*. Washington, DC: Central Intelligence Agency. Available: http://www .cia.gov/cia/publications/factbook/index.html

UNAIDS. 2002. *Epidemiological fact sheets by country*. Geneva, Switzerland: Joint United Nations Programme on HIV/AIDS (UNAIDS/WHO). Available: http://www.unaids.org/hivaidsinfo/statistics/fact_sheets/index_en.htm.

1. Aguilera Ribeaux, D. La violencia intrafamiliar. Tratamiento jurídico en Cuba. Ponencia presentada en el taller *Violencia contra la mujer. Un problema de todas y todos*, Cuidad de La Habana, 2001.
2. Alfonso Rodríguez, A. Del silencio a la palabra. Ponencia presentada en el taller *Violencia contra la mujer. Un problema de todas y todos*, Cuidad de La Habana, 2001.
3. Alfonso Rodríguez, A., y C. Sarduy Sánchez. *Género. Salud y cotidianidad*. Editorial Científico Técnica, Ciudad de La Habana, 2000.
4. Álvarez Carril, E. *Crecer en la pubertad* (Tesis de maestría en intervención comunitaria). CENESEX, La Habana, 2001.
5. Álvarez Suárez, M. Rodríguez, I., y otros. *Situación de la niñez, la adolescencia, la mujer y la familia en Cuba*. Centro de Estudios de la Mujer–UNICEF, 2000.
6. Artiles de León, I., y otros. *Mi proyecto de vida. Programa para Jóvenes*. Centro Nacional de Educación Sexual (CENESEX). Edita Pue y Educación, Ciudad de La Habana, 1998.
7. Artiles de León, y otros. *Violencia y sexualidad*. Editorial Ciencia y Técnica, 1998.
8. Artiles Visbal, L. Navarro Despaigne, D. Manzano Ovies, y B. R. Clmaterio. Cambios en la conducta sexual. ¿Estereotipo cultural o disfunción biológica? *Revista Sexología y Sociedad*, *10*, 1998.
9. Ascuy, Arelis. *Tesis de doctorado en ciencias pedagógicas*. Instituto Superior Pedagógico "Enrique J. Varona," Ciudad de La Habana, 2000.
10. Berjes Díaz, C. Violencia intrafamiliar. El grupo nacional de atención a la violencia. Ponencia presentada en el taller *Violencia contra la mujer. Un problema de todas y todos*, Cuidad de La Habana, 2001.
11. Castillo, J.; M. Goñi, L. Figueredo. Orgasmo femenino, resultado de una encuesta. *Revista Sexología y Sociedad*. Año 5, *12*:7, 1999.
12. Caño, M. del C. *Función económica de la familia. En caracterización del modo de vida de las familias obreras y de trabajadores intelectuales y el cumplimiento de su función formadora. Informe de investigación*. CIPS–ACC, 1989.
13. Castro Espín, M. *La educación sexual en Cuba. Nuevos retos*. Conferencia magistral. III Congreso Cubano de Educación, Orientación y Terapia Sexual. La Habana, abril 2001.
14. Castro Espín, M. *Crecer en la adolescencia. Sus características y resultados parciales en la provincia Santiago de Cuba* (Tesis de maestría en sexualidad). CENESEX, Ciudad de La Habana, 1997.

15. Castro Espín, M. *Sexualidad y desarrollo humano. El programa Cubano de educación sexual*. Ponencia presentada en el XV Congreso Mundial de Sexología, París, 2001.
16. Castro Espín, M., A. Cano López, y M. Rebollar Sánchez. *Crecer en la Adolescencia*. CENESEX, Ciudad de La Habana, 1995.
17. Castro Espín, M., L. Bardisa, y M. Córdova. *Cómo se aprende lo bueno del sexo*. Ponencia al X de FLASSES, octubre 2002.
18. CENESEX. *Informe de balance annual*, 2001.
19. Centro de Estudios de Población y Desarrollo, ONE. *Anuario demográfico de Cuba 2001*.
20. Centro de Estudios Sobre la Juventud (CESJ). *Factores psicosociales que intervienen en el comportamiento sexual de riesgo con énfasis en las ITS–SIDA 2000*.
21. CESJ. *Reflexiones y valoraciones de adolescentes y jóvenes cubanos sobre aspectos de la sexualidad a finales del milenio, 1997. Investigación representación social de la familia en un grupo de jóvenes cubanos*. Ciudad de La Habana, 2001.
22. CESJ. *Estudio exploratorio con muchachas con conducta sexual prostituida. Consideraciones del tema en sujetos no prostituidos*. Ciudad de La Habana, 1996.
23. CESJ. *Análisis de la prostitución en Cuba. Aproximación a su representación social*. Ciudad de La Habana, 1998.
24. *Constitución de la República de Cuba*, publicada en la *Gaceta Oficial*, en edición extraordinaria no. 7, 1 de agosto de 1992.
25. De la Torre, C. Conciencia de la mismidad. *Revista Temas* (La Habana), *2*:115, abril-junio 1995.
26. Díaz Álvarez, M. *El varón cubano antes y ahora* (Tesis de maestría en sexualidad). CENSEX, 1999.
27. Díaz, O., y I. López. Comportamiento de algunos aspectos de la sexualidad en trabajadores del Municipio La Lisa. *Revista Sexología y Sociedad*, Año 1, *2*:28, 1995.
28. Díaz, O. Necesidad de la educación sexual en los mayores de 60 años. *Revista Sexología y Sociedad*, año 2002, *18*.
29. Dixie, E. *La historia cíclica de la prostitución*. Entrevista realizada para SEM a Osmany Horta, investigador y profesor de la Facultad de Historia de la Universidad de La Habana, enero 2002.
30. Domínguez, R. *Sexualidad en los Ancianos de Consolación del Sur*. Congreso Internacional de Geriatría, 1998.
31. Elizalde, R. M. *Flores desechables. ¿Prostitución en Cuba?* Editora Abril, Cuba, 1996.
32. Elizalde, R. M. Prostitución ¿Crimen o castigo? *Revista Sexología y Sociedad*, *21*, enero 2003.
33. Espín Guillois, V. *Conferencia magistral*. III Congreso Cubano de Educación, Orientación y Terapia Sexual. La Habana, abril 2001.
34. Fernández Ríos, L. ¿Roles de género? ¿Masculinidad vs feminidad? *En Revista Temas* (La Habana), *5*, 1995.
35. Forteza Cordero, J. *Educación sexual de las madres y los padres a sus hijos(as), ¿Desconocimiento o resistencia?* (Tesis de maestría en intervención comunitaria). CENESEX, 2001.
36. García Álvarez. C. T. *Adolescente varón. Aspectos psicológicos, salud sexual y reproductiva*. Ponencia presentada en el CIMEQ, Noviembre 2000.
37. García Tirada, M. *Como viven su sexualidad las mujeres de mediana edad* (Tesis de maestría en intervención comunitaria). CENSEX, Ciudad de La Habana, 2001.
38. González Hernández, A., y B. Castellanos Simons. *Sexualidad y géneros. Una reconceptualización educativa en los umbrales del tercer milenio* (páginas 11 y 12). Cooperativa Editorial Magisterio, Bogotá, Colombia, 1996.
39. González, S. Identidad nacional e identidad de géneros: Sugerente asociación. *Revista Sexología y Sociedad*, *3*, Diciembre 1995.
40. Guerrero, N., y J. Alfonso. En Cuba: Jóvenes de los 90. Centro de Estudios de la Juventud, *Editora Abril*, La Habana, 1999.

41. Hernández Arias, N. *Roles de género y relación de pareja. Estudio de casos* (Tesis de maestría). CENESEX, Ciudad de La Habana, 1998.
42. Jiménez Berrios, S. Investigadora Centro de Investigaciones Psicológicas y Sociológicas del Ministerio de Ciencia, Tecnología y Medio Ambiente.
43. Ley No 1298 del 15 de Febrero de 1975, *Código de Familia.* Capítulo I Sección primera, Artículo 2. Editorial Orbe, 1980.
44. Lleo Jiménez, G., y E. Pérez Glez. Maltrato sexual. *Revista Sexología y Sociedad, 14.* Cuidad de La Habana, 2000.
45. Martínez, F., y otros. Orientaciones educativas sobre algunas conductas del niño preescolar. *Edita Pueblo y Educación,* Ciudad de La Habana, 1982.
46. Méndez Gómez, N., y otros. Pacientes con disfunción sexual. Una clasificación útil para un efectivo diagnóstico y tratamiento. *En Revista Sexología y Sociedad, 3,* 1995.
47. Ministerio de Educación (MINED). *Educación formal para una conducta sexual responsable. Programa realizado dentro del proyecto.* MINED–UNFPA, desde 1997.
48. Ministerio de Salud Pública de Cuba (MINSAP). *Anuario estadístico de salud,* 2002.
49. MINSAP. Programa Nacional de Control y Prevención del VIH-SIDA. *Editora de salud,* La Habana, 1997.
50. MINSAP. Atención integral al adolescente. Programa que se realiza por el MINSAP desde 1990. *Editora de Salud,* La Habana, 1990.
51. Moreno Álvarez, L., y M. Escobar Peraza. Función educativa en la familia en revista. *Sexología y Sociedad, 5,* 1996.
52. Morín González, M. M. Menarquia, y eyacularquia. Expresiones externas de la pubertad. *Revista Sexología y Sociedad, 14,* Ciudad de La Habana, 2000.
53. Oficina Nacional de Estadísticas (ONE). *Anuario estadístico de Cuba 2001 y 2002.*
54. ONE: *SABE: Salud y bienestar del adulto mayor.* 1998.
55. Ortiz, F. *El pueblo cubano.* Editorial Ciencias Sociales, La Habana, 1997.
56. Ortiz, F. *Etnia y sociedad.* Editorial Ciencias Sociales, La Habana, 1993.
57. Pérez González, E., y otros. Niños víctimas de delitos sexuales. *Revista Sexología y Sociedad, 6,* 1996.
58. *PNUD informe del desarrollo humano 2002.*
59. Proveyer Cervantes, C. Identidad femenina y violencia doméstica. Un acercamiento a su estudio. *Revista Sexología y Sociedad, 14,* abril 2000.
60. Reca, I., y otros. *Caracterización del modo de vida de las familias obreras y de trabajadores intelectuales y cumplimiento de su función formadora. Informe de investigación.* CIPS–ACC, 1989. Ídem.
61. Robledo Díaz, L. *Homosexualidad—Familia: Acoso y simetrías* (Tesis de maestría en sociología, página 53). Universidad de La Habana, Abril 2000.
62. Rodríguez Botti, R. *Sexualidad en el otoño de la vida. Estudio de la sexualidad en los ancianos de la provincia Guantánamo.* (Tesis de maestría en sexualidad). CENESEX, 2001.
63. Rodríguez Lauzurique, M., y O. Bravo Díaz. *Leiva marín, Y. Atención a los transexuales en Cuba. Investigación.* CENESEX, La Habana, 1994.
64. Rodríguez Jiménez, D. *La sexualidad adolescente desde lo grupal* (Tesis de maestría en intervención comunitaria). CENESEX, La Habana, 2001.
65. Rodríguez Maria, A. *Patrón sexual de un grupo de ancianos del policlínico 26 de Julio* (Tesis de grado para optar por el título de especialista de primer grado en psiquiatría). Facultad Finlay Albarrán, 2000.
66. Rodríguez Ojeda, M. *Manifestaciones sexistas en el contexto del aula. En Revista Sexología y Sociedad, 19,* agosto 2002.
67. Rodríguez Reyes, I. *Hombres y mujeres cuadros del turismo. Rol profesional y roles de materno y paterno en la familia* (Tesis de maestría en intervención comunitaria). CENESEX, La Habana, mayo 2002.
68. Roselló Manzano, R. *La pareja homosexual. Nuevo modelo familiar alternativo en el siglo XXI* (Tesis). Facultad de la Derecho Universidad de La Habana, 2003.
69. Rosete Silva, H., y J. C. Guanche Zaldívar. Entrevista a Aurelio Alonso Sociólogo, Investigador Titular del Centro de Investigaciones Psicológicas y Sociológicas del Ministerio de Ciencia, Tecnología y Medio Ambiente. *Revista Enfoques, 21,* noviembre de 2002.
70. Sánchez Almira, T., y N. Hernández Arias. Violencia conyugal. *Revista Sexología y Sociedad, 10.* Ciudad de La Habana, 1998.
71. Sierra Madero, A. *La nación sexuada.* Editorial Ciencias Sociales, La Habana, 2002.
72. Sobrado Rosales, Z. *La mujer cubana de mediana edad. Nueva mirada desde la metodología de los procesos correctores comunitarios* (Tesis de maestría en intervención comunitaria). CENSEX, Ciudad de La Habana, 2002.
73. Torres Betancourt, Ma. del Carmen. *La adquisición de la identidad de género en la edad preescolar con la ayuda de la expresión corporal* (Tesis de culminación de estudios en la licenciatura de educación preescolar). ISPEJV, 1994.
74. Thompson, W., y O. Díaz. Utilización de los exámenes complementarios en la consulta de sexología. *Revista Sexología y Sociedad,* Año 3, 7:12, 1997.
75. Valdés Padrón, C. C. *Percepción de la sexualidad de niños y niñas menores de un año* (Tesis de maestría en sexualidad). CENESEX, La Habana, julio 2002.
76. Vasallo, C. Consultas de disfunción y terapia sexual. *Revista Sexología y Sociedad.* Año 2, 8:8, 1997.

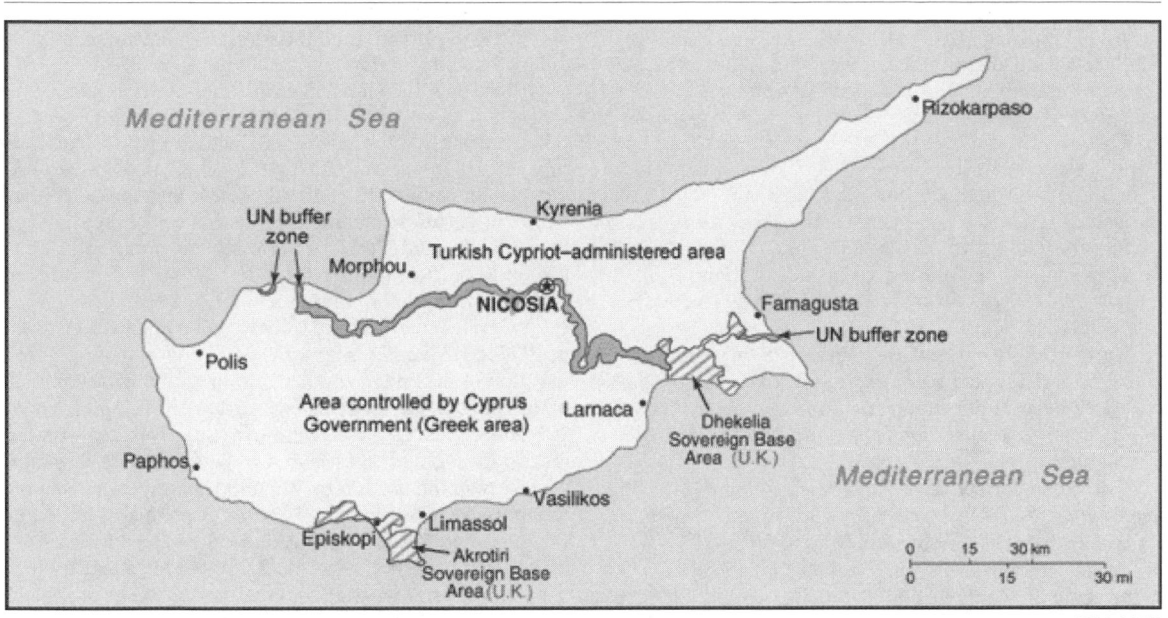

(CIA 2002)

# Cyprus

### (*Kypriaki Dimokratia*) (Greek) (The Democracy of Cyprus) (*Kuzey Kıbrıs Türk Çumhuriyeti*) (Turkish) (The Turkish Republic of Northern Cyprus)

*Part 1: Greek Cyprus*: George J. Georgiou, Ph.D.,*
with Alecos Modinos, B.Arch., A.R.I.B.A.,
Nathaniel Papageorgiou, Laura Papantoniou, M.Sc., M.D.,
and Nicos Peristianis, Ph.D. (Hons.)
*Updates by G. J. Georgiou and L. Papantoniou*
*Part 2: Turkish Cyprus*: Kemal Bolayır, M.D.,**
and Serin Kelâmi, B.Sc. (Hons.)

## Contents

## PART 1: GREEK CYPRUS

GEORGE J. GEORGIOU,*** with
ALECOS MODINOS, NATHANIEL PAPAGEORGIOU,
LAURA PAPANTONIOU, and NICOS PERISTIANIS

### Demographics and a Brief Historical Perspective

ROBERT T. FRANCOEUR

### A. Demographics

Cyprus, the third-largest island in the Mediterranean Sea, lies in the Middle East off the eastern shore of the Greek Islands, the southern coast of Turkey, and the western shore of Syria, with Lebanon, Syria, and Israel to the southeast. Mea-

*Communications*: George J. Georgiou, Ph.D., P.O. Box 2008, Larnaca, Cyprus; E-mail: drgeorge@avacom.net. Nicos Peristianis, ifi@intercol.edu. Laura Papantoniou, M.D., Ministry of Health, 10 Markou Drakou Street, 1448 Nicosia, Cyprus; laurapap@cytanet .com.cy.

**Kemal Bolayır, M.D., Post Office Box 597, Lefkosa, Mersin, Turkey; kbolayin@superonline.com. Serin Kelâmi, 27 Albert Road, London N 22 7AQ, United Kingdom; skelami@aol.com.

***Note*: The Greek authors welcomed the opportunity to prepare this chapter on Cyprus because very little has been published on Cypriot sexuality in the international literature. This has been because of the lack of adequate funding and professionals to conduct methodologically sound research on the island, a lack of a coordinating body, the difficulties involved in collecting data given a conservative and sexually inhibited society, the suppressive influence of the Orthodox Church on human sexuality, and other factors. We have collected, analyzed, and integrated whatever information we could find, including statistical data, the results of professional experience and clinical work, and anecdotal reflections from professionals in fields related to sexology.

suring 141 miles by 60 miles (227 km by 97 km) wide, the island's total land area is 3,570 square miles (9,250 km²), a little more than half the size of the state of Connecticut. The island is divided between Greek and Turkish regions, with 2,275 square miles (5,895 km²) comprising the Republic of Cyprus and 1,295 square miles (3,355 km²) in the Turkish Republic of Northern Cyprus. Two mountain ranges cross the island from east to west, separated by a wide, fertile plain.

In July 2002, Cyprus had an estimated population of 767,314, of which Turkish Cyprus had about 200,000. (All data are from *The World Factbook 2002* (CIA 2002) unless otherwise stated.)

**Age Distribution and Sex Ratios**: *0-14 years*: 22.4% with 1.05 male(s) per female (sex ratio); *15-64 years*: 66.6% with 1.02 male(s) per female; *65 years and over*: 11% with 0.77 male(s) per female; *Total population sex ratio*: 1 male(s) to 1 female

**Life Expectancy at Birth**: *Total Population*: 77.08 years; *male*: 74.77 years; *female*: 79.5 years

**Urban/Rural Distribution**: 70% to 30%

**Ethnic Distribution**: 99.5% of the Greek Cypriots live in the southern Republic and only 0.5% (about 500) Greek Cypriots in the Turkish-occupied territory; similarly, 98.7% of Turkish Cypriots live in the northern Turkish Republic and only 1.3% of Turkish Cypriots live in the south. The remaining 4.1% include: Maronites: 4,500 (0.6%); Armenians: 2,500 (0.3%); Latinos: 700 (0.1%); and other nationals, mainly British, Greek, European, Lebanese, and Arab: 23,000 (3.1%).

**Religious Distribution**: Greek Orthodox: 78%; Muslim: 18%; Maronite, Armenian Apostolic, and others: 4%

**Birth Rate**: 12.91 births per 1,000 population (18 per 1,000 for Turkish and 15 per 1,000 in the Greek Republic, according to G. J. Georgiou)

**Death Rate**: 7.63 per 1,000 population

**Infant Mortality Rate**: 7.71 deaths per 1,000 live births (12 per 1,000 for Turkish and 8.2 for Greek Cyprus)

**Net Migration Rate**: 0.43 migrant(s) per 1,000 population

**Total Fertility Rate**: 1.9 children born per woman

**Population Growth Rate**: 0.57%

**HIV/AIDS** (1999 est.): *Adult prevalence*: 0.1%; *Persons living with HIV/AIDS*: 400; *Deaths*: NA. (For additional details from www.UNAIDS.org, see end of Section 10B.)

**Literacy Rate** (*defined as those age 15 and over who can read and write*): 97% with nine years of compulsory schooling (1992 est.)

**Per Capita Gross Domestic Product** (*purchasing power parity*): Greek $15,000 (2001 est.), Turkish $7,000 (2000 est.); *Inflation*: Greek 1.9%, Turkish 53.2% (2000 est.); *Unemployment*: Greek 3% (2001 est.), Turkish 5.6% (1999 est.); *Living below the poverty line*: NA

**B. A Brief Historical Perspective**

Recent excavations on the island of Cyprus have yielded evidence of human society at least 10,000 years old. The Mycenean (Greek) culture flourished in the second millennium B.C.E. After Phoenicians colonized the island in the 10th century B.C.E., Cyprus remained a major *entre-pôt* for trade in the eastern Mediterranean. Annexed by Rome in 58 B.C.E., Cyprus later became part of the Byzantine Empire until the English King Richard I (Lion-Heart) established a crusader state there in 1191 C.E. The Lusignan dynasty ruled until 1489, when Venice annexed the island. In 1571, Cyprus became part of the Ottoman Empire.

In 1878, the Congress of Berlin placed Cyprus under British administration. After annexing the island in 1914, Great Britain made it a British colony in 1925. Between 1945 and 1948, the British used the island as a detention area for "illegal" Jewish immigrants trying to reach Palestine.

After 1947, the Greek Cypriot community expanded its longstanding agitation for union (*enosis*) with Greece, a policy strongly opposed by the Turkish Cypriot community. After violence in 1954 and 1955, Cyprus gained full independence under a 1960 agreement that forbade either *enosis* or partition and included guarantees of the rights of both Greeks and Turks. Efforts by the president, Archbishop Makarios, to alter the Constitution in favor of the Greek majority led to more violence in 1964.

A Greek Junta-inspired military coup against Makarios in 1974 led to Turkey's invasion of Cyprus and the *de facto* partition of the island and declaration of the northern 40% of the island as the Turkish Federated State of Cyprus. Some 200,000 Greek Cypriots were expelled from the Turkish area to the Republic, while many Turks fled the Republic for safety in the north. The Republic has experienced a return of political stability and economic prosperity, with agriculture, light manufacturing, and tourism leading the way. The economy in the Turkish sector has been generally stagnant, as the international community refused to recognize the 1983 declaration of independence by the Turkish Republic of Northern Cyprus. Tensions have eased since the United Nations-sponsored Greek-Turkish talks on Cypriot unity, even though little progress has been achieved thus far.

## 1. Basic Sexological Premises, and 2. Religious, Ethnic, and Gender Factors Affecting Sexuality

NICOS PERISTIANIS*

**A. Character of Gender Roles**

Ethnographic and anthropological accounts of Cyprus (Peristiany 1974, Markides et al. 1978) stress the importance of the nuclear family as the paramount institution of Cypriot society, so much so that "an individual exists only as a member of a family," and the self cannot be conceived independently from its familial roles. This is in marked contrast to Western "solitary" conceptions of the self (Mavratsas 1992). The family has acquired such significance, because it was, and still is to a large degree, the primary social, economic, and moral unit of Cypriot society.

*The Traditional Cypriot Family and Gender Roles*

The economy of Cyprus maintained its predominantly agrarian character well into the 20th century (Christodoulou 1992). The perennially heavy financial demands of conquerors and the especially hostile ecological factors—the strategic resources of water and land were always in limited supply, and diseases frequently destroyed crops—led to competition being a keystone aspect of life, and reliance on the family group being vital for survival. Economic activities were conducted by the entire household for the improvement of their common position, thus enhancing family solidarity and the strong distinctions between "insiders" and "outsiders."

In his survey of rural life in the late 1920s, Surridge, a British colonial officer, noted an internal division of labor within the family, with men being responsible for heavy agricultural work and women (aided by the older children) for the lighter work in the fields, as well as housework. Usually one of the girls would stay behind to look after younger children and help with some housework (Surridge 1930). At the same time, much as in Greece and elsewhere in the Med-

---

*Note*: This combined section on gender roles, marriage, family, and ethnic and religious factors was written by Nicos Peristianis, president of the Association of Cypriot Sociologists, based upon his research and that of his colleagues.

iterranean, there was a "moral division of labor inside the family," revolving around the cultural codes, or values, of "honor and shame" (Campbell 1983, Schneider 1971).

Honor (*timi*) refers to the value or worth of an individual—but since the individual exists as a "member of a family," whatever worth one earns for oneself automatically "spills over" to the family. Correspondingly, shame (*ntropi*) refers to a loss of honor, esteem, or worth, which brings humiliation, "staining" the individual and family.

It is important to appreciate the salience of these codes on the lives of individuals in traditional Cypriot society. Peter Berger has argued convincingly that contrary to modern societies' emphasis on "dignity," which implies a notion of the self devoid of institutional attachments and roles, more traditional societies put an emphasis on "honor," which "implies that identity is essentially, or at least importantly, linked to an individual's institutional roles." In fact, an individual in a "world of honor" "discovers his true identity in his roles." "To turn away from the roles is to turn away from himself" (Berger et al. 1973). What, then, were the roles through which individual Cypriot men and women discovered their true identities or selves?

The traditional role of the man in Cyprus was that of representing the family to the outside world. As head of the family, he engaged in all tasks necessary to protect and sustain the family. He was the main income earner who made decisions regarding production by obtaining knowledge about environmental conditions, resources, and markets. After work, he would spend time in the coffeehouse (*kafeneion*), where information was exchanged and contacts made, as well as views shared on political and village affairs. The highest value for man was "love of honor" (*philotimo*), that is, self-respect and self-assertive courage, which amounted to assertive masculinity, in all areas of social life, to protect the honor of the family.

The traditional role of the woman was to be responsible for the family inside the home. Her tasks revolved around three sets of duties: first, the duty of being a good mother, hence the tasks of nurturing and caring for the children; second, the duty of being a good housekeeper, responsible for cleaning the house, cooking, shopping, and looking after domestic animals; and finally, the duty of being a good wife, by being obedient, respectful, and submissive to her husband.

The separation of the sexes in traditional society, especially rural areas, was quite strict, even though it has lessened with modernization. A woman would keep away from public areas, which were the domain of men. Women would never enter coffeehouses or athletic clubs; similarly, they would rarely be seen passing through the central square of the village, where most male-dominated coffeehouses were concentrated. In churches, women would occupy the rear and upstairs sections, the front part being reserved for men only. Women could attain more freedom to circulate among men only when they were not considered sexually risk-bearing, i.e., young girls before puberty and elderly, no-longer-sexually attractive women (well past menopause). In these cases, women could walk in the streets more freely, pass through the central square, and converse with men. But in no case could women enter and contaminate in church the holy of holies where the altar is housed.

Women's avoidance of public spaces related to their need to avoid sexual shame. In fact, shame-avoidance was the principal value governing all female behavior in traditional society. In his classic study of a Cypriot highland village in the 1950s, Peristiany (1965) noted that a "woman's foremost duty to self and family is to safeguard herself against all critical allusions to her sexual modesty. In dress, looks, attitudes, and speech, a woman in the presence of men should be virginal as a maiden and matronly as a wife." A woman who behaves in conformity to the "code" regulating the behavior of her sex (femininity and passive modesty), is said to be an honorable woman (*timia gynaika*), whereas the one who doesn't is without honor (*atime*), or, what amounts to the same thing, without shame—shameless (*adiantrope*). Again, honor and shame, respectively, are not restricted to the woman, but "spill over" to her family. Thus, for instance, in the case of an unmarried woman, shame taints directly the father and brothers, "who did not protect or avenge her honor." After marriage, these responsibilities pass to the woman's husband.

Whether father, brother, or husband, men bear the responsibility of caring for the women of the family. Indeed, this will be their conformity hallmark that regulates the behavior of their sex ("manliness and assertion of masculinity"). In both cases of non-conformity to the code of honor ("an unmanly man" or "an immodest woman"), the perpetrators are guilty not of breaking an externally given rule, but of betraying their very nature, their *physis*—because it is considered in the nature of men and women to act in those ways (Peristiany 1974).

Gender roles are taught throughout the socialization process. A study of the lowland village of Lysi in the early 1970s provides an account of the different patterns of socialization for the two sexes (Markides et al. 1978). From a very early age, in their games, boys try to imitate their father's behavior and girls their mother's. Until the age of 6, children are free to play in the streets and visit neighbors' and relatives' homes. But after this age, girls begin to spend most of their time at home, playing with their sisters or other friends, but also learning how to clean, cook, sew, and so on. As they grow older, they may be allowed to visit relatives or friends, once they have secured their mother's consent. No such limitations apply for boys, who continue to be free to wander around and play in the streets, and to visit the *kafeneion* or other clubs and public places. Boys are encouraged to develop their masculinity as expressed through "physical courage, toughness, competitiveness, aggressiveness, and defending one's honor," whereas girls are taught to cultivate their femininity as expressed through "gentleness, expressiveness, responsiveness, tenderness and modesty" (Balswick 1973). The most important virtues that girls must learn are, again, those related to modesty and shame-avoidance. A girl must demonstrate that she is a virgin not only in the flesh, but also in spirit. She should avoid not only physical, but also social contact with men, because this could be associated with sexual desire. This entails accepting a number of social prohibitions, such as never to talk to a man in the street, unless he is a close relative; not to fraternize with men, and "when a man looks at her she should avert her eyes and blush; she should not laugh in front of men and if she does so, she must bring her hand in front of her mouth" (Markides et al. 1978).

If this behavior is maintained, her good name and family honor are preserved, which adds to her value as a future bride. Throughout socialization in the family and community, a girl learns to set marriage as the paramount goal of her life, since it allows her to become a wife and a mother. A woman who remains unmarried is destined to remain at the social and cultural periphery of the village, for she is not offered any role to play within the mainstream of society. Her destiny will, in fact, be to care for the elderly parents and the children of married sisters and brothers, and to engage in church-related activities.

Marriage and the creation of a family are also very important for young men, for it is only through them that they will be considered full and mature members of society with equal rights and responsibilities. A man reaches manhood only when he marries. Until then, he is still a *kopellin*, a "lad," which means he cannot hold any responsible position within the power hierarchy of the village.

## Social Change, Modernization, and Gender Roles

The roots of Cyprus's modernization can be traced back to the beginnings of British colonialism. Prior to British control, Cyprus had been subject to Ottoman rule for approximately 300 years, during which time the land was owned by the State; the peasants had the right to use the land in exchange for the appropriate taxes. British colonialism introduced a connection between individual production and the right to private property. Peasants could now own the land they cultivated; but they could also lose it! Indeed, for various reasons, such as bad agricultural years and overspending on their children's dowry, many peasants found themselves in heavy debt to insurers, to whom they had resorted for borrowing money, and to whom many eventually lost their land because they could not repay their mortgage.

Such destitute peasants sought employment in other sectors of the economy, namely the mines and small industries that started developing in the urban centers early on in the 20th century. After World War II, when Britain was forced to abandon her bases in the Middle East and to grant independence to India, Cyprus acquired enhanced strategic value. In response, the British constructed two large military bases on the island, at Episkopi and Dhekelia, with the resulting construction industry providing new employment opportunities. Furthermore, the increased needs of the British military and administrative personnel provided further jobs and new commercial possibilities.

During the 1950s, the final decade of British rule in Cyprus, the average annual rate of growth of the economy reached 12%, an indicator of the progress that was being achieved. Urbanization had also grown dramatically: Whereas at the beginning of British rule, the urban population was only 17%, by the time they left, it amounted to 36%. As Attalides (1981) showed in his study of social change and urbanization in Cyprus, the majority of the people who migrated to the towns were those who had no land of their own and no work, mostly unmarried men and women. Another major reason for migration was the decision to attend high school. This was because of the recognition that education provided a way out of the villages and hard toil in the fields, into "a better life" in the towns and employment possibilities in the newly created white-collar jobs.

Gradually, the urban centers became the foci of the economy as well as of social and cultural life. This, along with the emergence of a sizable urban middle class, led to a restructuring of power relations—a shift of power from the village to the city. As a result of these modernizing processes, the family underwent considerable change. Functions earlier performed by the family were gradually taken over by other institutions, even though not to the extent and with the consequences this had in the West. Thus, even though in many cases the family stopped being a production unit (as in the case of destitute peasants joining the working force in the mines or industry), in many other cases, money earned from work in the towns found its way back to the villages to help the family pay off debts and maintain its land and unity. In yet other cases, family businesses were set up in towns, so the family kept its production role in a new context (Argyrou 1996).

It is also interesting to note that, whereas in many other developing societies, urbanization led to a break-up of extended family systems into the nuclear system, in Cyprus there was somewhat of a reversal in the process. We have noted how rural Cypriot society was characterized by a nuclear family system; urbanization, in its early stages at least, had an expanding effect, since kin members were added to the nuclear core (usually younger relatives looking for a job in town). Thus, it does not seem that modernization and urbanization negatively affected family cohesiveness and strength (Attalides 1981).

There were, however, gradual changes in gender roles within the family. Two of the most important factors leading to these changes have been education and employment. Education became an important mechanism of social mobility, advancing both the status of peasants to that of white-collar workers and improving the status of women (Persianis 1998). The first primary schools were established by the Orthodox Church toward the end of Ottoman rule. Very few girls attended these schools because women's destiny was to marry and have a family at an early age. Besides, because there were only male teachers at the time, parents were unwilling to allow their daughters to stay in school beyond the age of 8 or 9. For the same reasons, this absence was even more pronounced in the case of the few secondary schools, which were concentrated in the towns. The first girls to attend schools came from the wealthier (bourgeois) class, which valued the cultural benefits of education, expecting their girls to be taught how to be "refined ladies," but also to remain "modest and quiet." It is from the 1920s onwards, the period in which we start having increasing rates of urbanization and industrialization, that we have sizable increases in student numbers, including girls. Most of these new students were children of the wealthier rural and, primarily, urban classes. The motives, henceforth, became mainly economic, because education was now considered instrumental in securing a job in the towns, in commercial shops, trading firms, banks, and similar work. Such motives were further strengthened in subsequent periods, when the economy grew at a faster pace, providing more and more opportunities for work. This was true after World War II, but especially after independence in 1960, when the service sector opened up. Cypriots thought service jobs to be more appropriate for women, since they more closely resembled their traditional roles.

The 1974 Turkish invasion brought destruction of biblical proportions to the Greek Cypriots. Almost 40% of the land came under Turkish control; a full third of the population became refugees and had to flee to the south for survival. Most of these ended up in refugee camps at the outskirts of the larger towns, creating a large new wave of "forced" urbanization. Women from such refugee families, especially of rural and working-class background, provided cheap labor for light manufacturing industries, mostly in shoes and clothing, which found unexpected opportunities for growth during this period. Furthermore, the expanded welfare and other state services, which tried to cater to the new needs, provided new opportunities for middle-class women, both refugee and non-refugee alike. The final pull was provided with the economic recovery and unprecedented boost, the "economic miracle," in the early 1980s, which created numerous new jobs in tourism and the wider service sector.

Throughout this period, women's employment increased by leaps and bounds, as did schooling for girls. By 1995, women's employment was 38.6% of the total, as compared to 35.17% in 1985. In both primary and secondary education, the ratio of girls was equal to that of boys, with some marginal differences at the tertiary level, where more boys than girls study outside Cyprus, whereas more girls than boys study at tertiary institutions in Cyprus.

All these changes have obviously transformed the Cypriot family and gender roles within it, although continuity with past patterns remains strong. Mothers, especially of the younger generations, are not only "allowed," but "expected" to work. Recent research by Papapetrou and Pendedeka in 1998 shows that family members believe the mother to be sensitive, permissive, and flexible toward children's demands. She is over-protective and worries a lot about her children, spending time in discussion with them, certainly more so than the father, which may explain why she demonstrates more empathy and understanding toward the children. This is seen to be related to the fact that she carries the care of the household and family, spends many hours at home, and thus has more opportunities to see each family member separately. This, it is speculated, may also provide her with the opportunity to "administer" or "rule," to know "what" and "when" something must take place. Such powers, however, are not tantamount to the role of "leader," which is reserved for the father. She is expected to work, but she is also expected to ungrudgingly interrupt her career to raise children. After all, woman's working role is seen as a secondary one, important for supplementing the family's income and not as the main breadwinner.

The father is the one considered to be really responsible for the economic well-being of the family. He is still considered to be the leader of the team and his opinions are "determinative" when it comes to "serious" matters, or matters which have an impact upon the whole family. He does very little in the house, his activity being mostly limited to heavy jobs (such as construction or repair-work) upon mother's requests. Usually, he does not spend much time at home, but prefers the coffee shop, a hobby, or a second job; when he stays at home, he usually watches television, especially news reports. He is thus seen as austere, strongly opinionated, and distant. Often he is "unexpressive," since man's socialization into masculinity (competitiveness, toughness, aggressiveness, physical courage, and defending one's honor) teaches him that expressiveness toward his wife and children is a "feminine" characteristic.

## Sociolegal Status of Males and Females, Children and Adults

The traditional social and moral order has been sanctioned by the Cypriot Orthodox Church. The family is considered to be a divine institution, relations between its members being comparable to the relations between God, Mary, and the Christ Child. Icons were traditionally kept in a specific holder (*ikonostasi*) of every home, with an oil-lamp constantly burning, symbolizing the divine protection of the institutions of marriage and family.

During the marital ceremony, considered to be one of the seven "Divine Mysteries" or Sacraments through which God's grace is bestowed to humans, St. Paul's Epistle to the Ephesians is read to the newlyweds, reminding them that, in their relationship, the wife must fear her husband and be submissive to him at all times, whereas the husband must love the woman, as Christ loved the Church. Obedience, respect, and submission to husband are moral imperatives that highlight the patriarchal nature of traditional Cypriot society.

Modernization of all spheres of Cypriot life and secularization of the religious sphere have certainly brought about important changes. The 1960 Constitution of the Republic of Cyprus enshrines modern democratic ideals, including equality of men and women before the law. It also specifically prohibits any "direct or indirect discrimination against any person on the ground of his [*sic*] community, race, religion, language, sex, political or other convictions, national

or social descent, birth, color, wealth, social class or any ground whatsoever . . ." (Article 28).

Nevertheless, as has been pointed out by Stavrou (1998), the patriarchal "logic" lurks behind some of the provisions of the supreme legal document of the country. For instance, in determining the ethnic community to which a citizen should "belong," after marrying someone from the opposite community (i.e., a Greek Cypriot marrying a Turkish Cypriot or vice-versa), the Constitution clarifies that: "A married woman shall belong to the community to which her husband belongs." Similarly, in the case of children under the age of 21 who are not married, a child "shall belong to the community to which his or her father belongs . . ." (Article 2: Par. 7).

This patriarchal logic pervades other sociolegal institutions and respective provisions or regulations. Thus, if an alien man marries a Cypriot woman, he does not automatically acquire Cypriot citizenship, unless he fulfills almost all the conditions that any other alien must fulfill in order to acquire citizenship. If, however, an alien woman is married to a Cypriot man, she thereby acquires his residence as well as his domicile.

While there are often no specific laws determining discriminatory social practices, traditional norms and values may produce such outcomes. For instance, there is no legal provision that regulates the name the parties in a marriage should assume. "The practice, however, as has been customary throughout much of the European Christian world, is that upon marriage a woman takes her husband's family name. Also, the children take their father's family name except in the case of illegitimate children, who take the name of the father of their mother" (Stavrou 1998).

In many other instances, the laws may provide for equality and prohibit discrimination, but traditional institutions and practices may still prevail. A most glaring case is that of divorce, traditionally governed by Church law, which entails different divorce provisions for husband and wife. Two reasons that may be invoked only by the husband as against his wife are: First, that the wife was found not to be a virgin on the night of the wedding, which has to be reported to the local Bishop the next day; second, that the wife spent the night with persons unrelated to her (unless she could not find a relative's house to stay for the night, after being ousted from the home by her husband).

The Constitution perpetuated these unequal provisions by declaring marriage and divorce matters as the domain of the Church. It was much later, when Civil Marriage Law 95/ 89 amended the relevant article of the Constitution, to allow free choice of civil weddings for Greek Cypriots, and to place matters such as divorce, judicial separation, and family relations under the governance of special family courts. The Church of Cyprus reacted strongly against these legal changes and exerts all kinds of pressure in order to retain control of the institution of marriage. Until today, the Church insists that civil weddings are illegitimate and refuses to offer perpetrators the services of baptism and other holy sacraments. These pressures by the Church, but also (and perhaps most importantly), the weight of long-adhered-to traditions, explain why the vast majority of Cypriots (more than 70%) still choose religious, instead of civil weddings. Indeed, civil marriages between Cypriots account for only 3.6% of total marriages.

A similar situation prevails with divorce. The procedures for securing divorce through the Church are not only long and laborious, but they are also much more exacting and discriminatory against women. Nevertheless, because of the Church's pressures and the special weight of adhered-to traditions, most Greek Cypriots prefer to put up with the difficulties of Church divorce instead of resorting to civil divorce. They are afraid of getting themselves entangled into a web of socially difficult or embarrassing situations. For instance, should one wish to remarry in church after a civil divorce, one may find oneself accused of attempting bigamy!

Interestingly, on the issue of abortion, women's span of control or available choices seems to be much greater than in many other countries, even of the developed West. This seems to have to do as much with historical circumstance as with current social realities. Up to the early 1970s, the Criminal Code completely prohibited the practice and provided severe penalties for perpetrators. Developments related to the 1974 Turkish invasion drastically changed the situation when many Greek Cypriot women became pregnant after being raped by Turkish soldiers during the hostilities. Obviously, Greek Cypriot society was not ready to accept the offspring of the "barbarians" into its midst. Many Greek Cypriot men found it difficult enough to accept the raped women themselves, who were violated or "shamed" publicly. Even though the women resisted this violation of their bodies, the public consequences of the rape indirectly brought shame on their families, and especially on their men. As a consequence, the relevant law was radically amended to allow medical intervention for the termination of unwanted pregnancy in such cases. In addition, a provision was made for pregnancy to be terminated if two doctors advised that the life of an expectant mother would be in danger should pregnancy be allowed to continue, or in cases in which a newborn baby would face the risk of serious physical or mental disability.

These loopholes in the law effectively opened wide the doors for abortions under almost any pretext. Although hard data are not available, there are many indications that a large number of abortions are carried out in modern-day Cyprus. This may appear strange for a society that is still quite conservative on a number of other counts. Even stranger is the fact that there hardly appears to be much anti-abortion talk from any quarters, let alone an anti-abortion movement. Finally, the Church, though in theory opposed to all forms of abortion, seems in practice to be only paying lip service to a cause it does not really care to fight for. One suspects that the main reason for this is that the Church cares mostly to control not the private decisions, but the public behavior and choices of Greek Cypriots, since it is the latter which serves as an index of its power.

Obviously, the historical circumstances, outlined earlier on, explain to some extent why abortions were initially "legalized," and why, consequently, once the legal prohibition was removed, the door was opened for abortions for all kinds of reasons. But why did the phenomenon grow to much larger proportions? It seems that social change and new realities in contemporary Cyprus account for the remaining part of the answer. Indeed, in recent decades there have been fast-paced and drastic socioeconomic changes, which seem to have eroded traditional values and norms without allowing the time for new norms to develop—the phenomenon of "cultural lag." This is evident in the area of sexual relationships. Many young people are experimenting with sex in their relationships, something that contemporary "open" or "liberated" Cypriot society seems to "allow." Yet the relationships of these young people with their parents (and teachers) do not seem to be so liberated as to allow for straight talk about sex and contraception—thus the many unwanted pregnancies and the use of abortion as an alternative to contraception!

Besides the young, many older people have problems with their marriage; hence the increasing rates of divorce. Both young and older couples also seem to be resorting to relationships outside marriage, which may again lead to unwanted pregnancies and abortions.

To the above must be added the fact that Cypriot males, and sometimes their women partners, seem to think that male contraceptives will somehow render lovemaking "less natural" and enjoyable. Thus, contraception ends up being the sole responsibility of women. And if she has not taken the necessary precautions, they end up with unwanted pregnancies and abortions.

The ease of abortions may be an important explanatory factor for the fact that children born out of wedlock are rarely found in Cyprus. To this, of course, we must add the prevailing conservative traditional values, which view unmarried mothers as immoral, since they are seen to be flagrantly violating the sexual code and carrying the "shame of dishonor." Because stigma is a certain outcome for childbearing outside wedlock, and because abortions are so easy to arrange, it is no wonder that illegitimate births are almost nonexistent.

Cyprus has, in fact, introduced legislation (Law 243/90) to bring itself in line with the provisions of the relevant European Convention. An interesting example, which highlights all the above issues, concerned a case in the mid 1990s of an unmarried woman working in the Church-run broadcasting station (Logos). When she decided to go against convention and not hide the fact that she was pregnant, she was soon fired, as she was seen to be a case of embarrassment for her employer and a bad moral example for all. The fired woman sued the station and managed to win the case and be awarded compensation (*Fileleftheros*, 9 May 1995).

Another recent law, which aims to protect women from the abuse of traditional norms, relates to the Prevention of Violence in the Family and the Protection of Victims of Violence (47(I)/94). Such a law was of absolute necessity in Cyprus, where many men consider it their legitimate right to uphold their power as husbands and/or fathers in the family through any means possible, including violence, whether it be physical or psychological violence against the wife and children, or sexual violence against the wife.

### The Sociolegal Status of Men and Women in Work/Employment

For many years, women in the labor force suffered various forms of discrimination as regards inequality in pay for similar work done, conditions of work, type of employment, and opportunities for advancement. Gradually, as a result of a number of factors, such as pressures from women's organizations and the trade unions, and political pressures emanating from the signing by the Cypriot government of various international treaties, the situation has substantially improved, at least as far as legal provisions are concerned. This has not, however, substantially improved the situation for all women, nor has such legal improvements dramatically improved the life of women.

A good example is that of social insurance legislation, enacted since independence, which provides for a marriage grant payable to working women when they marry, as well as a maternity grant and allowance, the former paid to a woman giving birth, the latter paid during a maternity leave of up to 12 weeks. Unfortunately, the plan does not cover self-employed women or unpaid family workers in agriculture, who comprise approximately a third of the total number of economically active women. Furthermore, it does not cover thousands of women involved with unpaid housework, as this is not considered "proper" work. This means that a great number of Cypriot women, particularly older women, have to remain in a state of complete dependence on their husbands. Social insurance legislation has been modified appropriately, after ratification of the International Labor Organization Convention 100, and the Equal Remuneration Law (158/89), to provide for equal pay for men and women for work of equal value. This has decreased the gap between male and female wages, although it has certainly not closed it, since equal remuneration is practiced only by the government and a few large corporations, mainly banks, but certainly not by the private sector at large. Among the laws that seek to improve the legal position of women in employment is the "termination of employment" law (24/87), under which sex, pregnancy, or maternity can never constitute reasons for the termination of employment. Again, however, evidence shows that many employers tend to ignore the law, and that in such cases few women proceed to take legal measures against the perpetrators (Varnavidon & Roussou 1995).

Another interesting example, which illustrates how small an effect changes in laws can have on actual social practices, is the abolition of the pre-independence law (180), which prohibited the employment of women during the night. For many years following abolition of this law, social resistance to the idea of women working outside their homes during the night has been such that few women still dare to do so. The result has been an intense shortage of women working in jobs for which night duties are essential, such as nursing and paramedical occupations. For this reason, private clinics have been given permission to employ women from foreign countries. Also, Cypriot women employed in the Cypriot Police Force and the National Guard, as well as those working in the thriving tourist industry, are exempt from night duties.

Lastly, we should underline the fact that in 1985 the Cyprus government ratified the United Nations Convention (34/180) on the Elimination of All Forms of Discrimination Against Women (Law 78/85). This symbolized Cyprus's commitment to eliminate all forms of discrimination against women in all spheres of life, be it education, politics, employment, family, or public life.

In summary, two major comments could be made about legislative change and its impact on Cypriot society. To begin with, most ratifications of international conventions and relevant laws were passed in the recent decades, after independence in 1960, but mostly after 1974. This suggests that, until recent times, concerns about equality and the protection of the rights of various underprivileged groups in society, including women and children, were not a primary issue, because traditional Cypriot society was based on conservative norms, values, and morals. Cypriot life revolves around the central social institution of the patriarchal family, with the father enjoying controlling power over the behavior of the other members of the family, especially women, as the preordained "order of things," legitimated by religion.

Modernization and socioeconomic change have contributed to an "opening-up" of society and the gradual espousal of more liberal values and norms. Thus, the introduction of the various laws outlined above. Yet, it seems that Cyprus is going through a period of transition, in which new values coexist with traditional ones. This, as well as the efforts of traditional male and clerical power holders to cling to their powers, seems to explain the persistence of inequality between the sexes and generations.

Women themselves have been slow to organize and push for their rights. Traditionally, the main domain of women's participation in public life has been that of voluntary institutions, especially charitable organizations. This is true especially for upper- and middle-class women, the roots of this phenomenon dating back to the formative stages of the bourgeois class in Cyprus and its ideals of keeping women away from the world of production, as "queens" in the private realm of the family, into which men would retreat after work. Women's involvement with charitable institutions was accepted and encouraged, because, in dealing with these, they could expend similar "feminine" services as the ones expended within the families themselves, namely care, love, and affection (Peristianis 1998). Voluntary organizations, and especially charitable ones, seem to have increased in numbers after the Turkish invasion of 1974, with the appearance of new social groups in need of support (Antoniou 1992). Interestingly enough, the leadership of most of these organizations is composed of men, with the exception of a handful of organizations, such as the Cyprus Red Cross and the Association for the Prevention of Violence in the Family.

Women from the working classes had a more prominent role in the trade unions, which started organizing early on in the 20th century. The oldest such union, PEO (Pancyprian Federation of Labor), is controlled by AKEL, the communist party of Cyprus. SEK (Federation of Cypriot Workers) is controlled by DISI, the right-wing party, and DEOK (Democratic Workers Federation of Cyprus), is controlled by the socialist party, EDEK. There are also strong autonomous unions representing government employees (PASIDI) and bank employees (ETIK).

In the labor history of Cyprus, women have fought alongside men for basic labor rights, such as social insurance, improvements in wages, and shorter working hours (Pyrgou 1993). However, trade unions do not appear to have actively pursued women's rights for equality in the labor market. In fact, trade unions have accepted pay discrimination against women in labor agreements with respective employers (House 1987). It is interesting that the first law (in 1961), which provided for equal pay for women in the public sector, was enacted, not after trade union pressure, but as a result of a private prosecution by a woman employee who sued the Republic of Cyprus for not upholding the Constitutional Law's provision for equal treatment of the sexes.

Cypriot women have never gone on strike in pursuit of their specific rights as women. One possible reason for this may be the fact that, whereas all unions have departments dealing with women's matters, policymaking of these departments is directed by men (Antoniou 1992). Overall, although women constitute more than a third of the total trade-union membership, they seem to exert little influence of their own.

A contributing factor is obviously the control of all general unions by the political parties, who are, once again, male-dominated, and whose primary objectives have to do with furthering their political ambitions. Even more surprising is the fact that women's organizations themselves seem to be controlled or strongly affiliated with political parties. Thus POGO (Pancyprian Organization of Women) is controlled by the communist party; Equal Rights and Equal Responsibilities is controlled by the right-wing party. The Socialist Feminist Movement and the Women's Organization of the Democratic Party are even more forthright in declaring their affiliation in their own names.

For decades now, the primary focus of concern for the political parties has been the ethnic conflict between Greek and Turkish Cypriots, "the Cyprus Problem." This has overshadowed all other issues, including those concerning women, equality of the sexes, and gender relations. Even though the higher officers of these women's organizations have the opportunity to participate in the decision-making processes of the political parties, their voices are seldom strong enough to make a real impact, as the leading teams are always male-dominated. This becomes even more obvious in times of elections, as women candidates seldom, if ever, make it on parties' lists. Because of prejudices and stereotypes, hardly any women who do make it onto ballots manage to attract enough votes to enter the House. In 1999, there were only three women members out of a total of 53 members. Women seem to do somewhat better in local government, where they appear to be increasing their numbers yearly. Of course, these posts hold negligible political power, so women's gains in this area do not amount to a serious improvement in their status or impact.

### General Concepts and Constructs of Sexuality and Love

In traditional Cypriot society, marriages were arranged by parents and had nothing or little to do with the personal preferences of the young people involved. Often a young man coming of wedding age would suggest to his parents a particular girl of his fancy (usually a girl he found attractive in external appearance but had little knowledge of—since girls were expected to practice "male-avoidance," in order to protect their reputation and honor). If the parents approved of their son's choice, they would proceed to sound out the parents of the girl, usually through the services of a mediator/matchmaker. If the parents disapproved of the choice, their objections usually prevailed, as they were supposed to "know best" because they were "older and more experienced." Obviously, the girl's opinion was rarely asked for and her freedom of choice was much more restricted than the young man's.

The paramount criteria for parents' preferences had to do with considerations of their family's best social and economic interests—thus, they had to be satisfied with the economic well-being of the girl's family, the status of her family in the social hierarchy of the village, as well as the moral reputation/standing of the girl and her family in the village. Obviously, a good choice for marriage would enhance both the material resources as well as the status of their family in the village community. Parents would give a "dowry" to the young couple as a material aid to help the newlyweds make a good start in their married life. The bride's family would usually contribute the house plus furniture, kitchen utensils, household linen, and similar items. The bridegroom's side would provide some land and animals. Attalides (1981) notes that marriage settlements imply a bargaining process of matching the assets brought to the new household by the respective partners. Moreover, the practice of giving equal inheritance to all children means that parents must be aware so that what they give to one child at the time of marriage does not jeopardize the share of any remaining children. "In this situation, it is understandable that control of premarital sexuality should be extremely strict for girls." Thus, if a girl acquires a "bad reputation," the bargaining power of a potential husband is enormously increased, allowing him the chance to make "virtually extortionate demands for a property settlement, thus incapacitating the domestic group from provision for further children" (Attalides 1981). Of course, property considerations were only one set of reasons for the adherence to a strict moral code of behavior for women, but they were surely an important set.

The above constitutes one more set of reasons why families had to always be vigilant of the reputation of their women. Young women had to maintain their chastity until their wedding day. If a woman's sexual purity was questioned, she risked her chance of ever marrying. Virginity was a necessary condition of a woman's moral integrity and the principal prerequisite for marriage. It should be remembered that virginity did not entail only the "physical purity of a girl," i.e., an "intact hymen," but implied that "the girl should avoid any social contact with men that is automatically associated with sexual desire" (Markides et al. 1978).

So important was the value of female purity that during wedding celebrations, the visual display of the bloodstained sheets, proving the bride's virginity, had central importance. It has been noted (Argyrou 1996) that the virginity rite "expressed female subjugation but also the wider subjugation of younger people of both sexes to their elders and in particular their parents," for the rite symbolized in a "tangible and indisputable way" that the parents had been managing and controlling the family well. Argyrou (1996) demonstrates how changes to the rite, leading to its disappearance, reflect changes in the power relations between the older and younger generations, as well as between the sexes. The first set of changes became visible in the 1940s, when new employment opportunities were created, giving young men the opportunity to move to the towns for jobs. The sons of wealthier parents moved to towns in order to obtain secondary education. Eventually, with mass education, this became true for all classes and for both sexes. Youngsters were now exposed to new ideas and values through books, magazines, and newspapers. Overall, opportunities for economic independence and education decreased the dependence of the young on their parents and eroded the latter's authority and powers of control, as children could be more knowledgeable or competent than their parents in some areas.

Other developments also contributed to the changing nature of power relationships between generations. For instance, a young man moving to a town often found it practical to stay with his in-laws, so that his fiancée and mother-in-law could look after him and he could also save money to contribute to the costs of building a house. This practicality made vigilant observation of the engaged youngsters difficult for the parents. It also meant that parents themselves chose to avoid the embarrassment of asking for evidence of a bride's virginity, whereas the couple itself increasingly considered the matter their private affair rather than a public spectacle. By the late 1960s and 1970s, "the practice of having fiancees move in with their in-laws became generalized" and "engaged youngsters were sleeping together with the parents knowledge and implicit consent." Loizos (1975) notes that, in fact, by the 1960s, "youngsters had acquired power to veto their parents' choice of marriage partner." Balswick (1973) points out that by this time, young people considered "romantic love" to be of primary importance, and this development was responsible for the challenging of parentally arranged marriages. The concept of romantic love was related to changing sexual standards. For if love was felt to be a prerequisite for marriage, then only the young people themselves could determine the existence of love, and this entailed a certain amount of familiarity with members of the opposite sex. Thus "dating" started becoming common.

Such developments cannot be taken to imply that youngsters have now been liberated from traditional values and that virginity and female chastity are no longer important to men. In fact, as Argyrou (1996) reminds us, what has changed has mostly to do with the "timing of sexual access to the bride." Furthermore, the traditional "double standards," requiring a woman to be a virgin until she marries but not so the man, are still prevalent in Cypriot society. Similarly, although some expected that modernization and romantic love would lead to the demise of the dowry system (Balswick 1973), the practice seems to be going strong with some minor changes. Nowadays, the bride's parents are still the ones who contribute to the house and most other items needed for setting up the new household. The groom's parents are expected to have invested considerably in their son's education, which will have led, or hopefully will lead in the future, to very good employment.

After 1974, with the displacement and impoverishment of a third of the population, who lost all their wealth and became refugees so they could not give any dowry to their children, the tradition suffered a setback. However, traditional values and expectations were so strong that the state was pushed to donate land or money to all unmarried daughters of refugee families as a form of dowry for establishing their own households in the free south. Besides, the economic recovery and boom after the 1980s has enabled Cypriots to continue with the practice (Stavrou 1992). Some analysts point out that the willingness of Cypriot parents "for deferred gratification" in order to invest in their children's dowry, may actually itself be one of the main reasons for the continued success of Cyprus's economy (Balswick 1973, Mavratsas 1992). The above realities may account for an interesting paradox, revealed by social surveys. On the one hand, young Cypriots claim that love is what is important in marriage and that the giving of a dowry is an outdated practice that they do not believe in. On the other hand, they say that parents should "help" with a house and in other ways so the young couple can make a start in life (Intercollege 1996). This seems to vindicate Argyrou's (1996) position that we are looking at developments in sexual mores and related practices, which are the result of "a struggle in which children won a dominated freedom and parents retained partial control through compromise."

## B. Religious Beliefs Affecting Sexuality

In Cypriot society, the religious attitudes and beliefs of the Greek Orthodox Church exercise a strong influence on the sexual attitudes and behavior of the people. Some insight into this factor can be gained from the responses of Greek Orthodox priests to a semi-structured questionnaire regarding seven sexual topics: a) adultery, b) premarital sex, c) masturbation, d) abortion, e) contraception, f) homosexuality, and g) coital abstention. There were 130 (23.2%) responses from the total of 560 questionnaires distributed to all priests on the island, followed up with face-to-face interviews of 27 of the priests (Georgiou 1990).

On the issue of premarital sex, the priests were asked for their pastoral response to the following "situation":

A young, engaged Christian couple who has been cohabiting for three years is very much in love, but they cannot marry immediately as they have a number of difficulties. As they do not want to have sexual intercourse before the marriage ceremony, but are involved in heavy petting, they approach a priest for advice. (Georgiou 1990)

For their pastoral advice, the priests chose the following:

- to separate immediately (0.8%)
- to stop all caring gestures (5.3%)
- to stop all passionate caressing that lead to sexual excitement (22.3%)
- to continue as they are now until they get married (21.5%)
- not to the cohabit together, and (8.5%)
- something else (32.3%)

A thematic analysis was performed using subjective responses based on 14 mutually exclusive general categories. The responses were: The couple:

- should get married immediately, no matter what (32.6%)
- should refrain from sexual intercourse until they get married as soon as possible (19.7%)
- should refrain from heavy petting (19.7%)
- should live in separate houses or sleep in separate beds (18.2%)
- should be reminded that sex outside marriage is considered a sin of fornication (15.9%)

- should continue as they are until they get married (14.4%)
- should get married after a very brief engagement, otherwise problems are inevitable (6.1%)
- should use the engagement as a time to know each other, allowing their relationship to mature until marriage, before having sexual intercourse (5.3%)
- could proceed with their committed relationship and have sexual intercourse (2.3%)
- should read religious literature to help them overcome their passions (1.5%)
- should not consider their sexual relationship sinful, since their goal is to get married (0.8%)
- should realize that there is a danger that they will have an abortion if they have sexual intercourse (0.8%)
- should separate immediately (0.8%)
- it is not the job of a priest to advise how an engaged couple should behave sexually (0.8%)

Face-to-face interviews with the 27 priests revealed what appeared to be a confused attitude toward premarital sex. They offered a variety of legalistic definitions of premarital sex, which dichotomized sexual acts into "acceptable" or "not acceptable." Some, for example, drew the line of "acceptability" at light kissing between a couple engaged to be married. Others drew the line at a light caress, rejecting all other sexual expressions as either unacceptable or sinful, and so on and so forth. There was also no consensus as to why premarital sex was a sin. The majority said that it was a sin because the Orthodox Church said so. None of the priests, however, could refer to any specific writings of the Orthodox Church to validate their claim. (See other responses from this survey of priests on homosexuality in Section 6B, on contraception in Section 9A, and on abortion in Section 9B.)

## 3. Knowledge and Education about Sexuality

### A. Government Policies and Programs

There are no specific government policies and programs for sex education. There are no formal sex education programs taught in schools beyond the biology lessons, which cover subjects such as the anatomy and physiology of the reproductive organs, fertilization, twins and genetics, sexually transmitted diseases, changes during puberty, and birthing. These lessons are normally taught by biology teachers, and it is left to their discretion to answer specific questions that may be raised in class. These lessons are taught from the age of 15 upwards.

### B. Informal Sources of Sexual Knowledge

There is an element of informal sex education from organizations such as the Family Planning Organization, but this only covers specific groups of people, such as married women seeking gynecological or family planning assistance, soldiers doing their National Guard service, and other minority groups. There is also some teaching in hospitals and schools, but limited staff does not allow for further expansion.

When the main author arrived on Cyprus from the United Kingdom in 1983, there were no explicit sexual articles published in the Cypriot media for fear of reprisals. I wrote my first article on Cypriot male sexuality during this period, but found it impossible to find an editor willing to publish it in their newspaper, as it contained words such as "penis" and "vagina." There seemed to be an inherent fear of publishing sexual articles of any nature, as the editors believed that there would be a volcanic eruption from the Church and the conservative people of Cyprus. They could not have been further from the truth! When a brave editor of a relatively small, radical right-wing newspaper decided to publish the article, there was applause from many sectors of society; one of the long-lasting, but superfluous taboos had been broken! Cypriots were thirsting to learn more about sexuality. After the newspaper editor's initial enthusiasm, I proposed a weekly column, which would allow people to write in their problems anonymously and receive replies in the newspaper. He agreed, and the first sexual column in the history of Cyprus was launched in 1984 in the newspaper *Alitheia* (*The Truth*). The sales of this particular small newspaper increased dramatically in just over a year!

The degree of sexual ignorance from the questions being received was apparent: "Can I get pregnant by swallowing sperm?" "What is the clitoris?" and many, many other questions touching on topics such as anal sex, transvestitism, telephone sex, and sexual problems. At least a dozen letters were received every day. The columns gave people from all age groups and all walks of life an opportunity to write their questions or problems about sexuality, and get a response published in the media for all to read. The weekly column in the popular magazine *To Periodiko*, which ran from 1984 to 1994, reached a peak audience in excess of 30,000 people weekly. More than 1,000 articles covering all aspects of sexuality were published during this period. This, along with a weekly radio program titled *Human Sexuality*, broadcast live every Saturday at lunch time by the author, covered a wide variety of sexual topics and provided a large part of the informal sex education of the population. After a few years, other newspapers began to publish articles, usually translated from foreign magazines. Beginning in September 1999, this editor completed a series of six television programs on human sexuality for EF-EM, a local TV station in Larnaca. (See Section 10, Sexually Transmitted Diseases, for survey data on the knowledge of adolescents regarding STDs.)

In the Knowledge, Attitudes, Beliefs, and Practices (KABP) Survey on AIDS (Georgiou & Veresies 1990, 1991; see also Sections 5B, Interpersonal Heterosexual Behaviors, Adolescents, 6A, Homoerotic, Homosexual, and Bisexual Behaviors, Children and Adolescents, and 10A, Sexually Transmitted Diseases and HIV/AIDS), 3,176 15- to 18-year-old schoolchildren gave us additional insights into their sources of sexuality information. The respondents reported receiving their first sexual information from five main sources: books and periodicals (24.1%), newspapers and magazines (15.4%), friends (12.0%), videos (12.3%), and television (12.2%). It is not clear from the questionnaire, however, who is actually providing this information in the sources mentioned. Sex differences showed that the boys were more likely to obtain their information from videos (9% vs. 3.3%), probably commercial pornography, while the girls were more likely to obtain their information from books and periodicals (14.7% vs. 9.4%) and mother (4.4% vs. 0.6%). It appears that newspapers and magazines are read equally by both. Subsequent sources of additional sexual information included: television (13.2%), schoolteachers (12.3%), and medical personnel (11.7%). The same-sex differences as those noted above emerged, with the exception of books and periodicals, which are again read equally by both sexes.

When asked, "Where would you prefer to get information about human sexual behavior? (Circle only your first choice)," the great majority of respondents preferred to obtain their information from books and periodicals (24.1%), followed by newspapers and magazines (15.4%), friends (12.6%), videos (12.3%), and television (12.2%). All the other responses were below the 5% level.

It should be noted here that there are no known sex education videos circulating in Cyprus, apart from the commercial pornographic videos that are freely available for rental in most video shops, certainly before the clamp-down on piracy came about. It therefore appears that 12.3% of the respondents are obtaining their information from pornographic videos. When asked to name their second preferred source of sexual information, students listed books and periodicals (16.1%), newspapers and magazines (14.2%), television (13.7%), videos (12.7%), and friends (11.4%). The remaining responses were below the 5% level. Sex differences showed that more males than females would prefer the radio as an important second source of sexual information (108 males vs. 46 females), newspapers and magazines (105 males vs. 70 females), television (224 males vs. 194 females), and videos (111 males vs. 38 females). More females than males would prefer sources such as books and journals (153 females vs. 137 males), mother (191 females vs. 56 males), and doctors and nurses (226 females vs. 143 males).

The survey gave no information regarding the specific books, videos, and magazines that students used, or how accurate the sex information was. Moreover, it is not clear how the students interpreted the question, "From where do you get information about human sexuality?" in a country where human sexuality courses have never been taught formally at school. Under the circumstances, the concept of "human sexuality" may be a difficult one for teenagers to interpret.

## 4. Autoerotic Behaviors and Patterns

### A. Children and Adolescents

The only data available on child and adolescent autoerotic behavior comes from retrospective histories taken with a clinical sample of 840 patients whom the main author saw in clinical practice between 1993 and 1996. While male masturbation in this sample is far more prevalent than female masturbation (85% vs. 15%), approximately 50% of masturbating females felt guilty about this behavior compared with 48% of males.

It appears that parents also have fears of the female losing her virginity if she is allowed to "play about down there!" Virginity is related to the "honor" (*timi*) of the family, and this is very carefully guarded. Males, on the other hand, are often encouraged and "cajoled" to continue, if they are caught fondling their genitals in infancy, as this is seen as a normal part of growing up. Given that the females get rather negative messages when caught masturbating, and indeed may be chastised for this behavior, then it is perhaps not a surprise to find that only 15% of the females in this sample masturbated.

Still, it may be a little surprising that such a large number of Cypriot girls begin masturbating at such a young age, before age 10. One of the factors is certainly the early growth spurt that females have in relation to boys, but there are probably other explanations also. Most males learn how to masturbate from their friends (77%) compared to only 26.5% of females. The majority of girls, however, learn to masturbate by themselves, through experimentation or accident (54%), compared to fewer boys (21%) that learn in this way. Again, more girls (19%) learn to masturbate from the media, books, magazines, and the like, compared to about 2% of boys. It appears that girls tend not to talk as openly as boys do with their peers about masturbating, and therefore, this is not the source of their information. Girls, it appears, prefer to find their sexual information from books and magazines, and self-experiment in the privacy of their own home.

The main author's clinical experience has shown that there is a widely reported incidence of childhood masturbation from infancy to nursery-school age. These cases are often reported by parents and are accepted by parents and caretakers if the child is male, and it is often joked about: "He's as potent as his father. Look, he's started young." If the child is female, such behavior is often frowned upon, with punishment as a consequence if it continues. Over the last decade, I have had a number of parents coming to the clinic to discuss the "normality" of their young infant daughter's masturbatory behavior, sometimes in horror that their little "innocent" should be capable of such "disgusting" actions! I have yet to see a parent come to discuss their son's masturbatory behavior!

## B. Adults

There are no data available for adult masturbation, but from anecdotal evidence in clinical practice I would say that adult masturbation in a stable relationship is quite rare for both sexes. There are the few occasions when masturbation is reported by a married man who has problems approaching his wife sexually because of marital discord, but this occurred in less than 1% of the clinical population. I believe that the Cypriot male views masturbation more as a "child's thing," and not the sort of thing that a "man" does, unless compelled to do so by circumstances.

Women, on the other hand, will often refuse to masturbate even when the husband is in therapy, believing that coitus is the "proper thing." They prefer not to become part of the therapy until it reaches a stage where coitus is allowed. It follows from this that the treatment of anorgasmia using the traditional European or American treatment protocols is doomed to failure in Cyprus, as masturbating to orgasm is the essence of this therapy. (In Cyprus, one has to be a very creative sex therapist to succeed!)

## 5. *Interpersonal Heterosexual Behaviors*

### A. Children

No data have been gathered to date regarding children's sexuality or sexual rehearsal play in Cyprus.

### B. Adolescents

The only systematic survey that has been conducted to date in Cyprus regarding adolescent sexuality involves a sample of 3,176 (1,528 male and 1,643 female) Cypriot lyceum students conducted by Georgiou and Veresies in 1990 and 1991. The Knowledge, Attitudes, Beliefs, and Practices (KABP) Survey was organized and completed along the lines of work carried out by the World Health Organization (WHO), the Global Programme on AIDS, the Social and Behavioral Research Unit (SBR), the Cyprus National AIDS Committee, the Ministry of Health, and the Ministry of Education in Cyprus. The whole project was headed by the main author of this chapter as the WHO Principal Investigator.

Even though the premise of the research was to look at the knowledge, attitudes, beliefs, and practices of Cypriot adolescents toward HIV infection and AIDS, many of the 177 questions in the survey touched on other aspects of human sexuality. There were two questionnaires, one for high school adolescents and another for head teachers. A multistage random-cluster sampling strategy was used to obtain data for the survey, using 27 schools—20 (79.2% of the sample) in urban areas and 7 (20.8%) in rural ones. The 177-question survey was answered anonymously, and covered the following areas: sociodemographics, sources of information on AIDS, knowledge of AIDS, attitudes and beliefs about AIDS, attitudes toward people with AIDS, knowledge of sexually transmitted diseases (STDs), leisure-time activities, perceived norms in certain health-related behavior, drinking and drug abuse, attitudes about condom use, and sexual behavior.

*Adolescent Attitudes and Behavior*
*Previous Heterosexual Experiences.* Students were asked to respond to a series of questions about individual behaviors

ranging from hugging to anal sex. Even though hugging, deep kissing, and petting are not considered sexual activities through which HIV is transmitted, they are often enough preliminary steps toward sexual intercourse. Therefore, the percentage of young people engaging in them indicates when these steps toward more-advanced sexual activity are first taken (see Table 1).

Three quarters of the adolescents (76.7%) surveyed have experienced hugging at least once. Of these, the majority were boys (1,340 boys vs. 1,075 girls). One in six (15%) of the boys and one third (32%) of the girls were "sexually inexperienced," not having engaged even in petting. About half of the students have experienced deep open-mouth kissing and some sort of petting above the waist. Again, the majority of these were boys (963 boys vs. 439 girls). About one third have petted below the waist (850 boys vs. 289 girls) and a further one third have slept together without sexual intercourse (628 boys vs. 242 girls). Sexual intercourse was attempted by approximately one quarter (18.6%) of the students (550 boys vs. 97 girls), which means that about 94% of the girls and two thirds (66%) of the boys were technically still virgins, even though they may have had other sexual experiences.

Judging from the figures for sex differences, it appears that the boys are not having sexual intercourse with the indigenous females. This raises the question of who their sexual partners are. Is it mostly with prostitutes, either local girls or imported "artists," or is it with tourist girls? This data does not answer these questions, but they are definitely worth further investigation because of the implications for HIV transmission.

A further 25% of the respondents reported experiencing oral sex at least once (563 boys vs. 103 girls).

There is no doubt that the most dangerous sexual activity in terms of contracting HIV is receptive anal sexual intercourse. Masters, Johnson, and Kolodny (1988) point out that the risk from a single episode of anal intercourse with an infected partner is considerably higher than with other sexual activities—probably on the order of one in 50 to 100. Just over 15% of the respondents reported experiencing anal or rectal sex. Of these, the majority were boys (424 boys vs. 41 girls). It would certainly be worth investigating further whether the boys had homosexual or heterosexual anal intercourse, whether they had used a condom, and whether they were the receptors or the penetrators. It is also not clear why there should be so many boys participating in anal intercourse. If a large majority of girls were involved, this would be understandable, given the patriarchal attitudes that prevail in Cyprus regarding the preservation of a girl's ("technical") virginity. Perhaps the males are using anal sex as a means of birth control.

### Table 1

### Sexual Behaviors with the Other Sex
### for 14 to 18-Plus-Year-Olds

|  | Never | 1-2 times | 3-6 times | 7 or more |
|---|---|---|---|---|
| Hugging | 23.3 | 26.7 | 13.2 | 36.2 |
| Deep (open mouth) kissing | 47.5 | 20.4 | 8.9 | 22.7 |
| Petting above the waist | 54.5 | 19.0 | 8.2 | 17.2 |
| Petting below the waist | 63.1 | 12.8 | 6.3 | 16.9 |
| Sleeping together (without sexual intercourse) | 71.9 | 13.3 | 5.0 | 9.1 |
| Sexual intercourse | 78.5 | 7.2 | 3.9 | 7.5 |
| Oral sex | 75.2 | 8.2 | 4.2 | 8.5 |
| Anal (rectal) sex | 84.4 | 8.0 | 2.3 | 4.4 |

Among the 19.4% of respondents reporting having had vaginal intercourse, 11.7% (296 males and 75 females) reported having had one or two sexual partners, 4% (123 boys and 5 girls) between three and six partners, and 3.7% (115 boys and 4 girls) admitted to seven or more partners.

### Table 2

**Age at First Sexual Intercourse Experience**

| Age | Percentage | Number of Males Versus Females | | |
|---|---|---|---|---|
| Under age 11 | 4.2% | 123 boys | v. | 11 girls |
| Age 12 | 1.3 | 37 boys | v. | 4 girls |
| Age 13 | 2.1 | 63 boys | v. | 3 girls |
| Age 14 | 4.7 | 145 girls | v. | 3 girls |
| Age 15 | 5.5 | 154 boys | v. | 22 girls |
| Age 16 | 4.2 | 96 boys | v. | 38 girls |
| Age 17 | 0.7 | 8 boys | v. | 15 girls |
| Age 18-19 | 0.6 | 14 boys | v. | 4 girls |

### Table 3

**Reasons Cited for First Sexual Intercourse**

| | Number Citing | Boys | Girls | Percent- age |
|---|---|---|---|---|
| I have not yet had intercourse | 2,275 | | | 71.6% |
| Love for the person | 232 | 160.0 | 72 | 7.3% |
| Physical attraction | 162 | 152.0 | 10 | 5.1 |
| Curiosity | 106 | 100.0 | 6 | 3.3 |
| To maintain a relationship | 99 | 88.0 | 11 | 3.1 |
| Got carried away by passion | 72 | 64.0 | 8 | 2.3 |
| It was expected by friends | 23 | 0.7 | | |
| I was physically forced | 13 | 11.0 | 2 | 0.4 |
| Under the influence of alcohol or drugs | 9 | 0.3 | | |
| Loneliness | 4 | 0.1 | | |
| Other | 99 | 55.0 | 26 | 3.1 |

### Table 4

**Frequencies of Coitus with Different Partners**

| | Freq. | Percent |
|---|---|---|
| Cypriot your age whom you have recently met | 146 | 4.6% |
| Tourist your age whom you have recently met | 249 | 7.8 |
| Cypriot your age whom you have known a long time | 434 | 13.7 |
| Tourist your age whom you have known a long time | 195 | 6.1 |
| Cypriot you had recently met who was much older than you | 111 | 3.5 |
| Tourist you had recently met who was much older than you | 132 | 4.2 |
| Cypriot you had known a long time who was much older than you | 118 | 3.7 |
| Tourist you had known a long time who was much older than you | 92 | 2.9 |
| Cypriot prostitute, man or woman, who has sex in return for money | 216 | 6.8 |
| Foreign prostitute, man or woman, who has sex in return for money | 140 | 4.4 |

Of those who reported vaginal intercourse, the most frequent age of first intercourse was 14 to 16 years old, 14.4% (see Table 2). Girls showed a marked increase in sexual intercourse starting at age 15, whereas for boys, a marked increase was noted after age 13. The figures for the 11- and 12-year-olds appear to be rather high on first impression and need to be examined further (see also Table 6.)

Table 3 shows the most common reasons given for having a first coital experience. Eleven males and only two females reported being raped; from anecdotal clinical evidence, male adolescent rape is uncommon in Cyprus.

*Contraceptive and Prophylactic Condom Use.* Knowledge and use of condoms is another important area of adolescent sexual behavior, with 2,298 (72.4%; 1,378 boys vs. 915 girls) admitting they had seen a condom, and 65.6% (1,312 boys vs. 771 girls) saying they knew how to use them. Of the roughly one-in-four teens who had had sex, 6.7% (168 boys and 45 girls) had never used a condom, 7.0% (193 boys and 7 girls) had used a condom sometimes, 3.6% (108 boys and 7 girls) most times, and 3.9% (110 boys and 15 girls) always.

These findings have dire implications for HIV and other STD transmission. Only one in five students who had had sexual intercourse at least once had always used condoms. Three out of four were unprotected sometimes or all of the time. Moreover, it is not clear from the question whether the condom was used correctly or not, whether it was placed on the penis before any type of intromission, or whether it was placed on the penis just before ejaculation for purely contraceptive purposes. It is also not clear whether the condom was used for other sexual practices, such as anal and oral sex, which are also high-risk behaviors. These issues can be incorporated into any safe-sex and health education program.

*Kinds and Duration of Relationships.* The disparity between a much higher incidence of sexual intercourse for Cypriot males and a much lower incidence for females raises the question about who the females are that these young men are having sex with. Questions were asked regarding the age of the sexual partner, the duration of the relationship, and the demographic identity of sexual partners. Given the very high influx of tourists every year—for the past six or seven years, tourists have outnumbered the indigenous Cypriots—questions were asked that differentiated between the kinds of sexual partners Cypriot men and women have. Table 4 analyses the responses to these questions.

It appears that there are a large number of longstanding relationships with indigenous Cypriots. A total of 434 students (13.7%) said that they had a longstanding relationship with someone their own age. Of these, there were many more boys than girls (346 boys vs. 88 girls). A further 146 (4.6%) admitted to having sexual intercourse with a Cypriot partner their own age whom they had recently met. Again, the majority of these were males (126 males vs. 20 females).

Another category of partner preference that has implications for HIV transmission are the large number of students who had sexual intercourse with tourists their own age whom they had recently met. The overwhelming majority of these were boys (236 boys vs. 13 girls). Another equally potentially high-risk behavior was with tourists their own age whom they had known a while, even though it is not clear how long a term is indicated by "a while." Of these, again the majority were males (181 males vs. 14 females). To the list of potentially high-risk partners could be added the students who had coitus with older tourists whom they had just met (120 males vs. 12 females), and the older tourists whom they had known for some time (77 males vs. 15 females). Further, potentially high-risk partners would include Cypriot prostitutes (212 males vs. 4 females) and foreign prostitutes (133 males vs. 7 females). It is not clear why there are a small number of females in the prostitute categories, as it is unlikely that they frequented a male prostitute. Perhaps they misinterpreted the question to mean that they themselves were paid for having sexual intercourse—there have been such known cases in Cyprus among the student population.

*Cohabitation.* In response to the question, "Have you ever lived with a man or a woman as a regular sexual partner without being married?" 148 (4.7%; 134 boys and 14 girls) said that they had cohabited with a sexual partner before marriage.

*Teen Pregnancy.* A total of 73 boys said that they had made their partners pregnant, and a further 11 girls admitted to being made pregnant by their boyfriends.

*Age of Marriage.* Table 5 summarizes the results of the question, "At what age would you like to marry?"

## C. Adults

The following data were obtained from a clinical population of 840 clients of varying ages and educational backgrounds (see Section 12, Sexual Dysfunctions, Counseling, and Therapies, for details on sample and methodology).

### Virginity

It is clear that far fewer males (9.4%) than females (69%) are virgins when they become engaged or marry. "Family honor" is at stake because of the prevailing belief that a nonvirgin or "soiled" bride should be considered a second-rate citizen in no way equal in social and ethical standing to a virgin bride. Indeed, many brides-to-be have been accused of not being a virgin by their fiancés on the first night. This often results in both families getting involved, taking the female by force to be examined by a gynecologist, and deciding whether the couple should stay together based upon the doctor's diagnosis. Needless to say, such affairs are extremely degrading for the female involved. Even if the couple decides to stay together, there is no guarantee their relationship will stabilize and survive. In my clinical practice, I have encountered many cases of males who believe that virgin females should bleed like a chicken with it's head chopped off! The males expect to see much blood on the sheets, and if this does not happen—which inevitably it does not—then the accusations will begin, and the horrid saga begins. (See also comments on premarital sex under Sociolegal Status of Males and Females, Children and Adults, in Section 1A.)

Nonvirgins before marriage who have slept with a partner before making a firm commitment to marriage will often visit a gynecologist and ask for a hymenorrhaphy or hymen-repair operation. This is one way of "fooling" the potential husband and avoid being ridiculed and belittled by the "expert" spouse who thinks that he has the ability to differentiate between a virgin and nonvirgin with his penis on the first night. My national live radio program at Radio Proto (1991 to 1992) and my advice column in the best-selling national magazine *To Periodiko* received many questions about hymen-repair operations. Gynecologists I spoke with admitted performing at least two or three such operations a week, for a total of thousands annually on the island.

Tables 6, 7, and 8 summarize some responses from the author's clinical population of 840 adults. There appears to be quite a range in the frequency of sex, with a fairly even spread between the sexes (Table 8). About two thirds of the sample have sex more than twice weekly, with the remaining third less than once weekly. Remember that this is a clinical sample that has come for sex therapy for some sexual dysfunction or other, which inevitably adversely affects the frequency of lovemaking. This picture may not be so

representative of the general Cypriot population. My guess is that, given our Mediterranean temperament, we Cypriots are generally more hot-blooded than this!

There is a clearly significant difference between the sexes regarding the number of sexual partners in their lifetime (see Table 9). Two thirds of the women tended to stick with only one partner mostly, compared to about 7% of males, while very few women have more than two to three partners com-

### Table 5

### Ideal Age for Marriage

|  | Number | Percent |
|---|---|---|
| Already married or engaged | 51 (26 males and 25 females) | 1.6% |
| Do not intend to marry | 52 (36 males and 16 females) | 1.6 |
| At age 18 | 190 | 6.0 |
| Between ages 19 and 20 | 797 | 25.1 |
| Between 22 and 25 | 1,455 | 45.8 |
| Between 26 and 30 | 360 | 11.3 |
| Between 31 and 35 | 43 | 1.4 |
| Age 36 or older | 18 | 0.6 |

### Table 6

### Age of First Sexual Intercourse

| Age | Male | Female |
|---|---|---|
| Up to 16 years | 26.3% | 11.7% |
| 17-19 years | 52.7 | 35.1 |
| 20-25 years | 18.3 | 44.1 |
| 26+ | 2.6 | 9 |

### Table 7

### First Sexual Partner

|  | Male | Female |
|---|---|---|
| Prostitute | 66.6% | 0% |
| Tourist* | 11.4 | 5.5 |
| Cypriot | 13.3 | 17.4 |
| Spouse/Fiancé(e) | 8.6 | 77.1 |

*Tourism is a unique phenomenon in Cyprus, with an annual flow of about 1.5 million tourists to 600,000 of the indigenous population.

### Table 8

### Frequency of Sexual Intercourse

| Times per Month | Male | Female |
|---|---|---|
| 1-2 | 16.7% | 18.6% |
| 3-4 | 16.6 | 18.6 |
| 5-8 | 24.7 | 19.9 |
| 9-12 | 26 | 25.5 |
| 13 or more times | 15.8 | 17.3 |

### Table 9

### Number of Sexual Partners in One's Lifetime

| Number | Male | Female |
|---|---|---|
| 1 | 6.8% | 66.3% |
| 2-3 | 18.6 | 25.9 |
| 4-10 | 41.8 | 6.3 |
| 11 or more | 31.9 | 1.3 |

pared to males (8% of females vs. 73% of males). Whether this reflects the difference between the sexes or the inhibitions and taboos that exist in the Cypriot culture is not clear; the editor's guess is that the taboo placed upon female "promiscuity" by family and society is certainly a hindrance to moving from one partner to the other. Certainly, females that are likely to have multiple partners that are known in society will be labeled with very nasty names, such as "used," "prostitute," "ethically free," and others. These females tend to have difficulties finding a marriage partner, particularly if their behavior is well known. Usually, when a marriage is about to take place, both sets of parents will begin conducting an informal "character" assessment by asking various individuals in the close community of the prenuptials for a character reference. If the girl has a "bad name" in this community, then this will be reported to the potential bridegroom's parents who will strongly advise their son not to proceed, and will continue to stand as an obstacle until their son "sees sense"! These societal norms and taboos are enough for young girls not to consciously want to repeat one mistake twice or more.

About one third of males and one fifth of females had never experienced giving or receiving cunnilingus (see Table 10). A very small percentage of males tend to dislike giving cunnilingus (7%), whereas a much larger number of females dislike the act (21%), which could be for a variety of reasons. The most common reason cited by women in

### Table 10

**Do You Enjoy Giving/Receiving Cunnilingus?**

| Reaction | Male | Female |
|---|---|---|
| Definitely not enjoyed | 1.9% | 6.8% |
| Not enjoyed | 5.3 | 14.2 |
| Moderately enjoyed | 11.9 | 16.8 |
| Enjoyed | 36.3 | 25.4 |
| Very much enjoyed | 7.1 | 18.1 |
| Never experienced | 37.2 | 18.5 |

### Table 11

**Do You Enjoy Giving/Receiving Fellatio?**

| Reaction | Male | Female |
|---|---|---|
| Definitely not enjoyed | 1.2% | 5.6% |
| Not enjoyed | 2.8 | 14.7 |
| Moderately enjoyed | 5.1 | 19.1 |
| Enjoyed | 45.8 | 30 |
| Very much enjoyed | 7.8 | 3 |
| Never experienced | 37.1 | 27.3 |

### Table 12

**Have You Ever Engaged in Anal Sex?
If So, How Often?**

| Given/Received | Male | Female |
|---|---|---|
| Never | 57.6% | 64.8% |
| Yes | 42.2 | 35.1 |
| **Frequency for Males and Females Who Have Engaged in Anal Sex** | | |
| 1-2 times | 25 % | 31.1% |
| 3-6 times | 29.3 | 35 |
| 7-8 times | 1.2 | 0 |
| 9 or more times | 44.3 | 33.7 |

this sample was the partner's inexperience, his ignorance about the clitoris, and his or her belief that the vagina is the most stimulating and sensitive of areas. Also cited were the inhibitions of females who feel that they are dirty "down there," or that coitus is the only "acceptable" form of sex.

Not surprisingly, very few males do not enjoy being fellated—these being in the older age groups, which tend to be a lot more conservative in their sexual behaviors. About a fifth of the women in this clinical sample did not like giving fellatio to their partners, again probably related to taboos and inhibitions rife within the Cypriot community. Over a third of the men and a quarter of the women had never experienced this sexual behavior, but again these tend to be in the older age groups above 50 years old in the lower working social classes. Certainly, one third of the women thoroughly enjoyed it, as did well over half of the men (see Table 11).

A majority of the men and women who reported experimenting with anal sex appear divided about equally between those who tried it once or twice and those who were a bit more persistent, trying it three to six times before deciding not to continue with this sexual outlet (see Table 12). A third of the women and 44% of the men who tried anal sex appear to have incorporated this outlet into their sex lifestyle on a perhaps more regular basis, despite the disapproval of this behavior by the Greek Orthodox Church and despite it generally being considered a "no-no" by most couples. Perhaps one of the reasons for its fairly widespread occurrence among both sexes is the availability and popularity of pornography. Additional questioning of this clinical population revealed that it is mostly the male who will "subtly coerce" his partner into trying it, mostly for the sake of experimentation, after viewing anal sex on a pornographic video. In many cases, the reaction of the wife will determine the frequency of anal sex thereafter.

Unfortunately, there has been no epidemiological study of the sexual behavior of Cypriots. This small clinical sample is the only data available at present and it is limited by focusing on details of sexual functioning among a group of people who at some point in their lives developed a sexual dysfunction. In my opinion, this does not necessarily mean that the sexual histories and behaviors of these particular people differ from those without sexual dysfunctions, as this sample of people were also likely "normal"—without dysfunction—at some point before they decided to seek sex therapy. Their dysfunctions did not exist all their lives. The ideal, of course, is to have a methodologically sound, longitudinal epidemiological study with a substantial random sample of subjects. The lack of funds at present has made this very difficult to impossible.

*Divorce, Extramarital Sex, Single Mothers, and Domestic Violence*

See comments under Sociolegal Status of Males and Females, Children and Adults, in Section 1A.

## 6. Homoerotic, Homosexual, and Bisexual Behaviors

### A. Children and Adolescents

*Previous Homoerotic or Homosexual Experiences*

Many adolescents have some kind of sexual interaction with same-sex peers. This fairly common behavior, particularly among young adolescent males, might best be referred to as "homoerotic" rather than "homosexual." Sorenson (1973) found that about 9% of young people in the United States had one or more sexuoerotic experiences with someone of their own sex between the ages of 13 to 19. The likelihood of homoerotic activities in adolescence is significantly greater among those who have had same-sex experiences prior to adolescence. Indeed, most adolescents have their first homoerotic experience with another adolescent.

In the Knowledge, Attitudes, Beliefs, and Practices (KABP) Survey (Georgiou & Veresies 1990, 1991), about 34% of the respondents reported having hugged someone of the same sex at least once. Of these students, the majority were girls (722 girls vs. 354 boys). A further 7.9% had kissed passionately and a further 5.3% had petted above the waist—of these the majority were males. Table 13 summarizes the frequency of various sexual activities with a same-sex partner.

The majority of students who reported experiencing same-sex anal intercourse were males (141 males vs. 9 females). It is not clear, however, how these 9 females could be involved in homosexual anal intercourse, unless it was taken to mean anal penetration by a homosexual boy or with a dildo, but the likelihood of this is probably very small. These results are probably because of a misunderstanding of the question, or ignorance regarding anal sex.

When asked, "With how many people of the same sex have you had oral or anal sex?" 88.7% reported never experiencing oral or anal sex with a same-sex partner. An additional 4.3% had attempted homosexual oral or anal sex with between one to two partners (119 males vs. 18 females), and 1.2% had with three to six partners.

It appears that the majority had their first homosexual experiences when they were between the ages of 13 to 16 (see Table 14). During these ages, 5.5% of the respondents reported having their first homosexual experience. There may be a latent period for homosexual experiences at the age of 12, but this cannot be confirmed by the data. It has been shown by Kinsey and his co-researchers that the age of puberty is related to the age of the initial sexual experiences, including homosexual ones. It is not clear from the data, however, when Cypriot boys reach puberty, even though it might be presumed that it is younger than 11 years old for some boys.

## B. Adults

### A Few Statistics

The author's clinical sample of 840 patients cited earlier gives us some idea of homosexual and bisexual behavioral practices in a group of men and women seeking help with some sexual problem or dysfunction. A second bias in this data is the gender balance, with 597 males to 243 females.

The respondents were asked during history taking if they had ever been approached sexually by another person of the same sex. This opening question was chosen as much less threatening than asking whether the client had actual same-sex experiences. If the response was "yes," then they were asked simply, "What happened?" Of the total number of responses, 12.4% of the sample admitted to some type of sexual contact to orgasm with a same-sex partner; 11.6% were male and 0.8% female.

In order to avoid polarizing the population into "homosexual versus heterosexual," the following clinical data were collected using the seven-point rating scale of heterosexual-homosexual attraction/behavior devised by Alfred Kinsey (1953).

It seems clear from the data that the majority of people who admitted to some type of homosexual contact or experience were Kinsey 1 or 2 (13.1%), with very few, 1.7%, in Kinsey 5 and 6. This indicates the transitory experiences of these people with a same-sex partner. Indeed, all of the male experiences, with the exception of 18 cases discussed below, were age 18 to 20, the age when all Cypriot males are required to do their National Guard training as a soldier in

an army camp for 26 months. It was during this period in the National Guard that most of these experiences occurred. Most of these young soldiers would be "picked up" by homosexuals "cruising" the scene and taken to their army camp. The deal would be struck in the car, and most of the time they were offered a small sum of money ranging from ten to 15 dollars (US) in exchange for "services," which meant the homosexual fellating the soldier, or the soldier

### Table 13

### Frequency of Sexual Activity with a Same-Sex Partner

| Behavior | Never | 1-2 times | 3-6 times | 7 or more times |
|---|---|---|---|---|
| Hugging | 62.4% | 14.0% | 4.5% | 15.5% |
| Deep (open mouth) kissing | 88.9 | 3.7 | 1.3 | 2.9 |
| Petting above the waist | 90.9 | 2.3 | 1.2 | 1.8 |
| Petting below the waist* | 89.8 | 2.4 | 1.5 | 2.8 |
| Sleeping together (without sexual/ anal intercourse) | 85.0 | 4.6 | 1.8 | 4.8 |
| Sexual intercourse | 91.5 | 1.5 | 1.3 | 2.5 |
| Oral intercourse** | 91.6 | 1.5 | 0.6 | 1.9 |
| Anal (rectal) sex*** | 91.6 | 1.9 | 0.6 | 2.3 |

*Of the approximately 7% who reported petting below the waist with a same-sex partner, 192 were males and 31 females.

**A further 4% of the respondents reported experiencing same-sex oral intercourse, with the majority of these being males (114 males v. 13 females). It is not known whether the respondents were giving or receiving oral sex. This is an important factor regarding HIV transmission, as the probability of contracting the virus is far higher for the person giving oral sex, particularly if semen is released into the mouth.

***The latter numbers probably indicate that there are between 2% and 3% homosexuals on Kinsey's scale 5 and 6 of his heterosexual-homosexual continuum. This is a little lower than what one would expect, compared with other research. Kinsey and associates (1948) reported that during early adolescence, about 28% of the early-adolescent boys were involved in same-sex activities. Sorenson (1973) in his study of adolescent sexuality reported that 11% of the boys and 6% of the girls in his sample had at least one active same-sex experience.

### Table 14

### Age of First Experience with Oral or Anal Sex with a Person of the Same Sex

| Age | Percent | | | |
|---|---|---|---|---|
| Never experienced oral or anal sex with a same-sex person | 91.6% | | | |
| Age 11 or younger | 2.0% | 61 boys | v. | 8 girls |
| Age 12 | 0.7 | 18 boys | v. | 3 girls |
| Age 13 | 1.0 | 29 boys | v. | 2 girls |
| Age 14 | 1.6 | 49 boys | v. | 2 girls |
| Age 15 | 1.9 | 47 boys | v. | 12 girls |
| Age 16 | 1.0 | 21 boys | v. | 10 girls |
| Age 17 | 0.3 | 6 boys | v. | 3 girls |
| Age 18 or older | 0.5 | 12 boys | v. | 4 girls |

| Kinsey Scale: | 0 | 1 | 2 | 3 | 4 | 5 | 6 |
|---|---|---|---|---|---|---|---|
| Male | 82% | 9 % | 4% | 0.9% | 2 % | 1 % | 0.3% |
| Female | 95 | 0.1 | 0 | 0.9 | 0.9 | 0.4 | 0 |

penetrating the homosexual anally, but not the reverse. With most soldiers, this activity was a one-time experience; with a few, it was repeated two or three times.

The five exceptions that had not had these types of army experiences had encountered homosexuals while studying abroad, and they behaved in a similar fashion to what has been mentioned above. The other 18 males had a specifically homosexual orientation, and their homosexual experiences were more varied and more frequent. These homosexuals had voluntarily entered same-gender relationships, and their interest in opposite-sex partners was very limited. The women were mostly patients who had come to specifically discuss their sexual orientation, and they were involved with a single partner with whom they had fallen in love. All were married at the time.

### Homosexual Life in Cyprus    ALECOS MODINOS*

For centuries, this island, which is now an independent country only 100 miles (160 km) from the coast of Lebanon, was a model of social and familial conservatism. Family ties were close, the patriarchal concept was entrenched, and strict social mores were enforced by both Church and tradition. The pattern of life, while not unduly exciting, was extremely stable nevertheless.

Abruptly, in just a few short weeks 25 years ago, the pattern of centuries was destroyed when Turkey invaded and occupied almost 40% of the country. A great percentage of the population lost their homes and jobs, and fled to the southern half of the country before the advancing armies. Thousands were killed or injured and another 200,000 became refugees.

In those short weeks, the entire social fabric of Cyprus was destabilized. Family ties were abruptly loosened or disappeared altogether in the chaos that followed, and even now, 25 years later, there are still over 1,600 missing persons as a result of the invasion. In a small island-state of less than 700,000 people, the effects of the invasion and continuing occupation were profound.

In May 1989, the following headline appeared on the front cover of a popular national magazine and in daily newspapers: "Homosexual Accuses Cyprus to the Council of Europe for Violation of His Human Rights." The article clearly demonstrated how many journalists were not only prejudiced, but knew very little about the subject. Cyprus is one of the few member countries of the Council of Europe that until very recently had not abolished its anti-homosexual laws. The existing criminal law, CAP 154, articles 171-174, considers homosexual acts a criminal offense punishable by 5 to 14 years' imprisonment. This law was influenced by the British Colonial occupation of the island between 1878 and 1960, and was incorporated in our legislation in 1929 in accordance with the British "Criminal Law Amended Act of 1885," a good reflection of the Victorian period! In Britain, the 1885 anti-gay law was abolished with the "Sexual Offenses Acts of 1967," but this had no effect in Cyprus, which by then was an independent state. Cyprus thus was left with an outdated colonial law that Britain had abolished 32 years ago. Homosexuality between women is not a criminal offense, but is completely ignored by the law as if it does not exist at all.

The first discussion on homosexuality was organized by the Pancyprian Mental Health Association in the fall of 1979. In the spring of 1982, a two-day seminar was organized by the same association on the same subject. About 500 persons

attended; the great majority were women, and the absence of men was obvious! As a result of the second seminar, five gay men began working together. Five years later, after many difficult and laborious efforts, 16 gay men and a lesbian founded the Gay Liberation Movement of Cyprus on December 10, 1987. As of January 2000, less than half-a-dozen persons have come out of their closet, while the remaining hundreds of gay men and women members of the Gay Liberation Movement still remain in the closet for fear of reprisals.

From 1989 onwards, with great caution, two radio stations arranged live interviews with a gay man who answered questions from listeners calling in. Between 1991 and 1992, in a regular weekly radio program titled *Human Sexuality* presented by the main author of this chapter, homosexuality was included as a topic on three separate occasions. After this initial exposure on live radio, homosexuality was more openly discussed on a few other private radio and television stations.

On December 6, 1990, the European Commission decided unanimously, with 15 Commissioners, in the case *Modinos vs. Cyprus*, that Cyprus was violating the human rights of homosexual people. The case went to the European Court, as the Government was reluctant to reform the law. Following a hearing on October 26, 1992, the European Court decided eight to one on April 23, 1993, that Cyprus was violating the human rights of homosexual persons, and ruled that the antiquated anti-homosexual law of 1885 must be abolished. The sole dissenting vote was cast by the judge from Cyprus.

The Greek Orthodox Church bitterly opposed this law reform and was supported by the majority of the members of Parliament. However, after a lot of pressure from the European Council of Ministers over a period of five years, a week before the third ultimatum given to the Government was to expire, the Cypriot Parliament very reluctantly reformed the law in May 1998.

The new law, made to the satisfaction of the Church and the majority of the opposing Members of Parliament, was found unacceptable by Amnesty International, the human rights organizations of the island, practically all the Pancyprian scientific organizations including the Family Planning Organization, the Gay Liberation Movement, and, on September 17, 1998, by the European Commission. The amended law, which the Cypriot government submitted in early 1999 to the European Council of Ministers, was rejected because it was full of discriminations. The Cypriot government planned to rewrite the law and submit it again in 2000.

The Cyprus government was obliged to revise the 1999 law in May 2000 because of the discriminations that were not accepted by the European Council of Ministers. During the voting procedure in Cyprus, 27 of the 40 Cypriot Members of Parliament walked out, and as the Cypriot media wrote, "it was not for purposes of micturation [urination]!" Of the remaining 13, two were against the law with the remaining 11 passing the amended law. The main points in the amended law included:

- The title, "Licentiousness Against the Order of Nature," has now become "Coitus Between Men."
- The age of consent for homosexuals has been made 18, whereas for heterosexuals it is 16. Cyprus is not the only country with this discrimination.
- Before, it was against the law for more than two homosexuals in the privacy of their homes to engage in sexual acts. This has now been amended to include more than two consenting adults.
- Article 174a stipulates that it is a criminal offense if homosexual males under the age of consent engage in homosexual acts.

---

*Note: The following perspective on homosexuality in Cyprus was provided by Alecos Modinos, B.Arch., A.R.I.B.A., president of the Gay Liberation Movement of Cyprus, and a chartered architect.

Homosexuality is still a subject very few Cypriots talk about, despite the great publicity through the media since 1989. Cypriots in general are sympathetic and sensitive people who oppose any violations to human rights. There is, therefore, no organized movement against homosexual persons at present. General attitudes toward gays are slowly changing in a positive way because of the European Court's decision and the great publicity given by the media to the gay law reform. However, parents are very unhappy and bitterly disappointed if they have a lesbian daughter or a gay son. Given the slow progress toward liberalization, there still exists a lot of prejudice and discrimination from all walks of life against lesbians and gay men, and this is why the vast majority still remain in the closet.

Besides the clinical data gathered by the main author, there are some anecdotal data regarding homosexual behavior gathered from members who attended the weekly meetings of the Gay Liberation Movement, but this is not in a presentable format that would make any scientific sense. There is clearly a need for further research on this important topic of human sexuality, but the lack of funding makes this difficult.

The difficulties that homosexual and lesbian Cypriots encounter stem from the great social stigma associated with the limits on open homosexuality in the small Cypriot society, the legal system, which still considers gays criminals, and the powerful Orthodox Church, which considers homosexual relationships "the gravest of sins."

Most Cypriot homosexuals conceal their identity behind the curtain of wedlock; it is estimated that about 80% of homosexual males are married with families. Marriage makes them feel accepted and secure in a patriarchal, very family-oriented society. Homosexual activities outside marriage are usually conducted with other married homosexuals, or indeed, married "heterosexuals" who are willing to "service" the gay partner with anal penetration without this being reciprocated. Other willing partners include tourists who frequent the island; there is a huge choice, given that Cyprus welcomes about 1.5 million tourists annually!

Because Cyprus did not have its own university until recently, a record number of young Cypriots study abroad. Away from home, they are free to join gay groups, become gay activists, take part in gay parades, and thoroughly enjoy a very active gay life, including one-night stands—a way of life forbidden to them at home. Some even develop long-term relationships. After finishing their studies, many settle down abroad. Those who return home have the same predicament that practically all gay people have in Cyprus. Very few of them remain free at home and travel abroad for holidays and business trips; the great majority will get married, have children, and lead a double life.

There are no organized gay bars or clubs on the island. However, there are a couple of bars/pubs in the main towns, usually owned by gay persons, that are known meeting places with a mixed clientele. Beaches, parks, and "cottages" in the main towns are listed in all European gay guides, but are best avoided because many people frequenting these places, especially during the summer months, land in trouble with plainclothes young policemen acting as "provocateurs." Cyprus's many exercise gymnasiums are another popular meeting place. Good cinemas and theatrical productions, recitals and concerts, as well as ballet performances from visiting companies, attract a number of gay men. Often, they socialize with other gay friends over coffee, sometimes for dinner, and most of the time with mixed groups of friends without anybody knowing, perhaps not even suspecting, they are gay.

The great majority of adult gay men and women who remain single and tire of one-night stands want to eventually settle down in a permanent relationship. Such relationships are much easier to achieve between women than men and are, thus, more numerous. The majority of adult lesbians have a lasting relationship. Cypriot men grow up to be strong and to conceal their emotions, and they find it very difficult to be tender and loving toward another man. The Gay Liberation Movement and specialists trained abroad, enlightened with the latest scientific discoveries concerning human sexuality, have assisted many gay persons who seek counseling, with the result that we now have over 30 male couples who have been living together for six to ten years in the main towns. Very few of these couples have talked this over with their family. For the great majority, there is unspoken understanding and silent acceptance, a practice terribly common between all who have a gay son or a lesbian in their families.

Lesbians are discriminated against both as women and as lesbians. Practically all get married and have children; very few of them will dare or manage to have a special friendship with another woman. In the past, they were active members of feminist organizations or women's groups, without letting anybody know of their homosexual inclinations. Unavoidably, special friendships were formed and, as a result, suspicion and prejudice made all such women's groups slowly disappear. Some lesbian couples in the main towns live together, but most live with their families or in separate flats, even though they have been together for several years. This provides them with good cover for family, friends, and colleagues alike.

The younger generation of lesbians today are somewhat more rebellious and daring. They refuse to get married, even to socialize with other young men as a cover-up, especially if they are economically independent. They usually live on their own, not with their families. They socialize with small groups of five or six other lesbians of the same age on the look-out for a partner. They usually form relationships lasting only a few months. Sometimes, they may meet the right person and settle down to a more permanent relationship, but many of these will have relationships on the side for quite a while before making a final commitment to one person.

Single lesbians, especially those who have given up hope of finding a permanent friend, avoid the company of straight men and often meet and socialize with gay young men who share the same interests. The necessity to socialize with the opposite sex brought many homosexual men and women together, thanks to the Gay Liberation Movement, which helped to disperse the myths and stop the prejudices that existed between them.

Recently, although they still dare not come out in the open, the women of very wealthy families who have studied abroad live their lives and form friendships with other women. They ignore the drawing-room gossip about them, much as that hurts and makes them and their families miserable. They often put up a fight with their own families, who may accept their sexual orientation, but they are concerned about what the other people say.

Practically all Cypriot gay men take holidays abroad, even those who can hardly afford it. They travel alone or with friends. They are out to enjoy themselves and have as many sexual relationships as possible, trying to make up for that which is forbidden for them at home. Greece is very popular, with the gay bars of Athens, the saunas, and the gay beaches of Myconos and other Aegean islands coming first. Amsterdam, Paris, London, and other European cities are always resorts for those who can afford them.

Homosexual men are not accepted or retained in the army if their homosexuality is discovered. Except for half a dozen or so cases, all members of the Gay Liberation Movement have served their national service and have excelled in the posts they were assigned by their officers.

Apart from occasional parties at Christmas and special occasions, where about 50 gay men and some lesbians are invited, there are few gay private parties. The first one was in December 1990 to celebrate the unanimous decision of the European Committee, when the 15 Commissioners condemned Cyprus for violating the human rights of homosexual people. The second took place in April 1993 to celebrate the European Court's decision against the Government for the same reason, and since then, two more to raise money for people with AIDS. About 350 gays attended these huge parties that were considered a great success by all who attended.

Cyprus is a divided country, proud to be a member of the Council of Europe and trying hard to become a member of the European Union. To achieve this, a first necessary step is the equality of all citizens in the eyes of the law. But this is a minimum demand. What must be achieved is true equality in the minds of all people in everyday life. To achieve this, we still have a long way to go!

In the main author's 1990 survey of Greek Orthodox priests (mentioned in Section 1/2B, Religious Beliefs Affecting Sexuality), the priests were asked for their pastoral response to a second situation involving an 18-year-old boy who is having a sexual relationship with another boy, and finding it rewarding and fulfilling. He has heard from someone that it is wrong, and approaches a priest for guidance and advice. The responses chosen by the 130 priests responding to the questionnaire were:

- to terminate this relationship immediately (38.5%)
- to terminate the sexual relationship, but maintain the friendship (10.8%)
- to continue as they are (0.3%)
- to visit a Christian therapist (21.5%)
- something else (28.9%)

The subjective responses given by the 27 priests interviewed face-to-face were analyzed using a thematic analysis consisting of 16 general categories, some of which are included below:

- the two boys should separate immediately (51.5%)
- homosexuality is considered a cardinal sin (40.2%)
- the boys should visit a Christian therapist, because they are sick and need help (27.3%)
- God destroyed Sodom and Gomorrah for the sin of homosexuality (17.4%)
- it would be advisable for this boy to find a woman to marry immediately (12.9%)
- they should visit a Spiritual Father for guidance and confess their sins (12.1%)
- this is an abnormal, unnatural act that can only be considered a disease (9.1%)
- they should remain friends and have no sex; if this is too much of a temptation, then they should separate completely (8.3%)
- God did not create only men or only women, he created both sexes so that they could be united in matrimony (5.3%)
- if the boy truly repents, his sins will be forgiven (3.8%)
- homosexuality was responsible for the spread of AIDS, etc. (2.3%)

The face-to-face interviews elicited more attitudes from the Cypriot priests that were similar to the survey responses cited above. There was a belief that all homosexuals are really promiscuous heterosexuals who choose same-sex partners for fun, as their passions have overrun them, and that this was definitely the work of the devil. The focus appears to be on the homosexual act, as opposed to the homosexual person. This was further reinforced by the belief that the homosexual person was seen to be the person who accepts being penetrated. This "true" homosexual was referred to by many of the priests interviewed as the *passive* partner, whereas the active penetrative partner was not seen as being homosexual by many priests. This appears to be congruent with St. Chrysostomos's belief of gender expectations, or men behaving inappropriately like women.

## 7. Gender Diversity and Transgender Issues

There is no information available on this topic. There are certainly a few transsexuals and transvestites living on the island, as they appeared in media interviews seven or eight years ago, but little is really known about their situation. The main author has also seen a couple of transvestites and one transsexual in clinical practice, mostly seeking advice regarding sex-change procedures and relationship problems.

## 8. Significant Unconventional Sexual Behaviors

NATHANIEL PAPAGEORGIOU*

### A. Coercive Sex
*Sexual Abuse of Children and Incest*

Because Cyprus is a close-knit community, it is difficult to conceal sexual abuse and incest with children. The police statistics cover only a minor portion of what happens within families. For example, there has only been one case of incest reported between 1995 and 1997. In the same period, 15 cases of sexual assault on a minor between ages 13 and 16 years old were reported, with 5 cases of assault on a minor younger than 13 years of age. From a sample of 840 patient interviews (see Section 12, Sexual Dysfunctions, Counseling, and Therapies, for details), 3.6% or 29 females and one male reported sexual encounters with relatives. These encounters were with a cousin (1.8%), uncle or grandfather (1.3%), father (0.4%), and brother (0.1%). This rather small sample of the general population indicates that the problem of incest is far larger than what is reflected in police statistics. It seems reasonable to assume that most such cases are "hushed-up" by the families and by the authorities to avoid shame for the family and having to face all the consequences thereafter. If such incestuous practices were known, the family would be stigmatized, and the chances of the female victim finding an appropriate partner for life would be severely affected.

*Rape and Marital Rape*

Of the 25 cases of rape reported to the police between 1995 and 1997, all involved tourist women visiting the island. Some of the rapes were perpetrated by Cypriot males "on-the prowl," while many others have been by foreigners living on or visiting the island. Most of the female victims were from Scandinavian countries, with a few from Europe. There is no doubt that there have been more such cases that were not reported for various reasons.

Perhaps the most common sexual assault is that perpetrated by husbands on their wives. The author has encounter many such cases, including sexual coercion and abuse. If these cases are reported to the police, they are usually covered up and do not go to the courts for fear of shaming the family and destroying its honor. Many times, the police and family members persuade the wife to keep this within the

*Note: The editor is grateful to Nathaniel Papageorgiou, Chief Superintendent in the Criminal Investigation Department (CID) of the Ministry of Justice and Public Order, for providing parts of this section on sexual crimes.

family and not to press charges. Even cases that are reported are often "struck-off" the record after intervention by family members concerned about the probable effect on family ties and honor. (See comments at the end of Sociolegal Status of Males and Females, Children and Adults, in Section 1A.)

*Sexual Harassment*

Sexual harassment is perhaps the most commonly occurring crime in the workplace and by Cypriot men harassing tourist women. Sexual harassment in the workplace has been a frequent topic of discussion by the local media, as this was a way of life here in Cyprus. In the workplace, it involves male supervisors using their position and power against women, or women who want to improve their work status or to obtain a promotion. This type of behavior still occurs, but not on the scale that it was once practiced.

A study involving sexual harassment was conducted in 1997 by the Research and Development Center of Intercollege, a large private college in Cyprus, using 1,500 questionnaires that were distributed anonymously to both men and women. About 85% of the sample felt that sexual harassment was a serious social problem in Cyprus. About 40% of the sample actually knew first-hand of people who had been victims of sexual harassment; most of these took place in nightclubs (cabarets) with strippers (96%), with foreign home workers (73%), in hotels (64%), in factories (38%), in shops and offices (28%), and at schools and colleges (17%).

## B. Prostitution

There has not been any systematic study conducted on the rather large population of prostitutes in Cyprus. Apart from the local indigenous prostitutes, there is a growing group of foreign artists who have been specially imported by cabaret and nightclub owners for "entertainment" in their clubs. These girls, from the Philippines, Russia, Bulgaria, and India, are given work-permits and visas by the Cypriot government to work as dancers in these clubs. It is estimated that there are over 1,000 foreign girls working on the island, plus an unknown number of Cypriot women. The latter are probably dwindling because of the growing number of foreign imports who are favored by the Cypriot males who frequent such clubs. These foreign girls are not officially registered to work as prostitutes, but it is often recognized by the authorities that this happens. These girls are monitored for sexually transmitted diseases on a regular basis by the authorities.

In the last few years, there have been cases where the owners of these clubs have been convicted of coercing these women to have sex with customers against their will. These cases are usually reported because of some dispute over pay for services rendered between the women and their boss. Most of these cabarets are frequented by Cypriot businessmen in groups who are out for a laugh and a bit of fun with their friends; most are married.

## C. Pornography and Erotica

Pornography and all types of erotica are freely available in Cyprus to those who want it. Before the ban on video piracy which the government implemented about two years ago, there were literally hundreds of video shops where anyone of reasonable age could go and ask for a porno tape "behind-the-counter." These tapes cover the whole gamut of sexual behavior, from straight heterosexual sex, to anal and oral sex, homosexuality, bestiality, sadomasochism, fisting, and all the other sexual behaviors in between. Cypriots can rent their usual thrillers or soap movies on a regular basis, and while in the video shop, pick up a porno movie to watch while the children are in bed. Many of these tapes were subsequently copied and are still circulating in many

households in Cyprus, often entertaining the children as well, who happen to find their hidden location while the parents are at work.

There were large groups of Cypriots who, out of sheer curiosity and fascination, were requesting harder and harder varieties of porn that consisted of acrotomophilia, anaclitism, anolingus, bestiality, bondage, coprophilia, fisting, klismaphilia, and much more. This surfaced about 12 years ago when the author had the opportunity to interview one of the main suppliers of pornographic material on the island. He mentioned that the more "perverse" or "deviant" the sex he could obtain on video, the greater his business!

## D. Sexual Crimes

[*Update 2003*: To the police and the public, sexual assaults, and especially sexual assaults against young children, are a major social concern. In Cyprus, sex crimes are not reported frequently. This is because of the conservativeness and closeness of the society in Cyprus. It is believed that the police statistics cover only a minor portion of sex crimes, especially of crimes that are committed in the family, for example crimes of incest and of partner violence.

[Even though changes in the social structure are taking place in Cyprus, it is still considered a shame to a family that experiences a rape case. Many families decide to either "hide" this crime, or to take no legal action, and bring the offender to justice, in order to avoid publicity of the case, and therefore shame. Because of the close-knit community in Cyprus, many people always avoid the possibility of getting stigmatized. This is the case especially for rape cases where the honor of the family is at stake. Therefore, it is assumed that the phenomenon of sex crimes might be larger than what the statistics show.

[There seems to be an increase in the rape rates since 1997. To be more specific, in 2001, 18 cases were reported involving rape cases, compared to 10 that were reported in 1997. In the year 2000, there were 12 rape cases reported and in the year 2001, 18. Out of these 30 cases, only 2 were committed by the partner of the victim.

[The majority of the other types of sex crimes showed a decrease since 1997. Comparing the statistical information of 1997 to the statistical information of the year 2001, there was a decrease in the following categories of sex crimes:

- Seduction of a female under the age of 16,
- Procuring,
- Indecent assault against a female,
- Indecent offense,

It should be noted that these types of sex crimes all showed a major decrease in the past four years.

[No cases were reported to the police for the following sex-crime categories in the year 2001:

- Seduction of a female between the ages of 13-16
- Pimping
- Solicitation

[The categories that showed relevant increases and decreases between the years 1997 and 2001 were, indecent offense and indecent offense exposure. These two categories have some commonalities between them. The category of indecent offense was the most prevalent of the others throughout the years 1997-2001. For example, in 1997, there were 101 cases of sex crimes reported, 24 of which were indecent offenses. Again, for the year 2001, there were 80 cases of sex crimes reported, 31 of which were indecent offenses. It should be noted that there has been an overall decrease in the cases concerning sex crimes by 20.8% (21 cases) between the year 1997 and 2001.

[Sex-crime cases where the perpetrator is a member of the family or the partner of the victim are rarely reported. For example, in the year 1997, there were only 8 such cases reported, and all of them were indecent assault against a female, while in the year 2001, there was only one case reported where a member of the victim's family was the perpetrator, and this was a rape case. This shows how the family in Cyprus in the 21st century is still afraid to bring a case of such nature in the court of law, or even report it to the police. This emphasizes how the "honor in the family" cliché discourages victims in Cyprus from reporting incest cases, or even rape cases to police, and thus not bringing the perpetrators before justice.

[Even though Cyprus is a small country, and it is not expected to have large numbers of sexual crimes, we believe that there is a dark figure to this category of crimes. In fact, until quite recently, the number of sexual crimes committed each year was negligible (see Table 15). (*End of update by G. J. Georgiou and L. Papantoniou*)]

## 9. Contraception, Abortion, and Population Planning

FAMILY PLANNING ASSOCIATION OF CYPRUS*
[*Update 2003*: *Mission*: The Cyprus Family Planning Association promotes the development of a society where all people can enjoy the basic human right to make free and informed choices in their sexual, emotional, and reproductive lives:

- Defends, protects, and advocates for the sexual and reproductive rights of all women, men, and young people.
- Provides high-quality informational, educational, and clinical services in the sphere of sexual and reproductive health in an accessible and affordable manner to all people, especially the marginalized, including sex education and family planning.
- Exercises a leadership role in sexual and reproductive health through committed, competent, and skilled volunteers and staff.

### Table 15

### Sex Crimes Reported During the Years 1995-2001

| Type of Crime | 1995 | 1996 | 1997 | 1998 | 1999 | 2000 | 2001 |
|---|---|---|---|---|---|---|---|
| Rape | 8 | 8 | 10 | 11 | 11 | 12 | 18 |
| Kidnapping | 3 | 0 | 3 | 6 | 4 | 2 | 1 |
| Seduction of a female under 13 years old | 1 | 1 | 3 | 2 | 1 | 1 | 0 |
| Seduction of a female from age 13 to 16 | 6 | 5 | 4 | 3 | 1 | 14 | 1 |
| Procuring | 0 | 11 | 17 | 17 | 7 | 8 | 10 |
| Indecent assault against a female | 24 | 14 | 19 | 7 | 16 | 6 | 17 |
| Indecent assault against a male | 2 | 3 | 4 | 2 | 3 | 1 | 0 |
| Pimping | 3 | 11 | 15 | 4 | 2 | 2 | 0 |
| Solicitation | 0 | 1 | 0 | 1 | 0 | 1 | 0 |
| Indecent offense | 32 | 20 | 24 | 38 | 20 | 35 | 31 |
| Indecent offense exposure ("unethical projection") | 8 | 4 | 2 | 7 | 15 | 4 | 1 |

*Note: The editor is grateful for information supplied for this section by the staff at the Family Planning Association of Cyprus.

[*Aims*:
1. To enlighten and educate the public on issues relating to family planning and sex education, emphasizing the role and responsibility of the parents to the family and the social welfare.
2. To support and promote means and services for providing advice and help on family planning issues, sex education issues, marital counseling, and other related matters appertaining to the institution of marriage.
3. To increase the understanding of the Cypriot people and government of the demographic issues regarding their own community and those of the world.
4. To advise the public on conception and contraception and to provide voluntary family planning services.
5. To ensure the maintenance of satisfactory standards in the delivery of voluntary family planning services.
6. To promote the provision of family planning information and services through other appropriate organizations
7. To take any and all other appropriate measures to further the above aims.

*"Youth Center"*: *The activities will be carried out in all parts of Cyprus where youth can potentially be reached.*

[*Summary*: The "Youth Center" project aims towards the provision of counseling, informational, and educational services, in the field of Sexual and Reproductive Health, to youth living in Cyprus. In-person counseling will be provided and, at the same time, a hotline will be established so that young people can have access to the psychological support they might need. Young volunteers, members of the "Youth for Youth" group, will receive comprehensive training in order to become able to run the center. Furthermore, youth will be able to obtain information regarding issues in S&R Health through a website. Concurrently, a massive distribution of relevant informational material will take place throughout the project.

[*Objectives*: The Cyprus Family Planning Association has assumed a leading role in the provision of services in the field of Sexual and Reproductive Health over the past three decades. Issues such as unwanted pregnancy, teen pregnancy, sexually transmitted infections, and abortion have surfaced as major social problems, especially among youth, in the past few years in Cyprus. Unfortunately, the increasing magnitude of these problems has not yet been measured scientifically. Expert observations, however, allow for great concern.

[Based on its ongoing effort to target young people, educate them, and provide them with psychological support and information in regards to Sexual and Reproductive Health, the CFPA strongly believes that the creation of a program such as the "Youth Center" will establish a more direct contact, strengthening its existing relationship with youth so that the above services are provided in the most effective way possible. Furthermore, sex education is not currently fully provided by the educational system in Cyprus. The Youth Center project aims to attempt to fill this gap through peer education, a tested and rewarding method of approaching youth. Young men and women, who live in rural areas, do not have easy access to free family planning services. Also, young people who live in tourist areas are more prone to exhibit risky sexual behavior, and therefore may become more exposed to sexually transmitted infections. CFPA will try to approach these youth and provide them with the services, the information, and the attitude needed to sustain a healthy sexuality.

[*Aim of the Project*: The main goal of the "Youth Center" project is to satisfy the unmet needs of young men and women throughout Cyprus with regards to their Sexual and Reproductive Health. (*End of update by G. J. Georgiou and L. Papantoniou*)]

## A. Contraception

In the main author's clinical sample, 33% reported using the condom and 21% used coitus interruptus. The IUD ranked third at 7.3%, followed by 6.7% for the contraceptive pill. Very few Cypriot women use the diaphragm, cervical cap, or contraceptive foam—only 0.1% for each. Cypriot women tend to have concerns about placing objects in their vagina, not necessarily because they may injure themselves, but because there is a repulsion to placing items in the vagina. This seems to be a cultural attitude reported in the sexual histories taken by the author. "Touching" the vulva seems to be out-of-bounds for most Cypriot women, and this is reflected in the relatively low frequency of women who masturbate. The IUD is slightly more acceptable because this is placed by the gynecologist and does not entail self-insertion. One in five survey subjects reported using no contraceptive, and 3.8% reported sterility. (See Section 5B, Interpersonal Heterosexual Behaviors, Adolescents.)

In the 1990 survey of priests conducted by the main author, the priests were presented with a case for pastoral counseling involving:

> a Christian couple with five children. The husband is 35 years old and the wife 30. Only the husband is working and earning a small income, which provides the essentials for the family. Under the circumstances, the couple has decided to use artificial contraceptives (that do not allow fertilization to take place), and go to a priest to discuss the matter. (Georgiou 1990)

The priests responded as follows:

- all contraceptive methods are disallowed (39.2%)
- the couple should sexually abstain (25.4%)
- contraceptives are allowed in exceptional circumstances (8.5%)
- contraceptives are freely allowed (6.2%)
- the couple should make love during the wife's infertile days (1.5%)
- something else (9.2%)

Older (over 65) and less-educated priests (junior school with additional training in the Theological School of the Cypriot Archbishopric) tended to be more against the use of contraception than the younger, more-educated priests ($p = 0.0002$).

The thematic analysis of the subjective responses included 17 mutually exclusive general categories, some of which are presented below:

- the Orthodox Church considers the use a contraceptive sinful, and therefore does not allow it (37.9%)
- the couple should coitally abstain during the fertile days (25.8%)
- God gave the command to multiply and fill the earth, which means that we should have as many children as possible (18.2%)
- the couple should humbly accept as many children as God sends them (16.7%)
- the idea would be to completely abstain from sexual intercourse, unless one wants to procreate (12.9%)
- there are many large families of eight to ten children who are healthy and content, so why not others? (8.3%)
- contraception is allowed in exceptional circumstances (7.6%)

- we should believe in God's Providence; He will help us raise our families if we have faith (6.8%)
- God cares for all the animals of the earth, so why would he not care for his people (6.1%)
- the state should provide assistance to large families (4.5%)
- procreation should not be the only goal in marriage (4.5%)
- contraception is freely allowed to be used by all (3.0%)
- the couple should avoid intercourse during the second to the eighth day of the menstrual cycle which are the fertile days [*Comment 2001*: In this self-generated response, the priests revealed their own misinformation about the menstrual cycle, because days 2-8 are not the fertile days. (*End of comment by G. J. Georgiou*)] (2.3%)
- it is better to use contraception than to have an abortion (2.3%)

## B. Abortion

Perhaps the fact that over half of the main author's sample do not use adequate contraception should lead us to the conclusion that many Cypriots have abortions or have numerous children. The latter is not the case, and epidemiological statistics for abortion are unavailable. Using the same clinical sample of 840 patients (see Section 12, Sexual Dysfunctions, Counseling, and Therapies), 21.5% said they had had an abortion. Examining the statistics from an unpublished Cyprus Family Planning Association study, 20% of the total sample of 496 women reported having at least one abortion during the years 1995 to 1997, with 19% having at least one from 1985 to 1987. Interestingly, in the 1980s, 25% of these women were single, 18% were engaged, and 19% were married, whereas in the 1990s, only 3% were single, with more married women (27%) having abortions than before. It is certainly difficult to be certain about precise figures, but a figure of approximately 20% of the female population during any one year would be a fair estimate of the incidence of abortion. In the same study, about 7% of women had two abortions between the years 1995 to 1997, compared to 11% of women who had two between 1985 and 1987. (See also Section 1A, Sociolegal Status of Males and Females, Children and Adults.)

It is known that there are about 10,000 births per year, and it has been estimated that there are probably 12,000 to 13,000 abortions yearly. It appears that many Cypriots use abortion as a method of contraception after all else fails. The majority of gynecologists on the island will freely give abortion upon demand, because of a loop-hole in the law amended after the 1974 invasion of Cyprus by the Turks, allowing abortions for women who had been raped by Turkish troops or based on medical grounds with the permission of two medical doctors. This law still exists and allows gynecologists to practice abortion upon demand. There are only two gynecologists on the island whom the author knows that do not perform abortions for ethical and religious reasons.

In the main author's 1990 survey, Greek Orthodox priests were presented with the following situation involving abortion:

> A Christian woman is pregnant with her fourth child, even though her doctor warned her not to have another child as she would be endangering her health. Presently three doctors have told her that if she continues the pregnancy there is a chance that she would die. She has been advised, therefore, to have an abortion. As she is a woman who believes in God, she approaches a priest for advice. (Georgiou 1990)

The responses selected by the priests were as follows:

- she should listen to the doctors and have the abortion (17.7%)
- she should not have the abortion under any circumstances (60.0%)
- something else (19.3%)

An additional 3.1% of the total sample of 130 priests avoided the question.

A thematic analysis of the subjective and "something else" responses produced 14 mutually exclusive general categories, some of which are examined below:

- she should have complete faith in God (43.2%)
- the Orthodox Church believes that abortion is an act of murder and is therefore a cardinal sin (25.0%)
- she should pray and ask for God's help and make up her own mind (16.7%)
- if the diagnosis is certain, then she should have the abortion so she will not leave her children and husband to suffer alone (15.2%)
- I've seen similar cases where the woman and child had both survived (11.4%)
- we must bear in mind that there are many cases where doctors have been proven wrong (10.6%)
- she should have the baby; I am certain that God will help her and the baby survive (9.1%)
- God is the wisest scientist (6.8%)
- the woman should follow the doctors' orders and she will be forgiven (5.3%)
- it is important not to listen to the doctors in cases like this (3.8%)
- if she presents a letter from her doctor to the Spiritual Father with the facts of the case, then he will allow her to proceed with the abortion (2.3%)
- she should die for the love of her child (1.5%)
- she should have the abortion, and she will be given a heavy penance (1.5%)
- the priest cannot take responsibility for any abortion (0.8%)

## C. Population Programs

The total population of Cyprus was estimated at 746,100 at the end of 1997, compared with 741,000 in 1996, having increased by 0.7%. In 1997, the number of births in the Government-controlled areas (the Greek Cypriot side) declined from 9,638 in 1996 to 9,275 in 1997, giving a crude birthrate of 14.2 per 1,000 in 1997 compared to 14.9 in 1996. Both the number of births and the crude birthrate have followed a declining trend in recent years. The total fertility rate (TFR), which describes reproductive behavior unaffected by changes in the age of the population, is 2.3, slightly above replacement level but declining.

Cyprus has one of the lowest rates of extramarital births in Europe, and fertility is almost exclusively marital fertility. In 1997, only 146 children were born out of wedlock constituting a mere 1.6% of the total number of births. The mean age of women at the birth of their first child was 25.8 years old, while the mean age at birth irrespective of the older child was 28 years old in 1997. Women in rural areas tend to start younger, compared to urban areas: 24.8 years and 26.3 years, respectively.

At the Special Session of the United Nations on Population and Development in New York, June 30 to July 2, 1999, the Cyprus Delegation reported that:

Cyprus is undergoing demographic changes worth mentioning. Fertility is falling below replacement level and shows no sign of recovery. Concurrently, mortality is on the decline and currently is at 7.9 deaths per 1000 population. Also, infant mortality is 8.0 per 1000 live births, while maternal mortality is practically zero. Moreover, life expectancy is 75 years for males and 80 years for females. These are indications that Cyprus is going through a period of nearly stagnant population growth, 1.0% per year in the last five years, a phenomenon of population aging. Although, aging does not mean an old population, still my Government is worried about the problems that come in its way and in particular the social and economic implications.

Indeed, the government certainly wants to increase the declining population of 600,000 Cypriots on the island, and is giving incentives to this effect. All parents who have four or more children, so-called "multi-sibling" families, receive monetary and social incentives. For example, each child is entitled to a child benefit allowance of about $60.00 per child per month, and mothers receive a "mother's allowance." Also, all health expenses are paid by the government, as well as subsidies on school fees, books, entrance to museums, theatres, low-interest loans for building or repair of existing home, reduction in months spent doing National Service, tax incentives, and others. There is even discussion in Parliament at present to offer a duty-free car of choice, which is a huge incentive for most families, as car duties can exceed 100% of the value of the car.

In Cyprus, reproductive health is integrated into the primary health care system, and is provided free of charge by public sector institutions and at affordable rates by the private sector. The total expenditure dedicated to health purposes, from all sources, is on the order of 6% of GDP, or 16% of all public expenditure. This compares very favorably with most developed countries.

In Cyprus family planning issues are entrusted to specialist doctors in the private sector, but more so to an NGO subsidized mainly by Government. The services provided are not confined within the narrow meaning of population control but also include access to information relating to sexual and reproductive rights, sexual education, including health issues, reproductive choice and gender equality; it also provides counseling on sexual relations and more recently on the prevention of HIV/AIDS. (United Nations Cyprus Delegation, June 30-July 2, 1999)

Some information regarding the work of the Cyprus Family Planning Association (CFPA) is provided in a recent unpublished study. The data were obtained retrospectively by examining 495 patient records of visits to the CFPA between 1985 and 1997. Most of the women visiting the CFPA were married between the ages of 21 and 41. The most commonly requested services were for birth control and cytology tests. The four major services that women requested were Pap tests, IUD insertions, breast examinations, and prescriptions for the contraceptive pill.

## 10. Sexually Transmitted Diseases and HIV/AIDS

### A. Sexually Transmitted Diseases

There are no systematic surveys that have been conducted regarding sexually transmitted diseases, as most of the population with STDs saw private practitioners who do not need to report these statistics. There are, however, some official statistics, which are based mainly on the monthly returns from the dermatology clinics of the four Government general hospitals. Although rare, certain cases may be reported by gynecologists, urologists, and possibly general practitioners in the private sector. The diseases recorded are those that are considered notifiable and reported to the

World Health Organization (see Table 16). The sharp increase in AIDS cases in 1997 is because of the adoption of a new case definition by the United States Centers for Disease Control in 1993. A workshop on epidemic preparedness was held in November 1999, during which the list of notifiable diseases was revised to include other STDs such as chlamydia.

From the KABP Survey on AIDS of 3,176 schoolchildren examining their knowledge, attitudes, beliefs, and practices related to AIDS, there were a few questions regarding STDs that would be worthy of note (Georgiou & Veresies 1990, 1991).

Twelve questions were designed to tap respondents' knowledge about syphilis, gonorrhea, chlamydia, and genital herpes:

- Close to half the teenagers surveyed had heard something about syphilis: 1,498 (844 boys and 654 girls, or 47.2%)
- Had heard something about herpes: 1,432 (700 boys vs. 732 girls, or 45.2%)
- Had heard something about gonorrhea: 965 (517 boys vs. 448 girls, or 30.4%)
- Only 236 (150 boys vs. 86 girls, or 7.4%) had heard of chlamydia, probably because it is not an STD that is often portrayed through the Cypriot media.

Overall, it appears that Cypriot school adolescents are relatively ignorant regarding STDs compared to their American, Canadian, and English counterparts. This relative ignorance, probably related to the fact that there is no formal sex or health education in schools, needs to be addressed.

Asked more specific questions regarding STDs, the great majority of students were "uncertain." Overall, it appears that less than 20 to 25% of the students have correct knowledge regarding ways of transmission, therapy, prevention, and asymptomatic status of STDs. Perhaps the most striking finding is the fact that only about 25% of the students were aware that condoms can protect against gonorrhea. The overwhelming majority (63.1%) were uncertain about the prophylactic use of condoms. There was also high uncertainty regarding syphilis transmission from an asymptomatic person (57.8%), and whether a person who has caught syphilis once can catch it again (64.3% uncertain, with 15% incorrect). It is clear that these issues need to be urgently addressed in any program on human sexuality.

## B. HIV/AIDS                                LAURA PAPANTONIOU
[*Update 2003*: *Note*: The following data for HIV/AIDS was abstracted by the Editor from the Ministry of Health, National AIDS Programme (NAP) December 2002 report prepared and provided to the Editor by Laura Papantoniou, M.D., National AIDS Programme Manager. Elements of Dr. Papantoniou's summary in the 2001 volume 4 of this *Encyclopedia* have been incorporated into this summary.

### Table 16

**Summary Statistics for STDs from 1995 to 1998 and for AIDS from 1994 to June 1999**

| STDs | 1994 | 1995 | 1996 | 1997 | 1998 | 1999 |
|---|---|---|---|---|---|---|
| Syphilis | | 23 | 32 | 32 | 33 | |
| Gonococcal urethritis | | 56 | 48 | 61 | 42 | |
| Non-gonococcal urethritis | | 220 | 206 | 166 | 114 | |
| Herpes genitalis | | 137 | 118 | 122 | 118 | |
| Genital warts | | 140 | 81 | 77 | 97 | |
| AIDS | 40 | 49 | 57 | 85 | 91 | 97 |

[*Dimensions of the Epidemic*

[Our current knowledge of the HIV/AIDS epidemic in Cyprus is based on epidemiological surveillance, which covers the period between the first reported AIDS case in 1986 and the end of December 2002. From 1986 on, this surveillance has included both cases of AIDS and cases of asymptomatic HIV infection. There has been an upward trend in the number of new cases of HIV infection diagnosed in each year until 1994, followed by a slight decrease until 1998. A small increase observed between 1999 and 2002 was mainly because of cases among foreign people and cases of clinical AIDS among repatriated Cypriots, who returned to Cyprus to continue their treatment that had been initiated abroad and was interrupted, mainly because of interruption of the supply of free drugs.

[A. Between 1986 and December 2002, 392 cases were reported to our program, 229 Cypriots and 163 foreigners. The great majority of the foreigners have left the country immediately after diagnosis, since the test was mainly done in order to obtain a stay permit, for work or studies.

[B. Among the group of seropositives who are Cypriots or foreign permanent residents, 203 are men and 42 are women, giving a sex ratio of five men for one woman.

[C. The main mode of transmission is sexual intercourse, which was reported by 91% of known seropositives. Homosexual intercourse was reported in 44.1% and heterosexual intercourse in 46.9% of cases. Blood transfusions accounted for 3.3%, but these are all cases that were diagnosed before 1987 and all of them were transfused or received blood products abroad. Another 1.6% reported illegal drug use and it is possible, though not confirmed, that they were infected through the use of infected needles. This percentage is very low by international standards, but we have to bear in mind that in Cyprus, drugs trafficking and use have increased significantly in recent years, and we need to be on the alert for the implementation of the necessary preventive measures. Perinatal transmission—from mother to child during pregnancy, delivery or breastfeeding—occurred only once in Cyprus, whereas, in four other cases regarding seropositive pregnant women, timely action with the administration of antiretroviral drugs to the mother during pregnancy and to the newborn has averted mother-to-child transmission. In 3.7% of cases, there is no information regarding the mode of transmission. However, these represent cases that were diagnosed at the initial stages of the epidemiological surveillance, when recording of information was less detailed.

[Mean age at diagnosis is rather advanced in Cyprus compared to most other countries, being 34.2 years. A proportion of 73.5% of seropositives were aged between 20 and 40 years at the time of diagnosis, and this is in concordance with the fact that the main mode of transmission is sexual intercourse.

[Monthly epidemiological reporting is based on data collected from the sources shown in Table 17. Table 18 shows the numbers of new cases of HIV infection by year. Since the beginning of the surveillance in 1986, 140 seropositives were AIDS patients at the moment of diagnosis or subsequently developed AIDS. Of those people, 52 subsequently died of AIDS.

[*Preparing Phase Two Response*

[When the strategic plan covering the period 1995-1999 ended, a workshop took place in October 2001 to prepare the next five-year plan, under the guidance of a WHO expert. The Phase Two plan, in its initial stage, is being designed to address the main groups that were identified by the workshop participants as being at risk for HIV infection: drug abusers, youth, and men who have sex with men.

[The evaluation and follow up of the 1995-1999 Programme was based on systematic epidemiological surveillance and on sentinel surveillance in selected populations. Behavioral studies have been initiated among selected sections of the population. A *Study on the Knowledge, Attitudes and Behaviour Regarding AIDS, Sex and Sexually Transmitted Diseases, Among the Adult Population of the Limassol Town and Rural Areas* was carried out in 2001. Preliminary results from this study are described below. Further statistical and sociological analysis of the results is planned. This is considered to be a pilot study that will serve for the carrying out of a nationwide study that will cover the remaining areas of the government-controlled part of Cyprus.

[Despite the low HIV prevalence in Cyprus at present, the potential for increase in the number of new cases is visible, particularly among persons with risky sexual behavior and among people who are making use of illegal drugs. The study was undertaken in order to obtain quantifiable data on the individual and public risk in Cyprus of becoming infected with HIV and other sexually transmitted diseases and on various ethical an social aspects related to HIV infection.

[This study is of the cluster type, based on WHO methodologies, regarding the sampling of communities and of individuals within these communities. The sampling frame used was the list of cumulative totals of the population of the communities included in the 1992 census, which *at the time* was the most recent census that has been conducted. The sample selected consisted of 505 individuals—243 men and 262 women.

[Eligible for participation were Cypriots and other permanent residents (over 3 months in Limassol District) aged 18 to 50 years. Foreign workers on contract, foreign students, and Cypriots who live permanently abroad were excluded but are eligible for a different study design that will probably be planned in the future.

[Out of 767 households visited, 601 households were eligible for participation to the study. There were 96 refusals and 505 participations, giving a participation rate of 84%. Results of the study are summarized below:

[*Survey Results: Knowledge.* Cypriots who participated in the *Study on the Knowledge, Attitudes and Behaviour Regarding AIDS, Sex and Sexually Transmitted Diseases* proved to be quite knowledgeable about the modes of infection with HIV, except in the case of perinatal transmission, which 20% of respondents failed to identify correctly. Ways by which HIV is not transmitted are less well recognized, with misconceptions ranging from a low 13.5% of those believing that eating with an HIV-infected person can expose one to the risk of infection with HIV, to a high 66% of those believing there is risk of acquiring HIV infection during the act of donating blood. The percentage of people who believe that insects can transmit HIV is 46.4%.

[When different ways of protecting oneself from HIV are considered individually, knowledge may be rated as medium to high, ranging from 63% for abstinence from sex, to 93.7% for avoidance of common use of needles. Correct condom use is correctly identified as protective against HIV infection by 93% of the respondents.

[Avoiding people who are HIV-positive and using the contraceptive pill (by women) are still considered by 27% and 23%, respectively, as ways of protecting oneself from HIV infection.

[Naming correctly at least two ways of protecting oneself from HIV is used for the estimation of Prevention Indicator a. The level of 90% specified for Prevention Indicator a (P.I.a) is not reached, since the highest percentage for naming correctly two ways of protection is 82%, represented by the combination of "avoiding common use of needles" and "correct condom use."

[Knowledge on the general features of HIV infection is medium to low. As many as 65% of respondents did not know that an HIV infected person can have a negative test for HIV, whereas 26% did not know that it is possible to be infected with HIV but have no external signs of it. A proportion of 83% did, however, recognize that the presence of another sexually transmitted disease increases the risk of HIV infection.

[*Survey Results: Attitudes.* Relatively low proportions of respondents consider that using a condom is a man's responsibility (53%) or a woman's responsibility (56%). (The possibility that the questions may have been misinterpreted should be explored and relevant corrections made before using the questionnaire in future surveys). Eighty-seven

### Table 17

### Sources of HIV Testing in Cyprus

| Source | Rate* | N |
|---|---|---|
| Contacts of HIV-infected people | 2.52 | 714 |
| Suspected AIDS patients | 80.22 | 91 |
| Routine diagnostic testing of in-patients in the public and the private sector | 0.03 | 91,320 |
| Voluntary testing in the government services | 0.16 | 64,324 |
| Routine testing of pregnant women in the public sector and partly the private sector | 0.003 | 37,536 |
| Foreign workers and foreign students | 0.32 | 20,815 |
| Foreign bar girls | 0.06 | 62,137 |
| Blood recipients** | 0.08 | 13,957 |
| Routine testing of STD patients of Government dermatology clinics— sentinel surveillance | 0.0 | 1,394 |
| Universal screening of blood donors | 0.003 | 458,288 |
| Registered Cypriot prostitutes | 0.0 | 1,078 |
| Child from HIV+ mother*** | 25.0 | |
| Intravenous drug users | 0.0 | 36 |
| Non-intravenous drug users | 0.0 | 48 |
| Prisoners | 0.06 | 6,309 |
| National Guard (recruits, sentinel surveillance, 1998) | 0.0 | 3,423 |
| Premarital testing group for thalassemia**** | 0.0 | 307 |

*Rate of infection per 100 persons tested.
**Multi-transfused only are recorded. All known cases were infected abroad before 1997.
***Based on 4 known cases of HIV+ pregnant women.
****1992-1993 sentinel surveillance; we are contemplating resuming sentinel surveillance.

### Table 18

### Numbers of New HIV Cases in Cyprus by Year

| | | | | | |
|---|---|---|---|---|---|
| Up to 1986: | 11 | 1991: | 22 | 1996: | 28 |
| 1987: | 17 | 1992: | 24 | 1997: | 27 |
| 1988: | 16 | 1993: | 24 | 1998: | 19 |
| 1989: | 24 | 1994: | 39 | 1999: | 23 |
| 1990: | 16 | 1995: | 35 | 2000: | 29 |

percent of respondents (86.4% of men and 87.5% of women) stated that they could get a condom any time they need it. People who believe they can protect themselves from HIV by avoiding risky sexual behavior represent 91% of the respondents. A proportion of 17.3% of respondents believe that a woman who carries a condom in her bag is loose, whereas 34.9% believe that a woman and 14.3% that a man should guard their virginity until marriage.

[It is believed by 85.1% of respondents that alcohol can lead to risky sexual behavior and by 81.3% that the intravenous-drug-related risk for HIV is high in Cyprus. Risk of getting AIDS from foreigners is believed by 83.8% to be increasing in Cyprus. The corresponding figure regarding Cypriots is 60.2% of respondents. As many as 77% of respondents (79% of men and 52% of women) consider that it is acceptable to donate blood so as to have a test for HIV at the same time.

[Positive attitudes towards people with HIV are noted on the whole. However, 6.2% believe that HIV-infected people got what they deserved and 5% believe that they should be isolated away from society. A proportion of 68% (72% of men and 65% of women) stated they could be friends with an HIV-infected person and 91% believe that free care for HIV should be provided by the State.

[Participants were asked to adopt (or reject by not marking) various statements about a) people with multiple sexual relationships, b) morality, and c) factors which control sexual behavior. Further analysis is needed, for better validation of the answers to this type of questions.

[*Survey Results: Behavior.* Data on the behavior of the participants identified various sexual activities and provide limited information on the use of drugs and alcohol. The main findings are as follows:

[Five out of six, 86.5%, of respondents stated that they had had sex (defined as penetrative sexual intercourse in the questionnaire). The proportion of people having had sex increases with age, whereas respective proportions for men and women are 92.1% and 81.4%, presumably because of the earlier onset of sexual activity in men. Mean age of onset of sexual activity is: 17 years for men with a range of 12 to 29 and 20 years for women with a range of 13 to 36. Moreover, 13% of men started sexual activity before the age of 15 and 50% between 15 and 17; 2.5% of women started sexual activity before the age of 15 and 30% between 15 and 17. On average, both men and women tended to have had sex for the first time with an older person than themselves.

[Forty-three percent of people out of those who stated that they had had sex, reported having had sex with a person other than their steady sexual partner at some time in their lives (respective proportions for men and women are 67.8% and 17.3%). (The question does not define what is meant by "steady sexual partner" and does not ask whether the intercourse with a non-steady partner took place while the respondent was in a steady, free relationship or in wedlock. In future surveys, inclusion of these clarifications will be considered).

[Among the people who answered that at some time they had had sex with a person other than their steady partner, 63.5% stated that they used a condom in the last sexual intercourse with a non-regular partner. Reasons cited for not using a condom during the last sexual contact with a non-regular partner include the partner's refusal (5%), not having thought to use one (22%), being dizzy from alcohol drinking (10%), and the belief that it decreases pleasure (58%). (The question did not include options for the participants to state whether they were "embarrassed to buy one" or "embarrassed to ask partner to use one," and this should be included in the questionnaire for future use). Of those having had sex with a non-steady partner, 48.3% stated that

they always used a condom with the non-steady partner, 33.8% stated they used one sometimes, and 17.9% stated they never used one.

[The proportion of people reporting use of intravenous drugs at some time in their life is 1.7% for all categories. For the 18-to-20 age-group category, this proportion is 4.3%. One in 40 respondents, 2.4%, reported having had a sexual partner who was a drug addict at some time in their lives. It is interesting to note that 11.3% of respondents—17.5% of men and 4.9% of women, as well as 25.9% of people aged 18 to 20 years—reported having been led at some time in their life to unchecked sexual behavior because of alcohol consumption. These figures are close to figures obtained from studies on drug use conducted in Cyprus among school youth.

[The mean number of lifetime sexual partners is 14 for men, with a range of 1 to over 100 (the latter reported by four people), and 2.5 for women, with a range of 1 to 20 (also one woman at 45). Some overreporting of sexual activity in men and some underreporting in women is to be expected, because of prevailing social norms and taboos. It is believed, however, that differences in mean number of sexual partners in men and women do exist and that men would tend to have sexual contacts with people not meeting the inclusion criteria to the study, such as foreign bar girls or visitors. This issue would have to be clarified in future research.

[It is interesting to note that the interviewers reported that on some occasions men tended to brag about their sexual achievements, leading presumably to an exaggeration in their recorded answers. Most of these cases concerned men who visit nightclubs and bars on a regular basis. On the other hand, some women seemed shocked that it was even considered possible that they engage in such activities. (It is specified that interviewers were asked to record on separate sheets of paper or to report verbally to us any interesting reactions and situations encountered in the households, and this has led to the collection of very interesting comments regarding the reactions of the participants. This information will have to be evaluated in the course of future study of the survey results. It is, also, reminded that, because of the methods used in data collection, identification of respondents and linkage of information to known individuals are quite impossible).

[Six percent (6.3%) of men and 3.8% of women stated that they had had sex with a person who was of the same gender as themselves at some time in their lives. These figures are very interesting, since the forbidden nature of the subject did not allow for much optimism as to the level of response to the question. It is very encouraging to have obtained even this level of response, though this figure should be considered a clear underestimate of the true level of homosexuality. It is noted, however, that it is comparable to some of the results obtained by Kinsley in his famous study, *Sexual Behavior in the Human Male*, conducted in 1948 in the USA on 12,000 males, at a time when acceptance of homosexuality was probably at similar levels as it is currently in our country. This issue is being examined in cooperation with the Gay Liberation Movement of Cyprus, for a more in-depth evaluation, in light of statistical and sociological information from the extensive international research.

[Six percent (6.3%) of respondents (5.7% of men and 7.0% of women) stated that they had at some time been forced to have sex. The question does not specify whether the event took place within or outside the family. It is interesting to note that in a recent study conducted by the Advisory Committee for the Prevention and Handling of Violence in the Family, 11% of respondents had admitted having been victims of violence in their family, but it is not specified which proportion had suffered sexual violence. Further evaluation is needed.

[It is very important to note the early onset of sexual activity and the large number of sexual partners reported by relatively large proportions of the respondents, and this information should be taken very seriously into consideration in the preparation of future preventive strategies against AIDS and other sexually transmitted diseases. All this information will have to be reexamined and evaluated, in cooperation with the authorities dealing with the study and management of the drug problem in Cyprus.

[*Costs and Financing of Treatment and Care*

[*Estimated Costs.* Care for HIV-infected persons and people seeking support from the National AIDS Programme includes free medical care (antiretroviral treatment and treatment for opportunistic infections and neoplasms), nursing care, laboratory support for the diagnosis of cases and the monitoring of treatment based on WHO guidelines, and counseling for HIV-infected individuals and their families and for people undergoing examination for HIV. These services are offered free of charge to all citizens of the Republic and for a fee to people who are not citizens of the Republic.

[Table 19 shows the cost of delivering antiretroviral treatment to patients from 1995 to 2002. The cost of other components of HIV/AIDS care include:

1. General treatment costs involving nursing, counseling, laboratory diagnosis and monitoring (including CD4 count and viral load), treatment for opportunistic conditions, and hospitalization costs. The costs for this component of care have not yet been evaluated.
2. Assistance from the Social Welfare Department: according to general terms applying to the general population. Social workers make home visits for social and financial support.
3. Assistance from the AIDS Fund: Christmas bonus per person ranging from £400 to £2,000 (US$800 to $4,000), according to socioeconomic evaluation.
4. Assistance from nongovernmental organizations: in close cooperation with the AIDS Programme (employment of a psychologist for AIDS Clinic needs, financial assistance in urgent cases, insurance for the education needs, and tuition fees of children of HIV-infected people).

[*Financing HIV/AIDS Care*
1. The healthcare expenses are covered through the Ordinary Budget of the Republic.
2. The expenses for the support of PWHIV/PWAIDS are covered in part through the AIDS Fund, and in part from the Social Welfare Department and voluntary activities, as mentioned above.

### Table 19

**Cost of Antiretroviral Treatments (Delivery Statistics)**

| Year | Pounds | Dollars |
|------|--------|---------|
| 1995 | £  20,114 | US$   40,228 |
| 1996 | 64,008 | 128,016 |
| 1997 | 244,908 | 489,816 |
| 1998 | 317,012 | 634,024 |
| 1999 | 333,610 | 667,220 |
| 2000 | 493,090 | 986,180 |
| 2001 | 612,334 | 1,224.668 |
| 2002 | 610,405 | 1,220,810 |

3. The educational campaigns and the research activities are undertaken in part by the regular personnel of the Ministry of Health and in part in collaboration with non governmental organizations. Preparation of health education material (including purchase of condoms) and research activities are financed through the AIDS Fund, through the Development Budget, and through the Publications Programme of the Public Health Information Office. The AIDS Fund is financed mainly through voluntary donations and in part through the government budget. This arrangement is not always adequate with regard to the basic needs of the NAP.

[*Future Requirements*

[Main concerns at present arc linked to risky sexual behavior, which has been the basic driving force of the epidemic until now, since over 90% of cases have been infected through sexual intercourse, and to the increasing use of illicit drugs, which has a potential for a sudden increase of new cases of HIV infection.

[*Health Education.* Based on the international experience that knowledge does not necessarily lead to behavior change, a new orientation is now being promoted, with the development of peer education projects in schools. Despite the fact that the first attempts were highly encouraging and successful, peer education has not yet been applied on a routine basis in schools because of a shortage of staff and time constraints. Most other health education activities are also focusing on the area of behavior change in youth and other sections of the population. Such activities are information kiosks, special events, lectures, messages and programs using mass media, youth meetings, and others.

[It should be noted that health education is facilitated by the fact that sex issues and the subject of condom use may be easily addressed in Cyprus because of the high level of knowledge and sensitization among the population. Opposition from certain society leaders, mainly the Church, is hampering full implementation of effective health education. New material is being constantly developed, such as brochures, booklets, posters, TV spots, videos, and various advertising items (key rings, T-shirts, etc.) as a necessary complement to these activities.

[Health education focuses mainly on sexual behavior, but all other important issues, i.e., compassion and avoidance of discrimination, safe blood donation, dangers of drugs and other habit-forming substances, and the hazards of perinatal transmission, are addressed as well.

[Based on the country situation and the recommendations from WHO/UNAIDS, the immediate requirements for the National AIDS Programme may be defined as follows:

1. Finalization of the next five-year strategic plan.
2. Restructuring of the National AIDS Committee to conform to current needs of the program.
3. Continuing and strengthening the provision of services already provided through the National AIDS Programme.
4. Ensuring a mode of steady financing for the AIDS Fund through the government budget.
5. Improving local expertise through relevant training (clinical, counseling, nursing, epidemiology, laboratory, and health education) and through an increase of the number of personnel where relevant (e.g., health visitors and counseling service).
6. Strengthening intersectoral collaboration by improving and increasing the involvement of key nongovernmental organizations and government services in program activities.

7. Expanding peer education programs to cover all final year students of secondary education and, at a later stage, students of lower grades.

8. Providing information to various groups who are inaccessible for purposes of peer education (Parents' Committees, army personnel, police, etc.), but may be approached through lectures, the media, special programs, and other events.

9. Reaching out to groups that are, for various reasons, difficult to approach (men who have sex with men, drug addicts, and sex workers).

10. Promoting further research in behavioral studies (knowledge, attitudes, and behaviors) and focus-group discussions, in relation to AIDS, sex, sexually transmitted diseases, and drug abuse among the general population and the school youth, in epidemiological monitoring (strengthening of routine monitoring and continuing/initiating sentinel surveillance among youth, adult males, and army recruits), and in evaluating the socioeconomic impact of the epidemic.

11. Strengthening the cooperation with the drug-abuse control program.

12. Strengthening the cooperation with the sexually transmitted diseases control program.

13. Upgrading the legislation with regard to HIV/AIDS.

*[Conclusions*

[In the light of the above epidemiological and general information, it is evident that the HIV/AIDS situation in Cyprus is comparable to that in other Western countries. Based on current epidemiological evidence, health education activities are focused mainly on prevention of transmission of HIV through sexual intercourse, with the main emphasis on abstinence, delayed sex, mutual faithfulness, and the correct use of condoms. Peer education in schools and in youth NGOs is being promoted, though at present, it has only been implemented on a pilot basis. Program evaluation is planned according to WHO guidelines and constitutes an integral part of the NAP, but has not been implemented to a satisfactory degree to date. (*End of update by L. Papantoniou*)]

[*Update 2002*: UNAIDS Epidemiological Assessment: This combined epidemiological assessment is for both the Turkish Republic of Northern Cyprus (TRNC) and the (Greek) Republic of Cyprus.

[HIV seroprevalence among blood donors has been reported below 0.01% in Cyprus since 1989. There was no evidence for HIV infection among pregnant women that were tested from 1998 until 2001, with the exception of one HIV case detected among 4,019 pregnant women in 1992 and one case detected among 2,422 pregnant women in 2001. HIV seroprevalence among bar girls remains below 1%. No infection has been detected among sex workers over the years. HIV prevalence among injecting drug users is reported to be between 0.1% and 0.3% between 1993 and 1999. Of clients of voluntary counseling and testing, 0.4% and 0.8% were found to be HIV-positive in 1999 and 2000, respectively.

[The estimated number of adults and children living with HIV/AIDS on January 1, 2002, were:

| | | |
|---|---|---|
| Adults ages 15-49: | < 1,000 | (rate: 0.3%) |
| Women ages 15-49: | 150 | |
| Children ages 0-15: | NA | |

[No estimate is available for the number of adults and children who died of AIDS during 2001.

[No estimate is available for the number of Cypriot children who had lost one or both parents to AIDS and were under age 15 at the end of 2001. (*End of update by the Editors*)]

## 11. Sexual Dysfunctions, Counseling, and Therapies

### A. The General Situation

There is scant information on sexual dysfunctions and therapies in Cyprus, mainly because of the lack of qualified, professional therapists who can systematically collect such data. As of 1999, the main author was still the only professionally qualified sexologist with doctoral training on the island. There were a few psychologists who attempted sex therapy using psychoanalytic techniques with very poor results. There were also a number of medically qualified dermatologists, STD specialists, and urologists who advertised as "sexologist," but are not qualified in any form of sex therapy and have no specific training in this field. Their treatments included mostly drugs and papaverine and prostaglandin penile injections for both erectile problems and premature ejaculation, regardless of etiology. In 1999, Viagra was granted an import license, and no doubt this will be used widely. The situation is quite sad really, as many patients fall victim to costly medical treatments without seeing any benefit.

Unfortunately, at present, Cypriot law does not regulate the training, certification, or licensing of sex counselors or therapists. Anyone can advertise freely on their signs whatever they wish, on the condition that they do not use the adjective "specialist." So "dermatologist-sexologist" is a legal sign, but "dermatologist-specialist sexologist" would be illegal if the individual does not have qualifications and clinical training in sexology. Few Cypriots are aware of this distinction and its inevitable consequences for the delivery of effective healthcare in this specialized area.

[*Update 2003*: The medical profession is quite determined to protect their self-interests and will not allow any other profession, even qualified clinical sexologists with doctoral degrees, to practice sex therapy on the island. The law regarding medical practice written in the 1960s and amended in 1979 clearly states that no one can diagnose or treat without being a qualified medical practitioner. The editor and author of this work has been arrested once and taken to court a second time based upon charges brought against him by the president of the Cyprus Medical Association. The charge was practicing medicine without being a qualified medical practitioner. On both accounts, the case was thrown out and nothing further was heard, but the Medical Association is far from happy with this situation. There are frequent "witch hunts" and publications in the local media about 'apparent sexologists' exploiting the public, and being called charlatans along with other 'titles.' This anachronistic legislation will be tested in a court of law in order to bring it in line with European standards. (*End of update by G. J. Georgiou*)]

### B. Some Limited Observations

*The Population and Its Problems*

The following observations have been culled from 840 clinical cases of Cypriots with sexual dysfunctions who sought treatment at the editor's Natural Therapy Centre in Larnaca between 1993 and 1996. Some additional insights came from a survey of sexual knowledge, attitudes, beliefs, and practices of 3,176 schoolchildren aged 14 to 18 years old conducted under the auspices of the World Health Organization (Georgiou et al. 1990), a study of the sexual attitudes of Greek Orthodox priests (Georgiou 1990), a 1995 book on the treatment of premature ejaculation by the editor, and *Homosexuality*, a book written in 1982 by the Pancyprian Society of Psychic Health after a seminar on homosexuality.

A quarter of the editor's clinical population were age 18 to 25, 40% between ages 26 and 35, 21% from age 36 to 45,

9% ages 46 to 55, 4% between the ages of 56 to 65, and the remaining 1% 66 and older. One percent of the sample had not completed elementary school, 12% had attended junior high school but not graduated, 12% had attended school to age 15, 40% had completed high school, and about 20% were university graduates. Two thirds of the subjects were married, 12% engaged, 2% separated, 1.5% divorced, 1% widowed, and 18% single. Some of the 840 attending were partnered, but individual histories were taken, and are presented here as such. The sample is quite representative of the spread of occupations on the island, and covers professionals (13%), technical—plumbers, electricians, and so on (9%), business people (20%), clerical (12%), civil servants (10%), housewife (6%), agricultural (11%), unskilled (9%), students (3%), unemployed (1.5%), waiters and hotel workers (5%), and others (4%). All clients completed a sexual-history questionnaire covering 75 topics or questions modeled on Wardell Pomeroy et al.'s *Taking a Sex History* (1982).

In terms of the whole sample of 840 patients, the most common problem was secondary erectile dysfunction (30%), with an additional 2% primary erectile dysfunction. Other male dysfunctions included premature ejaculation (24%), retarded ejaculation (2%), and male sexual desire disorder (5%). Secondary inhibited orgasm (7%) was the most common female complaint, with an additional 3% presenting with primary inhibited orgasm—the total of female inhibited orgasm: 11%. Other female dysfunctions included vaginismus/coital phobia (11%) and female sexual desire disorder (6.5%). One percent presented with problem paraphilias, mostly "flashing."

### Premature Ejaculation

Males suffering from premature ejaculation commonly postpone treatment for years, waiting until the stress and anxiety of the chronic situation makes the problem a lot worse and their marriage is threatened. Only 15% of premature ejaculators seek help within three years of onset. Thirty-seven percent wait four to ten years, 31% wait 11 to 20 years, and 4% wait more than 20 years. In comparison, men with erectile dysfunction are much quicker to seek help, probably because their problem directly threatens their male ego. Ninety-two percent of impotent men sought help within three years of onset, 4% within four to ten years, and 4% in 11 to 20 years. A strong majority of premature ejaculators recall ejaculating quickly from their early masturbatory experiences.

This appears to support Helen Singer Kaplan's (1983) theory of the ejaculatory reflex being conditioned to ejaculate early from the initial sexual experiences. Very few of the males recalled otherwise. Most of the males who came for treatment for premature ejaculation had the problem for many years, on average about ten years, but only decided to seek help when additional stress factors had exacerbated the problems to such a degree that many were ejaculating before intromission. Certainly the majority where finishing in 10 to 20 seconds, to the woman's growing frustration. At this point, additional coercion from the wife resulted in the men seeking help.

### Erectile Problems

Many cases of erectile problems began with an extramarital partner, and not with the wife or major partner. This may be because of the tremendous performance anxiety that is again related to the huge Mediterranean masculine ego to "conquer" the woman and show her that one is a "man." I have also thought that it may have been because of the anxiety related to the prickling of consciences, but having spoken at length to many of these men, this does not appear to

be the case. Indeed, many of them had come to me not so much to improve their relationship with their wives, but to help them "get it up" so that they could "prove" their manhood with their girlfriends. Many actually expressed satisfaction in the wish to "do it just once" with the girlfriend, and that would be enough! The shame, disappointment, anguish, and bruised ego was very apparent in many of these men. The vast majority of them had no sexual or relationship problems with the spouse—their motivation in pursuing an extramarital partner was purely to satisfy their ego, and not much else.

In addition to these psychological problems, I have found causes related to dietary stresses and abuses, smoking, nutritional deficiencies, subclinical hormonal imbalances, subclinical hypothyroidism, reactive hypoglycemia, toxic metal status, systemic toxemia, and others. These causes I would consider as "organic," but not in the traditional classical medical view of organic. There may not be any obvious pathology that can be measured on blood tests, Doppler, or morphological changes, but there is a continuum of health and disease, with a lot of gray areas in between. Many of these men have malfunctioning organs and tissues, which inevitably will affect penile functioning, unless one holds the view that the penis has its own will and personality and is totally independent of other bodily functions. Cognitive-behavioral sex theory is often quite effective in treating an erectile problem that is strictly psychogenic in etiology, but compound a psychological factor with smoking two packs of cigarettes a day, eating fast foods full of empty calories and fats, working a 12- to 18-hour day, drinking alcohol regularly to "destress," being anxious and insecure about the future, and so on, as many Cypriot males do, and it is obvious that something more than traditional cognitive-behavioral sex therapy may be indicated, including nutritional and homeopathic remedies.

### Vaginismus

A clinical incidence of 11% for vaginal spasms in Cypriot women is much higher that reported in other countries, where the reported incidence ranges between 1 and 4%. The origin of this difference, I believe, lies in the cultural dynamics, and specifically the sexual messages that both sexes receive while growing up in Cyprus. The male child gets messages based around: "You are a male, so it is normal, acceptable, and a sign of your manhood to pursue and conquer females sexually," whereas the woman gets a very different message: "You are a female and must remain a virgin, as this has direct links with your honor and that of your family—be careful as males are cunning and are only after one thing." Sixty-nine percent of the women in this clinical sample were virgins until they married, compared to only 9% of the men. The women had limited premarital experiences, and their sexual knowledge was obtained mainly from friends and media—with all the misconstrued ideas and prejudices that are inevitable from such sources, mixed with a high level of anxiety and neuroticism. A large majority of the vaginismic women reported dwelling on the fear of coitus, starting when some friend or cousin shared her initial "painful" sexual experiences, saying that the pain was unbearable, and that they had hemorrhaged. Without exception, these women had high scores on the Spielberger Trait Anxiety Inventory (SPAI), averaging at least one or more standard deviations above the mean for their age group.

### Dysorgasmia

There appears to be a problem with the statistics for dysorgasmia, which one would expect to be higher than the

10% reported in this limited clinical sample, particularly when 24% of the males have a chronic problem with premature ejaculation. Again, the answer may lie in cultural values and conditioning. Cypriot women are very reluctant to discuss their sexual lives with a complete stranger, even when that person is a competent professional in the sex field. Also, Cypriot women have been taught not to consider or make a fuss about the quality of their sexual pleasure, given that their male is performing like an *epividoras* (stud). Cypriot women tend to lament in silence, perhaps until things in the marriage get to such a point where frustrations can no longer be tethered. Other causes may include physical and mental fatigue from coping with home, work, and many children, an insensitive husband who is tender only in bed, limited sexual foreplay because of ignorance and inhibitions, marital discord, and certain "naturopathic" organic causes. Similarly, I believe the incidence of female sexual desire disorder, a scant 6.5% in my clinical sample, is not indicative of the actual incidence of female inhibited sexual desire in the general population. Cypriot women are not taught to expect much from their sexual relations, and so they suffer in silence. We simply do not see these people in clinical practice.

### Male Coital Phobia

A recent development in this limited clinical sample has been a three- to fourfold increase over the past two or three years (compared with five years ago) in the incidence of males seeking help with unconsummated relationships owing to their own coital fears. I have no explanation for this fascinating phenomenon, which is certainly worthy of being researched.

The main author's clinical experience with over 10,000 patients in the last 16 years in Cyprus suggests that the treatment of sexual problems in both sexes is getting more and more difficult. Modern Cypriots are more stressed and anxious, more concerned about finances, apprehensive about the future, concerned about personal safety, have less time for relaxation and leisure activities, are more affluent with all the consequences of bad eating and drinking leading to poor health, and more.

## 12. Sex Research and Advanced Professional Education

Certainly there is much research that needs to be done in the field of human sexuality on the island of Cyprus. Lack of funding for such research has left the island literally virginal territory for sexology.

The tertiary educational establishments on the island, and there are many, do not even have a single course geared to human sexuality. Perhaps the administrators and educators see it as unnecessary, or fear that it would take up additional space on a busy curriculum. Perhaps it is the inhibitions of the governing bodies to include such topics in the curriculum. Whatever the case, these topics do not exist, neither in the private institutions that award undergraduate and postgraduate degrees from external universities, nor in the one and only newly opened University of Cyprus. It goes without saying that there are no sexological journals and periodicals published in Cyprus, or indeed any national and regional sexological organizations. It is difficult to set these up with only one member!

Certainly the talent for research exists on the island. We have the second highest rate of university graduates per population ratio in the world, as well as the technology and infrastructure. We also have keen researchers who would love to participate in ongoing research. If someone will fund, research will progress.

## References and Suggested Readings

Alastos, D. 1976. *Cyprus in history: A survey of five thousand years* (2nd ed.). London: Zenou.

Antoniou, C. 1992. *The revolution of Cypriot women in society and their increased participation in civil engineering*. Unpublished Master of Philosophy thesis. London: University of London.

Attalides, M. 1981. *Social changes and urbanization in Cyprus: A study of Nicosia*. Nicosia, Cyprus: Social Research Centre.

Argyrou, V. 1996. *Tradition and modernity in the Mediterranean*. Cambridge, UK: Cambridge University Press.

Balswick, J. 1973. *The Greek Cypriot family in a changing society*. Lanarca, Cyprus: Department of Social Welfare Services, Ministry of Labour and Social Insurance.

Berger, P., B. Berger, & K. Hansfried. 1973. *The homeless mind*. London: Penguin Books.

Campbell, J. K. 1964. *Honor, family and patronage: A study of institutions and moral values in a Greek mountain community*. New York: Oxford University Press.

Christodoulou, D. 1992. *Inside the Cyprus miracle*. Minneapolis, MN: University of Minnesota.

Charalambous, N., & N. Peristianis. 1998. Ethnic groups, space and identity. Unpublished paper presented at the Space Syntax Second International Symposium, Brazilia, Brazil.

CIA. 2002 (January). *The world factbook 2002*. Washington, DC: Central Intelligence Agency. Available: http://www.cia.gov/cia/publications/factbook/index.html.

Department of Statistics and Research, Ministry of Finance. 1998. *Demographic report 1997*. Lanarca: Printing Office, Republic of Cyprus.

Georgiou, G. J. 1990. *Sexual attitudes of Greek Orthodox priests in Cyprus*. Dissertation for the degree of Doctor of Philosophy in Human Sexuality. San Francisco: The Institute for Advanced Study of Human Sexuality.

Georgiou, G. J. 1992. Sexual attitudes of Greek Orthodox priests in Cyprus. *The Cyprus Review*, 4:2. Nicosia, Cyprus: Intercollege.

Georgiou, G. J. 1995. *Premature ejaculation* (in Greek). Athens: Hellenic Letters.

Georgiou, G. J., & K. Veresies. 1990. *AIDS knowledge, attitudes, beliefs, and practices (KABP) pilot study undertaken in Cyprus: Preliminary report*. Geneva: World Health Organization (WHO).

Georgiou, G. J., & K. Veresies. 1991. *AIDS knowledge, attitudes, beliefs, and practices (KABP) study of Cypriot schoolchildren in Cyprus*. Geneva: World Health Organization (WHO).

House, W. J. 1987. *Population and labour force growth and development*. Nicosia, Cyprus: Department of Statistics and Research, Ministry of Finance.

Intercollege, Research and Development Centre. 1996. *Youth and leisure time in Cyprus*. Nicosia, Cyprus: Intercollege.

Intercollege, Research and Development Centre. 1997. *Sexual harassment in the workplace in Cyprus*. Nicosia, Cyprus: Intercollege.

Kaplan, H. S. 1983. *The evaluation of sexual disorders*. New York: Brunner/Mazel.

Kinsey, A. C., et al. 1953. *Sexual behavior in the human female*. Philadelphia: Saunders.

Kolodny, R. C., W. H. Masters, & V. E. Johnson. 1979. *Textbook of sexual medicine*. Boston: Little, Brown and Company.

Loizos, P. 1975. Changes in property transfer among Greek Cypriot villages. *Man* [U.S.], *10*:503-523.

Mavrastas, C. 1992. The Greek-Cypriot economic ethos: A socio-cultural analysis. *The Cyprus Review*, *4*:2. Nicosia, Cyprus: Intercollege.

Mavros, E. 1989. A critical review of economic development in Cyprus: 1960-1974. *The Cyprus Review*, *1*:1. Nicosia, Cyprus: Intercollege.

Markides, K. E., N. Nikita, & E. Rangou. 1978. *Lysi: Social change in a Cypriot village.* Nicosia, Cyprus: Social Research Centre.

Mylona, L., et al. 1981. *I Kipria ghineka [Cypriot woman].* Nicosia, Cyprus: Author.

Pancyprian Association of Psychic Health. 1982. *Homosexuality.* Nicosia, Cyprus: Author.

Papapetrou, S., & M. Pendedeka. 1998. *The Cypriot family: The evolution of the institution through time: Trends of change.* Unpublished paper presented at the Annual Conference of the Cyprus Sociological Association.

Peristiany, J. G. 1965. Honour and shame in a Cypriot highland village. In: J. G. Peristiany, ed., *Honour and shame: The values of Mediterranean society.* London: Weidenfeld and Nicolson.

Persianis, P. 1998. *Istoria tis ekpedefsis koritsion stin Kipro [History of the education of girls in Cyprus].* Nicosia, Cyprus: Author.

Pomeroy, W. B., C. C. Flax, & C. C. Wheeler. 1982. *Taking a sex history: Interviewing and recording.* New York: Free Press/Macmillan Publishing.

Pyrgos, M. 1995. *The Cypriot woman at a glance.* Nicosia, Cyprus: Author.

Schneider, J. 1971. Of vigilance and virgins: Honor, shame and access to resources in Mediterranean societies. *Ethnology, 1*:1-24.

Stavrou, S. 1992. Social changes and the position of women in Cyprus. *The Cyprus Review, 4*:2. Nicosia, Cyprus: Intercollege.

Stavrou, S. 1997. Cypriot women at work. *The Cyprus Review, 9*:2. Nicosia, Cyprus: Intercollege.

Surridge, B. J. 1930. *A survey of rural life in Cyprus.* Nicosia, Cyprus: Printing Office of the Government of Cyprus.

UNAIDS. 2002. *Epidemiological fact sheets by country.* Geneva, Switzerland: Joint United Nations Programme on HIV/AIDS (UNAIDS/WHO). Available: http://www.unaids.org/hivaidsinfo/statistics/fact_sheets/index_en.htm.

Vassiliadou, M. 1997. Herstory: The missing woman of Cyprus. *The Cyprus Review, 9*:1. Nicosia, Cyprus: Intercollege.

Yeshilada, B. 1989. Social progress and political development in the 'Turkish Republic of Northern Cyprus.' *The Cyprus Review, 1*:2. Nicosia, Cyprus: Intercollege.

## PART 2: TURKISH CYPRUS

KEMAL BOLAYIR and SERIN KELÂMI

### Demographics and a Brief Historical Perspective

ROBERT T. FRANCOEUR

### A. Demographics

In July 2002, Turkish Cyprus had an estimated population of 200,000 out of an estimated total Cypriot population of 767,000. All data are from the authors, and pertain to the Turkish Republic. Readers are invited to compare these figures with those in Part 1, Greek Cyprus, of this chapter.

**Age Distribution and Sex Ratios**: *0-15 years*: 29% with 1.04 male(s) per female (sex ratio); *16-64 years*: 65% with 1.2 male(s) per female; *65 years and over*: 10% with 0.77 male(s) per female; *Total population sex ratio*: NA

**Life Expectancy at Birth**: *Total Population*: 74.03 years; *male*: 73 years; *female*: 75 years

**Urban/Rural Distribution**: NA

**Ethnic Distribution**: 98.7% Turkish and 1.3% Maronites, Greeks, and other nationalities

**Religious Distribution**: 98.7% Muslim

**Birth Rate**: 17 births per 1,000 population. The rate is rather high because of the people who emigrated from Turkey.

**Death Rate**: 8 per 1,000 population

**Infant Mortality Rate**: 9.5 deaths per 1,000 live births
**Total Fertility Rate**: 2.2 children born per woman
**Population Growth Rate**: 0.4%
**HIV/AIDS** (2000 est.): *Adult prevalence*: 0.1%; *Persons living with HIV/AIDS*: 100; *Deaths*: NA. (For additional details from www.UNAIDS.org, see end of Section 10B.)
**Literacy Rate**: 94% can read and write
**Per Capita Gross Domestic Product** (*purchasing power parity*): US$4,000; *Unemployment*: 19%; *Inflation*: 51% (2001 est.)

### B. A Brief Historical and Cultural Perspective

Cyprus occupies a very important strategic position in the triangle of Asia, Africa, and Europe. Because of this strategic significance, several countries occupied the island of Cyprus during its history. Among these countries, the most important ones were the Phoenicians in the 10th century B.C.E., the Romans in 58 B.C.E., and the Ottomans, who were there for 300 years starting in the 16th century. After the division of the Roman Empire, the island became part of the Byzantine Empire. Cyprus was ruled by Britain during the Christian Crusades to the Holy Land. Later, the Lusignans and Venetians came to Cyprus.

In 1571, the island was occupied by the Ottoman Empire and ruled by them until 1878 when it was leased to Britain at the Berlin Congress during the Crimean War. In 1914, Britain annexed the island when the Ottomans participated in World War I on the side of the Germans. At the Lausanne conference in 1925, Cyprus became a British Colony and remained so until 1960 when independence was declared and a bi-communal Republic of Cyprus was established.

During the British administration, Cyprus was the scene of disturbances as a result of Greek Cypriots' campaigning and efforts for *Enosis* (the aspiration to unite the island with Greece). The Turkish community strongly opposed the union of the island with Greece. The first major uprising was in 1931 when the Greek Cypriots set fire to the Government House. The second move came in 1955 when again the Greek Cypriots launched the Eoka terrorist attacks.

The colonial government cooperated with the Turkish Cypriots and tried to suppress the Greek violence. The reason why the Turkish Cypriots cooperated with the British was because the only aim of the Greek Cypriots was the union with another country, Greece, not the independence of all the Cypriots.

The Republic of Cyprus had a short life of just over three years. In 1963, the island again became the scene of intercommunal strife, and the regime collapsed. On March 5, 1964, the United Nations (UN) Security Council recognized the Greek Cypriot faction of the government as the official government of the Republic of Cyprus. This UN resolution contributed to the continuation of intercommunal conflict resulting in ten thousands of Turkish Cypriots abandoning their villages and homes in the big cities and living as refugees in restrictive enclaves in the north.

In 1974, the Greek Junta joined hands with the fanatical Greek Cypriot elements and annexed the island to Greece (until the Junta was replaced by a democratic government). Because of this, Turkey exercised her right of intervention under the 1960 agreements and intervened in July 1974. Since then, the two communities have been living separately in two regions, the Turkish Cypriots in the north of the island and the Greek Cypriots in the south. The intercommunal talks for solving the Cyprus issue have not produced any positive results. However, the recent decision of the European Union (EU) to accept Cyprus as a member has perhaps created an opportunity for ending the division of the island. In

May 2003, the borders between the north and south were opened, signaling a new attempt at reunification.

## 1. Basic Sexological Premises

### A. Traditional Turkish Cypriot Family Life and Gender Roles

Since the beginning of the 20th century, Turkish and Greek people of Cyprus have engaged in agriculture and animal husbandry. In the cities, Turks opted to become civil servants, whereas the Greeks engaged in trade alongside with employment in government services.

As in other Mediterranean countries, Turkish Cypriot women traditionally occupied themselves with work at home while the male population undertook the role of the breadwinner. But, in time, these sorts of activities could not secure a prosperous life. It was difficult to have sufficient income and maintain a decent life for the family because of the lack of irrigation water and technical insufficiencies obstructing productivity, especially in the northern rural areas. This shortcoming affected the social life of the family. In due course, in order to obtain a better income, people had to move from villages to the big cities.

In the traditional Turkish community, the man was the head of the family. He was responsible for the protection of the family's honor and dignity and for ensuring a better life for all. The activities at home did not concern him very much. He spent most of his free time at coffee shops and clubs, which were only visited by men.

Women in the traditional Turkish family were responsible for all the work inside the home, looking after the children, cooking, washing, tending the domestic animals, and meeting the husband's various needs. Above all, she had to be honest and dignified and protect the family honor in every respect. Women and grownup girls normally stayed at home and did not frequent places visited by men, but visited other women friends in their homes. In mosques, women occupied specially prepared areas where men could not see them. Sexual relations between husband and wife were strictly secret, even kissing each other was not disclosed to third parties. Only very young girls and mature women could freely go around, as they were not considered to be sexually at risk. Women and grownup girls were fully familiar with the traditional sexual evasion. They knew how to dress, talk, and behave in public places where men were in the majority, without losing their honor and dignity.

Under the traditional Turkish Cypriot gender roles, girls and boys up to the age of 6 could easily play together in the streets. After this age, the parents dictated the conventional conditions to their children. Boys were given more freedom in their activities, while girls were told to be modest and not get involved in any disgraceful activity. They were told that they had to learn traditional behavior in their social life. If a girl was seen talking to a boy who was not her relative, this could have been interpreted as reflecting a sexual desire. The advice of the mothers and fathers to their daughter was that, when a boy looked and/or smiled at her, she should not smile or look back. She should close her mouth with her hand (if she had the urge to smile) and divert her glance elsewhere. A girl who obeyed the traditional rules, honored her family and had a better chance of a good marriage.

In the traditional Turkish Cypriot society, the roles of young girls and boys were very strict. Nowadays, these strict rules have changed, and the relations between the genders have become easier and more modern.

### B. Social Changes and Modernization

The influence of the British colonial administration and the increase of technical facilities around the world have forced Turkish Cypriots to move to the cities. Some members of the family, usually the main breadwinner and the young boys, try to find job in the cities. In 1950s, the Turkish Cypriots' preference was to get a job either in the British sovereign areas, or to find employment in the mining industry or the civil service. These were good sources of income.

The modernization in the Turkish Cypriot community started after the end of World War II. During this time, the people in the cities had a better source of income and a better social and cultural life. This alone led to the relocation of people from rural areas into the cities. This, in turn, led to increased education and, as a result of increased education, the philosophy of sexual strictness changed and became much more flexible.

Since 1960, important changes have taken place in the family structure. In the Turkish community, employment in the civil service became the most secure area of livelihood for both the male and the female. The significance given to education also increased. In the 1950s, kindergarten education was officially introduced (although there had been private kindergarten facilities long before that). During the late 1960s, the number of boys and girls in both elementary and secondary education was almost equal. However, after 1974, because of the influx of the population from Turkey to the northern part of the island, the number of boys in schools increased, as the Anatolian people traditionally give priority to the education of boys rather than girls.

In 2001, Dr. Ahmet Cavit carried out a research study on the communal structure of the Turkish Cypriots, including the immigrants from various parts of Turkey. According to this research (census of December 15, 1996), the total number of the population in Northern Cyprus was 200,857. Of these, 146,450 were citizens of the Turkish Republic of Northern Cyprus (TRNC), 30,702 were citizens of Turkey, and 5,425 were citizens of other nations.

This study indicates that the immigrants from Turkey also take part in the political life of Northern Cyprus. In the 1998 general elections, four out of 50 Members of Parliament were of mainland Turkish origin. According the statistics of the Research and Statistic Department of TRNC, 1,108 marriages took place in 1998. One third of these marriages were among the immigrants. Most of the married Turkish Cypriot couples had secondary or higher education levels. TRNC recorded 2,433 births during 1998. A breakdown of this figure indicates that the majority of the Turkish Cypriots preferred private clinics, whereas the immigrants frequented government hospitals because of their low economic position.

Because the immigrants give priority to the education of boys, their daughters rarely have secondary education, as their parents prefer to see them married and having children instead of carrying on to higher education. According to this study, Turkish Cypriots prefer government services, whereas immigrants find employment as manual workers and waiters.

Another important aspect is the increase of women in employment. A 1998 study revealed that 20 out of 100 women were employed outside the home. In 2001, this increased to 28%. Looking at the role of woman in modern life, the mother is still seen as more loving and tolerant than the father and often communicates better with the children. She devotes more time to the family, looks after the children, runs the house, and sometimes contributes to the family budget by working outside the house as well. The man is the breadwinner, head of the family, and has the final say in family affairs. Husbands rarely get involved with domestic affairs and spend most of their spare time at coffee shops or clubs. This is especially true in rural areas. As in most parts of the world, women and men in cities are successfully trying to achieve a sense of equality of the sexes.

## C. Sociolegal Status of Males and Females

Secularization has been an important factor in the life of the Turkish community since the early 1920s, when Kemal Atatürk introduced modern life and secularization in the Republic of Turkey, as well as introducing the right of women to vote. During the last 20 years of the British colonial administration, the family life inherited from the Ottomans underwent important changes. The 1960 Cyprus agreements also contributed to the modernization. Article 28 of the 1960 Cyprus Constitution provides for equality of the male and the female.

In the Turkish Republic of Northern Cyprus, if a foreign individual marries a Turkish Cypriot, he or she becomes a citizen after the lapse of one year from the date of the marriage. Marriage and divorce in the Turkish community is performed under the Turkish family law. It has no connection whatsoever with religious rules.

In Northern Cyprus, abortion is not legally allowed except under very special circumstances. However, it is common knowledge that abortions are possible in private clinics.

## D. Legal Status of Men and Women at Work

In Northern Cyprus, it is not a common practice in the private sector for men and women to receive equal pay even when they perform the same duties. Despite agreements between trade unions and employers to ensure equality for men and women, discrimination still exists. It is different at the civil services. Equality does exist there, and men and women have equal payment and equal chances for promotion. Another reality in the Turkish Cypriot community at the moment is that a large number of labor forces from mainland Turkey accept employment at very low wages, thus increasing the wage gap between the male and female by forcing the female to accept employment at still lower wages. According to Cavit's study, most of these workers are illegal immigrants.

Women in Northern Cyprus do not fight for their rights. The main reason for this is the fact that senior posts and political offices are mainly occupied by men. So far, women's efforts and desires to get a better place in the political arena have not produced any positive results. The existence of only four women MPs out of 50 in the Parliament is a proof of this.

## E. General Concepts and Constructs of Sexuality and Love

Traditional marriages in the Turkish Cypriot community were performed on the basis of *Görücü evliliği*, arranged marriages. The candidate bridegroom and his family visited the bride-to-be and her family to see the chosen woman (sometimes for the first time) and eventually ask for the hand of the woman in marriage. The decision of the youngsters was not of great importance in this system, although most families did at least ask their opinion. The choice of the elders was the decisive factor. Sometimes, a boy requested his parents to go and ask for the hand of the girl whom he had seen and liked physically without knowing her personality and/or educational level. It was always the boys who asked for the hand of the girls, never the other way around.

Usually, the family of the bride was chosen first, because the boy's parents wished for a bride from that particular family. The main criteria for the man's family in these marriages were the social and financial status of the woman's family. It had to be of the same background, rank, and social standing to theirs and occupy a position of respectability in the community.

If the impressions of both of the families were positive, then the marriage was agreed upon and the couple got engaged, usually during a ceremony including family and friends. The couple was seldom allowed to be alone together. Typically, a member of the family, this could even be a child, was sent along with them as a chaperon. The period of engagement was kept as short as possible. The families wanted to have the marriage ceremony as quick as possible. Traditionally, the engagement ceremony was paid for by the bride's family, and the wedding ceremony by the bridegroom's family.

This tradition is still mostly true, although recently, more and more families are sharing the cost, as weddings are getting more and more expensive. The woman was supposed to bring her dowry into the marriage, including all the furniture for the new house, and the man was supposed to supply the house in which they were to live in. At present, this, too, can vary, and there is no set rule, especially in the cities.

It is still customary for the bridegroom to give a piece of precious jewelry to the bride on their wedding day. This stems from the time when the bridegroom was only allowed to see his bride after the wedding ceremony was over. This present was called the *yüz görümlügü* (to see the face), as it was presented after the bridegroom had lifted the bride's veil, thus seeing her face for the first time.

Until the 1950s, marriages in the Turkish Cypriot community were performed on a religious level by a *Hodja*, a man of religion. After the enactment of the family law during the last years of the British colonial administration, these became civil marriages and were performed by marriage officers. All marriages performed prior to the enactment of the law were considered as performed under the law.

Until the 1950s, the woman's family was very strict with the virginity of their daughters. The girl was not allowed to have sexual relations before her marriage, not even during the engagement period. The men, on the other hand, were encouraged to "gather some experience" before their marriage. The day after the wedding, the bridegroom's family was anxious to see the red blood spot on the sheet, proving the virginity of the bride. This was mostly true in the rural areas and rarely in the cities. However, after the 1970s, this tradition was also widely abandoned, and the virginity of the bride was not the first prerequisite for the continuation of the marriage. But even today, an intact hymen is interpreted as belonging to an "untouched" woman.

After the 1960s, men and women preferred marriages based on mutual love and respect, preferring to choose their partners themselves, but hoping for approval by their parents. Families tolerated the decision of their children without imposing traditional rigid conditions. At present, dating and flirting has increased in the Turkish community. This has been made easier for most by the increased number of men and women studying and working together. Some go as far as to say that flirting is a must prior to marriage. There is even a modern version of arranged marriages, where the families choose the partner but agree to let the man and woman go out dating before they make up their minds. The engagement period can also take as long as it is necessary for the couple to make up their minds. Despite these developments and changes, there are still many people, especially in the rural areas, who believe that virginity is essential in the community. The enlightened youth, though, is starting to believe in the equality of the sexes, including their sex lives before marriage.

A difference is seen in the marriage understanding of the Turks who came to Northern Cyprus from Turkey after 1974. They are more conservative and prefer marriages among themselves, especially between relatives.

## 2. Religious, Ethnic, and Gender Factors Affecting Sexuality

Religion does not have any direct effect on sexuality in the Turkish Cypriot community. Though adultery, abortion, premarital sex, and homosexuality are a sin in Islam, most people are not influenced by this. During the holy month of Ramadan, sex, flirting, touching each other, kissing, and so on, is not permissible in the fasting time from dawn to sunset every day. In 1990, a respected *Hodja* offered the following advice to young people: "Get acquainted with each other prior to engagement. Afterwards, only get engaged if it is your own decision. It is not a sin for young people to get to know and talk with each other beforehand. Get married only if there are not any problems during the engagement period."

## 3. Knowledge and Education about Sexuality

This section was prepared from a study by Nuri Gökşn, M.D., Chief Medical Officer of the Turkish Hospital in Famagusta.

### A. Government Policies and Programs

In the TRNC, there is no sexual education in schools. The only information about sex given at schools is during biology lessons on an insufficient level. Teachers try to teach the students only the anatomic structure of the genital organs.

### B. Sexual Knowledge in the Turkish Community

To ascertain the level of sexual knowledge among the Turkish community, a three-stage study was carried out. These studies were undertaken at the encouragement of the late Prof. Dr. Alpay Kelâmi, who was a Turkish Cypriot andrologist/urologist working at the Free University of Berlin, Germany. The first stage was carried out among the 4- to 12-year-old age group by K. Bolayır and N. Cahit in 1990. The second stage was carried out among the 14- to 18-year-old and 18- to 24-year-old age groups by K. Bolayır, N. Gökşn, and E. Emekçi, in 1991. The third stage was carried out among the age group over 30 years of age by K. Bolayır and S. Özyigit in 1992.

In the 1990s, sexuality was not taken up in the media very much. Sexual words, such as "penis" or "in the vagina," could not be written in the newspapers. Teachers were reluctant to give sex education to the children in schools, because they themselves had insufficient knowledge on sexual issues. During the above studies, the schoolchildren made interesting comments when questioned on the subject of biology lessons. They said teachers avoided any reference to genital organs and sometimes boys were sent out of the classroom while a female teacher talked to the girls only, thus compelling the boys to ask the girls questions as to what the lesson was all about afterwards.

- Below are ten typical questions and answers from the 1,000 schoolchildren in the 4-to-12 age cohort: How did you come to the world? Answers: From the belly of my mother: 80%, My mother gave birth: 20%; Down my mother's legs: 5%.
- Do you sleep with your father and mother? 95% no, 5% yes.
- Do you prefer playing with boys or girls? 92% preferred playing with the same gender.
- Why do boys and girls not want to play with each other? 70% simply said 'we don't play' without giving any reason, 20% considered it wrong or because they might be thought of as sweethearts, 10% were afraid to be made fun of.

- To the boys: Were you afraid of circumcision? 10% yes, 90% were proud of it.
- To the girls: Has your mother said anything to you about menstruation? 80% yes, 20% no.
- Which scenes that you watched on TV have you tried on your friends? 20% only kissing scenes.
- What dirty words have you heard from your environment? 80% admitted hearing dirty words, but did not say what they were.
- Have you learned anything from what is written on the toilet walls and desks in school? 60% became acquainted with love affairs between the names mentioned.
- Between which relatives are marriages not allowed? 100% said that marriages were not allowed between brothers and sisters and first-degree relatives.

This study revealed that children are not immensely affected by traditions and taboos. Unfortunately, however, as time goes on, communal pressure will affect these children. During this study, in a TV discussion in 1990 with A. Kelâmi, Telaloglu, and Bolayır, the priority was given to the sex education of the parents and schoolteachers.

In 1991, in the first part of the second stage of this study, 980 schoolchildren 14 to 18 years old were questioned:

- Do you think that both testicles can be felt in the scrotum when a boy is born? 70% didn't know and 30% said yes.
- Can you speak about sexuality with your parents? 90% no, 10% yes.
- Do you have friends of the opposite sex with whom you can discuss sexuality? 75% yes, 25% no.
- Do you know what homosexuality is? 55% yes, 45% no.
- Do you know what sperm and ovum are? 70% yes, 30% no.
- Have you learned anything about sexuality from writings on restroom walls and school desks? 70% yes, 30% no.
- When you play with your sexual organs, do you do this in a feeling of fear and guilt? 70% yes, 30% no.
- Do you masturbate? boys 95% yes, girls 13% yes.
- Do you know that AIDS is the most dangerous sexually transmitted disease? 60% yes, 40% no.
- Do you know that a woman can have a child without having menstruation? 80% don't know, 20% yes.
- Have you watched any porno film? 90% yes.
- Do you flirt? 50% yes, 50% no.
- Do you have sexual education at your school? 98% no.

The second part of the second stage of the study surveyed 1,000 18 to 24 year olds in 1991, including the following questions:

- Can you speak with the older members of your family about sexuality? male: 90% no; female: 80% no.
- Can you discuss sexuality with your friends? 95% yes.
- Can you communicate with your teachers in school about sexuality? 98% no.
- Do you know that in females, menstruation occurs in the uterus and continues for about five days? male: 45% do not know; female: 95% yes.
- Are both testicles palpable in the scrotum when a boy is born? 60% do not know.
- Is the hymen the most valuable thing for girls? male: 60% yes; female: 80% yes.
- Are you against a marriage arranged by your family? male: 75% yes; female: 50% yes.
- Do you think that masturbation is not harmful? male: 87% yes; female: 50% yes.
- Do you think that a married couple should have a baby within a year if they desire so? male: 60% yes; female: 40% yes.

- Are you against premarital sex? male: 85% no; female: 30% no.
- Do you think that abortion should be legally permitted? 90% yes.
- Do you think that the main cause of erectile problems is psychological? 80% do not know.

A 1998 study of 800 persons in the age group over age 30 produced the following results:

- Who chooses the marriage partners in the Turkish Cypriot community? 40% the partners themselves; 60% chosen by the family.
- Do you think menopause is a cause for the reluctance to have sexual intercourse? 60% yes; 40% no.
- Do males continue to masturbate after 30 years of age? 60% yes; 40% no.
- How many women out of ten masturbate until 30? 70% said "2"; 20% said nothing.
- Do you agree that the sex knowledge of a newly married woman is sufficient? 80% yes.
- Do you agree that Turkish Cypriot women learn sex by experience after their marriage? 80% yes.
- Do sexual problems create a cause for divorce in the Turkish Cypriot community? 60% yes.
- How many married women and men out of ten have extramarital sexual intercourse in the Turkish Cypriot community? 70% of married men had one to three affairs; 10% of married men had only one or none; 35% of married women had one to three affairs; 30% of married women had one or none.
- What percentage of married partners discusses sexual problems between themselves? 50%.
- Can a man over age 70 have sexual intercourse? 50% yes.
- Can a cure be found for an impotent man? 50% yes; 50% do not know.
- Do you believe that pornographic films should be freely distributed? 75% yes.
- Do you think that women have as much desire for sexual intercourse as men? 60% no; 40% yes.
- Do you think that the man should always be the initiator of sexual intercourse? 60% yes; 40% do not know.
- Do you believe that the contribution of the woman is very important to the sexual quality and performance? 40% yes; 60% no.
- Is pregnancy possible during the menstruation? 90% don't know.
- Do you think that a spinster should also have a gynecological check-up, just like a married woman? 70% yes; 30% do not know.

Between 1990 and 1998, we examined the level of sexual knowledge in the Turkish Cypriot community. We tried to ascertain how and from where people got their sexual information. The answers given by 6 to 70 years olds reveal that the level of sexual knowledge in the community is very low.

It is a very important finding that 95% of youngsters do not discuss sexual issues with their parents and 98% of boys and girls also do not discuss sexuality with their teachers. Where do these boys and girls get their sexual knowledge? Young people of marriageable age learn about sex from friends, magazines, porno films and similar publications, and the media. In the past, males used to get their sexual experiences in brothels. Nowadays, nightclubs and pubs have replaced these places.

Porno films can be easily bought in Northern Cyprus. From Bolayır's clinical experience, the following are some of the main complaints of people watching porno films in the Turkish Cypriot community.

- When compared with those in the porno films, they find that their penises are smaller, and ask whether these can be lengthened.
- They also inquire about why their own sexual intercourse does not last as long as that in the porno films.
- He or she is also confused to see that anal sex is brought to the foreground in porno films, and then inquire about the dangers and harms of anal sex.
- Others find themselves in a state of great stress because men in porno films appear to be very powerful.
- The couples in porno films appear to be very energetic and hot blooded, whereas some of our patients say they are not the same when together with their wives.

## 4. Autoerotic Behaviors and Patterns

### A. Children and Adolescents

In a 1990 study among 980 young people, it was established that 95% of boys and 13% of girls masturbate. Girls in the Turkish Cypriot community are sexually under greater pressure and control than boys. Therefore, girls who feel guilty masturbate in secrecy and under very secure conditions as if doing something wrong. It appears that parents are always inclined to take great care to prevent their daughters from masturbating, and have a fear that they might lose their virginity if they are allowed to do so. Hence, we see that statistical data for girls are very limited. No clear-cut results have been obtained in these studies regarding the age at which girls and boys start masturbating. Generally, the girls are taught to be shy, which is probably another reason why they could not admit to masturbating. However, it can be said that many girls start masturbating at about the age of 11 years and boys at about age 13 years. As adolescents grow older, masturbation becomes more frequent, especially among boys. Our clinical experience has shown that parents accept masturbation if the child is male. In a sense, the parents are proud of their son's masturbatory behavior, saying their boy is a real man, like his father. Sometimes, parents refuse to discuss the normality of their daughter's masturbation. These parents never accept their daughter's masturbation and punish her as a consequence if she continues.

### B. Adults

There is no available data about adult masturbation in the Turkish Cypriot community. It is thought to be very rare in both sexes, but it is practiced by a number of married men who have problems approaching their wives because of marital conflict. Turkish Cypriot women say that they do not masturbate when their husbands are abroad or in therapy.

## 5. Interpersonal Heterosexual Behaviors

### A. Children

No study on the sexual rehearsal play among children has been made in the Turkish Cypriot community.

### B. Adolescents

There are no puberty rituals as such in the Turkish Cypriot tradition, but the start of menstruation for the girls and circumcision for the boys are both celebrated as milestones. When the female child starts menstruating, the mother is told. She in turn tells the father, the sisters and brothers, the grandparents, and the aunts and uncles. A great fuss and excitement surround the child, with everyone kissing and congratulating her on becoming a woman. The girl is usually embarrassed by all this commotion around her.

Every young boy knows that one day, he is going to be circumcised and "become a man." Traditionally, boys are circumcised between the ages of 5 and 7 years. Parents usually like to have the boys circumcised before they start elementary school. In the past, circumcisions were performed without any anesthetic by men called *sünnetci*, non-medical men specializing in circumcisions. The child was held firmly by two male family members (other than the father) while the *sünnetci* performed the operation. As soon as the child opened his mouth to cry out, a little piece of *lokum* ("Turkish delight candy") was put into his mouth and the whole procedure was over in minutes. Although these *sünnetci* still exist in rural areas, nowadays circumcisions are performed under anesthesia by urologists in hospitals. On the day of the circumcision, the boys are dressed in special costumes and hats. Depending on the family, they may then be taken around the village or the city on horses with accompanying traditional *Davul* and *Zurna* music drums and a kind of clarinet. The children and adults of the family, sometimes in cars and blowing their horns, follow this happy procession. On the eve of the circumcision, a party is given, and all the guests bring presents or give money to the circumcised boy. The boys continue to wear their long white shirts for about a week until they can wear trousers again.

No clear-cut studies have been carried out in the Turkish Cypriot community on sexual behaviors among adolescents. However, Bolayır's (1991) study of 230 adolescents (age 16 years.) revealed that 80% of the boys and 30% of the girls had experienced hugging, kissing, petting, and sexual intercourse. Boys and girls of this age consider themselves to be mature. Boys try to prove themselves by endeavoring to influence girls. On the other hand, girls are under the influence of physical and psychological changes and want to be loved. At this period, the young do not possess sufficient sexual knowledge, but they put on a brave face and attempt to think and act strongly.

In a 1998 study by Bolayır among 210 adolescents, it was established that 68% of the boys and girls in the 16- to 18-year-old age group had no sexual intercourse, 20% had only one such experience, and 10% more than one. Ninety percent of these youths knew what a condom was and 48% had used and knew how to use a condom properly. To avoid pregnancy, some boys and girls preferred anal sex. However, there is no available data about the extent of this practice.

The male adolescent's main sexual experience is with women working in nightclubs, pubs, and other entertainment places. These interactions are with payment, and the duration is short. The women in the nightclubs are commonly known as "Natasha." It is an interesting fact that 50% of the men who have paid for sexual relationships with "Natasha" are married and are mostly fathers. In the community, sexual relationships between Turkish Cypriot men and women and tourists are at a very low level.

## C. Adults

The study made in 1992 among 800 people of marriageable age revealed that virginity was an important phenomenon in the Turkish Cypriot community. According to our clinical findings, 11% of men and 77% of women were found to be virgins when first engaged or married. In the Turkish Cypriot community, one of the reasons for ending an engagement or marriage is when a bride is found not to be a virgin on the first night of her marriage or during her engagement. Sometimes, members of both families insist on a medical examination prior to marriage to prove the virginity of the girl, forcing the girl concerned to be examined by a gynecologist. This is an unfair, unacceptable, and disgraceful position for the girl. Several families have a hymnography operation—hymen reconstruction—performed on their daughters before marriage. As a result of this, the girl is compelled to have to resort to a deceitful marriage and build her life on unsound foundations. Nowadays, virginity has lost its importance in the cities, but unfortunately not in the rural areas or with the very conservative families.

This study also showed that 3% of the girls and 15% of the boys had their first sexual intercourse before the age of 16, and 75% of these males had their first sexual intercourse before marriage with prostitutes. Nine out of 10 Turkish women had their first sexual intercourse either with their fiancée or husband. It is expected that this rate has increased in recent years and, therefore, new research is necessary.

In the Turkish Cypriot community, 98% of married women and men do not have extramarital sexual relationships during the first years of their marriage. But in this male-dominant community, after a short lapse of time, and probably trying to prove their superiority over their wives, most men do not keep up this good record. The majority of the men who visited nightclubs to have sex insisted that they went there under the influence of alcohol and on the insistence of their friends. Some even infected their wives with sexually transmitted diseases from these extramarital sexual relationships.

In the Turkish Cypriot community, it is acceptable for men to easily and openly speak to their friends about their extramarital activities. They can also unreservedly speak with their doctor, telling him or her how and from whom they got the disease. However, this is not the case with women. Women who have extramarital affairs will possibly be labeled as prostitutes, whereas men are often considered as brave for acting in this way and are easily forgiven in the public eye. This is the traditional mentality of the community. In Northern Cyprus, 75% of the women tend to stick to only one partner in their life, but that is not true of the men, 75% of whom have one or more extramarital relationships.

Our clinical experience shows that 4 out of 10 men and 7 out of 10 women do not like oral sex. Three out of 10 women do not know what a clitoris is or what a clitoral orgasm is. They claim that the vagina is the only source of sexual pleasure. These findings show the level of sexual knowledge of the women in the community.

Another clinical finding is that in the younger generation, 70% of men and 30% of young women enjoy anal sex. Young Turkish Cypriots who are interested in and watch porno films often prefer anal sex.

In a close-knit small community such as Northern Cyprus, confidential information is not easily disclosed, so more funds are required to carry out detailed research.

## 6. Homoerotic, Homosexual, and Bisexual Behaviors

### A. Adolescents and Adults

To establish the ratio of homosexuality in a community of 200,000, it is essential to make a very detailed study. Traditional community principles and family pressure make this sort of study all the more difficult.

In a study made in 1992, clinical samples indicated that there were 16 homosexual cases, 14 boys and 2 girls. The average age was between 19 and 23 years. Eight of these boys were exposed during their military service. These homosexuals coerced their peers to have sex with them in return for money or valuable gifts. As soon as these cases were exposed, the army immediately discharged the involved homosexuals for misconduct.

Our studies show that these male homosexuals not only enjoy anal sex, but also all other sorts of activities, such as deep kissing, hugging, nipple stimulation, nongenital touching, oral-genital kissing, and hand-genital stimulation. Male homosexual orgasm is more commonly achieved by fellatio or mutual masturbation. Briefly, it can be said that not all male homosexuals necessarily engage in anal intercourse. It could also be ascertained that female homosexuals insert different phallus-like objects into their vagina during sex.

Looking at the reports of the Kinsey Institute, it is seen that the differences between homosexual and heterosexual findings are about the same. "The major difference between homosexual and heterosexual sex activities is that homosexuals cannot engage in penile-vaginal intercourse with a member of the same sex."

People in Northern Cyprus dislike talking about homosexuality. However, according to widespread belief among the Turkish Cypriots, this is not so among the Greek Cypriot community. Prior to 1974, parents even advised their children to always keep this in their minds in their relationships with the Greek Cypriots.

In the Turkish Cypriot community, it is a great disgrace to be a homosexual, which makes it very difficult to find out the exact number of homosexuals in the community. It is also very difficult for the homosexuals to seek any rights in the community. They have no clubs or places of assembly of their own. Parents never approve of their children's being gay or lesbian.

Homosexuals in the Turkish community escape from the community by either immigrating to other countries, or staying and struggling to have a place in the community. Those who flee aspire to have a better and easier life and enjoy homosexuality somewhere else. Those who stay and wish to have a place in the community, opt to marry someone from the opposite sex and carry on his or her homosexual activities in secret.

In 1986, when we started to examine the level of sexual knowledge in public schools, we encountered several problems from the Ministry of Education. It was indeed not easy to get permission to conduct this study, simply because the officials of the Ministry were of the opinion that such a study would provoke homosexual feelings among the students. In fact, this is not true. In our opinion, and also according to the Kinsey Institute, homosexuality is not an abnormality, nor an illness or a disorder.

Today, in the Turkish Cypriot community laws inherited from the British colonial administration are still in force on sexuality. Since 1974, the Turkish and Greek communities are living apart in Cyprus as a result of events started by Greek Cypriots in 1963. Negotiations are continuing, and there is hope for a peaceful solution. The Greek side has already enacted the relevant law legalizing homosexuality. The Turkish community has so far not done so. Nevertheless, homosexuality is legal in the European Union, which both communities are trying to join.

## 7. Gender Diversity and Transgender Issues

In Northern Cyprus, there are very few transsexuals. In 1996, five people, three women and two men, who were anxious to change their sex, were interviewed. Although they all wanted to have a surgical operation immediately, they all believed that if they stayed in Cyprus, they could be ousted from the community. All claimed that they could reach their goals easier abroad in developed, large countries.

## 8. Significant Unconventional Sexual Behaviors

### A. Coercive Sexual Behaviors

*Sexual Abuse of Children and Incest*

In small communities like the Turkish Cypriot community, any attempt of child sexual abuse can easily be uncovered and can have widespread repercussions. Such events are also given great coverage in the press.

According to the reports of the Criminal Department, only three incest cases occurred during 1995-1996 in Northern Cyprus. On the other hand, there were 12 cases of child sexual abuse. In fact, these figures are probably incorrect. In order to avoid scandals and disgrace, and to protect the family honor, events among relatives are not reported to the police.

*Rape and Marital Rape*

According to police reports, cases of rape have increased in the Turkish Cypriot community after the arrival of immigrants from Turkey. These reports claim that the numbers of such cases are 12. However, the opinion is that these do not reflect the real situation, as raped women are afraid of a bad reputation in the community and, therefore, prefer to remain silent.

Marital rape is even more common than anticipated, because violence in the family has always existed in both communities in Cyprus. Some cases of marital rape consist of attempts by men to have anal sex with their wives against their will. In most cases, men usually act only in accordance with their egocentric feelings and desires, and do not take into consideration the psychological feelings of their wives. Sometimes, men go to such extents, that woman have no other choice but to complain to the police. However, both the police and the members of the family do their best to avoid going to court. The main reason for this is the fear that during the trial period, family honor will be harmed, and the families of both the husband and the wife will be disgraced considerably.

Irrespective of the belief that the number of such cases may have decreased during recent years, it is essential to continue investigating these cases in the Turkish Cypriot community.

*Sexual Harassment*

In the Turkish Cypriot community, sexual harassment of women by men generally occurs at the place of work. The offer of promotion priority and higher payment is used as an excuse to sexually harass and violate the woman employee. Additional dangers await women subjected to this sort of sexual harassment. Other male employees might consider the woman as easy prey, risking the honor of the woman and her family.

In 1994, there was a report in the local press about the sexual harassment of a woman at her workplace. Following this publication, a questionnaire was sent to about 200 female employees in various workplaces. Three out of four women surveyed replied that sexual harassment was rather widespread in the Turkish Cypriot community. Women working as cleaners in private homes and belly dancers were also possible targets. Sexual harassment in schools and in government offices is less common.

### B. Prostitution

Although prostitution is illegal, it was common knowledge that, until recent years, prostitution was practiced in certain houses. However, nowadays, there are no local prostitutes, because girls known as "Natasha" from countries like Russia, Ukraine, Moldavia, Romania, and Thailand are in abundance operating as prostitutes, usually controlled and forced by the nightclub owners. These girls claim that they only get 25% of the money received from the customers in return for sexual intercourse, with the rest of the money being kept by the bosses.

## C. Pornography

See survey results at the end of Section 3B, Knowledge and Education about Sexuality, Sexual Knowledge in the Turkish Community.

## D. Sexual Crimes

The incidence of sexual crimes in the Turkish Cypriot community is very low. This number is so low that it is not worth dwelling on it. Kidnapping of children has not taken place during the last five years. According to police reports, there were 6 cases of rape in 1997, 5 in 1998, and 7 in 1999. Seduction, indecent assaults against women, and indecent offenses were also found to be very rare.

## 9. Contraception, Abortion, and Population Planning

### A. Contraception

To avoid pregnancy, males have learned to use condoms, and the females hormonal contraceptive pills and intrauterine devices (IUD). In extramarital sexual relationships, the males prefer to use condoms, as this is a precaution against sexually transmitted diseases and AIDS as well.

In the Turkish Cypriot community, the question as to which one of the couple is mostly responsible for the prevention of pregnancy during their marriage is very important. Is it the woman or the man? In fact, the best method for couples that do not wish to have children is for the man to have a vasectomy operation. This is the simplest and safest method (Kelâmi et al.). If the couple change their mind and wish to have children again at a later stage, the man can easily have a vasectomy-reversal (vasovasectomy) operation.

In a study carried out in 1996 among 100 couples, it was ascertained that only 2% have had vasectomies and 8% had tubal ligation. The same study showed that 15% of men used condoms and 20% had coitus interruptus, 35% of women used pills and 15% used the IUD. Five percent of the couples took no precaution. In these cases, tests revealed sterility in either the man or woman.

In contrast, most of the immigrant families from Turkey in the Turkish Cypriot community, take no precautions against pregnancy, so many of their families have between 5 to 10 children. However, when questioned about the number of children and their socioeconomic problems, their common reply was: "No problem, God will give the livelihood of the children."

### B. Abortion

Abortion is the only way to end undesired pregnancies. As stated previously, abortion is illegal except in very exceptional circumstances. However, it is quite possible to get an abortion in the private clinics in Northern Cyprus, despite the fact that this is considered a sin and crime in Islam. In a study carried out in 1999 by Bolayır and Gökşn among 300 women, it was determined that 21% of the women had had one abortion, 15% had had two, and 5% had had three or more abortions. There are no doctors in Northern Cyprus who will not perform abortions for ethical reasons.

### D. Population Programs

The total population of Cyprus is about one million. There has been no steady increase of the population of Northern Cyprus during the last 50 years. The reasons for this are the political problems and intercommunal conflict. These compelled a large number of Turkish Cypriots to emigrate from the island. However, after the Turkish intervention in 1974 and the agreement to relocate the Greek Cypriots from the North to the South and Turkish Cypriots from the South to the North, there has been a sudden increase in the population in the Turkish community. This is because of the arrival of immigrants from Turkey. In 1974, the Turkish Cypriot population was about 120,000; in 1999, it was 200,000.

In Northern Cyprus, there is no official department of the government to direct family planning. This is done by specialist doctors. People, too, have learned to keep a balance consistent with their socioeconomic condition. However, tax exemptions for children encourage people to have more than one child. Parents with more than one child also enjoy subsidies in school fees and facilities in hospitals.

## 10. Sexually Transmitted Diseases and HIV/AIDS

### A. Sexually Transmitted Diseases

In Northern Cyprus, people suffering from STD generally prefer treatment by private medical practitioners because they want to keep this a secret. Although it is a legal obligation to report such cases to the Ministry of Health, in general, medical practitioners, urologists, gynecologists, and dermatologists refrain from doing so. Therefore, there are no reliable records on STD in Northern Cyprus, except for AIDS, which is normally reported. The only available data is from our own clinical samples, results learned from our researchers, and from official statistical information given out monthly.

As stated earlier, the study carried out among 100 young people in 1990 confirmed that they had insufficient knowledge on sexually transmitted diseases. Faced with this finding, we were requested by schoolteachers to give talks to the students on all matters related with sex. Up to now, we are doing this task periodically. In the course of these conferences, it was discovered that AIDS was the main topic of interest. For instance, 98% of the participants did not know that the papilloma virus causes warts in the genital region. Another virus, the herpes genitalis, enters the body and remains there for the rest of one's life and causes painful sores on the skin of the genital organs that may reappear from time to time for many years. Also, chlamydia and gonorrhea, if not treated, lead to scarring in the channels of the genital organs. These scars might cause infertility in females and urethral stricture in men, as well as facilitate entrance of the HIV virus into the body.

In Northern Cyprus, men who have sexual intercourse with girls in nightclubs do not know whether the girls are drug users or recipients of blood transfusions, but they should at least know that they are risking exposure to HIV and/or some other STD.

During the period of 1996 to 1998, the number of cases officially reported are shown in Table 20. According to our clinical experience, Turkish Cypriot schoolchildren are anxious to learn more about STDs. But the question is, from whom are they going to receive this information? Although the young have learned to use condoms, the majority do not

### Table 20

**Official Number of Sexually Transmitted Disease Cases in Turkish Cyprus, 1996-1998**

|  | 1996 | 1997 | 1998 |
|---|---|---|---|
| Syphilis | 13 | 17 | 19 |
| Gonorrhea | 40 | 32 | 38 |
| Herpes genitalis | 98 | 80 | 90 |
| Genital warts | 110 | 120 | 119 |
| AIDS | Total of 15 cases | | |

know how and/or what type of condoms to use. Neither do they know the exact benefits of using a condom. It is obvious that sex education should be a must in every school. The question is how to introduce this information into the school curricula and train teachers to present the information.

## B. HIV/AIDS

AIDS is a frightful disease in Northern Cyprus as it is in the whole world, particularly because a person with this deadly infection is seldom aware of the infection and continues to have sex, thus transmitting the disease to others. Throughout the world, as well as in Northern Cyprus, there are thousands of undiagnosed individuals with HIV, as this infectious disease takes a long time to manifest itself. Thousands of tourists from various countries of the world visit Northern Cyprus every year, and certainly some of these have sexual intercourse with Turkish Cypriots. Even if only a fraction of these are unknowingly HIV seropositive, their partners can easily be infected.

The only way to find out whether one has AIDS is to have a blood test. The ELISA test (enzyme-linked immunabsorbant assay) is generally performed in the Burhan Nalbantoglu State Hospital, but there is no way to require Turkish Cypriots suffering from other sexual transmitted diseases and drug users to have the ELISA test. Such a requirement for arriving tourists is beyond any practicality. However, the application of the ELISA test in Northern Cyprus started in 1986. According to Dr. Tansel Dikengil, the head of the Microbiology Department of the State Hospital, 180,000 people are annually subjected to the ELISA test. This test is applied to every patient undergoing an operation, to newly married couples, and those who apply to become citizens. The test is also obligatory for individuals who are known to have had sexual intercourse with an HIV-seropositive partner. Under an agreement between the Ministries of Health of Northern Cyprus and Turkey, Refik Saydam health institute in Ankara also confirms the result of the tests that are found to be HIV seropositive in Northern Cyprus. The Ministry of Health of the TRNC (Turkish Republic of Northern Cyprus) reports these results to WHO at the end of each month. The results of the HIV-seropositive tests between the years 1987-1999 are shown in Table 21. The most recent number of seropositive persons in the TRNC is 87. Of these, 27 were Turkish Cypriots and 60 were foreigners; 70 were men and 17 women. The average age was 31.8 years. Out of the total 87 cases, 40 were heterosexuals and 47 were homosexuals. Three cases were the result of blood transfusions and five were drugs users.

In Northern Cyprus, of the 15 total cases of AIDS, 12 were male and 3 female. These patients received treatment in medical centers in Ankara and Istanbul. Three patients died in Northern Cyprus. The foreign patients, 80% of whom came from Moldavia, Russia, Ukraine, and the Far East, were sent to their countries at their request. In 1996, Gökşn carried out a test on 2,000 soldiers between the ages of 19 and 23 yrs. No cases of HIV seropositivity were found as a result of these tests. The ratio of 0.1% HIV in Northern Cyprus is rather low compared to other countries.

### Table 21

**Number of HIV-Seropositive Test Results in Turkish Cyprus by Year, 1987-1999**

| | | | | | |
|---|---|---|---|---|---|
| 1987: | 3 | 1992: | 7 | 1996: | 3 |
| 1988: | 6 | 1993: | 8 | 1997: | 9 |
| 1989: | 5 | 1994: | 9 | 1998: | 7 |
| 1990: | 8 | 1995: | 10 | 1999: | 8 |
| 1991: | 4 | | | | |

## Treatment, Prevention Programs, and Government Policies

In Northern Cyprus, the Ministry of Health educates the public on AIDS throughout the year, but especially on the first of December, which is worldwide "AIDS Day." Lectures, television and radio panels and interviews, and other activities are organized. The public is continuously reminded that the most important preventive measure for AIDS is the use of condoms. Brochures, leaflets, posters, key rings, and T-shirts are used in the anti-AIDS campaign to stress the fact that risky sexual intercourse without using condoms is the main factor of the AIDS infection, not forgetting blood transfusions and the hazards of prenatal transmission.

Cooperation with the World Health Organization and UNAIDS is an important issue in Northern Cyprus. The main criterion is the prevention rather than the cure of AIDS. The media plays an important role in all anti-AIDS campaigns. However, the difficulty is educating the homosexuals, drug users, and those frequenting prostitutes. It is emphasized that abstinence from sex and the correct use of condoms are very significant in preventing the spread of the disease among the community.

[*Update 2002*: UNAIDS Epidemiological Assessment: This combined epidemiological assessment is for both the Turkish Republic of Northern Cyprus (TRNC) and the (Greek) Republic of Cyprus.

[HIV seroprevalence among blood donors has been reported below 0.01% in Cyprus since 1989. There was no evidence for HIV infection among pregnant women that were tested from 1998 until 2001, with the exception of one HIV case detected among 4,019 pregnant women in 1992 and one case detected among 2,422 pregnant women in 2001. HIV seroprevalence among bar girls remains below 1%. No infection has been detected among sex workers over the years. HIV prevalence among injecting drug users is reported to be between 0.1% and 0.3% between 1993 and 1999. Of clients of voluntary counseling and testing, 0.4% and 0.8% were found to be HIV-positive in 1999 and 2000, respectively.

[The estimated number of adults and children living with HIV/AIDS on January 1, 2002, were:

| | |
|---|---|
| Adults ages 15-49: | < 1,000  (rate: 0.3%) |
| Women ages 15-49: | 150 |
| Children ages 0-15: | NA |

[No estimate is available for the number of adults and children who died of AIDS during 2001.

[No estimate is available for the number of Cypriot children who had lost one or both parents to AIDS and were under age 15 at the end of 2001. (*End of update by the Editors*)]

## 11. Sexual Dysfunctions, Counseling, and Therapies

### A. The General Situation in Northern Cyprus

During the 1980s the main author and his colleagues carried out a series of research surveys in the Turkish Cypriot community with the support of the late Prof. Dr. Alpay Kelâmi. The results of these studies indicated that the level of sexual knowledge was inadequate and that there were no qualified professionals to treat the individuals suffering from sexual dysfunction. People were mostly ignorant as to which physician was knowledgeable or involved in treating sexual dysfunction of either men or women. Most were inclined to visit general practitioners. In 2003, Cypriots who seek professional help with a sexual problem are limited to a few general medical practitioners, andrologists, and gynecologists who have expanded their interest and expertise to include some professional training in sexual counseling and therapy.

In the traditional mentality of the people in Northern Cyprus, the sexual organs were to be concealed at all times, The sexual organs were considered taboo, prohibited areas of the body that were not exposed or discussed, even with a spouse or physician. When it came to a disease or functional disorder of the sexual organs, nothing is disclosed to close family members. Even visits to the physicians are avoided, with the belief that the disorder may be temporary and might cure itself. If the situation continues for a longer time, the advice of the same-sex elders in the family or close friends of the same sex might be sought. A visit to a doctor is only considered when nothing else works. Sometimes, the treatment is made more difficult through the waste of precious time. If, however, the ailment were in any other part of the body, friends and family would be extensively asked for advice and the doctor visited immediately.

Understandably, the few pioneering physicians who have decided to address sexual issues in Northern Cyprus have come from the well-established fields of urology and gynecology, and the new field of andrology, the diagnosis and treatment of the dysfunction, function, and disease of the male genital organs.

In the field of andrology in general, and contributions to the sexual health of the people of Cyprus in particular, it is a great pleasure to stress the services of the late Prof. Alpay Kelâmi. Turkish and Greek Cypriot urologists attended courses on andrology and urology at the Free University of Berlin organized by Kelâmi. He also played a leading role in organizing numerous International uroandrological symposia in Northern Cyprus. Distinguished doctors, all authorities in their fields, from all over the world attended these international symposia and presented papers and had discussions on relevant subjects. Several Turkish Cypriot doctors, and doctors from Turkey and other countries had the opportunity to exchange views with the participating foreign specialists. Unfortunately, however, the Greek Cypriot authorities did not allow Greek Cypriot doctors to attend these symposia because of political reasons. Prof. Kelâmi also participated in TV and radio interviews after each symposium in Northern Cyprus between the years of 1980-1992 and enlightened the public on sexual issues. His innovative "Art and Andrology" exhibitions during the symposia were additional means of bringing the medical sexual issues to the attention of the lay public.

Having acknowledged the many contributions of the late Professor Alpay Kelâmi to the sexuality education of physicians and to the sexual health of Turkish Cypriots, because he was a urologist/andrologist, his focus in sexuality was on the male, and the treatment of women was more restricted to their procreative role.

## B. Diagnosis and Treatment of Sexual Dysfunctions

The first author of this chapter on Turkish Cyprus is a physician specializing in uroandrology with some 20 years experience in treating sexual dysfunctions. An associate professor of urology, he has presented papers on andrology, sexual therapy, and rehabilitation at three-dozen professional meetings and has organized several international conferences on urology and andrology. The observations offered here are based on the main author's clinical practice.

### Diagnosis and Treatment of Erectile Dysfunction

For many years, the cause of male impotence was believed to be solely psychological in origin. Even today, some physicians believe that the majority of cases of male impotence have some psychological origin. This is not correct. In fact, more than 80% are primarily of physiological origin, although many of these patients are affected psychologically later on.

In the past decade, clinical research in erectile dysfunction has demonstrated that penile erection is a vascular and neurological phenomenon. In our clinical experience, when we evaluate a male patient suffering from impotence, we consider that erection appears to be the result of three hemodynamic stages, the proper clinical evaluation and management of which requires an understanding in anatomic and physiologic aspects of these prerequisite events.

An impotent patient in Northern Cyprus is evaluated by a sensitive medical interview. The initial evaluation is based on doctor-patient communication during history taking together with the husband and wife/partner. Unfortunately, however, in Northern Cyprus, the visit of the husband to the doctor together with his wife/partner is an important problem. The Turkish Cypriot community is a small and conservative unit. The traditional mentality is that discussing sexual matters in the presence of a doctor will damage the family dignity. In fact, women are reluctant to discuss these matters with any person. Women in general shoulder so many responsibilities in the family that probably sexual affairs are ignored. In the traditional mentality, the women even refrain from discussing sexual matters with their husbands. So, many women over the age of 50 years never like to visit doctors to discuss sexual issues. However, in recent years, couples are beginning to visit doctors jointly to discuss their problems. This is a good omen for the future.

In taking the sexual history of the patient, Turkish Cypriots use a different sexual terminology than physicians, creating a communications problem that needs to be addressed and resolved. Questions are especially directed to verify the existence of an erectile problem, because sometimes patients describe impotence as lack of libido, or retarded or premature ejaculation. By the end of the interview, the physician should be aware of the patient's problem. History taking leads to identifying psychological and physiological factors that may affect erectile performance. Most cases involve both physiological and psychogenic erectile dysfunctions. These findings are confirmed by intracavernal injection tests and analyses of blood, urine, and hormones.

One common disease that causes erectile dysfunction in men is diabetes. In the Turkish Cypriot community, when looking at the patients who suffer from physiological erectile dysfunction, the following symptoms are seen; gradual loss of erectile ability, change of rigidity of the erection, and diminished morning erections. In contrast, if the suggestive diagnosis is primarily of psychological origin, predisposed individuals may be affected and the long-lasting rigid erections, as well as morning erections, may diminish and disappear for a long time. Our clinical experience has shown that, as in other communities, purely psychologically impotent men are very rare. Looking at the ages, we see that most of the impotent patients of psychological origin are under age 40 while patients with physiological impotence are over age 40.

When looking at the options of treating patients with erectile dysfunction, it can be seen that many advances have occurred, such as penile prostheses or the "miracle drug" sildenafil (Viagra). Patients with erectile dysfunction in Northern Cyprus received either nonsurgical or surgical treatments. Among the alternatives to surgical treatment for impotent patients are: intracavernous injections, vacuum devices, hormonal injections, behavioral sex therapy, and sildenafil (Viagra). If all these treatments fail to remedy the erectile dysfunction, then the patient is advised to have surgical treatment. In Northern Cyprus, we apply venous and arterial surgery for vasculogenic impotence or use penile prostheses in these patients. The majority of the impotent patients who received penile prosthesis in our clinic were diabetic.

Since 1980, 640 males were treated in our clinic for erectile dysfunction: 70% of these were cases of impotence, 17% of premature ejaculation, 7% of honeymoon impotence, 4% of sexual desire disorder, and 2% with retarded ejaculation.

### Honeymoon Impotence

This is normally seen in male patients with anxiety and a lack of sexual experience and knowledge. According to our clinical experiences, the custom in the conservative community of expecting a spot of blood on the sheet on the wedding night, plus the expectations of the family members of the bridegroom, can easily cause him increased anxiety and prevent him from having an erection. A few more unsuccessful attempts may lead the young groom to believe he is permanently impotent. An andrologist can easily diagnose this "honeymoon impotence" and the treatment of such cases is very easy in modern medicine. Between 1999 and 2001, 13 cases of honeymoon impotence were treated in our clinic. As all cases were found to be because of psychological impotence, the treatment results were very satisfactory.

### Early Ejaculation

According to our clinical experience, the patients who suffer from early or "premature" ejaculation have a good erection initially, but the duration of the erection changes from between 10 to 15 seconds up to 2 or 3 minutes. These patients do not like to receive early treatment, as they believe that this problem threatens their male ego. They prefer to continue to suffer from this situation rather than visit a physician. However, upon increased coercion from their wives, they eventually seek medical advice from an andrologist or sexologist. In these cases, men always visit their doctor on their own. It has to be stressed that sex therapy is very effective with this disorder.

### Drugs Affecting Sexual Function

According to our clinical experience, there are diseases that affect erectile dysfunction, such as diabetes, vascular diseases, hypercholesterolemia, alcoholism, heavy smoking, depression, and hypertension. Some of the pharmaceuticals used in the treatment of these diseases may affect erection. They may also affect sexual desire (libido) and ejaculation. Although there are numerous publications, both epidemiological and anecdotal, on the adverse effects of these drugs, many physicians are still not aware of these negative side effects.

### Dysorgasmia and Anorgasmia

Very few cases of male dysorgasmia have sought help in our clinic, Those who do are usually men over the age 40.

As noted earlier, women do not like to discuss their sexual problems with strangers, with family members, or with a specialist doctor competent in the field of sex. The majority of these women are unhappy and complain about their lack of sexual satisfaction, despite the insistence of their husbands to make love to them regularly. According to Özyigit, most sexual complaints from the females involved inhibited orgasm, vaginismus (vaginal spasms), and coital phobia, most cases of which can be traced back to negative sexual learning, misinformation, religious inhibitions and prohibitions, or lack of sexual knowledge.

Dysorgasmia among women is more frequent in a long-term marriage. This is believed to be because of the heavy burden of the women, housework, childcare, and the need to work outside the house, as well as contribute to the family budget. Men's insistence on making love whenever they desire, without taking into consideration the feelings of the women, and their failure to include enough foreplay prior to sexual intercourse, are among the reasons for women's dysorgasmia. In Northern Cyprus, the main cause that diminishes sexual desire for women is the lack of quality in the sexual foreplay. Many Turkish women are deprived of enjoying orgasm, but yet prefer to suffer in silence instead of speaking out. In brief, women avoid revealing or discussing their dysorgasmia or anorgasmia problem, and so suffer without relief.

### Sex Therapy

It is common knowledge that one of the most effective behavioral therapies for erectile dysfunction, the sensate focus exercises, is designed to reduce the performance anxiety that is interfering with erectile dysfunction. This requires the cooperation of both of the sexual partners. In Northern Cyprus, behavioral sex therapy is applied to all patients with erectile dysfunction as the initial choice of treatment. Between 1990 and 1994, 90 patients were evaluated, and those diagnosed with erectile dysfunction of psychogenic origin showed a good response to sex therapy.

In 12 out of 20 cases of early ejaculation, a combination of sex therapy and the sildenafil drug produced a very good response. Seventy percent of the patients who did not respond to sex therapy alone, received another type of combination therapy. This included intracavernous injections, vacuum therapy, the sildenafil drug, and sex therapy. According to investigations, these patients' disorder had physiological origins, and most had significant performance anxiety as well. In our cases, very few received sex therapy together with the intracavernous injection.

## C. Certification and Advanced Education

In many developed countries, in both Europe and North America, as well as both the Greek and Turkish communities of Cyprus, licensed physicians, psychologists, and psychiatrists can offer sexual diagnosis, counseling. and therapy as part of their healthcare expertise. In many countries, including both Cypriot communities, there is no further regulation, certification, licensing, or required training for sex educators, counselors, or therapists as such, apart from the standard licensing or certification of traditional healthcare professionals. If a political solution is found to the separation of Cyprus' two communities, and the island becomes a member of the European Union, these issues will then hopefully be solved.

## 12. Sex Research and Advanced Professional Education

Despite the research that has been done in Northern Cyprus since 1980 on sexual matters, we believe that further research is necessary.

Political, social, and economic problems prevailing in Cyprus for the last 50 years have had adverse effects on sexuality. These problems have caused several interfamily discords between the older and young generation. The research studies that we carried out in the Turkish Cypriot community have shown that sexual knowledge is insufficient. The young make use of foreign publications, magazines, journals, and TV programs. Because these publications are produced outside of Northern Cyprus, they address their own communities and do not generally meet the requirements of the Turkish Cypriot community. There is a definite need for periodic publications on sexuality produced within the Northern Cyprus community and similar material addressing the Greek Cyprus community. On the other hand, widespread intersectional research and surveys on sexuality have to be made in order to have reliable information for future planning. There is also need for a clear need for family, relationship, and sex counseling.

However, the prevailing political structure in Cyprus has so far prevented cooperation between the two communities. There is need for cooperation in the fields of dangerous diseases, such as AIDS and so on. Laws have to be enacted by both communities on patient's rights in keeping with the WHO requirements. Nongovernmental organizations in both the North and South have to cooperate and work more closely in every field of health. And finally, universities in Northern Cyprus have to contribute more towards sexual education.

## References and Suggested Readings

Bancroft, J. 1998. *Human sexuality and its problems.* Edinburgh Churchill Livingstone.

Bolayır, K. 2000. *Northern Cyprus.* Lefkoşa, Cyprus:Yeni Duzen matbaasi.

Bolayır, K. 2000. *Sexuality and our children in the Turkish Cypriot community.* Lefkoşa, Cyprus: Yeni Duzen matbaasi.

Bolayır, K. 2000. *Sexuality and adolescents in the Turkish Cypriot community.* Lefkoşa, Cyprus: Yeni Duzen matbaasi.

Bolayır, K. 2002. *Sexuality and adults in the Turkish Cypriot community.* Lefkoşa, Cyprus: Yeni Duzen matbaasi.

Diamond, J. 1997. *Male menopause.* Sourcebooks, Inc.

Gibbson, H. S. 1997. *The genocide files.* Charles Brovos Publishers.

Hashmat, A. 1993. *The penis.* Pennsylvania, USA: Lea & Febiger, pp. 167-168.

Kaplan, H. S. 1990. *The evaluation of sexual disorders.* New York: Brunnel-Mazel.

Kelâmi, A. 1980. *Atlas of operative andrology.* Berlin/New York: Walter de Gruyter.

Kelâmi, A. 1984. Urethral manipulation syndrome. *Urology International, 39*:352-354.

Lue, T. F., & E. A. Tanagho. 1987. Physiology of erection and pharmacological management of impotence. *Journal of Urology.*

Master, W. H., & V. E. Johnson. *Human sexual inadequacy.* Boston: Little Brown.

Moran, M. 1999. Sovereignty divided. Essays on international dimensions of the Cyprus problem. *Cyprep.*

Musher, J. 1990. Anorgasmia with the use of Fluoxetin. *American Journal of Psychiatry.*

Nelson, R. P. 1988. Nonoperative management of impotence. *Journal of Urology, 139*:2-5.

Papp, G. K. 1990 (April 12-15). Our results with Kelâmi-Syndrome. *International Urology.* Symposion–North Cyprus.

Reinisch, J., & R. Beasle. 1990. *The Kinsey Institute new report on sex.* New York: Penguin Books.

Rüstem, K. 1987. *North Cyprus almanac.* London: K. Rüstem & Brother.

Schover, R. N., & R. B. Jensen. 1988. *Sexuality and chronic illness. A comprehensive approach.* New York: Guilford Press.

UNAIDS. 2002. *Epidemiological fact sheets by country.* Geneva, Switzerland: Joint United Nations Programme on HIV/ AIDS (UNAIDS/WHO). Available: http://www.unaids.org/ hivaidsinfo/statistics/fact_sheets/index_en.htm.

Whitehead, E. D. 1990. Treatment of impotence. *Postgraduate Medicine, 88*(2):139-141.

Yesilada, B. 1989. Social progress and political development in the Turkish Republic of Northern Cyprus. *Intercolledge, 1*:2, Cyprus.

Zorgniotti, A. W., & R. S. Leufleur. 1985. Auto-injection of the corpus cavernosum with a vasoactive drug combination for vasculogenic impotence. *Journal of Urology, 133*(1):39-41.

# Czech Republic
## (*Česká Republika*)

Jaroslav Zvěřina, M.D.*
*Rewritten and updated by the Author*

(CIA 2002)

## Contents**

## Demographics and a Brief Historical Perspective
### ROBERT T. FRANCOEUR

### A. Demographics

The 30,450 square miles (78,866 km$^2$) of the Czech Republic are divided between the very hilly Moravia in the east and the plateau of Bohemia in the west surrounded by low mountains. Germany borders the Czech Republic on the north and west, Austria on the south, Slovakia on the east, and Poland on the north. The Czech Republic is slightly smaller than the state of South Carolina in the United States. From the administrative point of view, the Czech Republic is divided into 13 regions; the capital of the country is Prague.

In July 2002, the Czech Republic had an estimated population of 10.26 million. (All data are from *The World Factbook 2002* (CIA 2002) unless otherwise stated.)

**Age Distribution and Sex Ratios**: *0-14 years*: 15.7% with 1.05 male(s) per female (sex ratio); *15-64 years*: 70.3% with 1 male(s) per female; *65 years and over*: 14% with 0.63 male(s) per female; *Total population sex ratio*: 0.95 male(s) to 1 female

**Life Expectancy at Birth**: *Total Population*: 74.95 years; *male*: 71.46 years; *female*: 78.65 years

**Urban/Rural Distribution**: 66% to 34%

**Ethnic Distribution**: Czechs: 81.2%; Moravian: 13.2%; Slovaks: 3.1%; Polish: 0.6%; German: 0.5%; Silesian: 0.4%; Gypsy: 0.3%; Hungarian: 0.2%; other: 0.5% (1991 est.). The number of Gypsies is universally judged as underestimated because many Gypsies report themselves as Czech. The Gypsy ethnic population consists of about 100,000 people, approximately 1.0% of general population.

**Religious Distribution**: Typical for the Czech Republic is the high secularization of citizens, with 39.8% of respondents signing themselves as atheists. Religious affiliation is Roman Catholic: 39.2%; Protestant: 4.6%; Orthodox: 3%; and other: 13.4%.

**Birth Rate**: 9.08 births per 1,000 population

**Death Rate**: 10.76 per 1,000 population

**Infant Mortality Rate**: 5.46 deaths per 1,000 live births

**Net Migration Rate**: 0.96 migrant(s) per 1,000 population

**Total Fertility Rate**: 1.18 children born per woman

**Population Growth Rate**: –0.07%. The birthrate is about 1.13, and the balance sheet of population has remained negative for the last five years (in 2001 it was –18.091). Such a deficit is not fully compensated for with immigrants (about 8,000 people in 2001).

**HIV/AIDS** (1999 est.): *Adult prevalence*: 0.04%; *Persons living with HIV/AIDS*: 2,200; *Deaths*: < 100. (For additional details from www.UNAIDS.org, see end of Section 10B.)

**Literacy Rate** (*defined as those age 15 and over who can read and write*): Literacy is practically universal with nine years of compulsory education. In 2001, 16.5% of men and 29.1% of women had only a basic education. Meanwhile, 10% of men and 7.1% of women had a university degree.

**Per Capita Gross Domestic Product** (*purchasing power parity*): IS$15,300—about 70% of the GDP average within the European Union (2002 est.); *Inflation*: 5% (2001 est.); *Unemployment*: 9%; *Living below the poverty line*: NA. The Czech Republic is a member of NATO and one of the best-prepared candidate countries for the membership in the European Union (EU).

### B. A Brief Historical Perspective

Probably sometime in the 5th century of the Common Era, Slavic tribes from the Vistula basin settled in the region of the traditional Czech lands of Bohemia, Moravia, and Silesia. The Czechs founded the kingdom of Bohemia, the Premyslide dynasty, which ruled Bohemia and Moravia as the Great Moravian Empire from the 10th to the 16th century. This later became part of the Holy Roman Empire. Charles IV, one of the Bohemian kings and a Holy Roman emperor, made Prague an imperial capital and a center of

---

*Communications*: Asst. Prof. Jaroslav Zvěřina, M.D., Sexuologicky Ustav, 1. lekarske fakulty, Univerzity Karlovy Karlovo nam, 32, 120 00 Prague 2, Czech Republic; jaroslav.zverina@lf1.cuni.cz *or* zverina@psp.cz.

**Editor's Note: Because there was minimal information about the Slovak Republic in the original chapter in volume 1 of the *International Encyclopedia of Sexuality*, this revised chapter focuses only on the Czech Republic and omits the data on Slovakia.

Latin scholarship. In the 14th century, Prague was the cultural center of Central Europe.

Early in the Reformation Movement in the Christian Church, the Hussite movement founded by Jan Hus (1369?-1415) linked the Slavs to the Protestant Reformation and revived Czech nationalism, which had previously faded under German domination. After Ferdinand I, a Hapsburg, ascended the throne in 1526, the Czechs rebelled in 1618, precipitating the Thirty Years' War (1618-1648). Defeated in 1620, the Czechs became part of the Austrian empire for the next 300 years. Full independence from the Hapsburgs was not achieved until the end of World War I, following the collapse of the Austro-Hungarian Empire.

A union of the Czech lands and Slovakia was proclaimed in Prague on November 14, 1918, and the Czech nation became one of the two component parts of the newly formed state of Czechoslovakia. In March 1939, when German troops occupied Czechoslovakia, Hitler proclaimed Czech Bohemia and Moravia protectorates and declared Slovakia independent. The former government returned in April 1945 to power when World War II ended and the country's pre-1938 boundaries were restored. Communists became the dominant political party in 1946 and gained control of the Czechoslovakian government two years later. Soon thereafter, the former democracy was turned into a Soviet-style state. Nearly 42 years of Communist rule ended when Vaclav Havel, a highly respected writer and dissident, was elected president of Czechoslovakia in 1989 in what was known as "the Velvet Revolution." The return of democratic political reform saw a strong Slovak nationalist movement emerge by the end of 1991. Independence then became an issue for Slovakia. When the general elections of June 1992 failed to resolve the continuing coexistence of the two republics within the federation, Czech and Slovak political leaders agreed to separate their states into two fully independent nations. On January 1, 1993, the Czechoslovakian federation was dissolved and two separate independent countries were established, the Czech Republic and Slovakia. In March 1999, the Czech Republic joined NATO. The country's next goal in international relations is to gain entrance into the European Union in 2004.

## 1. Basic Sexological Premises

### A. Character of Gender Roles

The prevailing character of gender roles in the Czech Republic is traditionally European in accordance with the Judeo-Christian culture. Masculinity is connected with social dominance, and the socioeconomic status of women is still under the average status of men. The number of women employed outside the home is high and their role in family and childcare is underestimated. In 2001, about 58% of men and 46% of women were economically active. The employment rate for women is one of the highest in Europe.

### B. Sociolegal Status of Males and Females

Both men and women have the same political rights. In both civil and criminal law, both genders are traditionally equal in the Czech Republic. Basic schools, colleges, and universities are coeducational. The principle of nondiscrimination according to gender and sexual orientation is fully respected in accord with the Charter of Fundamental Rights.

### C. General Concepts of Sexuality and Love

According to the Judeo-Christian tradition, the couple concept of sexuality is dominant. Most couples base their sexual relationships on romantic love. Marriage is still very popular, which is in contrast with the very low fertility rate of 1.18 children born per woman and a negative population growth rate since 1998. Under the communist dictatorship, erotic and sexuality topics were kept out of the mass media. With the growing impact of HIV/AIDS and the changing political atmosphere after 1989, there has been a shift to more-open discussions about sex and sexual morals.

## 2. Religious, Ethnic, and Gender Factors Affecting Sexuality

### A. Source and Character of Religious Values

Christianity is still a dominant religious influence in the Czech Republic, with Roman Catholics in the majority. The Czech Republic also has an old tradition of Protestantism. In the 15th-century Protestant movement against the Roman Church, Jan Hus and Jan Žižka were very influential religious reformers and martyrs. In 1415, the Council of Constance condemned Hus to be burned at the stake. In the 16th and 17th centuries, Jan Comenius, a Moravian educational reformer and bishop, was a major religious reformer. In today's Czech Republic, religiosity has only a limited influence on the citizens. The country is very secularized, partly as a result of 50 years of atheist communist propaganda. Forty percent of Czech profess to be atheists. This situation seems not to be changing under democratic government within last ten years.

### B. Source and Character of Ethnic Values

In terms of ethnicity, the population of the Czech Republic is very homogenous. Practically all ethnical minorities (Polish, German, Slovak, and Gypsies) have very similar ethical and cultural values. Within the last ten years, more legal and illegal immigrants are living in the country, with most of them coming from countries of the formerly Soviet Union. The Czech Republic now has some communities of people from China and Vietnam.

## 3. Knowledge and Education about Sexuality

### A. Government Policies and Programs

Basic knowledge about sexual anatomy and physiology is provided as part of the basic school curriculum. Part of the official sex education is prevention of STDs and HIV/AIDS. However, information about sexual hygiene, safer sex practices, and contraception are not universally covered within such curricula. Almost universally ignored in sex education are topics like homosexuality, paraphilias, and sexual delinquency.

### B. Informal Sources of Sexual Knowledge

As a consequence of the insufficient formal education, children and young people get the major part of their information about sex from peer groups and mass media. Attitudes towards erotic explicit materials are very liberal in the Czech Republic. Most Czech journals and magazines have some columns devoted to sexual topics and problems.

According to our latest findings using a representative sample of 2,003 Czech respondents in 1998, a third of Czechs, 37% of men and 32% of women, listed their peers as their main source of sexual information. Books were the second most common source for 19% of men and 23% of women. Television and the mass media ranked third, for 21% of men and 16% of women (Weiss & Zvěřina 2001). The participation of schools in sex education is growing very slowly.

## 4. Autoerotic Behaviors and Patterns

In all sources of sex education, self-pleasuring (masturbation) is almost universally presented as an important and natural part of normal human sexuality. Myths about the unnaturalness and harmfulness of autoeroticism are only rarely mentioned, although letters of readers to sex publications indicate that, despite negative beliefs and fears, people do engage in autoeroticism. This applies to both children and adults. Sometimes, but rarely, parents complain to physicians about the masturbation practices of their children, but medicalization of this phenomenon is very rare.

In a representative sample of 2,003 Czech respondents in 1998, 84% of men and 58% of women reported masturbating sometime in their lives, with the average age of first masturbation being 14 years for men and 17 years for women. Only 5% of men and 10% of women said that masturbation poses some health risk (Weiss & Zvěřina 2001).

## 5. Interpersonal Heterosexual Behaviors

### A. Children

The sexual games of children are usually played in secret and ignored by parents if discovered. They are not the objects of particular sanctions in most Czech families.

### B. Adolescents

*Puberty Rituals*

There are no special or institutionalized rituals that recognize either puberty or the initiation of a nonmarital sexual relationship.

*Premarital Sexual Activities and Relationships*

First sexual intercourse usually occurs between ages 17 and 18. Criminal law sets the minimum age of consent for sexual intercourse at age 15 for both men and women. This law applies equally to both heterosexual and homosexual intercourse. Premarital sexual intercourse is very common, with 98% of women having had sexual intercourse before marriage. Premarital sex is quietly tolerated, but not openly accepted or endorsed by parents for women under age 18. The average number of premarital sexual partners is one or two for women and two to four for men.

In a representative sample of Czech adults over age 15 years, the average age reported for first coitus was 18.1 years for men and 18 years for women. More than 40% of these first experiences occurred in a cottage or outdoors; without contraceptives for 57% of the men and 64% of the women; and with an "occasional partner" for 34% of the men and 12% of the women (Weiss & Zvěřina 2001).

In 1993, the author of this chapter carried out a representative survey of the sexual life of Prague youths of age 15 to 29 years. Seventy-eight percent of the men and 83% of the women reported having had sexual intercourse, with the average age for first coitus 17.3 years for men and 17.4 for women. In this same survey, sexually active men reported an average of 8.1 coital partners, while women reported an average of 6.6 partners. Nearly two thirds of the men and 73% of the women reported having a sexual partner in the previous year. Nine percent of the males and 18% of the women reported only one sexual partner. One in five males and one in eight females reported having had more than ten sexual partners in their lives. The most common sexual expression was vaginal coitus (96% of sexually active men and 99% of sexually active women). Fellatio was refused by 16% of the women surveyed, while anal heterosexual

intercourse was reported by 22% of the men and 16% of the women (Weiss & Zvěřina 2001).

### C. Adults

*Premarital Courtship, Dating, and Relationships*

Courtship and dating customs are similar to those in other European countries and are based on the romantic model. There are no major differences in the dating and courtship patterns of young Czechs living in the cities or rural areas. There are no special courtship customs. Only in very small rural areas in South Moravia persisted in some engagement rituals in folklore.

Under the communist regime, the age of first marriage was relatively low, about 21 years, for most men, with their brides generally being about a year younger. During the 40 years of communist rule, the government supported early marriage with a system of government benefits and loans. Under communism, and down to the present, it has been extremely difficult for a single man or woman to obtain a flat or apartment. In addition, marriage and having a first child is an important social signal of having grown up and achieved adult status. During the 1990s, the average marriage age for men and women gradually crept upward. In 1990s, the age of first marriage was on average 24 years for men and 21 years for women. In 2001, it was 28 years for men and 25 years for women (ČSÚ 2002). This recent evolution has extended the gap between coital debut and marriage. Also more obvious today than ten years ago is the cohabitation of couples who live together without marriage.

In a 1994 study of Czech adults over age 15 years, men reported an average of 12.2 sexual partners, women 5.1 partners, with 1.8 and 1.9 partners, respectively, for the previous year. The average coital frequency in heterosexual partnerships was 8.4 times monthly. Three quarters of the men and 82% of women reported being "fully satisfied with their sexual life" (Zvěřina 1994a). In 1998, a similar investigation found men reporting an average of 10.1 partners and women 5.1 sexual partners in their lifetime at that point, and an average of 1.7 and 1.5 partners for men and women, respectively, in the previous year (Weiss & Zvěřina 2001).

*Marriage and the Family*

As in most parts of the world, heterosexual monogamy is the dominant pattern of sexual behavior in the Czech Republic. At the same time, and following the same pattern elsewhere in Europe and North America, serial or successive monogamy is becoming a common modification. The 1990 Czech marriage rate was 8.8 per 1,000 inhabitants; the divorce rate was 40.81 per 100 marriages. The average age of first marriage in 1990 was 23.7 for men and 21.3 for women. During the 1990s, this age has been continuously rising, as shown in Table 1.

Substantial rises in the age by first marriage and the age of mothers at the birth of a first child are indicators of changes in reproductive behavior after the "velvet revolution." Political and social changes have led to an extremely low fertility rate.

Several studies indicate the incidence of extramarital intercourse at between 25% and 35% of husbands and wives, with extramarital sex more frequent for men. Most of these extramarital activities are short-lived and infrequent. Rea-

**Table 1**

**Average Age by First Marriage in the Czech Republic, 1992-2001**

| Year | 1992 | 1993 | 1994 | 1995 | 1996 | 1997 | 1998 | 1999 | 2000 | 2001 |
|------|------|------|------|------|------|------|------|------|------|------|
| Men | 24.2 | 24.4 | 24.7 | 25.0 | 25.4 | 25.9 | 26.3 | 26.7 | 27.1 | 27.6 |
| Women | 21.6 | 21.7 | 22.0 | 22.4 | 22.8 | 23.3 | 23.6 | 24.1 | 24.6 | 25.0 |

sons for extramarital sex have not been studied, although it is likely that sexual variety and the attraction of a new experience are common motivations. Eighteen percent of men and 31% of women held that extramarital sex is "ethically unacceptable behavior" (Zvěřina 1994a, Weiss & Zvěřina 2001).

In recent decades, there has been an escalating problem of single-parent families, mostly divorced mothers with children. The divorce rate used to be relatively high—about 40%—with the average duration of marriage about ten years. More than 70% of marriages that end in divorce have a minimum of one minor child. Single mothers have a state-guaranteed minimum standard of living, plus the economic support from the father of their children. Czech and Slovak societies are not hostile to unwed mothers or divorced women. Surveys suggest that coital frequency for most married couples is one to three times per week.

As mentioned earlier, the Czech birthrate is low, with substantial decreases during the 1990s (see Table 2). The birthrate in 1978 was 18.4 per 1,000 inhabitants. In 1992, it had dropped to 12.2 per 1,000, and in 2002, it was under 9.0. The fertility rate was under 1.2 in 2002, one of the lowest in Europe. Most married couples plan to have one or two children. Planning for more than two children in a family is extremely unusual.

### Sexuality and the Physically Disabled and Aged

Sexual behavior and sexual problems of mentally and physically handicapped persons are only rarely mentioned in public. The same is true with sexologists and marriage counselors. Since the dissolution of communist control in the "velvet revolution" of 1989, there has been a growing activity of different nongovernmental organizations (NGOs) seeking to promote the care and well-being of the physically handicapped. Enhanced attention is paid to sexual and reproductive functions of people with transversal spinal injuries (Šrámková 1997).

As elsewhere, there are more single women than single men over age 60. Older women are less likely to find an acceptable partner than older single men. We know that interest in sex in the later years has a direct connection with the availability of an appropriate sexual partner. An additional problem in the republic is that the living standard in state facilities for older persons is not conducive to couples' maintaining intimate relationships. In most cases, the state facilities for the elderly are based on a collectivist model.

### Incidence of Oral and Anal Sex

Oral sex is widely accepted and practiced by Czechs and Slovaks. Respondents in several surveys indicated that about 70% of men and women engage in oral sex as a part of their sexual intimacy. In a 1994 survey, 74% of men and 67% of women acknowledge experience with some oral sexual practice. Figures from 1998 were similar (Weiss & Zvěřina 2001).

### Table 2

### Fertility and Abortions in the Czech Republic

|      | Births  | Induced Abortions | Spontaneous Abortions |
|------|---------|-------------------|-----------------------|
| 1990 | 130,564 | 111,268           | 14,772                |
| 1995 | 96,097  | 49,531            | 10,571                |
| 1996 | 90,446  | 48,542            | 11,420                |
| 1997 | 90,657  | 44,471            | 11,500                |
| 1998 | 90,535  | 42,959            | 11,128                |
| 1999 | 89,471  | 39,382            | 11,173                |
| 2000 | 90,910  | 36,300            | 11,070                |
| 2001 | 90,715  | 34,500            | 10,516                |

In 1994, 15% of men and 12% of women acknowledged experience with anal sex. In 1998, 20% of men and 17% of women reported experience with anal intercourse. In most cases, where reported, this activity was exceptional and infrequent.

Sexual practices are not the object of legal regulations. The sexual behavior of consenting adult partners is free from any restriction by criminal law.

## 6. Homoerotic, Homosexual, and Bisexual Behaviors

### A. Children and Adolescents

Same-gender sexual experiences are a natural part of the sexual play and exploration of children. However, their prevalence does not appear to be high. Only about 10% of men and 5% of women in the heterosexual population report having had same-gender experiences in childhood and early adolescence. In the population of gay men and lesbians, such experiences are, of course, more common.

### B. Adults

Attitudes towards homosexuality among the greater part of the Czech population are hostile or ambivalent. Homophobia and hostility towards homosexual people are more common among people in the lower socioeconomic classes. The pandemic of AIDS has brought some changes, mostly in the attitudes towards gays. It seems there is a greater tolerance of stable gay partnerships and couples, and the existence of gay clubs and associations. However, 33% of men and 41% of women in the 1994 adult survey considered homosexuality a disease. Twenty-two percent of both Czech men and women fully accept homosexuality.

In 1994, 3.4% of the men and 2.6% of the women reported sexual experience with a partner of the same sex. One percent of both male and female respondents self-identified as homosexual with another 1% unsure. In 1998, these figures were 6.2% and 4.4%, respectively. This means that sexual experience with a same-sex partner is becoming more frequent, or that respondents are more comfortable admitting this behavior. In more than 60% of male homosexual coitus, condoms were not used (Weiss & Zvěřina 2001).

In the penal law code, which went into effect in 1990, no distinction is made between heterosexual and homosexual behaviors. The age of legal consent to sexual intercourse was formerly 15 years for heterosexuals and 18 years for homosexuals. Now the age is the same for both heterosexuals and homosexuals, 15 years. This new code revoked the partial criminalization of homosexuality that existed in the previous code. At present, there is a movement to reduce the intolerance and inequities homosexual persons experience socially. These involve paying more attention to the situation of homosexual men and women in the workplace, in schools (both students and teachers), and in the army.

Most gay and lesbian associations are engaged in a movement to legalize the unions or marriages—also called "registered partnerships"—of homosexual couples. Important politicians support some kind of legalization of long-term homosexual partnerships. The attitude of the Catholic Church on homosexuality is, at present, still fundamentally rigid and hostile. Some Protestant Christian churches, on the other hand, are traditionally more liberal and less rigid.

Bisexual behavior is more common among homosexual persons than among the heterosexual majority. About 60% of the homosexual men surveyed and more than 70% of the lesbians reported having had heterosexual intercourse some time in their lives. Among heterosexual men and women surveyed, only 12% of the men and 5% of the women reported some same-gender sexual contacts. Most of the same-gender contacts reported did not involve coitus.

While homosexual men tend to be more sexually promiscuous than lesbians, the frequency of anonymous sexual contacts under poor aesthetic conditions is decreasing. One hopes that this is connected with the increasing sex and AIDS-prevention education programs. The prevailing pattern at present is stable, long-term gay and lesbian relationships.

Sexual practices among homosexuals in the Czech Republic are the same as in other parts of the Western world. Among homosexual men, active and passive (receptive), anal intercourse is common. Condoms and lubricant gels are used with growing frequency.

## 7. Gender Diversity and Transgender Issues

Fetishistic transvestitism is a paraphilia with seemingly low incidence among males in both the Czech Republic and Slovakia. In some cases, transvestite males bring their problems to sexological counseling centers. Most of these problems are connected with the partner's/wife's hostility toward the client's cross-dressing and its impact on their sexual practices.

The prevalence of transsexualism also appears to be low, as in other European countries. Interestingly, the sex ratio of transsexuals in the republics' sexological centers is the opposite of what it is in Western Europe. In the records of the Institute of Sexology at the Charles University in Prague, for instance, there are three times as many female-to-male transsexuals as male-to-female transsexuals. In most Western European gender clinics, twice as many male-to-female transsexuals are reported as female-to-male. Colleagues in Poland report a ratio similar to that in Prague. Different social conditions and gender viewpoints in east and west European countries may be a factor in this difference in ratios.

Treatment for transsexual persons follows the common step-by-step practice in respected gender clinics around the world. Initial counseling and screening is followed by months of psychotherapy and sociotherapy. In allowing the client to adapt better to a reversal in gender role, it is possible to change the patient's name to a gender-neutral one; in Czech, the given and family names usually indicate the person's gender. However, some names are gender neutral and the same for either a male or a female.

Following months of hormone treatment, the decision for anatomical sex reversal surgery can be made. Sex reassignment surgery, which involves plastic surgery and gonad removal with consequent infertility, is required for an official and complete sex-reversal procedure.

Sex-reassignment surgery is available for both female-to-male and male-to-female transsexuals as part of the health insurance system. From a medical point of view, transsexuals are seen as people with inappropriate development of secondary sexual characteristics. In the Czech Republic, about eight patients a year request official sex-change surgery.

## 8. Significant Unconventional Sexual Behaviors

### A. Coercive Sexual Behaviors

*Sexual Abuse, Incest, and Rape*

The statistics on criminal sexual delinquencies are low when compared with most western European countries or with the USA. Twelve percent of women in the 1994 adult Czech survey reported an experience with rape, while 5% of the men admitted forcing sex on a woman. In 1998, these figures were 13% and 5%, respectively. Most of these assaults were not reported to the police or other authorities.

In 2001, there was a substantial change in the definition of rape in the Czech criminal law. The previous law defined a rape as sexual violence, perpetrated by a man on a woman. The new definition removed the "gender-specific" description and now defines a rape as sexually motivated violence, without reference to the gender of the victim or perpetrator.

Sexological investigations of criminal sexual delinquents requested by the police and courts are generally grouped in three main categories: (1) indecent exposure, (2) sexual molestation or abuse of children and minors, and (3) rape and other sexual assaults.

Approximately 8% of women and 4.6% of men in 1994 stated that they had been the object of sexual abuse as a child. In 1998, it was 10.4% and 7.1%, respectively.

In recent years, greater attention has been paid to sexual abuse and incest. The common experience is that the most threatened individuals in terms of sexual abuse and incest are children in single-parent families. The most frequent perpetrator is a stepfather or the boyfriend of the mother of the victimized child.

The police subject a woman who reports a rape to a very careful and long investigation. Hearings and questioning of the woman can last up to five hours or more. Once a charge is made, the woman cannot withdraw it. Nor can she discuss the accusation with anyone other than the police. If she does, she can be prosecuted for false accusation. At the court hearing, the woman has to answer questions from the court, the defense attorney, and the accused male, in what can be a very traumatizing experience. Similar procedures are followed in cases of child abuse.

At present, there are only a few special centers for counseling and support of the victims of rape and sexual abuse founded and directed by NGOs.

When apprehended, perpetrators of sexual assault are examined both from psychiatric and sexological perspectives. In cases of psychopathological or paraphilic motivation, the court can commit the perpetrator to compulsory treatment in a hospital psychiatric department or in an outpatient clinic. Specialized sexological departments in most psychiatric hospitals are staffed with personnel trained in treatment of dangerous sexual delinquents.

### Sexual Harassment

Men can be sued for comments and sexually explicit (dirty language), but accusations and court cases involving accusations of men making sexual advances to women, using indecent language, or sexually harassing women are rare. [*Comment 1997*: A 1996 report by J. Perlez suggests that Central European countries and corporations are being slowly influenced by Western concepts of sexual harassment. In a high-profile case in the Czech Republic, a manager at a major state bank was dismissed after a secretary filed a sexual harassment complaint against him. In a 1995 case involving the same manager, the bank refused to act. (See additional comments in Section 8A of the chapter on Poland) (Perlez 1996) (*End of comment by R. T. Francoeur*)]

In 2002, the Czech labor law was changed to give the possibility of penalization for sex harassment in the workplace. Experience with the new legal statute is still limited.

### B. Prostitution

Prostitution is a common phenomenon in the Czech Republic. There are probably several thousand prostitutes working in Prague and in other greater cities. Some work in massage parlors and exotic clubs, but most frequent hotels, bars, and restaurants. Since the collapse of the Communist regimes, there has been a migration of Czech prostitutes to the West, and from Eastern European countries to the Czech

Republic. Street prostitution is concentrated at the borderline with Germany and Austria and along the highways. Nine percent of men in 1994 and 14% in 1998 reported paying at some time for sex. No men and only 3% of women had engaged in sex for money in our exploration of the sexual behavior (Weiss & Zvěřina 2001).

Prostitution, as such, in the Czech Republic is not penalized. Pimping and trafficking of people are, of course, criminal offenses.

Some Czech cities have great problems with street prostitutes and their negative influence on tourists and citizens. In this context, the possibilities of legal regulation of prostitution are frequently discussed. Some Czech politicians criticize contemporary abolitionist law. The government is trying to find a solution in partially regulating "sex workers."

Some nongovernmental organizations are active in social, health, and hygienic help for prostitutes, for example "RR" (Rozkoš bez Rizika: "Pleasure Without Risk").

### C. Pornography and Erotica

In comparison with the situation before 1989, the contemporary production and availability of sexually explicit materials has increased significantly. Soft erotica is free from restrictions. Hard-core magazines, book, and audiovisual materials are sold in special shops, which are restricted for minors under 18 years of age.

In our 1994 survey, 4% of the men and 8% of the women thought that pornography should be prohibited; 11% and 20%, respectively, thought pornography to be dangerous. In 1998, these figures were 9% and 14%, and 20% and 21%, respectively. More frequently, however, contact with explicit erotic materials could promote a greater sensitivity and more-negative attitudes.

### D. Paraphilias

Paraphiliacs at present have more opportunities for communication and contact than they had under the communists. Some sexual-contact magazines, advertisement services, and clubs now exist for these people. Most of the interest is in sadomasochism and fetishistic practices. Groups which produce pedophilic pornography, both heterosexual and homosexual, are repeatedly investigated by the police. Some paraphilic erotic materials are accessible on the Internet.

Some people with ego-dystonic paraphilias seek help at the counseling centers and sexological departments. More frequently, sexologists are called on to treat paraphiliacs who have been arrested as perpetrators of some sexual crime. In such situations, consultation with a psychothera-

pist is required, and treatment can be paid for from the national health insurance.

## 9. Contraception, Abortion, and Population Planning

### A. Contraception

The birthrate in the Czech republic is very low. About 49% of all children are not planned, but only 1.4% of all newborns are placed for adoption. The fact that almost half of all pregnancies are unwanted poses a major problem and challenge. In 1990, the most popular contraception in the Czech Republic was coitus interruptus, which 40% of the Czech women relied on at their risk (1991 data). A third of Czech women, 31%, used barrier methods, particularly the condom and IUD. The hormonal contraceptive pill was used by 8% and sterilization by 2%. The low incidence of hormonal contraception and surgical sterilization was a national problem. See Table 3 for a comparison of contraceptive use by men and women in 1994 and 1998.

### B. Teenage (Unmarried) Pregnancies

The number of pregnancies in women under age 15 is low. Slovak and Czech teenage women have limited access to contraception. Contraceptive pills can only be obtained from a gynecologist, and the attitude of many gynecologists toward hormonal contraception for young women is not always a positive one. Hormonal contraception is not paid by health insurance and could be relatively expensive for some young women.

As shown in Table 4, the share teenagers have in the total fertility of the Czech Republic has steadily decreased from 13.0% in 1990 to 5.6% in 2000. The number of pregnant women under age 18 is also low. Table 5 shows the number

### Table 3

**Contraception in the Czech Republic: Percentage of Men and Women Who Have Ever Used a Particular Method**

| Method | 1994 | | 1998 | |
|---|---|---|---|---|
| | Men | Women | Men | Women |
| Withdrawal | 79% | 75% | 76% | 64% |
| IUD | – | 31 | – | 25 |
| Condoms | 66 | – | 70 | – |
| Oral contraception | – | 63 | – | 60 |
| Natural/rhythm | 44 | 41 | 42 | 26 |

### Table 4

**Different Age Groups of Czech Women and Their Fertility in 1990-2000 (Percentage Share of Fertility in Particular Age Groups)**

| Age | 1990 | 1991 | 1992 | 1993 | 1994 | 1995 | 1996 | 1997 | 1998 | 1999 | 2000 |
|---|---|---|---|---|---|---|---|---|---|---|---|
| < 20 | 13.0 | 13.5 | 13.5 | 12.7 | 11.0 | 9.3 | 8.0 | 7.1 | 6.6 | 6.4 | 5.6 |
| 20-24 | 46.1 | 46.0 | 44.9 | 43.7 | 42.4 | 40.3 | 38.6 | 36.5 | 34.4 | 31.8 | 29.2 |
| 25-29 | 27.4 | 27.0 | 27.7 | 28.5 | 29.9 | 31.8 | 33.2 | 35.0 | 36.3 | 37.7 | 39.2 |
| 30-34 | 10.1 | 10.0 | 10.3 | 11.1 | 12.2 | 13.6 | 14.7 | 15.5 | 16.4 | 17.5 | 18.8 |
| 35 + | 3.4 | 3.5 | 3.6 | 4.0 | 4.5 | 5.0 | 5.5 | 5.9 | 6.3 | 6.6 | 6.2 |

### Table 5

**Number and Share of Children Born Outside of Marriage, 1993-2000**

| | 1993 | 1994 | 1995 | 1996 | 1997 | 1998 | 1999 | 2000 |
|---|---|---|---|---|---|---|---|---|
| Number of children | 15,434 | 15,570 | 15,013 | 15,367 | 16,194 | 17,284 | 18,532 | 19,868 |
| Share of children of all births | 12.7% | 14.6% | 15.6% | 16.9% | 17.8% | 19.0% | 20.6% | 21.8% |

and share of children born outside of marriage in the Czech Republic between 1993 and 2000.

## C. Abortion

The law regulating induced abortion in the former Czechoslovakia was liberalized in 1956. Between 1956 and 1986, women seeking an abortion had to present their request to special "abortion commissions." After 1987, pregnant women could obtain an abortion simply by requesting it. Induced abortion is legal until the 12th week of gestation. Abortion for medical reasons or to protect the woman's health is legal up to the 24th week of gestation. Illegal abortions are rare. In the 1994 adult survey, 60% of women and 58% of the men were fully "pro-choice." This situation was not changing in the repeat survey in 1998. Only 3% of both men and women believed the law should prohibit induced abortion.

In the last two years, the number of legally induced abortions has declined. More than 85% of all abortions are performed in the first two months of gestation as "mini-interruptions." RU-486 is not available.

The number of legally induced abortions per 1,000 women decreased from 1991 to 2001, from 111,268 to 34,500. Such a radical change is, of course, connected with all these dramatic shifts in different segments of the Czech society during the last decade.

From the point of view of the prevention of induced abortions, two things seemed to have great importance: The first is substantially better availability of modern contraception; the second is dramatic change in the value system of citizens, with great influence on the reproductive behavior of people.

## D. Population Programs

In the 20 years between 1970 and 1989, the communist Czechoslovak government made some efforts to promote population growth. All of these efforts utilized economic incentives. Money was provided for the support of each additional child at above the standard of normal living. Families with three or four children received increased support and benefits. All of these efforts had only a temporary effect, and no substantial long-term success.

At present, the state population policy is relatively liberal, based on the free choice and reproductive rights of people. The main goal is to enhance the social and reproductive responsibility of the people. The state supports some sexual educational and healthcare programs. Nongovernmental organizations also sponsor activities, including education programs aimed at improving contraceptive use and lowering the number of legally induced abortions for non-medical reasons.

One of the stable questions within domestic politics used to be state support for young families with children, which is now seen to be insufficient.

## 10. Sexually Transmitted Diseases and HIV/AIDS

## A. Sexually Transmitted Diseases

*Incidence, Patterns, and Trends*

At present, the incidence of STDs and AIDS is relatively low. In the young Czech citizens survey, only 7% of males and 16.5% of females reported some experience with a sexually transmitted disease. This is because of 40 years of communist policy, which, in a substantial way, restricted the free movement of people. After the frontiers were opened in 1989, the movement of people into and out of the country increased. This new mobility and migration is already increasing the number of STD cases in the larger cities and in regions near the western frontier.

*Syphilis.* In the 1980s, no more than four cases of syphilis were reported annually per 100,000 inhabitants. In 1991, the rate of new syphilis cases was 1.3 per 100,000, with more women than men affected; in 1995, it was 4.0 and in the 2001 already 12.5. Such a rapid elevation of STD prevalence is conditioned by greater migration, primarily from Eastern Europe, where the prevalence of STDs is very high. In the last decade, some small local epidemics of syphilis, imported from abroad, were registered.

*Gonorrhea.* In the 1980s, the annual incidence of gonorrhea was under 100 cases per 100,000 inhabitants. In 1991, 71% of all cases were men between ages 15 and 24. In 1992, the incidence of gonorrhea increased significantly in some regions on the north and west frontiers and in Prague. This is one of the first signs of a new STD epidemic developing under new social conditions. Contemporary prevalence of gonorrhea is officially very low. In 1991, it was approximately 70 cases per 100,000 inhabitants and in 2000 only 10 cases. This decline is only an estimate, based on the unwillingness of physicians to report these cases.

Actual clinical experience reveals a remarkable increase in the incidence of all other STDs, including genital warts, papilloma virus infections, genital herpes, nonspecific urethritis, pelvic inflammatory disease (PID), chlamydia, cervical dysplasias, and cervical carcinomas.

*Availability of Treatment and Prevention Efforts*

The law requires that all new cases of classical venereal diseases be reported to the Ministry of Health Care. Infected persons are also required by law to give health professionals information about all sexual partners. Diagnosis and treatment for STDs is easily available in all the larger cities, at dermatovenereological departments, clinics, and gynecological and urological departments.

The main factor in the primary prevention of STDs is responsible sexual behavior. Sexual education should be started at a very young age and should include information of the health risks of sexual behavior. Some particular groups, "at-risk populations," need special attention with specifically designed sexual education programs. Such programs would promote safer sex information among promiscuous heterosexuals, homosexuals, prostitutes, and highly mobile minorities (tourists and professional drivers). There are many nongovernmental organizations that are active in the sex education and the promotion of STD-prevention efforts. However, sexologists are not completely satisfied with the present situation in sex education. In the Czech Republic, sex education is a compulsory part of the educational programs in schools, but the level and quality of these programs varies widely. The involvement of the mass media, radio, and television in this area is not consistent.

## B. HIV/AIDS

*Incidence, Patterns, and Trends*

Thus far, the incidence of HIV infection in the republic is low. At the end of 1992, there were 143 known cases of HIV infection and 32 cases of AIDS in the Czech Republic, 93 of them being homosexual or bisexual men and 30 hemophiliacs or blood-transfusion recipients. Only one IV-drug user has registered. Ten cases involved heterosexual transmission and 9 cases had unknown sources. Of the 143 known cases, 11 were women and 7 were children under age 15.

In 1995, there were 249 HIV-positive cases, including 72 cases of AIDS; in 2001, 501 HIV-positive cases, and 149 cases of AIDS were reported. Most of the HIV-positives are men, approximately 80%, with the main source of infection being sexual contacts with men. Intravenous drug abusers are very rare in the Czech Republic, with only about 4% of HIV-positive cases being intravenous-drug users.

The low incidence of HIV infection is well demonstrated by the results of several preventive and anonymous screenings for HIV. In 2002, 800,000 HIV tests were conducted in the country, with positive findings in only 70 cases (including 21 foreigners).

Persons with suspected HIV infection or AIDS are protected under a special rule guaranteeing their personal freedom to seek or refuse testing.

For 96% of the Czech men and women, the main source of information about HIV/AIDS is the mass media.

### Treatment, Prevention, and Government Policy

The Czech Ministry of Health Care has a special program for the prevention and treatment of HIV/AIDS. This program has a self-contained budget. There are centers for HIV/AIDS investigation and treatment in all regional centers, and in the capital city, Prague.

Anonymous testing for HIV is available in all larger cities free of charge. Government policy fully respects the international standards of the World Health Organization. The national center for HIV/AIDS has been operating by the National Health Care Institute in Prague (www.aids-hiv.cz) for several years.

The Ministry of Health Care has been coordinating governmental activities with nongovernmental organizations and institutions. An AIDS-Help society, SAP [Společnost AIDS Pomoc], was founded in 1991. Sexual education is actively promoted by the Sexological society and by the Czech Family Planning Association [SPRSV–Společnost pro Plánování Rodiny a Sexuální Výchovu]. Many hotlines and telephone counseling services are operating with varying professional standards.

Programs for training counselors and health professionals are just being organized. Work with "at-risk" populations does not have a long tradition, because the communist government did not acknowledge such groups.

An organization for prostitutes was started in 1992 (RR–Pleasure Without Risk). Propagation of safer sex information among promiscuous homosexual men and promiscuous heterosexuals is possible with the collaboration of gay self-help groups like the Lambda Klub and through erotic magazines and video-rental clubs. SOHO is an NGO, which is trying to represent different gay and lesbian groups in the country.

The author's 1993 survey of 984 residents of Prague ($N = 485$ males and 499 females) between the ages of 15 and 29 contained 30 questions about past and present sexual behavior designed to elicit information on the risk of HIV infection. The most frequent sources of information about HIV/AIDS were books and magazines (for more than 50% of males and females). Parents and school were the main information source for less that 10% of the respondents. More than 90% of the male and female respondents were appropriately informed about HIV transmission, although 20% believed that insects, kissing, or sneezing could spread the virus. Five percent of the males and 2% of the women believed that hormonal contraception protects against HIV infection. One in four males and females felt threatened by the risk of infection. One in four males and one in five females had changed their sexual behavior as a result of this fear, with a decrease in sexual partners and an increase in condom use being the most common changes. Twenty-nine percent of males and 16% of females stated they would break with a partner if they learned that he or she was HIV-positive. Twenty-three percent of the men and 17% of the women believed persons with HIV/AIDS should be kept in isolation. Eleven percent of males and 20% of females had been tested for HIV infection at least once.

Preliminary results of the survey of Prague youth indicates that approximately a third of the youth of Prague are at very low risk for the infection, because of their monogamous lifestyle, avoidance of risky sexual practices, regular use of condoms, or complete sexual abstinence. Approximately 5% of the men and women were at high risk because of a combination of sexual promiscuity, risky sexual practices, coitus with IV-drug users, and failure to use condoms. Now that information about this risk group is on the record, it can become the subject of a government-sponsored prevention campaign.

[*Update 2002*: UNAIDS Epidemiological Assessment: By the end of 2001, a cumulative total of 551 cases of HIV infection had been officially reported. Estimated prevalence and incidence of HIVAIDS is still relatively low and the epidemiological situation seems stable. However, there are some changes in the pattern of HIV spread in the years 1995 to 1999. No HIV infection has been reported in blood donors since 1995. Heterosexual transmission of HIV is increasing and, as of the end of March 2000, was responsible for 35.7% of all registered HIV cases. The number of HIV-infected women is increasing, now comprising 20.2% of all registered HIV cases. The rate of HIV-infected pregnant women is also increasing, making up 7.1% of all HIV-infected women; during this period, the first two cases of mother-to-child HIV transmission were reported. HIV is also slowly penetrating to the subpopulation of injection drug users; at present, 4.2% of HIV infections are among injection drug users. The number of HIV infections registered among foreigners from Eastern Europe, especially from Ukraine, is increasing. The incidence of notified syphilis cases in the last few years is in the range of 3 to 4 per 100,000 population.

[The estimated number of adults and children living with HIV/AIDS on January 1, 2002, were:

| | |
|---|---|
| Adults ages 15-49: | 600  (rate: 0.1%) |
| Women ages 15-49: | < 100 |
| Children ages 0-15: | < 10 |

[An estimated less than 10 adults and children died of AIDS during 2001.

[No estimate is available for the number of Czech children who had lost one or both parents to AIDS and were under age 15 at the end of 2001. (*End of update by the Editors*)]

## 11. Sexual Dysfunctions, Counseling, and Therapies

The investigation and treatment of sexual dysfunction has a long tradition in Czechoslovakia. Since the founding of the Institute of Sexology at Charles University in Prague in 1921, sexual dysfunction has been one of the main interests. Czech sexologists have adopted a psychosomatic approach to couple sexual problems and sexual dysfunction. Strong emphasis is given to the quality of the therapeutic contact and to psychotherapeutic activities. Sexology was introduced as a particular medical specialization in 1975. Most of the clinical sexologists came into sexology from psychiatry, others from gynecology and urology. Prague has a long tradition of investigating the vascular etiology of erectile dysfunction. One of the pioneers of surgical treatment of vasculogenic impotence is Vaclav Michal from Prague.

The prevalence of sexual problems within the population was repeatedly studied in our survey. Global satisfaction with their own sexual life was expressed in 1994 by 76% of men and 82% of women. In the 1998 survey, overall satisfaction was expressed by 73% of men and only 70% of women. Very outstanding was the decline in the level of satisfaction level for women from 83% to 70%. For such a trend, we have no rational explanation, and further study of this phenomenon is needed.

Medical diagnosis and treatment of sexual dysfunction in both men and women are free of charge at present for all ages and social groups. Some medications, of course, are provided with partial payment by the patients. For example, recently introduced drugs for impotence (sildenafil, tadalafil, apomorphine—Viagra) are not covered from health insurance. Counseling and psychotherapy for sexual problems are available not only at the sexological clinics, but also at some psychological centers in the health system and in social institutions, particularly marriage-counseling centers that operate in all the larger cities in both countries.

## 12. Sex Research and Advanced Professional Education

The main center for sex research has traditionally been the Institute of Sexology at Charles University in Prague, founded in 1921. Research at this Institute has centered on behavioral sexology and on some andrological problems.

The founder of the Czech School of Medical Sexology, Josef Hynie (1900-1989), spent some time at several of the world-renowned centers of early sexology, particularly the Magnus Hirschfeld Institute of Sexology in Berlin. His successor, Jan Raboch (1915-2002), has made important investigations in both andrology and behavioral sexology. In 1977, Raboch was president of the International Academy of Sex Research (IASR). Prague has twice been the site of an annual meeting of the IASR (in 1977 and 1992).

Czech psychiatry is well known for its sexological research. In the early 1950s, Kurt Freund began his studies using penile plethysmography to investigate male sexual orientations. Ales Kolarsky and Josef Madlafousek, at the Prague Center of Psychiatric Research, extended Kurt Freund's work in penile plethysmography with important publications. Research on gender problems has been established at a new center founded by the Faculty of Philosophy of Charles University in Prague. The Czech Sexological Society used to regularly organize scientific conferences at least twice a year. "East-West" conferences on sexual abuse and sexual violence are organized every two years in Prague.

Undergraduate programs in sexology are included in some medical, pedagogical, and law faculties. Postgraduate study is available only in medicine. Admission to this postgraduate specialization is limited to those who have successfully completed the program in psychiatry, gynecology, or urology.

The main sexological institutions in the Czech and Slovak Republics are as follows:

Institute of Sexology, 1st Faculty of Medicine, Charles University, Prague. Address: Karlovo namesti 32, 120 00 Praha 2, Czech Republic. Tel./Fax: +420224966609.

Sexological Society (of the Czech Medical Society). Address: See Institute address above.

SPRSV (Společnost pro Plánování Rodiny a Sexuální Výchovu–National Family Planning Association). Address: Senovážná 2, POB 399, 111 21 Praha 1, Czech Republic.

Gay Initiative in Czech Republic. Address: Senovážné náměstí 2, 110 00 Praha 1, Czech Republic. www.gay.iniciativa.cz.

AIDS-Help (AIDS Pomoc) Society. Address: Malého 3, 180 00 Praha 8, Czech Republic. Phone: +420224814284.

## References and Suggested Readings

Český Statistický Úřad (Czech Statistical Office). 2001. Data from census. Praha (Prague).

CIA. 2002 (January). *The world factbook 2002.* Washington, DC: Central Intelligence Agency. Available: http://www.cia.gov/cia/publications/factbook/index.html

Stehlíková, M., I. Procházka, & J. Hromada. 1995. *Homosexualita, společnost a AIDS v ČR [Homosexuality, Society and AIDS in the Czech Republic].* Praha: Orbis.

Šrámková, T. 1997. *Spinal trauma from the sexological perspective [Poranění míchy pohledem sexuologa].* Praha: Svaz Paraplegiků.

UNAIDS. 2002. *Epidemiological fact sheets by country.* Geneva, Switzerland: Joint United Nations Programme on HIV/AIDS (UNAIDS/WHO). Available: http://www.unaids.org/hivaidsinfo/statistics/fact_sheets/index_en.htm.

Weiss, P., & J. Zvěřina. 2001. *Sexual behavior in the Czech Republic: Situation and trends* (in Czech). Praha: Portál Publ.

Zvěřina, J. 1994. *Lékařská sexuologie [Medical sexology].* Praha: Schering AG.

# Denmark

## (*Kongeriget Danmark*)
## (The Kingdom of Denmark)

Christian Graugaard, M.D., Ph.D., with
Lene Falgaard Eplov, M.D., Ph.D., Annamaria Giraldi,
M.D., Ph.D., Ellids Kristensen, M.D., Else Munck, M.D.,
Bo Møhl, clinical psychologist, Annette Fuglsang
Owens, M.D., Ph.D., Hanne Risør, M.D., and
Gerd Winther, clinical sexologist*

## Contents

## *Demographics and a Brief Historical Perspective*

ANNETTE FUGLSANG OWENS

### A. Demographics

Once the seat of Viking raiders and later a major European power, Denmark is located in northwestern Europe, with the southern tip of Sweden to its east, Germany to the south, Norway to the north, and Great Britain to the west. Denmark occupies the Jutland Peninsula north of Germany, and the major islands of Zealand and Funen, plus hundreds of smaller islands. The North Sea separates Denmark from Great Britain on the west, while to the north and east the Skagerak, the Kattegat, and the Baltic Sea separate it from Norway and Sweden. With a total landmass of 16,639 square miles (43,094 km²), Denmark is slightly less than twice the size of the state of Massachusetts in the United States and half the size of the state of Maine. The terrain is low and flat to gently rolling plains, and the climate temperate, humid, and overcast. Mild windy winters and cool summers predominate, interrupted by the occasional ice-winter, when islands can be reached by foot, and by periods of hot summer days, when air-conditioned facilities are longed for but rarely found. Whenever the sun shines, Danes are out to enjoy it.

In July 2002, Denmark had an estimated population of 5.37 million, with a quarter of the Danes living in metropolitan Copenhagen. (All data are from *The World Factbook 2002* (CIA 2002) unless otherwise stated.)

*Communications: Christian Graugaard: kack@post9.tele.dk; Lene Falgaard Eplov: falgaard@dadlnet.dk; Annamaria Giraldi: annamaria@giraldi.dk; Ellids Kristensen: ellids.kristensen@dadlnet .dk; Else Munck: else.munck@dadlnet.dk; Bo Møhl: bomoehl@ worldonline.dk; Annette Fuglsang Owens: info@cvillewellness .com; Hanne Risør: olerisor@post.tele.dk; Gerd Winter: gerd.winther @get2net.dk.

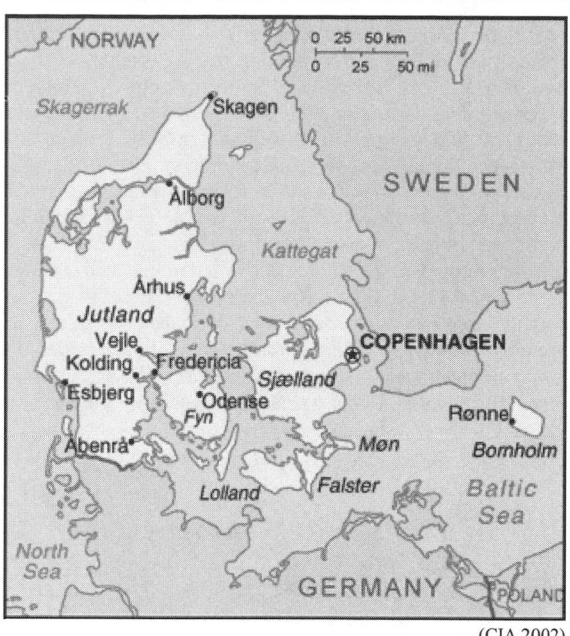

(CIA 2002)

**Age Distribution and Sex Ratios**: *0-14 years*: 18.7% with 1.05 male(s) per female (sex ratio); *15-64 years*: 66.4% with 1.03 male(s) per female; *65 years and over*: 14.9% with 0.72 male(s) per female; *Total population sex ratio*: 0.98 male(s) to 1 female

**Life Expectancy at Birth**: *Total Population*: 76.91 years; *male*: 74.3 years; *female*: 79.67 years

**Urban/Rural Distribution**: 61% to 39%

**Ethnic Distribution**: Scandinavian, Inuit, Faeroese, German, Turkish, Iranian, Pakistani, and Somali. Immigrants and their descendants constitute 7.4% of the total population.

**Religious Distribution**: Evangelical Lutheran: 95%; other Protestant, Roman Catholic, and Muslim: 5%

**Birth Rate**: 11.74 births per 1,000 population

**Death Rate**: 10.81 per 1,000 population

**Infant Mortality Rate**: 4.97 deaths per 1,000 live births

**Net Migration Rate**: 2.01 migrant(s) per 1,000 population

**Total Fertility Rate**: 1.73 children born per woman

**Population Growth Rate**: 0.29%

**HIV/AIDS** (2000 est.): *New cases*: 258; *Overall incidence*: 4.8 per 100,000 population; *Adult prevalence*: 0.17%; *Persons living with HIV/AIDS*: 4,300; *Deaths*: < 100. (For additional details from www.UNAIDS.org, see end of Section 10B.)

**Literacy Rate** (*defined as those age 15 and over who can read and write*): 100%

**Per Capita Gross Domestic Product** (*purchasing power parity*): $28,000 (2001 est.); *Inflation*: 2.4%; *Unemployment*: 5.3% (2000); *Living below the poverty line*: NA

### B. A Brief Historical Perspective

From 10,000 to 1500 B.C.E., the Danish population evolved from a society of hunters and fishermen into an agricultural one. The missionary Ansgar (801-865) and, later, king Harald Blaatand (?-985) Christianized the country in the 10th century. Bishop Absalon (1128-1201) is regarded as the founder of the city of Copenhagen, the Danish capital, situated on the east side of the country.

The Danes formed a large component of the Viking raiders in the early Middle Ages and, for centuries, the Danish kingdom was a major European power. Denmark's power began declining when Napoleon (whom the Danes supported) was defeated, and the Congress of Vienna in 1815 gave autonomy to Norway and Sweden. Schleswig-Hostein withdrew from a union with Denmark in 1864, although Northern Schleswig rejoined Denmark in 1920. Iceland declared its independence in 1944, ending a union that began in 1380. The Faeroe Islands and Greenland, the latter being the biggest island in the world, are still part of the Danish Kingdom, but with their own home rule. Denmark has been a member of the E.C. (now the European Union) since 1973. A monarchy for more than 1,100 years (one of the oldest in the world), Denmark is currently ruled by Queen Margrethe II. Nine political parties, collaborating in coalitions and led by the Prime Minister, share political power. Medical health is primarily socialized, with a small, but growing private sector.

## 1. Basic Sexological Premises

CHRISTIAN GRAUGAARD

### A. General Concepts and Constructs of Sexuality and Love

As other Western countries, Denmark has experienced a marked socioeconomic development over the last two centuries: from a classical agrarian society to a modern industrialized welfare state. Along with modernity came profoundly altered concepts of love, intimacy, sexuality, and gender, and broadly speaking, the process of sexual liberation came about in three distinct (yet historically closely intertwined) stages: the late-19th-century feminism, the inter-war sexual-reform struggle, and "the sexual revolution" of the 1960s. Today, Denmark is a peaceful and politically stable democracy, and although women in executive positions are still amply outnumbered by men, gender inequality is nowhere near bleak global figures. On the contrary, it can be argued that the "social gender" of Danes has been gradually obliterated over the past century, and in spite of persisting differences, it is generally acknowledged that males and females are *potentially* capable of discharging similar jobs and societal positions. Specific legislation on gender equality has existed since 1919, and currently the Ministry of Social Affairs is formally responsible for governmental surveillance of gender issues.

Today, Denmark is a predominantly secular country, and although well over 90% of the population belong to the Protestant Church, doctrinaire religious groups are scarce and have very little impact in public debate. In the rural areas of Jutland, however, Christian morals are still kept alive, having an impact on various levels of personal experience and conduct. On a whole, the Danish population is small (1.4% of the EU population), and uniquely homogeneous, and though issues of immigration have been vividly debated in recent years, immigrants and their descendents constitute only 7.4% of the population. Out of 5.3 million inhabitants, one fifth are below the age of 17, whereas 15% are older than 65. Seventeen- to 24-year-olds constitute slightly less than one tenth of the total population. Most Danes live in metropolitan areas.

During recent decades, Denmark, like other Western European countries, has been largely "postmodernized." Thus, "serial monogamy" has become a prevailing way of life, and a majority of adults cohabitate without being married. In 2000, 38,844 marriages were contracted, and the same year, a total of 14,394 couples were divorced. Unfaithfulness is generally frowned upon, but seemingly considerable numbers of Danes have had extramarital affairs: Among 60-year-old Copenhageners, 38% and 22% of males and females, respectively, stated than they had been engaged in extramarital relations at least once (Eplov 2002ab). A total of 1.4 million

adults live by themselves, and 120,000 (8.6%) of these have children. Thus, a growing subculture of singles has emerged among adult Danes. The availability of pornography has markedly increased since its decriminalization in the late 1960s, and similar to other Western countries, a certain "sexualization" of mass medias, art, and popular culture has occurred during recent years.

### B. Basic Outlines of Sexual Behavior and Knowledge

Along with profound socioeconomic changes, a gradual relaxation of sexual attitudes and behavior has taken place among Danes: The median age of coital debut among women and men born before 1920 was 21 and 20, respectively, as opposed to 16 for both women and men born in 1960 or later (Jaeger 2000). Similar figures were reported by Fog (1994). For females born before 1920 and after 1960, respectively, the median interval between menarche and coital debut has decreased from seven to three years. The median lifetime number of partners for women and men born before 1920 was 1 and 3, respectively, and 7 for both women and men born after 1960. For women and men above age 75, 1% and 17%, respectively, have had more than 10 sexual partners, as opposed to 42% of both women and men under age 35 (Jaeger 2000). In sum, a marked liberation of sexual behavior has occurred over recent generations in addition to a striking leveling of former sexual gender differences. In 1976, the age of sexual consent was set at 15 for both homosexual and heterosexual relations.

On a legislative level, too, an overall air of sexual *frisind* (Danish for "free-mindedness") is detected. Sex education in schools has been mandatory since 1970 (see Section 5A, Interpersonal Heterosexual Behaviors, Adolescents), abortion was decriminalized in 1973 (see Section 9B/C, Contraception, Abortion, and Population Planning, Abortion and Teenage Pregnancies), and in 1989, same-sex partners obtained (almost) the same legal status as heterosexual couples (see Section 6, Homoerotic, Homosexual, and Bisexual Behaviors). Moreover, Denmark was the first country in the world to legitimize written pornography in 1967 (followed by pictorial pornography in 1969) (Kutchinsky 1989). Prostitution is no longer a criminal offense in Denmark, and it is estimated that a total of 5,000 transactions with female prostitutes take place every day. Further, 13% of Danish males claim to have been with a prostitute at least once. Among 40- to 44-year-olds, this fraction rose to 17% (Melbye 1992). Equivalent numbers were seen by Jaeger (2000). Male prostitutes are believed to constitute a total of only a few hundred persons. The number of migrant sex workers is apparently low, but internationally, Denmark is sometimes mentioned as a transit country for women who end up in prostitution in neighboring countries such as Germany and Holland. Though not in itself prohibited, prostitution is considered illegal vagrancy if the prostitute has no other means of income. Prostitution of minors is rarely seen.

Generally speaking, sexual and reproductive rights are both acknowledged and appreciated in Denmark, and sexual autonomy is taken for granted by younger Danes. Sexual curiosity of juveniles is widely accepted (many kindergartens have "cushion rooms" for children to fight and cuddle in privacy), although heated debates on the alleged "pedophile threat" have swept over Denmark (as it has in the rest of Europe and the US) during recent years. As previously mentioned, sex education in schools has been obligatory since 1970. The current sexual knowledge of adolescents is supposedly good, even though up-to-date didactic methods are called for. Thus, a quarter of youngsters still don't use any contraception at their first intercourse (Rasmussen 1999), and rates of chlamydia and venereal warts among adolescents are a matter of medical concern (see Sections 5A, Interpersonal Heterosexual Behaviors, Adolescents, and 10A/B, Sexually Transmitted Diseases and HIV/AIDS, Basic Figures).

## C. Danish Sexology

Danish sexology was founded in the 1950s, and Dr. Kirsten Auken's 1953 dissertation on the sexual behavior of young women is often considered the starting signal of serious scientific efforts. Foremost, however, it was her protégé, Dr. Preben Hertoft, who—inspired by Masters and Johnson and Helen Singer Kaplan—pioneered modern sex therapy in Denmark. In 1986, a Clinic of Sexology was launched at the University Hospital of Copenhagen (Rigshospitalet), and for more than a decade, Dr. Hertoft functioned as its productive chief physician. Though two more clinics were originally intended, the Copenhagen clinic is currently the only service of its kind in Denmark.

As of early 2003, clinical sexology was not approved as a medical or psychological specialty by central authorities, but recent efforts have been made by the Nordic Association for Clinical Sexology (NACS) to certify and authorize sexological specialists on various levels (see Section 11, Sexual Dysfunctions, Counseling, and Therapies). The NACS hosts annual meetings rotating among member countries and, additionally, the Second Congress of the European Federation of Sexology was held in Denmark in 1994. Between 1983 and 1998, NACS published a periodical, *Nordisk Sexologi* [*Nordic Sexology*], subsequently replaced by the *Scandinavian Journal of Sexology*. Regrettably, this was given up in 2001. Currently, efforts are being made to relaunch a Nordic periodical of sexology.

The first Danish textbook on sexology was published by Dr. Hertoft in 1976. Though not revised since 1987, this book is still commonly used and has been translated into several languages (Hertoft 1987). In recent years, two thorough encyclopedias of sex and sexology have been published in Danish (Graugaard 2001; Hertoft 1989). A useful list of selected publications in non-Scandinavian languages (until 1994) was presented in a special issue of *Nordisk Sexologi* (1994, *12*:151-175).

## 2. Religious, Ethnic, and Gender Factors Affecting Sexuality

See Sections 1, Basic Sexological Premises, and 5B, Interpersonal Heterosexual Behaviors, Adults.

## 3. Knowledge and Education about Sexuality

See Sections 1, Basic Sexological Premises, 5A, Interpersonal Heterosexual Behaviors, Adolescents, and 10C, Sexually Transmitted Diseases and HIV/AIDS, Sex Education and Legal Measures.

## 4. Autoerotic Behaviors and Patterns

See Sections 5A, B, and C, Interpersonal Heterosexual Behaviors, Adolescents, Adults, and Sexual Attitudes and Behavior of Elderly Danes.

## 5. Interpersonal Heterosexual Behaviors

### A. Adolescents          CHRISTIAN GRAUGAARD
*Coital Debut and Sexual Behavior*

Classic studies of adolescent sexuality in Denmark were performed by Auken (1953) and Hertoft (1968), but since the appearance of the HIV/AIDS issue in the mid-1980s, several studies concerning sexual knowledge, attitudes, and behavior of youngsters have emerged (Wielandt 1993; Krasnik

1990). In 1999, a comprehensive questionnaire survey was carried out among 7,355 representative adolescent Danes, including more than 500 questions about sexual issues, such as experience and current behavior, use of contraception, sources of information, attitudes, and factual knowledge (Rasmussen 1999). This study provided healthcare persons, sexologists, and sex educators with valuable insights into the sexual world of young Danes, and the following is largely based on the major results of that survey.

The median age of coital debut (sexarche) among adolescent Danes is 16.8 years, and in all age groups from 13 to 25, girls tend to be slightly more experienced and active than boys. The age at coital debut has dropped about two years since the post-war period (Jaeger 2000; Fog 1994), but seemingly it has remained stable over recent decades. At the age of sexual consent (15 years), just about a third of both girls and boys have had their first sexual intercourse, whereas 7% to 8% of 13-year-olds claim to have had sex. At age 20, 8% and 13% of girls and boys, respectively, are still not sexually experienced. Despite Denmark being a small country, marked differences are seen between urban and rural youth—the former being significantly more experienced and active than the latter. Similarly, youngsters with an ethnic background (at least one parent not originally Danish) were considerably less sexually active than their same-aged peers with Danish parents. By far, this tendency was most striking for girls.

The primary motives for first sexual encounter included "being in love" (about two thirds) and "curiosity" (one third), but various kinds of pressure from partner or peers were also reported by around one third. A similar fraction claimed to be drunk at their sexual debut, whereas less than 5% were influenced by cannabis. Not surprisingly, sexual activity increased by age, and 56% of 20-year-old women (43% of men) claimed to have sexual intercourse at least once a week. A third and a half of girls and boys, respectively, had known their partner less than a month at their sexual debut, and similar fractions found it fully acceptable to have sex within a week of the first date. Only a small minority of youngsters had had more than 10 sexual partners—and a vast majority of both girls and boys insisted on (serial) fidelity.

Expectedly, the frequency of orgasm among girls increased with age. One third, reportedly, experienced an orgasm in the year of their sexual debut, whereas 60% considered themselves orgasmic five years later. No knowledge exists as to the masturbation habits of adolescent males, but among 13-year-olds, three fourths reported having ejaculated. Though still somewhat tabooed, masturbation is thought to be highly common among young Danes of both sexes. Less than 10% had anal sex on a regular basis, whereas the frequency of oral sex is unknown. Only about 5% reported having had intercourse with a partner of the same sex. Other same-sex experiences (i.e., petting and mutual masturbation), however, were not investigated and are believed to be quite common.

One fourth of youngsters did not use contraception of any kind at their first intercourse, whereas 61% used a condom; 14% used the pill, alone or combined with a condom. The lack of coital protection is a matter of great educational concern, and during recent decades, various safe-sex campaigns have been specifically targeted at adolescents (Wielandt 1993). The prevalence of unsafe sex decreased with age, and just 12% of all sexually active youngsters abstained from use of contraception on a regular basis. A considerable amount of sexually active youngsters (one third) had experienced failure of the condom, and one fourth of active girls had used postcoital prevention at least once. Just 7% of sexually active girls had had an induced abortion, whereas 9% and 5% of active girls and boys, respectively, had been diagnosed with chlamydia at least once. The last-mentioned number was considerably higher among youngsters with a minimum of 10 previous partners (see Section 10, Sexually Transmitted Diseases and HIV/AIDS).

*Sex Education*

Surprisingly enough, more than half of girls and 70% of boys reported that sexual topics were "never" or "rarely" discussed at home. On the other hand, a vast majority—96%—had received sex education in schools, and a total of 43% considered this both sufficient and relevant. By far, peers constituted the preferred forum for talks and discussions on sexual and emotional matters. As mentioned earlier, sex education has been mandatory in Danish elementary schools since 1970, but there are substantial differences in both quantity and quality of the didactic efforts made by single schools. Unfortunately, sex education only holds a scant priority at most teachers' colleges, and a majority of educators have actually never received formal pre- or postgraduate education prior to starting their teaching.

During recent years, efforts have been made to supplement official activities and, hence, reach youngsters with information and counseling by alternative means. In 1992, the Danish Family Planning Association launched an anonymous, nationwide hotline service for teenagers—the service is free of charge and it receives around 2,000 calls a year, mainly concerning "basic information" and "sexual problems." Considering the small population of Denmark, 2,000 calls to the FPA hotline is a substantial response. Moreover, interactive counseling on the Internet is gradually evolving, and a number of private or semi-private websites offer free sexual counseling to adolescents (Graugaard 1998). Gradually, new didactic methods are being developed for school purposes, too, including peer education, interdisciplinary teaching aids, and interactive computer games. The concept of *ungdomsmottagningar* (youth clinics) known in Sweden has not as yet gained ground in neighboring Denmark, but for many years, the Danish Family Planning Association has run a well-attended contraceptive service in downtown Copenhagen. Congenial clinics are found in other major cities.

As in other Western countries, youth culture has become increasingly diverse and polyphonic since the "youth revolt" of the late 1960s. Thus, no predominant or homogeneous trend is currently found within the teenage group, rather an ever-changing variety of mobile adolescent subcultures. Sexually, not least, conduct, codes, values, standards, role models, social conventions, self-staging, and modes of expression widely differ within various adolescent segments—from MTV-viewing "pop girls" to left-radical "autonomous," from Americanized hip hop boys to well-behaved, timid, middle-class girls. During recent years, concerns have been raised as to the possible pernicious effects of the increasingly "pornofication" of mass media and public spaces. However, the genuine harmfulness of late-modern conditions, including the shattering of gender roles and traditional family structures, still remains to be shown. On the contrary, it seems that Danish youngsters are competently coping with—and fully enjoying—the multitudinous cultural wardrobe of the Babylonian "fetish society." Moreover, teenagers seem to draw a clear line between the sexualized "kitsch" of the outside world and their own personal dreams, hopes, and expectations. Thus, in spite of their ever-increasing sexualized appearances (i.e., diminutive dress codes, defiant piercing, and harsh diction), many youngsters express surprisingly conservative, romanticized ideals and stereotypes, rather than any urge to engage in extreme sexual practices. (See also Sections 1, Basic Sexological Premises, and 9B/C, Contraception, Abortion, and Population Planning, Abortion and Teenage Pregnancies.)

## B. Adults         LENE FALGAARD EPLOV

*Sexual Attitudes*

Although officially a Protestant country, most Danes are brought up in a secular tradition with relaxed attitudes towards sexual matters. Only minor provincial communities maintain more-restrictive religious beliefs. The sexual attitudes of Danish people, however, are also influenced by old Nordic traditions, such as "night-courtship." Thus, for centuries, premarital sex has been common and accepted (Hertoft 1977). Altogether, Danes consider themselves sexually open-minded, and to some degree, this is supported by national legislation. As mentioned in Section 1B, Basic Sexological Premises, Basic Outlines of Sexual Behavior and Knowledge, Denmark was the first country in the world to legalize written pornography in 1967. In 1970, sex education in schools became mandatory. Abortion was legalized in 1973. And in 1989, registered same-sex partners obtained (almost) the same legal status as married heterosexuals.

Despite this liberal legislation, the sexual attitudes of adult Danes, however, cannot be substantiated by comprehensive, cross-sectional studies, and our current knowledge stems from smaller studies only. In 1996, the sexual attitudes of a representative group of 60-year-olds from Copenhagen County were examined. Around 60% of males found pornography to be stimulating. Fewer than 20% indicated that infidelity, group sex, sadism, masochism, homosexuality, transvestitism, transsexuality, and fetishism should be legally banned, whereas a vast majority indicated that zoophilia, pedophilia, exhibitionism, incest, and voyeurism should remain punishable (Eplov 2002a). Among women, 9% used pornography occasionally, whereas 60% claimed to be indifferent towards pornographic material. Around half of the women regarded infidelity as immoral, and 12% indicated that prostitution should be abolished. Practically all women labeled pedophilia, necrophilia, and zoophilia as "perverse," whereas two thirds labeled exhibitionism so. Around half of the women found sadomasochism, voyeurism, and group sex perverse, but less than 15% regarded homosexuality, transvestitism, and transsexuality as perverse (Eplov 2002b). These data among 60-year-olds cannot be considered representative for the general population, and results from studies among three female birth cohorts living in Copenhagen County indicated that younger women had more liberal attitudes towards sexual topics than older women (Fog 1994; Nielsen 1986ab; Garde 1980).

Sexual attitudes are obviously influenced by many factors, knowledge being one. Presumably, sexual knowledge has increased in the Danish population during the last decades, thus studies on the above-mentioned female birth cohorts (born 1910, 1936, and 1958) established that the fraction of people having received sexual information as juveniles decreased by age: 7% of the 1910 group, 6% of the 1936 group, and 61% of the 1958 group (Fog 1994). A nationwide study of adolescent Danes revealed that in the late 1990s, only 4% of youngsters had *not* received sex education in schools. Contrary to this, nearly a quarter of the girls and more than one third of the boys stated that they had not received sexual guidance at home (Rasmussen 1999).

*Sexual Behavior*

In Denmark, the patterns of intimacy have changed considerably over the past decades, from long-lasting marriages to serial monogamy. Figures from the National Statistics Department show that although the number of yearly marriages was a little over 35,000 in both 1951 and 2001, the number of divorces more than doubled, from around 7,000 to almost 15,000. Around 20% of the persons getting married in 2001 had been married before, and the average duration of a marriage was 11 years. As mentioned, registered partnership was legalized in 1989, and by late 2001, around 3,000 same-sex couples had been registered. Furthermore, an increasing number of Danes live alone, and in late 2001, around 37% of adult Danes, both men and women, lived by themselves (Danmarks Statistik 2002). See also Section 1, Basic Sexological Premises.

Concerning the number of sexual partners, Schmidt (1989ab) reported that 34% to 47% of Danish men aged 16 to 55 had had more than five female partners in their life. Within the past 12 months, 64% had had one female partner, 8% had two, 1% had 3 to 5, and 3% had more than five partners. In a study of almost 5,000 adult Danes, the median number of sexual partners was highest for men aged 30 to 34 (eight partners) and for women aged 25 to 29 (seven partners) (Melbye 1992). In a sample of Danes and Swedes, 1% and 17% of women and men over age 75, respectively, had had at least 10 partners in their lifetime. This was contrasted with 42% of both women and men under age 35 (Jaeger 2000).

The sexual behavior of Danes have only been well examined with regard to age of coital debut and risk behavior in relation to HIV/AIDS (Eplov 2002c). Since "the sexual revolution," one might expect that the age at sexual debut had decreased gradually, but studies reveal otherwise. Thus, the three female birth cohort study showed a decrease in sexual debut from women born in 1910 (average age at debut 21) to women born in 1958 (average age at debut 16) (Fog 1994). Representative studies among pupils in 9th grade in a municipality in Jutland showed no changes in the age of coital debut over 14 years (Boelskifte 2002b). Similar results were found in two representative studies among 16- to 20-year-old Danes from 1984 and 1989 (Wielandt 1993). In sum, a decrease in the average age at coital debut took place before 1980, with no real change in recent decades. See also Section 5A, Interpersonal Heterosexual Behaviors, Adolescents.

Since Danes have overall liberal attitudes towards sex, one might expect this to be apparent in their sexual conduct. The sexual activity of adult Danes, however, is only briefly illuminated by one nationwide study among citizens aged 18 to 88. This study demonstrated that a total of 81% were sexually active, falling off to 64% in the top age bracket (Ventegodt 1998). The incidence of masturbation, oral sex, and extramarital relations are only examined among metropolitan adults, whereas anal sex and the use of prostitutes are both examined in nationwide studies. Studies among 60-year-olds have shown that 11% of male respondents masturbated weekly or more; 27% masturbated at least monthly, whereas 33% stated that they did not masturbate at all. Among women, 4% masturbated weekly or more, 7% at least monthly, and 75% did not masturbate. The three female age cohort study showed an age-dependent increase in the number of women having ever masturbated—the youngest being the most experienced (Fog 1994). Among 60-year-olds, 55% of men had experienced fellatio, 79% cunnilingus, and 12% anal intercourse. On the female side, 63% had tried fellatio, 80% cunnilingus, and 20% anal intercourse (Eplov 2002ab).

A national cross-sectional study by Melbye and Biggar (1992) showed that 22% of women had tried anal intercourse, it being most common (36%) among those aged 30 to 34. Further, more younger than older women reported having engaged in anal sex within the last year. The practice of anal intercourse was associated with a high number of male partners. Notably, a study of 23- to 87-year-old Danes

and Swedes revealed that receptive anal intercourse was significantly more common among Danish (17%) than Swedish (3%) women (Jaeger 2000). Among 60-year-olds in Copenhagen County, 38% of males stated than they had been engaged in extramarital relations, while this was true for 22% of females (Eplov 2002ab). Figures from the three female birth cohorts revealed an increase in unfaithfulness from the oldest to the youngest women (Nielsen 1986ab, Garde 1980). In two representative studies, male use of female prostitutes was examined, showing that 13% to14% of respondents had had sexual contact with a prostitute once or more in their life (Melbye 1992; Schmidt 1989ab).

As for sexual satisfaction and frequency of sexual problems and/or dysfunctions among grownup Danes, Ventegodt (1998) found that 67% of females and 58% of males were "satisfied" or "very satisfied" with their current sex life. Eleven percent of women and 18% of men were "dissatisfied" or "very dissatisfied." A review from 2002 documented that even though the frequency of sexual problems and dysfunctions in the Danish population have been the issue of several studies, only one of these could comply with basic methodological requirements (Eplov 2002c). Subsequently, the frequency of sexual problems and dysfunctions among adult Danes is poorly established. In a representative sample of the Danish general population, Ventegodt (1998) found the following female complaints: reduced sexual desire (11%), pain/discomfort during intercourse (3%), anorgasm (7%), and vaginismus (less than 1%). Common male complaints were: reduced sexual desire (3%), erectile problems (5%), premature ejaculation (5%), and anorgasm (less than 1%).

## C. Sexual Attitudes and Behavior of Elderly Danes

BO MØHL

*Sexuality in Old Age*

In 2000, the mean life expectancy of Danes was 74 and 79 years for men and women, respectively. Because of improved standards of living, the numerical and relative fraction of old-aged persons in the Danish general population has increased dramatically during the 20th century (in 2000 15% of the population was 65 or older) and to quote the WHO, "years have been added to life" as well as "life to years." Thus, a growing number of elderly people experience more years in good health. Among 80-year-olds, however, there are five times as many women as men, obviously making it difficult for a widow to find a new male partner.

Despite the fact that modern Denmark holds liberal attitudes towards sexuality, there is a perpetual tendency to look down upon sexuality in old age. The sex lives of older people are often neglected or depicted as ridiculous or even disgusting. The reason is clearly a lack of knowledge, but presumably also because of children's profound resistance to acknowledge and accept the sexuality of their parents, extending their reluctance to any old person. Elderly people who identify with the cultural prejudices of asexuality will often repress their sexual impulses and desires, resulting in a subsequent loss of sexual capacity and self-esteem.

Only a few studies of the sexuality of elderly Danes exist. Recent surveys among 60-year-old women and men (Eplov 2002ab), however, describe attitudes and sexual lives of mature, urban people. A majority of both men and women had experienced different sexual practices during their lifetime, and relatively liberal attitudes existed towards sexual preferences such as homosexuality and transvestism. Pedophilia and incest, however, were deemed unacceptable. This is in accordance with the public opinion in Denmark and with the Danish edition of WHO's code of diagnoses (ICD 10), in which homosexuality and transvestism are no longer considered to be diseases.

Approximately, half of the women still felt spontaneous sexual desire once a month or more, and a similar number had intercourse at least once a month. Despite the fact that they had a partner, 11% of the women had no sexual activity. Further, in a sample of 66- to 75-year-old Danish and Swedish women, 45% were still coitally active, whereas the same was true for just 4% of the over-75-year-olds. A quarter of coitally active women in these age groups were still married. The same study revealed that just 1% and 17% of women and men over age 75 had had at least 10 lifetime partners, as contrasted with 42% of both women and men under age 35 (Jaeger 2000). In the above-mentioned studies of 60-year-olds (Eplov 2002ab), about half of the men felt sexual desire once a week or more. More than half of them had intercourse at least once a month. Eleven percent of women masturbated at least once a month, and 90% of these were fully orgasmic. Two thirds of men masturbated, 40% once a month or more.

### Sexual Dysfunctions

The most common sexual problem among 60-year-old females was vaginal dryness (29%). Approximately, every tenth man of the same age had serious erectile problems, while 47% had never experienced this sort of problem. Ninety-five percent of women were satisfied with the way they had sexual intercourse; 68% of the men were content with their sexual life in general. Both sexes described a good sexual experience as more than just a matter of physical satisfaction. The contact with the partner and the circumstances surrounding the intercourse were considered equally important. In a study of 70-year-old women, 11% reported having a current sexual problem as opposed to 22% of 22-year-olds and 36% of 40-year-olds. One in ten 70-year-olds expressed a need for sexological treatment or counseling (Fog 1994).

Approximately, 80% of elderly people have at least one impairment or chronic disease (i.e., diabetes, cancer, dementia, cardiovascular, or rheumatic disease), affecting their sexual life and well-being negatively. Besides, many elderly persons take prescription drugs (i.e., SSRIs, antihypertensives, or painkillers), which may have negative impacts on their sexuality. Lack of knowledge and misunderstandings about sexuality in old age result in additional sexual problems. The age-related physiological changes of the body make adjustments in sexual practice and coital positions necessary. Especially for old persons brought up with a puritanical and negative attitude to sexuality, a change of deeply rooted habits and routines can be very difficult (Møhl 2002a).

In Denmark, there is a condescending saying about mature/old age: "Forty, fat, and finished." Sexually speaking, however, this motto should be changed to "Eighty, fresh, and fiery," as the chance that an 80-year-old has sexual interests and desires is much greater than the opposite. Though presumably, there are considerable variations in the sexual lives of elderly Danes, the majority are certainly *not* asexual. The contrary might well be the case. A change in attitudes is therefore called for, by laypeople as well as professionals (Møhl 2002b), and during recent years a public debate has occurred as to the sexual rights of elderly in nursing homes.

## 6. Homoerotic, Homosexual, and Bisexual Behaviors

CHRISTIAN GRAUGAARD

### A. A Brief Historical View

During the Middle Ages, sexual same-sex relations in Denmark were solely a matter of church law, but after the Lutheran Reformation (1536), sodomy was tried by secular courts and punished in accordance with the Bible. Not until the Danish Code of 1683, however, was sodomy added explicitly to national statutes—it was considered a "contranatural act" and sanctioned by capital punishment. Interestingly, only a few cases of sodomy between males have been documented in the period before the penal code of 1835, and it seems that most sodomy cases were resolved discreetly by administrative means (for an informative overview, see von Rosen 1994). Between 1835 and 1866, 14 men were sentenced, but the death penalty was routinely commuted to hard labor by the Royal Chancery. The new criminal code of 1866 reduced the maximal penalty to six years of imprisonment, but in practice, punishment for sodomy between consenting adults was considerably milder, usually 8 to 12 months in jail. With the Civil Penal Code of 1930, adult same-sex relations were decriminalized, but not until 1976 was the homosexual age of consent lowered to the same level as the heterosexual, namely 15 years. Historically, sexual relations between Danish women have only been considered scarcely problematic and such behavior was never an object of specific legal interest.

As elsewhere in Europe, the early modern *époque* gave rise to "homosexuality" as a circumscribed social phenomenon with a distinct personality and lifestyle of male homosexual persons. Prompted by early continental sexology, the modern homosexual gradually came into being, and in Denmark, too, the views on same-sex relations shifted from a question of morality, sin, or crime to being strictly a medical and/or forensic concern. No longer was homosexual behavior something which deviant people *did*, but rather something they *were*. Inspired by the writings of Richard von Krafft-Ebing (1840-1902), Danish *fin-de-siècle* doctors considered "genuine" homosexuality (as opposed to moral depravation) a degenerative condition of the central nervous system, and most Danish psychiatric textbooks of the period offer detailed descriptions on the concept of "contraire sexual instincts." In the first decades of the 20th century, however, the medical focus shifted towards the internal glands, and ambitious theories about homosexuality as a hormonal disturbance were put forward. In Copenhagen, Dr. Knud Sand (1887-1968) substantiated these through an elegant series of gonad transplantations in rodents and birds. Like Austrian Eugen Steinach (1861-1944), Sand believed that (male) homosexuality could be cured by restoring a proper testosterone balance, and during the 1920s, a number of Danish homosexual men underwent surgical procedures with transplantation of "heterosexual" gonads. This hormonal-deterministic viewpoint culminated in 1929, when the Danish Parliament passed the world's first Act on Sterilisation. The primary aim of the new legislation was to sterilize on eugenic grounds, but the law also warranted surgical castration on sexual delinquents or simply on persons whose sexuality caused them "mental suffering" or "social disparagement." By the late 1960s, just over 1,000 men (and some 10 women) had been legally castrated. Out of these, approximately 100 homosexuals underwent castration solely on the grounds of "mental suffering." (See Sections 7, Gender Diversity and Transgender Issues, and 8, Significant Unconventional Sexual Behaviors.)

Though no way near the proportions of "neighboring" cities like Hamburg or Berlin, a male homosexual subculture (and a modest male prostitution) gradually evolved in late-19th-century Copenhagen. Little by little, certain bars, secret societies, and meeting points became notorious homosexual territories, and one of the central parks of Copenhagen (Ørstedsparken) is still frequently used as an "erotic oasis" for men seeking sex with men. Initially, this was barely tolerated by philistines, legislators, and law-enforcement officers, and several scandals swept over town before the outbreak of World War I. As late as 1947, an opinion poll revealed that 61% of Danes considered same-sex relations to be worse than drunk driving, burglary, forgery, and rape (Albaek 1998), and in the postwar decades, an overheated moral panic again focused on depraved and subversive gay men. Thus, in 1961, a change of the Civil Penal Code criminalized male prostitution for the paying party, when the prostitute was under 21 years of age. This led to a considerable increase in police harassment and enabled numerous cases of blackmail. This so-called Ugly Law (*Den Grimme Lov*) was abrogated by Parliament in 1965. In 1967, male prostitution, as such, was legalized.

In 1948, the first homosexual organization in Denmark, simply called The Association of 1948, was founded. The Association soon began publication of the periodical *Vennen* [*The Friend*], later succeeded by *Pan*, which is still published. In 1980, the original organization changed its name to Landsforeningen for Bøsser & Lesbiske (Danish National Association of Gays and Lesbians) and though never truly radical, the Association has successfully managed to put various gay-related issues on the political and societal agenda. In the beginning of the 1970s, more activist homosexual groups evolved, and especially Lesbisk Bevægelse (Lesbian Movement), to some extent succeeded in bridging hard-core feminism with a lesbian lifestyle.

## B. Danish Homosexualities

Public attitudes towards homosexuality and homosexual persons have changed considerably since the sexual revolution of the 1960s. Thus, today the human rights of Danish homosexuals are (almost) on footing with heterosexuals. In May 1989, the Danish Parliament passed a pioneer bill on registered partnership between same-sexed persons, and on October 1, 1989, Axel and Eigil Axgil were married at the City Hall of Copenhagen as the first homosexual couple in the world. From 1989 to 1997, just over 5,000 individuals (two thirds males) were officially registered as partners (Frisch 2003). Despite legal equality, homosexual marriages are still not sanctioned by the Danish church. However, the atmosphere among Danish bishops is sympathetic towards ecclesiastical weddings, and priests are free to bless registered partners in their church. Unlike Sweden, Danish homosexuals are still not allowed to adopt (except for their own stepchildren), and following a fiery debate in the Parliament, it was decided that the Danish healthcare system should not assist lesbians in having children, nor should doctors be permitted to perform fertilizations of female same-sex couples. Still, a number of clinics, typically conducted by midwives, offer fertilization to lesbians with anonymous donor semen. The topic is still under debate, and a change of legal statutes is expected within a few years. Danish legislation explicitly bans sexual discrimination, and incidences of severe harassment or "gay bashing" are rarely heard of. In rural areas of Denmark, though, homophobia still abounds, and the Danish National Association of Gays and Lesbians hosts a telephone hotline for youngsters fearing to come out of the closet. Among urban 60-year-old males, 6% believe that homosexuality should be legally banned (Eplov 2002a).

According to recent studies, only 1.1% and 1.4% of Danish 31- to 33-year-old males and females, respectively, label themselves as homosexuals, while 1.3% and 1.6% claim to be bisexual (Ventegodt 1996). In a study of 18- to 88-year-olds, just 1% reported being homosexual (Ventegodt 1998). Among males aged 18 to 59, an overall 2.7% reported to have had homosexual intercourse. This percentage, however, was almost doubled in men aged 40 to 44 (Melbye 1992). Among Danish teenagers, about 5% of girls and boys reported to

have had intercourse with someone of the same sex (Rasmussen 1999). Despite these marginal figures, the homosexual subculture in Denmark is broad and vivid, and in major Danish cities, several gay-friendly bars, cafés, clubs, saunas, and discotheques exist. Gay Pride Parades (so-called Mermaid Pride) are conducted every summer in the streets of the capital (in 1996, Copenhagen was the official European Pride City), and the World AIDS Day (December 1) is solemnized among both homosexuals and heterosexuals.

As in other Western countries, the gay and lesbian community is dispersed and manifold, with a virtual abundance of lifestyles open to view (Lofstrom 1998). Along with late-modern life conditions and the gradual demolition of sharp, mutually excluding sexual categories, homosexuality is being further de-dramatized. Thus, even though few Danes presently label themselves as homosexuals, it is generally agreed upon that same-sex relations will eventually appear in a more-relaxed manner among younger people considering themselves (and considered by others to be) heterosexuals. The modern homosexual man, therefore, may be a "ghost of the past," as more flexible and unpredictable sexual life forms evolve. This is a theme thoroughly investigated by the Danish sociologist, Henning Bech (1999ab, 1998ab, 1997).

## 7. Gender Diversity and Transgender Issues

ELSE MUNCK

### A. Brief Historical View

During the second half of the 20th century, knowledge of gender-conflicted persons has increased considerably in Denmark through art, literature, and the news media. Thus, as a predominant late-modern trend, the multiplicity of gendered roles, expressions, and behavior patterns are increasingly accepted, appreciated, and cultivated. Both individuals and subcultural groups are now challenging the traditional stereotypes of gender and curiously investigating and modifying the boundaries of traditional gender roles. Furthermore, transvestites, transgenderists, and transsexuals are no longer objects of prohibitions. There has been no Danish legislation against transgender behavior since 1966. A few years ago, the Ministry of Health even eliminated transvestism from the official diagnostic code.

In 1930, the Danish painter, Einar Wegener (1882-1931) became the first person in the world to undergo a partial sex-change operation in Dresden, Germany. Wegener was a patient of the German sex researcher Magnus Hirschfeld (1868-1935), and soon after the operation, he changed his name to Lily Elbe. Unfortunately, Elbe died following a subsequent operation, and though the circumstances remain unclear, it is possible that her death was caused by surgical complications. The first transsexual surgery in Denmark took place in 1952 on the American photographer George Jorgensen (1927-1988). Jorgensen had Danish ancestors and came to the country for hormonal treatment and possibly to have a sex-change operation. After the operation, she took the name of Christine Jorgensen, and the sensational affair became known all over the world—providing Denmark with a highly exaggerated reputation as a "transsexual paradise" for years to come (Meyerowitz 2002). Jorgensen later described "the Danish connection" in her autobiography (Jorgensen 1967).

### B. Current Perspectives

At present, about five to ten individuals undergo sex-change surgery each year in Denmark. During recent decades, gender-conflicted persons tend to be ever younger when they confront authorities with their desire to change sex, often as young as 16- to 18-years-old. The number of females wanting to change sex is on the rise, and currently, the male-to-female and female-to-male cases have almost equalized. Previously, the ratio was relatively constant at about three to one. As of early 2003, a total of about 200 individuals have undergone a legal sex-change operation in Denmark. Additionally, an unknown number of Danish transsexuals are operated in other countries, mostly Thailand, Belgium, or England—by personal choice or because they were not legally accepted for surgery by the Danish authorities (Sorensen 1982; Hertoft 1978; Sturup 1976).

No specific legislation for cross-gendered persons exists in Denmark. Access to sex-reassignment surgery is regulated by a law originally from 1929 concerning sterilization and castration (see Section 6A, Homoerotic, Homosexual, and Bisexual Behaviors, A Brief Historical View). This law warrants voluntary castration in cases of potential criminal behavior or a considerable amount of "social disparagement" or "mental suffering." The person must be at least 21 years of age. By tradition, however, the age of 25 has been recommended before sex-change surgery can be permitted. Admittance to sex-change surgery requires clinical/psychiatric visitation during at least two years, often more. In almost all cases, this takes place at the Clinic of Sexology in Copenhagen, which is the national center for sexological research, counseling, treatment, and education.

On the whole, the visitation for sex-reassignment surgery follows the guidelines drawn by the Harry Benjamin International Gender Dysphoria Association. The applicant is counseled by a multidisciplinary professional team evaluating medical, psychological, and social issues. The object is to ascertain whether the person has a strong and persistent cross-gender identification and a persistent discomfort with his or her assigned sex. During the "real-life diagnostic test"—that is living as the opposite gender during at least one year—the person's ability to adapt him- or herself to the new gender role is observed. After one year, hormonal therapy may be instituted. Some transsexuals only desire partial surgical correction and some female-to-male transsexuals just want mastectomia and hormonal treatment. The transsexual him- or herself applies to the Department of Civil Law (The Ministry of Justice) for permission to change sex. The Department of Civil Law then consults the Medical-Legal Council (a board of psychiatric experts) before deciding on the matter. If a person is rejected he or she can try again, but there is no board of appeal.

At present, sex-reassignment surgery can only take place at the University Hospital of Copenhagen (Rigshospitalet). All expenses are covered by the state. Prior to the operation, the person may change his or her first name to a gender-ambiguous one. Not until after the operation, however, can identity papers, passport, and civil registration number be altered. The person is now legally considered an individual of the newly assigned sex and shares (almost) the same rights as other Danish citizens. Thus, transsexuals can marry, but would hardly be allowed to adopt children.

There are various Danish organizations fighting for the civil rights of transsexuals, transgenderists, and transvestites—and a number of gender-conflicted persons are affiliated with the FPE-NE, the Danish branch of Phi Pi Epsilon. Transgender people, however, are still quite invisible in public spaces and, though not legally or socially stigmatized to any great extent, the whole area of cross-gendering is still somewhat ridiculed.

An often-debated issue is the legal situation of transgenderists and transsexuals who live as the opposite sex waiting for (or not desiring) a full sex-change operation. For many years, a legal sex change could not take place prior to surgical reassignment. However, in March 2003, it was permitted for people to change their sex-specific civil registra-

tion number, birth certificate, and so on, without (or before) surgical intervention. Moreover, it has been argued that sex-reassignment procedures should be further liberalized and surgical sex change made fully available for persons who are not psychotic or otherwise severely mentally disturbed. This, however, is still a matter of great medical and political controversy.

The medical, surgical, and psychosocial treatment of intersex people is not systematized in Denmark, but in many cases, the Department for Growth and Reproduction at the University Hospital of Copenhagen (Rigshospitalet) conducts the treatment and long-term follow-up of these patients. A nationwide study concerning the overall quality of life of intersex people was initiated at this department in 2001.

## 8. Significant Unconventional Sexual Behaviors

ELLIDS KRISTENSEN

### A. Coercive Sexual Behaviors
*Basic Statistics*

In Denmark, just under 3,000 cases of sexual crime are reported to the police every year, and in approximately one third of cases, legal proceedings are instituted. In 2001, a total of 912 charges were pressed: offenses against minors (including 38 cases of incest) 29%, offenses against decency (including exhibitionism) 49%, and rape 22%. Just over half of the charges (497) resulted in a conviction or other legal measures. Only eight charges were raised against women, emphasizing the well-known male predominance in sexual crimes. The charges against female perpetrators concerned incest and offenses against decency, and only two of these resulted in legal measures.

Because of both international and domestic focus on incest and pedophilia, public as well as governmental awareness of this problem has been raised considerably during recent years. Thus, in 2000, a center for treatment of sexually molested children was established at the University Hospital of Copenhagen (Rigshospitalet), and many Danish counties now have professional committees that can be consulted in suspected or factual cases of child sexual abuse. Additionally, many voluntary groups offer support to adolescents and adults who have been sexually abused recently or as juveniles.

*Child Sexual Abuse*

A study of child sexual abuse in the Copenhagen area was undertaken two decades ago (Merrick 1985), and two studies have recently been published (Strange 2002; Helweg-Larsen 2000). Moreover, Leth (1988) established that out of 2,000 demographically representative 18- to 50-year-old Danes, sexual abuse before the age of 18 was reported by 14% of females and 7% of males. More than one third of instances were reported to have taken place within the family. Also, the specific problems regarding child sexual abuse in Greenland have recently been evaluated (Curtis 2002). In 1998, a multi-center study of women sexually molested as children was launched at five psychiatric departments—400 women participated in this program and follow-up studies are still in progress as of early 2003.

Decriminalization of pornography in 1967 and 1969 also legalized child pornography, and not until 1980 was sale and propagation of this kind of material prohibited. In 1994, the possession of child pornography, too, was made illegal, and in 2002, additional types of drawings and computer-generated material were criminalized. The correlation between pornography and sex offenses has been studied for decades in a Danish context, and not least in the case of rape and child abuse, results have indicated that availability of pornography might decrease the number of offenses actually committed (Kutchinsky 1991, 1989, 1973).

*Rape and Sexual Harassment*

With a total of 202 criminal charges in 2001, rape is still a major problem. The difficulties of producing conclusive evidence in rape cases are illustrated by the fact that only one third of the charges result in a conviction. This is, however, an increase compared to 1975, where only 18% of charges resulted in an actual conviction (Helweg-Larsen 1985). In 2002, the maximum penalty for rape was increased to12 years of imprisonment. Since 1999, a number of shelters for male and female rape victims have been established. These have led to an upgrading in the medicolegal and psychological management of rape victims. Victim-compensation laws give rape victims the right to compensation for damages in connection with the sexual assault. The frequency of unreported "acquaintance rape" is not known.

In recent years, a number of cases have been brought to court regarding sexual harassment, often conducted by trade unions on behalf of one of their members. Regularly, these cases catch the attention of the public, particularly if they involve politicians or other well-known persons. However, as no controlled studies of sexual harassment exist, it is difficult to estimate the true number of cases. Following the recommendations of the European Union, the Danish legislation was changed in 2002. Earlier, the alleged victim had to prove that sexual harassment had in fact taken place, but now he or she just has to make probable that sexual harassment has occurred, leaving it to the alleged offender to refute the accusation in order to be acquitted of the charge.

*Treatment of Sexual Offenders*

In addition to normal punitive measures, the Penal Institution at Herstedvester (Copenhagen) for decades has been treating violent sex offenders. Between 1929 and 1970, surgical castration was used in a total of 1,000 cases (Sturup 1971, 1968), but since then, the predominant treatment of sexual offenders has been intensive psychotherapy. Since 1989, a subgroup of sex offenders (3 or 4 annually) has received additional treatment with anti-androgens (Hansen 1997; Ortmann 1980).

The Sexological Clinic in Copenhagen has offered psychiatric/sexological treatment to sexual offenders since its founding in 1986. In 1997, a nationwide visitation and treatment network was established by the Danish Parliament in order to extend the psychiatric/sexological treatment to all those who had been convicted for a sexual crime and were found suitable and motivated. About 100 sex offenders are treated every year. The treatment is based on collaboration between the Department of Justice, the Ministry of Social Affairs, psychiatric-forensic departments in Jutland and Funen, and the Sexological Clinic in Copenhagen (Kristensen 2000). A follow-up report concerning the first five years was in preparation in June 2003.

**B. Prostitution**

See Sections 1B, Basic Sexological Premises, Basic Outlines of Sexual Behavior and Knowledge, 5B, Interpersonal Heterosexual Behaviors, Adults, and 6A, Homoerotic, Homosexual, and Bisexual Behaviors, A Brief Historical View.

**C. Pornography**

See Sections 1B, Basic Sexological Premises, Basic Outlines of Sexual Behavior and Knowledge, 5B, Interpersonal Heterosexual Behaviors, Adults, and 8, Significant Unconventional Sexual Behaviors.

**D. Other Sexual Minorities**

CHRISTIAN GRAUGAARD

A Danish association for sadomasochists (SMil) was founded in 1979 and today, it has local branches in several Danish cities. SMil publishes a periodical, offers education and counseling, and hosts SM events of various kinds. Just like other sexual subcultures, sadomasochistic trends have been gradually mainstreamed through art, the media, and popular culture. Thus, public "fetish parties" have become quite popular in major cities during recent years, but it is unknown to what extent adult Danes engage in sadomasochistic behavior. However, it is suspected that mild forms of bondage are quite widespread, and a number of fetish shops have emerged in several Danish cities in recent decades.

Danish transsexuals and transvestites (see Section 7, Gender Diversity and Transgender Issues) are united in FPE-NE (the Danish branch of Phi Pi Epsilon), and associations for every conceivable sexual preference (such as infantilism, swinging, and all sorts of fetishism) abound. Because of the smallness of Denmark, however, these associations mostly have the form of private clubs, and only the Danish National Association of Gays and Lesbians—and to a lesser extent SMil—hold any genuine political and popular impact. A group of Danish pedophiles has launched Pædofilgruppen (Danish Pedophile Association), which hosts a website on the Internet (www.danpedo.dk). Though supposedly diminutive, the group has recently attracted vast public attention, and both political and non-political forces are currently trying to have it abolished.

See Section 5B, Interpersonal Heterosexual Behaviors, Adults, for other paraphilic behaviors.

# 9. Contraception, Abortion, and Population Planning

HANNE RISØR

**A. Contraception**

Generally, Danish people have good knowledge of contraceptives, and accessibility is satisfactory. The following contraceptives are readily available and commonly used: oral contraceptives (including progesterone-only pills), condoms, IUDs, hormone implant sticks, diaphragms, and oral postcoital contraceptives. High-quality condoms can be purchased at pharmacies, drugstores, supermarkets, gas stations, and from vending machines in many public toilets. In some bars and nightclubs, they are available for free, but normally one has to pay. Since July 2001, postcoital contraceptives ("emergency pills") are sold at pharmacies without a prescription. Subsequently, an increase in use has been detected and by early 2003, around 3,500 therapeutic doses were purchased every month.

No credible statistics exist regarding the use of contraceptives in Denmark, but from sales figures we know that around one third of fertile Danish women use oral contraceptives. Almost half of 20- to 24-year-olds use oral contraceptives. In a representative survey study among adolescents, more than two thirds of respondents used a condom at their coital debut, whereas 14% used contraceptive pills. Sadly, one quarter of youngsters did not use any kind of contraception at their first sexual intercourse—and 43% of sexually experienced boys deemed condoms unpleasant or difficult to use. Moreover, a quarter of sexually experiences girls had used emergency contraceptives at least once (Rasmussen 1999). IUDs and diaphragms are rarely employed by young women, and the general use of IUDs has been declining during recent years. Natural family planning methods are seldom used by youngsters.

If a woman wants personal (prescription) contraception, she must consult her general practitioner (Denmark has a GP for every 2,000 people) or go to a family planning clinic in one of the major cities. Counseling on contraceptive issues is an integrated part of the general health service, but contraceptive devices have to be paid for. Furthermore, Danes aged 25 or more can undergo a sterilization free of charge. Counseling, though, is mandatory prior to surgery. In 1999, 5,470 males and 5,370 females underwent sterilization (2 to 3 per 1,000 inhabitants).

Since 1966, youngsters who want medical counseling about contraceptives do not need the consent of their parents, and any GP can be approached anonymously and free of charge. In addition to obligatory sex education in schools, information about contraceptives are available through leaflets, women's magazines, telephone hotlines, and counseling on the Internet (Graugaard 1998). (See also the end of Section 5A, Interpersonal Heterosexual Behaviors, Adolescents.)

## B/C. Abortion and Teenage Pregnancies

The first bill legalizing abortion was passed by the Danish Parliament in 1939. This legalized abortion on tightly regulated medical or social grounds. A second bill was passed in 1971. This law allowed women over age 38 to have an abortion before the end of the 12th gestational week. Younger women who had more than four children under the age of 18, or presented serious medical or social issues, could also have an abortion before the end of the 12th gestational week. These rather restrictive laws forced many women to give birth to children that they could not manage, and for decades, a black market for illegal (and often hazardous) abortion flourished. It is estimated that some 18,000 illegal abortions were carried out annually during the 1950s.

On October 1, 1973, the Danish Parliament legalized abortion before the end of 12th gestational week. After this time, women can still obtain an abortion, but her application now has to be approved by a regional abortion council consisting of a gynecologist, a psychiatrist, and a lawyer. Dispensations are routinely given on medical, social, and psychological grounds. However, legal abortion after gestational week 20 to 22 is rarely approved. Only 2% to 3% of abortions take place after week 12. Adolescents below the age of 18 must have their parents' consent in order to apply for an abortion. Dispensations are sometimes given by the councils (usually on social grounds). All council decisions can be brought before a board of appeal.

Legal abortion must take place at a public hospital and is free of charge. A doctor can refuse to perform abortions on personal ethical grounds, but in practice this rarely happens. Medicinal (mefipristone or RU-486) abortions have been available at major hospitals for a couple of years and currently make up one third of all cases. Abortions are generally accepted and taken for granted, and a survey from 1995 established that 95% of 18- to 44-year-old Danes consider induced abortion before the end of the 12th gestational week a basic human right (Norup 1997). Religious groups regularly protest against the current legislation, but although a pro-life-inspired association exists (Retten til Liv [The Right to Life]), rabid abortion opponents are marginal and seldom heard of. Only one political party (the Christian Democrats, currently holding four of 179 seats in the Parliament) opposes legal abortion.

The number of abortions peaked in 1975 at 27,884, and since then, it has gradually decreased. In 2000, a total of 15,681 women had a legal abortion, a fifth of the total number of known pregnancies. The same year, 1,954 women between ages 15 and 19 had an abortion (abortion rate 14.3 compared to 12.5 in total). The relatively highest number of abortions is seen among 20- to 24-year-olds (abortion rate 19.9), whereas the abortion rate is around 18 for women aged 25 to 34. The abortion rate is predictably higher among urban women.

The number of teenage pregnancies in Denmark is relatively low, supposedly because of sex education in schools, counseling measures, and availability of contraceptives. Very few pregnant teenage girls want to carry through with the pregnancy, so a majority of these choose to have an abortion. In 2000, 216 women between ages 15 and 19 gave birth to a child, while 1,954 had an abortion. Among sexually experienced teenage girls, around 7% reported to have had an induced abortion (Rasmussen 1999). This pattern is seemingly different among second-generation ethnic minorities, who typically have their first child at a slightly younger age.

## D. Population and Family Planning

During the "baby boom" of the 1960s and 1970s, the population increase in Denmark was around 40,000 per annum. In the 1980s, however, it was just a few thousand. Thus, from 1965 to 1985, the number of newborns went down from 85,796 to 53,749. In 2000, 67,081 live babies were born and the population growth was 18,593. In 1800, the population of Denmark was a little less than one million, while it is estimated that there will be 6.2 million Danes by year 2040.

Currently, Danish women have their first child at an average age of 27 years, and on the average, every woman has 1.73 children. In the postwar decades, it was common for women to have their first child between ages 23 and 25, or younger. The current marked postponement is mainly thought to be because of socioeconomic circumstances (better contraceptives, legal abortion, educational changes, and gender equality), but a possible deterioration of the fertility has also been speculated to be of importance (Jensen 2002). In most families, both parents work and the majority of Danish preschool children are in daycare institutions. Family planning is encouraged by free access to counseling on contraceptives, and both sterilization and legal abortion are free of charge. All families with children under the age of 18 receive a government paycheck four times a year.

The Danish Family Planning Association (Foreningen Sex & Samfund) was founded in 1956 by Dr. Agnete Braestrup (1909-1992), and today it conceives itself as a "watchdog" of sexual and reproductive rights in Denmark and abroad. The purpose of the association is to sustain and enhance sexual possibilities and well-being for individuals of all ages and backgrounds, and domestically, STDs, contraceptives, and sex education in schools are among its top priorities. The Danish Family Planning Association runs a telephone hotline and a website targeted at adolescents (www.sexlinien.dk). Moreover, the association hosts a database on abortion and contraceptives (www.abortnet.dk), and a clinic offering anonymous and free counseling for Copenhageners. An educational service for school classes is also provided. Over the years, the association has published various information materials in different languages (i.e., Turkish and Arabic), in addition to books on sexual counseling and sex education. Since it foundation, the Danish FPA has been an active member of the International Planned Parenthood Federation (IPPF), and it currently conducts and supervises a number of projects in the developing world.

## E. Sexual and Reproductive Health and Rights

Denmark has officially participated in all United Nations' conferences on population and development since Teheran 1968. At the International Conference on Population and Development (ICPD) in Cairo in 1994, Denmark supported the Program of Action and sympathized strongly with the shift from traditional family planning to more comprehensive notions of sexual and reproductive health and rights. Traditionally, Denmark has been a major donor behind UNFPA and IPPF, and though recently struck by major domestic cutbacks, the governmental aid organization (DANIDA) funds extensive developing programs in the Third World. A number of these aim specifically at the empowerment of women. Unfortunately, there is much less focus on the followup of the ICPD's Program of Action today than in 1994. In general, HIV/AIDS has gotten a much higher priority than more-basic themes of sexual and reproductive health and rights. There is still a lot to do.

## 10. Sexually Transmitted Diseases and HIV/AIDS

CHRISTIAN GRAUGAARD

### A/B. Basic Figures

The incidence of classic sex diseases has been rapidly declining during the second part of the 20th century: Syphilis is hardly ever seen (51 cases in 2001), whereas the number of gonorrhea cases has decreased from over 10,000 in 1983 to just 309 in 2001. When it comes to chlamydia and venereal warts, however, numbers are considerably more worrisome: It is estimated that one fifth of sexually active adolescents are infected with HPV, and the number of diagnosed chlamydia cases has been on the rise for several years. The incidence of the latter was 283 per 100,000 in 2001, and out of 15,150 annually reported cases, two thirds concerned patients aged 15 to 24. It is estimated that 7% of sexually active youngsters currently have a chlamydial infection. (See also Section 5A, Interpersonal Heterosexual Behaviors, Adolescents.)

Like other European countries, Denmark was struck by the first AIDS cases in the early 1980s. Initially, an uncontrolled epidemic was feared, but although more extensive than in neighboring Sweden and Norway (Amundsen 2000), the spread of HIV has remained modest over the years. By June 2002, a total of 3,335 Danes had been diagnosed with HIV, and around 2,500 persons were then receiving treatment at one of five Danish HIV centers. Estimates show that the prevalence of HIV in the general population is 0.1% (0.03% among heterosexuals, 4.8% among homosexuals) (Smith 2003). In 2000, the overall incidence of HIV was 4.8 per 100,000 and in 2001, a total of 304 persons (213 males, 91 females) were diagnosed with HIV. Half of the newly diagnosed were aged 29 to 39, and nearly half resided in the greater Copenhagen area. In 2000, the annual HIV incidence here was 15.5 per 100,000, while it was below 5 per 100,000 in most rural areas. One third of the infected persons were men having sex with men, whereas almost half were infected heterosexually. The remainder caught the disease through intravenous drug abuse, blood transfusion, or from an infected mother. Slightly more than one third of newly infected persons were emigrants (especially from Eastern and Central Africa). One third of heterosexually infected persons contracted the disease abroad. The number of infected persons below the age of 25 has been declining between 1990 and 1999. In 2001, the median age at diagnosis was 37 and 29 for males and females, respectively.

In 1874, it became legally mandatory for venereal patients to seek medical treatment, and throughout the 20th century more or less restrictive laws sought to regulate the behavior and civil rights of persons infected with STDs. In 1988, however, the legislation on STD was completely abolished and Denmark became the only country in the world to base examination, treatment, and partner notification entirely on mutual trust between patient and doctor. Thus, full anonymity exists regarding STD and HIV/AIDS, the rationality of which is intermittently debated. Following a vivid public discussion, the Parliament in 1994 made it punishable for "known" HIV-positives to deliberately have unprotected sex.

HIV testing in Denmark is anonymous and free of charge and can be performed either by the family physician or at a public Venereal Clinic. In 2000, a total of 134,116 tests were performed. A central surveillance system exists for both STDs and HIV/AIDS, but registration is strictly anonymous (Smith 2003). Since the mid-1980s, several HIV campaigns have been launched by the central health authorities, and contrary to some European countries, it has been paramount to avoid the fear factor in favor of relaxed and matter-of-factly information—*not* emphasizing sexual abstinence, but focusing on thoughtfulness and the joys of "safe sex" (Wielandt 1993).

[*Update 2002*: UNAIDS Epidemiological Assessment: By the end of 2001, the cumulative total of 3,255 known cases of HIV infection was reported. An anonymous HIV case-reporting system was implemented in August 1990. Data collection includes information on risk behavior, previous testing and results, and on nationality. The number of HIV tests conducted are reported monthly. No routine screening programs exist except for blood donors. The annual number of voluntary tests done is around 130,000 (2.5% of population) and cross-sectional studies have shown that the rate of retesting is relatively high and increasing. The number of persons below 30 years of age seeking testing is high as well.

[All data indicate that HIV-incidence has been stable for many years, with an overall annual incidence of around 230 (4.3 per 100,000), 2.2 per 100,000 among men who have sex with men, 180 per 100,000 among injection drug users, and 2 per 100,000 among heterosexuals. However, because of the decreasing AIDS-morbidity and -mortality resulting from HAART, the number of people living with HIV is increasing, and reached the highest number ever by the end of 2001, with an estimate of 15 per 100,000 population. The infectious burden in Danish society is estimated to be increasing, although the annual HIV incidence is unknown and very difficult to estimate with the existing surveillance tools.

[Cross-sectional studies on knowledge, attitude, and behavior among men who have sex with men have been conducted since 2000. The first results indicate that many of them were still practicing unsafe sex that may expose them to HIV. Such results may have great implications for prevention work.

[Incidence of syphilis has been fairly low for many years, while the incidence of gonorrhea has decreased since the mid-1980s. But there was a slight increase in the last few years, mainly among men. The annual incidence of chlamydia has not changed in recent years and is still relatively high; it is highest among young women age 20-24, with an annual incidence of around 2.2%.

[The estimated number of adults and children living with HIV/AIDS on January 1, 2002, were:

| | | |
|---|---|---|
| Adults ages 15-49: | 3,800 | (rate: 0.2%) |
| Women ages 15-49: | 770 | |
| Children ages 0-15: | < 100 | |

[An estimated less than 100 adults and children died of AIDS during 2001.

[No estimate is available for the number of Danish children who had lost one or both parents to AIDS and were under age 15 at the end of 2001. (*End of update by the Editors*)]

## C. Sex Education and Legal Measures

Over the years, mandatory sex education in elementary schools has been tentatively expanded and improved, and surveys among Danish adolescents have continuously revealed a general high level of knowledge and an overall satisfaction with AIDS-education in schools (Rasmussen 1999; Krasnik 1990). However, around one fourth of youngsters still have sex the first time without using any contraception (see Section 5A, Interpersonal Heterosexual Behaviors, Adolescents). A state-funded AIDS hotline was launched in 1986, and in 2002, it received more than 9,000 calls. At the Adolescent Sexuality Hot-Line (run by the Danish Family Planning Association), around 12% of callers inquired on STD and HIV/AIDS related issues.

As in other countries, several organizations and services are specifically targeted at HIV-positive persons. These are increasing in number because of recent advances in antiviral treatment (and subsequent survival). Thus, in 1995, 43 per million inhabitants died of AIDS, compared with just 5 per million in 1998. The World AIDS Day (December 1) is solemnized in major Danish cities, but contrary to the USA, no Act Up movement exists.

## 11. Sexual Dysfunctions, Counseling, and Therapies

GERD WINTHER

### A. Availability of Sexological Counseling

Despite the fact that Scandinavia is often considered to be among the most sexually liberated countries in the world (Graugaard 1997; Rasmussen 1996; Westrup 1993), a fair share of Danes will experience sexual problems of some kind during their lifetime. Unfortunately, only few valid studies have been carried out concerning sexual problems, but some useful cohort studies exist (see Section 5, Interpersonal Heterosexual Behaviors). In these studies, the prevalence of self-assessed sexual problems in various age cohorts was reported to be between 5% and 22%, and one might suspect the frequency of unreported sexual troubles to be substantial.

Since the inter-war period, the Danish Parliament has discussed the possibility of creating public sexological clinics, but it took almost 50 years before the first one was established in 1986 at the University Hospital of Copenhagen (Rigshospitalet) (Hertoft 1991; Spanager 1987). As yet, this is the only clinic of its kind, although it was originally intended that similar clinics should be opened in the cities of Odense and Aarhus. A few other hospitals in Denmark provide minor sexological services free of charge. To some degree, general practitioners offer free psychological counseling to their patients, but only a slight minority of Danish GPs have any formal sexological training. Counseling on STDs and contraceptive issues, however, is almost completely carried out by the family physician. Furthermore, a range of private or semi-private initiatives exist: A nationwide telephone hotline and a counseling clinic are being run by the Danish Family Planning Association, and various sexual subcultures (i.e., homosexuals and sadomasochists) offer free and anonymous counseling, personally or by phone or the Internet. The availability of sexological treatment is considerably better in the metropolitan areas of Copenhagen, Odense, and Aarhus than in more-rural districts of Denmark.

As of early 2003, around 200 Danish sexologists are unionized in the Danish Association for Clinical Sexology (DACS), which offers a multidisciplinary environment for doctors, nurses, psychologists, social workers, midwifes, physiotherapists, and occupational therapists. Some members are in private practice, while others work part-time

with clinical, theoretical, and/or didactic sexology. DACS was founded in 1981 at a Copenhagen meeting of the Nordic Association for Clinical Sexology (NACS) (Jensen 1994). More than 400 people have been members of DACS since its foundation. The aims of DACS are to make sexological services more readily available in Denmark, to train professionals, and to provide them with a competent sexological forum through postgraduate courses and seminars, a scientific journal, and annual Nordic meetings (besides Denmark, NACS currently consists of Sweden, Norway, Finland, Iceland, and Estonia, a recent new member).

### B. Views on Sexual Dysfunction

The Danish healthcare system uses the WHO's ICD diagnosis system, but in the middle of the 1970s, when Dr. Preben Hertoft's team began treating people with sexual dysfunctions at the University Hospital of Copenhagen, a supplementary diagnostic system was developed, inspired by Helen Singer Kaplan's and Masters & Johnson's theoretical framework and diagnostic taxonomy (Winther 1990; 1982; Møhl 1988). During the 1970s, the most common sexual problems were female orgasmic dysfunction (61%) and male erective difficulties (73%) (Spanager 1987; Winther 1982). Throughout the 1980s and 1990s, the situation gradually changed, and a growing number of patients of both sexes now presented various desire problems. A much lower percentage (about 20%) was now women with orgasmic problems, while the percentage of men with erectile dysfunction remained about the same. Cases of premature ejaculation, on the other hand, were far fewer than in the 1970s, and today many of those treated for this problem are born outside of Denmark (Faber 1991). The spectrum of diagnoses and therapeutic procedures outside the Sexological Clinic is unknown. (See also the end of Sections 5B, Interpersonal Heterosexual Behaviors, Adults, and 5C, Interpersonal Heterosexual Behaviors, Sexual Attitudes and Behavior of Elderly Danes.)

Since the early days of modern Danish clinical sexology, the main therapeutic approach has been psychodynamic, especially inspired by the concepts and procedures of Helen Kaplan, supplemented by behavioral instructions *ad modum* Masters and Johnson. Treatments are preferably based on holistic biopsychosocial principles. From the very beginning of sexual dysfunction treatment in couples, marital dynamics have been an integral part of therapy and counseling. The Danish language has a word for the integration of marital and sex therapy, namely *samlivsterapi* ("cohabitation therapy"), which indicates that the total life situation of the couple is focused upon, rather than just their sexuality. Outside the academic world, private "sexological" services of every kind abound—from Tantric techniques to body-centered therapy. Moreover, a few urologists specialize in erectile dysfunction. Just one or two plastic surgeons offer penile augmentation surgery, thus genital reconstruction treatment is scarce and generally frowned upon by professionals.

### C. Sexological Training and Certification

Since 1972, voluntary sexological courses for medical students have been provided at the University of Copenhagen—originally lasting for one week, but later divided in two separate courses (Hertoft 1992; Wagner 1976). Until 1995, the medical school at the University of Aarhus (Jutland) also offered voluntary courses, while the medical school at the University of Odense (Funen) has had a mandatory sexology course since the late 1980s. Preben Hertoft wrote the first Danish textbook of clinical sexology in 1976 (third edition 1987), and this is still widely used. Sexology is a voluntary elective part of the training to become a general practitioner.

Starting in the late 1960s, psychology students at the University of Copenhagen had access to sexological lectures by Inge and Sten Hegeler (Hegeler 1963), and voluntary courses of basic sexology are still a part of the curricula at the Faculty of Psychology in Copenhagen. Furthermore, several institutions of higher education offer intermittent sexological courses, though a certain decline has sadly been detected over the past ten years. Educators and social workers dealing with disabled or mentally handicapped people typically have to pay for sexological training themselves. However, voluntary postgraduate training is sometimes offered free of charge by various Danish counties (Buttenschon 1994).

DACS has provided postgraduate therapy and counseling courses since 1982. Around 250 postgraduate students have completed such courses as of early 2003. In 2001, NACS passed a joint agreement on common rules for certification in clinical sexology and in sexual counseling (Fugl-Meyer 2001). Since then, DACS has launched a three-step postgraduate education (Basic Sexology, Clinical Sexology I, and Clinical Sexology II), which meets the inter-Nordic demands and is equivalent to two years of full-time university studies. Before achieving authorization in Clinical Sexology, students have to go through a formal psychotherapeutic education. A specialist board under DACS assesses all applications for authorization, and these later must be confirmed by a similar board under NACS. Finally, the student is authorized as Specialist in Sexological Counseling or Specialist in Clinical Sexology.

## 12. Sex Research and Advanced Professional Education

LENE FALGAARD EPLOV, ANNAMARIA GIRALDI, and CHRISTIAN GRAUGAARD

### A. Epidemiological Sex Research

Epidemiological sex research in Denmark is scarce despite the fact that conditions for exactly this kind of research are optimal: Every Dane is assigned a 10-digit civil registration number that follows the person lifelong, making register studies and prospective designs highly favorable. Furthermore, the population is small and homogeneous, and national registers of all sorts virtually abound.

Although the amount of epidemiological sex research in Denmark is not impressive, it all started out quite well. When Alfred C. Kinsey made his revolutionary research in the United States, the Danish psychiatrist Kirsten Auken (1953) interviewed 315 young Danish women about their sexual lives. Subsequently, Preben Hertoft (1968) studied the sexual lives of young Danish men. Inspired by the methodology of Shere Hite, Temte (1984, 1983) published two surveys in the early 1980s based on questionnaires distributed by a "word of mouth method." Although historically interesting, these studies do not meet strict epidemiological standards.

Moreover, a long Danish tradition exists as to the sexual attitudes and behavior of adolescents (see Section 5A, Interpersonal Heterosexual Behaviors, Adolescents), and this is naturally reflected in research. A few studies are especially worth mentioning:

- Three representative studies among pupils in 9th grade in a municipality in Jutland (Boelskifte 2002ab; Rasmussen 1994, 1987).
- A study among all pupils in the 8th, 9th, and 10th grades, in high schools, and similar youth education settings in Copenhagen (Rasmussen 1991).

- A nationwide study among adolescents (Rasmussen 1999).
- Two nationwide studies concerning risk behavior in relation to HIV/AIDS (Melbye 1992; Schmidt 1989ab).
- A longitudinal cohort study (The Glostrup Population Study) among adult Danes living in suburban Copenhagen (Eplov 2002abc; Fog 1994; Lendorf 1994; Solstad 1993ab; Garde 1980).

To picture the full scope of sexological epidemiological research in Denmark, a comprehensive review was conducted in 2002 (Eplov 2002c). Altogether, it was possible to identify 49 population studies, 34 of which were found to be representative. Among these, 14 had adolescents as a target group, and in six studies, the aim was to examine sexual behavior of people under the age of 30. Only 10 out of the 34 studies were nationwide, and out of these, six dealt with adolescents. Out of the remaining four studies, three examined risk behavior in relation to AIDS, one study only included men and one study studied mixed Danish/Swedish material. The last study only included five questions about sex.

In sum, it must be emphasized that additional epidemiological sexological research is needed in order to obtain a thorough picture of the sexual lifestyles of Danes. Thus, a comprehensive, representative population survey covering issues of sexual desire, activity, behavior, dysfunctions, and satisfaction is still lacking.

### B. Biomedical Sex Research

In Denmark, a long research tradition exists on reproductive physiology, andrology, urology, and sexology. In the area of male and female genital physiology, one of the pioneers is Dr. Gorm Wagner, who for decades was affiliated with the University of Copenhagen. In females, Wagner's research has focused on vaginal function and the changes during orgasm. This work was carried out in collaboration with Roy Levin from Great Britain. Wagner and Levin developed new methods to measure vaginal blood flow and lubrication, and in numerous articles they have described the mechanism underlying vaginal lubrication (Levin 1985; Wagner 1978). Their work has added tremendous insight into the physiological function of the vagina. In collaboration with a Danish gynecologist, Bent Ottesen, the research was expanded to cover the effect of various hormones, especially Vasoactive Intestinal Polypeptide (VIP) and its possible sexual role and distribution along the genital tract (Ottesen 1987, 1983).

Wagner has also been a pioneer in the area of male sexual function, especially erectile function and dysfunction. He has developed new methods to evaluate erectile function, in addition to research on various aspects of penile surgery and pharmacological agents. Much of this work was done in collaboration with several other prominent Danish researchers, i.e., Thomas Gerstenberg, Anders Uhrenholdt, Jorgen Ebbehoj, Peter Metz, and Giles Brindley from the UK. Over the years, the work done by these researchers has added tremendously to the understanding of erectile mechanisms (Wagner 1989, 1981; Ebbehoj 1985, 1974; Metz 1983). Gorm Wagner was one of the founders of the International Society of Impotence Research (ISIR) and the *Journal of Impotence Research.*

In the field of andrology and reproductive medicine, Niels E. Skakkebaek at the University Hospital of Copenhagen (Rigshospitalet) is one of the leading scientists. His department works in several areas, but especially the investigation of prenatal environmental exposures in testicular cancer and semen quality has attracted international attention during recent years. Skakkebaek's team has shown a low and decreasing sperm quality in Danish men (Auger

2001; Andersen 2000) and linked this to the recent decline in fertility rates in the industrialized world (Jensen 2002).

Fin Biering-Sorensen and Jens Sonksen have done extensive work on men with spinal cord injury, describing their sexual function and developing new methods to treat their erectile and ejaculatory dysfunction. The latter is of great importance in order to prevent infertility in this group of often younger men (Biering-Sorensen 2001).

Finally, an important research area in Denmark is the treatment of torture victims suffering from post-traumatic somatic and psychosexual problems (Lunde 1990; Larsen 1987). ETICA (Treatment Centre for Traumatised Refugees, Migrants, and Danes) offers treatment to torture victims and also participates in education, counseling, supervision, and research. One of their priorities is research on sexual torture.

### C. Humanistic Sex Research

As elsewhere in Europe, scientific sex studies were originally dominated by a biological discourse, and during the inter-war period, Danish investigators were among the pioneers of sex hormonal research (see Section 6A, Homoerotic, Homosexual, and Bisexual Behaviors, A Brief Historical View). In the post-Kinsey years, however, new perspectives on sexual behavior and interactions gradually came about, and in 1953, Kirsten Auken published an important thesis on the sexual lives of female adolescents (Auken 1953). Auken was openly inspired by Alfred Kinsey's reports and met with her acclaimed American colleague during his roundtrip of Scandinavia in 1955. Until her premature death in 1968, Auken maintained a sociological/humanistic angle towards sex research issues, and a number of her younger protégés published significant sexological work in the years following her dissertation. Not least, Preben Hertoft (1968) published a doctoral thesis on the sexuality of adolescent Danish men.

In the early 1970s, new approaches to body, sexuality, gender, and sexology emerged and, stimulated by (post) feministic and Foucaultian thinking, numerous constructionist studies of variable form and quality have occurred. Among the prominent sex researchers in the field of sociology and human science are the late criminologist Berl Kutchinsky (the societal effects of pornography), folklorist Karin Lützen (lesbian studies), historian Wilhelm von Rosen (gay studies), historian Bente Rosenbeck (female studies), historian Hans Bonde (male studies), historian Morten Thing (history of pornography), and art historian Rune Gade (aesthetics of pornography). Foremost, sociologist Henning Bech has published extensively on masculinity and male homosexuality (Bech 1999ab, 1998ab, 1997). During recent years, several queer-study-oriented scholars have emerged, and literary historian Dag Heede (2001) has launched an ambitious "queering" of the Danish literary canon—from Hans Christian Andersen to Isak Dinesen (Karen Blixen), from Nobel Prize-winning Johannes V. Jensen to contemporary Klaus Rifbjerg.

### D. Sexological Organizations

Denmark has a good number of special-interest sexological organizations. Four of the more important ones are:

Danish Association for Clinical Sexology (DACS), Gronhojgaardsvej 147, DK-2630 Taastrup, Denmark; tel./fax: 45/43 99 66 19; email: dacs@klinisksexologi.dk; www .klinisksexologi.dk.

The Danish Family Planning Association, Skindergade 28, DK-1159, Copenhagen K, Denmark; tel.: 45/33 93 10 10; fax: 45/33 93 10 09; email: danish-fpa@sexogsamfund .dk; www.sexogsamfund.dk.

Danish National Association of Gays and Lesbians, Teglgaardsstraede 13, DK-1007 Copenhagen K, Denmark; tel.: 45/33 13 19 48; email: lbl@lbl.dk; www.lbl.dk.

SMil (sadomasochists), P.B. 691, DK-2200 Copenhagen N, Denmark; tel.: 45/35 83 55 69; email: info.kbh@ sado.dk; www.sado.dk.

## References and Suggested Readings

Albaek, E. 1998. Frisindets graenser: Homoseksuelle mellem moralske dilemmaer og politiske hensyn [The limits of the "free spirit": Homosexuals between moral dilemmas and political considerations]. *Politica*, 30:405-422.

Amundsen, E. J., A. A. Aalen, H. Stigum, et al. 2000. Back-calculation based on HIV and AIDS registers in Denmark, Norway and Sweden 1977-95 among homosexual men: Estimation of absolute rates, incidence rates and prevalence of HIV. *Journal of Epidemiological Biostatistics*, 5: 233-243.

Andersen, A. G., T. K. Jensen, E. Carlsen, N. Jorgensen, A. M. Andersson, T. Krarup, N. Keiding, & N. E. Skakkebaek. 2000. High frequency of sub-optimal semen quality in an unselected population of young men. *Human Reproduction*, 15:366-372.

Auger, J., F. Eustache, A. G. Andersen, D. S. Irvine, N. Jorgensen, N. E. Skakkebaek, J. Suominen, J. Toppari, M. Vierula, & P. Jouannet. 2001. Sperm morphological defects related to environment, lifestyle and medical history of 1001 male partners of pregnant women from four European cities. *Human Reproduction*, 16:2710-2717.

Auken, K. 1953. *Undersogelser over unge kvinders sexuelle adfaerd* [*Studies on young women's sexual conduct*]. Rosenkilde og Bagger.

Bech, H. 1997. *When men meet: Homosexuality and modernity*. Polity Press.

Bech, H. 1998a. CITYSEX: Representing lust in public. *Theory, Culture & Society*, 15:215-241.

Bech, H. 1998b. A dung beetle in distress: Hans Christian Andersen meets Karl Maria Kertbeny, Geneva, 1860: Some notes on the archaeology of homosexuality and the importance of tuning. *Journal of Homosexuality*, 35:139-161.

Bech, H. 1999a. After the closet. *Sexualities*, 2:343-346.

Bech, H. 1999b. *Leisure pursuits: Studies in modernity, masculinity, homosexuality and late modernity. A survey of some results*. University of Copenhagen.

Biering-Sorensen, F., & J. Sonksen. 2001. Sexual function in spinal cord lesioned men. *Spinal Cord*, 39:455-470.

Boelskifte, J., P. M. Saval, & K. L. Rasmussen. 2002a. Unges viden om praevention og seksualitet gennem 14 aar [Sexual knowledge and sources of information in ninth grade pupils in the municipality of Viborg over the last fourteen years]. *Ugeskr Laeger*, 164:3203-3206.

Boelskifte. J, P. M. Saval, & K. L. Rasmussen. 2002b. Seksuel aktivitet og praeventionsvaner blandt unge gennem 14 aar [Sexual activity and contraception habits in ninth grade pupils in the municipality of Viborg during the last fourteen years]. *Ugeskr Laeger*, 164:3207-3212.

Buttenschon, J. 1994. Sexuality and handicap. *Nordisk Sexologi*, 12:137-145.

CIA. 2002 (January). *The world factbook 2002*. Washington, DC: Central Intelligence Agency. Available: http://www .cia.gov/cia/publications/factbook/index.html

Curtis, T., F. B. Larsen, K. Helweg-Larsen, & P. Bjerregaard. 2002. Violence, sexual abuse and health in Greenland. *International Journal of Circumpolar Health*, 61:110-122.

Danmarks Statistik. 2002. *Befolkningens bevaegelser 2001.* [*Vital statistics 2001*]. Danmarks Statistik.

Ebbehoj, J. 1974. A new operation for priapism. *Scandinavian Journal of Plastic Reconstructive Surgery*, 6:241-242.

Ebbehoj, J., & P. Metz. 1985. New operation for "krummerik" (penile curvature). *Urology*, 26:76-78.

Eplov, L. F., T. Weigner, & K. Solstad. 2002a. Danske 60-aarige maends seksualliv [The sexual life of 60-year-old Danish men]. *Ugeskr Laeger, 164*:4819-4823.

Eplov, L. F., A. Koster, & A. Garde. 2002b. Noegen ude paa graesplaenen-60-aarige danske kvinders seksuelle liv [Naked on the lawn. The sexual life of 60-year-old Danish women]. *Ugeskr Laeger, 164*:4815-4819.

Eplov, L. F., K. Garde, & A. Koster. 2002c. Danskernes seksualliv belyst ved befolkningsundersogelser [The sexual life of Danes illuminated by population studies]. *Ugeskr Laeger, 164*:4745-4752.

Eplov, L. F. 2002d. *Seksualitet–Belyst teoretisk og ved en prospektiv befolkningsundersogelse i Kobenhavns Amt med speciel fokus paa aldringens og personlighedstraeks betydning.* [*Sexuality–Examined theoretically and with a prospective population study in Copenhagen County, specially focusing on the significance of aging and personality traits*]. University of Copenhagen.

Faber B. 1991. *Socio-cultural differences in presentation of treatment of ejaculatio praecox.* Paper presented at 10th World Congress for Sexology, Amsterdam.

Frisch, M., E. Smith, A. Grulich, & C. Johansen. 2003 (In press). Cancer in a population-based cohort of men and women in registered homosexual partnerships. *American Journal of Epidemiology.*

Fog, E., A. Koster, G. K. Larsen, K. Garde, & I. Lunde. 1994. Female sexuality in various Danish general population age-cohorts. *Nordic Sexology, 12*:111-117.

Fugl-Meyer, K. S., E. Almaas, E. Benestadt, et al. 2001. Nordic sexology education and authorisation. *Scandinavian Journal of Sexology, 4*:61-68.

Garde, K., & I. Lunde. 1980. Female sexual behavior. A study in a random sample of 40-year-old women. *Maturitas, 2*: 225-240.

Graugaard, C., 1997. Sex in Scandinavia–A guide to the essentials. *Nordic Sexology, 15*:65-74.

Graugaard, C., & G. Winther. 1998. Sex counseling on the Internet. *Scandinavian Journal of Sexology, 1*:201-204.

Graugaard, C. 2001. *Sexleksikon–Fra abe til Aarestrup* [*Encyclopedia of sex–From Ape to Aarestrup*]. Rosinante.

Hansen, H., & O. L. Lykke. 1997. Treatment of dangerous sexual offenders in Denmark. *Journal of Forensic Psychology, 8*:1-199.

Heede, D. 2001. Queering the queer: Herman Bang and the pleasures and dangers of allegorical readings. *Scandinavica, 40*: 11-40.

Hegeler, I., & S. Hegeler. 1963. *An ABZ of love.* Medical Press of New York.

Helweg-Larsen, K. 1985. The value of the medico-legal examination in sexual offences. *Forensic Science International, 27*:145-155.

Helweg-Larsen, K. 2000. *Seksuelle overgreb mod born i Danmark. Problemets omfang og karakter vurderet ud fra litteraturstudier og en raekke danske datakilder* [*Sexual assaults against Danish children. The proportions and character of the problem valued from literature studies and a number of Danish data sources*]. Statens Institut for Folkesundhed.

Hertoft, P. 1968. *Undersogelser over unge maends seksuelle adfaerd viden og holdning* [*Studies on the sexual behavior, knowledge, and attitude of young men*]. Akademisk Forlag.

Hertoft, P. 1977. Nordic traditions of marriage: The betrothal system. In: J. Money & H. Musaph, eds., *Handbook of sexology.* Elsevier.

Hertoft, P., & T. Sorensen. 1978. *Transsexuality: Some remarks based on clinical experience. Ciba 99Foundation Symposium, 62*:165-181.

Hertoft, P. 1987. *Klinisk sexology* [*Clinical sexology*]. Munksgaard.

Hertoft, P. 1989. *Sexologisk opslagsbog* [*Sexological dictionary*]. Hans Reitzels Forlag.

Hertoft, P. 1991. *Sexology in a sexual liberal country.* Paper presented at the 10th World Congress of Sexology, Amsterdam.

Hertoft, P. 1992. *Clinical sexology and postgraduate education in Denmark.* Paper presented at the First Congress of the European Federation of Sexology, Taormina.

Jaeger, A. B., A. Gramkow, P. Sorensen, et al. 2000. Correlates of heterosexual behavior among 28-87 year olds in Denmark and Sweden, 1992-1998. *Archives of Sexual Behavior, 29*:91-106.

Jensen, S. B. 1994. The sensate focus of Danish sexology. *Nordic Sexology, 12*:67-77.

Jensen, T. K., E. Carlsen, N. Jorgensen, J. G. Berthelsen, N. Keiding, K. Christensen, J. H. Petersen, L. B. Knudsen, & N. E. Skakkebaek. 2002. Poor semen quality may contribute to recent decline in fertility rates. *Human Reproduction, 17*:1437-1440.

Jorgensen, C. 1967. *A personal autobiography.* Bantam Books.

Kristensen, E., & T. Lillebaek. 2000. Erfaringer fra samarbejde mellem behandlingsinstitutioner og justitsvaesen med hensyn til behandling af seksualkriminelle [Experience from a collaboration between treatment centres and the Department of Justice regarding treatment of sexual offenders]. In: S. Mossige, ed., *Personer som begaar seksuelle overgreb mot barn* [*Persons committing sexual assaults against children*] (pp. 125-134). TemaNord.

Krasnik, A., & M. Wangel. 1990. AIDS and Danish adolescents–Knowledge, attitudes, and behavior relevant to the prevention of HIV-infection. *Danish Medical Bulletin, 37*: 275-279.

Kutchinsky, B. 1973. The effect of easy availability of pornography on the incidence of sex crimes: The Danish experience. *Journal of Social Issues, 3*:163-181.

Kutchinsky, B. 1989. Legalized pornography in Denmark. In: M. S. Kimmel, ed., *Men confronting pornography.* Crown Publishers.

Kutchinsky, B. 1991. Pornography and rape: Theory and practice? Evidence from crime data in four countries where pornography is easily available. *International Journal of Law and Psychology, 14*:47-64.

Larsen, H., & J. Pagaduan-Lopez. 1987. Stress-Tension Reduction in the treatment of sexually tortured women–an exploratory study. *Journal of Sex Marital Therapy, 13*: 210-218.

Lendorf, A., L. Juncker, & P. Rosenkilde. 1994. Frequency of erectile dysfunction in a Danish subpopulation. *Nordic Sexology, 12*:118-124.

Leth, I., B. Stenvig, & A. Pedersen. 1988. Seksuelle overgreb mod born og unge [Sexual assaults on children and adolescents]. *Nordic Psykology, 40*:383-393.

Levin, R. J., & G. Wagner. 1985. Orgasm in women in the laboratory–Quantitative studies on duration, intensity, latency, and vaginal blood flow. *Archive of Sexual Behavior, 14*: 439-449.

Lofstrom, J., ed. 1998. *Scandinavian homosexualities: Essays on gay and lesbian studies.* Harrington Park Press.

Lunde, I., & J. Ortmann. 1990. Prevalence and sequelae of sexual torture. *Lancet, 336*:289-291.

Metz, P., J. Ebbehoj, A. Uhrenholdt, & G. Wagner. 1983. Peyronie's disease and erectile failure. *Journal of Urology, 130*:1103-1104.

Melbye, M., & R. J. Biggar. 1992. Interactions between persons at risk for AIDS and the general population in Denmark. *American Journal of Epidemiology, 135*:593-602.

Merrick, J., S. Asnaes, N. Michelsen, & M. J. Skov. 1985. Seksuelt misbrug af born. En descriptiv undersogelse af intrafamiliaert seksuelt misbrug af born fra Kobenhavns kommune 1970-1984 [Sexual abuse of children. A study in intra-familial child sexual abuse in Copenhagen 1970-1984]. *Ugeskr Laeger, 48*:3932-3936.

Meyerowitz, J. 2002. *How sex changed: A history of transsexuality in the United States.* Harvard University Press.

Møhl, B., & G. Winther. 1988. Group therapy with single males with erectile difficulties. In: W. Eicher & G. Kockott, eds., *Sexology.* Springer Verlag.

Møhl, B. 2002a. Seksualitet hos aeldre [Sexuality in old age]. *Ugeskr Laeger, 164*:4776-4779.

Møhl, B. 2002b. Aeldre og seksualitet [Old age and sexuality]. In: C. Swane, L. Blaakilde, & K. Amstrup, eds., *Gerontologi. Livet som gammel. [Gerontology. Life in old age]*. Munksgaard.

Nielsen, I. L., E. Fog, G. K. Larsen, J. Madsen, K. Garde, & J. Kelstrup. 1986a. 70-aarige kvinders seksuelle adfaerd, oplevelse, viden og holdning [Sexual behavior, experience, knowledge, and attitudes of 70-year-old women]. *Ugeskr Laeger, 148*:2863-2866.

Nielsen, I. L., E. Fog, G. K. Larsen, J. Madsen, K. Garde, & J. Kelstrup. 1986b. 22-aarige kvinders seksuelle adfaerd, oplevelse, viden og holdning [Sexual behavior, experience, knowledge, and attitudes of 22 -year-old women]. *Ugeskr Laeger, 148*:2866-2869.

Norup, M. 1977. Attitudes towards abortion in the Danish population. *Bioethics, 11*:439-449.

Ortmann, J. 1980. The treatment of sexual offenders. Castration and antihormone therapy. *International Journal of Law Psychology, 3*:4-451.

Ottesen, B., T. H. Gerstenberg, H. Ulrichsen, T. Manthorpe, J. Fahrenkrug, & G. Wagner. 1983. Vasoactive intestinal polypeptide (VIP) increases vaginal blood flow and inhibits uterine smooth muscle activity in women. *European Journal of Clinical Investigation, 13*:321-324.

Ottesen, B., B. Pedersen, J. Nielsen, D. Dalgaard, G. Wagner, & J. Fahrenkrug. 1987. Vasoactive intestinal polypeptide (VIP) provokes vaginal lubrication in normal women. *Peptides, 8*:797-800.

Rasmussen, K. L., & M. Munk. 1987. Seksuel aktivitet og praeventionsvaner blandt unge [Sexual activity and contraceptive habits among adolescents]. *Ugeskr Laeger, 149*: 46-48.

Rasmussen, K. L., & H. J. H. Knudsen. 1994. Skoleelevers viden om, behov for og brug af praevention for og efter AIDS-debatten [School pupils knowledge of, need for, and use of contraception before and after the AIDS-campaigns]. *Ugeskr Laeger, 156*:1447-1451.

Rasmussen, N. 1996. *Sexual and reproductive health and rights for youth. The Danish experience*. The Danish Family Planning Association.

Rasmussen, B. 1999. *Ung 99. En seksuel profil [Young 99. A sexual profile]*. Frederiksberg Kommune.

Schmidt, K. W., A. Krasnik, E. Brendstrup, H. Zoffmann, & S. O. Larsen. 1989a. Attitudes towards HIV infection and sexual risk behavior. *Scandinavian Journal of Social Medicine, 17*:281-286.

Schmidt, K. W., A. Krasnik, E. Brendstrup, H. Zoffmann, & S. O. Larsen. 1989b. Occurrence of sexual behavior related to the risk of HIV- infection. *Danish Medical Bulletin 36*:84-88.

Smith, E. 2003. HIV/AIDS surveillance in Denmark: The challenges ahead. *Journal of Acquired Deficiency Syndrome, 32* (Suppl.):S33-38.

Solstad, K., & P. Hertoft. 1993a. Frequency of sexual problems and sexual dysfunction in middle-aged Danish men. *Archives of Sexual Behavior, 22*:51-58.

Solstad, K., & M. Davidsen. 1993b. Sexual behavior and attitudes of Danish middle-aged men–Methodological considerations. *Maturitas, 17*:139-149.

Sorensen, T., & P. Hertoft. 1982. Male and female transsexualism: The Danish experience with 37 patients. *Archives of Sexual Behavior, 11*:133-155.

Spanager, B., & G. Winther. 1987. *Presentation of the first year of the first Sexological Clinic in Denmark*. Paper presented Eighth World Congress for Sexology in Heidelberg.

Strange, M. 2002. *Unge kraenkere [Young offenders]*. Socialforskningsinstituttet.

Sturup, G. K. 1968. Treatment of sexual offenders in Herstedvester Denmark: The rapists. *Acta Psychiatry Scandinavia*, (Suppl. 204):1-62.

Sturup, G. K. 1971. Treatment of the sex offender. Castration: The total treatment. *International Psychiatry Clin., 8*:175-196.

Sturup, G. 1976. Male transsexuals: A long-term follow-up after sex reassignment operations. *Acta Psychiatry Scandinavia, 53*:51-63.

Temte, R. 1983. *Seksualitet og kvinder. En slutrapport om kvindeundersogelsen [Sexuality and women. A final report from the female survey]*. Uakademisk Forlag.

Temte, R. 1984. *Seksualitet og maend. En slutrapport om mandeundersogelsen [Sexuality and men. A final report from the male survey]*. Uakademisk Forlag.

UNAIDS. 2002. *Epidemiological fact sheets by country*. Geneva, Switzerland: Joint United Nations Programme on HIV/ AIDS (UNAIDS/WHO). Available: http://www.unaids.org/ hivaidsinfo/statistics/fact_sheets/index_en.htm.

Ventegodt, S. 1996. Seksualitet og livskvalitet [Sexuality and the quality of life]. *Ugeskr Laeger, 158*:4299-4304.

Ventegodt, S. 1998. Sex and the quality of life in Denmark. *Archives of Sexual Behavior, 27*:295-307.

von Rosen, W. 1994. A short history of gay Denmark 1613-1989: The rise and the possibly happy end of the Danish homosexual. *Nordic Sexology, 12*:125-136.

Wagner, G. 1976. Sexology: A new university discipline? *British Journal of Sexual Medicine, 3*:14.

Wagner, G., & R. J. Levin. 1978. Oxygen tension of the vaginal surface during sexual stimulation in the human. *Fertility and Sterility, 30*:50-53.

Wagner, G., & R. J. Levin. 1980. Effect of atropine and methylatropine on human vaginal blood flow, sexual arousal and climax. *Acta Pharmacology & Toxicology, 46*: 321-325.

Wagner, G., & R. Green. 1981. *Impotence–Physiological, psychological, surgical diagnosis and treatment*. Plenum Press.

Wagner G, T. Gerstenberg, R. J. Levin. 1989. Electrical activity of corpus cavernosum (EACC) during flaccidity and erection of the human penis. A new diagnostic method? *Journal of Urology, 142*:723-725.

Westrup, A., & B. Kutchinsky. 1993. Healthy sex, healthy society: A view form Denmark. *Nordisk Sexologi, 11*:221-230.

Wielandt, H. B. 1993. Have the AIDS campaigns changed the pattern of contraceptive usage among adolescents? *Acta Obstetrics and Gynecology Scandinavia, 72*:111-115.

Winther, G., P. Hertoft, & S. B. Jensen. 1982. Some common problems of resistance in sex therapy. In: Z. Hoch, ed., *Sexology*. Excerpta Medica.

Winther, G. 1990. *Sensate focus as a psychotherapeutic tool*. Paper presented at the Dutch-Danish Sexology Meeting, Amsterdam.

# Egypt

## (*Jumhuriyah Misr al-Arabiyah*)
## (The Arab Republic of Egypt)

Bahira Sherif, Ph.D.*
*Updates by B. Sherif and Hussein Ghanem, M.D.*

## Contents

## *Demographics and a Brief Historical Perspective*

ROBERT T. FRANCOEUR

### A. Demographics

Egypt is located in the northeastern corner of Africa and the Sinai, a small Asian peninsula between the Middle East and northern Africa. Egypt's borders include a coastline of 1,523 miles (2,450 km) facing the Mediterranean Sea on the north and the Red Sea on the east. Israel is on the northeast border of Egypt's Sinai Peninsula, between the Mediterranean and Red Seas. On the south is Sudan and on the west Libya. Egypt's 386,660 square miles (1,001,450 km²) make it about one and a half times the size of the state of Texas. Almost all of Egypt is arid, desolate, and barren, with hills and mountains in the east and along the Nile River. The Nile River and its fertile valley, where most Egyptians live, stretches 550 miles from the eastern Mediterranean Sea south into the Sudan. Three percent of the land is arable and 2% is devoted to permanent crops; 2% of the land is irrigated.

In July 2002, Egypt had an estimated population of 70.71 million. (All data following are from *The World Factbook 2002* (CIA 2002) unless otherwise stated.)

**Age Distribution and Sex Ratios**: *0-14 years*: 33.96% with 1.04 male(s) per female (sex ratio); *15-64 years*: 62.18% with 1.02 male(s) per female; *65 years and over*: 3.86% with 0.84 male(s) per female; *Total population sex ratio*: 1.02 male(s) to 1 female

**Life Expectancy at Birth** (1999): *Total Population*: 64.05 years; *male*: 61.96 years; *female*: 66.24 years

**Urban/Rural Distribution**: 45% to 55%; Cairo: 9.7 million; Alexandria (El-Iskandriyah): 3.6 million (1999)

*Communications*: Bahira Sherif, Ph.D., Department of Individual and Family Studies, University of Delaware, Newark, DE 19716-3301 USA; Bahira.Sherif@mvs.udel.edu. Hussein Ghanem, M.D., Professor of Andrology, Sexology, and STDs, Cairo University; hmghanem@hotmail.com.

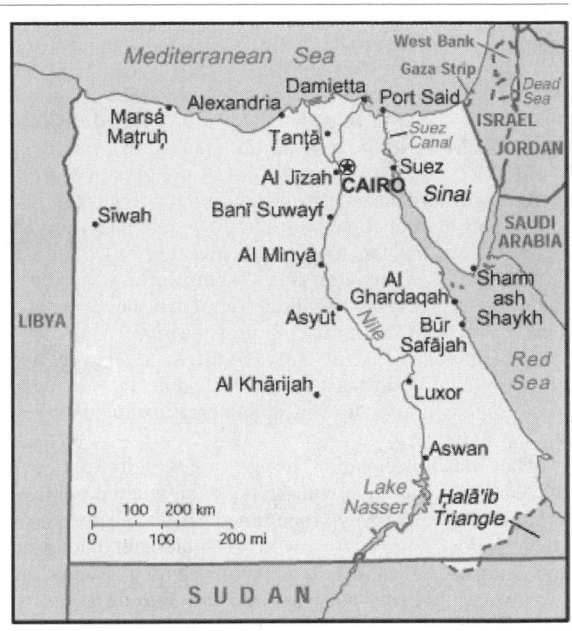

(CIA 2002)

**Ethnic Distribution**: Eastern Hamitic stock (Egyptians, Bedouins, and Berbers): 99%; Greek, Nubian, Armenian, and European (Italian and French): 1%

**Religious Distribution**: Official government statistics cite Muslim (mostly Sunni): 94%; and Coptic Christian and other: 6%. However, several outside authorities claim the Coptic Christian population is actually 15% to 20%.

**Birth Rate**: 24.41 births per 1,000 population

**Death Rate**: 7.58 per 1,000 population

**Infant Mortality Rate**: 58.6 deaths per 1,000 live births

**Net Migration Rate**: –0.24 migrant(s) per 1,000 population

**Total Fertility Rate**: 2.99 children born per woman

**Population Growth Rate**: 1.66%

**HIV/AIDS** (1999 est.): *Adult prevalence*: 0.02%; *Persons living with HIV/AIDS*: NA; *Deaths*: NA (For additional details from www.UNAIDS.org, see end of Section 10B.)

**Literacy Rate** (*defined as those age 15 and over who can read and write*): 51.4% (*male*: 63.6%, *female*: 38.8%) (1995 est.); *attendance for nine years of compulsory school*: 95% (education is free and compulsory from age 6 to 13)

**Per Capita Gross Domestic Product** (*purchasing power parity*): $3,700; *Inflation*: 2.3%; *Unemployment*: 12%; *Living below the poverty line*: 22.9% (2001 est.)

### B. A Brief Historical Perspective

Civilization and urban life were born around 5000 B.C.E. in the fertile valleys of the Nile, Indus, and Tigres/Euphrates Rivers. About 3200 B.C.E., King Menes established the first of many dynasties of pharaohs who gradually unified the country from the Nile Delta to Upper Egypt. The pharaohs produced a distinctive ancient civilization of great wealth and cultural brilliance, built on an economic base of serfdom, fertile soil, and annual flooding of the Nile Valley. The decline of ancient imperial power facilitated the conquest of Egypt by Asian invaders, the Hyksos and Assyrians. The last pharaonic dynasty was overthrown by the Persians in 341 B.C.E. Alexandrian and Ptolemaic Greek dynasties then replaced the Persians, who were in turn replaced by the Roman Empire. Egypt was part of the Byzantine Empire from the 3rd to the 7th centuries of the Common Era, when it was conquered by Arab invaders who introduced the Muslim religion and Arabic language. (The ancient Egyptian language is still used in the Christian Coptic liturgy.) Around 1250, the Mameluke dynasty, a military caste of Caucasian origin, replaced Arab control. In 1517, the Turks defeated the Mamelukes, and Egypt became part of the Ottoman Empire.

In 1798, Napoleon's armies invaded Egypt and occupied Cairo. His effort to block British trade routes to India and establish a francophone society was ultimately unsuccessful. Nevertheless, Napoleon's invasion had profound repercussions for the Arab and Muslim world, which continue to affect the region's political and social development. This was the first European conquest of a major Arab country in the history of Islam, and it signaled the rapid decline of Islam as a world political power. Some analysts even trace contemporary Muslim fundamentalism to this initial shattering defeat.

The French occupation, defeat, and withdrawal destabilized Egypt and left it vulnerable to an internal political struggle that was won by Mohammed Ali, an Albanian lieutenant in the Ottoman army, who set about modernizing the economic and educational structure of Egypt. However, the expansion ultimately put Egypt heavily into debt, and, at the end of the American Civil War with the resumption of American cotton production, initiated a major recession in Egypt's cotton industry. As a result of the economic crisis, the British began to assume greater control over the country.

The Suez Canal, built by a French corporation from 1859 to 1869, was taken over by the British in 1975. After the British Empire expanded into East Africa and the Sudan, the British established their *de facto* rule in 1882, although Egypt remained a nominal part of the Ottoman Empire until 1914. Egypt became a British protectorate in 1914 and a League of Nations Mandate in 1922. The autonomy of the Egyptian monarchy was strengthened in the Anglo-Egyptian treaty in 1936, although Great Britain continued its military presence in Egypt and its control of the Sudan.

After the heavy fighting of World War II, a growing nationalist movement led Egypt to abrogate the 1936 treaty in 1951. A military uprising the following year forced King Farouk to abdicate. Farouk was succeeded by Gamal Abdel Nassar when Egypt declared itself a republic. British troops were withdrawn from the Suez Canal Zone in June 1956, and the following month, Egypt nationalized the Canal. At the end of October, Israel invaded the Sinai Peninsula, and French and British forces came to Israel's aid. United Nations intervention maintained the peace between 1957 and 1967. Egyptian incursions into the Gaza Strip in June 1967 led to a full-scale war with Israel that continued through 1970, when Nassar died and was succeeded by Anwar Sadat. In October 1973, Egyptian forces crossed the Suez Canal and attacked Israeli positions. Eighteen days later, the Yom Kippur War ended in a ceasefire. Meanwhile, Soviet influence had risen with Russian contributions to the Aswan High Dam, and then waned. In 1974, Sadat's government became increasingly friendly to Western and American investment, and relationships between Egypt and Israel improved.

Sadat's economic "Open Door Policy" encouraged, in particular, the private sector to increase the productive capacity of the economy. However, as the government withdrew its commitment to guaranteed employment for all college graduates, unemployment increased. Women, in particular, were affected by this policy. While there had been an increasing expectation in the 1960s that women would increasingly enter the labor force, the Open Door Policy surprisingly worked against this expectation. The national dialogue about women's work started to shift, and the definition of women as primarily playing a role in the domestic arena gained ground. Justifying ideologies based on sexual divi-

sion of roles began to appear, supported by the newly emerging Islamic fundamentalist groups, which advocated that a woman's place was in the home (el-Baz 1997, 149). Further, a provision was added to Article Eleven of the 1971 Constitution, which declared the state's commitment to help reconciling women's family obligations and their equality to men in the public sphere, "provided that this did not infringe on the rules of the Islamic *shari'a* [the "Way" of Islam, including the law and governance]." The new Constitution represented an important divergence from the secular discourse of the 1960s and created opportunities for Islamic groups to oppose women's rights on the grounds that they were in opposition to Islamic principles (Hatem 1992, 241).

Throughout the 1980s, the Open Door Policy became increasingly institutionalized, eventually leading to the current economic Reform Policy. While this policy has been relatively successful on a macro level, it has had negative consequences for the more vulnerable sectors of society, namely the poor, and specifically, poor women and their children (el-Baz 1997, 149). As key resources, such as healthcare and education, have become scarcer, it has been lower-class women and children who have become least likely to have access to them. Also, affected by the economic restructuring have been individuals who would previously have been classified as middle class, namely civil servants and unemployed graduates.

While the pressures and tensions of a rapidly changing world in the last half of the 20th century have affected all the nations and peoples of the world, these tensions have been more obvious in the Islamic nations of the Middle East and southeast Asia. In particular, the growing Islamic fundamentalist movement symbolizes the tensions and conflicts between Western and indigenous traditions and beliefs. Further, in Egypt, this movement has centered much of its rhetoric around the "appropriate" roles for women in society. Gender issues thus constitute a principal mechanism for understanding issues of marriage and sexuality.

## 1. Basic Sexological Premises

According to Egyptian societal norms, sexuality and the ensuing children are part of marriage and creating a family, and do not, therefore, belong in any other sphere of life. With this ideology in mind, contemporary fundamentalists often point to the West and the "loose morality between the sexes" in order to legitimize their arguments about sexuality and gender roles. The essence of their arguments is that women should not work outside of the home and should instead take care of their husbands and children. The family structure emerges as all-important for maintaining a well-ordered society, practical morality, and channeling sexuality. As will be seen, gender roles, and in particular woman's role at the center of the family, thus acquire social importance and political relevance.

## 2. Religious, Ethnic, and Gender Factors Affecting Sexuality

### A. The Issue of Gender

Egyptian society is organized on the principle that men and women simply have different natures, talents, and inherent tendencies. This becomes most apparent in the realm of the family, where each gender has a different role to play. Men are created for going out in the world and are responsible for providing financially for the family. Women are suited for remaining within family boundaries, caring for the home, the children, and the husband. Further, women's inherent sexuality is believed to be constantly endangering the social harmony of society (specifically, men) and is, therefore, best controlled through women's modesty and women remaining as much as possible within the private sphere of family. This belief is reinforced through cultural and religious norms that increasingly advocate that family roles of both women and men are fundamental in maintaining societal structure. The dominant gender constructions therefore support keeping women in the home and oppose women working and abandoning their primary roles (Macleod 1991, 85). Nonetheless, contemporary images of women as economic assets and providers are rapidly coming into conflict with what are perceived as divinely inspired roles.

Gender roles in Egypt derive much of their legitimacy from the Qur'an. In particular, women are often the focus of quotes that supposedly refer to the appropriate roles and behaviors of women. References to the role of women are widely scattered throughout the Qur'an. Some passages focus on women's unique nature, some on women's place in society, and some on women's role within the general congregation of believers. As Fernea and Bezirgan (1977, 13) emphasize, even though the Qur'an is the central source of Islamic belief, there is considerable controversy about the meaning of each of these passages and their implications for the status of women. Consider the verse:

> O mankind! Be careful of your duty to your Lord Who created you from a single soul and from it created its mate and from them twain hath spread abroad a multitude of men and women. Be careful of your duty toward Allah in Whom ye claim [your rights] of one another. (Qur'an 4, 1)

This verse is used by some interpreters as evidence that women are considered equal within Islamic doctrine. Others, however, point to the following verse:

> Men are in charge of women, because Allah hath made the one of them to excel the other, and because they spend of their property [to support women]. So good women are the obedient. (Qur'an 4, 3, 4)

They cite this as evidence that women can never achieve equality within Islam (Fernea & Bezirgan 1977, 18). Selectively choosing Qur'anic verses can either undermine or support dialogues concerning the proper role of women.

Verses from the Qur'an, the *Hadith* (traditions about Mohammed, second only to the Qur'an in authority), and theological arguments about their relevance, are often used as empirical data for sociological explanations of a gender hierarchy in which women are subordinate to men (Mernissi 1987; Marcus 1992). Notwithstanding the powerful assertion that Muslim men and women utilize these sources as part of their hegemonic beliefs, contemporary scholarship has shown that, rather than determining attitudes about women, parts of the Qur'an are only used at certain times or occasions in order to legitimate particular acts or sets of conditions that concern women. The Qur'an is part of the way in which the gender hierarchy and sexuality are negotiated and enforced. It does not provide an explanation of gender roles; instead, it is part of a constant process of gender-role negotiation. While central to Islam, the Qur'an is neither the only nor the most important part of the beliefs and practices that influence the daily life of Muslim women and men. Differences between men and women are readily apparent in several aspects of Islamic law, which accords certain rights and capacities to both men and women. A Muslim's legal capacity (*ahliyyat*) begins at birth and ends with death. Legal responsibilities are assumed under one's legal capacity and are distinguished as a "capacity of execution" and a "capacity of obligations." A free Muslim man who is sane and considered an adult has the highest degree of legal capacity. A Muslim woman, even though she has certain rights, generally has half the legal capacity of a man. This difference only becomes apparent when men and women reach adulthood.

According to the Islamic legal point of view, an adult is a:

> legally and morally responsible person, one who has reached physical maturity, is of sound mind, may enter into contracts, dispose of property, and be subject to criminal law. Above all, he is responsible for the religious commands and obligations of Islam. (Lapidus 1976, 93)

When a Muslim man reaches maturity, his legal capacity becomes complete; neither his age nor marital status influences his legal rights, responsibilities, or capacity of execution.

A Muslim woman's legal identity also begins at birth, but in contrast to men, her legal capacity and status undergo various changes throughout her lifecycle. For a woman, her legal coming of age and her achievement of physical maturity do not necessarily coincide. She is a ward of her father or guardian as a child and, as an adult, is restricted in legal decision-making. Her legal persona and social status depend on the state of her sexuality, whether she is a virgin, married, divorced, or widowed. There is, of course, variation in different Islamic societies as to the perception of the different stages of femaleness. At different times in a woman's life she is treated differently both by the law and by the society. Societally and legally, the young woman (*shabba*) is the focus of a great deal of protection, and her freedom of movement is limited. In contrast, an old woman (*aguza*) is able to move with much greater ease, and may also move in places and participate in situations where the young woman is forbidden even to enter. It is, therefore, very important to emphasize the fundamental difference between the stability of mature men's status under the law versus the changing nature of women's status. This legal difference pervades and shapes the lives of women all over the Islamic world.

Existing side by side, and sometimes in contradiction to the reality of women's daily struggles in Egypt, is the cultural religious ideal of complementarity between the sexes. Within this concept, women are not devalued as persons, or somehow considered to be inherently lesser in value than men, or thought to be lacking in abilities. Instead, Egyptian women tend to emphasize that everyone—man, woman, or child—is thought to be part of an interrelated community, and that gender complementarity is part of the message of the Qur'an and *Hadith*. Even though men overwhelmingly act as the public spokespeople for Islam, as *ulama* (teachers and scholars of Islam), or as *sheikhs* (spiritual leaders), women tend to categorically emphasize that they are just as capable of spreading the word of Islam as men.

While women are clearly not always as much in the spotlight as men, they perform their duties in other ways. Women are valued as the first teachers of their children in the ways of Islam, both through their instruction and also by their example in daily life, which extends beyond the home. There are also many examples of women in Islamic history, beginning with the wives of the Prophet Muhammad and in folk Islam, who have become spiritual leaders in their communities (Ahmed 1992).

While both Muslim men and women are expected to be observant practitioners of religious rites, the actual practice of Islam among men and women in Egypt varies. According to the male view of Islam, all believers have the same responsibilities to God and the same duties to perform. This is supported by the Qur'an, which states: "And they [women] have rights similar to those [of men] over them in kindness, and men are a degree above them (2, 228)." In one sense, the Muslim community is made up of equals, and this is supported by the belief that all are equal before God. This doctrine is supported by reference to the Qur'an, and serves as the foundation for the assertion that Islam is egalitarian. However, while it is stated that all are equal before God, at the same time men are in charge of women. Mernissi (1987, 41) considers the Islamic community, *umma*, to be the male Muslim world, while women's world is the other portion, a kind of sub-universe. However, this is only partially accurate. There is an important distinction between the concept of the *umma* as the imagined moral community to which all people naturally belong, and the society of believers on earth. The two spheres of the moral community and the world of daily life are connected, but in a manner that may not be directly apparent.

## B. The Dangerous Sexuality of Women

A dominant gender ideology is an actively negotiated aspect of many Egyptians' daily lives. Contemporary constructions of what it is to be male or female are only partially shaped by Islamic beliefs. Western images, indigenous feminism, new Islamic views of women, and the requirements of the institutions of family and state all contribute to the creation of the ever-changing image of "proper" woman and man. Nonetheless, an Islamic framework is becoming ever more popular as the foundation for gender discourse in certain segments of Egyptian society. Fundamentalist discourse lends legitimacy and cultural authenticity to all positions in the argument. Much of this gender discourse is based on the "dangerous" nature of women and the evils of unbridled sexuality in society.

The contemporary sociologist Halim Barakat comments that, in the Arab world in general, "the prevailing religious ideology considers women to be a source of evil, anarchy [*fitna*] and trickery or deception [*kaid*]" (Barakat 1985, 32). Throughout Egyptian society, one finds the expression of a pervasive gender ideology that perceives women as posing extreme danger for men.

This same ideology prescribes modesty in the form of dress and behavior for women. Contemporary Egyptian beliefs regarding the modesty of women represent a convergence of ideology with customary practice and modern problems. In Egypt, as throughout the Arab world, descent is traced through the male line, and a woman remains a permanent member of her father's family. Even after marriage, a woman keeps her father's name and returns to him, or to another male relative on her father's side, if she is divorced or mistreated. She remains tied to the prestige structure of her father's family, even though she is incorporated into the household of her husband. The honor of the family is closely bound to the modest behavior of women, and honor is associated with the family group, not just with an individual. Thus, one finds that the actions of one family member affect the honor of everyone in that group. This leads to the complex situation that a woman's dishonorable actions before marriage threaten her father's whole family, but such actions after marriage threaten both her father's and her husband's family. As head of the family, a man must insure the integrity of family honor by watching over the behavior of the women of the group at all times.

One way in which these existing attitudes and practices are reinforced is by the recitation of passages from the Qur'an and *Hadith* that relate to women's modesty, and by interpreting them in a way that underscores the social values of keeping unrelated men and women separated from each other. For example, "And when ye ask of them [the wives of the Prophet] anything, ask it of them from behind a curtain [*higab*]" (Qur'an 33, 53). The word *higab* in some contexts is interpreted variously as a screen or a cloth used as a space divider in a tent, or in a metaphorical sense as modest dress or maintaining a decorous distance between

men and women. A key word relating to the modesty of women is *zina*, which is defined as adornment, ornament, or beauty. The Qur'an states:

> And tell the believing women to lower their gaze and be modest and to display of their adornment [*zina*] only that which is apparent, and to draw their veils over their bosoms, and not to show their adornment [*zina*] save to their own husband or father or husband's father, or their sons or . . . And let them not stamp their feet so as to reveal what they hide of their adornment [*zina*]. (Qur'an 24, 31)

This verse has been alternately interpreted as defining *zina* as adornment, such as makeup or jewelry, or all of a woman, except for her face and hands or natural beauty (Hoffman-Ladd 1987, 29). It has become increasingly common in Egypt to hear that a woman must cover all of her *zina* in the name of honor and for the protection of public morals. In a constantly changing world, women have thus become the locus for many of the debates that actually deal with wider issues in the society.

Much of contemporary Islamic discourse on women deals with the underlying preoccupation with what it means to be a Muslim in a changing world. As technological developments in transportation, communication, and the media become accessible to a wider segment of the Egyptian population, some Muslims are turning to the fundamentalist scriptural versions of Islam, which are unfamiliar to much of the population. In an attempt to validate their positions, these Muslims cite the works of medieval jurists as the basis for their views on the appropriate roles of men and women. These works provide some insight into current developments with respect to gender roles.

First, one should note that the Qur'an specifically encourages sexual relations in the following verses addressed to husbands:

> And when they [the women] have purified themselves, then go in unto them as Allah hath enjoined upon you. (Qur'an 2, 222)

> Your women are a tilth for you to cultivate so go to your tilth as ye will, and send [good deeds] before you for your souls. (Qur'an 22, 23)

Having said this, medieval jurists regarded women as a major site of disruption, *fitna*. This was based, in part, on the specific notion of the potential danger of women's sexuality. In their arguments, the presence of women presented society, i.e., men, with the ever-present threat of *fitna*. Nonetheless, this presence was relational. Even though the danger of *fitna* was located in women, it was not their actual being that represented disorder, but the possibility of their unregulated relationships with men. A popular *Hadith*, frequently cited in contemporary fundamentalist literature, states: "I have not left any disorder [*fitna*] more damaging to men than women." Thus, women's disruptive sexuality presented a constant danger to a harmonious society.

In their socialization of men and women, the medieval societies of the Islamic world presumed that the sexes needed to coexist. Nevertheless, men and women needed to interact in prescribed ways. This was based on an ideology that assumed that women were seductresses and men were susceptible to seduction (Bouhdiba 1988, 20-29). Based on an assumption of their innate abilities, men were accorded the responsibility to set limits for women, who were considered to be below them. Jurists based this assumption on the Qur'anic verses that state: "men are a degree above women" (2, 228). While medieval jurists' emphasis on *fitna* must have affected attitudes toward other concepts relating to women's modesty, these discussions were not by any means original or exclusive to the societies of that time.

The fear of *fitna*, which was posed by the visible presence of women, added an element of vested communal interest to the seclusion of women, an interest which was religiously sanctioned (al-Misri 1994, 512). Not only was women's modesty supposed to be guarded by men, who did so in order to guard the honor of their family, but women themselves were seen to bear a religious obligation to uphold their own modesty (*Ibid.*). Part of a woman's duty was to prevent *fitna*, to prevent men from feeling aroused, for if a man misbehaved as a result of arousal by a woman's physical presence, she, personally, was to blame. Furthermore, this was considered to be a woman's duty, not just toward her own family, but also toward society at large. Thus, Ibn al-Hajj, for example, writing in 14th century Cairo, suggests that in order for a woman not to cause havoc in society, she should leave the house three times in her lifetime: "at the time of her wedding; at the funeral of her parents; and at her own funeral" (1973, 1, 119). Any contact between men and women was deemed as potentially dangerous, as seen in another of his examples, where he warns the water-carrier to lower his gaze upon entering a house, because of the possibility of seeing an unveiled woman (1973, 3, 123). A spontaneous glance, in this case totally without forethought, was quite naturally assumed to lead towards seduction. These examples provide some insight into the underlying issues of gender ideology which are undergoing change in modern Egypt and reveal why women and sexuality remain a central focus of contention in contemporary debates about the centrality of marriage and family.

## 3. Knowledge and Education about Sexuality

### A/B. Formal and Informal Sources

There is no form of sex education in Egypt. While Islamic culture has a certain fascination with all sexual matters as evidenced in the bawdy nature of *A Thousand and One Nights*, in contemporary Egypt, no sexual issues are discussed, either in schools or in the media. This is also in contrast to Qur'anic teachings, which encourage married couples to have sex both for reproductive as well as pleasurable purposes. This is evidenced by an Islamic law that says that if, on the wedding night, the woman discovers that her husband's penis is smaller than the thickness of three fingers, she may divorce him on the grounds of impotence.

While discussions of sexuality are a common component in Egyptian social life, and part of the role of older men and women is to help younger men and women deal with their sexuality, these informal discussions take place within highly regulated spheres of interaction characterized by gender segregation and, among women, the virgin/non-virgin category.

## 4. Autoerotic Behaviors and Patterns

ROBERT T. FRANCOEUR

For Muslim men, the loss of semen in masturbation and nocturnal emissions is bound up, as is the menstrual flow of women, with the impurity associated with the evacuation of organic wastes, unlawful (*haram*) relations, and specific taboos of the *ihram* (ritual purity and dedication of the pilgrim), violations of which constitute a capital sin against *zina*. The life of an observant Muslim is a succession of states of purity acquired then lost, and of impurity lost and then found again in carefully specified purification rituals. Man is never ultimately purified, nor is he condemned to permanent impurity. Major impurity (*janaba*) results from

any emission of semen, menstruation, or the 40-day lochia (*nafas*, the liquid discharged from the uterus following childbirth). Minor impurity is contracted as a result of any excretion by the urethra or anus.

Faithful execution of prescribed purification rituals, following emission of semen, urination, defecation, and the menstrual flow, enable a good Muslim to face God. Whatever the body eliminates is impure and sullies the body, and that pollution must be cleansed each time. This has nothing to do with sin, because man's very life involves the pollution of elimination and excretion, and nothing else. The serious nature and detailed prescriptions of the various purification rituals following an evacuation of organic wastes are often a surprise to non-Muslims (Bouhdiba 1985, 43-57).

> The nature of the purificatory act is of a metaphysical order. It is the act of sublimating the body, of removing pollution and of placing it at the service of the soul and spirit. A material, physical, psychological or moral pollution is never final in Islam and the purpose of the purificatory techniques is to restore man to his original purity. (Bouhdiba 1985, 43)

Not surprisingly, in view of Egypt's Islamic culture and Islam's reticence in discussing sexual issues, female masturbation is not discussed, or even mentioned, in standard references on sexuality in Islam or Egypt. A single reference discovered by the editor in *Sexuality in Islam*, by Abdelwahab Bouhdiba (1985, 31), notes that, while both male and female homosexuality are equally condemned, female homosexuality (*musahaqa*) incurs the same reprimand as incurred by autoeroticism, bestiality, or necrophilia. Whether Bouhdiba would include female autoeroticism in this unspecified mention of masturbation is open to speculation.

## 5. Interpersonal Heterosexual Behaviors

### A. Children and Adolescents

*Gender Segregation of the Young*

An Islamic marriage contract entwines men and women in a set of mutual rights and obligations. The first obligation of marriage is faithfulness and chastity. Any involvement in an extramarital relationship constitutes adultery and is grounds for divorce. This stems from two Qur'anic verses:

> And who guard their modesty—save from their wives or the [slaves] that their right hands possess, for then they are not blameworthy. But who so craveth beyond that, such are transgressors. (23, 5-7)
>
> And all married women [are forbidden unto you] save those [captives] whom your right hands possess. It is a decree of Allah for you. Lawful unto you are all beyond those mentioned, so that ye seek them with your wealth in honest wedlock not debauchery. (4, 42)

Traditional practices throughout the Islamic world limit interaction between the sexes, based on the idea that contact encourages adulterous relationships to develop. Contact is thus limited between young boys and girls, and complete separation of boys and girls becomes the ideal after the onset of puberty. These ideals have become extremely difficult to uphold with the advent of large numbers of women working outside of the house, and are presently in a state of negotiation between the sexes.

Faithfulness and chastity also account for the extreme emphasis that families and prospective bridegrooms place on the virginity of the bride. Both sexes believe that virginity guarantees the faithfulness of the woman to the man after marriage: "She will not desire others if she has not known men before," is a common phrase that is bantered about. While customarily, these rules are not applied as stringently to men, men from "better" families will attempt (at least in mixed company) to portray themselves as very "moral" and as abstaining from women until marriage. It is commonly believed that one is able to predict future behavior based on the past.

Infractions of the moral code of faithfulness and fidelity are more common than is usually admitted by most middle-class Egyptians or than is cited in the literature on women and family. For example, Altorki writes, "In all the families studied, the fidelity of the wives was a principle that was strictly observed, and to my knowledge no infractions occurred" (1986, 63). While Egyptians also adhere to a similar belief system where the issue of faithfulness and fidelity is concerned, the reality may at times differ quite substantially.

## B. Adults

Egyptian society is characterized by a general sense of patriarchy as well as sexual frustration. Men dominate over women in all matters of sexuality, and children are from their first day brought up with very strict sexual guidelines. Girls are expected to be virgins at marriage and are not allowed to ask about sex before their weddings. For many young women (especially the less-educated ones), the actual sex act comes as a complete surprise on their wedding nights and often results in lifelong frigidity because of the shock of the experience. Further, because of cultural constraints, even if a woman comes to enjoy sex, she is not allowed to show this to her husband, who will otherwise become suspicious of her desire and suspect her of having sex with other men. Also, women are not allowed to be the initiators when it comes to sex. Women are expected to initially be completely innocent and then later to "endure" sex in order to be "respectable" in their husband's eyes.

Men have a different set of challenges. While they are expected to have some "experience" before marriage, men also are faced with maintaining their reputations so that they will be eligible to marry a "morally respectable" girl once they are financially set to do so. This entails secret sexual behaviors, since many men do not marry until their 30s. Further, it is difficult to find women to have sex with. Men, therefore, resort to encounters with prostitutes or with willing married women. However, most of this behavior occurs secretly and a man will never tell his bride about his experiences. Given the sexually repressive atmosphere of the society and the lack of sexual access to women, many men suffer from impotence and are extremely preoccupied with all sexual matters.

In addition, it must be pointed out that there are strong differences in degree between rural and urban areas, as well as class differences, in terms of interpersonal behaviors between men and women in the private sphere. Men from the south of Egypt (Saidi'is) are renowned for their jealous behaviors over their wives. Nonetheless, the rules depicted above apply in some degree to all individuals brought up in Egyptian society.

### Concepts of Beauty

The traditional idea that in order to be attractive, women should be pleasantly plump (*mirabraba*) is still around, but it is changing in the upper strata of society. For example, it is now possible to find diet Coca Cola and other diet sodas in Egypt. Also, hospitals have started treating obesity. There are no reported cases of bulimia or anorexia. "*Hilwa mirabraba*" or "pretty and plump" is a standard phrase, as if the two words are automatically attached. To call a woman "skinny as a stick" or a "drumstick" (referring to drums, not a chicken's legs) is an insult. Traditional lower-class women use a different insult, "you rusty needle" (*Iya ibra miSaddiyy*), as a standard insult.

As far as ideals of beauty are concerned, women spend a lot of money straightening kinky hair and trying to whiten their skin using various creams such as "Fair and Lovely" or "Fair Lady." There are commercials for these products on television all the time. Also, the male ideal of a woman in traditional sectors is blonde, with white skin and blue eyes. Women tend to find men who are somewhat taller, have a full head of hair, and again fair skin, as attractive. However, women do not attach great importance to men's looks if they have other favorable criteria, such as a job, good education, and respectable family background.

### Intimacy and Nudity        ROBERT T. FRANCOEUR

While the Imams and mullahs of Islam are very clear in their interpretations of the Qur'an and what is permitted and not permitted by tradition, there is often, as Perper points out in the Preface to this volume, a real discrepancy between "proper sex" and "formal values," what the authorities say should be done, and "smart sex" and "informal values," what men and women actually do in their private sphere. The comments of Abdelwahab Bouhdiba in *Sexuality in Islam* are a good example of this distinction applied to the issue of nudity. Bouhdiba (1985, 37-38) writes about formal values and proper sex according to the Qur'an:

> To be a Muslim is to control one's gaze and to know how to protect one's own intimacy from that of others.
>
> However, the concept of intimacy is far-reaching, for we are confronted here with the concept of '*aura*, which tradition divides into four categories: what a man may see of a woman, what a woman may see of a man, what a man may see of a man, what a woman may see of a woman.
>
> Between men and women, and also between men before their own wives, the part to be concealed from the eyes of others stretches from the navel to the knees exclusively, with a greater or lesser tolerance for the lower part of the thighs, especially in the case of youths. A woman must reveal only her face and hands. Between husband and wife sight is permitted of the whole body except for the partner's sexual organs, which one is advised not to see for "the sight of them makes one blind." However, this is allowed in cases where it is necessary, for juridical or medical purposes, to examine the sexual organs of the *zani* or woman in confinement.
>
> Certain *fugaha* authorize the partners to look at one another's sexual organs during intercourse. Zayla'i, armed with the opinion of Ibn 'Omar and Imam Abu Hanifa, even affirms that it increases one's ability to reach the quintessence of ecstasy.
>
> Total nudity is very strongly advised against, even when one is "alone." This is because absolute solitude does not exist in a world in which we share existence with the *djinns* [*spirits lower than angels*] and angels. "Never go into water without clothing for water has eyes," Daylami observes.

When the editor asked Bahira Sherif to comment on the above description of "proper sex" offered by Bouhdiba, she offered the following comment: "Public nudity in all forms is forbidden for both men and women. The most extreme case of this is that some ultraconservative men will cover their wife's feet with a cloth when she climbs in and out of a bus. Men and women *are* allowed to be intimate and to see each other's sexual organs."

### Islamic Law and Egyptian Marriage

In order to understand sexuality in Egypt, it is necessary to clarify the role of marriage in Islamic law (which remains in effect in all issues related to family in Egypt.) In all schools of Islamic law, marriage is seen as a contract whose main function is to make sexual relations between a man and a woman licit. The term *'aqd al-nikah* refers to the contract of coitus. A valid and effective marriage contract outlines certain respective legal rights and duties for wife and husband, together with other rights and duties common to both of them. Very superficially, these rights and duties can be summed up as dowry and maintenance for the wife and children, as well as the good treatment of the wife and children by the husband, the mutual right of inheritance between the conjugal couple, and the wife's obedience to her husband in lawful matters. At the time of marriage, other parties can stipulate certain conditions, provided that they are not contrary to the basis of marriage as defined by jurists.

The essential requirements for a valid Muslim marriage in Egypt are:

1. consent of the wife,
2. consent of the legal guardian or *al wali*,
3. two legal witnesses, and
4. payment of dowry or *mahr*.

While each of these elements must be present for a marriage to be considered valid, there are other features inferred from Islamic legal texts, which combine to make a legitimate, socially respectable marriage. Because marriage is a contract, both parties can stipulate certain conditions. For example, one condition may be the wife's right to divorce, but a condition that eliminates the husband's right to divorce would be void. Verma (1971, 97-104) has provided a list of valid and void conditions related to marriage.

Beyond its legal components, marriage is also regarded as a religious obligation and is invested with many ethical injunctions. This can be attributed primarily to the fact that any sexual contact outside marriage is considered fornication or a violation of *zina*, and is subject to severe punishment. Furthermore, Islam condemns and discourages celibacy. In this manner, marriage acquires a religious dimension; it becomes the way of preserving morals and chastity through the satisfaction of sexual desires within the limits set by God (Maudoodi 1983, 6-7). Muslim jurists have gone so far as to elevate marriage to the level of a religious duty. The Qur'an supports this notion in the verse that states, "And marry such of you as are solitary and the pious of your slaves and maid servants" (24, 32), which is commonly interpreted as advocating marriage in order to "complete the religion" (Bousquet 1948, 63). A common *Hadith*, still often quoted, particularly among men, states that "the prayer of a married man is equal to 70 prayers of a single man." Thus, all individuals are encouraged to marry, and societal provisions, such as the importance of family reputation, discourage being single.

Marriage remains at the center of contemporary Egyptian social life. It is the primary focal point in the lives of both men and women, followed only by the birth of a child. From a legal standpoint, the marriage contract establishes a series of rights and obligations between a couple which have a long-lasting effect on many aspects of their lives. An Islamic marriage contract naturally represents more than a mere exchange of money or material goods. It is a form of social exchange and is thus a legal, religious, economic, and symbolic transaction (Mauss 1967, 76). The contract is attended to with utmost seriousness and is preceded by a set of lengthy negotiations, almost all of which center around the material protection of the woman and her unborn children once she enters the state of matrimony. Nevertheless, the marriage contract may include conditions that are advantageous for either or both spouses. Conditions specified in the contract may range from the woman's right to dissolve the marriage, to an agreement that neither party may leave the town they agree to live in, and even that the husband may not marry another woman. The contract, as a matter of course, also acts as a medium for bringing the various members of the two families together and provides them with the opportunity to discuss in detail the preliminary workings of the marriage. Most importantly, the marriage contract symbolizes the public acknowledgment of the formation of a lawful sexual partnership that will be sanctioned both religiously and socially, and which marks the beginning of a family and the care and upbringing of children.

## Mut'a *or Temporary Marriage*

While *mut'a* or temporary marriage is not recognized as legitimate by any school of Sunni Islam, its acceptance and practice among the Shi'as highlight the contractual nature of Muslim marriages (Haeri 1989). However, Haeri's argument that all Islamic marriage contracts are basically an exchange of money for sexual intercourse, while thoroughly researched and argued, is incomplete. While that is one element of the exchange, Haeri ignores the other elements of protection of the woman and her children. Even temporary marriages require a contract based on the notion that should a child be fathered, even in a short-term union, the man must claim paternity. This can be observed by the fact that after the short-term-marriage contract expires, the woman is still required to observe the *'idda*, the period of waiting. A *mut'a* wife is not entitled to maintenance, but should children be conceived during a legitimate *mut'a* marriage, they are entitled to inherit from both parents.

For a *mut'a* marriage to be valid, the term of cohabitation must be fixed, and it may be a day, a month, a year, or a number of years; and a dower should be specified. However, it is still incorrect to draw conclusions about the nature of all Islamic marriage contracts based on *mut'a* marriage contracts. *Mut'a* marriages are outlawed among all other schools of law because they do not fulfill the purpose that the jurists argue is the fundamental reason behind marriage in the first place. While lawful sexual intercourse is one aspect of the contract, the legalities bound up with the relationship, I think, indicate the multidimensional nature of an Islamic marriage. The Sunni jurists emphasize that even under Shi'a doctrine, temporary marriage is not a proper marriage, since it establishes no maintenance or inheritance rights for the woman.

Modern Egyptian legislation dealing with marriage and its actual practice provides insight into the contemporary nature of the founding of an Islamic family through matrimony. Here we can only give a general summary of the issues dealing with marriage and divorce. A general examination of the legalistic intricacies of marriage is relevant to all schools of law in Islam and reveals the rights and obligations of both men and women that are established through the marital bond. It is not within the scope of this chapter to expound on the social and cultural customs that vary across the regions that are today primarily Islamic. While these variations are very important, they are not central to our discussion here, because of the prevailing uniformity of the legal issues. Few fundamental conceptual and legal differences exist among the various schools of Islamic law concerning the basic rights of women (e.g., dowry and financial maintenance), inheritance laws being the exception. Since the legal structure for marriage and divorce, which constitutes most of the laws dealing with women, is described in detail in the Qur'an (especially *suras*, chapters of the Qur'an, 2, 221-41; 4, 3-35; 65, 1-7), they are believed to be immutable. Historically, Islamic societies have avoided making changes to the structure of family law because of its derivation from religious text. Thus, it is of contemporary relevance to examine some of the legalistic aspects of marriage with respect to their derivations from the Qur'an.

Sources such as the Qur'an and Islamic law represent norms; they do not describe what is or what was, but what should be. They constitute the mechanism of an ideally functioning Islamic society, the goal being to provide for humankind the path to happiness and paradise. However, this does not mean that these sources have no relation to reality. In fact, they do from two aspects. On the one hand, the solutions that they suggest to human questions and problems are often derived, in particular relation to issues about marriage and family, out of the existing circumstances, even in those instances when they seek to change existing conditions. On the other hand, these guidelines influence the given society, leading to changes in social practice, including marriage, family, and gender roles.

### Sexuality Within Marriage

Islamic justification of sexual intercourse through the marriage contract can be seen in a variety of provisions (Bousquet 1948, 63-74). For example, a Muslim marriage only becomes completely valid when it has been consummated. If a man declares his wife divorced three times, he can only remarry her once she has contracted a marriage with another man and consummated the new marriage—a *Hadith* refers to this as "tasting a bit of honey."

[(*Comment 2001*) As Zeynep Gülçat, author of the chapter on Turkey in this volume, explained when asked about this by a graduate student in the Editor's class, this *Hadith* is meant to protect the wife from repeated, impulsive declarations of divorcing a wife for minor irritations and then remarrying her on reflection. (*End of comment by R. T. Francoeur*)]

Also, once husband and wife live together, the marriage is to be consummated within a certain period of time. The different schools of law vary on the specified time period, but one year seems to be the average (al-Misri 1994, 531). A woman may not refuse her husband's sexual advances at any time, even if she is menstruating, unless it will cause her discomfort. She, in turn, has the right, not just to sexual intercourse, but also to sexual satisfaction. It is said that if a woman pleases her husband sexually, she can be assured of paradise, and if she refuses him, she will be penalized both on earth and in heaven. If a man swears an oath that he will not touch his wife any more, then she has the right to divorce him after four months, unless he resumes sexual relations with her again (Qur'an 2, 226). All of these prescriptions indicate how important and potent Islam considers sexuality to be. Both men and women are to be satisfied sexually in order to prevent adultery and consequent chaos in the society.

The importance of sexuality in the married life of Egyptian women is very apparent in their conversations, which are often, by Western standards, very explicit. Married women will not speak of their sex lives in front of other men or unmarried young women. Nevertheless, once they find themselves alone with other married women, the conversations will become very detailed about the various strengths or weaknesses of their married lives. Women will advise one another on all aspects of sex and on how to best "deal with one's husband."

A major issue among married women is the issue of frequency of sex. Some women feel that their husbands place undue demands on them, given the fact that they work, have children, and are running a household. Interestingly, some other women have the opposite complaint. According to a couple of my informants, several of their husbands kept them on a strict schedule of sex. Thus, the men initiated sex with their wives regularly but in a limited fashion on, for example, Tuesdays and Thursdays, Thursdays being the most common night for sex before the holy day on Friday. Any attempts on the wife's part to deviate from this schedule were met with great opposition. Thus, women are constantly advising one another on "seductive" techniques to force their husbands to vary the schedule. Men, however, feel that it is necessary to preserve a strict regular sexual schedule in order to keep their wives' sexuality under control. Men tend to fear that, as they age, women may want or expect too much from them, and that once they are not able to perform as well, this could initiate a marital crisis. Furthermore, many men fear that anything beyond basic sexual knowledge could potentially make their wives "promiscuous" and "uncontrollable." A major complaint on the part of women is their ignorance about sex when they married and their husband's lack of interest in educating them in this matter.

While Thursday night is considered "sex night," Friday is traditionally known as bath day. This is the day that ritually men get cleaned up to go to Friday prayer. Because of the traditional association of sex with full ablutions required after a major impurity, water is strongly associated with sex. This can even be seen in the term *Imayya suxna*, hot water, a phrase used by parents for something that the children should not be allowed to hear.

Among many Egyptians, part of the role of older men and women is to help younger men and women deal with some of the fundamental aspects of marriage. While sexuality, within the legitimate institution of marriage, is an active, much-discussed component of Egyptian social life, these discussions take place within highly regulated spheres of interaction characterized by gender segregation and, among women, the virgin/nonvirgin category.

To an individual brought up in the West, Egyptian women's discussions of sexuality are striking because of the many allusions to the Qur'an. While many women do not actually know what the Qur'an says, they do know that it urges all individuals to marry and that sexuality is encouraged and considered of primary importance for both men and women. "The Qur'an says it [sexuality] is part of our nature," or, conversely, "sex is part of their [men's] nature," are common comments and complaints among women. Especially among older women, jokes and anecdotes about sex and their husbands are afternoon entertainment. Younger women tend to be quite proud of the new power they have over their husbands and again validate these feelings with religious references, such as, "the Qur'an urges us to reproduce—and we are helping them [their husbands] to become good Muslims," or, "We are helping them to fulfill their religious obligation." Some of the less-happily married women in my study (in particular the older ones) repeatedly emphasized to me that, even though they were not satisfied with their husbands, "this was God's will," and that they were trying to please their husbands in all aspects, including sex, "because it is part of our religion and we will be rewarded in the afterlife." Religious references are used by both older and younger women to validate their positive and negative marital experiences. Nonetheless, none of the women seemed to have concrete knowledge of the actual *suras* or *Hadith*.

The complete social prohibition of young people's sexual activities outside of marriage naturally leads to the almost nonexistence of illegitimacy among this societal group. Illegitimacy is only spoken of in hushed tones and is associated with unusual occurrences, such as a maid getting pregnant through the advances of one of the men in the household. The Western phenomenon of older, educated, unmarried women having children is unheard of and evoked expressions of extreme surprise among my acquaintances. "That is *haram* [forbidden]. Why would a woman do this to herself!" or "A woman bears children for her husband. Children need a father. How can this be?" A unanimously shared Egyptian belief is that reproduction belongs to the realm of the family and is thus, like sexuality, highly regulated by legal, as well as social rules and responsibilities.

## Divorce

Until 2000, Egyptian and Islamic law provided the wife with a very limited right to initiate a divorce, one of these being the right of the wife to divorce her husband on the grounds of impotence if she discovered when the marriage was consummated that his penis did not exceed the thickness of three fingers.

A major development occurred in late January 2000 when the 454-member Egyptian Parliament voted to allow women to divorce their husbands without first having to prove to a judge that they had been mistreated. Under the new legislation, which was quickly approved by President Hosni Mubarak, divorce will still be more complicated for a woman than a male (Sachs 2000).

[*Update 2002*: With the new law, enacted after a 15-year campaign, an Egyptian woman now has two choices. A woman can still use the often-protracted procedure, which requires her to have witnesses to provide a family court judge with exacting proof that her husband has committed adultery or has mistreated and abused her badly enough to justify divorce. In the end, the court procedure usually results in a ruling against the wife. The old law gives men appeal rights that can take years to exhaust. Under the old law, as little as an hour with the local marriage registrar is all that it takes for a husband to get a divorce, sometimes without even informing the wife. Prior to passage of the new law of 2000, a Muslim man in Egypt could end his marriage by saying three times, "I divorce you," or by filing with a government registrar a document testifying to his action. Despite these disadvantages, 1.5 million such requests were filed each year under the old law, and 290,000 divorces were granted, according to government statistics. In Cairo, where one fifth of Egypt's 70 million people live, roughly 15,000 women filed for divorce annually under the old law.

[Even with the new law giving women the option of seeking a divorce, and the likelihood that the courts will tie up a case for years examining a woman's claim, it is still preferable for the wife to prove cause, if only to retain the *mahr* (bridewealth or marriage payment) her husband brought to the marriage. The option of the quick divorce demanded by the wife allows the husband to file his own divorce request and make a quick exit with the *mahr*.

[The new option allows a woman to demand a unilateral, no-questions-asked divorce on the basis of incompatibility. The only restrictions are a required court-supervised attempt at mediation and a six-month wait for a woman with children, and a three-month wait if no children are involved. If a judge fails to reconcile the couple in this period and the wife still wants a divorce, the judge has to grant it. However, the woman has to return all money, property, and gifts she received in the marriage from her husband—her *mahr*— and forego alimony.

[One compromise during the debate over the new law eliminated a provision that would have allowed Egyptian women to travel with a husband's or father's permission, because it was too daring. In late 1999, the government repealed a controversial part of the criminal code that allowed rapists to avoid imprisonment if they offered to marry their victims.

[During the 15-year effort to change the old family law, the conservative religious element objected vehemently that the proposed reform would cause major social upheaval and set women at war with men, while advocates of reform argued that reform would make the legal system more efficient and in tune with contemporary concern over women's rights. In the end, a diverse coalition made reform possible. President Mubarak, whose wife has been active on social reform issues, along with legal reform activists, civil libertarians, and supporters of women's rights, all supported the reform. Perhaps most crucial were the Muslim scholars who agreed that there was justification within Islam for the proposed changes. It was, in fact, the justification of the new law on religious grounds that won it approval in a nation where family law, in particular, is seen as deeply rooted in *shari'a* (Islamic code). The activists for reform successfully argued that the Prophet Mohammed meant divorce to be a gender-equal—or at least nearly equal—opportunity for men and women to dissolve an unhappy marriage. When scholars at Cairo's Al Azhar University, the Muslim world's oldest seat of religious learning, agreed, the reform became a reality (Geissinger 2000; Schneider 2000). (*End of update by B. Sherif*)]

The situation of the 6% of Christian Egyptians remains as burdensome as before, because religious courts, which administer family law, rarely grant Christian women a divorce unless she can prove adultery.

Many leading clerics supported the change, including the government-appointed *mufti* (legal advisors on religious matters) and the sheik of Al Azhar University, the oldest Islamic teaching institution in the world. Supporters of the change point out that even the Prophet Muhammad allowed an unhappy woman to divorce her husband over his opposition, provided she first returned her dowry.

In the impassioned debate on the new law, opponents argued that Islam gives only men the right to initiate a divorce. Extending this right to women, whom they described both in Parliament and the media as emotionally capricious and vengeful, would lead to a massive breakdown of family life. "This will only lead to more and more splits within the society," Ayman Nour, a member of Parliament claimed; "This law will instigate women to be corrupt. A woman could just get together with another man and agree to divorce her husband."

Establishment of a woman's right to initiate a divorce is a major advancement for women in Egypt in light of the strong fundamentalist movement.

## Polygyny

While polygyny is allowed by the Qur'an, it is virtually nonexistent in Egypt. In contrast to the stereotypical Western image of Muslim men with multiple wives, Egyptian men bemoan the difficulties of supporting one wife in today's economy, and strong social sanctions work against their even considering polygyny as a viable option.

Male and female reactions must be seen in light of a 1979 ruling, also known as "Jihan's law," so named after Sadat's unpopular modernist wife, who introduced a decree outlawing polygyny as an option for men. Considerable debate ensued in the media and among secular and religious elites concerning the Personal Status Laws and their relationship to the *shari'a* (Islamic law). This amendment was eventually partially abrogated on procedural grounds in 1985. However, in June of that year, a similar law (Law No. 100) amending the 1925 and 1929 laws was enacted and is now the law in place (Karam 1998, 145). The new law stipulates that in the case of a polygynous union, the first wife retains the right to seek divorce, but it is no longer an automatic right. Instead, she now has to prove that her husband's second marriage is detrimental to her either materially and/ or mentally. Further, the first wife now only has the right to sue for divorce in the first year of the new polygynous marriage. It is socially unacceptable among the middle and upper classes for men to engage in polygynous unions and, in fact, is not seen as an option. The revisions in the law are important on a symbolic level in terms of giving men certain legal rights over women in the context of the family.

## 6. Homoerotic, Homosexual, and Bisexual Behaviors

While there is no public acknowledgment of homosexuality in Egypt, there is a largely hidden but thriving bisexual and homosexual community (Murray 1997c). Nevertheless, families will never acknowledge that one of their members is potentially homosexual. Men will remain living in their natal family for most of their lives and there will never be any public discussion about their reasons for not marrying. Islam condemns male homosexuality and popular culture further reinforces this message. In reality, homosexuality is widely practiced but is divided into two categories: the active versus the passive partner. The active partner has little stigma attached to him, or at least much less than to the *khawal* or passive partner, who is heavily stigmatized. According to one *Hadith*, there are three kinds of male homosexual: "Those who look, those who touch, and those who commit the criminal act" (Bouhdiba 1985, 32).

There is also traditional pederasty between older men and younger boys. Long-term domestic relationships between men are unknown, given social norms that force all unmarried individuals to remain in their natal families until they marry. Since there are many situations in which males can interact with other males, opportunities for male homosexual encounters are available. Egyptian culture, for instance, encourages intimate interactions between men, and it is common to see men holding hands, embracing, or kissing each other on both cheeks without, again, any sexual overtones.

There are no similar venues for women, who are under the constant supervision of their families. Thus, there is no information available on the prevalence of lesbianism in Egyptian society. Also, it is considered quite appropriate for women to interact with other women in very intimate settings (such as helping each other bathe) without there being any sexual overtones to these encounters (Murray 1997b).

After pointing out that the Islamic world rests on the bipolarity of the sexes and their union in marriage, Bouhdiba (1985, 30-33) notes that "homosexuality is a challenge to the order of the world as laid down by God and based on the harmony and radical separation of the sexes."

"God has cursed those who alter the frontiers of the earth." In these terms the prophet condemns any violation of the separation of the sexes. Tradition has it that four categories of person incur the anger of God: "Men who dress themselves as women and women who dress themselves as men, those who sleep with animals and those who sleep with men." Homosexuality [*liwat*] incurs the strongest condemnation. It is identified with *zina* and it is advocated that the most horrible punishment should be applied to those who indulge in it.

In the final analysis, *liwat* even designates all forms of sexual and parasexual perversion. Nevertheless, in Islam, male homosexuality stands for all the perversions and constitutes in a sense the depravity of depravities. Female homosexuality [*musahaqa*], while equally condemned, is treated with relative indulgence and those who indulge in it incur the same reprimand as those condemned for auto-eroticism, bestiality or necrophilia. (Bouhdiba 1985, 31)

[*Update 2003*: Although most Egyptians view homosexuality as heretical, it is not illegal. In the late 1990s, Cairo was gaining a reputation in Egypt's gay grapevine, and even in some nearby Middle Eastern countries, as having a rapidly expanding gay scene. Bars, discos, and plenty of public meeting places were opening up in the center of Cairo where it was relatively easy to socialize, exchange cellphone numbers, hold hands, and perhaps be more daring. The gay life flourished, either largely unnoticed amid more pressing issues, like terrorism and a government crackdown on radical Islamic activists, or tacitly tolerated.

[That changed dramatically in May 2001, when 52 men were arrested for "debauchery" in a police raid on the Queen Boat, a disco on the Nile known as a gay-friendly hangout. After the defendants were convicted in a November 2001 trial that caused international protests, President Hosni Mubarak ordered a second trial. In March 2003, a Cairo court convicted 21 of the 52 Queen Boat defendants of "debauchery" and sentenced each to three years in jail. Both highly publicized trials were widely criticized by human rights groups and Western governments. While homosexuality is not explicitly outlawed in Egypt, a section of the penal code dealing with "debauchery" that is rooted in Islamic law has recently been used to prosecute gay Egyptians. Activist lawyers and human rights activists estimate that 70 gay men have been arrested in recent months in addition to the 52 arrested two years ago.

[With the gay hangouts and clubs now closed down, gay men have turned to connecting on the Internet. But the police are now using sting operations on the Internet to track down gays. Government officials deny any harassment of gays. They also deny having targeted gays for arrest. However, several Western governments remain concerned about the treatment of gays and have been discussing the matter with Egyptian officials behind the scenes (Kershaw 2003). (*End of update by R. T. Francoeur*)]

## 7. Gender Diversity and Transgender Issues

There is no information available on transvestites or transsexuals because they cannot come out in public. This topic is not considered legitimate for discussion in Egypt.

## 8. Significant Unconventional Sexual Behaviors

### A. Female Circumcision

In the West, the most controversial and publicized issue concerning women's health in the Islamic world and Africa is the practice of female circumcision. This practice is extremely widespread in Egypt, especially among the poorer classes and in rural areas. It is considered imperative for girls to be circumcised because of cultural norms that stigmatize uncircumcised girls and prevent them from marrying. Estimates range from 50 to 90% of all Egyptian women are circumcised, but precise figures are not known. A recent study conducted by researchers from Ayn Shams University found that 98% of all girls in the Egyptian countryside and poor girls in Cairo had been circumcised, both Muslims and Coptic Christians, while the estimate for upper-class girls in Cairo was approximately 30% (Botman 1999, 106). The 1995 Egypt Demographic and Health Survey (EDHS-95) indicates that female circumcision is still a common practice despite government portrayals to the contrary. Among women with one or more living daughters, 87% report that at least one daughter has already been circumcised or that they intend to have the daughter circumcised in the future.

Most circumcisions take place before puberty; the median age at circumcision among both respondents and their daughters was 9.8 years. Traditional practitioners were responsible for more than eight to ten circumcisions among respondents, while trained medical personnel performed more than half of the circumcisions among the daughters of respondents.

The majority of women surveyed (82%) think female circumcision should be continued. Seventy-four percent believe that husbands prefer their wives to be circumcised and 72% believe that circumcision is an important aspect of religious tradition. Relatively few women recognize the negative consequences of circumcision, such as reduced sexual satisfaction (29%), the risk of death (24%), and the greater risk of problems in childbirth (5%).

This clinic-based study, one of the few of its kind, was carried out at five university hospitals, several rural hospitals, and two urban clinics. It included a total of 1,339 women for whom both questionnaires and physical examinations were completed. All clients coming to the sites for family planning or gynecological examinations were interviewed about their experience with female circumcision. In addition to the interview, pelvic examinations were conducted on all the women in the study. As part of the examinations, specially trained gynecologists determined whether there was physical evidence of circumcision and, in the case of circumcised women, the amount of tissue excised during the circumcision.

The results of the study permit a classification of circumcised women according to the type of circumcision performed. Because the interviews were conducted prior to the physical examinations, it was also possible to compare the woman's own report as to her circumcision status with the results of the physical examination. For 94% of the women in this clinic-based study, there was agreement between the reporting of circumcision and the findings of the subsequent physical examination.

While female circumcision is often presented as a requirement of Islam, this is in fact a fallacy. To the great embarrassment of the Egyptian government, the issue was raised at the 1994 International Conference on Population and Development in Cairo. Subsequently, a decree was issued to limit the practice to hospitals. The government refrained from completely outlawing the practice because of pressure by Islamic groups who deem female circumcision as necessary based on a saying by the Prophet Muhammad. Critics, however, point out that the Prophet's own daughters were not circumcised and that circumcision is not practiced in Saudi Arabia, the most conservative Islamic country in the Middle East. In 1997, under pressure from Islamic fundamentalist groups, the government lifted the ban on female circumcision. Despite international efforts to publicize the physical and psychological dangers of circumcision, the practice is gaining legitimacy as Islamists revive the belief that it is religiously mandated. The controversy around female circumcision is indicative of the tension between ingrained cultural values with respect to gender, Islamists' quests for "authenticity," and Western perspectives that advocate universal women's rights with respect to control of their bodies.

## B. Coercive Sexual Behavior

### Incest

Although all cultures have some kind of incest taboo, the boundaries restricting who is an acceptable sexual and marital partner vary. In Egypt, for instance, sexual relations and marriage between first cousins is not considered incestuous behavior and historically was very common. Even today, it is not uncommon for first cousins to marry. In fact, many families, particularly in the poorer and rural areas, consider this form of arranged marriage preferable to marrying outside of the family. The rationale for this includes the idea that one has an insider's knowledge about one's own family and, therefore, knows "what one is getting." Also, first-cousin marriages keep the land and wealth within the family.

### Rape

Incidents of reported rape are infrequent in Egypt, because young girls, especially from middle-class and upper-class families are very protected. They tend to only move in the company of members of their families and they themselves take great care to protect their reputations in order to remain "marriageable." Girls from poor families who work as domestic servants are at a much greater risk of rape, because they have little power to protect themselves from the advances of male family members. These cases tend to go unreported and are not of interest to most members of the society. Also, the surge in an underground drug culture has led to a greater risk for women to be sexually exploited.

### Unconventional Sexual Outlets

Although there are no recorded cases, some people claim that rural males occasionally use animals, such as sheep, as a sexual outlet. Especially in isolated villages, where sexual outlets for unmarried adolescents are lacking, sexual intercourse with animals is not uncommon.

## C. Pornography and Erotica

Pornography, as well as prostitution, are forbidden by Egyptian law. That said, there are attempts to smuggle in pornography from the West, in particular now through the Internet. A crackdown on this behavior has been advocated by the government to the extent that at Internet cafes, users must sign a form saying that they will not attempt to access or download pornography.

## D. Prostitution

Although information about prostitution in the religiously conservative nations of the Middle East is limited, prostitution is known to exist in most Arab countries, including the urban areas of Egypt (Inhotn & Buss 1993). Even though prostitution is outlawed in Egypt, Cairo is widely known as offering males access to many classes and types of prostitutes. With the increasing conservative climate in Egypt, the social phenomenon is increasingly hidden and not easily observed. Prostitution rings catering to traveling Western businessmen are known to operate out of private apartments, while other prostitutes frequent the large hotels with a high percentage of Western guests. It is difficult to regulate this form of prostitution because Egyptian prostitutes do not exhibit the same overt signals as their Western counterparts. There is no published data on prostitution in Egypt.

## 9. Contraception, Abortion, and Population Planning

Family planning is a problematic area even though Egypt has the longest history of contraceptive initiatives in the Middle East. In 1996, the former Ministry of Population and Family Planning was abolished and a new Ministry of Health and Population was created to underscore the renewed importance the government is giving to issues of population growth. Egypt's population problems are two-fold: rapid rates of population growth related to high fertility and an unbalanced population distribution. The highest fertility level is found in rural Upper Egypt, 5.2 births per woman, compared to a lower fertility level of 2.7 births per woman in urban Lower Egypt (Chelala 1996, 1651).

In order to help curb population growth, the government has consistently advocated the use of family-planning methods. However, the quality of family-planning services is often poor, contraceptives are not readily available, and, especially, poor and rural women are reluctant to use artificial birth control methods, which they have heard rumored are detrimental to women's health. Many unwanted pregnancies end in self-induced abortions because abortion is prohibited in Egypt, except in cases where pregnancy threatens the life of the mother. The 1995 Egypt Demographic and Health Survey, a nationally representative survey of 14,779 married women aged 14 to 49, shows a leveling off of the contraceptive prevalence rate at around 48% from 1991 to 1995. Although contraceptive use in Egypt doubled between 1980 and 1995, from 24% to 48%, most of the increase happened in the 1980s, with no significant change in the overall rate of contraceptive use between 1991 and 1995. The 1995 survey also revealed significant differences in the level of contraceptive use based on region, with women in Lower Egypt showing the lowest contraceptive use. This high discrepancy can be attributed, at least in part, to lower socioeconomic conditions and traditional practices and beliefs.

A primary issue discussed during the International Conference on Population and Development held in September 1994 in Cairo was the relationship between religion, family planning, and women's rights. Abortion turned out to be the most controversial topic. Muslims vehemently argue against abortion as a means of family planning but believe that abortion should be tied to the family unit. They believe that abortion may be practiced in exceptional cases where the health of either the mother or the fetus is in danger. The government's stance is that women must avoid abortion as a method of family planning, but the government does not provide treatment and counseling for women forced to resort to this measure.

Herbal and folk contraceptives are still popular, particularly in rural areas. Midwives are popular sources for information on preventing pregnancies and inducing abortions. Midwives are also often indirectly involved in the hymen-breaking ceremony of young virgins on their wedding night. Should a young woman not be a virgin or be worried about the intactness of her hymen, she may go to a midwife who will arrange for her to place a small sack with chicken blood into her vagina, so that when the marriage is consummated on her wedding night she will bleed.

Infertility, even though it is barely acknowledged or studied, is also an important problem that culturally afflicts primarily women in Egypt. In a society where it is imperative for women of all classes to bear children and, thus, attain social status through motherhood, the inability to bear children leads to serious social consequences. Alternatives to motherhood and domesticity are largely absent, and adoption is not allowed under Islamic law. Thus, for all women, biological parenthood is imperative, especially since under Islamic law a man has the right to replace an infertile wife through divorce or polygynous marriage. While polygyny is not an option that is exercised by upper- and middle-class men, the threat of divorce hovers over childless marriages. Among all classes and educational levels, women are typically blamed for reproductive failings, and they also bear the burden of overcoming this condition through a therapeutic quest that is often traumatic and unfruitful (Inhorn 1994, 5). Further, women face extremes of social judgment, for they are cast as being less than other women, as depriving their husbands and their husband's families of offspring, and as endangering other people's children through their supposedly uncontrollable envy.

## 10. Sexually Transmitted Diseases and HIV/AIDS

### A. Sexually Transmitted Diseases

Information about sexually transmitted diseases in Egypt is scattered and often anecdotal. Nevertheless, evidence suggests that sexually transmitted diseases are widespread in the general population. The only study, which provides some indication of the prevalence of sexually transmitted diseases, is research on reproductive morbidities, including reproductive tract infections, conducted among 502 women in two villages in rural Giza, 1989 to 1990. Sixty-four percent of the women sampled had a reproductive tract infection at the time of the survey, which may be in part because condoms are rarely used in Egypt. While solid data are lacking, the 1995 Demographic and Health Survey reported that only 14% of married women used condoms for family planning. It is, therefore, unlikely that condoms are commonly used in Egypt for disease prevention (Lenton 1997, 1005).

As in many other countries in sub-Saharan Africa, the migration–prostitution–STD triad is operative in Egypt. Studies indicate that, in particular, male labor migration, which is currently over 2 million, brings with it a variety of social ills, including STDs. Given strict cultural norms regarding women's premarital virginity and marital fidelity, Egyptian women find themselves on the receiving end of a variety of sexually transmitted infections. Their husbands, many of whom migrate for extended periods of time, contract gonorrhea, genital chlamydia, and other sterilizing infections, primarily from foreign prostitutes. Emerging studies from both rural and urban Egypt indicate that rates of various STDs are rising in similar proportions to the West. Often men contract STDs from either female or male prostitutes, and, given cultural norms that discourage this form of behavior, avoid seeing doctors. The infection, therefore, becomes chronic in men's prostates and they transmit the diseases directly on the first wedding night to their new brides. Women, thus, may start their marital lives with tubal infections that potentially lead to infertility. This has major societal implications, because infertile women face their greatest threat from their husbands, who have the right under Islamic law to replace an infertile wife through divorce or a polygynous remarriage. Such replacements are often encouraged by the husbands' families, who view an infertile wife as, at best, useless and, at worst, a threat to the social reproduction of the patrilineage (Inhorn 1996, 4).

Another factor that may influence the spread of STDs is the fact that Egypt remains a popular tourist destination, both for visitors to the pyramids and pharaonic treasures and, more recently, for seekers of sand, sea, and sex who visit Red Sea resorts. Despite the growing conservative fundamentalist movement, Egypt is still more liberal than other Arab states.

### B. HIV/AIDS

According to United Nations statistics, North Africa and the Middle East accounted for less than 1% of the total number of people infected worldwide with HIV. In this region, 27,000 people have died from HIV-related illnesses, compared to 170,000 in Europe and 46 million in sub-Saharan Africa (as of 1997). The National AIDS Program in Egypt recently published the number of units of blood that have tested positive for HIV in each of the seven years prior to 1997. The prevalence of infection is low and there is no real evidence of an upward trend. For example, in 1990, 136,422 blood units were tested and only 4 were positive for HIV; in 1996, a quarter of a million units were tested and only 3 were positive (Lenton 1997, 1005). The data from blood donations is particularly interesting, because all blood collected in Egypt's public-health facilities is voluntarily donated by family members of patients. There is no evidence of either voluntary or non-voluntary donor referral. Egypt's medical surveillance of blood units is, therefore, a good indicator of the prevalence of HIV in the adult population.

Despite worldwide increases in the AIDS epidemic, AIDS is so far not spreading in any perceptible numbers in Egypt. Nonetheless, factors that contribute to the spread of HIV definitely exist, and anecdotal evidence suggests that other sexually transmitted diseases are widespread in the general population. However, while reliable survey data is not available, Egyptian medical experts claim that the negligible spread of HIV infection and AIDS in the general population is possibly the result of the Islamic moral code, which forbids adultery, sex before marriage, and homosexual practices. This indicates that widespread adherence to this code could mean that, while HIV infection occurs in small groups practicing sexual behaviors that increase their chance of infection, only rarely do individuals in the general population come into contact with at-risk individuals. Nonetheless, research into patterns of sexuality is needed in order to explain the low prevalence of AIDS in Egypt. Also, the lack of reliable data makes it difficult to gauge the real situation from the picture presented by official sources.

[*Update 2002*: UNAIDS Epidemiological Assessment: Egypt appears to be at a low epidemic level. A small number of sex workers, men who have sex with men, and drug users have been tested yearly and the rate of HIV infection remains very low. In 1999, only one HIV-seropositive case was found out of 236 men who have sex with men who were tested. Likewise, there is still no evidence from reported data that HIV prevalence among injecting drug users is high. However, the problem of HIV and drug use in Egypt, as in many countries of the Eastern Mediterranean, should not be underestimated. In a recent study on the prevalence and patterns of drug use in Egypt, the rate of injecting drugs was around 13% of all practices of drug intake. HIV among sex workers is still below 1%. Clearly, with the current level of reported information about HIV in Egypt, and the obvious gaps in the surveillance system of high-risk groups, it is difficult to draw any conclusive remarks about the situation and the trends of HIV in the country.

[The estimated number of adults and children living with HIV/AIDS on January 1, 2002, were:

| | | |
|---|---|---|
| Adults ages 15-49: | 8,000 | (rate: < 0.1%) |
| Women ages 15-49: | 780 | |
| Children ages 0-15: | NA | |

[No estimate is available for the number of adults and children who died of AIDS during 2001.

[No estimate is available for the number of Egyptian children who had lost one or both parents to AIDS and were under age 15 at the end of 2001. (*End of update by the Editors*)]

## 11. Sexual Dysfunctions, Counseling, and Therapies

While there are no official studies on sexual dysfunction in the Egyptian population, it is widely known that Egyptian men are obsessed with enhancing sexual performance. While the men define enhanced sexual performance as prolonging intercourse, all remedies used suggest underlying occurrences of impotence. In recent years, Viagra has become very well known and popular in Egypt. During Ramadan 1999, better varieties of dates, which are very popular as one of the favorite foods for breaking the fast, were being sold under the names "Viagra" and "Monica" dates. Even melatonin, when it initially became popular on

the world market, was seen by Egyptian men as some kind of aphrodisiac, as a means for bringing one's youth back. Other remedies that are thought to be good for men are hashish, tea (but not mint or *karkadeh* or hibiscus tea), and other things which are "relaxing," for example, pigeon, sheep's feet, and also nutmeg. There are other more medicinal remedies available at the traditional pharmacies. In addition, there is *dahaan*, "ointments" of various kinds, local anesthetics also supposed to prolong erection. Many Egyptian men at the time of their wedding will seek advice on sexual aids in order to ensure that everything will "function properly."

Women's medicinal and folk medicinal remedies tend to center around issues of conception, pregnancy, and nursing. While many people are aware that female circumcision may lead to frigidity, as was mentioned above, it is still extremely common. Also worthy of mention is the cosmetic practice of hymen repair. Because of the fact that female virginity plays an enormous role in terms of the honor of a family and the bride involved, some doctors have developed the practice of sewing up ruptured hymens before an upcoming wedding night. This practice is particularly common among upper-middle-class and upper-class families, where the girls have been permitted more freedom in terms of their interactions with men before marriage, but where female virginity on the wedding night remains just as important as among the lower classes.

## 12. Sex Research and Advanced Professional Education

Sexological research is only in the initial stages in Egypt. While issues of family planning, mother and infant mortality, and women's reproductive concerns have been at the forefront of the Egyptian research agenda for quite a long period, other topics concerning sexuality are not. The growing fundamentalist movement further impedes any research that deals with issues of sexuality not directly related to reproductive issues.

There are no sexological organizations or publications in Egypt. The Egyptian Family Planning Association has its offices at: 66 Gazirat El Arab Street, Al Mohandissen, El Giza, Cairo, Egypt. Phone: 20-2-360-7329; fax: +20-2-360-7329.

[*Update 2003*: The Egyptian Society of Andrology (ESA) and the Pan-Arab Society of Impotence Research and Sexual Sciences (PASIR) are well established and popular societies in Egypt and the Middle East, working in the areas of erectile dysfunction and sexology. Egyptian consultants have also initiated several erectile dysfunction centers in Saudi Arabia and the Gulf area. Since 1985, the Andrology, Sexology, and STD Department at the University of Cairo has offered a doctoral degree, possibly one of the few in the world, in Andrology, Sexology, and STDs. The faculty have numerous publications in both national and international journals, including the *International Journal of Impotence and Sexual Research*. Most sexological work and publications from Egypt over the past 20 years have been done by members of ESA and PASIR—many of whom are members of both societies. Both societies maintain good relations and are supportive of each other's activities (www.family-clinics.com).

[Many eminent members of both societies have been active in local media to promote sexuality education and to fend off fundamentalist critics. Many are also working and actively educating against the practice of female genital mutilation (female circumcision), which is sadly still very popular in Egypt and many parts of Africa despite the laws passed against it. Others are working on updating the study curricula for undergraduate medical students and for postgraduate degrees in Andrology, Sexology, and STDs at Cairo University. ESA and PASIR members provide a variety of educational, scientific, and community services. They are also very popular and respected figures within our scientific community. (*End of update by H. Ghanem*)]

## References and Suggested Readings

Abdel Kader, S. 1992. *The situation analysis of women in Egypt*. Cairo: Central Agency for Population, Mobilization, and Statistics (CAPMAS) & UNICEF.

Abudabbeh, N. 1996. Arab families. In: M. McGoldrick, J. Giordano, & J. K. Pearce, eds., *Ethnicity and family therapy* (2nd ed., pp. 333-346). New York: Guilford Press.

Ahmed, L. 1982. Feminism and feminist movements in the Middle East: A preliminary exploration: Turkey, Egypt, Algeria, People's Democratic Republic of Yemen. *Women's Studies International Forum*, 5(2):153-168.

Al-Ali, N. 1997. Feminism and contemporary debates in Egypt. In: D. Cahtty & A. Rabo, eds., *Organizing women: Formal and informal women's groups in the Middle East*. Oxford: Berg Publishers.

Amin, Q. 1976. *Tahrir al-mara* [*The liberation of women*]. Reprinted in *Muhammad 'Imara, Qasim Amin: Al-amal al-kamila* (vol. 2). Beirut.

Anderson, J. N. D. 1968. The eclipse of the patriarchal family in contemporary Islamic law. In: J. N. D. Anderson, ed., *Family law in Asia and Africa* (pp. 221-234). London: George Allen and Unwin.

Badran, M. 1995. *Feminists, Islam, and nation: Gender and the making of modern Egypt*. Princeton, NJ: Princeton University Press.

Badran, M. 1991. Competing agenda: Feminists, Islam, and the state in nineteenth- and twentieth century Egypt. In: D. Kandiyoti, ed., *Women, Islam and the state* (pp. 201-236). Philadelphia: Temple University Press.

Badran, M., & M. Cooke. 1990. Introduction. In: M. Badran & M. Cooke, eds., *Opening the gates: A century of Arab feminist writing* (pp. xiv-xxxvi). Bloomington, IN: Indiana University Press.

Baron, B. 1994. *The women's awakening: Culture, society and the press*. New Haven, CT: Yale University Press.

Beck, L. G., & N. Keddie, eds. 1978. *Women in the Muslim world*. Cambridge, MA: Harvard University Press.

el-Baz, S. 1997. The impact of social and economic factors on women's group formation in Egypt. In: D. Cahtty & A. Rabo, eds., *Organizing women: Formal and informal women's groups in the Middle East*. Oxford: Berg Publishers.

*Beijing National Report*. 1995. Cairo: The National Women's Committee, National Council of Childhood and Motherhood.

Botman, S. 1999. *Engendering citizenship in Egypt*. New York: Columbia University Press.

Bouhdiba, A. 1985. *Sexuality in Islam* (A. Sheridan, trans.). London: Routledge and Kegan Paul.

Bousquet, G. H. 1948. La conception du nikah selon les docteurs de la loi musulmane. *Revue Algerienne*, 63-74.

Brooks, G. 1995. *Nine parts of desire: The hidden world of Islamic women*. New York: Anchor Books/Doubleday.

CAPMAS (Central Agency for Population, Mobilization, and Statistics). 1986. *National census*. Cairo: CAPMAS.

CAPMAS. 1990. *Labour force sample survey* (LFSS), Cairo: CAPMAS.

CAPMAS and UNICEF. 1991. *Women's participation in the labour force*. Cairo: CAPMAS and UNICEF.

Chelala, C. 1996. Egypt faces challenge of population growth. *The Lancet*, 348:9042, 1651.

CIA. 2002 (January). *The world factbook 2002*. Washington, DC: Central Intelligence Agency. Available: http://www.cia.gov/cia/publications/factbook/index.html.

Fernea, E. W. 1998. Egypt. In: *In search of feminism: One woman's global journey* (pp. 240-288). New York: Doubleday.

Geissinger, A. 2000 (February 1-15). New divorce laws proposed in Egypt raise unnecessary and damaging rumpus as usual. Available: muslimedia.com/archives/oaw00/ergy-women.

Haeri, S. 1989. *Law of desire: Temporary marriage in Iran*. London: I.B. Tauris.

Hatem, A 1992. Economic and political liberalization in Egypt and the demise of state feminism. *International Journal of Middle East Studies*, 24.

Inhom, M. 1994. *Quest for conception: Gender, infertility and Egyptian medical tradition*. Philadelphia: University of Pennsylvania Press.

Karam, A. 1998. *Women, Islamisms and the state: Contemporary feminism in Egypt*. New York: St. Martin's Press.

Kershaw, S. 2003 (April 3). Cairo, once 'the scene,' cracks down on gays. *The New York Times*, p. A3.

Lenton, C. 1997. Will Egypt escape the AIDS epidemic? *The Lancet*, 349:9057, 1005.

Macleod, A. E. 1991. *Accommodating protest: Working women and the new veiling in Cairo*. New Haven, CT: Yale University Press.

Mernissi, F. 1993. *Islam and democracy: Fear of the modern world*. Reading, MA: Addison-Wesley.

Mernissi, F. 1991. *The veil and the male elite: A feminist interpretation of women's rights in Islam*. Reading, MA: Addison-Wesley

'al-Misri, A. I. al-N. 1994. 'Umdat al-Salik wa-'Uddat al-Nasik. Reliance of the traveller: The classic manual of Islamic sacred law (In Arabic with facing English text, N. H. M. Keller (trans.), rev. ed.). Evanston, IL: Sunna Books.

Murray, S. O. 1997a. Male homosexuality, inheritance rules, and the status of women in medieval Egypt: The case of the Mamluks. In: S. O. Murray & W. Roscoe, eds., *Islamic homosexualities: Culture, history, and literature*. New York/London: New York University Press.

Murray, S. O. 1997b. Woman–woman love in Islamic societies. In: S. O. Murray & W. Roscoe, eds., *Islamic homosexualities: Culture, history, and literature*. New York/London: New York University Press.

Murray, S. O. 1997c. The will not to know: Islamic accommodations of male homosexuality. In: S. O. Murray & W. Roscoe, eds., *Islamic homosexualities: Culture, history, and literature*. New York/London: New York University Press.

Murray, S. O., & W. Roscoe, eds. 1997. *Islamic homosexualities: Culture, history, and literature*. New York/London: New York University Press.

Najmabadi, A. 1991. Hazards of modernity and morality: Women, state and ideology in contemporary Iran. In: D. Kandiyoti, ed., *Women, Islam and the state*. London: Macmillan.

el-Nashif, H. 1994. *Basic education and female literacy in Egypt*. Cairo: Third World Forum, Middle East Office.

Parrinder, G. 1980. *Sex in the world's great religions*. Don Mills, Ontario, Canada: General Publishing Company.

Sachs, S. 2000 (January 28). Egypt makes it easier for women to divorce husbands. *The New York Times*, International Section.

Schneider, H. 2000 (April 14). Women in Egypt gain broader divorce rights. *Washington Post*, p. A16.

Talharni, G. 1996. *The mobilization of Muslim women in Egypt*. Gainesville: University of Florida Press.

UNAIDS. 2002. *Epidemiological fact sheets by country*. Geneva, Switzerland: Joint United Nations Programme on HIV/AIDS (UNAIDS/WHO). Available: http://www.unaids.org/hivaidsinfo/statistics/fact_sheets/index_en.htm.

UNICEF. 1993. *Report on the state of women and children in Egypt*. Cairo: UNICEF.

Verma, B. R. 1971. *Muslim marriage and dissolution*. Allahabad, Egypt: Law Books Co.

# Estonia

## (*Eesti Vabariik*)
## (Republic of Estonia)

Elina Haavio-Mannila, Ph.D., Kai Haldre, M.D.,
and Osmo Kontula, Ph.D.*

## Contents

## *Demographics and a Brief Historical Perspective*

ROBERT T. FRANCOEUR

### A. Demographics

The northernmost of the three Baltic states, Estonia is located in Eastern Europe, north of Latvia and west of Russia. To the north of Estonia is the Gulf of Finland and Finland. Estonia's western border is formed by the Baltic Sea and Gulf of Riga. With a total area of 17,462 square miles (45,226 km²), including 1,520 islands in the Baltic Sea, Estonia is slightly smaller than the states of New Hampshire and Vermont combined. The terrain is marshy and lowlands, with maritime, wet, moderate winters and cool summers.

In July 2002, Estonia had an estimated population of 1.42 million, or 1.37 million in the last national census of 2000 (Estonian Board of Border Guard, Statistical Office, http://www.stat.ee/). (All data are from *The World Factbook 2002* (CIA 2002) unless otherwise stated.)

**Age Distribution and Sex Ratios**: *0-14 years*: 16.4% with 1.04 male(s) per female (sex ratio); *15-64 years*: 68.5% with 0.93 male(s) per female; *65 years and over*: 15.1% with 0.49 male(s) per female; *Total population sex ratio*: 0.86 male(s) to 1 female

**Life Expectancy at Birth**: *Total Population*: 70.02 years; *male*: 64.03 years; *female*: 76.31 years

**Urban/Rural Distribution**: 73% to 27%; 67.4% versus 32.6% in the 2000 national census

**Ethnic Distribution**: Estonian: 65.1%; Russian: 28.1%; Ukrainian: 2.5%; Byelorussian: 1.5%; Finn: 1%; Other: 1.8% (1998). The official language is Estonian, which be-

*Communications*: Elina Haavio-Mannila, Ph.D., Department of Sociology, P.O. Box 18 (Unioninkatu 35), FIN-00014 University of Helsinki, Finland; elina.haavio-mannila@helsinki.fi. Kai Haldre, M.D., Sexual Health Clinik, Suur-Ameerika 18A, Tallinn 10122. Estonia; kaihaldre@hotmail.com. Osmo Kontula, Ph.D., Population Research Institute, The Family Federation of Finland, P.O. Box 849, (Iso Roobertinkatu 20-22A), FIN 00101 Helsinki, Finland; osmo.kontula@vaestoliitto.fi.

(CIA 2002)

longs to the Finno-Ugric language family and is closely related to Finnish. English, Russian, and German, along with Finnish, are also widely spoken and understood.

**Religious Distribution**: Evangelical Lutheran, Russian Orthodox, Estonian Orthodox, Baptist, Methodist, Seventh Day Adventist, Roman Catholic, Pentecostals, Word of Life, and Jewish. Since the 16th-century Protestant Reformation, the Evangelical Lutheran Church has played the leading role in Estonia.

**Birth Rate**: 8.96 births per 1,000 population; 9.5 in the 2000 national census

**Death Rate**: 13.48 per 1,000 population

**Infant Mortality Rate**: 12.32 deaths per 1,000 live births

**Net Migration Rate**: –0.73 migrant(s) per 1,000 population

**Total Fertility Rate**: 1.24 children born per woman

**Population Growth Rate**: –0.52%

**HIV/AIDS** (1999 est.): *Adult prevalence*: 0.04%; *Persons living with HIV/AIDS*: < 500; *Deaths*: < 100. (For additional details from www.UNAIDS.org, see end of Section 10B.)

**Literacy Rate** (*defined as those age 15 and over who can read and write*): 100% (1998 est.); compulsory school attendance from 7 years to 16 years of age

**Per Capita Gross Domestic Product** (*purchasing power parity*): $10,000 (2001 est.); *Inflation*: 5.8% (2001 est.); *Unemployment*: 12.4%; *Living below the poverty line*: 25% (2000 est.)

### B. A Brief Historical Perspective    KAI HALDRE

In the area that now forms present-day Estonia, the first settlements occurred some 11,000 years ago, after the last ice cap retreated. During the 12th century, the Baltic region was in the hands of the Teutonic Knights. Estonia was incorporated into Christendom at the beginning of the 13th century, under the pressure of crusaders from Germany and Denmark. During the 14th century, the power shifted to the Hanseatic League, with several Estonian towns and cities belonging to the League, including Tallinn (Reval), which had received its city charter as early as 1248.

In the first half of the 16th century, the Protestant Reformation reached Estonia. Since that time, Estonia has remained a part of the Lutheran cultural space. From 1558 onwards, Estonia became the battleground for a war involving Denmark, Sweden, Russia, and Poland. Sweden won the war and Estonia remained under her sphere of influence until the beginning of the 18th century. During Swedish rule, the first university in Estonia was founded at Tartu in 1632. The Great Northern War left Estonia under Russian rule (1721). Estonia became a window through which Peter the Great wished to gain access to Europe.

In the 19th century, the winds of numerous national movements blew through the whole of Europe. In Estonia, the period of national awakening began with the publication of Estonia's national epic *Kalevipoeg* in 1862.

The Estonian Republic was declared on February 24, 1918. At first, this was merely a decision made on paper. True independence was fought for between 1918 and 1920, during the War of Liberation. The struggle was crowned with success, and a treaty was finally signed with Soviet Russia, which revoked in perpetuity all claims over Estonia. During independence (1918-1939), Estonia established diplomatic relations and made its existence felt throughout Europe. Independence was curtailed by the signing of the Pact between Nazi Germany and the Soviet Union in 1939.

Following the Soviet occupation in 1940, Estonia became part of Nazi Germany from 1941 until 1944. The Soviet Union incorporated Estonia in the fall of 1944. A large proportion of the population fled abroad. Many others were arrested and deported to Siberia. Those who remained had to adjust to a new way of life. Estonia succeeded in regaining its independence when the Singing Revolution was signed in 1988, with full independence once more since 1991.

## 1. Basic Sexological Premises

According to the Estonian sexologists Imre Rammul, Olev Poolamets, and Tõnu Ots (2000), the sexological premises behind contemporary sexuality and sexual life in Estonia has deep roots:

Before Christianity, Estonians were quite liberal about sexuality. It was not a sin for a woman to be sexually active before marriage, in some places it was appreciated to have a child already before the marriage as it indicated the reproductive capacity of the woman. Folk merrymakings contained orgiastic elements. Special holy places were defined to carry out fertility rituals, using totemistic items and figures of the Fertility Goddess, *Maaema*. Thunder and rain were connected with male Gods; fertility and the harvest were influenced by female Goddesses.

Something like trial marriage was accepted for a period of one year. However, it was more a trial of reproduction rather than a testing of psychological compatibility.

These liberties were mostly accepted silently for nonmarried people. Later the society, especially men, tried to keep genetic purity with repressions aimed at those not following the rules. It seems that later as a result of Christian attitudes and traditions, abortions and killing of newborns became more common. Though Estonians have had some gender role models similar to those in neighboring countries, the historical background did not contribute to the opposition between genders. The reason is probably that marriage had traditionally been more like a social agreement rather than a trade. Also, women in the Estonian household had more power than men who were more involved outside the household. Marriage was not complicated by the rule that the manor lord had the right to intercourse with the wife on the wedding night.

Bridal ransom has never been a tradition in Estonia, the reason for that being unclear. It was enough to bring a bottle of alcoholic drink to the parents of the bride while making the proposal. The parents also considered the economic capability of the man or made him work for the family. Even today the word to depict the son-in-law and the farmhand/servant is the same in Estonian and Finnish *sulane/sulhanen*. On the other hand, the bride was commonly required to have an amount of property—a special box that was called *veimevakk/dowry-chest*. Its contents included different handwork and jewelry and symbolized that the woman was industrious and not poor. In Estonia, many Christian sexual manners were combined with traditional paganistic habits.

Estonia was part of the Russian Empire in 1721-1918. It might sound surprising, but Russia, even before the beginning of the 20th century, was quite liberal in matters of sexuality. Probably, it was because of the early spread of atheistic ideas and later because of the attitude that during communism, everything is common (except one's own wife). Already in 1848, Shavrov issued his research about female sexual satisfaction. Later, Tarnadovski published *Female Sexual Disorders*. However, most research described statistics or deviant sexual behavior, mostly among men. A 1904 presentation by Nenadovitsh at Pirogov Institute in St. Petersburg, on "Anaesthesia sexualis mulieris" (including classification of female sexual dysfunction), was an early cornerstone of Russian, and hence Baltic sexology.

A widespread study of students' sexual behavior was carried out by Tshlenov in 1909. It was already influenced by the coming Revolution and remains one of the last studies in the country. The results of the study were confiscated by the police.

The period of independence in Estonia between the two World Wars was a sort of pre-revolution before the real sexual revolution in the 1960s, with contradictory attitudes. There was an increase in prostitution, the coming out of sexual minorities, and the cult of nudity, but this raised opposition, creating moral police and organizations to promote the moral way of life. There were also some medical publications taking a stand against masturbation and polygamy as harmful practices. At the same time, nice romantic literature became internationally popular in *The Ideal Marriage* (1930) by Theodore Van de Velde and other similar works. Meanwhile, sexuality in school and university curricula was limited to its medical aspects.

During the Soviet occupation, human sexuality was a taboo in Estonia as it was all over the Empire until the end of the 1980s. This taboo was illustrated by the TV bridge between the USA and Soviet Union at the end of the 1980s, when one Russian lady announced, "*There is no sex in Soviet Union.*"

In spite of that, already in the 1960s, several people tried to touch on sexual issues. For example, in 1964, urologist Mihkelsoo at Tartu University started to use human ribs to perform operations in the case of erectile dysfunction. At the end of 1960s, psychiatrist Heiti Kadastik from Tartu University started offering lectures on sexology for students. Kadastik also initiated translation and publication of a book by Finnish psychiatrist Martti Paloheimo, *Openly About Marriage*. This book, published in 1974, remained almost the only source of literature about sex for Estonians thereafter and became a cult itself. Psychoanalysis was represented by V. Vahing, who for several years had a private practice as well as taught students. Another key person in the development of Estonian sexology was psychologist Tõnu Ots, who started to answer questions about relationships in a youth magazine *Noorus* in 1971. He used the name Dr. Noormann, which remains a synonym for sexology counselor until today.

## 2. Religious, Ethnic, and Gender Factors Affecting Sexuality

### A. Source and Character of Religious Values

The dominant religion in Estonia is Evangelical Lutheranism. Estonians were Christianized by the Teutonic Knights in the 13th century. During the Reformation, Lutheranism spread, and the church was officially established in Estonia in 1686.

At the same time, Estonian culture and politics influenced the traditions of the church. The privileges granted to the Baltic-German nobility by the Russian Czarist powers in 1743 to supervise the church, the schools, and hospitals paralyzed church activities, as the church lost its relative independence. The 1832 ecclesiastical law reduced the Evangelical faith in orthodox Russia to the status of a "tolerated" religion. In 1919, in the newly independent Republic of Estonia, control of the church passed into Estonian hands. Religious freedom was granted to all persons and all denominations. The Estonian Evangelical Lutheran Church with an Episcopal-synodical structure was created and soon grew to be the largest church in Estonia, with 80% of the population as its members. In 1925, the church was separated from the state, but religious instruction remained in the schools and clergymen were trained at the Faculty of Theology at Tartu University.

With the Soviet occupation and the implementation of anti-Christian legislation, the church lost over two thirds of its clergy. Work with children, youth, publishing, and so on, was banned, church property was nationalized, and the Faculty of Theology was closed. Although some church services were tolerated (Sunday church services and presiding over funerals), by the 1970s, less than 10% of Estonians were prepared to publicly state that they were Christians. It was not until 1988 that the state's religious policies became tolerant, and by 1990, repressive legislation was annulled.

Today, the Estonian Evangelical Lutheran Church is the largest church in Estonia, with 169 congregations and approximately 175,000 members. Although Estonia has never had a "state church," the predominant position of Lutheranism is based on a centuries-long tradition. The next in size, also with long historical traditions, is the Estonian Apostolic-Orthodox Church, with 58 congregations and approximately 18,000 members. Other Orthodox in Estonia belong to the Russian Orthodox Church, whose activity has not yet been coordinated with local laws. Third in size is the Alliance of Estonian Evangelical Baptist Congregations, which consists of 89 congregations with 6,100 members. Although official statistics imply one congregation for every 2,700 inhabitants, only 16% of the population has formalized their ties to a specific congregation. Most Estonians do not belong formally to any religious community. According to the Estonian sex survey of 2000, 22% of Estonian-speaking men and 19% of Russian-speaking men, and 37% and 50% of respective women consider religion important in their life.

### B. Source and Character of Ethnic Values

Most of the religious adherents among the country's Russian-speaking population are Orthodox, while the Estonian majority is predominantly Lutheran. There is a deep-seated tradition of tolerance of other denominations and religions. Although the majority of citizens are nominally Lutheran, ecumenical services during national days, Christian holidays, or at public events are common. Tension between the ethnic Estonian and ethnic Russian populations generally do not extend to religious matters.

According to the population and housing census in 2000, there are 1.37 million people living in Estonia. 80% of them are citizens of Estonia, 6% citizens of Russia, 0.7% citizens of other countries, 0.6% with unknown citizenship, and 12% of the population are with undetermined citizenship. About 83% of Estonian citizens speak Estonian as their mother tongue, 15% speak Russian, and 1% speak other languages. One of the main priorities of the state integration program is to teach the state language, while at the same time creating opportunities for the different ethnic groups to learn their mother tongues. There are more than 140 ethnic groups represented in Estonia, forming around 32% of the population. The largest non-Estonian ethnic groups are Russians, Ukrainians, Byelorussians, and Finns.

The tensions between the ethnic groups in Estonia have culminated in citizenship laws. Estonian citizenship demands officially accepted Estonian language skills shown by a test. Non-citizens in Estonia are guaranteed basic rights under the Estonian Constitution, including the right to unemployment benefits and social services. Although they have no voting rights in Parliament elections, they can vote in local governance elections. This has caused problems in the process of joining the European Union, which will take place in 2004.

## 3. Knowledge and Education about Sexuality

In the late 1960s, a growing demand for sexual counseling initiated an idea to create a family counseling center in Tallinn. In 1975, this center started sexuality education lectures for the adult public and schoolchildren. Sexological counseling was provided by gynecologists, urologists, and psychiatrists. People from different specialties, mainly gynecologists and psychiatrists, could get postgraduate training in sexology in St. Petersburg (Leningrad), Moscow, or in Ukraine at Harkov or Kiev. Being a medical person gave a sort of "permission" to talk about sex. Educators generally lacked an interdisciplinary approach and presented the views of their own background.

Nowadays, sex education is included in the school health education curricula. There are nongovernmental organizations established in the first half of the 1990s, which provide information materials. Young people can visit the 15 youth counseling centers in different parts of Estonia to get individual counseling on reproductive and sexual health issues. Sexologists work in Tallinn and Tartu. Sex education had improved a lot at the end of the 1990s thanks, to NGOs and the empowerment of schoolteachers, the Internet, youth and women's magazines, and many other sources. These rapid recent developments are not yet reflected in statistics or research data. (See Section 5B, Interpersonal Heterosexual Behaviors, Adolescents, for survey data on sexual education and knowledge.)

## 4. Autoerotic Behaviors and Patterns

ELINA HAAVIO-MANNILA

### Children, Adolescents, and Adults

Masturbation is a common harmless practice. Nowadays, men and women with sexual problems are encouraged to masturbate in order to overcome their inhibitions (Kay 1992). People with a high interest in masturbation have been found to be less afraid of intimacy than those with no interest in masturbation (Rinehart & McCabe 1998). The way in which individuals view masturbation is linked to their perceptions of its nature and the consequences associated with it in a given culture, particularly during one's teenage years (Kontula & Haavio-Mannila 2002).

### Prevalence and Frequency of Self-Pleasuring

The Estonian sex survey of 2000 (see Haavio-Mannila & Kontula 2001) shows that 64% of men and 47% of women respondents had practiced masturbation at some time in their life. In the past month, 33% of men and 22% of women reported having masturbated. In a Multiple Classification Analysis (MCA) with five predictors: gender, age group, type of relationship, education, and national group, Estonian-speaking respondents reported self-pleasuring more often than Russian-speaking Estonians. Younger and more-educated respondents reported masturbating more often than older and less-educated subjects. Type of couple relationship (married, cohabiting, living apart together (LAT), and being single) had no statistically significant association with masturbation. Compared to Finns and Swedes in the 1990s, Estonians were less likely to report masturbation, whereas, compared to people in St. Petersburg (and Finland in 1971), they were more likely to do so.

In 1996, Eesti Kirjandusmuuseum (The Estonian Literature Museum–ELM) in Tartu collected sexual autobiographies in response to advertisements in 17 newspapers and journals. Sixty-two sexual life stories were received. Thirty-eight of them were translated into English. The examples cited here are from the translated autobiographies. In terms of autoeroticism, these Estonian sexual autobiographies, especially those written by men, included a lot of stories about autoerotic behavior. Women less often wrote about autoerotic behavior than men. [This collection of autobiographies was organized by Rutt Hindrikus, supported by a grant received by a grant to J. P. Roos from the University of Helsinki. Merle Karusoo edited 21 of the autobiographies into a book (Karusoo 1997).]

These stories confirmed the common-sense assumption that young Estonian males learn autoerotic behavior from other youngsters:

> Once one of my classmates invited me to their sauna. His two brothers, who were studying in technical school, and a boy from next door, would also be there. We five would have a real men's sauna! I went! The sauna was good and hot and soon all the youths were sitting lined up in a row, on the top step of the "stage," all naked of course. My classmate suggested we give ourselves erections and measure to see who has the longest tool. We had a wooden, folding ruler with clear numbers (meters). The erections were achieved with the help of soap and by sliding the foreskin back and forth until my tool was as taut as a bowstring (I felt it would snap any minute). My classmate and I measured 18 cm. His one brother's and the neighbor boy's measured 20 cm. and the third brother's was 22 cm. After we had finished measuring one of the older brothers said, let's jerk off and see whose sperm shoots the furthest. All five boys masturbated to climax and exploded with that great feeling and a huge spurt of white liquid. The first stream landed near the wall at the opposite side of the narrow washroom and every one thereafter increasingly closer until it merely trickled down the head of our shafts: Our tools were all swollen close to bursting—red, and with veins bulging. We were perspiring heavily and silent for a while, while we recovered. Then began the real sauna. We washed, birched and swam in the lake behind the sauna. This was the first time I had masturbated and have done so again later in life. (ELM 1996)

Getting intense pleasure from autoerotism makes the following young woman hypothesize that she will continue self-pleasuring also after marriage:

> In about the ninth form (or earlier) I discovered something pleasant! Taking a bath I accidentally found out that it was awfully pleasant to direct the spout of water on my clitoris (at that time I did not know what clitoris was). I felt how my body became tense; meanwhile the feeling was so strong that I could not direct the spout, and then the frantic end, and I was not able to continue that activity even for a moment. Soon I discovered that when to stop it for a while I could stand the feeling again. I was very happy about that discovery and thought that if the intercourse with a man was as pleasant, it was worth to be desired. I could take a bath several times a day and you may presume that someone might wonder why it took me so much time. I did not tell anyone about that, and even now that I am going to be thirty already I have confided in one friend only. I do not deny that I have to do that also when married. (ELM 1996)

Masturbation compensated for the lack of sexual commitment by men. Married and cohabiting men masturbated less often during the previous month (29%) than single men (40%) and men living in a separate steady relationship (36%). Nevertheless, having had intercourse during the past month was not connected to masturbation in the same time period.

Autoerotic behavior of women seems to be a more private, secret matter than that of men. Contrary to men, autoerotism and heterosexual activity during the past month were associated among women. Women who had had intercourse in the previous month masturbated more often than women who had not had intercourse—27% compared with 15%, respectively ($p < .003$).

The gender difference was also apparent when one looked at the masturbation of women in different types of couple relationships. Twenty-two percent of married and cohabiting women had masturbated during the past month, slightly more than had single women (19%). Women who were living apart together in a committed relationship (LAT) were most active in self-pleasuring. As many as 33% of them had masturbated in the previous month. These connections are partly because of the different age composition of the four couple-relationship types. Separately living and cohabiting women were, on average, ten years younger than the single and married women subjects.

### Predictors of Masturbation

Beyond the influence of gender, age, relationship type, education, and nationality on experiences of self-pleasuring during the lifetime summarized above, is our deeper study of how the social background and some characteristics of the present relationship predict recent masturbation using stepwise regression analysis. Because we wanted to explore the impact of relationship factors, we excluded from the analysis people not living in a couple relationship as married, cohabiting, or having a steady sexual relationship without living together (LAT).

We found that recent masturbation (seven alternatives; see Table 1) was connected to mutual oral sex[1] (standardized beta coefficients were, for men .17 and for women .29), and finding pornography arousing (both genders .15).

For men only, being an Estonian-speaker instead of a Russian-speaker (beta .19), dissatisfaction with sexual life as a whole (beta .18), practicing manual sex (.21), frequent use of alcohol[2] (.14), and having had parallel relations dur-

---

[1]*Oral sex.* A sum scale composed of the five response alternatives in the following two questions: "In the last five years, how often have you had oral sex in your sexual relationships, that is, caressing a man's penis or a woman's genitals by mouth? Partner has/I have done [it] mostly, sometimes, seldom, 1-5 years ago, and not at all" (range 2 to 10).

[2]*Alcohol usage.* The six alternatives were: Daily, twice a week, once a week, a couple of times a month, once a month, and once in two months or more seldom.

ing the present couple relationship (.13) predicted masturbation too.

For women only, masturbation correlated with young age (beta .12), number of sexual partners during the past year (.18), and wanting to have intercourse more frequently in the present couple relationship[3] (.11). In addition, masturbation was associated with low quality of the present couple relationship[4] (.12).

The regression model predicted 29% of the variation of recent masturbation by men and 22% by women. When the influence of all these variables was controlled for, masturbation was not statistically significantly explained by, for example, education and recent intercourse.

These findings indicate that recent masturbation among people having a steady couple relationship is part of a *liberalized and versatile sexual lifestyle* (oral and manual sex, accepting pornography, having had several sexual partners, and frequent alcohol use). It is also connected to *problems in the couple relationship*. For men living in a steady sexual relationship, this can be seen in the association of recent masturbation with dissatisfaction with their sexual life and having had parallel relations. For women in couple relationships, the compensatory nature of masturbation emerges as a connection between self-pleasuring and a low quality of the present steady sexual relationship and longing for more frequent intercourse with the permanent partner.

For single people, autoerotism is sometimes the only way to get sexual release, as is evident in the autobiographical passages above. According to the survey data, masturbation did not compensate for the single men's lack of a steady partner. Estonian men without a steady sexual partner practicing self-pleasuring were dissatisfied with their sexual life as a whole (beta .28). Their sexual lifestyle was versatile with recent experiences of oral sex (.30).

Among single women, the young ones (.30), those getting aroused by pornography (.24), and those having practiced oral sex (.24) had engaged in masturbation more recently than other women. Single women with recent experiences of masturbation were as satisfied with their sexual life as a whole as were the women who had masturbated a long time ago or never. For single women, masturbation seems not to be a desperate attempt to cope with the "misery" of not having sex with a partner, which may cause dissatisfaction. In sum, autoerotic behavior is part of a liberated sexual lifestyle more often for single women than for single men.

## 5. Interpersonal Heterosexual Behaviors

### A. Children

There is autobiographical, but no statistical information.

### B. Adolescents                    OSMO KONTULA

*Behavior and Knowledge*

After the incorporation of Estonia into the Soviet Union, sexuality was a taboo topic for decades, making it difficult to obtain sex information. As a consequence, the state of sex education in Estonia was poor until the 1990s. In the KISS (*Küpsemine Inimsuhted Sõbrad Sesksuaalsus*) survey (conducted in Estonia in 1994 among 1,080 schoolchildren at the 9th grade—15 year olds), a good level of sexual knowledge among Finnish boys was five times as high as among Estonian boys, and among Finnish girls eight times as high as among Estonian girls. In Estonia, the sexual knowledge level of the girls was lower than that of the boys. Adolescents with a low level of sexual knowledge mostly had not discussed these issues with their parents or friends, nor had they sought information from alternative sources (Papp et al. 1998).

Estonian society accepted adolescents' romantic feelings towards the opposite sex but disapproved of sexuality in the relationships of adolescents. Courtship in Estonia has had significantly less sexual intimacy than in Finland. Estonians had much less sexual intercourse in their courtship than did Finnish adolescents. A double standard for males and females was common: 18% of boys and 5% of girls reported that they had experiences of sexual intercourse. For masturbation, these figures were 14% and 6%, respectively. During the occupation, articles published, as well as programs of sex education for schools, presented masturbation to adolescents as a vice and recommended weaning oneself away from it.

In 1999, another KISS survey was conducted among 1,676 students in the 9th grade. In this survey, girls showed a marked improvement in their knowledge compared to 1994. The number of pupils with poor sexual knowledge had been cut in half. Topics concerning sexuality began to be discussed more frequently in schools during this period. However, a fifth of Estonian pupils and half of the Russian pupils said that questions concerning sexuality had not been discussed in the classroom in this or previous years. As a source of information, video films and pornographic magazines were popular among boys, and articles in women's and youth magazines among girls. Sexual intercourse was experienced by 9% of the 15-year-olds in 1994 and by 14% in 1999. The increase was much more pronounced among girls. Slightly over half of the respondents of Estonian origin had used a contraceptive (mainly a condom) in their first intercourse. Condom use had not increased during the five-year follow-up (Papp et al. 2001).

In a 2000 sex survey of adult Estonians, only 10% of the people who belonged to the middle-age group (35 to 54 years) and an equal proportion belonging to the old-age group (55 to 74 years) reported that they had received enough sexual knowledge from their parents. In the youngest generation, this proportion was almost a quarter. More-open discussion about sexual issues had started in homes, although only in exceptional cases.

According to the responses in the 2000 survey, there has not been much sex education in Estonian schools before the

### Table 1

### Time of Latest Masturbation Event, in Percent

| | Men | | Women | |
| | Estonian | Russian | Estonian | Russian |
| Masturbation | speakers | speakers | speakers | speakers |
|---|---|---|---|---|
| During the past 24 hours | 9 | 3 | 4 | 4 |
| During the past week | 15 | 8 | 7 | 6 |
| During the past month | 14 | 11 | 13 | 7 |
| During the past year | 11 | 9 | 14 | 15 |
| 1-10 years ago | 9 | 12 | 8 | 6 |
| Over 10 years ago | 11 | 10 | 4 | 3 |
| Never | 31 | 47 | 50 | 59 |
| Total | 100 | 100 | 100 | 100 |
| Number of respondents | 301 | 142 | 329 | 192 |

---

[3]*Wanting to have more intercourse.* The four alternatives were: I would like to have intercourse clearly more often, somewhat more often, I am satisfied with the present frequency of intercourse, and I would like to have it less frequently.

[4]The quality of the relationship was measured by a sum scale based on dichotomous variables of happiness of the couple relationship, open communication on sexual matters with the partner. The opposite of low-quality relationship is high-quality relationship, HQR (see Kontula & Haavio-Mannila 2003).

1990s. Only a few percent report that they have received enough knowledge in sexual issues in their school. Even in the youngest generation, this proportion was only around 10%; the comparable figure was two thirds in Finland. Even though the available knowledge and material (including pornography) have increased in the 1990s, there is still a major deficit in sexual knowledge in Estonia.

### Dating

Forty-eight percent of Estonian-speaking men and 43% of Estonian-speaking women had dated before they were 18 years old. For Russian-speaking men and women these proportions were 38% and 41%. The average age for the first dating was 18.2 years for men and 18.3 years for women. This age had decreased for both genders. In the oldest generation (age 55 to 74), the average age at first dating was 20.0 years.

Young Estonian men dated for the first time when they were around 17 years old, about the same age of their Finish cohort. Compared to their Finnish counterparts, Estonian women dated for the first time at an older age, having started dating, on average, at 17 years old. This was a year later than in Finland. Among Estonian women, the average age of first date was comparable to that one generation ago in Finland.

### Sexual Debut

According to the Family and Fertility Survey carried out in 1994 in Estonia, 40% of those age 20 to 24 had started sexual life by age 18, compared with 14% in the age group 40 to 45 years. The mean age of first sexual intercourse in these age groups was 18.4 and 20.1 years, respectively. According to the Estonian Health Interview Survey carried out in 1996, 40% of women in the age group 20 to 25 and 10% of women in the age group 40 to 45 had had intercourse by age 18 years.

In the 2000 sex survey, 42% of Estonian-speaking men and 29% of Estonian-speaking women had had intercourse by the age of 18. For Russian-speaking men and women, these proportions were 38% and 21%, respectively. A third of Estonian-speaking women and half of Russian-speaking women had experienced first sexual intercourse after they were 20 years old. The age of sexual initiation has been higher for those whose level of education has been higher than average.

The age of first intercourse has been changing in Estonia in much the same way as in most other European countries, only the timing of this transition has been one generation later than in most Western European countries. In the female generation born in 1927 to 1931, the average age of first intercourse was 22.3 years; in the female generation born in 1972 to 1976, intercourse came, on average, at 17.5 years. During these years, the average age of first intercourse had decreased by as much as almost five years. Among men, a similar decrease occurred from 19.7 years to 17.3 years, a smaller decrease of only two and a half years. A couple of generations ago, men had their first intercourse two years younger than women in the same age group. In today's youngest generation, there is no longer as much difference between genders in sexual initiation.

In comparison to the neighboring countries, young men in Estonia experienced their first intercourse almost at the same age as in Finland. The other men in Estonia had had their first experience when somewhat older than men in Finland, but roughly at the same age as men in St. Petersburg.

Estonian women had experienced their first sexual intercourse significantly later than women in Finland. In each age group, Estonian women had their sexual debut on the average of one or one and a half years later than Finnish women. This difference was even bigger between Estonia

and Sweden. The decreasing trend in Estonia has followed the trend measured in Finland, with a 20-year delay. The decrease in the age of sexual initiation started earlier in Estonia than in St. Petersburg.

Estonian women had a higher age for sexual debut than men, and they also married younger than men. In the 2000 survey, the average age at first marriage was 23.8 years for men and 21.8 years for women. This implies that, on the average, women have had several years less sexual experience than men before they marry. Almost half of women and a quarter of men married their first sexual partner. This proportion had been higher among Russian-speaking men and women than among Estonian-speaking men and women. It has also declined from one generation to the next.

The Western sexual revolution that reduced the average age of female sexual debut in Western European countries by two to three years from the 1960s to the 1990s, arrived in Estonia and Russia one generation later than in the West (Bozon & Kontula 1998; Kontula 2002; Kon 1995). This one-generation difference has been found, for example, in attitudes towards sexual activities of teenagers. Sexual initiation in Estonia has been more limited to engagement and marriage than in the other Western European countries, and young men have had more sexual freedom than young women. A sexual double standard still exists in Estonia. However, among the young generation, already four fifths of Estonian men and women approved of teenagers' sexual intercourse, provided they are going steady.

In a European comparison, the age of sexual initiation in Estonia was found to be fairly high, even though trends have followed the Eastern European trends. The Estonian male debut age in the last two generations has been one of the highest in Europe. The Estonian female debut age was as high as in Portugal, which had the highest debut age in Western Europe, but lower than, for example, in Romania, Moldova, and in some cities in Russia (Kontula 2002).

### C. Adults                                      ELINA HAAVIO-MANNILA

Here, we look at marriage and family structures and patterns in Estonia using several indicators: people's couple relationships at the time of the surveys, and then their lifetime relationship patterns (numbers of marriages, cohabitations, and sexual partners, and experiences of love at work). A brief passage discusses the number of sexual partners in the past year. A considerable part of this section is devoted to parallel or extra sexual relationships and attitudes toward marital fidelity. Finally, we look at the ideal sexual lifestyles of people in Estonia.

### Sexual Relationships

*Type of Couple Relationship.* More than 40% of the respondents in Estonia were married, one fifth was cohabiting, and one fifth had a permanent sexual relationship without living together—living apart together (LAT). About 20% of men and 30% of women were at present living without a steady sexual relationship. Estonian-speaking men were more often single (26%) than Russian-speaking men (15%). Compared to people in Sweden, Finland, and St. Petersburg, people in Estonia were less often presently married. There was, however, quite a lot of cohabiting and separately living (LAT) people. Thus, the proportion of people in a couple relationship (marriage, cohabitation, or LAT) was about the same as in the neighboring countries.

*Duration of the Present Relationship.* On the average, people in Estonia had lived 15 years in their present couple relationship. According to MCA, there was no statistically significant gender or national difference in the duration of the relationship. Self-evidently, the unions of younger people were shorter than those of the older ones. The unions of the officially married persons had lasted on the average of 20 years, those of the cohabiting people 11 years, and those of the people with a steady relationship living separately only 8 years. There was a weak association between the education of the respondent and the duration of his or her relationship. The unions of the least educated had lasted longer, 17 years, compared with 15 and 14 years for people with the middle and highest education, respectively.

*Number of Marriages or Cohabitations.* Quite a lot of Estonians were not with their original marital or cohabiting partner. Thirty percent of the ever-married or cohabiting Estonian-speaking men and 26% of Russian-speaking men in Estonia had been married or cohabiting more than once. For women, the proportions were 34% and 28%. On the average, the ever-married or cohabiting persons had been married or cohabiting 1.4 times. MCA showed that there was neither gender nor educational differences in the number of unions. Older, cohabiting, and Estonian-speaking people reported more marriages or cohabitations than the others.

In Finland in the 1990s and in St. Petersburg, fewer people than in Estonia had been married or cohabiting more than once. In the older age groups, multiple marriages were more common in Sweden, Estonia, and St. Petersburg than in Finland.

*Lifetime Sexual Partners.* The average number of sexual partners in a lifetime was 13 for Estonian men and 16 for Russian men in Estonia. In both ethnic groups, women had had, on average, 5 sexual partners. Very few, 12% of men and 22% of women, had had only one sexual partner. A large gender gap can also be seen in the finding that 40% of men and 17% of women had had at least 10 sexual partners. There were no significant age, educational, and national-group differences in the number of partners. Married and cohabiting people had had fewer partners (8) than the separately living (13) and single people (10).

Finding out the large number of partners of her partner was a shock to a 71-year-old woman teacher:

> I found his notebook, where he had put down the names and birthdays of his girls, and the dates when the relationship had began. My name occupied the 78th place. I cannot describe the disgust I felt reading that list. It was just as if I had sunk into deep, stinking and sticky mire; the taste of it was in my mouth. Where was the deep and happy first love, which should have given support in all hardships of life? . . . Oh how right had been my father, trying to persuade me to give him up. I told myself that as I had chosen that path myself, I had to bear my cross without letting anybody know about my sufferings. (ELM 1996)

For a 54-year old Estonian man, it was not a big deal to have several lovers:

> Anyway, that bottle of cheap, 1.60 rubles wine set me going on a merry-go-round of sex affairs, which did not stop for a number of years and involved a frequent change of partners. There were women whom I did not even ask the name and there were some who I kept seeing for a long time. The older I got, the more "luck" I had with women older than myself and married ladies. I liked the latter because with them there was no need to talk about love or promise to be true to the end of my days (which in fact I never did); it was enough to pay them some compliments and hear the usual story of a drinking, unfaithful or brutal husband and find the words of consolation. (ELM 1996)

The number of sexual partners in Estonia was about the same as in Sweden and Finland. Inhabitants of St. Petersburg

had had fewer partners. In Sweden and Finland, the middle-aged respondents reported the highest numbers of sexual partners in a lifetime, and oldest people the lowest numbers. Contrary to this, in Estonia and St. Petersburg, the number of partners of the youngest people was the largest. This indicates that sexual liberalization has been quite recent and most powerful among young Estonian and Russians in Estonia.

*Sexual Partners During the Past Year.* A majority of Estonians who had had intercourse in the past year had only one sexual partner: two thirds of the men and 85% of the women. One quarter of Russian men and 14% of Estonian men had had at least three partners. In Estonia, having had several sexual partners during the past year was much more common in the younger age group (average 2.1 partners) than in the middle and older age groups (1.4 and 1.6 partners). Married and cohabiting people had fewer partners (1.5 and 1.3) than people living apart together (2.5) and single people (2.6). Education did not predict the number of partners during the past year. In the past year, Russians in Estonia had had more partners (2.0) than Estonians (1.6).

*Love at Work.* In Northern Europe, most women work for pay and there are plenty of opportunities to find interesting love objects in the workplace. About every second Estonian had experienced "falling in love" at work, with a coworker or someone else met at work. Only 2% to 6% of the respondents were in an affair at work at the time of the survey; the others reported past affairs or infatuations. There were no statistically significant differences between men and women or in the type of their steady relationships. Middle-aged people, as well as those with higher education had fallen in love at work more often than the others. Estonian men had experienced a work romance slightly more often (51%) than Russian men, 51% versus 40%. The incidence of love at work in Estonia did not differ from that in Finland or in St. Petersburg.

*Incidence of Parallel Relations.* Having had parallel or extra sexual relationships in addition to a present marriage or cohabitation was more common among men than among women. In Estonia, 35% of Estonian men and 39% of Russian men had engaged in a parallel relationship during their present marriage or cohabitation, compared with only 24% and 21% of respective women. Most of the parallel relationships had been casual. Only 7% of Estonian men and 12% of Russian men in Estonia reported regular parallel relationships; for women it was 6% and 4%, respectively.

Age group, education, and nationality did not predict parallel relations, but the type of couple relationship did. As many as 43% of people living apart together had had a parallel relationship during their current LAT. Only 30% of the married and 17% of cohabiting persons had had parallel relations during their present union. Parallel relations of men were more common in St. Petersburg than in Estonia. The proportion was about the same as in Finland in the 1990s. Women in Estonia and St. Petersburg had been unfaithful more often than women in Finland.

The quality of the couple's relationship predicted faithfulness in marriage or cohabitation. This was especially true for men. For Estonian men with a "high quality relationship"—defined as a happy couple relationship with easy communication and mutual love (see discussion of Sexual Satisfaction below)—only 28% had been unfaithful during their marriage or cohabitation. For men with a poorer quality relationship, as many as 52% had had one or more affairs. For women, the proportions were 24% and 41%. Also in the sexual autobiographies, parallel relationships were often explained as a consequence of a poor marital relationship. The same connection between fidelity and the quality of the relationship was found also in St. Petersburg and Finland (Kontula & Haavio-Mannila 2003).

Four excerpts from the ELM archives illustrate the varieties of parallel relationships, starting with the most common type: *extramarital relations of men with non-married women*.

The following married male teacher was asked by a single woman to take her virginity and even make her pregnant:

> There was a girl from the Faculty of Medicine who was especially keen on helping me, even after her graduation. And what came out, she had been in love with me. She was already twenty-eight years old, but still a virgin. In the end, she asked me to help her to lose her virginity. I had never in my life had sex with a virgin before, I agreed willingly. We drove out of the town, it was June and a very beautiful day. It was near Tartu, on a nice grassy meadow, where we managed to get rid of her virginity. But that was not enough for that girl. Later, she asked me to give her a child; she promised to raise it herself, without bothering me. Now I regret it, but then I agreed. She chose the most suitable time for conceiving and got pregnant from the very first effort. She kept her promise and had a very fine son all by herself! Her son is a grown man already, a bright and energetic person, his mother is still grateful to me. (ELM 1996)

Affairs by *married women with unmarried men* were rare. The following story is from a married woman architect who had had a satisfying extramarital romance while studying abroad:

> In summer after my fourth year of university I had the chance to go abroad through the student exchange. We visited the Bratislava Art Institute. Half of the group was from Tallinn Art Institute and half from Kiev Art Institute. It happened somehow that I became friends with a young man from Kiev called Vassili. We went together through the wonderful art galleries of Prague and went walking in the evenings. We had our first sexual intercourse somewhere on the park-bench. I was awfully ashamed because I was married but Vassili said there was no difference if I was with him just once or more and so I went with him also to his hotel-room. Vassili was very good but I understood it really when I went to visit him in Kiev in my fifth year. Vassili liked to sex long and energetically. I do not know where he got his endurance. He trained himself at yoga. Maybe it helped? (ELM 1996)

Men enjoyed when they happened to have ample opportunities to get new women (and good food) through their work. A 68-year-old male teacher took advantage of tourist trips on which he met women traveling alone:

> In the Soviet Union I went on the tourist trips that took me all over the country, as a rule, these were quite long ones, and many women were traveling alone. I usually went in August, as the grapes and other fruits were ripe by that time. The fruits were helpful with sex too. And in the southern republics it was possible to taste all kinds of local wines, which was also very helpful in forming relationships. So I met plenty of willing women on those trips. The local women tended to appreciate a man from a Baltic country very much. (ELM 1996)

For some married women, it was difficult to abstain from sex because of the absence of the husband who was working or studying far away. A 69-year-old chauffeur writes about these women as follows:

> There is also another group of women and men who have extramarital affairs. These are women whose husbands

are away from home for a long time, they are either taking some courses, in the army or long business trips. They just need a partner who would be alive and there with them. I once met one such woman. She worked in our ministry. Her husband was sent to some course in Leningrad; it had something to do with the Communist Party. One day she dropped me a note to meet at our common friend's place. I went there but my friend wasn't home. The woman had a lot of difficulty explaining that she just wanted to make love. I freed her from tormenting herself. Through my wife I knew that some women have really bad time when they don't have a sexual partner. (ELM 1996)

*Attitudes Toward Marital Fidelity.* Attitudes toward temporary infidelity of a husband were more liberal than toward an unfaithful wife. In Estonia, men were more permissive than women, especially when it was a question of male unfaithfulness. A very clear ethnic difference could be seen in the attitudes of Estonians and Russians in Estonia in permitting temporary infidelity by a husband. As many as 60% of Russian-speaking men, but only 27% of Estonian-speaking men accepted it. On this issue, Russian men in Estonia were even more permissive than men in St. Petersburg. Also, in respect to temporary infidelity by a wife, Russian-speaking Estonians were very permissive compared to Estonians. The results of MCA showed that age group and education did not explain the attitudes of people in Estonia toward fidelity, but the type of couple relationship did. People in LAT relationships were more liberal than the others.

In comparing people in Finland and St. Petersburg, russophones in Estonia were very permissive in regard to marital infidelity. Only men in St. Petersburg were close to them in accepting male infidelity.

The attitudes of Estonians on infidelity were amply expressed in the sexual autobiographies. Most of those who gave their opinion on this issue were quite permissive. A 28-year-old unemployed man reports:

> Adultery? On the one hand I consider marriage to be a holy union, but on the other hand I do not think that husband and wife belong to each other only and are each other's property. Sexual intercourse can happen out of love of adventure or of friendship or it can just be a casual act between two people. A person is still a very many-sided creature, and why cannot s/he have friends outside of marriage, with whom occasionally to go to bed with? Simply one's feelings should be under control and not let the situation grow beyond oneself. But I still think that if one of the partners finds a new one for him/herself, there is still something wrong in the relationship and it should be an alarm signal. Before that, one should still think whether the "danger" exists and how serious it is. (ELM 1996)

The same opinion is expressed by a 68-year-old divorced woman worker:

> And I am not so negative about extramarital relations—that might sometimes improve the situation, the man or the woman might find that another partner is no better than the old one. (ELM 1996)

But there were also negative attitudes. The following 58-year-old woman teacher was ashamed of her extramarital relations and strongly condemned them.

> I, too, at first out of defiance, later simply because of opportunities had some extramarital affairs. . . . I would give much . . . to undo it. Out of my own experience it is perfectly clear to me that the highest value of a woman is her moral pureness, not the number of men whom she can get into her bed. On the basis of present-day attitudes I could

even look for justification. Maybe my marriage did not satisfy me. . . . [But] I am ashamed and regret until now, more than thirty years later. (ELM 1996)

*Ideal Sexual Lifestyle.* The ideal sexual lifestyle of Estonians varied a lot. The most-often-chosen lifestyle was living married without other sexual relationships. It was chosen by about 30% of men and 40% of women. The next-popular lifestyle was living together with a partner without marriage (cohabitation) and without other relationships—about 15% of both genders. Thirteen percent of men, but only 3% of women preferred marriage with parallel relations. Seven percent of men and 2% of women preferred cohabitation with parallel relations. Women were more likely to choose separate living as their favorite sexual lifestyle than were men— 12% versus 6%. Surprisingly, 12% of the women did not have any sexual relationship in their life; 4% of the men were also in a celibate lifestyle. The gender differences can be summarized by saying that men preferred marriage or cohabitation with other relations, women preferred separate living or no sexual relations. The differences between Estonians and Russians in Estonia were very small.

Compared to Swedish and Finnish men, Estonian men more often preferred as their ideal lifestyle marriage or cohabitation with parallel relations. Estonian women would choose celibacy as their sexual lifestyle more often than women in Sweden and Finland. (Haavio-Mannila & Kontula 2001, 150-151). This indicates that there may be some problems in the couple relationships in Estonia.

### Sexual Behaviors

Sexual behaviors were studied using the time since most recent intercourse, position in last intercourse, attitude toward women taking an initiative in sexual contact, manual and oral sex, orgasm in intercourse, and erection problems.

*Time Since Last Intercourse.* In answering the survey question "When was the last time you had sexual intercourse?" men reported more-frequent intercourse than women. Seventeen percent of the men and 12% of the women had had coitus in the last 24 hours; 34% and 27% in the past 2 days (cumulative percentages); 44% and 38% in the past 3 or 4 days; 56% and 46% in the past week; 66% and 55% in the past 2 weeks; 74% and 61% in the past month; 83% and 67% in the past 3 months, 90% and 73% in the past year; 93% and 78% in the past 2 years; 98% and 89% in the past 10 years; and 2% and 11% more than 10 years ago.

There was very little difference between Estonians and Russians in the time since last intercourse. Fifty-seven percent of the Estonian men and 54% of the Russian men in Estonia had had intercourse in the past week, of the women 48% and 44%, respectively. Younger people were more active than older people, persons living in a steady relationship more active than singles, and Estonian-speakers more active than the others. Education did not make any difference in sexual activity, when the influence of the other factors was controlled for in the MCA. Fewer Estonians had had intercourse in the past month than people in Finland and Sweden and men in St. Petersburg. Especially the older Estonians and Russians had stopped having intercourse when they have grown older.

*Position in Last Intercourse.* The most common position in sexual intercourse was laying face-to-face, man on top and woman underneath. As many as 37% of men and 40% of women in Estonia reported that this "missionary" position was the only position used in their last intercourse. The reverse position, with the woman on top and man underneath, was the only position used by 12% of men and 7% of women. Lying side by side was the only position in the in-

tercourse reported by 8% of both genders; 6% of men and 7% of women used other positions, and 30% of men and 28% of women used two or more different positions.

Using several positions in the latest intercourse did not differ by gender or national group. Young people had used versatile positions more often than the older ones. People in LAT relations had most often used several positions (42%, people with other types of relationships 25% to 28%). More-educated persons were slightly more likely to engage in different positions than the less-educated. People in Estonia used several positions in their last intercourse to the same extent as Finns in the 1990s and people in St. Petersburg (and clearly more than Finns 30 years earlier).

*Attitude Toward Gender Equality in Initiating Sexual Contacts.* In the Western world, initiation of sexual contacts by women has traditionally been rare; women were expected to be passive and men active in sexual interaction. In Estonia, 93% of Estonian-speaking men and 69% of respective women and 86% of Russian-speaking men and 67% of respective women totally or somewhat agreed with the statement: "Women have every right to take the initiative when they want sexual contact with men." Supposedly, it is taken for granted that men have this right. Thus, we take the attitude toward the statement as an indicator of attitudes toward gender equality in sexual initiation.

According to MCA, men were more favorable toward female initiative than women themselves were, young people more favorable than older people, people in a couple relationship more favorable than singles, and Estonian-speakers more favorable than Russian-speakers in Estonia. Compared to Finns, people in Estonia and St. Petersburg were less gender-equality oriented. Only the Finnish female respondents 30 years ago were as reluctant to give women the right to initiate sexual contacts with men as were women in Estonia and St. Petersburg.

*Oral Sex.* A majority of the respondents had engaged in oral sex. This was measured by the question: "How often have you had oral sex in your sexual relationships, that is, caressing a man's penis or a woman's genitals by mouth in the last five years." The response alternatives were presented separately for passive oral sex received from a partner and active oral sex given to a partner.

About 60% of the respondents in Estonia had received or given oral sex in the past five years. Men reported oral sex somewhat more often than women did. There was no difference between the Estonian and Russian speakers in Estonia. Younger people were much more likely to report mutual oral sex (81% of the 18- to 34-year-olds) than middle-aged (53%) and older people (13%). Living in a LAT relationship and having higher education were connected to the practice of oral sex. In Sweden and Finland, mutual oral sex was more common than in Estonia. In St. Petersburg, men reported mutual oral sex as often as in Estonia, but women less often. Among young people, national differences in having practiced oral sex were small. Estonia and St. Petersburg differed clearly from Finland and Sweden in the older age groups, where oral sex was rare.

*Manual Sex.* Giving a partner satisfaction by hands was quite popular in Estonia. Men reported it somewhat more often than women did: only 28% of men, but 37% of women had never given manual sex. Twenty-two percent of men and 16% of women had given manual sex to his or her partner during the past 7 days, 26% and 31% at most a month ago (cumulative percentage), 40% and 40% 1 to 6 months ago, 47% and 46% 6 to 12 months ago, 55% and 54% 1 to 5 years ago, and 62% of men and 63% of women more than 5 years ago. Younger people had practiced more oral sex than the older ones; people living in a LAT relationship more than the those living in the other types of sexual relationships; the more educated more often than the less educated, and Russian speakers more often than Estonian speakers. In Finland, manual sex was somewhat more common than in Estonia, especially in the older generation.

*Orgasm in Intercourse.* Having defined an orgasm as "sexual pleasure ending to relaxation and very good feeling," the question was: "Have you got an orgasm during sexual intercourse?" Men reported orgasm much more frequently than women did. Only one in ten women reported that they had always reached orgasm in intercourse, of the men about 60%. Russian-speakers reported orgasm more often than Estonian-speakers did.

Frequent orgasm in intercourse was, according to MCA, related to male gender, young age, living in a permanent sexual relationship, and higher education. The statistical significance between the national groups disappeared when the impact of the other variables in the model was adjusted for. International differences in getting orgasm (almost) always were very small, both among men and among women.

In Estonia, Finland, and St. Petersburg, getting an orgasm (almost) always in intercourse was more common among younger than older women, with the excerption that in the youngest age group (18 to 24 years), it was not very frequent. In Sweden, however, elderly women reported orgasm as frequently as middle-aged women.

*Erection Problems.* Two thirds of Estonians reported having at least sometimes encountered problems with male erection in their sexual encounters. The question was phrased as follows: "It is not uncommon that a man cannot enter into sexual intercourse because he cannot get erection or his penis becomes flaccid right when sexual intercourse is started. In the last year, has something like this happened to you/your partner?"

Men reported erection problems somewhat more often than women did for their partners. Estonian-speaking men had had more erection problems in the past year (49%) than Russian-speaking men (33%). Female respondents of both ethnic groups reported equally often that their male partner had had erection problems—38% and 32%. Erection problems strongly increased with age. The less educated reported them much more often than the more educated. Type of relationship was not related to erection problems.

Erection problems were a little more common in Estonia than in Sweden and Finland in the 1990s. There was a large regional difference in the share of men with erection problems among the 35- to 54-year-olds. More than 70% of people in Estonia, but only 50% to 60% of Swedes and Finns reported erection problems in the past year. Erection problems were very common among the 65- to 74-year-old Estonian speakers—96%.

Sexual behavior of the Estonian- and Russian-speaking people in Estonia was, in most respects, very similar. Russian respondents in Estonia reported more often to giving their partner manual sex, always reaching orgasm in intercourse, and having less often had erection problems than Estonian-speakers.

### Sexual Satisfaction

In the Estonian sex survey 2000, we asked about satisfaction with sexual life as a whole, satisfaction with the frequency of intercourse in the present couple relationship, pleasure derived from intercourse, quality of the steady relationship (happiness of the couple relationship, easiness of talking about sex with the partner, and mutual love), and sexual self-esteem (to what extent the respondent considers him- or herself to be sexually skillful, active, and attractive).

*Satisfaction with Sexual Life as a Whole.* About 25% of Estonian-speakers in Estonia and 33% of Russian-speakers were very satisfied with their sexual life as a whole. Forty-two percent of male Estonian-speakers and 40% Russian-speakers, and 36% and 22% of women, respectively, were fairly satisfied with their sexual life. About 20% found it unsatisfactory. The rest considered their sexual life as neither satisfactory nor unsatisfactory. Russian women in Estonia gave more-extreme responses (very satisfied or not satisfied) than Estonian women, but the average satisfaction of the two female groups was the same.

According to MCA, there was a bimodal relationship between age and sexual satisfaction in Estonia. The younger and older people were more satisfied with their sexual life than the middle-aged were. People with a steady sexual relationship were very much more satisfied than single people. People in Estonia were less satisfied with their sexual life as a whole than Swedes and Finns were. Estonian men of both ethnic groups were as satisfied as men in St. Petersburg. Estonian women were more satisfied than women in St. Petersburg.

In the four research areas, satisfaction with sexual life as a whole varied by age in different ways. In Sweden and Finland, age differences were small. In Estonia and St. Petersburg, there was a sharp decline from the age group 25 to 34 years to the 45- to 54-year-olds, but then an increase toward the oldest age groups.

*Pleasure from Intercourse.* Thirty-five percent of Estonian-speaking and 34% of Russian-speaking men considered their sexual intercourse very pleasurable; of the respective women 19% and 23%. A majority, about 57% of men and 61% of women, reported that intercourse is quite pleasurable. Six percent of Estonian- and 11% of Russian-speaking men, and 18% of women in both ethnic groups evaluated intercourse as not pleasurable.

Younger people in Estonia enjoyed coitus more than middle-aged and older people. Cohabiting and separately living people found intercourse more pleasurable (mean on a 5-point scale was 4.2 to 4.3) than married (4.1) and single (4.0) people. The more-educated people enjoyed intercourse more than the less-educated ones. An international comparison reveals that Finns found intercourse more pleasurable than people in Estonia and St. Petersburg.

*Preferences for Frequency of Intercourse.* Two thirds of men and 45% of women in Estonia would like to have more-frequent intercourse in their couple relationship than they have at present. This indicates that there is a lot of unsatisfied sexual desire in Estonia. Only 1% of men and 6% to 9% of women wanted to have intercourse less often. The rest considered the frequency of coitus to be suitable.

More younger and middle-aged (64% and 60%) than older (46%) people would have liked to have more-frequent intercourse with their steady partner, in spite of the fact that the younger and middle-aged persons actually had had more recent intercourse than older persons. People's level of aspiration in regard to frequency of intercourse seems to decline with growing age. Also, the generation one is part of may have an impact: In the older generations, people may have had learned to demand or expect less-frequent sexual activity. Type of relationship and education did not predict preferences for frequency of intercourse. Compared with Finland and St. Petersburg, more people in Estonia would prefer more-frequent intercourse in their couple relationship than they have at present. The wide gender gap in the attitude toward frequency of intercourse was visible in all research areas. Everywhere, men would like to have more frequent intercourse than women did.

*Quality of the Couple Relationship.* Three indicators of the quality of the couple relationship were used in the Estonian sex survey of 2000: mutual love, happiness of the couple relationship, and ease of communication on sexual issues with the steady partner.

About 55% of Estonians of both genders and both nationalities felt that there is a man or a woman whom they really *love*, and the same proportion thought that they are really loved by some man or woman. The very young ones least often felt love. In the middle-aged and older age groups, the feelings of love decreased with growing age among women, but in the older male groups, love did not decrease with age. On the contrary, the oldest men very often felt love and being loved. This may explain their satisfaction with sexual life, which will be described below.

Married and cohabiting people reported mutual love most often—66% of men and 67% of women. Women in LAT relationships told of mutual love more often (58%) than LAT men (46%). Single people very seldom (men 9% and women 7%) thought that they loved and received love. The feeling of love was equally rare in Estonia and St. Petersburg. In Finland in the 1990s, three quarters of the respondents felt love and being loved. In their lack of love, Estonians and Russians resemble Finnish men 30 years ago.

A 61-year-old woman teacher tells about companionate marital love that has lasted for a long time:

I have been loving my husband for almost 40 years. Our marriage is continuously directed and guided by mutual respect and decency but we have certainly had the moments of excitement, burning passion and exaltation. I have never liked ambiguous conversations on the topics of love and sex. . . . I know that he does not watch erotic shows on TV and is mostly at home. Only his two main hobbies, sports and fishing make him go out. He usually goes fishing with children. For us, mutual understanding, trust and support have been more important than sex. Yet, we have also enjoyed the happiness of a complete unification with a person you can trust as much as yourself. (ELM 1996)

People in couple relationships (married, cohabiting, or LAT) were asked about the *happiness of their relationship*. Men reported happiness a little more often than women did. Twenty-one percent of men and 16% of women considered their couple relationship as very happy, 46% and 44% fairly happy, and 33% and 40% neither happy nor unhappy. There was no ethnic difference in this issue.

*Discussing sexual matters with the partner* was considered not at all difficult by 46% of men and 42% of women. Gender and ethnic differences in the easiness of communication were small.

The indicators of mutual love, happiness of the couple relationship, and open communication on sexual matters correlated with each other. They were combined to an index of High Quality Relationship (HQR). There was neither gender nor national differences in the quality of the relationship in Estonia according to MCA. Younger people rated the quality of their relationship higher than the middle-aged and older people. Married and cohabiting people found more love, communication, and happiness in their present couple relationship than people living apart together (LAT). The more-educated people reported more quality in their relationship than the less-educated.

International comparisons revealed that the quality of the couple relationship was lower in Estonia and St. Peters-

burg than in Finland. In all three areas, more younger than middle-aged and older people reported that the quality of their relationship was high. The exception was that, in Estonia and St. Petersburg, the oldest respondents aged 65 to 74 years reported higher quality of relationship than the 55- to 64-year-olds.

*Sexual Self Esteem*

"What is your opinion about the following statements concerning your sexual life and characteristics: I am sexually skillful, I am sexually active, and I am sexually attractive." In Estonia, men considered themselves more often sexually skillful and active than women did. Women had a little more belief in their sexual attractiveness than men had. Russian-speaking men considered themselves more attractive than Estonian-speaking men. Otherwise, the ethnic groups were similar. The three indicators of sexual self-esteem correlated with each other. The reliability of the three-item sum-scale of sexual self-esteem was 0.78 (alpha).

In Estonia, according to MCA, men, the younger, and the more-educated people had a higher sexual self-esteem than women, older people, and the less-educated people. Cohabiting and separately living (LAT) persons reported more self-esteem than married and single people. When we compared the three areas in which sexual self-esteem was studied, we found that men in Estonia and St. Petersburg had about as high sexual self-esteem as people in Finland in the 1990s. Women in Estonia had a lower sexual self-esteem than women in Finland in 1999 and in St. Petersburg.

## 6. Homoerotic, Homosexual, and Bisexual Behaviors

ELINA HAAVIO-MANNILA

**History**

Male homosexuality was not punishable in the independent Estonian Republic before World War II. In spite of this, there is no information about gay structures in Estonia in that era.

During the Soviet occupation, male homosexual behavior—specifically anal intercourse between men—was forbidden everywhere in the Soviet Union. Homosexuality was considered as a psychiatric pathology. This repressive legislation prevailed until June 1, 1992. However, the situation seemed to be more liberal in occupied Estonia than in most other parts of the former Soviet Union. Gay men who had no public sex or political problems, were not persecuted. Usually, no more than 10 men were imprisoned per year. Up to the mid-1980s, there was an unofficial gay bar in Tallinn. Also, there was at least one cruising area in both Tallinn and Tartu.

A decisive year for Estonian homosexuals was 1990, when the International Scientific Conference on Sexual Minorities and Society in Twentieth Century Europe took place in Tallinn, the first of this kind in Eastern Europe. Also, during 1990, the first advertisements for gay and lesbian acquaintants were published in independent newspapers. The first gay/lesbian organization in Estonia was the Estonian Lesbian Union, founded in 1990, followed two years later by the Estonian Gay League.

According to A. Raudsepp, an expert in the field, the situation of homosexuals has changed with the overall liberation and democratization in Estonia. The position for gay and lesbian youth in 2003 seems to be very different from the situation, for example, at the end of 1980, when some people started to come out as gays. During the Russian occupation, there was no information about homosexuality other than rumors, penal code, and psychiatric manuals. It was very difficult to meet other gay people.

## Attitudes Toward Homosexuality

The ambivalence of the attitudes toward homosexuality is clearly shown in the sexual autobiography of a 49-year-old male chauffer written in 1996:

> In US homos want to become quite official. I just can't understand such people. Once one of my friends told me a story about them. He had a small joint-stock company and went to Cesis (in Latvia) to get some goods. He stayed the night with his Latvian business partner. At night this man came to his bed and behaved the same way that a man does when he starts making love to a girl. My friend tried to push him away but he kept coming back. This lasted half of the night. In the other room there was a nice pretty wife of this man; they probably even had children. I tried to look upon this as some kind of disease that should be cured. During the Soviet times they tried to cure this with prisons but this isn't probably right, except in cases where the other party is a minor. I can understand women who make love to each other even less. But this has been a taboo, so we don't know much about that at all. (ELM 1996)

In Estonia in 2000, 50% of surveyed men and 63% of women agreed with the statement "Homosexuality among adults is a private affair of the people concerned with which officials the law should in no way interfere." Twenty-one percent of men and 12% of women disagreed with the statement. Quite a number of the respondents, 29% of men and 25% of women, found it hard to say what their position was. Women considered homosexuality to be a private affair more often than men did. There was no difference between the national groups in the attitudes toward homosexuality. Younger people were more liberal than older people. Type of couple relationship and education did not affect homosexuality attitudes.

## Sexual Orientation

In 2000, 12% of people in Estonia reported homoerotic feelings, i.e., they were sexually interested in the same sex. Most of these people were also interested in the other sex, that is, they had a bisexual orientation. Only 2% of men and no women were interested only or mainly in the same sex. People with lower education reported same-sex interest more often (16%) than those with middle or higher education (9%). Age, type of relationship, and ethnicity were not associated with sexual orientation.

Compared to Sweden and Finland, homoerotic interest was more common in Estonia and St. Petersburg. The highest rates appeared among Estonian-speaking women in Estonia (13% of the 18- to 54-year-olds) and St. Petersburg women (12%). In Estonia, contrary to the other areas, middle-aged and older people reported homoerotic feelings at least as often as younger people.

## Same-Sex Experiences

In 2000, 6% of men and 8% of women in Estonia had had sexual experiences with persons of their own sex. These encounters were more common among younger (14%) than among middle-aged and older people (3% to 5%). Type of relationship, education, and ethnicity did not predict homosexual experiences.

A 55-year-old Estonian unemployed man was not sure of his sexual orientation. He had had sexual experiences with both women and men.

> I was still quite helpless in intercourse later, but my kissing had developed much and I would still enjoy it, even on "some other places" . . . A week after our encounter she started suffering from awful pains, which made her scream. She was taken away, and forever—she had leukemia and it

killed her. With her gone, my intimate world collapsed. I buried myself in sport, until the next sexual experience, which was with a man when I was sixteen. It may seem that I have been a homosexual already from an early youth, but that is not true. My sharpest and most exciting memories are still of those overwhelming kisses and the first entry into a vagina. . . .

> . . . We were lying on the mattress and talking about all kinds of things. Then he started caressing me, and as I had experienced it already from a man, I was quiet and a sort of expectation came over me. Gradually he moved closer and closer to my genitals, pulled down my underpants and took me into his mouth. A sudden rush of pleasure gave me a start and I almost moaned aloud. He sucked me very skillfully, taking almost the entire length of my penis into his mouth and licked the tip of it. Stroking my balls he put one finger into my anus, which also gave me a new kind of pleasure. I had the feeling that my member would truly explode, it was so full of blood, stone-hard, really painful. He went on, caressing and stroking my penis with his tongue. He felt the throbbing of my member and sucked it deeper and deeper into his mouth. I couldn't stand it any more and ejaculated into his throat. I heard him swallow and his satisfied grunting, and felt myself totally pumped out. He asked me whether I wouldn't want to do the same to him. I suppressed the thought that the same thing is used to urinate; besides, he smeared something sweet-tasting onto his penis. At the beginning it felt disgusting, but he continued rubbing me and I felt a sort of passion arise. His member was very big and veined, my mouth got tired, but he encouraged and taught me all the time. He said he wanted to ejaculate into my mouth too, and if I couldn't (or wouldn't want to) swallow it, I could pass it from my mouth into his mouth, he would swallow it himself. I tried to follow his teachings and do the thing as well as possible. In the end I felt his member grow even more, then it started to jerk and a kind of salty greyish-white slime came out of it like from a fountain. I couldn't help but swallowed some of it, but passed the rest over into his mouth. We kissed for a long time with our sperm-smeared mouths and all this was simply indescribable. I still want to stress once again that actually I am not a gay or bisexual, only the circumstances developed this way. (ELM 1996)

Homosexual or bisexual authors of some sexual autobiographies in Estonia complained about their alienation and mental health problems. One should notice that the majority of the population has a favorable attitude toward homosexual behavior between adults; it is seen as a private affair with which officials and the state should not interfere.

## 7. Gender Diversity and Transgender Issues

KAI HALDRE

*Health System.* After regaining independence, health reform was carried out in Estonia. The Sick Insurance Fund was formed on a solidarity basis—up to every salary (payment to a person), 33% of a sick insurance tax has to be paid. After that, the person becomes insured and can have the majority of health services either free or for a very small payment. All minors up to 18 years old and retired persons are automatically insured. A list of pharmaceuticals is defined, which are compensated to a different extent according to the diagnosis and drug. Together with health reform, a family doctors' system was introduced.

Currently, there is no legal regulation for organizing help for transsexuals. In October 2002, a new law on organizing medical services was adopted, and all old regulations are not valid any more. Helping transsexuals will be organized in accordance with the principles adopted in the European Council's Parliamentary Assembly session No 41 in 1989.

There is a draft of a new regulation, according to which an advisory committee for helping transsexuals is formed. The task of the committee is to be the final body that makes the proposal to the Minister of Health to change the gender of a person. It can happen only if the person has felt that he or she belongs to the other gender/sex group for at least two years, after any psychiatric illness is excluded and the genetic sex is defined. Then, the Minister gives a decree, according to which hormonal therapy and surgical therapy can be started. Both are not obligatory and the person can stop at any stage. The passport is changed only after two years of treatment. If the person wants to change back to the initial gender/sex, it is done according to her or his written directive.

Transsexuals are entitled to get both psychological help and buy medications in the same way as all other people who have sick insurance. If they decide to have surgery, this cost is not covered by health insurance and they have to pay for it by themselves. Treatment of intersexual persons (both medical and surgical) is covered by sick insurance.

## 8. Significant Unconventional Sexual Behaviors

### A. Coercive Sexual Behaviors

*The Legal Situation*

Until the year 2002, the old modified Soviet law regulated legal penalties for sexual crimes. There was a differentiation according to how natural or unnatural a sexual act was. Sexual abuse/coercion performed by woman was not possible. The new law active since 2002 is based on the principle of sexual freedom of the person—a person him- or herself has the right to decide with whom and how he or she has sexual relations.

The penalty for rape is five years imprisonment. If the rape was with a person less than 18 years old, carried out by two or more persons, if the victim's health was damaged or death caused, if the victim has taken to a stage of suicide or attempt of suicide, or if the offender had raped earlier, the penalty is 4 to 12 years imprisonment. If the rape was inflicted on a person less than 14 years, the penalty is 6 to 15 years imprisonment.

In 2000, there were 676 criminal acts against a person. Of these 676, 54 were registered as rape (in 1999, there were 58 cases registered as rape). Out of these 54, 39 person's court decisions were put into force. At the same time, while criminal acts against a person have been decreasing since 1995, rape and attempts of rape have remained the same.

The Bureau of Equality of Rights in the Ministry of Social Affairs and the Estonian Open Society Institute has carried out some research on sexual violence. In 2001, the Estonian Open Society Institute studied the incidence of violence in the family and against women. Twenty-one percent of women and 16% of male respondents answered "yes" to the question "Have you experienced against yourself either physical, mental, or sexual violence during the last 12 months?" According to this study, it is estimated that every day, 252 women experience physical violence and 33 women experience sexual violence. Two thirds of the violent acts take place at women's homes.

In terms of social response, sexual violence still seems to be quite a taboo topic. Many professionals (medical persons, police, teachers, etc.) feel themselves uneasy while meeting the problem. At the same time, a lot of education has been provided to different groups (including police,

medical personnel, etc.) since the mid-1990s. Two children's support centers have been established. They deal with counseling and rehabilitating mistreated children and families. The Children Support Center in Tartu has been active since 1995, while Tallinn's Children Support Center was opened in 1999. The Open Estonia Foundation is financing both centers. Additionally, specialists are being trained to work with children, and a network of specialists is being established for solving cases of child abuse.

A sign of immaturity in the Estonian legislation is perhaps that the law on Equal Gender Rights (*Soolise Vordoiguslikkuse Seadus*) was not adopted by the Parliament in 2002. Parliament declared it "unnecessary" and some members of Parliament ridiculed it. Since sexual violence is mainly a problem for women, an equal-rights law would help in fighting against it.

### Child Sexual Abuse, Incest, and Pedophilia

ELINA HAAVIO-MANNILA

*Incest.* In the Estonian sexual autobiographies, there is a detailed story by a 16-year-old girl about the sexual abuse by her father:

> It was winter. I went to school and had my 15th birthday in September. Father drank every day. One night when he came home he appeared in my room. I had heard nothing. I woke up when he touched me. I did not dare even to move and was breathing with difficulties. I pretended to be sleeping and was terribly afraid. My heart was pounding. He touched my breasts and thighs. We sleep on a "double-decked" bunk with my brother and it seems that my brother moved in his sleep. Father went away pulling the blanket over me before that. I could not sleep till morning. I went to school broken and sad; I could not concentrate at the lessons and was terribly tired. A few days passed and everything happened again. I thought I would lose my mind out of fear and was having constant nightmares. I did not venture to speak about all that to anybody. It all went rather far. He began kissing me, taking out his penis and caressing me until it hardened, then tried to enter me but I could not bear it any longer, moved myself and pulled the blanket over my head—I felt myself totally defenseless. Father left. Next night he tried it again, again luckily without any result. At last he satisfied himself between my buttocks. He wiped the sperm off his penis, covered me and went to sleep beside mother in the other room. I was awfully scared. I went to the toilet and wiped myself clean. I wept from fear.
>
> After some days he came again, I pressed my teeth together and thought I now would get up and scream but fear fixed me to the bed, I was afraid, paralyzed by my own ignorance. At the same moment mother came in. I let out an imaginary sigh of relief, at last it was all over. But no, that was but the beginning. It seems mother had felt it strange that father was lingering in the kitchen so long (for my father had a habit of eating at night) and had decided to come and have a look. The only thing she said was: "So it is the child you are at now." That was said with great bitterness. Mother seemed to collapse inwardly as if some huge waves had carried her away. She could say nothing else. (ELM 1996)

*Other Abuse of Children by Adults.* Sexual abuse of children by adults was frequently mentioned in the autobiographies. A 39-year-old Russian-speaking woman writes:

> When I was 10 or 11, the other bachelor who was about 20 and half-wittedly asked me to come to his room so that the neighbors would not see me. He promised to buy me

candy when I show him my "thing." Our life was poor and Mother used to borrow from the neighbors to buy us food. I must have wanted candy so much I agreed to climb in through his window so that the others did not see me. (ELM 1996)

*Peer Harassment.* A married 59-year-old retired male teacher with two children writes about the after-play of peer harassment of girls in his own school-age.

> Toilets were the centers of sex lore for boys. When the girls could break off from their tormentors, they ran into the girls' WC. It was called a sanctuary by angry boys, but the girls themselves also called it so, because it was a safe place. When the boys had touched and pawed girls in the classrooms or corridors, they were quite aroused and ran into the boys' WC, where they jerked off. It was quick, and then they compared, who could shoot higher. I was 8-9 at the time, and knew everything, watching the "real men" and learning the trade. (ELM 1996)

In addition to schoolmates, the members of youth organizations could harass each other, as the following story by a 40-year-old woman architect shows:

> There is also one unpleasant experience from form 7 after a game of pioneers that we had had. All the girls had probably gone home already; I remained there in the wood with boys, to come home together with them. I trusted them; they had always been my good fellows. Then suddenly they dragged me down to the ground and tried to get my trousers off. I didn't realize at all what's going on. There was someone holding his hands on my mouth to prevent me from crying and someone climbed over me and tried to stuff something between my legs.
>
> I don't remember how I escaped from there. I probably began to cry so loud that they had pity on me. Or maybe there was someone with more common sense to stand up for me. The more active ones threatened me that they would catch me with a net the next day after school and take me to the wood. It was such a terrible threat for me that I didn't dare to go to school for two weeks. Luckily, the boys had lost interest in me by then. (ELM 1996)

*Gang Rape.* Gang rapes of girls occasionally took place in Estonia, even though the formal and informal punishments were very serious. A 60-year-old locksmith told stories of gang rape by peers.

> The schoolboys were running after girls too, trying to "make them." I know an occasion, when an eleven or twelve-year-old girl was caught and gang raped in the forest, the boys were telling about it afterwards. They described how the girl had tried to fight them off, but couldn't, and later they often visited that girl, she even sort of expected it. So a gang of boys spoilt a girl, who was too afraid to tell about it. (ELM 1996)

*Adult Sexual Harassment and Rape*

According to the 2000 Estonian sex survey, 2% of men and 14% of women in Estonia had been sexually harassed, 0.4% of men and 8% of women had been raped, and 3% of women had been both harassed and raped. Russian-speaking women in Estonia had been sexually harassed or raped more often than Estonian-speaking women had been—30% versus 22%. Three percent of respondent men and 13% of respondent women reported being the subject of physical violence from a long-term partner.

In the ELM archives, there are many stories on physical violence in relation to sexuality. Kelly (1988) has divided these into five groups: 1) harassment from flassing to assault,

but not attempted rape, 2) pressurized sex against one's own will, 3) coercive and forced sex involving elements of threat or fear, 4) (attempted) rape, and 5) general mentions about violence including domestic violence. There are not many stories in the sexual autobiographies about the author perpetrating a rape, but most of the authors told about attempting rape of another person or animals.

*General Family and Sexual Violence*

Violence in the family was sometimes upheld by the older-generation family members. The following 61-year-old Russian-speaking woman teacher writes:

> When he came home again, I told him about money [the mother of the author had demanded her to ask money from the husband for the upkeep of the family] but he did not give me any. He simply lived with me, used me and beat me. Whenever he had had alcohol he found a reason to beat me, cruelly, with his feet. Once he beat me on the head with his fists and it seems I even lost consciousness. Mother watched and told him: "It is right to educate her, otherwise she will not listen to me any more and there is nobody who could tame her." Yes, that was my own mother who allowed her daughter to be beaten in such a cruel way and never came to help me, to rescue me from the drunkard with whom I had refused to go out because he was drunk.
>
> I thank God I was saved from that sadist [the husband was put in jail for killing a man]. I wish he had got death penalty but it was our child that saved him from that. I thought that from now on I could live peacefully but no . . . he began to write me from the prison, threatening me in his letters. I have lived in fear all my life. When I started receiving those letters I must have thought about seeking defense from somebody and also I was fed up with my mother's scolding. I wanted a home of my own; I wanted to marry, to find a father for my child. (ELM 1996)

Women were more often than men victims of sexual harassment and violence, as can be seen in the lack of autobiographic stories by men on general family and sexual violence.

**Prostitution**

Since the beginning of the 1990s, combined with fast socioeconomic changes, there was a rapid booming of prostitution in Estonia. Kristiina Luht (2003) estimates that more than 1,000 prostitutes work in Tallinn. Since a prostitute's working time during the life course is quite short, 5 to 10 years, many more than a thousand women and men are involved.

According to Juri Kalikov (2003), two main tracks can be followed: first, girls go to bigger cities (half of the prostitutes come from Russian-speaking northeast Estonia), and second, women are taken abroad—mainly to Finland, Sweden, Poland, Germany, Denmark, Holland, and Spain. The human trade can appear in different forms: to work as a prostitute, to work as an *au pair*, cleaner, and so on, to work as a dancer (striptease), escort, and so on, and getting married with the aim of making a person work for free or as a sex worker. The local criminal organizations profit from prostitution and work closely together with foreign club or brothel owners.

In the 2000 Estonian sex survey, people gave their opinions on the following statement: "I have nothing against people earning money by selling sexual services (prostitution)." Fifty-five percent of men and 30% of women agreed entirely or almost completely with this statement. There was no difference between the national groups. Young people accepted it more often than middle-aged and older people. Type of relationship and education were not significantly connected with prostitution attitudes. Compared to the neighboring countries, Estonia was the most permissive to prostitution. People in St. Petersburg were particularly very much against it. But in the sexual autobiographies, many authors expressed their negative attitudes toward prostitution. The following 71-year-old woman teacher supports legal, controlled brothels:

> I do not justify prostitution, but those who want to sell themselves always find ways to do it. But this shouldn't ruin our youth. The ads in the newspapers where girls invite men to have coffee with them, giving addresses and phone numbers should be condemned. When I read the ads in the newspapers where somebody wants to find a boy- or girlfriend for extramarital relationship, I think that these people should be mad.
>
> There should be a house in town, where those who cannot do without it, could find satisfaction. This house should be under medical surveillance and the persons working there should be issued passports of different color than the other citizens. This lush sex is disastrous for the nation. (ELM 1996)

Twelve percent of men and 28% of women in Estonia had been solicited to have sexual intercourse in return for money or equivalent economic advantages, but had refused to take it. Three percent of the Estonian-speaking men and 1% of Russian-speaking men accepted the financial offer, as did 2% and 5% of the women. Younger and Russian-speaking people had been offered money for sex more often than older and Estonian-speaking people. Type of couple relationship and education did not predict persuasion to have sex for money.

Taking money for sex was more common among Russian-speaking women in Estonia and St. Petersburg than in Sweden and Finland. As many as 14% of the 25- to 34-year-old russophone women in Estonia had accepted money or other economic advantages for sexual services.

Ten percent of men in Estonia had paid for sexual intercourse. Only 2% admitted that they had been offered money for intercourse, but had refused to take it. Two women, both Russian-speaking, had paid for sex. National differences were not significant. The younger and the middle-educated had offered money for sexual services more often than the older and the least- or most-educated people. Type of relationship did not have any impact on paying for sex.

In Estonia, fewer men had paid for sex than in Sweden (15%) and Finland in 1999 (13%). In St. Petersburg, 10% had done it. Contrary to the situation in Estonia, where mostly younger men had paid for sex, in Sweden and Finland, middle-aged men most often reported having paid for sex.

## C. Pornography and Erotica

During the stagnation times of the Soviet system, before 1991, all sexual literature, sex aids and substitutes, films, and so on, were strictly forbidden in Estonia, and there were legal codes and sentencing procedures for offenders. But it was not totally absent from the society as the following passage of the sexual autobiography by a 45-year-old man reveals:

> An acquaintance of two of my classmates was having a birthday party in Tallinn and we were all invited to go. I was sixteen. Nothing predicted the course of following events as it really happened. At the party, we ate and had a few drinks. The walls of the flat of that man were covered with all kinds of pornographic pictures, which excited us all a lot. For the first time I saw all kinds of positions of intercourse, group sex, oral and anal sex. It all had a very strong impact on me and for a long time I saw them in my

erotic fantasies. I don't know from where he had got those pictures, but Finland is only some 80-90 kilometres off Tallinn and it was possible to smuggle things in. (ELM 1996)

After the independence, pornography became legal and easily attainable. The following 27-year-old man uses it as educational material:

> Sex magazines, porno films? I don't buy them except when I come across them when I'm alone, I look them through, trying to remain independent. I am more interested in the contents, pragmatical advice that I can share with my wife. I would also like to watch realistic films of deep thoughts and ideas, including erotica elements, in case it does not embarrass my wife. But cheap, downright hardcore porno films I wouldn't watch more than just once. (ELM 1996)

In 2000, attitudes toward pornography were very positive: 68% of men and 55% of women considered pornography very or quite arousing. Young people enjoyed pornography more than the older persons. People in different types of couple relationship, educational, and national groups found pornography equally arousing. Estonians considered pornography more arousing than Swedes and Finns did in 1992. But in 1999, the Finnish attitudes resembled those of the Estonian people.

## 9. Contraception, Abortion, and Population Planning

KAI HALDRE and ELINA HAAVIO-MANNILA

During the last decade of the 20th century, major socio-economic changes took place in Estonia. At the same time, many reproductive and sexual health indicators abruptly changed: The beginning of sexual life took place at a younger age; the number of induced abortions and deliveries, including teenage pregnancies, decreased rapidly; the availability of contraceptive methods improved; and their use increased. Nevertheless, much less contraception is used in the first sexual intercourse than in other developed countries, and often the sexually active people used unreliable methods of contraception—coitus interruptus and the rhythm method.

### A. Contraception

*General Usage*

There are no systematic and accurate data about contraceptive usage in Estonia. According to the statistics given by the Estonian Ministry of Social Affairs, there were 182 users of hormonal contraception and 145 IUD users per 1,000 women of fertile age in 2001. These data are collected only about women who visit state women's outpatient clinics. The definition of which data should be included in statistics is not well defined, and the collection of the data is not on the same level in all of these institutions.

According to the available statistics, the number of women using hormonal contraception has increased about fourfold, and the number of women with an IUD has decreased a little, when compared with the year 1992 statistics of 39 and 209 per 1,000 women of fertile age, respectively. These statistics of hormonal contraception do not tell us whether the figures refer only to the combined oral contraceptive pills or include also usage of other hormonal methods (POP, depo progestogen, or levonorgestrel-IUS). Nor do they tell use about how constant is the usage. The statistics reflect the usage per 1,000 women of fertile age, but do not distinguish how many of these women are in need of contraception.

The Estonian Health Interview Survey carried out in 1996 shows that the usage of different family planning methods during the previous four weeks by sexually active women in age groups 20 to 24 years and 25 to 29 years was as shown in Table 2. From the EHIS 1996 data, one might conclude that every user of a contraceptive method used only one method at a time. Our practical experience does not support this conclusion, and it was possible to select two main methods while answering this particular question in the interview. One, then, cannot consider the EHIS data reliable. The data depicting contraceptive usage do not reflect how many of these women were pregnant, infertile, or wishing pregnancy at the time when the interview was carried out. No reliable methods were used by one quarter of the women; at the same time, there are no data about their plans in case of pregnancy. Twenty-five percent of the 20-to-24 age group and 21% in age group 25-to-29 did not have intercourse during the previous four weeks.

According to the Family and Fertility Survey carried out in 1994, the usage of different contraceptive methods among sexually active women during the previous month was 58% in age group 20-to-24 and 66% in age group 25-to-29, including, respectively, condom use 21% and 17%, contraceptive pills 5% and 5%, IUD 19% and 34%, coitus interruptus 9% and 7%, and other methods 4% and 2%; 25% and 19% in these age groups did not use any method. During the survey, 8% and 3% were pregnant in age groups 20-to-24 years and 25-to-29 years, respectively; 25% and 19% of women in these age groups did not have sexual intercourse during the last month.

We can compare this 1994 Family and Fertility Survey to the results of a Finnish survey carried out in 1994 of the age groups 20-to-24 and 25-to-29, in which 60% and 52%, respectively, of the sexually active women used contraceptive pill, 17% and 4% used condoms together with either the pill, IUD, or depo progestogen, 13% and 25% condoms alone, and 2% and 6% the IUD. The proportions of those not in need of contraception among sexually active women were 7% and 11% in age groups 20-to-24 and 25-to-29 years (cf. Table 3). Male and female voluntary sterilization is legally regulated by the "Law of Pregnancy Termination and Sterilization," adopted by the Estonian Parliament at the end of 1998. There are no data on how many people have used this possibility, and what is the potential amount of users in the near future.

In the middle of the 1990s, emergency contraception was introduced in Estonia. The prerequisite of successful usage of this method is good information about the method among public and medical personnel, and easy accessibility of the emergency pills.

### Contraception in First Intercourse

According to the Estonian Health Interview Survey in 1996, 62% of women in age group 20-to-24 years did not use contraception in their first intercourse. According to the Family and Fertility Survey in 1994, the proportion of non-users in the same age group was 67%. Additionally, about half of those who said that they had used the method had chosen "traditional methods" for avoiding pregnancy. We can compare this with the proportion of non-users of contraception at first sexual intercourse found in the KISS study in Finland already in 1988, where it was 27% among girls in the age group 15-to-16 years.

According to the Estonian sex survey conducted in 2000, in their first intercourse, 42% of Estonian-speaking men and 38% of respective women, and only 21% of Russian-speaking men and 33% of respective women had used some contraceptive method. The difference between the language groups was statistically significant for men, 42% versus 21%.

Coitus interruptus was the most-often-used method in the first intercourse. Twenty-one percent of the Estonian-speaking respondents had used it; of the Russian-speaking, only 10%. A condom was used by one tenth of the respondents, and the pill by only 1%. Two percent had used some other technique, and the rest could not remember what method of contraception they had used in their first coitus.

Very few Estonian autobiographers referred to contraception when they wrote about their first intercourse. This is probably because of the fact that no contraception was used, as the findings above indicate. Lack of knowledge on sexual matters, especially contraception, often made the first intercourse an unpleasant experience.

In Estonia, fewer people used some contraceptive in their first intercourse than Finns did 30 years earlier, not to speak of Finland in the 1990s. Only 10% to 13% of people in Estonia had used a condom in their first intercourse, compared with 28% in Finland in 1971, 52% in 1992, and 55% in 1999. Among the 55- to 74-year-olds, Estonian-speaking people (born before 1946) reported as much as, and even more contraception than the Finns did in 1992. This Finnish generation (born before 1937) grew up when contraception was not yet common in Finland.

### Contraception in Most Recent Intercourse

These statistics are more reliable than those for contraceptive usage in the first intercourse. Fifty-two percent of men and 54% of women surveyed—needing contraception and having had intercourse in past year—had in his or her latest sexual intercourse used one or several of the following contraceptive methods: condom, birth control pill, minipill, implant capsule or injections, intrauterine device (IUD), or sterilization. There was no age difference in the use of these contraceptive methods considered as reliable ones.

### Table 2

### Contraceptive Usage, in Percent

| Method | EHIS 1996 | | FFS 1994 | |
| --- | --- | --- | --- | --- |
| | 20- to 24-year-olds | 25- to 29-year-olds | 20- to 24-year-olds | 25- to 29-year-olds |
| Total usage | | | 58 | 66 |
| Condom | 22 | 12 | 21 | 17 |
| Oral pill | 11 | 6 | 5 | 5 |
| IUD | 21 | 35 | 19 | 34 |
| Natural methods | 13 | 16 | — | — |
| Coitus interruptus | 5 | — | 9 | 7 |
| Other methods | 1 | — | 4 | 2 |
| No methods | 27 | 24 | 25 | 19 |

### Table 3

### Usage of Contraceptive Methods During Last Four Weeks: Women, 20 to 24 Years, in Percent

| Contraceptive Method | Estonia 1994 | Finland 1994 |
| --- | --- | --- |
| Condom | 21 | 13 |
| Pill | 5 | 60 |
| IUD | 20 | 2 |
| Coitus interruptus | 9 | |
| Other methods | 4 | |
| Did not use | 25 | |
| Condom and pill depo/IUD | | 17 |
| Pregnant/infertile // no need* | 8/1 | 7* |
| Did not have sexual intercourse | 25 | |

(FFS 1994; Kosunen 2000)

A comparison of the contraception techniques in the four sexual relationship types shows that cohabiting people had used reliable contraception most often (67%) and single people least often (39%). Married and LAT people were in-between, with 53% and 57%. The higher the educational level, the more often was a condom, pill, IUD, or sterilization used. Of the least-educated persons, 46%, of those with the middle level of education, 54%, and those with the highest education, 63%, had used these reliable birth control techniques. Estonian-speakers had used reliable contraception more commonly (56%) than Russian-speakers in Estonia.

Of the different contraceptive techniques labeled as reliable, condoms were the most popular. Of Estonian-speaking men, 25% reported the condom as the main device used in the latest intercourse, of Russian-speaking men, 22%. For women, the percentages were 10% and 19%. The coil or intrauterine device had been used in the latest intercourse by 18% of Estonian-speaking men and 16% of Russian-speaking men, and by 31% and 19% of respective women. Use of birth control pills, minipills, hypodermic capsule, or injections was rare: 11% of the Estonian-speaking men and none of the Russian-speaking men reported their use, of the respective women, 9% and 3%. Use of contraceptive foam or cream was reported by no men and by 4% of Estonian- and 3% of Russian-speaking women. Three percent of the respondents told that they or their partner had been sterilized.

One reason for the infrequent use of reliable birth control techniques is exemplified in the following passage from a 53-year-old woman chauffeur in a cooperative farm:

> I had made a promise not to have more children. I had not enough strength any more. It was hard time to tell my husband so I went to a gynecologist and had a diaphragm entered but my body rejected it. I worked like a horse: when the baby was born on 4 September, I had to be in the field ten days later, harvesting potatoes, milk pouring down from my breasts. What a life! (ELM 1996)

Of the less reliable methods, 15% to 16% of the survey respondents had in their last coitus used coitus interruptus. About 7% of men and 15% of women had applied the rhythm method ("safe days"). Of Estonian-speaking men, 6%, and of Russian-speaking men, 6%, and of the respective women, 5% and 14% had used no contraception, even though they needed it. The rest, 1% to 4% of the respondents, did not remember what kind of contraception they had used in their last intercourse.

Lack of contraceptives in intercourse was very often mentioned in the Estonian sexual autobiographies reporting on sexual life after the first intercourse. For a steady-going couple, pregnancy was mostly not a catastrophe, as a 60-year-old male mechanic shows:

> From the beginning we agreed that I would not interrupt coitus but I would shoot ahead and if she got pregnant we would have a child in the family. We had sex constantly for three months until she told me that her menstruation had stopped. It was clear we had started a family. Once we tried to have sex with a prophylactic but didn't like it. It was artificial! (ELM 1996)

A 69-year-old male chauffeur writes about the successful use of the less-reliable birth control techniques, abstinence, and moralism in the social networks, in preventing unwanted pregnancies.

> In the thirties in Virumaa it was a matter of big shame when a single woman had a child. Although knowledge of sex was scanty boys and girls knew how to regulate their sex-life so that there were no love-children, or if there

were, there were just very few. Single people also didn't live so active sexual life and I had never heard that someone had divorced because of sex. I think life was much more private in these older days. When someone did something that was forbidden by popular law then there was much more putting to shame, reproaching and condemnation than now. (ELM 1996)

Compared to Finland, the surveyed people in Estonia needing contraception and having had intercourse in the past year had rarely used reliable contraception in their last intercourse. In St. Petersburg, middle-aged and older people used them even less often than the respective people in Estonia. There was no gender difference in the likelihood of having used reliable contraceptive techniques. In all research areas, the use of the condom, pill, IUD, foam, or sterilization was least common in the age group 55-to-74 years.

### Worry About Unwanted Pregnancy

Most people, especially women, in Estonia had in their lifetime been worried about unwanted pregnancy. For men, the proportion was 70% and for women 80%. Estonian-speaking men had been more often (74%) worried about unwanted pregnancy than Russian-speaking ones (61%). These proportions include the 44% of men and the 59% of women who had been worried at least sometimes; the rest had been worried scarcely ever.

## B. Abortion

### Legislation and Statistics

In the Soviet Union, abortion was prohibited from 1936 to 1955. In Estonia, it has been legal since November 23, 1955. There was no abortion law until 1998, although it was regulated by a decree of the Ministry of Health (now Social Affairs). Since 1994, abortion is partially paid by women having health insurance. Approximately one third of the cost of abortion is paid by the woman—currently 330 EEK. The main method is vacuum curettage; mifepristone is not available.

The 1998 Estonian abortion law states that abortion is allowed on request up to 11 weeks of pregnancy and for medical reasons up to 21 weeks of pregnancy. Therapeutic abortions and treatment for spontaneous abortions are free of charge. Abortion for girls up to 15 years and women over age 45 are also free of charge. Abortions are performed only in state or private-owned institutions having a special license for that procedure. Filling in an abortion form for the Abortion Registry is obligatory (including so-called mini-abortions—termination on an outpatient basis up to 21 days of absent menses). The Abortion Registry started in 1994 and data are available from the registry from 1996 on. In 1998, the quality of the Registry worsened when, for political reasons, it was not allowed to write the personal identification code on the registration forms.

Until 2000, more pregnancies ended with termination than with birth. The rates of legally induced abortions and the birthrate have both decreased remarkably in Estonia during the last 10 years. According to the data of the Estonian Abortion Registry and Medical Statistics Bureau, there were 69.6 induced abortions per 1,000 women of fertile age in 1992; the figure was 34.0 in 2001. The fertility rate per 1,000 women of fertile age was 48.6 in 1992 and 36.8 in 2001, according to the Estonian Medical Birth Registry.

During the last ten years, the proportion of repeat abortions among abortion patients has remained the same—in 1996 to 2001, about 68% of women had terminated two or more pregnancies. This is a high proportion compared to Finland in 1997, where the proportion of repeated abortions was 30%.

The proportion of teenagers among abortion patients has increased during the last 10 years, being 11% in 1992 and 13% in 2001. The proportion of teenage mothers has decreased during the last 10 years, being 15% in 1992 and 10% in 2001.

### Incidence and Consequences of, and Attitudes Toward Abortion

Of the male respondents of the 2000 sex survey who answered the question about abortion, 38%, and of the respective female respondents, 66%, reported that they themselves or their partner had had an abortion. There was no significant difference between the language groups. Thirty-three percent of the women who had had an abortion reported that they had had only one abortion, 34% two, 16% three, 6% four, 5% five, and 6% six or more abortions. Two women reported 26 abortions.

Compared to Sweden and Finland, the abortion rates in Estonia and St. Petersburg were very high. The discrepancy in the replies of men and women found in Estonia (men reported much fewer abortions than women) did not emerge in Sweden, Finland, and St. Petersburg. Estonian women may have kept their abortions secret from their partners, because of shyness and traditional Protestant morality. One explanation given to the consistency of the replies by men and women in St. Petersburg is that the father candidate had to pay part of the cost of abortion in the Soviet Union. Thus, it was necessary for a woman to reveal their pregnancy to her partner.

Reactions to and feelings about abortion varied by gender. In most cases, the surveyed women reported more consequences of abortion than men did.

Quite a number of both women (44%) and men (39%) who/whose partner had had an abortion reported that abortion made them feel guilty. Guilt feelings were more widespread among Estonian-speaking (men 42% and women 50%) than Russian-speaking people (men 30 and women 33%). According to a multiple classification analysis, young people had suffered from guilt feelings more often than older people had. Type of the relationship and education did not predict the guilt feelings of the respondents from abortion.

In Estonia, more women (19%) than men (7%) thought that an abortion had been degrading. Women considered abortion painful much more often (48%) than men did (10%). Russian-speakers reported pain in connection with abortion more often than Estonian-speakers did (Russian-speaking men, 20%, and Estonian-speaking men, 6%, and the respective women, 58% vs. 42%). Very few respondents (7% of men and 3% of women) reported that their or their partner's abortion had been easy.

Thirty-six percent of men legitimized the abortions of their partners by saying that they had been natural in the partner's situation. Of the women, only 22% stated that the abortions had been natural in their situation. There was no difference between the national groups in this respect.

The decision to have an abortion was often a difficult one, as a 39-year-old Russian-speaking woman told of deciding again an abortion at the last minute:

> When he learned about my pregnancy, he decided to go to sea, said he needed big money and told me I could do whatever I wanted—bear the child or not to bear. My colleagues learned about my pregnancy too and advised me to make an abortion. It may be he had even advised everybody to tell me that. One of my colleagues took me to the hospital and went to negotiate with the doctor. Until they discussed things in the doctor's study, I spent time reading the posters that hung on the walls. I learnt that if a woman

aborted her first pregnancy, she would risk being childless for the rest of her life. But I wanted to have children. So I gave up the abortion plans and bore the child. I was 17 when I bore my first child. (ELM 1996)

Another 40-year-old woman architect avoided abortion in spite of the request of her partner. Later, she anyway had an abortion. She seems to have had guilt feelings, because she thought that she was punished for it.

> The father of my child did not want any children but as I was 26 myself already, it was the last moment for me to become a mother. And I really did give birth to a sweet lovely boy, exact copy of his father. [Later] I had won a prize at an architectural exhibition and it included a voucher for a trip to Finland. Giving birth to a baby was an obstacle. My conditions to [my partner] were as follows: I shall bear the third child if he will marry me and we shall live together. He didn't agree on marrying and I had an abortion. . . . I had a bitter revenge from destiny for destroying this embryo. In June 1987 an inborn dilatation of a blood-vessel (aneurysm) that was predicted to break at the age of 30, broke in my head. It was God's providence it didn't happen during the birth of my children. (ELM 1996)

In the 2000 survey, attitudes toward abortion were measured by the statement "I do not accept free (legal) abortion." The responses were quite evenly distributed between the five alternatives ranging from agree entirely to disagree entirely. The average score for men was 2.9 and for women 3.1; women were thus slightly more favorable toward free abortion then men were. There was no statistically significant difference between the ethnic groups. In Estonia, 35- to 44-year-old people accepted legal abortion better than younger and older people. The higher the educational level, the more likely were the respondents to permit abortion. Type of the relationship was not associated with abortion attitudes. Attitudes toward abortion were more restrictive in Estonia than in Finland in the 1990s, and especially in St. Petersburg.

### C. Getting and Caring for Children

From the 1950s until the end of the 1980s "Singing Revolution," Estonia's annual birthrate was quite stable—about 20,000 births per year. In the aura of liberation at the end of 1980s, the birthrate increased, and then suddenly and dramatically decreased during the socioeconomic transformation of the 1990s. In the last year of the 20th century, 1999, Estonia saw a small blip in the annual number of births and the birthrate per 1,000 women of fertile age. Between 1992 and 2001, the average maternal age increased from 25.5 years to 27.1 years, and the age of first birth from 22.7 to 24.1 years. The total fertility rate is below replacement level: 1.27 children per fertile woman and 1.33 in 2001.

While it is assumed that the maternal age will continue to increase, Estonia can expect an increase in birthrates when it reaches the level of Nordic countries, as in Finland, Sweden, Iceland, and Norway. In the past decade, most deliveries in these Nordic countries were in the maternal age group 25-to-29, in Estonia in 2001, only 30% were in age group 20-to-24 and 30% were in age group 25-to-29; previously, the biggest group of mothers were of age 20-to-24. The perinatal mortality rate also decreased markedly from 20.1 in 1992 to 8.0 per 1,000 live births in 2001. Since the decreasing birthrate and an aging population are pointed out by different groups in society as main concerns, many political parties have tried to introduce their "population programs," none of which have been implemented effectively until now.

In Estonia, most children have not been deliberately planned. In earlier times, when reliable contraception was unavailable, many children were, nevertheless, likely to be born. Pregnancy was often a joyful event.

The autobiographies contained also stories about problems in becoming pregnant. A 69-year-old male teacher writes about the best position in intercourse for begetting a child:

> I have noticed that when using this position [see below], the woman conceives most easily, as the sperm directly reaches the orifice of the womb, which is very important. I was quite worried in the first years of my marriage, as all our efforts to have children were in vain. Then we discovered this position, which also gives much pleasure. Woman is on her belly and man on her back, in the end woman lifts his bottom. This position led us to the desirable results. I have given this advice also to my pupils when teaching the class of family and sexual education. I have even received some thanks from the people whom it has helped, there was a couple who had tried to have children for several years, and they followed my advice, and had one child after another, all in all five of them. I have talked on this subject with my former pupils, who have been of the same opinion. This is the position, which the animals use, that is why I call it an animal-position. (ELM 1996)

A high proportion of the surveyed people in Estonia, about 70% of men and 80% of women, had their own children. Of Estonian-speaking men, 21%, and of respective women, 20%, had at least three children; of the Russian-speaking men, only 12%, and of the respective women, 8% had at least three children. The average number of children for Estonian-speakers was 1.6, and for Russian-speakers, 1.3 (childless people were included in this calculation). The difference between the language groups may be related to the ardent campaign to increase the number of the Estonian-speaking population in the 1990s, after the independence.

Middle-aged and older people had more children than younger people. The obvious reason is that they had had more years for childbearing. Married and cohabiting people had more children (1.8) than LAT persons (1.3) and singles (1.0). The number of children for the less-educated people was higher (1.6) than for the middle-educated (1.5) and highest-educated people (1.3).

The international comparison shows that in Finland in 1999, there were more childless respondents (34%) and less respondents with only one child (15%) than in Estonia, where 25% had no children. Twenty-one percent of Estonian-speakers and 30% of Russian-speakers had one child. In St. Petersburg, more people (41%) than in Estonia and Finland had only one child. In Finland in 1999, 23% had at least three children, compared with 21% among Estonian-speaking people.

In comparing age groups, Swedish data have been included. In the age groups below 45 years, people in Estonia and St. Petersburg more often than those in Sweden and Finland had their own children. This was the case in spite of the high abortion rate in the areas of the former Soviet Union.

During the Soviet regime, the social conditions for having children were unfavorable. A 28-year-old university-educated unemployed woman tells about her own birth as follows.

> I was born in one of the small towns of Estonia in 1968, during the deep Soviet regime. At that time women had to complete their work tasks equally to men. Everybody was supposed to follow the example of the leading workers—women truck drivers, astronauts (Valentina Tereskova) etc. The main task and function of women at that time was neglected. After the birth of a child, women could stay home for 2 months only, not more. And also the occasions when the mother could stay home with a sick child were rare. Work was the most important thing. (ELM 1996)

In the 2000 survey, we asked parents of children in Estonia how the birth of the last child had affected their life. People reported more positive than negative consequences of getting a child. The most popular response was, "I became happy." Of men, 43%, and of women, 49% felt happiness on the birth of the child. This autobiographical sketch was by a 73-year-old medical nurse:

> In July 1949 the baby boy was born and we called him Viktor, considering that the name should suit both Estonian and Russian environment. The baby brought new feelings into our life; our happiness was more complete than ever. Now we already had a family! When the baby was two months old, I had to go back to work. Juhan's mother agreed to baby-sit. To ease the burden of the nanny and to get free days, I was willing to have night duties. At night Juhan looked after the baby and the boy slept well, too. So far I had breast-fed my child but when I went back to work, difficulties arose. The hospital was two kilometers away. To feed the baby, I had to walk home. Sometimes, because of the patients, I could not leave the hospital on time and when I reached home I found a fed and sleeping baby.
>
> We lived in a small bachelor's flat where my mother-in-law's bed was only a few meters away from ours. Moreover, she suffered from sleeplessness. Even the slightest movement made our wooden beds squeak. We had to enjoy sex, trying not to breathe. It often happened at the sweetest moments of love that she began to sigh and turn over in her bed. In the morning she used to tell us how she had not slept a wink at night. For me it was most embarrassing when she tried to advise me, saying that one had to have sex in moderation, and the norm she offered was twice a week, otherwise it might happen that later the husband had no potency left. (ELM 1996)

Thirty percent of the survey respondents of both genders felt themselves as a real man/woman as a result of the birth of the child. The term "real woman" was actually used in the story of a 53-year-old woman former chauffeur in a *kolhose* (a leading worker of the socialist society) with three older children.

> On an evening I felt pains inside, I was taken to hospital where I gave birth to a baby boy. It was a hard delivery; the child was in its mouth position. I was in despair, it is all over, the child's breathing disappeared, and there was no pressing, my own blood pressure 180. The doctors were hopeless, at that Kunda hospital. I was thinking, I gave myself a command, Aino, you are a woman, and you are a creator. Pull yourself together! I exerted all my strength. And really, as a result of it, a boy was born. I was so happy! I felt a real woman, a mother. Everything ended well, in a few days we were back at home. There I had to cope with everything, and I did.

Twelve percent of the surveyed women were satisfied because they did not have to go to work.

But the birth of the last child also had negative effects. Twenty percent of both men and women respondents of the survey reported that their economic situation worsened considerably because of the birth of the last child.

Fourteen percent of the survey respondents felt that the relationship with the partner suffered because of the birth of a child. The following autobiographical passage was written by a 68-year-old retired woman worker:

> Until the birth of our first child we lived really well, although we had only a borrowed stool and a mattress in our

hostel room. We spent all free time embracing each other and talked about how nobody had ever been so much in love. We obtained more furniture but it seemed like with every new piece we lost something of our feelings. When our child was born I felt that I was not paid so much attention any more and I did not understand that a part of me now belonged to my child. My husband started to be away from home, another child was born in a year, and after that I had an abortion. (ELM 1996)

Nine percent of female and 1% of male survey respondents felt that the child took all their energy.

Twenty-seven percent of the men surveyed and 31% of the women had children who needed daycare. When listing the usual caregivers of their children needing care, the respondents were allowed to mention several types of persons.

One third of men and 44% of women reported that, in their family, the wife usually takes care of the children, and one sixth that the husband does it. In every tenth family, parents or grandparents of the respondents were the main caregivers. In 1% to 2% of the families, the children or grandchildren took care of the children. Only 1% of the respondents reported that there were other caregivers in the family. The caregivers in Estonian- and Russian-speaking families were almost exactly similar.

The parents seem to be the main caregivers of children in present-day Estonia. The extended family is not such a support as one might have expected on the basis of the autobiographies. The following story by a 34-year-old woman reveals the truth about traditional gender roles in childcare:

After the birth of the child everything vanished, no tears and hysterics any more, no more humiliating scenes. We still matched well in bed, but that was the only thing that kept us together. I went to work when the child was three months old. My husband wanted to sleep late, so I had to drag the child, the carriage and a bag with the bottles and nappies all through the snow to the nanny we had. Our love diminished more and more. When I was again two months pregnant, my husband was taken to the army. We wrote each other long letters. My grandmother, with whom we had been living, told me that I was a fool. I was the fool, and gave birth to the second son. (ELM 1996)

The low birthrate in Estonia has been and remains a national worry. After the independence, public daycare services were neglected—but supported again since the late 1990s. Thus, it is no wonder that less than half of the parents in Estonia reported happiness because of the birth of a child. One in five had serious economic problems because of it. Nevertheless, from the perspective of sexual life, it is encouraging to learn that only 14% of the parents reported that their relationship with the partner had suffered with the birth of their latest child.

To illustrate the changing family model and value system, we can report that, according to the Medical Birth Registry in 1992, 66%, and in 2001, 43% of mothers were in a registered marriage. At the same time, the proportion of deliveries attended by the father (sometimes another family member) was 13% in 1992, when the possibility to do that became available, and 56% in 2001.

## 10. Sexually Transmitted Diseases and HIV/AIDS

KAI HALDRE

### A. Sexually Transmitted Diseases

Source data for this chapter are derived from healthcare institutions whose area of work includes the diagnosis and treatment of dermatological and venereal diseases. In 1999, there were 97 such institutions in Estonia. HIV-related information is from the Merimetsa Hospital and Health Protection Inspectorate. The increased incidence of syphilis and other predominantly sexually transmitted diseases is characteristic of many states that became independent after the collapse of the USSR (Health in Europe 1997). Major socioeconomic changes (unemployment, a boom in prostitution, growing drug abuse, expansion of borders, and increase of tourism) create a good soil for the spread of diseases.

For the third time after World War II, an increased incidence of syphilis poses a problem for Estonia. The greatest incidence rates in the postwar period were registered at the end of the 1940s (149.2 cases per population of 100,000 in 1949), the smallest in the 1960s and at the end of the 1980s, respectively, 2.0 to 4.6 (Communicable Disease Statistics in Estonia 1998). In the 1970s, a second wave of syphilis incidence occurred (42.4 in 1976), which can partly be explained by the peak of the organized inflow of labor at the turn of the 1960s and 1970s (Population 1997). Thirdly, the second-largest increase period has been the past ten years, in which the incidence rate has increased by 20 times, from 3.6 per 100,000 persons in 1989 to 72.4 per 100,000 persons in 1998, before starting to decrease to 30.6 in 2001.

Gonorrhea incidence has, in the past decades, been relatively stable (together with some fluctuations), although the trend has been downward from 1993 to 2001—from 233 registered cases per 100,000 persons to 50 cases, respectively. Compared with other European countries, the incidence of gonorrhea has always been very high in Estonia (Nordic/Baltic Health Statistics 1998). Since Estonia started to register cases of chlamydia in 1991, the upward trend of the first half of the 1990s represents an improvement in diagnostic facilities. The downward trends observed in the past years with several STDs (gonococcal infections, trichomoniasis, etc.) can partly be explained by changes in sexual behavior. The problem of the quality of registering incidences (STDs are underregistered) must be noted. The system that for years worked requires a new approach in the changing healthcare system.

One of the autobiographical stories in the ELM collection is told by a 34-year-old woman who tells about a STD, which she got at the age of 14, and about the problems she encountered in getting treatment.

One night, when I was sleeping naked, as the night was so hot, I woke up feeling somebody touching me. It was my cousin who was gently fussing with me.... Some time after this incident my periods started, and together with this came a brownish foul-smelling flow. To hide the smell I poured plenty of perfume over myself, being childishly naive. This, of course, made the things worse. I didn't dare to tell my aunt or to ask anybody for help. I couldn't wash my panties clean, so my aunt started to suspect something. She took me to town to see a doctor the diagnosis was trichomoniasis. Back home the interrogation started: where?, with whom?, when? We had never talked about private things with my aunt, so I told her nothing. She still suspected her son. I denied everything. The very first moment was when my cousin called me a stink bomb. I was alone with my trouble and sorrow. My aunt had given me the medicine and told me to treat myself. Unfortunately, I didn't manage, the large flow stopped, but I didn't get entirely well. My aunt didn't take me to the doctor again, it was such a shame to go to a gynecologist with such a young girl. (ELM 1996)

### B. HIV/AIDS

The first HIV infection was discovered in Estonia in 1988 and HIV diseases in 1992. As of December 31, 1999, there were 62 HIV-positive patients in Estonia, 54 men and 8 women. Five people (all men) diagnosed with AIDS were alive and 15 (one of them a woman) had died. Fourteen HIV patients had left Estonia. Although, only a couple of the HIV-positive patients were infected because of drug injections (*Health Promotion in Estonia 1997-1998*), increases in viral hepatitis, syphilis, and drug abuse are warnings of an increased spread of the HIV infection. The year 2000 marks the beginning of the explosive increase, as by the middle of December, more than 350 new virus carriers, mostly drug addicts, had been registered. Since then, the number of HIV patients reveals an explosive increase of 0.6 in 1999, 28.5 in 2000, and 108.1 cases per 100,000 inhabitants in 2001.

[*Update 2002*: UNAIDS Epidemiological Assessment: HIV testing is mandatory among blood donors and prisoners. HIV surveillance is done through screening and through a national HIV case-reporting system. Prevalence data come mostly from ongoing testing programs. UAT is not authorized in the country. By December 1999, 96 HIV cases had been reported, most of them living in the capital area. No HIV cases had been reported among injection drug users; numbers of cases among homo-/bisexual men and persons infected through heterosexual contacts were comparable. Women represented a small proportion of infected patients (16% in 1997 to 1999). Incidence of syphilis cases increased dramatically from less than 10 cases per 100,000 in 1982 to 1990 to 70 per 100,000 in 1995.

[In 2000 and 2001, the situation has become extremely alarming. In 2000, 390 HIV-positive cases and 3 AIDS cases were reported. In 2001, 1,470 new HIV-positive cases and 7 new AIDS cases were reported. Men make up 76% of the HIV/AIDS cases reported in 2001. New HIV/AIDS cases are concentrated among the young; 76% of all positives were among 15 to 24 year olds, and 89% among people under age 30. Of the cases reported in 2001, over 25% (382) were among prisoners. The cumulative totals for the country, at the end of 2001, are 1,940 HIV-positive cases and 7 AIDS cases.

[The estimated number of adults and children living with HIV/AIDS on January 1, 2002, were:

| | | |
|---|---|---|
| Adults ages 15-49: | 7,700 | (rate: 1.0%) |
| Women ages 15-49: | 1,500 | |
| Children ages 0-15: | NA | |

[An estimated less than 100 adults and children died of AIDS during 2001.

[No estimate is available for the number of Estonian children who had lost one or both parents to AIDS and were under age 15 at the end of 2001. (*End of update by the Editors*)]

## 11. Sexual Dysfunctions, Counseling, and Therapies

Sexual dysfunctions are diagnosed according to ICD-10. People with sexual dysfunctions can get help mainly from psychologists, psychiatrists, urologists, gynecologists, and sexologists. Those involved in treating sexological dysfunctions have received additional education in sexology besides their basic discipline.

There is currently no system of sexology education in Estonia. Postgraduate three-day courses about basics in sexology for gynecologists and family doctors are organized at Tartu University Medical Faculty (Department of Obstetrics and Gynecology).

After becoming members of Nordic Association of Clinical Sexology, those in the field have made attempts to start to implement the Nordic system of sexology education in Estonia.

The drugs for treatment of erectile dysfunction are not supported by sick insurance and people have to pay the whole price themselves. The same was true concerning oral contraceptive pills; sick insurance started to reimburse part of the cost only in the second half of 1990s. A majority of the cost of pills is reimbursed to women three months after an abortion and one year after delivery, and to school and university students. Surgical phalloplasty and prosthesis are available.

## 12. Sex Research and Advanced Professional Education

### A. Graduate Programs and Sex Research

Some institutes and programs for sexological research are presented in Section 1, Basic Sexological Premises.

### B. National and Regional Sexological Organizations

At the annual meeting of the Nordic Association for Clinical Sexology in 2000, Imre Rammul, Olev Poolamets, and Tõnu Ots presented the activities of the Estonian Academic Society of Sexology. According to them, there was a lot of sex and little information and discussion about sex in Estonia a couple of decades ago. Now sex is discussed everywhere and constantly in Estonia, but less sex is taking place in the bedroom. At least this can be speculated, looking at one aspect of heterosexual sex—the number of pregnancies has decreased many times during the last decade. To study the situation and promote sexual and reproductive health and rights, the Estonian Academic Society for Sexuality was founded in 1998, connecting different specialists: medical doctors, psychologists, teachers, lawyers, writers, and so on.

Rammul, Poolamets, and Ots intentionally used the word "academic" to stress the competency and reliability of the members. Since there is still a lot of "trash" information that is naturally mostly consumed by the youth, there is some inconsistency in legislation; sometimes specialists do not know how to find their colleagues and people in need of help do not know where and how to find help. All this provides a reasonable need for more reliable information and analysis of the situation.

Sexual violence and the sexuality of the disabled have been among the topics discussed at meetings of the society. Members of the society have also presented seminars with colleagues from Finland. Collaboration between the society, Tartu University, and the Family Planning Association has resulted in regular training in sexuality for medical doctors. In 2000, the Estonian Academic Society of Sexology became a member of the Nordic Association for Clinical Sexology.

The two main sexuality organizations in Estonia are:

Estonian Academic Society of Sexology, Suur-Ameerika 18 A, Tallinn, Estonia 10122; email: kliinik@amor.ee; www.hot.ee/eass.

Estonian Family Planning Association, Kotka 2, Tallinn, Estonia 11315; email: eppl@amor.ee; www.amor.ee.

## References and Suggested Readings

Bozon, M. & O. Kontula. 1998. Sexual initiation and gender: A cross-cultural analysis of trends in the 20th century. In: M. Hubert, N. Bajos, & T. Sandfort, eds., *Sexual behaviour and HIV/AIDS in Europe: Comparisons of national surveys* (pp. 37-67). London: UCL Press.

CIA. 2002 (January). *The world factbook 2002*. Washington, DC: Central Intelligence Agency. Available: http://www.cia.gov/cia/publications/factbook/index.html

*Eesti tervishoiustatistika 1992-1999* [*Estonian health statistics 1992-1999*]. 2000. Tallinn: Sotsiaalministeerium (Ministry of Social Affairs).

*Eesti tervishoiustatistika 2000-2001* [*Estonian health statistics 2000-2001*]. 2002. Tallinn: Sotsiaalministeerium (Ministry of Social Affairs).

Gissler, M., E. Vuori, A. Rasimus, & A. Ritvanen. *Lisäänty-mistilastot 2000* [*Reproduction statistics*]. Statistikrapport. Helsinki: STAKES.

Haavio-Mannila, E., & O. Kontula. 2001. *Seksin trendit meillä ja naapureissa* [*Trends in sexual life at home and in the neighboring countries*]. Helsinki: WSOY.

Haavio-Mannila, E., & O. Kontula. 2003 (In press). Single and double sexual standards in Finland, Estonia, and St. Petersburg. *Journal of Sex Research.*

Haavio-Mannila, E., & A. Rotkirch. 1998. Generational and gender differences in sexual life in St. Petersburg and urban Finland. *Yearbook of population research in Finland XXXIV 1997* (pp. 133-160). Helsinki: The Population Research Institute, The Family Federation of Finland.

Haavio-Mannila, E., O. Kontula, & E. Kuusi. 2001. *Trends in sexual life measured by national sex surveys in Finland in 1971, 1992 and 1999, and a comparison to a sex survey in St. Petersburg in 1996* (Working Papers E 10/2001). Helsinki: The Population Research Institute, The Family Federation of Finland.

Kalikov, J., http://www.enut.ee/KASULIKUDVIITED/INIMKAUBITSEMINE.

Karro, H. 1999. *Reproductive health and pregnancy outcome in Estonia: Association with different factors* (Dissertationes medicinae universitatis Tartuensis). Tartu: Tartu Ülikool.

Karusoo, M. 1997. *Kured läinud, kurjad ilmad* [*When cranes leave, the weather turns bad*]. Tartu: Eesti Kirjandusmuuseum.

Katus, K., A. Puur, & L. Sakkeus. 1995. *Eesti pere- ja sündimusuuring. Standardtabelid* [*Estonian family and fertility survey. Standard tabulations*]. Tallinn: Eesti Kõrgkoolidevaheline Demouuringute Keskus (Estonian Interuniversity Population Research Centre).

Kay, D. S. G. 1992. Masturbation and mental health–Uses and abuses. *Sexual and Marital Therapy,* 7(1):97-107.

Kelly, L. 1988. *Surviving sexual violence.* Cambridge: Polity Press.

Kon, I. S. 1995. *The sexual revolution in Russia: From the age of the czars to today.* New York: The Free Press.

Kontula, O. 2002. *Trends in teenage sexual behaviour, pregnancies, sexually transmitted infections and HIV infections in Europe.* European Population Papers Series No 14. Strasbourg: The European Population Committee (CAHP). Council of Europe.

Kontula, O., & E. Haavio-Mannila. 2002. Masturbation in a generational perspective. *Journal of Psychology and Human Sexuality* [The Haworth Press, Inc.], 14(2/3): 49-83.

Kontula, O., & E. Haavio-Mannila. 2003 (In press). Romanticism in an area of increasing individualism. In: G. Allen et al., *The state of affairs.*

Kontula, O., & E. Haavio-Mannila. 1995. *Sexual pleasures: Enhancement of sex life in Finland, 1971-1992.* Aldershot, Hampshire: Dartmouth.

Kosunen, E. 1996. *Adolescent reproductive health in Finland: Oral contraception, pregnancies and abortions from the 1980s to the 1990s* (Academic dissertation). Tampere: University of Tampere.

Leinsalu, M., M. Grintšak, & R. Noorkõiv. 1999. *Eesti terviseuuring. Tabelid* [*Estonian health interview survey. Tables*]. Tallinn: Eksperimentaalse ja Kliinilise Meditsiini Instituut (Institute of Experimental and Clinical Medicine).

Lewin, B., K. Fugl-Meyer, G. Helmius, A. Lalos, & S-A. Månsson. 1998. *Sex i Sverige: Om sexuallivet i Sverige 1996* [*Sex in Sweden: About sexual life in Sweden 1996*]. Stockholm: Folkhälsoinstitutet 11.

Lottes, I., & O. Kontula, eds. 2000. *New views on sexual health: The case of Finland.* Helsinki: The Population Research Institute, The Family Federation of Finland.

Luht, K. www.enut.ee/KASULIKUDVIITED/INIMKAUBITSEMINE.

*Nordic/Baltic health statistics, 1999.* 2000 Copenhagen: NOMESCO.

Papp K., K. Part, & S. Tõrik. 2001. *KISS Küpsemine Inimsuhted Sõbrad Seksuaalsus* [*The youth sexual maturation survey KISS*]. Tartu: Eesti Pereplaneerimise Liit, Tartu Noorte Nõustamiskeskus (Family Planning Association of Estonia, Tartu Youth Counselling Centre).

Papp, K., O. Kontula, & E. Kosunen. 1998. Teenage sexuality in Estonia and in Finland in the 1990s. In: I. Söderling, ed., *Yearbook of population research in Finland XXXIV 1997* (pp. 161-172). Helsinki: The Population Research Institute, The Family Federation of Finland.

Pettai, I. 2001. Naistevastane vägivald–tabuprobleem Eestis [Violence against women–A taboo in Estonia]. Kogumikust 2001. *"Vaikijate hääled"* [*From a collection "Voices of those who maintain silence"*]. Tallinn: Põhjamaade Ministrite Nõukogu Infobüroo. EV Sotsiaalministeeriumi Võrdõiguslikkuse Büroo. Eesti Avatud Ühiskonna Instituut (Information Bureau of the Nordic Council of Ministers. The Bureau of Equal Rights in the Estonian Ministry of Social Affairs. Estonian Open Society Institute).

Rammul, I., O. Poolamets, & T. Ots. 2000 (September 23-24). *Sexology in Estonia.* Presentation at the 23rd meeting of the Nordic Association of Clinical Sexology, Helsinki, Finland.

Rinehart, N. J., & M. P. McCabe. 1998. An empirical investigation of hypersexuality. *Sexual & Marital Therapy,* 13(4): 369-384.

Tellmann, A., H. Karro, & V. Serkina. 2001. *Eesti meditsiiniline sünniregister 1992-2000. Eesti Abordiregister 1996-2000* [*Estonian medical birth registry 1992-2000. Estonian abortion registry 1996-2000*]. Tallinn: Eksperimentaalse ja Kliinilise Meditsiini Instituut (Institute of Experimental and Clinical Medicine).

Tellmann, A., H. Karro, & V. Serkina. 2000. *Eesti meditsiiniline sünniregister 1992-1999. Eesti abordiregister 1996-1999* [*Estonian medical birth registry 1992-1999. Estonian abortion registry 1996-1999*]. Tallinn: Eksperimentaalse ja Kliinilise Meditsiini Instituut (Institute of Experimental and Clinical Medicine).

Tellmann, A., H. Karro, & V. Serkina. 2002. *Eesti meditsiiniline sünniregister 1992-2001. Eesti abordiregister 1996-2001* [*Estonian medical birth registry 1992-2001. Estonian abortion registry 1996-2001*]. Tallinn: Eksperimentaalse ja Kliinilise Meditsiini Instituut (Institute of Experimental and Clinical Medicine).

Tiit, E-M., E. Käärik, & A. Tellmann. 2001. *Eesti elanike seksuaal- ja reproduktiivkäitumine. Uurimisprojekti lõpparuanne* [*Sexual and reproductive behaviour of Estonians*] (Final report of a research project). Tartu.

Toomet, K., M. Loit, & A. Vatter. 2001. *Juhiseid tööks seksuaalvägivalla ohvritega* [*Guidelines for helping victims of sexual violence*]. Tallinn: Eesti Pereplaneerimise Liit (Family Planning Association of Estonia).

UNAIDS. 2002. *Epidemiological fact sheets by country.* Geneva, Switzerland: Joint United Nations Programme on HIV/AIDS (UNAIDS/WHO). Available: http://www.unaids.org/hivaidsinfo/statistics/fact_sheets/index_en.htm.

# Finland

## (*Suomen Tasavalta*)

Osmo Kontula, D.Soc.Sci., Ph.D., and
Elina Haavio-Mannila, Ph.D.*
*Updates by O. Kontula and E. Haavio-Mannila*

## Contents

## *Demographics and a Brief Historical Perspective*

ROBERT T. FRANCOEUR

### A. Demographics

Finland lies in northern Europe where Russia, Sweden, and Norway are its neighboring countries. It is also bordered by the Baltic Sea, the Gulf of Bothnia, and the Gulf of Finland. With a total area of 125,182 square miles (324,220 km²), Finland is slightly smaller than the state of Montana. The terrain is mostly low and flat to rolling plains interspersed with lakes and low hills. The climate is cold, potentially subarctic, but comparatively mild because of the moderating influence of the North Atlantic Current, Baltic Sea, and more than 60,000 lakes.

In July 2002, Finland had an estimated population of 5.18 million. (All data are from *The World Factbook 2002* (CIA 2002) unless otherwise stated.)

**Age Distribution and Sex Ratios**: *0-14 years*: 17.9% with 1.04 male(s) per female (sex ratio); *15-64 years*: 66.9% with 1.02 male(s) per female; *65 years and over*: 15.2% with 0.64 male(s) per female; *Total population sex ratio*: 0.95 male(s) to 1 female

**Life Expectancy at Birth**: *Total Population*: 77.75 years; *male*: 74.1 years; *female*: 81.52 years

**Urban/Rural Distribution**: 64% to 36%

**Ethnic Distribution**: Finn: 93%; Swede: 6%; Sami: 0.11%; Roma: 0.12%; Tatar: 0.02%. The population is ethnically very integrated. Separate cultures are not very conspicuous within Finnish society.

**Religious Distribution**: Evangelical Lutheran: 89%; Greek Orthodox: 1%; none: 9%; other: 1%

**Birth Rate**: 10.6 births per 1,000 population

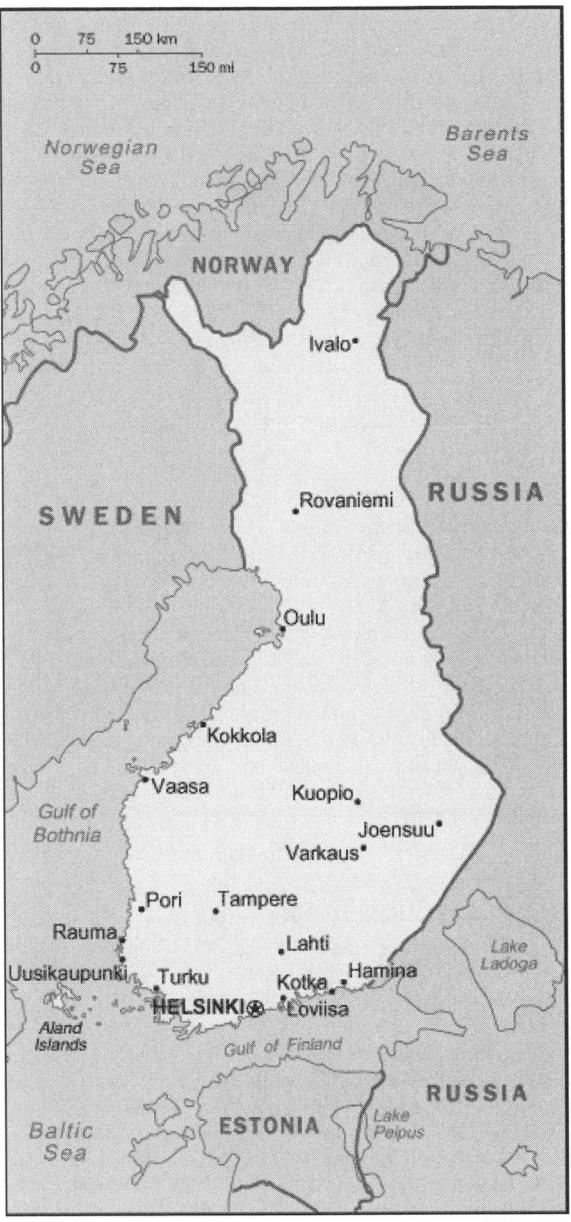

(CIA 2002)

**Death Rate**: 9.78 per 1,000 population

**Infant Mortality Rate**: 3.76 deaths per 1,000 live births

**Net Migration Rate**: 0.62 migrant(s) per 1,000 population

**Total Fertility Rate**: 1.7 children born per woman

**Population Growth Rate**: 0.14%

**HIV/AIDS** (1999 est.): *Adult prevalence*: 0.05%; *Persons living with HIV/AIDS*: 1,100; *Deaths*: < 100. (For additional details from www.UNAIDS.org, see end of Section 10B.)

**Literacy Rate** (*defined as those age 15 and over who can read and write*): 100%

**Per Capita Gross Domestic Product** (*purchasing power parity*): $25,800 (2001 est.); *Inflation*: 2.6%; *Unemployment*: 9.4%; *Living below the poverty line*: NA

Social services are well developed in Finland. People receive free counseling in contraception for family planning at the communal health centers, expectant mothers have been given free guidance in childcare centers for decades, mothers of small children have paid maternity leaves, and there are

*Communications*: Osmo Kontula, Ph.D., Population Research Institute (Vaestontutkimuslaitos), P.O. Box 849, Iso Roobertinkatu 20-22A FIN 00101 Helsinki, Finland; osmo.kontula@vaestoliitto.fi; Elina Haavio-Mannila, Ph.D., Sociology Department, Box 18 (Unioninkatu 35), University of Helsinki, FIN 00014 Helsinki, Finland; elina.haavio-mannila@helsinki.fi.

inexpensive communal daycare places for children and financial compensation for childcare given at home, as well as child benefits until the age of 18. As a result, Finnish women play as active a part in paid employment as Finnish men.

In 1992, the sexual life of the Finns was studied using nationally representative data on the 18- to 74-year-old population in Finland (Kontula & Haavio-Mannila 1993). The response rate for the 2,250 Finns in this FINSEX survey was 76%. Each of the respondents was interviewed personally and asked to fill out a questionnaire about the most intimate sexual matters. The questionnaire responses were not shown to the interviewers. The results of this study have been compared with a corresponding 1971 study (Sievers et al. 1974) to provide a detailed picture of Finnish sexual attitudes and behaviors in recent decades. Worldwide, the 1971 study was only the second population survey based on nationally representative data of sexual matters. (The first nationally representative sexual study was done in Sweden in 1967.) The results of this most recent FINSEX study will be discussed in different sections of this chapter.

[Update 2003: In 1999, the authors conducted a follow-up to the 1992 survey by a mailed survey (Haavio-Mannila, Kontula, & Kuusi 2001). This sex survey had 1,496 respondents. Because of this new data-collection technique, the response rate was 46%. By analyzing the distributions of several identical retrospective questions measuring sexual issues in different birth cohorts in the three Finnish surveys, Kontula (2001) showed that the low response rate in 1999 did not bias the recorded sexual histories of those who were under 55 years old. In the age group 55-to-74, the male respondents were more monogamous than those participating in the two earlier Finnish sex surveys. (End of update by O. Kontula)]*

## B. A Brief Historical Perspective

There is archeological evidence that Finland was inhabited already at least 50,000 years ago. In a better-known history, the early settlers of Finland probably arrived about 2,000 years ago from the Ural area to the southeast. Swedish settlers brought the country into the Kingdom of Sweden in 1154, where it remained until 1809, when it became an autonomous grand duchy of the Russian Empire. A strong national spirit emerged, with Finland declaring its independence in 1917 and becoming a republic two years later. Finland was invaded by the Soviet Union in 1939, forcing the Finns to give up 16,173 square miles (41,888 km²) of territory. Further cessions were exacted by the Soviets after World War II. Finland became a member of the European Union in 1995.

## 1. Basic Sexological Premises

### A. The Character of Gender Roles

Historically, Finland has a longer tradition of gender equality than most other countries of the world. This can be seen in the realm of politics, paid work, and in the division of labor at home.

In 1906, Finnish women gained parliamentary voting rights, second in the world after New Zealand. Finnish women also were the first in the world to gain the right to serve in Parliament. These rights were immediately implemented. In 1907, 19 women were elected to a Parliament of

---

*Editor's Note: Because most of the updates to this chapter are brief inserts to add the results of this third national survey in 1999 (Haavio-Mannila, Kontula, & Kuusi 2001), we indicate these only with brackets to avoid breaking the reader's attention; longer updates are in our standard format, i.e., beginning with Update 2003 and ending with the updaters' names.

200 members. At present, 39% of the MPs in Finland are women. In the 1994 presidential election, the female candidate got 46% of the votes, indicating that a woman can reach the highest positions of power in this country. [Update 2003: In the 2000 presidential election, a woman candidate was for the first time elected President of the Republic. (End of update by O. Kontula)]

Women in Finland are gainfully employed nearly as often as men. In 1991, some 72% of the women in the working-age population and 78% of the men were part of the labor force. In Finland, both women and men work on a full-time basis. In 1991, the proportion of women working part-time was 10% and that of men 5%.

The large proportion of gainfully employed women is also reflected in their high percentage of the entire labor force. In 1991, 48% of the labor force were women, and women made up 51% of the salary and wage earners. Unlike most European countries in the 1980s, Finland had a lower rate of undisguised unemployment for women than for men. However, the rate of unemployment among women over 55 has been higher than the rate among men of the same age.

Public offices are equally open to women and men, and under the Equality Act, no vacancy in the private sector can be announced exclusively for women or men on any other than weighty and acceptable grounds relating to the nature of the work. Nevertheless, the Finnish labor market remains somewhat gender-segregated. Women comprise approximately 60% of the labor force in the service sector, while the industrial and building sectors are dominated by men. The segregation extends to occupations and specific tasks. No dramatic change has taken place in the gender segregation of the labor market, although employees who have made nontraditional choices have entered practically every occupation dominated by the other sex. Another illustration of the gender-segregated labor market is the differences in the positions that women and men occupy in the official hierarchies. Men advance rapidly and attain higher positions than women (Haavio-Mannila & Kauppinen-Toropainen 1992).

Recent studies indicate that the quality of working life for women has deteriorated considerably in some respects. Time pressures and stress have become a more prevalent feature of jobs held by women.

The differences between women's and men's earnings diminished both proportionally and in real terms in the 1970s. In 1983, this development shifted, and the pay differentials between women and men began to grow in real terms in most sectors. In 1991, women's pay was 80% of men's pay.

Women are slightly more-often unionized than men, and their daily working hours, as well as the time spent working during a lifetime, are nearly the same. The characteristics of women workers—unionization, rise in educational standards, full-time work, and very short absences from the labor force—have not served significantly to narrow the pay differentials between the sexes.

As most women work for pay, it is necessary that men share household work with them. In international comparison, gender equality in the division of housework is high (Gershuny 1990). Nevertheless, women still do more domestic work than men, even though their share of it has declined from 67% in 1979 to 64% in 1987 (Niemi & Pääkkönen 1989). In the United States, the percentage was 67% in 1987 (Robinson 1988).

## B. Sociolegal Status of Males and Females

As the number of children in the families is small, children are valued as individuals. Even though there is a slight tendency to prefer boys when asked which gender one wishes the future child to be, girls are taken care of and loved as much as boys.

The provision of daycare for children is a municipal responsibility. The Day Care Act of 1973 aims at providing communal daycare for all children in need of it. Since 1985, parents have been able to choose between placing their child in communal daycare or receiving a homecare allowance for taking care of their child at home. This allowance may also be used to cover some of the costs of private daycare. Taking care of one's child at home with the help of a homecare allowance does not terminate employment or, since 1991, lower employee pension.

When the educational level of the entire population is examined, it is discovered that women and men are now at the same level. In 1989, half of those who had completed senior secondary school or vocational education or had a university degree were women. Women have reached a high level of general education. In the working-age population, women have a senior secondary school diploma more frequently than men, a circumstance that will prevail in the future, because 60% of senior secondary-level students are women.

Men still have the majority of masters' degrees (60%), but women are quickly catching up; since 1986, the number of women graduating from universities has exceeded that of men. For example, in 1989, women represented 54% of students who obtained a master's degree and 34% of those with a higher degree. The proportion of women who have a doctorate has been steadily increasing since 1976. The percentage of women in the senior faculty of universities remains small.

The choice of fields is segregated by gender. The proportion of women is the largest in healthcare, and quite considerable in the fields of pharmacy and veterinary science. Similarly, students in teacher training are predominantly women. At the university level, clearly the smallest proportion of women can be found in the mathematical and technical fields.

The dropout rate at the basic level of education is very low nowadays. The law provides for compulsory education until the age of 16. The dropout rate at the upper secondary level was 7% in 1988. Somewhat fewer women leave school prematurely than men.

Leisure pursuits are differentiated according to gender. Girls are more interested in arts, boys in sports. Attempts to achieve equality in training are made by offering girls and boys the same opportunities to engage in various kinds of arts and sports.

Women are more active than men as consumers of cultural services. They go to the library, theater, concerts of classical music, museums, and art shows more frequently than men, and form the majority of students in voluntary adult education. Men go to sports competitions more often than women, and somewhat more often to the cinema and to concerts of popular music.

Gender differences in drinking alcoholic beverages have diminished; women have started to imitate the drinking habits of men. This applies particularly to women working with men (Haavio-Mannila 1992).

While men and women are, in principle, equal in Finland, the position of men in the public sphere—in politics, work, and the economy—is still better than that of women. In the private sphere, at home, women have more power than men, but it also means a heavier workload there.

## C. General Concepts of Sexuality and Love

People in Finland have a positive attitude toward sexual behaviors as a health promoter—they do not see it as a threat to health. In 1992, 88% of Finnish men and 79% of women thought that sexual activity promotes health and well-being. A clear majority, 74% of men and 70% of women, believed that masturbation does not endanger one's health. [In 1999, these figures were 81% and 76%, respectively.]

Sex is considered to be an important aspect of a steady relationship. In 1992, most Finns, 86% of men and 78% of women, considered sexual life very important or important for happiness in their relationship. Among women, the strength of this opinion had declined from 1971 to 1992. In 1971, 40% of women aged 18 to 54 considered sexual life very important for happiness in their relationship, while only 21% held this view in 1992, a development that reflects the strong public preoccupation with sexual liberation 20 years ago. [In 1999, this figure had increased to 29%.]

Women are expected to be more restricted than men in their sexual behavior. These expectations are rationalized by referring to gender differences in sexual needs. In 1992, 51% of Finnish men and 61% of women thought that a grown-up man has a clearly or somewhat stronger sexual need than a woman. Forty-one percent of men and 33% of women considered the sexual needs of men and women as equally strong. Only 7% believed that the sexual needs of women are stronger.

In the case of marital fidelity, a double moral standard is not very strong. In 1971, 34% of men and 29% of women aged 18 to 54 said that one must be able to accept a husband's temporary infidelity, and 28% of men and 30% of women would accept a wife's temporary infidelity. In 1992, the corresponding liberal attitudes in regard to a husband's infidelity were 19% of men and 21% of women, and to a wife's infidelity by 22% and 23%, respectively. [In 1999, the corresponding figures were 23% and 13% related a husband's infidelity, and 21% and 15% related to wife's infidelity. Women's approval of sexual infidelity had decreased significantly.]

Even though attitudes toward many aspects of sexuality, for example, adolescent and homosexual sex, have liberalized with the course of time, attitudes toward marital unfaithfulness have become more conservative in the last 20 years. This may be because of the fear of AIDS, or to a general increase in familism in the society. It is easier to be liberal in issues not directly tied to one's own life than in matters related to the personal relationship.

[*Update 2003*: The trend toward increasing expectations of marital faithfulness represents a renaissance of romanticism in a time of increasing individualism. Sex belongs currently to a romantic script in which sexuality is highly valued. According to this approach, individual pleasures are integrated into romantic relationships. Romanticism does not mean an orientation toward the partner at the expense of oneself. The romantic ideas highly valued in traditional female culture have become transformed into valuing the relationship between the partners. This has happened especially among women and in the youngest generation. (Kontula & Haavio-Mannila 2003.) (*End of update by O. Kontula*)]

## 2. Religious, Ethnic, and Gender Factors Affecting Sexuality

### A. Religious Factors

In terms of religiosity, Finland is a uniform country, for about 87% of the people belong to the Evangelical Lutheran Church of Finland and about 50,000 people to the Orthodox Church. Both churches are considered state churches. Only a few thousand people at the most belong to each of a few other religious groups. About 8% of the Finns do not belong to any religious communities. The religiosity of the Evangelical Lutherans is, in most cases, rather passive; only a small percentage attends church services regularly. The influence of religion and religious values has declined significantly during the last few decades. Religious thinking does not have much meaning in the sexual lives of people, especially the younger generations.

Marriage is no longer considered a prerequisite to having a sexual life in Finland. The quality of the relationship has become more important than its religious or civil form. Sexual relations are accepted in steady dating relationships and most couples live together before marriage. A significant number of cohabiting people do not get married even after years of living together as a couple. The sexual life of single persons is also widely accepted. The percentage of single persons has gradually increased, with about 30% of the middle-aged not living with a sexual partner. One third of these single persons have a steady relationship with a person with whom they do not live.

## B. Cultural Factors

It is an essential principle in recent Finnish legislation concerning sexual issues that people may and can do privately all they want when it does not involve forcing another person. In this regard, Finnish legislation aims to respect the individual's right of self-determination. This was a decisive principle in the reform of Finnish legislation around 1990. This principle is also strong in the general population where liberal sexual attitudes prevail among the secularized and independent-thinking majority. This liberalization of sexual attitudes is a significant change, because those with liberal attitudes on sexual issues are usually more satisfied with their sexual life than are others.

The interval between publication of results from the 1971 national survey (Sievers et al. 1974) and the FINSEX survey (Kontula & Haavio-Mannila 1993) was marked by a great change in attitudes, values, and practices that began in the sexual revolution of the 1960s. Public discussion about the sexual revolution at the beginning of the 1970s in Finland concerned, to a great extent, the increased availability of sexual material and its commercial use in advertising and mass communication in general. The change could also be seen in legislation where the individuals' liberty to decide about their own sexual matters was increasingly recognized. While increased open discussion about sexual issues in society continued the erosion of some of the still-existing old taboos, a clear step was taken towards more-accepting attitudes to sexual issues as a whole. Today, the sexual life of unmarried people is almost as accepted as that of married couples.

A major factor in this shift to more-liberal attitudes has been a rise in the level of education, but even without this, the changes would have been significant. More-positive attitudes about the sexual rights of adolescents, women, and homosexuals have been matched by more-liberal attitudes regarding the acceptability of casual sexual relationships that are not based on love.

In 1971, two women out of three set the promise of marriage as the condition for beginning a sexual relationship; in 1992, only 16%, [and in 1999, only 11%] of Finnish women were of this opinion (see Table 1). Among adolescents, the revolution is even more apparent. Dating has replaced marriage as an institution, with sexual intimacy almost as accepted during dating as it was earlier only within marriage. As a consequence, very few young people marry their first sexual partners any more. As late as 30 years ago, 60% of women married their first sexual partners.

Attitudes have also become more positive towards casual relationships (see Table 2). About 70% of Finns think that even a casual sexual relationship can be happy and satisfying. The necessity of love as a premise for sexual intercourse has also diminished. Sexual intercourse without love was considered wrong by 42% of men and 64% of women in 1971. In 1992, the corresponding shares were 29% and 43%. [In 1999, they were almost unchanged: 28% and 42%.]

Still, 70% hold that living in a steady relationship in which sexual fidelity prevails is most desirable, compared with 10% who believe that living apart is most desirable. Twenty percent of men and 4% of women would like to maintain several concurrent and continuous sexual relationships. So, as far as their hopes are concerned, women are more monogamous than men.

Finns also take a more liberal attitude than before toward sexual relationships that are outside their own steady relationships. This shift is linked with the greater acceptance of sexual relationships among unmarried and single persons. Attitudes toward homosexual relationships are also significantly more accepting than before. In 1971, close to half of all Finns, 44% of males and 45% of females, regarded homosexual behavior between adults as a private affair with which officials and legislation should in no way interfere (see Table 3). In 1992, this opinion was supported by 59% of men and by 72% of women. [In 1999, the corresponding figures were similar: 58% and 72%.] On the other hand, attitudes toward extramarital relationships of spouses and pornography have become somewhat stricter, but only among women. Two thirds of the men and one third of the women considered watching pornography sexually arousing for themselves. The quite-free sale and distribution of pornographic films and videos were supported by 51% of men and by 24% of women.

Based on attitudes towards sexuality, equality of gender has made remarkable progress in Finland. Women's right to be the initiators at sexual intercourse when they want it so,

### Table 1

**Percentages of Men and Women by Age Who Think Adolescent Sexual Intercourse Is Acceptable in a Regular Relationship, 1971 and 1992**

| Age | Men 1971 | Men 1992 | Women 1971 | Women 1992 |
|-----|----------|----------|------------|------------|
| 18-24 | 75 | 91 | 59 | 91 |
| 25-34 | 64 | 94 | 40 | 93 |
| 35-44 | 52 | 88 | 20 | 86 |
| 45-54 | 38 | 80 | 14 | 71 |
| 55-64 |  | 72 |  | 49 |
| 65-74 |  | 56 |  | 43 |

1971: $N = 2,139$, with 738 men and 1,401 women
1992: $N = 2,244$, with 1,101 men and 1,143 women

### Table 2

**Percentages of Men and Women by Age Who Think That an Entirely Casual Sexual Relationship Can Be Happy and Satisfying, 1971 and 1992**

| Age | Men 1971 | Men 1992 | Women 1971 | Women 1992 |
|-----|----------|----------|------------|------------|
| 18-24 | 77 | 74 | 52 | 73 |
| 25-34 | 66 | 82 | 44 | 73 |
| 35-44 | 50 | 73 | 35 | 63 |
| 45-54 | 51 | 68 | 24 | 56 |
| 55-64 |  | 65 |  | 34 |
| 65-74 |  | 48 |  | 35 |

1971: $N = 2,132$, with 741 men and 1,391 women
1992: $N = 2,239$, with 1,101 men and 1,138 women

was supported by 94% of men and by 90% of women in 1992. This is a significant increase, especially among women. [In 1999, these proportions were still higher: 97% and 94%.] Three out of four women were of the opinion that a respectable woman could openly show her interest in sex.

The cohort analyses show that part of the changes in attitudes do not concern the oldest people at all, especially not the women. Women aged 55 to 74 approve of women initiating a sexual relationship, casual relationships, and sex without love as rarely as they did 20 years ago when they were 35 to 54 years of age. On the other hand, the attitudes towards gays and sexual relationships between steady-going adolescents have become more liberal in all the gender and age groups.

The differences in sexual behavior between Finland and the U.S.A. are not very big. However, Finns are significantly more liberal than Americans, at least, in their attitudes towards the beginning of sexual life with adolescents, homosexual relationships, and pornography (Smith 1990). A corresponding difference was observed 20 years ago between Denmark and the U.S.A. (Christensen & Gregg 1970).

## 3. Knowledge and Education about Sexuality

### A. Government Policies and Programs for Sex Education

Legal restrictions designed to control sexarche, the beginning of sexual coitus, which prevailed in Finland until as late as the 1800s, were gradually replaced by the moral education given by the Church and the school. This education with its religious morals gradually changed, giving way to medical views on sexual matters. In sexuality education, the main attention gradually turned from teaching about what is immoral and a sin to focusing on the prevention of pregnancies and the ill health effects caused by sexual relationships. Contrary to the custom in many other countries, giving information, advertising, or distributing contraceptives have never been officially prohibited in Finland.

In the 1920s and 1930s, sex education was considered a family responsibility. There was no sex education in the schools as yet. In 1944, the National Board of Education sent a letter concerning sex education to the schools, directing teachers of biology, hygienics, Finnish, and religion to give instruction in sexual matters.

In 1948, an expert board set up by the Ministry of Education produced a program for instruction and education in sexual morals. The program contained guidebooks both for teachers and students. These guidebooks were distributed to schools, colleges, municipal officers of health, church registry offices, and youth organizations at the public expense. Apart from information about personal relations and

sexuality, the program, with the guidebook to accompany it, also contained moral views about conditions in which sexual life was considered appropriate for young people.

In the early 1960s, the first summer university courses were held for teachers on family education. In the schools, sex education was still very scarce. In the 1970s, the National Board of Education set up a working committee to make a curriculum for the education in personal relations and sexual matters for the comprehensive school. The work was finished in 1976, but it did not lead to any wider reform of teaching. Instruction in contraception was, however, given in most schools.

From the 1950s on, Finnish municipalities have arranged equal school healthcare for all students, and sex education was already a part of this care prior to the 1970s. In practice, however, sex education has—and continues to be—concentrated on the anatomy and physiology of sexuality, contraception, and sexually transmitted diseases. Its outcome has largely depended on the personal interest of those teachers of biology and health education, together with physicians and nurses, who are responsible for the planning and the implementing of the educational experiences, most of which are aimed at the 15- to 16-year-old students in the 9th grade. However, in comparison with the 1960s, all young people have been included in this program, and other sources of information have also been available.

Since the early 1970s, the number of unwanted pregnancies and abortions among adolescents has decreased considerably. In part, the increased liberalization may have contributed to the decline in sex-related research efforts at the end of the decade.

Since 1972, the Primary Health Care Act has required municipalities to organize contraceptive counseling for all who want it, including schoolchildren, who were given access either to public clinics or to school physicians and nurses. When a physician or school nurse has found it necessary, girls have been provided with contraceptive pills.

In 1996, a comprehensive national study of sex education was started at the upper stage of the comprehensive school (grades 7 to 9). A questionnaire was mailed to the biology teachers in all upper-stage schools in Finland ($N = 603$) in February 1996. A total of 421 acceptable responses were returned from 70% of the target population.

The survey came during a period of transition in school sex education, for, in many schools, significant reductions have been carried out in the lesson hours reserved for Health Education. Family Education is about to disappear altogether and new self-governed curricula of the schools have recently been implemented.

Prior to the survey, sex education had been included in the curricula of most of the schools. Only 6% of the teachers reported otherwise. It has been given by a filtering method in connection with several other school subjects.

In the 9th grade, the biology teachers usually discuss the subject in connection with biology and the home economics teachers in connection with family education. In the 8th grade, the boys' and the girls' physical education teachers take up the subject in connection with health education. In addition, approximately half of the schools use school health nurses in sex education (as instructors in contraception) in each of the upper-stage grades.

In the 7th grade (aged 13 years), half of the schools had given instruction in the developments in puberty and menstruation. In the 8th grade, new items were: sexual intercourse, "the first time," contraception, sexually transmitted diseases, dating, and emotions, which had been dealt with in every other school. In the 9th grade, in addition to the above subthemes, nearly all the schools' sex education dealt with

### Table 3

**Percentages of Men and Women by Age Who Think That Official and Legal Interference in Homosexual Behavior Is Wrong, 1971 and 1992**

| Age | Men 1971 | Men 1992 | Women 1971 | Women 1992 |
|-----|----------|----------|------------|------------|
| 18-24 | 49 | 60 | 54 | 74 |
| 25-34 | 53 | 66 | 54 | 77 |
| 35-44 | 37 | 59 | 33 | 75 |
| 45-54 | 31 | 52 | 25 | 62 |
| 55-64 |  | 52 |  | 55 |
| 65-74 |  | 44 |  | 40 |

1971: $N = 2,126$, with 742 men and 1,384 women
1992: $N = 2,242$, with 1,101 men and 1,141 women

genitals and their functioning, ejaculations, conception, pregnancy, birth, and abortion. Other generally discussed new subthemes were sex roles, sexual minorities, sexual morals, sexual terminology, and sex life in adulthood.

Almost all the schools had used videotapes or films in the 9th grades. Textbooks had been used by four out of five, brochures of different kinds had been distributed by two out of three, and condoms had been given at least for examination in every other school. In one third of the schools, visits had been arranged to contraception or family planning clinics; and every tenth school had made visits to youth offices and/or to the congregation. A special event or happening related to sex education had been arranged in 16% of the schools within the school year.

According the survey, the most important objectives of school sex education were directing the growth to responsibility, transmission of correct information, promoting the growth of personality, and learning easy attitudes towards sexuality. On the other hand, teaching abstinence, finding the sexual experience nice and stimulating, as well as learning that casual relationships were unsatisfactory were considered the least important objectives. The chosen objectives emphasized promoting adolescents' readiness for couple relationships and sexual life. The teachers wanted to avoid moralistically intervening in adolescents' own choices or "feeding" them their own moral values. The teachers did not want to warn against sex too much; neither did they want to advertise it.

One of the objectives of the survey was to explain the possible differences in sex education across the country. As a whole, these differences were not strikingly great or systematic between the provinces. The perceived differences were mainly explained by the local governments' activity in arranging further training in this field or various campaigns.

The greatest problem in the Finnish school sex education is its timing: It comes too late for the stage in the adolescents' development. The present sex education given to the 9th graders (aged 15 years) should be provided two years earlier. Both the students themselves and the experts in this field agree unanimously that sex education in its full extent should already be given to the 12- to 13-year-olds. According the latest news, the syllabi of biology will cover sex education for the 8th graders (aged 14 years).

The strength of school sex education in Finland comes from the school healthcare, which brings out sexual matters in connection with annual physical examinations. Over a third of the girls and a fifth of the boys go to the school health nurse even at other times to talk about sexual matters. In most schools, they also give contraceptive pills. According to the survey, school health nurses also give proper lessons in sex education in at least every other school. Without the contribution of the school healthcare, the level of adolescents' knowledge of sexual matters would be significantly lower than what it is now.

[*Update 2003*: In 2002, health education was prescribed as a compulsory subject of the national primary school curriculum. Sex education was integrated in health education. This will harmonize and improve sex education in Finland.

[Teenage sexual knowledge was tested in Finland in 2000 (Kontula et al. 2001). Fourteen- and 15-year-old students of the 8th grade responded to the national sexual health knowledge survey. It was organized as a competition between schools. The survey had 30,000 respondents. It revealed that the quality of sexual knowledge was much poorer among the boys than among the girls. On the average, boys got 48 points and girls 57 points of the maximum 80 points. Girls had better knowledge in all areas of the sexual health topics. Because of more-limited sources of information, sex education

provided in the school is more important for the boys than for the girls. (*End of update by O. Kontula*)]

No detailed and effective public program for the development of sex education or other public services related to contraception can take credit for the quite-effective system of school sex education and the low teenage pregnancy rates in Finland. Rather, we would credit the liberal climate around adolescents and their sexuality for the teachers' natural willingness to teach the subject. Adolescents' need for information about sexual matters has been taken for granted. When sexual relationships between adolescents are accepted, it is clear that they are entitled to be prepared and well informed about various matters related to sexual life.

Public healthcare plays a significant role in sex education and advising on contraception. The system of maternity and childcare of the public health centers covers the whole country for almost all the expectant mothers and families with children. In the maternity centers, sexual life during pregnancy and contraception are discussed, among other things, and mothers and fathers are psychologically prepared to welcome the baby.

A liberal attitude towards sexuality may be reflected in the condom advertising found in the mass media, especially during the summer months. Women's magazines have also contained numerous sex-related articles that are read by both sexes.

## B. Informal Sources of Sexual Knowledge and Education

In the FINSEX study (Kontula & Haavio-Mannila 1993), people were asked if they had gotten information about sexual matters in their childhood homes in their youth or sex education at school. At the same time, the people were asked to evaluate the sufficiency of the information and education they had received and their willingness then to receive such information about sexual matters in general. Similar questions were asked both in 1971 and 1992.

Discussion of sexual matters has gradually increased both in the homes and in the schools. In their childhood home, information had been received about sexual matters by 39% of men and by 41% of women in 1971, and in 1992, correspondingly by 61% and by 64%. Ten percent of men and 14% of women in 1971 regarded the information received at home as sufficient. In 1992, the percentages were 29% and 32%, respectively. Until recently, most people have, thus, not been getting very much information about sexual matters at home, even if these matters have been more talked about.

In 1971, 28% of men and 33% of women reported having received sex education at school, and in 1992, 64% of males and 74% of females. [In 1999, these proportions were already 78% and 81%.] In 1971, 7% of men and 8% of women considered this information sufficient; in 1992, the percentages were 25% and 32% [and in 1999, 36% and 43%]. This shows that sex education in the schools has clearly improved, although only around 40% of the respondents considered the education sufficient. Close to 5% of the people said that they would not even have wanted such education. Slightly more people would have wanted to receive more education from the school than from the home.

Young people report clearly more often than others of having received sufficient information concerning sexual matters from the school or home (see Table 4). This suggests that speaking and teaching about sexual matters has clearly become more common, at least with those people who lived their youth in the 1980s. During the past 20 years, there was an especially clear increase in dealing with sexual matters. After 1971, the share of those who had received sex education in the school increased nearly threefold. Only a few people in the oldest age groups reported they had talked enough about sexual matters in their homes or at school.

The school has often tried to avoid taking the responsibility of giving sex education, maintaining that it is a question of family privacy with which the school should not interfere. This has been an attempt to cover the teachers' own feelings of insufficiency about the teaching of sexual matters. The homes again have shuffled off the responsibility upon the school. The young people in this awkward situation have had to find the information they needed from the most diverse sources. Such sources have been the mass media and sex-related literature, from which the information received has been spread from one to the other in the circle of friends. Boys often use sex magazines as a source of information—often as their only source—where they have found actual information about sexual practices. The girls again have been more interested than the boys in the medical facts about becoming pregnant and contraception. This information has often been found in the readers' queries sections of magazines.

The attitudes about the school's sex education are fairly trusting in Finland nowadays, since at least 63% of the men and women reported that they did not think sex education in the schools would induce the young to start their sexual life too early. Only 19% of the men and 22% of the women feared that sex education would induce young people to have intercourse too early. Those who supported this opinion were strongly concentrated in the over-55-year-old age group, where one in every two held this opinion. Since the people of this age group have had their say in the decision making of sex education in the schools up to now, it is no wonder there are still some deficiencies in the teaching.

## 4. Autoerotic Behaviors and Patterns

### A. Children and Adolescents

According to Kontula and Meriläinen (1988), between 2% and 3% of both the boys and the girls reported having started masturbating already before age 10. In childhood, touching genitals to cause pleasure cannot very often be connected with masturbation. In addition, adolescents often dare not report it in a survey such as this. The researchers, therefore, believe that the percentage of children practicing masturbation at an early age is surely more than 2% or 3%.

In the follow-up of the same survey (Kosunen 1993), 13- to 17-year-olds were asked if they had ever practiced masturbation and if they had masturbated during the last month. Of the 13-year-olds, 36% of the boys and 23% of the girls reported that they had sometimes practiced masturbation; of the 15-year-olds, 67% and 45%, respectively, reported this practice; and of the 17-year-olds, 79% and 59%. About 40% of the boys had masturbated during the last month and about 20% during the last week. With the girls, the corresponding figures were 20% and 5%. With age, the masturbation activity of the young increased.

### B. Adults

The proportion of adults engaging in self-loving, clearly more common among men than women, has definitely increased during the last 20 years, according to the FINSEX study. There has been an increase in the practice of self-loving both during the previous month and during the past year. In 1971, 28% of the men and 16% of women reported masturbating during the previous month. In 1992, the corresponding shares were 42% and 25% [and in 1999, already 60% and 37%]. The strength of the change can be seen in the percentage of women who had masturbated during the previous year. In 1992, this figure for women was higher than the corresponding data for men in 1971.

With the spread of a more-natural attitude towards self-loving, fewer and fewer people abstain from it entirely. In 1971, 49% of the women and 26% of the men had never tried this sexual outlet. In 1992, the corresponding figures were 23% and 10% [and in 1999, 14% and 6%]. So, a large majority of both women and men have engaged in self-loving at least some time in their life.

Self-loving is considerably more common with the young than with older people (see Table 5). This, however, is not so much because of age differences as it is to changes in the times. People seem to keep the frequency pattern of self-loving they adopted in their youth throughout their lives. There are no obstacles to this, since masturbation is in no way dependent on the presence of a partner. With the aging of the present middle-aged people, the incidence of self-loving will increase further in the population.

The increase in self-pleasuring is explained by the fact that fewer and fewer people believe in the unfounded arguments that it entails health risks, as booklets on sex education maintained as late as the 1950s. Two thirds of the women and over one third of the men who still believed in these risks, or were at least uncertain about them, had never engaged in this sexual activity. Very few of these women had masturbated during the last month. On the other hand, half of the men who had totally lost their belief in the health risks of masturbation, and nearly 30% of the women, had engaged in self-pleasuring during the last month. The spread of accurate information had been a major factor in encouraging people to feel free to enjoy their sexuality with self-pleasuring.

Having a steady sexual partner somewhat diminished the need for self-loving: The unmarried, the divorced, and the widowed engaged in self-pleasuring more regularly than did married people. The better-educated people engaged in self-loving more often than others. Religiosity did not relate to the incidence of self-loving, but those who consumed more alcohol were more likely to masturbate than others. During the past 20 years, the differences in the incidence of self-loving among the different age groups has disappeared, while the differences between the marital-status groups and alcohol-user groups had grown.

Young low-income men and women engage in self-pleasuring more often than others. This relation of the mas-

#### Table 4

**Percentages of People by Age Reporting That They Received Sufficient Sex Education at Home and at School, 1971 and 1992**

|  | 18-24 | 25-34 | 35-44 | 45-54 | 55-64 | 65-74 |
|---|---|---|---|---|---|---|
| School 1992 | 58 | 37 | 18 | 7 | 3 | 1 |
| Childhood home 1992 | 52 | 34 | 19 | 17 | 9 | 7 |
| Childhood home 1971 | 21 | 12 | 7 | 8 | | |
| School 1971 | 17 | 5 | 3 | 2 | | |

#### Table 5

**Percentages of Men and Women by Age Reporting That They Had Masturbated During the Past Year, 1971 and 1992**

|  | 18-24 | 25-34 | 35-44 | 45-54 | 55-64 | 65-74 |
|---|---|---|---|---|---|---|
| Men 1992 | 77 | 71 | 57 | 43 | 25 | 18 |
| Men 1971 | 64 | 44 | 30 | 14 | | |
| Women 1992 | 61 | 53 | 43 | 26 | 13 | 11 |
| Women 1971 | 45 | 28 | 16 | 11 | | |

turbation frequency to low income persists in middle-aged men. Further, this higher incidence of self-loving is related to the observation that low-income men enter into steady relationships less frequently than others. Masturbation thus serves them, at least in part, as a substitute for an intercourse-centered sexual life.

[*Update 2003*: One important finding of the current study is that masturbation does not necessarily decrease during the course of one's life. In fact, the three surveys in Finland show that masturbation remained almost at the same level in every birth cohort from one survey to another. This implies that the masturbation habits, which each generation adopted in its teenage years, tend to remain very similar throughout life, even over a 27-year time span. This tells us how important a generational approach is to understand differences between age groups in sexual attitudes and behaviors. Comprehensive sex education for teenagers would help new generations enjoy their sexuality free from unnecessary fears and anxiety (Kontula & Haavio-Mannila 2003b).

[According to studies of the sexual autobiographies of ordinary people, fears related to masturbation have been common among many generations in Finland, Estonia, and St. Petersburg. Several authors of the sexual life histories have been afraid of the negative consequences of masturbation after reading warnings in publications or after hearing about them from others. Fears (of becoming insane) and guilt related to masturbation were common especially before the 1970s. Some people explained how they had tried to stop masturbating because of these fears, usually unsuccessfully. Even among women in the youngest generations, feelings of guilt remained common (Kontula & Haavio-Mannila 1997; Haavio-Mannila et al. 2002). (*End of update by O. Kontula and E. Haavio-Mannila*)]

The use of pornographic materials has remained almost the same among men but decreased among women between 1970 and 1990. Even when sex videos were included in the printed publications in 1992, fewer people, on the average, had viewed such material during the previous year. During the past year, 50% to 60% of the men in the different age groups, and from 15% to 20% of the women, had watched a sex video or read a sex magazine.

Obviously, interest in pornographic publications was exceptionally high in 1971, because open nakedness had come, for the first time, into the pictures of the sex magazines at the end of the 1960s in Finland. The charm of novelty and the taste of "the forbidden fruit" made this material especially attractive. More recently, this high excitement and attraction have settled down. Besides, the so-called soft pornography is now within everyone's reach, for example, in the pictures in the afternoon tabloids, although it is no longer referred to as pornography.

[*Update 2003*: In 1999, the popularity of pornography had again increased: 64% of the men and 21% of the women had looked at sex magazines during the last year. For sex videos, these proportions were 57% and 27%, respectively. (*End of update by O. Kontula*)]

## 5. Interpersonal Heterosexual Behaviors

### A. Children

Small children often play sexual games (doctor games) and masturbate, during which they examine the genitals of both their own and the other sex. According to the KISS study conducted in Finland (Kontula & Meriläinen 1988), sexual games have been played by at least 40% of the young adults in their childhood, half of them more frequent than one or two incidents. These games may also include imitating and trying the sex habits the children had seen adults us-

ing. This cannot, however, be regarded as an actual initiation of sexual life, because it is not yet conscious activity that could be interpreted as sexual. Sexual meanings are not generally understood before approaching adolescence and the effects of pubertal hormones on the brain. Puberty brings a quite new kind of interest in sexual matters.

### B. Adolescents
*Puberty*

By age 13, about four out of five girls have had their first periods of menstruation and about 60% of the boys their first ejaculations. As a result, many young people show considerably more serious interest in the opposite sex than before. Over half of the boys of this age and one third of the girls have already viewed sex magazines and sex videos, and more than half of both boys and girls have kissed, according to the 1992 data. Many have experienced caressing over the clothing. Almost half of the 13-year-olds are ready to accept sexual intercourse in their peers' relationships. About as many report having already had a dating relationship with the opposite sex. Mostly, this means going around together with the dating partner as part of a group of young people. Sexual intercourse has been experienced by about 5% by the age of 13.

Between ages 14 and 15, most Finnish adolescents go to a confirmation class, a one-week church-sponsored camp, after which they are confirmed. This has become a kind of initiation rite for becoming a sexual adult.

Adolescence is a time of rapid changes, and, with age, sexual experience quickly grows. In Finland, the greatest changes in adolescent sexual behaviors occurred between 1960 and 1970. In 1992, Finns between ages 18 and 54 reported they had kissed for the first time, on the average, at the age of 14, had started dating at 17, and experienced their first sexual intercourse at the age of 18. Young people with a long education began sexual intercourse later than others.

Nowadays, young people mature, both physically and mentally, earlier than before. Because of the increased economic well-being, they live in a more grown-up way at a fairly young age, when they build their sexual identity through a multinational youth culture. As a result, the age of sexual initiation has fallen. On the other hand, the time spent in education has lengthened and the age of entering into marriage has risen. This explains why young people have more relationships, both successive and casual, today, and why marriage has been displaced by cohabitation, at least before having children.

In the 1992 FINSEX survey, one third of the 18- to 74-year-old women and a quarter of the men reported dating (going steady) by age 15. About four out of five had experienced kissing, and two out of three caressing over the clothing. Petting under the clothing had been experienced by one of every two younger Finns. Sexual intercourse before the age of 16 had been experienced by 31% of the girls and 19% of the boys according to the 1992 data (see Table 6). On average, Finnish girls begin having intercourse somewhat younger than the boys. This is quite understandable, because girls

### Table 6

**Percentage of 9th-Grade Pupils (15-Year-Olds) Who Had the Indicated Experiences, 1992**

|                     | Boys | Girls |
|---------------------|------|-------|
| Masturbation        | 67   | 45    |
| Kissing on the mouth| 72   | 81    |
| Light petting       | 66   | 70    |
| Heavy petting       | 45   | 53    |
| Sexual intercourse  | 19   | 31    |

often date boys from two to three years older than they themselves are. The boys are more eager to have intercourse than the girls, but the girls have better opportunities.

### Early Noncoital Experiences

The sexual life of young Finns does not generally begin with sexual intercourse, but with kissing and caressing. These behaviors are often associated with first dating relationships. It has been observed in Finland that four years, on the average, elapse from the first kisses and caresses of the young people to the first sexual intercourse (Kontula 1991). These experiences are surely as important to the young as the first intercourse. In the past, when a great number of people wanted or had to put off beginning sexual intercourse until marriage, kisses and caresses were the only forms of sexual life before entering matrimony.

A great number of people have already kissed before their first steady relationship, according to the 1992 FINSEX study. After the mid-1970s, about 60% of the men and 70% of the women were dating before the age of 18. About 40% of the present-day under-35-year-olds had had a steady dating relationship before the age of 16. Before the 1950s, it was quite unusual for women of this age to date. Nowadays, only 3% of the over-25-year-olds have never had a dating relationship. Since the 1980s, there have not been great changes in the onset of dating.

The age of sexual initiation has clearly fallen during the past few decades. Both first kisses and dating relationships are experienced at a younger age today than in the past. Four out of five have kissed before the age of 16, and two out of three have been going steady before the age of 18.

Characteristic of those adolescents who initiate a sexual life earlier than the others is a lifestyle that emphasizes a break with the norms of childhood and an orientation towards a freer social life. To these young people, free social life represents a means rather than a goal. The reverse is true for those who have less self-confidence and fewer sexual experiences. The acquired values and moral codes, such as associating love with family, lose their importance after sexual initiation.

Based on the KISS study (Kontula 1991), it can be said that the values associated with starting a sexual life early are today often connected with symbolic opposition or rebellion to authorities. Extended education with its upper-class values is ideal for arousing such opposition.

Sex is used to sell things and ideas to the young, but sex itself is rarely sold to them. Society and parents rarely provide adolescents with interpretations of sex (scripts) that would give a positive and an enjoyable picture of sexuality. Thus, adolescents, girls in particular, do not expect much good of their first sexual experiences, especially of sexual intercourse. Normally, organized education and instruction only provide warnings about the risks of getting pregnant, being infected with an STD or the HIV virus, getting a bad reputation, and similar dangers.

Moral values concerning reproduction and marriage have gradually been replaced by the values of satisfying one's social needs. This shift has contributed to a widening of interpretations relating to sexual interactions guided by strict Christian and conventional scripts towards "games," in which various tactics to achieve first sexual experiences are possible. The morals of satisfying social needs, which emphasize the importance of sexual life, give young people permission to initiate a sexual life in various practical situations. This widening of the sexual script towards "games" is one important reason for an earlier sexual initiation among Finnish adolescents during the last few decades (Kontula 1991). Tactics, interpretations, and values, which are all

part of sexual interactions, are, however, still strongly regulated socially and culturally.

### Dating

The age of first dating, like the age of first kisses, has lowered in recent years. In the 1930s, only half of the under-20-year-old people had dating relationships; currently, more than four fifths of the under-20-year-olds are dating. This increase stopped in the 1980s.

In the Finnish-Karelian culture area, "night courting or prowling" was a common way for young people to become acquainted until the early 20th century. In rural areas, it was customary for groups of boys to visit several girls during a single outing, since the girls belonged to the same social group. In going to the girls' sleeping quarters, "night courting" constituted a formal social venture or endeavor, with identifying knocks, introductions, overtures, seductive lines, and poetry. The choice of a conversation partner was made with the help of night proposal rites. The many customary rules and norms in night courting were aimed at the preservation of morality (Sarmela 1967). In their classic study *Die Einleitung der Ehe* [*The Introduction to Marriage*] (1937), K. Rob and V. Wikman divided night prowling into two main types: organized-group and individual courting. In group prowling, the boys watched, often very strictly, over each other's behavior. The girls could not refuse the visits of such groups. It was, nevertheless, in the power of the girls to decide which boys in the group would be allowed into their sleeping rooms in the storehouse or building where they were spending the summer.

### Sexarche

Sexarche, first sexual intercourse, requires finding an appropriate partner and becoming sexually aroused. What a person defines as "appropriate" is closely associated with the interpretations given by society. "An appropriate partner" may be understood as a partner with whom one has a love relationship and a relationship in which both partners feel "ready" for sexual intercourse. The importance of these social conditions is emphasized by the fact that about 20% of the 15-year-olds with steady partners would have liked to have sexual intercourse, but, for some reason, they had not had that experience. They had had both the chance and the willingness; nevertheless, all the social conditions had not been fulfilled.

At the age of 15, adolescents usually accept the sexual intercourse of their peers on grounds of love. Thus, an important condition for starting a sexual relationship is that two people love each other enough. The importance of love in legitimating sexual relationships of the young people is somewhat greater among farmers and the upper-middle class. This applies to both youths and their parents. This emphasis on love is closely connected with the demand for faithfulness.

Girls tend to value sex less, to masturbate less frequently, and to report considerably less desire for sexual intercourse than boys of their age. Girls who have never had a steady relationship with a boy are less likely to report a strong sexual desire. A female culture that emphasizes love does not attach a high value to sexual enjoyment in the expectations of Finnish girls. The dating institution, however, diminishes the effect of this romantic value that delays sexarche. Among the girls, the importance of sex quickly increases with an increase in experience. Dating clearly brings the expectations of sexual life closer to each other in boys and girls.

Twenty percent of Finns currently experience sexual intercourse before the age of 16, and approximately 50% by age 18. [*Update 2003*: According the latest results (2003), about three quarters of women and over half of men experience sexual intercourse before the age of 18. The mean age of first intercourse was 17.6 years for women and 18.1 years for men. (*End of update by O. Kontula*)]

Seventy percent of the women and half of the men reported that they had had their first experience of sexual intercourse with a steady partner. Only 60% of the women and 50% of the men reported being in love with their first sexual partner (see Table 7).

Among the older Finns surveyed, nearly half of the women had their first sexual intercourse after the age of 20. With the men, the corresponding share was about one fifth. Among younger Finns, about 10% have their first intercourse after age 20. Two percent of the over-30-year-olds reported that they had never had sexual intercourse.

The age of first sexual intercourse does not differ significantly in the provinces of Finland. Nor is it related to population density, although people living in the rural areas start having sexual intercourse somewhat later than urban youth, probably because rural living provides fewer opportunities for making social contacts.

A significant change has also occurred in the extent to which sexual intercourse is involved in the first dating experiences. When ages of first dating relationship and first sexual intercourse are compared, it appears that, as late as the 1930s, sexual intercourse was not generally a part of a steady dating relationship. Less than a third of the women who had been dating at a particular age had had sexual intercourse at that age. After the 1930s, there was a continuous even growth in the proportion of the women who experienced sexual intercourse while dating. By the end of the 1970s, the proportion of women dating who had had sexual intercourse grew to nearly 90%. During the 1980s, it dropped a little and is now about 80%.

Women's greater sexual initiative and willingness at the first intercourse has contributed to this change. However, for many women the first experience of sexual intercourse is still painful and a disappointment. Many women go through their first experience expecting it as a necessary routine in order to be able to start really enjoying their sexual life after this "puncturing."

The decreasing gap between the willingness of men and women to initiate sexual relations in the interval between the 1970s and 1990s is statistically very significant. In two decades, the share of the women who were reluctant at their first sexual intercourse fell from 40% to 10%. This increasing equality between women and men has been matched by an increase in equality in other sectors of life, such as education, work, politics, family, and leisure time. Part of this change may be because of the more-honest reporting of both men and women to these questions than before.

*Early Contraceptive Use*

The use of contraception at the first intercourse has increased considerably in recent decades (see Table 8). Only a

few percent of the over-55-year-olds had used contraception at the first time, and about 70% had been entirely without contraception. Withdrawal was the most common contraceptive method. The use of the condom as a contraceptive method at the first intercourse increased significantly with the under-55-year-olds, especially among the young after the middle of 1960s. In the 1970s, the use of the condom decreased slightly, according to age-group comparisons, but increased again in the 1980s, obviously because of the condom campaigns against AIDS. In the recent years, 60% of the men and 65% of the women had used the condom at the first intercourse. About 15% used no contraception at all. These proportions correspond well with results of the most recent surveys among adolescents.

## C. Adults

*Single Adults*

In 1992, 30% of Finnish men ages 18 to 74 and 34% of women were not married or cohabiting. One third of these had a steady sexual relationship. In the whole population covered by our survey, 11% of both men and women had a steady sex partner with whom they did not live.

The proportion of single adults, i.e., not having any steady sexual relationship, is highest in the youngest and oldest age groups (see Table 9). A large proportion of people under 30 years have not yet started to live together with a partner but will probably do so later. Many of the women over 60 years are single because of widowhood and the shortage of older men. Among men, singlehood does not increase with age because they less often get widowed and have more potential partners available.

Singlehood in Finland does not mean celibacy. A large proportion of single people have a regular sex life: 40% of all single men and 28% of single women had not experienced periods of at least six months without sexual intercourse over the course of the previous five years. On the other hand, 8% of single men and 30% of single women had not engaged in sexual intercourse during the previous five years.

More single adults never had engaged in sexual intercourse, 14%, compared with 3% of the total population. Single women started their sexual activity at a later age than other women, but for men, singlehood was not connected to the age of initiating sexual intercourse.

Single men have a more-varied sex life than single women. Forty-six percent of single men and 20% of single women reported sexual intercourse during the previous month. Thirteen percent of the single men and 3% of the single women had engaged in sexual intercourse at least once a week during the previous month.

Measured by the number of partners, the sexual life of single adults is also livelier than that of married and cohabiting people. Close to half of all single men and more than a

Table 7

**Percentages of Men and Women Who Had Their First Sexual Intercourse by the Age of 18, in Different Decades, Based on the Cohort Analysis, 1971 and 1992**

|            | 1933-1942 | 1943-1952 | 1953-1962 | 1963-1972 | 1973-1982 | 1983-1989 |
|------------|-----------|-----------|-----------|-----------|-----------|-----------|
| Men 1971   | 37        | 30        | 40        | 49        |           |           |
| Men 1992   | 35        | 41        | 36        | 47        | 58        | 50        |
| Women 1992 | 9         | 16        | 28        | 42        | 60        | 55        |
| Women 1971 | 6         | 18        | 21        | 34        |           |           |

Table 8

**Percentages of Men and Women by Age Who Used No Contraception at the First Sexual Intercourse, 1971 and 1992**

| Age   | Men 1971 | Men 1992 | Women 1971 | Women 1992 |
|-------|----------|----------|------------|------------|
| 18-24 | 26       | 17       | 24         | 13         |
| 25-34 | 39       | 24       | 46         | 22         |
| 35-44 | 58       | 29       | 60         | 18         |
| 45-54 | 57       | 40       | 60         | 42         |
| 55-64 |          | 67       |            | 68         |
| 65-74 |          | 82       |            | 70         |

1971: $N = 1,919$, with 669 men and 1,250 women
1992: $N = 2,048$, with 1,002 men and 1,046 women

third of single women had had more than one sex partner during the previous year.

For single adults living without a steady sexual relationship, their last sexual partner was usually a sexually unaffiliated person. Fourteen percent of single women and 9% of the men said that their last partner was a spouse or steady partner of somebody else. Of single men, 2% said that their last partner was a prostitute. One tenth of single men had, during their lifetime, had intercourse with a prostitute. This is the same proportion as for married or cohabiting men. No single women reported contact with a paid sex partner.

Single people do not use as varied sex techniques as cohabiting couples and other people having a steady relationship. The positions used in last intercourse resemble those of married people: the missionary position with the man lying on top and the woman underneath. In the casual sexual relationships of single people, the love play and coital positions are fairly traditional: There is little oral sex and stimulating of a partner's genitals by hand.

For women, the incidence of orgasm in sexual intercourse varies according to having or not having a steady sexual relationship. However, 26% of single women did not recall whether they had an orgasm during their last intercourse, perhaps because this may have been several years ago.

Single adults reported less satisfaction with their last intercourse than other people. Single adults also reported less satisfaction with their sex life as a whole than people having a steady sexual partner. Single people have a lower sexual self-esteem than other people; this may be one reason for their lack of sexual partner. People not having sexual relations do not receive positive sexual feedback, which might strengthen their self-esteem.

Slightly more single men have had some homosexual experiences during their lifetime than attached males, 7% compared with 4%. Single men also are more likely to have a homosexual identity or identify themselves as bisexuals than other men (see Section 6 on homosexuality and bisexuality). Single women are not more often lesbians than other women.

Masturbation is more common among single adults than other adults. Half of single men and one fourth of single

women reported self-loving during the last month, twice as high as married people. Self-loving is most common among single people living with their parents. Most of these are young people.

In addition to using self-loving to compensate for not having a steady sexual partner, singles watch sex videos. Forty percent of single men had watched sex videos at least a couple of times during the previous year. This is the same frequency as cohabiting men and more than married men. Only 5% of single women had watched sex videos during the year, less than cohabiting or married women had done. Similar differences were found in the use of pornographic books and magazines. Women with steady partners may get invitations from their partners to watch sex videos or read pornographic materials. Single women seem to be too shy to buy or borrow sex materials to use alone.

Sex toys and aids are generally not used as substitutes for sexual relations (see Section 8 on unconventional sexual behaviors). Vibrators are not used more by single than by other women—about 5% of all women had ever used them.

Alcohol is associated with the sexual life of single adults more than it is for affiliated persons. As many as 58% of single men and 26% of single women reported drinking alcoholic beverages before their last intercourse. For single men, this proportion is almost double that of other men, perhaps because the casual relationships of single adults often begin in restaurants and other social situations where alcoholic beverages are served.

Even though single adults suffer from feelings of loneliness more than people living in a couple relationship, not all of them long for a sexual partner. Many deny the importance of having sex or living with somebody.

### Cohabitating Adults

All over the world, families and couple relationships have changed in recent decades. In the developed countries, children move away from the parental home earlier than before, cohabitation has become a common form of starting a marriage, divorces have increased, and the number of children has declined.

Because of the higher standard of living, adult Finns today live less often with their parents than in earlier times and more often alone (see Table 10). The increase in unmarried cohabitation has decreased the proportion of married people in the population. In 1971, 64% of the respondents ages 18 to 54 lived together with their spouse and only a few percent with their fiancées or steady partners. The rapid growth of cohabitation can be seen from the 1992 survey: 16% of the 18- to 54-year-olds were cohabiting and only 53% of the population in this age cohort were married. [In 1999, 15% were cohabiting and 50% were married. Living apart together (LAT) relationships had increased; their proportion was already 13%.]

The increase in cohabitation has not meant that there are more couples living together than earlier. When one adds the percentages of married and cohabiting people together, their proportion only grew from 66% in 1971 to 69% in 1992. The main change is that nowadays more people delay or do not

### Table 9

### Percentages of Men and Women by Age in the Given Type of Couple Relationship, 1992

| Type of Relationship | Age, Years | | | | | | |
| --- | --- | --- | --- | --- | --- | --- | --- |
| | 18-24 | 25-34 | 35-44 | 45-54 | 55-64 | 65-74 | Total |
| **MEN** | | | | | | | |
| No couple relationship | 48 | 17 | 14 | 12 | 15 | 16 | 19 |
| Steady sexual relationship without living together | 29 | 12 | 4 | 5 | 7 | 8 | 11 |
| Cohabitation | 9 | 27 | 11 | 6 | 2 | 2 | 13 |
| Marriage | 4 | 44 | 71 | 77 | 76 | 74 | 57 |
| (*n*) | (159) | (249) | (266) | (203) | (308) | (96) | (1103) |
| **WOMEN** | | | | | | | |
| No couple relationship | 32 | 11 | 15 | 13 | 29 | 49 | 23 |
| Steady sexual relationship without living together | 32 | 11 | 8 | 9 | 6 | 3 | 11 |
| Cohabitation | 28 | 22 | 13 | 7 | 4 | 1 | 13 |
| Marriage | 8 | 56 | 64 | 71 | 61 | 47 | 53 |
| (*n*) | (164) | (233) | (250) | (191) | (157) | (149) | (1114) |

enter a formal marriage, and maintain an official status as single. In the past 20 years, the proportion of never-married people among the 15- to 54-year-old Finns rose from 35% to 40% for men and from 27% to 36% for women.

The developmental cycle of the present union greatly varied by age in 1992 (see Table 11). In the older age groups, 55 years and over, a large majority first moved in together after the wedding. In the age category 25-to-44 years, half of the people first lived together and then married. Four fifths of the less-than-35-year-old people living together with someone were cohabiting without marriage. At present, most Finns start their marital life as a cohabiting couple.

In 1992, the age at moving in together was for men aged 15 to 64 years, on average, 0.9 years lower than age at marriage in 1971, and among women 0.6. The increase in cohabitation thus made men, in particular, more inclined to move in together with their partner relatively early. Twenty years ago, the average age at first marriage was 24.6 for men and 22.3 for women—there are no data on when couples moved in together from that era. In 1992, men initiated cohabiting, or married for the first time, on average, at age 23.7 years, women at age 21.8. [The mean age of women at first marriage in 2000 was 28.0 years. This difference is because of the fact that, practically speaking, everybody cohabited before they married.]

Of all the men interviewed in 1992, 79%, and of the women, 83%, had lived in a matrimonial relationship. In the oldest age group, 65 to 74 years, there was a gender gap: 7%

### Table 10

**Changes in Household Structure of People Aged 15 to 54 from 1971 to 1992 (in Percentages)**

| Living Companions | Men 1971 | Men 1992 | Women 1971 | Women 1992 |
|---|---|---|---|---|
| Parents or other kin | 26 | 17 | 18 | 15 |
| Wife or husband | 62 | 52 | 66 | 51 |
| Cohabiting partner | 3 | 17 | 2 | 18 |
| Same sex companion | 3 | 1 | 3 | 1 |
| Other and no information | 2 | 0 | 4 | 0 |
| Lives alone | 4 | 13 | 7 | 15 |
| (*n*) | (744) | (877) | (1408) | (838) |

### Table 11

**Developmental Cycle of the Present Union by Gender and Age (in Percentages, 1992)**

| Cycle of the Union | Age, Years | | | | | | |
|---|---|---|---|---|---|---|---|
| | 18-24 | 25-34 | 35-44 | 45-54 | 55-64 | 65-74 | Kaikki |
| **MEN** | | | | | | | |
| From marriage to living together | 6 | 10 | 36 | 80 | 87 | 93 | 50 |
| From cohabitation to marriage | 11 | 51 | 51 | 12 | 10 | 4 | 31 |
| Cohabiting | 83 | 39 | 13 | 8 | 3 | 3 | 19 |
| (*n*) | (36) | (176) | (218) | (169) | (101) | (73) | (773) |
| **WOMEN** | | | | | | | |
| From marriage to living together | 5 | 17 | 43 | 78 | 85 | 94 | 51 |
| From cohabitation to marriage | 15 | 52 | 39 | 13 | 8 | 3 | 28 |
| Cohabiting | 80 | 31 | 18 | 9 | 7 | 3 | 21 |
| (*n*) | (59) | (182) | (193) | (150) | (101) | (72) | (757) |

of men and 13% of women never had cohabited or married. This is partly explained by the fact that single men die young and single women live long.

A longer life expectancy and the growing divorce rate have contributed to the fact that people have time to enter several unions during their lives. According to the 1971 study, 5% of the ever-married men and 6% of the women had been married at least twice. In 1992, the proportions were 17% and 22%, respectively, [and in 1999, 26% and 25%].

Cohabitation does not always lead to marriage, particularly among young people. One fourth of the 1992 respondents had been cohabiting without getting married to the partner. Among people under 35 years, the proportion was more than half.

### Marital, Extramarital, and Postmarital Sexual Behaviors

*Sexual Intercourse.* The frequency of sexual intercourse 20 years ago was almost as high as nowadays. Finns have sexual intercourse usually once or twice a week. The share of people who had had sexual intercourse during the last two days among the people ages 35 to 54 was higher in 1992 than in 1971 (see Table 12). Sexual relations seem nowadays to remain consistent and regular later in life than they did 20 years ago. The frequency of sexual intercourse does not decrease significantly until after the age of 55, especially among women. Even this change does not necessarily follow from aging but from generational differences.

[*Update 2003:* In the 1990s, the frequency of sexual intercourse had not changed significantly. In 1999, the number of intercourses per month in the age group 18-to-54 years was 6.3 for men and 5.9 for women; the annual totals for men was 75.9 and for women 70.3. (*End of update by O. Kontula*)]

Sexual intercourse has become more varied. While in 1971, as much as 68% of the most recent occurrences of sexual intercourse among 18- to 54-year-old people were the missionary position, in 1992, the proportion was 43%. The proportion of those who had used many different positions during their most recent sexual intercourse had increased in a very significant way, from 16% to 32%. [In 1999, this proportion was even higher: 44% of men and 36% of women.]

Twenty years ago, it was usual that the man was the sole initiator of sexual intercourse in 49% of the incidents. In 1992, only 37% of the most recent experiences of sexual intercourse were initiated solely by the man. Fifteen percent of the male respondents said that the woman was the initiator of the last sexual intercourse, but this figure was only 10% according to the women's responses. Women were slightly more likely than men to report that both partners took an equal role in initiating intercourse, 51% compared with 45%. Women may find it more difficult to admit that they have taken an active role in coitus.

Alcohol consumption before the last sexual intercourse became slightly more frequent in the past 20 years. In 1971, alcohol had been used by 21% of the men and 11% of the women; in 1992, this figure was 25% and 16%, respectively, [and in 1999, 34% and 23%, respectively]. This reflects an increased consumption of alcohol among Finns in general.

*Sex Styles.* Sexual satisfaction can be attained in many ways. Following a factor analysis of the 1992 data to measure variables associated with different sexual habits and partners, three sex styles were identified:

1. Sex in a sexual-intercourse-centered steady relationship (frequent sexual intercourse with a steady partner);
2. sex in casual relationships (many sexual partners, including relationships with foreigners and prostitutes); and
3. alternative sexual habits (anal and oral sex, manually stimulated satisfaction, acquaintance with sexual aids, the use of different sex facilities, and masturbation).

The connection of the social background with these sex styles was examined by regression analyses. As explanatory variables in the simple linear regression model, there were gender, age, place of residence, type of marital relationship, years of education, income, days on working trips, religiosity, and two variables about alcohol consumption: the frequency of alcohol use and of getting intoxicated.

Sex in a steady relationship, meaning frequency of sexual intercourse and familiarity of the last sexual partner, relate naturally to living in a steady relationship, but also to youth and high income with a lower level of education. This sex style is typical of ambitious couples. The regression model explained 41% of the variation in the steady-relationship sex.

Those who practice casual sexual relationships, or people who have numerous sexual partners and/or sex with foreigners and paid partners are men, city residents, well-paid, who travel a lot for their work. They are indifferent to religion and often consume alcohol. The people cohabiting or in a steady noncohabiting relationship more often than other people had transient sexual relationships. The typical male practitioners of casual sexual relationships may well be called "rich good-time boys" for their social background, even if they can be found in all age and gender groups. The regression model explained 18% of the variation in the casual sexual relationships.

Alternative sex was related to male gender, youth, frequency of alcohol consumption, and frequency of intoxication. The married and the single people did not engage in alternative sexual habits as much as the people living in cohabitation or in steady sexual relationships. Alternative sexual habits are related to the lifestyle of young go-ahead men. As much as 43% of the variation in alternative sex was explained by these social factors.

*Sexual Partners.* For Finns ages 18 to 54, the average number of sexual partners during their lifetime has risen from 7 to 10 during the last 20 years. In 1971, women of all ages had about 3, men about 11 partners, and in 1992, correspondingly, 6 and 14. In 1992, the male respondents between ages 25 and 44 years had the most partners, between 40% and 50% had at least 10 partners; of the women in the same age cohorts, about 18% had at least 10 partners (see Table 13).

[*Update 2003*: The number of sexual partners had somewhat increased in the 1990s. In 1999, the mean number of sexual partners was 16 for men and 7 for women; 43% of men and 25% of women had had more than 10 sexual partners in their lifetime. (*End of update by O. Kontula*)]

In both surveys, the large number of sexual partners is related not only to gender and age, but also to marital status, according to a Multiple Classification (multivariate) analysis: The married people had fewer partners than the un-

married, widowed, and the divorced. Those alienated from religion, as well as the frequent consumers of alcohol, had more sexual partners than the religious and temperate people. Those who had passed the matriculation examination had fewer partners than the less educated; this difference, however, was no longer statistically significant in 1992.

Worldwide, in all the sex surveys, men claim to have had more sexual partners than women. This survey refined this general data by separating out data on Finnish men and women who had foreigners, homosexuals, or prostitutes as partners. When those who had, at some time in their life, at least one foreigner, one homosexual, and one prostitute as a sexual partner, were separated from the data on under-56-year-old men and women, the men still had at least 10 sexual partners—about twice as many as the women. One explanation of this might be that the Finnish men subconsciously overestimate the number of their partners, while the women underestimate their contacts. Another possibility is that many of the men with multiple sexual partners who responded to the survey have as sexual partners a small group of women who, for the main part, were left outside the survey and were among the nonrespondents of the questionnaire.

Finns report a somewhat higher number of sexual partners than Americans (Laumann et al. 1994). This may partly be explained by the fact that in the United States, a greater proportion of survey respondents left the question concerning the number of partners during their lifetime unanswered.

In addition, during the prior 12 months, the Finns more often than the Americans had more than one partner. During the previous year, 21% of the Finnish men and 11% of the women had had two or more partners; the corresponding figure for Americans was 17% and 7%, respectively. Only 4% of the Finnish men and 7% of the women reported that they had had no partners at all during the prior year; in the United States, the proportions were 13% and 24% (see Tables 14, 15, 16, and 17).

These results suggest that the sexual life of the Finns is at least as active as that of the Americans. Indeed, fear of AIDS and traditional sexual attitudes may restrict the number of sexual partners in the United States more than in Finland.

*Extra or Concurrent Sexual Relationships.* The partners in the most recent sexual intercourse have mostly been steady

### Table 12

**Percentages of Men and Women by Age Reporting That They Had Sexual Intercourse Within the Past 48 Hours at the Most, 1971 and 1992**

|  | 18-24 | 25-34 | 35-44 | 45-54 | 55-64 | 65-74 |
|---|---|---|---|---|---|---|
| Women 1971 | 43 | 42 | 34 | 23 | | |
| Women 1992 | 37 | 46 | 46 | 38 | 14 | 3 |
| Men 1992 | 36 | 50 | 54 | 46 | 33 | 17 |
| Men 1971 | 34 | 53 | 36 | 31 | | |

### Table 13

**Percentages of Men and Women by Age Reporting at Least 10 Sexual Partners During Their Lifetime, 1971 and 1992**

|  | 18-24 | 25-29 | 30-34 | 35-39 | 40-44 | 45-49 | 50-54 | 55-59 | 60-64 | 65-69 | 70-74 |
|---|---|---|---|---|---|---|---|---|---|---|---|
| Men 1992 | 22 | 47 | 52 | 46 | 50 | 40 | 35 | 33 | 33 | 16 | 13 |
| Men 1971 | 21 | 32 | 28 | 16 | 21 | 28 | 29 | | | | |
| Women 1992 | 15 | 24 | 23 | 16 | 20 | 6 | 5 | 6 | 2 | 3 | 3 |
| Women 1971 | 3 | 4 | 5 | 3 | 1 | 2 | 4 | | | | |

partners or spouses in marriage or cohabitation. In 1992, only 6% of the men and 4% of the women in a steady sexual relationship had had someone other than the steady partner as the last partner. However, a greater and greater share of people have experiences of sexual relationships alongside their steady sexual relationships. Sexual relationships of this kind, including extramarital relationships, are called extra or parallel sexual relationships in the study.

The number of extra sexual relationships has approximately doubled during the 20 years among the Finns between 18 and 54 years old. In 1971, 24% of the men and 9% of the women who were married at the time of the survey stated that they had had sexual intercourse with some persons other than their spouses during their marriage. In 1992, 44% of the men and 19% of the women who were living in cohabitation or marriage had experiences of parallel sexual relationships during their cohabitation or marriage (see

### Table 14

**Number of Sexual Partners for Men During Their Lifetime in Three Countries in the Early 1990s in Percentage Share**

|  | None | 1 | 2-4 | 5+ |
|---|---|---|---|---|
| Finland | 3 | 13 | 25 | 60 |
| USA | 6 | 18 | 25 | 51 |
| Great Britain | 7 | 21 | 29 | 44 |

(Kontula 1993)

### Table 15

**Number of Sexual Partners for Women During Their Lifetime in Three Countries in the Early 1990s in Percentage Share**

|  | None | 1 | 2-4 | 5+ |
|---|---|---|---|---|
| Finland | 4 | 28 | 35 | 34 |
| USA | 5 | 39 | 34 | 23 |
| Great Britain | 6 | 39 | 35 | 20 |

(Kontula 1993)

### Table 16

**Number of Sexual Partners for Men During the Past Year in Four Countries in the Early 1990s in Percentage Share**

|  | None | 1 | 2-4 |
|---|---|---|---|
| Finland | 5 | 71 | 24 |
| USA | 15 | 66 | 20 |
| Great Britain | 13 | 73 | 14 |
| France | 11 | 78 | 11 |

(Kontula 1993)

### Table 17

**Number of Sexual Partners for Women During the Past Year in Four Countries in the Early 1990s in Percentage Share**

|  | None | 1 | 2-4 |
|---|---|---|---|
| Finland | 8 | 79 | 13 |
| USA | 27 | 64 | 8 |
| Great Britain | 14 | 79 | 6 |
| France | 17 | 78 | 5 |

(Kontula 1993)

Table 18). [In 1999, these proportions had somewhat decreased among men, but increased among women.]

In 1992, the respondents were also asked how many parallel sexual relationships they had had while in their steady relationship with their then or earlier partner. Of all the people aged 18 to 74 years who had sometimes lived in a steady relationship, 52% of the men and 29% of the women admitted having experienced at least one relationship of this kind. Even if the incidence of parallel sexual relationships has increased, attitudes to parallel sexual relationships have become stricter during the past 20 years. This discrepancy between liberated actual behavior and tightening attitudes may be related to the fear of AIDS and the growing conservatism in the society in general (Haavio-Mannila et al., 1997). [*Comment 2003*: It may also imply higher expectations for permanent couple relationships and a renaissance of romanticism in the 1990s. (*End of comment by O. Kontula*)]

*Incidence of Oral and Anal Sex.* In the 1992 data, stimulation of the partner's genitals (e.g., fondling and stimulating by hand) in order to give him or her satisfaction without sexual intercourse is a common form of petting and love play. It may or may not be linked to vaginal intercourse. A large majority, 86% of men and 76% of women, had at least sometimes during their lifetime stimulated a partner's genitals. [In 1999, these proportions were 84% and 81%.] During the past month, this had been done by half of men and more than a third of women. More than one year had gone by since the last incidence of stimulation by hand for 26% of men and 42% of women. Women thus have been less active than men in giving satisfaction to a partner without sexual intercourse. Maybe some men offer fondling and stimulation by hand to their partners who otherwise do not have an orgasm in intercourse.

Young people stimulate their partner's genitals by fondling much more commonly than do older people. Of women and men over 55, half of the women and 30 to 40% of the men have never done it, whereas the proportion among 25- to 34-year-olds is only 5%. This huge age gap indicates that fondling the genitals was not considered a part of a "normal" sex life to satisfy one's partner when today's older generation was in their youth. Vaginal intercourse was then the main sex technique.

Anal sex (sodomy) has been practiced throughout history for pleasure, birth control, and to avoid breaking a virgin's hymen. Including the anus in sexual activity is taboo in some cultures.

> Clinically there is no difference between stimulation of the mouth, ears, nipples, feet, or anus in the production of pleasure sensations to the brain. None of these activities have a direct role in reproduction so it seems inconsistent for people to accept some and not all points of arousal in sexual activity. (Love 1992, 10)

In Finland, anal intercourse is not illegal. Nevertheless, it seems not to have been an acceptable sex technique in earlier generations, as older people rarely admit having prac-

### Table 18

**Percentages of Men and Women Reporting More Than One Sexual Partner During the Past Year by Duration of the Relationship, 1992**

|  | 0-1 Year | 1-4 Years | 4-9 Years | 9-19 Years | 19+ Years |
|---|---|---|---|---|---|
| Women | 69 | 5 | 11 | 9 | 4 |
| Men | 68 | 15 | 15 | 21 | 16 |

ticed it. According to the 1992 survey, only 20% of men and 17% of women reported having ever practiced anal intercourse. Eight percent of men and 6% of women had done it several times. It had most often been practiced by 25- to 34-year-old persons, 31% of the men and 29% of the women. In this age group, one in ten had had anal sex several times. Only 2% of the women over 55, and 5% of the older men, had ever tried this sex technique.

[Anal sex had become much more prevalent in the 1990s. In 1999, 28% of men and women reported having ever practiced anal intercourse. In the age group 18-to-34, one third has practiced anal intercourse several times.]

Cunnilingus and fellatio are very common sexual practices throughout cultures and history. In the Finnish questionnaire, experiences of oral sex were inquired by the following question: "In the last five years, how often have you had oral sex in your sexual relations, that is, fondling a man's penis or a woman's genitals by mouth?" Men reported to have done cunnilingus to their partner more often, 78%, than women had done fellatio, 67% (see Table 19). More than half of the men and 42% of the women had done it often or sometimes. Men also had received oral sex more often, 73%, than women, 64%.

Oral sex was much more common among younger than older Finns. In the age group 18 to 34 years, almost all had done and received oral sex, whereas in the age group 55 to 74, only 35% of men had received it from and 46% had done it to the partner. Only one in five women admitted it either

### Table 19

### Percentages of Men and Women by Age Reporting Experiences with Oral Sex, 1992

| Partner has done oral sex to me | Age, Years | | | |
|---|---|---|---|---|
| | 18-34 | 35-54 | 55-74 | Total |
| **MEN** | | | | |
| Mostly | 20 | 9 | 2 | 12 |
| Sometimes | 43 | 34 | 12 | 34 |
| Seldom | 22 | 34 | 21 | 26 |
| Not at all | 15 | 23 | 65 | 27 |
| (n) | (371) | (395) | (163) | (929) |
| | | | | |
| **WOMEN** | | | | |
| Mostly | 22 | 9 | — | 12 |
| Sometimes | 45 | 28 | 7 | 29 |
| Seldom | 20 | 32 | 12 | 23 |
| Not at all | 14 | 31 | 81 | 36 |
| (n) | (377) | (408) | (241) | (1026) |
| | | | | |
| **I have done oral sex to partner** | | | | |
| **MEN** | | | | |
| Mostly | 23 | 12 | 5 | 15 |
| Sometimes | 46 | 41 | 14 | 39 |
| Seldom | 18 | 28 | 27 | 24 |
| Not at all | 3 | 18 | 54 | 22 |
| (n) | (370) | (395) | (136) | (901) |
| | | | | |
| **WOMEN** | | | | |
| Mostly | 18 | 6 | 1 | 10 |
| Sometimes | 45 | 30 | 5 | 32 |
| Seldom | 23 | 32 | 12 | 25 |
| Not at all | 15 | 31 | 81 | 33 |
| (n) | (378) | (368) | (159) | (905) |

way. The discrepancy in older men's and women's reports of oral sex may be because of the more common experiences of extra sexual relations with prostitutes and perhaps a less-inhibited extra partner.

The wide age differences in the practice of oral sex are connected to the varied sex practices of young people in general. Young people use more-varied positions in sexual intercourse, satisfy each other more often by hand and mouth, and have more often experimented with anal sex than older people. The liberated sexual behavior of younger people may be one explanation for their greater sexual satisfaction.

*Sexual Satisfaction.* Perhaps the most positive result of the Finnish sex survey is the observation that young Finns are more satisfied with their sexual lives than their elders are. Sexual intercourse was more generally regarded as pleasant in 1992 than it was in 1971. The amount of love play was considered more adequate, the steady relationship was experienced as happier, discussing sexual matters with the partner was more open and easier, and sexual life as a whole was estimated to be more satisfying than in 1971. Women had experienced orgasm somewhat more often in their last sexual intercourse, and men had had less problems with getting erections during the prior year.

From the viewpoint of sexual equality, it was remarkable that women considered their experiences of sexual intercourse clearly more pleasant than 20 years ago and nearly as pleasant as men. The gender gap in experiencing sexual intercourse as pleasant or as unpleasant decreased significantly. Men enjoyed their sexual life as a whole more than women, but in the pleasantness of the last sexual intercourse, there was no difference between the genders.

Women are now able to enjoy sex partly because there is practically no fear of an unwanted pregnancy. Only a quarter of the women reported that they had been pregnant when entering into marriage or cohabitation; 20 years ago the share had been 45%. The number of marriages-of-necessity has decreased as sexual education and contraception became more common.

[*Update 2003*: Respondents were less satisfied in their sexual life as a whole in 1999 compared to that in 1992. This was evident, although sexual intercourse was considered more pleasant than before, and sexual self-esteem had improved. This finding was explained by strongly increased desire to experience more sexual intercourse. As the frequency of sexual intercourse did not increase in the 1990s, satisfaction in one's sexual life also diminished, on the average of 5 to 10 percentage points. (*End of update by O. Kontula*)]

Sexual satisfaction as a whole is a combination of emotional and physical satisfaction. According to our 1992 survey results, the two aspects are equally important. Among women, the correlation between general sexual satisfaction and finding intercourse pleasant—measured by the sum of finding them in general pleasant and considering the last intercourse as pleasant—was 0.47 and 0.40 for men. Happiness in the present steady relationship, meaning emotional satisfaction, correlated with sexual satisfaction as a whole for women at 0.44 and for men at 0.36.

Happiness with life was more strongly connected to emotional sexual satisfaction—for men 0.52 and women 0.59—than to physical satisfaction—0.23 and 0.20, respectively. Emotional satisfaction prevents feelings of loneliness—for men 0.27 and women 0.30—more than physical satisfaction—0.16 and 0.15, respectively.

Sexual satisfaction is a socially constructed phenomenon. It is related to emotions, sexual practices, and relationships. In Table 20, correlation coefficients between emotional, physical, and overall sexual satisfaction, and a number of variables related to sexual feelings, practices, and partners are presented. Perhaps this analysis gives hints as to how to improve sexual life so that it will be more happy and enjoyable.

Loving and being loved is important for emotional, physical, and overall satisfaction in sexual life. Women in particular need love in order to be happy in their steady relationship. A loving relationship greatly increases satisfaction with sexual life as a whole. The quality of the present

steady sexual relationship also has an impact on sexual satisfaction. People for whom talking about sex with their partner is not difficult at all, but open and easy, are emotionally, physically, and generally satisfied with their sexual life.

The number of persons one has really fallen in love with only correlates with the unhappiness of men's, but not women's steady relationships; that is, men who have fallen in love often are not very happy in their present relationship. Perhaps they have known too many women with whom they can compare their present partner in order to feel totally happy with her. Or maybe falling in love very

### Table 20

**Correlations Between Sexual Satisfaction and Sexual Feelings,
Practices, and Partners (*r*) for Men and Women, 1992**

| | Sexual Satisfaction | | | | | |
| | Emotional | | Physical | | General | |
| Sexual Feelings and Behavior | Men | Women | Men | Women | Men | Women |
|---|---|---|---|---|---|---|
| **FEELINGS** | (Correlation Coefficients) | | | | | |
| **Love:** | | | | | | |
| Loves somebody right now | 0.26 | 0.38 | 0.23 | 0.26 | 0.32 | 0.38 |
| Receives love | 0.24 | 0.36 | 0.22 | 0.26 | 0.31 | 0.36 |
| Talking about sex with one's partner is easy | 0.16 | 0.22 | 0.23 | 0.23 | 0.23 | 0.28 |
| Number of objects of love during lifetime | −0.10 | ns | ns | ns | ns | ns |
| **Sexual self esteem:** | | | | | | |
| I have great sexual skills | ns | 0.16 | 0.26 | 0.30 | 0.26 | 0.31 |
| I am sexually active | ns | 0.28 | 0.21 | 0.35 | 0.27 | 0.35 |
| I am sexually attractive | ns | 0.18 | 0.16 | 0.24 | 0.19 | 0.21 |
| **Role of sex in life:** | | | | | | |
| Considers sexual life to be an important part of life | 0.17 | 0.19 | 0.25 | 0.37 | 0.23 | 0.28 |
| Sexual desire has increased in the last five years | ns | 0.24 | 0.17 | 0.35 | 0.11 | 0.20 |
| **Happiness:** | | | | | | |
| Considers one's life happy | 0.52 | 0.59 | 0.23 | 0.20 | 0.31 | 0.38 |
| Is not lonely | 0.27 | 0.30 | 0.16 | 0.15 | 0.30 | 0.29 |
| **PRACTICES** | | | | | | |
| **Intercourse:** | | | | | | |
| Frequency of intercourse (in general and during the last month) | 0.10 | 0.23 | 0.28 | 0.29 | 0.39 | 0.37 |
| Both took initiative to last intercourse | 0.12 | 0.12 | 0.11 | 0.25 | 0.13 | 0.16 |
| Considers the amount of foreplay in intercourse suitable | 0.11 | 0.24 | 0.11 | 0.29 | 0.18 | 0.33 |
| Several positions in last intercourse | ns | 0.14 | ns | 0.22 | ns | ns |
| **Other sex practices:** | | | | | | |
| Stimulated recently partner's genitals without intercourse | ns | 0.19 | 0.13 | 0.26 | 0.18 | 0.21 |
| Partner gives oral sex | ns | 0.20 | 0.16 | 0.25 | 0.16 | 0.19 |
| Gives oral sex to partner | ns | 0.18 | 0.19 | 0.25 | 0.18 | 0.18 |
| Has had anal intercourse | ns | ns | ns | ns | ns | ns |
| Masturbates often | ns | ns | ns | ns | −0.20 | −0.12 |
| Has used sex materials (videos, movies, magazines etc.) during last year | ns | ns | ns | 0.11 | ns | ns |
| Has ever used sex facilities (vibrators, lubricants, erection rings, sexy underwear etc.) | ns | ns | ns | ns | ns | ns |
| **PHYSIOLOGICAL REACTIONS** | | | | | | |
| Orgasm in intercourse in general | 0.07 | 0.20 | 0.62 | 0.79 | 0.14 | 0.41 |
| Orgasm in last intercourse | 0.07 | 0.15 | 0.74 | 0.87 | 0.21 | 0.29 |
| Experienced own or partner's impotence during last year | ns | −0.22 | −0.22 | −0.28 | −0.15 | −0.27 |
| **PARTNERS** | | | | | | |
| Number of sexual partners | ns | ns | ns | ns | ns | −0.10 |
| Number of extra sexual relations during present or previous steady relations | −0.20 | −0.16 | ns | ns | ns | ns |

many times in life is an indicator of problems in getting really attached to anyone.

Sexual self-esteem is also more important for women's than men's sexual satisfaction. Women who consider themselves as sexually active, having great sexual skills, and being sexually attractive are happy in their steady relationships, and especially satisfied with sexual intercourse and sex life as a whole. Men can consider their steady relationship quite happy irrespective of their own opinion of their sexual capacity. But for men's physical and overall sexual satisfaction, it is important to have a high sexual self-esteem.

The role of sexuality in life is connected more to women's than to men's sexual satisfaction. Considering sexual life as an important part of life is associated with emotional sexual satisfaction to the same extent for both sexes. Valuing sexuality counts more for women's than men's satisfaction with intercourse and, to some extent, their sex life in general. Denial of sexuality in life may prevent women from enjoying sexual intercourse, or vice versa; women who do not like physical sex, may undervalue sexual life as part of their whole life. The subjective experience of an increase in sexual desire in the last five years is more closely correlated with women's than men's sexual satisfaction.

Happy people enjoy their steady relations and also sexual intercourse. The relationship between happiness and sexual satisfaction is probably reciprocal: satisfactory sexual life contributes to feelings of happiness, and happy people are likely to find joy also in sexuality. Sexual partners are often good social companions. Thus, it is understandable that sexual satisfaction diminishes feelings of loneliness.

Sexual habits or practices have a stronger effect on physical than emotional sexual satisfaction. Most of them correlate more with women's than men's satisfaction. From the point of view of sexual satisfaction, the following sexual habits have a positive outcome: frequent sexual intercourse, equal activeness in initiating it, a suitable amount of kissing, petting, or other love play in connection with coitus, and use several positions in intercourse (applies to men only).

In addition to practices related to sexual intercourse, the study also investigated other techniques aiming at sexual satisfaction. Stimulation by hand and oral sex clearly increase women's emotional, physical, and overall sexual satisfaction, and also to some degree, men's physical and general, but not emotional satisfaction. Anal sex, masturbation, and use of sex materials and aids are only to a small degree related to sexual satisfaction. People, particularly men, who masturbate often, are not satisfied with their sexual life as a whole. Women who use sex materials—sex movies and programs on TV, videos, magazines, and wall calendars with naked pictures—are somewhat more satisfied with intercourse than women who do not use them. Perhaps sex materials help women to adopt new, more-rewarding sex techniques.

Orgasm during sexual intercourse is very strongly connected to finding sexual intercourse pleasant. The correlations are higher for women than for men. Also, general sexual satisfaction, and to some degree, happiness of the steady relationship, correlate with experiencing an orgasm during intercourse.

It is not uncommon that a man cannot enter into sexual intercourse because he cannot get an erection or his penis becomes flaccid when sexual intercourse is started. One's own or one's partner's erectile problem decreases physical sexual satisfaction for both sexes. It is also connected to the emotional dissatisfaction of women in their steady relationships.

The number of sexual partners during a lifetime does not correlate with sexual satisfaction except at one point: Women who have had many sexual partners report more dis-

satisfaction with their sexual lives as a whole than other women. Traditional gender roles may make women uncomfortable with a life in which sexual partners change frequently. This lifestyle probably includes a lot of brief casual relationships that women do not take as lightheartedly as men have been socialized to take them.

The number of extra sexual relations during present or previous steady relations is connected to unhappiness of the present steady relationship, but not to physical nor overall sexual satisfaction. Parallel relations indicate a wish to escape the unhappiness of the steady relationship, or they may cause jealousy on the part of the steady partner that might deteriorate the relationship.

Determinants of physical sexual satisfaction have earlier been analyzed by using path analysis (Haavio-Mannila 1993). In the path models developed for explaining satisfaction with intercourse for men and women, some more-general social factors than those presented in Table 20 were included. Some of them only had an indirect influence on sexual satisfaction, but some also had direct effects on it. The social factors studied contributing to physical sexual satisfaction were: irreligious and sexually open childhood home, early age at starting sexual life, liberal attitudes toward sexual issues, short duration of the present steady relationship, and young age. These social background factors correlated with the sexual variables increasing sexual satisfaction: the value of sexuality in life, sexual assertiveness, love, use of sex materials, frequency and variety of intercourse, and orgasm.

### Divorce and Remarriage

In 1986-1989, there were 11.6 officially recorded divorces per 1,000 mean population of married women, compared with 5.3 in 1966-1970. In 1989, 47% of marriages ended in divorce. The increase in divorces can also be seen in the survey data. In 1971, only 3% of the respondents were divorced or separated from their spouse at the time of the survey; 20 years later, the figure was 8%. [Altogether, 30% of both genders had experienced divorce, based on the results of the 1999 survey.] Even changes in the structure of families with children reflect the increased incidence of divorces. In 1971, 90% of the respondents reported that their parents had lived together throughout their childhood; 20 years later, the figure was 88%.

Cohabitation does not always lead to marriage; separation of cohabiting partners is relatively common, especially in the younger age groups. One in four respondents interviewed for the 1992 study had had a cohabitation relationship that had not continued as a marriage. This share was more than one in two in the age groups 35 or younger.

The increased lifespan and increasing occurrence of divorce allows people time to marry several times. According to the 1971 study, 5% of married men and women had been married at least twice. Two decades later, 17% of presently or formerly married or cohabiting men and 22% of the corresponding women had had at least two such relationships. [In 1999, these proportions were 26% and 25%.] Women had had a higher number of such relationships before age 54. In older age groups, men had been married more times than women.

### Sexuality, Disability, and Aging

There are no serious obstacles concerning values and attitudes in dealing with the sexual needs and activities. In 1992, only 5% of the respondents believed that elderly people should not establish sexual relationships. Most Finns, 75%, held that people in residential facilities ought to have a privacy room for intimate meetings. Although the majority also approve of sexual relationships for physically and mentally challenged persons, no actual studies have been carried out on sexual issues and the disabled.

There is currently some kind of generation gap between elderly and young Finns on sexual issues. Elderly people, especially women, are more conservative in their attitudes toward adolescents' sexual relationships, casual relationships, relationships without love, and women's right to take sexual initiatives. Elderly people have lived their childhood in a world where restrictions against free sexual pleasure were enormous. They have learned that sexual issues are not really important and that they have to be careful in order to avoid the problems and risks associated with fulfilling their sexual images and fantasies. They never had any knowledge and education, for instance, on how to satisfy the needs of their partners, such as young Finns have nowadays. They initiated their dating and sex life much older than the younger generations because sexual activities were interpreted to be as a part of marriage only. Many of them were, in practice, forced to abstain while married because there were almost no contraceptives available.

The frequency of sexual intercourse is increasing among older Finns. Most retired men have had intercourse during the past month, and they report their experiences to be as pleasurable as the younger ones. Elderly people are still not as actively engaging in sexual relationships as the younger people. More than half of retired women abstain from sexual intercourse because they are widowed and are not able or willing to engage to some new relationship—there is also a lack of older men. Old women are many times sexually quite inactive, because they have learned that sexual initiatives are men's duty.

The coital positions of elderly people do not vary very much and they quite seldom engage in oral sex, anal sex, or manual stimulation. They even abstain quite often from masturbation and pornographic products. Only 18% of men and 11% of women over 65 years have masturbated during the past year. [In 1999, these proportions were already 28% and 20%, respectively.] The sexual inactivity is explained only partly by aging and illness; the education and generation gap is the more-important reason for this finding. This can be seen, for example, in the data on the number of sexual partners during a lifetime that are much lower among elderly people. Elderly Finns have had much more time to engage in sexual relationships than younger Finns, but they seldom have experienced multiple relationships.

Because of their health status, elderly people have more sexual dysfunctions—lack of desire, and problems with having vaginal lubrication, erections, and orgasms—than younger generations. These problems will be discussed later in this chapter.

## 6. Homoerotic, Homosexual, and Bisexual Behaviors

Finnish homosexuals were studied by the snowball method in 1982 (Grönfors et al. 1984). More than 1,000 homosexuals answered a relatively extensive questionnaire. Two thirds of the respondents were men and one third were women. About 60% of the respondents reported that they were exclusively homosexual in their feelings and about 70% in their behavior. Finnish homosexuals were quite similarly distributed into Kinsey's categories (Kinsey et al. 1948, 1953). Feelings and behavior were in most cases consistent. However, it is not always possible to combine feelings with practice in real life. There were people who identified themselves as only or mostly homosexual, but behaved only or mostly heterosexually.

In the Finnish sex survey of 1992, there were ten questions about sex with same-sex persons. They refer to sexual identity, sexual experiences with persons of one's own sex, age at first homosexual experience, type and frequency of these experiences, number of same-sex partners, and orgasm in homosexual intercourse.

Homosexual identity was measured by a five-point scale ranging from exclusive homosexuality to exclusive heterosexuality (cf. Kinsey et al. 1948). The question was phrased as follows: "Besides being sexually interested in the opposite sex, people are sometimes also interested in their own sex. Are you at the moment sexually interested in only the male sex, mainly the male sex, both sexes equally, mainly the female sex, or only the female sex?"

In the population aged 18 to 54 years, the proportion of persons interested only or mainly in people of the same sex was 0.8% in 1971, in 1992 only 0.6%, [and in 1999, 1.1%]. When one takes into consideration all people who have at least some interest in people of the same sex, the proportions were 7.6% and 6.5%, respectively. When all people aged 55 to 74 years who were studied in 1992 are included, the proportion of the exclusively or mainly homosexually oriented persons was 0.7%, and that of at least partly bisexually oriented 6.4%. Men more often than women identified themselves as homosexuals, whereas there was no gender gap in the proportion of bisexually oriented people. Same-gendered experiences are more common than homosexual identity. According to the 1992 survey, 4.0% of the Finnish men and 3.8% of the women had had same-sex partners during their life. [In 1999, these proportions were 6.5% and 5.3%, respectively.] In the United States, in 1991, the proportions were 5.0% for men and 2.7% for women (Laumann et al. 1994). The gender difference is thus larger in the United States than in Finland where there is hardly any gender gap. American women may be shyer than Finnish women in admitting their lesbian behavior, or they may avoid lesbian practices deliberately in order to avoid the social stigma attached to them. In Finland, the liberalization of attitudes toward homosexuality in the last 20 years may have helped lesbians acknowledge and report on their homosexual experiences.

The number of homosexual partners during one's lifetime was on the average of 7.4 for men and 1.6 for women. Compared with the number of sexual partners in the whole population (10.6), these figures are small. This is because of the fact that most homosexual encounters only have taken place with one person: 53% of men and 72% of women had had only one same-sex partner. [These proportions were almost equal in 1999.] Many homosexual contacts took place a long time ago. Only 29% of the same-sex contacts of people ever having had one had happened during the last 12 months. During the last year, 1.3% of the Finns and 1.6% of the Americans had had a homosexual relationship. [In 1999, 2.6% of men and 1.3% of women had had a homosexual relationship.] This question had been left unanswered by a significantly greater proportion (23%) of the Americans than of the Finns (8%). This again suggests that there are more social taboos regarding homosexuality in the United States than in Finland.

The first homosexual experiences took place at the same age as first sexual intercourse—that is, on the average at the age of 18.3 years. Men started somewhat earlier than women. Eight percent of these experiences were probably sexual play as children, since they took place when the respondent was less than 10 years old.

The most common type of homosexual experiences were arousing fondling without touching genitals (54% of people having had homosexual experiences), stimulation of genitals by hand or rubbing genitals against partner's genitals (also 54%), and oral stimulation of the genitals (29%). Only 19% of men with homosexual relations had been engaged in anal intercourse.

Thirty-eight percent of men and 26% of women had had orgasm in homosexual intercourse. This is less than the proportion of orgasm in heterosexual intercourse (see Table 28 in Section 11, Sexual Dysfunctions, Counseling, and Therapies). Homosexually oriented and/or experienced men considered their sexual life as a whole somewhat less often very or quite satisfying (75%) than bisexually or mostly heterosexually oriented men without homosexual experiences (87%) and exclusively heterosexual men (85%). For women, the percentages were 77%, 61%, and 83%, respectively.

The lower sexual satisfaction of homosexuals may be related to the prevailing conceptions about the superiority of heterosexual love and sex (Jeffreys 1990). It may be more difficult to enjoy homosexual experiences as freely as heterosexual experiences because of their ambivalent status in sexual culture. This can be concluded on the basis of the fact that 28% of men and 38% of women interested in their own sex have sometimes been bothered personally by or fearful and worried about their own sexual deviation. This is three times as common as in the population on the average. Of men with homosexual experiences, 38%, and of women, 19% have felt that kind of fear. This fear still prevails, even though the attitudes toward homosexuality have liberalized during the last 20 years (see Table 3 in Section 2B, Religious, Ethnic, and Gender Factors Affecting Sexuality, Cultural Factors).

[*Update 2000/2002*: In December 2000, the government of Finland proposed legalizing gay partnerships, but with some limitations. In Parliament, the five government parties holding a majority were expected to approve the proposal. The Finnish Evangelical Lutheran Church, to which 85% of Finland's population of 5.2 million people belongs, opposed giving gay partners the same rights as married couples. However, Archbishop Jukka Paarma admitted that "the legal position of homosexual and lesbian couples should be improved."

[In April of 2002, gay partnerships were legalized, but without allowing them to adopt children or share a surname. Finland joined the four other Nordic countries, Sweden, Norway, Denmark, and Iceland, in legally recognizing gay partnerships. Denmark, Sweden, and Iceland also allow gay couples to adopt children under certain circumstances. Same-sex couples 18 years or older are able to make their union official in a civil ceremony, comparable to matrimony but nevertheless "a separate legal institution." Registered gay couples have the same rights as heterosexual couples who are married when it comes to inheritance and divorce. (*End of update by R. T. Francoeur and O. Kontula*)]

## 7. Gender Diversity and Transgender Issues

### A. Sociological Status, Behaviors, and Treatment

In Finland, the most conspicuous gender minority group has been the transsexuals, because their situation requires both therapeutic and juridical measures to be resolved. Society has indeed taken concrete measures to draft legislation and to develop a functioning healthcare system to meet this need. The Ministry of Social Affairs and Health has been preparing the legislation since 1991.

The National Research and Development Center for Welfare and Health (STAKES) gave the first report on the matter in 1992 and the second at the beginning of 1994. The second report had been drafted by a working committee that had been set up to develop a support and care system for the transsexuals in Finland. The aim is to create legislation to secure healthcare services for transsexuals, create a special expert healthcare system, and provide juridical protection for their gender reassignment and privacy. The legislation will also define the criteria for gender reassignment.

In Finland, there are an estimated 300 people who would benefit from sex-reassignment surgery. So far, the treatment of transsexuals has been quite haphazard. The information about the possibilities and places of treatment varies. The transsexuals get this information through their associations. As of early 1994, sex-reassignment operations were being postponed until the law comes into force. Male-to-female transsexuals have their operations abroad, mainly in London. Of necessity, female-to-male operations may be performed in the homeland, because Finns cannot obtain these operations abroad.

So far, the cost of the surgery has been paid by the patient, but it is the aim of the proposed new law to extend public healthcare to cover the cost of these operations. Those who have sought this corrective gender surgery have had to apply for a castration permit before having plastic surgery on their genitals. A psychiatrist's and an endocrinologist's certificate must be attached to the application. Because the castration law was not designed for use with transsexuals, attempts have been made to have it removed from their procedure.

Various sexual organizations have become active in support of sexual minorities. In Finland, SETA or Sexual Equality, a registered association, was originally a national organization for homosexuals and lesbians, but during recent years, it has also worked actively on behalf of other sexual minorities. SETA arranges group evenings for transsexuals and transvestites, where other sexual minorities have been welcomed. In addition, SETA has vigorously promoted some juridical matters for the sexual minorities, such as allowing a change of one's name and identity number as part of gender reassignment.

TRASEK, the transsexuals' own association, offers advice on the medical process in gender reassignment and surgery. It also provides a support person for those who need one and gives practical help in writing applications. Providing information by transsexuals who have been through the procedure is a major service of TRASEK.

[*Update 2003*: The Transgender Support Center (TSC) was established by SETA in 1994 with the financial help from the Finnish government. By close networking with the authorities and other relevant organizations, the expertise of the TSC has been an important part of the ongoing process of creating the new professional practices and consensus in medical, juridical, and psychosocial services.

[TSC gives psychosocial support services for people with transgender experiences. The clients are transsexuals, transvestites, and people between genders, as well as their partners and families.

[Psychosocial support has been arranged, both on a professional basis and by organizing volunteer individual and group self-help support. The TSC has played a significant role in strengthening the networking of the transgender community.

[In 2000, STM (the Ministry of Social Affairs and Health) started to give instructions for treatment and recommendations for legislation on transsexuals' legal status. Internationally, in 2002, a very progressive law and instructions for treatments were confirmed. They were then implemented at the beginning of 2003.

[The medical and juridical sex-reassignment process in the public services includes:

- psychiatric evaluation and diagnosis in Helsinki or Tampere (at least 6 months)
- hormone treatment
- psychiatric follow-up (2 to 5 years)
- treatment plan
- juridical change of name and social security number, together with a psychiatric follow-up (people can choose the right moment for the change of juridical name and social security number, but usually it is required for the Real Life test)
- possible treatments: epilation therapy, speech therapy or phoniatric surgery, breast mastectomy, and supportive psychotherapy
- consultation on the surgery and a place in the queue for surgery (1.5 to 3.5 years)
- castration and corrective genital surgery (2 to 6 operations) and surgery for silicone implants if needed (1 to 2 years)

The total period of treatment varies from 5.5 years to 11 years. In the future, the period of treatment is expected to be shortened to a maximum of 5 years. (*End of update by O. Kontula*)]

## B. Specially Gendered Persons

There are actually no *hijra* or *berdache* communities in Finland, but a so-called gender community that includes people from different gender groups, such as transsexuals, transvestites, transgenderists, and gender-blending people, does exist. There are so few people of each of the groups that they have not formed any subgroups of their own.

## *8. Significant Unconventional Sexual Behaviors*

### A. Coercive Sex

#### *Sexual Abuse, Incest, and Pedophilia*

Finnish women have been sexually abused as children more often than men: Under the age of 18, 17% of women and 8% of men had been sexually harassed by peers, other boys or girls, parents, or other adults. There was no clear age difference in the incidence of child abuse. Women most often were harassed by male peers and men, and men by female peers and women. Two percent of women had been sexually abused by their fathers. No reports of sexual abuse by a mother have been made.

#### *Sexual Harassment and Rape*

Incidence of sexual harassment was studied by using the following question: "In the last five years, has anyone laid hands on you or touched you in an offensive way (with a sexual purpose) either in your apartment or elsewhere, e.g., in a restaurant, workplace or at school?" Affirmative answers were given by 3% of men and 9% of women. Younger women reported more sexual harassment than older women. For men, age made no difference. Sexual harassment in most cases was described as approaches (men 88% and women 69%), but 0.4% of all women described the incident as rape, and 1.1% of all women defined it as attempted rape. Of all men, 0.2% described the harassment as attempted rape; no men reported actual rape. Regression analysis showed that becoming an object of sexual harassment was connected with being sexually abused as a child, young age, and female gender. Persons who were sexually harassed were more likely than other persons not to have steady sexual relationships and to have had extra sexual relations and homosexual experiences. Drinking to intoxication and having many sexual partners was also related to having been sexually harassed.

The harassers were mostly men. About half of the respondents knew the harasser before the incidence. Very few of the harassed—6% of the harassed men and 7% of women—had informed the police about the incident. The most common reason for not reporting sexual harassment to the police was that it was considered to be of minor importance. The second reason was that the respondent personally resolved the matter.

Becoming an object of sexual harassment increased sexual fears and worries. Other social factors influencing sexual fears were female gender, young age, lack of steady relationship, stress symptoms, casual and extra sexual relations, and sexual practices alternative to intercourse. One third of the variation of sexual fears was explained by these factors. In order to diminish sexual anxiety, it is worthwhile to discuss and control sexual harassment publicly.

### *Prostitution*

Prostitution itself is not illegal in Finland, but it is against the law to organize prostitutes' services, for example, by maintaining a brothel. Until the beginning of the 1990s, prostitution was scarce (Järvinen 1990). One of the consequences of the fall of the Soviet Union was that many Estonian and Russian women came to Finland to earn money as prostitutes.

Attitudes toward prostitution differ greatly by gender. In 1992, men more often (51%) than women (21%) had nothing against people earning money by selling sexual services in Finland. This activity was opposed by 34% of men and 65% of women. People over 50 years were most negative toward prostitution. [In 1999, 64% of men and 24% of women had nothing against people earning money by selling sexual services. Men had more favorable attitudes towards prostitution than before.]

There has been recurrent public discussion about establishing brothels under the control of the state as there were in the beginning of the 20th century in Finland. Brothels might be a means to fight problems connected with prostitution: i.e., liability of clients and prostitutes to venereal diseases and connections to criminality, particularly drug dealing. Approval of state-controlled brothels was greater among men than women: 42% of men, but only 17% of women approved public brothels, while 41% and 67%, respectively, opposed them. Middle-aged people were most favorable to brothels. Support for public brothels has clearly increased since a 1972 survey. At that time, only 20% approved establishing state-controlled brothels (Markkula 1981). [In 1999, 60% of men and 26% of women approved of establishing brothels under the control of the state. The proportions were higher than before.]

There is a certain amount of demand for paid sexual services in Finland. Twenty percent of women and 8% of men had during their lifetime been persuaded to intercourse by being offered money or similar economic advantages. [In 1999, the corresponding proportions were 17% of women and 11% of men.] Women under 35 years of age most often reported having received these kinds of offers. This indicates that they have increased with time. Only 0.2% of Finnish women and 1.5% of men admitted that they had complied with the request.

Men use paid sexual services more than women. Eleven percent of Finnish men and 0.3% of women had offered money or similar economic advantages for intercourse. One percent of all men and women said that their initiatives had not led to sexual activity. [In 1999, 15% of men had offered money for intercourse in their lifetime.] For Finnish men, traditionally, buying sexual services starts at about age 40 when men begin to have the economic resources for it. Having sex with prostitutes was connected with having many sexual partners, extra relationships, sex with foreigners, high sexual self-esteem, and few homosexual experiences. Using paid sexual services was not related to sexual satisfaction nor sexual fears.

[*Update 2003*: A quarter of the men who had bought sexual services in their lifetime, had done so during the last year. This means that: 4% of men had visited prostitutes during that year, 72% of men had visited foreign prostitutes abroad, 11% foreign prostitutes in Finland, and 14% Finnish prostitutes in Finland. Altogether, 4% of men had paid for sex in Finland, and 71% of men reported that they used a condom in the latest sexual intercourse with a prostitute.

[In 2002, there was a lively public discussion on the human rights problems related to the pimping of Russian prostitutes in Finland. This has led to proposals of criminalizing buying prostitute services in a similar way to what was done in Sweden some years ago. It is assumed that the government will give this amendment to Parliament in 2003. (*End of update by O. Kontula*)]

### Pornography and Erotica

In Finland, between 1971 and 1992, women's attitudes toward pornography became somewhat more negative, whereas men's attitudes have remained unchanged. This may be related to the contents of pornography becoming "harder" and less satisfying to women's expectations than before. The consumption of pornographic products has remained almost the same among men, but has decreased among women. Even when sex videos are included with the printed publications, fewer women, on the average, used pornographic materials during the year in 1992 than in 1971.

Interest in pornographic publications was exceptionally great in 1971 because open nudity had only recently become available in pictures in sex magazines. The charm of novelty and the taste of the forbidden fruit made people anxious to have and use them. Since this initial interest, the greatest excitement and attraction have settled. Besides, the so-called soft pornography has come within everyone's reach—for example, in the pictures of the afternoon tabloids. Such material, however, is no longer referred to as pornography. There are legal restrictions against hard pornography in Finland, but soft pornography and erotica are shown even on public television.

[*Update 2003*: Consumption of pornographic products increased in the 1990s. Use of sex magazines and sex videos was 5% to 10% more common in 1999 than in 1992. Pornography was also more valued than before. Four fifths of men and two thirds of women judged pornography sexually very stimulating. This proportion was even 25% higher among young women in 1999 than what it was in 1992.

[In 1999, phone sex was also studied. Of the men who were younger than 35 years, 15% reported using phone sex during their lifetime and 8% during the last year. Among young women, these proportions were 4% and 1%. (*End of update by O. Kontula*)]

Sex magazines published in Finland are forbidden by the Ministry of Justice to present pictures of anal and oral sex, sexual violence, sadomasochism, sex with children, sperm, paraphilias with sex models, and close-up pictures of genitals. All movies and video films are inspected by state authorities, and hard-core pornography, as listed above, is not allowed to be presented in cinemas or to be rented in video markets. However, in practice, hard-core videos can be bought or leased from specific sex shops. Films presented on TV are not under any legal regulations.

[*Update 2003*: In 2001, new legislation was implemented in Finland. Practically speaking, it gave legal status to pornography. The only exceptions are pictures that are related to pedophilia, sexual violence, and sex with animals. These forms of sexually explicit material are now defined as illegal. (*End of update by O. Kontula*)]

### Paraphilias

In Finland, the use of sexual aids and toys, such as a vibrator or vibrating penis, lubricants, pills or substances increasing potency, erection rings, a penis enlarger with a pump, ropes or gags, an artificial vagina, sexy underwear, sex dolls, and whips or handcuffs or fetters in masturbation or in sexual intercourse by the respondent or his or her partner is fairly rare.

Sexy underwear was the most commonly used aid: One fifth of people told about using it. In the younger age groups under 35 years, the proportion was about one third, and in the oldest age groups only a few percent. Lubricant was the next most popular aid: 17% of men and 15% of women had used it. Lubricant use increases with age, because it lessens problems connected with vaginal lubrication during intercourse.

Vibrators or vibrating dildos were used by the respondent or a partner according to the replies of 7% of men and 6% of women. These were most popular among those around 30 years old (10%). The interest of young people in vibrators indicates that their use will increase in the future. The other sexual aids listed above were each used by less than 2% of the respondents.

Use of sex aids did not correlate with sexual satisfaction except in one case: use of a pump penis enlarger and sex dolls was related to women's unhappiness in steady relationships. These devices are meant for fighting impotency or for compensating for lack of a human sexual partner. As mentioned in the section on sexual satisfaction, impotency and lack of partner indicate an unhappy steady relationship.

[*Update 2003*: In 1999, 8% of men and 7% of women reported that they had practiced bondage plays in their lifetime. Among young persons, this proportion was around 15%. Sadomasochistic experiences had been experienced by 3% of men and 1.5% of women. (*End of update by O. Kontula*)]

## 9. Contraception, Abortion, and Population Planning

### A. Contraception

A decline in birthrate has been a common phenomenon in most West European countries and in all the Nordic countries during the past several decades. In Finland, the birthrate was at its highest after World War II; for instance, in 1947, as many as 108,000 children were born. After this, there was an even decline, so that, after 1968, the birthrate has been lower than the replacement birthrate, which would be about 70,000 births per year. At its lowest, in 1973, the birthrate was 56,787 births. In the 1990s, it has been about 65,000 children per year. Unless immigration increased, the population had been estimated to grow until 1999, after which it would begin to decrease. [*Update 2003*: In the latest prognosis, the population is estimated to increase until 2013, after which it will slowly decrease. (*End of update by O. Kontula*)]

Contraception has been well taken care of in Finland. Young people may obtain contraceptives from their school healthcare services. The law or other regulations require that those who have given birth or had an abortion be given counseling in contraception. Generally, counseling and even the contraceptive methods themselves are easily available. There is also a variety to choose from, thanks to the development in the research and production of contraceptive methods. From an international viewpoint, Finland is considered a model country in organizing contraception.

In 1988, contraceptive use among 13- to 17-year-olds was surveyed (Kontula & Rimpelä 1988). No contraception had been used at the first intercourse by 27% of the 15-year-olds. Most of them, 66% of boys and 71% of the girls, had used a condom during the first intercourse. A few percent had used the pill. At the most recent intercourse, use of the pill was reported by 17% of the girls and 7% of the boys. At the same time, the proportion of those who used the condom had diminished to 59% with the girls. The share of those with no contraception had remained almost the same as at the first intercourse, about one in four.

Use of the contraceptive pill quickly becomes more common among the young as they settle into a relationship. As many as 44% of the 17-year-old girls in Helsinki had used the pill at their most recent sexual intercourse; the proportion using condoms remained at 45%. Nationwide, the proportion of 17-year-old boys relying on the pill was 25%; for girls, 56%. The differences in these responses stems from the fact that the girls usually have intercourse with boys some years older than themselves.

[*Update 2003*: In 2002, 61% of 15-year-old boys and 51% of girls had used a condom during the last sexual intercourse. Twelve percent of boys and 26% of girls had used contraceptive pills, while 18% of boys and 16% of girls used no contraception. Among 17-year-olds, these proportions were 27% and 43%, and 11% and 8%, respectively. (*End of update by O. Kontula*)]

According to the 1971 sex survey, only about 3% of those who needed contraception did not use any method. According to a study conducted in 1977, one in ten women who needed contraception did not use any method (Riihinen et al. 1980).

In 1992, 29% of the men and 18% of the women did not need contraception at their last intercourse (Erkkola & Kontula 1993). About one fifth of the middle-aged people reported that they did not need contraception. A very important reason is that about 12% of the 35- to 54-year-old women had undergone hysterectomy, which becomes more common with age.

The prevalence of contraceptive methods was surveyed by a question about the method used at last intercourse. Slightly over 3% of the men who had thought they needed contraception in their steady relationship had not used any method at their last sexual intercourse. No method had been used at the last intercourse by 5% of the 18- to 54-year-old women who thought they needed contraception.

The condom and contraceptive pill are popular with young people (see Tables 21 and 22). After the age of 30, the pill loses most of its users, although about one tenth of the women still use it after that age. This is in part because of the health officers' recommendations. The condom, however, holds its popularity fairly steady among users of all ages. This may be because of the protection the condom affords against diseases.

Use of the intrauterine device (IUD) increases considerably around the age of 30, at the same time as the popularity of the pill wanes. The IUD maintains its popularity until the age of menopause, after which it is naturally no longer needed. The IUD is used by about one third of women. The use of sterilization as a contraceptive method increases a little later than the use of the IUD. Sterilization is mostly used around age 40 years, with about 25% of middle-aged women using this method. Based on generation comparisons, it seems likely that the use of sterilization will clearly increase in the coming years.

The pill, IUD, and sterilization had been used by 59% of women; 27% had used the condom. Only slightly over 3% had used withdrawal or the rhythm method ("safe period"); the latter had been used by only a few women. About 4% of the female respondents had used two methods at their last intercourse, mostly the condom with some other method.

[*Update 2003*: The use of condoms decreased somewhat in the 1990s among the adult population: 27% of men and 28% of women had used a condom in their last intercourse. Also in temporary relationships, condoms were less popular than before. About half of the men and women used a condom with their last temporary partner. (*End of update by O. Kontula*)]

Laws relating to sterilization were enacted in 1970 and 1985. The spirit of the latter law is quite liberal, for, in practice, any person over age 30 may be sterilized if he or she so wishes. This law caused sterilization to rise threefold compared to previous years.

Regional differences in contraceptive methods used are fairly insignificant. There are hardly any regional differences in the use of the pill and the IUD, but the condom has been more used in the big towns than in the smaller localities, according to the women's responses.

Finns who had their last intercourse with a steady cohabitation partner or spouse and needed contraception had used the condom less frequently than others, 32% of the men and 27% of the women, compared with 46% and 28%, respectively, for those who had had their last intercourse with some other steady partner, and 68% and 45% of those with someone other than a steady partner. The condom was most often used at the most recent intercourse by men, 71%, and women, 39%, who had no steady partners. No contraception had been used by 5% of men and 10% of the women with the latest not-steady partner, although they reported that they needed contraception. The pill had been used by 28% and the IUD by 10% of the women with their latest not-steady partners. Slightly over 40% of those men and women who had had their last intercourse with somebody else's spouse or steady partner had then used the condom.

## Table 21

**The Contraceptive Method Used During the Most Recent Intercourse Among Men Who Need Contraception and Have Had Intercourse, 1992**

|              | 18-24 | 25-29 | 30-34 | 35-39 | 40-44 | 45-49 | 50-54 | 55-59 | 60-64 | 65-69 | 70-74 |
|--------------|-------|-------|-------|-------|-------|-------|-------|-------|-------|-------|-------|
| Condom       | 53    | 42    | 45    | 38    | 24    | 30    | 36    | 50    | 50    | 56    | 38    |
| Pill         | 44    | 45    | 28    | 13    | 8     | 15    | 7     | 4     | 7     | 6     | 0     |
| IUD          | 1     | 10    | 19    | 33    | 33    | 32    | 32    | 23    | 14    | 0     | 13    |
| Sterilization| 0     | 1     | 4     | 7     | 23    | 16    | 13    | 12    | 14    | 6     | 0     |

## Table 22

**The Contraceptive Method Used During the Most Recent Intercourse Among Women Who Need Contraception and Have Had Intercourse, 1992**

|              | 18-24 | 25-29 | 30-34 | 35-39 | 40-44 | 45-49 | 50-54 | 55-59 | 60-64 | 65-69 | 70-74 |
|--------------|-------|-------|-------|-------|-------|-------|-------|-------|-------|-------|-------|
| Pill         | 60    | 57    | 24    | 14    | 11    | 0     | 7     | 14    | 9     | 0     | 0     |
| Condom       | 38    | 25    | 30    | 25    | 26    | 29    | 43    | 32    | 14    | 20    | 31    |
| IUD          | 1     | 10    | 31    | 31    | 32    | 33    | 29    | 11    | 0     | 0     | 8     |
| Sterilization| 0     | 0     | 7     | 19    | 28    | 25    | 18    | 14    | 18    | 10    | 0     |

Having children changes quite decisively the type of contraceptive method used. This is most apparent in the shift away from the pill, the most common contraceptive method before having children. In many cases, the pill is replaced by the IUD, which is almost solely used by women who have given birth to a child. As the number of children rises, the percentage of those who have undergone sterilization considerably increases, and the share of the condom users decreases.

## B. Teenage Unmarried Pregnancies

Women under age 20 account for about 2,000 pregnancies each year, about 3% of the total number of 65,000 pregnancies. Teenage pregnancy and live births have been relatively one of the lowest of the whole world. The number of live births to unmarried women has been growing fast and is nowadays about 20,000 a year. The proportion of unmarried women giving birth is about 30%, a share that has doubled during last 20 years. There are no separate statistics of unmarried, noncohabiting couples. The estimated figure has been, according to surveys, about 5% of annual live births.

[*Update 2003*: The teenage fertility rate declined throughout the 1990s, slower in the second than in the first half of the decade. For 19-year-olds, the pregnancy rate continued to decrease until 1996, while among younger girls (aged under 18 years), the decrease leveled off two years earlier. Starting from 1997, the pregnancy rate has increased every single year in every age group among teenagers. In 2000, the mean age of women at the birth of their first child was as high as 27.4 years. (*End of update by O. Kontula*)]

## C. Abortion

In the earlier decades when prevention of pregnancies was poor and abortions illegal, the women in their despair resorted to infanticide in Finland. Nowadays, the situation is considerably better in this respect, but there is still discussion of the justification of abortions. In Finland, the situation is exceptionally good, for abortions had clearly decreased because of the improved contraception during the last 20 years, and abortions are exceptionally few by international comparison.

The current law regarding termination of pregnancies, which was preceded by a fierce debate, was enacted in 1970. As a result of this liberal law, abortion became practically free, and illegal abortions were believed to have almost entirely ceased. With the new Primary Health Care Act instituted in 1972, the cost of abortions was essentially paid by the municipalities.

A 1978 amendment to the abortion law required permission of the Central Administrative Board for termination of a pregnancy after 12 weeks. The latest law concerning abortions came into force in 1985, making it possible to terminate pregnancy prior to the 24th week of pregnancy on the grounds of the illness of the fetus, instead of the earlier 20th week. If the mother's life or health is at stake, termination of pregnancy is permitted at any stage of pregnancy, even after the 24th week. In practice, termination of pregnancy has been without restriction, at least prior to the 12th week of pregnancy, for the past over 20 years.

In the 1992 FINSEX survey, 57% of the men and 53% of the women supported free abortion, disagreeing with the statement, "I do not approve of free abortion (termination of pregnancy)." [In 1999, these proportions were 62% and 59%, respectively.] Agreement with this statement was expressed in 1992 by 28% of the men and 34% of the women [and in 1999 by 22% of the men and 29% of the women.]. Most abortion opponents were in the older age groups.

Opinions on abortion did not vary much in the other age groups, or between men and women.

There are hardly any opponents of abortion in Finland when the pregnancy would seriously endanger the woman's health or the child would probably be born abnormal. Mostly, people understand free abortion as the right of the married people or sexual partners to decide about having the child when the pregnancy is unwanted.

Men's attitudes on abortion mainly reflect their religious views and their general sexual liberality. With women, the acceptance of abortion relates to the modern urban lifestyle, which emphasizes women's right to self-determination in sexual matters. Free abortion is generally accepted by women with a long education and a white-collar background who live in big population centers. Again, free abortion is opposed by religious and conservative women who have had only one sexual partner in their lifetime. These women connect sexual intercourse with a faithful marital relationship that they had entered young; they do not regard women's sexual initiative as proper and they often use unsafe contraception. Becoming pregnant is generally not experienced as a problem when it happens in a steady marital relationship (Kontula 1993).

In 1992, 18% of the women of fertile age thought that they would terminate their pregnancy if they just then found out that they were pregnant. One in two woman thought that they would not want to terminate their pregnancy. If a pregnancy had been a current problem, 16% of the men would have supported their partner's abortion and 69% would have opposed it. Women want to have abortions clearly more often than men, especially after the age of 35. Women's desire to have children is clearly concentrated within narrower age limits than with men—around the early 30s. With women, wanting to have an abortion is most centrally related to their age. Almost half of the young women under 25 and women over 40 years of age want to have their pregnancy terminated.

As a result of the 1970 law, the number of abortions rose quickly, reaching its peak of over 23,300 abortions, about 41% of the births, in 1973. After that, the number of abortions declined evenly to 11,200 abortions, about 17% of the births, in 1992. Since the early 1980s, the relative number of abortions has been about 30% lower in Finland than in the other Nordic countries (Ritamies 1994). With young people under 20, abortions have also decreased after the early 1970s. Abortion is more than twice as common among young women in the United States than it is in Finland, 44 per 1,000 compared with 9 per 1,000.

[*Update 2003*: In 1995, the number of abortions fell below 10,000, varying thereafter between 10,000 and 11,000. In 2001, the number amounted to 10,696 or 8.8 abortions per 1,000 women aged 15-to-49 years. The most common reason for performing an induced abortion has been social (about 85%), meaning that the birth of the child would cause considerable strain to the mother in view of her living conditions. About 94% of induced abortions are performed before the end of the 12th week of gestation.

[Since 1994, the relative number of abortions among those under 20 has increased by 43% and the corresponding proportion under age 17 by 23%. The rise in both pregnancy and abortion rates from 1997 to 1999 strongly suggests that unplanned teenage pregnancies are increasing. (*End of update by O. Kontula*)]

Twenty percent of the women who had at some time been pregnant reported having had an abortion, 80% of these women having had only one. Thirteen percent had had two abortions; 4% three abortions; and 2% four abortions. Twelve percent of the men reported that a pregnancy resulting from their sexual relationship had been terminated. Sixteen percent of these men reported two or four abortions. The data suggests that in nearly half of the cases, the woman had an abortion without the man's knowledge.

In the big towns, about one third of the pregnant women had undergone an abortion. In smaller localities, only one in five pregnant women had an abortion.

Concerning the possible effect of abortions on the degree of gratification gained in sexual life, women who had had an abortion experienced orgasm at their last intercourse more often than women who had not had an abortion. Age was not a factor in this. The sexual life of the women who have experienced abortion is quite satisfying, according to these results.

### D. Population Control Efforts

Because of the low birthrate, Finnish population policies are directed to support families with children, not to limit the number of children. Child allowances, paid parental leaves, parents' right to stay at home for childcare without losing their job or pension benefits, high-quality municipal daycare service for children, and other family policies aim at encouraging childbirth. The birthrate has remained relatively stable, [the total fertility rate being 1.74,] and in the future, the population will decrease if fertility does not grow. There is some discussion about the compensation for the lack of births by loosening the strict immigration laws in order to avoid a population decline.

## 10. Sexually Transmitted Diseases and HIV/AIDS

### A. Sexually Transmitted Diseases

The 1992 FINSEX study shows that 15% of the men and 11.5% of the women surveyed had contracted gonorrhea, syphilis, chlamydia, condyloma, or the HPV, and/or genital herpes during their lifetime. Three percent of the men and 2.8% of the women had experienced at least two of these diseases. During the prior year, 0.7% of the men and 1.5% of the women had an STD infection. Based on the total population, these numbers suggest that 450,000 Finns had a some time suffered from an STD, more than one STD had been contracted by about 100,000 people, and during the year, about 38,000 people had been infected.

For the time being, the STDs have been somewhat more common with men than with women. Based on the under-35-year-old women's responses, women's morbidity is likely to surpass that of men's in the future. This change is because of the considerable spread of chlamydia and condyloma among young women. Among men, those who have had an STD appear rather evenly distributed in the different age groups because of gonorrhea, which has been prevalent among men since World War II. However, other STDs have replaced gonorrhea as the leading infections.

Compared to the corresponding study of the year 1971, morbidity among men only slightly rose; with women, the rise was fivefold. This can be explained by the fact that in 1971, only gonorrhea and syphilis were surveyed and diagnosed. In 1992, reports of chlamydia and condyloma greatly enlarged the share of the women who had experienced an STD.

One in ten middle-aged and older men has had gonorrhea. In the younger age groups, especially the under-25-year-olds, gonorrhea is significantly decreasing; none of these men had contracted gonorrhea during the prior year, and only 0.2% of the women. Earlier, gonorrhea had been relatively infrequent among women, but it has become more common in the younger age groups with the spread of other STDs. Genital herpes remains less frequent

than gonorrhea. The responses to the survey suggest that only a few thousand Finns had suffered from herpes during the prior year (see Table 23).

While data on chlamydia are not available for older Finns, one in ten of the under-35-year-olds has had this infection. During 1991, 1.3% of both men and women had been infected by chlamydia. This share very well corresponds to the statistical observation of about 12,000 chlamydia infections per year.

Condyloma is also mainly a problem for young adults. It is more common among women than among men. Only a few of the older Finns have had it during their life. Among the under-35-year-old women, one in ten has suffered from condyloma. During the prior year, condyloma has centered on men around 30 years of age and on women under 40. Of all the women, almost 1% had been infected by HPV during the prior year, and 0.5% of the men. This means about 25,000 infections for the year in the total population.

Of those who had at some time suffered from an STD, 8.3% had had an infection during the year prior to the survey. All men who had been infected by an STD, excepting herpes, during the prior year were under age 35. With women, there were infected women in all age groups under the age of 55, with the highest incidence among 18- to 24-year-olds and 35- to 44-year-olds. Condyloma and chlamydia were clearly the most frequently contracted diseases.

Those men who had had at least ten sexual partners during their lifetime had had 81% of the men's infections. The women of the corresponding group had 43% of the STDs. The women's lower number comes from the fact that only 15% of all the women had had more than ten partners, while 44% of the men had had that many partners. About 2% of the people had contracted an STD, although they had had only one partner during their lifetime. Keeping to one sexual relationship only does not always guarantee safety against the STDs.

Of the men who had had sexual intercourse with at least ten partners during their life, 29% had at some time had an STD and 7% had had more than one STD. With women who had more than five sexual partners, the corresponding figures are 35% and 14%. Half of those who had had 20 or more partners had been infected with an STD. Thus, in reality, most Finns have been spared an infection in spite of multiple partners.

Still, the number of sexual partners is directly linked with the risk of contracting an STD. The probability of the men's being infected by chlamydia or condyloma clearly increases after five partners; after ten partners for gonorrhea; and after as many as over 50 partners for herpes (see Table 24). In the group with over 50 partners, one half had had gonorrhea. Yet, even in this group, most of the people had escaped the other STDs.

With women, the risk of contracting chlamydia, condyloma, or gonorrhea grew significantly already with those who had had more than five partners (see Table 25). Almost one fifth of those who had had more than ten partners had had all the above-mentioned STDs.

### Table 23

**The Percentages of Those Men and Women of Two Age Groups Who Had at Some Time in Their Life Been Infected with Different STDs**

| Age | Gonorrhea | | Chlamydia | | Condyloma | | Herpes | |
|---|---|---|---|---|---|---|---|---|
| | Men | Women | Men | Women | Men | Women | Men | Women |
| 18-34 | 2.8 | 4.1 | 9.6 | 10.3 | 6.9 | 7.7 | 0.8 | 2.8 |
| 35-plus | 11.5 | 2.0 | 2.3 | 1.5 | 1.9 | 3.1 | 11.9 | 1.0 |

About 40% of those who contracted an STD during the last year had had only one partner during this time. Only one in ten had had more than five partners. This suggests that a great part of the STD infections still come from the steady partner and only a small share from people who continuously have many sexual relationships.

The reports of the men and the women on the sources of infection differ from each other greatly. The women suspect, more often than the men, that they had gotten the infection from the steady partner. The men estimate, more often than the women, that they got the infection from a casual partner or a prostitute. It seems obvious that a significant share of the infections the women got from their partners came from prostitutes. The number of prostitutes is not very great, but they often have infections. The large number of their partners offers them many occasions for spreading infections.

With women's sexual liberation and willingness to initiate, the sources of infection have been "equalized." More and more women are infected by casual partners or friends/acquaintances, and men by their steady partners. Almost half of the under-30-year-old women have been infected by casual partners. One third of the under-30-year-old men, again, have been infected by their steady partners. This reflects a change, particularly, in women's sexual behavior.

In earlier times, a significant part of the men's infections were contracted from foreign women. During the past few years, these infections have increased also with women. Twenty-nine percent of men and 27% of women who had at some time had sexual intercourse with a foreigner while in another country had had an STD. Seven percent of these men and 11% of these women had contracted more than one disease.

Fourteen percent of middle-aged men who reported an STD said they had been infected by a foreign woman, either by an acquaintance on a vacation or a prostitute. A foreign prostitute was the source of infection for 29% of the men who had had sexual intercourse with more than 50 partners during their life and had at some time undergone an STD.

The anxiety about AIDS had caused about one tenth of all the people to decrease the number of sexual partners, and a little more than one tenth reported that they would find out more about the people they were going to have sexual intercourse with. This opinion was supported by 34% of the men and by 39% of the women who had had several partners during the year. The risk of HIV influences people's sexual life even if they did not restrict the number of their partners. One tenth of the people had felt fear of AIDS during the last year. Even the people who have no actual risk of becoming infected are often afraid of AIDS.

One fifth of the people reported that they had kept to only one partner more strictly than before. These people were, however, not always those with only one sexual relationship. One third of these men and women had had several partners during the year. Certain sex practices, obviously most often anal intercourse, was avoided by 8% of all the men and 5% of the women.

The use of the condom had, as reported, increased with 20% of men and 12% of women. An increase in condom use was reported by 30% of those under age 25 years. Among those who increased their use of the condom because of AIDS, not all use it regularly. Only 46% of the men and 40% of the women who reported they had increased their condom use actually used a condom in their last intercourse.

About 30% of men and women under age 35 who had experienced an STD reported having decreased the number of their partners for the fear of HIV infection. Every other man and one third of the women reported increasing their use of the condom for the same reason. The condom had been used as the contraceptive method in the most recent sexual intercourse by 25% of the men and 20% of the women who had at some time undergone an STD. With the other men and women, the corresponding shares were 32% and 24%.

Of the men who had never been infected with an STD and whose sexual partner in the most recent intercourse had not been a steady partner, 67% had used a condom on this occasion. The corresponding share was 57% with the men who had at some time had an STD. Of the corresponding groups of women, 45% and 38% reported using a condom. Those who had at some time had an STD did not much deviate from others in their habits of condom use in casual relationships. A previous infection did not seem to "teach" anyone the use of the condom.

About half the men and women who had experienced an STD reported that a physician had advised them in connection with the treatment on how to avoid STD infection. One third had been left completely without counseling. About one tenth had been given a brochure, and about 5% had received counseling from a public-health nurse or a nurse. So, there is still much to improve within the public healthcare system on STD prevention.

[*Update 2003*: In the 1990s, the prevalence of STDs in a lifetime had increased by 2% to 3%. This increase was attributed to both chlamydia and condyloma. The proportions of gonorrhea and syphilis remained the same as before. Looking at the annual numbers of new infections in the 1990s, chlamydia was the most prevalent STD. After the mid-1990s, there was a sight increase in chlamydia infections. Similar increases have been found in syphilis and HIV, although the numbers are rather low. Gonorrhea decreased fast until the mid-1990s; in the second part of 1990s, these numbers have been stable (see Table 26). (*End of update by O. Kontula*)]

## B. HIV/AIDS

The first public statements about AIDS in Finland were issued in 1983, with a general discussion following in 1985 and 1986. Health officials were immediately involved, concentrating their efforts on general information about AIDS and its transmission and about other sexually transmitted diseases, strongly recommending the use of condoms in casual sexual

### Table 24

**The Percentages of Men Who Had Been Subjected to Different STDs During Their Lifetime According to the Numbers of Sexual Partners During Lifetime**

| Partners during lifetime | Gonorrhea | Chlamydia | Herpes | Condyloma | (*n*) |
|---|---|---|---|---|---|
| 1-3 | 1.6 | 0.3 | 0.3 | 1.0 | (307) |
| 4-9 | 2.3 | 3.3 | 0.5 | 3.3 | (214) |
| 10 or more | 17.4 | 10.9 | 2.7 | 6.7 | (403) |

### Table 25

**The Percentages of Women Who Had Been Subjected to Different STDs During Their Lifetime According to the Numbers of Sexual Partners During Lifetime**

| Partners during lifetime | Gonorrhea | Chlamydia | Herpes | Condyloma | (*n*) |
|---|---|---|---|---|---|
| 1-3 | — | 1.1 | 0.4 | 1.8 | (541) |
| 4-9 | 2.7 | 8.1 | 2.4 | 7.5 | (295) |
| 10 or more | 14.1 | 16.2 | 5.6 | 20.4 | (142) |

contacts. At the same time, together with communal health organizations, health officials also directed an effective information and support campaign for groups at special risk of AIDS. In schools, the AIDS issue was—and continues to be—associated with general sex education and the prevention of sexually transmitted diseases.

Public discussion and education concerning AIDS was at its strongest from 1986 to 1988, but the tone was considerably calmer than, for example, in the United States or the United Kingdom. By September 1990, the cumulative AIDS incidence rate per million of population was 14.3, compared with 66.3 in the United Kingdom.

By 1994, about 600 HIV infections had been diagnosed, and about 100 people had died of AIDS. The proportion of the HIV-infected in Finland has remained fairly small by international comparison. This is partly because of the scarcity of prostitution and intravenous drug use in Finland. [*Update 2003*: At the end of the 1990s, IV-drug use had become more popular in the Capital area. This caused some increase in HIV infections. In 2001 and 2002, this epidemic was already rather well controlled by the health authorities. (*End of update by O. Kontula*)]

In the FINSEX study, 6.4% of the men and 7% of the women reported having taken the HIV test on their own initiative by the beginning of 1992. [In 1999, these proportions had already about doubled to 12%.] Multiple tests were reported by 30% of these men (1.9% of all men) and by 16% of the women tested (1.1% of all women). At the beginning of 1992, about 250,000 Finns had been tested for HIV, and about 50,000 of those had had themselves tested several times. Multiple tests were most common among 30-year-old women. The young age groups had had themselves tested more frequently than older Finns. One tenth of young adults had taken the test.

Some of the HIV-tested had not had very many partners during their lives. One fifth of the men and one fourth of the women tested had had three partners at the most. About half of all the males tested had had at least 20 partners. Of the women tested, 40% had had at least 10 partners. Eleven percent of the men and 17% of the women with more than one partner were tested during the prior year. This shows that, with the risk of infection rising, women were quicker to have themselves tested.

Seven percent of current or past intravenous drug users and 16% of men and 19% of women with a previous STD infection had taken the HIV test on their own initiative. Of the other men and women, the test had been taken by 6%. Of those who had reduced the number of sexual partners or increased their use of the condom because of anxiety experienced because of AIDS or HIV, from 16% to 18% had taken the HIV test. Of the people who had sometimes used drugs intravenously, 7% had themselves tested for HIV.

[*Update 2002*: UNAIDS Epidemiological Assessment: As of the end of 2001, Finland had reported a cumulative total of 1,301 cases of HIV infection. Of 222 HIV cases reported in 1998 to 1999, 100 were injection drug users, which suggests a recent outbreak among this population. HIV testing is mandatory for blood donors but otherwise voluntary. Diagnosed HIV infections are recorded in a national HIV case-reporting system, using an identification code. Other data come from screening programs. An UAT survey in all pregnant women has been conducted nationally since 1993. Of five positive women identified through unlinked anonymous testing, three were already identified through voluntary testing. UAT surveys have been done also among injection drug users. The incidence of syphilis decreased from 2 to 1 case per 100,000 between 1985 and 1987, and remained stable until 1995. In 1996 to 1998, an epidemic of syphilis had occurred, and most cases identified were imported cases from neighboring countries.

[The estimated number of adults and children living with HIV/AIDS on January 1, 2002, were:

| | |
|---|---|
| Adults ages 15-49: | 1,200  (rate: 0.1%) |
| Women ages 15-49: | 330 |
| Children ages 0-15: | < 100 |

[An estimated less than 100 adults and children died of AIDS during 2001.

[No estimate is available for the number of Finnish children who had lost one or both parents to AIDS and were under age 15 at the end of 2001. (*End of update by the Editors*)]

## 11. Sexual Dysfunctions, Counseling, and Therapies

In Finland, sexual dysfunction can be treated—depending on its causes—using sexual counseling, sexual short-term therapy, intensive therapy, medicines, and/or surgery. Sexual advice is given both in communal healthcare centers and in medical and therapeutic service centers specializing in counseling. It is possible to get sex therapy all over the country.

In the FINSEX study, the prevalence of different kinds of sexual problems was surveyed, as well as the help sought to resolve these problems. Half of the men and 26% of the women in a steady relationship reported no lack of sexual desire during the prior year. Fifteen to 55% of women in a steady relationship in different age groups experienced a lack of sexual desire fairly often. The women had succeeded in concealing this lack of desire in many cases, since clearly fewer men than this, when asked about their partners' lack of desire, had experienced their partners' lack of desire as a problem in each of the age groups. The men's reports on their own lack of desire and the women's opinions about their partners' lack of desire fit well together. Five to 20% of the men had experienced a lack of sexual desire at least fairly often. [In 1999, this variation in different age groups ranged from 7% to 19% of men. Among women, it ranged from 27% to 56%. Lack of one's own sexual desire increased especially among middle-aged women.]

Married women clearly suffered from a lack of sexual desire more often than the women in other steady relationships. According to their own responses, 35% of the married women had experienced a lack of sexual desire at least fairly often during the prior year. For women in cohabitation and other steady sexual relationships, the corresponding share was 15%. A similar perception, though slighter, could be found in the men's responses, where 18% of the

### Table 26

**The Annual Number of STDs and HIV Infections in Finland in 1990-2000**

| Year | Chlamydia | Gonorrhea | Syphilis | HIV |
|---|---|---|---|---|
| 1990 | 12,567 | 2,326 | 32 | 89 |
| 1991 | 11,245 | 1,426 | 37 | 57 |
| 1992 | 11,462 | 993 | 33 | 93 |
| 1993 | 9,883 | 781 | 48 | 62 |
| 1994 | 8,289 | 493 | 63 | 69 |
| 1995 | 9,317 | 331 | 122 | 72 |
| 1996 | 9,438 | 182 | 148 | 69 |
| 1997 | 10,175 | 218 | 172 | 71 |
| 1998 | 10,654 | 269 | 187 | 81 |
| 1999 | 10,660 | 243 | 116 | 143 |
| 2000 | 11,731 | 287 | 212 | 145 |

husbands, 13% of cohabiters, and 8% of the men in some other steady relationship reported that their partners had had a lack of sexual desire at least fairly often during the past year. Partly, these differences are because of the fact that the married people are older, on the average, than those in other relationships, and a lack of sexual desire is noticeably frequent in over-55-year-old women.

In sexual therapy, it is presumed that love, trust, and security are generally needed as essential elements in the creation of sexual desire. Anxiety has been observed to inhibit sexual arousal from taking place (Kaplan 1987). Why then was there less desire in marriages that would appear more secure than other relationships? Important causes are certainly found in the effects of aging on sexual desire, the facilitation of marital relationships, and, in some cases, a sexual life changing into an obligation. Many speak about marital relationships turning into boring routine. Most passion has been observed in new and, in some respect, insecure relationships. Particularly longstanding marital relationships may be regarded as already too secure, thereby lessening the sexual excitement (Hatfield & Rapson 1987).

During the prior year, 58% of the women and 52% of their male partners reported some problem with vaginal lubrication. In this respect, the women's and the men's responses corresponded very well to each other. On the other hand, 15% of the women reported suffering fairly often, often, or regularly from insufficient vaginal lubrication, while only 5% of the men reported this problem. This suggests that it is sometimes difficult for men to notice the woman's problems with vaginal lubrication. Men notice only what affects the insertion of the penis, but, obviously, they do not actually know how much pain and discomfort insufficient vaginal lubrication may cause the partner during sexual intercourse.

With women, vaginal lubrication problems increased considerably with age. About one tenth of the middle-aged women reported fairly frequent problems with vaginal lubrication; after age 50, this rose to about a third, with hormonal changes a prime factor.

Many of the women who suffer from problems with vaginal lubrication experience intercourse as painful. Intercourse had fairly often been experienced as painful by 29% of the women who had suffered from vaginal dryness at least fairly often during the year. The corresponding proportion is 16% with the middle-aged and 40% with the aging. Of the same women, two out of three had experienced their sexual intercourse as painful at least sometimes during the year.

Almost half of the women who had suffered from problems with vaginal lubrication at least fairly often during the year, had obtained lubricant cream to facilitate intercourse and to remove the possibility of pain, according to both the women's and the men's responses. Lubricants had been of evident help, for a greater number of the women who used lubricants experienced orgasm during the last intercourse than those who did not use lubricants.

On the average, 3% of the under-45-year-old women had consulted a physician for problems of lubrication, and of the older women, more than 10%. About nine out of ten seekers felt they had been helped. The problem is thus quite easily resolved in most cases with the help of a lubricant.

Problems with vaginal lubrication have a strong connection with sexual desire and its possible deficiency. Half of the women who had experienced a lack of sexual desire at least fairly often during the year had also at least fairly often had problems with vaginal lubrication.

For the 1992 survey, 49% of the men who had intercourse during the prior year reported that they themselves had had at least some problems with having an erection during that year; 47% of the women reported the same about their partners. Six percent by the men and 9% by the women reported this as a fairly frequent problem, a fairly good convergent appraisal, although men obviously tend to conceal their more difficult erectile problems. Comparatively, it seems that men's erectile problems are slightly less frequent than women's problems with vaginal lubrication.

Two clear observations emerge when the results of the years 1971 and 1992 are compared: On the one hand, erectile problems seem to have diminished during the 20 years and, on the other hand, they are very much age-bound. In 1971, 4.3% of the under-55-year-old men reported having experienced erectile problems during the last year, and in 1992, 2.2%. The corresponding figures with women about their partners were 6.2% and 4.4%. Both vaginal lubrication and erectile problems become clearly more common after the age of 50. In the age group of the 70-year-olds, almost one third of the couples had at least fairly often suffered from them.

[*Update 2003*: In 1999, there was some increase in erection disorders compared to the 1992 survey. Of all men, 7% reported having had erection disorders at least quite often in the last year. Among women, the equal proportion (of their partners) was 12%. In the age group 55-to-74 years, these proportions were 19% of men and 32% of women's partners (of the respondents who had sexual intercourse in the last year). (*End of update by O. Kontula*)]

According to the 1992 survey, men's erectile ability is strongest around the age of 30, when two men out of three have no problems having erections, as reported by both the men and women. With the 50-year-olds, the corresponding share is about 40%, and with the 70-year-olds, about one fifth. So, a significant number of men live throughout their lives without experiencing any problems with having erections. Here, it may be of great importance what kind of partners men have intercourse with, among other things, and how healthy they themselves are.

Men were also asked about their experience with continuous erectile dysfunction during their life. The continuity was not defined except by options of varying spans of time, the shortest of which was the option of "a few weeks' time." Fifteen percent of the male respondents reported experiencing a continuous erectile dysfunction for a span of at least a few weeks at least once (see Table 27). The incidence of erectile problems increased significantly for those over age 50. Half of the 70-year-olds had experienced continuous erectile dysfunction. While erectile dysfunction remains a very common problem, it did decrease slightly between 1971 and 1992.

Fifty percent of all Finnish men had experienced no erectile problems during the prior year, nor a few weeks' continuous dysfunction prior to that. On the other hand, 5% of the men had fairly often had erectile problems during the past year as well as at least a few weeks' continuous erectile dysfunction during or prior to that time. About 9% of the men had had no erectile problems during the past year,

### Table 27

**Percentages of Men by Age Who Reported Having at Some Time Experienced Continuous Erectile Dysfunction, 1971 and 1992**

|          | 18-24 | 25-34 | 35-44 | 45-54 | 55-64 | 65-74 |
|----------|-------|-------|-------|-------|-------|-------|
| Men 1971 | 7     | 7     | 16    | 19    |       |       |
| Men 1992 | 3     | 7     | 7     | 18    | 35    | 53    |

although they had suffered periods of erectile dysfunction prior to that time.

Slightly under 4% of all men in 1992 had consulted a physician for erectile problems, about one third of the men who had reported having sometimes experienced continuous erectile dysfunction. Nearly half of the men who had suffered from at least half a year's continuous erectile dysfunction had sought a physician for help. In 1971, fewer men than at present, 16%, had talked about the matter with a physician. More than half of the men who sought help in 1992 and about one fifth of the men who sought help in 1971 felt that they had been helped. So, seeking treatment, and the efficiency of this treatment, improved during the 20 years.

Of the men whose partners had had problems with vaginal lubrication at least fairly often during the last year, 31% had themselves had problems with obtaining or maintaining an erection at least fairly often. Twenty-three percent of the women who had had problems with vaginal lubrication reported that their partners had fairly often had problems having an erection during the same time. So, one's partner's sexual problems had obviously had an effect on the other's sexual responses. If the partner does not seem really eager to have intercourse, one's own excitement may easily die halfway.

About 5% of the men who had at least occasionally suffered from erectile dysfunction told that they had sometimes used some substances or pills that increase potency. Rings to maintain erection or penis enlargers with pumps, on the other hand, had not been much used by the men who had erectile problems. Neither had vibrators or vibrating dildos been used by these men with their partners more often than by the others. These devices had not been sought to substitute for deficiency in obtaining an erection.

Experiencing orgasm is a focal matter in view of the gratification of sexual life. This is true even though the FINSEX study shows that many women reported enjoying their sexual life although they had not experienced orgasm or had seldom experienced it during intercourse. However, those who had experienced orgasm more regularly were clearly more satisfied with their sexual life and their partners than the others.

About half of the men and from 6% to 7% of the women reported, irrespective of age, that they always experienced orgasm at sexual intercourse. This shows that only a small share of women experience orgasm very easily and that orgasm is not a self-evident matter even for men, for instance, if—from their point of view—their coitus is interrupted. With women, having no orgasm is often a consequence of the quickness of their partner's "coming," after which the love play ceases.

Most men have orgasm during sexual intercourse, either always, almost always, or, at least, mostly. Less frequently than this, orgasm had been experienced by 8% of the 18- to 24-year-old men and 19% of the 65- to 74-year-old men. In the other age groups, from 1% to 2% of the men obtain orgasm during intercourse less frequently than "mostly." Thus, men remain without orgasm during intercourse mostly at the beginning of their sexual life and at retirement age when their physical condition is declining.

With women, experiencing orgasm is much more occasional than with men. Orgasm is experienced at least mostly during sexual intercourse by slightly over half of the women and by about 60% of the middle-aged women. When the incidences of women's orgasms in the 1971 and the 1992 surveys are compared, the regularity of experiencing orgasm had slightly increased with the over-35-year-olds. With women younger than this, no change had hap-

pened. At least mostly, orgasm had been experienced during intercourse by 53% of the under-55-year-old women in 1971, and in 1992, by 58%.

Comparing orgasm data of 50-year-olds in 1971 with the 70-year-olds 20 years later in 1992, experiencing orgasm had not decreased in spite of aging and the increased morbidity (see Table 28). So, the preconditions for sexual satisfaction seem to have improved in this respect. On the other hand, since a considerable number of women do not experience orgasm during intercourse, it is a clear sign of the many restraints that still are obstructing women on their way to enjoyment. And if the woman does not find real satisfaction in sexual intercourse, the man cannot enjoy himself to the full either.

A third of a percent of the men had not experienced orgasm during intercourse, and of the women, 4.4%. This is a relatively small percentage when one looks at the United States, for instance, where about 10% of women do not have orgasm during intercourse (Darling et al. 1991).

Orgasm during intercourse had been experienced seldom or never by 0.7% of the men and 10% of the women according to the 1992 data on 18- to 74-year-old Finns. In 1972, 12% of the women under 55 years old had experienced orgasm seldom or never. In 1992, 9% of the women under age 55 reported orgasm never or seldom; quite-seldom orgasm had been experienced by 30% of the women between the ages 18 and 74 years. Thus, sexual satisfaction has remained significantly deficient for a large number of women, and little improvement has been observed in this regard between 1971 and 1992.

Achieving orgasm reportedly is decisively important to finding sexual intercourse pleasant. Of the men who report that they always experience orgasm at intercourse, half consider sexual intercourse very pleasant, while only 18% of the men who have orgasm approximately on every other occasion or less frequently regard intercourse as very pleasant. With women, the corresponding shares are 65% and 15%. Some women considered intercourse very pleasant, although they had never experienced orgasm.

Ninety-two percent of the men and 56% of the women reported having experienced orgasm in the latest intercourse

### Table 28

**Percentages of Women by Age Who Reported Having at Least Mostly or at Most Seldom Experienced Orgasm During Intercourse, 1971 and 1992**

| Age | Mostly 1971 | Mostly 1992 | Seldom 1971 | Seldom 1992 |
|-----|-------------|-------------|-------------|-------------|
| 18-24 | 52 | 50 | 16 | 12 |
| 25-34 | 58 | 59 | 8 | 10 |
| 35-44 | 51 | 64 | 9 | 9 |
| 45-54 | 44 | 56 | 17 | 5 |
| 55-64 |  | 44 |  | 8 |
| 65-74 |  | 45 |  | 16 |

1971: $N = 1,231$; 1992: $N = 1,031$

### Table 29

**Percentages of Women and Men by Age Who Reported Having an Orgasm at the Most Recent Intercourse, 1971 and 1992**

|  | 18-24 | 25-34 | 35-44 | 45-54 | 55-64 | 65-74 |
|--|-------|-------|-------|-------|-------|-------|
| Men 1992 | 92 | 99 | 99 | 98 | 98 | 81 |
| Women 1992 | 62 | 69 | 62 | 57 | 34 | 33 |
| Women 1971 | 58 | 65 | 50 | 41 |  |  |

(see Table 29). There was a rise in this level of experiencing orgasm for all the women's age groups between 1971 and 1992. In 1971, 56% of the under-55-year-old women had experienced orgasm at their last intercourse, and in 1992, 63%. The possible change concerning men is not known, for in 1971, only the women had been asked questions about experiencing orgasm. With women, the level of experiencing orgasm had stayed at 60% until the age of 50, after which it had fallen to about one third.

[*Update 2003*: The frequency of orgasms in sexual intercourse had remained almost unchanged in the 1990s. In the last intercourse, orgasm was experienced by 62% of women and 94% of men. Two or more orgasms during that intercourse was experienced by 10% of women and 7% of men. Fifty-seven percent of women usually experienced an orgasm, while 5% of women had never experienced orgasm. Eighty-eight percent of men and 66% of women reported having orgasm via masturbation. (*End of update by O. Kontula*)]

Fifty-five percent of the married women, 71% of the cohabiting women, 64% of the women in other steady relationships, and 41% of the women with no steady relationship experienced orgasm in their latest intercourse. Perhaps it is surprising that orgasms are experienced less frequently within marriages than in other steady relationships, for it has been presented that having orgasm is in an important connection with the feeling of security experienced in a relationship (Kaplan 1987).

The regularity of the orgasms experienced by women in sexual intercourse is clearly related to their sexual desire and to the quickness of the partner's "coming" (see Table 30). The women who had reported having themselves suffered from a lack of sexual desire during the last year experienced orgasm less frequently than the other women. Also a great number of the women who feel that their partner "comes too fast" are usually left without orgasm.

The orgasm experienced in the most recent intercourse was about as strongly related to a person's own sexual desire as to the quickness of the partner's "coming." An orgasm had been experienced by 24% of the women who had very often felt a lack of sexual desire during the year, and by 73% of the women who had not had any lack of sexual desire at all. If the partner's "coming" was not felt to be too soon, 70% of the women reached orgasm in their most recent intercourse. If the woman herself is desirous and the

partner "considerate" in his speed, the woman mostly achieves orgasm.

The partner's sexual desire is also connected with the woman's orgasm. Only 38% of the women whose partners had at least fairly often suffered from a lack of sexual desire during the last year had experienced orgasm during intercourse at least mostly. That is clearly fewer women than average.

The orgasms experienced by women during their most recent intercourse have a clear connection with the sexual practices applied. The best practice at sexual intercourse, in this respect, had been using two or three positions; the second best had been the "woman-on-top" position. The shares of the women who had experienced orgasm in these cases was 72% and 67%, respectively. In the "man-on-top" position, 49% of the women had experienced orgasm. Practicing varying positions at intercourse and the woman's own activity thus greatly increase the probability of her experiencing orgasm.

A number of people experience their first orgasms before their first sexual intercourse during various kinds of petting experiences. Most of the men, however, have their first intercourse-related orgasm at the same time they have their first sexual intercourse. Less than a third of the women reported achieving an orgasm in their first intercourse. Half of the women and one tenth of the men had not experienced their first orgasm until a few years after their first experience of sexual intercourse. There has not been much change in this timing even in the younger age groups. With one tenth of the women, more than ten years had elapsed between their first intercourse and their first orgasm. Four percent of the women reported no orgasm at all.

With respect to sex therapists, there have been some informal courses for them in order to provide them some professional skills. However, anyone can start working as a sex therapist without any special training, certification, or licensing.

[*Update 2003*: After several years of educational discussions, the general assembly of the Nordic Association for Clinical Sexology (NACS) in September 1997 appointed a committee of three representatives from each of the countries, Denmark, Norway, Sweden, and Finland, to work on a Nordic educational project. The purposes were: to design and offer qualitatively high-standing educational programs structured into different levels and comparable between the different Nordic countries, and, to provide regulations for sexological authorization [certification] and act for authorization of those who are clinically active within the field of sexology. The Nordic Council ("Nordplus") supported the project financially.

[Between 1997 and 2000, the committee—which *per se* regarded itself as a network—met ten times. Analyses of the current sexological educational situation in the Nordic countries, as well as in other European countries and the United States, were performed. Thereafter, analyses of expected requirements, seen from the viewpoints of the prospective students of each country, the different countries, and the NACS followed. Consensus for Nordic educational programs for clinical sexologists took shape. These programs were, in 1999, approved at the NACS Annual Meeting in Grimstad, Norway. The Nordic training program has three levels: Sexology I: Basic sexology (20 points), Sexology II: Clinical sexology: Sexological counseling (20 points), and Sexology III: Clinical Sexology: Specialist in clinical sexology (40 points). This training has started in Finland.

[In order to secure the (basic) quality of sexological education and the clinical practice of sexologists, the NACS

**Table 30**

**Percentage of Women Reporting Orgasms During Intercourse by Their Sexual Desire and the Quickness of Partner's Coming, 1992**

| | Orgasm at least mostly | Orgasm every other time | Orgasm at the most quite seldom | (n) |
|---|---|---|---|---|
| **Lack of sexual desire** | | | | |
| Very often | 26 | 14 | 60 | (62) |
| Quite often | 45 | 18 | 37 | (161) |
| Quite seldom | 62 | 17 | 21 | (370) |
| Never | 73 | 13 | 14 | (205) |
| **Partner "comes too soon"** | | | | |
| Very often | 28 | 11 | 61 | (36) |
| Quite often | 35 | 23 | 42 | (141) |
| Quite seldom | 62 | 17 | 21 | (350) |
| Never | 73 | 12 | 15 | (250) |

Annual General Meeting in 2000 (in Helsinki, Finland) approved the authorization [certification] procedure based on the Nordic Association of Clinical Sexology's education requirements. In 2002, the first specialists in sexological counseling and clinical sexology were authorized in Finland, Sweden, Denmark, and Norway. This gives more official status to these professions. (*End of update by O. Kontula*)]

## 12. Sex Research and Advanced Professional Education

### A. Institutes and Programs for Sexological Research

In Finland, sexological research is conducted by individual scholars working at universities and research institutes or projects financed mainly by the state. A bibliography of sex literature for the time period 1549-1989 includes over 2,000 authors (Turpeinen 1991). Most of the articles and books listed are written by medical doctors, but some important sociological studies on sexual behavior were also published in the last century. [*Update 2003*: An updated bibliography covers years 1990-2000 and is available at: http://www.seksologinenseura.net/Palvelut/body_palvelut.htm. (*End of update by O. Kontula*)]

### B/C. Post-College Sexuality Programs and Sexological Publications

None currently exists in Finland. [*Update 2003*: A newsletter, *Seksuaaliterveys*, is distributed to the members of the Finnish Association for Sexology and to other persons belonging to the network of sex education and family planning. (*End of update by O. Kontula*)]

### D. Sexological Organizations

Three sexological organizations are active in Finland: SEXPO Foundation (Säätiö). Address: Malminkatu 22E, 00100 Helsinki, Finland; www.health.fi/sexpo.

Seksuaalinen Tasavertaisuus SETA ry (Sexual Equality Association). Address: Hietalahdenkatu 2 B 16, 00180 Helsinki, Finland; www.seta.fi.

[*Update 2003*: The Finnish Association for Sexology (FIAS) (Suomen Seksologinen Seura ry). The aim of FIAS is to improve qualifications of sexologists and to serve as a network for professionals who have an interest in sexual issues. FIAS is a member organization of the Nordic Association for Clinical Sexology (NACS), the European Federation of Sexology (EFS), and the World Association for Sexology (WAS). Address: Population Research Institute, Family Federation of Finland, P.O. Box 849, FIN 00101 Helsinki, Finland; www.seksologinenseura.net. (*End of update by O. Kontula*)]

## References and Suggested Reading

CEDAW Convention. 1993. *Second periodic report by Finland*. Helsinki: Ministry of Foreign Affairs.

Christensen, H. T., & C. F. Gregg. 1970. Changing sex norms in America and Scandinavia. *Journal of Marriage and Family*, *32*:616-27.

CIA. 2002 (January). *The world factbook 2002*. Washington, DC: Central Intelligence Agency. Available: http://www.cia.gov/cia/publications/factbook/index.html.

Darling, C. Anderson, J. K. Davidson, & R. P. Cox. 1991. Female sexual response and the timing of partner orgasm. *Journal of Sex and Marital Therapy*, *17*(1):3-21.

Erkkola, R., & O. Kontula. 1993. Syntyvyyden säännöstely [Birth control]. In: O. Kontula & E. Haavio-Mannila, eds., *Suomalainen seksi* (*Finnish sex*). Helsinki: WSOY, pp. 343-370.

Fugl-Meyer K. S., E. Almås, E. Benestad, et al. 2001. Nordic sexology education and authorisation. *Scandinavian Journal of Sexology*, *4*(1):61-68.

Gershuny, J. 1990. International comparisons of time budgets—Methods and opportunities. In: R. von Schweitzer, M. Ehling, & D. Schäfer, eds., *Zeitbudgeterhebungen—Ziele, methoden und neue konzepte*. Stuttgart: Metzler Poeschel.

Grönfors, M., E. Haavio-Mannila, K. Mustola, & O. Stålström. 1984. Esitietoja homo-ja biseksuaalisten ihmisten elämäntavasta ja syrjinnästä [Preliminary data on lifestyle and discrimination of homo- and bisexual people]. In: K. Sievers & O. Stålström, eds., *Rakkauden monet kasvot*. Espoo: Weilin+Göös.

Haavio-Mannila, E. 1991. Impact of coworkers on female alcohol use. *Contemporary Drug Problems*, *18*(4):597-627.

Haavio-Mannila, E., T. R. Harris, A. D. Klassen, R. W. Wilsnack, & S. C. Wilsnack. 1996. Alcohol and sexuality among American and Finnish women. *Nordisk Sexologi*, *4*(3):129-146.

Haavio-Mannila, E., & K. Kauppinen-Toropainen. 1992. Women and the welfare state in the Nordic countries. In: H. Kahne & J. Giele, eds., *Women's work and women's lives—The continuing struggle worldwide*. Boulder, CO: Westview Press.

Haavio-Mannila, E., & O. Kontula. 1997. Correlates of increased sexual satisfaction. *Archives of Sexual Behavior*, *26*(4):399-419.

Haavio-Mannila, E., O. Kontula, & E. Kuusi. 2001. *Trends in sexual life: Measured by national sex surveys in Finland in 1971, 1992 and 1999 and a comparison to a sex survey in St. Petersburg in 1996* (Working Papers E 10/2001). The Population Research Institute. The Family Federation of Finland. Helsinki.

Haavio-Mannila, E., O. Kontula, & A. Rotkirch. 2002. *Sexual lifestyles in the twentieth century: A research study*. Hampshire & New York: Palgrave.

Haavio-Mannila, E., J. P. Roos, & O. Kontula. 1997. Repression, revolution and ambivalence: The sexual life of three generations. *Acta Sociologica*, *40*(1):2-22 (in press).

Hatfield, E., & R. L. Rapson. 1987. Passionate love/sexual desire: Can the same paradigm explain both? *Archives of Sexual Behavior*, *16*(3):259-78.

Järvinen, M. 1990. *Prostitution i Helsingfors—En studie i kvinnokontroll* (*Prostitution in Helsinki—A study on control of women*). Åbo: Åbo Academy Press.

Jeffreys, S. 1990. *Anticlimax: A feminist perspective on the sexual revolution*. New York: New York University Press.

Kaplan, H. S. 1987. *The illustrated manual of sex therapy* (2nd ed.). New York: Brunner/Mazel.

Kinsey, A. C., W. B. Pomeroy, & C. E. Martin. 1948. *Sexual behavior in the human male*. Philadelphia: Saunders.

Kinsey, A. C., W. B. Pomeroy, C. E. Martin, & P. H. Gebhard. 1953. *Sexual behavior in the human female*. Philadelphia: Saunders.

Kontula, O. 1991. Sukupuolielämän aloittamisen yhteiskunnallisista ehdoista [Cultural terms of sexual initiation]. *Sosiaali-ja Terveyshallitus. Tutkimuksia* 14/1991. Valtion Painatuskeskus, Helsinki.

Kontula, O. 1993. Ketkä hyväksyvät vapaan abortin? [Who approves a free abortion?] In: *Suomalaisia mielipiteitä raskauden keskeytyksestä*. STAKES. Julkaisusarja Aiheita 34/1993, Helsinki, pp. 23-39.

Kontula, O. 1996. *Sex education in Finland*. Paper presented in the 39th Annual Meeting of the Society for the Scientific Study of Sexuality (SSSS) held in Houston, November 14-17, 1996.

Kontula, O. 2001. *Response rate and selection bias in a sex survey: An empirical test*. Paper presented in the IUSSP XXIV General Population Conference held in Salvador, Brazil, August 18-24.

Kontula, O., R. Cacciatore, D. Apter, K. Bildjuschkin, M. Törhönen, S. Koski, & L. Tiilo. 2001. *Nuorten tiedot seksu-*

*aaliterveydestä* [*Adolescent knowledge on sexual health*] (Väestöntutkimuslaitoksen katsauksia E 11/2001). Helsinki: The Family Federation of Finland.

Kontula, O., & E. Haavio-Mannila, eds. 1993. *Suomalainen seksi: Tietoa Suomalaisten sukupuolielämän muutoksesta* (*Finnish sex: Information of changes in sexual life in Finland*). Juva: WSOY.

Kontula, O., & E. Haavio-Mannila. 1994. Sexual behavior changes in Finland in the past 20 years. *Nordisk Sexologi*, *12*(3):196214.

Kontula, O., & E. Haavio-Mannila. 1995. *Matkalla intohimoon: Nuoruuden hurma ja käsimys seksuaalielämäkertojen kuvaamana* [*Along the way to passion: The joy and suffering of youth revealed in sexual autobiographies*]. Juva: WSOY.

Kontula, O., & E. Haavio-Mannila. 1995. *Sexual pleasures: Enhancement of sex life in Finland, 1971-1992*. Aldershot, Brookfield, USA, Signapore, and Sidney: Dartmouth.

Kontula, O., & E. Haavio-Mannila. 1997. *Intohimon hetkiä: Seksuaalisen läheisyyden kaipuu ja täyttymys omaelämäkertojen kuvaamana* [*Moments of passion: The longing for sexual intimacy and its fulfillment described in autobiographies*]. Juva: WSOY.

Kontula, O., & E. Haavio-Mannila. 2003a (in press). Renaissance of romanticism in the era of increasing individualism. In: G. Allan, J. Duncombe, K. Harrison, & D. Marsden, eds., *The state of affairs*. London: Erlbaum. London.

Kontula, O., & E. Haavio-Mannila. 2003b (in press). Masturbation in a generational perspective. *Journal of Psychology & Human Sexuality*, *15*(1):2003.

Kontula, O., & K. Kosonen 1996. Sexuality changing from privacy to the open—A study of the Finnish press over the years from 1961 to 1991. *Nordisk Sexologi*, *14*(1):34-47.

Kontula, O., & J. Meriläinen. 1988. Nuorten kypsyminen seurusteluun ja seksuaalisuuteen [Adolescents' maturation for social intercourse and sexuality]. Lääkintöhallituksen julkaisuja. *Sarja Tutkimukset 9*/1988. Valtion Painatuskeskus, Helsinki.

Kontula, O., & M. Rimpelä. 1988. Onko AIDS-valistus vaikuttanut nuorten seksuaalisuuteen 1986-1988? [Has AIDS education influenced the adolescents' sexuality 1986-1988?] *Suomen Lääkärilehti*, *43*:3493-3500.

Kosunen, E. 1993. *Teini-ikäisten raskaudet ja ehkäisy* [*Teenage pregnancies and contraception*]. STAKES. Helsinki: Raportteja, 99.

Laumann, E. O., J. Gagnon, R. T. Michael, & S. Michaels. 1994. *The social organization of sexuality*. Chicago: University of Chicago Press.

Love, B. 1992. *Encyclopedia of unusual sex practices*. Fort Lee, NJ: Barricade Books.

Markkula, H. 1981. *Maksettu nainen* [*Paid woman*]. Hämeenlinna: Kustannus-Mäkelä Oy.

Niemi, I., & H. Pääkkönen. 1989. Ajankäytön muutokset [Changes in the appropriation of time in the 1980s]. *Tutkimuksia* [*Research Reports*], *153*. Helsinki: Tilastokeskus [Statistics Finland].

Riihinen O., A. Pulkkinen, & M. Ritamies. 1980. *Suomalaisen perheen lapsiluku* [*The number of children in the Finnish family*]. Helsinki: Väestöntutkimuslaitos D.7.

Ritamies, M. 1994. *Finland: A comparative handbook* (pp. 85-99). Westport, CT: Greenwood Press.

Robinson, J. 1988. Who is doing the housework? *American Demographics*, *10*(12):24-28.

Sarmela, M. 1969. *Reciprocity systems of the rural society in the Finnish-Karelian culture area* (FF Communications No. 207). Helsinki: Academia Scientiarum Fennica.

Sievers, K., O. Koskelainen, & K. Leppo. 1974. *Suomalaisten sukupuolielämä* [*Sex life in Finland*]. Porvoo: WSOY.

Smith, T. W. 1990. The sexual revolution? *Public Opinion Quarterly*, *54*:415-435.

Turpeinen, T. 1991. *Suomalaisen seksuaalikirjallisuuden bibliografia 1549-1989* [*Bibliography of the Finnish sexual literature 1549-1989*]. *Kellokosken Sairaala, Mariefors Sjukhus and Sexpo ry*. Jyväskylä.

UNAIDS. 2002. *Epidemiological fact sheets by country*. Geneva, Switzerland: Joint United Nations Programme on HIV/ AIDS (UNAIDS/WHO). Available: http://www.unaids.org/ hivaidsinfo/statistics/fact_sheets/index_en.htm.

Wikman, K., & V. Rob. 1937. Die einleitung der ehe. *Åbo: Acta Academiae Åboensis. Humaniora*, *XI*:1.

# France

## (*Rèpublique Française*)

Michel Meignant, Ph.D.,* chapter coordinator,
with Pierre Dalens, M.D., Charles Gellman, M.D.,
Robert Gellman, M.D., Claire Gellman-Barroux, Ph.D.,
Serge Ginger, Laurent Malterre, and France Paramelle

*Translated by*
Genevieve Parent, M.A.

*Redacted by*
Robert T. Francoeur, Ph.D.**

Comment by Timothy Perper, Ph.D.; Updates by the Editors

## Contents

## *Demographics and a Brief Historical Perspective*

ROBERT T. FRANCOEUR

### A. Demographics

France's position in western central Europe has made it a major cultural force in European history for 2,000 years. France's neighbors are Belgium and Luxembourg on the north, Germany, Switzerland, and Italy on the east, the

(CIA 2002)

Mediterranean Sea on the south, Spain in the southwest, and the Atlantic Ocean and English Channel on the west. With a territory of 211,210 square miles (547,030 km²), France is about 80% of the size of the state of Texas in the United States. A wide plain covers more than half of the country. The northern and western regions of the country are drained to the west by the Seine, Loire, and Garonne Rivers. France's eastern border is marked by the Rhine River. A mountainous plateau, the Central Massif, marks the center of France. The Alps form France's eastern border with Switzerland and Italy, while the Pyrénées mark its border with Spain in the southwest.

In July 2002, France had an estimated population of 60 million. (All data are from *The World Factbook 2002* (CIA 2002) unless otherwise stated.)

**Age Distribution and Sex Ratios**: *0-14 years*: 18.5% with 1.05 male(s) per female (sex ratio); *15-64 years*: 65.2% with 1 male(s) per female; *65 years and over*: 16.3%

*Communications*: Michel Meignant, Ph.D., 2 B's Rue Scheffer, 75116 Paris, France; meignant@wanado.fr. Charles Gellman, M.D., 103, Avenue Charles de Gaulle, Neuilly-sur-Seine, 92200 France; gellman@psygestalt.org. Pierre Dalens, M.D., 25, Avenue de l'Entre deux Mers 33370 Fargues, Saint Hilaire, (Près Bordeaux), France; pierre.dalens@wanadoo.fr. Robert Gellman, M.D., 3, rue Copernic, Paris 75116, France. Claire Gellman, c.gellmanbarroux@free.fr. France Paramelle, France.Paramelle@wanadoo.fr. Laurent Malterre, 74, Rue des Gravilliers, 75003 Paris, France; laurentmalterre@ hotmail.com. Translator: Genevieve Parent, M.A., genevieve_ parent@hotmail.com.

***A Note from the Editors*: This chapter came into being after a ten-year frustrating search for a French sexologist to recruit and coordinate a team of experts to write a chapter about sexuality in France. Our breakthrough finally came in late 2001, six months after the Fifteenth World Congress of Sexology was held in Paris. The Congress was widely recognized for its strong therapeutic, psychoanalytic, and medical/pharmacological tenor, a good example *de le mirage complementaire* of French culture in general, and French sexology in particular. In early 2002, Dr. Michel Meignant accepted our invitation. Despite a tight editorial schedule, Dr. Meignant managed to recruit a team of France's leading sexologists and therapists.

At the Paris World Congress, Dr. Ludwig Fineltain, a neuropsychiatrist and psychoanalyst, reminded us that:

The history of French sexology has been closely linked with the beginnings of the Société Française de Sexologie Clinique. The idea arose between 1970 and 1974. Where? At La Couple, of course. In Paris, it is well known that great ideas are born in the literary *cafés* between Saint-Germain-des-Pres and Montparnasse.

As with all our contributors to *IES* and *CCIES*, Dr. Meignant and his team received our detailed eight-page chapter outline and guidelines, translated into French. The chapter on sexuality in France has its own unique flavor and gourmet accent. It is very different from the other chapters, with a very strong didactic, analytic, and ideological focus. That, in itself, is informative. Several years ago, when Dr. William Prendergast, one of our editorial consultants, analyzed the information on coercive sexual behavior (Section 8A) for the 32 countries in volumes one to three, he ended with an important observation relevant to all the information in the *Complete International Encyclopedia of Sexuality*, and particularly relevant to this chapter: "Often what is not said in these chapters is more informative than what is said."

The French texts provided by the eight creators of this chapter were ably translated by Genevieve Parent, B.A., M.A., a double graduate of the Sexologie Programme at the University of Quebec in Montreal (UQAM). She has held several positions as a sexuality teacher, clinical sexologist, psychotherapist, and certified sexual abuse counselor. Because this chapter is a composite created by eight different French sexologists, R. T. Francoeur, the editor, assumes responsibility of redacting the translation and integrating the different parts of the chapter.

with 0.69 male(s) per female; *Total population sex ratio*: 0.95 male(s) to 1 female

**Life Expectancy at Birth**: *Total Population*: 79.05 years; *male*: 75.17 years; *female*: 83.14 years

**Urban/Rural Distribution**: 74% to 26%

**Ethnic Distribution**: Celtic and Latin, with Teutonic, Slavic, North African, Indochinese, and Basque minorities. Following the breakup of its overseas empire, France received immigrants from its overseas colonies, particularly Vietnam, Morocco, Algeria, and Tunisia, and several Caribbean nations.

**Religious Distribution**: Roman Catholic: 83% to 88% (at least nominally); Protestant: 2%; Jewish: 1%; Muslim (North African): 3%; unaffiliated: 4%

**Birth Rate**: 11.94 births per 1,000 population

**Death Rate**: 9.04 per 1,000 population

**Infant Mortality Rate**: 4.41 deaths per 1,000 live births

**Net Migration Rate**: 0.64 migrant(s) per 1,000 population

**Total Fertility Rate**: 1.74 children born per woman

**Population Growth Rate**: 0.35%

**HIV/AIDS** (1999 est.): *Adult prevalence*: 0.44%; *Persons living with HIV/AIDS*: 30,000; *Deaths*: 2,000. (For additional details from www.UNAIDS.org, see end of Section 10B.)

**Literacy Rate** (*defined as those age 15 and over who can read and write*): 99%; schooling is free and compulsory from age 6 to 16

**Per Capita Gross Domestic Product** (*purchasing power parity*): $25,400 (2001 est.); *Inflation*: 1.7%; *Unemployment*: 8.9%; *Living below the poverty line*: NA

## B. A Brief Historical Perspective

Traces of 400,000-year-old covered wood shelters created by Neanderthal-type humans (*Homo erectus*) have been found in Nice, along with stone and ivory sculptures from 25,000 years ago. The remarkable, sophisticated wall paintings in prehistoric caves of southern France and northern Spain, particularly Lascaux and Altamira, date back to the Upper Paleolithic about 18,000 years ago and are evidence of some of the earliest modern-type humans (*Homo sapiens sapiens*). The Celtic tribes of ancient Gaul were conquered by Julius Caesar in 57 to 52 B.C.E., and remained under Roman rule for 500 years. The Franks, a Teutonic tribe, reached the Somme from the east around 250 of the Common Era. By the 5th century, the Merovingian Franks had ousted the Romans and defeated the Huns under Attila. Under Charlemagne (742-814), Frankish rule extended over much of Europe, including what is now France and Germany, as well as parts of Italy, Spain, and Austria. Charlemagne's grandsons fought over the empire, and in the peace of Verdun (843), divided the kingdom with Lothar becoming the Roman emperor. Pepin I became the king of Aquitaine, Louis II took over Germany, and Charles the Bald ruled France. The absolute monarchy reached its apogee in the reign of Louis XIV (1643-1715), the Sun King, whose brilliant court was the center of the Western world. The French Revolution of 1789-1793 overthrew the monarchy and plunged France into a bloodbath that ended with a new absolute rule under Napoléon Bonaparte, who became First Counsel in 1799 and Emperor in 1804. The defeat of Napoléon and the 1815 Congress of Vienna sought to restore the pre-Napoléonic order in the person of Louis XVIII, but industrialization and the middle class fostered under Napoléon pressed for change until a revolution in 1848 drove the last of the Bourbon kings into exile.

Napoléon's nephew, Louis Napoléon, declared the Second Empire in 1852, taking power as Napoléon III. His opposition to the rising power of Prussia ignited the Franco-Prussian War (1870-1871) and ended in his defeat and abdication.

France emerged from World War I as the continent's dominant power, but political instability and economic chaos stemming from the devastation of the war, plagued the postwar Third Republic. During World War II, northern France was occupied by the Nazi troops while southern France remained free. After World War II, as all the European empires with overseas colonies began to collapse, France withdrew from Indonesia in 1954, from Morocco and Tunisia in 1956, and from most of its African territories, including Algeria, in 1958 to 1962. Today, a few small overseas Departments and Territories remain part of France: the island of Corsica in the Mediterranean off the coast of Italy, French Guiana on the northeast coast of South America, the islands of Guadaloupe and Martinique in the Caribbean, and French Polynesia in the Pacific (see the chapter on French Polynesia in this volume).

## 1. Basic Sexological Premises

### A. Sexology in France

SERGE GINGER and MICHEL MEIGNANT

Sexology was born at the end of the 19th century with the publication of *Psychopathia Sexualis* by Richard von Krafft-Ebing in Suttgart in 1886. Havelock Ellis' work, *Studies in the Psychology of Sex* (1898, Philadelphia, USA), and Sigmund Freud's *Three Essays on Sexuality* (Vienna, Austria, 1905) were published around the same time, but showed very different conceptions of sexuality. This accounts for the hesitations of newborn sexology. In 1919, Magnus Hirschfeld created his famous Institute in Berlin. It was one of the first buildings to be plundered and burnt down by the Nazis in 1933. In the eyes of the Nazis, Magnus Hirschfeld had two reasons to be persecuted: He was Jewish and a homosexual. Pioneers in sexology have always had to confront conservative, racist, and fascist attitudes. In 1926, in the context of the liberal and democratic Netherlands, Theodore Van de Velde published *The Perfect Marriage*, endorsing the replacement of sex as a "conjugal duty" with an emphasis on sexual pleasure and happiness. The book was widely published in many countries, and in translations as recently as 1965, in about 50 editions.

In 1966, William Masters and Virginia Johnson published *Human Sexual Response*, documenting their revolutionary research, which became the foundation for modern scientific sexology. Masters and Johnson were the first to observe the physiology of sexual function, in the same way that Claude Bernard had observed the heart, respiratory, and digestive functions. In their laboratory, transformed into a fortress, 694 men and women masturbated or made love in front of cameras. They were heterosexual or homosexual. The subjects were fitted with electrodes and all sorts of sensors in order to record their heartbeat, rhythm of their breathing, and blood pressure. The erection of the penis, of the clitoris, of the breast and nipple, and the color of the skin were, among other things, also measured. Masters and Johnson then moved to the clinical phase of their work, with their book, *Human Sexual Inadequacy*, published in 1970. Following my experience in supervising the French translation of Masters and Johnson's *Human Sexual Inadequacy*, my own therapeutic methodology moved from experimental and behaviorist sexology into a humanistic sexology and a humanistic analytical sexology, to finally become a modality known as Amorology, with the publication of *L'Amourologue*, in 1992. The resulting methodology replaced the therapy of sexual function with a therapy of the love relationship. The symptom was thus set in the global context of the subject's relational problems.

In France, sexology is not considered to be a specific method of psychotherapy. Since its creation in 1974, the French Society of Clinical Sexology (Société Française de Sexologie Clinique–SFSC) has chosen an eclectic approach, under the coordination of Charles Gellman, Gérard Vallès, Michel Meignant, Georges Teboul, and others.

Thus, various trainings and specializations have developed in parallel, some inspired by psychoanalysis (Gérard Vallès and Georges Teboul)—enriched by "sexoanalysis" (Claude Crépault, from Montreal); some inspired by cognitive-behavioral therapies, following the work of Masters and Johnson (Mireille Bonierbale, and Robert and Claire Gellman); others inspired by Gestalt Therapy ("Sexo-Gestalt"—with Charles Gellman, Martine Masson, and Chantal Higy-Lang), and others inspired by hypnotherapy or the systemic approach.

## 2. Religious, Ethnic, and Gender Factors Affecting Sexuality

No information given.

## 3. Knowledge and Education about Sexuality

The Family Planning Association, France's national branch of Planned Parenthood/World Population, is the nation's main agency in providing sex education. The approach taken is a "preventative" approach, linked with the curricula in biology, health, and/or natural sciences. The model consists of pregnancy and STD prevention, teacher training programs, and lectures to the youth in the context of "Life Education." In 1994, in terms of public attitudes toward sexuality, using a scale of 1 for "opposed" to 9 for "well accepted," the Family Planning Association rated France as a 5 (Vilar 1994; Caron 1998, 68).

## 4. Autoerotic Behaviors and Patterns

No information given.

## 5. Interpersonal Heterosexual Behaviors

### [A. A French/U.S. Comparison: *Comment 2003*

TIMOTHY PERPER

[This comment briefly describes statistics relating to couple status and sexual partnering among men and women in France and in the United States for four age groups—19- to 29-, 30- to 39-, 40- to 49-, and 50- to 59-year-olds.

[The results are based on two large-scale and representative probability samples, both from 1992. The U.S. sample contained 3,432 adults, ages 18 to 59, from the *National Health and Social Life Survey* (Laumann et al. 1994). The French sample contained 4,580 adults, ages 18 to 59, from the *Analyse des Comportements Sexuels en France* (cf. Spira, et al. 1994). The French sample was obtained by telephone interviews, whereas the U.S. sample was obtained by face-to-face interviews. Readers interested in statistical and methodological details are referred to the original publication (Gagnon, et al. 2001).

[For the French sample, the percentage of men and women living in couples is lowest among 19- to 29-year-olds (38% for men, 46% for women) and then rises to a plateau among older men and women (from 82% to 89% among 30-, 40-, and 50-year-olds). In France, the percentage who are unmarried but living with a partner is largest among 19- to 29-year-olds (22% among men, 21% among women). These percentages drop steadily with age (16% among men, 12%

among women for 30- to 39-year-olds, and then to less than 10% among 40- and 50-year-olds). Comparable data from the United States show similar effects—proportionally more younger people (19- to 29-year-olds) are single or, if coupled, then unmarried, than among older people.

[These differences among age groups may have several causes. One is a cohort (or "generational") effect that might represent mores having changed in the youngest generation towards a decreased valuation or even avoidance of marriage (or coupling of any kind) among people born after 1970. Another possibility is an effect of age, in which couple formation normally occurs primarily among older rather than younger individuals. If so, then members of the youngest group will begin to marry when they reach their 30s. Both factors may play a role. Further research is needed to clarify these possibilities.

[Concerning sexual activity in these coupled individuals, in the French sample, the percentages reporting no sexual partner within the last year differ among the age groups. For coupled men, the percentage without a sex partner rises steadily from a low of about 2% for 19- to 29-year-olds to a high of 6% for 50- to 59-year-olds. Although small, the increase is statistically significant. For U.S. men living in couples, men reported a similar (and small) increase in living without a sex partner.

[However, the percentages of coupled women in the French sample who report no sexual partner changes very little with age—in fact, the lowest percentage reported (1%) was among the 50- to 59-year-old women. Unlike French women, U.S. women reported a steady increase with age in living without a sex partner. The origin of this national difference is unknown.

[In French men and women, a U-shaped relationship exists between age/cohort and the presence of a sexual partner. For men and women in France, 30- to 39-year-olds most frequently report having a sex partner, with younger and older individuals both less likely to report having a sex partner. This effect may represent two different processes—a tendency for younger people to live singly and to lack partners, plus a tendency for older people to remain coupled but celibate. However, these hypotheses require further study.

[By contrast, in the U.S. sample, the percentages of coupled men and women who report living without a sex partner increases steadily with age for both sexes. It is unknown why the French sample shows a U-shaped form whereas the U.S. sample does not.

[We turn next to sexual activity among coupled and noncoupled men and women of different ages. For the French and U.S. samples, most coupled individuals (more than 90%) report living monogamously with the partner in all four age groups. However, a far more complex pattern emerges for individuals not living in a couple. In the 20-, 30-, and 40-year-old ranges, about 30% of men in the French sample and about 50% of the men in the U.S. sample report having more than one sexual partner within the last year (both percentages decrease among 50- to 59-year-old men). So it seems that in both nations, a fair proportion of the younger non-coupled men tend to have had more than one sex partner within the last year.

[However, both age/cohort and national differences occur among women not living in a couple. In the French sample and across all four age groups, between 10% and 20% of uncoupled French women report having more than one sex partner in the last year. This is about one-half to two-thirds the rate reported by French men. In principle, for heterosexuality within a closed population, the number of partners must be equal for men and for women. It may be that men exaggerate and women minimize their self-reports about sex partners, or it may be that men and women define sex partner differently. Again, only further research can clarify these possibilities.

[Among uncoupled U.S. women across the age/cohort groups, the youngest women (19- to 29-year-olds) are most likely to report more than one sex partner in the last year (42%). This percentage decreases steadily among 30-, 40-, and 50-year-olds, to a low of 15% among 50- to 59-year-old women. These percentages are less than reported by U.S. men, again raising the question of why the percentages among men and women are not equal. Furthermore, the percentages of uncoupled U.S. women reporting more than one partner in the last year are consistently higher than percentages reported by French women. The origin of this national difference is unknown.

[The survey results indicate that most coupled respondents in France and in the U.S. report that their primary sexual activity was with their partner. However, complex differences between men and women, between France and the U.S., and among the age groups occur for uncoupled individuals. The most robust finding appears to be that for the youngest men and women in both France and the U.S., sexuality is not limited to marriage or living with a partner. Only further research and time will reveal what these patterns imply for the future of marriage and sexuality. (*End of comment by T. Perper*)]

## B. Heterosexual Behaviors in an Ethological
### Perspective          CHARLES GELLMAN

This chapter will mainly discuss sexual behaviors, using a behavioral and ethological approach. The study of ethology is done through the observation of animal behaviors, and is based on factors, which lead animals to adopt specific behaviors. The word "ethology" is very similar to ethnology, which is the study of human relations in a given society. Ethnology also provides a better knowledge of a variety of societies and cultures.

In order to write this section, we used a scientific approach without any preconceived ideas. We have been quite surprised to notice that very few French studies have been published on heterosexuality, all authors referring to homosexuality, often in a polemic manner. We consider it is possible to study heterosexuality on its own.

We will discuss later on the contention that homosexuality is not the opposite of heterosexuality. We consider heterophobia as the opposite to heterosexuality.

Also, a common mistake lies in the consideration that heterosexuality is a sexual identity. In fact, *sexual identity* or *gender identity* or *gender* refers to the male or female gender identity *and not to sexual orientation*. Male or female gender (or a neutral gender) is not an indication of the heterosexual or homosexual orientation, or of any other orientation. Identity and sexual orientation are two different concepts. On the other hand, once the sexual orientation is defined, it may become a part of the person's identity, but surely not of one's gender!

### Sexual Behavior

Sexual behavior includes all the actions surrounding sexual attraction (for example, the sexual parade [response]) and leading to the sexual act. In most species, sexual behavior serves reproduction purposes only. The human race and some monkey species are not only reproduction oriented. While the sexual act allows the fertilization of the egg, sexual behavior also includes certain parental roles, such as nest making and care of the newborn. Sexual and parental behaviors are caused by specific physiological states, such as

gonad maturation and certain hormones, all controlled by the nervous system.

Human sexual behavior has three aspects:

• The instinct: sexual urge or libido;
• The attachment bond, which influences interpersonal activities; and
• The passion: love.

### Pairing Up (Intimacy Between the Sexes: "What's Different Comes Together")

The search for sexual partners serves the purpose of heredity for both animals and humans. Many different mechanisms are used to facilitate interaction between sexes.

*Attraction*: the attraction of the male for the female. The female animal signals its interest to the male in an extraordinary variety of ways. Women, on their part, use perfumes, makeup, clothes and underclothing, jewels, tattoos, piercing, singing, and vocalization.

*Proceptivity*: the female search for the male. Different behaviors demonstrate the active female search for a male partner: closeness (females are more bodily active during estrus), hops, and facial expressions. The female then readjusts according to male signals. This phenomenon can also be noticed in nightclubs, where men and women mainly interact in a nonverbal way, despite the loudness of the music.

*Receptivity*: when the female accepts copulation, for example, lordosis in the female rat and a woman granting access to her vulva.

*Estrus*: the period during which mammals look for copulation; the state of being during this same period (female in rut = female in heat, from *rugitus*, roaring). It is the ovulation period.

### Heterosexual Orientation

As mentioned earlier, we should differentiate between heterosexual orientation—being sexually attracted by someone of the opposite sex—and one's gender identity. A person who has a male sexual identity can be either homosexual or heterosexual, depending on different factors. The heterosexual orientation can be expressed in different ways:

• Global heterosexual orientation;
• Partial heterosexual orientation, interest for specific body or psychological characteristics of the opposite sex (breast, buttocks, musculature, or personality traits, such as calmness, kindness, or aggressiveness);
• Strong orientation, or on the opposite, weak, fragile, or uncertain orientation;
• Positive orientation; or
• Defensive heterosexual orientation: homophobia.

All these concepts account for the different variations in the time and life of individuals.

Kinsey's report (1948), followed by Masters and Johnson in 1979, considers sexual orientation on a scale of seven, from an exclusive heterosexual orientation, to an exclusive homosexual orientation, with gradient bisexuality an in-between.

Bisexuality can be considered as either sequential or transitional (from 7, an exclusive homosexual orientation, to 0, an exclusive heterosexual orientation, or vice-versa, and the return to the primary orientation). It is considered "contemporary" when a person has sexual partners of both sexes within the same period of time. According to Berkey, Perelman-Hall, and Kurdek (1990), bisexuality can be serial or concurrent (simultaneous—with sexual intimacy at the same time with both a male and a female partner). These studies are limited in that they define sexual orientation through sexual behaviors.

Other studies refer to the self-identification process (identifying oneself as heterosexual, bisexual, or homosexual).

On the other hand, Klein (1985) considers sexual orientation as a dynamic process including different sexual variables: attraction, behavior, fantasies, emotional preference, self-identification, and lifestyle/affiliation.

Relying on Klein's concepts, Berkey, Perelman-Hall, and Kurdek identified six categories of bisexuality to replace the levels 3, 4, and 5 of Kinsey's scale. These categories are:

1. From an exclusive homosexual orientation to an exclusive heterosexual orientation;
2. From an exclusive heterosexual orientation to an exclusive homosexual orientation;
3. A primary homosexual orientation (frequent homosexual contacts or desires with a few heterosexual contacts or desires);
4. A primary heterosexual orientation (frequent heterosexual contacts or desires with a few homosexual contacts or desires);
5. A shared sexual orientation towards both sexes (desires and contacts are as frequent for both sexes within the same period of time): concurrent bisexuality; and
6. A shared sexual orientation towards both sexes (exclusive homosexual orientation followed by an exclusive heterosexual orientation), or a sequential bisexuality.

All this is rather complex, since homosexuality, following Kinsey and Masters and Johnson, is conceptualized as the opposite of heterosexuality. In this conceptualization, homosexuality and heterosexuality are located on the same scale.

We suggest the representation of this clinical reality is more accurately represented as being on *two different scales*. Accordingly, the opposite of heterosexuality is not homosexuality, but *heterophobia*. Again, the opposite of homosexuality is not heterosexuality, but *homophobia*.

This conceptualization underlines that these two scales exist in all human beings. An individual's heterosexual orientation is not something intangible, but rather a demonstration of his or her position in a given period and environment on these two scales. This conceptualization highlights also a defensive heterosexuality, as a consequence to homophobia.

### The Process, from Unconscious Fantasies to Sexual Intercourse: "Psychosexual Axis"

The source of our sexual life is in unconscious fantasies. They can be of multiple origins and can only be understood through psychoanalysis, psychotherapy, or with regression techniques (hypnoses, rebirth, or meditation). Many of these fantasies stem from childhood erotic experiences or from "first times" (first love, first masturbation, or first sexual contact). Unconscious fantasies vary depending on cultures, since they are compromises between taboos and cultural and religious interdicts.

Finally, some of the fantasies are genetically transmitted archetypes:

1. *Night dreams*: the royal way to the unconscious;
2. *Day dreaming* and *erotic fantasies*: sexual imagery which can be similar or very different from the behavior;
3. *Plans* and *projects*: the rational behind sexuality;
4. *Behaviors*: from thought to action; and
5. *Aptitudes and abilities*: because of its complex and unpredictable nature, sexual intercourse needs a learning, a special attention to the partner and the process, a capacity for adjustment, and creativity; in summary, a sexual intelligence.

### The Duration of Heterosexual Systems

*Monogamy*: The couple is stable at least until the children are fully grown up. Only 1.5% of mammals are monogamous (gibbons and wolves). In human beings, 10% of children are not fathered by the putative father. Social monogamy is facilitated when both parents are necessary for the youths' upbringing, for example, in the case of a premature baby.

*Polygamy* refers to two different situations: *polyandry* (several males for a female) and *polygyny* (a male with several females).

The second situation reflects *promiscuity*, meaning many copulations without real engagement. Out of 854 societies representative of all earth regions, we note 0.5% practice polyandry (in Tibet, the woman marries all the brothers of a same family, one after the other), 55% maintain monogamy, and 44% practice polygyny. In most monogamous societies, polygyny is tolerated.

## 6. Homoerotic, Homosexual, and Bisexual Behaviors

PIERRE DALENS and LAURENT MALTERRE

In recent decades, the evolution of homosexuality in France called for a clear distinction between homosexuality and bisexuality. This distinction requires a definition of these two realities, but first one needs to explore the real meaning of sexual activity.

Sexual activity can be consented if both individuals are not family or biologically related. In homosexuality, both individuals share the same gender. In bisexuality, the object of desire varies, sometimes being the same gender, sometimes being of a different gender. Pleasure is the primary concern, over procreation. However, the emotional and affective aspects play a major role in homosexuality as in bisexuality. In most cases, the homosexual relationship fulfills important affective and emotional needs. There are several degrees between sensoriality and affectivity.

The age of consent for homosexuals is 15 years of age. In 1985, France made it illegal to discriminate against homosexuals. France also prohibits discrimination against homosexuals and lesbians in the workplace. In late 1993, the French government directed insurance companies to accept joint insurance coverage for nonmarried couples.

### A. Homosexuality

Homosexuals are sexually attracted by individuals of the same sex. Some heterosexuals may have this fantasy but will never act on it. The reverse is also true for homosexuals: Some will have heterosexual fantasies but will never act on them. We can distinguish between an actualized homosexuality and a fantasized or latent homosexuality. We also have to consider whether the homosexuality is primary or secondary, or transitory. These concepts are particularly important in adolescence and early adult life, while the individual is still exploring his or her lifestyle and orientation. The partner choice is either homogender or heterogender. In this case, we define a reverse homogenderism as being a gender different from the biological identity. In summary, we consider the affective demonstrations and the sex of the partner, similar or different from the biological sex.

Up to now, no study has shown a neurological imbalance responsible for homosexual orientation. The physiological theories seem to apply only to a small number of individuals with a hormonal imbalance. The vast majority of homosexual behavior would be conditioned by psychosociological factors.

There is no difference between homosexuals and heterosexuals in the sexual response, which denies a genetic origin for homosexuality. The behavioral differences are highlighted in foreplay, being much more varied in homosexual couples than in heterosexual couples, partly explained by a coital preference in heterosexual couples.

## B. Bisexuality

Bisexuality is defined as the capacity to experience erotic feelings and have sexual desire for both sexes, with an uncertainty concerning the actual sexual orientation. Bisexual people act out their dual fantasy (heterosexual and homosexual), depending on the circumstances. The bisexual is clear with his object of desire and his sexual preference, but has ambivalence regarding his sexual orientation.

Ambisexuals or bisexuals emphasize the sexuality rather than the sex of the person. In all these homosexual and bisexual people, there is a triangulation between the object of desire, the desiring subject, and the rival model, which goes back to an unresolved preoedipal conflict. This situation is similar to the heterosexual preoedipal structure. The bisexual is considered incomplete and therefore in search of both the male and female identity, as in androgyny. The threat does not lie in homosexuality, but rather in the loss of gender identity. The bisexual is stuck in an unclear frontier between homosexuality and heterosexuality.

Even if bisexuality is still considered taboo, we should not think of it as being unclear. It is a variation in sexuality, not necessarily socially accepted, but at least more common or usual than in previous times.

Although fragile, this homeostasis possesses its own specificity, and should not be submitted to repressive and normative models, as other aspects of human sexuality were.

This homeostasis suggests a fragile equilibrium for bisexuals through their erotic investment in both sexes. Erotic is here taken in its global meaning, such as what brings two individuals together in terms of affects, emotions, senses, and the mind. It is not specifically limited to the sexual aspect. There are passages from the heterosexual states to the homosexual states. A state can be overly invested in bisexuality when there is a cleavage between the "archaic," the impulse and the senses, and, on the other hand, the affects, the emotions, and the mind. Bisexual maturity is attained when the individual recognizes his or her dual desire for same-sex and opposite-sex people, while considering the specificity of each relationship in terms of eroticism, affects, and emotions. This is why we believe that the term "bi" should be carefully used and defined in terms of the unique nature of each love story.

Bisexuality can take many faces. When an individual has difficulty acknowledging his dual desire, it will evolve in an interior battle. When a married person is sexually attracted to same-sex people, then feelings of guilt and shame through this experience may threaten his or her heterosexual identity, to the extent of unsettling couple relationships and family unity.

- It may be expressed in the avoidance of ambiguous behaviors and attitudes in a search for normalcy, which leads the individual to shut himself out with his suffering.
- It may be a married man living his secret life as a homosexual with difficulty.
- It may be a heterosexual man who constantly denies his sexual fantasies of being anally penetrated.
- It may be a man who considers himself homosexual and who relives his first love and sexual experience with a woman. The sensations and erotic codification are new and surprise him. Touches, contacts, odors, glow, and body forms are to be rediscovered. In this case, it is a bisexual identity hiding a strong homosexual orientation.
- It may be a love and affection between men and between women which brings them to question their identity.

They feel a psychological dissociation and ask themselves: "Who am I?"

- Finally, it may be this man or this woman who has no real desire for either sex, sometimes seducing males, sometimes females, questioning where his or her actual desire lies.
- It may also be the man experiencing repeated failures with women, who question his male condition and, consequently, his sexual desire and sexual normalcy.

## C. Sociological Aspects

The sociological aspects of homosexuality are worth studying because of the high incidence of HIV, the suicide rate among teenagers, and in the first years of active sexual life, the search for relational stability among homosexual couples. In France, a national cooperative of homosexual and bisexual associations, PACS (Pacte Civil de Solidarité), is major resource both for researchers and for individuals with a homosexual or bisexual orientation seeking to discover and eventually achieve a more stable orientation.

Since the sexual liberation movement in the 1970s, new lifestyles have emerged, which have led the French to rethink their identity again in building their community. This has given birth to the craziest [*sic*] and most-varied homosexual associations, the adoption of health issues as their own concerns—as in the battle against HIV, the emergence of a gay culture with its own novels, magazines, critiques, and studies, its goods, clothes, and underclothing specific to the gay community, the Techno music, and a rainbow flag. PACS: the Pacte Civil de Solidarité, coupled with a new gay ideology, has led the fight against the discriminations the homosexual community has always been victim of. The gay liberation movement asks for civil rights: In 1998, the rights of homosexual couples were fully recognized in terms of social rights, lodging, and fiscal matters.

However, this gay liberation movement has not enabled the gay community to be freed from its provocative myths and visibility concerns, since it is so worried about being assimilated by the heterosexual majority. There was a risk of being caught in a cultural ghetto, with no freedom concerning behaviors and discourse. The gay community does not consider the plurality of homosexuality, where some individuals are bisexual and others previously married. Bisexuality is not well-represented in French society, having only one association called BI. Thus, bisexuals are far from being seen and heard. The bisexual community runs the risk of repeating the same mistakes the gay community has made, namely to consider the group rather than the individual. In reality, each individual has to construct his own identity with his own sexual specificity.

## 7. Gender Diversity and Transgender Issues

PIERRE DALENS and LAURENT MALTERRE

The roots of ambiguity in the sexes can be found in organic or psychological problems, which lead to transgenderism or intersexuality.

## A. Intersexuality

The morphological division between the sexes may cause certain dysmorphological states: the intersexual states caused by problems in the biology of embryogenesis. Such pathologies are infrequent.

The intersexual pathologies are a type of organic pathology and show some dysfunction in the neurological and hormonal systems. In the embryological development of human sexuality, there could be dissonance between the biological sex and the physical appearance of the person.

There also exist other undifferentiated states. All these syndromes prevent an appropriate genital functioning. A real hermaphroditism, being male and female, does not exist.

More frequently, there are difficulties in the process of gender development, and sometimes to the extreme of transsexualism.

## B. Transsexualism

We define transsexualism as follows: The irresistible need for an individual to belong to the opposite sex, totally convinced that there was a mistake with his or her biological sex. Contrary to the transvestite, the transsexual is not sexually aroused by dressing up in the opposite-sex clothing. He is looking for a real sensorial and sexual transformation. The transsexual looks for a change in his morphological sex.

Transsexualism also includes individuals whose gender identity and sexual expression are unfixed and go beyond dual representation of male and female identity.

## C. Transgenderism

This category includes transgender and transvestite behaviors, either in a social way or in a fetishistic way, or in a search for physical comfort. There also exists some transgender individuals who have both male and female characteristics (androgyny), in order to feel comfortable. There are marked differences between transvestites, androgyns, and non-operated transsexuals. The latter live their life in the opposite gender identity without undergoing the sexual operation. On the other end of the continuum are the operated transsexuals who can only live their gender identity by undergoing the sexual surgery.

Gender dimorphism exists when a person experiences too few specific traits of an individual similar to his sex or too many specific traits similar to the opposite sex. There is then a dissonance between the body and the sociocultural realities. This amounts to a disturbance in the gender evolution. Only a few cases of transsexualism are what we would call "primary," unaffected from birth by the parents or society. Most transsexuals are secondary, from the age of 4, according to Stoller. This would often have to do with the mother's regret in not having a child of the opposite sex. The mother is most often the one to trigger the transvestitism. Slowly, the personality structures and the behaviors become seriously affected. This is when the fantasy evolution leads to the surgery, following predetermined steps ruled by the psychiatric norms in France. It is not possible to set a standard procedure, because each case is different.

With the male-to-female transsexual, one needs to consider the emphasis put on the female attributes and the return to an archaic androgyny. The mother-son relationship excludes any sexuality, but includes an asexual intimacy. This explains the low level of heterosexual desire for some operated transsexuals. On the other hand, female transsexualism has different motivations for the daughter. It may be that the female-to-male transsexual considers the male role to be more glorious?

Transsexualism is, therefore, an experimentation of personal identity and of relational and sexual psychology.

## D. Psychosociology

In French society, the transsexual's request to be considered according to his psychological identity and his gender identity, is often considered foolish, since we categorize individuals according to their biological sex. For the transsexual, the individual's gender identity should be given more importance than the biological factors. His discourse resembles the violence he is ready to endure in order to be castrated and, therefore, become incapable of experiencing pleasure. He claims there is a dissonance between his body and spirit. This raises the question of which should be given primacy: the anatomical sex or the gender identity. In the name of making men and women equal, can we transform a man into a woman and a woman into a man? Is sex a legal matter? In terms of achieving equality, do we give priority to sexual differentiation, or to gender differentiation?

In France, an estimated one in 5,000 is a transsexual. These numbers do not include the castrated and the eunuchs who have their own specific identity. The transsexual is totally convinced that he belongs to the opposite sex and not to his own sex. He or she asks for sex reassignment. There are other cases where people are uncomfortable with their social status and claim the social recognition of their psychosocial sex. In 1992, the European Court in Strasbourg said that it was an invasion of the private life to deny the right for sex change in civil matters. This modification of the sexes in civil matters has to be sorted out and evaluated by psychiatric expertise, which takes three years in France. The purpose is to establish whether it is a paranoid psychosis or a primary transsexualism. Statute law remains perverse, since it obliges a transsexual to undergo the sex surgery even if they do not want to have surgery in the first place. A transsexual does not need to be castrated to belong to the opposite sex; the clothing and the social appearance may satisfy their wish to be considered one of the opposite sex.

All this contributes to the emergence of a new conceptualization: the queers, the drags, and the transvestites are in a transhomosexuality, meaning that they go beyond global expressions of homosexuality. This new conceptualization avoids the bi-categorization, the dichotomizing, which leads to stress in many individuals who do not fit in. This is why it remains important to consider each case as different and deal with it according to its specificity. We should remember that etymologically, sex in Latin is *secare*, meaning "cut in two." This "sex-tion" pushes the individual to search for the other part of his missing "self." This search allows him to be in touch with his sex and the emergence of his desire in his quest for the other, for the encounter, and eventually, for the relationship.

## 8. Significant Unconventional Sexual Behaviors

FRANCE PARAMELLE

### Introduction

This section is a review of the different sexual infractions as described in the French criminal code.

France has experienced a significant increase in the charges of sexual assaults. Also, there has been an increase in the severity of the sentences that take into consideration the actual facts of the sexual assault reported, its circumstances, and the victim's state of being. There has also been an improvement for the victims of sexual crimes. Youths under the age of 18 are now protected by legislation, even within their family. Also, the rights of both men and women are given more consideration. The procedure of reporting and prosecuting is also facilitated by the sensitization of the police forces to the victims and the accusations made. Victims now play an active role throughout the whole procedure. If they wish to, they can assist in the whole procedure and make appeals concerning certain facts. They can also benefit from psychological support throughout the whole procedure. Indemnification funds have also been made available.

Even though all these measures may help the victims, the associations for victims' defense find these efforts insufficient. They state that most victims will not make accusations, in part because of all the media publicity around such cases, and also because they fear the offender will take revenge. Representatives of victims' support associations can attend the court with the victims if they wish to.

The court and jury are also preoccupied by the presumption of innocence. Because a person is considered innocent until proven guilty, the defense rights of the accused have also been amplified.

## A. Coercive Sex

Sexual aggression, in general, is defined in French law as every sexual attempt committed with the use of violence, force, threat, or surprise. French law makes a distinction between sexual aggressions with or without penetration. A second distinction is the adult or minor status of the victim. A subdistinction is made for a minor victim under age 18 and a minor under age 15, either of which is considered as an aggravating factor.

### Crimes Against Minors

*Child Sexual Abuse.* The corruption or sexual abuse of a minor occurs when the minor is induced to participate in "obscene acts." This definition does not include the seduction of a minor for the adult's satisfaction.

Article 227-22 deals with corruption acts towards minors under 15 years old. Whether or not the youth was corrupted before does not affect or cancel the accusation. The perpetrator cannot evoke the unawareness of the victim's age, unless he demonstrates his non-responsibility for this mistake. This crime is not necessarily related to monetary issues; the matter is considered to be a crime whether or not money exchanged hands. Criminal intent is the criterion for this offense, as the following examples illustrate:

- A woman who commits obscene acts in front of a minor girl to introduce her into the prostitution milieu.
- An adult or many adults who engage in sexual activity in front of children in order to initiate them.

Whether this happened once or many times, this offense is punishable by a sentence of 5 years in jail and a 500,000-franc fine. The following aggravating circumstances lead to a 7-year jail sentence and a 700,000-franc fine:

- The author met his victim by telephone or the Internet.
- The crime was committed in an educational establishment or in its surroundings.

The corruption attempt is also punishable. The corruption offense is different from the crime of sexual aggression and from attempted sexual aggression.

*Pedophilic Pornography and Minors.* Article 227-23, adopted June 17, 1998, addresses the recording and transmission of pornographic images of a minor. The transmission can be done in a variety of ways. Importing or exporting such images is punishable in the same way as the actual production or transmission of pornographic images involving minors.

Normally, the penalty is a 3-year jail sentence and a 300,000-franc fine. The use of a telecommunication network used by the general population to transmit the juvenile pornographic images is an aggravating circumstance calling for a 5-year jail sentence and a 500,000-franc fine. Unfortunately, this does not prevent the transmission through videotapes or the Internet, which in terms of statistics, represent real traffic.

*Messages Not Permitted for Viewing by Minors.* Article 227-24 concerns the fabrication, transport, and transmission of a violent or pornographic message, which can lessen human dignity when viewed by a minor. The sentence is 3 years in jail and a 500,000-franc fine. An example of this offense would be posting a violent or pornographic message without any precaution to keep a minor from seeing it. The analysis of the message and of its criminal character is judged by the court, which will apply the statute based on the mores and opinion of the time. Messages supporting sexual contacts between adults and minors are incriminating.

*Sexual Attempts on Minors.* This offense relates to the 1998 law and Article 227-25 of the criminal code. It applies to an adult who attempts to engage in sexual activity with a minor of 15 years old without the use of violence, force, threat, or surprise. The sentence is more severe than what it used to be. Currently, the penalty is a 5-year jail sentence and a 500,000-franc fine. This article also punishes any accomplice, including a person who introduces a minor to an adult perpetrator. Again, the unawareness of the victim's age is not excusable, unless the author demonstrates he is not responsible for this mistake.

Aggravating circumstances are detailed by Article 227-26 as follows:

- The perpetrator is a relative or an authority figure.
- The perpetrator abused authority given by his professional functions.
- The act was committed by a group of people, authors, and accomplices.
- The act involves a monetary payment, in which case the sentence is 10 years in jail and a 1,000,000-franc fine.
- The author met his victim by a telecommunication network for the general population (e.g., the Internet). The same aggravating sentence just mentioned applies here also.
- The same text of law is applied to minors of more than 15 years of age who are not married. The sentence is 2 years in jail and a 200,000-franc fine in the following cases:
  - The perpetrator is a relative or an authority figure.
  - The perpetrator abused the authority given by his professional functions.

The notion of authority is considered essential by the law and underlines the vulnerability of the victim.

### Sexual Aggression and Rape

*Sexual Aggression Without Penetration.* Article 222-22 of the criminal code covers nonpenetrative sexual aggression. The law penalizes the aggression against another person and not the sexuality in itself. The facts represent a sexual action on a person, without her consent. The perpetrator can surprise his victim in order to have a sexual contact with her, without her consent and without penetration. This article also applies when committed by a French citizen in another country, according to a law enacted June 17, 1998.

The penalties for conviction are 15 years in jail plus a 500,000-franc fine. A more severe sentence can be imposed in the following circumstances:

- There were injuries or lesions.
- The perpetrator was a relative or an authority figure.
- The perpetrator abused the authority associated with his professional functions/status.
- The act was committed by a group of people, both leaders and accomplices.
- When a weapon or the threat of a weapon was used.
- When the victim met the perpetrator by a telecommunication network for the general population (e.g., the Internet).

These aggravating circumstances stipulated in the Article 222-28 call for a jail sentence of 7 years plus a 700,000-franc fine. The law also considers the vulnerability of the victim when the victim is under age 18 or under age 15. Vulnerability may also be a factor when the perpetrator knows or should suspect the victim's old age, obvious sickness, physical or psychological disabilities, infirmity, or pregnancy. In these circumstanced, the sentence is also 7 years of jail and a 700,000-franc fine (Article 222-29).

Article 222-30 of the criminal code states a 10-year jail sentence and a 1,000,000-franc fine when the aggression is committed on victims described in the Article 222-28:

- Resulted in physical injuries or lesions.
- The perpetrator is a relative or an authority figure.
- The perpetrator abused of the authority given by his professional functions.
- The act was committed by a group of people: initiators and accomplices.
- When a weapon or the threat of a weapon was used.

The attempted sexual aggressions corresponding to Articles 222-27 to 222-30 are all sentenced the same.

Of interest for doctors, especially gynecologists, is a 1997 case in which a doctor was sentenced for having sexually caressed a female patient during a medical exam. The court stated that the accusation was true for two reasons: It was admitted by the doctor since he did not appeal, and the victim's friends testified they heard her scream "no" many times while they were in the waiting room. This example should lead doctors to adopt a rigorous code of ethics to prevent false accusations from being made.

*Rape (Sexual Aggression with Penetration)*

The definition of rape, or sexual aggression with penetration (Article 222-2), is very important. Technically, this act involves any act of sexual penetration, of any nature, committed on another person with the use of violence, force, threat, or surprise. In the simplest terms, rape is any act of sexual penetration involving the vagina, mouth, or anus. "On another person" implies either a man or a woman. Oral penetration is considered a rape by the law, whether the person submitted or was forced to act. The act of penetration can be performed with the penis, the fingers, the tongue, or an object with a sexual connotation, for example, a vibrator or a stick, as long as it has a sexual connotation. For example, the statute law recognized as rape a penetration performed with a stick with a condom on its extremity. If the stick had been used alone, it would have been qualified as an act of torture or barbarism.

The absence of consent is essential. The following situations have been stated as non-consenting:

- The victim was paralyzed by fear and could not escape or run away.
- The mental state of the victim (depression) led to the same consequences.
- The victim was under the authority of the perpetrator, in a state of vulnerability.
- An employer was sentenced for having raped a female employee known as timid and inhibited.
- Another example would be the vulnerability of a patient facing her doctor, during a medical exam, or in relation to a nurse in a hospital.

The law also accepts the reality of marital rape, as long as it can be demonstrated that force and coercion were part of the act. For rape, the intention of the perpetrator is a crucial element. The accused can be acquitted if he has mistaken the victim's intentions. On the other hand, statute law recognizes paralyzing fear and neurotic state as possible reactions for the victim, which enable her to express her non-consent.

Attempted rape is also considered. An "attempt" is usually defined as the intending and trying to force someone into a sexual act or to assault someone in a sexual way. Article 121-5, states: "The attempt is considered as is when in the process of execution, an act was stopped or enabled because of independent circumstances of its author." For example, an attempted rape exists when the perpetrator, after he had put on a condom, tried to penetrate his victim and only a momentary erectile deficit led him to give up on his project. The judges stated that the beginning of execution and the non-voluntary desistance justified an accusation of attempted rape.

The punishment for the rape crime is 30 years in jail when the victim dies following the aggression. Article 222-26: The rape crime brings a life sentence when torture or barbarian acts were committed before or during the rape. The torture and barbarism are defined as exceptionally severe acts, which led to severe suffering or pain. The acts also have a moral component: a wish to deny the human dignity within the victim. For example, the statute law named as barbarism forcing a victim to have penetration with a dog.

## B. Prostitution, Pimping, and Procuring

Prostitution, defined as having physical contacts to satisfy someone else's sexual needs in return for financial payment, is not a legal offense in France, but procuring for prostitution or benefiting from it is a crime. A prostitute is the only person who can benefit from her business transactions. She cannot use her earnings to purchase food or residence for her husband, children, or anyone beside herself. If she does, the beneficiaries of her trade can be prosecuted for procuring. Prostitutes are not allowed to solicit on a public highway. This tolerance accounts for many problems, such as the traffic of human beings, especially minors.

Article 225-5 deals with procuring or pimping (proxenetism). This applies to the action taken by anyone, in any way,

- To help, assist, or protect a person who is engaging in prostitution.
- To make money from the prostitution of a person, to share the benefits of it, or to receive subsides from a person practicing prostitution.
- To hire, lead, or pressure a person to prostitute herself.

Proxenetism carries a sentence of 5 years in jail and a 1,000,000-franc fine.

Article 225-6 deals with proxenetism and designates similar punishments. It covers the action of anyone, in any way,

- Who panders between the person who prostitutes herself and the person who pays for the prostitution.
- Who helps to pander to justify fictive resources.
- Who is unable to justify resources concerning one's lifestyle, while living with a person who practices prostitution, or to be in relation with people living by prostitution.

This includes an unemployed married man who maintains his lifestyle with money his wife gets from prostituting herself. It also applies to someone who rents a room for someone who does prostitution or who acts as the pander, even if not paid.

Article 225-7: Conviction for proxenetism carries a sentence of 10 years in jail and a 10,000,000-franc fine when the criminal activity is committed:

1. With a minor.
2. With a particularly vulnerable person in terms of age, physical or psychological disabilities, sickness, infirmity, or pregnancy.
3. With many people.
4. With a person who was recruited for prostitution outside France or before her arrival to France.
5. By a relative or an authority figure of the person, or someone who abuses the authority given by his professional functions.
6. By a person whose mandate is to fight against prostitution, protect public health, or maintain public order.

7. By a person carrying a weapon.
8. By the use of force, violence, or physical injuries.
9. By many people acting as authors or accomplices, without being members of an organization.
10. By the transmission of messages through telecommunication networks used by the general population (e.g., the Internet).

Article 225-8: The penalties for proxenetism described in Article 225-7 above increases to 20 years in prison and a 20,000,000-franc fine when committed within an organization. Article 225-9: The proxenetism committed with torture or barbarism carries a life sentence and a 30,000,000-franc fine.

Article 225-10 provides a sentence of 10 years in jail and a 5,000,000-franc fine for a person who, directly or with the help of someone else:

1. Owns, manages, exploits, or finances an establishment for prostitution.
2. Owns, manages, exploits, or finances a public establishment, while accepting or tolerating one or many people to prostitute or search for clients within the establishment.
3. Sells or rents rooms not used by the general population, knowing they will serve for prostitution

Article 225-11 provides similar punishment for a person who attempts to commit crimes related to proxenetism. Article 225-12 states that moral persons can be found criminally responsible for offenses described in Articles 225-5 to 225-10.

The laws against proxenetism are severe and aim to fight the Mafia traffic quite common in France and its territories. In practical terms, the owner of residential apartments can be charged with proxenetism if he rents to people without knowing they will do prostitution, and does not report this activity to the police or take action to stop the criminal activities when he becomes aware of them.

*Conclusion*

French legislation is concerned with the protection of minors, vulnerable persons, and the dignity of human beings. Laws are enacted to maintain public order and to protect the victims of pedophilia, pornography, and proxenetism. The fight against organizations behind these crimes is not easy and requires specific training of police forces and collaboration between different state agencies. Ignorance of the law is not an excuse in the eyes of the French law.

Article 122-1 mentions some causes for non-responsibility or diminished responsibility. The person who is affected by psychological or neuropsychological trouble, which would interfere with her judgment while engaged in a crime described in the above articles, is not criminally responsible. Such a person will still be sentenced, although her disability will be considered when the sentencing occurs.

For recidivists in sexual offenses, therapy can be suggested and will have a positive impact on the sentence. The psychiatrist can advise, but the accused remains free to accept or refuse the treatment. The psychiatrist will also judge the accused's responsibility in his actions.

### C. Pornography

[*Update 2003*: The legal age for viewing pornography in France is age 18. (Reekie 1994) (*End of update by the Editors*)]

### D. Exhibitionism and Sexual Harassment

*Exhibitionism*

Article 222-32 defines exhibitionism as the exposure of the sexual parts to a non-consenting person in a public place or an area which can be seen by other people. Sexual acts can be committed in public and private places. An example of a public place would be a sauna accessible to all after payment of an entry fee. An example of a private place would be a hotel room where the door was not completely closed, but half-opened so anybody could come in.

Harcélement *(Sexual Harassment)*

This law was enacted in 1998 and defines harassment of another person as ordering, threatening, forcing, or severely pressuring in order to obtain sexual gratification, by a person who abuses the authority given by his professional functions. Conviction carries a 1-year jail sentence and a 100,000-franc fine.

## 9. Contraception, Abortion, and Population Planning

### A. Contraception

[*Update 2003*: In 1993, France reduced the price of condoms to encourage young people to use them. More than two thirds of French women take the hormonal birth control pill. In 1996, the French Roman Catholic bishops broke with Vatican directives and approved the use of condoms to help reduce the spread of the HIV virus (Caron 1998). (*End of update by the Editors*)]

### B. Minors and the Availability of Free Morning-After Pills

[*Update 2003*: In November 2000, the French Parliament enacted a new law that allows school nurses to distribute the morning-after pill in junior and senior high schools. As of 2002, French pharmacists were authorized to provide teenage girls with RU-486 (mifepristone), the "morning-after contraception pill," free and without a prescription or parental authorization. In a decree published in the *Official Journal*, the government required that pharmacists speak briefly with the young women before giving them the pill to make sure they are using it correctly and in the right time frame. All girls under age 18 are eligible for the free pills. The pill is taken within 72 hours following intercourse and prevents pregnancy by blocking the implantation of a fertilized egg in the uterus. The government journal said pharmacists who distribute the pill should offer advice about regular birth control and encourage women to see a doctor regularly. (*End of update by the Editors*)]

### C. Abortion

[*Update 2003*: Abortion until the 10th week of pregnancy has been legal in France since 1979 and the cost of abortion is covered by national healthcare insurance. Parental consent is required for unmarried minors. In the early 1980s, Roussel Uclaf, a leading French pharmaceutical company, researched and marketed RU-486 (mifepristone), also known as "the morning-after pill." One in six of all abortions in France are performed with RU-486. Each year, more than 2,000 French women go to England for an abortion, many of them because they have passed the time limit for abortion in France (Henshaw 1996). (*End of update by the Editors*)]

## 10. Sexually Transmitted Diseases and HIV/AIDS

### A. Sexually Transmitted Diseases

No information given.

### B. HIV/AIDS

[*Update 2002*: UNAIDS Epidemiological Assessment: AIDS surveillance: A significant decline in AIDS-case incidence has been reported since 1996, primarily because of the wide-scale introduction of HAART, the anti-viral cocktail. Since 1998, the decrease in new AIDS cases has continued, although at a slower rate, among homo-/bisexual men and injection drug users. However, the decrease is no longer apparent among cases attributed to heterosexual contact. The stability of the heterosexual group is explained by an increase of AIDS cases among foreigners, especially among persons coming from sub-Saharan African countries who relocate mostly in the Paris area. More than 75% of AIDS cases diagnosed actually could have possibly been delayed or prevented by testing or access to treatment for those aware of their HIV-positive serostatus. Persons infected by heterosexual contact are more represented among AIDS cases resulting from a lack of access to care, more than a third of them originating from sub-Saharan countries.

[HIV testing: A national HIV reporting system has not been set up in France yet. Despite a stabilization of the HIV-screening activity in free and anonymous testing sites since 1995, the number of HIV-positive diagnoses has increased since 1998 among men and women in Paris. This increase concerns especially persons originating from sub-Saharan countries infected by heterosexual contacts. Other indicators give evidence of a relapse in behaviors in recent years. An increase in gonorrhea has been observed since 1998 through a national laboratory surveillance network. The number of syphilis cases increased in 2000 in Paris among gay men, half of whom were HIV-positive. The results of the study carried out in 2000 in gay venues in Paris show a high level of risky behavior; 30% of respondents with casual partners had unprotected anal sex with them. Several nationwide surveys among injection drug users, including a study carried out in 1997 and 1999 in over 1,000 social and medical centers specializing in the care of injection drug users, consistently found levels of prevalence in the range of 15% to 20%. These surveys were based on self-reported HIV status.

[The estimated number of adults and children living with HIV/AIDS on January 1, 2002, were:

| | | |
|---|---|---|
| Adults ages 15-49: | 100,000 | (rate: 0.3%) |
| Women ages 15-49: | 27,000 | |
| Children ages 0-15: | 1,000 | |

[An estimated 800 adults and children died of AIDS during 2001.

[No estimate is available for the number of French children who had lost one or both parents to AIDS and were under age 15 at the end of 2001. (*End of update by the Editors*)]

## 11. Sexual Dysfunctions, Counseling, and Therapies

ROBERT GELLMAN and CLAIRE GELLMAN-BARROUX

### A. Amourology Group Psychotherapy

SERGE GINGER and MICHEL MEIGNANT

*Methodology*

Amourology is meant to give support to individuals and couples who are searching for love and happiness. The main aim is to increase one's capacity for love, in order to reach a properly adequate level. It is a group process, with individual sessions in between the group sessions. There must be at least one individual session between every two group sessions, sometimes more, depending on the desire of the person, the clinical needs, or the hazards of life (a breakup, a death, an accident, or professional problems).

Amourology, according to Wolberg's definition, is: "a treatment in which emotional problems are dealt with thanks to psychological means. During this treatment, an experienced person has a professional relationship with a patient in order to suppress, change or diminish certain existing symptoms, alter disturbed behaviors; and encourage positive growth and the blossoming of personality."

A child naturally discovers the whole range of feelings in his family. Amourology incorporates this obvious aspect of the human condition into the context of group therapy, and thus offers many possibilities for experimentation.

*The Psychotherapists*

The therapeutic team is composed of:

• Two Amourologists. The referent psychotherapists are in charge of half the group, a male psychotherapist with male clients in the group, while the female therapist works with the female clients in the group.
• Two other Amourologists, who offer couple psychotherapy, run the couples groups and give personal sessions between the group sessions to people who come as a couple. Once a year, during the 9-day summer seminar, they run the practice of behaviorist exercises from the Masters and Johnson method. This practice is offered only to people who come for couple therapy.
• a person trained in the Milton Trager method.
• a psychotherapist specialized in creative methods. This practice is offered to individuals during the summer seminar, while couples are doing Masters and Johnson behavior-talk therapy.
• Trainee psychotherapists who come to work as assistants.

*The Therapeutic Context*

Each therapisand (client) signs, before the therapists and the whole group, a contract by which he or she commits him- or herself:

1. To participate in all the workshops programmed for the group:
   • Seven 24-hour weekends that take place in a venue equipped with a 32°C swimming pool for mind-body work.
   • Three 3-day groups: "Becoming a Man, Becoming a Woman, Becoming a Couple," during which couples work in a couples group and individuals work in a male or female unisex group.
   • A 3-day group for sexual education, with films from the National Sex Forum of San Francisco.
   • A 9-day seminar, which offers practice of the Masters and Johnson behavioral therapies for couples, creative and audiovisual work for individuals, and Trager Work for all.
   • A 6-day ecological workshop, experienced individually on one of two themes: "The humanist sea" and "The humanist island."
   • For couples only, on top of the individual ecological workshop, a 4-day workshop titled "The couple's humanist island."
   • A Christmas weekend retreat.
   • Two 8-hour groups of Trager Work, experienced individually.
2. To participate in evening workshops from 6:30 p.m. to 8 p.m. every week, if the clients live in the Paris area and can free themselves to come.
3. To have at least one individual session between each weekend workshop.

The clients or therapisands also commit themselves:

• not to see each other or write to each other or phone each other in between workshops.
• not to have erotic games or sexual intercourse during the workshops.

• not to drink alcohol during the workshops, and not to smoke inside the rooms or on the boats.

The first two restrictions naturally do not apply to people who come for couple therapy. The length of the therapy is not predetermined. It can vary from a few weekends to several years.

### The Therapists

Currently, there are about 50 trained Amourology therapists, roughly about 25 male and 25 female. They are between ages 18 and 70, come from 15 different countries, and belong to various races and religions. Most of them are heterosexuals, but there are some homosexuals. More than half of the group consists of people who work as couple therapists.

### The Therapeutic Methods Used

Amourology uses a variety of therapeutic modalities:

• Sexologic.
• Behaviorist (Masters and Johnson method).
• Analytical, based on Jungian as well as Freudian concepts.
• Humanist (using concepts and practices that belong to humanistic psychology: gestalt, bioenergy, and koula)
• Mind-body therapy (the Milton Trager method, sensitive massage, and work in swimming pools).
• Music therapy, using operas by Mozart, but also by Rossini, Verdi, and Offenbach, and Celtic and other kinds of music.
• Self-fulfilling (dance, creativity, music, and singing).
• Audiovisual. Each year, the therapisands see more than 20 feature films and around 10 short films. The therapisands are filmed during the ecological workshops, while they explore the Ponant Islands (Hoëdic, Houat, Belle Ile en Mer, and Groix), the Bay of Quiberon, and the Gulf of Morbihan.

All workshops are residential: They take place either in a seminar center or on a camping site. A lot of the work is actually done during the breaks, the meals, and by the very fact of living together 24 hours a day during the ecological workshops.

### The Trager Work

In 1975 and 1978, a group of 50 French participants attended to training session in California that consisted of:

• a video-gestalt-therapy workshop with Barry Goodfield in San Francisco.
• a Sexual Attitude Restructuring (SAR) workshop at the National Sex Forum, San Francisco.
• a bioenergy workshop with Alan Schwartz or a gestalt workshop with Betty Fuller at the Esalen Institute, Big Sur.
• a sensitive Californian massage workshop and an erotic massage workshop with Margaret Elke in her La Fayette Institute.

During the 1978 workshop at the Esalen Institute, California, Betty Fuller introduced us to the Trager Work, a very specific massage that integrates transcendental meditation. The massage is not at all erotic; however, it does bring the therapisand (client) to a delicious and tender regressive state. When practiced in a group, it is a gift to the giver as well as to the receiver. It is a way of differentiating need and desire. Eroticization is one of the major drawbacks of sensitive massage in the context of a group where sexual intercourse between the therapisands is forbidden. The Trager Work is a solution for the eroticization-frustration dilemma.

After a 1979 meeting in Hawaii, Milton Trager accepted an invitation to give two training sessions in France. A few years ago, a Trager Work school was created in France.

### The Amourology Workshop Cycle

This therapeutic regime includes:

1. *Residential weekends for groups*: In the early years, the therapeutic process consisted of one marathon weekend of 24 hours each month, with nothing in between. These weekends, therefore, constituted the core of the work. During this weekend, we offer an experience in hot water, adapted from Big Sur in California, where the mind-body work takes place in the natural 40°C hot springs of the Indian tribe of Esalen. This work can be regressive, but is most of the time playful and based on tenderness and relaxation. There is no erotic induction. Music that supports emotions or encourages dancing is also used. A general feature film is used as a basis for analytical group psychotherapy, not to debate the film, but to become conscious of one's emotions and identifications in viewing it. Each participant studies his own reactions, compares them with others', especially with the reactions of participants of the other-sex participants.

   Now that other workshops have been incorporated in the process, there are only seven of these weekend workshops, evenly distributed throughout the year. They take place at a venue where we have a 32°C hot water swimming pool for the mind-body work and that is close to a cinema complex for showing films.

2. *"Becoming a Man, Becoming a Woman, Becoming a Couple" workshops*. In these 3-day workshops, offered three times a year, couples work in a couples group and individuals work in unisex groups of men or women. Everyone has the opportunity to experience the Trager method in a group. A feature film or a documentary is shown each night and used as a basis for therapy. Working in unisex groups gives the therapisands the opportunity to express their feelings even more freely, without the fear of hurting or embarrassing someone.

3. *A Sexual Attitude Reassessment/Restructuring (SAR) workshop*. These 3-day sexual education workshops use films from the National Sex Forum of San Francisco, that are sexually explicit and educational but not pornographic. After seeing the film, there is a group discussion in which clients explore their emotional reactions and responses to the films.

4. *A July workshop*. This 9-day workshop enables participants to work with the Masters and Johnson method and with the Trager Work. Each night, a feature film is used as a basis for therapy work. It is the most powerful workshop in the process, mainly because of its length. Regression is more intense, and watching many films on the same topic reinforces the impact of the films. Sometimes films by Marcel Pagnol or Ingmar Bergman, and operas by Mozart, Verdi, or Rossini are used in the visual mix.

5. *A 4-day individual workshop* designed for individuals who choose to do both "the humanist sea" and "the humanist island" experiences.

6. *The Christmas workshop*, just before the New Year, involves working on giving with a spiritual therapeutic experience, a Celtic music concert, a conference on Buddhism, a meeting with a Tibetan monk, and a Christmas liturgy with a Dominican monk. Each participant has the opportunity to express his beliefs. This workshop takes the form of a party, and people can share their culinary skills cooking for a 'Christmas eve' supper.

7. *Evening workshops* are offered for therapisands who live in the Paris area. The workshop consists of a group talk preceded by 20 minutes of listening to Mozart.

8. *Individual and couple sessions* in between groups consist of face-to-face talk without mind/body work:
   • at least one individual session with the referent Amourologist between two workshops. Often the therapisands choose to have a weekly session.
   • each couple has at least one meeting with the couple Amourologists between the big groups they attend together.

*The Humanist Sea* was the first ecological workshop we created, but clients have the option between sailing and the "Humanist Island" experience, which takes place on Hoëdic Island, in Brittany, off the northwest coast of France. The Humanist Sea actively brings nature into the therapeutic process. In the past 20 years, we have offered the sea experience 36 times. Absolute priority is given to safety, with professional staff from the Cruising Training Centre (CFC) based in La Trinité-sur-Mer (Morbihan).

The workshop lasts for 6 days, during which the therapisands sleep and eat on board the ships. They form teams of 5 to 8 people, according to the size of the boat. A skipper chosen among the therapisands is in charge of each boat and all theripsands have their functions. The rocking of the sea invites deep sleep and is favorable to dreaming. The therapisand writes down his dreams in a personal notebook for later discussion and analysis.

Specific rules and safeguards have been developed to protect and enhance the therapeutic process.

• The therapists never sail in the same boat as the therapisands (clients).
• The sailing instructors have as little contact as possible with the therapisands. They only see each other for the sailing lessons and when boats are under sail. We ask the instructors to stay away from the therapisands during free time and meals or evenings. The instructors live on the staff boat, with the therapists.
• During times in port, the therapists themselves try to put some distance between them and the instructors. This is done by sleeping on shore as often as possible and by avoiding dining with the instructors. This ensures that each person's specific professional attributes and identity remain clear.
• The analytical work is done in small discussion groups. For example, if the fleet is composed of four boats hosting five therapisands each, two small groups of 10 are created and they meet in one of the boats under the supervision of one psychotherapist. This short working time is sufficient. It can be used to do analytical group therapy, or to work on life on board. It might deal with relational problems that have emerged because of living together, or it could be about maneuvers necessary to navigation.
• During the cruises, each therapisand has a notebook that provides a double record of dreams and impressions. The therapisand keeps the original and gives the copy to the psychotherapist, who can then follow the therapeutic process of each person.

The sun, the sea, the rain, the swell, the beauty of the landscapes, the call of the birds, meeting dolphins, the friendship, all this creates the context for an unforgettable psychological and therapeutic experience.

*The Humanist Island*. This workshop takes place on a small Ponant Island, the Island of Hoëdic (which means duckling in Breton). It is two and half kilometers (1.55 mi.) long and one kilometer (0.62 mi.) wide. There are about 100 inhabitants. The workshop lasts 6 days, including the 8-hour travel from Paris. Hoëdic is a bit like the end of the world. The therapisands' camp has *gîtes* (simple shelters) in which to cook, wash, and get warm if the weather is bad. The sea is always present, in the minds as well as in the activities. The therapisands are in small groups with a leader and someone responsible for supplies in each *gîte*. Those who do not want to camp out can have a bed in a room of a *gîte*.

## Conclusion

Amourology is one of several therapeutic modalities born on the American continent after World War II. At first, these methods seemed to question the principles of psychoanalysis, but in fact they use some of its tools. The therapists who practice these new methods have themselves undergone an analysis. Their practice was then transformed, through their personal work and through training. Just as doctors who practiced in Africa noticed that they had better results if they mixed traditional methods with European medicine, some psychotherapists have noticed that they had better results if they mixed a psychoanalytic approach with mind-body therapy and behaviorist methods.

## B. Couple Therapy PIERRE DALENS

Can therapists establish a relation between the notions of desire, pleasure, and love, what makes the love relationship possible within a couple, and what is its evolution in time?

The beginning of a relationship is often characterized by passion, through affective, emotional, and sexual components, which define an "unconscious couple." On the contrary, when the evolution of the couple results in a love relationship, a certain stability can be achieved, with less idealization, but with more durability and social adaptation.

We have to admit that the search for passion is very tempting, compared to the love relationship, which is a more-grounded notion.

We believe that the dysfunctional couple should not be considered as having a marital sickness, which needs to be cured because of physiopathological dysfunctions. Rather they should be viewed in the context of *Relational Eros*, an in-between of the honeymoon, which characterizes passion, and the maturation of an "unconscious couple."

Sexuality can only be integrated through the symbolic acceptance of what pushes a person towards another person, and where the affective, emotional, and sexual components define what will lead to a love relationship, a long-term stabilization.

The body-mind approach is well suited to understand these two relational levels. The psychological-sexological-somatotherapeutic analysis looks at the individual and relational dynamics and the way the emotions and affects are symbolized in the interrelations. The sexological-psychotherapeutic consequences will show in terms of relational dysfunctions and individual *sexoses*.

The goal of group sexotherapies is to establish a new body sensuality through the energetic approach and role play, the neo-Reichian and Gestalt techniques. This will allow the patients to integrate love better in their lives and feel even more alive.

In sexual dysfunctions, the sexual desire is often repressed, either by a denial of any erotic manifestation, by an indifference towards sexuality, or by an inhibited sexuality. On the opposite side, the loving state of being will lead the individual into a search for pleasure and exchange.

The genuineness of the pleasure leads to a real delight, in relation with the individual structure and the integration within the existential life, what G. Abraham called the *sensitive metabolism*, compared to the *fantasmatic metabolism*. The sensitive metabolism can be defined as the search for an experimentation of the sensation, which correlates the imaginary, the mental representations, and the dreams. The fantasmatic metabolism will mostly consider the imaginary. We are often preoccupied by the lack of sexual desire, called *"erotic aphasia"* by G. Abraham.

We would like to emphasize the problems of communication within the couple. When the love is still fixated at a sadistic-anal stage, it is characterized by possession and impulsiveness. On the contrary, a mature eroticism could relate the desire to the expression of feelings and affects.

Sexual dysfunctions, called sexoses, are considered as an imbalance within the symbolic and imaginary, emotional and pulsional functions. But the couple often puts into play the interaction between the neurotic aspects of the individuals and the repression of pregenital systems. (*Pregenital systems* here refers to the early embryonic "androgynous" stage lasting about 6 to 8 weeks from conception to development of the male and female genitals.) When there are dysfunctions and incompatibilities within the individuals, we can often observe problems in terms of communication, power and control issues, emotional dependency, and stress—and most often in terms of erotic and sexual disagreements within young couples. The marital relationship will be considered as having a durability over time, but also as having a confrontation through exchanges. The search for long-term durability will involve the search for the expression of sexual desire and pleasure through an erotic and passionate exchange.

If we use a *biological* metaphor, it is the indication of different modalities succeeding one another in sensation and sensuality, just as fantasies will coincide with a shared desire. Even if we often use technical and logical approaches to deal with couple difficulties, we will here emphasize the role played by individual structures.

### The Individual Structures

Prior to committing to a couple relationship, each individual had developed his own personal history and traumas. Each partner has a basic structure with which the other person will be confronted. Different typologies were created to explain these structures of character. We will consider two, the first one being the *bioenergetic structure of Lowen*, and the second being the *primary and secondary notions, as well as the introversion and extraversion notions of C. G. Jung*. The partners might experience more or less difficulties in accommodating these structures.

The structures of character as defined by A. Lowen consider the impact of the personal history, the couple entity, and the environmental influences on each other. They also study the impact of the lack of affection in the first months of a person's life on his psychosexual development. We associate the different neo-Reichian steps of Lowen, such as schizoidal, oral, psychopathic, masochistic, and rigid, to the couple structure through the energetic unification and affective maturation of partners in marital relationship.

### Biopsychological Theory

The notion of marking by Konrad Lorenz defines the importance of the early relational programming. The initial marking is biologically understood as the cerebral sex, inducted by cerebral sexual hormones and cerebral chemical mediators in the first weeks of the fetal life, combined with maternal stimuli. This neurobiological determinism can be reinforced later on a psychosociological level through the notions of gender identity and role identity. The notion of archaic psychological inscription refers to the individual mark in the couple as a mutual modeling of two identical marks.

Partners are brought together because of this first original inscription in the body. In the dyadic relationship, there would be two identical marks, but with different mind-body components. We then come up with a crossed identification of a unique bi-sexed being. This neurobiological mark retrieved in the couple brings up the understanding that a part of my own neuropsychological equipment is also in the other person. In the bi-sexed being that we are, it is the lost part of the androgyn we look for in the partner. We can therefore consider the romantic encounter as the start for this twin bonding. The couple becomes the ground for all the future symbolic projections.

### Psychoanalytic Theory

This therapeutic modality emphasizes the choice of the total object from the choice of the partial object. The unconscious initial choice of the partner and later on, the development of the couple dynamic, will create the internal structure of the couple based on the interactions between the ego and the unconscious of each partner.

The selection of the partner is based on the choice of sexual impulses as part of vital functions or on the choice of the narcissistic object, a search for the ideal ego. The emotional security, influenced by parental images or pregenital impulses, is very important in the establishment of the marital structure. Through crises, the couple will be confronted by the gap between desires and reality; the partners will have to resign themselves to accepting the distance between them and the reemerging of the repressed.

The crisis will happen when the subject expectations confront the object desires. The cultural and social background might add to the crisis, although this crisis can lead the couple to restructure their relationship, as long as each partner has a solid ego to facilitate autonomy for both partners.

The narcissistic partner can project his own desires on the other person, blocking the other person's impulses. This partner is actually searching for a bonding resembling the one he used to have with his mother as a child-mother relationship. The world of the castration and the oedipe is confronted by the symbolic and imaginary sublimation of the absorbing relationship with the partner. There appears a transitional period where the self does not exist, and the androgynic reunion will only become possible through orgasm.

When the intimacy becomes too intense, there is a need for distancing in the couple. This will modify their unit dynamic and preserve the self of each individual.

All the archaic desires will need to be expressed in the couple dynamic: *the oedipal desire* by assimilation of the partner as a parental figure, *the latent homosexual impulses* in the couple, and *the bisexuality concept* by a better understanding of the male and female polarities in each partner.

The pregenital stages in the psychosexual development are often expressed in the foreplay, such as in sadomasochistic, voyeuristic, and exhibitionist plays. These impulses can be definitively repressed or be expressed in fantasies; this repression is necessary to the stabilization of the couple union. The partners will be confronted to the idealization of the other and to the creation of an intimacy not available to the external world, as well as other possibilities for the couple and the partners to enter in relation with the external world.

### Homeostatic Relations Within the Couple

The choice of the partner is influenced by the value we put into love and its relation to the individual unconscious and to the social and cultural conditions. From the start, the couple will be faced with (confronted by) socioeconomic norms imposed by the social group.

The couple can serve as a refuge by overcompensating affective and emotional lacks of the individuals and be the center of communication and exchange. Fidelity and autonomy are components of a non-official contract about a physical and impulsive sexuality, as well as a fleshly and spiritual love.

The couple can be formed where the economic function and familial projects meet. It cannot be based on passion, since passion is of short duration. It is only after the passion is over that the partners can consider their capacity to form a couple together. The bond will be established with a narcissistic comfort and an erotic satisfaction. When two people form a couple, they can live their archaic issues through the other person with a certain distance of the self, allowing autonomy rather than isolation. The collusion of the partners gives an image of "couple personae" to the external world, while the shadow of this same couple lies within the marital desire.

All these structural and energetic factors within the dyadic communication make a certain "marital contract" possible, and even before, a "corporal contract." In the Middle Ages, this kind of contract existed between spouses, implying a certain debt in the sexual life of the couple.

### Marital Eroticism

Marital eroticism refers to nudity and the body relations. To be satisfying, the relationship has to integrate the physical and emotional sensations to lead to arousal, sensuality, and affective exchange. Marital eroticism puts the partners in contact with all the pleasurable body sensations from past experiences. All this exploration will bring more satisfaction within the couple sexuality, since the sexual exchange is not reduced to sexual intercourse. The beauty of the body will also play a role in seduction, which will bring a certain liberation of the body and a liberation of the mind within the couple relationship.

The marital contract implies pleasurable notions as well as a sexual responsibility. Here, sexual fidelity and extramarital affairs, both extremes of the same pole, have to be negotiated by the couple. The marital relationship involves a total commitment and an agreement on rules for both partners; on the other hand, extramarital affairs can also serve as an escape from responsibility of this same commitment. The corporal contract refers to a commitment to pleasure, within the couple, on affective and erotic aspects. When the couple has trouble exploring its sexual intimacy in different ways, it is a symptom that both individuals are incapable of facing the other person's needs.

The notion of commitment is a challenge to the value of liberty: How can we manage to introduce other people completely and significantly into our relationship? The answer will depend on the couple's maturity and on the corporal contract. The commitment will therefore clarify the notions of liberty, the allowed sexual liberation, with the feelings of jealousy and possession. In this context, researchers need to further explore the relationship between the need for emotional security and the sexual intimacy.

### Marital Conflict and Extramarital Sex

These can be understood in different ways. There are different aspects that have an impact on both the sexual and the sociocultural plan. Marital dysfunction will lead to sabotaging behaviors on different levels—sexual, affective, and relational—with the final consequence being an imbalance between the partners' desire.

The sociocultural level will condition competitive social structures in a narcissistic society where the most concrete consequences can be seen in the vicious cycle of "marital sickness," through manifestation of infidelity and jealousy. The nature of the extramarital affair can be based on the affinities two people share and their reciprocal identification. The affair can be seen as a complement to the marriage, but most often, it will lead to divorce.

The partner may admit having an affair without realizing it, but unconsciously pressured by guilty feelings. This can allow the couple to look for the deep causes and eventually find a compromise. There are many couple problems nowadays, but extreme jealousy can be found because of resentment towards the partner, needs for possession, and narcissistic devaluation of self-worth. This is the oedipal pathology to the extreme.

It is often one of the partners, usually the most suffering or the most demanding, who asks for help, either to do couple therapy with the partner or to deal alone with the couple difficulties. These therapies usually involve communication problems, and affective or sexual difficulties. Often, these requests are made too late, which makes results difficult to obtain.

For the last 20 years, we have offered groups for couples in a body-mind approach with the use of different body and psychological techniques to help the development of body energy, a body re-sensitization, a corporal and affective exchange through role play, neo-Reichian techniques, the emotional gestalt, and with the psychodrama, in the *psychosomatodrama* of W. Zaruchas. These groups for couples use both verbal and corporal analysis, suggesting an individual therapy as a complementary between the monthly group sessions. The evolution of couples is generally positive.

Masters and Johnson created co-therapy for couples, with two therapists, a man and a woman, as the "model couple." In France, only Robert and Claire Gellman from Paris still apply this type of analytical couple therapy.

The nature and function of sexuality make us wonder about the affective components of sexuality: Is the sexual union an exclusive and necessary condition? The answer would vary depending on the point of view, whether it is more traditional or liberal. It appears necessary that each partner keeps an intimate time for himself without feeling guilty; this rule should apply to both partners and be respected.

### A Clinical Example

In order to illustrate the different theoretical approaches discussed earlier, we will present the case of "Diane."

Her husband works in computers, she has two children. She lives in a beautiful property in the country and works in a laboratory. She wants to take better care of herself and express herself freely, give up her artificial role of entertainer, and stop living in someone else's shadow. This was her initial request for help.

Diane felt she was getting protection from her husband and intellectual challenge from her lover. After a couple of sessions, she admits having difficulty sexually initiating with her husband and being fulfilled with her lover because of the loving friendship they were living together. She decides to commit to an analytical psychotherapy in addition to a somatotherapeutic group.

She suffers from the lack of emotional expression in this stable and grounded family. Her husband represents an important "social personae." She complains about not receiving any tenderness outside the genital sexuality. She handles with difficulty the passive role her husband plays in their marriage, whereas he takes on such an active role outside their marriage. She realized they had made the agreement that she was "the chief" in the family. Because her behavior does not reflect her existential wishes in life, she wonders how she and her lover can live their love together.

Frustrated by the lack of affection, she looks for a different love, a manifestation of her oral impulses. Her bipolarity is expressed in her activity and feelings through archaic impulses on one side and an external and conscious masculine position on the other side. She is balanced between her fear of being abandoned and not being protected anymore, and her need for liberty and autonomy, which she prioritized over her fears. She feels the precariousness of her relationship with her lover, especially concerning the wife, who considers Diane as a friend and confidante, a strong and dynamic woman she has admiration for. Diane feels stuck between her lover, Robert, and his wife. She thus starts feeling guilty. She gets the impression of still waiting for something, which will not happen, just like she used to do in her childhood. She progressively loses interest for the lover and the couple, which allows her to get more autonomy. She meets a new friend from a different background who deals with things simply and naturally, and who does not make her feel inferior.

She leaves her husband, sells the property, and asks for a divorce, which she associates with her liberty. On the other hand, she is insecure about her new life, but feels a strong need to build a new existence. At first, she has difficulty to balance herself in the new couple between her fear of abandonment and the happiness she cannot find.

Through the relational exchange Diane experienced, she was dissatisfied both ways, with her husband being unable to fulfill her affective needs, since he prioritized the financial security, and her lover being unable to fulfill her erotic needs, since he prioritized the intellectual part.

The therapy made Diane realize all the lacks of affection she suffered in the past and the essential role they will play in her new relationship. This search for marital happiness will end with a stabilization of the couple in time, all initiated by Diane.

### Conclusion

The search for love and happiness implies a rediscovery of our archaic desires and our individuality, since joy is something we have little control over. Therefore, we find ourselves facing a hidden reality. The *love history* leads us through a transformation process, which will never end—a wisdom of the soul impossible to attain. It is an affective ritual of exchange through a symbolic operation to recreate *the mystic androgyn*. It is the energy behind this image that makes the external reality concrete.

## C. Therapeutic Model for Gender and Orientation Difficulties LAURENT MALTERRE

All human problems can be summarized as the attempt to reunify opposites. We can assume that most people go through this resolution of opposites in sexuality first, since it is probably the most extensive ground for polarities. It is the principal source of conflicts and a place for reunification of opposites, while allowing for all kinds of male and female expressions. While their interdependency is obvious, this does not mean that its resolution will be achieved necessarily through orgasm, but more through a search for a whole identity.

These polarities can be expressed through different forms, such as bisexuality, real or repressed homosexuality, or a desire for sex change often expressed through transvestism, or erotic interest in the breast or the anus. For others, this uncertainty between the two polarities will be expressed through sexual orientation problems.

### Objective

What kind of therapy can we offer to patients who suffer from sexual orientation and gender-identity problems? How do we help an individual to integrate a stable image of himself when all he sees is a fragmented, complex, and imprecise image. This calls for an ongoing evolutionary process through individual and group therapy with experimentation, understanding, and integration of fundamental steps, such as the androgyny, the psychological bipolarities, anima and animus, which synthesis is the love dimension.

### The Methodology

The individual and group therapies use approaches referring to diverse disciplines: analytic, somatotherapeutic, and sexologic. For each discipline, different authors are recognized as pioneers: Freud, Jung, and Lacan for the analytic approach, Masters and Johnson, Stoller, and Crepault for the sexologic approach, and Lowen, Reich, and Singer for the body-mind approach. All these approaches are used to form the whole therapy we offer:

- The somatotherapy and gestalt therapy work on the energy, the body sensations, the emotions, the affects, and the relations. They aim at repairing the affective lacks and traumas, to empower the individual in his expression of affects in the here and now, and to pass from a closed attitude to a relational opening.
- The bioenergy works through the analysis of body and character rigidity. Once the person learns to focus on her- or himself and to be in relation with others, she or he will become familiar with her or his emotions and sensations and be more in contact with both his or her body and pleasure.
- Sexoanalysis will study the orientation and identity difficulties through the analysis of the erotic imagery. The person develops capacities to symbolize and better integrate their erotic imagery and unconscious image of her or his body.
- Psychoanalysis will deal with the unconscious, the psychological functioning, the symbolism, the dreams, and archetypes. Words will serve to verbalize the sexual history and the affects and emotions related, in order to have a better understanding of the self.

This therapeutic framework allows for both the affective intimacy through role play, body contacts, relational touching, and the psychological intimacy through active listening of the partner's history, one's emotions and feelings, and the mental representations of the actual exchanges.

The goal of these therapies, whether they are done in individual or in group, is to facilitate the improvements and the reinvestment in one's existence: *How to be in contact with the self, the experiences, the sensations, and the emotions, to feel as a man or a woman, and to be in relationship with the partner without losing one's identity?*

These therapies aim at progressively reconstructing the imprecise or fragmented identity, the emotions, the affects, and the symbolization. This search for identity will lead the individual to transform his relationship and his perception of himself through the exploration of his internal representations of what it is to be a male or a female or an androgyn. This process is what the human being usually goes through in his psychosexual development. It will help the individual to gain a more realistic image of himself, a new identity, and eventually, a new way of loving.

A caring and secure environment will facilitate the emerging of real or latent homosexuality, bisexuality, or ambisexuality through transvestism and transgenderism.

### The Androgyny

The androgyny is opposed to the genital, and fights against the sex differences. It is oriented towards a narcissistic completion and a symmetrical illusion. It means to have both sexes. Plato defines the androgyn as being neither father, mother, man, or woman. It is all at the same time. It is a denial of differences and opposites.

The transsexual is considered the modern face of androgyny. He defends himself against the sex differences by disinvesting his own sex. In doing this, he tries to reunify the opposites by abolishing the duality between sexes. In being asexual, he avoids being confronted by the dual experience, that of being a man or a woman.

The bisexuals and transhomosexuals also go through a gender variability just living as transvestites, drags and queers, named trangenders. They often experience relational failures when facing the illusion they can reunify with their opposite.

In therapy, we work on the androgyny by:

* The integration of the body image, the body being often considered as asexual, in-between, or immature. All this variation in degrees between the male and the female poles can be seen through the gender dysphoria, the disgust of the body, the narcissistic fragility, and the desire to cross-dress. Each individual will identify his male and female components and look for his secret sexual identities. The therapist will help his patient to feel more grounded in order to reunify all his different components.
* Exploring this symmetrical view of a double of the self, referred to as homosexuality. The individual will learn to invest both an identical and different vision of the other. This way, the individual is able to recognize his own limits regarding his ideal self. It shows that the partner heals the feeling of emptiness by providing a feeling of continuity. Here, homosexuality and bisexuality tendencies may appear.

*Male and Female Polarities*

Identity and sexual orientation develop through identification processes with male and female components.

In order to feel at peace with one's identity, the individual has to find the equilibrium between the male and the female poles. This is very difficult to achieve nowadays, since the female entity is seen as the total antagonist to the male entity. All the male qualities are developed and privileged over female qualities, which is a real disaster!

In summary, as a society, we need to get rid of the phallocentrism, by giving the repressed female entity all the importance she deserves. It is a long road for both men and women. The man overemphasizes his male traits through macho and misogynist attitudes, as well as patriarchal structures. The female part of the woman is treated as being inferior, responsible for all sins. There has to be a serious awareness that the female component is an essential psychological reality. The male and the female components should work in harmony to contribute to the unification of the individual with himself. We need to get rid of all the male and female stereotypes in order to consider the resemblance between the sexes as a common psychological bisexuality.

The man can see the female entity through the anima. Some well-known models can portray this image, such as Eve, Sofia, Penelope, Marie, the Amazon, the Mother, Diane, the muses, and the fays. There also exist negative images, such as the prostitute, the witch, the employer, or the son's lovers. In these situations, the men are no longer in contact with their female entity, their Jungian anima. They are completely cut off emotionally and intuitively. They are those "rough" men, who degrade as soon as there is no maternal or female presence around. They are those noland men, with no ambition, the criminals. They can remain close to their animal impulses and block any expression of tenderness. They collect women to avoid being intimate with only one.

The male entity in the woman can be seen in the Jungian animus. These images can appear in dreams and through body expression. Often, the first animus images are quite negative. They refer to captured animals, criminals, and truckers. In these situations, their animus is opposing the man. When the images are ones of fragility, vulnerability, or castration, women cut themselves off from their sensitivity, and their female entity gets disguised in men caricatures. These women want to be in the head office. Fortunately, images change to become more positive animus, such as Tarzan, the knight, the teacher, the wise man. All these images are a reflection of a man being in contact with his female entity: his eroticism, his romanticism, his mental, and his spirituality. They also reflect women whose animus communicates openly and tenderly with the man's anima. The relationship is more human.

Each individual carries Eros, scars which are opened when a new partner arrives. The individual will have to re-establish the dialogue with Eros in order to overcome:

* What separates the man from his female entity and the woman from her male entity?
* Can the man accept that he will never be his female entity, and can the woman accept she will never be her male entity?
* Nowadays, on which figures do we project the female entity in the man and the male entity in the woman?

These questions about the female entity within the man and the male entity within the woman lead us to consider the question of entity as a whole. In fact, when the individual gets closer to his other half, does the relationship become stronger, deeper, and more human or, on the contrary, more destabilizing and fragmented?

We have to be aware of these male and female archetypes in order to integrate them into the psyche. The male and female entity within each individual can fluctuate over time, and be variable and varied in terms of proportions. The final result will be, according to Jung, "a union without fusion between the anima and the animus in the living individual."

The therapies provided allow the participants for the first time to put into play their male and female polarities, especially through psychodrama. It brings the individual through a scenario asking for different language, behaviors, and attitudes, to play fantasies, or situations related to homosexuality, bisexuality, androgyny, or transvestism.

These therapies also allow for an exploration of the body dynamic, the imaginary, and the balance between the male and female polarities, in order to come to terms with a unified identity. The opposite sides of gender identity, their complementarity, and variability will be explored.

On another level, the transvestite will experience his capacity to fit in the opposite-sex entity. He projects himself in the image he has of the opposite sex. Each individual will name his new personae, changing his attitude and his body movement in order to be in relation with someone who has opposite or complementary polarities.

Through his behavior, the transvestite will be able to explore:

* The variability in male and female polarities.
* The similarities and differences between the imaginary body and the real body.
* The way others perceive him, where feelings of attraction, repulsion, and fear can be experienced.
* The possibility to imagine, for women, they have a penis and, for men, they have a breast.

- The emerging of new and different sensations, through the investment of the opposite-sex body, the transvestite can be in contact with other secret identities.
- The role of one's sexual fantasies at a conscious and preconscious level in his relationships.
- One's place on the sexual continuum (heterosexual, bisexual, transhomosexual, asexual).

It is a deep transformation within, where the esthetical appearance is not a finality. While working on one's mental representations of what is male and female, the individual can recognize his or her own identity value. At first, the body image is fragile, imprecise, and becomes strong, powerful, assertive, seductive, erotic, and a new self, an erotic self. It is the search for the erotic self in homosexuality and transgenderism, which explains a loss of the self.

### Synthesis of Polarities: The Road to Love

This imaginary relation will allow the individual to develop a strong self-image, to repair his identity uncertainties, and to experience the emerging of desire. Relational difficulties will perpetuate themselves as long as the individual will not come to peace with his identity and orientation. Self-growth then becomes impossible. The relationship will make the individual aware of the partner's limits and his own limits, especially through sexual intercourse. In experiencing relational, emotional, and affective situations, both partners will learn to meet their own needs, while considering the ones of the partner, to achieve a certain harmony in their capacity to love and be loved.

The emphasis will be on the exploration of fusion, separation, and resolution experiences. Exercises on projection of aggressiveness, on domination, submission, and independent relations, will clarify the relational dynamic. Triangulation with a rival, and the jealousy and possessiveness it involves, refers to the unresolved oedipal triangulation.

### Conclusion

Between the group therapy sessions, we have to emphasize that the patient will work on his personal dynamics in individual therapy. All the emotions experienced in the group sessions will be explored in individual sessions.

The multiplicity of factors in homosexuality and transgenderism are considered in the individual and group therapies. Bisexuality, next to heterosexuality, comes to terms with a whole structured identity. All the other sexual problems, such as lack of desire, erectile dysfunctions, sexual addictions, love disorders, and marital conflicts, can also be resolved through a similar work than the orientation problems, meaning an exploration of the female and male internal representations and of the androgyny. Each individual will construct his own realistic image of himself.

As Freud said in *The Schreber President*: "All human beings balance between heterosexual and homosexual feelings; a deception or a privation on one side has the individual balance on the other side.

## D. Therapist Training & Certification

ROBERT GELLMAN and CLAIRE GELLMAN-BARROUX

The medical universities and nonprofit organizations specialized in teaching and ongoing education are responsible for therapist training and certification. The first sexology training in France was created in 1974 at the Necker Hospital in Paris. The French School of Sexology is partly responsible for the creation of the University Teaching at the René Descartes–Paris V University.

There are other sexology certification and training in the most important universities in France. They offer diplomas of Sexology Practitioners to doctors, and sometimes to psy-

chologists having a DESS in Clinical Psychology. Under the same conditions, diplomas in sexology can also be earned by paramedical workers (nurses, social helpers, kinesiotherapists, marriage counselors, educators, etc.).

[*Comment 2003*: Recently, a distinction has been proposed between medical doctors, physicians, "sexologists," and "sexotherapists," which include non-medical specialists who are psychotherapists, psychologists, marriage counselors, social workers, nurses, midwifes, and so on. Professional training is available in several universities in Bobigny, Toulouse, Nantes, and Paris, as well as in private associations, such as SFSC and the Gestalt Institut de Neuillly.

[Most of the practitioners incorporate biomedical or endocrinology interventions, behavioral therapies, studies of profound psychological problems, both intra- and interpsychic, as well as relationship-oriented problems of the couple. A particular variety of Sexotherapy is represented by the work with couples, notably within Gestalt Therapy (Anne and Serge Ginger, Charles Gellman, and Martine Masson). In order to emphasize the important role of the emotional and relational dimension within Humanistic Sexology, Meignant has proposed the term "*Amourologie*" (*End of comment by S. Ginger and M. Meignant*)]

## 12. Sex Research and Advanced Professional Education

### Sexological Organizations and Publications

Academie des Sciences Sexologiques, 20 Rue Vignon, Paris, 75009 France.

Association des Sexologues Cliniciens Francophones (ASClif), Présidente: Claire Gellman-Barroux, 3, rue Copernic F-75116, Paris, France; email: asclif@citeweb.net; http://asclif.free.fr/sommaire.html. Secretary General: Ursula Pasini, 62 bis Avenue de la Roseraie, CH-1205 Genève, Switzerland; fax: (+ 41 22) 346 77 01; email: ursulapasini@freesurf.ch.

Association Interhospitalo Universitaire de Sexologie (AIHUS), Dr. Robert Porto, 21 Place Alexandre Labadié, F-13001 Marseille, France; tel.: +33 (0) 491-76 44 89; fax: +33 (0) 491- 77 01 39; email: robert.porto@worldonline.fr.

Recherche Sexologique du Sud-Ouest (ARSSO),"Les Bons Enfants," Dr. Francis Robert, Bordeaux Rive Droite, Route Bergerac F-33370 Fargues-St.-Hilaire, France; tel.: (+33-56) 21 21 14.

Centre International de Formation et de Recherche en Sexualité (CIFRES), Dr. Rejean Tremblay, 14, Rue Bertrand-Gril, F-31400 Toulouse, France; tel.: +33- 62- 26 12 56; fax: +33- 62- 26 44 13.

Ecole Française de Sexologie; Dr. Robert Gellman, 3 Rue de Copernic, F-75116 Paris, France; tel.: +33-47- 27 96 67; fax: +33-47- 04 40 57; email: efsweb@citeweb.net; http://efsweb.citeweb.net/.

Enseignement de Sexologie, Faculté de Médecine de Marseille. 27, Bd. Jean Moulin, F-13005 Marseille, France; tel.: (+33) 91 83 43 25 or (+33) 91 83 43 26.

Faculté de Médecine Paris XIII Bobigny, Département des Enseignements Spéciaux, UFR Santé-Médecine-Biologie Humaine, Sexologie; Mme. Nadia Ouarti-Saighi/ Docteur Suzanne Kepes; 74 rue Marcel Cachin, F-93017 Bobigny Cedex, France; tel.: (+33) 48 38 76 11; fax: (+33) 48 38 77 7.

Fondateur de L'Association Mondiale de Sexology, 72, Quai Louis Bleriot, 75016, Paris, France; tel.: 30-40/50-38-99.

INSERM (Institut National de la Santé et de la Recherche Médicale), U 292: Recherches en Santé Publique: Reproduction, VIH/SIDA, Sexualité; Alain Giami, Hôpital de Bicôtre,

82, rue du Général Leclerc, F-94276 Le Kremlin-Bicetre Cede; tel.: +33-1-4521-2289; fax: +33-1-4521-2075; email: giami@vjf.inserm.fr.

Institut de Sexologie, Dr. Jacques Waynberg, 57 Rue Charlot, F-75003 Paris, France; tel.: +33-1-4271-1030; fax: +33-1-4271-5115; email: waynberg@club-internet.fr; http: //www.sexologie-fr.com.

Institute Européen de Psychsomatothérapies, Centre de Sexologie Clinique, 77 Rue Lakanal, F-37000 Tours, France.

*Sexologies–European Journal of Medical Sociology*, 21, Place Alexandre Labadie, 13001 Marseilles, France; tel.: 33-91/50-20-03; fax: 33-91/50-52-77.

Société Française de Gynecologie Psychosomatique, Dr. Sylvain Mimoun, 45 rue de Maubeuge, F-75009 Paris, France; tel.: (+33-1) 42 80 21 67.

Société Française de Pathologie Sexuelle, Dr. Henry Dermange, 61 Avenue de Passy, F-75016 Paris, France.

Société Française de Sexologie Clinique (SFSC), Dr. Marc Ganem, 85, Avenue Charles de Gaulle, 92200 Neuvilli s/Seine, France; tel.: (+33-1) 45 72 67 62; fax: (+33-1) 45 72 67 63.

Syndicat National des Médecins Sexologues (S.N.M.S.), 77 Rue Lakanal, F-37000 Tours, France.

Université d'Aix-Marseille, Administrative Office, Enseignement de Sexologie Faculté de Médecine 27, Bd. Jean Moulin, F-13005 Marseille, France; tel.: +33-91-83-4325 or 4326.

## References and Suggested Readings

Assoun, P. L. 1992. *Le couple inconscient*. Edition Economisa.

Bauer, A., & A. M. Ventre. *Les polices en France*. Ed que-sais-je PUF.

Brenot, Ph. 2001. *Inventer le couple*. Odile Jacob.

Caron, S. L. 1998. *Cross-cultural perspectives on human sexuality* (pp. 67-70). Needham Heights, MA: Allen & Bacon.

Chilland, C. 1986. *Changer de sexe*. Odile Jacob.

CIA. 2002 (January). *The world factbook 2002*. Washington, DC: Central Intelligence Agency. Available: http://www.cia.gov/cia/publications/factbook/index.html

Crépault, C. 1997. *La sexoanalyse*. Payot.

Crépault, C. 1997. *La sexoanalyse*. Payot.

Dalens, P. 1986. Homosexualités. *Cahier de Sexologie Clinique*, *12*(72).

Dalens, P. 1987. Lien entre désir, plaisir et amour. *Médecine et hygiène*. Genève.

Dalens, P. 1992. *Le couple et son désir*. La Louvière.

Dalens, P. 1999. *Les bisexualities*. PUQ.

Desportes, F., & F. Le Gunehec. *Le nouveau droit pénal*. Ed Economica.

Diaz, Ch. *La police technique et scientifique*. Ed que-sais-je PUF.

Duda, A.1996. *Comparative survey of the legal and societal situation of homosexuals in Europe*.

Eliade, M. 1962. *Méphistopheles et l'androgyne*. Gallimard.

Gagnon, J. H., A. Giami, S. Michaels, & P. de Colomby. 2001 (February). A comparative study of the couple in the social organization of sexuality in France and the United States (Statistical data included). *Journal Sex Research*, *38*:24-34.

Goode, E. 2001 (May 29). On sex, U.S. and France share a language. *The New York Times*, Science Section, p. 1.

Hatfield, E., & R. L. Rapson. 1996. *Love and sex: Cross-cultural perspectives*. Needham Heights, MA: Allen & Bacon/Simon & Shuster.

Henshaw. 1996 (March/April). Abortion services under national health insurance: The examples of England and France. *Viewpoint*, *26*(2):87.

Laumann, E. O., J. H. Gagnon, R. T. Michael, & S. Michaels. 1994. *The social organization of sexuality: Sexual practices in the United States*. Chicago: University of Chicago Press.

Lemaire, J. G. 1971. *Thérapie de couple*. Payot.

Lemaire, J. G. 1986. *Le couple: Sa vie, sa mort*. Payot.

Lemaire, J. G. 1998. *Les mots du couple*. Payot.

*Le mineur et le droit pénal* (sous la direction de Roselyne Nérac-Croisier). Ed L'Harmattan.

Mackay, J. 2000. *The Penguin atlas of human sexual behavior: Sexuality and sexual practice around the world*. New York: Penguin Reference.

Martinage, R. *Histoire du droit pénal en Europe*. Ed Que-sais-je PUF.

Mendes-Leite, R. 1996. *Bi-sexualité, le dernier tabou*. Calman Levy.

*Nouveau code pénal*. Ed 2001. Dalloz.

*Nouvelle revue de psychanalyse. Bisexualité et différences des sexes*. Gallimard n7.

Nuburger, R. 1997. *Nouveaux couples*. Odile Jacob.

Pasini, W. 1996. *A quoi sert le couple?* Odile Jacob.

Pradel, J., & A. Varinard. *Les grands arrets du droit pénal general*. Ed Dalloz.

Rassat, M.-L. *Droit pénal special*. Ed. Dalloz.

Reekie, A. F. 1994. *Age of consent laws in the Council of Europe States in 1993*.

Robert, J. H. *Droit pénal general*. Ed PUF.

Salomon, P. 1994. *La sainte folie du couple*. Albin Michel.

Sciolino, E. 2002 (October 13). The French spar over sex: There's a limit, no? *The New York Times*, International, p. 3.

Singer, Ch. 2000. *Eloge du marriage*. Albin Michel.

Soyet. *Droit pénal et procedure pénal*. Ed L.G.D.J.

Spira, A., N. Bajos, & the ACSF group. 1994. *Sexual behaviour and AIDS*. Aldershot, England: Avebury.

Stoller, R. J. 1998. *Recherche sur l'identité sexuelle*. Gallimard.

Teboul, G. 2000. Les couples et leur sexualité. *Cahier de Sexologie Clinique*, *26*(148).

Tordjeman, G. 1995. *Le couple: Nouvelles règles du jeu*. Hachette.

Tzitzis, S. *La philosophoe pénale*. Ed que sais-je PUF.

UNAIDS. 2002. *Epidemiological fact sheets by country*. Geneva, Switzerland: Joint United Nations Programme on HIV/AIDS (UNAIDS/WHO). Available: http://www.unaids.org/hivaidsinfo/statistics/fact_sheets/index_en.htm.

Veron, M. *Droit pénal special*. Ed Armand Colin.

Vilar, D. 1994. School sex education: Still a priority in Europe. *Planned Parenthood in Europe*, *23*(3):8-12.

Wolff, C. 1981. *La bisexualité*. Stock.

# French Polynesia

## (*Polynésie Française*)

Anne Bolin, Ph.D.
*Updates by A. Bolin and the Editors*

## Contents

## *Demographics and a Brief Historical Perspective*

ROBERT T. FRANCOEUR

### A. Demographics

French Polynesia encompasses five administrative areas representing five archipelagos with 130 islands and atolls in the South Pacific, approximately 5,000 miles (8,050 km) east of Australia. The Society Islands, the Gambier Islands, the Austral Islands, and the Marquesas are primarily volcanic islands, while the majority of the Tuamotu Islands are atolls. Oceania is divided into three broad cultural groupings, with Melanesia and Micronesia to the west and Polynesia to the east. French Polynesia as a political entity is situated within the indigenous culture area of Polynesia, which includes all the islands in a "triangle" stretching from Easter Island in the east to the Hawaiian Islands in the north and New Zealand in the southwest. It incorporates diverse societies of Polynesian peoples colonized by the French and declared a French Protectorate in 1842 (Stanley 1992). In 1957, this area became officially known as Polynésie Française. It is important to note that French Polynesia is not an indigenous or cultural subdivision, but is rather a modern neocolonial political subdivision.

The Society Islands consist of 14 atolls and volcanic islands and include the Windward Islands of Tahiti (1988 population 131,309), Moorea (population 8,801), Maiao, Tetiaroa, and Mehetia; and the Leeward Islands of Huahine (4,479), Raiatea (8,560), Tahaa (4,005), Bora Bora (4,225), Maupiti (96), Tubai, Maupihaa/Mopelia, Manuae/Scilly, and Motu One/Bellingshausen. Tahiti has a mountainous interior surrounded by a fertile coastline where cane and coconut are grown. Over half of the indigenous French Polynesians live on the island of Tahiti, along with French, Chinese, and genetic intermixtures of these groups.

The Marquesas Islands, popularized by Melville in *Typee*, consist of 11 islands, six of which are inhabited (1988 population 7,358). Gauguin is buried on Hiva Oa, the

Anne Bolin, Ph.D., Elon University, Sociology Department, Box 2115, Elon College, North Carolina, USA 27244; Anne.Bolin@elon.edu.

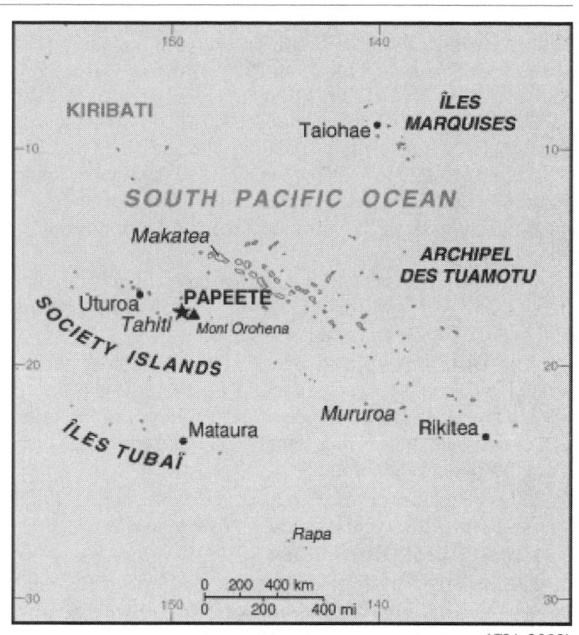

(CIA 2002)

most populated of the Marquesas Islands. Other inhabited islands include Tahuata, Fatuiva, Ua Pou, Nuku Hiva, Ua Huka, and Hova Oa. The Tuamotu Archipelago, which means "cloud of islands," situated north and east of the Society Islands, spans an arc of 80 coral atolls covering 1,100 miles (1,770 km), with a population of 7,547. Included among the 78 atolls in this group are: Tepoto, Napuka, Pukarua, Takaroa, Manihi, Rangiroa, Raroia, Rotoava, Tatakoto, Hao, Reao, and Pukapuka, among others. Copra and mother-of-pearl are important exports. The Gambier Islands are southeast of the Tuamotus and include three inhabited islands, of which Mangareva is best known (Suggs 1960). According to a 1987 report, it is estimated that only 1,600 speakers of Mangarevan remained on the inhabited islands, a result, in part, of heavy out-migration. Their livelihood consists of horticulture, with crops such as coconuts, taro, and bananas, along with fishing (HRAF 1991, 172).

The Austral Islands include five inhabited volcanic islands with a population of 6,509. One of these is Tubuai, and the group is sometimes called the Tubuai Islands. Islands include Rimatara, Rurutu, Ra'ivavae, and Rapa. The Rapanese cash crops are coffee and potatoes, which are exported, while farming and fishing are primary subsistence activities (Hanson 1991, 274). The Austral Island peoples are well known for their indigenous arts and temples.

It is difficult to ascertain the precolonial population of these five island groups, because European contact resulted in a massive population decline throughout French Polynesia, both indirectly through disease and directly through European attacks, e.g., in 1595, Mendana's crew was responsible for killing over 200 Marquesans. Thomas (1991, 188) estimates that the population of the Marquesas declined from 35,000 to 2,000 between the 18th century and the 1920s. By the mid-1980s, the population had increased to about 5,500. The Mangarevan population may have once been 8,000 people, but by 1824, it was only 1,275 (HRAF 1991, 172). According to Hanson (1991, 273), the island of Rapa, at contact, had a population of 1,500 to 2,000, but by 1867, it reached a low of 120. Today, there are only an estimated 400 remaining Rapan speakers. The population of the Tuamotu Islands was estimated at 6,588 in 1863, but declined by almost 2,200 by the 1920s. A report in 1987 establishes the Tuamotuan population at 14,400, with 7,000 of these in the Tuamotu, but most of the remainder living in Tahiti. The Raroian population declined from 260 in 1897 to 60 in 1926. It rose to 120 in 1950 (HRAF 1991, 276). Tahiti's population is believed to have declined from a 1767 estimate of 35,000 to 16,050 in the first missionary census in 1797. By 1869, it had declined to 7,169 (Oliver 1974, 1989, 67, 117). Stanley (1992, 5) cites the 1988 population of French Polynesia at 188,814, and the CIA *World Factbook 1999* estimated the total population as 253,506 (CIAO).

In July 2002, French Polynesia had an estimated population of 257,847. (All data are from *The World Factbook 2002* (CIA 2002) unless otherwise stated.)

**Age Distribution and Sex Ratios**: *0-14 years*: 29% with 1.04 male(s) per female (sex ratio); *15-64 years*: 65.7% with 1.09 male(s) per female; *65 years and over*: 5.3% with 1.01 male(s) per female; *Total population sex ratio*: 1.07 male(s) to 1 female

**Life Expectancy at Birth**: *Total Population*: 75.23 years; *male*: 72.88 years; *female*: 77.69 years

**Urban/Rural Distribution**: NA

**Ethnic Distribution**: Polynesian (*Mā'ohi*) 78%; Chinese 12%; local French 6%; metropolitan French 4%. This ethnic-identity breakdown has been critiqued and remains a major obstacle to interpretation of the data.

**Religious Distribution**: Protestant 54%; Roman Catholic 30%; other 16%

**Birth Rate**: 18.17 births per 1,000 population

**Death Rate**: 4.49 per 1,000 population

**Infant Mortality Rate**: 8.95 deaths per 1,000 live births

**Net Migration Rate**: 3.04 migrant(s) per 1,000 population

**Total Fertility Rate**: 2.23 children born per woman

**Population Growth Rate**: 1.67%

**HIV/AIDS**: *Adult prevalence, Persons living with HIV/AIDS*, and *Deaths*: NA

**Literacy Rate** (*defined as those age 15 and over who can read and write*): 98%. About 87% of Polynesians are literate in French and 64% to 68% are literate in one of the Polynesian languages. The official languages of French Polynesia are French and Tahitian or *reo Mā'ohi*. (The Tahitians refer to themselves as *Mā'ohi* or *Ta'ata Tahiti*.) Indigenously Polynesian languages form two major divisions: Western and Eastern Polynesian. In 1987, educational institutions included 176 primary schools, 7 secondary schools, and 18 high schools; the Université Française du Pacifique was established in 1987. The curriculum in public and private church schools alike is a French one.

**Per Capita Gross Domestic Product** (*purchasing power parity*): $5,000 (2001 est.); *Inflation*: 1.5% (1994 est.); *Unemployment*: 15% (1992 est.). Of the 64,000 persons counted in the 1988 census as "having employment" out of the total population of 188,814, two thirds of the employed were men and three out of four worked on the Windward Islands of Moorea and Tahiti. In the outer Leeward Islands, 80% of the women and no more than 73% of the men had jobs. Most employed *Mā'ohi* work either as civil servants or in the tourist industry. All Tahitians, even in the rural areas, are involved to varying degrees in the market economy, either in independent enterprises such as craft production, periodic wage labor, and/or cash cropping (Hooper 1985, 161; Elliston 1997).

European culture has had an impact on the indigenous culture of French Polynesia in a number of ways for over 200 years. This chapter presents an overview, integrating historically situated accounts of the traditional culture with perspectives on the influence of colonization and missionary activity on the expression, beliefs, and values related to

Polynesian sexuality over the course of time. When available, contemporary sexual data will be presented. The focus is specifically on the sexuality of the indigenous peoples of French Polynesia and does not address that of the Europeans or the other minorities, unless otherwise stated.

## B. A Brief Historical Perspective

The beauty of these islands has been captured in the paintings of Paul Gauguin and the writings of Herman Melville, Robert Louis Stevenson, Jack London, and W. Somerset Maugham, among other notables. Early explorers, such as Captain James Cook (1769) and Captain Bligh of Bounty fame (1788-1789), contributed to Tahiti's reputation as a sexual paradise. Indeed, the peoples of the area, particularly the Society Islands, became distinguished for their sex-positive attitudes and known by Europeans for taking a casual approach to sex. Although the Polynesian sexual mores varied greatly from those of the Europeans, they were not unregulated. Polynesians had clearly defined cultural rules structuring sexuality and marriage, including exogamy, hierarchy, chiefly structure, genealogy, and incest rules.

The Polynesians' ancestors arrived in the frontier areas of Fiji, then reached Tonga and Samoa about 3,300 to 5,000 years ago (Oliver 1974, 1989, 67, 117). Eastern Polynesian occupation occurred by 200 B.C.E. The Tuamotu Archipelago was probably occupied by voyagers from the Society Islands by about the 9th century, as were the Austral Islands (Suggs 1960, 140-141).

The 1,609 square miles (4,167 km²) of area became a French overseas territory under the French constitution in 1957 and is currently administered by a French High Commissioner assigned by France, and a 48-member Territorial Assembly, both in the capital city of Papeete on Tahiti, the largest of the Society Islands. The Territorial Assembly is composed of locally elected representatives from the Windward and Leeward Islands of the Society Islands, the Austral Islands, Tuamotu Islands, Gambier Islands, and the Marquesan Islands (Elliston 1996). "The Territorial Assembly has been granted more powers over internal affairs over the past 20 years, as a result of Tahitian calls for more 'internal autonomy'; the French High Commissioner, however, retains the right to overrule or modify any Assembly decision" (quote from von Strokirch 1993; Henningham 1992; Elliston 1996).

The islands that now constitute French Polynesia are linguistically of the Eastern division and originally included proto-Marquesan and proto-Tahitian. Dialects of Tahitian are spoken on the Austral, Tuamotu, Gambier, and Marquesas Islands. (Tahitian is part of the Austronesian language family that spread and diversified 6,000 years ago.) This linguistic division is also replicated in terms of two cultural groupings: Western and Eastern Polynesia, with the Marquesas and the Society Islands identified as the cultural epicenters of Eastern Polynesia (Goldman 1970, xxvii). Robert C. Suggs suggests that these two archipelagos were centers of population dispersion for the other islands in Eastern Polynesia (1960, 107, 137).

## 1. Basic Sexological Premises

### A. Character of Gender Roles

Because cultures operate as integrated systems, the basic sexological premises, such as gender roles, social status, general concepts, and constructs of sexuality and love, must be considered within the broader Polynesian cultural context. Research on the status of women in traditional Polynesian societies supports the view that their position was regarded as high (Howard & Kirkpatrick 1989, 82-83). High status prevailed in the face of a *tapu* system in which women and men were segregated and women were regarded as less powerful. (See Section 2A, Religious, Ethnic, and Gender Factors Affecting Sexuality, for a discussion of the concepts of *tapu* and *mana*.) In addition, although there was a division of labor between Polynesian women and men, it was different from the traditional Western gender bifurcation of public/domestic or inside/outside. In traditional Tahiti, men hunted pigs and fished, engaged in warfare, and built temples, while women fished for shellfish, gardened, and produced mats and bark cloth (Oliver 1974). However, role flexibility was differentially enacted among the various Polynesian societies (Howard & Kirkpatrick 1989, 82-83). To fully understand women's position in precolonial Polynesia, the context of the "chiefly structure" must be considered. Chiefly status could take precedence over gender, and consequently, women could also assume positions of power as chiefs (Elliston 1996).

Levy's work among the Tahitians from 1962 to 1964 suggests a culture in which attention to gender distinctions continues the precolonial trajectory (1973, 230-237). Evidence of this is found in the Tahitian language in which gender is linguistically underplayed. While gender-specific occupational divisions do occur, there is a great deal of role pliability and cross-over, e.g., although women do not hold office in the formal political sector, they have an important voice and interest in politics (Levy 1973, 233). The high position of Tahitian women continues a pattern reported early on by explorers. The traditional descent system of reckoning through either matrilineal or patrilineal lines provided women access to powerful positions in the social order. Levy's research concluded that a blurring of gender boundaries continues as a contemporary pattern in rural Tahiti. However, he found that in the more urbanized and Westernized setting of Papeete, this pattern of gender equality and blending was becoming polarized by the wage-labor economy in which men are the breadwinners and women the homemakers (Levy 1973, 232-237). Elliston (1996) suggests that this pattern has not come to fruition, but rather women's employability is increasing while men's is decreasing.

Some researchers have proposed that in traditional times, in Eastern Polynesia (including the Marquesas and Society Islands), women's status was considered low because they were *noa*: common, impure, and polluting in regard to *mana*. Shore's examination of the literature suggests this may be an oversimplification. He cites considerable evidence to the contrary (1989, 146-147). For example, Hanson and Hanson argue that women's menstruation was not regarded as "simply polluting, but as inherently dangerous because it represents a heightened time of female activity as the conduit between the worlds of gods and human" (1983, 93 in Shore 1989, 147).

In-depth discussions of gender roles in recent times are presented in Douglas Oliver's *Two Tahitian Villages* (1981), Greg Dening's *Islands and Beachers* (1980), and Robert Levy's *Tahitians: Mind and Experience in the Society Islands* (1983), among others.

Thomas (1987) has discussed Polynesian gender roles in order to highlight the dramatic effect of colonization and missionization on contemporary Marquesan women and men. Depopulation has had an impact on the Marquesans, as has the introduction of wage labor, which, in some areas, continues today as a mixed economy with subsistence, occasional copra sales, and/or intermittent wage work. The work of Marquesan women is *haka ha'e propa*, which means "to make the house clean." This includes a variety of domestic chores, childcare, clothes washing, and cooking. Men engage in agriculture and horticulture, fishing, cutting coconuts for copra sales, and/or paid manual work. The division of labor is flexible, and women may work in gardens or collect Tahitian chestnuts, while men may do some work in the house which consists primarily of cooking. Unlike Western practices, cooking, washing dishes, and clothes washing in the nonurban areas are done outside the home. Even if a family has a gas stove or washing machine, this is placed outside the home.

But this model of gender roles that continues in more-rural areas is changing in the more central, Westernized, and urbanized island locales, where the presence of schools, hospitals, post offices, and other administrative services, as well as greater opportunities for continuous employment, affect traditional patterns. Women participate in the workforce in these areas to a high degree, particularly in clerical positions, while men are employed primarily in the highway department with road maintenance. Women's pattern of employment is typically one in which they quit work to have children, but may later return to part-time positions. In contrast, men have a more consistent pattern of long-term, wage-labor employment (Thomas 1987).

Thomas (1987) suggests that these gender-role patterns and the division of labor is more likely a result of colonialism than a traditional Polynesian cultural pattern. The traditional pattern of gender roles in the early contact period (1790-1830) was quite different, according to Thomas. Like Polynesian societies generally, the *tapu* system was an important part of the social organization of the Marquesas, and it frequently involved segregation of the sexes.

Traditional activities for men included fishing from canoes, which continues today, while traditional women's activities included gardening, preparation of bark cloth, and making mats. Prior to missionization, women had other opportunities for enhancement of their status. Coexisting with a class of male chiefs and priests was a class of women shamans whose importance varied throughout Polynesia. In the Marquesas, these women priests occupied a privileged position in society as curers and diviners who received food or pigs as payment for their services. The old Marquesan role parameters provided women with opportunities and access to prestige and power.

The Western disparity in gender roles delineated by separate but unequal domains of the public and the domestic was not expressed in traditional Marquesan gender roles. The *tapu* system also mitigated against such a Western public/domestic split, since typically men ate meals with men, not with women. As Thomas (1987) has noted, today Marquesan gender roles reflect Western tradition and the imposed Christian gender polarization of men-public-provider and women-domestic-nurturer. The demise of the *tapu* system occurred unevenly, but seemed to have been eliminated by the 1880s, facilitated by French colonial rule in 1842, the political efforts of the Catholic and Protestant missions, and the decline of the indigenous population. Colonialism and missionization disrupted the hierarchical aspects of the social system and eroded the chiefly structure, along with the system of *tapu* and *mana* that sustained it (Elliston 1996). By the late 19th century, polyandry, which was probably only practiced by the highest-ranking females, had become almost extinct (Thomas 1987).

Major changes in the political economy resulted in the replacement of traditional landholding units and mechanisms of redistribution by autonomous groups engaged in their own subsistence. Missionaries felt that the traditional Marquesan practice in which women gardened was improper and unseemly to their sex. According to Christian dictates, the women should be confined to their homes while the men should work as the cultivators. This was successfully imposed on the Marquesan peoples and others in

French Polynesia. Lockwood reports a similar pattern in the division of labor, in which men are the farmers while women are responsible for the household and childcare on Tubuai (1989, 199).

The impact of Western missionization on gender roles was particularly effective in French Polynesia because of the large-scale disruption in the indigenous way of life. All these factors converged to influence indigenous gender roles. Yet, the continuity of women's precolonial status vis-à-vis men cannot be underestimated (Elliston 1996). However, this does not now mean that women cannot surmount the Christian ideologies that place men at the head of the household. Lockwood observes that Tahitian women are "socially assertive and are frequently willing to challenge male authority when in a position to do so." Oliver's description of ancient Tahitian women as "anything but a passive, deferential, submissive lot; certainly not in domestic matters and often not in 'public' affairs either" (1974, 604) could be applied equally to contemporary Tahitian peasant women (1989, 207).

## B. Sociolegal Status of Males and Females

The sociocultural status of Polynesians throughout the life course varies in terms of ages and expectations. Oliver's (1981) and Levy's (1973) work on Tahitian life stages is particularly valuable in this regard. The infant, an *'aiu* ("milk eater"), gradually becomes a child (*tamāri'i*) between 1 and 3 or 4 years old (also *tamaroa*, boy child, or *tamāhine*, girl child). Childhood is followed by *taure'are'a*, the period of pleasure. This stage is ushered in by signs of approaching puberty. Between the mid 20s and early 30s, one becomes *ta'ata pa'ari* ("a wise or mature person"). Old age is *rū'au* (old) and/or if an individual becomes senile, he or she is *'aru'aru*, "weak and helpless" (Levy 1973, 25), see also Oliver (1981, 340-400).

Traditionally, the status of individuals in many areas of French Polynesia was defined by a hierarchical pattern of genealogical ranking, sustained by the belief in *mana*, and encountered through the *tapu* system of behavioral rules and restrictions. The Polynesian system of genealogical ranking was one in which the firstborn child was of higher status than his or her siblings. Those in such a position, regardless of their gender, were in a state of *mana* and, according to some reports, were therefore secluded for certain periods. The aura of *mana* also extended to a lesser extent to other siblings as well.

In traditional Polynesian societies prior to disruption of the *tapu* system, children were regarded as highly potent and potentially dangerous. As a result, they had to undergo certain rituals to prepare them to interact in the secular world. All upper- and lower-echelon children were apparently imbued with this divinity. The Polynesian cosmology regarded this sacredness as a highly charged force that required precautions lest harm could befall the unprotected individual.

Jane and James Ritchie (1983) noted that the precolonial pattern of early-childhood indulgence, community concern, and an extended-family concept of parenting has continued, especially in the more traditional areas at the time of their research. Children learn to be autonomous and responsible for tasks and chores at an early age. This transition to responsibility and autonomy occurs when the child is around 2 to 3 years old. By the middle years of childhood, peers are accountable for most of the childcare. Polynesian groups, and French Polynesia is no exception, were noted for a pattern of fluid child adoption. This pattern still occurs today. Adoption may occur informally through kin networks that may bypass the legal adoption process. (See discussion below of marriage and the family.)

Gender was also conceived as an integral part of generalized Polynesian hierarchy, genealogy, and the status of the individual as adolescent and adult. Thomas (1987) has described Marquesan men as traditionally having *mana*, while women were *me'ie* (common or free of *tapu* in relation to men). The term *noa* is used in other parts of Polynesia. However, there were numerous situations in which women could become subject to *tapu* prohibitions. This represents the contextual aspects of the *tapu* system described earlier. Such contexts required precautions as well as certain restrictions on the individual, his or her possessions, and tasks. Certain kinds of activities were segregated by sex and locale, e.g., women learning a new chant, men making a net, or a woman placing herself under *tapu* to conceive or prevent a miscarriage. This kind of *tapu* involved communal eating, sleeping, and prohibitions on sexual activity for a particular period of time, or until the project was completed.

Thomas (1987) has also pointed out that *tapu* and *me'ie* were relational constructs, and that in the Marquesas, a man who was *tapu* in relation to a particular woman might be *me'ie* in relation to other men who were in a *tapu* grade above him. This same man would be *me'ie* in relation to women of chiefly status.

In addition to the elites in the Polynesian hierarchy, there were people who were low-status servants of the elites, as well as those who were nonlandholding tenant farmers. It was the commoners in the Marquesas who were most affected by the *tapu* restrictions, e.g., common men could only eat what was produced by women. Persons at the lowest level of the hierarchy were not affected by the *tapu* on food, since they were the servants and produced food for not only themselves, but for the elite they served. The elite were less affected, because they neither produced nor prepared the food they ate.

## C. General Concepts of Sexuality and Love

While sailors on the early European exploring ships regarded Polynesia as a sexual paradise, the missionaries they brought viewed the same cultures as dens of debauchery. Oliver (1989) cites a 1778 report of J. Forster who stated: "The great plenty of good and nourishing food, together with fine climate, the beauty and unreserved behavior of their females, invite them powerfully to the enjoyments and pleasures of love. They begin early to abandon themselves to the most libidinous scenes." Tahitians specifically, and Polynesians generally, became known for their sex-positive attitudes and open valuing of sexuality, although the cultural structuring and tacit rules for sexual expressions were not apparent to the Europeans. Sexual experience and expression for many Polynesians began early and continued throughout the life course.

Needless to say, the various explorers and colonial ship crews visiting the islands misunderstood Polynesian sexuality. For example, in the Marquesas, young naked girls swam out to the ships to engage in sexual trysts with the sailors. While the sailors took advantage of the sexual liberation of these young girls, they experienced some ambiguity, because their own Western sexual paradigm had no comparable framework or referent. While Polynesian girls were similar in some respects to the prostitutes or sex workers who typically greeted these sailors at other ports, they were also very different because of their youth, nakedness, and willingness to swim out to greet the boats. In addition, not all young women swam out to the boats or engaged in sex with the sailors. The young girls that came out to the ships were outside the *tapu* classes, so their relations with the visitors provided them access to status and wealth that they would not normally have. Foreign sailors and observers were not aware of the situational and contextual factors behind this behavior (Dening 1980).

Others who swam out to the ships were the Marquesan *Ka'ioi*. These were adolescents who were separated at puberty in order to be educated in the social conventions and skills necessary to become singers and dancers at *koina* (feasts). For girls, this was a period of intense sexual play and display. It involved learning songs and dances for the feasts, as well as the art of beautification, which included the application of oils and bleaches. High-status girls were not educated as *Ka'ioi*, nor did they swim out to the ships. However, it was this behavior among the Marquesans that also contributed to the Western stereotype of Polynesian sexual license (Dening 1980).

In their massive cross-cultural review of the ethnographic literature, Ford and Beach (1951) classified the Mangarevans, the Marquesans, and the Pukapukans as "permissive societies," characterized by tolerant attitudes toward sexual expression in the lifespan of the individual. According to Gregersen (1983), Polynesia is known for "public copulation, erotic festivals, ceremonial orgies and sex expeditions," which had disappeared by modern times. It should be pointed out that this does not imply a sexual free-for-all by any means, as noted by Douglas Oliver's account in *Ancient Tahitian Society* (1974). While missionaries were immediately struck by the Polynesian variance from Western Christian standards of sexual morality, it should not be assumed that Polynesian sexuality was without cultural rules. Like sexuality everywhere, Polynesian sexuality was structured and bound by norms, regulations, and sanctions—although these were different from those of the explorers, missionaries, and colonials. It was primarily the young and unmarried people who had the greatest sexual freedom; married people and the elite class had much less.

Although Polynesian societies condoned premarital sexual expression, access to partners was strictly structured. Gregersen (1983), for example, reported that on the island of Raroia in the Tuamotu Archipelago, there were only 109 people in 1951. Such a small population meant that seven of the nine women of marriageable age were prohibited from having sexual partners because of incest regulations. In the neighboring atoll of Tepuka in the 1930s, the young people were all related and had to journey to other islands or await the arrival of visitors to find a partner.

Specific laws were enacted with French colonization. In 1863, for example, the French administrators banned much of the traditional cultural practices that involved *tapu*, the religion, traditional songs and dances, warfare, naked bathing, wearing of perfumed oils, polygyny, polyandry, and other practices at variance with Christian morality. These laws did much to repress the precolonial culture, but, as Elliston (1996) points out, "Polynesians found ways around both the Church teachings against sex-outside-marriage, and against French laws."

## 2. Religious, Ethnic, and Gender Factors Affecting Sexuality

### A. Source and Character of Religious Values

Polynesians today are primarily Christian, with 54% Protestant, 30% Roman Catholic, and 16% other, including Mormon, animist (the indigenous system), and Buddhist. The impact of missionary activity in the Pacific is reflected in the high percentage of Christian religious affiliation. Depending on the particular historical situation, different denominations may predominate in an area, e.g., the Mar-

quesas Islands are over 90% Catholic; Protestantism dominates the Austral Islands and the Leeward Islands, while the Tuamotu Islands are two-thirds Catholic and one-third Mormon. Although Thomas (1987) suggests that Catholicism's antagonism to contraceptive use has resulted in typically large families, large families are more probably a continuation of an earlier pattern that existed prior to depopulation, rather than as the consequence of Catholic religious attitudes.

It is important to remember that once the Europeans arrived in Polynesia, the traditional culture began to undergo major change and disruption. Archival and historical research can provide important clues in unraveling the traditional patterns that have persisted despite European colonialism and missionary activity. Broadly speaking, the various denominations of missionaries found the Polynesian sex-positive cultures repugnant. They were appalled by the Polynesian joy of sex, and repelled by the marital practices that allowed for polygyny and even polyandry.

In discussing religion, it is inappropriate to segregate the sacred aspects of indigenous Polynesian life from the wider culture, since these societies are unlike the West, where there is a clear division between the sacred and the secular. In contrast, the sacred and secular are interwoven in an integrated fashion within Polynesian cultures. An attitude in which sex was highly valued was reproduced as part of the synthesis of the social and the sacred in Polynesian life. Sacred aspects of sexuality incorporated beliefs about reproduction, fertility, and fecundity that were symbolically expressed through ceremonial sex. Marshall (1961) reports evidence of public sex associated with sacred temples on the Island of Ra'ivavae. This was also recorded for Tahiti. Among Tahitians, the sacred temples, or *marae*, served as the center of daily life. The religious system was based on beliefs in spirits and gods. Humans and gods were in a relationship that permeated all aspects of the Tahitian's daily life. Even the gods were regarded as joyous and sexually playful in concert with the positive sex ethos of the culture.

The *tapu* (taboo) system regulated social behavior. It was based upon an important religious element, *mana*, a fundamental principal of divinity and sacredness, that has been likened to electricity, prevalent among some Polynesian societies. *Mana* provided a relational and contextual structure, as well as demarcated sacred boundaries around class, time, events, space, and people. "Theoretically mana is an inherited potential, transmitted genealogically, with greater proportions going to firstborn children. It is therefore a matter of degree—a gradient ideally coincident with kinship seniority. Ultimately it stems from the gods" (Howard & Kirkpatrick 1989, 614). *Mana*, however, must be demonstrated through acts and activities of an individual. Success demonstrated the strength of one's *mana*, while failure signified weak *mana* (Howard & Kirkpatrick 1989, 64). *Mana* was also associated with fertility, fecundity, and abundance—both reproductive and agricultural, according to Shore (1989, 142).

Shore suggests that this aspect of *mana* may account for the traditional Polynesian emphasis on the genitals of the chief. In the *mana*, relational and contextual construct power was somatically embodied in the head and the genitals, which were regarded as sacred. For the Marquesans, these were the bodily sites for the protection of the self (Dening 1980). Linton reports that in traditional times, "there was constant mention of the genital organs of the chief, which were given names indicating their vigor and size" (Linton 1939, 159, in Shore 1989, 142). The Marquesan concepts of sacred personhood and the autonomy of the individual apparently also transcended class and gender in some respects. All individuals were credited with an inherent divinity that granted them inalienable social respect. However, in terms of ranking, the chiefly group held a higher position, because it was believed that their personal *mana* far exceeded others. Nevertheless, regardless of rank or status, the individual was endangered if the *tapu* regions around the head and groin were violated.

Bradd Shore (1989, 137-173) has described *tapu* in depth. *Tapu* is a difficult concept for Westerners to understand. It is not directly translatable into our concept of taboo. *Tapu* has multiple referents. According to Shore,

> First, the term has two quite distinct usages, one active, the other passive. As an active quality, tapu suggests a contained potency of some thing, place, or person. In its passive usage, it means forbidden or dangerous for someone who is noa [not divine, common]. Moreover, it seems to combine contradictory properties, suggesting on the one hand sacredness, reverence, and distinctiveness and, on the other, danger, dread, and pollution. (1989, 144)

When people were engulfed by *tapu*, they were in sacred states, and consequently, restrictions and prohibitions were placed on their behavior as well as their person. *Tapu* was the system that structured behavior in relation to *mana*. For example, according to Nicholas Thomas (1987), females were considered *me'ie*, common or free of *tapu* in relation to men. This classification, however, did not mean that women could not have a high status or could not enter *mana* states. However, *mana* was a fundamental spiritual rationalization for segregation of the sexes that resulted in *tapu*, or restrictions on the interaction between the genders in certain domains.

Marquesan women were also regarded as potentially dangerous when menstruating, which provided them with certain kinds of power. For example, a woman could curse an object by naming it for her genitals or by placing the object beneath her buttocks. Similarly, *tapu* could be assigned to an object by naming it for one's head or placing the item above one's head. Among the Marquesans, who believed women were potentially dangerous, sexual restrictions were also placed on intercourse at various times. According to Thomas (1990, 67) "some aspects of femaleness seem to be at the center of the tapu system." This was not, however, a universal pattern in French Polynesia.

The religious aspects of indigenous sexuality were also evident in the Tahitian *arioi* cult (discussed later in greater detail and described by Oliver (1974).) Members of the *arioi* society, an organization of traveling Tahitian entertainers, dancers, and athletes, were permitted unrestricted sexuality. Their roles as entertainers included sexual titillation and celebration for the public. The sexual element of this cult was permeated by the religious, as the *arioi* were dedicated to the Tahitian god, 'Oro (Oliver 1974).

## B. Source and Character of Ethnic Values

The peoples of French Polynesia are part of the larger culture area of Polynesia, sharing linguistic and many other cultural characteristics (Burrows 1968, 179). However, in precontact times, there was much cultural variation and diversity among the five island groups making up French Polynesia. Today, unification by the French has provided "the Polynesians living in these different archipelagos and islands . . . new grounds for relating to one another, including the use of French and Tahitian languages" (Elliston 1996). However, it should not be assumed that variation has been lost. For example, Oliver's study in 1954-55 of two Tahitian villages, one on Huahine and the other on Mo'orea, led him to state: "I came to recognize that there were almost as many subspecific varieties of Tahitian societal cultures as there were communities" (1981, xii). In Elliston's (1996)

words, "Polynesians throughout the archipelagos continue to have a very strong sense of their own locally-based identities by which I mean that their contemporary identities are strikingly based on their islands and archipelagos of origin." Elliston explains this as "in part because Polynesians associate different characters, economic practices, even different cultures with different islands and archipelagos; where one is from encodes a great deal of information in the local signifying systems," noting that Polynesians themselves generally see a great deal of diversity in the islands.

Oliver spearheaded a research project in which the social organization of eight Tahitian communities were studied, two each by Douglas Oliver, Ben Finney, Antony Hooper, and Paul Kay. The social organization of these island peoples varied, as did their methods of food production, as adaptive responses to different environmental riches. In Eastern Polynesia, as in Western Polynesia, social organization was a ranked system. The precolonial social system was a chiefly structure and within it variance occurred. Therefore, unlike Western Polynesia in which rank was graded, Eastern Polynesia was stratified by class (Burrows 1968, 185). Four major kinds of socioeconomic ranking or "degrees of stratification" existed in the traditional chiefly structures of what is now constituted as French Polynesia.

Tahiti had a very complex ranking system that usually included hereditary statuses consisting of *ari'i* (aristocracy), *ra'atira* (gentry), *manahune* (commoners), *teuteu* (servant class), and a small nonhereditary slave class of *titi*, captured during warfare. The people of Mangareva had "two basic status levels with tendency to form a third," while the Marquesas had "two status levels," and the Pukapukans "two status levels; the upper containing very few members" (Sahlins 1967; Stanley 1992; Ferdon 1991). While class stratification continues in modern times, the traditional categories have been abandoned (Oliver 1981, 37).

These hierarchical aspects of Polynesian society were permeated with religious meaning since the chiefs and other elites were regarded as divine and rich in *mana*. *Tapu*, *mana*, the *arioi*, and a hierarchical chiefly structure were interconnected as aspects of the sexual system. For example, in Tahiti, as elsewhere, hierarchy was mandated by the gods and manifested in all levels of social organization. The kin-congregation or extended family had small *marae* to make offerings to spirits. Extended-family households were organized into neighborhoods that had larger *marae* with the chief's *marae*, which was the largest and most potent (Scupin & DeGorse 1992). It was believed that "the highest ranking chiefly family . . . was . . . descended from the first humans created by the creator god, Ta'aroa," and was, therefore, the most powerful spiritually (Scupin & DeCorse 1992, 31).

The bilateral kinship system was one in which the chiefly status and sibling order (first-born siblings ranked in status above others) determined one's social position. This was not necessarily limited through the patrilineage. Women, like men, could have access to chiefly positions. The practice of bilateral reckoning provided for flexibility in status and rank, facilitating affiliation through either the paternal or maternal line (Scupin & DeCorse 1992, 313). As a result of colonialism and Christianization, the traditional social-political organization of inherited rank no longer exists (Hooper 1985, 161).

## 3. Knowledge and Education about Sexuality

### A. Government Policies and Programs

Because Tahiti contains over 70% of the population, public health efforts are focused in this area. Not currently available at the time of this writing is information from a sexual survey conducted in Tahiti in November 1993 under the auspices of La Direction de la Santé Publique.

## B. Informal Sources of Sexual Knowledge

Informally, spatial organization and sleeping arrangements may contribute to sexuality education of the young. Ford and Beach (1951) reported that among the Pukapukans and Marquesans, families often slept in one room, thereby providing children an opportunity for sexuality education through clandestine observation. This, however, must be placed in cultural context. Parents were not putting on an open display for children; but, because families slept in close proximity, this provided children an opportunity to secretly observe their parents copulating. In these societies, discussions about sex with children were also very open and frank as part of a pattern of sex positiveness. For example, among the Ra'ivavaens studied by Marshall (1961, 241), children were aware of orgasm, the role of the penis (*ure*), and the clitoris (*tira*) in sexual arousal.

Other avenues for sexuality education included practices around childbirth. Oliver (1989) recounts that on old Raroia in the Tuamotu Archipelago, childbirth was a social event in which the whole community attended, including children, and even male members who also assisted in childbirth. This custom of including males in childbirth as assistants is notable, for in many parts of Oceania, as elsewhere, men are prohibited from participating in childbirth.

Indigenous beliefs about conception in French Polynesia are part of the informal system of education. In a study of the Marquesas in the late 1970s, Kirkpatrick (1983) reported the then-current belief that, although babies were conceived through the copulation of males and females, this was not sufficient. Divine intervention was also a necessary component.

The Tahitian ethnotheory of conception asserted that the fetus received physical and divine characteristics from both parents. The infant's sacred attributes were regarded as cynosure of its birth. In Old Tahiti, the genealogical system of ranking reckoned that the degree of divinity in each child was directly proportional to the degree of descent from his or her ancestral deities. The firstborn inherited more divinity or *mana* than the subsequent children, so that a genealogical line consisting of all firstborn children had more divinity than others. The amount of divinity was also synergistic, so that a firstborn of parents of equal divinity possessed more sacredness than either parent.

F. Allan Hanson (1970, 1444-1446) has written on the "Rapan Theory of Conception." This analysis focuses on the Rapanese ethnotheory that conception is most likely to occur in the three to four days following menstruation when it is believed women are most fertile. In order to prevent pregnancy, Rapanese couples abstain from sex during this three- to four-day period. While this practice is not an effective method for limiting family size, it can be understood as articulating with Rapan theories of physiology and reproduction.

The Rapanese woman, based on Hanson's survey of 85% of the population, has an average of 6.3 births and raises about five children per woman. This is considered burdensome by the Rapanese who would like to reduce family size to ideally two to three children. The Rapanese say that:

> a fetus is formed when semen enters the uterus and coalesces with the blood harbored there. The existence of ovaries, Fallopian tubes, and ova is not recognized. Menstruation ceases after conception, because all the blood goes to building the fetus. If conception has not occurred, the blood becomes stale after a month, is expelled in menstruation and is replaced with a fresh supply. The uterus opens and closes periodically, opening each month to allow the old blood to flow out. . . . Semen cannot enter when the uterus is closed, so there is no possibility of conception during the greater part of the cycle. (Hanson 1970, 1445)

This theory is also found in the Tuamotu Archipelago on Pukapuka. In the Huahine and Mo'orea villages studied by Oliver (1981, 334), as elsewhere in Tahiti, children were highly valued. Problems in conception were treated by a woman specialist who used an indigenous medication of hibiscus and green coconut.

## 4. Autoerotic Behaviors and Patterns

### A. Children and Adolescents

Among the Pukapukans, Mangarevans, and the Marquesans, during indigenous times prior to Christianization, a tolerant attitude was taken toward childhood sexual expression. Among the Pukapukans, children masturbated in public with no opprobrium. The parents apparently ignored their behavior (Ford & Beach 1953). Levy's research among Tahitians from 1962-1964, cites early explorer and missionary accounts of masturbation among adults and children (1973, 113-116). His work among rural Tahitians indicates children masturbate, although the Tahitian term used to describe masturbation refers to males, since it includes the morpheme for uncircumcised penis. Levy notes that "the emphasis on prepubertal male masturbation is striking" (1973, 115). It is considered a boy's activity outgrown with adolescence. However, adult censure of masturbation does occur and seems to be centered on the fear that the boy's foreskin might tear. Masturbation by post-superincised males is criticized as an indication that he cannot attract a female.

### B. Adults

According to William Davenport (1973), in traditional pre-Christian Tahiti, masturbation was sanctioned positively for young women and men.

## 5. Interpersonal Heterosexual Behaviors

It needs to be noted here that the three Euro-American developmental stages of childhood, adolescence, and adulthood may be of limited utility when encountering non-Western peoples. Adolescence is a fairly recent Western construct whose relevance and meaning cross-culturally will vary. For example, Kirkpatrick (1983) notes that the contemporary Marquesas islanders have an ethnotheory that encompasses four stages of human development: infancy, childhood, youth, and age.

### A. Children

During the traditional times, the Pukapukans, Mangarevans, and Marquesans permitted children open sex play (Ford & Beach 1953). The cultural practices of Marquesans and Pukapukans not only allowed open sex play among children but, as mentioned earlier, provided children clandestine opportunities to observe adult sexual behavior because of the sleeping arrangements. According to Oliver (1974) on Tahiti, coital simulation became actual penetration as soon as young boys were physiologically able. The Tahitians found children's imitation of copulation humorous. Other evidence suggests that young girls may have engaged in copulation before age 10 (Gregersen 1983).

Kirkpatrick's research (1983), based on 25 months of fieldwork in the Marquesas (primarily on Ua Pou and Tahiti during the late 1970s) provides much information on the lifecycle, gender identities, and the integration of traditional patterns with new cultural influences. According to

John Kirkpatrick, babies are massaged with oils and herbal lotions to make their skin smooth, and baby girls are given vaginal astringents to make the genital area sweet smelling. Such treatments for girls continue through puberty and include menstrual preparations as well. The application of fragrant oils, and the concern with cleanliness and personal hygiene, is tied into a wider Polynesian valuing of beauty and the body embedded in the traditional precontact culture. Suggs (1966, 25) comments that in traditional Marquesan society, girls may have had their first coital experience by age 10, and boys were circumcised between 7 and 12 years old.

Oliver's (1981) ethnography includes in-depth discussion of infancy, childhood, and other life-course stages in Tahiti (see the chapter on "Passing Through Life," pp. 342-400). In this regard, he notes that children played in mixed-gender groups until 13 or 14 years old. The Tahitian attitudes to children playing at copulation was one of amusement (1981, 366). However, as children approached the age of 11, adult parental attitudes shifted in regard to young females but not males. Oliver points out that parents objected to girls engaging in sex prior to marriage, an ideal that coexisted with an open and sex-positive attitude. Given Atean and Fatatan flexible definitions of marriage and the cohabitation of young people as a kind of trial marriage, the ideal of chastity in veiled-bride weddings accounted for only 8.9% of Atean and 22.5% of Fatatan weddings.

## B. Adolescents

In discussing adolescents, it is especially important to avoid ethnocentrism. Adolescence is a Western construct with specific age and social concomitants that is of limited use cross-culturally. A more culturally relevant approach for a discussion of Polynesian sexuality is marital status and hierarchy rather than age.

### Rites of Passage

Puberty rituals were practiced in traditional times among the Polynesians, including ceremonies in which male genitals were altered surgically, and females and males were both tattooed. These rituals defined the individual as having reached the age of procreation. Traditionally, superincision, along with tattooing, occurred some time after childhood, but before adulthood in the Society Islands.

Superincision continues to be part of contemporary Polynesian practices among some societies. One of the functions of the superincision is to make the penis hygienic and clean, just as vaginal astringents are used for cleanliness in young girls. This is part of the continuing traditional Polynesian cultural emphasis on beauty and cleanliness. It is believed that clean and sweet-smelling genitals make one more attractive as a partner (Kirkpatrick 1983).

However, the puberty ceremonies were and continue to be much more than male genital surgery. They are markers of a process of social-identity transformation as the youth approaches competence and adulthood. Kirkpatrick (1987) discusses Marquesan superincision as a "freeing or enabling event. It results in emergence into the world, rather than the incorporation of the subject into a new group or status" (1987, 389). Young Marquesan males take pride in being superincised for these reasons. Additionally, it is not considered proper for an unsuperincised male to have intercourse. In the Old Society Islands, Oliver (1974) notes that sex was allowed prior to the completion of the tattooing or superincision.

The superincision was traditionally done in the Marquesas by a local indigenous specialist. In the Old Marquesas, the superincision was performed after puberty, al-

though Kirkpatrick (1983) found that in the late 1970s, the age of superincision was expanded to include 11- to 18-year-old boys. Frequently, a boy or group of boys would request that a superincision be performed.

Levy (1973) describes Tahitian superincision in very similar terms. Superincision among Tahitians is part of a boy's entré into *taure'are'a* ("the time or period of pleasure"). Levy points out that this precontact pattern continues in modern times because of its association with Christian circumcision. Peer pressure, such as teasing about smegma, is the reason boys gave when asked why they pursued superincision. Reinforcing this is a belief that superincision enhances sexual pleasure. Linguistic evidence includes an indigenous term for "skin orgasm," which describes the unsuperincised male's orgasm as quick and unsatisfying (Levy 1973, 118-119).

In superincision, the foreskin is cut, various preparations may be applied on the wound, and then the penis is exposed to heat and salt water to heal. Young men will go to rock pools in the sea and expose their penis to the heat from sun-warmed rocks and then alternately bathe in the sea. When the incision is healed, the boys may return to their daily activities and wear shorts. This pattern is similar to the Tahitian regimen that has changed very little from traditional times. A group of boys gets together and asks a man known for his ability to operate on them. Parents are not told beforehand of the boys' plan to do this. A razor blade is now used to cut the skin, followed by bathing in the sea and application of herbal medicines. A fire is made with leaves, and the boys heat the penis from the vapors and then bandage it (Levy 1973, 118-119).

Marshall (1961, see below) reports that superincision, practiced among the ancient Ra'ivavaens, included sexuality education by a priest, as well as a training component in which the superincision scab was removed by copulation with an experienced woman. A boy cannot become a man, even among contemporary Ra'ivavaens, without the superincision. While specialists performed the superincision traditionally, any male with knowledge of the procedure may do so today. However, traditional elements persist in the technique, as well as in the removal of the scab through intercourse with the older experienced woman (Marshall 1961, 248).

Superincision is a characteristic Polynesian practice. Although the foreskin is only slit, the outcome of exposing the boy's penis is the same as in circumcision, according to Davenport (1977, 115-163). Although Davenport maintains that the dramatic ritual aspects of superincision have been lost, the genital operation continued at the time of his writing in 1976 in Polynesia.

Generally speaking, in the Polynesian area, women were not rigidly isolated when menstruating as in Melanesian groups. Like female puberty rituals throughout the world, the Marquesan girl's rite of passage is more continuous and less dramatic than the boys. Reproduction readiness was recognized by the growth of pubic hair. Kirkpatrick (1983) notes that if a menstruating female climbs a breadfruit tree, it is believed that the fruit will have blotched skin. In the Old Society Islands, there was no ritual around menstruation, although at puberty, girls did receive tattoos on the buttocks. Menstruating women were not to enter gardens or touch plants. Levy reports in his early 1960s research that some traditional beliefs persist regarding menstruation among Tahitians. Apparently, young women who were menustrating were told to avoid getting chilled or eating cold foods, as this could result in *ma'i fa'a'i* (the filled sickness). It is believed that if a girl does not menstruate, and/or if she remains a virgin, the blood will fill her body and head and make her crazy, also leading to *ma'ifa'a'i*. One act of intercourse was believed necessary to ensure good menstruation (Levy 1973, 124-126).

## Premarital Sexual Activities and Relationships

Among traditional French Polynesian societies, and for Polynesia generally, there were two standards for premarital sex that varied by status and rank, according to Davenport (1976). For example, among the Tahitians, firstborn daughters in lineages of firstborns were very sacred. As a consequence, their virginity was valued and protected until a marriage with a partner of suitably high status was arranged. Among these elite daughters, virginity was demonstrated, for example, by the display of a stained white bark cloth following coitus. Subsequent to the birth of their firstborn child, females of high rank were permitted to establish extramarital liaisons. On Pukapuka, according to Marshall Sahlins (1967), the chief kept a sacred virgin in his retinue as a symbol of his spiritual power.

Among the Margarevans and Marquesans, the only apparent restrictions on adolescent sexuality were incest, exogamy regulations, and/or the upper-class status of certain females. Premarital virginity was required for a chief's daughters but not for other youths. This pattern, according to Kirkpatrick (1983), continues even today, where concern for rules of exogamy and relatedness still persist among Marquesans. However, Marquesan youths may not be aware of their degree of relatedness to a potential partner when they begin a relationship, a source of concern to their elders.

Marshall's study of Ra'ivavae (1961), based on reports from the archives of ethnographer J. Frank Stimson, his own ethnographic research with elderly consultants, archeological, and linguistic analysis, presents a picture of a highly eroticized Tahitian culture that has been largely dismantled by colonialism and Christianity.

The clitoris, among ancient Ra'ivavaens, received a great deal of cultural attention. Marshall reports that the clitoris was elongated by the child's mother through oral techniques as well as tying it with an hibiscus cord. An elongated clitoris was considered a mark of beauty. According to Marshall's research, the king would inspect a girl's clitoris to see if it was sufficiently elongated for her to marry. The girls who were ready for marriage would display their genital attributes at a sacred *marae* (Marshall 1961, 272-273). Both cunnilingus and fellatio were practiced among traditional Marquesan youth and adults (Gregersen 1994, 272; Marshall 1961). Suggs (1966, 71-73) describes contemporary Marquesan sex as including virtually no foreplay and lasting five or less minutes.

For the indigenous population of French Polynesia, the *taure'are'a* period in the lifecycle is demarcated as a special status. *Taure'are'a* is part of a traditional pattern that continues today primarily in rural areas. In the Marquesas, adolescence includes a category known as *taure'are'a* that operates as a transitional period between childhood, *to'iki* (kid), and adulthood *'enana motua* (parent person). Kirkpatrick describes it as "errant youth" (1987, 383-385). *Taure'are'a* are characterized by their sexual adventures and same-gender peer orientation. *Taure'are'a* are known for brief sexual liaisons in contrast to adult sexuality, which is integrated within the larger context of domesticity. As a period in the lifecycle, *taure'are'a* is characterized by its pleasure-seeking goal and is looked back upon fondly by adults (Kirkpatrick 1987, 387). *Taure'are'a* is regarded as a temporary status that gradually evolves into adulthood. It is one in which brief sexual encounters are replaced by relations and cohabitation with their partners (Levy 1973, 123). It has also been argued that *taure'are'a* is a time of "testing

relationships" through cohabitation with one or more partners serially (Elliston 1996).

According to Kirkpatrick (1983), peers are very important for the Marquesan youth, especially the finding of a confidant with whom one can share secrets, including sexual ones. Of apparent equal interest is the establishment of heterosexual relationships. These sexual liaisons must remain secret because of the rigid Christian sexual prohibition against premarital sex. For example, if pregnancy were to occur, the girl would be either forced into marriage or her relationship would be ended, although this is not true of Tahiti or other areas of French Polynesia. Peer relations are not severed with marriage, although one's behavior is expected to mature. Sexual gossip is considered normal for youths but not for adults. There is some expectation of a double standard for youthful males and females. Youthful females are expected to act more coy than their male counterparts. In the Marquesas of the late 1970s, males were the sexual initiators, while it was considered inappropriate for girls to take the lead. However, it is a cultural value that both partners should desire and enjoy sex.

Levy also reports on the *taure'are'a* period among rural Tahitians. *Taure'are'a* for Tahitians during the 1960s was very similar to that described for the Marquesans. For girls, *taure'are'a* status converged with menstruation and the development of secondary sexual characteristics. According to Levy, the girls' *taure'are'a* period is less distinctive than the boys in terms of role contrast with childhood norms (Levy 1973, 117-122). For boys, *taure'are'a* status does not begin with superincision, but occurs gradually over the next year or two following it.

In Piri (a pseudonym), Levy notes that most youngsters had sexual intercourse between 13 and 16 years of age. Virginity was regarded as unusual for *taure'are'a* males and females, although shifting demographics, with the migration of *taure'are'a* girls to Papeete, seems to be having an impact on the prevalence of virginity. At the time of Levy's research (1962-1964), the *taure'are'a* male was the initiator in terms of making the arrangements for a sexual encounter (Levy 1973, 122-124).

Douglas Oliver's *Two Tahitian Villages* (1981), historically situated in 1954-1955, offers a detailed enthnography of social life, life stages, sexual behavior, courtship, marriage, and relationships in two rural villages on Huahine and Mo'orea. Oliver's male Tahitian consultants began having intercourse between the ages of 12 and 15 years old. According to Oliver, the standard position was male on top. Male foreplay, which typically lasted from five minutes to half an hour, included: "breast fondling and kissing, clitoral manipulation, and cunnilingus; mutual orgasms were expected and . . . nearly always achieved" (1981, 274).

Night crawling/creeping is a traditional practice that continues even today in various forms throughout Polynesia. It is known as *moe totolo* among Samoans and *motoro* among Mangaians and Tahitians. There is some controversy among anthropologists as to the function and meaning of this institution. Oliver (1989) regards night crawling/creeping as resulting from sleeping arrangements in which family members shared the same sleeping quarters. It seems to be embedded in the *taure'are'a* pattern for adventure by both females and males.

Night crawling is characterized by the efforts of a young man to sneak into the house of a sleeping young woman and copulate with her without her parents finding out. Apparently, this could be accomplished either with collusion from the young female or without her prior consent. In the latter case, the belief was that the suitor would penetrate the young female while she was asleep; and, if she awoke, she would enjoy it so much she would not want to scream and alert her parents. Oliver (1989) offers a different explanation, suggesting that the parents may have abetted the situation if their daughter was without suitors by making arrangements for a young man to sneak into their home, and then deliberately catching the couple and forcing them to get married. Levy reported that *motoro* continued among Tahitians in Piri at the time of his research, but that the pattern was on the decline (1973, 123).

## C. Adults

### Cohabitation, Marriage, Family, and Sex

Adult interpersonal heterosexual behaviors, like other aspects of French Polynesian sexuality, must be placed within its cultural context. Oliver (1974, 1981, 1989) has reported that the traditional Tahitians, both premaritally and maritally, experienced sexuality with great joy and gusto, and that this value was expressed in the wider culture through styles of interaction and verbal banter, religion, entertainments, mythology, and so on. This ties in with William Davenport's analysis of the "erotic codes" of Polynesia, defined as those symbolic aspects of culture that "both arouse sexuality and enhance its expression" (1977, 127). Davenport's 1977 essay on "Sex in Cross-Cultural Perspective" is very useful in summarizing this cultural framework and describing intracultural variations.

Marriage was traditionally restricted between individuals by status in the chiefly structure and lineage. Upper ranks were not permitted to marry lower ranks. Formal marriages were relegated to the upper and perhaps middle echelons (Oliver 1989b). Although couples of disparate status were not usually permitted to marry, they could cohabit, although they were dissuaded from having children (Oliver 1974). Divorce was traditionally handled flexibly with the couple returning to her or his own family. They were then free to remarry. There was no formal legal divorce in premodern Polynesia, according to Weckler (1943).

Beauty and sex were closely linked in Polynesia, although in Old Tahiti it was most pronounced. In Tahiti, because large size was a symbol of beauty, higher-ranked boys and girls were secluded, overfed, and prevented from exercise so that they could put on weight. Subsequently, they were displayed in all their pale and fat beauty so as to attract a potential spouse. According to Ford and Beach (1951), Pukapukans also liked plump builds on men and women. Apparently, the Tahitian's value on beauty was reiterated in the belief that a baby could have several biological fathers who would contribute their respective physical traits. Since extramarital, as well as premarital sex was accepted, women would select attractive and athletic young men as sexual partners. In the traditional Marquesas, Ford and Beach (1951) noted that elongated labia majora were considered attractive. Levy has uncovered an ethnotheory of relationships that suggests couples must have a physical compatibility. This is in contrast to one-night trysts in which one person may be as good as another (1973, 129).

In the mid-1950s Aeta and Fatata, Tahitian attractiveness norms favored physical types that were neither too thin nor too fat. Aside from the veiled-bride weddings in which chastity, or at least evidence of strong parental control over the daughter's social behavior, was a prerequisite, previous sexual experience was not unexpected (Oliver 1981, 291-292). See below for Oliver's (1981) typology of Tahitian weddings.

The sexual practices of indigenous French Polynesians include cultural-religious institutions. Gregersen's (1983) review of Oceanic sexual practices makes note of the *arioi* cult. This was an organization of Tahitian men and women divided into sects, located throughout the Society Islands, who traveled within the archipelago as singers, dancers, athletes, and sexual exhibitionists. Eroticism pervaded the Tahitian songs and dances of the *arioi* entertainers. The *arioi* members were allowed free sexual expression on their journeys, but they were not allowed to marry or have children. This organization was embedded with religious meaning and has been interpreted as a fertility cult. The *arioi* practiced abortion and infanticide, because having children was not permitted for the member. Should an *arioi* become a parent, he or she was humiliated and their participation in the cult limited. The *arioi* were well known for their sexual pursuits with one another and with noncult members encountered on their journeys. Members were selected on the basis of physical beauty and talent that transcended chiefly boundaries to include commoners as well.

Sex and eroticism were made public in other ways as well. Linton's 1939 report of the Marquesans revealed that naked dancing, along with public group copulation, was practiced as part of feasting and festivals as a pre-Christian traditional pattern. Linton disclosed that women would pride themselves on the number of men they had sex with. In ancient times, Pukapukans of the Tuamotu Archipelago would reserve places called *ati*, where men and women could go for sex parties. These were organized by a person who also acted as a guard, to prevent conflict by angry ex-lovers and husbands (Gregerson 1983).

One of Marshall's (1961, 273) Ra'ivavaen consultants contended that, in traditional times, public sex followed men's prayers in the sacred temples. According to this particular consultant, various positions were used, cunnilingus was practiced, and "sperm was smeared upon the face and in the hair as a kind of mono'i' (coconut oil)" (Marshall 1961, 273; Elliston 1996). Ceremonial copulation was integrated within the spiritual ethos, which, according to Marshall, was saturated with eroticism as a central theme. The erotic was related to fertility, reproduction, and the sacred.

Polynesian societies have been distinguished by a position for coitus at variance from the Western "missionary" position, as the Polynesians refer to the male-prone-above-prone-female position. According to Oliver (1989b), the "Oceanic position" was traditionally far more popular than the missionary position. The "Oceanic position" is one in which the couple sat facing each other. Other positions included the man squatting or kneeling between the woman's legs and pulling her toward him, lying side-by-side facing one another, or with the woman's back to the man's front. In the Marquesas, a sitting position was reported where the woman sat astride the man's lap or assumed a side-to-side lying position. A variety of sexual positions were used, although the woman on top seems to have been the more-prevalent position related to the generalized Polynesian concern for the sexual pleasure of women. The most common position taken today seems to be the missionary position, which is undoubtedly a result of Christian missionary efforts (Gregersen 1983).

Delayed ejaculation for the man was considered a valued expertise in Old Polynesia because it facilitated the female partner's pleasure. Multiple orgasms were valued by both partners in traditional Polynesia as well. Although there was a lesser emphasis on foreplay and more concern with intercourse, the Marquesans were known for practicing cunnilingus and fellatio. Coitus interruptus was also reported among the Marquesans. According to Ford and Beach (1951), the Pukapukans had no preference for sex during the day or at night; each was just as likely.

Kissing among Polynesians is a Western custom. The traditional Tahitian/Polynesian kiss (*ho'i*) consisted of mutual sniffing and rubbing of noses on the face. According to Levy (1973, 128),

> kissing on the mouth is still considered a mild perversion. Contemporary Tahitian foreplay according to younger male Pirians includes: "kissing, fondling the woman's breasts, and occasionally cunnilingus." Fellatio was considered a practice of "bad girls" in Papeete. (Levy 1973, 123)

Intercourse among Pirian youth continues the traditional pattern that emphasizes the female orgasm. A man is humiliated by not bringing his partner to orgasm. The role of the clitoris in women's pleasure, as in traditional times, still is part of people's sexual knowledge. In Piri, it is referred to as *teo*. Linguistic evidence provided by the term *'ami'ami* suggests a precontact focus on eroticism. It is considered a unique capability of some women who can contract and relax the vaginal muscles during coitus (Levy 1973, 128). Elliston (1996) notes that Sahlins makes reference to the Hawaiian term *'amo'amo* in *Islands of History*, writing: "Girls were taught the *'amo'amo*[,] the 'wink-wink' of the vulva, and the other techniques that 'make the thighs rejoice'" (p. 10).

Surveys on the frequencies of sex for traditional indigenous French Polynesians at various points in history are sparse, although qualitative reports found in the ethnographic literature are available for some of this area. Suggs's 1956-1958 study, *Marquesan Sexual Behavior* (1966), combines qualitative and quantitative data. Frequencies for Marquesan adolescents are sometimes said to be more than ten times in a single night. This may be compared to frequencies for older married couples that are reported of from five times a night to two to three times a week. Questions of accuracy and bias must be considered in evaluating this data. Levy's Pirian male consultants reported that sex occurred daily in the first year or two of a steady relationship, but dropped to about one to three times a week, declining after several years to once every two or three weeks or once a month. A sex-positive attitude is evident as there is no indication of sanctioning of sex among the elderly. Sex continues up to two to three weeks prior to childbirth and is resumed in one to two months. However, sex is prohibited during menstruation (Levy 1973, 125-126).

Data on contemporary sexuality in French Polynesia are not abundant. A sexual survey was considered in Tahiti under Le Direction de la Santé Publique in 1993, but had not been initiated as of early 1997. Spiegel and colleagues (1991) have provided recent sexual data collected between October and December 1990 on 74 sexually active women between the ages of 18 and 44 who were working in bars or nightclubs. It must be noted that this sample is not at all representative of the population at large. The median number of sexual partners among this group was 3 (range 1 to 200), and the median number of sexual encounters was 104 (range 12 to 1,095). This segment of the population is important because of their risk for contacting and spreading sexually transmitted diseases.

Marriage patterns in traditional French Polynesia included monogamy, serial monogamy, polygyny, and polyandry. For example, Oliver (1974) observes that elite chiefs were required to engage in monogamy; lower male chiefs could have two to three wives, although only one wife's children could inherit titles and property. The middle and lower classes of Tahiti were known to have been polygynous. The Marquesas were known for polyandry. An elite woman's household might include a primary as well as secondary husbands (*pekio*). The secondary husbands were subordinate to the primary husband and performed menial duties, although as members of elite households, they had privileges associated with the aristocracy (Goldman 1970, 142). According to Thomas's 1987 review of gender in the Marquesas, polyandry is better understood as part of domestic relations rather than conjugal relations *per se*. However, Goldman asserts that an unequal sex ratio of 2.5 men to one woman may account for the pattern (1970, 142). Commoners practiced cohabitation rather than the formalized marriages of the privileged classes.

The Marquesans traditionally engaged in a ritual in which the husband was required to have intercourse with his wife almost immediately after childbirth. Following expulsion of the afterbirth, the wife would bathe in a stream. It was believed that intercourse should then occur while the wife was in the stream in order to stifle the flow of the bleeding.

In contemporary French Polynesia, marriage is legitimized by the Church although most people are not formally married. The Protestant Marquesans must be married before membership in the Church is granted. The transition from the secret liaison to marriage signals a dramatic change from youth to adulthood (Kirkpatrick 1983). On Ra'ivavae, Marshall found that of 31 marriages, 29 couples had cohabited (1961, 275). This continues the traditional pattern of premarital sex despite a Christian overlay.

Nonlegalized adoption, a common pattern throughout Polynesia, must be interpreted in the context of the social organization of the family. Kirkpatrick (1983) has noted that the traditional Marquesans had a pattern of large multicouple households that included not only extended families, but also others not closely related. Such households may have been indicative of wealth. This pattern would also include children whose biological parents were unable to raise them for a variety of reasons. Although this kind of adoption or fosterage is not legal in colonial French Polynesia, it is socially instituted and informally practiced. It represents an old and more widespread Polynesian pattern of fluid adoption that may include close kin, more-distant kin, and even those not directly related.

The trend in the Marquesas in the late 1970s was toward nuclear conjugal family dwellings. This represents the influence of Catholicism as well as broader Western trends. However, the traditional pattern of foster parents and casual adoption still continues today. Kirkpatrick (1983) found that on Ua Pou, 19% of the individuals in the households were unrelated to the household head. Tahitians have a similar pattern of fosterage. Levy reports that 25% of the Tahitian children were not residing with their biological parents at the time of his research (1973, 474-483).

Polynesian childrearing patterns have continued to persist despite the social disruption caused by exploitation, missionization, and colonialism. The Ritchies (1983) have identified several common themes delineating traditional Polynesian childrearing. Among these are fosterage and adoption as part of a wider pattern of community investment in children. Because the community was traditionally composed of lineages of related people, parenting was a collective endeavor, unlike that in the West where it is exclusive to the nuclear family. Howard and Kirkpatrick note that adoption continues today to function as a mechanism to foster relationships between families at the community level and to create alliances at a more macro level (1989, 87). There are economic and ecological implications as well. Adoption of children may help a family with domestic labor since children have certain tasks to do. As they mature, they become important economic contributors for a household. Adoption is also "a powerful adaptive mechanism for equitably distributing people relative to resources, including land, in island environments" (Howard & Kirkpatrick 1989). In addition, early indulgence of infants was followed by an expectation of autonomy for children beginning around 2 to 3 years of age. Peer socialization began with sibling care and responsibility for younger siblings, and included larger community groups of peers who spanned a broad age range from 2 to 20 years old.

*Extramarital Sex*

Extramarital sex was also part of precolonial French Polynesian cultures. The Pukapukans celebrated a successful fishing expedition with extramarital sex. Apparently, women would initiate sexual joking as the men returned with their catch. This was followed by trysts in the bush. Both single and married people participated in these extramarital opportunities with no opposition from their spouse, provided they respected class and incest prohibitions (Oliver 1989b). Among the Tahitians, restrictions on sexuality occurred for upper-class women, sometimes before as well as after marriage, although men and women of common status were free to participate in extramarital sex (Oliver 1989b; Davenport 1977).

There were, therefore, two standards in effect for traditional Tahitians—one for commoners and others, and one for the very elite. Firstborn children, in genealogical lines of firstborns, were regarded as very high ranking and sacred. Purity of the genealogical line was important and controlled through rules against premarital and extramarital sex until, at least, the woman gave birth to a successor. Then, she was permitted extramarital freedom. For example, Douglas Oliver notes that married *ari'i* women were notoriously promiscuous (personal communication with Oliver 1994). Elite women were known to separate from their husbands and to establish their own residence and have lovers (Oliver 1974). Men and women of common status faced no restrictions on extramarital sex (Davenport 1976, Oliver 1989).

On Tahiti, according to Sahlins (1976), a male chief who produced an illegitimate heir practiced infanticide unless measures were taken to alter the status of the mother to be equal to that of the chief. On Mangareva, the chief's power was such that the rule of prohibition against marriage to a first cousin was often disregarded.

Extramarital sex was also institutionalized in the Society Islands in terms of sexual hospitality. Male *taiō* participated in a form of formal friendship relations where sexual intercourse was permitted with one's married *taiō*'s wife. *Taiō* of the opposite sex were not permitted intercourse because their relationship was a social siblinghood and prevented by the incest taboo (Oliver 1974; Ferdon 1981). Sexual hospitality is regarded by some researchers as a widespread Polynesian pattern (Gregerson 1983).

Among the Pukapukans, adultery was believed to cause delayed delivery, and women in such situations were expected to confess (Gregersen 1983, 255). Kirkpatrick (1983) did not find extramarital affairs practiced on Ua Pou, although Suggs (1966) reported that extramarital affairs were common in the Marquesas during his sojourn there. However, according to Goldman (1970, 585) precontact adultery could have dire consequences, resulting in murder by jealous husbands and possible suicide by the wife of an adulterous husband. Suggs (1966, 119-120) reveals that at the time of his research, although adultery was condemned, it still occurred. However, it caused jealousy and hard feelings among both sexes if found out.

Although adultery was the primary cause of breakups and divorce in Aeta and Fatata in the mid-1950s, it was not reason enough by itself. Oliver's Tahitian consultants regarded adultery as something any Tahitian, given an opportunity, would be likely to do (1981, 317). While church pastors in both villages declared adultery as a sin and cause for expulsion, the Tahitian attitude was more relaxed, reflecting a double standard of greater tolerance of male adultery than female (p. 334).

## 6. Homoerotic, Homosexual, and Bisexual Behaviors

### A. Children and Adolescents

Some Tahitian upper-class men, according to Douglas Oliver, kept boys in their household for sex, although this was not a widespread practice. Suggs (1966, 24) states that homosexual experiences among boys, and possibly girls, were common among Marquesan adolescents.

### B. Adults

Since first colonial contact, the indigenous peoples of Polynesia have been engaged in culture change and transformation. Indigenous systems of homosexual options may be influenced, or even reinvigorated, by the advent of Western homosexual identities. For French Polynesia, it is necessary to point to this complexity in order to understand homosexuality/bisexuality from a cultural perspective that is not a Western-based psychological model.

There were two forms of homosexual behavior in ancient Tahiti. Some Tahitian *ari'i* men, according to Oliver (1989), kept boys in their household for sex. The other context for homosexual expression was associated with the *māhū* status. The *māhū* was a transvestic tradition that included homosexual practices with nontransvestic males. It is important to note that since the *māhū* is a transgendered category, the term homosexual is not really an appropriate descriptor for *māhū* sexuality. Swallowing semen was believed by Tahitians to foster masculine vigor (Gregersen 1994, 274). The indigenous pattern of the *māhū* is not an equivalent to Western subcultural homosexuality or Western transvestism, but was an integrated part of the wider Tahitian culture. The homosexual aspects of the *māhū* status were not its most significant features, but rather it was the cross-gendered aspects of dress and behaviors that identified one as a *māhū*. The *māhū* is reported throughout Polynesia and was found among the Marquesans, where it was very similar to the Tahitian form, according to Oliver (1989). Ferdon (1981) found evidence that the *māhū* began dressing in women's attire while very young. (See Section 7 on gender diversity for further discussion.)

Data on Western-type homosexuality in contemporary French Polynesia is sparse. Chanteau et al. (1986) distinguish the presence of a male homosexual community of Polynesian men that frequented hotels, bars, restaurants, and nightclubs of Tahiti (presumably in Papeete). This population was considered at high risk for LAV/HTLV-III infection by Chanteau et al. who conducted a serological survey. (See discussion on HIV/AIDS below in Section 10.) The population recruited for the serological survey consisted of 50 transvestite homosexuals known as *raerae*. Forty percent of this population had only one partner and frequency of intercourse was once a week. Eighty-five percent of this group had intercourse only once a month. Some of this population had had plastic surgery and female hormone therapy. It is difficult from this report to assess the character of this population, since there are a number of possible gendered identities.

Spiegel and colleagues (1991) collected data from 156 male homosexuals aged 13 to 54 between October and December 1990. The annual median number of sexual partners was 9.5 (range 1 to 600) and the median number of sexual encounters was 156 (range 2 to 5,810). Of this population,

56.4% were transvestites. Unfortunately, it is not possible to place the transvestites in the cultural milieu, as sampling information was not provided by the researchers. Nor is it possible to determine the social identity of the transvestites in terms of the *māhū*, Western gay transvestism, a modern synthesis of both patterns, or some other identity (Williams 1986, 255-258). These transvestites are employed in bars, hotels, and nightclubs. Apparently a *raerae* subcultural expression is found in the Miss Tane and Miss Male beauty contests. It should be noted here that the Western term *transvestite* is not really appropriate in describing the complexity of transgendered identities and homosexualities of French Polynesia.

Levy also records the introduction of the term *raerae* to refer to homosexual and lesbian behavior. While Pirians maintained lesbian behavior (oral and mutual masturbation) did not occur on Piri, it was believed common in Papeete in the bar scene. It was not considered part of a lesbian orientation but rather context-specific. Women who engaged in lesbian encounters were not stigmatized, according to Levy (1973, 139-141), but more-recent research indicates that lesbian lifestyles are problematic in Tahiti (Elliston 1996).

## 7. Gender Diversity and Transgender Issues

In discussing transgendered individuals among indigenous populations, Western-based terminology, such as "transsexualism" or gender dysphoria, are inappropriate, since they refer to 20th-century Western psychiatrically derived categories. The expression of cross-gender or transgender roles needs to be understood in the sociocultural context and not viewed from the Western perspective as "deviant" behavior. Levy (1971, 1973) has provided some of the most significant research on this subject in his study of the *māhū* of Tahiti. The *māhū* was a transgendered role for males who dressed and took on the social and occupational roles of Tahitian women including taboos and restrictions. According to Levy, the *māhū* tradition has continued from precontact times, although attributes of the status have changed somewhat, so that today the *māhū* no longer cross-dresses, but still engages in work that is considered traditionally female, such as household activities. Levy considers the *māhū* a role variant for men. An interesting parameter of the *māhū* in rural Tahiti is that a man can be "*māhū*-ish" without being *māhū*. *Māhū* are regarded as being "natural," yet one does not have to remain *māhū* throughout the life course. There is a conception of effeminacy associated with *māhū*. *Māhū* are not stigmatized nor are their heterosexual male partners. According to Levy, "a *māhū* is seen as a substitute female" (1973, 34). In Piri, the *māhū* are not believed to practice sodomy, but are fellators of other men.

As mentioned previously, this institution was widespread throughout Polynesia. The *māhū* engaged in fellatio with nontransvestite male partners, but these partners were not considered *māhū* or homosexual. *Māhū* were also reported to have been sex partners of chiefs. This suggests that the Polynesian gender paradigm is one in which sex and gender are discrete categories and the *māhū* identity functioned to highlight gender differences. Levy suggests that the *māhū* may be analyzed as an embodied warning to other males on how to avoid nonmale behavior.

In neo-Tahiti, the *māhū* continues to be regarded as a natural phenomenon. While various explanations are offered for its occurrence, the *māhū* is generally a nonstigmatized status and accepted within wider Tahitian soci-

ety. According to Kirkpatrick (1983), the Ua Pou Marquesans note that there are no *māhū* in their area today because the *māhū* have migrated to Tahiti. Kirkpatrick describes the *māhū* as an ambiguous or disvalued status. The Marquesans also have a more recently introduced term, *raerae*, which is used interchangeably with *māhū*. The Marquesan *māhū* are not considered women, but rather men who want to act as women. The significant attributes for the Marquesan gender paradigm in terms of *māhū* status relate to occupation and appropriate peer relations, rather than homosexual behavior *per se*.

Kirkpatrick (1983) reports on the Marquesan *vehine mako*, or shark woman, which is a gender-variant identity for females. Unlike the *māhū*, the *vehine mako* is not based on relational or occupational criteria. Instead, the shark woman is characterized by an aggressive and vigorous sexuality. The defining feature of *vehine mako* woman is that she is a sexual initiator, an activity defined as masculine. Thus, both the *māhū* and *vehine mako* are defined in terms of the reversal of gender-role attributes. However, *vehine mako* is not a female equivalent of the *māhū*, or recognized as a form of female homosexuality. Levy regards the institution of the *māhū* as a boundary-maintenance mechanism that identifies the limits of what is considered conventional male and female gender behavior, i.e., masculinity and femininity. Whether this applies to the *vehine mako* must be determined by further research.

[*Update 2002*: In the text above written in 1996, I raised a cautionary note concerning the use of "Gender Conflicted Persons" as a subheading, which was used then for this section, because of its ethnocentric bias. That caution is even more important in light of the emergence of intersexed and transgendered persons in North America and Europe during the 1990s. It is even more important today that researchers avoid biased and ethnocentric wording that is rooted in the Greco-Roman philosophical dualism of male and female genders/sexes. The concept of "gender conflicted" is intertwined with Western medical/psychiatric derived categories whose applicability in the cross-cultural record remains to be determined. I have suggested substituting the terms "gender diversity" or "gender variance" generally, and the indigenous terms specifically, following Sue Ellen Jacobs recommendation for replacing the term *Berdache* with "two spirit" in reference to Native American gender diversity (1994, 7). The trend among anthropological researchers is to use less "culture-bound" terminology and to seek to understand gender variance within the extant gender paradigm.

[In the original text above, I reported on Robert Levy's (1971, 1973) substantial research on the Tahitian *māhū*. Levy considered the *māhū* a role variant for men, which operated as a negative identity for Tahitians in a society where there was little gender disparity in roles. The *māhū*, according to Levy's interpretation, serves as a clear model of what not to be. Although this research and argument are compelling, it is important to note that this research has not gone unchallenged. In his discussion of "Polynesian Gender Liminality Through Time and Space" (1996, 285-328), Niko Besnier makes a strong and persuasive argument that the *māhū*, although clearly not a third gender as found in the cross-cultural records elsewhere, is nevertheless something more and outside of a variant role for men, as Levy claims. Besnier suggests that the *māhū* is part of a wider Polynesian pattern of gender liminality (threshold) or gender-liminal personhood that occurs within a dimorphic gender paradigm. Besnier makes several important points regarding the Polynesian *māhū* in general, but argues for a historical particularistic interpretation of the *māhū* as gender liminality. He argues that although gender liminality:

is best viewed as a borrowing process rather than as a role or identity, it does give rise secondarily to a rather loosely defined identity. Fundamentally counterhegemonic, it can be a means through which some individuals stake a claim on certain forms of prestige, but at some cost, as evidenced in the low status with which it is associated in the politics of sexual encounters, for example. (Besnier 1996, 327)

[Thus, Besnier takes issue with Levy's functionalist interpretation of the *māhū* as located in Tahitian low sex-role disparity. Rather, Besnier points to a clear division of labor by gender in Tahiti and argues that the *māhū* "blurs gender categories rather than affirms them" in a society where ". . . gender boundaries are anything but blurred." (Besnier 1996, 307). The question of the character of Tahitian gender roles is an important one that has influenced subsequent research. Thus, Levy's perspective that Tahitian gender roles are relatively androgynous has informed subsequent literature on men's and masculinity studies, such as David Gilmore's *Manhood in the Making*, specifically his chapter, "Exceptions: Tahiti and Semai" (1990, 201-219). Gilmore provides a cultural-ecological explanation for Tahitian gender roles, wherein it is argued that in environs where resources are abundant and where there are no enemies and serious environmental challenges, Tahitian men have nothing to prove and no reason to separate their roles as radically different from women. Besnier (1996) argues against this view that Tahitian gender roles have little gender differentiation and rejects Levy's explanation of the *māhū* as related to androgynous gender roles.

[Besnier regards the *māhū* status as an extremely complex positioning that simultaneously incorporates ambiguity, conflict, and contestation. It is articulated within the Polynesian, and specifically Tahitian, concept of personhood as context oriented (Besnier 1996, 328; Nanda 2000, 70). While Besnier (1996) notes that the gender liminality is porous, it may be adopted as a temporary position. Elliston's research in Tahiti finds that long-term participation in gender liminality facilitates its legitimization (1999, 236).

[While commonalities may occur throughout Polynesia, there are also regional differences that prohibit the view of the *māhū* as a monolithic Polynesian presence, as testified in the work of Levy and Besnier. Indeed, further research is needed to understand regional context, but also the gender crossings with Western-derived identities such as gay and transgender. There is far less evidence of liminal females and that the identity may be of more recent origin (Besnier 1996, 288; Elliston 1999). Indeed, there is little research on this subject, most notably Kirkpatrick's (1993) ethnographic research of the *vehine mako* in the Marquesas, and recently, Elliston (2000) in Tahiti.

[However, Besnier reports "copious early accounts of *māhū* in Tahiti, . . . Hawaii, the Marquesas and New Zealand . . ." (1996, 294), and argues that there appears to be historical continuity in contemporary gender liminality, although she cautions that this needs more ethnographic and ethnohistorical research. For example, the *māhū*, whether in rural or urban settings, has proclivities towards occupations and tasks associated with women. The *māhū* is thought to have exceptional expertise in these areas. For example, in urban settings, *māhū* demonstrate skill as secretaries and as domestic workers. While some intermittent cross-dressing occurs on special occasions, such as dances, permanent crossdressing is not reported among *māhū*. However, Elliston's (1999, 236) research indicates that most Tahitian *māhū* men wear a *pareu*, a clothing item worn mainly by women. Gender-liminal persons also span social backgrounds. Historically, *māhū* have been reported as part of chiefly retinues,

acting as confidants to persons of chiefly rank and offering sexual services for male chiefs, although it is not clear if the *māhū* are actually of chiefly rank themselves (Besnier 1996, 297-298).

[According to Besnier (1996, 300), "sexual relations with men are seen as an optional consequence of gender liminality, rather that its determiner, prerequisite or primary attribute." Levy (1973) reports that the Tahitian *māhū* engages in fellatio with non-*māhū* men, who in return view the *māhū* as an accessible and unencumbered alternative to women for sexual release. However, same-sex relations with non-liminal men do not define the *māhū* (Elliston 1999). In contemporary Polynesia, erotic encounters with *māhū* do not commonly occur once a man has married, suggesting that sex with liminal men is a second choice to sex with a woman (Besnier 1996, 301-303). Thus, the meanings associated with sex with *māhū* vary from that of the heterosexual ideal, such that it is "viewed as promiscuous, transient and lacking in significance," contesting Levy's (1973) stance that the *māhū* is "nonstigmatized" (Besnier 1996, 302). Sex with liminal men can be conceived as embedded in wider Polynesian ideologies of illicit sexuality. *Māhū* sexuality is further complicated by Western-style gay identities, known as *raerae*, currently emergent in urbanized areas. This is considered a French importation (Nanda 2000, 65). Both Levy (1971, 1973) and Besnier (1996) offer provocative interpretations of the *māhū* in French Polynesia that deserve careful review before conclusions can be drawn. Serena Nanda (2000) provides an overview in "Liminal Gender Roles in Polynesia" that integrates Levy (1971, 1973), Besnier (1996), and Elliston's (1999) research. (*End of update by A. Bolin*)]

## 8. Significant Unconventional Sexual Behaviors

### A. Coercive Sex

Douglas Oliver's (1974) intensive research could not find evidence of rape in the precolonial Society Islands, and according to J. E. Weckler, "rape is practically unknown in (traditional) Polynesia" (1943, 57). However, today, rape does occur. According to one anthropologist with a research background in Tahitian culture, first encounters with a young girl are often forced by the young man. Levy's consultants argued that *haree* (rape) may have occurred in the past on Piri, but it does not occur today. Levy found no reports of violent rape on the island of Huahine in which Piri is located (1973, 124). More recently, Elliston (1996) reported rape and attempted rape on Huahine and in Papeete.

### B. Prostitution

Oliver reports that prostitution, as defined in the West, was associated with European contact and exploitation of the Pacific. In Old Polynesia, there were opportunities for women in the royal courts to entertain visitors sexually. These positions were not stigmatized in the least. One consultant reports that today, in the Westernized and urbanized city of Papeete, prostitution is not uncommon, although statistics were not available at the time of this writing. Stanley also reported that today there is evidence of male prostitution among some transvestites (1992, 34).

### C. Pornography and Erotica

Information was not available at the time of this writing. The sexual survey of La Direction de la Santé Publique (1995) is expected to address this (see address in Section 12B, Sex Research and Advanced Professional Education, Major Sexological Surveys, Journals, and Organizations).

## D. Paraphilia

It is especially important here to specify the culture of derivation in discussing unconventional behaviors. What is unconventional from Western perspectives is not necessarily regarded so from the indigenous view. Generally, the Pacific peoples have a low incidence of Western categories of paraphilia. In fact, Gregersen's review of the literature of Oceania revealed only the two rather suspicious reports described below. Archival data on which these reports are based may be inaccurate and even fanciful. It is with caution that these are presented here.

According to Gregersen (1983, 1987, 278), among the precolonial Pukapukans, a form of sexual contact with corpses was said to have occurred. In this group, a strong aversion to corpses was expressed in *tapu*. Contact with corpses was prohibited and friends were not even permitted to look at the dead. This *tapu* was mitigated in certain circumstances by the belief that the "grief of a cousin will be naturally so intense that the tabus will be broken—not only by looking at the corpse but even embracing it and sometimes having intercourse with it." This violation of the corpse *tapu* was referred to with a special term, *wakaavanga*. Although contact with corpses was *tapu*, such behavior was expected of cousins. Archival data on which this report is based may or may not be inaccurate and is subject to Western and historical bias.

Gregerson (1983) also notes that sexual contact with animals occurred among the Marquesans when partners were unavailable. Men were known to have sex with chickens, dogs, and even horses, while women were said to have lured dogs into performing cunnilingus on them. However, this account may also be in need of further investigation of its accuracy.

From the vantage of the indigenous peoples of French Polynesia, there was one behavior that was considered sexually deviant. The celibate role of the priest is considered at great variance with male Marquesan ways of being, according to Kirkpatrick (1983). This role is considered distinctive and deviant with the nature of Marquesan masculinity.

## 9. Contraception, Abortion, and Population Planning

### A/B/C. Attitudes, Practices, Teenage Pregnancies, and Abortion

In precolonial Tahitian times of the latter 1700s, discussion of teen pregnancies must be situated within the cultural and historical context. The *taure'are'a* was a period of sexual freedom during adolescence, and this, combined with fosterage, testifies that teenage pregnancy was not problematic and should not be interpreted in terms of Western concerns over teenage pregnancy, where the cultural ideal is delayed pregnancy until young adulthood. It was not unusual among traditional indigenous societies for pregnancy to occur during the teenage years; in many cultures, it was the norm. Today, according to one consultant with Tahitian cultural experience, grandparents may adopt the child, while teenage marriage is much rarer.

The precontact Tahitians practiced infanticide and abortion on occasion. The stratification by class was castelike and intermixing was strictly prohibited. The offspring of parents who were respectively from an upper- and lower-class status was strangled at birth. The *arioi* society members were prohibited from producing offspring, since children would be a hinderance to the many religious activities required by cult membership (Ferdon 1981). Abortion and infanticide were practiced not only by *arioi* members, but also in cases where *arioi* couples of two different class levels conceived. In these cases, infanticide had no connection with population control, but was practiced instead to counter a violation of interclass marriage. This was tied to the status system in which titles and positions were inherited through chiefly lineages. Infanticide was practiced in situations in which either a woman's child was conceived with a male of lower rank or in which a man's child was conceived with a woman of lower rank. Although, according to Goldman, male infanticide was more common on Tahiti, Marquesan female infanticide was prevalent enough to result in a ratio in which men far outnumbered women (1970, 563).

In the villages of Aeta and Fatata, mixed attitudes were voiced on contraception, although few, if any, used contraceptives regularly. According to Oliver, only "some [from both villages] . . . knew of the existence of contraceptive devices, mainly condoms" (1981, 341).

While attitudes about abortion was varied in these two Tahitian villages, it was generally viewed as the concern of the individual. A folk abortificient, a blend of green pineapple and lemon juices, was available from older women specialists and believed to cause miscarriage within two months (Oliver 1981, 34).

### D. Population Control Efforts

Information could not be obtained by the author at the time of this publication. See La Direction de la Santé Publique "Sexual Survey" (1995; see address in Section 12B, Sex Research and Advanced Professional Education, Major Sexological Surveys, Journals, and Organizations).

## 10. Sexually Transmitted Diseases and HIV/AIDS

### A. Sexually Transmitted Diseases

In Tahiti, testing for sexually transmitted diseases is available at STD and maternity public clinics. There is a dearth of information on the epidemiological study of chlamydia in the Pacific Islands, with the exception of one study in New Caledonia. Chungue et al. (1988) have examined the rate of *Chlamydia trachomatis* in three populations of at-risk individuals in order to illustrate the importance of specific diagnostic testing for monitoring of this infection. Chlamydia was found in 53% of 53 bar women (ages 15 to 45), 24% of 75 women attending a public maternity clinic for routine care (ages 14 to 40), and 37% of 71 men attending an STD clinic with acute or subacute urethritis (ages 17 to 37).

*Neisseria gonorrhea* infection was associated with chlamydia infection in 11.4% of the bar women and 18.3% of the men with urethritis. Of the chlamydia-positive women, 58.3% of the bar women and 23.2% of the women at the maternity clinic were without clinical complaints. Eight bar women (15%) were infected with *Trichomonas vaginalis*. This study proves that *Chlamydia trachomatis* is common in Tahiti and warns that asymptomatic women who are chlamydia-positive may be vectors for the spread of the disease. The authors have proposed routine testing for *Chlamydia trachomatis* in STD or maternity clinics.

According to a 1984 public health report by John A. R. Miles, in 1971, three cases of syphilis were reported, but by 1977, the rate was 23 per 10,000. The rate of gonorrhea is 27 per 10,000.

### B. HIV/AIDS

*Incidence, Patterns, and Trends*

Several important surveys have been conducted regarding HIV in the French Polynesian population. Chanteau et al. (1986) conducted a serological survey screening for anti-LAV/HTLV-III antibodies using Institut Pasteur and Abbot Laboratories immunoassay kits. Four populations considered high risk were tested. These included 80 homosexual and transvestite men of low-SES (socioeconomic status); 37 homosexual/bisexual men of Polynesian, European, and Chinese ethnic background of middle- or upper-SES, 35 female prostitutes, and 33 blood-transfusion patients. Four positive results were obtained from the group of 37 homosexual/bisexual men; three Europeans and one Chinese were positive. This group was a highly traveled population that appears to be the source of the introduction of LAV/HTLV-III in French Polynesia. Nicholson and colleagues (1992) measured the prevalence of HTLV-I using the ELISA test and confirmation by Western Blot in 19,975 blood samples from Australia and the western Pacific. No antibody was detected in the 198 sera from the French Polynesian population. However, a 1989 study by Alandry et al., a 1991 report by Spiegel et al., and research by Gras et al. (1992) all report evidence of HIV and AIDS in French Polynesia.

These researchers suggest that HIV was introduced in French Polynesia as early as 1973. Factors contributing to the introduction and spread of HIV include blood transfusions prior to August 1985, tourism primarily from continental France and the United States, and certain groups of individuals whose behaviors put them at risk.

The Allandry (1991) report on HIV is based on data collected over three years. In June 1988, 27,000 HIV tests were given, including to 16,881 blood donors. Of the 27,000, 45 were seropositive; none of the blood donors were HIV-positive. While an additional two children not older than 18 months were HIV-positive, these were not included in the study *per se*. The age breakdowns for the HIV-positive individuals are: 18 months to 6 years, 1; 20 to 29 years old, 24; 30 to 39 years, 10; 40 to 49 years, 8; 50 years and over, 2.

Of the 32 HIV-positive men and 13 HIV-positive women, 22 are of Polynesian ancestry, 19 are European, and 4 are Asiatic. Twenty-two are homosexual or bisexual males (48.8%), 12 are polytransfusions recipients (26.6%), 6 are partners of HIV-positive people (13.3%), 3 are heterosexuals with multiple partners, and 2 are former drug users. Based on this data, the rate of HIV-positives is 2.4 per 10,000.

Only 1 (0.7%) of the 147 homosexuals screened by Spiegel et al (1991) showed a positive result. A subsequent screening of 156 male homosexuals, among whom 56.4% are transvestites working in hotels, nightclubs, and restaurants, and 74 sexually active females working in bars, was conducted between October and December 1990. Among the male homosexuals 13 to 54 years old, 3 (1.9%) are positive for HTLV-I. Among the 74 females 18 to 44 years old, 3 (4.1%) are positive. The median number of sexual partners was 9.5 and the median number of sexual encounters was 156 in male homosexuals, while for the female population, the median number of partners was 3 and the median number of sexual encounters was 104 for the period of October to December 1990. Among the total population of 230 subjects, 2 are IV-drug users, but both are HTLV-I negative. The authors concluded that the risk for HTLV-I infection among male homosexuals is increasing, and the infection is also present in a female population at risk.

Gras et al. (1992) reported on 96 cases of HIV-positive and AIDS-infected persons. Of these, 78% were between 21 and 40 years old, 72 of the 96 had acquired HIV through sexual contact, and 94% live in Tahiti. The sex ratio was 2.8 males to 1 female. Fifty-five percent were Europeans, 38% Polynesians, and 7% Asiatic. Gras estimates the rate of new HIV infection at 20 new cases per year in a French Polynesian population of 200,000, with 150 cases of AIDS per 1 million inhabitants. The rate of prevalence of HIV-positive cases between 1987 and 1990 per 100,000 was a mean of

9.45, a median of 9.65, and the extremes of 7.2 and 11.4. As of June 21, 1993, 30 cases of AIDS were reported for French Polynesia, according to the regional office for the Western Pacific of the World Health Organization (1993, 9). Twenty-two cases were reported for 1979-1990, five AIDs cases for 1991 with a rate of 2.7, and three in 1992 for a rate of 1.6, with no cases reported as of July, 1993.

The ELISA test can be performed in only six laboratories on the Island of Tahiti. A Western Blot confirmation test is required for the HIV-positive cases. HIV-positive patients are provided sex education on condom use, and follow-up of asymptomatic individuals continues for six months. Treatment may be either by a private physician or under the Chef du Service de Medecine du Centre Hospitalier Territorial. A medical exam for the occurrence of opportunistic diseases is also available. Individuals with AIDS may be treated with AZT and pentamidine.

*Availability of Treatment and Prevention Programs*

Government policies contribute to the tracking of HIV through readily available testing at hospitals and public health centers. Testing may be done at the following centers: Le Centre de Transfusion Sanguine, Le Centre Hospitalier Territorial, L'Institut Territorial de Recherches Medicale Louis Malarde (Centre des Maladies Sexuellement Transmissibles, Centre de Lutte contre la Tuberculose). La Direction de la Santé Publique en Polynésie Française has been mandated by the Bureau d'Education to teach safe-sex practices. A December 1985 law requires testing of blood donors. In 1986, a consulting commission for HIV was formed, along with efforts at follow-up. Since 1987, condoms may be imported tax-free. In 1990, free and anonymous testing was made available to the public. In monitoring HIV, the French Polynesian Public Health Service and health authorities have implemented HIV-serum surveillance following World Health Organization guidelines. Twenty thousand screening tests for both HIV I and HIV II are done on a population of less than 200,000. Thus far, only HIV I has been found.

[*Update 2002*: There is very little information on current French Polynesian sexual behavior and HIV/AIDS available, with the exception of high-risk populations of *raerae* and bargirls (Beylier 1998). Confusion over terminology of *raerae* exists in the literature. Anthropologists, including Levy (1973) and Besnier (1996), define *raerae* as Western-style homosexuality in reference to a person "who does not perform a female's village role and who dresses and acts like a man, but who indulges in exclusive or preferred sexual behavior with other men" (Levy 1973, 140). However, in the report *Sexual Behavior and AIDS Prevention in French Polynesia* summarized below, "raerae" are referred to as transvestite or transsexual males (1999, 7).

[This confusion was recognized as a problem by the French Polynesian Health Department in its efforts to evaluate and direct HIV-prevention activities for the community-at-large. A study was conducted with the approval of the Territorial AIDS Control Committee in November 1998. The report was published in November 1999 by the Ministry of Health and Research, Health Department, and the Messager Contre le SIDA association, under the title: *Sexual Behavior and AIDS Prevention in French Polynesia. Papeete, Polynésie Française*. The objective of this invaluable research was to "describe sexual and prevention-related behavior in the population residing in French Polynesia and to gather information in an attempt to understand the social logic which leads certain people to protect themselves, but others not, when faced with a possible risk of infection" (1999, 2).

[The population surveyed included 1,043 people, 523 males from 15 to 35 years old and 520 females from 15 to 35 years old on Tahiti, Moorea, and the Leeward Islands. Respondents ranged from those with no schooling through those with senior high school education or higher. All ethnic groups and mixes thereof were included (1999, 6). Areas covered included lifetime number of partners, sexual orientations, first sexual experience, forced sexual activity, recent sexual activity including new partners and occasional partners, social acceptance of infidelity, social acceptance of homosexuality, preventative behavior with regard to AIDS and STDs including condom use over the lifetime, opinions about condom use and other preventative behaviors, screening for HIV antibodies among the population surveyed, knowledge and attitudes about AIDS, sources of information about sexuality, contraception, pregnancy, and abortion, comparing 1993 and 1999, and sexually transmitted diseases. Some of the important findings are listed below:

- "Over the last five years, almost half of young people used condoms during their first sexual experience" (1999, 3).
- The highest level of protection was with those most at risk, those who have intercourse with occasional partners, and homosexual or bisexual men.
- "The non-use or intermittent use of condoms with occasional partners by more than half of the subjects was a particularly high risk" (1999, 3).
- Men were most often the ones to take the initiative in condom use whereas women gave preference to relationship-based models of risk management, which tend to utilize careful selection of partners than on reducing risks with condom use in sexual intercourse (1993, 4).
- "People with little education had less access to prevention information" (1993, 4). Regardless of age group, the cost of condoms was regarded as an obstacle by half those surveyed.

[According to the World Health Organization, 54 cases of AIDS were reported for the years 1979-1996, with no cases reported for 1997 and 1998 (WHO Report 1999, 1). (*End of update by A. Bolin*)]

## 11. Sexual Dysfunctions, Counseling, and Therapies

### A. Concepts of Sexual Dysfunction

Sexual dysfunction must be considered within the cultural context. For example, sexual dreams with orgasm among Levy's rural Tahitians were thought to be the work of spirits and were regarded as "dangerous" (Levy 1973, 129). The concept of "dangerous" is not translatable as a sexual dysfunction, but neither is it considered desirable.

Hooper (1985, 158-198) collected ethnomedical data in two rural Tahitian communities on the Iles Sou-le-Vent, a group of islands northwest of Tahiti in the 1960s. Indigenous folk medicine continues despite the cultural disruption caused by missionization and colonialism and the introduction of Western medicine. Hooper describes a form of "ghost sickness" with sexual implications. Ghost sickness, *mai tūpapa'u*, is a special category of illness that is believed to be caused by *tūpapa'u*. Such illnesses are characterized by their "bizarre" aspects and can only be cured by an indigenous healer, a *tahu'a*. *Tūpapa'u* is an incorporal aspect of the self, distinct yet coexisting along with the Christian notion of the soul. Each person has a *tūpapa'u* that can travel during one's dreams. When an individual dies, his *tūpapa'u* continues to remain in the vicinity watching over his kin.

The *tūpapa'u* is regarded as having a personality and can be protective, but also vengeful and playful.

One form of ghost sickness entails visitations from *tūpapa'u* of the opposite sex. While erotic dreams are regarded as encounters with *tūpapa'u* of the opposite sex (no mention of same sex was made) and are therefore not really dreams at all, these are not regarded as problematic if they are occasional and the partners are varied. However, illness can occur if an individual becomes obsessed with a particular visiting *tūpapa'u*. In such a case of ghost sickness, the individual may lose weight, refuse sex with his or her spouse, and may be seen chatting and laughing with invisible *tūpapa'u*. Hooper describes the case of B, who refused sex with her husband. "She would bathe in the evenings, put on scented oil and special clothes, and lie on a separate bed, talking and laughing with a *tūpapa'u tāne* (male ghost)." A healer was called in who "commanded the *tūpapa'u* to leave and never return. B slept soundly for the rest of the night and had no more dealings with the male ghost again. According to . . . the healer . . . the ghost was 'ripped up' by his familiar" (Hooper 1985, 178).

Levy's Pirian consultants reported that frigidity and impotence did not occur. The only conditions acknowledged as leading to impotence were illness or getting chilled. The Tahitian theory of sexual attraction may explain this, and clearly points to the importance of a relativistic perspective when regarding Western categories of sexual dysfunction. A Tahitian man who does not have an erection with a woman in an intimate situation, assumes that he must not want to have intercourse (Levy 1973, 128-129).

## 12. Sex Research and Advanced Professional Education

### A. Sexological Research

Sexual research concerning indigenous peoples of the area of French Polynesia includes the work of Richard Levy (1971, 1973), as well as Douglas Oliver (1989ab, 1974), I. Goldman (1970), W. H. Davenport, R. Linton (1939), and R. C. Suggs (1966), among others. In addition, contemporary sex research with a focus on HIV and at-risk sexual behaviors has been conducted by G. Alandry et al. (1989), C. Gras et al. (1992), and Spiegel et al. (1991). La Direction de la Santé Publique conducted a sexual survey in November 1993. The results were to be available in 1995, but were not published at the time of this writing. The interested reader is encouraged to write for the survey. There is no organized advanced education in sexuality in French Polynesia.

### B. Major Sexological Surveys, Journals, and Organizations

A major sexological survey is the following:

Ministry of Health and Research, Health Department, and Messager Contre le SIDA Association. *Sexual Behavior and AIDS Prevention in French Polynesia*. Papeete, Polynesie Francaise. November 1999.

Journals and periodicals in which sexological information, research, and reports on French Polynesia may be found include:

La Direction de la Santé Publique "Sexual Survey," Epistat CMRS Laure Yen, BP 611, Papeete-Tahiti, Polynésie Française.

Counseil Economique Social et Cultural, Avenue Bruat, BP 1657, Papeete, Tahiti, Polynésie Française.

Ministry of Social Affairs, P. O. Box 2551, Papeete, Tahiti, Polynésie Française.

Institut Territorial de la Statistique, BP 395, Papeete, Tahiti, Polynésie Française.

Service d'Information et de Documentation, BP 255, Papeete, Tahiti, Polynésie Française.

Institut Territorial de Recherches Medicales, Louis Malarde, BP 30, Papeete, Tahiti, Polynésie Française.

*The Medical Journal of Australia*, Australasian Medical Publishing Company, 1-5 Commercial Road, P. O. Box 410, Kingsgrove, New South Wales, 2208 Australia.

*Medecine Tropicale*, Institut de Medecine Tropicale, Marseille Armee, France.

Oceania University of Sydney, Oceania Publishing, Mackie Building, Sydney, New South Wales, 2006 Australia.

*Bernice P. Bishop Museum Bulletins*, 1525 Bernice Street, Box 19000-A, Honolulu, HI 96817-0916, U.S.A.

*Journal of the Polynesian Society*, University of Auckland, Anthropology Department, Polynesian Society, Private Bag, Auckland, New Zealand.

*Journal de la Sociétédes Océanistes*, The Association for Social Anthropology in Oceania.

*The Journal of Pacific History.*

*Pacific Studies.*

*Australian and New Zealand Journal of Sociology.*

## Acknowledgments

I am deeply indebted to Dr. Douglas Oliver who gave generously of his time in reading and commenting on this manuscript. His expertise and many works have been an invaluable source of knowledge and inspiration to me. I would also like to thank Dr. Victoria Lockwood and Dr. Paul Shankman for their helpful suggestions for researching this subject. Dr. Deborah A. Elliston provided an extremely detailed commentary on this paper. Her research among the Tahitians has been critical in this review, as she provided thoughtful and up-to-date feedback. I am grateful to Linda Martindale for manuscript preparation, editing, computer magic, and reference research.

Acknowledgments for updates: I would like to thank Dr. Bruno Hubert, Medecin Coordinateur pour les Maladies Transmissibles, Direction de la Santé, Papeete, Polynésie Française, for making available to me a crucial document for this update: *Sexual Behavior and AIDS Prevention in French Polynesia* (Ministry of Health and Research, Health Department, and Messager Contre le SIDA Association, Papeete, Polynésie Française, November 1999). Thanks are due to Robert Francoeur for taking on and continuing this admirable endeavor of the *IES* and for being a wonderful mentor and friend. Special thanks to my intrepid Elon student researcher, Hillary Sherman, for locating the recent data on HIV and AIDS in French Polynesia.

## References and Suggested Readings

Alandry, G., et al. 1989. Infection par le virus de l'immuno-deficience humaine (VIH) en Polynésie Française. *Medecine Tropicale, 49*(1):71-72.

Besnier, N. 1996. Polynesian gender liminality through time and space. In: G. Herdt, ed., *Third sex/third gender: Beyond sexual dimorphism in culture and history.* New York: Zone Books.

Blackwood, E. 1986. Breaking the mirror: The construction of lesbianism and the anthropological discourse on homosexuality. *Journal of Homosexuality, 11*(3-4):1-17.

Blot, W. J., L. Le Marchand, J. D. Boice, & B. E. Henderson. 1997. Thyroid cancer in the Pacific. *Journal of the National Cancer Institute, 89*(1): 90-94.

Burrows, E. G. 1968. Polynesia: Culture areas in Polynesia. In: A. P. Vayda, ed., *Peoples and cultures of the Pacific* (pp. 179-191). Garden City, NY: The Natural History Press.

Chanteau, S., F. Flye Sainte, M. E. Chungue, R. Roux, & J. M. Bonnardot. 1986. A serological survey of AIDS in a high

risk population in French Polynesia. *The Medical Journal of Australia, 145*(2):113.

Chungue, E., et al. 1988. Chlamydia trachomatis genital infections in Tahiti. *European Journal of Clinical Microbiology & Infectious Diseases, 7*(5):635-638.

CIA. 2002 (January). *The world factbook 2002.* Washington, DC: Central Intelligence Agency. Available: http://www.cia.gov/cia/publications/factbook/index.html.

CIAO (Columbia International Affairs Online). Maps and country data. *The CIA world fact book 1999.* http://www.ciaonet.org. Retrieved October 10, 2000.

Davenport, W. H. 1977. Sex in cross-cultural perspective. In: F. A. Beach, ed., *Human sexuality in four perspectives* (pp. 115-163). Baltimore, MD: Johns Hopkins University Press.

Dening, G. 1980. *Islands and beaches.* Honolulu, HI: University of Hawaii Press.

Drage, J. 1995. The exception, not the rule: A comparative analysis of women's political activity in Pacific Island countries. *Pacific Studies, 18*(4):61-92.

Elliston, D. 1996/1997. (January 15). Comments re Bolin, Anne, 'The Polynesian Islands: French Polynesia.' Unpublished comments.

Elliston, D. A. 1999. Negotiating transitional sexual economies: Female mahu and same-sex sexuality in Tahiti and her islands. In: E. Blackwood & S. E. Wieringa, eds., *Female desires: Same-sex relations and transgender practices across cultures* (pp. 230-252). New York: Columbia University Press.

Ferdon, E. N. 1981. *Early Tahiti: As the explorers saw it 1767-1797.* Tuscon, AZ: University of Arizona Press.

Ferdon, E. N. 1991. Tahiti. In: T. E. Hayes, ed., *Encyclopedia of world cultures, vol. II: Oceania* (pp. 305-307). Boston: G.K. Hall & Company.

Ford, C. S., & F. A. Beach. 1951. *Patterns of sexual behavior.* New York: Harper & Row.

Gilmore, D. 1990. *Manhood in the making: Cultural concepts of masculinity.* New Haven, CT: Yale University Press.

Goldman, I. 1970. *Ancient Polynesian society.* Chicago: University of Chicago Press.

Gras, C., et al. 1992. Surveillance epidemiologique de l'infection par le virus de l'immunodeficience humaine (VIH) et du syndrome d'immunodeficience acquise (SIDA) en Polynésie Française en 1991. *Medecine Tropicale, 52*(1): 51-56.

Gregersen, E. 1983. *Sexual practices: The story of human sexuality.* New York: Franklin Watts.

Gregersen, E. 1994. *The world of human sexuality: Behaviors, customs, and beliefs.* New York: Irvington Publishers, Inc.

Grosvenor, M. B., ed. 1963. *National Geographic atlas of the world.* Washington, DC: National Geographic Society.

Hanson, F. A. 1970. The Rapan theory of conception. *American Anthropologist, 72*(6):1444-1446.

Hanson, F. A. 1991. Rapú. In: T. E. Hayes, ed., *Encyclopedia of world cultures, vol. II: Oceania* (pp. 273-276). Boston: G.K. Hall & Company.

Hays, T. E., ed. 1991. *Encyclopedia of world cultures. Volume II: Oceania.* Boston: G.K. Hall & Co.

Henningham, S. 1992. *France and the South Pacific: A contemporary history.* Honolulu: University of Hawaii Press.

HIV InSite 2000. *HIV/AIDS throughout the U.S.: The Pacific Islands area.* http://hivinsite.ucsf.edu. Feb. 19, 1997-Sept. 18, 2000. Retrieved October 12, 2000.

Hooper, A. 1966. *Marriage and household in two Tahitian communities.* Cambridge, MA: Harvard University (unpublished Ph.D. dissertation).

Hooper, A. 1985. Tahitian healing. In: C. D. F. Parsons, ed., *Healing practices in the South Pacific* (pp. 158-198). Honolulu, HI: The Institute for Polynesian Studies.

Howard, A., & J. Kirkpatrick. 1989. Social organization. In: A. Howard & R. Borofsky, eds., *Developments in Polynesian ethnology* (pp. 47-94). Honolulu, HI: University of Hawaii Press.

Howard, M. C. 1989. *Contemporary cultural anthropology.* New York: Harper/Collins.

Human Relations Area Files. 1991. Mangareva. In: T. E. Hayes, ed., *Encyclopedia of world cultures, vol. II: Oceania* (p. 172). Boston: G.K. Hall & Company.

Human Relations Area Files. 1991. Raroia. In: T. E. Hayes, ed., *Encyclopedia of world cultures, vol. II: Oceania* (pp. 276-277). Boston: G.K. Hall & Company.

Institut Territorial de la Statistique, Polynésie Française. 1988. *Résultats du recensement général de la population de la Polynésie Française du 6 Septembre 1988.*

Jacobs, S. E. 1994. Native American two spirits. *Anthropology Newsletter, 35*(8):7.

Kay, P. 1963. *Aspects of social structure in Manuho'e.* Cambridge, MA: Harvard University (unpublished Ph.D. dissertation).

Kirkpatrick, J. T. 1985. Some Marquesan understandings of action and identity. In: G. M. White & J. T. Kirkpatrick, eds., *Person, self, and experience: Exploring Pacific ethnopsychologies* (pp. 80-120). Berkeley, CA: University of California Press.

Kirkpatrick, J. T. 1983. *The Marquesan notion of the person.* Ann Arbor: UMI-University of Michigan Research Press.

Kirkpatrick, J. T. 1987. Taure'are'a: A liminal category and passage to Marquesan adulthood. *Ethos, 15*(4):382-405.

Le Marchand, L., J. Hankin , F. Bach, et al. 1995. An ecological study of diet and lung cancer in the South Pacific. *The International Journal of Cancer, 63*:18-23.

Levy, R. 1971. The community function of Tahitian male transvestism: A hypothesis. *Anthropological Quarterly, 44*:12-21.

Levy, R. 1973. *Tahitians: Mind and experience in the Society Islands.* Chicago: University of Chicago Press.

Linton, R. 1939. Marquesan culture. In: A. Kardiner, ed., *The individual and his society* (pp. 138-196). New York: Columbia University Press.

Lockwood, V. S. 1989. Tubuai: Women potato planters and the political economy of intra-household gender relations. In: R. R. Wilk, ed., *The household economy* (pp. 197-220). Boulder, CO: Westview Press.

Mann, J. M., D. J. M. Tarantola, & T. W. Netter. 1992. *AIDs in the world: The Global AIDs Policy Coalition.* Cambridge, MA: Harvard University Press.

Marshall, D. 1961. *Ra'ivavae.* Garden City, NY: Doubleday & Co., Inc.

Medecins Sans Frontires. 2000. *The health of the population of French Polynesia and nuclear testing* (pp. 1-15, 1995). http://www.oneworld.org/news/pacific/msf_report.html. Retrieved October 12, 2000.

Medecins Sans Frontires. 2000. *Health in French Polynesia—The effects of French nuclear testing* (pp. 1-3, 1995). http://canterbury.cybersplace.co.nz/peace/nuchealth.html. Retrieved October 12, 2000.

Miles, J. A. R. 1984. Public health progress in Polynesia. In: J. A. R. Miles, ed., *Public health in the Pacific* (pp. 157-173). Helmstedt, Germany: Geo Wissenschaftliche Gesellschaft.

Moorehead, A. 1966. *The fatal impact: An account of the invasion of the South Pacific 1767-1840* (Part I. Tahiti, chaps. 1-6, pp. 3-86). New York: Harper & Row.

Nanda, S. 2000. *Gender diversity: Crosscultural variations.* Prospect Heights, IL: Waveland Press, Inc.

Nicholson, S., et al. 1992. HTLV-I infection in selected populations in Australia and the Western Pacific Region. *Medical Journal of Australia, 156*(12):878-880.

Oliver, D. L. 1974. *Ancient Tahitian society.* Honolulu, HI: University of Hawaii Press.

Oliver, D. L. 1981. *Two Tahitian villages: A study in comparisons.* Provo, UT: Brigham Young University Press.

Oliver, D. L. 1989a. *Oceania: The native cultures of Australia and the Pacific Islands* (vol. I, part 1. Background and part 2. Activities). Honolulu, HI: University of Hawaii Press.

Oliver, D. L. 1989b. *Oceania: The native cultures of Australia and the Pacific Islands* (vol. II, part 3. Social relations). Honolulu, HI: University of Hawaii Press.

Pacific Region Acknowledges AIDS Epidemic. 2000. *Australian Nursing Journal, 6*(9):14, (electronic pages 1 and 2), April 1999. http://proquest.umi.com. Retrieved November 28, 2000.

Ritchie, J., & J. Ritchie. 1983. Polynesian childrearing: An alternative model. *Alternate Lifestyles, 5*(3):126-141.

Sahlins, M. 1967. *Social stratification in Polynesia.* Seattle, WA: University of Washington Press.

Scupin, R., & C. R. DeCorse. 1992. *Anthropology: A global perspective.* Englewood Cliffs, NJ: Prentice-Hall.

*Sexual behavior and AIDS prevention in French Polynesia.* 1999 (November). Papeete, Polynésie Française: Ministry of Health and Research, Health Department, and Messager Contre le SIDA Association.

Shore, B. 1989. Mana and Tapu. In: A. Howard & R. Borofsky, eds., *Developments in Polynesian ethology* (pp. 137-174). Honolulu, HI: University of Hawaii Press.

*Socio-demographic profile: French Polynesia.* Country Profiles United Nations Population Information Network (POPIN). http://www.undp.org/popin. Retrieved October 19, 2000.

Spiegel, A., et al. 1991. HTLV-I in French Polynesia: A serological survey in sexually exposed groups. *Medical Journal of Australia, 155*(11):718.

Stanley, D. 1992. *Tahiti-Polynesia handbook.* Chico, CA: Moon Publications.

Suggs, R. C. 1960. *The island civilizations of Polynesia.* New York: The New American Library.

Suggs, R. C. 1966. *Marquesan sexual behavior.* New York: Harcourt, Brace and World.

Tahiti Friendship Society. 2000. *Population 1988.* http://tahitinet.com/presense/population.html. Retrieved October 19, 2000.

Thomas, N. 1987. Complementarity and history: Misrecognizing gender in the Pacific. *Oceania, 57*(4):261-270.

Thomas, N. 1990. *Marquesan societies: Inequality and political transformation in Eastern Polynesia.* Oxford, England: Clarendon Press.

Thomas, N. 1991. Marquesas Islands. In: T. E. Hays, ed., *Encyclopedia of world cultures, Volume II: Oceania* (pp. 188-191). Boston: G.K. Hall & Company.

*United Nations statistics.* 2000. http://www.un.org. Retrieved Oct. 10, 2000.

Vayda, A. P., ed. 1968. *Peoples and cultures of the Pacific.* Garden City, NY: The Natural History Press.

von Strokirch, K. 1993. *Tahitian autonomy: Illusion or reality?* (Doctoral dissertation). Bundoora, Victoria, Australia: Department of Politics, La Trobe University.

Weckler, J. E. 1943. *Polynesian explorers of the Pacific* (Smithsonian Institution War Background Studies. No. 6). Washington, DC: Smithsonian Institution.

Williams, W. L. 1986. *The spirit and the flesh: Sexual diversity in American Indian Culture.* Boston: Beacon Press.

World Health Organization. 1993. The current global situations of the HIV/AIDs pandemic. *Global Programme on AIDS.* Geneva: WHO.

*WHO Report on global surveillance of epidemic-prone infectious diseases.* AIDS Cases Reported to WHO as of November 1999. http://www.who.int/emc-documents. Retrieved November 29, 2000.

*Worldmark encyclopedia of nations.* 1988. New York: World Press, Ltd.

# Germany

## (*Bundesrepublik Deutschland*)

Rudiger Lautmann, Ph.D., and Kurt Starke, Ph.D.
*Updates by Jakob Pastoetter, Ph.D., and
Hartmut A. G. Bosinski, Dr.med.habil., and the Editor*

## Contents

## *Demographics and a Brief Historical Perspective*

ROBERT T. FRANCOEUR

### A. Demographics

Located in central Europe, Germany embraces 137,847 square miles (357,021 km²) and is slightly smaller in size than the state of Montana. Denmark and the Baltic Sea mark its borders on the north, the Netherlands, Belgium, Luxembourg, and France on the west, Austria and Switzerland in the south, and Poland and the Czech Republic on the east. Germany's terrain includes lowlands in the north, uplands in the center, and the Bavarian Alps in the south. The climate is temperate and marine.

In July 2002, Germany had an estimated population of 83.25 million. (All data are from *The World Factbook 2002* (CIA 2002) unless otherwise stated.)

**Age Distribution and Sex Ratios**: *0-14 years*: 15.4% with 1.05 male(s) per female (sex ratio); *15-64 years*: 67.6% with 1.03 male(s) per female; *65 years and over*: 17% with 0.64 male(s) per female; *Total population sex ratio*: 0.96 male(s) to 1 female

**Life Expectancy at Birth**: *Total Population*: 77.78 years; *male*: 74.64 years; *female*: 81.09 years

**Urban/Rural Distribution**: 85% to 15%

**Ethnic Distribution**: German: 91.5%; Turkish: 2.4%; other, mostly Serbo-Croatian, Italian, Russian, Greek, Polish, and Spanish: 6.1%

**Religious Distribution**: Protestant: 38%; Roman Catholic: 34%; Muslim: 1.7%; unaffiliated or other: 26.3%

**Birth Rate**: 8.99 births per 1,000 population

**Death Rate**: 10.36 per 1,000 population

Rudiger Lautmann, Ph.D., Bremen University FB 8, GW 2, B 1460 28334 Bremen, Germany; LautmannHH@aol.com. Professor Dr. Kurt Starke, Hauptstr. 6 A, 04774 Zeuckritz, Germany; kurt@ starke.I.uunet.de. Jakob Pastoetter, Ph.D., Eichborndamm 38, D-13403, Berlin, Germany; Magnus Hirschfeld Archive for Sexology at Humboldt University, Prenzlauer Promenade 149-152, 13189 Berlin, Germany; jmpastoetter@compuserve.de.

(CIA 2002)

**Infant Mortality Rate**: 4.65 deaths per 1,000 live births

**Net Migration Rate**: 3.99 migrant(s) per 1,000 population

**Total Fertility Rate**: 1.39 children born per woman

**Population Growth Rate**: 0.26%

**HIV/AIDS** (1999 est.): *Adult prevalence*: 0.1%; *Persons living with HIV/AIDS*: 37,000; *Deaths*: 600. (For additional details from www.UNAIDS.org, see end of Section 10B.)

**Literacy Rate** (*defined as those age 15 and over who can read and write*): 99%, with 100% attendance in nine or ten years of compulsory schooling

**Per Capita Gross Domestic Product** (*purchasing power parity*): $26,200 (2000 est.); *Inflation*: 2.4%; *Unemployment*: 9.4%; *Living below the poverty line*: NA

### B. A Brief Historical Perspective

Julius Caesar defeated Germanic tribes in 55 and 53 B.C.E., but Roman expansion north of the Rhine River was stopped in 9 of the Common Era. After Charlemagne, ruler of the Franks from 768 to 814, had consolidated Saxon, Bavarian, Rhenish, Frankish, and other lands, the eastern part became the German Empire. The Thirty Years' War (1618-1648) split Germany into several small principalities and kingdoms. After Napoleon, Austria challenged Prussia's dominance in the area, but Prussia prevailed. In 1867, Otto von Bismarck, the Prussian Chancellor, formed the North German Confederation. After Bismarck managed the defeat of Napoleon III, he formed the German Empire in 1871 with King Wilhelm I as Prussian German emperor or Kaiser. The German Empire and its colonial possessions reached its peak just before World War I. The Republic of Germany (1919-1933) faced a disastrous economic collapse brought on by war reparations to France and its allies. The National Socialist German Workers' (Nazi) Party came to power with Adolph Hitler in 1933, and started World War II. In the aftermath of the war, Germany was split into an eastern portion under Communist control, and a western democratic republic.

The unification of the Federal Republic of Germany (West Germany—the "Old Lands") and the German Democratic Republic (East Germany—the "New Lands") in 1990 caused serious economic problems for the whole population. The long-lasting tension between richer and poorer regions will mask the remarkable differences that have developed in sexual habits. Possibly the unexpected unification, together with the increasing immigration, will lead to new turbulences on the sexual front.

Germany, as well as the predominantly German-speaking countries of Austria and Switzerland, has always received large numbers of immigrants. For many centuries, its geographic situation in the middle of Europe meant that the country functioned as a transit land and clearinghouse for people of other nations. Fascist rule with its tenet of Aryan purification interrupted this mobility for a dozen years and the Iron Curtain for four decades. Apart from these historic peculiarities, the German-speaking countries have always fulfilled the paradox of a "cosmopolitan province." Exportation and importation of ideas and persons created a melting pot. Diverse cultural traditions and ethnic backgrounds currently form a contradictory mixture, apparently productive as well as unstable.

In this region, the following events occurred within the 20th century: the invention of sexology, a sexual repression of extreme cruelty, and most recently, a fundamental sexual liberation. The leadership in sexual reasoning was suddenly lost when the Nazi government annihilated the symbiosis with the Jews, who until then had fruitfully and uniquely assimilated themselves into German culture. The leaders of German sexual science included Albert Moll (1862-1939), Iwan Bloch (1872-1922), Magnus Hirschfeld (1868-1935), and Albert Eulenburg (1840-1917). The German-speaking sexual science has never recovered from this loss of genius.

## 1. Basic Sexological Premises

### A. Character of Gender Roles

The structure of and changes in gender differentiation in Germany resembles that of other Western countries. The long-term trend, since the first feminist movement in the 1880s, exhibits an egalitarian tendency with regard to political, economic, as well as sexual participation. The trend was interrupted by the Nazi regime, which tried to push women back into household and nursing activities. The policy of "a child as a donation to the Fuehrer" was a remarkable failure. World War II brought women back into the industrial workplaces and to autonomous decision making in all social domains.

Today, there are many endeavors to emancipate women (and, possibly, men). Political rights and the wording of laws and official texts are strictly gender neutral. Affirmative action, quotas, governmental subsidies, and similar programs support and proclaim an egalitarian policy. But there are numerous barriers to putting these incentives into everyday practice (Lautmann 1990). Equality remains a task for generations to come. Still, the actual progress—sometimes in the economic, but mainly in the private sphere—is noteworthy.

### B. Sociolegal Status of Males and Females

Jurisprudence says that every human being from birth on is granted a status as a person with their own rights. Attention is even paid to children's decision making, according to their level of maturity. Family jurisdiction has to orientate itself around the child's welfare as its highest principle. Corporal punishment is strictly forbidden, abrogating a traditional customary right of adults. In practice, the children's autonomy contradicts their factual dependency and older ideas of "parents' property" and parental rights.

Formal education is gender neutral. Girls and boys are given equal opportunities at schools. The principle of coeducation has been implemented thoroughly. Some feminists are currently recommending a partial return to gender-specific classes in order to overcome certain problems in the learning of mathematics and technical subjects.

After puberty, men and women enjoy a high level of sexual autonomy. Some youngsters leave the parental house before majority (age 18) to share a flat with other adolescents.

The perception of gender roles is clear for many adolescents. They fixate on these roles, while other factors and, above all, their individuality, are neglected as one-sided. The actual or intended relationship between men and women is partly seen as threatening, especially in the west. The proportion of women with a habitual feeling of disadvantage on account of their sex is much greater in the west. At the same time—and this only appears to be a contradiction—girls in the west also reflect the advantages of their sex more than girls in the east.

Adolescents in the east see themselves to a lesser extent than in the west as men or women, and experience relations between the sexes as less conflict-ridden. Feminist thinking was hardly disseminated in East Germany and did not influence girls as they grew up to develop a critical perception of men, who in turn did not experience a resulting feeling of insecurity. They attribute events in their lives, their success and failure, less to their membership of one of the sexes and more to their overall personality.

[*Update 2001*: In terms of *Gleichstellung* (the promotion of equal status of men and women), the percentage of women in jobs increased from 47% in 1960 to 56% in 1998. However, in 1989, 81% of the women in the German Democratic Republic had a job. After the *Wende* (Union), the percentage of working women in the New Lands (former East Germany) decreased to 74% in 1995 because of a high unemployment rate.

[Although the percentage of women with *Abitur* (the highest school diploma) increased from 32.8% in 1950 to 39.4% in 1975 and reached 54.1% in 1998, and the percentage of female students at universities increased from 19.7% in 1950 to 44.3% in 1998, Germany still has few women in management positions. German women experience no discrimination in their academic or training period. They also do not have problems securing a good job. However, some time between their 30s and 40s, especially qualified women do experience an "invisible glass ceiling" and their career advancement stops. Because lower positions in the corporate hierarchy receive proportionately lower compensation, the "glass ceiling" means that women in the Old Lands (former West Germany) earn about 78% of the gross salary per hour that men receive. In the former East Germany, where many more women held full-time jobs and were paid equally before the Union, their salaries are now about 89.9% of male compensation. Although the share of female professors at German universities increased in the 1990s, they still constitute less than 10% of all professors. Only 5.9% of the university professors in the highest and best-paid rank of C4-professor are women.

[In recent years, more and more German women have formed networks to overcome the difficulties of an employment world that is marked by male interests and male work structures, like long work hours and few possibilities to combine job and rising children at the same time. In the 1990s, the number of "contact markets" and support groups for women organizing for equal rights in the business world increased from 75 to more than 300.

[Gender equality has also not penetrated family life. Although possible paternity leaves are often available to men, only 1.5% of *Erziehungsurlaub* (unpaid vacation with job guarantee) are taken by men. Men cite a variety of reasons for their disinterest in these leaves, including fears of damaging effects to their career, possible loss of their job, and the financial cost of an unpaid leave. German women can expect little help when it comes to running the household: 58% of working women between ages 25 and 45 say that they have to care for the household and children; the same is true for only 10% of men in the same age group.

[After the European Court decided early in 2000 that women cannot, in general, be excluded from armed units, the Ministry of Defense proposed that all careers in the armed forces would be opened to women beginning in 2001. As of 2000, women accounted for only 1.3% of the German Army, 4,300 out of 340,000 in active service, and these women were only in medical and musical units. (*End of update by J. Pastoetter*)]

### C. General Concepts of Sexuality and Love

In Germany, the basic ideologies and configurations of the erotic world do not differ very much from those found in western and northern Europe and in the WASP population of the United States of America. With respect to sexual behaviors, the most important cleavage runs between the two principles of Romantic Love versus Hedonism. Romanticism binds together personal love and sexual attraction. Without a "harmony of hearts," no orgastic fulfillment is possible. This principle is founded in the Christian idea that the spiritual community dignifies the genital encounter. The prosaic concept of hedonism emphasizes the erotic quality of the body and the satisfaction of desires. The sexual drive is a natural need. One may give way to it without making many preconditions, calculating only costs and gratifications.

Similarly, there are two ideal types of intimate partnership. *Affective solidarity* is the principle of a stable and universal relationship between two human beings whose individual disparities are balanced through a mutually complementary performance. On the other hand, *contractual partnership* is based on a calculation of mutual benefits. The relationship lasts as long as the balance remains positive for both participants. The contractual element allows for negotiations about sexual relations.

Sexual phenomena are generally conceptualized from a naturalistic point of view developed in the 19th century. The average person and most experts—outside sexology, of course—follow a version of naive biologism that reflects this naturalistic viewpoint. In this view, innate programs, hormones, and so on direct the sexual response. Psychoanalytic and sociological approaches are not prominent, with the exception of a behavioristic learning theory.

## 2. Religious, Ethnic, and Gender Factors Affecting Sexuality

### A. Source and Character of Religious Values

Since the Reformation in the 16th century, Germany has been the arena of fierce conflicts between the two main religious denominations, including long wars. Not until the 20th century could the two churches find an arrangement for coexistence—today 45% of the population are Protestant and 35% Catholic. A growing proportion of the population has left the Church—roughly 18%—and even more are only nominal members without much belief (but still paying the not-so-insignificant Church tax).

Thus, the sexual morals of Protestantism and Catholicism exist side by side with all their differences and similarities. Many surveys show that the sexual teachings of the churches do not effectively direct the behaviors of the sexually active population, although they may have some effect on the attitudes. Instead, the churches exert a considerable influence on sexual politics. They are accepted as an expert voice in moral debates, but to a diminishing extent. In the

new, controversial legislation since 1970, no-fault divorce, liberalization of abortion, and sexual autonomy, the ecclesiastical positions were overruled.

### B. Source and Character of Ethnic Values

The current growing immigration rate, which includes, for example, 1.7 million Turks now resident in Germany, may lead to new conflicts. The Islamic and paternalistic view of family values, gender differentiation, same-sex relations, and the like is opposed to the secularized Western view. Immigrants of the second generation experience tensions between intra- and extrafamilial worlds. Moreover, in combination with low social prestige, an explosive mixture arises, bursting with violence against women, gays, and other persons defined as weak

## 3. Knowledge and Education about Sexuality

### A. Government Policies and Programs

The parental family and the school have the mandate to give the necessary instructions about sexuality. To a certain degree, both institutions are reluctant to perform that task. They mutually suspect each other of being inefficient in advising and/or of being dangerous with respect to the contents. Sex education, if publicly discussed, immediately becomes a political controversy, where the right-left continuum corresponds to the poles of repressive versus emancipative doctrines.

School curricula provide for the instruction of sexual issues from the first elementary class onwards. Since there is no special course, the matter can be addressed in various fields, such as biology, religion, politics, and so on. The outcome, in spite of existing detailed syllabi, is a sporadic sex education. The teachers think of themselves as not being competent enough. As a matter of fact, the academic training is entirely insufficient; only a tenth of the pedagogic students are offered suitable courses. The parents' attitudes are of a similar uncertainty. They hesitate to speak frankly to their children; and many parents wish that teachers would refrain from doing so (Glueck 1990).

### B. Informal Sources of Sexual Knowledge

As in other Western countries, the mass media and peer-group conversation are the primary sources for spreading sexual knowledge. The censoring of magazines, books, and films does not occur, except for pornographic material. There are laws to prevent minors from being exposed to sexual matters, but the general media are full of instructive articles and illustrated stories. Public television has developed a high standard of feature programs dealing with sexual issues. Sex-related problems and questions are presented to audiences and discussed by experts. Presumably, these widely watched features and talk shows have raised the level of knowledge and value consciousness about most variants of sexuality.

## 4. Autoerotic Behaviors and Patterns

Nine out of ten men and seven out of ten women in Germany admit to having performed masturbation. Female activity in this field has been rising rapidly within the last decades (Clement 1986). Boys start mostly during puberty, girls during adolescence. Today, the majority of parents and teachers accept masturbation of young people as a normal and important experience (Glueck 1990).

The social construction of masturbation has undergone a radical change during the 20th century. Around 1900, the meaning of masturbation was associated with ideas of pollution, removing sexual tensions, depletion, risks for health, and moral dangers. Today the meaning of masturbation is principally satisfaction, to work out sexual fantasies, and to maintain inner balance; it bears no risks for physical and moral development. What has been considered to be a surrogate is now appreciated as a sexual expression in its own right.

## 5. Interpersonal Heterosexual Behaviors

The following findings are derived from various investigations of a social-scientific and sociosexual nature—in particular the relationship studies headed by Kurt Starke among 11,313 people aged between 16 and 48, and an east-west comparative survey of youth sexuality (Starke et al. 1984-1989; Starke 1991; Starke et al. 1993).

### A. Children

Children explore each other's intimate parts in games like doctor/nurse-patient. Even if informed parents know what their children are doing, these games are surrounded by a certain suspicion that they may be too early, or the fear that the children may become oversexualized. Picking up on these silent messages, the children tend to hide their encounters and games from their parents. Since there is no discussion of the morality of these activities, and their expressions have not been subjected to empirical investigation, one knows very little about their reality.

### B. Adolescents

*Puberty Rituals*

No significant rituals mark the passage from childhood to adolescent or young adult.

*Premarital Sexual Activities and Relationships*

Nowadays, young people become sexually mature on an average of three years earlier than at the beginning of the 20th century; menarche occurs at approximately the age of 12.8 years, while the ejacularche takes place at around the age of 13.9 years. This physical acceleration has been accompanied by a mental acceleration marked by the earlier inclusion of adolescents in adult society in terms of consumption and information. Young people now have a more dynamic lifestyle; their plans for life are becoming more diverse and open and, at the same time, more short-term and unpredictable. The perspectives of life are expanding with the increase of not only opportunities and alternatives, but also risks and imponderables. Sexual behavior, which is an integrated part of a personality's all-around behavior, is thus social behavior, and is learned in the same way. Sexual self-discovery, the search for a partner, and partner relationships represent important socialization factors and promote the personal development of adolescents.

Ninety percent of Germans at the age of 16 have already been in love. This feeling of being in love quickly brings with it an urge for reciprocation and the establishment of a pairbond. Infatuation without trying to organize further contact or vigorous efforts to achieve interaction are no longer characteristic. Being in love is not suppressed, hidden away, or enjoyed secretly, but is institutionalized (as long as mutuality is present).

Adolescents in Germany enter into steady relationships at an early age. About 80% of 16-year-olds have experience of a relationship, and at any one time a quarter of the males and half the females aged 16 have a steady boyfriend or girlfriend. This proportion used to be higher in East Germany. These days, young males in particular want to live without firm ties for the present, preferring to wait a while so that they can be open and flexible when planning their lives and careers. They do not necessarily long for the joys of having a partner and would rather avoid any risks, hassle, or pressure. However, even among those not currently involved with a long-term partner, the majority yearn for love and desire a steady relationship.

This is not merely the case among youngsters, but also true of older unattached people. The main reasons for being involuntarily single are that Mr. or Miss Right has not yet been found, or that one has not yet gotten over a recent broken relationship. People often hold themselves responsible for this; they expect too much or have contact problems and are less likely to see the causes in the objective circumstances of life. Those who are voluntarily single explain their lifestyle particularly by a shortage of time and the pressure to achieve good results at school or work. A good quarter of the males and exactly half of the females with no fixed partner say that they do not want to give up their sexual freedom, or even their freedom as a whole.

Emotional bonds in steady relationships are close. Even at the beginning, phrases like "I don't know" or "a feeling of ambivalence" are almost never used to describe emotional ties, and "we like each other" only occurs rarely; "being in love" or more commonly "love" are the order of the day. Most young Germans only enter into a bond and seek closeness and intimacy when they can classify the relationship as "love." Both males and females have a mental attitude of expectation and then a feeling of certainty that their partner is also at least as equally committed as they are. Finding a partner purely out of boredom or loneliness, in order to bolster one's own self-confidence or prestige, or for other reasons—sexual, for instance—has become completely untypical.

Relationships among adolescents are, as a rule, romantic attachments of a high standard and of very definite qualities. The dominating and overriding criterion, and simultaneously, the chief motive for the establishment of a pair group is mutual trust. This includes being able to trust one another, mutual empathy, harmony of the heart, mental and physical communication, and affection—all connected with mutual respect for the other person, recognition of her or him as an individual, and the acceptance of the other's need for personal freedom. By contrast, differences in desires, quarreling, fear of the other, the domination of one partner by the other, latent or actual interference in the other's affairs, and chiefly sexual liaisons are immediately regarded as negative and detached from love, and are rejected as unbearable.

It is not "any old relationship," but love that characterizes young couples. Love is also verbalized: Around 90% have already told their partner they love them and have, in turn, themselves heard the phrase "I love you." Young love in modern Germany, both in the east and in the west, is not silent, but rather a communicative relationship.

The romantic question, "Do you wish to spend your whole life with your partner?" was answered by half of the males and females asked in both eastern and western Germany with a hearty "Yes." However, a difference is to be observed among the other half. Whereas in western Germany, the more common answer is "No," those asked in eastern Germany give the answer "Undecided." This corresponds completely to a general strategic concept of life in the eastern regions—most youngsters, around 80%, want to remain with one and the same partner as long as possible, while the remaining 20% plan partner mobility. Hardly anybody wants to abstain from having a relationship their whole life long.

*Love as Condition for Sexual Intercourse*

Throughout Germany and equally among the sexes, love is not only the most important motive for a relationship, but also the decisive condition for sexual intercourse. Sexual intercourse without love is, particularly among females, just as much of an exception as anonymous sex. The major sexual experiences are not exotic and anonymous (although such do occur), but are shared by young people with a chosen partner. A steady romantic attachment is regarded as the ideal setting for sexual activity. In this sense, love and sex closely belong together in the thoughts and feelings of German adolescents. Despite the variety of lifestyles and current exceptions, their real behavior and sexual experience, their hopes and fears, and the prospective meaning of life and probable disappointments, are also determined by it.

A renaissance of romantic love is currently to be observed in Germany. In both east and west, the ideal of the one great love, exclusive and lasting a lifetime, is predominant. Adolescents do not fall in love temporarily or in order to try it out—they search for a steady, lasting relationship and devote themselves completely and unconditionally to their chosen partner, to whom they also intend to remain faithful. The ideal of eternal love is supplemented by the ideal of current fidelity. Partner mobility consequently does not represent a rupture of the idea of love and faithfulness, but a consequence of it (see the second subsection under Section C, Adults, below for a discussion of partner mobility). Similarly, the modern unwillingness to form close ties cannot be regarded as a countertendency. It, too, is a consequence of the ideal to allow oneself to get involved with just one particular beloved and loving partner.

### First Coitus

Romantic attachments quickly lead to sexual contact, including sexual intercourse. Longer-term phases of petting for its own sake are uncharacteristic, especially in eastern Germany. The first instance of sexual intercourse occurs among approximately half of males and females within the first three months of their going out together. Almost all adolescents tolerate premarital coitus and also practice it. Virginity is not regarded as a stigma, a success, nor as something special to be preserved. Sex has freed itself from the institution of marriage, but not, however, from a romantic attachment.

The first instance of sexual intercourse is based on love or being in love and 75 to 85% of the time takes place within a steady relationship. It is only rarely that sexual intercourse first takes place anonymously, by chance, or casually. Although the general tendency is for partners to be of the same age, the first coitus partner (especially among the girls in eastern Germany, who also start earlier) is usually a little older. The older partner, usually male, in many cases is equally sexually inexperienced.

Eight percent of 17-year-old males with experience of coitus from western Germany have had sex with a prostitute; the corresponding figure for males from East Germany is 0%. But, experience with a prostitute is almost never the first experience of sexual intercourse. Ideally, the intimate partner is the object of one's love, making the first instance of sexual intercourse an event that is mutually striven for and desired by both parties. If this is not the case, then young people would rather abstain from sexual intercourse.

The average age at which young males and females have sexual intercourse for the first time, about 17, has remained constant for about a decade. One difference that is to be observed is that boys in western Germany and girls in eastern Germany start somewhat earlier; in fact, one third of the latter have their first experience of coitus before their 16th birthday. Members of the lower classes start particularly early in western Germany, whereas the upper classes and future intellectuals are somewhat slower.

In both eastern and western Germany, young people have a place where they can be with each other undisturbed, exchange affection, and sleep together; this is nearly always their own room in the parental home or else their partner's home. Adolescents usually enjoy a close emotional relationship with their parents. The mother, and to a lesser extent the father, is the chief person in whom young people confide and the preferred communication partner, including in matters of love. Two thirds of young males and females say that they can often talk to their mother openly about sex. By contrast, communication between father and daughter is often either disrupted or only rarely touches on intimate topics, and only one quarter of daughters can talk openly with their fathers about sex. Most parents accept their children's partner relationships, allow them to sleep together, and know about their sexual contact. Sex does not take place somewhere outside in secret, but cozily in one's own bed.

## C. Adults

### Premarital Courtship, Dating, and Relationships

Men and women aged 22 have sexual intercourse around nine times a month; the frequency among 17-year-olds is six or seven times (six times for males, eight times for females). The figure falls only marginally among the over-30s and over-40s. Psychological and social factors are mainly responsible for intrapersonal and interpersonal differences in the frequency of sexual intercourse, especially the nature of the relationship, as well as external circumstances, such as separation from one's partner and living conditions. People who are happily in love have sexual intercourse more often.

The proportion of women experiencing orgasm increased sharply in the 1970s. About 75% of 16-year-olds, 90% of 18-year-olds, 95% of 22-year-olds, and 99% of 27-year-olds have experienced orgasm. The rate of orgasm during sexual intercourse and other intimate behavior has also increased. The sexual satisfaction of both men and women is judged as an invariant component of sex within a relationship. Affection is the most common aspect associated with love and sex, and sexual sensitivity is expected and appreciated. Sexual contact without a feeling of desire is generally not even undertaken by women.

Young women and men have partnership concepts of sexual relations and want their partners to be desirous of sex as well. People still experience being forced or pestered, and this is regarded as harassment; however, pestering or force have since come to contradict the morals of most young men. The initiative for sexual intercourse hardly ever comes from the man alone, and, in fact, it is now more common for the woman's desire to be decisive. Sexual interaction in a relationship among young people is rarely controlled by the male, but quite often by the female.

One in ten acts of coitus takes place outside a steady relationship. Four out of ten adults have had sexual intercourse with somebody else during their current relationship. In the 1980s, sexual contact outside the main relationship became more common—this increase being especially true of women—and the number of females experiencing sex outside their steady relationship quadrupled in this decade (whereas the figure for men merely doubled). There are no differences in this respect between married and unmarried people. Men have had an average of seven sex partners; women have had five on average, with a fifth having had only one and another fifth having had more than five. Apart from sex, other factors that affect the various numbers of previous sexual partners include conditions of origin and development, as well as of age. Furthermore, partner mobility is higher in an urban environment than in rural areas. In the past year, three out of ten men and two out of ten women have had more than one sex partner. Younger women are more mobile than older men.

The frequency of orgasm has not changed in keeping with sexual liberalization, but the attitude towards it, its experience, and its function within a relationship have changed. The sexist emphasis on male and female potency measured in terms of orgasm has become fragile, and the compulsion to have orgasm is being resisted. There is a growing aversion to orgasm achieved with all manner of tricks and used as a measure of male or female performance, celebrated as a victory in joint conflict, and feared as a stress-obsessed prestige event. Instead, the individual quality of a steady relationship is sought, linked with closeness, trust, warmth, carefree pleasure, and unpredictable, uncalculating, uncalculated affection within the total erotic form. Cuddling is back in fashion; compulsive or cheap commonplace sex is out.

There are many common aspects in partner and sexual behavior between western and eastern Germans. However, noticeable differences continue to exist. These differences are not so much on the level of behavior as on the level of desire, the experience of sex, and sexual attitudes. More eastern than western German females look forward to their first sexual intercourse and they start somewhat earlier. Sexually inexperienced boys and girls in eastern Germany clearly want to have more sexual experiences than those in the west. Females from eastern Germany begin sexual relations earlier than those of the same age in the west. Western German males, on the other hand, link sexual intercourse more firmly than males from eastern Germany to a steady relationship; then again, twice as many have sex with occasional partners. It is possible that they are quicker than eastern German males to detach sexuality from a person or relationship, at least occasionally.

More adolescent females in eastern Germany regard their sexual activity to be gratifying and enjoyable. This refers both to masturbation, which they experience with more pleasure, and especially to sexual intercourse. About 30% more young females in the east say that their latest incidence of sexual intercourse was enjoyable, was sexually satisfying, was a great experience, and that they were happy. The differences are not the frequency of orgasm, but rather the sexual experience, the joy of sexual arousal, the subjective quality of the entire erotic form, and the feelings of happiness experienced during intimacy. In both eastern and western Germany, young females are less appreciative of their latest incidence of sex if they did not achieve orgasm; however, the experience of eastern girls not experiencing orgasm is hardly less positive than that of western girls who do experience orgasm. In the west, some adolescent females feel sexually unsatisfied during sexual intercourse and are not happy, even though they had an orgasm. In eastern Germany, on the other hand, women are also sexually satisfied and happy, even if (on the last occasion) they did not experience orgasm. They are apparently less "fixated" on the orgasm, but are by no means less able to achieve orgasm. On the one hand, female adolescents in eastern Germany are more "conservative," in the sense that they (without disregarding other forms) are more strongly centered on sexual intercourse and orgasm with their lover. By contrast, they are not so strongly centered on the "autonomous" orgasm. At the same time, they are more "liberal," as they begin earlier than their western German counterparts. In addition, it can be seen that among eastern German adolescents, virtually all the differences between the sexes, as regards the experience of sex is concerned, have been dispelled, whereas they continue to exist among western German adolescents.

### Partner Mobility in Lifestyles

Four tendencies in the pattern of relationships that individuals adopt are to be observed:

1. Serial Monogamy—having a succession of steady relationships, especially at a young age. This is part of learning exercised by young people as they mature. It is connected with practicing partnership and sexual behavior—the search for the optimal liaison with high demands being made on its quality. The high demands also lead to the end of one relationship and the commencement of the next. This succession of relationships is an expression of increased sovereignty in the treatment of sexuality as the basis of social developments, which have led to a liberalization of sexual norms. Changing one's partner one or more times during the course of one's life is connected to the ideal of the unity of love and sex. Such a romantic love morality adheres less and less to the traditional model of lifelong marital monogamy, even though, or precisely because, great importance is attached to faithfulness within each relationship.

2. Sexual Nonexclusivity—sexual relations are entered into outside a steady relationship, either occasionally or continually. One reason for this—along with a thirst for adventure, an urge to undergo new experience, curiosity, and many other factors—is an unsatisfactory sex and emotional life in the primary relationship. This behavior has increased in the past 10 to 20 years, something that should be neither celebrated as an expression of libertarian norms, nor condemned as a violation of the traditional command of exclusive monogamy. It is self-contradictory and, above all, a product of the problems of long-term relationships. Having sex outside a relationship has traditionally been a male privilege. However, in modern society, where women enjoy a considerable amount of emancipation and independence, particularly in the professional sphere, the situation has been balanced out. Sexual contact outside the primary relationship almost always takes place with close acquaintances or friends. Anonymous sexual contact is a rare exception and is usually rejected.

   By and large, a moral assessment of either item 1 or 2 above cannot be based on the number of partners. Neither large nor small quantities of partners can provide a general expression of quality, performance, stability, satisfaction, or happiness. In addition, people's personalities and their activity in life's various situations are too different. If one follows these findings, then the appeal for fidelity in view of AIDS is just as justified as it is out-of-touch and repressive. Partner mobility alone does not constitute a risk in terms of AIDS, especially when the comarital relationships involve outercourse more than intercourse, as frequently occurs in such responsibly nonmonogamous relationships, as couples move beyond the raging hormones of youth. Hardly anybody sacrifices happiness in life for the sake of abstract faithfulness.

3. Commercial Sex—new partners can easily be obtained in the form of disposable items without the assumption of mutual responsibility, and lust can be quickly satisfied without any complications. Although forms of male prostitution exist, mainly for homosexuals, but also for women, female prostitution is the predominating form. The entire sex industry, including pornography, is chiefly aimed at men, and as a result, these sexual relationships, including long-term relationships and regular clients, are far more common among men than among women.

   In terms of prostitution, men can be divided into three habitual groups. The first group has no contact whatsoever with prostitutes, the second visits prostitutes occasionally, while for the third group, prostitution is an integral part of their lives. These groups are clearly separated from each other in terms of their sociological and psychological profile, and the borders dividing them are not fluid. The size of the groups varies among the various social subgroups, and also geographically.

4. Promiscuity. This refers to the very frequent change of sexual partners and the lack of a steady relationship. Further forms of partner mobility within a steady, long-term relationship include partner swapping and group sex.

[*The Single Life*        JAKOB PASTOETTER

[*Update 2002*: In 1999, only one in 25 Germans lived in a household with five or more individuals, while at the beginning of the 19th century, 44% did so. In the same time span, single households quintupled. In 1999, 36% or 13.5 million Germans were living alone. A third (12.6 million) were living with one other person, 15% (5.6 million) were living with two others, 12% (4.4 million) with three others, and only 4% (1.7 million) in households of five or more. Most of the latter are located in small communities of less than 5,000 people; most of the former live in the big cities with more than 500,000 people. Nearly half of the 1.2 million Berliners between 25 and 45 are single. In all of Germany in the early 1990s, 20% of Germans between ages 25 and 35 lived in a single household; in 2000, this rose to 25%. It appears likely that by 2010, a third of this age group will be living alone. In 1998, 17% of all children under age 27 lived with a single parent.

[Since the 1970s, Germany's modern postindustrial society has resulted in growing abundance, plenty of apartments, increasing urbanization, decreasing importance of marriage, sexual liberalization, integration of women into the workforce, increasing pressure for mobility to get a job, and last, but not least, better education for more people. Single females are more likely to earn the highest academic degree (*Abitur*), have a job, and a higher paid one. Single males and females live in bigger apartments than their married peers. Interestingly, they have about the same social network as married couples, and keep closer contact with their parents. In the New Lands, only 15% to 30% enjoy their single lifestyle enough to not wish to find a partner. Nearly half of them are convinced that it is important to have a family and children. One third experience the single lifestyle as being forced on them.

[Not being married or cohabiting is a high-risk factor for little sexual activity. In the New Lands, the 20- to 30-year-olds have sexual intercourse less often than the 50-year-olds. Ninety percent of all heterosexual sex acts take place in long-term relationships. About 50% of singles have no sex at all, according to the most recent survey by Gunter Schmidt (2000). Eighty percent of people in a steady relationship described the quality of their sexual relations as "high," in comparison with only 40% of the singles. As Schmidt notes: "The sexual world of the singles is rather depressing; they spend lots of time, energy, and money for little sex, and this sex is not very satisfying." Besides sex, the other major problem is loneliness. Here one finds that men have a harder time dealing with loneliness than their female counterparts because of their less-developed social and emotional skills, and their inability to make their apartment *gemütlich* (cozy).

[Catchwords and headlines like "Onanisation of Sexuality" (Alexander Schuller) and "Does Society Break Up into a Bunch of Masturbating Monads?" (*Der Spiegel*) reflect the uncertainty of German society in dealing with this development. The "Pioneers of the Modern Age" (Ulrich Beck),

once stylized as self-picked masters of the art of living, are now seen as narcissistic egoists unable to act responsibly. Although the number of longtime singles is quite high, the truth might be in between, since many are only living temporarily as singles. In 1991, 47% of the 25- to 55-year-old singles had had no partner for more than six years, 18% had been alone for four or five years, 20% for two to three years, and only 15% for a shorter period. (More recent numbers are not available.) (*End of update by J. Pastoetter*)]

[*Singles in Their Later Years*        JAKOB PASTOETTER

[*Update 2002*: A certain uneasiness exists regarding aging. In the near future, hundreds of thousands of singles will reach an age where traditionally younger family members take care of the older members. Although Germany has had a national nursing insurance for several years, many doubt it is sufficiently funded. Voluntary solidarity communities are an alternative, but the question is whether people who have lived their life for a long time alone will be able to share responsibility in a larger group. (*End of update by J. Pastoetter*)]

## Cohabitation Patterns

Most people who maintain a steady sexual relationship will live together in one residence, although not all men and women who share a residence are necessarily having sex with each other. The housing situation in Germany allows living together. Frequently, occupational mobility may lead to a separation of partners.

[*Update 2001*: In mid-1999, 2.1 million Germans were cohabitating, an increase of 47% since 1991. Increasingly, German couples, especially in the New Lands, prefer cohabitation to marriage. In mid-1999, 12% of all couples living together were cohabiting without being married. Both partners in 46% of all cohabiting couples were under age 35, and 29% were raising children. In cohabitation, women have more freedom to build their own career, especially if they are also childless. Eighty-seven percent of cohabiting women support themselves and 80% of those with children work outside the home. At the same time, 92% of all husbands hardly share the household work; 87% have never ironed clothes, 79% have never done the laundry, and 75% have never cleaned the windows. Meanwhile, public opinion is shifting in favor of cohabitation. Fifty-six percent of Germans would like to see equal status for couples with and without a marriage certificate, while 71% of young women between 16 and 29 cannot see any argument for a different status for married and unmarried couples. (*End of update by J. Pastoetter*)]

## Marriage and the Family

As regards the current family, the following model is preferred: "Man and wife both pursue their own profession and are equally responsible for housework and bringing up the children, so that both have the same amount of time for their career." Having one's own family with children remains a high aim in life, and only a few do not wish to have any children at all. Since unification, however, both the number of marriages in eastern Germany and the number of newborn children has drastically declined—within three years, the birthrate had fallen by 60%. Adolescent mothers and female students with children have suddenly disappeared as if by magic. The once-low marriage age has rapidly risen and is set to reach that prevalent in western Germany, with the result that the establishment of families is being delayed. What remain unchanged are the attitudes coordinating parenthood/family with career/employment.

Female and male adolescents in eastern Germany are more likely to have grown up with both parents employed full-time than their counterparts in western Germany, and this is, thus, the model on which they base their own lives. (Before unification, the number of women working full-time in East Germany was over 90%, compared to over 50% in West Germany.) Men and women have become accustomed to their respective partner's professional activity and regard it as an important aspect of life. The compatibility of parenthood and work does not at all only mean for them the adaptation of family necessities to the parents' work, but also the consideration of the family at work and the repudiation of the complete dominance of the job. Work and family are not seen as alternative, mutually exclusive values, but are only acceptable when organized in conjunction with each other. This is a demand being made on both society and the relationship.

[*Marriage and Divorce*        JAKOB PASTOETTER
[*Update 2002*: In April 1999, 39 million Germans lived as married couples. For the first time since 1991, the number of weddings in 1999 rose over the previous year: 430,000 couples married in 1999, an increase of 3.2% (13,500 couples) over 1998. In the Old Lands (former West Germany) the increase was 2.2%; in the New Lands (former East Germany), the increase was 10.3%. Experts suggest the increase was not the start of a new trend, but a blip because of the magic of the date 9/9/99, even though couples who marry on a *Schnapszahl* (funny number) date have an especially high risk of divorce.

[Married people encounter two disadvantages in the job market. Potential employers still regard married women as "being provided for," while "flexible" single men have better opportunities in the job market. The reasons for marriage have changed dramatically in the last ten years; love and partnership are no longer the most important factors, having yielded to economic stability. Couples without children also have a higher per capita income and a higher standard of living than couples with children.

[At the same time, there is a countertrend toward a "new high regard of the family as an emotional home," according to the Delphi-Study of value orientations by the Heidelberg Gesellschaft für Inovative Marktforschung (September 2000). Other surveys confirm this with findings that 72% hope to find Mr. or Miss Right, and 33% think that finding an ideal partner is the most important thing in life. Ninety-four percent of young people say they believe in true love, 70% hope for a single lifelong relationship, and only 4% say they are not interested in an intimate relationship (see Table 1).

[Television soaps depicting happy family life attract an average of 25 million fans. Sociologists and psychologists think that more and more people have learned through experience that a successful job life is emotionally less fulfilling than a satisfying relationship in filling the emptiness of their private lives. While the *Kettenehe*, chain marriage or serial monogamy, is popular, few German couples believe any longer that filing a declaration of divorce as soon as major marital problems occur is the only remedy for relationship problems. They realize that they will not only get rid of a husband or wife, but also of a good deal of their life together, friends and relatives included. The number of therapists who special-

ized in marriage therapy has increased significantly over the last 15 years. Catholic-sponsored offices for marriage therapy rose from 282 in 1985 to 349 in 2000 in the Old Lands. The Protestant Diakonische Werk now has 349 offices that offer free counseling. The share of divorced Old Lands people who remarried rose from 8% for men and 6% for women in 1960 to 21% for men and 24% for women in 1997.

[On the other hand, the probability of a marriage ending in a divorce increased by fivefold in the Old Lands since 1978, while in the New Lands, divorce decreased by a quarter. The New Lands divorce rate peaked in 1986 with 128.5 divorces per 10,000 marriages. The highest divorce rate in the Old Lands came in 1987 with 87.6 divorces per 10,000 marriages. The 1998 divorce rates were 85.7 in the New Lands and 105.7 in the Old Lands. Overall, the 1998 divorce rate rose by 2.5% over 1997. More than half of the divorces involved minor dependents. Four of five divorced husbands had another partner within ten months, while half of all women were still single after three years. Two thirds of all divorce petitions were filed by wives. According to sociologists, factors for the growing rate of divorce include a decline in the social stigma of divorce since the sexual revolution in the 1970s and the growing financial independence of gainfully employed women. Couples without a church wedding or children, and couples who do not own their home are more likely to divorce, with infidelity cited as the most frequent reason. Nine of ten German women and two thirds of German men hold fidelity as the most important value in a relationship. But the same percentage believes that it is not possible to remain faithful to the same person all life long. (*End of update by J. Pastoetter*)]

[*Living Apart Together (LAT) Relations*
                                JAKOB PASTOETTER
[*Update 2002*: Since two thirds of all singles have a stable relationship with another single, one needs to address the issue of LAT (Living Apart Together) relationships. This new term actually refers to a very old and traditional way of life. In the agricultural world of Old Europe, few newlywed couples possessed the financial means required to establish their own household. Only wealthy farmers, burghers, and aristocrats could afford to pay the brideprice or supply their daughters with a dowry sufficient for the newlywed couple to establish their own household. Most others fell into the mass of poor farmers, day laborers, and servants, the younger sons and daughters of aristocrats who in earlier times had to join a monastery or convent, the voluntary or involuntary spinsters and bachelors, and those who were allowed to marry but not to set up their own household. In a sense, LAT relations are only new if we forget history.

[The economy is the main factor for the growing number of LAT relations today. If a couple can only find work in different cities, it may well be more economical to maintain two separate households instead of absorbing the time and cost of daily commutes. LATs also include singles who share a committed relationship, but prefer to maintain their separate modest household, in which each has privacy and the flexibility of being together or apart. In Germany, more than 15% of all couples, married as well as unmarried, have this kind of "weekend relationship." Higher education and flexibility make it more likely that couples will live apart together. (*End of update by J. Pastoetter*)]

## Incidence of Oral and Anal Sex

Oral stimulation of the genitals, both fellatio and cunnilingus, has become a customary practice. Since hygienic standards and opportunities are high, there are no longer aesthetic scruples. For example, at least 60% of German

**Table 1**

**Happiness of Germans by Marital Status**

| Status | "Very Happy" | "Happy" |
|---|---|---|
| Married couples | 23% | 51% |
| Unmarried couples | 17 | 45 |
| Single persons | 10 | 33 |

students have practiced fellatio or cunnilingus. Anal intercourse has remained quite rare; less than 20% report this experience, most of them only occasionally. Personal hygiene education in early childhood blocks the unaffected dealing with this aperture of the body.

## 6. Homoerotic, Homosexual, and Bisexual Behaviors

### A. History and Legal Status

Same-sex genitality as an institution is rooted in a changeable history. Before the advent of Christianity, German tribes repressed such acts with capital punishment. From the Middle Ages on, there were meeting places in some metropolitan cities, such as Cologne, which, however, were not large enough, compared with London or Paris, to develop an urbanity suitable for a real subculture. From the early 19th century, Swiss and German writers gave expression to the voice of love between men. The term *homosexual* was created, interpretations of same-sex relations were published, and civil liberties for homosexuals were demanded.

The foundations for the modern concepts, lesbian and gay, were laid in Germany. In 1933, this hopeful development was suddenly interrupted by the Nazi government. The persecution was based on racial-biological and demographic beliefs. Enforced with jail and concentration camps, it was the fiercest ever seen in modern times. It was not until the 1970s that the gay and lesbian existence could recover from this knockout blow.

Today, homosexuality is societally established as never before in history. Not even the menace of AIDS has reversed the trend. Despite the numerous victims of HIV, one may say that the life chances of homosexual and bisexual people continue to be enhanced. Same-sex relations between consenting adult men were completely depenalized some 20 years ago. Same-sex relations among women were only criminalized in Austria in earlier decades. Currently, any differentiation between homosexual and heterosexual has been removed from the penal code, as is the case in Switzerland since 1992 and in the former East Germany since 1988. Contemporary political demands include an antidiscrimination amendment to the Constitution and the legalization of marriages of same-sex couples.

The state has long since abstained from open denial of rights and privileges, e.g., against teachers or civil servants, in the judiciary, public administration, social security, and the like. Many politicians, even conservatives, hasten to confirm that they will not "discriminate." That does not mean that the politicians are willing to grant equal rights to homosexuals. They are given as much equality, meaning tolerance, as necessary, but not as much equality as possible in terms of integration.

Residual discrimination remains in niches like the military and the Church. And it is difficult to intervene in the antihomosexual policies of the private sector of the economy. Homosexual lifestyles are possible even here, as long as they are restricted to the private sphere.

### B. Children

Children, before they "discover" the other sex during or after puberty, naturally look for friends and intimacy within their own sex. So there are many occasions for homoerotic feelings, even for sexual encounters between friends. The passage through such a temporary "youngster homosexuality" is no predictor of adult homosexuality. Most youngsters with homoerotic experiences will follow the path of "normalcy," with the sole difference that their antihomosexual prejudices are less negative than those of the general population. The same-gender contact of youngsters has been reduced, but has not disappeared, in the last decades, because of coeducational schools and acceleration, including the earlier start of heterosexual coitus (cohabitarche). Moreover, the age of coming out for homosexuals has been getting ever lower, so that today this often occurs during adolescence.

### C. Adult Psychology and Lifestyles

Turning to gender roles, the theory of the third sex proposed by Magnus Hirschfeld has faded away. Today, gays are thoroughly masculine, lesbians quite feminine. Sometimes, they play with the possibilities of cross-gender behavior, onstage or in subculture situations. But their personal identity is confined to their biological sex. One is a "faggot" for fun, for provocative purposes, i.e., in a voluntarily chosen role. In lesbian subculture, the rigid separation into butch or femme has diminished.

Uncertainties of gender, intergenerational longings, and love relations between the social classes are no longer the prerequisites of a homosexual preference. Transgression of class, generation, and gender frontiers contributed to earlier sex scandals, and even constituted their kernel. Today, the only and really subversive moment in homosexuality is its negation of compulsory heterosexuality.

The homosexual desire as it has crystallized throughout the 20th century signifies precisely the same-sex relationship. By this, homosexuals were confronted with the possibility and necessity of forming lasting partnerships. Meanwhile, a considerable portion of this population follows a quasi-conjugal lifestyle. Two men or two women establish one household, and share income, leisure time, and friends. Their descent families consider them as a pair; the partner of one's own offspring, after a certain time, will be treated as child-in-law and vice versa. The couple, especially a lesbian one, may enlarge to a family with children from a former marriage, sometimes from adoption or fostering.

There is no separation of rights, duties, and prestige according to the traditional roles of husbands and wives. Gay and lesbian couples attach great value to egalitarian decisions. On the other hand, their stability is endangered by the lack of institutionalization and public recognition. Too many details of daily life have to be negotiated. Most couples admit some form of sexual contacts with third parties. This sort of "legitimate infidelity" gives rise to erotic flexibility as well as a certain burden of jealousy.

Homosexuality as an accessible form of erotic preference enjoys a high degree of social visibility that was increased but not generated by the public reaction to AIDS. There are more occasions than ever before to learn about homosexuality, to discuss it, and to confront oneself with such experiences. In many sectors of everyday life, the questions of homosexuality are addressed: at school, in the family and peer group, at work, and during leisure activities. So a latent desire can quite easily manifest itself, and one can look for possible partners.

Many doors open to the homosexual world. A lot of newspapers—public or subculture—have a rubric for contact ads. Special guides list the commercial and the hidden places where homosexuals meet. Today, each city with more that 50,000 inhabitants has at least a gay bar and an anonymous meeting point in a public park or lavatory ("tea room"). Bigger cities have baths, numerous bars for special interests, bookshops, voluntary groups, and a "gay switchboard." The opportunity structure for a lesbian/gay lifestyle has an extraordinary density.

Nationwide associations address cultural and professional interests for Christians, adolescents, teachers, medical people, writers, and the like. On the one hand, only a tiny minority of this minority affiliates with such an organization. On the other hand, these few people operate as a real avant-garde to improve homosexuals' life chances.

Homosexuals have conducted numerous experiments with gender roles, forms of coupling, and techniques of sexual outlet. Some of their inventions have gained significance for nonhomosexuals: the social autonomy of women explored in the economically independent existence of lesbians; body image and sensitivity of men explored via some feminine components in gay performance; the remasculinization of men in the 1980s experienced in the so-called clone style. Homosexual relations, of course, are not a model for the general public; nevertheless, they give a striking example for the plasticity of erotic configurations.

[*Update 2002*: After the 1994 removal of §175 of the German Penal Code, which prohibited male homosexual activity, a second revolution took place on November 10, 2000, when the German Bundestag, with the majority of the Social Democratic Party (SPD) and Green Party coalition, approved a governmental legal initiative that homosexual couples should be treated equally with married heterosexual couples as far as certain legal rights are concerned. (Female homosexuality had never been prosecuted.) The law is already widely seen as "historic," since for the first time, homosexual couples can officially register their relationships in a way that comes quite close to traditional marriage. Since Article 6 GG of the German Constitution states that (heterosexual) marriage and family have to be especially protected by the state, the new family-law institution is called *Eingetragene Lebenspartnerschaft* ("registered partnership through life").

[According to sociologist Michael Bochow, about half of all German homosexuals already live in cohabitation, and although not all such couples will decide for an *Eingetragene Lebenspartnerschaft*, the legal possibility is widely seen as a good thing. The argument is that all social commitments and responsibilities should be strengthened in a time of progressive social fragmentation.

[The individual states (*Länder*) of the Federal Republic have the authority to decide where the couples have to go to get registered. The most probable choice will be the registry office (*Standesamt*) where all heterosexual marriages must be performed to be legal. The *Eingetragene Lebenspartnerschaft* will include such fundamental rights and obligations as the right to choose a common family name, the legal status of next of kin, the right to see the partner in hospital, the obligation to pay maintenance, a so-called *kleines Sorgerecht* (small law of custody for children in the partnership), and rulings for divorce, rent law, and inheritance. A homosexual foreign partner will have the same rights as a heterosexual foreign partner with regard to permission to work and immigration of family members.

[Still being decided are all regulations not subject to federal but to state legislation, such as the tax advantages of *Eingetragene Lebenspartnerschaften*. Income and inheritance tax laws, as well as laws pertaining to tax advantages for maintenance payments when a couple gets divorced, fall within the sovereignty of the 16 German states. Laws pertaining to these matters have to pass the second chamber, the German Bundesrat, where the conservative Christian Democratic Union/Christian Social Union (CDU/CSU) had the majority. On December 1, 2000, the Bundesrat, with its conservative majority, rejected the second law involving these ancillary rights. The main law was, however, passed in the Bundesrat. As for the ancillary rights, the ruling "Red-Green" coalition is prepared to further divide these, so that parts of their proposal can be passed.

[Most Germans see themselves as tolerant towards homosexuals. More than 70% of Germans under age 40 ac-

cept homosexuality, and already in a 1996 survey, 49% said they were in favor of a registry-office marriage, 93% wanted homosexuals to have the same job opportunities, and two thirds suggested a law to protect homosexuals against discrimination. (*End of update by J. Pastoetter*)]

## D. Bisexuality

Bisexuality, in the narrow sense of having homosexual and heterosexual relations during the same phase of a sexual biography, occurs quite often, presumably more often than exclusive homosexuality. Nevertheless, the concept is obscure and psychologically underdeveloped.

Most experts agree with the thesis that they have never seen a genuine bisexual, i.e., someone who reacts with equal sexual appetite to women and to men. Since this judgment refers mostly to a population of therapy clients, and since the universe of bisexual people has not yet been empirically investigated, the question of what types of bisexuality really exist remains open.

There are quite a few sexual biographies where phases of intimate relations with a woman alternate with relations with a man. Such a "successive bisexuality" is frequently reported by women, and there is no reason to suggest a "latency" of either homosexuality or heterosexuality.

## 7. Gender Diversity and Transgender Issues

For transvestites, there are no institutionalized roles in German society. The dichotomy of two and only two sexes is highly crystallized. So transvestites very seldom gain public attention. They are generally considered deviants, but do not constitute a social problem. The phenomena of transvestism, transsexuality, and homosexuality are today clearly separated. Behaviors of cross-dressing and making-up as the other gender do not irritate public opinion, and the individual reaction contains a greater degree of amusement than of worry. Furthermore, since the 1980s, some transvestites have won high prominence as entertainers in stage shows.

For some people, transgressions of the valid definitions of gender lead to a considerable amount of hostility. Transgenderists and transsexuals are, therefore, marginalized even today, when legislation, medicine, and the mass media have acknowledged their right to live as they are and accommodate their outward appearance to their gender identity.

German law provides some procedures for people who wish to change the sex designation ascribed to them shortly after birth. They may choose between officially changing their name or also altering their sex status. The second step presupposes the surgical adaptation of the genitals. In addition, the surgery presupposes expert evidence given by a psychologist or physician testifying that the person is able to live in the long term in the chosen gender role. Several hospitals in the country have specialized in this sort of medical support and are quite willing to deliver it.

At present, several juridical initiatives are being directed towards normalizing transsexuality. Support groups have been organized and receive state subsidies. New sociological research describes the life world of gender-changing people (Hirschauer 1993; Lindemann 1993). The leading German sexologist is pleading for depathologizing the phenomenon (Sigusch 1992). But this will remain a utopia as long as transsexuals themselves apply for medical help, psychotherapy, hormonal treatment, and surgery to gain a healthy condition.

[*Update 2002*: Since 1981, Germany has had a special law for transsexual issues, the *Gesetz über die Änderung der Vornamen und die Feststellung der Geschlechtszugehörigkeit in Besonderen Fällen Transsexuellengesetz TSG;*

*Transsexuals' Act*. It provides for two possibilities, which may be applied either successively or independently of each other. The first possibility is for a transgendered person to change his or her first name without changing the assigned sex. For this so-called "small solution," the law requires two expert opinions confirming the diagnosis of transsexualism for the past three years. The second possibility entails legal recognition of gender reassignment in all official documents including passport, birth certificate, and so on. This so-called "major solution" requires not only two mutually independent expert opinions, but also sex-reassignment surgery. Moreover, the applicant must be unmarried and must be permanently incapable of reproduction. Between 1981 and 1990, 1,422 judicial decisions were rendered in Germany on this basis, 683 of them involving the "small solution" and 733 the "major solution." Hence, one can estimate the frequency of transsexual applications within these 10 years as being between 2.1 and 2.4 per 100,000 German adults. The male-to-female/female-to-male ratio was 2.3 to 1 (Weitze & Osburg 1996).

[It is obvious that sociocultural factors (*Zeitgeist*) have a tremendous impact on the accessibility and acceptance of legal and medical procedures for changing the assigned sex in Germany (Hirschauer 1993). After decades of desperately split discourses between essentialists (see, for instance, Dörner et al. 1991) and constructionists (see, for instance, Sigusch 1992) regarding the origin of transsexuality, a biopsychosocial approach to the understanding of this phenomenon has been accepted in Germany (see, for instance, Bosinski et al. 1997; Beier et al. 2000). (*End of update by H. A. G. Bosinski*)]

## 8. Significant Unconventional Sexual Behaviors

### A. Coercive Sex

*Sexual Abuse of Children and Incest*

The criminal law prohibits sexual acts with young people under age 14 and under age 16 if the acts are exploitative. Moral crusades initiated by some feminist groups argue with increasing numbers of child sexual abuse cases. With some lag, the figures in the official statistics rose after decreasing for three decades. Actually, it is only the public and private awareness that has changed, and child abuse is a more or less stable phenomenon—about 60,000 cases per year. The common construction and terminology throws together three distinguishable interactions: parent-daughter (incest), men-children (abuse), and intergenerational love (pedophilia) (Lautmann 1994). These forms vary in ingredients and consequences.

*Rape*

Sexual violence against women is the other big topic exciting the public opinion during recent years. The punishment of rape in the roughly 2,000 convictions per year is quite severe. But many women do not go to the police even though officers have recently been taught sensitivity in dealing with victims. Legislation has hesitated to criminalize marital rape.

Many young people are afraid of sexual violence. A quarter of the 16- to 17-year-old males in western Germany, compared to a tenth of those in the east, and more than half of adolescent females in the west, compared to a third in the east, reported that they had personally experienced sexual violence, sexual molestation, or sexual interference. In the east, 4% of women said they were forced to engage in sexual intercourse against their will the first time they experienced coitus. The figure among homosexual men is 2%. A

fifth of women in eastern Germany have experienced rape or attempted rape.

*Sexual Harassment*

There are many cases of verbal and bodily molestation of women. Some women train in techniques of self-defense. The majority of men have not yet learned to pay complete respect to a woman's No.

Sexual molestation in the workplace or elsewhere is penalized as an insult, but seldom prosecuted. Some feminists are campaigning for legal recognition of a special offense of sexual harassment. However, the German legislature usually resists the demands to adapt the penal code to social problems addressed by moral crusades.

### B. Prostitution

More than 100,000 women offer sexual services to men, either as a professional or casual job, or to obtain money to buy drugs. The organization of the activity varies. The most respected form is to use an apartment with a telephone and to receive the visitors there after having advertised in a paper. Working in a brothel provides less autonomy for the women, but perhaps equal comfort. Other women wait in bars or hotels for clients. Dangerous, hard, and least profitable in comparison with the other forms is soliciting on the streets.

Male homosexual prostitution is not as common, but it is organized in quite similar ways. Some call boys offer their services equally to men and women. The demand from lesbians is extremely small, if any.

The social prestige of prostitutes has improved to a certain extent since they founded interest groups for "whores." They argue that, if they have to pay income tax (and they do), then they may claim social security and recognition for their vocation.

The law forbids prostitution only under special circumstances, in certain areas, in the neighborhood of schools, and the like. It is also forbidden to further prostitution and to recruit minors. These statutes are enforced in a very incomplete and selective way.

### C. Pornography and Erotica

All forms of sexual, pornographic, and/or obscene material are easily available in Germany—the soft variety from newsstands and television, the harder types in numerous shops where even the most extreme examples are available under the counter. The law forbids hardcore pornography that includes violence, children, or animals, and the sale of all sorts of sexual materials to minors. The debate about the character and danger of pornography has also taken place in Germany (Lautmann & Schetsche 1990).

[*Update 2002*: Germany leads all other European countries in the production of pornographic movies, with about 600 new German titles hitting the market every month. Consumption is also quite high, with more than 78 million hardcore videotapes rented in 1999. Eighty percent of the videotapes rented and purchased are of American origin. Germany is also the European leader when it comes to more explicit sex shows on television: *Liebe Sünde* [*Dear Sin—Love Sin*], *Peep!* and *Wa(h)re Liebe* [*True Love, Love as Consumer Item*] have been in competition for viewers since the early 1990s, with documentaries that mix sex education, voyeurism, and sensationalism. (*End of update by J. Pastoetter*)]

## 9. Contraception, Abortion, and Population Planning

### A. Contraception

Contraception is regarded positively and for the most part is correctly practiced throughout Germany. All but 1%

of Germans accept the prevention of unwanted pregnancy, without any differentiation as regards age, sex, origin, qualifications, or profession. Around 80% of women used contraception the first time they had sexual intercourse, and at least 90% used some method of birth control during the last incidence of coitus. Three quarters of 16-year-olds and nine tenths of 18-year-olds have experience with the contraceptive pill. Some sexually inexperienced females take the pill as a precautionary measure, while others prefer to refrain from sexual intercourse because they are not on the pill. Similarly, many male adolescents also avoid sexual intercourse if a condom is not available. Only 5% of those who have experienced sexual intercourse have never used contraception. Almost everybody regards contraception as a joint responsibility. The current types of contraception are well known among adolescents.

The most popular contraceptive is the pill, favored by 99%. The IUD and diaphragm are less popular. Ninety-four percent of eastern German women aged between 30 and 44 have taken the pill, usually over a protracted period of time, and 52% continuously. (The pill was easily accessible and free of charge in East Germany; it was prescribed by doctors, even to 14-year-old girls.) Two thirds have used condoms; one fifth have used the IUD. Another fifth prefer the rhythm method, a method half of all women have never exercised.

Although hormonal contraception is not decreasing in significance, and acceptance of the pill has actually increased among both men and women, the condom, which was completely out of fashion in East Germany, has been rediscovered as a result of AIDS. However, the condom has not become a rival to the pill or the IUD. It is normally used as an additional means of contraception, and also as a means of protection. The condom is, in fact, the preferred method in certain situations, but regular users are rare. What are sometimes referred to as "natural methods," such as the rhythm method, have decreased in popularity. Coitus interruptus is also widely shunned.

Safe contraception these days, even more than a decade ago, is regarded as an indispensable condition for sexual intercourse. The degree of care exercised, especially in eastern Germany, has actually increased as a result of the changes in values and the social risks, and a significant number of men and women in eastern Germany have taken the opportunity to be sterilized, something that has only been possible since German unification.

## B. Teenage Unmarried Pregnancies

Not more than about 1% of all live births are to minor mothers (under age 18), and half of these are unmarried. A considerable number of teenage pregnancies are terminated by abortion.

[*Update 2002*: Whether born in- or out-of-wedlock, German children are on equal legal status since 1998, when the last discriminations regarding custody, inheritance, and birth legitimacy were abolished. There is a large discrepancy between the numbers of out-of-wedlock births in the Old and New Lands. In the Old Lands, the rate is between 13% and 27%; in the New Lands, out-of-wedlock births account for up to 51%. In the former West Berlin, 29% of births are out-of-wedlock, while in the former East Berlin the figure is 52%.

[One reason for this development is a strong mistrust, mainly but not exclusively in the New Lands, against middle-class values and the romantic-marriage ideal, since many young adults know from experience in their own families that marriages are often unhappy in the long run—mainly for the woman—or lead to divorce. In addition,

there is hardly any material advantage in being married if one does not keep to the traditional role model of the husband earning the family income. On the other hand, there are many advantages in raising children as a single mother: social security, rent rebates, and other financial support by the state. Another factor in this demographic difference is the different self-awareness of women in the east who are less likely than women in the west to define themselves through their partner, and less likely to perceive a child as a reason to marry. In the New Lands, it was much easier to have a child out-of-wedlock, since the state also promoted lifestyles other than marriage. Single mothers got certain advantages, like smaller taxes and extra vacation. Ninety-five percent of women had children in the New Lands, compared to only 76% in the Old. (*End of update by J. Pastoetter*)]

## C. Abortion

The acceptance of contraception contains a critical, negative assessment of abortion as a method of birth control, although the principle of the legal option of the termination of pregnancy is supported. Only 2% are in favor of the complete prohibition of abortion, and the majority of Germans are in favor of at least allowing abortion within the first three months. A quarter of eastern German adolescents and a tenth of their western German counterparts are totally against any form of criminal legislation governing abortion. Most German youngsters support the concept of self-determined pregnancy and liberal legislation. Planned childbirth remains the ideal.

[*Abortion and* Donum Vitae    JAKOB PASTOETTER

[*Update 2002*: In 1998, 131,795 abortions were registered in Germany, for a ratio of 169 abortions per 1,000 live births. Eight of 1,000 women in childbearing age had had an abortion. This corresponds to 14% of all pregnancies, with West Germany reporting 12% and East Germany 23%. Most of the women in West Germany were between 18 and 24 years old and had no children; in East Germany, most women were between 30 and 34 years old and had already one or two children. One of the reasons for this discrepancy might be seen in the fact that East Germans do not worry as much as West Germans do about providing the government with more-or-less confidential information about themselves, as long as the government pays in part or in full for their medical costs, including abortions.

[The government supports consultation offices for pregnant women who are considering an abortion, since women need a *Beratungsschein* (proof of consultation) before getting a legal abortion. The consultation offices are run by the two main churches, the Protestant and the Roman Catholic, most of the latter by organizations like Caritas or the Social Service of Catholic Women, and ProFamila, the German offspring of Planned Parenthood. In January 1998, Pope John Paul II advised the German bishops to find a way to stop the practice of issuing *Beratungsscheine*. The German bishops agreed to an alternative, but still allowed the more than 260 consultation offices to issue the proofs. In September 1999, when the Pope ordered the addition of the phrase, "This Proof may not be used for carrying out an unpunished abortion," the bishops decided to obey. This prompted Catholic laypeople, with the support of the CDU/CSU and SPD politicians, to found a new organization, Donum Vitae [Latin for "Gift of Life"], to continue the pre-abortion consultations and the issuing of *Beratungsscheine*. On January 1, 2001, when all dioceses (except for Limburg) stopped the consultations, 90 offices of Donum Vitae were ready to carry on. (*End of update by J. Pastoetter*)]

## D. Population Control Efforts

A negative population growth holds only for "native" Germans. The secular trend of a sinking birthrate began here at the end of the 19th century. It has various causes, many of them grounded in the rationalization of the social structure and private life. Many children born in Germany do not become German citizens, because their parents are immigrants. The laws of citizenship follows the principle of *jus sanguinis* instead of that of *jus soli*.

Unification of Germany has unexpectedly resulted in the sharpest drop in birthrates in modern world history. Birthrates have been very low in West Germany for many years. In the last several years, slightly more west Germans have died than have been born. Birthrates in all five states of east Germany have fallen sharply. In Brandenburg, births have fallen by more than two thirds, from nearly 38,000 in 1989 to barely 12,000 in 1993. Birthrates are down by more than half in the other four states in the same period. In late 1994, Brandenburg announced it would begin immediately to pay parents $650 for every new child they have. This is in addition to both the national health insurance, which covers obstetric and other medical expenses, and a monthly allowance, called *Kindergeld* that is awarded on a sliding scale based on income. *Kindergeld*, which has been distributed in western Germany since 1955, can reach a monthly cap of $420 for a family of four (Kinzer 1994).

War, famine, and plague are the usual factors triggering such a precipitous drop in the birthrate. In Germany today, the rising rate of unemployment increasing the threat of poverty is the cause for the free-falling birthrate, which is accompanied by a drop in the rate of marriage and a more than tenfold increase in sterilizations. "Young people in east Germany used to think that the most important conditions for marriage were love and a good partnership," a recent report noted, "Now they are seeing that the crucial condition is a secure job." Prior to unification, the Communist system provided jobs and daycare for all and a strong social safety net prevented anyone from falling into poverty. If the current trend continues to 2010, there could well be fewer than half as many children in eastern Germany as there are today.

Nearly all the former Communist countries in Europe have experienced drops in their birthrates, though none match the drop in east Germany. Some countries, including Hungary and Poland, provide payments to the families of newborn babies, but they are much smaller than those initiated in Brandenburg. In the West, Belgium, Luxembourg, and Portugal pay the parents of new babies.

[*Update 2002*: Two phrases are relevant to any discussion of population programs in Germany: *Überalterung*, or the increase in the percentage of old people, and *kinderfeindliche Gesellschaft*, or the child-hostile society.

[According to a study of the United Nations published in early 2000, Germany would need an influx of an additional half million immigrants each year to keep the number of 15- to 64-year-old social security contributors at the level of 1995. To stabilize the number of people living in Germany, 17 million immigrants would be needed in the next 50 years. On the first of January, 1999, Germany had a population of 82.1 million. In all of 1999, 767,000 children were born (765,000 in 1995), while 844,000 people died (885,000 in 1995). In 1998, for the first time, the number of deaths surpassed the number of immigrants, 67,353 compared with 47,098, reducing the population of Germany by 20,000. Germany's birthrate was 1.35 per fertile woman in the west and 1.10 in East Germany, one of the lowest rates worldwide. At the end of 1998, 22% of the German population was age 60 or older; the average age was 39.1 years.

[Reasons for this development can be seen in a growing life expectancy, in the decline of immigrating younger people, and last, but not least, in what is referred to by Germans as *kinderfeindliche Gesellschaft*, or our "child-hostile society," meaning the combination of factors that make it difficult for young adults to think about having children. These factors include a high social pressure to give priority to one's career, difficulty in finding part-time jobs, and a society and environment that are perceived by aspiring parents as non-supportive or even hostile and dangerous to children. The latter includes the often-mentioned aversion against noise caused by children's play, a pessimistic outlook to the future in general, the high costs of raising children, gangs and drug use in the schools, and finally, high traffic-accident and death-toll rates. Children are even seen as "women trap Number One" that prevents self-fulfillment through job and leisure time. Especially in the east, many parents feel left alone, in comparison with the full-time care children received in the former German Democratic Republic.

[The German government tries to improve the financial and social position of parents with certain allowances and other privileges. Primary among these are the *Erziehungsgeld*, a child-support allowance with a maximum of US$300 per month paid until the child's second birthday, and the *Kindergeld*, a child allowance of about $130 a month for the first and second child, $150 for the third, and $175 for subsequent children. The *Kindergeld* is normally paid until the child reaches age 18, but it may continue to age 21 if the young adult is still without job, until age 27 if he or she is still in education, and lifelong if handicapped. There is also the right of *Erziehungsurlaub*, or unpaid vacation with job guarantee. In addition, the government has increased by $15,000 per child the amount of money a couple can invest tax-free into a special savings account to be used to build or purchase their own townhouse, condominium, or apartment. In Germany, and elsewhere in Europe, only 15% of couples own their own residence, while 85% rent. This is the reverse of the situation in North America, and the German government hopes that its *Eigenheimförderung* incentive, linking home ownership with family size, will encourage couples to have more children. (*End of update by J. Pastoetter*)]

## 10. Sexually Transmitted Diseases and HIV/AIDS

### A. Sexually Transmitted Diseases

The incidence of sexually transmitted diseases is incompletely known, since there is a legal obligation to report only four of the 20-some diseases. Presumably, the incidence of STDs equals that observed in other Western countries. That means it has remained quite high in spite of medical and hygienic progress. Within the medical profession, venereology is associated with dermatology. National and private health insurance pays for the cost of treatment.

[*Update 2001*: The figures for STDs have remained quite low in Germany for several years. In 1995, 4,061 new cases of gonorrhea were reported; this decreased to 2,412 cases in 1998. The largest drop came between 1984 and 1990, before Union, when the number of cases in West Germany decreased from 42,045 to 6,614. The same trend can be seen for other STDs, like syphilis, which decreased from 4,250 in 1984 to 868 in 1990. The annual number of new cases of syphilis increased to 1,138 in 1995 and has remained at this level since. The influx of prostitutes from Eastern Europe is likely to reverse this trend, since in the Russian Federation alone, the number of newly infected persons with syphilis has jumped to several hundred thousand. (*End of update by J. Pastoetter*)]

[*Update 2002*: In the first half of 2002, Germany recorded 1,116 new cases of syphilis, compared with 756 cases during the same time period in 2001, according to the Robert-Koch-Institut, the German equivalent of the American Centers for Disease Control. The increase in the number of new cases of syphilis was similar to that for other sexually transmissible diseases in the same time span. Health experts interpreted this as an "early warning" of an impending increase in new HIV infections, because it indicates a willingness by people to engage in unprotected sexual contact. Young people who did not witness the "AIDS shock" of the mid-1980s and do not fully comprehend the need to use condoms, appear particularly susceptible.

[Because advances in HIV/AIDS treatments have created false hopes of a cure among many people, health officials warn that prevention efforts must be redoubled. However, funding for HIV/AIDS programs in Germany has remained steady over the last three to five years, even though the number of new German AIDS cases has been increasing steadily. The growing concern is that a kind of "prevention fatigue" may reduce prevention efforts at the very time these efforts need to be increased, not just in Germany, but also in other European and North American countries (Stafford, Reuters Health, September 9, 2002; Kaiser 2002). (*End of update by R. T. Francoeur*)]

## B. HIV/AIDS

Among the people diagnosed as HIV-positive, men with homosexual experiences constitute the biggest category, about 70%, followed by IV-drug users, about 15%. Consequently, in Germany, AIDS is essentially understood as a venereal disease. The prevalence up to 1993—about 10,000 cases of AIDS—is lower than in some other European countries, not to mention the United States. Women constitute 10% of the cases. Eastern Germany is as yet a sort of developing country for HIV infection following the fall of the Iron Curtain, which served as a preventive measure.

The comparatively low incidence is a result of a policy that emphasized rational recognition instead of repression and denial. Campaigns in the mass media, at schools, and by street workers delivered preventative messages. Homosexual men changed some of their practices (Bochow 1993; Dannecker 1990). Since the rules of safer sex are not observed completely, some new infections still occur.

Because the official information applies to the whole population instead of just to special risk groups, it is understood that sexuality in general will be affected by the AIDS crisis. It may be that the recently identified return of young people to the ideal of romantic love results partly from official condemnation of promiscuity.

Approximately one tenth of adolescents with experience in sexual intercourse say they have on at least one occasion shunned some sort of sexual activity for fear of being infected with the HIV virus. For most young people, sexual contact is not normally connected with a current fear of being infected with AIDS, and when it is, there is some obvious reason, such as a suspected at-risk partner or unprotected intercourse. Despite the very different epidemiological situations reigning in eastern and western Germany—there are hardly any AIDS patients in eastern Germany and most of these are in Berlin—AIDS has produced equal degrees of consternation. This anxiety is rarely fear for one's own health or behavior, but rather a more general sense of concern, including sympathy for those infected by HIV and PWAs (persons with AIDS). Somewhat older and more-experienced young people, in particular, do not see themselves in danger as a result of their partnership activity and sexual behavior and know how to protect themselves in doubtful cases. The fear of AIDS among younger adolescents results from uncertainty, ignorance, and a lack of experience. It represents a sort of "mental barrier" to the adoption of sociosexual contact, which is subsequently dissipated during the relationship. The real dangers are often suppressed in daily sexual life.

Autistic concepts of safer sex are out of fashion, especially among younger people and, in particular, in eastern Germany. Sexuality is not idealized as aseptic sex without contact if at all possible (with the "enemy"), or as an anonymous service, or as isolated desire, but rather as firmly linked with the (beloved) partner. Both heterosexuals and homosexuals love a concrete person, enter into a relationship, and have sexual contact with them. The rates of masturbation are comparatively low. Although masturbation is accepted as a sexual activity, and inhibitions in this respect have been dispelled, partnership sex is still preferred.

[*Update 2001*: In 1999, 2,100 Germans were newly infected with HIV, about the same number as in 1998. Also the number of people diagnosed with AIDS (568) or died (close to 600) has remained constant in recent years. This marks a decrease from 1995, when 2,045 AIDS patients died, and is mainly because of improved medical treatment. According to an estimate from the Robert Koch Institute, Berlin, in 1999, an estimated 37,000 Germans were infected with HIV: 29,000 men, 8,000 women, and about 400 children. (*End of update by J. Pastoetter*)]

[*Update 2002*: UNAIDS Epidemiological Assessment: By mid 2001, a cumulative total of 16,769 cases of HIV infection had been reported in Germany. HIV testing is systematic among blood donors and recommended for pregnant women, with an estimated coverage of 50% to 80%. Since 1993, laboratories and, since 1998, clinicians report anonymously newly diagnosed HIV infections to a national HIV database. Clinician reports are provided for over 90% of cases and contain a name-based code to allow for detection of duplicate reports. Among cases reported in 1997 to 1999, 38% were homosexuals, 30% heterosexuals, 11% injection drug users, and 20% were reported with an undetermined mode of transmission.

[UAT of all newborns has been conducted since 1993 in Berlin and Lower Saxony and since 1995 in Bayern. HIV prevalence is low in the general population, in particular outside metropolitan areas. In Berlin, the city with the highest cumulative AIDS incidence, HIV prevalence in pregnant women is below 0.1%. No significant trends could be detected between 1993 and 1995. Since 1985, prevalence has decreased among injection drug users entering drug treatment centers; and varied in 1992 to 1993 from 6% to 4%. Other data, partly based on self-reported test results, showed a prevalence around 20% among users of syringe vending machines or storefront units (1992 to 1993). As in other Western European countries, prevalence in non-injection drug-using prostitutes is similar to that in the general population.

[The estimated number of adults and children living with HIV/AIDS on January 1, 2002, were:

| | |
|---|---|
| Adults ages 15-49: | 41,000 (rate: 0.1%) |
| Women ages 15-49: | 8,100 |
| Children ages 0-15: | 550 |

[An estimated 660 adults and children died of AIDS during 2001.

[No estimate is available for the number of German children who had lost one or both parents to AIDS and were under age 15 at the end of 2001. (*End of update by the Editors*)]

## *11. Sexual Dysfunctions, Counseling, and Therapies*

### A. Concepts of Sexual Dysfunction

Real fears of sexual joys exist. The most common fear in connection with sex among males and females and throughout Germany is that of unwanted pregnancy. Sexual diseases and AIDS are, by contrast, currently regarded as worry factors of lesser importance. Other fears refer to the anticipation of sex and the experience of sexuality.

Only one quarter of 16- to 17-year-old, sexually inexperienced females in western Germany have a desire for more sex, and only 10% of them want to have their first experience of sexual intercourse. They are afraid of disappointment, they are fearful of not finding the right partner who will meet their expectations, they are occasionally conscious of an aversion to men in general, not wanting to become a man's sexual plaything, and they are rather wary of both abstract and direct involvement in sex.

Male adolescents, especially those from western Germany, often abstain from sexual contact: Their sex drive is not that great. During their first incidence of sexual intercourse, only a good half of males from western Germany, compared to 80% from eastern Germany, said that a strong sex drive was a motive. They link sexual intercourse with a steady relationship and having a faithful girlfriend, and certainly do not want to get involved in something "wishy-washy," unpredictable, restrictive, or vexing only in order to establish a close bond or for reasons of sex.

Sexual experience: By no means do all females experience their sexual activity to be pleasant and enjoyable, especially those from western Germany. This refers both to masturbation, which they often do not find gratifying, and above all to intimacy with their partner and sexual intercourse. Half are sexually unsatisfied after sexual intercourse, and only the remaining half derive any pleasure from it at all. It is only a great experience for a quarter, and only a quarter have the wish to repeat it soon. Among eastern German females, almost two thirds find sex a great experience. This appraisal is acted on, as girls from eastern Germany have sexual intercourse more often than their counterparts from the west.

Men in the west suffer, in particular, from mental problems connected with sexual competence, sexual performance, their own attractiveness, and frustrations in love and sex, and these are connected with failure to cope with the pressure of norms or a fear of not being accepted without bias, but rather having to first fight as a man against a barrage of devaluation, mistrust, and prejudice.

[*Update 2001*: Impotence and lack of sexual desire are rapidly growing phenomena in Germany. The number of men without sexual desire quadrupled from 4% in the 1970s to 16% today. Most couples seem relieved when they learn that intense sexual libido rarely survives beyond the first few years of an intimate relationship. Most men and women also seem to accept the fact that having good sex means hard work: keeping in shape and learning from and respecting one another. In everyday life, the stress of work and the time and energy consumed in hobbies also affects the level of libido.

[For most couples, sexual satisfaction is less a matter of sheer lust and ecstasy as it is showing each other affection and love. Emotional intimacy, tenderness, and the feeling of belonging together are increasingly more important than sexual satisfaction. On the other hand, a trend towards less sexual activity, especially in long-term relationships, is not as new as it might look at a first glance. Early in the 20th century, psychoanalyst Carl G. Jung and the German poet and physician Gottfried Benn agreed that "marriage is an institution to paralyze the sex drive." At the end of the 20th century, three quarters of German wives married for 30 or more years reported a strong decline of the sexual interest of their partners. Only 12% of all couples think that sexuality is important or very important, and four of ten couples have stopped sexual intercourse all together. (*End of update by J. Pastoetter*)]

### B. Availability of Counseling, Diagnosis, and Treatment

Counseling and therapy in sexual matters is offered by a range of public institutions and private practitioners, most of them psychologists. However, this scene is not as widespread as it is in the U.S.A. Special certifications and licenses for sexual therapists do not exist. National and private health insurance pays a considerable portion of the costs.

### [C. Redefining the Meaning of Sex

[*Update 2002*: German men and women are becoming more and more similar in their attitude toward sex, as well as the quantity and quite-high satisfaction both get from their sexual activity. The percentage of women who say they have masturbated increased from 50% in the 1960s to 86% in 2000. The percentage of males who masturbate has been above 90% for decades. For 90% of Germans, love and sex belong together; only one in ten persons says that love is not decisive for sex. For 60% of Germans, touching, tenderness, and petting are the most important sexual behaviors. Overall, only one in three—50% of men and 25% of women—says coitus is the most important aspect of sex. (*End of update by J. Pastoetter*)]

## *12. Sex Research and Advanced Professional Education*

### A. Advanced Education and Research Institutes

Funding and support for sexological research in Germany are deplorably low considering the public demand for knowledge and the gravity of social and individual problems with sexuality. The funds available are far less, proportionately, than in the U.S.A. Consequently, Germany is throwing away its great tradition in sexology.

There are some small institutes within the medical departments of the universities of Frankfurt/Main, Hamburg, and Kiel. Empirical sex research is mainly conducted in Leipzig, pedagogical in Landau, and sociological in Bremen. Ideological cleavages cause controversies, which means that researchers do not cooperate very much. Frequently, they ignore and despise each other. The small sexological community is split into five organizations—which, in turn, contributes to the political weakness of the profession.

Postgraduate training exists at only one or two medical faculties. Graduate-level programs for the advanced study of human sexuality are unknown. Some private institutes for family counseling and birth planning offer courses for interested adults, that is, at the college level. What the Federal Bureau for Health Information (offices in Cologne) can do depends on the ruling party. The conservative government, in power since 1982, had an information pack destroyed soon after it had been developed by their liberal predecessors. This symbolizes how the evolution of sexology in Germany is impeded by the public moralization of sexual matters, even in the time of AIDS.

### B. Sexological Publications and Organizations

Only one sexological journal, a quarterly founded in 1988, is published in Germany: *Zeitschrift für Sexualforschung*. Address: Enke, Box 101254, Stuttgart.

National sexological organizations include:

Deutsche Gesellschaft für Sexualforschung, based at the Universities of Hamburg and Frankfurt/Main. Address: Martinistr. 52, 20251 Hamburg, Germany.

Gesellschaft für Sexualwissenschaft (Leipzig). Address: Bernhard-Goering-Str. 152, 04277 Leipzig, Germany.

Gesellschaft für Praktische Sexualmedizin (Kiel). Address: Hospitalstr. 17-19. 24105 Kiel, Germany.

Deutsche Gesellschaft für Geschlechtserziehung (Bonn/ Landau). Address: Westring 10A, 76829 Landau, Germany.

Deutsche Gesellschaft für Sozialwissenschaftliche Sexualforschung (Düsseldorf). Address: Gerresheimer Str. 20, 40211 Düsseldorf, Germany.

## Germany's Immigrants

JAKOB PASTOETTER

[*Update 2002*: Germany has 7.5 million immigrants: Turkish citizens account for 2.1 million (28.8%); citizens from the former Yugoslavia, 9.8%; and Italians, 8.4%. About one third have lived in Germany for 20 years or longer; about 20% were born here. The jobless rate for immigrants is about double that of native Germans. A major factor in this unemployment, according to the last biannual *Report of the Situation of Migrants in Germany* (3/2000), is the decreasing level of education among immigrant students. Another subgroup that deserves more interest is the rapidly growing number of senior immigrants, with half a million now over age 60.

[The immigration rate of Aussiedler, people with German heritage resettling from host countries like Russia, Poland, and Rumania after having lived there for several hundred years, has remained relatively constant, with 104,916 registered in 1999 and 103,080 in 1998. Meanwhile, the number of people becoming naturalized Germans increased rapidly from 61,709 in 1994 to 106,790 in 1998.

[Specific medical problems, like a higher rate of sexually transmitted diseases. and sexual problems, like inhibited ejaculation, are often the result of highly traditional gender roles and sexual traditions colliding with the values of a postindustrial, Western society. For people living in the conservative and patriarchal traditions of Islam, of Catholic Poland, or of the village societies in rural Eastern Europe, the confrontation with liberal sexual attitudes is a shock. It seems that immigrant males have more problems with the devaluation of their often highly ritualized and privileged position within their family, as well as in society. Women, however, experience the individual freedom of choosing their own lifestyle. German social workers, sex educators, and physicians have started to see some of these conflicts as cultural problems, and are trying to find cultural answers. For example, a German doctor would normally ask to see a male patient alone without the male friend or relative who accompanied him. Turkish men, however, are accustomed to have a male friend or relative present with them during the whole visit to the doctor. Another culture-related problem is the sex-information leaflets, which use a formal, impersonal German style and language, whereas Turkish men tend to prefer an informal and personal form of address.

[Migrant women and men alike tend to be less informed about sexual facts. They also have more difficulty in speaking about sex in general. Immigrant women, particularly those from the former Eastern Bloc, often see abortion as the preferred contraceptive; some have had as many as ten abortions during their reproductive years. Their men, in turn, have a strong dislike for condoms. Polish surveys find the same high level of double moral standard as in the United States; women are expected to enter marriage as virgins while men are expected to have multiple sexual "experi-

ences." That sexual experience male immigrants can achieve with German women at *Salsa* parties in discos and bars, which have developed as rendezvous places over the last ten years. This also sheds some light on how German women view their fellow countrymen as intimate partners, and on their high regard for Latin looks and temperament, which makes German women leaders in sex tourism to the Caribbean. As sex tourists, German men travel mainly to South East Asia.

[Sex education in school can only be a success with immigrant children if the parents are not informed in advance, because many parents do not allow their children to learn about sexuality at all. They regard the German culture as being unchaste and immoral—for Muslims even to talk about sex is "impure." Sex education for immigrant adults also runs into difficulties, because the women, in particular, fear that their peers, parents, or husbands will criticize them. Solutions for this information deficit and culturally conditioned hostility may be found in developing a range of cultural sensibilities and introducing peer-education strategies. (*End of update by J. Pastoetter*)]

## References and Suggested Readings

Becker, S., H. A. G. Bosinski, U. Clement, W. Eicher, T. Goerlich, et al. 1997. Standards of treatment and expert assessment of transsexuals by the German Society for Sex Research, the Academy for Sexual Medicine, and the Society for Sexology [Standards der Behandlung und Begutachtung von Transsexuellen der Deutschen Gesellschaft für Sexualforschung, der Akademie für Sexualmedizin und der Gesellschaft für Sexualwissenschaft]. *Sexuologie*, 4:130-138.

Beier, M., H. A. G. Bosinski, & Hartmann. 2000. Sexual medicine fundamentals and practice [Sexualmedizin–Grundlagen und praxis]. München: Urban und Fischer.

Bochow, M. 1993. Einstellungen und werthaltungen zu homosexuellen maennern. In: C. Lange, ed., *AIDS—Eine forschungsbilanz*. Berlin: Bohn.

Bosinski, H.A.G., P. M. Bonatz, G. Arndt, R. Heidenreich, M. Sippell, & W. G. R. Wille. 1997. A higher rate of hyperandrogenic disorders in female-to-male transsexuals. *Psychoneuroendocrinology*, 22:361-380.

Bundeszentrale für gesundheitliche Aufklärung (BzgA), Abteilung Sexualaufklärung, Verhütung und Familienplanung. 1995ff. *Research and praxis of sex education and family planning*, vol. 1-17 [*Forschung und praxis der sexualaufklärung und familienplanung*, Bde. 1-17]. Köln.

BzgA Forum Sexualaufklärung und Familienplanung 2. 1999. *Intercultural* [*Interkulturell*].

CIA. 2002 (January). *The world factbook 2002*. Washington, DC: Central Intelligence Agency. Available: http://www.cia.gov/cia/publications/factbook/index.html.

Clement, U. 1986. *Sexualitaet im Sozialen Wandel*. Stuttgart: Enke.

Dannecker, M. 1990. *Homosexuelle Maenner und AIDS*. Stuttgart: Kohlhammer.

Glatzer, W., H. Stuhler, A. Mingels, et al. 1997. Consensual unions: Marriage substitute or marriage alternative? State of research in Germany 1996-1997. [Nichteheliche lebensgemeinschaften: Eheähnlich oder eher alternativ? Stand der forschung in Deutschland 1996/97]. *Materialien zur Bevölkerungswissenschaft, 89*:87. Wiesbaden: Bundesinstitut für Bevölkerungsforschung.

Glueck, G. 1990. *Heisse Eisen in der Sexualerziehung*. Weinheim: Deutscher Studien Verlag.

Haeberle, E. J., & R. Gindorf. 1994/1998. *Bisexualitäten*. Stuttgart: Fischer-Verlag, 1994. *Bisexualities: The ideology and practice of sexual contact with both men and women*. New York: Continuum, 1998.

Hirschauer, S. 1993. *Die soziale Konstruktion der Transsexualitaet*. Frankfurt/M: Suhrkamp.

Jürges, H. 1998 (October). Vocationally motivated migration behavior in double-income households. An empirical analysis using GSOEP data [Beruflich bedingte umzüge von doppelverdienern. Eine empirische analyse mit daten des SOEP]. *Zeitschrift für Soziologie, 27*(5):358-377.

Karatepe, H. 1996. Sexual troubles of migrants [Sexualstörungen bei migranten]. *Sexualmedizin, 1*:20-21.

Kinzer, S. 1994 (November 25). $650 a baby: Germany to pay to stem decline in births. *The New York Times*, p. A3.

Lautmann, R. 1977. *Seminar: Gesellschaft und Homosexualitaet*. Frankfurt/M.: Suhrkamp.

Lautmann, R. 1994. *Die Lust am Kind*. Hamburg: Klein.

Lautmann, R., & M. Schetsche, 1990. *Das Pornographierte Begehren*. Frankfurt/M.: Suhrkamp.

Lindemann, G. 1993. Das Paradoxw Geschlecht. Frankfurt/M.: Fischer.

Mayer, K. U., & P. B. Baltes. 1996. *The Berlin study on aging* [*Die Berliner altersstudie*]. Berlin: Akademie Verlag.

Reinecke, J., P. Schmidt, & I. Ajzen. 1997 (May 1). Birth control versus AIDS prevention: A hierarchical model of condom use among young people. *Journal of Applied Social Psychology, 27*(9):743-59.

Schmidt, G. 2000. *The sexual revolution and her children* [*Die sexuelle revolution und ihre kinder*]. Gießen: Psychosozial-Verlag.

Sigusch, V. 1992. *Geschlechtswechsel*. Hamburg: Klein.

Starke, K. 1991. Jugend und Sexualitaet. In: W. Friedrich, & H. Griese, eds., *Jugend und Jugendforschung in der DDR*. Opladen: Leske.

Starke, K., & W. Friedrich. 1984-1991. *Liebe und Sexualitaet bis 30*. Berlin: Deutscher Verlag der Wissenschaften.

Starke, K., & K. Weller. 1993. West-und Ostdeutsche Jugendliche. In: G. Schmidt, ed., *Jugendsexualitaet*. Stuttgart: Enke.

UNAIDS. 2002. *Epidemiological fact sheets by country*. Geneva, Switzerland: Joint United Nations Programme on HIV/AIDS (UNAIDS/WHO). Available: http://www.unaids.org/hivaidsinfo/statistics/fact_sheets/index_en.htm.

Weitze, C., & S. Osburg. 1996. Transsexualism in Germany: Empirical data on epidemiology and application of the German Transsexuals' Act during its first ten years. *Archive of Sexual Behavior, 25*:409-425.

Winawer-Steiner, H., & N. A. Wetzer. 1982. German families. In: M. McGoldrick, J. K. Pearce, & J. Giordano, eds., *Ethnicity and family therapy*. New York: Guilford Press.

## Internet Sources

The Magnus Hirschfeld Archive for Sexology http://www2.hu-berlin.de/sexology/.

Bundeskriminalamt. http://www.bka.de.

Bundesministerium für Familie, Senioren, Frauen und Jugend. http://www.bmfsfj.de.

Bundeszentrale für gesundheitliche Aufklärung (BzgA). www.bzga.de.

Deutsche Gesellschaft für Sozialwissenschaftliche Sexualforschung. www.sexologie.de.

Robert Koch Institute, Berlin. http://www.rki.de.

Kaiser Health Report. 2002. *German health experts concerned that rising STD rates are 'early warning' of increase in HIV incidence*. http://www.kaisernetwork.org/daily_reports/rep_index.cfm?DR_ID=13377.

Shell-Studie "Jugend 2000." http://www.shell-jugend2000.de.

Statistisches Bundesamt. http://www.statistik-bund.de.

# Ghana

Augustine Ankomah, Ph.D.
*Updates by Beldina Opiyo-Omolo, B.Sc.* *

## Contents

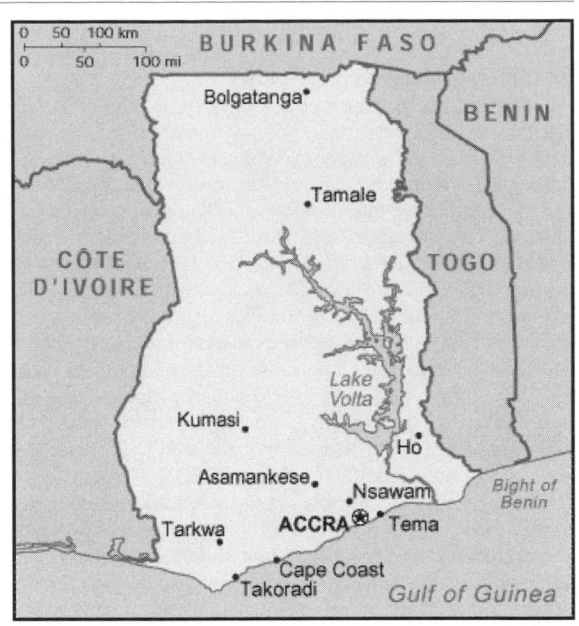

(CIA 2002)

## Demographics and a Brief Historical Perspective

ROBERT T. FRANCOEUR

### A. Demographics

Ghana, on the southern coast of West Africa, is a land of 92,098 square miles (238,533 km²), slightly smaller than the state of Oregon or about the size of the United Kingdom. Ghana has fertile plains of luxuriant vegetation in the forest zone in the south and much sparser savanna, woodland, and scrubland in the north. The south supports the growing of cash crops, like cocoa—the main export commodity—rubber, coffee, kola nuts, and coconut, and food crops such as maize, cassava, and plantain. The north is particularly suited for cereal cultivation and cattle rearing. Although the official language is English, Ghana's neighbors are all French-speaking nations: Burkina Faso on the north, Togo on the east, and Côte d'Ivoire (the Ivory Coast) on the west.

In July 2002, Ghana had an estimated population of 20.24 million. These estimates explicitly take into account the effects of excess mortality because of AIDS. This can result in lower life expectancy, higher infant mortality and death rates, lower population and growth rates, and different changes in the distribution of population by age and sex than would otherwise be expected. (All data are from *The World Factbook 2002* (CIA 2002) unless otherwise stated.)

**Age Distribution and Sex Ratios**: *0-14 years*: 40.4% with 1.03 male(s) per female (sex ratio); *15-64 years*: 56.1% with 0.98 male(s) per female; *65 years and over*: 3.5% with 0.91 male(s) per female; *Total population sex ratio*: 0.99 male(s) to 1 female

**Life Expectancy at Birth**: *Total Population*: 57.24 years; *male*: 55.86 years; *female*: 58.66 years

**Urban/Rural Distribution**: Slightly less that one-third are urban while a little over two-thirds live in rural areas

**Ethnic Distribution**: Black African: 99.8% with major tribes: Akan: 44%; Moshi-Dagomba: 16%; Ewe: 13%; Ga: 8%; European and other: 0.2%

**Religious Distribution**: Indigenous beliefs: 38%; Muslim: 30%; Christian: 24%; other: 8%

**Birth Rate**: 28.08 births per 1,000 population

**Death Rate**: 10.31 per 1,000 population

**Infant Mortality Rate**: 55.64 deaths per 1,000 live births

**Net Migration Rate**: –0.74 migrant(s) per 1,000 population

**Total Fertility Rate**: 3.69 children born per woman

**Population Growth Rate**: 1.7%

**HIV/AIDS** (1999 est.): *Adult prevalence*: 3.6%; *Persons living with HIV/AIDS*: 340,000; *Deaths*: 33,000 (For additional details from www.UNAIDS.org, see end of Section 10B.)

**Literacy Rate** (*defined as those age 15 and over who can read and write*): 64.5% (*male*: 75.9%, *female*: 53.5%)

**Per Capita Gross Domestic Product** (*purchasing power parity*): $1,980 (2001 est.); *Inflation*: 25% (2001 est.); *Unemployment*: 20% (1997 est.); *Living below the poverty line*: 31.4% (1992 est.)

### B. A Brief Historical Perspective

Ghana was named for an African empire that existed along the Niger River between 400 and 1240 of the Common Era. The country was ruled by Britain for 113 years as the Gold Coast. In 1956, the United Nations approved the merger of the Gold Coast with the British Togoland trust territory. In 1957, it emerged as the first country in black Africa to achieve independence from a European power. Since that time, Ghana has witnessed a seesaw of political power shared between military and elected governments.

In the years immediately following independence, schools, hospitals, and roads were built, along with hydroelectric power plants and aluminum plants by President Nkrumah, but the economic situation deteriorated between the 1970s and late 1980s. J. J. Rawlings, a flight lieutenant who took over the administration of the country through a military coup in 1979 and again in 1981, won the national election and was sworn in as president in 1993. However, Rawlings was defeated in a landslide victory in the 2000 presidential elections by the current President, John Agyekum Kufuor.

*Communications*: Augustine Ankoma, Ph.D.: *Not available.* Beldina Opiyo-Omolo, B.Sc., Department of Health, East Stroudsburg University of Pennsylvania, East Stroudsburg, PA 18301 USA; bopiyo@yahoo.com.

## *1. Basic Sexological Premises*

### A. Character of Gender Roles

In Ghana, the human world is basically a "man's world." Women are in a subordinate position in terms of decision making within the household. Women work both inside and outside the home. At home, they are responsible for mothering, cooking, washing, food storage, and processing. Outside, they participate in agricultural activities and farm different crops, but few hold titles to land. It is in the sphere of trading that the ingenuity of Ghanaian women is most displayed and apparent. Traditionally, they have maintained an autonomous economic role as market traders, and some of them in Accra and Kumasi are perhaps among the most independent women in Africa. Although women who work in the informal sectors may support themselves, their children, and sometimes the husband, decision making on sex and reproduction is still regarded as a man's prerogative. In 1988, three in ten households were female-headed, yet these heads have to refer issues relating to their children to the male kin. It can be said that in Ghana, women can achieve considerable economic autonomy, but the female power and prestige accruing from her economic independence at the societal level is unable to affect, to any considerable extent, the power relations within marriage.

### B. Sociolegal Status of Males and Females

*Children*

On the whole, Ghana is a pronatalist country and the value of children inestimable. To suggest that children are the *raison d'etre* of marriage is an underestimation: They are the *raison d'etre* of life. The specter of childlessness is indescribable, and it is felt by both men and women as the greatest of all tragedies and humiliations. Children are the sign of a woman's normality, femininity, and healthiness. Among some Akan groups in the not-distant past, a public ceremony of congratulation was performed for a couple when they had ten living children. A woman who has no children is open to various suspicions. The two most common are that she or a relative is a witch who has "killed" all her children or that she led an immoral life when she was young. The changing social and economic conditions have not diminished the traditional desire for children, although the number of children women consider as an ideal family size has been considerably reduced. For example, the ideal family size was found to be 6.1 children in 1979-80, but had dropped to 5.3 by 1988, both of which are still higher than actual current fertility. Today, the status of a family, to a very large extent, depends on how well they are able to support their children, rather than on the absolute number of children.

Unlike in some developing countries where sex preference is very strong, with dire consequences for the "unwanted sex," Ghanaians do not appear to have any strongly held bias for a particular sex. Ideally, every parent would like to have boys and girls in certain proportions, depending on whether the society is matrilineal or patrilineal. For example, among the matrilineal Akan, since descent and inheritance are reckoned through the mother's side, women provide the continuity of the lineage. A man without sisters is haunted by a sense of frustration.

There is no evidence of sex bias in the feeding or mothering of infants. A government survey in 1988 based on anthropometric measures found no differences between males and females. However, male children under the age of 5 years were more prone to illness and injury than their female counterparts.

An increasing number of school-age children roam the streets and lorry parks of Accra and other cities. This is gradually becoming a social problem. Children at risk include those from broken or extremely poor homes and migrants. Very little has been done in terms of research on these street children. The Ghana National Commission on Children (GNCC) was established in 1977 in response to the United Nations General Assembly's Declaration of 1976, which set 1979 as the International Year of the Child. The GNCC is the sole coordinator of issues relating to the development of children. In order to support such children, GNCC in 1987 established the Child Education Trust to enable needy dropouts to continue their education. Sustaining breastfeeding and promoting the use of locally produced weaning food products has also been one of the commission's achievements, as well as putting on the public agenda issues relating to child labor.

*Adults*

Although there are no legal barriers to female education, employment, and other formal aspects in the public sector, situational factors put females in a disadvantageous position. Parents are more likely to educate boys beyond basic education than girls who, it is thought, will soon get married or can earn a living through trading. Consequently, the proportion of females in secondary schools is about 30%; in the universities, the percentage has always been around 18%. Through education, many women have been able to embark on careers that were considered to be for men.

In Ghana, professional women—doctors, lawyers, administrators, headmistresses, and judges—are highly respected, and in their societies serve as role models. Parents are proud of such daughters and may boast to colleagues and friends about them. Women earn the same salary and have the same conditions of service in employment as their male counterparts, although there is a tendency for men (and some women as well) to feel reluctant to work under a woman boss. In general, women occupy subordinate positions in the Ghanaian society and are not regarded as equals of men, who still monopolize most positions of influence.

Given that the early socialization process is modeled along distinct sex roles, every Ghanaian grows up with the knowledge that it is the woman who cooks, does the washing up, and the laundry, and indeed is responsible for all household chores. Notwithstanding her level of education, profession, or schedule of work, a woman does not expect her husband to share in household chores. A few men in highly educated homes may occasionally assist their wives in the kitchen, but many will abandon whatever they are doing when there is a knock at the door, for it is considered disgraceful for outsiders, especially from the man's family, to find a man engrossed in feminine roles, such as cooking or washing up. Yet, it is the man who always has the lion's share. There is unequal allocation of food between husband and wife in the home, especially in the rural areas. Men are given the prime cut of meat, for example. The patriarchal nature of the Ghanaian society also has negative implications for the health of women.

### C. General Concepts of Sexuality and Love

The sexual culture of Ghana can be described as a paradox. Sexual matters are among the popular topics for conversation and gossip, but there is less evidence of serious societal debate about sexual issues. Though many cultural artifacts, Ghanaian traditional and "high life" music, dances, jokes, and gibes, are frequently woven around sex, the topic hardly comes into the forefront of any formal discussion, and blunt questions about sexual matters may encounter opposition. It must be stated that Ghanaian sexual mores, as elsewhere in Africa, can be well understood if one keeps in mind that sexual facts are significant, since they affect other spheres of life. In most traditional societies, there was a seemingly inseparable link between the sexual and the social.

In Ghana, public exhibition of emotions by lovers through kissing is frowned at. This does not imply that there is no love in Ghanaian sexual relationships as some foreign writers claim; however, love alone is not enough to persuade parents to approve of a relationship.

## 2. Religious, Ethnic, and Gender Factors Affecting Sexuality

### A. Source and Character of Religious Values

There are three main forms of religious practice in Ghana: traditional indigenous (38%), Muslim (30%), and Christian (24%), with 8% other (CIA 2002). In terms of religion, Ghana is a very tolerant country. There is little or no evidence of religious intolerance and fanaticism as are known in some African countries. As with most African countries, Ghanaians believe in the existence of one Supreme Deity, known by different names, whom they regard as far greater than any other being. Atheists are very rare.

In every Ghanaian town there are churches everywhere. The largest Christian denomination is the Catholics. There are Protestant churches like the Methodists and Anglicans, and also a growing number of Pentecostal and charismatic churches. Many members, especially those of the orthodox churches, still maintain some traditional practices that are unacceptable to their churches—such as polygyny—although more and more churches are becoming tolerant. Since it lacks literary documents, traditional religion is not systematic in doctrine. However, one basic characteristic is the belief in the spirits of the ancestors who influence the living in every conceivable sphere of life, and apply rewards and sanctions where appropriate. There are also lesser gods or deities with different powers who represent the Almighty God on earth. Compared with other West African countries, the proportion of Muslims in Ghana is low. Most of Ghana's Muslims are Sunnis, although there is a substantial group of Ahmadi Mission who are well established in Saltpond in southern Ghana. Apart from northern Ghana, the biggest concentration of Muslims is to be found in the two largest cities of Accra and Kumasi.

In a recent study in an urban center in southern Ghana, it was observed that religion has no relationship with female sexual behavior in terms of number of sexual partners and age at first sexual intercourse, although Catholics are more likely than other religious groups to have first sexual intercourse late in life.

### B. Source and Character of Ethnic Values

With over 90 ethnic groups, there is relative diversity not only in language, but also in customs, including sexual norms. The Akan, consisting of several tribes with closely related languages, are by far the largest. Inhabiting most of central and southern Ghana, they form 44% of the total population. The southeast is inhabited by the Ewes (13%). In northern Ghana, the ethnic situation is more diverse, and relatively few groups have been extensively studied. Other ethnic groups include the Moshi-Dagomba (16%) and Ga (8%).

One basic difference with significant implications for sexual values exists between the Akan and other ethnic groups. The Akan is a matrilineal group and the others patrilineal. In matrilineal societies, descent is traced through the mother's line and a person is therefore legally identified with his or her matrikin. A person inherits from the mother's line and thus children hold no claim whatsoever to their father's estate. As in many matrilineal groups, conjugal ties are weak and considered less important than blood ties. Con-

versely, in patrilineal societies, descent is traced from the father's line and children inherit from their fathers. The "luckiest" Ghanaian children are from intertribal marriages where the father comes from a patrilineal group and the mother from a matrilineal society. The reverse (father from a matrilineal and mother from a patrilineal) is the "worst" match, since children cannot inherit from either side. While all the matrilineal Akan groups generally share similar sexual values and norms, within the patrilineal societies there are striking variations in premarital, marital, and extramarital sexual ethos. Generalizations on "Ghanaian sexuality" is, therefore, very hazardous. As far as possible, where differences are striking, attention is drawn to them in this chapter.

## 3. Knowledge and Education about Sexuality

### A. Government Policies and Programs for Sex Education

The government's attitude toward sex education in Ghana, as in several other sub-Saharan African countries, can be described as ambivalent. In a survey in 1987, it was found that all the teachers agreed that there was a need for sex education in schools. When surveyed in 1991, secondary schools in Accra revealed some disturbing findings showing a high degree of ignorance, especially on questions relating to menstrual cycle and pregnancy. In a study by the Health Education Division of the Ministry of Health conducted in 1990, when junior secondary school (JSS) students were asked whether one can get pregnant the first time one had sex, 47% thought it was not possible. The situation is expected to be worse in rural schools. Yet, some people have argued that the Ghanaian society is open and that the children are not ignorant of human sexuality, and hence, it is unnecessary to handle the subject matter in the formal school setting. Others from a religious point of view are worried that sex education is likely to encourage sexual experimentation among sexually quiescent adolescents.

Theoretically, sex education should be covered, but in practice few schools have a comprehensive program on family life education. Policymakers, perhaps for the fear of arousing religious opposition, are ambivalent on issues concerning sex education. On the one hand, sex education is part of the school curricula in order to acknowledge official interest, yet on the other hand, most officials feel unconcerned that it is not effectively taught, thus pacifying the moral and religious critics. The establishment of junior secondary schools, which marks a radical change in Ghana's educational system, may result in a new approach towards the teaching of sex education. With the new educational structure, family life education at both junior and senior secondary school levels is to be covered in a new subject called Life Skills, and again at the senior level within Home Economics. [*Update 2003*: Despite a national reproductive health policy with specific provisions for adolescents, actual access to information and services is severely limited by adults' judgmental views of sexually active youth. Many community organizations have taken an interest in sex education. The Young Women's Christian Association is working with the U.S.-based Center for Development and Population Activists to involve parents and church leaders in counseling. (*End of update by B. Opiyo-Omolo*)]

### B. Informal Sources of Sexual Knowledge

Though a child's own relatives (mostly grandmothers, in the case of females) were responsible for his or her upbringing, they did not have exclusive right in the traditional society. The society as an entity had a system of preparing and training the young children for every aspect of future life, including sexual life. The training was given by traditionally recognized instructors, usually the elders. In most Ghanaian societies, the initiation or puberty rites were occasions where guidelines and instructions were provided. This was the traditional approach to sex education.

Rapid urbanization, increased mobility, education, and other agents of change have together undermined the traditional channels of sex education. With very limited access to sex education both at home and in the schools, coupled with long periods of schooling in an unmarried state, the gap between sexual and social adulthood has widened, and the modern Ghanaian adolescent faces a sexual dilemma. When in 1991, students in two secondary schools in Accra were asked to state their sources of knowledge on reproduction, the most frequently mentioned source was teachers—apparently as part of biology lessons. On the broad issue of sexual knowledge, students most frequently get their first information on sex from friends, and further from their teachers and relatives. According to Bleek's study in 1976, girls more than boys tend to rely on relatives, especially their mothers, for their first knowledge on sex education. Boys generally receive this information from male friends. The role of teachers appears to be equal for both sexes. In the urban centers, students also report magazines and books as an important source of sex information.

## 4. Autoerotic Behavior and Patterns

Information on self-pleasuring is hard to come by in Ghana. Kaye, in his impressionistic survey in the 1960s on how Ghanaian children are brought up, noted that parents strongly disapproved of their children engaging in self-pleasuring. They are sternly scolded or severely beaten. Even small boys who play with their genitals are warned to cease. Rattray, who wrote extensively in the 1920s on the Ashanti, an Akan subgroup, described the phenomenon with a phrase, *owo ne kote afeko* (he makes a pestle of his penis). In Ghana, self-pleasuring is not considered an alternative means of sexual expression and is abandoned or forgotten after childhood. This is supported by Bleek's study of schoolchildren in the 1970s, during which he did not observe the slightest hint of self-pleasuring. Adult male self-pleasuring is extremely rare, and local terms for this sexual behavior are hard to find.

## 5. Interpersonal Heterosexual Behaviors

### A. Children

The genitals of children, especially females, are not referred to directly. Special attention is given to children's genitals during bathing. The penis and vagina are washed clean to avoid sores. This is almost universal in Ghana. Warm water is dribbled into the girl's genitals (the opened vulva) and sometimes ground ginger is applied in some traditional homes to prevent disease, or sometimes as punishment for misbehavior.

Sex games in which children play the role of mothers and fathers are commonly practiced in Ghana. The games are not forbidden, but sexual exploration in the form of mutual examination of genitals may not go unpunished. Until puberty, boys and girls play together freely, and in towns and villages, especially on moonlit nights, clandestine affairs are sometimes reported.

### B. Adolescents

In traditional Ghana, as in most other African countries, the sexual transition from infancy to adulthood was not only a physiological phenomenon, such as onset of menarche, but also social. Adolescence as a reality, where a person is neither a child nor an adult, did not exist. Puberty in girls is a sign of approaching womanhood and special nubility rites for girls are performed after the first menstruation. The sociological function of initiation rites and ceremonies is to usher the child to adulthood without the period now called adolescence. In Ghana as a whole, girls' initiation ceremonies are culturally more widespread, interesting, and complex than boys' initiation. Girls' entry into womanhood, especially among the Krobo, are marked with complex ceremonies involving elaborate preparation and rituals. Generally speaking, Ghanaian boys enter manhood quietly: There are no initiation ceremonies or public ceremonies for boys.

At the end of the girl's initiation, she is gorgeously dressed and beautifully decorated. The initiate sets out with her retinue to thank all people in her village or town. She is now regarded as marriageable. If she is betrothed, her "husband" (fiancé) is formally informed to perform the marriage rites and take her as his wife as soon as practicable. If she is not already "engaged," then bachelors have a chance to have a closer look at her. During the initiation period, "sex education" lessons were provided by recognized older women who serve as custodians of instructions on motherhood. The sexual instructions given included: how to "sleep" with the husband, menstrual taboos, how to recognize pregnancy, and personal hygiene, especially of the genitals.

Unlike parts of East Africa, where there are cycles of initiation periods and ceremonies are performed for groups of persons, in Ghana with few exceptions, initiation ceremonies are mainly individual affairs, although two or three girls may begin their rites on the same day in one village. But, even here, the ceremonies are often separate, except where the neophytes are either closely related or are close friends. While puberty rites are still performed in some rural areas, they have lost a great deal of their pomp and pageantry, perhaps with the exception of the Krobo, the rural Ga, and the Adangbe, where it is still popular.

### Circumcision

Female circumcision is ritually unknown among all Akan groups in Ghana. On the whole, the practice is fairly common among the Frafra and other groups that inhabit the regions of northern Ghana. The practice is also reported in the areas in the city of Accra, such as Nima and Madina, with a large concentration of migrants from the north. In these societies, it performs a social function as a puberty rite. It is claimed by the local people that it is a precondition for marriage and a test of virginity. Most doctors are of the view that circumcised females stand a higher chance of experiencing problems during childbirth, and female circumcision has always been cited as one of the cultural practices negatively affecting women's health in Ghana.

There are significant differences in the practice of male circumcision among the various ethnic groups in Ghana. For example, the Ga of Accra and the Krobo have traditionally been practicing circumcision. A Krobo parent will not give her daughter in marriage to an uncircumcised man (apparently from an Akan tribe). Traditionally, among the Akan groups, however, male circumcision was not practiced, since it was considered as mutilation of the human body. The Akan have a rule that no one who has a scar can be elected a chief, and one already selected can be "destooled" (deselected) as soon as it is found that he has been circumcised—apparently because his body has been maimed in a way that disfigures him.

In spite of the traditional mores, male circumcision has become very popular. In boarding schools, uncircumcised boys feel shy and are unable to join others in the bathrooms, as they are constantly ridiculed and called *koteboto* (uncircumcised penis). They lack the confidence to profess love, since girls are known to shun them. The pressure may be so great that many young men are compelled to undergo a painful adult circumcision. These days, however, a great number of boys are circumcised shortly after birth.

## C. Adults

### Premarital Courtship, Dating, and Relationships

In Ghana, traditional norms involving attitudes to and acceptance of premarital sexual relationships differ from society to society. Among the Kwahu (a subgroup of the Akan), girls were not to engage in sex before they were married, and certainly not before their first menstruation. Rattray, who wrote in the 1920s, also stated that among the Ashanti, premarital coitus was forbidden. The official code on prenubility sexuality was rather strict. In olden times among the Akan, a girl was killed, or both parties banished, when she engaged in sexual intercourse prior to her puberty and initiation. In most societies in southern Ghana, since girls were usually married shortly after their initiation, many entered the conjugal union as virgins.

Among the communities in northern Ghana, the situation was different. Prenuptial chastity was not particularly valued. It is reported that among the Kokomba, for example, many women were already pregnant before marriage. The Tallensi, also of northern Ghana, explain that copulation and marriage are not the same thing. It can be said that while premarital sexual relationships have been permitted in most societies in northern Ghana, it arrived in the south as an influence of modernization. Chastity can mean two things in Ghanaian sexual mores: chastity before puberty rites and chastity after initiation, but before marriage. In olden days, both were thought important among most ethnic groups of southern Ghana. The attitude towards postpubertal but premarital chastity, however, has undergone substantial changes in many parts of Ghana.

The force of social change in Ghana resulting from education, increasing urbanization, and monetization of traditional economic systems, among others, have blended to produce changes in sexual culture. In Ghana today, it is clear that, even in societies where premarital relationships were not openly permitted, they are now at least condoned. In Ghana as a whole, the onset of sexual activity is fairly early. The median age at first sexual intercourse for females is 17 to 18 years, although one survey puts the mean age at 15. Although a substantial minority have multiple partners, for females, premarital serial monogamy with frequent partner-switching is the norm. Durations of sexual relationships are generally short and women do not appear to be worried about frequent partner-switching. In a study in one town in 1991, the mean duration of relationships was 13 months.

The underlying issue that shapes the duration of sexual relationships is basically pecuniary in nature. For many single women, especially in the urban areas, sexual relationships are means of additional income. A recent study in a town in southern Ghana has shown that personal sociodemographic variables are not significantly associated with parameters of sexual behavior, including the number of sexual partners and duration of sexual relationships. The strongest predictor of sexual behavior is women's attitude to material recompense for sex. Several anthropological studies in southern Ghana, especially, have shown that for women, economic pressures, among others, provide the background for most premarital sexual relationships. At present, the consumerist nature of premarital sexual relationships (but not formal prostitution) is generally acceptable, and it is its absence, rather than its presence, that is strange. It is interesting that most Western researchers mistakenly label this phenomenon as prostitution, apparently because some women obtain money and other gains from sexual relationships.

Premarital sexual relationships are essentially secretive in nature, although secrecy is always a matter of degree. Public show of love and affection through kissing and holding of hands while walking is hardly seen among lovers. This often misleads researchers from other cultures to misinterpret this to mean lack of love in Ghanaian "lover relationships." In Europe or America, dating couples may agree on the nature and extent of their relationships, for example, whether it is to be sexual or not. In most premarital relationships in Ghana, there is no such decision to be made. In both traditional and modern societies, premarital relationships are primarily sexual. Implicitly, male-female relationships are never nonsexual.

### Sexual Behavior and Relationships of Single Adults

Until recently, the term "single adult" was a misnomer in the Ghanaian sense. The puberty rites marked a graduation from youth to adulthood, and a woman was usually married out soon after into a relationship sometimes contracted by the couple's families prior to the initiation. The transition from childhood to adulthood was, therefore, definite and clear-cut.

The modern young adult is in a different social milieu. Modern schooling keeps boys and girls longer in an unmarried state. Some people after school spend some years looking for decent jobs. This has widened the gap between sexual maturity and married life. However, since the social position of a person, especially a woman, is often dependent on marital status, single adulthood as a chosen option is hardly acceptable. The normal pattern of Ghanaian life is to marry and have children. Any alternative lifestyle is highly questionable. Within the past few years, however, an increasing number of women do not conform to social norms and remain single.

It is worth noting that most of the few voluntarily single women are not without children. Some had unwelcome pregnancies at early ages, while others with experience from previous unions find married life distasteful and men untrustworthy. The fact that most single women choose to do so after having had children underscores the importance Ghanaian women attach to their reproductive roles.

The position of a male single adult, compared with the female, is perhaps even more untenable. While a single female adult can have children, and in the process, exhibit her fecundity to her family and indeed the entire community, the single man has no way of demonstrating his virility. Men who continue as single right up to late ages are viewed with suspicion, and may even be thought to be impotent. A middle-aged man who cooks on his own, or eats outside his home, is in an awkward position, because society does not tolerate his position as a single adult. In villages, children may refuse to go on his errands—a Ghanaian child is trained to go on errands—and some impertinent children can boldly tell him to have children of his own if he requires the services of those younger. He is normally regarded as irresponsible: He cannot assume responsibility of a wife and children. This may impair his social esteem, and can become an issue for gossip at his workplace, especially if he holds a responsible position.

### Marriage and Family

Marriage, perhaps the most important social institution in Ghana, is almost universal. Age-specific marital rates are very high and increase rapidly through successive cohorts. According to the Ghana Demographic and Health Survey of

1988, 98% of all women aged between 30 and 40 years were in marital unions. The median age at first marriage is around 8 years, and there has been no significant change since the 1970s. The national figure, however, conceals regional variations. The northern regions of Ghana together exhibit the highest rates, with over 84% of all women aged 15 to 19 in marital unions.

As elsewhere in Africa, marriage is not an individual affair, but rather a union between two families. Even today, highly educated urbanized men and women will go to great lengths to persuade an unwilling mother, but especially the father, to agree to their marriage. Costs involved in marriage differ from society to society and between families, depending on the status of the couple or their parents. On the whole, marriage among the matrilineal peoples is far cheaper. Bridewealth is considerably smaller, compared with the patrilineal groups, where husbands may be asked to pay dozens of fowls or cattle, which in terms of money is quite substantial.

In Ghana, there is legal pluralism of marriages. There are four basic ones: customary marriage; marriage under the ordinance; Christian marriage; and Muslim marriage. Eight out of every ten marriages are under customary law, under which a man can marry many wives (polygyny). Marriage under the ordinance is a British colonial legacy, which introduces attributes of legitimacy, monogamy, and inheritance into the Ghanaian context. To many, this has caused ambiguity in Ghanaian marriage law. For example, it precludes the husband from the practice of polygyny. In fact, only a small minority of Ghanaian marriages are contracted this way. Marriage types are not necessarily mutually exclusive. Persons who marry in church or in a registrar's office under ordinance do so only after they have performed the necessary customary rites.

In Ghana, as in other parts of Africa, a man, his wife or wives, and children do not constitute a family. Although the Western concept of the nuclear family can be distinguished, it is not the basis of social organization and community living. The extended family network consists of a long list of kinsmen who are matrilineally or patrilineally delineated.

In Ghana, cohabitation as a practice may be better referred to as a consensual union. In very many instances, marriages under customary practice do not take place as a single, definite event. It is rather a process that involves a series of presentations by the man's family to the family into which he proposes to marry. These presentations may be made at once, as among the Kokomba, or over a period of several years, as among the Akan. After the first presentation, a marriage may begin as a consensual union approved by parents of both partners and accepted as a proper marriage for all practical purposes. However, such unions have some drawbacks: For example, under customary law, the husband cannot claim damages if his wife commits adultery. This type of marriage is called *mpenawadie* (concubine marriage), and is less respected, and wives will put pressure on husbands to perform the final rites.

### Polygyny

In almost all Ghanaian societies, polygyny (where the husband has two or more wives) is socially accepted, and is even desirable. It is practiced in all the different customary marriage patterns. Although there are some variations, it is practiced in both urban and rural areas, and by literate and nonliterate people.

Many reasons are put forward to explain, if not to justify, polygynous marriages. These include long periods of post-partum sexual abstinence from anywhere between three months and two-and-a-half years. It is common for the pregnant wife to leave the husband's home in order to deliver among her kinsmen; she does not return until the baby is able to walk. To satisfy his sexual desires, a man is allowed to marry more than one wife. In the not-too-distant past, social status and economic prestige were the motivating factors. The large number of children from the different wives was useful in the husband's occupation, which was basically farming.

Polygyny demands some domestic residential arrangements. The most uncommon arrangement is the situation where all wives live separately from the husband who arranges periods for visits. Another solution is that in which the husband lives with all his wives in one house. This is not highly desirable, given the embedded rivalry and tension among cowives, which not infrequently results in brawling. The most favored option is that one wife (usually the first) resides with the husband, and the other(s) live on their own or with kinsmen. Cooking, "sleeping," and other wifely duties are arranged by the husband.

Polygyny is commonly practiced. Ghana's 1960 Population Census showed that 26% of all married men had more than one wife; in 1979-80, according to the Ghana Fertility Survey, 35% of all married women were in polygynous homes. The figure for 1988 was 33%. Younger women are less likely to be in polygynous unions than older women. Given that in Ghana an unmarried woman is an anomaly, polygyny affords all women (who desire) the opportunity of being attached in marriage to a man (who, unlike in the past, may not be necessarily supporting her in full). Ironically, polyandrous marriages (where one wife is legally married to more than one husband) is not practiced in Ghana or any studied society in Africa.

### Divorce

Marriages among the matrilineal groups in Ghana, strictly speaking, do not promote stability. The children and their mother are considered "outsiders" by the man's matrilineage. After the husband's death, the wife and the children are allowed up to one year to live in the deceased's property, after which they can be forcefully ejected—and many are. The man's children, until the introduction of the Intestate Succession Law in 1985, had no claim to their father's property. Given that the woman and her children are always welcomed back into their lineage after divorce, and the bridewealth, even where refundable, is fairly small, the incidence of divorce in matrilineal societies is higher than in patrilineal societies.

Under customary law, divorce is common, simple, and easily obtained. Both husband and wife can initiate divorce. Divorce in Ghana can result from several causes—the key culprit being infertility on the part of either partner. Other frequent reasons to merit divorce are: bad conduct, neglect of marital duties (such as a man's failure to provide money for food and family upkeep, popularly called "chop-money"), gossiping and tale bearing (usually on the part of the woman), laziness, accusation or suspicion of witchcraft, and interference in lineage affairs or lack of respect for in-laws. Adultery of a woman is grounds for divorce, but in customary law, the wife cannot enforce divorce on the grounds of her husband's adultery or his marrying more wives. The practice is that before an additional wife is married, the first wife is informed by the husband, who pacifies her with money or in kind.

There is usually a small and simple ceremony or ritual performed to legalize divorce. Among the Akan, it consists of the sprinkling of white clay before the woman's feet, thus formally loosening her from her former matrimonial bonds.

Although it cannot be exaggerated how easily and rapidly marriages dissolve with little trouble, it must be pointed out that, because marriage is a union between families, most divorces are preceded by family "arbitration." The aggrieved party will have to state his or her case before responsible men. The arbitrators deliver their finding after hearing each party, and then attempts are made to reconcile the couple. Unlike the matrilineal groups, traditionally among the patrilineal groups, especially the Ewe, there usually was stability of marriage. However, there have been significant changes due largely to the curtailment of the power of traditional authorities, which used to enforce the sexual morality of the people. Now, divorce is common among the Ewe, but perhaps not as frequent as it is among the Akan.

It appears the proportion of divorced persons is on the decline. In 1960, up to 20% of women aged over 44 years were divorced, compared with 13% in 1988. It is difficult, however, to obtain any useful idea of the frequency of divorce by examining the proportion of divorced persons in the population. Studies have shown that few women spend long intervals between marriages. They are usually in the process of contracting another marriage before the previous one has been formally terminated. Remarriage rates are, therefore, high, given that the society looks down upon single women.

### Extramarital Sexual Behavior

Among the Akan, extramarital relationships have been very common traditionally, and today are still practiced by married adults of both sexes and by people of all socioeconomic groups. There are some circumstances that are especially conducive to this phenomenon. Differences in status or age may demand different sexual or social habits that the partner is unable to provide. Given the high cost of living in Ghana today, some women engage in extramarital liaisons for material recompense, especially if the husband is unable to provide support. In a society where procreation is the main reason for marriage, the husband or wife may indulge in extramarital sex in the hope of having children when the other is infertile. Broadly speaking, women engage in extramarital relationships less than men.

An extramarital relationship by a married woman is regarded as adultery and both male and female culprits are liable to punishment and ridicule. Among the traditional Ga, for example, a man caught in the act of adultery with a married woman is severely beaten there and then by the family of the injured husband, their friends, and helpers. In villages, the distinctive sound of an adultery-hoot may be heard all over. A crowd gathers around the house where the adulterous act is claimed to be taking place. People begin hooting—*huu huu huu*—to emphasize the shameful behavior of the woman. The guilty man sensing danger may jump out the window. If he is lucky enough to avoid a severe beating by escaping into the bush, his family has to pacify the aggrieved husband in his absence. For his own safety, the male adulterer may avoid any public appearance until his family has completed all necessary rites to pacify the husband.

A wife's adultery, especially among the Ewe, is believed to cause not only her own death, but even that of her husband. Among the Anlo Ewe, for example, husbands, including highly educated ones, know well the risk to their lives of the infidelity of their wives. To prevent these misfortunes, many men have charms which help to strike terror in wives with adulterous intentions. Sometimes, adultery is believed to make childbirth difficult, and unless confession is made before or during childbirth—and some women do so in the rural areas—the adulteress may die with the child.

In Akan customary marriage, where a married woman is seduced, her seducer is bound to pay the husband, as damages, an amount which is fixed by law (called *ayefare* by the Akan), although one could seek divorce outright. Today, *ayefare* is not routinely claimed by men because of the shame attached to its acceptance. Many prefer that their wives' extramarital affairs are kept secret, but once it comes out in the open, divorce is sought rather than the claim of damages that may be considered embarrassing. The societal attitude to the extramarital affairs of men can be described as a double standard. The philandering of married men is generally accepted until a point is reached at which a wife feels she is suffering a grievous hardship; then she may ask her husband's family to restrain him. A woman who seeks divorce because her husband has an affair with another woman is considered to be overreacting, and she cannot expect much sympathy, let alone support, from her relatives, unless there is compelling evidence that the man is financially not supporting her and the children.

### Levirate

Levirate marriage, in the strict sense of a man marrying his deceased brother's wife and bearing children with her for the dead person, is practiced in very few ethnic groups in Ghana, among the traditional Ga, for instance. As a rule, levirate does not exist among the Anlo Ewe, where the husband's sexual rights are personal, nontransferable, and end with his death. His widow is then free to remarry any man of her choice, including the deceased's agnates. What is customary among the Akan groups, and is currently practiced in a few instances, is widow inheritance. Here, the brother of the dead man becomes the real husband of the widow, but the children by that marriage belong to him and not the deceased brother. Sororal polygyny, where a man marries two sisters of a family, is unheard of in Ghana.

### Sexuality and the Disabled and Aged

Ghana's 1984 population census recorded that about 3% of all the population aged 15 years and over were disabled, with the number of women twice that of men. No studies on the sexual adaptations of this segment of the population have been undertaken.

Very little, if at all, is known about the sexuality of the aged in Ghana. It is not uncommon to find an old man married to a young woman, although many of such women may still have sex with their former lovers or with other young men. In most villages, however, some situational factors may inhibit sexual relations of aged couples. As they grow old, children may be asked to sleep with the grandparents to give privacy for the young couple. This makes it difficult for the aged couple to have sexual intercourse, and they, therefore, slowly drift apart. While young widows normally remarry, remarriage for women over 50 is rare. They are unlikely to find marriageable single men, and many at this age are unwilling to be married as second or third wives to polygynous men. Secretive sexual exploits at this stage are very rare: it is considered disgraceful, not only to the aged person, but also to the children and grandchildren.

### Incidence of Oral and Anal Sex

Penile-vaginal penetrative sex with little foreplay is the normal sexual style in Ghana. Although among the well-educated youth, some form of foreplay is introduced, fellatio or cunnilingus is abhorrent. Even among prostitutes, vaginal sex is the norm; very few practice oral sex. Genital manipulation is hardly accepted and, traditionally, women feel shy to touch the penis—and most men are not interested in having their genitals manipulated anyway. Anal sex is considered a sexual depravity and is reserved for animals. It is abhorrent even to prostitutes. In a recent study in Accra, the capital city, only one respondent reported that she would engage in anal intercourse if the price was right.

## 6. Homoerotic, Homosexual, and Bisexual Behaviors

Any form of same-sex activities is hardly mentioned in Ghanaian society. Homosexual activities among boys is exceedingly rare. Even where homosexual activities are practiced by boys, they are considered basically "presexual," and are quickly abandoned as they mature. The situation may be different for female homosexuality. It is practiced in girls' boarding schools by a few students "who want to release tension," but are either afraid of getting pregnant or have no access to male partners, given the strict rules regarding male visits to girls' schools. But here too, it is basically situational and not an alternative means of sexual expression. It is quickly forgotten once the girls leave school. In Bleek's study in the 1970s, he observed that no reference whatsoever was made to homosexuality and no word gave a hint of its occurrence. It is the impression that homosexuality is so rare in Ghana that people hardly have any idea of it, even on university campuses. Young male adults may dance together at nightclubs, and may even imitate a couple, without any inhibition. If there existed a secret or clandestine practice of homosexuality, this would not be possible and boys would be too embarrassed to behave in such a way. It is virtually impossible to prove that homosexuality does not exist: What can be said is that homosexuality as a means of adult sexual expression hardly exists in Ghana, and it is not listed as a sexual offense because self-identified gay men are virtually unheard of.

## 7. Gender Diversity and Transgender Issues

There is no knowledge of gender-conflicted persons. Adult homosexuality is so rare that the sociolegal status of a homosexual is unthinkable. Transsexuals are virtually unheard of in the Ghanaian society.

## 8. Significant Unconventional Sexual Behaviors

### A. Coercive Sex

*Sexual Abuse*

Child sexual abuse is very rare in Ghanaian society. Those who engage in it may be regarded as perverts. Even in societies where daughters could be given in marriage at a very tender age in a form of betrothal, sexual intercourse is precluded until after the girl has undergone the initiation rites. Domestic maids often brought into the cities by middle-class families may in some instances be sexually abused by unscrupulous husbands, especially if there develops a marital discord or the maid becomes more and more beautiful as she grows up in the city.

*Incest*

Incest, sexual intercourse between parents and children or between full siblings, is abhorred, extremely rare, and culprits are severely punished. An incestuous act may be wider than imagined, depending on whether the society is endogamous (the Dagaaba of Upper West and the Ewe, for instance) or exogamous (the Akan), where sexual relationships within the large clan are prohibited.

The sexual mores defining what relationships are incestuous may appear strange to an outsider. For example, among the matrilineal Akan, while it is incestuous for a man to have sexual intercourse with his mother's sister's daughter, he is enjoined to marry his mother's brother's daughter or father's sister's daughter. Among the Ga of southern Ghana, it is so repugnant that in the early days, an incestuous man was punished by drowning and the woman driven away into the bush. To make sure that the practice was not condoned by the family, none of the relatives of the offenders was allowed to hold any post of importance for one generation. Today, it still is a family calamity. An offender is denied from using the family name and is forbidden to attend public festivals.

*Sexual Harassment*

Traditionally, a woman's body is considered special, and care should be taken in the way a man handles it. To pull or play with a woman' nose, ear, or any other part of the body, or tickle the palm of a woman's hand is considered highly indecent and immoral. If this is done to a married woman, it could be likened to adultery and the aggrieved husband may claim damages. In contemporary Ghana, few single women will consider any of these as sexual harassment. Rather, they are signs of a man showing interest, but lacking the courage to say so because "he has a mouth that is sewn."

It is, however, common to hear reports of young women, especially typists and secretaries, being sexually harassed by their bosses, or student girls by their teachers. Given the subordinate role of women, coupled with the fear of losing their jobs or being denied promotion when they tell others or decline the sexual advances, women are put under tremendous pressure. Some women are compelled to give in or blow the matter up by exposing the boss, who may become a reference point for public ridicule. It must be stated that sometimes the advances may also be made by women who think they can materially gain from a sexual relationship with the boss.

*Rape*

In Ghana, as elsewhere, indecent assault and rape are criminal offenses. Rape is defined in Ghana's Criminal Code as an unlawful carnal knowledge against any female, and when the assaulted woman is physically incapable of resistance to force, rape does not have to be proved. Its occurrence in Ghana is very rare, and a woman walking alone in a city late in the night may be afraid of mugging, but would hardly think of rape.

Very little research has been done on the issue. In 1977, 273 cases of assault and rape were reported. The victims were mostly house girls, babysitters, and were, like the offenders, mainly in the lower social class. The minimum sentence for rape is 12 months, which is considered too lenient by women activists. An attempt in 1993 by female members of Parliament to increase the minimum sentence to three years was opposed. The main national newspaper, the *People's Daily Graphic*, described the men's behavior as "sheer display of male chauvinism and lack of respect and understanding of women's sensitivity."

There is a variant of unconventional sexual behavior that is fairly common in the villages. This is an attempt to seduce a woman while she is sleeping in the night, not infrequently with the connivance of the woman, especially if she is married. Consent of the woman is immaterial if they are caught. The man can be so ridiculed that he may be compelled to move out of the village.

[*Female Ritual Slavery*

[*Update 1997*: In the isolated farming villages along the Volta River in southeastern Ghana, several thousand young women are caught in a religious tradition that condemns them to a form of perpetual ritual slavery. The *trocosi*, as they are known in the Ewe language, or "slaves of the gods," work in local religious shrines to appease the fetish gods for crimes committed by their relatives. In the local culture, justice and punishment are viewed in communal rather than individual terms. Thus, a young female who has no connection with a crime, and may not even know what it was, may be sent by her family to atone for a (male) relative's crime by serving the local fetish priest. Because the priest is a spiritual intermediary between worshipers and deities of the area's traditional Ju-ju religion, the *trocosi* can appease the fetish and keep them from punishing her whole family. Her life becomes one of unquestioned service to the priest, cooking, cleaning, weeding the shrine's farm, growing yams, manioc, and corn, and providing sexual favors to the shrine's priest. The *trocosi* gain nothing personally from their service; their families must even provide them with food. The people are convinced that without the protection provided by the *trocosi*, the gods may wreak vengeance on their entire extended family or community (French 1997).

[The *trocosi*, who must begin their service as virgins, can only be freed by the priest. A *trocosi* usually gains her freedom only when she is middle-aged, has borne the priest many children, and has lost her sex appeal. But freedom for one *trocosi* means enslavement of another virgin from the same family who must replace her. Thus, the slavery continues generation after generation in perpetual atonement.

[This form of ritual slavery, which is also found in neighboring Togo, Benin, and southwestern Nigeria, is deep-rooted in a very powerful superstition that will be difficult to eradicate. A government law banning the practice would have no effect, since the whole community is in agreement with the custom and firmly believes their survival depends on their freely sending a "scapegoat" *trocosi* to serve the local fetish priest when someone commits a crime. Recently, there has been increasing criticism from international human rights advocacy groups and from women's rights groups within Ghana. Individual women's rights advocates and private groups within Ghana have had some success in stopping the practice by negotiating with paramount chiefs and other prominent local leaders. One local group, International Needs, has persuaded several fetish priests and their shrines to abandon the custom in return for a gift of ten cows, a bull, a corral for the priest's new cattle, and cash given to the surrounding villages (French 1997). (*End of update by R. T. Francoeur*)]

## B. Prostitution

From the onset, it is necessary to distinguish between sexual exchange and prostitution in Ghanaian sexual culture. These two practices are often misunderstood by outsiders, who consider them as the same. Sexual exchange, a recent phenomenon, is a socially acceptable and pervasive practice in which sexual relationships, both premarital and extramarital, are contracted for material recompense. While implicit pecuniary gains underlie the relationship, it is worth noting that in sexual exchange, material rewards, especially money, are not given directly after sexual intercourse, as is the case with prostitution. The giving and receiving of gains is separate from the act of coitus. A girl is likely to be offended for being thought a prostitute, if she is given money immediately after sexual intercourse. Unlike prostitution, in sexual exchange, it is not the sexual act that is rewarded, but the relationship.

Prostitution, the exchange of sexual acts for money, is illegal in Ghana, and women who practice it are often harassed by the police and other officials of city or local councils. Nevertheless, it is openly practiced in many cities and towns. In Accra, for example, an area called Korle Wokon is noted for its prostitutes. Unlike sexual exchange, prostitution is unacceptable to the Ghanaian society—the only exception being perhaps among the Krobo—and constitutes an infraction of Ghanaian sexual mores. Those who engage in it often conceal their identities by working in suburbs where they are not likely to be recognized by familiar faces, and some may even change their names altogether.

Ghanaian prostitutes generally operate without pimps. At least two main groups of prostitutes can be identified: home-based prostitutes and hotel-based prostitutes. The former usually work in rented rooms or brothels and are of low class with little or no education. They are usually old, with an average age of around 40 years, divorced, and are heads of households with four or more children to support. They all cite acute financial problems as reasons for prostitution. They charge around $1 per client per sexual act or "round," and report an average of two or three clients a day.

Hotel-based prostitutes operate from hotels, nightclubs, and discos. They are sophisticated, are of high class, much younger, highly educated, and serve an equally high-class clientele. Their prices, which are generally higher, depend on the class of the hotel where they operate.

Tema is the major port and industrial complex of Ghana, and the visiting seamen, both Ghanaian and foreign, attract many prostitutes. With the scourge of HIV/AIDS infection, intervention programs, with support from Family Health International (FHI) and other international agencies, are being implemented to encourage prostitutes to use condoms, given that in 1986, about 60% of all prostitutes surveyed in Accra had never used condoms before.

## C. Pornography

Nudity is culturally repugnant. It is considered inappropriate for parents to undress in the presence of their children. Societal attitudes to nudity are more severe towards females than males. Women are expected to cover their breasts and thighs in public. In the Muslim areas, the rules are tighter. Even in Ghana's large cities, a lady wearing a pair of shorts in public is considered immoral. Any explicit display of erotic materials is highly unacceptable and magazines on erotica are not available. Television programs never include sexual material likely to be offensive. With the growing number of video rentals and show spots, there is an increasing concern about the sexually offensive nature of some films, although they come nowhere near the soft pornographic materials available in Western countries.

## D. Sexual Taboos

Apart from incest, there are other sexual taboos worth mentioning. These include sexual intercourse while a woman is in her menstrual period, with a widow less than a year after her husband's death, and sexual intercourse with a woman in the bush. The latter is called by the Akan *ahahantwe* (sexual intercourse in the leaves), and is considered antisocial because it threatens the life of the society. By being performed in the bush, sexual intercourse, upon which society depends for its perpetuation and, hence, is regarded as sacred, is reduced to the level of an act that is performed without regard to the environment. If it was done without the connivance of the woman, it could lead to death in the olden days. Today, however, if reported, it is treated as rape. But whether there is consent or connivance on the woman's part, the man is asked to provide a live sheep, which is sacrificed upon the spot where the adulterous act had taken place. This is currently practiced in most rural settings among the Akan.

## 9. Contraception, Abortion, and Population Planning

### A. Contraception

The present high level of Ghana's population is the result of persistent high birthrates and declining mortality rates over the years, leading to a high rate of natural increase. For a variety of social, economic, and cultural reasons, large families are attractive to many Ghanaians. The average Ghanaian woman in the 1990s is expected to have 6.4 children in her lifetime. Knowledge about contraception is high. According to the Ghana Demographic and Health Survey in 1988, 79% of currently married men and women had heard about contraception, but only 13% of the women were using any method of contraception (5% if restricted to modern methods). The pill and postpartum abstinence are the most popular modern and traditional contraceptive methods, respectively. For adolescents and young adults, however, the condom is the most popular.

There are some differentials in contraceptive knowledge and use by educational level, type of residence, age, and reproductive intentions. Modern contraceptives are available at several service delivery points owned by the Ministry of Health, the Planned Parenthood Association of Ghana (PPAG; an affiliate of International Planned Parenthood Federation), the Christian Council of Ghana, private maternity homes, contraceptive social marketing outlets, and pharmacies. However, about one in every five users obtained their supplies from friends or relatives. With the scourge of HIV/AIDS infection, condom promotion has been intensified through social marketing and community-based distribution.

### B. Teenage Unmarried Pregnancies

Births to adolescents accounted for 11% of Ghana's births in 1978-1980. Teenage premarital pregnancy is becoming an increasing social and health problem. One reason for low teenage (unmarried) pregnancies in the traditional societies was the observance of puberty rites, after which marriage followed almost immediately. Increased education and other forces of social change have eroded the traditional constraints. Unfortunately, no replacement has been found for these rites and the sex education it provided. Modern counseling is inadequate for teenagers, and access to family planning is limited.

When sexual relations between teenagers result in pregnancy, the boy's parents are informed. Pressure is exerted on the man to marry her, unless the girl's lineage does not want him as an in-law. In a few instances, a pregnancy can be used to persuade the elders of a lineage to approve of a relationship to which they would not have normally consented.

### C. Abortion

Abortion is illegal except for medical reasons, and very few Ghanaians would want this changed. Yet many pregnant student girls procure abortions in order to complete school or because their partners are not yet ready to father a child. While these are the official reasons women give, it appears that it is the fear of shame that is the dominant factor. Statistics of induced abortion are hard to come by and, even where they exist, are grossly defective. In a 1990-1991 study among secondary school students, 10% of male students who have had intercourse admitted having impregnated a girl, and for 61% of these, the girl concerned resorted to abortion. Induced abortion is reprehensible and always remains hidden. Although the official rules for procuring an abortion are not liberal, it is well known that, provided the client is able to pay, most hospitals will undertake it.

Many abortions, however, are performed outside of hospital premises by unqualified back-street abortionists, quack doctors, and self-induced or friends. In the last category, herbs and other incredible combinations of concoctions form the largest method. The knowledge of alleged abortifacients among young men and women is amazing. Bleek, in his study among the Kwahu in the 1970s, listed at least 53 different methods for procuring self-induced abortion, which included "modern" methods involving the use of assorted pills and herbs, such as the insertion of the twig of *nkrangyedua* (*Jathropa curcas*) or *menyenemenyeneme* (*Thevetia peruviana*) into the uterus. Many of these amazing methods are still in use. In a study in 1990-1991 among secondary school students, respondents' lists of abortifacients included: a mixture of sugar and lemon, *akpeteshie* (a very strong local gin), and Guinness ale.

The life-threatening risk arising from induced abortions is all too obvious. In 1973, for example, between 60% and 80% of all minor operations at Korle Bu Teaching Hospital, Ghana's largest hospital, involved abortion-related complications.

### D. Population Control Efforts

Currently, Ghana's population growth rate is 3.0% per annum, with 45% of the population below 15 years of age, thus epitomizing a high dependency burden. In 1969, Ghana was among the first countries in Africa to declare an explicit population policy. The Ghana National Family Planning Programme was established in 1970 to offer individual citizens the freedom to choose family planning and eventually slow down the rapid population growth. Not very much has been achieved, partly because of inadequate support from subsequent governments. Since the mid-1980s, however, Rawlings' government has reinforced Ghana's commitment to its population policy through the collaborative participation of international donor agencies. A National Population Council has been established, and it is likely that some decline in the fertility measures will be observed in the near future.

## 10. Sexually Transmitted Diseases and HIV/AIDS

### A. Sexually Transmitted Diseases

Very little is known about STDs in Ghana, but given that it is considered a cofactor of HIV infection, considerable attention is now being focused on its prevalence, prevention, and treatment. Although no reliable data are available, there is the consensus among experts that STDs are fairly common in Ghana, the most common being gonorrhea. There is a greater incidence of STDs among the 15- to 19-year-olds than among other age groups. This may be partly explained by the fact that STDs are considered as part of normal growing up when one begins sexual exploits.

Antibiotic treatment is available in hospitals and health centers, and there are also a few STD clinics, such as the Adabraka STD clinic. Still-infected persons, especially adolescents, are particularly slow to seek medical attention. Many tend to resort to traditional medicine or self-medication.

The government through the National AIDS Control Programme (NACP) has intensified efforts in STD control as part of the national HIV/AIDS control program. The European Economic Community (EEC) Task Force on AIDS is supporting the procurement of material, equipment, and reagents for a project on STD control.

### B. HIV/AIDS

Until recently, it was widely assumed that West Africa has been spared the social, economic, and health burdens of AIDS. Sadly, this optimistic view can no longer be justified. The first reported case of AIDS in Ghana was in 1986. At the beginning of 1995, there were some 12,500 reported AIDS cases. This is likely to be an underestimation since many cases are unreported. Over 80% of all cases of HIV infection involve persons infected through heterosexual intercourse. No other particular sexual practice has been implicated in the sexual transmission. As noted earlier in the chapter, homosexual practice and anal sex are unacceptable and extremely rare. The early phase of HIV transmission was among prostitutes with a history of outside travel. As in many other countries, this led to finger pointing at other countries. The current trend indicates that the diffusion has gone beyond the so-called risk group. There has been almost a fourfold increase between 1986 and 1990 in the number of AIDS patients without any history of foreign travel. It can be stated that the future spread of HIV in Ghana may largely depend not on formal prostitution, but on the socially acceptable and pervasive phenomenon of sexual exchange in which women constantly switch sexual partners in order to maximize material gains accruing from sexual relationships.

In Ghana, as elsewhere, AIDS is primarily a disease that affects the economically active group. For both sexes, adults in the age group 20 to 29 account for 70% of the cases. The pattern, however, shows female preponderance over males. At the early stage of the epidemic in Ghana, there was one male to every eight females, although this has narrowed down to a current level of 1:2. Ghanaian epidemiologists agree that the sex ratio is changing to the direction of 1:1, which is consistent with heterosexual transmission in most countries.

Another pattern of HIV/AIDS infection in Ghana is that the majority of cases were initially not reported from major cities. Recent data on seropositives, however, show a tremendous increase in the number of cases in Ghana's main cities of Accra and Kumasi, thus supporting the generalization that, in Africa, AIDS is primarily an urban disease. Three regions out of ten, Ashanti, Eastern, and Greater Accra, account for over 70% of all reported HIV cases. It is not clear, however, whether the regional variation results from the level of reporting, although the general impression is that certain sociosexual practices in these regions may facilitate HIV transmission.

No nationwide HIV seropositive studies have been conducted yet, apart from a few using convenience samples. However, a study conducted in 1989-90 among patients of Ghana's second-largest hospital, the Okomfo Anokye Hospital in Kumasi, found a prevalence rate of 12.6%. Although this apparently high figure should not be extrapolated to the rest of the country, it definitely indicates a serious problem for the immediate future. Up to June 1991, only 25 out of 2,474 reported AIDS cases were under 5 years. Given that a substantial and fast-growing number of women of childbearing ages may be infected, perinatal transmission will soon become an issue of grave concern in Ghana.

There is a National AIDS Control Program (NACP) within the Ministry of Health. NACP, through information and education campaigns, is attempting to reinforce HIV risk-reduction sexual behaviors by discouraging casual sexual relationships or having multiple partners, and encouraging relationships with one faithful partner (or partners in polygynous homes). Condom promotion has also been intensified through social marketing and community-based distribution. The care of AIDS patients is generally home-based, given the lack of trained counselors, a task now being addressed by the Counseling Unit of the NACP. The best-organized counseling program has been developed at St. Martin's Hospital in Agomanya by the Catholic Mission. Other international nongovernmental organizations, such as the World Vision, are also involved in providing physical and economic support for AIDS patients. [*Update 2003*: In November 2001, the Ghana Ministry of Education included HIV/AIDS education in the school curriculum as a move to curb the

spread of HIV among the youth. (*End of update by B. Opiyo-Omolo*)]

[*Update 2002*: UNAIDS Epidemiological Assessment: HIV surveillance information on antenatal clinic women is available since 1990. Information is available only from Accra in 1990, but by 1994, 20 sentinel surveillance sites were reporting HIV seroprevalence. Overall median HIV prevalence among antenatal clinic attendees was 2.4% in 1994, 3.4% in 1998, and 2.2% in 2000. There are three sites that are included as the major urban areas: Accra (2 reporting sites in 1997, 3 in 2000), Kumasi, and Tamale. In Accra, HIV prevalence increased from 0.7% in 1992 to 3.1% in 2000, while in Kumasi, HIV prevalence has been fluctuating and was 3.8% in 2000. In Tamale, HIV has slowly increased from 1.0% in 1994 to 1.3% in 2000. Outside of the major urban areas, HIV prevalence increased, from 1% in 1991 to 3% in 1998. In 1998, HIV prevalence among the 14 sites ranged from 2% to 12%. In 2000, prevalence at 18 sites ranged from 1% to 7.8%. Both HIV-1 and HIV-2 exist in Ghana with HIV-1 being the predominant type; information on HIV prevalence by type is not available. Implementation of the 2001-2002 antenatal clinic sentinel surveillance survey was underway at the time of this writing.

[HIV seroprevalence rates among sex workers increased from 2% in 1986 to nearly 40% in 1991. By 1997-1998, HIV prevalence in Accra and Tema had reached 74.2% among "seater" sex workers and 27.2% among the "roamer" sex workers. A repeat study in Accra and Tema in 1999 found "seaters" with a rate of 75.8% and "roamers" with a rate of 23.1%. In 1999, sex workers in Kumasi had an HIV-infection rate of 82%. HIV prevalence among STD clinic patients in Accra increased from 2% in 1988 to nearly 9% in 1991. In 1998, HIV infection among female STD patients tested in Adabraka, Greater Accra region, had reached 27%; in 1999, prevalence was 39%.

[The estimated number of adults and children living with HIV/AIDS on January 1, 2002, were:

| | |
|---|---|
| Adults ages 15-49: | 30,000 (rate: 3.0%) |
| Women ages 15-49: | 170,000 |
| Children ages 0-15: | 34,000 |

[An estimated 28,000 adults and children died of AIDS during 2001.

[At the end of 2001, an estimated 200,000 Ghanaian children under age 15 were living without one or both parents who had died of AIDS. (*End of update by the Editors*)]

## 11. Sexual Dysfunctions, Counseling, and Therapies

The most obvious sexual disorder is sterility. A barren woman is always in despair. The desire for children makes impotence in men even more disgraceful and pitiful. A childless couple is scorned and despised. Among the Akan, the man's penis is ridiculed as being flabby, and is nicknamed *kote kra* (wax penis). In the olden days, it is reported that an impotent man, after his death, had great thorns driven into his soles, and the corpse addressed: *woanwo ba, mma no saa bio* (you have not borne children; do not return again like that). Although family-planning centers and general hospitals may provide some advice and counseling, professional therapy is almost nonexistent. Given the embarrassment associated with impotence, very few men may accompany their wives to seek treatment from professionals in modern medicine. The source of childlessness is usually attributed to the wife, rather than the husband.

Traditional healers in Ghana, while conceding the superiority of Western biomedical medicine for certain diseases, have insisted that infertility and sexually transmitted diseases are believed to be more effectively treated by traditional medicine than modern medicine. The secret and highly confidential nature of their practice makes traditional medicine men, herbalists, Mallams, fetish priests, and others the main source of treatment. They are visited by people of different educational and economic status. Men who claim to have medicines potent enough to induce pregnancy soon become rich.

## *12. Sex Research and Advanced Professional Education*

Studies on sexuality in Ghana are particularly scanty. Until the onset of HIV/AIDS, all that was known was based on anthropological evidence gleaned from discussions on family, initiation rites, and other rites of passage. Although there are no special centers or institutes devoted to sex research, there has been a gradual interest in the subject, and surveys on sex have been undertaken. Specific groups surveyed in addition to the general population include; adolescents, young adults, return migrants, long-distance truck drivers, and secondary school students. The Departments of Sociology and Geography at the University of Cape Coast; the Institute of Statistical, Social, and Economic Research; and the Institute of African Studies, both at the University of Ghana, are all involved in sex research. The Institute of Population Studies, University of Exeter (U.K.), is also engaged in collaborative research, with local investigators on sexual behavior and HIV risk-reduction strategies in Ghana. One key methodological finding on sex research in Ghana is that, on the whole, respondents are more willing to discuss sexual matters and provide frank answers than it was first thought.

There is no professional association, nor are there journals for sexuality. Graduate programs devoted to sexuality are nonexistent. However, there is a Department of Guidance and Counseling at the University of Cape Coast that offers graduate programs. Perhaps the only major book of academic significance that deals exclusively with sexuality in Ghana is Bleek's (1976) *Sexual Relationships and Birth Control in Ghana: A Case Study in a Rural Town.* A well-written book based on participant observation and field survey, the study was done among only one group (the Kwahu), and, therefore, will not satisfy the needs of a student who wants a handbook on Ghanaian sexuality.

## *References and Suggested Readings*

Akuffo, F. O. 1987. Teenage pregnancies and school dropouts: The relevance of family life Education and vocational training to girls' employment opportunities. In: C. Oppong, ed., *Sex role, population and development in West Africa* (pp. 154-164). Portsmouth: Heineman.

Anarfi, J. 1992. Sexual networking in selected communities in Ghana and the sexual behavior of Ghanaian female migrants in Abidjan, Cote d'Ivoire. In: T. Dyson, ed., *Sexual behavior and networking: Anthropological and sociocultural studies on the transmission of HIV* (pp. 233-248). Liege: Derouaux-Ordina.

Ankomah, A. 1992. Premarital sexual behavior in Ghana in the era of AIDS. *Health Policy and Planning, 7*(2):135-143.

Ankomah, A. 1992. *The sexual behavior of young women in Cape Coast, Ghana: The pecuniary considerations involved and implications for AIDS* (Ph.D. thesis). Institute of Population Studies, University of Exeter (UK).

Bleek, W. 1976. *Sexual relationships and birth control in Ghana: A case study of a rural town.* Amsterdam: Centre for Social Anthropology, University of Amsterdam.

CIA. 2002 (January). *The world factbook 2002.* Washington, DC: Central Intelligence Agency. Available: http://www .cia.gov/cia/publications/factbook/index.html.

French, H. W. 1997 (January 20). The ritual slaves of Ghana: Young, female, paying for another's crime. *The New York Times,* pp. A1, A5.

Neequaye, A. 1990. Prostitution in Accra. In: M. Plant, ed., *AIDS, drugs and prostitution* (pp. 175-185). London: Tavistock/Routledge.

UNAIDS. 2002. *Epidemiological fact sheets by country.* Geneva, Switzerland: Joint United Nations Programme on HIV/ AIDS (UNAIDS/WHO). Available: http://www.unaids.org/ hivaidsinfo/statistics/fact_sheets/index_en.htm.

# Greece

## (*Elliniki Dimokratia*)
## (The Hellenic Republic)

Dimosthenis Agrafiotis, Ph.D.*, Elli Ioannidi, Ph.D.,
and Panagiota Mandi, M.Sc.
*Rewritten and updated in December 2002 by the Authors*

**Contents**

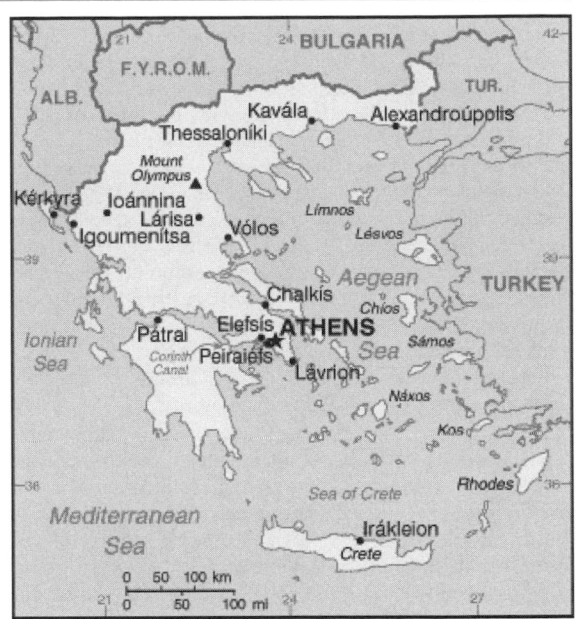

(CIA 2002)

## Demographics and a Brief Historical Perspective

ROBERT T. FRANCOEUR

### A. Demographics

In southern Europe, the Greek peninsula projects into the Mediterranean Sea from south of the Balkans. The mountainous, mostly non-arable land of the Greek peninsula is deeply indented by long sea inlets and surrounded by over 2,000 islands, of which only 169 are inhabited; these include Myconos, Lesvos, Chios, Samos, Kerkira (Corfu), Crete, and Rhodes. Greece's neighbors in southeastern Europe are Albania, Former Yugoslav Republic of Macedonia, and Bulgaria on the north and Turkey on the east. With an area of 50,942 square miles (131,940 km²), Greece is about the size of the state of Alabama.

According to the 2001 Census (May 2001), Greece has a population of 10.939 million, with 5.055 million males and 5.204 million females. (The demographic data below is an integration of the National Statistical Service of Greece 2002, and the CIA *World Factbook* 2002).

**Age Distribution and Sex Ratios**: *0-14 years*: 18% with 1.04 male(s) per female (sex ratio); *15-64 years*: 67% with 0.99 male(s) per female; *65 years and over*: 15% with 0.77 male(s) per female; *Total population sex ratio*: 1.02 male(s) to 1 female

**Life Expectancy at Birth**: *Total Population*: 77.92 years; *male*: 75.39 years; *female*: 80.59 years

**Urban/Rural Distribution**: 65% to 35%—more than 4 million in the two cities of Athens and Piraeus

**Ethnic Distribution**: Greek: 97%; other: 3% (2002 est.)

**Religious Distribution**: Greek Orthodox: 97%; Muslim: 2%; other: 1% (2002 est.)

**Birth Rate**: 9.55 births per 1,000 population

**Death Rate**: 9.80 per 1,000 population

**Infant Mortality Rate**: 6.15 deaths per 1,000 live births

**Net Migration Rate**: 5.99 migrant(s) per 1,000 population

**Total Fertility Rate**: 1.29 children born per woman (down from 2.2 in the 1980s)

**Population Growth Rate**: 0.97%

**HIV/AIDS** (2001): *Adult prevalence*: 0.2%; *Persons living with HIV/AIDS*: 5,676; *Deaths*: 1,273 people since the beginning of the epidemic. (For additional details from www.UNAIDS.org, see end of Section 10B.)

**Literacy Rate** (*defined as those age 15 and over who can read and write*): 95% (*male*: 98%, *female*: 93%) (1993 est.); nine years of schooling are compulsory

**Per Capita Gross Domestic Product** (*purchasing power parity*): $10,900 (1999); *Inflation*: 3.8%; *Unemployment*: 9.6% (National Statistical Service of Greece 2002)

### B. A Brief Historical Perspective

Because sexual identity, attitudes, and behavior are, in a large part, formed in a nation's sociocultural environment, it is important to sketch out the general ethnic, racial, and socioeconomic character of Greece.

In the past century, Greece has been a country searching for its national boundaries and identity, as well as its economic survival. Being a backward agrarian society, its economy has oscillated between self-subsistence and dependency on external markets. Since the advent of the 20th century, constant territorial and, consequently, demographic expansion has provided the foundations for a rapid development. Greece finally embarked on the process of industrialization, though considerably later than the rest of Europe, and under rather violent and short-lived stimuli. However, this rapid development has produced an imbalance between its economic and sociocultural level. This lack of correspondence is a common aspect of societies that are in a stage of development that is neither well articulated nor well defined, and of societies where coexisting economic, social, and cultural structures correspond to different modes of production. Thus, it can be said that Greek economy is characterized by heterogeneity due to the coexistence of "traditional" and "modern" components of technoeconomic activity. The social structure of institutions, groups, and relations is still in a state of inertia imposed by the past. Social groups and/or classes cannot eas-

*Communications*: Dr. Dimosthenis Agrafiotis, National School of Public Health, Sociology Dept., 196, Alexandras Avenue, Athens, 11521, Greece; agraf@compulink.gr.

ily and creatively articulate their role in the context of prevailing conditions and available opportunities. The cultural environment is under the pressure of imported models, while the traditional characteristics do not show any signs of endurance. There are clear indications that aspects of Greek social life are altering. For example, the Greek family, an institution that remains a core value and practice in Greek society, and gender roles do not share the characteristics of a specific family model, but are gradually altering and follow at a slow pace the Western European model (Maratou-Alibranti 1999). The "modernizing" trend in Greek society concerns the necessity for greater equality and a decline in patriarchy, where structural links increasingly give way to the negotiation of individualized interpersonal relationships. This may also be perceived as part of the individualizing process.

The achievements of ancient Greece in art, architecture, science, mathematics, drama, literature, philosophy, and democracy are acknowledged by all as the foundation of Western Civilization. Classical Greece reached its apex in Athens during the 4th century B.C.E. In 336, the kingdom of Macedonia, which under Philip II dominated the Greek world and Egypt, passed to his son Alexander. Tutored by Aristotle in the Greek ideals, Alexander the Great conquered Egypt, all the Persian domains, and reached India in 13 years. After his death in 323, his empire was divided into three parts: Egypt under the Ptolemaies, Macedon, and the Seleucid Empire. During the ensuing 300 years, the Hellenic Era, a cosmopolitan Greek-oriented culture permeated the ancient world from the borders of India to Western Europe. The sciences thrived, especially in Alexandria, where the pharaohs financed a great library and museum. Major advances were made in the fields of medicine, chemistry, hydraulics, geography, astronomy, and Euclidian and non-Euclidean geometry.

Greece fell under the domination of Roman rule in the 2nd and 1st centuries B.C.E. In the 4th century C.E., Greece became part of the Byzantine Empire, and, after the fall of Constantinople in 1453 to the Turks, a part of the Ottoman Empire. Greece gained its freedom from Turkey between 1821 and 1829, and became a kingdom. A republic was established in 1924, followed by restoration of the monarchy in 1935. In 1940, Greece was occupied by German, Italian, and Bulgarian troops. In the late 1940s, the Communist's guerrilla warfare ended with restoration of the monarchy; the monarchy was abolished in 1975.

Greece has experienced, although with some chronological differences, about the same population growth as most advanced countries have, despite the mass emigration during the two periods from 1900 to 1922 and from 1951 to 1973. Ever since, emigration has given way to repatriation and the entrance of refugees of Greek origins (*Pontioi*), as well as of foreign refugees and immigrants who came mainly from the former Communist Eastern European countries as well as from Asia and Africa. The massive immigration flow into the country took place in the late 1980s and, especially, after the fall of the Albanian regime in the early 1990s. Most of the immigrants came into the country illegally. Since a legalization process started in 1997, a third of a million migrants have asked for their legalization: 65% are Albanian and the rest come mainly from Eastern European countries.

## 1. Basic Sexological Premises

### A. Character of Gender Roles

In the last 20 years, Greece has been experiencing changes in gender relationships that are altering aspects of family life. Although the institution of the family remains a core value and practice, the foundations are less secure as individualism becomes a stronger force in Greek society.

There is wide agreement that the "traditional" type of patriarchal Greek family has been changing, in line with economic and modernizing forces. Gender relations are at the eye of the storm in these changes. One reason lies in what H. Kataki (1984) discussed two decades ago that is still relevant: the historical coexistence of different types of familial and gender formations and expectations. These, Kataki termed the traditional, the modern, and the postmodern identities of Greek families.

Although Greek society and the state still have patriarchal characteristics, at the family level, even within apparently traditional families, the actual nature of the power relations between men and women is very diverse (Papataxiarchis et al. 1992). Equality within the family has always been the outcome of a number of variables, including the ownership of property, social class, the relationship to nondomestic work, education, age, and the personalities involved. Thus, however "traditional" they might be, individual Greek men and women have always been aware of the flexibility and variations possible in gender relationships. Consequently, they often are not experienced with the patriarchal system at the personal level.

There are structured repercussions for gender relations from living in a patriarchal society, e.g., lack of power in political and economic life, but at the family or individual level, gender relations may be played out by the individuals in a far more equitable and nontraditionally gendered manner. Gender relations are constantly mediated through socioeconomic changes, as well as class and educational backgrounds.

### B. Sociolegal Status of Males and Females

From the legal viewpoint, Greek men and women enjoy the same rights as children, adolescents, and adults. Men and women have the same right to vote and equal rights for education and employment.

### C. General Concepts of Sexuality and Love

In Greek society, the expression of sexuality and "romantic" love are interdependent. Many people believe that sexual pleasure is realized only in a relationship governed by love (Apostolodis 1992; Ioannidis et al. 1991; Mandi et al. 1993). The ability to love is regarded as something special, and individuals who are indifferent to or unable to feel it are held in contempt. In a survey on sexual behavior that was conducted in 1998, 33.5% of the respondents reported that it was totally unacceptable to have sex with someone without loving him or her, and 30% said it was rather unacceptable (Ioannidi-Kapolou et al. 2001).

Some believe that although the sexual act is possible with someone else besides the "one and only," true passion and completeness become real only when there is mutual care and devotion.

## 2. Religious, Ethnic, and Gender Factors Affecting Sexuality

### A. Source and Character of Religious Values

In Greece, the majority of the population (97%) are affiliated with the Greek Orthodox religion. There are also some Catholics, a few Jews and Protestants, and a number of Muslims, mainly from Thrace. The Greek Orthodox Church is much more liberal than the Roman Catholic Church in some aspects, allowing divorce (up to three times normally) and remarriage in church. Although archbishops are not allowed to get married, the majority of parish priests are married.

Influenced by the Platonic and Stoic dualism and the Persian Gnostic tradition (Francoeur 1992), Christianity is governed by a dualistic opposition between the soul and the body, with the soul and mind seeking liberation from the prison of the flesh. Christian faith provides "a special kind of knowledge, gnosis, which the soul can use to transcend this earth and rise to the divine heavenly sphere." Thus, Christianity has awakened in each person the worry of saving one's soul, with this salvation depending on the value of one's personal actions, particularly in the sexual sphere. If the flesh is somehow the source of evil, all sexual practices that are not procreative in character are condemned.

However, there is no correspondence between the official teachings and daily practices, at least in present-day Greece. Greeks regard love and sex as a main part of their existence, as evidenced by the incidence of extramarital relations and abortion, both of which are condemned by the Church. Greece's abortion rate is among the highest in Europe. In reality, Greeks often indicate that they do not consider themselves particularly religious; however, there are the "faithful" who follow the Church's teachings, and the latter does intervene in the sexual life of couples.

## B. Source and Character of Ethnic Values

Until the late 1980s, 98.5% of the population was ethnic Greek. Apart from the Muslims, who comprised about 1% of the population, lived in a particular area, and followed their own religious and cultural patterns, there was ethnic homogeneity. With the massive immigration entering the country, Greece is slowly turning into a multicultural society, at least in the urban centers. At this stage, it is obvious that the country was not prepared to receive and integrate so many different cultures. There were 120 different nationalities registered among those asking for legalization, although 91% came mainly from Albania, Bulgaria, Romania, Pakistan, Ukraine, Poland, Georgia, India, Egypt, and the Philippines).

# 3. Knowledge and Education about Sexuality

## A. Government Policies and Programs

It is not an exaggeration to say that in Greece, sexual education is not the target of any systematic and well-planned governmental program. Even today, sexual education is not included in the school curriculum, although a limited few pilot projects have recently been introduced into a limited number of schools. Sporadic knowledge is given as part of lessons in such subjects as anthropology. However, this knowledge concerns more elements of physiology and anatomy than references to the external genital organs, the sexual relationship, or the search for and existence of pleasure in connection with the body and sexuality.

Currently, there is an effort and movement to include sexual education in the schools, although two Ministries, that of Health and Social Welfare and that of Education, have not made clear which one will be responsible for these matters. In recognizing the need for sex education, the government has taken some steps, starting in the early 1980s, by bringing Family Planning under the auspices of the Ministry of Health and Social Welfare. Prior to this move, contraceptive education was mainly handled by the Family Planning Association, a nongovernmental organization (NGO). The Ministry established 46 Family Planning Centers all over Greece to provide genetic counseling, sexual education, information about AIDS and sexually transmitted and gynecological diseases, contraceptives, and so on.

However, a 1991 evaluation of the efficiency and effectiveness of these centers made by the Family Planning Association has shown that the Family Centers in Greece meet the needs of only a very limited number of people. Their geographic distribution is not sufficient, and there does not appear to be any strategy for a systematic operation. A large number of the centers have departed from the initial aim of their operation and now focus their interest more on medical matters, such as Pap tests and gynecological pathology, rather than on sexual education.

## B. Informal Sources of Sexual Knowledge

The inadequacy of formal sexual education programs, and the resultant lack of sexual knowledge in the population, have been detected in a small number of studies carried out by the Department of Sociology of the Athens School of Public Health (Pantzou et al. 1991). Four different research projects, focusing on the general population and on pupils (a pilot study) using quantitative and qualitative methods, have indicated that:

- the mass media as a whole, and television in particular, seem to be the main sources of information for both the general population and young people on matters concerning health and AIDS,
- the majority of high school pupils receive no kind of information on sexuality and AIDS at school, and
- there is a need both for intensification of information on sexual contraception, sexually transmitted diseases, and AIDS, and improvement of the quality and specialization of this information.

# 4. Autoerotic Behaviors and Patterns

The data on autoerotic behaviors in Greece are very limited. The only available information is that which is derived from the K.A.B.P. (knowledge, attitudes, beliefs, and practices) study in relation to AIDS in the city of Athens (Agrafiotis et al. 1990). A section of this study was devoted to sexual practices, but only one question, in the section on sexual practices that someone engages in with his or her sexual partner, referred to autoerotic behaviors. According to the results, men reported twice the percentage of self-pleasuring than that of women (10.6% and 5.1%, respectively) when they were with their partner. Otherwise, the frequency and the attitudes towards self-pleasuring, both of children, adolescents, and adults have not been examined.

# 5. Interpersonal Heterosexual Behaviors

## A. Children

Sexual exploration by children between ages 3 and 5 in nursery school has been observed. The first discoveries are connected with gender and take place mainly among peers. Different kinds of games (playing doctor and nurse, mother and father, or king and queen) imitate adult roles, sometimes producing specific pleasure connected with stimulation of the genitals.

Later on, at the age of 10 or 11 years, children's interest is focused on details and confirmation of earlier knowledge on gender differences. At the prepuberty age, they are usually engaged in self-pleasuring activities that occur either in pairs or in groups of peers of the same and other gender, as well as alone.

## B. Adolescents

*Puberty Rituals and Adolescent Sexual Activities*

In the pubertal period, children are more interested in matters related to emotional/sentimental relations and sexuality. In a survey on "Attitudes of parents on the information of their children on HIV/AIDS and STIs" funded by the Center for the Control of Infectious Diseases (KEEL), 68.6% answered that the mother is the one who talks to children on issues relating to sexual behavior. It is also noticeable that parents avoid discussing with their boys topics such as masturbation, orgasm, and abortion, while, with the girls, besides masturbation and orgasm, they avoid discussing homosexuality (Ioannidi et al. 1997).

Although there are no particular puberty rituals, the occurrence of the first menstruation and the first nocturnal emission or ejaculation are the signs of sexual maturation. These events, however, are not celebrated in any particular formal way in the family or among relatives.

Premarital sexual activities, especially in large cities, are no longer socially condemned. In a survey of sexual behavior that was conducted on a national general population sample aged 18 to 49, it appears that people start their sexual activity between the ages of 16 and 20. There are differences among men and women, and this gap appears to be closing compared to the past where, in the 1950s, the difference was six years, while at present, it has diminished to two years. Thus, boys start at the age 16 to 18 and girls 18 to 20 (Ioannidi et al. 2000).

Research also showed that the most frequent types of contact are through hugging, deep (open mouth) kissing, petting above and below the waist, sleeping together (without sexual intercourse), and oral and vaginal sex.

In a 2002 survey on virtual sex among students aged 18 to 23 of technological colleges in urban cities, all of the respondents (100%) claimed that virtual sex (TV, Internet, or video) is an important source for sexual information; 95% of males and 89% of females believe that the Internet is the best way to communicate sexual information and to start sexual relations without fear with people of different cultures through the practice of Internet sex (Kampoura et al. 2002).

## C. Adults

### Premarital Courtship, Dating, and Relationships

In a society in which major social and cultural transformations are taking place, it would be misleading to present facts and opinions that seem definite and absolute. However, it does seem obvious and clear that there are great differences concerning premarital relations and courtship among urban and rural settings.

In today's predominantly urban and anonymous setting, young people often have access to automobiles that allow an exceptional degree of privacy in their courting. The practice of dating enables young Greeks to find out about one another, to improve their own interpersonal skills, to experiment sexually if they wish to, and, finally, to select a marriage partner.

In more "closed" rural communities and small villages, premarital relations and courtship are not yet the norm before marriage. Although freer than in the past, young adults, and especially women, do not have the opportunity of dating their future spouse. The idea of arranged marriages and matchmaking (*proksenio*) is still present; the difference is that now women have the right to choose which matchmaking will end in marriage. In some areas, a dowry (*prika*) is still required.

In anthropological literature on family life in Greek villages, reference has frequently been made to the importance of family honor—involving the sexual behavior of women, access in public and social life, and the successful execution of parental and spousal roles (Dubisch 1986). Strikingly, two generations later in a metropolitan center, reference to such values still appear to underlie some attitudes and behavior.

### Single Adults

Up until the last two decades or so of the 20th century, a large proportion of Greek men and women found their primary identification in their family, and moral approval was given to those who fulfilled traditional expectations of being "good" husbands and "housewives." The proportion of those who remained single was very low and, as a result, data on their sexual behavior and relationships are limited.

However, certain groups, mainly the younger and more educated people, are adopting more-contemporary attitudes towards family and marriage, giving greater priority to their personal rights and self-fulfillment as individuals. Nonetheless, the number of children born to unmarried women is the lowest in Europe. In 1999, the number of children born outside marriage was 3,890, compared to 96,753 who were born to married couples. In 1995, 5% of all the families were single-parent families (Kogidou 1995).

### Marriage and the Family

The Greek family seems to be going through a period of transformation, following the patterns of all other industrial societies. The number of marriages decreased from 7.78 per 1,000 people in 1953 to 6.41 in 1985, 5.77 in 1990, and 5.28 in 1998. On the other hand, the number of divorces is rising.

The typical Greek family unit is monogamous: Greeks may marry only one person at a time. Second, it is increasingly nuclear, although occasionally a grandparent or other relative may live with a family group. Third, it is increasingly egalitarian, with wives becoming much more assertive and husbands more flexible than they were even a decade ago.

### Divorce and Remarriage

The divorce rate, although low compared to other European countries, has been rising steadily in the last decade. Divorces more than doubled between 1979 and 1995—from 4,716 to 10,995, according to the Greek statistical service. The divorce rate has risen from 82.0 per 1,000 marriages in 1982 to 124.2 per 1,000 marriages in 1993.

According to the statistical data on the culpability of a divorce, it is evident that there has been a great change in the mentality and structure of the Greek family. In a total of 5,684 divorces reported in 1980, men were held culpable for the breakdown of 2,162 marriages and women for 1,144. In a total of 6,360 divorces reported in 1989, after amendment of the divorce law, the culpability numbers were 280 and 294, respectively. In addition, the above numbers indicate that "no-fault" divorces are on an upward trend, reaching about 75% of all divorces.

The majority of divorces are obtained after five to ten years of marriage. Also, the majority of divorcing couples have no children or only one child. In 1989, 1,730 divorced couples had no children and 1,520 had only one child. Although both divorced parties may experience difficult times, ex-wives, in particular, may face severe economic problems, especially if they have to raise young children. In the past, when most wives were not expected to work outside the home, courts frequently awarded alimony to divorced women. Now, after adoption of a new Family Law in 1983 that considers women capable of earning their own living, they receive alimony only for a period of three years. After this period, the alimony is automatically interrupted, without considering the possibility that a woman may not find a job. Courts award child custody to mothers rather than to fathers in most cases. However, the courts usually require that the fathers provide child support. A mother cannot retain the children's custody if she is a drug or alcohol addict, mentally or physically disabled, or psychopathic.

The Greek Orthodox Church allows a person to get married up to three times in his or her lifespan. Although there are no statistical data, it is estimated that 90% of those who obtain divorce will marry again—especially now that divorces are easier to get and provoke less social disapproval than ever before.

## Marital and Extramarital Sexual Behaviors

In a 1998 research study on the sexual behavior of the general population aged 18 to 49 in relation to the risk of HIV infection, respondents were asked if they were involved in a parallel relationship in the last five years. It is interesting that 214 men and only 47 women (in a sample of 2,000 people) admitted that they had a parallel relationship during this period. Among these 261 people who had parallel relationships, 82 described themselves as married (Ioannidi et al. 2000).

According to some opinion polls, however, both men and women, although satisfied with their sexual life, express their desire for even greater sexual activity. In addition, men, in higher percentages than women, report extramarital relationships with at least one partner. In addition, it can be said that there is a kind of tolerance on this matter. For instance, the extramarital relationships of important political persons do not constitute a cause for political disgrace or resignation, as is common in some other European countries.

## Incidence of Oral and Anal Sex

The survey conducted by the Department of Sociology of the National School of Public Health (Agrafiotis et al. 1990) has revealed some interesting results in relation to the sexual practices of the general population. The representative sample drawn from the general population of Athens, which really covers one third of the total Greek population, consisted of 1,200 people aged 16 to 65. Generally, for all practices, men reported higher percentages than women. This included vaginal sex (97.3% of men vs. 94.5% of women), oral sex (36.3% vs. 19.3%), and oral sex with body-fluid transmission (8.2% vs. 3.5%). Anal sex was also reported at double the rate of that of women (10.8% vs. 5.1%).

Women were less likely to respond to questions concerning sexual practices, (37% vs. 9%). Age groups also showed a considerable variation in sexual practices, with younger groups mentioning a wider variety of practices and a higher rate of them. Those who were 16 to 22 years old were less likely to practice vaginal sex (92.6% vs. 96%) and more likely to practice anal sex (14.9% vs. 8%). Oral sex was over 40% for the age group 16 to 30, but declined to 5.3% in age group 51 to 64. Of course, whether this difference is related to age, to religious and moral objections, or simply to an unwillingness by the older generation to admit to such practices is open to debate.

The above results were more or less confirmed by Malliori et al. (1991) with a representative sample of 1,980 Athenians of both sexes, 15 to 49 years old. According to these results, 95.5% of the females and 96.5% of the males employ ordinary intercourse, 35.6% of the females and 45.5% of the males use additional fellatio practices, 32% of the females and 40.5% of the males employ cunnilingus, and 10% of the females and 17% of the males use anal intercourse. Greek law contains no legal restrictions on fellatio, cunnilingus, or anal sex.

## 6. Homoerotic, Homosexual, and Bisexual Behaviors

According to the first scientific research conducted by the Athens Medical School (Hantzakis 1992) in an unrepresentative sample of homosexual men, about half of the sample of 213 men were single without ever being married, and either lived alone or with a parent or relative. The majority of these gay men's sexual activity is taken up in the three behaviors of self-pleasuring, fellatio, and anal intercourse. In addition, the majority claimed to have heterosexual contacts as well. This can be partly attributed to the fact that, in Greek society, there are different kinds of homosexuals (i.e., gays and bisexuals) and a mixture of tolerance and taboos coexist. As a result, many gay men are forced to get married and pass as heterosexuals, whereas, in reality, they are bisexual or psychologically and emotionally exclusively homosexual, although engaging in some heterosexual relations.

In a survey on gender identity and HIV risk among gay men (Vassilikou et al. 1999), it appeared that, with regard to sexual identity, young gay men frequently pass through an initial identity crisis, which harbors dangers both for their mental and physical health. There was no specific model of a gay man encountered, but rather many and diverse ways of living with being "different." It also emerged that the first disclosure (coming out) in most cases is made to another or other gay men, and their subsequent disclosures are to persons whom they believe will accept them anyway. Disclosure to the family is made either through a third person or through protracted persistent processes or not at all.

The legal age of consent for homosexual men is 17 years. The legislation of 1981 can force STD testing of homosexual men.

## 7. Gender Diversity and Transgender Issues

Greek society does not provide for any special gender roles, such as the *hijra* of India or the *berdache* among Native Americans. Among the registered prostitutes, 66 are transsexuals who had their surgery abroad, as, in Greece, these operations are not performed.

## 8. Significant Unconventional Sexual Behaviors

### A. Coercive Sexual Behaviors

#### Child Sexual Abuse and Incest

The phenomenon of child sexual abuse has only recently been surfacing in Greece as an issue of concern among professionals, researchers, and the public, following a long period of denial that continues to exist in many settings. This change can be partly attributed to the altering of society's general attitudes towards sexuality, as well as to the appearance of AIDS. The term "child sexual abuse" does not exist in Greek criminal law; there are, however, many provisions that specify offenses that infringe upon a child's purity. These offenses are rape, seduction of a minor, indecent assault, incest, and pimping. When the person culpable of such an offense is a parent, a teacher, or a minor's guardian, the punishment is particularly severe. In the seduction of a minor, the younger the child, the harsher is the punishment. If the child is less than 10 years old, the penalty can be at least ten years imprisonment; if the child is between 10 and 13 years, the penalty can be between five to ten years; the penalty is five years imprisonment for children 13 to 15 years of age. For the offenses of rape, incest, and pimping, the prosecution is automatic, *ex officio*, while for the rest of the offenses, the prosecution continues only if the sufferer or his or her legal representative brings a charge against the perpetrator.

In cases of child sexual abuse, it is not possible to ascertain the incidence of pedophilia, because this category is not included as such in the offenses that infringe upon a child's purity. There are no data on incest, and it is very difficult to estimate the extent of the phenomenon, as the cases registered in police records involve rape or pregnancy (Artinopoulou 1995).

All types of sexual offenses are socially condemned. Although there is no statistical evidence, a study of child sexual abuse among an unrepresentative sample of Greek college students, conducted by the Department of Family Relations of the Institute of Child Health (Agathonos et al. 1992), has shown that the phenomenon in Greece is unexplored and its magnitude very likely underestimated. Among the 743 respondents, 96 students (13 men and 83 women), or 13%, had experiences of sexual victimization, while 230, or 31%, had sexual experiences that did not contain the element of victimization. In one third of the group with the sexual victimization cases, the abuse had been intrafamilial; in one third of the cases, the perpetrator was known to the child. The remaining perpetrators were strangers. In men, perpetrators were, on average, 12 years older, while offenders were, on average, 22 years older than abused women.

*Sexual Harassment*

Although Greek legislation does not distinguish this category of behavior, sexual harassment, especially by males in the workplace, is not uncommon.

*Rape*

Although Greece, according to the statistical data of the United Nation's Report, had the lowest number of rapes per 100,000 women in 1992 (only 2 rapes compared to New Zealand with 254 rapes), scientific studies have shown that only 15% of rapes are reported to the authorities. From police records, the 6% associated with rapes is considered as a relatively low percentage according to an international bibliography (Tsingris 2000). However, it is not indicative of the situation, since many cases are never reported to the police.

According to the legislation, the penalty for rape is between five and 20 years imprisonment. As of early 2003, an ongoing discussion was expected to come to the Parliament for voting a law that includes the punishment of marital rape.

**B. Prostitution**

Prostitution has, for many years, been a socially accepted practice, especially for young Greek men. Given traditional rules of virginity for women and the expectation of masculine behavior, including sexual prowess, for men, prostitutes were both an outlet and schooling for many men. Nowadays, particularly in the urban centers, young men are more likely to have a girlfriend with whom they have sex.

In Greece, the number of professional prostitutes who are registered is 406. They have a health book and are obliged to report twice a month for health inspection at a special clinic of the Ministry of Health and Welfare. After 1990, with the entrance of illegal migrants into the country, especially from ex-Communist Eastern European countries, the number of unregistered sex workers has risen, and it was estimated that Greece then had as many as 17,000 sex workers. This estimate included Greek women, although the majority here are migrants (Kornarou et al. 2002). According to a survey on condom usage by non-registered prostitutes carried out during the period 1995 to 1997, where 1,805 prostitutes—560 Greeks and 1,245 foreigners—completed a questionnaire, the usage of condoms is low. More specifically, the usage is significantly lower among women of Albanian descent, the prostitutes of older age, and the heroin users (Nestoridou et al. 2002). Alongside the unregistered female prostitutes, there is also an unknown number of male and adolescent prostitutes, mainly in Athens and Thessaloniki.

**C. Pornography and Erotica**

Despite legislation that prohibits the production and distribution of pornography and erotica, both hard- and softcore pornography is easily accessible in Greece. In addition, during the last decade, there have been a few telephone "hotlines," which are extremely expensive. Many kiosks sell pornographic magazines, and pornographic videotapes are unofficially available to anyone over age 18. However, these tapes are not openly displayed, and there is an unwritten code of communications between the customer and the shop owner.

## 9. Contraception, Abortion, and Population Planning

**A. Contraception**

Unlike other countries, where a considerable amount of social research has been carried out on attitudes of the population towards contraceptive methods, in Greece until the appearance of AIDS, there were only a few studies on such issues.

There are no official data for the use of contraceptive methods. Research data suggest that condoms and coitus interruptus are the two most familiar methods used (Ioannidi et al. 2000). Estimated data from the Department of Family Planning in the Gynaecological Clinic of Areteio Hospital (Athens) concerning the use of contraceptive methods in the last 5 years in Greece present the following figures: condom 45%, coitus interruptus 20-30%, pill 2%, and IUD 10%.

Indicative of the situation are the findings of research carried out on a national sample of 4,560 women aged 15 to 44, concerning the socioeconomic factors that determine reproduction in Greece: 70% of the women reported withdrawal as the first contraceptive measure, and abortion, which is still considered as a contraceptive method, was reported by 42% of the women (Simeonidou et al. 1997).

In a study carried out by the Institute of Social Preventive Medicine (2001), 50% of the male population used the condom in their sexual relations, and 21.7% used coitus interruptus. Six in ten women admitted that they used the contraceptive method suggested by their partner. One in ten women used a method of their own choice (pill 4.8% and IUD 3.6%).

What is evident in comparison with other European countries is two particularities of the Greek situation in regard to the attitudes towards contraceptive methods. First, Greek society has not fully adopted the use of modern methods of contraception. According to the statistical data provided by the pharmaceutical companies (Margaritidou et al. 1991), such methods are not easily available and their use is relatively low (i.e., IUD sales are 20,000 annually). Thus, the condom, which is available through pharmacies, supermarkets, and kiosks, is still the most widely used method of contraception. Second, there is a tendency for many Greek couples to prove their fertility by not using contraception and resorting to frequent abortion. It is worth noting that while many countries reported that abortion concerns a very small percentage of women and is considered "marginal" behavior from a psychosocial point of view, in Greece repeated abortion and withdrawal are the most widespread methods of birth control (Agrafiotis et al. 1990).

As for education in the contraceptive methods, it can be said that the state or medical practitioners provided little systematic information until the founding of the Family Planning Centers after 1982. Some of these centers provide contraceptive methods free of charge to persons who are not insured, while the National Health Insurance organization does not cover the costs of contraception.

**B. Teenage Unmarried Pregnancies**

The recent doubling of the teenage pregnancy rate, and its continued increase, can be mainly attributed to several reasons. First is the lack of information on ways to avoid an undesired pregnancy. It has been estimated that in countries where adolescent sexual education is put into practice, the percentage of undesired pregnancies is kept relatively low. Second, biological maturation of girls now comes earlier than in the past. And third, premarital sexual activities start at a younger age now than they did in the 1940s and 1950s. Many of the expectant teenage mothers, however, decide to terminate their pregnancies, being fearful of both the medical and social consequences. Thus, parallel to the teenage pregnancies, teenage abortions are increasing. This was evident in recent research on European levels, where the U.K. and Ireland, for example, presented as a major problem the high incidence of births in adolescence, while in Greece, the problem focused on the increase of abortions in this age group (Ioannidi et al. 2002).

## C. Abortion

Since 1986, abortion has been legal in Greece, and a great number are conducted in the private sector. There is no official registration of abortions and the data provided by the National Statistical Service of Greece refers to abortions taking place in National Hospitals only, which is not a representative figure. According to the National Report of the General Secretariat of Equality in Greece (2000), the estimated number of abortions is 100,000 to 120,000 cases per year. The fact is that the abortion rates are high, and, according to estimates by gynecologists, the number of abortions equals the number of births (Kintis 1996). Greece possesses the highest percentage of abortions among the European countries.

In research carried out by the National Center for Social Research (E.K.K.E.) in 1988, it was found that the ratio between abortions and live births was nearly one to three. Forty-three percent of all Greek women in the sample reported at least one abortion or miscarriage. In the study conducted by the Family Center in Thessaloniki (Anapliotis 1985), it was found that a large number of women, around 64% aged 16 to 46 (and over), had an abortion, with the ratio between abortion and live births being 1:8 to 1:3 per woman, respectively. Thus, it can be said that repeated abortion is a "norm," a traditional form of birth control, especially for Greek women who have already acquired the desirable number of children.

The above evidence indicates that abortion in Greece is not considered a moral issue of any dimension, and there is a general lack of guilt about the subject. In a recent study (Ioannidi et al. 2001), only 26% of the general population considers abortion a totally unacceptable practice. One explanation provided for this behavior is that the traditional importance of the mother role, and the constraints concerning the expression of female sexuality, come into conflict with the symbolic and real meaning of modern contraceptives (Naziri 1988). Both men and women use the "unwanted" pregnancy that usually ends up in abortion as evidence of their continuing fertility, whereas modern contraception would create doubts about this.

The law allows for abortion until 12 weeks of pregnancy. The National Health System covers the expenses and provides the right of three days full-paid leave. Despite this, only a few women use the National Health System and their insurance fund for abortion, while there is still a substantive use of private gynecologists for unreported abortions. This can be partly attributed to the fact that private abortions are usually performed immediately, in contrast to the state system that requires some bureaucratic procedures and, therefore, involves delays. Finally, it must be stressed that only a vocal minority associated with the Orthodox Church was against the legalization of abortion, though, in general, the Orthodox Church, unlike the Catholic, is not so absolute in its teachings and is more tolerant in its attitudes towards people's practices such, as birth control, abortion, and so on.

## D. Population Control Efforts

In the last decade, Greece's population growth rate has dropped to 0.97% annually, compared to the rate of 12% to 13% before World War II (National Statistical Service 2000). The government's aim is to promote population growth with financial incentives, such as allowances, houses, and reduced military service. However, the birthrate still remains very low and is related mainly to sociocultural and economic aspects.

# 10. Sexually Transmitted Diseases and HIV/AIDS

## A. Sexually Transmitted Diseases
*Incidence, Patterns, and Trends*

There are no data available on STD prevalence. The only available data that EKEPAP (Centre for the Surveillance and Intervention of Epidemics 2000) could provide were the total numbers of reported cases in the year 2000 for the following STDs on which they keep a record: chlamydia: 66; gonorrhea: 103; syphilis: 100; and hepatitis B: 234. For these diseases, however, there are no data concerning the individuals' gender, age, and so on.

Despite the lack of official data, some conclusions can be drawn from a study that attempted to describe the epidemiology of several major sexually transmitted diseases in Greece during a 23-year period (1974 to 1996). The patient population examined included individuals that had visited the outpatient clinic of Andreas Syngros Hospital, which is a national referral center for venereal diseases. The selected STDs studied were syphilis, gonorrhea, nongonococcal urethritis, genital warts, and HIV/AIDS infection. According to these findings, the incidence rate by sex shows an overall decreasing trend, with slight variations during the study period. In contrast, the incidence of HIV-infected and AIDS patients follows a constant upward trend. The researchers concluded that the incidence of STDs in Greece is characterized by much lower rates than those observed in other countries around the world. These findings may, however, change in the next few years in view of the large number of individuals migrating into the country from Eastern European and other countries (Strategos et al. 2000).

As far as the tracing of STDs and HIV/AIDS, one should take into account the following: There is no compulsory registration of HIV/AIDS in pregnant women. Since 1994, KEEL, in the framework of its surveillance of HIV infection in our country, has suggested to gynecologists to report these cases. There is no compulsory testing for HIV in pregnant women; gynecologists usually suggest it to women and they decide whether they want to take the test or not. Moreover, there is no compulsory tracing to HIV-positive people, but health professionals try to persuade them to keep a contact with their physician. There is also no compulsory registration of STDs, either in pregnant women or the general population, although gynecologists suggest it, as in the case of HIV testing. According to EKEPAP, it is not in the priorities of the Department of Public Health to trace STD cases.

*Availability of Treatment and Prevention Efforts.*

In Greece, there are two public dermatological hospitals for the treatment of STDs, with 200 beds in Athens and 60 beds in Salonica.

In Greece, the Ministry of Health is responsible for the design and implementation of public health policy. In the case of STDs and HIV/AIDS, an independent body has been established, named the Hellenic Center for Infectious Diseases Control (KEEL), which has undertaken the task of implementing preventive policy on a national level. In 1992, KEEL was recognized as a legal entity subject to private law, and it operates in collaboration with other relevant departments of the Ministry of Health and other organizations, both in the public and private spheres. Priority on STDs and HIV/AIDS prevention and/or care policies, is given mainly to women sex workers and mobile populations (gypsies and migrants).

## B. HIV/AIDS

Epidemiological facts on STDs in general, and HIV/AIDS in particular, permit policymakers in Greece not to prioritize these issues as major public health problems. It should be noted here that the spread of infectious diseases in our country follows an epidemiological model that is different from the other Western countries, where a higher number of cases is reported among intravenous drug users along the zone that extends from Spain to the former Yugoslavia. In Greece, the number of homosexuals and heterosexuals infected is higher than the number of drug users. An important number of women have also been infected. A possible explanation for this exception can be attributed to the fact that a development of modern industry has emerged in the above-mentioned areas, which Greece did not follow. Thus, it can be said that "the socio-cultural difference is mirrored in the socio-epidemiological distribution rejecting in this way the myth of cultural homogeneity in the Mediterranean because of the difference among Greece and countries like Italy, Spain, France" (Agrafiotis 1991).

The reporting of AIDS cases in Greece is compulsory (A1/6824/4/7/83). The first surveillance system was initiated in Greece in 1987, four years after the first reported AIDS case in 1983. However, HIV case reporting was implemented in Greece in 1998. It is anonymous, confidential, and mandatory by law (B1/5295/7-8-1998). In KEEL (Center for the Control of Infectious Diseases), there is an office for the epidemiological surveillance of HIV/AIDS infection in our country. In 1998, EKEPAP (Greek Center for Epidemiological Surveillance and Intervention) was also established as a department of KEEL, attempting to keep a record of all STDs reported.

Every six months, an edition of KEEL is published, including the latest epidemiological data, where the following data were reported (June 2001).

The total number of people who live with HIV/AIDS in Greece in the year 2001 (June) is 5,676 persons, 60 of whom are below 15 years of age. The number of women who live with HIV/AIDS in Greece is 883, and most of them are 25 to 39 years old. It should be noted here that these figures might be differentiated slightly, if one takes into account a number of infected people who prefer to go abroad and have an HIV test in order to preserve their anonymity.

The total number of people infected with the HIV virus in the year 2000 was 552, of whom 519 were 15 years of age or older. Among them, 120 women were reported being infected with the HIV virus, all of them above 15 years of age, and the majority being 25 to 39 years old.

There is no official data on the number of people who lived with HIV/AIDS in Greece in the years prior to 2000, because systematic recording of HIV and AIDS cases has only been established from 1999 onwards (KEEL 2001)

The total number of deaths caused by AIDS in the year 2000 was 67 people, 53 men and 14 women, most of whom belonged to the age groups of 30 to 39 and 45 to 54 years. The total number of deaths caused by AIDS since the beginning

of the epidemic is 1,254 people, 1,104 men and 150 women. The majority of these people were 25 to 49 years of age.

As for the prevalence of HIV/AIDS-related routes of transmission, 378 people have declared transmission through heterosexual contact (181 men and 197 women); 19 cases referred to mother-to-child transmission, 1,248 homo-/bisexual male contact, 83 intravenous drug users (61 men and 22 women), and 435 cases (372 men and 63 women) by other routes of transmission.

Overall, sexual transmission accounts for the vast majority of reported HIV adult and adolescent cases. Most of them are men (40%) who have been infected through homosexual intercourse, and approximately 15% are men and women who have been infected through heterosexual transmission. There are signs of increasing trends in both homo- and bisexual men, and heterosexuals. Heterosexual transmission shows, in fact, a faster rate of increase in recent years, while the proportion of heterosexually infected women increases over time (KEEL 2000).

[*Update 2002*: UNAIDS Epidemiological Assessment: Through December 2001, a cumulative total of 5,859 HIV-seropositive persons, 2,254 AIDS cases, and 1,299 deaths from AIDS have been reported at the national level. Among newly reported HIV cases during the 2000 to 2001 period, 26.94% are men who have sex with other men, 17.78% are heterosexuals, and 2.98% are injecting drug users. The route of transmission is yet to be determined in 51.86% of cases.

[HIV prevalence is low among injecting drug users. During 2000 to 2001, no prostitutes were reported to be HIV-seropositive.

[HIV testing is mandatory and systematic in blood donors and recommended for pregnant women, STD patients, injecting drug users, and persons at high risk for HIV. Case reporting is mandatory and confidential by law for both HIV and AIDS cases at the national level. Infection Disease Units, HIV/AIDS Reference Centers, district, regional, university, and private-sector hospitals and laboratories report cases in real time. Retrospectively updated registries include cases since 1982.

[The estimated number of adults and children living with HIV/AIDS on January 1, 2002, were:

| | | |
|---|---|---|
| Adults ages 15-49: | 8,800 | (rate: 0.2%) |
| Women ages 15-49: | 1,800 | |
| Children ages 0-15: | < 100 | |

[An estimated less than 100 adults and children died of AIDS during 2001.

[No estimate is available for the number of Greek children who had lost one or both parents to AIDS and were under age 15 at the end of 2001. (*End of update by the Editors*)]

## 11. Sexual Dysfunctions, Counseling, and Therapies

### A/B. Concepts of Sexual Dysfunction and the Availability of Treatment

Even at the end of the 20th century, the sexual act in Greece seems to be shrouded by myths and antiscientific attitudes and approaches that lead to the superficial management of sexual dysfunctions.

It was only at the end of the last decade that some private institutions, both in Athens and Salonica, began to deal with sexual therapy. Having a better mechanism for preserving a patient's privacy, they brought the problem up for open discussion, recognized it, and helped in its demystification. The acceptable methodology for the diagnosis and therapy of sexual dysfunctions is based on the protocol of I.S.I.R. (International Society of Impotence

Research). Impotence is regarded as a symptom of both psychological and organic problems. According to the statistical data of the Andrological Institute, which specializes in male impotence, from a sample of 5,000 patients treated, 25.1% of impotence was because of psychogenic causes, 24.6% by organic causes, and 50.3% resulted from combined causes. The distribution of cases according to age has shown that problems exist in all age groups, with more cases between the ages of 40 and 50. In addition, the analysis of cases according to profession and social class has shown that the problem is present in all social classes with more or less the same frequency. From the same data, it is evident that one in four men in Greece has some kind of sexual dysfunction. (The name "Andrological" reveals the distinction of science into two specialties related to sex. From a sociological and cultural point of view, it is interesting to see how this will operate in Greece.)

## 12. Sex Research and Advanced Professional Education

Agrafiotis pointed out the need for sexual research in Greece in the early 1980s. But it was the advent of AIDS that forced these matters to emerge somewhat into the public consciousness and policy. In Greece, there are no institutions engaged in sexological research on a regular basis. Research on sexual matters is conducted occasionally and by different research teams without any national coordination. Among the teams engaged in various kinds of sexological research are:

University of Athens, Department of Psychiatry. Director: C. Stefanis. Address: 74 Vas. Sophias Avenue, Athens.

National School of Public Health, Department of Sociology. Director: Demosthenis Agrafiotis. Address: 196 Alexandras Avenue, Athens.

National School of Public Health, Department of Epidemiology. Director: A. Roumeliotou. Address: 196 Alexandras Avenue, Athens.

A Syngros Hospital. Address: 6 Dragoumi, Athens.

Family Planning Association (FPA) Address: Evrou & Pontoiraklia 1-3, Athens 115 28.

Athens Medical School, Department of Epidemiology and Hygiene. Director: D. Trixopoulos.

Hellenic Society of Paediatric and Adolescent Gynaecology (HSPAG). Director: C. Kreatsas. Address: 9 Kanarie str, Athens.

The Department of Psychiatry, the FPA, and the HSPAG offer sex education programs for parents.

Undergraduate courses are provided to doctors by the Medical School, but only as part of the general curriculum (knowledge of organic systems), and are not intended to be a study of human sexuality as such. There is no medical specialization in sexology, and the psychiatrists or gynecologists who wish to specialize in this field should go abroad. The question of sexology as a scientific field is not fully recognized, and there is always a controversy on this matter. As a result, psychologists, sexologists, psychiatrists, and psychoanalysts try to determine their domains of competence. On the other hand, the Department of Sociology of the National School of Public Health explores various issues related to sexuality, and, in general, the social sciences include sexuality and sexual issues in their area of research.

There are no Greek journals or periodicals on sexuality.

## A Final Remark

The issue of sexuality in Greece has yet to be adequately studied. Overall, there is an urgent need for a more systematic investigation of the coexistence of traditional and modern values because of the social particularities of the Greek society and their influence on current sexual attitudes and behaviors. As far as sexual relations are concerned, it appears that couples are well protected from STDs and HIV/AIDS, as the use of condoms is higher than in other European countries. This is explained by the particularities of Greek society, where modern contraceptive methods were never practiced.

Overall, although Greek society and the state still have patriarchal characteristics, there are clear indications that aspects of family life are altering. This is evident in the later age of marriage, increasing rates of divorce, the increase in female participation in the paid labor force, and the very slow increase in single parenthood. The power relations between men and women are very diverse and are played out by the individuals in a far more equitable and nontraditionally gendered manner.

## References and Suggested Readings

Agathonos, H., et al. 1992. *Retrospective study of child sexual abuse. Experiences among Greek college students*. Paper presented at the ISPCAN Conference, Chicago, USA, August 30 to September 2, 1992.

Agrafiotis, D. 1981. *Social and cultural development in Greece* (Scientific Report). Athens: Ministry of Health.

Agrafiotis, D., et al. 1990. *Knowledge, attitudes, beliefs and practices of young people. Pre-test* (*Research Monograph No. 26, Sociology of Health and Illness*). WHO/GPA/SBR (World Health Organization, Global Programme on AIDS, Social and Behavioural Research).

Agrafiotis, D., et al. 1991. *Knowledge, attitudes, beliefs and practices in relation to HIV infection and AIDS. The case of the City of Athens*. Athens: Department of Sociology, Athens School of Public Health.

Agrafiotis D., et al. 1997. *Egarsia Skia–AIDS*. Athens: Ypsilon Publ.

Apostolodis, T. 1992. *A cross-cultural investigation of sociocultural models on sexuality and love, between students in France and in Greece* (Unpublished thesis). University of Paris, France.

Artinopoulou, V. (1995), *Incest, theoritical approach and research data*. Athens: Law Library.

CIA. 2002 (January). *The world factbook 2002*. Washington, DC: Central Intelligence Agency. Available: http://www.cia.gov/cia/publications/factbook/index.html.

Creatsas, O., et al. 1991. Teenage pregnancy: Comparison with two groups of older women. *Journal of Adolescent Health Care, 15-17*:77-81.

Dubisch J., ed. 1986. *Gender and power in rural Greece*. Princeton, NJ: Princeton University Press.

Francoeur, R. T. 1992. The religious suppression of Eros. In: D. Steinberg, ed., *The erotic impulse*. New York: Tarcher/Perigee.

General Secretariat for Equality. 2000. 4th & 5th national report of Greece (1994-2000), for the UN's Committee for any kind of discrimination against women.

Hantzakis, A. 1992. Homosexuality in Greece. In: A. P. M. Coxon, ed., *Homosexual response studies. International report*. World Health Organization.

Ioannidis, E., et al. 1991. *Sexual behavior in the years of AIDS in Greece* (Lisbon Workshop, ECCA).

Ioannidi, E., V. Margaritidou, & Ch. Tselepi. 1997. *The attitudes of parents on the information of their children on HIV/AIDS and STI's* (Report for the Center for the Control of Infectious Diseases).

Ioannidi, E., I. Mitropoulos, & D. Agrafiotis. 2000. Sexual behaviour and risks of HIV infection in Europe. The case of Greece. *Hellenic Archives of AIDS. 8*(2):105-111.

Ioannidi-Kapoloulos, E., I. Mitropoulos, & D. Agrafiotis. 2001 (September-October). The attitudes and sexual practices of the Greek population in the prevention of HIV infection as a basis for intervention policy. *Health Review, 12*(72).

Ioannidi, E. I., et al. (2002). Greek national report. In: L. van Mens, et al., eds., *Prevention of HIV and STI's among women in Europe*. Utrecht: PHASE, PlantijnCasparie.

Kataki, H. 1984. The three identities of the Greek family. Athens: Kedros.

Kaklamani, E., et al. 1981. Syphilis and gonorrhea: Epidemiology update. *Paediatrician. 10*:207-215.

Kampoura, et al. 2002. *Approaching students of tertiary education on virtual sex*. Conference presentation, 14th National Conference on AIDS, 14-17 November 2002, Thessaloniki.

KEEL. 2000. *Half yearly edition of the Hellenic Center for Infectious Diseases Control*. Athens: Ministry of Health and Welfare.

Kintis, G. 1996. Socio-medical dimensions of abortions. In: A. Roumeliotou, E. Kornarou, & M. Gitona, eds., *Health and women*. Athens: Dept. of Epidemiology, National School of Public Health.

Kornarou, H., G. Lazos, & A. Roumeliotou. 2002. *The changes in the function of sex industry due to the entrance of women economic refugees and the risks of AIDS/STD's transmission, Public Health and Migration* (vol. 6, pp. 25-39). Athens: Ministry of Health and Welfare, National School of Public Health, INTERREG II for Public Health in the Balkans.

Malliori, M., et al. 1991. *Sexual behavior and knowledge about AIDS in a representative sample of Athens area*. Athens: Department of Psychiatry, University of Athens.

Madianos, M., et al. 1988. *Health and Greek society*. Athens: EKKE.

Mandi, P., et al. 1993. *Sexual patterns in contemporary Greece: A pilot study* (Research Monograph No. 9). Athens: Athens School of Public Health/Andrological Institute.

Maratou-Alibranti, L. 1999. *Family in Athens: Family patterns and spouse's practices*, Athens: EKKE.

National Statistical Service of Greece. 2002. Available: http://www.statistics.gr/Main_eng.asp.

Naziri, D. 1988. *Greek women and abortion. Clinical study of repeated abortion* (Unpublished thesis). University of Paris.

Nestoridou, A., E. Kornarou, G. Lazos, & A. Roumeliotou. 2002. Condom usage from non-registered prostitutes. *Hellenic Archives of AIDS, 10*(1):44-47.

Pantzou, P., et al. 1991. *The demand for health education on sexuality and AIDS based on sociopsychological research*. Second European Conference on Effectiveness of Health Promotion and Education.

Papaevangelou, G., et al. 1988. Education in preventing HIV infection in Greek registered prostitutes. *Journal of Acquired Immune Deficiency Syndromes, 1*:386-389.

Papataxiarchis, E., & Th. Paradellis, eds. 1992. *Identity and gender in modern Greece: Anthropological approaches*. Athens: Kapenioti.

Primpas Welts, E. 1982. Greek families. In: M. McGoldrick, J. K. Pearce, & J. Giordano, eds., *Ethnicity and family therapy*. New York: Guilford Press.

Roumeliotou, A., et al. 1990. *Prevention of HIV infection in Greek registered prostitutes: A five-year study*. 6th International Conference on AIDS, San Francisco, USA, June 20-24, 1990.

Simeonidou, Ch., et al. 1997. *Socio-economic determinant factors of fertility in Greece* (Vol. B). Athens: EKKE.

Tsingris, A. 2000. *Sexual crimes*. Athens: Sakkoula.

Strategos et al., 2000. The epidemiology of selected sexually transmitted diseases in Greece during the period 1974-1996. *Hellenic Dermato-Venereological Review, 11*:171-177.

UNAIDS. 2002. *Epidemiological fact sheets by country*. Geneva, Switzerland: Joint United Nations Programme on HIV/AIDS (UNAIDS/WHO). Available: http://www.unaids.org/hivaidsinfo/statistics/fact_sheets/index_en.htm.

Vassilikou, C., P. Pantzou, & D. Agrafiotis. 1999. *European project on identity, risk and AIDS* (Research Monograph 17b). Athens: Department of Sociology, National School of Public Health.

# Hong Kong
## (Special Administrative Region of the People's Republic of China)

Emil Man-lun Ng, M.D., and Joyce L. C. Ma, Ph.D.*
*Updates by M. P. Lau, M.D., and Robert T. Francoeur, Ph.D.*

## Contents

### Demographics and a Brief Historical Perspective

ROBERT T. FRANCOEUR

#### A. Demographics

Located at the mouth of the Pearl River about 90 miles (145 km) southeast of Canton (Guangzhou), the former British crown colony of Hong Kong is a very small but important Asian territory and hybrid culture now incorporated as a Special Administrative Region of the People's Republic of China. Hong Kong has 421.6 square miles (1,092 km²), including the 32-square-mile (83-km²) island of Hong Kong. Most of the island is hilly to mountainous with steep slopes, with lowlands in the north. The climate includes tropical monsoons, and is cool and humid in the winter, hot and rainy from spring through the summer, and warm and sunny in the fall.

In July 2002, Hong Kong had an estimated population of 7.3 million. (All data are from *The World Factbook 2002* (CIA 2002) unless otherwise stated.)

**Age Distribution and Sex Ratios**: *0-14 years*: 17.5% with 1.13 male(s) per female (sex ratio); *15-64 years*: 71.6% with 0.98 male(s) per female; *65 years and over*: 10.9% with 0.85 male(s) per female; *Total population sex ratio*: 0.99 male(s) to 1 female

**Life Expectancy at Birth**: *Total Population*: 79.8 years; *male*: 77.1 years; *female*: 82.69 years

**Urban/Rural Distribution**: NA

*Communications*: Dr. Emil Man-lun Ng, Queen Mary Hospital, University of Hong Kong, Psychiatry Dept., Hong Kong; hrmcml@ hkucc.hku.hk, nml@i.am. Joyce L. C. Ma, Ph.D.; joycelai@cuhk .edu.hk. *Note*: The editor gratefully acknowledges the careful review of this chapter and additional comments by M. P. Lau, M.D., a native of Hong Kong and coauthor of the chapter on China in this volume.

*Editors' Note*: Because of space constraints in volume 4 of the *International Encyclopedia of Sexuality* published in 2001, the original chapter on Hong Kong, like Norway, was not included. Instead, the Editors published them as "Supplemental Countries on the World Wide Web" at http://www.SexQuest.com/IES4/.

(CIA 2002)

**Ethnic Distribution**: Chinese: 95%; other: 5%

**Religious Distribution**: Buddhist or Taoist affiliation: 90%; Christianity: 7.8%; Hinduism: 1.8%; Muslim: 0.8%; and Jewish: 0.15%

**Birth Rate**: 11.13 births per 1,000 population

**Death Rate**: 6.02 per 1,000 population

**Infant Mortality Rate**: 5.73 deaths per 1,000 live births

**Net Migration Rate**: 7.76 migrant(s) per 1,000 population. Between 1949 and 1962, Hong Kong absorbed more than a million Chinese refugees.

**Total Fertility Rate**: 1.3 children born per woman

**Population Growth Rate**: 1.26%

**HIV/AIDS** (1999 est.): *Adult prevalence*: 0.06%; *Persons living with HIV/AIDS*: 2,500; *Deaths*: < 100. (For additional details from www.UNAIDS.org, see end of Section 10B.)

**Literacy Rate** (*defined as those age 15 and over who can read and write*): 92.2% (*male*: 96%, *female*: 88.2%), with over 90% attendance for 9 years of compulsory schooling (1996 est.); *attendance for nine years of compulsory school*: 95% (education is free and compulsory from age 6 to 13)

**Per Capita Gross Domestic Product** (*purchasing power parity*): $25,000; *Inflation*: –1.6%; *Unemployment*: 5.2%; *Living below the poverty line*: NA (2001 est.)

#### B. A Brief Historical Perspective

In 1841, the 32-square-mile (83-km²) island of Hong Kong was ceded by China to Britain. In 1860, Britain annexed Stone Cutters' Island (one-quarter square mile, 0.65 km²), 200 other islands, and the 3-square-mile (7.8-km²) Kowloon Peninsula. In 1898, Britain leased 355 square miles (919 km²) of agricultural land in the New Territories on the adjoining mainland. As a crown colony, Hong Kong was, despite its tiny size, a vibrant capitalist enclave and free port on the edge of China. In 1994, following two years of painstaking negotiation, the British and Chinese governments agreed that Hong Kong would return to Chinese sovereignty on June 30, 1997, when Britain's lease on the New Territories expired. The agreement specified that the territory would retain its social, economic, and legal system as a special administrative region of China under a unique "One Country, Two Systems" arrangement for the next 50 years. The agreement guaranteed freedoms of speech, press, assembly, association, travel, the right to strike, and religious belief. However, the chief executive and some members of the legislature are appointed by Beijing.

## 1. Basic Sexological Premises, and 2. Religious, Ethnic, and Gender Factors Affecting Sexuality

Different sexological premises coexist in Hong Kong, along with a variety and mix of ethnic and religious factors that affect sexual attitudes and behavior in Hong Kong.

### A. The Original Taoist-Confucian Premise

This most ancient sexological premise of the Hans, the major Chinese tribal group, has a documented history of over 5,000 years. It holds a very natural and utilitarian view of sex. The interaction of two cosmic forces, Yin and Yang, is thought to be universal and essential for the existence, change, and growth of all matters, and sex is just one mode of this interaction in living things. For their well-being and prosperity, human beings are advised to follow this natural interaction to the full, as long as it does not jeopardize social harmony, which is a Yin-Yang interplay of a higher order. Based on this doctrine, both the reproductive and pleasurable aspects of sex were given high consideration. Sex within marriage must serve the purpose of procreation, whereas sex outside marriage is for erotic satisfaction. Within marriage, therefore, contraception is discouraged, and infertility is a good-enough reason for divorce or for the husband to take a second wife or a concubine. Outside marriage, except for incest and rape, a wide range of sexual behavior is acceptable or at least tolerated, including homosexuality, bestiality, prostitution, fetishism, and pedophilia. This explains why, for the Chinese before the second half of the 20th century, prostitution, homosexuality, and pedophilia were openly practiced. Foot fetishism, taking the form of bound feet for females, had even been an open paraphilic custom in China for 1,000 years. From the beginning of the second millennium down to the early decades of the 20th century, some well-bred Chinese women had to undergo extreme pain in childhood to orthopedically deform their feet by means of cloth bindings, splints, and special shoes to a size and shape supposed to be sexually stimulating and fascinating to the men. [*Comment 1997*: While "bound feet" is a most-cruel custom, modern Western women wear high-heeled shoes, pluck their eyebrows, and have their ears pierced, liposuction, facelifts, and breast implants. Male and female ballet dancers wear special shoes and suffer through special exercises to achieve a lilting gait and sprint movements. (*End of comment by M. P. Lau*)]

### B. The Neo-Confucian Premise

During the Song Dynasty (960-1279 C.E.), a group of scholars started to reinterpret the original Confucian doctrine. The resultant Neo-Confucianism has been very influential on the Chinese concept of sexuality up to the present day. Selected books and passages in the Confucian teaching were given new and strict meanings to denounce sexual intimacy, pleasure, and all types of physical enjoyment. In this premise, the harm of sexual pleasure to bodily health and to spiritual pursuit was very much emphasized. Sexual chastity, especially for the females, had to be guarded at all costs, even at the price of one's life. Premarital sex, extramarital sex, and remarriages were seriously frowned upon. Socially, sex must not be discussed openly, dresses must be all-covering up to the neck, and males and females not belonging to one family must not touch one other under any circumstances. For example, even when a male physician had to ascertain the pulse of a female patient, he should only do it by feeling the tight extension of a piece of string tied to the patient's wrist.

### C. The Christian Premise

Christianity came into China as early as the Tang Dynasty (618-907 C.E.), but its influences became significant only after the 18th century when Western civilization, supported by a strong British military superiority, entered China with Western scientific technology and a different lifestyle. The fundamentalist Christian ideas of sex were sown, developed, absorbed, and practiced. They included the denunciation of sexual pleasure, the love-marriage-sex trilogy, and the exclusively monogamous marital system. As a result, at the establishment of modem China in 1949, monogamy replaced polygyny as the only legal marital system of the country. Although Christians represent less than 10% of the Hong Kong population, the influence of the Christian premise on the sexual ethos of the territory must not be underestimated. Up to June 30, 1997, Hong Kong had been under the governance of Great Britain. Hence, Christianity had a great advantage over other religions in promoting their ideology and practices in Hong Kong. For example, up to now, five of the roughly 20 government-designated public holidays have been Christian holidays. None of the government-designated holidays are Buddhist, Taoist, or Confucian holidays. Most of the elite schools in Hong Kong are Christian-affiliated and directed. Instruction in the Christian doctrine is standard and required for all students, whether or not they will ultimately become converted Christians. Many of these elite students become the ruling or influential class in Hong Kong and help to spread the Christian premise consciously or subconsciously.

### D. The Male Domination Premise

All the above three premises assigned a dominant role for men over women, making Hong Kong still a society tilted in favor of men. Although the participation rate of Hong Kong females in the labor market has increased from 36.8% in 1961 to 49.5% in 1993 and 49.2% in 1996 (Hong Kong Government 1996), their employment is mostly concentrated in traditional service industries (e.g., clerical and secretarial jobs, and manual and menial services with lower job status and lower payment in comparison with their male colleagues). Among all working women, less than 5% are in administrative and managerial jobs (Westwood, Ngo, & Leung 1997). The employment situation of Hong Kong women is more or less similar to that in the cities of mainland China and Taiwan.

The educational statistics also demonstrate this male dominance. According to the mid-census report in 1996 (Census and Statistical Department 1996), in 1986, 66.38% of students in degree courses in tertiary institutions were male and 33.62% were female, whereas in 1996, 57.15% were male and 42.85% were female. Although the gap had decreased, there was still a sizable 15% difference.

The suicide rate among Hong Kong women has increased from 4 to 8 per 100,000 between 1981 and 1994 (Yip 1995), which is lower than in mainland China, where the female suicide rate is 15.9 per 100,000 for urban women and 78.3 per 100,000 for rural Chinese women (Pearson 1998). In a survey of married women's gender views (FPAHK 1993), 22% of the respondents believed that their career achievement should not be higher than that of their husbands, and 17.9% indicated that they would get respect from friends and relatives by giving birth to a son. Because of the disadvantaged position of women in society, it is not surprising to find from a youth sexuality survey (FPAHK 1998) that 8.7% of girls between 18 and 27 wished they were the other gender, compared with 2.7% of boys of the same age range who wished they were female.

## E. The Liberalism Premise

Liberalism is a growing premise in Hong Kong. It could refer to sexual recklessness stemming from a lack of sexual knowledge and ethics, but it is more likely a summation of the confluence of ideas from a wide range of modern philosophies, which call for gender equality, human rights, elimination of sexual discrimination, scientific rationalism, democracy, and freedom. These individual philosophies go hand in hand with the general political change of the territory engineered by the British government before 1997, major examples being the decriminalization of homosexuality in 1991, and the establishment of the Equal Opportunities Commission in 1996. Less apparent changes can also be seen in the growing social tolerance of prostitution and sexually explicit materials. To live by the income of prostitution is illegal in Hong Kong, but patronizing a prostitute is not. Sexually explicit materials are subject to the monitoring and rating by the Obscene and Indecent Articles Tribunal, but only after the materials are published and distributed. Publishers are penalized only if they are found to have produced sexually explicit materials that are obscene or indecent, and distributed this material to readers in the inappropriate age range. It is commonly believed that sexually liberal ideas come from the West. This belief, however, may be too simplistic, at least for Hong Kong, because, as mentioned above, the Chinese culture has a long history of tolerance to varied sexual practices. Hence, modern liberal sexual ideas may be seen as a signal of the swinging back of the pendulum, gradually settling into a new equilibrium.

## 3. Knowledge and Education about Sexuality

### A. Government Policies and Programs

*Sexuality Education in Schools*

Hong Kong started public sex education in the 1950s, led by the Family Planning Association of Hong Kong (FPAHK). Various social service and volunteer agencies joined in afterwards (Ng 1988). Late in 1971, the Education Department issued a memorandum to all schools in Hong Kong to include sex education topics in their standard subjects and offered a summary of suggestions on what could be taught. In the subsequent years, efforts were made to include sex education as a part of the social education subject in the junior secondary grades. In 1986, the Department issued its *Guidelines on Sex Education in Secondary Schools* (Education Department 1986). It proposed an interdisciplinary approach to sex education and made further and more-detailed recommendations on resources and references. In the same year, a Sex Education Resource Center was set up by the Department to further assist in-school sex education. Frequent sex education seminars, lectures, and short courses have also been held to train the teachers. These efforts at sex education have received official applause. Some official statistics have also shown that changes do seem to be heading in a satisfactory direction (Pau 1991). A growing number of schools or teachers are reported to show an interest in strengthening sex education and have assigned teachers as coordinators. In 1990, 40% of the schools, which responded to a sex education survey conducted by the Education Department, felt that their sex education plans had been successful.

However, these official figures are far from being firm proof that sex education is making good overall progress. In 1989, the Family Planning Association of Hong Kong did a survey of sex education in schools. They found the topics taught were mostly the basic biological information like "puberty bodily changes" and menstruation. The teachers were unprepared for topics like contraceptive methods or prostitution, which are also very important (FPAHK 1989). In the in-school portion of the sexuality survey of the Association (FPAHK 1986, 1991a), it was found that the percentage of students who reported having acquired sexual knowledge from their teachers had decreased from 26.4% in 1986 to 21.4% in 1991. The percentage of students who reported they got sexual knowledge from seminars had decreased even further, from 58.4% to 31.6%. Most of them had turned to newspapers and magazines. How this drop has affected the students' sexual knowledge was shown by figures in the same surveys: Except for the question on the safety function of condoms, there was on the average a 12.4% decrease of students who were able to give correct answers to some simple sexual knowledge questions. The disconcerting fact is that, despite a lot of statistics and a lot of work by the educational bodies, they are not meeting the students' educational needs as it has been hoped for.

How this situation has come about cannot be discussed in detail here. The obvious problem is that the "sex education" efforts in Hong Kong so far have only been lip work and service, consisting of empty words much more than effective action or support. Memoranda, guidelines, resources, lectures, and theories abound without paying enough attention to practicality or feasibility. Restricted by the insistence that sex education has to be an interdisciplinary and, therefore, a shared and fragmented subject, sex education teachers in schools lack identity, promotion, and the prospect of any psychological or material reward. Because of the heavy content and examination pressure of other "more important" subjects, it is also impossible for them to squeeze enough sex education materials into the school curriculum to make their sexuality teaching continuous, meaningful, or interesting.

There seems to be little hope for much improvement in the foreseeable future, because the official bodies appear to be sitting tight with their established principles, and are hesitant to move forward. Their work plans are still geared toward setting up more resource centers, publishing more sex education bulletins, and organizing more piecemeal sex education seminars, lectures, and courses. As for the crucial issue of setting up sexuality education as an independent subject and assigning it more time and recognition, nothing substantial is likely to be done if one looks at the second, more recent *Guidelines for Sex Education Guideline* published by the Department of Education in 1997. In these guidelines, all secondary schools are advised to set a minimum amount of teaching time for sex education. The students of Form One to Form Three are to have an annual minimum of 20 hours of Life Education, the contents of which include civics, social ethics, politics, environmental protection, etc., etc., and among all these, also sex education! In view of the special difficulties in sexuality teaching, teachers are likely to continue using most, if not all, the time for the other "more important" content.

*Sexuality Information and Knowledge*

Surveys have been directed toward specific groups to evaluate their sex knowledge. In 1994, the Education Department carried out the Study on Knowledge and Attitudes of Secondary School Pupils on Sex and Sex Education with a sample of 4,087 pupils. In this study, a grade of 60 was considered a passing mark, and the average mark the students obtained was 68.4. The subjects showed that they were knowledgeable about AIDS and the risks associated with unprotected sex with an HIV-infected person. However, the students got low marks in two areas, which should be the concern of all secondary school pupils. Only 24.6% of the students stated correctly that the bad effects of masturbation come only from psychological guilt. Only 47.7% stated correctly that the size of the penis does not reflect the sexual ability of a man. For the self-evaluation of sexuality knowledge, only 41% of the pupils claimed to have sufficient knowledge, whereas 45.8% claimed their knowledge was insufficient, and 10.9% claimed it was very insufficient.

In a 1996 study of the sexual knowledge of couples preparing for marriage, Wong had 41 couples with a male age range of 19 to 37 (mean 28.5) and a female age range of 19 to 35 (mean 26.5). They obtained a mean score of 67%. The female respondents got a lower mean score than the males, but the difference was not statistically significant. Knowledge of female sexuality was particularly poor. Approximately half of the sample believed that women must have pain and bleeding at first sexual intercourse. The location of the clitoris was not known to one third of the respondents. Furthermore, the knowledge of those couples who had attended a premarital preparation course (23%) was not necessarily higher. The association between sexual experience and sexual knowledge was tested, but was found not significant, except for the association of experience with knowledge about female sexual arousal. Experienced subjects were more likely to understand that orgasm in women could be produced by various means of foreplay and clitoral stimulation, and not solely by vaginal intercourse. No association was observed between educational background and gender on the overall level of sexual knowledge. One exception was that the higher the level of education, the more correct answers could be obtained regarding the differences in the nature of female and male orgasms. Also, female respondents were generally ignorant about male erectile problems.

Knowledge about HIV/AIDS was studied by Chung and Fung (1999). In testing 1,160 women, ages 20 to 50, the average score of correct answers was seven out of ten. Only 55% of the respondents knew that HIV could be transmitted via breastfeeding. Only 11% of the respondents knew that the incubation period for AIDS was eight to 12 years, not seven years as formerly claimed. See also Section 3B below for data on informal sources of sexuality information.

*Sexual Attitudes and Values*

The Family Planning Association of Hong Kong (FPAHK) provides the most detailed, reliable, and longitudinal data on sexual knowledge, attitudes, and behaviors in Hong Kong. Since 1981, the Association has been conducting sexuality surveys of secondary school students once every five years (FPAHK 1981, 1986, 1991a, 1991b, 1996). In each of these surveys, to ensure comparability of data from different years, Hong Kong students in Form Three to Form Seven (age range 14 to 19) were sampled by stratified random sampling and given similar questionnaires to answer. Despite problems of non-response and other inevitable technical deficiencies of sexuality surveys, the data represent the most reliable that can be obtained in Hong Kong. Since 1986, the survey has a section added on for the out-of-school youths, graduates, and dropouts, ages 19 to 27, making it possible to trace the direction of change in the sexual knowledge, attitudes, or behaviors of the subjects when they grow older.

According to the FPAHK data, the sexual attitudes of Hong Kong youths are not as open or liberal as many people think. Also, being liberal or not seems to depend on which sexual attitude or value one is looking at. Although an overall picture can be drawn that the Hong Kong youths are increasingly more open and permissive in their sexual attitudes, there are items also showing that in some aspects they are

holding on to sexual repression and conservatism. In the in-school surveys, for example (FPAHK 1986, 1991a), an increasing percentage of males were found to be dissatisfied with their own gender, from 1.4% in 1986 to 2.9% in 1991. In the three out-of-school surveys, which spanned a period of ten years (FPAHK 1986, 1991b, 1996), roughly the same percentage of males could accept single males having sex with prostitutes (36.2% in 1986, 28.4% in 1991, and 30.7% in 1996).

Using and reanalyzing part of the 1986 survey data of the Family Planning Association of Hong Kong, Lui, Cheung, Chan, and Ng (1993) confirmed that different types of traditional sexual values in Hong Kong changed at very different paces. They examined three items in the survey representing three different sets of sexual values: sexual enjoyment, social conformity in sex, and sexual equality. It was found that social conformity in sex was upheld by a strong majority of the subjects (81.7%) and that it was quite resistant to social changes, because covariate analysis demonstrated the small contribution of the subjects' social contextual factors to any of its variation. An even more important finding is that in these subjects, their strong adherence to social conformity went in parallel with their support for the value of sexual enjoyment, which was also quite high (65.9%). The message is that, for whatever reason, even though the Hong Kong youths might increasingly recognize and accept the enjoyable side of sex, the recognition does not necessarily make them less socially responsible in sexual attitudes and behavior. [*Comment 1997*: When confronted with double messages, the youths were able to resolve their conflicts by prioritizing their choices and preferences. (*End of comment by M. P. Lau*)] The moralists could have been misled or misleading when they sounded out alarms simply based on a changing social attitude to the function and value of sex.

It is interesting to find that despite a high acceptance of the value of sexual enjoyment, compared with their counterparts in China, Hong Kong youths show a much more conservative sexual attitude in general. Of the Hong Kong secondary school students in 1991, 80.4% supported the idea of monogamous marriage and said they planned to get married in the future (FPAHK 1991). In the Shanghai secondary school students of 1988, however, only 49.5% had the same idea. As to pornography, only 39.5% of the Hong Kong secondary students of 1991 accepted its existence in the community. This compares with 63.5% of mainland Chinese secondary school students from a large variety of regions, who, in 1989 and 1990, accepted pornography as harmless, and maintained that they should be allowed to read it (Liu et al. 1997). Some scholars (Fan et al. 1995) found evidence that the greater sexual conservatism in the Hong Kong students were because of the greater Christian influences in the territory.

### B. Informal Sources of Sexual Knowledge

In the 1994 Study on Knowledge and Attitudes of Secondary School Pupils on Sex and Sex Education carried out by the Education Department with a sample of 4,087 pupils, the main sources of sexuality knowledge for secondary school students were the newspaper (54.1%), television, and biology and science classes at school. As for the sources of sexual knowledge about HIV/AIDS, Chung and Fung (1999) reported that 94% of the 1,160 women respondents, ages 20 to 50, cited television as an information source, 75% cited newspapers and magazines, and 67% cited radio.

## 4. Autoerotic Behaviors and Patterns

In the Family Planning Association of Hong Kong (FPAHK) 1996 survey of 4,116 students aged 15 to 18, 46% of the boys and 17% of the girls reported experiences of masturbation. Girls had more negative feelings and perceptions about masturbation than boys. About 36% and 51% of boys and girls, respectively, indicated that masturbation was immoral, and about 37% and 43%, respectively, thought it was not good for mental or physical health. Compared with the FPAHK surveys of 1991 and 1986, the percentages of subjects who masturbate have been rising, and those holding negative views about it have kept on decreasing. There are no data on the methods of masturbation. Clinical information suggests that simple manual manipulation is the most common method, followed by squeezing the genital by the thighs or pressing on the bed sheets. Sex aids are rarely used, although they are available openly in "adult shops," which are not very different from the "sex shops" in Western countries.

However, the survey indicated that the more common form of autoeroticism among the youths involved voyeurism and the consumption of sexually explicit materials. About 66% of the boys and 39% of the girls under 18 reported that they had seen pornographic movies, and about 60% and 39%, respectively, had bought pornographic comics. Other channels of consumption included videotapes and discs, the Internet, and sexual telephone services. This finding should be a surprise to some policymakers in Hong Kong, because by law, youngsters below the age of 18 are supposed to be prohibited from access to these materials or services. The degree of sexual explicitness or "obscenity" of all published media in Hong Kong is subject to rating by government officials in consultation with representatives from the public whom the government appoints. The law imposes heavy penalties for anyone who distributes "obscene" materials to anybody, or "indecent" materials to youngsters below the age of 18.

## 5. Interpersonal Heterosexual Behaviors

### A. Youths

By comparing the in-school surveys of the Family Planning Association of Hong Kong (FPAHK) in 1986, 1991, and 1996, a trend of increasing heterosexual activity can be identified among secondary school students. Dating behavior among the boys increased from 42% to 54.2%, and among the girls from 42.5% to 55.0% in five years. In terms of having experience with sexual intercourse, the boys' figure increased from 5.7% to 6.1%, and the girls from 3.5% to 4.3%. The frequencies of other types of physical intimacy increased much more. The out-of-school surveys further confirm the sexually permissive behavior among the youths. A greater number of these youths in 1991 perceived that their friends and relatives were sexually permissive in terms of premarital sex and visits to prostitutes or other "vice" establishments. A greater percentage of the boys, 32.8% in 1986 and 36.7% in 1991, reported having had sexual intercourse. The 1991 survey shows that 16.7% of the males and 15.1% of the females of age 18 to 19 already had sexual intercourse.

However, the out-of-school survey shows that, although the Hong Kong youths of 1991 were becoming more sexually active, they were also more cautious in many respects. For example, much more of those who had sex before marriage did so with their dating partners, 52.2% in 1986 compared with 79.8% in 1991, and much less with prostitutes (28.4% compared with 10.8%). The percentage of males who had ever used prostitutes decreased from 16% in 1986 to 11.7% in 1991. The percentage of males who used condoms in their premarital sexual intercourse increased from 64.5% to 84.2%, and for females from 50.6% to 76.5%, between 1986 and 1991.

With these findings, it would appear that the increase in sexual activities among Hong Kong youths has been moderate. The Hong Kong youngsters are not as promiscuous or reckless with sex as some moralists are trying to portray. The sexual self-control of Hong Kong youths is more obvious if they are compared with their counterparts in China, who are often thought of as very much under the influence of traditional sexual repression and conservatism. If Hong Kong youths are compared with their counterparts from all parts of China, their rates of sexual experience are higher. For example, in 1989, Liu, Ng, Chou, & Haeberle (1997) did a sexuality survey of 6,092 secondary school students in ten cities in China. It was found that only 461 (7.5%) of the Chinese youths had experienced sexual contact (kissing, embracing, petting, and coitus), and of these, 461, only 39 of the males and 95 of the females, reported having experienced sexual intercourse. However, if an equal degree of modernization is taken into account by comparing the Hong Kong youths with the Shanghai youths only, the story is different.

In 1991, the Hong Kong Tertiary Institutions Health Care Working Group did a sexuality survey on all university freshmen of Hong Kong and found 3.5% of the males and 1.4% of the females had experience with sexual intercourse. In the same year, Hong et al. (1994) did a sexuality survey on a random sample of the university freshmen in Shanghai. Their data showed that 6.3% of the males and 2.9% of the females had experienced sexual intercourse. The percentages were nearly double those of Hong Kong. For those who had sexual experience, 19.5% of the Hong Kong male students had sex with more than one partner. For Shanghai, the corresponding figure was 25.0%, also showing that the Shanghai students were more sexually permissive and active.

On the other hand, only 15.0% of the Shanghai males and 20.0% of the Shanghai females had the habit of using condoms, while the corresponding figures in Hong Kong were much higher at 69.5% and 37.5%, respectively. Although there are data to show that Hong Kong subjects are increasingly more open and permissive in their sexual behavior, this openness could just be part of a universal trend in modern cities. The magnitude of change is far below that of many Western societies, and not even up to that of China or Shanghai (Rosenthal 1999). If this change is a necessary adaptation for people in modernizing and developing societies, the slow change of Hong Kong sexuality should be a cause for worry rather than delight, because Hong Kong is supposed to be one of the more modernized of Asian cities.

[*Comment 2001*: History has provided many examples of overseas or expatriate groups clinging to traditional values and identities, while these same values and identities underwent changes in their places of origin. Consider the Romans in their colonies, the Mennonites, the Taiwanese Chinese (who still use the pre-pinyin characters in their alphabet), the Vietnamese Chinese (with their large family sizes), the United Loyalists in Ireland, and the Quebec separatists. Scandinavians in the American Midwest still cling to holiday customs popular with their ancestors when they came to the U.S. as poor immigrants generations ago—customs which their contemporary relatives in Scandinavia gave up long ago. The Marxists in China tried to put loyalty to the state ahead of loyalty to one's family and clan, or material productivity ahead of interpersonal, cultural, and spiritual needs. When loyalty to the central government becomes less intensive, there is a vacuum to be filled, or an anomie that may invite handy substitutes, such as wanton sexual gratification. (*End of comment by M. P. Lau*)]

### B. Adults

The only form of marriage now legal in Hong Kong is the Western Christian form of monogamous marriage. The old Chinese marital system that allowed a man to take an unlimited number of wives has been illegal since 1971, and arranged marriages are now hardly practiced. For two or more generations, Hong Kong people have subscribed increasingly to romantic love, freedom in dating, courtship, and choice of one's own marital partner. The nuclear family is the rule after marriage, although the older generations are still respected and supported.

The mean age of first marriage in Hong Kong in 1997 was 30 for males and 27 for females. The age has increased by three years in both sexes over that of 1981. The rising marital age is associated with a rise in cohabitation, casual sex, premarital sex, and prostitution, but the exact extent of these is not known.

There are signs that the monogamous marital system is not meeting the needs of those living in the Hong Kong culture. The annual number of divorce cases had doubled from 5,507 cases in 1989 to 10,492 cases in 1997, while the number of marriages in the same period dropped from 43,952 to 37,593 (Hong Kong Special Administrative Government 1998). In recent years, the high number of males who take mistresses in mainland China has caused a number of serious marital tragedies and become a social concern. In 1996, it was estimated that, out of the approximately two million married couples in Hong Kong, about 300,000 husbands had mistresses in China. If unfaithful wives and those husbands who have mistresses in Hong Kong or practice casual sex are included, one may estimate that at least about one third of the married couples are or have been affected by extramarital relationships (Rosenthal 1999).

The Family Service Division of the Hong Kong Council of Social Services Clientele Information Service, a major marital counseling center in Hong Kong, reported that extramarital affairs constituted 26.1% of their cases from 1988 to 1990. The Hong Kong Catholic Advisory Council reported that extramarital affairs occupied about 38% of their caseload in 1993, with husband's affairs accounting for 32% and the wives' for 6%. The Caritas Family Service in the same year reported a similar proportion, and 40% of the extramarital affairs involved a stable partner (Young et al. 1995).

[*Update 2002*: For thousands of years, Chinese emperors and government officials surrounded themselves with concubines, while traders and businessmen maintained a wife in every port. Under British rule (1841 to 1997), concubines were legal in Hong Kong. In the past generation, enough Hong Kong men had led the double-life to father an estimated 520,000 children. In 1999, a local Hong Kong court exercised its separate legal jurisdiction to grant Hong Kong residency to the half million children born to the second wives of Hong Kong men. That decision would have added significantly to Hong Kong's 6.5 million people packed into a very limited 422 square miles (1,092 km²). It also created some serious legal consequences for the "One Country, Two Systems" policy. Not surprisingly, a mainland Chinese court overturned the local decree.

[With Hong Kong and the former Portuguese colony of Macao now under mainland Chinese rule, the borders are increasingly porous, and concentrations of second wives and concubines are expanding in small cities and suburbs within commuting distance of Hong Kong and Macao and along the main rail lines from Hong Kong and Macao to Guangzhou, as well as across southeast China.

[Concerned about the negative effects of the concubine tradition on China's family-planning policies of one child per family in the cities and a tolerated two children in the rural areas, the government is now trying to eliminate or at least reduce concubinage. This will not be easy, for both economic and jurisdictional reasons.

[Mass migration and economic dislocation have made concubines a major problem across the country, wherever rural poverty meets the affluence of the new free market's restrained capitalist economy. For a modest $200 monthly rent in a village of concubines, a moderately affluent married businessman can enjoy the comfort of an attractive devoted second wife. Second wives are easy to find on farms just outside cities. There is also a flourishing business of go-betweens who recruit young women who are happy to trade the hard life on a poor farm in some distant province for the luxury of a two-bedroom apartment with some modern conveniences in the bustling suburb of a modern city.

[The government tries to combat migration from the farms to the cities by issuing every adult a work permit allowing that person to work legally only within a certain distance of their birthplace. Permits to migrate to a city are strictly limited. In becoming a concubine, a young woman can leave her rural home without a work permit and be supported by a "husband."

[A law introduced in 2000 in Shenzhen, just outside Hong Kong's Kowloon district, provides a prison sentence of 10 months for "factual bigamy"; a single act of adultery is still not a crime. Under a new law in Guangdong province, which includes both Shenzhen and Dongguan, long-term cohabitation by an unmarried couple is now a crime and can bring a two-year sentence at a labor camp. However, the police face a near-insurmountable obstacle proving long-term cohabitation when a monthly lease or no lease enables a man to move his second wife to a new apartment on very short notice.

[The current separate legal jurisdictions of Hong Kong, Macao, and China also make prosecution very difficult. If a Hong Kong woman wants to take her bigamist husband into a Chinese court, she must first make sure that the Chinese police can prove that the husband is living with his mistress somewhere in one of the populous mainland villages of concubines (Landler 2000; Luk 2002). (*End of update by R. T. Francoeur*)]

## 6. Homoerotic, Homosexual, and Bisexual Behaviors

Because of the influence of the British laws, up to 1991, male homosexual practices in Hong Kong were illegal. Anal intercourse was punishable up to life imprisonment, while conviction for any act of "gross indecency" could bring up to two years' imprisonment. After 1991, consensual sexual conduct between two males aged 21 or older was decriminalized, following the provision of the Sexual Offenses Act of England (1967). This decriminalization has permitted Hong Kong homosexuals to "come out," the opening of homosexual bars, and the founding of a number of new homosexual societies.

There are now more than ten well-known gay bars in Hong Kong. Together with some special discos and sauna baths, there are places where male homosexuals and bisexuals get together to meet friends and spend their leisure. Lesbians have fewer venues to patronize. These are limited to a few bars, so-called lesbian karaokes, in Causeway Bay, a well-known shopping district in Hong Kong. Some selected public toilets are popular places for male homosexuals to find suitable partners. There are also magazines with personal advertisements that help homosexuals find partners or establish friendships. Homosexual erotica is available in adult shops, as well as on cable or interactive television.

The gay societies in Hong Kong are all voluntary organizations established by homosexuals and bisexuals. They provide mutual support, information, and social activities to their members. The oldest of these societies is the Ten Percent Club, established around 1984, with an academic flavor. The Horizon, established in 1992, provides professional hotline or face-to-face counseling and produces regular publications for members. After 1997, the Horizon began to receive sponsorship from the Home Affairs Bureau, Government of the Hong Kong Special Administrative Region. The Satanga, established in 1993, gives medical and psychological advice on the health of the homosexuals. Two lesbian groups, the Female Homosexual Club and Homosexual Sisters, were founded in 1996. Around the same time, a Christian homosexual group and a Buddhist homosexual group were also formed. There are no formal governmental agencies that serve specifically the needs of homosexuals. The idea is that it is less discriminative if the life problems of homosexuals are helped through the usual services provided to the general public.

Despite decriminalization, homosexuals still do not enjoy equal rights with heterosexuals in Hong Kong. They cannot be legally married or adopt children, and are barred from certain types of employment. In 1996, the government of Hong Kong started a public consultation to propose legislation to ban some types of discrimination on the ground of sexual orientation. Public opinions received were divided and the matter is still under consideration.

## 7. Gender Diversity and Transgender Issues

Hong Kong had its first sex-change surgery in 1981. In 1986, a special team for the evaluation and assessment of patients requesting sex change was established in Queen Mary Hospital. The team of psychologists, social workers, endocrinologists, lawyers, geneticists, gynecologists, and surgeons is headed by a psychiatrist. They provide the standard assessment and test procedures practiced internationally for gender-conflicted persons (Green & Money 1969). By the end of 1998, a total of 78 gender-conflicted patients had been assessed. Forty-eight had received sex-revision surgery and seven were still under evaluation. The numbers of patients who come to the team have remained rather stable throughout the years and so is the percentage that passed the assessment and was given the surgery. Since there is only one team in Hong Kong doing sex-revision surgery, it might be assumed that the team receives most of the transsexuals in the territory. Based on this assumption, the prevalence of clinically presented transsexualism in Hong Kong is estimated to be about one per 200,000.

With certification by an attending physician, transsexuals can have their names and identity cards changed to agree with their chosen gender, but legally, the law only recognizes and abides by a person's chromosomal sex in case of any judicial disputes. Hence, a male-to-female transsexual cannot be raped according to the legal definition of rape. The law also does not recognize or permit a marriage if one of the partners involved is a transsexual, because the law only recognizes heterosexual monogamy. Because of this legal non-recognition, a transsexual runs the risk of losing many of the social rights enjoyed by ordinary citizens, such as public housing, tax deductions, and children adoption for married couples. Any documents or contracts they sign may become legally invalid if they do not state their chromosomal sex on paper.

The discrimination against transsexuals has caused a lot of suffering to this minority group. In the series of transsexuals who have undergone sex-revision surgery on the recommendation of the Gender Identity Team, none has regretted receiving the surgery and all have found the post-surgical complications mild and tolerable. It is the social and legal discrimination that has caused in them the greatest tragedies. A female-to-male transsexual was turned down by the Marriage Registry at the last minute, after he had announced his marriage to all relatives and friends. A male-to-female transsexual killed herself after her cohabitation with a male was widely publicized in the tabloids.

Along with the legislative proposal under consideration banning discrimination based on sexual orientation, the Hong Kong government has started public consultation to propose legislation to ban some types of discrimination against transsexuals. However, the proposal focuses on superficial and trivial matters only. It does not say anything about the discrimination created by the legal adherence to chromosomal sex, which is the root of many other discriminations against transsexuals. The Gender Identity Team has recognized its duty to enhance public awareness of the problem of discrimination and the need to correct it. It has also organized self-support groups for pre- and post-surgical transsexuals. But all this work is still at its infancy and far from being successful to a desirable degree.

Cross-dressing is not illegal in Hong Kong and the law does not actively interfere with transsexuals as long as their appearances or behaviors do not upset public peace. However, they are given a strange eye socially, are often the subject of gossip and ridicule, and are disadvantaged at work and in social rights.

## 8. Significant Unconventional Sexual Behaviors

### A. Coercive Sex

*Child Sexual Abuse and Neglect*

Little is known about the type and extent of unconventional sexual behaviors such as child sexual abuse, sex crimes, and spouse sexual violence in Hong Kong. The issue of child abuse did not receive public attention until 1979 when the first comprehensive survey of 22 organizations involved in treating child abuse was conducted, with the aim to understand the prevalence of the problem and to develop better coordinated service for the abused children and their families (Mulvey 1997). In the 1979 survey conducted by the Hong Kong Council of Social Services, a total of 358 cases were identified. Cases of child neglect, that is, the failure to provide the child with adequate supervision, guidance, and care, constituted the largest category, 80.7% of cases reported, while sexual abuse cases accounted for only 4.2% of cases studied. However, the percentage of sexual abuse reported has increased from 4.2% in 1979 to 17.9% in 1995 (Tang & Davis 1996). The increase may probably be the result of increased awareness and reporting.

In a 1992 review of 134 sexual abuse cases by Ho and Mak-Lieh, the typical victims of sexual abuse were females with the mean age of 12.2; 96.3% of the perpetrators were male. These perpetrators are: the victims' friends or members of their household ($n = 96$, 64.2%), strangers ($n = 50$, 37.3%), father ($n = 16$, 11.9%), elder brother ($n = 4$, 3.0%), stepfather ($n = 2$, 1.5%), parents' cohabiters ($n = 2$, 1.5%), and unknown relationship ($n = 7$, 5.2%). Vaginal intercourse ($n = 93$, 69%) and inappropriate fondling ($n = 59$, 44%) were the most frequent types of abuses reported. Although these studies give us some information about the rate, patterns, and characteristics of child sexual abuse in Hong Kong, one has to be cautious of a bias of underreporting in interpreting these data. Chinese families tend to protect the reputation of the family rather than to fight for the welfare of the victim. Hence, Chinese families would be hesitant and reluctant to report any sexual abuse incident to helping professionals or the police, to avoid the family losing "face" and suffering shame and pain during the investigation.

In recent years, the government and voluntary organizations have invested considerable energy and resources in public education to increase public awareness of the problem of child sexual abuse. This has enabled the social work and legal circles to improve their methods of investigation, identification, and tracking processes for child sexual abuse cases. At the same time, considerations are given to minimize false accusations and psychological trauma to the child during the investigation and trial.

### Sexual Assaults

The rate of sex crimes is a frequently discussed topic, because many local moralists keep trying to use it as a reason for purging commercial sexual institutions, prostitutes, and pornography. The fact, however, is that there are as yet no reliable data to show that the rate of sexual offenses in Hong Kong is on the rise. There are only two sources from which reliable figures of sex crime rates can be obtained in Hong Kong, the annual reports of the Royal Hong Kong Police (on rape and sexual assault cases) and the Family Planning Association of Hong Kong on victims of sexual assault counseled (FPAHK 1988-1992). The police figures (Royal Hong Kong Police 1988 to 1997) show that in the ten years from 1988 to 1997, neither rape nor indecent assault cases, reported or ending in arrest, showed any clear evidence of a rise (see Table 1). From the data on sex criminals below the age of 16, there is no evidence also to support the fear or claim that the age of sex offenders is getting lower.

It might be argued that these official figures could not reflect the actual situation because they depend very much on self-reporting, which could be affected by a lot of social, legal, or psychological factors. However, without more reliable figures or any clear evidence that people are more or less reluctant about reporting sex crimes, one is at least justified stating that there is no proof to show that sex crimes are on the rise in Hong Kong.

### Marital Rape and Spousal Abuse

Domestic sexual violence has been a topic of concern in recent years in Hong Kong. The exact rate of this type of violence before 1980 is unknown, because it had not been surveyed and few people reported it to the police when it happened. In the service statistics of institutions that provide

### Table 1

### Annual Sex Crime Rates in Hong Kong (Police Figures)

| Year | Prosecuted Rape | | Prosecuted Indecent Assault | | Reported Rape | Reported Indecent Assault |
|---|---|---|---|---|---|---|
| 1998 | 81 | (4)* | 768 | (110)* | 90 | 1214 |
| 1997 | 89 | (9) | 753 | (85) | 74 | 1114 |
| 1996 | 67 | (6) | 776 | (98) | 86 | 1214 |
| 1995 | 102 | (6) | 744 | (96) | 103 | 1099 |
| 1994 | 84 | (0) | 677 | (113) | 100 | 1066 |
| 1993 | 97 | (5) | 607 | (76) | 103 | 1030 |
| 1992 | 86 | (3) | 611 | (57) | 116 | 1099 |
| 1991 | 86 | (10) | 655 | (81) | 114 | 1101 |
| 1990 | 109 | (10) | 659 | (80) | 111 | 1078 |
| 1989 | 101 | (5) | 584 | (77) | 120 | 1019 |
| 1988 | 92 | (7) | 479 | (38) | 97 | 922 |

*Figures in parentheses are the numbers of offenders below age 16.
(*Source*: Royal Hong Kong Police Annual Reports 1988 to 1998)

counseling and asylum to battered wives, such as Harmony House and Wai On House, the average annual number of admissions was around 300 cases for 1986 and 1987 (Yeung 1991; Tang 1994). The official data may not reveal its actual prevalence in society. As estimated by a current survey among 246 female and 136 male undergraduate students at a local university (Tang 1994), 14% of the respondents' parents have made use of physical force against each other; the rate of spouse aggression is comparable to that reported in the United States.

Among the various forms of family violence, there has been an increasing number of spouses who reported having been sexually assaulted by their partners in recent years. In 1998, sexual violence occurred in 6.5% of all the spouse violence cases handled by Harmony House, and the assault was invariably associated with other types of non-sexual bodily or psychological violence. It took the form of forced sexual intercourse, genital injury, or other forced sexual behavior. The victims were predominantly female (96.08%) and mostly between age 30 and 40 (41.7%). Women experiencing spouse abuse ($n = 21$) were the most depressed and anxious, in comparison to those women seeking help from family service for other marital problems ($n = 20$) and the normal group ($n = 18$) (Tang 1997). Local scholars (Tang 1994, 1997) argue that patriarchal beliefs and values from traditional Chinese culture have legitimized and sanctioned men's use of violence toward their wives. However, Hong Kong people are also subjected to the influence of Western values, such as individualism, autonomy, and feminism. Spouse sexual abuse is a complex issue. It is likely to be the result of the interactions among forces at different levels: the individual, family, and society.

### B. Prostitution

Following Chinese tradition, prostitution was initially legal in Hong Kong. It was made a crime only after 1935 when Britain began to ban prostitution. However, the *Crimes (Sexual Offences) Ordinance* (Hong Kong Government 1980) is not exactly aimed at the prostitutes. It only punishes those who run brothels, or live wholly or partly on the earnings of prostitution. That means, if a prostitute appears to be just working on her (or his) own, she or he can still make a living without being prosecuted. Hence, although prostitution is illegal in Hong Kong, with the existence of the black market as well as independent operators, it is not difficult to find prostitutes. And, they do have rather good business. The Family Planning Association of Hong Kong (FPAHK) survey in 1996 showed that 10.2% of males up to the age of 27 got their first sexual experience with prostitutes and 13.9% had had sexual intercourse with at least one prostitute. (See also Sections 1/2A and E, Basic Sexological Premises and Religious, Ethnic, and Gender Factors Affecting Sexuality above.)

Pearson and Yu's study (1995) of eight prostitutes on the streets of a working-class area in Kowloon reveals that these women entered into the trade voluntarily in the face of negative life events, such as sudden widowhood or heavy gambling debts. Working on the street as a commercial sex worker enabled them to earn "quick" money, exert control in the choices of their customers, and, most importantly, to pay off the significant debts. Use of soft drugs or alcohol was common. Perceiving themselves as forever polluted, they hid their professional status from their spouses, children, and parents. Despite of the lack of trust toward their customers, a few of them could develop genuine affection with their customers.

Since the prostitutes have to practice semi-secretly, their business could only have very poor quality control. There is no way to obtain a reliable figure on their number in Hong Kong or to monitor their service to ensure their safety or that of their clients. The public generally looks down on the profession. Supported by this attitude, the law enforcers could still have many ways to legally harass the prostitutes, for example, by arresting them for aiding or abetting the commission of other offenses, for indecent behavior or exposure in public, or for "loitering" or soliciting for immoral purposes. In 1995, a well-intentioned social worker organized a small work-union type of association for the prostitutes to help them fight for civil and legal rights. The group is growing and its voices are heard more year after year.

[*Update 1997*: In 1997, investigative journalist Kate Whitehead and top Asian writer Nury Vittachi published *After Suzie: Sex in South China*, their report of the sex industry in and around Hong Kong. After reviewing the colonial history of prostitution, Whitehead and Vittachi detailed the state of the sex tourism business in the mid-1990s in Wan Chai at Mong Kok, Hong Kong's real sex center, the hostess bars, fishball stalls, and the world of expensive escorts and gigolos after the 1950-to-1970 days of Suzie Wong, Hong Kong's fictional prostitute made famous by Hollywood and Broadway. (*End of update by R. T. Francoeur*)]

## C. Pornography

Pornography is officially regulated by two government authorities, the Obscene and Indecent Articles Tribunal and the Television and Entertainment Licensing Authority (TELA). These two agencies interpret and apply two ordinances passed in 1995 toward the end of British rule (Hong Kong Government 1995ab).

The Obscene and Indecent Articles Tribunal monitors printed matters, exhibits, and electronic publications (such as videotapes and computer programs). It does not pre-censor materials, but has the authority to grade them to the effect of declaring whether they are suitable, if at all, to be made available to people of a certain age group. There are essentially three grades: the obscene grade that is totally unsuitable for any person, the indecent grade suitable for adults above 18 years of age only, and the all-age grade for people of any age. Any person found by the police, the tribunal staff, or any member of the public to have printed, published, or distributed materials of the obscene grade or of the indecent grade to underage people will be committing an offense punishable by law. Hence, before printing or marketing any sexually explicit materials, a publisher would be wise to apply for an examination and grading from the Tribunal beforehand unless he or she can judge from personal experience and knowledge of the public standard to which grading it is likely to belong. To grade material, the Tribunal calls upon a group of adjudicators consisting of a magistrate and two or more lay adjudicators appointed by the government from a list of volunteers from the general public. The grading takes about two weeks, and can be speeded up if necessary, for which the Tribunal charges a small fee.

The Television and Entertainment Licensing Authority (TELA) monitors movies, radio and television programs, shows, and theatrical and related productions. The grades for these materials are slightly different from those for printed matter. They include: the all-age grade, the parental-guidance grades A and B, and the adults-only grade that must not be shown or distributed to people below 18. Movies have to be censored before public showing. For other materials where pre-censorship is not practical, the principles for printed matters apply. That is, the producer will be punished and the broadcast terminated if found to have gone beyond an adjudicated grade. The TELA adjudicators are also appointed volunteers from the general public, but it

is different from the Tribunal, with their number for each production larger (nine nonofficial members and an ex-officio member, who is a secretary for Information Technology and Broadcasting). A magistrate is not required.

The sentiments of the adjudicators are supposed to represent the standard of the general public, but because each adjudication can be made by a different group of people, the standard cannot be perfectly uniform, and unexpected grading does come up from time to time. A work of art, e.g., a plain photograph of Michelangelo's *David* in a newspaper, was once rated to be indecent. Appeals for an adjudication review is time-consuming, expensive, and rarely successful. There are still frequent public debates on how to make this monitoring system more fair and reliable, with the least interference on the freedom of speech and publication. The authorities are willing to listen and are always finding ways to improve the system according to public needs.

Despite laws to prevent youngsters from having access to pornographic materials, the FPAHK Annual Report (1996) showed that they are not very effective. About 1% of the males surveyed reported that they started viewing pornography as young as 7 years old. The mode was 15 for males and 18 for females. Also, 34% of males and 6% of females had bought pornographic materials when under the age of 18.

# 9. Contraception, Abortion, and Population Planning

## A. Contraception

Contraception is widely practiced by Hong Kong people. This is partly because of the hard and successful publicity work of the Family Planning Association of Hong Kong (FPAHK), and partly because of the reality needs in a crowded city. The accepted motto to follow is, "Two (children) are enough." Couples of higher social status and education tend to want only one child. As a result, Hong Kong has kept its annual natural population growth down below 1% for more than 20 years. The 1995 total fertility rate for Hong Kong was 1.3 children per fertile woman, ranking Hong Kong 220 among 227 nations.

The most popular contraceptive method is the oral contraceptive pill, used by 50.1% of ever-users of contraceptives. The oral contraceptive is available over the counter, without prescription. The male condom is used by 32.4%, the rhythm method or natural family planning, by 5.9%, the intrauterine device by 3.9%, injections or implantables by 3.3%, and female sterilization by 1.6% (FPAHK 1993). Vasectomy is the least popular contraceptive method.

## B. Abortion

In essence, there are three conditions for legal abortion in Hong Kong:

1. approval from two medical doctors to verify that the pregnant woman or the child will be in physical or mental or social danger if the pregnancy continues or is allowed to come to delivery;
2. the pregnant woman is under 16 years old; or
3. there is evidence that the pregnancy is a result of rape or incest.

Most educated women know these conditions. Among those who have been pregnant, 22% have experienced an induced abortion and the rate is increasing. Younger females with lower income tend to have a higher incidence of having an induced abortion (FPAHK 1993). However, only about 45% of abortions that the women received were legal abortions, because illegal abortions are readily available and convenient in secret clinics in Hong Kong (15%) or in proper hospitals in mainland China (25%). An abortion round trip to China needs only one day. The laws there are much more lenient and the costs lower.

## C. Population Programs

As noted above, Hong Kong's total fertility rate of 1.3 children per fertile woman, well below replacement level, makes it one of the slowest growing countries in the world. In the future, the demographic shift from a youthful population to a graying population is bound to result in major societal disruptions and adjustments.

[*Update 2003*: While Hong Kong remains one of the most crowded cities on earth, it has become concerned with a steep decline in its birthrate; the current birthrate is 0.9 children per fertile woman, well below the replacement level of 2.1. In February 2003, the government announced a policy to begin accepting immigrants based partly on their wealth and talents. Adjustments in the tax policies were announced to offer the same tax deductions for all children and to end the current policy of offering smaller deductions for third and subsequent children.

[Employers of foreign domestic helpers will now be taxed, and the minimum wage for such helpers reduced by an equal amount. Hong Kong's population of 7 million includes nearly 240,000 foreign maids, mainly from the Philippines, and they are encountering resentment because of high unemployment among native-born residents.

[Hong Kong's immigration policies have long been criticized for allowing mainland residents to settle here permanently—150 a day, almost all spouses or children of current Hong Kong residents. Despite this emphasis on the reunification of families, mainland residents can wait up to a decade for permission to move here. There has been heavy intermarriage across the border since Britain handed over Hong Kong to China in 1997. Businesses claim this makes it hard for them to transfer experienced professionals here if they are mainland citizens. The new rules create a new category to permit mainland managers and professionals to move here. Immigrants, other than those from the mainland, will also be allowed to settle here if they invest at least $833,000. Singapore, Australia, Canada, Britain, and other countries also have special immigration rules for people who invest large sums, and the United States is discussing this approach (Bradsher 2002). (*End of update by R. T. Francoeur*)]

## *10. Sexually Transmitted Diseases and HIV/AIDS*

### A. Sexually Transmitted Diseases

Government statistics in Table 2 show that traditional types of sexually transmitted diseases are rather well con-

trolled in Hong Kong. This could be because of the generally effective therapies available and the good public knowledge about precautions. But government statistics are not reliable in this respect, because many people go to the offices of private practitioners for treatment and these cannot be recorded.

### B. HIV/AIDS

#### *HIV/AIDS Incidence*

The statistics on HIV/AIDS come from voluntary reporting since 1984. The cumulative number of HIV/AIDS cases as of June 1998, and some analysis, are shown in Table 3. The trend is an increasing number of HIV/AIDS cases reported year after year, with a continued narrowing of the male-to-female ratio of new HIV infections. Mother-to-baby transmissions have been found only in the last five years and number between one to two cases per year. The number of HIV cases in homosexuals and bisexuals has continued to rise, but its ratio with heterosexual cases was inverted after 1989.

#### *HIV/AIDS Prevention*

There are four basic components in the strategies for AIDS prevention, care, and control in Hong Kong. The first is to prevent its transmission by the providing of transmission information and education to bring about behavioral modification, as well as early detection and treatment of sexually transmitted diseases. Secondly, the AIDS-care programs aim to relieve physical and psychological suffering. A third component focuses on understanding better the dimensions and impact of HIV/AIDS in Hong Kong—epidemiological surveillance studies and monitoring are conducted regularly to obtain useful and accurate information about HIV/AIDS distribution in the community. The fourth component consists of partnerships, with the community and internationally, to bring about a coherent and constantly updated method of prevention and control. These strategies are carried out jointly by governmental and nongovernmental organizations (NGOs). The main governmental organizations come under the Department of Health. They are the AIDS Hotline, for public education, and the AIDS Unit, for

#### Table 3

**Cumulative Reported HIV/AIDS Statistics from 1984 to June 1998**

|  | HIV+ | AIDS |
|---|---|---|
| **Sex** | | |
| Male | 912 | 314 |
| Female | 154 | 35 |
| **Ethnicity/Race** | | |
| Chinese | 732 | 261 |
| Non-Chinese | 334 | 88 |
| **Age at Diagnosis** | | |
| Adult | 1,039 | 349 |
| Age 13 or less | 27 | 6 |
| **Exposure category** | | |
| Heterosexual | 579 | 200 |
| Homosexual | 239 | 82 |
| Bisexual | 58 | 24 |
| Injection drug user | 17 | 5 |
| Blood products | 67 | 16 |
| Perinatal | 6 | 2 |
| Undetermined | 100 | 20 |
| Total | 1,066 | 349 |

(Department of Health 1998)

#### Table 2

**Annual Number of New Cases of Gonorrhea and Syphilis Treated in Public Hospitals, Correctional Institutions, and Private Hospitals from 1990 to 1997**

|  | 1990 | 1991 | 1992 | 1993 | 1994 | 1995 | 1996 | 1997 |
|---|---|---|---|---|---|---|---|---|
| Syphilis | 87 | 100 | 78 | 94 | 133 | 147 | 129 | 153 |
| Male Deaths | 3 | 1 | 2 | 1 | 4 | 3 | 0 | 0 |
| Female Deaths | 1 | 0 | 0 | 0 | 2 | 0 | 0 | 1 |
| Gonorrhea | 22 | 11 | 11 | 8 | 20 | 17 | 12 | 19 |

(Hong Kong Government Department of Health statistics 1990-1997)

the screening and treatment of AIDS patients. On the non-governmental side, there are the Hong Kong AIDS Foundation, which centralizes and distributes public donations for running AIDS education, counseling, or research programs, AIDS Concern, to give assistance to AIDS patients and their relatives, and TeenAIDS, which runs AIDS educational programs for the youngsters. The government Secretariat has an Advisory Council, comprising AIDS experts from various fields, to advise on the implementation and coordination of all these organizations and strategies.

[*Update 2002*: UNAIDS Epidemiological Assessment: Since the first HIV/AIDS cases were reported in 1984, there has been a slow increase in reported cases in Hong Kong, China. At the end of June 2001, 1,636 cases (including 524 AIDS cases) had been reported. The best estimate of HIV prevalence as of 2000 was about 2,500. Although there is a steady increase in the number of HIV cases, the prevalence rate is estimated to be less than 0.1% in the adult population. The majority of reported cases occurred among men (82%). Mode of transmission was largely through either heterosexual contact (57%) or homo-/bisexual contact (24%).

[STDs are reported only from social hygiene clinics (SHC), with data showing an increase in reported STDs over time. Periodic surveys of private medical practitioners are conducted to complement passive STD surveillance. However, it appears that only about 20% of all STDs are taken care of by public doctors. Gonococcal antimicrobial resistance has increased. Data on HIV/STD risk behavior are available through monitoring of STD patients, methadone clinic attendees, and prison inmates.

[The estimated number of adults and children living with HIV/AIDS on January 1, 2002, were:

| | | |
|---|---|---|
| Adults ages 15-49: | 2,600 | (rate: 0.1%) |
| Women ages 15-49: | 660 | |
| Children ages 0-15: | < 100 | |

[An estimated less than 100 adults and children died of AIDS during 2001.

[No estimate is available for the number of children who had lost one or both parents to AIDS and were under age 15 at the end of 2001. (*End of update by the Editors*)]

## 11. Sexual Dysfunctions, Counseling, and Therapies

Before the advent of the modern sex therapies in the 1970s, the treatment and counseling of people with sexual dysfunctions relied mainly on folk medicine or traditional Chinese medicine. These treatment methods included the use of herbs, health tonics, physical exercise (e.g., Kung-Fu) or breathing exercises (e.g., Chi-Kung), acupuncture, acupressure, and sex aids. There is some evidence that some of these modalities are effective (Ng 1988), and they are still used by many in Hong Kong (Liu & Ng 1995; Rosenthal 1999). Supportive psychotherapy and anxiolytic drugs are also used.

The first sex clinic to offer the Western type of sex therapy in Hong Kong was established about 1979 as a part of the general psychiatric clinic in the Department of Psychiatry at Queen Mary Hospital. The clinic receives referrals from all other clinics for cases of sexual dysfunction, paraphilia, and miscellaneous sexual problems. Referrals in the early years were few, but they have increased steadily. The male-to-female ratio of initial presenters has also changed from 5:1 in 1977 to around 2:1 in 1997, showing a rising awareness and initiative among females in understanding and meeting their sexual needs and rights. There has been a gradual change in the types of cases attending the sex clinic too. For males, the most common cases have

changed from retarded or inhibited ejaculation to erectile dysfunction. For females, the shift has been from vaginismus to general sexual dissatisfaction. These changes are found to be associated with a diversification of referral sources, which indicates a general awareness by the medical profession and general public of the effectiveness of the Western type of sex therapy in dealing with a variety of sexual problems (Ng 1990b).

Despite this increasing demand, only one other formal sex clinic has been established. This clinic, established in 1997, will be discussed in the next section. Other less specialized or comprehensive sex therapy or counseling is offered by social workers or psychologists in private practice or in non-profit organizations, such as the Family Planning Association of Hong Kong, the Social Welfare Department, and agencies for the mentally or physically handicapped. Some psychiatrists, gynecologists, and family physicians have also gained a reputation for being able to provide sexual counseling. Urologists, of course, have always helped to manage a large share of erectile dysfunction cases that are principally of organic origin.

All types of medication found to be useful for erectile dysfunction are used in Hong Kong, including intracavernosal injection or urethral insertion of prostaglandin E1. Most recently, in February 1999, Sildenafil (Viagra) was approved and, as in many other places, the drug has caused sensational public reaction even before its approval, leading to abuses and illicit sales. However, there have not been any reported cases of death or severe complications because of the drug up to the time of writing (April 1999). The government has imposed strict regulations on the prescription and dispensing of Viagra to prevent abuses.

## 12. Sex Research and Advanced Professional Education

### A. Advanced Sexuality Education

There is no sex education on the advanced level. Different faculties in different universities run their own sex courses to meet the specialized needs of their students. The advanced sex education course with the longest history at a tertiary institution is the Human Sexuality Course in the Medical Faculty of the University of Hong Kong. It was started in 1981 by the Department of Obstetrics and Gynecology and was taken over by the Department of Psychiatry in 1990. Its aim is to provide the medical students with a basic understanding of the interdisciplinary nature of the study of human sexuality and its relation to the practice of medicine. The course is run at the end of the third year of the medical curriculum and lasts for five half-days (about 20 hours). The topics include introduction to medical sexology, Chinese sexual attitudes and practices, sexual philosophy, social construction of sexuality, psychosexual development and sex education, sexual variations, forensic sexology, sexual attitude reappraisal, sexual problems in medical practice, clinical sexual interview, introduction to sex therapy, sexology, and AIDS. The teaching format consists of lectures, video demonstrations, intranet computer-interactive teaching, group discussion, opinion polling, and role-plays. Besides medical practitioners, non-medical specialists, including a social worker, a philosopher, educators, and psychologists participate in the teaching significantly. Prominent sexologists from different parts of the world have been invited regularly to take part and to advise on the teaching as well. This has helped to ensure the quality of the course and to regularly update its contents. From the post-course feedback, it has been found to be one of the favorite courses for the students.

There are other sexuality courses in other departments or universities, but they are of shorter history and less systematic, usually focusing on areas of direct interest to the discipline concerned. For instance, in 1993-1994, a general education course known as Sexuality and Culture was started at the Chinese University of Hong Kong, with the aim to equip the undergraduate students with a cultural perspective on human sexuality. This course was stopped in 1995 and was reintroduced in 1998 upon the request of the students. The popularity of this course can be reflected by the fact that over 100 students attended.

Even less systematic are those short or part-time courses organized ad hoc by health or family planning agencies. These courses do not have set structures, formats, or content, but are run to meet immediate social or professional needs only.

Generally, although advanced sexuality courses in Hong Kong are improving both in quantity and quality, sexology in Hong Kong has not been recognized for its value and deserved status. There is no advanced sexuality program that can lead to a separately recognized degree in sexology or sex education, although a postgraduate student can take up a sexuality subject as a research project for a master's or doctoral thesis.

### B. Sexual Medicine and Research

Hong Kong has been proud of its medical services. It is the first Chinese community in the world to provide valuable and verifiable organized service for sexual problems. The excellence of this service has been well supported for a long time by statistics on obstetric care, infant mortality, neonatal care, population control, and the treatment and prevention of sexually transmitted diseases (Ng 1990a). The sex clinic in Hong Kong, set up in 1979, was the first in Chinese communities. It was also in Hong Kong that the first Chinese sexology association, the Hong Kong Sex Education Association, was set up in 1985. The Association was instrumental in the formation of the Asian Federation for Sexology in 1992. Despite an early start, the subsequent growth of sexual medicine in the territory has been slow. Besides the clinics run by traditional healers, there is only one sex clinic in the public hospitals in Hong Kong, established in 1997. Aside from the gynecologists and urologists with partial interests in sexual problems, only one new medical doctor has specialized in the field of medical sexology and sex therapy. A sex clinic needs not just a doctor and a consultation room, but also nurses, social workers, psychologists, technicians, and many other auxiliary personnel, as well as laboratories, drugs, reading materials, instructions, and treatment devices that can be easily accessed by the public. Patients also have to know where and when to come, and they need to not be too shy to come. All these require a sexually enlightened and open atmosphere.

[*Update 1997*: In understanding the uniqueness of sexology in Hong Kong and the conflicting currents that have inevitably had an impact on Hong Kong culture as its people moved from being a British colony into the People's Republic of China, it is important to remember that in democratic societies, the majority decides how the public should be governed, and the lay and nonprofessional perspectives prevail, as a safeguard against the pitfalls of professionalism and authoritarian government. Although the experts have the cutting-edge knowledge and skill, they need to be sensitive to the historical, political, and emotional elements involved in making public decisions.

[Frustrated as professionals may be at times by the obstacles and the resulting inclination to ventilate, influencing public health policy decisions requires another set of per-

spectives and skills. These include an understanding of the dynamics and processes involved in dealing with controversial and polemical political issues and in testing the applicability of new ideas in certain frameworks. More time, effort, and patience are required for more progress—as well as more communication, lobbying, the alignment of support groups, and the creation of new coalitions. Cooperative alliances are particularly effective, especially when they bring together the collaborative skills of professionals and laypersons and facilitate the exchange of ideas. (*End of update by M. P. Lau*)]

Like all other societies making a start on sex research, Hong Kong spends quite a lot of effort on sexuality surveys to understand the basic sexual characteristics of its people. These surveys have ranged from the broad knowledge, attitudes, beliefs, and practices surveys to specific ones focusing on the consumption of pornography, experience, and attitudes toward rape (Cheng, Ip, & Cheung 1984; Cheung, Audry, & Tam 1990), sexual harassment (Tang, Yik, Cheung, Choi, & Au 1995), child sexual abuses (Tang & Davis 1996), homosexuality, gender inequality (Westwood, Ngo, & Leung 1997), and sex among the disabled and the mentally handicapped. Some of these surveys are commissioned by the government to guide its social or health policies, some by voluntary agencies to evaluate their work, some by religious or political groups to support their views and affirmations, and some are sponsored by academics with theoretical interests. The quality of these surveys is very variable. The religious and political surveys are well known to be very unscientific. They use vague and broad definitions and unrepresentative samples. Good surveys should satisfy international standards and their data should be suitable for cross-cultural comparisons.

Clinical sexuality research has focused on the development and application of sex therapy, family therapy, and psychotherapy, drugs and devices in the treatment of sexual dysfunction, and transgender problems. There is also sexuality research into the biomedical aspects of sexuality, such as research on sexually transmissible infections, contraception, assisted reproduction, prostate and penile surgery, sex hormones, and women's health. As in most other countries, it is difficult to obtain funding for sexuality research in Hong Kong. Research studies on sexual behavior, psychology, and sexual minorities are often thought to be unimportant and unscientific, and attract little financial support unless they are done for specific political or ideological causes. This is a principal reason for the highly uneven quality of sexuality research in Hong Kong.

## *Conclusion*

Hong Kong is a very special place as far as the evolution of understanding sexuality is concerned. One finds Hong Kong very sexually open if one reads the newspapers, watches the "illegal" videotapes or disks that are easily available in street shops, listens to sexual discussions on the radio and television, experiences how easy it is to find casual or commercial sex, and follows the lifestyles of some of the movie stars and socialites. On the other hand, the laws are strict, voices for sexual conservatism are loud, and sex education activities or serious discussion of sexual matters are difficult to find. Such a sexuality split is found probably in many other communities around the world, but it is certainly very strong in Hong Kong. This could be because of the strong influences of both the Chinese and Western civilizations, which often clash vigorously with each other, creating difficult choices for the common people. Luckily, and probably because of the high level of mutual tolerance in the Chinese, open physical violence between antagonistic camps has rarely, if ever, occurred. This type of sexuality environment should make Hong Kong a particularly interesting place for sexologists to study, to see how sexual diversities can coexist peacefully and be properly managed and promote growth.

[*Comment 1997*: In commenting on this summary of sexuality in Hong Kong, M. P. Lau, coauthor of the China chapter and a native of Hong Kong, emphasized that "in spite of on-going conflicts and some set-backs, amazing progress has been made in Hong Kong so that there are many reasons to be optimistic and upbeat. Admittedly, the people of Hong Kong, and pioneers in sexology like Emil Man-lun Ng and Joyce L. C. Ma, have found themselves confronted with double messages, conflicting views, inconsistent commandments, and ambiguous role models, out of which they have struggled to emerge with decisions for action. Both professionals and laypeople in Hong Kong have witnessed the struggle and the dissonance, the casualties and sufferings, the resolution and reintegration, however idiosyncratic these may be. The crises and opportunities in Hong Kong, a crucible of diverse worldviews and ideologies, some very fascinating, invite further scrutiny and empirical endeavors." (*End of comment by R. T. Francoeur*)]

## References and Suggested Readings

Bradsher, K. 2003 (February 23). Hong Kong moves to raise birth rate and richer immigrants. *The New York Times*, p. A17.

Census and Statistical Department. 1996. *Population by census: Summary results*. Hong Kong: Hong Kong Government.

Chung, S. F., & E. Fung. 1999. *Survey on women and AIDS: AIDS knowledge, attitudes, opinions, about condom use and practice with spouse or sexual partner(s)*. Hong Kong: St. John's Cathedral HIV Information and Drop-In Centre.

CIA. 2002 (January). *The world factbook 2002*. Washington, DC: Central Intelligence Agency. Available: http://www.cia.gov/cia/publications/factbook/index.html.

Department of Health. 1998. *Hong Kong STD/AIDS update. 4: 3:2. 1998*. Hong Kong: Department of Health, Hong Kong Special Administrative Region Government.

Education Department. 1986. *Guidelines on sex education in secondary schools*. Hong Kong: Education Department, Hong Kong Government.

Education Department. 1994. *A study on knowledge and attitudes of secondary school pupils on sex and sex education*. Hong Kong: Education Department, Hong Kong Government.

Fan, M. S., J. H. Hong, M. L. Ng, L. K. C. Lee, P. K. Lui, & Y. H. Choy. 1995. Western influences on Chinese sexuality: Insight from a comparison of the sexual behavior and attitudes of Shanghai and Hong Kong freshmen at universities. *Journal of Sex Education and Therapy*, 21(3):158-166.

FPAHK. (Family Planning Association of Hong Kong). 1988 to 1998. *Annual report*. Hong Kong: Family Planning Association of Hong Kong.

FPAHK. 1981. *Hong Kong school youths*. Hong Kong: Family Planning Association of Hong Kong.

FPAHK. 1986. *Adolescent sexuality study*. Hong Kong: Family Planning Association of Hong Kong.

FPAHK. 1991a. *Youth sexuality study, in-school youth*. Hong Kong: Family Planning Association of Hong Kong.

FPAHK. 1991b. *Youth sexuality study, out-school youth*. Hong Kong: Family Planning Association of Hong Kong.

FPAHK. 1993. *Report on women's health survey*. Hong Kong: Family Planning Association of Hong Kong.

FPAHK. 1998. *Youth sexuality study 1996*. Hong Kong: Family Planning Association of Hong Kong.

Green, R., & J. Money, eds. 1969. *Transsexualism and sex reassignment*. Baltimore: Johns Hopkins Press.

Hong, J. H., M. S. Fan, M. L. Ng, L. K. C. Lee, P. K. Lui, & Y. H. Choy. 1994. Sexual attitudes and behavior of Chinese university students in Shanghai. *Journal of Sex Education and Therapy*, 20(4):277-286.

Hong Kong Government. 1980. *Crimes (sexual offences) ordinance*. Hong Kong: Hong Kong Government.

Hong Kong Government. 1995a. *Control of obscene and indecent articles ordinance (revised)*. Hong Kong: Hong Kong Government.

Hong Kong Government. 1995b. *Film censorship ordinance (revised)*. Hong Kong: Hong Kong Government.

Hong Kong Government and the Hong Kong Special Administrative Region Government. 1988, 1997. *Against child abuse society: 1988, 1997. Annual reports*. Hong Kong: Hong Kong Government.

Hong Kong Police. 1997, 1998. *Annual report*. Hong Kong: Hong Kong Special Administrative Region Government.

Hong Kong Special Administrative Region Government. 1998. *Hong Kong monthly digest of statistics: August*. Hong Kong: Special Administrative Region Government.

Hong Kong Tertiary Institutions Health Care Working Group. 1991. Survey on sexual behavior of students in tertiary institutions in Hong Kong. Unpublished data.

Landler, M. 2000 (August 14). Dongguan journal: For Hong Kong men, mistresses on the mainland. *The New York Times*.

Liu, D. L., M. L. & Ng. 1995. Sexual dysfunction in China. *Annuals of the Academy of Medicine of Singapore*, 24:728-731.

Liu, D. L., M. L. Ng, L. P. Chou, & E. Haeberle. 1997. *Sexual behavior in modern China—A report of the nationwide "Sex Civilization Survey" on 20,000 subjects in China*. New York: Continuum.

Lui, P. K., C. F. Cheung, K. L. Chan, & M. L. Ng. 1993. Differential erosion of three traditional Chinese sexual values in Hong Kong. In: M. L. Ng & L. S. Lam, eds., *Sexuality in Asia* (pp. 21-32). Hong Kong: Hong Kong College of Psychiatrists.

Luk, H. 2002 (August 29). Hard times for economy and amour. *Newark [New Jersey] Star-Ledger*, p. 2.

Ng, M. L. 1988. Transsexualism—Service and problems in Hong Kong. *The Hong Kong Practitioners*, 11(12):591-602.

Ng, M. L. 1990a. Sexual problems in Hong Kong—A medical perspective. In: M. L. Ng, ed., *Sexuality in dissent* (pp. 198-210, in Chinese). Hong Kong: Commercial Press.

Ng, M. L. 1990b. Sex therapy for the Chinese in Hong Kong. *Sexual and Marital Therapy*, 3(2):245-252.

Ng, M. L. 1998. School and public sexuality education in Hong Kong. *Journal of Asian Sexology*, 1:32-4.

Pau, W. N. 1991. Sex education in schools and its outcome. In: Hong Kong Federation of Sex Educators and Hong Kong Education Resource Centre, eds., *An analysis of Hong Kong education* (pp. 377-385, in Chinese). Hong Kong: Wide Angle Press.

Pearson, V. 1998. The mental health of women in China. *Hong Kong Journal of Psychiatry*, 8(1):3-8.

Pearson, V., & R. Y. M. Yu. 1995. Business and pleasure: Aspects of the commercial sex industry. In: V. Pearson & B. K. P. Leung, eds., *Women in Hong Kong* (pp. 244-275). Hong Kong: Oxford University Press.

Rosenthal, E. 1999, April 11. Seriously, China learning sex is fun. *The New York Times*, p. 6.

Royal Hong Kong Police. 1988-1997. *Annual reports*. Hong Kong: Hong Kong Government.

Tang, C. S. K. 1994. Prevalence of spouse aggression in Hong Kong. *Journal of Family Violence*, 9(4):347-356.

Tang, C. S. K., M. S. M. Yik, F. M. C. Cheung, P. K. Choi, & K. C. Au. 1995. How do Chinese college students define sexual harassment? *Journal of Interpersonal Violence*, 10(4):503-515.

Tang, C. S. K. 1997. Psychological impact of wife abuse—Experiences of Chinese women and their children. *Journal of Interpersonal Violence*, 12(3):466-478.

Tang, C. S. K., & C. Davis. 1996. Child abuse in Hong Kong revisited after 15 years: Characteristics of victims and abusers. *Child Abuse and Neglect, 20*(12):1213-1218.

UNAIDS. 2002. *Epidemiological fact sheets by country.* Geneva, Switzerland: Joint United Nations Programme on HIV/AIDS (UNAIDS/WHO). Available: http://www.unaids.org/hivaidsinfo/statistics/fact_sheets/index_en.htm.

Westwood, R. I., H. Y. Ngo, & S. M. Leung. 1997. The politics of opportunity: Gender and work in Hong Kong. In: F. M. Cheung, ed., *Engendering Hong Kong society* (pp. 41-100). Hong Kong: The Chinese University Press.

Whitehead, K., & N. Vittachi. 1997. *After Suzie: Sex in South China.* Hong Kong: Corporate Communications/A Chameleon Book.

Wong, W. L. E. 1996. *To talk or not to talk—A study of the knowledge, communication pattern and expectation about sex of couples preparing for marriage* (M.S.W. dissertation). Hong Kong: Department of Social Work and Social Administration, University of Hong Kong.

Yeung, C. 1991. Wife abuse: A brief historical review on research and intervention. *Hong Kong Journal of Social Work, 25*:29-37.

Yip, P. S. F. 1995. *Suicides in Hong Kong: 1981-1994.* Hong Kong: Department of Statistics, University of Hong Kong.

Young, K. P. H, B. C. H. Chau, C. K. Li, L. Y. Y. Tai, V. P. L. Yim, & W. Y. Cheung. 1995. *Study on marriages affected by extramarital affairs.* Hong Kong: Family Service, Caritas-HK.

# Iceland

## (*Lýðveldið Ísland*)
## (The Republic of Iceland)

Sóley S. Bender, R.N., B.S.N., M.S., Coordinator,*
with Sigrún Júlíusdóttir, Ph.D., Thorvaldur Kristinsson,
Haraldur Briem, M.D., and Gudrún Jónsdóttir, Ph.D.
*Updates by the Editors*

## Contents

## *Demographics and a Brief Historical Perspective*

SÓLEY S. BENDER

### A. Demographics

Iceland is an island nation located just south of the Arctic Circle in the North Atlantic Ocean. Geographically isolated until 870 when the first settlers arrived, Iceland's nearest neighbors are Greenland about 190 miles (305 km) to the northwest, Norway about 620 miles (1,000 km) to the east, and the United Kingdom 500 miles (800 km) to the south. Iceland's total land area is just under 40,000 square miles (103,000 km²), with a coastline of 3,100 miles (4,990 km), making it slightly smaller than the state of Kentucky. About 65% of the country is mountainous, with glacial rivers coursing through sandy deserts and lava fields. About 11% of Iceland is covered with glaciers (Hagstofa Íslands 1998).

There are innumerable hot springs both in the lowlands and in the mountains. Natural hot water is used to heat houses. There are many geysers in Iceland, the most famous being the Great Geyser in Haukadalur, which gives its name to geysers all over the world. The Gulf Stream makes Iceland's climate much warmer than the name suggests. Icelanders import grain and vegetables, but are self-sufficient in meat and dairy products.

In July 2002, Iceland had an estimated population of 279,384. (All data are from *The World Factbook 2002* (CIA 2002) unless otherwise stated.)

**Age Distribution and Sex Ratios**: *0-14 years*: 23% with 1.07 male(s) per female (sex ratio); *15-64 years*: 65.1% with 1.02 male(s) per female; *65 years and over*:

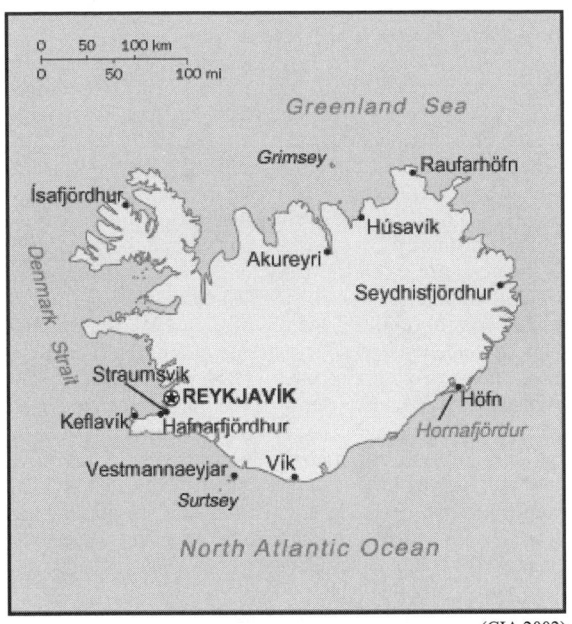

(CIA 2002)

11.9% with 0.81 male(s) per female; *Total population sex ratio*: 1 male(s) to 1 female

**Life Expectancy at Birth**: *Total Population*: 79.52 years; *male*: 77.31 years; *female*: 81.92 years

**Urban/Rural Distribution**: 92% to 8%. In 1999, 61.5% of Icelanders lived in the Reykjavík metropolitan area.

**Ethnic Distribution**: a homogeneous mixture of descendants of Norwegian (Norse) and Celtic settlers who arrived over 1,300 years ago

**Religious Distribution**: Evangelical Lutherans: > 90%; other Protestant and Roman Catholic: 3%; no affiliation: 1%

**Birth Rate**: 14.37 births per 1,000 population

**Death Rate**: 6.93 per 1,000 population

**Infant Mortality Rate**: 3.53 deaths per 1,000 live births

**Net Migration Rate**: –2.27 migrant(s) per 1,000 population

**Total Fertility Rate**: 1.99 children born per woman; in 1997, Icelandic women had a TFR of 1.8 children. The mean age of having the first child in 1998 was 25.1 years and the mean age of women in general to have a child was 28.8 (Hagstofa Íslands 1999b).

**Population Growth Rate**: 0.52%

**HIV/AIDS** (1999 est.): *Adult prevalence*: 0.14%; *Persons living with HIV/AIDS*: 200; *Deaths*: < 100. (For additional details from www.UNAIDS.org, see end of Section 10B.)

**Literacy Rate** (*defined as those age 15 and over who can read and write*): 99.9% (1997 estimate); schooling is compulsory from age 6 to 16. The language is Icelandic, which is actually similar to the language spoken by the Vikings who settled in Iceland in the early days. Most education is free. The number of women graduating from universities is rising, with 59% of the 1995-1996 graduates being women and 41% male, compared with a 93:7 ratio in the early 1950s (Hagstofa Íslands 1997).

**Per Capita Gross Domestic Product** (*purchasing power parity*): $24,800 (2000 est.); *Inflation*: 3.5%; *Unemployment*: 1% (April 2001 est.). Iceland's unemployment rate in 1998 was 2.7%, 3.3% for females and 2.3% for males (Hagstofa Íslands 1999b). The majority of Icelandic women, 83%, participate in the labor force, which is higher than in the other Nordic countries (Nordic Council of Ministers, 1999). *Living below the poverty line*: NA

*Communications*: Sóley S. Bender, R.N., M.S., Department of Nursing, University of Iceland, Eirberg, Eiriksgotu 34, 101 Reykjavík, Iceland; ssb@rhi.hi.is. Sigrún Júlíusdóttir, Ph.D., Department of Social Work, Faculty of Social Sciences, University of Iceland, IS-101 Reykjavík. Iceland; sigjul@rhi.hi.is.

## B. A Brief Historical Perspective

The first settlers of the volcanic island of Iceland were Vikings who arrived from Norway in 874 C.E. accompanied by a number of Scots and Irish. The Icelandic people are therefore mainly Scandinavian, genetically very homogeneous because of their longstanding geographic isolation. In 930, the Vikings established their legislative assembly, the Althing at Thingvellir, the world's oldest parliament. Christianity arrived in Iceland around the year 1000. In the year 1262, Iceland came under Norwegian rule. In 1380, it came under the rule of Denmark when the Danes gained control of all of Scandinavia. In 1918, Iceland became an independent sovereign state in union with Denmark through a common king. In 1944, with the Nazis occupying Denmark, Iceland deposed its king and declared itself a republic. The republic developed a Scandinavian-style welfare state, with comprehensive social benefits, that have produced one of the healthiest and best-educated populations (Olafsson 1989, 1990, 1999). Since 1944, Iceland has been an independent republic with the president chosen by a general election every four years.

## 1. Basic Sexological Premises

SIGRÚN JÚLIÍUSDÓTTIR

The character of gender roles, the sociolegal status of males and females, and general concepts of sexuality in Iceland are dealt with here as the product of the interaction between macroconditions and cultural values on the macro level, and lifestyle and adjustment on the meso or family level within Icelandic culture. These three basic sexological premises are discussed on the basis of statistics and research, as well as on clinical experience.

## A. Character of Gender Roles

The rather young and small Icelandic society is known for its ancient literature, the *Sagas*, from which some basic cultural values derive. From the 1,000-year-old Saga period, we have colorful and influential descriptions of powerful gender characteristics of men and women and their equally esteemed gender roles as Vikings and Valkyries.

The written sagas and their narratives reflect cultural-ethical values and social norms, which have been transmitted through the generations in written texts, oral history, and developing myths. They have brought with them strong ideas, or even ideals, for modern men and women, for good and for bad. Also, some of the old values linked to survival and social adjustment in a tough natural environment under poor socioeconomic conditions in earlier times are still today reflected in men's and women's tough attitudes to work, love, and children (Juliusdottir & Asmundsson 1987). Accordingly, the modern woman sees herself as strong and independent, but simultaneously, she still assumes almost single-handedly the responsibility for the internal life of the family, reproduction, emotional care, and survival. Modern young men still see themselves as socially and economically responsible for the family's external, reproductive, and economic survival.

A family study on coping strategies in Icelandic families with children includes an analysis of the interaction of old cultural values and modern lifestyle. The results show how the ties to earlier times shape a set of gender-based complementarity of responsibilities enchaining both sexes to old hidden loyalties, which often seem to be a stumbling stone to individual freedom and career goals (Juliusdottir 1993).

Strivings for equality in Iceland started more than a century ago with women's movements and activity in different social organizations. Several factors, such as different formal human rights early in the 20th century, have contributed to the development of a myth about the strong Icelandic woman. Icelandic women gained eligibility and the right to vote in 1915, and the first woman was elected to the Parliament in 1922 (Erlendsdottir 1993; Kristmundsdottir 1997). Other historical events are often referred to as verifying instances of gender equality and the somewhat special position of Icelandic women. These are the strong Redstocking Movement (for sexual equality) around 1970, the celebrated "Day of Women's Strengths and Solidarity" (*Kvennafrídagur*) on October 24, 1975, the Women's Slate Movement and the subsequent Women's Party from 1982 onwards, and the election of Vigdis Finnbogadottir in 1980 as the first woman president of a nation in the world. Also cited are the establishment of the Society for Sheltering Battered Women in 1979, followed by the first study of violence against women (Olafsdottir et al. 1982; Juliusdottir 1982), and the Women's Counselling Service in 1984. All these are evidence of the progress modern Icelandic women have made in their endeavors for solidarity with victims of violence and injustice.

Being strong, however, is not the same as being free and independent, a distinction that may apply to both men and women. In spite of the positive image of the strong Icelandic women, statistics give another picture. Figures on the low wages and occupational status of Icelandic women, and their poor participation and lack of recognition in the public sphere, in politics and the economy, show the opposite, i.e., a much lower status of women than men (Hagstofa Íslands 1999b, 67, 184).

The increasing pressures of globalization have reduced the historic isolating effects of Iceland's geographical distance from other countries. Modern electronic and computer/Internet media rapidly import new scientific knowledge and convey the latest ideas from abroad about gender equality and behavior patterns. Ideas about the personal freedom to choose and plan one's educational path, occupational career, children, and family obligations thus often collide with the persistent old values related to the virtue of personal sacrifice, hard work, and social adjustment in Iceland.

The labor force is in short supply and both professionals and qualified and unqualified workers are badly needed. Thus, the relatively few inhabitants are not only expected to contribute with long working hours, but also are simultaneously expected to find for themselves effective solutions for family matters, such as childcare and care for the elderly. A strong informal family network often comes into play when public services and support are lacking for dual-career couples. Another example of how social concerns are dealt with in the private sphere is the expectation that married couples will successfully negotiate their own marital/familial roles and responsibilities (Rafnsdottir 1994; Olafsson 1990).

There is strong social pressure to reach the goal of a first-class housing standard, high educational level, and modern material consumption pattern for all Icelanders. Simultaneously, the old values of still having many children, taking care of one's own parents, and other "old fashioned" family obligations often put young parents in a situation of heavy conflicts in their daily lives.

## B. Sociolegal Status of Males and Females

The small, traditionally rural Icelandic society changed rapidly after World War II. The process of urbanization with a civil environment and modern lifestyle did not appear until the 1950s. Iceland is supposed to share the welfare-state ideology of the Nordic countries. The implementation of constitutional and juridical issues is, however, somewhat different (Olafsson 1999, 1989). Iceland's healthcare expenditure is in line with the other Nordic countries and even higher in some cases. In Iceland, consumers of health services, however, pay a larger part of the medical costs themselves. The high-quality health-service results include the lowest infant mortality rate and the highest life expectancy in the Nordic countries (NOMESCO 1998, 67-69, 161, 164).

On the other hand, the government's economic contribution to social and family matters is much lower than it is for the health services. Thus, daycare centers and services for the elderly are insufficient to meet the needs of the people (NOSOSCO 1996). The difference is striking, when long working hours, the number of children, and the considerable number of three-generation households are taken into account. In spite of the high divorce rate, approximately 40% of the weddings, the strong and still increasing familialism with its emphasis on building families early and having many children, makes the percentage of intact families (married or cohabiting with their own children) up to 50% plus. At the same time, the number of single-parent households is 8.5% and 7.3% for stepfamilies (Hagstofa Íslands 1999b, 33, 60, 65; Juliusdottir et al. 1995, 40-41).

Statistics show that, on average, men between the ages of 25 and 54 have a workweek of 54-plus hours and women 45 hours (Hagstofa Íslands 1999b, 88). Ninety-six percent of the men and 85% of the women between ages 25 and 54 are actively employed (Hagstofa Íslands 1999b, 79). The choice of fields in this labor market is highly segregated by gender. The proportion of women is highest in public services, healthcare, and education, whereas that of men is highest in administration, special techniques, fishing, and agriculture (Hagstofa Íslands 1999b, 86). The wages of women are only 52% of those of the men, and that has not changed in recent years (*Heilsufar Kvenna* 2000).

Icelandic women have reached a high level of education. Among the 20-year-olds, 42.3% of the women and 28.5% of the men pass the matriculation examination. Also, proportionally more women than men are admitted to universities, and they graduate more frequently than men, both with undergraduate and graduate-level degrees (Hagstofa Íslands 1999b, 269). Women do not seem, however, to realize their potential in a vocational career to the same extent Icelandic men do, as already pointed out above.

After World War II, the work of Icelandic women outside the home increased and their educational level improved considerably. There has, however, been a significant difference between single and married women. The latter continued to give birth to many children and take care of their parents, although the daycare system and services for the elderly did not expand in proportion to the demand. As elsewhere, the social care services have developed as a gender issue, both regarding the employed and the families as consumers (Rauhala et al. 1997).

During the last decade, several improvements of crucial importance for equality have been legislated. One sign of progress for equality of the sexes was new legislation on parental leave of nine months at childbirth, which is to be implemented in steps in the next few years. It allows three months leave for the mother, three months for the father, and three months to be divided as the parents choose.

In 1992, Iceland was late in introducing legislation on joint custody for children of divorced parents. A new study on the experience of this alternative shows that parents who choose joint custody adjust in several ways better and more equally to their new life circumstances. Both parents and children report better health on average, and the frequency of depression and social isolation is less than among parents with divided custody. They use alcohol less often and the contact with families of origin is more frequent, especially

for the fathers. The parental responsibilities also came out more equal for both sexes than when custody was divided (Juliusdottir & Sigurdardottir 2000).

A recently established public Family Council, followed by the Year of the Family in 1994, has played a role in preparing an integrated and comprehensive family policy, recommending political initiatives, and facilitating actions in family matters, such as family planning and family life education. The Family Council is also supposed to serve as a consulting organ for the government.

The rapid socioeconomic evolution has caused a cultural lag, where families and couples are struggling with adapting to the new society's demand for consumption and self-realization, but at the same time taking on family obligations in the spirit of the still-alive old values and images.

Sometimes the loyalty to old values is beneficial and sometimes it restricts the changing character of Icelandic gender roles. The influences of the macro- and mesofactors mentioned above often appear strikingly in parental roles and in couples' intimate relationships affecting their emotional and sexual lives. A comparison between two Icelandic and Swedish counseling services shows that the reasons for seeking professional help are different. The Swedish clinical population in marital and family therapy seems more prone to seek help to improve couples' emotional relationships and communication when dealing with personal and interactional conflicts. This may, unlike the case in Iceland, have to do with the fact that Swedish parents are not so busy struggling with practical (e.g., financial, housing, working, and daycare) problems of daily life as Icelandic parents are. Such practical needs and the problems related to them are not so prominent in Sweden. They are, to a greater extent, taken care of through effective family policy with sufficient official family support (Juliusdottir 1993).

In modern European societies, where the public is generally well educated and conscious about qualities of life, there is also increasing emphasis on harmonious proportioning of work, private life, leisure, sex, and pleasure. In Iceland, some similar changes in cognitive attitudes are appearing. In a comparative European study, 66% of Icelanders agreed with the statement, "The government must offer extensive social services, even if it requires higher expenditures and increased taxes." This percentage of agreement was similar to that in other European countries. On the other hand, 79% in the Icelandic sample were strongly against the statement, "Social service is too expensive and must be cut down" (Olafsson 1999; Olafsson et al. 1998).

## C. General Concepts of Sexuality and Love

Icelandic constructs of sexuality related to family building, health, work, values, and moral attitudes provide a third domain of basic sexological premises.

The Icelandic population, in general, holds rather permissive attitudes regarding sexual relations and other related social-moral issues. Although the age of majority for males and females is 18 years, young people start working already at an earlier age and consequently identify with adult behavior in many regards. Icelandic adolescents, boys earlier than girls, start petting early in comparison to other countries, often before age 16, and have their first sexual intercourse, on average, at age 15 (Jonsdottir & Haraldsdottir 1998). Approximately 55% of 14-year-olds, girls more often than boys, have started smoking. A somewhat higher proportion at this age has started drinking. There is no difference between the sexes until the age of 17, when the proportion is significantly higher for the girls (Adalbjarnardottir et al. 1997). Another Icelandic study confirms these results, but also shows that young Icelandic adolescents in general use alcohol and drugs to a somewhat lesser extent than those in the other European countries (Thorlindsson et al. 1998).

Young people, on average, leave home at the age of 20-plus and start cohabitation or marriage, on average, about the age of 21. It is most common to start "going steady" at about the age of 18 and to have experienced two longer relationships before cohabitation. At least 40% start cohabiting in the housing of their parents or parents-in-law (Juliusdottir et al. 1995, 52).

The generally liberal attitudes of Icelanders are reflected in the Icelandic part of an international opinion study of a nationwide representative sample (Jonsson & Olafsson 1991). In some moral attitudes and values concerning sexuality and family life, Icelanders do not differ from the average on most items. Approximately 24% agree on a requirement of "totally free and unregulated sexual behavior," whereas the other Nordic countries are harder on that issue. Icelanders differ from other Scandinavians, on average, in holding more-positive attitudes towards divorce, abortion, and homosexuality. On the other hand, Icelanders are, on average, more negative than other Scandinavians when it comes to marital infidelity.

In the 1991 family study just cited, approximately 80% of responding husbands and wives said that it never occurred in their relationship. The respondents, however, reported that they would discuss it rather than see it as a reason for divorce. Asked about their attitudes to their own sexual life, they commonly reported that they have intercourse six to ten times per month (45% of the men; 49% of the women). They emphasized caring more than intercourse (45% men; 70% women), and preferred showing physical closeness and warmth (30% men; 21% women) (Juliusdottir 1993, 186, 190).

In an international study of 60 countries (Gallup 1999) with a representative sample of Icelanders, the respondents evaluated similar factors as the other Nordic countries as most important in life, specifically, good health and happy family life. A recent nationwide Icelandic opinion study on moral values and virtues showed similar results (Proppé 2000). What Icelanders saw as more important to care about and to pursue were family and friendship (50%) rather than education and vocational career (11%). This was especially true among younger people.

## 2. Religious, Ethnic, and Gender Factors Affecting Sexuality

SÓLEY S. BENDER

### A/B. Source and Character of Religious and Ethnic Values

In Iceland, about 89% of the population are registered members of the state Lutheran Church, 3.6% belong to the Lutheran free churches, 3.3% belong to other religious organizations, and of those, there are 1.4% Catholic (Hagstofa Íslands 1999b). There is not a strong religious influence on sexual life. According to the Lutheran religion, people should only have sex within marriage. In the earlier days, marriage was arranged between two clans. Both the bride and the bridegroom had to have enough money to be able to get married (Gudmundsson 1990).

In Thorvardarson's 1978 study, students in the age group 16 to 18 were asked about the importance of teaching about Christian values, especially regarding sexuality and marriage. Only 10% considered it very important to teach religious values in sex education. This issue had the lowest value when compared to other topics in sex education, such as sexually transmitted diseases (97%), contraceptive methods (92%), where to get information (86%), and sexual problems (61%).

Nowadays, marriage is not a prerequisite for living a sexual life. Cohabitation is common and some people never get married, although they may have several children. Icelanders widely accept single persons having a sexual life.

## 3. Knowledge and Education about Sexuality

SÓLEY S. BENDER

### A. Government Policies and Programs

In the 1950s, sex education in Iceland's schools was limited. For the most part, it consisted of two pages in the human health book. In many schools, the teachers skipped these two pages. In 1948, *Sexuality* by Fritz Kahn, M.D., was published in Iceland. It was a popular possession of many families at that time. Through the years, several books about sexuality have been translated into Icelandic. Some of these books have been used in teaching sex education. In 1976, *The Man, Birth, Childhood and Adolescence* was written by Icelanders to be used for sex education (Eiriksdottir et al. 1976). It has since been widely used for 5th and 6th graders (10- and 11-year-olds). *Human Reproduction*, published in 1983 (Kjartansson & Brynjolfsson), was another Icelandic addition to textbooks for sex education in the schools. It has been widely used in the schools for 13- to 16-year-old students.

The 1985 diagnosis of the first person in Iceland with AIDS raised the importance of preventive work in the schools. This meant increased emphasis on sexually transmitted diseases and the importance of condom use. Because of AIDS, new Icelandic educational material about sexually transmitted diseases was published in 1988 by the Ministries of Education and Health for use by teachers and others in sex education. In 1989, the Ministry of Education issued a curriculum plan for grades 1 through 9. In this plan, sex education was emphasized as a part of many subjects in the schools, like Christianity, sociology, and biology. Teachers in the schools and health professionals from the local community health center were encouraged to work together on sex education. In the fall of 1999, a new curriculum plan was released by the Ministry of Education for grades 1 through 10 and beyond. Presently, teachers in every school make their own teaching plan, and the number of hours devoted to sex education can vary considerably. Sex education is, therefore, in the hands of individual teachers and schools. Some schools have very good sex education, whereas others are very limited.

A standard curriculum for sex education was lacking for many years. It was not until 1991 that a holistic curriculum for sex education for the 8th through the 10th grades was introduced in the schools. This program, *Human Sexuality, Values and Choices*, was an American sex education curriculum from Minnesota. It was translated, adapted to Icelandic culture, and pilot-tested in seven schools in 1990 (Axelsdottir et al. 1990). The pilot test was based on an experimental design. It showed that there was a significant increase in knowledge among those in the experimental group compared to those in the control group, but it showed very limited changes of attitudes. This sex education curriculum is based on 15 lessons, with lessons about the biological facts of human sexuality, but also about feelings and intrapersonal relations. It does stress identity, feelings, how to make decisions, and knowing what to do when it comes to making decisions about sexuality. It has a comprehensive handbook for teachers, with objectives and the contents of the lessons, as well as projects for the students. It also has a video of 120 minutes that has short episodes of certain sex education sessions meant to facilitate group discussion. There is an additional handbook for parents.

The teachers are supposed to have three meetings with the parents about the curriculum. Many projects are intended to be completed by the students in cooperation with their parents or other adults. This program is now in use in many schools and it has made a considerable difference for sex education. A 1993 study showed that this curriculum was used by 63.6% of the 60 schools participating in that study (grades 8 through 10) (Palsdottir & Hardardottir 1993).

No comprehensive curriculum has been developed for students younger than 13 years old or for those older than 16 years old. There is no sex education in the junior colleges except when students arrange it themselves. Representatives from the Icelandic Association for Sexual and Reproductive Health have been asked to go to several schools to give sex education. Also lacking are regular training courses about sex education for teachers and school health nurses. The last time such a training course was offered was in 1992.

A regulation about health promotion in schools from 1958 is probably one of the oldest legal documents that deal with sex education. In addition, sex education is based on 1975 laws about information and counseling regarding sexuality and responsible parenthood, abortion, and sterilization, 1976 laws about gender equality, and 1978 laws about sexually transmitted diseases. A 1975 law stated: "Educational authorities should in cooperation with the chief school health physician give information about sexuality and moral issues regarding sexuality in the compulsory school system. Additionally information should be given in other educational programs."

In Thorvardarson's 1978 study, 6.4% of boys and 13.7% of girls in the 6th grade said that they received good enough sex education. In the 8th grade, the percentages were 2.9% for boys and 3.7% for girls. In the same study, 79% of the 6th graders and 96% of the 8th graders wanted the school to provide sex education. A nationwide study of sex education, based on a sample of 60 teachers in 60 schools, showed that the mean hours of sex education for the 9th grade was 19.7 hours, and for the 10th grade, it was 15.6 hours (Palsdottir & Hardardottir 1993). In this same study, participants were asked how they taught each issue. More teachers reported that they taught the contraceptive methods (condom, pill, diaphragm, IUD, etc.) well, than reported that they taught the STDs (gonorrhea, chlamydia, herpes, etc.) well (91% to 84% for contraception versus 62% to 81% for STDs). Eighty-eight percent thought they taught about puberty and human reproduction very well, and 81.8% felt they did well teaching respect for the decisions of others (Palsdottir & Hardardottir 1993).

Although the 1993 study showed that there were several issues considered by the teachers to be taught well, the survey results can give us only limited information about the actual sexual education on these topics. The study had a response rate of 60%, and it is a question whether the 40% who did not answer did not respond because they were not motivated to teach the subject or because of some other reasons. These study results do not agree with the results of three interviews with student focus groups, who frequently stated that they got very limited sex education in grades 8 through 10 (Johannsdottir 2000).

What needs to be done in the future is to have sex education as a compulsory subject in the school system, to have training courses on a regular basis, and to develop a curriculum for junior college (age groups 16 to 20).

## B. Informal Sources of Sexual Knowledge

People have had access to sexual information from books, magazines, films, and the media. There has been a considerable increase in the publication of educational material about sexual and reproductive health from the Director of Public Health, from the Icelandic Association for Sexual and Reproductive Health, and from the Icelandic Incest Center (Stigamot). In 1990, Ottar Gudmundsson wrote *Íslenska Kynlífsbókin* (*The Icelandic Sexuality Book*), the first comprehensive Icelandic book about sexuality. Before that time, the books that were available were translated from other languages and cultures. Over the last few years, especially after AIDS got into the picture, sexuality has been discussed more openly on television and on the radio.

## 4. Autoerotic Behaviors and Patterns
SÓLEY S. BENDER

There are many negative terms in the Icelandic language for masturbation, starting with *self-pollution* (*sjálfsflekkun*). In *Sexuality* by Fritz Kahn, which was translated and published in Iceland in 1948, masturbation was explained in a detailed manner for both genders. It was stressed that masturbation was not bad for the health and that this behavior was not related to diseases. Kahn mentioned that Simon André Tissot, who published a treatise on the vice of "onanism" in 1760, had a considerable negative influence on attitudes toward masturbation. Tissot described the terrible effects of masturbation, ranging from nervousness to insanity.

There is no Icelandic study that provides any information about masturbation. Today, it is stressed that masturbation is a good way to get to know oneself. It is considered important to know one's own body sensations before sharing it with someone else.

## 5. Interpersonal Heterosexual Behaviors
SÓLEY S. BENDER

### A. Children

No Icelandic studies have been done about the sexual explorations of young children.

### B. Adolescents

A 1977 study by Sigurgestsson showed that among 14-year-olds, 23.2% of the boys and 21.2% of the girls said they had had sexual intercourse. This was considerably higher than in countries like Denmark, and the difference between genders was less in Iceland compared to other countries like Norway. A 1990 study showed results similar to those reported by Sigurgestsson: 25.6% of 14-year-old boys and 22.5% of the girls said they had had sexual intercourse (Axelsdottir et al. 1990).

A study by Jonsdottir (1994) showed that the mean age at first sexual intercourse was higher among the older age group than the younger, suggesting that the age of first sexual intercourse has been going down. For 50- to 60-year-olds, the mean age at first sexual intercourse was 17.6 for males and 18.6 for females. For 16- to 19-year-olds, the mean age at first sexual intercourse was 15.1 for males and 15.4 for females. Among the 50- to 60-year-olds, 4.1% had never had sexual intercourse, 48.7% were 16 or younger when they had their first sexual intercourse, and 47.2% were 17 or older. Among the 16- to 19-year-olds, 25% had never had sexual intercourse, 64.3% were 16 or younger when they had their first sexual intercourse, and 10.7% were 17 or older. This is a considerable difference for the age group 50 to 60, where 3.3% had never had sexual intercourse, 32.9% had sexual intercourse at age 16 or younger, and 65.8% were 17 or older.

A 1996 study showed that the mean age of sexual conduct was 15.4 years for both genders. The main author of this chapter conducted this national study based on a random sample of 1,703 people in the age group 17 to 20 years old (Bender 1999a). Table 1 shows the age distribution for first sexual intercourse.

## C. Adults
*Marital Data*

Between 1961 and 1965, the rate of marriage per 1,000 population was 7.9; in 1995, this was 4.6 (Hagstofa Íslands 1997). In 1998, 34.5% were married or cohabiting, 56% were not married, and 9.3% had been previously married and divorced (Hagstofa Íslands 1999b). The divorce rate has been increasing, doubling from 0.9 in 1961 to 1.8 in 1995 (Hagstofa Íslands 1997). The mean age of people who get married has also been going up. In 1961 to 1965, the mean age was 24.4 for brides and 27.4 for bridegrooms. Thirty years later, it was 29.9 for brides and 32.4 for bridegrooms. The attitudes of people to having a child out of wedlock are quite relaxed. A Gallup study (1997) showed that 95% did not think this was wrong.

*Heterosexual Behaviors*

A study conducted in 1992 by Jonsdottir and Haraldsdottir (1998) about sexual behavior and knowledge of AIDS showed that the average number of sexual partners is nine over the life span. Men have more sexual partners than women (12 versus 6). There is an identical ratio of men compared to women who have had anal sex (16.2% and 16.3%). The majority of men, 62.7% of those between ages 16 and 60, had experience with cunnilingus.

Those who have had two or more sexually transmitted diseases have had much higher numbers of sexual partners (26.4%) than those who were infected by one STD (11.9%) or none (6.2%). Casual sex is most frequent among those who are 16 to 25 years old.

This same study asked if participants had or knew about someone close to them who had had an affair while married or cohabiting. The results showed that 71.8% answered yes to this question (Jonsdottir & Haraldsdottir 1998). This may not be very reliable or accurate information, but it is the only available information about extramarital affairs.

## 6. Homoerotic, Homosexual, and Bisexual Behaviors

THORVALDUR KRISTINSSON

As of late 2000, no study provided reliable information about the frequency of homosexuality in Iceland. A study conducted in 1992 came closest to this by asking the participants about the sex of their partners. This national study of sexual behavior and knowledge about HIV had a sample of 971 people 16 to 60 years old. The response rate was 65%,

### Table 1
### Age at First Sexual Intercourse

| Age | Percent | Cumulative Percent |
|-----|---------|--------------------|
| 12 or younger | 1.2 | 1.2 |
| 13 | 6.4 | 7.6 |
| 14 | 17.9 | 25.5 |
| 15 | 27.2 | 52.7 |
| 16 | 24.8 | 77.5 |
| 17 | 15.5 | 93.0 |
| 18 | 5.7 | 98.7 |
| 19 | 1.2 | 99.9 |
| 20 | 0.1 | 100 |

(*Source*: Bender 1999b)

with 53% of the respondents being women and 47% men. The percentage of people who reported having had sex with a person of the same sex ranged from zero to 1.8% for different age groups, with an overall average of 0.7%. In the age group 16 to 19, 1.8% reported a same-sex partner. Among 30- to 34-year-old respondents, only 0.6% reported a same-sex partner. Of those who had had homosexual experience, 0.3% were married, 2.2% single, and 5.6% divorced (Jonsdottir 1994; Jonsdottir & Haraldsdottir 1998).

Until the 1970s, lesbians and gay men were practically invisible in Icelandic society, which surrounded them with contempt and a massive silence. Their reaction was either to hide their sexual orientation completely, finding an occasional escape from the oppression while touring abroad, or to move to the metropolitan cities of continental Europe and North America. Many of those people never returned, being later referred to as sexual political refugees. The silence was first broken in 1975 when the first gay Icelandic man, influenced by the international liberation movement, revealed his sexual identity publicly in the media. Three years later, Samtokin 78, the organization of lesbians and gay men in Iceland, was founded by some 20 people. After 20 years, it has become the most powerful force in the gay liberation movement of Iceland with a little less than 400 members. Typical of the prejudice and hostility that met this small group on its way to visibility in its early years, was the case of a discotheque in Reykjavik, which in 1983 advertised in newspapers: "Everyone is welcome—except gays and lesbians." Another example from the same year took place in the Nursing School of Iceland, which forbade its students from meeting with the educational group of Samtokin 78, a meeting which the students themselves had organized after a gay student found himself forced to leave the school because of group harassment and hazing.

Nevertheless, the few who had the courage to speak up for homosexuals saw remarkable progress in the 1980s. They rejected, for instance, the commonly used derogatory Icelandic terms, such as *kynvilla* (sexual aberration) for homosexuality, a term analogous to the older word *truvilla* (religious aberration) for heresy. For a decade, they fought with the Icelandic State Radio against being labeled in such a derogatory manner, and suggested their own popular words, *lesbia* and *hommi* for themselves, and *samkynhneig*, a compound of same-sex and orientation, for homosexuality. Finally, they won.

Since then, gay activism in Iceland has been characterized by educational and legislative work with positive results. Several other gay associations have recently appeared, including an association of gay, lesbian, and bisexual students at the University of Iceland, and an association of gay junior college students (Stonewall), both founded in 1999. In 1983, a new political party, the Socialdemocratic Alliance, was the first one to place gay human rights on its agenda, and two years later, a recommendation was presented in the Parliament by four political parties demanding action to abolish discrimination against lesbians and gay men. It never passed, and it was not until 1992 that a similar recommendation passed Parliament, after the original recommendation had been reworked by five political parties. As a result of the research work ordered by this recommendation, a law on registered partnerships for same-sex couples passed the Parliament in 1996, although it denied same-sex couples any right to adopt children or to seek insemination in an official clinic. With this law, Iceland became the first country in the world to legalize common custody of children brought into a same-sex partnership from previous marriages. At the same time, the Protestant Lutheran state church did not approve of a formal church wedding, causing friction and open fights with the church authorities, which are still unresolved. In the year

2000, the Parliament passed a new law on registered partnerships giving same-sex couples the right to adopt stepchildren who are brought into the partnership. An antidiscrimination law passed the Parliament in 1996. It is worth noting that the parliamentary opposition in the debate preceding these legislative improvements was minimal, compared to the parliamentary opposition in other Nordic countries. To find an example of organized opposition, one has to go to the very small Christian fundamentalist congregations functioning outside the state church of Iceland.

Opinion polls nowadays show a surprising change of values in the society, and they express, in fact, more respect and tolerance towards gay men and lesbians than in other Western societies. When asked by an international opinion survey in 1990 about to what extent certain acts were justifiable on a one-to-ten scale, Icelanders expressed more tolerance than people in other nations regarding homosexuality, showing an average of 5.5. Other nations placed around 4.7 on the average, with the United States at a low 3.0. An international opinion survey of the same kind from 1984 gave the Icelanders an average rate of 3.3. This positive change is generally confirmed by what lesbians and gay men experience in their everyday life (Olafsson 1991). In a surprisingly short period of time, Icelandic society has left its homophobic attitude of the past and opened up for new visions and ideas.

## 7. Gender Diversity and Transgender Issues

SÓLEY S. BENDER

There is no study that provides information about Icelandic persons with gender conflicts or confusion. Given the clinical experience and incidence figures for gender-conflicted persons in nearby culturally similar countries, it seems reasonable to assume that a few hundred or more of the 280,000 modern Icelanders experience various forms of transsexualism, transvestism, hermaphroditism, pseudohermaphroditism, and intersexualism. Given the presence of support groups for gender-conflicted persons on the Internet and World Wide Web, one can reasonably assume that some gender-conflicted Icelanders may find local counselors and psychologists sensitive to their needs and explore possible medical help on the island and abroad.

## 8. Significant Unconventional Sexual Behaviors

SÓLEY S. BENDER and GUDRÚN JÓNSDÓTTIR

### A. Coercive Sex

*Sexual Harassment*

No prevalence studies have been done regarding the frequency of sexual harassment, but the Icelandic Office for Gender Equality has made some small surveys in a limited number of workplaces. They show that between 12% and 16% of the female workers have been subjected to sexual harassment in their workplace. In the last few years, employees have been better informed than before about their rights if they are victims of sexual harassment. However, many myths still exist regarding this issue.

*Sexual Abuse and Incest*

No prevalence studies have been conducted regarding sexual abuse and incest in Iceland. Even so, it was clear to a group of women who had been working as volunteers in different services for women that incest and sexual abuse of women and children is not unknown in Iceland. In 1986, these women formed a group whose purpose was to develop services for survivors of sexual violence. The group was named the Working Group Against Incest. In 1987, when an

office was opened half a day, the demand for the service increased steadily. The Stigamot (The Icelandic Incest Center), which opened in 1990, is the product of this movement. Stigamot is an information and counseling center for women and children who have experienced sexual violation. In its first decade, Stigamot helped a total of 2,811 persons, with 213 new individuals seeking help in 1999. The two main reasons women and children have come to Stigamot are incest (about 60%) and rape (about 30%). Those who use the service are mainly 19 to 49 years old (80.2%); the majority have limited education (Jonsdottir & Sigurdardottir 2000).

The Government Agency for Child Protection does coordinate and strengthen child protection in Iceland. In 1997, this agency recommended to the Minister of Social Affairs that a special Children's House (Center for Child Sexual Abuse) should be developed to coordinate the work of child protection authorities, social service, police, the state prosecution, doctors, and others when investigating sexual abuse, to improve the quality of the service for children, and to protect the child from having to go through many traumatic forensic interviews and possibly relive the difficult experience. In November 1998, this Children's House started as a two-year experimental project. In 1998, there were 21 children referred to this center and in 1999, there were 119. In 1999, laws were passed about new procedures for court cases, which gives the responsibility of the forensic interview to the judge (Gudbrandsson 1999). The experience has been that not more than 10% of cases go to court. The center also offers treatment services. On average, each child has about 14 interviews during the treatment process. This center serves the whole country. In late 2000, the future of the center was uncertain.

The criminal law about incest (1940) states that a parent who has sexual intercourse, vaginally or by other means with his child, shall get up to six to ten years in prison. Conviction for other types of sexual harassment by a parent towards a child can bring a prison sentence of up to two years and four years if the child is younger than 16 years old. Whoever has sex with a child younger than 14 years old can get imprisonment up to 12 years. Other types of sexual harassment and assault can lead to imprisonment up to four years.

In 1998, 58 legal charges of sexual abuse were brought in all of Iceland (Ministry of Law and Justice, personal communication, 4 July, 2000). Since 1981, the number of prison sentences stemming from sexual crimes has been rising. Between 1981 and 1985, there were 11 prison sentences and in 1998, there were 28. The mean number between 1985 and 1998 was 19.1 annually (Hagstofa Íslands 1999b).

*Rape*

In 1984, a group of women formed a group of counselors for survivors of rape. In the City Hospital in Reykjavik, a rape trauma center was established in 1993. As of mid-2000, 640 individuals had been attended to by the service. Seven were mentally retarded. In 1999, 103 individuals, 97 women and 6 men, used the service (Arsskyrsla Sjukrahuss Reykjavikur 2000). The majority of clients are females, but annually three to four men seek help. The clients range in age from 12 to 78 years, with 65% to 70% 25 years old or younger. The service is free of charge (Jonsdottir 2000). Rape is punishable under a 1940 law with imprisonment of between one and 16 years.

### B. Prostitution

Prostitution has probably been organized in Reykjavik, but valid information is hard to obtain. In recent years, several nightclubs offering nude dancing have opened both in Reykjavik and other cities. The women there have mostly come from abroad, particularly from Eastern European countries, to work as "dancers." This is probably hidden prostitution.

Sexual telephone service has become more and more obvious and is advertised in one of the main newspapers. This service was temporarily advertised with porno pictures. This was recently changed and now there is only text in the advertisements. These advertisements for sexual telephone services are also probably hidden prostitution services.

The 1992 study of sexual behavior and knowledge of AIDS showed that there were 71 individuals who had had sexual experience with a prostitute. Most of them were men and two were women. The majority were in the age group 25 to 39. The greater majority, 91%, had this sexual experience abroad (Jonsdottir & Haraldsdottir 1998). A person convicted of making a living by being a prostitute can get a prison sentence of two years. A person who gains a living from organizing the prostitution of others can get four years imprisonment. A person who encourages someone who is younger than 18 years old to work as a prostitute can get up to a four-year sentence in prison.

### D. Pornography and Erotica

Pornography and opposition to it have existed in Iceland for centuries (Gudmundsson 1990). In the 20th century, there has been some control over pornography in books and movies. Today, there seems to be very limited control. Books, magazines, movies, and videos showing pornography are easily available.

According to the 1940 criminal law, it is illegal to make, import, sell, and/or distribute pornographic material. It is also criminal to give pornographic material to a person younger than 18 years old. It is also not allowed to store pornographic material of children. These offenses can lead to a fine and/or up to six months in prison.

## 9. Contraception, Abortion, and Population Planning

SÓLEY S. BENDER

### A. Contraception

Contraception is available through Iceland's community health centers, gynecologists, and some hospitals. Around 1994, the only specialized family planning clinic, which served mostly young people, closed. In 1995, the Icelandic Association for Sexual and Reproductive Health started an information and counseling service for young people on sexuality, STDs, and contraceptives. As with the early clinic, mostly young women have used this service.

Few studies have been conducted about the use of contraceptives of women in their reproductive years. In the 1977 Sigurgestsson study, young people 14 years old gave information about their use of contraceptive methods at their first sexual intercourse. Overall, 40.6% of the respondents, 43.7% of the boys and 36.7% of the girls, said they had used contraception for their first full sexual intercourse. A 1990 study showed that the most frequent reasons for not using contraception were: not having thought about it, 61.7%; not daring to go to the community health center, 61.1%; being too shy to discuss this with their partner, 51%; and believing coitus interruptus was sufficient contraceptive protection, 49.2% (Axelsdottir et al. 1990). A 1996 study of 1,703 individuals ages 17 to 20 showed that 59% used contraception at first coitus. The methods most used were the contraceptive pill, 7.6%; condom, 61.7%; diaphragm, 0.58%; and other, 1.0%. After first coitus, the pill, the condom, and coitus interruptus were in that order the most frequently used methods (Bender 1999). There are no national studies of contraceptive use among the over-20 population.

Some data from the Cancer Society have been analyzed. This data shows that the most frequently used contraceptive method for younger women is the contraceptive pill and for older women the intrauterine device. In the 20-to-44 age group, 35% of contracepting Icelanders used the IUD and 18% the contraceptive pill (Geirsson & Gudmundsson 1988, 1987). In 1997, sterilization was used as a permanent method by 640 (83%) of contracepting women and by 130 (17%) of contracepting men. In 1983, this gender ratio was 95% for contracepting women and 5% for men.

A 1988 survey exploring information and counseling about sexual and reproductive health in Icelandic community health centers showed that the more-common subjects for counseling and information were: contraceptive methods, 84.4%; menopause, 72.8%; STDs, 72%; pregnancy tests, 67.1%; and premenstrual syndrome (PMS), 65%. Less frequently provided information dealt with: abortion, 23.4%; sexual problems, 29.8%; and sexual health, 30.2%. Most of these services were provided by family practitioners (Bender 1990).

The present legislation about contraception, abortion, and sterilization took effect in 1975. This 25-year-old law suggests that people should get subsidized contraceptive methods, but this has not been acted on.

### B. Teenage (Unmarried) Pregnancies

The incidence of teenage pregnancies is considerably higher in Iceland than it is in other Nordic countries. Table 2 compares the rate of teenage pregnancies in these countries. Table 3 compares the birthrates. Although the birthrate among young women in Iceland has been dropping significantly, from 73.7 per 1,000 in 1970 to 24.9 in 1998, it is still much higher than in the other Nordic countries.

The percentage of live births by mothers under age 20 as a percentage of all live births in Iceland declined from 15.3% in 1977 to 6.3% in 1998 (Hagstofa Íslands 1999b). Table 4 shows comparable Scandinavian percentages for 1998.

A recent study showed that the birthrate among young women in Iceland is considerably less in the capital area compared to other places in Iceland, but the abortion rate is

**Table 2**

**The Rate of Teenage Pregnancies per 1,000 Pregnancies in 1997**

| Country | Rate per 1,000 |
|---------|----------------|
| Iceland | 46.2 (1997) |
| Norway | 31.7 (1997) |
| Sweden | 25    (1997) |
| Finland | 19.2 (1997) |
| Denmark | 23.5 (1996) |

(*Source*: NOMESCO 1999)

**Table 3**

**The Birthrate among Young Women per 1,000 Pregnancies in 1998**

| Country | Rate per 1,000 |
|---------|----------------|
| Iceland | 24.9 (1998) |
| Norway | 12.7 (1997) |
| Finland | 9.0 (1998) |
| Denmark | 8.4 (1998) |
| Sweden | 7.2 (1998) |

(*Source*: NOMESCO 1999)

also higher (Adalsteinsdottir 2000). At the same time, as the birthrate among teenagers (15 to 19 years old) there has been declining, the abortion rate has been rising (5.8 per 1,000 in 1976 and 21.7 in 1997). Now, close to 50% of pregnancies end in abortion and 50% in childbirth. A descriptive study of the health of teenage mothers (15 to 19 years old) during pregnancy and the health of their newborns, compared to older mothers (25 to 29 years old) and their newborns, based on a sample of 50 mothers in each group and 50 newborns of both groups, showed that the mean numbers of prenatal visits were identical in both groups. Teenage mothers attended 11.0 times and the older mothers 12.0 times. The younger mothers did not start to attend the prenatal visits later than the older mothers did. Health problems, such as pre-eclampsia and anemia, were more common in the older age group. There were fewer medical and surgical interventions during the delivery for the younger mothers. The percentage of low birthweight was identical for both groups (6% in each). The younger mothers, on the other hand, smoked more than the older mothers (25.5% versus 18%) and had higher frequency of delivering before the 37th week of gestation (6.3% versus 2.1%). The easy access to and no cost of prenatal service seem to contribute to fewer health risks among young mothers (Lorensdottir et al. 1994).

Young people do encounter some hindrances in obtaining contraceptive methods based on their insecurity, shyness, and the cost of the product. They also consider the health service at the community health centers to be too expensive and difficult to obtain, in contrast with the no-cost and easy availability of prenatal care (Johannsdottir et al. 2000). Young Icelanders want sexual and reproductive health services that are organized according to their needs. They have special needs regarding open hours and are sensitive to the environment and the interactions with the healthcare providers (Bender 1999a). This was further verified in a recent focus group study. This focus group study was based on three interviews of young people 16 to 19 years old, and showed that their special needs were better service hours in the afternoons or evenings, healthcare providers who show respect to young people, and a friendly staff attitude and friendly environment. They want to have music channels on the television in the waiting room, but not educational movies about STDs (Johannsdottir et al. 2000).

Most young mothers are probably single. Often they get good support from their families. A study based on two focus group interviews with young mothers showed that it was their mother who mostly helped them. They sensed the great responsibility of being a mother. Their inexperience, however, was demonstrated in being intolerant to breastfeeding and not knowing what to do when caring for the child. In spite of that, they felt good about being alone with the child, but often sensed insecurity when they were with others. Oftentimes, they felt that adults were interfering with their childrearing practices. They sensed that they had little time for themselves, had less freedom, and often felt isolated from their friends. All of the participants had some future vision. Most of them wanted to go to school or to finish the school they were attending (Sveinsdottir & Gudmundsdottir 2000). These results show the need of young mothers for support and guidance about childrearing practices.

Based on the high teenage pregnancy rate, more preventive efforts need to be made. Sexuality education needs to be improved, and specialized sexual and reproductive health services for young people need to be developed.

## C. Abortion

The present law legalizing abortion took effect in 1975. Anyone can apply for an abortion for medical or social reasons or following a rape. Abortions can only be done within a hospital setting. According to the legislation, permission is required for the intervention to be performed. The application form needs to be signed either by a social worker and medical doctor or two medical doctors depending on the reason. Women who apply for an abortion report low use of contraceptives. In 1977 to 1980, about 30% of women seeking an abortion had used some type of contraception at the time of conception; in 1981 to 1984, contraceptive use rose to 37% (Oskarsson & Geirsson 1987). Because of the rising number of abortions, a contraceptive counseling service has been developed within the National Hospital for women before and after an abortion.

Abortion is free of charge, but there is small outpatient fee for the laboratory tests and physical examination before the operation. The majority of abortions are done for social reasons. The rate of abortions for all age groups has been rising over the last 24 years and is now identical to those in other Nordic countries; but their abortion rates have has been going down over the years (Bender 2000). Between 1976 and 1980, 472 abortions were preformed; in 1998, the number was 901. Table 5 shows the abortion rate by age group in 1998. Between 1976 and 1980, the abortion rate for the age group 15 to 19 was 9.4 per 1,000. In 1996, the abortion rate among 15- to 19-year-old Icelandic women was the highest among the Nordic countries.

There has been a group opposed to abortion in Iceland, but it has never been very active.

## D. Population Programs

Iceland is a pronatalistic country, as demonstrated by the positive attitude to having many children. In 1997, a Gallup study showed that about 70% of Icelanders wanted to have three or more children. Eighty-five percent of those surveyed considered it necessary to have a child to feel fulfilled. This pronatalism is also evident in the fact that there are no government-run teenage clinics. Teenage pregnancy is high and seems to be generally accepted. There is a trend of population movement from the rural to the urban areas.

#### Table 4

**Live Births by Mothers Under Age 20 per 1,000 Live Births in 1998**

| Country | Rate per 1,000 |
|---|---|
| Iceland | 6.3 |
| Norway | 2.7 |
| Finland | 2.6 |
| Denmark | 1.7 |
| Sweden | 1.3 |

(*Source*: Haagensen 1999)

#### Table 5

**Abortions in Iceland in 1998**

| Age Group | Abortions per 1,000 women |
|---|---|
| 15 to 19 years | 24.1 |
| 20 to 24 | 23.2 |
| 25 to 29 | 16.2 |
| 30 to 34 | 11.0 |
| 35 to 39 | 9.1 |
| 40 to 44 | 3.8 |
| 45 and older | 0.2 |

In some rural areas, there are recent efforts to increase the local population by using some financial incentives for young people to have children.

The discussion about the need for better contraceptive counseling services for people at reproductive age is new. The Icelandic Family Planning Association (The Icelandic Association for Sexual and Reproductive Health, or IcASRH) was established in 1992. This Association has been giving information to professionals and the public about these issues. One of these issues has been about emergency contraception. IcASRH published a special pamphlet about emergency contraception in 1996 and this has been widely distributed. The 1996 study about the attitude of young people to sexual and reproductive health services showed that only 35% of the 17- to 20-year-old participants knew what emergency contraception was.

In 1991, an infertility program was established at the National Hospital in Reykjavik. Before that time, people had to go abroad to have infertility treatment. The success rate of the Icelandic in-vitro fertilization (IVF) program has been high.

## 10. Sexually Transmitted Diseases and HIV/AIDS

SÓLEY S. BENDER

### A. Sexually Transmitted Diseases

*Incidence and Trends*

Iceland's national registration of sexually transmitted diseases does not provide accurate information about the prevalence of those diseases. The most accurate information about the rate of STDs is based on data from the Department of Infectious Diseases at the National Hospital in Reykjavik. Based on their information, there were 9,415 chlamydia cases between 1981 and 1990, about 941 annually. The number of positive tests for chlamydia has been dropping from 26% in 1981 to 11% in 1990 (Steingrimsson et al. 1991). From 1991 to 1997, the incidence of positive tests was 11 to 13%.

*Chlamydia trachomatis* has been the most frequent sexually transmitted disease in Iceland for several years. The number of gonorrhea cases has been dropping over the years, but herpes and condyloma have increased. The 1992 sexual behavior study showed that there were 9.3% who had gotten *Pediculus pubis* (pubic lice), 8.4% chlamydia, 8.0% scabies, 5.6% condyloma, 4.5% gonorrhea, and 2.5% herpes (Jonsdottir 1994). In the same study, 20% of the participants said they had had one STD, while 6.8% reported two or more infections, with men having a higher frequency at 9.3% compared with 4.7% for women (see Table 6).

*Treatment and Prevention Efforts*

There is one STD clinic in Reykjavik offering diagnosis and treatment. People can also visit their family practitioner at community health centers all over Iceland. The diagnosis and treatment is free for the client.

There are many aspects that need to be considered regarding prevention and risk-reduction efforts regarding STDs in Iceland. The 1992 study showed that about 8% of those surveyed had had casual sex once or more often in the last three months before the study was conducted. Casual sex was most frequent in the age group 16 to 24. About 10% of those who had casual sex were always or most often under the influence of alcohol or drugs during sexual intercourse (Jonsdottir & Haraldsdotttir 1998).

In the same study, 9% of men 16 to 24 said it was difficult to talk to their partner about the use of condoms; 5% of the women in the same age group shared this difficulty. Fifty-two percent of the men and 44% of women felt that the condom spoiled sexual pleasure. In the 16-to-19 age group, 23.1% of participants who had had casual sex in the last 12 months before the study never used a condom during that time. The average non-use of condoms for all other age groups was 14.9% (Jonsdottir & Haraldsdottir 1998).

STD preventive efforts in Iceland have been focused on the importance of increasing knowledge about STDs and influencing attitudes. There are several hindrances that make this preventive work not as effective as it could be. In Icelandic society, as in many other countries, there are not many healthy role models for young people regarding the use of condoms. Most movies show sexual intercourse without anyone mentioning the need for protection against STDs or pregnancy.

### B. HIV/AIDS

*Incidence and Trends*

As of January 2000, Iceland had 140 individuals diagnosed with HIV. The annual number of individuals diagnosed with HIV has ranged from zero to a high of 16. Most of those who became infected were homosexuals, but the number of infected heterosexuals is growing. Men have a higher frequency of HIV infection than women, as shown in Table 7. As of the end of 1999, a total of 50 cases of AIDS had been diagnosed and reported to the authorities; 33 Icelanders have died of AIDS.

*Treatment, Prevention Programs, and Government Policies*

In 1988, a national AIDS committee was formed by the Ministry of Health. The role of this committee included creation of guidelines regarding prevention of HIV. This committee decided to conduct a study about the sexual behavior of Icelanders and their knowledge about HIV/AIDS (Jonsdottir 1994; Jonsdottir & Haraldsdottir 1998). This study showed that Icelanders were interested in three ways to promote safer sex behaviors in order to reduce the risk of HIV infection: increasing the use of condoms, having fewer

### Table 6

#### Percentage Infected with STD

|  | All (*n* = 966) | Men (*n* = 450) | Women (*n* = 516) |
|---|---|---|---|
| Never infected | 73.1% | 70.2% | 75.6% |
| Once infected | 20.1 | 20.4 | 19.8 |
| Infected by two or more STDs | 6.8 | 9.3 | 4.7 |

(*Source*: Jonsdottir & Haraldsdottir 1998)

### Table 7

#### Incidence of HIV from 1985 to 1996 per 100,000 Population

|  | Total | Women | Men |
|---|---|---|---|
| 1985 | 7.5 | 1.7 | 13.2 |
| 1990 | 2.0 | — | 3.9 |
| 1991 | 3.9 | 1.6 | 6.2 |
| 1992 | 4.2 | 0.8 | 7.6 |
| 1993 | 1.1 | 0.8 | 1.5 |
| 1994 | 3.0 | 1.5 | 4.5 |
| 1995 | 1.9 | 1.5 | 2.2 |
| 1996 | 1.9 | 1.5 | 2.2 |

(*Source*: Hagstofa Íslands 1997)

casual sexual partners, and being more careful with the use of alcohol and drugs.

[*Update 2002*: UNAIDS Epidemiological Assessment: The HIV epidemic remains at a low level in Iceland. By mid 2001, a cumulative total of 148 cases of HIV infection had been reported. Testing is mandatory in blood donations; the first HIV-positive case was detected in 1995. Among 400 persons attending the HIV-testing site in the capital city between 1987 and 1992, 2 (0.5%) were detected positive. Diagnosed HIV cases are reported at the national level.

[The estimated number of adults and children living with HIV/AIDS on January 1, 2002, were:

| | |
|---|---|
| Adults ages 15-49: | 220 (rate: 0.2%) |
| Women ages 15-49: | < 100 |
| Children ages 0-15: | < 100 |

[An estimated less than 100 adults and children died of AIDS during 2001.

[No estimate is available for the number of Icelandic children who had lost one or both parents to AIDS and were under age 15 at the end of 2001. (*End of update by the Editors*)]

## 11. Sexual Dysfunctions, Counseling, and Therapies

SÓLEY S. BENDER

### A. Sexual Dysfunctions and Availability of Therapy

Since only very limited studies about sexual dysfunctions have been done in Iceland, very little is known on a national level about the prevalence of these problems. Sexual dysfunctions have been reported postpartum in relation to postpartum depression. Sexual dysfunctions are mostly presented in connection with other problems that people have when they visit their family practitioner. It therefore depends on the sensitivity of the attending physician to discover the oftentimes hidden problem. In general, people seem inhibited about discussing sexuality in general and sexual problems in particular. This reluctance often seems to apply to medical practitioners as well. The 1992 study about sexual behavior showed that 28.2% of the respondents had had some discussion with a family practitioner or a nurse at the community health center, and 16.8% had discussed sexuality with a healthcare professional in a hospital (Jonsdottir 1994). From the healthcare providers' perspective, 29.8% said they often and rather often provide information and counseling in the community health centers about sexual problems (Bender 1990). Psychiatrists, psychologists, social workers, urologists, and gynecologists are the practitioners most likely to be consulted or involved in diagnosing sexual problems. Some people turn to the IcASRH for advice about their sexual problems.

There is no one certified as a sexual therapist by the Ministry of Health or a professional association in Iceland, and no sexual treatment center run by the government of Iceland. In 1975, a treatment center was launched and functioned for about ten years. Information and counseling services about sexuality and its relation to diseases are lacking within the hospital setting. There is no therapist practicing in Iceland who has a master's or doctoral degree in sexology.

## 12. Sex Research and Advanced Professional Education

SÓLEY S. BENDER

### A. Graduate Programs and Sexological Research

No undergraduate or graduate sexology programs are offered at the University of Iceland or in other universities in the country.

Very few Icelandic studies have been done about human sexuality. Before the 1975 abortion law took effect, there had been considerable discussion about the issue, and members of Parliament were stressing the need for preventive work. Following this, Sigurgestsson completed a psychology dissertation in 1977 based on a sample of 1,420 young people and conducted among all 14-year-old students in the Reykjavik area. The response rate was 92%. This study was the first of its kind to explore sexuality among this age group. The focus of this study was on puberty, sexual activity, and sex education. A year later, in 1978, Thorvardarson conducted a study of sex education as part of a Bachelor in Education program. This study was based on a sample of young people in the 6th grade ($n = 460$), 8th grade ($n = 480$), and among 16- to 18-year-olds ($n = 345$).

Following the first cases of HIV/AIDS, the first national study about sexual behavior and knowledge of HIV/AIDS was sponsored in 1992 by the Directorate of Public Health (Jonsdottir 1994; Jonsdottir & Haraldsdottir 1998). The purpose of this study was to get information for the direction of preventive strategies regarding HIV and AIDS. This study was a cross-sectional postal survey based on a national sample of 971 individuals in the age group 16 to 59. As noted in Section 6, Homoerotic, Homosexual, and Bisexual Behaviors, the response rate was 65%; 47% of those responding were males and 53% females.

Another national cross-sectional study was done in 1996 based on a stratified random sample of 2,500 young people 17 to 20 years old, 20% being teenage boys and 80% being teenage girls. The crude response rate was 68%. This study explored the attitudes of young people to sexual and reproductive health services, sexuality and the use of contraceptives, and the use of contraceptive services (Bender 1999).

### B. Sexological Organization and Publications

The Icelandic Sexology Association was established in 1985 and was active for the first ten years. Its goal was to promote sexology and the cooperation of people working as teachers, therapists, and researchers in the field of sexology. It was a member of the Nordic Association for Clinical Sexology (*Nordisk Forening for Klinisk Sexologi*, NACS).

The Icelandic Family Planning Association (The Icelandic Association for Sexual and Reproductive Health, IcASRH) was established in 1992. The Association has been focusing on teenage sexuality and the special needs of young people. It has published several pamphlets, postcards, and a semiannual newsletter. It is a member of International Planned Parenthood Federation (IPPF) and belongs to the European Network of IPPF. The address of the Association is: P.O. Box 7226, 127 Reykjavik, Iceland; email: fkb@mmedia.is; www.mmedia.is/fkb.

Stigamot (The Icelandic Incest Center), discussed in Section 8A under Sexual Abuse and Incest, has a website at www.stigamot.is.

There is no Icelandic sexological journal or periodical published exclusively about sexology. There have been some articles published in the Icelandic medical and nursing journals about sexuality. The Icelandic Sexology Association published a few issues of a newsletter, and the Icelandic Association for Sexual and Reproductive Health currently publishes a newsletter two times a year.

## References and Suggested Readings

Adalbjarnardottir, S., S. Davisdottir, & E. M. Runarsdottir. 1997. *Áhættuhegun reykvískra unglinga* [*Risk behavior of adolescents in Reykjavik*]. Reykjavík: Félagsvísindastofnun (The Institute of Social Sciences) Háskóla Íslands.

Adalsteinsdottir, H. 2000. *Unganir, fæingar og fóstureyingar meal unglingsstúlkna.* [*Pregnancies, births, and abortions among teenagers*]. Unpublished Bachelor of Science degree thesis. University of Iceland, Department of Nursing.

*Almenn hegningalög, nr. 19/1940 me vibótar breytingum* [*General criminal law with additional changes*]. 1940.

*Arsskyrsla sjukrahuss reykjavikur* [*The annual report of the City Hospital*]. 2000. Reykjavík: Sjukrahus Reykjavikur.

Axelsdottir, A., A. Atladottir, H. S. Davidsdottir, K. Skuladottir, K. Rikhardsdottir, R. Runarsdottir, & S. Hedinsdottir. 1990. *Könnun á kynfræsluefninu Lifsgildi og ákvaranir* [*A pilot study of the curriculum, human sexuality, values and choices*]. Unpublished Bachelor of Science degree thesis. University of Iceland, Department of Nursing.

Bardarson, H. R. 1965. *Iceland.* Haarlem: Joh. Enchede en Zonen.

Bender, S. S. 1990. Fjölskylduáætlun í íslensku heilbrigiskerfi [Family planning within the Icelandic healthcare system]. *Heilbrigisskrslur* (Fylgirit nr. 2). Reykjavík: Landlæknisembætti (The Directorate of Public Health).

Bender, S. S. 1999a. Attitudes of Icelandic young people toward sexual and reproductive health services. *Family Planning Perspectives, 31*(6):294-301.

Bender. S. S. 1999b. *Study of attitudes of young people toward sexual and reproductive health services.* Unpublished report.

Bender, S. S., A. G. Bjornsdottir, G. E. Hermannsdottir, M. R. Jonasson, R. I. Bjarnadottir, & Th. E. Gudjonsdottir. 2000. *Skrsla um fóstureyingar og agengi a getnaarvörnum* [*Report about abortion and access to contraceptive methods*]. Reykjavík: Heilbrigis og Tryggingamálaráuneyti (The Ministry of Health and Social Security).

Broddadottir, I., G. Eydal, S. Hrafnsdottir, & S. Sigurdardottir. H. 1997. The development of local authority social services in Iceland. In: J. Sipilä, ed., *Social care services: The key to the Scandinavian welfare model* (pp. 51-77). Aldershot: Avery.

CIA. 2002 (January). *The world factbook 2002.* Washington, DC: Central Intelligence Agency. Available: http://www.cia.gov/cia/publications/factbook/index.html.

Denmarks Statistics. 2000. *Statistics across borders.* Denmark: Denmarks Statistics Trykkeri.

Eiriksdottir, E., H. Haraldsson, H. Kjartansson, P. Gardarsson, R. Bjarnason, & Th. Ketilsdottir. 1976. *The man, birth, childhood and puberty.* Reykjavík: Namsgagnastofnun (National Center for Educational Materials).

Gallup. 1999. *The Gallup millennium survey.* Reykjavík: Gallup Iceland.

Gallup Organization Princeton. 1997. Family values differ sharply around the world. Gallup Poll Release. Princeton, NJ: Gallup Organization.

Geirsson, R. T., & J. A. Gudmundsson. 1987. Er pillan betri en af er láti? [Is the contraceptive pill better than what is said?]. *Heilbrigismál, 4*:12-15.

Geirsson, R. T., & J. A. Gudmundsson. 1988. Lykkjan hefur kosti og galla (The IUD has its pros and cons). *Heilbrigismál, 4*:28-31.

Gudbrandsson, B. 1999. *A report of activities during 1995-1999.* Unpublished report.

Gudmundsson, O. 1990. *Íslenska kynlífsbókin* [*The Icelandic sexuality book*]. Reykjavík: Almenna Bókafélagi.

Haagensen, K. M. 1999. *Nordic statistical yearbook 1999* (vol. 37). Copenhagen: Nordic Council of Ministers.

Hagstofa Íslands [Statistics Iceland]. 1997. *Konur og karlar* [*Women and men in Iceland*]. Reykjavík: Hagstofa Íslands. (Home page: Iceland Statistics, www.hagstofa.is.)

Hagstofa Íslands [Statistics Iceland]. 1998. *Ísland í tölum* [*Iceland in numbers*]. Reykjavík: Hagstofa Íslands.

Hagstofa Íslands [Statistics Iceland]. 1999a. *Fréttatilkynning nr. 88/1999. Mannfjöldi á Íslandi 1. Desember 1999, Bráabirgatölur.* [*News release nr. 88/1999. Population of Iceland 1. December 1999, Estimations*]. Reykjavík: Hagstofa Íslands.

Hagstofa Íslands [Statistics Iceland]. 1999b. *Landshagir 1999.* [*Statistical yearbook of Iceland 1999*]. Reykjavík: Hagstofa Íslands.

Hagstofa Íslands [Statistics Iceland]. 1999c. *Iceland in figures.* Reykjavík: Hagstofa Íslands.

Hagstofa Íslands [Statistics Iceland]. 2000. *Landshagir 2000* [*Statistical yearbook of Iceland 2000*]. Reykjavík: Hagstofa Íslands.

*Heilsufar Kvenna* [*Health of women*]. 1998. Reykjavík: Heilbrigis-og Tryggingamálaráuneyti (The Ministry of Health and Social Security).

Johannsdottir, B. H., E. O. Gudjonsdottir, & H. R. Eyjolfsdottir. 2000. *Kynheilbrigisjónusta fyrir unglinga* [*Sexual and reproductive health service for teenagers*]. Unpublished Bachelor of Science degree thesis. University of Iceland, Department of Nursing.

Jonsdottir, E. 2000 (July). Hópnaugungum fer fjölgandi [Group rape is increasing]. *Dagblai Vísir,* bls. 4.

Jonsdottir, J. I. (1994). Könnun á kynhegun og ekkingu á alnæmi [A survey on sexual behavior and knowledge about AIDS]. *Heilbrigisskrslur* (Fylgirit nr. 2). Reykjavík: Landlæknisembætti (The Directorate of Public Health).

Jonsdottir, J. I., & S. Haraldsdóttir. 1998. Kynhegun og ekking á alnæmi [Sexual behavior and knowledge about AIDS]. *Heilbrigisskrslur* (Fylgirit nr. 5). Reykjavík: Landlæknisembætti (The Directorate of Public Health).

Jonsson, F. H., & S. Olafsson. 1991. *Lífsskoun í nútímalegum jófélögum* [*Values in modern societies*]. Unpublished manuscript. Reykjavík: Félagsvísindastofnun (The Institute of Social Sciences).

Juliusdottir, S. 1982. Váld i isländska familjer [Violence in Icelandic families]. *Nordisk Socialt Arbeid, 4*(2):3-15.

Juliusdottir, S. 1993. *Den kapabla familjen i det isländska samhället. En studie om lojalitet, äktenskapsdynamik och psykosocial anpassning.* [*The capable family in the Icelandic society*]. Reykjavík: University of Gothenburg/University of Iceland.

Juliusdottir, S., & G. Asmundsson. 1987. The emphasis on work and income in Icelandic families and its effect on family life. In: N. Schönnesson, ed., *Nordic intimate couples: Love, children and work* (pp. 45-65). Copenhagen: Nordisk Ministerråd/JÄMFO.

Juliusdottir, S., S. J. Gretarsson, F. H. Jonsson, & N. K. Sigurdardottir. 1995. *Barnafjölskyldur. Samfélag. Lífsgildi. Mótun* [*Childbearing families, society, values, and influences*]. Reykjavík: Félagsmálaráuneyti.

Juliusdottir, S., & N. K. Sigurdardottir. (in press). *Joint custody. A nation-wide comparative study on divorced parents' experience.* Reykjavík: Háskólaútgáfan.

Kahn, F. 1948. *Sexuality.* Reykjavík: Helgafell.

Kjartansson, H., & S. H. Brynjolfsson. 1983. *Human reproduction.* Reykjavík: Namsgagnastofnun (National Center for Educational Materials).

Kristmundsdottir, S. D. 1990. *Doing and becoming: Women's movements and women's personhood in Iceland 1870-1990.* New York: University of Rochester.

*Lög um jafna stöu og jafnan rétt kvenna og karla, nr. 65/1985* [*Law about equal status and equal rights of women and men*].

*Lög um rágjöf og fræslu varandi kynlíf og barneignir og um fóstureyingar og ófrjósemisagerir, nr. 25/1975* [*Law about information and counseling about sexuality and childbearing and about abortion and sterilization*].

*Lög um varnir gegn kynsjúkdómum, nr. 16/1978 Me vibótarbreytingum* [*Law about STD with additional changes*].

Lorensdottir, A. S., E. O. Sigurdardottir, G. Matthiasdottir, & G. A. Valgeirsdottir. 1994. *Ung og ábyrg fyrir nju lífi* [*Young and responsible for a new life*]. Unpublished Bachelor of Science degree thesis. University of Iceland, Department of Nursing.

NOMESCO. 1998. *Health statistics in the Nordic countries.* Copenhagen: NOMESCO (Nordic Medico Statistical Committee).

NOMESCO. 1999. *Health statistics in the Nordic countries.* Copenhagen: NOMESCO (Nordic Medico Statistical Committee).

Nordic Council of Ministers. 1999. *Women and men in the Nordic countries 1999.* Halmstad, Sweden: Bulls Tryckeri AB.

NOSOSCO. 1996. *Social tryghed i de nordiske lande [Social support in the Nordic countries].* Copenhagen: NOSOSCO (Nordic Social Statistical Committee).

Olafsdottir, H., S. Juliusdottir, & Benediktsdottir. 1982. *Ofbeldi í íslenskum fjölskyldum [Violence in Icelandic families].* Ge 	vernd, *17*:17-32.

Olafsson, S. 1989. *The making of the Icelandic welfare state. A Scandinavian comparison.* Reykjavík: Félagsvísindastofnun (The Institute of Social Sciences). *See also*: Variations within the Scandinavian model. Iceland in a comparative perspective. In: E. J. Hansen, H. Uusitalo, & R. Erikson, eds., *Welfare trends in Scandinavia.* New York: M.A. Sharpe.

Olafsson, S. 1990. *Lifskjör og lífshættir á Norurlöndum. Samanburur á jófélagi Íslendinga, Dana, Finna, Normanna og Svía [Living conditions in the Nordic countries. Comparison between Iceland, Denmark, Finland, Norway, and Sweden].* Reykjavík: Iunn.

Olafsson, S. 1991. *Lífsskoun í nútímajófélögum [Values in modern societies].* Reykjavík: Félagsvísindastofnun (The Institute of Social Sciences).

Olafsson, S. 1999. *Íslenska leiin. Almannatryggingar og velfer í fjöljólegum samanburi. [The Icelandic way. Public insurance and welfare in multisocial comparison].* Reykjavík: Tryggingastofnun Ríkisins/Háskólaútgáfan.

Olafsson, S., I. Kaldalons, & K. Sigurdsson. 1998. *Vihorf til velferarríkisins á Íslandi. [Attitudes to the welfare state of Iceland].* Unpublished manuscript. Reykjavík: Félagsvísindastofnun (The Institute of Social Sciences).

Oskarsson, Th., & R. T. Geirsson. 1987. Fóstureyingar og notkun getnaarvarna [Abortion and use of contraceptive methods]. *Læknablai [The Icelandic Medical Journal], 73:* 321-326.

Palsdottir, J. B., & Th. Hardardottir. 1993. *Könnun á hvernig kynfræslu er hátta í efri bekkjum grunnskóla út frá sjónarhóli kennara [Survey of sexuality education according to the teachers'perspective].* Unpublished Bachelor of Science degree thesis. University of Iceland, Department of Nursing.

Proppé, J. 2000. Dyggirnar og Íslendingar [The virtues of Icelanders]. *Tímarit Máls og Menningar, 61*(2):6-17.

Rafnsdottir, G. L. 1995. *Women's strategies against suppression. A discussion about female trade unions in Iceland.* Lund: Lund University Press.

Rauhala, P.-L., M. Anderson, G. Eydal, O. Ketola, & W. Nielsen. 1997. Why are social care services a gender issue? In: J. Sipilä, ed., *Social care services: The key to the Scandinavian welfare model* (pp. 131-156). Aldershot: Avebury.

Sigurgestsson, A. (1977). *Ungdom og seksualitet [Young people and sexuality].* Århus: Psychologisk Institute, Århus Universitet.

Steingrimsson, O., J. H. Olafsson, K. G. Kristinsson, K. E. Jonsdottir, & A. Sigfusdottir. 1991. Eru klamydíuskingsar á undanhaldi á Íslandi? [Are chlamydia infections reducing in Iceland?]. *Læknablai [The Icelandic Medical Journal], 77*:369-372.

Sveinsdottir, M. Th., & V. B. Gudmundsdottir. 2000. *Unglingsmæur, skynjun á móurhlutverkinu [Teenage mothers, their perception of motherhood].* Unpublished Bachelor of Science degree thesis. University of Iceland, Department of Nursing.

Thorlindsson, I. D. Sigfusdottir, J. G. Bernburg, & V. Halldorsson. 1998. *Vímuefnaneysla ungs fólks. Umhverfi og astæur [Drug use of young people: Environment and conditions].* Reykjavík: Rannsóknarstofnun Uppeldis-og Menntamála.

Thorvardarson, J. 1978. *Um kynferisfræslu [About sex education].* Reykjavík: Kennarahaskóli Islands.

UNAIDS. 2002. *Epidemiological fact sheets by country.* Geneva, Switzerland: Joint United Nations Programme on HIV/AIDS (UNAIDS/WHO). Available: http://www.unaids.org/hivaidsinfo/statistics/fact_sheets/index_en.htm.

United Nations Development Program (UNDP). 1999. *Human development report 1999.* New York: United Nations Development Program.

# India

## (*Bharat*)

Jayaji Krishna Nath, M.D.,* and Vishwarath R. Nayar
*Updates by Karen Pechilis-Prentiss, Ph.D.,*
*Aparna Kadari, B.A., M.B.A., and Robert T. Francoeur, Ph.D.*

## Contents

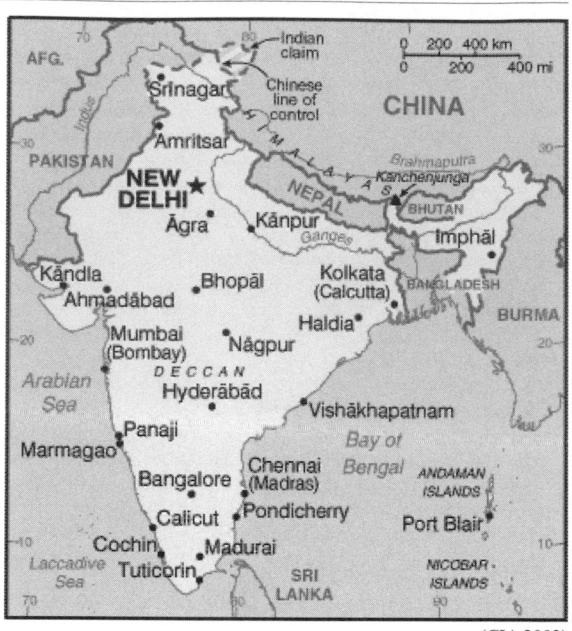

(CIA 2002)

## Demographics and a Brief Historical Perspective

ROBERT T. FRANCOEUR

### A. Demographics

India, with an area of 1.27 million square miles (3.29 million km²), is the largest democratic country in the world. India is one-third the size of the United States and occupies most of the Indian subcontinent in south Asia. In southern Asia, India's southern neighbor is the island nation of Sri Lanka. India borders on the Arabian Sea and Pakistan in the west and the Bay of Bengal, Bangladesh, and Myanmar in the east. China, Bhutan, and Nepal are on India's northern border.

The terrain is upland plains, the Deccan Plateau, in the south, flat to rolling plains along the Ganges River, deserts in the west, and the Himalayan Mountains in the north. Below the Indo-Ganges plain, which extends from the Bay of Bengal on the east to the Afghan frontier and Arabian Sea on the west, the land is fertile and one of the most densely populated regions of the world. The three great rivers, the Ganges, Indus, and Brahmaputra, have their origins in the Himalayas. With one quarter of the land forested, the climate varies from tropical monsoon in the south to near-Arctic in the north. The Rajasthan Desert is in the northwest; in the northeast, the Assam Hills receive 400 inches (1,000+ cm) of rain a year.

In July 2002, India had an estimated population of 1.045 billion people, giving it about 16% of the world's total population living on 2.4% of the earth's land area. Next to China, India is the most populous country in the world. (All data are from *The World Factbook 2002* (CIA 2002) unless otherwise stated.)

**Age Distribution and Sex Ratios**: *0-14 years*: 32.7% with 1.06 male(s) per female (sex ratio); *15-64 years*: 62.6%

with 1.07 male(s) per female; *65 years and over*: 4.7% with 1.03 male(s) per female; *Total population sex ratio*: 1.07 male(s) to 1 female

**Life Expectancy at Birth**: *Total Population*: 63.23 years; *male*: 62.55 years; *female*: 63.93 years

**Urban/Rural Distribution**: 28% to 72%. In 1991, one third of the 12.6 million inhabitants of Bombay were homeless, living on the streets or in squatters' camps built on putrid landfills. Bombay, India's most populous city, has 100,000 people per square kilometer (0.39 mi²).

**Ethnic Distribution**: Indo-Aryan: 72%; Dravidian: 25%; Mongoloid and other: 3% (2000 est.)

**Religious Distribution**: Hindu: 81.3%; Muslim: 12%; Christian: 2.3%; Sikh: 1.9%; other groups, including Buddhist, Jain, and Parsi: 2.5%

**Birth Rate**: 23.79 births per 1,000 population

**Death Rate**: 8.62 per 1,000 population

**Infant Mortality Rate**: 63.19 deaths per 1,000 live births

**Net Migration Rate**: –0.07 migrant(s) per 1,000 population

**Total Fertility Rate**: 2.98 children born per woman

**Population Growth Rate**: 1.51%

**HIV/AIDS** (1999 est.): *Adult prevalence*: 0.7%; *Persons living with HIV/AIDS*: 3.7 million; *Deaths*: 310,000. (For additional details from www.UNAIDS.org, see end of Section 10B.)

**Literacy Rate** (*defined as those age 15 and over who can read and write*): 52% (1995 est.) with schooling compulsory to age 14. The literacy rate is significantly lower for females than for males, 37.7% versus 65.5%.

**Per Capita Gross Domestic Product** (*purchasing power parity*): $2,500 (2000 est.); *Inflation*: 3.5% (2000 est.); *Unemployment*: 4.4% (1999 est.); *Living below the poverty line*: 25%; more than a third of the population cannot afford an adequate diet.

### B. A Brief Historical Perspective

Modern India is one of the oldest civilizations in the world. Excavations in the Indus valley trace civilization there back for at least 5,000 years. India's cultural history includes prehistoric mountain cave paintings in Ajanta, the exquisite beauty of the Taj Mahal in Agra, the rare sensitivity and warm emotions of the erotic Hindu temple sculp-

*Communications*: Jayaji Krishna Nath, M.D., National Institute for Research in Sex Education Counseling and Therapy (NIRSECT), 'SAIPRASAD' C5/11/0.2 Sector–4 (C.B.D.) Vivekanand Nagar, New Bombay 400615 India. Karen Pechilis-Prentiss, Ph.D., Drew University, Department of Religion, Madison, NJ 07940 USA; kpechili@drew.edu.

tures of the 9th-century Chandella rulers, and the Kutab Minar in Delhi.

Around 1500 B.C.E., Sanskrit-speaking Aryan tribes invaded the Indus valley from the northwest and blended with the earlier inhabitants to create the classical Indian civilization. Asoka ruled most of the Indian subcontinent in the 3rd century B.C.E. and established Buddhism; but, Hinduism experienced a revival and became the dominant religious tradition. The Gupta kingdom, in the 4th to 6th centuries of the Common Era, enjoyed a golden age of science, literature, and the arts. In the 8th century, Arab invaders brought the Muslim faith to the west, and Turkish Muslims gained control of north India by 1200. Vasco da Gama established Portuguese trading posts in 1503, and the Dutch followed soon after. Between 1526 and 1857, India was ruled by the Mongul emperors. In 1609, the British East India Company sought concessions for spices and textiles from the Mongul emperor, and subsequently gained control of most of India. The British curbed the rule of the *rajahs* around 1830 and supported the native rulers in the mutiny of the Sepoy troops in 1857-1858.

After World War II, the Indian National Congress joined with the Muslim League. Mohandas K. Gandhi, who had launched opposition to the British in 1930, emerged as the leader of the independence movement. In 1935, the British partitioned British India, giving India its own constitution and bicameral federal congress and establishing India as a self-governing member of the British Commonwealth. The partition created an independent Pakistan, triggering a mass migration of more than 12 million Hindu and Muslim refugees that was often violent and set the stage for a war in 1971-1973. This time, the massive migration involved some ten million refugees. Kashmir, a predominately Muslim region in the northwest, which has been in dispute with Pakistan and India since 1947, was divided in 1949, with Pakistan incorporating one third of Kashmir and India two thirds. India's new territory became the states of Jammu and Kashmir with internal autonomy. In 1952-1954, France peacefully yielded to India the five colonies of former French India, Pondicherry, Karikal, Mahe, Yanaon, and Chandernagor.

Ethnic violence accompanied several Sikh uprisings in the 1980s—the former British protectorate of Sikkim had become a protectorate of India in 1950 and was absorbed into India in 1974. Violence also broke out in the Pungab in 1988 and Assam in 1993. Also in 1993, the largest wave of criminal violence in Indian history jolted Bombay and Calcutta with devastating bombings.

## 1. Basic Sexological Premises

### A. Gender Roles
The family in Indian society provides for the satisfaction of the fundamental biopsychic drives of hunger and sex, and makes it possible to perpetuate the species through reproduction and the social heritage through the handing down of traditions from generation to generation. The function of preserving language, customs, and traditions is normally performed in collaboration with other social groups. Husband and wife, though, contribute to the maintenance of the family. There is a clear division of labor based on sex. The sex roles of a person consist of the behavior that is socially defined and expected of that person because of his or her role as a male or female. Rigid, mutually exclusive, conceptualizations of appropriate abilities or activities, tasks, characteristics, and attitudes are assigned differently to men and women in all Indian cultures. Because of rapid social and technological changes, it is observed that in the recent period, traditional gender-role differentiation is breaking down, espe-

cially in the fields of education and work. The historical analysis of the status of women shows that in Vedic India, as revealed by its literature, women were treated with grace and consideration. However, in the post-Vedic age, there was a slow but steady decline of their importance in the home and society. A decline, indeed a distinct degeneration in their status, is visible in medieval India. The *purdah* system of female seclusion, the *sati* tradition of immolating the widow on the husband's pyre (Weinberger-Thomas 1999), the dowry, and child marriages were obvious in the preindependence period. Following independence from England, however, there was a distinct, if uneven, and gradual liberal change in the attitude toward and status of women.

> [In India's] male-dominated tradition, and everywhere in Vedic, classical, medieval, and modern Hinduism, the paradigms in myths, rituals, doctrines, and symbols are masculine. But just as goddess traditions encroached successfully on the territory of masculine deities, so too has the impact of women's religious activity, the ritual life in particular, been of increasing significance in the overall scale of Hindu tradition. To put this another way, in traditional life the unlettered folk have always shaped Hinduism, and half of them have been women. It is not feminine roles in Hinduism that have been lacking but rather the acknowledgment of such in literature, the arts, and institutions such as the priesthood and temple and monastic administrations. Only now, in a world rapidly changing because of education opportunities, are such institutions and media beginning to reflect accurately the total picture of Hindu class, caste, gender, and regional life. (Knipe 1991, 10-11)

The urban/suburban environment has given birth to a fascinating mix of traditional and new male/female roles and role models among the affluent middle class. Bombay films are much more influential in creating new role models than the Hollywood films were in their early days in the United States. While the United States had one example of a film star succeeding in presidential politics, India has seen many famous film stars, both male and female, achieve political prominence. In 1966, Indira Gandi became prime minister of India, at a time when few Western nations would have accepted a woman head of state. And yet, India remains a very male-dominated society.

Despite new currents, very often in Indian culture a woman's body is not seen as an object of pride or pleasure, but as something that is made impure every day, an abode of sinfulness. Thus, a muted yet extremely powerful theme can be found in Hindu marriages: "the cultural unease, indeed, the fear of woman as woman." Women, as reflected in popular novels and clinical practice, frequently view their sexuality as a capacity to redress a lopsided distribution of power between the sexes (Kakar 1989, 13). The age-old, yet still persisting, cultural splitting of the wife into a mother and a whore, which underlies the husband-wife relationship and which explains the often-contradictory Hindu views of the woman, is hardly unique to Indian culture, though it may be more pervasive here than in other cultures (Kakar 1989, 17).

The social context determines whether the woman is viewed as divine, good, or bad—as partner in ritual, as mother, or as whore. In the context of ritual, women are honored and respected. In her maternal aspect, actual or potential, woman is again a person deserving all reverence. "It is only just as a woman, as a female sexual being, that the patriarchal culture's horror and scorn are heaped upon the hapless wife" (Kakar 1989, 17).

[*Update 2001*: In the complex of conservative and patriarchal Indian society, contemporary roles for and attitudes toward women are informed by traditional images of women from each of India's many religions. Across all of these traditions, women are expected to marry, to bear children, especially sons, and to be devoted to their husbands. This image of women's role and duty remains a tenacious traditional ideal in Indian society. What many people may not be aware of, especially in the West where journalistic reports detail the problems of Indian women seemingly without ever presenting the efforts to find solutions, is that contemporaneous with this traditional ideal are ongoing public discussions and activist mobilizations in contemporary Indian society on the issue of women's rights. Women's rights, especially women's equality, is an ideal espoused among educated middle-class Indians and the politicians they elect, but it is also growing in influence, especially at the grassroots level. In this discourse, the sexual oppression of women is openly discussed and opposed. What remains largely implicit in this discourse is the pleasurable side of women's sexuality: that women not only have the right not to be abused sexually, but that they have the right to enjoy themselves sexually. This reticence is certainly related to the slowly changing traditional attitude that sexual fulfillment is not a proper subject for public discussion or experience (for women). This aspect of sexuality may yet find a place in the ongoing organized attempts to change ingrained patterns of defining and relating to women. Many of these attempts cut across boundaries of religion and regional tradition. (*End of update by K. Pechilis-Prentiss*)]

[*Contemporary Use of Traditional Female Images*

[*Update 2002*: From the cries of "Mother India" during Independence to the comparisons of Prime Minister Indira Gandhi and the contemporary policewoman, Kiran Bedi, to the Hindu Goddess Durga, classical feminine images have had a prominent place in contemporary expressions of national aspirations and role models (Robinson 1999). In a recent article, scholar Lina Gupta has deconstructed the patriarchal image of the Hindu Goddess Kali, in order to assert that Kali is actually an emblem of women's intellectual, emotional, and sexual power: "The dark goddess is perpetually present in the inner and outer struggles faced by women at all times. Her darkness represents those rejected and suppressed parts of female creativity, energy and power that have not been given a chance to be actualized" (Gupta 1991, 37). With respect to its long and distinguished cultural history, as well as its contemporary multiculturalism, Indian society today actively engages tradition with modernity. (*End of update by K. Pechilis-Prentiss*)]

## B. Sociolegal Status of Males and Females

While it is mostly the husbands who are breadwinners, the women generally take care of the household activities, besides bearing and rearing children. However, because of widespread educational programs and improvement of educational facilities for girls, women nowadays are accepting jobs outside the home, and thus contributing financially to the family budget. Also, because of constant efforts in making women aware of their rights and the importance of their involvement in day-to-day family matters, the status of women has increased significantly. Because of all these measures, women nowadays actively participate not only in their family affairs, but also in social and political activities in the communities.

The occupations that were earlier monopolized by men are gradually being shared by women. Similarly, various professional courses, like engineering, architecture, and allied disciplines, are also studied by women. In spite of these changes initiated for the benefit of women in India, the people's attitude to equal status for women has not changed sig-

nificantly in actual practice, and in this regard, various educational programs for men are still in great need of changing their outlook. For instance, although the legal age of marriage for girls is set by the government at 18 years, people, especially in rural and tribal India, encourage early marriage for girls, mostly within a short time of their attaining puberty. Similarly, in the educational development, the dropout rate among females is very high.

## C. General Concepts of Sexuality and Love

Adult marriage is generally the rule in India. Usually, it is expected that a husband must be in a position to earn a living and his wife must be able to run the home, which they set up after marriage. The influence of the Hindu religion has resulted in some prepuberty marriages. The vast majority of regular marriages are still parent-made, arranged marriages. Irregular marriages do occur with the increasing influence of Western concepts of romantic love in the mass media of magazines and movies. In one form of irregular marriage, the two lovers run away and stay away until they are accepted by their families, which is done as a matter of course. In a second form, known as "intrusion," a girl confronts her chosen husband and his parents and presses their acceptance of her by living in the house. A third form involves "forcible application of vermilion," when a young man takes the opportunity at some fair or festival to place a vermilion scarf on his chosen girl's head. Sometimes, a betrothal ceremony takes place before the marriage proper is solemnized. Legally, marriage takes place only between those who have passed the puberty stage. At the marriage ceremony, the local priest is required to officiate and prayers and offerings are made to the gods.

Because of modernization and the influence of Western culture, arranged marriages are becoming less popular and common, especially in metropolitan cities. In its place, marriages based on the couple's choice, often crossing caste and/or religious boundaries, are becoming more common.

While sexual urges had to be subordinated to social norms in the joint-family system, except for rare rebellious behavior or outbursts, the present newly found freedom has instigated more openness and casualness in matters of sexual behavior. Expressions and feelings that would have been termed scandalous and in need of being tamed to adhere to socially accepted rules, values, and practices, are now accepted as natural.

Individualism, in its Western Euroamerican consciousness, is foreign to the traditional Indian social consciousness and experience. However, this is changing. Sudhir Kakar, a distinguished psychoanalyst who has taught at the Universities of Harvard, Chicago, and Vienna, and has written extensively on Indian sexuality, notes that "individualism even now stirs but faintly" in India (Kakar 1989, 4).

Traditional Indian folklore and stories, as well as modern novels, provide an important theme—the perennial, cosmic-based conflict between man and woman—that flows through much of male-female relationships in Indian culture and domestic life. Margaret Egnor sums this theme up in her study of *The Ideology of Love in a Tamil Family*. Based on her research in Tamil Nadu, Egnor observed that:

> Within the household, as well as in the domain of paid labor, there was a strong spirit of rivalry between many women and their husbands. Wives would not automatically accept submission. Neither would their husbands. Consequently, their relationship was often, from what I was able to observe, disputatious. . . . The eternal conflict between spouses is abundantly reflected in Indian mythology, especially Tamil which debates the issues of male vs female superiority back and forth endlessly on a cosmic

level in the form of battles and contests between deities or demons and their real or would-be mates. (Egnor 1986).

In Indian folklore, Shiva and Parvati argue interminably about who is the better dancer, while Vishnu and Lakshmi are constantly debating which is the greater divinity.

In most regions of the country, male folk wisdom traces the reasons for man's perennial war with woman to the belief that the female sex lacks both sexual morality and intelligence. The Punjabis and Gujaratis agree that "The intelligence of a woman is in her heels." Tamils maintain that "No matter how educated a woman is, her intelligence is always of the lowest order." The Malayalis warn that "One who heeds the advice of a woman will be reduced to beggary."

Men in southern India seem more resigned and willing to acknowledge their helplessness in the face of "general female cussedness and constant provocation." Kannada and Telugu men admit that "Wind can be held in a bag, but not the tongue of a shrew," while Telugu males confess that "Neither the husband nor the brother-in-law can control a pugnacious woman." By contrast, in the northern regions of India, folk sayings place "singularly greater emphasis on the employment of force and physical chastisement to correct perceived female shortcomings." "The place of a horse and a woman is under the thighs." Two proverbs from Gujarati echo this view: "Barley and millet improve by addition of salt; women through a beating by a pestle," and "Better to keep the race of women under the heel of a shoe" (Kakar 1989, 6).

Faced with this perennial conflict between husband and wife, the object of the wife's affectional and sensual currents traditionally has been the husband's younger brother in the joint or extended Indian family.

For a time in Indian social history, the custom of *nigora* officially recognized the erotic importance of the brother-in-law—in the sense that he would or could have sexual relations with his elder's brother's widow. The *nigora* custom has been traced back to the times of the Rig-veda, where a man, identified by the commentators as the brother-in-law, is described as extending his hand in promised marriage to a widow inclined to share her husband's funeral pyre.

Although the custom gradually fell into disuse, especially with the prohibition of widow remarriage, the psychological core of *niyoga*, namely the mutual awareness of a married woman and her younger brother-in-law as potential or actual sexual partners, remains very much an actuality even today (Kakar 1989, 13).

Kakar has added a perspective from clinical practice, noting that women who are on terms of sexual intimacy with a brother-in-law rarely express any feelings of guilt. Their anxiety is occasioned more by his leaving home or his impending marriage, which the woman perceives as an end to her sensual and emotional life (Kakar 1989, 13-14).

The fate of sexuality within marriage is likely to come under an evil constellation of stars. Physical love will tend to be a shame-ridden affair, a sharp stabbing of lust with little love and even less passion. Indeed, the code of sexual conduct for the householder-husband fully endorses this expectation. Stated concisely in the *smritis* (the Law codes), elaborated in the *puranas*, which are not only collections of myths, but also contain chapters on the correct conduct of daily life), modified for local usage by the various kinds of religiosi, the thrust of the message seems to be "No sex in marriage, we're Indian" (Kakar 1989, 19).

According to Hindu tradition, a husband should only approach his wife sexually during her *ritu* (season), a period of 16 days within the menstrual cycle. But intercourse is forbidden on six of these 16 days, the first four days, and the 11th and 13th. This leaves only ten days for conjugal relations, but since the all-important sons are conceived only on even nights and daughters on uneven nights, the days for conjugal relations shrink to five. Then there are the *parvas*, the moonless nights and those of the full moon when sexual relations lead either to the birth of atheist sons (*Brahma Purana*) or the "hell of feces and urine" (*Vishnu Purana*). Add to these taboos the many festival days for gods and ancestors, when erotic pleasures are forbidden. Sex is also beyond the pale during the day.

There is a general disapproval of the erotic aspect of married life, a disapproval that cannot be disregarded as a mere medieval relic; this general disapproval of the erotic, even in marriage, continues to inform contemporary attitudes. This is quite understandable, since changes in sexuality occur at a more gradual pace than transformations in the political and social sphere; sexual time, as Kakar suggests, beats at a considerably slower pace than its chronological counterpart. Sexual taboos are still so strong in some Hindu communities that many women, especially those in the higher castes, do not have a name for their genitals (Kakar 1989, 20).

Cultural taboos may not, despite their pervasive presence in Indian society, affect the sexual expressions of men and women across the economic and caste spectra of India. But they can, and apparently do, increase the conflicts around sexuality, sour it for many, and generally contribute to its impoverishment. This can effectively block many men and women from a deep, fulfilling experience of sexual love. Accordingly, the considerable sexual misery one can deduce as being reflected in the Indian marriage and family, from cultural ideals, prohibitions, and modern fiction, are the sexual woes expressed by middle- and upper-class women who seek relief in psychotherapy, and is also evidenced in the interviews Sudhir Kakar and others have conducted with low-caste, "untouchable" women in the poorest areas of Delhi.

Most of these women portrayed their experiences with sexual intercourse as a furtive act in a cramped and crowded room, lasting barely a few minutes and with a marked absence of physical or emotional caressing. It was a duty, an experience to be submitted to, often from a fear of beating. None of the women removed their clothes during intercourse, since it is considered shameful to do so (Kakar 1989, 21).

Despite these pervasive negative images of the conflict between the sexes in marriage, and the negative view of women and sexuality, it must be pointed out that Indian sexual relations are not devoid of regular pauses in the conflict between man and woman. Tenderness, whether this be an affair with the soul of a Mukesh song, that is much quieter than a plunge into the depths of erotic passion known in Western culture, or sexual ecstasy of a husband and wife who have found their way through the forest of sexual taboos, does exist in India (Kakar 1989, 22-23).

## 2. Religious, Ethnic, and Gender Factors Affecting Sexuality

### A. Source and Character of Religious Values

India is a multiethnic and multilingual society with wide variations in demographic situations and socioeconomic conditions. People in India practice different religions, and there are numerous cultural identities. The religious composition of India shows that a majority, 82%, are Hindu. The other religious groups are Muslim, 11.7%; Christians, 2.4%; Sihks, 1.9%; and other religious groups, 2%.

In a nation as religiously and ethnically diverse as India—the nation is commonly described as "a jumble of possibilities"—the people follow a wide variety of customs and have varied beliefs that ultimately mold their lifestyles. In the life of a Hindu male, for instance, marriage is regarded as necessary, because without a wife he cannot enter the *Grihasthasrama* (the life stage of a householder). In addition, without marriage there can be no offspring, and without a son no release from the chain of reincarnation in birth-death-rebirth. According to Hindu custom, which still prevails in most families, marriage must take place within one's caste or *Varna*, although marriages between members of different castes and communities are gaining acceptance. Hindu marriage, being a religious sacrament, is indissoluble.

The *purdah* system still prevails in the Muslim northern region of the country, where a female has to cover her face in front of other males and elders, but this custom is also slowly fading out. The Muslim male, who is allowed to have four wives, subject to specified conditions, is also realizing the wisdom in small families and monogamy (more so the educated, urban Muslim male). Marriage is solemnized by signing a legal document and can be dissolved. Divorce is almost exclusively the husband's privilege, although a divorcing husband has to pay the "Dower," a settlement made to the wife out of her husband's property to compensate her in the event of death and divorce.

Indian Christians are also influenced by the social practices of the region, but they tend to follow the pattern of a family as an independent unit, in which their lifestyles and interactions revolve around the community and the local church. They have more freedom in their general outlook and easily adapt to local conditions and trends.

The tribal people of India have varied religious and social practices, often with a more natural approach to sexuality and age-old practices of premarital sex and premarital experimental cohabitation.

Although there is a decreasing acceptance of orthodox beliefs and religious practices among India's younger generation, each of India's religious traditions maintains its own forms of observations of various practices, starting with birth and regulating life through marriage to the death ceremonies. The lifestyles of the people, including their sexual behavior, are generally governed by these prescribed practices.

### B. Source and Character of Ethnic Values

India's dominant ethnic element is the Indo-Aryan peoples with 72% of the population. The Aryans invaded India from the northwest between 2400 and 1500 B.C.E. and intermingled with already well-civilized native people. The Australoid Dravidans, including the Tamils, constitute 25% of the total population and dominate in southern India. Arab invaders established a Muslim foothold in the western part of the country in the 8th century, and Turkish Muslims gained control of northern India by 1200. These Muslims were in part responsible for the decline of the Chandella culture that dominated in northern India from c. 200 B.C.E. to C.E. 1200. The great "love temples" of northern India, including Khajuraho, were built in the 11th century and were in part destroyed by the invading Muslims (Deva 1986). In 1526, Muslim invaders founded the great Mongul empire centered in Delhi. This empire lasted, at least in name, until 1857. Today, 3% of Indians are of Mongoloid ancestry.

The Portuguese influence in Bombay and the Indian subcontinent dominated trade with Europe in the 1500s. In 1612, the English influence began to spread with the founding of the East India Trade Company. In 1687, the English took over Bombay, setting the stage for their defeat of the French and Islamic armies, and laying the foundation for the incorporation of India into the British Empire in 1858. English Victorian views of sexuality remain a strong influence in urban India.

In 1947, the Indian Independence Act was passed, and a new constitution establishing India as an independent democratic country was adopted in 1949. In the 1970s, a war in the north between East and West Pakistan ended with Indian intervention and establishment of East Pakistan as the new nation of Bangladesh.

## 3. Knowledge and Education about Sexuality

### A. Government Policies and Programs for Sex Education

Present-day children in India are more exposed to new areas of knowledge than their parents were. As a matter of fact, young people are simply deluged these days with movies, magazines, and books—all prime sources of sexual information and stimulation. Young people nowadays want to know more about the pros and cons of marriage, premarital and extramarital sexual relationships, venereal diseases, and so on. In a survey of college students conducted by the All India Educational and Vocational Guidance Association, it was reported that 54% of male students and 42% of female students stated that they did not have adequate knowledge regarding matters of sex. Though parents have the primary responsibility of imparting sex education to their children, it has been found that a majority of young people in India derive their information about sex and sex behavior largely from companions, street-corner conversation, movies, and magazines. The government is seriously contemplating introducing sex education as a part of the curriculum from the secondary school level onwards. One important reason for giving the school responsibility for sex education is that many parents feel unable to handle this task themselves. Many have inhibitions about discussing sex with their children; others admit that they do not have the technical knowledge to answer all the questions their children ask. In this situation, the teacher is a major factor in determining the success of any sex-education program. Serious efforts are under way in specifying the contents and components of sex education and the level at which this has to be taught. No information is available on the provision of sex education in special schools, such as those for mentally handicapped persons.

### B. Informal Sources of Sexual Knowledge

Parents give their young children sex education many years before they can begin to convey sex information verbally. The mother's behavior, attitudes, and roles are a clear model for the growing girl. Similarly, the father provides a role model for a son. The relationship, warmth, and responsiveness between parents provides for all children a model for their later marriage. By observing their parents, children see the basic qualities that make men and women different. Similarly, when the child is in the company of his friends, he or she learns through them the various facets of their life. The other important informal sources of sexual information for the child are peer-group influence, teachers, books, movies, magazines, and siblings.

Fifteen million Indians attend the cinema every day. Hindi cinema, perhaps more than the cinema of many other countries, provides fantasy, the stuff that dreams are made of. The cinema is the major shaper of an emerging, pan-Indian popular culture. As such, the mix of fantasy and reality, dreams and hopes, that permeates Hindi cinema is already a major factor in the remolding of Indian sexual values, expectations, and attitudes, as well as gender relations, marriage, and the family (Kakar 1989, 25-41).

## 4. Autoerotic Behaviors and Patterns

Masturbation is generally unacceptable among girls. For boys, however, it is considered a preparation for mature sex life. Though boys at the younger ages may masturbate together without shame, at little more-mature ages, they all give it up. This seems to be particularly so in the case of married men. In recent years, the availability of sexually explicit books, magazines, and videos has also acted as a major contributory factor for male autoerotic activities.

## 5. Interpersonal Heterosexual Behaviors

### A. Children

Indian children are pampered as much as possible, often until age 6 or 7. Before puberty, a natural approach to sexuality and nudity prevails, especially in rural areas. Daughters and sons are carefully prepared for their future domestic roles as mothers and fathers. Women are considered to be much more skilled than males in love and sexual pleasures. At puberty, most boys and girls are segregated. In some regions of India, pubescent girls are not even allowed to enter a house where a single young man is present.

Sexual views and behavior are somewhat more natural and less inhibited in India's rural villages, according to Dr. Promilla Kapur, a research psychologist and sociologist at New Delhi's India International Center. Some tribal groups practice totally free sex among adolescents.

Nowadays, with the advent of various satellite television programs, children are exposed at their early ages to various programs, including considerable sexually related material. This exposure often results in conflicting responses for girls raised in a society that represses or ignores female sexuality. In rural areas, adults sometimes talk loudly about their sexual experiences in the presence of children, and this provides opportunities for the young men to think more about sex. In urban areas, especially cities where housing shortage is very acute, adults in public places, like parks and cinema theaters, generally satisfy their sexual feelings through hugging or other noncoital sexual practices. These acts also provide learning opportunities for the younger ones. Sexual play, such as looking at another child's buttocks or genitals, genital touching games, sharing a bed with a child of the opposite sex, and so on, likewise provides children with opportunities for sexual exploration; the parents would not necessarily be aware of these acts of their children.

### B. Adolescents

Adolescents in India today face a number of problems related to changing value systems and social expectations. The sexual world of adolescents is becoming increasingly complex. In traditional Indian society, adolescents were initiated into their sexual roles, more or less, in a clearly defined period and by a series of ceremonies and rites. As in some other cultures, these included instruction on their sex roles, marriage customs, sexual morality, and acceptable sexual behavior. But with the influence of Western culture, the present generation of youth is facing a number of problems that are ultimately forcing them to violate the traditional norms as laid down by the society.

When Kakar and Chowdhary (1970) examined some aspects of sexual behavior among young men prior to marriage, they found that a lack of adequate information and opportunities prompted these young people to turn to literature (often pornographic), to experimentation with prostitutes, friends, or relatives of the opposite or same sex, to co-

vert observation of the sexual activities of others, and to masturbation. Reddy and his colleagues, in a 1983 study of young people, found that the sample youth had their first sexual experience between the ages of 15 and 24 years. Homosexual activities were also reported in this study: 38% of women in the sample reported that their first sexual activity had been with a partner of the same sex. The Family Planning Foundation of India undertook a study in 1990 among teenagers (between 14 and 17 years) and found that about one fourth of them expressed their acceptance of premarital sexual contact, "if the boy and the girl were actually in love." While a good number of respondents were aware of at least one contraceptive method, they had very little precise knowledge. Men were found to be more liberal in their views than women.

Mane and Maitra (1992) have rightly inferred that "relatively little is known about the sexual behavior and attitudes towards different aspects and forms of sexual activity in India." With changing conditions in India, the opportunities for risk-taking behavior among adolescents seem to be increasing. Coping with sex is a growing problem for young people. Today's teenagers are faced with an ever-widening gap between the age at which they are physically ready to have sexual intercourse and the age at which it is culturally acceptable for them to do so. Youngsters are, in fact, often sandwiched between a near-obsessive preoccupation with sex in the media and a veritable wall of silence from other sources of information on the subject. Sex education, including family planning and reproductive health management, has to be the cornerstone of any youth program that is attempted. The social, psychological, and emotional consequences to early sexual involvement also need to be carefully explained.

### C. Adults

*Premarital Courtship, Dating, and Relationships*

The marital bond involves a social sanction generally in the form of a civil or/and religious ceremony authorizing two persons of the opposite sex to engage in sexual relations and assume the consequent and correlated socioeconomic relationships and responsibilities society maintains for a married couple. Under the kind of social structure that caste has given rise to in India, there are certain restrictions in the limits beyond which the parents, in the case of an arranged marriage, and a man and a woman, in the case of a love marriage, cannot go in choosing a spouse; he or she must invariably marry outside his or her own *gotra*. (*Gotra* is the name of the ancestral head or father of the family.) A decision to marry is usually marked by an "engagement," where the elders of both the parties announce their intention to conduct the marriage to their family and friends.

Traditionally, premarital sex activity was controlled in India. As the marriages were mostly arranged by elders, premarital sex was not the accepted practice. Although premarital sex among the tribal societies of India has been widely reported, there is very little, if any, reliable data on this topic in either the rural or urban areas.

A recent study by Savara and Sridhar in 1992 showed that 30% of the respondents had experienced premarital sex, while 41% of unmarried men and 33% of married men had their first intercourse before attaining 20 years. In another study, they found that about one quarter of married women had sex with their husbands before marriage. Other premarital sexual partners for women were mostly friends, relatives, and work acquaintances. A majority of the respondents—43%—agreed that casual sex is all right, and it is acceptable to sleep with someone you have no plan to marry. It is clear that, although premarital sexual relationships are considered generally as immoral in contemporary India, the majority of the young generation do not find it objectionable. A gradual increasing openness about sex in films, video music, television, magazines, and so on, is clearly influencing the young in India to be more adventurous about premarital sex than their parents and elders were.

### Single Adults

Since marriage is strongly endorsed for all adults in India, the number of men and women remaining unmarried is very negligible. With the rapid increase in urbanization and industrialization, more and more young people are moving out of the rural areas into the urban areas, mainly in search of a livelihood. Mostly they move to urban areas by leaving their families, sometimes including a spouse, in their place of origin, because of the lack of proper housing facilities and the high cost of living in their new home. In the absence of their spouses, many married men turn to the brothel houses for satisfying their sexual urges. In so doing, they face many health problems, like STD and HIV.

### The Dowry Conflict

The centuries-old marital tradition of the dowry has recently become troublesome among some young married couples. Since females historically could not inherit property, parents would give their daughters money and property—a dowry—when they married. Young men came to depend on a good-sized dowry to start them off in a comfortable middle-class life. Although dowries were outlawed in the 1947 Constitution and in subsequent laws passed by the Indian Parliament in the 1970s, the new law has created serious problems for brides whose parents refuse to give a sizable gift—the equivalent of the traditional dowry—to the groom. In such cases, some new husbands and their families conspire to drive the young bride to suicide, or if this fails, even murder her (see Section 8A, Significant Unconventional Sexual Behaviors, Coercive Sex, on domestic violence and dowry deaths). In this way, a young man might marry several times and eventually accumulate enough in illegal dowries to live comfortably. But dowries remain important for Indian women today. Even though they can inherit and no longer depend on the dowry for financial security, Indian women still consider the dowry their right. In the mobile social strata of the cities, the size of a woman's dowry definitely affects her social status. In West Bengal, the groom and his family may demand dowry payments of as much as 60,000 rupees, or nearly $2,000, more than ten times the annual income of many rural families.

Effective enforcement of the antidowry law and protection of brides from abuse is difficult, despite the efforts of women's rights groups and special courts set up by the government. Many believe the only hope for permanent improvement lies in changing social attitudes, including the promotion of marriages based on love instead of arranged marriages.

[*Update 2003*: In May 2003, 2,000 guests gathered to celebrate the wedding of Nisha Sharma, a 21-year old computer student, and Munish Dalai, 25, in Noida, an eastern suburb of Dehli. According to later reports in major newspapers around the world, the father of the bride had already provided two Sony television sets, two home theaters, two air conditioners, and two sets of electrical appliances for the kitchen—one of each for the couple and the other for the groom's older brother, who had headed the household after the death of their father. A car for the older brother was also included in the unofficial dowry. All went smoothly at the wedding until, at the very last minute, the groom's older brother demanded 25,000 rupees in cash for their mother.

[As the media was quick to report, the free-for-all that erupted between the two families ended when "the bartered bride put her hennaed foot down, reached for her royal blue cellphone and dialed 100." When the police arrived, they spent an hour calming down the families and guests, which allowed the groom and his family plenty of time to escape. Three hours later, Ms. Sharma accompanied the police to the station and filed an official complaint against the groom and his family for demanding an illegal dowry. By chance, a television crew from *Aaj Tak* news channel happened to be in the station. As the bride's father later described what happened, "With the pressure of the media people, the police went to the boy's house and arrested him." The groom would be in jail until he could be arraigned and officially charged with violating the antidowry law.

[India's new 24-hour news stations then propelled Nisha to "Hindi stardom" and a media blitz was on. The *Times of India* headline admitted, "It Takes Guts to Send Your Groom Packing." *Rashtriya Sahara*, a major Hindi daily, wrote, "Bravo, Nisha, We're Proud of You." *Asian Age* hailed her "as a New Age woman and . . . a role model to many." Major newspapers and television news programs around the world picked up the story of the bride who refused to be bartered. In the next few days, Ms. Sharma was unfazed by the loss of her fiancé, as 1,500 supportive emails poured into a special number set up by the 24-hour news stations. She also received two-dozen marriage proposals by cellphone, email, and letter (Brooke 2003). (*End of update by A. Kadari*)]

### Marriage and Divorce

Despite an increasing modernization and shift to love-based marriages, most marriages in India are still arranged by parents. Family concerns take precedence over the interests of young couples, because Indian parents strongly believe that a marriage will be good only if the bride and groom come from similar backgrounds. The impetus for arranged marriages is respect for the wisdom of one's elders. To assure that their offspring marry within their own community or caste, many Indian parents use the classified advertisement sections of newspapers to make contact and arrange marriages for their children. In the villages and rural areas, distinctions in the caste system are much stronger and sharper than they are in the cities.

Although the tradition of arranged marriages has a practical value in preserving family traditions and values, it encounters some opposition as young Indian men and women learn of the Western tradition of romance and love. Urban middle-class Indians are most affected. Most Indian men and women attending college outside India are careful not to compromise their prospects back home by letting their family or parents know they have dated a foreigner.

While marriage is a sacred arrangement made in the presence of elders, divorce is legally possible. The incidence of divorce was very negligible in the past, mainly because of the low status of women in the society and the very low level of educational background of females, which left divorced women incapable of supporting themselves. Current trends show that the divorce rate is increasing in the recent past, especially in urban areas. This clearly indicates that women are becoming more aware of their rights, and more assertive in maintaining their individual identity in their employment and personal earnings without being submissive to men.

The joint or extended Hindu family, which dominated in the past, is gradually disintegrating. In the traditional Hindu extended family, the eldest male governed the entire family; the daily life of its members revolved around this huge family. The family head, in consultation with other elder males, arranged marriages in which the youngsters had little say. The females lived behind closed doors—"within the four walls" environs. Festive occasions were the only times when they had the opportunity to interact with others in the neighborhood or relatives. With the disintegration of this family unit into individual families, the problems of insecurity and social influences of the neighborhood have become common. This is indeed leading to the assertion of individual freedom in the choice of marital partners and lifestyles.

[*Update 2003*: Srinath Krishnan (2003) echoes the opinion of most South Asian Indians that arranged marriages "have been around in India as long as probably the institution of marriage itself." Indian marriages were and still are a family matter, with romantic love and the input of the young woman and man traditionally of minor concern. Older, and wiser, women in the family, known as "Aunt Bijis" in the Muslim community and "Aunties" among the Hindi, still bear the responsibility of investigating the family background and history of the potential bride and groom, his education, caste, religious persuasion, economic status, and career potential to find the most compatible young man for their daughter/niece. Once the Aunties select the groom, the daughter's mother usually shows her a picture of the young man, and then arranges for a brief formal meeting with the prospect and his family, followed by a brief engagement and the marriage, with the bride and groom having little opportunity to become acquainted along the way. Today, in some families, after the engagement the couple might have a few formal meetings or dates chaperoned by a family member. But the engagement is binding and seldom broken. A more formal meeting might also be arranged, in which the young man, his mother, and several other relatives visit the young woman and her family. "These formal meetings could be awkward, drawn-out affairs for which the young woman wore her best Indian outfit, a sari or elegant Indian pants and top. She sat quietly, which is almost impossible to fathom, considering her chattiness. When called upon, she poured tea, and then talked briefly to her potential mate in a side room" (Alvarez 2003).

[Over the centuries, the customs of arranged marriages have gradually evolved as social circumstances changed. This adaptation and change is accelerating in the diverse urban and rural communities of the Indian subcontinent, but they are more obvious in the tight-knit Indian communities in Britain, where second- and third-generation children of Indian expatriates are exposed to a very different culture. In the 1960s, after Aunties arranged for a young couple and their extended families to meet, the couple might meet alone several times, either with family members in another room or at a restaurant, before the couple decided to marry. Even then, the decision was heavily influenced by family responsibilities. Today, these pre-engagement meetings take place in public venues with the family encounter coming later. In recent years, the traditional role of the family and Aunties has been reduced, as young Indians take advantage of a boom in Asian marriage Web sites, Internet chat rooms, and personal advertisements. "Speed dating" for Muslims on one night at a local restaurant or bar, and Hindi on another night, are also becoming a popular way for young Indians to meet each other for just three minutes before moving on to the next potential mate. If a woman meets a suitable, interesting candidate, she can inform the matriarchs in her family, her mother and Auntie, and let them make further arrangements. An "assisted arranged marriage" is the new term for this changing pattern of courtship and marriage (Alvarez 2003).

[The advantages of an arranged marriage are still evident, since the matriarchs base their advice and recommendation not on passionate, romantic, lusty love, which can

"fizzle out," but on longer-lasting considerations of family and mutual compatibility. Not all Indian parents are comfortable or accepting of these changes, but parents and elders, eager to avoid alienating their children, making them miserable or seeing them go unmarried, are showing considerable flexibility, especially in middle-class and urban Indian communities. South Asian expatriate parents and elders in Britain and Europe have had to adapt, in large part because the number of potential partners is much smaller there than in their home countries. Rather than see an educated daughter go unwed, parents and elders have accepted these more modern approaches. But there is also a cultural exchange with changes in the courtship and marriage customs outside India gaining root in the urban middle class on the Asian subcontinent. (*End of update by A. Kadari and R. T. Francoeur*)]

*Family Size*

In India, the demographic transition is at the middle stage where both birth and death rates are showing a declining trend, but the death rate is declining at a faster rate, while the fertility rate is not declining as fast as expected. As marriage is almost universal, in almost all religious groups the age at marriage—especially of females—is very low. For instance, the average age for females at marriage is 18.3 years; for males, it is 23.3 years. Because women have a long reproductive span, Indian couples tend to have large families. The total fertility rate in India is 4.5 and the total marital fertility rate is 5.4. Various factors, such as a strong preference for a son, the low status of women, a high infant mortality, a high illiteracy level, inadequate healthcare facilities, and irregular follow-up services provided by the health staff play a major role in keeping couples from accepting contraception.

More than 80% of deliveries in India, especially in rural and tribal areas, are conducted by the traditional birth attendants, locally called "*Dais*." In the absence of a formal healthcare system within their reach in times of need, people in general depend on these indigenous people for their deliveries. These older women generally have very high credibility and act as good change agents in the community. Though in traditional societies, a joint family system is more commonly observed, nuclear families have become more common in the recent decades, mainly because of changes in the occupational structure and dispersal of family members in search of livelihood, and their movements into urban areas.

*[Sexual Abstinence*

[*Update 2002*: Abstinence from sex is a strategy within marriage adopted by some wives in order to assert their own control over domestic space and family life. Women's rights author and activist Madhu Kishwar (1997) profiles contemporary women from several different walks of life who self-consciously pursue this strategy. For some Hindu women, this abstinence is related to their role as a medium for the Goddess: They are both vehicles for the Goddess and thus subject to Her command, yet they enjoy status, influence, and control with respect to their families and to the devotees who solicit the Goddess' favor through them (Hancock 1999, 141-173).

[Abstinence can also indicate that a woman has chosen a life path distinct from marriage and childbearing; religion is one of the few established institutional avenues in India through which a woman may make such a choice. Jains in India possess a very well established and living tradition of nuns, who renounce all ties to their families in order to practice intense spiritual discipline. In Hinduism, there are many contemporary female gurus who are celibate; some are married, but are understood not to have consummated their marriages. The internationally famous female guru Anandamayi Ma (1896-1982) established an ashram exclusively for women to practice spiritual discipline, as well as a Sanskrit school for young girls, which "provide protection for girls who [do] not desire marriage and education for those who do" (Hallstrom 2000, 206). (*End of update by K. Pechilis-Prentiss*)]

### Sexuality and the Physically Disabled and Elderly

There are no organized attempts made so far to assess Indian attitudes about the sexuality of physically and mentally handicapped persons and elderly. Very little attention has been paid so far in sexuality training for the teachers and health personnel who work with these disadvantaged groups. Furthermore, there is no effort made by the institutions that serve these people to deal with the sexual needs of their residents.

### Incidence of Oral and Anal Sex

Vaginal intercourse is the norm for marital sexual activity. The incidence of fellatio and cunnilingus is not known in the Indian context. However, oral sex appears to be relatively uncommon.

## 6. Homoerotic, Homosexual, and Bisexual Behaviors

Heterosexual acts, the only socially acceptable sexual expression, is based primarily on the much wider contact and more common relationships between males and females in society. The family is promoted as the early valid social unit. Although homosexuals existed even in ancient India, they never attained social approval in any section of the Indian population. There was a reference to such practices in the *Kamasutra*, written by Vatsyayana more than 1,500 years ago and long admired as an extraordinary analytic treatise on sex and love.

Very little is known about the current practice of male or female homosexuality in India. Homosexuality is slowly gaining acceptance, in part because of the efforts of one or two organized groups in metro cities that are affiliated with a couple of activist homosexual groups connected to international bodies of gays. A regular voice of one organization, and of its homosexual members, is published in Bombay, titled *Bombay Dost*, or "Bombay Friend."

Savara and Shridhar (1992) reported that 12% of unmarried men and 8% of married men reported that their first sexual experience was with another man, and most of them had it before they were 20 years of age. About two fifths of them had a homosexual experience with one or two persons, while over a fifth had such experiences with more than ten persons. In their homosexual acts, only 21% of them had used condoms. Ahmed (1992), in his study of truck drivers, found that 15% of them admitted previous homosexual experience. Parasuraman et al. (1992), from a study in Madras, found that 3% of the homosexuals earned their livings as dancers and/or sex workers. It is further reported in this study that most of the men were between the ages of 21 and 30, and took both active and passive roles in unprotected anal and oral intercourse.

[*Lesbianism*

[*Update 2001*: The issue of women's sexual fulfillment was dramatized in Deepa Mehta's controversial film of 1996, *Fire*, in which a young urban middle-class woman marries, is neglected by her husband, and begins a lesbian relationship with an older married woman in the family whose husband also neglects her. While many felt the film was rather crude in its presentation of Hindu Indian tradition as a foil for the "modern" approach of lesbianism, in the process relegating lesbianism to a response to selfish men (Kishwar 1998), the film takes a very public stand that women have the need and the right to be fulfilled sexually. Currently, lesbian groups in India are campaigning to decriminalize homosexuality. In 1999, the Campaign for Lesbian Rights in Delhi issued a report describing the intimidation and difficulties of lesbians in India. (http://www.umiacs.umd.edu/users/sawweb/sawnet/news/news337.txt) (*End of update by K. Pechilis-Prentiss*)]

[*Update 1999*: As in other parts of the world, India has seen a growing lesbian and gay movement, one which has also received its share of media attention. In early 1998, when two policewomen in Madhya Pradesh decided to get married, the news was picked up by the press. This was perhaps the first occasion when lesbianism became a matter of widespread public debate. The furor created by this debate made it difficult to dismiss the issue as yet another Western aberration. As a political event, however, it also raised troubling questions for the women's movement and for the fledgling gay and lesbian politics, whose relationship to each other was far from clear. An important article highlighted the "elaborate apparatus of explication" evident in most reports of the marriage, which explained away the decision of the two women in terms of their suffering and victimhood at the hands of a patriarchal society, never allowing for the possibility of an affirmative, let alone sexual relationship.

[Over the last decade, the gay and lesbian movement has grown in visibility, with a mushrooming of groups and publications in India, and among South Asians in the West. Legal activism has extended from ongoing efforts to change the discriminatory legislation embodied in the antisodomy laws, to proposals to amend the Special Marriages Act to permit same-sex marriages. In a recent overview, Sherry Joseph has tried to plot the emergence of the identity politics of the gay and lesbian movement in its relations with similar movements in the West, as well as the specific dilemmas faced by lesbians within a movement that is male-dominated (John & Nair 1999). (*End of update by K. Pechilis-Prentiss*)]

## 7. Gender Diversity and Transgender Issues

Gender-conflicted persons are generally regarded as homosexuals. Traditional Indian society did not provide for special gender roles. In the case of transsexuals, it is not possible to alter one's birth certificate to change the sex designated at birth.

The *hijra*—an Urdu word for eunuchs—are the most notable example of gender variance in India (Jaffrey 1996; Nanda 1990, 1994, 1999, 2000). *Hijra*, who live predominantly in the larger cities, belong to a Hindu caste of males who dress as females. Their religious role is to perform as mediums for female goddesses, hence their role at weddings. Usually, they leave their families in their teen years to join adult *hijra* in a large city. Some may finalize their gender status by castration. Their societal role, and means of making a livelihood, involves providing entertainment at weddings and other festivals, sometimes uninvited but always expecting to be paid. They may also engage in sexual activity with men for money or to satisfy their own sexual desires. The most commonly used technique of the *hijra* is the anal-intercourse passive role without the use of condoms. Characteristically, according to Walter Williams (1986, 258-259), *hijra* are bitchy like American gay drag-queens—heterosexual transvestites are rarely or never bitchy. Insistent and bad-tempered, they wear no underwear and lift their skirts to expose themselves to the embarrassed guests if not paid. They tend to complain and frequently make demands on others in public, such as demanding (rather than politely asking) rich women for their clothes on the street (Weinrich 1987, 96).

[*Update 2002-2003*: India's third-sex caste, the *hijra*, who are neither male nor female, include males born with deformed genitals, hermaphrodites, self-castrated eunuchs, and gay cross-dressers. Early Hindu texts, like the *Kamasutra*, tell of these third-sexed persons who danced at weddings, cast spells, guarded harems, and entertained guests in the royal courts. In more recent times, India's estimated half a million to two million *hijra* have existed on the fringes of Indian society. That may be changing, in part because a Constitutional amendment in 1993 reserved a quota of seats in city and village councils for women and oppressed castes. In 2000, a dozen *hijra* were elected to city and provincial offices, including Asha Devi, mayor of Gorakhpur in northern India, Kamla Jaan, mayor of Katni, and Heera Bai, city councilwoman in Jabalpur, a city of 1.4 million. Formation of a national political party of eunuchs was announced early in 2001 as a voters' alternative to the major political parties (Bearak 2001).

[In February 2003, the High Court of Madhya Pradesh state upheld a lower court ruling that eunuchs are still male and cannot seek election to offices reserved for women. At issue was the election of Kamla Jaan, a *hijra*, as mayor of Katnia. The court noted that this mayoral office was set aside for women to encourage their participation in politics. Kamla Jaan announced plans to appeal to India's Supreme Court (Associated Press). (*End of update by R. T. Francoeur*)]

## 8. Significant Unconventional Sexual Behaviors

### A. Coercive Sex

*Sexual abuse*

Because of the pressures of social change and the loss of the holding power of traditional taboos, child sexual abuse seems to be increasing in India. However, there is a growing awareness about child sexual abuse in the society. Girls who are near to attaining their puberty, or have just attained it, are often objects of older men's attention.

Although it is socially disapproved, some instances have been reported where parents, because of their poverty, accept a brideprice for the marriage of a very young daughter to an older man seeking a young girl as a second wife. In spite of rigorous efforts by the government in educating the people, it is still an accepted practice, especially in rural areas, to arrange marriages of young girls.

*Incest*

Repressed sexuality has also been a factor in what in the West might be considered widespread incest. In India's extended family system, sex between brothers-in-law and sisters-in-law, for example, or between cousins, or uncles and nieces, or aunts and nephews is common, although hard statistics are not available. See Section 1C, Basic Sexological Premises, General Concepts of Sexuality and Love, for the tradition of *niyoga*, describing the relationship between a wife and the younger brother of her husband.

*Sexual Harassment*

Poverty forces many rural girls around 10 years of age to be employed as housemaids in rich and middle-class homes. In addition to the economic exploitation, some of these girls also face sexual harassment by males in these households. Since these girls are in no position to resist sexual advances, most sexual harassment acts are not reported or complained about to the police. College girls and young working girls face the problems of harassment. The problem of "Eve-teasing"—old-fashioned pinching, fondling, and other sexual harassment of women on the street—has become so serious in recent years that the government has had to promulgate a law prohibiting this behavior.

One small but significant incident that may signal a change in the pervasive acceptance of sexual harassment in Indian culture occurred in mid-1996, when a 61-year-old Punjab state official was convicted of "outraging the modesty" of a woman in public by slapping the backside of another senior Punjab official at a public event in 1988. After eight years of delays and alleged government coverups for the defendant, the court unexpectedly convicted the defendant, the former general of police for the Punjab district and a national hero for his suppression of the Sikh rebellion. While the sentence appeared insignificant, a mere three months in jail and a $20 fine, the court did stipulate that the defendant be subjected to what is known in India as "rigorous imprisonment," a harsh regimen generally reserved for serious criminals and hardly befitting a national hero. While recognizing this verdict as a small measure of justice, women's groups in India hailed it as a landmark because of the prominence of those involved, and the fact that appeals will keep this harassment case in the public view for some years to come.

*Rape*

Sexual exploitation of girls is another problem faced by females in India. Data on the crime of rape shows that a total of 4,919 rape cases were registered in the country in 1981, with an increase of 12.8% from 1980.

Few cases of rape are actually reported to the police because of the negative consequences to the future life of rape victims. Young Indian women who are known to be victims of rape are viewed as outcasts, and their families disgraced, even though they were not in any way responsible for the attack. The spread of Western culture, the disruption of urbanization, exposure to films with lots of sex scenes, and pornographic materials are all blamed for the increasing number of rape cases in India.

[*Update 2001*: Indian dimensions on rape include the serious reluctance of women to rely on the law for recourse, not only because of the publicity it would engender, thus ruining a woman's chances for marriage, but also because some of the most infamous cases have been perpetrated by police officials. In addition, rape is a frequent aspect of conflict between castes and between caste groups and tribals. In part because of these factors, women's groups have sought to address incidents of rape at the local level. For example, the Rural Women's Liberation Movement in Tamilnadu, south India, has brought cases before village councils, and received monetary compensation for victims of rape from their attackers (Kumar 1997, 136). (*End of update by K. Pechilis-Prentiss*)]

*Dowry Deaths*

[*Update 2002*: Some claim that the "dowry deaths" in India widely reported in the international news media maim or kill some 25,000 women a year, but most incidents of dowry-related bride-burning are concentrated in the city of Delhi and in the north Indian states (Menski 1998, xiv). Government statistics are much more conservative, claiming that husbands and in-laws angry over small dowry payments killed nearly 7,000 women in 2001 (Brooke 2003). Although the absence of accurate figures do not allow a comparison of dowry deaths in India with domestic violence in Western developed nations, feminist scholar Uma Narayan suggests that dowry murder rates in India are "roughly similar" to rates for domestic violence murders in the U.S. (Narayan 1997, 99). This means that the shocking and horrific incidents of murder over dowry, which attract the news media, must be seen in the context of patterns of domestic abuse of women in patriarchal societies. The dowry is very much a canvas on which male power and status are portrayed. The dowry enables the bride's father to publicly demonstrate his wealth and the groom publicly to confirm his own worth. These factors are the cultural context that drives the practice of dowry, even among wealthy Indian families who live outside of "traditional" India (Menski 1998, 163-174).

[Dowry murders are but one example of domestic violence; the more commonly occurring example would be wife beating: "Indeed, the term dowry has become a euphemism for wife-battering, a practice so familiar that such violence has become a key issue in practically all movements in which women have been active" (Kumar 1997, 116). The widespread occurrence of wife beating suggests that its dynamics of intimidation and submission are accepted as emblematic of husband-and-wife relations across much of the populace. Emergency measures, such as Western-style battered women's shelters, have been proposed, but their usefulness has been questioned, because of the pervasive attitude in Indian society that an unmarried woman is an object of shame. However, there are counseling and service centers for abused women in the major cities of India, including Delhi, Mumbai (Bombay), Chennai (Madras), Bangalore, and Calcutta. Since the mid-1970s, women's groups have held demonstrations, rallies, public denunciations of suspect families, and street plays to combat accepting attitudes toward domestic violence. One of the most active has been the Stri Sangharsh in Delhi, "whose campaign made dowry murder a household term" (Kumar 1997, 118). (*End of update by K. Pechilis-Prentiss*)]

[*Update 2000*: R. B. Ahuja, a surgeon and secretary of the National Academy of Burn Doctors in India, estimates that three-quarters of the injuries he sees are the result of deliberate wife-burning associated with dowry and the pervasive acceptance of wife-beating. Perhaps a quarter of the injuries he sees are the result of true accidents caused by the cheap pump-action kerosene stoves used mainly by the urban poor. Although all admit that the official statistics on burn "accidents" are hardly reliable, the fact that 1,280 men died of kitchen accidents, out of an official total of 7,165 kitchen deaths in 1988, would seem to lend credence to a role for the common, explosively dangerous but affordable pump-action kerosene stoves. While recognizing the problems of domestic violence and dowry-burnings, some activists are also calling for immediate government action to improve the safety standards for manufacture of these stoves (Diwan 2002; Dugger 2000; Grover 1990; Mukherjee 1999; Oldenburg 2002; Sen 2002; Weinberger-Thomas 1999). (*End of update by R. T. Francoeur*)] (See also Sections 1C, Basic Sexological Premises, General Concepts of Sexuality and Love, and 2A, Religious, Ethnic, and Gender Factors Affecting Sexuality, Source and Character of Religious Values.)

## B. Prostitution

Prostitution, the indulgence in promiscuous sexual relations for money or other favors, is an age-old institution in India. Purchasing young girls and dedicating them to temples, the Devadasi system, was an established custom in India by 300 C.E. These girls often served as objects of sexual pleasure for temple priests and pilgrims. The current knowledge about female sex workers is mostly gained from studies done in the red-light districts of metropolitan cities. Generally, prostitutes tend to come from the less-educated class of women, including single abandoned girls, and economically distressed women. Some of the studies on prostitutes in India revealed that a majority of them had STDs, tuberculosis, chronic infections, anemia, scabies, and parasite infestation. Most of them were treated by the local medical practitioners, who are quacks in their profession. Most of these women were either forced by gang members and others to take up this profession or were betrayed with false promises of a job. Both the central government and the state governments have enacted statutes to repress and abolish prostitution. The central act, the Suppression of Immoral Traffic in Women and Girls Act (SITA), 1956, has been amended as the Immoral Traffic (Prevention) Act (ITPA), 1956. However, these statutes have made little impact on the increasing traffic in persons and sexual exploitation and abuse (Pawar 1991).

[*Update 1997*: According to investigative reporter Robert I. Friedman (1996), there are more than 100,000 female commercial sex workers in Bombay, which he describes as "Asia's largest sex bazaar." In all of India, there are as many as 10 million commercial sex workers. According to human rights groups, about 90% of the Bombay prostitutes are indentured servants, with close to half trafficked from Nepal. One in five of Bombay's sex workers are under age 18—the government is aware of child prostitution, but generally ignores the problem. Child sex workers as young as 9 are sold at auctions, where wealthy Arabs from the Persian Gulf compete with wealthy Indian males who believe that having sexual intercourse with a virgin cures syphilis and gonorrhea. A major motivation in the bidding for and slavery of child virgins is the fear of AIDS. In this context, child virgins often bring up to 60,000 rupees, the equivalent of US$2,000. (See also HIV/AIDS discussion in Section 10).

[The commercial sex district of Bombay is actually two interconnected neighborhoods in the south-central part of the city, approximately three square kilometers (about 1+ mi²) sandwiched between immense Muslim and Hindu slums. It is also the home of the largest organized crime family in Asia. This red-light district is well served by two major railway stations just a half-kilometer away, and 25 bus routes. The district is laid out with 24 lanes of wooden-frame brothels with gilded balconies interspersed with car repair shops, small restaurants, liquor stories, 200 bars, numerous flophouses, massive tenements, three police stations, and a municipal school from which only 5% of the students graduate.

[Two thousand *hijra* work on Eunuch Lane. Dressed in short black leather skirts or saris, they are virtually indistinguishable from the female prostitutes, except many are extremely beautiful. Shilpa, a 30-year-old social worker with five years experience working in the red-light district, provides a fair description of this aspect of Bombay's sex workers:

[The eunuchs, or hijras, have deep roots in Hinduism. As young boys they were abandoned or sold by their families to a sex cult; the boys are taken into the jungle, where a priest cuts off their genitals in a ceremony called *nirvana*. The priest then folds back a strip of flesh to create an artificial vagina. Eunuchs are generally more ready to perform high-risk sex than female prostitutes, and some Indian men believe they can't contract HIV from them (quoted by Friedman 1996, 14).

[Female sex workers are often harassed by the police, although their madams pay the police weekly bribes to look the other way. To protect themselves, each girl services several police for free.

[Though on average the girls see six customers a day, who pay between $1.10 and $2 per sex act, the madam gets the money up front. By the time the madam deducts for food, electricity, and rent, as well as payment—with interest—on her purchase price, there is almost nothing left. So to pay for movies, clothes, makeup, and extra food to supplement a bland diet of rice and dal, the girls have to borrow from moneylenders at an interest rate of up to 500%. They are perpetually in hock (Friedman 1996, 16).

[Bombay's flesh trade is an efficient business, controlled by four separate, harmonious crime groups. One group controls police payoffs, a second controls moneylending, and the third maintains the district's internal law and order. The fourth group, the most powerful, manages the procurement of women in a vast network that stretches from South India to the Himalayas (Friedman 1996, 18). (*End of update by R. T. Francoeur*)]

## C. Pornography

All forms of sexually oriented publications are illegal in India. The government-appointed Central Board has the power to make cuts or ban the indecent or obscene scenes in films. Although pornographic books, magazines, and videos are illegal, their display and sales are casually noticed in urban areas, especially in the major cities.

## 9. Contraception, Abortion, and Population Planning

### A. Contraception

*Contraception and Population Control*

As wide differences exist among different regions of the country, the population distribution is also not uniform among these regions. Despite the wide variations of existing customs, beliefs, and socioeconomic development among India's 866 million, the people generally favor a large family size and therefore are not in favor of adopting modern methods of contraception. India is the first country in the world to realize the importance of controlling the population growth and therefore initiated the Family Planning Program as far back as 1952.

There are nearly 145 million married couples with wives in the reproductive age group of 15 to 44 years. Assessment of the Family Planning Program performance reveals that nearly 40% of the eligible couples were effectively protected by one of the contraceptive methods. The Family Planning Program in India is being promoted on a voluntary basis as a people's movement in keeping with the democratic tradition of the country. The services of the program are offered through Health Care Delivery System. The program makes extensive use of various mass-media sources including television, radio, newspapers, posters, and pamphlets, besides interpersonal communication, in its strategies for explaining the various methods of contraception and removing the sociocultural barriers that work against the program.

Since the majority of the population lives in rural areas, which lack a good infrastructure of healthcare facilities and an adequate Social Security System, these people almost universally perceive children and large families as an asset. Added to this is a strong preference for a son that acts as a barrier in limiting the family size. In spite of the availability of various contraceptive methods like sterilization, IUD, condoms, hormonal pills, and other temporary methods, the adopters of the program mostly opt for sterilization, more often tubal ligation or tubectomy.

Because of widely varying customs, beliefs, and the very low level of involvement of the wife in the decision-making process, it is the women who ultimately are adopting the method of contraception. It is not surprising to know in a male-dominated society, especially in rural areas, that people generally perceive that the program is mostly meant for the womenfolk, as they are bearers of the children. Some common beliefs, like "using a contraception reduces a man's masculinity" and "contraception impairs the health of working men," also acts as a barrier for the adoption of the program by men. Methodwise data of adopters generally reveals that the temporary methods are mostly utilized by people with relatively high educational backgrounds and those living in urban areas. The condom, a simple reversible and nonchemical method of contraception, is widely accepted by couples in the younger age group, mostly for spacing pregnancies.

The government has adopted a primary healthcare approach that uses various indigenous and local medical practitioners, traditional birth attendants, and religious and community leaders as change-agents in convincing the eligible couples to adopt family planning. The medical termination of pregnancy, which is legalized in the country, is also considered as one of the methods of family planning. In spite of vast investments in a supportive infrastructure and manpower, the achievements of the Family Planning Program have fallen short of its targets. Rigorous efforts are needed to implement the program more effectively.

*Selective Female Abortion and Infanticide; Unbalanced Sex Ratios*

Census counts in India have shown a disturbing pattern, moving from 972 females for every 1,000 males in 1901, to 934 in 1981 and 927 in 1991. In Haryana, a populous northern state surrounding Delhi, there were only 874 females for every 1,000 men, an unprecedented disproportion.

A law passed in 1994 by the Indian Parliament provides penalties of three years in prison and a fine of about $320 for those found guilty of administering or taking prenatal tests—mainly ultrasound scans and amniocentesis, solely to ascertain the sex of the fetus. The new law focuses on hospitals and clinics, but leaves the operators of mobile van clinics outside the law's purview. Charges for fetal screening tests can run as low as 150 rupees, about $5, in poor rural areas to ten times as much or more in more-affluent urban areas. Under Indian law, ending a pregnancy only because the fetus is female was illegal even before the 1994 law was enacted, even though the practice remains common. No reliable figures are available on the number of abortions performed every year solely to prevent the birth of girls. But, with some clinics in major cities like Delhi and Bombay admitting to conducting as many as 60,000 sex-determination tests a year, child welfare organizations estimate the nationwide figure at tens of thousands every year, possibly higher (Burns 1994).

Another concern among women's groups has been the fear that curbing sex-determination tests will drive many families back to the centuries-old practice of killing baby girls soon after birth, or so favoring boys with scarce supplies of food that girls die young. In a 1993 survey conducted by the National Foundation of India, a private group working on child welfare issues, it was estimated that 300,000 newborn girls die annually from what it called "gender discrimination" (Burns 1994).

[*Update 2000*: A United Nations survey of six nations bordering India, namely Pakistan, Bangladesh, Nepal, Sri Lanka, Bhutan, and the Maldives, published in 2000, revealed some 79 million women were "missing" in South Asia, because parents practiced female infanticide or used ultrasound scans and amniocentesis to selectively abort female fetuses. Most likely, India has a shortage of females similar to that reported in its six neighbors and the 40 million shortfall recently acknowledged in China. (*End of update by R. T. Francoeur*)]

## B. Teenage Pregnancies

Sexual activity at an early age but within marriage is common in India. The most obvious health risk of teenage sex among the young is pregnancy for girls who are not yet physically matured. Further, if the pregnancy is unwanted or illegitimate, the health hazards are likely to be compounded by the social, psychological, and economic consequences. In their study of infant and childhood mortality, K. Mahadevan et al. (1985) found that the mean age of women at first conception was only 16 years; further, they found that infant mortality was very high for the first, followed by the second birth order, and then tapered down subsequently. The findings reveal that the high incidence of infant mortality among the first two birth orders may be mainly because of teenage pregnancy and childbirth. In traditional societies where mothers marry young, there is family support for the young parents, although medical risks remain high. But in today's transitional society, the family support is gone, and many times, the teenage pregnancies lead to abortion and thus have dangerous consequences.

## C. Abortion

Abortion is not considered a method of contraception in the strict sense, although it is treated as one of the methods of family planning because of its dramatic impact on birthrates. The Medical Termination of Pregnancy Act (1971) has great importance. Attempts are continuously made to induce all women seeking abortion to accept a suitable method of family planning, although abortion is mostly advocated on health grounds. The main health reasons for recommending an abortion are: (1) when continuance of the pregnancy would involve a risk to the life of the pregnant woman or of grave injury to her physical or mental health; and (2) when there is a substantial risk that the child, if born, would suffer from such physical or mental abnormalities as to be seriously handicapped. Since the inception of the 1971 Act, the annual number of abortions is around 7.6 million. Despite the legalization of abortion, the lack of trained health personnel and termination by local *Dais* who abort by using unscientific instruments, the death rates for women who have undergone termination of their pregnancies are also high, especially in the remote rural and tribal areas. It is also observed that young unmarried girls who experience a premarital pregnancy and approach unqualified charlatans seeking an abortion also experience similar high risks of mortality and morbidity. Though official statistics on these situations are not available, these situations are common, and their incidence may well be in an upward trend because of modernization and Westernization.

## D. Population Control Efforts

See the discussion above in Section 9A, Contraception.

## 10. Sexually Transmitted Diseases and HIV/AIDS

### A. Sexually Transmitted Diseases

The spread of sexually transmitted diseases is affected by sexual promiscuity resulting from marital maladjustment, and in some distinct inadequacies in the social and economic life of India and its healthcare system. Gonorrhea, syphilis, and other sexually transmitted infections are major problems for young people, especially in urban India, where social change is rapid, marriage tends to be delayed, and traditional restraints on premarital intercourse are reduced. Many cases

of STD infections remain untreated, especially in the large urban areas, mainly because the sufferers do not know that they are affected, and also because they fear revealing their problem. The lack of scientific knowledge about the diseases among the infected also adds to the misery of the victims. In some communities, parents act as a major source of information on sex for their sons and daughters, but for most of the communities in India, sex is a taboo topic, and parents generally avoid communicating it to their offspring. Among most of the young people in India, even in urban areas, ignorance of the most basic facts about sexuality, conception, and contraception still continues to be the norm. The combination of the rapid social change in India and the ignorance on the basic information about sexuality are creating major and widespread health problems for the young generation.

### B. HIV/AIDS

The first confirmed evidence of AIDS infection in India came in April 1986, when six prostitutes from Tamil Nadu tested positive for HIV antibodies. Subsequent findings indicate that between October 1, 1985, and September 30, 1993, a total of 459 AIDS cases have been detected in India, of which 444 are Indians and 15 are foreigners. Data available in early 1995 indicate that, thus far, 1,898,670 persons have been screened for the HIV virus, and 13,254 were found positive to HIV by the Western-Blot test. The seropositive rate is 6.98 per 1,000.

An indication of the population at risk for HIV infection can be found in the millions of STD cases occurring in the country. In addition to being a marker for behavioral vulnerability to HIV infection, untreated STD cases facilitate HIV transmission. In Pune, the HIV infection rate among people seeking treatment for STD has increased from about 9% in 1991 to 17% in 1992. An infection rate of up to 25% was reported in 1992 from surveys among prostitutes in Bombay. Meanwhile, there is little public support for or interest in promoting safer sex practices and condom use among the prostitutes, who are generally viewed as outcasts in India's caste-bound society and deserving of any ills that befall them. Among Bombay's estimated 100,000 prostitutes, the HIV rates shot up to 52% in 1994, from 2% in 1988. The sale of young girls into sexual slavery in the Persian Gulf complicates the situation (Burns 1996).

The prevalence of HIV infection among the 5 million long-route truck drivers is also very high. Health officials believe that the drivers are at the center of an imminent explosion of AIDS among India's 970 million people. The problem is evident at Petrapole, 75 miles (120 km) from Calcutta, on the main road between India and Bangladesh. While grimy trucks line up fender to fender for miles, often waiting a week or more to cross the Broken Boat River, thousands of drivers, helpers, and hawkers mix with local women and teenage girls willing to engage in sex for as little as 10 rupees, about 28 cents. It is common for these men to buy sex every day, and sometimes several times a day, while they wait. Researchers estimate that the truck drivers average 150 to 200 sexual encounters with sex workers a year. A single sex encounter can earn a woman enough to feed her family for a day. They seldom use condoms. In late 1996, experts estimated 30% of India's long-distance truck drivers were HIV-positive. The impact on the family is already evident. In a 1994 study by the National AIDS Research Institute in Pune, 100 miles (160 km) southeast of Bombay, 14% of the married women who reported no sexual contact with anyone other than their husband tested HIV-positive (Burns 1996).

The United Nations estimated that by the end of the 20th century, over a million Indians will be sick with full-blown

AIDS, and 10 million will be HIV infected. A quarter of the world's projected infected will be in India. Some Indian experts paint a still grimmer picture, estimating that between 20 and 50 million Indians will be infected by HIV by the year 2000. In this event, there will be more AIDS patients in India than there are hospital beds (Burns 1996).

While the principle mode for transmission of HIV infection in India is by heterosexual promiscuity, the prevalence of the disease is also high in intravenous drug users, who share syringes and needles, in Manipur state, in India's far northeast, bordering with Burma (Myanmar), Laos, and Thailand, where studies have been conducted by the field-practice unit at the surveillance center for HIV infection in Imphal. The results show that the situation in this area is different from the rest of the country, primarily because injectable heroin is easily available here. After the first seropositive case in Manipur appeared in 1989, HIV infections soared among drug users to 54% within six months, By the beginning of 1992, 1,600 HIV-positive cases had been detected, most of them being intravenous drug users.

Apart from unprotected sexual intercourse and intravenous drug injections, contaminated blood transfusion is one of the main sources of infection. In India, the sale of blood for transfusion and for preparation of blood products is a big business and subject to very little control. Estimates of the incidence of HIV-infected mothers transmitting the virus to their children during pregnancy and delivery show that every year, 20,000 out of 24 million deliveries in India are likely to occur in HIV-positive women (Ramachandran 1992).

More than half of Bombay's sex workers are HIV-positive, according to Dr. Subhash Hira, an Indian-American, who runs as AIDS clinic in Bombay. Currently an estimated 5 million people in India are HIV-positive. Hira predicts that by the year 2000, as many as 20 million Indians will be HIV-positive. However, with the incidence of the virus currently doubling every year, it is more likely that the figure for HIV-infected people in India will be about 15%, or 160 million. This, according to Dr. I. S. Gilada, a leading Indian expert on AIDS, could bring a collapse in India's economy, set the country back at least 50 years, and pull it "into a black hole of despair unlike anything seen in this century" (quoted by Friedman 1996, 12). India's national politicians and public health officials refuse to recognize or discuss this crisis, often considering sex workers as an expendable commodity.

The government has proposed to set up a resort for AIDS Rehabilitation and Control as a preparatory measure to cope with the AIDS threat looming large over the Indian horizon. However, the nation's annual AIDS budget is only about $20 million, or slightly more than two cents a person. Despite an $85 million World Bank loan to set up a national AIDS control organization, India's expendures for the control of AIDS is woefully inadequate. In late 1996, with only a year of the program left to run, only $35 million of the $85 had be spent (Burns 1996).

Opponents of spending money on AIDS prevention, including many politicians and other opinion makers, argue that the government should give top priority to controlling diseases like malaria and tuberculosis, which kill tens of thousands of Indians every year. In a nation which spends six tenths of 1% of its $50 billion annual budget on all healthcare, there is little money for educational publicity and free condoms. Some programs have been able to distribute packets of four condoms at two rupees (three cents), about half the usual cost. There is no money for AZT and other drugs (Burns 1996).

Although the HIV virus apparently did not begin to circulate in the Indian subcontinent until about a decade after it arrived in the United States, where the disease was first recognized in 1981, the virus has spread much more rapidly in India than elsewhere. According to a July 1996 report at the 11th international meeting on AIDS, well over three million Indians were HIV-positive. This number easily surpassed South Africa with 1.8 million cases, Uganda with 1.4 million, Nigeria with 1.2 million, and Kenya with 1.1 million.

[*Update 2001-2003*: According to an October 2000 report from the United Nations, India had 3.7 million persons with AIDS and 34 million HIV-infected persons. Fourteen million had already died of AIDS. Assuming that treating an AIDS patient will cost 18,000 rupees or US$386 per month, Prakash Kothari, a prominent Indian doctor, has argued that even the most innovative budget planning could soon be useless unless India's government begins to take the AIDS crisis as serious as it takes its arch-enemy Pakistan: "There will simply be no resources available to finance anything else in this country of ours." Part of the solution, Kothari argues, could be to create a "Ministry of Sex" that would put dealing with the AIDS crisis on a par with national defense. Meanwhile, officials in the Indian state of Patna, on the border of Nepal, are so concerned about the rise of HIV/AIDS that they distribute free condoms at all transit points to Nepal and at truck stops along the National Highways and Grand Trunk Road. Health officials adopted the plan because truck drivers coming from the northeastern states are reported to indulge in multipartner sex without using condoms.

[Also, in late 2002, a special National Intelligence Council meeting convened by the independent Center for Strategic and International Studies identified India, Nigeria, Ethiopia, China, and Russia as countries facing devastation by a second wave of HIV/AIDS infections in the next decade (see Table 1). Analysts at the meeting predicted famines, civil war, economic reversals, and a collapse of social and political institutions in these countries by 2010 (Garrett 2002).

[The head of India's national AIDS program, Meenakshi Datta Ghosh, denounced the intelligence report as "alarmist," but admitted that at least four densely populated states already had infection rates above 1% of all pregnant women. India has set ambitious goals for its AIDS programs, but the country lacks a coherent infrastructure for implementing prevention and treatment efforts. At least two AIDS epidemics are raging in the world's second most populous nation. The first, centered in the south and west, is heterosexual, fueled by India's large prostitution industry, while the second, focused in the far eastern provinces, is an intravenous drug use-driven epidemic. If India's programs can be solidified, Ghosh projected that by 2006, the country will have 9 million people living with HIV. If those programs remain fragmented, the number could reach 14 million, with 1.9 million deaths annually by 2002 and 20 million to 25 million

**Table 1**

**Leaders in an Expanding Pandemic: Current and Projected HIV/AIDS-Infected Adults**

| | Current Number Infected | | 2010 |
|---|---|---|---|
| | Government Data (millions) | Expert Estimates (millions) | Expert Estimates (millions) |
| India | 4.0 | 5 to 8 | 20 to 25 |
| Nigeria | 3.5 | 4 to 6 | 10 to 15 |
| Ethiopia | 2.7 | 3 to 5 | 7 to 10 |
| China | 0.80 | 1 to 2 | 10 to 15 |
| Russia | 0.18 | 1 to 2 | 5 to 8 |

HIV-positive Indians by 2010, or 4% of the nation's adults (Garrett 2002). (*End of update by R. T. Francoeur*)]

[*Update 2003*: When the first case of HIV was discovered in Chennai in 1986, the Indian Government responded to it immediately. Under the Ministry of Health and Welfare, the Indian government constituted a committee in 1987. The land of *Kamasutra* was suddenly under the surveillance. HIV levels were high amongst sex workers and STD clinic attendees. The spread of HIV within India is as diverse as the societal patterns between its different regions, states, and metropolitan areas. India's socioeconomic status, traditional social ills, cultural myths on sex and sexuality, and a huge population of marginalized people make it extremely vulnerable to the HIV/AIDS epidemic. In fact, it has become the most serious public health problem faced by the country since the Independence.

[HIV infection in India is currently concentrated among poor, marginalized groups, including commercial sex workers, truck drivers and migrant laborers, men who have sex with men, and injecting drug users. Transmission of HIV within and from these groups drives the epidemic, but the infection is spreading rapidly to the general community. The epidemic continues to shift towards women and young people, with about 25% of all HIV infections occurring in women. This also increases mother-to-child HIV transmission and pediatric HIV.

[In India, as elsewhere, AIDS is perceived as a disease of "others"—of people living on the margins of society, whose lifestyles are considered "perverted" and "sinful." Discrimination, stigmatization, and denial are the expected outcomes of such values, affecting life in families, communities, workplaces, schools, and healthcare settings. Because of HIV/AIDS, appropriate policies and models of effective prevention remain underdeveloped. People living with HIV and AIDS continue to be burdened by poor care and inadequate services, while those with the power to help do little to make the situation better.

[India is in some respects a *gendered phenomenon*. Women are often blamed by their parents and in-laws for infecting their husbands, or for not controlling their partner's urges to have sex with other women. Children of HIV-positive parents, whether positive or negative themselves, are often denied the right to go to school or are separated from other children. People in marginalized groups (female sex workers, *hijra* [transgenders], and gay men) are often stigmatized in India on the grounds of not only HIV status, but also for being members of socially excluded groups. (*End of update by A. Kadari*)]

[*Update 2002*: UNAIDS Epidemiological Assessment: The first case of AIDS in India was detected in 1986. Since then, HIV infections have been reported in all States and Union Territories. With a population of one billion—about half in the 15- to 49-year-old population—HIV epidemics in India will have a major impact on the overall spread of HIV in Asia and the Pacific, as well as globally.

[The spread of HIV within India is as diverse as the societal patterns between its different regions, states, and metropolitan areas. The epidemics are focused very sharply in a few southern States, with most of India having extremely low rates of infection. An overwhelming majority of the total reported national AIDS cases-96%—were reported by only 10 of the 31 states. The major impact is being felt in Maharashtra in the west, Tamil Nadu in the south with adjacent Pondicherry, and Manipur in the northeast. The epidemics vary between states with heterosexually transmitted infections predominating in Maharashtra and Tamil Nadu, while infections concentrated among injecting drug users and their partners predominate in Manipur. With a high prevalence of tuberculosis infection in India, the problem of tuberculosis related to HIV infection also poses a major public health challenge.

[Between 1994 and 1997, HIV prevalence among STD clinic attendees in Maharashtra state increased from 6% to 36%, and prevalence among injecting drug users in Manipur increased from 25% to 61%. However, there were insufficient numbers of sentinel surveillance sites to get an adequate picture of the overall HIV situation. In 1998, the number of HIV Sentinel Surveillance sites increased from 55 to 180: 83 for STD, 89 for antenatal clinics, and 8 for injecting drug users. HIV prevalence data were collected twice in 1998, February to March and August to October. The 1998 HIV sentinel surveillance data from antenatal clinics in seven metropolitan cities showed HIV prevalence to be over 2% in Mumbai, more than 1% in Hyderabad and Bangalore, and below 1% in Calcutta, Ahmedabad, and Delhi. HIV-prevalence levels outside these major urban agglomerations were in general lower, and no infection was found in a number of rural HIV Sentinel Surveillance sites.

[In late 1998, NACO convened a group of national and international experts to review the results of the first round of the expanded HIV Sentinel Surveillance to produce state-specific and national estimates on HIV/AIDS. The new calculations provide greater consistency in making a national estimate of HIV prevalence in India. The national prevalence estimate was increased for 2001 to 3.97 million.

[The estimated number of adults and children living with HIV/AIDS on January 1, 2002, were:

| | | |
|---|---|---|
| Adults ages 15-49: | 3,970,000 | (rate: 0.8%) |
| Women ages 15-49: | 1,500,000 | |
| Children ages 0-15: | 170,000 | |

[No estimate is available for the number of adults and children who died of AIDS during 2001.

[No estimate is available for the number of Indian children who had lost one or both parents to AIDS and were under age 15 at the end of 2001. (*End of update by the Editors*)]

## 11. Sexual Dysfunctions, Counseling, and Therapies

### A. Concepts of Sexual Dysfunction

The concept of sexual dysfunction in the Indian context is defined differently with reference to the person's socioeconomic and demographic background. Generally, it is differentiated for men and women, young and old, rich and poor, and able-bodied and disabled persons.

### B. Availability of Counseling, Diagnosis, and Treatment

There are no legal or other restrictions on who may practice as a psychosocial or sexual therapist in India. Most of the persons with sexual problems who feel that they need some treatment, seek help related to their symptoms. What sexual therapy there is available deals with symptom relief and is generally regarded as successful if this is the outcome. Though there is no clear-cut, government-funded, psychosexual therapy services available in India, most of the health and family planning clinics provide one or more of these services to their clients. Counseling by some of the marriage counseling services, especially in cities, are also widely reported in the society. Quacks who pose as very knowledgeable in sexual therapy, and widely advertise about the effectiveness of their treatment, are commonly seen, especially in rural areas and small towns. Because many people do not understand the need for qualified training of sexual therapists, these fraudulent therapists and their clinics attract many of those who need proper counseling, and cash in on their weaknesses.

A prevailing Victorian sexual repression, left over from colonial times, still makes it impossible for many married couples to function well sexually, or even to function at all. Sex clinics around New Delhi and other large cities typically cater mostly to men, and offer advice, hormone injections, and herbal remedies at a cost of up to about $500 for a full course of treatment.

There is no organized data available on such incidences, nor on the effectiveness of their treatments. Moreover, with the topic of sex being a taboo in Indian society, people generally do not discuss their problems openly with others. In the process, they easily become victims of such quacks in their communities.

## 12. Sex Research and Advanced Professional Education

There is very little sexological research being carried out in India thus far. Very few institutions have concentrated any effort in this area of research or undertaken any formal program on this important topic. Although there is no graduate or postgraduate program on sexuality in any of the educational institutions, because of the recent widespread discussions of HIV/AIDS, sexually transmitted diseases, and a host of other problems like bride-burning and marital violence, there is a growing inclination to undertake research in the area of sexuality, and to impart proper sex education for the people in the society.

The National Institute for Research in Sex Education, Counseling and Therapy (NIRSECT) is the only official professional organization devoted to sexual research in India. Its address is: Saiprasad-C5/11/02, Sector-4, C.B.D. New Bombay, 4990615, India. The director is Dr. J. K. Nath, first author of this chapter.

Other important sexological organizations are:

Sex Education, Counseling, Research Training Centre (SECRT). Family Planning Association of India (FPAI). Fifth Floor, Cecil Court, Mahakavi Bhushan Marg, Bombay 400 039, India (Phone: 91-22/287-4689).

Indian Association of Sex Educators, Counselors, and Therapists (IASECT) 203 Sukhsagar, N.S. Patkar Marg., Bombay 400 007, India (Phone: 91-22/361-2027; Fax: 91-22/204-8488).

Parivar Seva Sanstha. 28 Defence Colony Market, New Delhi 110-024. (Phone: 91-11/461-7712; Fax: 91-11/462-0785).

## Acknowledgments

The original authors wish to acknowledge the assistance of Dr. S. N. Kadam, M.R.C.P.; J. V. Bhatt, M.D.; Dr. V. C. Prabhu, M.B.B.S.; S. Patil, M.D.; C. Prakasam, Ph.D.; M. C. Watsa, M.D.; Mrs. S. J. Nath; Mrs. S. V. Nayar; Mr. Khan at the MGM Medical College; Mr. V. S. Rajan; Ms. C. Prabha; and M. S. Pawar, Ph.D.

## References and Suggested Readings

Ahmed, S. I. 1992. Truck drivers are vulnerable group in northeast India. An abstract published in the *Second International Congress on AIDS in Asia and the Pacific*. Randwick, Australia: AIDS Society of Asia and the Pacific.

Alvarez, L. 2003 (June 22). Arranged marriages get a little rearranging. *The New York Times*, p. A3.

Bearak, B. 2001 (January 19). Katni Journal: A pox on politicians. A eunuch you can trust. *The New York Times*.

Bhende, A. A. 1994. A study of sexuality of adolescent girls and boys in underprivileged groups in Bombay. *Indian Journal of Social Work*, 55(4). Bombay: Tata Institute of Social Sciences.

Bhende, A. A., & L. Kanitkar. 1978. *Principles of population studies*. Bombay: Himalaya Publishing House.

Burns, J. F. 1996 (September 22). Denial and taboo blinding India to the horror of its AIDS scourge. *The New York Times*, pp. 1, 16.

Burns, J. F. 1994 (August 27). India fights abortion of female fetuses. *The New York Times*.

Brooke, J. 2003 (May 17). Dowry too high. Lose bride and go to jail. *The New York Times*, pp. A1, A7.

Chowdhry, D. P. 1992. *Women's welfare and development*. New Delhi: Inter India Publications.

CIA. 2002 (January). *The world factbook 2002*. Washington, DC: Central Intelligence Agency. Available: http://www.cia.gov/cia/publications/factbook/index.html.

Department of Family Welfare. 1992. *Family welfare programme in India*. New Delhi: Government of India, Ministry of Health and Family Welfare, Department of Family Welfare.

Deva, K. 1986. *Khajuraho*. New Delhi: Brijbasi Printers Private, Ltd.

Diwan, P. 2002. *Law relating to dowry, dowry deaths, bride burning, rape and related offences*. Universal Law Publishing Company.

D'Souza, A. A. 1979. *Sex education and personality development*. New Delhi: Usha Publications.

Dugger, C. 2000 (December 26). "Kerosene, weapon of choice for attacks on wives in India." *The New York Times*, pp. A1, A8.

Egnor, M. T. 1986. *The ideology of love in a Tamil family*. Hobart and Smith College, unpublished. Cited by Sudhir Kakar, *Intimate Relations*, (1989:11).

Family Planning Association of India (F.P.A.I.). 1990. *Attitude and perceptions of educated, urban youth to marriage and sex*. Bombay: S.E.C.R.T. (Sex Education Counseling Research Therapy Training) F.P.A.I.

Friedman, R. I. 1996 (April 8). India's shame: Sexual slavery and political corruption are leading to an AIDS catastrophe. *The Nation*, pp. 11-20.

Garrett, L. 2002 (October 15). AIDS seen as threat to world: Experts say five big nations face devastation by 2010. *Newsday* [New York].

Grover, K. 1990. *Burning Flesh*. South Asia Books.

Gupta, L. 1991. Kali, the savior. In: P. M. Cooey, W. R. Eakin, & J. B. McDaniel, eds., *After patriarchy: Feminist transformations of the world's religions* (pp. 15-38). New York: Orbis Books.

Hallstrom, L. L. 2000. *Mother of bliss: Anandamayi Ma (1896-1982)*. New York: Oxford University Press.

Hancock, M. 1999. *Womanhood in the making: Domestic ritual and public culture in urban South India*. Boulder, CO: Westview Press.

Jaffrey, Z. 1996. *The invisibles: A tale of the eunuchs of India*. New York: Pantheon Books.

John, M. E., & J. Nair. 1999 (April). Sexuality in modern India: Critical concerns. *Voices for Change. A Journal on Communication for Development*, 3(1):4-8, Location: SNDT Churchgate.

Kakar, S. 1989. *Intimate relations: Exploring Indian sexuality*. Chicago: University of Chicago Press. New Delhi: Penguin Books India (P) Ltd.

Kakar, S., & K. Chowdhary. 1970. *Conflict and choice: Indian youth in a changing society*. Bombay: Somaiya Publications.

Kapur, P. 1973. *Love, marriage, and sex*. Delhi: Vikas Publishing House.

Kishwar, M. 1997 (March-April). Women, sex and marriage: Restraint as a female strategy. *Manushi* No. 98. Available at SAWNET under "Articles": http://www.umiacs.umd.edu/users/sawweb/sawnet/index.html.

Kishwar, M. 1998 (November-December). Native outpourings of a self-hating Indian: Deepa Mehta's Fire. *Manushi, 109*:3-14.

Knipe, D. M. 1991. *Hinduism*. New York/San Francisco/London: Harper/Collins.

Krishnan, S. 2003 (June). Arranged marriages in India. Available from: Krishnan@tcad.ee.utl.edu.

Kumar, R. 1997, 1993. *The history of doing: An illustrated account of movements for women's rights and feminism in India, 1800-1990*. New Delhi: Kali for Women.

Mahadevan, K., N. S. Murthy, P. R. Reddy, P. J. Reddy, V. Gowri, & S. Sivaraju. 1985. *Infant and childhood mortality in India*. Delhi: Mittal Publications.

Majumdar, N., & T. N. Madan. 1956. *Social anthropology*. Bombay: Himalaya Publishing House.

Mane, P., & S. A. Maitra. 1992. *AIDS prevention: The sociocultural context in India*. Bombay: Tata Institute of Social Sciences.

Menski, W., ed. 1998. *South Asians and the dowry problem*. London: Trentham Books and School of Oriental and African Studies.

Mukherjee, G. 1999. *Dowry death in India*. South Asia Books.

Nair, P. S., M. Vemuri, & F. Ram. 1989. *Indian youth*. New Delhi: Mittal Publications.

Nanda, S. 1990. *Neither man nor woman: The hijras of India*. Belmont, CA: Wadsworth Publishing Company.

Nanda, S. 1994. Hijras: An alternative sex and gender role in India. In: G. Herdt, ed., *Third sex, third gender: Beyond sexual dimorphism in culture and history* (pp. 373-417). New York: Zone Books.

Nanda, S. 1999. *Neither man nor woman: The hijras of India*. Belmont, CA: Wadsworth.

Nanda, S. 2000. *Gender diversity: Crosscultural variations*. Prospect Heights IL: Waveland Press, Inc.

Narayan, S. 1988. *Social anthropology*. Delhi: Gian Publishing House.

Narayan, U. 1997. *Dislocating cultures: Identities, traditions, and Third World feminism*. New York: Routledge.

Oldenburg, V. T. 2002. *Dowry murder: The imperial origins of a cultural crime*. New York: Oxford University Press.

Parasuraman, R., et al. 1992. STD and AIDS in homosexuals. *Abstracts of the Second International Congress on AIDS in Asia and the Pacific*. Rand Wick, Australia: AIDS Society of Asia and the Pacific, p. 200.

Pawar, M. S. 1991. Prostitution and the girl child. *Indian Journal of Social Work, 52*(1).

Ramachandran, P. 1992. Women's vulnerability. *Seminar, 396*: 21-25.

Reddy, G., D. Narayana, P. Eswar, & A. K. Sreedharan. 1983 (September). A report on urban (Madras) college students' attitudes towards sex. *Antiseptic*, pp. 1-5.

Robinson, C. A. 1999. *Tradition and liberation: The Hindu tradition in the Indian women's movement*. New York: St. Martin's Press.

Savara, M., & C. R. Shridhar. 1992. Sexual behaviour of urban educated Indian women. Results of a survey. *Journal of Family Welfare, 38*(1):30-43.

SAWNET: South Asian Women's Network: http://www.umiacs.umd.edu/users/sawweb/sawnet/index.html.

Sen, M. 2002. *Death by fire: Sati, dowry death, and female infanticide in modern India*. New Brunswick, NJ: Rutgers University Press.

Tata Institute of Social Sciences. 1994 (October). *Indian Journal of Social Work* (Bombay), *55*(4).

Registrar General and Census Commissioner India. 1991. *Provisional population totals (Rural-urban distribution)* (New Delhi), paper no. 2 of 1991.

UNAIDS. 2002. *Epidemiological fact sheets by country*. Geneva, Switzerland: Joint United Nations Programme on HIV/AIDS (UNAIDS/WHO). Available: http://www.unaids.org/hivaidsinfo/statistics/fact_sheets/index_en.htm.

Watts, A. 1974. *Erotic spirituality: The vision of Konarak*. New York: Collier Books.

Weinberger-Thomas, C. 1999. *Ashes of immortality: Widowburning in India*. Chicago: University of Chicago Press.

Weinrich, J. D. 1987. *Sexual landscapes: Why we are what we are, Why we love whom we love*. New York: Scribners.

Williams, W. 1986. *The spirit and the flesh: Sexual diversity in American Indian culture*. Boston: Beacon Press.

(CIA 2002)

# Indonesia

## (*Republik Indonesia*)

Wimpie I. Pangkahila, M.D., Ph.D.* (Part 1)**
Ramsey Elkholy, Ph.D. (cand.) (Part 2)
*Updates by Robert T. Francoeur, Ph.D.*

## Contents

*Communications*: Wimpie I. Pangkahila, M.D., Ph.D., The Master Program in Reproductive Medicine, Udayana University Medical School, Jl. Panglima Sudirman, Denpasar, Bali, Indonesia; wim@denpasar.wasantara.net.id. Ramsey Elkholy, Ph.D. (cand.), 105 Fifth Avenue, Apt. #6E, New York, NY, USA 10003; relkholy@hotmail.com.

***Editor's Note*: The cultures of the eastern half of the island of New Guinea, the nation of Papua New Guinea, are covered under that nation by Shirley Oliver-Miller. In Part 1 of this present chapter, Wimpie L. Pangkahila and J. Alex Pangkahila provide insights into the national and urban perspectives of sexuality in Indonesia. In Part 2, Ramsey Elkholy reports on the Indonesian Orang Rimba minority group. Elkholy's report on Indonesian New Guinea and Oliver-Miller's discussion of the many indigenous groups of Papua New Guinea offer some interesting complementary insights.

## PART 1:
## NATIONAL AND URBAN PERSPECTIVES

WIMPIE I. PANGKAHILA and
J. ALEX PANGKAHILA

### Demographics and a Brief Historical Perspective

ROBERT T. FRANCOEUR

### A. Demographics

Located in the archipelago southeast of Asia along the equator, Indonesia comprises some 13,700 to 17,000 islands (depending on who does the counting). While only about 6,000 are inhabited, the island of Java is one of the most densely populated areas of the world. Besides Java, Indonesia includes four other major islands: Sumatra, the largest and most western of the Indonesian islands, Kalimantan (most of Borneo), Sulawesi (formerly Celebes), and the "Paradise Island" of Bali, as well as the western half of the island of New Guinea, formerly known as Irian Jaya. Indonesia's total area covers 741,100 square miles (1,919,440 km²) and is roughly three times the size of the state of Texas.

The mountains and plateaus on the major islands have a cooler climate than the tropical lowlands. In the eastern island of New Guinea, the mountain peaks may be snow-covered. The Indonesian archipelago lies southeast of the Asian mainland. Straddling the equator, Indonesia's neighbors are Malaysia to the north, Papua New Guinea to the east, Australia to the south of its western islands, and the Indian Ocean to the west. Situated in a part of the "ring of fire," Indonesia has the largest number of active volcanoes in the world. Earthquakes are frequent. The "Wallace line," a zoological demarcation, divides Indonesia, marking the separation of Asian and Australian flora and fauna.

In July 2002, Indonesia had an estimated population of 231.32 million. (All data are from *The World Factbook 2002* (CIA 2002) unless otherwise stated.)

**Age Distribution and Sex Ratios**; *0-14 years*: 30.26% with 1.05 male(s) per female (sex ratio); *15-64 years*: 65.11% with 1 male(s) per female; *65 years and over*: 4.63% with 0.78 male(s) per female (2000 est., *The World Almanac and Book of Facts* 2000)

**Life Expectancy at Birth**: *Total Population*: 68.63 years; *male*: 66.24 years; *female*: 71.13 years

**Urban/Rural Distribution**: 36% to 64%

**Ethnic Distribution**: Javanese: 45%; Sunsanese: 14%; Madurese: 7.5%; coastal Malays: 7.5%; Minahasans, Balinese, Bataks, Dayaks, Timorese, Papuans, Chinese, Arabs, Indians, Europeans, and other: 26%. Indonesia has more than 300 ethnic groups, most of which are very small minorities. Some very small ethnic groups still live in the jungles where they maintain their traditional cultures. Part 2 of this chapter examines the sexual culture of the indigenous hill tribe of the Orang Rimba. Each ethnic group has its own culture and language. Fortunately, there is one Indonesian language as a national language, so that people of the different ethnic groups, with the exception of small geographically isolated peoples, can usually communicate with each other.

**Religious Distribution**: Muslim: 88%; Protestant: 5%; Roman Catholic: 3%; Hindu: 2%; Buddhist: 1%; other: 1% (1998 est.)

**Birth Rate**: 21.87 births per 1,000 population

**Death Rate**: 6.28 per 1,000 population

**Infant Mortality Rate**: 39.4 deaths per 1,000 live births

**Net Migration Rate**: –0.21 migrant(s) per 1,000 population

**Total Fertility Rate**: 2.54 children born per woman

**Population Growth Rate**: 1.54%

**HIV/AIDS** (1999 est.): *Adult prevalence*: 0.05%; *Persons living with HIV/AIDS*: 52,000; *Deaths*: < 3,100. (For additional details from www.UNAIDS.org, see end of Section 10B.)

**Literacy Rate** (*defined as those age 15 and over who can read and write*): 83.8%; (*male*: 89.6%, *female*: 78%) (1995 est.); *attendance for nine years of compulsory school*: 95% (education is free and compulsory from age 6 to 15)

**Per Capita Gross Domestic Product** (*purchasing power parity*): $3,000 (2001 est.); *Inflation*: 9%; *Unemployment*: 15% to 20%; *Living below the poverty line*: 27% (1999 est.)

Indonesia is a developing country with major problems in the social, political, and economic areas. Most people still have a low-subsistence standard of living. However, the small middle- and upper-class populations have a very good standard of life. Some Indonesian businessmen even have their companies in some other countries. This means that there is a wide gap between the poor, as the majority, and the rich, as a very small part of the population. It is estimated that the country will join the developed countries in the near future.

**B. A Brief Historical Perspective**

It is generally believed that the earliest inhabitants of the Indonesian archipelago came from India or Burma (Myanmar). Later immigrants, known as Malays, came from southern China and Indochina. This later group is believed to have populated the archipelago gradually over several thousand years. Hindu and Buddhist civilizations reached Indonesia about 2,000 years ago, taking root mainly on the island of Java. In the 15th century, Islam was spread by Arab traders along the maritime trade routes and became dominant in the 16th century.

In the 17th century, the Dutch replaced the Portuguese as the dominant European power in the area. The Dutch gained control over Java by the mid-1700s, but the outer islands were not subdued until the early 1900s, when most of the current territory of Indonesia came under Dutch rule. On the other side, the Dutch and the Portuguese also brought Christianity to the Indonesian people.

After the Japanese occupation of 1942-1945, nationalists fought four years until the Dutch granted Indonesia its independence. Indonesia declared itself a republic in 1945. In 1957, Indonesia invaded Dutch-controlled West Irian (the western half of New Guinea); in 1969, tribal leaders voted to become part of Indonesia, a move sanctioned by the United Nations.

Indonesia also invaded and annexed East Timor in 1975-1976, as Portuguese rule collapsed. However, this annexation brought many internal social, economic, political, and security problems and tensions in Indonesia's international relations. After the fall of President General Soeharto in 1998, the transitional president, B. J. Habibie, proposed East Timorese vote on two options: independence or integration as a part of Indonesia. Through a self-determination vote under United Nations supervision in 1999, the East Timorese decided to be independent from Indonesia. The level of unrest and violence remains high in East Timor.

In the same year, the Indonesian people held the most democratic general election to that time to choose the people's representatives in the Parliament and Assembly. Through the Assembly, Indonesian people now have a legitimate president, K. H. Abdurrahman Wahid, and vice president, Megawati Soekarnoputri, for the period 1999 to 2004. This, however, does not mean that the country has already been freed from its major problems. These economic, political, and security problems are the major problems faced by Indonesians under the new legitimated government.

## 1. Basic Sexological Premises

### A. Character of Gender Roles

In traditional Indonesian society, women clearly occupy a lower social status than men. This is still the dominant value in Indonesian culture. The idea that a female's place is in the kitchen is still easy to find, especially in the villages. The husband-wife relationship is a chief-assistant relationship rather than a partnership.

Nevertheless, the role of women is improving in modern Indonesian society. Many women work outside the home, particularly in restaurants and in garment and cigarette factories, even though their wages are lower than those of males. Many female physicians, notaries, and lawyers are found in modern Indonesian cities. A few women have achieved high political positions as Cabinet and Parliament members. Vice President Megawati Soekarnoputri, elected in 1999 by the people's representatives in the most democratic general election, is a female.

In modern Indonesian society, the husband-wife relationship is also improving, with a gradual shift to a partnership. Husbands increasingly treat their wife as a partner rather than as an assistant. It is no longer strange to see a husband taking care of his baby while his wife is working outside the home. Unfortunately, this improvement mostly occurs in well-educated couples, which are only a small part of the population. Furthermore, sometimes the change of the husband-wife relationship results in the disharmony of the relationship, mostly because of the negative response of the husband. For example, the husband will feel unhappy if his working wife's salary is more than his, or he will get angry if his working wife does not prepare dinner for him (Blackburn 2000; Hancock 2000; Robinson 2000).

## B. Sociolegal Status of Males and Females

From the standpoint of national law, males and females enjoy the same rights in schooling and careers. However, in some areas, traditional and cultural laws discriminate against females. Only males, for instance, have a right to receive a legacy from their parents. This contributes to a higher status for males.

Another consequence of traditional values is that parents insist on having a son, even though the government has proclaimed a limit of only two children per family, regardless of sex. Many women come to clinics seeking male-sex preselection, even though there is no method that can give a 100% guarantee of having a male child.

In many families, parents give special treatment to the son over the daughter. For example, parents are more likely to support higher education for a son than they would for a daughter. This is based on the stereotype that females will ultimately end up working in the kitchen, while males, as the chief of the family, will work hard to gain money.

Another more serious consequence of the traditional law is that males feel they have a higher social status, and therefore feel more powerful than females. This effect appears in the relationship between a husband and wife where the husband feels he has power over the wife and acts as a chief in the family. Husbands also feel free to do what they want, including having sexual intercourse with other women.

However, among the Miharg Kabou of West Sumatra, females have a higher status than males. Unlike other regions of Indonesia where the male courts the female, Miharg women court the men (Blackburn 2000; Hancock 2000; Machali 2000; Robinson 2000).

## C. General Concepts of Sexuality and Love

Traditionally, Indonesian women connected sexuality with love and engaged in sexual activities only with the males they loved, specifically their husbands. A woman, it was believed, was not able to have sex with a male unless she loved him. In contrast, the traditional view fully accepted males as having sex with any female they liked. In essence, females were only sexual objects, designed for male pleasure.

This traditional view is changing in modern Indonesia. For many, sex and love are easy to separate and are frequently viewed as two different things. Many females, especially among the young, want to engage in sexual intercourse with anybody they like without the necessity of loving that person or without any interest in marriage. This concept, of course, is not well received by the older generation.

This concept change does not seem to occur only in the large cities, but also increasingly in the villages. Some studies performed of the young of the villages showed that there is no significant difference in sexual behavior between the young in the village and in the city. The difference is only in the physical environment and other circumstances that facilitate or permit sexual intercourse. Whether in the city or in the village, the young have the same perceptions about pregnancy, abortion, and family planning. The sexual knowledge and behavior of the young seem to be a new dimension, which is separated from the settings and culture of traditional social organization, family, and religion. The opinion

that the village is a traditional and homogeneous community, which holds strongly the cultural and religious norms and is not easy to change, is no longer a reality.

## 2. Religious, Ethnic, and Gender Factors Affecting Sexuality

### A. Source and Character of Religious Values

During the first few centuries of the Christian era, most of the islands came under the influence of Hindu priests and traders, who spread their religion and culture. Muslim invasions began in the 13th century, and most of the area was Islamicized by the 15th century. Today, 88% of Indonesians are Muslim, with Hindu, Buddhist, and both Protestant and Catholic Christian minorities. There is a commendable degree of religious tolerance among the people.

Evidence of the Hindu influence can be found in some large ancient temples, like Borobudur, Prambanan, Mendut, and Kali Telon in Middle Java, and Jago temple in East Java. The temple in Borobudur is ranked by many as one of the seven miracles in the world. Many reliefs in the walls of these temples portray erotic themes. In the wall of the Kali Telon temple, for example, there are relief figures of males and females having sexual intercourse. In the Mendut temple, people can see in relief figures a scene of a male and female petting.

Christian Portuguese traders arrived early in the 16th century, but were ousted by the Dutch around 1595. In the early 1800s, the British seized the islands, but returned them to the Dutch in 1816. After the end of the Japanese occupation and World War II, Indonesia declared its independence from the Dutch.

In the past, conservative religious and cultural values had a strong influence on sexual attitudes and behaviors. For instance, it was taboo for male and female adolescents to walk together in public. A daughter who became pregnant before marriage created disastrous consequences for her whole family.

However, the influence of religious and traditional cultural values has decreased in recent decades, most noticeably since 1980. This decrease can be seen in the fantastic changes in the sexual attitudes and behaviors of the people, especially among the young. The widespread distribution of contraceptives, which the government initiated as a national program in 1970, brought many changes in the sexual attitudes and behaviors of the people.

The incidence of abortion among the young, which is estimated at around one million per year in the whole country, shows that the strength of religious values has decreased in today's Indonesian society. On the other hand, attendance for all the different religious services is very high.

### B. Character of Ethnic Values

Each ethnic group has its own culture and sexual values. The Javanese, Sundanese, Minahasans, and Balinese, for instance, are more "modern" than the Dayaks and Papuans. In general, however, sex is considered something private and even secret. Sex is appropriate only between husband and wife. Women are like maids; they are only for their husbands' benefit. Wives are subservient to their husbands in everything, including sexual contact.

In a certain Javanese art community of East Java, known as the Reog Ponorogo, some men engage regularly in homosexual behavior, because they believe that they have supernatural powers that will disappear if they have sexual contact with women. These men, known as *waroks*, take care of young males called *gemblaks* who are treated as females. *Waroks* engage in homosexual intercourse with *gemblaks* instead of with females.

In relation to supernatural belief or culture, in a certain community sexual intercourse is practiced as a part of ritual. Many people, hoping to receive a blessing, visit a cemetery on Mount Kemukus in Central Java. However, to receive the blessing the visitors must fulfill one erotic condition. The condition is that the visiting petitioners have to engage in sexual intercourse with each other. They are forbidden to have sex with their own partners during the visit to the sacred cemetery. The other condition is that the sexual intercourse must be done in seven visits with the same partner. It is hard to imagine hundreds of couples having intercourse in the open air under the trees covered with clothes. This cemetery is still visited today by many people from different places, and the free sex among the sacred cemetery visitors continues to the present.

In certain isolated ethnic groups living in remote areas, there is a custom whereby a man may borrow another's wife. This custom is based on the fact that the number of females in the group is very limited and out of balance with the number of adult males. This custom allows a man to enjoy the other man's wife for a few days, but after that, he has to bring her back to her husband.

In today's globalization trends, sexual attitudes and behaviors are changing rapidly in all the cultures of Indonesia. Premarital sex, for example, is now common among adolescents. Even premarital pregnancy is easy to find and, for many parents, it no longer has the disastrous consequences it did only a generation or two ago.

There is a homogenous tendency in sexual perception, knowledge, and behavior, especially among the young, which crosses the ethnic and religious boundaries.

## 3. Knowledge and Education about Sexuality

### A. Government Policies and Programs

Sex education is not a priority in the government's program. Until the year 1999, school curricula did not offer students any education on sexual topics or issues. However, the Department of Education and Culture has recommended a book, *About the Sexual Problems in the Family*, by Wimpie Pangkahila, as a source of sexual information for high school students. This 152-page text, published in 1988, discusses many sexual problems that occur in Indonesian families as a result of misinformation, misunderstanding, and myths, such as the belief in the harmful consequences of self-pleasuring or the impossibility of pregnancy if sexual intercourse occurs only once a month.

The Indonesian Health Department and the National Coordinating Board of Family Planning have a program for Reproductive Health Education. This program, designed for young people, provides seminars on topics of reproductive and sexual health.

In recent years, some secondary high schools have introduced a small segment of sex education as part of their extracurricular offerings. Outside experts are invited to talk about sexuality in these seminars. The era of reformation in Indonesia has also changed the policy of the government on sex education. The new government, through the Department of Education and Culture, has legalized sex education for students under the title of "healthy reproductive education." Now sex education is formally a part of school curricula.

### B. Informal Sources of Sexual Knowledge

Despite public reticence about sexuality, the Indonesian people are eager for and need more information about the subject—hence, the popularity of public and semi-private seminars on sexual topics. Many social organizations for young people and women sponsor seminars for their members, with outside experts invited to speak about sexuality. The seminars are not only held in the big cities, but also in the small cities and suburbs.

Some magazines, newspapers, radio broadcasts, and TV stations also have columns or programs in which sexuality and sexual problems are discussed. Readers, listeners, and viewers write or call in asking about some sexual issue or problem they are facing or they want to know about. Television viewers can watch advertisements for condoms every day in the context of HIV/AIDS prevention.

With the advent of cyberspace, some Indonesian Web sites now offer popular sites for dialog about sexuality. The popularity of these sites among Indonesians makes it hard to believe the view of some people that sex is still a taboo topic among the Indonesian people.

## 4. Autoerotic Behaviors and Patterns

### A. Children and Adolescents

Autoeroticism is common among children in the phallic stage of their psychosexual development. Although some parents report that they watch their children pleasuring themselves to orgasm, many parents are afraid when they discover their children self-pleasuring because they believe this to be an abnormal act.

Autoeroticism is also common among adolescents as a way of tension release. One unpublished study by Wimpie Pangkahila found that 81% of male adolescents and 18% of female adolescents aged 15 to 20 years old engaged in self-pleasuring. Most reported using their fingers, sometimes lubricated with a liquid. Some rubbed against a pillow or mattress. Only a few females reported using a vibrator.

However, there is still considerable misinformation and misunderstanding about autoeroticism. Many adolescents still believe that autoeroticism or masturbation may result in various health problems, like decreased memory, erectile dysfunction, infertility, and decreased bone marrow.

On the moral side, many adolescents feel that autoeroticism is sinful. But they continue to practice this sexual activity. Questions about autoeroticism appear very often in many informal sources of information about sexuality, such as seminars, interactive Internet chat groups, newspapers, and radio programs. The questions are usually related to the consequences of autoeroticism for the practitioner's health.

### B. Adults

Autoeroticism is very common among adults, especially single adults. The pattern is the same as among adolescents. The use of sexual accessories, like various kinds of vibrators and doll partners, are becoming common even though these materials are still illegal. No legal sex shop can be found anywhere in the country, even in the larger cities. One sex shop did open early in 2000 in Surabaya (East Java), Indonesia's second largest city, but the police quickly closed it on the grounds that the sex shop did not have a license from the government and that such shops are contrary to Indonesian culture and morality. It is really difficult to understand such reasoning, especially when this episode triggered a flood of questions in various media—questions, such as "Why close a sex shop? Why don't the police shut down the prostitution?" However, some drug shops still sell those sex accessories illegally, and people can buy from them.

Masturbation among married men or women is practiced in certain situations, like when they stay apart from their partners, if they cannot reach orgasm by sexual intercourse, or if the partner is not able to engage in sexual intercourse for some legitimate reason. Some wives practice masturbation directly in front of their husbands after they have had sexual intercourse without reaching orgasm. A few of them use vibrators or other sexual accessories, whereas others do not want to do it in front of their husbands. The result is that the husbands often do not know that their wives are not reaching orgasm by intercourse and are relying on masturbation for this.

Even though autoeroticism is very commonly practiced among both adolescents and adults, many people still believe that autoeroticism is morally wrong and will result in harmful physical and mental consequences.

## 5. Interpersonal Heterosexual Behaviors

### A. Children

Sexual exploration and sex rehearsal play are common among children as a natural part of their psychosexual development. However, many parents are afraid of such behaviors, believing that the child is suffering from some sexual abnormality or that this behavior will result later in life in some sexual abnormality. Some parents bring their children to psychologists to find out whether their child has had actual sexual intercourse.

Many adolescents are afraid of not being virgins because they had sex rehearsal play a long time ago during their childhood. Some of them even come to the clinic to make sure that they are still virgins. Others seek answers to their questions about childhood sexual rehearsal play and virginity from the dialog columns on sexuality in the newspapers.

### B. Adolescents

*Puberty Rituals*

Some ethnic groups, especially in the remote areas and among tribal people, have ritual ceremonies for adolescents. These ceremonies differ greatly from one ethnic culture to another.

In certain areas, there is a ritual ceremony for the female on the occasion of her first menstruation. This ceremony is actually a way to inform the community that this young female now has become an adolescent and is ready to marry. In one area in East Nusa Tenggara province, male adolescents have to practice sexual intercourse after they are traditionally circumcised. For practical reasons, these male adolescents tend to practice with sex workers. With the unhealed penile cut, this practice, of course, can result in transmission of STDs. This practice also poses a high risk factor for the transmission of HIV/AIDS. However, these ceremonies are no longer practiced in most modern areas of Indonesian society.

*Premarital Sexual Activities and Relationships*

Premarital sexual activities are still generally considered taboo. In general, older persons and parents oppose all sexual activities engaged in before marriage. However, during the past decade, there has been a change in sexual attitudes and behaviors among adolescents. Some small studies in a few Indonesian cities reveal a growing trend among adolescents to engage in premarital sexual activities, such as necking, petting, and even intercourse.

These sexual activities are also becoming common among adolescents in the villages and suburbs. Today, there is no significant difference in sexual perception and behavior between the young in the big cities and the villages.

However, knowing that parents and the older generation oppose premarital sexual activities, young people hide their activities from them. On the other hand, parents frequently give their children more opportunities to be alone with their boy- or girlfriends, and many adolescents take advantage of these opportunities for sexual activities.

In their sexual activities, oral sex is becoming popular among adolescents. There are at least two reasons why adolescents prefer oral sex. First, with oral sex they can avoid the risk of premarital pregnancy. Second, the female feels secure, because oral sex leaves her hymen, a mark of her virginity, intact. A few adolescents engage in anal sex for the same reasons.

Unfortunately, the changes in sexual behavior, which tend to be freer today than in the past, are not accompanied by any increase in sexual knowledge. Most adolescents have many questions about their sexual lives and experiences, which, if expressed, bring negative responses from the older generation, who still believe that such questions are not appropriate for adolescents to inquire about. However, it seems that the general public tends to be more permissive of these changes. Of course, the lack of sexual knowledge results in some negative personal consequences for adolescent life: feelings of guilt and anxiety, unwanted pregnancy, abortion, and STD transmission.

[*Update 2003*: Alarmed by increasing teenage pregnancies in the 1990s, the Indonesian government started planning to incorporate sexuality education into courses such as biology. Similar concerns prompted NGOs, supported by the United Nations Population Fund (UNFPA), to train peers to provide reproductive health information and services to reduce the rate of unwanted teen pregnancies. UNFPA expanded its information and education materials to reach parents, policymakers, and community leaders, as well as teenagers. Under the theme "Having sex before marriage is not appropriate among youth," specific messages stress such issues as: "Responsible relationships between boys and girls," "The world of youth is free, but there are limitations," and "Youth must get correct and clear information about sexuality." The UNFPA and its cosponsors program use regional newspaper columns, a question-and-answer book on the 100 most-asked questions about adolescent reproductive health, leaflets, posters, stickers, calendars, and T-shirts, as well as radio and television talks for youth (UNFPA 2000). (*End of update by R. T. Francoeur*)]

### C. Adults

*Premarital Courtship, Dating, and Relationships*

Dating and premarital sexual relations among adults are very common in modern Indonesian society. The culture requires a particular kind of courtship when a couple wants to marry. In this courtship, the parents and family of the male approach the parents of the female to make the arrangements.

In some ethnic groups, a courtship document is signed when presents, such as cows, buffaloes, gold, and jewelry, are given. For many people in these groups, this custom is very expensive, because they need to save enough money to buy the presents for courtship. Presently, this custom is still practiced among certain ethnic groups, particularly those who live in the areas where they have little contact with outsiders. This custom actually implies that the male has bought and now owns the female.

However, traditional courtship customs are no longer practiced by people who live a modern lifestyle, especially those who live in big cities far from their original area. It is much more practical for them to abandon the traditional customs of courtship, which are both expensive and impractical. The simpler courtship custom of modern Indonesians calls for the parents of the young man to visit the parents of the young woman and agree to their children courting, but without expensive presents.

*Sexual Behavior and Relationships of Single Adults*

Self-pleasuring is a common sexual behavior among single adults, even though it is not allowed by religious and moral values. Sexual relationships among male and female single adults are also taboo. However, some data show that many couples engage in sexual relations before they marry. A 1991 study by Wimpie Pangkahila suggested a rate of 53% for urban couples. Another unpublished study of rural, pregnant women found a premarital intercourse incidence of 27%.

This incidence is now believed to be much higher because of more-liberal relationships, between single adults and adolescents as well. The term "the other man or woman" has become very popular in the last few years. It is no longer a surprise if somebody is said to have a relationship with an extramarital partner.

Many single adult males have sexual contact with prostitutes. Prostitution exists in many places in Indonesia, whether it is legal or illegal. The range of services comes in various classes from low/cheap to high/expensive (see Section 8B, Unconventional Sexual Behaviors, Prostitution, below).

### Marriage and Family

Indonesia has had a marital code to regulate marriages since 1974. The law requires that a marriage be performed in a religious ceremony and then be registered in the civil act office for Christians, Buddhists, and Hindus. The marriages of Muslims are registered in the Muslim Religion Affairs Office.

Generally, marriage in Indonesia involves the families of both partners. It is uncommon for a marriage to be conducted without involvement of the families of both spouses. In case the families cannot agree for whatever reason, there are two choices for the couple. Adult couples who insist on marrying can arrange their own marriage. The other choice is to delay or cancel the wedding. Couples who insist on marrying, even though their families do not agree, usually attempt to repair their relationships with their families.

Divorce is prohibited in Christianity. However, Christian couples who want a divorce may apply to a state court for a civil divorce. In Islam, Hinduism, and Buddhism, divorce is allowed for certain reasons, mainly infertility and adultery on the part of the wife.

In some areas, the incidence of divorce is very high because of financial problems, family conflict, and infidelity. For example, in Lombok Island (West Nusa Tenggara Province) there are many young widows with or without children. Of course, this becomes a serious social problem in the society.

Extramarital intercourse is common, especially among males. Many married men seek prostitutes or have sexual relations with single or married women. Extramarital intercourse is also found among married women, but at a lower incidence than among husbands. Although married women do have sexual relations with single and married men, most people consider this as very bad and unacceptable behavior. In a typical, double moral standard, extramarital sex by males is considered something usual, even though it is forbidden by religion, local morality, and law.

### Sexuality and the Physically Disabled and Aged

Most Indonesians believe that sex is only for physically normal and young people. Most feel uncomfortable when a disabled or aged person still thinks about or expresses an interest in sexual activities. A disabled young woman wrote her complaint and protest in a newspaper because she was discriminated against by a dating and marriage service. The manager of the organization had refused her membership because she was a disabled person. The male manager mentioned that nobody would be attracted to a disabled female.

Even though there is discrimination against disabled persons, marriages do occur between disabled persons, or

between disabled and able-bodied persons. Some disabled and many aged people do come to sexual clinics with their sexual problems for counseling and treatment.

The misinformation that sexual intercourse should not be performed after menopause may lead a male with a postmenopausal wife to seek sex with another woman—prostitutes included. Erectile dysfunction is the most common sexual complaint of older males. On the other hand, pain during sexual intercourse is the most common sexual complaint of older females.

### Incidence of Oral and Anal Sex

Generally, Indonesians do not accept fellatio, cunnilingus, and anal sex as foreplay or sexual outlets. Most people consider these behaviors as abnormal or sinful. On the other hand, many people do engage in fellatio and cunnilingus, but not with their own spouses.

Many men seek out prostitutes only for fellatio, because their wives refuse to engage in it. Some women do like to have cunnilingus, but refuse to perform fellatio for their husbands. Still, many couples enjoy both fellatio and cunnilingus as a part of their normal sexual activities.

Fellatio and cunnilingus are becoming popular among the new generation as a sexual alternative to vaginal intercourse, and as foreplay as well. Generally, they decide to practice fellatio and cunnilingus after watching this behavior on pornographic cable television or on videocassettes. Very few couples engage in anal sex.

## 6. Homoerotic, Homosexual, and Bisexual Behaviors

### A. Children and Adolescents

Homoerotic and homosexual activities are not common among Indonesian children, although some sexual exploration involving exhibiting the genitals is known to occur. Some children who experience homosexual experience with adults may be drawn into long-term homosexual behavior, but no data are available on the various outcomes of child-adult same-sex experiences.

Some adolescents engage in homosexual activities as a sexual outlet, while others engage in this activity for material gain as homosexual male prostitutes. In one Javanese society of traditional artists, known as Reog Ponorogo, some adolescents engage in homosexual activities to serve adult males who are believed to have supernatural powers (see Section 2B, Character of Ethnic Values).

### B. Adults

In general, Indonesians consider homosexuality and bisexuality as abnormal acts forbidden by morality and religion. Despite this taboo, thousands of adults engage in homosexual and bisexual relationships. An organization called the Functional Group for Gays and Lesbians exists, with branches in some of the larger cities. This organization also publishes a newsletter/bulletin to help homosexual persons keep in touch and build support.

Most gays and lesbians, however, hide their orientation and activities, because they know that most people oppose homosexual behavior. Only very few male homosexuals want to be open and frank about their sexual behavior. Some homosexual males hide their sexual orientation by marrying a woman for social status and conformity. Their wives only learn that their husbands are homosexual after the marriage occurs. Some of these marriages end in divorce, but some others remain intact for social or religious reasons.

Some men gradually discover their homosexual orientation during adolescence or early adulthood. Others may be drawn into a homosexual lifestyle, because they had homosexual experience during their childhood. Some engage in homosexual behavior strictly for profit as male prostitutes, and then discover that they have a homosexual orientation.

Since same-sex marriage is illegal, homosexual persons are limited to living-together arrangements and cohabitation without legal sanction. In terms of socializing, some of the larger cities offer places where homosexual persons can gather and meet each other. Sexual outlets among homosexual, lesbian, and bisexual-oriented adults include oral sex, anal sex, and mutual self-pleasuring. Some lesbians use vibrators or other sexual accessories. But, unlike male homosexuals, lesbians are much less obvious in this society.

## 7. Gender Diversity and Transgender Issues

There are no precise statistics on the incidence or sexual lives of gender-conflicted persons. It is commonly assumed by professionals in the field that there are thousands of male transsexuals in Indonesia. *Banci*, a slang term, and *waria*, an abbreviated combination of *wanita* (female) and *pria* (male), are popular terms for gender-conflicted persons in Indonesia. In Surabaya, the capital city of East Java, Perkumpulan Waria Kotamadya Surabaya, the Association of Waria in Surabaya, provides members with support, education, and career training as beauticians, artists, or dancers. These skills, they hope, will allow *waria* to support themselves and avoid a life of prostitution. Support groups also provide information about HIV/AIDS prevention.

In modern-day Indonesia, people can see many transsexuals working as beauticians, dancers, or entertainers. However, on the other hand, many of them also work as low-class prostitutes. This gives all transsexuals a negative image in the eyes of the wider Indonesian society.

Only a few male transsexuals, usually well-known artists, can afford to have surgery to change their sexual anatomy. The average cost for such surgery is the equivalent of 30 to 40 times a lower-class worker's monthly income, about US$2,000 to US$3,000.

## 8. Significant Unconventional Sexual Behaviors

### A. Coercive Sex

*Child Sexual Abuse, Incest, and Pedophilia*

There is no research on child sexual abuse, incest, or pedophilia in Indonesia. What is known about these issues comes from reports in the newspapers detailing some incidents of coercive sex involving children. Legal penalties exist for persons convicted of child sexual abuse, incest, and pedophilia. The social response to these acts is very negative, and the perpetrators are viewed as criminals.

Many street children, whether female or male, experience child sexual abuse. Many male street children are sexually abused by female lower-class prostitutes, who believe the myth that anyone who has sexual intercourse with children or adolescents will remain young.

Incest usually occurs among poor and uneducated families, although this may be a myth. The housing situation of poor families with a single bedroom facilitates the occurrence of incest. Some cases of incest come to public attention when the victims become pregnant and the perpetrators cannot hide the incident. Neighbors and family normally become angry and physically abuse the perpetrator when they learn of such incest.

In the last few years, as the terms pedophilia and sex tourism have become common in Indonesia, knowledge of the incidence of sex with children is increasing. The victims are children of poor families in the villages, while the perpetrators are foreign tourists from other countries. Parents of the children do not object to the foreign tourists who visit their family and offer to help their children. Frequently, the parents agree when the tourists want to bring the children to the city.

It is reported that the organizers are members of an international syndicate of promoters of pedophilia. A video of pedophilia involving Indonesian children is reported to be widely available in many countries.

However, it is necessary to study whether the tragedy inflicted on the children of poverty-stricken families is really the result of paraphilic pedophilia or whether it occurs more because of the belief that sexual intercourse is safer with children who are assumed to be "clean," free from STDs including HIV/AIDS.

*Sexual Harassment*

Even though there are no significant data about sexual harassment, it is believed that it is a common occurrence in Indonesia. Many women who work in factories or offices, or walk along the street, suffer from a variety of sexual harassments, although few women realize they are victims of sexual harassment. Conviction on a charge of sexual harassment may result in three to six months in prison.

Fortunately, in recent years, some women leaders have been trying to educate women, teaching them that sexual harassment is illegal and that women have the right to prosecute those who engage in it.

*Rape*

As with other forms of sexual coercion, there are no significant data on the incidence of rape in Indonesia. Rape incidents perpetrated by an acquaintance, boyfriend, or stranger, and rapes that end in murder are sometimes reported. However, most rapes reported to the police do not end up in a court trial. One of the reasons for this is to protect the victim from public embarrassment in the mass media. Another reason is that the punishment for rapists is considered to be very light.

Marital rape is not reported in the news media, although some wives in counseling or therapy do report being raped by their husbands when they refuse to have sexual intercourse. However, none of the wives want to report this to the police, because they never realize that it is a rape if done by a husband to his own wife. Some wives, however, resist their husbands and threaten to divorce them when forced to have sex against their will. [*Update 2003*: Indonesia has no law on marital rape, despite considerable debate between religious and legal experts on the subject (Idrus 2000). (*End of update by R. T. Francoeur*)]

Some taxi passengers are raped by the drivers, and have ended up being murdered. According to the confessions of the taxi drivers, at the beginning they only wanted to rob the passengers, but this in the end resulted in sexual arousal, assault, and murder. Some wives and their daughters become the victims of gang rapes perpetrated by robbers when they are discovered at home during a robbery.

### B. Prostitution

Prostitution is widespread and occurs in many locations from small to large cities, even though it is often illegal. In some jurisdictions and cities, where prostitution is illegal, the law may prosecute either the prostitutes or those who manage the business of prostitution.

In a few large cities, prostitution is legal. Many prostitutes ("sex workers") of different ages, from adolescence to middle-aged, can be seen. The sex workers are not only local or Indonesian females. There are also some foreigners working as prostitutes. They are divided into different groups based on their appearance, with low-, middle-, and high-class categories. The price of sexual services offered by the sex workers varies, depending on the class determined by their managers. It varies from only 25,000 Rupia (Rp.) (US$3) to Rp. 3,000,000 (US$400) for a short time and one coitus.

Beside legal and illegal prostitution, there is also a hidden prostitution. This is a form of prostitution concealed in another business, such as a massage parlor, beauty parlor, or karaoke place. In terms of STD transmission, this sort of prostitution is worse because the masseuses, the beauticians, or the karaoke escorts do not feel that they are prostitutes; on the other hand, the male customers do not feel that they have had sexual intercourse with sex workers. As a result, many males are unknowingly infected with STDs after they have intercourse with masseuses, beauticians, or karaoke escorts.

Childhood prostitution is often supported by wealthy tourists from the Middle East, Europe, Japan, and other countries, but it is not the extensive problem it is in neighboring nations, like Thailand, Cambodia, Myanmar, and Vietnam. The increase of childhood prostitution is related to the myth that children are "clean" and free from STD infections.

In a few large cities, male sex workers also operate. Their customers are widows, women of middle age or older, and female visitors from foreign countries. Some of them operate quietly as masseurs providing special services for women.

In certain tourist areas, such as Bali, some foreign tourists end up marrying a sex worker whose services they originally sought for pay.

### C. Pornography and Erotica

In keeping with our conservative Indonesian tradition, pornography is illegal throughout Indonesia. However, it is not difficult to find "blue" or hardcore video material. Some people sell pornographic books, magazines, and pictures, despite their being illegal. People, including adolescents, can easily rent pornographic videos and videodisks in many rental places for a low price because so many of them are illegal copies.

Police have caught some criminals who illegally produce or import copies of pornographic video material. However, the illegal business never stops, and people can always rent or buy such hardcore video materials. There is no protection for adolescents from pornographic materials, so they can rent or buy it easily. The video renters/sellers do not feel a moral responsibility to protect adolescents from the effects of the hardcore materials they sell.

In the era of cyberspace, it is much more difficult to protect adolescents from pornography, because it is very easy to access pornographic Web sites. In big cities, there are many places where people can gain access to the Internet and no one can control this access to pornographic Web sites on the Internet.

## 9. Contraception, Abortion, and Population Planning

### A. Contraception

Indonesia has a national program promoting contraception to help married couples plan their families. This program addresses only married people, and not adolescents or unmarried adults. Information on contraception is provided through women's social organizations, newspapers, and radio and television broadcasts.

In 1970, the government began providing free contraceptives at public health centers. In 1988, with an improving economic situation and people recognizing the need for family planning, the government gradually began reducing its support, encouraging people who could afford them to obtain contraceptives from physicians in private practice or midwives with reasonable fees. The poor can still obtain free contraceptive services at public health centers where the only charge is for an inexpensive admission ticket.

The most popular contraceptives are the oral hormonal pill, hormonal injections, and IUDs. Women have to be examined by a physician before they can obtain a prescription for oral hormonal pills, but renewal of such prescriptions is not limited. Hormonal injections and IUDs are administered by doctors or by midwives. The other contraceptives are hormonal implants and tubectomy. As for males, acceptance of contraception is very limited. There are at least two reasons for this resistance. First, perceived male social superiority results in males not accepting their responsibility for contraceptive decisions and use. Second, there are only two alternatives in choosing male contraceptives, condoms or vasectomy. Condom users account for only about 5% of the total number of contracepting men and women.

Despite the limiting of contraceptive information to married women, some adolescents and unmarried women also use contraceptives. They are available in pharmacies (apothecaries or chemists), and include the condom and vaginal film (tissue). Often the hormonal pill can be obtained without a physician's prescription.

In general, the people do not agree that unmarried people should have access to and use contraceptives. Thus, there is no formal education in the schools about contraceptives for adolescents. Sexually active adolescents and single adults have only informal sources of information about contraceptives: newspapers, television, radio programs, and seminars sponsored by interested social groups. As a result, not many adolescents understand how to prevent unwanted pregnancies. They do not even understand how to estimate their fertile period. However, with the government agreement on sexual education as a part of the curriculum in the schools, adolescents will have access to complete information about sexuality, including contraceptives.

### B. Teenage (Unmarried) Pregnancies

Unmarried pregnancies are not uncommon, but data are nonexistent. What little information is available from routine clinical statistics simply documents the number of unmarried pregnancies in different years. Unpublished data from one urban clinic, for instance, reported 473 unmarried pregnant women seeking aid in 1985-1986, a second clinic served 418 pregnant unmarried women in 1983-1986, and a third clinic reported 693 unmarried pregnancies in 1984-1990.

These reports provide only raw data with no perspective, and the frequency and incidence of unmarried pregnancies are much higher than these few studies indicate. Likewise, there are no data that would allow one to compare the incidence of unmarried pregnancies in the cities and rural areas. However, the incidence of abortions performed illegally by medical doctors or traditional healers suggests that unwanted pregnancies are not uncommon, either in the cities or in the rural areas.

Of course, not all unwanted pregnancies result in abortion. Some pregnant adolescents are forced to marry even though they do not want to. The unwanted babies born by unmarried adolescents or young adults that are taken care of in orphanages also indicate that unmarried pregnancies are not uncommon. Some unwanted babies are left by their mothers in the clinic after delivery. Others are simply left in front of somebody's house to be rescued.

Based on an estimated one million teenage abortions a year, and the fact that not all unmarried pregnancies result in abortion, it is believed that the actual number of teenage unmarried pregnancies is well over a million a year.

## C. Abortion

Abortion is illegal throughout Indonesia, except in rare medical cases to save a mother's life. It is impossible to obtain any realistic number of abortions performed in Indonesia, simply because it is illegal. However, many abortions are performed. In addition to abortions performed illegally by medical doctors, abortions are also performed by native or traditional healers, who use traditional methods that are often unsafe and result in complications. One such method uses the stem of a coconut tree leaf, which is inserted into the uterus through the vagina and cervix. This method, of course, is very risky, because it is not sterile and the healers do not understand the sexual anatomy. Some deaths are reported after abortions by native healers because of uterine rupture, bleeding, or infection.

Some doctors are caught by the police because they perform abortions in their clinics. A few of these cases were reported in the news media when police found many dead fetuses buried in the yard of a clinic or in plastic bags thrown into the garbage bins or dumps.

It is estimated that around 2.5 million abortions are performed each year throughout Indonesia, for both married and unmarried women. Of these, around one million are abortions performed on teenagers.

## D. Population Programs

The success of Indonesia's national program of family planning was recognized in 1989 when the United Nations gave its Population Award to the president of Indonesia. Efforts are being made to achieve zero population growth in the near future.

These efforts are particularly important considering that the island of Java is one of the most densely populated areas of the world with 2,100 persons per square mile (2.6 km$^2$) and over 100 million people on the island of 51,023 square miles (132,149 km$^2$). By comparison, the states of New York, North Carolina, and Mississippi are each roughly the same size as Java, but have only 18, 6.6, and 2.5 million people, respectively.

One important effort is to increase the participation of males in family planning. Up to now, their participation is very low. The involvement of males in family planning is only 6% of the contraceptors because of various factors. The male superiority is one of important factors that inhibit males accepting responsibility in family planning. Most males are not interested in using either condoms or vasectomy.

## 10. Sexually Transmitted Diseases and HIV/AIDS

### A. Sexually Transmitted Diseases

Although no survey and reliable clinical reports are available, it is the clinical experience of the authors and their colleagues that sexually transmitted diseases are common among Indonesian adolescents and young adults, indicating that the taboos against premarital sex are not observed. The incidence is highest among those between ages 20 to 24, and lower among the 25- to 29-year-olds and 15- to 19-year olds. As would be expected given the social customs, the incidence among males is higher than it is among females. The most commonly reported STDs are nonspecific urethritis, gonorrhea, ulcus molle, and genital herpes. Syphilis is no longer common, although it appears to be increasing in recent years.

Transmission of STDs is caused by unsafe and high-risk sexual behavior, including intercourse with sex workers. The use of condoms is not popular among males who are involved in high-risk sexual behavior.

Treatment for STDs is available at all health clinics throughout the country. Some years ago, the government sponsored a program to reduce the spread of STDs by providing prostitutes with penicillin injections. Unfortunately, the program is no longer available.

Currently, sex workers have taken the initiative in preventing STD transmission. However, their effort is often medically unsound because it is only based on misinformation from friends or other lay people. The most popular method employed by sex workers is consuming an oral antibiotic after sexual activity. The other is irrigating the vagina with antiseptic. These methods, they believe, can prevent STD transmission, including HIV/AIDS. On the other hand, the customers also believe that if the sex workers do not have any visible signs of an STD, they are not at risk of being infected even though they do not use a condom.

The prevention efforts by the government and nongovernmental organizations (NGOs) focus on providing information in seminars and the mass media, including the newspaper, radio, and television.

Some informal studies of STD prevention have found that most Indonesians do not understand well the nature and character of STDs. The obvious question, then, is whether the strategy and/or technique of prevention efforts have to be reevaluated, and probably even changed.

### B. HIV/AIDS

The first case of AIDS found in 1987 in Denpasar (in Bali) was a Dutch visitor. This incident scared many people, including the hotel staff where he stayed and the hospital staff where he was treated a few days before he died. Fortunately, in revealing that HIV/AIDS was indeed present and active in Indonesia, this incident raised the awareness of many Indonesians, including doctors and government officials.

Until the end of 1987, there were only 6 cases of HIV/AIDS reported in Indonesia. Thereafter, this incidence has increased rapidly as reported by the Indonesian Department of Health (see Table 1). In the first two months of the year 2000, 103 new cases were reported, suggesting the start of an exponential increase, with perhaps a tripling of cases to about 600 for 2000. The cumulative number of HIV/AIDS cases until February 2000 was 1,146, consisting of 853 cases of HIV positives and 293 cases of AIDS. However, it is believed that the real number of HIV/AIDS cases is much higher than the reported number. The real number of HIV/AIDS cases is estimated around 100 to 200 times greater than the reported number (Indonesian Department of Health 2000).

The 1,146 cases of HIV/AIDS reported as of February 2000 are spread throughout Indonesia's 23 provinces. These involve 679 males and 412 females, with the sex of 55 patients unidentified. Most of the HIV/AIDS cases in Indonesia resulted from heterosexual contact. Most of those infected

### Table 1

### Incidence of AIDS in Indonesia, 1988-1999

| Year | Cases | Year | Cases | Year | Cases |
|------|-------|------|-------|------|-------|
| 1988 | 7 | 1992 | 28 | 1996 | 137 |
| 1989 | 7 | 1993 | 113 | 1997 | 118 |
| 1990 | 9 | 1994 | 87 | 1998 | 200 |
| 1991 | 18 | 1995 | 89 | 1999 | 225 |

are between 15 and 39 years of age (Indonesian Department of Health).

Sex workers are believed to be one source of infection transmission, but the freer sexual behavior among today's people has also become a prominent factor. In the early years of HIV/AIDS transmission in Indonesia, it is estimated that some HIV-positive foreign tourists who came to popular tourist centers like Bali introduced the virus through sexual contact with sex workers or local people.

Prevention efforts have been provided for some groups of people, such as sex workers, both female and male, people who work in the tourism industry, university and high school students, long-distance truck and bus drivers, women leaders, and religious leaders. These efforts involve providing information, education, and training on how to reduce the spread of AIDS, and include blood tests for HIV infection. Campaigns to popularize the use of condoms are now conducted through the mass media, including newspaper, radio, and television. However, it is not easy to make people aware and encourage condom use if they engage in high-risk sexual intercourse.

The classical belief that using condoms inhibits the joy of sex is still fixed in the mind of almost all Indonesian males, as well as females. The simple distribution of condoms to sex workers does not solve the problem. Most males seeking sex workers do not want to use condoms because of the classic myth of inhibiting pleasure. Sex workers are in a very weak bargaining position, so they do not have enough power to refuse the customers who do not want to use condoms. If they insist and refuse the customer who does not want to use a condom, they will have to answer to their manager, and this could lead to further difficulties. No one seems to know what policy could best convince those who have sex with sex workers that condoms are a must in today's world. Indonesia very much needs a national policy to encourage men frequenting sex workers to use condoms, or to press sex workers not to do their job if the customer does not want to use a condom. If such a policy is not found and implemented effectively, Indonesia faces the distinct likelihood of an explosion of cases of HIV/AIDS in the near future.

[*Update 2003*: Indonesia faces a national health disaster, which belies its reputation as the world's largest, and quite conservative, Muslim community—an epidemic of IV-drug use that suggests needle sharing will soon surpass unsafe sex as the most common method of contracting HIV (*The Age* 2003).

[According to Henry Yosodiningrat, a Jakarta lawyer and member of the government's National Narcotics Agency, "This is an extremely serious issue for us. It's a threat that could kill an entire generation. There's not a school or district anywhere across the country where drugs are not used." In January 2003, Broto Wasisto, head of the Health Ministry's committee on drug control, and a member of the national HIV/AIDS control board, agreed that IV-drug use "is a national emergency as far as controlling the spread of HIV/AIDS is concerned." In February 2002, a report by Melbourne's Macfarlane Burnet Institute for Medical Research and Public Health estimated that there were between 1.3 million and two million IV-drug users in Indonesia, with up to one million of these injecting. Some local estimates put the number of users at four million—about one in every 50 Indonesians.

[In 1996, Jakarta's RSKO hospital, which specializes in treating drug addicts, dealt with 2,000 patients; three years later, the number had risen to 9,000. In the process, users are getting younger, with most now between the ages of 16 to 25. The full range of drugs available in the West, and more, is used here. Premium-quality marijuana from Sumatra, ec-

stasy, heroin, and methamphetamines are offered for sale. Shabu-shabu, a potent new form of methamphetamine that is injected, inhaled, or taken orally, increases the duration and intensity of sex and reduces inhibitions, making users fearless and prone to risk-taking. It is popular among prostitutes and their clients in Indonesia's massive sex industry and is cheaply produced in backyard factories. There is a caste system among Indonesian drug users. The middle class use ecstasy; poorer people use shabu.

[Despite the growing awareness of the problem, Indonesia faces unique obstacles and some reluctance in dealing with it. "Although the use of illicit drugs is increasing, political conflict, power struggles, and widespread corruption are influencing how the drug-related HIV/AIDS crisis should be tackled," the Macfarlane Burnet report concluded. A major obstacle in the anti-drug war is a mind-boggling array of other social, economic, and security crises competing for the government's attention. Then there are too many other pressing health problems: high maternal and infant-mortality rates, malaria, tuberculosis, and a multitude of diseases because of the lack of clean drinking water. All these obstacles are complicated by the free flow of money from the drug syndicates to buy officials, police, and the army. There is also evidence that elements of the underfunded police and military are themselves involved in the drug trade and are willing to fight public turf wars for their share of it. In October 2002, at Binjai in north Sumatra, soldiers in an army airborne unit tied up their officers and attacked police stations using rocket-propelled grenades, mortars, and automatic weapons, killing eight police and civilians. The soldiers were upset after the police arrested a drug dealer and seized 1.5 tons of cannabis.

[Meanwhile, the East Timor government and the UN have launched an AIDS-awareness campaign on television, radio, and print media, hoping the country can avoid the explosion in HIV/AIDS seen elsewhere in the region. East Timor, newly independent from Indonesia on May 20, 2002, has so far avoided an HIV/AIDS epidemic, but social dislocation, cross-border migration, high unemployment, illiteracy among the rural population, and low awareness about HIV indicate a significant risk. In 2002, preliminary estimates from the Ministry for Health showed the rate of HIV infection at 0.64% of people of reproductive age. Cambodia, Thailand, and Myanmar have HIV rates of more than 1%, according to UNAIDS (Reuters Health, 2002). (*End of update by R. T. Francoeur*)]

[*Update 2002*: UNAIDS Epidemiological Assessment: Until the end of 1998, all HIV/AIDS data collected in Indonesia from all sources indicated that HIV-seroprevalence rates were very low (below 0.1%), even in the highest heterosexual risk groups, such as female sex workers. The exception to this very low HIV prevalence was in Merauke (in West Irian) where relatively high HIV-prevalence rates were reported among female sex workers several years ago.

[Starting in 1999 and continuing in 2000, several HIV Sentinel Surveillance sites for female sex workers began to detect increasing numbers of HIV infections, and prevalence rates from 1% to 5% were found in several areas. Although injecting-drug-user populations were not included as a routine sentinel surveillance group, several ad hoc sero-surveys throughout Indonesia, especially in Jakarta, detected sharply increasing HIV prevalence (up to over 35% in Jakarta) among injecting drug users in late 2000. This increasing trend of HIV prevalence can be seen in blood-donor data from the Indonesian Red Cross from 1992 to 2000. In recent years, approximately 750,000 to 1,000,000 blood donors have been screened annually for HIV; a marked increase was seen in 1999 and 2000, probably reflecting the large increase among injecting-drug-user populations noted during the same time period.

[Indonesia is classified as a country with a concentrated HIV epidemic, primarily among its injecting-drug-user population. At the end of 2001, an estimated 120,000 people were living with HIV/AIDS. The estimated number of AIDS deaths for the year 2001 is about 4,600. Most of these AIDS deaths occurred in or around Jakarta, where the majority of the HIV-infected injecting-drug-user populations live.

[The estimated number of adults and children living with HIV/AIDS on January 1, 2002, were:

| | | |
|---|---|---|
| Adults ages 15-49: | 120,000 | (rate: 0.1%) |
| Women ages 15-49: | 27,000 | |
| Children ages 0-15: | 1,300 | |

[An estimated 4,600 adults and children died of AIDS during 2001.

[At the end of 2001, an estimated 18,000 Indonesian children under age 15 were living without one or both parents who had died of AIDS. (*End of update by the Editors*)]

## 11. Sexual Dysfunctions, Counseling, and Therapies

The diagnostic paradigm used by Indonesian sexologists is basically that of William Masters and Virginia Johnson, with presenting cases of inhibited penile erection (erectile dysfunction), early (premature) ejaculation, inhibited (retarded) ejaculation, male and female dyspareunia, inhibited female orgasm, and vaginal spasms (vaginismus).

However, the development in diagnostic tools has changed both the results of the diagnosis and the strategy of case management. With some diagnostic tools, like the erectiometer, Doppler pen, and Rigiscan, a more accurate diagnosis can be achieved. For example, before the new diagnostic tools were developed, most erectile dysfunction was considered to be psychological in origin. But after the development of new diagnostic tools, it is found that most erectile dysfunctions are organic. This finding, supported by the new medicines like sildenafil, has changed the strategy in the management of erectile dysfunction. Now the treatment of erectile dysfunction is divided into three steps: first-, second-, and third-line therapies. First-line therapy consists of sexual or psychosexual therapy, oral erectogenic agents (primarily Viagra), and a vacuum constriction device. Second-line therapy includes intracavernosal injection and intraurethral application. Third-line therapy is the surgical procedure of penile implant. These advanced treatments are available only to a small minority of Indonesians living in urban centers who can afford them.

A common psychological sequel for males with a sexual dysfunction is a feeling of inferiority with regard to their partner. This feeling is often what brings the male to seek treatment.

Many women, on the other hand, tend to hide their sexual problems and feel shy about seeking treatment. Many married women never have orgasm and never tell their husbands. At the same time, many husbands are unaware or do not even suspect that their wives never have orgasms. Many of them are simply unaware of their wife's sexual dysfunction even after the wife complains to a sexologist.

Out of 4,135 women who came for consultation at the authors' clinics for their own or their husband's sexual problem, 2,302, or 55.7%, have never had an orgasm, and 527, or one in six (12.7%), have experienced orgasm only rarely. Among those who never reached orgasm, 60 (2.6%) experienced dyspareunia, 67 (2.9%) experienced hypoactive sexual desire, and 27 (1.2%) suffered from vaginismus.

The high incidence of sexual dysfunction among Indonesian females is caused by poor communication between husbands and wives, poor sexual knowledge, and male sexual dysfunction. However, good diagnosis and treatment for sexual dysfunctions are available in only a few urban clinics, and are available only to those who can afford it.

## 12. Sex Research and Advanced Professional Education

A few Indonesian sexologists have finished their education and training in the United States, Belgium, and Australia. Some informal unpublished clinical studies of sexuality in Indonesia have focused on sildenafil and alprostadil for the treatment of erectile dysfunction, on sexual perception and behavior among the youth in cities and villages, and sexual knowledge, perception, and behavior of STD patients. Some studies are currently in progress, including management of erectile dysfunction using the new medications, and high-risk sexual behavior in relation to HIV/AIDS transmission.

Advanced education on sexuality is available only in the Master Program in Reproductive Medicine at Udayana University in Denpasar, Bali. This program offers sexology lectures and study as a part of the curriculum. As a postgraduate program, it requires a two-year study course in sexology, spermatology, experimental reproductive biology, reproductive endocrinology, embryology, family planning, and infertility management. Instruction in sexology includes perspectives on sexuality, gender and sexual behavior, childhood, adolescence, and adulthood sexuality, sexual fantasy, sexual variation, sexual dysfunction, sexual deviation, and premarital and marital counseling.

The mailing address of this center is: The Master Program in Reproductive Medicine, Udayana University Medical School, Attention: Prof. Wimpie I. Pangkahila, M.D., Ph.D., Jl. Panglima Sudirman, Denpasar, Bali, Indonesia.

## References and Suggested Readings

CIA. 2002 (January). *The world factbook 2002*. Washington, DC: Central Intelligence Agency. Available: http://www.cia.gov/cia/publications/factbook/index.html.

Idrus, N. L. 2000. Marriage, sex and violence in Bugis ciety. In: S. Blackburn, ed., *Love, sex and power: Women in Southeast Asia*. Clayton, Australia: Monash Asia Institute.

Hancock, P. 2000. Gender empowerment issues from West Java. In: S. Blackburn, ed., *Love, sex and power: Women in Southeast Asia*. Clayton, Australia: Monash Asia Institute.

Machali, R. 2000. Women and the concept of power in Indonesia. In: S. Blackburn, ed., *Love, sex and power: Women in Southeast Asia*. Clayton, Australia: Monash Asia Institute.

Pangkahila, W. 1981. *Changes in sexual perception and behavior in adolescence*. Presented at the National Congress of Sexology, Denpasar, Indonesia.

Pangkahila, W. 1988. *Sexual problems in the family* [in Indonesian]. Jakarta: PT Gaya Favorit Press.

Pangkahila, W. 1991. *Premarital sex in married couples: A survey* [in Indonesian]. Presented in many public and professional seminars.

Reuters Health. 2002 (April 4).

Robinson, K. 2000. Gender, Islam and culture in Indonesia. In: S. Blackburn, ed., *Love, sex and power: Women in Southeast Asia*. Clayton, Australia: Monash Asia Institute.

*The Age* [Australia]. 2003 (January 4). Indonesia is dancing with death. Available: www.theage.com.au.

UNAIDS. 2002. *Epidemiological fact sheets by country*. Geneva, Switzerland: Joint United Nations Programme on HIV/AIDS (UNAIDS/WHO). Available: http://www.unaids.org/hivaidsinfo/statistics/fact_sheets/index_en.htm.

UNFPA. 2000 (June 22). Sex before marriage not appropriate for youth, messages tell Indonesian adolescents. *UNFPA at work*.

## PART 2:
## THE INDIGENOUS ORANG RIMBA
## FOREST PEOPLE

RAMSEY ELKHOLY

### Demographics and a Brief Historical Perspective*

#### A. Demographics

The Orang Rimba are an indigenous minority population inhabiting the primary and secondary lowland forests of south-central Sumatra, the largest and most western of the Indonesian islands just south of Malasia. *Kubu* is the most commonly used exonym by local villagers and the general Indonesian populace, and it is the most common referent found in the anthropological literature (see Van Dongen 1906; Loeb 1942; LeBar 1972; Sandbukt 1984, 1988ab; Persoon 1989; Suetomo 1992). However, it is a title they resent being designated by, as it is a pejorative term connoting "savage" or "primitive."

They practice a nomadic or semi-nomadic form of hunting and gathering economy, occasionally supplemented with basic slash and burn (swidden) agriculture. Precise population figures are difficult to obtain, but 2,600 to 3,000 are realistic estimates, with the large majority living in Jambi Province, and nearly one third of the total population concentrated in the Tembesi-Tabir interfluve, where slash and burn agriculture has intensified in recent decades, thus leading to higher birthrates. Significant numbers are also found in South Sumatra Province, while remnant populations and new migrants can also be found in West Sumatra and the Riau Provinces.

Group sizes range from small nuclear domestic units to larger swiddening (slash and burn) camps, which can reach 100 or more persons (Sandbukt 1988a). In cases where residential groups consist of nuclear family dwellings, it is common for two or more kin-related families to consolidate their efforts by sharing game and other wild foods to compensate for their small group sizes. In recent decades, some groups have adopted a more sedentary life, shifting their economic orientation towards subsistence horticulture and rubber tree cultivation and tapping. This has led to higher birthrates among women, but infant mortality remains high, particularly in areas where deforestation has occurred, where they are coping with the transition to sedentism without proper healthcare and hygienic education.

#### B. A Brief Historical Perspective

For centuries, the Orang Rimba have avoided sustained contact with neighboring agricultural peasantries, preferring to trade only with a select few trusted villagers. Various historical accounts report that in certain areas they had practiced a form of "silent trade," whereby forest products were placed on the fringes of the forest to be collected by villagers, who would exchange these products with needed goods, such as

salt and metal for spear heads and machetes, by placing them in the same spot—both sides never meeting face to face (Boers 1838; Forbes 1885). This form of barter may have been replaced, in some cases, with face-to-face encounters with a Malay intermediary known as *jenang* or *bapak semang*. He was seen as a guarantor of their autonomy, and the forest products they forfeited to him (e.g., rattan, damar, "dragon's blood," and honey) were often of much greater value than the goods received (e.g., salt, tobacco, metal tools, and clothing), which were to be seen as gifts rather than direct equivalents of the goods offered (Sandbukt 1988b, 112-13). This system lasted until recent years and still persists in some areas, but in a less paternalistic and strictly economic form.

Such extreme xenophobia may have been a response to the fears of slave raiding in past times. According to Sandbukt (1988a, 111) and Marsden (1811, 41), slave raiding on the inter-local level was a real and serious threat to the Orang Rimba until only a few generations ago. Such dangers may have increased with the spread of Islam from the 14th century onwards. In the Islamic faith, it is forbidden to enslave other Muslims. The non-Muslim indigenous populations of the interior, such as the Orang Rimba, were, therefore, obvious targets for slave raids and other forms of persecution (cf. Denatan et al. 1997).

Their long history of avoidance of the outside world is deeply rooted in an ideology, passed down from their ancestors, that envisages the bifurcation of humanity into two types: Malays—who live in permanent villages and follow the dictates of Islam; and the Orang Rimba—who live in the forest and follow the traditions and customs of their ancestors (see Sandbukt 1984). This distinction is the inspiration and guiding principle of their lives, and any crossing or confusing of these two domains would be seen as a breach of the sacred mode of life passed down from their ancestors. The Orang Rimba identify all that is sacred with the forest and, concomitantly, view many of the Islamic customs practiced by their sedentary village-dwelling neighbors as somehow impure and, therefore, taboo. The coexistence of these two groups, the Orang Rimba and Muslim villagers, is an excellent example of what anthropologists call a "commensal relationship," two groups who can reside in the same area without competing, because they have independent or different values and customs. Commensality practices perfectly illustrate this. The foods commonly eaten by Muslim villagers, such as goats, cows, buffaloes, and chickens, are foods that are forbidden to the Orang Rimba, whereas certain forest game, such as wild boar, turtle, and snake, foods quite common to the Orang Rimba, are taboo to the Muslim villagers.

The Orang Rimba integrate and associate religion, the supernatural, notions of well-being, subsistence practice, and survival in general with their forest environment. Richly imbued with nurturing and life-giving qualities, their forest world is viewed as a pantheistic totality where a wide variety of deities reside under the auspices of a benevolent and omnipotent Godhead (*Behelo*). Forest deities are contacted regularly by experienced shamans who, while in trance, are endowed with the special ability to see and communicate with these otherwise invisible beings. Such sacred communication insures protection from physical and supernatural dangers and promotes success in hunting and the general well-being of the group. It also serves to maintain and regenerate the delicate dialectical balance between themselves and the forest, and the sacred mode of life practiced therein.

Despite their rich and complex system of beliefs, they are, nonetheless, considered pagan savages or "infidels" by their Muslim agriculturist neighbors. Moreover, these encompassing agricultural peasantries, along with a continual

---

*\*Editor's Note*: Because there are over 300 distinct indigenous ethnic groups in Indonesia, the authors of Part 1 of this chapter focus mainly on urban and village Indonesians, for whom some data are available. Here, in Part 2, Ramsey Elkholy, a sociocultural anthropologist, expands on this picture of sexuality among modern urban and village Indonesians with insights from his fieldwork with the indigenous Orang Rimba hunter-gatherer forest people of Sumatra, Indonesia. For additional insights into the sexual attitudes and behavior among other indigenous peoples, the reader is referred to the sections on the aboriginal people of Australia and Brazil, Canada's First Nation People, and the indigenous people of French Polynesia and Papua New Guinea in this volume.

influx of transmigrants from Java, continue to clear Orang Rimban forestland for their slash and burn fields. More threatening still to Orang Rimban environments are the large-scale logging operations that continue in both South Sumatra and Jambi Provinces. These days, many groups camp on the side of logging roads in order to gain easier access to outer-market goods and services. Exchange contacts have also increased and diversified as a consequence of their broadening knowledge of the outside mercantile economy, and they no longer accept the paternalistic relationships with Malay intermediaries whereby "gifts" are received for their labor and forests products. Although they are enjoying greater access to the wider market economy, which has provided them with unprecedented opportunities to amass personal wealth (usually measured in sheets of cloth, gold, currency, and outer-market goods), there are few, if any, Orang Rimba environments that are not somehow threatened by the forces of encroaching development.

Aside from the destruction of their forests, the Orang Rimba have been under increasing pressures from central and local governments to assimilate. In the 1960s, the Department of Social Affairs (Depsos) initiated an assimilation campaign in an attempt to settle the Orang Rimba permanently in Malay-style villages and encourage them to practice subsistence agriculture. In coordination with Indonesia's Department of Religion (Dinas Agama), and occasionally through missionaries—sometimes foreign—attempts have been undertaken with varying degrees of success to convert them to Islam, the nation's predominant religion. Christian missionaries have also played an active role in persuading the Orang Rimba to abandon their traditional mode of life in the forest and assimilate to Malay ways, which involves taking up permanent residence in or near one of the nearby villages. Since Indonesia's independence in 1945, most villages have established Government-sponsored primary schools, where Pencasilan national philosophy and modern Indonesian is taught. This has promoted a sense of nationalism and broader regional awareness that is largely absent among the Orang Rimba, who by and large still remain separate geographically and culturally, and continue to see the world from a purely provincial or local perspective.

While the pressures of deforestation and development are causing rapid social changes and challenging the resiliency of their traditional way of life, domestic practices, including gender roles and relations, have remained relatively unaffected, aside from higher incidence of male defection to local villages where intermarriage is sought. No known precedence has been set for villager males marrying into forest-dwelling Orang Rimban camps. As such, these groups remain ideal contexts for studying traditional internal social dynamics. However, the Orang Rimba's well-established history of avoidance behavior had, in the past, undermined many attempts at conducting in-depth anthropological investigation, particularly regarding sensitive matters such as gender and sexuality, which require intimate contact on the domestic level and access to women by researchers. The information reported here is based on a field study of close to two years, when the author lived among the Orang Rimba on the domestic level. The demands of local customs necessarily restricted the author's access to Orang Rimban women.

## 1. Basic Sexological Premises

### A. Character of Gender Roles

The Orang Rimba use kinship categories as the basic societal building blocks of their social organization. Kinship ties determine residential arrangements, distribution of resources, and key social alignments, in effect producing and reproducing their ideational ties and wider social order. Populations who may be separated by hundreds of kilometers will maintain contacts with their near and distant kin, either directly or through intermediaries. Through these "kinship networks," one enduring cultural type—however dispersed—may be said to exist. Gender relations are equally conditioned and affected by kinship relations and, therefore, kinship affiliation plays a fundamental role in shaping Orang Rimban social values and general modes of behavior.

Postmarital residence is uxorilocal. A male will marry-in to his spouse's group and, after an unspecified period of bride-service to his father-in-law, he will remain under his authority and be expected to provide his labor power and moral support indefinitely. He will eventually replace his father in-law's position, either by usurping his power when he is physically unfit or too old to make important decisions (e.g., resolving disputes, representing the group and their needs to outsiders, etc.), or when he finally dies. Marriage is normally a strenuous affair for in-marrying males as well as for most families involved. Most family members, fathers and brothers in particular, will fiercely resist any attempts by an outsider male to marry into the family. The outsider male must first gain the family's trust, and the suitor's bride-service is aimed at achieving this end. Cross-cousin marriage is preferred over unions with non- or distant kin, as trust has already been established through previous consanguinal relations between siblings.

An Orang Rimban man will commonly exhibit "macho"-like characteristics, asserting a "don't fool with me" status to other men. Such a disposition is largely because of the ever-present need to claim one's rights to women, particularly spouses, but also female children of marriageable age who are increasingly coming under the eyes of amorous young bachelors. While a male's masculinity is often exaggerated in manner, he may be openly affectionate and nurturing towards his young children, particularly infants. Men will also display affection openly by embracing and weeping upon uniting with long-separated male relatives. Group weeping (*bubughatongpon*) in cases where long-separated parties unite is also common, as well as in the event of death, in which case weeping may continue sporadically for weeks on end. Embracing, however, is restricted to the same sex, and it is more common that a woman will bow her head and sniff the hand of a male relative, which signifies respect during such greetings and farewells.

Traditionally, the role of an Orang Rimban man is that of "the hunter," the provider of meat, and the protector of women and children. A woman's role is twofold, that of "the gatherer" of wild food, which includes digging edible tubers, and that of "the nurturer" of the young. While Orang Rimban society appears to be male-dominated in most respects, women often enjoy considerable autonomy and hold considerable political sway over their spouses, particularly when their fathers and male siblings are nearby, where they can voice their complaints and thereby summon their support (see Sandbukt 1988a).

Domestic space is delineated by the male and female domains in their split-level shelters. The upper level is the male domain, where visiting men are welcome to sit, smoke tobacco, and pass the time of day; the lower level is strictly for women and children. The lower level physically marks off a boundary from the rest of the shelter and is strictly off limits to all adult males except for a woman's spouse.

These days, collecting forest products for external exchange is increasing, as the Orang Rimba's ever-growing dependency on outer-market goods, such as cigarettes, coffee, sugar, and rice increases. It is now more common for women to frequent village shops to buy supplies and to sell their forest products. In some areas, however, women are still fiercely protected from the perceived dangers of the outer world and are forbidden to enter the village without male accompaniment. In more-rare cases, where traditions still strongly prohibits contact with outsiders, women are forbidden from entering the village altogether.

Labor power is a central concern in Orang Rimban society, and every member, if able, is expected to contribute to the well-being of the group. Even child labor is utilized to its fullest extent. As soon as children can walk, they learn, mostly through imitation, the tasks appropriate to their gender. Girls will look after their younger siblings, fetch water, cook, weave sleeping mats, collect firewood, help clear swiddens, and other household chores. Boys will also help clear swiddens and follow older boys and adult males on fishing and hunting excursions.

Young girls will be expected to take care of and nurture younger siblings, and it is not uncommon for a 7-year-old to spend an entire afternoon looking after younger siblings while her mother is out collecting forest products. On other occasions, they may accompany her on short excursions to dig for edible tubers. At this age, a girl will mix freely with boys, but as she approaches menarche her domestic responsibilities will increase along with her increasing awareness of her sexuality. She will already understand and adhere to the social sanctions regarding excessive contact with males. When she reaches her menarche, and for the remainder of her pre-marriage years, the only men she will interact with will be her male siblings and father. It is not uncommon, however, for an adolescent or young-adult girl to eschew intimate contact even with her male family members, who, following the same code of conduct, may speak to her only when necessary.

Female children are particularly coveted and prized. Aside from helping with household chores, such as cooking, collecting firewood and water, nurturing younger siblings, and various other domestic tasks, they will someday fetch a brideprice or fine, often paid in sheets of cloth. In more recent times, gold and currency have also been used. Female children are also valued for the subsequent labor power of an in-marrying male they will bring. More pressure to be self-sufficient is brought to bear on boys, and they will be encouraged to collect forest products or go fishing at the early age of 7 or 8. As they approach their adolescent years, they will accompany men on hunting excursions and increase their proficiency in forest-product collecting. They will commonly give their earnings to their mother for safekeeping or for the group's immediate needs. The logic behind expecting young boys to produce and contribute to the camp's subsistence base lies not only in their inherent abilities, but also in the recognition that they will provide their labor power during their growing years, but eventually will leave the camp to marry-in to another group. Moreover, they will need such survival skills in order to seek a wife and support a family someday.

Obedience to adults, particularly fathers, is an enduring characteristic of Orang Rimban family life. Unlike most of the world's egalitarian hunting and gathering societies, where children enjoy great personal autonomy and are expected to respect, but not necessarily obey their parents (Denatan et al. 1997), Orang Rimban children are highly disciplined and are expected to both respect and obey their elders. A child that does not obey a parent is referred to as "evil" (*jahat*) and, in extreme circumstances, may be subject to physical punishment. This is more common among same-sex parent-child relations. For example, a father will not beat his daughter, and a mother will rarely, if ever, beat her son. More commonly, however, children are scolded verbally to invoke a sense of shame that is especially felt when their behavior is called into question publicly before the scrutiny of the camp.

## B. Sociolegal Status of Males and Females

*The Adult World*

As mentioned above, most of the world's hunting and gathering peoples are egalitarian in their social organization. The Orang Rimba are an exception in this regard, in that competition between men based on unequal access to women creates distinct inequalities between men. As a result, disputes commonly arise between men over their "rights" to women. Out of the need to protect one's claims to women, fathers over daughters and husbands over wives, the Orang Rimba have developed strong notions of law and social order. A male's voice is often oratorical and loud, and their strong sense of law and moral propriety is revealed in the content and character of their speech. In some areas, they have assimilated to an archaic Malay hierarchy, one which the Malays themselves no longer ascribe to, where various ranks preside under the authority of a high-ranking headman (*tumenggung*). These hierarchies most likely served as a mechanism through which they could be governed, however loosely, by the wider rural society, and to extract valuable forest products for external exchange. But they also serve as a legal mechanism through which serious disputes can be resolved. Incumbents are elected to office by their own kinsmen after demonstrating their mastery of formal *adat* customary law, which is exhibited through a public recital of its precepts. In areas where the Orang Rimba have not assimilated to this hierarchy, marked inequalities between men still persist, mainly as a consequence of uxorilocal postmarital residence and the requisite subordination of in-marrying male's to their father-in-laws.

A deep mistrust between distant or non-kin males regarding access to women is a pervasive characteristic of Orang Rimban social relations. Women are fiercely protected from outsiders, and restrictive taboos on interaction with women by non-kin males are strictly adhered to by all but the southernmost groups. Local residential camps, therefore, are usually comprised of only close kin. Groups with distant or no kinship ties, although cooperating occasionally, perhaps by sharing game or storing foodstuffs for one another, will occasionally suspect each other of wrong doings. The nuclear or extended family, therefore, is the core and basic building block of Orang Rimban social life. Constituting their domestic sphere, it is the fulcrum from which all notions of self and collectivity, as well as relations with others, emanate.

Women are normally regarded as legal minors (Sandbukt 1988ab); but while women are normally subordinate to either their spouse or male relatives, they do often enjoy considerable autonomy within the domestic context, holding considerable influence in private family matters and in the unconditional loyalty they receive from their children. In legal matters, however, in cases of dispute or whenever personal rights are called into question, women are always subordinate either to their male consanguines or affines. Adultery, "wife stealing," and excessive intimacy with an unwed girl (*gadis*) are the most serious breaches of Orang Rimban customary law, and severe punishments may be administered by a headman when such transgressions occur. In cases when a headman is not present, a male litigant, perhaps a father or male spouse, will demand payment of a fine outright, as compensation from the accused male. Such fines are commonly paid in cloth, gold, and cash currency. When disputes cannot be effectively resolved by the two parties concerned, a headman or local villager, perhaps a village headman, will be summoned to mediate. In most cases, the woman involved will not be held accountable. Her actions are more often viewed as a subconscious response to the male offender's sorcery or "love magic." Full responsibility, therefore, is brought to bear on the actions of men, while strict behavioral constraints are adhered to by both sexes in order to temper suspicions and prevent such transgressions from occurring.

### The World of Children

The legal status of children is called into question when a parent dies. For example, in instances when a mother has died, her brother, rather than her spouse, will claim legal custody of the children, as is prescribed by traditional *adat* law. This often leads to a dire situation for fathers, who are pressed to either run off with their children or mount a defense against their brother(s)-in-law for custody. Life-long discord between men often results out of such situations, leading to disputes that may never be effectively resolved. "Legally," however, a widowed male will be required to join the group of a brother-in-law and remain subordinate to him. A man who loses a spouse, therefore, also loses a degree of autonomy over his children and himself if he wishes to remain with his children without fleeing the area.

In cases when a father dies, men, particularly those wishing to acquire a second wife, will often assert their claim to the widowed woman. In such instances, a woman can be taken against her will if her male relatives are unable to ward off such men. This happens when the male siblings are too young or simply unable to effectively assert themselves. Having a second wife increases a man's prestige and contributes greatly to the labor force, particularly because child-labor is also utilized. Moreover, female children will one day fetch bride-service and the requisite subordination of any in-marrying male. Orang Rimban life, therefore, is highly political, and power relations between men very much hinge on their ability, or inability, to claim and maintain their "rights" over women and children.

In many cases, women are enjoying greater autonomy these days as contact with neighboring village populations increases. They often travel to village markets to buy supplies unaccompanied by men. This would have been unheard of only a decade ago when women were still fiercely protected against the dangers of the outside world. In some areas, the Orang Rimba still maintain such taboos regarding excessive contact with outsiders. In all cases, however, a woman will not travel to the village unless accompanied by another woman or by children. Unwed and newly wed women are particularly restricted from excessive contact with outsiders, and they often do not leave the general vicinity of the camp unless they are deep in the forest. Boys, however, are free to travel as they desire, shifting their residence as personal whim dictates, often without announcement. Only when a male marries will he be obligated to other persons.

### C. General Concepts of Sexuality and Love

There is only one word in the Orang Rimba's lexicon that corresponds to the Western notion of "love" (*sayang*). While translating literally into the English notion of "pity," it more accurately connotes empathy and endearment. Often asexual in its usage, it is most commonly used to describe feelings toward children and long-acquainted spouses, particularly where bonds have grown and strengthened throughout the years. Romantic love is a much less articulated notion, most probably because it commonly occurs among young persons and leads to tensions between the two families involved, who must negotiate a solution, such as marriage or payment of fines to the girl's family in cases where excessive intimacy, which can consist of mere flirting, has occurred. Where marriage is consummated between first cousins, strong bonds may quickly develop through the pre-existing stable relationship between families, particularly in cases where the spouses have been acquainted since childhood.

While the complexion of any relationship is highly contingent on the individual personalities involved, the ability to bear children and perform adequately in household and subsistence-related activities is a necessary prerequisite for both sexes in order to allow a stable union to develop. Both sexes will seek an industrious mate, but in many cases their families will assist, or even determine, their children's spouse, particularly in the case of females. In the female context, bearing and nurturing children, forest-product and tuber collecting, and general domestic efficiency are highly valued attributes. A barren woman is either divorced or relegated to the subordinate status of second wife. In the male context, good hunters and natural leaders who are brave in articulating the group's needs to outsiders, thereby politicking effectively, are sought out, and in some cases, are able to marry more than one wife.

Lust is considered a natural inclination among men, but is downplayed in women. Far from embracing a woman's natural sexual desires, the Orang Rimba see women as innately vulnerable and, therefore, in need of protection against the predation and charms of men. Strict rules prohibiting male-female contact outside of marriage serve to combat or remedy a male's natural proclivity to seek a female. Although sex is accepted as a human urge, its referent, *mengawan*, is rarely spoken in the presence of women. Sometimes, a young man's desire for a woman will prompt him to run off with a girl without the consent of her father, particularly in cases where he either does not wish to perform bride-service, does not have the resources to pay a brideprice, or is simply unable to gain the trust and acceptance of the girl's family (see Section 5B, Interpersonal Heterosexual Behaviors, Adults, on Courtship and Marriage). Whatever the method of consummation, strong emotional dependencies will develop through the course of a lifetime, and the losing of a spouse is met with uncontrollable weeping that can last for weeks on end. (Keep in mind the hardships and loss of status experienced by widowed men and women discussed above.)

## 2. Religious, Ethnic, and Gender Factors Affecting Sexuality

Among males, loincloths are worn that cover the genitalia while exposing the buttocks. Women wear wraparound skirts known as sarongs and often go bare-breasted, particularly if they are nurturing young children. No sense of embarrassment is felt by such bodily exposure, because domestic units are comprised of only close kin. However, while in the village to trade, Orang Rimba now adhere to village etiquette and wear Western-style trousers, Indonesian sarongs for women, and shirts. Back in their forest camps, however, they revert back to their traditional attire. Men these days, however, are increasingly wearing short pants, even while in their forest camps.

Since their introduction in recent decades, brassieres have been commonly worn by women, often with no shirt. In the past, women wore brassieres outside their shirts as decorative attire, ceasing only when local villagers explained the proper manner in which they are to be worn. Orang Rimban women, nonetheless, continue to wear only brassieres without shirts while in their forest camps to provide easy access for breastfeeding an infant.

Children will remain naked until they reach the age of 3 or 4. During these years, they will mix freely with few, if any, behavioral constraints relating to gender. At this early stage in a child's development, however, a boy's sexuality will be exalted. This is best exemplified by the playful attention a boy's genitalia receive from camp members. The foreskin of the penis is often squeezed and the residual odor on the fingertips is smelled with much fervor and delight by all, who will claim it smells "sweet." A female's genitalia, however, do not receive such attention; on the contrary, they are rarely, if ever, referred to. A male infant will also receive a kind of "erotic" nurturing from his mother, who will adore and kiss him by smelling or sniffing while breastfeeding, or massage his penis and anus with no inhibitions. Female children, however, do not receive such attention from either parent.

As children grow, maternal bonds weaken and they are encouraged to be independent, both economically and emotionally. They will increasingly seek the company of their age-mates, with whom they will play and venture into the forest to search for food and forest products. They will no longer be permitted to sleep with their mothers, not only in order to encourage independence, but also to discourage incestuous desires in the boys. By the time adolescence is reached, both sexes will be well versed in the particular modes of conduct appropriate to their gender. Boys avoid all contact with young unwed females, while the latter eschew contact with all men.

A girl will cover her breasts during her adolescent years, exposing them once again only after marriage, when she will need to nurture her young. Expressions of female sexuality and displays of femininity are, therefore, systematically discouraged; and whereas only men are held "legally" responsible for their actions, heavy responsibility also rests on women to uphold ideals of purity and chastity, a task which often proves to be increasingly difficult as they come of age and become the temptation for acquisitive young bachelors or older males wishing to acquire a second wife. Should a woman fail in upholding these ideals, a sense of shame and embarrassment will be brought to bear on herself and her family.

## 3. Knowledge and Education about Sexuality

### A. Government Policies and Programs

The vast majority of Orang Rimba live in geographically isolated areas outside the main network of roads that connect most larger rural villages and towns and, therefore, have little or no access to formal schooling. Only those settled groups that are near roads have access to the primary schools found in nearby villages. Even in these cases, however, attendance is sporadic, as children are often required to help their families with subsistence-related work and/or parents may be unwilling to permit children to attend for fear of enculturation into the "village-world," where Malay customs and Pencasillan national philosophy are taught. (Recall the Orang Rimba's staunch opposition to village ways described in the opening section on Demographics.)

In some cases, however, the Indonesian Department of Health (Dinas Kesehatan) has sent healthcare workers to those Orang Rimban settlements that are accessible by road to hand out hygienic supplies and offer advice on contraception and family planning (see Section 9, Contraception, Abortion, and Population Planning).

### B. Informal Sources of Sexual Knowledge

As camp life is normally public and informal in nature, unmediated by walls or strong notions of privacy, children are free to overhear whatever they may take an interest in.

Young children may overhear or see the silhouettes of their parents making love in the same shelter should they awaken in the middle of the night. As married men will always be on alert for any undue attention or sexual overture towards their spouses, they will rarely discuss matters that are sexual in nature with other married men so as to avoid attracting such attention to her. However, boys and young men may discuss sex among themselves, outside the company of women. While uttering the word *mengawan* (sex) in the company of females is forbidden, young boys commonly discuss young girls, as well as their own sexuality, among their close age-mates. Masturbation and female anatomy may also be discussed, often playfully, by young males. Girls may have similar discussions, albeit in a less explicit manner.

Almost all sexual knowledge, therefore, is gained in the informal context of the camp, either through overhearing adults or through rehearsal with their same-sex age mates. Such rehearsal or "play" may occasionally lead to homosexual behavior among boys (see Section 6, Homoerotic, Homosexual, and Ambisexual Behaviors). While girls may overhear the discussions of older women and are well aware of the process of conception, they are generally less experienced in terms of premarital sexual exploration, because of the considerable pressures they are under to uphold ideals of chastity. It is therefore most probably the case that women learn the techniques of sexual intercourse only after marriage, following the lead of their spouse. This may simply involve assuming the bottom position, as the act of coitus is always performed in the "missionary" position.

## 4. Autoerotic Behaviors and Patterns

As mentioned above, the genitalia of male infants and children are the object of much playful affection. As male children reach adolescence, and often in their prepubescent stage, they will begin to explore their own bodies and perhaps even the bodies of their male age-mates. Young boys who have developed intimate relations with one another are extremely uninhibited with their bodies in each other's presence, and it is not uncommon for young boys to touch and comment on the dimensions, size, and general qualities of an age-mate's penis. At the site where this author collected data for this report, preadolescent and adolescent boys were well aware of which boys could and could not ejaculate through masturbation. And while this was most commonly performed in private, they did not feel any sense of shame or embarrassment when detected by the author of this chapter or their peers.

Among adults, masturbation is looked upon as something natural to the male gender. Women, on the other hand, are expected to live up to the ideals of purity and loyalty to men, and are thus discouraged from showing any expression of sexual enjoyment outside of marriage. It is therefore unlikely that masturbation would occur with anything near the same frequency as found among males because of the behavioral restraints imposed upon them.

## 5. Interpersonal Heterosexual Behaviors

### A. Children and Adolescents
*Puberty Rituals, and Premarital Sexual Activities and Relationships*

Orang Rimba do not practice any formal puberty rituals or rites of passage. However, when both genders have demonstrated a degree of self-reliance, which for boys includes proficiency in hunting and forest-product collecting—the former a skill required to perform adequate bride-service and eventually feed a family, and the latter as a means of cash income—they will be accorded relative degrees of respect by their elders. An indication that a child or adolescent has reached a level of self-sufficiency may be when she or he has a personal debt recorded in a villager's debit book. This implies that debts will be paid for products credited (e.g., rice, cigarettes, sugar, coffee, flashlight batteries, etc.) without the help of the young person's parents. In some rare cases, parents will wait until the child reaches this degree of sufficiency before giving a name.

Other indications that a child has "come of age" might be smoking cigarettes bought with their own earnings with other males, and for girls, covering the breasts with a sarong. This may occur well before menarche is reached, as the girls become increasingly aware of their sexuality and the appropriate modes of conduct incumbent on them. Marriage, however, is the decisive indication of adulthood, perhaps more so for men than women. A woman achieves the full respect accorded to womanhood when her first child is born.

As noted earlier, adolescents and pre-adults are required to adhere to strict taboos on touching or flirting with the opposite gender, and any act perceived as constituting excessive intimacy is grounds for adults to convene in order to discuss the matter and administer a fine to the accused. Because of such fear of punishment, premarital affairs of any sort are uncommon and always secretive. In almost all cases, the male will be blamed for "corrupting" the girl and he will be required to pay a fine (*dendo*), most commonly in cloth, currency, and occasionally gold. In cases where sex has occurred between the couple, they will be required to marry, but only after the male endures a frenzied beating by the girl's younger siblings for the shame he has caused her family.

Any sort of premarital sexual activity, therefore, is very rare, as it is considered among the most serious of crimes in Orang Rimban society, and is punished accordingly. In most cases, men also have no sexual experience with a woman prior to marriage. These days, however, pre-adult males are in increasing contact with local villagers and, in one case that was reported to the author, young Orang Rimba men were beginning to seek the services of prostitutes for "unattached" sexual enjoyment.

## B. Adults

### Courtship and Marriage

Marriage is rarely consummated as a result of a woman's personal preference. She may, however, be able to refuse a male suitor, depending on the nature of her relationship with her family and their own position on the matter. In most cases, however, daughters will acquiesce to the wishes of parents, their fathers in particular, as after many years of segregation from males outside the immediate family, they have developed no other ties with men, romantic or otherwise, and, therefore, may see marriage as an opportunity to progress to the next stage in their development. They would rather enjoy the accorded prestige and status of marriage, rather than remain a subordinate member in their cognatic family. In other cases, however, girls may be afraid and apprehensive of leaving the security of their parents' guardianship to enter into a new and unfamiliar living arrangement with a man. This may be particularly true when girls are betrothed at an early age to a male that they are relatively unfamiliar with or do not have feelings for.

In many cases, marital unions will occur between first or second cousins, most preferably where their parents are siblings of opposite gender. It is considered a mild form of incest (*sumbang*) when persons descending from same-sex siblings marry. In such cases, the male suitor must pay a fine to the family of his bride. In cases where a woman's family approves of the union, the father will fix a brideprice, which will be paid to the father and, in some cases, be distributed to the bride's male siblings as well.

Loyalty is the most important quality sought in a son-in-law, and the latter's bride-service is aimed at gaining the trust of the bride's family. During this period, which can last months or years, the male suitor is scrupulously tested for his honesty and generosity, which he demonstrates by sharing the spoils of his hunting and whatever other resources he acquires, such as coffee, cigarettes, and other products bought with his earnings from forest-product sales. He is also expected not to be "proud" (*banga*), which might be revealed through not showing proper respect to the bride-to-be's family or "saying one thing and doing another." If he is unable to demonstrate proficiency in subsistence-related skills, including collecting forest products, the male suitor will be thought to be either insincere in his intentions of marriage or simply incompetent in his ability to support a family and, consequently, he will be deemed an unworthy candidate for marriage into the girl's family.

In many cases, after being refused marriage by a woman's father, and finding no other welcoming host families, a suitor is pressed to either run off with the girl or express his intentions of marriage to her in private, in an attempt to circumvent the authority of her disapproving family. In such cases, the union may take place, but only after he pays a fine and possibly endures a beating by the bride's female family members and younger siblings for his unduly intimacy with the girl (Sandbukt 1988b, 114-115). The bride may also be severely beaten by her mother for her defiance and the consequent shame she has brought upon her family.

Payment of a fine is preferred by the host family, as it does not carry implications of bride ownership as does the outright payment of a brideprice. This type of union, *kawin lari* (literally, "marrying on the run"), often brings a sense of embarrassment and shame to the family of the groom, but nonetheless occurs with at least the same frequency as arranged marriages. Elopement of this sort may also occur between first cousins where the bride's family does not approve of the union. In one recorded case, a young man threatened to defect to a nearby village and "enter Islam" if his male cousin, whose father was deceased thereby entrusting him by default with the authority to betroth his sister, refused to give her in marriage. This young man was competing with another cousin and with his own father, who wanted to take the girl as a second wife.

In extremely rare cases where marriage occurs between male villagers and Orang Rimban women, the couple will always take up residence in the village. As such, this sort of marital arrangement is deeply resented by the Orang Rimba, in terms of the loss of a female family member, the lost labor power of an in-marrying male, and perhaps most significantly, in the act of making the prohibited cultural crossing of forest and village domains. Consequently, the family will often break ties with the female defector.

In cases where a woman's father is deceased and her siblings are either too young or unable to assert themselves with an older, more dominant male, the latter may bring enough pressure to bear on the situation, that the girl will be taken by coercion, and he may simply pay a compensatory fine to her male siblings. Having no father-in-law to provide bride-service for or be subordinate to in an uxorilocal residential arrangement, he may simply adopt the new wife to live in his own group. As such, this sort of marital arrangement is highly undesirable to the family of the bride and, concomitantly, is much sought after by Orang Rimban men, as it provides them with a high degree of personal autonomy that would not otherwise be achieved until the death of a father-in-law.

In another instance, an adult male of approximately 24 years of age (Orang Rimba do not keep track of age or birth dates) violated the above courting and marriage customs on two separate occasions by expressing his intentions of marriage directly to the girl and, later, by approaching another girl's father and not adequately performing the incumbent bride-service duties or producing the specified brideprice at a later date. In the former case, he was fined five grams of gold, whereas in the latter, he was required to pay 60 sheets of cloth to the offended father. This young adult male, having exhausted all internal options for marriage, eventually defected to a nearby village and adopted Islam, albeit superficially, in order to increase his mating selectivity in a new social environment. In such cases of defection to local villages, Orang Rimba are considered only marginal members of the wider rural society and are treated accordingly. During the time of this writing, the aforementioned male had yet to find a spouse, because of what local villagers claimed was the typical Muslim man's unwillingness to betroth a daughter to an Orang Rimban male for fear of causing shame to the family, or producing "stupid" offspring. This reasoning is based on the assumption that intelligence, or lack thereof, is hereditary, and the Orang Rimba are inherently inferior with limited intellectual capacities.

Among some groups, particularly in the southern areas, newlyweds will leave the group to camp alone for several days. In some cases, a week of prohibition on sexual intercourse is observed (*pantangan*), during which time parents of the bride will bring food to the couple, who are also not permitted to leave their shelter to engage in subsistence-related activities. In all cases, newlyweds will construct a shelter in which they will cohabit, signifying the commencement of their new marital arrangement. Consisting of tree stalks for scaffolding and tied with vine with logs sometimes overlain with bark for flooring, these temporary shelters are not built with walls and are customarily constructed by women. The birth of the first child symbolizes a stable union, while inability to produce a child is commonly seen as infecundity on the part of the woman and may be grounds for divorce.

A married male will be required to remain subordinate to his in-laws, continually sharing resources and providing moral support while residing in the same camp. Occasionally, the couple will reside in another camp should resource distributions necessitate, but are nonetheless always required to share any captured game and other resources. They are expected to return eventually to the camp of the bride's family. This ensures the bride will have sufficient moral support while her family will reap the benefits of her spouse's labor.

In time, a wife's loyalty will grow toward her husband, but she will also be expected to devote her loyalties to her blood relatives. Occasionally, tensions arise when nuptial and consanguiness obligations conflict, such as in cases where a woman complains to her father or brothers of maltreatment or insufficient food provided by her husband. In such cases, a husband will feel betrayed and may threaten to kill his wife. It should be noted, however, that homicide among the Orang Rimba is virtually unheard of, and such displays of anger more commonly serve as mere outlets for one's frustration and/or a strategy for dissuading a wife from further pursuing the matter.

Polygamy is a common conjugal arrangement and second wives are most commonly divorcees, orphans, or lack a father and/or other male consanguines. In the latter cases, a woman's matrimonial value is decreased and she is also rendered a more vulnerable target because male support is lacking—a situation that males will capitalize on without exception. An upper limit of seven wives has been reported, while at one field site in this author's study, a man was cohabiting with five wives, the fifth wife being an adopted daughter. In most cases, however, monogamy is the most common arrangement.

When a second wife is taken, she must first endure a ritual beating by the first wife for the shame that has been caused to her that her husband would seek another spouse, and to assert her seniority in their new residential arrangement. The new wife is not permitted to strike back or retaliate at any time and she is expected to remain subordinate to the former indefinitely. Their shelters may stand as little as three feet from one another, and the husband normally alternates residence with no fixed pattern; his original wife, however, may be given preference. Should a first wife discover her spouse in the act of coitus or other intimate activity with a second wife, the latter may once again undergo a severe beating for arousing jealousies and her perceived insolence in displaying her affection.

Divorce is not uncommon but becomes increasingly rare after the first child is born. Divorce may be initiated by the family of the bride, often when a husband does not adequately provide for his wife and children, or does not share with or show the proper respect to his spouse's consanguines, particularly her father, but also her mother and brothers.

If a woman wishes to remarry, she will be expected to wait at least two to three years in order to avoid being perceived as overly eager in her desire to form a union with another man. If she has been proven guilty of adultery in the past, she may be forever stigmatized and forbidden to remarry, in theory at least. If a woman remarries shortly following her divorce, she will be fined 500 sheets of cloth by her ex-husband and may lose custody of her children. A man is expected to abstain from marriage for at east six months, and a lesser fine, perhaps 20 sheets of cloth, must be paid to the family of his first spouse in the event that he remarries too soon.

Wife stealing is a reported occurrence, and in such cases the woman in question may not be held liable (see Section 1B, Sociolegal Status of Males and Females). The "stolen" wife's family and spouse may prefer rather to accuse the male culprit of enticing or alluring the woman with sorcery or "love magic." In one instance, a male was known to have "stolen" four wives, all on separate occasions. The putative punishment would have been severe fines or death by the spear of the woman's male siblings or husband. In this case, purportedly, no male siblings or husbands were courageous enough to seek retribution, and the fearless offender, aside from being banished from the area, was said to only have endured a physical thrashing by the women's younger siblings. However, if it were perceived that the woman fled intentionally and was willingly cohabiting with another male, she would also be the subject of death threats made by her male siblings, father, and/or husband for her immoral conduct.

*Sexual Behavior*

Immediately after marriage, a couple will take up residence in the same shelter, but in many cases, sexual activity will not commence until a much later date, when the girl overcomes her initial fear of sex with her new spouse and gradually adjusts to her new residential arrangement. Such a disposition is created by years of avoidance of males, which in many cases has instilled a deeply inculcated sense of embarrassment towards men as well as her own sexuality. This may be particularly true in cases where girls marry at an early age. A newly wed wife, therefore, may require up to two to three years before she is comfortable with engaging in sexual intercourse.

Occasionally, couples will reside a short distance apart from the rest of the group for the sole purpose of conception. This is particularly so in polygamous marital arrangements, in order to remain out of the purview of other spouses so as not to arouse jealousies. In most cases, because their simple temporary shelters do not contain walls, the couple will engage in sexual activity discretely during the night while others are sleeping or camped a safe distance away. Once children are born, the couple must engage in sexual activity only when children are sleeping, or during their infancy years when they are too young to be aware of their parents' behavior. Recall the rule prohibiting children, once they reach the age of 5 or 6 from sleeping with their mothers. This also insures that a couple will have sufficient privacy to engage in sexual intercourse in the confines of the small family shelter.

In most cases, the male initiates sexual activity. His spouse will normally not refuse him, particularly in polygamous arrangements where time may be divided between wives. In cases where a male has been effectively subordinated to his in-laws, a woman may exercise her power to refuse him or voice her opinion regarding the matter. Also, where couples are first cousins, a considerable rapport may develop, thus creating an arrangement through which mutual compliance dictates their course of action regarding such matters.

Acts of fellatio and cunnilingus are unheard of within traditional modes of sexual intercourse. Coitus is always performed with the man on top and woman on bottom in the "missionary" position. As is the custom in most areas of the Indonesian archipelago, kissing is not performed with the lips but, rather, involves the smelling or sniffing of the nose and facial area. Incidentally, mothers and fathers also practice this behavior in their nurturing of infants and young children.

## 6. Homoerotic, Homosexual, and Bisexual Behaviors

Male homosexual behavior has been reported in rare instances among adolescent boys and young adult males, whereas it is practically unheard of among married men. The actual form and nature such relationships take is unclear, and in most cases may amount to mere sex rehearsal or exploration. One case, however, has been reported first hand to the author by two married men of their engagement in anal intercourse during their adolescent years. After being detected by an adult, they were each fined 20 sheets of cloth and stigmatized for a brief period. As married adults with children, both men recounted the episode with humor and expressed no shame or embarrassment. While no cases are known of married men engaging in homosexual activity, informants claim that this may have occurred in previous generations. They could not recall actual incidents, but claimed that the men involved must have been punished severely, perhaps even killed by the male members of the wives' families. (Recall that homicide is more commonly threatened and rarely actually occurs.)

Despite the lack of information regarding incidence of female homosexuality, the sense of shame and ideals of purity regarding the female body and sexuality that are so deeply inculcated in a girl during her years of development and throughout her entire life may inhibit any actual lesbian activity from occurring, even if such desires should arise. However, while questioning men regarding the issue, they claimed that such conduct would not be seen as a serious offense, most probably because it does not threaten the delicate balance of power relations between men as do other forms of sexual misconduct, such as adultery.

## 7. Gender Diversity and Transgender Issues

In the small Orang Rimbal population of less than 4,000 persons, incidence of gender-conflicted persons is statistically rare. No cases have been reported of transvestite, transgenderist, or transsexual individuals. Even if such tendencies are harbored in individuals, they may never be realized because of the ever-present pressures to assimilate. Cases of specially gendered persons, such as hermaphrodite, *hijra*, *berdache*, *xanith*, or intersexual, are also unreported.

## 8. Significant Unconventional Sexual Behaviors

### A. Coercive Sex

*Child Sexual Abuse, Incest, and Pedophilia*

Child sex abuse has not been reported, but informants claim that such occurrences may occur between men and adopted daughters, but never between men and their natural-born children. Purportedly, an offender would be speared or liable to pay severe fines if detected. Pedophilia involving two males, although virtually unheard of, is not considered a serious offense, mainly because the male body is not seen as an object of purity to be coveted. Death, however, is the stated punishment if such an occurrence involved a young girl. Again, it should be emphasized that actual cases of homicide are extremely rare, and it is more commonly the case that only death threats are made, but never actualized in violent action.

Incest taboos are strictly adhered to, and there are no known cases of sibling or parent-child unions or sexual relations. Indirect forms may occur, but are subject to varying interpretations as to whether they constitute actual incest. For example, the above-mentioned instance where a male married an adopted daughter was not seen as constituting incest by the former; but his sons, who were raised with the girl and considered her a natural sister in every way, strongly disagreed. Despite their attempts to prevent the union from taking place, which included a report to the chief of a nearby Malay village, their father insisted he was not committing incest, as the girl was not related to him by blood.

*Sexual Harassment and Rape*

Incidence of sexual harassment and rape is rare and always subject to interpretation by the parties involved. For example, in the above-mentioned cases where men elope with women in an attempt to bypass the authority of the latter's disapproving family, the family of the girl may claim that the she was carried off against her wishes or while under duress. If the daughter agrees that this was the case—which may be in her best interest in instances where she fears punishment—her family may claim abduction, or even rape, if it can be established that sexual intercourse had occurred. In such instances, the male would be required to marry the girl and pay severe fines, as well as endure a beating by the girl's younger siblings.

Other sorts of harassment initiated by men towards women will, almost without exception, be interpreted as sexual in nature. In one case observed by the author, an adolescent male was accused of following a girl in the forest while collecting forest products. During a series of meetings between both fathers, which lasted three days, the accused male claimed to have been coincidentally working in the same area of forest, while his father, knowing well that his son was attracted to the girl and was indeed following her, tried to "settle amicably" by suggesting the two marry. The father of the girl refused vehemently in typical Orang Rimban fashion, and the young male was fined 20 sheets of cloth for a kind of "sexual harassment," even though physical contact, or even verbal communication between the two, did not occur.

## 9. Contraception, Abortion, and Population Planning

Plant contraceptives and abortifacients are not used and infanticide is unheard of. A postpartum taboo on sexual intercourse is adhered to for several years after a child is born, in order to allow for a sufficient weaning period. During a swiddening cycle, taboos are more lax; hence, when groups revert back to nomadic foraging, a woman may have more children to feed than she can comfortably manage. "Blood money" (*bangun*) is paid to a woman's parents if a child is thought to have died of milk deprivation caused by closely spaced pregnancies, which are thought to disrupt an infant's weaning cycle (Sandbukt 1988ab).

Most groups are inaccessible to the Indonesian Department of Health's regional and local offices, which deal primarily with neighboring rural village populations. Groups of Orang Rimba living in government-sponsored settlements, or who have settled on their own accord, may be visited by Department of Health nurses, workers, and, occasionally, government bureaucrats. Advice on infant care and family planning is given, and most recently, contraceptive injections have been offered, but widely refused, mainly because of mistrust and disapproval on the part of their spouses, who would prefer that the government not get involved in private family matters. Their visits are seen as mere formalities with distracted objectives. Such meetings involve little or no evaluation and are sporadic with no routine follow-up visits. During these "courtesy calls," soap, combs, and other toiletries are handed out, which the Orang Rimba find insulting, along with biscuits and cigarettes! For this reason, the Orang Rimba, males in particular, may resent the efforts of representatives of the Department of Health, which they perceive as being insensitive to their true needs.

## 10. Sexually Transmitted Diseases and HIV/AIDS

### A. Sexually Transmitted Diseases

Not much is known about the incidence and types off sexually transmitted diseases among the Orang Rimba. Male informants can name at least three different classes of sickness attributed to sexual contact:

- *Koreng*, literally "scabies": symptoms include itching and skin irritation in or near the genitalia. Instances are said to occasionally lead to divorce in cases where symptoms have not dissipated.
- *Sakit bini/sakit laki* or *sakit koncing*, literally "wife/husband sickness" or "urinating sickness": symptoms include urinary tract infection characterized by a burning sensation during urination.
- *Buntal*, or "swelling," which is said to feel like biting crabs. Buntal can infect the urinary tract and eventually lead to erosion, with death in rare cases. A tale was recounted (whether symbolic or literal is unknown) of a man's father spearing to death his daughter-in-law for allegedly afflicting and eventually killing his son with this disease.

The Orang Rimba employ a limited range of plant remedies, mainly derived from bark, leaf, and root extracts. For venereal disease, however, only bamboo water is used. Normally for the treatment of *koreng*, pulp water is drunk directly from the fillings of a species of bamboo shoot (*aee kurung bamboo*).

### B. HIV/AIDS

Intermarriage with local village populations is rare, and in cases where intermarriages do occur, Orang Rimba will marry into the village rather than vice-versa. Their forest-dwelling populations, therefore, are somewhat pristine, from a genetic point of view. This, coupled with the very low incidence of sex outside of marriage, has rendered their populations relatively safe from the wide range of sexually transmittable diseases that may occur among the surrounding Indonesian populace. There are no reported cases of HIV or AIDS among forest- or village-dwelling Orang Rimba.

## 11. Sexual Dysfunctions, Counseling, and Therapies

Male impotency is a sexual dysfunction that is rarely reported; but inability to conceive when males do not suffer from impotence may also be considered a form of sexual dysfunction, for which a female spouse will most commonly be blamed. In cases where the woman is known to be fertile, as in second marriages where she has produced offspring during her first marriage, she may seek a divorce on the grounds of her spouse's infertility. In cases of male impotency, an aphrodisiac is used to induce penis erection. This remedy is a root extract from a species of plant locally referred to as *penyega*, and can be boiled and drunk with water, or eaten directly.

## [A Postscript on the Dugum Dani

ROBERT T. FRANCOEUR [*Update 2003*]

[In 1938, the Dutch government discovered the people of Dugum Dani living in a fertile valley of the New Guinea mountains. Aside from one basic sexual taboo, the Dani live a free, unpressured sexual lifestyle with a positive view of sex and intercourse. They have only one restriction—that a member of the Wida Dani should never have sex or marry a member of the Waija, although the two clans are friendly. Yet there is little sexual activity among either clan of the Dani at any age.

[Couples seldom engage in premarital intercourse, not because of any taboo, but because they really are not interested in sexual intercourse. Whatever premarital sex occurs is always between seriously courting couples. When the Dani do marry, they usually delay having intercourse for at least two years until they have established a new residence. (Within the village compound, Dani men and women continue to sleep apart, the men in one hut and the women and children in another. After a child is born, the couple may remain celibate for five or six years before having intercourse again, allowing the mother to concentrate her efforts on raising the child. Others breastfeed their children for several years, and some Dani women still breastfeed hungry piglets if the sow is nowhere to be found, although this is not as common now as when they were discovered 70 years ago. After the death of a spouse or a divorce, a person may wait months or years before engaging in sexual intercourse. There are no taboos against male or female masturbation, but the Dani seldom do it at any age. In all these situations, the society places very few if any restrictions or negative messages on any sexual expression as long as it occurs between two persons in the same clan.

[Generally, Dani women see no advantage in having a lot of children, because their only social function is to care for the pigs, and one or two children per family can easily do that. Often the women will end an unwanted pregnancy by having a skilled friend massage and pummel the uterus, even though inducing an abortion is frowned upon.

[The Dani's low interest in sexual activity does not relate to prohibitions, repression, or a negative attitude toward sex. They live in a "perfect" climate, have a good diet, and no endemic diseases. Their hormonal balance has been found to be normal, as is their fertility rate, considering how infrequently they engage in intercourse. It is also interesting to note that the neighboring tribes do not share the Dani's lack of interest in sex. Therefore, it can be assumed that this is not a type of behavior learned from other cultures.

[Their low sexual activity seems to be a reflection of a generally low-keyed life. They are not an emotional society. They rarely show overt anger or fight. Occasionally, they have ritual battles with other tribes, but the battles, while bravely fought, are usually short, lacking in intensity and excitement. One can conclude that this society invests little psychological or emotional energy in anything they do, a characteristic reflected in their sexual relationships (Gardner & Heider 1974; Lindholm & Lindholm 1981; Sims 2001). (*End of update by R. T. Francoeur*)]

## *References and Suggested Readings*

Boers, J. 1838. De Koeboes. *Tijdschrift voor Nederlandsch-Indie, 1*(2):286-295.

Collier, J. F. 1988. *Marriage and inequality in classless societies*. Stanford, CA: Stanford University Press.

Collier, J. F., & M. Z. Rosaldo. 1981. Politics and gender in simple societies. In: S. B. Ortner & H. Whitehead, eds., *Sexual meanings: The cultural construction of gender and sexuality*. Cambridge, UK: Cambridge University Press.

Dahlberg, F., ed. 1981. *Woman the gatherer*. New Haven, CT: Yale University Press.

Denatan, R. K., K. Endicott, A. G. Gomes, & M. B. Hooker. 1997. *Malaysia and the original people: A case study of the impact of development on indigenous peoples*. Boston/London: Allyn and Bacon.

Dongen, G. J. van. 1906. Bijdrage tot de Kennis van de Ridan-Koeboes. *Tijdschrift voor het Binnenlandsch Bestuur, 30*: 225-263.

Endicott, K. 1981. The conditions of egalitarian male–female relationships in foraging societies. *Canberra Anthropology, 4*:1-10.

Endicott, K. 1999. Gender relations in hunter–gatherer societies. In: R. Lee & R. Daly, eds., *The Cambridge encyclope-dia of hunters and gatherers*. Cambridge, UK: Cambridge University Press.

Forbes, H. O. 1989/1885. *A naturalist's wanderings in the Eastern Archipelago: A narrative of travel and exploration from 1878-1883*. London: Oxford University Press (original publisher unknown).

Gardner, S., & K. Heider. 1974. *Gardens of war: Life and death in the New Guinea Stone Age*. New York: Penguin.

Klein, L. F., & L. A. Ackerman, eds. 1995. *Women and power in Native North America*. Norman, OK: University of Oklahoma Press.

LaBar, F. M. 1972. Kubu. In: *Ethnic groups of insular South East Asia*. New Haven, CT: Human Relations Area Files Press.

Lee, R. 1982. Politics, sexual and non-sexual, in an egalitarian society. In: R. Lee & E. Leacock, eds., *Politics and history in band societies*. Cambridge, UK: Cambridge University Press.

Lindholm, C., & C. Lindholm. 1981 (January-February). The taboos of the Dugum Dani. *Science Digest, 89*(1):82-87.

Loeb, E. M. 1942. *Sumatra: Its history and people*. Vienna: Institute fur Volkerkunde der Universitat Wein.

Marsden, W. 1966/1811. *The history of Sumatra*. Kuala Lumpur/New York: Oxford University Press.

Murphy, Y., & F. Robert. 1985. *Women of the forest*. New York: Columbia University Press.

Persoon, G. 1989. The Kubu and the outside world: The modification of hunting and gathering. *Anthropos, 84*:507-519.

Sandbukt, O. 1984. Kubu conceptions of reality. *Asian Folklore Studies, 42*:85-98.

Sandbukt, O. 1988a. Resource constraints and relations of appropriation among tropical forests foragers: The case of the Sumatran Kubu. *Research in Economic Anthropology, 10*: 117-156.

Sandbukt, O. 1988b. Tributary tradition and relations of affinity and gender among the Sumatran Kubu. In: T. Ingold, D. Riches, & J. Woodburn, eds., *Hunters and gatherers I: History, evolution and social change*. Oxford, UK: Berg.

Shostak, M. 1981. *Nisa: The life and words of a !Kung woman*. Cambridge, MA: Harvard University Press.

Sims, C. 2001 (March 11). Stone Age ways surviving, barely. Indonesian village is caught between worlds very far apart. *The New York Times*, p. A8.

Strange, M. Z. 1997. *Woman the hunter*. Boston: Beacon Press.

Suetomo, M. 1992. *Orang Rimbo: A structural functional study*. Doctoral dissertation. Bandung, Indonesia: Universitas Pajajaran.

Turnbull, C. 1982. The ritualization of potential conflict between the sexes among the Mbuti. In: R. Lee & E. Leacock, eds., *Politics and history in band societies*. Cambridge, UK: Cambridge University Press.

# Iran

## (*Jomhoori-Islam-Iran*)

Paula E. Drew, Ph.D.*
*Updates and comments by Robert T. Francoeur, Ph.D.;***
*Comments by F. A. Sadeghpour****

## Contents

## Demographics and a Brief Historical Perspective

ROBERT T. FRANCOEUR

### A. Demographics

In the Middle East, the Islamic Republic of Iran occupies 636,363 square miles (1,648,173 km²) of mainly salt desert area, with many oases and forest areas, surrounded by high mountains. Iran is bordered by the former Soviet republics of Azerbaijan, Turkmenistan, and Uzbekistan in the north, by Turkey and Iraq in the west, Afghanistan and Pakistan to the east, and the Persian Gulf on the south. It is slightly larger than the state of Alaska. The climate is mostly arid or semiarid, with subtropical along the Caspian coastline.

(CIA 2002)

In July 2002, Iran had an estimated population of 66.62 million. (All data are from *The World Factbook 2002* (CIA 2002) unless otherwise stated.)

**Age Distribution and Sex Ratios**: *0-14 years*: 31.6% with 1.05 male(s) per female (sex ratio); *15-64 years*: 63.7% with 1.01 male(s) per female; *65 years and over*: 4.7% with 1.1 male(s) per female; *Total population sex ratio*: 1.03 male(s) to 1 female

**Life Expectancy at Birth**: *Total Population*: 70.25 years; *male*: 68.87 years; *female*: 71.69 years

**Urban/Rural Distribution**: 40% to 60%; an estimated 4 to 6 million Iranians reside outside the country, the majority of these in the United States

**Ethnic Distribution**: Persian: 51%; Azeri: 24%; Gilaki and Mazandarani: 8%; Kurd: 7%; Arab: 3%; Lur, Baloch, and Turkman: 2% each; other: 1%

**Religious Distribution**: Shi'a Muslim: 89%; Sunni Muslim: 10%; Zoroastrian, Jewish, Christian, and Baha'i: 1%

**Birth Rate**: 17.54 births per 1,000 population

**Death Rate**: 5.39 per 1,000 population

---

*Communications*: Paula E. Drew, Ph.D., 122 High St., Randolph, NJ, USA 07869; spid@nac.net.

**Editors' Note*: Of all the countries examined in this *Encyclopedia*, Iran is among the most controversial. Major factors in Western/Iranian misunderstandings include the history of British imperial expansionism into Iran, influence struggles between the Soviet Union and the West over oil-rich territories, post-World War II efforts of Iran to nationalize its oil production, and several decades of armed and unarmed conflict between Iran and the United States. Another factor in Iran's negative image in the West has been the Salman Rushdie affair. These circumstances conspire to make an objective and scholarly study of sexuality in Iran very difficult.

Fluent in Farsi, Dr. Paula Drew is a British-born-and-educated cultural anthropologist. While married to an Iranian, she held consecutive tenured positions at the University of Tabriz in northern Iran and the National University of Teheran between 1964 and the fall of the Shah in 1978. In these universities, she taught Iranian women French, German, English, and psychology. For three years, she served as academic and personal advisor to female students in the humanities. She also ran a clinic for mothers and babies in an Iranian oasis community for almost ten years. Her field-note observations formed the basis for her doctoral thesis in anthropology on arranging marriages in Iran. Dr. Drew presents her view of a society torn by

modernization, yearnings for traditionalism, undertows of ancient customs, conflicts between urban and rural segments, tensions between newly affluent classes and the historically poor, and the influx of petro dollars, all of these surmounted by intensely complex religiopolitical conflict and warfare. Since Dr. Drew left Iran in the late 1970s, Iran has seen a revolution, a major war with Iraq, and an upsurge in Islamic activism.

Several Iranian commentators, all men, reacted strongly to Dr. Drew's depiction of sexuality and gender in Iran. They provided important clarifications and alternative viewpoints. As Dr. Drew's essay makes clear, sexuality and gender have been crucially affected by large-scale changes in Iran's modern history. In a world torn as painfully as Iran, it is probably impossible to attain consensus about the recent tidal changes in sexuality, women's roles, and gender in Iran. In the editors' view, these disagreements exist in a matrix of conflicts between West/Middle East, developed/developing economies, native/foreign, Judeo-Christian/Islamic, and male/female perspectives. There is also a strong overtone of national pride in Iran and its achievements, both under the Shah and the Ayatollah.

This chapter represents a starting point for disentangling the web of changes that have affected sexuality, gender, women, and reproduction in Iran.

***Pseudonym for an Iranian historian and social researcher.

**Infant Mortality Rate**: 28.07 deaths per 1,000 live births

**Net Migration Rate**: –4.46 migrant(s) per 1,000 population

**Total Fertility Rate**: 2.01 children born per woman

**Population Growth Rate**: 0.77%

**HIV/AIDS** (1999 est.): *Adult prevalence*: < 0.01%; *Persons living with HIV/AIDS*: 3,473 reported through January 2002 (however, the U.S. Centers for Disease Control (CDC) estimated the more realistic figure was 19,000); *Deaths*: 350. (For additional details from www.UNAIDS.org, see end of Section 10B.)

**Literacy Rate** (*defined as those age 15 and over who can read and write*): 72.1% (1997 est.: 79%); (*male*: 78.4%, *female*: 65.8%) (1994 est.); education is free and compulsory from age 6 to 10

**Per Capita Gross Domestic Product** (*purchasing power parity*): $6,400 (2001 est.); *Inflation*: 13% (2001 est.); *Unemployment*: 14% (1999 est.); *Living below the poverty line*: 53% (1996 est.)

## B. A Brief Historical Perspective

Iran, once known as Persia, emerged in the second millennium B.C.E., when an Indo-European group supplanted an earlier agricultural civilization in the Fertile Crescent of the Tires and Euphrates Rivers. In 549 B.C.E., Cyrus the Great united the Medes and Persians in the Persian Empire. Alexander the Great conquered Persia in 333 B.C.E., but the Persians regained their independence in the next century.

When Muhammad died suddenly in 632, he had designated no successor (*caliph*). Despite the ensuing struggle over religious leadership, the second *caliph*, Umar (in office 634-644), captured the ancient city of Damascus, defeated the Byzantine Emperor Heraclitus, and annexed all of Syria. Jerusalem and all of Palestine fell to the Muslims in 638; Egypt in 639-641. Islam arrived in Iraq in 637, and in Iran between 640 and 649, replacing the indigenous Zoroastrian faith. After Persian cultural and political autonomy was restored in the 9th century, the arts and sciences flourished for several centuries while Europe was in the Dark Ages. The Caliphs of the Umayyad dynasty (661-750), who ruled from their capital in Damascus, masterminded and extended the great Arab-Islamic conquests of Palestine, Syria, Iraq, and Egypt, across North Africa, through Spain, and into France in the west. In south and central Asia, the Caliphs extended their rule to the Indus and as far north as the Jaxartes River. Turks and Mongols ruled Persia, in turn, from the 11th century until 1502 when a native dynasty reasserted itself. In the 19th century, the Russian and British empires vied for influence; Britain separated Afghanistan from Persia in 1857 (Denny 1987, 32-39; Noss & Noss 1990, 552-556).

When Reza Khan abdicated as Shah in 1941, his son, Mohammed Reza Pahlavi succeeded him. Under the Pahlavis' rule (1921-1979), Iran underwent major economic and social change, strongly influenced by Western culture. Despite the repression of political opposition, conservative Muslim protests led to violence in 1978. The Shah left Iran January 16, 1979, and was replaced two weeks later by Ayatollah Ruhollah Khomeini, an exiled conservative religious leader. An Islamic Constitution was adopted, setting up a theocracy with the Ayatollah Khomeini as the final authority, the sole contemporary representative of the last divinely guided Imam. The complete takeover by very conservative Islamic clerics brought revolts among the ethnic minorities, a halt to Western influences in society, and a tension between the clerics and Westernized intellectuals and liberals that continues to the present. The new regime quickly revoked the Family Protection Act, which, under the Shah, allowed mothers some custody rights of their children in cases of divorce, and restored the *Shar'ia* provisions giving child custody to the father. The war with Iraq (1980-1988) was particularly devastating to Iran. In addition to the death of thousands of young males, Iran's economy suffered severely following the 1979-1981 seizure of the American embassy and the break in international diplomatic relations.

Following the Persian Gulf War in 1991, some one million Kurds fled across Iran's northern border into Turkey to escape persecution. Following the 1989 death of the Ayatollah Khomeini, the Islamic authorities were faced with pressure from the business community and middle class to moderate somewhat their opposition to Western influences. In the 1992 Parliamentary elections, President Rafsanjani and his supporters easily won control of the government against the anti-Western opposition.

[*Update 1997*: In 1997, reform-minded Mohammed Khatami was elected president; he was easily reelected in 2001. The new President's powers, however, were severely limited, as hard-liners retained control of the judiciary, security forces, army, large economic centers, the press, and the government-run television. One of the most substantial obstacles to change has been the religious panel called the Guardian Council. Members of the panel are appointed by the supreme religious leader, Ayatollah Ali Khamenei, and are authorized to reject any legislation they consider counter to the Constitution or Islamic law. By mid 2002, with the Guardian Council frustrating Khatami's every effort at reform, the President openly challenged the Council and moved to regain powers assigned his office by the Constitution. In late 2002, the outcome of this challenge, and efforts to improve the status and freedom of women, was still uncertain (Fathi 2002c). (*End of update by R. T. Francoeur*)]

## 1. Basic Sexological Premises

### A. Character of Gender Roles

Gender roles in Iran must be discussed in terms of different stages of the lifecycle and in terms of different kin roles: mother, father, aunt, son-in-law, daughter-in-law, and so on. Iran is a dependency culture.

### B. Sociolegal Status of Males and Females

Children are raised to be dependent on other family members and to remain so throughout their lives. Children are taught to contribute their labor to the family as part of their duty, with no expectation of financial reward or praise. Teenage boys help their father, uncles, or grandfathers in their business. Girls help in the home and with the care of younger siblings. They make few choices with regard to their clothing or the way they spend their time, and have little or no access to money. Working outside the family is frowned upon.

At a suitable age, determined by the parents and other older kin, a husband or wife will be selected for a daughter or son by the mother. She will investigate the health, wealth, and character of the proposed spouse and bring about the agreement of the person's parents that the marriage will take place. She will also ensure the compliance of her son or daughter. The father will negotiate with the proposed spouse's male kin with regard to all financial aspects of the marriage.

Since loss of virginity invalidates these financial agreements, female offspring are physically supervised by older relatives from cradle until the post-nuptial proof of a hitherto-intact hymen. It is thus part of the female role, in the capacity of mother, aunt, or grandmother, to participate in the continual supervision of younger females, leaving no opportunity for behavior that might jeopardize nuptial agreements. Once the marriage occurs, the mother-in-law takes over from the bride's mother the responsibilities of supervising her new daughter-in-law, ensuring her fidelity as a wife. The importance of this particular role depends both on the education level of the groom son and the residential situation, i.e., whether patrilocal or neolocal. As a wife, a woman is subordinate to her husband and his older kin, particularly his parents and older sisters. Regardless of her age, a woman's friendships with males are confined to those with her father, brothers, and sons. This is particularly true for upper-class women; the greater her family's wealth, the more likely the female is to be controlled and supervised. At the same time, there is a strong emotional component in father-daughter and brother-sister relationships, including familiar touches Westerners would likely consider somewhat erotic, if not lightly sexual.

Like the female, the male has a set of gender-defined kin roles. He remains subordinate to his father, uncles, and grandfathers until the age when his own children are marriageable. As he ages, he acquires more say in the financial affairs of the family. His major arena of power until well into middle age is the control of his wife. His mother, maternal aunts, and older sisters act as allies in enforcing his rules when he is away from home. This makes opportunities for shirking household duties, unmonitored phone calls, or unaccompanied shopping expeditions highly unlikely—let alone opportunities for infidelity. In the 1970s, wives in college and the workforce were more often than not accompanied to and from their places of study or business by an older relative or the husband. At the National University of Iran, the guard at the gate would not allow a father or brother to escort a daughter or sister to class within the enclosed campus.

As a father, uncle, and father-in-law, a man's power of veto in family decisions increases with age. He is likely to exercise strong veto over the education of his daughters and the way they dress. In this respect, he sets the rules, and his wife carries out the necessary supervision. The gender roles are thus closely tied to maintaining the rules and upholding the honor of the extended-family unit.

When the Shah of Iran was ousted in February 1979, the country reverted from a legal system, based on that of Switzerland, to the *Shar'ia* or Islamic law, under which females are not considered legally or mentally the equal of males. A woman must be represented in all legal transactions by a man, by her father or brother if she is unmarried, or by her husband if she is married.

At any time, a woman is at risk of repudiation. Divorce—male-initiated, incontestable, and brought about in a matter of days—can bring the immediate loss of her children to the husband's family. Children under Islamic law are perceived as the "substance of the male," merely incubated by the female body without any biological or genetic contribution. Children thus belong to the male, and Islamic law reflects this by allocating custody of children to the father. It is thus part of a woman's concept of her own sexuality that it is inextricably linked with the production of children; she will love them but forever risk losing them through repudiation. To keep her children, she must not risk repudiation by her husband. In a culture that has not encouraged romantic attachments leading to marriage, and discourages affection and companionship between spouses, the fear of losing her children often sustains the woman's efforts—culinary, domestic, and sexual—to please the husband, at least until the children are into their 20s. This fear of repudiation is stronger today, because of the 1979 restoration of the father's rights to child custody.

This fear of repudiation is further exacerbated by the lack of acceptable societal slots for divorced women. In a country where houses are not rented to single people, especially female, a repudiated woman must inevitably return to the home and control of her parents. Remarriage usually means becoming the wife of a man with custody of children from a previous marriage, who will often address her and refer to her by the title *zan baba*, "Daddy's woman/wife." If the children by an earlier marriage are on friendly terms with the new wife, they may refer to her by her first name or a more appropriate title.

Legal adulthood has little practical meaning, because children are always the responsibility of the father, regardless of their age. The war with Iraq (1980-1988) saw compulsory conscription to active combat of all males over the age of 12, other than only sons of widows. If a man dies, his brother automatically takes on the financial burden and social responsibilities of the widow and children. In this dependency culture, custom, not law, compels him in this.

If children do not like the arrangements made for them, it is not their place to comment, nor are there social agencies to which they could appeal. Kinship binds more strongly than law. There is also little infrastructure concerned with legalities other than blatant criminality or property disputes.

It is apparent to the careful observer that the legal and social status and rights of Iranian women are very much in transition, creating an unexpected blend of "traditional Islamic" and modern Western values. While the government still warns against a return to the near-Western freedoms that women experienced in Iran under the Shah, the strict fundamentalist practices introduced by the 1979 Islamic Revolution have undergone a major shift. Iranian women are still subject to fines, and sometimes flogging, for not wearing the *chador* (veil); they also suffer from the persistent denial of gender equality in Islamic law. Still, many Iranian women maintain that wearing the *chador* is not repressive, but in fact protects them from sexual harassment when they go out in public.

[*Update 1997*: In November 1994, thousands of Iranian women marched in a Teheran stadium to celebrate Women's Week and show their support for women's rights and a shift in government policy which started in 1991. The celebrations for the 1994 Women's Week included exhibitions by female artists, award ceremonies for female factory workers, and amnesty for 190 women prisoners. In recent years, a dormant family-planning program has been restarted. State-approved prenuptial contracts allow women the right to initiate divorce proceedings. Restrictions banning women from higher education to become engineers and assistants to judges have been lifted. As a result of these and other developments, the number of women in the workplace and in institutions of higher education have increased. In 1994, 30% of government employees were women as were 40% of university students, up from about 12% in 1978.

[Faezeh Hashemi, the Iranian President's oldest daughter, has become the chief spokeswoman for the emerging women's movement. In 1993, the 31-year-old former volleyball coach organized the first Islamic Women's Olympics in Teheran in 1993. "Our goal was to give women a sense of self-confidence," Ms. Hashemi announced. "In most of the Islamic world, women have cultural problems. They are regarded as a commodity. For Iranian women, the values have changed." She does not see restrictions, such as wearing the *chador*, as necessarily impeding a woman's career.

[Iranian secularists are not satisfied by this slow return to women's freedoms. They compare an event like the Women's Olympics, which attracted 700 athletes from 11 countries, but was closed to men and photographers, as a continuation of harem seclusion. Meanwhile, fundamentalists are equally unhappy, warning against the subversion of traditional Islamic values by "obscene Western values."

[The younger generation among Iranian government officials and administrators, who are more open to the West, are working to create their own complete and comprehensive version of Islamic fundamentalism that will rival Western liberalism and be viewed as better than it and other alternatives (*The New York Times* 1994). (*End of update by R. T. Francoeur*)]

### C. General Concepts of Sexuality and Love

Iranian culture is quite comfortable with speaking openly about all the physical aspects of sexuality and sexual responses. This includes open teasing about the physical side of sexuality. There is, however, a strong taboo when it comes to mentioning or discussing the emotional aspects of relationships.

The onset of attraction to the opposite sex is generally spoken of in physical terms. Teenage boys are openly subjected by older kin to routine inquiries as to their health and capacity for erections as soon as hair appears on the upper lip. "Your mustache is beginning to sprout. Do you need a wife yet?" is a more coy version of the same inquiry. The physical maturation status for young girls is measured by the onset of menarche.

Among young people, feelings of love for a person of the opposite sex are, if suspected by older kin, thought of as something to be ignored or ridiculed away rather than respected and indulged. Such feelings are only considered if they are directed towards a person found suitable for marriage after investigation by the older kin. Love is not considered a basis or prerequisite for marriage, which in turn is the only acceptable social matrix for sex.

Popular Iranian songs speak of love. Soap operas on Teheran television make much of love matches thwarted by economically more viable arrangements made by parents. Both songs and soap operas reflect the social reality. Young people see and are attracted by the face and form of members of the opposite sex, but such feelings cannot be nurtured and encouraged by dating into a situation where emotional and physical inclinations coalesce, unless there is social and financial eligibility for an imminent marriage approved by the older kin on both sides.

Even where a boy and girl meet these requirements, they will be most carefully watched to make sure they do not anticipate financial settlements. A girl who loses her virginity before such financial matters are agreed upon is not considered as having behaved immorally, but as having given the other side an advantage in negotiations, in that the girl's parents cannot now threaten to withdraw from the match, however poor the terms offered. Emotional attachment in marriage is considered desirable on the part of the wife towards the husband, but not vice versa. The male's power and control over his wife is considered in jeopardy if he is overly fond of his wife. In the early months of marriage, the husband's father and older brothers will often set up competing demands on the young man's time should they become privy to any prior arrangements he has made with his new wife. A husband will be ridiculed if he shows the weakness of acceding to his wife's wishes. A man's mother and older sisters will also often erect barriers in the way of companionship and intimacy between spouses by their continual presence and superior claims on the husband's time.

## 2. Religious, Ethnic, and Gender Factors Affecting Sexuality

### A. Religious Factors

[*Update 1997*: Islam, the dominant faith of Iranians, has two traditions or divisions: Sunni and Shi'ite. The Shi'ites, who account for 93% of Iranians, regard 'Ali, the son-in-law

of Muhammad, as the founder's proper successor, while Sunni Muslims follow the three caliphs who actually succeeded Muhammad. Shi'ite Muslims believe that God guides them through the divine light descending through 'Ali and several Imams, or divinely guided "leaders" of Shi'ism. Shi'ites have never ceased to exercise *ijtihad*, the intellectual "effort" of Muslim jurists to reach independent religiolegal decisions. Shi'ite Muslims are generally considerably more flexible and adaptive than the Sunni Muslims. However, both Shi'ite and Sunni Muslims consider each other to be members of the same tradition of faith, order, and community. To understand the connection between Islam and sexual attitudes and behavior, it is important the keep in mind that the worldwide Muslim community or *Umma* can be compared with a triangle whose sides represent history, the religious doctrine/ritual, and culture. In different historical eras in Iran's long history, as well as in other Muslim countries and communities, the balance between these three elements varies. At times, doctrine and ritual are emphasized over culture and history. At other times, cultural and ethnic identity within particular regions have been emphasized. At still other times, Muslims have emphasized the ideal of certain historical eras of Islam. Still, all three dimensions are essential to the *Umma*. (Denny 1987, 5-12, 32-71; Noss & Noss 1990).

[While the number of Sunni Muslims in Iran is much smaller than that of the Shi'ites, they and other minorities of Christians, Jews, B'hai, Zoroastrians, Ismailies, Sikhs, and Buddhists quietly reside in isolated communities. There are also seven to eight million ethnic Kurds and Belouch, the majority of whom are Sunni Muslim (Denny 1987; Noss & Noss 1990). (*End of update by R. T. Francoeur*)]

Islam, like other monotheistic religions, prohibits pre- and extramarital sex. Sex between two adults married to others is condemned as the most serious of sins (*zina*)—under Islamic law, adultery and fornication incurs the penalty of stoning to death. Some Islamic countries have at different points in time lifted the death penalty for adulterous males, while retaining it for females. In Iran and probably most Islamic countries, adultery is rare, not because of Islamic prohibitions, but because of social mores that segregate the sexes and allow no privacy. [*Comment 1997*: In the upper classes, it is rampant, for both men and women! (*End of comment by F. A. Sadeghpour*)] The Islamic sense of pollution, which prohibits all acts of worship under certain conditions of spiritual and physical uncleanliness, makes public—and therefore amenable to control—otherwise private, biological events, such as menarche, menstruation, sexual contact, and ejaculation.

Males who have ejaculated, females whose external or internal organs have had contact with seminal fluid, and females who are menstruating may not pray or touch a copy of the Qur'an without first performing ablutions. Since these ablutions were not possible in the majority of Iranian houses in the 1970s, these necessary ablutions had to be performed at public facilities and were, therefore, open to public scrutiny. Prayers were said individually within the home, but audibly and in full view of others at the prescribed times of the day. Thus anyone who, through fear of committing sacrilege, had to abstain from ritual recitation of prayers or from the obligatory periods of fasting set down by the Islamic calendar, would be subject to scrutiny and interrogation by older family members about the reason for such abstention.

Most Iranian housing consists of a one-story, single large room, or two-story, two-room, with-curtain-hung alcoves, a private courtyard enclosed by a high wall, and a toilet/bath in one corner of the courtyard. The wealthy can afford to live in moderate high-rise apartments, but these are limited because of the danger of earthquakes. This architecture and the desert environment makes privacy a premium.

Menarche announces itself to the entire household when a young girl is unable to recite her prayers. This is often the signal for parents to conclude marriage arrangements, so that the girl can be wed before her second menstruation. Intercourse between married members of the household is similarly monitored. Conception or failure to conceive is similarly apparent to all. The approximate time of any woman's ovulation can be informally calculated by interested parties. Wet dreams and visits to houses of prostitution can be surmised by the family in the same way, by watching who does and does not pray and when. Wash basins or pools for routine washing of the face, hands, and feet are set in full view of all household members in the hallway or yard. Bathing the body under a shower takes place at the neighborhood bathhouse where abundant hot water is available for a modest sum. Taking a shower, for the most part, is seen not so much as a hygienic measure, but as a way of ridding the body of anything that makes it spiritually unclean and the person unfit to participate in religious activities. The body parts are washed in ritualized sequence with prescribed prayers. The bathing practices of family members reveal a great deal of otherwise private information to those interested in monitoring them. The rituals of Islam thus abet the older members of the family in their task of controlling the sexual behavior of all those potentially reproductive or sexually active within the household.

There is a strong resistance among older women to the growing practice of installing hot water systems in the home. Although simplifying their dishwashing and laundry tasks, an automatic hot water system interferes with their ability to supervise the bathing practices of their husbands, offspring, and daughters-in-law, and thereby keeping tabs on their sexual behavior. Even in houses with a shower, the matriarch of the household often controls the means of igniting the hot water system. Similarly, she controls the supply of laundered undergarments and towels, keeping them tied up in bundles so that nobody can retrieve these essentials without her help.

Although the Qur'an does not prescribe the covering of the head for women nor the separation of men and women in public places, Iranians follow a style of dress and segregation of the sexes characteristic of Islamic societies of the Middle East. In Iran, some cities have always been more conservative than others in this regard, but the Ayatollah Khomeini did much to bring about conformity to the strictest code by making violations subject to immediate physical punishment at the hands of the young revolutionary guards, the Pastoran. [*Comment 1997*: Commentators strongly agree with this observation. (*End of comment by R. T. Francoeur*)] The traditional veil or *chador*, which in many villages and towns often concealed only the back of the head and the general outline below the waist, is now supplemented with bandannas pulled low over the forehead, and thick stockings to conceal lower limbs not completely covered by loose pants. The outline of the ankle has to be obscured because its dimension is thought to be related to that of the vagina. The veil itself is pulled firmly across the face and chest, as was always the custom in Qum, Mashad, and most of Tabriz. Now "modesty" is a requirement for all girls over the age of 9. No hair must show around the face.

By custom, certain times of the day are "women's hours" on the streets and few men are about. At other times, only men throng the streets, so a woman would be conspicuous and likely to be harassed. Many stores have sex-segregated service lines, often with a curtain separating the two.

Public baths have days for women and days for men, identified by the color of the flag hoisted above the establishment. Schools, too, are segregated to the point that girls' schools employ only female personnel at any level. Places of worship are divided into men's and women's quarters with separate entrances. Informal prayer meetings are only for one sex or the other. Many celebrations and funerals in private houses send males and females into separate rooms. Women are barred from many places, such as some cinemas, restaurants, and teahouses. Other places, such as swimming pools and ski areas, allow families to enter but not young men or women, either singly or in same-sex groups. Young multiage groups of cousins might be allowed into a cinema, if several of the older males are obviously in charge.

The Iranian culture, especially now with its conservatism bolstered by the Islamic regime, is not one in which people of the opposite sex can meet casually. Clandestine meetings, for which there are few arenas, are made dangerous by the pervasive armed guardians of Islamic law, the Pastoran, who demand to see marriage certificates of couples on the street, at beaches, and parks.

## B. Ethnic Factors

Just over half of all Iranians are Persian, 25% Azerbaijani, and 9% Kurd. Although the vast majority of Iranians are Muslim, each has its own distinctive character with regard to the extent to which Islamic dress codes for women, and sexual segregation in streets and public buildings are enforced. [*Comment 1997*: For instance, the Baktiari, Quashquai, and Lore tribes, who live in the Zagros Mountains in the west, do not follow the Islamic dress codes or the practice of female segregation in public places. Although these tribes are Muslim, they do not comply with the Islamic regime's heavy handedness. (*End of comment by F. A. Sadeghpour*)]

## 3. Knowledge and Education about Sexuality

### A. Government Policies and Programs for Sex Education

Under the Shah's regime, which ended in 1978, the state school biology curriculum for the second year of high school included a section on human reproduction, showing the mechanics of meiosis, or egg and sperm production. Such information, revealing that males and females both contribute genetic material to the production of a fetus, runs counter to a central underpinning of Islamic law with regard to child custody, i.e., that the child is the product solely of male seed. When Islamic law was reinstated by the Ayatollah Khomeini, it was necessary to suppress any dissemination of the idea that males and females both contribute materially to the production of a child.

Even before the 1978 revolution, and despite the passage of the Compulsory Education Act of 1953, many female children were withdrawn from school before the onset of puberty. The Compulsory Education Act required children to remain in school until age 15. However, the birth of a newborn girl was commonly recorded as having occurred two years prior to her actual birth date among all but the educated elite. The parents then had government documentation in hand that their daughter was 15 and old enough to leave school, when in reality, she may not even have reached puberty. During the Shah's regime, efforts to curb this practice were frustrated by the fact that few births took place in a medical setting with personnel able to provide documentation.

The other chief formal source of information on human sexuality is provided by the compulsory religious instruction curriculum in the public schools. In religious instruction classes, students are taught the format of prayers to be said at the five daily prayer times prescribed by Islam, and the rules of purity and pollution surrounding them. Details of prerequisite ablutions of the genital and other orifices of the body provided information on anatomical differences between the sexes. Information is also given on the measures to be taken prior to prayer to counter the polluting effects of urination, defecation, expectoration, expulsion of nasal mucus, menstruation, childbirth, ejaculation, and penetration of the vagina (human and animal) to restore spiritual purity. These measures require that the student have detailed knowledge of the reproductive organs and sexual practices. The Islamic clergy, or *mullahs*, also disseminate this type of information on television, in the mosque, and in the many informal neighborhood prayer meetings.

The general trend of this information, whether given by lay teachers or *mullahs*, is to present sexual behavior as the most polluting form of elimination, which renders the participant spiritually and physically unclean. Sexual behavior of any kind obstructs spiritual readiness. Whereas the polluting effects on the body and spirit of urination or defecation can be washed away in a bathroom with a sink or a shower, orgasm or sexual contact with a person or animal requires a more ritualized bathing with accompanying spiritually cleansing words.

Television programs in Iran regularly deal with the finer points of Islamic observance, such as determining the readiness or otherwise for prayer in ambiguous situations such as nursing mothers, sufferers from vaginal discharges, and males awaking in a state of sexual arousal. Often, the format of the program is one in which viewers' letters are answered by experts in Islamic practice.

## B. Informal Sources of Sexual Knowledge
*Sexuality Education Within the Home*

The nature of Iranian family and social life offers a major informal source of sexual knowledge.

There is little coyness about the physical aspects of sex. Because it interrupts fasting and prayer schedules, menstruation is openly mentioned by men and women. Pregnancy's physical aspects are not only discussed in intimate detail, but the taboos against males' touching women are lifted during pregnancy, so that males can feel free to pat a pregnant woman approvingly on the abdomen. Breastfeeding is also subject to few social taboos. Women breastfeed in public places and in mixed company in private houses with no attempt to cover the breasts. A little milk, believed to be stale, is usually expressed quiet openly from each breast before beginning to nurse. So although faces and limbs are assiduously covered, the nursing breast is displayed quite blatantly. [*Comment 1997*: This is characteristic of provincial and lower-class urban Iranians. (*End of comment by F. A. Sadeghpour*)]

Little girls of all ages are kept well covered. In many provincial towns, girl babies are hidden completely under their mother's *chador* on the street. Toddler girls wear *chadors* often with only a pacifier protruding from its folds.

Little boys are often bare from the waist down, obviating the need for diapers outside. At any age, males may urinate openly in the street or at the roadside. Older males often seek the partial privacy of a tree or wall. Most, however, orient themselves in a way so as to avoid the sacrilege of urinating while facing Mecca, even if it then means facing an audience. Many men, subsequent to urination, bend down and bathe the head of the penis in any convenient pool or stream of water, to avoid the spiritual defilement of a drop of urine before prayer. Females' visual knowledge of male anatomy is derived largely from seeing little boys unclad and males of all ages urinating and washing in public.

Prior to puberty, male children gain a much more extensive knowledge of female anatomy at all stages of the lifecycle, and at all stages of pregnancy and lactation, by virtue of the fact that their mothers take them to the public baths with them on "women's day." The public baths consist of waist-deep bathing pools for communal bathing and private shower rooms for families. No one bathes completely alone. Women of all ages are unclad. Most wear loose drawers in the public areas, but are otherwise nude. Within the privacy of the shower rooms, little boys therefore observe their grandmothers, mothers, aunts, sisters, and female cousins taking showers and being depilated of all body hair. Female bath attendants, who assist in applying the leefah and pumice stone, also assist in the removing of facial and leg hair with a kind of scissor made of twisted threads, and in the shaving of the pubic regions and armpits. The bath attendants enter the cubicles wearing a *chador*, which they then remove to work in the nude. They themselves are devoid of all body hair. It is up to the bath attendants to decide, based on their own observations, whether a young boy is too old to be present on women's day. Clearly, men retain in adulthood images of what they saw in the bathhouse during childhood. Many speak openly, with disgust and derision, of the effects of pregnancy and the aging process on the female body. Females, however, lack this kind of longitudinal information on males, because fathers do not take children with them to bathe. [*Comment 1997*: These observations do not apply to upper- and rich-class families, which commonly have showers in their homes. (*End of comment by F. A. Sadeghpour*)]

Children are aware from an early age that an intrinsic part of wedding preparations is the setting out of the wedding night sleeping quarters for the bride and groom. The first night after the wedding has to be spent within the supervised setting of the family. Children learn, too, that something painful involving blood is going to happen to the bride, and that for her protection against excessive brutality on the part of the groom, older female kin have their bedding set out within earshot, often with only a curtain separating them from the bridal couple. (The prevalence of voyeurism, mentioned in Section 8, Unconventional Sexual Behaviors, below, also provides a rich informal source of sexual knowledge.)

Another informal source of sexuality information is American and European adult magazines such as *Playboy* and *Penthouse*. Until the crackdown of the Islamic regime, these magazines were on sale everywhere and openly displayed in homes. They were a source of pictures to decorate the walls in private houses, particularly in the kitchen and areas of the house off-limits to formal visitors. Although the magazines can no longer be openly sold, back issues still abound and old centerfolds still adorn some family rooms.

*Television as a Source of Sexual Information*

In the absence of many other forms of recreation, watching television has become a major urban pastime. Since there are only three Government-run television channels, and since their regular scheduled programming is often supplanted, without announcement, by religious broadcasts, satellite-dish television keeps the general public aware that the position of women, and patterns of courtship, marriage, and sexual behavior, are much more liberal outside Iran. In 1994, Iranian-made satellite antennae cost $700 and small, low-tech antennae sold through the black market for as little as $400. An estimated 200,000 Iranian families have dishes, but it is common for several neighboring families to reduce the cost even more by tying in their television sets to a single jointly purchased dish.

For some years, Iranian satellite dishes were able to bring in everything from late-night soft pornography films from Turkey to the BBC news. Most satellite programs were handled by the Hong Kong-based Star TV. The most popular satellite programs were "Dynasty," "The Simpsons," "Baywatch," "Moonlighting," "Wrestlemania," professional American basketball, and an Asian version of MTV. The Donahue and Oprah Winfrey talk shows, which regularly deal with sexual and relationship issues, were also very popular in a society where a woman's ankle cannot be exposed in public. Until December 1994, when the Government outlawed satellite television antennae, this source of sexuality information encouraged the adoption of Western ideas of fashion and relationships. [*Comment 1997*: For the rich, this has always been the norm. (*End of comment by F. A. Sadeghpour*)] Of necessity, even before they were outlawed, satellite antennae were carefully hidden from the representatives and enforcers of religiously conservative dictates from the Ministry of Culture and Islamic Guidance.

In 1994, threatened with a loss of their captive audience, the *mullahs* fought back with Government efforts to jam the satellite reception. Members of the popular militia, known as *bassijis*, began barging into homes to smash satellite receivers (Hedges 1994). On December 25, 1994, after months of debate, the Iranian Parliament ratified a ban on satellite dishes. Once the ban is routinely approved by the Guardian Council, dish owners would have 30 days to remove them or face confiscation and trial with unspecified penalties. The Interior Ministry and Secret Service agencies were ordered to prevent the import, distribution, and use of satellite dishes "with all the necessary means." Some lawmakers warned that, if people refused to comply with the ban, the forcible removal of satellite dishes would violate their right to privacy and could lead to serious political repercussions for the Islamic Government.

### Sexual Information on the Internet

In addition to their interest in controlling sexual information and sexually explicit material available to Iranians on satellite television, the government has very mixed feelings about allowing access to the Internet. *Sobh*, the monthly newspaper of the most puritanical clergy, has called for a ban on the Internet, similar to the ban on satellite-television antennae enacted in 1994. However, as of late 1996, the Parliament had yet to take up the issue. Rapid upgrading of telephone lines, growing pressure from scientists interested in communicating with colleagues around the world, and clergy interest in spreading the message of Islam by making computerized texts of both Sunni and Shi'ite law available on the World Wide Web are forcing the government to open up some access to the Internet. The government is trying to centralize all access through the Ministry of Posts and Telecommunications, which is struggling to screen the rapidly increasing number of sites on the World Wide Web, and block access to objectionable sites with a "firewall." The Ministry is constantly updating its list of banned Web sites and information, ranging from pornography sources like "playboy.com," to opposition groups like the Mujahedeen Khalq, based in Iraq, and abhorred religious faiths like the Bahai, as well as any information seen as Western propaganda (MacFarquhar 1996b).

Cost remains a major hurdle for most Iranians seeking information on the Internet. The Government charges large initiation fees, and bills Internet use at the same high rates as long-distance phone calls.

Outside the Government, a few services have established Internet links. Since 1994, much of the Iranian university system has depended on a trunk line established by the Institute for the Study of Mathematics and Science to a sister institution in Austria. But with an estimated 30,000 people having accounts, and the trunk line limited to six users at a time, getting through requires patience. There is also an ongoing feud between the universities and the Telecommunications Ministry over whether the universities will be allowed to keep their independent access once the government's system is operational. In 1996, Teheran's energetic Mayor, Gholam Hussein Karbaschi, had a municipal bulletin board and an email system that forwarded messages internationally, but exchanges often took at least 24 hours. Professors and students were suspicious that messages sent and received on this municipal service were screened and deleted when found objectionable, but the Mayor denied messages were vetted, blaming the huge backlog for lost exchanges. Government officials have already admitted they cannot control access to objectionable information on the Internet mechanically, so the future of access to sexuality information on the Internet remains uncertain.

### [Sexual Information in Iranian Cinema

[*Update 2001*: A report on "Subliminal Sex in Iranian Cinema" by Shakla Haeri describes how Iranian cinema has adapted to strict government censorship while accommodating the general interest of Iranians in sexual issues. The cinema has developed all kinds of symbols and codes so that the cinemagoers may assume sexual contact between lovers without any explicit mention or showing. Riding a motorcycle in tandem is one device. Another movie shows quivering lovers both holding on to the same branch of a tree, fully clothed, the girl neatly head-scarfed despite turbulent weather. The tree branch is briefly submerged in a torrent and emerges to show the lovers still perfectly kempt but devoid of former tension (*Anthropology News* March 2001). (*End of update by R. T. Francoeur*)]

## 4. Autoerotic Behaviors and Patterns

The subject of self-pleasuring is apparently taboo or unacknowledged, because its only reference appears to be within the context of preprayer ablutions requirements on the male after voluntary ejaculation.

## 5. Interpersonal Heterosexual Behaviors

### A. Children

Children do not play unsupervised. An invitation to a child to play at the house of a neighbor or a schoolmate always includes the mother. Such invitations are in any case rare, as are all social interactions with nonkin. Children, in general, play with their cousins under the watchful eye of all mothers. Female children are watched very carefully. Access to information on sex-rehearsal play would be severely hampered by cultural taboos on admitting anything detrimental about one's children, especially to nonkin.

### B. Adolescents
#### Puberty Rituals

The male puberty rite of circumcision, which formerly celebrated the onset of manhood, has for many years now been more customarily performed at the age of 5 or 6 for children born at home, and at two days old for those born in a medical setting. Boys circumcised after infancy wear a girl's skirt for several days, ostensibly to prevent chafing of the unhealed penis, but also to proclaim their status to others. By puberty, all Muslim Iranian boys must be circumcised if they are to participate fully in religious activities.

Female circumcision, common in African Muslim cultures, does not occur in Iran. For Iranian girls, there is some ambiguity about her societal status from the age of 9 on. In the Iranian brand of Shi'ite Islam, a girl of 9 is judged to have reached the age of understanding. She is therefore expected to say her prayers and abstain from food during periods of prescribed fasting. As a fully participating Muslima in many layers of society, she is expected to assume modest dress, i.e., the *chador*, if she has not already done so. More-conservative *mullah*s in Iran have construed the phrase "age of understanding" to mean age of readiness for marriage. The Islamic regime of the Ayatollah Khomeini has encouraged a return to this interpretation, promoting child marriages in which the 9-year-old girl joins her husband's household (patrilocal). The marriage, however, is not consummated until after her first menstruation. The child bride often shares a quilt at night with her mother-in-law, who, because of the prevalence of cousin marriage, is more often than not the bride's paternal or maternal aunt.

## Premarital Sexual Activities and Relationships

It can be said that there are no societally approved premarital sexual activities. The sexes are separated by adolescence. Young single males join male kin for most social activities. Young single females stay with the women in the family. Many young girls are married immediately after menarche. [*Comment 1997*: Several commentators questioned this broad generalization. (*End of comment by R. T. Francoeur*)]

A young virgin who joins a household as a live-in maid, is often required by both her parents and her employers to submit to a medical examination to establish whether her hymen is intact. Written into her employment contract is the amount of cash penalty payable by the employer should she lose her virginity (as determined by a second medical examination) during her employment. This contract protects her from the advances of male members of the household, as well as from male visitors to the house, by placing the onus on her employer to protect her and supervise her. In her subordinate capacity, she is extremely vulnerable to rape and seduction. Households employing young girls are also vulnerable to extortion by her parents. Her certificates of pre- and postemployment virginity are also documents that feature in her own prenuptial negotiations. Despite these precautions, young servant girls are usually considered fair game for sexual advances and harassment by males in general.

## [Teenage Runaways

[*Update 2000*: There are no official statistics on young Iranians who run away from home, although a November 2000 story in a Tehran newspaper estimated that the police round up close to 100 male and female runaways every day. The report also noted that runaways can be found in Iran's railroad and bus stations and public parks, where they often become prey of criminal gangs. For years, the government chose to ignore the problem of runaway youths, because problems of family honor should be dealt with within the family. But with more and more Iranian youth running away from home and falling prey to prostitution, crime, and addiction to cheap and plentiful heroin, the government has been forced to act. In early 2000, the city of Tehran funded the nation's only shelter for females who run away from their homes because of "divorce, addiction, poverty and the bizarre demands of parents."

[In addition to protecting the runaways from relatives bent on restoring their family honor by punishing or even killing the runaway, the shelter's main problem is to figure out what to do when a reconciliation with the runaway's family is not possible. If runaway girls are prostitutes, drug addicts, and go bareheaded, pretending that they are boys, they are turned over to the police and arrested. If they are just runaways, they are delivered to the shelter. The shelter has a strict regime, teaching basic math and language skills, a range of crafts, sewing, flower arranging, painting, and candlemaking. The hearty lunch is better than that served at many restaurants, and the girls can watch television, read newspapers, and listen to the radio (Sciolino 2000b). (*End of update by R. T. Francoeur*)]

## C. Adults

### Premarital Courtship, Dating, and Relationships

Courtship takes place in a supervised, formalized setting. All marriages are arranged, even those based on love matches and mutual inclination. Since male kin, especially the father, passes on the groom's portion of the family estate when he marries, the bride's kin have to know how much is involved before they consent to their daughter's betrothal. The older generation, therefore, controls all meetings between those seeking to marry each other.

A young man visits the girl he intends to marry accompanied by at least three older members of his family. He will be received in the dining room by her parents and relatives. The girl herself will often appear only fleetingly and not speak unless questioned directly. Marriage often follows betrothal by a matter of days. Often a contract is signed in the presence of a *mullah*, making the couple legally married and all financial agreements legally binding. The wedding celebration for the families is held off for up to a year. In some families, especially in Teheran, the couple is allowed to go out together between the official signing of the marriage contract and the wedding celebration. Sometimes the groom's family and sometimes the bride's family will prohibit such contact because, during negotiations, proof of virginity has been spelled out as a prerequisite to the finalization of property transfers. Urban and landless families usually have no such considerations.

Mild public displays of affection are tolerated between urban middle-class couples during the prewedding period. The couple, however, is seldom completely alone, even when allowed to go to the cinema or an ice cream parlor. Usually, there are siblings on either side in tow as a precaution against anything beyond hand holding or chaste kisses on the cheek.

### Marriage and the Family

*Temporary Marriages.* [*Update 2001*: The custom of "temporary marriage" (*mut'a* or *sigheh*) appears to be unique to Iran. Originally, it was meant to provide female companionship and domestic services for Muslim men on long trips, especially on pilgrimages to Mecca and while serving in the military. During the Shah's regime, it existed for a variety of somewhat similar circumstances. A temporary marriage could provide female companionship and comfort for businessmen traveling outside Iran who preferred to leave their wife or wives at home. In this case, the marriage contract had clearly specified a certain duration of days or weeks after which the marriage ended. While this form of marriage became more and more rare over time, its legal authority was never removed. After the Iran-Iraq war, *mut'a* allowed widowed women to find some financial support as "temporary wives" in a society not structured to deal with widowed women with no family support system. Temporary marriages were publicly approved in the early 1990s, when then-President Hashemi Rafsanjani endorsed it as a way to channel young people's sexual urges under the strict sexual segregation maintained by the Islamic Republic.

[The essence of the *mut'a* contract is its legal and binding character. It may be witnessed by a religious authority (*mullah*), who is paid a fee for his official witness, or it may be less formal, but equally as legal in effect, with anyone reading a verse from the Qur'an in the couple's presence. The *mut'a* contract specifies the legitimacy of any offspring conceived during the time of the contract and the inheritance rights of these legitimate offspring, with a claim to the father's support and a right to his name on the birth certificate. Normally, the woman receives some money for entering the contract.

[In 2001, correspondents in Tehran reported a revival and new application of the "temporary marriage" by unmarried consenting adults who just want to go out together in public without being arrested for doing so. The *mut'a* is particularly poplar now for two divorced people who are dating. The *mut'a* allows them to visit areas, such as restaurants and ski resorts, which otherwise would be closed to them as an unmarried couple. (Fathi 2002a; Sciolino 2000). (See also Update 2002 in Section 8B, Significant Unconventional Sexual Behaviors, Prostitution) (*End of update by R. T. Francoeur*)]

*Monogamy and Polygyny.* Monogamy has long been established as the norm for both urban and rural households. Traditionally, newly married couples were given quarters in the household of the groom's parents. This pattern persists in rural areas. Young couples in the cities now often rent an apartment, usually in close proximity to the groom's parent's house. The groom's mother, and sometimes the bride's younger sister, stay with the newlyweds for the first few weeks of marriage. The groom's mother sets her guidelines for the way the house is to be run. From the beginning, everything serves to compartmentalize the aspects of the marriage relationship and prevent any spillover of feeling to be expressed in physical expressions of affection or the companionship of shared daytime activities.

The bride is prepared for her wedding night at a prenuptial bath in which her pubic hair is removed for the first time. Her mother-in-law and her own mother will sleep in close proximity to the marriage bed on the first night. Both will inspect the specially prepared handkerchief, which will provide evidence of both a broken hymen and ejaculation. If a honeymoon trip is undertaken, the couple will seldom travel alone, but be accompanied by a couple of younger siblings, or maybe an older sister. Honeymoon companions are particularly common for females of the middle class and among university students.

At home, the couple cannot retire until the groom's mother deems it is a fit hour for everyone. Generally, sleeping arrangements are such that the couple cannot rely on uninterrupted privacy. Iranian houses do not have rooms set aside exclusively as bedrooms. Nothing prevents a mother-in-law from setting up her bedding adjacent to that of her son and his wife, or in such a way that she has an excuse to walk by during the night en route to the kitchen or toilet. A pattern is then set for sex in marriage to be quick and almost furtive with ejaculation of the male as the prime or even sole goal.

*Divorce.* [*Update 2002*: In August 2002, Iran's reformist Parliament approved a bill that would grant women a right to seek a divorce equal to that of men for the first time since the Islamic revolution in 1979. The bill requires approval by the hard-line Guardian Council to become law. While that approval seems unlikely, Parliament's approval of the bill was considered a major victory both for women and reformist politicians, who have consistently sought the support of women because it creates public pressure on the country's conservative Islamic rulers.

[Under the civil code adopted after the 1979 revolution, "a man can divorce his wife whenever he wishes." The new bill would replace that section of the code with a provision that gives men and women equal right to divorce, but sets the grounds on which a divorce could be sought—addiction, mental illness, or violent behavior. This would make divorce equally difficult for both men and women. Another provision of the bill would require a man to pay for healthcare if his wife became ill. At present, if a man refuses to pay for his wife's care, the case is sent to court, and judges have not consistently ruled in favor of the wives.

[Reformist women in Parliament have previously tried to change laws that discriminate against women, but their efforts have been blocked or altered by the clerical establishment. The Guardian Council, for instance, blocked a bill that would have raised the legal marriage age for girls from 9 to 15, contending that it went against *Shar'ia*, or Islamic law. After months of dispute, the Expediency Council, which resolves differences between Parliament and the Guardian Council, approved raising the minimum age, but only to 13. In another instance, women in Parliament proposed that Iran join the United Nations Convention on Elimination of All Forms of Discrimination Against Women, but members abruptly dropped consideration of the plan after hard-line clerics in the religious city of Qum declared that the convention was against Islam. (Fathi 2002ab). (*End of update by R. T. Francoeur*)]

### Incidence of Oral and Anal

The general lack of privacy inhibits all but the most perfunctory intercourse. Anal penetration of the female is a common means both of birth control and avoidance of possible contamination with menses. Khomeini's writings provide guidelines for preprayer ablution after penetration of the anus and animals under separate headings, though he considered the latter practice unworthy of practicing Muslims.

## 6. Homoerotic, Homosexual, and Bisexual Behaviors

In the same way that admissions about sexual behavior in children are impossible, homosexuality in a family member cannot be acknowledged. The derogatory term *cuni* (from *cun* = backside) is used to describe men outside the family, whose gait or voice is considered effeminate. Men who do not marry stay with their natal family all their life. Within the family, some such men are described as *na-mard* (not-men). Implicit in the term is a suggestion of phallic underdevelopment or dysfunction. Other older single men are described as not having found a wife yet, the implication being that they are physically normal but financially ineligible for marriage.

Male homosexuality is condemned by Islam and overt homosexuality is unknown. Just as most heterosexual relationships lack an emotional component, it is to be expected that homosexuality be predominantly physical and without an emotional component. Long-term, companionable homosexual relationships are rare. Two unmarried men (of whatever sexual orientation) would be unlikely to be able to set up house together, because of strong societal pressures against any unmarried person living beyond the pale of family control. However, since there are many exclusively male social arenas—teahouses, political and religious organizations, and men's days at the bathhouse—there are more opportunities both for male-male physical contact and for the setting up of clandestine meetings between males. Women, as noted earlier, do not have similar occasions for privacy in same-gender relationships. Iranian culture also allows men a great deal of public touching, embracing, kissing, and holding hands for prolonged periods while walking or in conversation.

[*Update 2003*: As indicated in the above comments of Dr. Drew, Iranian men who have sex with men do not fit the Western categories of homosexual or gay. Although somewhat closer to the cultural reality, the descriptor "bisexual" is also not accurate. In the Iranian mind, a man's masculinity and heterosexuality are not affected by the sexual relations he has, be these with women, men, or animals. As Zarit (1992, 56) notes, *kuni*, one of the Farsi words for "queer," reveals the importance of the role one plays in any sexual activity. A *kuni* is someone who gives himself in anal intercourse. Farsi has two complementary words for "pimp": *koskeš* means a procurer of vagina, while *kunkeš* means a procurer of ass (*kun*). Taking the active role in anal intercourse with a male is more acceptable than being the receiver in oral sex, which is better than being the giver of oral sex, though all three are enjoyed almost as much. Oral sex is considered a perversion introduced from the West. The acceptability of being the penetrator in anal intercourse—and oral sex—varies according to social class and religious conviction, according to Zarit. Because premarital virginity is so prized for women, a great many Iranians, particularly among the lower class, regard male-male anal sex as normal, particularly before marriage. The more educated and wealthy classes share this view, but tend to be more hypocritical about doing it, maintaining that sodomy simply does not exist in Iran. Vaginal intercourse, active anal sex, and penetrator in oral sex share one common character in Iran: They are equally and predominantly physical and without an emotional component. Long-term male-male sexual relations are very rare.

> Homosexual love hardly exists there, at least with foreigners, without some price tag on it: free meals, free jeans, or possibly help in getting a U.S. visa. In a sexual encounter Iranians rarely kiss, even more rarely on the lips, never with the tongue. . . . When it comes to oral sex, they find it better to receive than to give. And when they *do* get involved, they often literally 'come and go', zip sip. . . . [When an Iranian male was asked about having anal sex], he would respond, "But I was the man." (Reed 1992, 63, 65)

For the male who is the recipient of anal intercourse or takes the female role in fellatio, money is the lubricant that makes it excusable. (*End of update by R. T. Francoeur*)]

Other than among siblings, women do not enjoy an equal freedom. Although a similar situation applies to females with regard to touching and embracing, most are married or have marriages already being arranged for them before they reach a stage of physical/hormonal development at which they are aware of their own sexual orientation. Homosexual orientation in females has, therefore, little chance for expression.

Lesbianism is reported to occur in one of the very few residential situations for unmarried women, nurses' training hostels. It is possible that homosexually oriented females select a nursing career as one that allows opportunities for intimate contact with other women.

## 7. Gender Diversity and Transgender Issues

Since each person's behavior is strictly controlled by older family members, no overt expression of gender conflict, such as transvestism, would be tolerated. A child suffering from a physical or emotional deviation from narrow, accepted norms is generally kept from public view. Expression of any kind of individualism in unconventional dress or hairstyle is almost impossible, because of the power and the control of access to funds of the parent generation throughout the lifecycle of the offspring. The burlesque theater with its morality plays (*tazieh*) performed in the street or market place could provide a niche for gender-conflicted males, because female roles are played by tradesmen. This theater is largely thought of as a disreputable arena for the marginalized, providing a normal social framework for those without kin. This theater plays no part in upper-class mores.

## 8. Significant Unconventional Sexual Behaviors

### A. Coercive Sex

*Sexual Abuse*

Since marriages can be contracted at any point after a girl has reached the age of 9, it is legally feasible for a very little girl to be married to a man of any age, and thus be physically at his mercy. This no doubt constitutes the broadest category of potential sexual abuse of children. One of the strongest arguments made in Iran against the custody of children, particularly girls, being given to the mother, is that on her remarriage, the children will be in danger of sexual abuse from the new husband.

Sexual abuse of children, particularly little girls, often occurs at the hands of uncles and cousins staying under the same roof. In such cases, the child's mother is inevitably blamed for leaving her child unguarded, and little outrage is directed at the abuser. Sexual abuse of children in a family setting is not the concern of the police, nor are there any relevant social agencies to which it could be reported. A young servant boy would be withdrawn from the household by his parents if he were the victim of abuse. Only in the case of a young servant girl could the police be implicated, and then only if her virginity had been certified prior to employment.

*Incest*

Incest always requires a cultural definition at two levels. To be considered incestuous behavior within a culture, the sexual behavior must take place between people of the opposite sex who are not allowed to marry because of genetic or affinial relatedness. Secondly, the behavior itself must be considered erotic in nature and somehow shocking by the members of that culture. In Iran, marriage between cousins is the norm. Even the marriage between the offspring of two sisters, considered incestuous in most cultures, is very common in Iran, as it prevents the splitting up of parcels of land inherited jointly by two sisters by passing it on to their children at marriage. Within the same generation in a family, only brothers and sisters are off-limits to each other as marriage partners.

In Western cultures, certain zones of the body are described as erogenous, and any touching of these zones by another person is generally interpreted as sexually motivated behavior. Similarly, slow dancing, with bodies touching and the arms of one partner about the neck of the other, would be assumed to be motivated by either sexual attraction or a desire on the part of one or both of the partners to stimulate themselves or the other. In Iran, however, fairly intimate touching is common between opposite-sex siblings, although such behavior would not be tolerated among those of the opposite sex more distantly related. Teenage siblings of the opposite sex, even those who are married, have the license for close "accidental-on-purpose" body contact in rough-and-tumble play. They often display physical affection, kissing on the face, lips, and neck that border on the erotic. They may be seen grooming each other and, for example, anointing each other with suntan oil in a sensuous way. Such behavior continues with siblings until late in life. At any age, touching high up on the inner thigh or on the outer periphery of the breasts between opposite-sex siblings is allowable in public as a way of drawing attention to points made in conversation, even though it would be deemed indecent public behavior between nonsiblings.

Similarly, in large family gatherings, weddings for example, Western-style dancing is often mixed with Iranian-style dancing. Married couples, fathers and daughters, brothers and sisters, and occasionally mothers and sons, may be seen dancing together very closely. An Iranian would not interpret this behavior as incestuous or in any way distasteful, and would probably find any such suggestion rather warped on the part of the observer. This, of course, raises very interesting questions about what is and is not sexual behavior.

*Sexual Harassment*

The general pattern of sex segregation makes opportunities for sexual harassment rare. Should it occur and be mentioned, the female, and more particularly her mother, would be blamed for affording anyone the opportunity. The most common forms of sexual harassment are those of frottage and furtive pinching in crowded shopping areas.

*Rape*

The legal concerns of rape are not connected in Iran with the indignities suffered by the victim, but with the financial damages incurred to the family as a result of rupture of the daughter's hymen.

Opportunities for rape are rare. When it does occur, it is likely to involve the police at the instigation of the girl's parents. The police are empowered to force a man who has robbed a girl of her virginity, with or without her assent, to marry her legally. He is allowed to divorce her immediately if he wishes, but the legal procedures and documentation of marriage must be followed through. A divorced woman is more marriageable than an unmarried girl with a ruptured hymen. In the case of a servant girl, her parents may choose between a cash settlement from her employer or a forced marriage between the employer and their daughter, even if he already has a wife. Under the law, a girl can force into legal marriage any man with whom she claims to have had intercourse. The procedure is swift and uncomplicated, involving simple arrest and handcuffs. However, since the girl must be represented in this by her father, few girls would initiate this procedure frivolously or maliciously. This is especially true because there would be few legal repercussions against a father who killed his daughter for dishonoring the family.

Marital rape is not a legal category, in that a woman is her husband's property. If a woman shows signs of physical abuse, her male kin, especially older brothers, will threaten or assault her husband. In general, it is the duty of different members of the kin group to protect the females in the group. In most instances of sexual violence, punishment will be dealt out by the group without fear of intervention from police.

## B. Prostitution

Prostitution is one of the few subsistence slots available for women marginalized by the death of those kin vital to their functioning in society. Daughters of repudiated women and childless widows are particularly vulnerable. Every village seems to have its "fallen woman," who is rumored to serve as a prostitute. People speak too of brothels in the ba-

zaar area of large towns. Veiled women can be seen at night walking alone on the outskirts of towns. A woman walking alone at any time, particularly after dusk, unless obviously bent on shopping or an urgent errand, would be assumed to be a prostitute. Maids commuting from their place of employment carry large totes, a pair of men's shoes, or a garment on a hanger in a dry cleaning bag, so as not to be mistaken for prostitutes and harassed.

[*Update 2002*: Despite strong enforcement of anti-prostitution laws enacted after the Islamic revolution deposed the Shah in 1979, Iran's Parliament suggested establishing state-approved "decency houses" or "chastity houses" to reduce the explosion of "kerbcrawlers" (street prostitutes). The proposal surfaced in mid 2002 after eight members of the Iranian national football squad were sentenced to as many as 170 lashes of the whip after incriminating photographs of them turned up in a police raid on a whorehouse in the capital.

[About the same time, in a suburb of Tehran, a revolutionary court judge was jailed for ten and a half years for pimping young girls, including a 17-year-old who had been detained against her will. Conservatives, who still run the courts and security services, were quick to condemn the proposals as anything but decent, making it far from certain they will ever be put into practice. However, the very fact that they are being openly aired in the press shattered one of conservative Islam's strongest taboos and turned the proposals into an open discussion.

[The proposals being floated take advantage of the Shiite custom of "temporary marriage"—*mut'a* or *sigheh*. If the proposals are adopted, street prostitutes picked up by the religious police or other security forces would be given a choice: Take the assistance of social services to give up their profession, or accept placement in a state-sponsored "decency house" where they could contract temporary marriages with their clients. Such contracts may be for a few minutes or 99 years. Customers would pay a dowry, rather than a fee, and would be able to set the duration of the "marriage contract." The "decency houses" would only be open to males with identity cards proving they were bachelors, widows, or married to women incapacitated by physical or mental illness. Newspapers reported that certain Tehran hotels had already been earmarked for possible use.

[With Iran in the midst of an economic crisis and an estimated over 300,000 women supporting themselves as "kerbcrawlers," the proposals found some unlikely supporters, including the head of the Imam Khomeini Research Center, named after the revered founder of the Islamic Republic. The proposal for state-tolerated prostitution has precedent in Iran. In the days of the pro-Western Shah, when the country was awash with American advisors, the capital's Shahr-e-no district housed hundreds of brothels, which operated openly and legally. After the revolution, some supported keeping the brothels open and legal instead of driving them underground. Soon, however, the hard-line clergy forced their closure.

[After decades of severe repression by the police, Revolutionary Guard, and the courts, a string of high-profile prostitution cases in 2002 made it clear that the Islamic punishments handed out by the revolutionary courts have been and are ineffective. As conservatives put mounting pressure on the reformist administration of moderate President Mohammad Khatami, the whole question of prostitution was poised to become the keystone in elections to be held in late 2002, with the fate of the proposed "decency houses" being intimately connected to the fate of Khatami's government (Arabia.com 2002). (*End of update by R. T. Francoeur*)]

## C. Pornography and Erotica

During the Shah's regime, copies of American magazines such as *Playboy* and *Penthouse* were widely sold at newsstands, openly perused by men and women, and left lying around in full view in homes (see Section 3B on informal sources of sexual knowledge). Despite the Khomeini regime's ban on all depictions of the unclad human form and the sale of such magazines, this material is still available.

Displays of belly dancing in restaurants and private weddings and parties were staple entertainment prior to the Islamic regime. Although the dancers often showed great skill, male members of the audience clearly viewed them as prostitutes, or at least women with whom liberties could be openly taken. In mixed family audiences, older males often greeted their performances with exaggerated leering and lip-smacking. Young males would be inhibited by the presence of their parents. Middle-aged men, however, would tuck bills into the spangled brassiere or the low-slung waistband of the fringed skirts of the dancer as she passed their table.

[*Update 1997*: In December 1993, the Iranian Parliament approved legislation providing for capital punishment for the producers and distributors of pornographic videotapes. First offenders would receive a maximum five years' prison term and $100,000 in fines; "principal promoters" face the death penalty. Experts doubt that this attack on the "Corrupters of the Earth" will discourage the immensely profitable business. Videotapes of Western and pornographic films are already widely available through a network of unlicensed distributors. Also feeding the trade, according to official statistics, are three million Iranian homes with video recorders and 25,000 satellite dishes—analysts say the real figure is more like six million and 50,000, respectively (Hedges 1994). (*End of update by R. T. Francoeur*)]

## D. Domestic Sexual Controls

Living quarters in the cities are similar to private homes and apartments found in European countries. However, the traditional architecture of Iranian homes in small villages and the rural areas have curtained alcoves, rather than closets, for storing bedding and clothing. In these more traditional homes, people unroll mattresses and bedding from these alcoves to sleep at any convenient spot on the floor in any of the rooms, or on the roof or balcony. Often the choice seems to be dictated by the opportunity it provides for spying on others as they sleep or disrobe. Females, particularly those in their 30s, 40s, and 50s, seem particularly prone to spying on married couples, as well as on other women as they bathe, undress, or use the bathroom. Women gossip openly about information they have obviously garnered by such spying. Some intimate information is clearly used at times to discredit other females, as it is presented to listeners as if revealed by a male confidant with carnal knowledge.

There appears to be a strong interest, not only in details of other women's bodies and personal hygienic measures, but in the frequency and urgency with which they urinate. One who urinates often is spoken of in disparaging terms. Houses with outhouses often have no doors, with walls that conceal only the midsection of the occupant. It is considered a basic precaution to check that one is not being observed.

It is easy for a female to wander from room to room, from roof to balcony to yard without arousing suspicion as she goes about domestic tasks like rounding up soiled dishes and laundry. There are few internal doors in some Iranian houses and any stealthiness can be explained away as consideration for those engaged in the national pastime of brief and frequent naps.

Males do not have such freedom of movement in the house, and thus male voyeurism is less of a day-to-day problem in the typical large multigenerational household. Male voyeurism more often takes place outside the home. It usually takes the form of the male wearing a woman's all-concealing veil to insinuate himself into female enclaves or the bathhouse on women's day. While the success of such endeavors appears to be largely hearsay, there seems to be an acceptance of voyeurism as a far-from-infrequent fact of life embedded into the culture.

## 9. Contraception, Abortion, and Population Planning

### A. Contraception and Abortion

Condoms are openly sold on every street corner in the towns in Iran. Itinerant vendors display trays of condoms, together with cigarettes and chewing gum. Anal intercourse and coitus interruptus were previously the main male-initiated forms of contraception before the widespread distribution of condoms.

Abortion remains, in rural areas and among the urban poor, the most common female-initiated form of contraception. Untrained midwives induce abortion by introducing a chicken quill into the cervix. From the 1950s on, abortions were widely available in clinics, hospitals, and doctors' offices, restricted only by a woman's ability to pay. Neither male consent nor religious considerations seemed to be issues raised. The conceptus has neither legal nor spiritual status, nor, for that matter, has an apparently nonviable term-born child. Efforts are often not made to succor a weak newborn in the home. Mothers often abandon sickly babies born in a hospital. Only a viable offspring becomes a male concern and an object of his proprietary rights.

Tubal ligations are the contraceptive method of choice among the urban middle class. Contraceptive pills are freely available without prescription and are in common use by young, urban married couples.

### B. Population Control Efforts

Efforts on the part of the Iranian Women's Organization to educate women about safe contraception since the mid-1960s have been mainly aimed at improving female health rather than affecting the population size. Life for women among the rural and urban poor, until the 1960s, was more often than not one of an endless chain of pregnancies, spaced by prolonged and intensive nursing and unskilled, unsterile abortions. High infant-mortality rates in the villages, rather than contraception, kept the population size stable. The Shah set up a network of rural government clinics in the late 1960s and early 1970s to provide free primary healthcare, which included the distribution of contraceptive pills. This latter measure, together with the sudden widespread availability to all of antibiotics, had a dramatic effect both on the birthrates and the survival of those born.

[*Update 1997*: Between the Islamic revolution of 1979 and 1996, Iran's population almost doubled, from 35 million to more than 60 million. Faced with internal and external threats to the revolution, including the 1980-1988 war with Iraq, Iran's spiritual leaders regularly extolled large families as a way of preserving the revolution. The legal age of marriage was dropped to 9. Today, at least 43% of the population is under 17. Despite official support for larger families, many Iranians in the early 1980s found themselves faced with soaring inflation and eroding wages, a common deterrent to large families. Dr. Alireza Marandi, then Iran's Deputy Minister of Health and its current Minister of Health, recognized that Iran's population growth rate was rocketing out of control. At the time, considering the very conservative religious climate, Marandi did not deem it wise to bring the population issue into public debate. Instead, he quietly kept alive a prerevolutionary program of distributing free condoms and IUD's while maneuvering for an opening. One word from the Ayatollah Ruhollah Khomeini and all contraceptives would disappear throughout the country. In 1988, after the Cabinet approved birth control by a single vote, Marandi asked for a public statement supporting contraception. But the internal opposition was so strong, the Cabinet vote was not announced. Instead Ayatollah Khomeini suggested a public discussion that sent Muslim scholars digging through their texts for religious sanctions that could be cited in support of birth control.

[The debate culminated in a 1993 law that enshrined birth control and lifted subsidized health insurance and food coupons for any child after the third. Condoms, vasectomies, and the birth control pill are free. The state also introduced mandatory prenuptial birth control classes. Couples seeking a marriage license must submit a stamped form documenting their participation in an hour-long lecture on contraception. Abortion, however, remains illegal, except when the mother's health is in danger. As a result, Iran's population growth rate, which in the 1980s was 4%—one of the highest growth rates seen anywhere—declined to about 2.5%. Rural families still tend to have many children. Despite the fact that the nation's growth rate is now below 2.5%, Iran's population will pass the 100 million mark early in the 21st century (MacFarquhar 1996a). (*End of update by R. T. Francoeur*)]

## 10. Sexually Transmitted Diseases and HIV/AIDS

### A. Sexually Transmitted Diseases

The major endemic sexually transmitted disease has for decades been syphilis, although it is suspected that the term "syphilis" has become a generic one in Iran to include all sexually transmitted diseases. It is assumed that men contract syphilis from prostitutes and then infect their wives. Many babies in the villages are born with syphilis, contracted during the birth process. Standard neonatal ward procedure in hospitals involves medicating the eyes of newborns against the onset of syphilis-related infections. Part of the prenuptial inspection of prospective brides by the mother-in-law in the bathhouse is a search for what are thought to be symptoms of syphilis, notably patchy skin and thinning hair. Treatment for syphilis is available in clinics, but there is no government attempt to eliminate or track down sources of infection.

### B. HIV/AIDS

At present, there is no information on the prevalence or otherwise of AIDS in Iran. Although prostitution anywhere can bring about a spread of infection, there are cultural patterns in Iran that would minimize the spread of HIV infections. Consorting with prostitutes is not common for married men because of the strong cultural belief that variety adds nothing to the spice of sexual behavior. Since the main object of sex is seen as the relief of phallic tension, this goal is thought to be more safely achieved with one's wife. Advice to this effect is a common subject of sermons and religious writings. Visits to prostitutes are also seen as signs of immaturity, as "real men" have achieved the financial eligibility prerequisite to marriage and uninterrupted access to a woman.

[*Update 2002*: Until recently, the Health Ministry reported that the HIV virus was transmitted in Iran primarily by the sharing of contaminated needles. In 2002, the Health Ministry reported that HIV was increasingly being spread by sexual contact and prostitutes. This trend prompted Ayatollah Moussavi Bojnourdi to support establishment of "decency or chastity houses" where men could enter into temporary marriages with a prostitute. In August 2002, *Etemad*, a Tehran newspaper, quoted Bojnourdi as saying: "If we want

to be realistic and clear the city of such women, we must use the path that Islam offers us" (Fathi 2002b).

[Public health experts and epidemiologists have been ordered by the religious leaders to fight the spread of AIDS, but promoting AIDS-prevention programs to teach teenagers about safe sex without even whispering the word condom is not very effective. A pamphlet designed for adolescents by the Iranian Center for Disease Control suggests, for instance, that the "best way to avoid AIDS is to be faithful to moral and family obligations and to avoid loose sexual relations. Trust in God in order to resist satanic temptations." In mid 2002, the word condom was introduced to AIDS pamphlets for adults, although it continued to be banned on radio and television talk shows. Condoms are available in pharmacies. But the basic government point of view is that telling teenagers about them will inspire the youngsters to start having sex.

[Added to the limits on the mention of condoms is the fact that homosexuality is illegal. In view of Iranian macho and religious traditions, gay sex remains so deeply in the closet that few patients will even confide to their doctors that it could be the source of their disease. Premarital and extramarital sex are similarly hidden. Although drug addiction is now widely acknowledged, tolerance has limits. The Islamic revolution was supposed to eliminate all these social blemishes. To recommend condoms would be to admit the revolution was not a 100% success.

[Despite these restrictions, a small group of activist doctors are determined to exorcise the taboos that surround AIDS. Through January 2002, Iran had identified 3,438 people who were living with HIV, mostly male drug addicts, 35 persons with full-blown AIDS, and 350 who had died from AIDS. The Centers for Disease Control estimates the actual number of HIV-positive Iranians at 19,000, but other sources suggest higher figures. Although these are not epidemic statistics in a country with a population of 70 million, the potential for disaster looms, given widespread needle-sharing among Iran's 1.2 million confirmed drug addicts. Three years ago, Iran had identified just 300 people with HIV.

[In 2002, an anti-AIDS organization provoked outrage by suggesting that the prisons, where addiction is endemic, start needle exchanges. The idea was officially rejected as encouraging addiction. But the organization persuaded a few wardens individually to try it on the sly because the method has worked in lowering incidence of the disease in other countries.

[Government hospitals treat AIDS patients free, at a cost of $1,000 a week per patient for the cocktail that suppresses the disease. But Iranian doctors will not give AIDS medications to prisoners, because their compliance with the strict schedule of taking the medications is too random in the chaos of the overcrowded prisons.

[The practice of religiously sanctioned temporary marriage (*mu'ta*) has also been recommended by some clerics and members of Parliament. The hope would be that young men in a temporary marriage would be less likely to visit prostitutes who have a high rate of HIV infection (MacFarquhar 2002). (*End of update by R. T. Francoeur*)]

[*Update 2002*: UNAIDS Epidemiological Assessment: Based on the reported data, the HIV epidemic in the Islamic Republic of Iran appears to be accelerating at an alarming trend. According to reports by the National AIDS Program, the number 1,159 of newly diagnosed HIV infections and AIDS cases in 2001 shows a threefold increase in comparison to both years 2000 and 1999.

[This considerable increase may indicate another outbreak. The previous dramatic increase had occurred in 1997, when the number of HIV/AIDS cases had reached 815 new infections.

[Injecting drug use drives the epidemic in Iran. In 2001, 64% of AIDS cases were injecting drug users. The data on HIV seroprevalence among injecting drug users shows the highest rates of infection compared to all other tested groups. Injecting drug users were tested positive in 1996 and a prevalence was found of 5.7% of the cases in 1996, with 1.7% in 1997. The data are variable, as it relates to occurrence of well-known outbreaks among injecting drug users in prisons. Consequently, it is not surprising to note that HIV rates among prisoners rose up to six times higher in 1999 compared to 1996. Likewise, we observe a high rate of HIV-seropositive tests among attendees of voluntary counseling and testing centers, because these centers mainly serve drug users. The voluntary counseling and testing centers were introduced in 1999 and account for a considerable percentage of all annual HIV infections. The HIV prevalence rate among center attendees was around 3% in 1999 and 4% in 2001. There has been a significant increase of total numbers of reported STD cases in the country during the period of 1995 to 1998. Candidiasis, trichomoniasis, chlamydia and gonorrhea are the four main causes, accounting for over 60% of the total diagnosed cases.

[The estimated number of adults and children living with HIV/AIDS on January 1, 2002, were:

| | |
|---|---|
| Adults ages 15-49: | 20,000 (rate: < 0.1%) |
| Women ages 15-49: | 5,000 |
| Children ages 0-15: | < 200 |

[An estimated 290 adults and children died of AIDS during 2001.

[No estimate is available for the number of Iranian children who had lost one or both parents to AIDS and were under age 15 at the end of 2001. (*End of update by the Editors*)]

## 11. Sexual Dysfunctions, Counseling, and Therapies

### A. Concepts of Sexual Dysfunctions

In Iran, there is generally very little concern and a great deal of impatience with psychological considerations. Children who receive regular meals and are kept clean are considered well looked after, regardless of how happy or unhappy they are. A woman who complains about having nothing to wear would be taken more seriously than one who complains that her husband never talks to her or approaches her sexually. Sexual functioning and satisfaction are similarly measured without regard to the emotional component. Tenderness and attention to the state of arousal of the female are not valid considerations.

A male is judged to be sexually adequate if he is capable of erection and ejaculation, as proven by the presence of both semen and blood from the ruptured hymen of his bride on the nuptial handkerchief used on his wedding night. A female is inspected before marriage by her prospective mother-in-law to check for mammary development, nipples sufficiently protruding for nursing, and the width of pelvis for childbirth. The main proof of sexual adequacy, however, is her ability to conceive. Failure to conceive within two years of marriage is grounds for repudiation.

### B. Availability of Counseling, Diagnosis, and Treatment

Counseling in all marital matters is strictly a family affair. There is a strong taboo against discussing family problems of any kind with a nonfamily member. It is not even acceptable to admit, however casually, to a friend or person outside the circle of close kin, that anything is wrong with family, children, or finances. Iran is thus not very fertile ground for any kind of psychotherapy. On the one hand, the therapist would be perceived as a stranger and, therefore, not one to whom confidences should be made. Secondly, after long years of dictatorship under the Shah, backed up by the secret police, or S.A.V.A.K., and more than a decade of the repressive Islamic Republic with its brutal guardians of public morals, the Pastoran, no clear line would be seen between professionals of any kind asking questions and government officials collecting incriminating information.

Under the Shah's regime, gynecologists in Teheran and other major cities offered help to women with fertility problems. Western-trained medical personnel, however, for the most part fled from Iran after the ousting of the Shah. Most women in small towns and villages seek herbal and spiritual measures to overcome fertility problems. Bitter infusions, thought to aid conception, are concocted and drunk by the desperate. Large, old trees, thought in this mostly desert area to hold the power of fertility, often have their branches completely covered with little pieces of rag into which are knotted the prayers of supplicants who cannot conceive. Advice on the formulations of such potions and the text of such prayers is perhaps the closest one comes in Iran to therapy for sexual dysfunction.

## 12. Sex Research and Advanced Professional Education

Other than a concern with physical causes of infertility in women during the reign of the Shah, sexual research has been nonexistent in Iran. Surgical measures to correct reproductive dysfunction were widely available under the Shah. The psychosexual component of reproduction and sexuality itself were, even then, seldom considered to be of academic or medical interest.

## Conclusion

Within the family, sexual activity between married people can be alluded to in a jocular way. In mixed company, men may be teased for looking tired as a result of suspected sexual activity. Members of households exchange innuendoes about suspicious sounds heard during the night. However, alluding to extramarital sex is considered to be in extremely bad taste and discussion of one's sex life absolutely taboo. Friendships with nonkin are rare. The composition of marital households and informal networks is such that most social contact involves in-laws within the group. Discussion of anything intimate is thus inhibited. There are strong cultural constraints on revealing anything of a personal nature within the family, and even stronger ones on mentioning anything to strangers. Because of this lack of exchange of information, there tends to be an overestimate of the strength and longevity of the human sex drive, and a wildly exaggerated sense of the amount of sexual behavior that occurs in places, such as the U.S.A. and Europe, where Islamic cultural constraints are not in effect. This belief serves to reinforce the notion that such constraints are vital.

## References and Suggested Readings

Arabia.com. 2002 (July 29). Iran abuzz as Islamic Republic rethinks prostitution. *Tehran AFP.*

Beck, L. G., & N. Keddie, eds. 1978. *Women in the Muslim world.* Cambridge, MA: Harvard University Press.

Bouhdiba, A. 1985. *Sexuality in Islam* (Trans. by A. Sheridan). London: Routledge and Kegan Paul.

Brooks, G. 1995. *Nine parts of desire: The hidden world of Islamic women.* New York: Anchor Books/Doubleday.

Bullough, V., & B. Bullough. 1987. *Women and prostitution: A social history*. Buffalo: Prometheus Press.

CIA. 2002 (January). *The world factbook 2002*. Washington, DC: Central Intelligence Agency. Available: http://www.cia.gov/cia/publications/factbook/index.html.

Denny, F. M. 1987. *Islam and the Muslim community*. New York: Harper & Row.

Fathi, N. 2002a (August 26). Iran legislators vote to give women equality in divorce. *The New York Times*, p. A9.

Fathi, N. 2002b (August 28). To regulate prostitution, Iran ponders brothels. *The New York Times*, International Section, p. A3.

Fathi, N. 2002c (August 29). Iran's President trying to limit power of clergy. *The New York Times*, pp. A1, A14.

Haeri, S. 1980. Women, law and social change in Iran. In: J. I. Smith, ed., *Women in contemporary Muslim societies*. Cranbury, NJ: Associated University Presses.

Haeri, S. 1983. The institution of Mut'a marriage in Iran: A formal and historical perspective. In: G. Nashat, ed., *Women and revolution in Iran*. Boulder, CO: Wesyview Press.

Hedges, C. 1994 (August 16). Satellite dishes adding spice to Iran's TV menu. *The New York Times*, p. A11.

Jalali, B. 1982. Iranian families. In: M. McGoldrick, J. K. Pearce, & J. Giordano, eds., *Ethnicity and family therapy*. New York: Guilford Press.

Kafi, H. 1992. Tehran: Dangerous love. In: A. Schmitt & J. Sofer, eds., *Sexuality and eroticism among males in Moslem societies* (pp. 67-70). New York & London: Harrington Park Press, Haworth Press, Inc.

MacFarquhar, N. 1996a (September 8). With Iran population boom, vasectomy received blessing. *The New York Times*, pp. 1, 14.

MacFarquhar, N. 1996b (October 8). With mixed feelings, Iran tiptoes to the Internet. *The New York Times* (International Section).

MacFarquhar, N. 2002 (April 4). Unable to say 'condom,' Iran grapples with AIDS. *The New York Times*.

Mackey, S. 1996. *The Iranians: Persia, Islam, and the soul of a nation*. New York: Dutton.

Mernissi, F. 1993. *Islam and democracy: Fear of the modern world*. Reading, MA: Addison-Wesley.

Mernissi, F. 1991. *The veil and the male elite: A feminist interpretation of women's rights in Islam*. Reading, MA: Addison-Wesley

Naneh, K. K. 1971. *Women of Persia: Customs and manners of the women of Persia* (Translated by J. Atkinson). New York: B. Franklin.

Nashat, G. ed. 1983. *Women and revolution in Iran*. Boulder, CO: Westview Press.

*The New York Times*. 1994 (December 21). Iran offers an Islamic way to improve the lot of women,, p. A11.

Noss, D. S., & J. D. Noss. 1990. *A history of the world's great religions* (8th ed.). New York: Macmillan.

Parrinder, G. 1980. *Sex in the world's great religions*. Don Mills, Ontario, Canada: General Publishing Company.

Reed, D. 1992. The Persian boy today. In: A. Schmitt & J. Sofer, eds., *Sexuality and eroticism among males in Moslem societies* (pp. 61-66). New York & London: Harrington Park Press, Haworth Press, Inc.

Schmitt, A., & J. Sofer, eds. 1992. *Sexuality and eroticism among males in Moslem societies*. New York & London: Harrington Park Press, Haworth Press, Inc.

Sciolino, E. 2000 (October 4). Love finds a way in Iran: "Temporary marriage." *The New York Times*, p. A3.

Sciolino, E. 2000 (November 5). Runaway youths a thorn in Iran's chaste side. *The New York Times*.

UNAIDS. 2002. *Epidemiological fact sheets by country*. Geneva, Switzerland: Joint United Nations Programme on HIV/AIDS (UNAIDS/WHO). Available: http://www.unaids.org/hivaidsinfo/statistics/fact_sheets/index_en.htm.

Zarit, J. 1992. Intimate look of the Iranian male. In: A. Schmitt & J. Sofer, eds., *Sexuality and eroticism among males in Moslem societies* (pp. 55-60). New York & London: Harrington Park Press, Haworth Press, Inc.

# Ireland

## (*Eire*)

Thomas Phelim Kelly, M.B.*
*Updates by Harry A. Walsh, Ed.D., and the Editors*

## Contents

## Demographics and a Brief Historical Perspective

ROBERT T. FRANCOEUR

### A. Demographics

The Republic of Ireland—"Eire" in the Irish language—occupies five sixths of the island of Ireland in the North Atlantic Ocean west of Great Britain. Slightly larger than the state of West Virginia, Ireland has an area of 27,135 square miles (70,280 km²). The northeastern corner of the island is Northern Ireland, a part of the United Kingdom. The terrain is mostly level-to-rolling interior plains surrounded by rugged hills and low mountains, with sea cliffs on the western coastline. The climate is temperate maritime, moderated by the North Atlantic Current, with mild winters and cool summers. The island is consistently humid and overcast about half of the time.

In July 2002, Ireland had an estimated population of 3.88 million. (All data are from *The World Factbook 2002* (CIA 2002) unless otherwise stated.)

**Age Distribution and Sex Ratios**: *0-14 years*: 21.3% with 1 male(s) per female (sex ratio); *15-64 years*: 67.3% with 1.02 male(s) per female; *65 years and over*: 11.4% with 0.77 male(s) per female; *Total population sex ratio*: 0.98 male(s) to 1 female

**Life Expectancy at Birth**: *Total Population*: 77.17 years; *male*: 74.41 years; *female*: 80.12 years

**Urban/Rural Distribution**: 57% to 43%

**Ethnic Distribution**: Celtic and English

**Religious Distribution**: Roman Catholic: 91.6%; Church of Ireland: 2.5%; other: 5.9% (1998 est.)

**Birth Rate**: 14.62 births per 1,000 population

**Death Rate**: 8.01 per 1,000 population

**Infant Mortality Rate**: 5.43 deaths per 1,000 live births

**Net Migration Rate**: 4.12 migrant(s) per 1,000 population

**Total Fertility Rate**: 1.9 children born per woman

**Population Growth Rate**: 1.07%

(CIA 2002)

**HIV/AIDS** (1999 est.): *Adult prevalence*: 0.1%; *Persons living with HIV/AIDS*: 2,200; *Deaths*: < 100. (For additional details from www.UNAIDS.org, see end of Section 10B.)

**Literacy Rate** (*defined as those age 15 and over who can read and write*): 100% (1993 est.), with 96% attendance in nine years of compulsory school

**Per Capita Gross Domestic Product** (*purchasing power parity*): $27,300 (2001 est.); *Inflation*: 4.9%; *Unemployment*: 4.3%; *Living below the poverty line*: 10% (1997 est.)

### B. A Brief Historical Perspective

Celtic tribes invaded what is now Ireland about the 4th century B.C.E., bringing their Gaelic culture and literature. St. Patrick brought Christianity to these Celts in the 5th century C.E. The Norse invasions, which began in the 8th century, ended in 1014 when the Irish King Brian Boru defeated the Danes. English invasions began in the 12th century with bitter rebellions, famines, and savage repressions. The Easter Monday Rebellion (1916) failed, but was followed by guerrilla warfare and harsh repression by the English. When the Irish Parliament (Dail Eireann) reaffirmed their independence in 1919, the British offered dominion status to the six counties of Ulster and to the 26 counties of southern Ireland. The Irish Free State in the south adopted a constitution and dominion status in 1922, while northern Ireland remained a part of the United Kingdom. In 1937, a new constitution was adopted along with the declaration of Eire (Ireland) as a sovereign democratic state. In 1948, Eire withdrew from the Commonwealth declaring itself a republic. The British Parliament recognized both actions, but reaffirmed its control over the northeast six counties, a declaration Ireland has never recognized. Despite recurring violence and political shifts, both the British and the people of Ireland favor a peaceful resolution of the conflict.

## 1. Basic Sexological Premises

### A. Character of Gender Roles

The idea that there are definite and separate roles for the sexes pervades all aspects of Irish society. In this division of roles, the feminine is regarded as subordinate to the mascu-

---

*Communications*: Harry A. Walsh, Ed.D., 1201 Gulf Course Road, #1207, Monticello, MN 55362 USA; dialeat@msn.com.

line. The society is a patriarchal one where social power and control are associated with masculinity. The 1937 Irish Constitution reflected what was considered the main role of Irish women thus: "In particular the State recognizes that by her life within the home, woman gives to the State a support without which the common good cannot be achieved." This provision, and the attitudes underlying it, have been used to deny women equality in all spheres of Irish life.

[*Comment 1997*: The cult of the Virgin Mary is very strong in Ireland. Mary is depicted as a kind of Cinderella—confined to the kitchen with her dreams and fantasies. The model presented to the women of Ireland is seen at the Marian Shrine of Knock in western Ireland. In this vision, she was reported to have worn a long dress with a sash, a veil, and wearing the crown of a rich feudal lady. Yet, one of the best-selling prayer-cards at the shrine is "The Kitchen Prayer":

> Lord of all the pots and pans and things . . .
> Make me a saint by getting
> Meals and washing up plates.

[The image of the Virgin Mary held up before the eyes of Irish women reinforces the established cultural attitude: Women can have their dreams, but their place is in the kitchen. (*End of comment by H. A. Walsh*)]

[*Comment 2003*: However, the present generation of young mothers is quite different from their mothers. Getting a career outside the home in place before starting a family is quite common. They may be married, but they are in no rush to get pregnant the first year or, indeed, for several years after marriage. In the "old Ireland," tongues started to wag if a young wife failed to get pregnant within the first year or two after marriage. This, of course, raises the question: How are they avoiding pregnancy? The only reasonable conclusion has to be that they are using some method of artificial birth control. It is hard to imagine that all young couples are employing the natural family planning method of contraception—which suggests that young couples are making conscious decisions that fly in the face of the moral dictates of their Church. The fact that personal conscience is taking priority over institutional conscience is certainly a new feature of Roman Catholicism in Ireland.

[Another small, but significant, sign of the changing times can be seen in a practice that has become quite common today. Young females, when they marry, do not take their husband's name, not even as a second, hyphenated name. So, if Molly Malone marries, she stays Molly Malone. (*End of comment by H. A. Walsh*)]

At the same time, since the advent of the women's movement and Ireland's joining with the European Community in 1973, a number of legal reforms have been brought about, giving women more or less legal equality. But socially, economically, and politically, women are far from equal, although the gap has narrowed somewhat in the past 20 years. Women make up about 30% of the workforce, but in industry, their average earnings are only 67% of the average male earnings. Ireland has the lowest employment rate in Europe for mothers with children under 5 years of age. In 1991, 16.7% of married women were in the labor force, compared with 50% in Germany. There are no publicly funded childcare facilities. Discrimination against women is widely practiced, and as yet, they have no redress in law. The most powerful positions in politics, law, medicine, the military, police forces, industry, universities, and financial institutions are held almost exclusively by men. Although attitudes to equality have changed considerably in recent times, in the social sphere, actual practice lags far behind. For example, in a 1986 survey, 95% of the respon-

dents agreed that men and women should share housework. In reality, women do the lion's share.

## B. The Sociolegal Status of Males and Females

There are no differences between the legal status of male and female children. There are minor distinctions between male and female adolescents. For example, boys may work in bars at age 16 while women cannot work there until age 18. It is illegal for a male over age 14 years to have sexual intercourse with a girl under 17 years of age, but the girl commits no crime in the same situation. Homosexual acts under the age of 17 are illegal for males, but not for females. The government has recently promised legislation that will make discrimination on the grounds of sex illegal.

The social status of males and females is reflected in the gender roles demanded of each. From a very early age, girls begin to learn to prepare themselves for a traditionally feminine role in society and boys learn to prepare for a traditionally masculine role. The feminine role is regarded as having a sense of social value, while men regard themselves personally as superior to women. These attitudes are used as a justification for denying women equality and for the fact that political, social, and economic power is exercised by men.

## C. General Concepts of Sexuality and Love

The socialization process and gender-role stereotyping generally demands that sexual expressions belong properly to the married state of heterosexual men and women. The proper expression of sexuality within the marital union is limited to the act of penile-vaginal intercourse. An inability or lack of inclination to engage in coitus can be grounds for annulment of a marriage. Childless marriages are generally frowned on and the childless couple is considered selfish. Any overt or suggested sexual expression outside the privacy of the marriage bed is, at the very least, disapproved of. Within marriage, women are expected to be sexually available and to play second fiddle to their husband's sexual desires.

Sexual activity outside marriage in heterosexual relationships is tolerated to some degree, especially if it appears that the couple may eventually marry. However, different standards exist for men and women. Males are seen as sexual go-getters with instinctive sexual urges they cannot control. They are neither encouraged nor expected to take responsibility for the consequences of their behavior. Females are seen as sexually passive and in need of a male to awaken their relatively weak sexual desires. Because females are seen as more in control, they are held responsible for both their own and the male's sexual behavior. A further twist to the tale is that women must never undermine the male's dominant role in sex.

Romantic love is idealized and this ideal is perpetuated in all media forms. Romantic novels outsell all other types of fiction. Most people would say they married because they were "in love." People who say they are still "in love" after many years of marriage say so with pride.

The sexuality of children, disabled persons, the chronically ill, the elderly, those who live in institutions, and single persons without an opposite-sex partner is hardly acknowledged, let alone recognized and respected.

[*Comment 2003*: An older, Irish priest recalls the time when married women would confess to experiencing an orgasm when engaging in sex with their husbands. It was assumed that a woman engaged in sex just to satisfy her husband, and that she herself had low or no sexual desire. Consequently, women who experienced orgasm felt that this must have been the working of an evil spirit inside of them; therefore, she needed to confess and be forgiven. The young people of Ireland today would find it hard to believe that such a mentality existed just a generation back.

["Boys will be boys and girls will be sluts" was an imbedded, male attitude. All examples employed by preachers made it clear that the female was responsible if a couple had sex outside of marriage. Since she did not have any sexual desire worth talking about, she could maintain her composure and control the urges of the aggressive male. (*End of comment by H. A. Walsh*)]

## 2. Religious, Ethnic, and Gender Factors Affecting Sexuality

### A. Source and Character of Religious Values

The Irish are an outstandingly religious people. Over 90% of the population are Roman Catholic and 3% Protestant. Eighty percent attend church at least weekly and about 50% express a great deal of confidence in their Church. Among the younger generation, there is less acceptance of orthodox beliefs and religious practices, but the difference between generations is not nearly as great as that found in other Western countries.

Roman Catholicism greatly influences all aspects of Irish life. Since its foundation, the state laws have complemented Catholic Church laws. Until 1972, the Irish Constitution paid homage to the "special position" of the Catholic Church in Irish life. [*Comment 1997*: This resulted, until recently, in an unresolved issue of Church annulments vis-à-vis the constitutional prohibition against divorce. After the constitutional prohibition against divorce was revoked in a November 1995 referendum, it became possible for the estimated 80,000 separated Irish couples to obtain a civil divorce. The Church has, in recent years, granted annulments, dubbed "divorce Irish-style," and permitted remarriage, but annulments were and remain difficult to obtain from Church authorities. (*End of comment by H. A. Walsh*)]

[*Comment 2003*: Since the Irish are enjoying new wealth, the promise of "the grass of a goat and a cow" is ancient folklore to divorcing females today. If the divorcing husband has wealth, women are demanding their fair cut. Also, because of the new wealth of the country, thousands of Irish in America are returning home. Some are returning with second wives. The old put-down about "driving a second-hand car" (marrying a divorced person) has lost its sarcastic bite in today's Ireland.

State schools, which the majority of children attend, are mainly run by religious organizations. [*Comment 1997*: However, because of aging and a decline in vocations, many teaching and administrative positions in schools, once held by religious orders, are now filled by laity. This has caused some tension in recent years as lay educators become more conscious of having political clout. (*End of comment by H. A. Walsh*)] Religious bodies also play a major role in the provision of the country's nonprimary healthcare services.

This pervasive religious influence is reflected in the way sexuality is treated on political, social, and personal levels. It is reflected in the type of censorship of books, films, and television programs that prevails. It is reflected in the laws relating to human reproduction, the lack of sex education in the schools, and the absence of the study of sexuality in any academic institution.

On a personal level, sex is associated with fear and guilt for many people, and even in communal, single-sex showers, nudity is unusual. There is evidence, however, of some decline in religious influence over the past ten or so years.

The Irish people as a whole are characterized by conservatism—conservative in religion, in morality, in politics, and in their views on work, marriage, and the family. Many Irish people are at ease with a republic that is traditional, nationalist, and Catholic. However, a growing number feel alienated in such a society.

[*Comment 1997*: Ease of travel has made the young people of Ireland less insular and more impatient with the insular mentality of the older generation. The youth of Ireland think of London, Paris, Frankfurt, and even Boston and New York, as "neighboring cities," and have exposure to lifestyles and value systems that their parents never had.

[Catholicism and nationalism were synonymous in the minds of the previous generation. To be Irish was to be Catholic. Some of Ireland's greatest writers went into exile because, although thoroughly Irish, they were not seen as Catholic enough. The young Irish today do not see Catholicism as a necessary component of self-identity. They seem to understand where culture leaves off and real faith begins. Consequently, they can discard elements of Catholic orthodoxy with greater ease and feel no guilt about being un-Irish when they do so. (*End of comment by H. A. Walsh*)]

[*Comment 2003*: The Roman Catholic Church in Ireland faces an enormous challenge in today's Ireland. For one thing, the trust level between Church and people has been damaged seriously by revelations of clergy sexual abuse. In the former Ireland, the common thinking was: If you had a doctor in the family, you were blessed; if you had a priest and a doctor in the family, you were saved. Parents are not holding up priesthood as an ideal to their children as they used to do. (*End of comment by H. A. Walsh*)]

For some, the shift towards greater permissiveness and tolerance that began in the 1960s is progressing too quickly, for others too slowly. There is a constant tension between old and new ideologies, between Catholicism and nationalism on the one hand, and liberalism and materialism on the other. Until recently, the battle lines were clearly drawn, but now some are attempting a synthesis of these seemingly contradictory values. Foremost in this attempt is the Irish President, Mary Robinson.

[*Comment 2003*: It is true that the Irish of the last generation packed their churches on weekends. However, the drop-off in church attendance by today's youth would lead one to ask: What brought the previous generation to church in such great numbers? Was it faith or fatherland? There was a saying in Ireland: "It's easier to go to church than to stay away, because, if you stay away, everyone will be talking about you." It was the cultural thing to do. Also, Ireland had been touched by the Reformation Wars through people like Henry VIII, Oliver Cromwell, and Queen Elizabeth I. So, to go to church was a patriotic act, a defiance of English Protestantism. To be Irish was to be Catholic. To be Irish and Catholic was to be anti-British and anti-Protestantism. To say that the Irish packed their churches because of pure faith would be an exaggeration. Faith they had, but not in its purest form, because nationalism was part of the mix. Because faith is a unifying force, the fact that the "faith" of the British and the "faith" of the Irish kept them fighting each other for centuries surely makes one wonder how "faith-ful" either was. So, if Irish youth are not attending church as regularly as the generation ahead of them, it may not indicate a lack of faith but, rather, a search for a faith that comes without the trappings of nationalism and cultural pressures. Church leaders who are crying in their Guinnesses over the fact that youth are not coming to church as faithfully as their parents did, need to understand that the old Reformation Wars have no relevance for young Irish boys and girls today. The biases that still work with some success in Northern Ireland are irrelevant to young people in the Republic. (*End of comment by H. A. Walsh*)]

## B. Source and Character of Ethnic Values

[*Comment 1997*: In the 4th century B.C.E., Celtic tribes invaded what is now Ireland, where their Gaelic culture and literature flourished. The Celtic worldview was dualistic, dividing the world into two opposing subworlds, one of light, good, and spirit, and the other of darkness, evil, sin, and body. In the 5th century C.E., St. Patrick converted the Celts to Christianity. Some anthropologists have suggested that a major factor in the negative and repressive view of sexuality that pervades Irish culture may be traced to the adoption of the original Celtic dualistic philosophy by celibate Christian monks who found it congenial to their own apocalyptic vision. (*End of comment by R. T. Francoeur*)]

[*Comment 1997*: Monasticism introduced an ascetical element into Irish spirituality. To this day, thousands of Irish seek out the barrenness of mountains and islands to do penance for their sins of the flesh. Suffering is seen as meritorious, something to be "offered up" in union with Christ on the Cross or for the release of "the poor souls in purgatory." Since suffering was seen as meritorious, it was natural that pleasure would be suspect. Sex was "a stolen pleasure." (*End of comment by H. A. Walsh*)]

[*Comment 1997*: In the 17th and 18th centuries, Irish youth were trained for the clergy in France where they were strongly influenced by another dualistic current, French Jansenism. The Jansenists saw the world torn between two opposing forces of good and evil. Jansenism stressed the corruptibility of human nature and its sinful, evil tendencies, associated the body and emotions with evil, and glorified the ascetic denial of all "worldly" desires (Messenger 1971; Francoeur 1982, 58-60).

[English invasions and colonization started in the 12th century, and the resulting 700 years of struggle, marked by bitter rebellions and savage repressions, have left their mark on Irish culture. English taxation, limits on industrialization, and restrictions on the kinds of crops Irish farmers could raise helped create a society in which marriage of the offspring was delayed to provide manual labor for the farm and support for the parents. In the system of primogeniture, the first-born son inherited the entire paternal homestead, because dividing up the farmland among all the sons would leave none with a viable economic base. With few other economic opportunities available, the other offspring frequently became priests or nuns, or emigrated.

[This combination of religious dualism and economic pressures has resulted in a society strongly dominated by the clergy and religious, with late marriages for those who marry, and a sexually repressive value system that holds celibacy and sexual abstinence in great esteem (Stahl 1979). (*End of comment by R. T. Francoeur*)]

In 1922, Northern Ireland chose to remain part of the United Kingdom, while the Irish Free State adopted a constitution as a British dominion. In 1937, the Irish Free State rejected dominion status and declared itself a sovereign democratic state. In 1948, the Irish Free State withdrew from the British Commonwealth and declared itself a republic.

[*Editor's Note*: John C. Messenger has provided extensive ethnographic observations of "Sex and Repression in an Irish Folk Community" in a small island community of the Gaeltacht he calls Inis Baeg (see Marshall & Suggs 1971).]

## 3. Knowledge and Education about Sexuality

### A. Government Policies and Programs for Sex Education

Prior to 1984, the government had no formal policies regarding sex education. In that year, a 15-year-old girl and her baby died during childbirth in a field in the middle of winter. She had not told anybody that she was pregnant. Following this tragic event, sex education became a matter of public and political debate. The Minister for Education planned a reform of secondary level education to include personal and social skills training, including sex education, in the new curriculum. The government's Health Education Bureau began training teachers to teach this new aspect of the curriculum. However, this reform was not implemented because of political, religious, and pressure-group opposition. Nonetheless, over 2,000 teachers have been trained so far to deal with sexuality and personal relationships. A criticism of this training has been that it does not place enough emphasis on how political, religious, economic, and social factors shape sexuality, values, and personal relationships.

In 1987, the Department of Education issued guidelines to postprimary schools recommending that sex and relationship education be integrated into all subjects. These guidelines also recommended that such education should not be secular and would require a religious input. Parents were to be fully involved in the process. Whether or not and how schools implement these guidelines is not known, but it appears that few schools have adopted them. In a *Green Paper on Education* (1992), the government proposed that future curricula will provide for "sexuality education appropriate to all levels of pupils, beginning in the early stages of primary education."

The government-controlled Eastern Health Board has initiated a Child Abuse Prevention Program in primary schools. The program encourages children to exercise control, to be assertive, and to seek help for any problem. Critics claim that it dwells on negative aspects of sexuality, is too narrow in its scope, and places responsibility for avoiding abuse on potential victims rather than on adults.

It appears that there is wide variation in the ways in which individual schools provide sex education. Some provide none; others set aside a particular day or days and provide expert speakers. More frequently, it is incorporated into one or two school subjects, usually science and/or religion. Surveys reveal that the majority want a more comprehensive school sex education that begins early in schooling and is independent of religious instruction.

No information is available on the provision of sex education in special schools, such as those for mentally handicapped persons.

[*Comment 1997*: Higher education was not available to most Irish in the first half of the 20th century. The priests, schoolteachers, and local doctor, if the town had one, were the only ones with a higher education. This gave the clergy enormous power. Many of them were, for all practical purposes, mayors of the towns. With Irish universities turning out thousands of graduates today, the clergy have to deal with an educated youth. Older Irish people obeyed instinctively when the Church ruled on something. The young Irish today test the pronouncements to see if they make sense or not. If not, they say so. The older Irish were too superstitious to disagree with the Church ("God will get you for that"). The availability of higher education has resulted in young Irish men and women testing the ethical positions of Catholic orthodoxy. (*End of comment by H. A. Walsh*)]

### B. Informal Sources of Sexual Knowledge

*The Durex Report—Ireland* (1993), designed to be statistically representative of the adult population aged 17 to 49 years living in the Republic of Ireland, found that the following were the main sources of sexual information: own friends, 36%; mother, 23%; books and magazines, 12%; religious teacher, 10%; lay teacher, 10%; father, 5%; and sisters or brothers, 5%. Sixteen percent of this sample believed that the teaching of sex education should be directly influenced by their Church's teachings.

Another nationally representative survey carried out by *The Irish Times* (1990) found that 95% of urban dwellers and 92% of rural dwellers were in favor of providing sex education in the schools. A Health Education Bureau study in 1986 of a national random sample of 1,000 parents found that 64% learned about sex from friends, 37% from books, 23% from mother, 6% from both parents, 2% from father, and 11% from a teacher. Thirty-two percent stated that they had not themselves provided sex education for their children and one in three of these parents stated that they did not intend to do so.

Although sex education is firmly on the political and social agenda in Ireland, consensus has not yet been reached by those who control education on how it should be incorporated into the school curriculum. Meanwhile, the needs of children and adolescents go largely unheeded.

## 4. Autoerotic Behaviors and Patterns

### A. Children and Adolescents

The first Irish study of childhood sexual behavior (Deehan & Fitzpatrick 1993) assessed sexual behavior of children as perceived by their parents. It was not nationally representative and had a middle-class bias. More than half of the parents reported that their child had shown no interest in his or her own genitals. Boys were much more likely to show such interest, as were younger children. Thirty-seven percent reported that their child played with his or her genitals. Most parents said this occurred openly in the home. Sixteen percent described such play as self-pleasuring, most regarding this as a comfort habit or "nervous fiddling." It is probable that much childhood autoerotic behavior does not come to the attention of parents.

The impression that autoerotic behavior is common in adolescence comes from the frequency with which it is condemned by the clergy reacting to the frequency with which this "sinful behavior" is confessed, the high proportion of letters to "Agony Aunts" on the subject, and the frequent usage of slang words for self-pleasuring, particularly among adolescent boys.

[*Comment 1997*: Only 50 miles (80.5 km) separate Ireland from England, the home of Victorianism. During Victorian times, Ireland was occupied by England. The Victorian frenzy about masturbation crossed the Irish Sea, and with it much of the inaccurate "scientific" information about the health risks to those who masturbate, the so-called degeneracy theory. Both the Church and the medical profession reflected Victorian attitudes to autoeroticism in Ireland. Even the language of Victorian England crossed the Irish Sea, with masturbation being known as "self-abuse," "the solitary vice," and so on. However, the Irish have a way of molding the English language. While churchmen and physicians spoke of the "solitary vice" and "self-abuse," the native Irish began to speak of "pulling the wire" and "playing the tea pot." (*End of comment by H. A. Walsh*)]

### B. Adults

No studies have been carried out to indicate the extent or diversity of adult autoerotic behavior. There are indications that some men who engage in self-pleasuring during adolescence stop doing so when they reach adulthood because of the stigma of immaturity attached to it. This seems to be particularly so in the case of married men. In contrast, there are some indications that many women engage in self-pleasuring for the first time in adulthood. In recent years, there has been an increasing market for vibrators and other sex toys in Ireland. Sexually explicit books, magazines, and videos have become increasingly available in recent years, and these undoubtedly sometimes play a part in autoerotic activities. Unusual autoerotic practices sometimes come to light through the work of coroners and doctors. One of these is the use of asphyxiation techniques to heighten sensation during self-pleasuring. Other examples are the use of penile constricting devices, or "cock rings." It appears, too, that drug use is sometimes associated with autoerotic activities.

## 5. Interpersonal Heterosexual Behaviors

### A. Children

In Deehan and Fitzpatrick's (1993) study, less than half the parents stated that their child had shown interest in the bodies of others. Where interest was shown, 46% mentioned the interest was in the mother's breasts or genital area; 25% mentioned sibling's genitals as the focus of interest. Sexualized play that involved looking at another child's buttocks or genitals was reported by 23% of parents. However, parents always qualified their answers by adding that this had only taken place in a situation where the child would need to be undressed.

When parents were read a list of possible sex games their child might have engaged in, 7% reported genital touching games and 4% said that their child had been lying on top of another child in imitation of a sexual act. Simulated intercourse or kissing or licking of the genitals was not reported by any parents. Thirteen percent of the children were reported to share a bed, usually with siblings. This was distinguished from children going regularly to the parents' or sibling's bed, which was reported by 64% and 39%, respectively. Bathing or showering with other family members occurred in 78% of 3- to 5-year-olds, 68% of 6- to 9-year-olds, and 33% of 10- to 12-year-olds. These situations provide opportunities for sexual exploration of which the parents would not necessarily be aware.

### B. Adolescents

*Puberty Rituals*

There are no rituals to mark the milestone of puberty in Irish life. In the Deehan and Fitzpatrick (1993) study, parents reported having discussed breast development with 38% of daughters and 20% of sons, menstruation with 26% of daughters and 7% of sons, pubic hair development with 40% of daughters and 20% of sons, erections with 11% of sons and 5% of daughters, and wet dreams with 4% of sons and 3% of daughters. The vast majority of those children were prepubertal. An increasing number of primary school teachers are discussing puberty with their pupils.

*Premarital Sexual Activities and Relationships*

The only survey to date on premarital sexual activity in adolescence was conduced in 1991 by Ni Riordain among 2,000 female 12- to 17-year-old students in the province of Munster. It revealed that 25% of the 17-year-olds, 10% of the 15-year-olds, and 1% of the 12-year-olds had experienced sexual intercourse. In the same year, teenage extramarital births accounted for 26% of all extramarital births and 4.7% of all births. These figures suggest that the traditional religious and social taboos regarding premarital sex that were effective for so long are no longer so. It appears that adolescents are sexually active to a degree that would be unthinkable to their parents as adolescents. In addition to the change in adolescents' attitudes towards sex, there is the fact that today's teenagers also have greater freedom to meet and spend time with potential sexual partners. Mixed schools, teenage discos and other social events, trips away from home, and fewer social restrictions by parents provide sexual opportunities that were not heretofore available. The formation of couple relationships with an understanding of some degree of exclusivity seems to be occurring at a progressively earlier age.

## C. Adults

*Premarital Courtship, Dating, and Relationships*

The most common pattern in premarital heterosexual relationships is that of a series of more or less "steady" relationships leading eventually to engagement and marriage. A "steady" relationship usually involves a high degree of mutual affection and sexual exclusivity. Partners usually get to know and socialize with one another's family and friends.

Dances, workplaces, colleges and other postsecondary educational institutions, and social networks, appear to provide the most opportunities for meeting prospective partners, but parents, in particular, are not slow in letting a son or daughter know that they consider a particular person to be an unsuitable partner.

Between "steady" relationships, there may be a series of short-lived relationships, and "one-night stands" seem to be increasingly common. Otherwise, there may be periods of varying length where people show no interest in close heterosexual relationships.

A decision to marry is usually marked by an "engagement," when the couple announce their intention to family and friends. Rings are usually exchanged and a celebration party held. Most couples in steady heterosexual relationships appear to engage in sexual intercourse, though this fact would rarely be openly acknowledged within their families. When such couples spend the night in a family home, they are usually shown to separate bedrooms. More and more couples are choosing to cohabit, often causing considerable conflict with family, particularly for women.

*Single Adults*

Little is known about the sexual behavior and relationships of single adults. The cultural imperative to marry is so strong that older single adults, especially women, are often referred to in pejorative terms. Despite this, more and more adults are remaining single. In 1986, 39% of the adult population were single.

*Marriage, the Family, and Divorce*

Until the 1960s, Ireland provided an example of a Malthusian population, such that although fertility was high, population growth was controlled through the delaying or avoidance of marriage. Since then, Ireland has moved rapidly toward a neo-Malthusian type of population control, with generally increasing nuptiality and declining marital fertility. In 1961, the crude marriage rate was 5.4 per 1,000 population. This rose to 7.4 in 1973, but has been declining since to 4.6 in 1993. The median age of marriage shows a similar pattern. In 1945-46, this was 33.1 years for grooms and 28 years for brides. This fell to 25 and 23.2, respectively, in 1977, but by 1990 had risen to 28.6 for grooms and 26.6 for brides.

The crude birthrate per 1,000 population remained more or less constant at around 22 until 1980. However, between 1961 and 1981, marital fertility declined 37%, with a corresponding increase in the extramarital birthrate. Since 1980, the crude birthrate has fallen dramatically to 15 per 1,000. The extramarital fertility rate has continued to increase, accounting for 16.6% of live births in 1991, with 28.6% of extramarital births being to teenagers. Marriage has declined in popularity in the past 20 years; women are having fewer children and having them at an earlier age.

As extramarital births increase, so have single-parent families. The 1991 census revealed that at least 16% of households were single-parent families, with married couples with children making up 48% of the households. The vast majority of single parents are women. On average, they have lower incomes than other women with children and a higher risk of poverty. Most single parents are dependent on the state for their main or only source of income. Single mothers or fathers who cohabit are not classified as single parents.

Within two-parent households, there has been a change from the traditional pattern characterized by a dominant patriarchy, a rather severe authority system, and a generally nonexpressive emotional economy. There was a rigidly defined division of labor, with mothers specializing in emotionally supportive roles. The modern trend is toward a marriage where both husband and wife are expected to achieve a high degree of compatibilities based on shared interests and complementary differences. Rather than being defined and legitimized within closed communal systems, interpersonal relationships are geared toward individual self-development. Part of this trend is that an increasing number of married women are employed for wages, and more married men are assuming childcare and housekeeping duties.

*The Durex Report—Ireland* (1993) included questions regarding frequency of sexual intercourse, change in sexual behavior in relation to the awareness of AIDS, and the number of sexual partners in the previous 12 months. Daily coitus was reported by 2% of married and single adults. Forty-five percent of married and 25% of single people reported intercourse once or twice a week; 13% and 10%, respectively, reported a frequency of once or twice a month. Three percent of married and 36% of single people said they were not sexually active. Married men and women averaged 1.05 and 1.03 sexual partners, respectively, in the previous year. Single men averaged 2.72 partners and single women 1.25 partners in the previous 12 months.

Faithfulness within marriage is highly valued. In the 1983 *European Value Systems Survey*, 98% of the Irish respondents considered it as very important for a successful marriage. In the same study, 12% said they considered marriage to be an outdated institution; less than 1% were cohabiting. In law, a person may have only one husband or wife. Occasional instances of bigamy come to light.

In November 1995, Irish voters approved a referendum legalizing divorce. The original Irish Constitution had stated that "No law shall be enacted providing for the grant of a dissolution of marriage." A 1986 referendum on an amendment to allow divorce was rejected by 63.3% of the voters. Recent opinion polls suggest that the majority would now vote for such an amendment; the government proposed holding a second referendum in 1994. In the 1991 census, just over 2% of adults classified themselves as separated.

[*Comment 1997*: In December 1993, after a Matrimonial Home Bill had been approved by Parliament, the Republic's President, Mrs. Mary Robinson, sent the bill to the Supreme Court for a review of its constitutionality. This unexpected move appeared to be an effort to avoid a protracted battle in 1994, when the people were scheduled to vote again whether to legalize divorce. The matrimonial bill was intended to replace the traditional practice of almost always giving the home to the husband with joint ownership of homes in divorce settlements. After a year's delay, in November 1995, a scant majority of 0.4% of the voters, slightly over 9,100 votes out of more than 1.6 million votes cast in a country of 3.5 million people, legalized divorce. In mid-1996, the Supreme Court of Ireland rejected a challenge and confirmed the pro-divorce vote of November 1995. (*End of comment by R. T. Francoeur*)]

[*Comment 2002*: Divorce was forbidden by the Constitution. The referendum to amend the Constitution in 1996 led to a fight of Irish proportions. Anti-divorce campaigners ran with the slogan: "Hello divorce, goodbye daddy." The Catholic Church threw all its resources behind the anti-divorce campaign. Even the Pope intervened the day before the vote, calling on the Irish people to vote "no." Those favoring a change used some emerging, clerical sex scandals. They showed a picture of a prominent Irish Bishop who resigned after admitting that he had fathered a son in Connecticut. The caption read: "Let the Bishops look after their own families. Vote 'Yes.'" It seems that disgust over clerical sexual misconduct won the day—but not by much. The final vote was 50.3% in favor, 49.7% against. In round body numbers, the margin of victory was only 9,114 out of 1.6 million ballots cast. The one problem with the new Family Divorce Law is that its language is so incomprehensible that the average person will not be able to understand it, and it is so packed with clauses and subclauses, that even attorneys will have trouble interpreting it. It seems that all this padding was inserted to give the impression that a divorce would be difficult to get. Possibly the framers hoped that restrictions would make the bill more palatable. For example, the bill states that couples must be separated for four years before a divorce will be granted.

[Other indications that attitudes have changed in Ireland: It is no longer illegal for Irish women to travel abroad for an abortion; homosexuality was removed from the Criminal Code; between 1974 and 1992, the birthrate dropped by half; and, legal restrictions on the purchase of condoms were dropped. (*End of comment by H. A. Walsh*)]

*Sexuality and the Physically Disabled and Elderly*

Attitudes about the sexuality of physically and mentally handicapped persons and the elderly are generally negative. In the training of teachers and health personnel who work with the handicapped and the elderly, sexuality in given little or no attention. Institutions in general make little provision for the sexual needs of their residents.

*Incidence of Oral and Anal Sex*

The incidence of these sexual expressions is unknown. Oral sex appears to be relatively common and anal sex much less so. There are no legal restrictions on any of these activities.

## 6. Homoerotic, Homosexual, and Bisexual Behaviors

Representation of heterosexuality as the only acceptable sexual expression is directly linked to the wider relationships between the sexes in society. The family, based on marriage, is promoted as the only valid social unit. Homosexual men and lesbian women are seen as a threat, and are marginalized, ostracized, and discriminated against. They can be, and are, dismissed from jobs and denied promotions. In custody proceedings, they can have their children taken from them on the basis of their sexual orientation. They cannot adopt children. They are the targets of pervasive social prejudice, often amounting to open hostility and physical assault.

The societal messages to which young people are exposed almost entirely omit the experiences, desires, and hopes of young lesbians and gay men, as they do with all minority groups. Those images that do occur are almost always negative stereotypes and caricatures. Young homosexuals face an even greater burden of sexual guilt and confusion than is the norm in other societies.

While little or no research has been carried out on homosexual experiences, it appears that these are common in adolescence, particularly for males. It may be just as common for girls, but the greater general tolerance for male sexual expression makes it more likely that one becomes aware of the male homosexual.

Gay men and lesbians tend to meet in particular bars, discos, saunas, and clubs. These are concentrated in cities, particularly in Dublin. Relationships formed can include brief anonymous sexual encounters, a series of sexual friendships, an open relationship with a primary partner, or a closed monogamous relationship. Cruising, in which sexual partners are sought in public places, such as parks and toilets, seems to be limited to gay men. Bisexual married men also appear to favor these outlets.

Telephone support and information lines are run in the major cities by gay and lesbian organizations. They also provide facilities for meetings and social events. Gay and lesbian publications are widely distributed, and publications by the Gay Health Action organization have been in the forefront in keeping all segments of the community informed about HIV infection and AIDS.

In 1993, the government repealed the existing law making homosexual acts between men in public or private illegal, giving all such acts the same legal status as heterosexual acts. The extent of the reform surprised many, since a more limited reform would have resolved a ruling by the European Court of Human Rights in 1988 that Ireland's laws on homosexuality were in breach of the European Convention on Human Rights. The government has also initiated introduction of specific legislation to outlaw discrimination on the grounds of sex and sexual orientation in both employment and social areas.

## 7. Gender Diversity and Transgender Issues

Transvestism and transsexualism are so marginalized as to be almost invisible. However, people are generally aware of both phenomena and transvestism appears to be quite common. There are a number of transsexual people, but all would have undergone gender-reassignment surgery abroad. It is probable that most hospital ethical committees would not permit the procedure. At present, it is not possible to alter one's birth certificate to change the sex designated at birth. There are no legal restrictions on transvestism.

[*Comment 1997*: Transvestites have a way of acting out their transvestism that is culturally accepted. They can join a fife-and-drum band or belong to a troupe of traditional dancers, and wear kilts. (*End of comment by H. A. Walsh*)]

## 8. Significant Unconventional Sexual Behaviors

### A. Coercive Sex

*Sexual Abuse, Incest, and Pedophilia*

In the past decade, there has been a growing awareness that child sexual abuse is common and widespread in Ireland. A 1987 survey of Dublin adults revealed an incidence of 6% for males and females. However, this survey asked only about digital-genital and penile-genital contact. There has been much controversy and some denial concerning child sexual abuse, but there are now signs of official recognition of the problem. An integrated approach involving different disciplines is being developed in an effort to reduce its incidence and to treat victims. Following the success of a recent pilot project, plans are to introduce a full treatment program for abusers. A Child Abuse Prevention Program has been introduced in primary schools, but is not universally supported. One criticism has been that it places too much responsibility on children for prevention of such abuse.

A 1989 study of 512 confirmed cases of child sexual abuse in a health board area revealed only 55 criminal prosecutions (10.7%). Sentencing ranged from a seven-year jail term to application of the Probation Act. Police statistics for 1991 include only six reported or known incest offenses, a gross understatement of actual incidence. Legally, a male is prohibited from having sexual intercourse with his daughter, granddaughter, sister, or mother, and a female from having intercourse with her son, father, grandfather, or brother. When the victim is under 15 years of age, the maximum penalty for convicted males is life imprisonment and for convicted females, seven years imprisonment. When the victim is over age 15, the sentencing varies greatly.

There is very little public discussion of pedophilia and its incidence is not known.

### [Clergy Sexual Abuse

[*Update 2003*: In the spring of 2001 and March 2002, documentaries produced and broadcast by the British Broadcasting Corporation (BBC) television and state network RTE reported on the life and 1999 suicide of a priest from Wexford, Ireland, who faced 29 charges of sodomy, sexual assault, and gross indecency, as well as dozens of other cases of clergy sexual abuse. The documentaries shocked the very-Catholic nation, forced the April 1, 2002, resignation of Bishop Brendan Comiskey, the bishop of Wexford, and brought charges against Dublin's Cardinal Desmond Connell, the nation's primate. In 2001, the Catholic Church in Ireland agreed to pay $110 million in compensation to hundreds of people who were physically and sexually abused by priests and nuns in church-run, state-funded vocational schools. The Church and a special team of police and detectives appointed by the Prime Minister launched two internal investigations and one independent investigation. Early findings put St. Patrick's College in Maynooth, the country's most distinguished seminary, under a cloud following allegations that teenage pupils were sexually harassed by their teachers.

[The core of the scandal was that, despite hundreds of written and in-person complaints to the bishops, no action was taken by the priests' religious superiors. Also, in some cases reported after 1995 by church authorities to the Dublin police, the police took no action on the complaints. In many cases, as has happened in Australia, Canada, the United States, and elsewhere since the mid-1980s, the bishops responded by moving the accused priests to other parishes and jurisdictions. Some of the complaints dated back to the 1930s. In October 2002, the Government Minister for Health and Children said that a national investigation into abuse by Roman Catholic clerics would not be feasible. "How does one cope with the enormity of all of that? It could go on forever." At the same time, the head of the country's Bureau of Criminal Investigation said in an RTE radio interview that "Everything will be looked at, and it will be looked at systematically and collectively" (Lavery 2002ab; O'Brien 2002).

[On the last day of 2002, after a five-hour meeting with representatives of clergy sexual abuse victims, the Roman Catholic Archbishop of Dublin pledged the archdiocese's full cooperation with any police investigation into sexual-abuse allegations against priests. Cardinal Desmond Connell also promised the police full access to Church files, accepted a role for victims in shaping how the Church handles such matters in the future, and their involvement in improving structures for dealing with abuse and complaints (Hoge 2002). (*End of update by R. T. Francoeur*)]

### *Sexual Harassment*

Irish legislation does not specifically address the problem of sexual harassment. The Minister for Equality and Law Reform has indicated that such legislation will be introduced. Since 1985, victims of sexual harassment can pursue claims against employers under the Employment Equality Act. A survey of personnel managers, conducted by the Dublin Rape Crisis Center in 1993, found that incidents of sexual harassment had been brought to the attention of management in 40% of the companies. Half of the companies did not have a specific sexual harassment policy and 55% of these had no plans to introduce one.

### *Rape*

In 1991, 110 cases of rape were reported or known to the police, yet the Dublin Rape Crisis Center was aware of over 300 cases in the same year. Social and professional attitudes to victims of rape often encapsulate in stark form society's pervasive negative attitudes towards women. These very attitudes lead many victims not to report the crime. It is widely recognized that the number of rapes reported to the police represents a minority of the actual incidents.

The 1990 Criminal Law (Rape Amendment) Act extended the legal definition of rape to include penile penetration of the mouth or anus, and vaginal penetration with any object. This act also permits a married woman to charge her husband with marital rape. Conviction on charges of rape or other serious sexual assaults carries a maximum sentence of life imprisonment. Judges, however, possess complete discretion in sentencing, provided they take into account a Supreme Court ruling in 1988 that held that the normal sentence for rape should be a substantial prison sentence. Lenient sentencing is common and causes considerable public outrage.

### B. Prostitution

Female, and to a much lesser extent, male prostitution is practiced in the main ports, cities, and towns. Contact between prostitutes and clients occurs on the street, in massage parlors, and through advertising. Some prostitution is controlled by pimps.

Prostitution is not a criminal offense, but associated activities, such as soliciting in a public place, operating and managing a brothel, or creating a public nuisance, are felonies. The government has recently indicated that it intends to amend the laws on prostitution to make clients liable to prosecution for soliciting and to make "curb crawling" an offense. There is a high degree of tolerance towards prostitution in Ireland, as long as it is out of sight and mind.

### C. Pornography and Erotica

In 1926, the government appointed a Censorship Board with the power to prohibit the sale and distribution of material it considers indecent or obscene. Initially, books were its main focus of attention, and many works of literary merit, such as James Joyce's *Ulysses*, were banned. In 1946, an appeals procedure was introduced, and in 1967, the duration of each ban was reduced to 12 years. Customs and Excise officers are empowered to confiscate material they consider indecent or obscene. Pornographic books, magazines, and videos, mainly imported, are widely available, though they are not openly displayed or easily accessible.

## 9. Contraception, Abortion, and Population Planning

### A. Contraception

Until 1979, the law prohibited importation and sale of contraceptives, despite the fact that, in 1975, 71% of the adult Dublin population supported the view that birth control was a basic human right. *The Irish Times* survey in 1990 found that 88% of the 18- to 65-year-olds favored the provision of contraceptive information in health education courses in schools. For over 20 years, the discrepancy has been growing between Catholic Church teaching on contraception and the actual practice of many Catholics. Yet, the progressive liberalization of contraception law since 1979 has lagged behind the changing public attitude.

The absence of a comprehensive school sex-education program, combined with the reluctance of most parents to discuss contraception with children and adolescents, means that many young people begin having sexual intercourse with little knowledge, and even less use, of contraception. Little attention has been paid to the needs of adolescents in this regard, mainly because, up to now, the focus has been on meeting the needs of adults.

According to *The Durex Report—Ireland* (1993), the main sources of information on contraception for 17- to 49-year-olds were: books and magazines, 31%; friends, 20%; television and films, 7%; and lay teachers, 6%. The preferred main sources of information were: parents, 35%; lay teachers, 22%; books and magazines; 10%; and government health agencies, 5%.

[*Comment 1997*: Before the advent of "the pill" and condom, the most frequent form of contraception in Ireland was coitus interruptus. Many an Irish woman was shocked to find that she was pregnant even though "he pulled out in time." Also, men who could not get their hands on condoms were known to fashion their own from saran wrap. (*End of comment by H. A. Walsh*)]

All contraceptive methods are currently available in Ireland, although a person may have to travel a considerable distance for some methods, such as the IUD, diaphragm, or sterilization. Furthermore, the majority must pay for contraceptive services and supplies. Family planning clinics in the main cities and towns are the principle providers of comprehensive family planning services. These receive no government funding except for some educational and research projects. Some clinics have been providing recognized training for doctors and nurses for 20-some years, so that more and more family doctors are now providing fairly comprehensive family planning services.

A recent amendment to the family planning laws allows condoms to be sold to a person of any age with minimal restrictions. Male sterilization is provided in family planning clinics, some private and public hospitals, and by a few family doctors. Female sterilization is carried out in some private hospitals with varying preconditions. Many hospitals will not perform female sterilization for ethical reasons. Some voluntary organizations provide free instruction in natural contraceptive methods, the Billings cervical mucus, and related methods.

Respondents to *The Durex Report—Ireland* (1993) reported on contraceptive use as follows: condoms, 28%; the pill, 24%; natural methods, 9%; vasectomy and IUD, 3% each; female sterilization, 2%; diaphragm and other methods, 1% each. Fourteen percent reported using no contraception, and 12% reported not being sexually active. The condom is particularly popular among 25- to 29-year-olds, upper-social-class groups, and those living in urban areas. By contrast, natural methods are practiced almost exclusively by married couples over age 30 and those in rural areas. The pill is most popular among single women. (See additional comments in Section 1A, Basic Sexological Premises, Character of Gender Roles.)

No comparable survey has been carried out among adolescents. However, surveys in individual family planning clinics have repeatedly found that a high proportion of teenage, first-time clients had been having unprotected sexual intercourse, sometimes for up to three years.

**B. Teenage (Unmarried) Pregnancies**

In 1992, there were 2,435 live births to unmarried teenagers, representing 26% of extramarital births and 4.7% of all births. There has been a continuous rise in both extramarital and teenage unmarried births since 1981, even though the proportion of teens in the population has remained at about 13.3%.

Official statistics show that 700 unmarried teenagers of Irish residence had abortions in England and Wales in 1991. In addition, other Irish teenagers commonly give an English or Welsh address. There is no way of knowing how many unmarried, pregnant teenagers had miscarriages, illegal abortions, or concealed the birth of their babies.

Whatever the actual figures, an appreciable number of Irish teenagers are experiencing unplanned pregnancies each year. In contrast to former times, most pregnant teenagers do not marry. Most have and rear the child themselves, usually with the help of the family and/or partner. About 20% have an abortion and a small number give up the baby for adoption. All unmarried parents are entitled to a means-tested state allowance. In 1984, 42% of Irish teenagers who had an abortion in England or Wales had not used contraception on most occasions when they had sexual intercourse, and 83.4% were not using contraception at the time they became pregnant.

[*Magdalene Asylums for "Fallen Women"*

[*Update 2002*: In the 19th century, the Roman Catholic Church opened up what were called Magdalene Asylums as refuges for "fallen women." Some of the Magdalene women were prostitutes or unwed mothers, but others were committed to the asylums because, in some small way, they had violated the very conservative social mores of the time or ignored the Church's moral code, bringing shame and dishonor on their families. Operated with state approval by the Sisters of the Good Shepherd and other religious orders of nuns, the Asylums and orphanages were, in fact, self-supporting workhouses, functioning as commercial laundries for schools, prisons, and other institutions. Inmates worked long hours, seven days a week, and 364 days a year with only Christmas Day off. They received no pay, praying nonstop out loud, even while working, to prevent the girls from talking with each other. The women were so completely cut off from the outside world, many stayed in the Asylum until they died and were buried in unmarked graves in prison cemeteries. The babies of unwed mothers were given up for adoption or sent off to orphanages. Over the decades, some 30,000 young women were sent to the Magdalene Asylums. The Asylums were named after Mary Magdalene, the patron of prostitutes who repented and washed the feet of Christ.

[News stories about the 1996 closing of the last Asylum, coupled with the growing scandal of clergy sexual abuse and its coverup by both Church and state, triggered a series of biting exposés of the casual abuse and cruelty that characterized the Asylums, workhouses, and orphanages. One of the most influential of these documentaries was *The Magdalene Sisters*, which received the Golden Lion award for best film at the Venice Film Festival in 2002. The film was seen by over a million people, one quarter of Ireland's population (Lyall 2002). (*End of update by R. T. Francoeur*)]

**C. Abortion**

The Offenses Against the Person Act (1861) makes abortion illegal in Ireland. However, in 1992, the Irish Supreme Court ruled that abortion was permissible where pregnancy posed a real and substantial risk to the life of the pregnant woman. Both pro-choice and antiabortion groups campaigned for further action to clarify this ruling. A referendum followed in which the people rejected an amendment to the Irish Constitution that would allow abortion only where there was a real and substantial risk to the life of a pregnant woman, with the exception of a risk of suicide. At press time, legislation by the government was still pending to give effect to the Supreme Court ruling.

In 1983, the people had voted for an amendment to the Constitution that would have prevented any possible future legislation to allow abortion. Ironically, it was the wording of this amendment that facilitated the 1992 Supreme Court ruling.

Following the 1983 referendum, the court ruled that provision of information and counseling services concerning abortion were illegal. Legal opinion also held that a pregnant woman could be restrained from travelling abroad for an abortion. In 1992, an injunction was obtained prohibiting a pregnant 14-year-old alleged rape victim from having an abortion in England. This was appealed to the Supreme Court and led to the latest ruling mentioned above.

In the 1992 referendum, the people also voted in favor of amendments to the Constitution to allow dissemination of information on abortion and freedom of pregnant women to travel abroad for an abortion. Legislation giving effect to these amendments is also awaited. Opinion polls have indicated that the majority of Irish adults approve of abortion where the pregnant woman's life or health is at risk.

In 1991, 4,154 women who gave Irish addresses had abortions in England and Wales. It is not known how many Irish women giving other addresses have abortions each year. The majority of these women go to private, fee-paying clinics. Because of the ban in Ireland on providing abortion information, counseling, and referral, many of these women travel abroad unaware of and unprepared for what is ahead of them. Many have never been outside Ireland previously. Despite the ban, some organizations and individuals continue to provide nondirective counseling and abortion referral, although these sources will be hard to find for many women in need of such information. It is probable that many women experiencing complications following an abortion are afraid to seek help from medical personnel in Ireland.

[*Update 2002*: In March 2002, despite vigorous opposition from the Catholic Church, the Prime Minister, and the majority Flanna Fail party, Irish voters rejected a referendum that would have further tightened Ireland's already strict limits on abortion. This was the fifth time since 1980 that Irish voters have rejected such legislation. This latest referendum would have overturned a ruling that allowed abortion if the woman threatened suicide, and set a 12-year prison term for violations. It also protected existing rights of women to obtain abortions abroad and of women's advocacy groups to distribute information about overseas clinics, where an estimated 7,000 Irish women obtain abortions each year. As of 2002, Ireland and Portugal, both overwhelmingly Catholic, were the only European Union nations with strict laws against abortion (Gerlin 2002). (*End of update by R. T. Francoeur*)]

**D. Population Control Efforts**

The Irish government has no stated position on population growth or reduction. With the exception of the period between 1961 and 1986, the population has been decreasing since figures were first officially recorded 150 years ago. A high emigration rate has more than offset the traditionally high fertility rates. Almost every family in Ireland has a personal experience with emigration. In the past, most emigration has been motivated by the prevailing economic and social conditions.

## 10. Sexually Transmitted Diseases and HIV/AIDS

**A. Sexually Transmitted Diseases**
*Incidence, Patterns, and Trends*

All sexually transmitted diseases are officially reportable in Ireland. However, the number of cases reported to the Department of Health is low and widely acknowledged as representing only a small proportion of the total. A 1979 study by Freedman et al. estimated that reported cases of syphilis represented only 24% of the probable total and reported gonorrhea cases less than 10% of the probable total. The total number of reported STD cases increased from 1,823 in 1982 to 4,619 in 1988 before decreasing to 3,858 in 1991. Overall, there has been a rise of about 400% in the number of cases reported annually between 1972 and 1991. The majority of cases reported are those treated in STD clinics, and these represent a small proportion of all STD cases. Statistics from the STD clinic in the city of Cork show a decline in the number of new cases between 1985 and 1989, with a considerable increase each year since. Genital warts is the most common condition encountered in this clinic, increasing by 63% between 1985 and 1991, while gonorrhea decreased dramatically in the same period.

*Treatment and Prevention Efforts*

Treatment for STD is available free of charge at STD clinics in the main cities and towns. Treatment is also available from specialists in private practice and family doctors. Thirty percent of the population is entitled to free medical treatment by family doctors. Until the appointment of a full-time consultant in genitourinary medicine in 1988, clinic services were poorly developed, understaffed, and overcrowded. Since 1988, the situation has improved, but many parts of the country still have no clinical services.

Patients are encouraged to contact partners at risk. If they fail to do so, some clinics will make the contact themselves with the patient's permission. In the 1979 Freedman et al. study, one in five family doctors was interviewed by phone about treatment of STDs. Six percent had seen no STD cases in the previous 12 months. The vast majority had not seen a single case of syphilis or gonorrhea in a woman and a very small number saw more than two cases in the prior 12 months. More than half saw at least one case of male gonorrhea; 4% saw ten or more cases. At the time, the male/female ratio of syphilis and gonorrhea cases was 8.4:1 and 8.5:1, respectively. Over two thirds of the family doctors said they would diagnose and treat cases of STD themselves; 18% would use laboratory tests, and 51% would treat on the basis of clinical diagnosis alone. Unfortunately, there is no more-current data on STD treatment in Ireland.

Only in very recent years has an effort been made to educate the public about STD symptoms, treatment facilities, and prevention. Leaflets on these topics are now produced by the Department of Health, STD, and Family Planning Clinics. STDs are sometimes discussed on radio programs.

**B. HIV/AIDS**

By April 1993, over 70,000 HIV tests had been administered in Ireland. Of these, 0.5% were positive, with intravenous (IV) drug users representing 52% of those who tested positive, with homosexuals 18% and heterosexuals 13%. Among the 341 persons diagnosed as having AIDS, 40%

were IV-drug users, 35% were homosexual or bisexual, 10.5% were heterosexual, 7% hemophiliac, and 2.8% were babies.

All blood donors have been tested for HIV since the mid-1980s. Since November 1992, women attending antenatal clinics and pregnant women having blood tests for rubella status have had anonymous (unlinked) HIV testing. Consideration is being given to similar testing of IV-drug users and those attending STD clinics to ascertain the incidence of HIV infection in these populations.

The vast majority of those suffering from AIDS are treated at a Dublin hospital that is finding it more and more difficult to cope as the numbers increase. Efforts are now being made to concentrate medical care for AIDS patients in primary healthcare settings.

In Ireland, the gay community reacted swiftly and effectively to the AIDS epidemic. A 1989 survey of gay men found that there had been a major swing to safer sex practices, and that this had resulted primarily from education and information campaigns initiated by the gay community. For IV-drug users, the government has initiated a methadone-maintenance and needle-exchange program. This is concentrated in satellite clinics around Dublin. A national AIDS committee advises the Minister of Health on various aspects of AIDS. This has led to wider availability of condoms and government-sponsored advertising about HIV infection in the media. These prevention efforts are supplemented by school sex education programs, but the availability and effectiveness of these, as discussed earlier, is highly suspect. Many nongovernment bodies, such as trade unions, have initiated their own prevention programs.

[*Update 2002*: UNAIDS Epidemiological Assessment: By the end of December 1999, there were a cumulative total of 691 cases and 349 deaths. Injection drug users accounted for the largest number, 280 (40.5%), of cases of AIDS, homosexual/bisexuals accounted for 237 cases (34.2%), heterosexuals for 92 (13.3%), and the remaining 82 cases (11.9%) was composed of hemophiliacs, children, and others. By mid 2001, a cumulative total of 2,469 cases of HIV infection were reported. The latest breakdown of HIV infection data from the HIV Surveillance System showed at the end of December 1999 that 41.6% of the reported 295 cases were among injection drug users, 22.7% among homosexuals, 18.8% among heterosexuals/unspecified risk, and the remainder (16.9%) was made up of hemophiliacs, children, and other categories.

[The progress of HIV infection and AIDS is monitored through the National System of Surveillance in Ireland. The available data include the AIDS reporting system and the laboratory information on HIV Surveillance. The AIDS reporting system is based on clinical events that are reported by the regional AIDS coordinators to the Department of Health and Children. A number of laboratories throughout Ireland perform HIV testing, and confirmatory tests are carried out in the Virus Reference Laboratory. The HIV Surveillance System is supplemented by an anonymous unlinked antenatal HIV-testing project and a linked antenatal HIV-screening program introduced during 1999.

[The Irish data indicate a relatively low incidence of known HIV-positivity, with approximately 150 new cases per year in a population of 3.6 million (4 per 1,000). It is important that the HIV data reflect the true overall transmission rates, and in this context, the reporting system will include new developments. These include HIV case-based reporting, adjustments for reporting delays, and additional surveillance data, including HIV infection in high-risk groups, including prisons, drug treatment clinics, and sexually transmitted infection clinics. The most recent HIV statistics indicate that interventions with injection drug users are effective in reducing transmission rates in this group. While Ireland has a low prevalence of HIV/AIDS, transmission has increased significantly in the heterosexual category, and prevention programs are reflecting the new epidemiological data.

[The estimated number of adults and children living with HIV/AIDS on January 1, 2002, were:

| | |
|---|---|
| Adults ages 15-49: | 2,200 (rate: 0.1%) |
| Women ages 15-49: | 660 |
| Children ages 0-15: | 190 |

[Less than 100 adults and children died of AIDS during 2001.

[No estimate is available for the number of Irish children who had lost one or both parents to AIDS and were under age 15 at the end of 2001. (*End of update by the Editors*)]

## 11. Sexual Dysfunctions, Counseling, and Therapies

### A. Concepts of Sexual Dysfunction

Irish society defines healthy sexuality differently in many respects for men and women, young and old, rich and poor, and able-bodied and disabled persons. Consequently, cultural definitions of sexual dysfunction depend on who is doing the defining and which people they are talking about. Those who define sexual dysfunctions are often the same people who treat it. In many instances, the definitions current in professional circles in Ireland reflect and reinforce cultural stereotypes of what is considered socially appropriate gender and sexual roles. Those seeking treatment are usually as culture-bound as professionals in their concept of what is sexually dysfunctional or unhealthy.

### B. Availability of Counseling, Diagnosis, and Treatment

Kieran (1993) sent questionnaires to 201 organizations and individuals who appeared to practice psychosexual counseling and sex therapy. Psychologists, social workers, and doctors made up the majority of 75 respondents. Most worked in private-practice settings and doctors were the most common source of referral. The responses are the only perspective on sexual therapy in Ireland.

While there are psychosexual therapists who practice a more psychosomatic approach; they are in a minority. The most common theoretical element shared by the respondents was a behavioral approach.

In the survey, sexual problems were defined in terms of symptoms, for example, vaginal spasms, erectile dysfunction, and early ejaculation. Symptom relief is regarded as a successful outcome in sexual therapy. This symptom-oriented approach is also evident in the enthusiastic manner in which many people have embraced the latest "cure" for "erectile dysfunction," namely, pharmacologically induced penile erections.

Government-funded psychosexual therapy services are not available, except on an ad hoc basis by some public health personnel. Most family planning clinics provide this service, as do organizations such as the Catholic Marriage Advisory Council and the nondenominational Marriage Counseling Services.

There are no legal or other restrictions on who may practice as a psychosexual therapist in Ireland. Although all respondents to Kieran's survey stated that they had undergone training in counseling, no indication of the quality of such training was given. Forty percent of the respondents had received no specific training in psychosexual counseling or sex therapy; 70% were receiving supervision. Training, professional standards, and accreditation were the most common concerns of the respondents.

## 12. Sex Research and Advanced Professional Education

Little sexological research is carried out in Ireland. No university or other tertiary educational institution has a graduate or postgraduate program on sexuality. Nor is there any formal program for sexological research in any of these institutions.

The only sexological organization working in Ireland is the Ireland Region of the British Association of Sexual and Marital Therapists. Address: 67 Pembroke Road, Dublin 4, Ireland.

## References and Suggested Readings

*A.I.D.S. Action News.* 1989 (August). Dublin: Gay Health Action.

Cantillon, J., et al. 1993 (April). *Sexually transmitted diseases.* Newsletter of the Irish Association of Family Planning Doctors.

*The changing family.* 1984. Dublin: University College, Family Studies Unit.

*Child abuse statistics 1983-1991.* Dublin: Department of Health.

*Child sexual abuse in Dublin (Pilot survey report).* 1987. Dublin: Market Research Bureau of Ireland Ltd.

*Child sexual abuse in the Eastern Health Board region of Ireland in 1988.* 1993. Dublin: Kieran McKeown Ltd.

CIA. 2002 (January). *The world factbook 2002.* Washington, DC: Central Intelligence Agency. Available: http://www.cia.gov/cia/publications/factbook/index.html.

Deehan, A., & C. Fritzpatrick. 1993. Sexual behaviour of normal children as perceived by their parents. *Irish Medical Journal, 4*:130-32.

*The Durex report–Ireland.* 1993.

*First report of the Second Joint Committee on Women's Rights.* 1988. Dublin: Government Publications Office.

Francoeur, R. T. 1982. *Becoming a sexual person* (1st ed.). New York: John Wiley & Son.

Freedman, D., et al. 1981. Sexual transmitted diseases as seen by general practitioners in Ireland: Use of a telephone survey. *Sexually Transmitted Diseases, 1*:5-7.

Gerlin, A. 2002 (March 9). Irish voters strike down bid to further restrict abortion law. KRT News Service; *The Star-Ledger* [Newark, NJ].

*Guidelines on the development of sex/relationships education.* 1987. Dublin: Department of Education.

Hoge, W. 2002 (December 31). Irish Church to cooperate with abuse inquiry. *The New York Times,* p. A10.

*Irish values and attitudes: The Irish report of the European value systems study.* 1984. Dublin: Dominican Publications.

*The Irish Times/M.R.B.T. Poll.* May 28, 1990. Dublin: *The Irish Times.*

Kiernan, K. 1992. *School sex education in Ireland* (Thesis). Dublin: Trinity College.

Kieran, P. 1993. *Psychosexual counseling and sex therapy in the Republic of Ireland* (Thesis). University College Cork.

Lavery, B. 2002 (October 23). TV program raises new assertions of abuse by priests in Ireland. *The New York Times,* p. A5.

Lavery, B. 2002 (October 25). New Irish police squad to investigate all clerical abuse cases. *The New York Times,* p. A5.

Lyall, Sarah. 2002 (November 28). Irish recall sad homes for "fallen" women. *The New York Times,* p. A3.

McGoldrick, M. 1982. Irish families. In: M. McGoldrick, J. K. Pearce, & J. Giordano, eds., *Ethnicity and family therapy.* New York: Guilford.

Messenger, J. C. 1971. Sex and repression in an Irish folk community. In: D. Marshall & R. Suggs, *Human sexual behavior.* Englewood Cliffs, New Jersey: Prentice-Hall.

O'Brien, B. 2002 (March 30). Bleeding the Church. *World Press Review, 49*(6). Available: www.worldpressview.com/Europe/547.cfm.

*Report of the Garda Commissioner.* 1991. Dublin: Government Publications Office.

*Sexual harassment in the workplace.* 1993. Dublin: Dublin Rape Crisis Center.

Stahl, E. J. 1979. A new explanation of sexual repression in Ireland. *Central Issues in Anthropology (Journal of the Central States Anthropological Society), 1*(1):37-67.

*Summary of A.I.D.S./H.I.V. statistics.* 1993 (March). Dublin: Department of Health.

*Sunday Press/Lansdowme Market Research Poll.* 1993 (June 20). Dublin: The Sunday Press.

*Termination of pregnancy: England, women from the Republic of Ireland.* 1984. Dublin: The Medico-Social Research Board.

*Third report of the Second Joint Committee on Women's Rights.* 1991. Dublin: Government Publications Office.

*Venereal disease statistics 1982-1991.* Dublin: Department of Health.

UNAIDS. 2002. *Epidemiological fact sheets by country.* Geneva, Switzerland: Joint United Nations Programme on HIV/AIDS (UNAIDS/WHO). Available: http://www.unaids.org/hivaidsinfo/statistics/fact_sheets/index_en.htm.

# Israel

## (*Medinat Yisrael*)

Ronny A. Shtarkshall, Ph.D., and Minah Zemach, Ph.D.*
*Updates by R. A. Shtarkshall and M. Zemach*

## Contents

## Demographics and a Brief Historical Perspective

ROBERT T. FRANCOEUR

### A. Demographics

At the eastern end of the Mediterranean Sea, in the Middle East, Israel is a small nation, long and narrow in shape, about the size of the state of New Jersey. Its western border is the Mediterranean Sea. On all other sides are Arabic, predominantly Muslim, nations—Egypt, Syria, Jordan, and Lebanon, most of which are in a state of war with Israel since its declaration as a Jewish state in 1948. Israel's 7,847 square miles (20,324 km$^2$) include a western fertile coastal plain, a well-watered central Judean Plateau, and the arid Negev desert in the south. The climate is temperate, but hot and dry in the southern and eastern desert areas.

In July 2002, Israel had an estimated population of 6.02 million. (All data are from *The World Factbook 2002* (CIA 2002) unless otherwise stated.) The 6.02 million population includes about 182,000 Israeli settlers in the West Bank, about 20,000 in the Israeli-occupied Golan Heights, fewer than 7,000 in the Gaza Strip, and about 176,000 in East Jerusalem (August 2001 estimates).

**Age Distribution and Sex Ratios**: *0-14 years*: 27.1% with 1.05 male(s) per female (sex ratio); *15-64 years*: 63% with 1.01 male(s) per female; *65 years and over*: 9.9% with 0.75 male(s) per female; *Total population sex ratio*: 0.99 male(s) to 1 female

**Life Expectancy at Birth**: *Total Population*: 78.86 years; *male*: 76.82 years; *female*: 81.01 years

**Urban/Rural Distribution**: 90% to 10%

**Ethnic Distribution**: Jewish: 80.1% (Europe/America-born: 32.1%; Israel-born: 20.8%; Africa-born: 14.6%; Asia-born: 12.6%); non-Jewish: 19.9% (mostly Arab) (1996 est.). In 75 years, Israel's population has increased tenfold, while the Jewish population multiplied by fiftyfold from about 85,000 Jews in 1918 to more than 4,140,000 Jews in 1992.

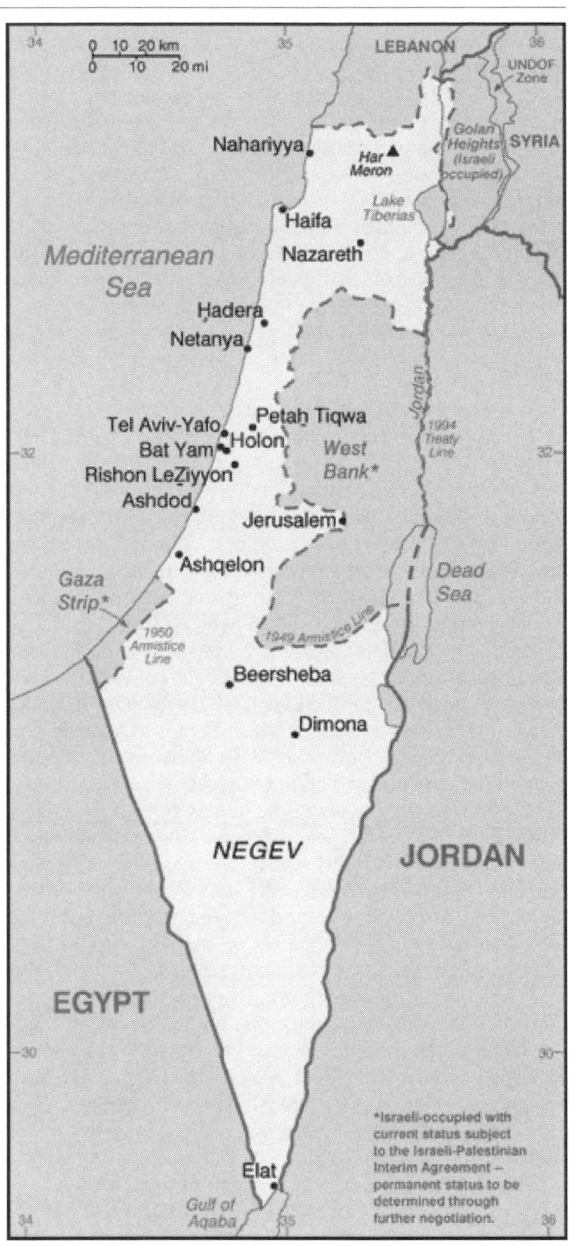

(CIA 2002)

**Religious Distribution**: Jewish: 80.1%; Muslim: 14.6% (mostly Sunni Muslim); Christian: 2.1%; other: 3.2% (1996 est.)

**Birth Rate**: 18.91 births per 1,000 population

**Death Rate**: 6.21 per 1,000 population

**Infant Mortality Rate**: 7.55 deaths per 1,000 live births

**Net Migration Rate**: 2.11 migrant(s) per 1,000 population

**Total Fertility Rate**: 2.54 children born per woman

**Population Growth Rate**: 1.48%

**HIV/AIDS** (1999 est.): *Adult prevalence*: 0.08%; *Persons living with HIV/AIDS*: 2,400; *Deaths*: < 100. (For additional details from www.UNAIDS.org, see end of Section 10B.)

**Literacy Rate** (*defined as those age 15 and over who can read and write*): 95% for Jews and 70% for Arabs; education is free and compulsory from age 5 to 15

**Per Capita Gross Domestic Product** (*purchasing power parity*): $20,000 (2001 est.); *Inflation*: 1.1%; *Unemployment*: 9%; *Living below the poverty line*: NA

*Communications*: Ronny Shtarkshall, Ph.D., 15 Yasmin St. (Box 1116), Mevasseret-Zion, Israel 90805; ronys@md2.huji.ac.il.

Israel is the only country where the society is predominantly Jewish and the Jewish culture dominates. This is a source of difficulty in understanding sexuality in Israel. First, Western cultures do not always appreciate the extent to which Christian teachings differ from Jewish teachings in matters relating to sex and sexuality. (Outside of Israel, large Jewish communities living within dominant Christian cultures have acquired some of the host culture constructs.) This problem is aggravated by a methodological difficulty: Some of the common analytical tools and theoretical frames of reference used to explain sexual issues, especially gender ones, are somewhat lacking, because they are anchored in alien, mainly English-speaking, cultures.

## B. A Brief Historical Perspective

In the southwest corner of the Middle East's ancient Fertile Crescent, the land of Israel contains some of the oldest evidence we have of agriculture and the earliest town life. By the 3rd millennium before the Common Era, civilization had made significant advances in the area. The Hebrew people probably arrived sometime during the 2nd millennium B.C.E. Judaism and the land of Judea prospered under King David and his successors between 1000 and 600 B.C.E. After being conquered by the Babylonians, Persians, and Greeks, Judea again became an independent kingdom in 168 B.C.E. However, within a century, the land was occupied by the Romans. Rome suppressed revolts in 70 and 135 of the Common Era, and renamed Judea Palestine, after the Philistines who had inhabited the coastal land before the Hebrews arrived.

Arab invaders conquered the land in 636. Within a few centuries, Islam and the Arabic language became dominant, and the Jewish community was reduced to a minority. During the 11th to 13th centuries, the country became a part of the Seljuk, Mamluk, and Ottoman empires, although the Christian Crusades provided some temporary relief from Islamic culture between 1098 and 1291.

During four centuries of Ottoman rule, the Jewish population declined to about a third of a million people in 1785. As the Ottoman Empire collapsed in World War I, Britain took over control of the land in 1917; the Balfour Declaration pledged support for a Jewish national homeland there as anticipated by the Zionists. In 1922, the land east of the Jordan River was detached.

Jewish immigration, which began in the late 19th century, swelled in the 1930s as Jews fled the rising tide of Nazi persecutions. At the same time, Arab immigration from Syria and Lebanon also increased. Arab opposition to Jewish immigration erupted in violence in 1920, 1921, 1929, and 1936. After the turmoil of World War II, the United Nations General Assembly voted to partition Palestine into an Arab and a Jewish state. In 1948, Britain withdrew from the country and Israel declared itself an independent state. The Arab world rejected the new state, and Egypt, Syria, Jordan, Lebanon, Iraq, and Saudi Arabia invaded, but were defeated by Israel, which incorporated new territories. In separate armistices signed with the Arab nations in 1949, Jordan occupied the Left Bank of the Jordan, and Egypt occupied the Gaza Strip in the south, although neither granted Palestinian autonomy.

An uneasy truce prevailed until the Six Day War of 1967 erupted when Egypt tried to reoccupy the Gaza Strip and closed the Gulf of Aqaba to Israeli shipping. The war ended with Israel taking the Gaza Strip and occupying the Sinai Peninsula to the Suez Canal, and capturing East Jerusalem, Syria's Golan Heights, and Jordan's West Bank.

Egypt and Syria attacked Israel on Yom Kippur of 1973. Israel drove the Syrians back and crossed the Suez Canal into Egypt. In the disengagement agreement of 1974, Israel withdrew from the Canal's West Bank. A second withdrawal followed in 1976, and Israel returned the Sinai to Egypt in 1982. In 1979, Egypt and Israel signed a peace treaty, ending 30 years of war. A 1978 terrorist attack from southern Lebanon led to an Israeli invasion. The violence and terrorism has continued, with Israel responding to the 1982 wounding of its ambassador to Great Britain by surrounding and entering West Beirut, and a military occupation by Israel of the West Bank and Gaza Strip.

Civilian unrest and military conflict has intensified in recent years marked by two Palestinian uprisings, called *intifadas* (literally, the shaking off). The First Intifada, 1987 to 1991, was followed by a period of relative quiet and reconciliation from the early to mid 1990s, with hope for a settlement to all Israeli-Palestinian hostilities. In September 1993, the Oslo Agreement was seen by many as groundbreaking and a first step to a firm and lasting peace. But after the 1996 assassination of Prime Minister Yitzhak Rabin by a fundamentalist Jew opposed to Israel giving up any of its occupied territory, the peace process slowed down to a grinding halt. The Palestinians living in the occupied territories did not see their living conditions improve. Additionally, Israel did not begin to withdraw from settlements in the occupied territories, which the Palestinians viewed as one of the largest obstacles for peace. Instead, their population almost doubled in the West Bank, even though few new settlements were constructed. This, along with sporadic attacks from Palestinian militant groups and the retribution from the Israelis, made the situation untenable.

The second intifada, the "al-Aqsa Intifada," began in 2000 with the death of the Oslo Agreement and the failure of a summit between U.S. President Bill Clinton, PLO Chairman Yassir Arafat, and Israeli Prime Minister Ehud Barak. In the wake of the controversial visit of Ariel Sharon to the Temple Mount, renewed violence erupted with a new wave of suicide bombers, and many more deaths among the Palestinians than among the Israelis, as the Israeli army reoccupied the West Bank enforcing strict military law, sealing off the Gaza Strip, and imposing economic and travel restrictions on the Palestinians. The Israeli security forces instituted targeted assassinations of Palestinian militants, and destroyed the homes of suicide bombers' families. With Mr. Arafat isolated by the Israelis, a new Palestinian prime minister was chosen. In mid-2003, with a new "road map" for peace, U.S. President Bush applied very strong pressure on Israel's Prime Minister Ariel Sharon and Palestinian Prime Minister Mahmoud Abbas, even as Palestinian opposition to Mr. Abbas increased and the prospects of peace appeared increasingly remote. At this writing, a new truce seemed at risk over the conflicting need for Israeli security and Palestinian demands for troop withdrawals and the return of prisoners.

## 1. Basic Sexological Premises

### A. Character of Gender Roles

Judaism paints an ambivalent attitudinal picture in regard to women. It is certainly patriarchal in nature. The prayer a man recites three times a day includes a blessing for not being made a woman. On the other hand, the Shabbat blessing includes a praise glorifying the woman of valor. She is described in a traditional role of wife, mother, and homemaker. When a person is commanded to honor his parents, mother and father are mentioned explicitly and not the general form or the masculine one. A man is ordered to leave his mother and father and literally "stick" to his wife, while she is never ordered to leave her parents.

Gender and gender roles are viewed in a more traditional manner in Israeli sociocultural reality than elsewhere in Europe or North America. Already mentioned are several unique conditions that contribute not only to the perception of gender roles and the division of labor that are the public domain of family life, but also to concepts of intimacy and roles in sexual relations.

Service in the army reserves also contributes to the fixation of traditional roles of men and women beyond the military service at young adulthood. Men serve in the reserve forces a significant part of their adult life, typically 7 to 8%, but some as much as 25% of their time, annually, until they reach the age of 45 to 50. This fact has to be coped with within the family, and essentially exerts its influence on the balance of family life emotionally, as well as on the division of labor within the family balance of power, and the burden of physical and emotional responsibility of women to the children. Many children grow up with the ongoing worry about the danger to the life of the father, but also with stories that include macho and aggressive overtones. The exemption of women from reserve service on their first pregnancy, understandable as it is, only stresses the role division (see also Section 5C, Interpersonal Heterosexual Behaviors, Young Adults).

## B. Sociolegal Status of Males and Females
### Children

Legally, the rights of male and female children are fully equal. They inherit equally, are viewed with no distinction in terms of rights for protection by state authorities, and have the same rights for education and welfare in case of need.

Another law that has a bearing on sexual and familial issues is the prevailing legal situation (both in civil code and religious law), that there is no flaw in the legal status of a child born out of wedlock. This is sometimes used by religious authorities as an additional argument against granting abortions for unmarried women.

The only gender difference in the legal status of children is part of the religious family law that favors giving custody over girls to the mothers, while favoring fathers in the case of boys over the age of 6.

### Adolescents

During adolescence, the legal status of boys and girls becomes somewhat different, mainly in regard to age of consent for sexual intercourse and the legal age of marriage, while their basic sociolegal rights remain equal.

The differences are in statutory rape laws—a concept that does not exist for boys. This creates an anomalous situation when a boy, who is more than two to three years younger than a girl of 14 or 15, has intercourse with her, opening him to the charge of rape in strict legal terms.

Despite this, the law does not distinguish between minors when it comes to sexual intercourse or molestation by authority figures, such as parents, caretakers, and professionals like teachers, psychologists, or physicians. Both males and females are considered under the protection of the law until age 21.

Another difference is the explicit permission needed to grant a minor girl an abortion without the knowledge and consent of her parents (see Section 9C, Contraception, Abortion, and Fertility Planning, Abortion). The practice is an extension of the rule that allows physicians to give minor girls treatment for preventing abortions, i.e., contraceptives, without the consent of their parents. This widespread interpretation of the law is never challenged in the courts.

### Adults

The situation becomes more complicated when females and males reach adulthood. In addition to the complications of family law and the interaction between a predominantly nonobservant population with state-enacted and enforced orthodox laws and legal system mentioned above, there are several other issues of personal standing in which the issues of gender arise.

Only a few years ago, the income tax laws were changed so that the designation of "head of family" was struck and married women acquired independent standing. Prior to that, women's earnings were treated as a joint income of the family. The term "head of family" was applied to the husband, unless it was a one-parent family headed by a woman.

An increased percentage of women participate in the labor force. While in 1967, only about 25% of the women worked outside their household, their number passed 40% in 1980 and reached 49% in 1992. Despite their increasing numbers in many economic branches, and higher positions, women still suffer from lower wages for equivalent work, and from lower chances for advancement within a specific area.

The equal opportunity law does not permit discrimination on the basis of gender, and even demands that advertisements for work be directed toward both genders.

There is a public campaign now for corrective or compensatory discrimination. Many men and women object to this proposal because they believe that women in Israel do have some offsetting advantage because they do not serve in the reserves, a fact that many employers appreciate.

Another point is the fact that several of the labor laws, especially those dealing with maternal leave, shorter working hours for mothers of small children, and the inability to fire pregnant women burden employers with additional expenses and restrict their ability to compete in an open market. This seems to be a case where what was perceived to be an advanced social law less than 30 years ago may be inappropriate in the new political climate.

Another economic burden and female advantage that both employers and politicians cite is the differences in the pension laws and regulations. Women, whose life expectancy at birth is 79, 3.6 years longer than men (75.4), retire five years earlier than men at age 60. In the public campaign to change the rules, women won the right to choose their age of retirement, but men still have to work until age 65 in order to earn their pensions. Thus, the time that pension funds expect to pay most women is almost nine years longer.

This condition is aggravated by the fact that pension rights to which the surviving member of a couple is entitled are strongly in favor of women, who can receive up to 40% of their partner's salary, while in the rarer cases of a man surviving his wife, he can receive about 15% of hers. Several advocates of labor reform claim that any such changes will need to deal at the same time with all the structural differences between men and women, otherwise the system will not be able to carry the economic burden, and will also move from one form of discrimination to another, instead of toward egalitarianism.

### [Issues of Sexual Rights

[*Update 2002*: The national elections of May 1999 and early 2001 illustrated a social phenomenon that has been emerging for a few years, a sectorial fragmentation of the Israeli society and the loss of power of a unifying common core. This is expressed in the political arena by the ideological parties losing their power. About 40% of the seats in the Parliament are held by sectorial parties acting as three large sectorial blocks: Arabs, immigrants from the former Soviet Union, and the religious party of Jews of Middle Eastern origin. On one hand, this has heightened the political power of organized religion; on the other, it has made the secular sector more militant. Nonorthodox religious movements embedded in the U.S.A., namely the reform and conservative movements, are gaining popularity and power and are using the Supreme Court to force some issues around marriage-divorce laws. This weakens the traditional ties between church and state. On the other hand, the public discourse is currently characterized not only by the intensity of the differences, but by exaggerations and sensationalism in their expression.

[Israel's Supreme Court is also the focus of change around other issues of sexual rights. The most recent case concerning the rights of homosexuals, decided in May 2000, was the registration of a child born to a lesbian woman as the adopted son of her female partner. The boy is now being raised by two official mothers, one biological and one adoptive. In the last two years, the Supreme Court also ordered the military to accept women into some of the most exclusive courses: flight and flight navigation training and navy ensigns. In 1999, two women graduated from flight school and one of them was already flying combat missions early in 2000. On the basis of that decision, a few women applied to be trained in the air force rescue team and to other combat units. This is a conceptual revolution in the military, which since the end of the war of liberation in 1949 excluded women from combat units. Three women are now one-star generals. A retired head of the women's corps was recently appointed to head the prison service. In the civilian domain, the court ordered affirmative action in appointing women as directors to companies which are fully or partially owned by the central and local governments until an equal number of men and women serve as government representatives on the boards of directors. Capitalizing on this decision, several institutions offered courses to train women to serve on boards of industrial, commercial, and public-service companies.

[Another factor in this changing scene is the increasing commercialization of the media and no-holds-barred wars held over ratings in both the printed and electronic media. In a long process, the media, which were mainly ideologically affiliated, are becoming increasingly commercialized. Cable TV was introduced into Israel in the 1990s and, only somewhat prior to that, a second television broadcasting network. Political, social, and, of course, sexual sensationalism are rising in a process that reminds one of the noise level in a restaurant. If the noise level rises beyond a certain point, people who want to talk to each other must raise their voices, which contributes to further increasing of the noise and so on. Thus, issues of rape, harassment, and incest are among the issues discussed and portrayed in minute and hyper-realistic detail in the media. (*End of update by R. A. Shtarkshall and M. Zemach*)]

## 2. Religious, Ethnic, and Gender Factors Affecting Sexuality

### A. Source and Character of Religious Values

The term "secular Jew" embodies the problematics and the uniqueness of the Israeli situation. One part of it—Jew—defines the national sociocultural and historical identity. The second part—secular—defines a relationship to Judaism as a religion and religious lifestyle, and the choice of a humanistic or secular democratic frame of reference over a religious one. These two parts can be naturally linked together only within Israel, the Jews' national home.

Only about 30% of the Jews living in Israel define themselves as religious. Most of the other 70% define themselves as secular, while about 17% to 23% define themselves as traditional. The latter observe a few selected rules of observance, mainly ritualistic ones, while living most of their lives according to a secular lifestyle. Despite that, the culture is strongly influenced by traditional Jewish religious values.

Three examples—1. Jewish thought and its vehicle, the Hebrew language; 2. the role of religious values in a predominantly secular society; and 3. religious politics—will illustrate the extent in which Jewish culture influences sexual constructs.

### The Hebrew Language and Jewish Thought

Language is the vehicle of abstract and analytical thought and therefore plays an important role in our psychosocial phenomena. Hebrew, the language of Jewish thought, exerts a very strong influence on Israeli Jewish thinking about sex and gender. The first expression of the place and meaning of sex in the world appears in the first chapters of the Old Testament, in a way diametrically divergent from Christian thought. In Genesis, the first time intercourse is mentioned in Jewish literature, the root of the verb used has multiple meanings: knowledge, consciousness, and intercourse. As far as is known, Hebrew is unique in using one root, and thus overlapping meanings, for sexual intercourse: knowledge and consciousness. The common root for knowledge, consciousness, and the verb for sexual intercourse indicates that sex is highly prominent in Jewish thought, and not necessarily in a negative way, especially when one recalls that Jews are known as the "people of the book."

This influence is apparent despite the fact that other layers were added over the biblical language and, until the 20th century, Hebrew was only intermittently used as a spoken language for secular, nonritual, or nonreligious studies. In modern, largely secular, albeit Hebrew-speaking Israel, very few people use the biblical term for intercourse in daily life. Current terminology ranges from the intimate (*make love*) through the neutral (*to perform sex* or *sexual relations*, *to lie with*) to the aggressive equivalents of *fuck*, *screw*, *shaft*, and so on.

Thus, unlike many Christian approaches, traditional Jewish thought views sex as intrinsically neutral. It is a human characteristic with an extremely strong potential (like knowledge and consciousness), which can be turned into either good or evil by three humanly determined acts of choice: the meaning one gives to sex (an act of piety), the context within which it is practiced (marriage), and the way one practices it (rules of conduct, including purity laws). In itself, sex—and the pleasure of sex—is not a sin. The harmony of flesh and spirit, an important tenet of Jewish culture, is expressed in married heterosexual relations. Its consummation on a regular basis, not necessarily for procreation, is a *mitzvah*—a combination of an obligation and a privilege—and pleasure is an important part of it. Those who abstain in marriage run the risk of religious sanctions. As role models, community leaders are to be married with numerous children. There is no monasticism, and abstinence is frowned upon.

Despite this, one can also find strong ambivalence about sex and the expression of sexuality in Jewish thought throughout the ages. Its instinctual nature and extremely high potential for evil needs to be guarded and curbed at all times. Some strong Christian influences are also apparent, especially among the Jews living in Europe for the last two millennia.

Another example of the role of the historical language's influencing modern sexual constructs is the fact that Hebrew is almost a totally gendered language. All the forms of speech—nouns, pronouns, verbs in all tenses, adjectives, and adverbs—take a gendered form. In contrast, English, the language of international research, is neutral, except for a few nouns describing animate objects. A comparative study among children of three different countries found that the gender prominence and dichotomization were ordinal according to the gender differentiation within the language,

Hebrew-speaking children having the highest gender awareness. Thus, Jewish children learn with their first abstractions how important it is to identify the gender of each object/entity and to look for the characteristics that distinguish one gender from the other.

### The Power of Religious Values in a Secular Society

The Judaic nature of the society is demonstrated by the role that even secular people ascribe to Judaism in the life of Israel. While most Jews are nonobservant in terms of Jewish orthodoxy, many of them define themselves as traditional. Debates on the relations between state and religion are a constant issue in Israeli politics and public life. Issues, like the definition of the Jew in the law of returning, the opening of public places, or the operation of public transportation on Shabbat (Saturday), support for religious educational systems, and the exemption of women and men studying in religious seminaries from army service, are argued regularly.

In many such debates, many secular people defer to religious demands, not as a surrender to their power politics, but because they view Judaism as having a special role in the life of the state. One of the basic tenets of Judaism is that it is a national religion with a role in both public and private life, with a unique historical role in preserving the Jews as a cohesive people. Sometimes, there is a feeling that in relating to religious demands in public life, secular people place themselves in an inferior position. This closely relates to this topic because marital and gender issues are an important part of the discourse and the complex relationship between state and religion.

### The Political Power of Religious Parties

The influence of Judaism on family, gender, and sexual issues is exerted not only through the subtler cultural and indirect sociocultural forces, but also through the political, social, and economic power of the religious minority of the population. While the political platforms of the religious parties are varied, they are united in their determination to preserve the power and lifestyle of Jewish orthodoxy in the public life of Israel. Their political leverage is far greater than their actual electoral power. While the left- and right-wing parties alternated as dominant political powers and formers of governments, religious elements have held the balance of power in all coalition governments because of a proportional electoral system.

In return for support on issues of defense, foreign affairs, and the economy, the secular parties give in to the demands of the religious parties on issues of secondary importance to them in many social areas, including those relating to family, sex, and gender. Thus, the judicial system that determines family matters is religious, although some aspects can be dealt with also in civil court. The religious influence is obvious in the reform of laws regarding abortion, homosexuality, and censorship of pornography.

The combination of religious Halachic canons with a public that is largely secular creates a conflicted situation. The reason for this conflict lies in several religious laws that impose great hardship on men and women, especially on those who do not adhere to the religious lifestyle. These include the law that forbids men who are descendants of the priesthood families of the temple from marrying a divorcée or a widow; a law forbidding an adulterous woman from marrying her partner in sin, even after she is granted a divorce from the husband; and similar laws.

These situations cause hardship also for religious people, but they suffer them because they adhere to the basic religious tenets. For the secular majority who encounter them, they are an imposition. This is one of the reasons for the strong tensions between the religious and the secular sectors, but the fear of schism is so intense that most people will look for compromise solutions instead of cultural war.

Nevertheless, while the secular and the religious parties have officially agreed to a token truce—the preservation of an ill-defined status quo—in reality, there is a constant political war fought in separate skirmishes on different fronts: in Parliament, the courts of law (especially the Supreme Court of Justice), local governments, and economic pressures. While many secular people feel that religion is gaining ground in public life, most of the religious sector feels on the defensive within the paradox of a secular Jewish state.

## B. Source and Character of Ethnic Values

### An Immigrant Society with Unifying Forces

Israel is an immigrant society with a common historical background and a melting-pot ethos acting as cohesive forces. The absorption of repeating masses of immigrants since the early 1950s has had a considerable impact on sexual behavior, sexual health, and public involvement in sexual issues. In 1990 and 1991, 400,000 people, 10% of the total Jewish population of Israel, immigrated from the former Soviet Union. Issues of increased rates of induced abortions, relatively low numbers of children, one-parent families, an alleged combination of alcohol consumption and sex, and a seemingly instrumental view of intercourse, quickly surfaced.

Also in 1991, 15,000 Jews immigrated from Ethiopia over one weekend, confronting Israel with issues of traditional medical practices, ritual isolation of menstruating women, and increased incidence of infectious diseases, including STDs and AIDS.

Unlike other societies where immigration leads mainly to social fragmentation, indications suggest that social cohesiveness forces within Israeli society also act in the opposite direction: as integrating agents even within the span of one generation (see below in marriage and fertility patterns). The melting-pot ideology is not just a whim. There are some strong basic and structural needs that contributed to its development: a belief in the continuity and unity of the Jewish people; a sense of threat of either political or physical annihilation or both; and, a sense of revival and modernization of an old culture that was suppressed or dormant by external conditions. Although many people perceive the melting-pot society not as a domination of one group over others, but as a continuous process of the evolvement in a new culture, others espouse a more pluralistic approach, advocating the preservation and even the development of ethnic characteristics.

In reality, one can see that many factors relating to dyadic relations and sexual behavior, fertility and fertility regulation, and other characteristics change in a relatively short time, and different studies show the emergence of common phenomena.

### Israel's Political Situation

Israel's political situation has a strong impact on sexuality and sexual issues. This small country, with a total population less than that of New York City, has been surrounded by enemy states and hostile populations since its founding. Until the 1979 treaty with Egypt, there was no land border that an Israeli Jew could legally cross. Even in mid-1994 when ongoing political processes set the stage for reducing the siege, Israel required a military service for all citizens that influenced sexual and related issues beyond that requirement.

Siege feelings and the need to keep national unity make many people accept compromises in striving for change, or at least lower the tone. This often changes the perspectives about priorities and leads to personal inner conflict between personal aspirations and internalized collective ones.

The influence of wars and physical danger on the sexual behavior of people, their marriages, and their fertility patterns are understudied. It is proposed here that, in critically dangerous situations, sex—which is biopsychosocially still connected to reproduction—may serve as a means to symbolically negate personal death. Such a hypothesis was used in attempts to explain diverse phenomena, like the frequently discussed increase in reproduction following military engagement, and the divergence from normative sexual behavior during times of active warfare.

Recent analysis demonstrates that the first phenomenon is only a rumor based on impressions and does not exist in reality. As appealing as the symbolic explanation is, the anecdotally reported departure from normative behavior during times of peace could alternatively be explained by feelings of disintegration during wars and irrelevance of social norms in those times. However, if this explanation were true, one would also expect widespread occurrence of phenomena like rape of the conquered population, which did not materialize in the wars in which Israel conquered land and assumed rule over large Arab populations.

### Military Service

Several characteristics of the general military service, which is dictated by the political realities, can affect, directly or indirectly, the nature of Israeli sexual constructs. The role of the Israel Defense Forces (IDF), both as an institution and as a life event for Israeli youth and adults, is larger than in other Western societies. Most people would view it as essential to both their physical and national existence. It is an existential event in the life of most Israelites, and most families are immediately involved with its realities and dangers.

*1. Gender Roles and the Status of Women.* Military service in Israel is general and compulsory for both men and women at the age of 18. Exemptions are granted for physical and mental health reasons, low educational level, criminal record, and religious reasons, but rarely for conscientious objections. However, men serve for three years and continue to serve in the reserves for 25 to 80 days annually until they are 50 years old. Women serve for approximately two years and are retired from reserve service when they bear their first child. This, in itself, is both a reflection and an enhancer of the more traditional role still ascribed to women in Israel (discussed in greater detail below). Other characteristics of the military service tend to accentuate the traditional gender roles.

Despite compulsory service, there is a strong element of volunteering in the army, as youth compete, sometimes fiercely, for service in elite units or prestigious tasks. This entails additional physical and mental hardship during compulsory service and, in many cases, an obligation to serve as many as six additional years. There is a strong element of macho psychology involved here, with both male status and preference by the young women at stake.

Women do not serve in combat, and their choice of professions is not only smaller, but also limited to the less prestigious tasks within the army. Being out of combat service also blocks them from advancing in the army to the higher levels of general staff commands.

As the IDF retires its generals at between the ages of 45 and 53, exemplary service in the army and a top-echelon position is one of the stepping stones to the higher levels of civil service, business, and political careers. This avenue for advancement is closed to women.

The hardships of service, especially in combat units, promote strong male camaraderie and individual friendships; annual service in the reserves to age 45 to 50 tends to reinforce them. These almost-exclusively male interactions can be transferred to civilian life in the form of enhanced networking and alliances.

It seems that the realities of the military can foster traditional gender roles in the minds of both men and women, and also influence their social positions. Other issues discussed below point in the same directions.

*2. Social Mobilization and Meeting Ground.* Sociologists have noted the IDF's role as a unifying factor and as contributing to the relative high mobilization within the Israeli society.

The IDF is involved in absorbing immigrants and in educational projects for women and men who otherwise would be unfit to serve. It also serves as a common meeting ground for people from different ethnic groups, allowing them to mix socially, and in many cases sexually. Many marriages can be traced to relationships formed in the army.

All IDF officers start as rank and file. There is a strong emphasis on advancement based on merit and achievement, and excellence is measured by a combination of mental, physical, and social characteristics. A meritorious service record is viewed as a strong character reference; in civilian life, young men from less-privileged strata have another chance for mobility.

*3. Rite of Passage or Moratorium?* It is hard to appreciate the influence of the IDF on sexual and family issues if one does not understand the role it plays in the general individual psychosocial development of Israeli youth, and its centrality in the life of many individuals. Most Israeli youth leave direct parental control to go into the army. This is only one factor that ties army service strongly to sexarche, choice of mates, and other sexual issues (see Section 5C, Interpersonal Heterosexual Behaviors, Young Adults). Developmentally, IDF service has some definite elements of a rite of passage—the physical and mental tests, the demand for initiative and resourcefulness judged by peers and veterans, the formation of group cohesion and social responsibility, the ability to deal with moral dilemmas in extreme conditions—and these serve to separate childhood from adulthood.

While not disputing the rite-of-passage elements in IDF service, or its positive effects, it was recently suggested that, at the same time, the nature of IDF service may also cause a long moratorium on the tasks of real life, and can even be viewed as causing some elements of infantile regression. These may have effects on dyadic relationships and gender roles within them (see below).

*4. Internal Conflicts, Trauma, and Violence.* A possible negative aspect of the military service that may have a bearing on sexuality and family life involves the nature of military engagement in the civilian uprising in the disputed occupied territories during the last six years. This forced the soldiers to confront civilians, rather than enemy soldiers, in a manner previously not experienced. These high-risk confrontations with civilians tend to create strong inner and normative conflicts. Those who raised the issue hypothesized long-lasting effects, among them proneness to violence (including domestic violence) and posttraumatic stress disorders. Claims had been made that, in such discussions, it is difficult to distinguish between political stands and professional opinions.

The possible contribution of these issues on the actual shaping of sexual and dyadic constructs will be discussed in several instances.

## 3. Knowledge and Education about Sexuality

### A. Government Policies and Sex Education Programs

The educational system in Israel is divided between the general educational system and religious ones. This necessitates separate discussion of the situation in the different sectors. Most of this discussion will be devoted to the secular educational sector.

*The Early Years (1930s and 1940s)*

Early attempts at sex education, in the late 1930s and early 1940s, were based on local initiatives. Although coming from two different directions, they converged around the dominant psychoeducational ideology of that period—Freudian psychoanalytical thought. The theoretical concepts, which had little direct field application, were largely that of mental health hygiene of a "preventive" nature, and were concentrated around the Psychoanalytical Institute of Jerusalem and the Public Health Services of a voluntary health service of the Jewish community (Hadassah).

At the same time, attempts were made to develop sex education programs at the educational institutions of the left-wing kibbutz movement "Hashomer Hatzair." The atmosphere in these institutions was highly experimental, and the issues of sex, sexuality, gender equality, and the control of individual urges and wishes—not only sexual ones—as part of socializing ethos, were central to the life of the movement at that time. For example, not only was the system coeducational, but boys and girls slept together in the same room, four to a room, until age 18, and bathed together until age 12 to 14. Contrary to the expected, this was a society with highly puritan values, at least when it came to youth, and the key concept of sex education and youth sexuality was borrowed from psychoanalytical literature—sublimation. There was high social control over behavior: purity and self-control were expected, not only in the area of sexuality, but also in areas like smoking and drinking. It is interesting to note that these two behaviors are clustered with precocious initiation of intercourse as "problem behaviors" in the modern research literature.

*The 1960s*

A revival of interest in sex education came in the early and mid-1960s, when several sex-education "guidebooks" were published by concerned professionals. These were not as yet part of an organized sex-education drive, but their almost simultaneous publication is significant, as was the foundation of the Israeli Family Planning Association in 1966. It seems that the main concerns during that period were the apparent increase of sexual behavior among youth and the alleged contribution of large families to low socio-economic status (SES) prospects and crime among young immigrants from Middle Eastern countries.

*The 1970s and 1980s*

The big organizational change happened in the early 1970s. Dominant among the incentives was the increase in the incidence of sexually transmitted diseases (STDs) among youth, following a wave of youth tourism to Israel after the 1967 war. This also coincided with some changes in the general ethos of the country from communal to individual, which may be attributed to filtration of the youth movements of the 1960s in Europe and North America, and with a relative economic boom following four years of recession.

A national study about sexual knowledge, attitudes, and practices was mandated and carried out in the early 1970s. The outcome of the deliberations of a multisectorial committee was an outline for a comprehensive general curriculum arranged chronologically by content areas and skill formation, and the formation of a Unit of Family Life and Sex Education at the Ministry of Education.

The original conceptual framework for this experimental unit was a mixture of preventive health (implying a high potential for adverse effects of sexual behavior), a developmental outlook, and normative boundaries. Its mandate was very wide and flexible and included the development of educational programs, the training of sex educators, and the implementation of non-mandatory sex education within the school system.

Two parallel units were formed, one to deal with the issues within the national-religious sector (which dropped the sex education out of its name) and the other one to deal with the same issue within the general (secular) national educational system.

*The National (Secular) Sex Education Approach.* The efforts concerning sex education in the secular (general) system developed in three main parallel directions: 1. the development of programs and educational materials for different content areas, ages, and skills; 2. training sex educators/facilitators; and 3. creating the infrastructure for the implementation of the programs within schools. The development of the programs and the training of sex educators was influenced by the humanistic approach to sex education of the Sexuality Information and Education Council of the United States (SIECUS), the American Association of Sex Educators, Counselors, and Therapists (AASECT), and Society for the Scientific Study of Sexuality (SSSS). Professionals from the United States of America, most notably Lester Kirkendall and Sol Gordon, helped with the first training courses and development programs in the late 1970s and early 1980s.

In 1978, the curriculum for family life and sex education was formally adopted and the unit ceased to be an experimental one. After several years of independent (precarious) existence, it was adopted administratively into the Psycho-Educational Services of the Ministry of Education. The infrastructure for supporting implementation of sex education now includes several regional trainers, with whom teachers can consult.

The appearance of AIDS on the Israeli scene in the mid-1980s was a mixed blessing for sex education. The rise in public interest in sexual behavior, the perception of youth as an at-risk group, and the feeling of inadequacy concerning sex education among many parents, acted together with other factors in 1989 to mandate sex education at least three times within the formal education span. In each stage, elementary, middle, and high school, pupils are to be given 16 hours of sex education. Unfortunately, this mandate was not accompanied by the necessary budgetary or time allotment for this purpose, so that its implementation still depends on local arrangements, the priorities of principals, and the difficulties of the staff in dealing with the subject.

On the other hand, the public interest in sex education took a swing from the developmental-humanistic approach back to the preventive-medical ones. Also, parties less interested in education jumped on the bandwagon and attempted to lead campaigns by playing on the fears of the public.

*The National-Religious Sector Approach (Excluding the Ultra-Orthodox Approach).* This educational system focuses on a moralistic approach and normative behavior within the boundaries of the religious framework. An integral part of this framework is the dichotomization between public and private behavior. While the Jewish practice allows for the fallibility of the individual and mitigating circumstances, it strongly forbids the a priori consideration or discussion of alternative behaviors. Thus, an educational discussion of the forces leading to premarital sexual behavior, decision making, and alternatives within such situations can be done only within a judgmental right-wrong framework in which abstinence is viewed as the only appropriate alternative.

Several religious educators have been dissatisfied with this approach and expressed their displeasure by participating in training courses for sex educators in the secular sector, contrary to administrative directives. They explain this by their wish to respond to the pressing needs of their pupils beyond the formal and normative guidelines and by a personal need for developing in this area.

*Ultra-Orthodox Educational Systems.* There is only indirect and fragmentary knowledge about sex education within the "Independent Educational System" run by the ultra-orthodox sector, because this system is not accountable to the administrator of the national curriculum (see Section 13B, National, Religious, and Ethnic Minorities, on Ultra-Orthodox Jews [*Haredim*]).

## B. Informal Sources of Information

### Parents as a Source of Information

Findings of a national study of youth sexuality from the 1970s, augmented by some later studies using convenience samples and limited populations studies, show that between the ages of 14 through 17: 1. parents in general were viewed as a low source of information on sexual issues; 2. daughters consulted more than sons with parents; 3. mothers are a much more common information source than fathers; and 4. both parents were a very low source of information for sons, although sons also consulted more often with their mothers than with fathers. Finally, the tendency to view parents as a source of information decreased with age—youth in the 10th and 11th grade were less likely to view their parents as a source of information than were 8th and 9th graders. This change was bigger for sons than for daughters. These results are supported by studies of unique populations, such as youth from problem families residing in boarding high schools, kibbutz youth, and by youth general health studies that included sexuality components. Even when similar pictures are different in important details, this can be explained by the unique conditions of the studied populations.

A possible explanation for the findings that girls interact more than boys with their parents, especially their mothers, on sexual issues, can be that the interactions are not initiated by the girls but by the mothers, who are both more concerned with the expression of female sexuality and more comfortable in approaching their daughters.

This finding that daughters consult parents more than sons conflicts with the findings that their objective knowledge is lower when compared to male youth. An explanation might be that the interaction of daughters with their mothers is more on issues of attitudes and consent than on information, or that the higher ambivalence of female adolescents about their sexuality does not allow them to benefit from the higher amount of interactions with adults.

A recent study using a limited convenience sample found a different picture that could be very important, if replicated in a more generalizable form. In a high-middle-class senior high school sample, parents were the second most important source of information for girls and third for boys.

This may indicate that urban middle-class parents are now finding it easier to talk with their children about sex. This may be part of the trend of increased acceptance of adolescent sexuality, or a reduction in the distance between parents and their adolescent offspring.

There is a question whether parents are an appropriate source of sexual knowledge for youth because of their emotional involvement and their heterogeneity in regard to reliable information. Popular sentiments, based on the general assumption that parental involvement in education is desired, regard as problematic the findings that parents are a low perceived source of information. Attempts are being made to change this situation by interventions directed toward both youth and their parents. However, the effort to increase parental involvement may also reflect adult ambivalence over youth sexuality and the desire to control it.

Even if one accepts the belief that increased parental involvement is desirable, these findings are insufficient grounds for designing interventions, many studies need to be deliberately targeted at more-defined specific subgroups before intervention programs are designed. It may be worth investing in programs to help parents to increase their role as a resource for their children and to help fathers talk with and be more available to their sons, only if the recent findings from the urban middle class are confirmed and the explanatory assumptions hold.

The findings from the boarding schools may indicate that in dysfunctional families, a parental substitute may be needed as a reliable source of information, especially for boys whose fathers are either physically or mentally absent and whose mothers find it difficult to interact with male adolescents about sexual issues.

### Other Sources of Information to Adolescents

Concern over parents' being a low resource is heightened when other sources of information are viewed. Peers and older adolescents are found to be the main source of information for both male and female adolescents. This may increase parental and adult perception of loss of control, as these are potential sexual partners. In addition, the reliability of this information resource is questionable because of the limited knowledge among older adolescents and because it is biased by the agenda of the resource persons.

While information from peers is in many cases unreliable or incomplete, its language and tone are acceptable to adolescents and young adults. It may, therefore, be beneficial to invest more efforts into developing systems of peer education and peer training.

An important information source is the written and electronic media. Unfortunately, much of the material directed to adolescents is sensationalistic, commercial in nature, and/or caters to the lowest common denominator. Thus, question-and-answer sections in youth magazines rarely deal with ambiguities and some questions that have no answers that are definite or generalizable.

Another source of concern is the fact that more children and youth report exposure to pornographic videos, especially among males, but also females, a result of cable television networks and the popularization of video. (Pornography is discussed in Section 8C, Significant Unconventional Sexual Behaviors.)

### Extent and Reliability of Sexual Knowledge

Although knowledge is insufficient to assure healthy or responsible sexual behavior, it is essential for their attainment. Knowledge is also essential during puberty and adolescence to help prevent adverse sequels of sexual behavior, like unwanted pregnancies and sexually transmitted diseases.

It should be noted that, unfortunately, some of the studies mentioned above used what is considered unsatisfactory measures of knowledge, i.e., subjective perception of knowledge rather than measurable objective ones. Studies by

Ronny A. Shtarkshall in convenience samples have shown a marked discrepancy between objective knowledge and the subjective perception of knowledge about contraception; for example, the fact that 90% of adolescents in a large study reported familiarity with at least one contraceptive did not mean that they really had the knowledge they needed to use it.

When objective measures of knowledge were used, a low level of knowledge was found among high school students, many of whom were either sexually active or on the verge of initiating intercourse. Generally, male adolescents demonstrated higher objective knowledge. Female adolescents had higher score on signs of pregnancy and abortions, possibly because of the personal concern with an unexpected pregnancy.

It is unclear why females who reported more interactions with adults demonstrate lower knowledge. As was hypothesized earlier, this could be because their contacts are on issues of conduct, but also because they and the adults are more ambivalent about female sexuality and sexual behavior during adolescence. This hypothesis is supported by limited findings from a high-middle-class study that showed that positive feelings about sex were positively associated with higher objective knowledge.

*Sexual Knowledge among Professional Students*

A study evaluating knowledge of professional students in medicine, social work, and law at the Hebrew University in their first and final years revealed rather alarming findings. First, medical school education had almost no effect on the knowledge of medical students; only one of five content areas, the biomedical, showed a positive effect. Second, the level of knowledge was rather low, especially considering the professional needs of physicians and social workers. Third, sexual experience was in marked and significant association with subjective perception of knowledge. Fourth, there were weak and inconsistent associations between sexual experience during adolescence and objective knowledge. The combination of the two findings is alarming. Since it is assumed that awareness of lack of knowledge is better than perceived knowledge that is erroneous, the finding that medical students are largely aware of their lack of knowledge was viewed as a mitigating sign. Finally, even at this stage, age was positively associated with both increased knowledge and a more adequate perception of knowledge. Extrapolating for a younger age, this finding supports the hypothesis that older adolescents are more ready, both cognitively and mentally, to enter into the sexual arena.

Several studies by Shtarkshall evaluated the lack of knowledge apart from mistaken knowledge, assuming that people who are aware of their ignorance are in a better situation than those who do not know, but mistakenly think that they do. The finding that professional students were largely aware of their lack of knowledge was viewed as a positive sign.

## 4. Autoerotic Behaviors and Patterns

There are no known sources that document autoerotic behavior patterns in the general population in a quantitative way. Even a publication of a recent general population survey on sexual function and dysfunction does not fill this gap.

Sexual history interviews with a large biased sample of help-seeking individuals and couples show the following patterns. Among the nonreligious, more men than women report masturbating either prior to sexarche or after it. Also, more men than women report direct manual stimulation, while fewer report indirect stimulation, like rubbing the thighs, or thrusting and rubbing against objects. These methods are more favored by women. There is a question

whether this is a difference in practice or a reporting bias, but this question cannot be resolved on the basis of these reports in themselves. Among the orthodox, and certainly among the ultra orthodox, the issue of reporting bias is more pronounced, as male masturbation is a serious sin, while female masturbation is only frowned upon and considered unhealthy.

There are many lay beliefs concerning masturbation that are expressed mainly by adolescents and youth, either as questions or comments within sex education sessions. These are mainly lay beliefs concerning general or reproductive health, and also the ability to identify a masturbating person. For men, the beliefs include depletion of the semen, blindness or shortsightedness, hirsutism on the palms, and an asymmetrical (bent) erect penis. Among women, there are admonitions about weak sight and about giving birth to retarded children as a consequence of masturbation.

## 5. Interpersonal Heterosexual Behaviors
### A/B. Children and Adolescents
*Pubertal Rites of Passage*

See remarks on IDF service as a kind of rite of passage for adolescents under Section 2B, Religious, Ethnic, and Gender Factors Affecting Sexuality, Source and Character of Ethnic Values.

*General Lack of Data*

Attempts to elucidate the patterns of sexuality, sexual behavior, dyadic relationships, and other sexual issues concerning adolescents and youth are hampered by sociopolitical restraints. The last study of sexual knowledge, attitudes, and practices in a national sample of youth was done in 1970. In 1991, a proposed study of adolescent sexuality was approved by a review system and then vetoed on educational and moral grounds by the Director General of the Ministry of Education and Culture, a political appointment of a religious minister. Even after the change of government at the end of 1992, a lengthy and tortuous negotiation process about the same study ended abruptly when the psychological services of the Ministry of Education "changed its research priorities" and excluded the survey from them.

Most of the available quantitative information is on secular youth with little on those who define themselves as traditional. All information about religious youth reported here is anecdotal, although it represents the cumulative shared experiences of a network of researchers, counselors, and educators.

*Puberty, Adolescence, and Psychosocial Development*

Very little research has been done on pubertal stages. All studies have used convenience samples of Jewish girls. The normal range for the onset of breast development in 1977 was from 8.22 to 12.38 years and the normal (corrected) age for pubic hair development 8.58 to 12.58 years. The normal range for reaching menarche is 11.09 to 15.49 years.

Several interesting effects associating pubertal stages and social class or ethnic origin have been observed. Girls from low socioeconomic class as defined by their fathers' occupations, whose mothers were poorly educated and who came from large families, reach the stages of puberty later than other girls. All three variables are highly and significantly associated with each other and with Middle Eastern/North African origin. Sample sizes did not allow a distinction between the contribution of ethnic origin (genetic) and social conditions (nurture) to this phenomenon.

It is possible that a secular trend is present, since a comparison of menarche in separate studies of similar populations have shown a drop of almost five months in mean age from 13.75 in the mid 1960s to 13.29 in the late 1970s. (This is not significant because of a large standard error in the more recent study.) During this period, there was a large increase in both the general standard of living and ethnic mixing.

The importance of individual and group differences in pubertal development in relation to psychosocial sexual development is well recognized but very difficult to study. Based on observations and anecdotal information, a hypothesis can be advanced that among Israeli female adolescents, there is an inverted J-curve relationship between age at puberty and the time gap between the onset of puberty and the first sexual intercourse, or sexarche, i.e., girls who develop earlier and later than their peers may go faster through a scale of the stages of sexual behaviors. (Information about male adolescents is insufficient even for development of a hypothesis.)

As for social-class differences in puberty showing that girls of low socioeconomic class reach pubertal stages and menarche at a later age, this may put some stressful pressure on them to act out sexually, especially in integrated schools, because the influence on psychosocial sexual development is exerted not through the abstract national norm, but through interactions with the significant peers. Another pressure on adolescents of low socioeconomic classes in schools, and especially in integrated ones, is the need to excel. There is enough information to suggest that low achievement, in comparison with a significant reference group, is associated with precocious sexual activity.

*[Ongoing Research on Adolescents*

[*Update 2001*: Several studies are currently in progress on the sexual behavior of adolescents and young adults. Another round of the *Health Behavior in School Aged Children* (*HBSC*), a study coordinated by the European Region of the World Health Organization, was scheduled for 2001. This long study contains a very brief section on sexual behavior. The results of the previous round, conducted in 1994 and published in December 1997 (Harel, Kani & Rahav 1997) were limited to the secular sector of the national school system and further limited only to the 10th and 11th grade section of the survey. Other behaviors were also studied among 6th to 7th graders and also in the National Religious Sector of the schools. Adolescents in Israel report having sexual relations to a lesser extent than those in the U.S.A., 27.8% and 13.9%, as compared to 53.5% and 53.1% for American males and females, respectively. The difference between the genders in reporting intercourse during adolescence, on which we reported earlier (in our original chapter in the *International Encyclopedia of Sexuality*), persisted even at the end of the 20th century. Preliminary results from other studies show that this difference continues to be true today. The two other studies are another study in the secular school sector, which focuses on sexual attitudes, norms, and behavior, and a study started in 1995, which looks cross-sectionally at successive groups of young adults. The latter also includes information about orthodox men and women. In the *HBSC* study, the researchers were able to demonstrate that risky behavior, coitus with more than one partner ever or in the last three months, engaging in unprotected coitus, and experiencing coitus under the influence of alcohol or psychoactive drugs is limited to a small subgroup of the adolescents, which may explain the picture of the spread of HIV/AIDS in Israel. (*End of update by R. A. Shtarkshall and M. Zemach*)]

*Premarital Sexual Activities and Relationships*

This discussion of sexual practices among Israeli youth focuses on two main issues: premarital intercourse and the context within which it occurs, and on sexarche or age at first intercourse.

The issue of premarital intercourse during adolescence is more complex than that of premarital intercourse in general. It includes adult attitudes toward adolescents' sexual expression and adolescents' response to it, the interaction between adolescents, peers, and significant adults on issues of control and separation. It is very hard to treat these different issues separately, and sometimes even to distinguish between them.

In general, studies up to the mid-1980s showed that attitudes of Israeli youth concerning premarital intercourse, self-pleasuring, homosexuality, and gender are more conservative than those of European and North American youth. Attitudes among adolescents towards premarital intercourse were associated with several independent variables: gender, age, modernity (socioeconomic status of the family of origin), and religiosity.

Degree of agreement with two extreme attitudes toward premarital intercourse—"Intercourse is forbidden before marriage" and "Intercourse is permitted if both partners want it" (not qualified by age, above 18, or by relationship status, in love or engaged)—are detailed in Table 1. In general, younger adolescents are more conservative about premarital intercourse. Both younger boys and girls are more accepting of the forbidding message than older boys and girls, while the situation is reversed for both genders in relation to the permissive attitude.

The findings indicate that, in general, younger adolescents are more conservative about premarital intercourse. 1. As expected, acceptance of the permissive message increases, and that of the restrictive message decreases, with age for both genders. 2. Comparing genders, one sees that in various adolescent age groups, more boys than girls accept the permissive message and more girls than boys accept the restrictive one. 3. Both boys and girls are more accepting of premarital intercourse if there is an emotional commitment, and more so if there is a formal public one, i.e., engagement. The commitment is much more important to girls than to boys. 4. The discrepancy between boys and girls that supports a behavioral double standard is more pronounced when males and females report their attitudes towards virginity at marriage. Both genders express more-permissive attitudes toward males' premarital intercourse. More than two thirds of females believe that girls should be virgins at marriage, while less than half expect this of their prospective partners. Among males, 10% believed that sex is forbidden before marriage, while 43% felt that a woman should be virgin at marriage. 5. There is also a discrepancy between attitudes and behaviors: Males are more permis-

**Table 1**

**Degree of Agreement in the Attitudes of Adolescents Toward Premarital Intercourse**

|  | Boys | | Girls | |
|---|---|---|---|---|
|  | Grades 9-10 | Grades 11-12 | Grades 9-10 | Grades 11-12 |
| Premarital intercourse is legitimate in adolescence if both want it | 35.3% | 53.3% | 14.1% | 24.4% |
| Premarital sex is forbidden before marriage | 18.1 | 10.2 | 51.1 | 35.2 |

*Editors' Note*: Percentages are approximations from the original bar graphs.

sive in their attitudes than their behavior and females are more permissive in their behavior than their attitudes.

These differences in premarital sex attitudes are more pronounced if one compares older boys with younger girls. As this is usually the pattern of pair formation, it can be a source of tension and discontent in dyadic relationships, prior to initiation of intercourse and after initiating it.

Mechanisms like denial and externalization used to cope with these discrepancies can cause difficulties on the individual and social level, including coercive behavior and problems in contraceptive behavior. They can also lead to a reporting bias about intercourse.

In the religious sector, public norms are against any premarital sexual expression, not just intercourse. Many structural and social controls attempt to enforce these norms because of the common belief that, while adolescents have natural urges, they lack the self control of adults—such beliefs are also common among the more conservative elements of the secular sector. The result is sometimes paradoxical: The constant warnings and controls make people more aware of the temptation. The results may be dire when those who transgress do not possess the range of skills that enable them to protect their own needs while doing so. Those who transgress also have very little chance of parental or even peer social support.

## Trends in Sexual Behavior, Premarital Intercourse, and Sexarche

Pooling the results of several different studies, one is able to conclude that the trend from the 1960s to the 1980s is for more youth to engage in premarital intercourse, and that a larger proportion of those who do so start at a younger age. The increase in the reported rate for younger women from the 1960s to the 1980s is three- to sixfold, the highest increase for both men and women of all ages.

Table 2 shows the trend to earlier sexarche among urban women in one study. Caution is needed in using this study, the only one giving data about premarital intercourse among urban Jewish women prior to 1965. This study has all the limitations of retrospective studies; the time span between the occurrence of the events and the reporting point varies, and the reporting may be influenced by a memory bias. In addition, it was limited to married women in their first marriage, and thus it does not represent the whole Jewish population. Both nonmarrying and divorce may be associated in more than one way with the timing of first intercourse.

### Table 2

**Cumulative Percentages of Women Initiating Intercourse at Different Ages, for Women Reaching Age 16 at Three Different Periods (Cumulative Percentages of Those Who Practiced Intercourse in a Calendar Year Prior to Their Marriage)**

| Age at Sexarche (Years) | The Period at Which the Women Reached Age 16 | | |
|---|---|---|---|
| | 1963-1969 | 1970-1975 | 1976-1982 |
| 14-15 | 1.5% | 3.8% | 3.2% |
| 16-17 | 14.2 | 23.9 | 26.9 |
| 18-19 | 50.2 | 60.1 | 70.1 |
| 20-21 | 80.2 | 85.1 | 93.4 |
| 22+ | 100 | 100 | 100 |

*Note*: The differences between the three studied periods are significant at the $p = 0.001$ level.

*Editors' Note*: Percentages are approximations from the original line graph.

Table 2 also demonstrates an interesting phenomenon. All three groups of women show a sharp rise between ages 16 to 17 and 18 to 19. Since most Israeli youth leave home at that age to go to the IDF, it seems that this is a critical age for the urban women.

In all studies of the urban population, more than 90% of the studied population—secular Jewish youth at high school, at any age more men than women—reported that they had already had sexual intercourse. However, the trend from the 1970s to the 1980s shows that the gender discrepancy in decreasing. The ratio of urban men/women reporting intercourse ranged from more than 8:1 for the 10th grade and 3:1 in the 12th grade in the 1970s, to 3-4:1 in the 10th grade and 2-3:1 in the 12th grade in the late 1980s.

In the mid to late 1980s, between 12% and 30% of urban females and 40% to 55% of males had reached sexarche by the end of grade 12; 2% to 11% of girls and 20% to 35% of boys were sexually active at the end of grade 10.

The discrepancy in proportions between men and women should be a source of concern. The three most widely used explanations in the literature are: 1. the presence of a small group of young women who engage in sex with many young men; 2. The initiation of young men into intercourse by older women; and, 3. reporting bias. As far as is known, the age gap between partners in most of the relationships among adolescents and young adults is either very small or in the opposite direction, the men being older than the women. There are no indications that there is a small group of women who initiate many men into sexual intercourse. Also, the tradition of initiation through sex-for-profit is relatively rare in Israel. It is thus probable that the normative pressures reported above are acting on youth of both genders to create reporting bias in the opposite direction: That is, more boys report having reached sexarche than those who actually do so, with fewer girls reporting it than those who do. An extensive experience with interactive sex education programs dealing with normative pressures and sexual behavior lend additional evidence to support this explanation.

## The Context of Sexarche

In studies of the context within which intercourse is initiated during adolescence, a high proportion of youth reported that intercourse is started within a steady relationship. This is more true for females (95% of those reporting premarital intercourse in a large-scale study) than for males (46% in the same study). The same picture is apparent when comparing the length of relationships: More girls initiate intercourse in longer relationships. Also, girls who were sexually active reported higher frequency of intercourse than boys, which would be the case if intercourse is practiced within a steady relationship.

Despite the general trend of initiating intercourse within a steady relationship, a phenomenon of initiating intercourse with a "sex object" is encountered in significant numbers. Youth of both genders report that they chose a person for the sole purpose of losing their virginity, mainly because "it was time." Sometimes, the chosen person is a different man or women from the one they are in a current dyadic relationship with. Sometimes, this happens when they play the role of a sexually experienced person in the beginning of a relationship and do not find a way out of the role; at other times, they set out deliberately to find a person "to do it" with. Attention should be paid to this group even if it is small, as they may be considered an at-risk group. Because communications may be hampered by conflicting agendas and pretending experience that is not there, and the commitment between the sexual partners may be lower, it can be hypothesized that protection within this group would also be lower.

Experience shows that youth who are able to consult with parents or other significant adults, more often engage in protected intercourse. Unfortunately, these are a minority, and those who do talk with adults are usually older and less in need of this support than the younger ones.

In looking at the length of relationship within which intercourse is initiated, a seemingly contradictory picture appears. A higher proportion of young women initiate intercourse within a steady relationship of more than 13 months as compared to the young men—41% and 27% respectively.

Several factors, acting separately or in unison, could contribute to this phenomenon. First, the study was done among high school youth, and it is possible that the steady relationship of the young women is with older men who are already out of school. This does not fit with the higher proportion of males reporting the initiation of intercourse during adolescence. Second, the study may be dealing with a double-barreled reporting bias: young women, who feel that it is desirable to initiate intercourse within a relationship, tend to overreport the duration of the relationship, or those who start intercourse early in a relationship refrain from reporting it. An additional contribution to this discrepancy is that a higher proportion of casual relationships are between younger males and older females.

*Premarital Courtship, Dating, and Relationships and the Prospects of Military Service*

The dyadic and sexual relations are highly influenced by the required military service, even long before they have to enter the IDF. Awareness of this future in the life of each and every youth comes in many ways, encroaching on the daily life of adolescents. Boys and girls are called for physical examinations at age 17. Many of the boys and some of the girls start even earlier on a road leading to one of the elite units or to a desirable military task. Membership in an elite unit means three things: first, a very high physical and mental competition requiring intense and long preparation; second, a much more strenuous and dangerous service; and third, a longer service, ranging from one to six years beyond the mandatory three years. Not all Israeli youth actually espouse this lifestyle; those who do are the pacesetters. The danger of getting killed or wounded in the army is small, higher in the combat units, and still higher in the elite units where even the training can be dangerous. The visibility and psychological impact on everyone are very high and out of proportion to the statistical reality when compared with road accidents or accidents in the workplace.

Working closely with youth and with facilitators of sex education, one frequently encounters two ways in which this reality influences youth in their midadolescence. First, lack of time to grow up and an unsure future are often brought up as reasons for hastening sexarche, mainly by boys, but also by girls who find it hard to face these realities. Girls bring these facts up as looming in their mind even when the boys do not raise them. While it is possible that some young men use these as manipulative arguments, many of them are also strongly concerned. This effect is also documented in fiction and films, especially those by young artists. The summer before army service is part of the cultural terminology that carries with it connotations far beyond the surface.

Also encountered was an effect acting in the opposite direction, to postpone initiation of intercourse. Girls from some conservative environments, especially of Middle Eastern origin, may postpone sexarche in expectation of the time when the family and social controls will be lowered, and also out of regard for their parents' feelings, honoring family values by waiting until they are out of the home prior to initiating intercourse. Most of these girls will not go to college, but

when they come back home after two years, the parents are already resigned to their new status.

*Age of Consent: Lowering the Social Controls Over the Sexual Behavior of Youth*

In the 1980s, the law of consent underwent a significant reform. Until then, the uniform age of consent—16—applied to women only. While some interpreted this as an expression of the wish to control the sexuality of women, others viewed it as expression of male threat to females' virtue. Toward the end of the 1980s, a change in the legal age of consent took into consideration some of the changes in the behavior of youth. While the age of consent remained 16—again only for women, intercourse between a girl aged 14 to 16 and a boy who was older than her by two years or less would not be considered statutory rape in the context of this relationship. On the other hand, the age of consent was elevated to 21 in cases of intercourse with someone under the guardianship or influence of a professional. The latter section applies to both men and women victims, but it is still not clear whether it applies to perpetrators of both genders.

## C. Young Adults

*Heterosexual Relations and IDF Service*

Life within the IDF strongly influences sexual behavior, the formation of couples, marriage patterns, and gender issues.

By and large, the IDF is an institution of young people, outside regular parental and adult social controls, with its own sets of norms and pressures. Its immediate formal rules, which can be very restrictive, are usually set and administered by people who are between two to seven years older than those obeying them. For most youth, the regularity of military life is highly irregular when compared to their previous lifestyle. On the other hand, outside of defined training and active military duty, life in the military leaves them with unregulated and unsupervised time in the exclusive company of their peers. Despite being a male institution, the IDF includes a high proportion of young women.

There are no formal or social restrictions on fraternization between officers and soldiers, and very little emphasis on military formality and distancing that to outsiders sometimes looks alarmingly like anarchy. Since most youth serve in the army, and all officers rise from the ranks, they are essentially of the same class and traditions.

These circumstances that offer many chances for intimate and sexual encounters, combined with a rite-of-passage situation, tend to give those who are not sexually initiated a chance to be so. This is especially true for those who refrain from dyadic or sexual relations because of external restriction. Many girls growing up in traditional families or communities consciously postpone their sexual debut until the army, as an act of honoring their parents. They view sex away from home as less encroaching on the parental values. It seems that, by mutual consent, the question is not discussed between parents and daughters. Most of these girls will not go to college, but when they return home after two years, the parents are already resigned to their new status, as noted above.

The conditions and situations within the army service are conducive not only to sexual relations, but also to pair formation and to experimentations in relationships (see Section D, Marriage Patterns, below). The IDF environment also creates two specific problems in regard to sexual behavior and gender roles.

First, the permissive environment can impose a strong hardship on youth from traditional backgrounds, especially those with lower educational achievements, who find it very difficult to deal with the relative lowering of parental control over sexual behavior, coupled with increased opportunities and the company of eligible mates. This is especially true of some young women, mostly from families of Asian/African origin, who put a great value on virginity, and who, finding themselves in an environment much more permissive than their home atmosphere, lack the personal, experiential, and social skills to cope with controlling their own sexual behavior. Add to this the fact that those behaving permissively, including other women, are the ones with the prestigious jobs and high social status, and one gets a problematic situation. To resolve this conflicted situation requires internal controls and social skills that some of these women do not possess because of their traditional sheltered upbringing. For some who feel that once they have lost their virginity they are tainted, the result is promiscuous behavior. For others, it is a contributing factor to their inability to use contraceptives resulting from externalizing what they are doing. Internal conflicts regarding the fact that they are engaging in intercourse are sometimes resolved by the feeling of being repeatedly subjected to it "unintentionally," a solution that also precludes the use of contraceptives. The majority of soldiers applying for abortions through IDF come from this background.

To counter this, the IDF women's corps targets women with low educational achievement as a priority group for sex education programs. These programs attempt to strengthen their self-image and internal controls and to allow those who initiate intercourse to preserve both their self-respect and health.

A second factor is that Israel is a geographically small country. With very strong family ties, most soldiers in the combat units get home regularly every second or third week for a long weekend. It is rare that they will not get home for a month or more. It is thus possible to preserve dyadic relationships and meet with girlfriends on a regular basis. On such weekends, the soldiers, who are both tired physically and under a lot of emotional stress, try to cram in as much eating and sleeping together as they can. Their girlfriends accept the role of supporters and nourishers, a traditional motherly role, because they know how much hardship the boys have to take. There is also a tacit agreement not to raise disagreeable issues. This creates a situation in which the partners establish a pattern of separate traditional roles at the early stages in the relationship. It may also create regressive symbiotic dependence, where one is feeding into the relationship different components and relies on the other to supply the missing ones.

*Cohabitation*

Unmarried cohabitation has become more prevalent in recent years. Its frequency is unclear, but it is certainly much more visible and acceptable, mostly among middle-class secular youth, either working or in higher education. This is a change from a generation ago when fewer couples cohabited, and then mostly after having decided to get married. Although this phenomenon has been little studied in Israel, the combination of anecdotal data and educational experiences suggest several points of interest:

1. While cohabitation is less binding than marriage and is often perceived as an experiment in dyadic relationships, the partners are expected to be monogamous.
2. Although somewhat more flexible than married ones, cohabiting couples adhere to traditional gender roles.
3. Cohabitation sometimes develops through an interim semi-communal stage, as when two or more boys or girls or a mixed gender group share an apartment for economic reasons. When one of them forms a liaison, the partner sometimes moves in and shares the bedroom in that communal arrangement. It is only at a later stage in the relationship that the couple sets out to find their own apartment. The initial stage is characterized many times by advertising it only among the peers and not sharing it with the parents, at least not immediately. The movement to the private apartment is usually done with parental knowledge and/or consent.

4. Parental consent, either implied or overt, is no refuge from the feelings of tensions or ambivalence on both sides. When interviewed, several women in such arrangements mentioned that either their father or mother had a difficulty in relating to either the bedroom or the shared bed when visiting their apartment.
5. It is possible that cohabitation is part of the larger phenomenon of extended moratorium that Israeli youth take after IDF service. Cohabitation creates an interim stage between the public announcement of the relationship and creating a formal commitment.
6. Cohabiting young adults who eventually marry, although not necessarily with the cohabiting partner, suggest some ambivalent attitudes to marriage. On one hand, there is dissatisfaction with the parental model of marriage and reluctance to perpetuate a similar pattern. On the other hand, the idealization of marriage and attachment to it as an institution drives them to aspire to an improved version. This may act against the crystallization of traditional gender roles.
7. There are anecdotal indications that cohabiting is, for a growing number of couples, an expression of shunning the rabbinical religious ritual and a rejection of the legal ramifications that it entails. Resolution comes either by using one of the tolerated civil arrangements or in postponing the religious ritual until the last moment when they plan to have children.
8. Breaking up a cohabiting arrangement seems to be more difficult than breaking up a noncohabiting relationship, and the phenomenon of feeling entrapped in a relationship is encountered also by cohabiting couples.
9. When deciding to marry, couples express it as either taking another step along the road or as wanting to formalize the relationship in order to have children. Many cohabiting couples marry when the women are already pregnant.

**D. Marriage Patterns**

*Legal Age of Marriage*

The legal age of marriage is distinct from the age of consent. It applies only for women, and currently it is 17. Ronny A. Shtarkshall was involved as an expert witness in an attempt to apply both age of consent and legal age of marriage to men also. This was barred in a parliamentary committee by a representative of a human rights party on the grounds that this will complicate things and that, while women need protection from men, men do not need protection from women.

*Age at First Marriage*

In comparison to other Western industrial countries, Israelis marry relatively young. This is true even if one looks separately at the Jewish population. In 1990, the median age at first marriage for Jewish brides was 23.2 and for grooms 26.0. It seems reasonable that many marriages at the younger age were initiated by encounters within the service in the IDF. In 1990, roughly 25% of all the men who married for the first time did so between ages 20 and 23, and a third of the women marrying for the first time did so between ages 20 and 22, the years immediately following the service.

Among the Arabs, Muslim women marry for the first time at the median age of 20.0, more than 3 years younger than their Jewish counterparts, while the men marry at 24.4, only about a year and a half younger than Jewish men. Among the Christian Arabs, the median age is only a year younger for women, 22.5, but a year later for the men, 27.5.

In Table 3, we show the changes in age at first marriage of the Jewish population over four decades. It is evident that between the early 1950s and mid-1970s, there was a drop of more than two years in the age at first marriage of Jewish grooms from 27 to 25. Among Jewish brides, the phenomenon is very similar, but smaller, a drop of about one year (23 to 22). This drop is because of the mass immigration from Muslim countries in the mid-1950s and early 1960s. The tradition of these Jewish communities favored early marriage, similar to the Muslim host cultures. This effect on the mean marriage age of brides is less pronounced—and in the median age even nonexistent—because traditionally, brides were younger than the grooms and were married at a very young age, 14 to 16. The Israeli laws forbade such marriages, raising somewhat immediately the marriage age of brides.

Since the mid-1970s, there is a steady rise in both mean and median age of first marriage for both brides and grooms. The rise is larger for women than for men. It is suggested that this rise is the result of educational changes, especially those affecting immigrants from Islamic countries that had a greater impact on women, who were educationally underprivileged in comparison to men. It is also possible that the social acceptance of cohabitation has contributed to the rise in age at first marriage for both genders.

## Marriage Formation

Among the Jewish population, most first marriages, especially those that do not deviate by more than a few years beyond the median age for first marriage, are based on personal choice and attachment. This is true for the secular, traditional, and orthodox segments of the Jewish population, the exceptions being the ultra orthodox and small groups of immigrants from Georgia, Ethiopia, and the Caucasus. Even among the immigrants, the pattern is changing, and many arranged marriages merely formalize previously formed attachments. Youths from some immigrant groups explain that they go through the motions in an attempt to preserve cultural traditions and avoid conflict within their families. The pattern of marriage formation among the ultra-orthodox Jews and among Muslims, the largest group of non-Jews, will be discussed in the special sections dedicated to them at the end of this chapter (see Section 13).

At an indeterminate point beyond the median first marriage, the pressure on the unmarried to conform increases. Participation in family weddings becomes a burden, as many people use the traditional well-meaning but stress-generating blessing, "Soon at your wedding." This is especially stressful to people with homosexual orientation and those whose self-image keeps them from initiating pair formation. At this point, families, especially mothers, sometimes turn to matchmakers and the young adults agree. The

young adults themselves sometimes resort to meeting people through advertising in the newspapers. It seems that these channels are used by a minority of the population.

## Interethnic Marriages among the Jews

It is estimated that 15% to 20% of the marriages of secular and traditional Jews are among those who originate from different parts of the world, mainly Ashkenazi Jews, originating mainly in Europe, and Sephardic ones, who lived during the last 500 years in Islamic countries. The rate is somewhat lower among the orthodox and lowest among the ultra orthodox. The melting-pot ethos, high mobility of the Israeli society, and the strong mixing effect of the army all contribute to this.

## Marital Variations: Polygamy

Polygamous marriages were prevalent among several Jewish ethnic groups, especially those immigrating from Islamic countries. During the peak immigration years of the 1950s, there was a great outrage about polygynous marriages, mainly from women's organizations, and they were outlawed almost immediately. This civil law contradicted both the Jewish Halachic law (as interpreted in these Jewish communities) and the Islamic law and tradition.

## Common Law and Civil Arrangements

The courts recognize the status of a "common-law spouse" for the purpose of property division, inheritance, pension rights, and carrying a name. It also recognizes civil marriages enacted in foreign countries by citizens of Israel, and cohabitation contracts enacted according to the civil code, even when the religious courts ban these specific unions. As a matter of fact, these arrangements evolved in order to solve cases that rise from the conflicts that have already been referred to between the Halachic canons and the secular public.

Other patterns of marriage, like homosexual marriages, are not recognized by Israeli law, and single people find it very hard to adopt children.

## Divorce

The Israeli divorce rate is lower than that of the U.S.A. and non-Catholic European countries. Still, the rates of divorce per 1,000 ever-married people aged 15 to 49 rose monotonously by 48% from 1973 to 1983, from 6.5 to 9.6, respectively, for husbands and from 5.3 to 8.2 for wives. In 1983, the denominator was changed to 1,000 married at all ages; comparison between the two periods is difficult. Since 1983, the rate has fluctuated, rising from 5.8 in 1983 to 6.4 in 1991 (new rates), about a 10% increase.

A time series analysis of rates of divorce after a specific duration of marriages reveal that the increase in rates of divorce is only because of an increase in rates of "late divorce." It is the rates of divorce after nine and 12 years of marriage that are still on the rise. The rate of divorce after two years of marriage did not rise at all since the early 1960s and may even have come down slightly. The rate of divorce after six years of marriage has remained stable since the early 1970s; see Table 4. These findings are somewhat puzzling, as formal marriages are almost universal, the percentage of secular people is similar to most western European countries, and the Jewish religion is more tolerant toward abortion than Catholic Christianity. The relative stability in Israeli marriages supports the claim that the family is a central theme in Israeli society.

One result of the increase of late divorce is an increase in the average duration of marriages that ended in divorce—a rise from 8.3 in the early

### Table 3

### Age (in Years) at First Marriage of Jewish Men and Women

|  | 1952 | 1960 | 1970 | 1975 | 1980 | 1985 | 1990 |
|---|---|---|---|---|---|---|---|
| Average male | 27.32 | 26.33 | 25.02 | 24.92 | 25.52 | 26.40 | 26.70 |
| Median male | 25.68 | 24.88 | 24.13 | 24.21 | 24.81 | 25.72 | 26.01 |
| Average female | 22.82 | 22.20 | 21.81 | 22.19 | 22.61 | 23.53 | 23.90 |
| Median female | 21.01 | 21.01 | 21.40 | 21.52 | 21.99 | 22.82 | 23.21 |

*Editors' Note*: Ages are approximations from the original line graph.

1960s to about 11 in the late 1980s and 11.9 in 1991. However, this increase in the duration of the divorcing marriages by almost 4 years was not accompanied by a similar increase of average age of divorce. For men, the average age at divorce for the same periods is 40.0, 38.6, and 39.4; for women, it is 35.1, 35.2, and 35.8, respectively.

This means that the proportion of the couples who marry at a younger age among the divorcing couples is higher than among other couples. This is a sobering observation regarding marriage at a younger age if one regards stable marriages as desirable.

### Extramarital Relations

Another measure for the quality of marriages is extramarital affairs. There is no reliable research evidence about the prevalence of extramarital affairs among married Israeli couples, but anecdotal evidence, the reports in the newspapers about extramarital affairs of celebrities of all kinds, and the citations in divorce cases lead one to believe that the prevalence is rather high. Evidence from counseling, and from extensive education and information work among adults, leads one to believe that extramarital affairs, even known ones, are not in themselves sufficient to destabilize marriages.

### E. Marital Law and the Status of Women

The law in Israel gives authority over personal issues to semiautonomous religious judicial systems of the recognized religious communities. Cases are tried according to the religious laws of each denomination. This is one of the reasons why conservative fundamentalist elements within the non-Jewish religions sometimes support Jewish religious parties, and even vote for them. Opponents of religious rule over personal issues sometimes refer to this as the "unholy alliance."

Marriage and divorce issues of Jews are, therefore, largely determined by the religious Halachic law, although the civil law may also be resorted to in issues of division of property and custody of children. For a secular Jew, the patriarchal nature of the Halachic law creates an asymmetrical and undesirable power balance between the marriage partners.

This situation should not be fully attributed to the power of religious politics. They have at least the passive support

### Table 4

**Couples Who Married in Israel and Divorced, by Year of Marriage and Selected Periods of the Duration of the Marriage**

| Elapsed Time: | Cumulative Percentages of Divorcing Couples[1] | | | |
|---|---|---|---|---|
| | 2 Years | 6 Years | 9 Years | 12 Years |
| **Years Married:** | | | | |
| 1964-1967 | 2.7 | 6.0 | 7.5 | 8.9 |
| 1968-1969 | 2.4 | 5.4 | 7.5 | 8.8 |
| 1970-1971 | 2.4 | 5.6 | 7.5 | 9.2 |
| 1972-1973 | 2.4 | 5.8 | 7.9 | 9.6 |
| 1974-1975 | 2.6 | 6.6 | 8.7 | 10.4 |
| 1976-1977 | 2.5 | 6.9 | 8.9 | 10.7 |
| 1978-1979 | 2.9 | 7.2 | 9.4 | 11.0 |
| 1980-1981 | 2.7 | 6.9 | 9.3 | |
| 1982-1983 | 2.7 | 7.1 | | |
| 1984-1985 | 2.6 | 6.6 | | |
| 1986-1987 | 2.9 | | | |
| 1988-1989 | 2.2 | | | |

[1] The formula used is: Number of couples divorcing after the specified interval from marriage period divided by the number of couples who married in a specific period times 100.

of large segments of the secular majority. Attempts to create a situation in which secular civil marriages will be recognized under the law have been defeated several times under different governments. The claim of orthodox Jews, who are a minority, that this will create a schism within the nation that will end up in a disaster, strikes a chord in the heart of many nonobservant Jews. On the other hand, several developments suggest that the power of the religious establishment is diminishing (see below).

Jewish religious laws and the practice of the religious courts place women in a highly undesirable position for those who do not accept the canonic tenets. They cannot be judges in the rabbinical courts or even testify officially; they can only present their case. According to the Jewish religious laws, the men have more sexual freedom, even within a marriage. The husband is the grantor of a divorce and the wife is the acceptor. Even the religious courts cannot force a husband to receive a divorce against his will. On the other hand, there are several reasons why a divorce can be enforced on a women, one of them being adultery. As the duty to procreate is placed on the man, he may be granted permission to marry a second wife, when his first one is infertile and refuses to accept a divorce after ten years of marriage.

### F. The Incidence of Oral and Anal Sex

Although anal intercourse was proscribed by law until recently, the restriction was almost never applied to heterosexual couples. A prosecution dealing with a heterosexual couple did result in a ruling by the then-Legal Advisor and Chief Prosecutor, that strongly restricted the legal control of sexual issues (see below).

There is no collected data on the prevalence of these practices, but the experience of counselors and therapists point to the fact that all are practiced by significant numbers of couples. It is interesting to note that several subgroups in the Israeli population, Jews and non-Jews, practice heterosexual anal intercourse as a means of keeping an intact hymen and as a birth control measure, where the loss of one and the appearance of the other can be highly stigmatizing, damaging, or even dangerous.

The approach of orthodox Judaism is expressed in the fact that it frowns upon these practices, but does not proscribe them. A Talmudic story illustrates this approach very clearly, although using metaphorical language. A woman approached one of the sages with a complaint: "I set a table for my husband and he turned it around." The sage answered: "What can I do, daughter, and the scriptures permits him." There is a question whether the story deals with the issue of anal sex or with vaginal rear entry, but at least some of the commentators agree that anal sex is the issue. This can be perceived on one hand as ambivalence, but on the other as a realistic view of human nature.

## 6. Homoerotic, Homosexual, and Bisexual Behaviors

### A. The Legal Situation

Until recently, homosexuality—or rather anal intercourse (sodomy), including heterosexual anal sex—was illegal in Israel. This was an inheritance of the British colonial penal code of 1936. According to gay organizations, victimization of homosexuals on the basis of this law was frequent.

Changes have occurred gradually and evolutionarily, starting in the early 1960s. Despite the illegality of anal intercourse, the then-Legal Advisor to the government and Chief Prosecutor and later Supreme Court Judge, H. Cohen, ruled that sexual intercourse between consenting adults, in private, cannot be a basis for prosecution. Since 1972, five attempts had been made by members of different parties to strike this sodomy statute from the penal code. In 1988, a political opportunity allowed its revocation. An amendment to the Equal Opportunity Law passed in 1990 also protects the rights of homosexuals to employment.

The attempts to change the law were accompanied by both public campaigns and many changes in public mood toward homosexuals and homosexuality. Until the mid-1970s, the IDF discharged homosexuals for psychiatric incompatibility and/or for being a security risk. This was changed prior to the 1988 legal change, and the IDF made several arrangements that allow homosexuals to serve without being exposed to undue difficulties.

Currently, several issues are being contested in the courts, mainly rights of cohabiting males that are usually granted to spouses under the rulings of common-law marriages. The issue is not as simple as it looks on first sight, especially when considering the regulations governing the pension rights of spouses when the principal owner of the rights dies. Male spouses have smaller pension rights as survivors than females. In the case of cohabiting gay men, this will give the couple an economic advantage over heterosexual couples.

## B. Public Atmosphere Concerning Homosexuality

Several factors combine to make issues of homosexuality very difficult to cope with:

1. The political power of the orthodox-religious sector within the Jewish population and the opposition/respect ambivalence of the secular sector are major factors. While shifting from viewing homosexuality as a crime to medicalizing it, the orthodox religious still strongly opposes its public sanction.
2. The high sex-role polarization in Israel is part of the perceived centrality of gender differences that have both cultural origin and social importance. Tolerance of Israelis to homosexuality is inversely related to their sex-role polarization, and lower than that of American students living in Israel in proportion to the differences in sex-role polarization. Homosexuality, especially male homosexuality, threatens the world picture of two dichotomized genders.
3. Homosexuality is perceived as incompatible with the familial structure, which is of central importance within Israeli society.

In early 1993, a gay/lesbian conference was held in the Knesset (Israeli Parliament), despite strong protests from members of religious and right-wing parties. Public response to the conference, and to the personalities who discussed their difficulties, created further changes in both attitudes and practice.

A still problematic issue is that of open gay cohabitation. Although possible and prevalent, many people feel uncomfortable about it, and some express opinions that this is part of homosexual activism attempting to influence heterosexuals.

[*Update 2002*: Jerusalem saw its first "gay/lesbian pride parade" and outdoor party in a public park on June 8, 2002. Despite strong protests from orthodox Jews, approximately 4,000 homosexual Israelis recognized Jerusalem's sanctity to Jews, Christians, and Muslims with a blessing in Hebrew, English, and Arabic, and then marched under rainbow flags and balloons provided by city officials. Similar parades have been held in recent years in the predominantly secular Tel-Aviv, where gays are more accepted and can socialize at an assortment of cafes, clubs, and bars that cater to them. There are only a handful of such gathering places in Jerusalem, where the first local gay community center opened in 1999 (Greenberg 2002). (*End of update by R. T. Francoeur*)]

## C. Homosexuality in Sex Education

Despite the fact that homosexuality is part of the sex-education curriculum, and several units deal with homosexuality in general and with homophobia in particular, it seems that both school administrations and sex educators still find it uncomfortable to deal with the issues properly. Many youths, therefore, go through school without encountering issues of homosexuality in sex education, a fact that in itself constitutes a very strong message to both homosexual and heterosexual youth, and especially to those who are still ambivalent about their orientation or wonder about it. Adolescents uncertain of their sexual orientation or gender identity will hardly find support within the school system, as there is no systematic training and recommendations on how to deal with these issues. Normative pressures to conform are high.

An interesting difficulty in facilitating issues of homosexuality in the schools was encountered during the training process of sex educators. Several educators justified their reluctance to deal with homosexuality, expressing fear of their own biases or stereotypical thoughts. Facilitators from the Association for Individual Rights, the Israeli equivalent of a gay task force, supported this position, claiming that only gay people are sufficiently unbiased and sensitive enough to facilitate educational programs on homosexuality.

## 7. Gender Diversity and Transgender Issues

Gender-conflicted persons find it difficult to be evaluated and cared for in an organized and controlled way. There is not one center that has a comprehensive program for sexually conflicted people, and the authors know of several occasions that surgical interventions were accomplished without going through a protocol of evaluation/care/treatment. Other cases, where the psychiatric and psychosocial questions were resolved properly, had to go abroad for the surgical procedures. Professionals may be wary to raise the issues, for fear of invoking restrictive regulations that will even lower the ability to supply the needs of these people.

## 8. Significant Unconventional Sexual Behaviors

### A. Coercive Sex

The categories in the criminal records of the *Statistical Abstracts* do not distinguish between subcategories of sexual crime and include sexual abuse, incest, and rape under sexual offenses. It is agreed by police, researchers, and activists alike that sexual offenses are probably one of the most underreported crimes. There is some disagreement as to the extent of underreporting as well as to the definition of criminal sexual offenses.

*Sexual Harassment*

The special circumstances of service in the army may create a convenient atmosphere and even stimulate sexual harassment. Since most officers in the three lowest ranks of IDF are not career soldiers, but extending their compulsory service, they are selected from the general mainstream of Israeli youth. Because IDF is in active combat, the selection of male noncommissioned officers (NCOs) and commissioned officers is based on, among other things, aggressiveness, charisma, initiative, and improvisation. These same officers, who are also in the closest working relationship with both men and women of the rank and file, are also older by two to five years, as compared to the compulsory service women—and in addition, are in a position of authority. Add to this the fact that IDF is organized mainly around values that are traditionally identified as male, and one gets an environment in which women are at a disadvantage. This creates situations that have a potential for sexual harassment on the one hand and manipulative relationships on the other.

There is another situation affecting older male officers of higher rank who are usually married. In combat units, the commanders are in direct daily contact with enlisted soldiers. As one of them phrased it in a group situation: "We grow older all the time, but they always remain at the same age, and we have to compete with them all the time." The context of this remark clearly indicated that women were part of the competition. It is unclear whether these officers are only in a power position or also in a very vulnerable one. Such environments and motivations have high potential for abuse of power.

The official stand of the army concerning harassment or misconduct is strong, with several structural arrangements that attempt to counterbalance the potential for abuse. First, all women's dormitories are out of bounds for men, including the officers commanding the camps. On any official supervisory visit, a male officer must be accompanied by an officer of the female corps. All female soldiers have direct access to an NCO or an officer of the female corps whose source of authority comes from an independent chain of command headed by a woman general. Complaints of sexual harassment, or any other issue of a sexual nature, are dealt with independently by the authority under which the woman is serving—the female corps—and if necessary, by the military police and prosecution. A highly publicized case is that of a general commanding the navy who was dismissed from the IDF for misconduct the day after he was acquitted in court of rape charges for lack of supporting evidence.

Despite this, it seems that harassment is prevalent and is a source of concern to both women and the military establishment. In a structurally male, aggressively oriented organization, there is strong ambivalence in treating sexual harassment issues, and there are documented cases of attempted minimalizing of complaints, especially when they concern officers with high military potential.

The difficulty lies in what is construed as harassment in the eyes of male and female soldiers. Moreover, many young women find it very flattering, even important, that high-prestige men in the immediate environment are attracted to them. There are also cases where such situations are used manipulatively by the women, this mainly with younger officers.

Several educational efforts are now in process to inform both genders about their rights and about the feelings and points of view of the two genders on this issue. It is believed that legal as well as educational efforts are urgent because, beside the individual aspect, sexual harassment can be used as a means to keep a disadvantaging power balance.

[*Update 2001*: In 2001, accusations of sexual harassment where brought up by a 23-year-old woman against a government minister and a political leader of his party. The man, a former army general and a Minister of Defense in a previous government denied the accusations. Police investigations prompted two other women to come forward, and a three-count indictment was submitted to the Knesset in order to revoke his immunity from prosecution. The case resulted in a strong public campaign against sexual harassment, especially in the military service.

[The issue of sexual harassment was also raised when several prominent therapists were accused of sexual abuse by clients. A psychologist was convicted of abusing female patients under a pretext of a treatment method. Accusations were also made in the press against another therapist, an out-of-the-closet homosexual and media expert of marriage and family, two years after his death. The latest case, in which hidden cameras and taping were used by one of the television investigative programs, involved a sex therapist who allegedly used the ruse of training males to become surrogates to sexually abuse them. This case was still pending in early 2001, but it brought into focus, along with the issue of sexual abuse by therapists in general, and sex therapists in particular, the issues of the precarious relationship between the media, the law enforcement authorities, and justice. (*End of update by R. A. Shtarkshall and M. Zemach*)]

### Incest

In Jewish tradition, incest is such a heinous act that, according to the *Halachah*, it is one of the only three crimes that a person should prefer being killed rather than commit. This may explain the shroud of silence and shame covering the issue of incest. For many years, this was an unheard-of crime.

In recent years, the changes in public climate, the establishment of child/youth investigators, and the change in the rules of evidence allowing the investigator to testify for the child, have increased the number of cases in which incest is reported and prosecuted.

Unfortunately, charges of incest (like battering) are sometimes used as weapons in attempts to get vacating orders and/or custody between divorcing couples.

There are some interesting research questions that need to be clarified, which will have strong bearing on preventive intervention and treatment: first, the differences between the legal definitions of family and of incest in different cultures prevailing in Israel; second, the contribution of the increase in nonbiological parents or siblings living together to the increase in the phenomenon.

### Rape

A marked change in public attitude in Israel toward rape and rapists occurred in the 1980s and early 1990s. This is mainly because of the activities of rape-crisis centers founded by the feminist movement and to their political and public campaigns. These campaigns resulted in changes in the rape and sexual assault laws, mainly the abolition of the need for additional material or other evidence, to that of the victim, in order to convict a sexual offender, an increase in the punishment range given within the law, and a redefinition of grave assaults done with the help of a weapon or gang rape. There were also some changes in the rules of evidence, making it impossible to bring into the trial the previous sexual behavior of an accuser or a witness.

There were also changes in the treatment of survivors. Special examination centers were arranged in emergency rooms in hospitals in each of the big urban centers, in which the staff were trained both by police, by professionals, and by the volunteers of the rape-crisis centers. There are special courses for police investigators, and the volunteers of the centers are allowed to accompany survivors throughout the police investigations.

These changes, which are by and large positive, nevertheless raise some problematic points: first, how to maintain the right to a fair trial and the principle that people are innocent until their crime is proved beyond reasonable doubt; second, the mixing of political and educational work aimed at eradicating rape, with prevention work in a society were rape is still prevalent, with crisis intervention, and with treatment of survivors, which can create some confusion and ambivalent messages.

A study presented at an international conference on victimology found some interesting phenomena that could cause some concern in this direction. The study compared the attitudes of two groups of professionals whose job was to treat rape survivors, police investigators, and emergency-room rape specialists, with those of helping-professions students and those of the volunteers of the rape-crisis centers. It was found that on several scales, the rape-crisis volunteers were more likely to take extreme positions, even when compared only to the women in the other groups. For example, they strongly disagreed with any assertion that there is a possible environmental involvement in the probability of rape, an attitude that seems to be problematic for prevention work. Despite the fact that they were one of the smallest groups, the standard deviation of their opinion scales was the smallest, indicating a very uniform norm. There is at least one case in which a woman who confessed in court that she had made a false accusation of rape against a man cited the pressure by the volunteers as the reason for the filing of the complaint. One has to be careful with such an allegation, because it may be an attempt to lighten the personal load.

Another issue of concern, debated in public, was the slogan that "every man is a potential rapist" proposed for a public service announcement spot. When challenged, it turned out that the intended messages were that one cannot distinguish by appearances a rapist from other men, and that rapists are "ordinary" people. While in itself a political statement open to argument, this is a far cry from the initial message, which was understood by many men and women alike as stating that in every man there exists a potential for rape.

[*Sexual Commerce and Sexual Slavery*

[*Update 2001*: For several years, especially since the waves of immigration from the former USSR began, which also brought with it some of the organized and unorganized crime, there were anecdotal reports of women imported from these areas for sexual commerce. As most of these women are illegal immigrants and illegal workers in the country, they are smuggled in as pilgrims to the Christian holy places, tourists, visitors of fictitious relatives, or through other coverups. If caught by the police, these women become victims again, as they are deported back to their countries as illegal employees. In early 2001, a human rights watch organization published a report, which attempted to describe the extent and implication of the phenomenon, and called it, justifiably, sex slavery. The report also condemned the Israeli authorities for not doing enough to eradicate this phenomenon. The authorities claimed that it is the human rights issue that prevents them from taking extreme measures against the perpetrators, because offers of immunity to the women for testifying against their "owners" are rejected by them when these ruthless criminals threaten their families in their counties of origin. (*End of update by R. A. Shtarkshall and M. Zemach*)]

## B. Prostitution

### The Legal Situation

Israeli law on prostitution is somewhat complicated. Prostitution itself is not outlawed, but soliciting is, and so are the operating of an establishment used for prostitution and living off the proceedings of prostitution.

As a result, there are several arrangements through which sex workers sell their services and there are "classes" of sex workers. Lowest on the ladder are the "street" or outdoor prostitutes, many of whom also perform the sexual act outside. Higher up are sex workers operating in hotels, especially in tourist hotels, and those operating through some of the escort services that are currently freely publicized

with advertisements on the fringe of legality. So, also, are massage parlors, which became a euphemism for sexual services with allusions to "relaxation."

There have been several media articles describing another kind of arrangement, which is reportedly limited to students, professionals, and middle-class women "supported" by a few men who are regular and exclusive clients. According to the reports, these arrangements are usually temporary, particularly among students.

Several attempts to change the legal situation by licensing prostitutes, putting them under medical surveillance, and allowing them to keep places of business, have failed mainly because of the opposition of the religious parties in the Parliament.

### Pimping: The Exploitation of Female Prostitutes

Although the pimps have traditionally belonged to the lower echelons of individual male criminals, they get most of the profits from prostitution. The women under their domination are kept in line by threats and the use of force.

There were several reports of specialists "hunting" young, runaway adolescents around the central urban bus stations, befriending them, and offering them shelter, and gradually moving them into prostitution. A more recent phenomenon in Israel involves importing women from the former USSR under forged papers and employing them in prostitution. This operation has many of the characteristics of organized crime, and the women are totally at the mercy of their "employers," as they are in a strange county with no valid documents.

### Homosexual Prostitution

Several areas in the urban centers are known to be mainly or exclusively the territory of male prostitutes. Several reports have shown that, as with female prostitution, many of the sex workers are early or middle adolescents. Apparently, despite the fact that homosexuality is no longer a criminal offense, the police are checking constantly on these areas, and there were some reports of them keeping "pink lists" of male prostitutes. These reports were denied by the police authorities.

### Transvestites

Several reports have revealed that some of the female sex workers are really male transvestites who are not gay and who do not cater to a gay clientele. These sex workers, some of whom have undergone hormonal treatment to grow breasts, pretend to their clients to be female prostitutes. They mainly provide fellatio; when asked to perform vaginal sex, they depend on their ability to stimulate the client to orgasm prior to penetration.

## C. Pornography and Erotica

### The Legal Situation

Until recently, Israel had at least nominal censorship on the theater and cinema. Written and audio materials were regulated only on grounds of security and not moral ones, and only public pressure created some restrictions. Abolishing censorship on the theater and cinema in 1990, part of an ongoing process of increasing the boundaries of freedom of expression as a basic human right, allows the production and dissemination of explicit sexual acts, and of violent ones, in print, film, and video formats.

Currently, despite the fact that there are fewer restrictions on moral grounds, there is a relatively recent law about displaying offensive materials in public that allows people to sue for damages if their feelings are hurt by specific items. Until now, the attempts to use this law have been restricted to religious issues. It seems that this does not include films or items otherwise displayed for a fee, especially if the public is warned about the presence of sexual materials. This is still vague, since different aspects of the law have to be tried through a full cycle of litigation before its extent and effectiveness are established.

Restrictions on importing pornographic materials in commercial quantities by customs control are inefficient, and developments in satellite television and videotaping make them obsolete. This, combined with the rise in VCRs during the 1980s and cable television in the early 1990s, expose much wider segments of the population to both soft and hard pornography. Another prominent development concerning the public treatment of sexual issues is the increased commercialization of sex that started in the mid-1980s and intensified in the early 1990s.

### Response of the Religious Sector

There is opposition to the increase of explicit materials aired in public from the religious sector. The more orthodox do not allow TV sets in homes and would shun those who do. Their reactions toward the treatment of sexual issues in public range from the economic boycotting of products promoted by what they consider offensive depictions in their advertisements (including dinosaurs!) to the defacing of commercial display windows and the burning down of bus stops. Because the glass/plastic walls of bus stops in Israel are used for displaying advertisements, conservative religious youths mounted a campaign of destroying bus stops displaying "offensive" ads. They later managed to persuade both advertisers and advertising firms, through boycotting, to change their policy and display different ads in areas where there is a large population of ultra orthodox.

### The Response of the Secular Public

Secular Jews are mainly concerned with two other aspects of pornography: sexual depictions that are demeaning or threatening to segments of the population and the effects of pornography on children and adolescents.

The influence of pornography on children and early adolescents is a source of concern to some parents, psychologists, and educators. Because sex is a very private matter, children and adolescents who are exposed to pornography have no objective criteria to compare it to and may believe that many or most of the things shown are part of normative behavior of adults. This may cause some difficulties in their emotional reactions to adult and parental sexuality. They are also unaware of the manipulations that are done in making these films, and that can create problems of self-image or fear regarding the sexual organs. There has been speculation that several cases of sexual violence among adolescents, especially those involved with group sex, are related to pornography. Despite the fact that there is no hard evidence to support this assertion, it cannot be ignored and should be researched appropriately.

Two issues are at the core of the secular political discourse. First, which of the following is the most prominent feature of pornography: the commercialized and dehumanized treatment of the human body, the linking of sex and violence, or its use by heterosexual males to dominate women and to perpetuate a sexist and heterosexist society? The second issue focuses on how to counteract the pernicious effects of pornography and whether censorship or social control are a remedy, or a worse disease.

### Sex Education and Pornography

Several efforts are being made to incorporate units dealing more effectively with pornography and its impact within the sex education programs in schools. The basic approach is that since there is very little hope of lowering the exposure of children and early adolescents to pornography unless there is a major social change, it is important to give them the skills to deal with its potential effects. The concern is focused on the explicitness of such units and on the claim that they may raise the interest in pornography or lower the barrier to exposure.

### Paid Services by Telephone

Privatization of the telecommunications monopoly in 1990 brought with it many new initiatives for marketing new services. One of these was caller-paid telephone (056) numbers offering medical advice, astrology maps, practical information, and in the sexual area, advice, introduction services, party lines, and sexual-talk bulletin boards. Each of these meets the different needs of people with sexual interests.

At their best, sexual-advice services supply minimal sexual information and a referral service. Callers have no idea of the expertise, knowledge, or training of the persons who provide advice. Some services attempt to do counseling, not the crisis intervention of hotlines, but on a more extensive, sometimes therapeutic level. It is questionable how helpful these procedures are. The service does supply the very strong need of some people who suffer from sexual doubts or problems, the need to get advice without the risk of exposure. If done properly, it could be helpful; however, it can also postpone the time that people will reach out for needed help. Also, lay people exposed to easy access and bad practices cloaked in professional claims may later doubt the ability of any professionals to give help.

Introduction services and party lines, unless they serve minors, have very little potential for damage. They mainly give an opportunity for people to create relationships at a safe distance with as many defenses as they wish. It also allows people some safety measures prior to creating non-mediated interactions.

The sex-talk, fantasy-activated lines operate on a different level, something that many people are unaware of. These services allow people to act out their fantasies in a partial manner, while interacting with a supposedly real person at a distance, allowing the imagination to add the missing elements of reality. For some people, especially sexually distressed ones, this could erode the line between fantasy and reality, creating a few features of virtual reality that may increase the distress instead of alleviating it. Another problematic feature is that commercial considerations demand that the service providers play the stereotypical roles, many of them demeaning and degrading ones, in order to please the customers. Whether these act as cathartic experiences or add themselves into a positive feedback loop is still a question.

Commercial sexual services ignore their potential for harm. They claim they sell a service that no one is forced to buy, and therefore should not be regulated in the name of freedom of speech. It is possible that serious studies undertaken jointly by the service providers and sexuality researchers, followed by self-regulation, will provide an optimal solution. Strong demands are being made by many organizations to limit the access to these services to customers who explicitly request it. Legal efforts are currently being challenged by the industry in courts on the basis of their rights to free speech.

## 9. Contraception, Abortion, and Population Planning

### A. Contraception

Modern contraceptives are easily accessible through several outlets within the health system: mainly the Mother and Child Primary Health Care (MCH) and ob/gyn clinics of the sick funds, including outpatient clinics in obstetrics departments. There is no legal restriction on the use of contraceptives.

### Adolescents

Despite the availability of contraceptives, several studies have found that the rate of their use by adolescents at first intercourse, and in general, is very low. One found that only half of the sexually active boys and a third of the girls were using contraceptives regularly. Another reported that only 40% of sexually active adolescents have ever used contraceptives. The level of knowledge, as measured in these studies, was not a limiting condition, as it was much higher than the rate of use.

A frequent characteristic of those with early sexarche is that they either use no contraception or rely on the traditional methods of withdrawal or rhythm, and that they are also lower contraceptors later on. Not only do they start without contraceptives, but they also take longer to achieve adequate protection. Whether there is any causal relationship at all between the two phenomena, and in which direction, is a very important research topic, but it seems to be consistent with the view that many of those initiating intercourse at a younger age do so as acting out or under personal and social pressures, and are therefore more prone to conflicts and their sequels. The fact that kibbutz youth with more egalitarian and permissive attitudes are also better contraceptors adds support to these interpretations; see Section 13C, National, Religious, and Ethnic Minorities, The Kibbutz Movement, for details.

### Married Women

Use of contraceptives among married Israeli Jewish women is given in Table 5 and demonstrates some of our arguments.

Sterilization is frowned on in the Jewish tradition. While more than two thirds of married Jewish women use medi-

### Table 5

**Current Contraceptive Use among Married Israeli Jewish Women (Aged 22-44 Years, Exposed Women Only,[1] 1988)**

| Method of Contraception | Number of Women (*n*) | Percent of Exposed | Percent of Total |
|---|---|---|---|
| **Effective methods** | **794** | **59** | **47** |
| Pill | 259 | 19 | 15 |
| IUD | 519 | 39 | 31 |
| Sterilization (male and female) | 16 | 1 | 1 |
| **Less-effective methods** | **138** | **10** | **8** |
| Condom | 66 | 5 | 4 |
| Diaphragm | 65 | 5 | 4 |
| Spermicides only | 7 | 0 | 0 |
| **Traditional methods** | **260** | **19** | **15** |
| Withdrawal | 175 | 13 | 10 |
| Rhythm | 71 | 5 | 4 |
| Others | 14 | 1 | 1 |
| **No method** | **152** | **11** | **9** |
| **Subtotal (exposed)** | **1344** | **99** | **80** |
| **Nonexposed** | **346** | | **21** |
| **Grand Total** | **1680** | | **101** |

[1] Exposure to contraception was determined by three independent variables: not-pregnant, not trying to become pregnant, and currently engaging in sexual intercourse.

cally prescribed contraceptives, the use of both male and female sterilization is less than 1%, very low compared to other industrial countries with comparable health systems. The demand for sterilization is low because of the importance of childbearing and other issues. But, even when requested, there are many barriers a man or woman needs to overcome to achieve their desire. The reasons given by physicians are the irreversibility of the process and distrust of the ability of people to make irreversible decisions without later regrets.

### Professional Control

The licensing, sale, and fitting of contraceptives are controlled through medical and medicopharmaceutical regulations. This highlights another issue, the power struggle between professions over controlling the availability and use of contraception. While in several Western industrial countries, IUDs and diaphragms are fitted by paramedical professionals, in Israel this is still the absolute prerogative of physicians. Insertion of IUDs is the only invasive procedure that is restricted by regulation to one type of physician, a gynecologist. Thirty years ago, the practice in most clinics was that before being fitted for an IUD, a woman had to have three or four children; later, the number came down to two and even to one. Today, most clinics still refuse to fit an IUD for nulliparous women, especially unmarried ones, on the basis of good medical practice and the wish not to endanger their fertility.

Other social restrictions are also exerted mainly through the medical/health system. A more subtle aspect of the professional power play is the disagreement about the role of psychosocial counseling in the fitting of contraceptives and the success or failure of their use.

### Family Planning

Fertility and family size are mainly a personal and familial decision shaped by normative forces, but they are also part of the public domain and strongly dependent on policy decisions, laws and regulations, authorizations, and financial support or constraints. Family planning and contraception in Israel can be viewed as part of a multidimensional domain built of several axes, of which the most important ones are: modernity, nationalism, and religiosity. While some people view religiosity as belonging to the axis of modernity, this is not always the case in Israel. While among Muslim women, high fertility is inversely associated mainly with modernity (women's education being a major component), in the Jewish population, it is mainly associated with religiosity. Among Jewish women, one finds a defined group of highly educated, professional women who espouse a combination of religiosity with nationalistic ideology, and pride themselves on having more than five or six children.

It is important to note here that while the commandment to "be fruitful and multiply" is taken almost literally, Jewish *Halachah*, which strongly opposes family planning, allows the use of contraceptives on the basis of individual need within the rather wide Halachic formulation of *Pikuach Nefesh* ("danger to the soul"). Moreover, some features of Jewish religious law create unique situations. The fact that many commandments, including "do not spill your semen in vain," bind men only, and allow women to use contraceptives, provided there is no direct damage to the men's sperm. Thus, while vasectomy, withdrawal, condoms, and spermicides are almost universally forbidden, pills, IUDs, and even diaphragms can be used within boundaries.

Apart from the personal position and family decision making, the public stand of Jewish orthodoxy has always been against organized family planning and the development of fertility control and contraceptive services.

### Public Policy and the Family Planning Movement

The movement for birth control or birth planning, and the utilization of modern contraceptives as an integral part of it, are relatively recent in Israel. The Israeli Family Planning Association (IFPA) was founded in 1966. Mother and Child Primary Health Care clinics (MCH), the mainstay of public health in Israel, received an official mandate to deal with birth control issues only in 1972.

The predominant approach to birth control and family planning in the late 1960s and 1970s was a mixture of demographic and health approaches with social/ethnic ideology. The main features concerned the national melting-pot ideology regarding immigrant groups, and the wish to better the situation of the groups with a low socioeconomic status through the control of their family size. From today's perspective, the latter component was not only flawed in its premises, but also parentalistic in its nature (Ronny A. Shtarkshall has coined the term *parentalistic*, as opposed to *paternalistic*, because of its less-sexist connotations). This approach was in conflict with two other important axes that strongly influenced family planning—the religious and nationalistic, both of which were pronatalist. Nevertheless, the strong medicalized approach to health in general, and pride in medical professionalism, resulted in one of the first field studies that heralded the introduction of IUDs for worldwide use.

Professionals in several disciplines, including health professionals, were dissatisfied with the medical/demographic framework and favored adoption of a human/family-rights approach. Implementation of this new approach has minimized the authority of the professionals, and focused on enabling the clients to take charge of their own needs and on adapting the counseling process to the need of specific groups. However, responses to recent immigrants from the former USSR and Ethiopia have shown that old habits die very slowly and can be resurrected easily when some service providers decide that they "know better" and intervene without appropriate preparation and adequate concern for sociocultural factors.

### Client-Oriented Services

The initiation of special counseling services for youth by the IFPA was also a step toward developing services adapted to the clients' needs. These are not only more accessible services that meet the unique needs of this population, but also a declaration that the sexual experiences of youth are not intrinsically negative. The informal approach, the environment, and the mode of counseling in these advisory centers aim at minimizing the feelings of adult social control of youth sexual behavior. Currently, many municipal services, sick funds, and other NGOs have established such services, so that the IFPA is phasing out direct service to youth and going into an advisory training role for developing such services.

### Groups at Risk for Unplanned Pregnancies

Some service providers and organizations view the 19% of the couples who want to postpone or terminate fertility, but use traditional, inefficient methods, as one of the main targets for family planning education. Several studies have shown that most of the married couples belonging to this group really want more-effective contraception, but are hindered from using it by lack of knowledge, suspicion, fear, and subjective difficulties in accessing services.

Unmarried adolescents and young adults, including soldiers in the service, students, and recent immigrants from the former USSR, are also the foci of family planning ef-

forts, because of underutilization or misuse of contraceptives and the high rate of unwanted pregnancies. (See Sections 13A and 13D, National, Religious, and Ethnic Minorities, for issues of family planning and contraception among Muslim women and couples, and among Russian and Ethiopian immigrants.)

As much as the contribution of the family planning services is appreciated, it cannot be ignored that the convergence of fertility rates among the second-generation immigrants was largely achieved, not through their action, but rather through intermarriages of Jews of different ethnic origin, the action of a universal, largely egalitarian, educational system, the unifying force of the IDF, and entry of women into the paid workforce.

## B. Unmarried Motherhood

Looking at the development of never-married mothers in the recent years, one concludes that, in Israel, for an increasing number of women, the drive toward childbearing is stronger than the convention that motherhood is only accepted within marriage.

The rate of live births per 1,000 never-married women aged 15 to 44 rose by 70% from 2.3 per 1,000 in the early 1970s to 3.9 per 1,000 in 1989. But the crude rates are not as informative as the age-specific rates: While the rates for the two younger age groups, 15 to 19 and 20 to 24, actually dropped (from 1.4 to 0.8, down 43%, and from 3.4 to 2.9, down 15%, respectively), the rates for the older aged groups increased significantly in the last two decades. In the two decades between 1970 and 1989, the rate has more than doubled for the 25-to-29 age group, from 4.1 to 9.1 per 1,000, tripled for the 30-to-34 group from 6.8 to 20.3 per 1,000, and more than quadrupled for the 35-to-39 group, 5.2 to 21.9 per 1,000.

The drop in the rate of birth of unmarried young women is probably the result of Article 2 in the abortion law that allows legal termination of pregnancy to unmarried women (see under Abortion below). Most abortions of unmarried women are concentrated in the 15-to-24 age group, where a sizable proportion of the sexually active women are still not only unmarried, but also in unfavorable conditions to marry or give birth. Since abortion is also available to unwed older women, the lower rate of abortion and higher rate of unwed motherhood among older women reflects the need of older unmarried women to exercise their right to childbearing.

By Jewish law, a child born to an unwed mother is legal, and there is no stigma attached to his or her birthright. It is the mother who carries the burden of shame, according to the religious ruling and much popular belief, and not the child. Obviously, an increasing number of women are willing to pay the price or do not feel the stigma.

There is no available information on the proportion of unwed women who choose to become pregnant by sexual intercourse or artificial insemination. Some institutions perform artificial insemination by donors with no requirement that the recipient be married, but several court cases reveal that at least some of women prefer impregnation by intercourse.

The issue came into public attention when women sued the fathers, some of them public figures, for child support. Several such cases included signed contracts waiving child support as part of the agreement by the men to impregnate the women. These contracts were declared void by the courts because the court is bound to decide in the best interests of the child even if both parents agree otherwise. In several cases, there were claims that the women misrepresented either their fertility status or the fact that they were using a specific contraceptive. The courts declared this argument to be irrelevant because, even if proven true, it had no bearing on the interests or the legal status of the child.

Several such involved fathers have formed an organization, "Fathers Not by Choice," and now lobby for the rights of fathers. They contend that the prevailing situation, giving them no custody rights in such cases, and in many cases no other rights, constitutes sex discrimination.

## C. Abortion

Several times in the short history of Israel, abortion has been a major public and political issue, with highly emotional and ideological arguments that embody tensions between different segments of the society, and a discrepancy between public policy and private practices. While playing a prominent role, the element of women's rights to their bodies was not as dominant as in some other countries. This may be because the issue of abortion touches on other issues highly important to the Israeli public: relations between religion and state, national identity and aspirations, and the collective memory of the annihilation of more than half of the Jewish people of Europe in the Holocaust.

Jewish religious laws, the *Halachah*, give precedence to the life of the mother over the life of the embryo/fetus until that moment of delivery when the head is fully out. An abortion because of danger to the life of the mother can be accepted by religious authorities, but only after consulting a Halachic authority. All other abortions are perceived to be murder. Abortion is presented by its opponents as the ongoing denial of life of its future children to a society that had lost one third of its people, 1.5 million of whom were children, and continues to suffer loss of young life by warfare and terrorism.

It has not helped that the professional view of family planning efforts within certain organizations providing abortions was predominantly biomedical. As a result, women seeking abortions were sometimes looked down upon as ignorant or failing to use medically available contraceptives properly. There was a feeling that they should have known better. This view is encountered mainly toward young unmarried women, though in the past it included women of low socioeconomic status who had already had several children. Recently, this attitude was revived in public discussion by the increased demand for abortions from the former USSR immigrants.

It is also possible that some vested economic interests were involved in the opposition to legalizing abortions. Some professionals objected to providing abortions in public hospitals as a waste of public money, while they or their colleagues were performing them privately for a fee.

During the abortion debate, reproductive health data was frequently misused. Those who objected to abortions exaggerated the health risk of abortions—both mortality and the risk to future fertility—as an argument against it. This was mainly done by comparing the mortality and morbidity rates from induced abortions to the successful prevention of pregnancy by contraceptive use, instead of comparing abortion mortality and morbidity with the risk incurred by carrying the pregnancy to term and its delivery. This argument is also facetious because, despite the fact that Israel has a very low perinatal morbidity and mortality, these are still much higher than the risks of abortions performed according to accepted medical standards.

Legally, abortion is still defined as a felony in the criminal code. As with most laws in Israel, abortions continue to be regulated by British colonial laws. For almost 30 years, 1948 to 1978, the only legal reasons for the performance of legal abortions were purely medical. Nevertheless, illegal abortions were widespread. Oddly enough, almost all the illegal abortions were performed by licensed gynecologists or general surgeons under accepted medical standards. Extremely few cases were prosecuted, and these only in cases where a woman lost her life.

Since the mid-1960s, several organizations, mainly human rights activists, the Israeli Family Planning Association, the women's segment of the Histadrut, the labor union, the feminist caucus, and organizations seeking to decrease the political power of the religious over individuals, have united in uncoordinated efforts to change the law. The fact that there was a vast difference between the law and the practice, and that the main barrier to seeking abortion was economic, has played a psychological role in paving the way to the change.

In 1977, the Knesset changed the abortion law (enacted January 1978). The main change was the establishment of hospital committees that could allow the performance of induced abortions under five clauses: age (women under 17 or over 40); pregnancy resulting from out-of-wedlock, adulterous, or unlawful relationships; medical conditions relating to the embryo (genetic or developmental malformations); medical conditions endangering the mother physically and/or mentally; and social or economic hardship.

The law stated explicitly that parental consent is not a condition for performing an abortion on a minor and that seeking abortion is free of regional restrictions on the dispensation of medical services. On the other hand, no physician is required to perform an abortion, even a legally authorized one. The establishment of committees in public and private hospitals that were medically authorized to perform abortions was at the discretion of the hospital management. Several hospitals did not establish such committees because of religious or other ideological reasons. The fact that permission for abortion is granted by a hospital committee does not mean that the hospital is required to perform the abortion. The committees are autonomous in determining their procedures and regulating their activities, provided that each committee includes at least one gynecologist, one social/mental health professional, and one woman. In most committees, the woman was also the social worker, thus combining two functions in one person who also has lower status in medical institutions. Some committees demand that the petitioning woman appear before the committee in person and answer questions; others only review a file prepared by the social worker. Some committees convene only once a week, others meet daily; some are known to be "liberal," while others are "hard."

This differentiation became highly important in 1980, only two years after enactment of the new law, when religious parties succeeded in striking out Article 5 allowing abortions for social or economic hardship. Since then, because there are no regional administrative restrictions on where women can seek an abortion, women have preferred to approach the more liberal committees. Thus, the demand for legal abortions among married women, and their performance, has not changed much in the years following abrogation of Article 5 (see Table 6). Only the reasons for which these abortions were granted have shifted. There was a fourfold increase in granting abortions for physical or mental medical reasons (from 8 to 36%).

As of late 1994, privately performed, illegal abortions are still performed largely by physicians under medically accepted conditions. The latest estimate by knowledgeable sources is that their number is 5,000 to 7,000 annually, about 25 to 33% of the total number of abortions performed. This estimate is for the period prior to the arrival of the large 1990-1991 immigrant wave from the former USSR (see Section 13D, National, Religious, and Ethnic Minorities).

In 1990, there was an attempt by religious parties to restrict abortions further by reducing the number of hospitals authorized to have committees and perform abortions, and to limit them to public hospitals only. Since the right-wing government at the time was favorable to this attempt for both ideological and political reasons, a coalition of family planning and health professional organizations, the feminist lobby, and human rights activists was needed to defeat this attempt.

Antiabortion organizations are active, especially among youth and among women seeking abortions. Their propaganda disregards the data and claims that every second or third pregnancy is willfully terminated, while the actual number is less than one in five, even if one counts the illegally performed abortions.

The IDF's attitude toward abortions is consistent with the wider tolerance toward premarital sex in late adolescence. In the past, a pregnant soldier was discharged whether she carried the pregnancy to term or terminated it. This caused many female soldiers who wished to continue their service to hide their pregnancy and have illegal abortions. This rule was changed, and currently a pregnant soldier can seek an abortion through the IDF and stay in the service. The rules still give the IDF an option to discharge a woman on the basis of incompatibility. As far as is known, this option is used only in the case of repeat aborters and if other adverse conditions exist.

As noted in Section 9B on unwed mothers, it seems that the decrease of unwed motherhood in the younger age groups is mainly because of the availability of legal abortions to unwed women. It would have been very interesting to be able to estimate how many "forced marriages" were avoided because of the availability of legal abortions to unmarried women. Research in Israel has shown that among marriages that suffer from abusive patterns, the rate of premarital conceptions is by far the strongest associated variable marking the difference between them and divorcing marriages that do not suffer from an abusive pattern.

A significant aspect of abortions in Israel is their cost. Prior to the 1978 law, abortions were very expensive, creating additional hardship for less-well-to-do women. Since 1978, the prices are between $250 and $600, between 40 to 100% of the minimal legal monthly wages. Only abortions performed for medical reasons in one of the public hospitals are covered by the sick funds; the foundation for children run by the Ministry of Welfare pays for abortions for women under 17; all abortions performed on soldiers are covered by the IDF. In all, an estimated 65% of all abortions are paid for by public funds.

Most abortions in Israel are first-trimester abortions by suction and curettage. Most hospitals use general anesthesia during induced abortion in order to minimize the psychological effects on the woman. Very few institutions perform second-trimester abortions (evacuation), mainly because of staff objections. Mortality and morbidity from induced abortions in Israel is very low.

The large immigration from the former USSR starting in 1989 and peaking in 1990-1991 changed the demand for induced abortions and, possibly also, the conditions under which some abortions are performed. First, it is estimated that these immigrant Jews will increase the demand for abortions by about 10% (over their proportion in the overall population). Second, since most Russian women seeking abortion are married, and the cost of out-of-hospital abortions, privately performed by a licensed physician is rather high, there is both statistical and anecdotal evidence indicating these women seek abortions from USSR-immigrant physicians who are unlicensed to practice medicine or surgery in Israel. They charge less for abortions, are highly proficient in their performance, but sometimes perform them in medically problematic conditions.

*[Trends in Termination of Adolescent Pregnancies*

[*Update 2001*: Requests for induced abortions from the hospital authorizing committees, and their outcomes, are reported to the Central Bureau of Statistics. Examination of the trend in the 13 years between 1985 and 1998 reveal that for girls up to age 14 and from age 15 to 19, there is a clear trend of decreasing demand for abortions. Since live births for these age groups have not increased, it is apparent that these youths are protecting themselves with greater success. The conclusion of experts from several fields interviewed for a major series of newspapers articles on this issue was that there is no one cause of this better protection, but an accumulation of several factors: better sex education, the availability of services dedicated to the needs of adolescents, and more social acceptance of adolescents' sexuality, resulting in some adolescents approaching their parents for help in contraception prior to initiating coitus. (*End of update by R. A. Shtarkshall and M. Zemach*)]

## D. Population Trends

### Uniqueness of the Jewish Population

The Jewish population of Israel has the highest total fertility rates (TFR, i.e., the average number of live children expected to be born to a woman during her lifetime, as calculated from the age-specific fertilities) among the Western industrial countries—2.6 for 1991. This fertility is far above that of other major Jewish communities, including Eastern Europe and Latin America, even though both populations are descendants of survivors of the Holocaust (as is a large segment of the Israeli population). This is well above the replacement value and reflects the importance of children in the Israeli-Jewish lifestyle, including but not limited to the orthodox and ultra-orthodox sectors. Among secular Jewish couples in Israel, it seems like the birth of the first two children is taken for granted, and family planning considerations are usually reserved for timing and for additional children.

Also, the second generation of Jews immigrating from different parts of the world to Israel change markedly in less than a generation, so that their fertility patterns resemble the Jewish-Israeli pattern more than the patterns in their countries of origin.

## Table 6

### Induced Terminations of Pregnancies Performed in Hospitals in Israel (1979-89)

| Year | Total Number of Abortions | Rates per 1,000 Women (Ages 15-49) | Rates per 1,000 Live Births |
|------|---------------------------|-------------------------------------|------------------------------|
| 1979 | 15,925 | 17.7 | 17.0 |
| 1980 | 14,708 | 18.0 | 15.6 |
| 1981 | 14,514 | 17.4 | 15.6 |
| 1982 | 16,829 | 19.8 | 17.4 |
| 1983 | 15,593 | 17.9 | 15.8 |
| 1984 | 18,984 | 19.1 | 19.2 |
| 1985 | 18,406 | 18.1 | 18.3 |
| 1986 | 17,110 | 16.8 | 17.2 |
| 1987 | 15,290 | 16.0 | 15.4 |
| 1988 | 15,255 | 15.6 | 15.2 |
| 1989 | 15,216 | 15.2 | 15.1 |
| 1990 | 15,509 | 14.9 | 15.0 |
| 1991 | 15,767 | 15.1 | 14.9 |

*Time Sequence of Fertility Changes*

Despite the just-mentioned facts, the fertility patterns over the last three decades do show a general drop in fertility among all the national and most ethnic groups in Israel, concomitant with modernization and the rise in both economic and educational level (see Table 7).

Closer analysis of the TFR in various Jewish ethnic groups reveals a more complete picture. While there is a consistent drop in the TFR for Jewish mothers born in Asia and Africa, for mothers born in Israel, and those born in Europe and America, there is a rise in the TFR until the first half of the 1970s and then a decline. The overall rate of increase for both latter groups was similar, 0.3 to 0.4 child per mother. If these trends—the rise in age at first marriage, the delay of age at first birth, and the lowering of the desired number of children—continue, the result can be a continuous decrease of the TFR among Jews in Israel. It is hard to predict to what levels they will go and what will be the forces acting to speed, slow, or reverse this trend. Whatever the situation, the TFR of orthodox and ultra-orthodox Jews will be a factor.

*Factors Shaping Israeli Fertility*

Forces shaping Israeli fertility changes in the last 40 years include: modernity, mainly women's education; changes in economic status and perspectives; entrance of women into the labor force; a general downgrading of the collective/national elements within the prevailing ethos; and a concomitant rise in the individualistic achievement-orientation components. Immigration was also a factor: Jewish women from Ethiopia contributed to a TFR rise in 1991, Russian immigrants to a drop in 1990, to where the TFR among Jewish women is below 2.

The pronatalist attitude prevalent in modern Israel explains the socialization toward marriage and parenthood that Israeli adults feel ill at ease to defy. Willed childlessness is not presented as a viable option and childless couples are considered to be in need of help.

*Fertility Services*

A direct consequence of this cultural climate is the demand for fertility services, and especially in vitro fertilization (IVF), as aids to married biological parenthood. In 1993, there was roughly one IVF clinic for every 30,000 Israelis, more than in any other country over the world, and lower by more than a factor of magnitude than the per capita rate in the U.S.A. The research in fertility, and especially in IVF, in Israel is disproportionately high, and several improvements on the methods originated here. Other fertility services are also highly developed in Israel, but the focus is mainly on the biomedical service, with minimal resort to accompanying psychosocial interventions. Several attempts in the latter direction report a marked increase in success rates of the biomedical interventions if they are done in conjunction with the psychosocial ones. Surrogate motherhood is still very rare and complicated by unresolved legal issues.

*Adoption*

Married couples who go down the fertility road to its limits without success resort to adoption. In an effort to protect the rights of the adopted children, adoption procedures in Israel are slow and cumbersome. These efforts sometimes backfire, as children drag for years through institutions, foster homes, and the courts without a stable environment and the ability to form lasting attachments. The processes are somewhat easier when older children or physically or mentally challenged children are involved, but in these cases, the adoption process can be much more difficult.

From the side of the petitioning couples, the waiting and procedures are sometimes intolerable, creating a large market in adoption of foreign children. Romania was a source, until government corruption and news of HIV infection in orphanages blocked this option. In several South American countries, what was a legal if costly process turned into illegal trade in forged documents, kidnapping, and extortion.

# 10. Sexually Transmitted Diseases and HIV/AIDS

## A. Sexually Transmitted Diseases

The public awareness of STDs in Israel in low. Syphilis, chlamydia, gonorrhea, and herpes genitalis are reportable diseases, but this regulation is not strictly enforced and not fully observed. A structural reason for this may be that Israel does not have STD clinics specializing in both care and prevention.

In the late 1960s, an apparent doubling in reported STDs, believed to be caused by the influx of volunteers after the "Six Days' War," caused the Ministries of Health and Education to recommend the study of sexual knowledge, attitudes, and behavior. This study, carried out in the early

### Table 7

### Total Fertility Rates of Jews and Non-Jews in Israel (1965-1989)

| Period | 1960-1964 | 1965-1969 | 1970-1974 | 1975-1979 | 1980-1984 | 1985-1989 | 1990 | 1991 |
|---|---|---|---|---|---|---|---|---|
| **Jews (total)** | 3.39 | 3.36 | 3.28 | 3.00 | 2.80 | 2.79 | 2.69 | 2.58 |
| Mothers born in Israel | 2.73 | 2.83 | 3.05 | 2.91 | 2.82 | 2.82 | 2.76 | 2.70 |
| **Muslims** | 9.23 | 9.22 | 8.47 | 7.25 | 5.54 | 4.70 | 4.70 | 4.70 |
| Jews (mothers born in Asian and African countries) | 4.79 | 4.35 | 3.92 | 3.40 | 3.09 | 3.14 | 3.09 | 3.27[1] |
| **Christians** | 4.68 | 4.26 | 3.65 | 3.12 | 2.41 | 2.49 | 2.57 | 2.26 |
| Jews (mothers born in Europe, America (N&S), Australia, and Southern Africa) | 2.38 | 2.59 | 2.83 | 2.80 | 2.76 | 2.66 | 2.31 | 2.05[2] |
| **Druze and others** | 7.49 | 7.30 | 7.25 | 6.93 | 5.40 | 4.19 | 4.05 | 3.70 |

The Total Fertility Rate (TFR) is the total number of live children born to a woman throughout her fertile period. It is based on the sum of age-specific fertilities for women between the ages of 14 to 49 and assumes that women of a specific group have the specific age fertility appropriate for their group when they are at that age.

[1] The rise in TFR among Jewish women born in African countries in 1991 is probably due to the wave of immigration of Jews from Ethiopia.

[2] The rather sharp drop in TFR in 1990 and 1991 among women born in Europe/America is probably because of the large wave of immigration from the former USSR where the TFR among Jewish women is below 2.

1970s, also recommended the introduction of a sex-education curriculum into the schools.

The current prevalence of STDs in Israel for 1993 in annual rates of preliminary notifications were 1.1, 0.0, and 0.3 per 100,000 for syphilis, genital chlamydia trachomatis, and gonorrhea, respectively. This is believed by researchers to be below the actual rate. For example, some estimates of chlamydia infection are as high as 10% of the women of 15 to 49 (2% of the population). Estimates of the prevalence of herpes genitalis are also quite high.

In 1988, a Society for the Study and Prevention of STDs was formed under the auspices of the Israeli Family Planning Association, with the aims of joining biomedical and behavioral efforts, integrating prevention with proper early detection and care, and for increasing the awareness of STDs and their risk to health among health professionals. It holds professional orientation and awareness meetings and formulates guidelines for better detection and care of various STDs. Its educational and public activities are conducted within the general framework of the IFPA.

## B. HIV/AIDS
### Situation Report
Currently, HIV/AIDS has a low prevalence/low incidence in Israel. The documented number of AIDS cases for May 1994 was 292—cumulative incidence of 56 per million—69 of which, 24%, are currently alive in Israel. As of June 1994, there were 1,152 people reported as HIV-seropositive who are not ill with AIDS, a cumulative incidence of 256 per million or 0.026%. It is believed that the reporting of cases is accurate. Tables 8 and 9 summarize the published data about both AIDS and HIV in Israel for June 1993.

The authorities cite the fact that incidence of new AIDS cases within Israel is flat as support for their claim that the situation is under control. They also claim that since half of the new AIDS cases are previously known as HIV cases, the actual number of HIV cases is probably twice the number of AIDS cases reported from all sources.

However, it may be that this perception is only the short-sightedness of politicians and policymakers who do not realize that this may be the lower flat part of an atypical hyperbolic curve, below the threshold of doubling. Several

facts apparent in these tables can be a cause for concern. First, the progression from HIV to AIDS may represent the transmission situation in the past five to ten years. Second, 30% of the HIV cases are of unknown risk factor, and almost 10% of all the people identified as HIV-seropositive are also of unknown gender; among those of unknown risk factor, 25% are of unknown gender. Since HIV testing in Israel is mostly voluntary, and there is no summarized and/or analyzed data about the people who have been tested for HIV, there is no information about over- or undertesting in important subpopulations like age groups or genders. This results in a puzzle with more holes than picture.

### Sociopolitical Issues
There are several troubling questions that relate to HIV/AIDS being a biopsychosocial construct, interlocking with sexuality and other social, political, and cultural issues.

The responsibility for dealing with all the aspects of AIDS has been allocated to the Ministry of Health with its mainly biomedical outlook. The decisions of the National AIDS Steering Committee, which is always headed by a physician, are only recommendations to the director general of the ministry. Thus, decisions to implement policies or actions that may have a strong psychosocial component can be taken up only from its biomedical end, resulting in a distinct bias with serious and unpredictable results.

A second issue is more pervasive. On the one hand, there is the perception that HIV/AIDS and infected persons are marginalized and stigmatized. This perception influences the ways in which people with AIDS or HIV and HIV/AIDS issues are treated. On the other hand, there is a proneness in the responsibility for public health to avoid discussing the fact that, in different situations and under different conditions, it may not only be responsible, but essential to undertake unpleasant or even restrictive measures. (In accordance with the traditional Judaic approach, the application is highly dependant on unique situations that need to be weighed from all sides and in relation to all those who are involved, even though the laws are general and cover everyone.) This chain of bias-guilt-avoidance is hardly suitable to deal with the sensitive issues of HIV/AIDS. It may also be responsible for the fact that Israel has yet to form a midrange plan to deal with the disease.

Another issue is the influence of organizational structures and vested interests on the nature of the efforts to stem the disease. Such phenomena affect the definition of prevention and the perception of appropriate behavioral interventions; they are also the source of the phenomenon that policies are formulated, and interventions designed and implemented, prior to ascertaining the behavioral patterns, psychological, social, and cultural determinants of behaviors involved in this disease.

Vested interests come into play, especially when dealing with allocation of budgets, human resources, control, and research opportunities. Thus, the AIDS centers that are located in eight hospitals, and that are treatment-oriented and medically controlled, strive to retain the overall responsibility for prevention, even of interventions that are community-oriented and those in which the behavioral, and even cultural components, are predominant.

### Table 8

**Cumulative Adult (Age 15+) HIV+ Cases in Israel (June 1993) Presented by Transmission Category (After Slater P. Sutton's *Law and AIDS Prevention in Israel*)**

| Transmission Category[1] | Males N | Males %[2] | Females N | Females %[2] | Unknown N | Unknown %[2] | Total N | Total %[3] |
|---|---|---|---|---|---|---|---|---|
| 1. Gay and bisexual men | 153 | 100.0 | — | — | — | — | 153 | 16.6 |
| 2. IV-drug users[4] | 97 | 78.2 | 14 | 11.3 | 13 | 10.5 | 124 | 12.6 |
| 3. Homophiliacs | 47 | 97.9 | 1 | 2.1 | 0 | 0.0 | 48 | 4.9 |
| 4. Transfusion recipients | 7 | 53.8 | 5 | 38.5 | 1 | 7.7 | 13 | 1.3 |
| 5. Heterosexuals | 199 | 58.0 | 139 | 40.5 | 5 | 1.5 | 343 | 34.7 |
| Subtotal (known risk group) | 503 | 73.9 | 159 | 23.3 | 19 | 2.8 | 681 | 68.9 |
| 6. Unknown transmission | 173 | 56.3 | 58 | 18.9 | 76 | 24.8 | 307 | 31.1 |
| Total | 676 | 68.4 | 217 | 22.0 | 95 | 9.6 | 988 | 100.0 |

[1] RS (the first author) would have preferred the use of risk practice or risk behavior to the use of transmission category or risk group. This would have changed the structure of this table. For example, the use of anal sex as risk practice (with subdivision for gay or heterosexual groups) could have clarified the relative role of this practice in heterosexual transmission in Israel, without loss of the ability to calculate the risk to encounter an HIV+ partner in sexual encounters within specific groups.

[2] Percentage of the total number of cases in this specific category.

[3] Percentage of this category in the total number of HIV+ in Israel at that date.

[4] Including drug users with additional risk factors.

Most of the HIV tests are done on these sites in which precounseling and postcounseling to the people who test seronegative is limited to printed brochures. The people who test seropositive receive a mixture of medical and social counseling with little organized support and few educational programs. Attempts to alleviate the situation, even with the help of volunteer services, meet with suspicion on the one hand, and financial constraints on the other.

*Priority Groups for Preventive Interventions*

The prioritization of groups, and development of educational interventions, have been done without prior behavioral and psychosocial studies or any organized decision-making process. Recently, the topic was discussed in an article with several published commentaries recommending the use of epidemiological data to determine priorities for interventions. This proposal would not be a step forward, because it does not give any consideration to behavioral patterns. It also does not distinguish between risk-group, at-risk group, and risk behavior. Thus, it did not consider hemophiliacs, the highest HIV-seroprevalent risk-group, and failed to notice that they are currently at a very low risk for passing on the infection, that most of them are under constant medical supervision and counseling for their primary disease, and that the at-risk group for infection are their sexual contacts.

The commentaries revealed deep differences between people who deal with AIDS, bordering on a communication gap. Thus, the head of the National AIDS Committee declared a commitment to implement a general AIDS education effort among adolescents in schools, while another commentator pointed out that there were still no behavioral data pointing towards that need, and suggesting that the existing epidemiological data, although scanty, favored the targeting of educational efforts to limited priority subgroups within youth.

The establishing of targeted priority groups is important not only because of the scarcity of financial and human resources, but also because of the need to target the educational messages to the specific needs and conditions of subgroups, if one is to expecting to make an impact (see below in AIDS Education Versus Sex Education). The general intervention efforts aim at the common denominators and, therefore, may be too diluted and unfocused.

The balance between targeting priority groups for interventions to lower the transmission within those groups, and support for those who are already HIV-seropositive, and stigmatizing these same groups, is very delicate, especially if the groups are marginalized or stigmatized to start with.

Recently, this issue raised its head when the educational and counseling efforts within an immigrant population suffering from high prevalence and incidence rates, and from a heterosexual pattern of transmission, were sensationalized in the media. The fear and shunning reactions of small segments of the population, combined with the sensitivity and shame within this traditional community, triggered reactions toward the professionals who were in close association with them, and set back some of the preventive efforts.

*Contact Tracing and Educational/ Counseling Programs*

Epidemiological follow-up and notification, support for people who are HIV-seropositive, and counseling interventions could be highly effective, if implemented professionally, compassionately, and discreetly. This was possible in Israel, as no anonymous testing is available, only confidential ones. Unfortunately, the system did not manage to make the essential accommodations to implement such policies.

In one case, when a whole group of immigrants from a country with a high prevalence of HIV was screened on entry, the recommendation for combined supportive and preventive interventions by case managers working within the community was postponed for more than two years. As transmission within the community continued, while people did not come in readily for voluntary testing, it is questionable whether the intervention can be as effective as if it had been implemented nearer to the screening date.

This immigrant community also posed the challenge of developing culturally appropriate educational programs and training personnel to deliver them. It also challenged the system with the necessity for cultural bridging, and the training of cultural mediators between professionals whose beliefs were embedded in biomedical models, and clients who used a combination of traditional lay beliefs and biomedical models.

This was achieved by creating an alliance between a group of professionals and a group of veteran immigrants who trained to become both educational agents and mediators while they also acted as cultural informants and consultants.

*AIDS Education Versus Sex Education*

This question, although general in nature, is especially relevant in Israel, a low-prevalence country in which adolescents can be defined by their moderate prevalence of heterosexual risk behaviors when compared to the U.S.A. and European countries, and very low prevalence of individuals being at-future-risk for HIV infection and not at-immediate-risk.

While today's adolescents do not face the probability of HIV infection, they do face a much more tangible risk of pregnancy and STD infection. In this context, attempts to motivate youth by fear of the small risk of HIV/AIDS or by fear of the future may backfire.

On a more theoretical basis, it is questionable whether it is appropriate to introduce youth to the issues of sex through risks of either a deadly disease, other diseases, or a pregnancy. It is proposed that early sex education, focusing on communication

---

**Table 9**

**Accumulative Adult (Age 15+) AIDS Cases in Israel (June 1993) Presented by Transmission Category (After Slater P. Sutton's *Law and AIDS Prevention in Israel*)**

| Transmission Category[1] | Males | | Females | | Total | |
|---|---|---|---|---|---|---|
| | N | %[2] | N | %[2] | N | %[3] |
| 1. Gay and bisexual men | 110 | 100.0 | — | — | 110 | 45.6 |
| 2. IV-drug users[4] | 43 | 84.3 | 8 | 9.8 | 51 | 21.2 |
| 3. Homophiliacs | 28 | 100.0 | 0 | 0.0 | 28 | 11.6 |
| 4. Transfusion recipients | 7 | 87.5 | 1 | 12.5 | 8 | 3.3 |
| 5. Heterosexuals | 26 | 74.3 | 9 | 25.7 | 35 | 14.5 |
| Subtotal (known risk group) | 214 | 92.2 | 18 | 7.8 | 232 | 96.3 |
| 6. Unknown transmission | 9 | | 0 | | 9 | 3.7 |
| Total | 223 | | 18 | | 241 | 100.0 |

[1] RS would have preferred the use of risk practice or risk behavior to the use of transmission category or risk group. This would have changed the structure of this table. For example, the use of anal sex as risk practice (with subdivision for gay or heterosexual groups) could have clarified the relative role of this practice in heterosexual transmission in Israel, without loss of the ability to calculate the risk to encounter an HIV+ partner in sexual encounters within specific groups.

[2] Percentage of the total number of cases in this specific category.

[3] Percentage of this category in the total number of HIV+ in Israel at that date.

[4] Including drug users with additional risk factors.

and decision-making skills, on responsibility for one's actions and health and also for the health and welfare of one's partner, and on alternative, noncoital sexual expressions, would be both more appropriate for adolescents and, in the long run, more efficient in lowering the transmission rates.

It is also important to note that the differences between cultures are not limited to "esoteric" immigrants, but can also be between "similar" industrial countries. Thus, the concept of "safer sex," which is embedded in the basic premises of a society that is highly individualistic and sometimes adversarial, may be insufficient or inappropriate in a culture that puts more emphasis on the sense of community and cooperation between individuals.

It is also questionable whether egoistic motivations, which are at the roots of safer sex, are sufficient in boundary conditions, where altruistic or secondary motivations are needed to augment the egoistic ones. Such considerations will call for alternative educational approaches. Dealing with issues of mutual protection and responsibility need a much more elaborate educational approach than focusing on barriers to condom use or on the mechanical skills of its use. These should be discussed in the wider scope of sex education.

The decision-making, communication, and protective skills learned in sex education are very similar and can be easily applied to protection against HIV/AIDS.

It is somewhat disappointing that the need for a comprehensive approach to sex education and the urgency of such implementation are wasted, because the interests of some politicians meet with those of educational entrepreneurs. The latter promote the use of shelf programs aimed at the largest possible populations and designed to offend as few people as possible. They are thus focusing on "clinical," nonoffensive, and nonsexual aspects of HIV/AIDS, demand minimal training of the implementers, and minimal hours for delivery. The interest of educational and health politicians is in "magic bullet" interventions that can be put in place speedily and with minimal fuss and objections from vocal political minorities.

Such ready-made AIDS-education programs allow them to shirk their responsibility, while pretending to fulfill it. It is only fair to say that some of these politicians do not know better and believe in what they are doing. The responsibility of the entrepreneurial professionals seems to be graver.

### [HIV/AIDS Education on the Internet

[*Update 2001*: In March 1999, the largest educational Internet network in Israel, Snunit, opened a site dedicated to sexuality and the prevention of HIV/AIDS. The site was jointly sponsored by the psychological counseling service of the Ministry of Education and the National HIV/AIDS Steering Committee. Its name, Yachad (Together), is significant, because it reflects the fact that the site is not dedicated to prevention in general or to HIV/AIDS in particular, but to couples and sexual relations (Yachad 1999). The launch of this site was a political event because, in order to be sponsored by the Ministry of Education and Culture, it had to be also approved by the National Religious Educational System. Beside information, chat rooms, and question-and-answer sections, the site includes educational activities through which adolescents can examine their attitudes and values, express opinions about the content of sex education in schools, and examine their exposure to risk through sexual behavior. (*End of update by R. A. Shtarkshall and M. Zemach*)]

### [Epidemiology

[*Update 2001*: Most new cases of HIV/AIDS reported in Israel are still people who were infected abroad, most of them in one country in which HIV is highly prevalent and from which immigrants are continuously arriving into Israel. At the end of October 1999, there were in Israel 605 cumulative cases of AIDS, out of which 155 were still living, and 2,051 reported cases of HIV, which had not yet progressed to AIDS (National TB and AIDS Unit 1999). The Ministry of Health and WHO estimate that Israel has 50% to 100% more HIV cases than reported. Out of the known cases, about two thirds are men. More than 50% were presumably exposed outside Israel by heterosexual contacts. The proportion is much higher for women than for men, 69% and 31%, respectively. Among those exposed abroad, the proportion of men to women is 1:1.

[Recently, two new phenomena have been emerging: the reporting of cases of HIV/AIDS among migrant workers and among immigrants from the former USSR. While the former are mainly sexually infected, the latter are infected through intravenous drug use, and many suffer also from advanced stages of alcoholism and untreated tuberculosis. Israel is a country with a National Health Insurance, which covers treatment of HIV through the most advanced diagnostics (viral load) and medications (cocktail therapy). Since immigrants are entitled to health insurance from the moment they arrive and are not tested outside the gates, there is an inducement for people from counties that do not supply therapy to move into Israel. Recently, some experts voiced concern whether this may increase the burden intolerably on a health system that is in a chronic financial crisis. (*End of update by R. A. Shtarkshall and M. Zemach*)]

[*Update 2002*: UNAIDS Epidemiological Assessment: By the end of 2001, a cumulative total of 3,333 cases of HIV infection were reported. Israel is a country with a low endemicity of HIV/AIDS. With the attribute of being a country of immigration, including significant immigration from African countries, rates of HIV are greatly dependent on the origin of the immigrants.

[An HIV/AIDS registry has existed since the beginning of the epidemic. HIV testing is systematic among blood donors and prisoners and among select groups of immigrants from HIV-hyperendemic countries. Testing is confidential and free of charge for any person requesting the service. Testing is done at all community clinics, all across the country.

[Health education programs are developed for both the general population and for groups with risk behaviors. Treatment and follow-up are specialized in regionally distributed AIDS centers, which can provide adequate follow-up and antiviral HAART treatment to all adherent patients.

[The estimated number of adults and children living with HIV/AIDS on January 1, 2002, were:

| | | |
|---|---|---|
| Adults ages 15-49: | 2,700 | (rate: 0.1%) |
| Women ages 15-49: | NA | |
| Children ages 0-15: | NA | |

[No estimate is available for the number of adults and children who died of AIDS during 2001.

[No estimate is available for the number of Israeli children who had lost one or both parents to AIDS and were under age 15 at the end of 2001. (*End of update by the Editors*)]

## 11. Sexual Dysfunctions, Counseling, and Therapies

### A. Concepts of Sexual Dysfunction and Therapy

Despite the fact that several of the founders of modern sexology in Germany had either passed through or settled in Israel after the rise of the Nazi regime to power, sexology did not emerge in Israel as a discipline until the early and middle 1970s. Treatment for sexual dysfunctions was limited either to medically oriented interventions or to analytically oriented psychodynamic therapies, which were imported by members of Freud's Psychoanalytic Institute who immigrated to Israel and founded a similar institute with his blessings in the late 1930s.

The medical approach focused on functional symptoms alleviation as a means to solving the sexual dysfunctions, e.g., the use of dilators for vaginal spasms or numbing creams for early ejaculation. While the psychoanalytic approach recognizes dysfunctions, and issues like orientation and gender confusion as separate diagnostic categories, and is interested in deep causes and their transformation, psychoanalysts did not treat them with the same methods and under similar basic assumptions as medical practitioners.

The development of sex therapy in Israel occurred mainly after Masters and Johnson and is, by and large, an import from the U.S.A. Most of the Israeli therapists are trained there rather than in Europe. Currently, there is a pluralism of approaches to the treatment of sexual dysfunctions, ranging from the purely medically oriented through the combined biopsychosocial approach, and the couple-oriented systemic approach to the psychodynamic.

## B. Availability of Diagnosis, Counseling, and Treatment

A World Health Organization (WHO) report counted, at the end of 1988, 13 centers offering sex therapy across the country. This list was not exhaustive even for that date, and since then, more services have opened up in different locations.

Most of the clinics are still located in public hospitals or specialists' clinics of the sick funds. Significantly, few of them have a freestanding status, and most are annexed to departments like Gynecology, Psychiatry, or Urology, depending on the medical training of the head of the clinic or on political considerations. These arrangements are typical of a situation in which sexology and sex therapy are still not considered a full-fledged, professional, and/or academic enterprise.

The clinics, even those in the public hospitals and sick funds, are very heterogeneous. A few have several staff members from different disciplines working full- or part-time with a wide range of services. These can offer a full biomedical and psychosocial evaluation and a variety of therapies. Usually, they will also treat orientation- and gender-confusion issues, including evaluations for sex change, e.g., the sexual function clinics at the Hadassah Medical Organization in Jerusalem and the Sheba Medical Center in Ramat-Gan. Most clinics focus on fewer aspects of the sexual functions or offer a smaller variety of services. Several sex-therapy clinics evolved in nonmedical family and marriage services. These offer mostly psychosocial evaluations and interventions. One of these clinics started in the early 1990s also offers surrogate therapy as part of its services. The male and female surrogates are selected and trained by the staff of that clinic.

Two centers specialize in rehabilitative sexology: Sheba and Beit-Lewinstein Rehabilitative Center. These offer both posttrauma and postdisease treatment of sexual concerns and functions.

A relatively recent development is the appearance of specialized private-enterprise sex clinics that use aggressive publicity and cater mainly to men with erectile dysfunctions. These clinics offer mainly treatment by medication, mostly penile injections. There are several reports that they offer rather poor psychological and dyadic evaluations and interventions, and at least one of them is under investigation by the Ministry of Health.

A national association of sex therapists (ITAM) was formed in the late 1980s in expectation of the therapy-licensing regulations. This is a rather loose association that did not take a public initiative in dealing with defending potential clients against exaggerated publicity claims or misconduct.

## 12. Sex Research and Advanced Professional Education

### A. Sexological Research and Advanced Education

There is not one academic department or academic program that focuses on sexual issues or sexology. All the research and training is done under the names of different "professions," with very little integration and/or interdisciplinary approach. One attempt to form an interdisciplinary group ended when the person who initiated it did not receive tenure and moved to Canada. Despite that, several studies concerning sexual function and dysfunction have been carried out in clinical and limited nonclinical populations. Other studies in the educational, psychosocial, and health fields have included issues of sexuality, sexual behavior, and attitudes. The rise of interest in HIV/AIDS issues has focused some attention to what is defined as sexual risk behaviors.

Only one of the four medical schools includes a course on sexuality and sexual behavior in their regular curriculum. The other three do so only as an elective or intermittently. It is possible to be board licensed in gynecology and urology without any course or internship in the psychosocial and behavioral aspects of sexuality. The only specialization that includes some issues of sexuality in the requirements for board certification is family practice. As a result, at least one of the postgraduate courses in this specialty offers a 32-hour unit on sexuality and sexual issues in the family practice and a 16-hour unit on family planning and contraception.

Several of the universities and colleges offer scattered academic courses on sexual issues within various faculties, schools, or departments. Such are the courses at the School of Social Work of the University of Tel-Aviv, sex education courses at the Kibbutzim teachers-training college, and others.

The Hebrew University of Jerusalem has several academic courses in family planning in various departments. One of them is an interdisciplinary course to train counselors in family planning, contraception, and sexuality-related issues. Although part of the M.P.H. curriculum, this course is considered to be an intervention course in the School of Social Work, and a skills course in educational counseling and psychology. Other courses there are those focusing on the biological, social, and psychological bases of gender differences.

Several courses in sex education are offered within university schools of education. These are nonacademic, in-service training courses held in cooperation with the Unit of Family Life and Sex Education of the Israeli Ministry of Education and Culture. Nonacademic courses, mainly in sex education and family planning, are offered by the Ministry of Education and the Israeli Family Planning Association (IFPA). These take the form of annual courses or concentrated workshops on general issues, on specialized populations (e.g., immigrants and challenged youth), or special issues (e.g., dealing with rape and coercive sex in the educational system, new methods in sex education, and cross-cultural issues).

Recent developments may herald some changes. First, one of the courses in sex education, which is coheaded by Ronny A. Shtarkshall, is currently considered for inclusion in the master of arts degree program by the School of Education of the Hebrew University of Jerusalem. This is a 168-hour course for training facilitators for interactive experiential work in sex education. The 56-hour, theoretical-academic component of this course will give, if approved, four annual credits at the graduate level. Second, the IFPA has initiated within the Post-Graduate Training Program of the Sakler Faculty of Medicine of the University of Tel-Aviv an interdisciplinary program in population, family planning, sexual health, and counseling. Third, the IFPA board of directors and council approved criteria for the training and recognition of sex educators. These include academic studies, skills training, sensitization and desensitization to sexuality issues, and supervised experience. It is expected that these developments will create some change in the attitudes toward professionalism in sexual issues.

## B. Sexological Organizations

Institute for Sex Therapy, Sheba Medical Center, Tel Hashomer, Israel; Phone: 972-3/530-3749; Fax: 972-3/535-2888

Israel Family Planning Association, 9, Rambam Street, Tel-Aviv, 65601, Israel; Phone: 972-3/5101511; Fax: 972-3/5102589

Ministry of Education and Culture, Psychological and Counseling Services, 2 Devorah Hanevia Street, Jerusalem, Israel; Phone: 972-02/293249; Fax: 972-02/293256

# 13. National, Religious, and Ethnic Minorities

## A. The Muslims

Muslim Arabs, the large majority of Arab citizens in Israel, constitute 14% of the population of Israel. Their situation is unique: a minority within a Jewish state and culture that has been at continuous war with its neighboring Muslim countries since its founding.

Despite that, some sense of group autonomy that transcends individual rights is recognized by the state, as matters like marriages, divorce, and family law are in the jurisdiction of the Muslim religious courts.

While the national and political aspirations of Muslim Arabs in Israel may be at odds with the mainstream of Israeli society, it is interesting that both the Muslim establishment and the population approve of the Israeli system that allows the religious courts of each denomination to govern its own population.

The religious courts are bound by the civil code, which takes precedence in matters in which the religious courts are at odds with it, like the ban on polygamy and the legal age of consent for marriage. Only recently, the Supreme Court ruled that the religious courts cannot ignore the rulings concerning division of property between husband and wife, which give women more rights than under the religious canons.

This indigenous control also gives the traditional establishment power over younger "upstarts." If there is a movement striving to free the Muslim society from the strong hold of the religious establishment, it is much less visible than among the Jewish segment of the population, perhaps as a result of the value placed on a uniform stance as a minority.

There are several other factors that affect sexual, marital, and familial issues in which the Arab-Muslim society differs from the Jewish mainstream. The Jewish majority is largely urban with an industrial and service-based economy, with high measures of modernity including women's education and their participation in the workforce. The starting point of Arab-Muslim society is largely rural, its economy is based on farming, and the determinants of modernity are rather low. This is rapidly changing, but there is still a wide gap. In recent years, both academics and some small activist organizations have broken the unified front by publishing studies about marriage patterns, sexual violence, and other disputed issues, and waging public campaigns against phenomena like murder for the honor of the family. These reports provide a good background for discussion of such issues.

### Marriage as a Public Transaction Between Families

The traditional view of marriage in the Arab, mainly Muslim, society is of marriage as a transaction between families, concerned mainly with strengthening the economic and political power of the extended family/tribe, the *Chamulah*. Love and sexual satisfaction have very little to do with marriage, but procreation is very important. This is typical of rural societies, depending on land for wealth and prestige and on unity for its preservation. Marriages are arranged between families, sometimes against the will of the bride or the groom.

Bride payment, *Mohar*, is paid according to the desirability of the bride and the purity of the name of the family daughters and the status of her family. The collection of appropriate *Mohar*, especially for a highly desirable bride from a prestigious family, is a very heavy burden on young men if they do not have the support of their well-to-do families or if they are poor. Thus, the practice of arranged marriages with high *Mohar* has acted not only to preserve the wealth, but to keep the younger men in line and preserve the social status quo. The payment of the *Mohar* has also represented symbolically the fact that the bride's family was losing a labor force, while the groom's family was gaining one, as well as a potential mother of children. Therefore, the fertility of the bride's mother, her aunts, elder sisters, and cousins has been a factor in her desirability and her *Mohar*. This contributes to the fact that the pregnancies and childbearing of each woman in the *Chamulah* is the business of every other woman. Women move into the husband's extended family, but her family of origin is still responsible for her proper conduct.

### Inbreeding

Several mechanisms exist to facilitate keeping the wealth, especially land ownership, within extended families. One is reciprocal marriages: Families exchange two pairs of their offspring, one male and one female from each family. These male-female pairs are often a brother and sister or first cousins. This saves the dowry payments for both families, but also creates double-kinship lines. A second mechanism is the marriage of first cousins, second cousins, uncle and niece, or aunt and nephew, although this is not as common today as in the past. The result is that 45% of all marriages in the Arab society in Israel are between relatives; 25% are of first-degree kin.

This happens despite the decrease in arranged marriages and their transformation into ritual formalization of voluntary pair formation. This seeming paradox can be explained by the fact that, despite modernization, the Arab society is still a closed one with low mobility. The available choices for marriage are limited and usually come from the same village built around extended families.

The health implications of these phenomena can be dire. Several villages, which are socially or geographically isolated, suffer from an extremely high incidence of specific genetic defects. Efforts are being made to lower the rate of genetic defects, even among the married relatives, by appropriate genetic counseling.

One such defect within the domain of human sexuality is the existence of a large number of pseudohermaphrodites of the dihydrotestosterone (DHT) or 5-alpha reductase deficiency. First reported and studied in the Dominican Republic, this recessive gene mutation has been traced to one family that migrated from the Syrian mountains about 150 years ago and continued to intermarry. A brief attempt to study these people and their environment, while extending them medical help, was cut short by the realities of the Israeli-Arab conflict. It was ascertained that the extended family is aware of the situation and of the peculiarity of these children. Yet, it was never clear whether this is an internal familial terminology or a public one. They almost invariably strive to become men because of the dominance of males in the Arab society. The very few individuals who live as females are servants within their own families.

### Polygyny

Another aspect of marriage among Muslim Arabs in Israel is polygyny. The Islamic religion allows a man four wives and as many concubines as his household can support. In reality, it was very rare that a man had more than two or three wives. One of the customs was for the older and dominant wife to choose a younger one for the husband, usually one that she could dominate.

Polygamy is banned by Israeli law. This ban was enacted mainly as a measure affirming women's equality, as a reaction to the custom of Jews who immigrated from Islamic countries. Acceptance of the law by Muslim Arabs in Israel was almost universal until 1967, when it became possible for men to have another wife either from or in the West Bank or Gaza district. Despite this, most Muslim Arabs obey the law and there are very few prosecuted cases of polygamy.

### Perceptions of Male and Female Sexuality

In Islamic cultures, the sexuality of men and women is perceived as moving in different directions during a lifetime, a picture somewhat in accordance with some modern sexological descriptions of the early peaking of male and later peaking of female sexual prowess.

According to this Muslim view, men's sexuality is uncontrolled in their youth before they marry. This is the time to keep guard on them, but also to allow them to fool around with women of ill repute. This is also the time to go to war or to forage (where women are seen as the spoils of war). After marriage, as men grow older, their appetites, while undiminished, become more controlled because of their added wisdom. In men, wisdom, cunning, and cool control over situations is usually associated with age.

The sexuality of a women is believed to be low in her youth and she is perceived as innocent. It is only after losing her virginity that the sexuality of women will grow and may get out of control. Therefore, married women are to be guarded at all times. A man's inability to satisfy his woman or to keep her in line is a very bad reflection on the husband's manhood, in addition to bringing shame to the woman's family of origin.

### Family Honor

Two concepts are strongly associated with family honor. The first is the public proof of intact female virginity at marriage; the second is punishment for its defilement. In a traditional wedding ceremony, the family of the bride, usually the mother and/or aunts, are expected to receive the sheet with the signs of hymen blood on it and exhibit it in public. Contrary to popular belief, this is not only a sign for the intactness of the bride's honor, but also proof of the groom's virility.

Sex therapists working with Arab populations encountered the male fear of slighting one's own manhood and family honor by failing to perform. On the other hand, there are reports that the literary description of shyness and reluctance, signifying a virginal nature that are expected to be conquered by force, are part of the construct of women's perception of the first intercourse. The emerging picture is that of a ritual choreography where each partner has to play his or her traditional role in order to bring it to its full destiny and honor both families.

Even in rural and highly guarded societies where marriages are arranged, young people find their ways to associate with each other. In recent years when schools became coeducational, when there is greater freedom of movement, and when Arab youth are attending universities together with a majority of Jewish students at the age of 18—they do not serve in the army—it is much harder to avoid romance and a certain amount of sexual play between youth. As already mentioned, family arrangements are many times a formalization of self-selection.

Despite this change, the symbolic meaning of virginity is still important. Two sexual practices help young people to keep the hymen intact while engaging in sex: interfemoral and anal intercourse. The first is more risky to the woman as she may become pregnant, and also the man may catch her off guard and penetrate the hymen. The second avoids both, but in the area of HIV/AIDS may be inadvisable. No research has been published on this subject among Israeli Muslims, although there is enough anecdotal information to say that both practices are prevalent.

"When the family honor is shamed, it has to be cleansed with blood." This is true not only of issues of honor relating to women, but also in other cases of honor, including blood feuds and ritual revenge. Both the annals of the courts and fiction are filled with such stories.

In cases of sexual honor, there are some revealing features. First, when family honor is shamed in matters of sex and marriage, the women carries the main burden of punishment and men rarely are blamed. One possible reason for this is that killing a man will touch on another matter of honor and start a blood feud that may last for generations. Second, when a transgression is made public, it is the woman's family that carries the burden of cleansing it with blood and killing the alleged transgressor. It was found that in many instances, the women of the family either incite the men to action, or even actively participate in its preparations or the actual deed. This is understandable in the light of the fact that an unpunished transgression reflects mainly on the good name of the women of the family, thus reducing the chances of the unwed ones to marry or to receive a good *Mohar*.

In 1992, a group of Muslim women activists publicly agitated against this practice for the first time. They even demonstrated in public against it, an unprecedented action. It is still unclear whether Jewish female and male activists, by joining in this campaign, will strengthen or weaken it. There is certainly strong expressed sympathy from Jews toward this campaign.

Unlike the practice in some Islamic countries, the courts in Israel do not accept the honor of the family as a mitigating circumstance. On the contrary, they have expressed their lack of sympathy for such customs and followed it with the maximum punishment under Israeli law, which is a life sentence.

### Fertility Patterns and Their Secular Trend

The total fertility rates (TFR) of Muslim Arab women in Israel (4.65 in 1993), is the highest among the national religious groups composing its population. Still, it has also undergone the most marked decline in the last three decades (see Table 7). The drop in TFR from 9.23 to 4.65 in 35 years is proportionally lower than that of the Christian Arab women (50% and 52%, respectively), but in terms of absolute family size, it is much greater. Christian women are having, on the average, only 2.6 children less as compared to 35 years ago, and their TFR is the lowest among the studied groups (2.09 in 1993), while Muslim women are having on the average 4.6 fewer children.

An attempt to study the contribution of different independent variables to this fertility change has revealed an interesting picture involving the cumulative effect of seven independent variables. At the time of the study (1988), the independent variables that were the most strongly associated with both the desired and achieved number of children were the mother's age group, her education, and a traditional arranged marriage with payment of a *Mohar.* Two other independent variables were associated with only one of the studied variables: Urban or rural locality was associated only with the desired number of children, while participation in the workforce was associated only with the achieved number of children.

Education seems to be the strongest of the associated variables, the difference in desired fertility between the two extreme educational categories being almost two children, and between the achieved fertility at a relatively young age (28.5) by one child. The type of marriage is a variable showing the second strongest association. The differences in the desired and achieved fertility between the two types of marriages are 0.6 and 0.5 children, respectively. The other variables, even when significant, showed much smaller differences. Prominent in their lack of association with either the desired or achieved fertility were religiosity and marital lifestyle (who gives up aspirations for the sake of the family).

The combination of the independent variables together show a better overall explanatory power for desired fertility than it did for the achieved fertility. One possible explanation of this discrepancy is the fact that the analysis was done with relatively young women who were still at an interim stage of achieving their fertility aspirations. Another explanation is that the study was dealing with cognitive conscious variables that associated with the verbal desired fertility, while achieved fertility is more associated with unconscious factors that are not available for this kind of analysis.

*Contraceptive Use*

Several studies have demonstrated that the availability and use of contraceptives, in themselves, were only weakly associated with the achieved fertility, the use of contraceptives, as an intermediate variable mediating between the desired fertility and the achieved one, being the behavioral means to space pregnancies or to terminate fertility. Table 10 compares the use of contraceptives among the Jewish population and Muslim Arabs. In order to get a better analysis, the study distinguished between women who do not use contraceptives because they are currently not exposed to additional pregnancies, and those who do not use them for other reasons. The former are pregnant women, women who try to conceive, infertile women, or those who do not practice sexual intercourse.

The first significant fact, in terms of fertility rates, is that the proportion of "non-exposed" women among the Muslims is much higher than among the Jewish women, 29.4% as compared to 20.6% of all the women, respectively. The bulk of the "non-exposed" are pregnant women and those trying to conceive. This means that at any one time, roughly 40% more Muslim women were in the process of having children (see Table 11).

The number of "nonusers" among the "exposed" is also very significant, 21.3% of the "exposed" Muslim women compared with 11.3% among the Jewish women—15.1% as compared to 9% of the total number of women, respectively. This number is very important because it marks the percentage of women among the "exposed" who do not want to conceive, but do not use means of protection from pregnancy. Therefore, these women may be a potential au-

**Table 10**

**Comparison of the Use and Non-Use of Contraceptives Among Married Jewish and Muslim Israeli Women (Aged 22-44 Years, 1988)**

| | Number of Women | Percent of Total | Percent of Exposed |
|---|---|---|---|
| **JEWISH WOMEN** | | | |
| **Users of contraceptives** | 1192 | 70.6 | 88.8 |
| **Non-users of contraceptives among exposed** (non-use for reasons of fear, reluctance, principle, family opposition, no intercourse, or ill-defined) | 152 | 9.0 | 11.3 |
| **Subtotal exposed** | 1344 | (80.0) | 100.1 |
| **Non-exposed non-users of contraceptives** (non-use because pregnant, want to become pregnant, recently delivered, infecund, or no intercourse) | 346 | 20.6 | |
| **Total non-users of contraceptives** | | 29.6 | |
| **Total number of women** | 1680 | 100.2 | |
| **MUSLIM WOMEN** | | | |
| **Users of contraceptives** | 258 | 55.5 | 78.7 |
| **Non-users of contraceptives among exposed** (non-use for reasons of fear, reluctance, principle, family opposition, no intercourse, or ill-defined) | 70 | 16.1 | 21.3 |
| **Subtotal exposed** | 328 | (70.6) | 100.0 |
| **Non-exposed non-users of contraceptives** (non-use because pregnant, want to become pregnant, recently delivered, infecund, or no intercourse) | 137 | 29.4 | |
| **Total number of women** | 465 | 100.0 | |

dience for family planning efforts. Another such group not shown here is the women who actually attempt to avoid conception, but who are using inefficient methods. Their percentage is also higher among the Muslim than Jewish women. The conclusion is that when looking only at the women who do not desire conception at a given moment, there is a strong need for family planning efforts among the Muslim Arabs in Israel in order to allow them to realize their desires.

*Fundamentalist Islam and Women's Status*

In the last ten years, the fundamentalist Islamic movement has gained power among the Muslim Arab population. The change is evident in both social phenomena and in the rise to power of the Islamic movement in the local elections. More women are seen wearing the traditional *chador* covering a woman from hair to toe at both high schools and universities. In previous years, such garb was limited to older rural women. Many mosques are being built in communities, boys and girls are separated in the schools, and there are overt attempts, some of them not so delicate, to bring women "back to their place," ban alcohol, permissive dresses, erotic films, and so on. The Islamic fundamentalists, who are politically most anti-Israeli, are similar in several respects to some Jewish ultra-orthodox groups.

*Sexual Violence Against Women and Children:
The Deep Silence*

The issue of sexual exploitation, coercion, and violence against women and children in the Arab sector has only recently been discussed in public; a first study has been published on the matter and crisis centers have been opened.

Because several characteristics of Arab society, especially in the sexual arena, make it against the self-interest of women, children, and concerned caretakers to make public accusations or seek help in situations of abuse, crisis support is mainly provided by telephone hotlines that allow the caller complete anonymity. A virgin woman who loses her virginity, for whatever reason, has a lower value in marriage and a taint on the ability of the family to guard the virtue of its daughters (which may reflect on the marriage value of other female members of the family). If a married woman is raped, the perception of nonvirgin women as tempters may cause people to blame her for what happened and not the man (over whom women may have sexual powers). A raped boy or man may keep quiet in order not to raise doubts about his manhood, which is highly valued in that society, and therefore in his ability to marry. Thus, the rape crisis centers that have counseling, intervention, and hotline programs in Arabic report that their contacts in the Arab sector are predominantly by phone, and that fewer callers will agree to identify themselves, make contact, or press charges, as compared to the Jewish sectors.

## B. Ultra-Orthodox Jews

The ultra orthodox, or *Haredim*, have an ambivalent existence as non-Zionist Jews, recognizing only divine rules yet living within a Jewish state. In some sense, it is more difficult for them in Israel than in the Diaspora under the rule of non-Jews. Judaism, as a national as well as an individual religion, prescribes rules of conduct not only within the private domain, but also in the public one. These rules do not apply to non-Jews, so it is only among Jews of differing practice that many conflicts arise about public observance of certain rules.

Many of the ultra orthodox live within a defensive spiritual perimeter, trying to isolate themselves and their children from the encroaching influence of secular temptations. They have a separate educational system that, although financed by the government, is totally outside of its educational supervision. Most of their youth do not go to the army, a highly significant experience in the life of secular and orthodox Israeli youth, which has an impact on dyadic, gender, and sexual issues. They also often feel strongly that secular Jews do not understand the importance of their way of life and, being in conflict with them over their own needs, hate or ridicule them. They, therefore, shun strangers, even the ultra orthodox who belong to other sects or communities. As their communities are very closely knitted, their life revolving around the synagogue, the ritual bath, and other public functions, it is very difficult to penetrate into their life.

It is even more difficult to penetrate into issues of sex and marriage that are not discussed in public. A very few windows have been opened into these areas in both fiction and nonfiction, written by people who were formerly ultra orthodox, in a study by a woman anthropologist among religious women, and in sexual counseling and therapy.

[*Comment 2003*: David S. Ribner (2003ab), a professor of social work at Bar-Ilan University in Ramat Gan, Israel, has identified six pervasive influences on the sexual behavior of Haredi Jewish couples, summarized briefly here:

• [*Holiness and sanctifying intimacy.* Because the Haredim see sanctity as infusing every aspect of human experience, all sexual behavior must be intentionally sanctified. By its very nature, sexual behavior cannot be neutral. A Haredi couple must consciously focus on creating an atmosphere of holiness through proper thoughts and some time-and-circumstance limits on behavior—the Sabbath eve is a preferred time for sexual relations which must always take place under the cover of a sheet. As Ribner (2003a, 55) notes, "Attempting to instill a feeling of sanctity while flooded with all the sensory in-

### Table 11

### Use and Non-Use of Contraceptives among Married Israeli Muslim Women According to Exposure/Non-Exposure to Pregnancy and the Reason Given for the Exposure/Non-Exposure (Aged 22-44 Years, 1988)

| | Number of Women | Percent of Total | Percent of Exposed |
|---|---|---|---|
| **Users of contraceptives** | 258 | 65.5 | 78.7 |
| Non-use on reasons of principle | 25 | 5.4 | 7.6 |
| Non-use because of reluctance, fear, ill-defined | 45 | 9.7 | 13.7 |
| **Non-users of contraceptives among exposed** (principles, opposition of family, reluctance, ill-defined) | 70 | 15.1 | 21.3 |
| **Subtotal exposed** | 328 | (70.6) | 100.0 |
| **Fertility-targeted non-use** (pregnant, want to become pregnant, or delivered recently) | 115 | 24.7 | |
| Infecund or no intercourse | 22 | 4.7 | |
| **Non-users non-exposed** | 137 | 29.4 | |
| **Total number of women** | 465 | 100.0 | |

puts of physical intimacy may prove a daunting goal indeed, one often doomed to failure."

- [*Time and the scheduling of intimacy.* Strict Jewish observance forbids any physical spousal contact during menstruation and the following week. This 'two weeks on/two weeks off' pattern of contact characterizes marital life until menopause, with uninterrupted contact permitted during pregnancy and nursing. Intercourse is strongly recommended on the Sabbath eve and the 'mikve' night (following the woman's ritual bath that marks the end of the two-week menstrual-related abstinence.

- [*Modesty in sex as in all else.* Any public contact or display of physical affection is prohibited. This means that Haredi children grow up without ever seeing any examples of parental affection. Sexual thoughts and fantasies about one's spouse are also forbidden. Sexual intercourse must take place in the dark, although the couple may use some indirect light during foreplay. It is not acceptable for the husband to look directly at the wife's genitals. The couple should be covered with a sheet during intercourse, but nothing should come between them. These modesty requirements often present major obstacles for newly-wed Haredi couples, and even couples married for some time, in shifting from an asexual lifestyle to marital relations with strict modesty requirements.

- [*Being together and becoming sexually active.* The abrupt shift from total abstinence to the initial physical contacts of marriage pose "a daunting challenge fraught with unknowns in a number of areas" for newlywed Haredi. In addition to the total lack of any opportunity to see someone of the other sex not completely clothed, either in person or in print, the little or no information about one's own sexual anatomy, the spouse's sexual anatomy, and what to expect in sexual arousal, "can create a potent problem-producing context. Difficulties in their purely physical realm may be as basic and as painfully awkward as neither husband nor wife knowing the location of the vaginal opening" (Ribner 2003a, 58). In addition, with minimal dating and conversation before the wedding, emotional intimacy and sexual communication with the spouse become problematic.

- [*Communications and the language of intimacy.* Everyday life in a Haredi community clearly militates against any exposure to or acquisition of language to describe the sexual parts of one's own body and the body of the other sex. Haredi women are encouraged to avoid being verbally explicit about their own intimate desires and to use nonverbal clues. Men have more leeway in this than women, but it is difficult for either men or women to be conscious of sexual desires when both have been taught to repress any sexual thoughts or fantasies about their spouse.

- [*Sexual isolation.* With no television, often no radio, no movies, no secular novels, and not even innocuous family or women's magazines to read, the Haredi couple is protected from any sexual information from the outside during the entire course of their marriage. The rules of modesty practically eliminate any possibility that either spouse will share his or her sexual concerns or questions with a friend, relative, rabbi, or physician. (*End of comment by R. T. Francoeur*)]

## Arranged Marriages: Potential, Yichus, Health, and Money

Marriage in the orthodox tradition is one of the most revered institutions. Many if not most of the religious rituals are familial, and it is assigned a most important role in transmitting the Judaic values from one generation to another.

Although Judaism allows divorces, they are highly stigmatizing; striving for the intactness of the family and keeping the peace within it are highly valued.

In the ultra-orthodox tradition, marriages are arranged, either through marriage brokers, or through interested parties in large family circles, or among friends. Four factors are highly important in arranging marriages. They are not necessarily the same for men and women, but they interact in more than one way. First, and probably the most important factor for a man, is his potential in Halachic scholarship. As marriages are arranged around the age of 18 to 20 for men and 16 to 18 for women, a realized potential is rare. The heads of the religious academies or seminaries—the *yeshivas*—will be looking for a suitable match for their most promising students. These will be decided by the second and third qualities: *Yichus*, for which the nearest translation is lineage and financial security. The first *yichus* concern focuses on finding a woman who is herself from a family of Halachic scholars, and thus will not only literally support her husband in his struggle for scholastic excellence, but also increase the chances of bearing and raising children who will be such scholars. This set of *yichus* issues also includes all the qualities of the lineage, not only the hereditary ones, but also ones like the "name" of the family, past divorces of other family members, and other such factors. The second *yichus* concern looked for in women is the ability of her parents to support the continuing studies of the husband in the *yeshivah* for years to come. Such support is contracted for in marriages and may place a heavy burden on the parents, as they can last for three, five, ten, or even more years. During that time, the parents can expect to support not only the young couple, but between three to six children. The quality of *yichus* is also a determinant in the men's eligibility, but not the financial one, if they are scholars. The financial status is important in men who are not scholars and who are in business or in trade.

Another highly valued factor is health, that of the bride and groom, and the health of their families. Thus, families strive to hide any "problematic" health problems like mental health, developmental disabilities, genetic disorders, or subfertility. They may hide such a son/daughter, even to the point of denying full care because of denial mechanisms.

Many things can detract from the value of a person in marriage, even having a brother or sister who has become less religious. Thus, gossip can be very harmful, and whisper campaigns pernicious. The admonitions against disqualifying gossip about brides and grooms are severe, which attest to the importance of the issue.

Sons and daughters of the big rabbinical families usually marry only within "proven" lines. Sometimes three or four such families remarry for several generations. Such marriages acquire the proportions of almost royal events.

Thus, marriages are viewed mainly not as an issue of the heart, but rational arrangements whose main purpose is to establish a viable, socially, and financially secure unit with a good potential for reproduction, continuations, and excellence.

### Rules of Conduct Regulating Intercourse

As stated before, in Judaic tradition, sex is an entity that intrinsically is neither good nor bad, but has a high potential for both. The nature of sex is dependent on its meaning, context, and practices.

For orthodox people, and certainly for the ultra orthodox, the context and practices are highly important and intermingled. The central role of intercourse is procreation in the spirit of the blessing "Procreate and multiply and fill the earth," although the Halachic basis for the rules and regulations covering the *mitzvah* to procreate are anchored elsewhere. On the other hand, it is important to note that sex is practiced as one of the marriage obligations of the husband, not only for procreation. Thus, contraception may be allowed either for spacing or for ending pregnancies, if one of several reasons recognized by the *Halachah* occur, even before the proscribed number of children is reached. During such periods, when procreation is not its reason, sex continues to be a *mitzvah*.

In terms of meaning, sex, as most other things, should be practiced for the glory of God and his creation. There are several degrees of elevation in practicing it, but if striving for a higher step disturbs one from fulfilling the *mitzvah* itself literally, then that person is really sinning and should change his or her ways. This sometimes has meaning in sex therapy, as the therapist encounters a phenomenon in which sexual dysfunction is explained by the need to strive for an elevation of the sexual act.

The context of practicing sex is restricted to the boundaries of marriage and to the prescribed period of the month that is determined by the woman's menstrual period (see below). The rules of conduct governing the actual act of intercourse are numerous, from the amount of light which is allowed into the room (only indirect), through the place of religious books during the act, through positions that are recommended and acts that are proscribed, to mention just a few. A most-proscribed act is, of course, the spilling of semen in vain, which determines the fact that condoms and withdrawal are religiously banned. There is a discussion whether, if in the course of transgressing other laws, the use of condoms is allowed for protection against AIDS. Another rule of conduct that is perfectly natural and understandable to those practicing Judaism in its ultra-orthodox variation is that women are prohibited from direct verbal initiation of intercourse, although they are allowed other means of initiation, including indirect verbal ones.

It is important to note that pleasure is considered an integral part of the act, and it is the duty of the husband to "please" his wife. This raises several interesting issues, some of which have a meaning in sexual counseling and therapy. First, what is the meaning of pleasing or pleasure in the differing minds of men and women? This will determine if at all, what, when, and how, they ask for pleasure in practice. This also poses a problem for a nonorthodox therapist who may interpret pleasure either in a culturally inappropriate manner, or neglect to include individual variations and needs within the stereotypical interpretation. A second question is what proportion of the couples practice intercourse strictly according to the rules, how prevalent are the private variations to the public norms and how far they go?

*Purity Laws: Periodic Abstinence, the Public-Private Dualism of Sexual Intercourse, and the Social Control Over Fertility*

Purity laws restrict the period in which a couple can practice intercourse to about half of the month. The cessation of not only intercourse, but any direct or indirect physical contact between husband and wife is determined by the onset of menstruation; this is called the *Nidah* period. Toward the end of her menstrual period, but not less than five days from its onset, the woman has to check with white cloth at the external opening of the cervix, whether she is still bleeding. When there are no signs of bleeding any more, she has to count seven "clean" days; at the evening of the last day, she has to cleanse herself in the "*mikveh*," literally a pool, which is the public ritual bath. On that same night, her husband is to approach her for intercourse.

This emphasis on purity and the high visibility of the dualism between impurity-purity in women's lives, raise several issues that can be viewed from different aspects.

Writings by religious people directed mainly at nonobservant people argue in a mixture of apologetic and aggressive modes that these laws protect the health of women in the time when her body is most vulnerable to infections through sexual intercourse, and that the periodic abstinence creates a healthy sexual tension between husband and wife, and not only increases the bond between them, but also puts some meaning into it. There are also claims that restrictions on intercourse, and the timing of the first intercourse after the abstinence, act not only to increase fertility, but also to the lowering of birth defects. Little evidence has been compiled that will be accepted as supporting the biomedical claim, in fact, and some of the evidence is cited wrongly or out of context. As for the psychological and dyadic claims, this may be true for some couples, but may be totally the opposite for others. Ronny A. Shtarkshall observed in a biased population of help-seeking couples that the purity laws were sometimes the focus of strong suffering on the side of women and a cause for conflict. Some women, for example, complained that the ban of touching was unbearable, especially when in a low or depressed mood or when one is ill or suffering. This was also true when the husband or an adolescent child is suffering. Women also complained that intercourse at the end of the *Nidah* period had a "mechanical" aspect to it, which causes both individual and interpersonal difficulties. The fact that this mechanical aspect of the intercourse— fulfilling a *mitzvah*—may have been only perceived or partially true is unimportant here. The important aspect is that it could cause difficulties and that it has to be addressed.

A highly important point of view is the feminist discourse that includes these laws as one of the determinants of the status of women in the Jewish religious society. Despite the fact that this discourse totally ignores the fact that purity laws also apply to men and to sperm emission, in a highly elaborate way, they point to some very important issues.

First is the issue of fear of contact with a *Nidah* woman unknowingly, which governs the rules of conduct of many orthodox men who will refrain from any casual touch or shaking hands with women. Thus, every woman is suspected to be impure unless proven otherwise. This may be the explanation for grandmothers sometimes being more "touching" than mothers when boys are concerned, and the readiness of the adolescent boys to accept this physical contact.

Second is the heightened awareness of adolescent girls of their bodies, its potential for impurity, and the need to examine it regularly. On the other hand, adolescent boys are introduced to the female issues from a totally "impersonal" point of view, through learning about it in their Halachic studies. The fact that boys also become aware of their own bodies through the need to keep a constant watch over themselves as not to spend semen in vain (which includes nocturnal emissions), and thus be in danger of defiling the religious scrolls, is not alleviating the potential harm that such awareness may impose on the development of girls.

It is important to emphasize that this discourse is mostly limited to nonreligious circles and to religious women of North American origin. Writings about these issues from this point of view, or from related ones, by orthodox women are generally not available.

An important point that is raised by both religious men and women, sometimes from different perspectives, is the public nature of intercourse and of fertility that is dictated by the use of the *mikveh*. Some recent ethnographic/anthropologic literature describe the feelings of women who go back home after visiting the *mikveh*, feeling in the look of every person in the street, especially the men, the knowledge of the expected intercourse. Thus, a very private act acquires a very public aspect. Both men and women in therapy for either lowered fertility or for sexual issues frequently comment on the fact that going to the *mikveh* is a public proclamation of the failure to conceive in a society where both internal familial and external pressures for procreation are very high, especially on young couples. Men and women commonly comment on the fact that it is public knowledge even before that, when people, especially parents and in-laws, can tell when they refrain from touching each other or making contact, even indirectly, through a dish. This may have several implications (see discussion of therapeutic issues below).

### Fertility Patterns

Although the high number of children born to ultra-orthodox families is obvious and an accepted fact which influences both perceptions and politics, there is little hard data on the fertility patterns of the ultra orthodox. This results from a combination of administrative restrictions and reasons embedded in the ultra-orthodox culture. While the religion of the parents is noted on the birth certificates of newborns, there is no notation of religiosity on documents that are the basis for all the statistical calculations of birthrates, age-specific birthrates, and TFRs. Thus, secular, traditional, orthodox, and ultra-orthodox Jews are in the same category. As the ultra orthodox tend to live in geographically cohesive communities, it is possible to get a handle on their fertility through statistical regions. The TFR for Jews in the city of Jerusalem, which has a high proportion of ultra orthodox (30% by municipal elections), is almost two children higher as compared to the TFR for Jews in the two other big urban centers—Tel-Aviv and Haifa—3.72 as compared to 1.86 and 1.91, respectively.

It is apparent even to naive observers that the fertility pattern is totally different both in spacing and in TFR, as it is common to encounter families with six to nine children and not uncommon to encounter families with ten to 14 children. Young couples usually aim at having the first child as soon as possible, within the first year of marriage. Studies have shown that this is such a prevalent and internalized norm that couples rarely discuss this issue. As a woman's menstruation and pregnancy are public knowledge, loving and concerned pressure is brought to bear on couples early in the marriage. Parents and in-laws are sometimes unaware that such pressures can be devastating both to the fertility and to the sexual functioning of the young couple.

Even in a fertility survey, it was difficult to look at the ultra orthodox separately, because their women tended to avoid being interviewed and were, therefore, underrepresented. The reasons for refusal, especially when the interview touched on issues of children, fertility, and family planning, are perfectly understandable from inside their cultural environment. First and foremost, children and fertility are one of the most precious things in the life of women. In a society where the future and planning for the future are the prerogative of God, any tampering, even a verbal one can be construed as tempting fate or courting punishment. Second, there is the fear of being misunderstood and/or stigmatized by outsiders, especially nonreligious Jews. Third, there is the fear of the evil eye resulting from jealousy.

### Contraception Versus Family Planning

Despite the strong emphasis on procreation, the Jewish *Halachah* allows contraception on the basis of individual needs and circumstances. As the principles of the *Halachah* do not recognize general rulings, each individual case has to be decided by a Halachic authority on the advice of medical opinion. On the other hand, there is a very strong public opposition to family-planning services. The delicate differentiation between family planning and the use of contraceptives lies in the realm of purpose. While family planning, as such, is a transgression, the use of contraceptives for religiously recognized purposes is allowed.

The religious rules govern not only the use of contraceptives, but also the types of contraceptives to be used. As already mentioned, two types of contraceptives are almost totally banned: male contraceptives and nonreversible contraception, whether male or female. Among temporary female contraceptives, currently the most acceptable ones are combined birth-control pills (for women with breakthrough bleeding), the IUD, and diaphragm. Again, there are personal variations, and medical opinions are sought and listened to.

The public opinion against family planning and contraceptive services is such that ultra-orthodox women, even those with strong need that will probably be acceptable to the Halachic authorities, refrain from seeking help. The tip of the iceberg was seen when women listeners started writing to a weekly radio program, "Not a Children's Game," devoted to reproductive health and family planning issues. A psychosocial analysis of the letters revealed that about half of the women writing in were from the ultra-orthodox community. Half of those were vociferously and almost violently against the program as promoting promiscuity and being antinatal; the other half were women desperately seeking help in dire situations. Religious authorities consulted by the producers assured them that these women could and should receive help according the *Halachah*. It was also evident that these women will be able to accept help only if it will be within the religious tenets. They were confidentially referred to both medical and religious authorities in the relevant geographical area. This public-private dichotomy is sometimes typical of the religious community.

### Transgressions

The fact that people adhere to many religious rules and live within a religious community does not mean that they do not transgress on any of its laws and rules. Transgressions on an individual basis are varied and should be only recognized and not discussed in such a paper. On the other hand, when cultural, ethnic, or other traditions within a religious community are in contrast with religious rules, or are in contradiction of the rules that these same people profess, these should be looked into.

One such example was mentioned above, when public and spousal pressure prevented women who probably deserved contraception within the *Halachah* from seeking and receiving help.

Another example that relates to contraception was noted in a study that examined the family-planning practices of a very orthodox community of immigrants from Yemen. While the women complained about unwanted pregnancies and the number of children, the husbands claimed that family-planning services should not be approached because of religious reasons. A study by family physicians revealed that the most prevalent family-planning practice in this community, one that the majority of couples used, was withdrawal—a grave sin according to the religious rules.

One can only conclude that, as strong as religious rules are among orthodox groups, cultural traditions sometimes modulate them in unexpected ways.

*Issues in Sex Therapy*

Nonobservant therapists working in areas with a concentration of ultra orthodox must resolve several therapeutic, ethical, and personal/professional issues.

First is the difference between the therapeutic paradigm and the basic tenets of the client(s) and their subculture. In essence, one can say that the place of sex in the worldview of the clients differs in some important points from that of the therapist and the therapeutic approach.

While the basic approach of sex therapy to sex is individual- and couple-oriented, hedonistic, and present-oriented, the approach of many of the clients is certainly different. While pleasure and fulfillment are not excluded from the constellation, they are certainly not at its center. The central themes of sex among the orthodox are its function in procreation and the preservation of the family; despite the strong shroud of secrecy and privacy, sex has several "public" aspects to it, especially within the extended families; through the centrality of procreation, sex acquires a strong future aspect to it.

In this domain, one can also include the egalitarian approach of sex therapy, implicit in many of its tenets and interventions. In the ultra-orthodox point of view there is a strong asymmetry in terms of initiative, responsibility, and the duty of husbands for the sexual act and the fulfillment of their wives.

A second issue can be viewed as environmental. While one of the basic means of sex therapy is to lower the burden of performance from the partner who carries it and the introduction of nonperforming sex, among the ultra orthodox, who view procreation as a central aim of intercourse, there is not only an objective criterion for performance, but also a regular almost public viewing of it, at least to other women—the visits of the wife to the *mikveh*.

A third issue is a more individual one. The use of exploration, inventiveness, and flexibility is an important part in the therapeutic intervention. Here the therapist encounters various degrees of rigidity/flexibility as in any other population. The uniqueness is the connection that the clients are making with the religious rules of conduct, a very powerful barrier to possible change. An approach that is embedded in their belief system is that transgression is a matter of choice, and it is an individual choice between sins.

The resolution of these issues lies in the recognition by therapists that any therapy cannot buck the basic belief system of the client and that changes can mostly be effected within that system. In the case of working with ultra-orthodox persons, the therapist must adhere to some self-imposed rules and restrictions. Some of these are harder than others. Such is the agreement to consult rabbinical authorities on issues within the therapy, when the client demands it, and to abide by their specific decision in working with the

specific client for which the question was asked. This raises issues like divided or shared authority and the use of consultations as escape routes. Other issues are the specialized knowledge needed even to ask Halachic questions and the use of the therapist's own rabbinical authority in phrasing them.

The basic rule seems to be the ability to feel true respect from outside and to grasp meanings from inside of a culture that is basically alien to the therapist's worldview.

It is difficult and inadvisable to talk about prevalence of sexual problems, not only because there are no adequate statistics, but because the reasons for seeking help may be totally different from that of the general population. The main complaint is subfertility, which is later diagnosed as a primary sexual dysfunction or the wish to have more children in the case of secondary ones.

## C. The Kibbutz Movement

The kibbutz movement comprises 2 to 3% of the Jewish population of Israel, a seemingly smallish part of the population to be dealt with separately. But this movement of collective communities, the first of which was founded 80 years ago, played an important role in the development of Israeli society. Several features of this subculture are highly important for the discussion of sexuality of youth, fertility patterns, and contraception. The first is that, even with the current changes in lifestyle, and the fact that most kibbutzes have changed sleeping arrangements so that children sleep at their parents' apartments instead of the communal children's homes, kibbutz youth live a life much more independent of adult control in general, and parental control in particular, from early adolescence on than any other group of Israeli youth. Second, despite the fact that the kibbutz society is not as egalitarian as people used to think, it is apparently very much so in many aspects. Third, the kibbutz society emphasizes self-reliance and internal locus of control in many aspects of life by minimizing economic secondary motivations. It is, therefore, not surprising that people take charge of their lives in many aspects, including sexual responsibility and sexual health.

On the other hand, in a seemingly contradictory vein, social pressures to conform are very high within the kibbutzes. It seems that the strongest effects occur when social pressures and the powers of the individual act in the same direction.

*Intercourse During Adolescence and Young Adulthood*

When comparing urban to kibbutz youth, it is apparent that beyond 10th grade (age 16), both kibbutz men and women report more premarital intercourse than others; they also start at a younger age. This difference is more pronounced for women than for men—the rate of reported intercourse for kibbutz men is either similar or slightly higher than that of urban young men. In contrast to urban youth, the ratio of kibbutz men and women reporting intercourse, among those who initiated it, was about 1:1 for all grades. Whether this is an egalitarian norm of reporting, or of initiating intercourse or both, needs further studies. These results have been verified in several independent studies over a period of about 25 years.

As reported earlier, it seems that since the mid-1960s, the age of sexarche in Israel is going down for those who practice premarital intercourse (see Table 2). This is true for both youth in both social settings, and is especially marked for urban women. However, as Table 12 shows, there is an interesting difference

### Table 12

**Comparison of Sexarche Between Urban and Kibbutz Women Who Reached Age 16 at Different Time Periods**

| Age at Sexarche (Years) | The Period at Which the Women Reached Age 16 | | | | | |
|---|---|---|---|---|---|---|
| | 1963-1969 | | 1970-1975 | | 1976-1982 | |
| | Kibbutz | Urban | Kibbutz | Urban | Kibbutz | Urban |
| 14-15 | 0.8% | 0.8% | 1.8% | 1.8% | 6.2% | 1.9% |
| 16-17 | 22.0 | 14.2 | 41.2 | 22.0 | 47.4 | 26.0 |
| 18-19 | 66.2 | 48.4 | 81.8 | 60.1 | 86.0 | 70.1 |
| 20-21 | 89.8 | 80.1 | 94.1 | 85.2 | 98.6 | 92.9 |
| 22+ | 100 | 100 | 100 | 100 | 100 | 100 |

*Editors' Note*: Percentages are approximations from the original line graphs.

between urban and kibbutz women. In all three cohorts of urban women, there is a break in the curve and a rise in the slope between ages 16 to 17, and 18 to 19. Among kibbutz women, this is true only for the older cohort, those who reached age 16 between 1965 and 1969. The two younger cohorts of kibbutz women, who reached age 16 in 1970 through 1975 and 1976 through 1982, show a straight line between ages 14 to 15 to 18 to 19 (significant at the 0.01 level for all three cohorts).

The "break" in the curve for urban women can be explained by the lowering of parental/social control for women who leave for the army at the end of 12th grade. There are several possible explanations for the fact that for the kibbutz women the curve is straight: first, kibbutz women may be relying more on internal locus of control and, therefore, are less influenced by the parental/social controls; second, less parental control being exerted on kibbutz youth than on urban youth; and/or more accepting and egalitarian norms of sexuality among kibbutz youth that allow more women both to practice intercourse and to report it. Several indications in the data and in the general structure of kibbutz life indicate all of these factors may be acting together.

### Fertility Patterns

A superficial analysis shows similarities between fertility patterns of urban and kibbutz women; closer analysis reveals a much more interesting picture. First, when comparing the TFR of kibbutz women to the segments of the population closer to them in composition, those of American-European origin, one finds that kibbutz women have more children. Second, when controlling for religion and comparing secular urban women with secular kibbutzes and religious (not ultra-orthodox) urban women with religious kibbutzes (a small minority), one can see that in each sector, the kibbutz women have 0.5 more children. Third, the patterns of fertility are different. Kibbutz women marry older, give birth at a later age, and lag behind the urban women in number of children until about age 30, although they continue to have children until a later age.

Another difference is that the interval between giving birth is longer for kibbutz women, when controlled for religiosity, education, ethnic origin, age, stillbirth, and natural or induced abortion. Kibbutz women had intervals two months longer between the first and second child, and three months longer between the third and fourth child. The two latter differences point to a relatively high degree of planning and control of fertility.

When looking at the differences between various types of kibbutz ideologies and diverse lifestyles that emerged during recent years—like young children sleeping at home instead of at communal children's homes—it was found that the personal differences between women within kibbutzes contribute to the differences in TFR, much more than the differences between kibbutz movements.

### Contraception

Does the fact that the kibbutz society: supplies all the material needs of its members, including health needs; shows high prevalence of egalitarian attitudes to sexual behavior of men and women; and puts a high value on planning and control, in fact lowers some of the barriers to family planning and to efficient contraception that are so prevalent among many other groups? If this is the case, then the use of contraceptives among kibbutz women, married and unmarried alike, should be consistently higher than for urban women across all other variables like religiosity, educational level, ethnic origin, and birth order of the children.

As early as first intercourse, kibbutz women show a different pattern from urban youth: 43% of secular kibbutz youth used some kind of contraceptive at sexarche, about half of them—21% of all the women practicing premarital intercourse—used the pill on first intercourse. This number is much higher than the rate for secular urban youth: 27% and 13%, respectively. The significance of this difference becomes more pronounced if one notes that it was already demonstrated that kibbutz women reach sexarche at a younger age than urban youth, and that age at first intercourse is a strong determinant of the ability of youths to protect themselves.

When comparing nonorthodox kibbutz women and urban women during their married life, it is clear that kibbutz women are more efficient and more consistent contraceptors. Only 15% of kibbutz women did not use any contraceptive prior to the first pregnancy, compared to 40% of the urban ones. During that period, only 12% of the kibbutz women relied on withdrawal as compared to 19% of the urban ones. The rates of pill use are reversed, 50% compared to 26%, respectively.

After first pregnancy, the differences are even more pronounced: 90% of kibbutz women contracept and only 8% use withdrawal or rhythm, compared to 28% noncontraceptors and 26% withdrawal or rhythm contraceptors among urban women. These differences remain pronounced in higher birth order intervals. Among variables that might explain differences in contraceptive use prior to first pregnancy within the kibbutzes, the only ones with significance were the birth cohort—older cohorts using fewer contraceptives and less-effective ones prior to the first pregnancy, and ethnic origin—women of Asian-African origin using less-effective contraceptives.

When comparing contraceptive use in 1987-1988, kibbutz women progress from 79% efficient contraceptors prior to the first pregnancy, through 81% after the first and second pregnancy, to 89% after the third pregnancy. Urban women progress from 24% through 62% to 64%, respectively. Not only is there a difference, but the pattern is different. It seems that urban women contact agencies that help them use efficient contraceptives only after giving birth to the first child, while the majority of kibbutz women do so prior to the first pregnancy.

Juxtaposing the patterns of contraceptive use with the patterns of fertility, and taking into account that kibbutz women who start having children at a later age and with longer birth intervals end up with more children over a longer fertile period, it seems that the group is very close to that of the ideal contraceptors—women who use contraceptives effectively to have as many children as they want at the time that they choose. This is also supported by information about much fewer reported unplanned pregnancies, most of which seem to be while using very safe methods.

### D. Immigrants and Immigration

Israel is, as indicated, an immigrant society, albeit with some strong internal and external cohesive forces. There are some indicators that demonstrate that these forces are acting toward creation of a common meeting ground, in which some unique characteristics develop.

Nevertheless, two groups of recent immigrants give us the opportunity to look at issues and processes that both immigrants and the host society undergo when faced with the phenomenon of people from an alien culture transplanted into an established one.

One can claim that the immigrants from the former Soviet Union (USSR) and those from Ethiopia have nothing in common. The Ethiopian immigrant group is small even by Israeli standards, the recent wave arriving since 1991 being 20,000 people and the whole community numbering 50,000. More than half a million immigrants, 10% of the total population of Israel, have arrived from the USSR since 1989. The "Russians" came from a mid-industrial European country with a high literacy rate, mainly from urban areas, having a high rate of academic profession-alization, and with many family ties with the established old-timers' society. As a matter of fact, the Mayflower founding parents of the Israeli society and state immi-grated from Tsarist Russia and its environments at the end of the 19th century and the beginning of the 20th. The im-migrants from Ethiopia came from a country with a rich but isolated culture, non-industrialized, with low literacy rates, mainly from rural-agricultural areas with low mobil-ity, an extended family structure, and very little family ties with the old-timers' establishment.

On the other hand, both groups had undergone, through the dual process of emigration/immigration, being uprooted from one's original culture and transplanted into a new alien one. But the similarities may even go deeper. Both groups came from societies that had very strong external social controls. While among Jews in Ethiopia, the controls were mainly familial and "tribal"—the forces of tradition within a small, isolated, and sometimes persecuted group—those of the USSR were political and institutional. Also, at the time of their immigration, both original societies were un-dergoing some very strong processes of disruptive transi-tions. So one is faced with a unique chance of looking at two groups of immigrants undergoing a very similar process, but with somewhat different starting points and cultural contexts.

Interest in the immigrants from Ethiopia and the former USSR is not one of explorers observing exotic cultures with mixed emotions, nor of amateurish anthropologists whose hidden agenda is asserting their own cultural superiority. We are involved and vested participant-observers, with a strong interest in ameliorating the difficult process of immi-gration and acculturation. Ronny A. Shtarkshall is already an intervener-observer involved in the study and develop-ment of integrating interventions.

Because these immigrations are quite recent, the initial processes of cultural integration, some of which are very painful, are still going on. Sensitivities are high and the po-tential for stigmatization is frightening. Hence, one cannot do more at this time than indicate that careful and sensitive work with these immigrant groups may well in the future provide a rich source for major new insights into the principles and functioning of a cross-cultural sex education program.

## *Glossary*

These are some Hebrew and Arabic words that are fre-quently used in the text, mainly for lack of an appropriately equivalent term in English (some of these terms are itali-cized throughout the text).

*Halachah*: The accumulated body of religious laws, dis-cussions, rules of conduct, interpretations, judicial deci-sions, and precedents that govern the life of an orthodox re-ligious Jew. Generally, the *Halachah* covers all the aspects of life of a religious Jew from birth to death, religious and secular, public and private. The more orthodox a person is, the more strict is the adherence to the Halachic rules and the more involved are the interpretations.

*Haredim*: A general name given to ultra-orthodox com-munities by secular people. Most people who use this name do not distinguish even between the major variations of ul-tra-Orthodox Judaism.

*Mikveh*: Literally, a place where flowing water will collect, the name of the ritual bath that serves for ritual pu-rification of both women and men when this is required ac-cording to religious regulations. It is mostly discussed, es-pecially by the secular population, in relation to the purifi-cation of women at the end of their impure period—*Nidah*. It should be noted that men should also purify themselves if they spill semen, and that many religious rituals require that men purify themselves in the *mikveh*.

*Mitzvah*: A combination of a religious law, personal ob-ligation, and a privilege. The Hebrew name for the reli-gious rules. The original biblical ones numbered 613 (not a small number in itself), but their development and inter-pretation in the Talmud increased their numbers several folds.

*Mohar*: Bride payment. Traditionally paid by Muslim grooms to the bride's father. *Mohar* can be paid in money or cattle. It is almost never paid with land.

*Nidah*: A period determined by the menstrual period and seven days after it, during which women are impure and un-touchable. The root of the word also means *ban* or *banish-ment*.

*Shabbat*: The seventh day. Among orthodox and ultra orthodox, it is strictly kept. Not only is no work allowed, but things like lighting a fire or an electric instrument, driving or riding in a car, picking a flower, writing, and tearing pa-per are banned. Although very holy and strictly observed, one is allowed to do most of the things if the purpose is to save lives. One of the things that is not only allowed, but recommended on Shabbat night, is intercourse.

*Yeshivah*: A high religious academy or a seminary.

*Yichus*: lineage.

## *References and Suggested Readings*

Antonovsky, H. 1980. *Adolescent sexuality*. Lexington, MA: Lexington Books.

Arieli, Y. 1992. Being a secular Jew in Israel. In: Y. Arieli, *His-tory and politics*. Tel Aviv: Am-Oved.

Birenbaum, M. 1993. *Survey of sex education in general na-tional education schools, 1991-1992*. Jerusalem: Unit of Family Life and Sex Education, Ministry of Education and Culture. (Hebrew).

Central Bureau of Statistics. 1993. *Statistical almanac, 1992*. Jerusalem: Governmentís Press (in Hebrew & English).

CIA. 2002 (January). *The world factbook 2002*. Washington, DC: Central Intelligence Agency. Available: http://www .cia.gov/cia/publications/factbook/index.html.

*Cross-National Study*. 1997 (December). Bar-Ilan University and Brookdale Institute.

Greenberg, J. 2002 (June 8). Gays in Jerusalem parade their pride. *The New York Times*, p. A7.

Haberman, C. 1993 (February 21). Homosexuals in Israeli army, no official discrimination, but keep it secret. *The New York Times*, p. A14.

Harel, Y., D. Kani, & G. Rahav. 1997. *Health behavior in school aged children (HBSC)*. World Health Organization.

Herz, F. M., & E. J. Rosen. 1982. Jewish families. In: M. McGoldrick, J. K. Pearce, & J. Giordano, eds., *Ethnicity and family therapy*. New York: Guilford Press.

Keysar, A. 1990. *Demographic processes in the kibbutzes of Is-rael* (Doctoral dissertation). Hebrew University of Jerusa-lem.

Nathan, M., & A. Schnabel. 1975. Changes in the attitudes of kibbutz children toward friendship and sexual relations.

*Note*: A more extensive list of references that were utilized in the preparation of this article can be obtained by writing to the first au-thor: Ronny A. Shtarkshall, Ph.D., 15 Yasmin Street (Box 1116), Mevasseret-Zion, Israel 90805; ronys@md2.huji.ac.il.

*Studies in Education* [*Iunim Bechinuch*]. *6*:117-132 (in Hebrew).

National TB and AIDS Unit, Israeli Ministry of Health. 1999 (November 1). *HIV/AIDS in Israel: Cumulative data update.*

Peritz, E., & M. Baras, eds. 1992. *Studies in the fertility of Israel.* Jerusalem: The Hebrew University of Jerusalem.

Ribner, D. S. 2003a. Determinants of the intimate lives of Haredi (ultra-orthodox) Jewish couples. *Sexual & Relationship Therapy, 18*(1):53-62.

Ribner, D. S. 2003b. Modifying sensate focus for use with Haredi (ultra-orthodox) Jewish couples. *Journal of Sex & Marital Therapy, 29*(2):165-171.

Sabatallo, E. 1992. Estimates of demand for abortion among Soviet immigrants in Israel. *Studies in Family Planning, 23*(4):268-273.

Sabatallo, E. 1993. The impact of induced abortion on fertility in Israel. *Social Science in Medicine, 36*(5):703-707.

Sabatallo, E. 1993. *Continuity and short term changes in patterns of fertility and abortions among immigrants from the former USSR.* Jerusalem: Social Security. (in press; in Hebrew).

Shtarkshall R. A. 1990. Formen und trends im sexualverhalten Israelischer jugendlischer. In: W. Melzer, W. Ferchhoff, & G. Neubauer, eds., *Jugend in Israel und in der Bundesrepublik.* Weinheim un Munchen: Juventa Verlag.

Shuval, J. T. 1992. *Social dimensions of health: The Israeli experience.* Westport, CT: Praeger.

Sketchley, J. M. 1991. *Psychosexual services in selected European countries.* Copenhagen: World Health Organization, European Region.

UNAIDS. 2002. *Epidemiological fact sheets by country.* Geneva, Switzerland: Joint United Nations Programme on HIV/AIDS (UNAIDS/WHO). Available: http://www.unaids.org/hivaidsinfo/statistics/fact_sheets/index_en.htm.

Yachad. 1999. http://www6.snunit.k12.il/yachad.

# Italy

## (*Repubblica Italiana*)
## (The Italian Republic)

Bruno P. F. Wanrooij, Ph.D.*
*Updates by B. P. F. Wanrooij*

## Contents

## *Demographics and a Brief Historical Perspective*

ROBERT T. FRANCOEUR

### A. Demographics

Italy is a large peninsula extending into the central Mediterranean Sea. It borders with France on the northwest, with Switzerland and Austria on the north, and with Slovenia on the northeast. The peninsula also contains the two small independent states of San Marino and Vatican City. Italy has a total of 116,306 square miles (301,230 km²), including the islands of Sicily with 9,920 square miles (25,700 km²) and Sardinia with 9,300 square miles (24,090 km²). The alluvial Po Valley drains most of the northern portion of the country. The rest of the country is rugged and mountainous, except for intermittent coastal plains like Campania, south of Rome. The Apennine Mountains run down the center of the peninsula. The island of Sicily, at the southwestern tip of the Italian peninsula, is 180 miles by 120 miles (290 km by 190 km) with a 1992 population of 5 million. A second major island, Sardinia, is about 115 miles (185 km) west of Rome and Naples, south of Corsica, which is a part of France. Sardinia had a 1992 population of over 1.6 million.

In July 2002, Italy had an estimated population of 57.7 million. (All data are from *The World Factbook 2002* (CIA 2002) unless otherwise stated.)

**Age Distribution and Sex Ratios**: *0-14 years*: 14.1% with 1.06 male(s) per female (sex ratio); *15-64 years*: 67.3% with 0.99 male(s) per female; *65 years and over*: 18.6% with 0.7 male(s) per female; *Total population sex ratio*: 0.94 male(s) to 1 female

**Life Expectancy at Birth**: *Total Population*: 79.25 years; *male*: 76.08 years; *female*: 82.63 years

(CIA 2002)

**Urban/Rural Distribution**: 67% to 33%; regionally, the north has 44.5% of the population, central Italy 19.2%, and the south 36.3%

**Ethnic Distribution**: An Italian majority with small clusters of German-, French-, and Slovene-Italians in the north, and of Albanian-Italians and Greek-Italians in the south. In recent years, most immigrants have come from Morocco, the former Yugoslavia, Albania, and the Philippines

**Religious Distribution**: Roman Catholic 78%; Protestant 5%; Muslim and other 10%; 7% profess no religion. The number of those adhering to other religions is increasing, partly as a result of immigration. Identification with a religion does not coincide with active participation: 8.7% of Italians never attend religious services; 39.6% do so only rarely.

**Birth Rate**: 8.93 births per 1,000 population

**Death Rate**: 10.13 per 1,000 population

**Infant Mortality Rate**: 5.76 deaths per 1,000 live births

**Net Migration Rate**: 1.73 migrant(s) per 1,000 population. The natural growth rate of a negative 0.8% per 1,000 population is offset by a positive immigration rate. The total number of immigrants legally present in Italy on January 1, 1999, was 1.1 million, about 2% of the total population. In recent years, family reunifications, mixed marriages, and the increase in the number of children born of foreign parents have led to a decline in the overrepresentation of young, single males among the immigrant population.

**Total Fertility Rate**: 1.19 children born per woman

**Population Growth Rate**: 0.07%

**HIV/AIDS** (1999 est.): *Adult prevalence*: 0.35%; *Persons living with HIV/AIDS*: 95,000; *Deaths*: 1,000. (For additional details from www.UNAIDS.org, see end of Section 10B.)

**Literacy Rate** (*defined as those age 15 and over who can read and write*): 98%; education is free and compulsory from age 6 to 13

**Per Capita Gross Domestic Product** (*purchasing power parity*): $24,300; *Inflation*: 2.7%; *Unemployment*: 10% (2001 est.)

Since World War II, Italy has changed from a rural society to an industrial or postindustrial society. Agriculture now contributes only 2.9% to the Gross Domestic Product, against 32.1% for industry and 65% for the service sector.

*Communications*: Professor Bruno Wanrooij, Syracuse University in Italy Program, Italian Politics and Cultural Studies, Coordinator, Humanities and Social Sciences Department, Piazza Savonarola, 15 50132 Firenze, Italy; bpwanroo@syr.fi.it; wanrooij@dada.it.

The service sector employs 60.1% of the labor force against 32.5% for industry and a scant 7.4% for agriculture. The per capita income in 1996 was $21,190, with clear differences in income, higher in the north and lower in the south.

## B. A Brief Historical Perspective

The earliest human settlements within the territory of present-day Italy date almost certainly to some 500,000 years ago and correspond to the Lower Paleolithic period. From the beginning of the 1st millennium B.C.E., there were increasing contacts with Phoenician and Greek colonists, and Italy entered the historical period. While the Greeks settled on the southern coasts of the peninsula, Etruscan civilization developed in central Italy. During the 4th and 3rd centuries B.C.E., the Roman state expanded its territory to the entire peninsula. Expansion continued, and by the end of the 2nd century B.C.E., Rome had become the major military power in the Mediterranean. Territorial expansion was accompanied by the growing importance of commercial activities in addition to agriculture and pastoralism. The following centuries saw a gradual decline of Italy's preeminence in comparison with other provinces of the Roman Empire. With the end of the Western Roman Empire in the 4th century of the Common Era, the Catholic Church sought to take over the authority and prestige of Rome, assuming the government in the territories under its control. In the 11th and 12th centuries C.E., agriculture, crafts, and commerce prospered, the latter two in particular becoming the foundations of an urban economy that was to produce the city states of central-northern Italy. Tuscan and Lombard bankers played an ever more important role in financing the military undertakings of European sovereigns and the papacy, thus increasing their own prestige and political influence. Arts and humanistic studies flourished, and during the Renaissance of the 13th and 14th centuries, Italy became one of the major cultural centers of Europe.

The lack of political stability and the frequent wars among the various Italian states, however, allowed the great European powers to intervene, and by the second half of the 16th century, Spain had established its predominance over Italy. What followed was a slow decline of the political role of Italy in Europe, and of its contribution to cultural and scientific developments. Spanish predominance in Italy, extending over some two centuries, had rather negative consequences for the country, in terms of economic decline and of a growing imbalance between part of the southern regions and other areas of the country.

The period of French rule, which followed the conquest of Italy by Napoleon Bonaparte, saw the reemergence of a sense of national unity among the intellectual and middle-classes. In 1861, after a number of wars of independence against Austria, the Risorgimento resulted in the creation of a United Kingdom of Italy governed by the House of Savoy. Rome was conquered only in 1870. The problems, which the new kingdom had to face, regarded the Catholic Church's refusal to recognize the new state, and, more generally, the integration of the older states, and the gap between the political elite and the lower classes of the population, especially in the rural areas.

After World War I, social tensions and the growth of New Socialist and Catholic Mass parties convinced the ruling groups to help the Fascist movement, lead by Benito Mussolini, to take over power. The Fascist regime pursued a policy of repression of the working-class movement while favoring at the same time colonial expansion. Family policies were inspired by the desire to increase the fertility rate and to reinforce the position of the male head of the family. This policy received full support from the Catholic Church

after the Lateran Treaty of 1929, which made Roman Catholicism the state religion until 1984, when a new agreement was signed between the Catholic Church and the Italian government that cancelled most of the privileges enjoyed by the Church.

Fascist family legislation remained valid in Italy even after World War II, and the national government, dominated by the Catholic party, Democrazia Cristiana, opposed changes in family and gender relations. However, developments in the late 1950s and 1960s, including growing industrialization, migration from the rural south to the industrialized north, secularization, and higher standards of education, brought the traditional structures under attack. The youth movement, the feminist movement, and the gay movement also played an important role in promoting profound changes, but maybe even more important was the diffusion of consumer culture.

While Italy in the 1990s has much in common with other European countries, some of the peculiarities of Italian society—the importance of the family, the strong regional differences, and the role of Roman Catholicism, among others—can only be understood in their historical context. For example, in the past in northwest and central Italy, the incidence of patrilocal residence and multiple family households was high. In these regions today, about one third of the population lives for some time in an extended family or in a multiple-family household, and contacts with the husband's family tend to be stronger (Barbagli & Saraceno 1997).

## 1. Basic Sexological Premises

### A. Character of Gender Roles

Sexuality, as we understand it today, is not merely a biological and "natural" fact, but above all a historical construction, resulting from the pressure by manifold forces, and, as such, it is the outcome of complex historical transformations. Gender roles, in particular, are not only based on physical or biological premises, but are primarily the result of the conditions of life of males and females in a given social class, time period, and geographical location.

During the last decades of the 19th century, emancipationist movements in Italy started to question the traditional gender roles, which were based on the identification of males with production and public affairs, and of women with reproduction and private affairs. The prescribed female gender role contrasted sharply with a reality, which—especially in the northern and central regions—saw an active participation of women in the production process. The need to maintain industrial production led to a further increase of the female employment rate in industry during World War I.

The Fascist regime, which came to power after World War I, tried to reinforce the role of the male breadwinner by introducing legislation favoring male employment and by introducing discriminatory measures against female workers. Women received lower salaries and had no access to certain positions in state administration. A quota system was introduced to limit the number of women working for private companies. The government measures failed to reduce significantly female employment, but public appreciation for the female role in the family contributed to strengthen already existing familist tendencies. The desire to conform to the traditional female role of mother and housewife explains the drop in the female employment rate coinciding with the economic boom of the 1960s.

Since this period, new ideals of independence and autonomy have created a trend of growing participation of women in the labor market. Nevertheless, in the 1990s, the female activity rate was still much lower than that of men, while, partly because of protectionist measures, female unemployment was higher. In addition, women were overrepresented on the "black" labor market, where wages are lower, working conditions worse, and social benefits and job security nonexistent.

In 1995, Italy ranked tenth on the United Nations world list of male-female equality. Since the 1960s, the level of education of women has rapidly improved, and today more women than men obtain a university degree. Also, in private business and in public administration, women in Italy have made important progress in the last few years, even though there is still a long way to go for real equality.

The participation of Italian men in household chores is relatively low. While the majority of men—especially in the northern regions—take an active part in the education of children, and a growing percentage is willing to cook, to set the table, and do shopping, very few men participate in activities like cleaning, doing the laundry, or ironing. On the contrary, almost all married women, both housewives and women with full-time employment, participate in domestic work.

### B. Sociolegal Status of Males and Females

Women received the right to vote in 1945, and in 1947, the Italian Constitution was approved, with Article 3 recognizing equal rights for men and women. According to Article 29 of the Constitution, however, the need to guarantee the unity of the family justified limits to the legal and moral equality of husband and wife. It took several decades to adjust the existing legislation to the principle of equal rights and to change traditional views about the role and position of women. Until 1968, adultery was considered a crime for women, whereas men could be punished for adultery only in special circumstances. Other discriminatory conditions deriving from the male position as head of the family survived until the general revision of family legislation in 1975. The new law, based on the principle of male-female equality and on the recognition of the rights of children, abolished the position of the head of the family, and attributes equal rights and duties to husband and wife in terms of residence, work, education of the children, and so on. Married women in Italy keep their own family name, and can add their husband's name if they wish to do so. Proposals are in discussion to give couples the choice to transmit to their children either the name of the father or that of the mother.

Legislation regarding crimes of honor—recognizing special mitigating circumstances for those who, enraged by an offense to their personal and family honor, killed their wife, daughter, or sister, or the person with whom their female relatives had an illicit sexual relationship—was canceled in 1981, but had become obsolete in most parts of Italy long before.

Discrimination against women existed also with regard to labor: Women were excluded from many positions and were paid less. This discrimination has been gradually abolished. In 1960, for instance, the Constitutional Court eliminated a law dating back to 1919, which excluded women from many higher-rank positions in the public sector. In 1977, a law was approved which guarantees equal rights for males and females in issues like recruitment and hiring, career, and the like.

### C. General Concepts of Sexuality and Love

In Italy, the prevailing ideology links love and sexuality. Love is presented as a necessary precondition for sexual relations, while happy sexual relations are generally considered necessary for the success of a love relationship. Yet, 60% of women and 74% of men admit sexual desires regarding persons for whom they feel no love (Sabatini 1988). In this case, the fact that the statistics were based on a questionnaire distributed among the readers of *Duepiu*, a progressive magazine with a clear pro-sex attitude, may have influenced the results. Later surveys, however, confirmed that, especially among young men, sexual relations without love were rather common.

Faithfulness is considered an important value for couples, but a recent survey among young people (Buzzi 1998) shows that about one third of young men and one sixth of young women had sexual relations with persons other than their partner. Adhesion to the values of romantic love and faithfulness thus often is more formal than real.

## 2. Religious, Ethnic, and Gender Factors Affecting Sexuality

### A. Source and Character of Religious Values

In Italy, the values of consumer society seem to have replaced religious values in many issues, especially among many young people who refuse to accept the moral guidance of the Catholic Church. In 1996, religious marriages made up 79.6% of the total number, compared to 20.4% of civil marriages. According to a recent survey, the religiosity rate—calculated on the basis of the importance of religion in personal life, and on participation in the activities of the religious community—is close to zero or low for 28.5% of Italians, and high only for 12.3% (Cesareo 1995).

Notwithstanding the ongoing process of secularization, the Catholic religion is still the main source of values affecting sexuality, and the public pronouncements of the Pope are widely discussed in the mass media. Because of the Catholic Church's opposition to a separation between procreation and sexuality, it has been impossible to introduce clear legislation regarding artificial insemination and other forms of medically assisted procreation. An administrative rule dating back to 1985, which applies only to hospitals and clinics falling under the public health system, admits medical assistance for procreation in case of married couples, but excludes the use of donors. Therefore, medically assisted procreation with the use of gametes from donors takes place only in private clinics, with possible health risks because of insufficient public control. Because of Catholic opposition, a new bill regarding medically assisted procreation, which was approved by the Commission for Social Affairs of the Chamber of Deputies in January 1998, still had not become law by the end of 1999.

### B. Character of Ethnic Values

Immigration to Italy is a relatively recent phenomenon, and as yet the values cherished by immigrants have not had much influence outside the various ethnic groups. In this sense, Italy is not yet a multicultural society. In a medium- or long-term perspective, there is no doubt that the presence of large ethnic groups which do not share many of the views about family values, gender relations, and extramarital sexuality commonly held by Italians, will be a challenge. Contrasting views may lead to greater appreciation of diversity, but may also become a source of growing social tensions and conflict.

## 3. Knowledge and Education about Sexuality

### A. Government Policies and Programs

The introduction of sexual education as part of the regular program of primary and secondary school has met with opposition from Catholics who question both the responsibility of schools in this area and the content of education. Catholics have changed their longstanding view that sexual education could lead to the premature arousal of sexuality in young people, but still insist that sexual education is, above all, the responsibility of parents. Moreover, they deny the value of an education that focuses on the physical aspects of sexuality if it does not place these aspects in a more general context, and if it ignores moral issues.

For these reasons, and notwithstanding the fact that a majority of Italians favor sex education in school at an early age (Durex 1998), until early 1999, sexual education occurred in schools only on the initiative of individual teachers. Only recently has the Ministry of Education decided to sustain these initiatives formally.

### B. Informal Sources of Sexual Knowledge

Peer-group conversation and the mass media are the primary sources of sexual knowledge. Parents, above all the mother, rank third as a source of information. Magazines and both public and private television offer instructive articles and programs dealing with sexual issues. Moreover, publishers have responded to market demands, and have supplied sexual information in printed form, in videocassettes, and on compact disks (CDs).

In contrast with the past, sexual education today is less focused on procreation and on genital activity, and tries to explore the relations between gender identity and sexual identity. Moreover, sexual education no longer wants to prescribe sexual behavior on the basis of ideological or religious principles, but rather aims at providing the cultural instruments for self-realization (Cipolla 1998).

Today, young Italians are generally well informed. It should be noted, however, that a high level of information does not automatically translate into sound practices. Knowledge of the risks of sexually transmitted diseases, for instance, does not always lead to the use of condoms.

## 4. Autoerotic Behaviors and Patterns

According to the most recent survey among young people, nine out of ten men, and four out of ten women, admit to masturbating (Buzzi 1998). However, earlier surveys give higher numbers for female masturbation, even though the number of women who never masturbate remains five times higher—20% against 4%—than that of men (Sabatini 1988). Men start masturbating earlier than women: 16.3% before age 12, and 33.3% between age 12 and 13. In any event, the vast majority—both men and women—consider masturbation part of the sexuality of every normal human being. This idea is the outcome of radical changes in the consideration of masturbation.

In the 19th century, masturbation was the object of severe repression, and was said to be the cause of numerous physical problems. Moreover, masturbation, especially if performed in the presence of other people of the same sex as might occur in boarding schools, was believed to lead to homosexuality. In the 20th century, opposition against masturbation was based, above all, on the idea that masturbation undermined the individual's capacity to use sexuality as a form of communication. Alternatively, masturbation was considered a substitute for "real sex," an act which could be performed by young people without stable partners, but which denoted a lack of sexual maturity in the case of adults. Still, in the 1978 sex survey by Giampaolo Fabris and Rowena Davis, 31% of males and 28% of females expressed the opinion that masturbation was unhealthy, while 26% of males and 36% of females expressed their moral condemnation of this activity. Today, even though taboos have not disappeared altogether, masturbation generally is rated more positively as a source of pleasure and as an experience allowing the increase of self-awareness and knowledge of the self (Rifelli 1998).

## 5. Interpersonal Heterosexual Behaviors

### A. Children

In the beginning of the 20th century, expressions of infantile sexuality were considered a form of perversion and were severely repressed. Today, on the contrary, most Italian parents acknowledge the sexual curiosity of children, but at the same time fear that games with a sexual overtone may lead to oversexualization. Moreover, Italian parents are afraid of the sexual abuse of children by adults, which is the object of general severe condemnation and repression.

From a legal point of view, sexual relations with minors under age 14 are considered statutory rape. The age limit is higher, 16, in the case when the adult person cohabiting with the minor is a relative, guardian, or other person with educational responsibilities over the minor. A minor who has sexual relations with another minor is not guilty of any crime, on the conditions that the younger partner is at least age 13, and the age difference between the partners is not more than three years.

### B. Adolescents
*Puberty Rituals*

In Italy, no specific rituals exist marking the passage from childhood to adolescence or adult age.

*Premarital Sexual Activities and Relationships*

Only a limited number of general surveys about the sexual life of the Italians exist, and most of them were based on the responses of a sample of a preselected population, such as the clients of public family advisory agencies. Most of the information about the sexual life of young people presented here comes from a survey of 1,250 persons aged 18 to 30 by the IARD Institute (Buzzi 1998).

According to this survey, males in contemporary Italy have their first complete sexual relations with penetration when they are 17 to 18 years old; the age of their first sex was not much different from that of their fathers. The average age for females is 18 to 19. The 1998 Durex global sex survey (Durex 1998) does not make a distinction between males and females, and indicates an average age for first sex at 17. The tendency to start sex at an earlier age began with the generation of women born in the 1950s and 1960s.

It is more common for young women aged 18 to 21 from central and northern Italy to have complete sexual relations than it is for males of the same age group (females 71% vs. males 66.3%). The opposite is true for females from the south: Only 51.8% of females aged 18 to 21 had complete relations compared with 64.8% of males from the south. For the age group 26 to 30, the percentages are 84.7% for females and 88.2% for males. Moral values determine why young females do not engage in sexual relations; for males the main reasons are the lack of opportunity or the refusal of the partner (Buzzi 1998).

The first sexual partner for both males and females in almost half of the cases is a person of the same age; the partner of 41.8% of females is somewhat older (21.6% for males), and is somewhat younger for 25.9% of males (4.7% of females). Major age differences are rare. Especially for males, it is very rare that the partner of their first complete sexual relations is their wife (0.8%); it is more common for females to have this experience with their husband (10%).

The "first time" is appreciated positively by 48.7% of males and by 38.6% of females, for whom embarrassment, fear of pregnancy, and pain play a greater role. Young women are also more prone to admit sexual passivity (10.7%), absence of sexual desire (8.8%), and major psychological difficulties (15.3%). Without making a distinction between the sexes, the Durex (1998) survey reports that first sexual intercourse was disappointing for 32% of Italians, and better than expected for 29%.

First-time intercourse is often at risk for pregnancy and sexually transmitted diseases: Condoms are used on this occasion by about 40% of Italians. Coitus interruptus is used as a method of birth control by 24%. The low incidence of teenage pregnancy in Italy is therefore not a consequence of better contraception, but of the fact that young Italian females start to have sexual relations at a later age than in other countries. [*Update 2003*: One consequence of the low incidence of teenage pregnancies is the fact that in Italy—contrary to trends existing in other European countries—the number of young unmarried mothers is decreasing. (*End of update by P. F. Wanrooij*)] Statistical data relating to premarital conception, extramarital pregnancy, and induced abortion showed a radical change in the ten years between 1969 and 1978, when the incidence of these events increased rapidly. The increase affected unmarried females of all age groups. In the following years, however, the growth in the number of extramarital pregnancies stopped, while the increase in premarital conceptions slowed down.

Stable relationships become more common with the increase of age, but a relatively high percentage of young people aged 26 to 30 have no stable partner (38.5% of males and 21.2% of females). Love, physical attraction, and trust are the elements that determine the creation and the duration of a relationship.

## C. Adults

*Premarital Courtship, Dating, and Relationships*

[*Update 2003*: In recent years, American television news magazines like *60 Minutes*, the International Section of *The New York Times*, and investigative reporters "discovered" an Italian premarital lifestyle that lent itself to what might be most accurately called a titillating cross-cultural comparison. The journalists knew that in the last quarter of the 20th century, after the 1960s' sexual revolution, the number of American unmarried couples living together rose dramatically from half a million in 1970 to 3.7 million in 1994. They also knew that one in seven American children who reported living in a single-parent household actually resided with a cohabiting unmarried couple. Cohabitation had become a part of American culture. "It was the modern way" (Bohlen 1996; Rodriguez 1997/1998; Stanley 1999).

[Young Americans, it seems, place an extremely high value on individual autonomy and the freedom to do what they please. Independence means living on your own or cohabiting without marital ties, and postponing marriage while you find a career and build your nest egg. Leaving home, taking time to live on your own, "helps one grow up, experience life, and be happy with yourself" (Whitehead & Popenoe 1998).

[Then there are young Italian men who find the idea of moving out of the parental home quite unacceptable and unnecessary. They continue living with their parents, into their 30s or 40s, despite being financially independent, and often in a serious ongoing relationship with a woman. In the Italian view, a man does not have to leave home to "be his own person and to do his own thing."

[This contrast between independent young American men and the Italian *mammoni*—simplistically translated "mama's boys"—was a bonanza for both Italian and American journalists.

[Personally, I prefer not to speak of *mammoni*, which has a pejorative meaning and suggests a morbid relationship between mother and son, which has little to do with the reality. A more appropriate term would be "long family." In my view, and that of many Italian men and women, living at home is not necessarily an indication of a lack of autonomy, unless one refers only to financial autonomy. For all other matters, young Italians are quite successful in negotiating a rather high level of independence while continuing to enjoy the "fringe benefits" of staying at home. In fact, my American students often are amazed by the freedom that their Italian friends enjoy in their families. According to them, American parents would never allow their daughters and sons to invite boyfriends or girlfriends over and sleep with them under the parental roof. Incidentally, I am told that the number of young Americans who return home after college is increasing as it is becoming more difficult to find a job or affordable lodging. I wonder how they will manage to convince their parents to become more accommodating to their personal intimate relationships.

[Which brings up a comment by Barbara Defoe Whitehead and David Popenoe (1998) in their study of unmarried, non-college-educated, young Americans:

[We were surprised by the high number of young adults living with parents. This may be due to the combination of available employment and scarce affordable housing in northern New Jersey. These young men and women are likely to find work close to their families but they may not find affordable rents—thus increasing the attractiveness of living with parents. Also, most of these men and women reported living in intact families at age 15, and perhaps their parents' marital stability increased the likelihood that they would have the option of returning home. . . . Interestingly, some women said that you had greater freedom living with your parents than living on your own or with a partner. Apparently, this form of dependence on parents is not incompatible with notions of personal independence.

[To make valid cross-cultural comparisons, one needs to avoid the simplistic description and, at the same time, understand and appreciate the subtleties of the social context in both cultures. (*End of update by P. F. Wanrooij*)]

Although there is no strong social condemnation of the cohabitation of unmarried couples, cohabitation is relatively rare, and marriage is considered the natural conclusion of a stable heterosexual relationship. In 1991, cohabiting couples made up 1.6% of Italian couples. The rate of cohabitation is significantly higher in the northern regions than in the south, for example, 4.1% in the region of Val d'Aosta against 0.5% in the Basilicata.

Notwithstanding a generally positive view of marriage, there is a tendency to delay the time of marriage, and, partly as a result of this, the nuptiality rate in Italy is low: In 1997, it was 4.7 per 1,000 population. The average age at a first marriage in 1994 was 29.3 for males and 26.5 for females; in 1984, it was 27.4 for males and 24.3 for females. Italians in the south are distinguished by a higher nuptiality rate: In 1994, it was 5.6 per 1,000 population against 4.8 in the regions of the north and the center, and at an earlier age at marriage, 25.6 for females and 28.7 for males (Barbagli & Saraceno 1997).

Most Italians leave the parental home only when they get married, and this holds true even for the older age groups: 68% of Italian males aged 35 and over and 63.3% of females who never married live with their parents. Divorce or separation often results in a return to the parental home: About 20% of divorced or separated Italians (25.2% of males and 17.1% of females) cohabit with their parents (ISTAT 1996)

"Long families" are the combined effect of the low cohabitation rate and a relatively late age of marriage: The majority of unmarried young people aged 18 to 34 continue to live with their parents (58.8% in 1998). It is more common for young men to stay with their family (66.5%) than for young women (50.9%). The percentage of young people living with their family is increasing, especially among young women: In 1983, only 40.4% of them were living with their family.

Economic circumstances, high unemployment among young people, and the difficulty of finding housing also contribute to the incidence of "long families," but do not offer a sufficient explanation for the fact that young people in Italy do not "strike out" on their own. "Long families" are in fact as common in the northeastern region, where unemployment is less a problem, but where 59.5% of young people aged 18 to 34 live with their parents, compared with the south, where economic problems are much more serious, and 59.8% of young people live with their parents. An alternative and more positive explanation of the growing incidence of "long families" is the democratic character of the modern Italian family, where young adults have the possibility to renegotiate their position. In this way, young adults are able to have a satisfactory level of autonomy and independence, while at the same time enjoying the "fringe benefits" of family life in terms of financial advantages and services (Barbagli & Saraceno 1997). For a high percentage of young people (57% in the northeast, 34.2% in the south), the reason for staying is that they are happy to stay and enjoy a fair amount of freedom. Satisfaction increases with age as the reasons for tension decrease (ISTAT 1999b).

The high level of interaction between married adults and their parents is further proof of the importance of the family network in Italy: 3.8% of married Italians under age 64 whose mother is alive live with their mother. Of those who are not cohabiting, 77.8% see their parents at least once a week and one third of them every day. One partial explanation of the high interaction with parents is the low level of geographical mobility: 28% of married Italians live at a distance of less than one kilometer (0.62 mi.) from their parents (ISTAT 1996).

## Marriage and Family

According to the 1975 family law, the legal age of marriage is 18 for both partners. Legal courts can give exemption from this requirement, provided that the partners are at least 16 years of age. Generally, the courts do not consider pregnancy a valid motive to grant permission for the marriage of minors. The same 1975 legislation abolished the possibility of reparatory marriage, which in the past had been used by persons accused of crimes like rape and forceful abduction, who could avoid punishment by marrying their victim.

The average frequency for sexual intercourse was 92 times per year (Durex 1998). According to an earlier survey, on average, men and women had sexual intercourse about eight times per month, but there were important differences according to age, with the highest levels of sexual activity in the age group 18 to 25 for women and 35 to 44 for men. The fact that females under 25 showed a higher frequency of sexual intercourse than males of the same age can be explained as a result of their earlier participation in stable relationships and marriage. A similar explanation is proposed for the fact that young women have more sexual partners than men, while the situation is inverted in the higher age groups. In this case also, the higher tolerance of male pre- and extramarital sexual relations may play a role (Fabris & Davis 1978). The more recent survey published by Carlo Buzzi (1998) confirms the higher sexual activity rate of young women, 33.8% of whom have sexual intercourse two to three times a week (against 27.4% for males). Also, the percentage of young women who had no sexual

intercourse during the previous three months turned out to be almost half that of men (12.4% against 23.5%).

According to the 1978 survey, women, more often than men, had sexual intercourse not because they desired to have it, but to please their partner. While 49% of males would like to increase the frequency of sexual intercourse, this was true for only 25% of females, most of whom were satisfied with the frequency (56% against 43% for males). Thirteen percent of females—mostly in the higher age groups—desired to reduce the frequency of sexual intercourse as compared with 3% of males. These gender differences may be explained as the result of a greater pressure on males for sexual performance, but also by the fact that more women found sex less enjoyable. Many of them, in fact, complained that before, during, and after sexual intercourse, men paid insufficient attention to their desires.

The brief duration of foreplay and sexual intercourse, limited almost exclusively to penetration, is more common among the uneducated, among more-religious couples, and among the higher age groups. The average duration of foreplay was about 13 minutes, and that of coitus about 9 minutes (Fabris & Davis 1978). A more recent survey indicates the duration of sexual intercourse, excluding foreplay, is 14.2 minutes (Durex 1998).

It should be noted that the statistical data regarding the frequency and duration of sexual intercourse, as well as other aspects of sexual life, should be treated with caution. Not only do the averages ignore important differences in individual reactions, but it is also possible that the responses are influenced by the desire of those interviewed to satisfy the presumed expectations of the interviewer, or—more generally—by the desire to make a positive impression. For these reasons, it is wrong to use these data as a measure of "normality."

Seventy-six percent of male partners and 72% of female partners in stable couples rated their sexual life "good" or "very good." More-negative judgments were expressed by 3% of males and by 7% of females. The degree of satisfaction with their sexual lives increased during the first ten years of the relationship, and remained the same or decreased thereafter (Fabris & Davis 1978).

According to the 1978 survey, 69% of males and 26% of females always experienced orgasm during sexual intercourse. About one fifth of women never or rarely experienced orgasm. Young, educated, and nonreligious women had a higher orgasm rate. Of the women who experienced orgasm, 29% experienced orgasm as a result of the oral or manual stimulation of the genitals, and 27% experienced it during penetration, whereas for 44% of these women, both activities resulted in orgasm.

At least 41% of Italian males and 14% of females have had extramarital sexual relations. Especially for women, the adultery rate increases with the level of education; it was 20% for women with a university degree. The adultery rate and the number of partners are lower for women, but the extramarital relationship is also characterized by a higher emotional investment (Fabris & Davis 1978). More recent figures indicate that 38% of Italians admit to having been involved in more than one sexual relationship at a time (Durex 1998).

## Divorce and Remarriage

Divorce became legal in Italy in 1970, and a 1974 referendum confirmed the existing legislation with a 59.1% majority. Between 1985 and 1996, the number of divorces increased from 15,650 to 32,717. In the same period, separations increased from 35,163 to 57,538. The numbers were highest in the region of Lazio, followed by the more industrial northwestern regions. The divorce rate was much lower in the south. Even though there is a clear tendency toward an increase in the divorce rate, the stability of marriage is higher in Italy than in any other European country. This impression remains true, even when taking into account both separations and divorces: In 1994 in Italy, 16 out of 100 marriages were dissolved as a result of legal separation, and 8 out of 100 because of divorce. In the same year, the divorce rate was 44% in the United Kingdom and Sweden and 29% in the Netherlands. In 1996, the divorce rate in Italy was 0.6 per 1,000 population against a European Union average of 1.8 (ISTAT 1999).

The main reason for the relatively low divorce rate is probably religion. Added to this factor is the importance of the family, not only as a source of emotional support and the context for the development of profound personal relations, but also for many other aspects of social life, from financial support to finding a job. Divorce is seen primarily as evidence of personal failure, and the end of the relationship is considered, above all, the beginning of a difficult period in personal life, rather than as a possible new start and an occasion to regain freedom and independence.

*Incidence of Oral and Anal Sex*

Oral sex, which in the past was condemned as "unnatural," is practiced more or less often by 55.2% of young Italians, and only rarely by 26.8%. Earlier surveys indicated that 47% of females and 58% of males experienced oral sex (Fabris & Davis 1978). Oral sex is a common element in the sexual fantasies of Italian males, especially during masturbation; this is less true for women. Both men and women prefer their partner to perform oral stimulation of their genitals, fellatio and cunnilingus, rather than performing these sexual acts themselves on their partners.

While anal intercourse is not part of the fantasies of the majority of women, it is part of the fantasies of 75 to 80% of men. However, the incidence of this practice is relatively low. According to the 1978 survey, 35% of males and 23% of females had experienced anal sex. A more recent survey among young people indicates that 78.6% of females and 62% of males never experience anal sex (Buzzi 1998).

## 6. Homoerotic, Homosexual, and Bisexual Behaviors

### A. History

With the noteworthy exceptions of the Kingdom of Sardinia and the regions under Austrian rule, the Italian states in the first part of the 18th century had no legislation against homosexual acts. After Unification, the repressive legislation of the Kingdom of Sardinia was extended to the other regions of Italy, excluding the territory of the ancient kingdom of Naples. With the introduction of a new penal code in 1889, regional differences in the treatment of homosexual acts were eliminated and homosexuality was decriminalized. Legal persecution of homosexuals continued, however, based on accusations regarding indecent acts, and so on. Especially in southern Italy, however, the general attitude regarding homosexuality was rather tolerant, and by the end of the 19th century, male homosexual communities existed on the island of Capri and in towns such as Taormina. In this same period, Italy attracted a fair amount of sex tourism from countries like the United Kingdom and Germany where existing legislation against homosexuals was applied more severely.

Homophobic attitudes were prominent in the nationalistic propaganda during World War I, which often made references to sexual scandals in the German imperial court, and used accusations of homosexuality against all those who opposed the Italian war effort, including neutralists and pacifists.

The attitude of repressive tolerance that characterized public reactions to homosexuality continued during the Fascist period, when attempts to introduce more-specific legislation were blocked to safeguard the virile reputation of Italian men. Homosexual communities were thus allowed to survive, but at the same time, police measures were used against homosexuals who dared to "come out." Especially after 1938, when racist legislation was introduced in Italy, many homosexuals were condemned to legal confinement.

While at the level of legislation, the situation remained unchanged after the fall of Fascism in 1945, during the 1950s, some isolated publications voiced the need to improve the social status of male and female homosexuals. These attempts, however, met with the opposition of medical doctors, and especially the Italian specialists of the new discipline of sexology, who insisted on considering homosexuality a perversion or disease, and advocated anything from sports and sexual encounters with prostitutes to electroshock therapy to cure homosexuals. During the 1960s, members of Parliament tried to introduce legislation against homosexuality, which would punish not only homosexual acts between consenting adults, but also any public discourse in favor of homosexuality. These attempts failed because of the prevailing attitude of repressive tolerance.

Within the context of the sexual liberation movement of the late 1960s, which in the first phase was not sympathetic to the problems of homosexuals, the first Italian group of organized homosexuals emerged. In April 1972, the Unitary Front of Revolutionary Italian Homosexuals (FUORI; the acronym also means "out") contested the power of medical science at a congress of sexologists. The lack of support from the traditional leftist parties and the radical opposition from the right-wing parties and from the Catholic party, Christian Democracy, convinced the leaders of FUORI in 1975 to establish institutional links with the Radical Party, which had a tradition of civil rights actions. However, the decision led to a split between the reformers and those who considered themselves part of a revolutionary movement; new groups with links to the extreme left-wing parties were then created. In 1982, FUORI was dissolved.

The first nucleus of a new organization of homosexuals, Arcigay, was created in Palermo in December 1980 as a reaction to the tragedy of a double suicide of two gay lovers who had become the victims of public ostracism in the small town of Giarre, when their story became public. The first national congress designed to unite the local groups, created with the support of a dissident Catholic priest, Don Marco Bisceglia, took place in Palermo in 1982. It saw the participation of the most important leaders of Arci, a leisure-time and cultural organization traditionally close to the parties of the left (the communist and socialist parties). The connection between the homosexual movement and the traditional parties of the left, created through Arcigay, was the result of the innovative political strategy of attention for new social groups, feminists and homosexuals, inaugurated by the Communist Party in 1977. This initial connection was followed by a debate on the conditions of homosexuals in the party press (Giovannini 1980). Finally, in 1985, Arcigay was given a more structured national organization, with the election at the second national congress of Franco Grillini as national secretary and Beppe Ramina as president.

The relations between lesbian women and gay men have not been easy, because of, among other reasons, the separatist tendencies of the most radical lesbian groups. In 1990, however, a group of lesbians created Arcigay Donna, and for the first time a woman, Graziella Bertozzo, was elected national secretary. In 1992, the association itself was rebaptized Arcigay Arcilesbica. In 1996, the association was once more restructured and became a federation of different groups; Arcilesbica chose to become autonomous. The most recent strategy aims at the construction of a gay and lesbian community offering services, institutional support, and the solidarity necessary to allow lesbian and gay persons to express their sexual identity just like non-homosexual persons. [*Update 2003*: In this context, it is important to note that according to a recent survey carried out by Marzio Barbagli and Asher Colombo (2001), the majority of homosexuals have never openly discussed their sexual orientation with their parents. Coming out on the job is considered even more of a problem, even though only 2% to 5% of those who did come out were confronted with serious acts of discrimination (*End of update by P. F. Wanrooij*)]

## B. Legal Status

Article 3 of the Constitution of the Italian Republic, approved in 1947, recognizes the equality of all citizens, and condemns discrimination based on sex, race, language, religion, political opinion, and personal and social conditions. The Republic has the obligation to remove social and economic obstacles, which *de facto* limit the full development of the human personality. While this can be interpreted as including the protection of the right of each individual not to be discriminated against on the grounds of his or her sexual orientation, there is no explicit mention of this in the Italian legislation. A campaign to introduce sexual orientation among the conditions mentioned in Article 3 of the Constitution started in 1998.

The creation of Arcigay has given more visibility to the problems of homosexuals in Italian society, and has made it possible to recognize and fight stereotypes, prejudices, and homophobic attitudes. The recognition of the role played by Arcigay in the defense of the interests of homosexuals became clear in 1987, when a group of members of Parliament attended the Third National Congress of the movement. Together with the fight against all forms of discrimination of homosexuals in Italian society, Arcigay has dedicated much energy to the issue of the recognition of the rights of homosexual couples. In 1997, a proposal was presented to Parliament in favor of the public recognition of relations not based on marriage. The proposal defines these so-called "civil unions" as relations between two consenting adult persons of any sex who have led for at least one year a common spiritual and material life. Legal recognition of these unions would entail the possibility of formal registration, and the extension to the partners of these unions of all rights commonly recognized to the partners of traditional couples, including unemployment benefits, compensation for injuries to the partner, priority access to public housing projects, the recognition of the right to reside in Italy for foreign partners, and so on.

A recent survey among Italian Catholics (Inchiesta 1998) indicated a 72.2% majority in favor of giving "*de facto* unions" the same rights as legal families. In this case, an insufficient understanding of the term "*de facto* unions" probably invalidates the results. However, according to a recent survey (Buzzi 1998), 47.1% of young people agree with the idea that "homosexual couples should have the same rights as heterosexual couples," while only 30% disapproved. The ideas that homosexuality is a disease or a form of sexual perversion that should be illegal obtained, respectively, the support of 17.4% and 8.3% of the respondents.

Notwithstanding this public support, the proposal for the recognition of "civil unions" has made no progress in Parliament, because of numerous groups voicing their objections and the opposition of the Catholic Church and its allies.

According to a 1988 survey, homophobic attitudes are strong, especially among the lower social classes and among the elderly. But 35.3% of all Italians declared that they would simply acknowledge the discovery of a homosexual relative, while 23% would try to help homosexual relatives to express their sexual orientation without anxiety (Fiore 1991). This relatively open-minded attitude at the individual level contrasts with the social rejection of homosexuality. Still, 11.2% of Italians proposed legal measures against homosexuality and, while 48.8% are in favor of the recognition of the equal rights and dignity of homosexuals, 45.3% of Italians see the diffusion of homosexuality as a social peril.

## C. Behaviors

Most males discover their homosexual desires during puberty, between the ages of 11 and 15 (42.6%), or adolescence, age 16 to 20 (20.9%). Females become aware of their desires at a later age. They also start having sexual relations at a later age (22.3% before age 15, against 42.1% in the case of males). Whereas homosexual contacts precede the acquisition of a homosexual identity in the case of males, in the case of females, the first homosexual experiences usually take place after the acquisition of a sexual identity. The main reaction in the case of females is happiness (64.5% against 47.2% in the case of males). However, fear and a sense of guilt continue to play a role. The high number of partners of male homosexuals—12.9% declared sexual contacts with over 400 partners—is in contrast with the declared preference for monogamous same-sex couples. [*Update 2003*: The number of partners per year is significantly lower for the generation born after 1972 than for those born before 1956. This may be explained in part by the fear of AIDS. However, it might also be the result of a generational change, because those coming of age in the 1980s and 1990s do not share the ideals of free love that were popular both among homosexuals and among heterosexuals in the 1960s. (*End of update by P. F. Wanrooij*)]

According to Fiore (1991), the most common sexual practices among homosexual couples are: mutual masturbation (practiced in all sexual contacts by 25% of males and 41.9% of females), followed by oral-genital contacts and penetration. Sadomasochistic practices are much less frequent. Generally speaking, sexual practices among homosexuals are polymorphous and depend on the partner, the place, and other specific conditions. [*Update 2003*: A recent survey by Barbagli and Colombo (2001) shows that similar characteristics apply to lesbian women: mutual masturbation and penetration of the vagina are the most common sexual practices, but practices vary widely depending on conditions like the level of emotional participation. (*End of update by P. F. Wanrooij*)]

## 7. Gender Diversity and Transgender Issues

During the late 1970s, a group of transsexuals created the Movimento Transessuali Italiani (MTI) (Movement of Italian Transsexuals or MIT). With the support of the Radical Party, this movement succeeded in 1982 in convincing Parliament to change the existing legislation. The original proposal would have made it possible to change one's sex simply by requesting a change in the sex indicators on official documents. The final approved compromise introduced a two-step procedure for changing one's sex. First, a court has to give permission for the surgical adaptation of genitals on the basis of medical and psychological evidence. Certification of the surgical intervention is then needed to change the indication of sex in the documents.

The law is based on the assumption that only two sexes exist, male and female, and, while acknowledging the right of transsexuals to recreate the unity of body and mind, the law offers no solution for transsexuals who intend to change their sex status without undergoing surgical interventions.

## 8. Significant Unconventional Sexual Behaviors

### A. Coercive Sex

*Child Sexual Abuse and Incest*

A number of serious crimes committed in Italy and abroad has brought the problem of sexual abuse of children to public attention. The activities of the telephone help service for children, Telefono Azzurro ("Blue Telephone"), have also contributed to making the problem better known to the general public.

Reacting to the increase in the number of cases of sexual abuse of children that have reached public attention, the Italian Parliament introduced in 1998 new legislation against the sexual exploitation of minors in prostitution, pornography, and sex tourism. The clients of prostitutes aged 14 to 16 risk a term of prison from six months to three years, or of four months to two years if the client is under age 18. Similar punishment is attached to the acquisition of pornography involving minors. The main innovations of the law regard more severe punishment for those who produce, sell, or transmit pornography depicting minors, and for those responsible for supporting the prostitution of minors. Those responsible for traffic in minors for prostitution risk a punishment of six to 20 years. The law can also be applied if the crimes are committed abroad, so that travel agencies have the obligation to warn their clients about the risks of sex tourism.

In order to combat sex tourism and the distribution of pornography involving minors, police forces are allowed to work undercover, participate in organized travel abroad, and create Internet sites and discussion groups.

The recent legislation has been criticized for confirming existing stereotypes and for calling for new crusades or "witch hunts." The main criticism centers on the fact that the law tends to focus on persons who are unknown to the child, whereas, in reality, in the majority of cases, those responsible for child abuse are family members or members of the community.

Indictment for incest involving two adults takes place only on complaint and in case of public scandal. Generally, police and judiciary authorities do not take action unless a formal complaint has been filed.

*Sexual Harassment*

The majority of Italian women aged 14 to 59 have been the victim of at least one of the following forms of sexual harassment: obscene telephone calls, acts of exhibitionism, physical harassment, and/or sexual intimidation on the job. The persons responsible for acts of sexual harassment are generally outsiders not known to the victims.

Proposals to clarify the legal status of some forms of behavior with a sexual connotation that are clearly offensive came up for open discussion, but early public opinion has resisted all attempts to introduce a more extensive notion of sexual harassment. In many cases, these attempts are considered part of a moral crusade imported from the United States.

*Rape*

The Fascist penal code defined rape as a crime that offended public morality and not as a crime against the person. Like many other parts of Fascist legislation, the articles regarding sexual violence remained valid during the first decades of the Italian Republic. Rape was considered a crime against morality, and no mandatory prosecution existed. The victim had to file a complaint, and often would be as much on trial as the perpetrator, because the defense would insist that the victim had provoked the crime. Evidence of the sexual history of the victim could be presented to the court. Moreover, the fact that the men responsible for this crime could escape punishment if they married their victims, often led to heavy pressure on the victim. In any case, punishment of the crime was relatively mild.

Given this legal situation, and taking into account the psychological problems that still today make it difficult to denounce acts of sexual violence, the statistics have no direct relation with the real incidence of the crime, but are linked with the attitudes prevailing in society, and especially among women. Until the early 1960s, the number of denunciations of rape was highest in the southern regions of Italy, where legal pressure was used to obtain extralegal solutions, like marriage, which could restore the honor of the family (Sabadini 1998).

During the 1970s, changes in sexual mores led to a decline of the number of denunciations in the south. The general increase of denunciations in the 1980s is linked with changes in public opinion, which had grown more aware of the importance of women's rights, while the police forces and judiciary system also changed their attitudes. Women's organizations have played an important role in this change. Already in the 1960s, women's organizations had started to campaign against the existing legislation, underlining the importance of sexual violence against women. The existence of anti-violence centers and of other assistance services organized by women, like the Telefono Rosa ("Pink Telephone"), convinced more women to denounce violence.

Still today, most cases of sexual violence are not denounced, and this is even more true when the person responsible for the crime is someone known by the victim, as is often the case. Only in 21.7% of the reported cases of sexual violence was the person responsible totally unknown to the victim; most other cases regarded friends, relatives, employers, and so on. Friends, relatives, and (ex-)boyfriends are responsible for 54.3% of reported incidents of sexual violence; violence on the job by employers or colleagues accounts for 10.7%. Street violence accounts for 22.5%.

In February 1996, new legislation was introduced. Sexual violence is now considered a crime against the person, and is punished more severely than in the past. By abolishing the distinction between rape (sexual violence with penetration) and other forms of sexual violence, Law n. 66 has eliminated the need for specific medical checks and for a detailed discussion of the acts. According to the new legislation, sexual violence, meaning sexual relations obtained with the use of physical violence, threats, abuse of authority, abuse of conditions of physical or mental inferiority, or deception, is punished with a term in prison from five to ten years. The punishment is six to 12 years if special conditions occur, as in the case of gang rape. Prosecution is mandatory only in special cases, such as when the victim is under age 14. In all other cases, it is necessary to file a complaint within a period of six months from the time of the crime. It is not possible to retract this complaint.

### B. Prostitution

In 1860, the new Italian kingdom followed the French and Belgian example of allowing regulated prostitution in closed houses, where prostitutes were subjected to mandatory medical control and deprived of many civil rights. Notwithstanding the opposition of the abolitionist movement and feminist groups, the system of regulated prostitution remained in vigor, with relatively minor changes, until 1958. The system was justified on the grounds that it gave young men a safe outlet for their sexual desires, and helped to avoid both masturbation and the socially more disruptive problem of the seduction of "honest" girls. Moralistic arguments played an important role as well in the discourse of the abolitionists, who refused to recognize that prostitution could be a choice for poor women for whom the alternatives offered by the labor market often were not much more attractive. Medical science viewed regulated prostitution as a necessary protection against the diffusion of sexually transmitted diseases. Moreover, positivist scientists like Cesare Lombroso (1836-1909), an Italian physician and criminologist, claimed that prostitution was the "biological destiny" of women who shared certain physical and psychological characteristics.

In 1948, Lina Merlin, a socialist member of Parliament, proposed a bill for the abolition of closed houses of prostitution. The proposal, which was not approved until 1958, met with the open opposition of brothel keepers who financed a campaign in the newspapers against the "Salvation Army mentality" of Lina Merlin, and accused her of disregarding male privileges. Protests were expressed also by the national association of venereologists, who warned that the abolition of mandatory medical checks on prostitutes would lead to a rapid increase of syphilis and other venereal diseases. The group of abolitionists was internally divided because some saw the abolition of organized prostitution primarily as a way to reconstruct the moral bases of male superiority, or as part of a more complex effort of moralization, including measures against premarital sex, adultery, and contraception. The main cause of the delay, however, was the silent opposition of the male members of Parliament who simply refused to put the issue on the agenda.

The new legislation, which was finally approved in 1958, did not make prostitution, as such, a crime, but punished only persons involved in procuring and in the exploitation of prostitution. Therefore, those who organized prostitution now ran most of the legal risks, while the prostitutes themselves had little to fear. The result has been that most prostitutes turned to streetwalking; only those prostitutes who could guarantee a high income, and who did not represent special risks of being minors or drug addicts, were employed in illegal brothels.

In the 1980s, prostitutes, or sex workers, started to organize themselves, and the year 1983 saw the first meeting of the Comitato per i Diritti Civili delle Prostitute (Committee for the Civil Rights of Prostitutes), created on the initiative of Carla Corso and Pia Covre. The main aim of this organization was to limit the extensive interpretation of the existing law against the exploitation of prostitution, which was often applied against the husbands and partners of prostitutes. An attempt was also made to reeducate the male clients, and to convince them of the necessity to use condoms.

The presence among prostitutes of drug addicts willing to accept lower prices and not requiring the use of condoms limited the successes of the organizations of prostitutes. In the early 1990s, the arrival of women from Eastern Europe and Africa created further problems. According to a report published by the Ministry of Internal Affairs in September 1997, the total number of women working as prostitutes in Italy is about 50,000. Thirty-five thousand of these women have migrated to Italy from abroad, with the major group coming from Albania. In 1996, 4,387 persons were denounced for the exploitation of prostitution.

Prostitutes can be divided into three categories, depending on differences between the level of personal autonomy, the prices paid for their services, the level of integration in

society, and age. At the top level are the call girls who are autonomous in the organization of their activities; they attract their clients through advertising in newspapers and in specialized magazines. Unlike the call girls, the second group of women, who work officially as actors, dancers, hostesses, strippers, and so on, cannot refuse clients who are procured by agencies or by the owners of nightclubs.

The working conditions of streetwalkers, many of them illegal immigrants, are worse, because their legal situation makes them easily exploited. Moreover, many of these prostitutes, especially those coming from Albania, are minors, and are forced to work on the streets. These young women are often exploited by criminal gangs, who force them to hand over all the money they earn. Moreover, they are the frequent victims of the violent actions of the procurers, especially when they stand up against their exploiters, and refuse to work as prostitutes. Streetwalkers also run more risks in their contacts with clients. Police actions against these forms of violence have been notably inefficient.

The rapid increase in the number of prostitutes and their growing visibility has led to a recent debate about the possible reintroduction of some regulation of prostitution. Proposals have been forwarded to force prostitutes to exercise their profession only in certain locations, and/or to allow them to organize themselves in cooperatives, without being accused of "favoring" the prostitution of their fellow sex workers. In 1998, many city councils introduced repressive legislation, using the existing rules regarding traffic and public order, to force prostitutes and their clients to change locations. At the national level, proposals were discussed to coordinate police actions against the exploitation of women and to create public facilities for prostitutes who want to abandon the streets. Moreover, illegal immigrants are offered the right to reside in Italy in exchange for their help in dismantling the criminal organizations responsible for the "traffic in women."

[*Update 2003*: In January 2003, the Italian government proposed a bill, which, in its intentions, will combat the increase of prostitution. The exploitation of prostitution by criminal organizations will be punished more severely, and more funds will be made available to assist the women who want to escape from these organizations. Streetwalkers who are not the victims of criminals will be punished with a fine plus a term of prison up to 15 days. Also, their male clients risk a fine. However, prostitution in private apartments will be legal. Moreover, prostitutes are encouraged to undergo frequent medical checkups, even though the bill does not introduce any formal obligation in this sense.

[The conservative government presented its bill as a way of promoting traditional family values, without reintroducing regulated prostitution. Members of the opposition and nongovernmental organizations, however, speak about a return to the system of "closed houses." They claim that the bill merely aims at eliminating the visibility of prostitution, without tackling the problem itself. (*End of update by P. F. Wanrooij*)]

Transsexuals and transvestites also participate in prostitution, where the two categories are often lumped together under the name *viados*. Male homosexual prostitution, which created Italy's reputation for sex tourism early in the 20th century, is concentrated in the major cities, and takes, above all, the form of streetwalking. As in the case of heterosexual prostitution, some of the prostitutes offering their services to homosexual clients are minors, and a relatively high percentage is recruited among (illegal) immigrants. Male heterosexual prostitution is less common, but according to journalistic sources, there is an increase in the phenomenon. Unfortunately, little research has been done on this. In recent years, the larger Italian cities have attracted Brazilian and other Latino transvestites, who can earn a much better living as prostitutes than they can in South America.

Not much information is available about the clients of prostitutes. Until 1960, about a quarter of Italian young men had their first complete heterosexual experience with prostitutes. Visits to brothels were considered part of the process of coming of age for young, unmarried men, even though in reality middle-aged married men made up a large part of the clientele.

Today, there is a growing demand for sexual services, which seems to be linked with the more general phenomenon of the commoditization of human relations. About 16% of sexually active Italian males have sexual intercourse with prostitutes, with a higher percentage in southern Italy (Cutrufelli 1996). The increase in the demand, however, has not kept up with the increase on the supply side. As a result, it has become ever more difficult for prostitutes to refuse certain clients or particular sexual acts. Also, the safety risk is higher, as the request to use condoms is often disregarded by clients.

A recent public opinion survey (Buzzi 1998) shows that most young Italians have a more severe judgment about the clients than about the prostitutes. Prostitution, however, is seen above all as a problem of public order, and 64.7% of young people agree with the idea of reestablishing brothels. Moreover, the majority of young men do not exclude the possibility of going with prostitutes.

### C. Pornography and Erotica

While it is difficult to find precise data about the production and commerce of pornography in Italy, there are no doubts about its diffusion. The gradual blurring of the distinction between pornography and other forms of erotica has led to a high level of social acceptance of pornography and opened new markets. In public debate, the anti-pornography position is weak, and pornography is often presented as a form of sexual liberation. Even some Catholic moralists have recognized that pornography can help couples to improve their sexual life as long as it does not replace "natural" sexuality.

The pornography market can satisfy most requests in genres from heterosexual and homosexual to transsexual, and from sadomasochism to sexual acts involving animals, and products including magazines, videocassettes, telephone services, and sex toys. A great diversification exists in the distribution system, which includes normal newsstands, video shops, porno shops, and mail-order services. From the economic point of view, the most important sector of the porno market is the sale of videocassettes, the success of which has been made possible by the wide distribution of videocassette players. With the increase in the sale of videocassettes, the importance of the so-called "red light" cinemas, with their almost exclusively male public, has decreased rapidly, from 122 in 1987 to 85 in 1992. Soft-core magazines, as well, have entered a period of crisis: The October 1991 issue of *Playboy* sold 51,000 copies, whereas during the late 1970s, the average sale had been about 120,000 copies. Hardcore magazines did not suffer the same decline, thanks to the greater diversification of their content. The total yearly sale of porno magazines is about 30 million copies.

Compared to porno cinemas, videocassettes offer the possibility of greater privacy, and cater to the needs of a more mixed public, including women and couples. Pornographic videocassettes are distributed primarily through video shops, where they can also be rented, and at the typi-

cal newsstand. The newsstands have fewer legal problems in selling the hardcore cassettes, which are formally attached to magazines, because, according to a law issued in 1975, the owner of the newsstand is not responsible for the content of the publications that he or she sells. This legal situation has made the newsstands the primary channel for the sale of pornographic cassettes, and has thus determined a high level of visibility for pornography. Video shops, however, offer the advantage of greater anonymity, especially, in the case of automatic dispensers, and the technical quality of the cassettes is usually higher. Estimates of the economic value of pornographic cassettes vary from 250 to 1,000 billion Italian lire per year.

The star system is a characteristic of hardcore pornographic movies produced in Italy, and actresses like Ilona Staller, Moana Pozzi, Jessica Rizzo, and Eva Henger have achieved some popularity also outside the world of pornography, thanks to their presence as guest stars in non-porno television shows. The best-known pornography stars have tried to exploit their popularity also, through the creation of pay sites on the World Wide Web. Not much is known about the consumption of pornography though Internet services, but the growing number of sites in Italian seems to indicate an expanding demand.

Surveys regarding the consumers of pornography (Eurispes 1993) indicate that about 50% of both males and females are sexuality excited by erotic films. However, whereas females prefer erotic films where sexual acts are embedded in a narrative context, males are more easily excited by viewing mere nudity and sexual organs. Earlier surveys (Sabatini 1988) defined the interest for pornography as predominantly male, and suggested that female curiosity increased with age. Moreover, female consumption of pornography seems to take place in the context of the couple, whereas for men it is more linked with solitary sex. The gender differences in the consumption of pornography are probably related to its male focus. Notwithstanding this, generally speaking, there are indications of an increase of the consumption of pornography by couples.

## 9. Contraception, Abortion, and Population Planning

### A. Contraception

According to a 1997 survey (De Sandre 1997), the most common method of contraception in Italy is withdrawal, which is used by 29.2% of women of fertile age with a stable relationship. The incidence of this method is highest among women in the age group 20 to 24 (38.0%), where the contraceptive pill ranks second with 32.9%, and in the age group 45 to 49 (39.6%). Condoms are the most popular method of birth control for women aged 35 to 39 (28.1%); the contraceptive pill prevails in the age group 30 to 34 (30.8%). Nine percent of women with a stable relationship do not use any method of contraception.

The situation is completely different among women without a stable relationship: 48.7% use the contraceptive pill, and 30.8% use condoms. Differences between the age groups are less important for this category, with the exception of women belonging to the age group 45 to 49, whose use of the contraceptive pill is equaled by the use of other modern methods of contraception (both 22.9%). Condoms are used by 7.6% of the 45-to-49 age group, whereas 38.9% of this group does not use any method of contraception. Differences between the age groups are less pronounced among women without a stable relationship. Only the women aged 45 to 49 distinguish themselves: The use of the contraceptive pill is lower for this group (22.9%), and the difference is even more striking for the use of condoms (7.6%). Thirty-nine percent of women without a stable relationship aged 45 to 49 do not use any form of contraception.

Condoms and other means of contraception were not easily available in Italy until World War I. However, the existing methods of birth control, sexual abstention and withdrawal, were not popular among men from the higher classes, who often preferred the sexual exploitation of domestic servants and peasant women. The ideals of neo-Malthusianism gained more popularity in the first decades of the 20th century when rubber condoms became available. In 1913, Luigi Berta and Secondo Giorni founded the neo-Malthusian League. The success of this movement was hampered by the advent of World War I, which seemed to show the need of population growth, and gave birth control an anti-patriotic image.

Eager to win the "demographic battle" in favor of population growth, the Fascist leaders introduced in 1930 legislation prohibiting publications and any other form of propaganda in favor of birth control. The production of condoms, as such, was not affected, because they were deemed necessary as a protection against venereal diseases. Subsidies and tax reductions for large families, jobs and better career chances for prolific fathers, higher taxation for bachelors, and healthcare for mothers and children were introduced in this period, but did not convince men, and above all women, to have more children. The main result of the prohibition of contraception was, therefore, an increase in the number of abortions. In addition, there was an increase in the number of illegitimate children, because economic hardship made it difficult to set up new households.

In the years after World War II, there was growing opposition against the Fascist legislation regarding contraception, which had remained valid in Italy even after the fall of Benito Mussolini. In 1956, the Italian Association for Demographic Education (AIED) was founded with the aim of defending the idea and the practice of a voluntary and conscious limitation of the number of children, and of combating the existing legislation against birth control. AIED had the support of the secular lay forces in Italy, of the socialists and of the communists, but its proposals were strongly opposed by the Catholics, who upheld the existing legislation. Still, in 1965, the Constitutional Court declared that detailed information about contraceptives should remain illegal because it offended public morality. In 1971, the legislation forbidding "propaganda in favor of birth control" was declared unconstitutional.

Since the legalization of contraception, the fertility rate has accelerated its decline. Notwithstanding the opposition of the Catholic Church, which has repeatedly reaffirmed its condemnation of contraception in the 1969 Encyclical *Humanae Vitae* of Pope Paul VI, the use of the contraceptive pill has increased, and almost tripled in the ten years between 1985 and 1996.

Some taboos survive, however. In 1997, the installation of condom dispensers in a public high school caused a major outcry in the conservative press. The official newspaper of the Vatican, *L'Osservatore Romano*, spoke about an act of arrogance committed by a minority, even though according to public opinion polls, 79% of the Italians were in favor of the initiative. Earlier, in 1993, an anti-AIDS campaign in high schools was blocked because it endorsed the use of condoms. Furthermore, a recent agreement among private and public television networks excludes publicity for condoms during prime time.

Especially among young people, who seem to be aware of the risks of unprotected sexual relations in terms of STDs and pregnancy, the use of condoms is limited, because it is

assumed that they make sex less enjoyable, because it is embarrassing to buy them, and also because the risk of not using condoms in contacts with occasional partners is judged acceptable. The low incidence of extramarital pregnancies is nevertheless an indication of the widespread use of contraception. The majority of unmarried women above age 20, in fact, have complete sexual relations, but only a few of them cohabit or have children. This is even more significant taking into account the distance between the age of first sex and marriage.

## B. Abortion

Although induced abortion was not allowed during the Fascist period, legal measures against contraception, and the high incidence of premarital sex in certain regions, made abortion a common method of birth control. The first exception in the general prohibition of abortion was made in 1975, when the Constitutional Court ruled that induced abortion should be possible in the case of serious health risks for the woman. After a campaign by pro-choice feminist groups, abortion was legalized in 1978, and women were granted the right to terminate a pregnancy upon request during the first trimester. However, the law contained a number of restrictions: Legal abortion is confined to women whose physical and psychological health are at risk or for whom social conditions, economic conditions, or the family situation make it extremely difficult to educate children. Further limitations regard the obligation to consult a medical doctor, and the mandatory waiting period of seven days between the medically certified decision and the actual intervention. Minors need to obtain permission of a parent or guardian. The male partner of the woman is involved in the decision process only if the woman wishes so.

After the first three-month period, induced abortion is legal only in case pregnancy or childbirth creates serious health risks for the woman, or when the fetus presents pathologies that entail serious risks for the physical and mental health of the woman. All induced abortions have to take place in public hospitals, where the medical staff has no obligation to cooperate if abortion is in conflict with their moral and religious convictions. Partly as a result of the limitations to the freedom of choice, illegally induced abortion has not disappeared in Italy. For obvious reasons, no exact data are available, but the Ministry of Health estimated that 50,000 clandestine abortions were carried out in 1993, 70% of which were in the south.

Attempts to change the existing legislation failed in 1981, when two different referenda, one aimed at eliminating the restrictions, the other designed to severely reduce access to abortion, were voted down by majorities of, respectively, 88.4% and 68%. Abortion remains controversial in Italy, however, and is severely condemned by the Catholic Church. The condemnation was reiterated in a recent Papal Encyclical on ethical questions, *Evangelium Vitae*. The Italian pro-life movement tries actively, but without much success, to convince the political leadership of the need to change the existing legislation. Most of its resources, however, are spent in providing alternative solutions and facilities for single mothers.

After the introduction of Law no. 194, abortion rates rose modestly, increasing from 13.7 abortions per 1,000 women aged 15 to 44 in 1979 to 16.9 per 1,000 in 1982. Since 1984, there has been a steady decline, reaching 9.8 per 1,000 by 1993. A similar pattern was displayed by abortion ratios (the number of abortions per 1,000 live births), which reached 213 in 1996 after having reached a peak of 389.5 in 1984. While the abortion ratios are relatively high because of Italy's low fertility rate, the general trends are similar to other western European countries. (Salvini Bettarini 1996). Abortion rates and ratios vary considerably according to regions. Since legalization, abortion rates have dropped most in the northern regions, where family planning services are more extensive, but both abortion ratios and rates remain higher in the northern and central regions than in the south.

As far as age patterns are concerned, the abortion rate is relatively low for young women (7.6 per 1,000 women at ages 15 to 19 in 1981, and 4.6 in 1991). This may be, in part, because of legislative restrictions, but it is also linked to the fact that Italian women start to have sexual relations at a relatively late age. Generally speaking, the trend in the distribution of age-specific abortion rates is shifting upward. In 1981, the abortion rate was highest among women aged 25 to 29 (25.3 per 1,000 women), whereas in 1991, the abortion rate was highest among women aged 30 to 34 (16.9 per 1,000 women), with women aged 26 to 29 coming second (15.7 per 1,000 women).

The most recent data (ISTAT 2000) show that the total number of voluntary abortions has stabilized at between 138,000 and 140,000 per year, after a slight increase in 1997 when the number of abortions was 9.5 per 1,000 women of fertile age. Thus, in the years 1980 to 1997, the average number of abortions per woman has diminished by 40.7% against a diminution by 29% of the fertility rate in the same time period. The decline in the abortion rate and in the fertility rate indicate a more frequent, or more efficient, use of techniques of birth control. The decline in the abortion rate is highest among married women in the most fertile age groups, 25 to 28 and 30 to 34. An opposite tendency can be noted among very young women, aged 15 to 19, among whom the abortion rate has increased since the early 1990s, reaching 6.6 per 1,000 in 1998. A more consistent increase regards the abortion rate of immigrant women, which reached the number of 32.5 abortions per 1,000 women in 1998.

## C. Population Programs

Under Fascism, public authorities shared the Catholic Church's positive view about large families, and after the fall of Mussolini, they were slow to change their position. Not until 1971 did the Constitutional Court declare that ideas about population growth dating back to the Fascist period were not sufficient to justify the existence of legislation against contraception. To advance information about contraception and to promote responsible parenthood are part of the duties of the public family advisory agencies created in 1975.

In the postwar period, population planning concentrated on various maternity benefits. The first important legal measure was taken in 1950 when employers were prohibited by law from dismissing pregnant women or mothers of small children. The same law prohibited employing pregnant women in activities that would endanger their health or the health of the unborn baby. Finally, a new law introduced a paid maternity leave of three months before childbirth and two months after childbirth. Mothers have the right to six more months of unpaid maternity leave, during which they retain their position. In the attempt to invalidate the attempt of employers to dismiss women as soon as the possibility of pregnancy increased significantly, a 1963 law specified that marriage was not a valid reason for dismissal. The rules regarding mandatory leave of absence for maternity were reaffirmed and elaborated on in Law n. 1204 of 1971.

Today, Italy's birthrate, expressed in Total Fertility Rate (TFR) is, with that of Spain, the lowest of 227 nations: 1.19 children per fertile woman. A TFR of 0.8 in the northern industrial city of Bologna underscores the social challenges Italy faces. The actions of the Italian governments in the field

of population planning are strongly influenced by the fear that this low fertility rate and a relative decline of the active population will make it impossible to finance pensions for the retired and other welfare projects. Most measures aim at improving the conditions of working mothers, and try at the same time to eliminate gender-specific discrimination, by extending rights, such as leaves of absence for the care of children to men. According to recent proposals, financial compensation for maternity, until now limited to employed women, will be extended to non-employed and self-employed women. Further measures focus on the creation and funding of childcare facilities, and, more generally, aim at reducing the financial burden of families with children.

## 10. Sexually Transmitted Diseases and HIV/AIDS

### A. Sexually Transmitted Diseases

Historically, sexually transmissible diseases (STDs) were seen primarily as a consequence of sexual contacts with prostitutes, and the legal interventions regarding prostitution and STDs were closely connected. The need to control the diffusion of STDs was one of the main arguments for the introduction, in 1860, of regulated prostitution. In 1870, the obligation to notify health authorities of infectious diseases was introduced, together with more specific laws regarding STDs. In 1888, the clinics for the mandatory treatment of infected prostitutes were reorganized and transformed into specialized clinics for the free treatment of contagious venereal diseases. New legislation, approved in 1901, defined syphilis, gonorrhea, and chancroid (*Hemophilus ducreyi*) as "venereal diseases." According to legislation approved in 1923, venereal clinics had to be created in all major cities. While reaffirming the principle of free treatment, Law 837 of 1956 and successive laws updated existing legislation and established a list of four diseases—syphilis, blennorrhagia (a profuse gonorrheal discharge), chancroid, and lymphogranuloma venereum (*Chlamydia trachomatis*)—for which there is an obligation to report. This law is still in effect. Moreover, the terminology used in official documents still refers to "venereal diseases," and has not yet adopted the broader term of sexually transmissible diseases (STD).

While venereologists denounced a rapid increase of venereal diseases after 1958, when the abolition of regulated prostitution made mandatory medical checks on prostitutes impossible, in reality the statistical data could be interpreted in various ways.

In 1972, responsibility for the diagnosis and treatment of STDs was transferred to regional governments. The result has been a growing differentiation in the treatment and operational conditions of various STD centers, with important differences both between regions and within the same region. In the past, venereology was associated above all with dermatology, but recent developments have shown the need for a more interdisciplinary approach.

The precise incidence of STDs is unknown, not only because there is a legal obligation to report only a few diseases, but also because medical specialists tend to disregard this obligation. The Higher Institute for Health (Istituto Superiore della Sanita, ISS) has estimated that the number of unreported cases is at least 100 to 150% higher than reported cases. In September 1991, a national STD surveillance agency was created to collect and analyze data coming from some 48 STD clinics. The aim is not to register the total number of cases, but rather to monitor developments and to gather the data necessary for a better description of STDs (Giuliani & Suligoi 1994).

The results of the first year of the survey confirmed the existence of important regional variations in the registration and/or recourse to STD centers for treatment: 67.4% of the 9,527 STD cases were registered in northern Italy, 19.3% in central Italy, and 33.6% in the south. In order to assist the large number of foreigners involved (10.4%), in 1992, a special project was created for the prevention and treatment of STDs among this group. Heterosexual contacts were responsible for 92% of the cases, and homosexual or bisexual contacts accounted for 8%. The most frequent pathologies were *Condyloma acuta* or venereal warts, 28%; nongonococcal urethritis, 11.2%; nongonococcal vaginitis, 18.6%; and quiescent seropositive syphilis, 10.4%.

## B. HIV/AIDS

The first case of AIDS in Italy was discovered in 1982, and until 1995, there was an annual increase in the number of persons diagnosed as being infected with HIV (see Table 1). HIV infection is unevenly distributed over the national territory, with the highest numbers in the regions of Lombardia, Lazio, Liguria, and Emilia Romagna. Between October 1997 and September 1998, the AIDS rate per 100,000 population was 6.5 in Liguria, 9.1 in Lombardia, 6.0 in Emilia Romagna, and 8.1 in Lazio, against 0.6 in the region of Molise and 1.2 in the Basilicata. In 1997, women constituted 23.2% of the cases.

Among the men diagnosed as being infected with AIDS, drug addicts are the major category (63.6%), followed by men with homosexual experiences (19.7%). Heterosexual experiences are held responsible for 15.2% of the cases of AIDS, but heterosexual contact is the second most important cause (34.2%) for HIV infection in women after the abuse of drugs (59.9%). The average age at which AIDS is diagnosed is increasing: In 1985, it was 29 for men and 24 for women, compared to 37 for men and 34 for women in 1997.

While at first, gay organizations interpreted the alarm about AIDS as an attempt of the medical professions to regain control and use the discourse about health risks to moralize "disorderly sexual conduct," the real dimensions of the problem soon became clear. In May 1985, Arcigay, together with the Abele group from Turin, promoted the publication of the first Italian book about AIDS, written by Giovanni Dall'Orto (1985). Since then, Arcigay has promoted many public debates and information campaigns about safe sex. Other initiatives included the free distribution of condoms and the creation of homosexual health centers managed by the association itself with the support of the Ministry of Public Health. The success of these actions is shown by the fact that homosexuals in Italy make up a much lower percentage of the victims of AIDS than in most other countries.

[*Update 2002*: UNAIDS Epidemiological Assessment: The incidence of new HIV cases diagnosed decreased from 19.18 per 100,000 in 1992 to 6.68 per 100,000 in the year 2000. Testing is mandatory for blood donors and systematically proposed in STD clinics and injecting-drug-user treatment centers. There are several regional HIV case reporting systems (e.g., Lazio (region of Rome), Veneto, Friuli, and the provinces of Trento and Modena). Universal Assessment Testing (UAT) surveys have been conducted in newborns in all regions since 1989, showing a mean prevalence of HIV seropositivity of about 1 per 1,000. Prevalence varies greatly by regions. In most of the population tested, prevalence is higher in Lazio, Lombardia (region of Milan), Emilia, and Liguria than most other regions. In addition, prevalence is higher in all regions of the north compared to the south in all populations tested, except blood donors, where the opposite is observed, probably due to the higher proportion of occasional blood donors. Geographical variations are even stronger among injecting drug users, where prevalence in the same region varied from 9% to 48% in 1985 to 86% in small cities. Overall, HIV seroprevalence among injecting drug users decreased from 30.8% in 1990 to 15.8% in the year 2000. Prevalence slowly decreased from 1990 to 1992 in pregnant women nationally, mostly due to a decline in prevalence in Lazio and Lombardia. In Lazio, about 2 of 1,000 women were found HIV infected before delivery, whereas prevalence was at least 2 times higher among those who underwent voluntary abortion.

[About 8,000 patients are diagnosed every year by the STD clinics (however, this number underestimates the burden of disease since STDs are diagnosed by private gynecologists in a large proportion of women). HIV prevalence among STD patients tended to increase from 9.3% in 1991 to 18.8% in the year 2000.

[The estimated number of adults and children living with HIV/AIDS on January 1, 2002, were:

| | |
|---|---|
| Adults ages 15-49: | 100,000  (rate: 0.4%) |
| Women ages 15-49: | 33,000 |
| Children ages 0-15: | 770 |

[An estimated 1,100 adults and children died of AIDS during 2001.

[No estimate is available for the number of Italian children who had lost one or both parents to AIDS and were under age 15 at the end of 2001. (*End of update by the Editors*)]

## 11. Sexual Dysfunctions, Counseling, and Therapies

### A. Sexual Dysfunctions

The notion of sexual dysfunction itself is subject to change, and definitions of sexual dysfunctions often mirror changing attitudes toward male and female sexuality. Thus, inhibited female orgasm (anorgasmia) was not considered a problem in a context where female sexuality was linked almost exclusively with procreation. Premature ejaculation became more of a problem with the emergence of the myth of simultaneous orgasm, and also the idea of (hetero-

### Table 1

### Annual Distribution of New Cases of AIDS and Mortality Rate

| Year of Diagnosis | New Cases | Mortality Rate |
|---|---|---|
| 1982 | 1 | 0.0% |
| 1983 | 8 | 87.5% |
| 1984 | 37 | 100.0% |
| 1985 | 198 | 93.9% |
| 1986 | 457 | 93.4% |
| 1987 | 1,029 | 93.0% |
| 1988 | 1,773 | 90.4% |
| 1989 | 2,480 | 90.8% |
| 1990 | 3,135 | 89.1% |
| 1991 | 3,826 | 88.7% |
| 1992 | 4,261 | 85.6% |
| 1993 | 4,818 | 77.6% |
| 1994 | 5,521 | 72.7% |
| 1995 | 5,654 | 56.9% |
| 1996 | 4,993 | 36.7% |
| 1997 | 3,728 | 20.7% |
| 1998 (to 30 September 1998) | 1,430 | 13.6% |
| Total | 42,899 | 67.5% |

(Instituto Superiore di Sanità, Notiziario, XI, 11 November 1998)

sexual) sex as pleasure-created pressures and tensions. Finally, the growing resistance to a compulsory idea of sexuality as necessarily linked with orgasm might eliminate the tendency to treat alternative expressions of eroticism as sexual dysfunctions.

About 11% of Italian males have erectile dysfunctions. More widespread are problems regarding orgasm: About one third of Italian males have had at least some experience with problems of early (premature) ejaculation. The most serious problem, however, is a decreased libido. The incidence of physical problems and, above all, psychological factors, like the identification of virility with sexual potency, and the desire to please the female partner, have created a market for new pharmaceutical products. Among women, the sexual dysfunctions with the highest incidence are painful intercourse (dyspareunia), vaginal spasms (vaginismus), and inhibited orgasm (anorgasmia). Also, among women the loss of sexual desire is common.

Recent research among young people aged 18 to 30 indicates that, among males, 10.2% presented erectile dysfunctions, and 30.1% presented problems of premature ejaculation. Inhibited orgasm was mentioned by 13.2% of young females, while painful intercourse was reported by 50.7%. Difficulties in experiencing orgasm were reported by 11.5% of males and 39.8% of females, while 14.1% of males and 28.4% of females complained about the lack of sexual desire (Buzzi 1998).

Other male problems involve fertility. A comparison of the results of sperm analyses of 4,518 men without fertility problems, carried out by the Centro di Andrologia based in Pisa between 1975 and 1994, has confirmed the thesis of a general decline of the number and of the motility of spermatozoa. In this 20-year period, sperm counts went down from 71 million to 65 million spermatozoa per millimeter. The decline of the motility was even more serious, as the number of spermatozoa with progressive motility decreased from 50% to 32%. Oxidation caused by environmental pollution is the main cause of this phenomenon.

## B. Counseling and Therapies

In 1948, the first Italian family advisory agency was opened in Milan by Don Paolo Liggeri. La Casa and its sister organizations functioned as a social movement, where volunteers tried to transmit values and ideals, not as a service agency where paid professionals offered their services to clients. For this reason, the use of American manuals for marriage counseling, with their pragmatic attitude, often created problems. Nevertheless, these Catholic marriage advisory agencies were often innovative, because they underlined the positive role of sexuality in marriage and favored a more active role of fathers in the education of their children. However, as far as the female gender role was concerned, they subscribed to more traditional ideas about the female biological destiny of motherhood, and women's generally more passive attitude in sexuality.

Law n. 405 of 1975 created a network of public family agencies, which were to offer psychological and social assistance to couples and families, and to assist couples in choices regarding procreation and responsible parenthood through information and the distribution of contraceptives. The same law allowed for the public funding of private family agencies. Both Catholic and feminist-oriented advisory agencies thus received funding. The prerequisite of client-oriented, non-directive counseling was satisfied, not by the single agencies, which maintained their ideological premises, but by the system as a whole.

Among the therapies often used in combination to combat sexual dysfunctions, it is possible to distinguish these:

psychotherapies focused on improving the understanding of sexual problems, and thus modifying reactions and behaviors; behavioral therapy using special assignments to modify and improve the perception of pleasure and the idea of sexual pleasure itself; and autogenous training and pharmacological therapies.

## 12. Sex Research and Advanced Professional Education

In 1921, the Società Italiana per lo Studio delle Questioni Sessuali was founded by Aldo Mieli, with the aim to improve the level of information about human sexuality. The journal published by the Society, *Rassegna di Studi Sessuali*, introduced in Italy the themes and ideas developed by progressive German sexologists, and greatly contributed to a more open discussion. The rise to power of the Fascists in 1922, however, reduced the possibilities for reformist action. This was one of the reasons why, in 1928, Mieli submitted his resignation as editor-in-chief of the journal and left Italy for France. By 1931, when Corrado Gini took over control, the journal had become an instrument of the Fascist population policy.

Sexology had to start again in the postwar period. In 1959, a group of medical doctors, headed by Professor Giacomo Santori, created the Centro Italiano di Sessuologia (Italian Center of Sexology, CIS), which is active, above all, in the sector of training and information. The CIS (Via O. Regnoli, 74, 40138 Bologna) promotes an interdisciplinary approach that draws on the results of medical science, psychology, and anthropology, and favors an interpretation of human sexuality that takes into account the biological and medical aspects, as well as the social and relational aspects, without excluding moral aspects. The CIS is a founding member of the World Association of Sexology (WAS), and a member of the European Federation of Sexology.

Aspects of sexology are part of medical training, and specialized schools are attached to some universities. Among these, the Center of Andrology of the University of Pisa, founded by Professor Menchini Fabris in 1975, deserves special mention. Numerous other institutes and associations do research and offer training in sexology, among them:

- Instituto Internazionale di Sessuologia, Via della Scala, 85, Firenze, Italy (founded in 1981).
- Instituto di Sessuologia Clinica, Via Fibreno 4, 00199 Roma, Italy.
- Società Italiana di Sessuologia Scientifica, Istituto di Sessuologia Clinica, Via Fibreno 4, 00199 Roma, Italy; publication: *Rivista di Sessuologia Clinica*.
- Società Italiana di Sessuologia ed Educazione Sessuale, c/o Prof. Gabriele Traverso, Via Circonvallazione 28, 10015 Ivrea, TO, Italy.
- Centro Italiano di Sessuologia (CIS), Via della Lungarina, 65, Rome, 00153, Italy; phone: +39-6-51-245-785.
- Instituto di Sessuologia di Savona, 17026 Noli, Via la Malfa, 5, Savona, Italy; phone: 39-19-748-5687; fax: +39-19-748-5687; Associazione per la Ricerca in Sessuologia (ARS), Via Angelo Cappi 1/8, 16126 Genova, Italy.
- The Centro Italiano di Sessuologia (CIS) is the publisher of the *Rivista di Sessuologia* (CLUEB, Via Marsala 24, 40126 Bologna, Italy; www.clueb.com).
- Other publications in the field of sexology are *Rivista di Scienze Sessuologiche* (Edizioni del Cerro, Via delle Orchidee 17, 56018 Tirrenia, Pisa, Italy) and *Rivista di Sessuologia Clinica* (Franco Angeli, Viale Monze 106, 20127 Milano, Italy; www.francoangeli.it; frang@tin.it).

The results of sexological studies often receive great attention in the mass media, and some sexologists—Willy Pasini, to name but one—have gained national popularity as guests on television talk shows and through their articles in the popular press.

## References and Suggested Readings

Barbagli, M., & A. Colombo. 2001. *Omosessuali moderni: Gay e lesbiche in Italia*. Bologna: Il Mulino.

Barbagli, M., & C. Saraceno, eds. 1997. *Lo stato delle famiglie*. Bologna: Il Mulino.

Bohlen, C. 1996 (March 1). At 30-something, leave home? Mamma mia, No! *The New York Times* (Foreign Desk), p. A4.

Buzzi, C. 1998. *Giovani, affettività, sessualità. L'amore tra i giovani in una indagine IARD*. Bologna: Il Mulino. (IARD Foundation, Via Soncino 1, 20123 Milano, Italy).

Cesareo, V. 1995. *La religiosità in Italia*. Milano: Mondadori.

CIA. 2002 (January). *The world factbook 2002*. Washington, DC: Central Intelligence Agency. Available: http://www.cia.gov/cia/publications/factbook/index.html.

Cipolla, C., ed. 1996. *Sul letto di Procuste. Introduzione alla sociologia della sessualita*. Milano: Franco Angeli.

Cutrufelli, M. R. 1996. *Il denaro in corpo. Uomini e donne. La domanda di sesso commerciale*. Milano: Marco Tropea.

Dall'Orto, G., with R. Ferracini. 1985. *AIDS*. Torino, Italy: Gruppo Abele.

De Rose, A. 1992. Socio-economic factors and family size as determinants of marital dissolution in Italy. *European Sociological Review*, 8(1).

De Sandre, P., et al. 1997. *Matrimonio e figli: Tra rinvio e rinuncia*. Bologna: Il Mulino.

Durex. 1998. *Global sex survey. 1998*. Available: www.durex.com.

Eurispes. 1997. *Terzo rapporto sulla pornografia 1992*. Eurispes, *L'Italia sotto la lente 1982-1997. Quindici anni di lavoro di ricerca sulla società italiana* [CD-ROM]. Roma: MGE Communications.

Fabris, G., & R. Davis. 1978. *Il mito del sesso. Rapporto sul comportamento sessuale degli italiani*. Milano: Mondadori.

Fiore, C. 1991. *Il sorriso di Afrodite. Rapporto sulla condizione omosessuale in Italia*. Firenze: Vallecchi.

Giovannini, F. 1980. *Comunisti e diversi. Il PCI e la questione omosessuale*. Bari: Dedalo.

Giuliani, M., & B. Suligoi. 1994. La sorveglianza in Italia delle malattie sessualmente trasmesse. In: M. Dolivo et al., eds., *Malattie sessualmente trasmesse* (pp. 245-255). Milano, Parigi, Barcellona: Masson.

Inchiesta. 1998. 'I diritti della famiglia e le 'unioni di fatto.' In: *Famiglia Cristiana*. Vol. LXVIII, n. 31.

ISTAT (Istituto Nazionale di Statistica). 1996. *Famiglia, abitazioni, servizi di pubblica utilità. Indagini multiscopo sulle famiglie. Anni 1993-1994*. Roma: ISTAT.

ISTAT. 1998. *Annuario statistico italiano 1998*. Roma: ISTAT.

ISTAT. 1999a. *Annuario statistico italiano 1999*. Roma: ISTAT.

ISTAT. 1999b. *Rapporto annuale. La situazione del paese nel 1998*. Roma: ISTAT.

ISTAT. 2000. *L'Interruzione volontaria di gravidanza in Italia. Evoluzione e tendenze recenti*. Roma: ISTAT.

Rifelli, G., & P. Moro, eds. 1989-1995. *Sessuologia clinica. Vol. 1, Sessuologia generale; Vol. 2, Impotenza Sessuale maschile. femminile e di coppia; Vol. 3, Consulenza e terapia delle disfunzioni sessuali*. Bologna: CLUEB.

Rifelli, G. 1998. *Psicologia e psicopatologia della sessualità*. Bologna: Il Mulino.

Rodriguez, H. 1997/1998. *Cohabitation: A snapshot*. The Center for Law and Social Policy.

Sabadini, L. L. 1998. *Molestie e violenze sessuali*. Roma: ISTAT. Available: www.istat.it.

Sabatini, R. 1988. *L'eros in Italia. Il comportamento sessuale degli Italiani*. Milano: Mursia.

Salvini Bettarini, S., & S. S. D'Andrea. 1996. Induced abortion in Italy: Levels, trends and characteristics. *Family Planning Perspectives*, 28(6):267-271.

Sgritta, G. B. 1988. The Italian family. *Journal of Family Issues*, 40(3):372-396.

Stella, R. 1991. *L'osceno di massa. Sociologia della communicazione pornografica*. Milano: Angeli.

Stanley, A. 1999 (November 16). Vastogirardi journal; Blissful bachelorhood and the shrinking village. *The New York Times*.

Tatafiore, R. 1994. *Sesso al Lavoro. Da prostitute a sex-worker. Miti e realtà dell'eros commerciale*. Milano: Il Saggiatore.

Trifiletti, R., A. Pratesi, & S. Simoni. 2001. *WP2 care arrangements in single parent families. National report: Italy*. Available: www.uta.fi/laitokset/sospol/soccare/report2.3.pdf.

UNAIDS. 2002. *Epidemiological fact sheets by country*. Geneva, Switzerland: Joint United Nations Programme on HIV/AIDS (UNAIDS/WHO). Available: http://www.unaids.org/hivaidsinfo/statistics/fact_sheets/index_en.htm.

Wanrooij, B. P. F. 1990. *Storia del pudore. La questione sessuale in Italia 1860-1940*. Venezia: Marsilio.

Whitehead, B. D., & D. Popenoe. 1998. *Why wed: Young adults talk about sex, love and first unions*. The National Marriage Project at Rutgers University. Available: http://marriage.rutgers.edu/pubwhywe.htm.

# Japan
## (*Nippon*)

Yoshiro Hatano, Ph.D., and Tsuguo Shimazaki*
*Updates and comments by Yoshimi Kaji, M.A.,
Timothy Perper, Ph.D., and Martha Cornog, M.S., M.A.,
and Robert T. Francoeur, Ph.D.***

## Contents

## Demographics and a Brief Historical Perspective

ROBERT T. FRANCOEUR

### A. Demographics

It was Marco Polo, a man from Venice, Italy, in the latter half of the 13th century, who wrote a book titled *Le Merveilles du Monde*, in which he introduced the country of Japan to the Western world as *Jipang*, "the land of gold." His book was actually a collection of his experiences and information about his journey through central Asia and China.

Japan is an island country, located to the east of the Asian continent in the northwestern part of the Pacific Ocean. The islands face the Pacific on the east and south sides, the Sea of Japan and East China Sea on the west side, and the Sea of Okhotsk on the north side. The islands form a bow-shaped

---

*\*Communications*: Yoshiro Hatano, Ph.D., Kyushuu University of Health & Welfare, Yoshino-cho, Nobeoka City, Miyazaki Prefecture, Japan; yhatano@phoenix.ac.jp. Tsuguo Shimazaki, Nippon Information Center for Sexology, Hobunkan Bldg. 6F 3-11-4 Kanda-Jinbo-cho, Chiyoda-Ku, Tokyo Japan 101-0051; nics@mail.at-m.or.jp. *Comments*: Yoshimi Kaji, M.A., Japanese Association for Sex Education, Miyata Bldg. 2F 1-3 Kanda Jimbocho, Chiyoda-ku, Tokyo 101-0051, Japan; ykaji@crocus.ocn.ne.jp. Timothy Perper, Ph.D., and Martha Cornog, M.A., M.S., 717 Pemberton, Philadelphia, PA 19147 USA; perpcorn@dca.net.

*\*\*Editors'Note*: Because of time and space constraints, the Editors have converted most of the extensive original bar and line graphs of the original chapter into tables or comments in the text. We have marked the textual material as 2003 comments following our standard notation in square brackets with the end of the comment referencing the original figure or table number and page number in *IES2*, i.e., the original chapter on Japan in volume 2 of the *International Encyclopedia of Sexuality*. Those figures that we have converted to tables contain this reference information in the new tables' footnotes. For those original line graphs that did not contain actual numbers, we have approximated the percentages, which are noted where appropriate. The reader is referred to the original figures in the original volume or on the Web at http://www.SexQuest.com/ccies/ies2-ref-figures.html.

(CIA 2002)

string stretching from the northeast to the southwest. In addition to five major islands, i.e., from the north, Hokkaido, Honshu or Main Island, Shikoku, Kyushu, and Okinawa, there are some 320 small islands over a square kilometer (0.39 sq. mi.) each, totaling 145,883 square miles (377,835 km²). Japan is slightly larger than Germany or the state of California, and smaller than Spain.

A relatively mild climate prevails, because of the location of most of Japan's islands in the Temperate Zone. With four distinctive seasons, there are variations because of the longitudinal distribution of the islands. Because of the mild climatic characteristics, natural features of the islands, and religious philosophy, the Japanese people have developed a sensitive and cooperative attitude to the relationship between nature and humankind, in contrast to Western culture, which is independent, and often exploitive or in opposition. Such views of nature and humankind may be regarded as characteristic of the Orient.

The landmass of Japan is rather small and approximately 87% of the land is mountainous. As a consequence, fields and basins of rather small scale are divided by mountain ranges. From the beginning, this geographic circumstance has isolated local communities—which in the early days were independent countries—producing different cultures, customs, and religious events in different areas. This situation persisted into the 20th century. Since the Meiji Era (1868-1912), the influence of Western cultures, along with economic growth and the development and popularization of the mass media system in recent years, has promoted an increasingly shared (common) education and culture, resulting in the current unification of the Japanese culture. Cultures imported from China and Korea since the 5th century, and from the Western world since the Meiji Era, have been well absorbed by the Japanese people. The Japanese always kept a flexible attitude in accepting foreign influences to amalgamate traditional and imported cultures, forming their own specific culture.

In July 2002, Japan had an estimated population of 127 million, double what it was in 1925. (All data are from *The World Factbook 2002* (CIA 2002) unless otherwise stated.)

**Age Distribution and Sex Ratios**: *0-14 years*: 14.5% with 1.05 male(s) per female (sex ratio); *15-64 years*: 67.5% with 1.01 male(s) per female; *65 years and over*: 18% with

0.73 male(s) per female; *Total population sex ratio*: 0.96 male(s) to 1 female

**Life Expectancy at Birth**: *Total Population*: 80.91 years; *male*: 77.73 years; *female*: 84.25 years

**Urban/Rural Distribution**: 77% urban to 23% rural and small villages, clearly indicating an extreme urban-centered social construction. In the second half of the 1900s, Japan's cities grew into metropolises as the focus of work. At the same time, the number of core (nuclear) families with a small number of children is increasing. As a result, the local community as the basis for human network activities and a humane life is often lost.

**Ethnic Distribution**: Japanese 99.4%; Korean: 0.6%. The government needs to pay attention, though, to the possible problem with minority races, such as Ryukyu (Okinawa) and Ainos, and the forced immigrants from the Korean Peninsula during World War II. At this moment, administrative policies and responsive movements of adherence and preservation of the respective cultures are effectively carried out.

**Religious Distribution**: observing both Shinto and Buddhist beliefs: 84%; others: 16%, including 0.6% Christian

**Birth Rate**: The estimated raw Japanese birthrate in 2002 was 10.03 per 1,000 population, compared with 51.8 in 1980, 63.6 in 1960, and 110.4 in 1950, only 45 years ago. The trend of decreased birthrate and increased longevity is already creating serious problems for Japanese society. Japan has a high-aged society that represents a heavy concentration of aged people in contrast to the working population. The current ratio is somewhere around one retiree for every four workers.

**Death Rate**: 8.53 per 1,000 population

**Infant Mortality Rate**: 3.84 deaths per 1,000 live births

**Net Migration Rate**: 0 migrant(s) per 1,000 population

**Total Fertility Rate**: 1.42 children born per woman

**Population Growth Rate**: 0.15%

**HIV/AIDS** (1999 est.): *Adult prevalence*: 0.02%; *Persons living with HIV/AIDS*: 10,000; *Deaths*: 150. (For additional details from www.UNAIDS.org, see end of Section 10B.)

**Literacy Rate** (*defined as those age 15 and over who can read and write*): 99%; attendance for nine years of compulsory school, although most Japanese children attend at least 12 years of school

**Per Capita Gross Domestic Product** (*purchasing power parity*): $27,200 (2001 est.); *Inflation*: –0.6%; *Unemployment*: 4.9%; *Living below the poverty line*: NA

## B. A Brief Historical Perspective

According to Japanese legend, the empire was founded by Emperor Jimmu in 660 B.C.E.. However, the earliest records of a unified Japan date from a thousand years later, about 400 of the Common Era. Chinese influences played an important role in the formation of the Japanese civilization, with Buddhism being introduced to the islands before the 6th century C.E.

A feudal system dominated Japan between 1192 and 1867, with locally powerful noble families and their *samurai* warrior retainers controlling local government, and a succession of military dictators, or *shoguns*, holding the central power. This ended when Emperor Meiji assumed power in 1868. The Portuguese and Dutch developed some minor trade with Japan in the 16th and 17th centuries. United States Commodore Perry opened American trade with Japan in an 1854 treaty. Japan gained Taiwan and other concessions following an 1894-1895 war with China, gained the south half of Sakhalin from a 1904-1905 war with Russia, and annexed Korea in 1910. During World War I, Japan ousted the Germans from Shantung and took over the Pacific islands con-

trolled by Germany. In 1931, Japan took over Manchuria, starting a war with China in 1932. World War II started with Japan's attack on Pearl Harbor, Hawaii, and ended with two atomic bombs being dropped on Hiroshima and Nagasaki in August 1945.

In 1947, Japan adopted a new constitution that reduced the Emperor to a state figurehead and left all the governing power with a Diet. In a few decades, Japan quickly moved to become a major world power and leader in economics, industry, technology, and politics.

## 1. Basic Sexological Premises

### A. Gender Roles

In Japan, a strict hierarchy of social classes and clearly defined traditional gender roles have their roots in over 2,000 years of cultural history. In terms of social classes, merchants or *chyonin* were beneath the farmers and artisans. *Samurai*, the social elite, were retainers in the service of the *shogun* and the *daimio*. The *samurai*, who represented the superior male, constituted a bureaucratic and conservative hereditary group. The *samurai* and his sword were more a class symbol than the fierce warrior pictured in American television mythology.

As for gender roles, Karel Van Wolferen (1989) gives a terse picture of the traditional/modern female gender role in *The Enigma of Japanese Power*:

> Although in reality Japanese tradition has never frowned on working women, and today the majority of working married women are obliged to help make ends meet in their families, the officially sponsored portrait of "wholesome" family life invariably shows that the proper place for women is at home. In a country where stereotypes are treasured, emphasis on the established proper roles of women is especially noticeable. It extends to demurely polite deportment, a studied innocent cuteness, a "gentle" voice one octave above the natural voice and always a nurturing, motherly disposition. The modern woman in the world of the salaryman [white collar workers] is a cross between Florence Nightingale and the minister of finance (as women are always totally responsible for household finances). Superior intelligence is a liability for girls and women, and must be disguised.

In early 1989, the Welfare Ministry launched a poster campaign to stress that the only difference between males and females is biological. The posters showed two romping, mud-splattered toddlers with the caption *Tamatama otokonoko, tamatama onnanoko*: "He just happens to be a boy; she just happens to be a girl." This notion gained little support from government ministries more closely allied to business and industry, who joined the politicians in upholding traditional gender-role values as a means of continually exploiting the diligence of the people (Bornoff 1991, 452).

In a 1982 opinion poll conducted by the Prime Minister's Office, 70% of the Japanese surveyed agreed with the statement that "Japanese women still believe a woman's place is in the home and that little girls should be brought up to be 'ladylike.'" In a 1989 multinational survey by the same agency on the theme "Men should work and women should stay home," 71% of the Japanese women either completely or somewhat agreed with the premise (see also discussion of Table 28 (*IES2* Fig. 34, p. 814) in Section 5B, Interpersonal Heterosexual Behaviors, The Sexuality of Adolescents). Critics suggest that respondents to government surveys may be inclined to give answers they believe the authorities want to hear, so it is important to balance these government survey results with similar surveys in the private sector. In one such survey conducted by a noted cosmetics firm, four fifths of the women found working women admirable, and 70% rejected the notion that a woman should quit her job after marriage (Bornoff 1991, 453). Still, the argument that traditional sex roles are strongly valued in Japan is persuasive when one considers that only 20% of Japanese firms offer female employees a year's maternity leave, in most cases without pay, and that daycare facilities are woefully inadequate. (One should recall, however, that the record of American corporations is not much different on these issues, and certainly lags far behind the policies in some European countries.)

Gender roles are clearly defined, although they are also being challenged in modern Japan.

At the two extremes of female and male in popular culture, one finds the geisha and the sumo wrestler: the dainty living doll standing for femininity and the mountainous icon of macho flesh with the little porcine eyes. Between the two bookends plenty of scope lies in a nebulous heaven of make-believe far from the constrictions of daily routine. Segregating the sexes during childhood and defining the contexts and nature of their encounters later on, Japanese society defines gender roles with adamantine rules. In the realm of the imaginary, the strict roles encapsulating male and female are broken, being transgressed in fantasies which can be singly and variously violent, sadistic, maudlin, sentimental or comical. Transcending the laws of society, authority and even gender, these fantasies reach apotheosis in the popular imagination with ethereal creatures as blessedly sexless as occidental angels. (Bornoff 1991, 437)

Gender definitions in Japan can transcend the anatomical; masculine and feminine attributes can fade or fuse through conventions. This is most clearly seen in public rituals, for instance, when the emperor becomes a female incarnation of the sun goddess Amaterasu during the *daijosai* enthronement ceremony (See Bornoff 1991, 15-16, for the legend of Amaterasu and Ama-no-Uzume, the Heavenly Alarming Female). Gender reversal is also common in both traditional theater and modern cinema. After centuries of evolution, *kabuki* became a sophisticated form of theater in which the all-male cast plays all roles. Kabuki theater has long found a female equivalent in certain *geisha* theatricals comprising dances and playlets in which some of the female cast adopt male roles. In Nobuhiko Obayashi's film *Tenkosei* [*Transfer Students*], a 1983 offbeat youth comedy hit about junior high school lovers who undergo a kind of Kafka-like metamorphosis when the girl's soul enters the boy's body, and vice versa, and are forced to confront their awakening sexuality, the characters adopt the physical and social gender roles of the other. Similarly, the famed Takarazuka Young Girls Opera, founded in 1914, embraces many older male-role superstars, with female actors performing in braided pantomime in military uniforms, tuxedos, cowboy garb, and *samurai* armor, blue cheeks, and mustaches. The Takarazuka Opera is part of a virtuous theme park called Family Land, "a florid world of Tinseltown baroque in pink, a feminine Disneyland with rose-colored bridges spanning artificial water courses." In 1987, when Takarazuka unsuccessfully pushed for recognition as a traditional art form to gain tax exemption, male traditionalists were quick to point out that *geisha* theater provided the proper traditional female counterpoint to male *kabuki* (see also Section 7 on cross-dressing, gender-crossing, and transsexualism; Bornoff 1991, 436-439).

[*Update 1997*: In ancient times, Japanese women wielded considerable authority. Until the 11th century, it was common for Japanese girls to inherit their parent's house.

The rise of Confucianism and a conservative moral movement that preached the inferiority of women in the early 18th century significantly reduced women's role. In some respects, Japanese women today have less power in society than they did a thousand years ago. Fewer than one in ten Japanese managers is female; women in less-industrialized nations, like Mexico and Zimbabwe, are twice as likely to be managers. Only 2.3% of Japan's key legislative body are women, compared with 10.9% in the U.S. House of Representatives. In this regard, Japan ranks 145 in a list of 161 countries, according to the Inter-Parliamentary Union.

[The public gender roles, however, are reversed when one steps inside the Japanese home. Typically, the wife handles and completely controls the household finances. She gives her husband a monthly allowance and has total control over the rest of the family income. Half of the husbands in one survey reported they were dissatisfied with the size of their allowance, but could do little if anything about it. While the husband and wife may have a joint bank account, and automatic teller machines are available, wives often do not share access to these with their husbands (Kristof 1996b). (*End of update by R. T. Francoeur*)]

[*Update 1997*: In the late 1990s, a new phenomenon appeared in Japan's vibrant, big-city nightlife that may echo other signals noted in this chapter suggesting that traditional Japanese gender roles are changing. A 1996 *New York Times* report by Miki Tanikawa focused on New Ai ("New Love"), the largest of Tokyo's estimated 200 "host clubs." The host clubs are a variation of the ubiquitous clubs where businessmen regularly unwind in the company of charming young women, except that the traditional gender roles are reversed and sex is not part of the host-club scene. In the host clubs, it is the women who are flattered and flirted with by attractive men of their choice. The clientele are usually the wives of wealthy men or hostesses at the businessmen's clubs where they spend their working hours pampering male clients. On a busy night, New Ai entertains more than 300 customers in its rooms elaborately decorated with rococo-style furniture, statues, and chandeliers. A band provides music ranging from standard jazz to Japanese love songs. Unlike their male counterparts, the host clubs are strictly for companionship and nonsexual entertainment. Still, an evening of flattery, chatting, drinking, and dancing can cost the equivalent of US$500 or more. Regular clients may run up monthly bills of $3,000 to $4,000.

[Traditional values are, nevertheless, evident in the absence of sexual activity and in the secrecy women are expected to exercise in their visit to a host club. Japanese men can have an open nightlife, including visits to the sexual hot spots known as "soaplands." Japanese women do not have this freedom (see discussion of soaplands in Section 8B, Significant Unconventional Sexual Behaviors, Prostitution). Despite their efforts to defy social conventions, clients of the host clubs often choose a host and remain devoted to him for years, sometimes showering him with expensive gifts to express their affection. (Tanikawa 1996; (*End of update by R. T. Francoeur*)]

## B. Sociolegal Status of Males and Females

An important insight into the status of women and men in the realities of everyday life and legal statutes can be found in the workplace. Female employees who pass the *tekireiki*, or marriage age, without getting married often encounter discrimination, despite the enactment in 1986 of an Equal Employment Opportunity (E.E.O.) Act. While firing such a female employee is against the law, the atmosphere may become so strained because of inquiries from supervisors and colleagues that the unmarried female may decide to leave the company. Women who remain employees and unmarried after *tekireiki* must be compensated as they climb, however unwelcomed, the corporate ladder. *Onna dakara* ("Because I am a woman") is a line often heard in the perennially popular and unabashedly sentimental Enka folk songs. Indeed, in a conservative country in which Confucian *samurai* ethics were resuscitated in the 1880s and fomented lucratively ever since in industrial disguise, being a woman can be difficult. Obligatory marriage and motherhood, and subservience to her husband and his family, would seem to have no place in a technopolitan economic supergiant in which half of the work force is female (Bornoff 1991, 452).

The E.E.O. law has been largely ineffectual because large corporations have a strong standing with the government, making enforcement of any measures against sexual discrimination unlikely. From the largest international firms to the smallest businesses, the widespread view is that sexual discrimination is unethical only according to concepts adopted in recent years, concepts that, to some, are quite foreign. The law entitles women to complain, but this more often than not results in "counseling" rather than action, and so few women complain. Even if filing a complaint could theoretically win a woman higher wages and guard her from dismissal, the action of filing a complaint would be viewed as a complete lack of loyalty to the firm and only earn her complete ostracism by her colleagues. Nevertheless, some major firms, including several banks, have recently moved to put ability before traditional stereotypes and hierarchical promotion, and stress greater sexual equality in the workplace. However, even when management gives female employees equality with males, the male business associates the women have to deal with are often uncomfortable or unwilling to deal with a woman as an equal (Bornoff 1991, 452).

[*Update 2002*: Japanese gender roles are still evident in most female names (which are formed using a word for child), in their limited career opportunities, and in the strong stigma and life of hardship women encounter if they divorce. It is still almost impossible for a woman to use her maiden name after she marries. Many women who are divorced face insurmountable obstacles in achieving financial independence. Even obtaining a credit card in her own name is very difficult. Gender-based restrictions affect women even after death. Under Japan's complex burial customs, divorced or unmarried women have been traditionally unwelcome in most cemeteries, where plots are still passed down through the husband's family and descendants must provide maintenance for burial sites or lose them. About a decade ago, this began to change, according to Haruyo Inoue, a sociologist of death and burial at Japan University. "The woman who wanted to be buried alone couldn't find a graveyard until about ten years ago." In 2002, there were close to 400 new cemeteries that serve single women only. According to Junko Matsubara, a popular writer on women's issues who is credited by many with igniting the trend to separate-sex burials in the late 1990s, "The point isn't simply to avoid being buried with one's husband, but rather to learn how we as women can lead more independent lifestyles."

[Western notions of women's liberation have never taken hold among Japanese women, which gives more social significance to what is quietly becoming one of the country's fastest-growing social trends. In a 2002 TBS television network survey, 20% of the women who responded said they hoped to be buried separately from their husbands.

[In another recent development, eight years after Princess Masako and Prince Naruhito married, and after fertility treatment following a miscarriage, Princess Masako produce a daughter on December 1, 2001. The newborn Princess Aiko could become a legal heir to the 2,000-year-old Japanese imperial line and Japan's first "test tube emperor," if the governing party decides to change the law of succession, which currently limits succession to the throne of the Sun Goddess to males (French 2001, 2002). (*End of update by R. T. Francoeur*)]

## C. General Concepts of Sexuality and Love

The Shinto religion recognizes neither good nor evil, so the concept of sin and personal guilt so commonly associated with sex in Western cultures does not exist in the Japanese tradition. The persistence of fertility festivals echoes the acceptance of sex and romance as a natural component of everyday life. Rooted in folk religions and primitive animism, these festivals are celebrated by revelers wearing traditional masks representing the more frankly sexual and comical denizens of Shinto myth and carrying oversized papier-mâché phalli and vulva through the streets (Bornoff 1991, 14-15, 89-90).

Apart from the persistent traditional culture of Japanese sexuality, it is true that Japan has also experienced a rapid modernization, especially in the 1950s and 1960s. As in other societies, modernization in Japan has brought a series of changes in the daily life and lifestyles and hence in human behavior. Table 1 provides a summary of such changes as a model of trends, problems, and issues in lifestyles and human life that are the result of a variety of primary and secondary changes (*IES2* Table 1, p. 771; Hatano 1972).

In general, technological development has resulted in a significant decrease in the amount of physical labor and inconvenient living circumstances. Development of scientific knowledge, along with popularization of education, brought more literacy and freer communications among the common people. The power of the patriarchal structure that originally gave an eccentric, unbalanced character to the family organization decreases as modernization proceeds. In this manner, communication within the family is being ignored. Modern Japanese family life has come to the point where many parents are not taking care of the children and the children are not establishing their self-identity. On the other hand, with only one or two children, parents, and particularly mothers, may be overly protective to the point of rendering their offspring indecisive and inadequate in their interpersonal relationships.

Such changes also cause significant shifts in the way human sexuality is experienced in modern Japan, including the sexual consciousness and sexual behaviors among the people (see also Table 2) (*IES2* Table 2, p. 772; Hatano 1991bc). The impact of the scientific development invited marked progress in the knowledge of biology and genetics. This in turn stimulated the development of sexology. For example, much of the mystery in childbirth, especially the superstitions that there are certain relationships between the behavior of the parents in the past and the physical nature of the newborn, has gradually disappeared. The promotion of science education in public schools has helped this tendency.

The next event in this line was the development of sexology and knowledge about sexuality, such as the separation of reproduction and other sexual behaviors, family planning, emancipation from traditional sex roles, and, subsequently, a more liberal attitude regarding sexual activities. Promotion of family planning after the war years played a decisive role in decreasing the yoke of the women in Japan. At some times, abortion was the most frequently used method of family planning, resulting in certain aftereffects on women's health. In these societal trends, religion no longer played a strong role in controlling the code of ethics because of the allergic reaction to the national control of religion during the dark days of World War II. However, at the same time, modern Japanese have often lost self-identity in terms of development of moral judgment and values.

The pre-modern Japanese had no choice but to accept and follow the lifestyles, behavior patterns, and basic philosophy of life of their parents or leaders in the society. Role models and lifestyle patterns were rather easily found among the family members, as long as one did not attempt to find something new in life. Modern Japanese people, confronted with an explosively large amount of information pouring into their brains, have had to learn how to sort and select this information before they can apply it to actual daily living. It is quite true that during the economic postwar prosperity period, Japan's economic growth almost became the standard of values for society, inviting severe criticism from people in other parts of the world.

Education in information selection systems or value systems—moral education, particularly in relation to sexual activities—has become a major necessity in formal and informal education. Likewise, education in sexual behavior, not in terms of instruction in a behavioral code but in terms of providing understanding of the stages of psychosexual development, will benefit the development of each individual's sexuality. Likewise, sexuality education is expected to enhance education for parenting. All of these needs share a common base as consequences of modernization. The current national *Course of Study* of the Ministry of Education does not include education for either value systems or for establishment of self- and sexual identity. Perhaps these aspects of education belong to the realm of family education. Unfortunately, in contemporary Japan, the national administration of public education is so well developed that the general public has almost forgotten the responsibility of family education. This is causing some serious social problems, particularly when parents expect the public schools to assume complete responsibility for teaching all the codes of ethics, including sexual behaviors.

## 2. Religious, Ethnic, and Gender Factors Affecting Sexuality

### A. Source and Character of Religious Values

According to the latest statistics from the Japanese Ministry of Education, 96.25 million Japanese believe in Buddhism, 109 million in Shintoism, and 10.5 million in other indigenous Japanese religions. A total of 1.46 million are members of various Christian churches. The sum of these statistics exceeds by 75% the total population of Japan. The explanation lies in a characteristic of the Japanese people's attitudes toward religion, which may not be easily understandable for the non-Japanese. The logic of this seemingly illogical trait of Japanese life may be explained in a typical example of Japanese parents who have a custom of visiting a local Shinto shrine to pray to all the 8 million divinities of Shintoism for the healthy growth and well-being of a newborn baby. In the same family, the same parents may have held their wedding ceremony at a Christian church and prayed there for happiness of their newly formed family. The same couple may read the holy scriptures in the Buddhism temple when a family member dies, praying for the dead one to be accepted in the heavenly world safely. Such inconsistency is widely accepted among the Japanese without much friction. Indeed, "three *different* bells ring in the valley," instead of "three bells ring in the valley." Having a mix of various religions in one's daily life is a common way of the Japanese lifestyle. In addition to these well-organized religions, nature worship, which is closely related to Shintoism, is another prevalent religious belief.

Regardless of the mix of religions practiced, which heavily influences the Japanese consciousness on culture, sex, and sexuality, one needs to understand the substantial connection between religion in Japan and the culture, value system, and attitudes toward sexuality. This understanding requires a brief sketch of the history of religion in Japan.

The results of archeological studies in Japan indicate a common practice of burying the dead with certain religious services and rituals during the Jomon and Yayoi culture periods, which ended somewhere around the 3rd or 4th century C.E. During the Jomon period, which lasted several centuries, especially in the eastern part of Japan, remains indicate the special attention the ancestors of the Japanese people then paid to sex and procreation. This is well demonstrated in the artificial designs of the earthed works that are frequently excavated. Throughout the Jomon period, people lived by hunting and gathering, and there was little evidence of any power struggles or the existence of social classes. The Yayoi period arose after the Jomon, around 100 B.C.E., mostly in the western part of Japan. This culture introduced rice crops and ironware from the Korean peninsula and Chinese continent. With these new cultural influences came a disparity of wealth and social

---

#### Table 1

**Trends, Problems, and Issues in Lifestyles as the Result of Primary and Secondary Changes in Societal Modernization**

| Primary Changes ⟶ | Secondary Changes ⟶ | Trends, Problems, and Issues |
|---|---|---|
| | | More leisure hours |
| | | Conformism |
| | | Impersonal society |
| | | Leaving hometown |
| | | Extinction of the fireside |
| | | Happy family circle |
| | Mass media development | Money-first philosophy |
| | Freer commuting | Longer adolescence |
| Technological development | Less concentric force in family | Lessened family concentric force |
| Industrial development | | |
| Universal education | Less physical labor | Fewer community activities |
| Decline of agricultural economy | More work outside of the home | Children leaving parents |
| Decline of patrimonial succession | Materialism | Nuclear family |
| | | Fewer social restrictions |
| | Longer school life | Lack of self-realization |
| | Emphasis on human rights | Lack of sincerity |
| | | Lonely crowd |
| | | Lack of communication |
| | | Less emphasis on individuality |
| | | Aimless life |
| | | Generation gap |
| | | Lowered moral code |

classes, which gradually spread throughout the society. (See Bornoff 1991, 7-16, for a helpful discussion of the sexual and coital implications of Japanese creation myths.)

Later, in the middle of the 6th century of the Common Era, Buddhism and Confucianism were introduced to Japan from Kudara in the Korean Peninsula. These religions rapidly spread nationwide, combining with the gradual permeation of a central government power ruled by the Emperor's family. Popularization of the new philosophy and new administration proceeded along with the preservation policy of these value systems by the central government. In adopting this new religion and culture, Japan followed a path distinctively different from that pursued in other countries. In most cultures, a religious war has been necessary before a newly introduced religion could gain acceptance. In Japan's case, the local religious practices and customs of the preceding culture were not abandoned; rather both old and new cultures and religions seemed to have coexisted quite peacefully.

From the early years until the end of the 16th century, the prevailing religion in Japan was an amalgamation of Buddhism, Shintoism, which is close to nature worshiping, and local religions. During the Muromachi Era in the 14th to 16th centuries, the Catholic form of Christianity was introduced and propagated to some extent by the Portuguese until 1590, when Toyotomi Hideyoshi issued a national policy prohibiting Christianity. In the next three centuries, during the Tokugawa (Edo) Era, the circumstances surrounding religion in Japan returned to the amalgamation of Buddhism, Shintoism, and local religions as before the Muromachi Era.

In 1868 when the Tokugawa Shogunate collapsed, the Meiji Era began with restoration of the emperor who held power within a new political system that promoted a policy of nationalism and who strengthened the nation's military force so that modern Japan could compete on even terms with other already modernized nations. As the spiritual basis of this strong Japan, the government pronounced that Shintoism would be the national religion. The emperor's family tree, it was claimed, could be traced back some 120 generations through more than 2,000 years of history. Whether or not the historical facts were twisted to some extent, the government goal was to integrate all the religions in Japan into one by national decree. This idea was pursued until the end of World War II in 1945. Aside from the intention of national power, among the common people the concept of traditional Buddhism and citizen's beliefs were substantially followed. This is another proof of the variability of the religion of the Japanese.

In the newly adopted Constitution of Japan after World War II, freedom of faith was promised, and thus the religious control of the national government was abandoned.

## Table 2

### The Development of Sexology Promoted More Demand for New Sexuality Education

| Events | Contents |
| --- | --- |
| Development of science and sexology | Biology and genetics |
| Broadening perspectives on sexual behavior | Family planning, separation of reproduction and sex, liberation from traditional sex roles, freer sexual activities |
| More demand for new sexuality education | Transmission of accurate sexual knowledge and information, value judgment education as standard of behavior judgment, education for life planning |

At the same time, the chaotic coexistence of various religions leaves the religious thoughts of today's Japanese more or less ambiguous.

## B. Source and Character of Japanese Ethnic Values Affecting Sexuality

While culture has been variously defined by different researchers, the concept is used here to indicate the complex of phenomena, ideologies, religion, and literature that provide the fundamental orientation for all sorts of behavior patterns of the Japanese people. As was mentioned earlier, deep in the Japanese mind, the structure of cultural consciousness includes a tendency to nature worship and local religions. This may be because of the roots of the Japanese consciousness in an agrarian culture that has been uniquely molded by archeological and historical processes. It can be said that the general belief among the Japanese that children are the natural gift from the divinities is an expression of the sexuality of the Japanese people. In the ancient days of the Nara and Heian periods, the *Man'yoshu*, a late 8th-century collection of 10,000 Waka poems, many of which are love songs, and the 11th-century *Romances of Genji*, 54 volumes of love stories by the woman novelist Murasaki Shikibu, strongly conveyed the attitude and message that love and sexuality were an important part of human thought and everyday behavior as a natural expression of human nature. In other words, sexuality was openly accepted among the early Japanese people.

In Japan's history, an aristocratic culture dominated the Nara (710-794), Heian (794-1336), and Muromachi (1336-1573) Eras. In the Sengoku (Turbulence) Period, many warlords competed with each other until the Tokugawa Shogunate was established and national integration begun in 1603. Various groups of the military commanders maintained control of the culture and the behavior of the Japanese people during the Sengoku and Tokugawa Eras. Therefore, the cultural construction and sexuality of the Japanese people operated in a double-layer system. More specifically, extremely strict moral ethics and control of behavior were enforced on children and adults in the families of the *samurai* class (soldiers and the commanders), who were influenced by the Confucianism originally introduced to Japan in the 6th century from China. In the feudal value system, as well as its family system, there was no room for any free expression of human passions and natural desires. Thus, not only romantic love, but also immoral and adulterous behavior of any kind were strictly prohibited, and severe penalties, including capital punishment, were instituted for any case that came to light.

While the *samurai* community kept to a strict behavior code of ethics, the commoners and the townspeople did not, except for the upper-class commoners who closely followed the *samurai* code of ethics. Romantic love was freely allowed among the commoners, and often an illegitimate child—a single mother and her child in today's sense—was accepted and reared without any prejudices in the community or tenement commune (Bornoff 1991, 83-149).

All of the *ukiyo-e* and *shunga* (pornographic paintings) by Utamaro, Hokusai, and Kunisada were produced from the commoners' culture. Yoshiwara, the sexual amusement quarter in the city of Edo, painted by Oiran, a prostitute and social entertainer of the highest class, for example, prospered in the middle and later Edo Era. Few examples of erotica in the world tell us as much about the cultures that produced them as the *shunga* tell us about the practices and fantasies of the Japanese. Among the more striking features of *shunga* is the common presence of children, indicating just how very uninhibited and frank the Japanese were about sex (Bornoff 1991, 184-86).

These examples of a dual-layered social and cultural construction during the *samurai* ruling periods produced a double standard of code ethics, each code composed of its own logical but superficial principles and real intention. These two codes are still actively practiced in contemporary Japanese society, making the understanding of the Japanese culture confusing and difficult.

It was during the very last stage of the Edo Era—in fact, only 130-some years ago—when the country of Japan abandoned its three-century-old policy of national isolation, that free trading and cultural exchanges began with the other countries of the world. As has been already discussed earlier, the modernization process of the nation at such an extremely rapid pace produced certain distorted periods in the history of modern Japan. These periods of turmoil and confusion include the collapse of the Tokugawa Shogunate political system, the restoration of the Imperial ruling system in the Meiji Era, the rise of nationalism in the Taisho Era, and the dominance of the militarism that collapsed at the end of World War II in the middle of the Showa Era.

During the Meiji Era, in order for the country of Japan to be able to compete evenly with the other nations in the world, Japan took a policy of economic enrichment based on development of heavy industry, strengthening of the military power, and placing the Imperial family in the sacred order. The value of each individual in this social system was extremely neglected, resulting in the idea that a man is to serve the nation and a woman is to bear children. Any consciousness of sexual equality was thoroughly repressed, and sexual discrimination—the ideas that higher education is not necessary for women or that childless women deserve to be divorced—were commonly expressed and adhered to. Under such circumstances, a very patriarchal sexual culture emerged in which specific male-centered sexual behavior was accepted without any argument. The proxy engagement system, in which it is mandatory for parents to choose the marriage partner of their child, and in which the matchmaking ceremony takes place only after the parents have chosen the marriage partner (distinctively different from the matchmaking practice seen in the modern times in which the young couple has the right to choose to proceed or not), were typical of such practices.

The cultural structure in the Taisho Era is often called Taisho Liberalism. As a temporal reaction of the Imperial-family-centered social structure of the Meiji Era, some opinion leaders advanced distinctly liberal ideas during this era. This was particularly evident in literary works, as some women writers and cultural leaders proposed the very first expression of the feminist movement in Japan. Others followed by advocating communism and the birth-control movement. The case of Senji Yamamoto, the first sexologist in Japan, was certainly an example of this liberalization trend. Yamamoto had spent some time in America while young and had been influenced by its culture. He was assassinated in 1902, at age 40 years, by an ultra-right-wing terrorist opposed to Yamamoto's promotion of birth control, labor liberalization, proletarian theory, and the anti-Law of Public Peace Maintenance. The national leaders of that time regarded a person like Yamamoto, who recognized the sexual rights of each individual, worked hard against poverty, and had a strong anti-power attitude, as dangerous.

The Taisho Era, which lasted only 15 years, was followed by the militaristic age of Showa, in which Japanese militarists initiated a series of wars, including the invasion of China and military actions in Southeast Asian countries and the Pacific area, leading up to World War II.

In the historical process of Meiji, Taisho, and Showa, Japan's primary national policy consistently focused on economic enrichment and strengthening of the military power. Within this societal atmosphere, children were regarded as a national treasure, and thus they were reared comparatively freely. In contrast with contemporary urban life, adolescents in the agricultural community life that dominated the Meiji and Taisho Eras, learned most of the manners and rules that were necessary to spend a normal life in the adult community by spending time together with peers in the local community. A good example of this peer learning was the *Shuku* or "dwelling-together practice."

This *Shuku* community group is roughly classified as either *Wakamono-shuku* for young males and *Musume-shuku* for young females. Within the local community, it was mandatory for each youth to join the *shuku* of their respective sex at a specified age. In the *shuku*, they worked together for the village in the daytime and learned the traditional codes of behavior of the community in the evening. Sexuality education in today's sense was definitely included in this community education system. Within the local community, the freedom of love was widely accepted, as those who fell in love with each other were usually allowed to get married. Children of the ruling-class families, such as village master and landowner, however, were not allowed to enjoy this freedom during their adolescent and youthful days.

In 1945, after World War II, the Japanese people were granted the right to experience democratic and liberal lifestyles because of the cultural influences of the Allied Western countries. The Japanese people have enjoyed this freedom in the subsequent 50 years, and yet, at the same time, the traditional Japanese consciousness of the societal system, moral codes, and fundamental attitude toward life and sex formed throughout the centuries still regulate their thoughts and behaviors today. The highly successful experience of 50 years of newly available pro-Western ways of life visible on the surface of Japanese culture today is definitely overpowered by the centuries-old value systems and views toward sex, human beings, religion, and society at the conscious level and deep in the mind. The sexuality of the modern Japanese is, therefore, formed in a double-layered manner that, in effect, defies clear description or understanding by outsiders. The world has become smaller as the consequence of the vast development in the transportation and media systems. At the same time, however, it is often pointed out that deep in the mind of the modern Japanese people, the national isolation policy is still alive.

## 3. Knowledge and Education about Sexuality

### A. Historical Perspectives

There are various opinions among the historians regarding the time of the establishment of Japan as a nation, but at least many agree that it was after the 6th century when the political system had gradually formed into a certain style, not in the modern sense, but in a way that was based on and facilitated by organized education run by Buddhist priests from their temples. With the coming of Buddhism in 538 or 552 C.E. (depending on the source cited), numbers of Buddhist priests came from Kudara on the Korean Peninsula. In addition, a likely larger number of Japanese priests went abroad to Korea and China to study. In these temples, education in Buddhist scripts and political administration was provided for the priests and the children of the national administrators.

It is commonly recognized that the first schools in Japan's history were the *Daigakuryo*, or College Dormitories, established in the nation's capital, and the *Kokugaku* or, National Schools, which were established in each major city, in accordance with the *Taihorituryo*, or Great Treasure Laws enacted in 701 C.E.

Subsequently, various educational systems were established to provide education exclusively for the ruling class, i.e., aristocrats, *samurai*, and priests. Even though the political systems and/or power structure changed from time to time, these educational systems persisted because the schools were established by the ruling *daimyo* (feudal lords or landlords) or *samurai* families. Education for the townsfolk and commoners, though not yet institutionalized, was initiated in the 13th and 14th centuries and continued afterwards in the Buddhist temples. During the Edo era (1603-1886), such private schools for elementary education became quite popular and were known as *Terakoya* or temple houses.

Education for women was not available in the rulers' schools, but was available to some extent in the "commoners' schools." Then, in the early 1700s, in the middle of the Edo Era, a unique educational organization developed as a function of the village and town community, for the education of the immature youths for daily life, including education in sexual behavior. These organizations were known as the *Wakamono-gumi*, or young men's activity group, and the *Musume-gumi*, or daughters' activity group. This system of community education was disbanded in the middle of the Meiji Era around 1890 in favor of promoting newly established public school systems.

In 1868, as the shogunate political system collapsed, Japan made its first step into the modern world when Emperor Meiji transferred the capital from Kyoto—formerly Edo, where the Shogunate was located—to Tokyo. In 1872, the new government announced a law known as *Gakusei*, or School System, based on the French school system, and launched a nationwide education for all. This educational law, intended to promote industrial development and the universal conscription system, was ultimately linked with the national policy of enriching the country and strengthening its armament. One may observe in this historic transition the germination of the Japan's militarism in the 20th century.

The Law of Education, enacted in 1879, took a liberal direction in using the American school system as its base. This was quickly amended the following year by the "Revised Law of Education," which put the emphasis on Confucianist morals as the fundamental spirit. This traditional vision was obviously necessary because of strong opposition within the government against Western liberalism. "Catching up with the already modernized nations in the world" was indeed the priority motto of the Meiji government, but in terms of practical education, the goal of producing guns and battleships outranked the education of humans. In 1903, the government took over supervision and authorization of textbooks in order to develop uniformity in people's thoughts and minds. As a result, Japan's education was overwhelmed by the moral and behavior codes of Confucianist ethics based on the emperor system and nationalism.

A short-lived liberal trend developed between 1912 and 1926, when Emperor Taisho was on the throne. This liberal movement, however, was not strong enough to change the government's educational policy, and in the long term, the militarists regained power.

The militarism, and later fascism, grew stronger and matured in the Showa Era beginning in 1926 and climaxing in education's dark period during World War II (1941-1945). After the 1945 defeat, Japanese education was completely transfigured with the adoption of a 6-3-3-4 year sequence, the first nine years being mandatory (six years of elementary school and three years of junior high school). This newly implemented system also brought to Japan substantially equal opportunity of education for boys and girls and all social classes.

The outstanding economic growth of Japan throughout the postwar years is regarded as a contemporary marvel. Along with it, education in Japan also made great progress quantitatively as well as qualitatively. Much of its content will be introduced in the following section. It should, however, be explained here that the Showa Era was closed in 1989 upon the passing of Emperor Showa, and now it is the era of Heisei.

## B. Sexuality Education in Contemporary Japan

### The Background Education System

As of 1994, Japan had a total of 65,000 schools of all kinds for its total population of 124.3 million. This includes approximately 25,000 elementary schools (grades 1 to 6), 12,000 junior high schools (grades 7 through 9), 5,500 senior high schools (grades 10 through 12), 1,100 colleges and universities (including two-year junior colleges), 6,700 vocational colleges (mostly two-year), 15,000 kindergartens, and 1,000 special schools for handicapped children. The rate of actual participation in required education has been as high as 99.9% since around 1910, although the length of mandatory education was much shorter before 1945. These statistics exclude some 1,200 heavily handicapped children and an estimated 100,000 prolonged absentees because of illness and unwillingness to participate.

The great majority of those who complete the required education of nine years by age 12 go on to three-year senior high school, specifically 94.3% of the boys and 96.4% of the girls. Advancement to colleges and universities is 36.3% for men and 39.2% for women. This trend to high academic achievement orientation has created stress and mental pressure in the "entrance examination war" all Japanese youths experience. Because of overemphasis on the entrance examination, many recognize the necessity of *Juku*, extracurricular schools in the evenings and on holidays, tutors, and/or correspondence courses to prepare for the examinations. Such practices are common in Japan these days, perhaps more so than in other countries, suggesting the need to discuss the effects and consequences of the *Juku* for the social life of Japanese adolescents and young adults.

The detailed curriculum in each school level, the general objectives of each subject, and aims and contents of each school year for each subject are precisely controlled by the national *Course of Study*. It may seem that the national government limits and controls the contents of education and its teaching methods; however, the *Course of Study* only presents the frame structure of the teaching, and the classroom teacher has the liberty of the details presented. The *Course of Study* is revised once every decade or so.

As in some other countries, the Ministry of Education provides a list of approved textbooks from which teachers select those to be used in their classes. It is true that sometimes court cases have arisen about the suitability of the national policy on textbooks, questioning whether the government is interfering with education, whether the examination/approval system conflicts with the Constitution, or whether the system infringes on the freedom of expression. However, so far the system is functioning well, with individual schools and teachers free to choose classroom content and presentations aside from government approval of texts and teaching materials.

### Sexuality Education

There is no distinct sexuality or family-life education course included in the subjects to be taught in the Japanese school system. The *Course of Study* does not require anything to be taught about sexuality, nor does the national government determine any objectives or the content of sexuality education wherever a local school or teacher decides to deal with this topic at any grade or school level. The official statement provided by the Ministry of Education states that "The contents of education regarding sex (and sexuality) are distributed in various respective subjects (relevant to biology, sociology and health, etc.) and sex (and sexuality education) is certainly expected to be integrated in all these subject matters at each school." Therefore, the promoters of sex (and sexuality) education, such as those involved in the Japanese Association for Sex Education (J.A.S.E.), have been advocating school instructional programs by developing and publishing *Sex Education Guidelines* for various school levels and various grades. J.A.S.E. was established and was officially approved by the Ministry of Education in 1972, and has since been the leading nonprofit organization in the field of sex education.

On the other hand, improvement in education for HIV and AIDS is increasing in Japan's schools because of the rapid spread of HIV and AIDS throughout the world since the late 1980s. This in turn has strengthened the importance of sex education in the Japanese schools.

Since 1992, as a result of revisions in the elementary school *Course of Study*, childbirth has been introduced into the science textbook, and physical and psychological changes of adolescence into the health education textbook, indicating that some changes can be made in the *Course of Study*. Any changes in the *Course of Study* automatically means definite changes in the instructional contents at every school. At present, all upper-grade elementary schoolchildren are expected to be exposed to the physiological and psychological aspects of human sexuality. However, so far no textbook describes any aspects of sexual intercourse, which has prompted some criticism from classroom teachers about the incomplete vision and unrealistic attitude of the Ministry of Education.

In the junior high school level, certain topics in sex education are dealt with in health education, science (biology), social studies, and domestic science. However, these are handled less candidly and actively than in elementary schools in the same system or district. The case is similar as well in the senior high schools; the reason perhaps being that classroom instruction is regarded much less as an education for human living than as a preparation for the next entrance examination, i.e., senior high school for the junior high students, and colleges and universities in the case of senior high school students.

"Education indeed is the greatest prevention" is the standpoint of the Ministry of Education regarding HIV and AIDS prevention. Because of this viewpoint, elementary school faculty are strongly encouraged to teach that HIV and AIDS are not transmitted by mosquito bites or by shaking hands with others, and that no person with HIV or AIDS should be discriminated against. It is greatly regretted by many educators and members of J.A.S.E. that sex education in Japanese schools currently needs to be improved so much and that teaching the fact that HIV can be transmitted through sexual intercourse is still not well accepted among the schoolchildren. This has an impact also on a number of cases in which hemophiliac patients have become HIV-positive because of contaminated blood transfusions. [*Update 1997*: By 1985, about 40% of all Japanese hemophiliac patients, more than 2,000 people, had contracted HIV through contaminated imported blood products. As of 1995, hemophiliac patients accounted for 60% of Japanese people with HIV. See Section 10B on HIV/AIDS. (*End of update by Y. Kaji*)] Even these patients are hesitant, because of public ig-

norance, to admit they are HIV-positive. As a matter of fact, voluntary admission of HIV-positive status is almost nonexistent in Japanese society. This is because, for most Japanese people, admitting to being HIV-positive is viewed as a kind of social suicide and societal discrimination is definitely expected.

Because of centuries of a national isolation policy that rejected anything that might endanger cultural and religious harmony, a person with any unusual handicap or disease like HIV was commonly treated as an enemy of society, or at least rejected. It is, therefore, difficult to judge whether appropriate HIV-related education would produce any effects in changing the attitudes of children of any age to HIV-positive persons. [*Comment 1997*: An added problem is the great reluctance, especially among elementary schoolteachers, to mention, let alone discuss, sexuality in their classrooms (*End of comment by Y. Kaji*)] Even in junior and senior high schools, where one might expect teachers to be more open in dealing with sexual issues, and students to be more open to education about discrimination prevention, the effectiveness of education in reducing discrimination against persons with HIV is unclear.

The content of the sex education actually received by students was studied in 1981 and 1987 surveys; Table 3 shows a breakdown in the content of sexuality education by subject (*IES2* Fig. 1, p. 784; J.A.S.E. 1988). When these subjects are clustered into three general categories, 1. physiobiological, 2. psychological, and 3. social, the youth surveyed reported that 29.4%—three out of every ten—had received no sexual education at all (type 0) while an identical figure of 29.4% received an education that covered all three general categories (type III). A little over 20% had sexuality education that covered only the physiological and biological aspects (type I), while 13.5% and 12.8% had instruction that covered the physiological-biological and social (type IIA), or psychological-biological and psychological (type IIB), respectively. In

### Table 3

**Subjects Actually Taught in Sex Education and the Percentages of Students Receiving Such Information by Sex, 1981 and 1987**

| Subjects | Females | | Males | |
|---|---|---|---|---|
| | 1981 | 1987 | 1981 | 1987 |
| Sex organs & functions | 63.7% | 77.3% | 73.2% | 83.9% |
| Menstruation | 92.6 | 98.4 | 64.9 | 78.3 |
| Ejaculation | 52.9 | 66.1 | 68.8 | 83.3 |
| Secondary puberty signs | 75.1 | 83.7 | 71.0 | 84.6 |
| Procreation | 64.8 | 83.3 | 56.6 | 75.8 |
| Gender selection & heredity | 37.0 | 50.3 | 38.3 | 53.2 |
| Psychological & behavioral differences between sexes | 28.4 | 25.7 | 27.3 | 23.1 |
| Sex roles & cooperation | 22.6 | 21.3 | 25.0 | 25.6 |
| Male/female friendship | 27.5 | 23.8 | 27.9 | 25.2 |
| Adolescent psychology | 30.9 | 40.1 | 32.6 | 48.0 |
| Friendship & love | 14.1 | 16.6 | 16.4 | 20.8 |
| Marriage meaning & premises | 19.1 | 25.5 | 18.5 | 22.3 |
| Population control & family planning | 31.0 | 48.5 | 26.8 | 40.0 |
| STDs and misconduct | 51.9 | 41.0 | 53.5 | 45.2 |
| Sex and culture | 7.1 | 11.6 | 12.7 | 19.7 |
| Sex morals | 11.2 | 11.8 | 16.7 | 17.6 |

(*IES2* Fig. 1, p. 784)

Table 3, the heavy concentration of responses on the top six items, which cover the physiological/biological background of sexuality, supports the conclusion that when Japanese children do receive sex education, it is more often limited to the facts of physiology and biology.

Table 4 presents the percentage of each type of sex education actually given to students of different school levels (*IES2* Fig. 2, p. 785; J.A.S.E. 1988). Naturally, the amount of education, particularly that of type III, increases as the level of schooling advances. In addition, it is shown that in junior high school, the psychological aspects of sexuality are emphasized. This may be an understandable trend since the biological and psychological aspects of pubescent events occur just before or in the early stages of adolescence.

As mentioned earlier, the contents of sex education in Japanese school systems are more or less centered around physiological aspects and are, therefore, cognitive-oriented rather than attitudinal-behavior-oriented. In order for sex education in Japanese schools to become the comprehensive sexuality education it needs to be, more consideration must be given to the psychological and sociological aspects of sexuality. HIV and AIDS education and prevention needs to be incorporated in this framework as a well-balanced education within the national *Course of Study*.

## C. Informal Sources of Sex Education

Teen sex magazines are popular and widely read by Japanese youth. They are noticeably different from their adult counterparts, comparatively wholesome, or at least harmless or insipid. Instead of the violent, sadistic, and degrading content common in adult pornography, teen sex magazines are filled with frivolous, inane, and unabashed boys' club talk and candid cheerleader squat-shots and near-nudist pictorials. Since true sexuality education is absent from Japanese education, and parents and the community no longer communicate this essential information to youths, these magazines do perform an important function, providing limited but basic information about sexual anatomy. Unfortunately, their popularity depends on adolescent titillation that ignores the need to provide information on STD prevention and contraception. Japanese television is also a major informal source of limited sexual information, particularly in the early evening television cartoon programs that cater to adolescent male curiosities about female anatomy (Bornoff 1991, 71).

### Table 4

**Types of Sex Education Actually Given and Percentage of Secondary and University Students by Sex Who Received Each**

| Age Group | Type 0 | Type I | Type IIA | Type IIB | Type III |
|---|---|---|---|---|---|
| **Males** | | | | | |
| Junior High Ages 12-14 | 47.1% | 24.0% | 3.4% | 15.1% | 10.4% |
| Senior High Ages 15-17 | 24.5 | 12.5 | 17.3 | 6.0 | 39.6 |
| University Ages 18+ | 25.6 | 10.5 | 19.3 | 5.5 | 39.1 |
| **Females** | | | | | |
| Junior High Ages 12-14 | 19.2 | 37.5 | 3.4 | 28.5 | 11.4 |
| Senior High Ages 15-17 | 8.7 | 15.0 | 22.2 | 8.4 | 45.6 |
| University Ages 18+ | 6.1 | 14.0 | 26.2 | 6.0 | 47.7 |

(*IES2* Fig. 2, p. 785)

(See Section 8C for comments on the *Roricon* or "Lolita complex" that is so widespread in Japanese sex magazines and can be said to constitute a national characteristic.)

## 4. Autoerotic Behaviors and Patterns

There are clear gender differences in terms of the masturbation fantasies and concrete activity that Japanese boys and girls pursue in their adolescent behavioral development. In reality, the great majority of the senior high school boys practice masturbation, while the majority of girls of ages 20 and 21 years still ignore masturbation after experiencing their first intercourse (J.A.S.E. 1994). The median 22-year-old female has not engaged in masturbation. This may indicate a difference in the degree of sexual drive between the two sexes. But another possible reason that females are not eager to engage in masturbation is the social pressure against the female's self-motivated sexual activities that are unrelated to procreation, although this belief is steadily becoming weaker. The majority of young Japanese women perhaps do not give serious consideration to autoeroticism because of the subconscious expectation that a good Japanese woman should always be modest in any sexual activity. [*Comment 1997*: This may be changing as young Japanese women increasingly reject traditional female roles. (See Section 5C on adult heterosexual behavior, marriage, family, and divorce, below.) (*End of comment by Y. Kaji*)] According to the 1981 survey results, females discover and first experience masturbation as a result of "incidental touching of the genital organ by something" and/or "reading erotic articles." For males, there is an indication that being "taught by some friend" is the more common inspiration.

[*Comment 2003*: In terms of the cumulative frequencies of masturbation experiences of Japanese youths in the 1987 and 1993 national surveys, 16% of the 1987 males had begun masturbating, while about 6% of the 1993 males and the same percentage of both 1987 and 1993 females had masturbated by age 12. For both groups of women, the cumulative totals rose slowly to about 13% at age 17, and then rose to 32% for 1987 females and 35% for 1993 females. After a sharp rise in masturbation experiences between ages 12 and 16, 1993 males held a plateau until age 19. Males surveyed in 1987 leveled off for a year and then moved ahead by 8% over their 1993 peers. At age 21, 92% of 1987 males, 95% of 1993 males, 34% of 1993 females, and 32% of 1987 females had masturbated (*IES2* Fig. 3, p. 786; J.A.S.E. 1994). (*End of comment by the Editors; percentages are approximations from the original line graph; see note at beginning of chapter.*)]

The teen sex magazines mentioned above in Sections 3C, Knowledge and Education about Sexuality, Informal Sources of Sex Education, and 8C, Significant Unconventional Sexual Behaviors, Pornography and Erotica, which are used primarily by young males as a masturbatory stimulant, pose many societal and cultural questions. [*Comment 1997*: The sex magazines and comics targeted to young females are also popular and raise many controversial questions. (*End of comment by Y. Kaji*; see also Perper and Cornog's observations on *manga* in Section 8C, Pornography and Erotica.)] Apart from their relatively healthy content in terms of normal psychosexual development, one controversy centers on the degree to which the staggering amount of these magazines produced and their extensive use by teenagers and older males for masturbation is all that wholesome. Do these magazines promote normal psychosexual development, or do they support and promote an unhealthy, introverted social isolation? Is the plethora of teen sex magazines an unhealthy substitute for many young men who have not developed the interpersonal skills they need relate to women on a mature and intimate adult level? (Bornoff 1991, 71).

## 5. *Interpersonal Heterosexual Behaviors*
### A. Childhood Play and Sexual Behaviors
*The Threat of a New Subspecies*

Since education in sexuality and education for parenting share a common basis, it may be helpful to sketch the possible role and position these two aspects of education hold in the natural developmental sequences of play and sexual behaviors children pass through as they mature (see Table 5) (*IES2* Fig. 4, p. 788; Hatano 1991bc). Throughout his or her growth and development, the child is expected to experience certain events and to develop certain skills, so that development of a mature consciousness and behavior will be promoted. Regular mother-child behavior like breastfeeding during infancy is believed to stimulate mental activity of the baby and to enhance a trustworthy relationship between parent and child. Based on this sort of relationship, the time spent in play and fun experiences between the two would promote a sense of playful exploration and form the basis of interpersonal relationships, as well as emotional security. This in turn enhances the ability of a child to play with other children and successfully join in peer-group activities.

Peer-group activities, especially involving play activities among young children, are believed to develop the social aspect of personality. It seems that social development of an individual includes acquisition of communication skills with others, procedures to maneuver human relations, leadership development within a group, and coping skills between boys and girls, between elders and the young, and between the strong and the weak. As a person grows and becomes ready to engage in heterosexual relationships and sexual behavior, these human relationship skills will become necessary to cope with the opposite sex. Likewise, the above skills are needed when a person becomes a parent.

Together with increasing urbanization and modernization, Japan, especially in recent years, is witnessing the emergence of a new type of young person—what may be termed *Neo homo sapiens*—who often does not accept traditional institutional human relationships and prefers living exclusively at the keyboard of a computer, communicating via networks, and avoiding direct human relations with the others. These young people are often cruel, lacking in interpersonal relationship skills in the sense of human relationships with the others, and unskilled in heterosexual or homosexual relations in later adolescent life. This is evidenced in the increase in older bachelors and in the increasing frequency of *Narita divorce*—divorce upon returning to Narita New Tokyo International Airport from a honeymoon trip outside of Japan—indicating the lack of patience, human relationship maneuvering skills, and inability to maintain a married relationship.

> What usually happens [in a Narita divorce] is that newlyweds take a honeymoon in a place like Australia or Hawaii, and the husband is so intimidated by overseas travel that he scarcely wants to leave his hotel room.
>
> The wife, on the other hand, has already taken several foreign trips with girlfriends and is much more comfortable with the idea of being abroad. She wants to spend her days scuba diving and her nights bopping in the disco, and she finds her husband a dreadful bore. So she dumps him at the end of the honeymoon, and they say a final good-bye at Narita. (Kristof 1996a)

The need for sexuality and parenting education is expected to increase as technology continues to transform Japanese society.

*The Past and Present Contrasted*

According to the latest national statistics, the average married Japanese couple has 1.6 children, definitely one of the lowest rates in the modern world. This tendency to a small number of children is a reflection of urbanization and a high-economic, growth-centered family life with the wife being a highly educated career woman. [*Comment 1997*: This tendency for Japanese couples to have fewer children may also reflect the lack of sufficient social welfare and public childcare systems, which pressures mothers to stay home and take care of their children. Many Japanese women are reluctant to have more children because of inflexible working hours required by Japanese companies, long-distance commuting to work, the high cost of housing, and the lack of childcare facilities. (*End of comment by Y. Kaji*)] Apart from the need and preference of each individual family, this trend is not necessarily a healthy phenomenon for society in general, particularly because

### Table 5

**Human Developmental Stages and Assignments of Play and Sexual Behavior and Positions of Sex Education and Education for Parenting**

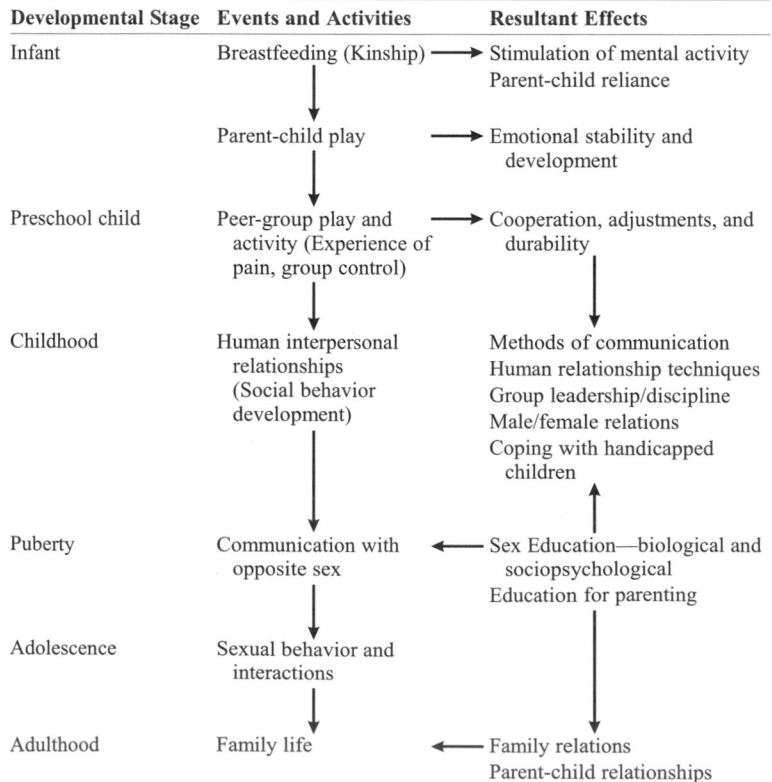

| Developmental Stage | Events and Activities | Resultant Effects |
|---|---|---|
| Infant | Breastfeeding (Kinship) → | Stimulation of mental activity<br>Parent-child reliance |
| | Parent-child play → | Emotional stability and development |
| Preschool child | Peer-group play and activity (Experience of pain, group control) → | Cooperation, adjustments, and durability |
| Childhood | Human interpersonal relationships (Social behavior development) | Methods of communication<br>Human relationship techniques<br>Group leadership/discipline<br>Male/female relations<br>Coping with handicapped children |
| Puberty | Communication with opposite sex ← | Sex Education—biological and sociopsychological<br>Education for parenting |
| Adolescence | Sexual behavior and interactions | |
| Adulthood | Family life ← | Family relations<br>Parent-child relationships |

(*IES2* Fig. 4, p. 788)

of the consequences of impediments that the individual single child encounters in his or her development (see the third column in Table 5).

In the past, the Japanese family was often situated in a large, family-tree system where several families related by kinship lived together on the same land but in different houses. This arrangement sometimes accommodated different families of three or four different generations. The children learned many important matters from the members of the various families, as well as from their own immediate brothers and sisters. With many children in each family, each child enjoyed excellent educational opportunities within the family community. Indeed, everyday life in the community functioned as the community education. The advent of modernization brought an urban life that forced the extended family and neighborhood community to abandon its educational function. In addition, the daily human exchanges and the network system with the neighbors were lost.

In the pre-modern community, children of similar ages formed peer groups and played together near their farm homes, in a backyard, an open field, or in the barn. The children often obtained interesting and helpful information related to sex from observing the farm animals; in this manner, sexuality education went on in an informal manner. The "doctor/nurse play" they often enjoyed within their peer group in a secret space provided sexual information and fantasy, which in turn helped them form a healthy sexual identity of their own.

Children in contemporary Japan, first of all, now have fewer brothers and sisters in their family so they seldom have opportunities to cope with a small baby, with a younger child, or with an older and stronger child. Some young children of 3 start special training in preparation for the entrance examination for kindergarten. In addition to public school, almost all elementary schoolchildren today attend *Juku*, or special training school, for entrance examination for some junior high school, that may provide a better opportunity for future school advancement. In addition, training in piano, ballet, and swimming, for example, is becoming a common practice among children of all ages. As a result, the children have very little time for spontaneous activities such as playing and spending time together with the children of the peer group. One's ability to live socially and peacefully with other people of different types and capabilities is usually cultivated in these childhood circumstances; however, contemporary Japanese children are not in the position to experience such education. It may not be surprising then to find young grownups today who lack the usual skills of living, playing, and communicating with young people of the same and/or other sex. Human relations require skills in sexuality-related behaviors, such as talking with and obtaining trust from the peers of the other sex, and these are skills that may not be attained by merely reading books or watching television programs.

Contemporary children, who are busy with *Juku* and extracurricular training programs, must watch television programs, play television/computer games, and read comic books during the precious free activity hours, perhaps an hour or so in the late evening, after finishing all the previously scheduled programs. While there is much information related to sex and sexual behaviors on television and in comic books, exposure to this information is not sufficient when they have to use it on their own, cognitively and affectively. They need to perceive this information in the context of actual human relations and experiences. In actuality, most contemporary Japanese children build their knowledge pertaining to sex in a passive manner that results in distortion and inflexibility. The sex-related knowledge should be actively acquired by each individual with a positive attitude in order for one to handle sexuality in later life constructively and with enjoyment. The reality in Japan today seems to be quite different from what it should be.

This is not to imply or suggest that today's children will grow up to become sexual deviants or criminals. However, it is obvious that attention needs to be paid to the fact that in Japan today, the psychosexual developmental processes of the infants and children are experienced in abstract textbooks rather than in actual experience-oriented activities.

## B. The Sexuality of Adolescents

### The Results of Four National Surveys

The office of the Prime Minister sponsored nationwide surveys of sexual development and sexual behaviors of Japanese youths in 1974, 1981, 1987, and 1993. The surveys, conducted by the Japanese Association for Sex Education (J.A.S.E.), mobilized nearly 30,000 youths of ages between 12 and 22 years each time. The reports provide a substantial picture of the sexuality of Japanese youth. The full reports were published in Japanese by J.A.S.E. (1975, 1983, 1988, and 1994) and summarized for the international community on several occasions by Yoshiro Hatano (1988, 1991ab, 1993).

[*Comment 2003*: In comparing the ages of menarche in girls and the start of ejaculation in boys, about 5% of all four groups had menstruated or ejaculated before age 10. According to the 1993 survey, a majority of 54% of the 12-year-old girls had already experienced their first menstruation. The menarche curve for girls then quickly declines to a few percent at age 16 and beyond; by age 19, close to 100% of the girls were menstruating. Girls mature a year or more earlier than the boys (*IES2* Fig. 5, p. 791; J.A.S.E. 1994). At age 12, 19% of males had experienced ejaculation. For boys, the peak ejaculation onset occurs at age 13, with about 38% of boys experiencing ejaculation for the first time at that age. At age 15, 76% of the 1993 boys and 64% of the 1987 boys were experiencing ejaculation. By age 21, 96% of the boys surveyed in 1993 and 84% of the boys surveyed in 1987 had experienced ejaculation (*IES2* Fig. 6, p. 792; Shimazaki 1994-95).

[In the cumulative frequencies of the development of "interest in sex" among Japanese youths in the 1987 and 1993 surveys, at age 13, 37% of 1987 girls and 42% of the 1993 girls, and 42% of both the 1987 and 1993 boys experienced an "interest in sex." Between ages 15 and 18 the cumulative total for boys rose from about 78% to 93%. At age 20, 100% of 1993 males and 96% of 1987 males expressed an interest in sex. Between ages 15 and 18, the cumulative male totals rose from 58% the 75%, peaking at about 90% at age 21 (*IES2* Fig. 7, p. 792; J.A.S.E. 1994).

[As for the cumulative "interest in approaching the opposite sex," 25% of 12-year-old males surveyed in 1993 and 34% of 1987 males were interested in approaching a girl, while 55.5% of 1993 girls and 48% of 1987 girls had experienced an interest in approaching someone of the opposite sex. At 16, the cumulative totals were 75% to 80%; by age 21, the cumulative totals for all four groups ranged from 89% for 1987 females to 91% for 1993 girls, and 94% for 1987 males and 96% for 1993 males (*IES2* Fig. 8, p. 793). As for the cumulative frequencies of "desire for physical contact with the opposite sex," the survey results are shown in Table 6 (*IES2* Fig. 9, p. 793). There is a clear difference between an interest in approaching a member of the opposite sex and the desire for physical contact, in that the boys are strongly interested in direct physical contact with the opposite sex while the girls are only interested in becoming closer with the other sex.

[Although these young people, both male and female, seem to start their adolescence with heterosexual "interests" by age 13 or 14, this interest does not have a concrete outcome in social activity, namely dating, for some years. In 1993, 3% of the males and 2% of the females reported dating. Twenty percent of both 1993 males and females started dating at age 14 or 15, and 40% of the Japanese youth, both males and females, surveyed in 1993 had their first dating at age 14 or 15. The tail for the age-of-first-date curve dropped to 7% at age 17 and to 1% at age 21, for both males and females (*IES2* Figs. 10 & 11, p. 794; J.A.S.E. 1994).

[In the 1987 and 1993 national surveys, between 5% and 9% of the males and females had experienced dating. From age 13 to age 21, cumulative statistics for males surveyed in 1987 lagged behind their 1993 counterparts by 3% to 8%. Females surveyed in 1993 led in cumulative frequency of dating experience at all age levels.

[Further analysis of these statistics suggests that the girls do not necessarily pursue real love-seeking activities, but prefer spending some time with a friend of the opposite sex. As a matter of fact, they are slow in becoming involved in sexual arousal experiences, while their male counterparts demonstrate a different developmental trend: Sexual arousal comes ahead of dating for males and after dating for the females. Between ages 12 and 14, males surveyed in 1993 have a significant lead of up to 12% over the same-age females in experiencing sexual arousal. At age 14, 1993 females overtake and surpass their male counterparts by about 5% until the two populations match at ages 20 and 21 in their experiences of sexual arousal and first dating.

[As for the onset of dating, nearly equal numbers of males and females surveyed in 1993 reported having their first date at the same ages, being neatly matched from age 11 to 21. Ages 14 and 15 marked the peak years for having one's first date, with 20% of males and females having their first dates at age 14 and another 20% at age 15. After age 15, the curve for first date gradually declines in the late teens. About 3% of the boys and girls surveyed in 1993 had their first date at age 10 or 11. Ages 14 and 15 were the most common ages for first dates, with 20% of boys and girls having this experience at age 14 and another 20% at age 15. About 6% of boys and girls reported their first dates at age 17.

[For the cumulative frequencies of being sexually aroused reported in the two national youth studies, see Tables 7 and 8 (*IES2* Fig. 12 & Table 3, p. 795; J.A.S.E. 1994).

[An examination of cumulative frequencies for kissing and touching the body of the other sex indicates that for boys, kissing and touching the body of the other sex occurs at the same age level, very probably with the two activities occurring as part of the same encounter. In the meantime, the girls are again slower in the physical-contact behaviors, and they perhaps consider kissing itself and their first kissing ex-

perience very seriously. Males and females demonstrate a difference in their developmental trend: Sexual arousal comes ahead of dating for males and after dating for the females (*IES2* Fig. 13, p. 795; Shimazaki 1994-95).

[Three percent to 8% of males and females in both surveys reported having their first kissing experience sometime by age 13 (see Table 9) (*IES2* Fig. 14, p. 796; Shimazaki 1994-95). (*End of comment by the Editors; percentages are approximations from the original line graphs; see note at beginning of chapter.*)]

Japanese youths, both male and female, show a remarkably slow development in sexual behaviors in comparison to other societies. There are no clear antisexual activity policies existent in the nation, nor any discouragement of male-female relations in the nation's limited sexuality education. The most probable reasons behind the slow psychosexual development lie in the traditional societal attitude toward the free sexual activities, particularly when they involve educated, upper-class women, and the society's strong respect for education, which results in suppression of sexual behaviors among the youths.

[*Comment 2003*: The 1987 and 1993 males were about even in experiences of touching the body of the opposite sex until age 16, after which the 1993 males reported between 6% and 11% more physical sexual contact with females than did the 1987 males. With some fluctuations, 1987 and 1993 females remained about on a par in touching experi-

### Table 7

**Cumulative Frequencies of "Being Sexually Aroused" for Japanese Youths in the 1987 and 1993 National Surveys**

| Age | 1993 Males | 1987 Males | 1993 Females | 1987 Females |
|---|---|---|---|---|
| 12 | 28% | 24% | 20% | 14% |
| 14 | 49 | 35 | 22 | 15 |
| 16 | 78 | 76 | 27 | 27 |
| 18 | 85 | 84 | 40 | 30 |
| 21 | 94 | 96 | 74 | 62 |

*Editors' Note*: Percentages are approximations from the original line graph (*IES2* Fig. 12, p. 795).

### Table 8

**Rate of Sexual Arousal and Desire to Touch the Body of Opposite Sex by School Classification (in Percentages)**

| | Junior High | | Senior High | | College | |
|---|---|---|---|---|---|---|
| | Male | Female | Male | Female | Male | Female |
| Sexual arousal | 47.5 | 21.2 | 81.1 | 30.4 | 92.5 | 54.7 |
| Desire to touch | 43.8 | 13.2 | 81.0 | 32.3 | 93.9 | 53.9 |

(*IES2* Table 3, p. 795)

### Table 6

**Cumulative Frequencies of "Desire for Physical Contact with the Opposite Sex" for Males and Females Surveyed in 1987 and 1993**

| Age | 1993 Males | 1987 Males | 1993 Females | 1987 Females |
|---|---|---|---|---|
| 12 | 17% | 31% | 11% | 7% |
| 13 | 33 | 33 | 11 | 7 |
| 15 | 70 | 60 | 22 | 22 |
| 17 | 84 | 80 | 37 | 27 |
| 19 | 84 | 94 | 50 | 30 |
| 21 | 97 | 97 | 70 | 53 |

*Editors' Note*: Percentages are approximations from the original line graph (*IES2* Fig. 9, p. 793).

### Table 9

**Cumulative Frequencies of First Kissing Experience among the Japanese Youths in the 1987 and 1993 Surveys**

| Age | 1993 Males | 1987 Males | 1993 Females | 1987 Females |
|---|---|---|---|---|
| 21 | 76% | 78% | 70% | 62% |
| 19 | 57 | 43 | 57 | 43 |
| 17 | 34 | 25 | 39 | 30 |
| 23 | 4-6 | 4-6 | 4-6 | 4-6 |

*Editors' Note*: Percentages are approximations from the original line graph (*IES2* Fig. 14, p. 796).

ences with males until age 19. At age 19, about 20% of both groups of females reported touching experiences. Between ages 19 and 21, the two female groups diverged with 1987 females, rising to 54%, while only 24% of 1993 females reported touching experiences (*IES2* Fig. 15, p. 796).

[A comparison of cumulative frequencies of petting and intercourse experiences by age progression shows a smooth curve for petting experiences for 1993 males and 1993 females, increasing with age to age 21, where females are about 11% below their male peers. The four curves for intercourse experiences are very similar up to age 16, when 1993 males and females show a distinct increase at age 16, a slowdown at 17, and a second increase from age 18, to 69% for 1993 men and 64% for 1993 women. For the 1987 men and women, the cumulative intercourse-experience curve shows a steady rise to age 17, when the male and female lines continue to rise but diverge (both with an increase at age 20), until the 1987 men reached 59% and the 1987 women reached 36%. Table 10 shows the cumulative percentages reported (*IES2* Figs. 16 & 17, p. 797).

[In comparing the male/female cumulative frequencies of kissing, petting, and intercourse (see Table 11), survey results for males show, as might be expected, an experience gap of 1% to 3% at ages 12 to 15, with the gaps between kissing experiences and petting/intercourse for ages 15 and 19 increasing to 10% to 15%. After age 20, the frequency gaps for all three experiences narrow. For males at all ages, cumulative experiences for petting are a few percentage points higher than for intercourse. There is no crossing over in the cumulative order, i.e., for males, kissing experiences are highest and intercourse lowest at each age. For females, survey results at all ages show a close approximation of the cumulative frequencies for petting and intercourse, with a 2% to 3% edge for petting over intercourse. At age 13, females reported slightly more intercourse experiences than petting experiences. Between age 14 and 15, petting and intercourse experiences were closely linked. At ages 16 and 18, females reported more experience with petting than with intercourse; at age 17, females reported more cumulative experience with intercourse than with petting. Overall, males reported a steady increase in all three experiences from age 12 to 21. Females showed a similar steady increase, with a slight slowdown in the upward curve for all three experiences between ages 17 and 18 (*IES2* Figs. 18 & 19, p. 798; Shimazaki 1994-95).

[Table 12 provides survey data on the total number of coital partners classified by sex and school levels (*IES2* Table 4, p. 799; Shimazaki 1994-95). As with previously cited results, these data indicate more-active behavior for males than for females. Psychologically, the girls seem to develop their interest in the other sex earlier in adolescence: By 12 years of age, 50% of girls already demonstrate a general interest in boys, as opposed to the 14-year-old median-age boy. But such interest in the other sex among the girls is more mental and fantasy-based, and not necessarily accompa-

nied by actual physical activities, such as physical contact, in which the boys are four years ahead of the girls, and sexual arousal, in which boys are five years ahead of the girls (see Table 13) (*IES2* Fig. 20, p. 800). (*End of comment by the Editors; percentages are approximations from the original line graphs; see note at beginning of chapter.*)]

The sexual difference in the cumulative experience rate of dating in the age progression does not seem to be very great, but the women's special activeness, far surpassing men's activeness, has been consistently noticed in all of the four surveys. The similarity between the sexes on this behavior very probably occurs because males and females of roughly the same age level are generally dating each other. On the other hand, the increased dating activity of females 15 years and older may have come about because older males start proposing dates to younger females who became more accepting than in earlier times.

In terms of actual heterosexual behaviors, the age differences between the sexes were rather small or nonexistent:

**Table 10**

**Cumulative Frequencies at Age 21 for
Petting and Intercourse Experiences**

|  | 1993 Males | 1987 Males | 1993 Females | 1987 Females |
|---|---|---|---|---|
| Petting | 73% | 66% | 62% | 45% |
| Intercourse | 69 | 59 | 64 | 36 |

*Editors' Note*: Percentages are approximations from the original line graph (*IES2* Figs. 16 & 17, p. 797).

**Table 11**

**Cumulative Frequencies of Kissing, Petting, and Intercourse
Experiences among the Japanese Males and Females in the
1987 and 1993 Surveys (in Percentages)**

| Ages: | 13 | 14 | 15 | 16 | 17 | 18 | 19 | 20 | 21 |
|---|---|---|---|---|---|---|---|---|---|
| **Males** | | | | | | | | | |
| Kissing | 4.2 | 5.0 | 10.5 | 21.0 | 30.5 | 40.6 | 55.7 | 63.0 | 77.0 |
| Petting | 2.0 | 3.0 | 9.0 | 10.6 | 21.0 | 29.0 | 39.0 | 55.0 | 72.0 |
| Intercourse | 1.0 | 1.5 | 4.8 | 8.0 | 17.2 | 23.0 | 37.0 | 51.5 | 69.0 |
| **Females** | | | | | | | | | |
| Kissing | 6.0 | 6.5 | 12.0 | 24.5 | 39.5 | 41.0 | 55.0 | 67.0 | 79.0 |
| Petting | 1.0 | 2.0 | 4.2 | 10.5 | 19.5 | 26.5 | 34.5 | 44.7 | 63.0 |
| Intercourse | 1.0 | 2.0 | 4.2 | 8.7 | 21.4 | 25.0 | 34.5 | 44.4 | 61.0 |

*Editors' Note*: Percentages are approximations from the original line graph (*IES2* Figs. 18 & 19, p. 798).

**Table 12**

**Total Number of Partners Engaged with Intercourse
Experiences (in Percentages)**

| Number of Partners | Junior High | | Senior High | | University | | Total | |
|---|---|---|---|---|---|---|---|---|
| | Male | Female | Male | Female | Male | Female | Male | Female |
| 1 | 52.6 | 43.3 | 49.7 | 48.7 | 31.3 | 50.0 | 38.8 | 49.0 |
| 2 | 5.3 | 16.7 | 15.9 | 19.6 | 18.1 | 17.9 | 16.7 | 18.5 |
| 3 | 5.3 | 13.3 | 10.3 | 8.9 | 14.0 | 8.0 | 12.3 | 8.8 |
| 4 | 0.0 | 0.0 | 2.1 | 2.5 | 6.6 | 8.5 | 4.7 | 5.5 |
| 5 | 5.3 | 0.0 | 4.1 | 3.8 | 6.2 | 4.2 | 5.4 | 3.8 |
| 6+ | 21.1 | 6.7 | 9.0 | 6.3 | 16.0 | 5.2 | 13.8 | 5.8 |
| Don't Know | 10.5 | 20.0 | 9.0 | 10.1 | 7.8 | 6.1 | 8.4 | 8.8 |
| Total % | 100.0 | 100.0 | 100.0 | 100.0 | 100.0 | 100.0 | 100.0 | 100.0 |
| Responses | 19 | 30 | 145 | 158 | 243 | 212 | 407 | 400 |

(*IES2* Table 4, p. 799)

dating (boys one year ahead), kissing (the same age), petting (boys one year ahead), intercourse (boys one year ahead), and dating (girls one year ahead).

The 1987 data were used to construct a developmental sequence model of sexual events and experiences of the Japanese youths (see Table 13) (*IES2* Fig. 20, p. 800); Hatano 1991). For the median male, experience of ejaculation and sexual curiosity occur within the same developmental year, and related experiences like masturbation and interest in the opposite sex occur in the next year. Indeed, for males, a series of physical and psychological pubescent events suddenly occur within a short two-year period. On the other hand, the social events of adolescence seem to need a certain time to mature, as it took three years after the stormy coming of these pubescent events for these boys to reach the first dating experience. Then three more years are spent before the first petting experience. The time between first petting and first intercourse is usually quite brief; sometimes the two experiences occur simultaneously, in which case both occur with the same partner.

For the median female, the first menstruation is a clear sign of puberty; however, other psychological and behavioral pubescent events are not as concentrated as they are with the male. A Japanese median girl takes about five years after menarche to reach the first dating experience, and another five years before the first experiences of petting and intercourse. In other words, the adolescent time of a boy is three years shorter than that of a girl.

In the case of a boy, sexual curiosity arises together with the ejaculation experience and quickly leads to masturbation. The pubescent male is thus mono-sex-organ-oriented (phallocentric). In the case of a girl, menarche occurs a good two years earlier than the first sexual development event of boys (i. e., ejaculation), but it does not lead to sexual curiosity for about two years on average, nor does it quickly move to masturbation, which comes towards the very end of female sexual development.

For a boy, the onset of dating leads to a sequence of heterosexual physical behaviors, such as touching the body of a member of the opposite sex, kissing, petting, and intercourse, within the short span of three years after the first date. Girls experience these events in the last three years of the five-year time span that starts with the onset of dating, two years after the average male.

Perhaps because girls traditionally do not initiate dates but rely on the male to take the initiative, and because it occurs one year earlier than in boys, there is a difference between them. At the same time, considering the data, the boy would have to date a different, slightly more mature girl after his first date partner in order for this hypothesis to be supported.

It should be noted that for girls, physical behavior, such as masturbation and touching a boy's body, occurs during the same last stage of development along with intercourse, whereas for a boy it is actually the key mechanism for the progression of subsequent development and is distributed over much earlier stages. The male experiences the series of physical changes and psychological developments in a shorter time span than the female, perhaps because of a strong sexual drive provided by male hormonal secretions. Male maturation is thus centered around more physical and concrete behaviors, and one event hurriedly leads to the next step. For the male, a sexual behavior means a direct phallic-oriented concrete activity, whether monosexual, such as sexual arousal and masturbation, or heterosexual, such as touching the body of a member of the opposite sex, petting, and intercourse.

Female masturbation, which occurs later than the male, seems to be more possible in relation to the aggressive behaviors of the male. A girl's maturation process is thus centered around vague, romantic loving; it is more psychological and, in the beginning and for some time, devoid of any concrete physical activities. Then, in its later stages, actual loving activities, such as kissing, petting, and intercourse, gradually proceed passively, along with concrete approaches made by the male.

The passiveness of the female in various heterosexual activities is demonstrated by the fact that the physical satisfaction/performance of the sexual activities, such as masturbation and touching the body of a male partner, is experienced at the same developmental time with intercourse and preceded by kissing and petting, which are only possible with a partner. This suggests that the sexually active male should change partners from one stage to the next, because the length of time devoted to the practice of one event varies between the male and female. Consequently, the male tends to seek a more permissive female as he moves rapidly along the developmental sequence. Thus, the typical Japanese male starts by dating a female a year younger than he, experiences the first kissing with a

### Table 13

### Sequential Developmental Model of Various Sexual Events and Experiences of the Average Japanese Youth as Seen in the Age of the Median Person for Respective Events
### (as of the 1988 Survey)

| Male | Age (Years) | Female |
|---|---|---|
|  | 12 | Menstruation / Interest in opposite sex |
|  | 13 |  |
| Ejaculation / Sexual curiosity | 14 | Sexual curiosity |
| Masturbation / Interest in opposite sex | 15 |  |
|  | 16 |  |
|  | 17 | Dating |
| Dating | 18 |  |
| Touching body of opposite sex | 19 |  |
| Kissing | 20 | Kissing |
| Petting / Intercourse | 21 | Petting |
|  | 22 | Masturbation / Touching body of opposite sex / Intercourse |

3 Years (male, 15–18); 3 Years (male, 18–21); 5 Years (female, 12–17); 5 Years (female, 17–22)

(*IES2* Fig. 20, p. 800)

same-aged female, and experiences his first intercourse with a third female, who is at least a year older than he is.

## Acceleration/Deceleration Trends in the Sexual Development Sequence

Changes in the timing of various sexual events and experiences for the average Japanese male and female in these four surveys, 1974, 1981, 1987, and 1993, are shown in Tables 14, 15, 16, and 17 (*IES2* Tables 5 & 6, pp. 805 & 806; *IES2* Figs. 21 & 22, pp. 803 & 804; Hatano 1991; Shimazaki 1994-95). In the seven-year intervals between one survey and the next, certain changes in developmental ages are observed, although the primary sequential order does not change. In particular, there was a slight acceleration tendency in the latter half portion of adolescence between 1987 and 1993. The steady and noticeable increase in the rate of actual sexual behaviors, like kissing, petting, and intercourse, especially among the college-level students, both male and female youths, is particularly noticeable. This "emancipation" tendency may be a sign of the modernization and Westernization of this age group. At the same time, one needs to consider the possible danger in the spread of STDs and AIDS, even though the latter was not really perceived as a threat in Japan as of mid-1995. (However, comments on the present and future of AIDS must be made with the utmost caution. The results shown earlier in Table 12 on the number of sexual partners, for example, already indicate that more than 60% of male and more than 40% of female college students admitted to having multiple intercourse partners.)

Accelerated physical growth is often observed when more-favorable circumstances are provided, a good example being nutritional improvement. Japanese Ministry of Education statistics suggest a sharp acceleration in physical growth starting in the early 1950s and ending by 1980 (*IES2* Figs. 23 & 24, p. 806; Hatano 1991bc). Apparently, the Japanese postwar growth acceleration because of greatly improved nutrition reached saturation around 1980. More specifically, little growth acceleration was observed in males and females after 1960. Since the changes in the biological phase of sexual maturation ended over three decades ago, the recent accelerating changes in sexual behavior patterns must be because of social changes and new pressures. Likewise, since there was no particular biological deceleration phenomenon during the past 50 years, decelerating behavioral changes can only be explained in terms of changes in social control.

Contemporary Japanese society is enjoying fully its freedom of creeds and beliefs, and rather radical liberal thoughts have been prevalent. As the scientific understanding of human sexuality spreads, people prefer more freedom in sex-related behaviors, as noted earlier in Table 2. This tendency involves college- and university-level students since they are treated as "adults" in Japanese society, and experience little social restriction on their behavior. Under the circumstances, it may be rather natural to find an ongoing behavioral acceleration among the youth of this age level. Changes in the rate of experiences of certain sexual events among university students in these four surveys are shown in Tables 14 and 15.

Contemporary Japan is an overly matured society, and thus certain pathological phenomena may be observed in relation with childrearing and the educational systems. One example is the over-controlling of children by parents, particularly by mothers who overly emphasize academic achievement and sacrifice spontaneous play of the children. Hence, children do not demonstrate autonomous development in their decision-making abilities or their interpersonal human relations. Some observers are increasingly anxious about the possible lack of developments in interpersonal human relations and decision-making abilities among contemporary Japanese children. It would not be a surprise if these children were to show deceleration ten-

### Table 14

**Changes in Rate of Experiences of Various Sexual Events among University Students in Four Surveys (20-Year-Olds; Junior College Students Included in the Data)**

|  |  | 1974 | 1981 | 1987 | 1993 |
|---|---|---|---|---|---|
| Kissing | Male | 45.2% | 53.2% | 59.4% | 63.4% |
|  | Female | 38.9 | 48.6 | 49.7 | 68.5 |
| Petting | Male | 29.7 | 40.3 | 53.3 | 57.0 |
|  | Female | 17.9 | 29.9 | 34.1 | 45.7 |
| Intercourse | Male | 23.1 | 32.6 | 46.5 | 52.7 |
|  | Female | 11.0 | 18.5 | 26.1 | 44.9 |

(*IES2* Table 6, p. 806)

### Table 15

**Comparison of Various Sexual Experience Rates among the Japanese Youths in Four Surveys**

| Experiences | School Level* | Male | | | | Female | | | |
|---|---|---|---|---|---|---|---|---|---|
|  |  | 1974 | 1981 | 1987 | 1993 | 1974 | 1981 | 1987 | 1993 |
| Menstruation (in females); Ejaculation (in males) | JHS |  |  | 37.8 | 46.7 |  |  | 75.0 | 80.3 |
|  | SHS |  | 87.1 | 83.8 | 86.0 |  | 97.2 | 95.5 | 95.1 |
|  | Univ. |  | 95.4 | 92.0 | 91.5 |  | 98.4 | 98.4 | 98.0 |
| Interest in sex | JHS |  |  | 52.5 | 53.9 |  |  | 45.5 | 48.6 |
|  | SHS |  | 92.8 | 69.6 | 89.9 |  | 75.0 | 71.4 | 70.5 |
|  | Univ. |  | 98.2 | 95.6 | 96.7 |  | 89.0 | 84.5 | 87.9 |
| Dating | JHS |  |  | 11.1 | 14.4 |  |  | 15.0 | 16.3 |
|  | SHS | 53.6 | 47.1 | 39.7 | 43.5 | 57.5 | 51.5 | 49.7 | 50.3 |
|  | Univ. | 73.4 | 77.2 | 77.7 | 81.1 | 74.4 | 78.4 | 78.8 | 81.4 |
| Masturbation | JHS |  |  | 30.0 | 33.3 |  |  | 6.9 | 10.1 |
|  | SHS | 84.1 | 77.1 | 81.2 | 80.7 | 21.6 | 17.2 | 10.0 | 12.6 |
|  | Univ. | 90.4 | 93.2 | 92.2 | 91.5 | 26.1 | 28.6 | 21.1 | 25.8 |
| Kissing | JHS |  |  | 5.6 | 6.4 |  |  | 6.6 | 7.6 |
|  | SHS | 26.0 | 24.5 | 23.1 | 28.3 | 21.8 | 26.3 | 25.5 | 32.3 |
|  | Univ. | 45.2 | 53.2 | 59.4 | 68.4 | 38.9 | 48.6 | 49.7 | 63.1 |
| Petting | JHS |  |  |  | 3.9 |  |  |  | 2.6 |
|  | SHS | 13.9 | 13.1 | 17.8 | 18.2 | 9.6 | 15.9 | 14.7 | 16.5 |
|  | Univ. | 45.2 | 40.3 | 53.3 | 60.6 | 17.9 | 29.9 | 34.8 | 42.8 |
| Intercourse | JHS |  |  | 2.2 | 1.9 |  |  | 1.8 | 3.0 |
|  | SHS | 10.2 | 7.9 | 11.5 | 14.4 | 5.5 | 8.8 | 8.7 | 15.7 |
|  | Univ. | 23.1 | 32.6 | 46.5 | 57.3 | 11.0 | 18.5 | 26.1 | 43.4 |

*Students: JHS = Junior High; SHS = Senior High; Univ. = University (*IES2* Table 5, p. 805)

dencies in their sexual behaviors because self-realization and individual independence are so important in the development of sexuality, and hence in the orderly development of sexual behavior.

Another example is the unnecessarily tight pressure of university entrance examinations. Since admission to a university of rank is often considered to be the decisive factor for the whole life of a Japanese, senior high school students are particularly repressed in their sexual behaviors in lieu of preparatory studies. Based on the same logic, parents, and perhaps classroom teachers too, are eager to require that the children concentrate only on schoolwork, and definitely discourage the sexual activity of the children. As a result, the onset of the pubescent developmental sequence, and the adolescent behavioral developmental sequence in general, are being decelerated at certain times. At the same time, because of the freer mode of sexual behaviors, particularly among post-senior high school youth, the last portion of the sexual development sequence is condensed to a shorter period of time.

How Japanese youth can cope with the shorter time span for adolescence and for sexual maturation and more-liberal sexual behavior patterns is an issue of concern for both society and for sex educators and sexologists.

### Thoughts and Attitudes Behind the Sexual Behavior of Youth

Certain data in the 1987 and 1993 national surveys suggest changes in the sociopsychological background of various sexual behaviors.

Table 18 shows the survey results about the primary initiator of the dating and intercourse behaviors among the Japanese youths in the 1993 survey (*IES2* Figure 25, p. 807; J.A.S.E. 1994). Between 40% and 49% of the male and female respondents reported that dating and inter-

course were jointly initiated. In the remaining cases, 46% of the males and 35% of the women saw the male partner as the initiator of dating, while 44% of the men and 60% of the women saw the male partner as the initiator of intercourse. Often, it is assumed that a female wants to pretend that she was forced to follow the male partner in certain sexual behaviors, even though such an attitude relieving the female of responsibility for her sexual behavior may be a reflection of a prevailing lack of self-identity in Japanese women. The ability to make one's own decisions in many important life events is one of the goals of sexuality education, and therefore, the situation is still quite challenging for sex educators.

Circumstances for the first sexual arousal experience in the 1987 survey are shown in Table 19 (*IES2* Figure 26, p. 808; J.A.S.E. 1988). The main source of sexual arousal for junior high school boys, ages 12 to 14, and to a lesser extent, girls of the same age, is watching sexual material on television and the cinema, 60% versus 45%, respectively. Among university students, on the other hand, 60% reported being sexually aroused—and only 11% by watching erotic visual material; 41% of university men reported being sexually aroused by watching erotic visual material.

The main rationales for the first kissing experience are shown in Table 20 (*IES2* Fig. 27, p. 809; J.A.S.E. 1988). Close to two thirds of both males and females found their justification for a first kiss in "liking the person." One in two males reported love or curiosity as their main motive, while significant numbers of women listed love, curiosity, being forced by the male partner, or no reason as their motive.

In terms of the partner's age at first intercourse, roughly equal numbers of university males reported their partner was older than, the same age as, or younger than they were,

Table 16

**Sequential Changes in the Developmental Model of Various Sexual Events and
Experiences of the Average Japanese Male in These Four Surveys as
Seen in the Age of the Median Person for Respective Events**

| Age (Years) | 1974 | 1981 | 1987 | 1993 |
|---|---|---|---|---|
| 13 | Ejaculation | Ejaculation / Masturbation / Sexual Arousal | | Ejaculation |
| 14 | Masturbation / Sexual arousal | | Ejaculation | |
| 15 | Desire to kiss | Desire to kiss | Masturbation / Sexual arousal | Masturbation / Sexual arousal / Desire to kiss |
| 16 | | | Desire to kiss | |
| 17 | Dating | Dating | | |
| 18 | | | Dating | Dating |
| 19 | | | | Kissing |
| 20 | | Kissing | Kissing | Petting / Intercourse |
| 21 | | | | |
| 22 | | Petting | Petting / Intercourse | |
| 23 | Kissing / Petting / Intercourse | Intercourse | | |

while more junior and senior high school boys indicated that their partners were either the same age as or older than they were (see Table 21) (*IES2* Fig. 28, p. 809; J.A.S.E. 1988). Regardless of education, about two thirds of the females reported their first sexual partner was older than they. The use of contraceptive devices by both sexes in their first intercourse increased with the level of schooling, reaching 73% and 85% for university males and females, considerably higher than in the United States (see Table 22) (*IES2* Fig. 29, p. 810; J.A.S.E. 1988).

Among the reasons cited for the first coital experience, overall roughly half of the males cited "sexual arousal" and "liking the person," and a third reported "curiosity" or "loving the person." Six out of ten females cited "liking the person" and 38% "loving the person," while 18% were motivated by "curiosity," 15% by "sport," and 13% by "coercion" (see Table 23) (*IES2* Fig. 30, p. 810; J.A.S.E. 1988). In breaking down these motives according to education, six out of ten senior high school and university males cited "liking the person," while junior high school girls mention coercion by the male partner more often than university females do (see Table 24) (*IES2* Fig. 31, p. 811; J.A.S.E. 1988). Table 25 (*IES2* Table 7, p. 811) clearly shows that more females than males think they love their first intercourse partner, and a great many more males than females have intercourse because they were sexually aroused or more curious about the event.

In terms of attitudes regarding premarital intercourse and its connection with anticipation of marriage, the largest number of female university students in the 1987 survey believed that premarital sex is acceptable when there are certain agreements between the partners; the second largest group found it acceptable when based on love (see Table 26) (*IES2* Table 8, p. 812).

Table 27 indicates the degree of concern about pregnancy and STD/AIDS reported by sexually active senior high school and university males and females in the 1993 survey (J.A.S.E. 1994). While both males and females expressed strong concern about pregnancy, 51% and 61%, respectively, and 42% and 34% were "somewhat concerned," their strong concern about the risk of STDs and AIDS was significantly less. This might suggest that the threat of STD/AIDS is not as high in Japan as in other countries, or that the youth are not aware of their actual risk (*IES2* Fig. 32, p. 813).

Throughout the four national surveys in these 20 years, sexually active Japanese youth showed a steadily increasing trend in their use of contraceptives from 56% in 1974, to 68% in 1981, to 69% I 1987 and then to 79% in 1993 (*IES2* Fig. 33, p. 813; J.A.S.E. 1994). Along with attaining "behavior emancipation," Japanese youths appear to be taking responsibility for protecting their own health and that of their sexual partners.

Across the education spectrum, Japanese males are more likely than not to agree that a man's role and place is to work outside of the home and a woman's role is to take care of the family. The split is more obvious among university students, with close to 60% agreeing and 40% disagreeing, indicating a conservative trend for more-educated males (see Table 28) (*IES2* Fig. 34, p. 814). Females were significantly more likely than males to disagree with this statement of roles, but university females also showed a clear conservative or traditional trend in their belief on this issue.

**Table 17**

**Sequential Changes in the Developmental Model of Various Sexual Events and
Experiences of the Average Japanese Female in These Four Surveys as
Seen in the Age of the Median Person for Respective Events**

| Age (Years) | 1974 | 1981 | 1987 | 1993 |
|---|---|---|---|---|
| 12 | Menstruation ⟶ | Menstruation ⟶ | Menstruation ⟶ | Menstruation |
| 13 | Interest in sex ⟶ | Interest in sex ⟍ | | |
| 14 | | | ⟶ Interest in sex ⟶ | Interest in sex |
| 15 | | | | |
| 16 | Dating ⟶ | Dating ⟍ | | |
| 17 | | | ⟶ Dating ⟶ | Dating |
| 18 | Desire to kiss ⟶ | Desire to kiss ⟍ | | ⟋ Desire to kiss |
| | | Sexual arousal ⟍ | | |
| 19 | Sexual arousal ⟋ | | | ⟋ Kissing |
| 20 | | Kissing ⟍ | Desire to kiss ⟍ | ⟶ Sexual arousal |
| | | | Sexual arousal ⟍ | |
| | | | ⟶ Kissing | |
| 21 | | Petting ⟶ | Petting ⟶ | Petting |
| | | | | ⟋ Intercourse |
| 22 | Kissing ⟍ | | Masturbation ⟶ | Masturbation |
| | Petting | | Intercourse ⟋ | |
| | Masturbation ⟍ | | | |
| | Intercourse ⟍ | | | |
| 23 | | Masturbation ⟋ | | |
| | | Intercourse ⟋ | | |

(*IES2* Fig. 22, p. 804)

Traditionally, Japanese married by age 25, but this expectation is clearly waning. Regarding their future plans of marriage, Japanese youth keenly reflect the current social trend toward later marriage. About one half of the young people indicated that they want to marry eventually, but are not concerned about the age at which they might marry. Only one in five wanted to marry soon (see Table 29) (*IES2* Table 9, p. 814).

## C. Sex and Sexuality of Japanese Adults
*Marital Sex*

The Japanese ethical and cultural views of sex could probably be summed up in a few words as something repressed, embarrassing, and simply not talked about. Thus, statistics representing the Japanese concerning frequency of sexual intercourse, sexual positions, and level of satisfaction are still not reported today. Similarly, statistics on oral and anal sex in Japan are not available. One could probably conjecture, however, that the number of Japanese practicing such forms of sex has increased over the past decade or two, because of the influence of more-open conceptions about sex or of adult-oriented comics and magazines.

#### Table 18

**Primary Initiator of Dating and Intercourse Behaviors among Japanese Youths in 1993**

| Age Group | Myself | Partner | Jointly |
|---|---|---|---|
| Dating | | | |
| Junior High Male | 46% | 10% | 44% |
| Junior High Female | 17 | 35 | 48 |
| Intercourse | | | |
| Junior High Male | 44 | 7 | 49 |
| Junior High Female | 0 | 60 | 40 |

(*IES2* Fig. 25, p. 807)

#### Table 19

**Circumstances for First Sexual Arousal Experience**

| | Junior High Students 12-14 years | Senior High Students 15-17 years | University Students 18+ years |
|---|---|---|---|
| Males | | | |
| Watching TV, video, movies, etc. | 60% | 47% | 41% |
| Females | | | |
| Watching TV, video, movies, etc. | 45 | 31 | 11 |
| Females | | | |
| During dating with opposite sex | 15 | 43 | 60 |

(*IES2* Fig. 26, p. 808)

#### Table 20

**Major Rationales for First Kissing Experience**

| Rationales | Males | Females |
|---|---|---|
| Sexual arousal | 21% | 2% |
| Liking the person | 65 | 60 |
| Loving the person | 26 | 19 |
| Curiosity | 25 | 16 |
| Forced by partner | 4 | 18 |
| No reason | 13 | 16 |

(*IES2* Fig. 27, p. 809)

In November 1990, *The Weekly Post*, which boasts the largest readership for a magazine in Japan, published the results of a survey in which a random sampling of 2,000 readers took part. Of those surveyed, 33.6% of the men and 23.0% of the women gave complete, valid responses. The average ages of these men and women were 44 and 41 years old, respectively. According to the survey results, which

#### Table 21

**Partner's Age Classified by Age at Coital Debut**

| Age Group | Older Partner | Younger Partner | Same Ages | Not Certain |
|---|---|---|---|---|
| Males | | | | |
| Junior High Ages 12-14 | 40% | 5% | 51% | 4% |
| Senior High Ages 15-17 | 31 | 13 | 54 | 2 |
| University Ages 18+ | 27 | 35 | 37 | 1 |
| Females | | | | |
| Junior High Ages 12-14 | 69 | 3 | 27 | 1 |
| Senior High Ages 15-17 | 60 | 3 | 36 | 1 |
| University Ages 18+ | 62 | 4 | 34 | 0 |

(*IES2* Fig. 28, p. 809)

#### Table 22

**Rate of Contraceptive Devices Used Classified by Time of First Intercourse Experience**

| Age Group | Device Used | Device Not Used | Ignorant about Devices | No Answer |
|---|---|---|---|---|
| Males | | | | |
| Junior High Ages 12-14 | 54% | 33% | 6% | 7% |
| Senior High Ages 15-17 | 71 | 26 | 1 | 2 |
| University Ages 18+ | 73 | 26 | 1 | 0 |
| Females | | | | |
| Junior High Ages 12-14 | 56 | 32 | 2 | 10 |
| Senior High Ages 15-17 | 70 | 29 | 1 | 0 |
| University Ages 18+ | 85 | 14 | 1 | 0 |

(*IES2* Fig. 29, p. 810)

#### Table 23

**Major Rationales for First Intercourse Experience**

| Rationales | Males | Females |
|---|---|---|
| Sexual arousal | 46% | 6% |
| Liking the person | 58 | 61 |
| Loving the person | 30 | 38 |
| Curiosity | 33 | 18 |
| Being a sport | 15 | 3 |
| Forced by partner | 4 | 14 |
| No reason | 9 | 9 |

(*IES2* Fig. 30, p. 810)

may or may not be relevant to our discussion, 85% of the men indicated having had sexual intercourse in the past month. Among these, 55% had had sexual intercourse in the past week. Of all respondents, 15% had not had sexual intercourse in the past month.

Among the men who indicated having sexual intercourse in the past week, 51% had had it once, 31% twice, and 13% three times, making the average number for the previous week 1.7 times.

In other survey responses, 51% of the men indicated that they practice oral sex, and 8% replied that they practice anal sex. Twenty-nine percent of the women said that they always experience orgasm when having sexual intercourse, 30% replied frequently, 24% replied occasionally, and 8% said almost never or never.

While this survey cannot be said to represent the average Japanese, it does provide a general picture of their sexual practices. The results of this survey, when compared to a similar survey conducted by the *Kyodo Press* in 1982, show an increased percentage in every category, which clearly indicates that sexuality in Japan is becoming increasingly more open.

### Marriage and Family

Dramatic improvement of women's status in society in the 50 years since World War II has resulted in great changes in the consciousness and attitude of the Japanese people toward marriage and family. Some obvious examples of such improvements are a steady increase in the number of women attending higher education institutions, a remarkable growth of professional and social activities by educated and enlightened women like Nora in Henrik Ibsen's 1879 *Et Dukkehjem* [*A Doll's House*], and development of a self-sustaining economic strength and expansion of independent life with individual decision making. The daughters of the traditional Japanese families, i.e., the Japanese female dolls wearing pretty kimonos, who used to be educated how to serve and follow the man (husband) and how not to express their own ego, desires, and needs are now nonexistent, having become a part of fairytales. [*Comment 1997*: An additional factor, mentioned in Section 4, Autoerotic Behaviors and Patterns, may be the slow-fading expectation that a good Japanese woman should always be modest and not initiate any sexual activity. (*End of comment by Y. Kaji*)]

The consciousness and attitude of the men regarding marriage and family life have also been forced to change greatly throughout the time of high economic growth and the current economic stagnation and collapse of the "economic bubble." The unbalanced economic life between consumer life and insufficient income, and extremely poor housing conditions that come from living in highly concentrated, dense metropolitan communities, are major examples of the forces that have caused changes in attitudes about marriage and family life. In 1950, the average age of first marriage of Japanese adults was 25.9 years for men and 23.0 years for women; by 1990, this was 28.4 and 25.8 years of age, respectively. This rather high age of marriage is not expected to drop in the near future.

According to a recent report from a survey of young adults' attitudes about marriage, the rate of those who indicated "marriage is not a must unless one needs to," and/or "living independently is more important than marriage," was 41% and 32.8% of women in their 20s and 30s, respectively, and 32.9% and 37.1% of men in their 20s and 30s, respectively.

The youth in older generations used to be concerned with a "get married to have sex and propagate" philosophy that was reflected in the statistical data. [*Comment 1997*: Ten years ago, in a survey conducted by the Ministry of Public Welfare in 1987, 91.8% of the males and 92.9% of the females aged 18 to 34 indicated that they wanted to get married. A 1986 survey of university students reported that their cohabitation rate was only 0.3% for males and 0.8% for females. (*End of comment by Y. Kaji*)] However, the

### Table 24

**Major Rationales by Age for First Coital Experience**

| Rationales | Junior High Students 12-14 years | Senior High Students 15-17 years | University Students 18+ years |
|---|---|---|---|
| Males Liking the person | 51% | 61% | 60% |
| Males Being a sport | 23 | 13 | 11 |
| Females Forced by partner | 16 | 14 | 10 |

(*IES2* Fig. 31, p. 811)

### Table 25

**Rationales of First Sexual Intercourse Event by School Level of Occurrence (in Percentage; Includes Multiple Answers)**

| MALES Rationales | Time of Event* | | | FEMALES Rationales | Time of Event* | | |
|---|---|---|---|---|---|---|---|
| | JHS | SHS | Univ. | | JHS | SHS | Univ. |
| Liking | 52.2 | 61.9 | 62.1 | Liking | 56.6 | 66.0 | 61.7 |
| Loving | 34.1 | 28.4 | 32.9 | Loving | 39.5 | 31.0 | 53.0 |
| Aroused | 45.6 | 48.1 | 48.6 | Aroused | 6.6 | 7.6 | 6.1 |
| Curiosity | 37.9 | 32.2 | 34.3 | Curiosity | 18.4 | 21.8 | 13.0 |
| Being sport | 23.6 | 13.5 | 11.4 | Being sport | 10.5 | 3.0 | 0.9 |
| No reason | 14.3 | 8.7 | 5.0 | No reason | 14.5 | 10.7 | 5.2 |
| Forced | 11.5 | 2.4 | 0.7 | Forced | 17.1 | 14.2 | 10.4 |
| Got drunk | 8.8 | 8.0 | 5.7 | Got drunk | 10.5 | 5.6 | 2.6 |
| Number used | 182 | 289 | 140 | Number used | 76 | 197 | 115 |

*Students: JHS = Junior High; SHS = Senior High; Univ. = University (*IES2* Table 7, p. 811).

### Table 26

**Relationship Between Attitudes on Marriage and Premarital Intercourse among University Female Students**

| Attitude on Marriage | Attitude on Premarital Intercourse | | | | Total N | Total Percent |
|---|---|---|---|---|---|---|
| | Unacceptable | Marriage Premise | Love Premise | Agreement Premise | | |
| Earlier the better | 11.1% | 25.8% | 31.7% | 36.1% | 208 | 100% |
| When time comes | 9.5 | 19.3 | 29.4 | 41.7 | 558 | 100 |
| No desire | 14.8 | 11.1 | 37.0 | 37.0 | 27 | 100 |
| No idea | 13.5 | 14.9 | 20.3 | 51.4 | 74 | 100 |
| Total (percent) | 10.5 | 19.0 | 29.4 | 41.1 | 757 | 100 |

(*IES2* Table 8, p. 812)

authors of this chapter believe that there is a trend among to-day's youths to move away from the traditional form of family life and marriage to accept cohabitation as a natural form of living in male-female cooperation. The majority simply hope that when all the conditions are fulfilled, it is not a bad idea to get married. [*Comment 1997*: Surveys need to be conducted to support or disprove this interesting hypothesis. (*End of comment by Y. Kaji*)]

The traditional matchmaking system as a prelude to marriage is well known. The system was developed under the feudalistic atmosphere and warriors' society in which the preservation of the family was of priority importance.

### Table 27

**Degree of Concern While Engaged in Intercourse among Japanese Youth in 1993 Survey**

| Age Group | Strong Concern | Somewhat Concerned |
|---|---|---|
| Pregnancy | | |
| Senior High & College Male | 51% | 42% |
| Senior High & College Female | 61 | 34 |
| AIDS & STDs | | |
| Senior High & College Male | 17 | 49 |
| Senior High & College Female | 22 | 60 |

(*IES2* Fig. 32, p. 813)

### Table 28

**Attitudes about the Hypothesis that "Man's Role Is to Work Outside the Home and Woman's Role Is to Take Care of the Family"**

| School Level | Male Agree | Male Disagree | Female Agree | Female Disagree |
|---|---|---|---|---|
| Junior High School | 52% | 44% | 40% | 58% |
| Senior High School | 53 | 46 | 38 | 62 |
| University | 58 | 40 | 46 | 54 |

*Editors' Note*: Percentages are approximations from the original line graph (*IES2* Fig. 34, p. 814).

### Table 29

**Opinions about Marriage (in Percentages)**

| Opinions | Junior High Male | Junior High Female | Senior High Male | Senior High Female | University Male | University Female | Total Male | Total Female |
|---|---|---|---|---|---|---|---|---|
| Want to marry soon | 20.3 | 22.3 | 17.6 | 23.1 | 19.6 | 27.9 | 19.1 | 23.7 |
| Want to marry eventually, regardless of age | 45.9 | 45.4 | 59.7 | 50.9 | 58.5 | 53.6 | 53.9 | 49.3 |
| No preference to marry or not | 14.3 | 18.7 | 13.1 | 17.7 | 15.6 | 14.1 | 14.0 | 17.4 |
| Will remain unmarried | 2.4 | 3.0 | 1.6 | 3.1 | 1.2 | 2.3 | 1.8 | 2.9 |
| Other | 1.2 | 0.7 | 1.1 | 1.1 | 0.9 | 0.8 | 1.1 | 0.9 |
| Cannot answer | 11.7 | 8.5 | 5.4 | 3.6 | 3.3 | 0.6 | 7.6 | 5.0 |
| Don't know; Not answered | 4.2 | 1.4 | 1.5 | 0.5 | 0.9 | 0.4 | 2.5 | 0.8 |
| Total (percentage) | 100.0 | 100.0 | 100.0 | 100.0 | 100.0 | 100.0 | 100.0 | 100.0 |
| Total (persons) | 1,008 | 1,008 | 1,008 | 1,008 | 424 | 488 | 2,440 | 2,504 |

(*IES2* Table 9, p. 814)

The so-called "middleman in honor" was asked by the parents of the young man or woman to find their child a proper partner in terms of the social level and position of the family. Traditionally, age was not a consideration.

This system is still widely practiced today, although the social status of the family and the respective person is increasingly becoming less important. In the 1960s, a survey analysis reported that 40.7% of all marriages were arranged in the manner mentioned above, and 57.0% were a freely made decision or love-oriented marriage. The rate of arranged marriage in a 1980s survey dropped to 22.8% for arranged marriages and rose to 71.8% for love-oriented marriages, leaving about a quarter of all marriages still arranged by a matchmaker. The newest trend in this system is an increase in the requests for arranged marriages among men over age 30, a reflection perhaps that these older bachelors tend to avoid the rather uneasy attempts to build a love-oriented heterosexual relationship. Marriage is not an easy life event for the young and middle-aged Japanese men these days, particularly considering a 1991 poll by the Asahi Shimbund that reported 60% of Japanese women consider Japanese men "unreliable" (Itoi & Powell 1992). (See also the discussion of the "Narita divorce" phenomenon in Section 5A above.)

*[Multiethnic Marriages*

[*Update 2002*: In the early 21st century, marriage and continuing the family line has become a major problem for many Japanese men. By the time a Japanese man reaches his late 30s or 40s, it is almost impossible for him to find a bride in her 20s or early 30s. Japanese culture celebrates youth as few other cultures do, and the 30- or 40-year-old male is out of the competition. Divorce has been uncommon until quite-recent times, and midlife marriages even rarer. Add in the fact that Japanese women are demanding a higher standard of living from prospective husbands and shunning marriage as noted above.

[As noted in the brief historical perspective, Japan has long been known as the quintessential insular country. Even today, Japan is a near-classless, mono-ethnic nation with 127 million people, of whom a scant 1.5 million are resident foreigners. Less than a million are Korean and Chinese who have lived in the country for generations. But, they are still considered outsiders and remain subject to Japan's exclusive cultural practices and arduous naturalization laws.

However, as more and more Japanese men find it increasingly difficult to find Japanese wives and Japan's population continues shrinking, some new thinking has taken root in recent years: Perhaps marriage with a foreigner is the best answer for these lonely men who want to continue their family line.

[The trend of young Japanese marrying non-Japanese spouses started in the 1970s with more Japanese women marrying foreign husbands. In the 1980s, increasing urbanization left many poor rice farmers with no Japanese women to marry as the women migrated to the cities in search of a more comfortable life. At first, the rice farmers turned to poorer Asian countries, particularly the Philippines, in their search for brides. In 1990, Korean women were very popular, but as Korea's economy improved, interest in Korean brides declined. In the 1990s, the number of Japanese men marrying Chinese women rose tenfold, despite past animosities and the ongoing political tensions between Japan and China. In 2003, China was the country of choice for foreign spouses, even if the spouse came from a far-western province of China.

[International marriages are now an urban phenomenon, fueled by exchange-student liaisons. And the boom is just beginning. In 2002, over 2,000 international marriage agencies were operating in Japan, with at least 107 specializing in Chinese spouses (see Table 30).

[International courtships usually depend on the Internet, with a few visits by the man to the woman's home and family, which may be several thousand miles distance in some remote western province of China. In many international courtships and marriages, communications are difficult, even after a couple have been together for some time. Communications often depend on an electronic dictionary, fragmentary sentences and phrases written with the Chinese characters that the Japanese and Chinese languages share (French 2002). (*End of update by R. T. Francoeur*)]

*[Japan's Changing Family Geometry*
[*Update 2000*: In the traditional Japanese family, the first-born son and his wife are expected to take care of his parents in their old age. A son is also critical for continuance of the family name. With Japanese families having only one or two children, the odds are that the parents may have no son and one or two daughters. In families with only a daughter or two, the future care of the parents depends on whether or not the daughter(s) adopt(s) her husband's family name, and on whether the daughters decide to live in the husband's parents' house or in her parents' house.

[The new family geometries evolving as a response to reduced fertility may involve the daughter keeping her own family name instead of adopting her husband's name, and the husband joining his wife's family and accepting responsibility for caring for her parents in their old age. This pattern of the husband living with the wife's family and assuming the burden of eventually caring for her parents is an arrangement almost unheard of just a generation ago. In "groom adoption," parents with a single daughter may adopt her husband, who will then take her family name, an old custom that is fading in popularity.

[The pressures behind these new geometries include falling birthrates, the world's most rapidly aging population, sky-high real estate prices, the inheritance of parental real estate, and persistent economic uncertainty after a decade-long recession. The result is often an increasingly open and sometimes raw tug of war between the parents of brides and grooms to determine which parents will be cared for in old age by their children, and who will maintain the family gravesite. As the beneficiaries of an economic golden age in the 1960s and 1970s, many of Japan's elderly have huge personal savings and immensely expensive urban real

estate. The contest between families for the allegiance of children has thus become inevitably intertwined with struggles over inheritance rights. Indeed, more and more men are being lured away from their own families to those of their wives by the promise of financial security. These struggles are increasingly eroding the male-driven family structure common in Japan. Ultimately, among the most important consequences of the economic power of the wife's family will be the strengthening of the role of women themselves in Japan and their growing equality with men (French 2000). (*End of update by R. T. Francoeur*)]

*[Fading Three-Generation Families*
[*Update 2002*: Despite impressions to the contrary, the practice of an extended Japanese family living under a single roof with the son bringing his wife home to live with him and his parents is relatively new in Japanese culture. It dates back only to the Meiji Era, from 1868 to 1912. Before the Meiji dynasty, most Japanese couples lived apart from their parents. However, as lifespans increased, the Meiji government wanted the household to become the unit of welfare, with the younger people providing all the care of their elders. In this system, the daughter-in-law's role is that of a submissive *yome* (or more politely, a *oyome-san*), who is ruled by her mother-in-law and has no independence of her own. Her main role is to take care of her husband's parents. This system continued after World War II, and began to weaken in the 1960s and 1970s.

[Today, the tradition of parents and children, sometimes three generations, living together has all but disappeared in urban areas of Japan, although it still observed in the rural areas. In 1999, people age 65 and older living on their own or as couples accounted for almost 46% of households, compared with 20% in 1972. In the same period, the number of three-generation families who live together under one roof has declined from 55.8% to 29.7% of all households.

[Among the many factors contributing to the demise of the *yome* are the lure of cities, the desire of more women to work outside the home, the independence of both young and old that comes with financial security, and the fact that increasing numbers of young women do not want to become *oyome-san* and take on the burden of caring for the elderly in their homes. To Japan's credit, the government now offers a huge menu of healthcare services for older people in their homes. The government provides workers to cook meals and bathe elderly family members, and nurses to administer injections. While the elderly have pensions that enable them to live independently, their children are not likely to enjoy this same freedom, as their public and private pension plans are grossly underfinanced (Strom 2001). (*End of update by R. T. Francoeur*)]

*Divorce*
The attitude of the Japanese people toward divorce has changed as much as their attitude toward marriage. Historically, the divorce rate in the Meiji Era (1868-1912) was higher than the current figure, very probably because men could divorce wives easily, since the social status and human rights of women were regarded as light as a feather. No statistics are available regarding marriage and divorce before Meiji (1868).

In 1946, divorce laws eliminated the old three-line letter whereby a man could dismiss his wife. Before World War II, Japan had one of the highest divorce rates in the world; that high rate is echoed in recent years, following after an all-time postwar low, with the difference that most divorces now are sought by women. Laws still leave alimony rather skimpy, but child-custody now favors the mother instead of

**Table 30**

**Japanese Men and Women with Foreign Spouses**

| Year | Japanese Wives with Foreign Husbands | Japanese Husbands with Foreign Wives |
|------|------|------|
| 1970 | 4,000 | 1,800 |
| 1985 | 5,000 | 7,000 |
| 1990 | 5,500 | 20,000 |
| 2000 | 7,500 | 28,000 |

the mandatory custody by the husband's family that prevailed before 1945.

Like many other democratic practices, the principle of male-female equality was first established throughout the legal structure of modern Japanese society in 1945. The Japanese people used to believe that ending a marriage in divorce for whatever reasons involved a loss of face and honor. Many, particularly among the older generations, still hold to this belief. In this respect, maintaining the marital structure, even when the husband-wife relations are practically broken, is socially acceptable and often the rationale for not divorcing. Considering this background, the divorce rate remained low during the 1950s and 1960s, less than 1.0 per 1,000. By the 1980s, the divorce rate had grown slightly to 1.5 per 1,000. The more recent rate is not much different from the 1980s rate. There are important differences in these general statistics. The divorce rate for couples in their early 20s was 17.0 per 1,000 in 1985, more than ten times the overall average. For couples in their 40s, the rate was 3.6 per 1,000, twice the overall rate. [*Update 1997*: According to Kristof (1996a), comparative divorce rates in the mid 1990s showed about 24 divorces for every 100 Japanese marriages, compared with 32 per 100 in France, 42 per 100 in England, and 55 per 100 in the United States. (*End of update by R. T. Francoeur*)]

The increased rate of divorce among the young people may come from their immaturity in the social-perseverance quality, while the rate among middle-aged people may be the result of changes in the male-female social strength relations. For the latter, factors to be considered include a rebellion of the women against the men-centered social structure, expansion of the economic independence of the housewives, and more promotion of women's emancipation. This, in turn, provides the starting point for a discussion about the husband/wife roles in the family life in the modern and future Japanese society.

[*Update 1997*: In an early-1990s survey conducted by the Dentsu Research Institute and Leisure Development Center in Japan, married men and their wives in 37 countries were asked how they felt about politics, sex, religion, ethics, and social issues. Japanese couples ranked dead last, by a significant margin, in the compatibility of their views. In another survey, only about a third of the Japanese said they would marry the same person if they could do it over. However, this incompatibility might not matter as much, because Japanese husbands and wives traditionally spend little time talking to each other. This is not unexpected, given the primacy most Japanese men place on their work, the disparate social positions and power of men and women in traditional Japanese society, and the suppression of emotions and feeling. The reality in many marriages is the "7-11 husband," so-called because he leaves home at 7 A.M. and returns home after 11 P.M., often after going out for an after-work drink or *mah-jongg* session with buddies. A national survey found that 30% of the fathers spend less that 15 minutes a day on weekdays talking with or playing with their children. Fifty-one percent of the 8th grade students reported they never spoke with their fathers on weekdays. In reality, then, the figures for single-parent Japanese families are deceptive, with the father in dual-parent families more often than not a theoretical presence (Kristof 1996a).

[Divorce, in Japan, has long been a simple matter, requiring little more than the signatures of both parties and filing the papers in city hall. Two major factors in Japanese culture have kept the divorce rate very low despite the lack of couple compatibility, communications, and emotional satisfaction. On the male side, shame is still a powerful social and financial sanction, especially in the workplace, where many companies are reluctant to promote employees who have divorced or have major problems at home. A divorce is always a negative factor in the employment world.

[Japanese women knew that this simple procedure carried with it many hidden consequences that made divorce psychologically, socially, and financially prohibitive in all but the most abusive situations. Family and relatives are socially embarrassed and shamed by a daughter who has rebelled against a life spent catering to a husband. In a shame-sensitive culture, the whispers of neighbors can be demoralizing. Also, court-ordered alimony was stingy, few jobs were open to middle-aged women, and banks often turned down applications for loans, mortgages, or even credit cards. While child custody goes to the mother in three quarters of all divorces, most Japanese mothers do not have a career or much in the way of financial resources. In the mid 1990s, only about 15% of divorced fathers paid child support (Kristof 1996a). (*End of update by R. T. Francoeur*)]

### [Divorce among the Middle Aged

[*Update 2003*: Although the overall divorce rate in Japan appears flat when compared with America and Europe, in the last few years, divorces among older people have been skyrocketing, reflecting profound changes in a traditionally conservative society. Fifteen years ago, middle-aged divorces were almost unheard of in Japan. But in the late 1980s and early 1990s, the divorce rate among younger couples was steadily creeping upward to levels comparable with many European countries.

[Some social-trend observers attribute the explosion in middle-aged divorce to a sort of trickle-up women's liberation, in which grown daughters, often still living at home, prod their mothers to stop putting up with emotionally barren or abusive relationships with their fathers. Concepts novel to Japanese culture, like individualism, materialism, and personal happiness, have been embraced by daughters and are now being picked up by their mothers, breaking down traditional values of the collective good, of harmony, and, above all, of *gaman*, or self-denial. Another factor has been a shift in the content of daytime television and advertising that reflect and energize changing attitudes surrounding middle-aged divorce. Sexy daytime dramas and Jerry Springer-style talk programs, known as "wide shows," have emerged to tutor women in issues like divorce, post-motherhood careers, and sexual freedom. Other roots of this phenomenon are profound social changes, like the demise of lifetime employment, later marriage, the collapsing birthrate, and a growing number of social-dropout younger adults, who drift between part-time jobs and live with their parents well into their 30s. Taken in combination, these changes are comparable to the seismic cultural shifts seen in the United States in the 1960s and 1970s (French 2003). (*End of update by R. T. Francoeur*)]

### *Sexuality and Older Persons*

Recently, surveys in Japan have enthusiastically taken up the topic of sexuality among the middle-aged and aged population. In 1979, Hideko Daikuhara, a public health nurse in Tokyo, conducted Japan's first-ever research on the actual condition of sexual activity among aged persons. Later, Yoshiaki Kumamoto and others at the Sapporo Medical School firmly established research on gerontology—in Japan, gerontology is a branch of andrology. Kumamoto reported the results of a survey on the relationship between sexual activity and aging that was conducted as a part of his research. The survey revealed that 14.2% of men in their early 60s were no longer sexually active. For men in their late 60s, the percentage of inactive males was 22.8, with

32.0% in their early 60s, 50.3% in their late 70s, and 62.6% of men aged 80 or older who were no longer sexually active. Of those who indicated being sexually active, 60% in their 60s, 40% to 55% in their 70s, and 30% 80 or older said they had sex once or twice a month.

Kumamoto's survey was given to 5,500 men. Although it would be difficult to say his survey is representative of middle-aged and aged men in Japan, it is sufficient reference for the trend of sexual activity in these age groups. "Human beings do not lose their sexual drive until they die," has been an expression heard among the common populace of Japan for many years. This is evidence that the Japanese have had sufficient knowledge of the sexual activity made evident in Kumamoto's survey. On the other side of the coin, the popular expression regarding men who are "forever chasing after women, in spite of their age" offers proof that Japanese have both an official and a private stance when it comes to sexuality.

*[Extramarital Relationships*

[*Update 1997*: Traditionally, the Japanese male has always had much more freedom for extramarital affairs than the women. In Japanese culture, there is no sin in sex. It is treated as a natural part of life by the Japanese, even more so than in European cultures. Few Frenchmen were upset when the widow and the former mistress of President Mitterand stood side by side at his funeral, because the whole affair was handled with proper decorum. Unlike the United States, Japanese culture has been even more accepting of the private extramarital affairs of high-ranking Japanese politicians, business executives, and ordinary husbands. Extramarital affairs traditionally posed no problem, unless the man either allowed this side of his private life to interfere with his duties or he lost face by not maintaining proper social decorum. One loses face and shames one's family by making public something that should be private (Bornoff 1991, 262-300).

[While no data are available on the incidence of extramarital sex and affairs, the incidence of such behavior is undoubtedly affected by several factors in the changing scene of Japanese male-female relations. While husbands have many avenues for extramarital sex available, with *geishas*, "soap ladies," and the sex workers who ply their trade via telephone clubs, pink leaflets, mobile van services (*Pinkku Shiataru*), lovers' banks, massage parlors, date coffee shops (*deeto kissa*), or on the street, the number of Japanese wives who seek a lover as a way of spicing up their lives with a bit of romance seems to be increasing. In the 1983 *More Report on Female Sexuality*, 70% of the women ages 13 to 60 surveyed reported being sexually unsatisfied. Add to this the fact that Japanese wives control the household finances and have considerably more leisure time than their husbands. Many of the part-time sex workers in Soaplands are female students and frustrated housewives who control their own work schedules and can use the extra money easily available in this work. A 1986 survey conducted by the Prime Minister's Office found that 10% of the 680 women sex workers arrested by the police were housewives (Bornoff 1991, 334). (See also Section 8B, Significant Unconventional Sexual Behaviors, Prostitution.) (*End of update by R. T. Francoeur*)]

## 6. Homoerotic, Homosexual, and Bisexual Behaviors

**[A. Homosexuality in Pre-Modern Japan**

[*Comment 1997*: Masculinity and virility were exalted in the ancient nature religions and in Shinto precepts and rituals that prepared the ground for the warrior culture. In the Shinto winter ritual of *hadaka matsuri*, males of all ages pu-

rified themselves with an icy dip in a mountain spring or waterfall, liberally consumed purifying *saki*, and then formed a pyramid of naked male bodies, a seething mass exaltation of manhood inside the temple. Masculinity was also exalted by the *samurai* and *shoguns* who kept legions of pretty young pageboys in attendance. Even among the Buddhist priesthood, where the injunction of chastity forbade all sexual contact of monks with women, homosexuality was considered an acceptable substitute, as it was elsewhere in Buddhist monasteries throughout the Far East. Each novice pledged himself to an older monk for a number of years. In exchange for tuition, the mentor provided his pupil with instruction in the sacred texts and the spiritual quest. The novice embraced the status of "sworn friend," serving his master, body and soul.

[During the long civil wars, violence and the warrior ethic reigned supreme and women were nothing more than a necessary incubator for progeny. Homosexuality was the ultimate criterion of virility and masculinity. In the stoic way of the warrior and the code of the *samurai*, *nanshoku* (male passion) was not a perversion, but a lofty ideal. Strict conventions limited the passive female role of recipient to youths and boys, while the older male played the active male role of inserter.

[For centuries, the traditional Japanese theater, another male preserve, also had an established current of same-sex behavior and relationships flowing through it. As soon as the female precursors of *kabuki* were banished from the stage in the early 1600s, the overwhelming majority of their male replacements were beauteous catamites and followers of Shudo, "the way of the youth" (Bornoff 1991, 422-433). (See also the discussions of male homosexuality in Section 6 of the chapters on Iran, Morocco, and Turkey.) (*End of comment by R. T. Francoeur*)]

[*Comment 1997*: Yanagihashi (1995) has identified four main characteristics evident in pre-modern Japanese homosexual traditions, namely:

1. The relationships are typically between an adult man and a minor;
2. The relationships tend to exist in contexts where contact with the other sex is limited;
3. Female homosexuality seems to be entirely nonexistent; and
4. The relationships were formed exclusively among members of the privileged classes.

[Homosexuality was understood as a substitute or supplement to heterosexuality in a fundamentally heterosexual and male-dominated society. (*End of comment by Y. Kaji*)]

### B. Male Homosexuality Today

[*Comment 1997*: Although Japanese culture has in its history a tradition of sexual love between men, and tolerates the expression of affection for the same sex at most levels of society, the contemporary Japanese attitude toward homosexuality is in general very negative. However, the issue has yet to be discussed as a social issue. For example, according to a nationwide survey of 188 university professors who are teaching subjects related to human sexuality, only 30 (15.8%) have ever addressed the issue of homosexuality in their curriculum (National Survey of Sexology and College Education 1995). Though many lesbians and gay men suffer from the prejudice and insensitivity of Japanese society, most heterosexual Japanese people may be unaware of the negative feelings that drive such prejudice and insensitivity. (*End of comment by Y. Kaji*)]

None of the larger urban entertainment districts in Japan is without its quota of gay bars and clubs. The laws against prostitution are fairly nebulous, but especially so when applied to homosexual prostitution. When a gay bar or club comes to grief from the law, it is usually because it employed boys under the legal age of consent or hired exotic youths from other lands who violate the provisions of their visa by working.

Until the specter of AIDS arose in the mid-1980s, many foreign homosexual men found Japan, with its very long, colorful, and venerable gay history, to be a paradise. The fear of AIDS and a touch of xenophobia have closed most gay facilities to foreigners. Exclusion of foreign gays from Japanese gay facilities provides the reassurance of freedom from the risk of AIDS if Japanese homosexuals associate only with other Japanese gays.

[*Comment 1997*: Japanese male homosexuals are called *okama* (august pots), a derogatory colloquial metaphor equating the common cooking pot with the human buttocks. Increasingly popular is the "Japlish" *gei*, or gay. In a 1981 survey, about 6% of male college students reported being active homosexuals; a third of high school boys surveyed reported latent homosexual inclinations. In a similar 1987 survey, both figures declined to 4.5 and 20%, respectively, with a proportionate increase in heterosexual activity.

[Apart from one gay support group with an overwhelming foreign membership, there are no gay activist groups uniting Japanese in coming out of the closet and political advocacy. Gay magazines, such as the famous *Bara Zoku* [*The Rose Tribe*], and gay comics are sold everywhere, but like the many heterosexual erotic publications, their emphasis is more on titillation than information, and certainly not on sociopolitical activism. Gay liberation parties on the political fringe do occasionally surface, especially at elections, but most Japanese gays would rather continue living their erotic lives contentedly in the closet, perusing their gay magazines, and attending gay bars or clubs when they can, rather than become involved in the risky business of political activism (Bornoff 1991). (*End of comment by R. T. Francoeur*)]

[*Update 1997*: This situation began to change in 1991 with the filing of the first court case pertaining to gay issues, the Association for Lesbian and Gay Movement vs. Tokyo Municipal Government. In this case, also known as the Fucyu Youth Activity Center Case, the Tokyo District Court reversed a decision by the Tokyo Metropolitan Government Board of Education that refused to allow homosexual groups to use a youth activity center. Beginning in 1994, the Annual Lesbian and Gay Pride Parade has been held in Tokyo. In 1995, about 2,000 people attended this event, which was cosponsored by 28 groups with predominantly Japanese membership. Also, in 1995, gay professional organizations, such as the Association of Gay Professionals in Counseling and Allied Medical Fields, were founded. (*End of update by Y. Kaji*)]

**[C. Lesbianism**

[*Comment 1997*: In ancient times, the neglected ladies of the *o-oku*, the *shogun*'s harem, were well known for taking consolation in lesbian relationships. Unlike the celebration of male homosexuality among the warriors and their pages, however, Japanese culture has preferred to ignore—neither condemning nor celebrating—lesbian relations. *Shunga* with a lesbian theme are relatively rare. There are *resuban sho* (lesbian shows) which are a staple in the modern striptease parlor frequented by heterosexual males, but more as a foreign import than indigenous expression. For a brief time in the early 1980s, Tokyo had a single lesbian bar, but given the contentedness of gay men in the closet and the pervasiveness of female submissiveness, there are even

fewer lesbians anxious to come out in public. While most gay bars exclude all women, some are known to cater to lesbians on certain days, and then only for a couple of hours. In modern Japan, lesbianism is shrouded in comparative obscurity (Bornoff 1991, 433-447). (*End of comment by R. T. Francoeur*)]

[*Comment 1997*: In Japan, as in most other cultures around the world, lesbians have been doubly stigmatized as homosexuals and as women. Lesbians have been typically viewed by Japanese society as a common element in the pornography targeted to men or as "gender-bending" and antisocial. A variety of colloquial terms are used for Japanese lesbians, all of them more or less derogatory. (*End of comment by Y. Kaji*)] [*Comment 1997*: Lesbians are sometimes known as *onabe* (stew-pot) in contrast with the male *okama*, or august pot, or more commonly by the "Japlish" *resz. Rezubiun* (lesbian) is the most commonly used term. The *otachi*, or butch, the actress playing male roles, and the *orneko nenne* or *neko* (cat), *Çnue*, or femme, mark the two ends of the lesbian spectrum. (*End of comment by R. T. Francoeur*)]

[*Comment 1997*: One uniquely Japanese custom of gender bending is found in the *joshi-puro* (women professional wrestlers). Elsewhere in the world, women wrestlers are shapely Amazons in bikinis intently watched by males. In Japan, women wrestlers mimic their male *sumo* counterparts, with some interesting twists. *Joshi-puro* stars, such as Chigusa, with a boyish hairstyle and tacky, gaudy leotards, serenades her audience of teenage and preteen girls with popular songs before climbing into the ring to attack, gouge, pummel, and drag her mountainous opponent around the rings. Commenting on the adulation Japanese girls show for their heroes in the All-Japan Women's Pro Wrestling Association, the director of AJWPWA has suggested that young girls see women pro wrestlers as very strong, ideal men, a substitute for boyfriends. They feel safe getting close to them because they are female. They provide vicarious thrills for the young girls, and models of aggressive champions of self-assertiveness (Bornoff 1991, 433-444). (*End of comment by R. T. Francoeur*)]

## 7. Gender Diversity and Transgender Issues

Except for the practices of certain ethnic groups in the world, cross-dressing, transvestism, gender-crossing, and transsexualism were, until about 50 years ago, generally considered "diseases" that either required medical treatment or were simply not practiced out in the open.

Reaction in Japan was similar, although there were some exceptions. *Kabuki*, Japan's traditional theatrical art, is one. All parts in a *Kabuki* play are played by male actors. Thus, cross-dressing and transvestism, at least in the theater, has long existed in *Kabuki* roles. One can easily imagine that the actor's psychological state, or mental makeup, walks a fine line between masculinity and femininity, as the actor tries to immerse himself in his role. Actors responsible for female roles were, from their early childhood, compelled to experience first-hand the everyday life, customs, and etiquette of the women they played. Although this extreme practice is not seen in the modern *Kabuki* world, it cannot be denied that an aesthetic sensibility exists in the mental makeup of Japanese in which importance is placed on the beauty of men acting in female roles. As a counterpart to *Kabuki*, Takarazuka Young Girls Opera, which began in 1914, has provided a stage for only female actresses and continues to enchant many women today.

These phenomena may provide a clue when considering gender-crossing, transvestism, and cross-dressing in Japan.

That is, the roles in both *Kabuki* and Takarazuka Opera have come to be viewed as a performance, something one sees only on the stage. Accordingly, occurrences in these fictitious worlds are not always so easily tolerated in the real world. A "drag queen" appearing on television, for example, lives in "television land," a world from which most people feel detached.

Gender-crossers and transsexuals have not yet been accepted into Japanese society. This is because the majority of people have a dualistic gender bias, believing that a man's role is to impregnate a woman and a woman's role is to bear children, while only a minority advocates a society where people are free to choose their gender.

In recent years, gatherings and study meetings on transsexualism and transvestism as a human issue rather than a moral issue have been provided in Japan as well. Saitama Medical School created a stir in July 1996, when its ethics committee approved female-to-male sex-change operations. There is no legal precedent for this in Japanese law and many problems remain concerning how society will accept those people who undergo a sex-change operation.

[*Update 2002*: In October 1998, five cases of sex-reassignment surgery were performed in Japan (four female-to-male and one male-to-female) by the medical group at the Saitama Medical University. Gender Identity Disorder has gained social recognition in Japan as a status needing medical treatment. A number of transgender support groups have been formed all over Japan. As of March 2000, Trans-Net Japan, a Tokyo-based support group, lists 41 transgender-related support groups all over Japan in their resource booklet. Also, the intersex status has been gaining some social recognition. An Osaka-based support group for the intersexual individuals and their families, PESFIS (Peer Support For InterSexuals) Japan was founded in August 1995 and is now active in Osaka, Tokyo, and Nagoya. In June 2000, Tokyo's metropolitan government drafted its *Guideline for Human Rights Public Policy Advancement*. Effective at the end of 2000, it became the first policy guideline in Japan to lists sexual minorities as human-rights-violated people. While the Governor's special task force committee was working on the draft, both gender identity disorder and homosexuality were listed as categories of people who need to be protected from discrimination. However, in the final draft, homosexuality was excluded. Gay organizations and their supporters quickly objected to this draft and are trying to make the case for including homosexuality in the listing. (*End of update by Y. Kaji*)]

## 8. Significant Unconventional Sexual Behaviors

### A. Coercive Sexual Behaviors

*Rape*

Rape, according to Japanese law, is described as having sexual intercourse with a woman through force or against the woman's will, but there is no clear legal definition for rape. According to Article 177 of the Criminal Code, "if a girl of 13 years or more is forced to have sexual intercourse by means of a violent act or threats . . . or if sexual intercourse is performed with a girl not yet 13 years of age, regardless of the method or whether there was mutual consent," the offender will be punished. However, the victim or her parent or legal guardian must file a complaint in order for the rape to be recognized as a criminal act.

In 1994, when victims of rape were required to go through this vague and complicated procedure, 1,616 cases of rape were reported. The number of cases actually dropped between 1980 (1,800 cases) and 1990 (1,500 cases), but re-

cent years have seen a slight increasing trend. In Japan, many feel that, because rape is an offense subject to prosecution only upon complaint, few cases come to light. The actual number of cases is sometimes said to be five to ten times the number reported. This is really the problem we should be concentrating on in our discussions, while striving to settle on a clear legal definition of rape. Although sexual crimes, such as indecent assault, sexual abuse, and sexual harassment, were not until recently taken up as social problems, we can at least say that surveys and case studies on these topics are being performed, and that the formation of a nationwide study network is anticipated for the future.

[*Child Sexual Abuse*

[*Update 2001*: A Child Prostitution and Child Pornography Prohibition Law, effective November 1999, prohibits both buying and arranging prostitution of minors who are under 18 years old. It also prohibits making, possessing, carrying, importing, exporting, selling, renting, and displaying child pornography. (*End of update by Y. Kaji*)]

*Sexual Harassment*

In 1986, Japan passed an equal-opportunity law for women that was purely advisory and only asked companies to make "an effort" to prevent discrimination against women. The 1986 law provided no penalties for companies that discriminated; it did not even mention the term "sexual harassment." In December 1996, a Labor Ministry panel recommended putting teeth into the 1986 law by publicizing the names of violators and specifically barring sexual harassment. The panel said that the revised law should expressly forbid gender discrimination instead of simply recommending efforts against it and should ban advertising that describe jobs as "open only to women." Despite these efforts, protection against sexual harassment in Japan lags far behind American and European standards.

*Incest*

According to Japanese myth, Izanami and Izanagi, the god and goddess couple credited with creating the islands that make up Japan, were in fact siblings who then married. Also, many stories have been handed down from the 4th and 5th centuries concerning consanguineous marriages (incest) in Japan's Ruling Family (thought by some to be the ancestors of today's Imperial Family, but this is uncertain). However, since that time, incest has been taboo and avoided in Japan, as in the Christian spheres of America and Europe.

Yet, reports of incest between a mother and son have become a phenomenon in the last few decades. Such reports have come mostly from volunteer groups that provide counseling over the telephone. Frequent situations in the reports include: 1. a mother who sees her son masturbating in his bedroom and begins helping him, which leads to sexual intercourse; and 2. a boy in a stupor or irritated from studying for exams who is embraced by his mother, who feels sorry for him, leading to sexual intercourse. Many psychologists hypothesize that the anonymous nature of the telephone counseling may result in calls that provide an outlet for the expression of fantasies peculiar to young people. However, there is no reason to totally discount the findings from this counseling method. We look forward with great anticipation to future surveys and studies.

### [B. Prostitution

[*Comment 1997*: Prior to 1948 and the enactment of the Law for the Regulation of Businesses Affecting Public Morals, prostitution was not a criminal offense. The 1956 Prostitution Prevention Law granted the country's red-light districts a year's grace, after which the estimated 260,000 sex workers in the 50,000 hitherto-licensed brothels would have to find other means of earning a living. The 1956 law also banned sexual slavery and the practice of selling daughters into the brothel trade. New revisions of the public morals were added in 1984.

[While the commercial sex industry has undergone many changes, it has retained much of its vitality and varied character.

Both before and after the new law, however, the operation of sex-orientated businesses was, and is subject to obtaining "prior permission" from the police and local authorities. This at once casts doubt upon how illegal such things actually are and just what kind of arrangements operators are expected to make in order to open shop. The fact is that bars, cabarets and other concerns employing hostesses are free to operate, provided their services abide by official-dom's favorite old (and sometimes highly coercive) chestnut of "voluntary restraint." "Most of the sex industry is illegal, yet it goes on just the same," the editor of a Tokyo magazine focusing on the *mizu shobai* recently affirmed. "As in the strip theaters, people usually know when the police are coming to raid them. In businesses like these, there's a lot of money changing hands under the table." (Bornoff 1991, 332)

[According to the 1984 *More Report of Male Sexuality*, the majority of men over 30 had their first sexual intercourse experience with a prostitute, whereas those in their 20s tended to have their first encounters with a girlfriend. (*End of comment by R. T. Francoeur*)]

*[Soaplands*

[*Comment 1997*: It is still quietly accepted and understood that a Japanese husband may join business associates or friends for a visit to a "Soapland" red-light district. The "Soapland" districts in Japanese cities are not an ordinary European or American red-light district. Like the fantasy land of the "love hotels" which provide much-needed romantic privacy for young couples living with parents or with their children in tiny living quarters with no privacy, a "Soapland," like Kobe's venerable Fukuhara district,

leaves nothing to be desired in terms of local color, and works up a merry throng on Saturday nights (the streets are nearly deserted on weekday nights). In Fukuhara's unimaginably gaudy streets, the predominant bordello architecture would put even the most fanciful love hotels to shame. The usual shoguns' castles are dwarfed by edifices with stucco baroque façades arrayed with colorful *son et lumière*, and the odd rickety little old Japanese brothel is eclipsed by adjacent chrome-and-smoked glass pleasure domes and sci-fantasy ferroconcrete extravaganzas from some Babylonian lunatic fringe. Here and there touts in proper *yakuza* uniform lounge in front of the doorways, all short-cropped frizzy hair and neon lights winking kaleidoscopically in their dark glasses. Otherwise pandering seems undertaken entirely by the descendants of the old *yarite*, aging women sitting on chairs and hailing passers-by.

Fukuhara's Soapland foyer interiors have to be seen to be believed. Sprayed fluorescent pink, statuary modeled after Botticelli's Venus rising from the waves stand blushing outlandishly beneath a red roof evoking a Shinto shrine; traditional Japanese cranes in chromium wing their way across a back lit diorama of the Château de Chenonceaux. . . . In the interests of mandatory discretion, the showy façades completely conceal the executrixes within. Upon crossing the threshold, it becomes apparent that Soapland ladies join the employees of cabarets and pink salons in a great variety of fancy dress: old-time

courtesans in florid kimono, nurses, airline flight attendants, bunny girls, Suzy Wongs in high-necked mini cheongsams slit up the sides, SM leather goddesses and Buddhist and Catholic nuns (Bornoff 1991, 271, 263-264)

[The leisurely ritual of a Soapland visit, as described by Bornoff, starts with a ceremonial undressing, followed by a relaxing sudsy sponge bath and gentle massage, a rinse, and a lather dance (*awa-odori*) or body-body massage in which the *Toruko-jo* (female) or *Sopu-reedi* (Soap-Lady) massages every part of her client's body with every part of her body on a king-size inflated rubber mattress. Another rinse and a skillful *shakuhachi*, in which the Soap-Lady displays her charms, lead into an artistic performance of sexual arousal that culminates in intercourse. All this occurs with a curious single-minded determination and absolutely no pretense of emotional involvement.

[The old-style, leisurely coital sex play with *geishas* and Soap Ladies, however, is declining in favor of quick, cheaper (and hence, more frequently affordable) masturbation, oral sex, and voyeurism. The equivalents of "fast food," non-coital sexual release for males now account for nearly half of the commercial sex trade. *Herusu massagi* and *fashon massagi*, health and fashion massage, are increasing in popularity. Independent women work in the videogame halls, discos, date coffee shops (*deeto kissa*), mobile van services (*Pinkku Shiataru*), lovers' banks (telephone date clubs), nude photo studios (popular in the 1970s and in decline since), or wait for calls responding to the pink leaflets (*pinkku bira*) they post in appropriate public places or drop in private mail boxes (see Section 8D, Significant Unconventional Sexual Behaviors, Prostitution, in the chapter on the United Kingdom for a British parallel to *pinkku bira*). One factor in this shift is the high-pressure life and lack of leisure in the male business world; most white-collar workers (salarymen) do not have a lot of leisure time or spare money to spend on the traditional commercial sex. Another factor, of course, is a recent growing awareness and concern about AIDS (Bornoff 1991, 282-300).

[According to a 1981 survey, younger prostitutes remained in the trade for three to four years; another small survey of sex workers in the Senzoku-Yoshiwara area in 1988 showed the average age was 26 and careers lasting about 16 months. In the 1986 survey conducted by the Prime Minister's Office, nearly 10% were housewives, another 10% office employees, and 4% students. More than half cited "making a living" as the motivation, 14% were doing it "for the sake of the family," 11% were doing it to pay off debts, while others cited money for clothes, travel, and leisure (Bornoff 1991, 273, 334). (*End of comment by R. T. Francoeur*)]

## C. Pornography and Erotica

Arguments over the definition of pornography in Japan tend to converge on the issue of what is obscene. The Japanese courts define obscenity as that which "excites or stimulates sexual desire to no purpose, causes harm to a normal person's sense of sexual shame, or goes contrary to a good sense of sexual morality." However, it would be reasonable to say that an interpretation of this correlates with social and cultural changes of the times. In fact, when D. H. Lawrence's novel, *Lady Chatterley's Lover*, was translated into Japanese and published in 1957, it was deemed obscene and banned. Now, in 1996, the same fully translated book is published without problem. In addition, until just a few years ago, photogravures of nude models in which the pubic hair can be seen were never printed in magazines. Now, however, seeing the pubic hair of nude models in Japan's weekly magazines that target adult readers is no longer a novelty.

When discussing pornography in the context of Japanese culture, one cannot leave out the *shunga* genre of the Edo period (1603-1867). *Shunga* is an art form that enjoyed high regard among the people of its time, but at the same time was kept secret. That is telling of the great artistic impact *shunga* had on society and, consequently, the ambivalent state of people's sense of shame, which was attacked by this shocking art form. Even Japanese today are most likely divided in their opinions of whether or not *shunga* is pornographic or obscene.

Turning our attention to modern times, Japanese who live in the big cities frequently come across shops that specialize in "adult goods," similar to what one might see in Europe or America. These adult shops house rows and rows of magazines and videos for the purpose of showing explicit sexual activity, although the sexual organs have been painted black or obscured. The reality is that even a junior high school student, albeit one big for his age, could enter such a store and make a purchase. Thus, one could say that Japan is completely open to pornography.

Japanese are often described as ambiguous, neither black nor white, but in a nebulous state of indecisive gray. They do not denounce the adult stores nor do they speak of them in good terms. They merely let the situation stand in a state of ambiguity. Once a year or once every few years, the police crack down on these stores, at which time the media raises a fuss over the issue for a short time, and then once again the problem is forgotten.

Recently, some mothers' and women's groups began a campaign to banish pornography from the viewpoint that it is degrading to women. How to effect a change in the male consciousness in order for such grassroots activities to take root is now a major topic, albeit one which is only being discussed among women.

## Sexually Violent Fantasies in Comic Books

A contribution to a local newspaper in the summer of 1990 complaining that the contents of comic books had become grossly obscene sparked debate between freedom of expression in Japanese comic books and the negative influence these magazines have on young people. This debate has grown into a major social issue. It is certainly true that a great many scenes in the comic books read by young boys and girls would trouble sensible adults. It should be noted that the authors or publishers of these comics have exercised self-imposed control concerning sexually explicit matter. However, there has been apparently no control from either party in limiting scenes containing violence.

This tolerance of violence is because of the norms of Japan's male-dominated society and to its long history in which violence was condoned as a symbol of manliness. As a result, the sexual content of comic books aimed at young people has been curbed, whereas the authors and publishers have been given free rein in depicting violence (Bornoff 1991, 69-71). The past few years, however, have seen an active increase in movements, spurred on largely by women's groups, to denounce sexual violence in the media. As a result, major enterprises, publishers, and television stations have revised their presentations of sexual violence. However, there are always people, in any society, eager to make a profit through work in the underground. It is an undeniable fact that comic books depicting sexual violence can be found in Japan today. Now, many people are crying out that urgent attention be given to sex education, in order to confront the sexism, gender bias, and sexual depravity found in such people as the authors and editors of these comic books. (*Editors' Note*: See also the following two sections on "Ladies Comic Books" and

Perper and Cornog's discussion of Sex, Love, and Women in Japanese Comics.)

## ["Ladies Comic Books"

[*Comment 1997*: One type of popular Japanese erotic comics (*ero-manga*) is the "ladies comic books" that seem to glorify sexual violence and rape. These are not a tiny fringe phenomenon—*Amour*, the leading such comic, has been published for six years and claims a sales circulation of 400,000. *Amour*, *Taboo*, *Cute*, *Scandal*, *Love*, and other similar *ero-manga* have a greater impact than their substantial sales would indicate because copies are often passed around among friends. Even so, these magazines are also not standard fare for the average Japanese woman.

[The paradox of these "ladies comic books" lies in the fact that, although their readers are overwhelmingly women mostly in their 20s and 30s, the cartoon stories glorify sexually passive women, sexual violence, and rape. Ninety of the 316 pages in the December 1995 issue of *Amour*, for example, contained rape scenes. Despite the growing independence of Japanese women, these comics portray passive women being brutalized rather than assertive women who control their own lives. When interviewed by a *New York Times* reporter, Masafumi Mizuno, editor of *Amour*, admitted that "Sometimes we carry stories where the woman takes the initiative, and those kinds of stories have their fans. But most readers seem to prefer when the women are in a passive position." Mariko Mitsui, a former politician and active feminist, finds it puzzling that many young Japanese women really do not want to be liberated. "They want to escape independence, and so for them to be raped seems better" than negotiating their own sexual encounters.

[Another popular comics theme, particularly in those aimed at teenage girls, deals with romances between gay men. These are less graphic and more sentimental than stories of heterosexual romances. They are also erotically engaging without being personally threatening for teenagers who are just discovering their sexuality (Kristof 1995). (*End of comment by R. T. Francoeur*; see a detailed account of *manga* comics in the following section.)]

## [D. Sex, Love, and Women in Japanese Comics

TIMOTHY PERPER and MARTHA CORNOG

[*Comment 2003*: In this comment, we address the sexual content of modern Japanese comics (illustrated books), an art form known as *manga* ("manga" rhymes with "conga"). *Manga* represent a non-Western, non-Christian, often quite erotic art form widely read in Japan and increasingly popular in the United States. *Manga* are very different from the Western comic book because they are deeply rooted in the Buddhist and Shinto belief systems, and antagonistic to the Neo-Confucian patriarchal social structure, which few non-Japanese readers and analysts understand or appreciate. Hence, Hatano and Shimazaki's descriptions of Basic Sexological Premises (Gender roles, Sociological status of males and females, and General concepts of sex and love) in Section 1 of this chapter and their reflections on religious and ethnic factors affecting Japanese sexuality in Section 2 are vital to our comments on *manga* (Perper & Cornog 2002).

[*Manga* are unfamiliar to many (especially older) non-Japanese readers, and the English-language scholarly literature about it is small (exceptions include Schodt 1986, 1996; Shigematsu 1999; Shiokawa 1999; and a recent monograph of our own, Perper & Cornog 2002). Yet in Japan, *manga* are read by millions of people of all ages and represent some 30% to 40% of Japan's total yearly print output (Schodt 1996). Translated *manga* comprise the fastest-growing component of comics marketed in the U.S. (Boyd 2001). However, U.S. media coverage quite typically misrepresents the content and meanings of *manga*. For example, the dictionary in the word processing program we are using defines *manga* as "a Japanese style of comic book or animated cartoons, often very violent or erotic" (Encarta 1999). This sort of description is also widespread in newspaper articles (Kristof 1995; Rutenberg 2001), but is nonetheless very wide of the mark. We believe that readers must understand sexuality in *manga* in its own terms rather than as reflected through fundamentally inaccurate media reporting.

[But far more is involved than simply correcting media misrepresentations. *Manga* derives from Japanese aesthetic and erotological traditions, and both are very different from what Westerners may believe is universal about sexuality.

[*The Japanese Cultural Background of* Manga
[*Aesthetic Traditions.* Japan has at least an 800-year-old tradition of "serial art"—stories told in sequences of pictures (Schodt 1986). Early examples were drawn on scrolls, and include illustrated romances (*emonogatari*) and illustrated versions of the Tale of Genji (originally written approximately a thousand years ago by Lady Murasaki Shikibu; Hirota 1997). These graphic traditions flourished throughout Japanese history, culminating perhaps during the Tokugawa Shogunate (1600-1868) in the polychrome woodblock prints of Hokusai, Hiroshige, and Kuniyoshi. As a genre, these include prints of cities, markets, and landscapes, as well as pictures of the "floating world" (*ukiyo-e*) and its courtesans, performers, and everyday dramas (Lane 1999). Notable also are sexually explicit *shunga* prints, which achieved mastery of art and eros rarely if ever seen in Western art (Fagioli 1998; Kronhausen & Kronhausen 1978, Vol. 1, pp. 260-312; Vol. 2, pp. 211-270). Iconographies of female beauty emerged, for example, in the work of Utamaro and Harunobu, in which female loveliness is irresistibly compelling, not merely sexy or pretty, but transcendent (Hájek n.d.; Kobayashi 1993; Kondo 1956).

[With the opening of Japan to widespread Western influences in the late 1800s, Japanese artists drew on Western graphic traditions to reshape Japanese art, but these developments were truncated—or even aborted—by the rise of nationalist, militarist, and imperialist power in Japan. With the end of World War II in 1945, Japan rebuilt its state institutions, including virtually complete prohibition of censorship. These factors interacted with the need for public entertainment in the desperate years after the war and with the introduction of Western comics and cartoons into Japan, processes that collectively set the stage for a rebirth of Japanese popular art. One result was the emergence of an ever-increasingly diverse art form today called "*manga*" (for a tabular view of this history, see *Manga* 1999, pp. 158-159).

[*Manga* can be classified by market niche: *shojo manga* for girls, *shonen manga* for boys, *seinen manga* for young adult men, including erotica for male readers, and *redi komi* or *redisu*, romantic/erotic *manga* drawn by women for adult women readers. Each has its own styles, audiences, and popular magazines. Many *manga* for adults—and not a few for adolescents and young adults—deal explicitly with sexuality (Dixon & Dixon 1999; Perper & Cornog 2002; Schodt 1986; Smith 1991). In fact, many *manga* have sexual content, even if not explicit.

[*Erotological Traditions.* Japan has long held beliefs about sexuality and about women that will seem startlingly liberal to Westerners. These combine with Japanese artistic traditions to yield some of the finest erotic art being produced in the modern world. Of particular interest are the roots of *manga* in Japanese erotological and religious traditions.

[Yet it is here that Western, particularly American, readers will have the most trouble. To Americans, sexually explicit depictions fall into either of two—and only two—categories: clinical material or pornography. Clinical material is marked by its emotional detachment, and pornography by its focus on producing sexual arousal. Neither is notable for artistry nor for sensitivity to the array of emotions and social contexts that swirl around sexuality. Indeed, Western pornography excels in decontextualizing sexuality in images of interpenetrating genitals and concupiscent intermingling. For some Americans, such images are unsavory, exploitative, or downright dangerous to individuals and families. To others, they are enjoyable and exciting, partly because the loss of context offers an escape from the sex-negative norms of everyday life. Within these Western social and historical frames for sexuality, it can be difficult—very difficult—even to imagine that a sexually explicit art could exist that does *not* decontextualize, exploit, or escape from everyday reality.

[One result is of considerable importance for understanding how *manga* (and Japanese animated video films) with erotic content have been received in the United States. Erotic *manga* is most often presented in the media, by marketers, and on the Internet as "*hentai*," a Japanese word meaning "perversion," but which has become a catchall word for anything sexually explicit from Japan. The outcome can be strange—for example, Yoshiaki Kawajiri's 1992 animated film *Wicked City* has been called *hentai* even though its basic premise and narrative are religious redemption and motherhood. However, to the American eye, redemption cannot coexist with sexually explicit depictions and, by default, such images are sluiced into the categories of pornography.

[Yet, Japan is in fact very different from the West. Because the main Japanese islands were never successfully occupied by invaders until the end of World War II, Japanese society retains complex and continuous connections with its ancient historical origins in agrarian life. Japan's native religion—Shinto—centers on nature and its immediate connections to human existence, mediated through a multiple pantheon of spirits, divinities, and supernatural beings collectively called *kami*. Nor does Shinto or the many forms of Japanese Buddhism have the notion of original sin. Neither religion has a single Deity who acts as Law-Giver and Eternal Judge of human wrongdoing. Japan lacks—and has lacked throughout its history—an organized, hierarchical, and centralized church for which sexuality is thought to be a sure path to damnation. In many ways, modern Japan retains—and aestheticizes—an open "peasant frankness about things sexual" (Adler & Wolf 2000, 227, 469, 569). This is not to say that Japan is a peasant society—it is nothing of the sort. Instead, Japan is the only major industrialized nation that has *not* demonized sexuality under the rubrics of sin, danger, and pollution.

[Japanese sexual traditions and customs have origins in native Shinto beliefs and in Chinese Taoism, which both consider sexuality a positive moral and medical good for men and especially for women. Examples range from the Taoist-derived erotology of the *Ishimpo*, dating from the late 900s C.E. (Levy & Ishihara 1989), to Dr. Sha Kokken's 1960 illustrated sex manual *Seiseikatsu no Chie* [*Hints for Sex Life*], which sold millions of copies (Sha 1964). These traditions are alive and well in *manga*, particularly in *redi komi* or *redisu*, sexually explicit *manga* drawn by women artists for women readers.

[*Women's Place in Society.* American readers unfamiliar with the complexities of Japanese society tend to think that Japanese women are oppressed, repressed, and disempowered by long-entrenched patriarchal rule. This is the image of the timid and submissive Japanese woman tip-toeing with eyes downcast behind her husband. But like all media- and movie-derived clichés about Japan, this view is profoundly oversimplified, if not downright inaccurate when viewed within Japanese social and historical traditions (McClain 2002, 93-98).

[The Shinto pantheon includes powerful female *kami*, like the sun goddess Amaterasu Omekami, whose shrine at Ise is among the most beautiful in Japan. In legend, Amaterasu is the foremother not only of the Imperial line, but of the Japanese people themselves. Likewise, Japan's animist traditions have powerful priestesses and shaman- esses (Ellwood & Pilgrim 1992, 50-51, 56-58, 72-73, 90). Images of female supernatural and spiritual power appear repeatedly in *manga* and will be incomprehensible if the reader insists on seeing Japan through Western stereo- types of the subordination of Japanese women.

[Likewise, women's literacy. Japanese is written in two native syllabaries—*hiragana* and *katakana*—plus charac- ters called *kanji* borrowed from written Chinese. From the 9th century onward, *hiragana* was used by women and was called *onna-de*—"woman's hand" (*Japan* 1999, 619). Women's literacy was initially the possession of a courtly class, like the Heian-era women writers, Lady Murasaki Shikibu and Sei Shonagon. But as urban merchant classes developed during the Tokugawa period, women's literacy increasingly became the norm, not merely because women worked in shops with their families (the wife or daughter who keeps books and accounts must be literate), but also because women read novels (Beasley 1999, 179). From the mid-1600s on, shrine and village schools began to pro- liferate, and McClain (2002, 84) shows a contemporary woodblock print of two women teachers instructing a class of children in calligraphy. One little fellow is busily pok- ing his brush into a friend's nose, but another is studiously practicing *hiragana* while the teacher guides his hand. By 1907, the percentage of girls entering school had reached 96% (Kaneko 1995).

[Another factor conducive to gender equality was the development of agrarian small land holdings during Toku- gawa Japan and later, in which members of a nuclear family farmed a small plot of land (Smith 1959; on p. 103, a Tokugawa-era print shows two men and a woman working next to each other threshing wheat). In these forms of family labor, men and women worked together in the fields, for ex- ample, planting and harvesting rice. The direct involvement of women in farm production seems to have left a powerful egalitarian imprint on gender relations: Planting rice may be back-breaking work, but in a nuclear farming family, the collaborative labor of both women and men was essential for survival. Hayao Miyazaki's beautiful and evocative 1993 animated film, *My Neighbor Totoro*, contains a num- ber of segments showing the essential role—and great im- portance—of women in farm life as recently as the 1950s, the decade of the film's setting.

[These agrarian traditions are associated with sexual customs. Anthropologist John Embree described open sex- ual joking and flirtation in village life (1939/1995), and the 1999 Kodansha Japanese encyclopedia notes that "night visiting" and multiple liaisons long continued in the prov- inces (Embree 1939/1995, 193-194; *Japan* 1999, 413). In some areas, such as fishing villages in Western Japan, it re- mained customary for teenage boys and girls to sleep in communal lodges until the young people paired up and mar- ried (a custom called *neyado*; Yoshizumi 1995, 191, 197). It follows that traditions of open sexual expression were not merely the prerogatives of a "promiscuous" Heian nobility of a thousand years ago—as Morris (1964/1994, Ch. 8, e.g.,

pp. 225-228) seems to suggest—but have survived as living traditions in Japanese agrarian culture.

[These traditions remained alive as the three great urban centers of Japan developed—Kyoto, Osaka, and Edo (later renamed Tokyo). *Ukiyo-e* and *shunga* prints document not only a widespread urban acceptance of sexuality, but also an aesthetic principle that still reigns in *manga*: Women em- body a variety of physical, emotional, and spiritual beauties and powers cohering in one person.

[Against these erotophilic and female-positive social forces have been arrayed a set of beliefs in male superiority and attempts to limit sexual activity. These broadly center on Neo-Confucianism. Neo-Confucianism was not a popu- list or grassroots movement, but was adopted by the upper and ruling classes, especially during the Tokugawa Sho- gunate, as providing a warrior- and duty-centered social system for the *shogun* and his high-ranking *samurai* retain- ers (Beasley 1999, 173; Hall 1968/1991, 181-185). From this vantage point of power, its adherents sought to impose Neo-Confucian doctrines top-down on Japanese society. The late 18th-century Neo-Confucianist ideologue Hosoi Heishu wrote, "When she is young, a girl must obey her par- ents. When she is married, she must obey her husband. When she grows old, she must obey her sons" (McClain 2002, 95). This social and political philosophy centers on obedience to one's superiors and ultimately to imperial power: The woman owes obedience to father-as-emperor within the family and to husband-as-emperor within a marriage.

[Neo-Confucianism and its underlying principles of male superiority and erotophobia had effects outlasting the fall of the Tokugawa Shogunate in 1868. Its tenets remained central to the militarist, nationalist, and imperialist policies that emerged in Japan of the 1930s. Kimura and Yamana (1999) trace the effects on women's rights, which declined for upper-class (noble) women during the Tokugawa peri- od, then declined in general during the period of Meiji constitutionalism and later militarism, but rose sharply after World War II (see also Yoshizumi 1995). But even so, West- erners living in Japan before and during World War II stress the power and importance of women in local Japanese soci- ety, for example, in the village (Maraini 1959, 143, 260).

[It appears that Neo-Confucianist ideology was con- tested throughout its history and was never fully assimilated throughout Japanese society. Today, Japanese feminist writers stress the need to eradicate the last vestiges of Confucianist patriarchalism (Sodei 1995, 216). But despite these vestiges, and despite the misogyny of some Japanese social circles, modern Japan seems much more similar to its pre-militarist traditions about women and sex than to any- thing that would please the Neo-Confucianist.

[A number of factors, therefore, combine to create a dis- tinctively non-Western view of sexuality in Japan. These include medical and intellectual traditions that consider sexuality a positive good, religious beliefs that bring people into close conjunction with nature and its fruitional capaci- ties, farming traditions that treat sexuality as normal and natural, and, in the cities, urban traditions of entertainment, theater, and the arts that bring sexuality and female beauty to the forefront. Equally important is the absence of reli- gious erotophobia, in particular, the notion familiar to West- erners that sexuality is sinful in all but a very few contexts. Likewise, the failure of Neo-Confucianism to seize the pop- ular mind and, later, the defeat of the militarists in World War II, reopened Japanese traditions of erotophilia and the view that sexuality is a positive good. Combine all these with traditions of sexually explicit art, and the erotic con- tent of *manga* seems inevitable and unsurprising.

[*The Sexual Content of Manga*

[Not all *manga* are sexually explicit, but most *manga* we have seen contain material of considerable sexological interest. Sexual representations range from lighthearted love comedy and satire to very serious dramatic fiction, and include virtually all forms of sexuality—romance, flirtation, kissing, courtship, sexual intercourse, oral sex, female and male homosexuality, sadomasochism, prostitution, orgies, transvestitism, hermaphroditism, incest, bestiality, voyeurism, and rape. Throughout these representations, sexuality in its many forms is contextualized by character, plot, and setting, so that it is not isolated from social and psychological meanings contained in the narrative. The result is an extraordinary diversity of content, emotional tone, and drawing styles in *manga* with sexual content.

[The discussion below is summarized from a monograph (Perper & Cornog 2002) in which we described the erotic content of *manga* translated into English and commercially available in the U.S. from 1999 to the present, supplemented by a smaller sample of untranslated *manga* available in Japanese-language bookstores. Readers interested in the details of the sample, together with a complete list of translated *manga* surveyed, are directed to the original paper. In the descriptions below, publishers are given in parentheses, and *manga* are categorized according to how important sexuality is to the narrative. The categories we use overlap more or less, and the reader should not take these categories as a rigid taxonomy. The range of depictions is considerable, from *manga* without any hint of sexual intercourse to stories that focus primarily on sex.

- [*Category 1*: No sexual intercourse.

  Sexual intercourse is neither depicted nor implied. Other content of considerable sexological interest may occur, such as transvestitism or intense emotional depictions of adolescent or adult romance. Occasionally, partial or incidental nudity may occur, but is not the focus of the story. By definition, rape does not occur in this category. (Perper & Cornog 2002, 102)

[Included here are *manga* for boys (*shonen manga*) and for girls (*shojo manga*), plus a variety of specialized *manga*, e.g., about *mah jongg* or boxing (Schodt 1996) or about firefighters in modern Tokyo (Masahito Soda's *Firefighter! Daigo of Fire Company M*, Viz Communications). But also included here are stories about adolescent and young adult romance that deal humorously or seriously with sexuality and its meanings.

[One subgenre is the love comedy, like Rumiko Takahashi's *Lum\*Urusei Yatsura* and *The Return of Lum\*Urusei Yatsura* (Viz) and Ken Akamatsu's *Love Hina* (Tokyopop/Mixx). These stories typically focus on the endless vicissitudes of the protagonists' affections, usually presented as comedies of miscommunication and confused lust. Lum is a very pretty 16-year-old alien princess with a volatile temper and a tiger-striped bikini and matching boots, who comes to Earth as part of an alien invasion. When the invasion fails, she immediately finds herself an Earth boyfriend, Ataru Moroboshi, with whom she lives in his parents' house (Lum and Ataru also attend the same high school). Ataru's gaze and hands are constantly wandering towards other girls, and Lum is equally constantly zapping him with electric rays or throwing things at him.

[In *Love Hina*, the male protagonist, Keitaro, has failed his college entrance examinations and is at loose ends until he inherits a boarding house from his grandmother. It turns out to be a girls' dormitory, and although Keitaro never deliberately makes advances on the young women, he continuously finds himself in compromising positions, like wandering by mistake into the women's side of the hot springs. In another episode, the young women—none of whom have boyfriends—are talking about kissing, and mischievously start kissing each other. But they are all very quick to retaliate against Keitaro if *he* overstrays the boundaries of propriety.

[Stories like these have a comic, even satiric, view of adolescent sexuality and its emerging emotions, embodied desires, and virtually complete lack of social skills. These narratives are comic because they often exaggerate the silliness of adolescence and because they drive the plot to deliberately absurd conclusions. But underlying the silliness is what can be called "selective realism." If the story never explains who feeds these always-hungry adolescents or who pays the rent, it never veers far from the deeper experience of adolescence as a period of genuine uncertainty about sexuality. Below the comedy, an adult reader will sense the fumbling confusion and mixed-up embarrassments of coming of age. Such plots caricature and displace adult sexuality onto the safer and less serious venue of adolescence.

[In another subgenre of young romance *manga*, feelings of anxiety, alienation, and disorientation come to the forefront. Miwa Ueda's *Peach Girl*, Fuyumi Soryo's *Mars* (both Tokyopop/Mixx), and Tomoko Taniguchi's *Aquarium* (CPM Manga) are far from amusing—indeed, they are quite compelling dramas. In depicting loss and anxiety, these narratives center on worlds in which girls bully each other, sometimes viciously, in which boys are never really trustworthy emotionally or sexually, and in which a girl's self-mutilation is not at all impossible (in *Aquarium* and in Mohiro Kito's *Shadow Star*, from Dark Horse Comics).

[Other examples include *shojo manga* such as Naoko Takeuchi's *Sailor Moon* and Clamp's *Cardcaptor Sakura* (Clamp is a group of four women artists from Osaka; both from Mixx). Both have heroines with superpowers, and both are immensely popular as *manga* and as animated videos. Ten-year-old Sakura has obtained her superpowers from a set of magical cards. But together with coming to peace with her magic, she must sort out her feelings for two boys who like her, and a young man, Yuki, who makes her feel "all floaty," a good description of Sakura's growing recognition that perhaps she loves Yuki and perhaps might someday marry him.

[In these stories and others like them, the absence of overt sexuality underscores not a world of asexual children or adolescents, but the reality that genuine sexual involvement is yet ahead of them. These narratives show young people who are still trying to organize and make sense of their sexual feelings, a task made harder because they may not even recognize that their feelings *are* sexual.

[Also of considerable interest are depictions of gender fluidity, including a variety of male-female interconversions. Rumiko Takahashi's *Ranma 1/2* (Viz) and Hiroshi Aro's *Futaba-kun Change* (Studio Ironcat) portray the mix-ups and confusions that attend the magical and repeated transformation of the protagonists, Ranma and Futaba, from male into female and then back. Because these are comedies, transformations always occur at maximally embarrassing moments—for example, when Ranma-female or Futaba-female morph into their male forms in the ladies' bathroom, or when Futaba, now in female form, discovers that "she" is menstruating.

[Transvestitism also occurs in *manga*. Early examples include Osamu Tezuka's *Princess Knight* (from the 1950s and 1960s; Schodt 1986, 95-96, Fig. 114) and Riyuko Ikeda's *Rose of Versailles* (1972-1974), whose apparently male "hero," Captain Oscar Franois de Jarjayes of Marie Antoinette's palace guards, is actually a woman (Schodt 1986, 215). *Cardcaptor Sakura* contains a charming example, when Sakura gets to play the Prince in a school performance of "Sleeping Beauty" wearing an elegant doublet, cape, high boots, plumed hat, and sword.

[In Masukazu Katsura's *Shadow Lady* (Dark Horse), the 17-year-old heroine, Aimi Komori, has an alter ego, the supersexy and superpowered cat burglar Shadow Lady. In one episode, the all-male Anti-Shadow Lady Squad of the police force wears wigs and dresses in an attempt to capture her in a department store late one night. But she is vastly amused by the hairy legs and distinctly unfeminine figures of the "female" mannequins that surround her in the cosmetics section. So she strips to her underwear and gleefully flaunts her real femaleness before the frustrated men, who of course cannot capture her.

[Junko Mizuno's *Cinderalla* (from Viz; note spelling) is a satiric noir retelling of the classic fairytale, where Cinderalla's father operates a bizarre *yakitori* restaurant (*yakitori* being a kind of skewered chicken dish). He dies but returns as a bright-green zombie with a new zombie wife and her zombie daughters, one of whom complains (or boasts) that she never wears a bra because her breasts are too large. Cinderalla tries to cope by making bras for her new stepsister, and *yakitori* sauce for the restaurant (from spider eggs and rice wine). But then she falls in love with a zombie idol singer named The Prince. A helpful fairy disguises Cinderalla as a zombie—very pretty, and also bright green with flesh coming off in green blobs. Thus transformed, Cinderalla attends a concert by The Prince, who falls in love with her. As dawn comes, Cinderalla runs away, losing not a slipper but an eyeball. The Prince mounts a search for the eyeball's beautiful owner, and eventually The Prince and Cinderalla are united, with The Prince now singing at the restaurant. The characters are all very cute—in Japanese, *kawaii*—but overall, the story is an acid satire of the pretensions of love and family.

[Although sexual interactions are not depicted explicitly in these stories, sexuality is always present in one form or another. Rather than artificially desexualizing life, these stories see sexuality as intrinsic to human existence, sometimes funny, sometimes dangerous, but never to be denied.

• [*Category 2*: Sexuality is an on-going presence, but is as yet not explicit.

Sexual intercourse among the main characters is not depicted explicitly but may be mentioned or joked about. Other sexual dynamics may occur in on-going manner, either jokingly or seriously. Rape may occur. (Perper & Cornog 2002, 102)

[This category blends into the first, but typically the protagonists are older or are more deeply involved with their social settings. A good example is Katsuhiro Otomo's six-volume *manga*, *Akira* (Dark Horse), which became famous as an animated film. It is an extremely complex story about a post-apocalyptic world in which mutant telepathic and telekinetic children vie with neo-imperialists for the control of a war-devastated Tokyo. The imperial soldiers—little more than teenage thugs—wander through the wreckage, raping and pillaging in desperate drug- and power-induced hallucinations. For the antihero, Tetsuo, the only solace is his sexual liaison with a young woman, but not even sex is an anodyne for the catastrophic destruction of society. [Yukito Kishiro's nine-volume masterpiece, *Battle Angel Alita* (Viz), is likewise set in a post-apocalyptic future city, called Scrapyard. Here too rapists abound, as do piles of

junk and trash, dysfunctional cyborgs, insane cybersurgeons, and a deadly game of rebellion and war with a ruling class that lives in the floating city of Tiphares. Alita herself is a cyborg warrior, discovered by cybersurgeon Doc Ito as a half-destroyed body in a junk heap. The story traces Alita's path of self-discovery from her early love for Hugo, a human who is killed trying to reach Tiphares, to an end in which Alita becomes a *bodhisattva*-like savior of the world.

[Like *Akira*, *Battle Angel Alita* centers on a world that has collapsed into chaos, in which personal epiphanies through sexuality or drugs cannot repair the damage. *Battle Angel Alita* deals with karma, in the sense of a sequence of events set into ineluctable motion as the past reverberates into the future. The almost off-handed presence of sexual themes creates a sense of adult realism in these stories that transcends noir fantasy.

[Clamp's *Clover* (Mixx) is among the most beautiful *manga* ever drawn. It is apparently unfinished, but centers on Suu, a young woman with immense telekinetic powers, and a soldier, Kazuhiko, who is commissioned by a military council of wizards to bring Suu to an amusement park. Unbeknownst to Kazuhiko, Suu is apparently trying to find a beautiful young singer named Ora, who had been Kazuhiko's lover before she died. We do not find out if Suu's quest succeeds, but the depiction of Ora and Kazuhiko is among the masterpieces of erotic art, not for being explicit (it is not), but for its evocation of intense erotic love. Here too, sexuality is woven into the fabric of life.

[Likewise, Hiroyuki Utatane's *Seraphic Feather* (Dark Horse) is a masterpiece of drawing and design. It is set in a city being built on the moon, where a wrecked alien starship has been discovered. The protagonists are Sunao Oumi, a fretful young man, and Kei Heidemann, a virginally lovely girl whom Sunao rescues from a terrorist bomb explosion in the spaceport. Their growing love arises from Kei's mysteriously forgotten childhood friendship with Sunao, and is set amidst corrupt corporations and politicians, assassins, plus strange alien robots and their ambitious master, Kei's brother-in-law, Apep.

[But Utatane's crowning achievement in *Seraphic Feather* is United Nations Special Investigator Attim M-Zak. She has the augmented powers of body and mind of an "Angel Class" agent, and is simultaneously erotic, beautiful, proud, and inwardly melancholy. Her sexuality glows through her every action, not as consummated sexual intercourse, but as a source of her power and pride.

[Certain themes link Shadow Lady, Alita, Ora, and Attim M-Zak together. Their openly powerful sexuality does not weaken them nor make them the helpless playthings of men. None is submissive, and none is passive. Neither does their femaleness make them second-best copies of men—for example, female characters who imitate male superheroes. Instead, in these depictions, femaleness is a self-complete state of being. These women do not need or want men to guide them or rule over them. Attim and her heroine sisters act for themselves, and therein we sense not merely resistance to Neo-Confucianist themes of women's subordination, but their final demise.

• [*Category 3*: Sexuality is increasingly important and explicit.

Sexual intercourse is explicitly depicted or clearly implied in the drawings. Other sexual activities, including rape, may also occur. All are significant to the story, but are not its central focus. (Perper & Cornog 2002, 102)

[Once again, the range and diversity of narrative is striking. Naoki Yamamoto's *Dance Till Tomorrow* (Viz) is an ironic view of an alienated generation of slackers, *yakuza* gangsters, relatives scheming over an inheritance, and a woman hired to seduce the presumptive heir, all admixed with dry humor, explicit sex, and a crazed roster of characters. By contrast, Hideo Yamamoto's *Voyeur* and *Voyeurs, Inc.* (both Viz) are grimly realistic depictions of a firm of young private detectives. In the first major episode of *Voyeurs, Inc.*, they are hired to spy on a high-school girl who, it turns out, is running a prostitute ring starring the services of her classmates. (The story is based loosely on real-life high-school prostitution that began, it is said, in Tokyo's Shibuya High School; Kimura & Yamana 1999, 75-87.) Matters are much worsened when they discover that her father wants to seduce her. *Paradise Kiss*, by Ai Yazawa (Tokyopop/Mixx), is a stylish and elegant story about high-school senior, Yukari, her decision to become a fashion model, and her love affair with George, a young fashion designer at the Paradise Kiss boutique. Yukari has never even dated a boy, let alone kissed one, when she decides that she will sleep with George—and she does.

[Historical *manga* like Kazuo Koike and Goseki Kojima's *Lone Wolf and Cub* (Dark Horse), Sanpei Shirato's *The Legend of Kamui* (Viz), and Takehiko Inoue's *Vagabond* (Viz) likewise incorporate sexuality into their narratives. Sometimes as rape, sometimes as consensual intercourse, sexuality cannot be avoided in the kind of aesthetic realism sought by these artists.

[But the significance of sexuality is not limited to satire or to aesthetic realism. Picaresque fantasies, like Johji Manabe's *Outlanders* and *Drakuun* (both Dark Horse), portray sexually enthusiastic heroines, for example, sword-swinging Princess Kerula with her lover Dard in *Drakuun*. When Kerula assassinates Emperor Gustav, she starts a major war between the Empire and her homeland, the tiny kingdom of Ledomiam. In the last published episode, a now-pregnant Kerula and Dard, Kerula's sister, Rosalia, and her rifle-toting female lover, Rua, plus a crew of other malcontents, are about to invade the Empire in an effort to topple Gustav's evil successor. In *Outlanders*, Princess Kahm is the daughter of the Galactic Emperor, which does not stop her from finding, bedding, and marrying a young Earthman named Tetsuya. In the end, her Imperial father kidnaps her, causes her to forget Tetsuya with a magical spell, and then orders her to kill him. But her memories return. She turns on her father in fury and kills him, not her husband, as the imperial world collapses into flaming debris. It is hard to imagine narratives better designed for subverting Neo-Confucianist ideologies of women's obedience to father and emperor.

[Rumiko Takahashi's masterpiece, *Maison Ikkoku* (Viz), is a 14-volume study of love, sex, and marriage in modern Japan. Like novelist Jane Austen, Takahashi depicts her characters in finely wrought detail, from Kyoko Otonashi's blinding grief at her husband's death after only six months of marriage, to her suspicious doubts about Yusaku Godai's motivations and protestations of love, and finally to her admission to herself and him that she returns his love. In parallel, Takahashi explicates the intricacies of an arranged marriage between Asuna Kujo, the daughter of a high-ranking and fabulously wealthy family, and Shun Mitaka, a young tennis coach from an equally wealthy family, who also loves Kyoko. For Kyoko and Yusaku, and for Asuna and Shun, the denouement centers on love and sexuality played out through complex machinations of family and class.

[Shun is skillfully maneuvered into marrying Asuna by both their families, who hold dynastic interests above everything else, and by Asuna herself. Asuna makes her marital intentions very clear—she arrives at his apartment one night ready to sleep with him. Although he is too drunk to respond sexually to her or to remember what happened, and she soon leaves, he certainly understands what it means that she has left breakfast for him in his refrigerator. In delicate but unmistakable symbols of domesticity and food, she has said that they are already married. He cannot ignore her invitation—her chauffeur knew where she was, and therefore so does her family. As rumors start that she is pregnant (she is not), he yields to the social and emotional forces that surround him and soon makes a formal proposal of marriage to her family, which is accepted. Their story ends with the birth of twins and their recognition of their growing love for each other.

[The tapestry of events leading to Kyoko and Yusaku's marriage is different. Overwrought with anxiety about Yusaku's feelings, and having just refused Shun's proposal of marriage, Kyoko accuses Yusaku of having an affair with someone else. Stumbling through his furious denial and through their mutual uncertainties, they end up in a love hotel, only to discover that memories of her late husband prevent them from having intercourse. Painfully, they must set their feelings to rest. The later scene where they triumphantly do make love is one of the most powerful in all *manga*. They too marry, and *Maison Ikkoku* ends with the birth of their daughter, Haruka.

[In stories like these, sexuality and sexual intercourse are depicted as they exist in actual life, within complex webs of feelings, intimacies, doubts, pleasures, and responsibilities. Sex is intrinsic to the narrative because it is inescapable in life itself.

- [*Category 4*: Sexuality is central.

  Explicitly depicted sexual intercourse and other forms of sexuality are a major narrative focus. (Perper & Cornog 2002, 102)

[Virtually all forms of sexuality occur in this category, and their diversity is hard to summarize. However, a few generalizations will be useful.

[Erotophilic consensual intercourse is typically loud, ecstatic, and drenchingly wet, especially for women. Women are often portrayed as erotic, powerful, and very beautiful (we have identified at least five modalities used in *manga* for depicting female beauty and sexual allure; Perper & Cornog 2002). Female sexuality is virtually never a source of shame or punishment, perhaps most notably in the sexually explicit *redi komi* subgenre drawn by women artists for women readers.

[Our sample contains relatively few depictions of male homosexuality, but the fan-drawn genre of YAOI, with its beautiful young men passionately in love with each other, is very popular in both Japan and the U.S. (YAOI-Con 2002). Female-female sexuality occurs more frequently in commercial *manga*. Some are casual encounters, but other stories depict the two women as partners and lovers in long-term relationships (Pamila and Pfil in Kondom's *Bondage Fairies* from Eros Comix, Princess Rosalia and Rua in Johji Manabe's *Drakuun* from Dark Horse, and Sheila and her friends in Ryo Yuuki's *Sheila's Diary*, from RedLight Manga). Sometimes, female-female sexual attraction is only suggested by gazes, touches, and intense emotional bonding, for example, between Utena and Anthy in Chiho Saito and Be-Papas' *Revolutionary Girl Utena* (Viz). However, in Kunihiko Ikuhara's brilliant 1997 animated film of *Revolutionary Girl Utena*, the love affair between Utena and Anthy is not only depicted, but is the heart of the film.

[Because space is limited, we will focus on three themes—comedy and satire, spirituality, and alienation and rape.

[*Comedy and Satire*. Two artists come to mind when writing about explicit sexual humor in *manga*—Toshiki Yui and Haruka Inui. Yui's stories are populated not only by cheerfully erotophilic and very pretty young women, but also by incompetent demons, eccentric gurus, and puzzled young men, all enmeshed in wildly escalating plots. In Yui's "The Contract" (in *Misty Girl Extreme*, from Eros Comix), Misty is hoping for sexual ecstasy when she summons a demon. Although he promises to drive her mortal mind insane with pleasure, he manages only one premature ejaculation, and disappears muttering and mumbling as Misty loudly expresses her disgust at how useless he is. Yui's *Wing-Ding Orgy* (Eros Comix) is a five-part parody about virginal Keisuke, his reluctant girlfriend, Michiko, and two female spirits, Ruki and Mana, who materialize to assuage his sexual desires. After the malfunction of a magical dildo obtained from a lunatic psychic guru, Keisuke seeks the help of a sex therapist, which only makes matters more complex, as Michiko, Ruki, and Mana coalesce into a single ultrasexy female. In Yui's "My Little Darling" (in *Hot Tails* from Eros Comix), a suave demon makes a pass at Miki. When her angry boyfriend, Tetsuya, threatens him, the demon shrinks Tetsuya down to three inches tall and stalks off. Miki and the now-tiny Tetsuya discuss this problem in a coffee shop, and Tetsuya asks to sit on her lap. There he discovers that he can climb into her vagina. While she squirms in embarrassed orgasms, the demon returns and inveigles her to a love hotel. But when the demon's penis enters her vagina, it encounters the now enraged Tetsuya, who bites this intruding monster and sends the demon through the hotel's ferroconcrete wall. He regains his full size in a later episode, but for now, Tetsuya is happy with the advantages of his miniaturization.

[Inui's *Ogenki Clinic* (Studio Ironcat) is a long-running, slapstick parody of sex therapy. Therapists Dr. Sawaru Ogekuri and Nurse Ruka Tatase are sex-positive, but their treatments are unconventional, to say the least. Dr. Ogekuri's penis looks exactly like him, including carefully parted hair and eyeglasses (an example of genital personification, Cornog 1986). Yui and Inui's stories, among others, have female characters with penises and testicles (in Japanese, *shii meru*). In *Ogenki Clinic*, even a *shii meru* woman can have a personified penis, but this one has her face and long hair, and is therefore a *female* penis (Perper & Cornog 2002, 30). *Ogenki Clinic* was one of several *manga* considered harmful by Japanese authorities during the early 1990s (Kinsella 2000, Ch. 5, notes 1 and 2, p. 211), but from the perspective of the year 2003, it seems more satiric than dangerous.

[In an untranslated example by Oida Cute (from *Penguin Club Comic*, Issue 11, 2001), Hana-chan and her boyfriend are leaving a bar, and Hana-chan is quite drunk (little bubbles keep floating over her head). Once outside, she happily reassures him that she is fine—and then throws up all over him. They end up at a hotel, where Hana-chan falls asleep fully clothed while hugging a pillow. Then she wakes up, decides she wants sex, and begins to masturbate. She and her boyfriend go on to intercourse, but then she throws up again. The story ends with them both taking a shower together and laughing.

[These stories satirize male libido and its blundering desires, the frustrations and complex desires of women, and the vagaries of sex in an imperfect world. The root of the comedy is that sex is constantly running out of control—in the family, in Wolf Ogami's *Super Taboo* (Eros Comix); in the workplace, in Tetsu Adachi's *Weather Woman* (CPM Manga); and in the entire cosmos, in Ai Ijima and Takeshi Takebayashi's *Time Traveler Ai* (CPM Manga). In such goings-on, even the deities are laughing.

[*Spirituality*. Serious spiritual themes are not uncommon in sexually explicit *manga*. An example is *Zashiki Bokko*, by Senno Knife (from *Sepia* No. 2, Studio Ironicat), which opens with a note: A *zashiki bokko* is "a female ghost inhabiting an old inn." Young Masao has just returned to his family's hot spring spa (*onsen*) after graduating from college. The welcoming party is well under way, and someone asks him if he will decide to work here at the inn. And peeking at him from behind a sliding paper wall is a very pretty girl. "Koyuki!" he murmurs. The relatives joke that he has no cousin named Koyuki. "Must be a ghost," they laugh. In a flashback, he remembers years ago when they met in the hot springs, both naked. She stroked his back as he nestled between her legs, and he protested, "It's getting hard. Stop that!" But she pressed her face to his: "Don't be ashamed about it. When the time is right, I'll do it with you."

[Now alone in his bed, he wonders if she even remembers. But she peeks into his room and then enters and takes his hand. Together, they go to the *onsen*. "Do you remember the promise?" she asks as they swim together naked. They make love, entwined in the warm water, kissing and caressing. He wonders who she is, and decides that it doesn't matter. He wants to be with her always.

[Next we see his mother and grandmother talking—Masao has decided to stay and maintain the family inn. "It must be that ghost," says grandmother. "They say when you have a *zashiki bokko* then business will thrive." The final drawing shows Koyuki alone in the *onsen*, naked and beautiful: "I'll protect this inn as long as you are here with me." With her, the inn is protected against fire, bandits, storm, and desolation. She is the *kami* of the *onsen*, not a ghost in the Western sense, but a semi-divine female protective spirit—beautiful, erotic, and powerful.

[There are other examples of explicit sexuality, spirituality, and the supernatural. One is Hiroyuki Utatane's elegantly drawn "Ryu-Ho" (in *Countdown: Sex-Bombs*, Eros Comix), which retells the legend of Ryu-Ho, the first emperor of China's Han dynasty, whose mother was a mortal woman and father a dragon. Another is Jiro Chiba's *Were-Slut* (Eros Comix), about a young woman whose magical sexuality heals her lovers. A similar theme occurs in *Wolf*, by Harumi Shimamoto (in *Space Dreams*, from Studio Ironcat). An untranslated example is Iruka Banto's *Toga-Oi Byakuni* (roughly, "To the Nun, the Harm," from *Cute*, Issue 10, 1999), set in 1910, about the murderous hatred between young and beautiful Yukiji Wakao and her mother-in-law, Ohkura. Yukiji's family is high nobility but presumably impoverished, whereas her husband's family is nouveau riche (*narikin*) but without rank or status. Ohkura poisons Yukiji after learning that Yukiji has been having an affair with one of her husband's business associates. But as the supernatural enters the story, Yukiji returns to life, triumphant and transcendently beautiful, and it is Ohkura who dies.

[*Alienation and Rape*. These themes of spirituality draw on Japanese folklore and religion to create images of sexuality interwoven into the fabric of the universe itself. And yet, sex has a dark side. It leads to art delving not only into sexuality, but also into social chaos and disintegration.

[Such narratives set sex into a grim modernity in which loss of self, identity, and security is the norm. Stylistically, such stories lend themselves to an aesthetic realism recognizable by both content and drawing style—serious themes directly involving social issues and negative emotions portrayed in a gritty, edgy style emphasizing the absence of beauty and prettiness in the characters' lives (sexually explicit examples include the work of Benkyo Tamaoki, Ronin Tenjiku, and Akira Gatjaw, among others). This sort of realism descends from the *gekiga* style pioneered in the 1960s and 1970s by artists like Sanpei Shirato (see Randall 2002ab, for a brief history and examples), but is also influenced by cyberpunk, e.g., William Gibson's 1984 pioneering novel *Neuromancer,* and by film noir, like Ridley Scott's 1982 *Bladerunner.* Now we encounter sexuality set in an alienated and anomic modern world or, more often, in post-apocalyptic worlds of social disintegration (*Akira* is an example). In those worlds, women's sexuality emerges not as pleasurable eroticism nor as passive victimization nor as a source of further chaos, but as *resistance* to death and disintegration.

[Masahi Shibata's *Sarai* (ComicsOne) is set in a post-apocalyptic world of social chaos and genetic disintegration. Sarai is a "guard maid," one of a group of young women who act as bodyguards and warriors. Sarai carries a *samurai* sword, traditionally a man's weapon, a visual trope that Neo-Confucianist masculinity can no longer protect society. But Sarai and the other guard maids can, or can try, to prevent utter chaos, sometimes by dispatching rapists and other vermin, and sometimes by saving the lives of their friends.

[One of the most extraordinary examples of a woman armed with a *samurai* sword is Saya, the protagonist of Benkyo Tamaoki's *Blood* (Viz), which combines themes of alienation, sexuality, and Japanese folklore into a sexually explicit horror story. It has a subplot involving explicit female-female sexuality, but *Blood* centers on the premise that a breeding program has existed for some 150 years for hybridizing human beings and ogres in an effort to obtain for humans the genes that confer immortality on the cannibalistic ogres. The program, ill conceived to begin with, has failed—the hybrids are worse killers than either parent species. Now the terrified human beings have bred Saya as an ogre-hunter, and although her American handlers treat her with great contempt—between assignments they keep her handcuffed and naked in a cell—they are quite willing to use her for exterminating the hybrids.

[Saya locates a motorcycle-riding gang of ogres in Yokohama ("sluts and thugs," someone calls them), and encounters their psychopathic gang-leader. She tracks him down to a wrecked and abandoned hotel, where he transforms into a monster who wants to rape and kill her, and devour her corpse. Saya beheads him with a single, sudden sweep of her sword.

[But she also encounters her counterpart, Maya, who, like herself, was bred from human and ogre stock as an ogre-hunter. But Maya is defective, and she needs human blood and flesh to live. Yet, it is Maya who tells her of their common ancestry and offers herself as a sacrifice for Saya to eat, thereby to fuse with each other and create their own future, independent of human beings. As Maya commits *seppuku,* Saya holds her dying body, waiting to complete Maya's request. Saya escapes, kills her American handlers, and, in the last images, walks through the dark streets of Tokyo seeking her and Maya's future.

[It trivializes the intensity and power of these images to dismiss them as fantasy or science fiction. Instead, we see women and their sexuality as embattled. Subjected to rape or to scientific but utterly wrongful breeding, these women find weapons and use them. When—to give another example—Attim M-Zak uses a sword to cut the arm off a man attacking her, the narrative has moved far beyond clichés of submissive Japanese women. Instead, we are in the territory of open resistance. But Saya's reaction to the rapist and to her handlers is not the resistance of a frightened child, nor even of an angry, defiant child having a tantrum. Saya is an adult, trained in the craft and use of a death-dealing weapon, and her purpose is to kill. Her ability to resist comes not

from a child's fear, but from her status as a mature and powerful woman.

[As *Blood* implies, no situation better illustrates themes of women's resistance and power than *manga* that deal with rape. Many critics of *manga* in the United States and Japan argue that it condones and glorifies rape. However, the data from our sample suggest the exact opposite (Perper & Cornog 2002, 45-54, 80-86). We identified 87 examples of sexual assault or rape in our translated sample. In them, we encounter a theme widespread in sexually explicit *manga*: rape followed by bloody revenge against the rapists. First we give several examples, and then some statistics.

[In "Dead Angela" by Kaz Yamane (in *Verotik 2: Verotika Fast,* published by Verotik), pretty and blonde Angela is the assistant to Professor Devore, an archeologist who has excavated a hitherto unknown bipedal skeleton somewhere in South America. Local terrorists invade the laboratory and machine-gun Professor Devore and then tie up Angela and repeatedly rape her. The terrorist leader shoots Angela, and her body falls backward against the skeleton. Its eye sockets start to glow, and it extends bony protrusions that surround her naked body. Now standing, its skeleton an armored carapace around her, she hears its voice in her mind: It is a living symbiont. "Master Angela, from now on, we are one. Your life is my life, your blood is my blood, your death is my death." She attacks the rapists, and, with one bloody sweep of her now-armored hand, she rips the head off the man who raped and shot her. The last panel shows her naked in her symbiotic armor, an icon of vengeance. The caption reads, "I am restored to life. We are not alone."

[Yuichiro Tanuma's *Princess of Darkness* (Eros Comix) is similar. It is a complex tale of dreams and demons centering on female art student, Maki Kurohara. In episode 4, she is sexually assaulted by five thugs, but invokes a murderous naked female demon armed with knife-bearing gauntlets who slashes the five men to ribbons.

[One of the most remarkable examples of rape-revenge occurs in Koh Kawarajima's *Immoral Angel* (published by Manga 18). Disgusted with humanity, the gods have decided to destroy the world. A man named Nekozo Kyusu, gifted with supernatural powers, is building an ark to save a selected number of his fellow humans (he contemptuously calls them lemmings). He kidnaps a high-school girl, Reimi, to be his mate and repeatedly rapes her. She resists each time, screaming and fighting, but his strength is too great. Finally, he abandons her, pregnant with his child.

[As the anger of the gods increases, the world is wracked by earthquakes, tidal waves, and other disasters. Nekozo abducts and rapes another young woman, but Reimi seems to reappear, naked. She reveals herself to be his and Reimi's grown daughter Rema, winged and vengeful. As father and daughter battle, his attacks go awry, and Rema taunts him with her mother's hatred and with his own powerlessness. Avowing that her one and only filial duty to him is to destroy him, Rema tears her father to shreds. She then destroys the ark, obliterating him and his life's ambitions.

[*Immoral Angel* deals not merely with rape-revenge, but also is explicitly anti-Confucianist. Earlier scenes of the mother's repeated rapes are balanced by the daughter's revenge. The conclusion, like that of most rape-revenge stories, is that rape is virtually a cosmic crime that demands and receives profound retribution and retaliation.

[An untranslated example is Go Nagai's *Devilman Lady* (KC Comics), about a woman martial artist who is also a demon. A ravening monster attacks and rapes a woman, but Devilman Lady counterattacks, first castrating him and then killing him. As other monsters attack a group of children, she then destroys them in scenes noteworthy for their bloodiness.

[In the 87 cases of rape in our earlier sample, 80% or 92.0% show the woman or her friends taking violent and most often, murderous revenge against the rapist. An additional five (5.7%) showed rape as criminal, but did not include revenge. This gives (80+5)/87 or 97.7% of the examples that are rape-negative. Only two stories (2/87, or 2.3%) showed rape as something that the woman desires. (See Perper & Cornog 2002, Appendix 2, for a complete annotated list of all 87 cases.)

[Since then, we have located a number of additional examples of rape-revenge, including *Blood, Immoral Angel,* and *Devilman Lady*. The occurrence of rape-revenge is a major trope in sexually explicit *manga*. It is not an artifact arising from our use of a translated sample, because the rape-revenge theme occurs in untranslated *manga* and in Japanese film, like Takashi Ishii's 2000 live-action *Freeze Me* and Yoshiaki Kawajiri's 1992 animated *Wicked City*. These conclusions are in line with Diamond and Uchiyama's (1999) well-documented argument that no correlation exists between pornography and rape in Japan, and also with Schodt's suggestion that *manga* may itself help reduce violent sexual crime (1996, 49-53). Rape-revenge *manga* rise in inexorable emotional intensity, which is released only when the rapists are destroyed and balance is restored between sexuality and the cosmos.

[*Conclusions*

[The sexual content of *manga* ranges over a wide spectrum of activities, emotions, and meanings. These include cheerful and humorous erotophilia, serious sexual and erotically expressed love, and revenge and resistance to rape. Most often, sexuality is contextualized by character, narrative, and setting, so that it is portrayed as a fully human activity rather than being restricted to genital couplings.

[At its best, *manga* contain some of the finest erotic art in the modern world. Japanese traditions have not been lost in these portrayals. Much *manga* holds the reader's attention not only for the sheer beauty of the drawing, but as comic and dramatic narrative. Modern *manga* continues Japanese erotic traditions in representing sex as a positive and healthful good for both sexes. Strong, powerful women characters, innovative and unconstrained treatment of sexual themes, excellent artwork, and powerful plots make *manga* a force to be reckoned with as the medium gathers more and more readers worldwide. (*End of comment by T. Perper and M. Cornog*)]

### E. Sadism and Masochism

It is well-known that sadism and masochism (S&M) have been taken up in Japan's literature and paintings. A number of works by Seiu Ito on the subject of *shibari* (bondage) are famous examples. One depicts a woman being tortured while a drooling jailer looks on in delight. Another shows a naked woman suspended upside down, while under her an old man is enjoying a drink of *saki*. These are typical of Seiu Ito's works. Of course, works such as these are not part of Japan's mainstream literature or paintings, but rather are learned of only in the quiet mania of the back streets.

It is uncertain how many people are interested in this type of sadism and masochism today, but their numbers are not few. Roughly 10,000 magazines dealing in S&M are thought to be sold each month, by which one could estimate the number of interested people to be perhaps two or three times that number.

On the other hand, in the Japanese media's typical fashion of trying to stimulate the reader's interest, some minor weekly magazines print photographs or articles that depict situations with a sadistic mistress and a masochistic man.

Naturally, most of these depictions are contrived, as people who really practice S&M do so in secret, hidden from public view. Both Tokyo and Osaka have nightclubs in their busiest nightspots that make money off of S&M. Still, experts say that the people who go to such places probably realize it is all just an act.

## 9. Contraception, Abortion, and Population Planning

### A. Contraception

Various contraceptive devices became available in the democratic days after the war, including use of the pessary (diaphragm), contraceptive jelly and foams, and so on. Nearly 80% of Japanese people still choose the condom as their most favorable contraceptive device. This choice, however, is conditioned by the government's near-total ban on the oral contraceptive pill. [*Update 1997*: As of January 1997, only a medium-strength form of the pill was available in Japan for medical (non-contraceptive) purposes. However, some women were using it as a substitute for the low-dose contraceptive pill normally taken by American and European women. Originally, the Ministry of Health and Welfare cited the possible link between the hormonal pill (OCP) and cardiovascular disease, weakened immunity, cervical cancer, and thrombosis as its reason for not approving distribution of the pill in Japan. In 1996, new research studies undermined this objection, and the Ministry of Health and Welfare gave signs that it might remove its over three-decade-old ban on the OCP, perhaps even by the end of 1997. The Ministry admitted to some continuing concerns about removing the ban. There is a fear that, with the birthrate at 1.4 live births per woman, pushing the OCP might drop the birthrate even lower. More realistic is the fear that use of the OCP rather than the condom would increase the spread of AIDS among those who use the pill. More basic to the cultural values of Japanese men and women is the fear that Government approval of the OCP may send a signal of promiscuity and upset the delicate dynamics in male-female relationships. Even married women tend not to discuss contraceptives openly with their husbands. Traditionally, Japanese men are accustomed to taking the lead in relationships, especially when it comes to sex. Japanese women frequently express their awe at the independence of American women who make their own decision to use the pill. Nevertheless, after decades of public and national administration debate, approval of the OCP may be expected in the near future (WuDunn 1996). (*End of update by R. T. Francoeur*)]

Japanese contraceptive practices naturally reflect this limitation. According to the latest statistics, 77.7% of contracepting Japanese use a condom; one in five, 21%, use the Ogino method/rhythm method/BBT method; 7.1% use withdrawal (coitus interruptus), 7% rely on surgical sterilization, and 3.7% on the intrauterine device. The rather high popularity of condom usage among the Japanese people is because of the strong policy of the Imperial Army Administration throughout the militarist period, when it was consistently used to prevent various venereal diseases.

Margaret Sanger (1883-1966), the American nurse who eventually organized the International Federation of Birth Control, visited Japan early in the Showa Era, the late 1920s, to promote the birth control movement in Japan. At the time, the national administration disliked this idea because of its own policy of promoting childbirth for national security reasons. Thus, the government publicly opposed the birth control movement. Nevertheless, because the military widely promoted use of the condom for prevention of venereal diseases, it eventually was firmly accepted by the common people in Japan as an effective method of birth control. Later, in the post-World War II years, this positive attitude of the Japanese people toward the condom functioned effectively in promoting the family planning movement.

Condoms are often sold to housewives by door-to-door "skin ladies." In 1990, moralists were disturbed when, after a marked increase in teen abortions, a condom company targeted the teenage market with condom packets bearing pictures of two cute little pigs or other cartoon animals and names like "Bubu Friend" (Bornoff 1991, 337).

The greatest obstacle in Japan to contraception is the national control of the contraceptive pill (OCP). In the 1970s, the promoters of feminism were openly against induced abortion and thus started a movement to make the OCP available. However, when they recognized that high-dosage OCPs had side effects, they changed their position and strongly opposed its free use. As is widely known now, the majority of current low-dosage OCPs pose little danger. Consequently, some of the current feminist promoters in Japan are not against expansion of choices by making low-dosage OCPs widely available. Nevertheless, the great majority of Japanese feminists still maintain their skepticism about the use of OCPs.

*[The Female Condom and "the Pill"*

[*Update 2001*: In June 1999, the 35-year-old government ban on the oral contraceptive pill was finally removed, prompted by serious criticism against the sexual double standard of the government regulatory board that approved Viagra in January 1999, an unusually brief six months after application from the pharmaceutical company. In November 1999, Japan's regulatory body approved the female condom, which clinical tests found to be 97% effective in preventing pregnancy. The female condom also received a very favorable relative overall acceptability rating of 89% (Reuters Health, November 12, 1999). (*End of update by Y. Kaji*)]

### [B. Unwed Teenage Pregnancy

[*Update 1997*: Japan has consistently maintained one of the world's lowest incidences of out-of-wedlock births, well below 5% (Lewin 1995). A 1995 study by the Population Council, an international nonprofit New York-based group, reported that only 1.1% of Japanese births are to unwed mothers, a figure that has been virtually unchanged for 25 years. In the United States, this figure is 30.1% and rising rapidly (Kristof 1996a). (*End of update by R. T. Francoeur*)]

### C. Abortion

As has been mentioned earlier, the national policy of Japan after the Meiji Era, when Japan's modern national structure emerged, was to strengthen the nation. Thus, children were considered to be the treasure of the nation, and abortion was naturally deemed illegal.

With the rebounding of the post-World War II social order, the Eugenic Protection Law was implemented in 1948, and induced abortion became a fully legal and allowed method of birth control in Japan. The law set out certain premises to be satisfied for abortion to be permitted, but many accepted it quite readily. Thus, induced abortion became the most popular method of family planning in Japan in the mid-1950s, with 1.2 million abortions a year, an extremely high rate of 50.2 per 1,000 women annually. Later, the rate and the number of the induced abortions declined rapidly, dropping from 1.1 million cases in 1960, to 730,000 cases in 1970, and 457,000 cases in 1990. By 1990, the abortion rate was 14.9 per 1,000 women a year, less than a third of the rate of 40 years ago. This significant and important change came about because of the special effort of advocates of a sound family planning movement and the increased use of

condoms. It should be noted that this reduction in abortion and the popularization of family planning were achieved despite the unavailability of the oral contraceptive pill and a quite-low IUD usage rate.

Even though the current rate of induced abortion is becoming acceptably low, there are still disturbing elements in the statistics, mainly a gradual increase of abortion among teenage youths. In the 1970s, the total number of abortions for teenage pregnancy was approximately 13,000. This number increased to 14,300 in 1970, 19,000 in 1980, and 29,700 in 1990. The rates of abortion among women under 20 years of age increased as follows: 3.2 per 1,000 in 1960 and 1970, 4.7 per 1,000 in 1980, and 6.6 per 1,000 in 1990. Keeping in mind that the sexual activity of young people in this nation is increasing, it is apparent that more-efficient education of the youth for pregnancy prevention is strongly needed. For one thing, sex education within the public education system is far from being well developed in this country. The traditional value systems about sex and sexuality, such as the theory of purity education that prohibits and condemns premarital sexual activities as a crime, for example, creates burdens for the young people, even though two thirds of them accept premarital relations. Such beliefs often affect the sexual behavior of the young and interfere with their acquisition of knowledge and skills about pregnancy prevention.

[*Comment 1997*: Japan has no debate over the morality of abortion, and no politicians taking political stands for or against abortion. In fact, virtually everyone believes that abortion is each woman's own private business. Despite this wide acceptance of abortion, there is ambivalence about abortion among many Japanese women and men that reflects the dualism one finds throughout Japanese sexual attitudes. At Buddhist temples around the country, one finds galleries of hundreds, even thousands of tiny memorial statues dedicated to aborted fetuses, miscarried and stillborn babies, and those who died as infants. These *mizuko jizo* are dressed and visited regularly, sometimes monthly, by Japanese women who have had an abortion or lost a baby and feel a need to atone for their loss. Japanese women, and sometimes men, visit their *mizuko jizo* to express their grief, fears, confusions, and hopes of forgiveness for ending a human life so early, however rational and necessary that decision may have been.

[The concept of the *mizuko jizo* did not develop until after World War II and has since been linked more and more with abortion rather than miscarriages, stillbirths, or infant deaths. Even some gynecologists who perform abortions regularly visit the temples to purify themselves in a special Buddhist ritual. In former times, fetuses and even newborns were not believed to be fully human or to have a spirit or soul until the newborn was ritually accepted into its family and linked with its ancestors, so abortion and even infanticide was accepted matter of factly. The recent tradition of the *mizuko jizo* appears to satisfy many of the emotions and feelings traditionally suppressed in the acceptance of abortion (WuDunn 1996). (*End of comment by R. T. Francoeur*)]

### D. Population Control

From ancient times, population control, particularly in each village community, has been maintained publicly perhaps as part of the wisdom of the public welfare. In premodern days, the actual method often involved certain techniques related to primitive religions and/or incantations "turning childbirth changing into stillbirth." What in Western culture is termed infanticide was not necessarily considered illegal or unreasonable according to the faith and/or ethics of that era. According to authentic ancient belief and practice, the baby belongs to God until the very moment of its first cry. Therefore, suffocating the newborn before it cried, before it was "really born," and returning the incipient life to God was not considered wrong. Western culture would consider this culpable infanticide, but such was not the case in ancient Japanese beliefs; see the discussion of abortion and *mizuko jizo* in the preceding paragraph. [*Comment 1997*: Similarly, in many regions of China, a newborn infant is not considered "fully born" and human until the whole extended family gathers three days after the infant's birth to celebrate its "social birth" and official recognition by the family's patriarch and, through him, by the whole extended family and their ancestors. (*End of comment by R. T. Francoeur*)]

By 1995, the Japanese government had become so concerned about its plunging birthrate—1.53 per woman and declining—that the Institute of Population Problems, a part of Tokyo's Health and Welfare Ministry, sent out questionnaires to 13,000 single Japanese citizens asking them what they thought about marriage, families, and children. In view of the plunging birthrate and a heating up of the war of the sexes, Japan is facing a demographic time bomb. As the population ages and the birthrate shrinks, the tax burden on the Japanese workforce will rise. Economists also suggest that Japan's famously high rate of savings will increasingly have to support its retired population, and not factories and other productive investments (Itoi & Powell 1992).

[*Update 1997*: With its birthrate plunging to 1.4 in 1996—Tokyo's birthrate was 1.1—Government projections suggested that within a hundred years, by 2100, Japan's population will tumble to 55 million, from 125 million today. That would be the same population Japan had in 1920. At 55 million, Japan would have a population density five times that of the United States today, but its position as a global power would certainly be reduced, when in 2050 Japan's population drops to just one quarter of America's projected population. By the year 3000, it could drop to 45,000, according to a weekly magazine projection. To counteract this trend, many Japanese cities are paying women residents a bonus, up to $5,000, when they have a fourth baby. Among the other incentives being considered are: cash upon marriage, cut-rate land for childbearing couples, importing Philippine women of marriageable age, and cash grants to parents when their children turn 3, 5, and 7, which are all auspicious birthdays in Japan. Because of the discouraging cost of childrearing, some have recommended an annual financial bonus. In 1995, when Prime Minister Hashimoto was Finance Minister, he suggested a novel way of encouraging fertility: Discourage women from going to college.

[In 1996, the average Japanese woman marries at 27. Seventeen percent of women in their early 30s are still unmarried. One of the reasons cited by women who chose not to marry was a common negative view of the Japanese male as a desirable mate (Kristof 1996c). (*End of update by R. T. Francoeur*)]

[*Update 2001*: With a 1998 Total Fertility Rate of 1.38 children per fertile woman, Japan is struggling to persuade couples to have more children and help avoid many long-term social problems. Japan's current population of 126 million is expected to drop to 105 million by 2050. In those 50 years, the median age will increase from 41 to 49 and those age 65 and older will double from 17% to 32%.

[Prior to June 2000, salaried parents with an annual income below US$67,000 and self-employed parents with an annual income less than US$43,000 received a monthly $50 subsidy for each of their first two children, and $100 monthly bonus for subsequent children under age 3. The $50 bonus covers 25% of basic monthly expenses for a child under age 3: food, clothing, and utilities. In June 2000, a

new law extended this bonus to children under age 6, more than doubling the number of parents who qualify. Similar past efforts have had scant effect. Social observers suggest that the major factor in Japan's low birthrate is the increasing number of Japanese women graduating from universities, obtaining well-paid jobs, enjoying their independence, and marrying later in life. Another is the fact that Japanese men traditionally avoid any participation in household work and leave the whole burden to their wives.

[This trend, coupled with the rising number of legal and illegal immigrants attracted by Japan's shortage of workers, will have serious repercussions for Japan's future economy and workforce, In 2000, about 1.5 million foreigners resided and worked legally in Japan. But thousands of undocumented aliens are also pouring into Japan, from China, Korea, South America, and Ghana. In 1990, Japan had an estimated 110,000 undocumented immigrants; this rose to half a million in the year 2000. In 1989, 4,159 Japanese who had immigrated to Brazil a generation or two back returned to Japan. In 1998, 222,217 returned from Brazil. In 1989, 864 Peruvian *Nikkeijin* returned to live in Japan; in 1998, 41,317 returned to Japan. In Oizumi, a small industrial town 50 miles (80.5 km) from Tokyo, nearly 12% of the population is Latino.

[As Japan's birthrate plummets and legal and illegal immigration accelerates, many aspects of Japan's traditionally insular homogeneous monoculture are already changing, including the context and character of sexual attitudes and behavior. (*End of update by Y. Kaji*)]

[*Update 2002*: In March 2002, the Japanese Cabinet issued a report signaling concern over Japan's plummeting birthrate and the aging population. In May 2002, Prime Minister Junichiro Koizumi ordered his top aides to draw up policies outlining plans to make parenthood more attractive and affordable for the country's swelling ranks of childless 20- and 30-year-olds. Echoing the need for new social strategies to promote parenting, Health Minister Chikara Sakaguchi predicted that company employees would have to pay nearly 25% of their salary to pension premiums to maintain the current payout in 2025. Japan's population is expected to peak at around 127 million as early as 2005. After 2005, Japan's population is expected to fall rapidly over the next 50 years to roughly 100 million. Meanwhile, the "graying" of Japan will accelerate until, by 2050, 35.7% of Japan's population will be over age 65, more than double the percentage in 2000. Demographers and economists do not agree on the effectiveness of new policies to encourage more young people to have more babies as a long-term viable solution. Faced with similar futures and failure of efforts to raise the birthrate, European and North American countries have stabilized their populations with immigrants (Greimel 2002). (*End of update by R. T. Francoeur*)]

## 10. Sexually Transmitted Diseases and HIV/AIDS

### A. Sexually Transmitted Diseases

Japan's Venereal Disease Prevention Law has remained unchanged since it went into effect in 1958. However, venereal diseases (VDs) common at the time this law was established, along with genital herpes, chlamydia, trichomoniasis, and HIV/AIDS, have come to be called sexually transmitted diseases (STDs) in Japan, as well.

Of these STDs, HIV/AIDS excluded, typical VDs of the past, such as syphilis and gonorrhea, have followed a steady decline year after year. The number of gonorrhea cases, for example, reported to the Ministry of Health and Welfare, in line with the Venereal Disease Prevention Law, declined from its peak of 178,000 cases in 1950 to 4,000 in 1964. Slight peaks in the number of cases reported were seen thereafter, with 12,000 in 1967 and 13,500 in 1984, but between 1970 and 1980, the number hovered between 5,000 and 7,000 cases. As concern for HIV/AIDS began to intensify in Japan in the 1990s, the number of gonorrhea cases showed a steady decline from 3,465 cases in 1992 to 1,724 cases in 1993 and 1,448 cases in 1994. As for the number of syphilis cases reported to the Ministry, a steady decrease can be seen from 6,138 cases in 1970 to 3,635 in 1975, 2,081 in 1980, 1,904 in 1985, 1,877 in 1990, and only 804 cases in 1993.

On the other hand, the actual number of herpes, chlamydia, and trichomoniasis cases is unclear since reporting of these diseases is not required. However, the Ministry of Health and Welfare began collecting data in the late 1980s from selected hospitals, with reports gathered from about 600 hospitals throughout Japan. This data suggests the following trends: Trichomoniasis and condyloma acuminatum have shown a decrease, albeit slight, but the same cannot necessarily be said for chlamydia and herpes. Reports indicate that the number of infections among people in their teens or 20s has become particularly striking. Such reports cannot be said to be unrelated to the increase in sexual activity among Japan's youth. Since sexual activity among these youths is expected to become even more prevalent in the future, it is obviously desirable that we tackle countermeasures for these STDs in earnest.

[*Update 2001*: The first sentinel surveillance of STD in Japan was conducted in 1998. Woman-man ratios of infection rates per 100,000 persons for each STD, and high woman-to-man ratios for overall STD incidence (1.40), condyloma acuminatum (1.11), genital herpes (2.25), chlamydia (2.31), and nongonococcal and nonchlamydial infection (1.51), challenge the current Japanese common understanding that STDs are mainly a male health problem treated by urologists. STD prevention and treatment in Japan should focus more on female patients (Kumamoato 1999). (*End of update by Y. Kaji*)]

## B. HIV/AIDS

Japan has not been quick to respond to the HIV/AIDS problem in its own country. Patients showing signs of Kaposi's sarcoma and *Pneumocystis carinii pneumonia* for which no cause could be found began to appear in America in 1981. The following year, the United States Centers for Disease Control and Prevention (CDC) began calling the syndrome AIDS. In 1983, it became known to the world that a virus, named HIV, was the cause.

At last, Japan's Ministry of Health and Welfare was moved to action, forming an AIDS research task force, which began surveillance for occurrences of AIDS in Japan. The first AIDS patient that the surveillance committee found was a homosexual returning briefly from America in March 1985. In May of the same year, they announced that AIDS patients contracting the disease through blood transfusions had been confirmed. In 1996, the country became embroiled in an extremely serious debate, in which the government or several committee members of the AIDS research task force and pharmaceutical companies were suspected of a secret pact to cover up the outbreak of "the real first" AIDS patients who had contracted the disease through unheated blood products. This problem was resolved in July of 1996 when the government and the pharmaceutical companies apologized to these victims and paid them an out-of-court settlement. However, not everyone feels that the agreement reached is a complete solution to the problem.

Turning to the situation of HIV/AIDS in Japan, current as of the end of May 1996, 3,642 people had been infected

with HIV (including those with AIDS symptoms), of which 1,806 contracted the disease through unheated blood products. Although these numbers are extremely low compared to those of other countries, one cannot discount that the HIV/AIDS problem in Japan is a large one. For example, only 13,703 people underwent examinations for HIV in 1995, just one third of the 37,774 tested in 1992, when the number of people taking the examination reached its peak. In Japan, the number of people taking the test has declined over the past three years, from which one could assume Japanese feel the danger of contracting HIV/AIDS is becoming more and more remote.

For those unlucky enough to contract AIDS in Japan, there are 203 AIDS-authorized hospitals throughout the country where one can receive treatment. However, the names of nearly half of these hospitals are currently not being made public. Furthermore, some hospitals, even some of the AIDS-authorized hospitals, refuse treatment to AIDS patients, as reported by the Osaka Plaintiffs in AIDS Litigation Organization.

Of course, not everything about the HIV/AIDS problem in Japan is negative. For instance, until recently, major newspapers and other companies serving the public, such as NHK Television, had not directly taken up sexual problems. However, with the current situation, including the HIV/AIDS problem, even the most straitlaced newspapers and television stations have begun to use such words as condom, homosexuality, and anal sex. Such a trend has engendered the makings of informative reports on human sexuality. This issue is not felt in the media alone; it is also having a great impact on Japan's educational system. HIV/AIDS is clearly introduced in junior high school textbooks on health as an infectious disease. Thus, all children in Japan are now learning about HIV/AIDS.

Furthermore, teachers of social studies, home economics, and homeroom classes are actively educating students about HIV/AIDS in order to dispel any prejudices and discriminations the students may have. Naturally, this education is not only aimed at HIV/AIDS discrimination, but is related to sexual discrimination, as well. Although sex education in Japan is not sufficient in its current state, this education aimed at HIV/AIDS and discrimination may be the breakthrough Japan needs, and perhaps a golden opportunity to firmly establish sex education in the schools. This can certainly be viewed as a positive influence.

[*Update 1997*: As of August 1995, the reported number of AIDS-related deaths was 626. The cumulative number of reported cases of HIV infection was 3,423 among Japanese persons and 881 among non-Japanese. Among this number were 1,803 hemophiliac patients who contracted HIV as a consequence of the use of contaminated blood products in their daily treatment.

[The incidence of AIDS in Japan is still very low, although some suggest that the official figures underplay the actual incidence and danger. Only 15 deaths from AIDS were reported in 1986 for a population of 120,000,000. By mid-1988, the death toll had risen to 46 with an additional 34 confirmed in hospitals, and 1,038 persons who tested seropositive.

[The initial response of the Japanese gay community to the AIDS epidemic in the early 1980s was misguided. Because the number of Japanese gay men infected with HIV had been comparatively low, many Japanese gay men, like the rest of the Japanese people, found it easier to view AIDS as an exclusively foreign phenomenon. Discrimination against foreign, especially Western, gay men by Japanese gay men was widespread. One consequence of the fear of AIDS is that homosexuals visiting Japan report that many former gay paradises, particularly the no-holds-barred male sauna, are now closed to non-Japanese. (*End of update by Y. Kaji*)]

[*Update 2001*: As of June 2000, Japan had an accumulative reported 5,058 persons infected with HIV and 2,367 AIDS patients. This number included 1,434 HIV-infection cases and 631 AIDS cases where the virus was transmitted by use of tainted blood products. Most HIV/AIDS cases in Japan are because of sexual transmission. Reported HIV/AIDS cases transmitted by IV-drug abuse or mother-to-child transmissions are less than 1% of the total cases. (*End of update by Y. Kaji*)]

[*Update 2002*: UNAIDS Epidemiological Assessment: HIV prevalence rates in Japan continue to remain well below 1% for most HIV-risk-behavior groups, except among female sex workers of foreign nationality (2.7% from 1987 to 1999). Most reported HIV/AIDS cases in Japan during the mid-to-late 1980s and early 1990s were because of HIV-infected blood products that were imported for the treatment of hemophilia patients; a third of the AIDS cases (33%) reported in 1988 were in hemophilia patients infected through imported blood coagulation factor products.

[The high percentage of hemophilia AIDS cases is still the distinctive characteristic of HIV infection in Japan and is not seen in other countries in the world. However in 2000, about 78% of newly diagnosed HIV infections appear to have been acquired through sexual contact. One of the characteristics in recent years is that the infection through sexual contacts in Japan is getting higher among Japanese men. Almost all HIV infections in Japan are related to imported infections (including hemophilia infections), and then some limited transmission from these infected persons to their regular sex partners. Behavioral data show low condom use, both in the general population and among female sex workers (6% to 25%).

[Estimates suggest that, by the end of 2001, 12,000 persons were living with HIV, a prevalence of 0.02% among people aged 15 to 49 years.

[The estimated number of adults and children living with HIV/AIDS on January 1, 2002, were:

| | | |
|---|---|---|
| Adults ages 15-49: | 12,000 | (rate: < 0.1%) |
| Women ages 15-49: | 6,600 | |
| Children ages 0-15: | 110 | |

[An estimated 430 adults and children died of AIDS during 2001.

[At the end of 2001, an estimated 2,000 Japanese children under age 15 were living without one or both parents who had died of AIDS. (*End of update by the Editors*)]

## 11. Sexual Dysfunctions, Counseling, and Therapies

Unfortunately, no compiled information is currently available on sexual dysfunctions in Japan. However, by drawing inferences from many researchers on the subject, certain facts come to light. The most common dysfunction, accounting for about half of all informally reported sexual disorders, is erectile dysfunction. Other common dysfunctions include sexual phobias, sexual avoidance, decreased sexual desire, dyspareunia (painful intercourse), female orgasmic disorder, vaginismus (painful vaginal spasms), homosexuality, and gender identity disorder.

One dysfunction that has become an issue of late is that of sexual inactivity among couples. Dr. Teruo Abe, a psychiatrist who studied under the American Helen Singer Kaplan, defines the term sexually inactive couples as "couples who do not engage in consensual sexual intercourse or sexual contact for a period of one month or longer, despite the lack of special circumstances, and who can be expected to remain sexually inactive for a long period after that." Abe reports that the number of such sexually inactive couples during the period from 1991 to 1994 increased by 2 to 4 times the number between 1985 and 1990. Yet, over a ten-year period, only 303 patients with this dysfunction came to seek Abe's assistance. Assuming that there are about 50 institutions in Japan that treat this sexual disorder, estimating generously, then only about 12,000 to 15,000 people have visited doctors for this sexual disorder over the past ten years. While there are probably many opinions on whether this number is large or not, the number reflects the current state of the disorder in Japan.

There are no types of sexual dysfunctions peculiar to the Japanese. The most common dysfunctions are treated by such specialists as gynecologists, urologists, and psychiatrists, or clinical therapists and counselors. Unfortunately, these fields of medicine remain too isolated from one another in Japan. It would be desirable, therefore, for the medical institutes themselves to gain an understanding of all aspects of human sexuality.

In 1976, the Japanese Red Cross Medical Center was the first public medical institution in Japan to establish a sexual counseling center. Although before that time, sexual treatment was carried out in the gynecology, urology, and psychiatry departments of private and university hospitals, such treatment was mainly for functional disorders. It was very rare for these hospitals to provide treatment from the perspective of total human sexuality.

Japanese doctors, counselors, psychologists, and sociologists who first became aware of the importance of sexual counseling and treatment met and formed the Japanese Association for Sex Counselors and Therapists (JASCT) in July 1979. The Association welcomed Patricia Schiller, founder of the American Association of Sex Educators, Counselors, and Therapists (AASECT), as honorable chairman and adopted the ideology of her organization. The JASCT proceeded to take charge of sexual counseling and therapy in Japan and continues to do so today. JASCT's objective is to carry out surveys and research with the help of sex counselors and doctors who treat sexual disorders. They do not issue licenses in recognition of qualifications.

From what limited information is available, it certainly seems that Japan is very active in the treatment of sexual dysfunctions, but unfortunately the reality is that a lot more problems remain unsolved. Underlying those problems in Japan is the popular notion that sex is not something you talk about, and the belief that, except in cases of extreme pain, as long as you can tolerate the problem, it will heal in time and you will not have to bother others about it. Recently, however, an increasing number of people in their 40s or younger, who have been exposed to a more sexually open society in their youth, are moving away from this tendency and seeking sexual counseling and treatment.

## 12. Sex Research and Advanced Professional Education

### A. Research and Advanced Education

With the exception of such scientific subjects as reproduction and birth taught in the fields of biology or medicine, Japan's institutions of advanced education have only made sex a direct topic of research in the past two or three decades. Traditionally, sex has not been made a subject of learning in Japan's academic world. Thus, on the rare occasion that someone has pursued the study of human sexuality, that person has been seen as an outcast, and, at times, ostracized, as was the case with Senji Yamamoto, who taught in the Biology Department of Doshisha University and, early in the 20th century, was Japan's first sexologist.

Although Japan became a democratic society in 1945 allowing for the freedom to study human sexuality, even in institutions of advanced education, a wall remained standing in the academic world inhibiting such freedom, and the wall was high and thick. No reason exists for the academic world to be separated from society. It has become gradually understood that sex education is necessary in higher education in order to address the various problems in Japanese society, such as sexual problems among youth, information on sex provided by the media, the issue of STDs and HIV/AIDS, and the phenomenon of more couples opting to rear fewer children.

Universities for training teachers and departments of education were the first to show an interest in teaching sex education at the university level. Regardless of its quality, sex education in Japan's elementary and junior high schools and institutes of advanced education is usually taken up in the health and science curricula. Therefore, it was natural for sex education to be first taught to those interested in teaching. Recently, an increasing number of departments of human science have been established in Japanese universities, wherein study of basic human sexuality has become abundant.

Still, sex education in universities and other institutions of advanced education cannot be said to be functioning sufficiently. Take, for example, the estimate that only about 5% of Japan's 1,150 universities and junior colleges provide lectures on human sexuality. One can assume that developing more programs on sex education in universities and other institutions of advanced education will become a major issue in Japan's educational system.

## B. Sexological Organizations and Publications

Until mid-1996, the authors of this chapter, Yoshiro Hatano, Ph.D., served as Director, and Tsuguo Shimazaki as Secretary of the Japanese Association for Sex Education (J.A.S.E.).

Japanese Association for Sex Education. Address: J.A.S.E., Miyata Building, 2F, 1-3 Kanda Jinbo-cho, Chiyoda-ku, Tokyo, 101 Japan. Tel.: +81-3-3291-7726; Fax: +81-3-3291-6238. J.A.S.E. publishes *Sex Education Today*, a monthly journal.

In mid-1996, Tsuguo Shimazaki established the Nikon Information Center for Sexology (NICS). Address: N.I.C.S., Hobunkan Building, 6F, 3-11-4 Kanda-Jinbo-cho, Chiyoda-ku, Tokyo 101 Japan. Tel.: +81-3-3288-5900; Fax: +81-3-3288-5387. N.I.C.S. publishes *Sexology Updater* (ten times a year).

Other Japanese sexological organizations and publications include:

Japanese Association of Sex Educators, Counselors, and Therapists (JASECT), JASE Clinic, 3F Shin-Aoyama Bldg (West),-1 Minami–Aoyama, 1-chome Minato-ku, Tokyo 107 Japan.

The Japan Family Planning Association, Inc. (JFPA). Address: Hokenkaikan Bekkann, 1-2, Ichigaya Sadohara-cho, Shinjuku-ku, Tokyo 162 Japan. Tel.: +81-3-3269-4041; Fax: +81-3-3267-2658. JFPA publishes the journal *Family Planning and Family Health* (monthly).

Japan Federation of Sexology (JFS). Address: c/o Nikon Information Center for Sexology (NICS), Hobunkan Building, 6F, 3-11-4, Kanda-Jinbo-cho, Chiyoda-ku, Tokyo 101 Japan. Tel.: +81-3-3288-5200; Fax: +81-3-3288-5387.

Japan Institute for Research in Education, 4-3-6-702 Kozimachi Chiyodaku, Tokyo 7102 Japan. Tel.: 03-5295-0856; Fax: 03-5295-0856.

Japanese Organization for International Cooperation in Family Planning, Inc. (JOICFP), 1-1, Ichigaya Sadohara-cho, Shhijuku-ku, Tokyo 162 Japan. Tel.: 81-3/3268-5875; Fax: 81-3/3235-7090.

Japan Society of Adolescentology (JSA). Address: c/o Japan Family Planning Association, Hokenkaikan Bekkann, 1-2, Ichigaya Sadohara-cho, Shinjuku-ku, Tokyo 162 Japan. Tel.: +81-3-3269-4738. JSA publishes the journal *Adolescentology* (four times a year).

The Japanese Society for Impotence Research (JSIR). Address: c/o First Department of Urology, Toho University School of Medicine, 6-11-1, Omori-nishi, Ota-ku, Tokyo 143 Japan. Tel.: +81-3-3762-4151, extension 3605 or 3600. Fax: +81-3-3768-8817. JSIR publishes the *Journal of the Japanese Society for Impotence Research*.

Japanese Society of Sexual Science (JSSS). Address: c/o Hase Clinic, Shin-Aoyama Building, Nishikan 3F, 1-1-1, Minami-Aoyama Minota-ku, Tokyo 107 Japan. Tel.: +81-3-3475-1789. Fax: +81-3-3475-1789. JSSS publishes the *Japanese Journal of Sexology* (semiannually).

## References and Suggested Readings

Adler, S., & S. Wolf. 2000. *Fodor's Japan* (15th ed). New York: Random House.

Asayama, S. 1979. Sexuality of the Japanese youth: Its current status and the future prospects. *Sex Education Today*, 36:8-16 (in Japanese).

Beasley, W. G. 1999. *The Japanese experience: A short history of Japan*. Berkeley, CA: University of California Press.

Benedict, R. 1954. *The chrysanthemum and the sword–Patterns of Japanese culture*. Charles E. Tuttle Co.

Bornoff, N. 1991. *Pink Samurai: Love, marriage and sex in contemporary Japan*. New York: Pocket Books.

Boyd, R. 2001. On second thought, there is a need for Tenchi. *Comics Journal*, 238:93-99.

CIA. 2002 (January). *The world factbook 2002*. Washington, DC: Central Intelligence Agency. Available: http://www.cia.gov/cia/publications/factbook/index.html.

Cornog, M. 1986. Naming sexual body parts: Preliminary patterns and implications. *Journal of Sex Research*, 22:393-398.

Diamond, M., & A. Uchiyama. 1999. Pornography, rape and sex crimes in Japan. *International Journal of Law and Psychiatry*, 22:1-22. Available: www.afn.org/~sfcommed/Pornography.htm.

Dixon, D., & J. K. Dixon. 1999. A serious look at the amazing phenomenon of erotic comic books. In: J. Elias, V. D. Elias, V. L. Bullough, G. Brewer, J. J. Douglas, & W. Jarvis, eds., *Porn 101: Eroticism, pornography, and the First Amendment* (pp. 427-36). Amherst, NY: Prometheus.

Earhart, H. B. 1984. *Religions of Japan*. New York: Harper and Row.

Ellwood, R. S., & R. Pilgrim. 1992. *Japanese religion: A cultural perspective*. Englewood Cliffs, NJ: Prentice-Hall.

Embree, J. F. 1995. *Suye Mura: A Japanese village*. Ann Arbor, MI: Center for Japanese Studies, University of Michigan. (Original work published 1939).

Encarta. 1999. *Encarta world English dictionary* [CD-ROM]. Microsoft Corporation/Bloomsbury Publishing.

Fagioli, M. 1998. *Shunga: The erotic art of Japan*. New York: Rizzoli/Universe Publishing.

French, H. W. 2001 (December 5). Japan: An equal opportunity throne. *The New York Times*, p. 6.

French, H. W. 2002 (May 9). Death does them part (Wives make sure of that). *The New York Times*, International Section, p. A3.

French, H. W. 2002 (July 31). For more Japanese, love is a multiethnic thing. *The New York Times*, International Section, p. A3.

French, H. W. 2003 (March 25). As Japan's women move up, many are moving out. *The New York Times*, p. A3.

French, H. W., S. Isett, & C. Sygma. 2000 (July 27). New pressures alter Japanese family's geometry. *The New York Times*, International Section, p. A3.

Greimel, H. 2002 (May 22). Tokyo's new task: To turn singles into married parents. *Newark* [New Jersey] *Star-Ledger*, p. 2.

Hájek, L. (n.d.). *Harunobu*. London: Spring Books.

Hall, J. W. 1991. *Japan: From prehistory to modern times*. Ann Arbor, MI: University of Michigan Press. (Original work published 1968).

Hatano, Y. 1972. L. A. Kirkendall: His platform for sex education and its background. *Bulletin of Tokyo Gakugei University*, 24(5):164-177 (in Japanese).

Hatano, Y. 1988. Sexualerziehung von kindern und jugendlichen in Japan. In: N. Eicher, et al., eds., *Praktische sexual medizin* (pp. 34-42), Verlag Medical Tribune (in German).

Hatano, Y. 1991a. Changes in the sexual activities of Japanese youth. *Journal of Sex Education and Therapy*, 17(1):1-14.

Hatano, Y. 1991b. Education for parenting viewed from education of sexuality. In: Japanese Ministry of Education, ed., *National women's education center*.

Hatano, Y. 1991c. Child-socialization and "parenting" education. In: *International seminar on family education proceedings*, pp. 272-92.

Hatano, Y. 1993. Sexual activities of Japanese youth. *Journal of Sex Education and Therapy*, 19(2):131-144.

Hatano, Y, & R. Fujita. 1976. Sexual behavior of selected college and vocational school students in Tokyo. *Bulletin of Tokyo Gakugei University*, 28(5):262-72 (in Japanese).

Hirota, A. 1997. The tale of Genji: From Heian classic to Heisei comic. *Journal of Popular Culture*, 31:29-68.

*IES2*. 1997. Hatano, Y., & T. Shimazaki. Japan (*Nippon*). In: R. T. Francoeur, ed., *International encyclopedia of sexuality* (vol. 2, pp. 763-842). New York: Continuum. [This is the original version of the current chapter for readers who wish to refer to the original graphs, which were converted to tables or text here. See the footnote at the beginning of this chapter.]

Itoi, K., & B. Powell. 1992 (August 10). Take a hike, Hiroshi. *Newsweek*, pp. 38-39.

*Japan: Portrait of a nation* (Rev. ed.). 1999. Tokyo: Kodansha.

Japanese Association for Sex Education (J.A.S.E.), ed. 1975. *Sexual behavior of Japanese youth*. Tokyo: Shogakukan Press (in Japanese).

Japanese Association for Sex Education (J.A.S.E.), ed. 1983. *Sexual behavior of Japanese youth*. Tokyo: Shogakukan Press (in Japanese).

Japanese Association for Sex Education (J.A.S.E.), ed. 1988. *Sexual behavior of junior high school, senior high school and university students in Japan*. Tokyo: Shogakukan Press (in Japanese).

Japanese Association for Sex Education (J.A.S.E.), ed. 1994. *Sexual behavior of junior high school, senior high school and university students in Japan*. Tokyo: Shogakukan Press (in Japanese).

Kaneko, S. 1995. Women's place: Cultural and historical perspectives. In: K. Fujimura-Fanselow & A. Kameda, eds., *Japanese women: New feminist perspectives on the past, present, and future* (pp. 1-14). New York: The Feminist Press of the City University of New York.

Kinsella, S. 2000. *Adult manga: Culture and power in contemporary Japanese society*. Honolulu, HI: University of Hawai'i Press.

Kimura, Y., & A. Yamana. 1999. *What Japanese women are really like*. Tokyo: Katsuyuki Hasegawa.

Kobayashi, T. 1993. *Utamaru: Portraits from the floating world*. Tokyo: Kodansha.

Kondo, I. 1956. *Kitagawa Utamaro*. Rutland, VT: Charles E. Tuttle.

Kristof, N. D. 1995 (November 5). In Japan, brutal comics for women. *The New York Times*, Sec. 4, pp. 1, 6.

Kristof, N. D. 1996a (February 11). Who needs love? In Japan, many couples don't. *The New York Times*, pp. 1, 12.

Kristof, N. D. 1996b (June 19). Japan is a woman's world once the front door is shut. *The New York Times*, pp. A1, A8.

Kristof, N. D. 1996c (October 6). Baby may make three, but in Japan that's not enough. *The New York Times*, p. 3.

Kronhausen, P., & E. Kronhausen. 1978. *The complete book of erotic art: Erotic art, Volumes 1 and 2*. New York: Bell.

Kumamoato, Y., et al. 1999. *Sexually transmitted disease surveillance in Japan. 1998*.

Lester, R. C. 1987. *Buddhism*. New York: Harper and Row.

Lane, R. 1999. Ukiyo-e: An introduction to the floating world. In: R. Faulkner, *Masterpieces of Japanese prints: Ukiyo-e from the Victoria and Albert Museum* (pp. 11-23). Tokyo: Kodansha.

Levy, H. S., & A. Ishihara. 1989. *The tao of sex: The essence of medical prescriptions (Ishimpo)* (3rd ed.). Lower Lake, CA: Integral Publishing.

Lewin, T. 1995 (May 30). Family decay global, study says. *The New York Times*, p. A5.

*Manga: Une plongée dans un choix d'histoires courtes du 12 Octobre au 18 Décembre 1999*. 1999. Paris: Maison de la Culture du Japon à Paris.

Maraini, F. 1959. *Meeting with Japan*. London: Hutchinson.

McClain, J. L. 2002. *Japan: A modern history*. New York: W.W. Norton.

*More report on female sexuality*. 1983. Tokyo: Shueisha.

*More report on male sexuality*. 1984. Tokyo: Shueisha.

Morris, I. 1994. *The world of the shining prince: Court life in ancient Japan*. Tokyo: Kodansha. (Original work published 1964).

National survey of sexology and college education. 1995. *Sexual Science*, 4(1):27-68.

Perper, T., & M. Cornog. 2002. Eroticism for the masses: Japanese manga comics and their assimilation into the U.S. *Sexuality & Culture*, 6:3-126 (Special Issue).

Randall, B. 2002a. Hey kids! Gekiga! Part one. *The Comics Journal*, 244:91-120.

Randall, B. 2002b. Hey kids! Gekiga! Part two. *The Comics Journal*, 245:107-111.

Rutenberg, J. 2001 (January 28). Violence finds a niche in children's cartoons. *The New York Times*, pp. 1, 19.

Schodt, F. L. 1986. *Manga! Manga! The world of Japanese comics*. Tokyo: Kodansha.

Schodt, F. L. 1996. *Dreamland Japan: Writings on modern manga*. Berkeley, CA: Stone Bridge Press.

Sha, K. 1964. *A happier sex life: Study in modern Japanese sexual habits* (R. Y. Tatsuoka & S. Kozuka, trans.). Tokyo: Ikeda Shoten.

Shigematsu, S. 1999. Dimensions of desire: Sex, fantasy, and fetish in Japanese comics. In: J. A. Lent, ed., *Themes and issues in Asian cartooning: Cute, cheap, mad, and sexy* (pp. 127-163). Bowling Green, OH: Bowling Green State University Popular Press.

Shimazaki, T. 1994-95. Upon completing the fourth youth sexual behavior investigation. *Monthly report sex education today*, 1994, 12:9-12, and 1995, 13:1-3. Tokyo: The Japanese Association for Sex Education (in Japanese).

Shiokawa, K. 1999. Cute but deadly: Women and violence in Japanese comics. In: J. A. Lent, ed., *Themes and issues in Asian cartooning: Cute, cheap, mad, and sexy* (pp. 93-125). Bowling Green, OH: Bowling Green State University Popular Press.

Smith, T. 1991. Miso horny: Sex in Japanese comics. *The Comics Journal*, 143:111-115.

Smith, T. C. 1959. *The agrarian origins of modern Japan*. Stanford, CA: Stanford University Press.

Sodei, T. 1995. Care of the elderly: A women's issue. In: K. Fujimura-Fanselow & A. Kameda, eds., *Japanese women: New feminist perspectives on the past, present, and future* (pp. 213-228). New York: The Feminist Press at the City University of New York.

Strom, S. 2001 (April 22). On the rise in Japan: Assertive daughters-in-law. *The New York Times*, International Section.

Tanikawa, M. 1996 (September 8). Clubs where, for a price, Japanese men are nice to women, *The New York Times*, Styles Section, p. 49.

UNAIDS. 2002. *Epidemiological fact sheets by country*. Geneva, Switzerland: Joint United Nations Programme on HIV/AIDS (UNAIDS/WHO). Available: http://www.unaids.org/hivaidsinfo/statistics/fact_sheets/index_en.htm.

Wolferen, K. Van. 1989. *The enigma of Japanese power*. New York: Macmillan.

WuDunn, S. 1996 (November 27). Japan may approve the pill, but women may not. *The New York Times*, pp. A1, A10.

WuDunn, S. 1996 (January 25). At Japanese temples, a mourning ritual for abortions. *The New York Times*, pp. A1, A8.

Yanagihashi, A. 1995. *Traditional homosexuality in Japan* (OCCUR, Association for the Lesbian and Gay Movement). A paper submitted to the 12th World Congress of Sexology, Yokohama, Japan.

YAOI-Con. 2002. *YAOI-Con convention guide, October 18-20, San Francisco, California*. Available: www.aestheticism.com; www.yaoicon.com.

Yoshizumi, K. 1995. Marriage and family: Past and present. In: K. Fujimura-Fanselow & A. Kameda, Eds., *Japanese women: New feminist perspectives on the past, present, and future* (pp. 183-197). New York: The Feminist Press at the City University of New York.

# Kenya

## (*Jamhuri ya Kenya*)

Norbert Brockman, Ph.D.*
*Updates by Paul Mwangi Kariuki and
Beldina Opiyo-Omolo, B.Sc.*

## Contents

## Demographics and a Brief Historical Perspective

ROBERT T. FRANCOEUR

### A. Demographics

Most African nations, being political artifacts of colonialism, are multiethnic and multilinguistic. Patterns of sexual behavior are, therefore, quite varied, the result being complexity rather than uniformity. Economic and social factors that have an impact upon sexual patterns, therefore, include traditional cultures (initiation, courtship, and marriage customs), colonial imports (Christian and Islamic values, and education), and contemporary Western influences (consumerism and the media). Nowhere is this more clearly demonstrated than in Kenya, an east central African nation that lies across the equator, with Sudan and Ethiopia in the north, the Somalia in the northeast, the Indian Ocean in the southeast, Tanzania in the southwest, and Lake Victoria and Uganda in the west. With a total area of 224,960 square miles (582,650 km²), Kenya is slightly smaller than the state of Texas in the United States. The north is arid, but the land supports large game reserves and contains the fertile Lake Victoria Basin in the west. The climate varies from arid in the interior to tropical along the coast.

In July 2002, Kenya had an estimated population of 31.14 million. These estimates explicitly take into account the effects of excess mortality because of AIDS. This can result in lower life expectancy, higher infant mortality and death rates, lower population and growth rates, and changes in the distribution of population by age and sex than would otherwise be expected. (All data are from *The World Factbook 2002* (CIA 2002) unless otherwise stated.)

**Age Distribution and Sex Ratios**: *0-14 years*: 41.1% with 1.02 male(s) per female (sex ratio); *15-64 years*: 56.1% with 1.01 male(s) per female; *65 years and over*: 2.8% with

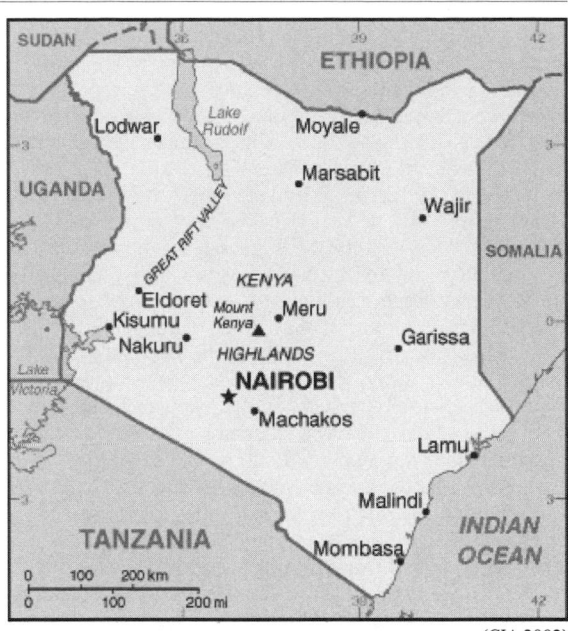

(CIA 2002)

0.77 male(s) per female; *Total population sex ratio*: 1.01 male(s) to 1 female

**Life Expectancy at Birth**: *Total Population*: 46.2 years; *male*: 46.2 years; *female*: 47.85 years

**Urban/Rural Distribution**: 35% to 65% (1994 est.)

**Ethnic Distribution**: Kikuyo: 22%; Luhya: 14%; Luo: 13%, Kalenjin: 12%; Kamba 11%; Kiii and Meru: 6% each; other African: 15%; non-African (Asian, European, and Arab): 1%

**Religious Distribution**: Protestant: 38%; Roman Catholic: 28%; indigenous beliefs: 26%; Muslim: 7%; other: 1%. A large majority of Kenyans are Christian, but estimates for the percentage of Muslims and adherents to indigenous beliefs vary widely.

**Birth Rate**: 27.61 births per 1,000 population

**Death Rate**: 14.68 per 1,000 population

**Infant Mortality Rate**: 67.24 deaths per 1,000 live births

**Net Migration Rate**: –1.48 migrant(s) per 1,000 population

**Total Fertility Rate**: 3.34 children born per woman

**Population Growth Rate**: 1.15%

**HIV/AIDS**: *Adult prevalence*: 13.95% (2001 est.); *Persons living with HIV/AIDS*: 2.2 million (2000 est.); *Deaths*: 180,000 (1999 est.). (For additional details from www.UNAIDS.org, see end of Section 10B.)

**Literacy Rate** (*defined as those age 15 and over who can read and write*): 78.1% (*male*: 86.3%, *female*: 70%) (1995 est.)

**Per Capita Gross Domestic Product** (*purchasing power parity*): $1,000 (2001 est.); *Inflation*: 50% (2000 est.); *Unemployment*: 40% (2001 est.); *Living below the poverty line*: 22.9% (2001 est.)

One in four Kenyans lives in modern urban areas, notably the capital, Nairobi, which has become a melting pot for all Kenyan cultures, and Mombasa, a tourist mecca on the Indian Ocean. Kenya is the leading Black African tourist destination, with splendid coastal areas, highly developed wildlife-viewing opportunities, and an infrastructure that has been very safe, comfortable, and competently run.

Nairobi, the capital and center of industrialization, has a population of more than one million. Mombasa, Nakuru, Eldoret, Kisumu, Nyeri, Embu, Meru, and Thika are other

*Communications*: Norbert Brockman, Ph.D.: *not available*. Updates: Beldina Opiyo-Omolo, B.Sc., Department of Health, East Stroudsburg University of Pennsylvania, East Stroudsburg, PA 18301 USA; bopiyo@yahoo.com.

large cities with a diversity and employment opportunities that attract many people from the rural areas, creating the usual urban problems. [*Update 2003*: In December 2002, Kenya went through a historic election in which political veteran Mwai Kibaki took a lead in landmark elections that marked the end of President Daniel arap Moi's 24-year rule. President Mwai Kibaki, a leader of the National Rainbow Coalition (NARC), defeated Uhuru Kenyatta, who had been handpicked by Moi to be the flagbearer for the Kenya African National Union (KANU), Kenya's long-ruling party since independence. (*End of update by B. Opiyo-Omolo*)] [*Update 1997*: In the 1990s, unrest with political tribal clashes have occurred primarily in the Rift Valley region from which the former president hails. Kenya has, since independence, had only one political party. The advent of multiparty politics in 1992 was decried by the president as a Western idea that would divide the people along tribal lines and plunge the country into lawlessness and anarchy. At the same time, legislators from the Rift Valley started preaching and demanding publically a change from the "Majimboism" (federal) system. Many tribes have coexisted peacefully in the Rift Valley for many years. These legislators asked the indigenous people, the people who originally owned the land before it was sold to others, to drive out these other people. With strong backing from the government, this effort resulted in a deadly, indiscriminate massacre of defenseless citizens, loss of property, and increased poverty, because a good percentage of the country's corn and pyrethrum is grown in this area. The children lost out on educational opportunities when the schools were closed and no teachers were willing to work in these areas. Nevertheless, the current situation is calm, and the churches and opposition parties have kept up their significant work for peace, restoration, and reconciliation. (*End of update by P. M. Kariuki*)]

### B. A Brief Historical Perspective

When the vast Bantu migration of the late medieval period—perhaps the largest human movement in history—turned south at Lake Victoria, it found small groups of well-entrenched Hamitic tribes and a few bushmen. The Bantus also encountered large Nilotic tribes that had arrived from the north, and these racially diverse nations settled into an uneasy relationship around the Lake region. Their descendents number about 25 million in Kenya, which straddles the equator on the east coast of Africa. Arab colonies exported slaves and spices from the coast of today's Kenya from the 700s on. Britain took over the country in the 19th century. In 1959, the Mau Mau uprising swept the country. British colonialism brought half a million East Asians and about a quarter million Caucasians in the early 1930s, both settler families and short-term expatriates connected with commercial, missionary, and international organizations.

[*Update 1997*: The agenda of the Mau Mau organization was to gain independence from the British, win control of their land and self-rule, and obtain the release of Jomo Kenyatta, then in British detention. Violence was widespread as the Mau Mau forces in the forests fighting the British were supported by a nationwide network involving the majority of Kenyans, both men and women. Defectors, traitors, and those who collaborated with the British were killed.

[For two decades, following Kenya's independence in 1963, the country was politically stable and prosperous, with a steady growth in its industry and agriculture, under Presidents Jomo Kenyatta (1963-1978) and Daniel arap Moi (1978-2002), under a modified private-enterprise system. In 1982, the military Air Force attempted to overthrow the government. Since then, government corruption, top-level scandals, the employment of unqualified people in upper-level positions, serious inflation, and the collapse of government services and systems have resulted in low morale throughout the workforce and an unstable economy. (*End of update by P. M. Kariuki*)]

## 1. Basic Sexological Premises

### A. Character of Gender Roles

Social reinforcement maintains clear gender roles in all Kenyan societies. Western education has produced a small female professional class, but expansion of women into new spheres of activity occurs only in Western roles that were unknown in traditional society: Western medicine, education, and bureaucracy. The Kenyan government has given strong support to educated women, appointing government officials, diplomats, and leaders from among them.

### B. Sociolegal Status of Males and Females

Among many Kenyans, there is strong belief in the existence of ancestral spirits. The ancestors assume functions of social control and must be placated when offended. There is a bond between the worlds of the living and the dead, and a mutual interdependence. It is important, therefore, to maintain a balance in populations between the two worlds by having children. The "living dead" need descendants to perform rites in their honor. Add to this the economic incentive of having large numbers of children in order to provide for old age, and the cultural resistance to population control becomes apparent. In the African family, children are received with delight and treasured. The firstborn is especially important in the family. The orphaned are taken in by their extended families. [*Comment 2003*: Institutional orphanages were almost unknown until recently, when the HIV/AIDS scourge has been killing many parents and leaving young children with nobody to take care of them. Most of these children whose parents have died of AIDS end up in the too-few orphanages. (*End of comment by B. Opiyo-Omolo*)]

Infanticide was practiced in traditional culture, but is now illegal and practiced rarely and surreptitiously. A baby may be killed if it is the result of an incestuous union or, in different ethnic groups, if an albino, triplets, or born feet first. The newborn of an uncircumcized Nandi girl is exposed to die if no one adopts it.

Life from childhood is organized around progress through age sets within a kinship system, each with its own preparation and responsibilities. These stages vary from tribe to tribe, but always include childhood, an initiation period leading to junior adulthood, marriage, family building, and the status of elder.

### C. General Concepts of Sexuality and Love

Sexuality is always a part of the kinship system, controlled within it, and subject to its purposes. Love is recognized and accepted as part of personal relationships. One may choose a marriage partner because of personal attraction, even though arranged marriages continue. Nevertheless, love is not a high value in itself. In polygamous marriages, junior wives will often be chosen by the first wife to meet work needs.

A great deal of sexual freedom for both sexes is allowed within these social controls. Unmarried boys and girls slept communally in many Kenyan societies, and several provide youth huts. [*Update 1997*: In a number of tribes, the Kikuyus, for instance, young men and women are allowed to dance, play, and even sleep together at certain organized times (*guiko*, among the Kikuyus), but no sexual activity is allowed although it may occur in these situations. Generally, premarital pregnancy disgraces a girl. Love, as an emotionally expressed feeling, was never valued in the tribal tradition. Today, it is treated as a Western idea and viewed with a lot of suspicion, especially by the older people. However, love as an act of the will has always existed. (*End of update by P. M. Kariuki*)]

## 2. Religious, Ethnic, and Gender Factors Affecting Sexuality

### A. Source and Character of Religious Values

For Africans, religion is a natural, present, and pervading influence deeply interwoven with culture. Everyday life is nowhere secularized as in the West, and religion as a personal and private activity is quite foreign to African sensibility. This is indicated by the presence of a mere 0.1% atheists and nonreligious persons in the country (see Table 1). The importance of religion for sexuality, therefore, is far beyond the issues of moral behavior so dominant in Western thinking.

Both Catholic and Protestant churches are very conservative theologically and morally, the former because of dependence upon expatriate (Irish and Italian) missionaries, and the latter because of a mass evangelical movement that has dominated Protestantism for several generations. Kenya is a center for the independent church movement, with over 500 groups ranging from African denominations to prophetic cults. Many allow polygamy and permit women prophetic figures, but are intolerant of abortion, contraception, sex education, and social equality for women. [*Comment 2003*: President Mwai Kibaki is a member of the Catholic Church, while former President Daniel arap Moi is a member of an evangelical Kenyan denomination, the African Inland Church. (*End of comment by B. Opiyo-Omolo*)]

Many Kenyan Muslims are East Asian disciples of the Aga Khan. African Muslims, primarily Swahilis on the coast, follow a moderate, relaxed form of Islam, and their numbers are declining.

### B. Source and Character of Ethnic Values

The ethnic distribution in Kenya in 1995 was: Kikuyu 21%, Luhya 14%, Luo 13%, Kalenjin 12%, Kamba 11%, and the remainder divided among Europeans, Asians, and Arabs. There are essentially two layers of cultural influences in every Kenyan. The first is the traditional tribal value system, and the second consists of Western influences. Sexual values, traditions, and behavior arise from the matrix of these influences, which vary among individuals. One family may speak a tribal mother tongue, continue traditional practices of initiation, bride wealth, and taboos, while another may speak Swahili or English predominantly, take many values from Christianity and the media, and feel free of tribal tradition. Several factors influence these differences: degree of urbanization, tribal intermarriage, religion, and level of education.

#### Table 1

#### Estimated Religious Distribution in Kenya

| Religion | Percentage of Population |
|---|---|
| Roman Catholics | 29 |
| Protestants and Anglicans | 27.4 |
| African independent churches | 21 |
| Orthodox | 2.6 |
| Christian Total | 80 |
| Traditional animists | 12 |
| Muslims | 6 |
| East Asian religions | 2 |

Moral strictures within Kenyan societies tend to be based on shame rather than on guilt. Disapproved sexual behaviors cast shame upon one's age group, clan, or tribe, rather than produce feelings of personal unworthiness through guilt. There is a strong social element to all ethical norms, including sexual norms. Sexual behavior in Kenyan societies is significant only in terms of the social realities of childbearing and family alliances. Consequently, where ethnic influence breaks down, as when a Kenyan moves to an urban area outside the tribal milieu, the inhibition of shame may be removed, resulting in behavior that by Western standards seems promiscuous and irresponsible.

There are contrasts in sexual norms among different ethnic groups. In some groups, such as the Luo, women who give birth before marriage are disgraced, while in other groups this is seen as a valuable sign of fertility. Virginity in women is highly prized in some groups, such as the Somali, Maragoli, and Luo, and regarded as unimportant in others, among the Kisii, Kikuyu, and Nandi. Among the Kikuyu, an infertile or impotent husband may provide another sex partner for his wife. Among the Nandi, a married woman can continue to have sex with her former lover or other members of her husband's age set. In contrast, the Maragoli regard extramarital sex as adultery. Therefore, the sexual culture shock in urban areas comes not only from contact with Western ideas and media, but also from interaction with diverse traditional value systems.

## 3. Knowledge and Education about Sexuality

### A. Government Policies and Programs for Sex Education

Sex education is treated with great ambivalence in Kenya. School curricula are nationalized, and there is no curriculum for sex education. Nevertheless, the idea is endorsed, and units of Family Life Education (FLE) are integrated into various curricula. These have been designed by nongovernmental organizations (NGOs), particularly the National Christian Council of Kenya, the Kenya Family Planning Association, the YMCA, the Kenya Catholic Secretariat, and the National Women's Federation (Maendaleo wa Wanawake). All of these organizations also provide various training programs for sex education teachers.

When tested in 1991 on six topics—menstruation, wet dreams, pregnancy, contraception, STDs, and AIDS—80% of the adolescents had received instruction on at least one topic between the ages of 12 and 15. Further testing on specific issues, however, showed that only 23 to 37% had practical knowledge on specific topics.

The government attempted to use television for sex education in the late 1980s, developing a popular soap opera series in Swahili. After several episodes, President Moi ordered the program stopped, endorsing instead traditional sex education by tribal elders. The fact that today, fewer youths live in rural areas or undergo traditional initiation, was never broached. Media such as television, comic books, and now radio and local comedian actors are used well in AIDS education, but this is the only topic systematically dealt with.

[*Update 1997*: The issue of sex education has become a major issue in Kenya. As mentioned, the government has made some efforts to introduce it in the schools, but this has met with considerable resistance from religious groups, particularly the Muslims and the Catholic Church. The Boy Scout movement, with the help of pathfinder funds, published a book on family life education for their members. This book discussed topical issues on sex education, human anatomy, and abortion. Subsequently, the government used this book as the basis for a sex education syllabus to be taught in the schools. Following much resistance and criticism from the religious groups and parents, the President ordered the book's withdrawal from all bookshops and stores in 1985.

[The issue of AIDS, which is alarming, has complicated the issue of sex education for several reasons. For one thing, the people do not take the AIDS threat seriously. {*Comment 2003*: The Kenyan government did not consider HIV/AIDS a priority until 1999, when the former President Daniel arap Moi declared AIDS a natural disaster. Since then, HIV/AIDS has been put on the priority list, with organizations like the World Bank and UNAIDS funding several HIV/AIDS projects. (*End of comment by B. Opiyo-Omolo*)}. The problem is with the level of information given, coupled with and complicated by the prevention methods advocated. The people in the churches who could be most effective in communicating the needed information believe the information about condom use as a way to reduce the spread of AIDS is scientifically false and that the people are not being told the truth. They are also aware of the economic factors in the sale of condoms: The manufacturers are out to make money with ineffective condoms while the users continue to die as AIDS spreads. There is a widespread belief that the whole issue is linked with a eugenics movement whose aim is to produce a "thoroughbred" race through genetic engineering. Africans are aware that some have classified them as a lower race. This belief in a eugenics-oriented link is supported by the requirement of the World Bank and the International Monetary Fund that 20% of every loaned dollar go to the provision of contraceptives and abortifacients. Government hospitals and clinics like the Maria Stopes clinics are flooded with these drugs, while there are absolutely no other drugs available to treat other ailments. The government preaches ensuring good health for everyone as a national goal. But when the only drugs the people find available are for AIDS and pregnancy prevention, they question the credibility of the government and its policies, and lose faith in anything it tries to advance.

[As a result, the main religious groups organize protest marches through the major towns, where thousands of people, young and old, attend. These marches are climaxed with the burning of condoms and sex education books. These people call for telling the truth about the effectiveness of condoms. They advocate that sex education be left to parents, and that parents be involved in any decision that would affect their children. They also advocate AIDS prevention through abstinence and chastity. For married couples, they call for "zero grazing," strict marital faithfulness. (*End of update by P. M. Kariuki*)]

[*Comment 2003*: Sex education for teenagers in Kenya has been largely stymied by the protests of religious groups. Teenagers are not told that condoms can protect against HIV. Instead, they are taught that abstinence is the best method of safe sex, with nothing mentioned about condoms and other contraceptives. Students only learn about AIDS in career subjects like biology, where the basic facts about this killer disease are taught in a very clinical way. (*End of comment by B. Opiyo-Omolo*)]

**B. Informal Sources of Sexual Knowledge**

Traditionally, sex education was undertaken as part of the initiation process. It began, however, much earlier in the extended family and social structures of particular ethnic groups.

Sex instruction does not often come from parents. In the presence of their children, they are expected to avoid any words, acts, or gestures of a sexual nature. The rules of shame might allow openness about sexual matters with a grandparent, however, and among the Kisii a grandmother could be the confidante of her grandchildren on their sexual experiences.

A small child will remain with its mother until about age 7. At this point, in some tribes, boys move in with their father or older boys. In other groups (Maragoli and Luo), both boys and girls go into separate huts with older children or into the homes of an elderly couple. These village dormitories provide socialization, sex education, and opportunities for sexual experimentation. The last is conducted in secret, although girls often "fail to notice" a youth visiting in the girls' dormitory. Two lovers might also go into the bush. A father and older sons might build a private hut for a son who reached puberty, especially since initiation ceremonies might be held only every few years. Under these circumstances, young men have free rein to engage in sexual activities. In slang, these huts are sometimes referred to as "the office," and "going to the office" means having a girl over for sex.

These patterns of sex education have continued into present-day society, where studies show that parents are a negligible source of information, while 31% of girls and 38% of boys indicate teachers as the most important source. This does not reflect organized sex education in the schools, but the influence of proctors and teachers in boarding-school settings.

## 4. Autoerotic Behaviors and Patterns

In Kenyan tradition, self-pleasuring is unacceptable among girls, and was part of the motive for clitoridectomy. For uninitiated (uncircumcized) boys, however, self-pleasuring is considered a proper preparation for a mature sex life. Boys in the same age group may engage in self-pleasuring together without shame, but all such activities are to be given up with initiation.

Adult male self-pleasuring is regarded as immature and childish after initiation, even for the unmarried. It is therefore surrounded with taboos. A man who has been circumcized is regarded as unready to assume adult responsibilities if he engages in self-pleasuring.

## 5. Interpersonal Heterosexual Behaviors

**A. Children**

Living in the unmarried men's hut, a boy has ample opportunity to listen to sexual conversations and observe older boys with their sweethearts. The degree to which an older boy may "play sex," as youth slang puts it, depends upon social custom. An uncircumcized Nandi boy rarely has an opportunity for intercourse, because of the strict controls of the warrior age set. Maragoli girls often participate in sex play with boys, although intercourse does not take place until after puberty. The Kisii tolerate extensive sex play among smaller children, although shame taboos require that after about age 7, such activities are not to be seen by parents.

Western influences have rendered many of these customs invalid. Many children are sent to boarding schools, where socialization is controlled by older children with little supervision. Nocturnal visits that are manageable in a traditional setting often turn into rape under these circumstances. Older youths who are not part of a tribal social system often feel little responsibility for younger children, and certainly not for female students who include no sisters or members of tabooed clan groups.

The urban family must dispense with age-set socialization entirely and keep their children in the home. Grandparents are seldom available for counseling or instruction. Other children and youths come from differing cultures, so that peer influences rarely reinforce traditional values.

## B. Adolescents

The sexual world of the Kenyan adolescent is extremely complex, combining traditional initiation rites, Western values and ideas, and a changing set of social expectations.

In traditional society, adolescents were initiated in a clearly defined period and by a series of events. In all cultures, these included instruction in male/female roles within the tribe, marriage customs, morality, and acceptable sexual behavior. Bantu cultures included circumcision for men, and usually for women. The Luo are the largest group not practicing circumcision. Among the Maasai and Samburu, after initiation, the new warrior could take a mistress from among the unmarried girls.

Initiation was done by age sets that were given distinctive names and provided a strong sense of bonding. While there were differences among ethnic groups, the pattern was essentially the same. Age sets went through various stages of adulthood together and shared a common responsibility for one another. In a few cases (Nandi and Maasai), it was not regarded as adultery if a women slept with an age mate of her husband. Elsewhere, the opposite is the case—adultery within the husband's age set would be incestuous, and there are taboos against the marriage of a son or daughter to one of another age-set member. However different cultures interpreted it, the age-set bond defines sexual and marital relations.

Male circumcision is an important sign of adulthood, responsibility, and bravery. When performed as a part of an initiation ritual, the boys are expected to receive the surgery without flinching, lest they disgrace their families. It is preceded by a cold dip in a river to deaden the senses. Circumcision is such a public symbol, it is not unusual to hear a man say "I have been to the river," to mean "I know what I am talking about." Because of the social significance, youths who do not undergo initiation, either because the family lives away from the tribal area or they are in school, will arrange for private circumcision from a doctor or clinician. After his teens, an uncircumcized male is the butt of ridicule and at considerable disadvantage in finding sex partners. A youth who cries out during the surgery is disgraced for life and will be able to find a wife only among the handicapped, elderly, or those with illegitimate children.

Female circumcision will be discussed under Section 8D, Unconventional Sexual Behaviors.

Although custom severely restricts adolescent intercourse, in reality a certain amount of sexual activity takes place. This is most marked in mixed situations (e.g., in cities and boarding schools), but it is also the case in traditional settings. In several cultures, elaborate sex play is institutionalized. Neither penetration nor touching of the genitals is allowed to either partner. Among the Kikuyu, the girl wears a leather apron during this activity, which is conducted in a special hut set aside to provide privacy to young people. Breast fondling is the main stimulant, as well as frottage. The Luo use a method of interfemoral intercourse. Where intercourse is tolerated, the main technique of avoiding pregnancy seems to have been withdrawal.

Detribalized youths experience considerable social pressure to become sexually active, without balancing social support that might make sexual abstinence a viable option.

Two 1987 studies reported age at first sexual intercourse to be 14 in the cities, and 13.7 for boys and 14.8 for girls in the rural areas. By age 20, 42% of rural females and 76% of rural males had had intercourse. Almost all of these involved multiple partners. Forty-one percent of rural girls have had intercourse with more than one partner (mostly for money from married men), 17% with three or more. The figures for boys are 72% and 51%, respectively. A 1991 cross-cultural study of in-school adolescents reported 48% of primary school males, 69% of secondary, and 77% of vocational to be sexually experienced. The comparable figures for young women are 17%, 27%, and 67%. No studies record preferred sex partners, but the widespread prevalence of prostitution is not to be discounted for the disparity between males and females in comparable settings.

Correlates of sexual activity among adolescents are peer influence (males with sexually active peers are seven times more likely to be active themselves); weak religious commitment; risk-taking behaviors (smoking, disco attendance, and alcohol use); dysfunctional family situations (for females); attending boarding school (for males); and attending a rural school.

Only 5% of the general adolescent population use any form of contraception. In striking contrast, the figure for students is slightly less than 15% who use contraception regularly, indicating that birth-control use is strongly influenced by educational status. It must be remembered that somewhere around 90% (statistics are imprecise) of youths terminate schooling after Standard Eight at about age 14 to 15. Correlates of contraceptive use among school girls are high academic achievement and upper socioeconomic status—each of these triples the likelihood of contraceptive use. There is only one correlate for boys, a sexual relationship with a girl supportive of contraception, which doubles the likelihood of contraception.

## C. Adults

### Premarital Courtship, Dating, and Relationships

Traditionally, premarital sex activity was circumscribed and controlled. A youth who impregnated a girl was liable for brideprice to her father, and might be punished in addition. While a few nomadic peoples like the Maasai institutionalized mistress relationships for unmarried warriors, this was the exception. Those practicing female circumcision usually demanded proof of virginity at marriage.

Courtship is dominated by brideprice. All marriages involve brideprice or bride wealth, regardless of whether they are traditional or among the educated elites. The origins of this payment to the father's family is recompense for the lost economic services of the daughter. Brideprice was paid originally in cattle and goats, but today usually involves money. Negotiations are often protracted, and various members of the extended family receive gifts over a period of time which corresponds to the Western engagement period. One Kenyan manufacturer uses a television ad showing the suitability of its blankets for brideprice gifts. A woman with education or skills is highly prized, while someone of low status— a housemaid, single mother, or orphan—might bring only a small bride wealth, and be viewed as appropriate only as a second or third wife.

[*Update 1997*: The payment of the brideprice has several functions beyond compensating the family of the bride for their investment and loss of the daughter's economic services. Part of the ceremony is to announce to all the intention of the couple to marry. After the traditional goats and bananas are offered, the clan members of the man and woman meet to negotiate issues like who the daughter is, what her skills are, her level of education, and the general duties she will undertake in her new home. The purpose here is to give the visitors, the man's relatives, a general overview of the woman's family, their status, and prosperous attitude as reflected in the daughter. This gives them a better reason to offer something substantial to compensate for the work done by the family on their daughter.

[The brideprice agreed to is always on the high side. This insures that the ties between the two families will never end. A Kikuyu aphorism states that the brideprice never ends. This underlines the purpose of the brideprice in maintaining the clan/family bond. Other ceremonies, involving a goat slaughter, sharing of the meat, and a traditional liquor between the clans, reinforce this bonding. While the brideprice ceremonies differ from one tribe to another, the principle and purpose remain the same. Among the social elite, the primary function may be the economic benefit, but for most Kenyans this is secondary. (*End of update by P. M. Kariuki*)]

If a marriage is not successful, the bride wealth is to be returned. Kenyan men marry at a later age than women, in part because of the burden of bride wealth. In Kenya, however, difficulties in acquiring bride wealth do not prevent marriage as it has in neighboring Uganda, and the Kenyan government continues to support the practice. Brideprice is a further indication that marriage is primarily seen as the alliance of families rather than an interpersonal commitment based on love. Marriage is cemented by the bride wealth, giving a large number of the bride's family a material stake in the perseverance of the marriage, a form of marital insurance.

## Sexual Behavior and Relationships of Single Adults

This area of life has undergone great change. In traditional society, male youths became warriors after initiation, protecting the tribe and its herds. With this function lost, unmarried youths have no clear position in the kinship system. Those fortunate enough to pass rigorous examinations usually attend boarding schools, separated from the influence of their extended families. This has had disastrous results for identity, producing alarming rates of promiscuity, premarital pregnancy, and AIDS. Substantial numbers of women in the university and professional schools drop out because of pregnancy, a tremendous economic loss for the country and a major force holding back the advancement of women. A 1988 government study estimated that 400 to 500 women drop out of normal schools each year because of pregnancy. Pregnancy screening is now a condition for admission to teachers' colleges, and random screening is conducted among students after admission.

Working-class youths suffer similar dislocation. About 90% of young people terminate schooling by the end of Standard Eight, around age 14. [*Update 1997*: While the 90% figure just cited seems high to me, it is clear that the average age of terminating education varies from region to region. Today, the higher percentage of young people end their education by the end of form four (high school) and fewer by the end of Standard Eight (grade or elementary school). In the central region where I worked as education secretary for seven years, the majority ended their education with the completion of high school. (*End of update by P. M. Kariuki*)]

Where traditional initiation has lapsed, circumcision of boys takes place in a clinic or by bribing a clinic worker to perform the surgery at home. Girls' circumcision is now illegal in Kenya. The sexual information imparted at initiation is not given, and sex education is dominated by peers. Youths have evolved an argot of Kiswahili known as "Sheng," a street language seldom understood by adults. Kiswahili has a very restricted, even prudish, sexual vocabulary, but Sheng is rich in sexual slang.

Huge populations live in massive slum areas surrounding Nairobi and a few other major towns, and these have become breeding grounds for prostitution, venereal disease, and sexual abuse. Radically altered social conditions have shattered traditional mores in the cities, while providing no alternative social controls.

## Marriage and Family

Most Kenyan societies are patrilinear, meaning that descent is reckoned in the father's line and authority over children rests with the father. In matrilinear societies, children are in the descent group of their mothers, but under the headship of the males in that line. The only significant implication of this presently is in marriage. In matrilinear societies, males are limited in their search for a wife, since they will bear responsibility for children in their sisters' families.

Matrilinear groups usually also practice levirate marriage, in which a man must take his brother's widow and children as his own. If the dead man has left no children, the brother may father children in the dead man's name. This aspect of African traditional law has been accepted into Kenyan jurisprudence in a contentious case involving a deceased Luo lawyer whose widow, from a prominent Kikuyu family, refused to accept Luo traditional law. When she lost the case, the brother's family seized the body to bury it in traditional fashion. By refusing to attend this ceremony, or to accept her brother-in-law as her new husband, she was regarded as divorced, and the deceased was buried as an unmarried man.

Of the five recognized forms of marriage in Kenyan law, three are monogamous—Christian, civil, and Hindu marriages. Islamic marriages are potentially polygynous, and African customary marriages are polygynous. Although the precise word for marriages of single husband/multiple wives is "polygyny," Africans use the broader term "polygamy," and it will be so used here.

## Polygamy

A man may take junior wives only if he is able to support them, which limits polygamy. Bride wealth alone inhibits polygamy, but the increasing cost of educating children is equally daunting. A man may take a second wife as a display of wealth or prominence, to provide an assistant in farm work for the first wife, or to begin another family. Each wife has to have living quarters for herself and her children. In practice, men arrange a small plot of land that the wife works to support the children.

A polygynous husband is expected to be sexually active with all his wives. In some groups, she is entitled to a visit between each menstrual period. More commonly in the rural areas, a man will sleep with his wives in rotation, several weeks at a time.

In contemporary society, the husband may take a job in the city, and visit his wife or wives from time to time. It is not uncommon today for a man to live apart from his legal wives for many years in this way.

In some cases, one or more wives may live on the *shamba*, or garden plot, while another stays in the city, caring for her husband. In addition, many men will take a "city wife," a form of concubinage in which the man supports the woman in the city while not having a legal relationship with her. Many wives living on the *shamba* prefer this to another legal wife or the probability of her husband's resorting to prostitutes. Children born to a "city wife" are the father's, and are raised by his wife.

Polygamous marriages were never in the majority, and today are declining under economic pressures. At the same time, other less-formal arrangements have become common. These include the phenomenon of the "city wife" and polyandrous mistresses. This latter arrangement involves several urban men who jointly support a woman. None of them live with her, but she shares a sexual relationship with each. In one case known to the author, one man paid the woman's rent, another her food bills, and a third paid for her clothing. Her arrangement was known to her peers since she held a professional position, and she was not regarded as a prostitute. Any children born of such arrangements are regarded as fatherless. [*Update 1997*: I am not aware of this polyandrous relationship involving a wife openly maintaining a sexual relationship with two or more men. However, a wife or mistress may have sexual relationships with more than one man for the purpose of obtaining money from each. When the men eventually learn about the multiple relationships, the result is a breakup that may escalate with a thorough beating of the woman or fighting between the men involved. (*End of update by P. M. Kariuki*)]

In the tradition, a marriage must be fruitful. The advanced stages of elderhood are marked by fathering children, having them come to the age of initiation, and having grandchildren. Among the Kisii, an impotent husband could recruit an *omosoi nyomba*, literally "warmer of the house," to impregnate his wife. He was preferably chosen from descendents of the same grandfather, and any children are the husband's heirs, not the biological father's. A childless widow could also make the same arrangement.

Since childbearing is such a central condition of sexuality, female orgasm is not sought in itself. Nevertheless, it is approved and acceptable. Male orgasm, however, is a sign of potency, and men will seek sexual relief even when abstaining from intercourse. Abstinence is observed from the time pregnancy is obvious until some time after birth, and during menstruation. During this period, if a man has only one wife, he may engage in other forms of sex, including fellatio. Kikuyu men, conditioned to breast stimulation, often center on this activity.

An interesting birth practice is found among the Luo, who are Nilotic and not Bantu. Several days after parturition, when a woman is to leave the birth hut with the newborn, her husband must have intercourse with her. Before this act, she may have no contact with anyone who has had intercourse, including midwives or relatives. To do otherwise would afflict the child with *chira*, a spiritual curse resulting in the child's death or the parents' sterility.

## [*Wife Inheritance*

[*Update 2003*: In August 2000, an Anglican bishop in west Kenya called on the women belonging to his church to reject *joter*, a widespread African tradition with some similarities to the Levirate Law, which in biblical times required the brother of a married man who died without a male heir to have sexual intercourse with the widow to provide the dead brother with an heir. In the African tradition, the widow becomes the wife of another member of her deceased husband's family. The term *joter* may be used to mean "wife inheritance," or it may refer to the male relative who inherits a widow. *Joter* is traditional among the Luo people of Nyanza Province of western Kenya. The Luo people are often polygamous, so several widows may be inherited by a single male family member. Another element of this tradition is the practice of holding a "cleansing" ritual, in which the widow has sex with an outsider before being given to her brother-in-law or other family member. The bishop called for creation of a new ritual of "symbolic inheritance," which would transfer responsibility for the support of the widow to a male relative without giving him sexual access to the widowed wife. *Joter* and other patterns of multiple sexual partners are, along with female circumcision and "salt cuts," a factor in the heterosexual spread of HIV/AIDS.

[Some males, seeking to profit from taking on an extra wife or two, are now becoming professional *Joters*, with offices where they advertise themselves for prospective clients (widows) in return for a small fee. Most of these men now demand payment to *inherit*. Because of this, some widows now demand that these *Joters* undergo a blood test for HIV first before they pay them.

[An early 2003 Human Rights Watch report condemned the traditional African practice of wife inheritance, which is common throughout Kenya, and extends far and wide in sub-Saharan Africa, in which a widow is transferred to a male relative of her deceased husband. Typically, the new husband takes control of the property with or without the consent of the widow.

[Traditionally, according to the report, wife inheritance ensured that the extended family would take care of widows. But critics maintain that it strips women of their property rights and exposes them to sexually transmitted diseases like AIDS. "Wife inheritance is often portrayed as an act of generosity, in that the widow will have a man to 'look after' her and confer the legitimacy of being in a male-headed household. But men clearly benefit, not just from their inherited wife's labor and childbearing potential, but also from the property the deceased husband leaves behind."

[The report found that widows have little recourse to retain family property after the death of their spouses or as a result of separation or divorce. Taking their claims to the judicial system is costly, and judges, relying more on tradition than law, do not necessarily side with the women. "It should be remembered that a wife is married into the husband's clan," a Kenyan judge ruled in a 1997 separation case. "The matrimonial home, in most cases, lies within the clan land. It would, therefore, not be in keeping with our culture for the husband to be made to vacate the clan land for the wife." Husbands may orally will their property to their widows, but they are often reluctant to put this in a written legal form, because they might hasten their death. Researchers for the Human Rights Watch report described many women who found relatives descending on their homes immediately after the burial of their husbands to take everything the widow owned.

[The report called on the government of President Mwai Kibaki, which has pledged better treatment of women, to overhaul the legal system so that women have the same rights to property as men. The report recommends that judges and police officers undergo training on the issue and that a legal aid system be set up to assist destitute victims (Lacey 2003). (*End of update by B. Opiyo-Omolo*)]

## *Sexuality and the Disabled and Aged*

The Kenyan government estimates that 5% of the population is physically disabled, mostly with deformed limbs and eye afflictions resulting from poor birth-delivery conditions. No studies of the sexual adaptations of this group have been reported, but the disabled can be observed in all types of relationships, married and otherwise.

Since childbearing so defines a married woman's importance, later sex is not spoken of. In at least one tribe, parental sex was supposed to stop when the first child was married. A wealthy man might take a young junior wife when his first wife reaches menopause, causing him to cease having sex with her.

## *Incidence of Oral and Anal Sex*

Vaginal intercourse is the norm for marital sexual activity, with little foreplay. Anal sex is associated with homosexual rape, not unknown during civil strife, and both anal and oral sex are culturally abhorrent, though fellatio is acceptable in a few cultures during periods of abstinence, such as the lactation period.

## 6. Homoerotic, Homosexual, and Bisexual Behaviors

### A. Children and Adolescents

Certain types of same-sex activity were tolerated in tribal tradition, but only as childish behaviors unworthy of an initiate. In tribes where initiation involves long periods of separation from female contact along with powerful emphasis on male group bonding (Maasai), situational homosexuality is not uncommon. When limited to mutual self-pleasuring, it is regarded as merely unmanly. Oral or anal intercourse can, however, result in expulsion from the age set, severe beatings, and disgrace. One finds some nonpenetrative homosexual behavior among Maasai *askaris* (guards) who have migrated to Nairobi or the coast.

Urban poverty has created an underclass of abandoned street youth, almost all male, ranging in age from 7 to the late teens. These "parking boys" survive by protecting parking spots, begging, petty crime, and scrounging for garbage. Though the older protect the younger, situational homosexuality is normative.

### B. Adults

Self-identified gay Africans hardly exist in Kenya, although homosexual activity is not unknown. There are no homosexual gender roles, such as the *berdache* in Native American societies, or the effeminate *gà 'tuhy* of Thailand. Because homosexuality profoundly violates the traditional social pattern, it has been tabooed to the point that subcultural social norms have never developed.

Kenya has retained many aspects of the colonial British penal code, and homosexuality continues to be illegal as a "crime against nature." It is regarded with disdain and disgust by the majority of the population, and persons arrested for homosexual activity are treated harshly by the police. In some traditions (e.g., Kikuyu), homosexuality could be punished by death.

Kenyans discriminate against same-sex behaviors. Self-pleasuring with a partner or spouse present is regarded as childish, but relatively harmless, particularly between friends. While socially and legally tabooed, playing the inserter role in same-sex acts does not define a man as homosexual. Accepting insertion, especially in anal intercourse, is regarded with extreme disgust.

There are no gay venues nor any overt gay presence in Kenya. A small white, predominantly British, homosexual society exists in Nairobi. Most expatriate white homosexuals avoid African partners because of the drastic consequences, and confine themselves to sexual activity on trips to Europe.

Male prostitutes are readily available on the streets of Nairobi and Mombasa, usually catering to tourists. They are well dressed in order to be able to enter international hotels. Male prostitution serving an African clientele does not seem to exist. The prostitutes themselves are probably bisexual, many having girlfriends or wives, and consider themselves heterosexual. All religious groups abhor homosexuality and condone its complete suppression. There are no gay activist or support groups in Kenya, nor any gay publications. Foreign gay publications are proscribed.

Lesbian and bisexual relationships are either so rare or so hidden as to be unnoticeable. The "woman-to-woman" marriage discussed in Section 8 should not be confused with lesbianism, even if an occasional sexual exchange may occur.

Homosexuality is often ascribed to the coastal Swahili, Arabs, and Muslims generally as a racist slur, and the few Africans involved are said to be exploited by these groups. The sexual act in these accounts is always sodomy, which, as an image of rape and political dominance, effectively excludes mutuality in same-sex relationships. Male homosexuality is politically interpreted in terms of racist, anti-black exploitation by whites (former colonial masters) and Arabs (former slavers).

This pattern, both expatriate and African, is typical of sub-Saharan Africa except for the Republic of South Africa. Although the dramatic AIDS pandemic has generated interest in research on same-sex behavior, almost no such research has been done in Africa. A 1995 study indicated that such research is almost unknown in sub-Saharan Africa. In Kenya, all survey research designs must be approved by the Office of the President, a sufficient damper on any same-sex studies. The National AIDS Programme has no literature or outreach to homosexuals in Kenya.

The imposition of Western social notions of homosexual/gay patterns tends to obscure any true picture of same-sex activities in Africa. To say that there is no organized gay community in Kenya does not mean that there is no homosexual activity. There are cliques of men who are predominantly or exclusively homosexual, but who limit their sexual activities to their acquaintance group. In this sense, in urban concentrations such as Nairobi and Mombasa, these serve as homosexual analogs to age-set groups. Occasionally, one finds a group organized as a brotherhood or fraternity, a form of homosexual support group providing casual, although not promiscuous, pairings. A 1995 survey indicated that violent assault was either likely or possible for homosexuals in Africa—at 69%, the highest in the Third World. This helps to explain the closed nature of homosexual society in Kenya and other African countries.

## 7. Gender Diversity and Transgender Issues

Gender-conflicted persons are regarded as homosexuals and treated as criminals. Suppression is so complete as to make such persons, to the extent that they exist, invisible.

Kenyan traditional societies did not provide for special gender roles. During the independence movement, sodomy was practiced by some in the Mau Mau society, with the sole intent of making the participants ritually unclean and thus unable to participate in normal society. This is the only ritual use of homosexual behavior known.

## 8. Significant Unconventional Sexual Behaviors

### A. Coercive Sex

*Sexual Abuse*

Child sexual abuse seems to be increasing, and is part of a generalized child abuse resulting from pressures of social change and loss of the holding power of traditional taboos. An alarming new development, however, has appeared with the rise of AIDS. This is the exploitation of pubescent girls by older men, hoping to find inexperienced partners who are unlikely to be infected. The image of the prosperous "sugar daddy" is a stock figure in Kenyan humor, accompanied by his *ndogo-ndogo* (literally, "little-little").

*Incest*

Incest is as socially condemned in Kenya as in the West, and seems to be rare. The Kisii sometimes excuse it because of drunkenness, but in other societies, it would be severely punished by mob justice. In some cases, children conceived incestuously would be killed.

## Pedophilia

True pedophilia, involving sexual contact between adults and prepubescent children, is rare in Kenya, scorned, and severely punished. Girls between 12 and 14 are often objects of older men's attentions, however, even though this is socially disapproved. Peasant fathers may accept bride wealth from men seeking a young wife, and this is not regarded as selling one's daughter. The government has campaigned against the practice, but has not been able to eradicate it in rural areas. In one district in 1988, only one girl completed Standard Eight, all the rest of her class having been married before completing elementary school.

## Sexual Harassment

The forms of sexual harassment found in Western society are probably as common among the professional class of Kenyans as elsewhere. There is also a serious problem of sexual exploitation of schoolgirls by male teachers.

Poverty forces many rural girls as young as 10, to be employed as housemaids and child minders in middle-class homes. Besides the economic exploitation they endure, sexual harassment by males in the household is common. Being from rural areas, often speaking only a tribal language, these girls have no power to resist sexual advances. If they become pregnant, they are cast out and often forced into prostitution.

## Rape

Reports of rape have been increasing in Kenya, although exact statistics do not exist. Practically speaking, only violent stranger rape is acknowledged as criminal. Neither Kenyan law nor general attitudes accept the concept of marital rape. Rape of such subordinate women as prostitutes or housemaids is regarded very lightly.

Sexual exploitation of girls in boarding schools and universities is common. A young woman who enters into a social relationship with a male student is expected to be available sexually. Because women have been conditioned to serve men and accept their orders from childhood, refusal of sexual overtures is difficult. In 1991, incidents involving mass rapes in secondary schools, in one case leading to several deaths, brought international publicity leading to government attempts at reform.

[*Update 2003*: The concept of sexual harassment is not Kenyan, and there is no vocabulary for sexual harassment in the local languages. So many times, this will be swept under the rug as the issue arises. Yet, there are so many unwelcome sexual behaviors, insults, remarks and jokes, unwanted physical contacts, requests, and even threats that create daily discrimination against so many women, particularly in Kenyan universities. In these universities, harassment occurs all the time. For example, women students are being groped and fondled as they queue for meals at the cafeteria. The result is that women students virtually end up retreating into their residence halls, and hence, their social life on campus is curtailed. They then cook and eat from their rooms, use the library sparingly, attend classes when it is an absolutely necessary, and avoid social functions on campus. Sexual guidelines do not exist on these campuses. (*End of update by B. Opiyo-Omolo*)]

## B. Prostitution

Female prostitution is widespread and patronized by both tourists and Kenyans. Technically illegal, it is tolerated by the authorities. Prostitutes tend to come from the less-educated class of women, including single mothers, junior wives driven out of their homes by first wives, abandoned girls, and economically distressed women. A working-class prostitute earns the equivalent of one U.S. dollar

per encounter, less in the poorer slums. Under these conditions, by 1990, almost 85% of Nairobi prostitutes tested positive for HIV. With weak economic inducement for remaining in prostitution, however, church programs such as Maria House in Nairobi teach cottage-industry and market skills that make it possible for women to earn a comparable living outside the sex trade.

Despite Kenyan government disapproval, sex tourism is promoted by German operators, including a "Sun and Sex Safari" that includes an antibiotic injection on return! Sex tourism in Kenya has never approached the exploitive level found in Thailand and the Philippines, but it is an ever-present element.

Male prostitution is a phenomenon of sex tourism, and is found mostly in coastal resort areas, such as Mombasa and Malindi.

## C. Pornography

All forms of erotica and sexually oriented publications are illegal in Kenya and not available for sale. This includes publications featuring nudity, which is culturally offensive.

## D. Female Circumcision

Female circumcision is practiced by Nilotic and some Bantu peoples. [*Update 2003*: Among the groups that practice female circumcision, it is thought that the procedure benefits girls. There is a widespread belief among those who practice it that ancestors will curse girls who have not undergone the procedures. Many believe that the cut reduces female promiscuity, ensuring virginity at marriage and marital fidelity. (*End of update by B. Opiyo-Omolo*)] It still continues widely among the Somali and Turkhana, and surreptitiously among others. Its purpose is to reduce female sexual pleasure, and make women docile to their husbands and less likely to engage in adultery. Women not circumcised are referred to by traditionalists as "unclean" or as "prostitutes." As a Kikuyu girls' circumcision song concludes, "Now we can make love, for our sex is clean."

The Kikuyu, Maasai, and Meru only removed the clitoris (clitoridectomy) during initiation at puberty. The Turkhana and Somali practice pharaonic circumcision, removing the clitoris and the labia minora. The wound is then sutured (infibulation), leaving a tiny hole for menstrual flow. This is often inspected at betrothal as a sign of virginity. Pharaonic circumcision is performed on girls between the ages of 3 and 7.

The Anglican Church strongly opposed female circumcision, and it has been illegal since the colonial period. The campaign reached a crisis in 1929, when the Church of Scotland Mission made opposition a condition of employment and school entry. This politicized the question and gave rise to the Kikuyu resistance, and the independent church and school movements. In 1930, an elderly female missionary died after rape, forced circumcision, and mutilation. Jomo Kenyatta, the Father of Kenya, made resistance a cornerstone of liberation, declaring that female circumcision "symbolizes the unification of the whole tribal organization."

After independence, Kenyatta permitted female circumcision, but President Moi again outlawed it in 1982 after the deaths of 14 girls. He reaffirmed this in 1990 after a widely publicized tribal ceremony. There are indications that the practice is waning.

[*Update 2003*: The practice is now illegal in Kenya, even though there are people who still practice it secretly in some communities. The government is now cooperating with a dynamic and broad-gauged campaign against the practice across Kenya being waged by NGOs and donor organizations in those areas where this is still being practiced illegally. There are now organizations that specifically provide protection to women or girls who wish to avoid this practice, for example, the Kenya Maendeleo Ya Wanawake, Federation of Kenyan Women Lawyers (FIDA), and Coalition on Violence Against Women in Kenya (COVAW), among others. Some churches and schools do offer occasional refuge to victims and potential victims of this practice. (*End of update by B. Opiyo-Omolo*)]

### [E. "Dry Sex" and "Wet Sex"

[*Comment 2003*: In Africa, as in cultures elsewhere, there are certain sexual practices and topics that Africans simply do not discuss or acknowledge with non-Africans, because they are very sensitive, sometimes taboo, and many times very racially charged. Even within an individual tribal culture, some sexual topics and behaviors are not open for discussion between men and women, or between children and their parents. Unless one lives within a native community and becomes very, very close to the people, Africans balk at discussing these issues, and "dry sex" is one such practice.

["Dry sex" is not something new. It is a well-established and more or less widespread practice in various subequatorial African cultures. It is very common in Southern Africa, particularly in Zimbabwe, Zambia, Malawi, some parts of Nigeria, some parts of Uganda, in Southern Sudan, and even in Kenya and Botswana. The only difference is in what these women use for drying up their vaginas. However, you will never hear about these practices, unless you are a woman who lives within the community for some extended time and the women learn to trust you.

[In the northwest part of Tanzania and neighboring regions, "wet sex" is widely known and practiced. "Wet sex" consists of foreplay, where there is intense stimulation by the male partner on the woman's labia and clitoral regions. This stimulation results in copious production of secretions (thought to come from Bartholin's glands). People talk about it openly, sometimes mixed with a sense of humor and intertribe jokes. Some researchers have blamed this practice for the high incidence and prevalence of HIV and STDs. The implications of this kind of information for action plans (resource inputs and sociocultural issues) are enormous. Now that these behaviors have been brought into public attention, a well-thought-out survey that is representative of different segments of the populations becomes essential for an effective public health policy (Tanzania Personal communication 2003).

[In March 2003, when Dr. Francoeur, editor of this *Encyclopedia*, inquired whether "dry sex" was observed in Botswana, Dr. Ian Taylor replied; "'Dry sex' is common in Botswana as well and leads to vaginal tears and lesions which help spread HIV/AIDS, it is true."

[Personally, as I was growing up in the rural town of Kisumu, Kenya, there were many practices and myths that we were taught by some of our peers and even older women that we were to do to attract men. Some of them were good, but some of those things I do not feel comfortable talking about to this day. We were told that if you want your breasts to grow fast, you had to rub a certain poisonous leaf on your breast or let boys touch them, so that you could have them grow faster and more round. Many African men like women with large buttocks as well. As a result of this, many girls tried to do whatever they could to have big buttocks. One technique to accent the buttocks was to tie their belt so tight that the lower parts of their body stood out.

[Even today, many African men have three to five wives. These women compete among themselves to be the best cook for the man of the house, or the best in bed. This is obvious and was determined by where the man slept most of the time. Some women consult traditional healers and witch-doctors, who sell them love potions so they can out-do their co-wives. Some of these love potions come in the form of soil mixed with baboon urine, or even salt, that women use before they have sexual intercourse with their husband. It is the traditional healers who teach these women about the importance of drying their vaginas as a way to please their husbands. These concoctions also make their vaginas swell and become very hot, making it tighter so that when a man inserts his penis, he feels "big" and therefore, a "real man."

[Until recently, very few people knew about these practices. Unless one grew up in the village or became very, very close to the people, you can never know what goes on. As the HIV/AIDS epidemic devastates subequatorial Africa, and non-Africans have become aware of female genital mutilation, taboos about other sensitive sexual practices have weakened. In 2000, Mark Schoofs discussed the implications of dry sex in the spread of AIDS in his eight-part Pulitzer Prize-winning report on "AIDS: The Agony of Africa. Death and the Second Sex." In the chapter on Nigeria, Uwem Edimo Esiet, a public health physician, and his wife Nike Esiet, M.P.H, (Harvard), a former public relations officer for the Society for Women and AIDS, have raised the issue of "salt cuts." But these new insights into the complexity of the HIV/AIDS epidemic only came after considerable trust was achieved. (*End of comment by B. Opiyo-Omolo*)]

### F. Woman-to-Woman Marriage

Some 30 Bantu societies provide for marriage between two women, including a dozen Kenyan ethnic groups. Among these are several large tribes—the Kisii, Nandi, Wakamba, and Kikuyu. In other parts of Africa, this was characteristic of status women, such as royals or political leaders, but in East Africa, it ordinarily represents a surrogate female husband who replaces a male kinsman as jural "father." The wife may bear children for her husband, in whose clan line they then belong. In other cases, women marry women to achieve economic independence, and brideprice is paid. These autonomous female husbands are accepted as men in male economic roles. This dual-female marriage is economic, and illustrates the separation of sex and gender in African societies (Amadiume 1987).

There is no evidence of lesbianism in any of these marriages, and the wife is often provided with a male sexual partner to raise the children. She is not permitted to refuse him when he visits the household for this purpose. The husband figure is henceforth forbidden to have sex with a man, because this would constitute homosexuality because of her legally male status. She may become an elder, and among the Nandi, may attend circumcisions, forbidden for females.

Although Westernization has made female marriages embarrassing, they were confirmed in customary law by the Kenyan courts in 1986, and are subject to divorce legislation. [*Update 2003*: In January 2000, a Kenyan court granted an 80-year-old tribal woman a divorce from her wife on the grounds of cruelty and molesting her daughter. In 2002, a Kenyan woman went to court, demanding the right to inherit a piece of land belonging to her deceased "husband"—another woman. Grace Wanjiru Ndungu, 70, was told by her "husband's" relatives to leave the farm, on which she had been living with her children for more than 40 years. Ms. Ndungu claimed she was a widow, and the only difference is that her husband happened to be a woman. Traditional inheritance law, her attorney argued, holds that in the event of death, the woman like Ms. Ndungu and her children are entitled to inherit the property of the dead woman "husband." The lawyer admitted that his client faced a tough legal battle, because this would be the first time such an argument had been heard in a Western-style court. (*End of update by R. T. Francoeur*)]

### G. Bestiality

Among pastoral groups and nomads, occasional instances of bestiality take place. When they involve uncircumcised youth, they are punished with a beating. Initiated males are treated more harshly. They are so disgraced after the public judgment of the elders that they would most likely go to a city. For a married man, bestiality is sometimes punished by death by mob justice.

## 9. Contraception, Abortion, and Population Planning

### A. Contraception

[*Comment 2003*: Only about one in every five women in Kenya uses at least one method of contraception. This means that a large number of women are open to the risk of unsafe pregnancy. (*End of comment by B. Opiyo-Omolo*)]

Foreign birth-control agencies cooperate with the government population-control program. Condoms are distributed at hospitals and clinics, supplied in large numbers by the U.S. Agency for International Development (USAID) and by such nongovernmental organizations (NGOs) as the United Kingdom's Marie Stopes Institute. The government has forbidden their distribution in schools, and school contraceptive education is severely limited. Condom use runs counter to the common taboo forbidding a wife to touch her husband's penis with her hand.

[*Comment 2003*: There is a strong belief in Kenya that condoms should be used only in sexual contacts outside marriage. The idea of using condoms with a marriage partner is rejected by most men since "Condom use in marriage suggests unfaithfulness, which leads to mistrust." (*End of comment by B. Opiyo-Omolo*)] Because of cultural resistance to condom use, Natural Family Planning (NFP), using the Billings Method, has had some modest acceptance by combining NFP with traditional periods of abstinence, such as during lactation. Operating throughout the country in both mother tongues and Kiswahili, NFP has promotion and training teams made up of unmarried youth and married couples practicing NFP.

Contraceptive methods requiring medical intervention, IUDs and the pill, are beyond the means of most Kenyans, and limited to the elite and expatriates.

### B. Teenage Unmarried Pregnancies

Having a baby outside marriage is unacceptable in much of Kenyan society where tribal customs are very strong. Teenage pregancies reported among schoolgirls between 1985 and 1990 ranged from 6,633 to over 11,000. These rough figures of only a small segment of the adolescent population indicate a serious problem.

### C. Abortion

Abortion is illegal unless the mother's life is at risk or unless two doctors certify that the pregnant woman is mentally unstable and incapable of caring for a child. It is likely to remain so in the foreseeable future. Former president Moi strongly disapproves of abortion, and no religious tradition accepts it. Under the law, anyone convicted of assisting in an abortion or killing of an unborn child can face 14 years in prison.

With abortion illegal and the widespread practical ignorance about contraception—and cultural proscriptions that prohibit its use—thousands of Kenyan young women and teenagers are forced every year to turn to illegal and unsafe abortions, which are a lucrative underground business, especially in the sprawling squatter slums of Nairobi.

Statistics are unavailable, but Nairobi's Kenyatta National Hospital with 2,000 beds treats 40 cases of incomplete abortion daily. About 50% of its gynecological admissions are because of complications from induced and incomplete abortions. Dr. Khama Rogo, a gynecologist at the private Agha Khan Hospital, has estimated that at least 187,500 illegal abortions were performed in Kenya in 1993. One third of Kenya's maternal deaths are because of unsafe abortions. With an extensive hospital and clinic system throughout Kenya, this represents only a tiny fraction of botched abortions. [*Update 1997*: Kenya has both government-run and church-managed nursing schools. While the church-run schools do not permit abortion, the state schools require that nurses record and document how many abortifacients they have inserted in patients to pass their licensing examination. In one state school I visited, the principal informed me that if the student nurses do not do this, irrespective of what they believe, they fail the examination. In the same school, a number of back-door abortions were carried out by the students for money. (*End of update by P. M. Kariuki*)]

The Marie Stopes Center, a grassroots organization with 10 clinics, is one of the few to provide counseling and abortion under the mental health provisions. These clinics also provide family planning and medical care (Lorch 1995).

### D. Population Control Efforts

Kenya's population growth rate is among the highest in the world, currently between 3.8 and 4% annually, at the current rate doubling every 17 years. With only 13% of its land arable, there is considerable population pressure. The government endorses population control as a national goal, and foreign-aid donors commonly demand active population-control programs as a condition for full assistance.

Kenya has succeeded in increasing contraceptive use to 27% of married couples, as compared with 10% throughout sub-Saharan Africa. Lifetime number of births per woman went from 7.7 in 1984 to 6.7 in 1989, but this still remains higher than the 6.4 figure for sub-Saharan Africa generally.

[*Update 1997*: The idea of population control has been unpopular among Kenyans for several reasons. Traditionally, children are embraced as a great blessing: They continue the family and clan lineage and also take care of the aged. The majority of Kenyans are firm in their Muslim or Christian faith, and all the religious sects have worked very hard to decry the Western methods of population control, which are viewed with great suspicion. Most Kenyans view the arguments for population control as overstretched and many times exaggerated. Most of the land is underutilized, and the real solution to the country's economic ills is not to reduce the population growth, but to provide good political governance and a sound economic system. With proper government and economy, Kenya can support its current growth rate. (*End of update by P. M. Kariuki*)]

## 10. Sexually Transmitted Diseases and HIV/AIDS

### A. Sexually Transmitted Diseases

Syphilis and gonorrhea are widespread among certain ethnic groups (e.g., the Maasai). Nomadic tribes are heavily infected, as are urban prostitutes, street youth living rough, and the residents of the most degraded squatter slums in Nairobi. Antibiotic treatment is available at all hospitals and clinics, and mobile clinics treat nomadic peoples, who are especially at risk. [*Comment 2003*: However, most people do not seek treatment because of the stigma attached to the STDs. (*End of comment by B. Opiyo-Omolo*)]

## B. HIV/AIDS

Because it borders Uganda and Tanzania, two countries with an extremely high incidence of AIDS, Kenya is vulnerable to AIDS. Since tourism is the greatest hard-currency earner, however, the government downplays the incidence of the disease. The first AIDS case was diagnosed in 1984, but the first death ascribed to AIDS was listed in 1984. In 1992, a powerful party leader argued in Parliament that "it is not in the national interest to release alarming AIDS figures." The Director of Medical Services in the Ministry of Health was dismissed for revealing that 700,000 Kenyans were diagnosed HIV-positive, with 40,000 confirmed AIDS cases, in an estimated population of 28 million. Current (1994) estimates are 800,000 HIV-positive Kenyans, including 30,000 children; an estimated 100,000 have AIDS. Dr. Frank Plummer of the University of Manitoba, who has done fieldwork in Nairobi for several years, calculates the infection rate among urban youth at 12% (see also Section 3, Knowledge and Education about Sexuality). The numbers are about equally divided between males and females, and heterosexual contact is the primary source of infection.

In Kenya, AIDS programs are based on a threefold attitude toward the significance of the disease. It is seen simultaneously as a health problem, a threat to the tourist industry, and as an insult to national pride.

Traditional initiation customs encouraged safe-sex practices among youths and limited intercourse outside marriage. With Westernization and urbanization, these controls have lapsed, however, and promiscuity is widespread. Condoms are readily available in the urban areas, but most traditions do not accept them. Christian and Islamic groups both disapprove, and in 1991, a prominent Muslim leader was disgraced when a condom was found in his luggage during a search by militant Islamic youth. The influence of religious groups is high, especially as Former president Moi was an evangelical Christian. When attempts were made to use television for safe-sex promotion, he personally stopped them. [*Comment 2003*: The use of condoms to prevent HIV/AIDS among Catholic faithful in Kenya is still out of question. They insist and believe in total abstinence for the unmarried and total faithfulness between spouses. In August 2002, the Anglican Church challenged the stigma associated with HIV as "a sin before God and humankind." They thus ended the silence surrounding HIV/AIDS by supporting the use of condoms in the fight against AIDS. (*End of comment by B. Opiyo-Omolo*)]

Despite political misgivings, the Ministry of Health has embarked on an extensive AIDS-education program since 1990. Devised by a national committee that has been relatively free of political pressure, it has centered on educating basic health providers and community leaders. This includes professionals such as physicians and nurses, but also herbalists, midwives, ritual circumcisers, and "market mamas," the influential local traders. Consequently, grassroots understanding of the causes of AIDS is high. For the future elites, use is made of the national service period, which is a condition for admission to higher education. Sex and AIDS education (with condom distribution) is included, and given in mother tongues. Studies done by the Marie Stopes Institute have shown that even university-educated youth respond to safer-sex education when it is given in their mother tongue, even though they may be fluent in English and Swahili.

Blood supplies have been screened for HIV since 1985. Despite this, as a further reassurance for the skittish tourist industry, special safari insurance was introduced, providing for air evacuation of injured tourists to Europe if necessary.

The implications of AIDS are very serious for the tourist industry. In 1987, the United Kingdom Ministry of Defense banned holiday use of recreational facilities on the Kenya coast to British troops. Resultant publicity in Europe caused extensive cancellations at resort areas, with loss of 20 to 50% of all bookings that season. Because of the catastrophic effect of this on the economy, the AIDS question is a delicate political issue.

Kenya, like many African countries, has been deeply offended by speculative Western theories that AIDS originated in Africa. This is ascribed to racism and colonialism, and has prompted denials and a defensive attitude towards AIDS and AIDS research. Conversely, it has spurred support for research leading to an "African solution." The government has strongly supported the work of Dr. Davy Koech of the Kenya Medical Research Institute (KEMRI) on oral alpha interferon (Kemron). Unfortunately, when Kemron was tested by the World Health Organization (WHO) and a Canadian NGO, Dr. Koech's positive results could not be replicated.

U.S. Agency for International Development (USAID) projections in 1993 show Kenya with 1.2 million cases of HIV/AIDS by 1995, 1.7 million by 2000, and 2 million by 2005. The government has acknowledged the problem and admitted that its educational program has not brought about behavioral changes. What seems to have created the crisis mentality in the government is the realization that HIV/AIDS is disproportionately high (and rising) among the best-paid workers, the base of the middle class. This includes urban business and long-haul truck drivers.

The Kenyan government healthcare budget for 1993 was $60 million in a falling economy, with 20% earmarked for AIDS prevention. Of this, Kenya contributed only $77,000, the rest coming from foreign donors. The United States doubled its $2 million contribution in 1994, but Western pressures to reduce foreign assistance make this source an unreliable one for the future.

There has been a recent shift in attitudes in the national leadership. Both former president Moi and current President Mwai Kibaki and his Health Minister, Honorable Mrs. Charity Ngilu, now regularly address AIDS prevention, although they do not speak out with the candidness of President Yoweri Museveni of neighboring Uganda, who openly endorses condom use. Although condoms are available in clinics, the government has not yet allowed them to be distributed to the young in schools. Since the great majority of high school and university students live in dormitories, this effectively removes the largest at-risk group from condom education.

According to a July 1996 report at the 11th International Conference on AIDS, Kenya ranked fifth in the world with 1.1 million people infected with HIV.

[*Update 2002*: UNAIDS Epidemiological Assessment: HIV information among antenatal clinic attendees has been available from Kenya since the mid-1980s. Nairobi and Mombasa are the major urban areas. In the major urban areas, HIV prevalence among antenatal clinic attendees tested increased from 2% in 1985 to 19% in 1995. In Nairobi, HIV prevalence increased from 2.7% in 1987 to 6.6% in 1990. By 1995, it had reached 25%. In 1999, HIV prevalence among antenatal clinic attendees in Nairobi was 17%. HIV prevalence among antenatal clinic attendees in Mombasa increased from 10.2% in 1990 to 16.5% in 1993 and then 17.8% in 1998. In Kiwi, a periurban area of Mombasa, HIV infection rates doubled from 12.2% in 1989 to 24.1% in 1995; in 1999, the rate was 23%. Information on age-specific HIV prevalences is not available.

[Outside the major urban areas, HIV information became available in 1988 from Machakos and from Kajiado in 1989. By 1990, 12 sentinel surveillance sites were reporting

HIV information. Among antenatal clinic attendees tested in these sentinel surveillance sites, median HIV prevalence increased from less than 1% in 1988 to 13% in 1997. In 1997, HIV prevalence ranged from 6 to 35% among 15 sentinel surveillance sites. In Kisumu, a town near the Uganda border, HIV prevalence plateaued between 1990 to 1993 at about 20%, and then shot up to 30% in 1994, 34.9% in 1997, before decreasing to 27% in 1999. In Busia, another border town, the rates increased from 17.1% in 1990 to 34% in 1999.

[Female sex workers tested in Nairobi were found with an HIV prevalence of 60.8% in 1985 and, by 1992, the rate had gone up to 85.2%. In 1993 to 95, 55.2% of sex workers tested in Mombassa were HIV-positive. HIV prevalence among male STD clinic patients tested in Nairobi increased from 16% in 1985 to 28% in 1991 to 1992, while among female STD patients, HIV prevalence increased from 33.3% in 1991 to 47.2% in 1998. In 1998, HIV prevalence among female STD clinic attendees tested in Nairobi was 29%. Nine percent of STD clinic patients tested in 1994 in Mombasa were HIV-positive.

[The estimated number of adults and children living with HIV/AIDS on January 1, 2002, were:

| | | |
|---|---|---|
| Adults ages 15-49: | 2,300,000 | (rate: 15%) |
| Women ages 15-49: | 1,400,000 | |
| Children ages 0-15: | 220,000 | |

[An estimated 190,000 adults and children died of AIDS during 2001.

[At the end of 2001, an estimated 890,000 Kenyan children under age 15 were living without one or both parents who had died of AIDS. (*End of update by the Editors*)]

## 11. Sexual Dysfunctions, Counseling, and Therapies

Professional therapy is a serious lack in Kenya. The University of Nairobi has a post-M.D. psychiatric training program, but it includes very little preparation for dealing with sexual dysfunctions, and has only a few graduates. The services of psychiatrists are also beyond the means of all but the wealthy.

Kenyan cultures exalt the dominant virile male. Erectile dysfunctions are, therefore, considered serious and deeply shameful. Impotence is often a symptom of the pressures on men from traditional backgrounds who attempt to succeed in a competitive, capitalist, and urban milieu. Successful Western therapies that involve progressive levels of sensate and sexual exploration are seldom successful, since men rarely admit impotence to their wives. Male dominance allows them to assert that they have an outside "girlfriend" and, thus, no further interest in their wives. The average Kenyan wife would not challenge this. The level of marital communication is very low.

Male self-pleasuring is regarded as a dysfunction after initiation, but an acceptable release before. It is seen as a symptom of immaturity and sexual failure, and is rarely admitted by adult men.

An American Catholic missionary group has established the Amani Counseling Center in Nairobi, where a wide spectrum of services is available on a sliding-fee scale. The most commonly reported presenting issues of a sexual nature are male impotence, sexual abuse of subordinate women (e.g., maids and students), male self-pleasuring, and fear of homosexuality. Amani also sponsors a weekly newspaper column from letters received from around the country.

The Kenyatta National Hospital has operated a sex therapy clinic one afternoon a week since 1981, treating about 30 patients a year. Presenting problems are: erectile failure, 46%; ejaculatory problems, 25%; and reduced libido, 29%.

With no licensing requirements for therapists, charlatans abound. While witchcraft is illegal and vigorously suppressed, traditional healers and herbalists advertise cures for impotence, AIDS, and homosexuality, and are eagerly sought out.

## 12. Sex Research and Advanced Professional Education

Research on sexual matters is conducted either through the Ministry of Health or the Kenyatta National Hospital. Quality surveys of adolescent sexual behavior have been done, and statistics are kept on AIDS. There are no centers engaged in sex research on a regular basis, and there are no courses at the university level on human sexuality.

Research by expatriates must be approved in advance by State House, the office of the president. This is regardless of topic, and a condition of getting an entry visa. In addition, the results of all approved research may be released only with government approval. Approval for sex research has been rare, and only when of benefit to national policy. A Canadian medical group has been allowed to study the incidence of AIDS among prostitutes.

There are graduate-level programs in counseling (United States International University—Africa, and Catholic University of East Africa), pastoral counseling (Amani Center), and psychiatry (University of Nairobi). All include courses in sexuality or marital therapy, but there is no program devoted to sexuality.

There is no professional association for sexologists, and there are no journals on sexuality in East Africa. However, a related organization, the Family Planning Private Sector Programme, is a possible source of information; address: Fifth Floor, Longonot Place, Kijabe Street, P.O. Box 46042, Nairobi, Kenya. (Phone: 254-2/224646; Fax: 254-2/230392).

## References and Suggested Readings

Amadiume, I. 1987. *Male daughters, female husbands*. Atlantic Highlands, NJ, USA: Zed Books.

CIA. 2002 (January). *The world factbook 2002*. Washington, DC: Central Intelligence Agency. Available: http://www.cia.gov/cia/publications/factbook/index.html.

Kenyan Community Abroad (KCA), P.O. Box 5635, Washington, DC 20016-5635, USA; Tel: (301) 622-0423; Fax (301) 622-0423; info@kenyansabroad.org; http://www.kenyansabroad.org.

Lacey, M. 2003 (March 5). Rights group calls for end to inheriting African wives. *The New York Times*.

Lorch, D. 1995 (June 4). Unsafe abortions become a big problem in Kenya. *The New York Times*, p. 3.

Molnos, A. 1972-73. *Cultural source materials for population planning in East Africa*. Nairobi: University of Nairobi Press. (This four-volume study contains comparative studies of 16 Kenyan ethnic groups on sex life, marriage, and pregnancy.)

Schoofs, M. 2000. AIDS: The agony of Africa. *The Village Voice* [New York, NY, USA]. (A Pulitzer Prize-winning, 8-part series.) Available: www.villagevoice.com/specials/africa/.

Stillwaggon, E. 2001 (May 21). AIDS and poverty in Africa. *The Nation*, pp. 2-25.

Tanzania. 2003 (March-May). Personal communications between Yusuf Hemed and R. T. Francoeur.

UNAIDS. 2002. *Epidemiological fact sheets by country*. Geneva, Switzerland: Joint United Nations Programme on HIV/AIDS (UNAIDS/WHO). Available: http://www.unaids.org/hivaidsinfo/statistics/fact_sheets/index_en.htm.

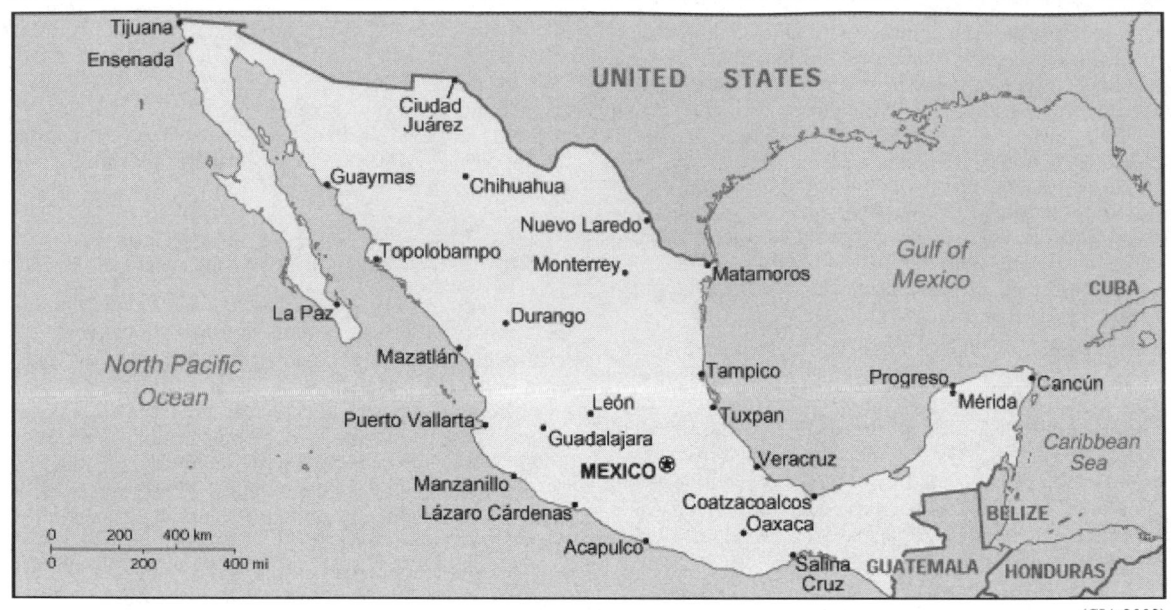

(CIA 2002)

# Mexico

## (*Estados Unidos Mexicanos*)
## (United Mexican States)

Eusebio Rubio, Ph.D.
*Updates by the Editors*

## Contents

## *Demographics and a Brief*
## *Historical Perspective*

ROBERT T. FRANCOEUR

### A. Demographics

Mexico, with the official name of United Mexican States, is a country of 761,606 square miles (1,972,550 km²) located in North America, bordered by the United States to the north, and Guatemala and Belize to the south. Mexico is bordered on the east by the Gulf of Mexico and on the west by the Pacific Ocean. It is the third-largest country in Latin America, three times the size of the state of Texas, and a republic formed by 31 states and one Federal District. Sandwiched

*Communications*: Eusebio Rubio, Ph.D., Pestalozzi 1204-705, Colonia del Valle, Mexico D.F. 03100 Mexico; eusebio@internet .com.mx, rubioa@servidor.unam.mx.

between the Sierra Madre Oriental Mountains on the west coast and the Sierra Madre Occidental Mountains on the Gulf coast is a high, dry, temperate central plateau. The coastal lowlands are tropical. About 45% of the land is arid.

In July 2002, Mexico had an estimated population of 103.4 million. (All data are July 2002 estimates from *The World Factbook 2002* (CIA 2002) unless otherwise stated.)

**Age Distribution and Sex Ratios**: *0-14 years*: 32.8% with 1.04 male(s) per female (sex ratio); *15-64 years*: 62.7% with 0.95 male(s) per female; *65 years and over*: 4.5% with 0.8 male(s) per female; *Total population sex ratio*: 0.97 male(s) to 1 female

**Life Expectancy at Birth**: *Total Population*: 71.03 years; *male*: 68.99 years; *female*: 75.21 years

**Urban/Rural Distribution**: 72% to 28%. In 2002, 20 million people lived in metropolitan Mexico City, making it the most populous city in the world.

**Ethnic Distribution**: Mestizo (Amerindian-Spanish): 60%; Amerindian or predominantly Amerindian: 30%; white: 9%; other: 1%

**Religious Distribution**: nominally Roman Catholic: 89%; Protestant: 6%; other: 5%

**Birth Rate**: 22.36 births per 1,000 population

**Death Rate**: 4.99 per 1,000 population

**Infant Mortality Rate**: 24.52 deaths per 1,000 live births

**Net Migration Rate**: –2.71 migrant(s) per 1,000 population

**Total Fertility Rate**: 2.57 children born per woman

**Population Growth Rate**: 1.47%

**HIV/AIDS** (1999 est.): *Adult prevalence*: 0.29%; *Persons living with HIV/AIDS*: 150,000; *Deaths*: 4,700. (For additional details from www.UNAIDS.org, see end of Section 10B.)

**Literacy Rate** (*defined as those age 15 and over who can read and write*): 89.6% (*male*: 91.8%, *female*: 87.4%), with ten years of compulsory schooling (INEGI 1992a)

**Per Capita Gross Domestic Product** (*purchasing power parity*): $9,000 (2001 est.); *Inflation*: 6.5%; *Unemployment*: 3% in the urban centers, plus considerable underemployment. Among most of Mexico's rural population and urban poor, who constitute by all measures a majority of the population, the standard of living is close to subsistence. In 1990, 63.2% of adult Mexicans reported a monthly income below the minimum wage, a measure of income that in 1993 corresponded to a yearly income of approximately $3,000 (INEGI 1992a). *Living below the poverty line*: 40% (2001 est.)

## B. A Brief Historical Perspective

Mexico was the early site of advanced indigenous civilizations, starting with the Olmecs (1500 B.C.E. to 300 B.C.E.) and the Mayas, who also began as early as 1500 B.C.E. As they moved north from the Yucatan to Mexico, the Mayas brought with them their advanced agriculture. They built immense stone pyramids and invented a very accurate calendar. Classic Mayan civilization collapsed between 790 and 900 C.E. The Aztecs, who overcame and replaced the Toltecs, built their capital city, Tenoochtitian, in 1325 on the site of present-day Mexico City. The Aztec civilization collapsed following its first encounter with Spanish conquistadors under Hernando Cortes, between 1519 and 1521.

After three centuries of Spanish rule, the people rebelled under the leadership of two priests and a general, the latter declaring himself Emperor Augustin I in 1821. A republic was declared in 1823. At the time, Mexico's territory extended into the American southwest and California. In 1836, Texas revolted and declared itself a republic. After the Mexican-American War (1846-1848), Mexico gave up all claim to lands north of the Rio Grande River. French support helped put an Austrian archduke on the throne of Mexico as Maximillian 1 (1864-1867), but American pressure forced the French to withdraw. Porfirio Diaz headed a dictatorship between 1877 and 1880 and again between 1884 and 1911.

In 1917, rival forces agreed to social reform and a new constitution. Since then, Mexico has developed large-scale social programs of social security, labor protection, and school improvement, although many segments of the population, including the indigenous natives, barely manage to subsist.

## 1. Basic Sexological Premises

### A. Character of Gender Roles

Gender roles are changing. Some 50 years ago, gender roles in Mexico could be easily described as the traditional separation, magnification, and stereotyping of male and female differences. Women were dichotomized into the two double-moral-standard subtypes of the princess and prostitute, and men were instructed to be the impenetrable and insensitive provider who exercised his power over women.

Today this is changing. In a sample of 10,142 high school students representative of the whole country, the National Population Council conducted a national survey on various aspects of sexuality (CONAPO 1988). In 1988, 83.1% of the respondents thought men and women had equal legal rights (as they do), 69.7% thought that authority at home should be shared by men and women, and only 13.2% thought housework to be the exclusive responsibility of the woman. In another survey among 2,983 male and female 15- to 24-year-olds, Morris et al. (1987) found that only 6.6% of females and 13.7% of males thought that a woman who works outside the home is deceiving her husband and not fulfilling her obligations as a wife. In 1984, Rubio et al. (1988) found in a sample of 521 first-year medical students that only 17.7% agreed with the statement that women are naturally passive, and 91.3% thought it is equally important for men and women to pursue professional educations.

The process of recognizing the equality of women and men has clearly begun, although it is also true that, in practice, women have more disadvantages than men. Women are overrepresented in the lower-income levels and underrepresented in the higher levels. Only 19.6% of Mexican women are engaged in paid work compared to 68% for males (INEGI 1992b). It is also a fact that most working women have, in fact, two jobs: the paid one and the housework.

### B. Sociolegal Status of Males and Females

The fourth Article of the Constitution explicitly recognizes the equality of men and women. In 1974, a revision of all legislation was effected to eliminate any gender discrimination, and there are several other laws and a national program aimed at evaluating and promoting the integration of woman in the nation's development. Despite these efforts, there are a number of areas where women are at a disadvantage. The expansion of industrial labor has benefitted males more than women. Inequality also shows in other areas of work: 74.1% of professionals are men, 80.6% of the executive positions in the government belong to men, and only 3.4% of those who work in domestic jobs are men (INEGI 1992b).

Technically, male and female children and adolescents enjoy equal benefits as far as education, healthcare, and social significance go within society and the family. However, gender-dimorphic training begins early. In general, lower-socioeconomic-level families tend to transmit the older values. As the social class and education level of the parents increase, one observes a tendency toward transmitting an egalitarian ideology.

### C. General Concepts of Sexuality and Love

There have been attempts at picturing empirically the constructs people have of sexuality and love. In general, it can be said that both sexuality and love are seen as positive and desirable aspects of life both for men and women, but ambivalent feelings on sexuality are often encountered. Díaz Loving's (1988) nonrandom sample of 300 individuals in Mexico City found that love, although seen positively, has many interpretations. Romantic love is seen as an idealization, passionate love as being vulnerable. Furthermore, there are important differences in how males and females perceive love: Females tend to see love more positively, while men tend to think of it as genital and sexual; men more often than women see it as an unattainable utopian dream.

In the CONAPO (1988) survey, the participating students thought that the aims of sex were: intimate communication 63%, mutual pleasure and satisfaction 37%, and having children 15.5%. In another survey effected in Mexico City with 613 individuals randomly selected from households, De la Peña and Toledo (1991a) found that respondents mentioned the following objectives for sex: enjoyment 48%, physical outlet 29%, and having children 18%. In a subsequent report (1991c), the same authors reported that, of the sexually active respondents, only 3% of males and 6% of females think of sexual intercourse as something unpleasant or have an indifferent attitude towards it. A survey of medical students found that the majority, 69%, disagree with the statement that procreation is the most important goal of sex (Rubio et al. 1988).

## 2. Religious, Ethnic, and Gender Factors Affecting Sexuality

### A. Source and Character of Religious Values

There are two sources of religious values in Mexico: European Hispanic Catholicism and the indigenous religions that dominated the area prior to the arrival of the Europeans. Both have blended in the course of almost 500 years of interaction. Religiosity has followed the same pattern of other cultural phenomena in the history of Mexico. Rather than one system giving up in favor of the other, a complex mixture of both cultures has generated a new and unique culture. In 1990, 90% of the population was Catholic, but the Catholicism practiced is different from the Catholicism of other countries. As with the ethnic blending, religiosity has gone through a process of syncretism. The best example of this is the cult to the Virgin of Guadalupe, which quickly gained popularity because it could be integrated with preexisting cults of Aztec gods.

To complicate the picture, the prehispanic source was not a single one. There were at least four major cultures with important religious differences: Olmec, Toltec, Mayan, and Aztec. The Aztecs dominated much of the land that is now Mexico when the Spaniards arrived, but they were the dominant political power and empire, not the only culture.

The Aztec religion was characterized by a view of the universe where a constant fight for cosmic order took place between the forces of the sun and the forces of the moon and the night. Light, endurance, sobriety, and sexual self-constraint were on the sun's side; cowardice, drunkenness, and sexual incontinence worked for the moon, the night, and the evil forces (Wolf 1975). Sex was seen as something to be controlled, but its value in procreation and as a source of pleasure in both men and women was also recognized. Polygamy was common among the wealthy and divorce rare but regulated.

An interesting aspect in the Aztec religion is the place that childbirth held in the culture. Childbirth was seen as a combat in which the woman was the warrior. A woman who died in childbirth received war honors at burial.

Moderation in every aspect of life, including sexuality, was central in the ideology of the education (Morgan 1982). In other aspects, religion and society were highly repressive: Homosexuality was severely punished, although practiced; the official penalty was death (Lumsden 1991).

The other religious components in this synergistic interaction were the beliefs and behavior patterns brought to Mexico by the Catholic Hispanic conquistadors. Historical documents clearly indicate that the Church teachings were not the norm of behavior among the people. The Council of Trent (1545-1563), a response to Protestantism, served as a basis for the teachings of the clergy in charge of indoctrinating the indigenous population. A document from the 17th century written by Fray Gabino Carta, summarizes the Church's sexual teachings: There were seven ways in which lust could appear, all conducive to mortal sin: 1. simple fornication (intercourse out of wedlock), 2. adultery, 3. incest, 4. ravishment (forcing a woman to participate in sex), 5. abduction of a woman, 6. sins against nature (masturbation, sodomy, which usually meant homosexuality, but sometimes applied also to "unnatural" heterosexual coital sexual positions—different from the man above the woman lying on her back, and bestiality), and 7. sacrilege (Lavrin 1991).

**B. Source and Character of Ethnic Values**

The ethnic composition of Mexico is complex. The majority of the population, 55%, is *mestizo* or *mestee*, a mixture of the European, mainly Spanish, with the indigenes that populated the area before the arrival of the Spaniards. Creoles, descendants of persons born in the New World from parents born in Europe, still constitute an important segment of the population, 37.5%. Being European in origin and not racially mixed, they can be considered Caucasian. A third group consists of a very heterogeneous minority called Indians. These indigenes are composed of 56 linguistically differentiated groups. In 1990, the indigenous population was 5,282,347, that is, 7.5% of the total Mexican population (CNP 1989).

It is difficult to pick out a single overriding characteristic in the ethnic values in Mexico. In the background, we have the original cultural sources that still can be observed today in many aspects. However, what is Mexico today only began to constitute itself some hundred years ago. There are many traces of the conquered culture. The resulting culture, best described by Octavio Paz (1950), is hermetic, inscrutable, full of resentment, and searching for refuge and finding it in the Virgin Mother María de Guadalupe-Tonantzin. According to Paz, Mexican culture is also hiding, always behind masquerades like the macho role where men attempt to calm their fears of being penetrated in a sexual way. Yes, but more importantly, Mexicans also hide in their inner self, behind a very sophisticated strategy of simulation and lies. Almost every foreigner soon learns when dealing with people of low social level that words and promises do not mean what they normally mean. When Mexicans lie or simulate they feel protected and safe. The cult of the Virgin of Guadalupe, the macho attitude, the propensity to simulate and to lie are the results of a process lived by a culture that, instead of being eliminated, was dominated.

[*Comment 1997*: In addition to the value of *machismo* mentioned above, Mexican sexual attitudes and behaviors are strongly influenced by three other values—*marianismo*, *ediquetta*, and *pronatalism*—which are commonly shared with some minor variations across the Latino world of South and Central America. To avoid duplication in several chapters, these four basic values are described in detail in Section 1A, Basic Sexological Premises, in the chapter on Puerto Rico. The reader is referred to that material later in this volume. (*End of comment by R. T. Francoeur*)]

But the Mexico of 1995 is by no means well depicted by the above comments. The process of the last two-plus decades has exerted a profound impact on the character of Mexican culture. Proximity to American culture is a major factor. The American dream is at the same time desired, hated, and feared, but the shaking of economic structures during the 1980s has led to a new identity search that is currently in the process of being delineated. This is evident in the sexual attitudes and behavior of people, as can be seen below.

## 3. Knowledge and Education about Sexuality

### A. Government Policies and Programs for Sex Education

In the last five to ten years, the need for sex education has been recognized and accepted by most sectors of the population. There are, however, differences about what this education should include and how it should be effected, depending on the ideology of the subsector of the population one considers. Both the government and the Catholic Church have stated that there is a specific need to pay attention to the educative process of sexuality.

Education in Mexico is centralized. The Ministry of Education is in charge of developing programs for all basic school levels—the first ten years of education. This it implements with free schooling in an extensive system of public schools. Official textbooks are provided for these schools and their use is compulsory. Private schooling does exist, but their programs have to cover the official program material.

This situation has facilitated the inclusion of sex education themes. Since 1974, when the official population policy changed from a pro-procreative to a policy promoting low population growth, sex education has been seen as an important element of this policy. A National Population Council was established to pursue actions necessary to implement the new policy. One of the early programs undertaken was the National Program for Sex Education. As a result of this program, the content of the official programs and textbooks began to include sex education themes.

Initially, the sexual contents were limited to basic biological information. This raised considerable opposition, but after almost 20 years, the general public has come to accept the need for sex education and to demand more completeness in the program.

Most adolescents, especially females, now have access to information about puberty through the school system. The contents of sexual education programs now include psychological, family, and community considerations of sexual development. Meanwhile, sex education has been integrated into a more general framework of population education (Saavedra Arredondo 1986). The major shortcoming is the lack of adequate training for the teachers who apply these programs.

## B. Informal Sources of Sexual Knowledge

In the last ten years, an increase in the role of parents as reliable informants has being observed. Friends, popular literature in the form of comics with stories, and television and radio constitute the alternative sources of information. Popular literature deserves a special comment because it is probably the material more frequently read by Mexicans. Unfortunately, it is one of the means of perpetuating sexual myths and ambivalence towards sexuality. In the last four years, there has being a growing interest in the mass media to include sexuality themes in their broadcasts. In general, this has become a new source of scientific information for most people.

## 4. Autoerotic Behaviors and Patterns

### A. Children and Adolescents

Children frequently engage in self-pleasuring, but it still causes anxiety in many parents. The exploratory activities of children are well recognized and tolerated, but more explicit practices of sexual arousal are repressed. There are no figures of the incidence of this phenomenon.

Adolescent self-pleasuring is also very common. Reactions to it vary with the social context. In 1984, in a survey of single university students nonrandomly selected for a comparative study with American single students (mean age in both groups 20), Rubio (1989) found an incidence of 50.8% that, interestingly, was not different from the American incidence. In another study among younger students (17 to 19 years of age), Rubio et al. (1988) found a rate of 65% with an important gender difference: 88% for males and 39% for females. In a more recent study among 728 students 17 to 26 years of age, Ordiozola-Urbina and Ibañez (1992) found similar numbers: 83% of males and 22% of females.

Attitudes towards self-pleasuring are not clearly oriented towards accepting or denouncing it, but a tendency to view it as a natural act and not a sick one is clear. Morris et al. (1987) found that 46% of adolescent females and 75% of males said that autoeroticism was OK once in a while, but 34.5% of the females and 49% of the males said that self-pleasuring was bad for the health. Rubio et al. (1988) found less-restrictive attitudes, but the respondents were medical students: Only 29% agreed that self-pleasuring is not a healthy practice.

### B. Adults

There is less systematic information on adult autoeroticism and attitudes about it. Among Mexico City adults, De la Peña and Toledo (1991b) found that 75% of males and 20% of the participating females said they had engaged in self-pleasuring. Interestingly, more than half of those who were currently engaging in this sexual outlet at the time of the study said they liked it very little or not at all. My own personal experience with the mass media on this issue indicates that self-pleasuring is still one of the most anxiety provoking of all sexual issues.

## 5. Interpersonal Heterosexual Behaviors

### A. Children

Sexual exploration and sex rehearsal play occurs very often in children. There are forms, like doctor's play, which are tolerated and understood. More-explicit sex play is not tolerated and is usually repressed by parents and other caretakers, such as teachers.

### B. Adolescents

*Puberty Rituals*

There are no widespread rituals of initiation to puberty.

*Premarital Sexual Activities and Relationships*

During early adolescence, 11 to 15 years of age, most adolescents begin to explore in a form of ritualized relationship called *noviazgo*, formally a relationship period prior to marriage. However, during early adolescence, *noviazgos* are commonly established without marriage as a goal. For young adolescents, it is a social way to regulate interpersonal relationships. It appears that the major part of early dyadic sexual exploration takes place in this form, though no formal data exist. At this early age, *noviazgos* are usually of short duration. Once an adolescent has had his or her first *noviazgo*, it is not difficult for either a male or female to continue with subsequent *noviazgo* relationships. Intercourse is usually deferred to a later age.

The possibility of having had the first intercourse increases after 15 years of age: The CONAPO (1988) survey found that the typical age for first intercourse is 14 to 17 years of age for males and 16 to 19 years for females, but only 23% of participants had had sexual intercourse. Figures from other studies are higher: In a 1984 group of unmarried students, Rubio (1989) found a figure of 40%. Also in 1984, among medical students (17 to 19 years of age), Rubio et al. (1988) found 46% had had intercourse (59% of males and 31% of females).

The last decade may have seen an increase in early sexual intercourse, especially in the big cities. In their Mexico City study, Morris et al (1987) collected information from 2,983 youngsters in 1985 and found among the group of 15 to 19 years: 13.4% of the females and 44% of males had had intercourse, with 39% and 85%, respectively, for the 20- to 24-years-of-age group. More recently, Ordizola and Ibañez (1992) found among 728 university students that 31% and 74% of males had had sexual intercourse.

### C. Adults

*Premarital Courtship, Dating, and Relationships*

De la Peña and Toledo (1991c) studied adults in Mexico City and found that 76.3% of their respondents had had premarital intercourse. In another study by the same authors on adults living in the state of Baja California bordering the United States, the figure for premarital intercourse was 93% for males and 54% for females.

Those who will marry follow a clear set of rules for courtship, with a formal *noviazgo* that includes several assumptions: mutual exclusivity of sexual interaction, regular scheduling of dates, and, when the decision to marry has been taken, many activities to prepare the couple for the common life. Sexual intercourse is common in these adult relationships as the institution of *noviazgo* has gained autonomy in the past 30 to 40 years, and surveillance by an older woman in the family, the *duana*, has declined. In the larger cities, the *noviazgo* often has much less restrictive rules than it did in the past. Economic difficulties may delay or make the marriage plans impractical. One result is that a significant number of persons elect a single life as the style of life, either never marrying or after one or more marriages. These individuals may establish *noviazgos* where marriage in fact is not considered for the future.

Although not prevalent, there are some forms of courtship and premarital sexuality that deserve mention. In many communities, some close to Mexico City, a man and woman may decide to live together, but the man is said to "steal" the woman from her family. Depending on the economic possibilities, the woman goes to live with the man's family or the couple establishes a home of their own. After some years, and some children, the couple may decide to marry, and a wedding takes place, usually with a long series of festivities that may extend to several days. In some communities of the state of Oaxaca, the tradition of arranged marriages persists, many times in a less definitive form because the opinions of the man and woman are considered. In other instances, the man or the woman may spend some time, usually months, living with the family of the spouse-to-be to gain approval of the family to proceed to marriage.

## Marriage and the Family

Two types of marriage exist in Mexico: civil and religious, and, since one type does not have validity in the other domain, people tend to have both types. The 1990 data of the census indicate 45.8% of those 12 years or older are married, 7.4% live together but are not married, 40.6% are single, 1.9% are divorced or separated, and 3.6% are widows (INEGI 1992a).

Mexican families have varied structures, with the extended and nuclear family patterns dominant. Extended families include father, mother, and children with the addition of some other relatives, such as grandparents, uncles, aunts, or others. One form of extended family, characterized as "unstable" because some of its members, aunts and cousins, spend only a limited time with the family, is also very common. López-Juárez (1982) describes this family style as typical. The extended family functions as a social-support mechanism, substituting for other forms of social support that are nonexistent, or exist on a very low scale, in Mexico (e.g., unemployment insurance and care for the elderly). The extended family used to be the norm, but the frequency of nuclear families, groupings limited to father, mother, and children, increases as social class rises higher and urban living spreads. The mean number of household members dropped from 5.8 in 1970 to 5.0 in 1990 (INEGI 1992a).

As indicated above, cohabitation is frequent but not the norm. Monogamy is the rule and bigamy is penalized with jail. Although some individuals do in fact have two or more concurrent marriages, discovery entitles the concerned ones to send the guilty party to jail, and there are cases of this. While there are no recognized forms of plural marriage, it is important to note that this refers to formal marriage. Informal liaisons that include sexual interaction and forms of economic support, and cohabitation where one or both of the concerned have other concurrent liaisons, are not infrequent.

## Divorce and Remarriage

There are two forms of civil divorce: an administrative divorce, where the couple agrees, and the necessary divorce, where one of the spouses has incurred a legally recognized cause of divorce. Divorce statistics are not reliable,

but a general feeling is that it is becoming more frequent than it used to be some 50 years ago. The fate of the divorcee appears to differ according to gender: Males tend to remarry more than females. A trend observed in my own clinical practice is that the stigma and social barriers associated with divorce have decreased in the last ten to 20 years.

## Extramarital Sexual Relations

Marital sexuality, surprisingly, is not the most frequent form of sexuality, at least in Mexico City. De la Peña and Toledo (1991c) found that, of their respondents who had had sex in the month previous to the survey, only 45% were married. In another report (1991d), the same authors found that among the 613 adult respondents in Mexico City, extramarital behavior was reported by 29.7% (50% of males and 10% of females). In a report on the state of Baja California (De la Peña & Toledo 1992b), the figure was 40% of males and 15% of females.

[*Update 1997*: A form of concurrent liaison that used to be common occurs between a married man and his female lover who, after some time, acquires a higher status than a simple love affair and establishes herself in a separate household, usually helped or totally paid for by the man, who has a kind of second family with her. This relationship may include children and practically all the elements of a family, except for the legality of marriage and for the daily cohabitation, because the previous marriage is maintained. This phenomenon is known as *la casa chica*, literally, "the small home"—the term is also used to refer to the paramour. In January 1997, a prominent Mexico City politician, president of the Democratic Revolutionary Party, may have witnessed a change in public attitude when he called on his fellow politicians to abandon their widely known, and renown, custom of maintaining several *casa chicas* and commit themselves to marital fidelity.

[Deterioration of economic standards of living seen in the last two decades appears to have made this pattern of liaison less common today than in the past. Mexico's economy shrank by 6% in 1995 when inflation was expected to top 50%, banks were charging an astronomical 70% interest on credit cards, and corporate benefits and largess for executives and middle managers dried up, leaving males unable to support their usual number of *casa chicas* and paramours.

[Although this custom is widely practiced and has a long standing in Mexican culture, such relationships usually leave the woman totally unprotected by the law when it comes to inheritance and separation rights (food, pension, alimony, etc.). While most Mexican wives would likely be happy to see the mistresses out of work, economists are greatly troubled by estimates that tens of thousands of single women who have relied on the *casa chica* tradition for much of their livelihood will be added to the swelling unemployment lines. Most of these women have few if any marketable skills.

[The paramours are taking steps to cope, forming support groups, sometimes called *Las Numero Dos*, to help rebuild their lives and find jobs. Although Mexico's economy remained seriously depressed into 1997 and many middle-class and wealthy males were obliged to reduce the number of paramours they supported in separate houses, the resilience of the tradition and the adaptability of Mexican males is evident in the booming popularity of "pass-through hotels," which charge couples by the hour. However, Carlos Welti, a demographer who has been studying Mexican sexuality for 20 years, reports that the decline of the *casa chica* has been part of an evolution in sexual mores that has followed fundamental changes in the condition of women, including increased education and growth in the number of women working outside the home. Also, because of easy access to birth control, the average Mexican woman today bears about three children instead of the 6.8 average that prevailed in 1976 (Padgett 1995; Dillon 1997). (*End of update by R. T. Francoeur*)]

*Sexuality and the Physically Disabled and the Aged*

The prevailing attitude is that disabled and older persons are nonsexual and have no need for sexual intimacy. Only recently, and then in very small ways, has this public attitude begun to change with a slowly growing awareness of these special populations' needs.

*The Incidence of Oral and Anal Sex*

De la Peña and Toledo (1991a, 1992a) have provided some information on attitudes toward oral and anal sex: 44% of Mexico City respondents think oral sex is an acceptable practice, 41.2% think anal sex is acceptable. In the Baja California study (1992b), the corresponding figures were 33.3 and 22.2%.

Behavioral information gives similar rates: De la Peña and Toledo (1991ab) report 45.3% of respondents as practicing oral sex: more than 50% of males but only one third of women in the Mexico City study, and 42% of males and 40% of females in the Baja California study. Among Mexico City students, Ordiozola and Ibañez (1992) found that active oral sex was practiced by 21% of females and 51% of males, while 22% of females and 52% of males had engaged in passive oral sex. In a study of younger single university students, I found a figure of 28% (Rubio 1989).

Anal sex is slightly less common than oral sex: 32% of males and 26% of females (De la Peña & Toledo 1992b); 7.4% of female university students and 13.8% of males (Ordiozola & Ibañez 1992); and 18.5% of participants in my study of single university students (Rubio 1989). There are no legal restrictions to practice oral or anal sex.

## 6. Homoerotic, Homosexual, and Bisexual Behaviors

### A. Children and Adolescents

The values of mainstream Mexican culture are highly homophobic, as would be expected in a culture derived form two homophobic precursors, the Hispanic European and Pre-Columbian cultures. There is little evidence of the incidence of homoerotic or homosexual behavior during childhood and adolescence, but it is my clinical impression that these behaviors occur in an important number of people during development, especially during adolescence when identity formation is helped by closeness to same-sex friends in both males and females.

### B. Adults

Homosexual behaviors are infrequently studied by Mexican sexual researchers. The studies of De la Peña and Toledo (1991ab) report homosexual behavior in 3.3% of the respondents: 5% of males and 2% of females for the Mexico City study, and 9% of males and 5% of females for the Baja California study. I found a percentage of 6.2% of single students with some form of homosexual behavior (Rubio 1989).

Attitudinal information is also scarce. A tendency toward tolerating the homosexual person seems to be emerging, but few people think this is an acceptable form of sexual behavior. Only 9.9% of males and 9.7% of females in the De la Peña and Toledo (1992) study thought homosexuality was correct. While I found that 58.7% of medical students do not think legal measures should be taken against homosexuals, 40.3% nevertheless think homosexuality is a

degeneration. Still, 58.2% of female and 56.1% of male adolescents in the Morris et al. (1987) study thought it was no problem to have a homosexual friend.

According to my clinical and professional experience, there are no fixed patterns of selection of one of the traditional gender roles in male and female homosexual persons. Lumsden (1991) notes that Mexican homosexuals do not suffer the degree of loneliness typically experienced by American and Canadian homosexuals, because friends and families stay close to the individual.

The courtship patterns in the homosexual individuals have adopted an American pattern: organizing support groups, well-established spots in the cities, specialized bars, and gathering sites. An important number of homosexual and bisexual individuals, however, suffer from the restrictions of a society that is highly homophobic, and undergo a long period of isolation before integrating themselves in the homosexual social network. There are no legal restrictions for homosexual behavior, although lower-level authorities, i.e., local police, sometimes exert repression against the homosexual individuals, a manifestation more of internalized homophobia than institutionalized persecution.

During the past 15 years, homosexual persons have organized a variety of support groups. There are homosexual groups in almost every city of size. These groups work for the recognition of the legal and human rights of homosexual persons, and with AIDS prevention, education, and support.

## 7. Gender Diversity and Transgender Issues

### A. Transvestites, Transsexuals, and Transgenderists

There is no systematic information on the incidence of transvestism, transsexualism, and transgenderism. The three situations do occur and the number of people who have these conflicts is not small. The following comments reflect my impressions.

Transvestism occurs in four distinct forms. First, the fetishistic transvestite, who is generally a heterosexual who cross-dresses to achieve sexual arousal, usually with complicated rituals forming part of the arousal process. When this situation generates conflict with the partner, the individual may seek treatment, usually on an individual basis with a private professional. One private institution offers help at low-cost rates for these and other sexual problems (see Section 13, Research and Advanced Education, below). Second, the professional transvestite, who may be heterosexual or homosexual, who impersonates females working in transvestite shows. Third, the homosexual who sometimes likes to cross-dress as a means of expression of his sexual preference. Some of these individuals find in prostitution a way of living; other male prostitutes just cross-dress in order to gain more customers. The fourth type is the truly gender-conflicted person who finds relief for an internal craving to express his gender identity/role by cross-dressing for variable amounts of time during his daily life. Psychological adjustment of this last subtype varies. These people usually go through a period of high satisfaction cross-dressing and then suffer from various forms of anxiety that make them seek help from a mental health practitioner.

Transsexuals in Mexico suffer from a lack of systematic attention and knowledge on the part of most health professionals. They are often mistakenly diagnosed as homosexuals in conflict; the usual response from the medical profession is rejection. I have participated in the psychotherapeutic treatment of some transsexual individuals, but, until very recently, I was without any resource in the official health system to offer any help beyond psychological and behavioral counseling. In 1993, one public hospital agreed to pursue the medical and surgical treatment of transsexuals in collaboration with psychotherapeutic supervision by staff at Asociacion Mexicana para la Salud Sexual A.C. (AMSSAC). There are major needs in this area still uncovered by official health policy.

### B. Specially Gendered Persons

Mexican mainstream cultural expectations are very dichotomized in considering individuals either male or female. This is reflected in the difficulties encountered by gender-dysphoric patients described above, and by the lack of any kind of third gender or sex as found in some cultures.

I have one verbal report from a student some 15 years ago that in a region of Oaxaca near the Tehuantepec Isthmus, there are communities where a third gender is considered, with social norms ascribing to the effeminate man activities in the household and prohibiting him from pursuing more-typical male activities. I have not had the opportunity to corroborate this information.

## 8. Significant Unconventional Sexual Behaviors

### A. Coercive Sex

*Sexual Abuse and Incest*

All sexual behavior of an adult with a preadolescent (prepubertal) child is considered a crime. Around 1985, the government of Mexico City established special police offices dedicated to working with victims of sexual crimes and to legally prosecuting the perpetrator. Before this change, regular police handled these crimes, and many victims avoided contact with the police fearing further mistreatment. Some other states have adopted this new policy.

Recent information suggests the level of child sexual abuse, although underreporting can be assumed. During three months in 1991 in the Mexico Federal District, 122 cases of sexual crimes where the victim was under 12 years of age were investigated: In 53%, the crime was rape, and in 91%, the aggressor was known previously by the victim (the father was the aggressor in 12% of the cases) (Muñoz Gonzalez 1992).

Incest is a taboo for most of Mexican society. Among some low-level socioeconomic-class communities, it is evident only when the daughter delivers a child fathered by her own father, and this is acknowledged by the neighborhood as one more of the facts of life. Scientific knowledge of this phenomena is very limited and far from satisfactory.

Among some isolated ethnic groups that have conserved their purity of race by not mixing with outsiders, incest may be an acceptable way of organizing and perpetuating society. This is the case, at least, among the Huicholes, a group of some 8,000-9,000 people living in West-Central Mexico. According to Palafox Vargas (1985), various forms of incest are practiced and accepted in the community.

*Sexual Harassment*

Sexual harassment is considered a crime only in modifications to the law effected in 1990 after intense participation of feminist leaders. Sexual harassment, both in labor and academic settings, seems to be common, but it has been difficult to document cases. Penalties are possible for sexual harassment, but there is very little experience in applying the law.

*Rape*

Rape, forced sexual intercourse with a man or a woman, has long been considered a crime. Recently, the penalty for rape was increased to seven years in jail, which prevents early freedom for convicted perpetrators. Still, the crime is not adequately or sufficiently prosecuted. In Mexico City between January 1992 and November 1993, 1,645 rapes were reported to authorities (Casorla, in press). This figure of about 900 reported rapes annually in Mexico City is far below the estimates of authorities there of a yearly figure of reported and unreported rapes between 15,000 to 20,000. The figure for the whole country is difficult to estimate, but some authors put the figure at about 60,000 rapes per year (Ruiz Harrel 1979).

### B. Prostitution

Prostitution is a common practice in Mexico. There are no legal penalties for the prostitute, but there are for anyone who exploits her or him. The pattern of prostitute activities has varied with changing policies of the governments. Some 50 years ago, there were zones in the cities where open prostitution was accepted and regulated by authorities. This still is the case for several cities, but in Mexico City, the law now prohibits open acceptance zones. This policy has generated a lack of control of where and when prostitution is practiced.

There are many levels of prostitutes, from the street girl or boy to the sophisticated call girl, and even some specialized services where the contact is established by phone and arrangements made beforehand. Since these more sophisticated and organized forms of prostitution are illegal, it is difficult to find any information on the extent of the business.

In recent years, prostitutes working independently in the streets have organized themselves in groups to fight for their rights. Claudia Colimoro, the leader, now has a full program being pursued in the political arena. She estimates the number of street prostitutes in Mexico City at about 15,000 (Colimoro 1993).

### C. Pornography and Erotica

There are vague legal restrictions to the commercialization of pornographic material, vague because the material has to be considered obscene to be forbidden, and there are no clear criteria for this. Despite restrictions, softcore pornography circulates openly and legally, and hardcore is widely available. Softcore publications are produced in Mexico mainly through joint ventures with large American companies such as Playboy and Penthouse. Hardcore is not produced in Mexico, although American, and sometimes European, videotapes are illegally copied and distributed very efficiently to street markets, making them very easy to obtain. The dimension of this illegal business is unknown to anyone not inside it, but it is certainly a profitable and large business. In the last year, the Playboy subsidiary began mail distribution of legally authorized hardcore videotapes produced in the United States, but for the first time with translations in subtitles.

## 9. Contraception, Abortion, and Population Planning

### A. Contraception

Contraceptives are easily obtained by anyone seeking them. They are offered free of charge through the official healthcare system and can be purchased at any drugstore with few restrictions. This fact speaks about the informal values of Mexican society and the nominally Catholic people: The Catholic Church officially opposes the use of contraceptives, but this opposition is not reflected in the usage rates of the Catholic population. The Morris et al. 1987 study of a representative sample of adolescents in two sections of Mexico City clearly shows that the attitudes of youngsters do not correspond to Church positions: Only 22.3% of females and 15.5% of males thought God should decide the number of children to be procreated by the couple. The CONAPO survey documented that a majority of youngsters who have had sex actually use contraception: 64.6% of young males and 58.2% of young females, with condoms used by 38.8% and oral contraceptives by 23.8%. Women reported 23.9% using condoms, 23.3% rhythm, and coitus interruptus 21.5%.

Adult use of contraceptives is common. According to the information from the National Survey of Health and Fertility, the percentage of women in a marriage, cohabitation, or other sexually active relationship who use contraceptives is 52.7%, up from 30.2% ten years ago (Secretaría de Salud 1990).

## B. Teenage Unmarried Pregnancies

Adolescent pregnancy occurs frequently. An annual rate of 56 births for each 1,000 women in the 15- to 19-years-of-age group is reported (Urbina-Fuentes 1992). The fate of these pregnancies is not clear. Eskala et al. (1992) followed 189 pregnant unmarried adolescents at one of the main centers of high-risk pregnancy care in Mexico City, reporting that most unwed mothers decided to live with the father of the child. This option was much less popular for mothers with high education expectations. Since abortion is illegal, there is no reliable information on what percentage of pregnant adolescents terminate their pregnancy and what percentage carry through to birth.

## C. Abortion

Voluntary (on request) abortion is not legal in Mexico. The law permits abortion in cases of rape or when the health of the mother is at risk. However, the legal procedure is so complex that in practice it is almost impossible. Illegal abortions are, nevertheless, widely practiced. A source of the Mexican Social Security Institute, a huge social medicine system that provides medical care to everyone who has a formal job, estimated there were about two million during 1989 (IMSS 1990). According to some not-very-systematic reports, abortion is the fourth cause of death, although this does not show up in the official statistics because cause of death is recorded under another category, such as generalized infection (Abasolo 1990). This same source estimated that for each 100,000 babies born, 5.7 women, most of them adolescents, die from abortion complications. De la Peña and Toledo (1991d) reported that a third of their female respondents said they had had an abortion. The National Survey of Health and Fertility reported that 14.3% of Mexican women had had an abortion (Secretaría de Salud 1987).

Abortion is one of the most controversial issues in Mexico. Among the Mexico City respondents of De la Peña and Toledo (1991a), 30.3% approved abortion if there was a medical reason and 28.9% if a woman wishes it for social reasons; 17.1% said they would never accept it. Givaudán and Pick de Weiss (1992a) interviewed 500 persons in two groups in Mexico City and found that most respondents approve the decriminalization of abortion, 60% think abortion is a decision of the woman only, 62% think public hospitals should offer abortions, and 76.2% think legalization would reduce maternal deaths. The opinions of men and women in these studies did not differ significantly. In a second study, Givaudán and Pick de Weiss (1992b) interviewed 300 people representative of the two most important cities in the state of Chiapas where, in 1990, abortion was legalized briefly. After some days, the local congress reversed its position and suspended the new law. While the opinions reported were more divided than in the Mexico City survey,

half of the respondents think abortion is a woman's decision and that the Catholic Church should change its point of view. Half of the respondents also think abortion services should be provided by public hospitals; slightly more than half think depenalizing abortion would reduce maternal deaths.

## D. Population Control Efforts

Official policy is clearly oriented towards reduction of population growth. The policy changed 21 years ago from a pro-growth policy. In 1974, the government recognized that a low population growth would be favorable for national development. As a result, there has been a major campaign to achieve the new goal, and there are many indications that the efforts have been conducive to concrete results. The current population growth rate is 2.6, down from 3.2 between 1950 and 1970. Efforts include actions at many levels: free family planning at public hospitals, education and information programs at many levels, programs for women looking for an increase in the quality of life, and actions to promote a better distribution of population and many others.

## 10. Sexually Transmitted Diseases and HIV/AIDS

### A. Sexually Transmitted Diseases

Evaluation of the available data on the incidence of sexually transmitted diseases is difficult because not all the cases are reported. The data reported by the healthcare system include the following figures for 1991: gonococcal infections: 15,681 cases (18 per 100,000 habitants), genital herpes: 3,480 (4 per 100,000), and syphilis: 3,282 (3.8 per 100,000) (Secretaría de Salud 1992). There are no statistics for the other sexually transmitted diseases, except AIDS. Despite the problem of underreporting, investigators have come to some interesting conclusions: The rate for gonorrhea has been declining, from 230 cases per 100,000 inhabitants in 1941 to the current rate of 18 per 100,000. Researchers who have attempted to document prevalence among these diseases consistently report higher figures, suggesting that the problem is much more frequent than the levels reported by official statistics (Del Rio, in press). STDs are more frequently a problem for males between 20 and 24 years of age and women between ages 18 and 24.

### B. HIV/AIDS

AIDS (SIDA) was first diagnosed in 1983 when 17 cases were identified. Since then, the increase in diagnosed cases can be divided into three phases: from 1983 to 1986, the growth was moderate; from 1987 to 1989, a rapid growth period was observed where cases doubled in only a few months with an exponential increase in identified cases; and from 1989 to the present, when there has being a slower, yet still exponential, growth in the number of cases. As of December 31, 1993, the total number of cases reported to the Health Ministry was 17,387 cases. However, estimates of the real number of cases, correcting for late reporting and underreporting, takes the figure to 27,000 cases (Del Rio, in press).

Another alarming point in these statistics is a doubling of the number of cases in women, from 7.9% of all the cases in 1987 to a current 14.8% of all cases. The current male-female case ratio is 6:1 (INDRE 1994). (Table 1 shows the numbers of reported cases from 1983 to 1993.)

Most of the cases are because of sexual transmission. Thus, it is clear that education is the only preventive measure available. The severity of the AIDS epidemic has not escaped officials, but the effectiveness of preventive measures remains under discussion. Early in the epidemic, the government set up a special office to deal with the problem: the Consejo Nacional para el Control y Prevención del SIDA (CONASIDA). This agency has launched several campaigns in the mass media to increase the awareness of the general public of the risk posed by AIDS, but the campaigns have being criticized by both those who say they are offensive to the moral conscience of people and those who argue the contents of the messages are not clear enough. There has been an upsurge in the number of independent nongovernmental organizations (ONGs) that devote themselves to preventive and educative work, but their efforts are restricted by financial limitations. In the beginning, these organizations focused their work on the gay community, which was the hardest hit in the early stages of the epidemic. In the recent years, many of these ONGs have included actions to reach all the sexual orientations.

Public attention to the problem has increased considerably in the last three years, and the mass media has both responded and been responsible for these. It is common for radio stations, television, and the print media to devote space to discussions and informative programs on AIDS.

[*Update 2002*: UNAIDS Epidemiological Assessment: There is some information available on HIV prevalence among antenatal women in Mexico since the late 1980s. HIV testing of antenatal women in Mexico City in 1987 resulted in no evidence of HIV infection. HIV test results from ten states in 1990 also showed no evidence of HIV infection among antenatal women. In 1991, HIV testing in 12 states resulted in a prevalence of 0.1% and, in 1994, 0.6% of antenatal women tested were HIV-positive.

[HIV information among sex workers is available since 1986. Among the major urban areas, HIV information is available from Mexico City, Guadalajara, and, in 1987, Monterrey. Between 1986 and 1996, HIV prevalence among sex workers tested has remained below 0.5%. Outside the major urban areas, HIV information is available from Merida, Acapulco, Tijuana, and the states of Chiapas, Jalisco, and Michoacan from the late 1980s and from the 18 states through 1997. HIV prevalence among sex workers tested in the 18 states reached 1% in 1996.

[In 1995, 6% of intravenous drug users tested in Chihuahua were HIV-positive. In 1997, 1% of intravenous drug users tested in Tijuana were HIV-positive.

### Table 1

### New Cases of AIDS per Notification Year and Sex, 1983 to 1993

| Year | Cases per 1,000,000 | Incidence | Ratio Male: Female | Percentage of Cases in Women |
|------|------|------|------|------|
| 1983 | 6 | 0.07 | 6:0 | 0.0 |
| 1984 | 6 | 0.07 | 6:0 | 0.0 |
| 1985 | 29 | 0.3 | 14:1 | 6.9 |
| 1986 | 246 | 2.9 | 30:1 | 3.2 |
| 1987 | 518 | 6.6 | 12:1 | 7.9 |
| 1988 | 905 | 10.6 | 6:1 | 13.5 |
| 1989 | 1,607 | 18.3 | 6:1 | 15.2 |
| 1990 | 2,588 | 31.8 | 5:1 | 16.2 |
| 1991 | 3,167 | 37.9 | 5:1 | 15.4 |
| 1992 | 3,220 | 37.5 | 6:1 | 15.2 |
| 1993 | 5,095 | 58.5 | 6:1 | 14.8 |
| Cumulative data from 1983-1993 | 17,387 | 200.00 | 6:1 | 14.8 |

*Source*: INDRE 1994.

[In 1999, the information on HIV prevalence among STD clinic patients resulted in a very high prevalence in one site: males having sex with males (30.0%), male IV-drug users (8.0%), male sex workers (48.5%), as results of patient autoselection.

[The estimated number of adults and children living with HIV/AIDS on January 1, 2002, were:

| | |
|---|---|
| Adults ages 15-49: | 150,000 (rate: 0.3%) |
| Women ages 15-49: | 32,000 |
| Children ages 0-15: | 3,600 |

[An estimated 4,200 adults and children died of AIDS during 2001.

[At the end of 2001, an estimated 27,000 Mexican children under age 15 were living without one or both parents who had died of AIDS. (*End of update by the Editors*)]

## 11. Sexual Dysfunctions, Counseling, and Therapies

### A. Concepts of Sexual Dysfunction

The concept of sexual dysfunction as a health problem is only recently gaining acceptance in Mexico. The traditional approach ignored the quality of sexual interaction of people. If one interprets the decisions of the official health system on healthcare policies, attention to these problems was considered either unnecessary or a luxury. The assumptions were that problems of sexual dysfunction were always in the realm of psychoanalysis and traditionally outside the realm of possibilities available to the majority of Mexicans because of the high cost of treatment. Also, emotions of shame and undue guilt prevailed among those who had such problems, preventing any search for help. This panorama has changed in the last 15 to 20 years. I have had the experience of people who at 50 years of age ask for help for problems they have been aware of for 30 or more years, and who express their relief at the change they experienced in society. It is now easier to admit that one has a sexual problem and to seek help. The resources to provide effective help are still limited to a few private organizations with limited resources. I have been in the forefront of this change, because the institution (AMSSAC) where I work devotes its efforts specifically to the treatment of sexual dysfunction among economically restricted individuals, and to providing formal training in sex therapy to professionals.

In the minds of lay people, the concept of sexual dysfunction is still very vague. Most people immediately identify terms such as impotence and frigidity with the lack of ability to complete intercourse and to experience pleasure and orgasm. In more-professional settings, increasing attention is being paid to sexual dysfunction. Medical associations and medical schools are beginning to include themes on sexual functioning in their curricula and in their programs for congresses and professional meetings.

As a frame for clinical treatment and research, the following concept of sexual dysfunction has been proposed: a series of syndromes where the erotic processes of the sexual response occur recurrently and persistently in a way that results undesirably for the individual or the social group (Rubio & Díaz, in press). There is no information on the incidence and prevalence of these problems among the general population, but there are a number of indirect indicators that show the problems to be very common. In six years, the sexual dysfunction clinic set up at AMSSAC has been used by close to 700 individuals, around 30% of whom seek help as a couple. This number is surely much lower than the total number of people seeking help at AMSSAC, because patients requesting treatment are requested to wait a long time before their treatment can begin. The data in Table 2, reported by González in 1993 and based on 195 initial-intake diagnostic interviews during an 8-month period, give an idea of the relative frequency of the sexual problems encountered at AMSSAC. Generalization, however, is difficult, because the center is a specialized center in Mexico City. Comparative information from other regions of the country is not available.

### B. Availability of Counseling, Diagnosis, and Treatment

Specialized treatment for sexual dysfunctions is available, but the few trained professionals and treatment centers severely limit this. This is particularly true in the smaller cities and rural areas. In the big cities such as Mexico City, Guadalajara, and Monterrey, individual professionals who have obtained specialized training both in Mexico and aboard—mainly the United States—offer sexual therapy privately. However, this is far from sufficient for the size of the population. The situation in more critical in the official health system where sex counseling and therapy is not offered in any systematic way. Some professionals working for the official health system have been trained in sexual counseling, and they do provide this service, but with no organized structure.

As mentioned above, AMSSAC is involved in the training of sex therapists, and some already trained professionals offer their services within the sexual dysfunction clinic at AMSSAC. This clinic, although privately run, serves only patients whose economic situation prevents them from seeking help in a private clinic. Much work is needed before it can be said that the Mexican population has the ability to solve its sexual dysfunctions via professional treatment. Unfortunately, one result of the above situation is the proliferation of street therapists and fraudulent remedies to which many people still look for help.

## 12. Sex Research and Advanced Professional Education

Sexual research is conducted as a formal activity by very few researchers. However, their work is beginning to give a panorama of what goes on in the country. This has reduced the need for constantly referring to foreign research and literature.

There are researchers working now at every level of the sciences that deal with aspects of sexuality. Basic physiological research in animals is conducted following state-of-the-art methodologies in highly specialized centers. Psychological research, conducted basically by a group in the Universidad Nacional Autónoma de México, has produced interesting information on the sexual behavior of young people, some of which is reviewed in this article. Anthropology researchers have also produced original work on gender issues in both the Universidad Nacional Autónoma de México and in El Colegio de México. Clinical research on sexual problems is just starting, but some information is beginning to appear. The systematization of these efforts into a body of sexual science, however, is far from being realized. Sexology, as a formal discipline, is only recently being considered, and this with considerable reticence.

Advanced education in sexology has been offered by private institutions for some 25 years, but these efforts have been concentrated in Mexico City. Recently, a number of private and public universities have opened up the possibility of short programs on sexology, focusing on sex-education issues. The list below reflects the efforts and achievements of the main groups that have participated in the construction of the human sexuality body of professionals.

The Asociación Mexicana de Educación Sexual (AMES), a private nonprofit organization, was the first to offer systematic training in sex education, with good foundations in sexology. This organization has offered courses for professionals—usually professionals trained in other disciplines, such as education, psychology, and medicine—courses of approximately 180 hours, since 1974. Other institutions, such as the Instituto Mexicano de Sexología, followed this pattern, although with modifications in length and format of the courses offered.

Then, organizations with a focus on special problems, such as adolescent contraception, and family planning, followed. Among the latter, the Fundación Mexicana para la Planificación Familiar (MEXFAM) has distinguished itself in systematizing the training in sexuality via postgraduate courses in sex education and sex counseling. This organization has promoted the institutionalization of training in public universities in other cities in addition to Mexico City, in what has become known as the Diplomats in Sexuality.

Training in sex therapy has being available since 1987 in our institution, Asociación Mexicana para la Salud Sexual (AMSSAC). Training includes clinical experience and formal lectures and readings over two years, with 650 hours of instruction.

Official institutions have included courses on sexology in the medical and psychological curricula, but no formal graduate courses are offered, with the exception of the aforementioned Diplomats in Sexuality. No formal degrees in sexology are offered.

**Table 2**

**Frequencies of Diagnosis of Sexual Dysfunction in 195 Diagnostic Interviews at the Sexual Dysfunction Clinic, Asociacion Mexicana para la Salud Sexual, A.C. (AMSSAC)**

| Diagnosis | Males (138) | | Females (57) | |
|---|---|---|---|---|
| | *n* | % | *n* | % |
| Hypoactive desire | 67 | 26.07 | 7 | 29.13 |
| Hyperactive desire | 2 | 0.78 | 0 | 0.00 |
| Inhibited excitation | 86 | 33.46 | 36 | 28.35 |
| Anorgasmia | 10 | 3.89 | 38 | 29.92 |
| Pain syndromes | 9 | 3.50 | 5 | 3.94 |
| Premature ejaculation | 77 | 29.96 | 0 | 0.00 |
| Sexual phobia | 6 | 2.33 | 7 | 5.51 |
| Vaginismus | 0 | 0.00 | 4 | 3.15 |

*Source:* González 1993. Patients may have more than one diagnosis.

## References and Suggested Readings

Abasolo, G., Director of Social Communication of the Medical Services of the México City Government. 1990 (June 19). Quoted in a newspaper note: *Uno más uno*.

Casorla, G. (In press). Conductas sexuales delictivas: Violacion, incesto, abuso sexual, hostigamiento sexual y lenocinio. In: Consejo Nacional de Poblacion, ed., *Antologia de la sexualidad humana*. México.

CIA. 2002 (January). *The world factbook 2002*. Washington, DC: Central Intelligence Agency. Available: http://www.cia.gov/cia/publications/factbook/index.html.

CNP–Consejo Nacional de Población. 1989. *Programa nacional de población 1989-1994*. México City: Secretaria de Gobernacion.

Colimoro, C. 1993 (June). Personal Communication. México City.

CONAPO–Consejo Nacional de Población. 1988. *Encuesta nacional sobre sexualidad y familia en jóvenes de edu-*

*cación media superior, 1988.* Consejo Nacional de Población, México.

De la Peña, R., & R. Toledo. 1991a (May 26). El sexo en México (Part 1). *El Nacional Dominical.*

De la Peña, R., & R. Toledo. 1991b (June 2). El sexo en México segunda de cuatro partes: Debutantes y solitarios. (Part 2). *El Nacional Dominical.*

De la Peña, R., & R. Toledo. 1991c (June 9). Vida ¿en Pareja? El sexo en México. Primer informe (Part 3). *El Nacional Dominical.*

De la Peña, R., & R. Toledo. 1991d (June 16). El sexo en México. Primer informe. (Part 4): Cuerpos y susurros. *El Nacional Dominical.*

De la Peña, R., & R. Toledo. 1992a (March 1). Primer informe sobre sexualidad en Baja California. (Part 1). *El Nacional Dominical.*

De la Peña, R., & R. Toledo. 1992b (March 8). Primer informe sobre sexualidad en Baja California. (Part 2). *El Nacional Dominical.*

Del Rio, C. (In press). Enfermedades de transmisión por contacto sexual. In: Consejo Nacional de Poblacion, ed., *Antologia de la sexualidad humana.* México.

Díaz Loving, R. 1988. Desenredando la semántica del amor. In: *La psicología social de México: 1988.* México: Proceedings of the Congess of Social Psicology.

Dillon, S. 1997 (January 22). How to scandalize a politician: Bare a love affair. *The New York Times,* p. A4.

Eskala, E., et al. 1992. La adolescente embarazada y su relación de pareja. *Psicología social de México III. Proceedings of the Congess of Social Psycology.* México.

Falicov, C. J. 1982. Mexican families. In: M. McGoldrick, J. K. Pearce, & J. Giordano, eds., *Ethnicity and family therapy.* New York: Guilford Press.

Givaudán, M., & S. Pick de Weiss. 1992. Encuesta de opinión sobre el aborto inducido y su despenalización en el estado de Chiapas. *Psicología social de México III. Proceedings of the Congress of Social Psycology.* México.

Givaudán, M., & S. Pick de Weiss. 1992. Encuesta de opinión sobre el aborto inducido y su despenalización en la ciudad de México. *Psicología social de México III. Proceedings of the Congress of Social Psycology.* México.

González, G. 1993. Panorama sociodemográfico del servicio de preconsulta de la clínica de salud sexual AMSSAC. *Gaceta Amssac, 1*(1):2-5.

IMSS–Instituto Mexicano del Seguro Social. 1990. *Síntesis IMSS.* México.

INDRE–Instituto Nacionál de Diagnónstico y Referencia Epidemiológicos. 1994 (January). *Boletín Mensual SIDA/ETS* [México], *8*(1):2576-2593.

INEGI–Instituto Nacionál de Estadística Geografía e Informática. 1992a. *Estados Unidos Mexicanos: Perfil sociodemografico XI censo general de poblacion y vicienda, 1990.* México City: INEGI.

INEGI–Instituto Nacionál de Estadística Geografía e Informática. 1992b. *Estados Unidos Mexicanos: Resumen general XI censo general de población y vivienda, 1990.* México City: INEGI.

Lavrin, A. 1991. La sexualidad en el México colonial: Un dilema para la Iglesia. In: A. Lavrin, ed., *Sexualidad y matrimonio en la America Hispana: Siglos XVI-XVIII.* México D.F.: Grijalbo.

López Juarez, A. 1982. Familia y sexualidad en México. In: Consejo Nacional de Población (CONAPO), ed., *La educación de la sexualidad humana. Familia y sexualidad.* México City: CONAPO.

Lumsden, I. 1991. *Homosexualidad, socedad y estado en México.* México: Solediciones Canadian Gay Archives.

Morgan, M. I. 1982. La sexualidad en la sociedad en la sociedad Azteca. In: H. Carrizo, ed., *La educacion de la sexualidad humana: Sociedad y sexualidad.* México City: Consejo Nacional de Poblacion.

Morris, L., et al. 1987. *Young adult reproductive health survey in two delegations of Mexico City.* México City: Centro de Orientación Para Adolescentes.

Muñoz Gonzalez, L. 1992 (October). Departamento de Atención an Victimas: Procuraduría de Justicia del Distrito Federal. Personal communication.

Ordiozola-Urbina, A., & B. Ibañes-Brambila. 1992. Actitudes y conducta sexual en estudiantes universitarios. *Psicología social de México III. Proceedings of the Congress of Social Psycology.* México.

Padgett, T. 1995 (September 18). The end of the affair: Mexico's threat to an institution—Mistresses. *Newsweek,* p. 59.

Palafox Vargas, M. 1985. *Violencia, droga y sexo entre los huicholes.* México: Instituto Nacional de Antropología e Historia.

Paz, O. 1950. *El laberinto de la soledad.* México: Fondo de Cultura Economica.

Rubio, E. 1989. *A cross-cultural investigation of sexual behavior, religiosity and familism among American and Mexican urban single college students.* Doctoral dissertation. New York, NY: New York University.

Rubio, E., et al. 1988 (March). Caracterización de las opiniones y experiencias sexuales de los alumnos de primer ingreso a la carrera de médico cirujano. *Salud Mental, 11*(1):25-34.

Ruiz Harrel, R. 1979. Personal Communication. México City.

Saavedra Arredondo, G., ed. 1986. *La educación en población: Marco de referencia.* México: Consejo Nacional de Población.

Secretaría de Salud. 1987. *Dirección general de planificación familiar.* México: Encuesta Nacional Sobre Fecundidad y Salud.

Secretaría de Salud. 1990. *La salud de la mujer en México. Cifras comentadas. Dirección general de salud materno infantil.* México: Programa Nacional Mujer Salud y Desarrollo.

Secretaría de Salud. 1992. *Compendio de estadísticas de morbilidad 1991.* México: Dirección General de Epidemiología.

UNAIDS. 2002. *Epidemiological fact sheets by country.* Geneva, Switzerland: Joint United Nations Programme on HIV/AIDS (UNAIDS/WHO). Available: http://www.unaids.org/hivaidsinfo/statistics/fact_sheets/index_en.htm.

Urbina Fuentes, M. 1992. Jóvenes reproductores. In: H. Bellinghausen, ed., *El nuevo arte de amar.* México: Cal y Arena.

Wolf, E. 1975. *Pueblos y culturas de Mesoamerica* (3rd ed.). México City: Biblioteca Era.

# Morocco

## (*Le Moroc*) (French)
## (*al-Mamlaka al-Maghrebia*) (Arabic)
## (The Kingdom of Morocco)

Nadia Kadiri, M.D., and Abderrazak Moussaïd, M.D.,*
with Abdelkrim Tirraf, M.D., and Abdallah Jadid, M.D.
*Translated by*
Raymond J. Noonan, Ph.D., and Dra. Sandra Almeida
*Comments by Elaine Hatfield, Ph.D., and
Richard Rapson, Ph.D.; Updates by the Editors*

## Contents

## *Demographics and a Brief Historical Perspective*

ROBERT T. FRANCOEUR

### A. Demographics

Morocco is situated on the northwestern coast of Africa. It shares its borders with Algeria to the east and south, and with Mauritania to the southwest. It is bordered on the west by the Atlantic Ocean and on the north by the Mediterranean Sea, the two expanses of water being separated by the Strait of Gibraltar, which is situated to the north of Morocco. The area of Morocco is 172,410 square miles (446,550 km²), slightly larger than the state of California. About 20% of the land of Morocco is arable. Fertile plains extend the length of the Atlantic coastline: in the regions from the center-north, the plain of Fès-Saiss; to the south, the plain of Souss-Massa; and to the south-southwest, the Tadla. To the east of these plains, the Atlas Mountains, which peak at 4,165 meters (13,665 ft.) (Toubkal), extend from the southwest of Morocco to the confines of the Algerian borders in the northeast. To the north, the Rif Mountains connect the northwest coast of Morocco to West Algeria (l'Ouest Algérien). Of the great wealth of Morocco, along with farming and its human resources, is the mining of phosphate, which is found in great abundance in the central regions of Morocco, the city of Khouribga, and in the Moroccan Sahara. Until 1976, the Mo-

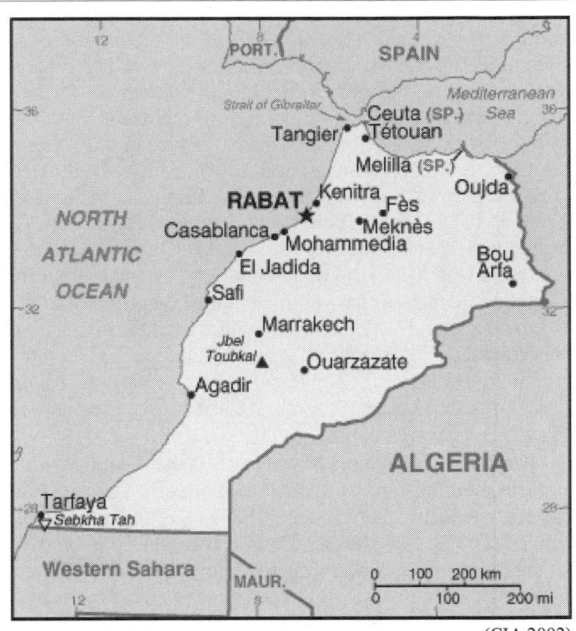

(CIA 2002)

roccan Sahara represented one of the last vestiges of French colonialism in Morocco.

In July 2002, Morocco had an estimated population of 31.17 million. (All data are from *The World Factbook 2002* (CIA 2002) unless otherwise stated.)

**Age Distribution and Sex Ratios**: *0-14 years*: 33.8% with 1.04 male(s) per female (sex ratio); *15-64 years*: 61.5% with 0.99 male(s) per female; *65 years and over*: 4.7% with 0.82 male(s) per female; *Total population sex ratio*: 1.0 male(s) to 1 female

**Life Expectancy at Birth**: *Total Population*: 69.43 years; *male*: 67.2 years; *female*: 71.76 years

**Urban/Rural Distribution**: 53% to 47%

**Ethnic Distribution**: Arab-Berber: 99.1%; other: 0.8%; Jewish: 0.2%

**Religious Distribution**: Muslin: 98.7%; Christian: 1.1%; Jewish: 0.2%

**Birth Rate**: 23.69 births per 1,000 population

**Death Rate**: 5.86 per 1,000 population

**Infant Mortality Rate**: 46.49 deaths per 1,000 live births

**Net Migration Rate**: –1.09 migrant(s) per 1,000 population

**Total Fertility Rate**: 2.97 children born per woman

**Population Growth Rate**: 1.68%

**HIV/AIDS** (1999 est.): *Adult prevalence*: 0.03%; *Persons living with HIV/AIDS*: NA; *Deaths*: NA. (For additional details from www.UNAIDS.org, see end of Section 10B.)

**Literacy Rate** (*defined as those age 15 and over who can read and write*): 43.7% (*male*: 56.6%, *female*: 31%) (1995 est.); *attendance for nine years of compulsory school*: 95% (education is free and compulsory from age 6 to 16)

**Per Capita Gross Domestic Product** (*purchasing power parity*): $3,700 (2001 est.); *Inflation*: 1% (2001 est.); *Unemployment*: 23% (1999 est.); *Living below the poverty line*: 19% (1999 est.)

### B. A Brief Historical Perspective

Morocco is rich in Paleolithic remains, particularly in parts of North Africa and the Sahara, which were populated until the Neolithic era. The people who settled in the region soon after that were probably natives of Europe and Asia. They became the ancestors of today's Berbers. In the 7th

*Communications*: Nadia Kadiri, M.D., Professor of Psychiatry, Centre Psychiatrique Universitaire, Rue Tarik Ib Ziad, Casablanca, Morocco; nadiakadiri@hotmail.com *or* n.kadri@casanet.net.ma *or* nadiakadiri@yahoo.com. Abderrazak Moussaïd, M.D., 38, Boulevard Rahal El Meskini, 20 000 Casablanca, Morocco. Elaine Hatfield, Ph.D., University of Hawaii, Psychology, 2430 Campus Road, Honolulu, Hawaii 96822 USA; elaineh1@aol.com.

century B.C.E., the Phoenicians laid the foundations of commerce on the Mediterranean coast of North Africa at sites having Berber names that became the great ports of Tingi (Tangier), Melilia (Russadir), and Casablanca. The conquest of Carthage by the Roman Empire in the 1st century B.C.E. assured Roman domination of the entire African Mediterranean coastline to the Straits of Gibraltar. From 25 to 23 B.C.E., Juba II, a Berber sovereign, administered the Berber kingdom of Mauritania (Algeria, Morocco, and a part of Mauritania). Around 42 C.E., the emperor Claudius I annexed the whole empire of Mauritania to the Roman Empire. In 429, Morocco underwent the invasion of the Vandals. The Byzantine general Bélisaire regained the region in 533. After the conversion of the emperor Constantine I the Great in the 4th century, Christianity expanded in the Roman regions.

It appears that Islamic troops reached the Atlantic Ocean in 681 under the command of Oqba Ibn Nafii. The real conquest started later on, between 705 and 707, under the direction of Moussa Ibn Nousair. The Muslim establishment was in the meantime long and difficult. Many Muslim dynasties, claiming Arabic origins for religious reasons or prestige, ruled in various areas of the country. In 788, Idriss I, descendant of Ali, son-in-law of the Prophet, founded the dynasty of the Idrissides. It is from this age that dates the founding of the city of Fès, which became an important religious and cultural center of the Islamic world under Idriss II. The rigorist Almoravide warriors of Islam went on to dominate the region beginning in 1062, the date at which they founded Marrakech as the crossroads of commercial routes between the Arab world and the Sahara. A new reform movement, the Almohades (the Unities), launched by Ibn Toumart in the first half of the 12th century, put an end to the Almoravide empire in 1147, marking the triumph of the seated Berbers of the anti-Atlas under the aegis of Abd Al-Moumen (1130-1163). The Almohades exercised their authority over what are currently Algeria, Tunisia, Libya, and part of Portugal and Spain.

In 1269, the Mérinides of the Arabic Berbers took over the throne, but they could not maintain the unity of the North African empire of the Almohades. During the reconquest of Spain, which exiled the Arabs and the Jews, the great majority of Spanish Muslims found refuge in Morocco they took over. In 1415, Ceuta (Sebta) was occupied by the Portuguese. In 1497, Melilia fell to the Spanish. The intrusions of the Europeans provoked the rise of the Beni Saâd (or Saâdiens), who became masters of the country in 1554. Moroccan Saâdiens, aided by Moorish and Jewish refugees from Spain, created a prosperous and unified country. In this period, Moroccan architecture and arts flourished. In 1664, Maulay Rachid founded the Alaouite dynasty, which still reigns to this day in Morocco. The Alaouite dynasty knew its apogee under the sultan Moulay Ismail (1672-1727), the builder of the city of Meknès. His reign was followed by a long period of family rivalries. At the end of the 18th century, only the northern third of Morocco remained under the administration of the sultan.

On March 30, 1912, the sultan recognized the French protectorate. Spain, for its part, assumed control of the north of Morocco, from the enclave of Ifni (southwest) and from the Moroccan Sahara (west). The occupation of the country was not total until 1934. After World War II, the Moroccan nationalist resistance forced independence in 1956, opening the era of the constitutional monarchy in Morocco. The last vestiges of European colonialism persisted until the recent past. The enclave of Ifni was not returned to Morocco until 1964, and the Moroccan Sahara was not recovered until 1976 at the end of a popular nationalist march called the "Green March." Two other enclaves, small ports situated on the Mediterranean coast west of Tangier, Ceuta and Melilia, are still occupied by Spain.

## 1. Basic Sexological Premises

### A. Character of Gender Roles

The traditional family structure remains very faithfully attached to the archaic patriarchal scheme. The father is, in general, a patriarch who inspires respect and to whom one owes obedience and acknowledgment. The mother is the housekeeper "wife-mother" who does everything. She is the one who makes the decisions in the social sphere. But she prepares her own strategy for managing her ecosystem by imposing a strong personality in the household. She reveals herself to be more conservative than the man. When a woman becomes a mother, she is always considered a potential danger, because she is perceived as having a devastating effect on the man. However, our Islamic religion adopts an ambivalent attitude toward women. On one side, she is considered as being more wily than *Iblis* (Satan) whom she incarnates in our collective unconscious; on the other side, the *Hadith* (*Words of the Prophet*) considers woman as a simple being of spirit, whose faith is incomplete. This notion is largely predominant in the rural population, whereas city women have begun to rebel against this state of things (Moussaid 1992; Naamane 1990). [*Update 1998*: In terms of Moroccan cultural change, there are continuing tensions between the people of the *magzken* in the urban organized government and the people of the rural and tribal *bled*. These tensions often focus on the differences between modern Western sexual and marital values and the age-old customs and values espoused by the tribal and rural cultures (Fernea 1998, 63). (*End of update by R. T. Francoeur*)]

### B. Sociolegal Status of Males and Females

In the legal sphere, the rights of the individual man or woman are governed by the penal code, the code of commerce, and the code of family (personal) law (*mudawana*). Morocco's penal and commercial codes are identical in scope, with men and women sharing the same rights and obligations. To the contrary, the code of family law, which regulates man-woman relations in the domains of marriage, repudiation, filiation, custody of the children, guardianship, and inheritance, is far from being equitable (*Statut du Code* 1996).

[*Update 2000*: A first step in reform of the *mudawana* came in the early 1980s, when the Union de l'Action Feminin and other groups gathered over a million signatures in support of a petition urging the King to reform the family law regulating marriage, divorce, inheritance, child custody, and polygamy. There is still no central office to deal with alimony or child support. The new code is known as the *Statut du Code Personnel "Mudawana"* (1996) (Fernea 1998, 106, 113, 120). (*End of update by R. T. Francoeur*)]

If the penal and commercial codes are inspired by French law, the Moroccan code of family law is inspired by the *Chariâ* (*Islamic Law*), especially that of the Malékite rite. Although the *Chariâ* accepts polygamy with up to four legitimate wives, Moroccan law adopts some restrictions with the view of limiting the practice of polygamy, and poses conditions of equality in the treatment of the co-spouses. Polygamy is to be avoided when a disparity is to be feared (Article 30.1).

On the other hand, Moroccan women still have not been able to reach a real emancipation and autonomy vis-à-vis men, despite the important changes observed in our modern society. The Moroccan woman still commonly estimates the man to be superior to her, tolerates work of a temporary nature, judges having children, especially boys, as all important for inheritance, thinks that virginity is of major importance, and accords a great place to the ceremony of marriage. The woman in our society is a woman in evolution, but she remains linked to the group (Amir 1988; Kacha 1996; Moussaid 1992). This woman is opposed to the total transformation of those who might lead us toward an insecure situation. This opposition is because of internal resistance that is linked to the educational and external schemas in the measure where the social milieu brakes this desire for change (Amir 1988; Kacha 1996).

On March 12, 2000, two rival demonstrations by several hundred thousand Moroccans bore testimony to the transitional tensions and evolution evident in our country. The issue of both demonstrations was a government plan for a variety of social and human rights reforms proposed by the new King, Mohammed VI, who came to the throne after the death of his father, King Hassan II, in July 1999. Among other reforms, the government plan would fully replace with a court divorce the practice of repudiation, in which the husband can divorce his wife by a triple verbal declaration. The reform would also provide for equal division of money and property in a divorce, and support a literacy program for rural Moroccan women, over 80% of whom are illiterate. In the capital, Rabat, 200,000 to 300,000 members and representatives of women's groups, human rights movements, and political parties ended their march supporting the reform with a concert. In Casablanca, at least 200,000 men and women marching in separate columns—some claimed twice that number—denounced the reform (Associated Press 2000).

[*Update 2000*: In terms of judiciary power, Morocco is far ahead of Egypt, with 20% of its judges being women, compared with no Egyptian female judges. On the other hand, whereas Egyptian President Sadat appointed 35 women to his country's Parliament in 1981, Moroccan women had to wait 37 years following independence to have two women elected to the Moroccan Parliament (Fernea 1998, 117). (*End of update by R. T. Francoeur*)]

## C. General Concepts of Sexuality and Love

In Islam, the love of God occupies a big place in the heart of the believer with regard to carnal love. This has not prevented sexuality from flourishing with the advance of Arab-Islamic civilization, across the different dynasties, in passing through the great sociocultural cities of Damas, Baghdad, and Cairo (Malek 1995). Since those early times, the arts, knowledge, amorous poetry, and sexual culture have not ceased to deteriorate. This degradation puts in relief the contradictions that exist between the religious law and the traditions that are a part of what is prescribed by Islam concerning sexuality and what is forbidden within the family, in the extended community, and in the whole society. While the Muslim religion is more permissive, in contrast to Christianity, it gives primacy to carnal pleasure within the framework of marriage as a means of union with the other and with God. This glorification of sexual pleasure is a necessary ornament to the existence of the believer. Sexual abstention is, consequently, advised against, almost forbidden: "Rahbaniatan: The monasticism that they [Christians] have created has not ever been recommended or enjoined by us," the Koran tells us. The *nikah* (marriage), the religious and judicial framework in which sexuality exerts itself, organizes the sexual connections, their breaks, their changes, and the practical consequences that they entail.

## 2. Religious, Ethnic, and Gender Factors Affecting Sexuality

[*Comment 1998*: To understand Moroccan culture, one needs to have some sense of the Spanish, French, Portuguese, Berber, and Arabic influences that have been blended together to create modern Moroccan linguistic heritage and customs. In Moroccan civil law, we are dealing with Islamic law, local customary law, and the resonance of tribal law, Spanish and Portuguese customs, and the French penal code. Attitudes toward women, for instance, come not only from Islam, but also earlier presences, such as the Tuareg nomads in the south and the mountains. When Herodatus spoke of the "blue men of the desert," he commented on how socially strong the Tuareg women were, and called them Amazons. When the Tuaregs became Muslims, they kept their tribal laws (Fernea 1998, 63-64). (*End of comment by R. T. Francoeur*)]

## A. Cultural Factors

The sexual behavior of humans is largely influenced by their sociocultural context. In our societies, to bring up the subject of sexuality is *hchouma*. This word is delicate to translate: On the one hand, it means "disgrace," on the other hand, it means "modesty." It is a code to which one conforms without reflecting on it and which legislates all the situations of existence. *Hchouma* presents itself thus like a thick veil that separates two worlds in total opposition: The one is governed by local customs and excludes every possibility for a being to affirm oneself as an individual, except for the social model. The other universe is done in silence and in secret. It is the world of the person beyond the conventions (Naamane 1999).

In the Arab world, sexuality remains a taboo, the oppression of women keeps their appearance more archaic; however, many voices are being raised against this state of things. Thus, many voices are being raised to denounce the situation of women in the Arab world and especially the sexist discrimination: polygamy, the wearing of the veil, and their non-participation in public life (Attahir; Cherni 1993; Kacem 1970).

In Morocco, the role of the woman and her status varies as a function of her ethnic origin, of her rural or urban setting, and of her socioeconomic and intellectual level, among others. Thus, according to the last census (1997), only a quarter of the urban women are illiterate, compared with 89% of rural women. Likewise, with the practice of polygamy, which varies according to the regions. The Berbers and the Fassis are less polygamous than the inhabitants of the Chaouia (region of the center). Women of the Moroccan Rif and of certain regions of the north work in the fields, assuming the rougher tasks, while men are generally passive. However, these women benefit from more experience, the right to education, and the right to work. But despite the recent changes in women's personal status [*mudawana*], more limits are emphasized in the persistence of polygamy, no right to divorce (the husband's prerogative), and no equality for inheritance, where a daughter inherits half of what a son receives.

However, misogyny remains common currency in Morocco; the woman holds a social status of second rank. She often remains less desired at birth than the boy. She frequently has less access to education. If she works, she has to do double work: professional activities and household activities. And she owes obedience to her husband.

## B. Source and Character of Religious Values

Knowing that 99% of Moroccans are Sunni Muslims, a remark must be made immediately: Islam is far from being the religion most repressive of feminine sexuality as it is current to believe; well to the contrary, Islam's view of sexuality takes more of the sense of a sacred duty, where erotic practices are encouraged, pleasure is pursued, and the satisfaction of the woman is indicated. Islam distinguishes itself in this way from the Judeo-Christian culture, where sexuality is a "regrettable necessity," a moment of victory of the body over the soul according to classical duality (body/soul, good/bad).

In considering woman as an erotic and seductive being, but also deceptive, Islam creates fears of the ominous role she can play in destabilizing society. Thus the prophet said: "I will not let this point be the cause of worse discord for men than for women."

Mernissi (1983) writes in this framework: For Islam, the woman is an invincible seductress; the undoing of the man is inevitable if he does not have recourse to God. The prophet orders his disciples: "Do not visit the women alone, Satan will seize you" (Berrada et al. 1999). In order to avoid the ominous consequences of that sensual and seductive tyranny over the social equilibrium, the Koran has foreseen the following measures:

- *Prohibition of Coeducation.* However, in Morocco, co-education in the primary and secondary schools and universities is a current practice. Women have the right to enter any profession or job. Just recently can one find women employed as traffic police.
- *Wearing of the Veil.* In Morocco, one finds great freedom regarding the wearing of the veil. Despite the extremist events that have occurred over the years, Morocco has witnessed a rise of integration and accommodation. Although the number of women who wear the veil has increased greatly, the wearing of the veil is a trivial act, neither rejected nor required.
- *Sexist Discrimination and Oppression of Women.* Islam has attributed to women the status of minors. During all periods of life, it is the man (father, husband, or son), who manages her life. She owes him obedience and submission. She can be beaten in the case of disobedience (*Les Femmes IV*: Sourat 38).
- *Polygyny.* Islam gives to man the right to have four wives at the same time (*Les Femmes IV*: Sourat 3). In defense of this right, the Imam Ghazali explains: "There are some men whose sexual desire is so ebullient, that a single woman does not satisfy them and does not protect them against the risk of becoming adulterous. It is desirable in this case that they marry several women (from one to four)" (Al Ghazali 1992). Thus, on the one hand, for Islam, it is the woman who is a seductress and nymphomaniac. On the other hand, it is the man who needs four women to appease his needs! Mernissi (1983) poses the question whether it is not the dreaded polyandry that is at the base of the conclusions regarding the erotic nature of women. The sexual satisfaction of women is taken into account by such laws that made sexual satisfaction of the woman a conjugal right in the case of polygamy and that authorized divorce in the case of the impotence or abstinence of the husband. Thus, the sexually satisfied woman will not try to look for sexual pleasure in illicit extramarital relationships.
- *Control of Women's Sexual Practices.* Islam constrains the woman to make love with her husband every time that he wants. In the case of refusal, she exposes herself to the curse of God. The prophet, reported by Boukhari, said: "The woman who refuses to satisfy the needs of her husband is cursed until she accepts."

Islam gives the woman the right to accept sexual pleasure. Thus, "the preliminary games [loveplay] (*mulaaba*) are warmly recommended by the prophet," "caress your women until they are tender." These preliminaries are destined for the satisfaction of the woman, just as the sexual act is not a bothersome duty, but the happiest gift from heaven (Boudhdiba 1986).

The frequency of marital contact has also been regulated. Thus, the Imam Al Ghazali (1992) recommends that Muslims make love with their wives as frequently as possible. He proposes for the polygamous at least one contact every four days.

Sodomy is prohibited. "Cursed are those who take the woman by the anus," said the prophet (Al Ghazali 1992). Sexual contact during menstruation is forbidden by the Koran (*The Génisse II*: Sourat 22). Masturbation, even though not forbidden, is not recommended. It is permitted only in the case of the risk of adultery or in the event marriage is not possible. Sexual contacts outside of marriage are prohibited.

## 3. Knowledge and Education about Sexuality

### A. Government Policies and Programs

Sexual education, such as is seen in European and North American countries as part of the programs of academic study, does not exist in either primary or secondary academic programs. What is taught is provided in the form of scientific knowledge of the anatomy of the sexual organs and of the biology of fertilization. This sexual education is centered on procreation and prevention of sexually transmitted diseases.

### B. Informal Sources of Sexual Knowledge

The expression "sexual education" is part of the multiple taboos that characterize our society. The subject frightens and worries Moroccans, because there has always been confusion between sexual education and sexual freedom. Discussing sexuality with parents remains a strong taboo in Morocco. A certain difference exists between the two sexes. For all young children, boys are encouraged to display their genital organs, whereas girls are supposed to hide their intimacy. At the time of preadolescence, the girl has discussions with her mother, who believes her role is to inculcate in her daughter the obligation to preserve her virginity and to avoid all sexual contact before the bonds of marriage. During these discussions, she prepares her daughter for puberty. The principal role of the mother is to obligate her to preserve her virginity with a talk full of modesty and *hchouma*. On the other hand, the preadolescent boy is left to his own devices, and has no one with whom to talk about his bodily transformations other than his friends and companions. A study in 1992 (Naamane 1999) showed that in 360 Moroccan men, divided equitably between the urban and rural areas, no man had ever gotten information from his father. In one case, the father made an allusion to the puberty of his son to ask him to begin to fast. Thus, in these situations where the young lack total communication about anything sexual with their parents and elders, it remains only to the young of their age, the media, and popular speech.

## 4. Autoerotic Behaviors and Patterns

Autoeroticism, in its broadest sense, is not condemned by the *Fikh* (religious law). Moreover, no Koranic verse mentions masturbation as a prohibited practice, so it is both a quite common and well known sexual outlet. The point of contention concerns the obligation of ablutions after involuntary touching of the genitals (Rissala in Malek, 1995, p. 29). In the rural areas, masturbation, as much as zoophilia, remains the instrument most used in a male youth's apprenticeship in sexuality. Adolescents masturbate themselves, often in a group, making from this event a competition that consecrates the one that ejaculates quickly and most strongly. If masturbation among adolescents is hushed, ignored, but not tolerated, that of adults is almost a sacrilege. It is a *hchouma*, more than a disgrace, without being truly illicit. In the popular mind, the fingers of the hand can symbolize the spelling of the word *Allah*: The little finger indicates the letter *A*, the ring and middle finger represents *LL*, and the closed index finger and thumb represents *H*, so the hand symbolizes *Allah* and must not be used as a sexual instrument.

## 5. Interpersonal Heterosexual Behaviors

### A. Children

Infantile sexuality absolutely is said not to exist in our context. Instead, from early childhood, one inculcates an implicit sexual education totally antagonistic to the consideration of the two sexes. The sexuality of a boy is praised and valued. He must forge his virility from his young age; he must be the stallion who must get hard in the presence of a woman (Malek 1995). The sexual education of girls is done traditionally by the women of the family, by mothers, aunts, and older sisters. The older women tell the young girl what is forbidden and what is recommended in terms of repressing their sexuality.

### B. Adolescents

Female adolescence is dominated by the repression of sexuality with the objective of preserving an intact hymen, the symbol of chastity, until the wedding day. The education of the senses of the body is negative and tends to block the personality of the girl on both the physical and psychic planes. The adolescent girl carries the mark [*prégnante*] of *hchouma* (disgrace) and honor, which crystallizes itself in the obsession with virginity (Naamane 1990). This education is perpetuated by the mothers, who make each step of the evolution of the girl a shock lived in anxiety. However, a study in the urban areas observed that "in three decades, the proportion of women initiated in the elementary principles of their sexuality changed from 38% to 55%." This initiation touches on two essential questions, menstruation and the gaining of knowledge of sexual contact (intercourse) (Naamane 1990). Paradoxically, in the large cities like Casablanca, girls have access to sexual information at a precocious age.

### C. Adults

The sexuality of adults is only conceived of within the framework of marriage. The couple is then an inescapable notion and an obligation that brings one to social conformity. However, the stakes of control in this institution are varied. Contrary to the apparent patriarchy, there are many households that are managed by women with strong personalities. This reality is reinforced by the number of children: The more children a woman has, the greater is her power. And it is not by chance that polygyny is predominant in certain regions more than others.

[*Update 2001*: In the northern coastal region of the Rif, patterns of authority in the traditional Moroccan family are changing because of a major economic reality. Local unemployment has drawn 60% of the fathers and sons in the Rif to Europe in search of employment, leaving many households headed by women. At the same time, Morocco is witnessing an increase in the number of young and middle-aged women choosing to remain single. Almost invariably, these singles by choice are economically self-sufficient and well educated (Fernea 1998, 104, 116)

[The preliminaries to a traditional Islamic marriage negotiation are concerned with class, family histories (blood), and the dowry. Marriage in Morocco today involves new concerns about common goals, joint religious faith, educational background and career potential, and love and romance. In the High Atlas Mountains, the Ait Haddidou tribe follows a very different set of marriage customs. During the annual *moussem* or festival season in Imilchil, men and women arrive looking for mates. The divorced, single, young, and middle-aged come in hopes of finding true love or at least a suitable partner. The village notary publics register the couples, so there is some record, but it is commonly understood that the couple can split up after a day or a month or a year, with no cost, no hard feelings, and no religious stigma (Fernea 1998, 64, 88-89, 104). (*End of update by R. T. Francoeur*)]

[*Comment 2003*: In Morocco, as in other cultures in which traditional tribal rural customs come into conflict with Western urban values, one of the most frequent and often-complex conflicts finds the family and older generation expecting the traditional arranged marriage, while the younger generation is being influenced by contact with the romantic marry-the-one-you-love view of marriage. Coping with this conflict of expectations and values requires some kind of compromise if the individuals and families involved are to avoid a major tragedy. (The reader is referred to Section 13 of the chapter on Sweden where the Editor summarizes the 2002 tragedy of Fadime Sahindal, a 26-year-old Kurdish woman who fell in love with a Swedish man and became the victim of an "honor killing" by her father.) Here we provide an abbreviated account of a Moroccan-tribal versus modern-marriage conflict that ended in a compromise. (The original 1987 account can be found in Roger and Terri Joseph's *The Rose and the Thorn*.) The Josephs' vivid descriptions of Moroccan family life make it clear that, even in Morocco, compromise is often required. In most of the world today, prospective brides and grooms, parents, elders, and the extended family have to consult with one another before arranging a marriage. Even in the most traditional of societies, parents and husbands have generally been forced to balance conflicting interests.

[The Moroccan tribal world, for example, is definitely a man's world. Men possess absolute authority over their wives and children. They have the power to take several wives. They often promise their sons and daughters to potential allies at very young ages. Yet, if you think of your own family, you will surely observe that things do not always go as they are "supposed" to. Some fathers are impossible. Eventually, family members learn that it is easier to give in than to try to argue. Some aunts are strategic geniuses—they can enlist an army of relatives to plead, threaten, and haggle on their behalf.

[Hamadi and Fatima, for example, were going along, happily married, when Hamadi decided that it was time to acquire a second wife. Within days, everyone in his immense, extended family was squabbling. Fatima threatened to divorce Hamadi if he married again. She refused to share her house with another woman. Fatima's brothers warned Hamadi that if Hamadi and Fatima got a divorce, they would reclaim all the land she had brought into the marriage. (Hamadi had spent years planting fruit and nut trees on the property.) Fatima threatened to take their twin daughters to her brother's house as well. Technically, Hamadi's family "owned" the infants, but because they were still nursing, he would have to wait two years to collect them. In Morocco, twins are considered to be *baraka* (good fortune); if Hamadi's daughters left, people might conclude that good fortune had left Hamadi's house. To add to Hamadi's woes, Fatima issued a final warning. If Hamadi divorced her, she would march bare-breasted to the weekly market. This left him badly shaken. Things got worse. One of Fatima's brothers had married Hamadi's cousin. He announced that if there was to be bad blood between the two families, he would divorce his wife. Hamadi's mother complained that the money Hamadi had saved for a second wife should be spent on Hamadi's son, Ali, who had just turned 15. He needed money for his wedding. Finally, a tired Hamadi surrendered. He concluded, "Women are to be gotten around, but I guess I won't get around these" (Joseph & Joseph 1987, 55).

[When other "all powerful" Moroccan fathers tried to force their children into unappealing marriages, sympathetic family members employed an avalanche of strategies to thwart them. Young lovers persuaded mothers, uncles, brothers, neighbors, and business partners to plead on their behalf. One fond mother slyly hinted that a prospective bride her son secretly disliked was bad tempered, lazy, and had a bad reputation. When his father forced Abdallah to marry a woman he disliked, Abdallah claimed his wife was a witch. He divorced her and married the woman he had been attracted to in the first place. After that, his poor father's alliances were really in shambles.

[One young woman threatened to kill herself if she were forced to marry. Many relied on witchcraft or magical charms to get their way. One woman warned an unappealing suitor (Haddu) that she had visited a *dhazubrith* (witch) and obtained a spell that was guaranteed to make him impotent. The marriage took place, but the hapless Haddu was unable to "become stiff" (p. 49). He tried counter-charms, but to no avail. He finally agreed to dissolve the marriage. Sometimes, these desperate stratagems worked; sometimes they did not. (*End of comment by Hatfield & Rapson, 1996, 47-48)*)]

As for extramarital relations, they are illicit. But socially, the "treachery" of the woman is much more condemnable than that of the man. In reality, after 30 or more years of marriage, the woman often becomes much more demanding with regard to her husband and does not hesitate to get involved with extramarital relations. In urban areas, despite the traditional norms and ideals, marriage is more and more inaccessible because of material constraints, particularly, the high cost of living and high unemployment, which make marriage impractical for many young men. The "detribalized" urban space creates intense sexual needs, but offers very few possibilities to satisfy them (Dialamy 1995).

In 1971, the average size of households was over 5.6 persons; this rose to 5.9 persons in 1982. In the same year, 1982, the rate of occupation was 2.3 persons per room. Many couples do not have a private bedroom. Thus, the beginning of a couple is hypothetical because of the absence of this exclusive and independent space that permits the spouses to isolate themselves during their sexual play, the condition imposed by the *Chariâ* and tradition.

Divorce by "repudiation" is an absolute weapon available only to the man, who can use it when he desires, even though the last modifications of the code of family law (1993) tend to humanize it more. The custody of children remains the full right of the mother, who to receive it should remain single until the boy is 12 years old and the girl is 14, the age at which a child has the right to choose the parent with whom he or she wants to live. When the mother remarries, the custody of the children returns automatically to the father (*Statut du Code* 1996).

Access to sexual pleasure is an inalienable right, prescribed by our religion, for both spouses to the same degree. Consequently, pleasure opens the path to all sexual practices. Only sodomy is prohibited by all the theological traditions. Instead, according to irrational popular ideas, the missionary position alone is well accepted. The other positions are seen as being generators of disorders and diseases.

## 6. Homoerotic, Homosexual, and Bisexual Behaviors

### A. Homosexuality

Homosexuality (*liwat*) derives from the name of Lot, whose person and tribe is mentioned on numerous occa-

sions by the sacred books (Malek 1995). In Morocco, male homosexuality is considered a punishable offense by both the *Chariâ* and the civil penal code. This attitude pushes homosexual practice into a clandestine realm, with all the obvious consequences associated with such social denial. Conformity to all-important social rules requires a male, regardless of his sexual orientation, to get married and have children. Within this façade of social conformity, homosexual males create well-closed spaces, cafés, cinemas, nightclubs, and so on, where they can meet other like-minded males without endangering their façade. They are completely sealed to all who come to these places for encounters.

Female homosexuality or *sihaq* is not mentioned in the Koran. It is prevalent in certain regions of Morocco, particularly the north, but remains hidden, unmentioned, and unstudied.

### B. Homoeroticism

Westerners consider certain behaviors of Arabs in general as signs of latent homosexuality. It is a matter of certain completely acceptable male behaviors, like holding hands, putting an arm around another man's shoulder, embracing the face, bathing together (Moorish bath), and masturbating in a group during adolescence in rural areas. From our point of view, these behaviors have nothing to do with being sexual. They are part of our everyday culture.

## 7. Gender Diversity and Transgender Issues

No scientific work has been performed in the transgendered field. The real transsexual subject is rarely seen as anything other than an isolated entity. They are generally confused with homosexual persons or persons with other deviant behavior. Casablanca has been known for a long time as a city where transsexuals came from all over the world for sex-change surgery. Although available, these operations were always practiced in a clandestine way.

However, cases do arise in the course of psychological consultations, in which the young behave in school or during everyday life in a manner opposite their sexual identity. In the course of follow up, some of these persons experience depression syndromes because of this conflict between their sexual identity and their social identity. Management of such cases is difficult in Morocco, where there is a complete legal void concerning this clinical entity. (See Section 8D below for transvestism.)

## 8. Significant Unconventional Sexual Behaviors

Sexology in our context must take account of sexually deviant or perverse behaviors. The particularity comes from the fact that what is perverse for us in the East may not be considered so in the West and vice versa. In this framework, it is the conformity to the prevailing social rules that sets the criteria for normality. All behavior that does not obey the said social criteria, is considered in our society as an offense. The question that is posed then is: Why are we seeing many transsexuals and transvestites in the West and very few in our Islamic countries, and then only in very specific and close circles? In our point of view, the answer lies in the close relationship between behavior and the system (society and power) in which we are living. If the social system is too liberal, too permissive, it will favor easy access and freer expression of more sophisticated "perversities." At the same time, a too rigid and repressive system will favor the appearance of a meager, weak, and repressed sexuality (Moussaid 1997). See also the discussion of transvestism in Section 8D, Paraphilias, below.

## A. Sexual Abuse of Children

The sexual abuse of children seems to be frequent, but is usually hidden by the families. In the legal field, these abuses are very seriously punished whether that abuse involves a male or a female child.

## B. Prostitution

Prostitution or *zina* has always existed in our Arab-Muslim landscape, as it has in all historical civilizations. In the recent past, at the time of the French protectorate, prostitution was regulated and supervised in brothels. Today, it is repressed and constitutes an offense, which leads to other negative effects and risks. In effect, there is a "sexualization" of different social factors, which are becoming more obvious in our country. This "sexualization," evident in the prostitution relationship (giver-receiver), is generated by the material concerns and the crushing weight of the entire social system, which neglects the woman to the point where she is reduced to her body and to her sexual appeal, and is forced to rely on prostitution to survive. Prostitution may sometimes be ignored, because it is occasional, but even then, it does raise some problems. This appearance of sexual freedom is in fact a kind of slavery of the young girl who has affairs with many men, some old, some rich, some strangers, some unfaithful spouses, and some dissatisfied husbands (Moussaid 1997; Naamane 1990).

## C. Pornography and Erotica

The pornographic industry, *khalâa*, as it exists in the West, is not present in Morocco. Instead, consumer spending has become more and more widespread, even while it is limited to certain social classes that are in contact with the Western world. The intrusion of the media, particularly satellite television and videocassettes, in our audiovisual field, has changed the previous situation by giving all levels and social classes access to pornographic images and materials. Meanwhile, the possession of pornographic documents, films, magazines, and so on, constitutes a criminal offense. On the other hand, Morocco was unique in the Arab world, being the only Arab country where the ancient works of Arab erotology of the 14th century, *The Perfumed Garden*, and so on, were available. These books, which deal with sexual behavior and erotic pleasures, are now perceived as true pornographic documents, especially by young adolescents.

## D. Paraphilias

*Frotteurism*

Frotteurism is a very prevalent behavior in our country, generated by the great frustration of the citizens. This frustration is a consequence of the years of repression, which censures all sexual relations outside the bonds of the marriage. The favorite place for this practice is the crowded public transportation system.

*Zoophilia*

In rural areas, zoophilia is still very widespread and not blameworthy. With masturbation, it constitutes an obligatory passage in the adolescent male's apprenticeship of sexuality. Although this practice has never been mentioned in the Koran, it is prohibited without question by the *Chariâ*: "He who has copulated with a beast, kill him and kill the animal."

*Transvestism*

*Takhanout* is more or less tolerated, insofar as in the past, women were absent from the artistic scene, and crossdressing men played the role of women. This practice has always existed and exists still in certain domains where women have not yet gained access. These transvestites are, in general, homosexuals who practice without any impunity, as long as there is no public act.

# 9. Contraception, Abortion, and Population Planning

## A. Pregnancy Outside of Marriage

Pregnancy outside of marriage is prohibited and remains punishable by law and religion. It appears that such pregnancies are more frequent in the urban than the rural areas, but no statistical study has touched this problem. However, there exist a not insignificant number of abandoned infants born out of wedlock, of which the state takes temporary charge in anticipation of their being adopted by welcoming families.

## B. Abortion

Only therapeutic abortions are authorized and practiced in a hospital setting. Non-therapeutic abortions are practiced secretly by physicians in private practice following standard medical methods. There are no accurate official statistics. Moreover, considering that contraceptive methods are not taught to young girls who get involved with illicit sexual relationships, their pregnancies are candidates for the voluntary interruption of pregnancy (IVG, *interruptions volontaires de grossesses*). These IVGs are also frequent among married women who utilize IVG in case of undesired pregnancies.

## C. Family Planning

Family planning is a program integrated within the healthcare system. It is based on the spacing of births and not on their limitation. It has contributed to reducing considerably the risks of morbidity and maternal and infant mortality. It is also an essential component of the strategy of the socioeconomic development of the country. The principal actors are the state in the public sector, the private sector, and the ONGs (*organisations nongouvernementals* or nongovernmental organizations, NGOs), in particular the Moroccan Association of Family Planning. The latest study documents the results of their efforts: 99% of married women have heard of at least one contraceptive method, and 92% know where to obtain information or services for at least one method.

By decreasing order, the best-known family planning methods are the pill, the intrauterine device, tubal ligation, condoms, the injectables, and the vaginal methods. The pill remains the contraceptive method the most used, with 64% in 1995 compared to 68% in 1992. The rate of contraceptive use has increased significantly since 1980. In effect, in 1995, 50% of married women utilized some contraceptive method compared to 41.5% in 1992, 35.9% in 1987, and 19.4% in 1980 (all methods combined).

The principal objectives of Morocco's family planning program are:

- To respond to the expressed and potential needs of the population concerning family planning and contraception;
- To attain a contraceptive prevalence in favor of the long-term methods;
- To modify contraceptive use in favor of the long-term methods;
- To involve the societal agents of the different agencies in our society—youth, sports, social affairs, agriculture, etc.—to participate in the promotion of the concept and methods of family planning; and
- To augment participation of the private sectors in the supplying of contraceptives to attain a balance between both

private and public sectors, a kind of social marketing project. At the present time, the private sector accommodates 38% of the demand for contraceptive products.

## 10. Sexually Transmitted Diseases and HIV/AIDS

### A. Sexually Transmitted Diseases

The sexually transmitted diseases (*maladies sexuellement transmissibles, MST*) and AIDS (*SIDA*) are illnesses known all over the world, and Morocco and the Arab Muslim countries are not exceptions.

At the present time, there is the Program to Fight Against STD and AIDS under the direction of the Epidemiology and the Fight Against Illness Division of the Ministry of Health, which organizes those activities in coordination with elected leaders, the local authorities, and the ONGs (NGOs). Table 1 lists the incidence of several STDs since 1991.

The incidence of STDs is progressively increasing; it increased from 50,567 cases in 1991 to 189,021 cases at the end of 1997 and 100,827 cases in the first half of 1998, despite the underreporting of cases in the public sector and its almost complete absence in the private sector.

The incidence of vaginal discharges (leukorrheas) is much higher than that of urethral discharges. In the early 1990s, syphilis outranked chancres (*Hemophilus ducreyi*), but this has been reversed in recent years. Eighty percent of the cases reported occur among 15- to 44-year-olds, with females accounting for 71% of the cases.

A variety of factors have contributed to the increase in STDs in Morocco, including:

- More than half the population is young;
- Tourism jobs in the country;
- The proximity of Europe and the important number of Moroccan nationals returning from abroad;
- The low socioeconomic level;
- The delay in the average age of marriage, which now approaches 30 years old;
- Self-medication by carriers of STDs;
- The anarchistic, unregulated prescription of antibiotics; and
- The poor use of condoms among those with extramarital relationships.

In 1999, the Ministry of Health launched a new public policy and strategy for taking charge of the STDs. This strategy adopts the syndrome approach, based on treating the patient at paraclinics without waiting for the results of biological tests. This approach, which seeks to intervene immediately to break the chain of transmission of these diseases, is based on epidemiological public health considerations, following the USAID project strategy, with the contribution of AIDSCAP and the University of Washington. In coping with the STDs in Morocco, one should not ignore the fact that half of the carriers of STDs self-medicate with antibiotics. This poorly advised and unregulated use of antibiotics is the cause of atypical and asymptomatic, highly contagious forms of STDs (*Note Ministérielle No. 26* 1997).

### B. HIV/AIDS

The first case of AIDS was diagnosed in Morocco in 1986. Its appearance was one of the elements that has allowed the very wide development of programs for the prevention of STDs using all the latest approaches. Tables 2 and 3 summarize the AIDS statistics in Morocco.

The age group predominantly affected is from 15 to 40 years old (69%). Ninety percent of the HIV-positive children are infected perinatally. Males account for 70% of the cases. The other particulars of AIDS in Morocco are: 42% are bachelors; 35% are married women; 85% were infected while living in Morocco; and 15% are recent immigrants.

Transmission modes include: heterosexual, 61%; homosexual, 10%; intravenous drug use, 9%; multi-risk, 8%; transfusion, 4%; perinatal, 4%; and unknown, 4%. Before the 1990s, the main modes of transmission were homosexual contact and IV-drug use; at present, the dominant mode of transmission is heterosexual intercourse.

In 1995, males with AIDS outnumbered females by three to one. The age distribution of AIDS cases was: 15 to 29, 24%; 30 to 39, 43%; and 40 to 49, 12%. STD patients, tuberculosis patients, and pregnant women showed an approximate seroprevalence of AIDS of 1 per 1,000. Eighty-three percent of the cases were urban, with the most cases reported in Oujda, Rabat, and Tangier. The transmission by blood products has noticeably diminished thanks to the screening by the Centers of Transfusion of the Kingdom, from 11.4% to 4% in 1998. However, the prevalence rate of HIV among blood donors, which was 1.3 per 10,000 in 1996 and 2 per 10,000 in 1997, had changed to 8 per 10,000 at the end of June 1998.

The actual prevalence rate of AIDS disease is 0.02%, which places Morocco among countries less touched, at the same level as the countries of the Maghreb in the western extremity of the Islamic world (northern Africa) and the Middle East.

In April 1998, the Ministry of Health adopted a national strategy to take charge of the HIV/AIDS challenge (*Circulaire Ministérielle No. 7* 1998). This strategy defines the modalities of the diagnosis of HIV, the prescription and utilization of the antiretrovirus (ARV) medications, the biological follow up, and the reporting of cases. The program is

### Table 1

### Statistics on STDs in Morocco, 1991-June 1998

| Disease | 1991 | 1992 | 1993 | 1994 | 1995 | 1996 | 1997 | 1998 (June) |
|---|---|---|---|---|---|---|---|---|
| Yeast/fungal | 26,646 | 68,176 | 69,119 | 102,214 | 106,621 | 108,621 | 133,716 | 72,886 |
| Urethritis | 14,402 | 23,207 | 19,948 | 27,012 | 28,260 | 32,397 | 35,603 | 17,916 |
| Syphilis | 4,952 | 5,506 | 5,635 | 5,226 | 5,015 | 5,084 | 5,226 | 2,507 |
| Chancre | 2,161 | 2,981 | 3,153 | 3,720 | 4,742 | 4,289 | 5,807 | 3,081 |
| Condyloma | 761 | 775 | 429 | 451 | 804 | 1,138 | 662 | 285 |
| Hepatitis | 792 | 1,594 | 1,195 | 1,367 | 948 | 1,138 | 2,008 | 1,024 |
| Genital herpes | 598 | 651 | 477 | 502 | 458 | 574 | 561 | 220 |
| Other STDs | 225 | 544 | 1,108 | 2,013 | 3,793 | 2,722 | 5,438 | 2,902 |
| Total | 50,567 | 103,434 | 101,065 | 142,505 | 150,541 | 156,722 | 189,021 | 100,821 |

(*Note Ministérielle No. 491* 1996)

financed in its majority by the Ministry of Health, as well as by certain ONGs (NGOs).

The new program is based on two major, well-equipped facilities, the Hospital Ibn Sina in the capital city of Rabat, which serves the north of the country, and the Hospital Ibn Rochd in Casablanca, which covers the southern part of the country. These two centers work in close collaboration with referring centers at the regional level. Reporting cases of HIV/AIDS is obligatory in accordance with the 1995 decree of the Ministry of Public Health. In Morocco, because the country has endemic tuberculosis, the early pursuit of the *Koch bacillus* bacterium is systematic among seropositive patients.

Another aspect of the campaign against HIV/AIDS are sensitization and education programs, especially those for women, which are reinforced every year on December 1, on the occasion of the worldwide day of the fight against AIDS. Sensitization programs have also been implemented for healthcare professionals. HIV-detection equipment at all centers for blood transfusions has clearly improved the quality of donated blood. At the same time, a considerable effort was made to educate all professionals traditionally at high risk, such as barbers and dentists. More basic in the prevention of STDs and AIDS is the improvement of the socioeconomic level of the country.

[*Update 2002*: UNAIDS Epidemiological Assessment: According to the HIV Sentinel Surveillance, in 2001, the HIV-prevalence rate in Agadir, Marrakech, and Casablanca was high compared to previous years. But these latest data were not confirmed by the HIV Sentinel Surveillance conducted in 2001. So, we cannot conclude that the infection rate has considerably increased in these areas.

[The results of the HIV Sentinel Surveillance in 2001, in pregnant women were: in Agadir 0.20%, in Marrakech 0.00%, and in Casablanca 0.37%.

[At the end of 2001, the number of AIDS reported cases was 963, of which 69% were because of heterosexual transmission and 6% because of injection drug use in all cases. Among 963 AIDS cases reported, 620 were in males, of which 59% were because of heterosexual transmission and 9% because of injection drug use.

[Concerning STDs, 600,000 new cases of STDs are estimated, but had not been registered. The number of STD new cases registered in 2000 was 307,040, and in 2001 was 347,655. Of the STD registered cases in 2000, 39.6% were young adults between ages 15 and 29, and 44.2% were among those 30 to 44. In 2001, of the STD registered cases, 39.4% were young adults aged between 15 and 29, and 44.8% were among those 30 to 44.

[The estimated number of adults and children living with HIV/AIDS on January 1, 2002, were:

| | |
|---|---|
| Adults ages 15-49: | 13,000  (rate: 0.1%) |
| Women ages 15-49: | 2,000 |
| Children ages 0-15: | NA |

[No estimate is available for the number of adults and children who died of AIDS during 2001.

[No estimate is available for the number of Moroccan children who had lost one or both parents to AIDS and were under age 15 at the end of 2001. (*End of update by the Editors*)]

## 11. Sexual Dysfunctions, Counseling, and Therapies

### A. Female Sexual Dysfunctions

Although female sexual dysfunctions are frequent in our society, they are usually concealed by society. Vaginismus represents the most frequent motive for a sexological consultation, because it puts the life of the couple's relationship in danger. Women who suffer from vaginismus do not consult a professional counselor or therapist until they are driven to do so by the partner and/or the family. In Morocco, the causes of vaginismus are, most often, a restrictive religious education, negative beliefs relative to the anatomy of the hymen, misconceptions about the mechanism of penetration, and sexual assault traumas (rapes and attempted rapes), which, unlike in the West, are rarely reported.

Anorgasmia, or inhibited female orgasm, is also frequent, but rarely constitutes a motive for a sexological consultation. Here, as with vaginismus, the causes are restrictive education, negative beliefs relative to female sexuality in general, the awkward behavior of the man, a lack of the development of fantasies [*agénésie fantasmatique*], and the prohibition of childhood and adolescent masturbation.

### B. Male Sexual Dysfunctions

Erectile dysfunctions (ED) are very frequent among men and affect all ages and all social classes. An epidemiological study in the general population with a representative sample ($N = 651$) showed that globally, 54% of the men presented some erectile dysfunctions, distributed as mild in 38.8% of men, moderately troubling in 15.1%, and severely troubling in 1.1% (Berrada et al. 1999). But only a small minority of males who admitted to ED were willing to take responsibility and seek treatment. That is because of their socioeconomic conditions and certainly because of the feeling of disgrace and devaluation that the patient experiences when he sees in the therapist a rival who will judge him. Also keeping the patient from seeking help for ED are the irrational folk ideas that accompany sexual impotence, which suggest that it is because of *tqaf*, a form of sorcery, which is treatable by a faith healer (*marabout*). Apart from the well-known organic causes of diabetes, high blood pressure, cardiopathies, cholesterol, iatrogenicity, smoking, and so on, the psychogenic causes are more frequent for men over 40 years old. These may include conjugal monotony associated with the lack of fantasizing, and may be aggravated by performance anxiety. In effect, the process of fantasizing, in our society, is associated with adultery, and accordingly, are

---

**Table 2**

**The Epidemiology of AIDS in Morocco, as of June 30, 1998**

| | |
|---|---|
| Cumulative number of cases of AIDS disease | 510 |
| Number of declared cases in 1997 | 92 |
| Number of declared cases (June 1998) | 46 |
| Number of adults affected (15-40 years) | 351 |
| Number of children affected (age < 15 years) | 21 |
| Cumulative number of deaths from AIDS | 139 |

---

**Table 3**

**The Incidence of AIDS over Time**

| Year | New Cases | Accumu- lated Cases | Year | New Cases | Accumu- lated Cases |
|---|---|---|---|---|---|
| 1986 | 1 | 1 | 1993 | 44 | 172 |
| 1987 | 9 | 10 | 1994 | 77 | 249* |
| 1988 | 14 | 24 | 1995 | 57 | 306 |
| 1989 | 20 | 44 | 1996 | 66 | 372 |
| 1990 | 26 | 70 | 1997 | 92 | 464 |
| 1991 | 28 | 98 | 1998 | 46 | 510 |
| 1992 | 30 | 128 | (June) | | |

*19 of the 77 new cases reported in 1994 had been previously counted as ARC (AIDS-Related Complex)

prohibited and inhibited for the majority of men. Among young adults, the relationship of circular causality, where various psychogenic factors—for the most part, religious and educational—interact, is a common cause of erectile dysfunction (Bonierbale 1991).

Premature ejaculation is beginning to become a very frequent symptom and a motive for consultation, more than before, when it was considered an indication of virility that one learns in the course of the collective masturbation during adolescence. At the present time, men are becoming more and more conscious of the frustration of their wives, and are thus beginning to take responsibility for it. A very frequent symptom in our cultural context is an association of premature ejaculation with the feeling of having a small penis. Constrained to conceal his assumed handicap, the subject will ejaculate quickly in a hurried sexual encounter.

### C. Therapies

The therapeutic modalities available for male and female sexopathies are varied. Therapy is available from general practitioners, urologists, psychiatrists, endocrinologists, gynecologists, and so on, as well as by sexologists and andrologists, who are a small minority in the healthcare community. However, almost all of the patients will consult first, if not in an exclusive way, with the traditional faith healers (*marabouts*). The therapeutic arsenal from which medical personnel can draw is rather rich. The most recent products, intracavernous injections (IIC), Viagra, and aphrodisiacs, were available in Morocco before the majority of European countries made them available in the market.

## 12. Sex Research and Advanced Professional Education

The domain of teaching and of sexological research is still timid in our country. The Moroccan Association of Sexology (L'Association Marocaine de Sexologie, AMS) began an ambitious program in this domain after 1994. This program rests on the organization of an annual congress, with the participation of numerous experts in the sexological world, and of roundtables on a particular theme. Meetings and congresses of the AMS are organized in a different city and under the aegis of a different university each year. Among the objectives of the AMS is the installation of a program of teaching or a course of sexology within a university framework, and the organization of fundamental research oriented especially toward anthropological, psychological, psychoanalytic, sociological, neurological, biological, judicial, medicolegal, physiological, pathological, experimental, and therapeutic aspects of sexual behavior. This research should result in a conceptualization of sexology that is adapted to our Moroccan context. Given that the actual sociopolitical climate is not favorable, the AMS has decided to limit this discipline to the medical domain (sexual pathology). This adoption of sexology by the medical sciences may be only beneficial in the short run. The focusing on sexual behavior, in the long term, needs a reaffirmation and an acceptance of this science by society and by the medical community. Because sexology carries at the present time a pejorative connotation, research on sexual behavior is marginalized (Moussaid 1997).

Three professional organizations deal with sexological issues in Morocco:

The Moroccan Association of Family Planning (Association Marocaine de Planification Familiale, AMPF), 6, Rue Ibn El Kadi Casablanca, Morocco.

The Moroccan Association of Sexology (L'Association Marocaine de Sexologie, AMS), Abderrazak Moussaid,

M.D., 38, Boulevard Rahal El Meskini, 20 000 Casablanca, Morocco; +212-2-298-381 or +212-2-298-331; fax +212-2-221-114; psych@casanet.net.ma.

Les Orangers, E. Abdel Krim Hakam, Executive Director, Rabat RP, Morocco (or BP 1217, Rabat RP, Morocco); +212-7-721-224; fax: +212-7-720-362; cable: FAMPLAN RABAT.

### References and Suggested Readings

Al Boukhari. *Al jamii assahi.h*. Egypt: Imprimerie Principale: Livre 67, Bab 85.

Al Ghazali. 1992. *Attib annabaoui* (in Arabic). Beyrouth: Dar AL Fikr.

Amir, A. 1988. Conditions sur la situation psychosociologique actuelle de la femme algérienne. *Présence Femme*, pp. 133-136.

Associated Press. 2000 (March 12). Moroccans and women: Two rallies. *The New York Times*, (March 13), p. 8.

Attahir, H. *Notre femme dans la législation "Charia" et la société* (in Arabic). Tunis: Société Tunisienne d'Édition.

Badran, M. 1995. *Feminists, Islam, and nation: Gender and the making of modern Egypt*. Princeton, NJ: Princeton University Press.

Beck, L. G., & N. Keddie, eds. 1978. *Women in the Muslim world*. Cambridge, MA: Harvard University Press.

Berrada, S., N. Kadiri, & S. Tahiri. 1999 (Unpublished). Dysfonctions érectiles, étudee au Maroc (*N* = 651).

Bonierbale, M. 1991. L'homme impuissant. Le premier entretien. *Sexologies*, *1*(1).

Bouhdiba, A. 1996/1986. *Sexuality in Islam* (trans., A. Sheridan). London: Routledge & Kegan Paul. *La sexualité en Islam*. Paris: PUF.

Brooks, G. 1995. *Nine parts of desire: The hidden world of Islamic women*. New York: Anchor Books/Doubleday.

*Circulaire Ministérielle No. 7*. 1998 (February 4).

Cherni, Z. 1993. Les dérapages de l'histoire chez T. Haddad. *Les travailleurs, Dieu et la femme* (pp. 137-147). Tunis: Édition Ben Abdallah.

CIA. 2002 (January). *The world factbook 2002*. Washington, DC: Central Intelligence Agency. Available: http://www.cia.gov/cia/publications/factbook/index.html.

Dialmy, A. 1995. *Logement, sexualité et Islam*. Casablanca: Edition Eddif.

Fernea, E. W. 1975. *A street in Marrakesh: A personal view of urban women in Morocco*. Prospect Heights, IL: Waveland Press.

Fernea, E. W. 1998. Morocco. In: E. W. Fernea, *In search of feminism: One woman's global journey* (pp. 62-143). New York: Doubleday.

Giami, A. 1991 (December). De Kinsey an SIDA. *Sciences Sociales et Santé*, *9*(4):23-55.

Hatfield, E., & R. L. Rapson. 1996. *Love and sex: Cross-cultural perspectives*. Boston: Allyn & Bacon.

Joseph, R., & T. B. Joseph. 1987. *The rose and the thorn*. Tucson, AZ: University of Arizona Press.

Kacem, A. 1970. Libération de la femme (in Arabic). Le Caire: Dar maarif Egypte, p. 87.

Kacha, N. 1986. L'algérienne et le changement. *Présence Femme*, pp. 137-140.

Malek, C. 1995. *Encyclopédie de l'amour en Islam*. France: Payot.

Mernissi, F. 1983. *Sexe, idéologie et Islam*. Paris: Tierce.

Mernissi, F. 1991. *The veil and the male elite: A feminist interpretation of women's rights in Islam*. Reading, MA: Addison-Wesley.

Mernissi, F. 1993. *Islam and democracy: Fear of the modern world*. Reading, MA: Addison-Wesley.

Moussaid, A. 1992. Les motivations de la polygamie: Mémoire de le fin d'études de sexologie, University of Paris XIII (unpublished lecture), Casablanca, Morocco.

Moussaid, A. 1997 (September). La sexologie un concept à redéfinir: Communication au 1er Congrès de l'Association de Sexologie (unpublished lecture), Casablanca, Morocco.

Murray, S. O. 1997. Woman-woman love in Islamic societies. In: S. O. Murray & W. Roscoe, eds., *Islamic homosexualities: Culture, history, and literature*. New York/London: New York University Press.

Murray, S. O. 1997. The will not to know: Islamic accommodations of male homosexuality. In: S. O. Murray & W. Roscoe eds., *Islamic homosexualities: Culture, history, and literature*. New York/London: New York University Press.

Murray, S. O., & W. Roscoe. 1997. *Islamic homosexualities: Culture, history, and literature*. New York/London: New York University Press.

Naamane Guessous, S. 1990. *Au-delà de toute pudeur*. Casablanca: Eddif Maroc.

Naamane Guessous, S. 1999. *Enquête sur la puberté, la ménopause et l'andropause*. In press.

Naipaul, V. S. 1998. *Beyond belief: Islamic excursions among the converted peoples*. New York: Random House.

*Note Ministérielle No. 26 du 23/06/1997*. DELM/35.

*Note Ministérielle No. 491 du 18/03/1996*. DELM/35.

*Note Ministérielle No. 1491 du 02/09/1996*. DELM/35.

*Note Ministérielle No. 1957 du 12/12/1998*. DELM/35.

Parrinder, G. 1980. *Sex in the world's great religions*. Don Mills, Ontario, Canada: General Publishing Company.

*Recensement général de la population et de l'habitat au Maroc de 1994. Caractéristiques socio-économiques et démographiques*. 1996 (January). Rabat: Direction de la Statistique.

*Statut du code personnel "mudawana."* 1996. Casablanca: Edition Dar Attaqafa.

UNAIDS. 2002. *Epidemiological fact sheets by country*. Geneva, Switzerland: Joint United Nations Programme on HIV/AIDS (UNAIDS/WHO). Available: http://www.unaids.org/hivaidsinfo/statistics/fact_sheets/index_en.htm.

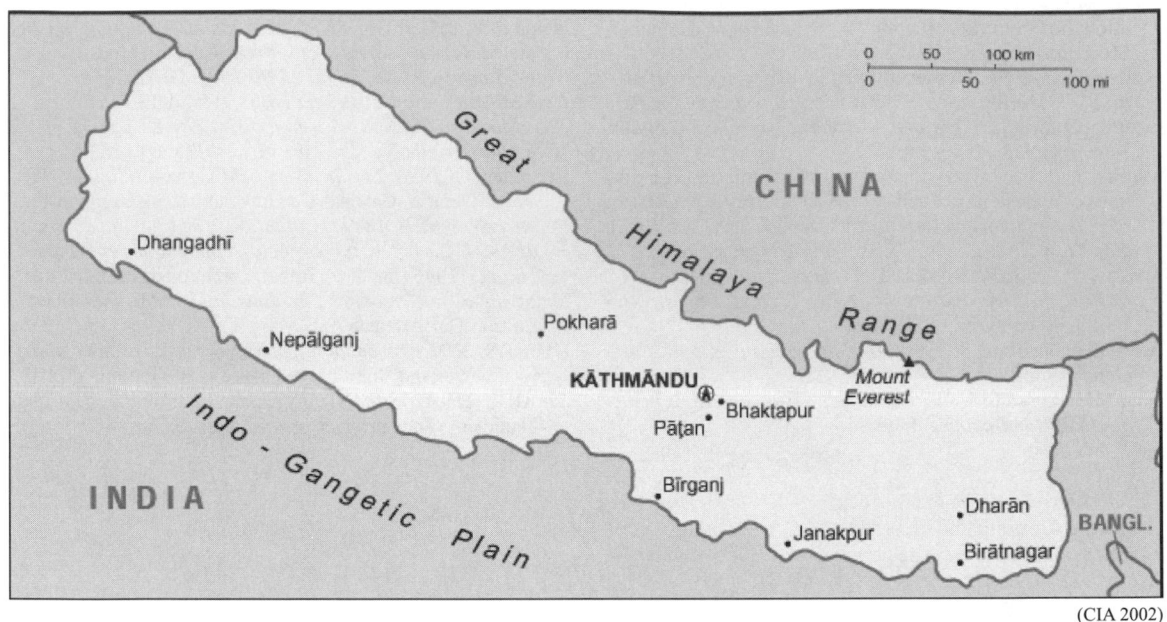

(CIA 2002)

# Nepal

Elizabeth Schroeder, M.S.W.*

## Contents

## Demographics and a Brief Historical Perspective

ROBERT T. FRANCOEUR

### A. Demographics

The Kingdom of Nepal is the world's only official Hindu nation. The landlocked kingdom is bordered on the north by the Tibet autonomous region of China, and on the west, south, and east by India, countries with the world's highest population rates. Nepal measures approximately 54,360 square miles (140,800 km²). As a comparison, Nepal is about the size of the state of Arkansas in the United States. However, the state of Arkansas has a population of only 2.7 million people to Nepal's 25 million. Of the world's 10 highest mountains, eight stand between Nepal and Tibet, including Mount Everest. The country has three different regions with three different geological terrains: the mountains, the hills, and the *terai* or "plains." The climate varies from cool summers and severe winters on the mountain slopes of the north to subtropical summers and mild winters in the southern plains.

In July 2002, Nepal had an estimated population of 25.3 million. (All data are from *The World Factbook 2002* (CIA 2002) unless otherwise stated.)

**Age Distribution and Sex Ratios**: *0-14 years*: 40% with 1.07 male(s) per female (sex ratio); *15-64 years*: 56.4% with 1.05 male(s) per female; *65 years and over*: 3.6% with 0.97 male(s) per female; *Total population sex ratio*: 1.05 male(s) to 1 female. Nearly 30% of the country's population are adolescents or teenagers. Much of the available data about sexuality and relationships are, therefore, from adolescents.

**Life Expectancy at Birth**: *Total Population*: 58.22 years; *male*: 59.01 years; *female*: 58.2 years

**Urban/Rural Distribution**: 11% to 89%. Nepal's most densely populated areas, with nearly half of the country's entire population, are Kathmandu, the capitol, Chitwan, and Sunsari.

**Ethnic Distribution**: Burman: 68%; Shan: 9%; Karen: 7%; Rakhine: 4%. There are over 70 ethnic groups throughout the country speaking nearly 50 different languages. These different groups are classified loosely into two main categories: Indo-Aryan and Tibeto-Burman. The Tibeto-Burman groups are predominantly Buddhists, although many are still Hindu. Among these groups are Brahman, Chetri, Newar, Gurung, Magar, Tamang, Rai, Limbu, Sherpa, Tharu, and more. Caste and ethnicity are terms that are often used interchangeably to describe the population. The refugee issue of some 100,000 Bhutanese in Nepal remains unresolved; 90% of these displaced persons are housed in seven United Nations Offices of the High Commissioner for Refugees (UNHCR) camps.

**Religious Distribution**: Hinduism: 86.2%; Buddhism: 7.8%; Islam: 3.8%; other: 2.2%. As of 1995, Nepal was the only official Hindu state in the world.

**Birth Rate**: 32.94 births per 1,000 population

**Death Rate**: 10.22 per 1,000 population

**Infant Mortality Rate**: 72.36 deaths per 1,000 live births

**Net Migration Rate**: 0 migrant(s) per 1,000 population

**Total Fertility Rate**: 4.48 children born per woman

**Population Growth Rate**: 2.29%

*Communications*: Elizabeth Schroeder, M.S.W., 45 Essex Ave., 2nd Floor, Montclair, NJ 07042, USA; ElizSchroe@aol.com.

**HIV/AIDS** (1999 est.): *Adult prevalence*: 0.29%; *Persons living with HIV/AIDS*: 34,000; *Deaths*: 2,500. (For additional details from www.UNAIDS.org, see end of Section 10B.)

**Literacy Rate** (*defined as those age 15 and over who can read and write*): 27.5% (*male*: 40.9%, *female*: 14%) (1995 est.); school education is free and compulsory from age 6 to 11

**Per Capita Gross Domestic Product** (*purchasing power parity*): US$1,400 (2001 est.); *Inflation*: 2.1%; *Unemployment*: 47%; *Living below the poverty line*: 42% (2001 est.) Nepal is among the world's poorest countries, with the majority of sources estimating an annual per capita GDP between US$200 and US$250. However, the *World* and *Time Almanacs* and *World Factbook* estimate the per capita GDP between $1,200 to $1,300.

## B. A Brief Historical Perspective

The earliest recorded history of Nepal goes back to somewhere around the 7th or 8th century B.C.E. in the fertile Kathmandu Valley. The people of the time were known as the Kiratis, but there is little other information about them, beyond knowing that they were sheep farmers. Prince Siddhartha Gautama was born in this region around 563 B.C.E. After Gautama achieved enlightenment as Buddha, he and his disciple, Ananda, established the Buddhist religion. In the 12th century C.E., the Nepali rulers ended their long patronage of Buddhism in favor of Hinduism, reflecting the growing influence of India. Buddhism all but disappeared as the Licchavis invaded from northern India, overthrew the Kiratis, and introduced Hinduism. Hinduism included a social caste system, which continues today.

Four successive dynasties prepared the way for Nepal to assume its present boundaries and be united under King Prithvi Narayan Shah in 1768. Treaties in 1792 and 1816 brought contact with Britain, which recognized the absolute independence of Nepal in 1923. After 100 years, during which hereditary prime ministers of the Rana family maintained political power, the king assumed all power in 1951 and proclaimed a constitutional monarchy.

When the British withdrew from India in 1948, the Ranas lost their major source of support and power. The people took advantage of the weakened state of the Ranas, and rebels rose up in opposition. In 1951, King Tribhuvan was crowned, and the government became a combination of Ranas and the newly established Nepali Congress Party. In 1959, the first democratic elections for a national assembly were held. However, King Mahendra declared parliamentary democracy a failure 18 months later, and instead established a "partyless" or "*panchayaat*" system. The monarch retained absolute power, with the King having sole authority over all governmental institutions, including the Cabinet and Parliament.

In 1990, King Birendra, a widely popular and adored king, dissolved the *panchayaat* system, lifted the ban on political parties, and released all political prisoners. The new government, with a prime minister, was comprised of members of the Nepali Congress Party, the communist parties of Nepal, royal appointees, and independents. A new constitution was established later that year, focusing on protecting fundamental human rights and establishing Nepal as a parliamentary democracy with a constitutional monarch. The King technically rules over the Parliament, but is not involved generally with day-to-day activities. The King has the power to grant pardons or to suspend, commute, or remit any sentence handed down by any court.

In June 2001, the crown prince assassinated the beloved king and queen and a good portion of the royal family be-

fore killing himself. Soon after, the Maoist insurgency that had been growing since 1996 took advantage of the turmoil created by the assassinations and increased its efforts to overthrow the Nepalese government. Since then, the country has lived in political and social instability, with high-level party resignations, strife throughout Parliament, and violence. The King, with the approval of Parliament, declared a state of emergency, and the government called out the army to help fight the Maoists. The violence has resulted in more than 7,000 deaths on both the Nepali army side and the Maoist side, with some civilian deaths occurring as well, and with the numbers continuing to grow. Attempted peace talks have been unsuccessful to date. Ceasefires continue to be broken, and Maoist bombings and violence between the two sides continue.

## 1. Basic Sexological Premises

### A. Character of Gender Roles

Gender roles are very well defined in Nepal. Expectations of girls and boys and women and men are clearly outlined, from social interactions to family communication to examples in school textbooks. Generally speaking, boys are valued higher than girls. Stories remain of families seeking to abort female fetuses, although these tend to be related by word of mouth. Men are usually the patriarchs of their families—although women have power within a social context. In many areas, men are expected to work outside of the home, and women are expected to tend to the home and the children. These values differ, however, based on the location of an individual community. In some of the hill communities, women may travel, while men remain in the community to tend to the home or family. In these communities, tasks are not gendered in any evaluative way. Folk beliefs about witchcraft remain in some areas, especially in the Terai (the southern plains). These generally target women, particularly elderly and/or widowed women, who are sometimes beaten publicly as part of an exorcism ceremony.

Some people report that seclusion rituals for girls and women during menstruation still exist in the rural areas. The most common ritual reported is having a girl or woman gather a week's worth of food and water and enter a hut where she stays for the duration of her menses. Other people maintain that these rituals are no longer practiced. However, menstruation is still seen as dirty. A menstruating woman is not supposed to cook or come into contact with anyone's food or water except her own.

### B. Sociolegal Status of Males and Females

As children and adolescents, boys have much more access to just about everything than girls do, from recreational activities to education to job opportunities. The literacy rate is significantly lower for girls than for boys. As adults, women face systematic, society-wide discrimination in many facets of life. This is particularly true in rural areas, where religious and cultural tradition, lack of education, and ignorance of their legal rights keep women from accessing such basic rights as voting or holding property in their own names. Access to jobs is much more limited for women than for men, and salaries for women are significantly lower—even though the Constitution specifically requires equal pay for equal work.

Part of the impediment to equal pay and treatment is that the Government has not taken enough action to implement its own provisions, even in government industries. Of the 265 members of Parliament, 21 are women. These women are only members of Parliament because a quota was established guaranteeing this many female representatives. More and more nongovernmental organizations (NGOs) are pressing for increased women's rights. Aside from the teaching profession, women seem much less likely than men to progress in their jobs. An increase in female volunteers in the health sector has increased awareness among women, and has encouraged more women to seek out health services. At the same time, however, they are unpaid and untrained in medical or health service provision.

According to legal experts, there are over 20 laws that discriminate against women. For example, the law on property rights also favors men in its provisions for inheritance, land tenancy, and the division of family property. The Citizenship Law discriminates against foreign spouses of female citizens, and denies citizenship to any children they may have together, even if those children are born in Nepal. Many other discriminatory laws still remain.

This is an area in which NGOs in Kathmandu are currently working to change. Over the last decade, efforts at increasing women's rights and equality have redoubled. In 2001, the Nepalese government created a National Women's Commission, designed to promote women's "active participation in the development of the nation" and promote women's rights. In addition, a law passed in September 2002 allows women for the first time to inherit property from their parents.

## C. General Concepts and Constructs of Sexuality, Love, Marriage, and Family

Virtually all sexuality in Nepal is seen within a heterosexual context; therefore, all examples in this chapter will be about heterosexual relationships unless otherwise indicated.

The concept of love and sexuality are quite romanticized, fed in part by the images presented in the Indian media that is prominent in Nepal. Young people tend to meet at social functions, become interested in each other, and decide to meet in secret. Part of the appeal is the secretiveness, and their behaviors might involve kissing, intimate touching, or sometimes, sexual intercourse and other sexual behaviors. Clearly, this behavior is normalized for boys much more than for girls; while many boys in a focus group said they had or knew someone who had had sex with a girl already, none of the girls would acknowledge that they had. If they knew of a girl who had engaged in premarital sex, it was through gossip.

Girls are more likely to romanticize love and marriage than boys. It is expected that young people will not have sexual intercourse outside of marriage, resulting in one of three outcomes: either young people will sneak off and get married at young ages, they will get married with their parents' support or intervention at a young age, or they will go ahead and have sexual relationships outside of marriage. While incidences of boys and girls running off together is more common in the rural areas of the country, it also does occur in the city. Often, the discovery that a boy and girl are having a romantic relationship will cause the parents of both young people to arrange for the adolescents' marriage. In fact, among the reasons for early arranged marriage is to protect a girl's reputation, which can become tarnished by public association with a boy.

In sexual and romantic relationships, men are expected to be the initiators. Women are expected to remain faithful to their husbands. Husbands, however, may have extramarital sexual relationships. In particular, men who travel for their work may seek out sex workers during their travels. Infrequently using condoms, these men often contract sexually transmitted infections, return home, and continue to have unprotected intercourse with their wives. A wife usually does not have the social power, clout, or right to insist that her husband use condoms—particularly if they have never used them before in their relationship. To do so could

raise questions about her own fidelity, rather than reflect the reality of her husband's sexual activity.

Childbearing is also valued highly in Nepal, although strains on natural resources, threats to women's health, and a desire for a higher quality of life have caused individuals, the government, and NGO professionals to focus on family planning methods. In one study, the vast majority of adults believed that a couple should wait at least two years before trying to conceive a child, with others favoring a wait of at least three or even four years. The reason behind this is to enable the couple to raise enough money to ensure that they can provide for the infant. At the same time, however, they do not believe that a married couple should use contraception immediately after marriage. The reason for this is a mistrust in family planning methods, and a concern that using, in particular, hormonal methods, will affect a woman's fertility once she is ready to have children. Therefore, pregnancies do occur shortly after marriage. Adults who push for pregnancy as soon after marriage as possible do so because having a child creates a family. Adults living in the urban setting tend to support fewer children, one or two per couple. Rural parents tend to favor larger families of at least four or five children.

There are different views from adolescents on friendships between the genders. Girls are not to do things alone, nor is it a good idea for a girl to have male friends. Once a girl is noticed or seen with a boy, questions are raised immediately about the nature of their relationship. Some report having friends of different genders outside of the context of romantic connections, while others do not believe that boys and girls can be friends.

Finding the language for talking about sexuality and reproductive health in Nepal remains an enormous challenge for Nepalese professionals, as well as professionals from other countries working on programs in-country. One U.S.-based professional working in Nepal reflected on the language of sexuality. She found:

> Nepalis discuss sexuality in terms of kinds of relationships and ways of being sexual. Terms for specific sexual acts and body parts are a subset of this vocabulary, but not its core. Instead, the Nepali vocabulary for sex includes terms for sanctioned and unsanctioned relationships (marriage, elopement, lovers) and roles (husband/wife; patron/mistress; boyriend/girlfriend; seducer; virgin; "loose" woman, etc.) It also consists of terms for feelings of love, sexual desire, arousal and attraction and an array of verbs for seducing, wooing, flirting, and the like. All these words are powerful, value-laden terms that immediately bring to mind elements of the social context, such as power relations between men and women, that are relevant to AIDS prevention efforts. These words, in and of themselves also draw attention to the fact that to be involved in a socially sanctioned sexual relationship has very different implications from being involved in a hidden or illicit relationship. Words relating to love, flirtation, seduction, and sexual coercion make evident the various ways people might come to be drawn into sexual relationships. (Pigg, n.d.)

Other professionals have found that talking about sexuality in Nepali to be impolite, and substitute English words as necessary.

## 2. Religious, Ethnic, and Gender Factors Affecting Sexuality

### A. Source and Character of Religious Values

Religion is important in Nepal. The Kathmandu Valley has more than 2,700 religious shrines, which appear to exist together with mutual respect and without conflict. While

Nepal is referred to as a Hindu nation, Hinduism is not the "state" religion. A recent breakdown of religious representation put the Hindu population at 89.5%, Buddhists at 5.3%, Muslims at 2.6%, and others, including Christians, at 2.6% of the population. Buddhist and Hindu shrines and festivals are respected and celebrated by most people, regardless of their religious affiliations or beliefs.

Hinduism's role in the social status of women in Nepal depends on how liberally or conservatively one observes Hindu tradition. Women's sexual roles, as being either "maiden, married woman, or widow" are defined within the context of their relationship to men. Some sects do not consider women to be human, responding to the birth of a female child by stating, "nothing was born." Others vehemently assert equality between men and women, and support the role of women in maintaining Hindu tradition.

Hinduism's greatest social effect on Nepal is that it is the source of the caste system. The caste system continues to have a strong influence in society, even though it is prohibited by the Constitution. At Hindu temples, for example, members of the lowest castes have not historically been permitted to enter. There has been a growing desire, however, to change this. In 2001, the Prime Minister spoke out emphatically against caste-based discrimination, including barring access to temples. Since then, members of the lower castes have successfully entered many temples, including Pashupatinath, the most sacred national site to Hindus.

Buddhism has a fundamentally egalitarian view of men and women. As a result, Buddhism has offered social liberation to some women, if they have felt free to adopt the religion. As mentioned earlier, the beliefs and celebrations of Buddhism and Hinduism are equally celebrated and respected in Nepal.

Both Hinduism and Buddhism have teachings on sexuality, and there is extensive writing on both—including Tantric sex, practiced by some Buddhist and Hindu individuals. However, there is not as much literature specific to the effects of these teachings on the sexuality values in Nepal. It seems clear that some Nepalese individuals will base their values around sexuality on Hindu and Buddhist teachings, and others will not. Resources for further reading on Hindu and Buddhist teachings on sexuality are included at the end of this chapter.

### B. Cultural Values and Sexuality

In Nepal, parents are seen as a vital source of cultural values, including those around reproductive health and sexual behavior. As in other countries, research in Nepal has shown that parents who are actively involved in their children's upbringing, and communicate their values clearly and openly, end up with children whose values are congruent with theirs. When it comes to sexuality, this translates into young people who postpone sexual involvement until they are older or married, and who are able to avoid pregnancy and sexually transmitted infections if they do not remain abstinent.

Modern Nepal is a society, like others, that is faced with conflicting messages and values around sexuality. There is a generation gap in comfort and knowledge levels around sexuality, with adolescents speaking more openly about sexuality issues if not often knowing more themselves. There is also an increase of sexual images in the media, because in great part of television programming from India, which includes Western programming and MTV India. As cable television grows, individuals in Nepal who can afford television will be "treated" to such "American" television shows as *Baywatch* and *Beverly Hills 90210*. The irony is palpable in Nepal as it is in other cultures: As a society, individuals can barely discuss sexuality issues, yet the culture ends up bombarded by explicitly sexual media images and messages that can throw a culture into social chaos around sexual values.

Another example of the cultural values relating to discussing sexuality came when I was conducting a meeting with adult women living in Kathmandu. My plan was to conduct a brief activity about the menstrual cycle. The professionals with whom I worked recommended that when I was done, I was to apologize to the group for discussing such a personal subject with them. When I apologized after my talk, the group of women forgave me, and then apologized themselves for not knowing some of the details I had discussed.

### B. Source and Character of Ethnic Values

The terms "ethnicity" and "caste" are often used interchangeably. There may be larger populations of members of certain castes in particular parts of the country, and the available sexuality research data have revealed differences in sexuality values based on geographic location. Therefore, it is a reasonable assumption to make that different castes and ethnic groups will often have different values and beliefs around sexuality. At the same time, it is difficult to gather accurate information about people of different castes and ethnic groups for a number of reasons. First, geographic location often makes it challenging to obtain data from certain groups of people. Second, it is often challenging to obtain data from members of the highest caste, because they do not feel they need to participate in community-based programs. These programs are, they believe, for people of lower castes.

## 3. Knowledge and Education about Sexuality

### A. Government Policies and Programs

Changing times and changing values are causing Nepali professionals and parents alike to face the task of talking about sexual and reproductive health issues with their children and other young people in the community. Most Nepalese teens say they would like to receive additional information about these issues. While some say they would like to be able to talk with their parents about these topics, others say they would be too embarrassed to speak with their parents and would prefer to learn from television, radio, and social clubs. Community-based programs and studies have found that young people have more information than one might think—but at the same time, the information has been filtered through unreliable sources (such as peers) to create misinformation.

General education is a highly valued aspect of Nepalese society. However, it is not compulsory. Young people are expected to go to school, and parents will often sacrifice their needs in order to ensure that as much money is allocated to the children's education as possible.

When it comes to sexuality, there is a curriculum titled, *Health, Population and Environmental Education*, that is used in the 9th and 10th grades. This curriculum includes reproductive health, family life education, and "safe motherhood." Teachers are widely undertrained in sexuality issues, and often extremely uncomfortable about discussing the topic with young people in class. While some schools require teaching about reproductive health, teachers have been known to assign the chapters without allowing time for in-class discussion or questions. Teachers who do address the topic tend to stick to easier topics, including biology, without discussing emotions or more challenging topics. They are also more likely to lecture on this topic rather than taking a more interactive, participatory approach. Some teachers believe that sexuality information should only be accessible by adults—and still others believe it should only be available to married adults. Local and international NGOs have been increasing efforts to provide teacher training on sexuality and reproductive health topics.

Most parents say they support some kind of sexuality education for their children, although some opposition remains. Supporters believe that this kind of education will keep young people pregnancy- and disease-free; opponents believe that providing information about sexuality will encourage young people to have sexual relationships.

### B. Informal Sources of Sexual Knowledge

As mentioned earlier, Nepali parents support information for their children about sexuality issues. However, one survey found that only one in ten parents had actually discussed these issues with their children themselves. Discussions that did take place differed, based on the gender of the child. In the urban areas, parents were more likely to talk with both their sons and daughters. In the rural areas, parents were more likely to talk with their daughters than sons.

Many parents, particularly those living in the rural areas, are unaware of where they can access this information. According to one group of parents living in the urban areas, sources of sexuality and reproductive health information are government hospital (85%), private doctor/clinic (49%), and pharmacies (28%). Parents in the rural areas named health post (76%), health workers (17.9%), and pharmacies (13%) as sources for this type of information and support.

Local organizations, like the BP Memorial Health Foundation, have been working to establish language that can be used with individuals in the community that are both medically accurate and culturally respectful. In addition, international organizations, such as Family Health International and EngenderHealth, have been working in collaboration with local organizations to provide accurate, respectful sexuality information. Research conducted by EngenderHealth and the International Center for Research on Women revealed that young people want to receive information about sexuality and reproductive health, particularly from their mothers, older sisters and brothers, and sisters-in-law. However, they say they do not feel comfortable approaching these individuals with their questions, nor do they feel confident that these identified family members would be comfortable or well equipped to answer. Young people, in particular, have questions and concerns about the menstrual cycle, nocturnal emissions, and dealing with feelings of sexual arousal that are heightened during puberty. As a result, young people and adults alike are likely to ask questions of the local pharmacist—although concerns about confidentiality remain high.

Another effort came from the Family Planning Association of Nepal, when they introduced a confidential telephone hotline in Kathmandu to answer questions about sexuality and reproductive health. In the first two months, they received over 200 phone calls on this line, which was staffed by a trained counselor. FPAN has also published materials, including *Your Queries: Our Answers*.

## 4. Autoerotic Behaviors and Patterns

Masturbation is, like many other sexuality topics, generally not discussed. This is changing among younger people. In one focus group of teenagers throughout the country, professionals found that masturbation was discussed, but only by boys. These young men saw masturbation as a sign of a boy's maturity and approaching adulthood. If masturbation is discussed among girls or between girls and their mothers or older sisters, they do not share this publicly.

## 5. Interpersonal Heterosexual Behaviors

Having the word "heterosexual" before the word "behaviors" when discussing sexuality and Nepal is assumed.

Homosexuality is rarely discussed, and the assumption is that people are or should be heterosexual. When referring to relationships and/or sexual behaviors, heterosexuality is implied by default. This will be discussed more in Section 6, Homoerotic, Homosexual, and Bisexual Behaviors, below.

Sexual exploration by children is not discussed, if it exists. Conversations and concerns tend to arise when a young person reaches puberty. This is because of perceptible physical changes, and the understanding that pregnancy can happen.

According to one study, 40% of unmarried men who are 19 or older are sexually active. Most of these men report having their first sexual relationship during adolescence. A study in Kathmandu found the average age of first intercourse for males to be 21 and for females to be 20. (UNICEF Nepal & UNAIDS 2001). Adolescents and teens with less education and from more-marginalized ethnic groups are more likely to engage in early and premarital sex than those who are educated and have a high potential for achieving their life goals.

Not surprisingly, young men are much more likely than young women to report having multiple sex partners, of those acknowledging that they were sexually active. Of those males who report being sexually active before marriage, more than 50% report having multiple sex partners. Of adolescents reporting to be virgins, more than a third say they engage in some kind of non-intercourse behavior, such as mutual masturbation or oral sex.

Most teenagers say they know that parents frown upon premarital sexual relationships. However, nearly 20% of teens in a survey conducted by UNICEF Nepal and UNAIDS (2001) believed there to be nothing wrong with a premarital sexual relationship. There is a significantly higher acceptance of premarital sex among teen boys than among teen girls, and a higher rate of sexual behaviors among boys than among girls. This suggests any of three things: that teen boys are being sexual with older women, that teen boys are being sexual with commercial sex workers, and/or that teen girls are not truthful in reporting their sexual experiences because of social mores that frown much more upon girls' sexual activity than boys' engaging in sexual activities.

In Nepal, there is an expectation from childhood that a person will be married at some point. Marriage is seen as the greatest rite of passage in a person's life, the true sign that a person has gone from being a child to an adult. Marriage is highly valued, as is childbearing. One study of parental attitudes around marriage found a majority of parents favoring early marriage for girls and later marriage for boys (Moktan 2001). Attitudes toward this tend to differ in urban and rural areas. Most parents say they would prefer their children to be at least 18 before getting married, although younger marriages do take place. In the rural areas, marriage is common between young girls (ages 14 to 16) and much older men. Women who are unable to become pregnant are often ostracized or thought to be "improper." The assumption is widely held that if a woman cannot get pregnant, there is something wrong with her. Rarely does one explore the possibility that a man could be infertile. In some situations, men will take second wives in order to partner with a woman who can bear them children. A man may take on several wives, even if a pregnancy does not occur, rather than consider his own potential infertility. It is not known how widely this type of polygamy exists.

Arranged marriages are common in Nepal. The average age at marriage for girls is 16, with over half of these girls becoming pregnant by the time they are 20. The majority of parents surveyed say they favor arranged marriages, although 25% of parents living in the urban center expressed support for love marriages as well.

Divorce is possible, however, it is not socially sanctioned. While there are still reports of men having more than one wife—particularly in situations where one or more wives are unable to bear the man a son—the practice of polygamy seems to be less and less frequent. There are also reports of women having more than one husband, although if this were to occur, it tends to be in the more remote areas of the country.

## 6. Homoerotic, Homosexual, and Bisexual Behaviors

Information about same-sex behaviors and relationships is rare. According to both professionals and other individuals living in Kathmandu, homosexuality "does not exist" in Nepal. I was, therefore, not to include discussions on sexual orientation in any of my meetings or training manuals. To have done so would have been culturally irrelevant. The International Lesbian and Gay Association states that same-sex sexual behavior between two men is against the law in Nepal. As in many other countries, sexual activity between two women is not mentioned. People visiting the country who are caught engaging in same-sex behaviors can face expulsion.

The true prevalence, real or perceived, of same-sex relationships and sexual behaviors in Nepal depends on the person with whom you speak. Some will acknowledge that "these types of relationships exist," but that there is no community for it. Others will say that there is an underground community in Kathmandu. Still others will insist that there are no lesbian, gay, or bisexual people in Nepal. Health professionals, however, are beginning to acknowledge same-sex behaviors, at least between men. This is happening primarily within the context of screening for HIV. Physical intimacy, however, appears to be common between people of the same sex. Adult men and women may walk arm-in-arm or hand-in-hand. A teen girl might sit with her head on a female friend's shoulder; two male adolescents might sit with fingers interlaced, lovingly stroking one another's fingers. However, there was no perceptible identity attached to these behaviors as being homoerotic or implying anything about a person's sexual orientation. The extent to which intimacy translates into same-sex sexual behavior is unknown.

The first Nepalese gay rights group, the Nepal Queer Society, was created in 1993. However, there is no readily available information on whether the group is still in existence, or what their activities are or have been. The Internet has also begun to provide a source of information and support for lesbian, gay, and bisexual Nepalese individuals. Gay Cyber Nepal and Queer Nepal are two sites created for gay or bisexual men. Other websites have been created by South and Southeast Asian individuals not living in Nepal or India, which seem to provide more of a community for people living abroad than there would be in that region.

## 7. Gender Diversity and Transgender Issues

In my fieldwork in Nepal, I had no conversations with Nepali professionals about transgender individuals, and there is very little written information specifically for transgender people in Nepal. There are, however, a growing number of transgender websites and organizations covering South and Southeast Asia, which may serve as sources of support for transgender individuals throughout the region, including Nepal.

## 8. Significant Unconventional Sexual Behaviors

It is virtually impossible to document this aspect of Nepali society beyond the presence of commercial sex work. Discussions of non-coercive fetishes or sexual behaviors are infrequent, so that admitting to, let alone discussing, any type of unconventional behavior would be virtually unheard of. Perhaps the most unconventional behavior would be a man who avails himself of a commercial sex worker—and even if the sex worker fulfills a non-traditional sexual fantasy, this type of work has not been reported on in the literature about Nepal.

It is estimated that there are 25,000 women engaged in commercial sex work in Nepal. UNICEF estimates that over 40% of the commercial sex workers in the Kathmandu Valley are between the ages of 15 and 19. Other studies indicate that nearly two thirds of commercial sex workers in Nepal are infected with some kind of sexually transmitted infection.

### A. Rape, Sexual Abuse, and Human Trafficking

According to the United States State Department, Nepali laws against rape carry prison sentences of 6 to 10 years for the rape of a woman under 14 years of age and 3 to 5 years for the rape of a woman over 14. The law prescribes imprisonment for one year or a fine for the rape of a prostitute. The law does not forbid spousal rape. A 2001 survey found that 39% of rape victims who reported the crime to police were under the age of 19. Of the reported rapes, 25% resulted in convictions and jail sentences.

Statistics relating to domestic violence are as sketchy as the many other statistics relating to Nepal. However, in 2001, the *Kathmandu Post* reported that Nepalese nongovernmental organizations believe 75% of the female population have been subjected to some kind of domestic violence. Included in these figures are physical assault, harassment, and incest. When an adolescent girl is married off to an older man, this age difference is often seen as a cause or contributing factor to the domestic violence. In addition, citizens, law enforcement officials, health professionals, and government authorities tend to minimize the severity of violence against women. Forty-two percent of respondents in one survey said that they experienced medical practitioners to be uncooperative or negligent in cases of violence against women and girls.

Sexual abuse and incest are not discussed as much. In fact, before September 2002, there were no laws against sexual abuse of a child. The new law carries penalties of up to 16 years in prison for pedophilic acts. Teenagers surveyed in Kathmandu overwhelmingly expressed disagreement with domestic violence. Some, however, both male and female, did say that they thought that a man had the right to beat his wife under certain circumstances. These include a woman who does not look after her children well, or who is disrespectful to her in-laws.

When working with teenagers in Kathmandu, there was much discussion of "teasing," which translates in Western terms to "sexual harassment." The term "sexual harassment" was not used, because it does not translate, both in terms of language and in terms of its significance. It is used in Western cultures as a legal concept—a term that describes behaviors and situations that can result in legal actions and remedies. Nepal, as other cultures, may use the phrase "sexual intimidation" or "teasing." According to Nepali professionals, this is not to minimize the experience—it is culturally more accurate. Discussions have begun, however, in the media about sexual harassment of women in the workplace. These discussions, as the discussions of teen-to-teen harassment, tend to focus more on what the people being harassed should do to avoid giving mixed signals, and less on teaching men more appropriate, respectful behaviors.

Human trafficking is an issue that has gained wider attention over recent years, particularly in South and Southeast Asia. Nepali law prohibits human trafficking, with penalties of up to 20 years' imprisonment for breaking this law. However, trafficking in women and girls remains a serious problem in several of the country's poorest areas. Girls are sold into sexual slavery by their parents, or leave for India thinking that they are going to get married or have a decent paying job. NGOs working on this topic in Nepal believe that parents do not understand the true consequences of trafficking until it is too late—and that if they did, there would be less done. Organizations like Maiti Nepal are working to provide alternatives to trafficking, such as viable job options, and to help bring trafficked girls and women home from India, to where the vast majority are sold. There are very little, if any, data on the prevalence of young boys who are sold into sexual slavery in Nepal.

A common statistic puts the number of girls and women currently trafficked from Nepal into India at 200,000, with approximately 3,000 girls being trafficked out of the country each year. A children's human rights group states that 20% of prostitutes in the country are younger than 16 years old. Many of the girls who are sold into the commercial sex trade in India return to Nepal, which creates a number of problems. Cultural attitudes toward returned victims of trafficking are often negative and the Government response often reflects that bias. In addition, girls who return to Nepal often have sexually transmitted infections (STDs). In fact, of the 218 girls rescued in February 1998, somewhere between 60 and 70% were HIV-positive. Testing for STDs, including HIV, is a rare occurrence, particularly for young, unmarried girls. The stigma associated with visiting a healthcare provider of any kind, let alone one relating to reproductive or sexual health, far outweigh a young person's concern about diseases. As a result, trafficking not only does extensive physical, psychological, and emotional damage to the young women being trafficked—it also puts a great segment of the population at risk for STDs.

While the vast majority of trafficking is for sexual exploitation, women and girls are also sold for domestic service, manual or semi-skilled bonded labor, or other purposes. In some cases, parents or relatives sell women and young girls, especially if they are destitute and do not see their daughters as marriageable. Unverified estimates say that approximately 50% of trafficking victims are lured to India with the promise of good jobs and marriage, 40% are sold by a family member, and 10% are kidnapped. If prevention programs are established in a particular district, traffickers simply move to other areas and continue their work.

The Human Trafficking Control Act of 1986 prohibits selling persons in the country or abroad, and provides for penalties of up to 20 years' imprisonment for traffickers. However, there are many social and legal obstacles to successful prosecution, and convictions are rare. Since border guards commonly accept bribes to allow contraband and trafficked girls in or out of the country, many professionals are pessimistic about significantly reducing the trade without true government and legal support.

There are more than 40 NGOs in Nepal combating trafficking, several of which have rehabilitation and skills-training programs for trafficking victims. These groups commonly use leaflets, comic books, films, speaker programs, and skits—short plays with a few actors—to convey anti-trafficking messages and education. Some organizations involved in the rehabilitation of trafficking survivors

state that they have been threatened and their offices have been vandalized because of their activities.

## 9. Contraception, Abortion, and Population Planning

### A. Contraception

The government of Nepal has a Ministry of Health, which oversees its national health policies. The most recent, 1997-2017 long-term National Health Policy, includes mention of access to reproductive health, as well as the benefits to having "small families" by accessing family planning information and services. The government also developed guidelines for national maternal health (the National Maternity Care Guidelines and the National Safe Motherhood Plan of Action). These guidelines provide a blueprint for how women should receive care during their pregnancies and postpartum, and how babies should receive care once they are born. The programs, as other health programs in Nepal, have been focusing much more on increasing training for healthcare professionals. There are still a low number of women who seek antenatal care and services, and home deliveries for infants, without a trained professional present, remain the norm.

The National Reproductive Health Strategy of Nepal (adopted in 1997) was designed to make integrated reproductive health services available to all people in Nepal by focusing on the following:

- Family planning;
- Safe motherhood, including newborn care;
- Child health;
- Prevention and management of complications of abortion;
- RTI (reproductive tract infections)/STD/HIV/AIDS;
- Prevention and management of infertility;
- Adolescent reproductive health; and
- Problems of elderly women, particularly cancer treatment at the tertiary level/private sector.

Contraception is available in Nepal, gaining in use and access dramatically since the 1970s, when approximately 3% of couples were estimated to use contraception. More current figures put this at approximately 33%. At the same time, however, access to contraception depends greatly on where a woman or couple lives.

According to the Center for Reproductive Law and Policy, the country's family planning policies tend to favor the use of the IUD and injectible hormonal methods.

Any reproductive health service that can be accessed in Nepal is most likely to happen in the urban areas, and the rural areas closest to the cities. As one moves farther and farther away, up through the hills and into the mountains, the quality and access to healthcare diminishes dramatically. Problems exist with staffing reproductive or any other health facility in remote areas, as well as with non-appearances of the staff who have been hired. As a result, inhabitants of the more-remote areas receive even less care than those in the urban areas.

Because of insufficient prenatal care, it is estimated that nearly one in ten pregnancies are terminated spontaneously. This translates to roughly 90,000 miscarriages in Nepal per year. Nepal also has one of the highest maternal mortality rates in the world. Most of this can be attributed to unsafe abortion practices, as well as to pregnancy-induced hypertension and/or other illness occurring during pregnancy. In addition, only half of pregnant women obtain any kind of prenatal care, only 14% have some kind of trained medical professional present during the birth, and only 9% of babies are born in some kind of healthcare setting.

## B. Abortion

Nepal's abortion laws were historically among the most restrictive and punitive in the world. Providers are neither trained nor skilled in performing abortions because of these laws. The result has been up to 12 women dying every day—or nearly 4,500 every year—because of unsafe abortions.

Nearly 5,000 women appear at Maternity Hospital in Kathmandu each year with an incomplete abortion, necessitating the completion of the procedure. Statistics on abortion-related deaths, as most statistics about Nepal, range depending on the source. According to JHPIEGO, 15% to 30% of all pregnancy-related deaths were attributed to abortions that were unsafe, incomplete, or spontaneous. Other sources of data do not mention spontaneous abortions specifically, but state that nearly half of all pregnancy-related deaths were caused by unsafe abortions. Even in situations where a woman obtains an illegal abortion, she runs the risk of being jailed afterward—possibly reported by the very family member or friend who brought her to the provider in the first place. In fact, the Center for Reproductive Law and Policy estimates that one out of five women in Nepal who are in jail are there for obtaining an abortion. Girls and women living near the border to India have historically crossed the border in order to obtain a legal abortion there.

In September 2002, King Gyanendra approved a law legalizing abortion up to 12 weeks on demand, and up to 18 weeks if the pregnancy is a result of rape or incest. Abortions will be allowed at any time if the woman's life or health is in danger, or if the woman learns that she is going to give birth to a disabled child. (The types of disabilities were not specified. This may raise a whole other range of concerns relating to people with disabilities in Nepal.)

Although this law is a significant victory for women's rights, two challenges remain. First, women already in jail for having obtained an abortion remain there, and the government has not mentioned anything about whether they plan to release them. Second, access to abortion services remains a challenge. In addition, the so-called global "gag rule" of the current Bush administration (USA) restricts any international organization receiving United States funds from discussing abortion. This, therefore, forces Nepalese reproductive health professionals to choose between direly needed U.S. funds and providing information and services to women seeking abortion.

According to the 1996 Nepal Health Survey, approximately half of all girls begin having babies by the time they are 19. While most teenage boys and girls report that they know what condoms are and where to get them, only about two thirds of teenage boys in one survey reported using condoms during premarital sexual relationships (UNICEF Nepal & UNAIDS 2001). When a pregnancy does occur out of wedlock, the father of the child is not usually seen as partially responsible, although this varies depending on where the couple lives. In some areas, the male is forced to marry his female sex partner, or, if he refuses, must either pay a fine or spend time in jail. As with the likelihood of sexual initiation, the likelihood of condom use was higher with boys living in Kathmandu and who were educated.

## 10. Sexually Transmitted Diseases and HIV/AIDS

### A. Sexually Transmitted Diseases

A major challenge in tracking STD incidence is obtaining local data. The World Health Organization estimated that in 1999, there were 340 million new cases of curable STDs throughout the world—specifically syphilis, gonor-rhea, chlamydia, and trichomoniasis. Of these, nearly half, or 151 million, were said to have happened in South and Southeast Asia alone. Specifically, this breaks down to 43 million new cases of chlamydia in this region, 27 million with gonorrhea, 4 million with syphilis, and 76.5 million with trichomoniasis. Statistics specific to Nepal about STDs other than HIV are difficult to come by accurately.

There is much stigma surrounding STDs. People who think they might have an infection are unlikely to seek out medical treatment, often exacerbating an easily treatable or curable infection. In one survey, adolescent and teen boys who ended up with an STD say that they are more likely to go to a pharmacy and purchase medicine in an effort to treat themselves, than they are to go to a family planning clinic to be diagnosed and treated appropriately by a health professional.

The majority of information and data available around infections relates to HIV and AIDS, described in the next section. Of the limited information about infections, there is information about syphilis within one population. In 1997, 1,800 women who went in for prenatal screening tested positive for this infection.

Culturally, myths and misinformation about STDs abound. One is the concept that a man who urinates on the grounds of or against a temple will be stricken with an STD as punishment. There is also a strong sense of invulnerability among males if they do not engage in sexual behaviors with a commercial sex worker. Unprotected sexual behaviors with a girl or woman who is not a commercial sex worker is, therefore, not seen by men and boys as risky. Unprotected sexual behaviors may be seen by young girls and women to be risky; however, they usually do not have the option of insisting that their partners wear condoms.

### B. HIV/AIDS

As with other health issues, there are little updated, reliable data about the incidence and prevalence of HIV and AIDS in Nepal. However, professionals can say with certainty that the HIV epidemic is increasing, and has been since the first HIV/AIDS case was recorded in 1988.

As in many parts of the world, the AIDS epidemic has forced previously silent countries to start addressing sexuality issues more directly and explicitly—although nowhere nearly as explicit as is done in many Western countries. As in other parts of Southeast Asia, it is estimated that HIV and AIDS cases are much more prevalent and are spreading much more rapidly than the limited statistics currently report. According to one source, the government will confirm that there were only about 500 HIV or AIDS cases over an eight-year period, something that most professionals in Nepal will say is a gross underestimate. Family Health International (FHI) estimates that between 30,000 and 50,000 individuals are currently infected with HIV; the World Health Organization puts the number at around 33,500. The CIA *World Factbook* estimated in 1999 that there were approximately 34,000 people living with HIV or AIDS and 2,500 AIDS-related deaths, numbers that many professionals believe to be a gross underestimate. According to UNAIDS, 10,000 of these cases are among women ages 15 to 49, and 930 are among children ages 0 to 15. UNAIDS also estimated that there were 2,500 AIDS-related deaths in Nepal in 1999, with approximately 2,200 children living as orphans as a result of losing one or both parents to an AIDS-related death. Without appropriate interventions, FHI estimates that the number of people living with HIV could reach between 100,000 and 200,000 by the year 2010.

The source of many HIV cases in Nepal are from sexual encounters with sex workers, both in Nepal and in other countries, such as India and Thailand, when men are traveling for business. Among the main locations for such encounters is the north-south highway that runs from Nepal to India. Rest stops, teahouses, restaurants, and other types of lodges along the highway and in border cities provide significant venues for prostitution, leading to significant transmission of HIV. At the same time, however, it is important to note that sex workers would be more likely to access health services. Other individuals at high risk for HIV and other STDs do not avail themselves of testing and other health and/or preventative services. There is a concern, therefore, that commercial sex workers will be held exclusively responsible for spreading HIV and other STDs, when they are not the exclusive conduits for the rise in HIV in Nepal. In fact, according to UNAIDS, the incidence of HIV among intravenous drug users in Kathmandu alone increased from nearly 0 in 1993-1994 to 50% in 1997.

According to a survey conducted by UNICEF of 1,400 Nepalese teens, the majority surveyed reported that they know what HIV is, but only about three quarters said they knew to use a condom during sex. A higher reported rate of sexual activity for boys rather than girls suggests that boys who are sexually active are doing so with commercial sex workers, putting them at higher risk for HIV and other STDs if they do not have knowledge of or insist upon using condoms.

Injection drug use is seen as being among the greatest causes for the increase in HIV in Nepal. According to UNICEF Nepal (2001), the incidence of HIV increased in intravenous drug users by 48% within a short four-year period. Since the majority of these drug users are in the 16- to 25-year age range, the implications for sexuality education and prevention services for adolescents and teens are significant.

HIV has overcome the conservative attitudes toward discussing sexuality issues. Media campaigns starting in the mid-1990s raised public awareness and touted the importance of condom use. Radio ads, public service announcements, and even a comic book discuss the dangers of HIV and the importance of using condoms. An annual observation of World AIDS Day on December 1st has also begun in Nepal. However, these campaigns are not consistent because of a number of factors, including the expenses involved in airing the ads, and the conflict between promoting the government-supplied free condoms and the concern from merchants selling condoms that they will lose money as a result. In addition, discomfort and modesty often keeps people from purchasing condoms and merchants from selling them. Yet, interestingly enough, Nepalese parents cite TV and radio as among the most important sources of sexual health information for young people.

[*Update 2002*: UNAIDS Epidemiological Assessment: As with virtually all other countries in Asia, the first cases of AIDS or HIV infection were detected during the late 1980s and early 1990s, either in a foreign visitor or in a citizen who returned from international travel. During the early 1990s, HIV seroprevalence surveys detected HIV infections among STD patients and female sex workers throughout most regions in Nepal. As a result, there has been great public health concern that extensive spread of HIV, similar to that in the neighboring countries of Cambodia, Myanmar, Thailand, and India might occur. Injecting drug users in Nepal were initially believed to share injection equipment in relatively small and isolated networks. However, since the mid-1990s, an explosive increase in HIV infection has occurred, infecting about half of all injecting drug users throughout the country.

[Large numbers of young Nepalese girls are recruited as female sex workers to Indian cities, and large numbers of young Nepalese males working in India frequent female sex workers there and within Nepal. Thus, in addition to the increasing number of HIV infections occurring among persons with high HIV-risk behaviors in Nepal, there are also increasing numbers of Nepalese female sex workers and young male Nepalese workers who have been infected with HIV in India, and who have or will be returning to Nepal. The estimated HIV prevalence in Nepal in 2001 was 58,000 or close to 0.5% of the total 15- to 49-year-old population. Asian countries with the highest HIV prevalence (from 2% to 3% of their 15- to 49-year-old populations) in the region all have brothel-based female sex workers as a dominant factor. Because Nepal's pattern of female sex workers is primarily non-brothel based, it appears likely that its HIV prevalence may not reach such high levels. Effective public health programs capable of increasing consistent condom usage levels in female sex workers and their male clients to 80% to 90% may be capable of keeping HIV prevalence in Nepal to less than 1% (i.e., less than 100,000) of the 15- to 49-year-old population.

[Based on an estimated HIV prevalence of about 34,000 in 2000, the number of AIDS deaths that can be expected in the year 2000 is close to 3,000 and this figure is projected to more than double (about 6,000) in 2005. It is estimated that these AIDS deaths will increase total deaths in the 15- to 49-year-old age group by about 4% in 2000, and account for close to 20% of total deaths in this age group in 2005.

[The estimated number of adults and children living with HIV/AIDS on January 1, 2002, were:

| | | |
|---|---|---|
| Adults ages 15-49: | 56,000 | (rate: 0.1%) |
| Women ages 15-49: | 14,000 | |
| Children ages 0-15: | 1,500 | |

[An estimated 2,400 adults and children died of AIDS during 2001.

[At the end of 2001, an estimated 13,000 Nepalese children under age 15 were living without one or both parents who had died of AIDS. (*End of update by the Editors*)]

## 11. Sexual Dysfunctions, Counseling, and Therapies

The scope of sexual dysfunctions is widely unknown, because of, in great part, the lack of information and education, and taboos about discussing sexuality, especially for women. If girls do not know what to expect when going into their marriage or sexual relationships, it is unlikely that they will know that something painful or pleasureless is not simply part of their duties as wives. And it is even less likely that a woman would request information about sexual behaviors or pleasure. Male sexual dysfunction is not discussed either, although men are less likely to be seen as "responsible" for their dysfunction or stigmatized for it.

## 12. Sex Research and Advanced Professional Education

Data are sorely lacking in Nepal. Organizations that conduct research are often able to survey only a small population at a time. As in the United States, data appear to be much more easily collected from individuals in urban settings and from individuals and families with a lower socioeconomic status.

As a result, Nepal's true diversity is often lost in research methodology. Census screening does not begin to show the true diversity of multicultural relationships and families. In Nepal, it is difficult to reach the many different ethnic groups who speak different languages and have different social norms. This means that presenting data on a typical Nepalese adult or teenager is virtually impossible. The research available about sexuality and sexual health in Nepal is quite limited in scope. What is available is primarily collected about men and boys, with more information being found more recently on girls and women. Statistics are unreliable, but they provide a preliminary snapshot of some of the issues facing Nepal.

There are no university programs or scientific journals specifically focusing on sexuality issues. However, the following organizations either do work on sexuality-related issues in Nepal, or maintain statistics on sexual and reproductive health. Several of these groups are Nepalese, while others are based outside of the country and work collaboratively with NGOs in Nepal.

Didibahini, GPO Box 13568, Anamnagar, Kathmandu, Nepal; www.didibahini.org; info@didibahini.org, didibahini @wlink.com.np.

EngenderHealth, 440 Ninth Avenue, New York, NY 10001 USA; www.cngenderhealth.org; info@engenderhealth .org.

Family Health International, P.O. Box 13950, Research Triangle Park, NC 27709 USA; www.fhi.org; services@ fhi.org.

Family Planning Association of Nepal, Pulchowk, Laitpur, P.O.Box: 486, Kathmandu, Nepal; www.fpan.org; fpan @mail.com.np, fpandg@mail.com.np.

International Planned Parenthood Federation, Regent's College Inner Circle, Regent's Park, London NW1 4NS UK; www.ippf.org; info@ippf.org.

Maiti Nepal, P.O. Box 9599, Gaushala, Kathmandu, Nepal; www.maitinepal.org; info@maitinepal.org.

Ministry of Population and Environment, Nepal; www .mope.gov.np.

The Population Council, One Dag Hammarskjold Plaza, New York, NY 10017 USA; www.popcouncil.org; pubinfo @popcouncil.org.

Care International, Boulevard du Regent, 58/10 B-1000, Brussels, Belgium; www.care-international.org; info@care-international.org.

The Centre for Development and Population Activities, 1400 16th Street NW, Suite 100, Washington, DC 20036 USA; www.cedpa.org; cmail@cedpa.org.

UNAIDS/WHO Working Group on Global HIV/AIDS and STI Surveillance, 20, Avenue Appia, CH-1211 Geneva, 27, Switzerland; www.unaids.org; surveillance@UNAIDS .org.

United Nations Population Fund, 220 East 42nd Street, New York, NY 10017 USA; www.unfpa.org.

## References and Suggested Readings

Bennett, T. 1999 (September). Preventing trafficking in women and children in Asia: Issues and options. *Impact on HIV*, *1*(2).

Cameron, M. 1998. *On the edge of the auspicious: Gender and caste in Nepal*. Chicago: University of Illinois Press.

Center for Reproductive Law and Policy. 2002. Nepal legalizes abortion: Next step is to release women in prison for abortion. *CRLP Press*. Available: http://www.crlp.org/pr_02_0314nepal.html.

Center for Reproductive Law and Policy. 2001. Mother's day: Life-threatening conditions for pregnant women. *CRLP Press*. Available: http://www.crlp.org/pr_01_0511mothers .html.

Center for Reproductive Law and Policy. 2001. *Emergency contraception: An analysis of laws and policy around the world*. Available: http://www.crlp.org/pub_art_icpdec2 .html.

Center for Reproductive Law and Policy and Forum for Women, Law and Development. 2002. *Abortion in Nepal: Women imprisoned*. Available: http://www.crlp.org/pdf/nepal_2002 .pdf.

CIA. 2002 (January). *The world factbook 2002*. Washington, DC: Central Intelligence Agency. Available: http://www .cia.gov/cia/publications/factbook/index.html.

Family Health International. 2001. *Nepal program overview*. Available: http://www.fhi.org/en/cntr/asia/nepal/nepalofc .html.

Family Health International. 2000. *Final report for the AIDSCAP program in Nepal*. Available: http://www .fhi.org/en/aids/aidscap/aidspubs/special/countryprog/ nepal/nepal3d.html.

Family Health International. 1999. *Fact sheet: Screening for contraceptive use by village health workers in Nepal*. Available: http://www.fhi.org/en/fp/checklistse/chklstfpe/ nepalfct.htm.

Gartoula, R.P. 2000. Anthropological perspectives on sexual behaviour and practices. *The People's Review: A Political and Business Weekly*. Available: www.yomari.com/p-review/ 2000/01/20012000/health.htm.

Guraubacharaya. 1997 (September). Ritual values that shape society. International Planned Parenthood Federation's *Real Lives*, Issue 2.

Johns Hopkins Program in Education and Gynecology. 1996. *JHPIEGO technical report FCA-25, June 1996*. Available: http://www.jhpiego.org/pubs/tr/tr625sum.htm.

International Planned Parenthood Federation. 2001 (July 19). *Testimony of Dr. Nirmal K. Bista, Director General, Family Planning Association of Nepal, before the Senate Foreign Relations Committee*.

International Planned Parenthood Federation, & International Women's Rights Action Watch. 2000. *Reproductive rights 2000*. Available: http://www.ippf.org/pubs/wallcharts/ reproductiverights2000/pdf/chart1.pdf.

Malhotra, A., S. Mathur, M. Mehta, P. Lal Moktan, & R. Bhadra. 2000 (March 23-25). *Adolescent reproductive health and sexuality in Nepal: Combining quantitative and participatory methodologies*. Paper presented at the Annual Meeting of the Population Association of America, Los Angeles.

Mathur, S., A. Malhotra & M. Mehta. 2001. Adolescent girls' life aspirations and reproductive health in Nepal. *Reproductive Health Matters*.

Ministry of Population and Environment, Nepal. 2000. *The state of population–Nepal, 2000* (chap. 4: Status of health system). Available: http://www.mope.gov.np/status/popstat/chapter4 .html.

Moktan, P. L. 2001. *Young people's reproductive and sexual health: Perceptions of parents and adult family members*.

National Planning Commission Secretariat. 1998 (December). *The gender challenge. Kathmandu, Nepal*. Available: http:// www.panasia.org.sg/nepalnet/socio/gender_chal.htm.

Pigg, S. L. n.d. *Translating AIDS awareness messages into south Asian contexts: Some comments on the sexual words exercises*. Simon Fraser University. Available: http://www .hsph.harvard.edu/Organizations/healthnet/SAsia/repro2/ sex_words_exercise.html.

Pokharel, T. 2001 (March 9). Severe penalty proposed against in-house perpetrators. *The Kathmandu Post* (Eng. ed.).

Rana, P. 2000 (August). Nepal: Knowledge is power. International Planned Parenthood Federation's *Real Lives*, Issue 5. Available: http://mirror.ippf.org/regions/sar/rl/issue5/ knowledge.htm.

Scovill, N. B. 1995. *The liberation of women: Religious sources*. Washington, DC: The Religious Consultation on Population, Reproductive Health and Ethics. Available: http://www .religiousconsultation.org/liberation.htm.

Simhada, P. 2002. *Trafficking and HIV/AIDS: The case of Nepal. Research for sex work #5*. Available: http://www.med .vu.nl/hcc/artikelen/simkhada.htm.

Thapa, D., J. Davey, C. Waszak, & R. Bhadra 2001. *Reproductive health needs of adolescents and youth in Nepal: Insights from a focus group study*. Kathmandu, Nepal: Family Health International.

UNAIDS. 2002. *Epidemiological fact sheets by country.* Geneva, Switzerland: Joint United Nations Programme on HIV/AIDS (UNAIDS/WHO). Available: http://www.unaids.org/hivaidsinfo/statistics/fact_sheets/index_en.htm.

UNICEF Nepal, & UNAIDS. 2001. *A survey of teenagers in Nepal for life skills development & HIV/AIDS prevention.* Available: http://www.unicef.org/programme/lifeskills/assets/nepal_teen_survery.pdf.

United States Department of State. 2001. *Background note: Nepal.* Available: http://www.state.gov/r/pa/ei/bgn/5283.htm.

United States Department of State. 2002 (March 4). *Country reports on human rights practices 2001.* Released by the Bureau of Democracy, Human Rights, and Labor. Available: http://www.state.gov/g/drl/rls/hrrpt/2001/sa/8234.htm.

Waszak, C., & S. Thapa. 2001. Gender discrimination and gender roles: Perspectives of urban Nepalese youth. *Nepal adolescents and young adults report series.* Kathmandu, Nepal: Family Health International. Available: http://pisun2.ewc.hawaii.edu/ayarr/ayarr_public_html/reports_materials/completepaper/GenderRoles.PDF.

Watkins, J. C. 1996. *Spirited women: Gender, religion, & cultural identity in the Nepal Himalaya.* New York: Columbia University Press.

World Health Organization. 2001. *Global prevalence and incidence of selected curable sexually transmitted infections: Overview and estimates.* Geneva, Switzerland. Available: http://www.who.int/HIV_AIDS/GRSTI/who_hiv_aids_2001.02.pdf.

# Netherlands and the Autonomous Dutch Antilles

## (*Koninkrijk der Nederlanden*)

Jelto J. Drenth, Ph.D., and A. Koos Slob, Ph.D.*
*Updates by the Editors***

## Contents

## Demographics, a Brief Historical Perspective, and Dutch Sexology

### A. Demographics
ROBERT T. FRANCOEUR

Located in northwest Europe on the North Sea, the Netherlands' 16,030 square miles (41,525 km²) are roughly the size of the states of Massachusetts, Connecticut, and Rhode Island combined. Belgium borders the Netherlands on the south, Germany on the east, and the English Channel and the United Kingdom on the west. The Kingdom of the Netherlands includes the Dutch Antilles, the autonomous Caribbean islands of the West Indies. Curacao, Aruba, and Bonaire are near the South American coast; St. Eustatius, Saba, and the southern part of St. Maarten are southeast of Puerto Rico. (The northern two thirds of St. Maarten island belong to French Guadeloupe). Combined, the six islands have an area of 385 square miles (995 km²).

*Communications*: Koos Slob, Ph.D., Erasmus University, Faculty of Medicine, P.O. Box 1738, 3000 Dr. Rotterdam, Netherlands; slob@endov.fgg.eur.nl. Jelto J. Drenth, M.D., Visserstraat 39, 712 CS Groningen, Netherlands.

Much of the basic information in this chapter is based on the 1991 Special English Issue of the *Tijdschrift voor Seksuologie*, published on the occasion of the Tenth World Congress for Sexology, Amsterdam, June 18-22, 1991. We gratefully acknowledge the authors of this volume and the editors for their kind permission.

**Editors' Note*: Because of time and space constraints, the Editors have converted most of the original bar and line graphs of the original chapter into tables. We have referenced the original figure or table number and page number in *IES2*, i.e., the original chapter on the Netherlands in volume 2 of the *International Encyclopedia of Sexuality*, in the new tables' footnotes. For those original graphs that did not contain actual numbers, we have approximated the percentages, which are noted where appropriate. The reader is referred to the original figures in the original volume or on the Web at http://www.SexQuest.com/ccies/ies2-ref-figures.html.

(CIA 2002)

In July 2002, the Netherlands had an estimated population of 16 million. (All data are from *The World Factbook 2002* (CIA 2002) unless otherwise stated.)

**Age Distribution and Sex Ratios**: *0-14 years*: 18.3% with 1.05 male(s) per female (sex ratio); *15-64 years*: 67.9% with 1.03 male(s) per female; *65 years and over*: 13.8% with 0.7 male(s) per female; *Total population sex ratio*: 0.98 male(s) to 1 female

**Life Expectancy at Birth**: *Total Population*: 78.58 years; *male*: 75.7 years; *female*: 81.59 years

**Urban/Rural Distribution**: 88% to 12%

**Ethnic Distribution**: Dutch: 91%; Moroccan, Turks, and others: 9%

**Religious Distribution**: Roman Catholic: 31%; Protestant: 21%; Muslim: 4.4%; other: 3.6%; unaffiliated: 40% (1998 est.)

**Birth Rate**: 11.58 births per 1,000 population

**Death Rate**: 8.67 per 1,000 population

**Infant Mortality Rate**: 4.31 deaths per 1,000 live births

**Net Migration Rate**: 2.34 migrant(s) per 1,000 population

**Total Fertility Rate**: 1.65 children born per woman

**Population Growth Rate**: 0.55%

**HIV/AIDS** (1999 est.): *Adult prevalence*: 0.19%; *Persons living with HIV/AIDS*: 15,000; *Deaths*: 100. (For additional details from www.UNAIDS.org, see end of Section 10B.)

**Literacy Rate** (*defined as those age 15 and over who can read and write*): 99%; education is free and compulsory from age 5 to 18

**Per Capita Gross Domestic Product** (*purchasing power parity*): $25,800 (2001 est.); *Inflation*: 4.5%; *Unemployment*: 2.4%; *Living below the poverty line*: NA

### B. A Brief Historical Perspective

ROBERT T. FRANCOEUR

In 55 B.C.E., Julius Caesar conquered the Celtic and Germanic tribes that inhabited the region that is now the Netherlands. After Charlemagne's empire fell apart in the mid-800s, the Netherlands—then what is today Holland, Belgium, and Flanders—was divided among dukes, counts, and bishops. Holland soon passed through the Duke of Burgundy to King Charles V of Spain. In the later 1500s, as the area drifted toward political freedom and Protestantism, William the Silent, prince of Orange, led a confederation of the northern provinces that declared independence from Spain in 1581. The United Dutch Republic's rise to naval, economic, and artistic eminence came in the 17th century, only to end in 1795 when Napoleon made his brother Louis king of Holland. Napoleon annexed the country in 1810, but the French were expelled in 1813 and the kingdom of the Netherlands, including Belgium, established. The Belgians seceded and formed a separate kingdom in 1830.

The Netherlands remained neutral in World War I, but was invaded and brutally occupied by the Germans between 1940 and 1945. After several years of fighting, Indonesia gained its independence in 1949; West New Guinea was turned over to Indonesia in 1963. The independence of former Dutch colonies was followed by mass emigrations to the Netherlands.

## C. Dutch Sexology

JELTO J. DRENTH and A. KOOS SLOB

To understand Dutch sexology, one needs to keep in mind five general characteristics of our society that crystallized in the latter half of the 19th and first half of the 20th centuries:

1. The role of the family and the position of men and women is central in Dutch society. Excluded from the labor process, women were supposed to derive their task, fulfillment, and satisfaction from marriage and family. Together with Ireland and Sicily, the Netherlands has the lowest rate of working wives and economically independent women. Even today, many politicians support this inequality of social roles. In recent decades, however, the position of the housewife has gradually declined, a factor that may have an impact on sexual problems for women and men.

2. Since the origin of the Netherlands in the 17th century, there has been a strong segregation between Catholicism and Protestantism, with many subdivisions among the latter. In the 19th century, humanism, socialism, and liberalism were influential. As a result, the Netherlands now has a very strong compartmentalization or "denominational segregation." Some 40 different organizations and over 25 political parties have access to television broadcasting and the elections. Because of different, sometimes very powerful religious influences, extreme contrasts in social and sexual behavior exist between various groups. For instance, one fundamentalist Protestant political party still discriminates against women in membership and office eligibility, although over half of those voting for this party are women. On the positive side, this compartmentalization has resulted in a willingness to cope with differences in opinion and a rather liberal attitude towards varying social groups and lifestyles. The pedophile movement, for example, openly expresses its views on child-adult sexual relations. Our homosexual movement is widely respected, and our national organization for homosexuals even received royal assent. The Protestant University of Amsterdam houses the world's only chair of transsexology.

3. Holland in the west was rich and industrialized with extensive colonial ventures; the east was less prosperous and mainly agrarian. The west is the focus of political, economic, cultural, and social development, including a large group of sexologists. This geographic separation also influences differences between groups in Dutch society.

4. When the Dutch East Indies became independent, Indonesia in 1949, several hundred thousand people came from this culture to the Netherlands. A similar immigration occurred in 1975 when Dutch Guiana became independent Suriname. The Netherlands has also received its share of labor from the Mediterranean. A second and third generation of Turkish and Moroccan origins, most born in the Netherlands, still struggle with the problem of being rooted in two cultures. Political refugees are the latest contribution to our multiethnic society. Some 7% of our population was born in other countries. The result is a profoundly multiracial society in which sexual rules and values sometimes differ greatly, presenting a major challenge for sexological research and treatment.

5. Sociosexological research in the Netherlands has been quite extensive since the 1960s. Initial research focused on problems resulting from a restrictive sexual morality. During the 1970s, attention shifted to the rapid process of sexual liberalization and its practical consequences, such as the need for family planning education and services. The past decade has been dominated by research on sexual abuse and the spread of STDs and AIDS. Published mostly in the Dutch language, this research has not had a significant impact outside Holland, despite the fact that open and permissive sexual attitudes give Dutch sexology a unique position, not just in terms of attitudes and behavior, but also in terms of research possibilities. More international comparative and collaborative research would benefit all.

Research on sexual behavior, attitudes, and related subjects began in 1968, when the largest women's weekly, *Margriet*, commissioned a national *Seks in Nederland* (SIN) survey using a representative sample of 1,284 men and women ages 21 to 65, and 809 youngsters ages 16 to 20 (Noordhoff et al. 1969). This study was repeated in a modified and extended way in 1974 (with teenagers only) and in 1981 and 1989. These surveys present a fairly accurate description of major social and demographic correlates of sexual attitudes and behavior, and the changes in these variables over time.

While strongly inspired by the 1948/1953 Kinsey studies, the 1968 Dutch study reflected the main interests and concerns of Dutch society at that time, namely self-pleasuring, premarital and extramarital sexual contacts, sexual desires, prostitution, homosexuality, contraception, and (illegal) induced abortion.

Kooy (1975) analyzed the 1968 SIN survey, putting the data in a theoretical perspective of changing family relationships, declining moral influence of religion, and growing social equality between the sexes. The second SIN survey (in 1981) had the character of a trend report (Kooy et al. 1983). The main trends observed were growing tolerance towards different kinds of sexual behavior and more equality between partners in heterosexual relationships. Secularization seemed to be the most important background factor in these changes. The 1989 survey was strongly influenced by fear of AIDS and a need for knowledge to underpin prevention programs.

In part, the study of adolescent sexuality parallels the adult studies, including sexual development, relationship development, sexual education, prevention of unwanted pregnancy, and induced abortion, and recently STD and AIDS prevention. In 1974, the first SIN survey was repeated for adolescents only. De Haas (1975) interpreted and reported the data from an educational viewpoint; Kooy (1976) used a sociological perspective. The 1981 adolescent data were not analyzed before they were used in the framework of the much larger 1989 study (Vogels & van der Vliet 1990). The 1974 and 1981 studies included 600 and 800 youngsters ages 15 to 19, while the 1989 study included 11,500 youngsters and 11- to 14-year-olds. Finally, both the 1989 adolescent and 1989 SIN adult surveys were motivated by the fear of the HIV epidemic.

## 1. Basic Sexological Premises

### A. Character of Gender Roles

It is difficult to generalize on gender roles in the Netherlands. Dutch society has become so diverse that, at any given moment, different groups will be influenced differently. Yet, in all but the most isolated groups, an awareness of the variation in social and sexual role responsibilities must have led to a rise in tolerance for less-conventional behaviors.

The classic Western role separation, men being providers and women housekeepers and caregivers, has been criticized intensively. Some feminist principles have found almost universal support. Holland is subject to Europe's legislation against sex discrimination, and today it is hard to find examples of sex discrimination in the workplace. Government policy includes a "positive action" plan: In some segments of paid labor, women will be favored in the job-application process to bring down the underrepresentation of women in these professions. The government has funded a mass-media campaign intended to raise girls' awareness of preparing for financial independence.

Countering these conscious efforts, mass-media influences, such as soap operas and commercials, are often extremely conservative in their depiction of role ideals. The impact of this on the general public's role awareness is hard to estimate.

### B. Sociolegal Status of Males and Females

In recent years, legislation reforms have tended to equalize legal rights for men and women, homosexuals and heterosexuals. For instance, a 1991 reform of rape laws encompassed male and female rape. Children under age 12 are protected against all sexual contacts; for 12- to 16-year-olds, sexual contacts are legal offenses only if the adolescent, his/her parents(s) or guardian, or the Child Welfare Court files a complaint. Existence of a dependency relation between the adult partner and the adolescent is an exception to this. The law's intention is that the child's own judgment outweighs the parent's.

In the Netherlands, bypasses are available for teenagers to obtain oral contraceptives and abortions without parental permission.

### C. General Concepts of Sexuality and Love

As oral contraception has uncoupled sexuality and procreation, so the possibility of uncoupling sexuality and love has also been recognized. Large groups of Dutch men and women sympathize with the need for sexual gratification of people who are not in steady relationships. Self-pleasuring and "recreational" sex are no longer taboo. Virginity is disappearing as an ideal. Self-pleasuring as a variation within a steady relationship is also no longer universally scorned.

Yet, love is still probably the most-valued principle in Holland. Almost all Dutch men and women believe that steady relations must be built on love, and that sexuality with love is more satisfying that without it.

## 2. Religious, Ethnic, and Gender Factors Affecting Sexuality

### A. Source and Character of Religious Values

Denominational segregation, 34% Roman Catholic and 25% Dutch Reformed, has not played an important role in Dutch sexuality. The Dutch Society for Sexual Reform (NVSH) found its Protestant counterpart in the Protestant Society for Responsible Family Planning (PSVG) and a Catholic Bureau for Sexuality and Relations. But these religiously inspired organizations are small and limited to providing written information and educational materials. NVSH has separated into a laypersons' organization for political action and education, and a professional organization, the Rutgers Foundation, for medical and psychological help. The Dutch government funds the foundation's counseling centers and participation of foundation administrators and staff in international organizations, such as the International Planned Parenthood Federation.

Religious motivations have played an important role in our legal reform. The Dutch abortion law adopted in 1985 permits abortion on request with the sole restriction of a five-day waiting period. Opposition from fundamentalist Catholics has little support. Moreover, the Pope's regulations on contraception is almost universally ignored by Dutch Catholics, as are restrictions on homosexual behavior and the sexuality of the handicapped. Catholic and Protestant groups have played important roles in the acceptance of gays and lesbians, with some churches celebrating ceremonies of gay and lesbian unions. (See "Update 2001" in Section 6, Homoerotic, Homosexual, and Bisexual Behaviors, on the legalization of marriage for homosexual couples in Holland.)

### B. Source and Character of Ethnic Values

Most Muslims in the Netherlands came from Turkey or Morocco as "guest laborers" in the booming economy, women and children following the men after they settled in. The Netherlands now has a second generation and a third on its way. Tension between Muslim traditions and the Western way of life is common. Islamic traditions emphasize family honor, with specific restrictions on sexual behavior and distinct social roles for men and women.

Arranged marriages are common and the confrontation of two cultures sometimes leads to conflicts between parents and children who, raised in the Western world, want to choose their own spouse. Muslim tradition includes the ultimate measure of kidnapping to force a marriage. Incidents of this, and of Muslim girls running away from home to avoid an arranged marriage, are common, leading to the establishment of a shelter home for Muslim girls only. Muslim honor sometimes conflicts with the Dutch legal system, leading to tragic misunderstandings in the law courts. Helping professionals are only slowly learning how to handle such problems without trespassing on Muslim taboos. Relevant for sexological practice are the following:

- A male doctor will not be allowed to perform a physical examination of a Muslima in the absence of her husband;
- A male patient will often be embarrassed if asked about his sexual problems by a female doctor;
- Self-pleasuring is an almost-absolute taboo and should not be advised as a therapeutic modality;
- Prostitution is much less forbidden for Muslim men; and
- Direct communications are uncommon—a metaphorical presentation of the most distressing problems, infertility and erectile failure, is the rule.

Comparative research data on the influence of religious background on sexual topics include:

- Muslim adolescent boys commonly initiate all types of sexual activity earlier than their Christian and nonreligious male and female peers; Muslim girls are considerably less experienced;

- Christian and nonreligious adolescents tend to prefer sex in steady relationships, Muslim adolescents tend to have more casual sexual experiences and less steady relationships;
- Attitudes toward premarital sex in steady relationships are more accepting in Christian and nonreligious adolescents (80%) and less so in Muslim adolescents (40%). Muslima are very restricted.
- Muslim adolescents tend to advocate abstinence as the best way to avoid HIV infection, and are less willing to use condoms for this purpose (Sandfort & van Zessen 1991).

While incidence figures for induced abortion are generally low in the Netherlands, some ethnic groups have a higher risk of unwanted pregnancy and abortion (see Section 9, Contraception, Abortion, and Population Planning). Among autochtonous* women, unwanted pregnancy is mostly because of contraceptive method failure; among Caribbean, Mediterranean, and refugee women, nonuse or inconsistent use of contraceptives is the more likely cause. A 1990 study of unwanted pregnancy among Caribbean women (Lamur et al.) identifies three groups with distinguishing attitudes towards contraception:

- Among women born in the six Caribbean islands, the strongest influence on sexual attitudes and practices is the Roman Catholic Church. Information on sexuality is extremely scarce. Strong negative moral and practical feelings toward contraception are common. The pill and IUD are often seen as severe health hazards; when used, physical complaints are common.
- Creole women from Suriname (formerly Dutch Guiana) also have little access to sexual information, but this is changing for Creole women born after 1960. In this younger group, middle-class women from stable families are mostly highly career-oriented and very concerned about unwanted pregnancy. Lower-class women are often familiar with a pattern of single women having children with fathers who are more or less distant. Among middle-class Creole families in the Netherlands, sexual information is more adequate and attitudes towards sex and protection less taboo-burdened. Yet, these women are less constant in their choice of contraceptive methods and tend to have more physical complaints when using the pill. For all Creole women, abortion is not an easy solution for unwanted pregnancy. Despite a high abortion rate in this group, moral restraints are strong and abortion is definitely not seen as a normal contraceptive method.
- Hindustani women of Suriname descent have very strict family rules, and honor (*Izzat*) is a leading principle. Premarital sex is an absolute taboo. Education is highly valued and often considered part of a girl's dowry. In recent years, information on sexuality and contraception is provided to Hindustani girls, but effective premarital contraceptive use is rare. A sex taboo seems to prevent information from being absorbed adequately for practical use.

The problems of political refugees have not yet been researched. Dutch Amnesty International workers have some experience with the atrocious problems of sexual torture and humiliation some refugees have experienced.

A particular problem causing some public discussion is clitorectomy. A modified form of clitorectomy, incision of clitoral prepuce, has been under consideration as a result of requests mainly from Somalian women. The Dutch government recently prohibited all forms of clitoral mutilation. Incidentally, Islamic and Hindustani women commonly consult Dutch gynecologists for hymen reconstruction, as part of preparation for marriage.

## 3. Knowledge and Education about Sexuality

### A. Government Policies and Programs for Sex Education

The Netherlands has the lowest rate of unwanted teenage pregnancies of all the industrialized nations. Some attribute this to a relatively effective use of contraceptives, especially the pill, among teenagers. This effective use is explained, at least in part, by a pragmatic and liberal attitude towards sex education, the high quality of information and education on sex and contraception in secondary schools and the mass media, and the wide availability of confidential and low-cost contraceptive services.

These results, however, are no reason for self-satisfaction or complacency. For one thing, contraceptive behavior among ethnic minorities and young adolescents is still ineffective, and the abortion rate among adolescents is still about 45 per 100 pregnancies. In terms of AIDS, about half of the sexually active teenagers appear to engage in risky behavior.

The Dutch government finances a number of sexuality organizations, including the Netherlands Institute for Social Sexological Research (NISSO), the Rutgers Foundation for contraceptive information, sexological education, and STD prevention, and the Foundation for the Study of STD. Recently, the government policy has tried to integrate these special service organizations into the general health institutions. The Rutgers Foundation, which has for decades provided the easiest access for teenagers to contraceptive information, has been forced to concentrate its services in seven offices in large cities and start a training program to share the foundation's specific knowledge and skills with physicians, mental-health workers, and educators.

In recent years, the government has strongly encouraged and promoted prevention programs. Health promotion is now obligatory in secondary schools, even though, traditionally, Dutch schools have formed their own curricula. Numerous educational courses and an amalgam of materials on sex and AIDS have been developed by several local and national organizations. Special materials have been developed for Catholic, Protestant, and nonreligious schools. Despite underlying philosophical differences, most of these programs are very similar in terms of goals, methods, and materials.

On a national level, knowledge of the proportion of schools providing sex and AIDS education, what teachers teach, and what methods and materials they use is limited. A late 1980s survey suggests that some sex and AIDS education was provided by about 85% of the Dutch secondary schools, generally by hygiene or biology teachers. The major topics covered were biological-physiological aspects of puberty and unwanted pregnancy. Topics such as intercourse and sexual desire received lowest attention. As for AIDS education, practical guidelines for reducing risk were the main topics covered, along with attitudes towards homosexuality. The way teachers covered these topics, however, varied widely, depending on the teacher's area of expertise and teaching methods. Biology-hygiene teachers seemed to fo-

---

*Note: In Dutch sociology, "autochtonous" means "of Dutch descent," including Dutch nationality, Caucasian, and raised in Western traditions. "Allochtonous" includes immigrants and their next generations from former Dutch colonies, immigrants from Mediterranean countries who came to Holland seeking work in the 1960s and 1970s, and political refugees from all over the world.

cus on transmission of knowledge of biological and physiological aspects. Sociology teachers and counselors seemed to emphasize relational aspects, such as gender-role patterns, cohabitation patterns, friendship, sexual orientations, and being in love.

Eighty percent of Dutch secondary schools offer a mean of four to five hours of AIDS education. Forty percent use one of four AIDS courses developed for national use on AIDS, though often not according to the specific methodological guidelines. More time is devoted to knowledge transfer than to training in social skills. Teachers were not sufficiently trained or supported to implement these courses, and the materials are not tailored to normal school practices.

Criticism of teachers' training in providing sex and AIDS education is widespread. Yet, there was for some years in the mid-1980s, a three-day in-service postgraduate course for secondary schoolteachers, during which about 500 participants were trained (Schraag 1989). A unique feature of this course was that teachers and pupils worked together to express their underlying convictions and wishes about sex education in school and to develop a program for sexual education. The course program and contribution of the trainers have been evaluated on many occasions, leading to continuous adjustments and corrections.

Although it is frequently argued that health education should be a systematic process, most sex-education courses and materials have not been developed in a systematic way. Very few consider behavioral determinants, and little is known about the effectiveness of the various courses and materials. Besides, only two of the evaluative surveys on sex- and AIDS-education classes have used an adequate experimental design. Both surveys concluded that the courses under scrutiny produced only an increase in knowledge and minor changes in some attitudes, results similar to evaluations of United States sex-education programs and the more general results of health education. Besides knowledge transfer, health education should offer students the opportunity to involve their social environment and develop skills necessary for an adequate performance of the desired behavior. In the 1990s, organizations responsible for implementing educational innovations in health and sex education were encouraged to cooperate with groups responsible for development of educational programs (Kok & Green 1990). Future research should clarify how interventions based on behavioral science theories can improve diffusion and adoption of health-education programs.

Government-financed mass-media campaigns are an important means of educating the public. In 1987, the first campaign to alter social norms of condom use focused on a number of Dutch celebrities who use condoms themselves. In 1988, a second campaign focused on "Safe Sex for Holidays," followed in 1989 by ironically confronting 18- to 24-year-olds with irrational beliefs and popular excuses for risky behavior. "Sleep well" was the final comment on each poster and the campaign's title. A pretest/posttest evaluation proved that the majority of respondents had noticed the poster campaign and understood its irony. Those who had noticed the campaign differed from the pretest group by better acknowledgment of the personal risks they took and a lower endorsement of three popular excuses. Condom use in this group rose slightly. Yet, only half of the group ever used condoms, and a quarter were inconsistent in their use.

A 1992 addition to government involvement in sex education and prevention is a mass-media campaign directed at child sexual abuse. This campaign, "There Are Secrets You Should Talk About," is designed to reach children in abusive situations and make the public aware of the reality of child sexual abuse. A second mass-media campaign, "Sex

Is Natural, But Never Self-Evident," addresses boys and men on the topic of coercion in sex. Evaluative data on these campaigns are not yet available.

### B. Informal Sources of Sexual Knowledge

Veronica, a Dutch broadcasting company, has had a Sunday-afternoon, three-hour phone-in radio program on sex and related subjects since 1985. Themes discussed on program "Radio Romantica" range from light-hearted to serious, including sexual fantasies, falling in love, rape, incest, sexual abuse, safe-sex techniques, coping with AIDS, unwanted pregnancies, homosexuality, bisexuality, and pedophilia. A professional sexologist hosts the program with a liaison officer and a team of students and graduates trained in psychology and social work. The program draws about 250,000 listeners.

In a less systematic way, almost all Dutch broadcasting companies have programs dealing with sex and AIDS. Since the sexual revolution of the 1960s and 1970s, sexuality has provided prime topics for radio, television, and magazines. Books on sex education, for adults and adolescents, are numerous, and vary widely in quality. Pornography is easily available, although the information and messages propagated in these magazines is a matter of concern for many educators. The impact of pornography as an educational source has not been evaluated. (Section 10B deals with numerous mass-media campaigns on AIDS and safe sex.)

## 4. Autoerotic Behaviors and Patterns

### A. Children and Adolescents

Research on child sexuality is relatively underdeveloped. In 1990, readers of the magazine *Ouders va Nu* [*Parents Today*] responded to a questionnaire about their children's sexual behavior and their own attitudes concerning sexual education (Cohen-Kettenis & Sanford 1991). The children's ages ranged from 0 to 7. The results of this survey on child autoeroticism are shown in Table 1.

In the 1989 adolescent study, 88% of 12- to 13-year-old boys and 77% of the girls reported at least one sexual fantasy. Frequency of sexual fantasy correlated strongly with self-pleasuring experience. Self-pleasuring according to age is shown in Table 2.

### B. Adults

In the 1989 research (Sandfort & Van Zessen 1991), questions on personal habits disclosed a distinct sex difference on several issues.

### Table 1

**Percentages of Childhood Self-Pleasuring Behavior**

| Behavior | Boys | Girls |
|---|---|---|
| Touches genitals with the hand | 96% | 94% |
| Self-pleasures by hand | 58 | 39 |
| Self-pleasures using an object | 13 | 21 |

### Table 2

**Percentages of Boys and Girls Engaging in Self-Pleasuring**

| | Ages 14-15 | Ages 16-17 | Ages 18-19 |
|---|---|---|---|
| Boys | 81% | 90% | 91% |
| Girls | 43 | 55 | 62 |

*Source*: Vogels & van Vliet (1990, 37, Fig. 3.2). *Editors' Note*: Percentages are approximations from the original line graph (*IES2* Fig. 1, p. 906).

- 55% of the women and 23% of the men had never read sexually explicit books or magazines;
- 71% of the women and 47% of men had never watched sexually explicit videos or movies;
- 30% of the women and 5% of the men never looked at an attractive man with sexual intent, 26% of the men reported this behavior "often";
- 77% of the women and 90% of the men were familiar with sexual fantasies. Men tend to fantasize more often and have a more positive view of fantasies. Fantasies featuring power balance and violence were uncommon.
- 92% of respondents reported a positive attitude toward self-pleasuring; only 16% opposed self-pleasuring in a steady relationship. Autoerotic behavior was related to sex, age, and current relationship status. (See Tables 3, 4, and 5.)

## 5. Interpersonal Heterosexual Behaviors

### A. Children

In the *Parents Today* study (Section 4A, Autoerotic Behaviors and Patterns, Children and Adolescents), many questions referred to childhood sexual behavior. Table 6 gives a selection of the data. In this study, Dutch parents reported considerably more sexual behavior than United States parents in similar studies, so U.S. data are not useful as criteria in diagnosing child sexual abuse in Dutch children.

### B. Adolescents

*Puberty Rituals*

There are no common puberty rituals among autochtonous Dutch groups, although as a result of the more open attitude towards sexual development in some progressive families, young girls will have their menarche greeted by some festive, yet intimate, parental or family attention.

It has been argued that in modern Western society, parallel to individualization tendencies, rituals have disappeared, leading to loss of emotional anchors. In psychotherapy, the use of individually tailored rituals is quite often recommended.

*Premarital Sexual Activities and Relationships*

The 1989 survey of children ages 11 to 19 involved more aspects than previous studies, and the presentation of many subjects that were put into longitudinal perspective. Data suggested an expanding "sexual moratorium," a period in which the adolescent is sexually active, but not in a steady relationship open to procreation. In recent years, it has been increasingly common for young adults to go through a period in which they have a number of sexual partners in more or less steady relationships (see Table 7).

Survey responses revealed a common pattern of four years between the first French kiss and sexual intercourse. The sequence of steps in this personal development is remarkably uniform and showed no sex difference (see Table 8).

In earlier studies, the concept of a "stepwise interaction career" was developed by Straver and coworkers (1986), based on Glaser and Straus's (1980) elaboration of symbolic interactionist theory and Simon and Gagnon's (1980) approach to psychosexual development. This approach emphasizes the active role of youngsters in shaping their own sexual identity and their sexual relationships. Rademakers (1992) later used this theoretical framework in her study of the causes of ineffective contraceptive behavior at initial sexual contact among adolescents (see Section 9, Contraception, Abortion, and Population Planning).

Going out to bars or discotheques is a major factor affecting sexual experiences, increasing sexual experiences at all ages and in all aspects. Young people with lower educational levels showed less permissiveness and less experience in communication, but experienced sexual inter-

### Table 3

**Percentage Frequencies of Self-Pleasuring According to Sex**

|  | Men | Women |
|---|---|---|
| Never | 17.5% | 44.2% |
| Less that once a month | 19.0 | 29.2 |
| About once a month | 30.0 | 19.5 |
| About once a week | 28.0 | 7.2 |
| Daily | 4.0 | 1.9 |
| More than once a day | 1.4 | 0.4 |

(Men: *n* = 418; Women: *n* = 574; Ages 18-50). *Source*: Sandfort & van Zessen (1991, 129, Table 4.10). *Editors' Note*: Percentages are approximations from the original line graph (*IES2* Fig. 2, p. 907).

### Table 4

**Percentage Frequencies of Self-Pleasuring According to Age**

| Ages | Never | Less than once/week | More than once/week |
|---|---|---|---|
| 18-21 | 30% | 46% | 24% |
| 22-25 | 24 | 50 | 26 |
| 26-29 | 30 | 54 | 26 |
| 30-33 | 27 | 51 | 22 |
| 34-37 | 38 | 46 | 16 |
| 38-41 | 30 | 60 | 10 |
| 42-45 | 48 | 46 | 6 |
| 46-50 | 47 | 47 | 6 |

(*n* = 982; Ages 18-50). *Editors' Note*: Percentages are approximations from the original line graph (*IES2* Fig. 3, p. 907).

### Table 5

**Percentage Frequencies of Self-Pleasuring According to Relationship Status**

|  | Never | Less than once/week | More than once/week |
|---|---|---|---|
| Casual Relationship | 9% | 41% | 50% |
| No Sex | 27 | 54 | 19 |
| Steady Relationship | 38 | 49 | 13 |

(*n* = 982; steady relationships, 75%; casual relationships, 13%; no sexual contact in past year, 12%). *Source*: Sandfort & van Zessen (1991, 129, Table 4.6). *Editors' Note*: Percentages are approximations from the original line graph (*IES2* Fig. 4, p. 908).

### Table 6

**Percentages of Childhood Heterosexual Behavior**

| Behavior | Girls | Boys |
|---|---|---|
| Interested in the opposite sex | 63% | 63% |
| Plays doctor-and-nurses games | 44 | 43 |
| Tries to see nude people | 44 | 43 |
| Touches genitals of others | 39 | 32 |
| Tries to undress other people | 30 | 22 |
| Shows genitals to adults | 15 | 25 |
| Shows genitals to children | 16 | 24 |
| Kisses with tongue out of mouth | 13 | 16 |

(*IES2* Table 2, p. 908)

course at an earlier age than adolescents with more education.

Responses to the question "Do you ask your partner what he/she likes in love making?" suggest that boys take responsibility for their partners' satisfaction more often, especially at an earlier age (see Table 9). Assessing personal limits is another competence aspect; girls more than boys seem to consider this to be their task at all ages (see Table 10).

Sexual contacts between children and adults have been examined in several Dutch studies. Unlike most such research data, these contacts were not considered abusive by definition. Sandfort (1982) studied the experience of 25

## Table 7

**Trends in Women's Median Age at First Menstruation, First Sexual Intercourse, and First Marriage or Cohabitation by Year of Birth**

| Year of Birth | Median Age | |
|---|---|---|
| **First Menstrual Period** | | |
| 1922 | 14.3 | |
| 1952 | 13.5 | |
| 1963 | 13.2 | |
| **First Intercourse** | | |
| 1908 | 24.3 | |
| 1911 | 24.0 | |
| 1938 | 20.4 | |
| 1952 | 19.5 | |
| 1964 | 18.2 | |
| 1972 | 17.7 | |
| **First Cohabitation** | | |
| 1948 | 22.5 | |
| 1953 | 22.0 | |
| 1967 | 22.7 | |
| **First Marriage** | | |
| 1908 | 25.0 | |
| 1926 | 24.6 | "Roarin' 20s" |
| 1928 | 24.9 | |
| 1932 | 24.7 | Great Depression |
| 1936 | 24.0 | |
| 1943 | 23.5 | World War II |
| 1947 | 22.9 | |
| 1952 | 22.7 | |
| 1962 | 24.0 | "Sexual Revolution" |
| 1967 | 25.4 | |

*Source*: van der Vliet (1990, 54). *Editors' Note*: Percentages are approximations from the original line graph (*IES2* Fig. 5, p. 909).

## Table 8

**Sexual Development Age at Which Half of the Respondents Had Experienced Some Behaviors (*n* = 11,500)**

| | Median Age |
|---|---|
| French kissing | 13.7 |
| Touching under clothes | 14.6 |
| Nude petting | 16.4 |
| Intercourse | 17.8 |

*Source*: Vogels & van Vliet (1990, 39, Fig. 3.3). *Editors' Note*: Percentages are approximations from the original line graph (*IES2* Fig 6, p. 910).

boys, ages 10 to 16, involved in sexual relationships with adult men. Almost all the respondents indicated the sexual contact was predominantly positive and did not have a negative influence on their general sense of well-being. The friendships also fulfilled several of the boys' personal needs. Although these results do not have general applicability, they counterbalance the predominant notion that all adult-child sexual involvement is abusive. In a later study, Sandfort (1991) used a much broader design to study the possible influences of voluntary, as well as nonconsensual, sexual experiences before age 16 in a random sample of 283 male and female subjects aged 18 to 23 years, who had had sexual experiences with adults. Controlling for other factors, these sexual experiences seemed to have positively influenced sexual desire, arousal, and anxiety irrespective of the partner's age. Nonconsensual experiences seemed to have caused sexual problems in later life, as well as more-general psychosomatic complaints. The more severe these experiences, the stronger were the negative effects. Nonconsensual contacts with peers seemed, on average, to be less severe than nonconsensual experiences with adults. Using the same data, Goddijn and Sandfort (1988) showed the importance of the opportunity to express one's feelings about traumatic experiences in order to diminish the psychosocial complaints in later life. Studies on involuntary sexual contacts are dealt with in Section 8A, Significant Unconventional Sexual Behaviors, Coercive Sex.

## C. Adults
*Some Demographic Outlines*

Remarkable changes in the popularity of marriage have occurred in the Netherlands in recent decades (Beets et al. 1991). Before the end of World War II, the Dutch tended to marry at a relatively late age. In the years of rapidly expanding economic possibilities in the 1970s, more men and women married at a younger age. In 1945, only 18.5% of 20- to 24-year-olds were or had ever been married; in 1974, the figure was 41.8%. Since 1974, marriage has again declined in popularity, especially for the young, as cohabitation became more popular. The mean age of first marriage was 22.8 in 1970; in 1990, it was 28.2 for men and 25.9 for women. Data on cohabitation are scarce, but what data are available provide some insights.

## Table 9

**Percentage of Respondents Who Ask Partner What He or She Likes While Making Love Always or Most of the Time, According to Age and Sex**

| Age | 14-15 | 16-17 | 18-19 |
|---|---|---|---|
| Boys | 30% | 36% | 37% |
| Girls | 14 | 20 | 30 |

*Source*: Vogels & van Vliet (1990, 45, Fig. 3.9). *Editors' Note*: Percentages are approximations from the original line graph (*IES2* Fig. 7, p. 911).

## Table 10

**Percentages of Respondents Who See to It That Lovemaking Does Not Get Out of Hand Always or Most of the Time, According to Age and Sex**

| Age | 14-15 | 16-17 | 18-19 |
|---|---|---|---|
| Boys | 18% | 14% | 10% |
| Girls | 56 | 45 | 30 |

*Source*: Vogels & van Vliet (1990, 45, Fig. 3.9). *Editors' Note*: Percentages are approximations from the original line graph (*IES2* Fig. 8, p. 911).

- Around 1985, almost half of all 20- to 24-year-olds who were living together were not (yet) married, and in the 25-to-34 age group, 20% were not married;
- 70% of the unmarried said their living together would be long term; 40% of a cohort were still in the same relationship at a three-year follow-up;
- Cohabiting couples have fewer children than married couples; the wish for children is often the motive for marriage.
- Until 1975, only 2% of the children born annually were born out of wedlock. Since then, the figure has risen to 10.6%. "Extramarital birth" today can have several meanings: a child of cohabiting parents (about two thirds of all extramarital births); a child in a Living Apart Together (LAT) arrangement, a lesbian couple's child, or a homosexual or heterosexual unwed mother who intends to raise the child alone. By 1989, 10% of unwed mothers were single women and lesbian couples who were artificially inseminated with donor semen (AID). In the past decade, self-insemination has gained in popularity, probably equaling physician-managed AID today.
- The classic unwed mother who had an unwanted pregnancy is almost extinct in Holland, forcing the Dutch organization for the support of unwed mothers to reorganize with new goals to support one-parent households and the victims of sexual violence (and their mothers).

Combining cohabiting and married couples, there is a recent slight decrease in the number of Dutch men and women living in two-person households. Divorce rates have gone up fast since 1968, from 11% of marriages in 1970 to 28% in 1988. One out of six children in the 1970s marriage cohort will experience their parents' divorce before age 21. One-parent families are also increasing. Ten years ago, 19% of Dutch mothers were raising their child(ren) alone. Divorcees outnumbered widows and never-wed mothers in this group, with most single mothers holding full-time employment outside the home.

Divorced persons are increasingly postponing a second marriage. In 1990, the mean age for males entering a second marriage was 42.7, and for women, 38.8 years. In 1990, 77% of all marriages were first marriages for both partners. In 23%, one or both partners were divorced, and in 10%, one or both were widowers.

Fertility rates have been decreasing, from 3.2 in 1964 to stabilize at just over 1.5 since 1976. In 1988, 4% of all 20-year-olds had one or more children, 32% of the 25-year-olds, 67% by age 30, and 87% by age 40. Government policy aims at zero population growth, a goal that seems feasible even though it will bring a considerable increase in the proportion of senior citizens. In 1990, 13% of the total population was over 65, compared with only 8% in 1950.

### Single Adults

Prompted by a need for data and insights useful in AIDS prevention, the 1989 SIN adult study was the first to pay specific attention to the sexual behavior of singles.

In this survey, 13% of male respondents ($n = 421$) and 11% of females ($n = 580$) reported no sexual contacts in the year before the interview. Some 40% were sexually inexperienced. Part of this group could be adequately characterized as "late starters," but at age 30, 8% of males and 4% of females were inexperienced in heterosexual intercourse. The higher percentage of male homosexuals in the sample may only partly explain the high figure of inexperienced males, because half of the male respondents who labeled themselves as homosexuals had in fact had sexual intercourse. Men tended to be more dissatisfied than women with being single, 70% versus 57% preferring to have a re-

lationship. In the larger cities, the proportion of respondents with no sexual relationships is slightly lower. In their solo-sex experiences, this group differs only slightly from couples: 18% never fantasize sexually, and only 19% more than once a week; 28% never engage in self-pleasuring and 26% do so more than once a week.

In the 1989 study, "singles with sexual contacts" were defined as: no steady relationships of at least one year at the time of interview, and one or more casual or short sexual contacts. By definition, this group must include a certain number of persons with new relationships that will eventually turn out to be long term: 10% of women and 18% of the men fell into this category. Respondents under 25 contributed most to this group, with respondents 33 to 50 rarely in this group. Singles with sexual partnerships tended to live in larger cities. Like the group with no sexual experiences in the last year, they, too, tended not to be politically involved. One-night stands were uncommon: only 13% had casual sex (defined as once or twice); 50% of men and 25% of women had casual sex besides one or more longer partnerships (the latter with a mean of 25 sexual encounters). Males reported a higher number of partners in the past year (mean 2.4 versus 1.8 for women, with a maximum of ten for men and five for women). Vaginal intercourse was the most popular technique for men (96%), but women preferred manual stimulation to vaginal intercourse, 95% to 86%. Anal intercourse was quite unpopular. Men used condoms in only 31% of their coital acts; women scored even lower with 21%.

### Adults in Dyadic Relations

In 1989, mean coital frequency for men and women in stable relations was seven times a month, higher than in 1968 and 1981, but respondents in the earlier surveys were aged 20 to 65, while the 1989 sample was 18 to 50 years old (see Tables 11 and 12). Length of the relationship is more

### Table 11

**Duration of Living Arrangement in 751 Stable Relationships**

| Age Group (in Years) | Mean Duration of Relationship (Years) | Married (%) | Cohabiting (%) | Living Apart (%) |
|---|---|---|---|---|
| 18-25 | 4.0 | 24 | 33 | 43 |
| 26-33 | 8.8 | 73 | 20 | 7 |
| 34-41 | 14.1 | 86 | 5 | 9 |
| 42-50 | 22.4 | 97 | 1 | 2 |

(Men: $n = 276$; Women: $n = 452$). *Source*: Sandfort & van Zessen (1991, 65, Table 3.3). (*IES2* Table 3, p. 915)

### Table 12

**Percentage Frequencies of Making Love in 751 Stable Relationships**

| | Men | Women |
|---|---|---|
| Less than once in 2 months | 3.5% | 3.5% |
| Once a month | 5.0 | 5.0 |
| About 2-3 times a month | 15.0 | 12.0 |
| About once a week | 19.0 | 23.0 |
| About twice a week | 40.0 | 40.0 |
| Three or four times a week | 15.0 | 16.0 |
| Five or more times a week | 2.0 | 2.0 |

*Editors' Note*: Percentages are approximations from the original line graph (*IES2* Fig. 9, p. 915).

important than age for coital frequency (see Tables 13, 14, and 15). In all groups, women tended to be content with their current frequency and men more likely to want more. Men were more affirmative in thinking their sex could be better. Women were more likely to admit to making love without the desire to do so and engaging in sexual acts they did not really like. Other satisfaction-related statements on which men and women gave similar responses included: general satisfaction with sex, conflicts about sex, admitting gender differences in sexual desire, admitting being pressured to engage in sexual contact, and communications on sexual preferences. On a 1-to-10 scale, the mean rating of men for their satisfaction with their own sex life was 7.3; for women 7.5.

Abstinence in these stable relations is nonexistent, when defined as refraining from all sensual body contact (hugging, kissing, and cuddling). When sexual contact is defined as genital contact, 0.5% of these relationships were abstinent; when defined as vaginal intercourse, 4% were abstinent during the past year (see Table 16).

### *"Extramarital" Sex*

Marriage was the only form of stable relationship studied in 1968 and 1981. In the 1989 study, questions regarding sex with more than one partner were edited differently to include cohabitation and stable Living-Apart-Together (LAT) relations. Moreover, the 1968 and 1981 studies focused on 21- to 65-year-olds, whereas the 1989 study dealt with 18- to 50-year-olds. Longitudinal comparisons must therefore be done with some caution.

In 1968 and 1981, men were more tolerant than women on extramarital sex, with a shift for both genders toward more tolerance. In 1981, 13% of the men and 6% of the women had no objections at all, with 48% of the men and 39% of the women accepting extramarital sex in certain situations. In 1989, more questions were included on this topic. Seven percent of the men and 5% of the women agreed that partners in a stable relationship should allow each other to have sex with a third party; 82% of men and 88% of women firmly opposed this (see Table 17).

Since extramarital sex is taboo more than other behaviors, underreporting cannot be ignored. In 1989, the fear of AIDS seemed to be a more potent motive for denying extramarital sex than moral restraints in general. Marriage is the type of stable relationship that contributes most to monog-

### Table 13

#### Mean Frequency of Sexual Contact in Steady Relationships by Age

| Age Group (in Years) | Mean Frequency of Sexual Contact, per Month |
|---|---|
| 18-25 | 7.4 |
| 26-33 | 7.0 |
| 34-41 | 6.9 |
| 42-50 | 6.8 |

(*IES2* Table 4, p. 916)

### Table 14

#### Mean Frequency of Sexual Contact by Duration of Relationship

| Duration of Steady Relationship (in Years) | Mean Frequency of Sexual Contact, per Month |
|---|---|
| 1-2 | 8.5 |
| 2-5 | 7.5 |
| Over 5 | 6.8 |

(*IES2* Table 5, p. 916)

### Figure 15

#### Satisfaction with Frequency of Making Love, by Sex and by Three Groups of Frequency

| Frequency of Making Love | Prefer Less Often | Content with Current | Prefer More Often |
|---|---|---|---|
| **Men** | | | |
| About 3x/month | 2% | 46% | 53% |
| 1-2x/week | 1 | 73 | 26 |
| About 3x/week | 2 | 86 | 12 |
| **Women** | | | |
| About 3x/month | 2 | 76 | 22 |
| 1-2x/week | 1 | 91 | 8 |
| About 3x/week | 7 | 91 | 2 |

*Source*: Sandfort & van Zessen (1991, 107, Fig. 4.2). (*IES2* Fig. 10, p. 916)

### Table 16

#### Sexual Behaviors in Stable Heterosexual Relationships, According to Sex

| Behavior | Sex | Never | Sometimes/ Regularly | Often/ Always |
|---|---|---|---|---|
| Kissing | Men | 0.0% | 26.0% | 74.0% |
| | Women | 0.0 | 28.0 | 72.0 |
| Hugging & Cuddling | Men | 0.0 | 23.0 | 77.0 |
| | Women | 0.0 | 27.0 | 73.0 |
| Masturbation of Woman | Men | 2.2 | 35.3 | 62.5 |
| | Women | 5.0 | 56.8 | 38.2 |
| Masturbation of Man | Men | 5.0 | 46.5 | 48.5 |
| | Women | 7.0 | 44.5 | 48.5 |
| Cunnilingus | Men | 19.5 | 60.5 | 20.0 |
| | Women | 35.0 | 54.0 | 11.0 |
| Fellatio | Men | 27.0 | 27.5 | 35.5 |
| | Women | 27.0 | 61.0 | 12.0 |
| Vaginal Intercourse | Men | 4.5 | 16.5 | 79.0 |
| | Women | 4.5 | 16.5 | 79.0 |
| Manual Anal Stimulation | Men | 68.5 | 29.0 | 2.5 |
| | Women | 66.0 | 30.0 | 4.0 |
| Anal Intercourse | Men | 94.0 | 0.0 | 6.0 |
| | Women | 78.0 | 14.0 | 8.0 |

(Men: $n = 276$; Women: $n = 452$. An * indicates a significant sex difference.) *Source*: Sandfort & van Zessen (1991, 67, Fig. 3.2). *Editors' Note*: Percentages are approximations from the original line graph (*IES2* Fig. 11, p. 917).

### Table 17

#### Extramarital Sexual Contacts in 1968, 1981, and 1989, in Percentages

| | 1968 | | 1981 | | 1989 | |
|---|---|---|---|---|---|---|
| Frequency | Male | Female | Male | Female | Male | Female |
| Occurred often | 1 | 0 | 3 | 2 | — | — |
| Occasionally | 10 | 2 | 11 | 7 | 12 | 7 |
| Never | 78 | 86 | 80 | 86 | 88 | 93 |
| Not answered | 11 | 12 | 7 | 5 | 0 | 0 |

*Source*: Sandfort & van Zessen (1991, 751, Table 3.10). (*IES2* Table 6, p. 918)

amy: In the total group of respondents in a stable relationship for over one year, 14.6% of the men and 9.2% of women reported sexual contact with more than one partner. In the year preceding the interview, 6.4% of the men and 2.8% of the women had engaged in sex with a second partner; 2.1% of the men and 3.7% of the women were aware of their partner's extramarital relations. Three quarters of the men keep their extramarital sex a secret; three quarters of the women informed their partners of their affair. "Extramarital sex" was casual in 50% of the cases; longstanding affairs were limited to one out of six. Prostitution and sexual contacts abroad were only a small proportion of the reported extramarital-sex contacts.

## Sexuality and the Disabled and Chronically Ill

In the early 1970s, when Heslinga gained national and international notoriety with his plea for better information and sex education for the handicapped with his book, *Not Made of Stone: Sexuality of the Handicapped People*, these services were not routinely provided by doctors, and empirical research was also scarce. Today, close to 100 organizations provide support and written information on the sexual consequences of such conditions as adrenogenital syndrome, anorexia nervosa, breast cancer and mastopathy, depression, diabetes, gynecological cancer, incontinence, ostomy, multiple sclerosis, premenstrual syndrome, postmenopause, posthysterectomy, and schizophrenia patients and their families.

Direct sexual services for the handicapped are available through the National Foundation for Alternative Partnership Mediation. In one ongoing research project, the Rotterdam sexology department and the department for industrial design at Delft Technical University developed a water-driven self-pleasuring aid for manually disabled men and women to be used in the bath or under the shower.

Mental-health institutions have also gained some awareness of their residents' sexual problems and the tension between controlling and understanding patients' sexual needs. Professionals in homes for the mentally handicapped seem more eager to take additional courses in sexual education. Awareness of the high figures for past sexual abuse among patients is growing rapidly, and competence in addressing these problems is probably also expanding.

In the past decade, Dutch sexologists have carried out longitudinal research on sexual rehabilitation of 1. women with ovarian, cervical, endometrial, and vulvar cancers, 2. men with testicular cancer and Peyronie's disease, and 3. men and women with diabetes, various ostomies, chronic kidney disease, and skin diseases. Because of the uniqueness of these studies, a summary of their findings follows.

1. *Cancer of the Female Genitals* (*Main sources*: Leiden and Groningen universities gynecology departments). The Dutch Cancer Foundation has funded a steady series of research programs on treatment for female genital cancers. Bos-Branolte used a semistructured interview and questionnaire to evaluate psychosexual functioning of 69 women treated for ovarian (29), cervical (24), endometrial (12), and vulvar (4) cancers. Posttreatment follow-up ranged from six months to seven years. Results showed a decrease in sexual activity (59%) and intimacy (22%) with an increase in need for intimacy (19%), emotional support (30%), and open communication (23%). In addition, 33% reported a negative change in their partner's sexual activity. Many women had the impression that, although their partners needed emotional support during their illness, they did not receive this help. Intimacy, emotional support, and open communications seemed to contribute more to a positive relationship than sexual expressions.

In 1984, Weijmar Schultz and Van de Wiel started a series of research projects with a pilot study of ten women treated for vulvar cancer. A self-report questionnaire evaluated sexual functioning some two years after treatment. Despite many problems, eight of the ten couples resumed sexual contacts, with or without restrictions. Sufficient information, coping, and communications did not guarantee complete sexual rehabilitation. Motivation for sexual expression and mutual affection might be more important than any physical restriction imposed by surgery. A small-scale prospective longitudinal study of the sexual functioning of women treated for vulvar cancer tested this observation. Ten couples and an age-matched control group were interviewed and filled out questionnaires at admission and at six, 12, and 24 months posttreatment. Only at six months could an increase in sexual dissatisfaction be detected. Over the remaining period, in spite of persisting poor perception of genital symptoms of sexual arousal, the women's satisfaction did not differ from pretreatment satisfaction and control-group ratings. Satisfaction with sexual interaction under these circumstances appears to be more dependent on intimate aspects than on physiological arousal, suggesting information and counseling as the most promising focus for intervention.

A more detailed assessment of seven of these women at 12 months posttreatment confirmed that although, in the patients' own opinion, cancer and its treatment had caused rather dramatic changes in their sexual life, comparison with the age-matched group revealed only minor differences in sexual satisfaction, behavior, and motivation. The only significant differences were in experienced sexual arousal and orgasm. The authors hypothesized that sexual rehabilitation itself is guided on a higher level by a more general striving for balance in the relationship. Interventions to prevent or reduce sexual problems after treatment for cancer of the female genitalia should be directed toward both the patient and partner.

A similar design was used for 13 couples with wives treated by simple hysterectomy for benign gynecological disease and 13 age-matched control couples. At a one-year follow-up, all patients reported some disruption in the sexual response cycle, whereas current behavior and motivation for sexual interaction were within the normal range. The women clearly expressed general satisfaction with their sexual functioning and little relational dissatisfaction. Here too, arousal experience is found not to be the sole reason for sexual motivation and satisfaction. The authors stress that posttreatment counseling should not be limited to hysterectomy patients with a cancer diagnosis. A more-detailed examination of 11 cervical cancer patients at six months posttreatment revealed that sexual interaction was valued significantly less than control subjects, while no changes in overt behavior occurred. The most important psychosexual variables underlying this reduced sexual valuation were found to be a considerable decrease in the self-image of oneself as a sexual partner. Apparently, women try to cope by conforming to the sexual demands of their partner and to prevailing norms. Cervical carcinoma treatment appears to have a strong negative effect on the sexuality of the patients, and often amplifies an already existing ambivalence toward sexual interaction common in many women.

Sixteen partners of patients treated for female genital cancer were interviewed one year posttreatment on two general themes: involvement and support, and sexuality and relationship. Many men reported experiencing the process of providing support as stressful, and had serious doubts about the efficacy of their efforts. Furthermore, these men appeared to have extensive sexual problems, which could not be adequately solved. It was hypothesized that the disease and its treatment also poses a crisis for the partner, which leads to a regression towards a more rigid, male-stereotypical way of coping. Consequently, while treating the patient, the partner and their communication patterns should be the focus of attention too.

Finally, data on seven vulvar cancer patients and 25 cervical cancer patients were analyzed for prognostic variables for future sexual adjustment. The small sample size allowed only a few cautious conclusions. Overt sexual behavior after treatment can be predicted quite accurately by past sexual experience. Satisfaction, motivation, and sexual response are less predictable. This outcome supports the conclusion from the comparative study on cervical cancer treatment and simple hysterectomy, that psychological variables are more decisive than physical ones in predicting future sexual rehabilitation.

2. *Testicular Cancer Treatment* (*Source*: Groningen University urology department). Nijman et al. studied sexual functioning of 101 patients following bilateral retroperitoneal lymph node dissection for stages I and II nonseminomatous testicular cancer. All patients were without evidence of disease after at least four years' follow-up. Twelve men experienced antegrade ejaculation, while 89 experienced retrograde ejaculation ("dry" orgasm). In 75 of the 101 men, urine analysis after intercourse or self-pleasuring showed retrograde ejaculation in 55 men, and lack of ejaculatory emission into the urethra in 20 patients.

Seventeen patients had diminished sexual desire (especially after radiotherapy), 12 experienced difficulty reaching orgasm, and six complained of erectile dysfunction. A second study of 56 men with nonseminomatous testicular cancer stages II and III, before and after treatment (surgery and chemotherapy), showed that two years after completing therapy, 54% experienced sexual dysfunctions. Greatly reduced or absent antegrade ejaculation was reported by 26 patients; 18 of them had undergone retroperitoneal lymphnode dissection in varying degrees of extensiveness, whereas eight had not. Chemotherapy may have caused ejaculatory disorders in 30% of the patients. Only two reported a change in quality of erections; seven experienced a markedly reduced libido, and five reported their orgasms had changed in a negative way. The remaining testis showed signs of atrophy in 21 patients.

3. *Diabetes Mellitus* (*Source*: Rotterdam University sexology department). Slob et al. recorded subjective and objective psychophysiological responses to erotic visual stimulation for 24 women with diabetes mellitus type I and ten control women. No significant differences in subjective response (general sexual arousal and genital arousal) were reported. The objective response (thermistor readings from one minor labium) varied with the height of the initial temperature. Since the initial temperature was significantly higher in the patient group, the subsequent rise during erotic visual stimulation was less in diabetic women than in controls. When samples of the two groups were matched for initial temperature, the difference in increase of labial temperature was no longer significant. When women with high initial temperatures (37° C/98.6° F) were excluded, there was in both groups a significant correlation between the degree of subjective arousal and the rise in labial temperature. Patients with serious neuropathy and/or angiopathy did not participate in this study.

4. *Peyronie's Disease* (*Source*: Groningen University urology department). Van Driel studied surgical treament, compared with the natural course, in 32 patients with Peyronie's disease and 12 with a congenital penile curvature. Subjective symptoms were recorded by checklist, and objective symptoms by means of Polaroid photography during erection at home. Patients were seen at three-month intervals until a steady state was reached. In 23 patients, spontaneous recovery was sufficient. When pain persisted longer than one year, a Nesbitt operation (surgical shortening of the contralateral side) was performed; 21 patients were treated this way. All were satisfied with the functional and cosmetic outcome, although a completely straight penis was not accomplished in four. No complications were met. Conservative management in cases of bent penis seems preferable; however surgery is a good and safe alternative when complaints and dysfunctions persist.

5. *Ostomy* (*Source*: Groningen University sexology department). The first step in Dutch research on sexological sequelae of ostomy operations was a study in which readers of a stoma patients' monthly were asked to complete a questionnaire: 995 men and 512 women gave a retrospective account of changes in their sexual life following ostomy. Results confirmed that men are more hampered in their sexual functioning by ostomy than women, and that colostomy had a stronger negative effect than ileostomy. Results suggest the most serious impact on sexual functioning is found with urostomy, especially in men. Prospective confirmation is needed.

6. *Chronic Kidney Disease* (*Source*: NISSO). Van Son-Schoones used a semistructured interview and psychometric questionnaires to evaluate psychosexual functioning in 70 men and 47 women with chronic kidney disease; 34 male partners and 47 female partners were included. Evaluation included the effect of treatment method (hemodialysis, continued ambulatory peritoneal dialysis, or transplantation) on sexual functioning, personal well-being, and coping with the disease, as well as the quality of information and counseling. Few differences were found between the three treatment modalities. Organic sexual dysfunctions, psychosocial problems, and acceptance problems were most frequently found in the hemodialysis group. Partners, irrespective of treatment, did have more sexual problems and were less satisfied with the sexual relationship. The quality of information and counseling appeared to be insufficient.

7. *Skin Disease* (*Source*: Leiden University dermatology department). In 1990, a research study was initiated to quantify the well-known sexual problems of patients with psoriasis and constitutional eczematous rash: 52 psoriasis patients (28 men and 24 women, mean age 37) and 25 eczema patients (9 men and 16 women, mean age 28) completed extensive anonymous questionnaires: 10% had no partner, and 3% had only incidental partners. Men felt most ashamed in social situations of partial nudity, and women were more ashamed in sexual situations. Sexual motivation was lower than average, and women scored lower than men. On sexual satisfaction, only women scored below average. Facial skin symptoms were most embarrassing. One third had difficulties initiating contacts and entering a sexual relationship, and felt shame in an intimate relation. Psoriasis patients felt more inhibited than eczema patients. Many expressed the conviction that a good sexual relationship is beneficial for the skin disease.

The authors advocate more discussion of sexuality in the care for skin-disease patients, especially when young and inexperienced in sexual relations. Women, psoriasis patients, and patients with facial symptoms are most in need of counseling.

*Incidence of Oral and Anal Sex*

Growing concern about HIV transmission and recognition that anal intercourse is high-risk behavior have attracted researchers' attention to anal sex. In 1989, 12% of women and 6% of men in steady heterosexual relationships reported being more or less experienced in anal intercourse. Anal sex seemed to be nonexistent in casual and extramarital heterosexual relations.

In the Amsterdam large-scale longitudinal cohort research project on homosexual behavior and seroconversion, the proportion of men who engaged in anal intercourse slowly declined from 88.6% in 1984-85 to 62.4% in 1987-88.

There are no legal restrictions on anal sex in Holland; social attitudes towards this form of eroticism probably show wide variation. The idea that anal sex is not an exclusively homosexual variation, but can be part of heterosexual lovemaking as well, is gradually being acknowledged in the general public.

In 1989, experience with fellatio and cunnilingus was the rule for both men and women (see Table 16 above).

## 6. Homoerotic, Homosexual, and Bisexual Behaviors

In the United States, the Kinsey-scale differentiation between exclusive homosexuality and exclusive heterosexuality based on combined sexual behavior and erotic experiences dominates most orientations theory and research. Historical, sociological, and psychological studies of homosexuality in the Netherlands lean toward a different paradigm in which homosexuality is seen as a design for living in which erotic and sexual attraction is embedded in a wider context. Dutch study of homosexuality thus focuses on gender and gender development, family studies, and lifestyle and lifestyle management. Changing social attitudes to homosexuality made this paradigmatic change possible.

### A. Children and Adolescents

The large-scale 1968 and 1974 studies of adolescent sexuality paid only limited attention to homosexual behavior and feelings. Tolerance towards homosexuals had grown considerably: In 1968, 55.3% believed that homosexuals should be free to lead their own lives; in 1974, 84.9% held this position. In 1968, 18.6% of male respondents said they had at least one self-pleasuring experience with peers; in 1974, this was 16.1%. In 1968, 5.5% reported being mostly or exclusively attracted to the same sex; in 1974, 1.8%. Some attraction was indicated by 10% in both surveys.

Information useful in AIDS prevention was a major objective of the 1989 study of 11,431 12- to 19-year-old boys and girls. On self-definition, 47% of the 12- to 13-year-olds reported not knowing the meaning of "homosexuality" and "bisexuality"; 6% of 18- to 19-year-olds were ignorant on this subject. Slightly less than 1% of boys and girls defined themselves as exclusively or predominantly homosexual; 1.3% of boys and 0.8% of girls defined themselves as bisexual; 8% of boys and 15% of girls reported fantasies of a homosexual nature. Such fantasies produced uncertainty on self-definition in only a minority; the youngest age group is most often uncertain on the subject of self-definition (60% of 12- to 13-year-olds did not know how to self-label).

Percentages of respondents experienced in homosexual behavior were low: boys 1.5% and girls 1%. Anal intercourse was practiced by half of these boys—among heterosexual 14- to 19-year-olds, 7% had at least one experience with anal intercourse. Bisexual experience was reported by 64% of the boys and 70% of the girls.

In the 1980s, several studies of homosexualities examined the process that homosexuals go through in self-defini-

tion. A large difference was found between males and females. More than 50% of men called themselves homosexual by age 17, 50% of women self-identified around age 23. Half of the boys experienced their first same-gender attraction by age 8; girls did so by age 14. In the process of sexual-identity formation, behavioral, psychic, erotic, and sexual responses appear more important for self-definition for boys. For girls, relational factors are characteristic, with identity formation and identity management centered on social, instead of sociosexual aspects. Defining oneself as a homosexual for boys means the coding of erotic and sexual responses, and for girls, the coding of feelings of intimacy, bonding, and togetherness. These are relative differences and one could predict that, as soon as gender differences in development become less important, the gap between a gay and lesbian development of the self will disappear. This accounts for intergenerational differences and the positive influence of a warm and permissive climate at home on identity development. In a theoretical perspective, in families without polarized sex roles, not only do male-female differences become less important, but also the distinction between homosexual and heterosexual differences. What counts is the capacity for management of social interactions.

Of special interest are Dutch studies on the construction of intergenerational male intimacy. Sandfort (1987) described how this developed in the gay movement and how concepts of male homosexuality and male homosexual pedophilia changed between 1946 and 1981. In a monumental two-volume work, *Loving Boys* (1988, 1990), Brongersma maintained that intergenerational male intimacy has a biological as well as a sociological foundation. At the beginning of puberty, boys tend not to interact sexually with girls. In this period, the sexual drive is high, so boys enter into sexual contact with peers and with older men. This view of man-boy relationships uses a theoretical framework that relies heavily on historical and anthropological material. These relations are seen as a *rite de passage*, emotionally loaded by images of becoming male, not homosexual. Another sociohistorical illustration was presented by Maassen, who described the work and life of Gustav Wyneken, an influential pedagogue of pre-Nazi Germany, accused of having had sexual relations with some of his pupils.

In a 1992 special women's issue of *Paidika*, the journal of pedophilia, some Dutch authors described woman-child intimate relations, of which the majority was homosexual and in some way pedagogic. While woman-girl relationships appear rare in Holland, Wekker describes a special kind of woman-girl relationship in Suriname Creole working-class women (*mati*) who are self-supporting and have children by men with whom they are in more or less steady relationships. They become familiar with homosexual contact in their teens and are mostly initiated by older women, and large age differences are common at all ages in this cultural group. One wonders whether the subject of adult-child sexuality is changing under the influence of coeducation, the development of youth cultures, and the acceptance of sexual relationships in early adolescence. Nowadays, adolescents can have sexual contacts with peers of both sexes, so the motivation for erotic commitments with adults may decline or disappear.

### B. Adults

*Gender Roles and Relationship Patterns*

Tielman's *Homosexuality in the Netherlands* (1982) describes the Dutch Gay Emancipation Movement between 1911 and 1982. Warmerdam and Koenders (1987) described the homosexual organization COC between 1946 and 1966. Detailed oral histories of the discrimination against homosexuals and their emancipation are available. There are numerous impressions, accounts, and photographs available, and a lot is analyzed in *Homologie*, a scientific and cultural bimonthly. Still missing, however, is a broad and thorough study of the homosexual and lesbian subcultures in these periods from a nonpolitical perspective.

Hekma (1987) analyzed how during the 19th century, Dutch physicians and psychiatrists, influenced mainly by German and French ideas, constructed a homosexual identity with specific bodily and mental characteristics. This widely accepted image of gay and lesbian identity was disputed by Muller (1990), who showed that most German physicians relied heavily on personal statements of their clients, who in their self-confessions constructed homosexuality themselves. The theoretical issue is, as in other psychiatric cases of alcoholism and anorexia, who has the power in the discourse: Who "invents" the images, the categories, the definitions of the self? It seems that in the 19th century, the "making of the homosexual" was mainly an interaction of physicians and their patients. In the 20th century, homosexuals discovered themselves as a community.

Dutch research on gay and lesbian relationships took root in our tradition of research on alternative relationships. Instead of focusing on differences between marriage and alternatives, Dutch researchers try to understand the dynamics of different forms of relationships. Straver (1981) found that among unmarried couples—heterosexual, homosexual, and lesbian—some couples structure their relationship in a traditional, strong role differentiation, while others accentuate complete togetherness with a tendency towards independence. Still others emphasize self-development. Living together is no longer an essential condition in forming a relationship. Straver does not present a correlation between these models and sexual orientation.

Schreurs (1990) compared lesbian, cohabiting women (above average in education, income, and professional activity, and mainly in their 20s and 40s) with a similar group of heterosexual couples. Analysis produced Stravers' types of relationships, except for the strong role-differentiation type. Relations characterized by togetherness led to the highest scores for relationship satisfaction; couples in autonomy relations expressed satisfaction with autonomy as well as with togetherness. A group characterized by distance scored identical on autonomy, but lower on togetherness. In comparison with heterosexual couples, only emotional and recreational bonding scored lower in heterosexual couples, and men scored lower on satisfaction with emotional bonding.

Schreurs criticizes current theories in which lesbian relations are considered a risk for symbiosis (i.e., high bonding with loss of autonomy). In lesbian relationships, a high degree of emotional bonding obviously is possible without loss of autonomy, an important consideration for therapists working with lesbian couples.

In a similar study, Deenen (1991) analyzed 320 men in steady homosexual relationships: 69% lived together; the mean relationship duration was 8.2 years (10-39 months: $n = 88$ with mean age 30; 40-199 months: $n = 138$ with mean age 36; 120-446 months: $n = 93$ with mean age 45). He found no support for the phasic developmental model of McWhirter and Mattison (1984), who hold that sexual and emotional satisfaction depend on the time of a relationship between two men. Deenen found differences between short- and long-lasting relationships, and a difference between men younger than 30 years and older men. Both variables, relationship duration and partner's age, predicted relationship satisfaction and sexual satisfaction better than the phasic developmental model.

For women and men in homosexual relationships, emotional intimacy is the best predictor for relationship satisfaction. Sexual contact seems more important for men, but this difference may disappear if one relies on a less-strict definition of sexual contact and replaces it by affectionate bodily contact. One can go even further, seeing the whole erotic and sexual attraction embedded in the more general context of living, a line of reasoning also found in Dutch studies of sexual identity and identity development.

## Social Status; Legal and Religious Restrictions

In the late 1960s, Dutch research on homosexuality was characterized by a social-scientific perspective in which the changing of social attitudes towards homosexuality was a primary objective. In 1968, 36% of Dutch adults believed that homosexuals should be restricted in leading their own way of life. In 1980-1987, this figure stabilized around 6 to 7%.

Until 1971, the legal age of consent for homosexual acts was 21 years of age; for heterosexual acts, it was 16. This statute was abolished in 1971, mainly on the argument that scientific research showed that people did not become homosexual by seduction at puberty or in adolescence. The new law and general tolerance had a great impact on the counseling of people with problems of homosexuality. Gradually, the image of homosexuality as a psychiatric symptom disappeared completely. In the 1980s, newly established departments of gay and lesbian studies at the Universities of Utrecht and Amsterdam triggered a diversity of studies on homosexuality. Studies of genetic, hormonal, and neural factors are insignificant, the emphasis being placed instead on history, sociology, and social psychology.

While tolerance certainly has increased, this does not exclude all sorts of gross and subtle discrimination, including violence. For decades, youth gangs have beat up gay men in cruising areas. It took the homosexual movement a long time to persuade the gay victims (often men seeking anonymous sexual contacts while they were still "in the closet") to accuse their assaulters in court and to convince police officials that this form of violence should be taken seriously.

Two legal topics are currently under discussion, legislation against discrimination and legal recognition of gay unions. Legislation against discrimination on grounds of race, sex, sexual lifestyle, and so on, has taken more than a decade. During these years, religiously inspired parties have tried successfully to introduce exceptions based on conflicting interests. The central issue is always whether Christian schools will dismiss or refuse to hire homosexual teachers.

Although Dutch civil laws do not specify the heterosexual essence of marriage, no gay or lesbian couple has been able to enter a legally recognized marriage. Two recent efforts to gain this recognition have been turned down by the high court with the suggestion that the matter should be studied by the government and a law reform prepared. All political parties support this opinion. (See "Update 2001" below.)

Discrimination and homophobia are expected in macho cultures such as the military. Since 1971 and the abolition of the penalty for homosexual acts after age 16, homosexuality has been tolerated in the military. A 1992 NISSO study of homosexuality in the military concluded that:

- Drafted men did not differ from the general population in homosexual feelings and experience;
- Male professionals less often reported homosexual feelings and experience;
- Female professionals more often reported homosexual feelings and experiences—women are not drafted for military service in Holland.

- In all branches and at all levels, respondents were aware that discrimination was not tolerated; female soldiers were more tolerant than their male colleagues. Yet, distancing and isolation in some form was a common reaction, and unconditional support was often withheld from homosexuals. When open about their sexual orientation, homosexuals were excluded from the comrade culture. Homosexuals tend to be isolated much more than allochtonous soldiers.
- Excesses, from abusive language to physical attacks, are not uncommon in the army.
- Homosexuals tend to mask their orientation while in service. In their immediate environment, homosexuals have little support—the Foundation Homosexuality and the Armed Forces functions only on a national level.

This 1992 NISSO research marked a milestone in the development of attitudes towards homosexuality in the military. COC, the national organization of homosexuals, gave the Dutch Minister of Defense and the Foundation Homosexuality and the Armed Forces its annual award. In 1993, a national confidential counselor on homosexuality in the military was instituted.

There is not much information on homosexuality in other organizations, e.g., prisons. Coercive homosexual contacts in institutions, as is known from reports in the United States, are reported incidentally, but these acts are definitely not prison routine. Homosexual rape is seldom reported to the Dutch police. A few cases of male pedophilic or incestuous offenses are brought to trial each year, but cases involving adult victims are rare.

*[Gay Marriages Approved*

[*Update 2001*: In 1998, the Dutch enacted a law allowing same-sex couples to register as partners and to claim pensions, social security, and inheritance. In September 2000, the Dutch Parliament voted to convert the country's "registered same-sex partnerships" into marriages, complete with divorce guidelines and wider adoption rights for gays. The Dutch law allows same-sex couples even more rights than the Danish law, which also recognizes gay marriages. When effective early at midnight, March 31, 2001, Dutch couples were able to marry at city hall and adopt. They are also able to divorce through the court system. As of March 2001, Iceland, Finland, Norway, Sweden, France, and Germany allowed legal registration of gay partnerships. The only restriction is that one of the two must be Dutch and live in the Netherlands.

[The new Dutch law had unusual and overwhelming support from all three parliamentary factions in the governing coalition in the 150-seat Parliament. Only a few small Christian parties opposed the law. Both Protestant and Roman Catholic churches rejected the change. At midnight, March 31, 2001, three gay male couples and one lesbian couple had their marriages witnessed by the Mayor of Amsterdam. Because gay Dutch couples may run into trouble traveling in countries where homosexuality remains illegal, the Foreign Affairs Ministry planned to offer legal assistance in such cases. (*End of update by R. T. Francoeur*)]

*Prevailing Patterns in Sexual Behaviors*

The 1989 survey showed that homosexual and bisexual people tend to be the most permissive on the subject of sex in general (Table 18 gives results for 421 male and 580 female respondents).

Physical attraction for same-sex partners was felt at a mean age of 14 for male and 19 for female respondents. This difference was smaller in the younger age groups. Respondents reporting attraction to same-sex partners generally were confused and worried by these feelings. After a mean duration of three years, these feelings subsided in about half of the men and two thirds of the women. Men who are attracted to men tend to have had some form of sexual contact at least once; in women, attraction led to sexual behavior in only a minority. The time from first sexual attraction to sexual contact was shorter for men than women (see Table 19).

Homosexual and bisexual men had a much larger number of sex partners; for women, total numbers were too small to form conclusions. For homosexual men, the mean number of partners in the past year was 9.1; in the past five years, 48.6, and in their whole life, 270.3. In comparison, heterosexual men reported means of 1.1, 1.4, and 3.9 for the same periods. Bisexuals reported numbers between these two extremes.

Long-term relationships (mean duration, six years) were reported by two thirds of the homosexual respondents. Of the men, half of this group had an open relationship with incidental contacts tolerated. The mean for such incidental contacts was 12, which is not different from the mean of homosexual men not engaged in a steady relationship. In steady re-

**Table 18**

**Homosexual Experiences**

| Experience | Male | | Female | |
|---|---|---|---|---|
| | Number | Percent | Number | Percent |
| Ever felt physical attraction | 54 | 13 | 59 | 10 |
| Ever been in love | 25 | 5 | 18 | 3 |
| Ever has thought to be homosexual | 33 | 8 | 19 | 3 |
| Ever had sex with a person of the same sex | 50 | 12 | 25 | 4 |
| More than incidentally had sex with a person of the same sex | 24 | 6 | 13 | 2 |
| Same-sex attraction is currently present | 24 | 6 | 19 | 3 |
| Feels to be (primarily) homosexual | 17 | 4 | 2 | 0.4 |

*Source*: Sandfort & van Zessen (1991, 4, Table 2.3). (*IES2* Table 7, p. 929)

**Table 19**

**Current Sexual Orientation, by Self-Labeling and Behaviors, in Percentages**

| Criteria | Males | Females |
|---|---|---|
| **Self-labeling** | | |
| Exclusively heterosexual | 89.5 | 92.9 |
| Almost exclusively heterosexual | 4.5 | 4.1 |
| Mainly heterosexual | 1.9 | 2.1 |
| Equally homosexual and heterosexual | 0.0 | 0.5 |
| Mainly homosexual | 0.7 | 0.9 |
| Almost exclusively homosexual | 1.9 | 0.2 |
| Exclusively homosexual | 1.4 | 0.2 |
| **Behavioral** | | |
| Exclusively heterosexual | 81.7 | 88.4 |
| Bisexual | 1.9 | 0.5 |
| Exclusively homosexual | 3.6 | 0.3 |
| Never had sexual relations | 12.8 | 10.7 |

(*IES2* Table 8, p. 930)

lations, anal intercourse was common (82%) and condom use was extremely rare. In incidental homosexual encounters, anal intercourse is practiced by a quarter of the men, with condom use uncommon. Gay bars and cafes, saunas and Turkish baths, some well-known highway parking places, and parks were the main sites for incidental contacts. All sorts of subculture variations are available, especially in Amsterdam, including leather and S-M, piercing, and tattooing.

In Deenen's 1991 gay-couples research, high frequency of sexual contact correlates with short duration of the relationship (but not very strongly) and with younger age (especially in longer-standing relationships) (see Table 20). A positive evaluation of the sexual interaction correlates with higher frequency, but less so in beginning relations. Dominance as a self-reported trait correlates with high frequency of sexual contact. No correlations were concluded for emotional distance, intimacy in the family of origin, or positive self-image.

### Bisexuality

Bisexual respondents in the 1989 study are relatively young. They tend to self-label as heterosexual and their behavior pattern is similar to heterosexuals with short-term relations. Anal intercourse is rare and, when practiced, condoms will be used, contrary to vaginal intercourse in which condom use is rare.

It is remarkable that there has never been a research study on homo(bi)sexuality in marriage in Holland. The 1968 and 1981 studies showed that 2.3% and 3.3%, respectively, of male respondents with predominant or exclusive homosexual attraction were, or had been married. Married homosexuals sometimes will seek help from professionals, but the only organization for marriage and homosexuality is the self-help group, Orpheus.

## 7. Gender Diversity and Transgender Issues

The first and most important clinic specializing in gender dysphoria is the Academic Hospital of the Free University of Amsterdam. The Dutch Gender Foundation was established in 1972. After several years of informal contact with the Free University Hospital, the ethics committee gave its approval to the medical treatment of transsexuals. The clinic started in 1976, mainly with hormonal treatment and a small number of surgical corrections. In 1982, a multidisciplinary team was formed, following the guidelines of the Harry Benjamin International Gender Dysphoria Association. Medical treatment is covered by health insurance. Support and peer-group contact are provided in some large cities by the Dutch Society for Sexual Reform (NVSH) and the Organization for Humanistic Help. Self-help groups often include transvestites. Special groups for parents and other family members have been organized recently. The most recent, and tragic, expansion of self-help for transsexuals is a group of persons treated with sex-reassignment surgery who regret the operation.

There are few legal barriers to the sex change after a legal reform that took place in 1985. A transsexual's sex may be corrected on the birth certificate if a medical declaration states that the person is irreversibly bodily corrected to the other sex and is permanently infertile. Married transsexuals must divorce before the birth certificate can be changed. At the same time (or sometimes earlier), a person's given name may be changed.

Thus far, some 1,500 transsexuals have been assessed by the Amsterdam gender team; approximately 150 sex-reversal surgeries (SRS) have been performed. In 1988, the Free University founded a chair for transsexology, which was awarded to Louis Gooren. Utrecht professor Peggy Cohen-Kettenis, whose chair (installed in 1992) is dedicated to gender development and psychopathology, works in close collaboration with the Amsterdam team. In some adolescent cases, treatment began before the patient's pubertal maturation process was fully completed; some 20 patients completed their SRS before or shortly after age 18. These teams also carry out training and research activities. Two smaller gender teams are active in Groningen and Arnhem, but, unfortunately, they are not active in research.

The incidence of male-female transsexuality has been estimated at 1:12,900; and for female-male 1:30,400. Scientific attention to further diagnostic specification is expanding, especially for the concept of primary (aware since early childhood) versus secondary (awareness developing later in life) transsexuality.

Kuiper (1991) has provided the most extensive evaluation of the Amsterdam SRS treatment approach, reporting on 105 male-to-female and 36 female-to-male transsexuals, all at least in the phase of hormonal treatment. In a long-term follow-up, 50% of male-to-female and 75% of female-to-male transsexuals participated, with mean duration since the start of hormonal treatment being over ten years. The main conclusion is that there is no reason to doubt that SRS is effective in ameliorating the patient's gender-related distress. Other personal and social problems were much less influenced by SRS, and female-to-male transsexuals were found to be better adjusted socially (criteria: relations, work, sexual satisfaction, and loneliness). Psychic functioning was characterized by high scores on negativism, shyness, and psychopathology (delusional, paranoid, and bizarre thoughts), and this did not change after SRS. For male-to-female transsexuals, SRS proved to be a major health risk: In a group (mean age 37), 11 out of 105 had died at eight-year follow-up, with myocardial infarction as the most common cause. There is a great need for psychological help on nongender issues, such as loneliness and shyness.

Verschoor (1990), a founder of the Amsterdam gender team, reported on a comparison of biographic questionnaires from SRS clients, transvestite members of the NVSH self-help groups, members of the homosexual organization COC, and controls. The youth of the transvestites appeared less conflicted than those of the transsexuals and homosexuals. Two thirds of the transvestites are married, often with resulting major problems in the relationship. Cross-dressing is sexually arousing for most transvestites. Progression towards transsexual wishes is uncommon—the transvestites in this group are certainly a selected group. For some transvestites, there is a link with S-M.

In 1984, Slijper studied female Congenital Adrenal Hyperplasia (CAH) patients (aged 6 to 16), comparing them with type I diabetes patients and controls. Diminished sex dimorphism in behavior correlated with severity of health problems (e.g., more pronounced in the salt-losing variant

#### Table 20

#### Frequency of Sexual Contact in Steady Same-Sex Relationships

| Frequency | Percentage |
|---|---|
| None | 4.1 |
| Once in a while | 6.9 |
| 1-3 times a month | 17.3 |
| 1-2 times a week | 43.1 |
| 2-5 times a week | 25.2 |
| 6 or more times a week | 2.2 |

*Source*: Deenen (1991). (*IES2* Table 9, p. 931)

of CAH) and with the degree of their parents concern with the illness, especially the gender-confusion aspect. Genital virilization itself does not correlate with degree of tomboyism. In 1992, ten patients aged 16 to 33, were reevaluated on sexual and relationship experience and sexual anatomy. Self-pleasuring was frequent in seven. While gender-role behavior had been masculine throughout primary and secondary school, self-expressed sexual orientation was heterosexual in all. Yet, falling in love and sexual experience with partners was very rare. Only three women menstruated regularly. In contrast with the patients' conviction that their genitalia were normal, adequate functional anatomy was found in only four.

## 8. Significant Unconventional Sexual Behaviors

### A. Coercive Sex

*Child Abuse, Incest, and Pedophilia*

Years of feminist activities directed at sexual violence resulted in 1982 in a large-scale government-organized conference to develop policies for future years. Since then, sexual violence has been high on the political agenda. Research flourished, volunteer movements were supported financially, the concept of expertise through personal experience was widely acknowledged, public attention was raised by mass-media campaigns, a network of confidential doctors for the anonymous reporting of child abuse was set up, and education for helping professionals was made available all over the country. In psychiatric hospitals, a more profound interest in the patient's sexual-abuse history is growing. Knowledge of the more complicated reaction patterns of childhood abuse, such as dissociative disorders, is expanding. More incest cases were brought to court, and perpetrators were sentenced to heavier penalties—the legal maximum being six years. A modest attempt with outpatient psychological help for perpetrators of sexual abuse was started, as an adjunct to the already existing residential compulsory programs for mentally disturbed violent sex offenders. A systems approach was introduced, in which all family members are supported by their own therapist, who work together to integrate the therapeutic process.

In the mid-1980s, Draijer (1990) carried out a nationwide representative study of female child sexual victimization by family members with in-depth interviews of 1,054 women, ages 20 to 40. This was 50% of all women approached. Intrafamily sexual abuse before age 16 was reported by 15.6%. For 25%, this study was their first discussion of these events. On a severity scale, 55.6% were found to be mild or not severe; 44.4% were classified as severe or very severe. (Step)fathers were the most inclined to commit more-intrusive forms of abuse. The level of education, level of professional occupation, religion, and geographical isolation were insignificant predictors. Family backgrounds that correlated significantly with incest included: conservatism in male-female roles, restricted sexual norms, child emotional neglect, lack of physical warmth in childrearing, discontinuity in family life, physical aggression, illness, depression, emotional instability of the parents, and the father's possessiveness and controlling tendency. Sexual victimization correlates with problems in later life in a much higher degree than all other negative family dynamics. Only 13% had no negative effects whatsoever.

Child sexual abuse outside the family has gained less attention (see Section 5B, Interpersonal Heterosexual Behaviors, Adolescents). In the 1970s, because of society's greater tolerance for all sexual expressions, pedophilia was for some years less tabooed. A public discussion about adult-child

sexual contact on a nonexploitative base was then possible. Since the legal reform of 1991, adult sexual contacts with boys aged 12 to 16 are felonies only if the boy or his legal representative wants prosecution: The maximum penalty is six years. Gender equalization of pubertal sexual rights was also part of this reform.

Following a low in child sexual abuse cases reported in 1983, there has been a steady increase in both reported cases and the percentage of cases prosecuted. In 1989, cases of child sexual abuse by nonfamily members or authority figures was 1.9 per 100,000 inhabitants.

Male victims of childhood sexual abuse come out of the closet much later than females. The double taboo on homosexuality and powerlessness results in massive shame and repression. Volunteer and professional help for male victims is more difficult to find. Some child-abuse cases attract a lot of the general public's attention, especially the difficulties in truth finding, e.g., the use of interviews with the so-called anatomically correct dolls.

### B. Sexual Harassment

Since the 1982 government conference on sexual abuse, sexual harassment has been recognized as a major problem in all sorts of organizations, including schools and business organizations. It has certainly become easier for workers to lodge complaints. Confidential counselors have been introduced in schools, and training of personnel managers and administrators on this issue is available all over the country. Verbal and physical misconduct on gender-related issues is extinct, but the general public's recognition of the intolerability of such behavior is widely acknowledged.

One special type of sexual abuse requires mention: the sexual contacts between (para)medical professionals and their patients or clients. It has been found that women abused in childhood were often revictimized during therapy. Recently, extra attention has also be given to the mentally and physically handicapped. In the 1980s, ethical codes on this particular type of misconduct were formulated. In the 1991 law reform, medical and social work professionals were included with civil servants, teachers, youth leaders, and prison wardens in those faced with a maximum penalty of six years for abuse of authority.

### C. Rape

Rape was an early target for the feminist movement in the 1970s. It took some years to convince police and the courts that rape cases deserved much more attention, and rape victims much more sensitivity during interrogation. Some rape characteristics shocked the general public, for instance, the almost universally denied fact that date/acquaintance rape is more common than stranger rape. A government-financed mass-media campaign in 1992 addressed young men on sexual coercion: "Sex is natural, but never self-evident." Until 1991, Dutch law did not allow prosecution for marital rape. Sexual assault, meaning all other forced sexual acts except vaginal intercourse, is a criminal offense between husband and wife. This law reform has been a major target for emancipation action. Rape victims have also profited from the victim movement's help initiatives and its achievements in training professional social and psychotherapeutic workers.

Maximum penalty in rape cases is eight years. The number of rape cases brought to the police is steadily rising. In 1991, 1,333 accusations (9 per 100,000 inhabitants) resulted in 858 rape cases (65%), 746 suspects being cleared, a rather stable percentage over the years. For sexual assault, 2,427 accusations (16 per 100,000) resulted in 1,060 cases (43.7%) and 632 suspects being brought to court by the police.

## D. Prostitution

Studies on prostitution are numerous, but almost all data are nonrepresentative. In Holland, prostituting oneself is not illegal, but creating the opportunity for prostitution, e.g., profiting from a brothel, is. In 1993, a legal reform lowered the sanctions and allowed local governments to formulate their own policies. Prostitute activists are dissatisfied with this reform, arguing that the new situation will not improve the prostitute's legal position. In the last decade, a movement to abolish exploitation and improve working conditions (safety, hygiene, and privacy) was initiated. Prostitutes fear that the new legal situation will lead to registration and taxing (including a Value Added Tax [VAT]), which will again force the weaker group members into evading the law. Today's urgent problems include the trade in women from Third World nations, exploitation, illegal immigration, and fraudulent parental claims by Antilles men for South and Central American girls intended to legalize their working for Dutch brothels, and violence.

The total number of prostitutes in the Netherlands has been estimated at 15,000 to 20,000, the vast majority being women. Some 10% are supposed to be streetwalkers, 30% in window prostitution, 30% working in a sex club, 15% in an escort service, and 15% work in their private residence. Drug addicts, including drug tourists, are numerous in the streetwalker group. Window and club prostitution are dominated by Caribbean, South American, African, and Asian women. In recent years, condom use among these groups has been promoted by means of audiotaped messages. It is generally believed that today, most prostitution intercourse is protected, with drug-addicted streetwalkers as the most likely exception.

In 1968, more than half of all single men and 12% of husbands refused to answer questions about paid sexual encounters. In both groups, 12% admitted to having visited a prostitute at least once. In 1981, refusal was almost nil and 11% admitted to having visited a prostitute at least once. Moreover, 19% of the married group, especially the younger-age group, had visited a sex club at least once. In 1989, 13.5% of the male respondents reported having paid for sex at least once; 2.6% had had at least one paid sex experience in the past year.

In the 1989 study, visiting prostitutes seemed to be motivated more by the desire to maintain independence than by social inadequacy. For men in steady relationships, common motives are variation or a strong desire for special forms of sex their partner refuses them. Condom use seems almost to have doubled as a result of the safe-sex campaigns.

Male heterosexual prostitution is extremely rare in Holland, but one study of escort boys was published in 1989. In recent years, male strippers ("Chippendales") have made a remarkable appearance in the entertainment world.

Male homosexual prostitution is estimated to count some 1,300 men, of which a large group must be relatively young. Some consider themselves true professionals, with a professional pride in working according to their own standards. Others are motivated largely by drug addiction and homelessness. Sexual orientation is problematic: Most boys consider themselves to be heterosexual, which suggests limits on the behaviors they consider acceptable or not. Fortunately, these restrictions result in a rather low prevalence of unsafe sex; homosexual prostitution seems to be a minor risk factor in the AIDS epidemic. Unfortunately, this discrepancy between self-perceived sexual orientation and behavior can lead to resentment and violent outbursts. A boy who feels trapped, especially when a man wants to perform anal penetration, will sometimes commit violent acts against his customer, as this behavior is most threatening to his masculinity.

In ten years, 18 murder cases with this dynamic were reported in Amsterdam. Moroccan boys were overrepresented, and this may reflect high vulnerability for threats to their masculinity as a result of their Islamic culture.

## E. Pornography

Pornography as a subject of public decency laws has almost completely disappeared from the legislative discourse since the 1960s sexual revolution movement. Feminist criticism of the misogyny obvious in a lot of pornography has been heard throughout the nation, but this did not influence legislation to any substantial degree. In the latest reform, the protection of children and women in the pornography-producing business has gained more impetus than the decency aspect. Penalties up to three months can still be given for public exposure of indecent materials, exposure to children under 16, and selling child pornography. Child-abuse laws are often applied in cases of the production of child pornography; the maximum penalty is six years.

Child pornography has been under scrutiny as a result of allegations from the U.S.A., implying that enormous amounts of these materials were being imported from the Netherlands. It cannot be denied that in the mid-1980s, Holland produced and exported child pornography, some of which, especially heterosexual material, clearly qualified as hardcore. Yet, the American interest in Dutch pornography has all the characteristics of a witch hunt, exaggerating the numbers of victims. In 1989, six child pornography cases led to convictions.

The use of pornography is quite common. In the 1989 study, only 23% of the men and 55% of the women had no experience at all with erotic magazines or books, while 54% of the men and 12% of the women had watched pornographic movies or videos. The "new kids on the block" are erotic pay-phone lines (06-numbers); 12% of the men and 4% of the women reported having phoned a sex line. This erotic option has become an addiction for some Dutchmen. Recently alcohol-and-drug services have begun treating some of their patients for 06-phoning problems.

## F. Other Unconventional Behaviors

Some paraphilic behaviors are well embedded in society. Transvestites, for instance, have formed groups, often with transsexuals, for mutual support and opportunities to cross-dress without the risk of ridicule or violent reactions. People interested in sadomasochistic sexual contacts have formed two national organizations, and numerous sex clubs offer opportunities for expression. Gay and lesbian S-M groups are also active, and one occasionally sees some very aesthetic expressions of the S-M preference, especially in photography.

Indecent exposure is the most common sex crime; in 1990, 1.8% of all women were confronted with an act of exhibitionism. The number of reported cases shows a slow decline: 3,840 in 1991 (26 per 10,000). Only 30.5% were brought to court by the police. Exhibitionism complaints often result in a warning, and when brought to court, suggestions for some sort of therapy will often be the judge's sentence. Unfortunately, no studies of results of court-ordered outpatient treatment of exhibitionists are published.

## 9. Contraception, Abortion, and Population Planning

### A. History

Contraceptive advice in Holland started in the 1880s. The inspiration for a Neo-Malthusian League was imported from the United Kingdom by Alette Jacobs (1854-1929). This remarkable woman, the first Dutch woman ever to enter secondary school, the university, and become a medical doctor, was strongly influenced by feminist ideals and a heartfelt concern for the poor. The League, founded by Jacobs and two other doctors, found little support and more often violent opposition in medical circles.

After Mensinga invented the diaphragm in 1881, this became the main weapon in the struggle against large, poor families. Free clinics started in Amsterdam in 1882, and soon afterwards in Rotterdam and Groningen. The Neo-Malthusian League produced leaflets and books in enormous numbers. Some midwives joined the clinics, and from the 1890s on, laywomen were trained in instructing and prescribing the diaphragm. The clinic network expanded rapidly, as condom quality improved and more precise information on the Ogino-Knaus method of periodic abstinence became available.

In 1939, the Neo-Malthusian League performed Holland's first sociosexological research, distributing 26,010 questionnaires to its members; 7,788 were returned and analyzed (Nabrink 1978); see Table 21 for some results of this survey.

When the Germans occupied the Netherlands, the Neo-Malthusian League was abolished. After World War II, a new organization replaced it, the Dutch Society for Sexual Reform (NVSH). Again, a chain of consultation bureaus was established and education for the general public gradually became more accepted. The ideals of the NVSH became more political, and the sexual revolution further radicalized the movement.

Following the introduction of the oral contraceptive in 1962, general practitioners and gynecologists were initially reluctant to prescribe the pill, sometimes for reasons blatantly moralistic. The NVSH consultation bureaus soon became a well-known alternative for teenagers, unmarried couples, married couples who wanted to postpone procreation, widows, and divorcees. Professional expertise in the NVSH bureaus was also on a higher level in those pioneering years. In 1969, the society separated into a professional organization for the management of the consultation bureaus, the Rutgers Foundation, and a layman's organization for political action, education, and discussion and self-help.

Since the mid-1970s, contraceptive advice has become part of the regular physician's routine; gynecologists play a minor part in contraception in Holland. The Rutgers Foundation still was a useful alternative for girls and women who sought extreme discretion (e.g., young girls and women in extramarital relations whose spouses had vasectomies) and for more specialized questions on contraception and "second opinions." Since 1992, the Rutgers Foundation has concentrated its services in seven large cities, and guides its

efforts more to educating the regular providers of contraceptive and sexological services.

From the mid-1960s on, contraceptive use and attitudes have been major research issues. Unwanted pregnancy and induced abortion caused major social, medical, and political concern. Accordingly, in the past two decades, questions about contraceptive use and the prevalence of unwanted pregnancy were almost always included in surveys, particularly those for adolescents.

Several studies directly addressed the issue of family planning. Initially, research was mainly done by general practitioners and family-planning doctors. Social scientists entered the field a few years later. A 1974-75 representative study, involving 1,200 men and women, revealed that modern methods of family planning had been rapidly accepted, irrespective of social status or religion. NISSO did several studies in close collaboration with Stimezo-Nederland, the national abortion federation, which began its own research program in 1974. The role of induced abortion in society was studied as it related to changing patterns of family formation, sexual behavior after the "sexual revolution," and emerging modern contraceptive behavior. An international comparative investigation of the consequences of legal changes regarding abortion in Western Europe and the U.S.A. was followed by a study of contraceptive behavior throughout Western Europe (Ketting 1990).

In 1986, NISSO started a new research program on family planning, concentrating on specific groups. Studies published prior to 1993 include:

- Anthropologically inspired in-depth interviews on sexual and contraceptive behavior of Turkish immigrants;
- A similar study on Caribbean immigrants;
- An in-depth study of the social and psychological mechanisms underlying the effectiveness of contraceptive behavior of young girls at the start of their sexual careers;
- A study on the rather new phenomenon of women's ambivalence towards childbearing; and
- A representative study of the experiences of 1,200 women with, and attitudes towards, oral contraception.

### B. Some Data

Vogel and van der Vliet's 1990 study on adolescent sexuality gave a lot of information on contraceptive use and the various motives for the use of condoms. They concentrated on contraceptive motives, although this distinction is not always possible.

Mean age for first coitus in this survey was 17.5. In this first coital experience, 57% used a condom. The earlier first coitus occurred, the higher the proportion of condom users. Allochtonous youngsters scored lower, especially when not born in the Netherlands. In the older age groups, as relations become steady, oral-contraceptive use is the rule, and condom use for STD/AIDS prevention loses most of its impetus.

Many girls are using oral contraceptives before their first coitus. One in five girls are taking the pill by the time they start petting naked. (A prescription for medical reasons, e.g., menstrual discomfort, may account for a proportion of this number.) Two thirds of all girls with some coital experience have at some time used the pill; 60% were using oral contraception when interviewed. When first intercourse was experienced at an early age (11 to 13), the percentage was lower (just over 10%); in the oldest group, almost three quarters were current users.

In keeping with the Dutch slogan, "If you take care of the condoms, I'll take care of the pill," combined use of the pill and condom was practiced by 13% of respondents (boys: 18%; girls: 9%) in their last intercourse experience. The 14-to-15 age group is most conscientious in this regard,

#### Table 21

**Contraceptive Use and Failures in 1939 Neo-Malthusian League Survey (*n* = 7,788)**

| Method | Females | | | Males | | |
|---|---|---|---|---|---|---|
| | *n* | Failures | % | *n* | Failures | % |
| Coitus interruptus | 155 | 29 | 18.7 | 165 | 46 | 27.9 |
| Diaphragm | 1,484 | 75 | 5 | 1,409 | 44 | 3.2 |
| Condom | 1,105 | 67 | 6 | 1,036 | 79 | 6.7 |
| Cervical cap | 95 | 19 | 20 | 91 | 12 | 13.2 |
| Patentex jelly | 56 | 20 | 35.7 | 61 | 20 | 32.7 |
| Periodic abstinence | 56 | 12 | 21.4 | 53 | 17 | 32 |

(*IES2* Table 10, p. 938)

22%. The use of no contraception at all is rare; only 11% of 16- to 19-year-olds used no contraception in their last sexual intercourse (see Table 22).

### Adults

Van Delft and Ketting (1992) have reported the most recent number data from 1988: Of the 18- to 37-year-old women, 43% used an oral or injectable contraceptive, 22% no contraceptive, 7% each for the condom or vasectomy, 5% each for vasectomy and IUD, and 3% tubal ligation. Only 13% of the married women, 5% of the cohabiting women, and 14% of the women in steady relationships used no contraceptive (see Tables 23 and 24).

No Dutch data are available on contraceptive failures for different methods. While a number of unplanned pregnancies are accepted after discovery, it is known from various sources that over 90% of all children born in the years 1981-88 were planned. A comparison of Dutch failure data with U.S.A. figures reveals that each method, except for periodic abstinence, is more reliable in Holland and the difference is enormous. Three sources of confusion are mentioned by van Delft and Ketting:

- American data often report method failure in the first year of use. Most methods gain in reliability in time.
- The "morning after pill" is easily available in Holland and is used by women who are aware something has gone wrong with their usual method.
- Some American data may be distorted by including users who deliberately stopped using the method.

It is generally acknowledged that U.S.A. data on method failure cannot be used for Dutch educational materials (see Table 25).

Estrogen dose-dependent side effects, especially cardiovascular ones, led to the introduction of the so-called sub-50s in 1975. In five years, they became the leading oral contraceptive. Today, most physicians prescribe sub-50s. This seems to work reasonably well: Abortion data show that women on 50s and sub-50s have comparable risks of unwanted pregnancy.

Concern over the pill's side effects around 1980 led to a short but sharp decline in pill use. Introduction of sub-50s largely removed this concern. Today, most women are aware of positive side effects. Nevertheless, total oral-contraceptive use once again showed a slight decrease in 1990. Condom use for STD and AIDS prevention may have led some women to stop or postpone oral contraception. The decline in popularity of hormonal contraception led to a short increase in IUD use (see Table 26).

Gynecologists and the Rutgers Foundation were the early providers for IUDs. From 1983 to 1987, the Dutch industry producing the most popular IUD ran educational workshops for physicians, increasing the use of IUDs. Early on, there was an awareness of negative side effects, menstrual discomfort, and a rising number of extrauterine pregnancies.

Because condom use has been so strongly motivated by disease prevention, it is discussed in Section 10 below.

### Table 22

**Pregnancies per 1,000 Unmarried Women, Grouped According to Consequences, 1980-1988**

| Year | "Forced" Marriage | Birth Out of Wedlock | Abortion | Total |
|------|------|------|------|------|
| 1980 | 2.8 | 2.4 | 5.3 | 10.5 |
| 1981 | 2.9 | 1.9 | 5.3 | 10.1 |
| 1982 | 2.5 | 2.1 | 5.1 | 9.7 |
| 1983 | 2.3 | 2.2 | 5.3 | 10.0 |
| 1984 | 2.1 | 2.0 | 4.4 | 8.5 |
| 1985 | 1.9 | 2.0 | 4.4 | 8.4 |
| 1986 | 1.9 | 2.1 | 4.1 | 8.1 |
| 1987 | 1.6 | 2.3 | 3.8 | 7.7 |
| 1988 | 1.6 | 2.3 | 3.8 | 7.7 |

*Source*: Van Delft & Ketting (1992, 61, Table 22). (*IES2* Table 11, p. 941)

### Table 23

**Current Contraceptive Method, by Age, in Percentages (1988)**

| Contraceptive Method | Age of Women (in Years) | | | | | Total 18-37 |
|------|------|------|------|------|------|------|
| | 18-19 | 20-24 | 25-29 | 30-34 | 35-37 | |
| Oral-injectable | 45 | 59 | 48 | 31 | 22 | 43 |
| IUD | 1 | 2 | 5 | 9 | 6 | 5 |
| Tubal ligation | 0 | 0 | 1 | 6 | 11 | 3 |
| Vasectomy | 0 | 0 | 3 | 12 | 23 | 7 |
| Condom | 5 | 5 | 9 | 9 | 8 | 7 |
| Other methods | 4 | 6 | 4 | 5 | 3 | 5 |
| No contraception | 45 | 24 | 19 | 16 | 15 | 22 |
| Pregnant | 0 | 3 | 9 | 6 | 2 | 5 |
| Infertile | 0 | 1 | 2 | 6 | 9 | 3 |

*Source*: van Delft & Ketting (1992, 10, Table 1). (*IES2* Table 12, p. 941)

### Table 24

**Current Contraceptive Use, by Relationship Status, in Percentages (1988; Ages 18-37)**

| Contraceptive Method | Married | Cohabiting | Steady Relationship | No Male Partner |
|------|------|------|------|------|
| Oral-injectable | 35 | 68 | 67 | 28 |
| IUD | 7 | 7 | 3 | 1 |
| Tubal ligation | 5 | 2 | 2 | 1 |
| Vasectomy | 13 | 3 | 1 | — |
| Condom | 9 | 6 | 6 | 4 |
| Other methods | 4 | 5 | 6 | 4 |
| No contraception | 13 | 5 | 14 | 58 |
| Pregnant | 9 | 4 | 1 | 0 |
| Infertile | 5 | 1 | 1 | 3 |

(*IES2* Table 13, p. 942)

### Table 25

**Distribution of Hormonal Contraceptive Use by Type of Method, 1980-1989, in Percentages**

| Year | Sub-50 Combination | Tri-phasic | 50(-plus) | Injectable | Others |
|------|------|------|------|------|------|
| 1980 | 41.9 | 0.1 | 46.7 | 4.3 | 7.0 |
| 1981 | 47.5 | 5.6 | 36.5 | 4.8 | 5.6 |
| 1982 | 55.6 | 10.1 | 25.3 | 4.7 | 4.3 |
| 1983 | 57.2 | 14.8 | 20.4 | 3.9 | 3.7 |
| 1984 | 58.7 | 18.8 | 16.6 | 2.8 | 3.1 |
| 1985 | 69.7 | 20.8 | 14.5 | 2.4 | 2.6 |
| 1986 | 61.0 | 22.1 | 12.5 | 2.2 | 2.2 |
| 1987 | 61.4 | 23.8 | 11.2 | 1.8 | 1.8 |
| 1988 | 61.7 | 25.2 | 8.2 | 1.6 | 2.0 |
| 1989 | 62.8 | 25.2 | 8.2 | 1.6 | 2.2 |

*Source*: van Delft & Ketting (1992, 26, Table 11). (*IES2* Table 14, p. 943)

The diaphragm was never very popular after World War II, being used predominantly by women in steady relationships and dissatisfied with alternatives. It has its place in a lifestyle characterized by conscious living with health risks. In small circles, modified and perfected forms of periodic abstinence are also used. We have no reason to suppose that Roman Catholics are a large proportion of abstinence users. In 1992, the woman's condom (Femidom) was introduced. Among 300 women, ages 21 to 40, who were regular users of oral contraception, IUD, or sterilization during the trial period, 155 women reporting using Femidom on at least three occasions. Both men and women appear reasonably satisfied with the Femidom.

Surgical sterilization peaked in 1979, when 132,000 men and women had vasectomies or tubal ligations. The proportion of men is growing steadily, because it is well known that sterilization is much easier in men. The operation is most often performed between ages 35 and 44. Since 1985, the percentages of sterilized men and women in each age group has been rather constant. In the 35-to-39 age group, 18% of women and 20% of men are sterilized; in the 40-to-45 age group, about 25% of women and men are sterilized; about 30% of men and women 45 to 49 have been sterilized. Forty percent of all couples aged 30 to 49 have one spouse sterilized.

In recent years, sterilization has decreased in the younger age group, most probably because of an ongoing tendency to postpone having a first child. Also, some couples are debating for a number of years whether or not they want to have children at all. This has led to an expanding group of last-chance mothers with considerable fertility problems caused by a more-advanced age. This group of doubters, combined with a growing conviction that oral contraception is not a major health risk, will likely lead to a further decline in sterilizations.

Interception with the "morning after pill" (MAP) and the "morning after-IUD" (MA-IUD), along with abortion, is one of the adjuncts of planned contraception. The MAP is easily available for use after unprotected intercourse, as well as for backup for incidental failures with the regular method. The largest group using MAP is the 16- to 18-year-olds. Around 1980, when the negative attitude toward the pill peaked, use of MAP also peaked. The original MAP (5 x 5 mg ethinyl estradiol) has been replaced with the Yuzpe regime (100 mg ethinyl estradiol plus 500 mg norgestrel repeated after 12 hours) introduced in 1982. By 1986, the Yuzpe MAP accounted for 85% of MAP prescriptions. In 1986 and again in 1992, some doubt was cast on the effectiveness of the Yuzpe regime, leaving the future of this method open to question.

## C. Abortion

Just over 30,000 abortions are performed yearly in Holland, a quite stable number in recent years. More than 90% are done in abortion clinics, almost all under local anesthesia; the rest are done in gynecology departments, 80% under total anesthesia. Among women living in Holland, 69% have their abortions within six weeks after conception; 2.2% were pregnant longer than 15 weeks in 1989-90. Large numbers of abortion patients (35 to 40%) visit our clinics from western Germany, Belgium, Spain (showing a sharp decline since 1988), and numerous other countries.

Separate data are available from women in Holland, Suriname, the Dutch Antilles, Turkey, and Morocco. Abortion rates in these groups show significant, but rather stable differences, with a slight increase for the Moroccan and a slight decrease for Suriname, Antilles, and Turkish women (see Table 27). Moroccan women tend to be relatively young, primigravidae, and unmarried; it is supposed that the rising number for Moroccan women indicates some alienation from their traditional culture. For Turkish women, data suggest that abortion is used mostly to put an end to the expansion of the family. Allochtonous women have used abortion more often than autochtonous women, and it must be assumed that this implies more user failures. Moreover, one third of these women had used no contraception at all, compared with 20% for Dutch women. For allochtonous women, some 25%, the abortion in 1989-90 was not their first. For Suriname and Antilles women, it is recognized that they show more fear for unhealthy side effects of oral contraceptives. This leads to an eagerness to stop taking the pill, for instance, when a relationship falls apart.

Teenagers as a group are constant in their risk of abortion in recent years, around 4 per 1,000 girls aged 15 to 19. Teenagers have shown a slight increase in live birthrates in recent years.

As Dutch couples conceive later in life, the number of prenatal diagnostic tests for fetal malformation and disease will rise, and so will the decision for an abortion to resolve an unfavorable outcome. Precise numbers of such abortions are not available.

## D. Government Policies on Contraception and Population

In 1970, the Dutch Parliament decided that medical contraception and the cost of medical contraceptive advice should be included under general health services. Condoms are the only contraceptives that are not covered. Even in AIDS-prevention campaigns, a recommendation to include condoms has been ignored. In the recent economic recession, with a growing need to reduce health expenses, hormonal contraception is quite often mentioned as one possibility to cut costs. Thus far, these suggestions have led to

### Table 26

**Total Number of IUDs Sold in the Netherlands and Estimated Duration *in Situ*, 1980-1990**

| Year | Number Sold | Mean Years *in Situ* |
|------|-------------|----------------------|
| 1980 | 100,000 | 2.00 |
| 1981 | 97,000 | 2.25 |
| 1982 | 79,000 | 2.50 |
| 1983 | 78,000 | 2.75 |
| 1984 | 77,000 | 3.00 |
| 1985 | 67,000 | 3.25 |
| 1986 | 48,000 | 3.50 |
| 1987 | 45,000 | 3.75 |
| 1988 | 40,000 | 3.75 |
| 1989 | 39,000 | 3.75 |
| 1990 | 38,000 | 3.75 |

(*IES2* Table 15, p. 943)

### Table 27

**Abortion Rates, per Ethnic Groups, Ages 15-44, per 1,000**

| Ethnic Group | Rate |
|--------------|------|
| Autochtonous | 3.4 |
| Surinam | 28.8 |
| Antillies | 31.1 |
| Turkey | 17.8 |
| Morocco | 12.4 |

(*IES2* Table 16, p. 945)

strong reactions, especially because risk groups, such as minors and allochtonous women, will be the first to suffer the consequences of unwanted pregnancy and abortion.

In 1979, the Dutch government endorsed its State Committee on Population Questions recommendation that all Dutch couples were free to decide their number of children and the time they wanted to have them. Since then, the government has supported effective contraceptive behavior by stimulating and financing research, general education, and low-level professional help. The effectiveness of Dutch contraceptive practice is based on the opportunity for almost all young people to get the pill. Today, most general practitioners are able to handle the delicacy of prescribing the pill to young girls, even if their parents are not informed. In coming years, it will be learned whether or not unwanted pregnancy will increase as a consequence of the Rutgers Foundation's concentration in seven cities.

Abortion was a criminal offense in the Netherlands until a long-awaited legal reform took place in 1982—1953 was the last time a physician was prosecuted for performing an abortion. In 1969, Stimezo, a national organization for medically qualified induced abortion, was formed. Stimezo standards of good advice and care have found their way into today's practice. On the insistence of the religious parties, the 1982 law includes one aspect contrary to the practice of that time, e.g., a waiting-and-reconsideration time of five days after the initial consultation with a doctor. Since that law passed, abortion has been free for all Dutch citizens. Minors living with their parents need their parents' consent, but a legal alternative is available.

Population planning is not an active concern of the Dutch government. Zero growth is accepted, and a changing population stratification (young groups shrinking, elderly groups growing) causes only moderate concern. Will the future active group be able to support a large retired population? In gynecological circles, some concern is growing about the tendency of couples to postpone having children until an age when fertility definitely is lower. A popular slogan, "A smart girl plans her pregnancy in time," is a variation of an earlier advertisement by the Institute for Idealistic Propaganda: "A smart girl is prepared for a future for herself."

## 10. Sexually Transmitted Diseases and HIV/AIDS

### A. Sexually Transmitted Diseases

*Incidence, Patterns, and Trends*

According to Mooij's (1990) history of STD, gonorrhea and syphilis were rare in the Netherlands in comparison with the surrounding countries—until 1942. During World War II, a rapid increase was reported, with a peak in 1947. In 1952, numbers were again as low as they were in the 1930s. A steady decline was observed until 1960; but, since then, a second, and longer, epidemic has occurred, with rapid increases in the 1970s. Undoubtedly, these growing numbers were the result of a new enthusiasm for sexuality, the sexual revolution, supported by the general public's knowledge that STDs were now easily cured. Public education almost forgot primary prevention in these years.

The sexual revolution certainly changed the medical and health professionals' ideas on specific risk groups. Prostitutes were no longer the main source of concern; homosexuals, teenagers, foreigners, and Dutch tourists who had sex while vacationing abroad became new targets for information campaigns. It is remarkable that these predictions, based on information from abroad, were not confirmed by Dutch experience, except for homosexuals, and recently Turkish and Moroccan men.

The neglect of primary prevention gradually ended when hepatitis B and herpes, which are not curable by penicillin, appeared. Herpes caused considerable panic in heterosexual circles. Alarming data from the U.S.A. were uncritically transposed to Holland and connections with cervical cancer and neonatal disease exaggerated. The number of diagnoses peaked in 1985, perhaps biased by a more widespread availability of diagnostic services and an antiviral medication that might have prompted people in fear of herpes to be finally tested. In this peak year, the number of herpes cases at the Amsterdam free clinic was 25% of the number of gonorrhea cases. Today, herpes is infrequently diagnosed and the attention paid it by the general public and media is insignificant. However, it is reasonable that herpes promoted a growing concern for primary prevention in the 1980s, as the sharp decrease in STD diagnosis started some years before AIDS appeared.

Two STDs are among the infectious diseases for compulsory notification to the National Health Inspection: gonorrhea and syphilis. Unfortunately, only about 35% of all cases are reported. Free clinics have a more complete reporting, including data on location of the disease (urethral, rectal, and/or pharyngeal), ethnic background, sexual preference, prostitution, and earlier infections. Unfortunately, they have no information on the characteristics of groups using their services, and whether or not this group's composition is stable or changing.

National registration numbers for gonorrhea steadily decreased from 13,199 in 1983 to 3,024 in 1989. The peak year for men was 1981 (140 per 100,000 inhabitants), and for women, 1984 (65 per 100,000). An increase in 1990 was followed by the lowest number ever in 1992. In free clinics, similar trends were observed. The fastest decreases were among male homosexual and bisexual men, since 1984. Female prostitutes showed a little slower decrease, and later—since 1985. For homosexual and bisexual men, 1989 already showed some increase, including more anorectal infections, and, unfortunately, this trend has continued into 1990 and 1991. Moreover, these patients tend to be slightly younger in recent years.

For the Amsterdam free clinic, repeaters are a growing population in the total numbers. Percentagewise, homosexuals are declining and prostitutes are increasing. In all years, the peak age for male infections is 25; for women, it is age 20.

The percentage of Penicillinase-Producing Neisseria Gonorrhoeae (PPNG) in Dutch patients is steadily increasing. The first cases of PPNG were reported in the Netherlands in 1976; in 1990, 29% of all gonococcal infections was caused by PPNG. Since 1985, a rapid increase in Tetracycline-Resistant Gonorrhea (TRG) has been observed. In 1989, 40% of PPNG cases also involved TRG.

Syphilis was still decreasing in 1992, with only 190 new infections reported. In Amsterdam free clinic, in 1987, an increase in syphilis incidence was reported in heterosexual men, and some increase in female prostitutes. In that year, heterosexuals for the first time outnumbered homosexuals. In 1989, homosexual men in Amsterdam also showed an increase in new cases of syphilis, similar to tendencies in gonorrhea and seroconversions, perhaps because of a decrease in safer-sex practices.

In Holland, since the early 1950s, all pregnant women are screened for syphilis in the first trimester. In the Amsterdam area, 1985-89, only 55 out of 3,520 blood samples were positive for both TPHA- and VDRL-tests. Only four cases of congenital syphilis were reported in 1990. However, screening is still cost efficient in Amsterdam, and a second screening later in pregnancy should not be introduced as a routine restricted to women having many partners during pregnancy.

Chlamydia trachomatis probably is the most widespread STD today, but information is scanty on this subject since reporting it is not mandatory. The most thorough research took place in 1986-1988. In a 1986-1988 Amsterdam free clinic survey of 1,000 clients (65% male) at the free clinic, chlamydia was found more often than gonorrhea: 14.3% versus 11.5% in men, and 19.2% versus 6.3% in women. Combined infections were found in 2% of men and 2.6% of women. Combination infections were low in homosexual men. In men, signs for urethritis were found in all but one, with negative tests for gonorrhea and chlamydia in 41% of the cases. In the department of gynecology of a large Amsterdam hospital, 1985-1989, the incidence of gonorrhea dropped from 1.1% to 0.4%, and chlamydia from 8.6% to 4.1%.

While chlamydia definitely is the most common STD in Holland, there are good grounds for concluding that the epidemic has peaked. However, the serious consequences for fertility justify further efforts to control the disease. In 1986, in the Tilburg Infertility Clinic, of 77 women receiving their first treatment, tubal abnormality was thought to be the cause of infertility for 69; 54% had significant titers for chlamydia.

Data on condylomata acuminata are rarer, with indications that incidence is in the same range as herpes, increasing slightly up to 1985 and decreasing in recent years. Tropical STDs are rarely diagnosed in Holland, with occasional small epidemics of *haemophilus ducrei*.

Allochtonous men are a growing proportion of free clinic customers. Data suggest that Turkish and Moroccan men are six to ten times more at risk for contracting STDs. Turkish men have gonorrhea in a high proportion and a high proportion of PPNG. They also report prostitution as the source of their infection in a higher percentage. Suriname and Antillian men show a higher proportion of syphilis.

### Government Policies Concerning STD

The Dutch government has recognized STDs as a special group of diseases, with associated shame and stigma calling for special forms of illness management. Alternatives for discreet and anonymous help have been financed. Local health services provide free clinics in all large cities; the Rutgers Foundation is another alternative for STD diagnosis and treatment. For syphilis and gonorrhea, a service is offered to assist patients anonymously in contacting the sexual partners they think they have infected or been infected by.

A national organization for STD control, the SOA Foundation, produces a scientific bimonthly and contributes to the discussions in medical and political circles and to prevention programs. In the last decade, physicians' organizations have produced consensuses for standard medical care. More intensive health and STD education programs have been incorporated in a framework of sexuality and relationship management in schools. STDs other than AIDS have never been the target for specific primary prevention programs until recently. The SOA Foundation has applied for funding for a Chlamydia Public Information campaign, but this has not been forthcoming. Target groups other than teenagers in schools also have never been defined for prevention programs on STDs other than AIDS. Special attention to allochtonous groups can be justified by these groups' higher infection rates, and their higher proportion of PPNG.

### B. HIV/AIDS

*Incidence, Patterns, and Trends*

Unlike syphilis and gonorrhea, notification of AIDS cases to the National Health Inspection is voluntary. While syphilis and gonorrhea cases are underreported, AIDS reporting tends to be almost complete because of the serious nature of the epidemic. Many intravenous drug users die of health risks inherent in their lifestyles before their HIV-positive status is detected. Starting with 5 new cases of AIDS in 1982, 437 cases were reported in 1991 and 419 in 1992. Only 10 cases of HIV-2 infection were reported. Homosexual men, followed by IV-drug users (male and female), and heterosexual men and women, account for most AIDS cases, with the incidence remarkably stable through the years. Men ages 30 to 45 and women 25 to 35 are most at risk. Survival time has increased from nine months in 1982-1985 to 22 months in 1989, because of earlier diagnosis and better treatment (see Tables 28 and 29).

The number of HIV-positive persons in Holland is unknown. Individuals may be tested anonymously, in which case their status is not reported. Some data is available on segments of the population from research groups studying pregnant women, drug users (30% of whom are IV users), clients at the Amsterdam free STD clinic, Amsterdam prostitutes and their customers, and voluntary applicants for blood donation.

In a national prospective research project on HIV-infection in pregnancy, testing is voluntary and the percentage of women choosing to be tested varies widely for different hospitals. Between September 1, 1985, and January 1, 1991, 55 women were found to be positive: 60% were not born in Holland. In 58%, intravenous drug abuse was the risk factor; in two of the 22 women supposed to be heterosexually infected, blood transfusion was also reported. Ten were born in an area where AIDS is endemic; seven had at-risk male partners. Of 36 women for whom test results were known before 20 weeks of gestation, two had spontaneous and ten had induced abortions.

Among the estimated 2,500-plus hard-drug users in Holland, only 30% are IV users. IV use varies from practically zero among allochtonous groups to 70% for "heroin tourists." Combining results of a cohort survey among injectors in Amsterdam started in 1985 with reported AIDS numbers,

### Table 28

**Number of Newly Diagnosed AIDS Patients per Year**

| Year | New Patients | Year | New Patients |
|------|--------------|------|--------------|
| 1982 | 5 | 1988 | 321 |
| 1983 | 19 | 1989 | 389 |
| 1984 | 31 | 1990 | 413 |
| 1985 | 66 | 1991 | 437 |
| 1986 | 136 | 1992 | 419 |
| 1987 | 242 | Total | 2,478 |

*Source*: National Health Inspection (1993). (*IES2* Table 17, p. 950)

### Table 29

**Number of AIDS Patients, According to Risk Group and Sex**

| Risk Group | Male | Female |
|------------|------|--------|
| Homosexual-bisexual | 1,930 | — |
| Intravenous drug user | 145 | 67 |
| Homosexual-bisexual + IVDU | 26 | — |
| Hemophilia | 40 | 1 |
| Blood transfusion | 20 | 15 |
| Heterosexual | 108 | 74 |
| Mother-to-child | 2 | 9 |
| Rest/unknown | 33 | 8 |
| Total | 2,304 | 174 |

*Source*: National Health Inspection (1993). (*IES2* Table 18, p. 951)

resulted in an estimation of 750 to 800 HIV-positive IV-drug users in Amsterdam as of July 1, 1991. Even more rough is an estimate of HIV-positive IV-drug users outside Amsterdam, ca. 500. Local differences are large and unexplained: Participants in a detox clinic in the Hague were all seronegative, while their injection behavior was no more risky than an Amsterdam group. Prevalence of seropositivity among all IV-drug users is estimated at 25 to 27%. Specific preventive measures include a syringe-exchange program and condom promotion, especially for those active in prostitution (some 80% of all female IV-drug addicts).

In an Amsterdam free STD clinic, during ten weeks in 1991, 90.5% of all the patients accepted testing: 22% of the homosexual men were positive, as were 12% of the male and 41% of the female IV-drug users. Prevalence in heterosexuals without other risk factors was 0.5% (5 of 997) for men and 0.1% (1 of 771) for women.

When prostitutes and their customers were tested in Amsterdam in 1991, three (from Ghana, Nigeria, and the Dominican Republic) of 199 prostitutes were HIV-positive. One customer who admitted to homosexual contacts was HIV-positive.

Blood-donor volunteers in any HIV risk group are asked not to donate. In 1985, 15 donors were found to be HIV-positive; in 1990, the new discouragement policy resulted in only five infected donors. This procedure does not totally exclude HIV transmission by blood transfusion, because of latency between infection and seropositivity. Blood products for hemophiliacs have been heat-treated since 1985, so this is no longer a risk group. Early in the epidemic, about 13% of hemophiliacs were infected.

### Effectiveness of Prevention Education Programs

In a sample of 1,013 homosexual men in Amsterdam followed since 1984, an extensive change in behavior has been documented in two directions: a decrease in the number of sex partners and a lower prevalence of anogenital contact. These behavior changes resulted in a decline in seroconversions to almost zero in 1987. However, since the end of 1989, there is an increase in the incidence of HIV infection in the same cohort. Interviews with this group revealed that higher percentages of both seropositives and seronegatives had had anogenital sex without protection, especially in casual sexual relations.

In recent years, AIDS health promotion has changed its message from "avoid anal sex" to "avoid unprotected anal sex." The availability of special condoms for anal intercourse has been a major factor in this development. Recently, condom efficacy was studied among cohort members. Condom failures (torn, slipped) were seen more often when vaginal condoms were used or when no lubricants, or oil-based lubricants, were used. Personal efficacy prevents failure by slipping, but not by tearing the condom. In-depth interviews with men who seroconverted indicate the significant role of the use of alcohol and other drugs, as well as the divergent individual background of each seroconverter. Personality factors, like coping styles and health locus of control, seemed to be almost completely unrelated to behavioral change. Preceding sexual behavior seems to be the best predictor of actual behavior.

In a quasi-longitudinal telephone survey, changes in beliefs, attitudes, and behaviors related to AIDS were followed from early 1987 onwards. Knowledge regarding the use of condoms to prevent HIV transmission increased to a level that can be considered sufficient by the end of the 1980s. The general population seems to opt for monogamy and condom use as preventive measures. The use of condoms rose, especially among teenagers and persons in nonsteady relation-

ships. These observations were confirmed by condom sales figures and STD incidence. However, there seems to remain a discrepancy between the inclination to use condoms and the actual use.

In the 1989 study, sexual behavior of 1,000 respondents is described in the context of HIV transmission as it relates to potential risk, awareness, knowledge, and endorsement of misconceptions on transmission. Based on sexual behavior, 12% should be considered to have taken at least some risk in the year preceding the interview. Of these 124 subjects, 58% completely ruled out the chance that they might have been infected. In general, the level of knowledge is rather high. The knowledge of the subjects who have been at risk ironically is slightly greater than average. This might imply that more intensive prevention strategies should be directed at subgroups who are relatively more at risk.

In the 1989 teen study, sexual mores are found not to be changed by AIDS. To avoid HIV infection, teens prefer postponing sex until one has found the right partner or using condoms during intercourse. In general, however, in fact, youngsters do not postpone their first sexual contact. Only a few of those who advise the postponing of sex have had unsafe sexual contacts. Half of those recommending the use of condoms do not stick to their own advice. Condoms are used especially in the beginning of affairs; but later on, many couples switch to oral contraceptives to avoid pregnancy. Moreover, a questionnaire survey among schoolchildren revealed that intentions of consistent condom use for HIV prevention decreases with the amount of actual intercourse experience. They seem to ignore the fact that their relationship career will most likely be characterized by serial monogamy. This research suggests more attention to efficacy aspects of condom use: buying them, raising the topic with a new partner, and so on.

Based on a theory of sexual networks, 60% of the 18- to 19-year-olds seem to run no risk whatsoever of getting infected with HIV. This network analysis research is a promising new branch of sociosexual study. Other new approaches are studies on negotiations between male and female prostitutes and their customers to find out to what extent they could take health-promoting measures.

### Treatment, Prevention Programs, and Government Policies

Since the onset of the AIDS epidemic, an elaborate system of care and prevention for homosexual men has been developed in the Netherlands. The gay community took the initiative for the first nationwide AIDS education campaign (1983) aimed mainly at homosexual and bisexual men. Also in 1983, an ambulatory venereal disease and AIDS clinic for homosexual men was started in Amsterdam, the Supplementary Services Foundation (StAD), supplementing regular services.

In 1984, as the AIDS epidemic spread among gay men, the StAD started a small-scale primary prevention course for gay men aimed at altering sexual habits. This was modeled after an American example and was successful throughout the country. The foundation still organizes numerous prevention activities aimed at gay men, such as safe-sex workshops, video workshops, shows in gay bars, and activities in gay cruising areas (parks, public toilets). Postgraduate education programs and material on AIDS have been produced by StAD and a number of Amsterdam physicians who have many AIDS patients. Doctors employed by the StAD support some of the doctors in Amsterdam with the heaviest burden of AIDS patients by taking over office hours and home visits.

Another important gay healthcare institute is the Schorer Foundation. In the AIDS field, the foundation has offered psychosocial care for gay men and their friends and families since 1984. It also initiated, and now coordinates, the "buddy" homecare projects all over the country. This project offers AIDS patients free volunteer support at home. The foundation also produces education programs and training courses for workers in psychosocial healthcare.

Although these gay organizations are important care providers, most gay men with AIDS make use of general health institutions, such as general practitioners, district nurses, hospitals, psychiatrists, and social workers. Therefore, gay (and other) lifestyle elements need to be included in postgraduate education for all caregivers to prevent communication problems. After all, HIV has no precedent as an extremely serious health and culture problem in the gay community.

The total number of women infected is smaller, but the progression is faster in women. Attention to women and AIDS seems to be restricted to their role as infectors (prostitutes, IV users, and pregnant women). In December 1990, on World AIDS Day, which was dedicated to women, it was observed that women should be the target for more and better campaigns for the prevention of AIDS, and that care for women should be improved. For some years, the Rutgers Foundation has provided short-term support and education groups for HIV-infected women.

Care for HIV-positive IV-drug users is often complicated by aggravated addiction behavior, which often makes these patients difficult to deal and make appointments with. Municipal health centers and general practitioners in the big cities, and local clinics for the addicted, monitor a substantial percentage of IV-drug users. This includes health education, education on HIV prevention, assessment of physical condition, and often also the prescription of methadone, a heroin substitute. A needle/syringe exchange program is an important part of prevention. Education for hemophiliacs and support for those infected have been helped by the very active national hemophilia patient association.

Treatment for HIV is evaluated nationally. Recently, a national consensus on early Zidovudine (AZT) treatment was published. In the early years, testing was thought to be of limited value because no health gain was to be expected, and for preventive measures, the individual's serostatus was supposed to be of no importance: Safe sex should be practiced by seronegatives as well as seropositives. Today, early detection is expected to be effective, even if it does not change the patient's sexual habits. Testing is always on a voluntary basis, and if the patient wants to be tested anonymously, this is always possible.

A policy decision currently under discussion is the desirability of contact tracing and notification in heterosexually infected cases of HIV, as is common practice for gonorrhea and syphilis. Because of low heterosexual prevalence, this approach might be highly cost effective.

[*Update 2002*: UNAIDS Epidemiological Assessment: HIV testing is systematic for blood donors and for some specific insurance applicants. A screening program in pregnant women was first conducted in a few hospitals and then extended to all hospitals in Amsterdam and to 16 of the 21 midwifery practices in the area (estimated coverage of 70% to 75%). From 1992, screening was restricted to high-risk hospitals. Systematic screening of pregnant women has been under discussion. There is no national HIV case-reporting system.

["Unlinked anonymous testing-consent" surveys have been conducted among women seeking abortions in Amsterdam, among injection drug users from the street or treatment centers in several cities, and nationally among readers of the popular gay magazines. Since 1991, repeated surveys

have been done in STD patients in Amsterdam. Among pregnant women, several cases of HIV-2 have been found, especially in women attending abortion clinics (about 40% of all HIV infections). Overall, the HIV prevalence (HIV-1 or HIV-2) was around 0.1% and remained unchanged between 1989 and 1991. Prevalence varied between 0.2% to 0.4% in women attending hospitals considered at high risk, and about 10 times higher in women seeking abortions (except in 1993). The HIV prevalence in injection drug users was as high as 37% in Amsterdam, while much lower in other cities (11% in Rotterdam, 5% in Utrecht, 9% in the southern regions (Maastricht), and 2% in Arnhem (east region). It remained relatively constant over time. A cohort study on 675 initially seronegative injection drug users showed a decrease in incidence from 8.9 per 100 person-years in 1986 to 2 to 3.6 per 100 in 1991-1995. HIV prevalence among gay magazine readers was in 1991 13% in Amsterdam, 7% in the rest of urban areas, and 3% outside urban areas. In homosexuals attending HIV-testing sites in Arnhem (considered as outside major urban areas), prevalence was 8% and remained constant over time. In STD clinics of Amsterdam, prevalence in homosexuals reached 21% in 1991 and 17% in 1992. A cohort study on 770 initially seronegative homosexuals showed a decrease in incidence from 7.2 per 100 person-years in 1985 to 1 per 100 in 1995. HIV prevalence in non-injection-drug-using prostitutes was around 2% in 1991. Comparison of prevalence over time needs to be looked at according to the city or area referred to by the data. Indeed, prevalence varies considerably from one area or city to another. Among pregnant women, HIV prevalence refers to HIV-1 or HIV-2 infections, while it only refers to HIV-1 in other populations.

[The estimated number of adults and children living with HIV/AIDS on January 1, 2002, were:

| | | |
|---|---|---|
| Adults ages 15-49: | 17,000 | (rate: 0.2%) |
| Women ages 15-49: | 3,300 | |
| Children ages 0-15: | 160 | |

[An estimated 110 adults and children died of AIDS during 2001.

[No estimate is available for the number of Dutch children who had lost one or both parents to AIDS and were under age 15 at the end of 2001. (*End of update by the Editors*)]

## 11. Sexual Dysfunctions, Counseling, and Therapies

### A. General Views

Dutch clinical sexological practice follows the international framework of diagnosis and the *DSM-III-R*, with some hesitance about the normative aspects of such procedures. Feminism and emancipatory trends have had an enormous impact on Dutch sexology. Health Care for Women projects have been substantially financed by the government with sexuality a major area of concern. In recent years, most of these projects have been integrated, sometimes unwillingly, into the general mental healthcare institutions. Health Care for Women is situated methodologically between self-help and professionalism. Group approaches are highly valued and the group-therapy approach is used more often than for men.

Another concern inherited from Health Care for Women is the power issue in heterosexuality. Since the early 1970s, there has been a passionate plea for better help for sexual-violence victims, stimulated by independent nonprofessional self-help organizations. Dutch sexologists have responded by initiating discussion on professional standards and ethical codes on therapist-client sexual contact. Current interests include: sexual abuse of the mentally and physically handicapped, and introduction of sexological diagnostic and treatment approaches as an adjunct to personality-oriented diagnosis.

*Desire problems*: There is a modest amount of literature on desire discrepancies. The interactional aspect, the incapacity for intimacy, has gained most attention, along with unrealistic expectations and the balance of power. There is no literature available comparing male higher-libido with female higher-libido.

*Arousal problems*: The medical-sexological approach used with many cases of male erectile dysfunction has resulted in numerous articles but no relevant quantitative data. While clinical criteria are set by the Dutch Society for Impotence Research, concern is growing about overuse of methods prompted by cost and patient acceptance. Psychophysiological methods and pharmacoDuplex scanning are the most widely used methods; neurourophysiological, hormonal, and invasive methods are restricted to specific indications. It is widely recognized today that psychological inhibition can prevent the reaction on intracavernous vasoactive drugs, and that an erotic atmosphere enhances the reaction. Regarding treatment, a preliminary, cautious conclusion might be: Dutch men seem to be rather reluctant to accept prosthesis as a solution for erectile failure; intracavernous injections are acceptable for a larger group with a high discontinuation rate; vacuum devices are used, but here, too, discontinuation is high.

There is no specific literature on arousal dysfunction in women, except for a study on diabetes.

*Orgasm problems*: In 1977, the Utrecht psychology group enriched sexological theory by contrasting the "interaction phase" with the "solo phase" and emphasizing surrendering to one's own feelings as essential during orgastic release. Lonnie Barbach's group treatment is widely used for primary female anorgasmia, but there are no outcome studies. For female secondary and/or situational orgasm difficulties, sex therapists tend to prefer couple therapy. After analyzing 1,112 respondent questionnaires, De Bruijn (1982) tried to describe backgrounds of female anorgasmia. Among her conclusions: To some women, orgasm is simply not important in lovemaking; those regularly having orgasms during partner interaction tend to use techniques similar to their self-pleasuring techniques; in interaction, some women simply do not get stimulation long enough to attain orgasm; and orgasm by following the male's movements in intercourse is the only stimulation technique in which orgasm is linked to feelings of love and intimacy. Her findings, published in a bestseller, have been widely acknowledged by both professionals and the general public. Ironically, the 1939 survey of NVSH members reported female respondents attributing differences in satisfaction found in men and women to the short duration of intercourse. *Plus ça change, plus c'est la même chose.*

Inhibited and premature male orgasms have received less attention. Premature ejaculation is common and treated by standard modalities, but no treatment results are published.

*Coitus problems and genital phobias*: Vaginismus, dyspareunia, unconsummated marriage, and phobic avoidance of vaginal penetration are subjects of intense interest, characterized by an increasing tolerance of the symptom's hidden meaning. As early as 1917, Treub concluded that fear is the main cause, and refrained from incision of the perivaginal muscles; in the 1960s, Musaph stressed the usefulness of psychoanalytical interpretations. During the 1979 World Congress of Sexology in Mexico City, Dutch women sexologists vented their annoyance with sexology's neglect of sex-role bias. Cohen-Kettenis criticized medical and behavioral sexologists for having only one goal in the treatment for vaginismus: consummation. Bezemer was the first to report on group treatment for women suffering for vaginismus, together with other primary dysfunctions in one group. Moch (1987) broke the taboo on reporting relapse after successful treatment for vaginismus. Drenth (1988) pointed out that for some couples, vaginismus is a fertility problem and can be treated as such by artificial insemination. In 1989, Drenth also identified genital fears, phobias, and obsessions as the male counterpart of vaginismus, pointing out that phobic avoidance of genital play can result in pseudo-phymosis. In 1989, the Dutch Society for Sexology organized a symposium on "Vaginismus and Dyspareunia: The Dutch View."

## B. Availability of Diagnosis and Treatment

Historically, treatment for sexual problems in the Netherlands began in the Neo-Malthusian League. In the League's counseling centers, psychoanalytic treatment of sexual problems was strongly influenced by Van Emde Boas and Musaph, pioneers in the Sexual Reform movement, until the 1970s. In 1969, when the Rutgers Foundation separated from the Dutch Society for Sexual Reform (the League's postwar successor), treatment of sexual problems was very much still part of its activities. As demand increased, the foundation reorganized its staff in multidisciplinary teams.

Dutch gynecologists also played a major role, led by the internationally renowned Theodor van der Velde. His book, *The Perfect Marriage* (1925), was the first such work to find a large general public. Fertility studies led to the formation of the Society for Psychosomatic Obstetrics and Gynecology in 1979. All academic hospitals now have a sexological outpatient department. Unfortunately, these clinics are much too small, except for Amsterdam and Leiden. Since psychiatry departments pay little attention to sexual problems, a Society for Impotence Research (NVIO) was founded in 1986.

The work of Masters and Johnson opened the sexological territory for social scientists. Between 1975 and 1986, Utrecht trained psychology students in the practical applications of group and couple sex therapy. Since then, some psychologists and social workers in private practice provide treatment for couples with sexual problems. The sexological knowledge of helping professionals has certainly expanded in recent years. However, specialized sexological help is sometimes hard to find for many patients. The total number of sexologists is small and concentrated in certain areas. Health insurance will pay for sexological help if a physician refers. Clients almost always have to pay their own sliding-scale bills for treatment by psychologists and social workers in private practice and by Rutgers Foundation sexologists.

## C. Therapist Training and Certification

Sexology is not a regulated profession in Holland, so full-time sexologists are rare, and reliable sexologists and therapists will always have other basic training in medicine, psychology, psychiatry, or social work, perhaps with some postdoctoral education in sexology. Sexological education in Holland lacks cohesion and formal recognition. A very small number of professionals has been educated in the Flemish University of Leuven Sexology Department, where one can earn a doctorate in sexology.

Recently, the Dutch Society for Sexology (NVVS) started to regulate sexological training. Since 1992, an introductory course in sexology is provided by the NVVS and Erasmus University Rotterdam. Specialized curricula for medical-sexological workers, educators, prevention workers, and researchers will follow. An applications course for psychopathic rapists will be the next step in regulating sexological training. Recently, the Amsterdam Psychotherapy Training Institute included sexology in behavioral psychotherapy training. A register of trained members and establishment of set standards for the education of professional sexologists are short-term goals for NVVS.

## 12. Sex Research and Advanced Professional Education

### A. Sexological Research

The Dutch Institute for Socio-Sexual Research (NISSO) has been the center of surveys on sexual behavior, sometimes in collaboration with other organizations. Considerable research has been done on contraception, abortion, sex and disabilities/illness, homosexuality in the armed forces, and prostitution. Other areas being explored are: the (in)adequacy of sexual help by different groups of helping professionals; an interview study on respondents of earlier surveys who reported exceptionally positive sex lives; child sexual development; forensic sexology; and construction of sexologically relevant psychometric scales.

The multidisciplinary nature of Dutch sexology is illustrated by the diverse backgrounds of the professors holding the six chairs dedicated to sexology in Dutch universities: endocrinology (Gooren, Amsterdam), psychiatry (Hengeveld, Utrecht), medicine (Van Dijk, Amsterdam), psychology (Frenken, Leiden), psychology (Cohen-Kettenis, Utrecht) and physiology/biology (Slob, Rotterdam).

The Psychology Department at Utrecht University has examined the therapeutic effect of different behavioristic treatment methods for sexual dysfunctions in individuals with different sexual orientations. The Utrecht University Gay and Lesbian Studies group has ongoing studies in: historical research on lesbian lives; various subjects on discrimination and homosexuality-related violence; homosexuality and education; and homosexuality in healthcare. The Amsterdam Psychology Department initiated Dutch psychophysiological research, including the effects of sexual imagery on sexual arousal, women's reactions to male- and female-made pornography, the effect of mood induction on subsequent visual stimulation, and the effect of subliminal visual stimuli. In Rotterdam, psychophysiological research includes study of the effects and interaction of visual and vibrotactile penile stimulation; the effect of papaverin-induced tumescence on perceptual threshold of penile stimulation in sexually functional and dysfunctional men, and the effect of menstrual phase on sexual arousability in women. In Groningen, research has included vaginal sensitivity in nonerotic conditions. Almost all academic urology departments are in some way active in research on erectile failure.

Animal sexology, centered in the Utrecht Department of Comparative Physiology, is an important aspect of Dutch sexology. Research at Utrecht and Rotterdam has focused on mating strategies in natural and semi-natural conditions: wolves, plains zebras, chimpanzees, orangutans and long-tailed macaques, savanna baboons, and stump-tailed macaques. The Rotterdam and Amsterdam groups have studied female initiative and hormonal influences on proceptivity and receptivity in rats, reward and aversive components in female sexual experience (including homosexual versus heterosexual preference conditions), hormone-dependency of self-stimulation behavior in the medial preoptic area; brain and behavior gender differentiation, and

the determination of the different influences of various steroids. The sexually dimorphic nucleus of the preoptic area is also being researched.

### B. Postgraduate and Advanced Programs

Treatment of human sexuality in medical, psychological, and social work curricula is subject to considerable variation, with the personal interest of faculty determining the impetus sexuality will have in the programs. Precise requirements and interdisciplinary training are defined in psychiatry and gynecology. There are no university sexology programs in other areas such as education, prevention, or research. In 1992, the Dutch Society for Sexology (NVVS) started a postgraduate training program (see Section 12C, Therapist Training and Certification, above).

*Journals*

*Tijdschrift voor Seksuologie* (*Journal of Sexology*). Faculty of Medicine, Erasmus University, P. O. Box 1738, 3000 DR Rotterdam, The Netherlands.

*SOA Bulletin* (*Journal of STD*). P. O. Box 19061, 3501 DB Utrecht, The Netherlands.

*Sekstant* (*Journal of the Dutch Society for Sexual Reform* [NVSH]). P. O. Box 64, 2501 CB Den Haag, The Netherlands.

*Sexuality in Society*. International newsletter of the NISSO. NISSO, da Costakade 45, 3521 VS Utrecht, The Netherlands.

*Organizations*

A. de Graaf Foundation. (Prostitution), Westermarkt 4, 1016 DK Amsterdam.

Interfacultaire Werkgroep Homostudies (Department of Gay and Lesbian Studies), Utrecht University, Heidelberglaan 1, 3584 CS Utrecht, The Netherlands.

Dutch Centre for Health Promotion & Health Education, P. O. Box 5104, 3502 JC Utrecht, The Netherlands. Tel.: 31-70/35-56847; Fax: 31-70/35-59901.

Jhr A. Schorer Foundation. (Consultation bureau for homosexuality), Nieuwendijk 17, 1017 LZ Amsterdam, The Netherlands.

NISSO (Netherlands Institute for Social Sexological Research), da Costakade 45, 3521 VS Utrecht, The Netherlands.

NVIO (Dutch Society for Impotence Research), Department of Psychology, University of Amsterdam, Weesperplein 8, 1018 XA Amsterdam, The Netherlands.

NVVS (Dutch Society for Sexology), Zijdeweg 17, 2811 PC Reeuwijk, The Netherlands.

Rutgers Foundation (Contraception information and sexuality education), Groothertoginnelaan 201, 2517 ES Den Haag, The Netherlands.

Rutgers Stiching, Postbus 17430, Croot Hertoginnelaan 201, 2502 CKs Gravenhage, The Netherlands. Tel.: 31-70/363-1750; Fax: 31-70/356-1049.

Stimezo (National organization for induced abortion), Pieterstraat 11, 3512 JT Utrecht, The Netherlands.

## References and Suggested Readings

*Note*: The Special Issue of *Tijdschrift voor Seksuologie* issued for the Tenth World Congress for Sexology contains an exhaustive list of literature.

Beets, G., et al. 1991. *Population and family in the low countries 1991*. Amsterdam/Lisse.

Brongersma, E. 1988, 1990. *Loving boys, 1 & 2*. Elmhurst, NY: Global Academic Publishers.

CIA. 2002 (January). *The world factbook 2002*. Washington, DC: Central Intelligence Agency. Available: http://www.cia.gov/cia/publications/factbook/index.html.

Cohen-Kettenis, P. T., & Th. G. M. Sandfort. 1991. Sexual behavior of young children: Observations of 665 parents. Paper presented at the Tenth World Congress for Sexology, 1991, Amsterdam.

Deenen, A. A. V. M. 1991. *Intimacy and sexuality in gay male relationships* (Dissertation). Utrecht.

Draijer, P. J. 1990. *Seksuele traumatisering in de jeugd. Lange termijn gevolgen van seksueel misbruik van meisjes door verwanten.* Amsterdam: SUA.

Gianotten, W. L. 1988. Sexology in the Netherlands: The past and the present. *Nordisk Sexologi, 6*:202-209.

Glaser & Straus. 1980. Cited in C. Straver, *Jong zijn en contact zoeken* [*Being young and seeking contacts*]. Zeist: Nisso.

Heslinga, K., A. Verkuil, & A. M. C. M. Schellen. 1973. *Wij zijn niet van steen* [*Not made of stone: Sexuality of the handicapped people*). Leiden: Noordhoff stafleu.

Ketting, E. 1990. *Contraception in western Europe.* Carnforth: Parthenon.

Ketting, E., & K. Soesbeek, eds. 1992. *Homoseksualiteit en krijgsmacht.* Delft: Eburon.

Kooy, G. A. 1975. *Seksualiteit, huwelijk en gezin in Nederland.* Deventer: Van Loghum Slaterus.

Kooy, G. A. 1976. *Jongeren en seksualiteit.* Deventer: Van Loghum Slaterus.

Kooy, G. A. 1983. *Sex in Nederland.* Utrecht/Antwerpen: Spectrum.

Kuiper, A. J. 1991. *Transseksualiteit. Evaluatie van de geslachtsaanpassende behandeling.* Utrecht: Elinkwijk.

Lamur, H., et al. 1990. *Caraibische vrouwen en anticonceptie.* Delft: Eburon.

Mooij, A. 1991. De ziektes van de revolutie. In: G. Hekma, et al., eds., *Het verlies van de onschuld.* Groningen: Wolters-Noordhoff.

Nabrink, G. 1978. *Seksuele hervorming in Nederland.* Nijmegen: SUN.

Noordhoff, J. D. et al. 1969. *Sex in Nederland.* Utrecht/Antwerpen: Spectrum.

Rademakers, J. 1992. *Abortus in Nederland 1989-1990.* Utrecht: Stimezo.

Sandfort, Th. G. M. 1987. Pedophilia and the gay movement. *Journal of Homosexuality, 13*:89-111.

Sandfort, Th. G. M. 1991. The argument for adult-child contact. A critical appraisal and new data. In: O'Donohue & Geer, eds., *The sexual abuse of children: Theory, research and therapy.* Hillsdale, NJ: Lawrence Erlbaum Associates.

Sandfort, Th. G. M., & G. van Zessen 1991. *Seks en AIDS in Nederland.* Den Haag: SDU.

Schraag, J. A. 1989. Sexual education in schools: Concepts and possibilities. *International Journal of Adolescent Medicine and Health, 3&4*:239-250.

Schreurs, K. 1990. *Vrouwen in lesbische relaties. Verbondenheid, autonomie, en seksualiteit.* Utrecht: Publikatiereeks Homostudies.

Simon & Gagnon. 1980. Cited in C. Straver, *Jong zijn en contact zoeken* [*Being young and seeking contacts*]. Zeist: Nisso.

Slijper, F. M. E. 1992. Evaluation of psychosexual development of young women with congenital adrenal hyperplasia: A pilot study. *Journal of Sex Education and Therapy, 18*: 200-207.

Straver et al. 1986. Stepwise interaction career: First elaborated in J. Rademakers and C. Straver, *Van fascinatie naar relatie* [*From fascination to relation*]. Zeist: Nisso.

UNAIDS. 2002. *Epidemiological fact sheets by country.* Geneva, Switzerland: Joint United Nations Programme on HIV/AIDS (UNAIDS/WHO). Available: http://www.unaids.org/hivaidsinfo/statistics/fact_sheets/index_en.htm.

van Delft, M., & E. Ketting 1992. *Anticonceptiege-bruik in Nederland.* Houten: Bohn Stafleu van Loghum.

van der Vliet, R. 1990. De opkomst van het seksuele moratorium [*The rise of the sexual moratorium*]. In: G. Hekma & B. van Stolk, eds., *Het verlies van de onschuld* [*The Loss of Innocence*]. Groningen: Wolters-Noordhoff.

Verschoor, A. M. 1990. *Een dubbel bestaan: Travestieten en hun omgeving.* Amsterdam/Lisse: Swets en Zeitlinger.

Vogels, T., & R. van der Vliet. 1990. *Jeugd en seks.* Den Haag: SDU.

# Nigeria
## (The Federal Republic of Nigeria)

Uwem Edimo Esiet, M.B., B.S., M.P.H., M.I.L.D.,*
chapter coordinator, with
Christine Olunfinke Adebajo, Ph.D., R.N., H.D.H.A.,
Mairo Victoria Bello, Rakiya Booth, M.B.B.S.,
F.W.A.C.P., Imo I. Esiet, B.Sc, LL.B., B.L., Nike Esiet,
B.Sc., M.P.H. (Harvard), Foyin Oyebola, B.Sc., M.A.,
and Bilkisu Yusuf, B.Sc., M.A., M.N.I.
*Updates by Beldina Opiyo-Omolo, B.Sc.*

## Contents

## *Demographics and a Brief Historical Perspective*
### ROBERT T. FRANCOEUR**

### A. Demographics

Nigeria is located on the southern coast of the horn of northwest Africa. Its 356,669 square miles (923,768 km²) makes it about twice the size of the state of California. Benin lies to Nigeria's west, Niger to the north, Chad and Cameroon to the east, and the Gulf of Guinea to the south. Geographically, the country is divided into four east-to-west regions: In the south is a coastal mangrove swamp 10 to 60 miles (16 to 96 km) wide; in the north is a semi-desert. In between are a tropical rainforest 50 to 100 miles (80 to 160 km) wide and a plateau of savanna and open woodland. Nigeria is currently made up of 30 states plus the Federal Capital Territory of Abuja; 16 of the 30 states are situated in

(CIA 2002)

the northern Muslim-dominated part of the country and the other 14 in the predominantly Christian south. The climate varies from equatorial in the south to tropical in the center and north. The Niger River enters the country in the northwest and flows south through tropical rainforests and swamps to its delta in the Gulf of Guinea.

Like all African nations, Nigeria's boundaries are the capricious result of European and other colonial conquests and power struggles that ignored ancient tribal and ethnic distributions. To understand sexual attitudes, customs, and behavior in Nigeria, one must be aware of the diversity of tribal, ethnic, and religious traditions among its 130 million people.

In July 2002, Nigeria had an estimated population of 130 million. Demographers expect the population to double by the year 2025, to 238.5 million. These estimates explicitly take into account the effects of excess mortality because of AIDS. This can result in lower life expectancy, higher infant mortality and death rates, lower population and growth rates, and changes in the distribution of population by age and sex than would otherwise be expected. (All data are from *The World Factbook 2002* (CIA 2002) unless otherwise stated.)

**Age Distribution and Sex Ratios**: *0-14 years*: 43.6% with 1.01 male(s) per female (sex ratio); *15-64 years*: 53.6% with 1.04 male(s) per female; *65 years and over*:

*Communications*: Dr. Uwem Edimo Esiet, Action Health, Inc., P.O. Box 803, Yaba Post Office, Lagos, Nigeria; ahi@linkserve .com.ng. Beldina Opiyo-Omolo, B.Sc., Department of Health, East Stroudsburg University of Pennsylvania, East Stroudsburg, PA 18301 USA; bopiyo@yahoo.com.

**Editor's Note*: This chapter presented an unusual editorial challenge, in that on most issues, two or more contributors chose to provide complementary insights and information. This is particularly valuable because the contributors approached the topic from different gender, professional, religious, and ethnic (tribal) backgrounds that clearly enrich the views and interpretations presented. In Section 8A, Significant Unconventional Sexual Behaviors, Coercive Sex, Christine Olufunke Adebajo, Deputy General Secretary of the National Association of Nigerian Nurses and Midwives, and Imo I. Esiet, a member of the Nigerian Bar Association, present not only their own respective views as a Nigerian woman and man, but also the two complementary views of two women's rights advocates, one

a healthcare professional and the other a lawyer. To identify the contributors of these varied views, their name or names are given at the beginning of a section or in brackets [name] at the end of individual paragraphs.

This rich diversity of perspectives on one of Africa's major nations is also apparent in the unusual comparisons of tribal and regional differences on sexuality education, menstruation, sexual intercourse, conception and pregnancy, menopause, homosexuality, and male and female circumcision presented in this chapter. The information in these comparisons is based on the responses of local healthcare professionals who met in Lagos in January 1999 under the aegis of Action Health, Inc, headed by the main author of this chapter, Uwem Edimo Esiet, with Nigerian government leaders, nongovernmental organizations (NGOs), and international United Nations agencies. The comments are from many healthcare professionals and social workers based on their field observations and experiences with clients in their own regions (Francoeur, Esiet, & Esiet 2000).

2.8% with 1 male(s) per female; *Total population sex ratio*: 1.02 male(s) to 1 female

**Life Expectancy at Birth**: *Total Population*: 50.59 years; *male*: 50.58 years; *female*: 50.6 years. By 2010, experts expect that the HIV/AIDS epidemic will reduce life expectancy in Nigeria to age 47 compared with 61 before the arrival of AIDS (Garrett 2002).

**Urban/Rural Distribution**: 40% to 60%. By the year 2001, half of Nigeria's youth were expected to live in cities, searching for better living and job opportunities.

**Ethnic Distribution**: Nigeria has over 250 different and distinct ethnic groups: 20% Hausa; 20% are Yoruba; 17% Ibo; and 9% Fulani; while the remaining one third belong to other ethnic minorities.

**Religious Distribution**: 50% Muslim and living mostly in the north; 40% Christian and living mostly in the south; 10% follow indigenous beliefs.

**Birth Rate**: 39.22 births per 1,000 population

**Death Rate**: 14.1 per 1,000 population

**Infant Mortality Rate**: 72.49 deaths per 1,000 live births

**Net Migration Rate**: 0.27 migrant(s) per 1,000 population

**Total Fertility Rate**: 5.49 children born per woman

**Population Growth Rate**: 2.54%

**HIV/AIDS** (1999 est.): *Adult prevalence*: 5.06%; *Persons living with HIV/AIDS*: 2.7 million; *Deaths*: 250,000. (For additional details from www.UNAIDS.org, see end of Section 10B.)

**Literacy Rate** (*defined as those age 15 and over who can read and write*): 57.1% (*male*: 67.3%, *female*: 47.3%) (1995 est.); education is free and compulsory between ages 6 and 15, with about 42% of the youth attending elementary school

**Per Capita Gross Domestic Product** (*purchasing power parity*): $840 (2001 est.); *Inflation*: 14.9%; *Unemployment*: 28% (1992 est.); *Living below the poverty line*: 45% (2000 est.)

## B. A Brief Historical Perspective

Between 500 and 200 B.C.E., the Nok culture, in what is today's Nigeria, was one of the richest and most advanced ancient civilizations in West Africa.

Around 1000 C.E., the Muslim Kanem civilization expanded into northern Nigeria. By the 14th century, the amalgamated kingdom of Kanem-Bornu took northern Nigeria as its political center, dominating the Sahel and developing trade routes that stretched throughout northern Africa and as far as Europe and the Middle East. During the 15th and 16th centuries, the Hausa Songhai empire rose to power. The Hausa Songhai were overthrown by the Fulani Muslim leader, Uthman Dan Fodio, who created the Sokoto caliphate.

At the same time that the Muslim Kanem civilization expanded into northern Nigeria, around 1000 C.E., southern Nigeria was dominated by the Yoruba, whose Oyo kingdom was centered at Ife. The Oyo kingdom gave rise to the Benin civilization, which flourished from the 15th to the 18th centuries. The Benin culture is famous for its brass, bronze, and ivory sculpture.

The Portuguese established trading stations on the Benin coast in the 15th century. Initially, the contact and trade relations were cordial, and Benin became well known in Europe as a powerful and advanced kingdom. However, with the rise of the slave trade, which began with the cooperation of the Benin kings who brought slaves from the interior, relations became hostile, and Benin declined under European pressure. The Dutch, British, and other Europeans competed strenuously with Portugal for control of the slave trade. Britain seized the port of Lagos in 1861 during a campaign against the slave trade, and gradually extended its control inland with the exploration of the Niger River until about 1900. By the end of the 19th century, because Britain had suppressed the slave trade, they transported the slaves they captured aboard European ships to Freetown in Sierra Leone.

In 1861, Nigeria became a British colony. Despite native resistance, the colony was expanded in 1906 to include territory east of the Niger River, which was called the Protectorate of Southern Nigeria. The two areas were administratively joined in 1914.

During the 1920s, Britain began to respond to Nigerian demands for local self-rule. In 1946, the colony was divided into three regions, each with an advisory assembly. In 1954, the colony was reorganized as the Nigerian Federation, and the regional assembles were given more authority. Nigeria became independent on October 1, 1960, and a republic on October 1, 1963. Attempts to partition the country along tribal lines for administrative purposes provoked controversy, and charges of corruption and fraud in elections held in 1964 and 1965 led to violence and rioting. In January 1966, civil war broke out when Ibo army officers overthrew the central government and several of the regional governments. Prime Minister Balewa was killed, along with many other political leaders in the northern and western parts of the country, and the Ibo forces took control of the government

The new government abolished the country's federal structure and set up a strong central government dominated by the Ibo. Anti-Ibo riots broke out in the north, and many Ibos were massacred. In July 1966, the Ibo leader was assassinated by a group of northern Yoroban army officers, who formed a new military government. The people in the eastern region refused to acknowledge the new government. In 1967, they seceded, proclaiming the eastern region as the Republic of Biafra. This plunged the country into a devastating civil war that left over a million dead, including many Biafrans (Ibos), who died of starvation despite international relief efforts. The war ended in 1970, and within a few years, the Ibos were reintegrated into national life.

A civilian government returned to power in 1979 after 13 years of military rule. Four years later, a military coup ousted the democratically elected government, and has remained in power ever since under various leaders. Revenues from the export of crude oil have made possible a massive economic development program, but agriculture has lagged.

## 1. Basic Sexological Premises

### A/B. Gender Roles and the Sociolegal Status of Nigerian Females with Implications for the Male

IMO I. ESIET

*Issues of Nigerian Constitutional Law*

The social and legal status of women has, over the ages, been a cause for grave concern in every culture and clime. In some areas, this concern has passed the stage of sympathy and has entered an era of aggressive feminism (Oputa 1989, 1). In Nigeria, as in other countries, the time has come to recognize that denial of rights solely because one is a woman is a human rights violation. Practices that expose women to degradation, indignity, and oppression on account of their sex need to be independently identified, condemned, compensated, and, preferably, prevented (Cook 1994, 228).

A wide range of evidence can be cited for a constructive trend in modern legislation on women's rights that are relevant to Africa and to Nigeria. Examples of this trend include the Convention on the Elimination of All Forms of Discrimination Against Women, the International Covenant on Economic, Social, and Cultural Rights, the 1981 African Charter on Human and Peoples' Rights (which endorsed the United Nations Declaration on Human Rights and the Human Rights Covenant), and the 1979 Constitution of the Federal Republic of Nigeria. Although the clear trend is to establish women's equality with men before the law, the battle against sex-based discrimination and for equality of opportunity, equal pay for work, equal privileges, and equal access to political, social, and religious power is still raging with unabated fury in Nigeria (Oputa 1989, 4).

According to Rebecca J. Cook, the term

discrimination against women shall mean any distinction, exclusion or restriction made on the basis of sex which has the effect or purpose of impairing or nullifying the recognition, enjoyment or exercise by women, irrespective of their marital status, on a basis of equality of men and women, of human rights and fundamental freedom in the political, economic, social, cultural, civil or any other field. (Cook 1994, 235)

The constitutions of most African countries today affirm the right to nondiscrimination on the basis of sex. Other rules of law and legislation may, however, discriminate against women in certain instances. Even where provisions of law are not overtly discriminatory, their application to women may yield discriminatory results, because of women's economic and social positions in society (Ilumoka 1994, 341). In this section, we examine the constitutional provisions for and cultural rights of Nigerian women. (Legal provisions related to marriage, sexual coercion, and prostitution in Nigeria are dealt with in Sections 5C, Interpersonal Heterosexual Behaviors, Adults, and 8A and B, Significant Unconventional Sexual Behaviors, Coercive Sex and Prostitution.)

The Constitution of the Federal Republic of Nigeria (1999) succinctly highlights the fundamental human rights to which all persons are entitled. These are the usual civil and political rights contained in most modern constitutions (Ilumoka 1994, 314). Chapter 4, section 39, of the Nigerian Constitution provides that:

1. A citizen of Nigeria of a particular community, ethnic group, place of origin, sex, religion, or political opinion shall not, by reason only that he is such a person,
   a. be subjected either expressly by, or in the practical application of, any law in force in Nigeria or any executive or administrative action of the government to disabilities or restrictions to which citizens of Nigeria of other communities, ethnic groups, places of origin, sex, religions, or political opinions are not made subject; or
   b. be accorded either expressly by, or in the application of, any law in force in Nigeria or any such executive or administrative action, any privilege or advantage that is not accorded to citizens of Nigeria of other communities, ethnic groups, places of origin, sex, religions, or political opinions.
2. No citizen of Nigeria shall be subjected to any disability or deprivation merely by reason of the circumstance of his birth.
3. Nothing in subsection (1) of this section shall invalidate any law by reason only that the law imposes restrictions with respect to the appointment of any person to any office under the state or as a member of the armed forces of the Federation or a member of the Nigeria Police or to an office in the service of a body cor-

porate established directly by any law in force in Nigeria.

Section 39 renders all laws, including customary and religious laws, subsidiary legislation, regulations, and official government practices that permit discrimination against women unconstitutional, null, and void. The only exception, stipulated in subsection 3, relates to appointments in the public service, the armed forces, and the police force. In effect, Nigerian women, therefore, have all the human rights stipulated in the Constitution, including the right to nondiscrimination on the basis of sex. However, they enjoy no positive rights specifically addressed to their particular needs or vulnerabilities, nor is there any statutory recognition of the need for such rights (Ilumoka 1994, 316).

Chapter 2 of the Nigerian Constitution, "Fundamental Objectives and Directive Principles of State Policy," contains principles of economic, social, and cultural rights relating to equal access to resources, provisions of basic needs, an adequate means of livelihood, provision of adequate health facilities for all, and free education. The State has a duty to conform to, observe, and apply these principles and provisions, but cases of alleged nonobservance cannot be tried in court (Ilumoka 1994, 314). The distinction made between the internationally accepted economic, social, and cultural rights guaranteed by the "Fundamental Objectives and Directive Principles of State Policy" and the fundamental human rights in the Nigerian Constitution clearly indicates that there was no intention to enforce them. Accordingly, Jadesola Akande asserts that:

The Nigerian Constitution has entrenched fundamental rights and made them justiciable* but economic and social rights have been reduced to a mere declaration of pious hopes because it is believed that they can only be achieved progressively according to available resources of the Nation and the policies pursued by the Government. (Akande 1989, 123)

In addition to the various constitutional provisions guaranteeing fundamental human rights, Nigeria subscribes to various international declarations and charters, which aim at eliminating discrimination against women (Oyajobi 1986, 16). Article 18(3) of the African Charter on Human and People's Rights became national legislation with Nigeria's Ratification and Enforcement Act of 1983. This Act provides that "the State shall ensure the elimination of every discrimination against women and also ensure the protection of the rights of the woman and the child as stipulated in international declarations and conventions." To be able to ascertain how much real emancipation women have received in Nigeria, we need to examine the treatment of women in Nigeria by the laws of the land (see also Sections 5C, Interpersonal Heterosexual Behaviors, Adults, and 8A and B, Significant Unconventional Sexual Behaviors, Coercive Sex and Prostitution).

### Specific Issues of Sex Discrimination

*Women's Property Rights.* The unmarried woman has the same right to hold property as any Nigerian male under both customary and statutory law. Also, since the passage of the Married Woman's Property Act of 1982 (Otaluka 1989) as amended in 1993, a married woman has the right to contract as a *femme sole* [single woman] to the extent of her separate property. However, it has been a longstanding custom that women in some areas of Iboland cannot acquire immovable property like land. Iboland women are devoid of such con-

---

*Any breach of such entrenched fundamental rights can be referred to the court for necessary redress.

tractual capacity (Otaluka 1989). This issue does not arise in Yoruba custom, where both married and unmarried women have the full capacity to contract, acquire, and dispose of all forms of property, including land.

*Women's Rights in Sureties.* Although there are no legal provisions that distinguish along sexual lines between the rights and/or capacity of any citizen to stand as surety for another in an application for bail, Nigerian police regularly deny women this right. This obviously contradicts every legal provision regulating bail practices; it also violates section 39(1)(b) of the Nigerian Constitution, which prohibits any executive or administrative practice that discriminates along sexual lines. The arguments for exempting women from the category of "fit and proper persons" are usually not based on any objective criteria.

*Women and Income Tax Law.* The Nigerian law on personal income tax discriminates largely against women. The tax system does not treat individuals within the marriage structure as persons in their own right. For instance, it is often generally assumed that the children of the marriage belong to the husband, and so it is to him that tax relief is granted. Married women who wish to claim tax relief for expenses related to rearing children are required to show documentary evidence of those expenses and evidence that the father of the children is not responsible for their upkeep. Men are not required to produce such documents. Although the Joint Tax Board justifies this practice by saying that these measures are designed to discourage duplication of claims, the present assumption in favor of the man is discriminatory and groundless.

*Women's Inheritance Rights.* Under the Yoruba customary law of intestacy, the succession rights of a male who dies without a will devolve not only on his children, but also on his brothers and sisters. The Ibo and Bini Customary Laws are governed by the primogeniture principle, so that on the death of a male without a will (intestate), the eldest son succeeds to his estate. The widow, however, has no customary right to inherit her intestate spouse's property. Although death does not necessarily terminate a common (customary) law marriage, the rights of a wife to retain membership in her husband's family, and possibly maintenance, remain only insofar as she remains in her matrimonial home. This holds whether or not she chooses to marry her husband's kin, except where the latter is not raised as an option, but is made mandatory.

Islamic law discriminates in the amount of entitlement granted the deceased intestate's children along sexual lines. The male children acquire in equal shares, whereas the daughters receive only a half share each. In a case where the deceased is survived by a single daughter, she would be entitled to only half the net estate, whereas an only son would take the whole estate. The widow is allowed a quarter of her husband's estate, whereas a widower takes half the net estate of the deceased wife (*Lewis v. Bankole* 1909; *Adedoyin v. Simeon* 1928).

*Women and Passports.* When a married woman applies for a passport, she is as a matter of practice required to submit a letter of consent from her husband. Similarly, a woman cannot apply to include the name(s) of her child(ren) on her passport without a letter of consent from her husband. There is, however, no such requirement for male applicants.

*Conclusion*

It cannot be argued more that there is an urgent need for a reappraisal of the status of women in Nigeria. The need to make all the constitutional rights of women a practical real-

ity that would continually guarantee that they have their fair share of power, education, financial resources, positions, and so forth in our society cannot be overemphasized.

## C. General Concepts of Sexuality and Love

UWEM EDIMO ESIET

Whereas sexuality is not openly discussed in Nigerian life, it is an underlying activity that is commonly displayed at publicly celebrated festivals. In most tribal cultures, dance dramas convey sexual values and attitudes as well as other more-general messages. Similarly, folk tales and drama are used to depict specific tribal sexual values and expectations. This is particularly true of the tradition of early marriage, whether consented or forced, which is the most accepted means of containing adolescent sexuality. Issues of love of children, especially of males who will perpetuate the family name and heritage, also run deep within the family and society in most cultural settings.

In times past, the virginity of the female at her marriage called for a family celebration with appropriate gifts and visits from the in-laws. In some cultures, especially among the Yorubas, where "hawking" (street vending) and "night marketing" is common, young girls are learning to receive "passes" from men and acquire skills in dealing with these. Since the introduction of Western values and education in Nigeria, women have continued to acquire skills in dealing with males in a culture in transition. This has led to an increased tendency to delay marriage and an increased incidence of premarital sexual relationships. In some tribal cultures, in fact, it is more common today to demand pregnancy rather than virginity as a prerequisite for marriage. This is especially true among the educated young.

Also, most of the popular music and advertisements glamorize sexuality, even though there is still a strong disapproval of open discussion of sexuality.

## 2. Religious, Ethnic, and Gender Factors Affecting Sexuality

BILKISU YUSUF and RAKIYA BOOTH

### A. An Overview and a Christian Perspective in Southern Nigeria
RAKIYA BOOTH

Religion and culture in Africa are closely interrelated. While religion has at times been used to oppress and exploit people, it has also been appropriated to enhance political liberation.

Maduro (1989) defines religion

> as a structure of discourse and practices common to a social group referring to certain forces (personified or not, multiple or singular) that believers consider as anterior and superior to their natural and social surroundings in whose regard they express their sense of a certain dependency (through creation, control, protection, threat, or the like) and before which they consider themselves obligated to a particular pattern of conduct in society.

Every religion is situated in a specific human context in a concrete, determined geographical space, historical moment, and social milieu. Members of a religion share certain collective dimensions—social, economic, political, cultural, educational, military, and so on. Religion is, therefore, closely linked and interrelated with all the dimensions of the life of a community. Because religion is part of a society, it follows that anything that affects people's lives will affect their religion. Hence, religion affects sexuality.

Nigerian society is dominated by two religions: Islam and Christianity. They are the main source of our Nigerian religious value systems, which affect sexual attitudes and behavior. Christianity, for instance, expects men and women to hold in high esteem the religious value of sexual purity. Girls are expected to be virgins at the time of marriage. Islam allows female children to be given in marriage before the age of puberty. These practices ensure that the female child is a virgin at marriage. Similarly, Christianity and Islam emphasize that adultery is unacceptable. However, our culture expects men to do what women are not to do. Our culture allows and even encourages a man to contract polygynous marriages. While extramarital sex is publicly frowned on, a man who engages in extramarital sex is privately hailed for his behavior. The same culture deals severely and ruthlessly with married women caught in adultery. In both the Islamic and Christian religions, a man can ask for and be granted a divorce if his wife is confirmed to have committed adultery. This is not, however, the case if a wife discovers her husband's illicit affairs with other women.

Generally, Nigerian men believe that because woman was created out of a man, a woman must be subservient to man in all spheres of life at all times. Women are described as having a small brain in comparison to men's, being deficient in logic, analytical abilities, and critical thinking. In fact, this is the guiding principle that governs the behavior of Christian women who are the most submissive. While women constitute a larger portion of the church membership, women are not allowed to preach or take leadership positions in Nigerian Christian churches. As a result, women have been consistently kept passive and denied equal status with men in decision-making, both in the family and at the national level. Men believe that the only things women control are fertility and the sex of the child. Thus, quarrels and even divorce arise where a marriage does not produce a child or where only female children are born.

Similarly, it is a taboo in the Islamic religion for a woman to lead prayers or pray jointly with men. Besides, local interpretations of both the Islamic and Christian faiths forbid men to accept sexual advances from their women. That is to say that sexual advances should be made by men, and not women.

## B. The Muslim Hausa of Northern Nigeria

BILKISU YUSUF

The Hausa people constitute one of the most numerous and influential ethnic groups in West Africa. The majority of Hausa live in northern Nigeria, and in Nigeria's three neighbors, the Niger and Benin Republics and the Cameroon. There is also a large population of Hausa living as immigrants in the Sudan Republic. Their language, Hausa, is widely spoken by about 50 million people in West Africa (Coles & Mack 1999, 4).

Hausan history dates back to the 8th century when city-states and empires flourished in Western Africa (Crowther 1972). Tradition traces the establishment of the seven Hausa city-states to Abu Yazidu (Bayajidda), a prince from Arabia, who fled his homeland after a succession struggle. On reaching Daura, he killed the snake that had troubled the inhabitants of the city, and Daurama, the Queen of Daura, impressed by Abu Yazida's bravery, married him. They had seven sons who established the seven Hausa states (*Hausa bakwai*), Daura, Kano, Biram, Zazzau, Gobir, Katsina, and Rano.

The single most important factor that influenced the development of Hausa culture was their interaction with the peoples of North Africa through the Trans-Sahara trade. After Islam was introduced to the land of the Hausa by Arab traders, it gradually became the religion of the ruling class, and later the religion of the majority of Hausans. However, pockets of non-Muslim Hausa (*maguzawa*) still survive today and have retained their traditional religion. Although

other ethnic groups, such as the Fulani and Kanuri, have mixed with the Hausa for centuries, the Hausa culture has retained some of its original features.

Hausa culture today is predominantly Islamic, making it difficult to distinguish tribal Hausa cultural norms from Islamic injunctions. Although Hausa culture has remnants of non-Islamic and distinctly indigenous practices that are part of their rites of passage, a marriage of convenience has evolved between Islamic injunctions and aspects of Hausa cultural norms that do not conflict with the religion.

Islam is a way of life for its adherents, with rules and regulations guiding all aspects of life. Its strong moral code emphasizes chastity, and prohibits loitering, soliciting, and unnecessary intermingling of the sexes. Islam permits women to go out of their houses only to pursue lawful needs, such as the acquisition of knowledge or to work and contribute to societal development. Marriage before age 18 was the norm among Muslim Hausa girls before the colonial era and the introduction of secular education. Most parents in those days preferred to marry off their daughters at age 12.

The Qur'an, the basic source of Islamic law, allows the marriage of girls who have not started menstruation (*Qur'an Suratul Talaq*, verse 4). It is common among the Hausa to marry off preadolescent girls and delay the consummation of the marriage. Although the marriage of minors is lawful, the various schools of Islamic jurisprudence have guidelines about how such a marriage must be performed for it to be valid. Hammudahah Abd al'Ati (1982, 70-84) clearly outlines the arguments for and against it. According to jurists and the schools of law, a minor cannot give herself away in marriage. Her marriage must be arranged by her father and her consent sought. Others argue that the father may give his daughter away in marriage with or without her consent if she is underage, i.e., 9 years or younger, a virgin, and is given in marriage to a suitable and socially equal husband. The father in such a case is also her guardian (*wakil*), and Islamic law stipulates that the *wakil* must be legally and religiously qualified. As a legal guardian, he has authority to do only what is beneficial to his daughter or ward.

Arranged marriages were and are still common among the Hausa. In the past, some were actually arranged through pledges made by the parents while their children were toddlers. It is also quite common for the educated elite and royalty to arrange their children's marriages. Cousin marriages are also widely practiced among both Hausa and Fulani commoners and royalty, particularly so among the latter.

Marriage age in Hausa society is now gradually changing, shifting away from child marriages contracted at 7, 8, or 9 years of age, which were quite common in royal households in the past, and away from teenage marriages contracted at 12 years of age among the other classes. With the increase in the number of females attending school, the average marriage age is now 16 or 17 for secondary school graduates and 13 for those who drop out of school. However, the marriage age may be lower in rural areas, where fewer females attend school. It is a common practice for the formal Islamic marriage (*dauphi aure*) to be performed early, after which the girl continues her schooling for several years and completes it before the Hausa cultural ceremony (*hiki*) takes place and the marriage is consummated.

## C. Character of Ethnic Values

Ethnicity develops and is expressed in multiethnic situations where a sense of "us" and "them" leads an individual or group to behave in exclusionary ways. This presupposes the existence of more than one ethnic group, an ethnic group being a group of people set apart from others by language, culture, political organization, territory, and myth of common descent. These shared group values constitute the basis for conscious identity and behavior by members when they relate with people from another group. However, it is important to point out that ethnic groups, such as those in Nigeria, are not necessarily homogeneous entities. Quite often, an ethnic group that contains several subgroups, languages, dialects, and cultural variations is classified as a homogeneous entity by bigots who emphasize selected specific traits as representing the whole group.

As with the Islamic, Christian, and indigenous religious traditions, the culture and norms of every ethnic group in Nigeria affect not only the sexual attitudes and behavior of its members, but all spheres of life. All ethnic groups in Nigeria believe strongly in sexual purity. Girls who are virgins at marriage are praised and showered with gifts. Married women are expected to avoid adultery. Although the same is expected of men, cultural norms give room for men to do otherwise. In a study of concubinage conducted among the Ngwa Igbo in southern Nigeria, such norms are viewed as cultural discrimination, especially in a polygynous society that deprives women of sufficient sexual satisfaction and emotional security.

However, the idea of eliminating this discrimination would definitely be considered offensive by decision-makers, both at the family and legislative levels. Such a move, if ever contemplated by a woman, would end the marriage in divorce. Cultural values clearly demand that, because they are family-oriented, women must be honest with their husbands and endeavor to prevent family disruption.

Studies have shown that women are more worried than men are by post-divorce problems. Furthermore, the wife's inability to initiate a divorce, the stigma of divorce, and a divorced woman's alienation from her natal descent group, along with early child betrothal and the payment of bride wealth, only increase women's subordination and resignation into acceptance of men's decision-making role in the family.

The subordination of women is most manifest in the family. It is in the family that one finds attitudes and behavior that give priority to education of males over females. Our culture believes that men have stronger sexual drives, need more sex than women do, and have greater control over sexuality. It is tradition and culture that socializes women to be sexually submissive to men. Moreover, it is the family and cultural attitudes that define the attributes of a good wife and, through sanctions, force females to fit into these qualities. To a girl, marriage is the ultimate goal. Hence, following cultural and family dictates, she has to appear less intelligent than men and behave with a certain amount of diffidence in dealing with men if she is to achieve that aspiration.

Economically, Nigerian women are expected to be dependent on men, in line with their traditionally assigned roles of wives, mothers, and homemakers. Whereas men are trained for remunerative employment outside the home, the process of socialization prevents, limits, or demobilizes women in their march to economic emancipation. Men are regarded as the breadwinners of the family. Because "he that pays the piper dictates the tune," men make all major decisions in the family. For instance, development efforts that provide men access to factors of production simultaneously deny women access to production inputs, such as credit, ownership of land, and skill training. As the family breadwinner, the husband's domain includes all major decisions, such as number of children the spouse should have, the spacing of births, the couple's sleeping arrangement, use of contraception, and even the type of contraceptive used. Although this is a general cultural value, it does vary with the couple's level of education.

Generally speaking, Nigerian women are sexually submissive to men because of the culturally determined masculine roles performed by men. Men pay the house rent and children's school fees, provide kerosene or firewood for cooking, and fulfill other chores that steer men towards leadership responsibilities and give them the legitimacy of decision-making in the family and in the larger society. Still, the internalization and perpetuation of sex roles are achieved through socialization processes. Although Nigerian role stratification is unequivocally male-oriented, as principal actors in child socialization, women unfortunately are used as instruments for its propagation, enforcement, and perpetuation. There is a thriving attitude in Nigeria that a male child should, among other things, exhibit decision-making skills, whereas a female child is expected to be passive, submissive, and portray the "nice girl" image, an image which attempts to control women socially through value construction.

The Ibo culture gives women more freedom of assertion than either the Yoruba or Hausa cultures. Ibo and other cultural groups agree that household activities, such as the pounding of yam (*fufus*), sweeping, and similar domestic chores, should be jointly done by male and female children. The Yoruba, on the other hand, see such tasks as female responsibilities, thus creating gender gaps in the division of labor in the family. The Ibo allow some women to seek divorce, whereas the Yoruba encourage them to engage in extramarital sex. In both ways, ethnic values affect the sexual attitudes and behavior of people.

Both religious and ethnic values are thus intimately interwoven and most profoundly affect the sexual attitudes and behavior of Nigerians in all spheres of our social existence.

## 3. Knowledge and Education about Sexuality

### A. Sexuality Education

UWEM EDIMO ESIET and FOYIN OYEBOLA

Because of the culture of silence on sexuality, there has been little or no structured way of teaching Nigerians about sexuality. In the late 1950s and early 1960s, family planning education was introduced in some areas of Nigeria. However, this met with considerable opposition from cultural traditions and religious institutions. At the time, the only way a wife could have access to family planning services was with the prior consent of her spouse. This situation has changed in recent years and married women can now obtain family planning information and services without the husband's consent.

The government has been working to get POP/FLE (population and family life education) into the schools' curricula, and this effort is ongoing. However, adolescents continue to be denied access to sexual information and services on a national scale. There have been some efforts by nongovernmental organizations (NGOs) to assure that marginalized groups have access to sexuality education. This effort is increasing, as data from studies continue to show that five out of ten girls and seven out of ten boys have had sexual intercourse at least once by the time they leave secondary school.

In 1996, this effort culminated in the production of *Guidelines for Comprehensive Sexuality Education in Nigeria*. This effort by about 20 government and nongovernmental organizations was publicly released by the then-Minister of State for Education chief, Mrs. Iyabo Anisulowo. Despite this laudable effort, the government still did not take the bold step of ensuring access to this education of our youth out of deference to the interests of religious leaders. However, in

March 1999, at the Forty-Sixth Session of the National Council on Education, a resolution to integrate comprehensive sexuality education into Nigeria's school curricula, sponsored by the Federal Ministry of Education, was unanimously ratified. As a result, the federal Ministry of Education made a historic commitment to implementing sexuality education throughout Nigerian schools. (National Guidelines Task Force 1996; SIECUS 2000). [U. E. Esiet]

The majority of Nigerians have the misconception that sexuality is equivalent to coitus. This has been a major obstacle to the integration of sexuality education into school curricula and other youth-related activities. Because of this equation of sexuality education with intercourse, the focus tends to be on the biological components. [F. Oyebola]

### Sexual Education and Discussion: A Regional/Ethnic Comparison

The following summaries of the attitudes and practices regarding sexuality education and the discussion of sex of several ethnic groups in eight geographical regions of Nigeria were compiled by the authors during a meeting with healthcare professionals in January 1999 (Francoeur, Esiet, & Esiet 2000) (see Editor's Note at the beginning of this chapter).

1. Regions: Ipoti-Ekiti, Oyo, and Yorubaland. Ethnic Group: Yoruba

   Sexual knowledge is acquired through storytelling myths, from peers, schools, apprenticeship centers, television, films, romantic novels, magazines, and overheard adult conversations. There is no positive attitude regarding sexuality education. Educated adults see nothing bad in sexual education, but the uneducated say it is an abomination and such things should not be heard of. Sex is freely discussed in the beer parlor, at home when husband and wife are quarreling, or during marriage preparation in the church or mosque. Otherwise, sexuality issues are never discussed and people are repulsed by sexual talk. When compelled to discuss sexuality issues, the uneducated are very shy and hardly give any correct information of participation. More-educated persons discuss sex mostly among peers and with persons of the same gender.

2. Regions: Kano, Katsina, and Kaduna. Ethic Group: Muslim Hausa

   Most children in these states learn about sexuality through their peer groups, media, and films. Parents do not discuss sex with their children. Parents are very negative about sexuality education in the schools because of the misconception that it will negatively affect the children. People will discuss sexual topics freely among friends and peers.

3. Region: Borno

   Sexual information is acquired from peers as well as parents. The general attitude towards sexuality education in schools is negative. Talking openly about sexuality is clearly taboo.

4. Region: Benue. Ethnic Groups: Tiv, Idoma, and Isala

   Children learn about sex from their peers, and through storytelling and the cultural practices of gender roles. Sexual intercourse is learned by experimentation. Mothers tell their daughters about the consequences of sexual intercourse when they start menstruating. They usually provide no knowledge on hygiene. People are generally not comfortable with sexuality education. Spouses rarely communicate about sexuality. They are, however, beginning to discuss family planning. Talking about sex is considered "wayward."

5. Regions: Akwa-Ibom and the Cross River: Ethnic Groups: Efik and Ibibio

   Children acquire sexual knowledge by listening to stories told by their elders, by eavesdropping on adult talk, and from older sisters, cousins, house helpers, school peers, and electronic and print media. Young people also learn about sex during moonlight activities with their peers. In these activities, known as *Edibe Ekok* (hide and seek), children make a ring with a broomstick with a sand heap in the middle, around which they sit, mostly naked. They try to locate a ring in the sand heap. When found, they are joyous and exchange pleasant times, which sometimes results in sexual activity. Knowledge about sexuality is considered inappropriate for children but acceptable for the married. Sexuality education is seen as a way of corrupting the children. People do not discuss sexual topics, but this can be done in private and secretly.

6. Region: Delta State. Ethnic Groups: Uhobod, Ibos, Ijaws, Isaw, and Itsekirus

   Children learn about sexuality from their peers and from the media in urban areas. Most people view sexuality education negatively because they believe it initiates the young ones to sexual relationships. Discussion of sexual topics is taboo. Males do, however, discuss sexuality—especially when they want to tell their peers how many girlfriends they have had intercourse with.

7. Region: Edo

   Children in Edo learn about sex through their parents, but mostly through peers. The general attitude toward sexuality education is negative. Discussion of sexual topics is avoided because it is believed that discussing the subject will result in promiscuity and exposure of adolescents to bad influences. People do not easily discuss sexuality topics because it is considered a taboo.

8. Regions: Imo, Enugu, and Anambra States. Ethnic Group: Ibo

   Knowledge about sexuality is picked up accidentally—mostly from peers. There is no formal sexuality education. Parents teach their children through their own attitudes and behavior. Knowledge comes mainly from peers. The Ibo believe talk about sexual matters is vulgar, sexual education should not exist, and sexuality should never be discussed.

### B. Sexuality Education among the Hausa

MAIRO V. BELLO, RAKIYA BOOTH, and BILKISU YUSUF

Sexuality education among the Hausa is imparted by parents and by the Qur'anic schools (*Islamiyyah*). Parents teach the rudiments emphasizing the gender roles expected of men and women, while the details of sexuality are left to the Qur'anic schoolteachers who instruct the children in *fiqh*, the law of Islamic jurisprudence. The *fiqh* curriculum for children and adults of both sexes includes lessons on the onset of puberty, menstruation (a sign of maturity for girls, when fasting becomes obligatory), and ritual purifications after menstruation, sexual intercourse, and childbirth. For the boys, instruction includes the discussion of wet dreams and voice changes as marks of the onset of puberty, when fasting becomes obligatory. Boys are also instructed in the requirement of a purification bath after sexual intercourse and wet dreams. All Muslim Hausa children routinely attend *fiqh* lessons, which prepare them for the prayers and fasting, the two fundamental requirements for Muslim men and women. *Fiqh* lessons also focus on what constitutes sexual intercourse, the virtue of abstinence for unmarried people, and what the law stipulates about fornication and adultery. [B. Yusuf]

Although adolescents in the predominantly Muslim Hausas are expected to learn about sexuality in *fiqh*, many Hausa boys, and most of the Hausa girls, are withdrawn from school, both Qur'anic and public, before they get to the stage of learning about *fiqh*. Those girls and boys who stay in school to the stage when *fiqh* deals with sexuality, often find that the instruction does not include much, if anything, beyond the rituals, purification baths, marriage, and divorce, because of shyness that is part of the societal culture and the culture of silence that surrounds sexuality issues in the Hausa society. [M. V. Bello]

*Fiqh* teaches that married couples are entitled to sexual satisfaction from their partners, and the absence of sexual satisfaction is a valid reason for divorce. Likewise, *fiqh* enjoins Muslims to maintain their chastity and avoid high-risk sexual behaviors. Affliction with a communicable disease, such as leprosy, and perhaps by extension one could add HIV/AIDS, is also a valid reason for divorce. [B. Yusuf]

Among Hausa parents, sexuality education is constrained by the cultural practice of *kunya* or modesty, whereby parents are too embarrassed or shy to impart sexuality education to their children. The observance of *kunya* varies from parents who do not show affection in the presence of their children and do not talk to their first child, to those who only refrain from calling the child's name and/or feel too shy to discuss sexual and reproductive topics with their children. In the extreme cases, *kunya* ensures that the child grows up without knowing who his mother is, with the father, stepmother, or grandparents filling the communication and affection vacuum created by the *kunya*-observing mother. The practice of *kunya* is being gradually eroded by the interaction of the Hausa with other ethnic groups, and young Hausa mothers these days refrain from observing *kunya*, calling their first children by their names and openly showing them affection. [B. Yusuf]

However, an aspect of sexuality education solely entrusted to parents in Hausa society is the expression of sexuality during courtship and marriage. Both Islamic and Hausa culture do not permit dating, but the suitor is allowed to visit the girl in her parents' house, discuss with her gifts (*zance*), and give her token money or presents (*toshi*). During such visits, the young couple is not allowed to stay alone in a secluded place. Although Hausa sexuality education and socialization is replete with measures designed to prevent premarital sexual intercourse, such attempts are being steadily undermined by the prevalent Hausa practice of sending children and young girls to hawk (*talla*). These hawkers (street venders) run the risk of early exposure to sexual overtures, sexual abuse, and harassment from unscrupulous men posing as buyers of their wares. [B. Yusuf]

## C. Sexuality Education among Christian Nigerians
FOYIN OYEBOLA

In Nigeria, the Catholic Church provides some limited sexuality education, emphasizing abstinence education for unmarried persons and the Natural Family Planning method for married couples, and condemning other forms of contraception. Other Christian groups, especially the indigenous Christian churches, emphasize menstrual hygiene and the separation of women during menstruation as described in the Old Testament. These churches tend to be more liberal on premarital sex and polygyny. The modern-day Pentecostal churches tend to be more receptive to contraceptive use within marriage, while emphasizing premarital abstinence. Overall, the Christian churches have yet to pay sexuality education its deserved attention. [U. E. Esiet]

It would be incorrect to say that sexuality education is not being provided in Nigeria. However, what is taught is not as comprehensive as it should be. Whatever is provided can be called moral education. Most adults are not comfortable with the concept of "sexuality education," because of the ambiguity of the term *sex*, and because of the low level of knowledge about sexuality among adults. [F. Oyebola]

However, in recent years, challenges to societal values and serious public health issues and problems have made sexuality education increasingly acceptable everywhere, including the Christian communities and informal sources. The Christian churches have been recognized as an agent of socialization for young persons in Nigeria. Consequently, most of the churches, especially in the urban centers, have been sensitized by the relevant NGOs through seminars and workshops, while some of the key religious leaders have been trained as counselors and educators. [F. Oyebola]

The integration of increasingly comprehensive sexuality education into church activities is a slow process for now, but it is expected to pick up with time. Most of the churches plan various activities and invite experts to make presentations on such topics as "Adolescent Sexuality: Making Responsible Decisions," "Bridging the Parent-Child Communication Gap on Sexuality Issues," "Teenage Pregnancy and Abortion: Consequences and Prevention," "Sexually Transmissible Infections," and "Developing Positive Self-Esteem with Others." [F. Oyebola]

[*Update 2003*: In August 2002, the Catholic Church in Nigeria developed a curriculum on sexuality education for use in homes and parishes. The adoption of the curriculum was the outcome of a workshop on sexuality education organized in Enugu by clerics in collaboration with Community Life Project, a nongovernmental organization. The curriculum gives guidelines on how to teach sex education to married couples, adults, youths, and couples preparing for marriage. The curriculum makes it obligatory for the priests to include sex education in their preachings. (*End of update by B. Opiyo-Omolo*)]

## D. Informal Sources of Sexual Knowledge
UWEM EDIMO ESIET and FOYIN OYEBOLA

There is a definite increase in the informal sources of sexual knowledge in Nigeria. Young people have access to a lot of information, including both foreign and local magazines, television shows (more foreign than native), books (mainly foreign), and peers. There is also what we refer to as "environmentally available sources of sexual knowledge" that accompany and are associated with the prevalence of poverty and unemployment, the increase in commercial sex work, and the international trafficking in commercial sex workers. Sexual knowledge is also picked up in the course of everyday living at neighborhood gatherings, affiliations, and at home as a consequence of the lack of privacy in many housing patterns. In general, the underground information network on sexuality has acquired greater prominence in the lives of Nigerians.

## 4. Autoerotic Behaviors and Patterns
UWEM EDIMO ESIET and FOYIN OYEBOLA

### A. Children and Adolescents

It is not unusual for the growing child to engage in thumb sucking and some self-body massage. Both behaviors are commonly frowned on by adults, and parents try to discourage both "bad" behaviors. Pacifiers are encouraged as a substitute for thumbsucking, but parents tend to punish masturbation. [U. E. Esiet]

Masturbation is a common sexual behavior in Nigeria among adolescents and adults alike. However, it is more common in adolescents, who rely on masturbation to satisfy their sexual urges. This they do by fondling the clitoris, breast, nipple, or penis. Masturbation is common in girls-only schools where same-sex relations occur. [F. Oyebola]

## B. Adults

While adults may engage in masturbation, they do not openly admit to this practice, because the whole topic of sex is a taboo. However, some counselors and healthcare providers are beginning to encourage an open discussion of masturbation and recommending it as an alternative to risky sexual behavior. [U. E. Esiet]

## 5. Interpersonal Heterosexual Behaviors

### A/B. Children and Adolescents

MAIRO V. BELLO, NIKE ESIET, FOYIN OYEBOLA,
UWEM EDIMO ESIET, BILKISU YUSUF,
and RAKIYA BOOTH

*Puberty, Menstruation, First Sexual Intercourse, and Marriage*

The northern area of Nigeria has the lowest age for first marriage. Local studies conducted among Hausa communities in Kano State, in Zaria (Kaduna State), and in Dutse (Jigawa State) have confirmed the prevalence of early marriage. Clara Ejembi, a staff member at Ahmadu Bello University, Zaria, found that 83.4% of girls in the Zaria Local Government Area were married before 14 years of age and 98.5% before age 20. A study by Adolescent Health and Information Project (AHIP) in Kano and Jigawa States confirmed that 75.5% of girls who do not have formal education got married before the age of 13 years of age, while 99.5% were married before 16. Most Hausa adolescent girls are married before or as soon as they enter puberty, which occurs between ages 12 and 15 (Goddard 1995). [M. V. Bello]

In an AHIP study of adolescent socialization, most respondents confirmed that they had their first menstrual period in their husband's house, suggesting that they were taught nothing about puberty before their first experience with menstruation. Research by the International Reproductive Rights Research Action Group (IRRRAG) found that the few young women who learned anything about menstruation before their first experience got their information from friends, books, or schoolteachers. [M. V. Bello]

Recently, however, the increased rate of Western-style education, a downward turn in the country's economy that has made marriage very expensive, and the terrible rate of inflation are affecting the age of marriage for young people. Many girls now get to finish their secondary school, and learn a little about puberty, their bodies, and life in general from school, friends, and the media before they marry. The boys now think that they cannot take wives, because they do not have jobs, and families no longer live in communal settings, where feeding is centrally handled. Young Hausans are fast adopting the nuclear-type family setting because they think it is more convenient for them. [M. V. Bello]

According to the 1990 Nigerian Demographic and Health Survey, the median age at first intercourse for girls is just over 16 years. By age 18, 63% of women have experienced intercourse; by age 20, approximately 80% have experienced intercourse. Thirty-four percent of 15- to 19-year-old females are married and 27% of adolescent married women are in a polygynous union, with rural and northern women more likely to be in such a union. A 1992 study by Makinwa-Adelzusoye also showed that among urban youth aged 12 to 24, over 20% of the females are married compared to 3% of the males. [B. Yusuf]

A common though not recent pattern of marriage among the Hausa is for girls to have many suitors (*samari*) from whom she selects her mate. Yet, it is not unusual to find forced marriages (*auren dole*) made out of monetary or other considerations in contemporary Hausa society. Victims of forced marriages may accept the union. However, there are instances when such brides leave the husband and return to their parents' home (*yaji*) or go to court to get a divorce. Forced marriages are now on the decline and are usually limited to girls who have not attained the age of puberty or do not attend school. Some girls are also withdrawn from school by their parents and given out in marriage. The prevailing economic hardship has made education too expensive for poor parents, who view marriage as a means of reducing the burden of maintaining their daughters in school (Goddard 1995; see also Section 2A, Religious and Ethnic Factors Affecting Sexuality, An Overview and a Christian Perspective in Southern Nigeria, for information about childhood and arranged marriages among the Hausa). [B. Yusuf]

*Menstruation: A Regional/Ethnic Comparison*

The following summaries of the attitudes and practices regarding menstruation of several ethnic groups in eight geographical regions of Nigeria were compiled by the authors during a meeting with healthcare professionals in January 1999 (Francoeur, Esiet, & Esiet 2000) (see Editor's Note at the beginning of this chapter).

1. Regions: Ipoti-Ekiti, Oyo, and Yorubaland. Ethnic Group: Yoruba

   In Yorubaland, menarche is seen as coming of age, and a young girl is then advised not to be close to a man because she may get pregnant. There are quite a number of taboos associated with menstruation. Powerful people, such as warriors and traditional leaders, are not supposed to copulate with their wives during this period because it neutralizes the efficacy of any charms they are using. Albinos are believed to be the result of conception occurring during the menstrual period. In Ipoto-Ekiti, a menstruating woman is considered dirty and people will not associate with her during this time.

2. Regions: Kano, Katsina, and Kaduna. Ethic Group: Muslim Hausa

   The social and cultural beliefs of the Muslim Hausa treat menstruation with silence. It is simply not discussed. If a single girl starts menstruating in her father's house, she is quickly given off in marriage to any available man. This is referred to as *Sadaka*. Menstruation prior to marriage is considered a bad omen. When a young girl begins menstruating in her father's house, her mother-in-law is faced with the task of teaching her all she needs to know about menstruation. During menstruation, women do not sleep with their husbands, do not say their five daily prayers, and are also not allowed to fast.

3. Region: Borno

   There are no special taboos or rites relating to menstruation in the Borno State.

4. Regions: Tiv-Benue. Ethnic Groups: Tiv, Idoma, and Isala

   There are no rites or taboos related to menstruation in the Tiv-Benue State, except that a family must give a daughter in marriage when she begins menstruating. This early-marriage tradition, however, is weakening.

5. Regions: Akwa-Ibom and the Cross River: Ethnic Groups: Efik and Ibibio

   Some people in this region see menstruation as an unclean process. They consider a woman dirty during her period. Hence, she should not cook or serve food at this time. Some churches and cults refuse to let women attend services during their period. Young menstruating women must hygienically and properly dispose of used sanitary napkins; otherwise, the enemy may use them to charm the individual. Sexual intercourse during menstruation is taboo. Menstrual cramps are relieved by using hot water to massage the waist and lower abdomen, by drinking illicit gin, and by taking a hot pepperish sauce to flush out the bad blood.

6. Region: Delta State. Ethnic Groups: Uhobod, Ibos, Ijaws, Isaw, and Itsekirus

For people in these tribal groups, menstruation is a welcome development and a sign of attaining womanhood. In some parts of the Delta State, no special attention is paid to menarche, apart from the mother telling her daughter that she has become a woman and should not "go near men." In other regions, a girl who is already betrothed is visited by her prospective husband as a sign of homage to her family. In some areas, a menstruating woman is not restricted to any area within the compound; in other regions, she cannot stay in the main house with her husband and others. Instead, a mat is used to construct a hut for her, where she stays for about seven days. Some fathers may exempt their daughters from such restrictions. But if they do, the father must perform a ritual cleansing when the daughter's menses end.

7. Region: Edo

During menstruation, women are forbidden to prepare meals for their husbands. In fact, they must refrain from doing anything for their husbands during this period. A menstruating woman must not sleep in her husband's room, or even in their main house. People believe the husband may die if she doesn't comply.

8. Regions: Imo, Enugu, and Anambra. Ethnic Group: Ibo

In the past, a menstruating woman could not cook for her husband. This is no longer taboo. She cannot, however, have sexual intercourse during her period.

## Courtship

When courtship reaches an advanced stage, the Hausa suitor indicates his intention to marry the girl by sending money. He also sends cosmetics and items of clothing (*kayan zance*) and money to her parents (*Gaisuwan uwa da uba*). Before the bride is conveyed to her husband's house, the groom's family sends *kayan sa lalle*, a combination of food and cosmetic items, such as henna (*lalle*), sweets, perfumes, sugar, millet, and head ties. The millet and sugar are used to prepare *tukudi* for the bride. *Tukudi* is a porridge prepared from dates, millet flour, yogurt, cheese, spices, and herbs that contain aphrodisiac substances given to the bride a few days before she is conveyed to her husband's house. Because a lot of emphasis is placed on chastity, retaining one's virginity is a virtue. Hausa culture makes it desirable, if not compulsory, for the groom to send a gift to the bride's parents after the consummation of the marriage (*kama hannu*) in appreciation of the fact that she remained a virgin until her wedding night. The Islamisation of Hausa culture is steadily eroding the practice of the forceful consummation of marriage and the publicity given to a private marital affair between a couple. *Fiqh* teaches that the couple's sexual experiences are confidential matters to be disclosed only to a marriage counselor for counseling purposes. In contemporary times, especially among city dwellers, nobody asks questions about the wedding night and the status of the bride. [B. Yusuf]

## Premarital Sexual Activities and Relationships

MAIRO BELLO, BILKISU YUSUF, and FOYIN OYEBOLA

In urban Nigeria, premarital sexual intercourse can be defined as sexual relations prior to the time a woman is socially recognized to be married. Premarital sexual relations with the man a woman eventually marries, as well as with other men, are included in this definition, as long as the sexual activity takes place before the time societal norms confer on the woman the right to have a sexual relationship. Premarital relationships in the Nigerian setting are guided by normative principles and beliefs, whose baseline is premarital chastity. [F. Oyebola]

Anecdotes drawn from living Yoruba heritage and sexual networking in Ekiti District showed how the traditional Yoruba society attaches a high degree of importance to female virginity. Every new Yoruba bride is expectcd to be a virgin at the time of consummation of her marriage, that is, during the first night when the woman and the husband sleep together. A virgin bride has been a source of real pride to the family. [F. Oyebola]

In the Ibo tradition and the attitude towards virginity in urban Nigeria, it is said that "A woman never forsakes the man who breaks her virginity." Other informal studies of the Ekiti in Ondo State confirmed that virginity was so important that two women waited outside the couple's room on the wedding night to take the good news to her parents that the bride had been intact. In traditional Fulani and Yoruba societies, a white cloth was spread on the bed on the night of marriage consummation; in the morning, the cloth was examined for blood marks. The husband sent a gift of money and kola nuts to the bride's parents if the new bride was found to be a virgin. However, in order to forestall any departure from this norm, some girls were betrothed in childhood. [F. Oyebola]

With the advance of Western values, however, the situation has changed. Previous informal studies have indicated a gradual erosion of the traditional premarital sexual norms. This change in the norms may be a consequence of the transformation taking place in the institution of marriage itself and, in particular, the transition from family-arranged to individual-choice marriages. [F. Oyebola]

Informal networking among sexuality workers in the Ekiti District of Nigeria revealed that sexual activity begins at about 17 years of age for both males and females, and that while 33% of rural females were virgins at marriage, only 25% of the urban females were virgins at marriage. [F. Oyebola]

Other possible reasons identified for the erosion of the traditional premarital sexual norms are the education of young adults, the rural-to-urban drift, and, most recently, the poor socioeconomic situation in Nigeria, which has thrown many female young adults into prostitution or commercial sex work. [F. Oyebola]

With the breakdown in the traditional value system, the value placed on virginity is gradually decreasing. Among the Yorubas, the practice of spreading a white bed sheet on the couple's bed on the night of betrothal has almost stopped, especially in the urban centers. In the case of the Hausa-Fulani society, it has been reported anecdotally that the new bridegroom now sends money and nuts to the bride's parents whether or not the new bride is found to be a virgin. This observation suggests that attitudes towards premarital sexual relations are becoming more positive. [F. Oyebola]

Also, the longer period of schooling, the increasing divorce rate, and the fact that there is no longer insistence on the traditional virginity test indicate that the Ibo may not take a bride's virginity seriously anymore. Westernization has therefore shifted the emphasis on virginity from a reality to an ideal. [F. Oyebola]

This picture of an increase in premarital relations is confirmed by the 1990 Nigerian Demographic and Health Survey, which revealed that by age 18, 63% of Nigerian women had had intercourse, while only 56% had married [F. Oyebola]. The 1988 Ondo State Demographic and Health Survey revealed greater exposure of young urban people to sexual activity. This was related partly to the influence of the mass media, as well as the availability of effective modern contraceptive methods that greatly reduce the risk of pregnancy in premarital relations. Other reasons why young people engage in premarital sex include:

- Ignorance about sexuality—it is still a taboo to educate young people about sexuality;
- The urge to experiment during adolescence without considering the consequences;
- For the fun of it and for sexual enjoyment;
- Peer pressure—doing it because others did it;
- Girls giving in to boys to show their love in the hope of marriage; and
- The influence of alcohol and drugs at parties, clubs, or drinking places. [F. Oyebola]

Traditionally, there were strict codes of sexual behavior and strict penalties were prescribed for transgressors. Indeed, the traditional custodians of society's values went to great lengths to ensure parallel but separate development of teenagers. Boys and girls were usually educated in separate institutions supervised by teachers of their own sex. In recent years, however, more and more schools are becoming coeducational. In addition, according to a 1992 study by Professor Makinwa-Adelzusoye, Nigerian youth today are maturing at younger ages and are doing so in an urban milieu that permits them a great degree of freedom from adult supervision. Add to this new environmental mix longer time in school, later marriage, urban mobility and independence, and financial hard times, and it is clear why premarital sexual intercourse is increasing among teenagers. As a result, today's young Nigerians are exposed to a lot of dangers, especially from unsafe sex, sexually transmitted diseases (STDs), HIV/AIDS, unwanted pregnancies, and unsafe abortions. [M. V. Bello]

In addition, Hausan youth appear to possess little knowledge of and considerable misinformation about contraceptives and their use. Less than 30% of Hausan youths used a contraceptive for their first intercourse. This proportion only increased to about 40% for currently young, unmarried, sexually active Hausans. These percentages are, however, higher than national rates as revealed by the Nigeria Fertility Survey (1981/1982). [M. V. Bello]

Many older Nigerians and religious leaders express anxiety about the moral decline reflected in premarital sex among adolescents and the increasing number of teenage pregnancies among students. Islam enjoins Muslims to remain chaste. To satisfy their sexual needs, Muslims are enjoined to marry. Although marriage is not compulsory, it is highly recommended as a very strong *sunnah* or custom in the tradition of Mohammed, the prophet of Islam. Muslims who have reached marriageable age and can afford it are enjoined to marry. Indeed, child and teenage marriage is often urged as a precaution against premarital sex and teenage pregnancies. [B. Yusuf]

*Forced Marriages*

In its proposal for a new social order for Kano State, the 1987 Committee for Women's Affairs identified forced marriages (*auren dole*), which are often contracted before

puberty, as one of the causes of high divorce rates and prostitution. Young girls forced into marriage not infrequently flee their marital homes and seek refuge in brothels (*gidan karuwai*) in urban centers. When this happens, these girls are believed to have "disappeared" into the world (*shiga duniya*) or to have become their own mistresses (*mata masu zaman kansu*). There have been cases of young girls threatening to *shiga duniya* (disappear) if and when they are forced to marry husbands they do not love. [B. Yusuf]

Early fertility and early childbearing are linked to teenage and child marriage in Hausa society. According to Makinwa-Adelzusoye and Feyiset (1994, 99), the fertility rate for women ages 15 to 19 is much higher in the largely rural north than it is in the south: 196 births per 1,000 in the northwest, 212 per 1,000 in the northeast, and 71 per 1,000 in the southeast. The Nigerian Demographic and Health Survey of 1990 showed that one half of all women became mothers before age 20. Ten to 12% gave birth before age 15, and 21 to 28% gave birth between ages 15 and 17. [B. Yusuf]

## C. Adults

MARIO BELLO, IMO I. ESIET, UWEM EDIMO ESIET, FOYIN OYEBOLA, and BILKISU USUF

### *Premarital Relations, Courtship, and Dating*

FOYIN OYEBOLA

Nigerian youths start dating at about age 16. Most of them date without knowing what dating entails, hence they do not know how to comport themselves during dates. There is a general belief that sexual intercourse must take place during dating. Most young people do not see dating as a first stage of courtship. Courtship in the real sense starts when young persons are in the tertiary institutions preparatory to marriage. Generally, the duration of most courtships is relatively short, and the courtship is kept secret from the parents, so there is no parental guidance. (See Section 5A/B, Interpersonal Heterosexual Behaviors, Children and Adolescents, above, for additional details on dating, courtship, and engagement.)

### *Conception, Pregnancy, and Sexual Intercourse: A Regional/Ethnic Comparison*

The following summaries of the attitudes and practices regarding conception, pregnancy, and sexual intercourse of several ethnic groups in eight geographical regions of Nigeria were compiled by the authors during a meeting with healthcare professionals in January 1999 (Francoeur, Esiet, & Esiet 2000) (see Editor's Note at the beginning of this chapter).

1. Regions: Ipoti-Ekiti, Oyo, and Yorubaland. Ethnic Groups: Oyo, Yoruba, and Ipoti-Ekiti

    The Oyo do not allow premarital sexual relationships. They also view "modern" (non-male-above) techniques of coitus as abnormal and unmentionable. They think sexual intercourse is solely for procreation; pleasure comes second. They prefer male offspring because they will carry on the family name. The Yoruba culture also prefers male offspring. In fact, a Yoruba man will seek a new wife if his current wife produces only girls. Sexual relations are male-dominated, with the male initiating it and dictating the pace. Female response or satisfaction is not considered important. Coitus takes place at night and in the dark. Among the Ipoti-Ekiti, premarital sex is a taboo. The male-above position is standard, and coitus is for procreation and not really for pleasure. Male children are preferred.

2. Regions: Kano, Katsina, and Kaduna. Ethic Group: Muslim Hausa

    These cultures frown on premarital sexual relations. Sexual foreplay before coitus is also frowned on;

sexual intercourse usually occurs in the dark or semi-dark. The man indicates his readiness to penetrate by clearing his voice. This tells the wife to position herself. The woman always remains clothed or at least semi-nude. At the end of sexual intercourse, both partners have a ritual bath called *Ghusul Janabat*. Male children are preferred because they continue the family name, help with the farming, and assure inheritance.

3. Region: Borno

Premarital sex is a taboo. Contraception is not acceptable. Female children are appreciated more than males.

4. Region: Benue. Ethnic Groups: Tiv, Idoma, and Isala

Premarital sex is not encouraged. A divorced woman, however, is free to have sexual relations with any man. Sexual relations are for procreation; hence, polygamy is acceptable. Women abstain from sexual relations while breastfeeding. There is no foreplay before coitus and techniques for coitus are not even discussed. A wife must allow her husband to have a girlfriend, a "sister," from his own clan. The wife relinquishes the bed for "the sister" and must treat her nicely. A man is always unhappy when his wife has a female child. The wife is believed to be responsible for determining the sex of the child. Fathers are responsible when children are well-behaved and mothers are responsible when a child misbehaves. Aleku is a traditional god of the Idomas. When a man marries, his wife takes an oath to Aleku, who oversees women and checks on their fidelity. During the Aleku festival, the men are allowed to have sex with any girl or woman who has not taken an oath to Aleku.

5. Regions: Akwa-Ibom and the Cross River. Ethnic Groups: Efik and Ibibio

Premarital sexual relations are considered an abomination. The male-superior position is conventional and foreplay is highly valued. However, because intercourse is for the man's satisfaction and for procreation, a childless wife has no place in her own home. Because women are believed to determine the child's sex, a woman who has only daughters is often thrown out of the home. A badly behaved child is usually blamed on its mother. Among the Efiks and Ibibios, during the "fattening period" before marriage, an engaged girl is taught how to manage and keep a clean home, take care of her husband, help him to reach orgasm, treat in-laws respectfully, care for babies and children, cook delicious meals, maintain personal hygiene, and do a full body massage. In this culture, there is no preference for male or female offspring; inheritance is by seniority and is hereditary. In the river communities, a female is preferred for the first child, whereas the inland communities prefer the first child be a male. This has to do with the fishing and farming activities of the men. Wives visit their husbands in the fishing ports, like Bakasi, where the husbands also keep mistresses.

6. Region: Delta State. Ethnic Groups: Uhobod, Ibos, Ijaws, Isaw, and Itsekirus

In some regions of the Delta State, sexual intercourse is sacred; in others, it is not a big deal. Premarital sex is taboo and shameful in areas where virginity at marriage is cherished, but it is allowed in other areas. A girl is expected to become pregnant soon after marriage. There is a preference for male children, and a woman who has only daughters is in trouble. More often than not, her husband and his family will hate her. Such husbands may take another wife.

7. Region: Edo

Wives must respond to their husbands' sexual demands. Male children are preferred. Premarital sexual relationships are accepted depending on the girl's age. It is discouraged in the teen years. The male-above position is preferred and intercourse is for procreation and to feel good. Pregnancy should occur in the first year of marriage, and the first child should be male. Female children are not warmly welcomed, although children are considered God-given and many children are a blessing.

8. Regions: Imo, Enugu, and Anambra. Ethnic Group: Ibo

Even though premarital sexual relations were previously prohibited, in some areas of Anambra it is no longer a crime. Pregnant teenage girls are quickly married because it shows they are fertile. The male-above position is preferred. Intercourse is for procreation. Conception is a thing of joy, but male offspring are preferred. Any odd behavior is inherited from the mother; the father only passes on good traits. Pregnant women are forbidden to eat certain foods, like snails and grass-cutter meats (herbivores), because they are believed to cause excessive salivation and prolonged labor.

*Women and Marriage in Nigerian Law* IMO I. ESIET

Nigerian marital laws have helped to consolidate sex-role discrimination in the family. Traditional customs, known as the "customary law," is still accorded recognition in the area of family law, and in fact plays a very dynamic role in determining related issues.

*Women and Parental Consent in the Brideprice and Marriage.* According to Nwogugu, "For a girl, parental consent is mandatory under customary law even where she has attained majority, . . . on the other hand, an adult male may contract a valid marriage without the consent of his parent" (Nwogugu 1974, 20). The reason given for this inequality is that the brideprice, which is an essential characteristic of customary marriage law, cannot be properly paid, nor can the formal giving away of the bride be properly effected without parental consent. The brideprice has been described variously as a gift in kind or monetary payment to the parent/guardian of a female person on account of marriage to that female person (Nwogugu 1974, 50). Although brideprice is supposed to be a token of appreciation for the worth of the female chosen as a bride, the amount of the modern brideprice is less a token of appreciation than evidence that a daughter is regarded as an investment property whose total market value and capital outlay should be realized at the time of disposition. This situation has led to the intervention of the law in some jurisdictions, although the laws are hardly enforced. In 1956, for instance, the Eastern Region enacted a Limitation of Dowry law to regulate the amount that can be demanded as the brideprice. The reality of this transaction having an economic and investment nature is evident in the entitlement of the husband to a refund of the brideprice upon dissolution of the marriage.

*Women and the Right to Consortium.* By virtue of marriage, spouses acquire a right to associate in matrimonial circumstances (known as *consortium*) and enjoy certain incidental rights that flow from that marital/spousal relationship. Any interference with this right is actionable against a third party.

1. *Enticement and Harboring.* A spouse may bring an action against a third party for enticing, procuring, or inducing the other spouse to violate the duty to provide consortium to him or her. Whereas a husband can file a

tort against another man for "harboring" his wife, a wife cannot make an actionable claim against another woman for "harboring" her husband (*Adv v. Gillison* 1962, 390).

2. *Loss Due to Tort of a Third Party.* Whereas a husband can recover damages from a third party for loss of consortium and accompanying benefits or services of his wife as a result of that third party's action, a Nigerian woman does not have this same right and may not recover for the actual loss of consortium. She may, however, receive damages awarded for matters which are somewhat incidental to the loss of consortium (Nwogugu 1974, 66).

3. *Adultery.* Under statutory law, the right of claims in cases of adultery is mutually enforceable, because it is tied up with divorce grants based on adultery and there can be no separate civil action for adultery. However, in most parts of Nigeria, customary law recognizes only the husband's right to file claim against a third party who commits adultery with his wife. Hence, the husband can claim damages from the third party whether or not he uses the adultery to file for divorce from his wife. According to customary law, a wife can only apply for divorce if she claims adultery as the grounds for the breakdown of her marriage (Nwogugu 1974, chap. 7). In reality, Nigerian customary laws derive from the traditionally prevalent view that the wife is owned by her husband, whereas the husband is owned by no one but himself. Hence, adultery with the wife offends against the husband's proprietary interest, and payment of some kind must be made to compensate. On the other hand, adultery by the husband does not offend the wife because he belongs to himself (Oyajobi 1986, 30).

*Women and Maintenance under Customary Law.* Although customary law recognizes the duty of the husband to maintain his wife, it does not provide any judicial machinery for enforcing this duty, except for the rules of the Maliki School of Islamic Law, which allows an Alkali court to issue an order to the husband. However, when a husband fails comply with this duty, even when ordered to comply, the Alkali Court, which is a customary Court, can do no more than grant dissolution of the marriage. The High Court, on the other hand, can enforce compliance to such duty.

*Mothers and Child Custody.* In the past, customary law gave the father absolute right to the custody of his legitimate children. This position, however, has been altered by recent statutes, particularly the Infants Law 1978 (Oyo State, Section 12, 1). Also, the Matrimonial Causes Act (Section 71) places the parents of a child on equal footing, and the decision of the court is to give paramount regard to the interests of the child.

However, the customary legal systems on custody still discriminate against the woman. The right to custody of children is vested in the father, although the child's welfare is considered when the child is of tender years. In this particular case, although the mother may be given physical custody (when the parents are separated), Nwogugu notes that "the father's right is merely in abeyance" (Nwogugu 1974, 260).

*Women and the Matrimonial Home.* Property disputes, especially regarding the matrimonial home, may arise between a couple anytime during the life of a marriage. Oftentimes, there are complaints from women that although they contributed to the acquisition of matrimonial property, their husbands disregarded their interest at later dates and dis-

posed of the property without their consent. The property is usually purchased in the husband's name only. Efforts have been made in other countries to remedy this position; for instance, in 1967, England passed the Matrimonial Homes Act recognizing the rights of a spouse to occupy a matrimonial home whether or not that spouse is entitled by any legal right devolving on contract, by enactment, or estate (Section 1(1)). This was designed to protect a spouse who is not a legal owner against the power of the other spouse to dispose of the property and also against a third-party purchaser. The spouse's right of occupation ceases on the termination of the marriage, except if an application is made to the court while the marriage subsists to direct otherwise by an order. Given the years of British colonial rule in Nigeria, legislation such as this protecting women's rights in England is used by women's rights advocates in their efforts to improve the legal status and protection of Nigerian women.

Since the right of occupation terminates with a divorce, the matter becomes one of property adjustment, and the court can be called upon by virtue of section 7(1) of the Matrimonial Causes Act to resolve distribution of the property in a way it considers just and equitable. Because of the special and domestic nature of the marriage relationship, transactions between couples are not evidenced in the same way as commercial transactions. But the position of the courts in Nigeria, as held in *Nwanya v. Nwanya* (NWLR 1987, 3, 697), is that a claimant for settlement must show evidence of her contributions.

## Marriage and Family　　　　　UWEM EDIMO ESIET

Individual married couples stipulate their sexual norms and values, protected by the male decision-making role and the custom of total silence regarding sexuality. Menopause may bring a major change, but the extent and nature of this effect has not been researched. Within the family, incest is not accepted.

## Menopause: A Regional/Ethnic Comparison

The following summaries of the attitudes and practices regarding menopause of several ethnic groups in eight geographical regions of Nigeria were compiled by the authors during a meeting with healthcare professionals in January 1999 (Francoeur, Esiet, & Esiet 2000) (see Editor's Note at the beginning of this chapter).

1. Regions: Ipoti-Ekiti, Oyo, and Yorubaland. Ethnic Group: Yoruba

   Menopause means a woman has finished her sexual activity. She can neither give birth nor give sexual pleasure to her husband. It is the end of her womanhood, and her husband hardly gives her any emotional attention. A menopausal woman "is old and should be preparing for the grave." Women don't talk about menopause because there are no issues attached to it and it is not celebrated. Menopause often results in the man taking another, younger wife. Menopausal women are looked at as old people and are recognized as mothers, but not as wives.

2. Regions: Kano, Katsina, and Kaduna. Ethic Group: Muslim Hausa

   Special considerations regarding menopause are unknown.

3. Region: Borno

   "Menopause is like having a sleepy pregnancy." (There is no indication of whether this is good or bad.)

4. Region: Benue. Ethnic Groups: Tiv, Idoma, and Isala

   Menopause is rarely recognized, as life goes on normally. It simply means that a woman is getting close to retirement.

5. Regions: Akwa-Ibom and the Cross River. Ethnic Groups: Efik and Ibibio

This culture does not accept or see menopause as a natural aging process. It is attributed to the attacks of witchcraft. When this happens, the man starts looking for a younger wife, while the woman starts seeking a traditional treatment or cure. During menopause, women become psychologically unstable, suspicious, erratic, irritable, and talkative. Menopause means the woman has outlived her reproductive role and her usefulness in the home. A menopausal woman is not expected to continue sexual relations with her husband, so she arranges for a younger girl to live with her husband.

6. Region: Delta State. Ethnic Groups: Uhobod, Ibos, Ijaws, Isaw, and Itsekirus

Menopause is seen as the end of a woman's reproductive and sexual life. Her husband may take another wife to satisfy his sexual urges. Menopausal women often become depressed when they feel they are no longer useful and therefore not cherished by their husbands.

7. Region: Edo

Men do not find a menopausal woman useful or productive. People feel that the "bad blood" lost during menstruation now collects in the body, causing problems.

8. Regions: Imo, Enugu, and Anambra. Ethnic Group: Ibo

Menopausal women gain more respect because they are now considered men. There are usually no acceptance problems for menopausal women. As for the men, they like running away from their menopausal wives, although our society frowns on this.

### *Cohabitation, Monogamy, and Polygyny*
UWEM EDIMO ESIET

In the past two decades, an increase in the incidence of cohabitation has been observed. However, this is far from being the norm as it has become in Euro-American countries. Because this is a new phenomenon in Nigerian culture, the partners are left to work out their own terms and conditions as appropriate, without benefit of or guidance from the legal structure.

Monogamy has been the hallmark of Christian marriages, even though a few indigenous Christian churches allow or endorse alternatives. Polygyny has been a traditionally accepted marriage pattern in Nigeria and it continues to have some support among Islamic adherents and members of some indigenous Christian churches.

### *Divorce, Remarriage, and Extramarital Sex*
UWEM EDIMO ESIET

"'Til death do us part" has long been the Christian marital ethic. However, this is increasingly being flouted, as spouses are now insisting on their personal rights within marriage, including the right to love and be loved, and have mutual respect and care for each other. Despite the Christian ethic, there is an increased incidence of divorce in contemporary Nigeria. Remarriage after divorce is also becoming more acceptable, especially within traditional tribal norms and Islamic practices and tenets.

Extramarital sex is permissible for the man but not for the woman. However, with the downturn in the economy and women being more assertive, such occurrences are becoming more realistic even for women.

### *Sexuality and the Physically Disabled and Aged*
UWEM EDIMO ESIET

The physically disabled have not been overtly discriminated against, as most children and families wish that their disabled family members could have children as a compensation for their efforts in contributing to the family.

The elderly enjoy their sexuality within their sociocultural norms and values, and like all Nigerians, are left to deal with their sexual desires and needs within the code of silence regarding all sexual matters.

### *Attitudes on and Incidence of Oral and Anal Sex*
UWEM EDIMO ESIET

Anal penetrative sex is frowned on even now, particularly in view of the HIV/AIDS risk. Although oral sex is practiced, it is not glamorized as it is in other countries, primarily because of the general culture of silence on sexual topics.

### *Aphrodisiacs*
BILKISU YUSUF

Traditional aphrodisiacs are quite common in Hausa culture. They vary from those used as food to special chemical preparations. There are different types used by men and women to increase libido and vaginal lubrication, and to ensure that married couples derive maximum sexual satisfaction from their partners.

While a variety of male aphrodisiacs exists, the most widely used among Hausa men is *Gaggai*, a root which is either boiled, powdered, and mixed with spices and eaten with meat, or soaked with spices to make a drink. For women, *tukudi* is routinely prepared for brides; its content depends on the local aphrodisiac herbs available in a particular area. *Hakin maye*, very common among Hausa in the Sokoto and Kebbi States, is a combination of herbs used as food additives mixed with chicken broth, sprinkled on yogurt, or mixed with honey.

The herb *Gyadan mata*, which grows in the wild and looks like a nut, is chewed by women. Two groups of aphrodisiacs, known as *Ko gida* and *Ko mota*, are popularly hawked by women: One is taken orally, whereas the other, used as a topical application, is used to tighten the vaginal muscles. *Maganin mata* (women's medicine) is a more general term used in a variety of female aphrodisiacs that include local herbs, a white sweet substance imported from Arab countries, and a dark substance called *laximi* imported from the Indian subcontinent.

It is quite common to see local female herbalists (*'yar mai ganye*) hawking these aphrodisiac herbs in the markets. Those who prepare aphrodisiacs for brides and other users buy their herbs from the local female herbalist or her male counterpart. After they prepare their special variety of ingredients, they sell their mixes wholesale to retail hawkers, *dillalai*, and it is not unusual to see these aphrodisiac hawkers making brisk business at social gatherings and sharing in hushed voice with friends their experiences on the efficacy of their own brand of tried and tested aphrodisiacs. There is no existing research on these traditional Hausa aphrodisiacs, but their usage is widespread. Dealers in Sokoto, Nigeria, and in Maradil in neighboring Niger Republic are known for their virtual monopoly on some of the most popular brands.

## *6. Homoerotic, Homosexual, and Bisexual Behaviors*
UWEM EDIMO ESIET

### A. Children and Adolescents

From what little is known, the incidence of same-sex sexual behavior among children and adolescents is very low. Incidents have been reported within same-sex institutions.

### B. Adults

More adult homosexual behavior is being recorded. One reason cited for this behavior is the myth that homosexual relationships enhance one's personal wealth acquisition. Persons who engage in homosexual behavior tend to be bisexual, because exclusive homosexuality is greatly frowned on.

### Homosexuality: A Regional/Ethnic Comparison

The following summaries of the attitudes and practices regarding homosexuality of several ethnic groups in eight geographical regions of Nigeria were compiled by the authors during a meeting with healthcare professionals in January 1999 (Francoeur, Esiet, & Esiet 2000) (see Editor's Note at the beginning of this chapter).

1. Regions: Ipoti-Ekiti, Oyo, and Yorubaland. Ethnic Group: Yoruba

   The people believe that homosexuality does not exist, only heterosexuals. People who engage in same-sex acts are seen as outcasts.

2. Regions: Kano, Katsina, and Kaduna. Ethic Group: Muslim Hausa

   Homosexuals exist. They are not accepted and keep their sexual activities hidden.

3. Region: Borno

   Both homosexuals and bisexuals exist, but such behavior is taboo.

4. Region: Benue. Ethnic Groups: Tiv, Idoma, and Isala

   The people may hear about homosexuality and bisexuality, and it may occur, but no one has ever seen it.

5. Regions: Akwa-Ibom and the Cross River: Ethnic Groups: Efik and Ibibio

   There are no forms of homosexuality or bisexuality in this culture: These acts are forbidden. Anyone known to be engaging in this activity is stigmatized and regarded as outcast.

6. Region: Delta State. Ethnic Groups: Uhobod, Ibos, Ijaws, Isaw, and Itsekirus

   Special considerations regarding homosexuality are unknown.

7. Region: Edo

   There are no forms of homosexuality or bisexuality allowed in this culture.

8. Regions: Imo, Enugu, and Anambra States. Ethnic Group: Ibo

   People say they know nothing about homosexuality in this culture.

## 7. Gender Diversity and Transgender Issues

Gender-conflicted persons are not recognized in our culture, which maintains a strict either/or belief regarding male and female gender. Transvestitism is neither acknowledged nor encouraged.

## 8. Significant Unconventional Sexual Behaviors

### A. Coercive Sex

CHRISTINE OLUFUNKE ADEBAJO and IMO I. ESIET

*Coercive Sex and Nigerian Law: An Overview of the Current Status* CHRISTINE O. ADEBAJO

Sexual abuse, assaults, and harassment all involve violence against women or men. Any of these forms of coercive sex can occur in the home, workplace, or in public. And each, as an issue, remains complex, ambiguous, interwoven, and extremely dangerous in the traditional Nigerian society. They all entail subjugation of the victim and the stripping of her (or his) autonomy and self-esteem. The occurrences against women are more pronounced because such acts are encouraged by the societal perception of a woman's low status. In Nigeria, as described above, women are subject to several dehumanizing and oppressive traditional values, which ultimately dictate how women are regarded, treated, and acknowledged.

As a traditional, tribal-based society, Nigeria has mechanisms that legitimize, cloud, and deny sexual abuse, assaults, and harassment as forms of violence against women in particular. In many instances, even when a particular act of violence is deplored, some conventional institutions, such as the family structure, as well as religious and traditional rulers, protect the status quo, making it more difficult to challenge. For example, most Nigerian communities, if not all, believe in male supremacy; hence, any of these acts is perceived as an acceptable exercise of the male's prerogative over women's sexuality.

Within the context of women's almost helpless social position, ridiculous scenarios and rhetorical questions are widely used in casual conversations to make light of the reality of oppression and subjugation that these acts inflict on women. For example, men and women alike ask, "Why should a man not chastise his wife for an offense?" Note that such "chastisement" can include physical assaults of varying degree. Another question usually asked involves female genital mutilation (female circumcision): "Why should a woman choose to be uncircumcised, or make her daughter an 'outcast' by not allowing her to be circumcised?" This act is not considered sexual abuse, when in reality it is indeed just that. In fact, one would like to ask who and what makes an uncircumcised woman an outcast? Obviously, it is the society. In this perspective, it could be concluded that sexual abuse, assaults, and harassment affecting women are in most cases not accidental; instead, they serve the sociopolitical function of keeping women subordinate. They are most often expressions of power that connote an unequal relationship between male and female sexuality.

The occurrences of sexual abuse, assaults, and harassment against men in Nigeria are very negligible. When such incidences do occur at all, they occur among children and adolescent males. Ironically, when any act of this nature is directed against a male, it is viewed with great seriousness. In some communities, the same powerful institutions that downplayed these acts perpetrated on women view them as an abomination when directed at a male.

Socially, sexual abuse, assaults, and harassment against women are subtly tied to sexism and women's oppressed status, particularly their sexuality. The law is seemingly insensitive to these acts, whether it is dealing with marital rape (see below) or with other more clear and documented cases. A typical case in which the courts evaded and ignored the need for redress is the outcome in the case of *Jos N. A. Police vs. Allah Nagari, Nigeria*, in which a 7-year-old girl gave evidence against the man she claimed raped her. Her bloodstained clothes were produced as evidence while a medical report confirmed injury to her genitalia. Despite this evidence, the man was not convicted because a clause in the law stipulates that any child less than 8 years of age needs her case corroborated, before the court can rule in her favor. Unfortunately, cases like this abound, even though requiring a witness to the rape makes a mockery of the law's professed lack of bias between the sexes.

Even though economic deprivation in Nigeria affects all groups, ages, and sexes, the worst hit are women and children. Women in particular suffer from unequal and inequitable access to vital development resources, such as education, employment, housing, and so on. Yet, women are mainly responsible for raising the children. This dependency exposes mothers and children to prostitution and other forms of sexual abuse. They are also prone to assaults and harassment from frustrated husbands and fathers. With the father's situation highly precarious because of the prevalence of unemployment, male frustration is common in the Nigerian home. Nigerian wives can easily be sexually exploited by their husbands for the benefit of their family. Also, fathers at times encourage their daughters to prostitute themselves, either directly or while hawking goods in the marketplace, in order to help the family's economic stress.

### Ethnic Variations CHRISTINE O. ADEBAJO

Although sexual abuse, assaults, and harassment occur among people of all ethnic, cultural, religious, and social classes, their pattern and causes can only be understood and remedied in specific social and cultural contexts. However, in all ethnic regions of Nigeria, almost all reported cases of sexual abuse, assaults, and harassment are perpetrated by men. For example, in a study conducted by Francisca Isi Omorodium between 1982 and 1988 in Benin City, Edo State, all cases of battering reported to the Social Welfare Department were perpetrated by men. The same study showed that the men who battered their wives were between the ages of 20 and 45 years, while their wives were between the reproductive ages of 18 and 36 years.

The study went further to ascertain that battering was not limited to level of education or class. It showed that 50% of the men and 30% of the women involved had attained at least a primary school certificate. More frustrating was the finding that 40% of the men and 30% of the women involved had an educational level ranging from secondary school to college. The findings portrayed a further worrisome fact that most of the cases reported to the Social Welfare Department were from the lower strata, while most of the upper-class cases went unreported and were kept secret by the victims.

Certain acts that qualify as sexual abuse, assault, and harassment are seen in some Nigerian communities as normal and hidden under the umbrella of traditional practice, culture, and beliefs. Examples include female genital mutilation, nutritional taboos in pregnancy and children, body scarification, seclusion in labor, hot baths during the six weeks after birth, and a host of others. Some of these acts are perpetrated as a societal norm. In the case of child battering, some communities believe that parents or guardians have a prerogative over their children and thus can scold and beat them to any degree without interference from a third party. In such a circumstance, a child can be ill-treated and badly injured without it being seen as battering. In certain communities where the wife is viewed as the man's property to be used as he desires or sees fit, beating one's wife is therefore nobody else's business. Worse still, in the same communities, a wife who expresses a need or seeks a favor from her husband can be seen as purposely aggravating the husband to beat her. This is because it is believed that such a domestic scuffle would be settled by the husband offering a gift.

### Current Data CHRISTINE O. ADEBAJO

Statistical information on the extent of sexual abuse, assaults, and harassment in Nigeria is very scanty, as most data have been compiled in small studies. This data therefore provides only a small insight into the incidence, and the data cannot be used as concrete indicators on the extent of these acts in Nigeria as a whole. However, some of the available studies portray serious health, emotional, and physical consequences that cannot be ignored.

For example, after a 1985-1986 study of the national prevalence of female genital mutilation (FGM), Christine Adebajo reported that female genital mutilation was ac-

tively promoted and advocated in 21 out of the 30 states in Nigeria. The prevalence within the newly adjusted state boundaries and newly created states indicated that 35% to 90% of the women in 18 states are mutilated, while in nine other states the percentage of mutilated women was 90% or higher.

Other documented cases of sexual assaults, abuse, and harassment include the following:

- In 1987, 12-year-old Hauwa Abubakar from northern Nigeria died after having both legs amputated by her husband after the girl made several attempts to run away from her forced marriage.
- A case of rape of a 10-year-old girl by a police officer was reported in Benin City. The police officer grabbed the girl who was returning from an errand, locked the door, and threw her to the floor, tearing her underclothes. Before her cries could attract a passerby, she had been raped. The only redress was a fine of 2,500 Naira (roughly $2,500 U.S.) which was never paid by the offender.
- In June 1995, some neighbors brought a 37-year old married woman to my husband's private hospital with a fractured collarbone. She had just been mercilessly beaten by her husband, because he suspected that their son told her about his infidelity. Despite the fact that she did not react, the husband's guilt could not hold him back from challenging his wife for knowing of his infidelity. The husband was, of course, reported to the police by the hospital, but the case was eventually thrown out of court as a mere family squabble that should be settled out of court.

These few cases typify the outcome of many reported cases of assault, sexual abuse, and harassment in Nigeria. Unfortunately, the majority of abuse/assault cases are not reported and do not get public notice. A culture of silence seems to be responsible for the inadequacy of documentation and population-based data. In addition, the sociocultural and legal barriers on the issue of violence, particularly relating to sexuality, make it almost impossible to acquire accurate data on any of the acts. Nevertheless, the few available data and several deafening whispers of daily occurrence of violence are sufficient to justify increased attention to this issue.

### Sexual Abuse, Assault, and Harassment

CHRISTINE O. ADEBAJO

In this discussion, we have tried to discuss the various forms of sexual abuse, assault, and harassment, respecting the ways in which these are perceived and categorized in Nigeria. However, sexual abuse, assault, and harassment are so interwoven that one can hardly talk of one without overlapping into the other. Clear operational definitions are difficult to come by, because the distinctions are often subtle and varied according to the interpretations of the victim, varying cultural perspectives, and differences in the way males and females view individual occurrences. The application of definitions, even when such are clearly delineated, is often difficult or impossible, because particular cases frequently involve a combination of various actions which cannot be separated out. Whatever form these actions take, they usually share a common motivation: to gain and sustain dominance and control over the victim. Sexual harassment, abuse, and assault in Nigeria constitute a major component of violence against women, since it is often associated with male dominance, although a variety of assaults are common among adolescents, peer groups, and adults of either gender.

*Sexual Abuse.* [Christine O. Adebajo] Sexual abuse is here defined as someone forcing another to engage in sexual activity, or interfering with someone's sexuality, against his or her will and without his or her consent. Such abuse, which may involve a male and a female or persons of the same gender, may result in, or is likely to result in, physical, sexual, or psychological harm or suffering to the victim. Abuse, in private or in a public place, can range from being kissed without one's consent to touching the sex organs to forced sexual intercourse. Sometimes, sexual abuse can occur between an adult and a child or teenager. Most commonly, however, sexual abuse occurs among people with a personal relationship or where they have had such a relationship in the past. While terms such as sexual assault, sexual coercion, and sexual aggression are sometimes used as synonyms for sexual abuse, in Nigeria sexual abuse includes the following acts: verbal aggression/assault, unwanted physical touch, rape, incest, child prostitution, female genital mutilation (FGM), and *Yankan Gishir* (salt cut)—these variations are discussed below individually.

*Unwanted Physical Touching.* [Christine O. Adebajo] It is not uncommon in public places such as work and school, especially colleges, for women to experience physical touch with a sexual connotation. This can involve patting the buttocks (bum-patting), open display of sexist images, rubbing of the body, and more-overt molestation. In Nigeria, it is difficult to take these particular types of abuse too far, because they are not viewed with any legal seriousness. Perhaps one of the reasons for this is the fact that Nigerians are known to be warm and close people, where touching is generally seen as an act of kindness and friendship. However, where it involves an adult male touching the genitalia of a child, particularly of the opposite sex, it is viewed with more seriousness.

*Verbal Assault.* [Christine O. Adebajo] Verbal assault or aggression occurs when words are used to control, dominate, and intimidate the victim by yelling, insulting, speaking unkindly, and name calling. Other forms of verbal assault involve judging and criticizing; discounting what the other says, feels, or thinks, and in repeatedly disagreeing with the victim. Verbal assaults can be very psychologically damaging, making the victim feel dehumanized and belittled. This can lead to serious emotional health problems. Verbal abuse also very often leads to physical assaults. Unlike other forms of violence, verbal assaults are not primarily limited to males against women; they are perpetrated by both sexes and in all age groups.

*Indecent Assaults.* [Imo I. Esiet] Section 360 of the Criminal Code provides that: "any person who unlawfully and indecently assaults a woman or girl is guilty of a misdemeanor, and is liable to imprisonment for two years." However, according to section 353 of the same Code, this felony is punishable with three years imprisonment when the victim is a male, rather than two years as in a case of female victims. A fundamental principle of criminal law is that all persons should be equally protected from harm of like degree. It is hard to see any justification for creating different offenses with different penalties to cover the same conduct for persons of different sexes.

*Sexual Harassment.* [Christine O. Adebajo] In Nigeria, harassment can be categorized under two headings as direct or indirect. Direct sexual harassment, including verbal assault and unwanted touches, such as bum-patting, sexist remarks, open display of sexist images, and more-overt molestation, is a major gender issue, particularly in the work setting and in colleges where it can manifest in the form of victimiza-

tion and/or molestation. Indirect sexual harassment/abuse occurs as a result of traditional practices or beliefs referred to as "harmful traditional practices" (HTP); see Section 8D, Female Genital Mutilation and Other Harmful Practices.

In Nigeria, as elsewhere around the world, sexual harassment is commonly perpetrated by men against women. However, a few cases have been reported of Nigerian female executives harassing their subordinates. Also on record are a few cases of sexual harassment by female college students against their male lecturers. Even though it is common knowledge that sexual harassment of females by males occurs in public spaces, such as the workplace, school, market, and street, it is often very difficult to prove such in a traditional society such as Nigeria, where the behavior correlates with the society's gender power differentials.

In the workplace, sexual harassment has been manifested in limiting the female to designated sex roles through blackmail or other means. For example, in labor unions, an assertive woman unionist is looked on as defiant. This also occurs when women try to move into professional jobs that are believed to be the exclusive preserve of men. In a research work very applicable to the Nigerian situation, Dr. Madeline Heilman of New York University showed that there is a general consensus that pretty career women have problems on the job. Heilman found that when an attractive woman is looking for lower-level jobs, her looks could earn her a plus. However, when she is in a managerial position, competing with a good-looking man puts her at a disadvantage. A good-looking man is seen as competent, tough, decisive, and hard-nosed, whereas an attractive woman with the same qualifications, background, experience, and recommendation is dismissed as gentle, soft, and indecisive.

Because of the nature of Nigerian social codes and values that stress male dominance of women, sexual harassment often goes unnoticed. This societal posture makes the victim unwilling to report cases of sexual harassment. It has also been observed that victims are not sure of what constitutes sexual harassment.

*Domestic Violence and Spousal Abuse.* [Christine O. Adebajo] These are aggressive acts, such as pushing, kicking, slapping, hitting, punching, grabbing, biting, throwing objects, burning, wounding, or in the extreme, killing. Even though physical assaults are perpetrated by both genders, the worst recorded cases are those perpetrated by males against females, particularly those associated with domestic violence. Domestic violence usually leads to severe injury and, in a few cases, to death. Unfortunately, this problem is not receiving adequate recognition from the society, which does not consider it a problem worth addressing. Physical assaults within the family are central to the violence in Nigerian culture at large. It is embedded within the traditional values that place men above women, and the concept that domestic violence is a private matter between husband and wife or man and woman. There is a quiet willingness to accept it.

Case studies of wife battering in some parts of Nigeria have documented that the injuries sustained by battered wives include: facial bruises, blackened eyes, cuts on the mouth, loss of teeth, fractures, and severing of hand(s). Another study, conducted by the Akwa-Ibom State branch of Women in Nigeria (WIN), listed the following major causes of violence in-home in terms of descending importance:

- arguments over money;
- jealousy and fear of the partner's infidelity;
- a partner's attempt to intervene in the punishment of children;
- arguments over drinking habits;

- being overburdened with family chores;
- in-law interference;
- a partner being blamed for the children's behavior;
- a spouse's desire to go for further studies or to advance her career;
- ignoring a spouse;
- frequent demands for sexual relations; and
- disputes over the number of children wanted.

The same survey went further to elucidate steps taken by spouses to protect themselves. Among the coping mechanisms used were:

- reporting the assault or abuse to parents, in-laws, the police, social welfare agencies, or a religious leader;
- doing nothing;
- leaving the home with the children;
- praying to God to change him; and
- keeping quiet until it is over.

The majority of the respondents considered domestic violence as natural and not to be questioned or challenged. Victims were optimistic that their partners who had shown a violent tendency would change with time, although all of them confirmed that their health was affected when violence occurred. The majority, who see acts of domestic violence as wrong, still feel that they should stick to their marriage, because:

- divorce and separation are considered shameful;
- there is no place to keep the children; and
- they do not want the children to have different fathers.

Thus, it appears that many marriages have seriously deteriorated, although things are patched up on the surface. Even when physical injury is not inflicted, many women live in perpetual emotional turmoil, obviously with impaired health.

*Domestic Violence and Spousal Abuse.* [Imo I. Esiet] Although much of spousal assault involves wife battering and is exploitative and abusive of the marriage relationship, keeping in mind the fact of female subordinance in Nigerian society helps one understand the peculiar social setting that exposes the married woman to such an attack on her physical person.

One of the reasons often given to justify wife battering is the right of the husband to chastise his wife and an erring wife's need of discipline. This defense and claim to moral justification is based on the view that by consenting to marriage, a woman consents to revert to the status of a minor. The provisions of law which allow a defense to assault on grounds of reasonable chastisement gives the right only to parents or those who stand *in loco parentis*. In essence, then, this defense places the wife in the same position as her children in relation to the husband's supreme authority. In most cases, we may safely assume that the wife would have attained civil majority. So the question becomes one of whether an adult woman loses her maturity and capacity to be responsible simply because she has married, and her husband decides to discipline her like a child when she errs.

*Rape.* [Imo I. Esiet] Section 357 of the Nigerian Criminal Code defines rape as "unlawful carnal knowledge of a woman or girl, with or without her consent, or if the consent is obtained by force or by means of threats, intimidation of any kind, or by fear of harm or by means of false and fraudulent misrepresentation as to the nature of the act or in the case of a married woman, by impersonating her husband." The offense is punishable with life imprisonment with or without whipping. This definition in section 357, however, needs to be read with section 6, which excludes forced sexual intercourse between spouses. Marital rape is not recognized in Nigerian law. The customary law reasoning for this exclusion was succinctly stated by Hale (in Smith & Hogan 1983), when he said, "The husband cannot be guilty of a rape committed by himself upon his lawful wife, for by their mutual matrimonial consent and contract the wife has given up herself in this kind unto her husband which she cannot retract."

It would appear from the above definition of rape that rape is deemed to differ qualitatively from the act of mutual and reciprocal lovemaking only on the issue of consent. According to Nigerian law, in consenting to contract marriage, a married woman gives up any right to refuse sexual intercourse with her husband, even when he forcibly imposes his will on her (Oyajobi 1986, 18). This legal position has prompted one commentator to ask: "If the law recognizes the need to protect the wife from other physical assaults from her husband, why should she not be entitled to protection simply because the assault this time is of a sexual nature" (Oyajobi 1986, 18; Criminal Code sections 335, 338, 351, 352, 362).

There are, however, some situations in which it has been ruled that a husband should be held liable for raping his wife (Oyajobi 1986, 19). These situations are where:

- a divorce decree has been given, even though the marriage is still in existence;
- the spouses are living apart under a court separation order;
- one spouse has filed papers to commence divorce proceedings;
- a husband has been given a court order not to return to his wife;
- there has been a separation by agreement; or
- there is a court order prohibiting molestation of the wife.

It is important to note that legally the sexual history of the victim is inextricably tied to the issue of whether or not the party gave consent to the alleged forced intercourse. Section 210 of the Evidence Act allows evidence of previous sexual dealings of the accuser with other persons as well as the accused. But the fact that the plaintiff gave consent to having sex with the accused on a previous occasion may not be conclusive evidence that consent was given on the alleged occasion.

Corroboration of evidence regarding the plaintiff's alleged previous behavior is not an express requirement of the law of rape in Nigeria. However, following the customary law trend, our courts have evolved the rule of practice of warning juries about the danger of convicting based on uncorroborated evidence. The difficulties inherent in providing corroboration in rape cases are obvious. This is not unconnected with the fact that these offenses take place in private, and it is unlikely that there will be any human witnesses apart from the parties themselves.

*Another View of Rape.* [Christine O. Adebajo] In addition to marital rape and stranger rape, Nigerian women have been subjected to brutal rape as part of war and violence against refugees. This experience was documented during the Nigerian Civil War with Biafra (1966-1970).

The Nigerian Criminal Code section 221 stipulates that it is a criminal offense if a man has sexual intercourse with a woman:

1. without her consent;
2. with her consent given under fear of pain or death threat; or

3. if the female is under 14 years of age or of unsound mind, whether with or without her consent.

Ironically, the age of consent for sexual intercourse varies from one part of the country to another. Specifically, the Nigerian Criminal Code puts the age of consent for boys at 14 and for girls at 16 (unless she is married). It will be seen that the law itself can be open to a lot of abuses. Law enforcement agencies are usually not sensitive to sexual rights violations, often making it difficult to establish a case of rape. The record shows that very few cases of rape offenders have been prosecuted. On the other hand, a child victim is often labeled as being sexually aggressive, even by the courts of law.

This unfavorable societal outlook on the issue of rape has not helped in the proper documentation of its incidence. Victims are reluctant to report rape cases because they feel ashamed that the society might insinuate that they made themselves a target of attack. They are also afraid of repeated occurrences by the perpetrator, because the victim is not sure of adequate redress by law enforcement agents. In some cases, victims have been driven to commit suicide because of the stigma and possible dishonor, particularly in cases of illegitimate pregnancy.

A common form of rape in Nigeria occurs with domestic help, usually a teenage girl, when she is molested by her master or by a teenage male child or relation of the master.

Nongovernmental organizations (NGOs) and other groups and individuals need to agitate for law reform that will provide adequate redress for victims. Such a law should also facilitate the prosecution of offenders, more so because the present provision under the criminal code makes a case of rape lapse if prosecution does not commence within two months of the offense. The other obstacle is the requirement of providing an eyewitness when the offense itself can hardly be committed in the presence of anyone.

*Incest.* [Christine O. Adebajo] It is difficult to provide a clear definition for incest in the Nigerian context, because its meaning varies from community to community. For example, certain ethnic groups permit marriage between cousins. Neither the criminal nor penal codes make provision for incest as a categorical form of crime. Sexual intercourse between father and daughter is illegal and regarded as an infringement on the daughter's sexual rights. Documentation of incest is almost totally lacking. Nevertheless, unreported cases do exist in almost every community. It is known that victims who were abused by their fathers or stepfathers, whose abuse involved genital contact, and whose molestation involved force, are at greater risk of long-lasting effects that can include: nightmares, flashbacks, disassociative responses, emotional numbing, and so on. It has also been established that the long-term psychological complications usually manifest as physical complaints, some of which may be linked with chronic pelvic pain, headaches, asthma, and gynecological problems (Koss 1987).

As with rape, a substantial number of cases of incest do occur among cousins, even in communities where cousin marriages are not allowed. The majority of these cases occur among teenagers. Most are never allowed to reach public notice, as the parents collude to "bury" such incidences within the family to avoid "dishonor." Other common cases involve sexual molestation of stepdaughters by their stepfathers, and of stepsisters by their stepbrothers. In recent times, it has been observed that teenage girls are increasingly more likely to initiate incestuous relationships. This development is perhaps linked with two facts: Girls mature biologically at a younger age than boys, and today's society allows girls more freedom, which exposes them to opportunities of early sexual interaction.

## B. Prostitution

*Adult Prostitution*                    IMO I. ESIET

Adult prostitution is on the increase, especially with the downturn in the economy. The connection between increasing prostitution and increased incidence of HIV/AIDS in this group has created considerable interest among healthcare providers. Several nongovernmental organizations are now working with prostitutes to get them to practice safer sex.

Section 1 of the Criminal Code defines prostitution as "the offering by a female of her body, commonly for acts of lewdness for payment . . .," whereas, by virtue of sections 222A, 223(2), and (4) of the Criminal Code, the male can only be liable for the offense of procuring a female to become a prostitute.

According to Ayo Oyajobi (1986, 23), there is hardly any moral justification or logical reasoning for the exemption of males from the definition of who can be a prostitute, while asserting that there is no reason why a man cannot offer his body for acts of lewdness for payment. The truth is that men in fact do so more often than we would like to admit. This assertion is based on the increased obviousness of homosexual activities by males, in which case male prostitution has become more common and evident. But in reality, only less economically fortunate women in Nigerian society find themselves policed and labeled for subsequent discriminatory treatment by the law (Oyajobi 1986, 24). Although, economic factors cannot adequately explain prostitution, they must not be treated as marginal considerations. Insofar as our male-dominated society offers relatively limited opportunities for women to earn a good living wage, win promotions, achieve a secure career, and generally attain economic independence from men, women will be only too willing to give their bodies to achieve these ends (Oyajobi 1986, 24).

*Child Prostitution*               CHRISTINE ADEBAJO

Child prostitution, which used to be a taboo, is now a reality in Nigeria. Since the economic downturn that is hitting every family, child prostitution has increased steadily. The practice comes in different forms. In certain situations, parents actually encourage their teenage daughters to prostitute themselves.

In a survey carried out in some cities of Nigeria by a soft-pornography magazine, *Hints* (March 1996), most children interviewed confirmed that their mothers, the majority of whom are prostitutes themselves, introduced them to prostitution in an attempt to augment the family's earnings. The age range of these girls is from 8 to 13 years. The same survey revealed that secondary-school girls between the ages of 10 and 13 hang around hotels and streets soliciting male patronage. Others who appear physically mature take older men, referred to as "Sugar Daddies," for boyfriends. These men, in return for sexual gratification, assist the girls with their school fees. Another form of child prostitution occurs when young girls aged 8 to 15 are sent by their parents or guardians to hawk goods on the streets. Some of these children are easily seduced by older men and are paid for any contracted sexual act. More worrisome in recent times are a few reported cases of child-prostitute exporters and importers. This is most often perpetrated by foreigners.

In Nigeria, child prostitution and child pornography are illegal. Any such act that reaches the notice of law enforcement agents is handled with seriousness. Although one would have expected constant raids on perpetrators because they usually have specific designated areas, such raids are very sporadic where they exist at all. Child prostitution is a gross sexual abuse because the act is illegal, and most of the time, the act is forced on the prostitutes either by some older person or by circumstances beyond their control.

## C. Pornography and Erotica

See Section 3D, Informal Sources of Sexual Knowledge.

## D. Female Genital Mutilation and Other Harmful Practices  CHRISTINE ADEBAJO

Female circumcision (FC), or female genital mutilation (FGM) is a traditional practice in Nigeria in which an unskilled person or a health worker cuts off parts or whole organs of the female external genitalia. This practice is tied to culture, religious belief, and myth. Beyond this, it is a gross sexual abuse, which infringes on a woman's rights with abundant negative consequences (Goddard 1995).

The type of FGM performed varies from community to community, mostly based on their beliefs. In a nationwide survey carried out between December 1985 and May 1986 by Christine Adebajo for the National Association of Nigerian Nurses and Midwives (NANNM), the following facts were established:

- In the 21 states in Nigeria (out of 30 states) where FGM is carried out, it is believed that an uncircumcised woman is usually promiscuous. In Anambra, Bendel, Imo, Ondo, and Oyo States, more than 90% of the women have had some form of female circumcision, compared with only 30% in Lagos, the capital.
- In states where type III FGM (infibulation or pharaonic circumcision) is practiced, it is done to preserve virginity. Type III FGM involves surgical removal of the whole of the clitoris, the labia minora, and part of labia majora, and the stitching together of the two sides of the vulva, leaving tiny openings for the flow of urine and menstrual products. In parts of Edo State, FGM is carried out on a woman when she is about seven months pregnant. In 1985-1986, over 30% of the women in Bendel and Imo States had infibulation.
- Type II FGM (called reduction or excision) involves removal of the prepuce and the glans of the clitoris, together with adjacent parts of the labia minora or the whole of it. People believe that if the head of a newborn baby touches the clitoris, the baby will die. In 1985-1986, Bendel and Imo States had, respectively, a 55% and a 60% prevalence of excision.
- Among the 1,300 individuals who reported performing female circumcision, only 5% were skilled health professionals.
- In some eastern parts of the country, FGM is carried out as part of a pubertal rite. In this case, the extent of mutilation varies, depending on the circumciser's "expertise" and associated beliefs.
- In the western parts of the country, FGM is performed for cosmetic reasons, the belief being that if the female genitalia, particularly the clitoris, is not trimmed, it will grow and elongate like a penis.
- In some areas, Type I FGM (*Sunna*), which involves the removal of the prepuce or foreskin of the clitoris, is performed. In 1985-1986, three quarters of reported female circumcisions were *sunna* circumcisions.

Some of the health consequences of FGM include: injury to surrounding body parts, severe bleeding, shock, fainting during the mutilation, infection, and the inability to pass urine. Other long-term health hazards include: tetanus, blood poisoning, infection to the urinary and reproductive tracts, menstrual disorders, complications during childbirth, scar formation, painful sexual intercourse, and infertility because of fibrosis of the vagina. There is also a wide range of emotional and psychological effects, which may include embarrassment resulting from deformity of the vaginal area, anxiety and irritability, depression, marital problems of varying degrees, sometimes because of painful sexual intercourse, and psychosis as a result of frustration, particularly when one is unable to have intercourse.

Basically, FGM can be traced to a desire of the society to control female sexuality. Behind the various superstitions that perpetuate FGM, what seems to have sustained the practice is that men will not marry uncircumcised women, because they are believed to be unclean and promiscuous.

### Male and Female Circumcision: A Regional/Ethnic Comparison

The following summaries of the attitudes and practices regarding male and female circumcision of several ethnic groups in eight geographical regions of Nigeria were compiled by the authors during a meeting with healthcare professionals in January 1999 (Francoeur, Esiet, & Esiet 2000) (see Editor's Note at the beginning of this chapter).

1. Regions: Ipoti-Ekiti, Oyo, Ile-oluji, and Yorubaland. Ethnic Group: Yoruba
   Both male and female circumcision are traditional practices in Oyo State. Normally, circumcision is done in the first three months after birth. In the old days, one hardly heard of any complications, infections, or other harm to health. Now, because there are many incompetent people handling circumcision, we hear of complications, infections, and harmful effects. Some educated persons in the medical field now discourage female circumcision. In Yorubaland, male circumcision is generally practiced on the eighth day after birth. Male circumcision is accepted traditionally and is encouraged by the dominant religions in this region. In Ipoti-Ekiti, male and female circumcisions are usually carried out on the eighth day after birth. Female circumcision is practiced in some areas and not in others—in Ondo, Ilesha, and Ekiti towns, but not among the Ijebus. Female circumcision reduces a woman's sexual desire and the temptation to promiscuity. It also prevents the death of the child during delivery. It is believed that the child will die if its head touches the clitoris during birth. In Ile-oluji, female circumcision is an initiation into womanhood.

2. Regions: Kano, Katsina, and Kaduna. Ethic Group: Muslim Hausa
   Only male circumcision is practiced in these regions. Males are circumcised at age 6 to 7 years, when they realize that a male must endure pain. An elderly person, a *Wanzami*, carries out this procedure with locally made tools (*Aska*) and medicinal herbs. He begins with some incantations and digs a hole in the ground for the blood to flow into. He then holds the boy's legs apart with two sticks and circumcises him. Afterwards, the cloth the boy sat on, the soap used for washing hands by the *Wanzami*, as well as money and other gift items, are given to the *Wanzami* as presents. The circumcised boy is fed with special food and taken to a home different from his own to recover. The boy is showered with gifts from well-wishers and relatives. These days, the rate of infection from circumcisions has decreased, because the *Wanzami* now boil their instruments to disinfect them (although some infections still occur).

3. Region: Borno

Male circumcision is usually done sometime after age 7 years. Unsterilized instruments are used, leading to infections; excessive bleeding can result in death. Females are not circumcised but may participate in other traditional rituals.

4. Region: Tiv-Benue. Ethnic Groups: Tiv, Idoma, and Isala

Males are usually circumcised eight days after birth, but some are circumcised at age 4 or 5. Traditional leaders or ordinary people who have gained some skill in male circumcision perform this both in hospitals and in the villages. Males sometimes become infected as a result of poor hygiene.

5. Regions: Akwa-Ibom and the Cross River. Ethnic Groups: Efik and Ibibio

Among the Efiks and Ibibios, males are circumcised as babies. Female circumcision is done for aesthetic reasons, to avoid promiscuity, and to maintain virginity before marriage. People believe that if females enjoy intercourse, then they are likely to seek it from different men. Females may be circumcised during infancy or childhood, as a pubertal initiation, or just before marriage in "the fattening room," or not at all. Only the clitoral hood is removed. If done with unsterile instruments or by an inexperienced person, female circumcision can be harmful and life-threatening, or not at all. Some believe that female circumcision helps the fetal head descend smoothly during labor. In female circumcision, some practitioners drink illicit gin and spit it on the new wound; some use iodine on it, whereas others use a feather to spread fresh palm oil or engine oil to commence the healing process. Circumcision at birth has no rituals, but at other ages, feasting is usual for those who participate in the ritual as a sign of respect and acceptance or as initiation into the age group. Infections, tetanus, formation of keloids and fibrosis, extensive tears during labor, postpartum hemorrhage, social stigma, psychological trauma, and frigidity, are reported consequences of female circumcision.

6. Region: Delta State. Ethnic Groups: Uhobod, Ibos, Ijaws, Isaw, and Itsekirus

Males are usually circumcised within a few weeks of birth. Female circumcision is no longer common in some parts of the Delta. In other parts, however, it is still routinely practiced with a lot of importance attached. People see it as a sign of a girl's honor, a sign of maturity, a source of parental pride, and for the prevention of promiscuity. Usually the girl is between 13 and 21 years of age. In some areas, it occurs when the girl is expecting her first baby. In areas where female circumcision is common, the whole community celebrates and other young girls with their waists beautifully beaded come to stay with the circumcised girl for ten days. She does not do any work and is given tender, loving care by all. If she is engaged to a man, he comes to pay homage to the family, brings gifts, and helps the girl, including grinding her food. Depending on how it is done, both male and female circumcision can result in infection and other conditions that are harmful to health.

7. Region: Edo

Males and females are circumcised seven days after birth to reduce promiscuity. Even though new razor blades are used, males sometimes experience infections, wounds that do not heal, and excessive bleeding. Circumcision of females may interfere with normal sexual desire. In some cases, female circumcision results in injury to the major and minor labia, or a vesico-vaginal fistula (VVF) that can lead to difficult delivery and other complications.

8. Regions: Imo, Enugu, and Anambra. Ethnic Group: Ibo

In Enugu and Anambra, males are circumcised eight days after birth. Previously, in certain areas, like Nsukka, female circumcision was practiced, but generally no longer. When performed for cosmetic purposes or to reduce promiscuity, female circumcision may be done with the low-risk orthodox method or a high-risk crude native method. Complications of the native crude method include infections, vesico-vaginal fistula, and the narrowing of the vaginal opening leading to painful intercourse. In Imo and Anambra States, a male child must be circumcised within eight days after birth. There are no rituals attached to male or female circumcision.

## [Mating Practices: Dry Sex and Wet Sex

[*Update 2001*: As noted earlier, in both Christian and Muslim cultures in Nigeria, sexual relations are male-dominated, with the male initiating and dictating the pace. Female response and satisfaction are not considered important. Coitus takes place with no foreplay. The male-above position is standard, and marital coitus is for procreation, not for pleasure. Women in many African cultures do not even know what female orgasm is, and have never experienced it. In describing mating customs in the chapter on Ghana, Augustine Ankoma reports that penile-vaginal penetrative sex with little foreplay is the normal sexual style. Although among the well-educated youth, some forms of foreplay are gaining a foothold, fellatio and cunnilingus are still abhorrent. Genital touches and caresses are hardly accepted, and, traditionally, women feel shy about touching the penis, and most men are not interested in having their genitals manipulated.

[Male-oriented cultural values, such as those in Ghana, Nigeria, and Kenya, are echoed throughout the traditional cultures of Africa. They underlie what is appropriately termed "dry sex," a common practice throughout sub-Saharan Africa. The "dry sex" mating behavior fits comfortably with the Nigerian/Ghanaian distaste for vaginal secretions, foreplay, and disinterest in female sexual arousal and orgasm. In this setting, males quickly reach orgasm and satisfaction. Women are left with painful intercourse, no arousal, and no orgasm.

[In many African cultures, women prepare themselves to pleasure their husbands with a dry vagina by mixing the powdered stem and leaf of the *Mugugdhu* tree with water, wrapped in a bit of nylon stocking, and inserted in the vagina for 10 to 15 minutes before intercourse. Other women use *Mutendo wegudo*, soil mixed with baboon urine, which they obtain from traditional healers. Still others use detergents, salt, cotton, or shredded newspaper. These swell the vaginal tissue, make it hot, and dry it out. The women admit that sexual intercourse is "very painful . . ., but our African husbands enjoy sex with a dry vagina" (Schoofs 2000).

[The inevitable results of "dry sex" include increased friction, vaginal lacerations, suppression of the vagina's natural bacteria, and torn condoms (when these are used). All these consequences increase a woman's risk of STD and HIV infections. Fortunately, the tradition of "dry sex" is waning among the educated urban young, but any change in this traditional mating behavior is also resisted, because of rejection of Western gender roles (Stellwaggon 2001). (*End of update by R. T. Francoeur*)]

[*Comment 2003*: In Africa, as in cultures elsewhere, there are certain sexual practices and topics that Africans simply do not discuss or acknowledge with non-Africans, because they are very sensitive, sometimes taboo, and many times very racially charged. Even within an individual tribal culture, some sexual topics and behaviors are not open for discussion between men and women, or between children and their parents. Unless one lives within a native community and becomes very, very close to the people, Africans balk at discussing these issues, and "dry sex" is one such practice.

["Dry sex" is not something new. It is a well-established and more or less widespread practice in various subequatorial African cultures. It is very common in Southern Africa, particularly in Zimbabwe, Zambia, Malawi, some parts of Nigeria, some parts of Uganda, in Southern Sudan, and even in Kenya and Botswana. The only difference is in what the women use for drying up their vaginas. However, you will never hear about these practices unless you are a woman who lives within the community for some extended time and the women learn to trust you.

[Personally, as I was growing up in the rural town of Kisumu, Kenya, there were many practices and myths that we were taught by our peers and even older women that we were to do to attract men. Some of these practices were good, but some I do not feel comfortable talking about to this day. We were told that if you want your breasts to grow fast, you had to rub a certain poisonous leaf on your breasts or let boys touch them so that you could have them grow faster and more round. Many African men like women with large buttocks as well. As a result of this, many girls tried to do whatever they could to have big buttocks. One technique to accent the buttocks was to tie their belt so tight that the lower parts of their body stood out.

[Even today, many African men have three to five wives. These women compete among themselves to be the best cook for the man of the house, or the best in bed. Some women consult traditional healers and witchdoctors who sell them love portions so they can outdo their co-wives. Some of these love portions come in the form of soil mixed with baboon urine, or even salt, that women use before they have sexual intercourse with their husband. It is the traditional healers who teach these women about the importance of drying their vaginas as a way to please their husbands. These concoctions also make their vaginas swell and become very hot, making it tighter so that when a man inserts his penis, he feels "big" and, therefore, a "real man."

[Until recently, very few people knew about these practices. Unless one grew up in the village or became very, very close to the people, you can never know what goes on. As the HIV/AIDS epidemic devastates subequatorial Africa and non-Africans have became aware of female genital mutilation, taboos about other sensitive sexual practices have weakened. Mark Schoofs (2002) discussed the implications of dry sex in the spread of AIDS in his eight-part Pulitzer Prize-winning report on "AIDS: The Agony of Africa. Death and the Second Sex"; see also Stillwaggon (2001). In the section below, the main authors of this chapter, Uwen Edimo Esiet, a public health physician, and his wife Nike Esiet, M.P.H, a former public relations officer for the Society for Women and AIDS, raise the issue of "salt cuts." But these new insights into the complexity of the HIV/AIDS epidemic only came after considerable trust was achieved.

[In the northwest part of Tanzania and neighboring regions, "wet sex" is widely known and practiced. "Wet sex" consists of foreplay where there is intense stimulation by the male partner on the woman's labia and clitoral regions.

This stimulation results in copious production of secretions (thought to come from the Bartholin's glands). People talk about it openly, sometimes mixed with a sense of humor and intertribal jokes. Some researchers have blamed this practice for the high incidence and prevalence of HIV and STDs. The implications of this kind of information for action plans (resource inputs and sociocultural issues) are enormous. Now that these behaviors have been brought into public attention, a well thought-out survey that is representative of different segments of the populations becomes essential for an effective public health policy (Tanzania Personal communication 2003).

In March 2003, when Francoeur, coeditor of this *Encyclopedia*, inquired whether "dry sex" was observed in Botswana, Dr. Ian Taylor replied; "'Dry sex' is common in Botswana as well and leads to vaginal tears and lesions which help spread HIV/AIDS, it is true." (*End of comment by B. Opiyo-Omolo*)]

### Yankan Gishiri *or Salt Cut*

This traditional "cure," practiced mainly in the northern part of Nigeria by the Hausa in Kaduna, Kano, and parts of Borno, involves a different kind of mutilation of the female genitalia. It is a traditional surgical cut in the vaginal wall of a women who has been diagnosed by a traditional healer or traditional birth attendant (TBA) to be suffering from *gishiri* disease. *Gishiri*, a Hausa term, refers to a wide range of conditions or symptoms, including: pruritis vulvae (itching vulva), amenorrhea (absence of menstruation), infertility, obstructed labor, anemia, malaria, and any condition that presents the symptoms of headache, edema, fainting attacks, or dyspareunia (painful intercourse). Unfortunately, health workers have found it difficult to associate *gishiri* with any clinical condition.

The "salt cut" is usually made on the anterior vaginal wall; repeated cutting over a period of time may extend the incision area to the posterior vaginal wall. The *gishiri* cut is also performed when certain changes occur during pregnancy, such as hypertrophy of the vaginal muscle and vaginal discharge. The cut is performed by a traditional birth attendant (TBA) or healer, few of whom are knowledgeable of the anatomical structure of the area they are cutting. There is no scientific basis for the *gishiri* cut, and despite the fact that it effects no cure, the practice goes on unabated. A *gishiri* cut leaves behind both immediate and long-term health complications, such as hemorrhage, infection, shock, and scar formation. Some of the most debilitating effects include a breakdown in the wound-healing process. This is caused by repeated cuttings, which can be done anytime any of the above-mentioned symptoms surface. Damage can also be done to the bladder, leading to vesico-vaginal fistula (VVF) or damage to the rectum causing recto-vaginal fistula (RVF).

This practice, which has no benefit whatsoever, illustrates the minimal value placed on female sexuality in Nigeria. No Nigerian male would suggest similar pelvic cuts to cure symptoms of *gishiri*, which occur as often in males as in women.

### Other Traditional Practices Harmful to Women

There are widespread cultural practices in Nigeria that pose serious health concerns to female victims and can be classified under gender harassment. Some of these include: nutritional taboos associated with pregnancy, childbirth, lactation, and the six weeks following childbirth; forced feeding; rites associated with widowhood; preferences for a male child; inheritance rights; hot bath during the six weeks following childbirth; and discrimination against female infertility, to name a few. In each of these, depending on the ethnic region, women are pressured to go through harmful practices in order to satisfy societal biases.

In the case of nutritional taboos, pregnant women are forbidden to eat specific foods that are rich in vitamins and protein because of the erroneous belief that such foods reduce contraction strength during labor. Other vital foods are prohibited during puerperium for other superstitious beliefs. For example, eating of salt and pepper or palm oil are forbidden for at least seven to nine days after birth, depending on the baby's sex. Some communities forbid breastfeeding, whereas others forbid eating of all kinds of nuts for fear of hemorrhoids. As expected, none of all these taboos has any scientific basis.

Forced feeding is a traditional practice whereby an adolescent is made to eat with the intention to fatten her up. This practice occurs during pubertal rites in preparation for marriage. This practice occurs also in areas where it is not acceptable for a man to marry a slim woman. The weight of the woman, not her personality or other characteristics, is the basis of choice. Unfortunately, the women who are subject to this practice live an obese life with all the health risks thereof.

Widows in some parts of Nigeria are forced to go through various dehumanizing rituals that can affect their physical and psychological health. These include sleeping on a concrete floor for upwards of 40 days to three months after their husbands' death, drinking the water used to bathe her husband's corpse, and the shaving of her hair, among others. Another form of gender-based cultural belief is the preference for a male child. A male child gets all the family attention, including educational opportunities. The female child, on the other hand, is forced to assist in all domestic chores while the male child is free to play.

The widely documented gender biases and discriminatory harm to Nigerian women resulting from the prevalence of violence and abuse against women, and the fact that few such cases are reported, and fewer still are addressed appropriately in the legal system, clearly indicate that there is a serious need for more research into the factors that favor these acts in order to be able to develop appropriate strategies and programs to combat the resultant problems. Health professionals also need to be exposed to specialized training that will enhance their knowledge when dealing with such cases. There is a need for special counseling units in health institutions where victims can be assisted. More nongovernmental organizations (NGOs) in Nigeria need to focus on these unconventional behaviors, with the aim of helping victims to seek redress, as well as combating the problems. The underlying cultural beliefs and social structures that perpetuate these behaviors must be challenged. NGOs should also sponsor laws that criminalize these behaviors in a more direct manner than the present legislation does, which glosses over them.

[*Sexual Rights and* Sharia *Death Penalties*

[*Update 2003*: Since 1999, more than a dozen states in predominantly Muslim northern Nigeria have adopted Islamic law or *Sharia*, with its penalty of death-by-stoning for those convicted of fornication, adultery, rape, and other crimes. Since 2000, local Muslim courts in northern Nigeria have sentenced several women, and men, to death-by-stoning after they were convicted of fornication, adultery, or rape. In Sokoto State, on March 22, 2002, a *Sharia* court of appeals dismissed, on technical grounds, a death-by-stoning sentence for Safiya Hussaini Tungar-Tudu, a 33-year-old mother of five convicted of adultery (Sengupta 2003).

[The most celebrated case, which captured international attention in 2002 and 2003, was that of Ms. Amina Lawal

Kurami, a 31-year-old divorced mother living in her father's house in Kurami. When someone reported she had borne a child out of wedlock, the man she identified as the father of her child denied the charge and swore to his innocence on the Holy Qur'an. The court accepted his oath as proof of his innocence and her guilt—under Qur'anic law, the only way Ms. Lawal could have proven her allegation would have been to produce four eyewitnesses of the fornication. The court postponed her execution until she weans her child in 2004.

[In an October 2, 2002, radio and television broadcast marking Nigeria's 42nd anniversary of independence, President Olusegun Obasanjo said that Ms. Lawal and others under sentence of death-by-stoning should appeal their Muslim court decision to Nigeria's Supreme Court, where they will be guaranteed justice. Nigeria's Constitution bans capital punishment. "We have never entertained doubts that whatever verdict a lower court may give, the appellate courts will ensure that justice is done. We fully understand the concerns of Nigerians and friends of Nigeria, but we cannot imagine or envision a Nigerian being stoned to death. It has never happened. And may it never happen" (*Agence France-Presse* 2002; Sengupta 2003).

[In late 2002, Muslim opposition to holding the Miss World contest in Abuja, the Nigerian capital, erupted across northern Nigeria. Ensuing riots in nearby Kaduna left an estimated 220 dead and 400 injured. To prevent further deaths, the contest was moved to London, where there was a pause in the show at the contestants' request in tribute to Ms. Lawal, then under sentence to death by stoning. Once before, in 1996, the Miss World contest provoked violence in Bangalore, India, when police fired teargas and rubber bullets at stone-throwing protestors (Hoge 2002).

[Nigeria's position as Africa's largest nation and a secular democracy guarantees that however these conflicts between religious freedom and secular democracy are resolved, such conflicts will continue in this age of transition in Nigeria and in other African nations. (*End of update by B. Opiyo-Omolo*)]

## 9. Contraception, Abortion, and Population Planning

### A. Contraception

*Contraception among the Hausa*

BILKISU YUSUF and RAKIYA BOOTH

Hausa society frowns on too-frequent and poorly spaced pregnancies (*Kwanika*), and nursing mothers who get pregnant before they wean their babies are sometimes derided. There are many traditional methods of contraception among the Hausa, such as *rubutu*, Qur'anic verses written on a wooden slate (*allo*) with black ink (*tawada*), which is washed off with water that is then administered orally. Others include *guru*, a string of leather, which the woman wears around her waist, and a Qur'anic verse written on a sheet of paper, bound with leather and worn as an amulet. No research has yet been conducted on the efficacy of these contraceptive methods. However, the Hausa practice one of the surest methods of contraception, voluntary abstinence from sexual intercourse. The pregnant Hausa wife leaves her husband's house to live with her parents when her pregnancy reaches an advanced stage, usually seven months; she remains there until she delivers. During this period, known as *goyon ciki*, the young mother is given lessons in pregnancy management, breastfeeding, and childcare. The length of the stay varies from 40 days to several months, while some remain in their parents' home until the child is weaned. Voluntary abstinence from sexual intercourse promotes child spacing. *Goyon ciki* has no basis in Islamic jurisprudence.

Islam recommends contraception, not through voluntary abstinence from sexual intercourse as *goyon ciki* promotes, but by breastfeeding their babies for two years. The *Hadith* also recommends *azl* (coitus interruptus) as a method of preventing pregnancy by mutual consent of the couple.

According to scholars of the Federation of Muslim Women's Associations in Nigeria (FOMWAN), family planning, which is permissible in Islam, should be geared towards child spacing to promote the health of the mother, rather than limiting childbirth out of the fear of poverty. Family planning can only be practiced with the full agreement of both spouses, who are free to choose any suitable method. FOMWAN specifically prohibits all methods that are harmful to the body, such as oral contraceptives, sterilization, and the injectibles. Condoms are recommended in addition to coitus interruptus (the *azl* recommended by the *Shariah* (Muslim laws and governance).

According to the Nigerian Demographic and Health Survey of 1990, nationwide, 5.9% of 15- to 19-year-old females currently use contraception. Two thirds use traditional methods, including rhythm and withdrawal. One percent uses oral contraceptives, less than 1% uses condoms, foaming vaginal tablets, or IUDs.

## B. Teenage Pregnancies and Hausan Maternal Health Practices

BILKISU YUSUF and RAKIYA BOOTH

Teenage marriage poses some health problems for Hausa society. When the husband of a young girl marries a man who is not patient enough to wait before consummating the marriage until she has matured and her body has fully developed, she runs the risk of getting pregnant before she is old enough to take care of the child. These minors, especially in the rural areas, are susceptible to superstitions. Pregnant teenagers living in the rural areas cannot attend pre- and postnatal clinics, and, where poverty and ignorance are rampant and healthcare facilities either not available or affordable, these young girls are left solely in the hands of untrained, traditional birth attendants (*Ungorzoma*).

There is a sociocultural preference for home delivery among the Hausa, and most husbands are adverse to the idea of male healthcare personnel attending to their wives. With the onset of labor, these girls are supposed to observe *kunya*, exhibit bravery and silently endure pain. It is considered shameful among the Hausa for women to cry, shout, or express pain during labor (*Nakuda*) and childbirth (*Haituwa*). Yet, protracted labor lasting for days is quite common. The local preventive measure is to give the pregnant woman one of several bitter herbal mixtures that prevent development of *zaki* (amniotic fluid). Literally translated, *zaki* means "sweet." There is a widespread superstition among Hausa that *zaki* obstructs delivery. Hence, pregnant women drink bitter herbs or *tsamiya* (tamarind) soaked in water to reduce the amniotic fluid, and thereby ease labor pains and hasten childbirth. They are also advised to avoid eating sweet foods in order to control *zaki*. This web of cultural practices does not ease the protracted labor nor the trauma most pregnant girls undergo.

Local birth attendants cannot handle other complications of pregnancy, such as eclampsia, which requires monitoring of the blood pressure, and pelvic malformations, which require a cesarean operation. These complications go undetected and often lead to the death of the mother and child; the Nigerian infant mortality rate is 70 to 87 per 1,000

live births. Use of unsterilized instruments by the local birth attendants also leads to life-threatening infections. In some cases, the placenta is not expelled after childbirth, leading to hemorrhaging, infection of the uterus, and death. When a lot of blood is lost, local birth attendants are ill trained and unequipped to provide blood transfusions. Cases of retained placenta and hemorrhage are often referred to hospitals from the rural areas when the patient's situation is critical and hopeless. The 1995 statistics released by the National Council for Population and Environmental Activities (NCPEA) show that Nigeria's maternal mortality rate of 15 per 1,000 births is one of the highest in the world. Teenage girls also account for almost 25% of maternal deaths in Nigeria.

Certain Hausan practices also lead to maternal morbidity. During labor, particularly a prolonged one, the local birth attendant performs a local episiotomy to facilitate delivery of the baby. These *gishiri* cuts are incisions made by the local midwife to cut off membranes in the vaginal region during labor, oftentimes using unsterilized instruments. Subsequent infection and the extension of the cut to the anal and urethral areas may damage the muscles that control the passage of the urine, resulting in a vesico-vaginal fistula (VVF). VVF research by Lawanson (1993) has revealed that the Hausa also believe that, in addition to facilitating childbirth, *gishiri* cuts also alleviate amenorrhea, infertility, and painful intercourse. However, these VVF patients often experience involuntary seepage of urine, a defect that requires a costly and complicated operation to correct. (See additional discussion in Section 8D, Significant Unconventional Sexual Behaviors, Female Genital Mutilation and Other Harmful Practices, above.)

Many pregnancy complications go untreated because of inadequate medical facilities and sometimes ignorance on the part of the patients, who fail to seek hospital treatment. Those who do seek treatment at a hospital usually compete for treatment, waiting for years for their turn. The seepage of urine makes the VVF patients undesirable, and they are often abandoned in hospitals or treated as outcasts by their families, especially husbands who desert them. These women, most of them in their teens, are thus condemned to living a life of misery. There are currently 200,000 reported cases of VVF in the country, with a heavy concentration in the northern states of Kano, Jigawa, Katsina, Sokoto, and Borno. Several cases have also been reported in the southern Nigerian state of Akwa Ibom.

## D/E. Abortion and Population Planning

FOYIN OYEBOLA and UWEM EDIMO ESIET

Abortion is a criminal offense in Nigeria except when the life of the woman is endangered by the pregnancy. It is not, therefore, an approved method of population planning and family limitation. Nevertheless, the abortion rate is high in Nigeria. Unsafe illegal abortion is one of the leading causes of maternal death in women of reproductive age. Also, abortion affects adolescent women who lack basic information about reproduction and the prevention of pregnancy, as well as the information and resources necessary for obtaining safe abortions. [F. Oyebola]

The Campaign Against Unwanted Pregnancy (CAUP) conducted a study recently in collaboration with the Alan Guttmacher Institute of the United States of America, focusing on the incidence of induced abortion in Nigeria ("Incidence of Induced Abortion" 1998). In each year studied, Nigerian women obtained approximately 610,000 abortions. Most of these women resorted to abortion as an outcome of an unwanted pregnancy. Sixty percent of the abortion seekers were age 15 to 25 years old, with a third of them being students, and 63% never being married. The study recommended better policies to improve access to contraceptive services to reduce unwanted pregnancy and abortion, as well as greater access to safe abortion to help preserve the health and lives of Nigerian women. [F. Oyebola]

Abortion has continued to generate controversy in Nigeria. Whereas Nigeria has one of the highest maternal mortality rates in the world, over 800 maternal deaths per 100,000 women, consensus as to how the issue of abortion should be addressed has not been agreed on. The 1998 report by the Campaign Against Unwanted Pregnancy mentioned above further corroborated this need. Thus far, the government has not taken appropriate steps to address this scourge, preferring the ostrich approach of burying its head in the sand and wishing the problem were over. There is no doubt that contraceptive usage is low, especially among adolescents, and that sexual ignorance is very high, with about 60% of Nigerian youth not knowing that pregnancy is possible at first intercourse. [U. E. Esiet]

In a 1994 countrywide report submitted by the Federal Ministry of Health and Social Services, Nigerian adolescents accounted for 80% of Nigeria's unsafe abortions. The government has responded to Nigeria's high fertility rate of six children in a woman's lifetime by formulating a National Policy on Population for Development, Unity, and Self-Reliance. Unfortunately, this 1988 document is not gender-sensitive. It recommends that each woman should have no more than four children, and that the minimum age for female marriage be 18 years. The document is silent on the age of marriage for men, and takes no notice of the well-known fact that many men have more than one wife and, therefore, father more than four children in their lifetime. Also, the issue of reducing early marriage is not supported by any appropriate legislation, education, or mass mobilization. It is obvious that the gender-interest perspective was not utilized in making this policy—not unexpected in a patrilineal society. Attempts have since been made to link population with Family Life Education in a POP/FLE effort (see Section 3A, Sexuality Knowledge and Education, Sexuality Education). In 1999, this resulted in a paradigm shift on the federal level, with a reproductive health strategy that addresses the people's needs primarily, and then hopes that this will empower the people to address the population issue. All of these strategies are going to be within the framework of a primary healthcare strategy. It must be acknowledged that government has done much within its new purview, without ignoring the fact that still more needs to, and can be done. Civil societal groups, especially the NGOs, have continued to make family planning services available, accessible, and directed at people's needs. [U. E. Esiet]

## 10. Sexually Transmitted Diseases and HIV/AIDS

### A. Sexually Transmitted Diseases

Data on sexually transmissible diseases (STDs) in Nigeria are limited. The prevalence of syphilis among antenatal clinic attendees in 1993 from sentinel surveillance was 3.8%.

STD clinics are underutilized because of stigmatization and the lack of appropriate facilities and specialists in STD management. Manuals for training health workers, and for syndrome management, have been produced with the support of donor agencies and specialists. Several health workers have been trained, and others are being trained to use these manuals. Appropriate drugs and condoms have been made available, and information and education about STDs is being incorporated into Primary Health Care facilities. It is, however, important for Nigeria to have baseline data, so that adequate and appropriate planning and education can be carried out.

Government support has been far below expectations, and it is hoped that NGOs will participate more actively in the near future in Information, Education, and Communication (IEC) activities and training.

Recommendations from various workshops and meetings are that measures aimed at control and prevention should be integrated into other development projects, such as Family Planning and Maternal and Child Health Services. This will ensure that women and children with STDs are treated in the same clinic by the same service provider in one hospital visit. Nigeria needs intensive IEC advocacy and mobilization of specific groups. We also should promote the best practices as a concept and as a tool for effective and expanded responsiveness to STDs (Family Health International 1996; UNAIDS 1994).

### B. HIV/AIDS

UWEM EDIMO ESIET

*The Current Status*

Nigeria reported its first case of AIDS in 1986. However, based on the most recent published data by the National AIDS and STD Control Programme, Nigeria can now be identified as a major locus of HIV infection in sub-Saharan Africa, with a national seroprevalence rate of 4.5%. The progression has been 1% in 1990, 1.2% in 1991-1992, 3.8% in 1991-1992, and 3.8% in 1993-1994. It has been estimated that one new infection of HIV occurs every minute in Nigeria. Esiet cites data suggesting that 95% of all infections are by heterosexual intercourse, 4% are through blood transfusions, and 1% are through mother-to-child transmission. Nigerian population surveys from both urban and rural areas indicate a seroprevalence rate of 5 to 8% in the general population, with a preponderance of HIV infection in females age 15 to 19, whereas for males, the peak age is 20 to 29 years old (WHO 1997; National Symposium 1998; Lagos State Seminar 1999).

Data from population and hospital-based studies indicate that about 80% of HIV transmission occurs through heterosexual intercourse while 10% occurs through blood transfusions. Vertical transmission (mother-to-child) is also becoming a significant route with the increase of HIV prevalence among women of reproductive age.

Factors responsible for the rapid spread of HIV in Nigeria include:

- low-risk perception, especially among youths;
- cultural and religious attitudes, which make it difficult for women to make decisions about reproductive health issues;
- myths and misconceptions about HIV/AIDS;
- the worsening economic situation;
- low acceptability, availability, and use of condoms;
- lack of appropriate medical care for STDs, opportunistic infections, and AIDS;
- lack of data management for planning and decision making; and
- lack of voluntary testing and counseling services.

All these factors mitigate against the behavioral changes needed for a decrease in the incidence of HIV/AIDS in Nigeria. At the same time, government efforts at all levels to address the epidemic over the past ten years have been grossly inadequate, and certainly not commensurate with the magnitude of the problem (Akinsete et al. 1997, 1999; Akanmu & Akinsete 1999; Federal Ministry of Health 1999).

Many NGOs are involved in the fight against HIV/AIDS, especially in the areas of information, education, and communication, and a few are involved in home-based care for people living with HIV/AIDS. However, their resources are limited, although several donor agencies support many of them. Sustainability of programs is a major problem.

The government response has included formulation of a National Policy on HIV/AIDS, the syndrome management of STDs, sentinel surveys, massive mobilization and AIDS awareness, and a national conference on HIV/AIDS, at which programmatically workable solutions were addressed. It must be acknowledged that despite all these efforts, HIV/AIDS programs continue to remain underfunded. However, NGOs have also been complementing government efforts in all areas that include IEC and service provision to people with HIV/AIDS. Despite all these efforts, a lot of Nigerians have yet to be reached with the appropriate information and support necessary to bring about altered behavior changes. Condom use is still low, and the abilities of women to negotiate safe sex also low. Even though it has been introduced, the female condom is quite expensive when viewed from the income level of the people.

## Gaps, Future Challenges, and the Way Forward

Nigeria is still going through a phase characterized by denial, stigmatization, panic, and political instability. The financial and material resources committed by the government fall far below the level required to adequately and effectively deal with the magnitude of the HIV/AIDS epidemic in Nigeria. AIDS cuts across all aspects of life, and therefore, the responses must be multisectoral and multidisciplinary (National Conference 1998).

There is a need to intensify advocacy at all levels, private, public, and community, and to prioritize responses. The priorities for action are:

- Promoting rational responses and priority-setting by the government, NGOs, and donor communities based on knowledge and information (accurate data) rather than anecdotes and prejudice. This makes it imperative that accurate assessment of the magnitude of the problem be undertaken for planning and decision making.
- Assembling usable economic data and knowledge to facilitate decisions about where best to spend limited resources.
- Advocating for appropriate budget allocations for HIV/AIDS/STD activities by the government at all levels and by donor agencies.
- Ensuring that there is a fair spread of resources allocated for HIV/AIDS/STD, which includes both prevention, care, and support activities by all stakeholders.
- Promoting the care and support agenda by government, donors, the community, traditional healers, and the public and private health sectors.
- Linking care with prevention at all levels.
- Encouraging private-sector sensitization, advocacy, and mobilization in support of intervention programs in the workplace.
- Increasing acceptability, availability, and access to condoms through condom social marketing supported by government and donor agencies.
- Finding funds to support Health Care Systems in dealing with conditions that increase vulnerability to HIV/AIDS, e.g., sexually transmitted diseases (STD), tuberculosis (TB), and malnutrition, through capacity-building for medical personnel. The promotion and support of such services, and their integration into reproductive health services, are necessary.
- Identifying and supporting income-generating activities and credit plans to reduce vulnerability to the poverty that accompanies and abets the epidemic.

- Promoting activities aimed at addressing issues of gender inequality, e.g., developing negotiation skills for women, knowledge of human rights, and income-generating projects for women.
- Providing access and linkages to counseling services and other activities that address the emotional and spiritual needs of both adults and children.
- Supporting and catalyzing groups of people living with HIV and AIDS, and encouraging their involvement in HIV/AIDS programs.
- Supporting activities that advocate legal rights for HIV/AIDS-affected persons, particularly women and children. AIDS intervention must address issues that promote the marginalization of some sectors of the society, thus increasing their vulnerability.
- Recognizing the rights of all individuals to care, as well as legal, economic, and inheritance protection.
- Encouraging accessibility and affordability of drugs for treatment of opportunistic infections and antiretroviral drugs.
- Preventing vertical transmission through breastfeeding.
- Preventing the transmission of HIV through blood transfusions by educating and recruiting voluntary non-remunerated blood donors, screening of blood for HIV, and the training of personnel.
- Promoting programs that are integrated into other routine activities, e.g., schools, cultural and media reporting, agricultural extension programs, and so on, because these are more effective in internalizing the epidemic than programs specifically focused on AIDS.

## Conclusion

As the HIV/AIDS epidemic continues to spread worldwide, we are learning more about how individuals, households, families, communities, organizations, government, and the nation are affected. Strategies to prevent the spread have been focused on the promotion of condoms, the reduction of multiple sexual partners, and the treatment of STDs.

Many of these interventions have failed to address the social, economic, and gender issues, as well as the care and support of persons living with HIV/AIDS, adolescent reproductive health, and the disabled. Future interventions need to take into consideration all these factors in all planning. There is a need to be forward-looking, if responses are to keep pace with the speed and impact of this epidemic.

Evidence from different countries, not just industrialized nations, has clearly shown that prevention works. In Nigeria, we need a multisectoral, multidisciplinary approach, as well as political commitment at all levels of our government.

[*Update 2002*: In late 2002, a special National Intelligence Council meeting, convened by the independent Center for Strategic and International Studies, identified Nigeria as one of five countries facing devastation by a second wave of HIV/AIDS infections, with famines, civil wars, and economic reversals predicted. The projection was for the collapse of social and political institutions in Nigeria, Russia, China, India, and Ethiopia by 2010 (see Table 1; Garrett 2002).

[Nigeria and Ethiopia are pivotal to the future of Africa, because of their large populations and strategic influence. Nigeria, the world's sixth-largest oil producer with a sizable well-educated elite, is second only to South Africa in military, cultural, economic, and intellectual influence over the continent. According to the director of Nigeria's AIDS control programs, about 6% of the population was infected in 2002, with an infection rate over 15% among 15- to 30-year-olds in some areas. Experts also predicted a growing orphan population. Nigeria and Ethiopia are home to 130 million and 64.5 million people, respectively, or about half of Africa's total population. Considered the most strategically important country in West Africa because of its large population and vast oil reserves, Nigeria is experiencing a rapidly growing heterosexually transmitted HIV epidemic. By 2010, experts predict that 11% of Nigerian children will be orphans, 40% of them because of AIDS. (*End of update by R. T. Francoeur*)]

[*Update 2002*: UNAIDS Epidemiological Assessment: Median HIV prevalence in Nigeria has steadily increased from 1.8% in 1991 to 5.8% in 2001. In 2001, the range of HIV prevalence from 85 sites across the 36 states and the Federal Capital Territory was from 0.8% to 16.4%. Twenty-one out of the 86 sites were rural, where HIV prevalence ranged from 2.2% to 16%; the sites with the highest prevalence in the 2001 sentinel survey were both rural. In 2001, HIV prevalence among the 15- to 19-year-old antenatal clinic attendees tested was 5.9%, among the 20- to 24-year-olds, the rate was 6.0%, and among the 25- to 29-year-olds, 6.3%. Of the antenatal clinic attendees who were HIV-positive in 2001, 97.5% had HIV-1, 0.4% had HIV-2, and 0.1% had both HIV-1 and HIV-2 infection. In the major urban areas, HIV prevalence among antenatal clinic attendees has increased from 1% in 1991 to nearly 5% in 1999; in 1999, HIV prevalence ranged from 3% to 8%. Median HIV prevalence among antenatal clinic attendees tested at sites outside the major urban areas increased from less than 1% in 1991-1992 to 5% in 1999; the range of HIV prevalence rates went from less than 1% to 21%. In 1999, peak infection occurred among those women less than 25 years, where 6% were HIV-positive. Categorization of HIV-prevalence data by major urban and outside major urban areas was not available for 2001. No antenatal clinic surveillance survey was conducted in 2000.

[Two percent of sex workers tested in Lagos in 1988 to 1989 were HIV-positive, increasing to 12% in 1990-1991; by 1993-1994, 30% of female sex workers tested were HIV-positive. In 1991-1992, sex workers tested in seven sites outside of the major urban centers had a median HIV prevalence of 13% with a range of 0% to 44%. By 1995-1996, 15 sites were reporting a range of prevalence among sex workers of 7% to nearly 70% of sex workers tested. In 1994, 5% of STD clinic patients tested in the major urban areas were HIV-positive. HIV prevalence among STD clinic patients tested from 21 sites outside of the major urban areas increased from 7% in 1993-1994 to 12% in 1995-1996; in 1995-1996, HIV prevalence ranged from 1% to 70%. In 2000, median HIV prevalence among STD patients tested in a survey covering 10 states was 11.5%, with a range of 5.6% to 23%. In 1993-1994, 4% of long-distance truck drivers tested in Anambra State were HIV-1 infected. Among the TB patients tested in the 2000 survey, median HIV prev-

alence was 17%, ranging from 4.2% to 35.1%. In 2000, HIV prevalence among IV-drug users surveyed was 8.9%; among non-injection drug users, the rate was 10%.

[The seroprevalence of syphilis among antenatal clinic attendees tested at 72 sites in 1999 was 2.3%, while in 2001, the seroprevalence of syphilis from 86 sites ranged from 0.3% to 2.99%.

[The estimated number of adults and children living with HIV/AIDS on January 1, 2002, were:

| | |
|---|---|
| Adults ages 15-49: | 3,200,000 (rate: 5.8%) |
| Women ages 15-49: | 1,700,000 |
| Children ages 0-15: | 270,000 |

[An estimated 170,000 adults and children died of AIDS during 2001.

[At the end of 2001, an estimated one million Nigerian children under age 15 were living without one or both parents who had died of AIDS. (*End of update by the Editors*)]

## 11. Sexual Dysfunctions, Counseling, and Therapies

UWEM EDIMO ESIET

The introduction of Viagra has opened up a public discourse on sexual dysfunction by providing a new, effective therapy for the primary sexual-dysfunction concern of Nigerian males, functional impotence. In Nigeria's traditional societies, many therapies have long been available to most Nigerians for dealing with functional impotence and other sexual dysfunctions. Some of these remedies have already been described by Bilikisu Yusuf in Section 5D, Interpersonal Heterosexual Behaviors, on aphrodisiacs. The efficacy of these traditional remedies has yet to be clinically ascertained. Sexual dysfunctions of women are hardly discussed, because, for the majority of Nigerians, the prime objective of sexual intercourse is not sexual pleasure but procreation. Therefore, the issue of counseling and therapy is not as profound as it should be in our society. Professionals need to educate the Nigerian public about sexual dysfunctions other than male erectile dysfunction, so that both men and women will seek appropriate counseling and therapies. Hopefully, as the study of human sexuality and sexology becomes more developed in Nigeria, challenges such as these will be addressed.

## 12. Sex Research and Advanced Professional Education

There is no sexological organization or publication in Nigeria. Nor is there any basic research unless it has practical health applications that address the major health issues facing our nation. The contributors to this chapter gained their expertise from training abroad, including the International Women's Health Coalition in New York (USA), and from their extensive fieldwork among the people.

Nigeria has three organizations that deal with sexuality issues. These are:

Action Health Incorporated, Youth Center, Plot 54 Somorin Street, Ifako, Gbagada, Lagos, Nigeria; Tel./Fax: 234-1-861-166; AHI@linkserve.com.ng.

Association for Reproductive and Family Health (ARFH), 13 Ajayi Osungbekun Street, Ikolaba GRA, Ibadan, Nigeria; Tel.: 234-1-820-945.

Planned Parenthood Federation of Nigeria, 224 Ikorodu Road, Palmgrove, Somolu, PMB 12657, Lagos, Nigeria; Tel.: 234-1-820-526.

## References and Suggested Readings

Abd al'Ati, H. 1982. *The family structure in Islam.* Lagos: Islamic Publications Bureau.

**Table 1**

**Leaders in an Expanding Pandemic: Current and Projected HIV/AIDS-Infected Adults**

| | Current Number Infected | | 2010 |
|---|---|---|---|
| | Government Data (millions) | Expert Estimates (millions) | Expert Estimates (millions) |
| India | 4.0 | 5 to 8 | 20 to 25 |
| Nigeria | 3.5 | 4 to 6 | 10 to 15 |
| Ethiopia | 2.7 | 3 to 5 | 7 to 10 |
| China | 0.80 | 1 to 2 | 10 to 15 |
| Russia | 0.18 | 1 to 2 | 5 to 8 |

*Agence France-Presse.* 2002 (June 4). Nigeria: Respite for woman who faces stoning. *The New York Times.*

Akanmu, A. S., & I. Akinsete. 1999. *Epidemiology of HIV/AIDS in Nigeria.* (Publisher not known).

Akande, J. O. 1989. A decade of human rights in Nigeria. In: A. Ajomo, ed., *New dimension in Nigeria law* (Law series no. 3, p. 123ff). Lagos: Nigeria Institute of Advanced Legal Studies.

Akinsete, I., A. S. Akanmu, & C. C. Okany. 1999. *Infected adults at the Lagos University Teaching Hospital—A five year experience.* (Publisher not known).

Akinsete, I., S. N. Gwarzo, N. Koita, J. Nnorom, K. Asiedu, T. Rehle, & E. Williams. 1997 (April). AIDSCAP (AIDS control and prevention). *Nigeria Program Review.*

Beck, L. G., & N. Keddie, eds. 1978. *Women in the Muslim world.* Cambridge, MA: Harvard University Press.

Bouhdiba, A. 1985. *Sexuality in Islam* (A. Sheridan, trans.). London: Routledge and Kegan Paul.

Brooks, G. 1995. *Nine parts of desire: The hidden world of Islamic women.* New York: Anchor Books/Doubleday.

CIA. 2002 (January). *The world factbook 2002.* Washington, DC: Central Intelligence Agency. Available: http://www.cia.gov/cia/publications/factbook/index.html.

Coles, C., & B. Mack, eds. 1991. *Hausa women in the twentieth century.* Madison, WI: University of Wisconsin Press.

Cook, R. J. 1994. State accountability under the convention on the elimination of all forms of discrimination against women. In: R. J. Cook, ed., *Human rights of women: National and international perspectives.* Philadelphia: University of Pennsylvania Press.

Crowther, M. 1972. *The story of Nigeria.* London: Faber and Faber.

Family Health International. 1996 (May). STD prevention: New challenges, new approaches. *The AIDS Control and Prevention (AIDSCAP) Project, Project No. 936-5972, 31-4692046, 3(1).*

Federal Ministry of Health and Human Services. 1992. Focus on AIDS. *Bulletin of Epidemiology, 2(2):15-16.*

Federation of Muslim Women's Associations in Nigeria (FOMWAN). 1986. Communique of the First National Conference on Family and Society, Queen's College, Lagos, July 24-27, 1986. (Conference summary).

Fernea, E. W. 1998. *In search of feminism: One woman's global journey.* New York: Doubleday.

Francoeur, R. T., U. Esiet, & N. Esiet. 2000 (April/May). Ethnic views of sexuality in Nigeria. *SIECUS Report, 28*(4):8-12.

Garrett, L. 2002 (October 15). AIDS seen as threat to world: Experts say five nations face devastation by 2010. [New York] *Newsday.*

Goddard, C. 1995 (May). Adolescent sexuality in Nigeria. Advocates for Youth (Available from: 1025 Vermont Avenue, NW, Suite 200, Washington, DC 20005).

Hoge, W. 2002 (December 8). World pageant goes ahead over protests; A Turk wins. *The New York Times.*

Ilumoka, A. O. 1994. African women's economic, social and cultural rights. In: R. J. Cook, ed., *Human rights of women: National and international perspectives.* Philadelphia: University of Pennsylvania Press.

The incidence of induced abortion in Nigeria. 1998. *International Family Planning Perspectives, 24*(4):156-164.

Koss, M. P. 1987. Hidden rape: Incidence, prevalence, and descriptive characteristics of sexual aggression and victimization in a national sample of college students. In: A. W. Burgess, ed., *Sexual assault* (vol. 3). New York: Garland Publishing.

Lagos State Seminar/Workshop on HIV/AIDS and Malaria. 1999 (March). Eko Hotel, Lagos.

Lawanson, J. 1993. Vaginal fistulas. *International Journal of Gynaecology and Obstetrics, 40:14.*

Makinwa-Adelzusoye, P. 1992. Sexual behavior, reproductive knowledge, and contraceptive use among young urban Nigerians. *International Family Planning Perspectives, 18:67-69.*

Makinwa-Adebusoye, P. K., & B. J. Feyiset. 1994. The quantum and tempo of fertility in Nigeria. In: *Fertility trends and determinants in six African countries: DHS regional analysis workshop for anglophone Africa.* Calverton, MO: Macro International Inc.

Mernissi, F. 1991. *The veil and the male elite: A feminist interpretation of women's rights in Islam.* Reading, MA: Addison-Wesley.

Mernissi, F. 1993. *Islam and democracy: Fear of the modern world.* Reading, MA: Addison-Wesley.

*Michigan State sexual offences act.* 1974. Ann Arbor, MI: The State Legislature.

Murray, S. O., & W. Roscoe, eds. 1997. *Islamic homosexualities: Culture, history, and literature.* New York/London: New York University Press.

Murray, S. O. 1997a. The will not to know: Islamic accommodations of male homosexuality. In: S. O. Murray & W. Roscoe, eds., *Islamic homosexualities: Culture, history, and literature.* New York/London: New York University Press.

Murray, S. O. 1997b. Woman-woman love in Islamic societies. In: S. O. Murray & W. Roscoe, eds., *Islamic homosexualities: Culture, history, and literature.* New York/London: New York University Press.

National Conference on HIV/AIDS in Nigeria. 1998 (December). *Lessons learnt and the way forward.* Lagos, Nigeria.

National Council for Population and Environmental Activities (NCPEA). 1995. *Population and maternal and child health.* In a press kit titled *Nigeria: Family planning and population activities*, released August 22, 1995, Lagos.

National Guidelines Task Force. 1996. *Guidelines for comprehensive sexuality education in Nigeria.* Lagos: Action Health Incorporated.

National Symposium/Workshop on HIV/AIDS in Nigeria. 1998 (June 2-5). Organized by Federal Ministry of Health (NASCP) in collaboration with Roche Nigeria Limited, Lagos, Nigeria.

*Nigerian demographic and health survey.* 1990. Columbia, MD: Department of Health Services. Cited in *Fact Sheet on "Adolescent Sexuality in Nigeria."* Washington, DC: Advocates for Youth, 1995.

Nwogugu, E. I. 1974. *Family law in Nigeria.* Lagos.

Oputa, C. 1989. Women and children as disempowered groups. In: *Women and children under Nigerian law.* Lagos: Federal Ministry of Justice.

Otaluka, A. O. 1989. Protection of women under the law. In: *Women and children under Nigerian law* (pp. 98ff). Lagos: Federal Ministry of Justice.

Oyajobi, A. 1986. Better protection for women and children under the law. In: *Women and children under Nigerian law.* Lagos: Federal Ministry of Justice.

Parrinder, G. 1980. *Sex in the world's great religions.* Don Mills, Ontario, Canada: General Publishing Company.

Schoofs, M. 2000. AIDS: The agony of Africa. *The Village Voice* [New York, NY, USA] (A Pulitzer Prize-winning 8-part series). Available: http://www.villagevoice.com/specials/africa/.

Sengupta, S. 2003 (January 26). A stoning case proceeds, Nigeria stands trial. *The New York Times*, p. A3.

SIECUS (Sexuality Information and Education Council of the U.S.). 2000. Approval of 'Guidelines for comprehensive sexuality education in Nigeria' for Nigerian schools. *Making the Connection, 1*(1):1-2.

Stillwaggon, E. 2001 (May 21). AIDS and Poverty in Africa. *The Nation*, pp. 2-25.

Tanzania, 2003 (March-May). Personal communications between Yusuf Hemed and the editor, R. T. Francoeur.

UNAIDS. 1994. *Management of sexually transmitted diseases. WHO/GPA/TEM/94* (1 Rev. 1). World Health Organization.

UNAIDS. 2002. *Epidemiological fact sheets by country.* Geneva, Switzerland: Joint United Nations Programme on HIV/AIDS (UNAIDS/WHO). Available: http://www.unaids.org/hivaidsinfo/statistics/fact_sheets/index_en.htm.

*Views and comments of the Kano State Government on the report of the Committee for Women Affairs.* 1988. Kano, Nigeria: Kano Government Printer.

WHO. 1997 (December). *UNAIDS—WHO computer epimodel estimate for HIV infection* (FSE/6). World Health Organization.

Yusuf, B. 1995 (January 21). *Impact of Islam and culture on marriage age in Hausa society.* Paper presented at the Seminar on Problems of Early Marriage in Nigeria, organized by Women in Nigeria (WIN), Kaduna State Branch, at the British Council Hall. Kaduna, Nigeria.

# Norway

Elsa Almås, Cand. Psychol., and
Esben Esther Pirelli Benestad, M.D.*
*Updates by E. Almås and E. E. Pirelli Benestad*

## Contents

## Demographics and a Brief Historical Perspective

ROBERT T. FRANCOEUR

### A. Demographics

Norway occupies the western half of the Scandinavian peninsula, stretching about 1,100 miles (1,770 km) from the North Sea in the south along the Norwegian Sea to 300 miles (480 km) above the Arctic Circle, the farthest north of any European country. Slightly larger than the state of New Mexico, Norway's eastern neighbor is Sweden, with borders on Finland and Russia in the northeast. Nearly 70% of Norway's 125,180 square miles (324,220 km²) is uninhabitable, covered by mountains, glaciers, moors, rivers, and deep fiords cut into the coastline of 12,000 miles (19,300 km). Along the western coast, nearly 50,000 islands form a breakwater and safe coastal shipping channel. Norway also administers four largely uninhabited island clusters, Svalbard in the Arctic Ocean with a declining population of about 3,000, Bouvet Island south of the Cape of Good Hope, Jan Mayen Island between Norway and Greenland, and in Antarctica, the region of Queen Maud Land and Peter I Island.

In July 2002, Norway had an estimated population slightly over 4.5 million. (All data are from *The World Factbook 2002* (CIA 2002) unless otherwise stated.)

**Age Distribution and Sex Ratios**: *0-14 years*: 20% with 1.06 male(s) per female (sex ratio); *15-64 years*: 65% with 1.03 male(s) per female; *65 years and over*: 15% with 0.71 male(s) per female; *Total population sex ratio*: 0.98 male(s) to 1 female

---

*\*Communications*: Elsa Almås, Cand. Psychol., MPAT-Institute, Storgaten 42, 4876 Grimstad, Norway; elsa.almaas@sexologi.com. Esben E. P. Benestad, M.D., MPAT-Institute, Storgaten 42, 4876 Grimstad, Norway; esben.benestad@sexologi.com *or* esther.pirelli @sexologi.com.

*Editors' Note*: Because of space constraints in volume 4 of the *International Encyclopedia of Sexuality* published in 2001, the original chapter on Norway, like Hong Kong, was not included. Instead, the Editors published them as "Supplemental Countries on the World Wide Web" at http://www.SexQuest.com/IES4/.

(CIA 2002)

**Life Expectancy at Birth**: *Total Population*: 78.94 years; *male*: 76.01 years; *female*: 82.07 years

**Urban/Rural Distribution**: 73% to 27%

**Ethnic Distribution**: Norwegian (Nordic, Alpine, and Baltic); Sami (Lapps): 20,000

**Religious Distribution**: Evangelical Lutheran: 86% (State Church); other Protestant and Roman Catholic: 3%; other: 1%; unaffiliated or unknown: 10% (1997 est.)

**Birth Rate**: 12.39 births per 1,000 population

**Death Rate**: 9.78 per 1,000 population

**Infant Mortality Rate**: 3.9 deaths per 1,000 live births

**Net Migration Rate**: 2.1 migrant(s) per 1,000 population

**Total Fertility Rate**: 1.8 children born per woman

**Population Growth Rate**: 0.49%

**HIV/AIDS** (1999 est.): *Adult prevalence*: 0.01%; *Persons living with HIV/AIDS*: 1,600; *Deaths*: 8. (For additional details from www.UNAIDS.org, see end of Section 10B.)

**Literacy Rate** (*defined as those age 15 and over who can read and write*): 100%; education is free and compulsory from age 6 to 16

**Per Capita Gross Domestic Product** (*purchasing power parity*): $30,800 (2001 est.); *Inflation*: 3.1%; *Unemployment*: 3.6%; *Living below the poverty line*: NA

### B. A Brief Historical Perspective

The ancestry of Norwegians, like the Danes and Swedes, has been traced back to early Germanic or Teutonic tribes that settled in the Jut Land, the Danish peninsula, in the 4th century B.C.E., although there have been found traces of settlements in Norway that are at least 6,000 years old. The Norsemen, or Vikings, emerged as a power in Europe when Norway's first ruler, Harald the Fairhaired, led the sacking of Lindisfarne, Ireland, in 793. Between the 8th and 11th centuries, Norse Vikings raided all the coastal lands and navigable rivers of Europe from Germany to Spain, often occupying widely scattered territories. In the beginning of the 10th century, Harold I united the petty kingdoms of western Scandinavia and extended his rule as far as the Orkney and Shetland Islands. Viking nobles fleeing his conquests strengthened and expanded the Norse duchy of Normandy in France.

Christianity arrived under Olaf II (Saint Olaf) early in the 11th century. Medieval Norway reached its zenith of power and prosperity under Magnus VI (1263-1280), but lost its independence in 1319 when Magnus VII, king of Sweden, also assumed the Norwegian throne. Under the Kalmar Union of 1397, Norway and Sweden merged with Denmark under Danish rule. In 1814, Denmark, which had sided with France in the Napoleonic wars, was forced by the victors to cede Norway to Sweden. Within a year, Norway attempted to assert its own independence from Sweden, but failed. The Norwegians had nevertheless made their own constitution, which was declared on May 17, 1814. May 17 was later to become the Norwegian day of independence. A compromise was reached in 1815 when Sweden acknowledged Norway's independence "in perpetual union with the Swedish crown." The union of Norway's merchants, fishermen, sailors, and peasants with Sweden, dominated by an aristocracy with large estates and tenant farmers, was never a happy one. In 1905, Norway's legislature deposed Swedish King Oscar II and declared its independence, with Prince Charles of Denmark ruling as Haakon VII for 52 years.

Neutral during World War I, Norway declared neutrality at the start of World War II, but was occupied by German troops from 1940 to 1945. By 1948, Norway's economy had returned to prewar levels. A founding member of the United Nations, Norway joined the NATO alliance in 1949 and the European Union in 1994. The 1980s were marked by turmoil in the oil market and a temporary downturn in the economy that brought questions and challenges to Norway's strong welfare state and large wage increases. Long a world leader in social experimentation, Norway has recovered in recent years, as the country became the second-largest net oil exporter after Saudi Arabia in 1995. Norway has chosen by binding referendum not to become a member of the European Union. By the onset of 2003, discussions on a new application for the Union are emerging.

## 1. Basic Sexological Premises

Tracing the origin of Norwegian sexology through the written record is like trying to understand the lives of our ancestors by studying footprints preserved in Paleolithic clay. The Norse warrior culture that gave rise to the Vikings recorded its feats in the *Sagas*. It is in *Gunlaug's Saga* that we find the first instance of individual love and passion in northern European literature. In this tale, Gunlaug and Ravn fight a duel (*Holmgang*) for the love of a woman. After Gunlaug defeats Ravn, he fetches water to his dying opponent in a heroic act of mercy. As Gunlaug approaches, the treacherous Ravn dishonors all the laws of *Holmgang* by giving him a deadly wound to the head. Gunlaug sinks to his knees and asks, "Why?" Ravn answers, "I could not bear the thought of her being in your arms." It seems that the Nordic record of love begins with tragedy.

The Feudal Age that followed the breakup of the Roman Empire persisted for approximately a thousand years in Norway. Sigrid Undset, the daughter of one of Norway's foremost philologists, was a prescient observer of medieval life. Her two masterpieces, *Kristin Lavransdatter* and *Olav Audunsen I Hestviken*, depict a probable texture of life in Norway during the 13th and 14th centuries. The drama of life is played out against a backdrop of warfare and perilous voyages for men and the bearing of children and household management for women. Olav and Ingunn are betrothed as children. Later, Olav flees the land after slaying a man and joins the war band of a Viking chieftain. He returns to Norway, marries Ingunn, and takes her to his ancestral manor.

Childbearing and the hard work of running a household soon crush the fragile Ingunn, and Olav is left to raise the children alone. We are left to speculate what sexual interactions were really like in a world dominated by incessant war, the betrothal of children, marriages arranged to advance feudal interests, long separations of spouses, and the absence of birth control. While faith, love, and nature's beauty must have had an elevating effect, medieval life in Norway was lived out in a newly Christianized society, where sexuality came to be viewed as an unholy temptation. The highest value was placed on chastity and celibacy, and this earthly life was regarded as a pause between Heaven and Hell. Nonetheless, the population continued to grow, and Norwegian folk tales and songs with erotic themes were widely popular. They are preserved in a collection called *Erotic Folk Tales* (Asbjørnsen & Moe 1977).

The period between 1319 and 1814, when Norway was part of the Danish Empire, was called "The 400 Years' Night." In the literature of this period, very little can be found of an explicitly sexual nature. The first formal study of sexuality in Scandinavia was done in Norway by Eilert Sundt (1817-1875), a theologian from the staunchly religious southwest coast. Sundt (1976) embarked on a study of Norwegian morality by systematically recording the instances of extramarital births throughout the country. His primary purpose was to investigate the living conditions of the poor; the orderly methods by which he undertook these studies has caused Sundt to be honored as one of the pioneers of Norwegian sociology and sexology. The analysis of data from these studies, however, must have profoundly shocked 19th-century Norway, which was influenced by the repressive morality of Victorian England. Sundt found lively and widespread sexual activity throughout the country, especially around Tromsø, Trondhjem, and Oslo.

Although the 18th-century Swedish biologist Carl von Linnée (Linneus) (1969) described women's desire and pleasure in the sex act in a most sensuous way, Victorian morality denying the sexual nature of women was widespread. As in many other countries, however, just below the surface, a widely different and more primordial form of sexual behavior was thriving. In his book *Love and Lovesickness*, John Money writes about the Nordic legacy:

Today's adolescents who establish their sex lives by breaching the doctrine of the virgin bride and the double standard are, whether they know it or not, adopting a modern counterpart of another very ancient tradition, one which undoubtedly covered an area much wider than the term Nordic or Scandinavian would imply. This is the tradition of betrothal and sexual egalitarianism. It is called Nordic because it survived longest in Scandinavia. There it resisted the incursion of the Mediterranean system, which spread into Northern Europe as an adjunct to Christianity. . . . There, especially in rural areas, it still can be traced. As its name implies, the betrothal system is one in which not the marriage, but the betrothal of a young couple is the ceremony that marks the high point of their beginning as a breeding partnership. . . . The season for the betrothal began with the advent of spring, for in the winter a typical farm family and its hired hands survived the sub-zero nights by sleeping in the big kitchen around a fireplace or heating stove. In spring, the loft became sleeping quarters for the young, unmarried women. To admit visitors, they either unlatched the inside trap door or hung a rope from their upstairs window. When it happened that a boy and girl became romantically interested in each other, it was proper for their friends to allow them to meet alone. Thereafter they followed a prescribed routine where the boy would spend the night with his girlfriend, but sleeping with his clothes on and above the covers. Step by step, visit by visit, he got under the covers, and then under the covers with his clothes off, at which point the couple announced to their families their intention to be betrothed. The betrothal would lead eventually to marriage, but only if pregnancy had ensued. Marriage itself was a confirmation of parenthood rather than coition. (Money 1981, 57-58)

In 1841, Lord Acton published *The Functions and Disorders of the Reproductive Organs in Youth* in England. This book became influential in learned circles in Norway. Lord Acton was a specialist in diseases of the urinary tract who advocated a program of sexual abstinence before marriage, suppression of onanism (masturbation), and rigid control of sexual activity in marriage as the means of preventing inevitable mental and physical deterioration caused by excessive semen loss. This pseudoscientific doctrine reinforced the prevalent belief that sexuality was harmful to manly virtues and could lead to the degeneration of society.

The Norwegian Dr. August Koren was a dedicated follower of Lord Acton's philosophy. He became an active member of Sedelighetsforeningen (Moral Guardians) and fought energetically against public prostitution in Norway. He had his work cut out for him; during the second half of the 1800s, a virtually uncontrollable epidemic of venereal disease was spread by prostitutes in Norway, particularly in Christiania (later to be named Oslo). In 1880, 1,200 cases of gonorrhea were reported, which indicates that 4% of the male population between the ages of 15 and 60 years old caught the disease in one year. At the same time, 1% of the adult male population was infected by syphilis. It was at this time (1881) that Henrik Ibsen wrote his play *Ghosts*, which deals exactly with the effects of inherited syphilis. Peculiarly enough, the play was poorly received and not really performed until long after that.

The population of Christiania had grown enormously during the 18th century, and prostitution grew right along with it. The debate over prostitution grew heated by the end of the century, and many authors and members of the arts participated in it. Christian Krogh, a well-known author and painter (1852-1925), wrote a novel that denounced the hypocrisy of society and the control of prostitution by the police. *Albertine* is the story of an innocent young girl who comes to grief when she is seduced by a police officer, then is forced to become a prostitute. The novel was confiscated by the order of the minister of justice the day after it was published, but it sparked a heated debate that resulted in the renewed prohibition of public prostitution. Although the ban on this novel has never been removed, it was included in a collection of Krogh's works and subsequently published in 1921. The works of Hans Jæger (1854-1910), another popular author during this period, were confiscated in the 1890s because of their frank descriptions of sexuality. They were not published again until 1969.

The debate about prostitution ceased abruptly around the turn of the 19th century. This about-face was most likely a result of the more liberal attitude concerning sexuality that can be traced to three basic causes: the revolutionary theories of Sigmund Freud, the entry of women into the world of work during the Industrial Revolution, and the availability of birth-control devices.

Prior to the work of Freud, the origin of mental illness—"hysterical" behavior and "phobias"—was attributed to neurological impairment of unknown origin, or simply to possessions of demons. It was not until Sigmund Freud began to publish his findings in the late 19th century that subconscious disturbances were identified as the underlying cause of many behavioral disturbances or "psychopathologies." What was truly revolutionary about Freud's theories was his belief that libidinal energy (the Id) manifested itself from earliest infancy; that the Id's goal was to obtain satisfaction (the Pleasure Principle), which, if thwarted by external or internalized repressions from the Superego, resulted in a psychological disturbance or neurosis, which in turn destabilized the self (the Ego). These disturbances, which were often traceable to trauma experienced in some early stage of psychosexual development, tended to manifest themselves in hysteria, physical paralysis, anxiety, dream imagery, inadvertent speech, and ego defenses. By expanding the parameters of the libido to include the subconscious and unconscious, Freud put the realm of sexology on the scientific map.

The working class may not have been privy to the wonders of Freud's discoveries, but they were exposed to a number of technological and social innovations that transformed their existence. The first was the mechanization of production that accompanied the Industrial Revolution in Norway in the middle of the 18th century. Rural populations were drawn to the new industrial sites, and women and children were encouraged to join the workforce. It is worth noting that women and children were actually preferred to men wherever possible, because they were weaker, more docile, and could be paid less. For the first time, the manly virtues of strength and aggression were bested by the female virtues of timidity and subordination. In fact, it was in the impersonal new order of the industrial environment that no basic distinction was made between the sexes. In the new industrial environment, women were subjected to the authority of men other than consanguine males, found themselves in close proximity to men who were strangers, and gained a measure of financial independence. As a result, traditional family bonds changed, as did traditional standards of modesty. The demands of regulated work hours took priority over spontaneous sexual expression and procreation. Workers had to rush sex in the morning before work, or have sex at night, when they were tired. Even childbearing conflicted with the demands of productivity.

The historical record shows that methods to terminate unwanted pregnancies were frequently employed, often with tragic results. Infanticide was a second desperate measure resorted to by impoverished parents. The means to improve this situation, fortunately, were soon available. The technological process of vulcanizing rubber made the production of condoms possible. By the 1860s, "rubbers" were being sold in England and Germany. In 1890, Dr. von Gelsen published *Nødvendige Lægeråd til Nygifte*, which provided advice to those who wished to avoid pregnancy, but the book was banned by the Fredrikshald Chief of Police. Lars Oftedal, a well-known clergyman from Stavanger, appealed this decision in the Norwegian parliament (*Stortinget*), but the ban was upheld by a small majority, and it remained illegal to advertise or promote the use of contraception until the 1920s.

In reaction to the emerging trend of sexual liberation, a wave of pietism swept through many rural areas of Norway. Music and dancing were condemned as sins, and women were branded as temptresses whose carnal wiles, unless curtailed, would lead the spirit of men astray. Although the radical negativity of these views seems absurd, they have survived in many religious subcultures until today, underwriting the suppression of sexuality and propagating the myth of male superiority. There was also widespread anxiety about masturbation and the supposed ill effects that resulted from its practice. In a widely circulated paper presented in 1895 by Dr. Klaus Hansen, this "unnatural" way to satisfy sexual urges was condemned; it was claimed that "self-contamination" resulting from this practice led to a host of diseases that impaired the central nervous system.

A notable proponent of sexual freedom was Karl Evang (1902-1981), who became the most active advocate of public sexuality education in the 1930s. Evang became the Director of Public Health in Norway, and published the popular and informative *Magazine for Sexual Information*, which for many years provided the public with a source of information concerning sexuality. Evang took umbrage with the notion that the loss of human semen caused deleterious physical effects. He once stated that this belief was as ridiculous as claiming that the loss of spit led to physical and spiritual degeneration. Evang was one of the cofounders of the World Health Organization (WHO), and presided over its Second General Assembly in 1949. During his career, he made major contributions to the contemporary understanding of drug abuse, work-related illnesses, and contraception.

Psychoanalytic theories gained momentum when Wilhelm Reich fled to Norway in 1934 to escape persecution by the Nazi regime in Germany. Reich was a substantial influence in Norwegian psychology and sexology. At the Nordic Association of Clinical Sexology (NACS) meeting in Oslo in 1983, Rolf Groenseth presented a summary of the Reichian view: Sex is a natural and health-promoting human drive. In *The Function of the Orgasm* (1927), one of his major works, Reich postulated that sexual fulfillment was key to emotional stability and physical health. Reich believed that every human being had a "healthy core" that served as a natural defense against cultural repression. Although Reich's sexual theories met with acceptance, his research on Orgone and the effect of cosmic fields was considered eccentric. He gradually lost support and had to leave Norway in 1939. Ola Raknes, one of Reich's most prominent Norwegian proponents, did extensive research on the results of the socialization of sexuality in childhood. Raknes was able to identify many adult sexual problems that were related to the repression of the natural sexual urge in childhood.

Because of the severe disruptions caused by World War II, not much was written on the topic of sexology in the 1940s. The German invasion of Norway, and the atrocities that took place throughout Europe, dealt deathblows to the legitimacy of war as an extension of foreign policy. The anachronistic myths of the proud warrior and the nobility of combat were cast upon the trash heap of history. Women around the world, who faced up to the rigors of war and the challenge of taking over tasks previously considered "men's work," found true freedom in self-sufficiency. When the war ended, this habit of self-sufficiency persisted, and women demanded equality in sexual, as well as domestic matters. This new woman, a full-fledged personality with the capacity to make choices, became one of the central characters in Agnar Mykle's controversial 1956 book, *Sangen om den Roede Rubin* [*The Song of the Red Ruby*]. In Mykle's novel, a young man is torn between his love for his mistress and the devotion he feels for his father. It is finally the admirable personal qualities he perceives in the woman that empowers him to leave his father, become an adult, and find a fulfilling new life with her. At the time of publication, the radical theme and explicit sexual descriptions were considered obscene, and both Mykle and his editor were forced to stand trial for foisting pornography on the public. Upon appeal, the Supreme Court decided that the book was not immoral, and Mykle was exonerated.

In 1964, *Profil*, a literary magazine, began to publish the work of a number of talented young radical authors. The un-

derlying purpose of their innovative and sexually explicit material was to permeate the watertight neurotic system of bourgeois morality. A number of sexuality education books were also published by PAX, a Norwegian publisher specializing in political and controversial books, in addition to a collection of erotic short stories.

Jens Bjørneboe was a controversial author whose well-crafted, revelatory books about the school system (*Jonas*), the postwar legal settlements, and the penal system were popular in Norway. When his book, *Uten en Traad* [*Without a Fiber*] was published in 1966, it sent a reactionary convulsion through conservative circles. Authorities confiscated the book and Bjørneboe was brought to trial for attempting to circulate pornography. The trial ushered in an intense debate to determine which descriptions of sexuality were to be considered illegal. The debate continues to this day.

## 2. Religious, Ethnic, and Gender Factors Affecting Sexuality

For several decades, conceptual influences on Norwegian sexology have come from a growing number of sources. A primary influence was the Sexual Revolution of the 1960s and 1970s, which served as a means of correcting societal norms for human sexuality that were too narrow and exclusive. One example would be the refusal of gay men and women to allow society to condemn their behavior or to label it abnormal. Unmarried heterosexuals, freed for the first time in history from the threat of unwanted pregnancy by "the Pill," began to view the opportunity to interact sexually as a form of liberation guided by choice and freed from the stigma of sin. This new freedom from biological and moral constraints shook the prevailing norms imposed by church and academia, which had formally labeled all sexual activity not in the service of procreation and marriage as either lewd or abnormal. Prototypes of appropriate behavior founded upon married couples tending their offspring, the economic dependency of women upon men, and the conceptualization of masculinity and femininity as monodimensional opposites, have all been challenged by the dissemination of this transformative concept of sexual freedom. The voices of previously ignored "unfit" sexual minorities, physically and mentally challenged individuals, the aged, children, and people in hospitals and institutions, were heard for the first time as they gave their own bold testimonies. However, the state-supported Lutheran Church still refuses to allow practicing lesbians and homosexuals to hold consecrated positions. At the turn of the millennium, this is one of the most heated religious debates in Norway. Likewise, religiously influenced views of erotica and pornography are being challenged by new insights into the possible harms and benefits of these phenomena. There is a growing awareness in many religious circles of sexuality as a force of good rather than one of evil.

There has been a significant shift in focus among feminists since women began to populate the universities in the 1960s. At first, there was a tendency to adopt male ideas and values in pursuit of the goal of entering previously male-dominated professions and fields of study. Subsequently, a gynocentric phase has ensued in which feminist theories have focused upon the substitution of masculine ideals with woman's values. It seems that success in "a man's world" has inspired women to find their own center of gravity. Women's self-help groups, women's issues, such as single motherhood and affirmative action in hiring practices, women's literature, and even women's rock bands are all examples of this trend.

## 3. Knowledge and Education about Sexuality

The first person to become known as a "sexologist" in Norway was the psychiatrist Berthold Grünfeld. He has long been considered a pioneer in sex information, and has held a central position on the team that enacts and performs gender-reassignment procedures. Grünfeld must also be honored for his effort on behalf of women's rights in the question of abortion. He has questioned the wisdom of those who assume that their opinions on sexual issues are infallible, and has warned against the indiscriminate use of male labels in gender-related terminology.

Although general knowledge about sexuality in Norway is high, the problem is that this knowledge is based on traditional masculine values, pornography, and the absence of women as spokespersons for sexuality. The authorities have played a rather passive and hesitating role in the spread of sex education after World War II (1945), and sex education has been a cause for politically radical people and pioneer groups. The Norwegian Society of Clinical Sexology was founded in 1982, and even if it has not been able to influence the authorities, it has been an important forum for those who have been interested in sexological education and sex information. In 1998 and 1999, the Nordic Sexological Societies received government support from the Nordic Minister Council to develop guidelines for the authorization of clinical sexologists in the Nordic countries, and to make an outline for sexological education. Norwegian politicians have begun to show an interest in sexological education, which gives rise to optimism about sexological education and the integration of sexology into clinical practices.

With the spread of HIV/AIDS, the National Organization Against AIDS was founded with government support. This organization has played an important role in spreading information about homosexuality and in the rapid change in attitudes towards homosexuals. Even as the most heated debate about homosexuality in Norway today is whether homosexuals should be allowed to perform holy services in the State Church, it is encouraging that one by one, the bishops have expressed positive attitudes towards homosexuals in church.

According to government plans for education, there is not much sex education during the first ten years in school. In the 9th grade, under the subject of science of nature, the pupil should be taught about how hormones work in the body. In the 10th grade, there is a topic called sex and cohabitation, which is taught as a subject under education in religion and philosophy of life. Tenth-grade pupils are also taught about contraceptives, sexually transmitted diseases, procreation, love, sexuality, sexual identity, and other topics concerning sexuality. This is far from the ideal that sexuality should be taught as an integrated part of many aspects of life throughout school. Young people are left to learn about sexuality from the media and their peer groups. Many parents still find it difficult to talk to their children about sexuality; they hope that the school will take care of this. Even if the school system does not take very good care of sex education, young people seem to be quite knowledgeable about the basic principles of sexuality and the use of contraceptives and sexually transmitted diseases. We believe, however, that this knowledge is poorly integrated in young people's emotional life and behavior. There are still too many negative effects of sexual activity among young people, like unwanted pregnancies, abortions, and sexually transmitted diseases. Studies show that such statistics vary with the level of sex education. Very good statistics from the Netherlands clearly support this conclusion, as well as the

benefits of extensive sex education at all levels of education. The Netherlands has become a model for many other countries that want to reduce the negative consequences of sexual activity, teenage abortions, and sexually transmitted diseases.

## 4. Autoerotic Behaviors and Patterns

In two surveys with identical questions, one carried out in 1987 and the other in 1997, a representative group of the Norwegian population was asked about the importance of masturbation. In 1987, an average of 24% (men 32%; women 17%) found this kind of sexual stimulation "very important" or "rather important." The corresponding number from the 1997 survey was 35% (men 44%; women 28%). In both surveys, self-pleasuring is more important for men than for women (Norwegian Society for Sexology 1987ab).

A mailbox sexual information service in a Norwegian men's magazine (*Vi Menn*) regularly receives questions from men concerning the normality of self-pleasuring activities. The notions of self-stimulation as unhealthy and even perverse still exist, but on the whole, the attitudes within Norwegian society are increasingly permissive. A recent newspaper discussion concerning the Norwegian armed forces disclosed attitudes to the effect that Norwegian soldiers should not masturbate during their 12 months of compulsory service. In the discussion, these attitudes were gently refuted by general insights and multiple personal experiences.

The psychologist Thore Langfeldt, one of Norway's sexological pioneers, has engaged himself in the teaching of masturbatory techniques through the erotic magazine *Cupido* (Personal communication 1984, 1985). Several textbooks on female masturbation are on the shelves of Norwegian bookstores. Norwegian textbooks of sexology offer instructions for female and male sexual self-pleasuring.

## 5. Interpersonal Heterosexual Behaviors

Heterosexual life in Norway is still influenced by heterosexist views and belief systems. At the same time, sexual life as such is constricted by notions of sin and deeds of darkness. Progress has, however, been remarkable. Magazines for women and men have open, professional, and permission-giving columns for questions on sexuality and sexual matters. There is a growing awareness of the beneficial effect of a satisfactory sexual life for most of human sexual diversity. For instance, there is a group working for the removal of the psychiatric diagnosis of paraphilias like fetishism, sadomasochism, and transvestic fetishism. While conservative views about sexuality still exist, the public debate is increasingly marked by liberal views. The general interest in sexuality as such is increasing; the debate focuses on the social construction of sexuality, pair bonding, and sexual relationships. One of the new topics is discrimination against singles in the debate around the organization of sexuality in relationships.

### A. Single Persons

*Age of First Intercourse*

According to studies, Norwegians seem increasingly to have their first sexual intercourse at younger and younger ages. The median age of first intercourse is between 17 and 18 years for people below the age of 30. For older groups, the median age of first intercourse gradually increases up to age 21. There seems to be a tendency for those who had their first intercourse when they were very young to have more sex partners thereafter. They also report more extramarital sex than those with a higher age for first intercourse (Seksjon for Epidemiologi 1993). Træen, Lewin, and Sundet (1992) reported that boys had more coital partners than girls, but girls had had intercourse more often than boys.

*Premarital Sex*

Premarital sex has gradually come to be regarded as a normal part of sexual development. Even if more-conservative Christian societies still regard sex after marriage as the preferred option, more and more Christians have come to question this as a sound moral guideline, as marriages are more and more based on love and partnership, and less on economic and social dependence. As people are free to divorce, people also seem to be more cautious getting married. It now seems to be a general attitude that people want to get to know each other before they get married. Also, the old Norwegian tradition, where people marry after they get pregnant or have had children, seems to be having a revival. The new moral seems to be that people put more effort into marrying the right partner, than they do in following any tradition that demands that at least the woman be a virgin before marriage.

*What Turns Norwegians On?*

In the surveys by the Norwegian Society of Clinical Sexology (NSCS) and Markeds of Media Instituttet (MMI) in 1987 and 1997, the respondents were asked who and what turned them on sexually. In 1987, 91% of the population reported that they were turned on to some degree by individuals of the other sex (men 95%; women 87%). The corresponding number from 1997 is 94% (men 95%; women 92%). The general increase in sexual interest that seems to have developed during the ten-year span is even more apparent when we look at those who turn on to the opposite sex "to a very large degree." In 1987, 34% of the women and 49% of men reported that they were turned on by the opposite sex "to a very large degree." The corresponding numbers from 1997 were 47% for women and 62% for men. There has been a tendency over the ten-year time span towards an increase in sexual and erotic interest, especially among women.

The most important sexual activity among all couples, homosexual couples included, was bodily closeness. In 1987, an average of 64% (men 59%; women 68%), and in 1997, an average of 66% (men 60%; women 70%) selected the option "very important" to describe this form of sexual activity or intimacy. Mutual genital contact was the second most-important sexual activity. In 1987, an average of 54% (men and women both 54%), and in 1997, an average of 54% (men 57%; women 53%) scored this activity as being "very important." Foreplay and petting was the third most-important sexual activity, with an average score on "very important" in 1987 of 48% (men 39%; women 57%), and in 1997, an average of 48% (men 45%; women 50%). Kissing was also rated rather high as a "very important" sexual contact or stimulation. In 1987, an average of 34% (men 29%; women 38%) chose this option. The proportion increased during the ten years that followed. In 1997, the number was 45% (men 35%; women 44%). Oral sex also had a high score of 15% in 1987 (men 17%; women 13%), and in 1997, an average of 22% (men 23%; women 21%).

*Number of Sex Partners*

To no one's surprise, the number of sex partners increases with chronological age, but it is also possible to see the effect of the so-called "sexual revolution" in the fact that men between 30 and 49 years have had more partners than men who are older than 50. Whereas in the group of men between 18 and 29 years old (who have had at least one sex

partner), 31% report having had more than ten partners, in the group of men between 50 and 60 years, 51% report having had more than ten partners. Among men between 20 and 39 years, 64% report having had more than ten partners, and in the group of men age 40 to 49, 62% have had more than ten partners. In all age groups, it is more common to have had between two and five sex partners in a lifetime.

Women, in general, have had fewer partners than men. Among women aged 18 to 29, 24% report having had more than ten partners in their lifetime. Among women age 30 to 39 years, 51% report having had more than ten partners, whereas in the older groups, among women age 40 to 49 and age 50 to 59, 41% and 26%, respectively, report having had more than ten partners (Seksjon for Epidemiologi 1993).

## B. Couples

*Marriage*

Norwegians are increasingly marrying at a later age. The mean age for men and women at first marriage in 1961 was 26.4 and 23.4, respectively. In 1997, this had increased to 30.6 and 28.3. The number of Norwegians who are not married, divorced, or single is also increasing. In 1961, 7.6% of all men and 3.6% of all women at age 50 where unmarried. In 1997, the corresponding numbers were 37.2 and 32.1, respectively (*Statistisk Årbok* 1999).

*Frequency of Intercourse*

There seems to be a continuous interest in the question: "How often do people do it?" Table 1 shows the results of a study from 1992 (Seksjon for Epidemiologi 1993) for men and women who had sex with another person, but who did not live with a partner. This study also reported that the number of intercourses per year for people who did not live with a partner declined in 1992 compared to 1987 (see Table 2). When we look at the frequency of intercourse for all people, with and without a partner, there is no difference in 1992 compared to 1987. Table 3 shows the combined distribution for men and women. Couples who have cohabited longer seem to have a lower frequency of intercourse than couples who have lived together for a shorter length of time.

In the survey done by NSCS/MMI in 1997, 28% (homosexuals not excluded) had had sexual contact/intercourse between two and four times in the past four weeks, 22%

### Table 1

**Frequency of Intercourse for Men and Women Who Lived with a Partner, 1992**

| Number of Intercourses Last Month | Men | Women |
|---|---|---|
| 0 | 58% | 57% |
| 1-2 | 10 | 13 |
| 3-4 | 10 | 12 |
| 5-10 | 11 | 10 |
| > 11 | 10 | 9 |

### Table 2

**Comparison of Frequency of Intercourse for Years 1987 and 1992**

| Number of Intercourses Per Year | 1987 | 1992 |
|---|---|---|
| 0 | 17.9% | 20.2% |
| 1-9 | 27.2 | 37.0 |
| 10-49 | 29.8 | 22.5 |
| 50+ | 25.1 | 20.3 |

stated five to ten times, and 13% eleven times or more. There were more women in the group of five to ten times. Otherwise, the numbers were equal for men and women.

Norwegian men and women both like variety in the locations where they have sex. Close to 50% often or sometimes had sex outside the bedroom in 1997. Correspondingly, about 40% wanted the same variety in 1987. In spite of a climate that often offers temperatures below comfortable, Norwegians are not adverse to outdoor sexual activities. As many as 24% of the men and 18% of the women are in favor of "sex outdoors in nature" either often or sometimes. The higher proportion of men may indicate outdoor activities are more popular among homosexual men than among heterosexuals and lesbians (Dalen 1987, 1997)

### Divorce and Remarriage

Twice as many individuals lose their partner by death than by divorce in Norway. While the number of widowers has stayed relatively constant, the number of divorces increased steadily until 1991. In the years since 1991, the divorce rate has oscillated between 11.2 and 11.7 per 1,000 married couples. The percent of men and women who have been widowed or divorced and remarry is rather constant. In 1961, 43.7% of men and 38.3% of women remarried. In 1997, 44.9% of men and 41.1% of women remarried (*Statistisk Årbok* 1999).

### Extramarital Sex

Official statistics show that there is a weak tendency towards fewer extramarital sexual affairs among Norwegian couples. This is a marked tendency in the younger groups, whereas there is a tendency towards more extramarital sexual affairs in the older groups (see Table 4). In two studies by the Nordic Association for Clinical Sexology (Dalen 1987, 1997), a representative group was asked whether they had ever had sex with others while they lived in a steady relationship. The tendency seems to be that people have more extramarital sexual affairs (see Table 5). When we look at the different age groups, we see that people between ages 40 and 59 have the most extramarital affairs (see Table 6). While more people seem to have extramarital affairs, more people seemed to be unfaithful only once in 1997 compared to 1987.

### C. Sexuality and the Elderly

While an Egyptian philosopher allegedly said, "Old age is the worst of all diseases that can happen to a person," in northern European countries old age is not regarded as an age of wisdom to be honored, as in some African countries. An older man expressing sexual desire is looked upon as a "bold pig" rather than as a remarkably strong and potent man in his old age. This situation is slowly changing, as most people learn that sexuality is not limited to procreation. As we learn that sexuality is to be enjoyed from childhood throughout old age, our attitudes and practices are challenged, and new practices in institutions for older people are changed to allow older people more privacy and opportunities to enjoy love and sexuality with their life partner or with a new partner. Elderly people who are asked what love and sexuality means to them say that coitus is no longer so important. Instead they appreciate tenderness, satisfaction, and mutual trust. Instead of orgasm, they appreciate intimacy and sensuality.

### D. Challenged People

Many people with chronic diseases and people with physical and mental handicaps encounter extra difficulties in their love relationships and sexual lives. Not many studies have been done to get more knowledge about these groups, but we experience an increasing demand from people who work with these groups to have more education in sexual matters, and people with chronic diseases and handicaps themselves ask for help in their sex life. In all communities in Norway, there are supposed to be places where people who need it can go for special devices that are necessary to be able to have sexual activity alone or together with a partner. Ethical discussions arise as to what extent or in what way people who work with these groups are obliged to assist their clients in obtaining sexual satisfaction.

#### Table 3

#### Frequency of Intercourse by Age Group

| Frequency | Age 18-29 | Age 30-39 | Age 40-49 | Age 50-60 |
|---|---|---|---|---|
| Less than once a day | 1.1% | 0.5% | 0.6% | 0.7% |
| Daily | 2.7 | 1.1 | 1.2 | 0.3 |
| 5-6 times a week | 6.9 | 3.0 | 2.6 | 2.0 |
| 3-4 times a week | 27.9 | 18.6 | 15.4 | 5.8 |
| 1-2 times a week | 38.9 | 47.6 | 48.6 | 38.9 |
| 2 times a month | 13.6 | 18.2 | 17.9 | 24.5 |
| Once a month or less | 4.3 | 5.1 | 6.2 | 12.6 |
| Never | 4.8 | 5.9 | 7.4 | 15.3 |

#### Table 4

#### Percentage of Men and Women by Age Group Having Extramarital Sex

| Age | Women 1987 | Women 1992 | Men 1987 | Men 1992 |
|---|---|---|---|---|
| 18-22 | 16% | 8% | 8% | 3% |
| 23-27 | 13 | 6 | 21 | 14 |
| 28-32 | 16 | 10 | 18 | 15 |
| 33-37 | 14 | 11 | 24 | 19 |
| 38-42 | 12 | 15 | 27 | 26 |
| 43-47 | 13 | 12 | 25 | 25 |
| 48-52 | 8 | 18 | 14 | 24 |
| 53-60 | 6 | 10 | 22 | 27 |
| All ages | 13 | 11 | 22 | 21 |

#### Table 5

#### Percentage of Men and Women Who Ever Had Extramarital Sex in Two Studies

| Number of Times | Women 1987 | Women 1997 | Men 1987 | Men 1997 |
|---|---|---|---|---|
| No, never | 68% | 59% | 57% | 53% |
| Yes, once | 15 | 22 | 12 | 20 |
| Yes, more than once | 13 | 15 | 25 | 21 |

#### Table 6

#### Percentage of Men and Women by Age Group Who Ever Had Extramarital Sex

| Number of Times | Age in 1987/1997 | | | | | | | |
|---|---|---|---|---|---|---|---|---|
| | 15-24 | | 25-39 | | 40-59 | | 60+ | |
| | male | female | male | female | male | female | male | female |
| No, never | 54% | 64% | 63% | 50% | 62% | 56% | 75% | 70% |
| Yes, once | 17 | 15 | 16 | 28 | 13 | 19 | 6 | 9 |
| Yes, more than once | 16 | 10 | 21 | 18 | 25 | 22 | 12 | 11 |

## 6. Homoerotic, Homosexual, and Bisexual Behaviors

It is estimated that approximately 5% of the Norwegian population is exclusively homosexual. Table 7 shows the results of a study from 1992 (Seksjon for Epidemiologi 1993) concerning people who have had at least one sexual contact, and who reported to have had sex with a person of the same sex.

Of men who lived with a partner, 1.3% lived with another man, and 1% of women who lived with a partner, lived with another woman. However, only 36% of these men and 52% of these women reported that they had had sex with a person of the same sex. This should be interpreted to mean that single people live together with people of the same sex without being sexual partners. Of women who lived with a man, 2.7% reported having had sex with another women, while 2.4% of men who lived with a woman reported having had sex with another man. Of those who lived alone, 6.4% of men and 4.6% of women reported having had a homosexual experience.

The first center for sexological counseling in Norway for people who find themselves attracted to people of the same sex was opened at the Counseling for Homosexuals at the Public Health Council in Oslo in 1983. This vital service was greatly expanded in response to the AIDS epidemic. Nils Johan Ringdal, a historian, writer, and himself a homosexual, has pointed to the tremendous impact of the AIDS campaign to augment the general public's awareness of homosexuality. Ringdal feels that it has not been unduly difficult to be homosexual in the last half of the 20th century (personal communication, December 2, 1993). In his history of the police in Norway during the German occupation in World War II, Ringdal (1994) notes that although homosexuality was officially forbidden, homosexuals were seldom punished unless they were engaged in sexual liaisons with Germans, or were found guilty of sexual offenses involving minors.

The Organization of 1948 was founded by Norwegian homosexuals inspired by a Danish organization for gay activists. Throughout the 1950s and 1960s, homosexuals courageously expanded their subculture. According to Ringdal, many homosexuals today become extremely nostalgic when they recall those exciting years. Section 213 of the Penal Code, which considered homosexual relations between men to be a criminal offense, was repealed in 1972. In 1979, Norway followed the example of the American Psychiatric Association by removing homosexuality from its list of mental diseases. In 1981, the Ministry of Justice passed a proposal that provided legal protection to homosexuals.

During the 1960s, Norwegian homosexuals were influenced by the sexual revolution that led to the "Golden Age of the Seventies." In the 1980s, HIV and AIDS caused the "Great Backlash" of increased caution and discretion. A recent publication from the Ministry of Children and Family Affairs (1999) states that, although homosexuality is now considered a variety of normal sexual behavior, most homosexuals remain reluctant to "come out" to their families, tend to live alone, and are likely to seek places of residence in the anonymity of the big cities. When interviewed, most respondents stated that they wished to live as a partner and want to bond with another. The findings indicate that a strong degree of alienation results from a homosexual orientation. This alienation may be ameliorated by the Law of Partnership, which gives Norwegian homosexuals equal rights to form legal partnerships. This law was passed in April 1993 and was effective August 1, 1993. The law allows people of the same sex the right to form formal partnerships with the same legal rights as married heterosexuals. They were, however, not given the right to a church blessing. Some priests have on their own given Christian blessing to homosexual couples. Although these partnerships may not be blessed by the church and do not confer the right to adopt children, the legal rights conferred upon homosexual unions represent a tremendous victory in the struggle for social acceptance. Mette Sorensen, information secretary of the Organization of 1948, was asked to comment upon the likely outcomes of the new law. She said that since the law was passed (April 1993), it was too soon to tell. However, there is every indication that Norwegian partnerships will prove to be at least as stable as heterosexual marriages. Sorensen believes that homosexuals and heterosexuals have essentially the same needs, to love and to bond. She adds that the purpose of marriage is not only to make and safeguard babies, but to make a life choice and have it recognized by one's society. Official statistics show that in 1995, 98 couples entered into partnership. In 1996 and 1997, the numbers were 127 and 118. So far, twice as many male as female couples have entered partnership.

## 7. Gender Diversity and Transgender Issues

[*Update 2003*: Norway has two organizations for transpeople. The older is FPE-NE. It was founded in 1968 to meet the needs of "heterosexual transvestites." Today, members of the FPE-NE include a continuum from classical part-time cross-dressers through self-defined bi-gendered and transgendered persons to transsexuals. By 2002, FPE-NE organized 142 individuals.

[LFTS, the younger organization, was founded in January 2000 with three purposes, the most urgent being to seize offers of the government to pay for gender-confirming surgery for transsexuals seeking this. The second was the willingness of some transsexuals to display themselves as transsexual women and men, thus generating the power to influence on most levels in society, including the arenas of politics and media. The third reason was the need for transsexuals to come in contact with other transsexuals and/or with other transpeople, to generate a context where each could find friendships, insights, and addresses of approved therapists in the field. LFTS was by 2002 organizing 120 individuals. There is an option of a supportive membership with cheaper dues for parents, siblings of transpeople, and for any other that may find such a membership meaningful. LFTS is receiving economic support from the Norwegian state, but is not yet securely financed. A bill to enforce the rights for transsexuals to receive optimal medical treatment is proposed, but was not ratified by the beginning of 2003. (*End of update by E. Almås and E. E. Pirelli Benestad*)]

Norwegian transsexuals over age 18 are offered professional assistance by a centralized team in Oslo. The team generally follows the standards of care recommended by

### Table 7

**Number of Men and Women by Age Group Who Reported Having Sex with a Same-Sex Partner, 1992**

| Age | Men | Women |
| --- | --- | --- |
| 18-29 | 5.1% | 3.9% |
| 30-39 | 6.3 | 5.1 |
| 40-49 | 4.0 | 2.0 |
| 50-60 | 3.4 | 0.9 |

the Harry Benjamin International Gender Dysphoria Association. The degree of pre- and postsurgical support is lower than wanted and needed by many transsexuals. Very little is done concerning children and adolescents who display transgendered feelings and behaviors. A Norwegian child psychiatrist, Trond Diseth, recently presented a thesis on the problems of addressing children with ambiguous external genitalia (Diseth 1998). One of the authors of this chapter, who is both a professional and a transgendered person, Esben Benestad/Esther Pirelli, has been a frequent oral and written presenter on transgender issues both nationally and internationally. He/she is presently working on a clinical project on how to address children and adolescents with unusual gendered feelings and/or expressions. Benestad/Pirelli also points out that most of the transgendered adults do not suffer from gender dysphoria, but are dysphoric about a body that does not affirm their ego syntonic experience of gender identity. Working with gender issues and problems concerning gender, we have found it most useful to apply the term "gender belonging" (gender identity) to the process by which a person develops a sense of belonging that is both generally appropriate and self-confirming within the parameters of cultural roles, erotic preferences, body status, and the subjective synthesis of sexual experiences. Work with male transvestites has provided ample material to discuss alternative gender belongings, including male, female, male and female, and others still not named. Dr. Benestad/Pirelli has found the individual experience of gender belonging to be a dynamic state of interaction between internal "beliefs" and external affirmations, decisively influenced and confirmed by subjective gender reference, body consciousness, body picture, gender-role behavior, and erotic preference.

Professor Per Schioldborg at the University of Oslo has done significant research on gender roles. He has based much of his research on Sandra Bem's scales, and his proposal, presented at the NACS meeting in 1983, represents an important development in the way we perceive masculinity and femininity. Schioldborg (1983) proposed that we regard masculinity-femininity as two orthogonal dimensions, rather than one. This concept is projected as a model with four groups: androgynous (high on both variables), masculine, feminine, and undifferentiated (low on both variables). Although the term "identity" is virtually ineluctable, we believe that it is too inflexibly linked to traditional thinking that defines sexual roles as being *either* male *or* female. Quite a few cultures give other possibilities of belonging to individuals that are "somewhere in between." We could call them "both-and" solutions. Even though deviation from the two approved gender stereotypes has been categorized in the psychiatric literature as "gender identity disturbances," "gender dysphoria," "perversions," or by John Money's term "paraphilias," we are inclined to ask whether the individuals in question really are disturbed, or whether they have a gender that disturbs their surroundings.

Since Freud introduced his trauma theories, psychiatric professionals have attempted to explain gender differences as the result of traumas suffered in childhood. In the last few years, clinicians have developed reservations about this. We believe this is because of the fact that transsexuals and transvestites themselves are increasingly active in scientific sexology as professionals. It is painfully obvious that much of the pathology that transsexuals and transvestites bring to the therapist's office is caused by culture-induced pain and rejection, rather than childhood traumas. There is reason to be optimistic about the future because of a widening acceptance of gender differentiation, a trend already manifesting itself in the growing acceptance of homosexuality.

## 8. Significant Unconventional Sexual Behaviors

### A. Coercive Sex
*Incest and Child Sexual Abuse*

In Norway, as in many other countries, only a small proportion of reported cases of incest and sexual abuse leads to conviction. It is, therefore, difficult to get exact statistics about how frequent these phenomena are. While some studies report that 20 to 25% of all children have been victims of sexual abuse of some kind, researchers in this field suggest that 5% is a more likely estimate. The public discussion now is whether the molester should have treatment or punishment or both. Today, not even the victim is granted relevant treatment, because of a shortage of therapists.

[*Update 2003*: In 2002, the Norwegian police, in collaboration with police forces in several other countries, unraveled a league of child pornography users and distributors. The number of individuals involved lies between 100 and 200. Still, the case is under investigation and more individuals may be involved. (*End of update by E. Almås and E. E. Pirelli Benestad*)]

*Rape*

The numbers of reported rapes were relatively stable during the early 1990s, but since 1996, there has been a steady increase. In 1994, 366 rapes where reported, according to official statistics (Ukenst Statistikk, Statistisk Sentralbyrå); 57 of these resulted in convictions. Estimates suggest that 90% of all rapes are not even reported. In 1998, 456 rapes were reported. In the period between 1989 to 1994, the severest penalties were between five and ten years in prison. The mean penalty was 2.4 years. The maximum penalty is now ten years in prison. If the victim dies as a result of the rape assault, the highest penalty is 21 years in prison.

*Sexual Harassment*

The Danish sociologist, Henning Bech describes the characteristics of sexual relationships in different cultures as follows:

> In most English-speaking countries, it is a question about power. In the Nordic countries, except Denmark, it is a question of prohibition. In Denmark, it is a question of ability to play the game. This may be one of the reasons why the question of sexual harassment has been such a big issue in the United States, but not in the Nordic countries. (From an interview in the Danish newspaper, *Politiken*, April 11, 1999)

However, some studies have been done concerning unwanted sexual attention in Norway. In 1992, a group of female researchers conducted a study based on a questionnaire printed in *Kvinner og Klær*, a women's magazine. The results showed that 20% of the women between 18 and 50 years reported that they had experienced unwanted sexual attention that had resulted in psychological, physical, or work-related problems (Brantsæther & Widerberg 1992). Another study showed that 8% of women had experienced unwanted sexual attention during the last six months. Table 8 shows the results of the NACS/MMI studies from 1987 and 1997. It is difficult to explain why these numbers are so low, compared, for instance, with American studies. One explanation may be that general attitudes toward sexual attention are more positive and not so thin-skinned in Norway.

### B. Prostitution
In 1993, a Scandinavian Conference on Prostitution was held at Lillehammer with a number of prostitutes actively participating in the dialogue. On the agenda were legal issues

involving sexual legislation, contemporary morality, the organization of brothels, and the need for a societal consensus regarding sex workers. The politicians were encouraged to adopt a "harm reduction" approach, which accepts prostitution as a time-honored societal phenomenon, rather than to persist in the more harmful and costly punitive approach, which criminalizes prostitution. Liv Jessen, leader of the PRO-Center, a prostitutes group in Oslo, emphasizes the importance of addressing the problems associated with prostitution on a structural meta-level, rather than belligerently attacking the prostitutes and condemning the existence of brothels. In response to the feminist activist Women's Front raid upon brothels, Jessen asks whether it is more immoral to prostitute oneself under a roof rather than on the street. Jessen stresses the need for more reflection and awareness, rather than for slogans and headlines, which merely stigmatize prostitutes. From her work with men who seek prostitutes, Liv Jessen concludes that sexuality is in difficult straits in our society. The typical "john" Jessen interviewed confided that, although he desires to experience an adventurous and loving sex life with his wife or girlfriend, he feels rejected and attempts to experience fulfillment by acting out fantasies with prostitutes (1993-1994).

Jessen reports that many men lose respect for themselves when they buy sex and usually experience a bad conscience. By neglecting to frankly express their sexual needs to their partners, these men are asking too little. In Jessen's opinion, the entire therapeutic community remains victimized by repression, and the reluctance to take sexual issues more seriously is because of the ubiquitous inhibition still hampering many clinicians.

## C. Pornography and Erotica

When standards regarding the appropriate depiction of sex-related subjects are discussed, the first question that comes to mind is whether the subject is pornographic or erotic. Although these terms have been used interchangeably, there is a significant difference between them. Pornographic is defined as the depiction of obscene or unchaste subjects in literature or art, while erotic pertains to the depiction of love.

Terje Gammelsrud, editor of a popular erotic magazine, *Cupido*, for many years the only legal magazine devoted to sex in Norway, informs us that the term "erotic" is preferable to most people, because it has a less lewd connotation. Also, it is easier to discuss sexual subjects when they are presented as erotica, rather than as pornography. Gammelsrud notes that, in his view, the difference between good and bad pornography is obvious once we determine whether the subject is expressing passion in an authentic state of sexual arousal, or whether the subject is acting out some form of sexual behavior that conforms to a predetermined stereotype of what

sexual arousal would look like if it were actually taking place. Gammelsrud expresses surprise at the absence of reaction from feminist activists when new magazines depicting the overtly sexual involvement of women are published. He wonders whether this lack of protest is because of a sense of resignation or to a more open and positive acceptance of sexuality (1993-1994).

Gammelsrud raises the important question: What is the price our society pays for not having a sexual politic? It surely amounts to billions if we factor in the costs spent in healthcare, the judicial system, the social system, and reduced work productivity. There is also the commonly invisible cost in human suffering and exploitation. As of January 2001, there were two bills that might change the present Norwegian law, which prohibits any depiction of sex organs in motion. One is a bill from the Sex Crime Committee that suggests that pornography should be prohibited, but defined as an unacceptable depiction of sexuality, using children, animals, or coercive sex. The other bill is from the Freedom of Speech Committee, which will move the responsibility from the state authorities to the editors. Both of these reforms are heavily debated.

## D. Paraphilias

Since 1997, a committee has been working to remove sexual turn-on patterns from the lists that classify mental diseases. The most influential such lists in Norway are the *DSM* (*Diagnostic and Statistical Manual*) and *ICD* (*International Classification of Diseases*) systems. There are several diagnostic categories related to gender identity and role that can and are being questioned. In terms of orientations, homosexuality was taken out of the classification of mental disorders in Norway in 1979, but it can still be found as subcategories in the description of "Gender Identity Disorders in Adolescents and Adults" in *DSM-IV*.

Sexual turn-on patterns are still considered mental diseases, if we look at *DSM-IV* and *ICD-10*. It is interesting to see how ideas about sexual behavior have developed, but are still defined on the basis of fulfillment of procreation. Sexual deviation has been specified on the basis that it does not serve the act of fertilizing the egg. As a consequence, we have long lists of sexual deviations regarded as mental diseases in both *DSM-IV* and *ICD-10*, including:

*DSM-IV*: 302.4 Exhibitionism; 302.81 Fetishism; 302.89 Frotteurism; 302.2 Pedophilia; 302.83 Sexual masochism; 302.84 Sexual sadism; 302.3 Transvestic fetishism; 302.82 Voyeurism; 302.9 Paraphilia not otherwise specified. *ICD-10*: F65 Disorders of sexual preference, including paraphilias: F65.0 Fetishism; F65.1 Fetishistic transvestism; F65.2 Exhibitionism; F65.3 Voyeurism; F65.4 Pedophilia; F65.5 Sadomasochism; F65.6 Multiple disorders of sexual preference; F65.8 Other disorders of sexual preference; F65.9 Disorders of sexual preference, unspecified.

Instead of being classified as mentally ill persons, people who regard themselves as fetishists or having a different gender identity now claim themselves to be normal healthy people, as far as these matters are concerned. In addition to having a specific sexual turn-on pattern, some might have developed mental problems because they think of themselves as "wrong" in the eyes of society, or because it is difficult to find a partner that matches one's sexual needs.

*Exhibitionists: Male Artists vs. Female Entertainers*

[*Update 2002*: Under Norway's strict gender-equality laws, men and women can demand equal treatment for doing the same job, even if it involves disrobing on stage. In November 2002, Norway's Gender Equality Ombudsman, Kristin Mile, investigated a complaint that tax authorities

### Table 8

**Percentage of Men and Women Who Reported Having Experienced Unwanted Sexual Attention During the Previous Six Months in Two Studies**

| | Percentage Experiencing Disagreeable Sexual Attention at Work | | | |
| --- | --- | --- | --- | --- |
| | Women 1987 | Women 1997 | Men 1987 | Men 1997 |
| Often | 1% | 1% | 0% | 0% |
| Sometimes | 1 | 4 | 2 | 3 |
| Rarely | 10 | 11 | 4 | 11 |
| Never | 59 | 66 | 74 | 71 |
| Irrelevant | 30 | 18 | 21 | 15 |

define female strippers as entertainers while male strippers pay a lower tax rate because they are considered artists. Mile told *The Associated Press* (2002) she had received a complaint from Norwegian booking agent, Magnus Morland, complaining that the all-male American Chippendales only had to a pay a 15% artists tax for their November tour of Norwegian concert houses, while his female strippers, also foreigners, had to pay a 24% tax on their tickets. "It seems like they are doing the same job," Mile suggested to the press. "This is pure discrimination," Morland told the Oslo newspaper *Dagbladet*. (*End of update by R. T. Francoeur*)]

## 9. Contraception, Abortion, and Population Planning

Positive attitudes toward sexuality and positive information about sexuality documented throughout all levels in public schools are related to a lower frequency of undesirable consequences of sexuality, like unwanted pregnancies and abortions. In this respect, Norway still has a long way to go, in spite of the positive ways we ordinarily present ourselves internationally. The government proudly announces full support of family planning and that services are provided in maternal and child clinics and other health outlets free of charge. All contraceptives are widely available, and contraceptive use is high. Nevertheless, Norway is one of the countries in Europe with the most abortions among teenage girls. Compared to the Netherlands, one of the "winners" on these statistics, Norway has three times as many births among teenage girls and five times as many abortions.

The most heated part of the family planning debate of Norway concerns the issue of self-determined abortion. The decision is now left with the pregnant woman herself, which has been regarded as a victory in the struggle for women's independence. First-trimester abortion on request has been legal since 1975, and three years later, the woman was given the right to make the decision herself. The government holds that family policy is based on and strengthens gender equality. The importance of governmental and nongovernmental collaboration in this field is also emphasized as essential. Men's participation in childcare, both in the family and at work, is encouraged by paid maternity leave for the father. In practice, few men use this opportunity because of the decrease in income. Another factor is the amount of time needed to change attitudes. Whereas some men take this opportunity, the majority still holds traditional attitudes and prefers to leave childcare to the mother.

## 10. Sexually Transmitted Diseases and HIV/AIDS

### A. Sexually Transmitted Diseases

A study done by the National Institute of Public Health in Norway in 1992 shows that 18% of men and 16% of women, among those who have had sexual relations, reported to having had a sexually transmitted disease at least one time in their life. The current incidence of STDs is shown in Table 9. In the group that has had homosexual experience, 36% have had an STD during their lifetime, 42% of the women and 32% of the men. The incidence pattern is shown in Table 10.

[*Update 2002*: The state of STDs is as follows:

• [Chlamydia: In the year 2001, more cases of chlamydia were diagnosed than in any year since 1991. The reason may be linked to more spread, better diagnostic tools, more test-focused professionals, or combinations of these factors.

• [Gonorrhea: 358 cases of gonorrhea were reported in 2001 compared to 252 in 2000; 82% of these patients were born in Norway. Of the total, 258 were men and 70 were women. (*End of update by E. Almås and E. E. Pirelli Benestad*)]

*Chlamydia trachomatis* was registered the first time in Norway in 1959, but was not recognized as a distinct disease until the 1970s. Today, this disease is the most common STD and is probably the most common cause of infertility. The infection is most common among sexually active people under the age of 25. The 1997 incidence in Norway was 9,889 (women 5931; men 3958). The incidence of gonorrhea has fallen drastically during the last few years. The highest incidence of gonorrhea in Norway was reported in 1975 and 1976, with approximately 15,000 cases yearly; the incidence in 1997 was 193. Presently, there seems to be an increase in primary and secondary stages of syphilis, mainly among homosexual men in Oslo. Medical authorities are following closely this trend. In 1998, the incidence of gonorrhea was the lowest ever registered in Norway. There is, however, reason to be worried about the increase in the number of cases of gonorrhea among men who have sex with men and in people who travel to Thailand, because this is an indication of unsafe sex, which also can give an increase in HIV infections.

### B. HIV/AIDS

There has been a steady increase in voluntary HIV testing in Norway. In the 1993 study (Folkehelsa 1993), 16% of the men and 13% of the women had been tested. More people with higher education (17%) than lower education (14%) had done so, and more people in urban districts (21%) than rural districts (10%) had been tested. Thirty-eight percent of the men and 28% of the women who had had sex with a person of the same sex had been tested. During the first six months of 1999, 70 new cases of HIV were detected, compared with 49 new cases in 1998. The increase is mainly attributed to people coming as refugees from pandemic African countries. In other risk groups, there have been few changes from year to year. As of June 30, 1999, a total of 1,932 HIV-positive persons (1,427 men and 505 women) were registered in Norway.

Since 1998, there has been a major decrease in the incidence of AIDS, which is explained by new treatment methods that has been available since 1996. Even with the present reports of increasing problems concerning therapy failure and the development of resistance and serious side effects, this positive development in the AIDS situation has continued throughout 1998. During the first six months of 2000, 85 new cases of HIV were detected; in the same period in 1999, 70 new cases were detected. The increase is mainly attributed to people coming as refugees from pan-

#### Table 9

**Incidence of Sexually Transmitted Diseases, 1992**

| Chlamydia: | 7% | Gonorrhea: | 6% | Genital warts: | 4% |
|---|---|---|---|---|---|
| Herpes: | 2% | Other STD: | 2% | Unknown STD: | 1% |

#### Table 10

**Incidence of STDs among Homosexual Men and Women, 1992**

| Chlamydia: | 17% | Gonorrhea: | 16% | Genital warts: | 11% |
|---|---|---|---|---|---|
| Herpes: | 7% | Other STD: | 5% | Unknown STD: | 3% |

(Seksjon for Epidemiologi, 1993)

demic African countries. In other risk groups, there have been few changes from year to year. As of June 30, 2000, a total of 2,095 HIV-positive persons (1,528 men and 567 women) were registered in Norway. Up to June 30, 2000, Norway had a total of 672 diagnosed AIDS cases (558 men and 114 women). Of this total, 672 cases registered since 1983, and 519 have died (Meldingssystem for Smittsomme Sykdommer 1998, 2000). [*Update 2002*: The recent increase continues to be mainly attributed to people coming as refugees from pandemic African countries. In other risk groups, there have been few changes from year to year. (*End of update by E. Almås and E. E. Pirelli Benestad*)]

[*Update 2002*: UNAIDS Epidemiological Assessment: HIV testing and case reporting: HIV testing is systematic for blood donors, pregnant women (including women having abortions), and STD patients. Diagnosed HIV cases are reported in a national HIV database using an identifying code. By the end of 2001, 2,323 HIV cases were reported. Among the cases reported in 1997 to 2000, 61% are heterosexuals, 27% are homosexual men, and 8% are intravenous drug users. Prevalence data come mostly from ongoing testing programs.

[The estimated number of adults and children living with HIV/AIDS on January 1, 2002, were:

| | | |
|---|---|---|
| Adults ages 15-49: | 1,800 | (rate: 0.1%) |
| Women ages 15-49: | 400 | |
| Children ages 0-15: | < 100 | |

[An estimated less than 100 adults and children died of AIDS during 2001.

[No estimate is available for the number of Norwegian children who had lost one or both parents to AIDS and were under age 15 at the end of 2001. (*End of update by the Editors*)]

## 11. Sexual Dysfunctions, Counseling, and Therapies

Many psychotherapists have persisted in the hopeful notion that sexual problems tend to become resolved automatically along with other personal problems as the client progresses in therapy. Clinical experience has indicated that this view is overly optimistic. We know that people without any psychopathology may develop sexual problems. Many such individuals resist seeking traditional psychotherapy where sex therapy is not available. In the late 1970s and early 1980s, a number of Norwegian therapists began to utilize the techniques developed by Masters and Johnson and Helen Singer Kaplan in treating sexual dysfunctions. In the beginning, there was a high level of enthusiasm for these innovative methods. However, many therapists found that they were handicapped by a daunting level of inhibition when it came to openly discussing sexual matters with clients. Working through these taboos together with colleagues was one step in facilitating communication.

Another step in guiding the helping professions to improve their sexological efforts has been in the application of the PLISSIT model as an effective paradigm developed by the psychologist Jack Annon in Hawaii. The aforementioned acronym is composed of the four levels of therapeutic intervention: Permission, Limited Information, Specific Suggestions, and Intensive Therapy (Annon & Robinson 1978). The model is originally illustrated as a funnel, but this has been turned upside down, and the PLISSIT model is in Norway shaped like a pyramid: The foundation is composed of the most frequently utilized intervention. *P* indicates permission to be in touch with one's sexuality and to discuss sexual matters, while *LI* focuses on providing limited information about these matters in question. It is impor-

tant for any therapist or professional to become comfortable enough to give his or her clients permission to talk freely about sexual problems. The levels of specific suggestions (*SS*) and intensive therapy (*IT*) involve the actual working through of the specific sexual problem. The counselor or therapist operating on the highest level, intensive therapy, requires highly specialized training and skills to be effective, whether this be in counseling, psychotherapy, psychiatry, or medicine and endocrinology.

## 12. Sex Research and Advanced Professional Education

Thore Langfeldt, a pioneer in the field of sexology in Norway, began his scientific career in research on sex and aggression in cats. He went on to investigate the neurophysiological function of the temporal lobes, then began his groundbreaking research with children. During the 1970s, he supervised several students, Jens Skaar, Bjørn Helge Gundersen, and Per Steinar Melås, in their task of collecting information from parents and nursery staff about the sexual behavior observed among children. The findings, published in *Hverdag*, caused a public protest against the invasion of the pristine world of children by lewd professionals. The debate initiated by this research showed the necessity to work with adult attitudes as well as with the lack of educational practices and guidance of childhood sexuality. Langfeldt (1993-1994) has criticized the trend of contemporary psychotherapy to focus on pathologies rather than sexual health. In a paper published in *Nordisk Sexologi* in 1983, Langfeldt drew attention to the work of Earl Barnes, an American psychologist who, as early as 1892, questioned the emphasis upon sexual abnormality. Barnes, cited by Langfeldt from Kern, 1973), stated: "None make any attempt to trace the normal development of sexual feelings and ideation in children, nor to examine the condition of sexuality actually existing in children's lives." Langfeldt's contribution to the increased awareness of the nature of sexual behavior in children has been considerable. Today, he lectures in numerous seminars and courses in childhood sexuality for professionals all over the world. His studies on unresolved sexual problems arising in childhood, and their consequent manifestation in adolescence, have made his work the focus of international attention since he began to publish his theories around 1980. Subsequently, Langfeldt has devoted his energies to the rehabilitation of juvenile sexual offenders and has founded the first sexological institute in Norway concentrating on this work.

The Norwegian Society for Clinical Sexology has been working for many years to integrate sexology into professional education for health professionals, without overwhelming success. (The current president is Elsa Almås, Storgaten 42, N-4890 Grimstad, Norway.) The problem seems to be that there is no room for new fields in the already existing curricula. As a consequence, the Nordic Association for Clinical Sexology (NACS), which represents Denmark, Finland, Iceland, Norway, and Sweden, has applied for and been granted money to develop guidelines for sexological certification/licensing and education. With these guidelines, it will be possible to develop inter-Nordic courses on different levels of sexological education. The programs, presented at the NACS meeting in 1999, build on three different levels of sexological education: The first level is a one-year, half-time university course in basic sexology. The second level is a one-year, half-time course for health professionals in sexological consultation. The third level is a two-year, half-time course in sexological therapy. These guidelines must be implemented in different ways in different countries. In Norway, politicians have recently become much more interested in sexological education, prevention, and treatment, and there are reasons for moderate optimism regarding the possibilities of developing sexology as a new field adding to the existing health professions in Norway in the future.

Today, research in sexologically related fields is scattered and dependent on money that follows time-limited projects that are politically motivated. It seems that a lot of this research has too few resources to secure the quality essential for publication internationally and even nationally. As in many other countries, the Norwegian government has granted money for some years to describe risk behavior for the spread of HIV/AIDS. When the situation seemed to be under control, much official funding disappeared. There also seems to be some money in projects that aim to prevent unwanted pregnancies and abortions, but reports on such research are difficult to find. Easily found, however, are national statistics with their options and limitations.

The e-mail address for P. O. Lundberg, editor of the *Scandinavian Journal of Sexology* is: PO.Lundberg@ neurologi.uu.se. The journal's website is: http://www.dpf .dk/defSCANSEX.htm.

## Conclusion

Sexuality is a powerful human force within the context of human culture. In compiling information for this overview of Norwegian sexology, it has become obvious that the most important body of knowledge, that which teaches us how to be comfortable with our sexuality, remains incomplete. We have observed that the male-dominance complex was an inevitable outcome of the institution of warfare. Now that Norway is committed to peaceful coexistence with its neighbors, indeed has evolved into a catalyst for international accord, the barbaric anachronism of sexual inequality has lost its *raison d'être*. The liberation of sexual minorities, homosexuals, transgendered people, and fetishists, has kept pace with the nascent equality of women; we view these developments with grateful optimism.

There are several volatile foci that require all of our professional acumen and personal courage if we are to accurately deal with them. One such area is the sexual molestation of children; a second area is a scrupulous inquiry into the differences between male and female sexuality. If our goal involves defusing repressive taboos, child molesters, who stand in the shadow of a long tradition of dark deeds, shall benefit the most. If we can combine open-mindedness and willingness to address this highly interactive malady with a more professional approach, we shall be more able to bring this fearful issue into balance. The women's liberation movement has immensely improved the status of women in our society, and has made it unacceptable to discriminate against women on basis of gender. In the justifiable efforts toward equality, the unique aspects of women's sexuality have frequently been overlooked. In our opinion, the full equality of women awaits the full awareness of women's uniqueness.

As a result of the enormous changes brought about by the sexual revolution, sex education, and the advances made in sex therapy, we may occasionally feel like acceding to the temptation to relax our efforts. An antidote to this kind of thinking is to remind ourselves that centuries of repression and limited access to educational resources have caused many people to fear and conceal their sexual feelings. Only yesterday, the notion of social equality for women, acceptance of homosexual behavior as a form of normal sexual expression, ecological activism, and systems theory were unthinkable. They became realities as a result of the unremitting efforts of many dedicated individuals. There is still a great deal of work to do, and many people in grave need of help. In reality, the history of sexology in Norway has only just begun.

## Acknowledgments

The authors wish to acknowledge personal communications from Berthold Grunfeld, Per Harbitz, Reidar Marmoey, Steven Neichin, Laila Nygaard, and Jan Henrik Pederstad.

## References and Suggested Readings

Acton, Lord W. 1857. *The functions and disorders of the reproductive organs in youth, in adult age, and in advanced life; Considered in their physiological, social and moral relations* (1st ed.). Philadelphia: Blakiston.

Almås, E. 1994. Sexology in Norway: Conceptualization of sexuality. *Nordisk Sexologi*, 2:78-95.

Almås, E., & E. Benestad. 1997a. *Sexologi i praksis*. [*Sexology in practice*]. Oslo: Tano-Aschehoug.

Almås, E., & E. Benestad. 1997b. Væren i systemene. [Being in systems], *Fokus på Familien*, 3-4:207-221.

Almås, E., & E. Benestad. 1999. Ord og begreper kjønn, kjønnstilhoerighet, kjønnsidentitet og seksuell orienteering [Words and concepts about sex, gender, gender belonging, gender identity and sexual orientation]. *Impuls*, 3.

Annon, J. S., & C. R. Robinson. 1978. The use of vicarious learning in the treatment of sexual concerns. In: J. LoPiccolo & L. LoPiccolo, eds., *Handbook of sex therapy*. New York/London: Plenum Press.

Asbjørnsen, & Moe, eds. 1977. *Norske folkeeventyr [Erotic folk tales]* (O. Høgseth, trans.). Oslo: Universitetsforlaget.

*Aschehoug og gyldendals store Norske leksikon*. 1986. Oslo: Kounnskapsforlaget.

Associated Press News Release. 2002 (November 29). *Norway strippers claim unfair tax rules*.

Bem, S. 1974. The measurement of psychological androgyny. *Journal of Consulting and Clinical Psychology*, 42(2):155-162.

Benestad, E., & E. Almås. 1993. Bekreftelsesmodell for kjønnstilhørighet. *Nordisk Sexologi*, 4:209-216.

Benestad, E., B. Grünfeld, & B. Krøvel. 1986. Heterofil transvestismc. *Tidsskrift for Den Norske Lægeforening*, 25:2069-2071.

Bjørneboe, J. 1966. *Uten en tråd*. Oslo: Scala Forlag (Published anonymously the first time).

Blystad, H. 1999. *Smittevernhaandbok for kommunehelsetjenesten 1999-2000*. Oslo: Folkehelsa.

Brantsæther, M. K., & K. Widerberg. 1992. *Sex i arbeidet*. Oslo: Tiden Forlag.

CIA. 2002 (January). *The world factbook 2002*. Washington, DC: Central Intelligence Agency. Available: http://www .cia.gov/cia/publications/factbook/index.html.

Dalen, E., Undersøkelse om Seksualvaner. 1987 (November). *Rapport utarbeidet for Norsk forening for klinisk sexologi*. Oslo: MMI Markeds og Mediainstituttet a.s.

Dalen, E., Undersøkelse om Nordmenns Seksualvaner. 1997 (May). *Rapport utarbeidet for Norsk forening for klinisk sexologi*. Oslo: MMI Markeds og Mediainstituttet a.s.

Diseth, T. 1998 (March). *Kan vi bestemme barns kjønn? [Can we govern children's gender?]*. Paper presented at Konferanse om Klinisk Sexologi [Conference on Clinical Sexology], Oslo: Soria Moria, 12-13.

Faleide, A., R. Groenseth, & B. Urdal, eds. 1975. *Det levande i muskelpanseret*. Oslo: Universitetsforlaget.

Gammelsrud, T. 1993-1994. Personal communications in preparation for "Sexology in Norway: Conceptualization of sexuality." *Nordisk Sexologi*, 12:78-85.

Gelsen, C. 1890. *Nødvendige lægeråd til nygifte*. Kristiania (Oslo): Folkeskriftselskapet.

Hansen, K. 1895 (May 5). *Foredrag om kjønnssykdommer.* Lecture in Bergen Turnhall in Bergen.

Hoegset, O., ed. 1977. *Asbjoernsen og Moe: Erotiske folkeventyr.* Oslo: Universitetsforlaget.

Hverdag. 1977. Barns seksualitet. *Temahefte,* 8.

Jessen, L. 1993-1994. Personal communications in preparation for "Sexology in Norway: Conceptualization of sexuality." *Nordisk Sexologi, 12*:78-95.

Kern, S. 1973. Freud and the discovery of child sexuality. *History of Child Quarterly, 1*:117-141.

*Læreplanverket for den 10-årige grunnskolen.* 1996. Oslo: Det Kongelige Kirke, Utdannings og Forskningsdepartement.

Langfeldt, T. 1980. Child sexuality, development and problems. In: J. M. Samson, ed., *Childhood and sexuality.* Montreal/Paris: Edition Etudes, Vivantes.

Langfeldt, T. 1983a. Aspekter ved barns seksuelle utvikling of problemer. *Nordisk Sexologi, 1*:45-52.

Langfeldt, T. 1983b. Norsk forening for klinisk sexologi. *Nordisk Sexologi, 1*:59.

Langfeldt, T. 1984. Runkeskolen del 1. *Cupido.* Hverdag, *3*: 46-49.

Langfeldt, T. 1985. Runkeskolen del 2. *Cupido.* Hverdag, *1*: 42-44.

Langfeldt, T. 1993-1994. Personal communications in preparation for "Sexology in Norway: Conceptualization of sexuality." *Nordisk Sexologi, 12*:78-95.

Linnée, C. von. 1969. *Om settet att tilhopa gaa. Seksualforelesninger av Carl von Linnée, utgitt etter et haandskrift.* Goeteborg: Zindermans.

Meldingssystem for Smittsomme Sykdommer [Report System for Contagious Diseases]. 1998. *MSIS meldingssyst smittsom sykd MSIS 08/99: Seksuelt overførbare sykdommer i 1998 [Sexually transmitted diseases in 1998]*.

Meldingssystem for Smittsomme Sykdommer [Report System for Contagious Diseases]. 2000. *MSIS meldingssyst smittsom sykd 2000, 28*:30.

Money, J. 1981. *Love and love sickness: The science of sex, gender difference and pair-bonding.* Baltimore/London: Johns Hopkins University Press.

Mykle, A. 1956. *Sangen om den røde rubin.* Oslo: Gyldendal Norsk Forlag.

*The Norwegian act on registered partnership for homosexual couples.* 1993. Oslo: Ministry of Children and Family Affairs.

Norwegian Society for Clinical Sexology [Norsk Forening for Klinisk Sexologi], Dalen, E. 1987. *Undersoekelse om Nordmenns Seksualvaner,* November 1987. *Survey on the sexual habits of Norwegians,* November 1997. Oslo: Markeds of Mediainstituttet a.s.

*P-2 documentary* [Radio program]. 1993 (October 2).

Ringal, N. J. 1994. A history of Norwegian police during the German occupation, *Nordisk Sexologi, 12*:78-95.

Sætre, M. 1997. *Omfanget av vold—HiO-notat, 1997* (nr. 7 notat 9). Available: http://www.hioslo.no/formidling/rapport/not_1997_7/notat9-4.htm#E10E9.

Schioldborg, P. 1983. Meeting of the Nordic Association for Clinical Sexology (NACS), Oslo, Norway. September 28-30.

Seksjon for Epidemiologi. 1993. *Rapport fra Seksualvaneundersøkelsene i 1987 og 1992.* Oslo: Statens Institutt for Folkehelse.

*Soga om Gunlaug Ormstunge.* 1968. Oslo: H. Aschehoug and Co. (W. Nygaard).

*Statistisk årbok,* 1999. 118. Aargang. Oslo: Ad Notam Gyldendals Forlag.

Sundt, E. 1976. *Verker i utvalg (IV): Om saedelighedstilstanden i Norge.* Oslo: Gyldendal.

Træen, B. 1993. *Norwegian adolescents' sexuality in the era of AIDS.* Oslo: National Institute for Alcohol and Drug Research.

UNAIDS. 2002. *Epidemiological fact sheets by country.* Geneva, Switzerland: Joint United Nations Programme on HIV/AIDS (UNAIDS/WHO). Available: http://www.unaids.org/hivaidsinfo/statistics/fact_sheets/index_en.htm.

Undset, S. K. 1920. *Kristin Lavransdatter.* Oslo: H. Aschehoug & Co.

Undset, S. O. 1925/1979. *Olav Audunsen i Hestviken.* Oslo: H. Aschehoug & Co. (W. Nygaard).

# Outer Space and Antarctica

## *Sexuality Factors in Extreme Environments*

Raymond J. Noonan, Ph.D.*
*Updates and new material by R. J. Noonan*

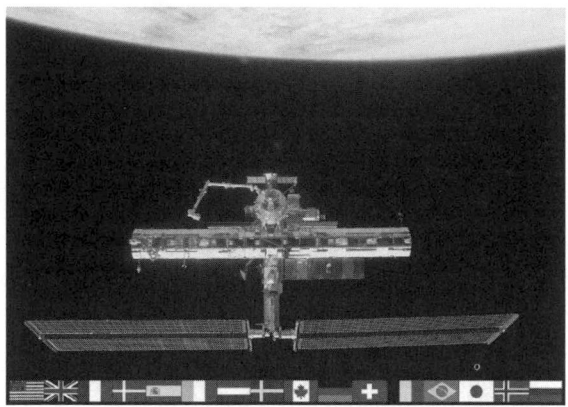

International Space Station (NASA/JSC 2003)

## Contents

## *An Introduction to Life in Extreme Environments*

Antarctica and outer space are considered two of the most extreme environments with which human beings have to contend. Because of certain similarities, these two are well-suited to being addressed in one chapter because of their common elements, which allow one—Antarctica—to be a research environment studied to find solutions to potential problems in the other—space habitats. In fact, numerous authors continue to consider them together in the human factors realm (e.g., Harrison, Clearwater, & McKay 1991; Stuster 1996; Palinkas, Gunderson, Holland, Miller, & John-

son 2000; Dudley-Rowley, Whitney, Bishop, Caldwell, & Nolan 2001). Sexuality in extreme environments is often a second thought—or later, if it is even thought about at all—for good reason: These environments are such that they require meeting the most basic of human needs in terms of immediate survival. In Maslow's (1970) motivational hierarchy of needs, this would include the lowest levels of survival and safety. Sexuality is at a higher level on the scale, and entails needs that, of necessity, would come later once the others have been adequately met. For additional analysis of this thesis, see Noonan (1998a). In addition to this are the corporate or state-sponsored interests in these endeavors (because of the costs and the technologies involved), which typically ignore or discourage sex-related behaviors because they are conceptualized as potentially (or likely to be) disruptive.

Extreme environments are not limited to space and the polar regions of Earth. Studies—particularly those in the psychosocial realm—focus on those factors that push the envelope of human survival and performance, because of environmental-system extremes in the physical, psychological, and social spheres. They have high barriers and sharp boundaries that limit both life and effective performance under normal circumstances, many of which require technological advances and intensive training for adaptation success. In addition to Antarctica and the space environment, extreme environments include arctic and other isolated environments, undersea operations and deep-ocean submarining, high-performance and general aviation, the armed services and special forces, caving, mountaineering, and vulcanology, and mining and hazardous-substance work, as well as medical, emergency, police, and firefighting scenarios in natural and man-made disasters. Essentially, extreme environments are those in which humans, either individually or in groups, have to perform under highly stressed, complex, and challenging conditions. The difference between space and Antarctic environments, however, is much less than the difference between those two and most of the other earthly pursuits listed above, and will be detailed more fully later in this chapter. Of particular importance to the success or failure of a particular space mission or polar expedition that makes the consideration of sexuality factors necessary, is the fact that these environments entail day-to-day living and working, and thus increase the likelihood that sexuality factors could have a determinative impact.

Suffice it to say that the physical enviroment of space has several important characteristics that Antarctica does not have: microgravity, high electromagnetic and particle radiation levels, high vacuum conditions, lack of oxygen, and extremes in temperature and pressure. Although it has extended periods of extreme cold and lack of humidity, Antarctica is protected by the Earth's mass, which provides a magnetic

---
*\*Communications*: Raymond J. Noonan, Ph.D., Health and Physical Education Department, Fashion Institute of Technology of the State University of New York, 27th Street and 7th Avenue, New York, NY 10001 USA; 212-217-7460; rjnoonan@SexQuest.com.
In addition to updates, this chapter now includes a new section on life in extreme environments and a new section on Antarctica.

field, called the magnetosphere, that deflects most of the charged particles that are carried by the solar wind, which give rise to the Van Allen radiation belts surrounding the globe as well as the polar auroras. In both environments, it is necessary to construct ecologically more-or-less closed, self-sustaining habitats for protection, and it is difficult if not impossible to effect a quick rescue in the case of an emergency.

Psychosocial factors are the key items of interest, however, in terms of scientific research relating the two environments. These include: isolation, remoteness, hazardousness, and extremely confining quarters—and the resulting high levels of emotional and physical stress that accompany them, including decreased motor function, fatigue, and unpredictable and potentially life-threatening occurrences. It is here that sexuality factors could have an impact, potentially both positive and negative, that need to be considered.

The Society for Human Performance in Extreme Environments (http://www.hpee.org/) is the organization for professionals involved in these fields. The Society publishes *Human Performance in Extreme Environments*, a journal devoted to fostering knowledge of and improving the levels of human performance in these environments.

## OUTER SPACE

### *Demographics and a Brief Historical Perspective*

#### A. Demographics

At this point in history, only a few hundred men and women from more than 25 countries have traveled and lived for some period of time in space.* With the advent of the new millennium, and despite the catastrophic loss of the Space Shuttle Columbia on February 1, 2003, the permanent human presence in space has become firmly entrenched, with the sixth crew of three beginning its stay on the new International Space Station (ISS) in November 2002. The largest cooperative scientific program in history, the ISS was developed jointly by the United States, Russia, Canada, Japan, and Brazil, and the participating nations of the European Space Agency (ESA): Belgium, Denmark, France, Germany, Italy, Netherlands, Norway, Spain, Sweden, Switzerland, and the United Kingdom (NASA 2003). Because of this virtually unprecedented mixing of cultures in a peacetime endeavor, we must expect that participants' cultural backgrounds will have an impact on gender interactions and any sexual relationships that will inevitably develop in space environments. Certainly, our common biological nature will have a different set of challenges in the sexological realm that will have to be met as well. Evidence for this comes from recent studies by Italian researchers that found that levels of the sex hormone testosterone are temporarily decreased in male astronauts by exposure to space, along with a concurrent decrease in sexual drive or libido (Strollo et al. 1998).

The "territory" of outer space, the study of which broadly comprises the domain of cosmology and astronomy, is open to interpretation. As Fazio (1997) has noted, where space begins depends on the physical properties of the area in question, specifically the problems that need to be resolved to allow humans to travel and live there. For example, extreme cold occurs, and sufficient air to breathe is lost, at considerably lower altitudes rising from Earth than the oxygen

needed to power a jet engine. Thus, humans would require physical protection much sooner than they would need a rocket engine, which does not require atmospheric oxygen to fly. In addition, at various points in space, we would be faced with the potential effects of microgravity, several types of radiation, extremes in temperature and pressure, a near-complete vacuum, and the impact of meteorites. Therefore, for men and women to live and work effectively and safely in various space environments, engineers either have or will design vehicles and habitats, including spacesuits, with countermeasures to protect spacefarers from some of these extreme conditions. Others are pervasive, however, like radiation, which could have serious consequences outside of the protection of the Earth's magnetosphere, in which lie the Van Allan radiation belts, and microgravity, which will likely have an impact on sexuality factors.

Perhaps the most critical aspect of space with which we have to contend, however, is a psychosocial environment that is "characterized by isolation (a separation from the normal or daily physical and social environment), confinement (restriction within a highly limited and sharply demarcated physical and social environment), deprivation, and risk" (Connors, Harrison, & Akins 1985, 7). In fact, they said that in space, ". . . the physical environment, when not terrifying, is likely to be bland" (p. 9). Pesavento (2000), in a very recent study of the psychological and social effects of isolation in space and during space-simulation analog studies on Earth, said that these may be the ultimate barriers to extended human spaceflight. He noted those factors that have yet to be resolved, including: "depression-like symptoms on orbit [(which Russian space physicians have named "neuresthenia")]; less-than-encouraging social interactions with mixed-gender and mixed-foreign-national groupings; sensory deprivation; as well as the emotional and sexual affects of close confinement on crew members" (p. 1; see also Cabbage 2001).

Yet, many astronauts have also described the profound sense of spiritual and philosophical awareness they gained being in space and viewing the awe-inspiring panoramas, especially looking back at the Earth (White 1987). Some have noted the absence of geographical boundaries, other than land and sea, and the meaning they ascribe to it in terms of the absence of political boundaries and the unity of humanity. Almost certainly, our collective sense of the fragility of Earth's environment has come from some of the widely published photographs taken in space.

For the foreseeable future, however, the laboratory for this grand human experiment will be the International Space Station (ISS), the largest and most complex scientific endeavor ever attempted on an international scale, which began assembly in orbit in late 1998 and had its first sustained trio of inhabitants in November 2000. When finished, the ISS will have a mass of over 1 million pounds (454,000 kg), measuring about 360 feet (110 m) across and 290 feet (88.5 m) long, with almost an acre (4,000 m$^2$) of solar panels for electrical power. Flying at an altitude of 250 statute miles (400 km) with an inclination of 51.6°, at which it can be reached by all of the international partners, the ISS will be able to observe 85% of the globe, covering 95% of the Earth's population. It will be the site of a wide range of scientific endeavors and research (NASA 1999).

#### B. A Brief Historical Perspective

The realization of the fantasy of space travel is a distinctly 20th-century phenomenon, having its antecedents in the age-old fantasy of human flight dating at least from the ancient Greek story of Daedalus and Icarus. Combining the human need for exploration and discovery with the political

---

*Citizens from the following countries have flown in space: Afghanistan, Austria, Belgium, Bulgaria, Canada, Cuba, Czechoslovakia, France, Germany, Great Britain, Hungary, India, Israel, Italy, Japan, Mexico, Mongolia, Netherlands, Poland, Romania, Russia, Saudi Arabia, Syria, Ukraine, USA, and Vietnam.

realities of striving for nationalistic prestige and military advantage, and now, with the possibility of vast economic returns, the spaceflight revolution began during World War II with the development of the first V-2 ballistic rockets used by Germany against Great Britain. One of the fascinating stories surrounding the end of the war involves the race, won by the Americans, with the then-Soviet military to capture these rockets after the fall of Nazi Germany, which, in 1946 and 1947, were used by the U.S. to carry its first biological payloads into space (Bushnell 1958). It was the V-2 rocket that made human spaceflight a theoretical possibility, and this, in turn, both stimulated an interest in suborbital test flights and spurred the development of space biology, as well as space medicine, which was first discussed by leaders at the U.S. Air Force School of Aviation Medicine in 1948 (Nicogossian, Pool, & Uri 1994). Thus began the pervasiveness of a military culture, with its similarities yet distinct dissimilarities with the wider culture of which it is a part, which once dominated but still persists in national space programs.

Test flights by the U.S. continued, including two primates in V-2 rockets prior to 1950, various animals in rockets until 1952 and high-altitude balloons from 1950 through 1954, and two men in balloons in the summer of 1957. Similar ballistic rocket flights by the Soviet Union from 1949 through 1957 used dogs as subjects. The Space Age proper is said to have begun with the launching by the Soviet Union in October 1957 of Sputnik-1, the first artificial satellite to orbit the Earth. This was followed a month later by Sputnik-2 carrying a dog named Laika, the first animal in orbit. The U.S. responded with the February 1958 launch of Explorer 1, which detected what would be named the Van Allen radiation belts. Subsequently, both the U.S. and the Soviet Union launched a number of animal flights, using mice, rats, monkeys, dogs, or other small animals, sometimes to test systems that would later contain humans. In April 1961, the Soviet cosmonaut Yuri Gagarin became the first man to orbit the Earth, with Gherman Titov being the second in August 1961. Following two manned suborbital flights by the U.S., John Glenn was the first American to reach orbital flight in Mercury's *Friendship 7* in February 1962. In June 1963, Soviet cosmonaut Valentina Tereshkova became the first woman in space.

It would be almost two decades later, August 1982, before the second woman, cosmonaut Svetlana Savitskaya, would fly; she would later be the first woman to conduct an EVA (extravehicular activity) in July 1984. Although it is widely accepted today that women will always be a part of the American space program, it was over 20 years, almost to the day from Tereshkova's historic flight, before the first American woman, Sally Ride, would fly on the space shuttle in June 1983, and October 1984 for the first EVA by an American woman, Kathryn Sullivan (Cassutt 1993; Nicogossian et al. 1994). Although it is interesting to note that Tereshkova's flight was considered by many at the time to be a Cold War public-relations ploy by the Soviet Union (Santy 1994), the United States had tested women as potential astronauts as early as 1960 (Atkinson & Shafritz 1985; McCullough 1973), although this fact is not widely recalled today. When news of it reached the press, it was treated with skepticism and flippancy. In fact, these women had been systematically barred from the space program, even though it was thought by some in the scientific community that women might be better suited, both physically and psychologically, for the severe requirements of those pioneering spaceflights (Levin 1989). These events illustrate an example of the collision of prejudice (sexism) with scientific knowledge that occurs all too often with sex-related issues (see Noonan 1998a).

Santy (1994) expressed her belief that a contributing factor to women's finally being selected as astronauts, although less obvious, was the fact that the first private toilet had recently been designed for use on the space shuttle:

> The issue of privacy, linked as it was to sexuality and personal hygiene, had been a big factor in NASA's reluctance to include women as astronauts, and the development of the private toilet—probably more than any other reason—encouraged NASA to believe that females could finally (and without embarrassment to the agency) be integrated into Shuttle missions in a way impossible during the earlier missions. In *Gemini* and *Apollo* missions, the spacecraft required that crew members live side by side without even the most minimal capability of providing privacy for personal activities. (p. 51)

In 1978, the first group of astronauts to include women and male minorities was chosen. It was considered a watershed event, signaling a change in the way in which future astronauts would be recruited and selected (Atkinson & Shafritz 1985). In fact, it was probably our first experience with what would later be called the "development of space cultures" (cf. Harris 1996), given that racial and ethnic minorities have distinct cultural attitudes and behaviors, and many regard males and females as having different cultures as well (Francoeur 1997, 1998). Cultural factors later became important in the Space Shuttle Program, which first flew in April 1981, and in the Shuttle-*Mir* Program, including Shannon Lucid's current-American-record 188-day stay on *Mir*, which resulted in unprecedented cooperation and trust between the U.S. and Russian space programs. The Shuttle-*Mir* Program, in which several Americans flew on *Mir* between 1995 and 1998, was designed in part to elicit some of the possible psychological, psychosocial, and human performance aspects of multicultural crews in preparation for the International Space Station (Morphew & MacLaren 1997). All of these experiences led to the present ISS, first known as *Alpha*, with its historical antecedents in the early space stations of the U.S. (*Skylab*) and USSR (*Salyut*) in the 1970s.

At the present time, international treaties govern the use of space, including the Outer Space Treaty of 1967, the Liability Convention of 1973, the Moon Agreement of 1979 (which was never signed by the U.S. or Russia), and others, under the auspices of the United Nations Committee on the Peaceful Use of Outer Space. Also, other agreements have been entered into in the telecommunications realm (Harris 1996). In addition, in the United States, Congress and the President determine space policy. Federal agencies also affect space activities, including NASA (the National Aeronautics and Space Administration), the Federal Communications Commission, and the Departments of State, Defense, Transportation, Commerce, and Energy, as well as the military, as noted earlier. Similar national organizations function in other countries. The Space-World Bar Association (Smith 1997) is working further to develop a prototype Lunar Economic Development Authority that would coordinate the planning of more extensive uses of space resources, not the least of which are the mineral resources expected to be mined and the microgravity environment expected to make possible new manufacturing opportunities.

Space tourism, in fact, is expected to be a very important, although initially expensive venue in which ordinary citizens will be able to visit space habitats for their vacations. Just as air travel has become common today with its mass-market availability and the concurrent affordability resulting from it, a few entrepreneurs are already creating private companies to offer the service. One expected attraction is what a former U.S. congressman called widespread public attention to: the honeymoon in space (Gingrich 1995). Such ideas, of course, echoed similar predictions by science fiction writers, such as the space visionary, Arthur C. Clarke (1986), but this was the first time that such an inherently sexbound human activity was included in a political vision for future Americans (if not for the bulk of humanity).

## 1. Basic Sexological Premises

### A/B. Character of Gender Roles, and Sociolegal Status of Males and Females

Early in the space programs of both the United States and Russia, men were virtually the only ones recruited for space missions. Although this has been attributed to the fact that the Eisenhower Administration in the U.S. directed that military test pilots be the first to attempt these early missions because of their skills in testing new aircraft designs, and the inherent danger they entailed, women had been considered as early as 1960 (see Section B, A Brief Historical Perspective, above). At present, women have been an integral part of the various space programs, including commanding the space shuttle, although there is still not a gender-balance in the ranks of astronauts. In addition, some authors have noted that sexist attitudes have been a part of the experience of some women, as well as attitudes that some women still have to prove themselves because they are women (Casper & Moore 1995; Connors et al. 1985). The issue with regard to the development of the toilet, noted above, serves as an example of the constraints surrounding the biological aspects of our differing anatomies, and psychological differences have been cited as well (see Noonan 1998a).

### C. General Concepts of Sexuality and Love

*Conjecture on the Influence of Spaceflight on Sexological Issues*

Levin (1989), a British consultant on reproductive and sexual physiology, has written the most extensive review of the possible effects of space travel on these human systems. In surveying the research literature, he wrote:

> Despite th[e] large number of people who have been exposed to space flight with all its attendant hazards, our knowledge about the effects of space travel on the human reproductive system, and human sexuality, is sparse, bordering on the non-existent. Some of the most elementary questions seem not to have been investigated, indeed in some respects not even to have been asked. For example, it appears that no programme to evaluate the effect of space travel on human spermatozoa was ever initiated despite the obvious hazard of exposure of astronauts to radiation, stress and G forces. Even if asked, answers have not yet appeared in the open literature. (p. 378)

With regard to the lack of research on the behavioral aspects of human sexuality, Levin provided additional insight:

> In some respects this near-complete avoidance of what is a sensitive area of human behaviour represents a significant failure to investigate fully the possible reasons for the known stresses of living in isolated, confined environments. It is remarkable that there is no study as to whether human sexual activity, *or its loss* [italics added], can influence the adverse effects of such environments e.g. boredom, listlessness, sleep disturbances, fatigue, impaired cognition, irritability, hostility, depression and deterioration of personality. (p. 382)

Despite these concerns expressed within the space science literature—and readily available in their headquarters

library in Washington, D.C.—little research has been done by NASA, whose typical response has been that sex is not yet an issue (Date 1992; Vaughan 1992). It is my contention that much of this official response to sexual expression and to sexual research by the U.S. space establishment has been guided by attitudes distorted by a conceptualization of human sexuality as a capacity to be feared, avoided, sensationalized, problematized, or trivialized unless considered within the traditional boundaries of American sexual propriety. Similar negative views of human sexuality have failed to alleviate many of the perceived problems of people on Earth—and, in fact, have created many more problems because of ignorance and irrational fear (see Francoeur & Perper 1997; Weis 1997). Americans, after all, whether educated scientists or the generally scientifically ignorant general public, are Americans first. As such, we have been profoundly influenced by cultural values publicly accepted and promulgated by those who define society's norms, even if those norms have often been privately ignored by significant numbers of people, including, often enough, the very leaders who promote them.

In 1998, the first comprehensive analysis of human sexuality factors in relation to extended spaceflight, *A Philosophical Inquiry into the Role of Sexology in Space Life Sciences Research and Human Factors Considerations for Extended Spaceflight* (Noonan 1998a), was published, in which the author explored the issues and constraints surrounding the study of sex in space and conjectured about the potential impact of our sexual nature on mission success or failure. It suggested new terminology, the *human sexuality complex*, as a useful construct in which to consider the various sexuality factors in which human beings interact in and with their various environments.

The complexity of human sexuality, human sexual relationships, and sexual responses suggests the advantages of adopting a complex systems approach, one that draws on chaos and complexity theories, in future research on sexual phenomena and the interactions of its various components conceived as systems (Noonan 1998ab). Research on human sexuality in space, it would seem, could definitely benefit from the systems perspective, much as it was essential in developing our space programs. It also seems worthwhile and reasonable to consider the space environment to be a culture in itself, a "microsociety in a miniworld," as Connors et al. (1985, 2) described it, although it is also influenced by the outside cultures that sponsor it, much as any organization or workplace develops an indigenous culture, and the cultures of birth and subsequent origin of the individual crewmembers. In time, of course, any group will develop its own culture and norms that may be independent and/or an intricate mix of the others.

[*Update 2003*: Stuster (1996, 180-181) discussed the reluctance of NASA to deal with sexual behavior mainly because of concerns about media reactions, and noted historical parallels with some earlier explorers (restricted to commanding officers and expedition leaders when it occurred) who took wives or mistresses with them on long voyages. He cited Kanas and Federson (1971), who "tongue in cheek" discussed "Tension Reduction" associated with a multiyear mission to Mars:

> The question of direct sexual release on a long-duration space mission must be considered. Practical considerations (such as weight and expense) preclude men taking their wives on the first space flights. It is possible that a woman, qualified from a scientific viewpoint, might be persuaded to donate her time and energies for the sake of improving crew morale; however, such a situation might

create interpersonal tensions far more dynamic than the sexual tensions it would release. Other means of sexual release (masturbation, homosexuality) would be discouraged because of the confined quarters and the lack of privacy on such a mission. Thus, it appears that methods involving sublimation are more practical than these more direct alternatives. (p. 38)

[Stuster (1996) also noted how women contributed a stabilizing influence to the isolated Antarctic research stations when they were first introduced to the continent and became a regular part of expeditions. In contrast to the men's previous boisterous and disruptive behavior, he wrote:

Winter-over crews now tend to be less disruptive and more concerned about their behavior or, more accurately, how women in their groups perceive their behavior. More important, the groups are believed to be more productive now than they were in the male-only days of Antarctica. Several experienced Antarctic managers confirm this observation. (p. 178)

[Thus, it appears that this behavior is similar to ordinary American life. (*End of update by R. J. Noonan*)]

On the International Space Station or future space habitats, it is likely that conflicts will occur when the status of women and men are inherently unequal, or if there is a perception of sexual deprivation among some members of a crew when others are in a sexual relationship there, as has occurred in Antarctica analogs (see Noonan 1998a). An anecdotal story tells of a Muslim passenger on an international spaceflight who had to take directions from a woman. Whenever she addressed him, he ignored her, because his cultural heritage, influenced by his religious beliefs, prohibited such contact between men and women. As a result, directions needed to be given by the woman to a male colleague who then repeated them to the man who then carried them out.

## 2. Religious, Ethnic, and Gender Factors Affecting Sexuality

### A/B. Source and Character of Religious Values, and Character of Ethnic Values

The experiences of U.S. astronauts on *Mir* are well-known examples of some of the problems encountered by international crews of different ethnicities. Pesavento (2000) and Harris (1996) highlight the potential impact that cultural differences have had or might have on future missions. Of particular importance with respect to cultural and religious factors would likely be the compatibility of crewmembers' worldviews, as Francoeur and Perper (1997) have elucidated. The example previously noted of the Muslim crewmember's inability to interact with women as a partial result of his religious beliefs about innate differences between the sexes would also be relevant here. Of equal or greater importance might be the organizational (i.e., NASA's) stance and corporate-cultural beliefs about sexual issues that are transmitted to crewmembers (probably reinforcing similar beliefs in the astronauts), although such beliefs may have the same questionable effectiveness long-term as similar ones do generally in the U.S. and in other societies today.

## 3. Knowledge and Education about Sexuality

### A/B. Government Policies and Programs, and Informal Sources of Sexual Knowledge

The impact on extended spaceflight is likely to occur as a result of policies that resist the study of both the potential positive aspects inherent in the human sexuality complex

as well as the potential negative ones. There may also be problems in failing to communicate the findings—and their importance—to the space community, Congress, and the American public as a whole, once they have been studied. The sexual myths of individuals at all levels of the scientific, administrative, and other parts of space organizations and their contractors or subcontractors are also likely to have a negative impact, as the myths become the guiding principles that are incorporated in the organizational philosophy. Perhaps another benefit of the space program (the so-called spinoff effect) could be the furthering of sexual knowledge by combining sexuality education and space education. Young people are very interested in both, and each subject could be used to impart knowledge about the other, particularly in the realm of science.

## 4. Autoerotic Behaviors and Patterns

### A/B. Children and Adolescents, and Adults

Today, masturbation is believed to be a generally healthy and normal part of the experiences of human beings throughout their lifecycle. Nevertheless, we are still influenced by some of the beliefs of the 19th century, that masturbation (and ejaculation in general) depletes certain personal mental and energy reserves, such as when coaches sometimes suggest that neither be engaged in prior to competing. Money (1985a) has shown that this now-discredited degeneracy theory of masturbation, which some people thought could be counteracted by proper fitness and nutrition, prompted prominent health proponents, such as John Harvey Kellogg and Sylvester Graham, to develop foods they believed would extinguish sexual appetite and masturbation. Today, two of these foods remain associated with their creators, Kellogg's corn flakes and graham crackers, respectively, although their original purpose is long forgotten. Nevertheless, some religious traditions continue to oppose masturbation as moral degeneracy. Both of these traditions—the medical and the religious—are likely to be important in the context of space, because they have and will prevent the study of masturbation as a sexual activity that will likely be practiced in space, in the unlikely event that it has not been already. Among other things, it can help to counteract boredom and stress, and the environment is amenable to it, in that sufficient privacy can be found in which to practice it. Pesavento's (2000) recent study noted that in the early 1970s, a physician suggested that masturbation would be an effective countermeasure to maintain prostate health and avoid urinary tract infections for astronauts on *Skylab*, the longest mission of which lasted 84 days. Children and adolescents will, of course, practice masturbation when they become a part of settlements in space in the distant future, just as they will have hetero- and homosexual experiences, as they do on Earth in various societies today.

## 5. Interpersonal Heterosexual Behaviors

### A/B/C. Children, Adolescents, and Adults

Heterosexual behavior encompasses a wide variety of possibilities: in specific activities, such as kissing, oral and anal intercourse, and vaginal-penile intercourse, for example, and in the variety of ways in which they can be done. A device has been patented, the "Belt to Paradise," to enable sexual intercourse in microgravity (McCullough 1992). In addition, there are numerous fantasy behaviors that can be acted out with a partner or imagined alone. Any of these heterosexual activities are very likely to occur in space at some point in the future, if some have not occurred already. Pesavento (2000) has discussed some of the rumored pairings that have occurred, although everyone officially denies that anything happened. However, it seems likely that sexual intercourse and oral sex have already occurred in space. It is likely because, in our culture, sex is pervasive, gender awareness is ubiquitous, and the astronauts are mostly young, healthy people. However, given the current political climate, it is not possible nor expedient to prove that sexual behavior has occurred because of the potential harm to the astronauts involved, as well as to the space program as a whole. Speculation at this time may be the best approach until the next sex-positive cultural phase, which, if Reiss (1990) is correct in his characterization of sexual revolutions as being cyclical, will probably occur early in this century, that allows and emphasizes healthy sexual experience as the predominant social norm (see also Noonan 1996, 1998b).

Given our experience on Earth, it is also very likely that at least a few astronauts have entertained the notion of being the first to "do it" in space—unknown to the world, but still a shared, cherished, intimate secret. In addition, there has long been evidence that higher levels of intelligence and overall education—characteristics selected-for in astronauts—increase the likelihood that certain sexual behaviors will be experienced (Hunt 1974). At this point in the space program, the astronauts are a large-enough population so that individuals would likely be able find appropriate partners. Privacy and space in which any sexual activity can occur, albeit scarce, can be made available with appropriate planning. Sexual intercourse can also be done rather quickly, if need be, with very satisfactory results.

Our experience on Earth with some of the heterosexual subcultures, such as multiple sexual partnerships, also would imply that, although they have been sometimes problematic when flaunted in an atmosphere of sexual deprivation for other crewmembers in the analogous Antarctic settings (see also Stuster 1996), in the more-normal conditions of typical urban, suburban, and sometimes rural settings, extramarital affairs, multiple relationships, and even group sex, have the potential to coexist with the more traditional expressed norms of heterosexual monogamous marriage (Libby & Whitehurst 1977). When these alternative relationship patterns are successful (i.e., functional), it is usually because the couple and the subcultural network in which it functions have adopted it, and group norms have evolved that define their expression, often in contrast to how they perceive the outside world's views of their subculture's behavior. In space, because there will be limited populations for the foreseeable future, both with and without a balanced gender mix, the various diverse alternative sexual lifestyle patterns might be an avenue of inquiry to minimize potential problems. Again, given the current political and social climate in the country, it may be necessary to keep it an internal group secret. Nevertheless, a television news magazine reported the possibility that group sex had occurred in space (Anderson 1992).

[*Update 2003*: The first wedding took place in space on August 10 between International Space Station commander, Yuri Malenchenko, a Russian cosmonaut, and Russian-born Ekaterina Dmitriev, an American citizen, in Texas. A quirk in Texas law allows a person to get a marriage license and to get married by proxy if one of the parties is not in the state. Malenchenko was present via a video downlink, with a lifesize cutout of him also used in the ceremony in a Johnson Space Center meeting room. Neither the Russian space agency nor NASA was enthusiastic about the marriage, however—Russia because, as a colonel in the air force, he needs prior clearance for changing his family status, and NASA because of the use of ISS resources. They will need to remarry when they return to Moscow, because the marriage is not recognized as valid by the Russians. (Boyle 2003; Stewart 2003). (*End of update by R. J. Noonan*)]

## 6. Homoerotic, Homosexual, and Bisexual Behaviors

### A/B. Children and Adolescents, and Adults

Connors et al. (1985) considered the possibility of homosexual relationships in space, although they considered heterosexual relationships to be the more realistic problem. At this time, it appears that homosexual activities in their varied forms are significantly less likely to have occurred in space, even if there are gay astronauts, simply because the majority of their colleagues are likely to be heterosexual; in addition, the process of coming out (making their homosexuality known to others) would very likely be the end of their career. However, homosexual sex may have occurred, because individuals are often able to find each other by conscious and unconscious subcultural cues. Then, allowing for the accidents of time and scheduling, potential homosexual partners may have been assigned to the same flight, guaranteeing training together for the mission and allowing them to be together in space for sex to occur. Again, it would not be politically expedient to prove that homosexual activities have occurred for the same reasons noted above for heterosexuals, but in this instance, there would also be the potentially greater harm that might come to a gay astronaut if his (or her) sexual orientation were unintentionally made public (although losing one's career would likely hold true for heterosexuals as well, if the activity occurred outside the accepted bounds of marriage).

The number of women who are astronauts would make lesbians even less likely to be represented in the astronaut corps than gay men, and thus would make it less likely that lesbian sexual activity has occurred. Nevertheless, both lesbians and gay men are represented in other aspects of the space program. The likelihood of bisexuals who might be astronauts is more difficult to assess, because many bisexuals typically do not identify themselves as a distinct subculture, but tend to shift between heterosexual or homosexual affiliations. Bisexuals, female and male, who are attracted equally to females and males are less common than those who tend to focus on one sex or the other. With regard to multiple pairings, my comments with reference to heterosexual astronauts would also likely apply, although in the case of gay astronauts, more or less their whole sexual persona would need to be kept secret in the present social climate.

## 7. Gender Diversity and Transgender Issues

At present, this issue probably has no relevance in the space programs.

## 8. Significant Unconventional Sexual Behaviors

### A. Coercive Sex

*Sexual Harassment and Rape*

Sexual harassment has been cited as a significant problem in the military, and, although it is often used now as a means of extortion or harassment itself, trivializing its actual victims as well as obscuring its real meanings and incidence in general, there is little information as to whether it has been a problem in the training or other professional or social settings involving the astronauts; it could be a problem in a space setting where significant levels of stress might precipitate that or other antisocial behavior. The same might be said for rape, although it is less common than sexual harassment. Clearly, we have not yet found the solutions to these problems in many of Earth's cultures.

Casper and Moore (1995), noting the instances of friction in the analog and space environments that have occurred as a result of the psychosocial stresses covered earlier, at one point highlighted the possible sexual violence that might occur because of these stresses. Apparently rejecting the evidence that shows that mixed-sex groups function more effectively in many ways than single-sex groups (Bishop 1996ab; Pierce 1991; Stuster 1996), they wrote:

> These accounts raise compelling questions about the limits of the "complementary sexes" model proposed by NASA as leading to more harmonious and productive work. Psychological disturbances raise the specter of sexual violence, racial violence, and other serious interpersonal conflicts resulting from stress induced by long missions. It is somewhat disturbing to us that sexual behavior in space is assumed to be "total consenting adult freechoice sex." Given contemporary gendered power dynamics, this seems naively idealistic. Yet, an interesting research question is presented by the possible effects of weightlessness on expressions of sexual and other types of violence. For example, how would physical/bodily deterioration affect an individual's capability to overpower, force, and/or injure another astronaut? What does force look like in a 0-gravity context? Despite these concerns, issues of sexual violence are rarely raised with respect to long-term travel, and when we mentioned this possibility to informants they seemed vaguely puzzled. (p. 325)

Coercive sexual behaviors and blatant sexual harassment are not likely to be a problem in space, except in the event of a complete breakdown of the microsociety within the space culture. As Pierce (1991) noted, such microaggressions are usually more verbal and do not result in explosive violence. Rather, Casper and Moore frame outcomes of sexual expression as likely to be negative, reflecting the prevailing antisexualism of our culture, and is a clear example of the concerns noted by Money (1995b) regarding the effects of the pseudoscience of victimology today.

Nevertheless, Pesavento (2000) noted that an attempted sexual assault did occur in a more-than-six-month-long simulated *Mir* mission module at the Institute for Biomedical Problems in Moscow. Alcohol was involved, as it occurred during a New Year's celebration. Still, it is important to emphasize that possibility does not equal likelihood. [*Update 2003*: Dudley-Rowley and her colleagues (2001/ 2002) continue to look at crew and mission characteristics that might affect deviance, conflict, and dysfunction in extreme environments. (*End of update by R. J. Noonan*)]

### B. Prostitution

Prostitution will likely find its way to space settlements once commercial exchange becomes established there, but it will not likely be an issue in any scenario until some time later in this century. It may well be a part of the expected sex-tourism industry that is expected to occur in the not-too-distant future.

### C. Pornography and Erotica

It seems reasonable to expect that there would be a place for pornographic and erotic materials during a long flight. Bluth (1985) has noted that at some Antarctic research stations, "the men liked to watch pornographic films and it's best if a woman is not offended by pornography" (p. 143). This brings up questions of a sexological nature that may have relevance to extended spaceflight. If sexually oriented materials have the ability to relieve stress under extremely trying conditions, then they should be studied to determine if, in fact, they do. They also may serve as a morale booster.

In addition, they may have value in places where there is currently a disproportionate ratio of women to men. The issue of sexual harassment would also be a factor when women are also members of the crew, because many courts have adopted the standard that such material sexualizes a workplace because some women (and some men) are offended by it. Although it is unlikely that it in fact does typically sexualize an environment, this position fails to take into account the sexually oriented materials marketed to gay males or lesbians, nor the feminist-produced corpus of literature and films for women. As a result, the ban on such materials as an expression of sexual harassment is typically applied only to materials oriented to heterosexual males.

Recently, Pesavento (2000) revealed that pornographic films were available to cosmonauts on the space station *Mir*, which Russian space psychologists recommended viewing only in the later stages of an individual cosmonaut's flight. He also described the surprise that American astronaut Norman Thagard had when he found that these soft-core French and Italian erotic videos were there. Pesavento also described plans for a movie to be made on *Mir*, in which sexual activity would be filmed, for which the Russian Space Agency had already been paid millions of dollars for training the actors for their time in space. However, the filmmakers were not able to raise the additional millions needed to save the *Mir* from its planned deorbiting, which occurred at the end of March 2001.

### D. Paraphilias

The paraphilias are those behaviors that are dependent on atypical or socially unacceptable things for sexual arousal, such as inanimate objects or parts of the body or events that are linked erotosexually to a person's childhood. They are thought to arise out of a traumatic or similar event that affects psychosexual development at critical periods during a child's life. Nevertheless, one may speculate that a generally sexually repressive environment would, at the same time, facilitate the expression of paraphilias. In relation to spaceflight, therefore, it would be incumbent upon space officials to create and maintain a sexually positive environment to avoid the problems associated with paraphilic behaviors.

## 9. Contraception, Abortion, and Population Planning

### A/B. Contraception and Abortion

Effective contraception is essential for long-term space travel for heterosexual couples, and efforts need to be undertaken to develop safe and effective contraceptive techniques, both for use on Earth and in space. Pregnancy is currently a contraindication for spaceflight because we do not know what effect the space environment would have on a fetus conceived on Earth. Abortion would probably be required in the event of failed contraception while in space, because of mixed results found with the development of fertilized eggs of various animals, although the morning-after pill could be available as an alternative of first choice. Because abortion at the earliest stages is relatively simple to perform, the necessary equipment for a menstrual extraction or for a later suction curettage should be available in the medical station, as well as appropriate pregnancy-testing kits. Returning to Earth would simply not be an option, at least for the foreseeable future, given that we do not know whether human development *in utero* is possible, nor what would occur later in life if a birth did occur after conception in space.

In an series of articles dealing with the effects of space on humans posted at one time on NASA's website, Jenks (1996) noted that "NASA has not studied the subject of human reproduction in space." It was the first sentence of an article mistitled "Sex in Space," which went on to briefly discuss developmental biology and plant and animal reproduction. However, it did, perhaps, unintentionally serve to highlight the pronatalist bias that persists in many societies' conception of the primary purpose of sexuality, that is, its procreational aspects. The more-common (and probably more important at the individual level) recreational and relational aspects of sexual behavior, on the other hand, were simply ignored, likely because of the erotic components that tend to fuel them (Noonan, 1998a).

### C. Population Programs

Population planning will become an issue when settlements are needed to be designed for lunar, Martian, or other outposts, and in that case, it is likely to be at the level of engineering the social environment around the professional expertise needed for the various parts of the mission (Harris 1996).

## 10. Sexually Transmitted Diseases and HIV/AIDS

The typical Earth-bound STDs with which we have to contend may present additional problems in space. This is because there is evidence that the immune system is compromised by spaceflight, although Sherr and Sonnenfeld (1997) wrote that some results are difficult to interpret. However, if this is found to be true, they thought it could severely limit long-term human spaceflight. Certainly, additional studies are needed to clarify this possibility, as well as to continue to learn more about our immune systems to be able to meet these challenges. There might also be the possibility that other disease organisms could mutate and become new STDs. The same is true for HIV/AIDS as well. In addition, there is the possibility that studies that gain a better understanding of the human immune system in space may have direct application for dealing with HIV/AIDS. It is also possible, given that drugs are expected to be manufactured in space because crystals form more purely in microgravity, that space science could assist in eradicating AIDS, as well as the STDs and other diseases and conditions.

## 11. Sexual Dysfunctions, Counseling, and Therapies

Sexual response can be viewed physiologically as essentially a series of cardiovascular and muscular events resulting in a buildup of vasocongestion and myotonia to a psychophysiological peak and release known as climax or orgasm—coupled with a buildup and release of muscular tension. In the human sexual response cycle, as sexual stimulation progresses, blood engorges the vascular tissues of the clitoris, penis, and other parts of the body in the process called vasocongestion, while the buildup of muscle tension (myotonia) occurs. This is usually accompanied by an increase in respiration and metabolic activity. Orgasm releases and is typically considered the climax of this vasocongestion and myotonic buildup of sexual tension, in a paroxysmal, rhythmic, reflexive discharge of energy, typically resulting in a feeling of relaxation throughout much of the body.

Among the most visible physiological effects of spaceflight are the shifts in body fluids, most importantly the blood, which rises from the lower extremities to settle into the chest cavity and head. In time, the cardiovascular system acclimates itself to the new environment. At the same time, with less blood volume and no longer the need to pump blood against gravity, the heart muscles begin to relax

somewhat, and the process of deconditioning begins (unless exercise is used to compensate for the loss by forcing the heart to pump harder). A similar condition occurs with overall body muscle tone, especially the large, weight-bearing, anti-gravity muscles that allow us to walk erect and maintain an upright posture. Therefore, we can probably expect a change in our perception of the various physiological phases of the sexual response cycle.

Anecdotal stories confirm that erections can and do take place in space, although a characterization of the quality of these erections has not been done. Information about whether women have experienced clitoral erections and vaginal lubrication has not been forthcoming, although the homologous nature of this aspect of the sexual response cycle would support the conclusion that they have. NASA could be easily monitoring this while the astronauts slept. One may conjecture that both female and male astronauts, when they are not asleep, would perceive a difference in their genital responses from their normal preflight experiences. Using Masters and Johnson's (1966) four-phase model of the human sexual response cycle, each phase might be affected in the following ways. During the excitement or arousal phase, penile erections in men may not feel as physically strong, particularly as the time in space gets longer and the body continues to adapt to weightlessness by deconditioning. The increase in respiration—the heavy breathing or hyperventilation, along with the increase in blood pressure and heartrate experienced during arousal through the plateau phase to orgasm—may also take more effort and feel more tiring as time progresses for the same reason. In women, clitoral erections and vaginal lubrication are likely to be similarly perceived.

Both vaginal lubrication in women and the erection of the clitoris and its homologue in men, the penis, are essentially vasocongestive in character. Vasocongestion forces the lubricating fluids through the pores of the walls of the vagina. This response varies with age, decreasing as women get older. This is likely to have an impact on astronauts who eventually travel to Mars, because older individuals are now thought to be among the prime candidates for such a trip because of the higher exposure risk to radiation in interplanetary flights. The main idea is that because the radiation effects are usually manifested many years later, it would be more likely that the astronauts would approach the natural end of their lives before the radiation effects would become evident. In addition, it is likely that the older astronauts would be well past the stage of starting families than younger ones would, given the impact of the possible and probable effects of radiation on gamete production.

The myotonia, the increase in muscle tension also characteristic of the sexual excitement and plateau phases, is likely to be experienced by the astronauts as being less intense during spaceflight than they normally experience on Earth, particularly in the voluntary muscle groups over which we have conscious control. This effect may increase as the time in space increases because of the progressive deconditioning of the muscles. Sexual activity, thus, might be an ideal part of an exercise program that people would very likely want to do regularly to maintain overall body and sexual fitness.

All of the effects on the human sexual response cycle just described provide possible mechanisms for a breakdown at some point in the cycle. Thus, there is the distinct possibility that any of the sexual dysfunctions experienced by men and women on Earth may increase or be aggravated in the space environment. But, just as Masters and Johnson (1966) indicated with respect to human sexual functioning on Earth, the range of normal functioning in space will need to be clarified before mechanisms and ameliorative actions for sexual dysfunctions can be described. Counseling practices will also need to take into account the unique psychosocial environment and the total space experience to be effective. In addition, countermeasures found to treat space-related sexual dysfunction should have application to the same problems on Earth.

Recently published data support the speculation that there would likely be some effect on sexual functioning, although deconditioning was not the focus of the study. Strollo et al. (1998) measured hormone secretion in four male astronauts pre-, in-, and postflight to test their hypothesis that stress-induced hormone changes might impair gonadal function by reducing testicular androgen (especially testosterone) secretion. In addition to its many roles in the differentiation of the fetus and the development of the secondary sex characteristics at puberty in males, testosterone stimulates the sex drive (libido) in both sexes. Strollo et al. found that "[s]exual drive was reduced inflight and postflight as compared with preflight (p < 0.05)" (p. 135), which correlated with a decrease in testosterone levels in the men. In addition, they noted that there were no endocrine signs of acute stress, in that the levels of adrenocorticotropin (ACTH) and cortisol (CS), although high from the preflight anticipation that astronauts typically feel, did not change inflight, although interstitial-cell-stimulating (i.e., luteinizing) hormone (LH) levels unexpectedly increased. LH stimulates the secretion of testosterone in the testes. The researchers also found that testosterone levels recovered dramatically one day following the astronauts' reentry from space. Thus, they noted, "For the first time, space life sciences research has shown reversible primary hypoandrogenism in man during exposure to microgravity" (p. 136). Nevertheless, although testosterone levels recovered quickly (as measured in the saliva), they noted that 15 days after reentry, other measurements suggested that more than two weeks were required for complete recovery at the cellular level. The timeframe for libido recovery, however, was not revealed in the article, or even whether it did recover. The authors stated that further research was needed to clarify whether fluid shifts or altered androgen distribution in the body because of microgravity was responsible for the results.

## 12. Sex Research and Advanced Professional Education

In the space arena, the time will eventually come when sexological concerns are recognized as legitimate topics for research in support of extended spaceflight missions. Administrators at the top levels of management and those with influence within the space life sciences of national and international space agencies, such as NASA, the Russian Space Agency, and the European Space Agency, need to encourage and support relevant biomedical, psychosocial, and human factors professionals within their organizations to receive advanced sexological training. These professionals should be urged to make contact with colleagues in sexology to find out the advances and concerns within this discipline that might have relevance to their spaceflight responsibilities, as well as to offer their knowledge from the space program that might be relevant to the work of sexologists. The Society for the Scientific Study of Sexuality (SSSS), with its international membership, would be the professional organization of sexologists whose expertise in sex research, counseling and therapy, and education would provide the best interdisciplinary support that would benefit the work of space life scientists. In addition, training programs for space life scientists should incorporate sexological information into their curricula, and sexologists have the expertise necessary to provide knowledgeable input at all levels of the educational spectrum, including advanced medical training for physicians.

## Conclusion

It should be clear that the integration of various human and mission components work synergistically to provide the context in which space missions will function and how they might be affected by the human sexuality complex. At the same time, it is not yet as clear that humans on Earth will soon come to terms with their own sexualities, as Perry (1990) has noted, and this should be a cause for concern. Despite this truism and the demonstrated evidence that various space life scientists and others have projected that sexuality factors are likely to have an impact on future long-term space missions, the intersection between the two scientific specialties whose domains encompass either the space life sciences or sexuality and gender has scarcely begun to be investigated. This should serve as a call to action to prepare adequately for meeting the challenges expressed here. One focus of intervention will need to be directed toward the managers and mission planners; the other focus will need to be on the individual crewmembers, as well as their families and intimate partners. My earlier work (Noonan 1998a) might well serve as a rationale and an outline for action for the managers and planners in the space endeavor. Certainly, wherever humanity goes, our sexuality will surely follow.

To me, possibly the most important conclusion to come out of my study was embodied in the new terminology I coined, the human sexuality complex, that conceptualized the various factors of human sexuality to be components of a unified system, one that has characteristics ascribed to chaotic, complex systems. Such a conceptualization, I believe, will allow scientists in both the sexual and space life sciences, as well as policymakers in the public domain, to better understand and address both the potential problems of sex and the role that healthy sexual expression has in society and in space. Once we are effectively able to do that, the consideration of the human sexuality complex in the closed ecological environments of space will appear more justified, and so a space sexology might well be established.

## References and Suggested Readings

Anderson, G. 1992 (May 15). Is NASA secretly experimenting with sex in space? *Now it can be told* (Geraldo Rivera television program) [Official transcript]. Livingston, NJ: Burrelle's Information Services.

Atkinson, Jr., J. D., & J. M. Shafritz. 1985. *The real stuff: A history of NASA's astronaut recruitment program*. New York: Praeger Publishers.

Bishop, S. L. 1996a (May). Psychosocial issues in spaceflight. In: R. J. Noonan (Chair), *Space Life Sciences Symposium*. Symposium conducted at the 15th International Space Development Conference (ISDC), May 24, 1996, New York, NY.

Bishop, S. L. 1996b (November 15). Psychosocial issues of mixed-gender crews in space. In: R. J. Noonan (Chair), *Women and men in space: Implications for the space and sexual sciences*. Symposium conducted at the 39th annual meeting of the Society for the Scientific Study of Sexuality (SSSS), November 15, 1996, Houston, TX.

Bluth, B. J. 1985. *Space station/Antarctic analogs* (ITT, Antarctic Services Contractor Reports NAG 2-255 and NAGW-659). Reston, VA: Space Station Program Office, NASA.

Boyle, A. 2003 (July 18). Space wedding faces complications. *MSNBC News: Technology and Science*. Available: http://www.msnbc.com/news/940767.asp?0bl=-0&cp1=1.

Bushnell, D. 1958. *History of research in space biology and biodynamics at the Air Force Missile Development Center, Holloman Air Force Base, New Mexico, 1946-1958*. Holloman Air Force Base, NM: U.S. Air Force Missile Development Center.

Cabbage, M. 2001 (March 11). Lust in space: Study tells all. *Orlando Sentinel*. Available: http://www.orlandosentinel.com/news/custom/space/orl-space031101.story?coll=orl%2Dhome%2Dheadlines.

Casper, M. J., & L. J. Moore. 1995. Inscribing bodies, inscribing the future: Gender, sex, and reproduction in outer space. *Sociological Perspectives*, *38*(2), 311-333.

Cassutt, M. 1993. *Who's who in space: The International Space Year edition*. New York: Macmillan.

Clarke, A. C. 1986. *Arthur C. Clarke's July 20, 2019: Life in the 21st century*. New York: Macmillan.

Connors, M. M., A. A. Harrison, & F. R. Akins. 1985. *Living aloft: Human requirements for extended spaceflight* (NASA Publication No. SP-483). Washington, DC: U.S. Government Printing Office (Scientific and Technical Information Branch, National Aeronautics and Space Administration).

Date, S. 1992 (June 6). The birds and the bees head into outer space. *The Orlando Sentinel*, pp. A-1, A-6.

Dudley-Rowley, M., S. Whitney, S. Bishop, B. Caldwell, & P. D. Nolan. 2001/2002. Crew size, composition, and time: Implications for habitat and workplace design in extreme environments (Paper 2001-01-2139; AIAA 2002-6111). 1st Space Architecture Symposium (SAS 2002), Houston, TX, USA, October 10-11, 2002. Reston, VA: American Institute of Aeronautics and Astronautics. Available: http://pweb.jps.net/~gangale/opsa/CrewSizeCompositionAndTime/2001-01-2139.pdf.

Fazio, G. G. 1997. Vacuum, temperature, and microgravity. In: S. E. Churchill, ed., *Fundamentals of space life sciences* (pp. 3-9). Malabar, FL: Krieger Publishing Co.

Francoeur, R. T., ed. 1997. *International encyclopedia of sexuality* (Vols. 1-3). New York: Continuum.

Francoeur, R. T., ed. 1998. *Sexuality in America: Understanding our sexual values and behavior*. New York: Continuum.

Francoeur, R. T., & T. Perper. 1997. General character and ramifications of American religious perspectives on sexuality. In: R. T. Francoeur, ed., *International encyclopedia of sexuality* (Vol. 3, pp. 1392-1403). New York: Continuum.

Gingrich, N. 1995. *To renew America*. New York: HarperCollins.

Harris, P. R. 1996. *Living and working in space: Human behavior, culture and organization* (2nd ed.). New York: John Wiley & Sons.

Harrison, A. A., Y. A. Clearwater, & C. P. McKay, eds. 1991. *From Antarctica to outer space: Life in isolation and confinement*. New York: Springer-Verlag.

Hunt, M. 1974. *Sexual behavior in the 1970s*. Chicago: Playboy Press.

Jenks, K. 1996. *Sex in space*. Houston, TX: Space Biomedical Research Institute, Johnson Space Center, NASA. Available: http://www.bway.net/~rjnoonan/humans_in_space/sex.html.

Levin, R. J. 1989 (August). Effects of space travel on sexuality and the human reproductive system. *Journal of the British Interplanetary Society*, *42*(7), 378-382.

Libby, R. W., & R. N. Whitehurst, eds. 1977. *Marriage and alternatives: Exploring intimate relationships*. Glenview, IL: Scott, Foresman and Co.

Maslow, A. H. 1970. *Motivation and personality* (2nd ed.). New York: Harper & Row.

Masters, W. H., & V. E. Johnson. 1966. *Human sexual response*. Boston: Little, Brown & Co.

McCullough, J. 1973 (September). The 13 who were left behind. *Ms.*, pp. 41-45.

McCullough, N. 1992 (November). Sex in space. *True News*, pp. 24-26.

Money, J. 1985a. *The destroying angel: Sex, fitness & food in the legacy of degeneracy theory, Graham crackers, Kellogg's corn flakes & American health history*. Buffalo, NY: Prometheus Books.

Money, J. 1995b. *Gendermaps: Social constructionism, feminism, and sexosophical history*. New York: Continuum.

Morphew, M. E., & S. MacLaren, eds. 1997 (June). Voyage to discovery: American astronauts aboard Russia's Mir space station [Introduction]. *Human Performance in Extreme Environments*, *2*(1), 39-61.

NASA. 1999. *NASA facts: The International Space Station: An Overview* (NASA publication IS-1999-06-ISS022). Houston, TX: Johnson Space Center, NASA.

NASA. 2003. *Human spaceflight*. Available: http://spaceflight.nasa.gov/station/reference/partners/index.html.

NASA/JSC. 2003. *Human spaceflight: International Space Station*. Available: http://spaceflight.nasa.gov/gallery/images/station/crew-6/inflight/ndxpage1.html.

Nicogossian, A. E., S. L. Pool, & J. J. Uri. 1994. Historical perspectives. In: A. E. Nicogossian, C. L. Huntoon, & S. L. Pool, eds., *Space physiology and medicine* (3rd ed., pp. 3-49). Philadelphia: Lea & Febiger.

Noonan, R. J. 1996. Survival strategies for lovers in the 1990s. In: P. B. Anderson, D. de Mauro, & R. J. Noonan, eds., *Does anyone still remember when sex was fun? Positive sexuality in the age of AIDS* (3rd ed., pp. 1-12; 2nd ed., pp. 1-12). Dubuque, IA: Kendall/Hunt Publishing Co. (Original work published 1992).

Noonan, R. J. 1998a. *A philosophical inquiry into the role of sexology in space life sciences research and human factors considerations for extended spaceflight*. Doctoral dissertation, New York University (UMI publication number 9832759). Information at http://www.SexQuest.com/SexualHealth/rjnoonan-diss-abstract.html.

Noonan, R. J. 1998b. The psychology of sex: A mirror from the Internet. In: J. Gackenbach, ed., *Psychology and the Internet: Intrapersonal, interpersonal and transpersonal implications* (pp. 143-168). New York: Academic Press.

Noonan, R. J. 2000 (September 11). The 200 mile high club. *The Position* [online journal of the Museum of Sex]. Available: http://theposition.com/.

Palinkas, L. A., E. K. Gunderson, A. W. Holland, C. Miller, & J. C. Johnson. 2000 (June). Predictors of behavior and performance in extreme environments: The Antarctic space analogue program. *Aviation, Space, and Environmental Medicine*, *71*(6):619-625.

Perry, M. E. 1990. Preface. In: J. Money & H. Musaph, eds., *Handbook of sexology*. M. E. Perry, ed., *Vol. VII. Childhood and adolescent sexology* (p. v). Amsterdam/New York: Elsevier.

Pesavento, P. 2000. From *Aelita* to the *International Space Station*: The psychological and social effects of isolation on Earth and in space. *Quest: The History of Spaceflight Quarterly* [University of North Dakota], *8*:2:4-23.

Pierce, C. M. 1991. Theoretical approaches to adaptation to Antarctica and space. In: A. A. Harrison, Y. A. Clearwater, & C. P. McKay, eds., *From Antarctica to outer space: Life in isolation and confinement* (pp. 125-133). New York: Springer-Verlag.

Reiss, I. L. 1990. *An end to shame: Shaping our next sexual revolution*. Buffalo, NY: Prometheus Books.

Santy, P. A. 1994. *Choosing the right stuff: The psychological selection of astronauts and cosmonauts*. Westport, CT: Praeger.

Sherr, D. H., & G. Sonnenfeld. 1997. Response of the immune system to spaceflight. In: S. E. Churchill, ed., *Fundamentals of space life sciences* (pp. 121-129). Malabar, FL: Krieger Publishing Co.

Smith, M. L. 1997 (January). The compliance with international space law of the LEDA proposal. *Space Governance: The Journal of United Societies in Space & The World-Space Bar Association*, *4*(1), 16-18.

Stewart, R. 2003 (August 10). Cosmic wedding goes off from JSC without a hitch. *HoustonChronicle.com*. Available: http://www.chron.com/cs/CDA/ssistory.mpl/topstory/2040806.

Strollo, F., G. Riondino, B. Harris, G. Strollo, E. Casarosa, N. Mangrossa, C. Ferretti, & M. Luisi. 1998 (February). The effect of microgravity on testicular androgen secretion. *Aviation, Space, and Environmental Medicine, 69*(2), 133-136.

Stuster, J. 1996. *Bold endeavors: Lessons from polar and space exploration.* Annapolis, MD: Naval Institute Press.

Thagard, N. 1997 (June). Additional comments from Norm Thagard. Sidebar to: Astronaut draws attention to psychology, communication (pp. 42-47). *Human Performance in Extreme Environments, 2*(1), 47.

Vaughan, D. 1992 (December). Sex in space: The final frontier. *Penthouse Forum,* pp. 48-53.

Weis, D. L. (1997). Adolescent sexuality [The United States of America]. In: R. T. Francoeur, ed., *International encyclopedia of sexuality* (Vol. 3, pp. 1479-1498). New York: Continuum. [The updated version also appears in this volume.]

White, F. 1987. *The overview effect: Space exploration and human evolution.* Boston: Houghton Mifflin Co.

## ANTARCTICA

### *Demographics and a Brief Historical Perspective*

The continent of Antarctica at the southern pole of the globe encompasses 10% of the world's landmass, about the size of the United States and Mexico combined. Covering 5.4 million square miles (14 million km²), it is the fifth-largest continent, with only 108,000 square miles (280,000 km²) ice-free. It is the coldest place on Earth with temperatures ranging from about –25° C to –80° C (–13° F to –112° F), with the lowest recorded temperature of –89° C (–129° F). It holds 90% of the world's ice and 70% of its fresh water. It is a landmass with an average ice thickness of 1.24 miles (2 km) and can be as thick as 2.97 miles (4.776 km). For about six months of the year, there is no sunlight at the pole. Most activity there occurs during the brief Antarctic summer from November to early February, although summer storms with temperatures as low as –60° C (–76° F) and blizzard conditions can occur. Chile, Argentina, Australia, and South Africa are the countries closest to the continent, which is surrounded by the Southern Ocean, which meets the South Atlantic, the South Pacific, and the Indian Oceans (Cornelius 1991; Taylor 1991; John Splettstoesser, polar consultant, personal communication, April 25, 2003).

In July 2002, Antarctica had an estimated winter population of 964, about one quarter of the summer population of 3,687. No other demographic data are available, other than the number of individuals representing each country that is a party to the Antarctic Treaty; these data are available in *The World Factbook 2002* (CIA 2002).

### B. A Brief Psychohistorical Perspective

There is no indigenous human presence. However, both men and a few women have been part of the pioneering exploratory efforts over the years since interest in Antarctica began in 1892. Since the 1957 International Geophysical Year (IGY), there has been a continuous human presence on the continent, which no country owns and which has been set aside for scientific and peaceful uses by treaty. As such, approximately 27 nations* have research programs in Antarctica, either in the summer or year-round, of which those of the United States, Chile, Argentina, Russia, and Austra-

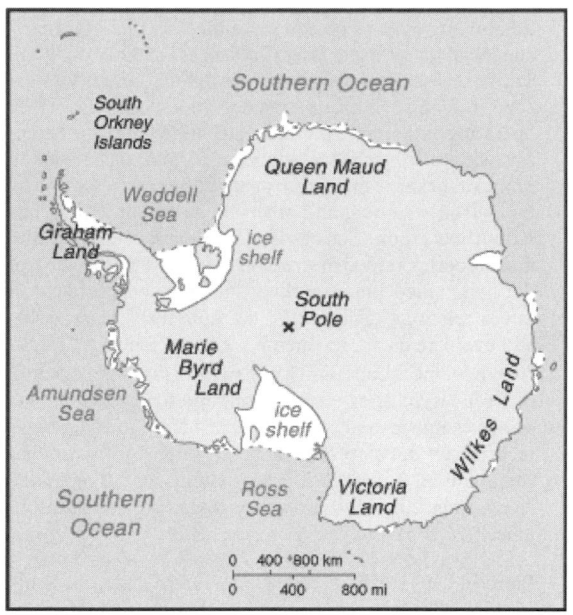

(CIA 2002)

lia were the largest in terms of number of people in 2002 (according to the CIA data). Although a novelty in the beginning, women are now an integral part of life there.

Once the arduous task of reaching the continent was accomplished for the first time, scientific discovery became the major focus. Often-introspective accounts written in diaries by the early explorers provide valuable knowledge about their psychological experiences and social interactions. These introspective reports gave way after World War II to formal behavioral studies. During the winter season between February and November, the stations are closed to outside travel. Cornelius (1991) described the isolation, which can vary, depending on the station and its distance from the pole, from about seven to nine months:

> The isolation is almost complete: no mail, no visitors, no leaving, and no fresh supplies. Outside contact is primarily by the high-frequency radio and sometimes by a satellite link. The first-ever midwinter airdrop at [Amundsen-Scott] South Pole [Station] was accomplished with a C-141B (refuelable version) in June of 1981 and has been done almost every year since. (p. 10)

The airdrop brings mail, fresh fruit and vegetables, movies, and other items. Cornelius expressed his view that this somewhat diminished the totality of the isolation. He also noted that the radios and other transmissions were sometimes unavailable because of solar storms. Today, the Internet and email provide better communications capabilities than ever existed before, although they too can be sporadic. In 1999, the first midwinter rescue from the United States' Amundsen-Scott South Pole Station was attempted that succeeded in the emergency evacuation of Dr. Jerri Nielsen (2001), who diagnosed and treated her own breast cancer before being airlifted out, which made headlines around the world.

Antarctica is often described as an extreme environment, and human performance in extreme environments is just one major focus of research being explored there today. Pierce (1991) wrote that Antarctica was an environment (like space) in which people would experience the stressful effects of prolonged isolation, confinement, uncertainty, and hazard. In addition, he described other sources of stress and the potential results:

---

*The nations with research teams in Antarctica at various times include: Argentina, Australia, Belgium, Brazil, Bulgaria, Chile, China, Finland, France, Germany, India, Italy, Japan, Netherlands, New Zealand, Norway, Peru, Poland, Russia, South Africa, South Korea, Spain, Sweden, Ukraine, United Kingdom, USA, and Uruguay.

Inhabitants in both places are subject to important psychosocial stresses that affect the success of the expedition. These include lack of privacy, boredom, inability to escape, forced socialization, anxiety, and nostalgia. While operating under these burdens, each individual must comply with a welter of regulations, formal and informal. Some of these are imposed by outside authorities, some by the person's culture, and others by developing traditions within the group. Sensitivity to obligations and regulations is compounded in stressful environments because of the heightened importance of vigilance and leader-follower relations. Constantly, the individual must assess and evaluate each crewmember's entitlements.

Under these conditions, orders from the outside world, differences in lifestyle, differing preferences for such things as music, and conflicts over the use of an exercise facility can develop compliance frictions. This psychosocial travail can yield offending slights, or microaggressions, rather than full-blown explosions or social turbulence. (p. 126)

Pierce (1991) also listed a number of other possible physiological and psychosocial disturbances that could result in some people at some point during their stay. These included: sleep disturbances, anxiety, increased territoriality, decreased performance, reduced motivation, impaired mental efficiency, withdrawal, and occasionally, augmented suggestibility and biological dysrhythmia. However, he noted, unlike the space environment in which space motion sickness has been a recurring problem, no polar-peculiar illnesses or derangements have yet been found. The reader is referred to Harrison, Clearwater, and McKay (1991abc) for a comprehensive review of other Antarctica research that is being applied to space habitability issues (see also the Outer Space section of this chapter).

In terms of possible ramifications for the human sexuality complex (Noonan 1998ab) in extreme environments, it is interesting to compare the occurrence of these microaggressions with similar minor problems that many couples living in more-normal situations experience after living together or being primarily focused on each other over extended periods of time. These microaggressions are usually expressed as verbal, often subtle comments, which can be perceived as insults that sometimes build up to what often appear to be major arguments over minor issues. The apparently almost-universal occurrence of this friction on some level in almost every group in the close quarters of the Antarctic stations (in the apparent absence, at least presumably in most cases, of any sexual interaction) might provide us with some insight into the phenomenon, both on Earth as it so commonly occurs with intimate couples and small workgroups, and its potential occurrence in space. In addition, it might be worth looking to the results of research that seeks to discern the mechanisms for its occurrence and the efforts that are being sought to prevent it, and apply them to everyday life on Earth. In those groups that had both men and women, certain frictions surrounding the actual or presumed heterosexual activity of others have been highlighted by a few reports, which I will review shortly.

Nevertheless, as with any frontier, national prestige factors entered into some of the very early attempts to be the first to reach the "white continent," similar in many respects to that which motivated the explorations that found the New World centuries earlier. Pierce (1991) noted that commerce, science, defense, and politics are the factors that are of strategic importance today for both Antarctica and space exploration, of which Antarctica is considered an analog for scientific research purposes, because both environments are characterized by isolation, confinement, deprivation, and risk, as noted earlier. In addition to space-based experience (Boeing Aerospace Company/National Behavior Systems 1983a; Bluth & Helppie 1986/1987), space scientists rely on information learned about human behavior in so-called analog environments found here on Earth. Analog environments are those that scientists believe closely approximate some of the key conditions found in space, such as the research stations in Antarctica, which are also remote and hazardous. Studies include those in Antarctica (Bluth 1985; Harrison, Clearwater, & McKay 1991a) and underwater habitats such as long-range nuclear submarines (Boeing Aerospace Company/National Behavior Systems 1983b). The descriptions of Antarctica by Cornelius (1991) and Taylor (1991) highlight why it is considered the best Earth analog for studies of the psychosocial processes that will occur during long-term space missions. Based on such analog studies, extended space missions, like Antarctic expeditions, are expected to follow what might seem to be a quite-obvious pattern, i.e., they have a beginning, a middle, and an end, each with varying durations. Yet, each has specific characteristics with distinct psychological ramifications for the participants, regardless of the full length of the entire mission. Of primary importance are the coping mechanisms that the individuals use to deal with the stresses at hand (Palinkas 1989, 1991, 1992; Palinkas & Browner 1995).

## 1. Basic Sexological Premises

### A. Character of Gender Roles

For most of the 20th century, the primary organization that supported exploratory and scientific expeditions to Antarctica for the United States was the U.S. Navy, although civilians conducted virtually all of the exploration and science after the 1957 IGY (John Splettstoesser, polar consultant, personal communication, April 25, 2003). As such, the old military's attitudes toward women were decidedly exclusionary—and all-male cultures were the norm. As women began to intrude in this all-male world, attitudes slowly changed, although then-current biases were tenacious. Today, private contractors conduct most of the American research in Antarctica, under the auspices of the National Science Foundation (NSF), and women are a regular part of the programs. Kanas (1992) has noted that during long-term Antarctic expeditions, status leveling occurs, in which leadership diverges into domains of expertise, such as emotional support functions, out of which conflicts may arise (of which some may be gender-based).

Similarly, other nations' expeditions originally consisted exclusively of men. Conditions were considered so severe that only men were thought to be able to withstand the rigors of Antarctic life. Finally, after a number of women—always vastly outnumbered by men—joined expeditions over many years, in 1984, an expedition consisting solely of women was sponsored by Germany. Since then, women have begun to approach, but have not yet fully achieved, parity with men in terms of their number and job functions. Today, it appears that women make up about 25% to 40% of most expeditions, with a higher percentage of women in the summer than who winter over, although some still consist of all men.

Robin Burns (2001) provides important insights into this history through the lives of women, mostly Australian, who have lived and worked in Antarctica, providing at the same time important insights into various aspects of the character of gender roles there. A summer expeditioner herself, she interviewed 130 women who spent some time there. Although the timeframes of the expeditions of most of the women were the 1980s and 1990s, some traveled there in the 1960s and

1970s, with a few going there even in 1959. Thus, Burns gives us a sense of the changes that have occurred as reported by these women, as she highlights the history of women on the continent. She also provides a look at the hardships faced by women and the impact of the extended separation from their families, which probably apply to others as well. She writes:

> Even with modern communications between Antarctica and Australia, twelve to fifteen months is a long time for couples to be separated. New relationships can form that are difficult to explain, and each may find it hard to understand the experiences of the other; for example, the intensity of life in Antarctica, or the new-found independence of the partner left at home. (p. 18)

She also discussed the difficulties in keeping up with younger children's development, although the use of the Internet now enables closer contact and the exchange of photos.

Burns's subjects tend to say that, although things have changed for women, in many ways the traditional roles of men and women are still in effect, with some men still viewing Antarctica as the "last frontier . . . where men go to prove they're men" (p. 25). Yet Burns also sees Antarctica as beneficial in breaking down some women's stereotypes of men. In some ways, there seems to be some hope of moving toward an interdependence between men and women.

## 2. Religious, Ethnic, and Gender Factors Affecting Sexuality

Although Antarctica has a multinational appearance, it is really largely a collection of national "neighborhoods," each station being staffed and run by its sponsoring country. As such, religious, ethnic, and other cultural factors tend to reflect, in varying degrees, the composition of the respective countries. One could anticipate, then, that these cultural factors operate in a similar manner to the way they do on their native soil, and, thus, their impact on sexuality factors might be assumed to operate in large measure the same way. Research has yet to be carried out to determine whether the physical and psychosocial environments peculiar to Antarctica mitigate their impact on people's sexuality in any significant way. As noted earlier in the Outer Space section of this chapter, idiosyncratic local cultures at the various stations are likely to develop as well, which will likely have an important impact as well. A good example follows:

Cornelius (1991) described the use of a ritualized nudity activity that was conducted every year at one Antarctic station, usually just past the midpoint of winter. The 300 Degree Club is a South Pole Station custom, whose name came from the fact that the temperature in midwinter (in September) drops below −100° F (−73° C) and there is a sauna that is set to 200° F (93° C) for the event. The crew would sit in the sauna wearing nothing but footwear and build up a profuse sweat. They would then dash out into the cold to the marked site of the geographic South Pole (about 325 feet, or 100 meters), pose for a quick picture, then dash back. The trick is not to fall, as the ice would burn like dry ice; the quick freezing of the sweat actually protects the body. Cornelius did not detail whether or how this was done when women were part of the crew. However, a 1996 Discovery Channel documentary reported a similar custom at another Antarctic station in which the members, male and female, after leaving the sauna took a quick dip in the water in a hole that was cut in the ice, before running back inside. This was described as a rite of passage that signified a major turning point of the expedition. This is also relevant to this discussion because of the common idea that many people have of

confusing nudity with inviting sexual activity. However, in both of these cases, there is apparently no overtly sexual significance involved.

Given the realities of sexuality today and the widespread perception that being associated with it somehow compromises one's professional standing and credibility, it is necessary to look at ways in which researchers can release the results of any sex-related research that might be done. Gender-related research does not carry the additional burden that specifically sex-related research does, and is thus being released and results presented at conferences often today (e.g., *Gender on Ice: Proceedings of a Conference on Women in Antarctica*, Edwards & Graham 1994; "Gender-Based Differences in the Cardiovascular Response to Standing," Gotshall, Tsai, & Frey 1991). This may be partly because gender has become neutered, in effect allowing it to be "uncontaminated" by sex, (i.e., the "clean" part above the belt vs. the "dirty" part below), as hypothesized by John Money (1995). In fact, today, it is common to use *sex* and *gender* as if they were synonymous, when sex is actually the biological (genetic, hormonal, and morphological) basis of gender, and gender is the cultural manifestation of sex.

With respect to gender factors, it is clear that, generally, women tend to change the environment in positive ways, because men appear to behave differently than they do in all-male groups (Bishop 1996; Stuster 1996). Nevertheless, Pesavento (2000) has noted that less-than-encouraging social interactions can occur in mixed-gender groupings. (See Section 5, Interpersonal Heterosexual Behaviors, below.)

## 3. Knowledge and Education about Sexuality

Antarctica is by and large an all-adult world, and children and adolescents are not part of most expeditions. Thus, sex education is not and probably will not be relevant in American or most other stations in Antarctica for the foreseeable future. Chile and Argentina, however, do have families, including children, living there year-round, with schools and other small-town facilities (John Splettstoesser, polar consultant, personal communication, April 25, 2003). The children are taught by teachers who come from their respective countries, although it is not known what kind of sex education might be taught. It is thought that the settlements were established to support territorial claims by these two countries should the Antarctic Treaty be dissolved, although none of the claims of the seven countries who make such claims are currently recognized by any others.

## 4. Autoerotic Behaviors and Patterns

No studies have been found that discuss masturbatory behavior in Antarctica. It can be presumed, however, that it is and has been practiced there, not only because of our human nature, but because, in the past, it would have been expected if no (heterosexual) partners were available in all-male crews (although it is normal behavior in individuals in couples in ordinary environments as well). It can also be expected in high-risk environments, in which it can function as a stress-reducer.

There is some anecdotal evidence, however: In all-male groups, masturbation was often the subject of a lot of jokes. At some Australian stations, stories were told of Wednesday nights being "wank night," although they may have been made in jest (Desmond Lugg, former head of polar medicine, Australian Antarctic Division, personal communication May 9, 2003). Dr. Lugg also related the story of how, when he gave the same preparatory lecture to new expeditioners prior to going to Antarctica (after having been admonished by some women that they get the same information as the men), one woman said, "We wank too."

## 5. Interpersonal Heterosexual Behaviors

Intimate relationships do develop, some quite open and some quite secret. I might expect that the open or secret nature might parallel the experience of people in ordinary workplaces or small towns, where group norms establish its acceptability and the positive, negative, or neutral impact on the individuals involved in and around them. There are no data available on the incidence or prevalence.

In an American Antarctic analog study commissioned by NASA for the Space Station Program (Bluth 1985), several aspects of heterosexual interaction were noted under a subheading called "Sex Roles." Among the issues discussed were the benefits and drawbacks of having married couples in the crew and the effects of fraternization, as well as of men's attitudes toward women. Some findings were that fraternization did occur at stations and that it "did not seem to be a problem as much when a woman remained with one person and did not flaunt or change relationships" (p. 141). The comments of one man indicated that those men who did not have a partner felt upset and resented those crewmembers who were indiscreet about sexual relations. Many of the women who wintered-over said they became the victims of gossip. The men also had a variety of other attitudes toward the women, some positive and some negative. One finding recommended that women need to be able to deal with male sexual attention.

Stuster (1996) echoed these observations and provided additional information about mixed-sex pairings:

> Promiscuity has had a rare but occasionally disruptive effect at Antarctic stations. Winter-over personnel have reported that if a woman chooses to have a relationship during her stay in Antarctica, it is usually with one man. Senior personnel are typically selected over junior staff, and clean-cut Navy men tend to be favored over the civilian construction workers, which can contribute to friction between military and civilian members of a remote-duty crew. In most cases, the other men tend to respect the decision once a woman makes a choice or makes clear her unavailability. Persistent, unwanted attention has occurred, however, with negative consequences to individual adjustment and group solidarity. Particularly disruptive problems develop when a woman and the station leader are involved in a relationship. In these circumstances, others in the group tend to claim that the leader has an unfair advantage. (pp. 178-179)

Stuster went on to suggest that leaders of space missions should avoid such involvements, but added that "it might be unwise for mission managers to dictate how crew personnel conduct this aspect of their personal lives" (p. 179).

Bluth (1985) also identified the "Antarctic Queen Syndrome," in which "every woman is beautiful," which "[s]ome women take advantage of . . . and play man against man" (p. 142). The Antarctic Queen "flirts with all the males, . . . always asks for favors [and] attention, . . . [and], "[i]f they need help . . . honey up to one of the guys, [which] causes problems between people and groups" (p. 142). Clearly, many of the situations noted can occur in non-isolated environments as well; however, in the latter situations, there are alternatives outside the group that can mitigate the frustration and problems that can occur.

Nevertheless, the benefits of both men and women working together appear to outweigh the disadvantages, as noted by Bishop (1996) and Stuster (1996). Bishop noted that in Earth-based studies, mixed-sex groups appeared to perform workgroup tasks better than all-male groups. She also reported that in military mixed-sex interactions, aggressive behavior appeared to be lessened, disciplinary cases were fewer, and the problems with sexual liaisons and pregnancies anticipated by critics failed to materialize. She also said that the addition of women tended to normalize group functioning, in that the presence of women seemed to enable or encourage the men to engage in a greater range of expression and cooperative behavior than in all-male crews. Women and men on extended spaceflights are likely to experience similar pressures and benefits, even though the crew sizes for the foreseeable future will remain smaller than on most Antarctic stations today. Law (1994) anticipated that many of the problems would not be solved until a more even balance of women and men is achieved. Lugg noted that women's entry into Antarctica after the transition from all-male to mixed-sex expeditions caused disruptions at times, but that it depended on the leadership and other factors (personal communication May 9, 2003). All this suggests that sexuality factors will still likely be stresses that will need to be addressed in both Antarctic and space environments.

Careful planning of living quarters with the assumption that sex is likely to take place is just one aspect that needs to be considered. In describing the differing characteristics of the Palmer Station, which is located near the coastline and so enjoys slightly less harsh conditions than the South Pole Station, which is located deeper in the interior on the high ice plateau, Cornelius (1991) noted in passing that the design of that station was poorer than that of the South Pole Station. In describing the crew's private quarters at Palmer, he wrote that, as a result of the station's poor design, which caused additional problems and stress, the acoustic privacy left much to be desired: "One can hear the crewmember in the next room breathing, making love, or listening to *his* music" (p. 14). In a follow-up article by ABCNews.com (2001) discussing Dr. Jerri Neilsen's outcome of her breast cancer and her planned return to Antarctica to work as a doctor on a cruise ship, she was quoted as saying that there were little of either sex or romance for similar reasons. Thus, some acceptance that sexual activity will take place, and a little foresight and planning, can help to alleviate some future problems with respect to sexuality factors.

Nevertheless, Burns (2001) has written that sexual relationships do happen in Antarctica. She noted that one third of the women she interviewed had been in Antarctica at the same time as their current partner, although fewer than half of these had started the relationship there. She noted that women entered sexual relationships for two reasons: One was to share the special experience of being in Antarctica with an intimate partner; the other reason was to handle the various pressures that had to be addressed.

In addition, Burns (2001) described the psychosocial aspects of relationships, such as dealing with male competition and the sexual activities of women who are known to be married, and the impact these can have on the men who might resent the fact that women have a choice of partners, whereas they do not. With respect to the married woman, it may arouse fears about what their wives at home may be doing. It appears that many of these dynamics, which are not uncommon outside of Antarctica, may be heightened in the extreme environment there. These dynamics might be useful for space mission planners in their Mars mission planning, for example, as the trip is expected to take maybe three years with far fewer people, which could exacerbate these effects further. It will be important to ascertain the differences between the two environments, however, as well as the psychosocial relationship variables that are different to more accurately gauge what can be done to minimize any potentially negative impact and to maximize the positive potential.

## 6. Homoerotic, Homosexual, and Bisexual Behaviors

### A. Adults

It is unlikely that there have been no gay Antarctic participants, and Burns (2001) has noted that "differences in ethnicity, class and sexual preference, as well as gender, are all reasons for not belonging" for women "to the male hierarchy" (p. 87). Thus, we might assume that this might apply to gay men as well. In my early research on this topic (Noonan 1998a), I came across Lugg (1991), who, writing of Australian expeditions, wrote that descriptions of "groups who lisped or used 'quaint' language" (p. 32) are part of the folklore of the Australian experience. I took this as a possible reference to the use of stereotypical American gay-male behaviors, which are often used for either ridicule or self-parody, although they are not typically used in everyday life by gay men. In a subsequent conversation, Dr. Lugg noted that it really was not related to gay caricatures, but rather that the language in the group mimicked the lisping of jokes that circulated one year at one Australian station, as well as the quaint language (i.e., old British-style accents and such) of old movies, which they would watch without the sound and the men would provide the dialogue imitating the actors. Thus, this is a good example of how different cultural behaviors and their meanings can lead to misunderstandings. He noted further, with respect to the lisping, that the language of the men had changed—they had developed their own language (inflections, meanings, and vocabulary) because of the isolation and their response to the environment. For the same reason, dogs at the station would sometimes be personified and become quiet partners in conversations. A parallel can be seen in less-isolated workgroups, and especially in intimate couples, where private languages often develop because of their insular nature.

Law (1994), a leader of 28 all-male Antarctic expeditions for Australia from 1947 to 1966 that established that country's three Antarctic stations, speaking at an Australian international conference on women in Antarctica, said:

> So far as I know there was no overt homosexuality at our stations. We of course, went to some pains to avoid homosexuals in the selection process. I heard that one man, a bisexual ex-naval rating, did some soliciting early on, but there were no takers, so that sort of fizzled out. Whether there was any covert homosexuality I would not know, but it would have been very difficult at a station to have kept secret such a liaison, and I was never informed by any of our men that anyone knew of anything of that sort happening. (p. 72)

Despite these comments, he appeared not to be necessarily opposed to homosexual behavior, however, as he qualified his statement:

> In that regard, however, I must point out that if we are to advance arguments justifying heterosexual behaviour at ANARE [Australian National Antarctic Research Expeditions] Stations now that women are admitted as expeditioners, then for the same reasons we shall have to accept possible homosexual behaviour and modify our selection processes accordingly. (p. 72)

He added, "It is important to stress the need for discretion in both heterosexual and homosexual behaviour at stations. Overt behaviour is objectionable for a number of reasons." He went on to say that the role of the leader in the event of

sexual behavior was important and could have a "considerable effect in moderating undesirable behaviour" (p. 72). Puskeppeleit (1994), the leader of the first-ever all-female expedition to Antarctica that was sent by the German Polar Institute, also speaking at the women-in-Antarctica conference, did not address the possibility that homosexual behavior was an issue at all for the women. She did note, however, that all of the women "would have preferred a mixed overwintering team" (p. 80), which the Institute would not allow.

Even today, potential problems could emerge with crewmembers who discovered that one of their team was homosexual or bisexual—just as they have when certain behaviors have been perceived as inappropriately heterosexual.

## 7. Gender Diversity and Transgender Issues

Although intersexual issues may become an issue in Antarctica in the future, it appears not to be so now, although it is known that men, as in some other all-male analog environments, sometimes dress up and act as women for parody and entertainment. The explanation seems to be that it occurred when there were no women who were part of the expeditions, and the men missed the company of women and sought to "normalize" the social environment. Burns (2001, 83-84, 91) noted, however, that "cross-dressing, 'girlie' posters and magazines, regular blue movie nights and 'page three girls' in the daily station news bulletins have been part of the tradition" at Australian stations, "and all have become contentious in recent years."

## 8. Significant Unconventional Sexual Behaviors

### A. Sexual Harassment, Rape, and Prostitution

Personal accounts of those who were in Antarctica when women first arrived suggest that mild forms of what has come to be known as sexual harassment, i.e., constant attention and cajoling for dates and such, appear to have taken place. As noted by Stuster (1996) in Section 5, Interpersonal Heterosexual Behaviors, apparently more-recent persistent, unwanted sexual attention has occurred, with negative consequences to individual adjustment and group solidarity. No reports of real (quid-pro-quo) sexual harassment, as opposed to the current social construction of "sexual harassment," or rape were found. Prostitution does not seem to occur.

### B. Pornography and Erotica

Cornelius (1991) noted that the ways in which the crew decorated common areas, such as with a large mural of a forest, probably helped to relieve stress during the period of isolation. This is likely to be true for the individual crewmember's small private quarters as well, in which he noted the "[m]any nature scenes and posters of the opposite sex" (p. 13). Law (1994) further noted that the Australians were always astonished at the number of nude photos on the walls of the American stations. The role of the use of sexually oriented materials in the leisure activities of the crew is, however, an issue that was not addressed in any of the analog studies, except that of Bluth (1985), who noted that at some of the stations, "the men liked to watch pornographic films and it's best if a woman is not offended by pornography" (p. 143).

Also, stories are told of how, along with Russian fur hats, American *Playboy* magazines, when they were banned in many countries, would become a valuable local currency in trade. In fact, *Playboy* centerfolds became part of the history of one station in the 1950s, where they were used to cover a ceiling, nicknamed the "Sistine Ceiling."

Anecdotal reports say that when women first became part of the expeditions, they tended to ignore the pornographic pictures or pinups (typically less sexually explicit), although they were eventually taken down from common areas. Private areas were considered private, and so these images usually stayed. In the late 1980s and early 1990s, when anti-pornography feminists came in and sexual harassment laws became common, they caused much acrimony and angst at the stations, as pinups and other materials had to be removed. For example, an uproar in the Australian press occurred over one explosive episode when a female leader banned the private posting of this type of material in one's personal area.

## 9. Contraception, Abortion, and Population Planning

### A. Contraception and Abortion

In a report prepared by George Washington University and Analytic Services Inc. (GWU/ANSER 1994a) on potentially difficult and sensitive events, including pregnancy, that might occur in space prepared for the National Aeronautics and Space Administration (NASA), the GWU/ANSER (1994b) team reviewed the Australian and U.S. Antarctic analog environments, and found the following related information. Both countries' stations have reported that pregnancies have occurred during expeditions. The policy they followed was that the woman be evacuated at the earliest possible time. "It is interesting to note," according to these authors, "that the father is not also sent home. The implication of this policy is not that sexual relations resulting in pregnancy are condemned but that the pregnant woman represents a medical liability unsuited for an extreme, isolated environment" (p. 30). They noted that an incubator was available at the Australian station in case the baby was born before evacuation was possible, and that abortions will not be performed there because of legal liability concerns, even though abortion is legal in Australia. However, they noted, pregnancies do not often occur in Antarctica, "[p]erhaps because birth control is readily available at all of the stations studied" (p. 30). The possibility that heterosexual relationships did not occur was discounted with the statement: "As one [Australian] female crew member reported, 'Just about every woman ends up in a relationship'" (p. 40).

CNN.com (2001) reported that New Zealand's Scott Base, located on the Ross Ice Shelf, installed their first two condom machines in anticipation of the influx of visitors in August 2001 in preparation for the warmer spring season in October. The supplier was quoted as saying, "It's pretty much a little village down there where everyone knows everyone, so if they can walk into a loo and buy a condom, it's a lot easier than going to the local shop and buying them, when everyone knows what's going on." It was expected to serve about 400 people, as well as about 1,200 Americans at their nearby McMurdo Base.

## 10. Sexually Transmitted Diseases and HIV/AIDS

It appears that most if not all countries do some screening for various diseases and conditions, and, if one is found with a condition, he or she is not allowed to go to Antarctica, so many diseases apparently do not appear there. Nevertheless, as noted above, condoms are now being sold in vending machines at New Zealand's Scott Base, which are also expected to serve the needs of the U.S.'s McMurdo Base nearby. UNAIDS.org (2002) does not list Antarctica among its list of countries for which it offers an epidemiological assessment, so HIV/AIDS does not appear to have reached that continent.

Various epidemiological data on STDs in Antarctica also suggest that STDs may not be an issue, although STDs have been taken to Antarctica in a number of national expeditions, but were not passed on to others within the group (Desmond Lugg, personal communication May 9, 2003). This suggests that those who had them got them earlier, perhaps in one of the South American entry points or their homelands. Screening specifically for STDs is not done. HIV screening is done through walk-in blood banks, and is provided as an ancillary finding. Because of the possibility of an HIV-infected person converting to full-blown AIDS, that person would probably not be allowed to go to Antarctica, because of the lack of medical support to treat it. It is unknown what would happen with someone who got an HIV-positive test result once there.

Some studies suggest, further, that the polar environment does depress the human immune response in otherwise healthy individuals, although specific environmental factors have not been identified that contribute. I would conjecture that stress is a likely candidate, and it would be interesting to compare the results of any studies on stress-hormone levels with Strollo, et al.'s (1998) study of male astronauts, which showed decreases in libido and testosterone levels while in space, which returned to normal postflight. No similar effects—or reports of sexual dysfunction specific to the polar region—have been reported in Antarctic settings.

Dr. Nancy Chin, a medical anthropologist from the University of Rochester School of Medicine who is studying social interactions in Antarctica, has noted that many summer participants clearly have an away-from-home attitude about being in Antarctica, and being there for sexual exploration is part of the Antarctic experience. However, she noted that sexual diseases are not screened out at the U.S. stations prior to arrival, and so, contrary to some myths, Antarctica is not the safest place in the world to have sex. For the most part, the same risks they faced at home were possible in Antarctica as well (personal communication August 12, 2003).

## 11. Sexual Dysfunctions, Counseling, and Therapies

Cornelius (1991) highlighted some of the major psychosocial factors that contribute to stress in Antarctica:

For example, absent are windows, privacy, living green things and animals, the sun, thick moist air to breathe, freedom to travel, or freedom to leave a rumor-infested, isolated human outpost. The "rumor mill" can be quite potent. Cliques can develop and be quite cruel and stressful to an individual with a different background than the rest of the crew. Cliques can also be quite insensitive to their own kind. Lack of acoustic privacy in the small "private" rooms can also lead to stress. Privacy becomes a cherished commodity. Time away from the group alone is very important for "charging one's batteries." Lack of a partner of the opposite sex can also lead to stress. Married couples who have wintered tend to handle the isolation much better. Constant low light levels can cause stress, too. It was observed that much higher light levels inside the dome at South Pole Station during the isolation period seemed to increase the morale of the crew. The higher light levels tend to decrease stress. (p. 10)

Thus, we can see that the level of stress, which is a major factor in disrupting interpersonal couple relationships and small-group interactions, can be quite high. In addition, stress is a major factor in many sexual dysfunctions. Therefore, we can expect that although stress can affect overall sexual performance and relationships, at the same time some undelineated aspect of the marital relationship (perhaps sex) tends to mitigate against the effects of stress for some married couples. It has been noted that most of the American work being done in Antarctica is being conducted by private contractors, who often send married couples to Antarctica.

In Antarctica, the value of off-duty leisure activities has been documented (Kelly & Kanas 1994). Such activities can provide the crew with a welcome respite from the monotony and stress of the long winter. Cornelius (1991) noted that, although they depend on the individual, they can include: conversation, watching movies and videos, listening to music, short excursions outside, looking out the windows if there are any, or doing group projects (e.g., building a jacuzzi at South Pole Station). He noted that they also try to find an excuse for a party, not only the standard birthdays and holidays, but also to celebrate midwinter (which signifies roughly the halfway point of the expedition) and the sunset and sunrise (there is only one sunset, corresponding roughly with our vernal equinox, and one sunrise, at about our autumnal equinox, in the interior parts of the continent each year).

Still, anecdotal stories have been told that suggest that some marriages have failed as a result of the Antarctic experience. Stuster (1996) confirmed this when he wrote:

> It is true that extremely disruptive and even dangerous relationships have developed among mixed-gender crews at both large and small Antarctic stations. Many relationships, including long-standing marriages, have dissolved while one or both parties were on the ice; other situations have been so bizarre that it is remarkable that the individuals were capable of coping with the experience. (p. 179)

He suggested that careful crew selection (as opposed to screening) was important, as well as special training about the many potential problems associated with life in isolation and confinement, which would allow most of the concerns about mixed-sex crews to dissipate.

Lugg has noted that marriages have been performed in Antarctica, and he also noted that some married couples have separated during their stay in Antarctica (personal communication May 9, 2003). He noted anecdotal stories that reveal that occasionally expeditioners may become involved with a new partner from the group, which can add additional stress to an already-stressful situation affecting established relationships. Today, people have psychological support services available by satellite phone, and doctors and many section leaders can also counsel those who winter over. Often, as well, the participants themselves can give useful support to those within the group who might need it.

## 12. Sex Research and Advanced Professional Education

It appears that no specifically focused sex research has been done in Antarctica. However, as can be noted from the previous sections, research has been done for NASA that has looked at the interpersonal relationships that occur in research stations there to help suggest what impact the psychosocial environment, in terms of isolation, confinement, deprivation, and risk, might have on extended spaceflights. In addition, personal accounts of expeditioners have drawn some attention to sexuality factors. Together, both can begin to suggest avenues of sex research that might be done in both environments, which, as I have argued elsewhere (Noonan 1998a), can be used to improve the sexual lives of everyone.

## References and Suggested Readings

ABCNews.com. 2001 (July 19/31). *PrimeTime: Survival at South Pole: Doctor rescued for cancer treatment to return to Antarctica*. Available: http://more.abcnews.go.com/sections/primetime/2020/primetime_nielsen_010719_feature.html.

Bishop, S. L. 1996 (November 15). Psychosocial issues of mixed-gender crews in space. In: R. J. Noonan (Chair), *Women and men in space: Implications for the space and sexual sciences*. Symposium conducted at the 39th annual meeting of the Society for the Scientific Study of Sexuality (SSSS), November 15, 1996, Houston, TX.

Bluth, B. J. 1985. *Space station/Antarctic analogs* (ITT, Antarctic Services Contractor Reports NAG 2-255 and NAGW-659). Reston, VA: Space Station Program Office, NASA.

Bluth, B. J., & M. Helppie, 1986/1987. *Soviet space stations as analogs* (2nd ed. with MIR update). Reston, VA: Space Station Program Office, NASA. (Original work published 1986)

Boeing Aerospace Company/National Behavior Systems, 1983a. *Space station habitability report* (NASW-3680/CC0081). Reston, VA: Space Station Program Office, NASA.

Boeing Aerospace Company/National Behavior Systems, 1983b. *Space station/Nuclear submarine analogs* (U.S. Naval submarine interview report/Space station crew system interface study). Reston, VA: Space Station Program Office, NASA.

Burns, R. 2001. *Just tell them I survived! Women in Antarctica*. Crows Nest, NSW, Australia: Allen & Unwin.

CIA. 2002 (January). *The world factbook 2002*. Washington, DC: Central Intelligence Agency. Available: http://www.cia.gov/cia/publications/factbook/index.html.

CNN.com. 2001 (August 2). *Sex in Antarctica no longer on ice*. Available: http://www.cnn.com/2001/WORLD/asiapcf/auspac/08/02/antarctic.sex/.

Cornelius, P. E. 1991. Life in Antarctica. In: A. A. Harrison, Y. A. Clearwater, & C. P. McKay, eds., *From Antarctica to outer space: Life in isolation and confinement* (pp. 9-14). New York: Springer-Verlag.

Edwards, K. & Graham, R. (1994). *Gender on ice: Proceedings of a conference on women in Antarctica, held in Hobart, Tasmania, under the auspices of the Australian Antarctic Foundation, 19-21 August 1993*. Canberra: Australian Government Publishing Service.

Gotshall, R. W., P.-F. Tsai, & M. A. B. Frey. 1991. Gender-based differences in the cardiovascular response to standing. *Aviation, Space, and Environmental Medicine, 62*, 855-859.

GWU/ANSER. 1994a. *Policy issues in space analogs* [Final report of the June 1992 Workshop]. Washington, DC: Space Policy Institute, George Washington University, and Arlington, VA: Analytic Services Inc.

GWU/ANSER. 1994b. *Policy issues in space analogs: Prepared for the GWU/ANSER Workshop 16-17 March 1994*. Washington, DC: Space Policy Institute, George Washington University, and Arlington, VA: Analytic Services Inc.

Harrison, A. A., Y. A. Clearwater, & C. P. McKay, eds. 1991a. *From Antarctica to outer space: Life in isolation and confinement*. New York: Springer-Verlag.

Harrison, A. A., Y. A. Clearwater, & C. P. McKay, eds. 1991b. Introduction. In: A. A. Harrison, Y. A. Clearwater, & C. P. McKay, eds., *From Antarctica to outer space: Life in isolation and confinement* (pp. 1-5). New York: Springer-Verlag.

Harrison, A. A., Y. A. Clearwater, & C. P. McKay, eds. 1991c. Conclusion: Recommendations for future research. In: A. A. Harrison, Y. A. Clearwater, & C. P. McKay, eds., *From Antarctica to outer space: Life in isolation and confinement* (pp. 395-401). New York: Springer-Verlag.

Kanas, N. 1992. *Interpersonal issues affecting international crews on long duration space missions*. Paper presented at the World Space Congress, 43rd Congress of the International Astronautical Federation (IAF), Washington, DC, August 28-September 5, 1992. (IAF paper IAF/IAA-92-0243).

Kelly, A. D., & N. Kanas. 1994. Leisure time activities in space: A survey of astronauts and cosmonauts. *Acta Astronautica, 32*(6), 451-457.

Law, P. 1994. The all male expeditions 1947-66. In: K. Edwards & R. Graham, *Gender on ice: Proceedings of a Conference on Women in Antarctica*, held in Hobart, Tasmania, under the auspices of the Australian Antarctic Foundation, 19-21 August 1993 (pp. 67-73). Canberra: Australian Government Publishing Service.

Lugg, D. J. 1991. Current international human factors research in Antarctica. In: A. A. Harrison, Y. A. Clearwater, & C. P. McKay, eds., *From Antarctica to outer space: Life in isolation and confinement* (pp. 31-42). New York: Springer-Verlag.

Money, J. 1995. *Gendermaps: Social constructionism, feminism, and sexosophical history.* New York: Continuum.

Nielsen, J. 2001. *Ice bound: A doctor's incredible battle for survival at the South Pole.* New York: Miramax Hyperion Books.

Noonan, R. J. 1998a. *A philosophical inquiry into the role of sexology in space life sciences research and human factors considerations for extended spaceflight.* Doctoral dissertation, New York University (UMI publication number 9832759). Information at http://www.SexQuest.com/SexualHealth/rjnoonan-diss-abstract.html.

Noonan, R. J. 1998b. The psychology of sex: A mirror from the Internet. In: J. Gackenbach, ed., *Psychology and the Internet: Intrapersonal, interpersonal and transpersonal implications* (pp. 143-168). New York: Academic Press.

Palinkas, L. A. 1989. Sociocultural influences on psychosocial adjustment in Antarctica. *Medical Anthropology, 10,* 235-246.

Palinkas, L. A. 1991. Group adaptation and individual adjustment in Antarctica: A summary of recent research. In: A. A. Harrison, Y. A. Clearwater, & C. P. McKay, eds., *From Antarctica to outer space: Life in isolation and confinement* (pp. 239-251). New York: Springer-Verlag.

Palinkas, L. A. 1992. Going to extremes: The cultural context of stress, illness and coping in Antarctica. *Social Science and Medicine, 35*(5), 651-664.

Palinkas, L. A., & D. Browner. 1995. Effects of prolonged isolation in extreme environments on stress, coping, and depression. *Journal of Applied Social Psychology, 25*(7), 557-576.

Pesavento, P. 2000. From *Aelita* to the *International Space Station*: The psychological and social effects of isolation on Earth and in space. *Quest: The History of Spaceflight Quarterly* [University of North Dakota], *8*:2:4-23.

Pierce, C. M. 1991. Theoretical approaches to adaptation to Antarctica and space. In: A. A. Harrison, Y. A. Clearwater, & C. P. McKay, eds., *From Antarctica to outer space: Life in isolation and confinement* (pp. 125-133). New York: Springer-Verlag.

Puskeppeleit, M. 1994 The all-female expedition: A personal perspective. In: K. Edwards & R. Graham, *Gender on ice: Proceedings of a Conference on Women in Antarctica*, held in Hobart, Tasmania, under the auspices of the Australian Antarctic Foundation, 19-21 August 1993 (pp. 75-81). Canberra: Australian Government Publishing Service.

Strollo, F., G. Riondino, B. Harris, G. Strollo, E. Casarosa, N. Mangrossa, C. Ferretti, & M. Luisi. 1998 (February). The effect of microgravity on testicular androgen secretion. *Aviation, Space, and Environmental Medicine, 69*(2), 133-136.

Stuster, J. 1996. *Bold endeavors: Lessons from polar and space exploration.* Annapolis, MD: Naval Institute Press.

Taylor, A. J. W. 1991. The research program of the International Biomedical Expedition in the Antarctic (IBEA) and its implications for research in outer space. In: A. A. Harrison, Y. A. Clearwater, & C. P. McKay, eds., *From Antarctica to outer space: Life in isolation and confinement* (pp. 43-55). New York: Springer-Verlag.

UNAIDS. 2002. *Epidemiological fact sheets by country.* Geneva, Switzerland: Joint United Nations Programme on HIV/AIDS (UNAIDS/WHO). Available: http://www.unaids.org/hivaidsinfo/statistics/fact_sheets/index_en.htm.

# Papua New Guinea

Shirley Oliver-Miller*
*Comments by Edgar Gregerson, Ph.D.*

## Contents

(CIA 2002)

## Demographics and a Brief Historical Perspective

ROBERT T. FRANCOEUR

### A. Demographics

Papua New Guinea (PNG) occupies the eastern half of the island of New Guinea, the world's second-largest island, in the southwest Pacific Ocean, north of eastern Australia's Captain Cook Peninsula. The Indonesian province of Irian Jaya occupies the island's western half. To the east are the Melanesian and Solomon Islands and the Coral Sea. North and east of New Guinea are about 600 islands in the Bismarck Archipelago, including Manus, New Britain, New Ireland, Bougainville, and the northern part of the Solomon Islands, which are also part of Papua New Guinea. The total territory of Papua New Guinea is 178,700 square miles (462,840 km²), making it about a tenth larger than California in the United States. Most of the main island, especially the interior, remains isolated from outside contact by rugged mountains, deep gorges, and swamps. The mainland's high plateau climate is temperate, contrasting with the tropical climate of the coastal plains. Two major rivers, the Sepik and the Fly, are navigable to shallow-draft vessels.

In the past, the very rugged topography of Papua New Guinea made communication and movement from one place to the next very difficult. This resulted in extraordinary variations in attitudes, behavior, ethnic groups, culture, traditions, customs, religion, and linguistics throughout the country. There are more than 850 spoken languages in Papua New Guinea. Only 1% to 2% of the people speak English, the official language, but Tok Pigin English is widely spoken. Only 15% of Papuans live in the few cities, about a quarter of a million in the administrative center of

Port Moresby. The majority of the people make their living in small-scale agriculture, although only 1% of the land is devoted to permanent crops and a negligible percent of the land is arable. The large majority of Papuans live in villages with settlements averaging about 800 persons. Many live in scattered homesteads with residents numbering no more than five to ten. The average-size village is about 200 to 300 people, located within a half-hour's walk to other neighboring villages.

In July 2002, Papua New Guinea had an estimated population of 5.17 million. (All data are from *The World Factbook 2002* (CIA 2002) unless otherwise stated.)

**Age Distribution and Sex Ratios**: *0-14 years*: 38.6% with 1.03 male(s) per female (sex ratio); *15-64 years*: 57.7% with 1.07 male(s) per female; *65 years and over*: 3.7% with 0.9 male(s) per female; *Total population sex ratio*: 1.05 male(s) to 1 female

**Life Expectancy at Birth**: *Total Population*: 63.46 years; *male*: 61.39 years; *female*: 65.64 years

**Urban/Rural Distribution**: 15% to 85%

**Ethnic Distribution**: Predominantly Melanesian in the northeast, and Papuan mainly in the south and the interior, with some Negrito, Micronesian, and Polynesian.**

**Religious Distribution**: indigenous religions: 33%; Roman Catholic: 22%; Lutheran: 18%; other Christian: 28%

**Birth Rate**: 31.61 births per 1,000 population. Experts project that if the high rates of fertility persist, the population will double by the year 2020.

**Death Rate**: 7.75 per 1,000 population

**Infant Mortality Rate**: 56.53 deaths per 1,000 live births

**Net Migration Rate**: 0 migrant(s) per 1,000 population

**Total Fertility Rate**: 4.21 children born per woman

**Population Growth Rate**: 2.39%

*Communications: Shirley Oliver-Miller, 6 Calumet Court, Dix Hill, New York 11746 USA; somatppnyc@aol.com. Comments: Edgar Gregerson, Ph.D., 302 West 12th Street, NYC 10014, USA; eagqc@qcvaxa.acc.qc.edu.

This overview of some attitudes and practices of the people of Papua New Guinea as they relate to sexuality is based on the author's own work experience in PNG over three years, her interviews with Papua New Guineans, studies done in Papua New Guinea, and current anthropological literature.

**Melanesians, Micronesians, and Polynesians constitute the three main ethnic groups in Oceania in the central and south Pacific. The brown-skinned Polynesians occupy the most-eastern islands of Oceania, from Hawaii to New Zealand, including Tahiti, Samoa, and Hawaii. The Micronesians inhabit the islands north of the equator and east of the Philippines, including the Mariana, Caroline, and Marshall Islands. The dark-skinned, frizzy-haired Melanesians occupy the islands in the south Pacific northeast of Australia.

**HIV/AIDS** (1999 est.): *Adult prevalence*: 0.22%; *Persons living with HIV/AIDS*: 5,400; *Deaths*: 450. (For additional details from www.UNAIDS.org, see end of Section 10B.)

**Literacy Rate** (*defined as those age 15 and over who can read and write*): 52%, with 65% of the children attending primary school and 13% in secondary school. Illiteracy is disproportionately high among females.

**Per Capita Gross Domestic Product** (*purchasing power parity*): $2,200 (2000 est.); *Inflation*: 10.3%; *Unemployment*: NA; *Living below the poverty line*: 37%

The country's health indices remain an abiding source of concern. Less well documented quantifiably, but widely acknowledged by healthcare providers and researchers, is the rapid proliferation of sexually transmitted infections (STIs/ STDs) and AIDS, as random sexual contacts both within and outside marriage increase.

Like other developing nations, internal migration from rural communities has resulted in rapidly expanding urban populations. Although 85% of Papua New Guinea's population lives in isolated rural areas, urban values exert very strong influences in the village communities. People seeking a better life in the city find few employment opportunities. Many have resorted to crime as one way to survive. Today, violence in Papua New Guinea has become a dominant and critical reality in the country.

## B. A Brief Historical Perspective

New Guinea, the world's second-largest island, was settled many thousands of years ago by waves of Papuans and Melanesian migrants. These many waves of immigration developed into hundreds of diverse, mutually hostile tribes of hunters and small cultivators, each with their own language. The eastern half of the island of New Guinea was first visited by Portuguese and Spanish explorers in the 16th century, but the Europeans did not become established there until the 19th century, when the island was divided between the Dutch in the west (the current Indonesian Irian Jaya), and the Germans and the British to the east. In 1884, Germany declared the northern coast a German protectorate. Britain followed suit in the south. Both nations then formally annexed their protectorates. In 1901, Britain transferred its territory to the newly independent Australia. During World War I, Australian troops invaded German New Guinea and maintained control under a League of Nations mandate that eventually became a United Nations trusteeship that incorporated a territorial government in the southern region known as Papua.

Australia granted the territory limited home rule in 1951, and autonomy for internal affairs in 1960. The country attained independence September 16, 1975, when the United Nations' trusteeship under Australia ended. In February 1990, guerrillas of the Bougainville Revolutionary Army (BRA) attacked plantations, forcing the evacuation of numerous workers. In May, the BRA declared Bougainville's independence, triggering a government blockade of the island until a peace treaty was signed in January 1991. However, the independence rebels still threaten and limit foreign investment on Bougainville.

## 1. Basic Sexological Premises

### A. Character of Gender Roles

The societies of Papua New Guinea are male-dominated and the attitudes of men toward women, on the whole, are poor. Women are valued as objects to be owned by men along with pigs and gardens; hence, few women exercise any real sort of power or control over their lives. Men are hunters and warriors; women are laborers, gardeners, and mothers who bring food to the men's house. The penis makes a man incapable of doing onerous gardening and tending the crops of edible sweet potatoes. Cultural tradition makes women subservient and responsive to male needs.

Whereas women's roles are clearly defined, men suffer from the loss of their traditional roles in defending their clan and land. The government of Papua New Guinea has now usurped these powers. Many young men find themselves unemployed and alienated from the society at large. Their capacity to produce income, the single most important prerequisite to securing a lasting relationship, remains the most difficult objective to achieve. These factors combine to make a very negative climate for gender equity both within and outside sexual relationships.

There are many examples of the low status of women in Papua New Guinea, not the least being the extent of violence used against them by males who exert authority and control, batter, and rape them. These social dynamics also contribute to the high risk for STD, including HIV infection, as well as adolescent pregnancy. While babies born out of wedlock are generally absorbed into the extended family without rancor, many girls drop out of school and otherwise foreclose their life options in terms of education and employment. Despite increasing educational opportunities, women continue to take a back seat to men in many aspects of development. Most men view women's development as breaking a longstanding taboo tantamount to entering "a man's house" in a rural culture where men and women, including married couples, often live segregated lives.

Although government officials and community members alike express private concern over adolescent sexual behavior and teen violence in general, a larger programmatic response has yet to be forthcoming.

### B. Sociolegal Status of Males and Females

Whereas the vast majority of cultures around the world and in Papua New Guinea adhere to a gender- and sex-dimorphic paradigm in which only males and females are recognized, the Sambians of Papua New Guinea's eastern highlands are among the interesting minority of societies that accept three sex categories: male, female, and a "third sex" or hermaphrodite. Classic examples of "third-sex persons" include the *hijra* of India, the *berdache* of American Indian and Eskimo societies, the *acaults* of Myanmar, the *kathoey* of Thailand, the *vehine* of Polynesia, and the *fa'afafine* of Samoa.

The Sambian third-sexed persons, known as *kwolu-aatmwol* ("male thing-transforming-into-female thing") or *turnim man* ("expected to become a man"), are the result of a rare genetic variation known as delta-4-steroid-5-alpha-reductase deficiency, or DHT (dihydrotestosterone) deficiency, first reported in the Dominican Republic as *gueve-doces* by Imperato-McGinley (1974) (Francoeur et al. 1995; Herdt 1981, 1984a, 1987, 1990; Money & Ehrhardt 1972). Individuals with DHT deficiency lack the gene necessary to produce the 5-alpha reductase enzyme that converts testosterone into dihydrotestosterone (DHT), the hormone that causes the undifferentiated external genitals of a fetus in its third month to differentiate as a penis and scrotum. As a result, during pregnancy, the external structures differentiate more or less as a female clitoris and labia. Given this pseudo-female appearance at birth, Sambian parents of such a child may identify and raise the newborn as female or male. However, the pubertal surge of testosterone causes the pseudo-female external genitals to more or less convert to male structures, along with the deepening of the voice, male facial, pubic, and axial body hair, penile enlargement, and labio-scrotal fusion (Gregersen 1996, 84).

Unlike the Dominican society, which celebrates the pubertal conversion of a *guevedoces* "daughter" into a son, the patriarchal Sambians are much less comfortable with their third-sexed offspring, even though their ability to function as a male would seem to be considerably more attractive in terms of personal power and prestige. Sambians, however, regard a newborn with ambiguous genitals as a boy with a defect, who is rejected by both parents, teased, and humiliated. After transformation at puberty, the male becomes the fellator (giver) in the sequential bisexual life of a male. When raised as males from birth and later married, they were rejected by their wives as unsatisfying. When raised as girls and married, they were soon rejected by their outraged husbands who found testes and a small penis within the labia when they attempted to have vaginal intercourse (see Section 6, Homoerotic, Homosexual, and Bisexual Behaviors).

### C. General Concepts of Sexuality and Love

In several highland Papuan societies, incest restrictions dictate that wives must be taken from other clans. But, because relationships between different clans are often so hostile as to verge on warfare, men who abduct women from hostile clans trigger armed retaliation and counter-abductions, which result in an endless cycle. "Marriage in these societies, and the sexual relationships within marriage," according to Davenport (1997, 126), "are always fraught with fear, hostility and anger."

The Dobo, who live on a small island off the coast of the main island, live in constant fear of sorcery from their wives. Because they believe that they are particularly vulnerable during intercourse, Dobo men have to continually weigh their need for sexual gratification against the possibility of sorcery when they try to satisfy their sexual need (Davenport 1997, 126)

## 2. Religious, Ethnic, and Gender Factors Affecting Sexuality

### A. Source and Character of Religious Values

After a century of Christian missionary influence, most of the indigenous ethnic-based rituals and customs described in the next section no longer exist. Today, Christianity dominates in Papua New Guinea, although a third of the people still practice traditional indigenous religions, especially in the remote mountainous areas.

### B. Character of Ethnic Values

Before the 1900s, no Papuan traveled too far from home for fear of being killed or even eaten by more distant neighbors, suggesting that marriage patterns were likely to have been locally endogamous. As most villages are composed of multi-clan hamlets, one might marry a spouse from another hamlet within the same village. The most common marriage pattern was based on the requirement that one must marry outside of one's clan, most of which were patrilineal. For the most part, marriage patterns still show couples come from the same contiguous villages. In the past, unmarried people from neighboring villages gathered together in courting rituals that included dance, song, and pair bonding. Married men looking for a second or third wife also participated in this ritual.

The following examples illustrate the wide range of traditional ethnic factors influencing the sexual attitudes and behavior of the diverse groups in Papua New Guinea. Contact with Western and other outside cultures are altering many of these patterns classic in the anthropology literature of the area, but to what extent in individual tribal cultures is not evident from the anthropological record pieced together over the last century.

- In the Eastern and Central Highlands, elders chaperoned festivities, which allowed young people from neighboring villages to sit opposite each other in pairs and rub legs, cheeks, or noses while they engaged in singing.
- In the Simbai areas of the Highlands, men adorned with heavy shiny beetle-decorated headdresses came together to dance in a ritual that lasted all night. A woman could take her pick of men during the night and the couple would then disappear into the nearby bushes. In the morning, women carrying men's headdresses were clearly visible. Each couple then went to the man's house, and word was sent to the woman's parents to come to discuss a brideprice. She may have never seen the man before that evening, but, as they were all from nearby villages, the sexual pool was still quite localized.
- In the Trobriand Islands of Papua New Guinea, courting parties were openly explicit sexual events. Boys were called out from villages A and B to have sex with the girls from village C; the host and guest roles were reversed on the next occasion. Public events of sexual mixing among adults were also permissible in some areas. These open sexual events took place only on special occasions, as rituals of reversal, fertility, or renewal, allowing people to have sex with those with whom they ordinarily had no sexual rights, e.g., the spouses of other men and persons within proscribed kinship relationships.
- Plural copulation or group sex was also a traditional pattern in some areas, and took the form of a single woman having sexual intercourse with a series of men in tandem. Among the Ok of the Highlands and the Sepik on the North Coast, this was done as a punitive measure (e.g., Ok, Highlands, and Sepik, North Coast) and in others, it was an honor (e.g., Papuan Coast).
- In the Eastern Highlands, Papuan Plateau, and Papuan Coast, there were also male initiations, which required insemination, either anally or orally, by elder males initiating younger males.
- Every Banaro man has a "ritual brother" as a sort of alter ego with whom he shares mutual access to each other's wives. The Banaro also require that a bride's first intercourse be performed by her husband's father's ritual brother (Davenport 1977, 144).
- Among the Fasu of the Southern Highlands, older males had sex with younger males with less ceremony, but still within the context of traditional relationships and ideology.
- The Enga of the Highlands firmly believed that men and women differed in many fundamental ways. Because of these fundamental differences, contact with menstrual discharge could contaminate a man and cause illness, weakness, and even death. But reality told them they could not avoid all contamination, so males and females were highly segregated. The Enga men needed some sexual outlet, for their own release and to produce offspring, so single men almost never engaged in heterosexual intercourse, and married men only reluctantly did so with their wives. Purification rituals were important (Davenport 1997, 136).
- The Wógeo added to the Enga menstrual taboo the belief that men in a trance or sacred state were dangerous to women. The sacred state was in fact an imitative menstruation, induced by hacking the penis until it bled freely and was thus purified. This periodic male bleeding rid the body of contaminations received from women. Unlike the Enga, the Wógeo did not avoid heterosexual intercourse to avoid contamination (Davenport 1977, 136).
- The Manus treated all aspects of sex as ugly and shameful. Even marital intercourse was sinful, degrading, and

to be engaged in only in strict privacy. Women considered intercourse an abomination they endured, however painfully, until they produced a child. The sexuality of men was considered brutish. Sex outside marriage offended the sensibilities of watchful spirits and triggered supernaturally ordained punishments. Sexual talk was not heard, and women were so secretive about their menses that Manus men denied women ever experienced such a thing as a monthly period (Davenport 1977, 115, 123-124).

In the exuberance of mid-20th-century anthropological research, considerable cultural data, much of it related to sexual beliefs, attitudes, and behavior, were gathered by cultural anthropologists, led by Bronislaw Malinowski (1927) and Margaret Mead (1930, 1935).

One of their favorite subjects was the Melanesian matriarchal Trobriand Islanders, off the eastern end of New Guinea. Trobriand Islanders not only view the expression of sexuality with great favor, they are also quite comfortable with pre- and extramarital affairs, provided these respect certain incest and age taboos. Trobriand Islanders make frequent and open use of love magic to make themselves irresistibly attractive to desired partners. With a few slight alterations in the love magic formulae, they have an equally irresistible aid for their famous overseas exchange system known as *kula* (Davenport 1977, 131, 245; Gregersen 1996, 268).

Most of these tribal patterns of sexual activity were rationalized as mechanisms to gather the spiritual force residing in sexual fluids, i.e., sexual power, and redirect it to social and material aims, such as improving the growth of boys or strengthening the clan's reproductive powers, both human and agricultural. These belief systems nearly always had within them a strong component of female pollution and associated behavioral taboos. Colonial contacts in the 19th century and expanded contact with outsiders in recent decades have changed many of the tribal customs so carefully documented by anthropologists. Whatever the extent of enculturation, and regardless of how unchanged these customs remain in the remote and inaccessible regions of Papua New Guinea, their record is important in understanding how sexual diversity plays out within the social fabric of individual functioning societies.

## 3. Knowledge and Education about Sexuality

### A. Government Policies and Programs

Recently, the Papua New Guinea government implemented a pilot Adolescent Sexuality and Reproductive Health Project, which targets adolescents, church groups, and teachers/lecturers. The program addresses a myriad of issues around sexuality, morality, reproductive health, STDs/AIDS, prevention of rape/child molestation/domestic violence/drug abuse, value clarification, decision making, and how to talk about sex (traditionally a taboo topic) with others. The project is the first of its kind in Papua New Guinea. Although it is too early to tell what impact the project will have, thus far, students, teachers, parents, and the church community (interdenominational) have welcomed the opportunity to learn more facts about sexuality, reproductive health issues, and the skills to communicate with others about sensitive topics.

### B. Informal Sources of Sexual Knowledge

It is important to acknowledge that sexuality education to a greater or lesser degree has always existed in cultures around the world. Culture and traditions are vehicles by which sexuality information and knowledge are transmit-

ted. We tend to forget that there have always been systems that controlled sexual behaviors. The erosion of cultural norms, coupled with today's health concerns about teen pregnancy, maternal and child spacing, sexually transmitted infections, AIDS, rape, child molestation, and domestic violence, have made talking about sex very controversial. It is clear that former systems no longer provide effective approaches to addressing social problems.

Parents make an effort to teach their children what is socially acceptable and what is not in all areas of life, including the sexual. When young people go away to school, it is very difficult for parents to maintain constant input over the years when their children are becoming sexually mature. Instead, their peers have the most influence. Even when children remain at home, peer pressure is often stronger than the influence of parents.

This is true in most societies today. Some parents attempt to strengthen their teachings about proper morality by insisting their children attend church. When parents themselves are sincere followers and doers of the teachings of the church, this has the most effect. But where the church is simply used as another means of control by parents who themselves practice behaviors considered improper by the church, children will not listen. Although sex is a biological drive, all sexual behavior must be learned.

In some communities, young people have few examples of responsible sexual behavior to follow. From childhood, they repeatedly hear tales about who slept with whose wife, who was raped, and who got pregnant out of wedlock. These events are often the subject of public discussions at court hearings and in community gossip. The usual outcome is that someone must pay someone else a fine. Single or married men who make a young girl pregnant are rarely publicly criticized, even though people may talk about them behind their backs.

Knowledge about sexuality and reproductive health is generally low throughout Papua New Guinea at all ages. Younger people have slightly better access to information than did most of their parents. Information levels are higher in cities and towns than in villages. Some parents, especially in the villages, persist in telling their teenagers as little as possible about sex and reproduction. They continue to say that babies come from the garden or from stones, or offer other fanciful explanations. Unfortunately, parents' notions that keeping their children ignorant about sex will keep them from trying sex is completely without foundation. In all areas, the average age at first sexual intercourse is about 15 or 16 for both sexes. This means that many try their first sexual intercourse quite a bit younger than 15, as well as some at ages 17 to 19. [*Comment 2000*: The age of first intercourse is likely earlier than just stated. (*End of comment by E. Gregerson*)] Few enter a sexual relationship with any knowledge of contraception or STDs.

After a girl has her first menstruation, throughout the country, she is warned to stay away from boys or it will lead to pregnancy. But little else is revealed. Sometimes a grandmother or other relative decides to give a traditional contraceptive spell or herb to a young woman. This is reported to be more common if the girl is in school. Occasionally, a schoolteacher or a kinswoman who is a nurse explains more to a young woman and even helps her obtain modern contraception. But, for the vast majority, the early years of sexual activity are the most dangerous, because the elders have not considered sex one of life's most powerful drives, as a topic to be discussed with young people. With few exceptions, neither the schools nor the churches carry out adequate sex education early enough to be of any value. By the time sexual reproduction is discussed in high school, nearly half of the young people have already begun having sexual intercourse. The health services do not make contraceptives accessible to young people. The result is many unwanted teenage pregnancies and STDs, including HIV. The known age distribution of HIV and AIDS cases up to 1995 in Papua New Guinea, compared to other islands in the Pacific with numerous cases, demonstrates this clearly.

Arguments against sex education, whether in the home or within an institution such as a school or church, focus on the fear that information will increase the desire for sexual experimentation. Evidence from studies conducted in several different countries point in the opposite direction. If young people are given adequate sex education, those who have not yet begun often delay starting, and those who have started do not increase their sexual activities. In either case, both groups are better informed about the pleasures and risks of sex. If sex education is carried out properly, they will then know how to have safer sex.

In *Sexual Networks and Sexual Cultures in Contemporary Papua New Guinea*, Carol Jenkins (1996), principal research fellow with the Papua New Guinea Institute of Medical Research (in Goroka), noted that:

> only a minority of young people reported learning about sex through the school system or from their parents. Most girls and boys first learn from older female or male relatives or friends. Sitting around and telling stories about sex is a favorite pastime of teenagers of both sexes. More than any other factor, this activity spurs the imagination. Many times older young people deliberately try to persuade younger ones to try sex. Cousins, in particular, often help set up the first sexual encounters for their younger relatives. Sometimes cousins are the first sexual partners. On a world scale, this pattern is not unusual. It is unlikely, however, that older relatives and friends raised under similar conditions represent a good source of information.

Until recently, Papua New Guinea has remained isolated from the rest of the world. Today, Papua New Guinea struggles with all the influences and trappings of modern-day society, including radio, television, drugs, computers, videos, MTV, written literature, pornography, rape, child molestation, domestic violence, commercial sex workers, and so on. As more and more people are exposed to modernization, there is an emerging culture whose sexual practices are becoming fairly homogenized.

Agricultural and mining industries require travel to and from rural areas, and this greatly contributes to the diffusion of new ideas. Media, especially video and pornographic magazines, also play a large part in changing sex practices and attitudes. Some copy what they see and learn in urban centers, whereas others condemn what they see. In either case, the eroticism of more complex and commercial societies, both Asian and Western, presents issues of contention in sexuality to Papua New Guinea.

## 4. Autoerotic Behaviors and Patterns

Although it is seldom discussed, masturbation is widespread and generally considered harmless but wasteful, particularly for boys. Therefore, the overwhelming pressure, when sexually aroused, is to find a partner of the opposite sex immediately. In some cases, this may lead to rape. Rape is very common in Papua New Guinea and can occur without the aid of pornography, simply because violence against women in Papua New Guinea is widespread and unopposed by strong cultural or legal norms (see Section 8A, Significant Unconventional Sexual Behaviors, Coercive Sex, below).

## 5. Interpersonal Heterosexual Behaviors

### A. Children

Trobrianders, and likely other Papua New Guinea societies, approve of imitative copulation or sex rehearsal play about age 10 or 11 (Davenport 1977, 150).

### B. Adolescents

*First Intercourse and Premarital Sex*

The initiation of first sexual intercourse among young people today takes place around the age of 15 for both girls and boys in both urban and rural areas. In general, virginity is not highly valued, but rather society denounces premenarcheal sexual intercourse for girls and getting pregnant before proper marriage arrangements, i.e., a brideprice, are made. In rural areas where traditional menarcheal seclusion ceremonies are still maintained, young men, often accompanied by their parents, begin to seek a young woman's interests as soon as she is allowed out of seclusion. Unless she is in school, a young woman is considered ready for sex and marriage immediately after menarche. And, as the age of menarche declines, so has the age of first sexual experience. Most rural girls experience their first sexual encounter willingly with young men slightly older than themselves from nearby villages. Others are forced into sex or raped. According to one study, 17% in a sample of 116 women said their first sex was with a boy they had just met, while only 8% had their first sex with an older man.

Studies conducted by the Papua New Guinea Institute of Medical Research indicate that nearly half of all adolescents in the country are sexually active by the age of 16, and by the age of 20, nearly a third studied reported having had at least one STD. Evidence suggests that sexual activity occurs among girls as young as 14, whose physiological immaturity and poor coping skills place them at particular risk for STDs and HIV.

Following the first experience of sexual intercourse, options for new and different sex partners increase. Young women fantasize that they will be rescued from the labor of rural subsistence farming, and hope for a man with a job, a permanent house, and car in town. Poor rural parents also want their daughters to "marry up," which usually means marrying a man from town. Approximately 25% of young women take married men as partners. Half of the women between the ages of 15 and 24 in our recent study of youth stated that they accepted cash, gifts, or both in exchange for sex. In the national study conducted in 1991, 66% of the women under 25 ($n = 33$) and 43% of those over that age ($n = 37$) had exchanged sex for goods. These young women do not see themselves as sex workers, although they say they earn some of their income through sex (see also Section 8B, Significant Unconventional Sexual Behaviors, Prostitution).

Young men are equally subject to earlier biological maturation, and the adolescent male is no longer subject to the dominating control of elder males as expressed through male initiation rituals. Few societies have maintained these rites of passage, and where they do exist, they are very much altered. Consequently, boys are free to experiment with sex more or less as they choose. Older siblings frequently teach a younger boy about sex in explicit ways, sometimes setting up a woman with whom he can "try his luck," often in a group situation. Two studies suggest some boys first have anal intercourse with each other several years before having intercourse with a female.

Whereas parents are concerned about the health of the mother and infant, they are more concerned about ensuring economic commitment from the purported father of the child.

Young people receive subliminal messages that say, a little sex is all right, but not too much with the same person. Long-term sexual involvement with a single partner implies the likelihood of pregnancy and is definitely to be avoided unless one is ready for commitment. Many people believe that pregnancy cannot take place unless a man has sexual intercourse with a woman at least six or more times. Hence, many girls and boys are taught to change partners frequently.

The sexuality of young, unmarried women is placed under fewer constraints than married women. Young women recognize this and seek to enjoy as many partners as possible while they remain unmarried. Whereas most Papua New Guinea societies do not allow a young girl to have sex before the onset of menstruation, Trobriand Islanders allow sex before menarche. First cousins may have temporary premarital affairs but can never marry (Davenport 1977, 145). [*Comment 2000*: However, certain kinds of first-cousin marriages may be permitted, such as a marriage with a child of one's mother's brother or one's father's sister (*End of comment by E. Gregerson*)]

### Courtship

Although Papua New Guineans still have widespread traditional sexual beliefs, practices, and unique customs, which differ by region and language areas, traditional courting customs have often been replaced with disco dances, CDs, cassette players, loudspeakers, alcohol, marijuana, and other recreational drugs. Anyone can enter a disco. This marks a major shift from the controlled courting practices in the past.

### A Puberty Ritual: Obligatory Universalized Transitional Homosexuality

Gilbert Herdt (1981, 1984a, 1987, 1990) and other anthropologists have reported on a pederastic puberty ritual shared by 30 to 50 Melanesian and New Guinea cultures that may be historically related to similar practices that developed among aboriginal Australians some 10,000 years ago. The focus of intense speculation by anthropologists and fierce opposition from Western governments and missionaries, these ritualized homosexual relationships are a necessary part of the coming-of-age training for boys. Their basis is the belief that boys do not produce their own semen and must get it from older men by "drinking semen," i.e., playing the recipient role in oral-genital sex or anal sex before puberty and during adolescence. This is the opposite of the traditional Western view in which the recipient (insertee) of anal or oral sex is robbed of his manhood.

Societies with this ritual practice characteristically maintain:

1. extreme social differences between men and women, with women clearly in an inferior status;
2. the blood of men and women are not ritually differentiated, but their semen and milk are; and
3. marriage often involves men exchanging sisters with no special marriage payment.

Other societies in the same area that do not share these beliefs or ritual pederasty are more likely to view menstrual blood as extremely dangerous and/or require a "bride price" to legitimize a marriage (Gregersen 1996, 274-276).

According to the Sambian people of the Eastern Highlands of Papua New Guinea, a young boy must be fed women's milk in order to grow until he approaches puberty, when the men of the village must rescue him from the society of women and feed him men's milk (semen). To trigger puberty and enable a youth to become a mature macho head-hunter, he needs the semen of mature youths and unmarried

men provided by young bachelors. After eight to ten years of exclusive homosexual relationships, the 19-year-old youth has completed his defining rite of passage and is ready to marry (McWhirter et al. 1990, 42-43) (see Section 6, Homoerotic, Homosexual, and Bisexual Behaviors).

### C. Adults

*Marital Relationships and Sexuality*

See Sections 1C, Basic Sexological Premises, General Concepts of Sexuality and Love, and 2A, Religious and Ethnic Factors Affecting Sexuality, Source and Character of Religious Values.

*Marriage and "Ritual Brothers"*

Among the Banaro of Papua New Guinea, every male has a "ritual brother," a kind of alter ego, as a companion and support throughout life. Every ritual brother is allowed sexual access to his "brother's" wife. This is not, in our Western sense, "extramarital" sex, because the ritual brother is in some ritually real way the other man, the husband, and so is entitled to have sex with his alter ego's wife. The ritual brother also plays a role in Banaro marriages. The bride's first intercourse after marriage must be performed by the ritual brother of her husband's father, i.e., the father-in-law's ritual brother). In the Banaro society, it is the social father, not the procreative or biological father, who is important (Davenport 1977, 144).

*Coital Positions*

Christian missionaries are commonly credited (or blamed) for trying to impose the male-superior coital position on the natives they evangelized, because they considered it "the natural and normal coital position." However, they do not deserve credit for its origins, which historians have traced back to the Stoics of ancient Rome and the early Egyptians, [*Comment 2000*: despite some modern assertions to the contrary. (*End of comment by E. Gregerson*)] Although popular in Western cultures, the male-superior position has not been adopted by the people of Oceania, despite Western advocates. In fact, the people of Oceania commonly view the male-above position as impractical and improper, placing too much weight on the woman, and are uncompromising in recognizing only two natural copulatory positions. The Dobuana and the Wógeo of Papua New Guinea prefer the rear-entry position, with the man standing behind the woman while she bends over and rests his hands on her knees. Also popular is the "Oceanic position," in which the man squats or kneels between the spread legs of his partner who lies on her back. He then pulls her towards himself and completes the intercourse. In a variation of this position, the woman lies on her back and keeps her knees up (Davenport 1977, 150).

One benefit of this position is that it can be carried out with minimal body contact, "which encourages young people to have sex with ugly and older partners. On the other hand, as Malinowski has expressed it: '. . . where love exists, the man can bend over the woman or the woman can raise herself to meet him and contact can be as full and intimate as is desired'" (Davenport 1977, 148; Gregersen 1996, 5, 67). The Tallensi point out another possible advantage (or disadvantage), in that this position enables the woman to push the man over with a kick.

*Premarital Pregnancy, Ritual Multiple Intercourse, and Extramarital Sex*

A single mother often gives her child to her parents or another relative to rear and she continues with her single lifestyle. When a married man sleeps with a woman other than his wife, it is hardly noticed. If a woman is caught having sex with a man other than her husband, she is beaten. On the whole, sexual infidelity does not cause martial breakups and life continues. In some communities, other sexual issues are more disturbing than sexual infidelity.

Colonial influences have changed the lives of the Marínd-aním, a former headhunting people of southern Papua New Guinea, but some of their customs likely continue in remote areas. One tradition involved an unusual ritual of extramarital sex. Traditionally, Marínd-aním men and women live in separate housing in their small villages, even after marriage, and always engage in marital sex outside in the bush. Immediately after a wedding ceremony, a few older women take the bride to a place they have prepared outside the village, where the bride has sexual intercourse with the male members of her husband's clan before the groom is allowed to copulate with his wife. These ritual multiple intercourses, *otiv-bombari*, may extend over several nights. Although not particularly satisfying for the wife, this sequential group sex is repeated at various specified occasions, when a woman returns from her seclusion after delivering a baby, when her husband's friends come to visit, or when another man gives the husband a gift of tools or food.

> Apart from this custom, most [Marínd-aním] marriages are monogamous and break up rarely. The rule is apparently that affection and love exist between the spouses, and the husband may get violently jealous if his wife should have secret sexual relations with a man without prearrangements and the husband's consent.
>
> Extramarital relations are not supposed to become love affairs. They have the character of a ritual. The birth rate is low. *Otiv-bombari* are supposed to make women fertile. They are also used to collect semen, for semen is considered the essence of life, health and prosperity. Semen discharged from the vagina is ritually prized. After an *otiv bombari* it is collected in a coconut bowl to be used in food or medicine, and for body creams. . . .
>
> Contemporaneously with marriage and heterosexual relations, men have also homosexual relations with young and adolescent boys while the younger ones are passing through an institutionalized phase of homosexuality. Here then one has a society in which the men but not the women are bisexual in experience, with some overlap from the homosexual to the heterosexual phase. (Money & Ehrhardt 1972, 132-135)

## 6. Homoerotic, Homosexual, and Bisexual Behaviors

### A. Children and Adolescents

Same-sex activities, boys with boys or girls with girls, are common in many Papuan societies, but they are generally viewed as play and meaningless, though somehow wrong. However, the ritualized pederasty for Sambian adolescents and their postmarital exclusive heterosexuality (see Section 5B, Interpersonal Heterosexual Behaviors, Adolescents) does raise a major question about the development of sexual orientation, or at least a question about the nature of erotic arousal.

> On the one hand, Herdt (1984, 1987) suggests that among the Sambia only about 5% of the male population become exclusively homosexual—virtually the same percentage Kinsey found for the United States where all homosexual acts are tabu. On the other hand, to discount homosexual arousal altogether in these institutionalized semen transfers seems unrealistic; slavish performance of a ritual does not produce erection and ejaculation unless an erotic component exists as well. (Gregersen 1996, 276)

[*Update 2002*: In the 1980s, classic anthropological reports of the Sambians of Papua New Guinea described a society in which young men fellated their elders in order to receive the masculinizing force of semen and thereby become men. When the boys grew up, they married, but now became the recipients of fellation by younger boys who ingested their semen. General terms like "ritualized homosexuality" and "semen drinking" were widely used by cultural anthropologists, even though attempts to describe this phenomenon with Western terms as a cultural lifecycle passing from "homosexuality" to "bisexuality" and "heterosexuality" suggested the inaccuracy of such terms/concepts. At the time, this "ritualized homosexuality" was conceptualized as a cultural rather than a sexual phenomenon. In his early studies of the Sambians, Gilbert Herdt (1981, 1987) viewed this sexual lifestyle as a classic social constructionist phenomenon that emphasized the *dissimilarity* of "gay types" across cultures. Herdt's follow-up studies in the late 1990s appear to support a modified essentialist view that emphasizes a *similarity* of "gay types" across cultures. In this more recent view, the ingestion of semen is not a variety of "homosexuality," but rather a variety of cultural masculinity.

[During fieldtrips back to Papua New Guinea in the 1990s, Herdt and his colleagues conducted interviews, gathered more data, and discovered that, in fact, there were some boys who had a real fondness for ingesting semen and who later had a real fondness for having their semen ingested, and did not marry. In other words, in the Sambian culture, all males were the recipients of "ritualized masculinization" in their adolescent years. As adults, they were expected to marry although they were now the ritual givers of semen. In this more nuanced description, most Sambian men can best be described as heterosexual males despite their teen years of "drinking masculine milk," their adult role as providers of masculinity, and their cultural distaste for marital relations. At the same time, there are also some Sambian males who can be described as homosexual in the Western use of that term, males who really enjoy giving and receiving fellatio with other males in a sexuoerotic way. (Herdt 1981, 1984ab, 1987, 1993, 49, 432-441, 444, R. Norton 2002 Personal communiqué via SexNet listserv). (*End of update by R. T. Francoeur*)]

[*Comment 2003*: Linguists and anthropologists have suggested that several thousand years ago, several different tribal groups arrived in New Guinea. Because they shared a similar language, they also shared some sexual practices in common, such as the belief that drinking semen is essential for a boy to become a man. The Sambians are not the only tribal group that practices semen drinking.

[Sometimes extensive taboos on heterosexual coitus exist, but none on homosexual contacts. This is true of the Étoro (Étolo) of New Guinea who taboo heterosexual contacts for between 205 and 260 days a year (an earlier account suggested as many as 295 days). Although hard and fast statistics are lacking about the degree to which these taboos are observed, the seasonal clustering of births suggests general compliance with the rules.

[None of these taboos holds for homosexual acts among the Étoro. In fact, they are positively encouraged because semen is seen as a life force, of which men have only a finite amount. Boys are believed to have no semen at all at birth. It is through oral insemination by older men that they acquire the necessary semen to become men and to provide life for their offspring. Consequently, boys between the ages of 10 and the mid-20s are continually inseminated by older men. Among the neighboring Marínd-aním, the cultural preference for homosexuality has allegedly helped produce so low a birthrate that to sustain the tribe, large numbers of children must be kidnapped from other groups and raised to become Marínd-aním.

[It is sometimes suggested that such homosexual rituals function as a kind of birth control. But more plausibly, they seem to provide a sexual outlet for males in an area with an unbalanced sex ratio (too many males) and the practice of older men of having many wives—very much like the situation among the Zande in Africa, who formerly had institutionalized pederastic marriages (Gregerson 1996, 276). (*End of comment by E. Gregerson*)]

An additional insight, offered by John Money suggests that:

> Institutionalized homosexuality, in serial sequence with institutionalized heterosexuality and marriage, as among the Sambia and other tribal peoples, must be taken into account in any theory that proposes to explain homosexuality. The theory will be deficient unless it also takes heterosexuality into account. Culturally institutionalized bisexuality signifies either that bisexuality is a universal potential to which any member of the human species could be acculturated or that bisexuality is a unique potential of those cultures whose members have become selectively inbred for it. There are no data that give conclusive and absolute support to either alternative. However, genetically pure inbred strains are an ideal of animal husbandry, not of human social and sexual interaction. Therefore, it is likely that acculturation to bisexuality is less a concomitant of inbreeding than it is of the bisexual plasticity of all members of the human species. It is possible that bisexual plasticity may vary over the life span. Later in life it may give way to exclusive monosexuality—or it may not. (Money 1990, 43)

Another aspect of this complex-orientations picture is the fact that in many South Pacific societies, for example, the Marínd-aním of southern Papua New Guinea and the (fictionally named) East Bay Melanesians, pubescent and adolescent boys are free to engage in homosexual relations with their peers and/or older married men. Unlike with the Sambia, these relationships are seldom exclusive or obligatory. In such societies, most men are more or less bisexual, and the women assumedly heterosexual (Beach 1976/1977; Marshall & Suggs 1971; Gregersen 1996, 276).

### B. Adults

The Trobriand Islanders admitted to Malinowski that homosexuality is contemptible, but also that it was formerly practiced (Gregersen 1996, 274). In general, the people of Papua New Guinea view homosexuality in a negative and unacceptable light. They cannot understand how a man might enjoy having sex with another man.

## 7. Gender Diversity and Transgender Issues

See the discussion of Sambian hermaphrodites, 5-alpha-reductase boy-girls, in Section 1B, Basic Sexological Premises, Sociolegal Status of Males and Females.

## 8. Significant Unconventional Sexual Behaviors

### A. Coercive Sex

*Rape*

To most young women today, a man with money, a car, or even a schoolboy with promise, is a far more attractive prospect than a poor boy with no obvious future. For many young men, having no money with which to buy sex

directly, or simply with which to make a girlfriend happy, is a frustrating state of affairs. Some such men state that there is no opportunity for them to have sex at all, unless they rape a woman. Group rape is less likely to lead to trouble than individual rape, although most men who state they rape women do both. Gregersen (1996, 149, 358) includes the Trobriand Islanders among the societies that simply prefer to ignore rape altogether.

Rape of any sort is disturbingly common in all areas of the country, rural, town, and city. In addition to commercial sex, there is the issue of "line-ups" or pack rapes. Often associated with "six-to-sixes" (clubs that remain open from 6 p.m. to 6 a.m.) or video showings that run from evening to dawn in both rural and urban areas, a group of men/boys take turns in forcing a woman to have sexual intercourse with them. As they watch each other, the sexual dynamics of rape and homosexuality mix to produce, for some, a highly erotic event. In some communities, line-ups are reported to take place every weekend. Older men, many of whom are married, are also frequently involved. Younger men and even boys of 11 or 12 are able to join with their elders in sexually abusing a woman. One young fellow of 17 years told me about his village:

> In here rape and forced sex exists just like in other parts of the province. It happens especially during disco nights and video shows. When we brought our village girls to the disco or video show, the boys from other places came and took our girls for dance and sometimes take them home to sleep with and have sex with. We thought they slept only with their friends, but somehow the boys arranged it with their village boys and made single file on them [line-up]. When the girls come back they never tell us about it because they are afraid and ashamed. Then we do the same to their sister in return. (Author's field notes)

This type of sexual behavior is extremely dangerous because the men involved are exposed to the semen of many of men, thus raising their risk of acquiring STDs and AIDS, not from the woman, but from the other men involved. The woman is placed at extremely high risk of acquiring STDs and HIV as well.

Many Papua New Guineans do not like to admit that such things are going on, but there is now a great deal of evidence from studies conducted in selected urban areas (i.e., Daru, Port Moresby, Lae, and Goroka) and many rural villages, indicating that such sexual activities are widespread. These sexual activities are highly dangerous from a public health point of view because they spread diseases very quickly, not just among the people who participate in them, but among all those other persons, wives and husbands, new and old boyfriends and girlfriends, with whom these people have sex. These activities are also responsible for many STDs, including HIV, among newborn babies.

### B. Prostitution

Across the country, people are complaining that more and more young women are having sex earlier, and often with older, married men. The lure of social status, drinking beer, going to dances or parties, the institution of the "six-to-six" clubs, and, increasingly, payment in cash and/or gifts, are drawing women into commercial sex. Papua New Guinea does not yet have a major brothel-based commercial sex industry, but it does have a large, highly dispersed population of women who are willing to sell sex and men willing to buy it.

Much of the activity among women is driven by poverty, some of which is severe. Single mothers, widows of all ages, urban married women whose husbands do not bring home enough money, and teenage girls everywhere are often poor in cash. There is little shame attached to selling sex in some communities, especially where the woman brings home the cash and food. Brothers, husbands, and other men in the family are often very willing to help a woman find a man who will pay for sex, especially if they can share the rewards. Young women are more saleable, and sometimes very young girls are offered to adult men for sex.

From their earliest contacts, outsiders and missionaries misinterpreted as promiscuity and/or prostitution the "casual" sexual relations and small gifts Trobrianders, and Papuans in general, offer their female partners. This is not the view of the Papua New Guinea people themselves, for whom sexual relations and small gifts do not carry the cultural messages of Western standards and norms. [*Comment 2000*: The contrast here is between the meanings and values insiders attach to some behavior and the way outsiders interpret this behavior from their "objective" perspective. The "objective" views of the outsiders represent what anthropologists label an etic view. In many, perhaps the majority, of customs, the "objective" etic view is quite different from the emic (insider) view of persons within the culture (Reiss 1997). (*End of comment by E. Gregerson*)]

### C. Pornography and Erotica

In most areas of Papua New Guinea today, pornographic magazines, picture books, and videos are available, despite laws to the contrary. Many adults and young people seem to enjoy looking at pictures of people having sex. They consider it educational, and given the dearth of printed or other media on sex, this is hardly surprising. To some young people, however, the experience is frightening, because they find themselves sexually aroused with little understanding of how to manage their desires.

### D. Paraphilias

In spite of fairly extensive reporting of sexual behavior in general, the paraphilia level for Oceania seems to be fairly low. Sexual contacts with animals has been reported in a few cultures, including the Marquesans, but such contacts are denied, condemned, or apparently unknown among the Wógeo and Trobrianders (Gregersen 1996, 278).

## 9. Contraception, Abortion, and Population Planning

### A. Contraception

Although male control over women is a significant factor in extramarital pregnancies and teen pregnancies, alcohol use by women and their inability to plan for protected intercourse are also factors. Condoms are readily available, but are deemed inappropriate for women to carry. Other contraceptive methods are unavailable and prohibitively expensive.

### B. Abortion

Abortion is illegal in Papua New Guinea and is considered to be morally wrong by the majority of the people. However, illegal abortions are increasing. It is not unusual to hear about young girls and older women inducing abortions. Many of these self-induced abortions result in serious infections and, on occasion, death. The methods of inducing abortions are done by ingesting certain mixtures or herbs, or inserting things into the vagina.

### C. Population Programs

Papua New Guinea health indices remain an abiding source of concern, with maternal mortality projected as high as 800 per 100,000 births and infant mortality at an underestimated 80 per 1,000 live births. Within the Action

Plan of the 1994 Cairo Conference on Population and Development, adolescent reproductive health is identified as a priority area. Hence, the government of Papua New Guinea, in collaboration with donor organizations, are launching programs to combat the spread of STDs, HIV/AIDS, and unplanned pregnancy, especially among young people.

## 10. Sexually Transmitted Diseases and HIV/AIDS

There is a National AIDS Committee in Papua New Guinea responsible for increasing public awareness and advocating prevention of HIV/AIDS and other sexually transmissible infections. Advocacy is done through media campaigns, advertisements, radio spots, local television, school curricula and classrooms, peer-education programs on university campuses, and community-outreach efforts, including training religious leaders about sexual and reproductive health issues.

Condoms are free but not always available. Efforts are presently underway to break through the walls of silence around issues related to sexuality and reproductive health. Although cultural taboos make this a challenging task, educators and service providers are making inroads by using culturally relevant videos and dramas on STDs and HIV/AIDS, and other related topic areas, to educate people about the facts.

[*Update 2002*: UNAIDS Epidemiological Assessment: The first HIV infections in Papua New Guinea were reported in 1987, with HIV prevalence increasing annually throughout the early 1990s. Reported cases are equally distributed among men and women, and infection appears to be concentrated in the capital city of Port Moresby. Prevalence remains low among blood donors (0.015% in 1997) and pregnant women (0.37% in 1998). The trend in the annually reported number of AIDS cases has continued to rise more sharply each year since the mid-1990s. Much higher levels of infection were found in female sex workers (17% in Port Moresby and 3% in Lae in 1998) and among patients attending STD clinics (7% in 1999, increasing from 3% in 1998 in Port Moresby, and from 0.7% to 1.2% in four other locations in 1997 to 1999). The estimated HIV prevalence in Papua New Guinea is, as of the end of 2001, about 16,000, or 0.5% of the total 15- to 49-year-old population, and continues to increase slowly, primarily because of heterosexual transmission.

[A wide range of social, economic, and cultural factors in Papua New Guinea have led to an environment in which sexual risk behaviors, including low levels of condom use in casual partnerships, are widespread. There have been a few behavioral surveys carried out recently. Among sex workers, the proportion reporting consistent use of condoms was around 15% in Port Moresby and Lae in 1999. The mean number of clients per sex worker was from three to five per week.

[STD prevalence surveys in Papua New Guinea show a high STD prevalence among both high-risk and low-risk groups. A 15% prevalence of gonorrhea among Highland's populations and 36% among sex workers were found. Chlamydia prevalence was up to 26% in Highland's populations, and 31% in sex workers. Prevalence of syphilis was 4% in Highland populations and 32% in sex workers.

[The estimated number of adults and children living with HIV/AIDS on January 1, 2002, were:

| | | |
|---|---|---|
| Adults ages 15-49: | 16,000 | (rate: 0.7%) |
| Women ages 15-49: | 4,100 | |
| Children ages 0-15: | 500 | |

[An estimated 880 adults and children died of AIDS during 2001.

[At the end of 2001, an estimated 4,200 Papuan children under age 15 were living without one or both parents who had died of AIDS. (*End of update by the Editors*)]

## 11. Sexual Dysfunctions, Counseling, and Therapies

Over the last few years, the author has conducted several training seminars on sexuality and reproductive health, including issues related to sexual dysfunctions. Common concerns among men were premature ejaculation, small penises, and erectile difficulty. Women complained of vaginal discharges, unpleasant odors, pain during intercourse, and dissatisfaction with their sex lives. Women reported that their husbands or partners use them for their own pleasure.

As in most developing countries, sexual diagnostic counseling is a luxury that most people cannot afford. However, through reproductive health interventions, information is being shared about the various types of sexual dysfunctions and treatment. In many instances, people need basic information about how the body responds sexually. Educators talk about some of the physical and psychosocial factors which can have an impact on sexual performance, including the negative effect that alcohol and other drugs can have on sexual performance. Other important issues that get discussed are gender roles, gender inequities, poor hygiene, and violence.

## 12. Sex Research and Advanced Professional Education

Despite the obstacles of geographic isolation and linguistic diversity until recent times, anthropologists, like Margaret Mead, Bronislaw Malinowski, Clelland S. Ford, and William Davenport, psychologists, such as Frank A. Beach, and others managed to gather considerable ethnographic data on the peoples of Papua New Guinea. Only recently, as modern transportation and electronic communication have broken down some of the obstacles, the HIV/AIDS and population/family planning crises have brought some limited and focused sex research. Sexological research, however, is just beginning to appear in very limited ways in Papua New Guinea, as it is in most other developing countries.

The main organization promoting sexological research is the Papua New Guinea Institute for Medical Research, P.O. Box 60, Goroka, Papua New Guinea.

## Conclusion

Although most societies and cultures around the world are experiencing major social change and tension, few are experiencing the transformation more intensely and radically than the people of Papua New Guinea. However, as Papua New Guinea moves into the new millennium, there is a great deal to be optimistic about. First, people are hungry for information and are open to learning new things about sexuality, as well as other aspects of life. Second, the government is working with agencies to prevent the spread of HIV/AIDS, and to educate the masses about population health issues. Third, the Ministry of Education, the Ministry of Health, and the faith-based communities in Papua New Guinea have developed curricula that address the issues of sexuality and reproductive health. Educators are being trained in sex and sexuality, family life education, reproductive anatomy and physiology, sexual and personal health, family planning and contraception, prevention of STDs and HIV/AIDS, prevention of sexual abuse and violence, and gender equity.

As Papua New Guinea continues to embrace the values and ways of the Western world, there will be many gains and losses. Culturally speaking, Papua New Guinea stands to gain information that will help to save lives. But, Papua New Guinea will no doubt experience all the problems and contradictions associated with Western society. Papua New Guinea's challenge is to maintain its cultural integrity as it struggles to become part of the modern world.

## Acknowledgment

We gratefully acknowledge Edgar Gregersen's helpful review and additional comments on this chapter.

## References and Suggested Readings

Beach, F. A., ed. 1976/1977. *Human sexuality in four perspectives*. Baltimore, MD: Johns Hopkins University Press.

CIA. 2002 (January). *The world factbook 2002*. Washington, DC: Central Intelligence Agency. Available: http://www.cia.gov/cia/publications/factbook/index.html.

Davenport, W. H. 1977. Sex in cross-cultural perspective. In: F. A. Beach, ed., *Human sexuality in four perspectives* (pp. 115-163). Baltimore, MD: Johns Hopkins University Press.

Ford, C. S., & F. A. Beach. 1951. *Patterns of sexual behavior*. New York: Harper, Colophon Books.

Francoeur, R. T., M. Cornog, T. Perper, & N. Scherzer. 1995. *The complete dictionary of sexology* (pp. 160-161). New York: Continuum.

Gregersen, E. 1996. Chapter 16. Oceania. *The world of human sexuality: Behaviors, customs, and belief*. New York: Irvington Press. pp. 263-281.

Herdt, G. 1981. *Guardians of the flute: Male initiation in New Guinea*. Berkeley, CA: University of California Press.

Herdt, G. 1984a. *Rituals of manhood: Male initiation in New Guinea*. Berkeley, CA: University of California Press.

Herdt, G. 1984b. Ritualized homosexuality in the male cults of Melanesia. 1962-1982. An Introduction. In: G. Herdt, ed., *Ritualized homosexuality in Melanesia* (pp. 1-81). Berkeley, CA: University of California Press.

Herdt, G. 1987. *Sambia: Ritual and gender in New Guinea*. New York: Holt, Rinehart and Winston.

Herdt, G. 1990. Mistaken gender: 5-alpha reductase hermaphroditism and biological reductionism in sexual identity reconsidered. *American Anthropologist*, 92.2:433-446.

Imperato-McGinley, J., et al. 1974. Steroid 5 alpha-reductase deficiency in man: An ingerited form of male pseudo-hermaphroditism. *Science*. 191:872.

Imperato-McGinley, J., R. E. Peterson, T. Gautier, & E. Sturla. 1985. The impact of androgens on the evolution of male gender identity. In: Z. DeFries, R. C. Friedman, & R. Corn, eds., *Sexuality: New perspectives*. Westport, CT: Greenwood Press.

Jenkins, C. 1996 (April 14-17). *Sexual networks and sexual cultures in contemporary Papua New Guinea*. An unpublished paper presented at the conference, "Reconceiving Sexuality: International Perspectives on Gender, Sexuality, and Sexual Health," in Rio de Janeiro, Brazil.

Malinowski, B. 1927. *Sex and repression in savage society*. Cleveland, OH: Meridian Books.

Marshall, D. S., & R. C. Suggs, eds. 1971. *Human sexual behavior: The range and diversity of human sexual experience throughout the world as seen in six representative cultures*. New York: Basic Books.

McWhirter, D. P., S. A. Sanders, & J. M. Reinisch, eds. 1990. *Homosexualty/heterosexuality*. New York: Oxford University Press.

Mead, M. 1930. *Growing up in New Guinea*. New York: Dell.

Mead, M. 1935. *Sex and temperament in three primitive societies*. New York: Dell.

Money, J. 1990. Agenda and credenda of the Kinsey Scale. In: D. P. McWhirter, S. A. Sanders, & J. M. Reinisch, eds., *Homosexualty/heterosexuality* (pp. 41-60). New York: Oxford University Press.

Money, J., & A. Ehrhardt. 1972. *Man & woman, boy & girl: Differentiation and dimorphism of gender identity from conception to maturity.* Baltimore, MD: Johns Hopkins University Press.

Reiss, I. L. 1997. An introduction to the many meanings of sexological knowledge. In: R. T. Francoeur, ed., *The international encyclopedia of sexuality* (vol. 1, pp. 21-30). New York: Continuum.

UNAIDS. 2002. *Epidemiological fact sheets by country.* Geneva, Switzerland: Joint United Nations Programme on HIV/AIDS (UNAIDS/WHO). Available: http://www.unaids.org/hivaidsinfo/statistics/fact_sheets/index_en.htm.

# Philippines

## (*Republika ng Pilipinas*)

Jose Florante J. Leyson, M.D.*
*Updates by J. F. J. Leyson*

## Contents

## *Demographics and a Brief Historical Perspective*

ROBERT T. FRANCOEUR

### A. Demographics

The Philippines is an archipelago of about 7,107 islands that stretch 1,100 miles (1,770 km) north and south in the Pacific Ocean off the southeast coast of Asia. With 115,830 square miles (300,000 km²) of total land area, the landmass of the archipelago is about the same size as the state of West Virginia, but slightly smaller than the British Isles. The Philippines is located northeast of Malaysia and Borneo, east of mainland China and Vietnam, south of Taiwan, and a distant west of the Hawaiian Islands in the Pacific Ocean. Ninety-five percent of the 1999 estimated 79.345 million Filipinos (Pilipinos) lived on the 11 largest islands, which are mountainous, except for the heavily indented coastlines and the central plains of Luzon. Slightly over half the nation's population live in the cities—in Manila, the former capital, with a 1990 estimated population of 1.6 million, in Quezon City, the new capital, with 1.7 million, and in Cebu City with 612,000. The Philippines is divided into three major regions: Luzon in the north, Visayas in the center, and Mindanao in the south.

In July 2002, the Philippines had an estimated population of 84.53 million. (All data are from *The World Factbook 2002* (CIA 2002) unless otherwise stated.)

**Age Distribution and Sex Ratios**: *0-14 years*: 36.6% with 1.04 male(s) per female (sex ratio); *15-64 years*: 59.7% with 0.98 male(s) per female; *65 years and over*: 3.7% with 0.8 male(s) per female; *Total population sex ratio*: 0.99 male(s) to 1 female

**Life Expectancy at Birth**: *Total Population*: 68.12 years; *male*: 65.26 years; *female*: 71.12 years

**Urban/Rural Distribution**: 55% to 45%

**Ethnic Distribution**: The large majority of Filipinos are Malays, either Christian- (91.5%) or Muslim- (4%) affili-

*Communications*: Jose Florantes Leyson, M.D., 6 Ranney Road, Long Valley, NJ 07853 USA; Phone: +908-876-5482.

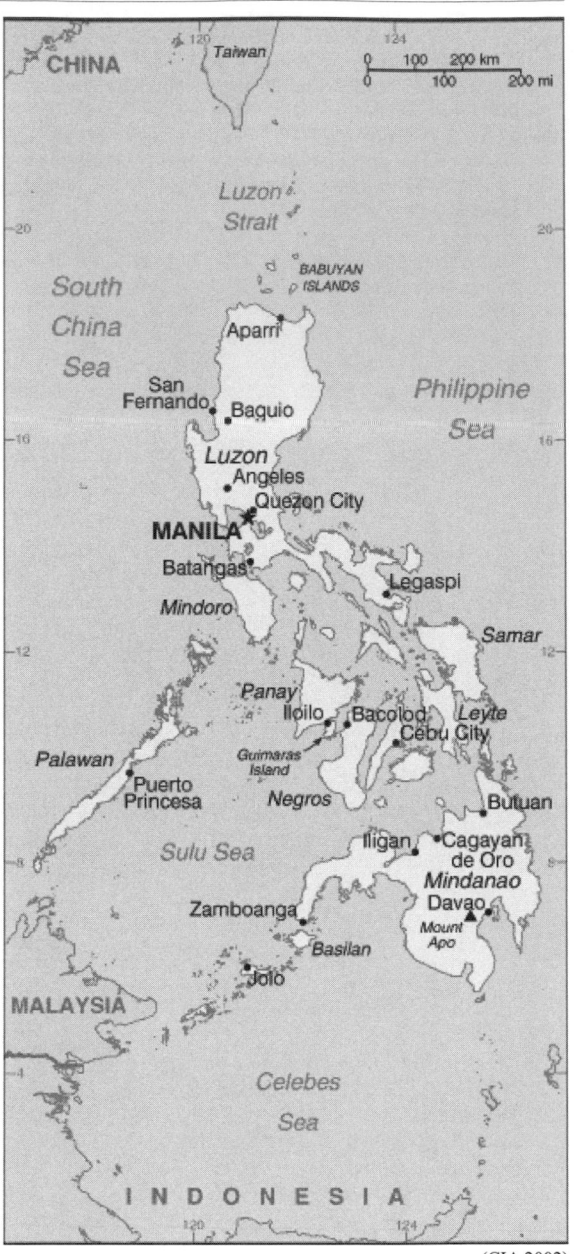

(CIA 2002)

ated, with small minorities of Chinese, American, Spanish, and Indian. Twelve percent constitute the ethnic and cultural minorities that include Aetas, Negritos (north), Ifugaos, Igorots, the "hill people" (north central), and the Muslims in the south.

**Religious Distribution**: Roman Catholic: 83%; Protestant: 9%; Muslim: 5%; Buddhist and other: 3%

**Birth Rate**: 26.88 births per 1,000 population

**Death Rate**: 5.95 per 1,000 population

**Infant Mortality Rate**: 27.87 deaths per 1,000 live births

**Net Migration Rate**: –1 migrant(s) per 1,000 population

**Total Fertility Rate**: 3.35 children born per woman

**Population Growth Rate**: 1.99%

**HIV/AIDS** (1999 est.): *Adult prevalence*: 0.07%; *Persons living with HIV/AIDS*: 28,000; *Deaths*: 1,200. (For additional details from www.UNAIDS.org, see end of Section 10B.)

**Literacy Rate** (*defined as those age 15 and over who can read and write*): 94.6%, with 97% attending primary (elementary) school and 55% attending secondary school. Education is free and compulsory from age 6 to 15. The Philippines also has the distinction of having one of the oldest universities in the modern world, Santo Tomas University, founded in 1645, 25 years before Harvard University, the oldest university in the United States. Although ten major languages (Cebuano, Bicolano, Ilocano, Pampangino, Spanish, English, etc.) are widely spoken, and there are 80 different dialects, Tagalog (Filipino) became the national official language in 1937. English is still widely used today throughout the country, and it is the medium of instruction beyond the 6th grade.

**Per Capita Gross Domestic Product** (*purchasing power parity*): $4,000 (2001 est.); *Inflation*: 6%; *Unemployment*: 10%; *Living below the poverty line*: 41% (2001 est.)

In 1997, *Time/World News* reported a 7% economic growth for the Philippines, with a per capita gross domestic product of $2,600, and considered the Philippines as one of the 10 leading major Asian countries in a business boom. However, in 1999, because of global economic crises, the country was trying to recover and survive in agriculture, aquaculture, and industry.

## B. A Brief Historical Perspective

Several waves of Malay peoples arrived in the Philippine archipelago from Southeast Asia long before the arrival of Europeans. These tribal societies and petty principalities coexisted with links to China, the East Indies, and countries in the Indian Ocean. Discovered by Magellan, who was killed there in 1521, the islands were named Las Filipinas (the Philippines) in 1559 by the Spanish explorer Ruy L. de Villalobos in honor of Prince Philip of Asturias, who later became King Philip II of Spain. The first Spanish settlements came in 1564, and a colonial capital, established at Manila in 1571, quickly became the key transit point for trade between Mexico and the Far East. Under Spanish rule, a majority of Filipinos became Catholics, except in the southwest islands where the people remained Muslim. In the shadow of a tepid colonial administration, the Catholic Church grew in power and wealth.

A nationalist movement gained strength in the late 19th century, leading to an armed uprising in 1896, the Spanish-American War, and defeat for Spain. In 1898, Spain ceded the Philippines to the United States for $20 million. When the nationalist movement declared the islands an independent republic, the United States refused to accept the declaration. A six-year war followed between 1899 and 1905, in which American troops brutally repressed the guerrilla uprising. In 1916, the Filipinos elected a Senate and House of Representatives, but the President was an American governor general. In 1935, a Philippine Commonwealth, modeled on the U.S. constitution, was established.

Japan brought the United States into World War II by attacking and then occupying the Philippines in December 1941. On July 4, 1946, the Philippines became the first Asian colony of the United States to gain independence, in accordance with an act passed by the United States Congress in 1934. In the 1970s, Muslim (Moro) secessionists fought repeatedly for their autonomy from the Christian majority on the island of Mindanao. In 1972, President Ferdinand Marcos declared martial law to combat riots by radical youth groups and terrorism by leftist guerrillas and outlaws. Despite some land reform and control of inflation, opposition continued, as a high population growth rate was aggravated by both poverty and unemployment. Opposition to Ferdinand Marcos continued despite his lifting of martial law and his election in 1981 to a second six-year term as president. The 1983 assassination of Benigno Aquino, the prominent opposition leader, sparked demonstrations calling for the resignation of the president. When Marcos declared himself victor in the bitterly contested elections of 1986 despite widespread charges of fraud, Corazon Aquino, the widow of Benigno Aquino, proclaimed herself president and announced a nonviolent "active resistance" to overthrow the Marcos government. The 20-year rule of Marcos ended in February 1986, with the recognition of Aquino as the new president by the United States and other nations. A weak economy, widespread poverty, and communist insurgents kept the political scene unstable between 1987 and 1990. Government forces were able to put down an attempted coup in 1989 with help from the United States military stationed in the Philippines. In 1994, the government signed a ceasefire agreement with Muslim separatist guerrillas, although some rebels have refused to abide by the agreement.

## 1. Basic Sexological Premises

### A/B. Character of Gender Roles and Sociolegal Status of Males and Females

The traditional gender roles in Filopino society are strongly influenced by centuries of Islamic culture, Chinese mores, and 425 years of deep-rooted Spanish Catholic traditions. However, since the 1960s, traditional Filipino gender culture has been transformed by tremendous Western—European and American—influences, except in the Muslim-dominated southern islands, which have been much less influenced by Western contacts. Polygamy, the wife as the husband's chattel, and deferential behavior of women in the presence of men are still strong values in the Muslim-dominated areas. The Muslim ideals of feminine behavior still produce a dependent, inferior, passive, and obedient woman.

In traditional Chinese society, women were to be obedient to the father and elder brothers when young (single), to the husband when married, and to their sons when widowed. For Filipinas of Chinese ethnic origin, marriage was the only means to economic survival. Arranged marriages are still common, with the clear expectation of male offspring who will maintain the "family business" interests and continuity. A wife's position and security within her husband's family remains ambiguous until she produces a male heir. These women have no right to divorce or to remarry if widowed. Those who try to defy these traditions have been ostracized and sometimes driven to depression or even to suicide.

The traditional colonial Filipina was supposed to reach marriage in a virginal state. She was expected to take care of the domestic tasks, go to church, bear and educate children, and support her man in his political, professional, and economic endeavors. The oppressive attitude of colonial Spain toward the Filipinas was first challenged by Mechlora Aquino (Tandang Sora), a nonviolent intellectual woman. In the mid-1800s, she was considered as the equal of the French "political" heroine, Joan of Arc, for leading both a political and cultural revolt against the suppression of women's rights. However, the colonial government quickly extinguished the local revolt, and the treatment of Filipinas as second-class citizens remained in force until Spain ceded the Philippines to the United States in 1898.

In the early years of the American occupation, 1900 to 1930, both females and males were provided with free elementary education. However, only the children of the rich had access to a high school and college education. Although women's social standing was improved, it was not until the late 1950s that the majority of women achieved equal rights; but this also happened mainly in the urban areas. For a long time, this double standard of colonial mentality was accepted without open criticism. That has changed since the Philippines gained its independence from the United States, with the democratic government taking steps towards recognizing the social and political rights of women. The Western influences on women have resulted in sociocultural independence from parents, spouses, and/or lovers. Women with a college education and businesswomen have started painstakingly to open spaces in the country's political, economic, legal, and administrative positions. On February 21, 1986, Mrs. Corazon Aquino became the first woman president of the democratic Philippines.

Today, Filipinas occupy key positions in university and medical schools, hospitals, both local and national government, large corporations, research-pharmaceutical companies, journalism, and all fields of the arts. However, discrimination against women and special privileges granted to men continue to exist simply because the males benefit from a deeply rooted and longstanding "male buddy" (*compare*) network.

## C. General Concepts of Sexuality and Love

Virginity is no longer a universally expected prerequisite for the marriage covenant. The 1994 *Young Adult Fertility and Sexuality Survey* (*YAFSS*) of 11,000 young people, ages 15 to 24 years, conducted by Dr. Z. C. Zablan, professor of demography at the Population Institute of the University of the Philippines, revealed that 18% of Filipino youths approved of premarital sex, 80% disapproved, and 2% were neutral. Today, sexual attitudes are more liberal and accepting of radical changes in sexuality and love because of the influences of the media and global communications. The same *YAFSS* survey showed that a large number of female college graduates residing in urban areas (35%) were exercising their liberal roles, both in their personal and professional lives with flexible sexual attitudes, while 40% were more likely to employ contraception. Filipinas in all classes are trying to balance their responsibility as mothers and lovers with some real class distinctions. The mothering role of the middle- and upper-class Filipinas is often supported by housemaids, professional babysitters, and grandmothers. In general, sophisticated, well-educated Filipinas are more comfortable than older women in taking the initiative in foreplay and learning new erotic techniques to introduce a variety of sexual techniques in their sexual lives. Also, these younger middle- and upper-class wives try to increase both the depth and scope in the emotional and intellectual communications within the couple. On the other hand, the 65% of Filipinas who live in the rural areas are less educated, more conservative in their sexual lifestyles, less likely to use contraception, and less independent in their personal lives.

The Philippines is a third-world country that enjoys the benefits of a young population, with 37.6% under age 15 and 47% between the ages of 15 and 49 years. There are also more women than men, with the surplus women finding support as maids or "nannies." The Latino tradition of single women serving as surrogate mothers for infertile wives is morally and legally unacceptable in the Philippines. For some males, especially in the rural areas and in minority groups, it is often difficult to internalize the impact of the women's liberation movement both in their sexual and professional lifestyles. In my observation, most well-educated males, especially urban dwellers, are starting to perceive that they enrich the relationship by participating in the rearing and education of their children, and the sharing of two incomes are beneficial to the family. The sophisticated professional men are also learning to relax during lovemaking, enjoying alternating passive and active roles, and accepting the fact that they can also be seduced and excited.

The majority of the Filipino urban population today is clearly Westernized, but still very conservative in its public and legal sexual values. Because of the dominant and pervasive influence of the Catholic Church, the only sexual behavior considered legal and moral is heterosexual intercourse within a monogamous marriage. Every other imaginable sexual variation is explicitly condemned. Thus, prostitution, pornography (nudity), polygamy (except in some minority groups and the Muslim south), premarital and extramarital sex, cohabitation, homosexuality, and other variant sexual behavior are all illegal. However, quiet homosexuality and heterosexual cohabitation seem to be more socially acceptable today, especially when they involve celebrities and politicians.

## 2. Religious, Ethnic, and Gender Factors Affecting Sexuality

### A. Source and Character of Religious Values

Although 83% of the Philippine population are Roman Catholic, 8% are members of the Mormons (Church of the Latter-Day Saints of Jesus Christ), Seventh Day Adventists, Four Square Church, Philippine Independent Church (Aglipan), Church of Christ, Jehovah's Witnesses, and Iglesia ni Kristo. Five percent are Muslim, and 4% follow Hinduism, Buddhism, Taoism, or the traditional nature worship of the aborigines or hill people. Taoism was introduced to the Filipinos by Chinese merchants during the 10th century. Taoism has both a philosophical and a religious tradition. Before the Spaniards came to the Philippines in the 16th century, in 1521, Taoism had some definite ideas about sex. For example, the wife's purpose is to please the husband and conceive more children. If the wife is barren, the husband can have a concubine or mistress to bear children, especially sons, for him. As the traditional Chinese population has aged, Taoist temples are increasingly seen only in a few major cities where they serve as tourist attractions, not religious symbols and sites. As octogenarian males are dying and their religion is fading away, modern Chinese males are being Westernized or practice a more popular religious persuasion.

Buddhism was probably first introduced to the Philippines during the 18th century from India through the Malaysian peninsula and China. Chinese Buddhism, based on the Mahayana (Great Vehicle, Wide Path) school of India, was handed down from generation to generation by both Chinese traders and immigrants. This form of Buddhism is very similar to Taoism. More recently, Buddhism has become more of a social ceremonial practice rather than a religion, and its temples have become a tourist curiosity. The "fat-bellied" Buddha statue is a symbol of the family's wealth and fertility that bedecked a Chinese house's foyer or living room.

Nature worship, the traditional indigenous religion of the Philippines, has been practiced from prehistoric times by the aboriginal Aetas, Negritos, Ifugaos, Igorots, and the hill people. Their constant struggle with the forces of nature for their survival has led to a closer relationship with their ancestors and the elements of nature. This form of religion has little if any systematic doctrine. However, there is one basic characteristic: the belief in the spirits of their ancestors who influence the living in every conceivable sphere of life and apply rewards and sanctions where appropriate. These religions also have lesser gods and deities with different powers related to physical health and fertility. The majority of tribal peoples believe that the first woman came from the "split" of the bamboo node, a kind of a tropical, tall, and slender palm with sequenced "nodes" in the trunk. Some tribal customs allow sexual activity as early as puberty, comparing this early exploration with sweet and tender young bamboo shoots. On the other hand, the expectation of virginity—the absence of penile/vaginal intercourse—with the assumed "tight vaginal entrance"—as "tight" like the nodes of an adult bamboo stalk—is favored for marriage.

Islam is practiced by 5% of the population, with the majority residing on Mindanao at the southwestern tip of the archipelago. Islam reached the Jolo and Zulu Islands in the Philippines, a century before the Spanish colonialists arrived, through Arab and Persian merchants arriving from the Malayan peninsula. Despite the fact that the Philippine government legally approves only monogamy, local Muslims, known as "Moros," are allowed to have several wives provided they can afford them.

American settlers brought Protestantism to the Philippines after 1898. The sexuality attitudes of both old and new Protestant tenets are based on the basic Judeo-Christian doctrines. However, two offshoots of the Protestant tradition are homegrown: one established in 1902 by the Aglipay family, the Filipino Independent Church, and the other in 1914 by the Manalo family, Iglesia ni Kristo (Church of Christ). These two Filipino Protestant churches have sexuality restrictions similar to the basic Judeo-Christian principles, but each has added rules imposed by personal preferences from their Filipino religious founders.

The influence of the Roman Catholic Church was and still is hegemonic over 90% of the Filipino population. Throughout Filipino history, the political powers have been submissive to the Catholic Church. The Church is determined to maintain its hold on important aspects of civil life, such as education, the availability of contraception and abortion, and even the registration of major events in the lives of the people, like births, marriages, child adoptions, and deaths. A very conservative interpretation of Catholic decrees about sexuality and marriage have been inscribed in the minds of the Filipino people, in a way that has proven difficult to alter or delete. Outstanding among these are the Church's views on the social roles of males and females, its insistence that any form of masturbation or premarital intercourse is sinful, and condemnation of homosexuality as unnatural behavior. The Church also places great emphasis on virginity as a prerequisite for matrimony, citing the example of the Virgin Mary, the Blessed Mother of Jesus Christ, who conceived her son without the need of sexual intercourse or a biological father. This sexual innocence and purity is clearly symbolized in the white clothing worn at baptisms, first communions, confirmations, and weddings. Catholicism also offers young men and women a celibate life that is supposedly more spiritual and rewarding in the priesthood and religious life.

**B. Character of Ethnic Values**

Before the arrival of the Spaniards in 1521, the Philippine islands were inhabited by fierce, indomitable tribes that valued their freedom and had learned to survive by adapting to the climate and resources of the different islands (regions) of the archipelago. It is believed that the chain of islands was a geological product resulting from volcanic eruptions from coastal/mainland China. However, the aborigines came by land and/or ice bridges from the Malayan peninsula. The indigenous people were mostly nomads who fished and hunted wild game. But the "hill people," the Ifugaos, who settled mainly in the north central part of the country about 1,000 years ago, developed and retain to this day unique sexual and marital ethnic values along with advanced engineering land cultivation. For instance, some tribal customs consider breast size and prominence of the hips to be financial assets that equate to the value or size of the dowry; large breasts and wide hips in the prospective bride would make a dowry of a few pigs or chickens unacceptable. The Rice Terraces of the "hill people" are considered one of the wonders of the world still existing today.

When the Portuguese explorer, Ferdinand Magellan, funded by Spain, discovered the Philippines in April 1521, he accidentally landed in the central part of the island country called Limasawa. Literally, "Lima" means five and "asawa" means wife. Limasawa, then, translates into "five wives." Magellan noticed that the natives were practicing polygamy. Most of the men have five or more wives. He did not realize that polygamy was a common marital ethnic norm in most of the indigenous tribes throughout the whole archipelago.

During the 10th century, China was trading regularly with different Philippine tribal clans led by a merchant known as Limajong, who introduced monogamy. The arrival of Chinese traders resulted in about 10% of intermarriages with the indigenous peoples. There was also a great variety in the way religious values and sexual customs developed in different ethnic groups and tribal traditions. For example, Islam takes on a slightly different expression among its many followers in the southern part of the country where ethnic plural marriages occur. Most of the ethnic minorities—Negritos, Aetas, Ifugaos, and Igorots of the north—practiced monogamy. The sexual values of these ethnic minorities often allow marriage by the age of puberty, about age 13 or 14 years for girls and age 15 and 16 for boys.

On the other hand, Catholicism, introduced to the islands by colonial Spain in 1521, considers males not mature or ready for marriage until age 20 or 21 years, and girls only at age 18 or 19. Masturbation is prohibited by the Church as sinful, "dirty," immature, narcissistic, and unnatural. In recent years, the traditional awareness of and opportunities for sexual initiation among adolescents have been relaxed, with male sexual exploits provided by an abundance of social opportunities, including birthday and college fraternity parties, community celebrations (*fiestas*), and public dances, which generally encourage sensual and erotic relationships.

The socioreligious education of women in traditional Catholic Filipino society encourages them to play the "cat and mouse" game. Young women are expected to develop social strategies that produce maximum enticement and individual satisfaction. This continual erotic stimulation and the hyper value of masculinity drives young men into the "courting game," leading hopefully to marriages. A young woman's ability to employ her virginity as a "bargaining tool" makes males inevitably impatient. The young male is then caught in an expensive web of socially productive and profitable engagements associated with courtship that resolves itself in betrothal to the young woman and "marrying" her, coupled with the expense of building his masculine image and sexual experience with prostitutes.

## 3. Knowledge and Education about Sexuality

### A. Early Sex Education Programs

For some 425 years, Spanish colonial rule afforded the Filipinos little political freedom and individual dignity. This began to change in the 1880s, when a multi-talented physician, Dr. Jose P. Rizal, broke through political, racial, and sociocultural barriers by studying medicine in Spain and Germany. Returning to the Philippines, Rizal established architectural and ecological parks, and local health education. He also advocated interracial marriages and later married an Irish woman before his political execution in 1896. At that time, only the most sophisticated elite and rich Filipino students were admitted to the oldest university of the Philippines, the University of Santo Tomas. At the time, only a few colleges offered limited science and social courses, and absolutely no sexuality or health education. All university and college courses placed a heavy emphasis on religious subjects. Between 1600 and 1824, the colonial Catholic Church had a total monopoly over education that kept the people ignorant of the advances in science, technology, and political organization that were taking shape in the Western world.

In 1898, when Americans colonists replaced the Spanish, public education was drastically altered and some individual freedoms were granted. In 1916, the Filipinos elected a Senate and House of Representatives, with its president an American governor general. He was interested in economic growth and political participation. Gradually, in the 1910s and 1920s, free secondary education was introduced in the big cities. In the 1930s, college education was free only in national colleges. With political modernization and the advent of the Philippine Commonwealth of 1935, Filipino society became increasingly Westernized, specifically Americanized. However, there was still no formal sex education or published material on the subject. Sex education was completely limited to information about pregnancy and childcare passed on by word of mouth among the women in families.

When Japan invaded the Philippines on December 8, 1941, at the start of World War II, the political and educational climates changed hands. Between December 1941 to October 1944, the Japanese occupation was characterized by political oppression and indoctrination. The Japanese military government was interested in total sociopolitical suppression, not in education.

The "re-Americanization" of the Philippines began when U.S. Army General Douglas McArthur liberated the islands on October 20, 1944. Two years later, the Philippines was granted its independence on July 4, 1946. Prior to independence, the educational system was reorganized and further modernized. United States soldiers who held educational degrees acted as model teachers and a catalyst for future Filipino teachers. From 1946 to 1968, there was rapid population growth, but still no formal sex education. What was not taught in the classrooms, the students would learn from their families at home and in the streets, although this information was often distorted, incomplete, or outright erroneous.

In 1969, in an effort to reduce the world population, the United Nations, through the World Health Organization in cooperation with the Filipino government, instituted a family planning and birth (conception) control program. In 1970 to 1971, this author was one of the principal instructors and trainers in the family planning program in the suburban and rural areas. The program consisted of teaching basic biology, conception/pregnancy, and the different options for contraception, but mainly the "pill." Although the Catholic Church was overtly opposed to contraception, particularly the "pill," the Church covertly supported this education in order to reduce the family's burden of childrearing because of poverty. In 1970, the educational (college) system was rocked by a widespread explosion of "student unrest" demanding more student rights and an expanded curriculum. The author was again one of the medical student leaders who demanded students' rights in a peaceful protest rather than a confrontational or violent demonstration. The college administrations finally settled and included in their curriculum science courses, such as expanded public health, that included information on sexually transmitted diseases and limited information on human sexuality.

During this era, sex education was left to the biology teachers, both in high school and college, who gave very limited information as part of the classes in the biological sciences. In a few cases, when the teacher decided to do so, this instruction was more or less a description of the reproductive organs in plants and animals, with perhaps some references to the role of the ovaries and testes in human reproduction. Explicit mention or pictures of the male and female genitalia were unacceptable and forbidden by custom.

## B. The Present Situation

In 1972, President Ferdinand Macros declared martial law and proclaimed a new sociocultural reform, the "New Society," which purported to reduce crime, enhance land reform, and augment economic stability. During this period, the government also approved a program, and directed that formal sex education be taught in all levels of education. Sex education courses were offered, starting at the elementary level in science and biology (human development and population). The high school equivalent to the 10th grade in the American system and college courses included elementary basic-level biological information, plus discussion of family planning and separation—divorce being illegal. The information on legal separation (*de facto* separation) was more in-depth in the public schools because of its high incidence in the lower class as compared to the middle and upper classes (professionals), who sent their children to private schools. In the 1980s, the medical schools supplemented the courses on human sexually with seminars and an international conference in which the author was one of the main speakers. In the 1990s, the government sponsored kindergarten classes. Research on population control, sexually transmitted disease (STD), premarital sex, sexual harassment, and AIDS are ongoing. (See Section 5B, Interpersonal Heterosexual Behaviors, Adolescents, for additional insights into sexuality education for adolescents and medical school students.)

Despite the government's crackdown on illegal sex publications, which was supported by Catholic Church authorities, it is obvious to any careful observer that informal sources of sexual information—television talk shows, soap operas, radio phone-in programs, and different kinds of adult journals and magazines commonly found in metropolitan and other urban areas—are widespread in the Philippines and cannot be controlled by either the government or religious authorities.

## 4. Autoerotic Behaviors and Patterns

The Catholic Church still maintains its condemnation of self-pleasuring (masturbation), teaching that any sex outside marriage is sinful. At present, a majority of Filipinos still believe that frequent masturbation can cause neuroses, premature ejaculation, and even blindness. In 1969 and 1970, the author conducted an informal sex survey in Central Region colleges and universities, which revealed that only 22% of the students, mainly males, engaged in masturbation. Another survey done in 1995, limited to medical school students, showed that 32% of the males and 8% of the females practiced masturbation (total $N = 280$).

## 5. Interpersonal Heterosexual Behaviors

### A. Children

In Filipino society today, it is not unusual for preteenage boys to engage in exploratory "sex" games with other boys and girls. Such exploratory play allows the child to reassure him- or herself of the normality of his or her body. This kind of childhood sexual rehearsal games was more common in the past and in rural areas, when violence and drugs were not as devastating as they are now in the urban areas. In some cases, boys would observe couples kissing and hugging in the park. Occasionally, they sit in the balconies of movie theaters where couples are engaging in heavy petting. In the rural areas and *barrios*, boys commonly compare their bodies with a friend, relative, or schoolmates. Generally speaking, parents and other adults have a mildly negative response when they discover child sexual play, ranging from warnings to spankings.

## B. Adolescents

Our knowledge of the sexual attitudes and behaviors of the Filipino youth is limited to a very few anecdotal reports, most of which deal with middle- and upper-class urban teenagers rather than the rural poor and urban street children. In this very limited context, my personal experience was the basis of my premedical school thesis on "First Night Sexual Experience of Young Boys—1968." This study consisted of personal interviews with 80 adolescents in the rural areas of Cebu during social dances and summer festivals. The majority of these teenagers were interested in obtaining information regarding nocturnal emissions, love, sexual intercourse, and, for women, contraception and pregnancy. Most of the males' ideas on sexuality were derived from older boys, brothers, and their uncles. On the other hand, the girls were too timid or shy to answer the sexuality questions.

During the author's return visit to the Philippines in July 1995 as an invited speaker at a college sociocultural conference, he arranged an impromptu meeting with middle and high school students, grades 7 through 10. They informed me that most of their teachers believed that they were too young to hear about sex education. The teachers did not allow questions from their students during the lecture on "family education." Most instructors were too insecure and embarrassed, and so were unable to facilitate any in-depth dialogue. In Catholic Filipino society, the Christian dogma still has a strong influence on the teachers' moral and religious values, so that, despite the presence of a government-mandated educational climate, sexuality remains taboo in public discussion. Unfortunately, these teenagers were afraid to elaborate further, confessing only that it is attitudes like this, repeated in their conservative homes, that make them view society and family cynically.

In Christian colleges and universities, being pregnant out of wedlock can result in expulsion. In most public nonsectarian universities, sex education is still mostly nonexistent except for those basic biological courses and family planning programs mandated by the government in 1972. However, in the largest government-run university, the University of the Philippines, sex education courses are more in-depth and liberal, because of the sophistication of the instructors and department heads who are Westernized and comfortable with controversial and sensitive ideas.

Although still limited—some might say elementary—sexuality courses in most urban medical schools are generally open to updating because of the infusion of new ideas from visiting professors and experts in periodic international forums and conferences. The best medical school students can graduate as doctors at the young age of 23, a factor that makes their communications with patients about sexual issues difficult at best.

### Pubertal Rites for Boys

The anatomical and physiological changes that herald puberty are universal to the human race. However, in Fili-pino society, the sociocultural pubertal rites are expressed in a variety of customs and traditions depending on the particular subculture and its religious orientation. In the Christian tradition, the custom is to circumcise all males. Male circumcision is performed either by a medical doctor trained in this surgery or by a traditional medicine man. Filipino boys may be circumcised as newborn infants or somewhere around age 8 to 10 years, when they are in the 3rd or 4th grade. City dwellers and the sophisticated elite have their newborn males circumcised before they are discharged from the hospital. Working-class and poor families seldom have their newborns circumcised, but usually wait until the boys are 9 or 10 years of age. The medicine man is not a medical doctor, but a man of ordinary skills who has learned the art of circumcision handed down from his father or grandfather.

Circumcision is done in two ways. In superincision, a dorsal-mesal cut is made along the length of the upper surface of the penis, from the base to the foreskin, or only on the top of the foreskin. In the coronal technique, the excess foreskin is removed with a circular incision, as is the practice in Europe and North America. When a medical doctor performs either of these types of circumcision, the incision is closed by sutures and oral antibiotics are prescribed to avoid postoperative infection. The medicine man, on the other hand, only performs the dorsal slit circumcision, using a specially "cleaned" (not sterilized) sharp knife or a modified slender "machete" as scalpel. The medicine man uses neither antibiotics nor anesthesia.

This pubertal initiation traditionally occurs in the spring or when the schools begin summer recess, somewhere in May or June. The ceremony commences when boys, aged 8 to 12 years old, march in procession, usually in groups of 10 to 12, to the medicine man's house. The medicine man, with the parents' knowledge and consent, will then lead the boys to a secluded place, a clearing in a thicket or on a farm to insure privacy. The boy, with pants removed, is seated on the edge of a rock or stump of a tree, while the medicine man sharpens and cleans the knife. Despite this tension-producing buildup, the boy must remain calm and composed to show that he is brave and ready to enter the new realm of adulthood and can handle the rigors of manhood. The medicine man places the knife's sharpest side underneath the tip of the excess prepuce (avoiding the glans penis). He instructs the boy to look up, saying "look for a bird or a plane," diverting his attention. In a split second, a piece of wood or a branch is struck down against the knife, resulting in a midline cut or dorsal slit of the prepuce. Bleeding may be profuse or minimal. The juice of a certain tropical palm plant (*nipa palm*) is squeezed over the wound as a post-surgical anesthetic and caustic agent to stop the bleeding. No wound dressing is applied to cover the fresh and rugged incision. A clamp of cobwebs or a mesh scraped from the underside of a coconut palm branch over the incision serves as a bandage and additional clotting agent (to stop further bleeding). In some parts of the Philippines, the medicine man spits on the wound pre-chewed tobacco or a concoction of guava (a tropical peach-like fruit) leaves to act as a clotting agent. Both the cobwebs and coconut palm scrapings act as mechanical meshes to trap blood platelets in order to stop bleeding. The guava leaves mixed with saliva has papase, a chemical agent that medically can minimize post-operation swelling and sometimes arrest bleeding.

After circumcision, the boys walk home without a sound of complaint or grimace of pain. It is interesting to note that a particular gait can be discerned before and after the circumcision. The boys naturally walk normally on their way to the medicine man's house. When they walk back to their homes, their gait is characterized by a "frog-like" walk, in which the knees are spread away from each other in order to avoid the thighs touching the newly circumcised genitalia. For three to five days, the circumcised boys stay home. Some wear skirts borrowed from their sisters or mothers, not pants, so that clothes do not touch or accidentally hit the sensitive, partially exposed glans (head) penis. Despite daily wound washing in the ocean, a river, or stream, about 90 to 95% of these cases of nonsterile circumcision become infected. It takes about six to eight weeks for the wound to heal, usually without ugly scars or deforming penile skin adhesions.

In the 1970s, Muslim boys were not usually circumcised unless their parents were well-educated and health-aware of Westernized attitudes of that time. In the early 1950s, boys of minority families in the north were not circumcised. However, with the arrival of foreign Christian missionaries and their conversion to Christianity, most of the boys are now circumcised either by a medicine man or a physician.

### Puberty Rites for Young Females

Christian girls undergo two phases of social transition to womanhood: ritual ear piercing and a *cotillion* or debutante's ball. Ear piercing is neither a religious nor a pubertal rite. It is just a custom, a traditional "tribal" rite of socially announcing that the person is a girl. The piercing of the ear is usually done between one month after birth and 2 or 3 years of age. In some parts of the country, the girl is much older. Ear piercing is usually done by a hairstylist, a "medicine woman," or medical person. Outpatient procedures by medical personnel use properly sterilized needles. Oftentimes, however, no anesthesia or antibiotic is given when the piercing is done by a hairstylist or a medicine woman. In general, however, infections from ear piercing are not as common as in male circumcisions done by a medicine man with an unsterilized knife. Phase two, the debutante's ball or *cotillion*, is a social introduction of young females ages 16 to 18 years in the form of an elaborate party or dinner dance. The hostess of this social event is an 18-year-old female usually from the rich families. *Cotillion* is an old Spanish tradition, dating back to colonial days, when the daughters of foreign dignitaries or tenured Spanish government officials were introduced to the eligible bachelors of the equally rich in order to secure the daughter's future financial and sociopolitical status as eligible and eminently suitable future wives.

In the Muslim or Moros community, about 10% of the Filipino population, the ear-piercing ritual is the same as among Christians. In the early 1950s, the older girls would wear a veil. At present, young females seldom use veils or cover their faces. Some Muslims include the *cotillion* in their rite of passage, but for others, dancing or any form of partying is absolutely prohibited and considered sacrilegious.

The minorities, Ifugaos, Kalingas, Igorots, and others, account for 3 to 5% of the population. These females, like most Filipinas, have their ears pierced at any early age. However, in some tribes, family wealth and status are demonstrated by the number of earrings or the layers of necklaces worn. No form of female circumcision or genital mutilation has been recorded. Anecdotal reports suggest that during the pre-Hispanic colonial days, some tribal females wore multi-appendage rings, nose, and lip rings. These tribal cultures do not observe the *cotillion*.

### Premarital Sexual Activities

Sexual attitudes and behavior differ from one group of Filipino youth to another, depending on their social class, educational level, and place of residence. In metropolitan and large cities, Manila, Quezon, Cebu, Iloilo, Davao, Dumaquete, and Zamboanga, adolescents and young adults are exposed to the cosmopolitan life and consequently receive more information on sex and sexuality. They are also freer to experience numerous options than are less-educated youths. Youth in small towns have narrower and more restricted ideas on sexuality, because of the family's and Church's strong control and influence. Furthermore, youngsters in big cities have easy access to adult magazines and entertainment, in which sexuality is openly discussed or shown, even though their parents and the Church try to hide such information from them. The majority of urban youth knows about contraceptives and can acquire these from pharmacies or from friends without problems. Despite the guilt and shame associated with sex, middle- and upper-class urban youth often engage in sexual contacts with girlfriends, household maids, and even prostitutes. For the youths of the poverty belts around the big cities, the situation is compounded by the lack of money and self-control. Even if they would prefer to use a contraceptive, they cannot afford them and there are no places where they can get them free. Oral contraceptives are only given free to married women for family planning purposes by government-run city and municipal health clinics. Although condoms were distributed freely in public high schools in the early 1990s on a mandate from the Secretary of Health as part of an STD and HIV prevention program, this practice was later discontinued because of a public outcry that it was ineffective and because of the Church's persistent objections.

The situation for rural (*barrios*) youth is quite different. They learn and receive information about sex and sexual behavior from observing farm animals, from magazines, from clandestine "boys only" meetings, and from the relations between parents and other family members in homes where there is little privacy. The prevailing Catholic dogma on sexual morality is written deep in the unconsciousness of every boy and girl. Only a few years ago, 98% of the youth associated premarital sex with guilt and sin. Only recently has this begun to change. In 1994, the *Youth Adult Sexuality Survey* (Zablan 1994) revealed that about 18% accepted premarital sex, although a majority of 80% still believed it was a sin and morally unacceptable.

Only a few general surveys about the sexual life of younger Filipinos exist; most of what is known is based on anecdotal reports. The author's experiences are with interviews of preselected groups of the youth population conducted during periodic sojourns back to the Philippines. The samples mainly consist of middle-class youth, ages 17 to 22, who were encouraged to bring to the meeting problems related to their sexual lives and development. Repeatedly, they expressed regret that these aspects of their lives that engender so much anguish and fears could not be explicitly discussed in the intimacy of their household.

It is becoming increasingly clear that first premarital sexual activities are initiated at an earlier age, especially for those in metropolitan areas, where the basic family structure often disintegrates because of a lack of parental supervision, with both parents working or the father absent and perhaps working overseas. Young males pursuing college and graduate studies in the city are often detached from parental supervision and frequently succumb to the lure of metropolitan temptations, go-go bars, and adult-entertainment houses. Twenty to 25% have their first sexual experiences with prostitutes, either out of peer pressure or curiosity. In a few cases, youths in smaller communities who impregnate their girlfriends may be forced to marry them or make an amicable financial arrangement with parental approval. The woman usually keeps the child in her parents' home instead of giving it up for adoption.

In the Muslim communities, premarital sex is absolutely prohibited. But young girls, ages 14 to 16, can be betrothed through the usual (parental) marriage arrangement, mainly to affluent and much older bridegrooms.

Among girls, the memories of being deflowered were somewhat different from those of the boys. Because of guilt and shame, the majority of young females did not bother to get prior information about sexual intercourse and the possible consequences of their first sexual encounters. They perceived their first intercourse as the fulfillment of young love, motivated by peer pressure to keep their boyfriends, and at the same time as a "challenge" to parental authority or a gross transgression of a religious or social taboo. For the well-educated and sophisticated city dwellers, it was a calculated act to get rid of the old-fashioned social taboo (virginity), which they perceived as an obstacle to entering into a more mature and fulfilling sexual life, or plainly to catch the men of their dreams. It is interesting to note that, compared with the United States and other industrialized nations, Filipino teenagers are probably less sexually active; thus, teenage pregnancy is less of a problem than elsewhere.

Most of the children born to single mothers are kept in the teenager's mother's home, instead of being given up for adoption. In the 1970s, a pregnant teenager was a social outcast and was subjected to severe parental scorn. However, in the 1990s, because of Western influence and financial difficulties, a pregnant teenager is somewhat more tolerated, and her parents are less condemning and more accepting of any financial help the teenage father might offer.

## C. Adults

### *Courtship, Dating, and Relationships*

As mentioned previously, Chinese influence runs deep and the majority of Filipinas adhere to its simple social dictum, "Get married at a marriageable age." Marriage is considered the natural conclusion of a stable heterosexual relationship. Recently, however, Filipinos have started to replace their old-fashioned social concepts with ones that recognize that the right to remain single is as much a personal right as the right to marry. Because of the Western influence on women's liberation, to be a single older woman is no longer considered a social disgrace or the result of any personal inadequacy.

### *Cohabitation*

The colonial view of the sacredness of marriage includes a strong social condemnation of cohabitation for unmarried couples. Thus, cohabitation was relatively rare during the 1940s. The social and legal implications of "common-law marriage" (cohabitation) are not significant in a society of less affluence and resources. Furthermore, the definition of unmarried used in compiling official statistics makes it difficult to estimate the popularity of this behavior in the sense it is understood in the Western Hemisphere. Beginning in the late 1980s, the increased tolerance of nonmarital cohabitation in the West began to influence the middle-aged and younger generations. During the author's 1996 visit in the provinces of Cebu, Leyte, and metropolitan Manila, there was an estimated increase of half a percent and an estimated 340,000 couples in unmarried cohabitation. The majority of cohabiting couples in the provinces are separated from their legal spouses because divorce is illegal and they cannot be civilly or religiously married. The rest are college students, youth, artists, and intellectuals who are attracted to this lifestyle.

[*Update 2003*: In a recent survey conducted by a polling agency, the Social Weather Station (SWS), in late November 2002, 35% of the respondents considered cohabitation a "good idea" prior to marriage. This was virtually unchanged from 1998. However, an estimated twofold increase in cohabitation is expected by the year 2005, especially in the entertainment industry and among college students in metropolitan areas. The main reasons are financial and novelty. (*End of update by J. F. J. Leyson*)]

Courtship is a cherished Filipino tradition with certain specific rules based on religious, sociocultural, and family values. There are five widely shared rules or "commandments" associated with courtship:

1. Say "yes" to the first invitation.
2. It is a prerequisite to have an escort, either a friend or next of kin, on the first date (no escort is necessary for a woman 28 years or older).
3. It is all right to publicly demonstrate decent affection, such as kissing, touching, and caressing.
4. A young Filipina should reserve criticism after the first date, be discreet about her feelings, and the man must cover (pay for) all expenses.
5. If dating leads to marriage, one must remember that marrying entails marrying into the spouse's whole family as a clan.

The majority of young men and women believe that love, physical attraction, similar religious beliefs, and trust are the basic essentials in creating and maintaining a stable relationship.

### *Adults, Marriage, and the Family*

The marriage ceremony is usually preceded by an engagement. For the rich and middle class, betrothal is marked with elaborate parties. On the other hand, the low-income class concludes the occasion with a firm handshake and/or a sip of a local wine or homemade ferment. The engagement and wedding are usually a happy, festive occasion. However, if questions of family honor and shame arise, the outcome may be violent and deadly, as happened at the time of this writing, when a male's family massacred the bride-to-be's family because she slept with another man two days before the wedding. The community accepted the outcome as a proper punishment for the betrayal and unbearable shame caused to the bridegroom's family.

Whereas the legal age for voting is 21 years for both males and females, the legal age for marriage is 21 for males and 18 for females. In the Muslim community, the parents of a girl between ages 14 and 16 may betroth her to an older man. Generally, in the Christian community, the courts do not consider pregnancy a valid motive to grant permission for the marriage of a minor. Legislation has also abolished the possibility of reparatory marriage; in the past a person accused of rape or forceful abduction could avoid punishment by marrying the victim. In the southern end of the archipelago, where the majority of the Muslims live, a dowry is agreed on before a formal marriage arrangement is signed. The dowry, given by the bride's parents to the groom, may be a large sum of money, property, or a sizable wedding present.

Muslim marriages are conducted by a judge or an *imam* (a religious cleric), Christian marriages by a priest or pastor. Civil marriages are recognized and accepted in both the Christian and Muslim communities when conducted by judges and commercial chiefs, such as pilots and ship captains.

Although polygyny had a long history in pre-colonial Filipino civilization and was common in the Muslim community prior to the 1970s, polygynous marriages are the exception today. The majority of sophisticated, highly educated males, whether Muslim or Christian, choose to be monogamous for financial reasons. Middle- and upper-class Filipino families also elect to have fewer children, two on average, as compared to three or more for the less educated and low-income families.

With the advance of information technology, foreigners seeking brides with traditional values can now surf the Internet for a modest fee. Companies also advertise "mail order brides" in different magazines and specialty journals. There are currently about 100 companies competing to lure mail-order bride customers, such as "Cherry Blossoms," "Asian Rose," and "Exotic Girls." The service charge can range from a basic $150 to upwards of $2,500. For $150, the bridegroom-to-be will receive a brief biographical sketch and a photo or video of the woman. He can correspond with her in letters or even phone calls. He can arrange to go to the Philippines and see her at his own expense. For $2,500, the services include airfare, hotel accommodations, and a two- or three-day tour to personally interact with the candidate bride(s). The client is introduced to different women during a party and the couples can interact socially.

A major shortcoming of this venue for finding a mate is that the interested males are not screened properly. These men can be psychopaths, criminals, or worse. In some cases, a syndicate of "Internet bride-merchants" sells young women aged 14 to 18, oftentimes with fake birth certificates, for a mere $3,000. These women are admitted to the United States on a fiancée's visa. Parents with severe income hardship frequently sign the contract believing that their daughters will either be given a job opportunity or be future brides of these unscrupulous foreigners. Recently, a congressman from the state of New Jersey sponsored a bill in the United States Congress to severely restrict the issuing of these "fiancée's visas" and to stop the practice of "bride-to-be/sex slave" businesses. Newspaper reports and embassy communiqués have documented that many young Filipino mail-order and Internet brides are held captive, raped, divorced, and then pressed into prostitution.

There are no credible published data on marital sexual satisfaction or on the status of Filipino marital life. According to the author's informal survey and radio-talk-show interviews in 1995, 15 to 20% of Filipinos are unhappily married. Women, more often than men, reported having sexual intercourse not because they desired it, but to please their spouses. Whereas 35% of males would like to increase the frequency of sexual intercourse, especially those in their 20s and 30s, most of the women were satisfied with the frequency of sex; only 5% of the females were interested in more frequent sex. These gender differences may be explained as the result of a greater pressure on males for sexual performance to maintain their macho image and maintain total control over women.

A majority of women complained of the brief duration of foreplay and premature ejaculation. Sexual intercourse is limited almost exclusively to penetration, which is more common among the less educated, more devotedly religious couples, and the older age groups. The average duration of foreplay is about five minutes, that of coitus about five to six minutes. On the other hand, the more educated, sophisticated, younger age group, and the "unchurched" have a longer duration of sexual foreplay and coitus, about 22 minutes. Although premature ejaculation is not uncommon among males, very few men seek medical help. Husbands generally do not consider premature (early) ejaculation a problem.

In the Christian community, sexual activity is not prohibited during any religious event or celebration. In some cases, Christian women make the personal choice of not having sex during their menstrual period. On the other hand, Muslim custom does not allow any sexual activity during the menstrual period, between sundown Friday and sundown Saturday, and during *Ramadan*, the month-long period of daytime fasting.

It is difficult to gather data on female orgasm because of religious repression and personal shyness. It is believed that Filipinas' sexual satisfaction is based on cultural and religious grounds. The husband's satisfaction is primary and the wife's orgasm clearly secondary. Young, educated, and less religious or unchurched women have a higher orgasmic rate as compared to their older, less-educated, (oftentimes) more religious, and shy counterparts. It is believed that for a majority of women who experienced orgasms, it was more a result of psychological and religious expectation and not so much because of oral or manual genital stimulation. However, the barrage of media and Western influences has increased the proportion of Filipinas who prefer both psychic and physical stimulation. Filipinas are bombarded by the mass media and performing arts with messages about more openness in sexual matters, greater gender equality, information about new techniques for lovemaking, new roles within the couple, and new opportunities for extramarital relationships. These issues are also conversation matter among friends and families, at business meetings, and at almost any social-civic gatherings.

*Divorce and Remarriage*

The Catholic Church does not allow divorce of any kind, but it will grant annulments, which most Filipinos find socially distasteful. However, generally, we find civil decrees of legal separation, divorce, and annulment are becoming more socially acceptable for Christian and Muslim Filipinos. A civil divorce requires that the ex-husband support the children and provide some assistance to the ex-wife along with household maintenance.

[*Update 2003*: A recent survey by *Filipino 2.0* (2003) magazine revealed that most Filipinos are satisfied with their family life, but the survey also found a "significant" minority who agree with divorce despite a ban on the practice by Philippine law and the dominant Roman Catholic Church. According to the Social Weather Station (SWS) survey of 1,200 Filipinos nationwide, 36% agreed that "divorce is usually the best solution when a couple can't seem to work out their marriage problems." On the same question in SWS's survey the year before, 29% agreed that divorce might be the best solution. In the 2002 poll, 50% of the respondents disagreed with divorce, down from 61% in the 2001 survey.

[Asked about satisfaction with family life, 27% said they were satisfied, 29% said they were completely satisfied, and 31% claimed they were very satisfied. Only 6% said they were fairly, very, or completely dissatisfied, while another 2% said they were neither satisfied nor dissatisfied; the remaining 5% had no opinion. On the question whether married people are generally happier than unmarried people, an overwhelming 61% agreed while 19% disagreed.

[In January 2003, the Philippines Solicitor General (the equivalent of the U.S. Attorney General), A. Benipayo, said that judicial officials are considering reforms that will make it easier for estranged couples to have their church marriage annulled. The Philippine Constitution states that "marriage is an inviolable social institution and the foundation of the family, and shall be protected by the state." Under the proposed reform, special family courts handling annulment cases would no longer be required to gain the consent of the Solicitor General's office before voiding a marital union.

Benipayo remarked that he favored the new proposal, which came from a judicial reform committee created by the Supreme Court, that his office should stop representing the state in annulment cases. The reform would also be empowered to invalidate marriages on specified grounds, including psychological incapacity. The office of the Solicitor General received on average 410 annulment cases every week. Benipayo added that the special court judges are "already properly guided by the law and pronouncements and interpretations of the Supreme Court" to handle the reform (Bascug 2003). (*End of update by J. F. J. Leyson*)]

Slightly more acceptable are consensual separations. What is popular today is having a court declare a marriage null and void under the Family Code (Executive Order 209, Article 36). The Family Code has adopted the grounds of "psychological incompatibility" as a basis for civil annulments. This was the criterion for annulment articulated by the Catholic Church 40 years ago after the Vatican II Council, when annulments became much more common. A civil annulment dissolves the marriage and leaves both parties free to remarry. With the incidence of annulments clearly increasing in the mid-1990s, Filipino Senator A. D. (Nikki) Coseteng introduced in the legislature a pro-marriage anti-divorce bill (No. 179), which now legally defines marriage as an inviolable social institution and the foundation of the family.

The incidence of remarriage is not presently known. However, both in the rural and metropolitan areas, cohabitation is on the upswing because of Western influences and financial problems. In major cities, younger, more sophisticated, and affluent women have more chances for remarriage, but priests will not officiate at a second marriage ceremony unless the Catholic Church has annulled the previous marriage. Despite liberalization in the dissolution or annulment of marriages, the main reason why the divorce rate is still relatively low, when compared to the industrialized countries, is most likely the pervasive influence of the Catholic Church and parental moral values. The importance of extended family norms derives, not only as a source of emotional support and the context for the development of profound personal relations, but also for many other aspects of social life, from financial support to finding a job. Legal separation, divorce, and annulment are still frequently perceived as evidence of personal failure and as a "social anomaly." The end of the relationship is not viewed as freedom and independence, but as the beginning of a different period in one's personal life.

### Extramarital Sexual Activities

Most of the causes of legal separation involve extramarital affairs. Adultery or extramarital sex is vehemently condemned by the Catholic Church and is socially detested. However, there is an issue of legal terminology and social definition. Under Filipino penal laws, a man does not commit adultery unless he violates the law against concubinage. To be guilty of concubinage, a man must:

1. keep a mistress within the conjugal dwelling;
2. have sexual intercourse with another woman under scandalous circumstances; or
3. cohabit with another woman outside the conjugal dwelling.

Having sexual intercourse with a women who is not one's wife does not in itself violate the law of concubinage. Nor is the ban on concubinage violated if a man fathers a child with a woman who is not his wife. A wife commits adultery simply by having sexual relations with a man who is not her husband, regardless of the circumstances.

The provisions of the Penal Code on female adultery and male concubinage are glaring examples, not only of the inequality between the sexes, but also of the inequity between erring spouses. The law provides a maximum penalty of four years imprisonment for the erring husband. The concubine shall be meted a penalty of *destierro*, wherein she is prohibited from setting foot within the man's residence. A wife found guilty of adultery, on the other hand, may be imprisoned for a maximum period of six years. Some lawmakers have pointed out that it is easier to send a female to jail and that this violates the constitutional provision on equality of the sexes. In simple terms, the law does not criminalize the sexual infidelity of a married man except under certain circumstances. This, some lawmakers point out, seems to imply that the extramarital affairs of men are acceptable as long as they are discreet in handling them—a clear reflection of the double-standard mentality of society with regard to sexual infidelity.

A 1996 survey conducted by an advertising and research group revealed that out of 485 married men in metropolitan Manila, 51% admitted having had extramarital affairs. The survey results reflect the machismo culture in the Philippines, wherein a man's worth, among other things, is also equated with his ability to lure other women. In an attempt to correct this inequality in 1997, Senator M. Santiago filed a bill simplifying marital infidelity. In her measure, she proposed that the extramarital sex by either the husband or wife be called *adultery*, whether the extramarital partner is of the other or same sex. The House committee made amendments to her bill and put the marital offense under a single crime called "marital infidelity," eliminating the separate provisions on concubinage and adultery, and the consideration of whether the infidelity occurs within the couple's home or elsewhere. Congress proposed a maximum penalty of six years for all parties concerned. Speaking for the Women's Legal Bureau, a nongovernmental organization (NGO), E. Ursua claimed that imposing criminal liability on the offenders is not the answer. "We do not think criminalizing is the proper solution. We can't force someone to be faithful."

The new law penalizes the guilty party with imprisonment, regardless of the reasons behind the infidelity. A woman escaping from an abusive or violent relationship, or one who simply falls out of love and finds growth and fulfillment with another person, is treated no differently than a man who keeps several mistresses. In effect, the law also punishes individuals who get out of marriages that are bereft of love, respect, and trust. Some legal organizations propose a modified "divorce" law and/or a new bill to decriminalize sexual infidelity. But Senator Santiago countered that this might send a "subliminal message" to the youth that the state is encouraging "free love."

In the Muslim world, adultery is severely punished, with the perpetrators either made social outcasts or, in rural villages, stoned to death in public. This "fatal justice" is carried out clandestinely as an expression of community justice that government magistrates (*datu*) can do nothing to either prevent or punish. The whole village maintains a "code of silence," because this punishment is written in the Muslim moral marital law. There is no witness to interrogate or testify.

During the Spanish colonial days, 1775 to 1899, rich Filipinos who owned *haciendas* (estates or a large parcel of land) and employed several female domestic helpers could easily have extramarital relations with their female employees, with or without the knowledge of their wives. Today, we still find married men in all walks of life who maintain a longstanding relationship with a second woman, oftentimes with the knowledge and approval of their spouses, and even of their grown children. In some cases, an extra-marital affair can end a politician's career; in other cases, an affair, even when its makes headlines, may have no po-litical consequences. Some couples find extramarital af-fairs a solution that keeps their marriage alive. The man may be freed to satisfy sexual needs he does not dare, be-cause of religious restrictions, reveal to his wife, while the wife is relieved of any pressure to change her sexual behav-ior. Most wives who adopt this compromise have limited horizons in their lives and a very low sexual appetite. Less common is a marriage in which both the husband and wife have extramarital relationships by mutual knowledge and agreement. In such cases, usually the husband has a job that keeps him abroad for long periods of time, with periodic visits to wife and family. Occasionally, Filipinos who mar-ried, found employment abroad, immigrated for a few years, and married a second woman while abroad, bring their second wives back when they return and set up a sec-ond household in a different dwelling. Discovery of this bigamous affair can be costly if the courts become in-volved. Legal penalties for bigamy can bring up to four years in prison and fines for moral and psychological dam-ages between US$500 and $1,300.

These relationships pose a serious problem in Philippine society because many of these men resist the use of con-doms, do not practice safe sex, and pay no attention to the possibility that their regular or occasional partner(s) may be HIV-positive.

### Incidence of Oral and Anal Sex

Both the Christian and Islamic sects abhor oral and anal sex acts. The Muslim tradition specifically requires the hus-band to enter the wife by natural means in penile-vaginal in-tercourse. Oral sex, which in the past was condemned as "unnatural," is practiced more or less by educated Chris-tians who live in the metropolitan areas. From the 1950s to the 1970s, when there was no constant supply of electricity in many towns and areas of the country, professional cou-ples enhanced their sexual lives by using pornographic and specialty magazines. In the 1970s and 1980s, with electric-ity more widely available, middle-class and upper-class couples used film projectors, and later videocassette play-ers, to enhance their sexual repertoire and learn about alter-natives to penile-vaginal intercourse that could bring re-newed vigor to their routine sex lives.

Anecdotal reports suggest that oral sex is practiced by 10 to 15%, and tried by 20% of the professional couples (i.e., doctors, lawyers, and businesspersons who travel a lot). The majority of Filipinos, however, still consider oral sex as dirty and unnatural. For the few who engage in oral sex, cunnilingus is acceptable, but Filipinas will only very rarely engage in fellatio. In general, older and lower-class Filipinos have a more negative view of oral and anal sex.

Modern Filipino youth, however, seem to be taking a new look at Westernized sexual expressions, according to what they said at the author's impromptu meetings. Al-though no general survey data are available, a segmental study of metropolitan youths revealed two groups of young women based on their responses. One group accepts and practices oral sex as a way of avoiding the risk of preg-nancy, maintaining their technical virginity until marriage, and/or as a form of safer sex. For the second group, oral sex was a more intimate form of sexual relationship, somehow more "romantic" than genital intercourse. Youths holding the latter view believed that oral sex should be only engaged in with a stable (engaged to be married) partner and not in the first few exploratory encounters or dates. Some other older girls joined some boys in rejecting this way of ex-pressing love, and thought that only prostitutes could prac-tice fellatio on boys.

Whereas anal intercourse is not part of the fantasies for the majority of devout Christian women, anecdotal reports revealed that 30 to 40% of males fantasized about having anal sex with women other than their wives. Prejudices against anal sex are even stronger in less educated youths. Most of the youths I spoke with do not accept anal sex even after marriage, perhaps influenced by the increasing inci-dence of AIDS in the Orient. Older boys agreed that a woman will never ask for it.

## 6. Homoerotic, Homosexual, and Bisexual Behaviors

Early Christian and Muslim colonists brought their reli-gious views of homosexuality as either sinful or at least un-natural and immoral. Today, the Philippines is still, to a large extent, a macho society, and macho men detest gays, whom they see as effeminate and "strange." For a majority of the population, including locally trained physicians, psy-chologists, and social workers, homosexuality is viewed as a perversion and a disease. Teenagers who feel a strong at-traction to persons of their own gender at first experience confusion about their feelings and sexuality. Gradually, as their orientation becomes clearer in their minds, they awake to the unpleasant reality of belonging to a group that Filipino society marginalizes.

Homosexuality in the Philippines, however, is increas-ingly being tolerated, and a gay movement is gaining strength and demanding their rights. Twenty years ago, this would have been unthinkable. The scorn for gays is stronger among low- and middle-class men than in the upper class. There always were artists, beauticians, fashion designers, writers, and medical and dental professionals whose homo-sexuality was known among the elite, but which was care-fully kept out of scrutiny from the media and the masses. Lesbians are still not too visible in Filipino society, in keep-ing with the Christian and Victorian tradition, which never wanted to think about sexual activities in a relationship be-tween two females. To be gay or lesbian in a repressive en-vironment whose stereotypes are the macho man and the submissive reproductive woman is not an easy task. Any-one who deviates from strict heterosexual behavior is ridi-culed: A gay is not a man and a lesbian is a degenerate woman. The Filipino Armed Forces does not allow gays to join the military and expels them when they are discovered.

To be bisexual, however, is not so annoying, as long as one's same-gender behavior is kept very private. In the early 1970s, it was common for Filipinos to identify or classify two types of gays: those who engage in homosexual sex activities and those who act effeminate but do not en-gage in homosexual acts. However, in the early 1990s, the former group has been active in promoting gay rights for the whole gay community. Although the "Gay Organization for Liberty and Dignity" is not yet a formal organization, they speak for both the visible and the invisible, helping the latter to openly assume their identities. Part of the emergence of gay and lesbian subcultures are masseurs who advertise their services in the most important papers and magazines and in metropolitan "gay" bars, discos, and hair salons. Some vocal gay groups lobby to influence politicians for future legal status and/or political clout.

Most Filipino gays prefer to mix with the heterosexual mainstream in their own social class and not form exclu-sively or predominantly homosexual neighborhoods. Those who have a well-defined and highly visible economic or po-litical role are still in the closet. The same is true for members of the Armed Forces and the clergy. To admit their homosexuality would be unthinkable or suicidal. On the other hand, among artists, writers, movie producers, TV personalities-actors, dancers, some doctors and dentists, and university professors, to openly admit they are gay may bring rejection from the most conservative members of society, but they may end up being accepted and sometimes even see their popularity increase. In the medical community, homosexuality is still generally viewed in Freudian terms as a condition originating in conflicts and childhood sexual conflicts, which can be cured by psychotherapy. Whereas members of the locally trained medical community, with limited experience abroad, view homosexuality as a violation of the laws of nature, the general public continues to believe that homosexuality is a result of growing up effeminate in a family without a masculine image or male role model.

[*Update 2003*: In December 2002, the continual suppression of gay activity by the Catholic Church was further reinforced by the Philippine government's refusal to issue a special non-immigrant visa to a "female spouse" of a female bank executive, even though the two women were legally recognized as "domestic partners" in the U.S.A. Then Justice Secretary H. Perez said that the Philippine Constitution and Family Code were "very categorical" in stating that marriages are only between a man and a woman. However, the Justice Secretary also said that "their (gay couple) marriage cannot be countenanced under Philippine laws for reason of public policy." In his view, "determinations or conventions agreed upon in foreign countries" do not override local laws.

[As recently as 2002, the public's reaction to lesbian activities was mixed, ranging from the firing of a medical school dean and professor for having a "romantic" involvement with a medical student, to the acceptance of a movie star's son as a macho gay topless dancer. In spite of the public's "conditional" acceptance of Filipino gays in early 2003, Oscar Atadero, a spokesperson for ProGay Philippines, again accused the Catholic Church of family anti-gay hatred. He referred to the exclusion of Filipino homosexuals from the Fourth World Meeting of Families, which was held in Manila in 2003. At the time, Manila's Archbishop Cardinal Sin warned that Christian family values were being eroded by advocates of same-sex marriages, divorce, the modern media, and technology. In response, Atadero declared that homosexuals are "not calling into question the existence of the family or staging a rebellion," but are merely asserting that they should be given "the same love and legal rights that other children of God have" (*Filipino Express* 2003). (*End of update by J. F. J. Leyson*)]

## 7. Gender Diversity and Transgender Issues

Despite the prevailing Spanish machismo mentality, the advent of democracy and Westernized media messages are slowly changing traditional attitudes. Thus, the "eccentric" minorities have had a chance to come out of their closets and express themselves. For the moment, the public reacts with curiosity rather than violence or acceptance. In the world of beauticians, dressmakers/designers, and performing artists, there are well-known transvestites. Because these persons are celebrities in Filipino culture, the public, especially the women, accepts them with smiles and gentle jokes. There is an annual summer parade of transvestites in Manila, where some men are indistinguishable from real women in physique and even "beauty." This event is similar to gay, lesbian, and transgender pride parades in San Francisco and New York City's Greenwich Village. In his younger days, this author would cross-dress with other

young professionals to entertain hometown guests during *fiestas* and Christmas celebrations. On the superstitious side, folklore in the North Central and Central parts of the archipelago holds that, when someone is confronted by a witch or travels through a haunted region, it is advisable to cross-dress so that the witch or the devil does not recognize you. In some rare cases, transvestites have acceptance from their mates, and sometimes from their children, when they live in metropolitan cities, cross-dress in the privacy of their homes, and maintain the macho stereotype in their work and social environment.

If life is not easy for non-effeminate gays or non-masculine lesbians, it is more difficult for those who identify themselves as the opposite sex in manners and clothing, and even more so for those who want to see their bodies change towards the features of the other sex. Persons who want to change their physical sex and be socially recognized as being of the other sex have not been seriously considered in the Philippines. The Philippine Medical Association and the Philippine College of Surgeons have not officially reported any case of transsexualism. Transsexuals are provided with psychiatric treatment, not transsexual surgery. The courts have not addressed this situation, and any person who desires to undergo medical (pre-surgical) and transsexual surgery treatments has to seek such services abroad.

## 8. Significant Unconventional Sexual Behaviors

### A. Coercive Sex

#### Sexual Abuse of Children and Incest

There are no statistics on the incidence of incest in the Philippines. However, it is quietly known that adolescent girls are often raped by older male family members, and fathers often use them as sexual objects after the death of the mother, or when the wife's work takes her outside the home for long periods. Abusive males are usually unemployed people with a past history of family violence, high consumption of alcohol, social inadequacy, and impulsive behavior. Although less frequent, cases of incest are also known in which the male is the head of an upper-class household and respected by his community. Cases of incest in middle- and upper-class families seldom surface while the victim is a minor. The trauma may emerge during private sexual therapy with an older woman, but there is a strong reluctance on the part of most victims to make formal charges. Generally, indictment for incest by judicial authorities does not take effect unless a formal complaint has been filed or in cases of public scandal.

Reacting to the increase in cases of child sexual abuse reported in the media, law enforcement agencies and the courts have started taking this situation seriously. Sexual exploitation of minors is more frequent in the cities, in the form of child prostitution, child pornography, and sex tourism. The clients and supporters of child prostitutes and those who produce, sell, or transmit pornography involving minors risk heavy fines and imprisonment. Crimes of sex tourism are difficult to prosecute because they originate or transpire outside the geographic borders and legal jurisdiction of the Philippines. There is, however, an organization, Hand Extending Love to the Philippines (H.E.L.P.), based in Phoenix, Arizona, USA, whose primary mission is to help sexually abused Filipino children, provide counseling for pedophiliacs, and prevent teenage pregnancy.

#### Sexual Harassment

The Euro-American concept of sexual harassment has no place in the tradition of Filipina subservience to males that is part of *marianismo*, the symbiotic culture to *machismo*. However, the experience of sexual harassment is emerging in the social consciousness, as Filipinas respond to Western influences and begin to assert their personal and political rights. Women from the *barrios* and small towns are easily intimidated, but it is the sophisticated and well-educated women who challenge the "old-boy buddy" system and file complaints. Sexual harassment is punished through an administrative indictment that may end with a dismissal from public service. The administrative procedure, however, does not preclude legal action by the alleged perpetrator. The strength of the current law shows that Filipinas are expanding their political presence/clout, and winning the support of men, who know the problem well from inside the system.

[*Update 2003*: In December 2002, Rodolfo Stavenhagen of the United Nations Human Rights Council issued a complaint to the Philippine government on the sexual harassment perpetrated on indigenous Filipinos by the Philippine Army. The report claimed that native Filipinos were physically abused and sexually harassed if they were suspected of being terrorists or communist guerillas. The report cited destruction of houses, herding the people into hamlets, torture, and sexual abuses. The sexual harassment consisted of sexual innuendos, poking guns into female vulvas, and frottage by intoxicated government soldiers.

[In order to put more legal teeth into preventing or reducing sexual harassment, the 12th Philippine Congress (2002) passed a more comprehensive anti-sexual harassment law. It provides more protection for victims and severe punishments for perpetrators. The law is gender neutral, applying to male-to-female and female-to-male cases. But, it does not clearly define or include same-gender sexual harassment. Despite the passage of this new law, the incidence of sexual harassment cases has not changed. A January 2003 incident is unfortunately still typical: A female vice-governor (American lieutenant governor equivalent) was groped by a businessman during a public works bidding. At the same time, groping (frottage) of female passengers on the MetroManila Light Railway train was so serious that the LRT assigned coaches exclusively for female passengers in order to protect women from physical sexual harassment. The all-female coaches are installed behind a special section reserved for the elderly, pregnant, and disabled passengers, and adults with infants or young children. To avoid confusion, security guards are assigned at the platforms to guide female passengers who want to use the all-female coaches. Women are not required to use the all-female coaches and can ride alone or with a male companion in the mixed-gender coaches. Sixty percent of the estimated 320,000 daily passengers are female. (*End of update by J. F. J. Leyson*)]

*Rape and Family Violence*

Despite a long colonial period during which wealthy *hacienderos* controlled and regularly exploited their indigenous female employees without fear that the victims might find some recourse in the justice system, recent educational reforms and the transition to a democratic government are producing a more humane society. However, there is still considerable violence within Filipino households perpetrated by the male head of the household. Abuse of this kind is seldom reported to police, because women know that the male police usually behave in the same way in their homes.

In the poorest households, girls are conditioned from infancy to accept the violent behavior of their fathers, particularly when they return home intoxicated. The initial physical abuse may lead to sexual intercourse that amounts to marital rape. Faced with a society that until recently did not recognize the possibility of marital rape or a woman's basic rights, abused women capitulate, repress their feelings, retreat into their taciturn dreams, and continue laboring for the survival of their families, especially their offspring. Even then, if she does not manage to hide at least some of her earnings, the husband may spend them with another woman or drinking with friends. Local newspapers occasionally report domestic incidents when a wife inflicts serious genital damage on her husband while resisting his violent carnal advances. Philippine Department of Social Work and Development (DSWD) statistics reported that in the first three quarters of 1998, there were at least 1,152 cases of rape and attempted rape, 656 cases of incest, and 400 cases of lasciviousness.

The seriousness of rape against an individual female was brought to the public eye by the media when a famous actress was "gang raped" in the mid-1960s. The public demanded the severest punishment, the death penalty, and they got it. Execution by hanging, electrocution, or lethal injection as a penalty for rape has been on the books since 1924. The death penalty was abolished in 1987 but reinstated in 1994. There are currently about 900 persons on death row, including a former member of Congress convicted in 1998 and awaiting execution for rape. Even though no actual executions for rape have taken place, the law has been instrumental in helping reduce such incidents.

After nine years of debate, the House of Representatives finally, in 1997, approved the bicameral conference report on a new law that heavily penalizes rape and makes it easier for government prosecutors to prosecute rape cases. This anti-rape law reclassifies rape from "a crime against chastity" to "a crime against a person." Thus, if the victim is a minor and refuses to accuse the perpetrator, only the minor's legal guardian or the court can file a suit. This new law also penalizes marital rape, but opens the door for the spouse to forgive her husband, in which case the charge is voided. The new law also redefines the nature of rape, expanding the traditional definition of forced penile insertion in the vagina to include unwanted insertion of the penis, or any object or instrument, in any bodily orifice of another person. These "other acts" are now part of "sexual assault." The law in the Revised Penal Code also eliminates the gender bias, so that a woman can now be charged with raping a man. Finally, the law makes it possible to present evidence in court, in which presumption is created in favor of a rape victim, so that any overt physical act manifesting resistance in any degree can now be accepted as evidence of rape. Similarly, evidence that the victim was in a situation where she or he was incapable of giving valid consent can now be accepted as evidence of rape.

### B. Prostitution

Tribal wars between the aborigines in the Philippine islands turned the vanquished into slaves for labor or cannibalism, but not sexual slaves. When Chinese merchants started trading with the inhabitants of the archipelago in 960 C.E., they intermarried with native women, but did not sexually exploit the women. With the advent of Spanish colonists in the late 1500s, a flourishing slave trade was established between the Philippines, the Caribbean, and Spain. Anecdotal reports revealed that some Filipina slaves were sold as "exotic sex objects" or prostitutes to European brothels. When Pope Gregory XIV abolished slavery in the Philippines in 1591, middle-class Europeans started to immigrate to the archipelago, but the sexual exploitation of Filipinas by the Spanish colonists continued.

During World War 11 (1941-1944), the Japanese Imperial Army forced Philippine women from Manila and surrounding towns to serve as "comfort girls" (military prostitutes) to provide sexual favors to all Japanese soldiers serving in the Philippines and in the Pacific region. In the 1990s, with international (legal) backing, these comfort girls were partially compensated for their humiliation and moral sufferings. When the American troops liberated the Philippines from Japanese imperialism in October 1945, many American soldiers left illegitimate Amerasian children behind. The mothers of these children and their Amerasian children were social outcasts. In order for these mothers to survive, they became part-time prostitutes in the rural areas for single laborers and traveling salesmen and in the cities with all kinds of customers. In 1947, President Roxas signed a military agreement granting 22 military bases to the United States. In the following year, the two largest U.S. military bases in the Far East, the Naval Subic Bay and Clark Air Force Base, were established north of Manila. Angeles City, located near Clark Air Force Base, later became the "Mecca of Sex Trade," the military adult-entertainment capital of the Philippines, with every variety of prostitution, exotic bars, pornography, and sex tourism conceivable.

With the advent of information technology and global travel, the old part-time prostitutes have moved to the big cities. Prostitution survives because of poverty, the commercialization of human relations, and the sustained carnal demand. Although for different reasons, all social classes made their contributions to the trade in sexual services. The rich are looking for entertainment and diversity of sexual practices that they would never dare to ask from their wives. These respectable matrons are assigned by society only to bear and raise children, manage households (sometimes businesses), and organize social activities. The out-of-town students, immigrant workers, and wayward youths may be looking for their first sexual experiences and to combat the loneliness of being separated from their family for the first time. The poor frequent the brothels to affirm their masculinity by using many women or to relieve their loneliness.

As in most other countries, there are three types of prostitutes or sex working girls in the Philippines: streetwalkers, entertainment girls (*hostitutes*), and call girls or high-class prostitutes. Streetwalkers are not common, are usually self-employed, and many have pimps. Their safety is at jeopardy on the streets. The majority of the prostitutes fall under the category of entertainment girls. These *hostitutes* include bar girls, nightclub hostesses (waitresses), masseuses, exotic dancers, and those that work in brothels. They are usually business employees and have contact managers (sophisticated pimps). Their safety is secure because they work inside an establishment. However, they cannot refuse clients who are produced by agencies and their managers. They cannot set the prices for their services. Some massage parlors are commercial fronts for prostitutes who offer their services from oral sex to regular intercourse (US$25 to $65). Call girls comprise approximately a third of the female sex-worker population. Self-employed or autonomous, they usually do not have managers. They advertise their services in specialized magazines disguised as escort services for sophisticated gentlemen and sometimes ladies. *Hostitutes* and call girls advertise their services through word of mouth, by taxi drivers, bar bouncers, club managers/owners, and hotel bell captains. These agents receive part of the price in exchange for referring clients. In the large sophisticated hotels, the bell captain may have an album with pictures of different prostitutes from which guests may choose. In 1997, a new phenomenon emerged, the *Japosakis*, Filipina *hostitutes* who return home from sex work in Japan and continue serving their Japanese special

clientele or sugar daddies on their periodic "business" trips to the archipelago. Recently, there are also reports of an increasing number of *gigallos* or *toy boys* who provide escort services and pleasures for lonely matrons and wealthy widows.

Although prostitution is still illegal, Filipino society believes that some regulation is always needed, based on the premise that prostitution is regulated in order to minimize the damage to society. Local city councils may require filing an application with the city to establish a brothel, indicating the location for legal reasons and/or tax purposes. Local authorities may also restrict brothels to certain areas and regulate any signs that would identify it as a brothel. Prostitutes cannot reside anywhere other than at the brothel itself, which is her official domicile. Brothels also have to have a bedroom for each working woman. The women cannot show themselves at the balconies or in a window, nor can they solicit in the streets. In order to work in a brothel, a woman has to register with the sanitary-health authorities (Bureau of Health). The authorities will check whether she is a victim of deceit or coercion and advise her that help and assistance is available from legal authorities.

Each prostitute is given a "sanitary notebook" with her picture, personal data, registration number (if any), and the main articles of the decree that concern her rights as a provider of a service. Her rights include being free to stay or quit the brothel in which she lives and works, debts cannot be used to compel her to stay in a given brothel, and no one can subject her to any abuse. Each prostitute has to undergo mandatory monthly medical examinations for sexually transmitted diseases (STDs). If an STD is diagnosed, the brothel pays for medical treatment. The sex worker must show her sanitary notebook to any customer that asks to see it. The manager of the brothel cannot accept any "prostitute-candidate" or applicant who has not first registered and passed a medical examination. The manager also has to report immediately to the sanitary authorities whenever a prostitute is ill, be this an STD or nonsexual disease.

It is easy to imagine the rampant corruption that this naive attempt to protect customers and suppliers of contractual sex alike has produced. Police protection is bought, violations are ignored, and politicians and judges are bribed, often on the pretext of protecting the free practice of a fully consensual sex by the client and sex worker. In reality, this law and its application or lack thereof does little to protect the health of the women and their clients. The women have no protection from customers already infected. The prostitutes can request that their clients wear condoms, but cannot demand the performance of safe sex practices. The clients are not subject to compulsory medical "control," and many may be infected but not show any symptoms, while others suffer in silence and continue practicing unsafe sex with other prostitutes, lovers, and even wives.

Transvestites also participate in prostitution, especially with unwary foreigners. Male homosexuals and child prostitutes who created Asia's reputation for sex tourism are concentrated in major metropolitan cities.

### Sex Tourism

The Philippines has always been known as the "Pearl of the Orient Seas," the Land of the Three *S*s—Sun, Sand, and Sea. A fourth "S," Sex, sold in "coolly" wrapped packages, has emerged to the point where it has already warranted the United Nations' attention: sex tourism involving child prostitutes as young as 6 years old.

Angeles City in Pampanga, north of Manila, once home of the mighty Clark U.S. Air Base, is now being developed as an international airport. But the new airport has also become the center of sex tours to the Philippines, openly promoted abroad, arranged by Filipino tour operators and their foreign counterparts, with attractive come-ons for men seeking sexual activities with "virginal" or child prostitutes who they hope are free of STD and HIV infections.

While the government is making major arrests in this trade, and sex establishments are regularly closed down, the front page of major dailies show bikini-clad young girls being led away by operatives, but never the brothel owners, the tour operators, their cohorts, and pimps. The Philippine Congress is still struggling to pass a law making a customer of a child prostitute criminally liable, even if he does not engage the services of a pimp. An increase of the maximum punishment for child labor and exploitation to 20 years was sought. The 1995 law set the punishment for child prostitution at 20 years in prison; the punishment for pornography and pedophilia, however, remained unchanged.

Sex tourism is the third-highest money-making industry in the Philippines. But the current penalties and enforcement policies do nothing to have an impact on the business. As in many other countries, the prostitutes are arrested, but not the clients, managers, and others whose enormous profits make this business so attractive. The punishment for committing prostitution is a US$500 fine or 12 years in jail. While this law, in effect for three decades, applies to women dancing in the nude or in scanty bikini tongs, a major element in the prostitution trade, arrests are seldom made because of corruption and bribery.

In order to reduce the negative moral and economic effects of prostitution, government and some nongovernment agencies are working together to rehabilitate former prostitutes or entertainment girls who retire or change their "profession." The government's Department of Social Welfare and Development has programs to teach these ex-prostitutes other work alternatives and technical skills as a means to a decent living. A civic action and rehabilitation group, Marriage Encounter, is also training married former prostitutes to help them move back into mainstream society and divert single women from the sex trade by improving their personal skills for future relationships and family life. But funds and enthusiasm for such social programs are too limited.

## C. Pornography and Erotica

Under Spanish colonial rule, the Dutch (in 1600), and the British (in 1762), Filipinos were concerned about their personal freedom rather than freedom of the press. In 1820, the Spanish Cortes (government) granted the Filipino freedom of the press, but it was not until 1887, 67 years later, that Dr. Jose P. Rizal, a Philippine national hero, published in Germany the first Filipino novel, *Noli Me Tangere* [*Touch Me Not*]. This literary masterpiece exposed the Spanish political, economic, and sexual abuses in the Philippines. However, it was not until the early 1900s that Filipino romantic novelist Francisco Balagtas published *Florente at Laura*, his Filipino variation on the Romeo and Juliet theme.

In 1946, when the Philippines became a republic after 48 years of American colonialism, American and foreign magazines started to pour into the country. Pornographic magazines were illegal, but the rich and some devoted collectors managed to import literary exotic pieces (erotica). By the 1960s, changes were visible in the social attitudes and private interests of Filipinos. Women's magazines are now found everywhere, in homes, hair salons, physician's offices, and in businesses. And in almost every issue, there are articles about sexuality and eroticism. These articles also cover a variety of subjects, such as contraception, the influ-

ence of a healthy sexual life on physical and mental well-being, and how to improve a marital relationship.

Although there are no precise data on the production and commerce of pornography in the Philippines, there is no doubt about its widespread distribution and availability. The gradual blurring of the distinction between pornography and other forms of erotica has led to some level of social acceptance of pornography and opened new markets. In public debates, the anti-pornography position is weak, and pornography is often presented as a form of sexual liberation. Even some Catholic moralists have recognized that pornography can help couples to improve their sexual lives, as long as it does not replace the "natural" (romantic) sexuality.

Three types of Filipino magazines deal with sexuality and eroticism:

1. Magazines dealing with sexual issues, but avoiding pornographic images and full nudity, (e.g., *Superstuds*, *Gossips*, *Intrigue*, *Expose*, *Teen Stars*, and *Soap Opera Stars*). They are moderately to expensively priced, have quality printing, and are directed at informing a public that accepts a scientific (although popular rather than academic) language. *Sex Forum* magazine, published by a lawyer in the mid-1980s, provided sexual information reviewed and approved by the author of this chapter. Among the topics discussed in *Sex Forum* were techniques to enjoy an intense sexuality, to make your bedroom a more erotic place, to renew sexual passion without changing partners, safer sex practices, and ways of taking care of yourself without handicapping your pleasure.
2. Magazines of literary and sexual humor, with pornographic texts, advice columns, letters, and partial or total nudity (e.g., *Tik-Tik*, *Playboy*, and *Penthouse*).
3. Magazines and packages of playing or picture cards, clearly pornographic and devoid of artistic quality, some with scatological content.

In reality, a wide range of pornography and erotica is readily available, with distribution handled by regular newsstands, video shops, porno shops (major cities only), and mail-order services.

From the economic point of view, the most important sector of the Filipino pornography market is the sale of videocassettes, fueled by the wide distribution of videocassette players-recorders. In the 1960s, before video players, rich couples viewed adult films with an eight- or super-eight-millimeter portable film projector in the privacy of their own homes, or at some occasional college students' "stag parties." Videocassettes offer the possibility of greater privacy, and cater to the needs of middle-class and even poor men, women, and couples. Most of the pornography is produced abroad and imported for rental through video shops and typical newsstands. The legal situation seems to favor the newsstand as the primary channel for the rental/sale of these cassettes. Video shops, however, offer the advantage of greater anonymity and the higher technical quality of the cassettes. The sale and distribution of these pornographic materials are illegal. Although enforcement of the anti-pornography law is weak, sometimes it will produce a dramatic example. In April 1999, a 61-year-old Filipina grandmother was arrested for selling pornographic tapes on the streets of a metropolitan city.

Filipino pornography also comes in the form of "Live Sex Shows" arranged through special parties held in motels or hotels. The movie *UHAW* (*Sexual Hunger*), a softcore film in the early 1970s, was the first erotica production with the lead female role played by a former national Philippine beauty queen. Hardcore videos, although poor in quality, are also homemade, but lack the better quality of American and foreign imports. The advent of the Internet has brought a wide variety of sexual information and visuals, including local Web sites, like *sex maniacs* (*manyakis*, www.mayakis.com), with a modest monthly access fee.

The author's informal survey of consumers of pornography indicates that about 85% of the males and 15% of females are sexually excited by such films. Females prefer erotic films where sexual acts are embedded in a narrative context, whereas males are more easily aroused by simply viewing mere nudity and sexual organs. Female consumption of pornography seems to take place in the context of the couple, whereas for men it is more linked with solitary sex. Generally speaking, there are indications of an increasing trend toward increasing consumption of softcore (clean) pornography by educated, sophisticated, and professional couples.

### [Body Painting and Piercing

[*Update 2003*: The aboriginal civilization of the Philippine natives has flourished simultaneously with other native populations of Eastern Asia, Africa, and Mexico. While the Incas, Mayans, and Aztecs were erecting their temples, the aboriginal Filipinos were sculpturing rice terraces along the mountainsides that are considered one of the engineering wonders of ancient civilizations. At the same time, these ancient people perfected body painting (tattoos) for religious reasons and sexual attraction as an art form using primitive tools and different plant dyes. The tattoo artists, sometimes a medicine man, etched exquisite patterns mainly on the faces of females and on the extremities of the males as "spiritual armour" to scare evil spirits or their enemies.

[In the late 1970s, when "liberal nudity" was appearing in the cinema, body tattooing underwent a revival. With Americanization in the 1980s, young Filipino urbanites followed the trend set by young actors and entertainers, applying tattoos in some strategic sexual parts, buttocks, inner thighs, umbilicus, and breasts. On the other hand, young females in the *barrios* have modified their simple makeup into elaborate "facial painting." Body tattooing is limited to male college students and only on the body parts covered by clothing.

[Body piercing is as primitive as body painting for the Filipino aborigines. Both sexes subject themselves to ear piercing solely for sexual attraction. However, anecdotal reports indicate that cannibalistic natives also pierced their noses with animal or human bones for decoration or as a trophy of their conquest.

[In the late 1980s, when the majority of young Filipinos were concerned with finding a date or romantic interlude, eroticism was still considered a sexual taboo until they entered college. With the advent of global communications, the use of body piercing as a form of eroticism was popularized by young artists and Filipinos living in the metropolitan areas. The traditional ear piercing expanded to eyebrows and the umbilicus. In 2001, this author (a surgeon) had to surgically remove an infected "umbiliring" from a female patient to avoid the spread of an infection. Young Filipinos, and others, who decide to have body piercing and umbilical rings need to be clean the umbilicus and ring regularly to avoid infections. Also rings are more dangerous in the inverted ("inny") umbilicus than they are in the everted ("outty") umbilicus.

[At present, the art of body piercing as a form of eroticism has intensified and expanded to other parts of the torso, the tongue and lips, and the genitals, labia, clitoral hood, and penile glans. The presence of erotic rings and balls in strategic sensual body parts will continue to pose a health hazard in the future. (*End of update by J. F. J. Leyson*)]

## 9. Contraception, Abortion, and Population Planning

### A/B. Population Planning and Contraception

[*Update 2003*: In the 1970s, Thailand and the Philippines each had populations of about 50 million and economies of similar sizes. Three decades later, Thailand has grown by 10 million to 60 million, while the Philippines has exploded exponentially to 85 million. Experts expect the Philippine population to double again to 130 million by 2025. Meanwhile, Thailand, Indonesia, South Korea, and Taiwan have brought their population growth under control. The Total Fertility Rate in the Philippines is 3.6 children per fertile woman, among the highest in the world outside Africa. Most of the larger families reside in the villages and *barrios*, especially among poor families. Families of 10, 12, or more children are the greatest source of pride. "If you have many children you are a great man," is a common belief. A few years back, when Cardinal Jaime Sin was asked about the country's population, his response was simple: "The more the merrier." The topography of the Philippines has made agriculture the main source of livelihood. This agrarian living needs workers. In order to provide "cheap" labor, it is advantageous for a Filipino family to sire more children, mainly boys, as workers and helpers in the agribusiness and aquaculture.

[The only contraceptive method accepted by the Catholic Church, the rhythm/cervical mucus or Natural Family Planning method, has a very low effectiveness rate because of menstrual irregularities. But in March 2003, President Gloria Macapagal Arroyo affirmed her backing for the "rhythm method." Mrs. Arroyo suggested that the rhythm method would promote family values by bringing spouses together, with the wife observing her body temperature, vaginal secretions, and menstrual cycle, and her husband writing them down on a chart. She also stated her belief that this natural contraceptive method would help teach patience, responsibility, and self-control. In the real world, critics say that the rhythm method is unreliable, complicated to follow (especially for the uneducated), and requires unusual restraint on the part of husbands. Another major barrier to the effectiveness of the rhythm method is the reluctance of Filipinas to check their cervical mucus, and their limited understanding of the physiology of fertility among those with limited school education.

[In 2003, Church officials announced they would be more vigorous in opposing all contraceptive programs, and would campaign in future elections against any politicians who support family planning, calling them "adulterers, fornicators and terrorists." Meanwhile, the Church has begun intimidating retail stores that offer condoms for sale. The Seven-Eleven grocery chain, for instance, stopped selling condoms following a Church-instigated boycott and picketing. Despite the fact that the government cannot educate, provide health services, and feed its present population of 85 million, let alone a population of 130 million 20 years from now, the Church continues its campaign in favor of large families and its ban on all artificial contraception. Family planning has become increasingly popular since World War II.

[Thirty years ago, between 1968 and 1970, the United Nations, through the World Health Organization and Planned Parenthood, initiated a massive population-control program, distributing contraceptive pills to Filipino families. As one of the trainer/instructors, this author gave public lectures and provided training to all municipal healthcare personnel. The pills were given free to all married women. Fortunately, there was no strong opposition from the Catholic Church. However, after two years of implementation, because of government mismanagement of funding and pill distribution, there was no significant reduction in the pregnancy rate. With the increasing number of couples living together out of wedlock, the number of illegitimate children will double by the year 2005. Before the government started the "aggressive and formal" family planning in the late 1960s, middle-class couples learned the use of contraception through specialized pamphlets, magazines, and private channels (family doctors and pharmacists). Today, with the government restricting public education about contraception, the most effective teaching tools are the American television programs *Sex and the City* and *Friends*.

[Nowadays, in the large cities, contraceptives of all kinds—pills, condoms, diaphragms, IUDs, and vaginal spermicides—are available. These contraceptives can be freely bought in pharmacies without prescriptions. Women who can afford to pay can use the services of private physicians to help them acquire the correct kind of diaphragm or to insert an IUD. But two out of five Filipinos, 41% of the people, live below the poverty level, on less than a dollar a day. Jobs, food, and farmland are increasingly scarce. Urban slums are teeming with poor families with a dozen children (Mydans 2003). (*End of update by J. F. J. Leyson*)]

The situation is more difficult for women who live in scarcely populated distant rural areas. There, both the birthrate and infant mortality rate are still high when compared to the urban figures. In these less-developed areas, the government has been trying to organize family planning services as part of its program of mother-child care including kindergarten classes. The number of abandoned children in metropolitan cities has increased. The Catholic Relief Services and other nongovernmental organizations are trying to house these children and provide contraceptive-control classes, including newspapers and television advertisements regarding practical birth controls for women and families who live in the city's slums and newly arrived urban immigrants. In 1997, faced with declining official development assistance from developed countries, the government requested increased funding for population programs. Former President F. Ramos suggested that developed countries must meet the United Nations target of committing 0.7% of their gross national product (GNP) to population control, and that this aid must follow the 20-20 formula on environment and development endorsed by the 1995 Copenhagen World Summit on Social Development.

[*Update 2003*: It is the Filipino women who bear the burden of raising large families and often seek to control their pregnancies. But the United States Agency for International Development reports that one fifth of women who want contraceptives do not have access to them. One reason, the agency reported, is that two thirds of the Philippine population cannot afford to buy condoms. The problem is immense: The use of modern contraceptive methods would have to rise by 40% for women to achieve the family size they want (Mydans 2003). (*End of update by J. F. J. Leyson*)]

According to recent studies, the Philippines has nearly 1.5 million street youth. At the same time, 74% of all unintended pregnancies in the Philippines occur in women 15 to 24 years old and 18% of Filipino youths engage in premarital sex. In late 1999, the Family Planning International Assistance office in Bangkok, Thailand, and the Reach Out Reproductive Health Foundation announced the start of Barkadahan, a new project designed to curb the spread of sexually transmitted diseases and unintended pregnancies among Philippine's street youth, and have launched a program to address their reproductive health needs with sexuality education, treatment for HIV and STDs, and family planning options (World Reporter Asia Intelligence Wire 11/1/1999).

## B. Abortion

From 1581 on, the Spanish colonists suppressed women's rights, including the right to an abortion. Filipinas were considered second-class citizens until 1937, when a plebiscite on women's suffrage gave them the right to vote. For the first time, Filipinas could have some impact on decisions regarding their health. In the 1930s, abortion was controversial and performed in rural areas by quack doctors with improvised instruments and herbal concoctions. These crude gynecological procedures often led to serious complications including death. After World War II, the American influence resulted in most abortions being performed by physicians. However, abortion today is illegal in the Philippines and is severely condemned by the Catholic Church. This condemnation was reiterated in a recent Papal Encyclical on ethical questions, *Evangelium Vitae*. The current criminal code penalizes with prison sentences women who have an abortion and the professional who performs this service. Abortions are allowed in only two situations, when the pregnant woman is mentally deranged and the pregnancy is a result of rape or incest, and when the pregnancy endangers the woman's life. The Catholic anti-choice movement tries actively, but with limited success, to convince the political leadership to tighten the existing legislation and its enforcement. Muslim law supports the national law on abortion.

Abortion is a last resort everybody knows about, but nobody talks about. Instead of fighting against the powerful forces that arrogate to themselves control over women's bodies, Filipino society prefers to tolerate the officially condemned practices with a mischievous twinkle of tacit agreement among professionals and citizens. Criminal prosecution and denunciation of abortion practices are rare, and only occur when a woman dies as a consequence of an abortion performed by a non-professional. Given these conditions, the Ministry of Health has no exact statistics for abortion, but it is believed that its practice is not as widespread as previously thought. In the major cities, women who typically seek medical help for abortion are unmarried, mature women who already have several children or single high school and college students. These women resort to abortion mainly to put a stop to an unwanted pregnancy or to reduce the family size.

Although morally wrong, pregnant teenagers are now being gradually accepted by their parents. They do not resort to abortion, but agree to keep the child in their parents' house despite embarrassment and peer ridicule. Studies on the relationship between abortion and socioeconomic position suggest that middle-class professional women resort to abortion more frequently than high- or lower-class women. Studies in Manila and Cebu City during the 1980s and 1990s revealed that the highest rate of abortion was among women with a college education or college students who temporarily reside in college dormitories on city-owned housing. There are no written records of abortion among the lower classes because they are usually not performed by healthcare professionals, and the women deny having them to avoid problems for themselves and for those who help them in the procedures.

The morbidity rate associated with illegal abortions, especially those performed by non-professionals, could be reduced if the Church and the government would provide appropriate sexual education and promote the proper use of contraceptives, and expand the socioeconomic criteria/indications for legal abortion. In addition, the government and nongovernmental organizations should appropriate extra funding to provide better accessibility to well-equipped provincial or regional hospitals to treat the complications of abortion.

## 10. Sexually Transmitted Diseases and HIV/AIDS

### A. Sexually Transmitted Diseases

The estimated one million foreign women sold into prostitution in Japan, Singapore, Europe, the Middle East, and Southeast Asian countries and sex tourism are a major source of STD. In metropolitan Filipino cities, the most frequently reported STDs are gonorrhea, genital chlamydia, chancroid, genital herpes, papillomas, and AIDS. There is an alarming increase in the number of cases with the traditional STDs, particularly gonorrhea, herpes, and syphilis. Because of global travel, resistant strains of gonorrhea and trichomoniasis have been reported in some pockets around large Filipino cities with international connections. The lack of appropriate sexual education among mostly the lower social class, an attitude of indifference to prophylactic measures, and a poorly funded medical care system combine to increase the rate at which STDs are growing in the Philippines. The nationalistic policies of the government have meant that doctors are trained and medical services organized to take special care of pregnant women and newborns, not for the prevention of STDs.

Management of STDs is organized on three levels. The first and most advanced environment is provided by private medical practitioners in their offices. In this privileged setting, only prejudice or ignorance can prevent doctors from providing timely prophylactic advice, early diagnosis, and appropriate treatment of STDs. The second environment is industrialized medicine, clinics established by big corporations and specialized businesses. While the quality of care in this setting depends on the training and qualifications of the medical staff, the availability of consulting specialists, dermatologists, urologists, and gynecologists has helped a large number of workers and their families by educating patients about the risks of STDs and encouraging them to seek early detection and treatment. The third environment is provided by municipal health clinics and provincial and/or regional hospitals. These hospitals are entrusted with two missions: to provide medical services to the poorest sectors of the population and to serve as training grounds for medical students from both private and public medical schools and universities. Initially, these services were totally free, but because of escalating labor-management medical costs, these facilities now charge a small fee or donation to defray the recurrent and management costs. This small donation and transportation difficulties may further discourage Filipinos from the shantytowns in the poverty belts around the large cities from seeking early diagnosis and treatment of STDs.

Prostitutes form another subpopulation in the larger cities that requires special focus in terms of being a reservoir of the diseases and implementing measures for prevention. Children and young adults, especially women from the *barrios*/rural areas, pour into the city and become prey to drug traffickers and pimps. Through shared needles and sexual activities, they are infected with all kinds of STDs, further contributing to the spread in their original milieus and city at large. Because of poor record keeping, there are no precise data or information regarding the incidence of STDs from city health offices. But anecdotal reports from the last ten years revealed that a small percentage of women who came to a medical office or made hospital appointments for gynecological problems, contraception, or family planning are infected with STDs. However, with the increasing population growth and the advent of sexual liberation, young Filipinos are vulnerable to STDs. The government and nongovernmental organizations (NGOs), including the Church, must marshal all their informational-educational resources to counteract the spread of STDs. Schools should incorporate STD-prevention information, with intense mandatory sex education starting in the 6th grade or earlier. Information provided by schools, social workers, health clinics, and NGOs should go well beyond this to help the youth develop a positive attitude towards the body, without shame and guilt about one's sexual nature, and to recognize their instinctive drives and develop an ability to establish tradeoffs between instinctual urges and the social moral constraints. Poor peasants and sophisticated urbanities can both understand a well-delivered message that these tradeoffs do not mean a repression of one's erotic life, but rather its enhancement by seeking to make it free of disease.

### B. HIV/AIDS

The current epidemiological explanation of the origins of HIV traces it to a mutant strain of SIV (simian immunovirus) found in "green monkeys" of the sub-Saharan regions of Africa. Two thousand years ago, the ancient Filipinos supplemented their rice and vegetarian diet with meat from a variety of game animals, including native Philippine monkeys. These simian creatures are the main prey of another world-famous carnivore, the Philippine monkey-eating eagle. In spite of their carnivorous appetite, the Filipino aborigines did not contract the HIV virus. Even today, there are Filipinos who still savor exotic menus of Philippine monkeys. Nevertheless, the HIV virus has reached the Philippines by other routes.

Acquired immune deficiency syndrome (AIDS) was first described in the U.S.A. in 1978. In 1988, an anecdotal report indicates that one infected Filipina prostitute from New York City came home to die in the Philippines. Twenty years after AIDS was diagnosed in California, the first 20 cases of AIDS were diagnosed in the Philippines (1990). Epidemiologists believe a major factor in the spread of HIV is the U.S. military personnel who frequented the sex bars and bordellos in the towns surrounding Clark Air Force Base and the Naval Base in Subic Bay. In 1992, it was estimated that 234 people were infected; by 1994, there were 834 cases. According to L. B. Duchene (1997) of Doctors Without Borders (Médicins Sans Frontières, MSF), 1,234 Filipinos were infected with the AIDS virus in 1997. But the World Health Organization (WHO) estimated that the true figures of Filipinos with AIDS in 1998 was approximately 23,350 persons. The dramatic increase in AIDS cases is attributed by MSF to exposure and infection of the virus through prostitution (heterosexual activities), the prohibitive cost of medicines, malnutrition, economic depression, untreated STDs, and limited access to modern medical care. Contrary to the experience in the industrialized nations, mortality is almost 82% in the first year of infectivity and 98% in two years. WHO and MSF estimated the Philippines would have 30,112 cases by the end of 1999, and about 39,780 cases by the year 2000. That is a 70% increase in the incidence of AIDS in just two years in a population of 79 million people.

The Department of Health AIDS Registry showed that 53% of the victims are men, 38% are women and 9% are children. Among persons diagnosed as being infected with AIDS, 55% are drug addicts, 40% were infected by heterosexual activities (mainly with prostitutes), and 5% by homosexual activity. Approximately 1.8 million Filipinos, 50,000 in Cebu City alone, are involved in the illegal drug trade, a US$6.6 billion business. According to Duchene (1997), the drugs and AIDS situation in the Philippines is, for unknown reasons, less serious that it is in India and Cambodia. As of 1999, 90% of the world's 33 million HIV/AIDS cases were found in Africa, Latin America, and Asia. Furthermore, the WHO figures estimated that there would be 38 to 40 million people living in the world with the HIV virus by the year 2000.

[*Update 2003*: One puzzle in the Philippines, where condoms are not widespread, is the nation's extremely low rate of HIV infection. According to government figures, just 1,810 cases have been reported. The United Nations estimate is higher, but still miniscule at 9,400 cases. Experts warn of an explosion to come. According to local studies, only 23% of sexually active young men reported using a condom, and only 4% said they use condoms regularly (Mydans 2003). (*End of update by J. F. J. Leyson*)]

While the gay community initially interpreted the alarm about AIDS as an attempt by the medical profession to regain control and use the discourse about health risks to moralize against "disorderly sexual conduct," the real purpose of this crusade was to reduce the risks and mortality for gays who are sexually active. Government and NGOs are more actively engaged in the education and prevention of HIV/AIDS.

It is now clear that any plan to decrease the social and economic impact of AIDS in the Philippines, as in any society, requires an emotional engagement that facilitates an important paradigmatic change of beliefs and behavior. This paradigmatic change is essential to practicing abstinence, to increasing the use of condoms, decreasing promiscuity, promoting the use of disposable needles among drug addicts, understanding and respecting those who suffer, and helping individuals everywhere to enjoy sexuality while minimizing the risks for one's self and society.

In addition to emotional engagement, changes in individual attitudes require the active and creative support of social groups to which the individual belongs; namely families, schools, private businesses, and churches. In 1995, a private civic organization hired Magic Johnson, a famous American basketball superstar, to give talks to Filipino youth about HIV prevention and living a responsible and healthy sex (safe) life.

[*Update 2002*: UNAIDS Epidemiological Assessment: The Philippines remains a low HIV-prevalence country. Since the first cases of HIV/AIDS were reported in 1984, 1,515 HIV infections, including 508 AIDS cases and 196 HIV/AIDS-related deaths, had been reported as of June 2001. An estimated 9,400 people were believed to be living with HIV at the end of 2001 (prevalence less than 0.1% in people aged 15 to 49 years). The estimated rate of reporting of HIV infection is low (5%). HIV in the Philippines is predominantly sexually transmitted (90%). The number of HIV/AIDS cases is not expected to increase substantially over the next few years.

[There is a high prevalence of STD among sex workers, with the prevalence rate of selected STDs—predominantly chlamydial infections—reaching more than 40%. The prevalence rate of STDs among women attending antenatal clinics was less than 1% for STDs other than chlamydia (5.6%). Gonococcal resistance to penicillin, tetracycline, and cipro-

floxacin is high. Most of gonorrhea isolates (89.3%) were resistant to penicillin and 38% were resistant to quinolones in 2000.

[Behavioral surveillance data in 1997 and 1998 indicated high prevalence of HIV/STD risk behavior. Sharing of needles was reported by 52% of injection drug users in 2000, and unprotected sex (non-condom use during the last sex with a non-regular sex partner) was reported by 75% of men who had sex with men and 34% of female sex workers.

[The estimated number of adults and children living with HIV/AIDS on January 1, 2002, were:

| | |
|---|---|
| Adults ages 15-49: | 9,400  (rate: 0.1%) |
| Women ages 15-49: | 2,500 |
| Children ages 0-15: | < 10 |

[An estimated 720 adults and children died of AIDS during 2001.

[At the end of 2001, an estimated 4,100 Filipino children under age 15 were living without one or both parents who had died of AIDS. (*End of update by the Editors*)]

## 11. Sexual Dysfunctions, Counseling, and Therapies

### A. Concepts of Sexual Dysfunction and Treatment

The Philippines is a conservative society in which definitions of sexual dysfunctions often mirror the changing attitudes towards male and female sexuality. Thus, in the 1970s, inhibited or absent female orgasm (anorgasmia) was not considered a problem in a context where female sexuality was linked almost exclusively with procreation. Premature ejaculation became more of a problem in the 1980s with the emergence of the myth of simultaneous orgasms, promoted by the Western media, and the idea of heterosexual sex as spontaneously pleasant, which taken together created a new set of pressures, expectations, and tensions. Finally, the growing public rejection of the conservative attitude of the Church linking emotionally stable sexuality with orgasm might reduce the tendency to treat alternative expressions of eroticism as sexual dysfunctions.

Prior to the mid-1950s, Filipino physicians had no better knowledge or understanding of human sexuality than the sophisticated Filipino citizen. Both could, but seldom did, read Kinsey's works and Masters and Johnson's book *Human Sexuality*. Even after some sexuality education was introduced into medical training, the information they received was prejudiced and biased. The departments of obstetrics and gynecology in the public health and urology section taught the pathologic aspects of genitourinary (sexual) organs and reproductive mechanisms, but refused to consider with the same vigor or objective the sexual behavior of healthy males and females. In my interviews with medical students and young doctors during my periodic visits to the Philippines in 1984, this author perceived that two years later, the physicians still did not feel comfortable discussing healthy sexuality issues. Some of these doctors even felt personally offended, especially in being asked to deal with the "sexually oppressed" minority social groups, such as the aging, homosexuals, and the mentally and physically disabled (handicapped).

Gynecologists, psychiatrists, urologists, and general practitioners often have limited knowledge when people come for advice on sexual problems, such as frigidity, impotence, ejaculatory dysfunction, painful sex, sex during pregnancy and after delivery, consequences on sex life from drug/alcohol abuse, sex among the aged and physically handicapped, and sexual surgical procedures. Although their scientific information about sexuality is limited and incomplete, they perceive that science and common sense conflict with their ideologies and cultural-religious beliefs. The internal battles between these two opposing patterns of thinking and behavior only add confusion and distress to ignorance.

In 1990, this author initiated the creation of sexuality programs in major Filipino universities and medical schools. *Sexual Rehabilitation of the Spinal Cord Injury Patients* (Leyson 1991), by this author, was introduced, along with other resources, and quickly became popular among medical and paramedical personnel along with judges, lawyers, and teachers who are increasingly more aware of their need for advanced education on sexual topics/issues.

## B. Sexual Counseling and Therapies

Prior to the 1960s, the management of sexual dysfunctions was based mostly on folklore and "witchcraft." In the 1970s, management was a mixture of traditional folklore and medical science. In the rural areas, marital dysfunctions (sexual and reproductive) were treated with exotic concoctions and herbal remedies. In the urban areas, impotence was mainly treated with psychotherapy, occasional antidepressants, and hormones. Premature ejaculation was managed by psychotherapy. In 1998, the most common male sexual problem was impotence, followed by premature ejaculation, decreased libido, and infertility. Premature ejaculation was managed by antidepressants and psychotherapy, with perhaps some behavioral sex therapy. Impotence was treated with nonspecific vasodilators, sex therapy, and, for those who could afford it, penile prostheses. Libido disorder and infertility were treated with psychotherapy and pharmacological remedies. Among women, the most common sexual problems were painful intercourse (dyspareunia), vaginal spasms, and inhibited orgasm (dysorgasmia). Occasionally, older women complained of a decrease of sexual desire. Dyspareunia was treated with psychotherapy and sex therapy. The other sexual dysfunctions were grouped into one disease and managed with sex therapy and pharmacological remedies.

From 1995 to the present, sexual dysfunction management is almost the same as in the United States and Europe for those able to afford it. Most urologists and gynecologists have taken additional training in sex education and therapy. A few American- and European-trained sexologists have opened offices in major cities. With the infusion of new ideas and discoveries in sexology, management of sexual dysfunctions consists of behavioral therapy, sensory amplifications, advanced psychotherapy, and sex therapy. Modern impotence treatment includes erection vacuum devices, oral and intraurethral medications, intrapenile injection medicines, and solid and inflatable penile prostheses, as well as sexual performance medications like Viagra. However, some herbal remedies for impotence, infertility, and libido disorders have also been revived. The Church and NGOs with social services offer premarital and marital counseling, although the official Catholic position still maintains the traditional female role of motherhood, and perpetuates a generally more passive attitude towards sexuality and pleasuring even in marriage.

## C. Sexual Counseling for Emigrant Filipinos

Sexual counseling and therapy for Filipinos who immigrate to other countries presents some unique problems. The "Filipino Blend," which represents the majority of Filipinos, is the result of racial diversity and genetic pooling involving over 1,300 years of infusions from China, Indonesia, Malaysia, Indochina, India, Borneo, Java, Spain, and the United States. The profound psychological and cultural result is a Filipino self-concept of being powerless and inferior. This perceived sense of dependency on the benevolence of envied Western masters detracted from the development of a strong national identity and solidarity, perpetuating a subservient mendicant role and passive resistance. A different generation of Filipinos immigrating to the United States and Canada are subjected to a variety of traditional and Westernized cultural and ethnical (values-communication styles) conflicts. This clash of values and behaviors may result in a cultural psychodynamic conflict, a kind of cultural baggage, which may include any or all of the following:

1. The primacy of family and small-group affiliation over the individual, a strongly held value that inhibits free expression of dissent and tends to detract from the creativity and autonomy that are highly prized by Americans.
2. A strict adherence to gender-role stereotypes and patriarchal family structure that goes against the egalitarian norms in the American family.
3. A primacy given to smooth interpersonal relationships that conflicts with the American ideal of openness and frankness.
4. An attitude of "optimistic fatalism" or *bahala na*, that is opposed to American beliefs in future orientation, careful planning, and the drive for excellence and economic development through determined effort.
5. A sensitivity to slight and criticism, which springs from an exaggerated need for self-importance, *amor propio*, and often leads to withdrawal and/or vengeance, in direct opposite to the American style of directness and sportsmanship.
6. A fear of *hiya* (devastating shame) that often inhibits competitiveness. This concern over face-saving is fostered by the use of ridicule and ostracism in child training.
7. The practice of *delicadeza*, or nonconfrontational communication, most evident among females, that is ineffectual in Western societies, where directness is appreciated and competitiveness is encouraged.
8. *Utang nang loob*, or reciprocity of favors, that derives from a sense of gratitude and belongingness, is incongruous in societies that give primacy to individualism and the "bottom line."
9. A strict adherence to Catholic belief on virginity, abortion, contraception, and homosexuality, which can nourish a self-righteous judgmental stance that is out of place in a pluralistic society with emerging alternative lifestyles.

The stress of immigration and acculturation have extracted a heavy toll on Filipinos, which can result in psychological and/or sexual dysfunctions and symptoms of depression, schizophrenia, and paranoia. These adjustment disorders may show up in family and marital conflicts, extramarital affairs, embarrassment from inadequacies in work situations, estrangement from the Filipino family, and even divorce. Unemployment and underemployment weigh heavily on the Filipino male's sense of his own masculinity, and he frequently takes his frustration out on his spouse and children. Filipino women may internalize their frustration against male dominance by developing symptoms of depression and/or arousal or orgasmic dysfunctions.

Santa Rita (1996) emphasized the need of professionals providing sexual and relationship therapy for native and émigré Filipinos to understand the psychodynamics and cultural and ethnic background of the Filipino personality and their families. The therapist should try to discard the "cultural baggage" of the Filipino colonial mentality by utilizing alternative Filipino cultural norms and practices in the therapeutic role. Such role playing can be used to suggest alternative, more functional ways of interacting as individuals within a family and as a family in a changing Filipino culture or in a different culture. These stage scenarios might include:

1. A scenario for role playing *Lakas ng loob* (assertiveness) may be used to contrast *mahinhin* (self-effacing) and long-suffering, passive behaviors of Filipinos with assertive behavior. Assertiveness is an alternative to playing the martyr, which exacts such a high psychological price in the form of depression and other medical symptoms.

2. *Tinikling* (a bird in a bamboo trap) is the traditional Filipino dance simulating how a bird skips and jumps its way through clashing bamboo poles. This dance can be used to remind the family that, like the bird, Filipinos can be resilient and resourceful, and thereby escape whatever traps the colonial masters might concoct. This resourceful dancing-bird image suggests an alternative to maintaining *amor propio* (need for self-importance) and *hiya* (shame) at all cost. These traits are so often exaggerated in both Filipino men and women, that failures and disappointments often lead to depression and adjustment disorders, including arousal and erectile dysfunctions.

3. "God helps those who help themselves" is a study theme that can utilize the religious theme of "actively working with God" through one's labor and accomplishments to "glorify" Him. This biblical view suggests an alternative to *Bahala Na* (fatalism) that may result in lack of initiative and impedes economic and social mobility.

4. "In my father's house, there are many mansions" is another basic religious theme common among Filipinos that can be used as an exercise in "hospitality"—welcoming one's fellow human beings. This thesis of "Christian welcome" may help Filipinos become more accepting of other people's beliefs and lifestyles, especially on very emotion-laden issues like contraception, abortion, premarital sex, homosexuality, and bisexuality.

The marital and psychogenic sexual dysfunctions of immigrant Filipinos stem from their sense of vulnerability over their perceived, often acutely subordinate status as a minority in a pluralistic society that reminds them of their colonial history. Culturally sensitive therapeutic approaches are important in order to neutralize the Filipino family's low image of self and provide the family and the individual an opportunity to discover its inner strengths and resources including the gaining of self-respect (Santa Rita 1996).

## 12. Sex Research and Advanced Professional Education

### A. Advanced Education

In August 1887, while on a trip to America, Dr. J. P. Rizal, a foreign-trained eye surgeon and "the Liberator of the Philippines," deplored the American prejudice against Asians and African-Americans and was especially appalled by the laws against interracial marriages in some states. At the time, over 100 years ago, the Spanish religious teachings were solely limited to family life, and sexual issues were totally suppressed. Despite the declaration of independence from Spain by Filipino nationalists on January 12, 1898, sex education was not formally taught in colleges until the American colonial rule. In the late 1940s, sexuality was introduced to the Filipino educated elite in the form of family planning and topics on reproduction and birth through pamphlets and specialized magazines.

Since the 1980s, despite the proliferation of medical schools, human sexuality courses have been limited to sexuality-related professional degree programs in nursing, psychology, and medicine. In 1996, through the author's encouragement, three medical schools in Manila, Cebu City, and Quezon City established some form of sexuality courses in the gynecology, urology, and public health sections. Today, there is only one so-called accredited postgraduate program in sexuality and humanities, offered by the Population Institute of the University of the Philippines in Quezon City. The Ministry of Health regularly trains nurses and midwives in family planning and contraception through the municipal health clinics. The Philippine Psychiatric Association and the Philippine Urological Association are updating their diagnostic codes for the diagnosis and management of sexual dysfunctions.

### B. Research

Most of the government research dollars and interest have been earmarked for the prevention and treatment of childhood diseases, population control, and combating the spread of HIV/AIDS. The limited research resources from private and civic organizations are directed to traditional medical illnesses, such as heart diseases, hypertension and stroke, and tuberculosis. Some international, foreign medical associations and the Association of Philippines Physicians in America (APPA), and medical alumni associations sponsor research projects that relate to social and practical sexual issues, including:

1. Sexually transmitted diseases and HIV/AIDS;
2. Birth control—the effectiveness of new contraceptives and their side effects;
3. Management of sexual dysfunctions—old treatment and new alternatives; and
4. Sexual attitudes and behavior: child prostitution, sexual violence (rape, incest, and spousal abuse), extramarital sex, homosexuality, and the sexuality of minority groups (blind people and the handicapped).

## Conclusion

The peoples of the Philippine archipelago, both indigenous and immigrant, Muslim, Christian, and other, reflect the cultural attitudes and behavior of their mixed Malaysian and Chinese ancestries. There are also wide variations because of the sociocultural and linguistic mix. However, the dominant Catholic Church, the legislative body, and the educational system are essentially an amalgam of the old Hispanic dogma and the modern Western flavor with the present public sexual morality reflecting the values of these enduring institutions.

## References and Suggested Readings

Austria, T. 1999. *Sexual customs and attitudes of Filipinos.* New York: Library of the Philippine Consulate.

Avento, G. P. 1982. *Sexuality: A Christian view.* Mystic, CT: Twenty Third Publications.

Bascug, A. 2003 (February 13). *Marital laws and other social bills.* Member 11th Congress, Manila, Philippines.

Baxter, J. 1992. Power attitudes and time: The domestic division of laborer. *Journal of Comparative Family Studies, 23*: 165-182.

Birk, L. 1970. Shifting years in treating psychogenic sexual dysfunctions, medical treatment, sex therapy, psychotherapy and couple therapy. *Psychiatry Clinics North America,* 3:153-172.

Bonoan, R. J. 1996. Jose Rizal, liberator of the Philippines. *America,* 20:18-21.

Bradley, E. 1996 (October 27). R and R in South East Asia. *60 Minutes* [Television news magazine]. New York: CBS Television.

CIA. 2002 (January). *The world factbook 2002.* Washington, DC: Central Intelligence Agency. Available: http://www.cia.gov/cia/publications/factbook/index.html.

Duchene, L de B. 1997 (December 8-14). AIDS cases in the Republic of the Philippines. *The Filipino Express* [Jersey City, NJ].

Evaristo, F. 1995 (August 1). Sex tours: A tourism come on. *Manila Bulletin,* 80.

Fernandez, T. 1995. *Prostitution, sexuality transmitted diseases, AIDS in Cebu.* Cebu City, Philippines: Chief City Health Officer.

*Filipino Express.* 2003 (February 2). Filipino homosexuals accuse Church of family anti-gay hatred [Jersey City, NJ], p. 9.

*Filipino 2.0.* 2003 (February 9). Happy with family life; more open to divorce. [New York], p. 4.

Freud, S. 1965. *Standard edition of the complete psychologic works of Sigmund Freud.* London: Hogarth.

Highlights of Philippine history. 1999. *Filipino yellow pages.* New York: The American Kayummanggi Communication, Inc.

Leyson, J. F. 1965. *First night.* Unpublished psychological thesis. Cebu City, Philippines: Cebu Institute Of Technology.

Leyson, J. F. 1982 (June 10-12). *Sexuality for Filipinos update in medicine.* Paper presented at the annual alumni meeting of the Cebu Institute of Medicine, Cebu City, Philippines.

Leyson, J. F. 1987 (May 17-23). *Comparative study between oral and intrapenile vasoactive drugs in the management of impotence.* Paper presented at the annual meeting of the American Urological Association, Anaheim, CA.

Leyson, J. F. 1988 (December 2-3). *Future options in impotence management.* Paper presented at the American College of Surgeons Meeting, Ashbury Park, NJ.

Leyson, J. F. 1991. Controversies and research in male sexuality. In: J. Leyson, ed., *Sexual rehabilitation of the spinal cord injury patients* (pp. 483-531). Clifton, NJ: Humana Press.

Leyson, J. F. 1995 (July 6). AIDS and Filipino sexuality. TV Talk Show *Medicine.* CBS, Channel 3, Cebu City, Philippines.

Leyson, J. F. 1996 (June 2 and 3). Sexual dysfunction management for the year 2000. Radio Talk Show *Dyrc and Dyss.* Cebu City, Philippines.

Laurel, S. H. 1999 (January 29-February 4). Malolos Republic glazed first democracy in Asia. *Turning Point Filipino Reporter Newspaper* [Jersey City, NJ].

Loach, L. 1992. Bad girls: Women who use pornography. In: L. Segal & M. McIntosh, eds., *Sex exposed: Sexuality and the pornography debate.* London: Virago.

Moore, S. W., & D. A. Rosenthal. 1991. Condom and coitus, adolescents' attitudes to AIDS and safe sex behavior. *Journal of Adolescence,* 14:211-227.

Morrison, A. 1988 (September 22). HIV may be a 200 year old infection. *Oncology and Biotechnology News,* 2.

Mosher, W. R. 1996 (February 6). *Visionaries.* New Jersey Television Channel, Trenton, NJ.

Mydans, S. 2003 (March 21). Resisting birth control, the Philippines grows crowded. *The New York Times.*

Paez, M. S. 1999 (March). Department of Social Work seeks NGOs' help to stem rise of child abuse cases. *The Filipino Express* [Jersey City, NJ], p. 10A.

Philippine population—Increased funding population programs sought. 1997 (December 10). *The Filipino Reporter* [Jersey City, NJ], p. 14.

Saludo, A. G., Jr. 1999 (March 22). The first Holy Mass in Limasawa as the embodiment of our faith and reaffirmation of history. Congressional Privilege Speech, House of Representatives Assistant Majority Leader, Philippine Congress, Manila, Philippines.

Santa Rita, E. 1996. Pilipino families. In: M. McGoldrick, J. Giordano, & J. Pearce, eds., *Ethnicity and family therapy* (2nd ed.). New York: Guilford Press.

Sison, J. 1996. Adultery by any other name. *Mr. and Mrs. Magazine* [Manila, Philippines], 19:14.

World Bank. 1993. *World development report.* New York: Oxford University Press.

Zablan, Z. C. 1994. *Young adult fertility and sexuality survey (YAFSS).* Quezon City, Philippines: Population Institute, University of the Philippines.

UNAIDS. 2002. *Epidemiological fact sheets by country.* Geneva, Switzerland: Joint United Nations Programme on HIV/AIDS (UNAIDS/WHO). Available: http://www.unaids.org/hivaidsinfo/statistics/fact_sheets/index_en.htm.

# Poland

## (*Rzeczpospolita Polska*)

Anna Sierzpowska-Ketner, M.D., Ph.D.
*Updates by the Editors*

## Contents

(CIA 2002)

## Demographics and a Brief Historical Perspective

ROBERT T. FRANCOEUR

### A. Demographics

Poland borders on the Baltic Sea, Lithuania, Byelorussia, Russia, Ukraine, the Czech Republic, Slovakia, Kaliningrad Oblast (Russia), and Germany. The national frontiers contain an area of 120,725 square miles (312,685 km²), making it slightly smaller than the state of New Mexico in the U.S. The terrain is mostly flat plain, with mountains along the southern border.

In July 2002, Poland had an estimated population of 38.63 million. (All data are from *The World Factbook 2002* (CIA 2002) unless otherwise stated.)

**Age Distribution and Sex Ratios**: *0-14 years*: 17.9% with 1.05 male(s) per female (sex ratio); *15-64 years*: 69.5% with 0.99 male(s) per female; *65 years and over*: 12.6% with 0.62 male(s) per female; *Total population sex ratio*: 0.94 male(s) to 1 female

**Life Expectancy at Birth**: *Total Population*: 73.66 years; *male*: 69.52 years; *female*: 78.05 years

**Urban/Rural Distribution**: 62% to 38%

**Ethnic Distribution**: Polish: 97.6%; German: 1.3%; Ukrainian: 0.6%; Byelorussian: 0.5% (1990 estimates)

**Religious Distribution**: Roman Catholic 95%, about 75% practicing; Eastern Orthodox, Protestant, and other: 5%

**Birth Rate**: 10.29 births per 1,000 population

**Death Rate**: 9.97 per 1,000 population

**Infant Mortality Rate**: 9.17 deaths per 1,000 live births

**Net Migration Rate**: –0.49 migrant(s) per 1,000 population

**Total Fertility Rate**: 1.37 children born per woman

**Population Growth Rate**: –0.02%

**HIV/AIDS** (1999 est.): *Adult prevalence*: 0.07%; *Persons living with HIV/AIDS*: NA; *Deaths*: < 100. (For additional details from www.UNAIDS.org, see end of Section 10B.)

**Literacy Rate** (*defined as those age 15 and over who can read and write*): 99%, with 97% attendance during eight years of compulsory education

**Per Capita Gross Domestic Product** (*purchasing power parity*): $8,800 (2001 est.); *Inflation*: 5.3%; *Unemployment*: 16.7% (2001 est.); *Living below the poverty line*: 18.4% (2001 est.)

### B. A Brief Historical Perspective

Local Slavic tribes converted to Christianity in the 10th century and Poland became a great power from the 14th to the 17th centuries. The country was partitioned among Prussia, Russia, and Austria in 1772, 1783, and 1795. After World War I, in which it was overrun by the Austro-German armies, it declared its independence in 1918. Large territories in the east were annexed after a 1921 war with Russia. In 1939, at the start of World War II, the country was invaded and divided by Germany and Russia. Some 6 million Polish citizens were killed by the Nazis, half of them Jews—practically all the Jewish population of the country. After Germany's defeat, Poland declared its independence and was recognized by the United States, while the Soviet Union pressed its claims. Following a 1947 election dominated by the Communists, Poland ceded 70,000 square miles (181,300 km²) to the Soviet Union and received, in turn, 40,000 square miles (103,600 km²) of German territory east of the Oder-Neisse, Silesia, Pomerania, West Prussia, and part of East Prussia.

After 12 years of rule by Stalinist Communists, workers in Poznan rioted to protest rising prices, nationalization of industries, collectivization of the farms, secularization of the schools, and imprisonment of Church leaders. A new, more independent Polish Communist government, which came to power in 1956, reversed some of these conditions. In 1970, new riots broke out in several cities, protesting new incentive wage rules and price rises. In 1980, after two months of labor turmoil crippled the country, the government met the demands of striking workers at the Lenin Shipyard in Gdansk. Following a nationwide referendum that favored establishing a non-Communist government, the government declared martial law and arrested the lead-

*Communications*: Polish Sexological Society, Sex Research Department, ul. Marymoncka 34, 01-813 Warsaw, Poland. (Correspondence: ul. Londynska 12m 31, 03-921 Warsaw, Poland.)

ers of the opposition. An accord was reached in 1989, and a non-Communist government elected in 1990. A radical economic program, designed to introduce a free-market system, led to protests from the unions, farmers, and miners over inflation and unemployment. In 1993, former Communists and other leftists returned to power.

## *1. Basic Sexological Premises*

### A. The Character of Gender Roles

The pervasive presence of gender-role stereotypes, consensual expectations about the fashion in which males and females behave, is likely to have a strong and continuing impact on male/female behaviors and on feelings about that behavior in Polish society. Gender roles in Poland were evolving away from the traditional stereotypes after World War II because of the very common situation when women had to look for work outside their homes.

Women now comprise 45% of total number of employees and 52.6% of the unemployed. However, their part in the workforce creates a semblance of equality between the rights of men and women. The average pay for women is 30% lower than that of men. In Poland, one can observe a visible feminization of certain professions, mainly education and social welfare, because they are so poorly paid. Although the paychecks for men in these professions are the same as women's, men usually try to find better-paying jobs because of their traditional role as providers. During the Communist regime, women had a number of privileges that protected their professional situations. For example, they could retire five years earlier than men and could obtain a leave of absence to take care of a sick child. In the present transition to a market economy, these apparent privileges significantly reduce women's chances in the work market.

Women's efforts to find employment were clearly connected with economic pressures and did not reflect the real situation of women in Poland. The part played by women in the political and social life of the country is rather marginal. Women, for instance, comprise only 10% of the members of Parliament. Feminist organizations are small and not particularly popular, playing an unimportant role in society.

### B. Sociolegal Status of Males and Females

From the legal viewpoint, as children, adolescents, and adults, Polish men and women enjoy the same rights. Men and women have the same right to vote and equal rights for education and employment. Children and adolescents attend coed schools.

Current political changes in Poland have created a danger in favor of conservative understanding of social roles, especially for women. The recently propagated family model has a patriarchal character, with the woman professionally inactive and playing only the role of mother. Very restrictive antiabortion legislation has produced a particularly heated discussion of women's rights that is assuming the form of a political campaign. [*Comment 1997*: Election results in late 1995 shifted political power away from the Church-supported government and back to former Communist politicians, in part as a rejection of the Church's antiabortion and anticontraceptive stance. (*End of comment by R. T. Francoeur*)]

### C. General Concepts of Sexuality and Love

In Poland, one can find two models of sexuality and love: both restrictive Catholic and permissive European models. While the sexual attitudes of Poles vary depending on gender, age, region of residence, and religious attitude, these two models have existed separately for several decades and have collided occasionally. At present, with the increasing influence of religion and the Church on political and social life, they are the subject of acute confrontations.

The rural population and city dwellers of rural origin characteristically have strong links with Catholic religious ceremonies and the deep influence of the Catholic Church. This group is also characterized by a low level of education. This group is very numerous, because of the extermination of highly educated Poles during World War II and intensive migration from rural areas to the towns after the war. This group is the main standard bearer for the traditional model of sexuality in which sex and love can be fulfilled only in marriage. In this model, all premarital and extramarital sexual contacts are condemned, only the rhythm or so-called natural methods of family planning are accepted, and the use of other contraceptive methods, such as the hormonal pill and condom, are prohibited.

Among Poles with a higher level of education, one finds sex education based on publications, an acceptance of varied forms of petting and premarital sexual contacts, extramarital sex, liberal attitudes towards different sexual orientations and behaviors, the use of varied forms of contraception, and greater criticism of traditional sexual standards.

In comparing attitudes towards sexuality and love among Poles of different educational levels from different regions of the country, one seems to be dealing with two different societies, the first being attached to traditional attitudes and the second expressing permissive values and attitudes that are more and more popular in the West.

## *2. Religious, Ethnic, and Gender Factors Affecting Sexuality*

### A. Religious and Political Factors

Since the end of World War II, the people of Poland have generally shared a single ethic, and one religion, Roman Catholicism. According to 1990 research data, 94% of Poles are Roman Catholics and 79% of adult Poles considered themselves religious or deeply religious.

The Catholic faith has been predominant among Poles since the recorded beginnings of the state in the 11th century. The period of the Reformation did not change this situation, despite the proximity of German Lutheranism. The multiethnic Jagiellonian Poland of the 15th and 16th centuries, and the Commonwealth of the Two Nations, as the union of Poland and Lithuania was called until the 17th century, were comprised of at least one-third ethnic minorities who, to a great degree, represented religions other than Roman Catholic. In the first half of the 20th century and during World War II when eastern territories were lost and western lands added, one third of the country's population comprised Jews, Ukrainians, Germans, Byelorussians, and others. These ethnic minorities professed mainly the Jewish, Greek Catholic, Protestant, and Eastern Orthodox religions.

Catholicism has become one of the main elements of the national self-determination and self-image of Poles, possibly as a result of the historical destiny of Poland in the last few centuries, and especially since the 19th-century partitions. Religious ceremonies thus became the occasion for expressing national and political views, which were often of greater social and psychological importance than the pure religious feelings. Also in the 1980s, the Solidarity period, subversion of the totalitarian Communist regime and appointment of a Pole as Supreme Pontiff of the Church in Rome strengthened the political authority of the Church in Poland.

It should be stressed here that Poland is currently undergoing significant changes associated with the democratic processes common in countries of the late Communist regime. At this turning point in our history, the situation of sexology in Poland is determined by two opposing tendencies: the increasing influence of religion and the Church on Polish political and social life, and European tendencies, which are coupled with the reality-based social attitudes to sex and sexual behavior. These opposing influences mark the main line of controversy on moral and legal policy in Poland today. Although there is a visible divergence between sexual behaviors and the formal religious views of society, the restrictive attitude of the Catholic Church is more and more evident, affecting most legal and medical problems as well as sex education.

## B. Ethnic Factors

According to unofficial data, ethnic minorities comprise about 5% of the population. Most of them are Byelorussians and Ukrainians. As a result of the invader's policy during World War II, and the change of borders after the war causing the loss of one fourth of the country's eastern territory, most ethnic minorities have disappeared. The remaining minorities, at present, do not demonstrate any particularly characteristic sexual attitudes or behaviors.

## 3. Knowledge and Education about Sexuality

It needs to be emphasized that sexual education has always been a kind of taboo in Poland. This was clearly reflected in the language used by the state in the past, referring to sexual education as "preparation for the life in a socialistic family." After 1989, sexual education was halted in the schools without any national debate about the relationship between the state and the Church, and the only textbook specially prepared by sexologists for school use was definitely forbidden. This was subsequently followed by introduction of religious instruction in all Polish schools.

Research in 1992 with a nationally representative sample revealed that friends were reported as the principle source of sex information with half of the men and one third of the women surveyed. The second source, reported most frequently by young people in large cities, was publications. Parents hardly ever wanted to provide input into sexual education, preferring to have their children obtain this information in school or from publications. Still, less than 10% of the respondents approved of school as a source of sex information.

## 4. Autoerotic Behaviors and Patterns

### A. Children and Adolescents

Retrospective research on the autoerotic behaviors of Polish children and adolescents has been carried out on a few select groups. M. Beisert (1990) found that about 15% of the girls and 29% of the boys remembered touching and manipulating their genitals in a repeated manner during childhood to evoke some pleasant feelings. In most children, an intensification of autoerotic behaviors is observed at ages 5 to 6, during nursery school education. The main purpose of autoerotic behaviors is to awake some positive emotions in oneself. Up to 80% of all children who engage in self-pleasuring consider the pleasure obtained as an autonomous value, while about 12% treat that pleasure as a side effect of fulfilling the need connected with what is termed a stimulation deficit, the deprivation of the need of receiving new and attractive stimuli from the surroundings.

Research demonstrates that there are two types of autoerotic behaviors: one open, observed in children who are unaware of the common negative valuation of that behav-

ior, and the other hidden and characteristic of children who are aware of the forbidden character of that behavior. An important source of information about the need to hide autoeroticism from parents is the child's peers. According to investigations, 80% of parents have never learned about the autoeroticism of children.

Polish literature dealing with sexual education presents two opposite views: an opinion that self-pleasuring is a normal stage of psychosexual development in human beings, and the contrary view that self-pleasuring is a sin reflecting in a negative way on human development. These opinions lead to two contrary educational recommendations. Adolescents appear to be aware of these contradictory views and their implications. Survey data indicate that 90% of adolescent boys and 45 to 75% of girls engage in self-pleasuring. At the same time, 20% of girls and 32% of boys reported fears accompanying their self-pleasuring. Half of those investigated were afraid of parents, siblings, or other people learning about their self-pleasuring practices. The correlation of self-pleasuring and religiousness was not statistically significant in adolescents.

### B. Adults

In a 1991 nationally representative survey, 28% of the women and 64% of the men reported engaging in autoerotic behaviors. In other research with university students, 99.1% of the men and 42% of the women reported autoerotic behavior.

## 5. Interpersonal Heterosexual Behaviors

### A. Children

M. Beisert's 1990 investigation reveals an undulatory character in the child's interest in sex. The first inflow is observed before the end of 5 years of age with the next during the prepubertal period, about the age of 10 and 11.

Contacts with other children in nursery school are conducive to some exploratory activities. Up to 56% of investigated adults place their first discoveries connected with gender at that period. The most important source of knowledge are other children, particularly peers. The first discoveries are connected with playing together, bathing, and other hygienic activities. However, the awareness of a strict injunction not to stare at the naked bodies of others, and particularly their genitals, is passed down at a comparatively early age and is widely popularized. The division between erotic play and cognitive activities is a difficult one, especially since sexual curiosity is at the bottom of much of children's play. However, when children want to study their own bodies, they often do it openly and clearly state their interest. In approximately 2.8% of childhood sexual exploration, coercion is a factor.

The cognitive methods are a bit different in families with many children of both genders. When the children in a family are close in age, or when the age interval is larger but older children participate in taking care of the younger, sex differences are not particularly exciting nor do they offer any special discoveries. The situation is similar when a child has no siblings but is brought up in a family with liberal attitudes towards sex.

Many different children's games include an erotic element or produce specific pleasure connected with stimulation of the genitals. Nearly 70% of students surveyed remembered not only the fact of such games, but also all the details accompanying them. Gender was not a factor in such games. Considering all the functions fulfilled by erotic games, such as pleasure, learning, and stimulation, they were grouped separately from other forms of childhood activities. The essence of most games is to imitate a fragment of adult life. The most popular games imitate adult roles that create an opportunity of mutual touching, undressing, and body manipulation, playing doctor, hospital, nurse, mother and father, king and queen, convalescent home, masseur, or the theater, ballet, and striptease. Among other inspirations for childhood games, direct observation of adult life takes place first, then movies, fairytales, and stories told by others. Imitations of such adult activities that provide excuses for body contact are the most important children's games.

A particular, qualitatively different variety of games is among those designed for only two children. In such games, watching and touching meet the needs of demonstrating a mutual bond. Children embrace each other, kiss, and touch. Such pairs are accepted by their peers, and their range of behavior does not differ from the behavioral patterns of groups. Solitary play also provides an outlet for sexual curiosity and rehearsal, as when a child enacts erotic scenes using dolls, draws pictures of naked girls and boys, or plays scenes that evoke pleasurable excitement.

The second period of interest occurs during the pre-pubertal age. Up to 35% of children report gaining knowledge about gender differences at the age of 10 or 11 years. The interest is focused on details and confirmation of earlier knowledge and intuition. Watching and touching is limited mainly to the genitals, and the aim is to gain pleasure along with a clear understanding of gender differences. These games occur in pairs, and sometimes in groups of peers of the same and other gender. Boys, for instance, may compare penis length or compete in urination contests. Girls concentrate on bust observations or dressing as adult women. Often pair games are clearly directed at pleasure, and consist of genital exploration and touching without the pretext of playing doctor or hospital.

According to survey data, most Polish children are well aware of the forbidden nature of these erotic games. The punishing attitude of parents towards erotic games reaffirms the fear of childhood eroticism and the unfavorable attitude towards self-pleasuring. Parental dissuasion and limiting the child's time with peers are more-mild forms of unfavorable reaction. However, two thirds of parents who catch their children in such games threaten them, punishing them verbally and/or physically for engaging in them. About 1% of parents do not adopt a punishing attitude, but quietly maintain their differing opinion of such games. Only 10% of parents treat these games as a normal stage in childhood development.

## B. Adolescents

### Puberty

The period of puberty involves three phases dominated by changes connected with biological, mental, and finally social maturity. In girls, signs of physical maturation generally appear at the age of 10 or 11. About a year earlier, mothers usually take some steps to prepare their daughters for their physical maturation and menarche. Research shows that nearly all unprepared girls react in a negative way to their maturation. Girls in this group usually start menstruating at an early age, around 10 years, and are easily distinguished from their peers by their physical maturity. Not knowing the purpose and course of the pubescence process, they exaggerate the significance of the physical changes, interpreting them as pathological symptoms.

The reactions of boys to the signs of maturation follow a different pattern. Only a small percentage of boys react negatively to the changes. Their negative reaction is usually conditioned by a lack of proper preparation. The male response to puberty shows greater uniformity, with a greater acceptance of manhood often compensating for some neglect in their sex education.

Research shows that the first menstruation in girls and the first nocturnal emission or conscious ejaculation in boys cause a strong emotional reaction. In these specific experiences, the reaction is unfortunately negative, irrespective of gender. Most often, the girls inform their mothers about their first menstruation. However, about 20% try to hide the fact. On the other hand, few boys inform their parents, preferring to boast about it among their peers.

The appearance of a new sexual behavior, namely petting, also marks the pubertal period. Up to 50% of Polish girls admit that an emotional bond with a boyfriend prompted them to start petting. Only an emotional involvement would make them agree to physical contact, although that agreement does not indicate a real need for relieving their sexual tension or taking the initiative to do so. Only a small percentage of girls admit their strong sexual tension and the need to relieve it. Among the reasons reported by girls, curiosity played only a small part in their decision. Much more important was the pressure exerted by the partner, although they did not consider the decision to start petting as being imposed on them. In their opinion, it was the natural consequence of their feelings towards their partners and not the consequence of sexual pressure. Boys more often explained the decision to start petting by their sexual tension. The need to relieve this tension resulted in less sensitivity in choosing their partner. Even a girl they scarcely knew would be acceptable. Polish boys try to start petting at the age of 16 and girls a year later.

Petting sets the stage for first sexual intercourse. According to data from a nationwide representative sample, 12.5% of the men and 6.6% of the women have sexual intercourse before age 16. By age 19, 54% of the men and 43% of the women have had coitus. Every fifth man and every third woman has first sexual intercourse after age 20. For 73% of the women, emotional involvement is the prime reason for initiation. Men most frequently cite emotion and love (41%), curiosity (35%), and the need to become an adult (16%). Only 40% of the women and 46% of the men rate their first sexual intercourse as a positive experience.

## C. Adults

The first statistical investigations of sexual behavior were carried out in Poland at the end of the 19th century when Z. Kowalski examined the attitudes of Warsaw University students. More-recent sexological studies were carried out in the 1960s and 1980s with selected groups of students, soldiers, and workers. In 1963, H. Malewska studied the sex life and its determinants in Polish women. The first research of sexual behavior using a nationally representative sample of 1,188 adults was carried out in 1991.

### Premarital Relationships

According to 1991 data, 72% of unmarried adults admit to premarital relations. Among married people, premarital relations were acknowledged by 80% of the men but only 50% of the women. This reflects the attitude of women towards virginity. Contrary to men, women paradoxically more often reveal their belief in the need to preserve virginity until marriage.

### Single Adults

Data on sexual behavior of single adults in Poland are limited, mainly because of the strong pressure on sex for reproduction within marriage. In 1988, 85% of Polish women aged 37 to 49 were married, 6% were singles who had never married, about 6% were divorced, and 3% were widows.

## Marriage and Family

In the 1970 research of Trawinska on values in marriage, adolescent and adult respondents gave priority to fulfillment of emotional needs, love, sex, the chance for self-realization, and achievement of economic success. People who had been married for several years placed the relative lack of conflicts and stability of the union on a par with emotional ties, respect, love, and sex.

The courtship period is short, and up to 60% of marriages are contracted between ages 20 and 24. Despite early marriage, the time of reaching social and economic independence with a separate apartment is delayed. Since the prewar period of the 1930s, the stage of marital childlessness has become shorter. One fourth of all women are pregnant when they marry. As in most European countries, the model of a small family is becoming a standard. A family with two children is usual, less often three children. In a family of two children, procreation is over in three years; with three children, it usually ends in five or six years.

## Monogamy

In Poland, marriage is monogamic in character. In the 1991 survey, nearly half of the women and one fourth of the men had had only one sex partner. Monogamic behavior is more common among people from small towns with a primary or secondary school education and a strong religious affiliation. Eighty-five percent of wives and 56% of husbands reported no extramarital sexual experiences. Sporadic extramarital sex was acknowledged by 10% of men and women. Less than 1% of respondents had more than ten sexual partners during their marriage. Extramarital sexual relations are more frequent in respondents over age 40, living in large cities, with a higher education, and better economic status.

Data on attitudes to sex show that for over 85% of respondents, sex is an expression of love and bonding. Sex without any emotional ties is accepted by 14% of women and 35% of men. The frequency of marital intercourse for most respondents ranged from a few times a week to a few times a month.

## Divorce

In 1991, Polish courts granted 34,000 divorces. A peak of 53,000 was reached in 1984. The most frequent reported causes for divorce are infidelity (30%), excessive drinking, and incompatibility of character. Usually it takes four to six months to obtain a divorce. Most often, couples seek a divorce after five to ten years of marriage. Usually the divorcing couple has no children or only one child. In three out of four cases, the mother retains custody. About 1% of children in divorces are placed in children's homes or with foster families.

## Incidence of Oral and Anal Sex

According to 1991 data, oral-genital sex, usually cunnilingus, is practiced by 30% of Polish men and women. Anal sex is acknowledged by 2.4% of respondents. There are no legal restrictions on fellatio, cunnilingus, or anal sex in Polish law.

## 6. Homoerotic, Homosexual, and Bisexual Behaviors

The Polish legal code of 1932, as well as the current code of 1969, are among the most progressive in respect to sexuality. Homosexuality was always legal in Poland. The current criminal legislation does not mention homosexuality or homosexual relations at all. As with heterosexual contacts, only the homosexual intercourse of an adult with a partner under 15 years of age, or forcing a person to have intercourse against his or her will are against the law and liable to penalty.

There is a divergence between liberal legislation and the degree to which homosexual persons openly take part in the social life. The first homosexual movement and organizations started in 1985. At that time, representatives from Warsaw and Wroclaw joined the International Lesbian and Gay Association. Programs and discussions with homosexuals appeared on television and the radio. The press published articles about the problems encountered by homosexual persons. The following years marked the appearance of official organizations and clubs for homosexuals in big cities in Poland. Also a homosexual section was organized to fight the spread of AIDS. Until this time, the public had little knowledge of homosexual issues.

In surveys, 4.4% of the women and 6% of the men acknowledged being homosexually active. So far, there has been no research in Poland investigating the character of homosexual relations, behaviors, and sexual patterns. A few publications on this subject have been based on West European and American research. Thus, the main source of information about homosexual issues and lifestyles is the gay press, which provides several local and national publications.

The Catholic Church in Poland maintains a restrictive attitude towards homosexuality. It is described as a "moral disorder," and homosexual activities are condemned as contradictory to the procreative purpose of sex. In the Church's opinion, sexual relations are morally right only in marriage. The Church also maintains that there are many ways to restrain a person from fulfilling his or her unnatural sexual desire.

## 7. Gender Diversity and Transgender Issues

An estimated 1,000 Poles are transgenderists or transsexuals. The research of J. Godlewski indicates there is one male-to-female transsexual for every seven female-to-male transsexuals. Five hundred persons have had hormone treatment and 400 surgery. The development of therapy for transsexuals started in the 1980s. In Poland, there are about 100 unions or cohabiting couples in which one partner is a transsexual and five where both partners are transsexuals. Two marriages were contracted legally.

Polish legislation, in principle, allows the change of gender, but no law regulates the surgical treatment of a transsexual. According to the Polish Criminal Code, it is comparatively easy to have one's sex/gender and name corrected in a birth certificate. A correction in the birth certificate is a necessary condition for further surgical treatment.

There are no legal restrictions on transvestites. However, transvestism is a marginal phenomenon in Poland.

## 8. Significant Unconventional Sexual Behaviors

### A. Coercive Sex

*Sexual Abuse, Incest, and Pedophilia*

Child sexual abuse has only recently forced its way into the social consciousness and scientific research. Investigations in 1991 revealed that 5% of the girls and 2.5% of the boys under the age of 15 years had had sexual contacts with family members, and 7.5% of underage girls and 17% of boys with virtual strangers.

In Poland, sexual contacts (coitus and coital equivalents) between children and their siblings (including adopted sibs), parents, and grandparents are subject to legal punishment. The penalty for incest ranges from six months to five years imprisonment.

Polish criminal law forbids sexual contacts with minors under 15 years old. The term "sexual contacts" includes coitus and coital equivalents, fellatio, cunnilingus, anal sex, and digital-vaginal/anal penetration. The penalty for such contact can be up to ten years imprisonment. However, sentences of six to 24 months are not uncommon.

In cases of sexual abuse of a minor, it is impossible to ascertain the incidence of pedophilia because this sexological category is not included in the diagnosis. In these cases, some perpetrators exhibited a pedophilic character. In other instances, the victim would not be considered a child, being a postpubertal adolescent.

## [Clergy Sexual Abuse

[*Update 2002*: In early 2000, the Vatican received several complaints that Archbishop Juliusz Paetz, of Poznan, Poland, had been sexually molesting seminarians in the Poznan seminary. The Archbishop was a longtime friend of Pope John Paul II and had spent more than a decade in the Vatican, including four years working in the Papal household. In November 2001, after the initial complaints from seminarians to newspaper editors brought no action and the Vatican ignored written complaints, Wanda Poltawska, an 81-year-old Polish psychiatrist and longtime friend of Pope John Paul II, brought the matter to the Pope's attention. However, the Vatican did not act until local priests issued a call for the archbishop's resignation, and the seminary rector forbade the archbishop to visit the seminary unless he was accompanied by one of the seminary priests. When a subsequent Vatican investigation found the claims were credible, the Pope accepted the archbishop's resignation on March 31, 2002 (Allen 2002; Tagliabue 2002abc). (*End of update by R. T. Francoeur*)]

## [Domestic Violence

[*Update 2002*: In 2000 and 2001, the Open Society Institute (OSI, Budapest) sponsored a series of media campaigns to combat violence against women. Although a third of women in Poland acknowledged that they had been victims of domestic violence, OSI claimed that Polish authorities had failed to recognize it as a grave social problem. On the contrary, after a new government entered into power in the fall of 1997, the situation deteriorated. Violence against women was neglected and presented, even in the international arena, as an issue of marginal importance. The result was a failure to implement comprehensive legal and policy changes aimed at preventing and combating violence against women more effectively.

[Despite some positive changes, the criminal justice system remains, in general, unresponsive to women's needs. The police continue to treat domestic violence as a family matter and either refuse to intervene or provide only ineffective intervention. Although domestic violence was sometimes publicly prosecuted, the police frequently collected evidence improperly and left the burden on the woman's effort. Victims filing complaints usually have to wait several years before their case is tried in court. In the meantime, the perpetrator usually continues to live under the same roof with the victim, even if they are divorced, which leaves the women vulnerable to further violence and other forms of pressure from the perpetrator. Convicted perpetrators usually receive the lowest possible sentence, which in 90% of the cases is then suspended. Legal actions taken against perpetrators of domestic violence often perpetuate further violence, and the rate of recidivism in these cases is very high.

[There is no doubt that the existing legal and institutional framework does not provide adequate protection to women and children victims of domestic violence. On the other hand, however, OSI argues that the existing laws need to be applied and enforced. Existing gender-based stereotypes and prejudices against women have a negative impact on the performance of the criminal justice system in domestic violence and rape cases. Too often, men's violence against women is justified, while women are perceived as provocateurs and, in fact, responsible for the violence they experience.

[While OSI and other civil rights groups work to increase awareness of domestic violence and its prosecution, social awareness that domestic violence constitutes a major threat to women's health, and even lives, remains very low in Poland (Open Society Institute 2001). (*End of update by R. T. Francoeur*)]

## Paraphilias

There are no statistics on cases or the incidence of paraphilias in Poland.

## Sexual Harassment

As of 1995, Polish legislation did not distinguish this category of behavior. [*Update 2002*: By late 1996, however, the situation had changed somewhat as central European countries and corporations began to be influenced by publicity in the news media and by the policies of Western European and American companies conducting business in Eastern Europe. In 1996, Poland's main government television channel ran a prime-time docudrama about sexual harassment, followed by a discussion with a studio audience and telephone calls from viewers. Despite the message to women workers that if they took their case to court, they could win, Poland has weak labor and civil-rights laws that have been largely untested in court because so few sexual harassment cases have been filed. Only 5% of those responding to a 1996 Polish newspaper poll said they had encountered cases of sexual harassment at work. Adding to the reluctance of Polish women to report cases of sexual harassment is a heritage of 40 years of Communist rule in which they accepted and endured sexual harassment as the norm. Today's harsh economic circumstances also encourage women not to complain. "We have a long way to go in raising the consciousness of women and men and making them realize what is not appropriate," Ursuzula Nowakowska, director of Warsaw's Women's Rights Center, a pro-bono group of lawyers, has reported. In the summer of 1996, Ms. Nowakowska appealed to the visiting lawyer-wife of U.S. President Clinton, Hilary Rodham Clinton, to help by urging large Western corporations to drop what she called their "double standard." She was referring to the tokenism of many Western and American corporations which issue policies against sexual harassment for all their offices worldwide, but then seldom let the employees in Western European branches hear of these policies and fail to enforce their policies when charges are brought (Perlez 1996). (*End of update by R. T. Francoeur*)]

## Rape

In Polish law, rape refers to coitus or coital equivalents (fellatio, cunnilingus, anal sex, and digital-vaginal/anal penetration) using force, violence, threat, or taking advantage of someone's vulnerable situation. The penalty for rape is between one and ten years imprisonment. A person under the age of 15 years cannot give legal consent to sexual intercourse. The concept of statutory rape does not exist. Within the legal category of rape, two types of rape are singled out: rape involving qualified cruelty involving brutal injuries to the body or mind; and collective or gang rape. Application of the law prohibiting marital rape requires real evidence of the use of force or coercion.

The minimum penalty for convicted rapists is three years imprisonment. However, depending on the type of rape, the prison sentence can range from six months to over five years. According to the data collected by Polish sexological expert witnesses, the majority of convicted rapists were drunk when they committed the crime.

## B. Prostitution

In Poland, neither heterosexual nor homosexual prostitution is subject to criminal penalty. However, in 1952, Poland signed the United Nations Convention, undertaking an obligation to abolish prostitution. Inducing or soliciting another person to prostitution or profiting from another person's prostituting him- or herself are subject to legal penalties of one to ten years.

There has been a steady decline in the demand for prostitutes since 1987 because of the growing concern about AIDS. Statistics on the total number of prostitutes in Poland are not available. The police estimate that there are about 12,000 prostitutes working in Poland. There are no houses of prostitution, but there are call-girl agencies, massage parlors, and other avenues of contact.

## C. Pornography and Erotica

The development of democratic liberties in Poland since 1989 has been accompanied by a growing access to pornography and an increasing number of pornographic publications on the market, even though the law prohibiting production and distribution of pornography is still in force. Despite legislation, both hard- and softcore pornography are easily accessible in Poland today.

In recent discussions, there has been some pressure to extend the meaning of pornography to include erotica and introduce more-rigid restrictions. The controversy is complicated by the lack of a clear definition of pornography. Some forensic experts, referring to the criterion of social harm, want to limit the meaning of pornography only to materials dealing with sexual relations with animals and children, and cruel or violent material. The dispute over pornography is part of the more general discussion about sexual liberalism or rigorism.

## 9. Contraception, Abortion, and Population Planning

### A. Contraception

The lack of sexual education in recent decades has affected negatively contraceptive behavior. Data from a 1988 POLL survey with a nationally representative sample, from the Polish Family Planning Association and other sources, revealed that the number of women who used oral contraceptives and intrauterine devices (IUDs) was not higher than 10%. About a third of those polled reported using coitus interruptus as their contraceptive method. Another third used a method based on the menstrual cycle, sometimes only the calendar method. A lack of information about contraceptive methods and prejudice against contraception has created favorable circumstances for acceptance of the so-called natural methods promoted by the Church. In a 1988 study by W. Wróblewska of a nationally representative sample of 1,266 teenage mothers, about 90% had no knowledge whatsoever about contraceptive methods.

### B. Teenage Unmarried Pregnancies

In the 1988 study of 1,266 teenage mothers published by the Family Planning Association in 1992, W. Wróblewska reported that the youngest mother was 13 years old and nearly 50% were age 19. At the time of childbirth, one fourth of the teenage mothers were unmarried. Polish law makes it difficult for girls to contract marriage at the age of 16 or 17. Girls who wish to marry at that age must obtain a special license. Girls who are not yet 16 cannot marry.

Prior to getting pregnant, a large group of these mothers, 41.2%, were professionally active. One third, 37.6%, were attending school. The research did not confirm the hypothesis that these mothers had poor relations with their parents and were using pregnancy as an excuse to leave home. Only 9% of the teen mothers described the atmosphere in their homes and family relations as not too good or even conflictive. Over 80% of the teenage mothers came from two-parent families and 80% of the parents of teenage mothers had at least an elementary education. Generally, the girls were brought up in large families and had many siblings. The mothers of most respondents had started their own procreation earlier than other women of their generation.

Nearly 40% of the teenage mothers did not anticipate the possibility of becoming pregnant, or even realize such a possibility, when they became sexually active between the ages of 11 and 19. Only 15% of the respondents knew anything about contraceptive methods. Only 10% mentioned the contraceptive pill, IUD, condom, and calendar method. They were totally unfamiliar with other contraceptive methods. Only a third of these teenage mothers had even the minimum knowledge of how to protect themselves against pregnancy when they first engaged in sexual intercourse. Books, publications, and magazines were the basic sources of information for 61% of the mothers. Friends and acquaintances provided information for a third of the respondents. Slightly under a third, 28.2%, learned about contraception in school. Sexual partners were the source of information more often than parents. Only one in ten teenagers reported parents as a source of knowledge. More rarely cited was a doctor or nurse.

### C. Abortion

Under Communist rule, from the end of World War II to 1989-1990, abortion was legal and widely used by Polish women despite the opposition of the Catholic Church. A restrictive law, enacted in March 1993, was overturned in October 1996. The situation, however, remains volatile and unpredictable.

Between 1956 and March 1993, abortion was legal for medical indications, when the pregnancy resulted from a crime, mainly rape, and for social reasons, such as the difficult circumstances of the woman. This law allowed for abortion in the first 12 weeks of pregnancy.

According to official statistics, the incidence of abortion remained stable for 15 years prior to 1993, with about 133,000 abortions per year, or 19 abortions per 100 live births. This statistic does not include abortions done in private clinics. Some sources estimated that an additional one million abortions were performed each year in private clinics, with about 30,000 of these being for women under the age of 18 years.

In 1992, pressure from the Catholic Church supporting a repeal of the liberal abortion law was evident in a new Ethical Code adopted for physicians. This code allowed abortion only when the mother's health or life was in danger, or when the pregnancy resulted from rape or incest. In practice, this code eliminated all prenatal fetal examinations and abortion of malformed fetuses. In addition, contraceptive information was to be given by the physician only when required by the patient or in special cases. The new Ethical Code was a real paradox, because it was much stricter than the then-existing liberal law.

Also in 1992, the Parliament rejected by majority vote a liberal proposal prepared by the Women's Parliamentary Group and instead accepted the antiabortion proposal of the Catholic Nationalist Party (ZChN), which forbade abortion. The sole exception was that of a danger to the pregnant woman's life. The proposal for a national referendum was not accepted by the Parliament. Meanwhile, research revealed that 56% of Poles were definitely in favor of abortion rights for women, 24% approved of some such rights, and only 13% were definitely against abortion rights.

In March 1993, the increasing influence of the Roman Catholic Church on Polish social life was a major factor in parliamentary enactment of a new law that replaced the 1956 liberal abortion-rights law with the most restrictive abortion law of any Eastern European country. A year after enactment of the 1993 restrictive law on abortion, critics pointed out that the number of clandestine abortions had increased, with unscrupulous physicians offering to provide an abortion for any women able to pay the equivalent of US$350 to $1,000. The average monthly income was only about $200, with half of the population earning below the poverty line, defined as $80 a month. Some travel agents offered "abortion trips" to the Ukraine at 8 million zloty, or about $400.

The 1993 law permitted abortion only when the pregnancy threatened the life or "seriously threatened" the health of the mother, when there was "serious and irreversible malformation of the fetus," or when the pregnancy resulted from "criminal action" (i.e., rape or incest). These provisions were further limited by many restrictions. For example, in the case of danger to the mother's health, supporting statements were required from two physicians independent of the acting doctor. And while prenatal tests were required to prove that the fetus was malformed, another section of the law appeared to allow for extensive prenatal tests, such as amniocentesis, only when there was reason to suspect a serious problem, as when a pregnancy occurred in a family with a history of genetic illnesses.

In March 1995, Poland's strict antiabortion law faced a painful test in court when a 37-year-old divorced woman, who was already supporting a 10-year-old child, persuaded a doctor in private practice to terminate her pregnancy. The physician was brought into court to face charges of violating the 1993 abortion law. If convicted, he could have spent two years in prison and had his medical license suspended for up to ten years. The woman's lover, who could only contribute about $10 to the child's support but gave her the equivalent of $125 for the abortion, faced up to two years in prison. Like other incidents of illegal abortion, this case became a legal issue when the child's father reported the woman's abortion because she refused to have his child (Perlez 1995).

In August 1996, the lower house of Parliament moved to liberalize Poland's restrictive abortion law, despite strong opposition from the Roman Catholic Church and its political allies. The bill, backed by the former Communists who dominated the Parliament after the November 1995 elections and a leftist opposition party, would allow women to end pregnancies before the 12th week if they could not afford to raise the child or had other personal problems. Early amendments, however, required counseling and a three-day waiting period for women seeking an abortion, and penalties of up to ten years in jail for aborting a woman against her will, or after the fetus can survive outside the womb. Opinion polls suggested that most people favored this liberalization, although 90% of those polled were nominally Catholic. (In 1993, President Lech Walesa, a devout Catholic, had vetoed a similar bill.)

In October 1996, despite a huge campaign against the bill including a silent march on Parliament by 30,000 Poles, the lower house overturned a veto of the new law by the Senate with a 228-to-195 vote and 16 abstentions; Aleksandr Kwasniewski, the president, had already promised to sign the new bill.

Under this legislation, women would again be able to end pregnancies before the 12th week if they face financial or personal problems. However, abortion is available only after counseling and a three-day waiting period. The law also provides for sex education in the schools and less-expensive birth control. Despite enactment of the new law, polls suggested that antiabortion sentiment has been rising, and that Poles, about 90% of whom are at least nominally Roman Catholic, are almost equally divided on the question. The future of abortion legislation in Poland, thus, remains uncertain.

[*Update 2002:* According to government figures, the number of legal abortions in Poland plunged from 11,700 in 1992 to 1,240 in 1993, when the restrictive law went into effect. In 1999, the latest year for which figures were available at press time, there were only 151 legal abortions in Poland. Women's rights groups have estimated that as many as 200,000 women have illegal abortions each year in Poland, often paying exorbitant fees and subjecting themselves to dangerous procedures. Efforts to revise the 1993 law and remove some of the restrictions failed in the legislature in 2001 (CRLP 2001). (*End of update by R. T. Francoeur*)]

**D. Population Control Efforts**

The model of a small family is at present predominant in Poland. There are certain premises for the advisability of a pronatal population policy with a model of families with two, or to a lesser degree, three children. The opposite model of uncontrolled fertility is promoted by the Catholic Church and is related to the Church's campaign to limit contraception and sexual education and prohibit all abortions.

## 10. Sexually Transmitted Diseases and HIV/AIDS

**A. Sexually Transmitted Diseases**

The epidemiological situation of STDs was investigated by H. Zielinski and A. Stapinski in 1992. In the first years after World War II, there was a significant increase in venereal diseases, especially syphilis, which was epidemic. At the time, there were an estimated 100,000 to 150,000 cases of syphilis a year in a population of 23 million. The therapeutic program, the so-called Action W, which included education, prevention, and outpatient clinics in every city, produced positive results and the epidemic was controlled. By 1954, early symptomatic syphilis had decreased to about 2,200 cases annually, about 8 cases per 1,000 people.

Between 1963 and 1969, there was another rapid increase in syphilis to 52 per 1,000 people, and the incidence of early syphilis (symptomatic and asymptomatic syphilis stages 1 and 2) to 66.6 cases per 1,000 people. The incidence of gonorrhea, which reached a low level of 80 per 1,000, also increased, although not so rapidly, to exceed 153 cases per 1,000 in 1970.

A new program of syphilis and gonorrhea control produced positive results. In the 1980s, the incidence of syphilis decreased steadily until 1989. In 1989, the number of new cases diagnosed was 4.6 per 1,000; in 1990, it was 4.8. In 1990, new cases rose to 4.9 per 1,000, a 5% increase. The 1991 incidence of early symptomatic syphilis remained stable from 1990, 2.8 per 1,000. However, the 1991 incidence of early asymptomatic syphilis was 9% higher than in 1990, while the incidence of late syphilis decreased by 16%. Similarly, the 1991 incidence of diagnosed gonorrhea decreased by 34% from 1990, less than 10% of what it was in 1970. In 1991, nongonococcal infections of the urogenital tract was 14% less than it was in 1990.

Information about the incidence of condyloma and genital herpes are fragmentary and have been included in the statistics only since 1990.

### B. HIV/AIDS

Serological examination for HIV status for people at risk was inaugurated in Poland in 1985. Of the 2,426 cases of HIV infection detected by November 1992, 1,776 were drug addicts. The real number of carriers is at least three times larger. Between 1985 and November 1992, 118 cases of AIDS were diagnosed. In this group, 58% were homosexual or bisexual, 30% heterosexual drug addicts, 10% heterosexual, and 2% unknown. Over half the 118 had died as of November 1992.

In 1989, A. Stapinski et al. published the data of the Institute of Venereology in Warsaw on the prevention of HIV infection in drug addicts. Noting "that the infection spreads rapidly in this population," the authors predicted "a further rapid spreading of this infection in this risk group," and recommended providing addicts with free syringes, needles, and condoms. They also recommended systematic intensive training of personnel in drug treatment and rehabilitation centers, as well as extensive informational education of all adults.

Also in 1989, D. Weyman-Rzucidlo et al. reported on the prevalence of HIV infection in a group of 1,297 homosexuals. In Poland, as in Western Europe and the United States, "homosexual and bisexual males are the group of high risk for HIV infection."

Dermatovenereological outpatient clinics provide HIV testing for anyone who wants to be tested and medical care for those needing it. Provincial clinics are also engaged in training health-service workers and providing health education in their own districts.

A program for AIDS prevention and control prepared by A. Stapinski in 1988 includes multidimensional activities: staff training, diagnostic facilities, research units, and prevention of infection by sexual contact, blood, needles, and syringes. Much attention was given to protecting health-service workers against infection, and to health education for at-risk groups and the general population, especially adolescents. Voluntary testing for HIV antibodies is encouraged, and stress is placed on preventing discrimination against persons who are HIV-positive and have AIDS.

[*Update 2002*: UNAIDS Epidemiological Assessment: By the end of 2001, 7,303 HIV infections have been reported. Most of the infections are seen in Warsaw, Gdansk region, and Katowice (south). Injecting drug users are systematically screened in treatment centers, outpatient clinics, and residential homes. All other groups are tested on a voluntary basis. Diagnosed HIV-infected cases are registered in a national HIV database using the name for identification, excluding those testing anonymously. A switch to anonymous reporting is being planned. From 1995 to 1999, annual numbers of newly diagnosed HIV infections were relatively stable, ranging from 539 to 638. Among HIV cases reported in 1997 to 1999, 53% were injecting drug users, 6% homosexuals, 3% heterosexuals, and 37% not determined. Underreporting is estimated to be 25% and has been increasing in Gdansk region; estimates for the number of cumulative HIV infections at the end of 1996 have been put at 10,000 to 12,000.

[Prevalence data comes mostly from ongoing testing programs. Prevalence among injecting drug users is esti-mated between 15% and 50% in Warsaw, and is probably lower elsewhere. Since known positive injecting drug users are not retested, data presented cannot be used as an estimate of prevalence, nor can they be used as incidence estimates, because seronegative persons can be tested several times and seropositive persons may have been infected for several years. The numbers of drug users have reportedly been increasing in recent years. However, there is a shift from injection drug use to oral and inhaling practices; nevertheless, since 1993, there is an increasing number of HIV infections among injecting drug users in some parts of the country.

[No data on pregnant women were provided. Nationwide, levels of reported STDs have been stable and relatively low in the recent years. However, in some western regions of Poland, there is an observed increase in STD levels. Prostitution has substantially increased at the borders of Poland and Czech and German borders; levels of STDs in those areas have increased as well. In a survey of homosexual men, very few reported having had an HIV test. In addition, there is still stigma associated with homosexuality, reflected in the low number of those voluntarily identifying themselves as homo-/bisexual; the number of infections in this subpopulation may, therefore, be underestimated.

[The estimated number of adults and children living with HIV/AIDS on January 1, 2002, were:

| | |
|---|---|
| Adults ages 15-49: | 14,000  (rate: 0.1%) |
| Women ages 15-49: | NA |
| Children ages 0-15: | NA |

[No estimate is available for the number of adults and children who died of AIDS during 2001.

[No estimate is available for the number of Polish children who had lost one or both parents to AIDS and were under age 15 at the end of 2001. (*End of update by the Editors*)]

## 11. Sexual Dysfunctions, Counseling, and Therapies

The diagnostic criteria developed by Masters and Johnson are accepted by some Polish sexologists, while others follow the *DSM-III-R*. Clinicians specializing in sexology require personality evaluation before sexological diagnosis. Sexual dysfunctions are viewed in the psychodynamic categories and diagnosis connected with the evaluation of neurotic mechanisms and personality disturbances.

There are two departments of sexology associated with the medical schools in Warsaw and Krakow. Outpatient clinics in all the larger cities and towns provide diagnosis and treatment for sexological patients. These clinics employ some 70 medical doctors with clinical specialization in sexology, and also some psychologists.

## 12. Sex Research and Advanced Professional Education

### A. Institutes and Programs for Sexological Research

The following are organizations for sexological research in Poland:

The Polish Medical Association, Medical Center of Postgraduate Education, Department of Sexology and Pathology of Human Relations, Director: Kazimierz Imielinski, M.D., Ph.D. Address: ul. Fieldorfa 40, 004-158 Warsaw, Poland.

The Medical School of N. Copernicus, Department of Sexology, Director: Julian Godlewski, M.D., Ph.D. Address: ul. Sarego 16, 31-047 Kracow, Poland.

The Academy of Physical Education, Sexual Division of Rehabilitation Faculty, Director: Zbigniew Lew-

Starowicz, M.D., Ph.D. Address: ul. Marymoncka 34, 01-813 Warsaw, Poland.

Polish Sexological Society, Sex Research Department, Director: Anna Sierzpowska-Ketner, M.D., Ph.D. Address: ul. Marymoncka 34. 01-813 Warsaw, Poland. Correspondence: ul. Londynska [n'] 12/13, 03-921 Warsaw, Poland. Programs are offered on sex offenders, sexual dysfunctions, transsexuals, and the handicapped and sexuality.

Postcollege, graduate programs and courses are provided for psychologists and medical doctors by the Medical Center of Postgraduate Education, Department of Sexology and Pathology of Human Relations. A medical specialization in sexology has been available since 1985 for psychiatrists and gynecologists. Training is also provided by the Polish Sexological Society, with certification of Clinical Sexologists since 1991.

## B. Publications

The Polish Sexological Society publishes the quarterly *Sexology*. Correspondence: Londynska 12/13, 03-921 Warsaw, Poland.

## *References and Suggested Readings*

Allen, J. L. 2002 (March 15). Polish prelate accused of sexual abuse. *National Catholic Reporter*, p. 1.

CIA. 2002 (January). *The world factbook 2002*. Washington, DC: Central Intelligence Agency. Available: http://www.cia.gov/cia/publications/factbook/index.html.

CRLP (Center for Reproductive Law and Policy) Press. 2001 (July 20). The Impact of Poland's anti-abortion law.

Mondykowski, S. M. 1982. Polish families. In: M. McGoldrick, J. K. Pearce, & J. Giordano, eds., *Ethnicity and family therapy*. New York: Guilford Press.

Open Society Institute–Budapest Network Women's Program. 2001 (June). http://www.osi.hu/vaw/Projects/Poland.htm.

Perlez, J. 1995 (April 2). A painful case tests Poland's abortion ban. *The New York Times*, p. 11.

Perlez, J. 1996 (October 3). Central Europe learns about sex harassment. *The New York Times*, p. A3.

Tagliabue, J. 2002a (March 27). Polish priests press Vatican on case against bishop. *The New York Times* (Ideas and Trends).

Tagliabue, J. 2002b (March 31). Polish bishop resigns. *The New York Times*.

Tagliabue, J. 2002c (April 21). Europe has problems, but not like America's. Maybe. *The New York Times*.

UNAIDS. 2002. *Epidemiological fact sheets by country*. Geneva, Switzerland: Joint United Nations Programme on HIV/AIDS (UNAIDS/WHO). Available: http://www.unaids.org/hivaidsinfo/statistics/fact_sheets/index_en.htm.

# Portugal

## (*República Portuguesa*)

Nuno Nodin, M.A.,*
with Sara Moreira, and Ana Margarida Ourô, M.A.
*Updates by N. Nodin*

## Contents

## *Demographics and a Brief Historical Perspective*

ROBERT T. FRANCOEUR

### A. Demographics

Portugal occupies the western part of the Iberian Peninsula in southwestern Europe. With the Atlantic Ocean on its western border and Spain to the north and east, Portugal has a land area about the size of the state of Indiana, 35,670 square miles (92,390 km²). It is crossed by many small rivers, and by three large rivers that originate in Spain and flow through Portugal to the Atlantic, dividing the country into three geographic areas. Between the Minho River, which forms part of Portugal's northern border, and the Douro River is a mountainous region with the city of Porto in the southwest corner. Between the Douro and the Tejo Rivers, the mountains yield to plains. South of the capital, Lisbon (Lisboa), and the Tejo River are the rolling hills of the drier Alentejo region. Culturally, the northern region is more traditional and religious and the southern region is more secular and less restrictive in gender and sexual matters.

The nine islands of the Azores stretch over 340 miles (550 km) in the Atlantic, about 900 miles (1,450 km) east of Cape da Roca in mainland Portugal. The Azores is a strategic station on the cross-Atlantic air routes. Madeira, Porto Santo, and two groups of uninhabited islands lie in the Atlantic about 535 miles (860 km) southwest of Lisbon.

In July 2002, Portugal had an estimated population of a little over 10 million. (All data are from *The World Factbook 2002* (CIA 2002) unless otherwise stated.)

**Age Distribution and Sex Ratios**: *0-14 years*: 16.9% with 1.06 male(s) per female (sex ratio); *15-64 years*: 67.3% with 0.96 male(s) per female; *65 years and over*: 15.8% with 0.68 male(s) per female; *Total population sex ratio*: 0.93 male(s) to 1 female

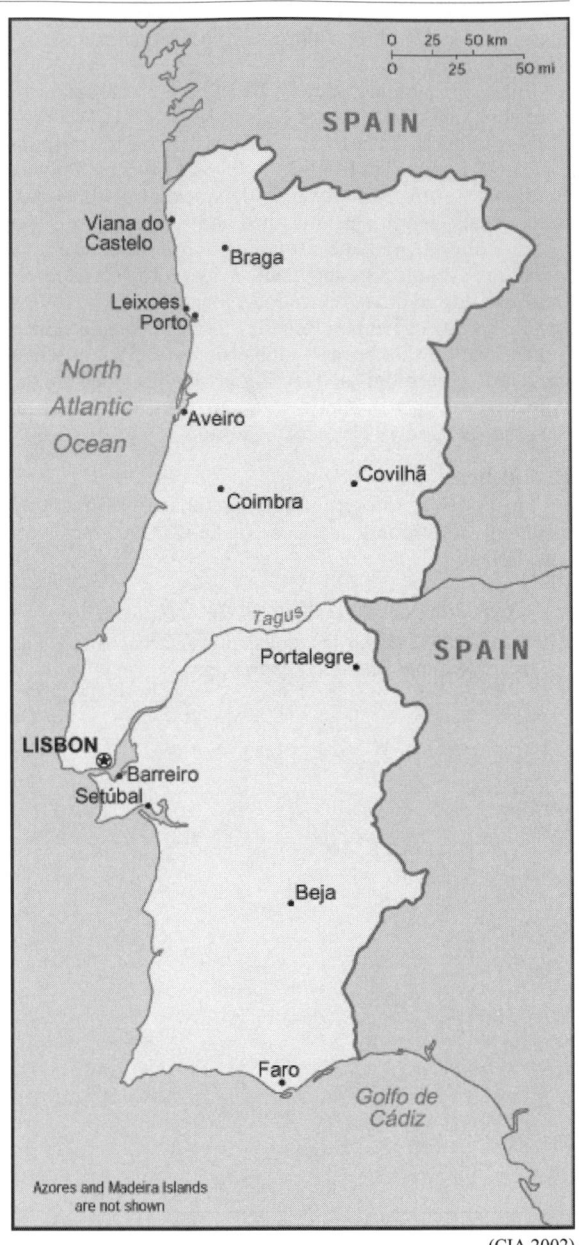

(CIA 2002)

**Life Expectancy at Birth**: *Total Population*: 76.14 years; *male*: 72.65 years; *female*: 79.87 years

**Urban/Rural Distribution**: 36% to 64%

**Ethnic Distribution**: Homogeneous Mediterranean stock with less that 100,000 citizens of black African descent who immigrated to the mainland during the independence movements in the colonies after World War II

**Religious Distribution**: Roman Catholic: 94%; Protestant 6%

**Birth Rate**: 11.5 births per 1,000 population

**Death Rate**: 10.21 per 1,000 population

**Infant Mortality Rate**: 5.84 deaths per 1,000 live births

**Net Migration Rate**: 0.5 migrant(s) per 1,000 population

**Total Fertility Rate**: 1.48 children born per woman

**Population Growth Rate**: 0.18%

**HIV/AIDS** (1999 est.): *Adult prevalence*: 0.74%; *Persons living with HIV/AIDS*: 36,000; *Deaths*: 280. (For additional details from www.UNAIDS.org, see end of Section 10B.)

---

*Communications*: Nuno Nodin, M.A., Av. Fontes Pereira de Melo, 35, 11-B Edificio Imaviz, 1050-118 Lisbon, Portugal; nunonodin@mail.teleweb.pt.

**Literacy Rate** (*defined as those age 15 and over who can read and write*): 87.4%; education is free and compulsory between ages 6 and 15

**Per Capita Gross Domestic Product** (*purchasing power parity*): $17,300 (2001 est.); *Inflation*: 4.4%; *Unemployment*: 4.4%; *Living below the poverty line*: NA

## B. A Brief Historical Perspective

Portugal's roots reach back to the warlike Lusitanian tribes of Roman times. Having gained independence in the 12th century by the hand of King Afonso Henriques (1128-1185) from a rebellion against his own Castillian mother, Teresa, Portugal was created at the expense of the conquest of territory from the Moors of Morocco who occupied part of the Iberian Peninsula until the 16th century. The country gained its final form after the conquest of the Algarve (Portugal's southernmost region) in the 13th century, and its frontiers have been kept almost untouched up to today. Prince Henry the Navigator (1394-1460) brilliantly coordinated Portugal's expansion that led to a period of great prosperity for the country. In 1488, Bartholomew Diaz reached Africa's Cape of Good Hope. Vasco da Gama followed by reaching India in 1498. By the middle of the 16th century, Portugal had colonies in West and East Africa, Brazil, Persia, Indochina, and Malaya.

In 1581, Philip II of Spain invaded Portugal, precipitating 60 years of occupation and a catastrophic decline in Portuguese commerce. By 1640, when the Portuguese dynasty was restored, the Dutch, English, and French had taken the lead in colonizing the world, although Brazil remained under Portuguese rule until 1822 and the African colonies until the 1970s. After years of weak governments, a 1926 revolution brought a strong, but repressive government into power under the rule of Antonio Salazar. The colonial wars of the 1960s placed a terrible strain on Portugal's economy, adding to the country's standing as Western Europe's poorest country. A successful military revolution in 1974 brought a socialist government into power. Fifteen years later, a "democratic economy" was introduced and industries were denationalized. In 1985, Portugal joined the European Community and, between that date and 1992, the per-capita income tripled so that Portugal was no longer the poorest country in Europe.

## 1. Basic Sexological Premises

### A. Character of Gender Roles

In Portugal, there is an influence of traditional Latin perspectives on male and female roles in society, so that social status is still, in part, related to biological sex. Nevertheless, some significant changes have been occurring in recent years. Traditionally, women were expected to have a passive role in society, although generally assuming a leading position at home, taking care of children, and, in many cases, being responsible for the management of the domestic economy. The male was the decision maker in what concerned major issues at the community level and the main provider of financial maintenance for the household. Women were "naturally" supposed to be good housewives, mothers, and wives.

This situation, a reality for the majority of cases at all socioeconomic levels of society, was maintained and reinforced by the fascist government that ruled in Portugal until 1974. The political and ideological principles of this period, which lasted for 48 years, was strongly influenced by the Catholic Church and also determined social and sexual roles of the male and female. The worship of the Virgin Mary, the *Marianismo*, symbolically reflected the feminine ideal of maternity without sexual involvement to which every women should aspire (Rodrigues 1995).

The Catholic and traditional ideals of the politics and social structure of this era are still a reference for the older generations, but the modernization of Portugal and of the Portuguese society in recent years has brought new values and realities. Women are more and more actively taking part in the social life, and they are also currently the vast majority of the university student population—about 80% of all university students are female. The *machismo*, once a value strongly associated with the male, is now considered a fault more than something positive.

Although it has been commonly accepted for several decades that women should also be gainfully employed outside the home to help support the family, gender differences exist here despite Portugal having one of the highest percentages of working women in Europe. The distribution of males and females according to professional categories, as well as to hierarchical levels, is unequal. Females mostly assume unskilled and lower-level positions and have the lowest salaries (Amâncio 1994). This fact is quite obvious in the Portuguese Parliament, in which after the 1999 elections only 19% of the commissioners were women. However, given the significant increase of college-graduate females, a shift should be expected in the near future.

The professional situation of men and women is not the only area in which gender differences can be found. It is easier for a parent to let a teenage son out at night than it is for a girl to have the same kind of liberty. The so-called sexual double standard also prevails and expresses itself through a more permissive attitude towards men's sexual behavior and a more conservative and repressive posture towards women's sexuality (Machado & Almeida 1996). This way, it is expected and somewhat valued that a male has several sexual partners, whereas the same is disapproved of in a female. However, this double standard has in recent times lessened, with a growing acceptance of female sexuality and the changing in the character of gender roles.

Among a new generation of couples and families, it is possible to find evidence of this change, as young men are more willing to share domestic tasks and are happy to take care of their children. These fathers are proud of their paternity and are assuming the traditional functions of the mother, which is reflected in publicity that uses images of young fathers changing diapers and playing with their infant sons and daughters.

### B. Sociolegal Status of Males and Females

According to the Portuguese Constitution, all men and women are equal before the law. Legal majority is achieved at 18 years of age or with marriage after 16. Marriage is allowed at age 16 with parental consent. Nevertheless, as previously mentioned, despite legal gender equality, several differences still exist at various levels of society. To reduce this gap, in 1991, a commission, Comissão para a Igualdade e para os Direitos da Mulher (CIDM, Commission for the Equality and for the Rights of Women) was formed, succeeding a previous organization that had a key role in changing the legal status of women and in achieving gender equality before the law. The main objectives of CIDM are:

- to allow the same opportunities for men and women;
- to reach the same level of responsibility for women and men in what concerns family, professional, social, cultural, economic, and political life; and
- to contribute to the recognition of maternity and paternity as social functions.

Although this commission is mainly concerned with feminine problems and rights, it contemplates the work with men as a way of achieving equality, which is most obvious in the attention given to the questions of paternity.

In October 1999, a new ministry, the Ministério da Igualidade (Ministry of Equality) was created. As in similar ministries in other European countries, the goal is to achieve equality at different levels of society. Gender equality will obviously be one of its main areas of action. [*Update 2003*: In 2001, critics of the Ministry of Equality managed to have this agency eliminated, despite praise from some who originally considered it a useless organization.

[No other relevant event has occurred since 2000 concerning the sociolegal status of males and females except, even if ever so slightly, the fact that it is increasingly obvious that women are taking a more visible role in public and political life, adding strength to the trend previously suggested. Nevertheless, after the March 17, 2002, elections for the Parliament, only 17% of deputies and two Ministers (of Justice and Finances) are women. (The Finances Minister is at the same time the State Minister and has, therefore, the role of supporting the Prime Minister's activities. These two women account for 12% of the 16 ministers in the Portuguese government. (*End of update by N. Nodin*)]

## C. General Concepts of Sexuality and Love

As in many other parts of the world, sex and sexuality are uncomfortable topics for most people. Sex and sexuality are mostly discussed between friends, using jokes as a way to lighten the tension involved in these issues. However, in sexual education programs or when asked about sexuality for research purposes, most people will participate and show an interest in the topic. Sex-related issues, such as homosexuality, abortion, and AIDS, are also regular subjects of talk shows and programs on television as well as of reports in the press. Nowadays, a wide range of information and services are available and this has, in turn, influenced and reshaped the general Portuguese conceptions of sexuality in recent years. This fact does not necessarily mean that the Portuguese are very open-minded about these issues. A certain resistance exists towards minority forms of sexual expression, which are more likely to be tolerated than truly accepted.

Love and the existence of steady relationships are considered previous conditions for sexual intimacy with a partner, especially for women. Men, as well as individuals from the younger generations regardless of gender, value the hedonistic and pleasurable aspects of sex the most (Pais 1998). One has to assume that there are significant gender and generational differences over what is or is not considered a steady relationship, and also over other general conceptions of love and sex. In any case, the general picture shows us clearly that sexuality is no longer associated with procreation and that relationships are based on affection towards the partner, rather then in formal structures, such as engagements and weddings.

The two tendencies in love and sex in the Portuguese mainstream society, i.e., the importance of romantic love and the sexual pleasure ideals, are somewhat in conflict: The first implies monogamous relationships and the second reinforces the search for different and multiple sexual partners. However, it is known that a gap exists between what is said and what is done and, when confronted with a choice, most frequently, the romantic ideals lose in favor of a greater sexual freedom.

## 2. Religious, Ethnic, and Gender Factors Affecting Sexuality

### A. Source and Character of Religious Values

Portuguese society has in the past been greatly influenced by the Catholic Church. In the 15th century, the clergy was one of the supporters of the colonial "discover-ies" that led to a period of great prosperity for the country. One of the reasons for this support was the opening of new possibilities of evangelism and the spread of the influence of the Church throughout the world. This eventually happened in many parts of the world, in Brazil, India, Macao (China), and Japan, where the Portuguese were the first Westerners to arrive and to introduce the Catholic religion.

The Portuguese Church grew, enriched and hegemonic, especially after the expulsion of the Jews from the country in 1496, which came by royal order, but with a strong Catholic influence. The Holy Inquisition (Tribunal do Santo Oficio), established in the 16th century, was for a long time a powerful means of political and ideological repression that was also used to persecute people with sexual behaviors that were considered deviant, like prostitutes and homosexual men. Women who lived their sexuality freely were often considered witches, especially in the interior of the country. Many of the charges of witchcraft against women were, in fact, the consequence of revenge related to cases of adultery.

The Marquis de Pombal (1699-1782), the prime minister during the reign of King Joseph, ruled the country despotically, but introduced many reforms and turned the big earthquake of 1755 that destroyed part of Lisbon into a chance to rebuild the capital according to modern principles. He reduced much of the power and importance of the Church and of the Inquisition that was finally extinguished in 1821. This was also the beginning of the end of much of the religious influence in civil society, which was only again regained during the government of Salazar, in the period called the Estado Novo (1926-1974). The three mottoes of this time were *Pátria, Deus, Família* (Fatherland, God, Family) that, like the Holy Trinity, were the moral references of the Estado Novo. This period left several marks in Portuguese society that still has an influential Catholic community.

Of the majority Catholics, 26% go to church regularly and have some degree of religious influence in their lives, whereas 65% are nonpractitioners (Pires & Antunes 1998). Nonpracticing Catholics are believers that do not attend religious rituals, such as the Mass, or go to confession very often.

There is an important difference between the practicing and the nonpracticing Catholics that can help us understand different positions in Portuguese society, and not just those related to sexuality. In general, practicing Catholics have more-conservative positions on such different things as marriage, social intervention, drug addiction, nudism, and tax evasion (Pires & Antunes 1998). Usually in Catholic families, behavioral norms are stricter than in non-Catholic families, and there is a greater concern over the upbringing of children according to religious principles. Most practicing Catholic children go to religious schools that are generally considered among the best private education institutions. The Catholic University is also one of the most prestigious universities in Portugal.

This conservative perspective of the practicing Catholics obviously influences their views on sexuality. In general, they are more repressive over the expression of sexuality, less tolerant towards sexual minorities, and have more-traditional ideas on contraception and abortion. Religious practice is also negatively associated with sexual experience and permissiveness among university students, while the simple fact of being or not being a believer is not a condition to explain these kinds of differences (Alferes 1997). What does influence the beliefs about these issues is, again, the assumption of a practicing or nonpracticing Catholic position.

Lately, some criticisms have emerged among the Catholic community towards the stagnant position of the Church on different subjects related to sexuality. One such criticism is that the Church still associates several different subjects with sin, this way repelling Catholic couples and individuals who do not find in the Church the answers they are looking for in what concerns their private lives (Ferreira 1993). In 1993, an organization of Catholic students, Movimento Católico de Estudantes (MCE), published a document that considered the ideas of the Church on sexuality inadequate and detached from the scientific speech. It also condemned the use of power in ways that affect the individual experience of one's sexuality in areas such as homosexuality, premarital sexual activity, and masturbation (MCE 1993). Despite these critical movements, the Catholic Church still has considerable influence in Portuguese society, and is economically powerful. This became quite obvious in the recent referendum over the legalization of abortion.

As for other religious beliefs and practices, they also have a strong effect on the permissiveness towards sexual behavior. Little is known about these minorities, but one researcher tells us that people that follow these beliefs have attitudes towards sexuality even stricter than the Catholic majority, especially in what concerns prostitution and adultery (Pais 1998). However, more research is needed in this area in order to study the effect of these attitudes on the behavior of people belonging to these groups.

### B. Character of Ethnic Values

Portugal is one of the oldest nations in Europe and its actual frontiers are almost the same since the 13th century. There has also been a considerable stability in the constitution of the population in its majority Caucasian character over the centuries. Although having been influenced by several races and cultures throughout history, the Portuguese are essentially a Latin people, with concepts of gender roles and sexuality similar to those existing in other south European Latin countries like Spain and Italy.

After the revolution of 1974 and the independence of the colonies of Guinea-Bissau, Angola, Mozambique, Cape Verde, S. Tomas, and Principe, about half a million Portuguese who lived there returned to the mainland (in fact, many had been born and always lived in Africa). This mass return of people with a different experience and kind of living was socially quite problematic, and a certain xenophobic climate appeared against the newcomers who were pejoratively called the *Retornados* (the ones that returned). The *Retornados* must have had an influence on the concepts and practices related to sexuality of the rest of the Portuguese, for in Africa, there were not as many restraints as the ones that existed on the more conservative mainland. However, to our knowledge, there are no studies about this subject.

[*Update 2003*: Portugal has historically had a tradition of emigration, most significantly during the Age of Exploration/Discovery in the 1500s, when the aim was to conquer new lands and to explore their richness, and in the 20th century, between the 1950s and 1970s, when many Portuguese left the country in search of better living conditions not possible under the then-current political regime. With the recent economical revival and development of the country, this process has practically disappeared, replaced by a mass influx of immigrants from Eastern European countries. However, to our knowledge, no investigation has been conducted on the sexual attitudes and lifestyles of these immigrants from poorer countries, the influence they are having on the Portuguese, or on how these new people are affected and influenced by the culture of their new home. (*End of update by N. Nodin*)]

## 3. Knowledge and Education about Sexuality

### A. Government Policies and Programs

The history of sex education in Portugal begins in the 1960s. Before that, the Catholic Church was responsible for the moral orientation of education, separating boys and girls in public schools, and repressing the study or teaching of sexuality. It was only with the Vatican II Council, which brought new ideas and a different approach to several areas within the Church, that sex education began to be discussed. It was also at this time that new values and attitudes emerged, together with democratic ideals and expectations of liberty.

A new course, "Sexuality, Love, Marriage and Family," started being taught at a seminary in Lisbon, and several articles about sexuality appeared in Christian magazines and newspapers. In public schools, in the existing class "Religion and Morality," mainly taught by priests, the discussion of sexuality was included as a way to guarantee long-lasting and happy marriages for future adults. However, this approach was non-systematic, had no scientific basis, and was frequently inadequate.

In 1967, the Associação para o Planeamento da Família (Portuguese Family Planning Association, or APF) was created, supported by the International Planned Parenthood Federation, which was interested in reaching southern European countries. This organization is not very well accepted by the government, by the Church, or by the most conservative sectors of society, but it has initiated several actions aimed at the training of professionals, as well as implementing a service of family planning for the population.

In the early 1970s, the Ministry of National Education created the Commission for the Study of Sexuality and Education. This commission advocated the abolition of separate education of boys and girls and focused on the need for a different approach, integrated and not fragmented, to the human body in schoolbooks (Roque 1999). This commission became extinct one year after its creation.

The revolution of 1974 that ended the dictatorship in Portugal brought a rapid change to society. But although sex education could be and was, in fact, publicly discussed and defended at this time, the disturbed post-revolutionary atmosphere was not favorable to its introduction in the educational system. Other issues, such as abortion and the equality between men and women, were the main concerns over which new legal and practical measures were brought together. The APF became the main organization responsible for sex education in the school context, with actions carried out by professionals. However, these efforts were very limited and could not respond to the real needs of young people. Teachers were trained as a way to enlarge the reach of its intervention, and later, at the beginning of the 1980s, new programs aimed at young people and supported by the United Nations Fund for Population Activities (UNFPA) were put to into action outside the school context. There was an urgent need to legally regulate sex education, and this came with the 3/84 Law, 24 of March 1984. According to this law:

- The state guarantees access to sex education as a basic educational right;
- The state is the responsible entity for the promotion, diffusion, and organization of the juridical and technical means necessary for a responsible maternity and paternity;
- The school curricula should include scientific knowledge about the anatomy, physiology, and genetics of human sexuality, and should also allow the overcoming of the social discrimination based on biological sex and of

the traditional division of duties between the male and the female;

- Teachers should be trained in sex education as a way to be able to respond to the needs of young people; and
- Parents should also be supported concerning the sex education of their children.

Although approved and authorized, the means to apply it in the school context were never standardized. Children and adolescents only had access to sex education because of the initiative of some teachers and other organizations. These initiatives were never truly systematic. In the meantime, new activities and classes, like "Personal and Social Development," where created to facilitate the discussion of subjects directly related to the reality and practical needs of young people (Vaz 1996). This allowed a more regular introduction of sex and sexuality in the school system, frequently as a response to the requests of the students themselves. Programs for the prevention of HIV also started, because sex education is considered as a way to fight the growing spread of AIDS. Proposals for including sex education in different branches of education have been made and pilot projects have been introduced in some schools.

In 1998, a commission formed by representatives of several ministries presented a report proposing a plan of action for sex education and family planning, in which practical measures are proposed in several areas. Its goal is to provide students with access to sex education and to insure the availability of family planning services. New laws and initiatives are emerging, but a lot of work still needs to be done concerning the regular and effective availability of sex education for the young and also for the general population.

[*Update 2003*: A year later, in 1999, this commission issued a special report (*Relatório Interministerial para a Elaboração de um Plano de Acção em Educação Sexual e Planeamento Familiar—Interministerial Report for the Elaboration of an Action Plan on Sex Education and Family Planning*) that was then approved by the government. In this report, sex education is considered as a part of education and a vital part of health promotion in general. The *Report* also established new goals for sex education in the school context.

[In August 1999, a new law was published (Law 120/99) whose main objective is to affirm the right that every citizen, especially children and adolescents, have to sexual and reproductive health. This law contains the topics that should be addressed in any sex education program in a school setting. These are:

- Human sexuality,
- Reproductive anatomy and physiology,
- AIDS and other STDs,
- Contraception and family planning,
- Interpersonal relations, and
- Gender equality and sharing of responsibilities

[The legal framework existing in Portugal with regard to sex education now contains a number of norms for its application:

1. That sex education should be treated in an interdisciplinary way, i.e., included within all the previously existing disciplines,
2. That all sex education programs should include an articulation between the school and the community (including health services and parents), and
3. That teachers should have specific training for teaching such matters.

However, these norms have not been applied in any systematic way, which means that empirical work and subsequent results are still very scarce, and effective actions are often dependent upon teachers' initiatives.

[Following a political turn to the right after the 2002 Parliament elections, the government is valorizing a conservative approach to the questions of sex education in schools and has signed a protocol with the Movimento de Defesa da Vida (Movement for the Defense of Life), an NGO, that has a known and active social position against abortion. According to this protocol, this organization will be responsible for the training of teachers in matters of sex education. This protocol substitutes a previous one that the Ministry of Education had with the Portuguese FPA (Associação para o Planeamento da Famlia), whose positions are much more liberal. (*End of update by N. Nodin*)]

## B. Informal Sources of Sexual Knowledge

Sex and sexuality have become common subjects of television programs and are frequently presented in the media. There is a concerted effort to invite experts to talk about these issues in the media, so that the information that reaches the public is usually of a fairly good quality. A popular and light-reading magazine, called *Maria*, is famous for having a section of responses about the sexual problems of the readers. In the past, this was a major source of informal knowledge on sexuality when very little, if any, information was available from other sources.

Several books about sexuality by both national and foreign authors have been published in Portugal and are easily available. Different institutions working in the field frequently publish and distribute brochures and leaflets on subjects such as contraception, special care during pregnancy, and sexually transmitted diseases. Since the appearance of AIDS, many of these leaflets have also appeared aimed at specific groups of the population, such as women and gay men.

When asked about the sources of sexual information accessed or preferred, most young people will refer to the media, with television at the top of the list. Other significant sources mentioned are friends and the partner or consort (Pais 1996). In fact, sexuality is in great part played and learned in a relational context, both with peers in informal situations and with the sexual partner. In adolescence and even in young adulthood, the information obtained from friends is not always the most correct and is frequently filled with popular false beliefs. However, given the known importance of peer influence, some of the most recent health-promotion and HIV-prevention programs developed in Portugal integrate this new approach through the training of young people. It is expected that these programs will produce a positive influence from peers, instead of a negative one.

Intervention in the influence of the sexual partner is more difficult because it occurs in emotional and intimate situations that are hard to change. A person who has information on how to prevent HIV infection or an unwanted pregnancy might, in any case, engage in risky sexual behavior with a partner because of feelings of inadequacy, low self-esteem, or simply because of forgetfulness in the heat of the moment. It should also be mentioned that a high percentage of young people (about 80%) think they do not need to be enlightened or to have technical support on sexual issues (Pais 1996). Although this percentage is higher among younger adolescents who are not sexually active and tends to get lower as the age increases, these numbers are still very disturbing. They show a great feeling of self-sufficiency in these youngsters that can be the first step to high-risk behaviors because of a lack of correct knowledge.

A significant percentage of young people get information on sexuality (60.6%), contraceptives (49.7%), and HIV

(30.4%) from their parents, with the mother being the most frequently mentioned source of information. A great part also report they would like to have more information from either one of their parents.

In June 1998, a free and confidential telephone helpline, *Sexualidade em Linha* (*Sexuality on Line*), opened to serve the information needs of young people. In its first year, 50,000 phone calls were answered and many more went unanswered because the amount of phone calls far exceeded the service's capability of response. The great majority of callers were between 13 and 18 years of age, and over half were girls (55.9%). The questions that led to the calls were varied. In most cases, the objective was to get information about sex (oral and anal sex, masturbation, virginity, etc.), contraceptives, and counseling for relational problems with the partner (GAEP 1999).

[*Update 2003*: Since pornography is currently easily accessible both by cable television and through the Internet, it is common that teachers in the classroom discover that children as young as 3 or 4, even if more commonly later, view such material. However, because many of the teachers and parents are ill at ease with the subject of sexuality, important opportunities for sex education using the viewing of such material by children are wasted. One consequence is that these children are often left with incorrect sexual information (and sometimes with anxiety) driven by the pornographic material they have viewed. (*End of update by N. Nodin*)]

## 4. Autoerotic Behaviors and Patterns

### A. Children and Adolescents

Autoerotic behavior is common in children and adolescents, but is usually repressed by parents and society, and condemned by religion. This induces some anxiety, especially for the adolescent who masturbates just the same, but often with guilty feelings about it. Adolescents sometimes request counseling over masturbation to know whether it causes illness, impotence, infertility, or pimples, or if it is bad for the health. All these questions reflect popular beliefs about this behavior.

### B. Adults

Although also slightly influenced by repressive religious-based ideas about masturbation, Portuguese adults are more and more open to this behavior. A recent survey shows that it is accepted by approximately 40% of the population, although another 40% feels it should not be accepted (Pais 1998). However, these figures do not coincide with the percentage of individuals who admit masturbating. In a different survey, 69% of adults reported having practiced masturbation (Marktest 1995). This percentage was surprisingly steady in all age groups studied, 18 to 45, but significantly different between men and women, the former reporting a much higher practice of masturbation than the latter.

In a study conducted by Valentim Alferes (1997) with college students, 74% of the males and 27% of the females reported having masturbated in the month previous to the inquiry. It was also possible to determine that men who had had intercourse masturbated just as much as men who had not. As for women, the number of the ones who had not had intercourse and masturbated, more than doubled the ones who had had intercourse and masturbated. Apparently this means that for men, sexual activity is no impediment to masturbation, whereas for women, genital self-stimulation is more frequent in the absence of sexual intercourse, and rarer in its presence.

Men have a more open attitude about masturbation, but individuals of both sexes have a similar level of acceptance over the performance of masturbation by men and women.

Differences exist over the acceptance of masturbation according to religious position, age, and social status: The more religious, the higher the age, and the lower the social and economic status, the less accepting will the individual be towards masturbation (Pais 1998).

## 5. Interpersonal Heterosexual Behaviors

### A. Children

*Sexual Exploration and Sex Rehearsal Play*

Childhood exploration of the body of one's self and others is common, although usually repressed by parents and caregivers. Most Portuguese adults still have some difficulty admitting that children are sexual persons and are thus curious about sex, especially when the adult is not at ease with his or her own sexuality. This is important because sex education directed at children is basically nonexistent in the school system and is not done at home. However, from a very early age, children try to get information about sex as they can, usually through their peers.

In some cases, sexual experiences start in childhood or early adolescence. In a survey conducted in an urban sample, 15% of the males reported having had their first sexual intercourse before 13 years of age (Marktest 1995). This, however, happens only in the case of the male population, probably caused by early curiosity and partner availability; in most cases the female partner is older.

Among younger adolescents, from age 9 or 10 on, a game called *Bate Pé* (Foot Stomping) is played in small- to medium-sized groups. In this game, each girl and boy alternatively proposes a number to an element of the opposite sex. Each number is related to a given behavior, e.g., number one is a handshake, number two is a kiss on the face, number three is a kiss on the mouth, number four is a French kiss, number five is touching the breasts, and so on. The higher the number, the more daring is the behavior, with sexual intercourse being the upper limit. When the recipient of the proposal refuses, he or she will stomp the foot—hence the name of the game. This game is a common starting ground for the discovery of the opposite sex and of rehearsal without compromise. Needless to say that boys rarely stomp their feet and the numbers rarely pass beyond four or five at age 9 or 10.

### B. Adolescents

The fast progress and improvement of life in recent years have affected the lifestyle of Portuguese youth. Major international fashion trends and influences reach Portugal within a few months from the rest of the world. The influence on youth is strongest for music. However, a gap exists between the urban and the rural youth. In the cities, access to leisure and information resources is much easier than in the interior and less-developed rural areas of the country. This makes it difficult to discuss Portuguese youth as a single group, because this cohort contains, in fact, a great range of different people. This should alert the reader to the fact that general information, like most of what we present here, can sometimes be misleading in terms of adolescents who live in different contexts. This fact should also be considered when interpreting information about adults and other groups of the Portuguese population.

*Dating*

Affective relationships in adolescence are frequent, and dating is common, usually starting at 14 or 15 years of age, at least in Lisbon (Silva, Dantas, Mourão, & Ramalho 1996). Dating is not seen as a first step towards marriage, but as a period of experimentation and discovery of the relationship. This pattern is accepted by the majority of young people and is slowly replacing the more traditional ideas about how relationships should be, i.e., a phase leading to marriage. Nevertheless, the large majority of young people (92% between 18 and 20 years of age) have marriage in their plans, even if this is an idea that diminishes as age increases (87% at 21 to 24, and 81% at 25 to 29) (Vasconcelos 1998). This probably happens because of social and economic difficulties perceived as obstacles to marriage or simply because marriage is no longer considered a necessary condition for being with a consort.

*First Sexual Intercourse and Premarital Sex*

Some decades ago, boys usually had their first sexual experience with prostitutes, whereas, for girls, marriage was a condition for starting their sexual experiences (Miguel 1987). The severe social laws that ruled peer and couple relationships at that time strongly disapproved of sex before marriage, but tolerated the sexual behavior of men who used professionals or "easy women" for their first sexual contacts. These easy women were not necessarily prostitutes, but also girls and women who, without great pressure from men, agreed to have sex without being married. These women were, of course, not seen by men as the traditional "marrying type" and were severely socially reproved.

By the end of the 1980s, sex outside marriage was still seen as reprehensible or even as a dangerous behavior, especially for girls (Figueiredo 1988). Ten years later, only 6% of young people considered marriage as a condition for starting their sex life (Pais 1998). Today, affection is the main reason for the sexual initiation of the young, and in fact, most of those who have already had sexual relationships were in love at that time (Alferes 1997). Nevertheless gender differences can still be found in these conceptions, although not as much in behavior. The importance of an emotional involvement with a partner is not considered a prerequisite for sex in the case of boys, as much as it is in the case of girls. This will also influence the psychological situation in which the "first time" takes place. In many cases, there is a strong pressure from the boy to have sex, and the girl will allow it to happen as a proof of her love, even though she might not feel ready for it. For boys, the erotic and hedonistic aspects of love are more important, whereas for girls, romance and love between the partners are the most valuable things.

In any case, sexual foreplay is frequently used as a way to discover sexuality and the body of the partner. There is a sense of inevitability connected with sexual activity in adolescents, for whom their sex life is something that can happen at any time, and often does. However, AIDS is considered one of the main general concerns for these young people, and 96.9% are moderately or very concerned with it (Sampaio 1996).

Despite the fact that sexual activity can, in some cases, be found at ages as early as 12, virginity is still considered something precious for many girls, who are sometimes anxious about the possibility of having lost it because of masturbation, sexual rehearsal, or sexual abuse during childhood. Also, the concept of virginity is not always very clear, and the absence of bleeding during the first intercourse can be interpreted as one still being a virgin.

## C. Adults

*Premarital Relations, Courtship, and Dating*

The pattern of love and sexual relations of younger adults is much like the one of teenagers. People usually get together and date with people they like, even if it is against their parents' wishes. There is a growing acceptance of premarital sexual activity, so that the absence of marriage is not considered a reason for not having sex with a loved one. Most people think that sex without love has no meaning, and this reason is often the determinant of sexual activity among young adults (Vasconcelos 1998).

This also explains the fact that the average age for the start of sexual activity has slightly decreased, at least for women. Thirty years ago, the average age for women starting sexual activity was 21.5 years; presently it is 19.8 years. For men, the average age for the start of sexual activity has been quite stable at around 17.5 years (Instituto Nacional de Estatística 1997). However, this gender gap tends to weaken as age advances. By 25 years of age, the great majority of people have already started their sexual activity, and the difference between the males and the females who have had sex is practically nonexistent.

As for young adults who still have not started their sexual activity, it is mainly because they have not yet found the right person, because they feel they are too young, or simply because they have not yet had the opportunity (Vasconcelos 1998). The start of sexual activity does not happen until certain conditions are met, foremost being a certain perceived level of self-development and the presence of the "right" situation or person.

Nevertheless, the so-called "one-night stands" do happen, 3.3 times more frequently for males than for females (Alferes 1997). Consistently, men are found to have much more positive attitudes towards casual sex and greater expectations regarding the number of future sexual partners. Real or imagined infidelity is also more common in males.

*Marriage and Family: Structures and Patterns*

The family is the stage where life and social relations play out, and where the major influences of the society become more acute. This means that the characteristics of gender roles discussed earlier achieve their clearest expression. Traditionally, women are responsible for taking care of the house and children, but their growing participation in the workforce has also granted them an important role in the economic sustenance of the family. Their husbands are increasingly involved in domestic tasks. Relationships between the couple, as well as between parents and children, have become more equilateral and democratic (Vicente 1998).

There is a strong consensus among the Portuguese of different generations on considering the family the most important social organization in everyday life, couple life, procreation, relationships between parents and children, as well as the role of the female inside and outside the house. These findings are counter to the idea, sometimes defended, that there is a crisis in the institution of the family.

Crisis or not, demography shows us that changes are occurring in the Portuguese family. The median number of family members has decreased substantially, in great part as the result of a smaller number of children being born, from four in the traditional family to a current average of two (Instituto Nacional de Estatística 1997). Divorce rates have increased to 11% in younger generations, and new forms of family are emerging, such as single-parent families, reconstituted families (families formed by partners previously divorced and most times bringing together children from the previous marriages), and cohabitation. The number of families in which the female is the sole adult responsible for the family has grown to about 5%, greater than the number of single-parent families headed by a male, currently less than 1%.

All of these new realities exist peacefully and are generally unquestioned. The notion of family itself has changed and has integrated these alternative organizations of the household. An example of this is the acceptance of cohabitation as a valid alternative to marriage or, at least, as a first step prior to marriage (Vasconcelos 1998). Actually, cohabitation is more easily accepted than it is practiced.

Family has truly become a place of relational and emotional belonging, and is no longer a rigid and institutional structure that has its own right to existence. This is true mostly for the younger generations, in which there is a rejection of the traditional institution of weddings associated with a clear gender difference, the functional division of the house tasks, and the idea of the irreversibility of the relationship. For many younger Portuguese, the main principles are freedom of association between the couple and the right to end the relationship when it no longer has any meaning for the persons involved.

Arranged marriages were never popular in Portugal, although they sometimes took place in the past, mainly in rural and interior areas. Frequently, however, marriage was a guarantee of economic sustenance, and it was also maintained for the same reason, mostly for women who depended on their husband to survive. Nowadays, the economic importance of the wedding has not disappeared, but it now has a different meaning since women have established their place in the workplace. Most Portuguese men and women consider economic stability a prior condition for getting married. Usually, couples do not get married before having a stable job or economic situation, although some will still rely on the parents for help and financial support.

Nevertheless, love is the main reason why two people get married. Marriage is thus seen as a public institutionalization of an affective relationship between two individuals, but it is sometimes also a way to legalize a situation of cohabitation when children are born (Vasconcelos 1998). One should not forget that the figure of the *bastardo*, a child born out of wedlock that previously was socially stigmatized, only disappeared from the Portuguese law in 1981, and still plays an important role at a more unconscious level, even among more progressive people.

Marriage is considered as a life project planned by both members of the couple, even if some concessions are involved. It is also considered as an engagement for life, which, curiously, is opposite to the idea of the reversibility of the relationship that most individuals defend. While romantic love is the basis for the marital relationship, its loss is also reason for ending a marriage. Separation or divorce is generally accepted and considered a way to reach the happiness that can no longer be obtained in the marriage. This fact might explain the growth of divorce rates in recent years.

## [*Cohabitation*

[*Update 2003*: In 2000, after heated debates in the media and the public sphere as well, a law recognizing cohabitation was approved by the National Assembly. According to this law, two people who can prove that they are living together for a period of at least two years can have access to some of the privileges that are traditionally granted by marriage, such as tax benefits and the possibility of not going to work to support a consort who is ill. One of the main issues in this discussion was the fact that this law considered equally the cohabitation of heterosexual and of gay couples. This led to discussion of several other proposals, some more conservative. In the end, the more progressive law was approved.

[Also worthy of note are new laws designed to protect maternity and paternity (Law 17/95 of June 9, 1995, later modified by Law 18/98). According to these laws, workingwomen have the right to a maternity leave of 120 days. In case the mother has twins, this leave may be extended an additional 30 days for each twin. This leave is mandatory for at least 14 days. The father has the right not to work for two days after the birth of a son or daughter, or to the same amount of days as the mother in cases in which she is physically or mentally unable to take care of the child, in the case of maternal death, or by joint decision of both the parents. (*End of update by N. Nodin*)]

## *Sexuality and the Physically Challenged*

In its Rule Number 9 dedicated to the Family Organization and Personal Dignity Dimension, the United Nations calls our attention to the fact that disabled people should not be denied the possibility to enjoy their sexuality, to engage in sexual intercourse, and to have children. It notes that, because of the fact that disabled people may have difficulties in getting married and in having a family, governments should encourage the existence of the appropriate counseling services for this matter. Therefore, disabled people should have access, as other citizens should, to family planning methods and to reliable information regarding the sexual functioning of their body (Secretariado Nacional de Reabilitação 1998). This concern is also present in the lines of the "Rehabilitation Coherent Policy for Disabled People," a European Council Recommendation signed by the Portuguese Council of Ministries in April 1992 (Secretariado Nacional de Reabilitação 1994).

As in other European countries, the United Nations 45/96 Resolution, that establishes the rules regarding Equalization of Opportunities for Disabled People, led to the constitution of Law 9 (of May 9, 1989), called "Prevention, Rehabilitation and Integration for Disabled People," which emphasizes the Basic Principles of the Portuguese Constitution (Secretariado Nacional de Reabilitação 1999). As a result of this law, a permanent national organization included in the Social Security and Solidarity Ministry was created in Portugal. This organization, the National Commission for the Rehabilitation and Integration of Disabled People, is responsible for the planning and general coordination of the National Rehabilitation Policy in cooperation with nongovernmental organizations and the sectarian systems of the Portuguese Public Organization.

As an Information Supplier, this commission organized a national Disability Inquiry, and its last results were published in 1996 (Secretariado Nacional de Reabilitação 1996). They included the situations of 142,112 persons and 47,020 families in the Portuguese continental territory. This *National Inquiry of the Incapacities, Disabilities, and Disadvantages* was very important for understanding the Portuguese reality in this area and made it possible to identify particular priorities and strategies.

Its conclusions, elaborated with the support of the National Statistical Institute and the Instituto Nacional de Servicios Sociales of Spain, showed a national disability rate of 9.16%, similar to that of other countries in Europe. It draws attention to the considerable disability rates in children under the age of 9, and also to its major incidence in the periods of the end of the productive life, earlier retirement and retirement (45 to 54 years of age). Also, the disability incidence, especially regarding locomotion, was directly proportional to age.

The *Inquiry* also stated that, in Portugal, the rehabilitation and integration actions are insufficient and centered in the medical-functional dimension, despite the increased number of organizations dedicated to intervention in disability. Furthermore, there is no structured national program associated with the managing of sexuality in the disabled, in particular for those physically disabled, despite the partial actions associated with the intervention of the organizations dedicated to disability, sexology, and family planning (see Section 13D, Research and Advanced Education, Important National and Regional Sexological Organizations).

*Incidence of Anal Sex, Fellatio, and Cunnilingus*

There is no legal restriction on the performance of oral or anal sex between consenting adults. Both are practices that can take place between couples, married or not, and apparently their incidence is growing. This might be because of the liberalization of sexual practices and the consequent curiosity over alternative forms of sexual experience.

Most people are pleased with the idea or practice of oral sex, either fellatio or cunnilingus, and over 60% report having practiced one or the other (Marktest 1995). Other studies have found values for the practice of oral sex as high as 67%, with no significant differences between males and females (Alferes 1997). In research conducted by one of the authors in a sample of young adults, 46.2% reported having practiced oral sex at least once with a regular partner, while 11.3% had practiced it with an occasional partner and about 1% with a prostitute (Nodin 2000).

The practice of simultaneous oral sex, also known as "69," is also documented, with 58.2% of respondents expressing enthusiasm or pleasure in anticipation of this activity, and a smaller proportion, 51.5%, reporting having practiced it (Marktest 1995). In this case, there is a slight difference between the attitude towards the behavior and the engagement in the behavior, which may happen because the ones who would like to practice it do not have the chance to do it, perhaps for lack of a willing partner.

Opinions are split on anal sex between the male and the female. The proportion of persons who anticipate it with enthusiasm or pleasure, 35.1%, is just about the same as the proportion of those who consider it unpleasant or disgusting, 35.0%, with 22.8% being indifferent about the subject (Marktest 1995). However, 43.3% have tried this sexual practice, especially men.

In the same sample of young adults mentioned before (Nodin 2000), 15.8% report having practiced anal sex at least once with a regular partner, 5% have tried it with a casual partner, and 1.2% with a prostitute.

## 6. Homoerotic, Homosexual, and Bisexual Behaviors

### A. Children and Adolescents

Studies of homosexuality in children and adolescents have not been done, and thus, little is known about its incidence or character.

### B. Adults

*Incidence and Relational Patterns*

There is no consensus regarding the percentage of homosexual individuals in the population. Different studies have arrived at different proportions: 0.7% (Nodin 2000), 1% (Lucas 1993), and 7.8% (Marktest 1995). Others only have specific data related to the incidence of same-sex experience, 2.9% in women and 5.2% in men (Alferes 1997). The marked differences found in these surveys are probably more because of the methodology used to assess the sexual orientation than to a real oscillation of its occurrence in the population. The highest results are obtained in studies made of urban samples, where it is possible to report that individuals who have had a sexual experience with someone of the same gender are mostly in their 30s, have lower educational backgrounds, and are married, cohabiting with a partner, or are divorced or widowed (Marktest 1995).

The prevailing patterns in relationships between homosexual individuals have not been studied, but it seems that it is very close to the heterosexual one, i.e., based on romantic feelings, affection, and sexual attraction towards the partner. This pattern is probably related to the devastating effects of AIDS in the gay community that led to a slow but obvious change in the relational behaviors of this population.

Bisexuality is admitted as a behavior or tendency by a larger proportion of individuals, although sometimes it is a way to dissimulate a homosexual preference. Many bisexuals marry as a way to have a socially acceptable facade, but maintain a secret double life. The existence of this group was highlighted by the advent of AIDS and its spread to women by sexual contact with boyfriends and husbands previously infected in homosexual contacts. These men usually have problems dealing with their sexual orientation and are thus difficult targets for HIV-prevention programs.

*Social Status*

For over 70 years, homosexuality in Portugal was considered by the law as a behavior against nature and was considered equivalent to the crime of vagrancy. Individuals accused of this crime were kept, sometimes for years, in the *Mitras*, institutions for prostitutes, homeless, and other excluded persons. Others were blackmailed with the threat of being "outed." Prior to 1974, no form of organization or group consciousness existed for gays and lesbians, although some meeting points existed, like bars, mainly for individuals from the upper social classes. It was only during the national revolutionary process, in 1975, that the first organization of gays and lesbians, called CHOR (Revolutionary Homosexuals Collective), appeared, claiming dignity, freedom, and political rights for this minority (Vitorino & Dinis 1999). This collective had some impact in the community, but also had difficulties in gaining associates within a group that had but a vague consciousness of what the gay identity really was. Two years later, CHOR had disappeared.

The 1980s were a decade in which several things changed in the Portuguese society, among them, the questioning of the restricted sexual morality the country lived with for several decades. Echoes of the gay movements in other countries started to appear and the propagation of gay bars influenced a growing awareness of a national gay community.

A new lifestyle appeared, but unlike in other countries, there were no community organizations to support the minority in its needs and rights. In 1991, a homosexual work group (Grupo de Trabalho Homossexual) appeared inside a small left-wing party (Partido Socialista Revolucionário) that became the face of the gay movement in Portugal. However, because of its political association, it could only work as a group of reflection and public intervention.

It was only with the upcoming of AIDS and its impact in the gay community, together with the nonexistence of an active and effective government policy to control this disease, that a slow but growing alert to a need for action appeared. Several nongovernmental organizations appeared in the fight against AIDS, many of them integrating gay individuals. It was within these organizations that a group of people, with support from international organizations, created the ILGA–Portugal (International Lesbian and Gay Association), which quickly gathered a considerable amount of members. Its growth was also largely a consequence of the pioneer use of the Internet, which made it possible to reach gay individuals all over the country. ILGA is responsible for the organization of several successful events, such as the Gay Pride Festival and the Gay and Lesbian Lisbon Film Festival, with consistent support from the Mayor of Lisbon. ILGA, which launched an unprecedented awakening of the gay and lesbian community in Portugal, was followed in late 1997 by another institution, Opus Gay.

These institutions have played an active part in trying to change the several existing discriminatory laws against homosexual individuals. Although Portugal has signed international conventions, such as the Amsterdam Treaty, and is a member of organizations that recommend the elimination of legal discrimination based on sexual orientation, it still exists. Most of the time, this discrimination in the Portuguese law is not explicit, excluding homosexual people by omission. Marriage, for instance, is not possible between two people of the same gender, which also makes it impossible for a gay or lesbian couple to adopt children, because, according to the Civil Code, only married couples can adopt children. A gay couple who live together is excluded from the recently proposed laws regarding the creation of cohabitation rights similar to those of married couples. Other legal differences can be found, for instance, the consenting age for same-sex sexual relations is 16 years compared with 14 for heterosexual persons. Individuals who admit to being homosexual are considered unable to enter a military career or the police force, and are also not allowed to donate blood (ILGA–Portugal 1999).

Socially, there is also a lot to be done. All forms of sexual behaviors and lifestyles considered different from the mainstream are usually not very well accepted by the common Portuguese. In a recent survey, a large majority of the population (86.1%) reported negative feelings towards homosexuality (Marktest 1995), although, in general, women were more open than men about the subject. Almost half the people, 48.5%, also think sexual relations should only be allowed between men and women (Pais 1998). Gender identity and sexual orientation are frequently confounded, even among professionals from the social and medical areas, and homosexuality is often associated with effeminate behavior.

Generally, Portuguese people have negative attitudes towards sexual minorities, but demonstrate some degree of acceptance when it comes to people they are familiar with. Perhaps the best word to describe this is not acceptance, but tolerance, which is a general attitude of the Portuguese also in other issues. In this particular case, the tolerance is usually related to the affection that one holds towards the homosexual individual, and that sometimes becomes incongruent with the ideas and positions otherwise held. This, however, is not seen as an internal conflict and is thus not resolved either way. Some degree of tolerance also exists towards public displays of affection between two people of the same sex, even though these are not very common. Gay bashing is almost unheard of in Portugal.

In the specific case of lesbians, they face the double discrimination of being women in a Latin country and of having a homosexual orientation. The lesbian community has much less visibility than the gay community. It is in any case easier for a couple of women to have a relationship or to live together and go unnoticed.

It is only recently that the lesbian community has started to get organized, with the publication of its first lesbian magazine, *Organa*, in 1990, and three years later of *Lilás* (Vitorino & Dinis 1999). The publication of these magazines, and the debate they launched in the lesbian community, allowed the organization of meetings and of small groups that stood for the rights of lesbian women in Portugal. Today, ILGA includes a group of women that integrates many of the members of those previous organizations and that is actively involved in working towards a greater acceptance and demanding of specific rights for lesbians.

## 7. Gender Diversity and Transgender Issues

### A. Sociolegal Status, Behaviors, and Treatment

There are no specific laws in the country regarding transgenderism or transsexualism, only a few court deci-

sions that serve as references about the latter, and these are sometimes contradictory (ILGA–Portugal 1999). According to one of these court decisions, someone that goes through the process of sex change cannot truly become someone of the other gender. The explanations are, in the case of a male-to-female transformation, that the individual cannot get pregnant or maintain sexual intercourse in the same conditions as a woman. Sex change is seen as an error and transsexuals are considered mentally unhealthy people. These ideas are a step back regarding a previous sentence (in 1984), according to which the moral personality of the individual should be respected, the sex change recognized, and the name change accepted by the civil registration.

In fact, name change is possible for any citizen who wishes it and is a relatively accessible procedure, but only when the new name belongs to the same gender category as the previous one or to a gender-neutral name. This last alternative is the one chosen by some transsexuals in order to avoid the complicated procedure to have gender identity recognized. For this, the person has to go through a complicated legal process, and it can only occur with the decision of a court of law.

It is only since 1996 that sex-change operations are possible and occur in Portugal, because the Portuguese Medical Order allowed it to happen. However, no information is available regarding the real number of operations performed in the national territory. The Santa Maria Hospital in Lisbon is the institution that has the major experience with these kinds of operations. Nevertheless, the process to have a sex-change operation is long and implies a severe psychological and psychiatric evaluation to verify whether the candidate is eligible for the process. This difficult process usually takes about two years. Before 1996 and still today, many Portuguese transsexuals went to other countries, like Morocco, or more recently to England, to have their operations done, sometimes under unsafe conditions.

In a study conducted with a sample of approximately 50 transsexual individuals, some of whom were sex workers and others working in various professional areas, the great majority came from rural parts of the country (72%), and many had changed from their birthplace because of their sexual orientation (28%) (Bernardo et al. 1998). This gives us important information regarding the problems that these individuals have to face related to their social adjustment. Besides, most of them do not benefit from social security.

Important problems were identified in risk behaviors and situations. Thus, 30% of these transsexuals knew they were HIV-positive, although only 61% always used a condom. Seventy percent abused alcohol, tranquilizers, or heroin on a regular basis. Fifty-seven percent of this transsexual sample were prostitutes, some having started to work as early as age 11. Eighty-six percent of the transsexual prostitutes were street workers. As this study concluded, "The transgender community in Portugal is an unknown reality, ignored by the public health system. A large majority of its members having a profession that is considered illegal, they do not benefit from any kind of social and medical assistance" (Bernardo et al. 1998).

Besides, transgender persons are not viewed in a positive light by Portuguese society, and so can be ignored, as well as discriminated against. However, as in the case of homosexuality, the traditional Portuguese tolerance is usually prevalent in personal contact with transgendered individuals.

For a couple of years now, several institutions working in the field of HIV prevention and gay rights have organized an annual transvestite gala on the first of December (World AIDS Day) to gather funding for the fight against AIDS. This gala has considerable impact in the media and is also changing the mainstream idea about the transgendered community. Regardless of that, during Portugal's widely celebrated Carnival holiday, it is common to see men dressed as women without that being considered strange.

## 8. Significant Unconventional Sexual Behaviors

### A. Coercive Sex

The present Portuguese Legal Code was designed to protect a recent legal accomplishment: sexual self-determination and freedom. Freedom is understood not only as the free use of sex and of the body for sexual purposes, and the individual sexual freedom of option and action, but also as the right of anyone not to endure actions of a sexual nature against one's will. Coercion and public displays that adversely affect a third person or disrespect a person's sexuality are grounds for charging someone with the crime of violating another person's sexual (rights and) liberties.

The behaviors that qualify by law as sexual crimes are:

- A relevant sexual act specified in the penal code;
- Nonconsensual intercourse (coitus);
- Non-consenting artificial procreation;
- White slave traffic;
- Those who profit from adult prostitution
- Child prostitution;
- Exhibitionist actions;
- Pornography (when it involves child corruption); and
- Homosexual actions as specified in the penal code.

Sexual crimes fall under two categories: *Crimes against sexual freedom* and *Crimes against sexual self-determination*. The former involves child sexual abuse (Article 172), adolescent and dependent individual sexual abuse (Article 173), stuprum (Article 174), homosexual actions with minors (Article 175), and prostitution of minors (Article 176). The laws regarding crimes against the sexual self-determination of a child victim distinguish between a minor under age 14 years, a minor between ages 14 and 16 years, and a minor between 16 and 18 years. The penalties for conviction of a crime against self-determination depend of the age of the victim.

Justice statistics show that, during 1995, 306 individuals were convicted for sexual crimes, from a total of 433 victims (62 males and 371 females), of whom 155 were minors under age 14 and 57 between 15 and 19 years of age. However, it is well known that these figures do not correspond entirely to a social reality because of the characteristics of these phenomena: shame, taboo, hidden practices, and the need for medical evidence in order to have a legal process. According to the Legal Medicine Institute, from 1989 to 1993, of the alleged examined victims of sexual abuse, 460 or 76.4% were children or adolescents. From the total of the population studied, 380 or 63.1% did not present evidence of physical sexual abuse during observation. This absence of physical evidence, in part because of the long period of time that passed before medical observation, does not automatically exclude the possibility of abuse. This absence should be reconciled with cognitive, emotional, and affective signs and symptoms (Costa Santos 1998).

[*Update 2003*: After the most recent revision of the law concerning sexual crimes, the distinction between crimes against sexual freedom and crimes against sexual self-determination endures, but the categories considered underneath each of these two distinctions have slightly changed. The updated list is as follows:

[Crimes against sexual freedom:

- Sexual enforcement (Article 163)
- Violation (Article 164)

- Sexual abuse of person incapable of resistance (Article 165)
- Sexual abuse of person in an institutional setting (Article 166)
- Sexual fraud (Article 167)
- Non-consenting artificial procreation (Article 168)
- White slave traffic (Article 169)
- Taking profit from adult prostitution (Article170)
- Exhibitionist actions (Article 171)

[Crimes against sexual self-determination:

- Child sexual abuse (Article 172)
- Sexual abuse upon dependent minors (Article 173)
- Sexual actions with adolescents (Article 174)
- Homosexual actions with adolescents (Article 175)
- Taking profit from minors' prostitution and white slave traffic. (*End of update by N. Nodin*)]

### Child Sexual Abuse, Incest, and Pedophilia

No generally accepted definition of what constitutes sexual abuse exists in Portugal. In what concerns pedagogic, therapeutic, penal-juridical, and social intervention, several models of intervention coexist and are applied. However, three criteria are commonly accepted on the base definition of sexual abuse: age differences, power differences, and types of behavior. The different intervention models establish as criteria the maximum age of the victim as 15 or 17 years. Above this age, the action is considered rape or sexual harassment. According to Felix López (1991), child sexual abuse can be singly based in age asymmetry. The age difference implies a biological maturity as well as different expectations and experiences. To João Seabra Diniz (1999), a Portuguese priest and psychoanalyst, the age asymmetry is in itself a violation. It is conceived that the child has desire, but the pathology lies in the fact that the adult is taking advantage of that desire. Children do not have the physical, mental, or symbolic experience that allows them to understand the adult's sexuality.

In Portugal, the child's complaint is followed by the need for evidence. This is a long and painful process for the child. The bureaucratic machine involves a hard interinstitutional process in the several areas of intervention.

The studies published in this area are recent and use professionals as the main research population. These studies are not theoretical but practical, analyzing the national situation and characterizing the cases of sexual abuse. In the report *Violence Against Children in Portugal* (Nunes de Almeida et al. undated), the number of maltreated children is analyzed according to the family context. From the 755 cases of family violence, 13.5% or 102 cases involved sexual practices with female children. The more-affected ages are 10 to 14 years, followed by 6 to 9 years and 4 to 5 years.

The General Health Department, in collaboration with the Family and Child Support Project, implemented yet another investigation, according to which, during 1996, each of 384 health professionals from Health Centers identified at least one case of child abuse involving a minor between infancy and age 19). A second questionnaire revealed that close to half of the victims (47%) were between 10 and 14 years of age, and 28% between ages 5 and 9. When the victim was a female, 48% of the cases occurred between 10 and 14 years, and when the victim was a male, the large part of the cases occurred between 5 and 9 years of age. It is important to mention that 17% of these cases involved a mentally or physically disabled child. In 68% of these situations, there was a family tie between the perpetrator and the victim.

The Justice Ministry Studies and Planning Office (GEPMI) reveals that, during 1996, 137 children under 14 years of age and 65 adolescents between 15 and 19 years of age were sexual crime victims. Of 23 individuals tried for minors' sexual abuse, only 15 were convicted. Of a total of 137 children, 44 were rape victims, 58 coercion, abuse, and sexual fraud victims, 5 were human trade and prostitution victims, 17 were sexual abuse victims, and 13 were victims of other crimes against freedom and sexual self-determination. However, the professionals' experience reveals that many more cases exist besides the ones that were exposed. The fact is that there is a serious increase of cases and a larger visibility of the phenomenon.

In 1990, Portugal signed the Children's Rights Convention in New York and approved it to ratification through the Republic's General Assembly Resolution n° 20/90 in June of the same year. Later, in August, the President of the Republic ratified it. According to Article 8 of the Portuguese Constitution, this convention is a part of Portuguese Law and has an imperative character, which means that it can be applied by the courts. However, because of its generality, it is only used as a reference in the interpretation of the Portuguese laws.

In the sexual child abuse area, we draw attention to Article 19°—*Child protection measures are needed against sexual violence in the family performed by those who are close or by the ones that have legal paternal power.* It is also important to reflect on the 34° Article—*The states should take the adequate measures against all forms of sexual exploitation and violence at the national, bilateral and multilateral level, in order to prevent the child from being drawn to perform sexual illicit activities, to be exploited or involved in other illegal sexual practices and exploited in pornography.* In accordance with these international principles, the Portuguese Law establishes in the 69° Article of the Constitution that *children have the right to be protected by the society and by the state, in order to allow their complete development, specially against all forms of abandonment, discrimination, oppression and also against the abusive exercise of authority in the family and other Institutions; The state gives specially attention to orphan children or children that are abandoned or deprived of a typical family environment.* The law establishes that in cases of sexual abuse, the courts can take the necessary and essential measures that are nevertheless unspecified. These measures are often limited to the total or partial inhibition of paternal power, because most cases of sexual abuse take place within the family and are committed by relatives or by people very close to the child.

The Family Court or the Family and Child Court are the entities responsible for putting in action the needed measures in cases of child abuse. Any person with paternal power (meaning a relative) or someone having child custody can request it, as also can the Public Ministry. A special division of this Ministry that works inside the courts, called Minors Curator, defends and promotes child rights, protecting their complete development and rights. The Public Ministry also defends the state's public interest in the protection of people who are vulnerable and incapable of exercising their rights. According to the law, a situation of sexual abuse must be communicated to the Public Ministry, which will take action using the civil-protection structures and penal actions available against the abuser.

[*Update 2003*: Besides the previously mentioned mechanisms associated with interventions in child abuse situations, there are also special commissions—the Comissões de Protecção de Menores (Commissions for the Protection of Minors) that are nonjudicial official institutions aimed at the prevention or interruption of situations that may negatively affect the physical or moral integrity and welfare of the child or adolescent. These commissions are staffed by a psychologist, a physician, and by representatives from the local political authorities, from the health, education, and social security services, as well as from the court. Their intervention is dependent upon parental (or parental-figure) consent, except when that is not possible, in which cases the court may have a direct intervention. (*End of update by N. Nodin*)]

## Sexual Harassment

Sexual harassment is a recent concept in Portugal. For some, it is the result of the changes in the traditional gender roles and of a growing equality between males and females. The fact that women are leaving the house and trying to get a job can be considered as an invasion of the masculine world. Sometimes, the professional dignity of women is the target of abusive behavior.

In Portugal, sexual harassment is all the manifestations of a sexual nature towards someone without that person's consent. The national newspapers and magazines regularly carry stories in which women in particular are victims of sexual discrimination and abuse. This happens mainly in institutions where males are in control. The level of dependency, the threat of unemployment, and the rightful wish to professional accomplishment reveal the exercise of a male power that often works as a barrier to the established equality of rights and opportunities in the professional world. This problem is spreading in a disturbing way, as revealed by the growing number of complaints filed, even though not always ending in legal incriminations. There are no statistics that detail this phenomenon. However, it is calculated that in Portugal, one in three women has already been a victim of this particular type of violence.

It is also common for women to be harassed on the streets by men who consider it as a sign of masculinity. However, this is becoming a rarer behavior, as new values are replacing those associated with the *machismo* culture.

As in the case of sexual abuse, sexual harassment is also based in asymmetries, not only the hierarchical, social, or economic ones, but also on age asymmetries, with the discrepancy being a particular form of power. This is apparent in cases of sexual harassment happening in Portuguese schools. Sometimes girls allow abusive behaviors from teachers in order to get higher grades or simply because they are afraid of retaliation. However, these situations are usually covered by fear and shame, leading to high levels of secrecy. As the Portuguese say: *hidden pussycat with its tail out.*

## [Domestic Violence

[*Update 2003*: In 2000, a new law concerning domestic violence was approved. According to this law, domestic violence is considered a public crime, which means that a complaint (charge) from the victim is no longer necessary for legal action to be taken. Legal action can now take place after the denunciation by a concerned neighbor or anyone else. (*End of update by N. Nodin*)]

## Rape

The crime of rape in Portugal is directly related with the exercise of power. Being perpetrated by the consort or by a stranger, it is punished with imprisonment. When it happens within marriage, it can be the cause of divorce or litigious separation. Rape, like sexual abuse, is not a statistically studied situation as it also involves some secrecy. When it happens inside the family, it is sometimes associated with domestic violence. Fear, embarrassment, and the will to forget, all joined up with self-guilt, keep the victim from filing a complaint. However, the crime does exist, and at a governmental level, there are several projects aimed at the facilitation of the denouncement process, including the training of police officers to deal with rape victims. There is also a concern over the necessity of interinstitutional articulation in the cases of rape and violence among other situations.

New associations, like the Associação Portuguesa de Apoio à Vitima (Portuguese Association of Victim Support, APAV) or the Associação das Mulheres Contra a Violência (Women Against Violence Association) try to act in a coordinated way to provide support and guidance for the victims. This process tries to protect the victim from a double victimization and the consequences of a long process. In 1995, the APAV assisted 1,238 victims; in 1996, this number almost doubled to a total of 2,300. Adding to this number are all the victims who do not search for help. The majority of people who seek help from these associations are women victims of violence and of physical offenses. In Lisbon, most of these women are between 25 and 35 years of age; in Porto, the situation occurs mostly with women between 36 and 45 years of age.

## B. Prostitution

During the 19th century, Lisbon was the capital of an intensive bohemian life. The cultural traditions of this city were characterized by deviant behaviors forbidden by the society. The moral and decency imperatives of a society that lived on public virtues and private habits were exposed by an accepted marginality that went along with popular traditions, such as *fado vadio* (the national song), bullfighting, and a spread of popular language. During this period, the city nightlife had some preferential spaces, particularly the traditional quarters of the Bairro Alto, Alfama, and Mouraria, which were gathering places for devotees of specific socially deviant behaviors. In these quarters, the participants, prostitutes, *fadistas* (*fado* singers), *marialvas* (extravagant, indolent people, usually males), bullfighters, vagabonds, and sailors from all social backgrounds, maintained an open get-together, where all the social distinctions, values, and rules were apparently minimized (Pais 1985). The animation of these times and places is well characterized by popular songs such as this one:

> *Correi a ver em cena as putas grulhas, Do Bairro Alto a corja dos pandilhas, Os fadistas pingões e bigorrilhas, Que de noite incomodam as patrulhas* (Run to see the whores, in Bairro Alto, the gangs, the drunken *fadistas*, by night disturbing the patrols).

These Lisbon night places are presently neighborhoods with a significant popular traditional history. Bairro Alto and Alfama are still important local references in the traditional and modern Lisbon night. However, the changes in the entire social process that occurred in Lisbon with the turn of the 20th century had its effects on bohemian life and prostitution. The places of prostitution and bohemia survived the beginning of the 20th century, but slowly, everything related to them—words, language, body, and movements—started to have a strong commercial value (Pais 1985).

The Portuguese legal code does not penalize the act of prostitution, but only a third party who profits by it. The prostitute occupies a marginal legal and social status, a sort of no-man's land, which can be more or less accepted. There are no specific data on how many people engage in this practice, but it is a well-known fact that prostitution has increased in recent years. This phenomenon daily involves thousands of individuals—prostitutes (women, men, or children), pimps, and clients. With the spread of services with sexual connotations, such as erotic phone lines and luxury prostitution (also existing in Portugal), we could draw wrong conclusions about this activity. As in the beginning of the 20th century, prostitution is not viewed as an individual act, but as a commercial enterprise that involves three individuals (the prostitute, the pimp, and the client). In some cases, prostitution occurs in environments involving specific social and economic situations, such as:

- Growing up in large families;
- Child labor;
- Abandonment and emotional privation;
- Parental alcohol-abuse problems;
- Familial disintegration;
- Rape; and
- Unemployment.

Prostitution raises issues of human rights, especially when it involves the sexual abuse of minors. The rising number of children in prostitution—boys and girls in their early teens—is the result of a large demand mostly by married men from all social classes, usually in their late 30s. Frequently, these men are still burdened with some taboos towards sexuality, but they find in prostitution a way to break away from tensions existing in their strict and conservative familial structure. On the other side, the demand for prostitution by young people has been diminishing. Before the 1970s, it was a tradition in Portugal for a young man to initiate his sexual life with a prostitute, sometimes with the father guiding that visit. This process marked the social role of the prostitute. Presently, information and counseling services in sexuality, sex education, and the fear of HIV/AIDS, have brought young people to initiate their sexual life earlier than in the past, but now in the context of an emotional involvement. One exception to this new pattern are young men from the interior of the country who enter compulsory military service and are stationed in the major Portuguese cities like Lisbon and Porto. These two cities are Portugal's main centers of prostitution, as well as a strategic entry passage for women and children from African and Latin American countries who become involved in prostitution.

Although the issue has not been studied, it is a fact that Portugal's strategic location between the rest of Europe and the countries of Latin America and western Africa, along with its tourism industry, make it a key element in the international child-prostitution nets. At present, a large number of prostitutes are also drug addicts who find in this activity a way to make money. Addiction and prostitution thus become a vicious circle of slavery. Although many think prostitution is a highly profitable activity, the fact that it is a marginal activity means that all profits are immediately used to pay bills. There are no credit lines.

Several social solidarity organizations are dealing with this problem, working side by side with prostitutes in their own activity places, providing humane and therapeutic assistance, and working for the social reinsertion of the prostitutes through professional and career training. Others provide medical support, information, and assistance. Drop-in centers exist, as well as mobile units that take professionals to places where prostitutes work. The abolition or legalization of prostitution is a hot topic of discussion. Legalization could be a way to provide effective legal, psychological, and medical support for this work group that otherwise cannot access it.

## C. Pornography and Erotica

As in other industrialized countries, pornography has gained an important place in Portugal. One has only to open the advertisement pages of a Portuguese newspaper or magazine to realize the numerous pornographic materials available. Sexuality has become a major, greatly magnified social factor, invading our lives through television, films, and magazines.

Before 1974, any kind of public or private display of pornography was forbidden and severely punished. As a result, the local production of pornographic magazines and videos did not develop in Portugal, so today, Portugal is more an importer than a producer of pornography. In the 1990s, markedly amateur pornographic films became a commercial venture. At the same time, Portugal was increasingly chosen by many foreign filmmakers and magazine owners as a cheap place to produce pornographic material.

The current visibility of pornography has made it the center of a heated debate in Portugal. Despite the fact that the first sex shops opened only a half-a-dozen years ago in Lisbon, pornographic films and magazines have been available for a long time in different kinds of shops (even in supermarkets) or through mail catalogues. There is even a cable network that broadcasts pornographic films three nights a week. While these broadcasts are popular with a considerable number of Portuguese, including teenagers, the older generations strongly oppose this development.

In general, Portuguese men have a more open attitude towards pornography, which they view as a way to improve their sexual life and as a source of diversion and entertainment. Women tend to consider pornography as immoral, and think it can degenerate in pernicious habits, and should thus be forbidden (Pais 1998). Sexual liberation seems stronger among younger age groups and also among people from higher social classes for which pornography is seen as a diversion that can improve the sexual life.

In a society just starting to develop its sex education programs, and still fighting against all kinds of anti-sexual prejudices—cultural, moral, and religious—pornography is still viewed as pernicious because of its contents.

## 9. Contraception, Abortion, and Population Planning

### A. Contraception

Contraceptives are widely available at pharmacies, hospitals, and health centers. Since 1985, contraceptive pills, IUDs, and condoms have been freely distributed at the various family planning services available. Condoms are also distributed by institutions involved in the prevention of HIV infection. The emergency contraceptive pill, depoprovera, which was not well known until quite recently, became available in late 1999 after some resistance from some public and private sectors of the society. However, unlike the contraceptive pill that can be easily bought in Portugal without a medical prescription, the emergency contraceptive has to be prescribed by a doctor. RU-486 or mifepristone is considered an abortifacient, and is therefore illegal.

The female condom was available in the past, but is not presently, mainly because they were not profitable. Sterilization is also available, and in the Maternidade Dr. Alfredo da Costa, one of the oldest and most important women's hospitals in Portugal, it is performed only after a careful evaluation of the request by a team of a gynecologist and a clinical psychologist.

More recent methods of contraception, like hormonal implants or injections, are available, but used only by a minority. The great majority of Portuguese women use the pill. In the youngest age group, 15 to 19 years of age, studied by the 1997 Inquiry on Fertility and the Family (Instituto Nacional de Estatística 1997), the pill was used by 55% of women, while in the following age group, 20 to 39 years, it is the method used by 70% of the women. In any case, the pill is followed in popularity by the condom among women, whereas for men, the condom is the most used method from

adolescence on. A significant proportion of individuals use the IUD. It is the method chosen by 10% of all women, although older women use it more than younger ones.

Among adolescents, where sexual activity is frequently unplanned and occasional, coitus interruptus has been used by as many as 37% of all individuals (Pais 1996). In those conditions, most times it is the only method available. Nevertheless, young adults will also use it, as well as the rhythm method, both easily fallible methods used because of the lack of knowledge related to their real efficacy to prevent a pregnancy. The first of these two is reportedly used by 9.5% of all individuals, whereas the second, many times not used in a proper way, is reported by 3.2% in the same age group (Nodin 2000).

The percentage of individuals who have not used contraceptives in their first sexual contact is very high, 65% of women and 73% of men. However, it is clear that in the younger generations, the gap between the first sexual intercourse and the first use of contraception is decreasing, when compared with older generations (Instituto Nacional de Estatística 1997).

### B. Teenage (Unmarried) Pregnancies

Portugal has a severe problem with teenage pregnancies and it has one of the highest rates of adolescent mothers in Europe. This situation is because of several factors, some of which are external and some of which are internal to the adolescent. Among the external factors, one can point to the nonexistence of sex education in schools, the difficulty that many parents have in talking about sexuality, and the lack of resources aimed at youngsters regarding family planning, especially in the rural areas where they are most needed. The internal factors are related to the idea that contraceptives are hard to obtain and to an inhibition related to the discussion of contraceptive use with the sexual partner, among others.

Among today's younger generations, the proportion of women who had their first child before 20 years of age is 3% (Instituto Nacional de Estatística 1997). In the past, this figure was significantly higher, but the social context was also significantly different. In fact, people got married younger, and because of this, many teenage pregnancies occurred within wedlock and thus in a more favorable context for the mother and child.

Almeida (1987) conducted a large research study with teenage mothers in a women's hospital. He found that the civil status of the mother had an important influence both socially and emotionally. Unmarried teenage mothers had more problems with the family and a greater intention to have an abortion. Besides that, they also had important medical complications, such as hypertension, pre-eclampsia and eclampsia, premature babies, and small babies for gestational age. However, when the father of the child was positively interested and not absent from the situation, these problems were alleviated.

Teenage pregnancies are generally not well accepted by the Portuguese family, and there are cases of girls being thrown out of their parent's home when their condition is discovered. For these, the solution is to move in with their boyfriend or with his family, or to resort to one of the existing institutions that shelter single pregnant women and mothers who have no place to go. However, in most cases, the family eventually accepts the pregnancy of the girl and tries to find the resources to receive the newcomer. This usually is done with the help of the grandparents or great-grandparents of the baby. Nevertheless, the pregnancy has a significant impact on the life of the girl, often leading to the abandonment of immediate plans of having a proper education.

Among girls who come from lower social backgrounds, in which one of the main life goals is the constitution of a family, pregnancy during adolescence means gaining status. Maternity, in these spheres, is a way to become socially accepted and recognized as a woman (Vilar & Gaspar 1999). Teenage pregnancy might challenge the traditional sexual morality, but it can also be a way for the girl to get closer to her family, to her baby's father, and most of all to her child. The child becomes, for many, a reason to be.

[*Update 2003*: The frequency of unplanned sexual intercourse, as well as of unwanted pregnancy leads to frequent abortions being used as a "contraceptive" method. This situation is also the result of a true lack of effective family planning programs and sex education. Many of these pregnancies, especially those that happen during adolescence, can be of serious risk to the mother or unborn infant, if not followed up medically. (*End of update by N. Nodin*)]

## C. Abortion

The Portuguese law on abortion was created in 1984 and changed in 1997. Currently, abortion is allowed at different times of gestation, according to the reason behind the decision to interrupt the pregnancy:

- Before 12 weeks, when a serious and lasting effect to the physical or psychological health of the pregnant women is present;
- Before 16 weeks, in the cases in which the pregnancy resulted from a rape; and
- Before 24 weeks, when there are strong indications of serious disease or malformations of the unborn baby.

Several attempts have been made to change the law to make it more extensive, but without any success. The strongest of these attempts occurred in 1998, when a national referendum, the first in the history of the Portuguese democracy, was conducted over the legalization of abortion after 12 weeks by request of the mother. This referendum launched a large-scale public debate over abortion, and several movements were formed for and against this law. Catholic sectors of the Portuguese society, in particular, responded very strongly against any kind of liberalization of abortion. However, participation in the referendum was very weak, below 50%, and the results showed a clear split in public opinion over this subject, with the number of responses against the liberalization only slightly outnumbering those in favor.

The existence of a restrictive law on abortion doesn't mean that women will not resort to it when confronted with an unwanted pregnancy. In fact, a recent national study showed that, for young adults, abortion was the option of 74.3% of women faced with an unwanted pregnancy (Nodin 2000). According to the national statistics, 5% of all Portuguese women have used abortion at least once (Instituto Nacional de Estatística 1997). However, in this area, as in others, the actual number is very likely higher than the reported number. Most times, women will not admit to having resorted to abortion as much as they really have. This is still a subject restricted to the privacy of couples and families and not spoken out loud. The legal penalty for abortion, which can be up to three years in jail for the woman, has been applied only a very few times. More often, the abortion provider has been prosecuted and convicted. But even in these cases, a legal charge or complaint is necessary for the process to begin.

While the number of legal abortions performed in hospitals in 1995 and 1996 were less than 300 annually, it is estimated that an average 20,000 to 22,000 occur every year in illegal situations (Rosendo 1998). These illegal abortions are the frequent cause of serious health problems and subsequent hospitalization of the women involved. Some, but not the majority, of the providers of illegal abortions have medical or nursing training. The use of traditional techniques, such as the insertion of objects into the uterus or the ingestion of toxic substances, is not as common as it was in the past, but it still occurs. Many Portuguese women also resort to abortion clinics in Spain, where, curiously, the law is very similar to the Portuguese law, except that there it has had a more liberal application that allowed the opening of abortion clinics. In 1998, 30% of all clients in one Spanish abortion clinic close to the border were Portuguese women.

Abortion is more frequent in women after the age of 20, which is also the average age for the start of the sexual life of the Portuguese. The incidence of abortion increases after age 35, and after age 45 about 70% of all pregnancies end up interrupted (Instituto Nacional de Estatística 1997). Abortion is also more common in women with a low socioeconomic status and education. However, these are also the ones who have more conservative attitudes towards abortion (Vasconcelos 1998).

[*Update 2002*: The issue of illegal abortions made news headlines in January 2002, when Maria do Ceu Ribeiro, a nurse, was sentenced to an eight-and-a-half-year prison term for running an abortion clinic and performing illegal abortions in a town north of the city of Porto in northern Portugal. Her clinic and its services were an open secret in the area. Most of her 42 codefendants, including 17 women charged with having an abortion, were acquitted by a panel of four judges. Six people who provided a referral network, and one woman who admitted to getting an abortion, were ordered to pay a fine or spend three months in prison. The trial produced considerable discussion and debate in this nation of 10 million, which has the strictest laws on abortion of any nation in the European Union outside Ireland. Abortion-rights advocates claim that between 20,000 to 40,000 illegal abortions are performed each year, and some 5,000 Portuguese women show up at hospitals each year with complications from illegal abortions (Lyall 2002). (*End of update by R. T. Francoeur*)]

## D. Population Programs

Unlike other industrialized countries where fertility rates started to decrease at the end of the 19th century, in Portugal this tendency is quite recent. It started in the 1960s, but the decrease was quite significant, and in less than 20 years, between 1970 and 1989, the fertility rate that was one of the highest in Europe dropped from 2.8 to 1.5 children per women (Bandeira 1994). One reason for this is the changes in the mating and marrying patterns of the population, formerly restricted by social norms, but recently replaced by individuals and couples taking control over their fertility. Women are delaying the birth of their first child, many times in favor of a professional career.

Another significant demographic phenomenon affecting Portuguese society is the aging of the population. Until 1960, the proportion of people 65 years of age or older was a constant 5% to 6%; in 1991, it was 14%, and still growing. Nevertheless, there are significant differences between the rural interior and the urban littoral, the former having more older people than the latter. This situation is mostly related to migratory movements that led a considerable proportion of the rural young population towards the cities and towards other countries, like France, Germany, Switzerland, the USA, Canada, and South Africa, in search of better living conditions (Barreto & Preto 1996).

Bandeira (1994) has interpreted the aging Portuguese demographic situation as decaying and entering a potentially irreversible process. According to this author, serious actions need to be taken in order to deal with this situation, but not much has, in fact, been done. He also argues that it is the government that should be responsible for a turnover in politics, facing the reality of the situation and supporting the high costs of having and rearing offspring, as well as creating the conditions for the resettling of the population in the interior.

Some of the more recent actions aimed at the promotion of population growth are related to the protection of maternity and paternity. New laws protect women against discrimination at work based on pregnancy, and grant them bigger maternity leaves, to a minimum of 6 weeks and maximum of 100 days. The working mother's right to breastfeed her child for at least a year after birth is also now guaranteed. For the first time in Portuguese legal history, the father now has the right to a work leave of up to 20 days subsequent to the birth of a child, and also has the possibility of absence from work to feed the child in case breastfeeding is not possible. Similar rights have been granted to grandparents when they are the baby's caretakers.

## 10. Sexually Transmitted Diseases and HIV/AIDS

### A. Sexually Transmitted Diseases

In Portugal, the sexually transmitted disease surveillance and treatment history goes back to the 19th century with the March 27, 1879, founding of the Consulta de Moléstias Syphilíticas e Venéreas of the Desterro Hospital in Lisbon, under the direction of the prominent Portuguese physician, Thomaz de Melo Breyner. Later, in the second decade of the 20th century, the Lisbon and the Porto Dispensários Centrais de Higiene Social centralized the surveillance of venereal diseases according to Law 14-803 of December 13, 1927.

Since the 1980s and the demise of the free and confidential Central Dispensaries, monitoring STDs has become the responsibility of the Reference Health Services. Two of these services are the Dermatology service of the Curry Cabral Hospital in Lisbon and the Sexually Transmissible Diseases service in the Lapa Health Center, also in Lisbon. Nowadays, in Portugal, notification is compulsory for gonorrhea, syphilis, and the soft ulcer, all of them bacteriogenic STDs.

In 1993, the results, conclusions, and recommendations of a descriptive, cross-section, longitudinal, and retrospective study regarding sexual behavior in Portugal were published. This report, known as *Portuguese Unprotected Sexuality* (Lucas 1993), focused on the adult population, ages 18 to 49, living in cities with 10,000 or more inhabitants in the continental territory. It was supported by the World Health Organization (Social and Behavioral Investigation Unit of the AIDS Global Program) and by the National Commission Against AIDS. It showed that 12% of those surveyed admitted to having had a sexually transmitted disease. The results showed that STDs were more prevalent in the metropolitan areas of Lisbon, Porto, and in the Algarve (in the south of the country), and more common after the age of 25. The incidence of the various STDs was 5% for gonorrhea, 4% for hepatitis, 2% for herpes, and 1% for cases of syphilis and urethritis (Santos Lucas 1993). It is important to note that the data were self-reported and so it can underestimate the reality.

At the end of 1997, the Dermatology service in the Curry Cabral Hospital and the Lapa's Health Center noted the stabilized number in cases of syphilis and the lower incidence of gonorrhea and *Chlamydia trachomatis*. It is, however, important to note that the 1997 data of the STD service in Intendente, an area of Lisbon traditionally associated with prostitution, draws attention to the fact that only 20% of the prostitutes were not infected with an STD, and the percentage of gonorrhea and chlamydia infections was above 30%.

Regarding the future of STDs in Portugal, Cardoso (1997) pointed out some difficulties related to the surveillance and treatment of these diseases that are responsible for our intermediate position between developed and less developed countries. These difficulties should be overcome by the reorganization of the STD services in Portugal, with real accessibility and confidentiality of the medical services, with free complementary exams for diagnosis and medication, with the epidemiological evaluation (overcoming sub-notification), and also with counseling.

### B. HIV/AIDS

In Portugal, human immunodeficiency virus infections and AIDS have been reported since 1983. The Epidemiological Vigilance Center of the Portuguese Health Institute in Lisbon collects the national data respecting the universal criteria of the Centers for Disease Control in the U.S. The Comissão Nacional de Luta Contra a SIDA (National Commission Against AIDS, or CNLCS.), an organization connected to the Ministry of Health, characterizes the national situation and organizes the national policy, priorities, and strategies in accordance with the United Nations AIDS (UNAIDS) policy.

According to the quarterly and annual information of this Commission, Portugal has had an annual increase of AIDS-related cases since 1983, the first year of notification (Carvalho Teixeira 1993). The official national values do not totally characterize the Portuguese reality, because they do not include untested, undiagnosed, and unreported people.

Since 1985, the year of the first 18 notified cases (and not the time of the primo-infection or first diagnosis), most cases have been related to homosexual and bisexual individuals, the same tendency as in the majority of European countries. This remained the case into the 1990s. Before 1993, the second most affected group were the heterosexuals who were not IV-drug users, as was already the trend in the rest of the Europe. After 1993, the heterosexual transmission of the virus in African emigrants from the Portuguese ex-colonies was overtaken by the greater number of reported cases of HIV/AIDS in IV-drug users (Prista Guerra 1998).

At the end of the first three months of 1999, the national percentages of accumulated cases according to the mode of viral transmission were distributed as follows: 45% homosexual or bisexual, 27% heterosexual, and 12.5% IV-drug abuse related. In 1996 and 1997, IV-drug users represented 53.8% and 61% of the total affected people, respectively (Ministério da Saúde 1997). The rates provided by the Comissão Nacional de Luta Contra a SIDA (1999abc) for the third quarter of 1999 also showed a significant increase in the HIV-infection rate in IV-drug users (46.9% in September, 46.5% in June, and 45.8% at the end of March 1999).

In the period between January 1, 1983, and September 30, 1999, 26.1% of the total number of AIDS-related reported cases was from heterosexual transmission, 19.2% was from homo-/bisexual transmission, and 1% was from vertical transmission (mother to child).

Since the beginning of the AIDS-epidemic situation, Portugal had, as of September 30, 1999, a total of 6,263 reported cases, of which 3,928 had already died because of the disease (86.2% with opportunistic infections, especially tuberculosis). Of the affected individuals, 85.8% were between 20 and 49 years.

Another existing trend in the national data is the increasing incidence of cases in the female population, although affected men still represent the large majority, as in the rest of Europe at the end of the third quarter of 1999, with the proportion 84.2% for men and 15.7% for women.

Even though the majority of Portuguese cases are HIV-1 infections, there is a great impact of HIV-2 infections and of infections with both viruses. Most European countries do not have specific numbers for HIV-2 infections, because it is almost nonexistent in those countries and the rare cases are simply combined with HIV-1 cases. In Portugal, 4.5% of cases are HIV-2 and 1.7% are infections with both viruses. Most of the notified cases until 1999 were concentrated in the capital, Lisbon, in the second major Portuguese city, Porto, in the north, and in Setúbal, approximately 30 km (18.6 mi) south of Lisbon.

Because of the epidemiological surveillance, several centers for HIV testing are available, as well as information sources from nongovernmental organizations (NGOs) and social solidarity institutions, such as Abraço (the Hug Association), Fundação a Comunidade Contra a SIDA (Foundation to the Community Against AIDS), and the Liga Portuguesa Contra a SIDA (Portuguese League Against AIDS), among others (see list at the end of the chapter). Several therapeutic resources are also available in the central and local health institutions.

Finally, it is important to note the national specificity and intervention priorities in the prevention and treatment areas of the HIV infection. In less than two decades, Portugal ranked highest regarding the dissemination and impact of HIV in Europe, and does not yet follow the stabilization trend of central and northern Europe.

Prevention, the most important weapon against AIDS, will be achieved by the reduction of risk behaviors on an individual level, but mostly by decisive investment in serious improvements in socioeconomic conditions, as well as in the educational and cultural arenas, i.e., in reducing risk situations on a community level.

These objectives imply a global Health Education Policy reaching the individuals who are considered the most vulnerable according to the data, such as homosexual and bisexual men, women, young people, children, drug users, prostitutes, people in jail, and ethnic minorities. Aspects of extreme relevance are condom access and their systematic use, with national information and promotion campaigns, free condom distribution, and initiatives created by drug-abuse prevention programs; real access to anti-HIV antibody testing; a generalized respect for informed consent and confidentiality; and the systematization of multidisciplinary structured responses for the affected persons, and particularly the creation of psychological and socioeconomic structures, such as domestic support. All of these are factors that reduce the personal, social, and financial costs of the AIDS phenomenon (Machado Caetano 1997).

[*Update 2002*: According to the latest data published in late 2002 by the Centro de Vigilância Epidemiológica das Doenças Transmissíveis (Center for the Control of Contagious Diseases, or CVEDT), from July 1 until December 31, 2001, 1,282 cases of HIV infection had been detected (of which 709 were of non-symptomatic individuals, 94 of AIDS Related Complex (ARC) and 479 of AIDS). Of these, 615 were caused by drug use, 517 were caused by heterosexual intercourse, and 104 by homo- or bisexual intercourse.

[During 2001, 2,543 cases of HIV cases were registered by medical doctors (incidence rate of 257.5 per million inhabitants), with 1,045 cases of AIDS (incidence rate of 105.8 per million inhabitants), and 469 of AIDS-related deaths reported. The most common way through which people were infected was via drug use (1,339 cases), followed by heterosexual intercourse (955 cases), and finally, by homo- or bisexual intercourse (179 cases). There were also six cases of vertical transmission and one case of AIDS in a child.

[The main tendency of HIV infection in Portugal is that of a growing number of infections because of intravenous drug use, and a diminishing number of infections because of heterosexual intercourse. The exception to these numbers is that of the infections by the HIV-2. Of the total group of seropositives (76.6% of which are between 20 and 39 years old), 54.6% belong to the "drug addicted" category of infection and 30.2% to the "heterosexual" group. Something similar happened to the total group of people with ARC, that is, 45% of these belonged to the first category of infection and 29.7% to the second.

[Until the end of 2001, there were 8,710 deaths related with AIDS, of which 342 were associated with the HIV-2 infection and 126 associated with the combination of HIV-1 and HIV-2 infection.

[The prevalence of HIV infection is higher in major urban centers like Lisbon, Oporto, Setúbal (because of the region's low economic situation and elevated number of drug users), and Faro (because of it being a high tourist region). Taken altogether, these urban centers have an average of 200 cases for each 100,000 inhabitants. Besides the cities, other areas of high incidence are those close to the border with Spain.

[According to UNAIDS, the estimate of HIV infections in Portugal is between 30,000 and 50,000 persons. Because of this fact, one of the designated areas of priority intervention for the CNLCS (Comissão Nacional de Luta Contra a SIDA—National Commission Against AIDS) is identification of the epidemiological character of the HIV infection, in particular, for small but vulnerable groups such as pregnant women, people in prison, young school-age people, drug users, sex workers, ethnic minorities, and mobile populations, in order to implement adequate actions of information and education. (*End of update by N. Nodin*)]

[*Update 2002*: UNAIDS Epidemiological Assessment: The HIV/AIDS Surveillance System in Portugal started in 1985 and some cases were identified retrospectively. At the beginning of the epidemic, notifications were predominantly of AIDS cases, but gradually clinicians reported cases in all stages of disease progression.

[Portugal has both HIV-1 and HIV-2 circulating in the general population, and notified AIDS cases attributed to HIV-1 are 94.6% and cases attributed to HIV-2 are 3.9% of the total; dually infected AIDS cases (1.4%) have been reported.

[The overall incidence of AIDS and the annual number of reported deaths rose steadily until 2000. The HIV/AIDS epidemic shows a mixed pattern, with the proportion of AIDS cases decreasing in injecting drug user cases and with a noticeable increase in cases attributed to heterosexual contact. Trend analysis of surveillance data reflects the diversity of the HIV/AIDS situation in the country, but young adults are most affected.

[The estimated number of adults and children living with HIV/AIDS on January 1, 2002, were:

| Adults ages 15-49: | 26,000 (rate: 0.5%) |
| Women ages 15-49: | 5,100 |
| Children ages 0-15: | 350 |

[An estimated 1,000 adults and children died of AIDS during 2001.

[No estimate is available for the number of Portuguese children who had lost one or both parents to AIDS and were under age 15 at the end of 2001. (*End of update by the Editors*)]

## 11. Sexual Dysfunctions, Counseling, and Therapies

### A. Concepts of Sexual Dysfunction

The diagnosis of sexual dysfunctions is usually done according to the existing specialty international disorders classification systems, such as the *DSM* and the *ICD*. However, despite the fact that several sexuality surveys have been conducted in the Portuguese population, questions about dysfunctions are usually left out of them. This reflects the secretive way that the Portuguese deal with these difficulties. Sexuality is a difficult subject to discuss of its own right, and all the problems affecting it are even more. The most frequent strategy used to deal with sexual difficulties is silence. It is only with some difficulty that someone will talk to a physician about a premature ejaculation problem or vaginismus, and when they do, it is usually with a professional that they trust. However, it is estimated that a large number of sexual dysfunctions go unreported.

There is a significant gender difference in the experience of these problems. For men, for whom sex is yet a means to prove their masculinity and virility, sexual problems are a major concern, especially impotence. Men make a great investment in their sexual performance and abilities, and when something goes contrary to expectations, catastrophic scenarios are built and self-esteem is severely affected. As for women, in the past they were supposed to serve their husbands sexually disregarding their own sexual pleasure. This way, many times there was not even the awareness of the existence of a sexual dysfunction when orgasm was not experienced. Today, women are more aware of their own sexuality and are able to seek help when they feel they need it, even though they are not as likely as men to seek help. In the Alferes 1997 survey of sexually experienced individuals, 100% of men had experienced orgasm, but only 88.5% of women had. In the portion of people who had not had sexual relations, all of the males had experienced orgasm, while only 35.5% of women had experienced it.

The sexological tradition in Portugal is strongly connected to a cognitive and behavioral perspective of sexuality. Nevertheless, nowadays, the different institutions working in this field have a broader approach to sexuality. The echoes of the International Conference for Population and Development held in Cairo in 1994, in which major emphasis was given to sexual and reproductive health, are having its effects at different levels. A greater concern is being devoted to the special sexual and reproductive needs of individuals in a holistic approach to the problems they face. To accomplish these goals, true efforts are being made especially by nongovernmental institutions (NGOs).

### B. Availability of Diagnosis and Treatment

Diagnosis and treatment of sexual dysfunctions are available in hospitals in the main urban centers. The cities where specialty sexology services can be found are: Porto, Coimbra, Leiria, Lisbon, Faro, and Ponta Delgada (in the Azores). Many private practitioners, either medical doctors or psychologists, offer their services in other parts of the country. However, not all the people can afford to go to these consultations, nor do they frequently know of their existence. In 1998, the Portuguese Society of Clinical Sexology (Sociedade Portuguesa de Sexologia Clínica, SPSC), together with a pharmacological company, created a telephone helpline called SOS Dificuldades Sexuais (SOS Sexual Difficulties) aimed at an adult public with sexual dysfunctions. The main goal of this helpline is to provide counseling for people with sexual problems, and also to work as a guiding service to indicate which services, both public and private, are available for these kinds of problems.

### C. Therapist Training and Certification

Until the 1990s, no specific sexological training was available in Portugal. There was a hospital tradition that provided practical and also theoretical training for psychiatrists, gynecologists, and professionals from other medical specialties that had an interest in sexuality. Others had their training abroad in countries where this kind of training was available. Many of the great names of sexology in Portugal today, like António Pacheco Palha, Francisco Allen Gomes, José Pacheco, Júlio Machado Vaz, or Júlio Silveira Nunes, had their training as part of their specialty training or abroad.

In 1984, following the first Portuguese Congress of Sexology, a commission was formed to create a Society of Sexology, which the following year had a total of 116 members. One of the main and primary goals of this society was to promote and regulate the scientific training in sexology in Portugal. In 1992, the society began seriously exploring the legal, practical, and pedagogical aspects of organizing a postgraduate course that would grant a certified title of sexologist.

The first postgraduate course in sexology was a two-year program started in 1995 with a group of 14 medical doctors, psychologists, and nurses; a second course started in 1998. This course, organized by the SPSC, is actually the only one that grants a certificate for Sexual Therapist in Portugal. This course is interdisciplinary and aimed at professionals with some experience in the area. It has a duration of two years divided into four semesters: The first semester is solely theoretical, the following two are theoretical and practical with the discussion of clinical material provided by the students and teachers, and the last semester is devoted to the elaboration and execution of a research project.

## 12. Sex Research and Advanced Professional Education

### A. Institutes and Programs for Sexological Research

As in other behavioral areas, there is little sexological research. The tradition of research is incipient and lacks appropriate articulation between universities and companies that would provide financing and practical application of the results of the research. The few research studies that exist within Portuguese sexology occur mainly in universities, usually associated with psychology, medicine, and sociology, and also in the hospitals and centers that offer specialty services in human sexuality.

### B. Post-College and Graduate Programs in Sexology

There is no graduate level course on human sexuality. There are some initial efforts in short-duration advanced courses on the subject, but they are infrequent and irregular. There are, however, two postgraduate courses on human sexuality in the country, one of them a master's degree course.

The first postgraduate course in human sexuality ever to occur in Portugal was organized by the SPSC in 1995 (see Section 12C, Therapist Training and Certification, above). In the meanwhile, a private university, Universidade Lusófona, organized a master's degree course in sexology that started in 1998. Many of the teachers of this course are connected to the SPSC and are, thus, the same as the ones in the postgraduate course provided by that society. The master's degree is, however, mostly theoretical and does not grant the title of sexual therapist as the postgraduate course does. The theoretical areas discussed in the master's degree are:

- The historical, social, cultural, and anthropological aspects of sexuality;
- The human sexual response;
- Gender identity and its disturbances;
- AIDS and other sexual transmitted diseases;
- Research methods in sexology;
- Diagnosis and evaluation of the disturbances of the human sexual response;
- Treatment of the disturbances of the human sexual response;
- Minority sexual and erotic preferences;
- Couple therapy;
- Sex education and family planning; and
- Data analysis techniques in sexology.

Although these courses have played an important role in extending the offering of sexological training programs in Portugal, professionals from different areas recognize the need for a more appropriate approach to sexual problems. Many have to deal with these kinds of problems and have no appropriate training to handle them.

## C. Main Sexological Journals and Periodicals

*Acta Portuguesa de Sexologia*, Hospital de São João, 4200-319 Porto, Portugal; Tel:/Fax: +351-225-508-384; email: psiquiatria.fmp@mail.telepac.pt.

*Sexualidade e Planeamento Familiar*, Rua da Artilharia Um, 38, 2º Dto., 1250-040 Lisboa, Portugal; Tel: +351-213-853-993; Fax: +351-213-887-379; email: apfportugal@mail .telepac.pt.

There are also some periodicals related to AIDS worthy of note:

*Abraço*, Tr. do Noronha, 5, 3º Direito, 1250-169 Lisboa, Portugal; Tel: +351-213-974-298; Fax: +351-213-957-921.

*Informação SIDA*, Apartado 1980, 1058-001 Lisboa, Portugal; Tel: +351-213-129-290; Fax: +351-213-129-299.

## D. Important National and Regional Sexological Organizations

Sociedade Portuguesa de Sexologia Clínica, Serviço de Psiquiatria, Hospital de São João, 4200-319 Porto, Portugal; Tel:/Fax: +351-225-508-384; email: psiquiatria.fmp@ mail.telepac.pt.

Associação para o Planeamento da Família, Rua da Artilharia Um, 38, 2º Direito, 1250-040 Lisboa, Portugal (with branches in Porto, Coimbra, Lisbon, Alentejo, Algarve, and Azores); Tel: +351-213-853-993; Fax: +351-213-887-379; http://www.apf.pt; email: apfportugal@mail .telepac.pt.

*Telephone Helplines:*
Sexualidade em Atendimento (APF), +351-222-001-798.
Sexualidade em Linha, 800-222-002; Ap. 1191, 1054 Lisboa Codex, Portugal; email: sexualidade@ipj.pt.
SOS Dificuldades Sexuais, 808-206-206.

*Lesbian, Gay, Transgender, and Bisexual Organizations:*
Grupo de Trabalho Homossexual (Partido Socialista Revolucionário), Rua da Palma, 268, 1100 Lisboa, Portugal; Tel:/Fax: +351-218-882-736.

ILGA–Portugal, Rua de São Lázaro, 88, 1150-333 Lisboa, Portugal; Tel: 218-873-918; http://www.ilga.portugal .org; email: ilga-portugal@ilga.org.

Opus Gay, R. Ilha Terceira, 34, 2º, 1000 Lisboa, Portugal; Tel: +351-213-151-396; http://homepage.esoterica.pt; email: anser@esoterica.pt.

*HIV/AIDS Organizations:*
Abraço, Travessa do Noronha, 5, 3º Direito, 1250-169 Lisboa, Portugal; Tel: +351-213-974-298; Fax: 213-957-921; http://abraco.esoterica.pt; email: abraco@mail .telepac.pt.

Associação dos Direitos e Deveres dos Positivos e Portadores do Vírus da SIDA, Quinta das Lapas, Monte Redondo, 2560 Torres Vedras, Portugal; Tel: +351-261-312-331; Fax: +351-261-312-322.

Centro de Respostas Integradas de Apoio à SIDA, Avenida da Imaculada Conceição, 153, 4700-034 Braga, Portugal; Tel. +351-253-261-500; Fax: +351-253-609-994.

Comissão Nacional de Luta Contra a SIDA, Palácio Bensaúde, Estrada da Luz, 153, 1600-153 Lisboa, Portugal; Tel: +351-217-210-360; Fax: +351-217-220-822; email: CNLCS@cnlcs.min-saude.pt.

Fundação Portuguesa a Comunidade Contra a SIDA, Rua Andrade Corvo, 16, 1º, Esq. , Portugal; Tel: +351-213-540-000; Fax: +351-213-160-000.

Gabinete de Apoio a Doentes com SIDA, Rua João António Gaspar, 40, Bairro Marechal Carmona, 2750-380 Cascais, Portugal; Tel: +351-214-861-429; Fax: +351-214-861-420.

Liga Portuguesa Contra a SIDA, Rua do Crucifixo, 40, 2º, 1100-183 Lisboa, Portugal; Tel: +351-213-225-575; Fax: +351-213-479-376.

Movimento de Apoio à Problemática da SIDA, Avenida Cidade Hayward, Blocos C1 e D2, Caves Vale Carneiros, 8000-073 Faro, Portugal; Tel: +351-289-864-777; Fax: +351-289-846-598.

Projecto STOP SIDA, Centro Laura Ayres, Rua Padre António Vieira, 12, 3000-315 Coimbra, Portugal; Tel: +351-239-828-771.

SOL Associação de Apoio a Crianças Infectadas pelo Vírus da SIDA e Suas Famílias, Rua das Praças, 55, r/c, 1200-766 Lisboa, Portugal; Tel: +351-213-625-771; +351-213-625-773.

*Disability and Rehabilitation Organizations:*
Liga Portuguesa dos Deficientes Motores, Rua Sítio Casalinho da Ajuda, 49 Frente, 1300 Lisboa, Portugal; Tel: +351-213-633-314.

Secretariado Nacional de Reabilitação e Integração das Pessoas com Deficiência, Avenida Conde Valbom, 63, 1050 Lisboa, Portugal; Tel: +351-217-929-500.

*Sexually Transmitted Diseases Organizations:*
Centro de Saúde da Lapa, Consulta de Doenças Sexualmente Transmissíveis, Rua de São Ciro, 36, 1200 Lisboa, Portugal; Tel. +351-213-957-973.

*Prostitution Support Organizations:*
Associação "O Ninho," R. Actor Taborda, 30, 3º Dto, 1000-008 Lisboa, Portugal; Tel: +351-213-426-946.

Centro "Drop In," Travessa do Maldonado, 3, 1100-329 Lisboa, Portugal; Tel: +351-218-853-249; Fax: +351-218-869-784.

Espaço Pessoa, Travessa das Liceiras, 14/16, 4000 Porto, Portugal; Tel: +351-222-008-377.

*Child Sexual Abuse Support Organizations:*
Associação Chão dos Meninos, Bairro António Sérgio, Avenida da Liberdade nº 100, 7000 Évora, Portugal; Tel: +351-266-731-079; Fax: +351-266-371-079.

Instituto de Apoio à Criança (IAC), Largo da Memória, 14, Portugal; Tel: +351-213-624-318; Fax: +351-213-624-756.

*Domestic Violence Support Organizations:*
Associação de Mulheres Contra a Violência, Al. D. Afonso Henriques, 78, 1º esq, 1000 Lisboa, Portugal; Tel:/Fax: +351-218-124-048.

Associação de Apoio à Vítima, Rua do Comércio, 56, 5° esq, 1100 Lisboa, Portugal; Tel: +351-218-884-732, Fax: +351-218-876-351.

Comissão para a Igualdade e Direitos das Mulheres, Avenida da República, 32 1° andar, 1093 Lisboa, Portugal; Tel: +351-217-983-000.

## Acknowledgments

For their assistance and valuable help, the authors wish to thank: Ana Paula Manteigas, Delegação Regional de Lisboa da Associação para o Planeamento da Família; Clara de Jesus, Associação para o Planeamento da Família; Francisco Allen Gomes; Jó Bernardo; Mário Lourenço, Sociedade Portuguesa de Sexologia Clínica; Sergio Vitorino, Grupo de Trabalho Homossexual—Partido Socialista Revolucionário; and Sofia Verissimo.

## References and Suggested Readings

Alferes, V. 1997. *Encenações e comportamentos sexuais [Sexual stagings and behaviors]*. Lisbon: Edições Afrontamento.

Almeida, J. M. R. 1987. *Adolescência e maternidade [Adolescence and maternity]*. Lisbon: Fundação Calouste Gulbenkian.

Amâncio, L. 1994. *Masculino e feminino: A Construcção social da diferença [Masculine and feminine: The social construction of the difference]*. Porto: Edições Afrontamento.

Associação para o Planeamento da Família. 1998. *1° Seminário nacional sobre abusos sexuais em crianças e adolescentes [Sexual abuse in children and adolescents: Contributions from the 1st National Seminar]*. Lisbon: Associação para o Planeamento da Família.

Bandeira, M. L. 1994. Envelhecimento demográfico e planeamento familiar: Que relação? [Demographic aging and family planning: What relationship?]. *Sexualidade e Planeamento Familiar* [Lisbon], *3*(2):15-18.

Barreto, A., & C. V. Preto. 1996. *Portugal 1960/1995: Indicadores sociais [Portugal 1960/1995: Social indicators]*. Lisbon: Cadernos do Público.

Bernardo, J., et al. 1998. *The Portuguese transgender community: An unknown reality*. Paper presented at the 12th World AIDS Conference–Bridging the Gap, Geneva.

Cardoso, J. 1997. O futuro das doenças sexualmente transmissíveis em Portugal [The future of sexually transmissible diseases in Portugal]. *Sexualidade e Planeamento Familiar* [Lisbon], *15/16*:17-22.

Carvalho Teixeira, J. C. 1993. *Psicologia da saúde e SIDA [Health psychology and AIDS]*, Lisbon: Instituto Superior de Psicologia Aplicada–CRL.

CIA. 2002 (January). *The world factbook 2002*. Washington, DC: Central Intelligence Agency. Available: http://www.cia.gov/cia/publications/factbook/index.html.

Comissão Nacional de Luta Contra a SIDA (CNLCS) do Ministério da Saúde. 1999a (March 31). *A situação em Portugal a 31 de Março de 1999 [AIDS: Portugal's situation at 31 March 1999]*. Lisbon: Informação Centro de Vigilância Epidemiológica das Doenças Transmissíveis, Instituto Nacional de Saúde Lisboa.

Comissão Nacional de Luta Contra a SIDA (CNLCS) do Ministério da Saúde. 1999b (June 30). *A situação em Portugal a 30 de Junho de 1999 [AIDS: Portugal's situation at 30 June 1999]*. Lisbon: Informação Centro de Vigilância Epidemiológica das Doenças Transmissíveis, Instituto Nacional de Saúde Lisboa.

Comissão Nacional de Luta Contra a SIDA (CNLCS) do Ministério da Saúde. 1999c (30 September). *A situação em Portugal a 30 de Setembro de 1999 [AIDS: Portugal's situation at 30 September 1999]* (Doc 117). Lisbon: Informação Centro de Vigilância Epidemiológica das Doenças Transmissíveis, Instituto Nacional de Saúde Lisboa.

Comissão para a Igualdade e para os Direitos das Mulheres. 1998. *Guia dos direitos das mulheres [Guide to women's rights]*. Lisbon: Presidência do Conselho de Ministros, Colecção Informar as Mulheres n° 10.

Costa Santos, J. 1998. Prova médica–Que prova? Reflexões sobre os exames periciais em matéria de abusos sexuais de crianças e adolescents [Medical evidence–What evidence? Reflections on the specialty examinations in cases of sexual abuse of children and adolescents]. In: Associação para o Planeamento da Família, ed., *1° Seminário Nacional sobre abusos sexuais em crianças e adolescentes [Sexual abuse in children and adolescents: Contributions from the 1st National Seminar]*. Lisbon: Associação para o Planeamento da Família.

Direcção Geral de Saúde. 1998. *Estudo exploratório de abusos sexuais em crianças e adolescentes [Sexual abuse in children and adolescents–An exploratory study]*. Lisbon: Divisão de Saúde Materna e Infantil e dos Adolescentes/Divisão de Promoção e Educação Para a Saúde.

Ferreira, A. C. 1993. Sinais dos tempos [Sign of the times]. *Planeamento Familiar* [Lisbon], *61/62*:16.

Figueiredo, E. 1988. *Portugal nos próximos 20 anos [Portugal in the next 20 years]* (vol. II). Lisbon: Fundação Calouste Gulbenkian.

Fundação Portuguesa a Comunidade Contra a SIDA. 1998. *As mulheres e a SIDA [Women and AIDS]*. Lisbon: Fundação Portuguesa a Comunidade Contra a SIDA.

GAEP. 1999. *Sexualidade em Linha–Um ano de funcionamento [Sexualidade em Linha–One year of functioning]*. Lisbon: Gabinete de Apoio, Estudos e Planeamento da Secretaria de Estado da Juventude.

Gameiro, O. 1999. *Aspectos sociais e políticos da população homo e bissexual em Portugal [Social and political aspects of the homosexual and bisexual population in Portugal]* [WWW document]. http://www.ilga-portugal.org/portugues/index.html.

ILGA–Portugal. 1999. *Situação portuguesa [The Portuguese situation]* [WWW document]. http://www.ilga-portugal.org/portugues/index.html.

Infante, F. 1998. *Comissões de Protecção de Menores: Síntese dos relatórios de actividade, 1997 [Minors' Protection Commissions: Resume from the activity reports, 1997]*. Lisbon: Ministério da Justiça Centro de Estudos Judiciários–Jurisdição de Menores e da Família.

Instituto Nacional de Estatística. 1997. *Inquérito à fecundidade e à família [Inquiry on fertility and the family]*. Lisbon: Instituto Nacional de Estatística.

López, F. 1995. *Prevención de los abusos sexuales de menores y educación sexual [Prevention of the sexual abuse of minors and sex education]*. Salamanca: Amarú Ediciones.

Lucas, J. S. 1993. *A sexualidade desprevenida dos portugueses [Portuguese unprotected sexuality]*, Lisbon, McGraw-Hill.

Lyall, S. 2002 (January 19). Portugal gives abortionist an 8½-year prison term. *The New York Times*, International Section, A4.

Machado Caetano, J. A. 1997. *SIDA em Portugal: Que perspectivas? [AIDS in Portugal: What future?]*. Lisbon: Fundação Portuguesa a Comunidade Contra a SIDA.

Madeira, J. & J. Costa Santos. 1998. Prova médica–Que prova? Reflexões sobre os exames periciais em matéria de abusos sexuais de crianças e adolescents [Medical evidence–What evidence? Reflections on the specialty examinations in cases of sexual abuse of children and adolescents]. In: Associação para o Planeamento da Família, ed., *1° Seminário Nacional sobre abusos sexuais em crianças e adolescentes [Sexual abuse in children and adolescents: Contributions from the 1st National Seminar]*. Lisbon: Associação para o Planeamento da Família.

Marktest. 1995. *Estudo sobre comportamento sexual dos portugueses [Study on the sexual behavior of the Portuguese]*. Lisbon: Marktest–Departamento de Estudos Especiais.

Miguel, N. 1987. A sexualidade na adolescência [Sexuality in adolescence]. In: F. A. Gomes, A. Albuquerque, & J. S. Nunes, eds., *A sexologia em Portugal* [*Sexology in Portugal*] (vol. I). Lisbon: Texto Editora.

Ministério da Saúde Direcção Geral da Saúde. 1997. *A saúde dos portugueses 1997* [*The Portuguese health in 1997*]. Lisbon: Ministério da Saúde Direcção Geral da Saúde.

Movimento Católico de Estudantes (MCE). 1993. *Documento sobre moral sexual* [*Document on sexual morality*]. Planeamento Familiar [Lisbon]. *61/62*:17.

Nodin, N. 2000. *A saúde sexual e reprodutiva. Resultados de um estudo nacional sobre factores de riscopara o VIH para gravidez não planeada em jovens adultos* [*Sexual and reproductive health. Results from a national study on the risk of HIV and of unwanted pregnancy in young adults*] [Master's degree thesis in Health Psychology] Lisbon: Instituto Superior de Psicologia Aplicada.

Nunes de Almeida, A. No date. *Maus tratos às crianças em Portugal* [Violence against children in Portugal]. Lisbon: Instituto Superior de Ciências do Trabalho e da Empresa.

Pais, J. M. 1985. *A prostituição e a Lisboa Boémia do século XIX aos inícios do século XX* [*Prostitution and Bohemian Lisbon from the 19th to the beginning of the 20th century*]. Lisbon: Editorial Querco.

Pais, J. M., coordinator. 1998. *Gerações e valores na sociedade portuguesa contemporânea* [*Generations and values of the contemporary Portuguese society*]. Lisbon: Instituto de Ciências Sociais da Universidade de Lisboa.

Pais, M. 1996. *Sexualidade in jovens de hoje e de aqui*. Caderros Estudos Locais Loures: Dept Socio-Cultural, C. M. Loures.

Pessoa, A. A. 1976. *Os Bons velhos tempos da prostituição em Portugal* [*The good old times of prostitution in Portugal*]. Lisbon: Arcádia.

Pires, L., & M Antunes. 1998. Vida religiosa [Religious life]. In: J. M. Pais, coordinator, *Gerações e valores na sociedade portuguesa contemporânea* [*Generations and values of the contemporary Portuguese society*]. Lisbon: Instituto de Ciências Sociais da Universidade de Lisboa.

*Planeamento familiar e sexualidade* [*Family planning and sexuality*] [journal]. 1996. Lisbon: Associação para o Planeamento da Família, *11/12*.

Prista Guerra, M. 1998. *SIDA: Implicações psicológicas* [*AIDS: Psychological implications*]. Lisbon: Editora Fim de Século.

Rodrigues, J. A. 1995. *Continuidade e mudança nos papeis das mulheres portuguesas urbanas. O aparecimento de novas estruturas familiares* [*Continuity and change in the roles of urban Portuguese women. The appearance of new family structures*]. Lisbon: Comissão para a Igualdade e para os Direitos das Mulheres.

Roque, O. 1999. *Educação sexual nas escolas portuguesas: Realidade virtual* [*Sex education in the Portuguese schools: Virtual reality*] (monograph paper). Lisbon: Univeridade Lusófona de Humanidades e Tecnologias.

Rosendo, G. 1998 (June 26). Decisões com consequências [Decisions with consequences] (magazine article). *Revista do Expresso* [Lisbon], 56-64.

Sampaio, D., coordinator. 1996. *Escola, família e amigos* [*School, family and friends*]. Lisbon: Programa de Promoção e Educação para a Saúde.

Seabra Diniz, J. 1998. O abuso sexual como rutura do processo de desenvolvimento [Sexual abuse as a rupture of the development process]. In: Associação para o Planeamento da Família, ed., *1° Seminário Nacional sobre abusos sexuais em crianças e adolescentes* [*Sexual abuse in children and adolescents: Contributions from the 1st National Seminar*]. Lisbon: Associação para o Planeamento da Família.

Secretariado Nacional de Reabilitação e Integração das Pessoas com Deficiência 1994. *Uma política coerente para a reabilitação das pessoas com deficiência* [*A coherent policy for the rehabilitation of people with disabilities*] (SNR N° 1 Conselho da Europa). Lisbon: Cadernos.

Secretariado Nacional de Reabilitação e Integração das Pessoas com Deficiência. 1996. *Inquérito nacional às incapacidades, deficiências e desvantagens. Resultados globais* [*National inquiry regarding incapacities, disabilities and handicaps. Global results*] (SNR N° 9). Lisbon: Cadernos.

Secretariado Nacional para a Reabilitação e Integração das Pessoas com Deficiência. 1998. *Normas das Nações Unidas sobre igualdade de oportunidades para pessoas com deficiência* [*The Standard United Nations rules on the equality of opportunities for persons with disabilities*] (SNR N° 3, 2ª Edição). Lisbon: Cadernos.

Secretariado Nacional para a Reabilitação e Integração das Pessoas com Deficiência. 1999. *Lei de bases da prevenção e da reabilitação e integração das pessoas com deficiência* [*Law on the prevention, rehabilitation and integration of people with disabilities*] (SNR N° 6, 2ª Edição). Lisbon: Folheto.

Silva, M. L., A. M. Dantas, V. Mourão, & H. Ramalho. 1996. *Promoção de saúde dos jovens na optica da prevenção primária do consumo da droga* [*Health promotion of young people regarding the primary prevention of drug addition*]. Lisbon: Fundação Nossa Senhora do Bom Sucesso.

UNAIDS. 2002. *Epidemiological fact sheets by country*. Geneva, Switzerland: Joint United Nations Programme on HIV/AIDS (UNAIDS/WHO). Available: http://www.unaids.org/hivaidsinfo/statistics/fact_sheets/index_en.htm.

Vasconcelos, P. 1998. Práticas e discursos da conjugalidade dos jovens portugueses [Behaviors and opinions of the conjugality of the young Portuguese]. In: M. Cabral, A. Fernandes, J. Nunes, & P. Vasconcelos, eds., *Jovens portugueses de hoj*. Oeiras: Celta.

Vaz, J. M., ed. 1996. *Educação sexual na escola* [*Sex education in school*]. Lisbon: Universidade Aberta.

Vicente, A. 1998. *As mulheres em Portugal na transição do milénio* [*The Portuguese women at the turn of the century*]. Lisbon: Multinova.

Vilar, D., & A. M. Gaspar. 1999. Traços redondos (A gravidez na adolescência) [Round traces (Pregnancy in adolescence)]. In: J. M. Pais, ed., *Traços e Riscos na Adolescência* [*Traces and Risks During Adolescence*]. Porto: Ambar.

Vitorino, S., & G. Dinis. 1999. *Lesbian, gay, bisexual and transgender (LGBT) politics in Portugal: The awakening of a new social movement*. Paper presented at the Euro-Mediterranean Conference of Homosexualities, Marseilles.

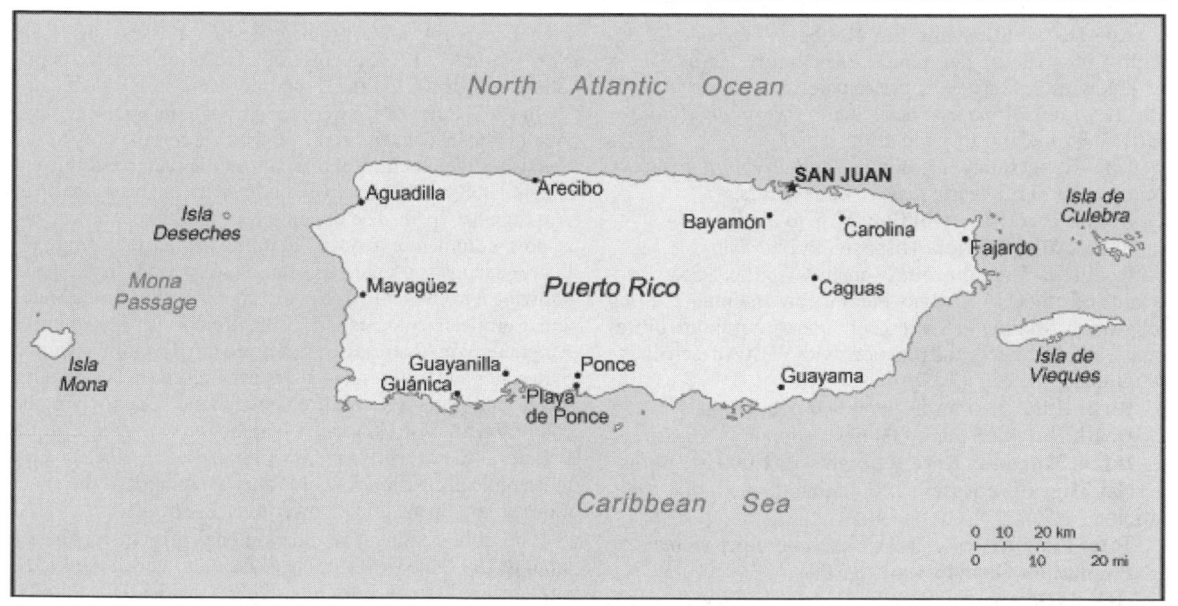

(CIA 2002)

# Puerto Rico

## (*Estado Libre Asociado de Puerto Rico*)

Luis Montesinos, Ph.D., and Juan Preciado, Ph.D.
*Redacted and updated by Felix M. Velázquez-Soto, M.A.,
and Glorivee Rosario-Pérez, Ph.D., and Carmen Rios*

## Contents

### *Demographics and a Brief Historical Perspective*

**A. Demographics**          ROBERT T. FRANCOEUR**

Puerto Rico is the easternmost island of the West Indies archipelago known as the Greater Antilles. Cuba, Hispan-iola (Haiti and the Dominican Republic), and Jamaica are larger islands in this group. Puerto Rico is a commonwealth of the United States. It is bordered by the Atlantic Ocean on the north and the Caribbean Sea in the south. Puerto Rico has a landmass of 3,515 square miles (9,104 km²), and is slightly smaller than the state of Rhode Island in the U.S. The climate is tropical marine and mild with little seasonal temperature variation. Three quarters of the island's land surface is mountainous, and the coastal plain belt has been used for urban development and contains most of the metro-politan area. Most of the municipalities and small towns are located in the mountainous area.

In July 2002, the island of Puerto Rico had an estimated population approaching 3,816,901 persons, based on data provided by the State Planification Board. An additional estimated 2.7 million Puertoricans [or Puertorricans] live in the United States mainland, mainly in the New York and northern New Jersey metropolitan area, where they are known as *NYRicans* [also *Nuyoricans/Newyoricans*] or *Jerseyricans*. There are Puertoricans throughout all the states, including Hawaii, where a large group was estab-lished between the 1940s and 1950s. Major migration to the New York area occurred in the 1950s and 1960s be-cause the people were looking for better occupational op-portunities. Since the mid-1970s, there has been a reverse migration back to the island. The present report will com-bine insights on the sexual behavior and beliefs of people living in the island commonwealth and in the New York/New Jersey metropolitan area. Puertoricans on the island maintain constant contact with relatives in the eastern U.S. cities where the HIV infection rate is high (Robles et al. 1990). The so-called yo-yo migration between the island and the mainland is a significant factor in the incidence and prevalence of the AIDS (SIDA) epidemic in Puerto Rico (Castro-Alvarez & Ramirez de Arellano 1991). (Un-less otherwise noted, all data in this section are July 2002 estimates from *The World Factbook 2002*, CIA).

---

*\*Communications*: Luis Montesinos, Ph.D., Psychology Depart-ment, Montclair State University, Montclair, New Jersey, USA. Juan Preciado, Ph.D., quetzalo1@aol.com. *Updates*: Felix M. Velázquez-Soto, M.S., and Glorivee Rosario-Pérez, Ph.D., Biology Depart-ment, University of Puerto Rico at Cayey Campus, Cayey, Puerto Rico, USA 00736; f_velazquez1@hotmail.com, glorivee@hotmail .com. Carmen Rios, LUPE Program, Raritan Bay Medical Center, 530 New Brunswick Avenue, Perth Amboy, NJ 08861 USA; crios@ rbmc.org.

---

**The reader is encouraged to check the other chapters in this *Encyclopedia*, which provide different perspectives on the variet-ies of Latino culture that complement those provided here, specifi-cally the chapters on Argentina, Brazil, Colombia, Costa Rica, Cuba, and Mexico, and the discussion of Latinos in mainland United States.

**Age Distribution and Sex Ratios**: *0-14 years*: 23.5% with 1.05 male(s) per female (sex ratio); *15-64 years*: 65.8% with 0.92 male(s) per female; *65 years and over*: 10.7% with 0.74 male(s) per female; *Total population sex ratio*: 0.93 male(s) to 1 female

**Life Expectancy at Birth**: *Total Population*: 75.96 years; *male*: 71.5 years; *female*: 80.66 years

**Urban/Rural Distribution**: 67% to 33%

**Ethnic Distribution**: Hispanic, Puertorican

**Religious Distribution**: Roman Catholic: 85%; Protestant and other: 15%. Many Puertoricans maintain a strong religious affiliation to Santeria or voodoo, a mixture of Roman Catholic beliefs and practices with West African native religions.

**Birth Rate**: 15.5 births per 1,000 population

**Death Rate**: 7.6 per 1,000 population

**Infant Mortality Rate**: 9.9 deaths per 1,000 live births

**Net Migration Rate**: –2.12 migrant(s) per 1,000 population

**Total Fertility Rate**: 1.9 children born per woman

**Population Growth Rate**: 0.51%

**HIV/AIDS** (on the island): *People living with AIDS*: 10,301; pediatric: 174; adult and adolescents: 10,127 (Puerto Rico Surveillance Report, December 31, 2002). (For additional statistics on HIV/AIDS on the island and in the New York metropolitan area, see Section 10B.)

**Literacy Rate** (*defined as those age 15 and over who can read and write*): 89% (1980 est.); 8.2% of the gross national product is devoted to education.

**Per Capita Gross Domestic Product** (*purchasing power parity*): $11,200 (2001 est.); *Inflation*: 5.7%; *Unemployment*: 9.5%; *Living below the poverty line*: NA

## B. A Brief Historical Perspective          CARMEN RIOS

Christopher Columbus and his crew were the first Europeans to discover the island of Puerto Rico. Arriving in November of 1493, during their second voyage to the New World, they found the island populated by about 60,000 Arawak natives, peaceful people thriving on their fishing and agricultural skills. In 1508, Spanish colonists arrived and the Arawak natives were either decimated by diseases brought from Europe by the colonists or quickly killed off by the colonists.

The Spanish newcomers originally named the island San Juan Bautista in honor of St. John the Baptist, and named the capital Puerto Rico, which means rich port. Later, the names were switched, making the capital San Juan and the island Puerto Rico. Puerto Rico also includes four other smaller islands (Vieques, Culebra, Mona, y Caja de Muerto). The city was later used as a transshipment port for gold being mined in Puerto Rico and gold and silver from South America being stored in the city for shipment on to Spain.

Concerned about threats from European enemies, Spain began constructing massive defenses around the city of San Juan in 1521. The strengthening of El Morro, San Cristóbal, San Gerónimo, and El Cañuelo forts, as well as the city walls, were the stronghold elements of these successful defenses. Sugar cane was introduced to the island in 1515 and became Puerto Rico's most important agricultural product, helping establish a thriving economy. African slaves were imported in 1518 to handle the cane harvest. Puerto Rico's gold mines were exhausted by the late 1500s. During the 1600s, Puerto Rico's settlements expanded with the establishment of such areas as Arecibo, San Blas de Illescas (later renamed Coamo), and Ponce. The 1700s brought hurricanes, droughts, plagues, and a constant threat of attack on the island's shores, because the British, Dutch, and

French were intent on capturing Spain's possessions in the New World. By 1776, the official census reported the population had grown to 70,210 people.

In 1809, Puerto Rico was recognized as an overseas province of Spain with the right to send representatives to the Spanish government. Political unrest characterized this era and, in 1868, a small group of landowners in Lares rose up in arms against Spain. The uprising was quickly put down, and is now commemorated as "El Grito de Lares." In 1897, Puerto Rico was granted a Letter of Autonomy from Spain, allowing it to enter into free commerce with the United States and European colonies. In 1898, following the Spanish-American War, Puerto Rico became a territory of the United States. Legend has it that in 1898, just before the last Spanish governor of Puerto Rico surrendered to the U.S. troops at the end of the Spanish-American War, he took a last look at La Fortaleza (the executive mansion) grandfather clock and hit it dramatically with his sword, thus stopping it at the exact moment the Spanish lost power over Puerto Rico.

The 20th century saw phenomenal growth for the island. In 1917, the U.S. Congress granted Puertoricans U.S. citizenship. Two decades later, U.S. President Franklin D. Roosevelt launched the Puerto Rican Reconstruction Administration, which provided agricultural development, public works, and electrification of the island. By 1951, Puerto Rico acquired the right to establish a government with its own constitution and, in 1952, was declared a semiautonomous commonwealth territory of the United States. The island then entered two decades of unprecedented economic development as it heavily promoted and attracted manufacturing plants primarily from the U.S. mainland. By the 1960s, the development was being referred to around the world as the "Puerto Rico Miracle," as other developing economies looked to the island as an example of industrialization. The 1970 census showed Puerto Rico was mostly urban for the first time in its history.

During the last quarter of the 1900s, as Puerto Rico's economy diversified into commerce and services, the island's status once again dominated its politics. The Pro-Commonwealth Consensus that had ruled since 1952 broke down. Supporters of commonwealth and statehood are now at rough parity, with independence holding a 5% share of electoral support. Status plebiscites in 1993 and 1998 were inconclusive, and both the public and political leadership remain deeply divided. This dispute has not hindered the island from growing, however, because life in Puerto Rico largely resembles most U.S. mainland states in business, education, commerce, dining, day-to-day activities, and more.

The role of the women as political leaders is marked at the second half of the 20th century. San Juan, the capital of Puerto Rico, has the first mayor woman, Doña Felisa Gautier Benítez. Puerto Rico's first woman governor, Doña Sila María Calderón, was elected in 2000. Today, a large number of women have entered politics as a career. Mayors, senators, and representatives are changing from an almost exclusively men's area to gender equality.

## 1. Basic Sexological Premises

### A. Character of Gender Roles

In describing the sexological premises commonly ascribed to by Puertoricans, it should be noted at the onset that differences still exist within the society where the population tends to agree with the more traditional values. Puertorican culture, like other Latino societies, stresses a very strong gender difference from birth on that is reflected in every aspect of sexual expression and male-female interaction. The predominant value of *machismo* sees males as superior and females as sexual objects whose aims are to fulfill men's desires and needs (Burgos & Diaz-Perez 1985). Outside the Latino cultures, the terms *macho* and *machismo* carry a common pejorative implication of a chauvinistic, tyrannical male domination. However, in Spanish, the terms refer to male pride. *Machismo* has been defined as the set of attitudes and beliefs that sees males as physically, intellectually, culturally, and sexually superior to females (Pico 1989). Puertorican boys are indoctrinated in the importance of being *macho* from a very early age. New realities have emerged in the last 15 years. Formal sex education programs contribute to and increase the trends toward the quality of life for both men and women. In the professional population, the trend is that a larger group of women are elected, designated, and occupy positions at the same level and over men.

One way the male child is socialized and reminded of his maleness in the rural cultures of Puerto Rico and the Dominican Republic is by his parents and other adults admiring and fondling the baby's penis. Little boys are valued for being male from the moment they are born into the family. Even if there are older sisters, the male sibling is the dominant figure, both in the eyes of the parents and in sibling interactions. Mothers train their daughters early on to play "little women" to their fathers, brothers, and husbands, while they train their sons to be dominant and independent in relationships with their wives as well as other women (Medina 1987). Education within the family supports and maintains traditional male and female roles, but at the school level, the equality is evident between males and females. Also, throughout the educational system, the number of female teachers is higher than for male teachers.

Research about *machismo* carried out before 1975 demonstrated that males were having sex with as many females as possible. By emphasizing their capacity as procreator and their willingness to have as many children as possible, preferably males, Puertorican males demonstrated their *machismo* (Mejias-Picart 1975). There was practically no societal control over male sexual behavior. Meanwhile, female sexuality was openly repressed. It was expected that the males assume the active role, initiate sexual activity, and be responsible for the satisfaction of the female. This aspect of the sexuality has evolved in recent years. Females have become more active and assertive. One detail that demonstrates this trend is the attitude toward the protection from STD and condom use. Sex education in Puerto Rico promotes equal responsibility between males and females.

The female equivalent of *machismo* is *etiqueta*, a complex value system that requires Latinas to be both feminine and pure and, at the same time, very sensual and seductive. Little girls are taught to hide their genitals and not to focus much attention on their vagina. Yet girls are valued for and taught to enhance their sexual appeal. From birth on, girls are adorned with earrings, bracelets, and special spiritual amulets. Their very feminine dress makes Latina girls extremely seductive and even provocative. However, a woman's virginity is highly valued, and families are careful to protect the virginity of their daughters.

When Puerto Rico was dominated by the Catholic Church, girls were constantly reminded of their inferiority and weakness, since a vital aspect of *etiqueta* is the concept of *marianismo*, the model of the obedient and docile female. Maria is by far the most popular female name. It was common that several daughters in the same family have the first name Maria and a different second given name, a reminder that all women should model themselves on the Virgin Mary, the mother of Jesus. Women were expected to sacrifice their own needs for the sake of their children and husband (Comas-Diaz 1985). Under an incorrect interpretation of Church rules, men expected their wife not to enjoy sex or to seek it—she was there simply and solely to please her husband. Females were expected to be passive, ready to respond to the male requirements, and not to assume responsibility for their own pleasure. A good woman was always ready for her man, but she should never be comfortable with sexual issues or with sexual intercourse. To do otherwise suggests a lack of feminine virtue. In a recent survey, almost 80% of the husbands surveyed were found to initiate sexual activities almost all of the time, while 90% of household chores (cooking and cleaning) were carried out by the wives (Vazquez 1986). All of these expectations and values are part of the history of sexual repression of Puertorican women. Today an increasing number of people in Puerto Rico accept that women are more than a sexual artifact. The sex educator promotes and claims that the women must enjoy sexual activities and Puertoricans must change this negative aspect of their sexual attitudes.

The Church promotes a strong pronatalist value in Puerto Rico. However, small families with one-to-three children are preferred. The surveillance statistics in Puerto Rico for girls who have a child outside marriage is 19.2%, alongside of which we have a common sexual education in pregnancy. Abortion in Puerto Rico is legal. There are some female healthcare clinics that provide counseling about choices. The clinics offer the opportunities for pregnant women to get into an adoption program if they so choose. Abortion is common among married women and among religious people. The pronatalist value is supported by the anticontraception and antiabortion position of the Catholic Church. Nevertheless, both contraception and abortion are commonly used by Puertoricans.

The Civil Rights Commission in 1973 concluded that discrimination against women outside and inside the home existed and subtle discriminatory practices occurred. In 1984, a study done by the Puertorican Senate found that the same pattern of discrimination continued to exist ten years later. Although there have been some changes in the recent past, oppression, control of women, male power, and heterosexuality continue as the dominant parameters of the Puertorican society (Zorrilla et al. 1993). The controversies about abortion, marriage, contraceptive devices and treatments, homosexuality, and sexual education, are ongoing.

Women themselves are in part responsible for the preservation of this situation, since they continue to accept the sole responsibly for childrearing, and play an essentially domestic role. However, this situation is changing, and the men are becoming more responsible in participating in childcare. There are laws that make women and men responsible to provide resources for childcare even if they do not live with the other parent. But this form of sexism is also "imprinted" in children who are socialized to accept the stereotypic roles from early childhood, where the main role of the female is to be mother, in spite of also working outside the home. Dependency, obedience, and submission are reinforced in daughters, while independence, aggression, and lack of emotion are reinforced in males (Burgos & Diaz-Perez 1985; Mock 1984). Females are socialized to be submissive, passive, attractive, compliant, obedient, and dependent, and they are expected to behave this way in their sexual interactions (Santos-Ortiz 1990). The fight against these stereotypes occurs continually on the professional level. Many psychologists, physicians, religious teachers, and a large group of professionals work in favor the elimination of the sexual stereotypes and look for the compliance of responsibility associated with the position of their job.

During the school years, gender roles are reinforced by a biased curriculum. A study on the illustrations and content of social sciences texts used in primary schools (Pico 1989) found that men were portrayed as relevant and superior, while females were relegated to a secondary role, and when depicted appeared in more-traditional stereotypical roles. Men and boys appeared more frequently than girls and women, in spite of the fact that females constitute over half of the population. Women appeared mostly working in their home or engaged in passive activities, such as reading, praying, and playing with dolls, and were rarely depicted outside of the home. This is epitomized by a page in a text under the title, "What I most enjoy doing." There are pictures of sliding, swimming, bicycle riding, skating, and other activities—all of them performed by boys; not a single girl appears in those activities. Although this research was done in the early 1980s, there is no reason to think that the pervasiveness of the gender stereotypes has changed at all. At the same time, in 1992, the State Department of Education established a program to train its personnel and to develop gender-equal curricula for sexual education in schools (Mock 1992).

Fortunately, today, education professionals exist who can manage the information and teach about the qualities of male and female. The Puertorican sex educators, counselors, and therapist associations, and nonprofit organizations, prepare and offer training to a large group of teachers about sex education. A group of teachers have been certified as sex educators and, under the concept "train the trainer," they are offering training to their peers. The State Education Department is requesting that all teachers get into the continuing education program to satisfy and increase their knowledge according to their needs as educators. For the last 15 years, the University of Puerto Rico at Cayey has been offering a University Sexual Education Symposium focusing on teachers and health professionals. The symposium provides the newest information about sex education trends and treatments for sexually related conditions. This training and education is offered free to the community in Puerto Rico and the United States.

## B. Sociolegal Status of Males and Females

The number of common-law partnerships has increased consistently during the last few decades, in spite of the fact that they are not recognized and consequently do not have any of the entitlements of legally married couples. Children, however, are recognized as legitimate offspring of the parents and have the right to be supported by them until they are 21 years old. Legal custody of children is almost always awarded to the mother, but legal responsibility is shared. No matter who has the child custody, the other parent has to provide economic support.

## C. General Concepts of Sexuality and Love

The basic values of *machismo*, *marianismo*, and *etiqueta* are evident in various sexual behaviors. In a 1985 survey, 60% of working-class women and 50% of professional women reported faking orgasm in order to end intercourse soon or to avoid the husband's questioning about their achieving orgasm. The great majority of women surveyed did not disapprove of self-pleasuring, and very few women engage in autoeroticism, or admit to this in surveys (Burgos & Diaz-Perez 1985). Things have been changing. It is now common that women and men buy sex toys, films, and publications to improve their sexual lives and autoerotisms. The number of stores that offer this kind of merchandise is increasing rapidly. One of the stores, Condom World®, has expanded to 20 stores in the past decade on the island.

Latino men still often express their discomfort with sex in ridicule and rejection of anything that hints of homosexuality. Even in the Latino culture of Brazil, where boys are encouraged to explore everything sexual, all men—even those who in the United States would be considered bisexual or homosexual—see themselves as *homens*, men in the sense of always taking the active phallic sexual role (Medina 1987; Parker 1987). Attitudes toward homosexuality are changing. The homosexuals are leaving the closeted life and gaining their place in Puertorican society. Like other Puertoricans, they pay taxes, have a job, and form families headed by a same-sex couple. There are cases in which homosexual couples have adopted a child legally. The State Department of Family is against adoption by homosexual families. The court, however, has been hearing cases under state law applied or created for heterosexual couple relationships. Today, there are homosexuals in all organizations, agencies, public and private institutions, professional roles, and in the churches.

As more women enter the workforce and pursue an education, the traditional maternity role has changed and continues to change. This is evidenced by the large number of Puertorican women who postpone marriage and childbearing until their late 30s. As mentioned before, out-of-wedlock partnerships have increased in popularity, especially among white-collar workers and educated Puertoricans.

## 2. Religious, Ethnic, and Gender Factors Affecting Sexuality

### A/B. Source and Character of Religious and Ethnic Values

The early pre-colonial inhabitants of Puerto Rico migrated either from Florida in the north or from the Orinoco River delta in Columbia, South America. When the Spaniards arrived in 1493, the island was inhabited by the peaceful Arawaks who were being threatened by the neighboring Carib Indians. The island was finally invaded and conquered for Spain in 1509 by Juan Ponce de Leon.

Introduction of sugar cane cultivation in 1515 was quickly followed by the importation of African slaves to work the cane fields. Although slavery was finally abolished in 1873, the impact of the forced African immigration can still be felt today in Puertorican society. Indigenous, Spanish, and African elements permeate Puertorican culture even today, with the Spanish influence dominant, since they occupied and controlled the island for nearly 400 years, until 1898.

It appears that in the island pre-Colombian societies, women had more power and were highly respected. Pre-Colombian women are also believed to have had an active sexual life. Men, especially those in the upper classes, were allowed to be polygynous.

Later on, the Spaniards introduced their patriarchal society with its values of *machismo*, *marianismo*, *etiqueta* (emphasizing female virginity), and a pronatalist familism. The popular traditions and doctrines of Catholicism introduced by the Spanish have played a major role in the shaping of the society's sexual values and attitudes. However, this influence, as will be seen, is more formal than real when it comes to some private decisions. Even though 80% of Puertoricans today identify themselves as Catholic, most are not highly active in the Church (Burgos & Diaz-Perez 1985).

Although the culture seems sexually repressive, in reality Puertorican society is quite erotic and exalts sexuality in pervasive and subtle ways. Sexual themes permeate Puertorican popular music and dance (salsa), radio and television communication, as well as nonverbal communications. Perhaps because of this, research about sexuality is uncommon in Puerto Rico, and there are very few written articles about sexuality. Consequently, very little is known about sexual behavior and attitudes of Puertoricans (Burgos & Diaz-Perez 1985; Cunningham 1991). (See parallel discussion of *machismo* and Cuban values in the chapter on Cuba).

The reproductive function of sexuality is seen as its natural goal, while its pleasurable aspects are viewed as a necessary incentive for accomplishment of this goal. All other sexual behaviors apart from penile-vaginal intercourse are generally seen as immature and undesirable (Mock 1984). At the same time, for most Puertoricans all versions of sexuality and sex are acceptable inside the marriage, with the sole provision that they be mutually accepted by the couple. Nevertheless, sexuality is commercialized and widely available in both pornography and prostitution (Mock 1984). Pornography and prostitution are against the law in Puerto Rico. Recently, the prostitution houses were closed by governmental order, but prostitution still exists.

As stated before, although the influence of the Catholic Church is felt in all aspects of sexuality, studies indicate that Catholics have as many abortions as non-Catholics (Ortiz & Vazquez-Nuttall 1987), and that religious affiliation has no bearing on the use of contraceptive methods, including sterilization and the pill (Herold et al. 1989).

## 3. Knowledge and Education about Sexuality

### A. Government Policies and Programs

As a result of *marianismo*, the Church's opposition, and the reluctance of society and families to acknowledge female sexuality openly, many girls experience their menarche with no formal education about it. And although males are expected to have their first sexual experience before marriage, they do not receive any formal sex education either. Obviously, neither females nor males have any knowledge about the health implications of various sexual practices (Burgos & Diaz-Perez 1985).

There are no systems or districtwide sexuality education programs such as exist in most, if not all, the mainland States. A program to train sexuality education teachers has been proposed and was being developed in 1994. As in other places where formal programs have not been developed, individual teachers may take the initiative into their own hands and incorporate various aspects of sexuality education into their standard courses, such as biology and health.

### B. Informal Sources of Sexual Knowledge

The media also plays a role in perpetuating sexist stereotypes and prejudices against women. A study found that articles in the popular media usually portrayed women as submissive, and presented acts of violence against women as normal (Maldonado 1990).

The same kind of sexual information portrayed in movies, television, and radio in the mainland United States is also available in the commonwealth island of Puerto Rico. The ready access to cable television and videotapes has permitted islanders to be exposed to the same kind of information that is available to individuals living on the mainland.

[*Update 1999*: In September 1999, concerned about the rising rates of pregnancy, AIDS, and chlamydia among adolescents aged 13 to 29 years, Puerto Rico's governor proposed a bill that would "give adolescents access to sex education and treatment for reproductive health, including contraceptive methods, without the knowledge or consent of their parents." The bill would require the health and education departments to offer STD treatment, reproductive health services, counseling, prenatal care, and birth control. The bill provoked a storm of protest from conservatives. Leaders in

the Legislature predicted the bill would go nowhere, but the Health Secretary and Education Secretary vowed a fight in the Capitol to push the bill through. In the end, it was rejected, and the community programs have picked up the requested services. (*End of update by Carmen Rios*)]

## 4. Autoerotic Behaviors and Patterns

When asked about self-pleasuring in a 1985 survey, a great majority of women did not disapprove of it. However, they reported not practicing it themselves. A survey of 191 adolescents found that 32% (61) of them engaged in self-pleasuring, 53 of them males and only 8 of them females (Burgos & Diaz-Perez 1985). But, self-pleasure has been promoted as a practice to prevent HIV infection, either alone or within the couple relationship. The discovery of erogenous areas in each person's body as a sexual therapeutic technique is recommended to increase the couple's sexual relationship. A common cause of divorce exists when couples do not understand their bodies and do not recognize that there are other sexual behaviors besides vaginal intercourse that promote a healthy couple relationship.

## 5. Interpersonal Heterosexual Behaviors

### A. Children

Childhood sexual rehearsal play and sexual exploration no doubt occur in private as they do in many other cultures, but there are no statistics or information on their incidence or extent. There is some indirect information about sex education and activities for and in childhood. Some teachers are including sex education concepts in the classroom, because the knowledge about sexuality is available on TV, Internet, radio, and, in general, in the media. Teachers know that there are needs; they know about the incidence of adolescent pregnancy and are reacting by promoting sex education and sex hygiene. Outreach programs have also seen that the sexuality information provided at home and in schools is not adequate, and most of the time, it is erroneous when it is offered out of the classroom by unprepared people in the community. Sex education projects are offering services in the community to prevent STD and pregnancy.

### B. Adolescents

*Premarital Sexual Activities and Relationships*

Studies of adolescents in public schools have found that a good number of them are sexually active before the age of 15 and that most of them do not use contraceptives to prevent pregnancy and/or sexually transmitted diseases (Mock & Ramirez 1993). Adolescent pregnancy is 19.2% as reported in surveillance statistics for 2002. The government policies are against comprehensive sex education and they have requested that schools include abstinence education as the rule. The contraceptive education is offered outside of the academic services. We believe that comprehensive sex education has to be offered if we want to control the adolescent-pregnancy incidence. In those areas where the adolescent pregnancy rate is high, the schoolteachers are assuming responsibility and are offering sex education.

As mentioned before, the fact that more females are postponing marriage and that more couples are opting for common-law partnerships as opposed to legal marriage, has resulted in an increase of individuals engaging in premarital sex. It is estimated that almost 50% of young Puertoricans are sexually active (Cunningham 1991). The general trend in the world is to establish couple relationship with freedom for all components. Puerto Rico, for instance, has a swingers group, based in Puertorican values that accept this sexual behavior.

*Premarital Courtship, Dating, and Relationships*

Courtship and dating behavior is governed by strong and clear gender-dimorphic roles and rules. It is very difficult for young people, particularly young women with older brothers or male cousins, to escape the pervasive pressure and surveillance of family members that enforces the dual standards of behavior expected of Puertorican males and females. The custom of a chaperone's accompanying a young woman disappeared long ago, since no one young or old recalls it.

Young Puertoricans attending colleges and universities are very similar to their student counterparts elsewhere in the world. However, some relevant differences are worth addressing here. Surveys done by Cunningham and collaborators (1991), with randomly selected students at the University of Puerto Rico, show that almost half of them are sexually active, 70% of the males and 40% of the females. Of those sexually active, 80% had experienced vaginal intercourse, more than 50% had tried oral intercourse, and over a third had tried anal intercourse.

Eighty-five percent of those practicing vaginal intercourse and 84% of those practicing oral sex reported having only one partner during the three-month period before the study. With respect to the use of condoms, 55% of the sample declared they had used one at least once; only 16.8% of the males and 13.6% of the females declared they always used a condom (Cunningham & Rodriguez-Sanchez 1991).

## C. Adults

*Marriage and the Family*

It used to be that the divorce rate was very low, probably because of the strong influence of the Catholic religion. However, there has been a dramatic increase in the rate of divorce during the past decade, as well as an increase in the number of households headed by women. In 1960, it was 18.7%; by 1980, the incidence was 25% (Vasquez-Calzada 1989). More recently, an increasing numbers of single mothers have been noticed (20.9% in 1980 to 32.9% in 1989) (Castro-Alvarez & Ramirez de Arellano 1991). In 1988, the percentage of teenagers giving birth was 17.4%, while those out of wedlock reached 32.8%.

*Extramarital Sex, Cohabitation, and*
*Single Mothers*

As in any strongly patriarchal culture, the double moral standard allows males much more freedom than it does females. Macho men, but not women, are allowed and expected to have extramarital sexual relationships. However, as is happening in other cultures, the increasing incidence and recognition of cohabitation and single mothers is definitely weakening this pattern.

*Sexuality and Disabled and Older Persons*

There is little if any discussion, and no statistics, on the sexual needs or behaviors of physically and mentally challenged persons and older persons.

*Incidence of Oral and Anal Sex*

Unexpectedly, 35% of university students surveyed in 1989 and 37% of those surveyed in 1990 had participated in anal intercourse. Approximately 40% of the males who had engaged in this activity were homosexual. And although those who practice anal intercourse do it less frequently and tend to use condoms in higher percentages, they also tend to have more partners than those who practice other types of sexual activity. Results show that almost 36% of those who practice anal intercourse (22% of the females and 46.5% of the males) had two or more partners during the three months previous to answering the survey. The reasons for engaging in this practice were different for males and females, while

the males reported they did it for pleasure, females reported that they did it mostly to satisfy their partners.

No data are available on the attitudes towards or the incidence of either anal or oral sex among non-university students, and single or married adults.

## 6. Homoerotic, Homosexual, and Bisexual Behaviors

In Puerto Rico, as in most societies of the world, being openly gay carries a negative stigma and in consequence, most of the gay community remains "invisible." Thus, no reliable information about the percentage of the population with homosexual or bisexual orientation or experience is available (Cunningham & Cunningham 1991).

There is a strong rejection of homosexuality, especially male homosexuality. [*Comment 2003*: Lesbians face even more discrimination and persecution than gay men in the island's culture. Lesbians lead even more-hidden lives than gay men, particularly if they have custody of their children. Under Puertorican law, lesbians can lose custody of their children. As of early 2003, repeated efforts by many groups to remove this law from the books have all failed, and the law remains in effect. (*End of comment by Carmen Rios*)] This negative attitude is present even in Puertorican males living in the New York area. In fact, law-enforcement officials tend to harass those who have sexual relationships with someone of their own gender or commit a crime "contrary to nature."

Because of the AIDS (SIDA) epidemic, homosexuals affected by the disease have organized support groups and have started to acknowledge their sexual orientation publicly. Within these groups, two distinct reactions have been observed: One group of individuals has reacted by increasing their sexual activity, while others have abstained almost completely from it (Ortiz-Colon 1991). However, in Puerto Rico, the main mode of transmission of HIV has been through intravenous drug use and increasingly through heterosexual contact.

There is a history of more than 20 years of gay and lesbian civil rights movements. The Comunidad de Orgullo Gay (Pride Gay Community) was founded in 1973; since then, other organizations have been established. The Coalicion Puertoriquena de Lesbianas y Homosexuales, created in 1991, publishes a bimonthly magazine dealing specifically with issues of discrimination and encouraging support among lesbians and gays. Because of the AIDS epidemic, other groups that deal specifically with this issue have been established in different parts of the island.

## 7. Gender Diversity and Transgender Issues

As in other parts of the world, transvestites and transsexuals do exist in Puertorican society. Transvestites have been portrayed in the media and television for a long time, and this style of dressing has become a style of street life. There are transvestites in school, universities, and in social night style. There are male sex workers who cross-dress at night and revert back in the morning. Transsexuals are not common in Puerto Rico. But their small group makes a loud noise, with some transsexuals appearing on television and participating in top television shows to demonstrate the lifestyles and changes faced by transvestites and transsexuals. Some physicians have participated on television shows to talk about the anatomical, social, psychological, and physiological changes involved in transsexualism.

[*Comment 2003*: Many transgender Puertoricans visit the United States to participate in the annual Fantasia Festival in

Provincetown on Cape Cod and other transgender events in the New York metropolitan area. Transgender Puertoricans also maintain and participate in Internet websites, and network with transgender groups on the mainland. Transgender persons living in California and Mexico travel to the island and have been particularly supportive by helping establish transgender support groups on the island. However, scientific data on the extent of this population and its practices are unavailable. (*End of comment by Carmen Rios*)]

## 8. Significant Unconventional Sexual Behaviors

### A. Coercive Sex

*Sexual Abuse and Incest*

There are no reliable statistics about the incidence of family violence, including the sexual abuse of women and children and incest, but a center to protect victims of family violence, Casa Protegida Julia de Burgos, reported almost 500 cases of spouse abuse in 1984 and the Department of Social Services reported over 5,000 cases of abuse and neglect of children in 1985. The Centro de Ayuda a Victimas de Violación reported 181 cases of rape and 21 cases of incest for the period 1984-1985 (Burgos & Diaz Perez 1985).

*Sexual Harassment*

This is a relatively new concept that has not been widely accepted in Puertorican society. Most people believe that these are the natural behavioral patterns in the relationships between men and women (Alvarado 1987). Sexual innuendoes, jokes, and repeatedly asking for dates are all expected in male-female interactions (Martinez et al 1988).

Recent studies have found harassment rates of 44% among women attending a conference on women in the workplace, to as high as 73% for women working in the healthcare sector (Alvarado 1987; Martinez et al. 1988). The great majority of these women had been harassed by supervisors (over 60%) or coworkers (almost 30%). Although more than 60% of the women confronted the harasser, only 13% reported the situation to their superiors (Alvarado 1987).

Although there is no specific law in Puerto Rico against sexual harassment in the workplace, there is a law that prohibits discrimination in any form at the workplace. Current efforts focus on raising the public's awareness of the nature, pervasiveness, and social unacceptability of sexual harassment in a culture where it has been universally accepted and expected as an important part of the behavior of *macho* males.

*Rape*

Outside of the scattered and nonrepresentative statistics mentioned above on incest, child sexual abuse, and spouse abuse, no data exist on the incidence of rape.

### B. Prostitution

As in other parts of the world, prostitution is tolerated in Puertorican society, although it is considered illegal and immoral. Males are encouraged to seek prostitutes as sexual outlets so as to maintain the purity of those whom they will eventually marry. This, however, is changing, as more and more young adults are engaging in premarital sexual relationships. Prostitution is not as common throughout the island as it is in metropolitan areas. Prostitution places have been eliminated in San Juan by a governmental action. However, street prostitution has increased as the control loosened. For many years, health education programs, STD prevention programs, and HIV testing were available to the prostitutes and their clients in places devoted to prostitution. With the elimination of brothels, there is now no site to offer these services.

In the early 1990s, the increase in AIDS among heterosexuals was attributed in part to heterosexual men having sex with prostitutes (Mock & Ramirez 1993). This is no longer true, because the homosexual has been alerted and taken control with prevention programs focused on their lifestyle. While some heterosexuals keep with their risky style, they are also exposed to another main transmission mode, IV-drug use.

### C. Pornography and Erotica

Erotic elements appear to be very common in writings (novels), and popular songs and dances. Pornography, however, is not as developed as it is on the mainland. Pornographic magazines and television channels, such as the Playboy Channel and other adult channels, are also available with cable television easily available. There is little, if any, indigenous pornographic material since a variety of such material is easily brought home by Puertoricans traveling back and forth between the island and the mainland to visit family and relatives. There is no frontier boundary between Puerto Rico and the world. For some people, pornography as erotic material is accepted, but others are concerned about how pornographic material affects young people. There are no controls for cable television Adult stores with pornographic material are common in Puerto Rico, but at the same time, some rules do exist. For instance, by custom, most stores do not sell adult material to people under 21 years old, or young people in student dress or school uniform.

## 9. Contraception, Abortion, and Population Planning

### A. Contraception

The first attempts to establish birth control services in Puerto Rico date to 1925, when a group of professionals, headed by Jose A. Lanauze Rolon, a physician, founded the Liga para el Control de la Natalidad (Birth Control League) in the city of Ponce. This venture paralleled Margaret Sanger's efforts on the mainland. In fact, Mrs. Sanger sent Dr. Lanauze the necessary forms and information for them to affiliate with the American Birth Control League. The goals were then the same: dissemination of information for women regarding safe and available contraceptives and maintaining appropriate statistics and studies demonstrating the negative consequences of overpopulation. Consequently, the league was very active in providing public birth control services, arguing not only from the negative consequences of overpopulation, but also from the positive outcome of reducing the high rate of abortion. However, because of strong opposition from the Church and the lack of funds, the clinic founded by the league, as well as two others founded in San Juan in the early 1930s, were eventually closed.

Federal agencies established contraceptive services in the 1930s, but these were also closed during the later years of the Roosevelt Administration because of dissatisfaction with their results and the strong opposition of the Catholic Church.

Today, contraceptive use in Puerto Rico is widespread. It is estimated that three fourths of Puertorican women have used contraceptives at least once (Davila 1990). Despite the purported influence of the Catholic Church, religious affiliation has no bearing on contraceptive use. Data show that Catholics use contraceptives as often as non-Catholics. Furthermore, studies have found that the level of contraceptive use is similar across socioeconomic classes, educational levels, and urban versus rural regions (Vazquez-Calzada 1988; Herold et al. 1989). It should be noted, however, that a significant number of university students were found to have little knowledge of contraception, especially regarding barrier methods that may decrease the spread of STDs and AIDS (Irrizarry 1991). Overall, birth control usage reflects the prevalent belief that birth control is the main responsibility of women (Davila 1990).

The most widely used contraceptive by women who intend to have more children is the pill. Studies indicate that about half of the married women have used the pill at least once (Davila 1990). The pill is less popular nowadays, with usage decreasing from 18.9% in 1968 to 11.9% in 1982 (Vazquez-Calzada 1988).

The IUD and the diaphragm are used significantly less than the pill (Robles et al. 1990). It has been reported that about one-third of the women had used these methods once (Davila 1990). The rhythm method is used much less, 18%. However, it should be noted that the popularity of the rhythm method increased from 2.9% in 1968 to 7.7% in 1982 (Vazquez-Calzada 1988). The use of condoms is not very high. About 6.6% of women reported that their partners used condoms as a means of birth control in 1968. About the same rate was reported in 1976 and again in 1982 (Vazquez-Calzada 1988). Researchers have suggested that religious beliefs and culture norms in Puerto Rico may be responsible for men's low usage of condoms and women's inability to demand the use of condoms from their partners (Menendez 1990). The HIV/AIDS epidemic has become a way to promote the use of condoms, not only as a contraceptive method, but for HIV and STD prevention. Finally, the female condom is now available, and its use is increasing.

## B. Teenage Unmarried Pregnancies

Statistics for the year 1985 show that 17% of all pregnancies occurred among adolescents between the ages of 10 to 19 years (Mock & Ramirez 1993). The rate increased dramatically; 19.2% of pregnant Puertorican women are adolescents (2002).

## C. Abortion

It has been estimated that between 50,000 to 75,000 abortions are performed every year in Puerto Rico (Pacheco-Acosta 1990). Abortion is more common in single than in married mothers. Furthermore, studies have found no differences between Catholics and non-Catholics in abortion incidence (Herold et al. 1989). It has been suggested that Catholics may prefer abortions to contraceptives because the former involves only one violation or sin and one confession, while the ongoing use of contraceptives requires repeated confessions in which absolution might be refused because of the lack of true repentance and the unwillingness to discontinue using contraceptives. If the abortion can be kept secret, the person in question can continue to go to church, whereas if the pregnancy were brought to term, everybody would know about it (Ortiz & Vazquez-Nuttall 1987).

## D. Population Control Efforts

Population-control policies in conjunction with migration—almost a third of Puertoricans live outside their country—have been long-term basic tenets of economic development on the island. This has permitted constant experimentation with contraceptives among Puertorican women. They served as human "guinea pigs" for testing the first contraceptive hormonal pill that was later withdrawn from the market because of its severe negative side effects (Davila 1990).

During the 1940s and 1950s, family planning and population control were supported by the government, and sterilization became a common practice. By the 1970s, Puerto Rico had one of the highest rates of sterilization in the world, and it was estimated that at least 35% of the women of reproductive age were sterilized (Acosta-Belen 1986; Robles et al. 1988). Data from recent decades indicate that sterilization increased from 56.7% in 1968 to 58.3% in 1982 (Vazquez-Calzada 1988). Sterilization remains the most accepted method of family planning among Puertorican women and the island continues having one of the highest rates in the world (Vasquez-Calzada et al. 1989; Robles et al. 1988). The same study showed that women who had Cesarean sections also requested tubal ligation. Despite the strong influence of the Catholic Church, sterilization is as prevalent among Catholics as it is among non-Catholics (Herold et al. 1989).

It has been suggested that the high incidence of female sterilization is another manifestation of *machismo/marianismo*; since women are not expected to enjoy sexuality, they are not expected to give much importance to their sexual organs (Burgos & Diaz-Perez 1985).

Vasectomy seems to be more common now than it was a few decades ago. There has been an increase from 2.4% in 1968 to 6.6% in 1982 (Vazquez-Calzada 1988). Vasectomy is more popular among educated males living in urban areas.

## 10. Sexually Transmitted Diseases and HIV/AIDS/SIDA

### A. Sexually Transmitted Diseases

Only partial data on the incidence of sexually transmitted diseases are available. The rate for syphilis (all stages) was 33.92 per 100,000 in 2001-2002. Available data on the absolute number of cases show a decline from 1,526 cases in 1998 to 1,292 cases in 2002. The rate for gonorrhea in 2002 was 13.65 per 100,000. The cumulative number of cases reported for four years show a dramatic increase from 388 cases in 1998 to 520 cases for 2002.

The greater proportion of reported cases of sexually transmitted disease is chlamydia. The cumulative number of cases reported for the last four years shows an increase from 2,008 cases in 1998 to 2,867 cases for 2002 (data obtained from Vigilancia de Enfermedades de Transmisión Sexual, Departamento de Salud de Puerto Rico, OCASET, División de Epidemiología 2002).

The statistics also indicate that sexually transmitted diseases occur most frequently among adolescents and young adults (15 to 45 years). Adolescents and young single adults are a common high-risk group in most societies today, where barriers to adolescent sexual behavior are falling without society's recognition of the need for education in reducing the risks of sexually transmitted diseases (Mock & Ramirez 1993).

### B. HIV/AIDS/SIDA

*Adolescent and Adult HIV/AIDS*

The first case of AIDS in Puerto Rico was reported in 1982 and the vigilance/prevention program was started in 1983. Initially, because of physicians' reluctance to report the cases they diagnosed as being HIV-positive or having AIDS, the reported rates were very likely serious underestimates of the true number of cases. By December 2002, a total of 24,700 cases had been reported.

The greater proportion of deaths from AIDS on the island occurred among people between 20 and 39 years of age, an age of great productivity and active social and sexual life. In 1987, it was reported that AIDS was the primary cause of death for women between ages 25 and 39 and for males between 30 and 39 years of age (Cunningham 1991). In 1989, 3.7% of all deaths in Puerto Rico were because of AIDS. However, in comparison to those living on the island, Puertoricans living in New York City have a five-times greater chance of dying from AIDS—this is true both for men and women (Menendez 1990).

In Puerto Rico, the use of intravenous drugs constitutes the most important risk factor in the development of AIDS (Marrero-Rodriguez et al. 1993). In fact, the largest concentration of intravenous (IV) drug users among AIDS cases in the United States is found in Puerto Rico (Colon, Robles, & Sahai 1991). It is estimated that more than 51% of AIDS patients on the island are addicted to intravenous drugs. Among males, 54% of AIDS cases are associated with IV-drug use compared to only 38% for mainland women (until December 2002). The relevance of this risk factor makes the epidemiology of AIDS different in Puerto Rico from what is encountered in other parts of the world. It is estimated that there are 100,000 drug addicts in Puerto Rico, 2.7% of the total population, 80% of who are IV-drug users (Rivera et al. 1990).

Most of the 100,000 drug users are young heterosexual and homosexual males, who continue being sexually active and practicing high-risk behaviors. Thus, one can expect that their partners would be infected through sexual contact. Epidemiological data show that IV-drug user's male partners account for 84% of heterosexual transmission in women. It has been suggested that the geography of Puerto Rico, which is a relatively small island, creates an opportunity for knowing and contacting a lot of people, and thus facilitating the spread of the disease. Furthermore, given the high rate of sterilization among women, a significant number may find no incentives to use barrier methods that may decrease the risk for contracting AIDS and other STDs (Robles et al. 1990). An additional factor may be that men expect women to be responsible for birth control, and these may prefer the use of methods, particularly the pill, which in turn may decrease the possibility of men using condoms (Davila 1990).

The second most common mode of HIV transmission, and one that is on the rise, is heterosexual activity. The data until December 2002 show that heterosexual infection increased from 6% in 1988 to 24% in 2002. By 2002, heterosexual transmission had increased to 6,533 cases, 3,753 (60%) of whom were women. Heterosexual transmission in women is increasing at a much faster rate than in men. The problem of heterosexual transmission seems to be worsened by the existence of *machismo* and the subordinate role that women are expected to play in sexual matters. Within such cultural beliefs, women have little power to negotiate safer sexual behavior with their partners. Yet, women who become infected must care for and financially support their infected male partners as well as their children (Santos-Ortiz 1991). See Tables 1 and 2.

The cumulative cases of AIDS in Puertorican adults and children on the island as of January 1, 2002, were:

Adults ages 13-49: 24,272
Women ages 13-49: 6,301
Children ages 0-13: 401

As of July 31, 2003, Puerto Rico had 28,637 confirmed cases of AIDS. In the west, Aguadilla had 881 cases and Mayaguez 1,378. In Mid-island, Arecibo had 2,003 cases, Ponce 4,827, and Bayamou 4,804. In the east, San Juan had 6,911, cases, Area Metro 3,362, Caguas 3,395, and Fajardo 934 (Vigilancia SIDA División de Epidemiología).

## Pediatric AIDS

The first pediatric AIDS case in Puerto Rico was reported in the San Juan Municipal Hospital in 1984. By November 1991, 190 cases had been reported. This figure clearly underestimates the magnitude of pediatric AIDS, because for every one diagnosed case, there are between two and ten children who are infected, but have not been diagnosed (Beauchamp et al. 1991).

It has been estimated that 1.4% of the cumulative AIDS (1998-2002) cases are acquired perinatally. Pediatric AIDS occurs equally in female and male newborns, with a ratio of one to one. The profile shows that more than 93% of the pediatric cases acquired the disease from their infected mothers. A protocol was developed in Puerto Rico to treat serological-positive to HIV pregnant women to prevent mother-to-newborn infection.

Interestingly, most of the HIV-infected children who have been orphaned by AIDS now live with their extended family members—aunts, uncles, and grandparents. Apparently, prior to their death, infected parents make private arrangements with extended family members to insure that their children will be taken care of and legal custody established. The care of HIV-infected children is often burdensome to an extended family that may be overwhelmed by the extra services and care needed by the orphan. Shelter care for HIV-infected children is often unavailable.

### Table 1

**Adult/Adolescent (Ages 13 to 49) AIDS Cases among Hispanics in Puerto Rico, by Exposure Category, Reported in July 31, 2003, Department of Health Statistics**

| Transmission Modes | Men No. | Men % | Women No. | Women % | Total No. | Total % |
|---|---|---|---|---|---|---|
| Men who have sex with men | 4,661 | 22% | 0 | 0% | 4,661 | 17% |
| Injection drug use | 11,768 | 54 | 2,431 | 37 | 14,199 | 50 |
| Men who sleep with men and inject drugs | 2,063 | 10 | 0 | 0 | 2,063 | 7 |
| Heterosexual contact | 2,889 | 13 | 3,920 | 60 | 6,809 | 26 |
| Blood transmission* | 49 | 0 | 6 | 0 | 55 | 0 |
| Risk not reported or identified | 157 | 1 | 54 | 1 | 211 | 1 |
| Totals | 21,678 | 100% | 6,525 | 100% | 26,195 | 100% |

*Hemophilia/coagulation disorder or receipt of blood transfusion, blood components, or tissue

### Table 2

**Reported Cases of AIDS and Case Fatality Rates by Year of Diagnosis**

| Year of Diagnosis | No. of Cases | No. of Deaths | Case-Fatality Rate |
|---|---|---|---|
| Before 1990 | 4,648 | 3,848 | 83.0% |
| 1990 | 1,890 | 1,540 | 81.5 |
| 1991 | 2,375 | 1,902 | 80.0 |
| 1992 | 2,451 | 1,892 | 77.0 |
| 1993 | 2,694 | 1,986 | 74.0 |
| 1994 | 2,369 | 1,622 | 68.0 |
| 1995 | 2,093 | 1,311 | 60.5 |
| 1996 | 2,085 | 1,067 | 51.0 |
| 1997 | 1,735 | 713 | 41.0 |
| 1998 | 1,453 | 583 | 40.0 |
| 1999 | 1,265 | 484 | 38.0 |
| 2000 | 1,155 | 439 | 38.0 |
| 2001 | 1,146 | 370 | 32.5 |
| 2002 | 915 | 240 | 26.0 |
| 2003, January-June | 313 | 25 | 6.0 |
| Totals | 26,637 | 18,011 | |

On the mainland, mothers infected with HIV are treated with a great variety of drugs to maintain low levels of the viral load. Before and during pregnancy, these treatments reduce significantly the vertical transmission of HIV.

Pediatric cases among school-age children present an additional challenge in Puerto Rico. There is a law that protects the confidentiality of all persons with HIV/AIDS. Students, teachers, and administrative personnel do not have to inform others of their status about serological conditions. On the other hand, state and federal regulations request that any school or employer provide information and workshops about blood pathogens including, HIV/AIDS and hepatitis. Employers are asked to establish a program to advise, prevent, and protect their employees against blood pathogens. In Puerto Rico, as on the mainland, prejudice and discrimination exist, so that some schools have tried to protect confidentiality by denying access to the records of children who have revealed that they are HIV-infected. Nonetheless, it should be noted that the Department of Education in Puerto Rico has an AIDS (SIDA) policy that adequately addresses the needs of HIV-infected children in the schools.

## 11. Sexual Dysfunctions, Counseling, and Therapies

### A. Concepts of Sexual Dysfunction

The data on types of sexual dysfunction are limited to small nonrandom samples. A 1985 report by Mock states that the most common sexual dysfunction among males was erectile dysfunction, followed by lack of sexual desire and premature ejaculation. For females, the most common problem was inhibited female orgasm, relationship problems, and lack of sexual desire.

In Mock's opinion, the male dysfunctions are in part because of three main factors: the belief that it is the male's responsibility to satisfy his partner, masculinity as defined by the ability to obtain and sustain erection, and the fear of homosexuality. In the case of the female, issues such as inhibitions to express their sexuality freely and the fear of losing a partner seem to play important roles in sexual dysfunctions.

### B. Availability of Counseling, Diagnosis, and Treatment

There are several private practitioners in Puerto Rico, most of whom have been trained in the United States and possess doctoral degrees as well as certification as sex counselors and/or therapists. Most of them are members of professional organizations in the United States, such as the Society for the Scientific Study of Sexuality (SSSS), the American Association for Sex Educators, Counselors, and Therapists (AASECT), and the Society for Sex Therapy and Research (SSTAR).

## 12. Sex Research and Advanced Professional Education

Human sexuality courses are part of the academic offerings in the colleges and universities in Puerto Rico. Major universities, such as the Universidad de Puerto Rico, conduct research in sexuality and AIDS (SIDA).

In the past 15 years, sex education has become a real need for teachers who deal with children and adolescents who have needs, problems, and questions related to their sexuality. The universities have prepared and offered courses in sexuality to satisfy the needs of the teachers. The University Sex Education Symposium provides the opportunities for educators and health professionals to obtain continuing education in sexuality. Unfortunately, most helping professionals do not have the opportunity of benefitting from formal courses in sex education, because there is a deficiency of such courses in the professional curricula. Efforts are underway in Puerto Rico to introduce a sex education curriculum into the professional schools in the universities.

Because of the relevance of AIDS in Puerto Rico, there are numerous organizations and centers providing services and conducting ongoing research in this area. Worth mentioning are two publications: *El SIDA en Puerto Rico*, edited by a group of scholars working at Rio Piedras of the Universidad de Puerto Rico (Cunningham et al. 1991), and the second one by Mock & Ramirez (1993) titled *SIDA: Crisis o Reto Transformador.*

The most important center for research on general aspects of sexuality is the Instituto Puertorriqueno de Salud Sexual Integral (Address: Center Building, Oficina 406, Avenida de Diego 312, Santurce, Puerto Rico 00909; telephone: 809-721-3578). There are also several centers and associations that deal with specific aspects of sexually transmitted diseases and AIDS (SIDA).

## Final Comments

In summary, sexual behavior and attitudes in Puertorican society reflects the social, political, and economic conditions of the country. A model of economic development based in population control and immigration has resulted in high rates of sterilization and the use of its population, especially the female, as involuntary experimental subjects for contraceptives such as the pill. This same pattern has been reported with the use of hormones to feed poultry and livestock, which has also had an impact on the health status of the inhabitants of the island.

The so-called yo-yo migration and high rates of intravenous drug use have resulted in a high incidence of AIDS (SIDA), with heterosexual transmission being more important than other means of contracting the virus.

The institutionalized inequality of women on the island contributes not only to high rates of AIDS (SIDA) among them and their newborn, but also to the repression of their sexuality and their engagement in high-risk behaviors only to satisfy their partner or because of a fear of losing them.

## References and Suggested Readings

Acosta-Belen, E. 1986. *The Puerto Rican woman, Perspectives on culture, history and society.* Rio Piedras: Universidad de Puerto Rico.

Alvarado, M. R. 1987. El hostigamiento sexual en el empleo. *Homines, 10*:192-196.

Amato. A. 1993 (October 31). Multiplying in smaller numbers. Santiago, W.: *The San Juan Star.*

Beauchaump, B., L. Flores, L. Lugo, L. Robles, & I. Salabarria. 1991. *SIDA pediatrico: Experiencia en el Hospital Pediatrico Universitario. El SIDA en Puerto Rico: Acercamientos multidisciplinarios.* Rio Piedras: Universidad de Puerto Rico, Instituto de Estudios del Caribe.

Burgos, N. M., & Y. I. Diaz-Perez. 1985. *La sexualidad: Analisis exploratorio en la cultura puertorriquena.* Puerto Rico: Centro de Investigaciones Sociales.

Castro-Alvarez, V., & A. B. Ramirez de Arellano. 1991. The health status of Puerto Rican women in the United States and Puerto Rico. Paper presented at the Public Health Service Conference, "A Celebration of Hispanic Women's Issues," San Antonio, Texas.

Castro-Alvarez, V., & A. B. Ramirez de Arellano. 1992. The reproductive health of Puerto Rican women in the United States and Puerto Rico. *Journal Multi-Cultural Community Health,* 2:9-14.

CIA. 2002 (January). *The world factbook 2002.* Washington, DC: Central Intelligence Agency. Available: http://www.cia.gov/cia/publications/factbook/index.html.

Colon, H. M., R. Robles, & H. Sahai. 1991. HIV risk and prior drug treatment among Puerto Rican intravenous drug users. *Puerto Rican Health Sciences Journal*, *10*:83-87.

Comas-Diaz, L. 1985. A comparison of content themes in therapy. *Hispanic Journal Behavioral Sciences*, *7*:273-283.

Cunningham, I. 1991. La mujer y el SIDA: Una vision critica. *Puerto Rican Health Sciences Journal*, *9*:47-50.

Cunningham, E., & I. Cunningham, I. 1991. La metafora del SIDA en Puerto Rico: El reportaje de una epidemia. In: Cunningham, Ramos-Bellido, & Ortiz-Colon, eds., *El SIDA en Puerto Rico: Acercamientos multidisciplinarios*. Rio Piedras: Universidad de Puerto Rico, Instituto de Estudios del Caribe.

Cunningham, I. & H. Rodriguez-Sanchez. 1991. Practicas de riesgo relacionadas con la transmision del VIH y medidas de prevencion entre estudiantes de la Universidad de Puerto Rico. In: Cunningham, Ramos-Bellido, & Ortiz-Colon, eds., *El SIDA en Puerto Rico: Acercamientos multidisciplinarios*. Rio Piedras: Universidad de Puerto Rico, Instituto de Estudios del Caribe.

Davila, A. L. 1990. Esterilizacion y practica anticonceptiva en Puerto Rico, 1982. *Puerto Rican Health Sciences Journal*, *9*:61-67.

Garcia-Preto, N. 1982. Puerto Rican families. In: M. McGoldrick, J. K. Pearce, & J. Giordano, eds., *Ethnicity and family therapy*. New York: Guilford Press.

Herold, J. M., et al. 1989. Catholicism and fertility in Puerto Rico. *American Journal Public Health*, *79*:1258-1262.

*HIV/AIDS surveillance reports*. Available from the Centers for Disease Control (CDC) National Prevention Information Network, Atlanta GA, USA.

Irrizarry, A. 1991. Conociminetos, creencias y actitudes hacia el SIDA en jovenes puertorriquenos. *Puerto Rican Health Sciences Journal*, *10*:43-46.

Maldonado, M. A. 1990. Violencia contra la mujer por ser mujer. *Puerto Rican Health Sciences Journal*, *9*:11-116.

Marrero-Rodriguez, et al. 1993. HIV risk behavior and HIV seropositivity among young injection drug users. *Puerto Rican Health Sciences Journal*, *12*:7-12.

Martinez, L., et al. 1988. *El hostigamiento sexual de las trabajadoras en sus centros de empleo*. Universidad de Puerto Rico, Centro de Investigaciones Sociales, Facultad de Ciencias Sociales, Recinto de Rio Piedras.

Medina, C. 1987. Latino culture and sex education. *SIECUS Report*, *15*(3):1-4.

Mejias-Picart, T. 1975. Observaciones sobre el machismo en la America Latina. *Revista de Ciencias Sociales*, *19*:353-364.

Menendez, B. S. 1990. Mortalidad por SIDA en mujeres puertorriquenas en la Ciudad de Nueva York, 1981-1987. *Puerto Rican Health Sciences Journal*, *9*:43-45.

Mock, G. 1984. La sexualidad femenina: Reflexiones para reflexionar. *Pensamiento Critico*, 16-20.

Mock, G. 1992. Personal Communication.

Mock, G., & M. Ramirez. 1993. *SIDA: Crisis o reto transformador*. Marrisonburg, VI: Editorial Cultural.

*MMWR–Morbidity and mortality weekly reports. 1989*. Centers for Disease Control: Summary of Notifiable Diseases, *38*(54):4-9.

*MMWR–Morbidity and mortality weekly reports. 1990*. Centers for Disease Control: Summary of Notifiable Diseases, *39*(53):4-8.

*MMWR–Morbidity and mortality weekly reports. 1991*. Centers for Disease Control: Summary of Notifiable Diseases, *40*(54):4-9.

Ortiz, C. G., & E. Vazquez-Nuttall. 1987. Adolescent pregnacy: Effects of family support, education, and religion on the decision to carry or terminate among Puerto Rican teenagers. *Adolescence*, *22*:897-917.

Ortiz-Colon, R. 1991. Grupo de apoyo con hombres homosexuales VIH positivo: Un estudio de caso en Puerto Rico. In: Cunningham, Ramos-Bellido, & Ortiz-Colon, eds., *El SIDA en Puerto Rico: Acercamientos multidisciplinarios*. Universidad de Puerto Rico.

Pacheco-Acosta, E. 1990. El aborto inducido en Puerto Rico: 1985. *Puerto Rican Health Sciences Journal*, *9*:75-78.

Parker, R. 1987. Acquired immunodeficiency syndrome in urban Brazil. *Medical Anthropology Quarterly*, n.s. *1*(2): 155-175.

Pico, I. 1989. *Machismo y educacion*. Rio Piedras: Editorial Universidad de Puerto Rico.

Quiroz, J., et al. 1991. Perfil sociodemografico y medidas del crecimiento fisicos en pacientes pediatricos con el sindrome de inmunodeficiencia adquirida seguidos en el Hospital Municipal de San Juan: 1986-1990. *Boletin de la Asociacion Medica de Puerto Rico*, *83*:479-484.

Rivera, R., et al. 1990. Social relations and empowerment of sexual partners of IV drug users. *Puerto Rican Health Sciences Journal*, *9*:99-104.

Robles, R., et al. 1988. Health care services and sterilization among Puerto Rican women. *Puerto Rican Health Sciences Journal*, *7*:7-13.

Robles, R., et al. 1990. AIDS risk behavior patterns among intravenous drug users in Puerto Rico and the United States. *Boletin de la Asociacion Medica de Puerto Rico*, *83*:523-527.

Santos-Ortiz, M. C. 1990. Sexualidad femenina antes y despues del SIDA. *Puerto Rican Health Sciences Journal*, *9*: 33-35.

Santos-Ortiz, M. C. 1991. El SIDA y las relaciones heterosexuales. In: Cunningham, Ramos-Bellido, & Ortiz- Colon, eds., *El SIDA en Puerto Rico: Acercamientos multidisciplinarios*. Universidad de Puerto Rico.

*Sexually transmitted diseases statistics, 1984*. Issue 134, U.S. Department of Health and Human Services. Washington, DC: Public Health Service, Center for Disease Control (U.S. Government Printing Office).

Vazquez-Calzada, J. 1988. *La poblacion de Puerto Rico y su trayectoria historica*. Rio Piedras: Escuela Graduada de Salud Publica, Recinto de Ciencias Medicas, Universidad de Puerto Rico.

Vazquez-Calzada, J. 1989. Variantes en la estructura del divorcio del hogar puertorriqueno. *Puerto Rican Health Sciences Journal*, *8*:225-230.

Vazquez-Calzada, J., I. Parrilla, & L. E. Leon. 1989. El efecto de los partos por cesarea sobre la esterilizacion en Puerto Rico. *Puerto Rican Health Sciences Journal*, *8*:215-25.

Vasquez, M. M. 1986. The effects of role expectations on the marital status of urban Puerto Rican women. In: E. Acosta-Belen, ed., *The Puerto Rican woman: Perspectives on culture, history and society*. Rio Piedras: Universidad de Puerto Rico.

Vasquez, S. M. 1985. Homophobia among college students of Puerto Rican descent as a function of residence and acculturation factors. Institute of Advanced Psychological Studies, Adelphi University.

Zorrilla, L. D., J. Romaguera, & C. Diaz. 1993. Recomendaciones para el manejo de mujeres con infeccion VIH. *Puerto Rican Health Sciences Journal*, *12*:55-61.

(CIA 2002)

# Russia

## (*Rossiyskaya Federatsiya*)

Igor S. Kon, Ph.D.
*Updates by I. S. Kon*

## Contents

## *Demographics and a Brief Historical Perspective*

ROBERT T. FRANCOEUR

### A. Demographics

Russia's 6.6 million square miles (17.1 million km²), over three quarters of the total area of the former Union of Soviet Socialist Republics, makes it the largest country in the world. Russia stretches from Finland, Poland, Norway, Latvia, Estonia, and Ukraine on the west, to the Pacific Ocean in the east, spanning ten time zones. Its southern neighbors include Georgia, Azerbaijan, Kazakhstan, China, Mongolia, and North Korea.

*Communications*: Igor Kon, Ph.D., Vavilova Str., 48-372, Moscow, Russia 117333; Igor_kon@mail.ru, igor_kon@yahoo.com, *or* http://konigor.hypermart.net.

In July 2002, Russia had an estimated population of 145 million. (All data are from *The World Factbook 2002* (CIA 2002) unless otherwise stated.)

**Age Distribution and Sex Ratios**: *0-14 years*: 16.7% with 1.04 male(s) per female (sex ratio); *15-64 years*: 70.2% with 0.94 male(s) per female; *65 years and over*: 13.1% with 0.48 male(s) per female; *Total population sex ratio*: 0.88 male(s) to 1 female

**Life Expectancy at Birth**: *Total Population*: 67.5 years; *male*: 62.29 years; *female*: 72.97 years. Life expectancy in Russia appears to be decreasing significantly and rapidly because of the deteriorating quality of the country's infrastructure and economics. Russia's healthcare system is in decline because of serious economic troubles since the breakup of the Communist system. Many hospitals are poorly equipped and most are poorly supplied with necessary medicines.

**Urban/Rural Distribution**: 73% to 27%; Moscow has close to 9 million, St. Petersburg, 5 million, and Samara and Nizhny Novgorod, 1.5 million inhabitants each.

**Ethnic Distribution**: very socially and culturally heterogeneous, with over 100 distinct ethnic groups. Russian: 81.5%; Tatar: 3.8%; Ukranian: 3%; Chuvash: 1.2%; Bashkir: 0.9%; Byelorussian: 0.8%; Moldavian: 0.7%; other: 8.1%

**Religious Distribution**: Russian Orthodox, Muslim, and other

**Birth Rate**: 9.71 births per 1,000 population

**Death Rate**: 13.91 per 1,000 population

**Infant Mortality Rate**: 19.78 deaths per 1,000 live births

**Net Migration Rate**: 0.94 migrant(s) per 1,000 population

**Total Fertility Rate**: 1.3 children born per woman

**Population Growth Rate**: –0.33%

**HIV/AIDS** (1999 est.): *Adult prevalence*: 0.18%; *Persons living with HIV/AIDS*: 130,000; *Deaths*: 850. (For additional details from www.UNAIDS.org, see end of Section 10B.)

**Literacy Rate** (*defined as those age 15 and over who can read and write*): 98%; education is free and compulsory from age 7 to 17

**Per Capita Gross Domestic Product** (*purchasing power parity*): $8,300 (2001 est.); *Inflation*: 21.9% (2001 est.); *Unemployment*: 8.7% with considerable underemployment (2001 est.); *Living below the poverty line*: 40% (1999 est.)

[*Update 2002*: Since the collapse of communism in 1991, a rapidly growing economic crisis, increasing alcoholism, violence, the lack of and high price of housing, and an increase in infectious diseases and the lack of medicines to treat them have all been factors in a drastic decline in Russian life expectancies, the quality of life, and the rates of marriage, divorce, and birth. In the early 1990s, life expectancies plunged, then rose steadily under Gorbachev from 1995 to 1998, and then again declined. In 1999, the last year for which statistics are available, life expectancy at birth was 59.9 years for males and 72.4 years for females. In the 1990s, Russia's marriage rate decreased by 25% while the divorce rate rose by 50%. In 2002, Russia's rate of HIV infection was almost double that of the United States.

[Meanwhile, after Russia's birthrate crept slowly downwards for decades, it fell by another 10% in the mid-1990s. Russia's birthrate in 1999 was 8.4 births per 1,000 people, compared with 13.4 in 1990. The average number of babies a Russian woman could expect to bear fell from 1.89 in 1990 to 1.17 in 1999. In the 1980s, Russia had Europe's highest fertility rate; in 1999, it ranked with Spain and Italy with the lowest birthrate. A United Nations report estimated that Russia's current population of 145 million would decrease to 121 million by 2050, the level of the country in 1960. In 2001, the Research Public Health Institute predicted a decline to 80 million people in 2050, 10 million fewer than the country had at the time of the 1917 Revolution. (*End of update by I. S. Kon*)]

**B. A Brief Historical Perspective**

Slavic tribes began migrating into Russia from the west in the 5th century of the Common Era. The first Russian state was founded in the 9th century with centers in Novgorod and Kiev. In the 13th century, Mongols overran the country. The grand dukes of Muscovy (Moscow) led the Russians in recovering their land; by 1480, the Mongols were expelled. Ivan the Terrible (1692-1725) was the first to be formally proclaimed Tsar. Peter the Great (1672-1725) extended the domain and founded the Russian Empire in 1721.

Under the aegis of Empress Catherine the Great (1729-1796), European culture was a dominant influence among the Russian aristocracy, particularly in the years prior to the destruction of the monarchy in the French Revolution. In the 19th and early 20th centuries, Western ideas and the beginnings of modernization spread through the huge Russian empire. Political evolution, however, failed to keep pace.

Military reverses in the war with Japan (1905) and in World War I undermined the Tsarist regime. In 1917, sporadic strikes among factory workers coalesced into a revolution that deposed the Tsar and established two brief-lived provisional governments in sequence. In brief order, a Communist coup placed Vladimir Ilyich Lenin in power. Lenin's death in 1924 led to a struggle from which Joseph Stalin emerged as the leader. Purges, mass executions, mass exiles, and even a famine engineered in the Ukraine marked Stalin's regime and resulted in millions of deaths, according to most estimates.

Although Russia and Germany signed a nonaggression pact in 1939, Germany launched a massive invasion of Russia in June 1941. Counterattacks during the brutal Russian winters of 1941-1942 and 1942-1943, coupled with the Nazi failure to take and hold Stalingrad, started the German retreat and eventual defeat. After Stalin's death in 1953, the "De-Stalinization" of Russia began under Nikita Khrushchev. In 1987, Mikhail Gorbachev began a program of reform that included expanded freedoms and democratizing the political process. This openness (*glasnost*) and restructuring (*perestroika*) was opposed by some Eastern-bloc countries and hard-line Communists in the U.S.S.R. In August, Gorbachev resigned and recommended dissolution of the Communist Central Committee. By the end of 1991, 74 years of Communist government had ended, with declarations of freedom from the Russian, Ukraine, and Kazakhstan republics, and the Union of Soviet Socialist Republics was dissolved. This opened the door for the many recent changes in the sexual lives of Russians detailed in this chapter.

## 1. Basic Sexological Premises

[*Update 2002*: At virtually every moment of its history, Russian sexual culture was described by both foreigners and by Russians in a highly polarized manner, and these contrasting images are reproduced in contemporary scientific literature (Kon 1995, 1997ab, 1999).

[On the one hand, medieval and early modern Russia was a patriarchal society in which women were brutally suppressed, and wife beating was considered an expression and proof of conjugal love even by the women themselves. The attitudes and practices of gender inequality, aggravated by centuries of serfdom, are abundantly reflected in Russian folklore and literature. On the other hand, Russia had always had a "powerful woman syndrome." Since the time of Hegel, German romanticism, and the Russian Slavophiles, philosophical tradition has considered the "Russian soul" or "national character" as feminine rather than masculine.

[Equally contradictory is the Russian bodily canon and body politic, including soul/body opposition, social representation of the body, attitudes to nudity, and the rules of decency. On the one hand, the Russian character, lifestyle, and mentality are often represented as a realm where spirituality is predominant (*dukhovnost*), in sharp contrast to Western materialism, pragmatism, and "body-boundedness" (*telesnost*). This ideology of disembodied spirituality, with a corresponding underestimation and denigration of the body and its physiological functions, is most clearly shown in Russian Orthodox religious art. Russian Orthodox icon painting, when done according to the Byzantine canon, is much stricter and more ascetic than Western art. Secular nude painting also appeared much later in Russia, and was under more stringent social control than in the West. On the other hand, Russian everyday life, popular culture, and language have always been anything but modest. Foreign observers of the 1600s to the 1800s expressed surprise and shock at the Russian custom of nude mixed bathing in bathhouses and rivers, and at the richness and openness of Russian obscene language (*mat*).

[This exaggerated soul/body contrast is further projected into the incompatibility between romantic love and "carnal lust" (sexuality). The normative image of love in classical Russian literature is extremely inhibited, chaste, and opposed to sexual, carnal pleasure. On the other hand, Russian folklore, language, and everyday culture have always been openly and crudely sexual. "Peasant society might be sexually repressive, but it was rarely sexually prudish" (Engel 1990, 700). As Charles-Francois Masson, an early 19th-century French diplomat, wrote:

> Nowhere did so many women arrogate to themselves the right of making the first advances, and being the active party, in affairs of love. . . . A Russian youth will never feel his blood boil, and his heart palpitate, at the idea of a rising bosom. He never sighs after secret charms, at which he scarcely dares to guess; for from his infancy he has seen and examined everything. The Russian maiden will never have her cheek overspread with an involuntary blush at an

indiscreet idea or curiosity, and her husband will have nothing new to show or to teach her, nor will marriage have any novelty for her. Love is here a stranger to those delicate and exquisite approaches that constitute its true charms, and to those preludes to pleasure more delightful than pleasure itself. Where poignant sentiments do not ennoble the happiest of human passions, it becomes mere momentary impulse, too easily gratified to be highly prized. (Masson 1805, 263, 266-267)

[The "civilizing process" of cultural modernization and secularization in Russia was also somewhat different from early modern Western Europe. Insofar as it was related to and associated with the development of capitalism, urbanization, and the emergence of the middle classes, the "civilizing process" in Russia was belated and labeled as "Westernization." Because of the peculiar strength of Russian absolutism, new forms of socializing and etiquette were often introduced from above, by the Imperial court, not as mere examples for more or less voluntary imitation, but as arbitrary and compulsory prescriptions, to be carried out under close administrative supervision, and with the utmost contempt and disregard for individual preferences and tastes. There is a sort of continuity between Peter the Great's masquerades and compulsory shaving of the *boyars* and the Communist party's 1950s-to-1980s crusades against long hair, beards, miniskirts, wide or narrow pants, and so on. Ideologically, these policies were quite opposed—in the first case, this was compulsory Westernization, and in the second—anti-Westernization, but the compulsory administrative methods and social-psychological consequences of both policies were similar. Since it was introduced mainly through external and repressive means, the civilizing process in Russia tended more to rigid conformity and uniformity than to pluralism and diversity.

[Because of the dual censorship by Church and state, and the conservative public opinion, any artist or writer who attempted to initiate sexual-erotic discourse simultaneously came under withering attack from both right and left. This seriously hampered the emergence in Russia of any lofty, refined erotic art with the appropriate language and vocabulary, without which sexuality inevitably appeared vile and sullied. The predominantly negative social attitudes to sexuality and erotica began to change only in the last years of the 19th century, when "the sexual question" (*polovoi vopros*) suddenly became one of the most urgent issues in philosophy, education, politics, and the arts.

[Yet "Silver Age" erotica, like its European counterpart, was openly decadent. Its enchantment with unusual, strange, deviant, somber, violent, "perverted" forms of sexuality was liberating, but at the same time repulsive and shocking. Decadent art openly declared itself to be both immoral and amoral, and it was generally regarded as socially and educationally subversive. After 1917, it was very easy to eradicate it.

[Ultimately, the Bolsheviks had two alternative strategies in regard to sexuality: acceptance or suppression. The first and more liberal viewpoint was formulated by Alexandra Kollontai, but it was always marginal. The second, more rigid and dogmatic stance was taken by Aron Zalkind. Zalkind admitted the existence of a biological sexual drive in human beings and the harm of "sexual self-corking." At the same time, however, he proposed the wholesale subordination of sexuality to the proletariat's class interests.

[The ideological justification of these repressive attitudes varied. In the 1920s, sexophobia had been reinforced by arguments about "class interests" and by mechanistic theories about the need to channel individual "sexual energy" into more-exalted social goals. Later, a moral concern

for marriage and the family was emphasized. Sexual intolerance became an essential aspect of global social intolerance and totalitarian control over the personality; the most important steps here were the recriminalization of homosexuality (1933), and bans on pornography (1935) and abortion (1936). But the liquidation of erotic culture produced not so much a desexualization of public and private life as its impoverishment and vulgarization. Sexuality, driven underground and degraded to the level of a "sex instinct," became a strong anti-Soviet and anti-Communist symbol, forcing people to make their choice—and their choices were often against the regime. (*End of update by I. S. Kon*)]

## A. Character of Gender Roles

Soviet Russian general attitudes to gender roles and sex differences can be defined as a sexless sexism. On the one side, gender/sex differences have been theoretically disregarded and politically underestimated. The notions of sex and gender are conspicuously absent from encyclopedias, social science and psychology dictionaries, and textbooks. On the other side, both public opinion and social practices have been extremely sexist, all empirical sex differences being taken as given by nature.

## B. Sociolegal Status of Males and Females

A paramount slogan of the October 1917 Revolution was the liberation of women and the establishment of full legal and social gender equality. The Soviet regime revoked all forms of legal and political discrimination against women. A host of women were attracted into industrial labor, education, and public activities.

Like all other actions by the Bolsheviks, however, the program was naive and unrealistic. Gender equality was interpreted in a mechanical way, as a complete similarity. All historical, cultural, national, and religious-based gender differences were ignored, or viewed merely as "reactionary vestiges of the past," which could and had to be removed by political means (Kon 1995, 51-127).

Soviet propaganda boasted of the fact that women, for the first time in history, had been drawn into the country's sociopolitical and cultural life. By the time Soviet history reached its peak, women comprised 51% of the labor force. The percentage of women with university educations was even higher than that of men and, in such professions as teaching and medicine, women absolutely predominated.

Yet, it was not so much an equalization as a feminization of the lower levels of the vocational hierarchy. Women occupy the worst-paid and less-prestigious jobs and they are grossly underrepresented on the higher rungs of labor. Women's average salary was a third less than that of men. With the transition to a market economy and the overall economic collapse of recent years, the position of women has deteriorated sharply. Entrepreneurs simply do not want to take on pregnant women or mothers with large families.

Russian public life remains dominated and governed by men. Women remain socially dependent. Seventy-three percent of the unemployed population are women, and women receive only about 40% of men's salaries. Women are also underrepresented in political bodies (Kon 1995, 129-157).

In the family, the situation is more contradictory. About 40% of all Russian families may be considered largely egalitarian. Russian women, especially urban women, are more socially and financially independent of their husbands than at any time in the past. Very often, women bear the main responsibility for the family budget and for resolving the main issues of domestic life. Russian wives and mothers are frequently strong, dominant, and sure of themselves. On the other hand, their family load considerably exceeds that of the man and is sometimes absolutely unbearable. The length of the workweek was the same for women as for men in the 1980s. Yet, women had to spend two or three times more hours than men on household work.

The fair distribution of household duties is a paramount factor in satisfaction with and the stability of marriage. Mutual recrimination and arguments about who is exploiting whom are a typical feature of Russian press comments going back many years. Women passionately and sorrowfully bemoan the lack of "real men," while men complain about the dying breed of women who show feminine tenderness and affection.

The overall trend in Soviet history has been towards the demasculinization of men. Given all the ethnic, religious, and historical variations, the traditional male lifestyle and stereotyped image have always emphasized such virtues as energy, initiative, and independence. These qualities are extremely important for male self-esteem. Yet, the economic inefficiency of the Soviet system, the political despotism, and bureaucracy left little room for individual initiative and autonomy. At any moment in his life, from the cradle to the grave, the Russian boy, adolescent, or man felt socially and sexually dependent and frustrated.

This social dependency was intensified by the global feminization of all institutions and processes of socialization. As a result of the high level of undesired pregnancies and divorces, every fifth child in the U.S.S.R. was brought up without a father or, at least, a stepfather. In the mid-1980s, some 13,500,000 children were being raised in so-called single-mother families. Yet, even where the father was physically present, his influence and authority in the family, and his role in bringing up the children were considerably less than those of the mother.

Thus, from the start of his life, the Russian boy is dependent on a loving but dominant mother. In the nursery and at school, the major authority figures are women; male teachers are extremely rare. In official children's and youth Communist organizations recognized by adults, the Pioneers and the Komsomol, it was also girls who set the tone. Junior and senior boys only found kindred spirits in informal street groups and gangs where the power and the symbols of power were exclusively male. As in the West, many of these male groups exhibit strong antifeminist tendencies.

When a young man marries, he has to deal with a solicitous, but often very dominating wife, much like his mother once was in his youth. The wife knows much better than he how to plan the family budget and what they need for the home and family. The husband ends up merely carrying out her instructions.

Finally, in public life, absolutely everything came under the control of the powerful maternal care of the Communist Party, which knew better than anyone what was best for its citizens and was ever ready to correct a citizen's mistakes by force if necessary.

This has produced three typical reactions: 1. Psychological compensation and overcompensation through the acquisition of a primitive image of a strong and aggressive male, affirming himself through drunkenness, fighting, and both social and sexual abuse; 2. The combination of humility and subservience in public life, with cruel tyranny in the home and family directed at the wife and children; and 3. Social passivity and learned helplessness, a flight from personal responsibility to the careless, play world of eternal boyhood.

All this is equally bad for both men and women. Aggressive sexism as a means of compensating for social helplessness gives rise to sexual violence. Many Russian women are obligated to withstand patiently the vulgarity, drunkenness, and even physical abuse of their husbands, thinking that it cannot be otherwise. Sometimes, they even see in that the manifestation of love, as it was in Ancient Rus: "A man who doesn't beat his wife doesn't love her." An intelligent and educated women frequently sacrifices her own professional and public career to maintain the family, but also because she is afraid of surpassing and thereby offending her husband.

As a result, opposition to the idea of gender equality has been mounting and widening since the 1970s. Men find it painful to lose their old privileges and accept the uncertainty of their social status. Women feel themselves deceived because they are under a double yoke. As a consequence, there is a mighty wave of conservative opinion dreaming of turning the clock back to times that were not only pre-Soviet, but prior to the industrial revolution and Peter the Great. Of course, a return to the pre-medieval (*Domostroi*) household rules is a conservative utopia. However tough life is for present-day Russian women, the overwhelming majority would never agree to reduce their social roles to being only a wife and mother. Younger and better-educated men also have more egalitarian social views and take on a greater domestic, including fatherly, responsibility.

[*Update 1997*: The collapse of Soviet rule changed everything in Russia, except the relationship between the sexes, which has deteriorated significantly. Expectations in heterosexual relationships have been and are low, but divorce rates remain high, and the number of single mothers, either divorced or never married, keeps growing. In contrast with the United States where single mothers have become the hallmark of the poorest urban areas, Russian women from all walks of life, domestic and factory workers, college graduates, university professors, and professionals alike, have grown inured to raising their families without men, relying on a support network of mothers, sisters, and aunts in a kind of matriarchal society with a downward spiral of poverty and limited horizons. Paternal absence and neglect is a reality widely shared by Russian women, regardless of background, aspirations, or income.

[Even in Communist times, the unhappiness of Russian families was hard to hide. The divorce rate in the 1970s was 40%; now it is 51%. In the past, sociologists blamed Soviet life—its regimentation, oppression, and lack of individual freedom—for men's alcoholism and apathy to work and family. Today, the major factor appears to be an economic freefall that humiliates men who cannot provide for their families, to the point where they just walk away with little social censure. An estimated 15% to 20% of all Russian families are now headed by a single parent, 94% of whom are women. This number is not significantly higher than those in Western and Eastern Europe and far lower than in the United States, where sociologists estimate 27% of mothers are single.

[Some Russian sociologists suggest that single mothers are not much worse off than married mothers, because so many single mothers—31%—live with their mothers or relatives. Others point out that single mothers generally do not want to live with relatives, but have no other choice. In a study begun in 1991 comparing Russian single mothers with European single mothers, half of the single mothers in countries like Switzerland were living with boyfriends, whereas only 5% in Russia had found a new partner. In addition, Russian divorce law does not allow joint custody, and child-support payments, while required by law, are difficult to collect and increasing. Given the free-market economy, men are better off hiding their real income from tax collectors and ex-wives. Many single mothers in the larger cities do not have residency permits and cannot apply for state welfare help, minimal as that is. While Parliament is drafting a new law aimed at providing absent fathers with more-flexible child-support payments, few expect the government to have much impact on this deeply rooted social problem (Stanley 1995). *(End of update by R. T. Francoeur)*]

## C. General Concepts of Sexuality and Love

Contrary to an opinion widespread in the U.S.A., Russians are very attached to the ideal of romantic love, which is considered a necessary precondition of marriage and even sex. In a 1992 national public opinion poll, 53% of the men and 49% of the women said that they have experienced "real love." "Sex without love" was approved as normal by only 15% of the respondents, while 57% strongly disapproved of it (Kon 1995, 19-25, 52-53, 158-175).

But such attitudes may be unrealistic and reflect the contradictions of a classical Russian excessive romanticism that was formulated in Chekhov's short story "Ariadna" (1895):

We are not satisfied because we are idealists. We want the beings who give us birth and produce our children to be higher than us, higher than anything on earth. When we are young we romanticize and idolize those we fall in love with; love and happiness are synonyms with us. For us in Russia, loveless marriage is scorned, sensuality is mocked and induces revulsion, and those novels and stories where women are beautiful, poetic and elevated enjoy the most success. . . . But the trouble is as follows. Hardly do we marry or hit it off with a woman than, give or take a couple of years, and we feel we've been disappointed, let down; we try other women and again we find disillusion, again horror, and ultimately we convince ourselves that women are liars, petty, vain, unjust, uneducated, cruel—in a word, even immeasurably lower, not simply not higher, than us men.

According to 1990-1992 research of Russian university students, they, especially women, have more-pragmatic and less-romantic attitudes about marriage, particularly a readiness to marry without love, than their American, German, and Japanese counterparts. Nevertheless, as everywhere in the world, their real sexual-erotic motivations are mixed, contradictory, and heterogeneous. Also, general developmental trends in Russia are more or less similar to those occurring in Western countries:

- Earlier maturation and sexual initiation of boys and girls;
- Growing, and more or less universal, social and moral acceptance of premarital sex and cohabitation;
- Weakening of the traditional double standard for men and women;
- Growing recognition of the importance of sexual satisfaction for individual happiness and for marital stability;
- Growing public interest in all kinds of erotica and a demand for sexual freedom;
- Growing generational gap in sexual values, attitudes, and behaviors—many things that were considered deviant, unacceptable, and even unmentionable for parents, are normal and desirable for their children (Kon 1995, 158-175).

As in any other large country, sexual values and attitudes are heterogeneous, depending on gender, age cohort, education level, social milieu (whether the person lives in a large city, a small town, or in the countryside, and where he or she spent childhood and adolescence), ethnic identity, and religious affiliation.

Younger and better-educated people are more prone now to accept sex for pleasure only, without relation to love and marriage. On the other hand, as a reaction to this new individualism, normative anomie, and the weakening of family ties, some conservative and religious writers and philosophers criticize not only hedonistic eroticism, but even classical romantic, passionate love, which, they claim, should be subjugated to the quiet, conjugal love and traditional family values.

Because of the economic collapse, the institution of marriage is in a deep crisis. In 1992, there were 20% to 30% fewer new marriages concluded in Russia than in 1990. In the same period, the number of divorces has risen by 15%. About half of all Russian men and women have at least one divorce during their lifetime. About a third of the divorced are young couples who live together less than five years.

## 2. Religious, Ethnic, and Gender Factors Affecting Sexuality

### A. Source and Character of Religious Values

Despite the 74-year effort of communism to promote atheism, 25% of the people still adhere to Russian Orthodox Christianity. While approximately 60% of Russians were nonreligious when the communist regime fell, Christianity and Orthodoxy are experiencing a mild revival. Among the non-Russian populations, Islam and Buddhism are widespread.

Ancient Slav paganism was rich with sexual symbols and associations. Sexuality was believed to be a general cosmic force. There were numerous openly sexual rites and orgiastic festivals at which men and women bathed naked together, the men symbolically fertilizing the earth and the women exposing their genitals to heaven in order to invoke the rain. In spite of the Church's efforts to eradicate certain "devilish" pagan sex rituals, some of these survived among Northern Russia peasants until the end of the 19th century (Kon 1995, 11-49).

The Christianization of Russia, beginning in the 9th century, introduced a new philosophy of sexuality, but this influence has been slow and superficial. The Russian Orthodox Church, *volens nolens*, had to accommodate ancient sexual practices in numerous regional and ethnic diversities. On some issues, like clerical celibacy, it was more lenient, or rather, more realistic, than the medieval Catholic Church. While complete abstinence from sexual relations, even in marriage, was officially classified as a "holy deed," in everyday life, sexual activity in marriage was fully accepted. While celibacy was obligatory for the monks from whom the highest Church leaders were chosen, ordinary priests were obligated to marry and to have children. Unable to eradicate certain ancient pagan customs, the Church concentrated more on matters of social representation and verbalization.

Hence, we have the persistent normative conflict between the naturalistic pagan attitudes to sexuality in the "low" everyday peasant culture and the extreme spiritualism and otherworldly asceticism of the official "high" culture. Everyday life was openly sensual, cruel, and carnal. Debauchery, drunkenness, sexual violence, and rape were quite common. Russian folk tales are filled with polygamous heroes. Various sexual exploits, such as the rape of a sleeping beauty, are sympathetically described. It was permissible and noble, for example, "to dishonor" or rape a virgin girl in just revenge for her refusal to marry the hero. There was no place for modesty and privacy in the lives of peasants, and the nude body was often unwillingly and deliberately (ritually) displayed. Russian communal bathhouses, where men and women often washed together, surprised and shocked more than a few foreign travelers in the 16th and 17th centuries.

At the same time, the limits on symbolic, artistic representation of the body were extremely narrow. In Western religious painting since the Renaissance and even in the late Middle Ages, the entire human body was represented as real, living flesh. Only the genitals were veiled. In the Russian icons, only the face is alive. The body is entirely covered or outlined in an emaciated and ascetic manner. Nothing similar to the paintings or sculpture of Michelangelo, da Vinci, or Raphael was permitted. Secular paintings of nudes did not appear until the end of the 18th century.

Sexually explicit art emerged in Russia only in the middle of the 18th century, under the direct influence of French "libertines." The Imperial Court of Catherine the Great (1729-1796) was highly eroticized. The first explicitly sexual Russian poetry by Ivan Barkov (1732-1768) was deliberately crude and arrogant. It lacked the elegance of French "libertine" literature and was never published legally. Russian nobility took lovers and read pornographic literature (mostly imported) (Kon 1995, 23-38).

In the West, the Church and clerical forces were a major foe of the erotic art and culture of pleasure. In Russia, the Church was particularly powerful because of its close relations with the state. Russian censorship was stricter and more pervasive than in Western countries.

## B. Source and Character of Secular and Ethnic Values

Three facts are important for understanding the specific features of Russian eros.

First, the contrast between the official high culture and the low everyday culture of the common people was considerably greater in Russia than in the West. The official high culture was sanctified by the Church and antisexual by its very nature, while the low culture of the common people accorded sexuality a positive value common to all medieval European Christian cultures.

Second, refined, complex erotic art came into being and gained acceptance much later in Russia than in the West. And it is only through the medium of erotic art that sexuality could be included in high culture at all.

Third, the development of civilized forms of everyday social life was, in Russia, more closely associated with state power than with the civil society. Because new rules of propriety were often introduced by political authorities, there was more pressure towards uniformity of everyday conduct than towards individualization and diversification; and without some established and reasonably diverse subcultures, there can be no basis for normative pluralism, one manifestation of which is sexual tolerance.

These three factors are interconnected both historically and functionally.

In addition to the religious influence, one special factor has powerfully influenced sexuality in Russia: 19th-century, left-wing radical revolutionary-democratic literary criticism. Young aristocrats of the early 19th century received a good secular home education from early childhood. Whatever their moral and religious convictions, they tried to distance themselves from official bigotry and were not afraid of their own sexual feelings and experiences. The most revered Russian poet, Alexander Pushkin (1799-1837), wrote some elegant and witty erotic poetry.

For the next generation of Russian intellectuals, who came mainly from a clerical background and were often themselves former seminarists, such freedom was impossible. While breaking with some of their parent's principles and values, they were unable to overcome others. Constant inner battles against their own unconventional sexual practices and feelings, particularly self-pleasuring and homo-eroticism, turned into a global moral and aesthetic rejection and denunciation of sexuality and hedonism as something vulgar, dangerous, and unworthy. Only broad social objectives, such as liberation of the poor and oppressed, were morally justified. Everything that was private or personal was considered secondary—and egotistical.

These antisexual, antihedonistic attitudes have become an integral part of a definite ideological trend in Russian culture. As in the West, it was a moral expression of the middle-class, bourgeoisie opposition to aristocratic individualism. In Russia, however, this opposition was more radical. While religious bigots condemned eroticism as godless and amoral, populists rejected it as politically incorrect, vulgar, and nonaesthetic.

Any artist or writer who dared to walk up that "slippery slope" came under immediate attack both from the right and from the left. This seriously hampered the birth and development of a lofty, refined erotic art and language, without which sexual discourse inevitably appears base, dirty, and squalid. Inhibitions against sexuality and sensuous pleasure are generally typical for Russian classical literature. Sex is presented as a tragedy or quasi-religious revelation, very rarely as a pleasure.

On the eve of the 20th century, the Russian cultural climate began to change. Leo Tolstoy's *Kreutzer Sonata* (1891) stimulated a philosophical dispute about the nature and relationship of love, sex, marriage, and erotica, with prominent Russian writers like Anton Chekhov and philosophers like Vladimir Solovjev, Nikolai Berdjaev, and Vassilij Rozanov taking part. While this metaphysics of sexuality tried theoretically to rehabilitate eroticism, it had no place for real, everyday, routine sexual pleasure (Kon 1995, 39-49).

While sophisticated erotic art and literature did appear in Russia in the early 20th century, the artists of that era were seeking more a legitimization of eroticism than portraying sexual enjoyment. Exceptions, like the poet Mikhail Kuzmin and the painter Konstantin Somov, only confirm this general pattern. Whatever its aesthetical and moral value, early-20th-century Russian erotic art was marginal both to the official and popular cultures. It was looked upon as decadent and was equally denounced with vehemence by the right and by the left.

In the early 1900s, the first sexual surveys were conducted among students at Moscow and other universities. Sexual concerns were raised within the disciplines of medicine, history, ethnography, and anthropology. The word "sexology" as a name for a special subdivision of science was suggested by Rosanov in 1909.

The October Revolution of 1917 liberated sexuality from its traditional religious, moral, and institutional restraints. No longer was sex a taboo subject. On the contrary, traditional sexual morality and marriage as a social institution were themselves suspect. Everywhere, there were fierce discussions of "free love" and debates over whether the proletariat needed any sexual restrictions whatsoever. The first net result, however, was sexual anarchy, the growth of unwanted pregnancies and births, induced abortions, sexually transmitted diseases, rape, and prostitution (Kon 1995, 39-49).

"The sexual question" being politically important, the Soviet government in the 1920s sponsored some sociological, biomedical, and anthropological sex research, as well as elementary sex education. Yet, the elitist, individualistic, and "decadent" erotic art was absolutely incompatible with the new revolutionary mentality. Sexual pleasure was only a hindrance and distraction from the goals of the Socialist revolution. In the 1920s, a few liberal Communists, like Alexandra Kollontai, suggested "to make way for winged Eros," but that was against the mainstream.

Already in the 1920s, erotica was treated as morally and socially subversive. The only legitimate function of sexuality was reproduction. According to the influential party educator and sexologist, Aaron Zalkind, "sexual selection should proceed according to the line of a class revolutionary-proletarian consciousness. The elements of flirtation, courtship, and coquetry should not be introduced into love relationships" (1924). In the article on "Sexual Life" in the first edition of the *Great Soviet Encyclopedia* (1940), the emphasis is exclusively on social control: The dangers of "unhealthy sexual interest" are discussed, and the aim of sex education is clearly described as the "rational transmission of sex drive into the sphere of labor and cultural interests."

Another historical factor that has affected the sexuality of the Russian people is their rather prudish approach to nudity and bodily functions. Thirty years ago, there was controversy about wearing any kind of shorts in public, including at beach resorts. Now, walking shorts are no longer prohibited in the western regions. The attitudes of Muslims in the eastern republics are even stricter. Body exposure by Muslim women is still strictly forbidden, and violating the taboo can lead to severe punishment. In these regions, shorts even on men are considered indecent.

Bodily functions are not openly acknowledged in Russian culture. Direct reference to the need for a toilet is considered impolite. Russians will just quietly disappear from a meeting or social gathering, or, at most, will simply refer to their intention to walk in a particular direction. Even young people who are dating and know each other well often make up artificial explanations before excusing themselves to find a toilet.

An additional contributor to the avoidance of overt discussion of bodily functions may be the sorry state of the country's plumbing. Part of the general breakdown of material goods and services in Russian society following the 1991 revolution includes the public restroom facilities, which are no longer free and often broken or dirty. Washbasins may stand idle, or may yield only a dribble of cold water. Toilet tissue is scarce; its substitutes include newspaper, magazine pages, used office papers, and even cardboard.

Despite the attention to cleanliness paid by many citizens, the combination of bodily inhibitions and inadequate material resources have combined to threaten their overall health, making personal hygiene difficult. Even the interest in improving physical fitness through better diet and exercise is only beginning, despite a long history of purported government commitment.

The Russian ambivalence toward nakedness, bodily functions, intimate hygiene, and sexuality combined with a history of heavy censorship and the contemporary lack of material resources to make the impact of these factors on everyday life and sexuality even greater.

Sexual enjoyment and freedom have been incompatible with totalitarian state control over personality. As George Orwell put it in *1984*:

> It was not merely that the sex instinct created a world of its own that was outside the Party's control and which therefore had to be destroyed if possible. What was more important was that sexual [de]privation induced hysteria, which was desirable because it could be transformed into war-fever and leader-worship. . . . For how could the fear, the hatred, and the lunatic credulity which the Party needed in its members be kept at the right pitch, except by bottling up some powerful instinct and using it as a driving force? The sex impulse was dangerous to the Party, and the Party had turned it to account.

The history of the Soviet regime was one of sexual repression. Only the means of legitimation and phraseology of

this suppression was changeable. In the 1920s, sexuality had to be suppressed in the name of the higher interests of the working class and Socialist revolution. In the 1930s, self-discipline was advocated for the sake of the Soviet state and Communist Party. In the 1950s, state administrative control was gradually transformed into moral administrative regulations, this time for the sake of stability of marriage and the family. But with all these ideological differences, the practical message regarding sex remained the same: DON'T DO IT! The Communist image of sexuality was always negative, and the need for strict external social control was always emphasized. The elimination of sexuality was beyond the abilities of the Soviet regime. But the net result of this sexophobia was an extermination of all sorts of erotic culture and the prohibition of sexual discourse, whether in the area of sex research, erotic art, or medical information. No wonder that the breakdown of the Soviet regime in 1991, and even earlier with the advent of *glasnost*, sexuality became one of the most important symbols of social and cultural liberation.

## 3. Knowledge and Education about Sexuality

### A. Government Policies and Programs for Sex Education

As in the former U.S.S.R., Russia today still has virtually no systematic sex education, although some efforts have been made to develop school-based programs since the early 1980s. Table 1 shows the responses in a late-1989 national public opinion poll to the question, "What channels of information on sexual life do you believe are the most acceptable and efficient?"

Clearly, a majority of the Russian people favor organized sex education. But the Communist Soviet government did not want it, and the present Russian government has no money for anything. However, an experimental 12-hour sex-education course for adolescents, based on a program from the Netherlands, was to have begun in eight schools in 1995 (Kon 1995, 75-76, 95-100, 108-110, 117-118, 192-193).

[*Sex Education, Religion, the Clergy, and the Anti-Sex Education Crusade*

[*Update 2002*: Naturally, since the collapse of the central Communist government, the new sexual freedom has been used by communists, the clergy, and nationalists as a political scapegoat. The first phase of the clergy/communist coalition's antisexual crusade was an unsuccessful attack on pornography (described below in Section 8C, Significant Unconventional Sexual Behaviors).

[The second crusade aimed at sex education has been much more successful.

#### Table 1

#### Preferred Sources of Sexual Information (in Percentages)

| Source of Information | Percentage |
|---|---|
| Special school course | 46 |
| Special educational literature | 43 |
| Special educational films or TV | 29 |
| Conversation with a physician | 22 |
| Conversation with parents | 21 |
| Personal experience | 6 |
| Discussion with peers | 5 |
| No need for sex education | 3 |

[Systematic sex education is long overdue in Russia. It has been discussed in the mass media since 1962. An attempt to introduce a special course in the early 1980s was welcomed by parents, but failed because teachers were not ready to teach it.

[The idea that sex education can be done by parents themselves runs counter to all of the international experience (Rademakers 1997). In Russian families, intergenerational taboos on sexuality discourse are very strong. According to the National Center for Public Opinion Research (VTsIOM) representative national survey in 1990, only 13% of parents have ever talked to their children about sexual matters.

[According to our 1997 survey, today's students have much more information about sexuality at their disposal than did their parents. For their parents' cohort, the main source of information about sexuality was conversations with peers. Today, printed materials and electronic media are most important, and the main sources of knowledge of sexuality are newspapers, books, and magazines. However, this often means merely replacing one source of misinformation by another, 'virtual' one.

[Until 1997, Russian public opinion generally favored sex education. In all national public opinion polls conducted by VTsIOM since 1989, the vast majority of adults, between 60% and 90%, depending upon age and social background, strongly supported the idea of systematic sex education in schools. Only 3% to 20% were opposed to it (Kon 2001). But who will, in fact, undertake to do this work? And what exactly should be taught?

[Teachers thought that parents should provide sex education for their children. In our 1997 survey, 78% of the teachers agreed with this. However, this same survey showed that the family cannot take on this responsibility. Only about one out of five teenagers considered it acceptable to discuss problems of sexuality with his or her parents. Parents themselves only reluctantly initiate such topics of conversation with their children. More than half of them never initiated such talks, another quarter had taken the initiative only once or twice, and only one in five mothers had such conversations with their children several times—the fathers did not do so at all. The primary inhibiting factors were a lack of psychological and educational readiness. More than three quarters of the parents said they needed special books explaining what should be told to children and how this should be done. About two thirds of the parents think it would be useful to have seminars for parents about sex education in the schools their children attend.

[But the school is also incapable of doing this. Three quarters of the teachers were convinced that form teachers (persons who are primarily responsible for social and moral education) should discuss issues of gender and sexual relations with their students. However, 65% of the teachers reported never having done this, and another 15% had done so only once or twice. It is clear why this is the case: Only 11.5% of teachers feel that they are well prepared for this task. Eighty-five percent were in favor of special courses on the fundamentals of sexology in teachers' colleges.

[In general, respondents in the 1997 survey were unanimous that sex education courses in schools must be launched. It might be expected that such courses would become one of the favorite curriculum subjects for students. Sixty-one percent of 7th grade students and 73% of the 9th graders said that they were eager to attend such classes. Only 5% of students would prefer to avoid them. There were much more serious disagreements among the interested groups, however, with respect to the content of sex education. Teachers would like to offer a detailed treatment of anatomy, physiology, and ethics, whereas students are more interested in practical issues and in sexual pleasure (see Table 2).

[In 1996, at the request of the Russian Ministry of Education, the United Nations Population Fund (UNFPA) in collaboration with UNESCO awarded a three-year grant for experimental work in 16 selected schools to develop a workable curriculum and textbooks "for classes 7, 8 and 9, considering the importance of the fact that young people should be able to make informed and responsible decisions before reaching the age for potentially starting sexual activities." There was no cultural imperialism or any attempt to invent something uniform and compulsory for the entire country. The introduction to the project emphasized that "to ensure cultural acceptability, the curricula and textbooks will be developed by Russian experts, making use of knowledge and experience from other countries, and with the input of technical assistance from foreign experts."

[The "UNESCO project" was formally initiated in October 1996. Its first step was a sociological monitoring, an attempt to assess sexual values, attitudes, and information levels of children, parents, and teachers of a few pilot schools on a strictly voluntary basis. Similar monitoring was also planned for the next stages of the experiment. Unfortunately, without consulting the experts, Ministry of Education officials announced the commencement of this sensitive undertaking without any political and psychological preparation. Even worse, the Ministry sent to 30,000

## Table 2

**Students' Preferences Regarding Topics for a Course in Sex Education**
**(Those Who Indicated a Topic as 'Very Necessary,'**
**in Percentages, in the 1997 Survey)**

| Topic | Grade 7 | | Grade 8 | | Grade 9 | | Total | |
|---|---|---|---|---|---|---|---|---|
| | Male | Female | Male | Female | Male | Female | Male | Female |
| Psychology of gender relationships | 54.6 | 60.8 | 59.8 | 69.8 | 62.2 | 67.0 | 59.8 | 66.4 |
| Conception, prenatal development, and childbirth | 49.7 | 64.9 | 45.5 | 52.7 | 39.6 | 54.3 | 43.6 | 56.2 |
| Sexual orientation, homosexuality, etc. | 27.9 | 26.8 | 27.0 | 24.4 | 18.8 | 24.3 | 23.3 | 24.9 |
| Sexual techniques: how to receive more pleasure from sex | 44.3 | 32.5 | 55.7 | 41.5 | 59.9 | 43.5 | 55.2 | 40.4 |
| Sexual anatomy and physiology | 45.4 | 42.8 | 43.0 | 46.5 | 44.4 | 45.8 | 44.2 | 45.3 |
| Marriage and family life | 63.4 | 79.4 | 58.2 | 70.2 | 56.6 | 66.5 | 58.6 | 70.5 |
| Sexual hygiene | 58.5 | 59.8 | 53.7 | 52.3 | 55.6 | 50.0 | 55.7 | 52.9 |
| Methods of birth control | 47.5 | 63.4 | 51.6 | 67.4 | 62.2 | 69.3 | 55.8 | 67.4 |
| Sexual abuse and avoidance of sexual harassment | 50.3 | 72.2 | 47.5 | 74.8 | 51.0 | 76.8 | 49.8 | 75.1 |
| Prevention of sexually transmitted diseases and AIDS | 72.1 | 82.5 | 76.6 | 83.3 | 78.7 | 84.0 | 76.6 | 83.5 |
| Improvement of sexual health | 55.7 | 49.0 | 56.6 | 52.7 | 62.4 | 52.8 | 59.2 | 51.9 |

schools a package of five self-made, sloppily edited, and unrealistic—some of them of them required more than 300 class hours—"alternative" sex education programs. Although these programs had never been tested in the classrooms and had nothing to do with the UNESCO project, they were perceived to be part of it.

[Before it was even born, the project came under fire and was labeled as a "Western ideological plot against Russian children." An aggressive group of Pro-Life activists complained to the communist-dominated Parliament's National Security Committee. In some Moscow districts, people in the streets were asked: "Do you want children to be taught in school how to engage in sex? If not, please, sign this petition to ban this demonic project." Priests and activists told their audiences that all bad things in Western life were rooted in sex education, that Western governments are now trying to promote it, and that the corrupt Russian government, at the instigation of the "world sexological-industrial complex" was acting against the best interests of the country. All this was supported by pseudoscientific data and lies, such as, "In England, boys begin to masturbate at 9 years of age, and at 11 they are already completely impotent."

[At an important roundtable in the Russian Academy of Education on March 6, 1997, influential priests declared that Russia does not need any sex education whatever in the schools at all, because this had always been successfully done by the Church. Church authorities claimed that up to 80% of the time people spent in the sacrament of confession was dedicated to sexual matters. Some prominent members of the Academy also attacked the "Western" spirit. As Professor Khripkova put it, "We don't need the Netherlands' experience, we have our own traditional wisdom." The President of the Academy, Dr. Arthur Petrovsky, strongly dissociated himself from this nationalist position, as well as from the suggestions to reintroduce moral censorship. But the general decision was to freeze the UNESCO project, and instead of "sexuality education," to improve moral education "with some elements of sex education" (this opportunistic formula had been used in 1962). Prof. Dmitry Kolessov proclaimed that instead of children's "right to know," educators should defend their "right not to know" (*pravo na neznanie*).

[After lengthy debates, a special academic commission for the preparation of a new program was formed (in which I refused to take part), but the new, openly conservative project was equally unacceptable to the clergy, and nothing came of it. In the Academy's recent program statements on children, neither sexual health nor sex education is even mentioned. The Ministry of Education formally cancelled its previously approved programs. Now it is very dangerous for Russian school principals to introduce any elements of sex education, even at the local level on their own initiative.

[During the 1999 parliamentary elections, the Communist Party of the Russian Federation (CPRF) presented this "anti-sex education" campaign as its most important political victory. The official position of the Russian Orthodox Church, which is trying to put itself in the shoes of the former Agitprop, denounces any form of sex education. Any form of sex education is formally denounced by the Russian Orthodox Church. With the help of some prominent scientists, such as the President of the Russian Academy of Sciences, Dr. Yuri Ossipov, and the Rector of Moscow State University, Professor V. A. Sadovnichij, the Moscow Patriarchy is even attempting to introduce the teaching of theology into the state-owned secular universities, which is unconstitutional and opposed by liberal intellectuals.

[For some Russian newspapers, anything that smacks of sex education is like a red flag before a bull. Militant sexophobia is raging not only in the communist, fascist, and clerical mass media, but also in many liberal and official media outlets. One of their main targets is the Russian Planned Parenthood Association. Since 1991, this is the only organization that took action to reduce the rate of abortion and to promote sexual and contraceptive knowledge. Now, it is being denounced by Christian fundamentalists as a "satanic institution," propagating abortion and depopulation. The official slogan of RPPA, "The birth of healthy and wanted children, responsible parenthood" was presented in communist *Pravda* and in religious newspapers as *One Child Per Family*. The booklet *Your Friend the Condom*, published for young adults and teens, is described as if it were addressed to first-grade children.

[Since there is no sex education in Russian schools, or even in the universities, the antisexual crusaders created another target: so-called valeology (from Latin *valeo*, meaning good health). I do not know if such a discipline has ever been institutionalized anywhere in the West. Russian valeology looks like a hybrid of social hygiene and preventive medicine, with some strange and even exotic ideas. A serious criticism and discussion of it would certainly be of use. But, for the fundamentalists, any "science of health" which is not approved by the Church is anathema. Like their U.S. allies, they are absolutely indifferent to real issues of public health, social hygiene, and STD or HIV prevention. They claim that "valeology" is simply another name for "sex education," and violently attack it for being "Western, non-Orthodox and prosexual."

[Even the medical profession is split. In 1997, the Ministry of Health and the leading experts in gynecology, pediatrics, and other medical disciplines strongly supported the need for family planning, contraception, and sex education. But scholars and state officials are worried about their moral and political reputations. In January 1999, *Meditsintskaya Gazeta* (a professional newspaper for medical doctors) published an open letter to the Minister of Education, signed by 130 medical experts, clergymen, teachers, and writers, against valeology and sex education. The dominant values of its editor-in-chief, Andrei Poltorak, are clearly expressed in the title of his recent interview: "Honor the doctor . . . since it was God who created him" (Poltorak 2000).

[The antisexual crusade is openly nationalistic, xenophobic, sexist, misogynist, and homophobic. Everything Russian is presented as pure, spiritual, and moral, and everything Western as dirty and vile. Sex education is treated as the most serious attempt there is to undermine Russia's national security, more dangerous then HIV. In the 1980s, Soviet propaganda attributed HIV to the Pentagon.

[The deputy editor-in-chief of *Rossiiskaya Gazeta*, Victoria Molodtsova, quotes a phrase from an unnamed educational program stating that "to become a real man, the male must not only be brave and courageous, but also acquire some traditionally 'feminine' qualities . . .," such as sensitivity, compassion, and understanding. The journalist's commentary was: "A Vologda peasant male doesn't need feminization; the educators arguing for the 'feminization' of Russian males are really trying to promote homosexuality, and are being paid for their subversive activities by Western secret services."

[The crusade against sex education is extremely militant and aggressive. The clerical site (orthodoxy.ru) features the slogan: "Attention! Danger! Be prepared for the most energetic means of self-defense!" According to this site, the main dangers for Russian children and their parents are not abortions, HIV, or syphilis, but the International Planned Parenthood Federation (IPPF), which expresses the interests of the contraceptive industry and the United Nations Population Fund, which is interested in the depopulation of Russia so that the West can appropriate its natural resources. Parents are being taught how to sabotage any attempts to introduce sex education, even including taking their children out of the schools. They are told that condoms are inefficient against HIV or STDS and also against pregnancy.

[The Moscow Patriarchy published a special formal address to adolescents, formulated in words, which would be more appropriate for the General Staff or State Security than for a Christian Church:

> Children! The enemies of God, enemies of Russia for hundreds of years have tried to conquer our native land with the help of fire and the sword, but each time they were shamefully defeated and sent to their graves in the boundless fields of Russia. Now they have understood that it is impossible to conquer Russia by military force. . . . Now they want to annihilate our people with the help of depravity, pornography, drugs, tobacco and vodka—by the same means by which THEIR forefathers annihilated American Indians. (*Slovok Podrostkam* 2000)

Militant Orthodox fundamentalism is not limited to sex education. There is even a protest movement against the introduction of national social security code numbers (these codes are named INN, so the movement is called "INN jihad"—Muslim sacred war). Its radical wing claimed that "the idea of a compulsory INN code for the total outside control of the population of Russia was born as a result of joint actions of the US secret services, members of Satanist organizations and of international Zionist [Russian euphemism for Jewish] financial groups (Verkhovsky 2001).

As a consequence of recent changes in adolescent sexual behavior, similar to the Western sexual revolution of the 1960s but compounded by the breakdown of state medical services and the general criminalization of the country, there exist some dangerous trends in Russian sexual life. These include but are not limited to the spread of STDs and HIV. The only reasonable answer to this challenge is sex education. But since 1997, all efforts in this direction have been blocked by a powerful antisexual crusade, organized by the Russian Communist Party and Russian Orthodox Church, and supported by "Pro Life." Its main targets are sex education, women's reproductive rights, and freedom of sexuality-related information. Especially vicious attacks are aimed at homosexuals. The campaign is openly nationalistic and xenophobic. In the long run, it goes against the dominant values of the young generation, and also has disastrous public health consequences. (*End of update by I. S. Kon*)]

### B. Informal Sources of Sexual Knowledge

According to a 1992 national survey, only 13% of Russian parents talk with their children about sexuality. The main sources of sexual information for teenagers, therefore, are their peers and the mass media. For adults, some medical and psychological information services are available in the larger cities. Several popular Western books have been translated, and a few have been written by Russian authors after 1987. Sexual issues are now often discussed on television and in the newspapers. But there is neither strategy nor money to do this effectively. The main source of sexual knowledge for many people are pornographic magazines and erotic newspapers. The monthly newspaper *SPID-info* (AIDS-information) has the second-largest print run in the country, 4.5 million. It says little about AIDS, but gives popular information about sexuality and erotic topics.

## 4. Autoerotic Behaviors and Patterns

Children and adolescents normally have their first sexual experience through self-pleasuring. Boys generally start to engage in self-pleasuring at the age of 12 or 13, reaching a peak at age 15 to 16. Girls begin to self-pleasure at a later age and do it less frequently. According to a 1982 survey by V. V. Danilov, 22.5% of the girls had engaged in self-pleasuring by age 13.5, 37.4% by age 15.5, 50.2% by age 17.5, and 65.8% by age 18.5.

Until the late 1970s, official attitudes to self-pleasuring were completely negative. Children were told that it results in impotence, deterioration of the memory, and similar harmful consequences. As an antidote, there was a clandestine teen ditty: "Sun, fresh air, and onanism reinforce the organism." Nevertheless, many Russian teens and adults still have strong anxieties regarding it. Many sexual dysfunctions are attributed to self-pleasuring experiences, and adults are terribly ashamed of it (Kon 1995, 43-44, 189-199).

## 5. Interpersonal Heterosexual Behaviors

### A/B. Children and Adolescents

*Puberty*

The overall trends in the psychosexual development of Russian children and adolescents are the same as in Western countries. Above all, there has been a substantial acceleration of sexual maturation. The average menarche age fell from 15.1 years to 13 among Muscovite girls over a period of 35 years, from 1935 to 1970. Similar trends are also typical for the boys.

Sexual maturation confronts the teenager with a host of bodily and psychosexual problems. Many boys are worried about delay in emergence of their secondary sexual attributes in relation to their peers—shortness of height or of the penis, gynecomastia (transitory female-breast development), and so on. Girls are concerned about hirsuteness, being overweight, the shape of their breasts, and so on (Kon 1995, 194-209).

*Premarital Sexual Activities and Relationships*

There is clear evidence that sexual activity is beginning earlier for today's Russian adolescents than in past generations. The mean age for first coitus dropped in the last ten years from 19.2 to 18.4 for males, and from 21.8 to 20.6 for females. According to the only survey of teenagers ages 12 to 17 (Chervyakov, Kon, & Shapiro 1993), sexual experience was reported by 15% of the girls and by 22% of the boys. Among 16- to 17-year-olds, 36% were sexually experienced; among 14- to 15-year-olds, 13%; and under 14 years, only 2%. Boys are generally more sexually experienced than girls, but the difference gradually disappears with age. Just as it was in the West in the late 1960s, early sexual experience is related to some form of deviant or counter-normative behavior: drinking, smoking, drug use, lower academic grades, poor school discipline, and closer association with peer group. Psychologically, sexually active 16-year-olds are more prone to be involved in different sorts of risky behavior, and some of them are from socially underprivileged families (Kon 1995, 62-63, 166-169).

The largest percentage of young people become sexually active between ages 16 and 18, with the incidence of intercourse reported in various studies ranging from 22 to 38% of the boys and 11 to 35% of the girls. "Love" is reported by many young people to be the primary motivator for sexual activity, about 30% of males and 45% of females. "Desire for enjoyment" or "pleasure" are reported by 20% of males and 10% of females. Many young people separate sexual motives from those involving marriage and engagement.

[*The Sexual Revolution and Russia's Young Adults*

[*Update 2002*: In the former Soviet Union, sexuality was a taboo, almost nonexistent topic. After 1987, the taboo was broken and sex became a fashionable subject for both private and public discourse (Kon 1995, 1997ab, 1999ab). Despite the official silence, general trends in Russian sexual behavior have been similar to those in Western countries.

[According to our 1993, 1995, and 1997 surveys (the first of which took place in 1993 with 1,615 secondary school and vocational school students aged 12 to 17 in Moscow and St. Petersburg), the sexual behaviors and attitudes of urban adolescents are changing rapidly (Chervyakov & Kon 1998, 2000; Kon 2001). In 1993, 25% of 16-year-old girls and 38% of boys had coital experience; in 1995, the respective figures were already 33% and 50%. Among 17-year-olds, the respective increase is from 46% to 52% (for females) and from 49% to 57% (for males) (see Table 3). Similar overall changes took place both in secondary and in vocational schools (see Table 4).

[Similar overall changes occurred in both the secondary and vocational schools. This suggests that changes in the age of sexual debut cannot be treated as an artifact caused by changes in the sample design. We found further evidence of a dramatic change in sexual behavior between 1993 and 1995 when we analyzed answers to the question about age at first intercourse independently for different age groups within one and the same sample (survey of 1995). Among 16-year-old women, there were twice as many sexually experienced girls than among the 19-year-old respondents when they were 16 (23% vs. 11%). The same difference was found between the 17-year-old and 19-year-old women who were sexually experienced at 17 (45% vs. 24%, respectively). The same tendencies were observed among male students, although the changes were not as large.

[The absolute figures are not surprising and are quite comparable to the U.S. and West European data. But in Russia, the change is occurring very rapidly, and adolescent sexuality, which is strongly related to social class, is often violent and aggressive. Uncivilized and uncontrollable early sexual activity has serious moral and epidemiological consequences.

[Thanks to medical efforts, the abortion rate has declined in recent years. According to official figures, in 1990, women aged 15 to 49 reported having 114 abortions per 1,000 women; in 1992, 98 abortions, and in 1995, 74 abortions. Yet the figure is still very high. Child prostitution and sexual violence are flourishing. For about 10% of teenage girls, their first sexual initiation is associated with some degree of coercion. (*End of update by I. S. Kon*)]

## C. Adults

### Premarital Courtship, Dating, and Relationships

The overall trend is towards a reduction in age and a rise in moral toleration of premarital sex and cohabitation. Among the university students surveyed by Golod in the 1978-1979 academic year, four out of every five men and every second woman had had sexual experience by the time they were surveyed. A total of 3,741 students from 18 colleges and universities were asked why they thought young men and women entered into sexual relations nowadays. The responses are shown in Table 5 (Golod 1984).

[*Update 2002*: The liberalization of Soviet sexual morality began long before *perestroika*, back in the 1960s and 1970s (Bocharova 1994; Kon 1997a; Haavio-Mannila & Rotkirch 1997). According to Sergey Golod's surveys in Leningrad-St.Petersburg, in 1965, only 5.3% of sexually experienced university students reported having first had intercourse before the age of 16; in 1972, this figure was 8%, and in 1995, it had risen to 12% (see Table 6) (Golod 1996, 59).

[The breakdown of the Soviet regime brought the Russian people their long-desired sexual liberation. But, as was also the case with the economy and politics, sexual freedom was immediately transformed into anomie and anarchy, and became a controversial symbol of social and personal liberation and the object of political speculation. By the 1980s, there were two poles: conservative traditionalists, nationalists, and communists, which blended together sexophobia,

### Table 3

**Proportion of Sexually Active Respondents by Age and Gender, 1993 and 1995 Surveys (in Percent)**

| Survey | 12 | 13 | 14 | 15 | 16 | 17 | 18 | 19 |
|---|---|---|---|---|---|---|---|---|
| Male | | | | | | | | |
| 1993 | 2.3 | 4.1 | 11.4 | 17 | 38.2 | 49.3 | — | — |
| 1995 | — | — | — | — | 50.5 | 57.1 | 69.8 | 77.5 |
| Female | | | | | | | | |
| 1993 | 0 | 1.8 | 3.7 | 11.8 | 25.5 | 45.8 | — | — |
| 1995 | — | — | — | — | 33.3 | 52.4 | 50.8 | 54.8 |

### Table 4

**Proportion of Sexually Experienced Secondary School and Vocational School Students, by Age and Gender, 1993 and 1995 Survey Samples (in Percent)**

| | Secondary School | | Vocational School | |
|---|---|---|---|---|
| Survey Year | 16-Year-Olds | 17-Year-Olds | 16-Year-Olds | 17-Year-Olds |
| Male | | | | |
| 1993 | 35.7 | 42.9 | 41.2 | 55.9 |
| 1995 | 44.1 | 44.1 | 62.7 | 71.9 |
| Female | | | | |
| 1993 | 16.4 | 29.0 | 39.3 | 58.5 |
| 1995 | 23.9 | 40.3 | 46.0 | 60.8 |

### Table 5

**Motivations for Sexual Relationships (in Percentages)**

| Motives | Men ($N = 1,829$) | Women ($N = 1,892$) |
|---|---|---|
| Mutual love | 28.8 | 46.1 |
| Enjoyable pursuit | 20.2 | 11.4 |
| Desire to obtain pleasure | 18.1 | 9.2 |
| Desire for emotional contact | 10.6 | 7.7 |
| Intended marriage | 6.6 | 9.4 |
| Self-affirmation | 5.5 | 3.6 |
| Prestige, fashion | 4.1 | 4.8 |
| Curiosity | 4.9 | 5.6 |
| Extending sense of freedom, independence | 1.8 | 2.2 |

### Table 6

**Age of the Sexual Debut of the Leningrad/ St. Petersburg University Students (Percent of Those Who Have Had Sexual Experience)**

| | Year of Survey | | |
|---|---|---|---|
| Age | 1965 | 1972 | 1995 |
| Younger than 16 | 5.3 | 8.2 | 12.2 |
| 16-18 | 33.0 | 30.8 | 52.8 |
| 19-21 | 39.5 | 43.8 | 30.7 |
| 22-24 | 19.5 | 16.0 | 3.2 |
| Later | 2.7 | 1.2 | 1.1 |

(from Serguei Golod's surveys)

homophobia, anti-Semitism, and anti-Americanism, on the one hand, and liberal "Westerners" on the other side.

[The first and undeniable achievement of the current Russian sexual revolution is that sexuality has become visible. It is openly discussed and represented in the mass media and advertising. A lot of erotic publications are available. Sexuality is recognized as an important element in culture and individual life. Questions about sexual attitudes and behaviors are included in national public opinion polls. People have become much more outspoken about sexual issues. Sexual tolerance is growing. After a long debate, homosexuality was decriminalized in 1993. Despite high levels of homophobia, same-sex love is no longer a taboo topic, and public tolerance, as reflected in the polls, is growing, especially among younger, better-educated, and urban people. Several voluntary associations for the promotion of sexual knowledge and safe-sex practices, including a Russian Planned Parenthood Association and a few local centers for sex education, have been formed (with Western financial help).

[At the same time, sexual liberation entails many difficult social problems. Contemporary Russian sexual culture is completely commercialized, and this is highly frustrating for parents, teachers, and intellectuals.

[There is also tension between the processes of liberalization and gender equality in sexual values and practices. "In Russia, liberalization began during the Soviet Union and was speeded up by the free press and the commercialization of the 1980s and 1990s. In the Nordic countries, liberalization reached its height in the 1970s. Today, liberalism and permissiveness are sometimes questioned from the perspective of gender equality and/or a new morality. In Russia, on the contrary, liberalism has undermined the arguments for gender equality from the Soviet era" (Haavio-Mannila & Rotkirch 2001, 13). (*End of update by I. S. Kon*)]

It is clear from these data that certain gender differences still persist in sexual behavior and motivation; men are more likely than women to justify sex merely for pleasure and to engage in premarital sex, not only with the beloved one, but also with some occasional partners. And, in fact, the men do have more sexual partners than the women (Kon 1995, 158-177).

*Marriage and the Family*

As in the West, individualization and intimization of the marital relationship have been taking place in Russia over recent decades. Sexual harmony is playing an increasingly important role here. According to Golod's (1984) surveys, sexual harmony invariably takes third place among factors contributing to perceived marital success and stability, after spiritual and psychological compatibility among spouses who have been married for up to 10 years, and after spiritual and domestic compatibility for those who have been living together for between 10 and 15 years. Sexual satisfaction and general satisfaction with the marriage are closely interrelated. Practically all couples maximally satisfied with their marriages believed they were sexually compatible, while only 63% were sexually compatible among the maritally dissatisfied (Kon 1995, 158-177).

Gender inequality and sexism manifest themselves in the marital bed as well (Kon 1995, 129-157). The natural and widespread disharmony of sexual-erotic needs and desires between wives and husbands, which should be the subject of exploration and discussion, is often seen by Russian spouses and those about them as a manifestation of an ineradicable organic sexual incompatibility; the only way out is divorce. Even in the professional literature, this problem is often discussed not in process terms—how the spouses adapt and grow accustomed to each other—but in

essentialist terms—whether spouses and their individual traits are compatible to each other.

The woman is almost always the first to suffer from poor sexual adaptation. The lack of a common language and the sexological ignorance create a mass of communication difficulties among married couples. Instead of exploring their problems together or going to a doctor, the spouses run off to their same-sex friends.

Another major problem is the lack of privacy, the shortage of housing, and poor housing conditions. Millions of Russians spend many years, or their whole lifetime, living in dormitories or communal flats, sometimes several families in one room, where every movement is seen or heard by others. Among 140 Soviet immigrants living in the U.S.A. asked by Mark Popovsky in 1984, "What hindered your sexual life in the Soviet Union?" the absence of a separate apartment was mentioned by 126 (90%), the absence of a separate bedroom by 122 (87%), and the excessive attention from the neighbors living in the same apartment by 93 respondents (66%). The lack of privacy is an even worse problem for nonmarital sex. "Where?" is the desperately important and difficult question to answer. Lack of privacy is detrimental for the quality of the sexual experience and produces anxieties and neuroses.

The divorce rate is very high; approximately one marriage of three ends in divorce. More than half of all divorces are initiated by the wife.

Cohabitation is more and more widespread among younger couples. Sometimes, it is a first stage of marriage, until children are born, and sometimes an alternative form of marriage. Public opinion, especially among younger people, is gradually becoming more and more tolerant of cohabitation.

Extramarital sex, both casual and long-term, is quite common; according to S. Golod (1984), more than three quarters of the people surveyed had extramarital contacts in 1989, whereas in 1969, the figure was less than half. But public opinion is critical of extramarital sex. In the VTsIOM 1992 survey directed by Professor Yurt Levada (Kon 1995, 275), only 23% agreed that it is okay to have a lover as well as a husband or wife, while 50% disagreed. Extramarital affairs seem to be morally more acceptable for men than for women (Kon 1995, 21, 45, 63, 166-167).

*Sexuality and the Physically Disabled and Aged*

Because of poverty and poor medical services, the sexuality of the physically disabled and the aged person has not so far attracted professional or public attention. Nothing is done to help these people.

*Incidence of Oral and Anal Sex*

Younger and better educated Russians often complain about the poverty of their sexual techniques. Anal and oral sex are legal and quite widespread, though some people believe these behaviors are sexual perversions. In some legal documents, both anal and oral sex are referred to as unnatural forms of sexual satisfaction.

## 6. Homoerotic, Homosexual, and Bisexual Behaviors

Although the Russian Orthodox Church has always severely condemned sodomy and other forms of male and female homosexuality—especially when it threatened the monasteries—the state tended to turn a blind eye to such things in everyday life. In 16th- and 17th-century Russia, homosexuality was not an unmentionable subject; it was, in fact, often the subject of very frank discussion and ribald jokes.

The first state laws against *muzhelozhstve* (male lechery, buggery) appeared in military statutes drawn up on the

Swedish model during the 18th-century reign of Peter the Great. The initial punishment of burning at the stake was changed to corporal punishment. The criminal code of 1832 based on the German model punished sodomy (buggery) with deprivation of all rights and exile to Siberia for four to five years. New criminal legislation adopted in 1903 reduced punishment to incarceration for no less than three months or, in aggravating circumstances, to three to eight years.

This legislation, however, was employed extremely rarely. Many Russian aristocrats, including members of the imperial family, as well as eminent artistic figures of the turn of the century openly led homosexual or bisexual lifestyles. A few lesbian couples were also quite well known at the time. Homoerotic poetry, literature, and painting began to appear. Same-sex love began to be debated seriously and sympathetically in philosophical, scientific, and artistic literature.

After the February 1917 Revolution and the demise of the old criminal code, the legal persecution of homosexuals ceased. In the Soviet Russian Criminal Codes of 1922 and 1926, homosexuality is not referred to at all, but in those parts of the old Russian Empire where it was most widespread—the Islamic republics of Azerbaijan, Turkmenia, and Uzbekistan, as well as in Christian Georgia—the legislation remained in force. In the 1920s, homosexuality was treated as a sickness rather than a crime.

Up to the 1930s, the situation of Soviet homosexuals, who frequently called themselves "blues," was reasonably bearable and many played a prominent part in Soviet culture. However, the opportunity for an open, philosophical and artistic discussion of the theme, which began at the turn of the century, gradually diminished.

In 1933, male homosexuality (*muzhelozhstve*) again became a criminal offense and literally an unmentionable, even in scientific literature, vice in the U.S.S.R. Conviction of this crime was punishable by deprivation of freedom for up to five years, or up to eight years if compulsion, violence, a minor, or abuse of a dependent was involved. This law (Article 121 of the RSFS Criminal Code) was frequently used up until the 1980s against dissidents and to extend terms in labor camps. Application of the law has always been selective. As long as they did not fall foul of the authorities, certain homosexual cultural and artistic celebrities enjoyed relative immunity. If they overstepped the mark, however, the law descended upon them with a vengeance.

Gay men in confinement have to endure absolutely unbearable conditions. A person who ended up in prison or labor camp under Article 121 usually became straightaway a "no-rights odd-bod" and recipient of constant taunts and persecution from other prisoners. Further, the rape of adolescents and young men is widespread in both prisons and labor camps; after such assaults, the victims forfeit all human rights, become "degraded," and have to act submissively to their violators. The status of the "degraded" is even worse than that of voluntarily passive homosexuals, who, to a certain degree, select their own partners and protectors (who perform an active, "male" sexual role that is not stigmatized and is even encouraged). The "degraded," on the other hand, are fair game for anyone. (Some Russian medical experts still make a "fundamental" division of homosexuals into "active" and "passive," depending on preferred sexual positions; moreover, they associate "passive" with "inborn" and "genuine," and "active" with "acquired" homosexuality.)

In the 1980s, the AIDS epidemic worsened matters for homosexuals. When AIDS arrived in the U.S.S.R., health officials referred to morality and risk groups, especially gays, portraying them as carriers, not only of the dreaded virus, but of just about every other vice. This hypocritical moralizing and the search for scapegoats instead of a real

sociohygienic policy helped to increase HIV infection already at a high level because of contaminated blood transfusions for hemophiliacs.

While the possibility of decriminalization of homosexuality has been debated by lawyers since 1973, these arguments have been secret and did not spill over into the newspapers until 1987. Since 1987, the popular press, particularly youth papers, radio, and TV, have discussed homosexuality: What is it? How should one relate to "blues"? Should they be treated as sick, criminal, or as victims of fate? From journalistic articles and letters from gay men and lesbians and their parents, ordinary Soviet people have, for the first time, come to recognize the scarred destinies, the police cruelty, the legal repression, the sexual violence in prison, labor camps, and armed forces and, finally, the tragic, inescapable loneliness experienced by people living in constant fear and unable to meet any of their own sort. Each publication has provoked a whole stream of contradictory responses that the newspaper editors have just not known how to handle.

After the breakup of the Soviet Union, some republics, beginning with Ukraine, Estonia, Latvia, Moldova, and Armenia, revoked their antihomosexual legislation. On April 29, 1993, Russian President Boris Yeltsin signed, and lawmakers approved, a decree repealing Article 121.1 dealing with consenting adult relations. Article 121.2 regarding minors and force remains in effect. The repeal did not address gay women since lesbianism was not acknowledged by previous Soviet governments (Kon 1995, 239-264). A new 1997 criminal code may well restore the former repression of gays.

Nevertheless, homosexuals remain the most hated and stigmatized social minority. In the VTsIOM 1992 survey directed by Levada (Kon 1995, 275), the question "How ought we to act with homosexuals?" produced the following spread of answers: 33% favored exterminating homosexuals, 30% favored isolating them from society, and 10% said leave them alone. Only 6% favored helping homosexuals.

The Communist, chauvinist, and fascist media methodically and consistently lumps together Zionism, democracy, and homosexuality. With few exceptions, Russian sexopathologists and psychiatrists still regard homosexuality as a disease, and repeat in their writings the negative stereotypes prevalent in the mass consciousness. Thus, parents are likely to be both worried and defensive when they confront behavior in one of their children that might lead to questions about homosexuality. If an adolescent appears to have a "crush" on a classmate or peer of the same gender, his or her parents may consult a physician or psychiatrist who is almost certain to discourage it directly, or attempt to eradicate the feelings and prevent any erotic activity.

Most gay and lesbian adults attempt to keep their orientation a secret from family, friends, and colleagues in the workplace. The risks of public scandal and humiliation, loss of a job, and other complications are too great. Gay men and lesbian women are often physically assaulted in the streets, beaten, and even murdered.

Nevertheless, the situation is rapidly changing. By 1989, after public discussions of homosexuality began in the mass media, on television and radio, sometimes quite sympathetic, gays and lesbians themselves initiated a struggle against discrimination. In 1990, the first openly gay and lesbian organization was formed in Moscow. As of mid-1994, there were several such organizations. In 1993, the National Union of Gays, Lesbians, and Bisexuals was formed. Gay activists take part in the AIDS-prevention work. Gay themes are now represented in the theater and movies. Several legally registered gay and lesbian newspapers (*Tema, Risk, 1/10*, and others) are published. In Moscow and St. Petersburg, there are gay discos, bars, and restaurants. Special consulting services are being organized. But all these effects suffer from the shortage of both money and professional personnel, as well as the lack of internal cooperation. Political activists quarrel among themselves and have little influence in the mainstream culture and mass media.

[*Update 2002*: In April 2002, the People's Deputy bloc introduced legislation that would reinstate an old Soviet law that provided for prison terms for gay and lesbian sex. A phone-in poll (2,813 calls recorded in a five-minute period) by Moscow's Ekho Moskvy radio station found most people divided on the idea, with 53% of those polled opposed to the People's Deputy proposal; 47% said that homosexual acts should be illegal.

[Oleg Mironov, a Russian human rights commissioner, called the proposal to return to Soviet sexuality laws "ridiculous. The Criminal Code does in fact contain criminal provisions for homosexual acts, where they constitute rape or they involve a minor and adult. However, I do not think that we should return to the old Criminal Code in which voluntary relations of this type were punishable in law." However, Mironov did support raising the age of consent for homosexual relations to 16 rather than its current 14 years. At the moment, it is legal to have such relations if a person is 14 years old.

[The new antisexual crusade is extremely homophobic. Despite the decriminalization of homosexuality in 1993 and its formal "depathologization" in 1999, some leading Russian psychiatrists still believe that homosexuality is an illness (Tkachenko 1999, 355). (*End of update by I. S. Kon*)]

## 7. Gender Diversity and Transgender Issues

Among the native populations of Siberia and the Far East regions of Russia, the tradition of the *berdach*, a spiritual leader who is neither male nor female but a third gender, was widespread in the beginning of the 20th century as an aspect of shaman behavior. The present situation of this custom is unknown.

In 1960, Professor Aron Belkin began biomedical (psychoendocrinological) research on transgenderists and transsexuals. However, the psychological and social factors of gender dysphoria are largely ignored. An Association of Transsexuals was formed in 1992 in Moscow to work for the human rights of transsexuals.

## 8. Significant Unconventional Sexual Behaviors

### A. Coercive Sex

*Child Sexual Abuse, Incest, and Pedophilia*

Reports of child sexual abuse were extremely uncommon in the Soviet press. Officially, incest did not exist as a societal problem. Indeed, any kind of child abuse and violence in the family—and it is very widespread—is only beginning to come to the attention of authorities and the professional community (Kon 1995, 215-218).

Some health professionals and others have begun to uncover evidence of various kinds of sexual activity between adults and children, as well as between children of different ages in orphanages, youth camps, and even families. The data on sexual harassment, child abuse, and violence in Moscow and St. Petersburg are largely anecdotal and unreliable, but the problem is serious. In the 1993 adolescent sexuality survey conducted by Vladimir Shapiro and Valery Chervyakov of 1,615 students aged 12 to 17 years in Moscow and St. Petersburg, 24% of the teenage girls and 11% of the boys said they had experienced some sort of sexual pressure, someone pushing them to go further sexually than they themselves wanted to go. Six percent of those under the age of 14 years reported such pressure, as did more than 27% of the 16- to 17-year-olds. Sometimes the perpetrators are older youths, sometimes parents and other adults. Professional medical and psychological help for the victims is at its very beginnings (Kon 1995, 276).

[*Update 1997*: While sexism was admittedly common during the Communist regime, sexual harassment, defined as a boss demanding sexual favors from subordinates, was a crime; it was a seldom-prosecuted offense. The current lack of laws protecting employees from exploitation and harassment, coupled with the heady sense of permissiveness fed by pornographic videos, sexy advertising, nightclubs, casinos, beauty contests (Waters 1993), nude pinups, and open prostitution, have raised the level of sexual harassment to epidemic proportions, according to aggravated feminists. Some male observers counter that women simply view their bodies as a way of furthering their careers, while most Russian men, including husbands, dismiss the issue of sexual harassment as yet another silly Western hang-up. Most employers stress youth and sex appeal in advertising for office help; some include as a prerequisite *bez kompleksov* or "without inhibitions" in their advertisements. Despite a few attempts to battle sexual harassment and initiate lawsuits in 1994, an unemployment rate for women three times higher than for men, and a decline in their wages from 75% of male salaries in 1991 to 40% in 1997 have provided fertile ground for sexual harassment (Stanley 1994). (*End of update by R. T. Francoeur*)]

*Rape*

The number of rapes and attempted rapes is growing very fast. Since 1961, the increase in reported assaults has been 60%; since 1986, the increase has been 21.3% (Kon 1995, 207-222).

Most recorded rapes occur on the street or are gang rapes. Most date and marital rapes are not recorded in criminal statistics and remain unpunished. Of 333 persons who applied in 1992 to the St. Petersburg Helping Center for rape victims, only four also reported the crime to the police. The reasons for this unwillingness have been fear of the psychological trauma of investigation and trial; fear of information being spread in school and among acquaintances; doubts about the possibility of legal help; and fear of personal safety. All of these fears and doubts are quite justified. Even when the victims are children, the police are often unwilling to open a criminal investigation or even to initiate a medical examination.

According to criminal statistics—and these are unreliable—male youths between ages 14 and 17 commit 30% of all reported rapes; 37% of perpetrators are between ages 18 and 24; 19% between 25 and 29, and 15% over age 30. Two thirds of rapists are under age 22, with the most dangerous age being 16 to 17. Every fourth reported rape is a group or gang rape. The younger the rapists, the more often their assaults are carried out in a group. Some 40% of rapists have previous criminal records, and two thirds had been drinking prior to the attack.

The global socioeconomic, political, and spiritual crisis that Russia is now experiencing invariably causes a rise in violence and crime. Sexual violence is just one of its aspects, closely related also to the sexist psychology and cult of aggressive masculinity.

The psychological profiles of rapists are very similar to those provided by Western researchers. Sixty-one percent of convicted rapists are psychologically normal, but they perceive women as hostile, aggressive, and dominating figures towards whom they experience an unwanted sense of passivity and dependence. Sexual aggression and rape are often a manifestation of "adolescent rebellion" against women in general.

Much of the male rape that occurs in correctional institutions is carried on to establish and maintain a social hierarchy. Coercive sexual activity is also widespread in the military, at schools, and in the arts.

At this time, Russian society is not equipped materially or attitudinally to confront these problems in a creative manner. Many Russian citizens simply lament the liberalization of traditional morality and blame the influence of "Western capitalism" and pornography. The current state of the Russian economy precludes economic or technical support for remedial services or preventive programs. The very first telephone "hotline" service for rape victims was established in 1992 in St. Petersburg. Specialized professional help focusing on sexuality is largely unavailable for sex offenders. The first registered rape recovery center and a crisis hotline for abused women opened in Moscow in 1994.

### B. Prostitution

Until 1987, the existence of prostitution in the U.S.S.R. was often publicly denied. Now, it is one of the most popular professions. It is highly stratified, beginning with those working exclusively with foreigners for hard currency, and ending at the very bottom of social life. Some prostitutes are professionals. For others, it means additional income for a family budget. Male prostitution is increasing. Prostitution is closely linked with organized crime. [*Update 1997*: Entrepreneurs have been quick to take advantage of the economic plight of young women in the former U.S.S.R., recruiting them to service the sexual needs and fantasies of middle- and upper-class males in some of the relatively affluent Middle Eastern countries. See parallel discussion in the chapter on Ukraine. (*End of update by R. T. Francoeur*)]

The legal status of prostitutes is unclear. Attempts to fight it with administrative measures have failed, but at least now, the issue can be discussed (Kon 1995, 42-43, 62-64, 222-229).

### C. Pornography and Erotica

Stalinist sexophobia had practically exterminated all Russian erotic art. Now there are two trends: 1. the revival of genuine erotic art and literature, including translations of classical novels of D. H. Lawrence, Vladimir Nabokov, Henry Miller, and others, old Chinese and Hindu treatises, and erotic films from the West, and 2. a torrent of pornographic and semipornographic books, films, and videos. All of this is very new and unusual for the Russian people (Kon 1995, 113-116).

In the spring of 1991, the Communist Party tried to use this situation for its own political purposes, initiating a big antipornography crusade. In whipping up a moral panic in the country, the Communist Party pursued very clear political goals. The antipornography campaign was used to divert popular attention from the pressing political issues and to blunt awareness of the government's economic failures. In flagging its defense of morality and the family, the Party was deflecting blame from itself for the weakening and destruction of both morals and the family. On that basis, the Party leaders were able to cement the developing alliance between the Party and conservative organizations, including the Russian Orthodox Church and blatantly fascist groups. Antipornography slogans have been used by the Party to direct popular fury and frenzy against *glasnost* that was so hated by the Party *apparatchiks*, by branding the democratic mass media as being part of a Jewish-Masonic conspiracy intended to corrupt the morals of young people, destroy traditional values, and so on. Under the pretext of concern for young people, the Party was endeavoring to restore its lost control over them.

However, the campaign failed when the people did not swallow the bait (see Kon 1995, 1997a). Public opinion polls show that the majority of Russians do not like pornography, but are positive about erotica. But to differentiate between the two is difficult, and there is a deep generation gap on this issue. Purely repressive police measures taken by some local authorities are ineffective. Instead of the former taboos on sexuality, it is now vulgarized, commercialized, and Americanized. The current Russian government is trying to bring the situation under control, but without much success.

## 9. Contraception, Abortion, and Population Planning

### A. Contraception

One of the most disturbing consequences of the lack of sexual culture in Soviet society has been the exceedingly limited contraception culture, as a result of which induced abortion was, and remains today, the major method of birth control and family planning (Kon 1995, 61-62, 178-193).

Already in the early part of the 20th century, Russian doctors officially recognized that the development of effective contraceptive methods was the only alternative to induced abortion with all its dangerous consequences. Soviet medicine also understood this. In 1920, induced abortion was legalized. Until the end of the 1920s, the U.S.S.R. was a leading world country in its family policies.

Nevertheless, in 1936, induced abortion was banned and no other means of birth control introduced. After the ban was lifted in 1955, induced abortion remained the principal form of birth control.

According to Andrei Popov (1992), Soviet family planning was distinguished by the following general traits right up to 1988:

- Although the right to family planning was formally proclaimed *de jure* in accordance with international conventions, this right was never *de facto* realized;
- Services were inaccessible or nonexistent owing to a total lack of information, an absence of qualified personnel and specialized medical services, and the unavailability of modern contraceptives;
- The only easily accessible method of family planning was and continues to be induced abortion; and
- Family planning behavior varies widely by region, according to the ethnographic, demographic, and socioeconomic realities within each region.

Without the necessary scientific information, modern contraceptives, and the ability to use them, the Soviet public was doomed to employ traditional and largely ineffective methods (see Table 7).

Until 1987, the Soviet Ministry of Health conducted a major propaganda campaign against oral contraceptives. Most Soviet citizens are relatively ignorant about the more sophisticated forms of contraception.

Since 1987, the negative consequences of this situation have begun to be officially acknowledged, highlighting two obvious problems: the material shortage of modern hormonal, chemical, and barrier contraceptives, and the lack of information and psychological sophistication regarding sexual and reproductive practices.

In 1993, experts of the World Health Organization (WHO) found that both physicians and women in St. Petersburg were convinced that hormonal pills are terribly dangerous. And only 11% of Russian gynecologists recognized the right of teenagers to confidentiality, a condition *sine qua non* of the effective contraceptive services for teenagers.

The government survey in 1990 demonstrated that 30.5% of all girls under age 15 had no knowledge whatsoever about contraception. In the 16- to 17-year-old age group, this percentage was 24.6, and among 18 to 23 year olds, 11%. Over 96% of 16- to 17-year-old girls never used any contraceptives. Most teenage sex—and their sexual activity is growing—still goes unprotected.

## B. Teenage Unmarried Pregnancies

As a consequence of the lack of contraceptives, the number of unplanned pregnancies and unwanted births is growing, despite the prevalence of abortion. According to national statistics, the rate of extramarital births was about 10% in 1987; in 1992, it was 17%. The rates are even higher in the largest cities. The rate of premarital conception of firstborn children among married couples in Leningrad rose from 27% in 1963 to 38% in 1978. Similarly, one study in the early 1980s found that, of 1,000 first pregnancies reported in a large Russian city, 272 were aborted, 140 births occurred out of wedlock, and 271 births took place in the first months of marriage—leaving only 317 children actually conceived within marriage (Kon 1995, 169, 181-182).

[*Update 2002*: As a consequence, in 1989, Russia was a world champion as far as unwanted pregnancies and induced abortions were concerned. Thanks to efforts by medical personnel, the abortion rate has declined in recent years. According to official figures, in 1990, women aged 15 to 49 reported having 114 abortions per 1,000 women, compared with 98 in 1992 and 74 in 1995. Despite the significant decrease, the figure is still very high. Child prostitution and sexual violence are flourishing. For about 10% of teenage girls, their first sexual initiation is associated with some degree of coercion. No more than 5% to 7% of rapes are formally reported, and even these cases are often ignored. (*End of update by I. S. Kon*)]

## C. Abortion

The total annual number of abortions in the late 1980s, according to official data, amounted to 6 to 7 million. That was virtually a fifth or even a fourth of all abortions performed in the world. The number of "backstreet abortions" was estimated at 12% of the total, according to official estimates, but at 50% to 70% according to independent experts. Thus, the aggregate number of abortions in the U.S.S.R. came to 10 to 11 million a year. Even without these adjustments, the number of abortions per 1,000 women of reproductive age in 1985 surpassed by six to ten times the analogous figures for Western Europe. On average, every woman

in Russia has four to five abortions during her lifetime (Kon 1995, 61-62, 73-75, 178-193).

In 1989, a voluntary association, the Family and Health, was organized and affiliated with International Planned Parenthood World Federation to raise public awareness of family-planning options and to improve the image of contraceptive methods other than abortion. Since 1991, it is supplemented by the Russian Family Planning Association. Mass media, particularly television, have begun to deal directly and positively with birth-control issues.

Unfortunately, but not surprisingly, this work is not very effective. According to the VTsIOM 1992 survey, most women indicated that they had used some form of contraception during the last five years (Kon 1995, 275). Only 18% did not use any contraception. Most likely not to use contraception are women between the ages of 15 and 20 (40%), the unmarried (29%), the poorly educated (24%), and those living in rural areas (22%) (see Table 8).

Modern contraception tends to be popular largely with the younger (under age 25) and better-educated women, while the rest commonly employ traditional, less reliable, but more-accessible methods. A 1990 survey of Soviet-German students (average age 25) showed that 15% of the female students had already had an abortion, 6% more than once. In 1992, 297,029 Russian teenage girls had an abortion; of these 16,320 were illegal.

The most-preferred contraceptive method was the IUD, most favored by half of the women and the second choice for 25%. The pill was less popular, favored by 18% as first choice and 25% as second choice. The pill is still believed to be unsafe and unreliable. The condom was the third-ranking first choice.

If the current plans of the government to make women pay for abortions, except when medically indicated, materialize, this situation will become much worse. Even now, according to the St. Petersburg Yuventa Reproduction Center, in spite of the general availability of professional abortion services, 80% of women who contact the abortion clinics do so only after they have tried to do something, often dangerous, themselves.

## 10. Sexually Transmitted Diseases and HIV/AIDS

### A. Sexually Transmitted Diseases

The customary hypocrisy did not allow the Soviet people to talk openly about STDs. STDs have been consistently regarded throughout the 20th century as shameful. This attitude has hampered health education, especially when new infections are confronted (Kon 1995, 229-231).

### Table 7

**Percentage of Users of Specific Contraceptive Methods (Moscow Sample Surveys, 1965-1983)**

| Method | Year of Survey Publication | | | |
|---|---|---|---|---|
| | 1965-1966 | 1978 | 1982 | 1983 |
| Withdrawal | 32 | 34 | 14 | 25 |
| Rhythm (calendar) | — | 18 | 28 | 27 |
| Condom | 46 | 42 | 22 | 24 |
| Diaphragm | — | 1 | 1 | .1 |
| IUD | — | 8 | 11 | 10 |
| Oral contraceptives | — | 4 | 4 | 2 |
| Spermicides | 1 | — | 3 | 3 |
| Rhythm (temperature) | — | — | 2 | — |
| Douche | — | 23 | 17 | 8 |
| Combinations | 12 | — | — | 12 |

*Note*: Respondents were allowed to indicate more than one method used.

### Table 8

**Contraceptive Methods Used During the Last Five Years (in Percentages)**

| Method | Frequency Used | | |
|---|---|---|---|
| | Always | Sometimes | Not Used |
| IUD | 37 | 11 | 52 |
| Condom | 18 | 51 | 31 |
| Rhythm | 17 | 31 | 52 |
| Coitus interruptus | 14 | 46 | 40 |
| Vaginal douche | 10 | 29 | 61 |
| Pill | 10 | 19 | 71 |
| Spermicidal | 2 | 14 | 84 |
| Spermicidal + condom | 1 | 4 | 95 |
| Diaphragm | 0 | 1 | 99 |

Nonetheless, free state medicine provided treatment in special dermatological and venereological clinics, with mandatory official registration identifying the source of infection, and doctors assisted by police endeavored to follow the entire chain of dangerous contacts. Treatment was compulsory, and any infringement of that, or willful infection of anyone with an STD, was punishable under the Russian Criminal Code. This policy enabled the state to confine the danger within certain limits.

In the early 1980s, physicians noted a substantial rise, especially among young people, in the so-called minor venereal diseases that often occur without symptoms. Russians had practically no knowledge of genital herpes or chlamydia until they encountered it in their own experience.

The demise of the Soviet system has acutely affected the epidemiological situation for the worse. Extensive sexual contacts with different partners, given the ignorance and lack of observance of elementary safety and hygiene rules, is dangerous in itself. State medicine is now debilitated, and in some areas collapsed, because of lack of funds, medicine, and equipment. Private medicine is not available to all, and, when available, it is less effective, especially when it comes to maladies requiring lengthy treatment with subsequent supervision. Administrative supervision is now worse, and official statistics have become even less reliable.

So there is an increase in sexually transmitted disease, particularly among young people. People are becoming infected at a younger age. A sharp increase in the incidence of syphilis began in 1988, followed by gonorrhea in 1991. In large cities, such as Moscow, these diseases have already reached epidemic proportions. Virtually half of that increase is accounted for by children and adolescents. According to the U.S.S.R. Health Ministry figures for 1985-1987, the number of under-17 women infected by STDs increased by virtually a third throughout the country.

The overall STD picture is still not as bad as it is in many other countries. According to Russian statistics, the rate of syphilis infection is on the increase, with 9,873 cases in 1991 and 7,178 cases in the first six months of 1992. The gonorrhea rate has fallen slightly, from 180,883 in 1990, to 175,020 in 1991, and 87,724 in the first six months of 1992. These statistics do not take into account that many people use home treatment or seek help from a variety of private practitioners who are not part of the official statistical records.

A special epidemiological investigation by Olga Loseva shows that in 1991, the number of registered syphilis sufferers in Russia rose by almost 34%, in Moscow by 17% in 1991, and by another 50% in the first quarter of 1992 (Kon 1995, 277). This is primarily because of the rise in child and teenage prostitution that often begins between ages 10 and 12 for girls and age 14 for boys. No less than half of the infected go to unregistered medics for treatment.

What is to be done? There are two competing strategies. The first demands more stringent administrative measures, namely enforcement of the law prohibiting private doctors from treating STDs. The second strategy would take the social and psychological reality into account. Patients should have the right to choose whether to go to a private doctor or use the state medical system. But the private doctor must report disease cases to the epidemiological services so the epidemiological situation can be correctly evaluated, trends forecast, and preparation made for future needs.

[*Update 2002*: There has been an enormous growth of STDs and AIDS. Between 1990 and 1996, the incidence of syphilis increased 50-fold in Russia, and 78-fold among young people. In 1996, 265 new cases of syphilis were diagnosed per 100,000 of population. The 1999 figures for syphilis were lower (185.4 per 100,000), but those for gonorrhea

rose to 14.5% since 1998. Fourteen percent of the syphilis and 19% of the gonorrhea sufferers were 15- to 19-year-olds. See also the updates in the following section on HIV/AIDS. Both show the the the importance of a sex education strategy. (*End of update by I. S. Kon*)]

## B. HIV/AIDS

Because of its relative social isolation in the past, the former Soviet Union, for a number of years, was spared the effects of the HIV-related diseases. Even now, the number of people infected and ill is much lower than in most Western countries (Kon 1995, 203-38, 261-62).

On April 1, 1994, the number of HIV-positive persons in the Russian Federation was 740, of whom 286 were children infected in hospitals and maternity homes. The number of AIDS sufferers was 124, of whom 96 were children.

However, this lead-time on the HIV epidemic has been wasted by government authorities and medical professionals. Instead of preparing the country for the inevitable increase in infection rates, the Soviet Ministry of Health and government-sponsored mass media waged an ideological campaign in the early 1980s—even accusing the Pentagon and CIA of inventing the virus as a form of germ warfare! Next, the blame was put on homosexuals and drug addicts. Hopes for control of the disease were placed on the prisons (for homosexuals) and on moral exhortations in favor of monogamy (for the addicts and the remainder of the population). Unfortunately, this strategy continued even after the disease had claimed its first victims. As late as 1988, an appeal to explore the social and psychological aspects of AIDS, including the dangers of an AIDS-induced public hysteria, brought violent attacks in the conservative media.

The major high-risk group in Russia turned out not to be gays, drug addicts, or prostitutes, but newborn children infected in maternity homes through lack of disposable syringes and the negligence of medical staff. Now the children and their families have become victims, not only of this terrible disease, but also of an AIDS-phobia. Medical personnel are scared of treating them, coworkers do not want to work with members of their families, and some schools are demanding their removal.

Since AIDS-prevention politics are completely in the hands of epidemiologists, millions of rubles are spent on diagnostics, HIV-tests—25 million were tested in 1993, and so on, but there is no money for prevention programs and sex education. Education and prevention programs are mainly in the hands of different voluntary organizations.

[*Update 2002*: In addition to the increases in STDs (see update in the previous section), the incidence of HIV has also begun to grow nearly exponentially. The cumulative number of HIV-infected persons reached 24,600 in 1999. The total number of registered HIV infections more than doubled to 177,354 in 2001 from 87,177 in 2000. Experts believe that the real figures are much higher, perhaps double. In some districts, like Irkutsk, HIV has already attained epidemic proportions. These facts suggest that something must be done, and that the first step could be sex education. (*End of update by I. S. Kon*)]

[*Update 2002*: The spread of the HIV virus did not reach epidemic proportions in Russia until the mid-1990s, when the social and economic ills associated with the collapse of communism fed an explosion of intravenous drug use. By 2002, it was clear that sexual transmission of the virus was starting to rival and overtake IV transmission. In Kaliningrad, a Russian enclave between Lithuania, Poland, and the Baltic Sea, only 4% of new infections were because of sexual contact in 1996. Five years later, in 2001, the percentage of new infections in Kaliningrad attributed to sexual contact jumped to nearly 30%. In the same year, in all of Russia, sexually transmitted HIV infections accounted for little more than 5%. Epidemiologists believe that Kaliningrad is a bellwether, marking a shift from transmission by IV-drug use to infections spread by prostitution and sexual contact. The projection is that sexual transmission will easily overtake transmission by needles through all of Russia by 2006, as young women drug addicts increasingly depend on prostitution to support their drug addiction. In 2001, an estimated 3,000 women work as prostitutes in Kaliningrad, but new clusters of prostitution have appeared on Kaliningrad's boarders with Poland and Lithuania, where they serve long lines of motorists and truckers waiting to cross. Money from the World Health Organization, the French, and private donors is supporting new clinics that distribute condoms and pamphlets on safer sex to the prostitutes (Myers 2002). (*End of update by R. T. Francoeur*)]

[*Update 2002*: UNAIDS Epidemiological Assessment: During 2000-2001, the country experienced a further dramatic increase of HIV incidence. By the end of 2001, a cumulative total of 173,068 cases of HIV infection had been reported, of which 86,000 were reported in 2001. Prevalence at the end of 2001 was 118.2 per 100,000 population. Large outbreaks of HIV in injection drug users have occurred since 1996. In 1998, 42% of the cases reported were among injection drug users and 48% were reported with undetermined transmission mode.

[Until 1995, HIV/AIDS surveillance was organized mostly through mandatory screening in most subgroups of the population, together with contact tracing. Since then, testing has remained mandatory only for blood donors, prisoners, and professionals exposed to HIV. The number of tests done has decreased by 43% between 1994 and 1996, in part because of the change in testing policies and reduced funding; there was a decrease of 33% and 54% among blood donors and prisoners for whom testing policies remained the same. Diagnosed HIV infections are reported by name in a national HIV case-reporting system.

[Prevalence data come mostly from the ongoing screening programs. Incidence of syphilis cases increased dramatically from less than 30 cases per 100,000 in 1978 to 92 to 172 per 100,000 in 1995. Incidence of gonorrhea cases increased from 75 cases per 100,000 in 1987 to 236 cases per 100,000 in 1993, and then decreased to 165 cases per 100,000 in 1995; underreporting of gonorrhea is estimated to be substantial.

[The estimated number of adults and children living with HIV/AIDS on January 1, 2002, were:

| | | |
|---|---|---|
| Adults ages 15-49: | 700,000 | (rate: 0.9%) |
| Women ages 15-49: | 180,000 | |
| Children ages 0-15: | NA | |

[An estimated 9,000 adults and children died of AIDS during 2001.

[No estimate is available for the number of Russian children who had lost one or both parents to AIDS and were under age 15 at the end of 2001. (*End of update by the Editors*)]

## 11. Sexual Dysfunctions, Counseling, and Therapies

The traditions of pre-1917 Russian sex research were completely lost in the 1930s and 1940s. Revival of medical sexology (sexopathology) as an area of clinical medicine that studies the functional (behavioral, personal, and social) aspects of sexual disorders began in the 1960s with a series of seminars under the leadership of Professor N. V. Ivanov in the city of Gorky (Nizhny Novgorod) and later in Moscow at the Sexopathology Department of the Moscow Psychiatry Research Institute. In 1973, this department gained the status of an All-Union Scientific Center on Sexopathology.

Initially, a monodisciplinary approach dominated Soviet sexopathology. Urologists, and to a lesser extent the gynecologists and endocrinologists, set the tone. Subsequently, however, when the neuropathologist Profesor Georgi Vasilchenko took charge of the center, the picture changed. Vasilchenko maintained that sexopathology should not take the "brigade" approach, where the urologist treats "his" pathology, the psychiatrist "his," and the endocrinologist "his," while the sexopathologist operates as a transport controller. His approach viewed sexopathology as an independent, interdisciplinary clinical discipline. It was in this spirit that the first Russian handbooks for doctors were written under his editorship—*General Sexopathology* (1977) and *Special Sexopathology* (1983).

Professor Abram Svyadoshch set up the first Sexological Center in Leningrad. His book *Female Sexopathology* (1974) enjoyed three editions and became a genuine bestseller. The Leningrad psychiatrists Professor Dmitri Isayev and Dr. Victor Kagan began to study the formation of sexual identity and problems in juvenile and adolescent sexuality. They published the first Soviet guide for doctors *The Psycho-Hygiene of Sex among Children* (1986).

Soviet sexological service was based on the principle of ambulatory assistance, preserving a normal living pattern, carrying on normal work, and sexual activity. The need for hospitalization arises only in cases of acute psychopathological disorder (where a patient will be placed in a neurosis unit or a daytime inpatient psychoneurological clinic), vascular insufficiency of the genitalia (admission to an angisurgical unit), acute urological illness (a urological unit), and specific endocrinopathy (an endocrinological unit). Inpatient treatment is normally followed by a period of ambulatory sexual readaptation by the partners.

Analysis of visits to sexological clinics reveals that the bulk (70 to 75%) of patients have sexual problems of a psychological nature. Women's visits to a sexopathlogist account for no more than 10% of the total number of patients. The percentage of patients who come because of misinformation or distorted knowledge about sex is fairly high, up to 10 or 15%.

In 1988, in the large cities, special family medical-psychological consultation units were introduced for:

- consultative-diagnostic selection of patients needing observation and treatment in the unit;
- comprehensive therapy of patients with sexual disorders through psychotherapy, physiotherapy, reflex-therapy, pharmacotherapy, and specialized procedures;
- psychological diagnosis and correction methods for family relationship disorders; and
- hygiene-educative and psychotherapeutic work with the public and, first and foremost, with people just entering marriage and couples divorcing.

## 12. Sex Research and Advanced Professional Education

### A. Russian Sexology

Historically, the professional training of sexopathologists was delayed in favor of other priorities. The first department of sexology was organized in the Leningrad (St. Petersburg) Institute for Advanced Medical Training only in 1989. Students at other medical colleges receive no sexological training at all.

The beginning of the 1990s saw extensive promotion of individual medical activity and group work. Numerous medical cooperatives and profit-making centers are increasingly advertising the services of sexopathologists. The development of this type of medical practice reflects the public's demand for it. The professional level of this practice is sometimes problematic.

The Russian Sexological Association Health and Culture was established in February 1991, to promote an interdisciplinary investigation of sexual behavior, sex education, and sex culture. But, like many other post-Soviet voluntary organizations, it exists only on paper and serves as a cover for private commercial activities like sex shops. Somewhat more efficient is the medically oriented Soviet Sexological Association.

## B. Recent Soviet and Russian Sexual Surveys

Because not one Soviet or Russian sexual survey was ever published in the normal scientific way, with all tables, questionnaires, and methodological discussions, sexologists, such as the present author, are forced to rely on published papers and summaries, as well as whatever unpublished data, raw tables, and so on they can obtain from colleagues (Kon 1995, 275-277). Below is a short description of the most important recent Russian surveys.

1. The VTsIOM "Culture" Poll of June 1992, was conducted by Vsesoyuznyi (since 1992, Vserossiiskii) Tsentr Izucheniya Obshchestvennovo Mnenia (VTsIOM, All-Union [since 1992, All-Russia] Center for Public Opinion Research), with Professor Yun Levada as director.

    This poll involved a representative sample of about 3,500 persons in three different areas: Slav (Russia and Ukraine); Baltic (Estonia and Lithuania); and Asiatic (Uzbekistan and Tadzhikistan). In the Slav area, the population was surveyed without regard to ethnic origins or "nationality" (that is, not only ethnic Russians, but also Tatars, Jews, Germans, and others were questioned), while in the other two regions, only members of indigenous nationalities were surveyed (that is, in Estonia, Estonians but not Russians).

    Questionnaires were completed by the respondents in the presence of a professional interviewer. Among many other questions, some were related to sexuality: Are people happy in love and family life? What are their family values, their attitudes to premarital and extramarital sex, conjugal fidelity, erotica, sex education, and so on?

2. The VTsIOM "The Fact" June 1993 Survey involved a representative sample for the Russian Federation, 1,665 persons. Demographics for this survey included 746 men and 909 women, aged from 16 to 84 (16-25 years, 285; 24-40 years, 546; 40-55 years, 383; and 55-84 years, 461), from 13 different regions. The subjects' educational level was: 235, university level; 803, high (secondary) school; and 616, fewer than 9 years of secondary school. The occupational demography was: nonworking pensioners, 409; manual workers, 330, professionals, 284; technicians, 136; other employees, 120; and students, 87. The subjects' place of residence included: capitals and regional cities, 604; towns, 614; and villages, 344. All standard procedures normally used in public opinion polls were used.

    Some of the questions concerned attitudes toward the following aspects of sexual behavior (on 5-point scales, from "It deserves censure" to "I don't see anything wrong in it"): masturbation, premarital sex, frequent change of sexual partners, marital infidelity, viewing of pornographic films, group sex, homosexual contacts, induced abortions, and so on. There were also a few questions about personal sexual experience,

such as age at the first sexual contact, number of lifetime sexual partners, and present sexual activities. About 40% of respondents did not answer these personal questions.

3. The Adolescent Sexuality Survey published in 1993 and conducted by Vladimir Shapiro and Valery Chervyakov, Institute of Sociology, Russian Academy of Sciences, with Igor Kon as a consultant and Mana Gerasimova as the research organizer. This survey used an adapted version of American sociologist Stan Weed's questionnaire. The data were collected in late 1992 and early of 1993. The sample involved 1,615 students (50.4% boys and 49.6% girls) from 16 high (secondary) schools and eight vocational schools in Moscow and St. Petersburg. The students' ages ranged from 12 to 17 years, and their grade levels from the 7th to 11th grades.

    The questionnaire contained 135 questions about aspects of sexual experience and attitudes: dating, going steady, age at, and the motives for, the first sexual intercourse, sources of sexual information, communications with parents and peers, moral and religious values, involvement in deviant behavior, and some personal psychological characteristics. The schools were selected to represent different social strata of the two cities' populations. Questionnaires were completed in the classrooms, anonymously, voluntarily, and individually, in the presence of a professional interviewer. The permission of the school administration was obtained, but none of them had access to this confidential information. There were no refusals from students to take part in the research, but some respondents did not answer certain questions. Detailed statistical analysis may be available by the time this chapter is published; however, a general popular overview of the results was published by Igor Kon, Valery Chervyakov, and Vladimir Shapiro in 1994.

4. A second survey of adolescent sexual attitudes, representations, and practices was conducted by Igor Lunin (1994) of the St. Petersburg Crisis Prevention Service for Children and Adolescents between May and September of 1993. The sample population for this survey was 370, (185 boys and 185 girls, secondary (high) school 10th graders and vocational school students from three socially and economically different districts of St. Petersburg). The average age was 15.9 years.

    In this study, an anonymous questionnaire was preliminarily reviewed in teenage discussion groups. Participation, on the school premises, was individual and voluntary. Questions concerned sexual values and behavior, main sources of sexual and contraceptive information and the evaluation of its availability and reliability, sexual harassment, violence, and rape experience, and attitudes to condoms and to different forms of sex education. (In addition to Lunin (1994), see also Igor Lunin, Thomas L. Hall, Jeffrey S. Mandel, Julia Kay, and Norman Hearst, *Adolescent Sexuality in St. Petersburg: Russia in the Era of AIDS* (in press).) A detailed statistical analysis is also in progress.

5. A telephone survey was conducted by Dmitri. D. Isayev in St. Petersburg between September and December 1993. The sample for this survey was 435 people, 16 to 55 years old; 155 men (average age, 35.4 years and 67.5% married), and 280 women (average age, 37.3 years with 67% married). Questions were asked about personal sexual experience and attitudes, number of partners, safe-sex practices, and AIDS-prevention measures.

6. An epidemiological study was conducted in 1991 by Olga Loseva, a Moscow venereologist. This unpublished dissertation summarized 15 years of research of sexual behavior and sexual values of syphilitics. Loseva collected data on 3,273 heterosexual men and women at a venereological clinic in Moscow: 300 medical histories and about 3,000 questionnaires. The data came from 1,782 infected patients and 1,191 in a control group of persons without sexually transmitted diseases, plus 120 teenage girls. Sociologically, the samples were not representative, but a comparison of three control groups, divided by five-year intervals, is informative for the shifts in sexual attitudes and practices.

## Conclusion

Sexuality is just beginning to be thought of as a subject worthy of consideration and study by Russian researchers. Clearly, sexual behavior is diverse in societies as large and heterogeneous as Russia and the other republics of the former Soviet Union. Although certain values are strong within and between these societies, there is no single standard of "normal" sexuality for family members. Marriage is valued as a primary arena for sexual expression; however, sex-related ideas, attitudes, and activities are extremely diverse. Citizens are exposed to sexual information and images from a variety of public sources. Naturally, their reactions to these differ, and the impact upon their behavior is varied. Parents seem concerned about the proper sexual development of their children. Yet, some of these same parents respond by suppressing expressions of sexuality in the family, others by obsessively explicating sexual guidelines, and still others by supporting social programs of sex education in schools and community institutions (Kon 1995, 265-272).

To develop effective public policies that encourage responsible sexual expression by citizens without reactionary negativism, and to accommodate pluralistic diversity without succumbing to crippling ambivalence—these will be the challenges common to our countries as they enter the 21st century.

[*Update 1997*: A March 1997 Russian Academy of Education conference clearly indicated the Russian Orthodox Church is rapidly assuming the Communist ideological mantle of sexual repression. Attacking all sex education in schools and any expression of sexuality as "satanic," Orthodox clergy have demanded a United Nations-sponsored sex education project be stopped immediately because it is a Western conspiracy to depopulate Russia. Although a few medical efforts and the Russian Planned Parenthood helped reduce the abortion rate since 1991 by 50%, teen syphilis rates increased 30-fold and teenage coital experience increased and began earlier. Orthodox clergy preach that they alone can provide proper sex education for the people, claiming that Westerners are trying to exterminate Russian culture by reducing its birthrate with abortion, contraception, sexual excesses, masturbation, and homosexuality. Mass media freedom is also threatened as legislators seek to outlaw "any products of mass media, other printed and audiovisual products, including advertising, messages and materials transmitted and received by computer networks, as well as things and means satisfying needs related to the sexual drive, except for medical drugs and products." (*End of update by I. S. Kon*)]

[*Update 2002*: What may be the possible results of the current Russian sexual counterrevolution?

[Basically, this is only the tip of the iceberg. Under the guise of a moral renaissance, these people want to restore censorship and administrative control over private life. In the long run, this goal is virtually unattainable. Sexual attitudes and practices in Russia are already highly diversified by age, gender, education, and regional, ethnic, and social background. In the near future, this heterogeneity will probably increase and may produce new cultural tensions. But in the long run, it is the younger, urban, and better-educated people who will have the upper hand in defining what is right and what is wrong. Any attempts by the state, Church, or local community to forcibly limit their sexual freedom is doomed to failure, and will be detrimental to the authority of the institutions making such an attempt.

[The Communist Party, which has waged this new holy war, belongs to the past; it is a party of old men. The militant position of the Orthodox clergy also may have a boomerang effect. They seem to have forgotten an old Soviet joke: "How can you make art flourish and religion decay? It is very easy, you simply disconnect art from the State and make religion compulsory."

[Yet, the crusade against sex research and sex education has very dangerous practical social consequences. Without professional sex education, it is impossible to solve such urgent public health issues as teen pregnancy and STD-HIV prevention. Effective family planning is equally impossible without sexual knowledge. And, last but not least, the antisexual crusade widens the generation gap, which is already vast and yawning. (*End of update by I. S. Kon*)]

## References and Suggested Readings

Attwood, L. 1990. *The new Soviet man and woman: Sex-role socialization in the U.S.S.R.* Bloomington, IN: University of Indiana Press.

Bocharova, O. A. 1994. Seksualnaya svoboda: Slova i dela. *Chelovek*, 5:98-107.

Borisenko, K. K., & O. K. Loseva. 1994. Zabolevaemost molodyozhi boleznyaimi, peredavaemymi polovym putyom. *Planirovanie Semyi*, 4:20-22.

Chervyakov, V. 2000. Russia: Study looks at youth sexuality knowledge and sexuality education. *Making the Connection* [New York: Sex Education and Information Council of the United States–SIECUS], *1*(1):3-4.

Chervyakov, V., & I. Kon. 1998. Sex education and HIV prevention in the context of Russian politics. In: R. Rosenbrock, ed., *Politics behind AIDS policies: Case studies from India, Russia and South Africa*. Berlin.

Chervyakov, V., & I. Kon. 2000. Sexual revolution in Russia and the tasks of sex education. In: Th. Sandford et al., eds., *AIDS in Europe: New challenges for social sciences* (pp. 119-134). London: Routledge.

Chervyakov, V., I. S. Kon, & V. Shapiro. 1993. Full citation not available.

CIA. 2002 (January). *The world factbook 2002.* Washington, DC: Central Intelligence Agency. Available: http://www.cia.gov/cia/publications/factbook/index.html.

Engelstein, L. 1992. *The keys to happiness. Sex and the search for modernity in fin-de-siecle Russia.* Ithaca, NY: Cornell University Press.

Flegon, A. 1976. *Eroticism in Russian art.* London: Flegon Press.

Gessen, M. 1994. *The rights of lesbians and gay men in the Russian Federation: An International Gay and Lesbian Human Rights Commission report.* San Francisco: I.G.L.H.R.C.

Goolod, S. I. 1984. *Stabilnost semi: Sotsiologichesky i demografichesky aspekty.* Leningrad.

Goolod, S. I. 1996. *XX vek i tendentsii seksualnykh otnoshenii v Rossii.* St. Petersburg: Aleteya.

Haavio-Mannila, E., & Rotkirch, A. 1997. Generational and gender differences in sexual life in St. Petersburg and urban Finland. *Yearbook of Population Research in Finland, 34*: 133-160.

Haavio-Mannila E., & Rotkirch, A. 2001. Gender liberalization and polarisation: comparing sexuality in St. Petersburg, Finland and Sweden. Unpublished manuscript.

Karlinsky, S. 1989. Russia's gay literature and culture: The impact of the October Revolution. In: M. B. Duberman, M. Vicinus, & G. Chauncey, Jr., eds., *Hidden from history: Reclaiming the gay and lesbian past*. New York: New American Library.

Kon, I. S. 1989. *Vvedenie v seksologiu [Introduction to sexology]* (2nd enlarged ed.). Moscow, Russia: Translations: Bulgarian (1990), Chinese (1990), Ukranian (1991).

Kon, I. S. 1995. *The sexual revolution in Russia: From the age of the czars to today.* New York: Free Press.

Kon, I. S. 1997a. *Seksualnaya kultura v Rossii: Klubnichka na beryozke [Sexual culture in Russia].* Moskva: OGI.

Kon, I. S. 1997b. Russia. In: R. T. Francoeur, ed. *The International Encyclopedia of Sexuality* (vol. 2, pp. 1045-1079). New York: Continuum.

Kon, I. S. 1999a. Sex als spiegel der russischen revolution. In: H. Steiner & W. A. Jadow, eds. (Hrsg), *Russland–Wohin? Russland aus der sicht russischer soziologen* (pp. 330-342). Berlin: Trafo Verlag.

Kon, I. S. 1999b. Sexuality and politics in Russia (1700-2000). In: F.X. Eder, L.A. Hall, & G. Hekma, eds., *Sexual cultures in Europe. National histories* (pp.197-218). Manchester University Press.

Kon, I. S. 2001. *Podroskovaya 'seksualnost' na poroge XXI veka.* Moskva: Feniks.

Kon, I. S., V. Chervyakov, & V. Shapiro. 1994. Podrostki i seks: Utrata illuzii. *Ogonyok*, 2.

Kon, I. S., & J. Riordan, eds. 1993. *Sex and Russian society.* Bloomington, IN: Indiana University Press. Includes chapters on "Sexuality and Culture," I. Kon; "Patterns of Birth Control," L. I. Remennick; "Sex and the Cinema," L. Attwood; "Sexual Minorities," I. Kon; "Soviet Beauty Contests," E. Waters; "Sex and Young People," S. Golod, and "Medical Sexology," L. Shcheglov.

Lenhert, P., I. Pavlenko, L. Remennick, & A. Visser. 1992 (May). Contraception in the former USSR: Recent survey results on women's behavior and attitudes. *Planned Parenthood in Europe, 21*(2):9-11.

Levin, E. 1989. *Sex and society in the world of the orthodox Slavs, 900-1700.* Ithaca, NY: Cornell University Press.

Loseva, O. K. 1991. *Seksualnoe povedenie bolnykh sifilisom (Epidemiologicheskie i mediko-sotsialnye problemy).* Avtoreferat Dissertatsii na soiskanie uchenoi stepeni doktora meditsinskikh nauk. Moscow: Tsentralnyi Nauchno-Issledovatelskii Kozhno-Venerologicheskii Institut.

Loseva, O. K., 1994. "Sotsialno-meditsinskie aspekty boleznei, peredavaemykh polovym putom, u detei i podroskov," Rossiyskaya Assotsiatsyia "Planirovanie Semyi," Pervaya natsyonalnaya konferentsya *"Problemy Planirovania Semyi v Rossii" (Materialy konferetnsii). 7-9 dekabrya 1993, Moskva, Moscow. Kvartet,* 89-96.

Loseva, O. K., & I. N. Bobkova. 1999. Dobrachnoe, brachnoe i vnebrachnoe seksualnoe povedenie i orientatsii muzhchin i zhenshchin: Sravnitelnoe panelnoe issledovanie bolnykh sifilisom i zdorovykh. Chast' 1. *Infektsii Peredavaemye Polovym Putiom,* 6:18-24.

Loseva, O. K., & I. N. Bobkova. 2000. Dobrachnoe, brachnoe i vnebrachnoe seksualnoe povedenie i orientatsii muzhchin i zhenshchin: Sravnitelnoe panelnoe issledovanie bolnykh sifilisom i zdorovykh. Chast' 2. *Infeksii Peredavaemye Polovym Putiom, 1:*16-22

Loseva, O. K., T. V. Chistyakova, A. V. Libin, & E. V. Livin. 1991. Seksualnoe povedenie podrostkov, bolnykh sifilisom. *Vestnik Dermatologfi i Venerologii,* 2:45-49.

Lunin, I. I. 1994. Seksualnoe prosveshcheme kak faktor profilaktiki seksualnykh posyagatelstv. *Problemy planirovaniya semyi v Rossii. Pervaya Natsionalnaya Konferentsia Rossiiskoi Assotsiatsii "Planirovanie Semyi."* Moscow, 96-105. See also Lunin, I., T. L. Hall, J. S. Mandel, J. Kay, & N. Hearst. *Adolescent sexuality in St. Petersburg: Russia in the era of AIDS* (in press).

Maddock, J. W., M. J. Hogan, A. I. Antonov, & M. S. Matskovsky, eds. 1994. *Families before and after peristroika: Russian and U.S. perspectives.* New York/London: Guilford Press.

Masson, C. F. P. 1805. *The secret memoirs of the Court of Petersburg.* London.

Molodsova, V. 1999 (10 June). Seks: Razvrashchenie vmesto prosveshchenia. *Rossiiskaya Gazeta.*

Myers, S. L. 2002 (July 21). Alarming portents on frontier of Russia's AIDS crisis. *The New York Times,* 4.

Poltorak, A. 2000 (15 April). Pochitai vracha . . . ibo Gospod' sozdal ego. *Mir za Nedeliu,* 16.

Popov, A. 1992. *Induced abortions in the U.S.S.R. at the end of the 1980s: Basis for the national model of family planning.* A paper for the Population Association of America 1992 Annual Meeting (Denver, Colorado, April 30-May 2, 1992).

Popov, A., A. Visser, & E. Ketting. 1993 (July/August). Contraceptive knowledge, attitudes, and practice in Russia during the 1980s. *Studies in Family Planning, 24*(4):227-235.

Rademakers, J. 1997. Adolescent sexual development: A cross-cultural perspective. *Sexuality beyond boundaries* International Conference, Amsterdam, 29 July-4 August 1997.

Seksualnoe i reproduktivnoe povedenie podroskov v Rossii. 2001 (March 26-April 8). *Demoskop Weekly,* 13-14. Available: http://www.demoscop.ru/weekly/013.

*Slovo k podrostkam.* 2001. Available: http://pms.orthodoxy.ru/uz/raps/s6.htm.

Stafford, P. 1967. *Sexual behavior in the Communist world. An Eyewitness report of life, love, and the human condition behind the Iron Curtain.* New York: Julian Press.

Stanley, A. 1994 (April 17). Sexual harassment thrives in the new Russia climate. *The New York Times,* 1, 8.

Stanley, A. 1995 (October 21). Russian mothers, from all walks, walk alone. *The New York Times,* A1, A5.

UNAIDS. 2002. *Epidemiological fact sheets by country.* Geneva, Switzerland: Joint United Nations Programme on HIV/AIDS (UNAIDS/WHO). Available: http://www.unaids.org/hivaidsinfo/statistics/fact_sheets/index_en.htm.

Tkachenko, A. A. 1999. *Seksualnye izvrashchenia–Parafilii (Sexual Perversions–Paraphilias). Moscow: Triada X.*

Verkhovskii, A. 2001. *Problema INN grozit raskolom No ne Tserkvi, a pravoslavnym fundamentalistam.* Available: http://www.polit.ru/documents/401411.html.

Waters, E. 1993. Soviet beauty contests. In: I. S. Kon & J. Riordan, eds., *Sex and Russian society.* Bloomington, IN: Indiana University Press.

# South Africa
## (The Republic of South Africa)

Lionel John Nicholas, Ph.D.,* and
Priscilla Sandra Daniels, M.S. (Part 1)
Mervyn Bernard Hurwitz, M.D. (Part 2)
*Updates by L. J. Nicholas, Ph.D.***

## Contents

### Demographics and a Brief Historical Perspective

ROBERT T. FRANCOEUR

#### A. Demographics

The Republic of South Africa is situated at the southern tip of the African continent and extends over an area of 471,011 square miles (1,219,912 km²), about twice the size of the state of Texas. The country surrounds the nation of Lesotho and is bordered on the north by Namibia, Botswana, and Zimbabwe, and by Mozambique and Swaziland on the east. The large interior plateau has few major lakes

*Communications*: Lionel Nicholas, Ph.D., University of the Western Cape, Centre for Student Counseling; (home address: 601 Villa D'Este Private Bag X17, 257 Beach Road, Bellville, 7535 South Africa; LNicholas@uwc.ac.za.

** The updates by Dr. Nicholas are based on the preliminary report of the South African Demographic and Health Survey completed in September 1998. The survey is nationally representative and the sample was selected from the 1996 census data. A total of 12,247 households were surveyed and 11,735 women were individually interviewed.

(CIA 2002)

and rivers. Rainfall is sparse in the west and plentiful in the east. The climate is mostly semiarid with subtropical along the eastern coast. Days are sunny and the nights cool.

In July 2002, South Africa had an estimated population of 43.65 million. These estimates explicitly take into account the effects of excess mortality because of AIDS. This can result in lower life expectancy, higher infant mortality and death rates, lower population and growth rates, and changes in the distribution of population by age and sex than would otherwise be expected. (All data are from *The World Factbook 2002* (CIA 2002) unless otherwise stated.)

**Age Distribution and Sex Ratios**: *0-14 years*: 31.6% with 1.01 male(s) per female (sex ratio); *15-64 years*: 63.4% with 0.94 male(s) per female; *65 years and over*: 5% with 0.6 male(s) per female; *Total population sex ratio*: 0.94 male(s) to 1 female. The age profile for whites is more evenly spread across age categories. Half of the black population and a third of the white population are under 20 years of age. There are many more children between the ages of 5 and 9 than in any other age group. The white population is aging, with 13% over the age of 60, whereas only 6% of the blacks fall into this age cohort.

**Life Expectancy at Birth**: *Total Population*: 45.43 years; *male*: 45.19 years; *female*: 45.68 years. [*Update 2001*: According to a UNAIDS projection, by the year 2010, the AIDS epidemic will have reduced the average life expectancy of South Africans to 36 years, a drop of 47% from the average life expectancy of 68 years projected without AIDS. (*End of update by L. J. Nicholas*)]

**Urban/Rural Distribution**: 63% to 37%, with 90% of whites and coloreds, 95% of Asians/Indians, and over 60% of blacks living in urban areas.

**Ethnic Distribution**: Black: 75.2%; white: 13.6%; colored: 8.6%; Indian: 2.6

**Religious Distribution**: Christian: 68% (including most whites and coloreds, about 60% of blacks, and 40% of Indians); Muslim: 2%; Hindu: 1.5% (60% of Indians); indigenous beliefs and animists: 28.5%

**Birth Rate**: 20.63 births per 1,000 population

**Death Rate**: 18.86 per 1,000 population

**Infant Mortality Rate**: 61.78 deaths per 1,000 live births

**Net Migration Rate**: –1.56 migrant(s) per 1,000 population

**Total Fertility Rate**: 2.38 children born per woman
**Population Growth Rate**: 0.02%

**HIV/AIDS** (1999 est.): *Adult prevalence*: 19.94%; *Persons living with HIV/AIDS*: 4.2 million; *Deaths*: 250,000. (For additional details from www.UNAIDS.org, see end of Section 10B.)

**Literacy Rate** (*defined as those age 15 and over who can read and write*): Overall: 81.8; whites: 99%; Asians: 69%; coloreds: 62%; Africans: 50%. Only 10% of blacks have a secondary high school education and only 6% have any education beyond high-school level. In 1993, there were 105 colleges with 60,000 students, 21 universities with 337,120 students, 15 technical colleges with 130,000 students, and 128 technical colleges with 93,000 students (Cooper et al. 1994).

**Per Capita Gross Domestic Product** (*purchasing power parity*): $9,400 (2001 est.); *Inflation*: 5.8%; *Unemployment*: 37% (unemployment is a major and ever-increasing problem); *Living below the poverty line*: 50% (2000 est.)

South Africa's first democratically elected government is currently grappling with unemployment, violence, illiteracy, and numerous other problems. It does, however, have tremendous natural resources, a well-developed industrial, educational, and transportation network, and enough skilled workers to start redressing the economic havoc apartheid has wreaked on South Africa. Many diverse ethnic, cultural, and religious groups make up the South African landscape, and these groups continue to influence one another, as they are in turn being influenced by the international community. Internal migration is a problem in South Africa, as socioeconomic and political factors force large segments of the population to leave rural areas and crowd into the cities.

**B. A Brief Historical Perspective\***

The roots of today's Republic of South Africa stretch back to the Dutch East India Company's arrival on the Cape of Good Hope in 1692. By the end of the 18th century, Boer or Afrikaner colonists numbered only about 15,000. Britain occupied the Cape colony in 1814 at the end of the Napoleonic wars, bringing another 5,000 settlers. Anglicization of the government and the freeing of black slaves drove about 12,000 Afrikaners to make the "great trek" northeast into African tribal territories, where they established the republics of the Transvaal and the Orange Free State. The discovery of diamonds in 1867 and gold in 1876 brought an influx of "outlanders," whose presence spurred Cecil Rhodes to plot annexation of the British Cape and Natal colonies. A three-year war between the Boers and the British, 1899 to 1902, resulted in 1910 in the formation of the Union of South Africa, joining the two former republics and the two colonies.

South Africa became a charter member of the United Nations in 1945, but refused to sign the Universal Declaration of Human Rights. Apartheid—racial segregation—dominated domestic politics as the nationalists gained power and imposed greater restrictions on the Africans, coloreds, and Asians. In 1949, apartheid became national policy. Afrikaner opposition to South Africa's membership

*\*Editors' Note*: This unique history poses a different kind of challenge for sexologists. Fortunately, Mervyn Hurwitz, the only South African member of the Society for the Scientific Study of Sexuality, accepted the editor's invitation to prepare a chapter on his country. Equally fortunate—and unexpected—Ted McIlvenna, founder of the Institute for the Advanced Study of Human Sexuality, introduced the *IES* editor to Lionel Nicholas at the 1994 meeting of the Society in Miami, and Dr. Nicholas agreed to work with a woman colleague to provide a black perspective that complements the perspective provided by Dr. Hurwitz. The two parts of this chapter are two windows on sexuality in South Africa.

in the British Commonwealth ended on May 31, 1961, with the declaration of the Republic of South Africa and the severing of all ties with the Commonwealth. In 1963, South Africa established the Transkei, the first of four partially self-governing republics, territories, or "homelands" for blacks. The Transkei consists of three discontinuous enclaves in the southeast. The seven areas of Bophuthatswana were joined in a northern Homeland in 1977. The Venda Homeland, with two discontinuous areas in the northeast, was established in 1979. In the southwest, Ciskei became a homeland republic in 1980. None of these territories has international recognition as a republic. In 1991, following negotiations between the government and the African National Congress, the Parliament scrapped the country's apartheid laws that limited ownership of property, required registration of South Africans at birth by race, and supported minority rule.

# PART 1:
## A PERSPECTIVE ON THE PEOPLE OF COLOR
LIONEL JOHN NICHOLAS and
PRISCILLA SANDRA DANIELS

## *1. Basic Sexological Premises*
### A/B. Gender Roles and the Sociolegal Status of Males and Females

South Africa is a strongly male-dominated society where violence against women is at a high level. Gender equality and freedom to express one's sexual orientation is enshrined in the new constitution of South Africa, but it is widely acknowledged that we have far to go before getting near to this ideal.

In general, women and men negotiate their lives differently, as well as express their sexual vulnerabilities differently. In a patriarchal society like South Africa, one may expect these differences to be more prevalent than reported in the relevant international literature. Sex counseling will have to take into account the differing sexual socialization experiences of women and men in societies that institutionally and structurally accept the dominance of men, and where many women and men may also have accepted sexist stereotypes (Nicholas 1994a, 6).

### C. General Concepts and Constructs of Sexuality and Love

The concepts and constructs of sexuality and love differ markedly between urban and rural communities for all groups in South Africa. Much of this difference is influenced by the greater visibility of particular love or sexual behaviors and observable traditional practices in rural areas that are protected from new urban practices. The following example of peer pressure to have sexual intercourse is cited from Preston-Whyte and Zondi:

> They laugh at you and say you are old-fashioned not to sleep with a boy, and they tell you that you are not in the country now, with the peer group watching to see you only do ukusoma—that was 'external' intercourse. No mothers in town examine one to see if you are a virgin—just let them try! (Preston-Whyte & Zondi 1992, 235)

African and colored groups are likely to have developed a larger range of "nontraditional" sexual behaviors because of the massive efforts to destabilize these communities, including removing parental figures through an enforced migratory labor system and high mortality rates. White and Asian groups have had more-intact family and extended-family systems in both urban and rural settings, which increased the capacity of these groups to monitor and regulate sexual practices of their members. These groups do, however, experience the same challenge to the concepts and constructs of sexuality and love mainly informed by religious guidelines of chastity.

Loubser (1994) reported that Afrikaner junior high school pupils regularly watched pornographic videos and engaged in sexual intercourse, and many of those who were virgins anticipated that their status would change in the near future.

While all groups would consider the seduction of a young woman as a situation where reparation has to be made, the acceptable reparation would differ widely across groups, especially if a pregnancy has resulted from the seduction. The different African groups have elaborate formal negotiations involving family members on both sides. A go-between would also negotiate the amount of bridewealth on behalf of the man's family before marriage takes place.

## 2. Religious, Ethnic, and Gender Factors Affecting Sexuality

### A. Source and Character of Some Typical Religious Values

According to the 1996 census, non-Christian religious affiliation was only 3.8% (Islam 1.5%, Hinduism 1.5%, Judaism 0.2%, and other faiths 0.6%). Some 12.9% indicated no religion. The largest religious groups were Zion Christian 10.7%, Dutch Reformed 9.8%, Apostolic 9.8%, Catholic 9.5%, Methodist 7.8%, and Pentecostal/Charismatic 6.1%. Hindu, Islamic, and Jewish traditions are also major influences in particular geographic areas. The most vociferous support for censorship has come from representatives of a range of religious denominations led by the Dutch Reformed Church. The religious-influenced taboos around sexuality are particularly strong in South Africa. Public discourse on sexuality has been severely restricted by legal, political, religious, and social norms. Stringent censorship has been a central and a bizarre feature of South African life. For example, in 1965, a film, *Debbie*, was initially banned because the chairman of the censor board believed that Afrikaner women do not get pregnant while unmarried.

Every month, bookshops and libraries throughout South Africa receive a list of banned books and objects that also contains recently unbanned materials and those undergoing review. The two main foci of censorship have been sex and politics. The work of sex counselors, and access to accurate sex information, have been most adversely affected by the draconian censorship on sexuality. Liberalization of the censorship laws was presented to Parliament in 1995. The draft legislation advocates a ban on: 1. child pornography, defined as involving children younger than 16, 2. the depiction of extreme violence including rape, 3. depiction of bestiality, and 4. promotion of religious hatred (Swayer 1994).

The history of South Africa's only recently discarded miscegenation laws and prohibitions on a wide range of books on sexuality have effectively exacerbated the sex-related problems experienced, through the official encouragement of ignorance about sexuality. For example, in 1992, several books on sexuality, vibrators, and objects, such as a penis tip attached to a condom, were banned by the censor board.

Standard methods of intervention with sexual problems have not been available to sex counselors and their clients in South Africa. One cannot advise the use of a vibrator to assist in treating inhibited orgasm, because it may be illegal to own a vibrator. Similarly, the range of informative books on sexuality easily available in other countries are not available in South Africa. Some films were restricted to those over 21 years of age; films that included birth scenes or sex education had to be shown to male or female audiences separately. Certain films were also limited to whites.

A censorship board, appointed by the President of South Africa, for example, made the decision that: "a massage instrument whose manufacturers obviously intend it to be used for purposes of masturbation does therefore not fall under the Act unless it is shaped for example like a male organ" (Van Rooyen 1987, 22). The implication here is that it is the duty of the censor board to disapprove of masturbation, but it will enforce its legal powers only if provoked.

The controversy around formal sex education is predicated on the erroneous belief that instruction about sexuality will increase premarital sexual behavior. It may in fact, however, make visible the sexuality that parents try to deny that children possess, and vice versa. When parents are considered as the ideal location for the dissemination of sex information, it is often overlooked that many children do not have both parents available to them, and that fathers have always had minimal involvement in the transmission of sex information in two-parent families.

Nicholas and Durrheim (1994) reported that negative attitudes towards homosexuality were significant, but only weakly associated with negative attitudes toward AIDS, high knowledge of AIDS, and high religiosity in a study of AIDS and knowledge, attitudes, beliefs, and practices of 1,817 black South African students. The sample was divided into those with high or low scores on Rohrbaugh and Jessor's (1975) religiosity scale (excluding virgins) by selecting individuals falling below the first quartile of the distribution of religiosity scores. The low scorers experienced their first sexual intercourse at a younger age ($M = 15.92$ years) than did the high scorers ($M = 17.25$ years). The high religious group was also less satisfied with their first sexual encounter, less likely to intend to be sexually active, less likely to make use of safe-sex practices, engaged in sexual intercourse with fewer partners during high school, and used condoms less frequently than the low religious group.

In a survey of 2,206 black South African students (Nicholas 1994a), 16.3% (361) of respondents indicated that they did not use condoms during sexual intercourse, because it was against their religion. While sexual stereotypes of the various ethnic groups in South Africa flourish, the paucity of research on sexuality in South Africa precludes any firm conclusions on various ethnic sexual practices. Black students who have consulted the first author have ascribed folk religious practices as being the cause of their sexual problems. It would not be uncommon to find a client consulting an indigenous healer for a sexual problem ascribed to witchcraft, in the belief that many approaches to the same problem would bring more-effective relief. These beliefs could be located within Christian faith healing, Islamic faith healing, or African herbal or psychic remedies.

[*Update 2003*: Sishana and Simbayi's (2002) national household study found that 35% of males were circumcised, with the mean age of circumcision being 15 years. Some 3.4% of married respondents ($n = 3,594$) reported that they were in polygamous relationships. Some 50.2% of those who were married ($n = 3,374$) reported that *lobola* or dowry had been paid when they got married. Some 57% of widows ($n = 467$) indicated that they were required to abstain from sex during the mourning period and 53% (256) indicated that they were required not to have any relationships with men. (*End of update by L. J. Nicholas*)]

### B. Source and Character of Ethnic Values

The sociopolitical context of South African blacks, and South African black higher education students, renders them very vulnerable to sexuality-related problems. Most black schools provide very poor guidance to their pupils, and sex education is the exception in schools. This lack of guidance and other resources is politically determined, in that the bulk of the financing for these resources had been reserved for whites. Even in 1993, there still existed a disparity in the allocation of resources to blacks and whites at all educational levels. Political decisions have also ensured that blacks lived in extremely crowded conditions by legally allowing blacks residential access to only 13% of the land of South Africa. These factors contribute significantly to sexual abuse, divorce, age-inappropriate exposure to sexual contact, and other high-profile sexuality problems prevalent in the black community (Nicholas 1994a, 4).

## 3. Knowledge and Education about Sexuality

### A/B. Government Policies and Programs, and Informal Sources

Failure to use contraception is a critical problem on university campuses and in schools. While sex counseling is being neglected at schools in South Africa, it is likely to take up an increasing amount of resources elsewhere. For example, parents and religious leaders attacked the introduction of sex education in South African Indian schools as a pilot program in 1993, expressing fears that their children would be corrupted. Such programs had not been taught before in these schools (Chothia 1993). Cilliers (1989) found that all the school departments he consulted supported the idea of the school as a means for AIDS prevention, yet it is evident that sex education does not have similar support (Kagan 1989). Some sex and AIDS education programs have been initiated in the 1990s, but these are experiencing some opposition from parents and others (Gevisser 1993). In 1992, service points at which family planning was provided numbered 65,182 (Cooper et al. 1994). As a result of these programs, 2,301,152 women were using contraceptives.

#### Intrafamial Communications

The following findings regarding intrafamilial communication about sex in South Africa were obtained in 1990 from 1,902 black first-year students at a South African university (Nicholas 1991).

*Age at Which Sex Information Was Acquired.* Table 1 shows how respondents to questions on age at which sex information was acquired reflect the small percentage of students who first learned certain concepts before the age of 10 years, and the relatively large per-

centage who learned about these sexual concepts when they were 16 years and older.

Statistically significant gender differences existed in the acquisition of sex information for the terms shown in Table 1, except for the acquisition of information on pregnancy, female prostitution, and male and female homosexuality.

*Manner in Which Sex Information Was Acquired.* Males and females in this sample acquired their initial learning about these concepts from different sources (see Table 2). Friends and the mass media are consistently ranked as the major source of initial sex information for this study, whereas school training showed severe limitations.

*Preferred Source of Information about Sexuality.* The preferred source of sex information for this sample is school training, 27.5%; friends, 26.7%; and mother, 17.7%. Fathers were chosen as the preferred source only by 5.1%: 4.5% of male respondents and 0.6% of females. The high percentage of students with a preference for friends points to the potential value of peer counseling programs for sexuality-related issues.

*Parental Provision of Sex Information.* Thirty-eight percent of respondents indicated that they had received no sex information from their mothers; 8.2% of females and only 3.8% of males indicated that they received much information from mothers. As expected, 65.5% of respondents indicated that fathers had given no sex information; 4.5%, 3.1% of males and 1.4% of females, reported their fathers provided much sex information.

*Provision of Sex Information at School.* Sixty-two percent of respondents indicated that they received no sex information at primary school, whereas only 10.9% indicated that they received no sex information at high school. Guidance teachers seem to provide much of the sex information at school, with 30.3% of respondents indicating that they received much information from guidance teachers.

*Approval for Sex Education.* A large percentage of students are against the provision of sex education in kindergarten (69.5%). Almost a quarter of respondents (23.4%) are against provision of sex information in primary school, 1.8% are against sex education in high school, and 2.6% are against sex education at the university.

*Attitudes Toward Premarital Intercourse.* Forty-five percent of respondents disapprove of premarital intercourse

### Table 1

**Age at Which Sex Information Was Acquired (in Percentages)**

| Topic | Before Age of 10 | After Age of 16 |
|---|---|---|
| Sexual intercourse | 17.6 | 1.8 |
| Pregnancy | 16.6 | 21.9 |
| Abortion | 1.8 | 36.6 |
| Venereal disease | 0.6 | 44.8 |
| Menstruation | 3.8 | 22.9 |
| Female prostitution | 4.7 | 32.4 |
| Erection | 12.9 | 32.5 |
| Condoms | 1.0 | 43.3 |
| Male homosexuality | 2.6 | 42.4 |
| Female homosexuality | 1.3 | 45.5 |
| Fertilization | 1.7 | 42.9 |

### Table 2

**Main Sources of Sexual Information (in Percentages) for 1,902 First-Year Black University Students**

| Topic | Mothers | Schools | Friends Same Sex | Friends Other Sex | Mass Media | Other |
|---|---|---|---|---|---|---|
| Intercourse | | | 33.4 | 20.7 | | |
| Pregnancy | 28.7 | | | 24.3 | | |
| Males | 8.3 | | | | | |
| Females | 20.4 | | | | | |
| Abortion | | 21.2 | | c. 21.7 | 30.1 | |
| STDs | | 28.5 | | c. 17.1 | 27.2 | |
| Menstruation | 28.2 | | | c. 33.0 | | |
| Erection | | | | c. 38.0 | | 20.8 |
| Female prostitution | | | | c. 27.3 | 37.0 | |
| Male homosexuality | | | | c. 20.9 | 43.0 | |
| Lesbianism | | | | c. 23.5 | 57.0 | |
| AIDS | | | | c. 4.5 | 61.0 | |

(17% male and 28% female). As expected, males have significantly higher approval ratings for engaging in premarital intercourse than females.

*Sex Myths.* The endorsement of sex myths by male and female students were statistically significantly different for 30 of 49 myths included in the survey. Large percentages of students also indicated "don't know" to many of the questions, with females indicating "don't know" more frequently than male students for most of the questions. The "don't know" responses are consistent with the lack of sex-information resources, the inadequacy of sex education programs in the schools where they exist, and the writer's experience of counseling and teaching hundreds of university students who did not possess extremely basic sex information.

*Summary.* Because males and females do experience sexual socialization differently, it can be expected that females will endorse sex myths differently, or discuss sexuality differently, from men. Programs designed to intervene in problem behaviors stemming from beliefs in sex myths may have to target male and female students separately. A large percentage of students used the "don't know" option, indicating that hardly any discussion on those topics had taken place for those students within the family or school system, and that they may be genuinely uncertain.

South African students in this sample are less knowledgeable about sexuality and AIDS than North American students as indicated by North American research studies. South African students have less access to a range of sexuality resources that may better inform them, and researchers have to acknowledge that many students may simply not have been exposed to sex information in a number of areas related to sexuality.

Mosher (1979) contends that there may be more "heat" than "light" in the sex lives of university students in the U.S.A., making the point that the North American student may not be very knowledgeable about sexuality even with access to a variety of resources. It is clear from the results of this study that South African students are even less knowledgeable about sexuality than North American students.

Male students were more knowledgeable at the age of 9 or younger about all the terms listed than female students in this sample, except for menstruation. Very few students had acquired knowledge of these terms by age 10 compared to similar EuroAmerican studies. The percentage of knowledgeable students in this sample ranged from 0.6% for knowledge of venereal disease to 17.6% for knowledge about sexual intercourse.

It is generally assumed that children and young people are learning about sex at considerably younger ages than did their parents and grandparents. Gebhard (1977) verified this assumption, comparing unpublished data collected by the Kinsey Institute for Sex Research between 1938 and 1960 with data collected in the mid-1970s. No such earlier South African data exist to compare with the recent study, but comparison with the two samples in Gebhard (1977), called the "Kinsey Sample" and the "Recent Sample," illustrates the comparatively late acquisition of sex information of the 1990 South African sample on all items of sex knowledge acquisition. Initiatives are therefore necessary to establish the extent of late acquisition of sex knowledge and its implications for safer-sex practices and the development of sexuality-related problems, and they should enjoy high priority among research initiatives.

The implications of this study for research and education point to the potential usefulness of same-sex peer sexuality counseling as a primary method of prevention and intervention. Those who have not had access to sex resources

may more readily accept advice in same-sex groups or present themselves for participation in such groups on sexuality.

This study confirms the fathers' lack of involvement in intrafamilial communication about sexuality, and emphasizes the need for research on South African fathers in this regard. Mothers are the most-preferred source of information about sexuality for female respondents, and school training is the most-preferred source for all respondents. The dynamics of mother-daughter communication about sexuality requires investigation in the South African context, as mothers may be a useful resource to school- and university-based sexuality programs, either by supporting such programs or through actively becoming part of campus-based extracurricular programs.

The overwhelming disapproval of the provision of sex education in kindergarten by 69.5% of respondents reflects the myth of the asexual child. A priority of sex education and sexuality courses should, therefore, be the acknowledgment of childhood sexuality. Myths that parents and teachers may hold in this regard also need to be investigated.

Forty-eight percent of respondents indicated experience in premarital sexual intercourse, while only 30% approve thereof. It is likely that the number of first-year students who experience premarital sex will increase during their first year of study on campus. Counselors are required to prepare students for that probability and offer resources to facilitate decision making about engaging in premarital intercourse.

Of respondents, 75.6% consider abortion as an unacceptable means of terminating pregnancy. Yet a number of respondents will find themselves either pregnant or responsible for a pregnancy, given the high pregnancy statistics at the campus serving as a site for this study. Abortion is illegal in South Africa and counselors cannot, therefore, advocate this as an option, except in rare cases. Providing information and resources to promote safer sex should therefore be a high priority for campus counselors in South Africa.

These studies present findings of significant differences between male and female students in their experience of a range of sexuality-related problems. In South Africa, where sexuality programs are not well established, counselors may be advised to structure intervention groups on a same-sex basis in the first stage of intervention for some problems.

The significant differences for gender that have been found for most sexuality-related concerns in this study require that a sex-counseling program includes a focus on particular gender-related needs of students. More emphasis may need to be placed on homophobia, prejudice, contraception, and belief in sex myths for male students, and emphasis on sex and AIDS knowledge acquisition, safety, and assertiveness for female students in such a program.

A 1994 study of 1,737 black South Africans in their first year attending a university conducted by the first author adds to the understanding of sexual education and the sources on sex information among black South Africans (Nicholas 1994a). The mean age of the subjects was 20.4 years with a range from 16 years old to 50 years old. Peers were reported as the overall primary first source of learning about sexual intercourse (see Table 3). Male and female respondents received the information much more from opposite-sex friends, 35% and 25.2%, respectively, than from same-sex friends, 18.2% and 19%, respectively. Together with reading, this accounts for 73% of the sources of learning for this topic.

Although peers are still ranked as the preferred source of information about sexual intercourse, approximately only half of the respondents who indicated peers as their first source of knowledge also include it as their preferred source (see Tables 4 and 5). The respondents indicated a much greater role for the school or guidance teacher (18.3%), mothers (18.2%), and fathers (5.1%). Peers are the preferred source of sex information for only a quarter of respondents. Peers are also supplanted by "reading" as the most important source of sexuality information. The father's current role in imparting important sexuality information is negligible, but he is the preferred source for 8.1% of males, rivaling the same-sex peer that is the preferred source for 8.3% of male respondents.

## 4. Autoerotic Behaviors and Patterns

A survey of 1,896 black university students revealed that 34.2%, 348 males and 288 females, worried about the

### Table 3

**Sources of Learning About Sexuality (in Percentages):**
**Most Important Source of Sexuality Information**

| Source | Male | Female | Total |
|---|---|---|---|
| Reading | 33.0 | 27.2 | 30.3 |
| Same-sex friend | 17.0 | 14.0 | 15.5 |
| Opposite-sex friend | 14.1 | 12.7 | 13.5 |
| School/guidance teacher | 17.0 | 19.4 | 18.1 |
| Mother | 4.8 | 13.4 | 8.9 |
| Mass media | 7.5 | 3.9 | 5.8 |
| Other | 2.6 | 0.4 | 4.4 |
| Other relative | 1.8 | 2.2 | 2.0 |
| Father | 2.2 | 0.7 | 1.5 |

Statistically significant gender differences: $\chi^2 = 37.34$; $df = 8$; $p = 0.0000$

### Table 4

**Preferred Source of Sexuality Information**
**(in Percentages)**

| Source | Male | Female | Total |
|---|---|---|---|
| Same-sex friend | 8.3 | 9.8 | 9.5 |
| Opposite-sex friend | 19.8 | 11.5 | 15.9 |
| Reading | 19.8 | 22.8 | |
| School/guidance teacher | 21.1 | 17.2 | 19.3 |
| Mother | 8.4 | 29.2 | 18.2 |
| Father | 8.1 | 1.7 | 5.1 |
| Mass media | 6.6 | 2.5 | 4.6 |
| Other | 4.4 | 3.9 | 4.2 |
| Other relative | 2.4 | 1.5 | 2.0 |

Statistically significant gender differences: $\chi^2 = 89.63$; $df = 8$; $p = 0.0000$

### Table 5

**First Source of Information about Sexual**
**Intercourse (in Percentages)**

| Source | Male | Female | Total |
|---|---|---|---|
| Same-sex friend | 18.2 | 19.0 | 18.6 |
| Opposite-sex friend | 35.0 | 25.2 | 29.3 |
| Reading | 21.3 | 29.2 | 25.1 |
| School/guidance teacher | 7.2 | 10.2 | 8.6 |
| Mass media | 9.0 | 3.7 | 6.5 |
| Mother | 2.7 | 6.7 | 4.6 |
| Other | 5.2 | 4.0 | 4.6 |
| Other relative | 3.4 | 1.2 | 2.4 |
| Father | 0.0 | 0.7 | 0.4 |

Statistically significant gender differences: $\chi^2 = 36.28$; $df = 8$; $p = 0.0000$

effect of masturbation (Nicholas 1993b). Of these students, 28.7%, 348 males and 190 females, also believed that women commonly insert foreign objects into the vagina. Over half, 51.9%, did not know whether or not masturbation causes pimples and acne, while 8.5% believed it does have these consequences. Fourteen percent of respondents believed that sexually fulfilled, mature adults do not masturbate, while 54.5% indicated "don't know." Similarly, 16.5% believed that most adults do not masturbate, and 58% indicated they did not know on this point.

## 5. Interpersonal Heterosexual Behaviors

### A/B. Children and Adolescents

A 1995 survey of South African teenagers by a national newspaper revealed the following. Of respondents whose average age was 16 years,

- 41% considered sex before marriage as unacceptable,
- 54% accepted it only with someone they cared about,
- 5% said it is something to experience with as many people as possible,
- 81% considered contraception as both partners' responsibility,
- 80% considered gay-bashing unacceptable,
- 10% indicated that they had a gay experience, and
- 71% thought that they will make a better job of marriage than their parents.

Sixty-seven percent of the respondents were female, but the number of respondents was not indicated in this anonymous 1995 report.

A 1992 survey of 7,000 adolescents found that 17% had engaged in sexual intercourse, with a median age of 15 years at first intercourse (Cooper et al. 1994). (Dating customs, sexual activities, and relationships before college are described in the discussion of first-intercourse experiences.)

Some insights into the sexual behavior of adolescent black South Africans can be drawn from a study of first intercourse and contraceptive experiences of 1,737 black South Africans conducted during their first year in a university (Nicholas 1994a). The mean age of the 754 females and 959 males was 20.4 years (with 24 missing cases). The age range was 16 years old to 50 years old. Of the sample, 37.7% spoke an African language, 28.1% spoke Afrikaans, 27% spoke English, and 7.2% indicated "other." Of respondents, 96.5% indicated that they were single. This discussion will focus on the 894 single students, 47.1% male and 52.9% female, who indicated that they had experienced sexual intercourse.

While females experienced first intercourse with a partner who was 2.5 years older, males reported experiencing first intercourse with a partner who was 1.0 year younger. Male respondents' mean age at first intercourse was 15.5 years and their partners' age was 14.5 years old. Female respondents' mean age was 17.8 years and their partners' mean age was 20.3 years old. Obviously, the first sexual partners of the female respondents were mainly outside the research group.

Most respondents indicated that they experienced their first intercourse with a steady friend. Males were, however, much more likely than females to have had their first intercourse experience with an unknown partner or casual acquaintance. It is a cause for concern that 4.1% of the sample indicated that first intercourse was experienced with a close relative (see Table 6).

Males were more likely than females to have sexual intercourse again with their first partner (see Table 7). Although most respondents had further sexual intercourse with their first partner, 35.5% of females reported no further intercourse with their first partner, as compared to only 20.6% of the male respondents. Almost 70% of respondents had sexual intercourse between 1 and 5 times with the first partner, which points to the short-lived nature of the sexual relationship with the first sexual partner for most respondents. First intercourse may have, therefore, influenced the relationships of the 60.6% of respondents who indicated "steady friend" as their first intercourse partner, because for at least half of this group, sexual intercourse occurred only 1 to 5 times during the "steady" relationship. Of respondents, 46.3% had had one sexual partner in high school and 20.8% had had the first intercourse experience after leaving high school, but before entering university (see Table 8). Males reported significantly higher numbers of high school partners than females.

Twice as many males as females indicated that they greatly enjoyed their first sexual intercourse experience (see Table 9). A third of respondents disliked or greatly disliked their experience of first sexual intercourse, 14.4% of males and 56.9% of females.

[*Update 2000*: Only 3% of teenagers surveyed in the 1998 South African Demographic and Health Survey were married. More than half of the respondents indicated never having had sexual intercourse, and 60% indicated having no sexual partner in the year prior to the interview. About one in five teenagers had sex in the month preceding the survey. Average age at first intercourse was reported as 18 years and age at menarche for most teenagers was below 15 years. By age 19, 35% of all teenagers have been pregnant or have had a child. One in eight teenage deliveries is by cesarean section. Among sexually active teenagers, almost two thirds are currently using a modern contraceptive, with injection/implants being the most popular (50%). One in every five teenaged women reported using a condom in their last sexual intercourse. Sishana and Simbayi (2002) found that some 24.7% of females and 30.3% of males used a condom during their last sexual intercourse. Younger respondents and those with multiple partners were more likely to use condoms than others. (The 1998 South African Demographic and Health Survey was a nationally representative sample selected from the 1996 census data. A total of 12,247 households were surveyed, and 11,735 women were individually interviewed.) (*End of update by L. J. Nicholas*)]

### Table 6

**Partner Relationship in First Sexual Intercourse (in Percentages)**

| Relationship of Partner | Male | Female | Total |
|---|---|---|---|
| Engaged partner | 6.7 | 5.7 | 6.2 |
| Steady friend | 44.6 | 75.5 | 60.6 |
| Casual acquaintance | 24.0 | 5.7 | 14.5 |
| Unknown partner | 8.4 | 2.6 | 5.4 |
| Close relative | 5.3 | 3.1 | 4.1 |
| Other | 5.4 | 7.5 | 9.2 |

Statistically significant gender differences: $\chi^2 = 89.40$; $df = 9$; $p = 0.0000$

### Table 7

**Times Intercourse Took Place with First Partner (in Percentages)**

| Number of Times | Male | Female | Total |
|---|---|---|---|
| Once | 20.6 | 35.5 | 27.2 |
| 2-5 times | 46.4 | 36.0 | 41.8 |
| 6-10 times | 10.4 | 8.4 | 9.5 |
| 11-25 times | 4.9 | 6.1 | 5.4 |
| 26 or more times | 17.6 | 14.0 | 16.09 |

Statistically significant gender differences: $\chi^2 = 23.30$; $df = 4$; $p = 0.0001$

### Table 8

**Number of High School Sexual Partners (in Percentages)**

| Number of Partners | Male | Female | Total |
|---|---|---|---|
| None | 13.4 | 29.4 | 20.8 |
| 1 partner | 37.6 | 56.3 | 46.3 |
| 2-5 partners | 30.4 | 12.4 | 22.0 |
| 6-10 partners | 8.5 | 0.7 | 4.9 |
| 11 or more partners | 10.1 | 1.2 | 6.0 |

Statistically significant gender differences: $\chi^2 = 134.9$; $df = 4$; $p = 0.0000$

### [*Puberty Rituals and Male Virginity Testing*

[*Update 2002*: Traditionally, boys in one of South Africa's biggest townships, KwaMashu, north of Durban, undergo virginity testing, a controversial custom widely carried out among girls in KwaZulu-Natal. The idea of extending female virginity testing to teenage and unmarried males on a monthly basis is being promoted by Isivivane Sama Siko, a group promoting African traditional cultures and a return to traditional customs. Traditional beliefs claim that young boys have a kind of hymen, a white lacy skin on the foreskin. If the foreskin on the penis slips away easily, it means this "hymen" is gone. If the foreskin is sore and hard to move, then it means he is still a virgin. Other methods include checking for a certain vein on the penis. The only time the vein can disappear is when a boy sleeps with a virgin, because her vaginal opening is still tight. Local belief also holds that a boy is a virgin if he can urinate straight up into the air. If the urine sprays, he has had sex before. Another clue used by male virginity testers is the color of the knees: If a man's knees are dark, it is believed he is not a virgin.

[Local physicians maintain: "There is no scientific basis for this. Men don't have hymens and what happens if a guy masturbates, . . . it makes the foreskin looser. Some men are very hygienic and retract the foreskin to clean the penis; they are very diligent with cleaning under the foreskin and get rid of those secretions—then the foreskin will also slip back easily." Dr. Suzanne Leclerc-Madlala, a lecturer at the University of Natal, noted that one effect of virginity testing is to "create fear" among teenagers to prevent them from having sex. "Virginity testing in no way helps halt the spread of AIDS unless part of the testing is done with sex education." (Kenya Community Abroad 2/19/02. kca-aids@ yahoogroups.com). (*End of update by R. T. Francoeur*)] (See also Section 1, Basic Sexological Premises).

### Table 9

**Characteristics of First Sexual Intercourse and High School Sexual Experience (in Percentages)**

| Satisfaction | Male | Female | Total |
|---|---|---|---|
| Greatly enjoyed | 40.5 | 10.2 | 26.3 |
| Enjoyed | 45.1 | 33.0 | 39.4 |
| Disliked | 10.7 | 39.0 | 23.9 |
| Greatly disliked | 3.7 | 17.9 | 10.3 |

Statistically significant gender differences: $\chi^2 = 196.5$; $df = 3$; $p = 0.0000$

## C. Adults

### Sexual Behavior and Relationships of Single Adults

Very little published South African data are available on various interpersonal heterosexual behaviors. Much of the data currently cited, especially in anthropology texts, do not accurately reflect current sexual practices that have been tremendously influenced by modern Western practices. In ten years of sex counseling, the first author found that various sex practices, like anal sex, fellatio, and cunnilingus, were not uncommon. Approximately 40% of these clients had tribal affiliations.

### Marriage and Family Structures

The migratory labor system has been undeniably destructive for the black African marriage and family structure. A consequence of introducing wage earners, forced to live in single-sex hostels in close proximity to impoverished communities with high levels of unemployment, is the inevitable bartering of sex and domestic chores for food and bed; similarly, with long-distance truck drivers and their "traveling wives."

In South African women's magazines, the problems of comarital and extramarital relationships, sexual satisfaction, and sexual outlets and techniques are openly and regularly discussed in advice columns. Among Muslims and Africans, polygamy is still being practiced.

[*Update 2003*: For whites and coloreds, more marriages were solemnized by religious ceremonies than by civil ones, with the reverse for Africans and Indian/Asians. The non-recognition of traditional and religious rites forces these couples to also have a civil ceremony. The number of officially recorded marriages in 1999 was 155,807, an increase of 6.2% on the 1998 figure. This excludes marriages solemnized under customary and religious rites. The 1996 census estimates that 32.2% of all marriages are traditional and that 46.5% of African marriages are traditional. After 2000, these marriages have been included in the civil registration system, enabled by the Recognition of Customary Marriages Act (Statistics South Africa). (*End of update by L. J. Nicholas*)]

### Sexuality and the Disabled

The sexual needs of the disabled are still very much a neglected topic, and the sexual rights of the disabled are not very well served in South Africa (Nicholas 1994a).

### Divorce

[*Update 2003*: In 1999, 37,098 divorces were officially recorded, some 83.4 per 100,000 of population, involving 45,360 minor children. The highest percentage of divorces occurs for marriages lasting between five and nine years of marriage, 28.1%, followed by those lasting between zero and four years. Of the registered divorces occurring among Africans during 1999, 31.1% were for marriages that had lasted 5.9 years, and 18.7% were for marriages that had lasted zero to four years. This divorce peak at five to nine years of marriage is found among all the other population groups, except for whites, where the peak number of divorces is for marriages lasting zero to four years (Statistics South Africa). (*End of update by L. J. Nicholas*)]

## 6. Homoerotic, Homosexual, and Bisexual Behaviors

Isaacs and McKendrick (1992, x) claim that an estimated one out of ten South Africans has a homosexual identity, even if this identity is disguised, denied, or suppressed. The formal gay movement, as represented by the Gay Association of South Africa (GASA), is now defunct as a result of

political and social divisions. Splinter nonracial groups, such as the Gay and Lesbian Organization of the Witwatersrand (GLOW) and the Organization of Lesbian and Gay Activists (OLGA), attempt to address gay issues in parallel with human rights (Isaacs & McKendrick 1992, 158). *Link/Skakel*, the most widely read local newspaper published by GASA, ceased publication in 1985 (Isaac & McKendrik 1992, 157). David Moolman initiated the publication of a private gay newspaper, *Exit*, which was criticized for its sexist, homoerotic, and political biases (Isaacs & McKendrick 1992, 157). A new column called "Outspeak" was introduced to expand coverage of the subject matter in *Exit*, and dealt more explicitly with issues of gay liberation and organization (Gevisser & Cameron 1994, 227).

There are only two formal organizations in South Africa that deal specifically with homosexual crises from the perspective of the crisis-intervention model. These are the Radio 702 Crisis Clinic and the GASA 60-10 Counseling Center in Cape Town (Isaacs & McKendrick 1992, 220). Homosexuals now feel safer about declaring their sexual preferences, and there have been gay-pride marches advocating gay and lesbian rights in the major cities of South Africa.

The first South African gay telephone directory was launched in Johannesburg, and the listing includes gay and gay-friendly businesses and services. The directory allows gay people to make use of the services of people who do not object to their lifestyle (Naidoo 1994).

There are not many referenced accounts of bisexual life in South Africa, but according to Zubeida, it is extremely difficult to be bisexual in a heterosexual society. The following excerpt from an interview with her illustrates her feelings:

> I guess I feel oppressed as a bisexual person. Most lesbian and gay organizations don't really cater for bisexuals—I think largely because bisexuals are even less visible than homosexuals. There is also so much distrust of bisexuals in the homosexual community. Sometimes we are seen as sitting on the fence and enjoying the best of both worlds; usually we are seen as being unable to come out of the closet. (Gevisser & Cameron 1994, 191)

Local university counselors are frequently confronted with ignorance about homosexuality in the campus environment, which may exacerbate the problems their homosexual clients present. A 1990 study of 1,902 first-year students at a black university revealed the following about homophobia and prejudice. Forty-three percent of the sample, 25.5% of the males and 17.9% of the females, believe that homosexuality is immoral. Twenty-seven percent of the sample, 13.7% of the males and 13% of the females, believe that a homosexual person cannot be a good religious person. Forty-six percent, 20.8% of the males and 19.4% of the females, believe that homosexual people could become heterosexual if they chose to. A quarter of the males and 21.8% of the females believe that homosexuality is not an acceptable orientation. A campus environment pervaded with highly homophobic beliefs such as these, is hardly one that provides support for homosexual clients or those struggling with their sexual identity (Nicholas 1994a, 73-74).

## 7. Gender Diversity and Transgender Issues

A survey of 2,209 black university students in 1994 revealed that 8.8% of the respondents (*n* = 194) indicated a moderate need for help with issues of sexual identity, and 8.3% (*n* = 183) of the respondents indicated a high need for help with sexual identity (Nicholas 1994b).

The Groot Schuur Hospital in Cape Town offers medical services for transsexuals who would like to undergo surgery to change their sex. The program includes an assessment by a psychiatrist who evaluates the candidate and makes a recommendation whether or not the surgery should be performed. After surgery, the patient continues counseling with a psychologist and social worker. Medical services for intersexual children are provided at the Red Cross Children's Hospital. The child's sexual orientation is assessed by a psychiatrist who makes a recommendation of the sex that would be most suitable for child. Again, postsurgery counseling and support are provided.

## 8. Significant Unconventional Sexual Behaviors

### A. Sexual Coercion

*Rape and Sexual Abuse*

In 1992, 15,333 cases of child abuse were reported to the Child Protection Unit. Of this number, 3,639 involved rape and 4,135 involved sexual abuse, including sodomy, incest, and other forms of sexual assault (Cooper et al. 1994). [*Update 2003*: Some 52,860 cases of rape and attempted rape were reported (120.1 per 100,000) (Kane-Berman 2002). The Early Sexual Experiences checklist was completed by 1,434 South African first-year students in 2002 to assess their victimization by pedophiles and exposure to sexual abuse (43%). Some 268 respondents (18.7%) indicated that they had had unwanted sexual experiences before their 16th birthday, and 97 respondents (0.68%; 62 female, 31 male, and 4 missing data), met the *DSM-IV-TR* criteria for experience of pedophilia; some 148 indicated abuse after the age of 16. Of respondents, 62% indicated that they were moderately to extremely bothered by the experience when it occurred, and 59% indicated that they were still moderately to extremely bothered by the experience.

[Neither the relationship between gender and the perpetrator relationship nor the number of times the behavior occurred was significant. The relationship between language group and the perpetrator relationship is significant. The biggest differences between observed and expected frequencies arc in the relative and friend/acquaintance categories of Afrikaans, the friend/acquaintance category of English, and the relative and stranger categories of African language. When all those who indicated abuse, 416 (205 males and 204 females), are analyzed, a different picture emerges. Women respondents were more bothered at the time, and when completing the questionnaire, than male respondents. Those experiencing relatively severe experiences were more bothered than those experiencing relatively less-severe experiences at the time, though this was not the case currently. Language remained not significant in relation to how bothered respondents were by their experience. The long-term negative effects of sexual abuse are borne out by this study for both relatively severe and less-severe victimization (Nicholas 2002). (*End of update by L. J. Nicholas*)]

The inquiry into legislation on rape (Havenga 1985) was regarded as presenting resistance to genuine reform. This inquiry was launched in May 1982, and was found to have certain inadequacies, mainly the emphasis on sexual aspects in the definition of rape (in contrast with the feminist emphasis on the violence aspects), the failure to make the definition of rape gender-neutral, and the failure to include oral and anal sex and penetration by means of an object. The recommendation that the law stating that a man could not be found guilty of raping his wife be rescinded was qualified by the requirement that prosecution in such cases cannot proceed without permission from the attorney general. The

previous sexual history of a rape victim/survivor can still be entered in evidence in camera.

The convictions for child sexual abuse for the years 1989 to 1992 were as follows: 1989, 1,086; 1990, 1,061; 1991, 1,345; and 1992, 1,124.

[*Update 2003*: In 2000, 21,438 rapes and attempted rapes of children under the age of 18 were reported. Some 113 cases of incest and 4,027 cases of indecent assault were reported (Kane-Berman 2002).

[The South African Law Commission made the following final recommendations regarding rape to the Justice Minister:

1. Intentional nondisclosure of infectivity by a life-threatening STD prior to sexual intercourse amounts to sexual relations by false pretenses, and would, therefore, constitute rape.
2. The definition of rape would be broadened to include anal penetration.
3. Men could be rape victims and women could be convicted of rape.
4. The state would no longer have to prove lack of consent, but that penetration occurred under coercive circumstances.
5. Two new crimes will carry the same penalties as rape:
   a. where any object was used to penetrate the anus or genital organs in conditions similar to rape.
   b. Oral-genital sexual violation, where genital organs or that of an animal penetrates the mouth in rape-like circumstances (SAPA 2003, 1, 3). Hiding HIV could turn sex into rape. (*End of update by L. J. Nicholas*)]

[*Update 2001*: According to the South African Demographic and Health Survey (1998), 4% of women who had ever been pregnant reported that they had been physically abused during pregnancy. One in eight women reported having been beaten by a partner, 6% reported abuse in the last year, and of these, 43% reported needing medical attention. Only 4% of all women reported ever having been raped. (*End of update by L. J. Nicholas*)]

### B. Prostitution

Prostitution is illegal in South Africa but has flourished in all major cities and townships for decades. In Cape Town, up to 200 prostitutes were allowed to work in the harbor area and were registered by the authorities as "port hostesses." They were recently banned from plying their trade, ostensibly because of safety concerns such as smoking on board ships carrying hazardous cargo (Underhill 1995). Daily newspapers have several columns devoted to advertisements for "escort services" that are fairly explicit offers of sexual services.

The socioeconomic status (SES) of black students has an influence on whether they are tempted to trade sexual favors for financial or educational gain. The difference in the SES between teachers and pupils led them to believe that they could have access to this perceived affluence through a sexual relationship. Pupils who trade sexual favors for financial gain are sworn to secrecy by allies and co-conspirators. In one case we are familiar with, Moses acknowledged that sex had taken place between a group of boys of whom he was one and their male teacher, but that they would "get" anyone who spoke out, as they were all "paid well."

Socioeconomic circumstances can lure pupils into prostitution, as in the case of five standard eight girls (age 15 to 16 years old) who were absent from school for three months and were subsequently found at a brothel. Female students also mentioned trading sex for grades. While these reports may not be completely accurate, it is sufficient for such allegations to gain currency in a school to damage seriously the confidence of pupils in the grading system. The lack of opportunities to discuss sexuality openly in school would, therefore, further exacerbate this serious problem (Nicholas 1994a, 4-5).

### C. Pornography and Erotica

South Africa now has local versions of *Penthouse*, *Playboy*, and *Hustler*. The censor board keeps a vigilant eye on these and other similar publications and recently lost a case against *Hustler* under the new constitution's freedom-of-speech provision. A new swingers' magazine, *Xpose*, with graphic closeups of male genitals and female vulvas, was recently launched (Chapel 1995). Pornographic movies are not openly available, but have a wide underground distribution. See also comments in Section 1A/B, Basic Sexological Premises, Gender Roles and the Sociolegal Status of Males and Females, above.

## 9. Contraception, Abortion, and Population Planning

### A. Contraception

In a study of 1,737 first-year black South African students, first intercourse was primarily characterized by the lack of contraceptive use, with 35.7% of the males and 32.8% of the females indicating non-use of contraceptives, and 12.3% of the males and 7.1% of the females indicating "don't know" (see Table 10). A further 6.2% reported using the unreliable withdrawal method (Nicholas 1994a, 88-94).

The major reasons given for not using a contraceptive were that the first sexual intercourse was unplanned (36.8%) and that no thought was given to contraception at the time of the first intercourse act (38.1%) (see Table 11). The belief that if one only has intercourse "a few times," contraception is not essential, was endorsed by 31.6% of respondents. The erroneous belief that having sexual intercourse only once or a few times protects one from the risks associated with unsafe sex, may significantly influence students to make the transition from virginity to nonvirginity without using contraceptives.

The opinion of significant others also influenced respondents' use of contraceptives. Male and female respondents almost equally were uncomfortable being too prepared (23.6%). Mothers' discovery of contraceptive use was cited by 18.8% of respondents, and fathers' displeasure was cited by 17.9% of respondents, as reasons that prevented contraceptive use. Of respondents, 18.1% indicated that contraceptive use was impractical when engaging in "many rounds of sex." Most safer-sex messages assume a single encounter requiring a single condom and neglect those who continue sexual activity after the first orgasm.

This study revealed that 54.2% of female respondents and 55.5% of male respondents had experienced sexual intercourse. Darling et al. (1992) cite relevant research indicating that, while males experience first sexual intercourse at a younger age than females, the average age for females is also declining to around 16 years of age. Further research is required to establish a trend towards gender convergence among South African students. Female respondents in this sample experienced first intercourse at 17.8 years old, compared to Darling et al.'s (1992) report of 17.7 years old. Male respondents initiated first intercourse at 15.5 years old, 2.3 years younger than the sample of Darling et al. (1992). No similar South African studies on first intercourse have been done to facilitate local comparisons.

This study found that many students do not use contraception during first intercourse. Similar to other studies, this reflects the unplanned nature of first sexual intercourse. Peers are reported as the primary first source of learning about sexual intercourse and are also considered the preferred source by respondents. "Reading," however, was indicated as the most important source of information about sexuality. More emphasis should be placed on the gender differences for peers' provision of sexuality information. This study found that opposite-sex friends are more likely to be the first source of sexuality information, as well as the preferred source of sexuality information. The same-sex friend was, however, considered the most important source of sexuality information. Peer sexuality programs could be guided by the preferred source of sexuality information in relation to gender.

The provision of information on safer sex has been found to be inadequate in facilitating desired behavior change (Keeling 1991). Those students who have not developed a

### Table 11

**Factors Preventing Contraceptive Use During First Sexual Encounter: Response to Statement, "What Prevented the Use of a Contraceptive During Your First Sexual Encounter?" (Rank Ordered; in Percentages)**

| Reason Given | Male | Female | Total |
|---|---|---|---|
| I used a contraceptive | 18.0 | 23.2 | 41.2 |
| I did not think about it | 21.6 | 16.5 | 38.1 |
| I did not intend to have sex | 14.8 | 22.0 | 36.8 |
| I only did it a few times | 18.0 | 13.6 | 31.6 |
| I feared the side effects | 12.6 | 11.8 | 24.2 |
| I was uncomfortable being too prepared | 11.6 | 12.0 | 23.6 |
| There was none available | 15.2 | 8.2 | 23.4 |
| It is against my religion | 9.8 | 9.8 | 19.6 |
| I feared that my mother would discover my use of contraceptives | 7.6 | 11.2 | 18.8 |
| It is impractical for many rounds of sex | 14.1 | 4.0 | 18.1 |
| I feared my father would be displeased | 8.1 | 9.8 | 17.9 |
| It makes sex unpleasant | 13.0 | 3.8 | 16.8 |
| It is not my responsibility | 6.5 | 8.2 | 14.7 |
| I thought it was the wrong time of the month | 2.9 | 5.4 | 8.3 |
| It is too expensive | 5.6 | 2.0 | 7.6 |
| I thought I was sterile | 4.0 | 2.7 | 6.7 |
| I was drunk | 3.6 | 0.3 | 3.9 |
| I wanted to cause a pregnancy | 2.4 | 1.3 | 3.7 |

### Table 10

**Contraceptive Practices at First Sexual Intercourse (in Percentages)**

| Contraception Used | Male | Female | Total |
|---|---|---|---|
| No method | 35.7 | 32.8 | 34.3 |
| Pill | 14.6 | 22.8 | 18.5 |
| Condom | 19.5 | 13.3 | 16.6 |
| Withdrawal | 7.4 | 4.8 | 6.2 |
| Rhythm | 1.1 | 0.5 | 0.8 |
| Condom & contraceptive | 6.8 | 11.9 | 9.2 |
| Other | 2.7 | 6.9 | 4.7 |
| Don't know | 12.3 | 7.1 | 9.8 |

pattern of risky sex practices may be more amenable to early intervention before high-risk patterns of sexual behavior set in. Students who have yet to make the transition to non-virginity, as well as those who have had only a few sexual experiences, may be more open to establish patterns of safer-sex behaviors through early intervention by counselors.

Starting in 1990, the first author and several colleagues have conducted an annual survey of first-time entry, first-year university students enrolling at a predominantly black university (Nicholas 1994b, 1993a, 1993b, 1992, 1991, 1990; Nicholas & Orr 1994; Nicholas, Tredoux, & Daniels 1994; Nicholas & Durrheim 1994). All consenting first-year students who attended the orientation program completed a structured questionnaire on intrafamilial communication about contraception. In 1990, 1,986 students completed questionnaires that included 829 male students and 948 female students (18 missing cases). In 1991, 2,069 students completed questionnaires, 1,029 males and 1,040 females. In 1992, 1,558 students completed questionnaires that included 684 male and 834 female students (32 missing cases).

Forty-eight percent of the 1990 sample (885) indicated that they had had sexual intercourse. Fifty-four percent of the 1991 sample (1,115) indicated that they had had sexual intercourse. Fifty-three percent of the 1992 sample (793) indicated that they had had sexual intercourse. Less than 30% of the total sample indicated approval of premarital sexual intercourse, while more than 50% of the sample indicated nonvirgin status.

Approximately twice as many respondents felt that their mothers would be understanding about a problem concerning contraceptive matters, as opposed to fathers (see Table 12). The percentage of students responding affirmatively about their mothers' understanding increased from 28.5% in 1990 to 38.3% in 1992. The percentage of respondents responding affirmatively about their fathers' understanding increased by only 4% from 1990 to 1992. Most students, therefore, do not consider their parents as understanding about a problem concerning contraception. Gender differences are significant at the probability level greater than .00001 ($p. > .00001$) level for respondents surveyed in all three years.

Over three quarters of respondents indicated that their fathers had not given them any information about contraception, compared to approximately 55% of respondents who indicated that their mothers had not provided such information (see Table 13). There was no significant difference for gender in the 1991 and 1992 samples. For the 1990 sample, $p = .0004$. Slightly more males than females had received information about contraceptives from their fathers. On average, more than twice the respondents received this information from mothers than fathers. More males received information about contraception from mothers than fathers, emphasizing the lack of involvement of fathers in these discussions.

More students preferred that their fathers not know about their use of contraceptives than they did their mothers (see Table 14). Twice as many female respondents disagreed with this statement than did male respondents. Gender differences are significant at the $p < .00001$ level for all three years.

Approximately three quarters of respondents indicated that they had not discussed contraception thoroughly with their mothers, and almost 90% of the respondents indicated this to be the case in relation to fathers (see Table 15). Fathers were conspicuously absent as far as thorough discussion of contraception is concerned. Gender differences are significant at the $p < .00001$ level for all three years.

Approximately a third of respondents believed that their mother's estimation of them would not decrease if the mother knew they were using a contraceptive (see Table 16). Approximately a quarter of respondents be-

### Table 12

**Response to Statement, "If I Had a Problem Concerning Contraceptive Matters, I Could Count on My Mother/Father to Be Understanding"**

| | Sample Year | | | | | |
|---|---|---|---|---|---|---|
| | 1990 | | 1991 | | 1992 | |
| Response | Mother | Father | Mother | Father | Mother | Father |
| True | 532 | 273 | 712 | 349 | 585 | 284 |
| | (28.5%) | (14.7%) | (35.2%) | (17.5%) | (38.3%) | (18.8%) |
| False | 736 | 977 | 698 | 991 | 545 | 803 |
| | (39.4%) | (52.8%) | (34.5%) | (49.8%) | (35.7%) | (53.2%) |
| Don't know | 600 | 601 | 615 | 650 | 396 | 423 |
| | (32.1%) | (32.5%) | (30.4%) | (32.7%) | (26.0%) | (28.0%) |
| Column Totals | 1,868 | 1,851 | 2,025 | 1,990 | 1,526 | 1,510 |
| | (100%) | (100%) | (100%) | (100%) | (100%) | (100%) |

### Table 13

**Response to Statement, "My Mother/Father Has Never Given Me Any Information about Contraceptives"**

| | Sample Year | | | | | |
|---|---|---|---|---|---|---|
| | 1990 | | 1991 | | 1992 | |
| Response | Mother | Father | Mother | Father | Mother | Father |
| True | 1,060 | 1,424 | 1,123 | 1,563 | 835 | 1,160 |
| | (56.5%) | (76.4%) | (55.3%) | (77.6%) | (54.6%) | (76.6%) |
| False | 747 | 346 | 853 | 384 | 673 | 306 |
| | (39.8%) | (18.6%) | (42.0%) | (19.1%) | (44.0%) | (20.2%) |
| Don't know | 68 | 94 | 56 | 66 | 22 | 48 |
| | (3.6%) | (5.0%) | (2.8%) | (3.3%) | (1.4%) | (3.2%) |
| Column Totals | 1,875 | 1,864 | 2,032 | 2,013 | 1,530 | 1,514 |
| | (100%) | (100%) | (100%) | (100%) | (100%) | (100%) |

### Table 14

**Response to Statement, "If I Were to Use a Contraceptive, I Would Prefer That My Mother/Father Not Know about It"**

| | Sample Year | | | | | |
|---|---|---|---|---|---|---|
| | 1990 | | 1991 | | 1992 | |
| Response | Mother | Father | Mother | Father | Mother | Father |
| True | 921 | 1,090 | 944 | 1,169 | 711 | 871 |
| | (49.5%) | (58.8%) | (46.5%) | (58.5%) | (46.6%) | (57.5%) |
| False | 666 | 404 | 826 | 477 | 628 | 376 |
| | (35.8%) | (21.8%) | (40.7%) | (23.9%) | (41.2%) | (24.8%) |
| Don't know | 275 | 359 | 258 | 352 | 186 | 268 |
| | (14.8%) | (19.4%) | (12.7%) | (17.0%) | (12.2%) | (17.7%) |
| Column Totals | 1,862 | 1,853 | 2,028 | 1,998 | 1,525 | 1,515 |
| | (100%) | (100%) | (100%) | (100%) | (100%) | (100%) |

lieved their father would not disapprove if he knew. Gender differences are significant at the $p < .0001$ level.

Three times as many respondents were encouraged to use contraceptives by mothers as by fathers (see Table 17). Most students, however, have not been encouraged by parents to use contraceptives. Gender differences are significant at the $p < .00001$ level.

Few students indicated that they shared the same ideas and beliefs about contraceptives as their parents, with more of such sharing being evident in relation to mothers than fathers (see Table 18). A large percentage of respondents also indicated "don't know," indicating the basic lack of communication between parents and children.

### Table 15

**Response to Statement, "I Have Discussed My Contraceptive Use Thoroughly with My Mother/Father"**

| | Sample Year | | | | | |
|---|---|---|---|---|---|---|
| | 1990 | | 1991 | | 1992 | |
| Response | Mother | Father | Mother | Father | Mother | Father |
| True | 302 | 84 | 377 | 118 | 302 | 86 |
| | (16.3%) | (4.6%) | (18.9%) | (6.0%) | (20.0%) | (5.7%) |
| False | 1,417 | 1,610 | 1,518 | 1,758 | 1,138 | 1,345 |
| | (76.3%) | (87.7%) | (76.1%) | (89.1%) | (75.3%) | (89.7%) |
| Don't know | 137 | 142 | 99 | 98 | 71 | 68 |
| | (7.4%) | (7.7%) | (5.0%) | (5.0%) | (4.7%) | (4.5%) |
| Column Totals | 1,856 | 1,836 | 1,994 | 1,974 | 1,511 | 1,499 |
| | (100%) | (100%) | (100%) | (100%) | (100%) | (100%) |

### Table 16

**Response to Statement, "If My Mother/Father Knew I Used a Contraceptive, Their Estimation of Me Would Go Down"**

| | Sample Year | | | | | |
|---|---|---|---|---|---|---|
| | 1990 | | 1991 | | 1992 | |
| Response | Mother | Father | Mother | Father | Mother | Father |
| True | 576 | 638 | 566 | 643 | 487 | 543 |
| | (31.0%) | (34.7%) | (28.6%) | (33.0%) | (31.9%) | (36.0%) |
| False | 611 | 435 | 711 | 467 | 542 | 367 |
| | (32.8%) | (23.6%) | (35.9%) | (24.0%) | (35.5%) | (24.3%) |
| Don't know | 673 | 767 | 703 | 838 | 498 | 599 |
| | (36.2%) | (41.7%) | (35.5%) | (43.0%) | (32.6%) | (39.7%) |
| Column Totals | 1,860 | 1,840 | 1,980 | 1,948 | 1,527 | 1,509 |
| | (100%) | (100%) | (100%) | (100%) | (100%) | (100%) |

### Table 17

**Response to Statement, "My Mother/Father Has Encouraged Me to Use Contraceptives"**

| | Sample Year | | | | | |
|---|---|---|---|---|---|---|
| | 1990 | | 1991 | | 1992 | |
| Response | Mother | Father | Mother | Father | Mother | Father |
| True | 301 | 113 | 380 | 116 | 327 | 109 |
| | (16.2%) | (6.1%) | (19.2%) | (5.9%) | (21.5%) | (7.2%) |
| False | 1,460 | 1,583 | 1,510 | 1,734 | 1,116 | 1,308 |
| | (78.5%) | (85.6%) | (76.3%) | (88.9%) | (73.4%) | (86.8%) |
| Don't know | 99 | 154 | 89 | 101 | 78 | 90 |
| | (5.3%) | (8.3%) | (4.5%) | (5.2%) | (5.1%) | (6.0%) |
| Column Totals | 1,860 | 1,850 | 1,979 | 1,951 | 1,521 | 1,507 |
| | (100%) | (100%) | (100%) | (100%) | (100%) | (100%) |

In a study to identify barriers to condom use among 700 high school students, Abdool Karim et al. (1992) found that the students were not using condoms to any significant degree, felt that condoms limited sexual pleasure, felt that condom use indicated a lack of trust in one's partner's faithfulness, challenged the male ego, and/or may indicate that one has an STD. Condom use was not well understood, and they were not accessible or available when required. Oral contraceptives cost about $30 per month and condoms $3 a piece. Both are available free at community clinics.

*Implications for Counselors*

Sex counseling as a discipline is not widely practiced in South Africa. The university's obligation to provide such a resource has been de-emphasized, influenced by the unresolved debate on the appropriate location of sex-counseling resources and the taboos around sexuality. The possibility that intrafamilial communication about contraception might make a major contribution towards eliminating unwanted pregnancy is slim, given the minimal involvement of parents in the provision of information about contraception, especially that of fathers. Schools are unlikely to make any major contribution to contraceptive education, and the thousands of university-bound students requiring guidance on contraception will become the responsibility of campus counselors.

The effective shouldering of this responsibility requires a knowledge of local circumstances and resources. For example, until 1996, abortion was illegal in South Africa, so counselors' efforts had to be largely focused on prevention. This would include facilitating programs that involve larger groups of students gaining access to contraceptive information, while still remaining accessible to individual clients. Knowledge of the incidence of sexual-related problems at a particular university is crucial in making students aware of the risks of unprotected sexual intercourse that could directly affect them. The availability of postcoital contraception for use up to 72 hours after sexual intercourse should also be made widely known in the campus community.

Advice on condom usage by counselors has to be specific as to local availability and practices. Sidley (1991) found that choosing a brand of condoms in South Africa is bedeviled by a range of factors. Only one brand is produced locally, Crepe de Chine, and the rest are imported without being subjected to tests before being placed on the market. The 24 brands, which the South African Bureau of Standards (SABS) tested two years ago, failed. Up to 33% of the condoms tested by the Johannesburg City Health Department failed the trials.

The SABS tests for dimensions, mass, tensile strength, elongation, breaking point, aging, freedom from holes, and leakage, but does not make a standard mark compulsory. None of the imported brands bear the quality mark of their country. Three suppliers meet SABS specifications: Vulco, which is South African, F.T.C. Aircraft, manufactured in Thailand, and

Freedom, made in Korea. One spermicide, Rendells, contains oil that can cause a rubber condom to blister and burst (Sidley 1991). Counseling clients with regard to condom usage, whether for prevention of pregnancy, STDs, or HIV transmission, has to take into account the many risks associated with condom usage (Masters & Johnson 1986). These include the care that has to be taken in avoiding having preejaculatory fluid spilling onto the labia, spillage of semen when the condom is removed or during detumescence, and the residue of semen on the penis that may come into contact with the vagina.

Effective contraceptive programs for university students must, however, not stop at providing accurate information about contraception. The acceptance of self and others as sexual beings, and of contraception as primarily a sexual rather than a reproductive decision, is essential for effective contraception programs among South African blacks.

[*Update 2001*: Half of the women in the South African Demographic and Health Survey (1998) are currently using a contraceptive method, and almost all women who have ever used contraception have used a modern contraceptive. The most widely used method is the injection/implantable (27%), followed by the pill and female sterilization (9%). Asian women are most likely to use contraception, followed by whites, coloreds, and Africans. Asian and white women tend to use the pill and female sterilization, while African and colored women tend to use injections. Male sterilization is commonly used by white couples. Only 53% of women were aware that abortion is legal in South Africa. (*End of update by L. J. Nicholas*)]

### B. Teenage (Unmarried) Pregnancies

In a survey at a local hospital, Sapire (1988) found that 75% of the pregnancies were unintended and 20% of the pregnant women were under 19 years of age. The seriousness of the problem is exemplified by requests for pregnancy tests and the morning-after pill at black universities (Nicholas 1994a, 63).

In Cape Town in 1987, of 2,800 teenage mothers, 2,300 were unmarried. The biggest increase in illegitimacy was among whites, where the percentage has doubled since 1982. In 1986, the percentage of white illegitimate births was 11.3% of all white births in Cape Town; in 1987, this increased to 17.2%. For coloreds, the number of illegitimate births increased from 6,700 in 1986 to 7,100. The percentage of illegitimate babies born to black, colored, and Asian women in Cape Town was 47.5% in 1987 (Stander 1988). A special clinic was instituted at a local hospital for pregnant teenagers, 90% of whom were unmarried, so that they would not have to attend with married women (Burman & Preston-Whyte 1992). Ample evidence exists that a stigma is attached to teenage pregnancy while unmarried for both the mother and child in all sections of South African society. Pregnant pupils consequently conceal their pregnancy from parents who are often absent. Burman (1992, 31) quotes a nurse in this regard:

> Parents or teachers may discover when she gets labor pains that she is pregnant, and it is only then that she can be rushed to a hospital. Schoolgirls don't want to book in advance as this will require them to attend clinics on certain days, which will mean that they are absent [from school] . . . The focus will be on them and the classmates can guess their problem and will laugh at them. They don't want to be seen by neighbours frequenting the clinic as they will talk badly of them (Interview of November 23, 1988).

While stigma is attached to teenaged pregnancy, fertility also has a cultural value, as is illustrated in the following example of a 17-year-old African girl who became pregnant at 16:

> I knew I might get a baby, and the sister at school warned me also. But I had been going with my boyfriend for over a year and my girl friends were beginning to laugh at me. They whispered that I must be inyumba—that is, how you say, sterile. Even my boyfriend asked why I was not having a baby. Then, when I did get pregnant, my mother and father were very cross, but I was pleased as it showed everyone I can have a baby after all. (Preston-Whyte & Zondi 1992, 237)

### C. Abortion

The Abortion and Sterilization Act No. 2 of 1975, which was the law until late 1996, allowed abortions only for instances of rape, incest, or when there is a danger to the physical health or life of the woman. The procedure for allowing a legal abortion was often so cumbersome that many who qualified opted for illegal abortion or went to another country where abortion is legal to have the operation performed.

In November 1996, a new abortion law passed its final legislative hurdle, clearing the way for President Nelson Mandela to replace one of the world's toughest abortion laws with one of the most liberal. The Choice of Termination of Pregnancy Bill was approved by a vote of 49 to 21 in the South African Senate. Twenty senators were absent when the vote was taken. The African National Congress insisted that members who could not support the new law absent themselves from the vote. The white-separatist Freedom Front, the National Party, and the Inkatha Freedom Party opposed the measure, as did Doctors for Life, which promised an immediate appeal to the Constitutional Court.

Under the new law, women and girls are entitled to a state-financed abortion on demand during the first 12 weeks of pregnancy if they have no private medical insurance. This support also applies between 12 and 20 weeks of pregnancy, subject to widely defined conditions. Physicians and midwives are required to advise a minor female to consult her parents, but the law specifically states that abortion cannot be denied if the minor refuses to inform her parents.

In 1986 and 1987, respectively, 770 and 810 legal abortions were performed in South Africa. During the same period, 26,062 and 35,882 operations for the removal of residues of a pregnancy were performed. These opera-

#### Table 18

**Response to Statement, "I Think That My Mother's/Father's Ideas and Beliefs about Contraceptive Use Are Very Similar to My Own"**

| | Sample Year | | | | | |
| | 1990 | | 1991 | | 1992 | |
| Response | Mother | Father | Mother | Father | Mother | Father |
|---|---|---|---|---|---|---|
| True | 735 | 507 | 716 | 473 | 617 | 417 |
| | (39.5%) | (27.4%) | (36.3%) | (24.3%) | (40.6%) | (27.7%) |
| False | 407 | 472 | 423 | 504 | 326 | 396 |
| | (21.9%) | (25.2%) | (21.5%) | (25.8%) | (21.4%) | (26.3%) |
| Don't know | 718 | 871 | 832 | 969 | 578 | 692 |
| | (38.6%) | (47.1%) | (42.2%) | (49.8%) | (38.0%) | (46.0%) |
| Column Totals | 1,860 | 1,850 | 1,971 | 1,944 | 1,521 | 1,505 |
| | (100%) | (100%) | (100%) | (100%) | (100%) | (100%) |

tions usually follow an illegal abortion and account for an unknown proportion of illegal abortions in South Africa. In 1992, 1,027 legal abortions had been performed in the first nine months, and 82 people were convicted between July 1988 and June 1991 of performing illegal abortions. [*Update 2003*: Some 155,624 abortions were performed in public hospitals and clinics between February 1997 and January 2001 (Kane-Berman 2002). (*End of update by L. J. Nicholas*)]

Of the 1,902 first-year students at a South African university, 75.6% were against abortion (35.8% male and 39.8% female). Only 15% of respondents felt that abortion is an acceptable way to terminate a pregnancy (8.6% male and 6.4% female).

## 10. Sexually Transmitted Diseases and HIV/AIDS

### A. Sexually Transmitted Diseases

In South Africa as elsewhere, sexually transmitted diseases (STDs) constitute a major public health problem. The annual caseload seen only at state/municipal clinics and in private practice is estimated at more than a million patients in a population of 40 million. Management of this endemic is worsened by the wide range of STDs encountered in South Africa, where the common Western STDs of syphilis, herpes, gonorrhea, and nongonococcal urethritis (NGU) coexist with tropical and subtropical entities like chancroid, lymphogranuloma venereum (LGV), and granuloma inguinale (Donovanosis). This poses a considerable number of diagnostic and therapeutic problems, especially among the people of color, the poor, and rural people.

In South Africa, considering the character of the primary healthcare and its context where access to laboratory facilities is limited, diagnosis and treatment are based more on a clinical pathology grouping of ulcerative, discharge, lymphadenopathy, and pelvic inflammatory disease (abdominal pain and infection) than on laboratory tests for specific causative organisms. Diagnosis in South Africa is often by exclusion of other similar infections (gonorrhea), as laboratory facilities are often limited or inaccessible. Combination treatment of NGU and gonorrhea is usually cheaper than the laboratory costs.

Table 19 shows the results of research on STDs at a South African university for the years 1989 to 1991 (Nicholas 1994a).

Black secondary and post high-school students are at high risk of acquiring STDs, because they are mostly single and the highest incidence of infection occurs in people between the ages of 15 and 24. Studies have shown, however, that the STD-infection rate decreases as education increases. Still, STD-infection rates for nonspecific urethritis, trichomoniasis, and herpes may be more common in college-educated people (Nicholas 1994a, 35).

#### Table 19

**New Cases of Sexually Transmitted Diseases
(First Infection by Year)**

| Disease | 1989 | 1990 | 1991 |
|---|---|---|---|
| Syphilis | 47 | 46 | 31 |
| Gonorrhea | 337 | 325 | 312 |
| NGU | 67 | 79 | 107 |
| Other | 202 | 239 | 479 |
| Total cases | 653 | 687 | 929 |

Total student population: 13,000

A sample of general students surveyed reported a prevalence rate of STD of 18%. Studies at another South African university revealed an STD-prevalence rate of 19.9% to 23.8% for the years 1991 and 1992. For both years, the prevalence of STD was higher than the 13% reported by the nearby general local hospital.

In another study of 1,902 black first-year students at a South African university, 17% believed that only promiscuous people contract STDs; 11% did not believe that people are ethically bound to warn potential sexual partners if they have a sexually transmitted disease, 82% of students would not have a relationship with someone who had an STD, and 35% of students indicated that if they found out someone close to them had an STD, it would negatively affect their opinion of him or her (Nicholas 1994a).

### B. HIV/AIDS

The total South African AIDS budget decreased from $6,076,337 in 1992/1993 to $6,045,556 in 1993/1994, a real decrease of 11%. According to the World Health Organization (WHO), South Africa should be spending $40 million a year on AIDS (Preston-Whyte 1995; Schoepf 1995).

Between April and September 1993, 488 cases of AIDS were reported in South Africa. Of these reported cases, 81% were African heterosexual men and women and 7% were infants. In nearly all the new cases of AIDS, the virus had been transmitted by heterosexual intercourse, in comparison with the period 1982-1986, when 88% of cases of the virus had been transmitted by homosexual intercourse. The Department of National Health and Population Development has reported that 550 people in South Africa were being infected with HIV daily in 1993. About 7,000 people were expected to develop AIDS in 1993. In 1995, the rate of HIV infection was expected to rise to 2.8% for men and 4% for women (Cooper et al. 1994). Table 20 provides an overall picture of HIV infection and AIDS in South Africa.

#### Table 20

**AIDS Cases According to Method of Transmission, Race, and Sex: 1982-1993 (Cooper et al. 1994)**

| | Homo- & Bi-sexual | Hetero-sexual | Hemo-philiac | Other Blood Trans-fusion | IV-Drug Users | Pedi-atric | Total |
|---|---|---|---|---|---|---|---|
| African | | | | | | | |
| Male | 3 | 313 | 3 | 4 | 1 | 99 | 423 |
| Female | 0 | 336 | 0 | 0 | 0 | 82 | 418 |
| Unknown | 0 | 6 | 0 | 0 | 0 | 4 | 10 |
| Colored | | | | | | | |
| Male | 21 | 13 | 1 | 1 | 0 | 0 | 36 |
| Female | 0 | 12 | 0 | 1 | 0 | 0 | 13 |
| Indian | | | | | | | |
| Male | 4 | 1 | 0 | 0 | 0 | 0 | 5 |
| Female | 0 | 0 | 0 | 0 | 0 | 0 | 0 |
| White | | | | | | | |
| Male | 61 | 14 | 13 | 12 | 1 | 0 | 401 |
| Female | 0 | 4 | 0 | 4 | 0 | 0 | 8 |
| Unknown | 0 | 1 | 0 | 1 | 0 | 0 | 2 |
| Total | | | | | | | |
| Male | 389 | 341 | 17 | 17 | 2 | 99 | 865 |
| Female | 0 | 352 | 0 | 5 | 0 | 82 | 439 |
| Unknown | 0 | 7 | 0 | 1 | 0 | 4 | 12 |
| Grand Total | 389 | 700 | 17 | 23 | 2 | 185 | 1,316 |

Analyzing results of an anonymous structured questionnaire designed to obtain baseline data on knowledge and attitudes of first-year black university students about AIDS and their attitudes towards homosexuals in 1990, 1991, and 1992 (ns = 1,902, 2,113, and 1,558), it is obvious that the students' knowledge of AIDS was inadequate, and misconceptions about AIDS transmission abounded. Prejudiced and exclusionary beliefs about people with AIDS were also common. Little difference was evident on any of the scales over the three-year period (Nicholas et al. 1994).

An AIDS-knowledge survey of 2,209 black university students in 1994 revealed striking misinformation about the risk of contracting AIDS by giving blood (41.5% said yes, 10.5% were unsure), contracting AIDS from a toilet seat (6% said yes, 8.1% were unsure), by masturbating oneself (2.9% said yes, 26.2% were unsure), and a high risk through blood transfusion (57.4% said yes, 22.5% were unsure (see Table 21).

In 1994, the newly appointed national AIDS director stated that previous AIDS-awareness programs only served to heighten fear and increase the stigma attached to AIDS,

resulting in infected people's being reluctant to disclose their status. She promised to rebuild the AIDS program (St. Leger 1994). (See also Section 10B, HIV/AIDS, in Part 2 of this chapter.)

*[The Incidence of HIV/AIDS in South Africa*

[*Update 2003*: The first antenatal survey in 1990 provided a baseline from which HIV trends have been assessed annually. Anonymous, unlinked, cross-sectional surveys were conducted among first-time pregnant women attending public antenatal clinics during October. October was selected because surveys undertaken by Statistics South Africa indicated that, during this period, the population tends toward more stability and is less mobile. A weighted, systematic-cluster, random sample was used, which, in 2000, surveyed 16,607 women from 400 sites. Public antenatal clinics are attended by 80% of pregnant women in South Africa, of whom 85.2% are African (Tshabalala-Msimang 2000). In the Western Cape, 4% of attendees refused to be tested (Shaikh & Adendorff 2000). Of the 16,607 women, 24.5% were infected with HIV, an increase from 22.8% in 1998 and 22.4% in 1999. Blood specimens were tested with

### Table 21

### Responses to Knowledge of AIDS Scale Items

| All items commence with "Do most experts say . . ." | Yes % | (n) | No % | (n) | Unsure % | (n) |
|---|---|---|---|---|---|---|
| 1. . . . there's a high chance of getting AIDS by kissing someone on the mouth who has AIDS? | 7.1 | 156 | 84.3 | 1,851 | 8.6 | 189 |
| 2. . . . AIDS can be spread by sharing a needle with a drug user who has AIDS? | 88.9 | 1,947 | 7.0 | 132 | 5.1 | 112 |
| 3. . . . you can get AIDS by giving blood? | 41.5 | 907 | 48.0 | 1,049 | 10.5 | 229 |
| 4. . . . there's a high chance that AIDS can be spread by sharing a glass of water with someone who has AIDS? | 3.6 | 78 | 89.9 | 1,969 | 6.5 | 143 |
| 5. . . . there's a high chance you can get AIDS from a toilet seat? | 6.0 | 132 | 85.8 | 1,879 | 8.1 | 178 |
| 6. . . . AIDS can be spread is a man has sex with a woman who has AIDS? | 97.6 | 2,137 | 1.4 | 31 | 1.0 | 21 |
| 7. . . . AIDS can be spread if a man has sex with another man who has AIDS? | 84.6 | 1,855 | 3.0 | 65 | 12.4 | 273 |
| 8. . . . a pregnant woman with AIDS can give AIDS to her unborn baby? | 96.4 | 2,116 | 1.7 | 37 | 1.9 | 41 |
| 9. . . . you can get AIDS by shaking hands with someone who has AIDS? | 1.4 | 30 | 96.9 | 2,124 | 1.8 | 39 |
| 10. . . . a woman can get AIDS by having sex with a man who has AIDS? | 96.6 | 2,116 | 2.8 | 62 | 0.6 | 13 |
| 11. . . . you can get AIDS when you masturbate yourself? | 2.9 | 64 | 70.8 | 1,546 | 26.2 | 573 |
| 12. . . . using a condom (rubber) can lower your chance of getting AIDS? | 92.4 | 2,020 | 3.7 | 80 | 4.0 | 87 |
| 13. . . . there's a high chance of getting AIDS if you get a blood transfusion? | 57.4 | 1,255 | 20.1 | 440 | 22.5 | 491 |
| 14. . . . prostitutes have a higher chance of getting AIDS? | 89.7 | 1,958 | 3.1 | 68 | 7.2 | 158 |
| 15. . . . eating healthy foods can keep you from getting AIDS? | 7.2 | 158 | 77.0 | 1,684 | 15.8 | 345 |
| 16. . . . having sex with more than one partner can raise your chance of getting AIDS? | 96.2 | 2,104 | 2.3 | 50 | 1.5 | 32 |
| 17. . . . you can always tell if someone has AIDS by looking at them? | 3.5 | 76 | 84.1 | 1,837 | 12.4 | 272 |
| 18. . . . people with AIDS will die from it? | 86.8 | 1,898 | 7.9 | 173 | 5.3 | 115 |
| 19. . . . there is a cure for AIDS? | 5.3 | 115 | 86.6 | 1,805 | 12.1 | 265 |
| 20. . . . you can have the AIDS virus without being sick from AIDS? | 54.4 | 1,188 | 18.1 | 395 | 27.5 | 601 |
| 21. . . . you can have the AIDS virus and spread it without being sick from AIDS? | 52.2 | 1,138 | 20.0 | 437 | 27.8 | 607 |
| 22. . . . if a man or woman has sex with someone who shoots up drugs, they raise their chance of getting AIDS? | 55.9 | 1,218 | 12.9 | 282 | 31.2 | 679 |

Sample: 889 women; 1,318 men; Mean age: 20.6 years (sd = 4.2)
Mean Total Knowledge of AIDS Scale Score: 17.1 (sd = 3.3) N = 2,209

one ELISA (enzyme-linked immunosorbent assay), except in the Western Cape, where two ELISAs were used because of the low HIV-prevalence rate. Given these results, it is estimated that approximately one in nine South Africans are infected with HIV (Tshabala-Msimang 2000). (See Table 22.)

[*Update 2003*: Sishana and Simbayi (2002) conducted the first national household HIV/AIDS prevalence study. The cluster sampled 14,450 potential participants, of whom 13,518 were visited. Some 9,963 (73.7%) persons agreed to be interviewed, and 8,840 (65.4%) provided an oral-fluid specimen for an HIV test. The results for whites, adults and youths, living in informal settlements, should be treated with caution, because the estimates are at the statistical borderline. Some 32% of white households declined to be listed in phase 1 of the study. The researchers found an estimated prevalence of 11.4% (females 12.8% and males 9.5%). Some 5.6% of children were HIV-positive, 0.3% of those between 15 and 24 years old and 15.5% of those over age 25 years. Table 23 shows the overall prevalence of HIV by sex and race. The study found that the HIV-infection rate among men is 74% that of women, and the HIV prevalence in pregnant women is much higher than in nonpregnant women (24.0% vs. 14.5%). HIV estimates in South Africa that have been based on antenatal surveys have, therefore, overestimated HIV prevalence in the general population. HIV prevalence is also lowest in rural areas and highest in urban areas, particularly urban informal settlements. Statistics South Africa (2002) reported the following for a 12% stratified random sample of death notification forms for 1997 to 2001, yielding 279,581 death records. The proportion of deaths because of HIV nearly doubled from 4.6% in 1997 to 8.7% in 2001. (*End of update by L. J. Nicholas*)]

[*Infant Mortality and Pediatric AIDS*

[*Update 2001*: In 2000, South Africa's infant mortality rate was estimated to be 45 deaths per 1,000 live births. One in about every 22 children born in South Africa died before reaching its first birthday. The infant mortality rate has shown an upward trend after declining before the 1990s, mainly because of HIV/AIDS infection. Only 8% of women reported that their partner had used a condom during their last intercourse. This figure doubled for those whose last intercourse was with a casual acquaintance or a boyfriend, but this is still very low. Overall, condom use is highest among African women and lowest among Asian women, who are, however, more likely than colored or white women to use condoms with their husbands. (*End of update by L. J. Nicholas*)]

[*AIDS Prevention and the Churches*

[*Update 2002*: According to a news release of the European News Service, the Religious Coalition for Reproductive Choice launched a church-based HIV/AIDS initiative in South Africa in conjunction with local churches and Jewish groups. The Anglican primate of the Church in the Province of Southern Africa endorsed the initiative, saying that "discussing issues of faith and religion in relation to HIV/AIDS gives new hope."

[The coalition, established in Cape Town, opened in February 2002 with a staff coordinator assisted by a corps of volunteers. Modeled on the coalition's successful Black Church Initiative, the South African program will assist churches in reducing teenage pregnancy and AIDS infections among youth, and hold forums for clergy to introduce the initiative. Training workshops will be offered for "Keeping it Real!" the coalition's faith-based sexuality education curriculum. Plans are to expand the initiative beyond Cape Town to other major cities, such as Johannesburg, Port Elizabeth, and Durban in the next two years. (*End of update by L. J. Nicholas*)]

[*HIV Prevention Programs*

[*Update 2002*: In February 2000, Lionel Mtshali, head of the provincial government of Kwa-Zulu-Natal Province, Durban, defied the national government by announcing his plan to distribute lifesaving drugs to every pregnant woman infected with the AIDS virus in this province in an effort to save their newborn babies. This announcement reinforced a widening campaign to challenge the national government's policy of restricting the distribution of AIDS drugs in public clinics and hospitals. Meanwhile, a small number of doctors and nurses began quietly distributing generic AIDS drugs purchased in Brazil in open defiance of South Africa's patent laws. National health officials have limited the drug to a handful of sites in each province, even though research has shown that it significantly reduces a pregnant woman's risk of transmitting HIV. Every year, 70,000 babies are born HIV-positive in South Africa, which has more people infected with the AIDS virus than any other nation. One tablet of nevirapine taken during labor—along with a single dose for the newborn—can reduce the risk of transmission by as much as 50%.

[The national government's program to distribute the drug reaches about 90,000 women a year, about 10% of those who give birth annually. In December 2001, a High Court judge ordered the government to expand the program, after advocates for AIDS patients sued. The government appealed that decision, saying it needed time to set up HIV testing and counseling and to assess the safety of the drug. Advocates for AIDS patients suspect that the government's position reflects President Thabo Mbeki's concerns about the side effects and toxicity of AIDS drugs and his widely publicized musings about whether HIV really causes AIDS. The cost of the drug is not a factor, since the drug's Belgian manufacturer has offered nevirapine for free.

[By early 2002, some government officials had acknowledged that the public outcry was mounting, as doctors, ministers, and politicians demanded a rapid expansion of the nevirapine program. These advocates say government officials are keeping a desperately needed program out of hospitals that could provide testing, counseling, and support. Government critics

### Table 23

**Overall HIV Prevalence by Sex and Race, South Africa 2002**

| Sex and Race | N | HIV+ (%) | 95% CI |
|---|---|---|---|
| Total | 8,428 | 11.4 | 10.0-12.7% |
| Male | 3,772 | 9.5 | 8.0-11.1 |
| Female | 4,656 | 12.8 | 10.9-14.6 |
| African | 5,056 | 12.9 | 11.2-14.5 |
| White | 701 | 6.2 | 3.1-9.2 |
| Colored | 1,775 | 6.1 | 4.5-7.8 |
| Indian | 896 | 1.6 | 0-3.4 |

### Table 22

**HIV Trends in Prevalence Percentages in the Western Cape, KwaZulu-Natal (KZN), and National for the Decade of 1990 to 2000 (Adapted from Tshabalala-Msimang 2000)**

| | 1990 | 1991 | 1992 | 1993 | 1994 | 1995 | 1996 | 1997 | 1998 | 1999 | 2000 |
|---|---|---|---|---|---|---|---|---|---|---|---|
| West Cape | 0.1 | 0.1 | 0.3 | 0.6 | 1.16 | 1.66 | 3.1 | 6.3 | 5.2 | 7.1 | 8.7 |
| KZN | 1.6 | 2.9 | 4.5 | 9.5 | 14.4 | 18.2 | 19.9 | 26.9 | 32.5 | 32.5 | 36.2 |
| National | 0.8 | 1.4 | 2.4 | 4.3 | 7.6 | 10.4 | 14.2 | 16.0 | 22.8 | 22.4 | 24.5 |

have pointed out that nevirapine was approved and found safe by the United Nations and the World Health Organization (WHO).

[With an estimated 36% of adults infected with HIV based on antenatal studies in Kwa-Zulu-Natal, Mtshali approached his provincial health minister and asked him to expand the nevirapine program, which is only available in two large sites here. This health minister explained that the national government would only consider expanding the program in 2003. Faced with this postponement, the provincial government announced plans to rapidly roll out the nevirapine program by the end of 2002. The national government—which expressed reservations at first—has accepted the plan. Other provinces, including the Western Cape and Gauteng, have also forged ahead with the government's permission. Still other provinces, with fewer resources and fewer established hospitals, will adopt a slower timetable (Swarns 2000). (*End of update by R. T. Francoeur*)]

[*Update 2002*: UNAIDS Epidemiological Assessment: National sentinel surveillance surveys of antenatal clinic attendees have been conducted in South Africa since 1990 and surveillance data is available by province and at the national level. Antenatal clinic HIV prevalence in South Africa increased rapidly from 0.7% in 1990 to 10.5% in 1995, and then to 22.8% in 1998. HIV prevalence among antenatal clinic attendees was 22.4% and 24.5% in 1999 and 2000, respectively. Age-specific analysis shows a modest decline in HIV-infection rates among 15- to 19-year-old antenatal clinic attendees from 21% in 1998 to 16.5% in 1999, and continuing to decline in the year 2000. However, antenatal clinic attendees in their early 20s still exhibit HIV prevalence of over 25%. In KwaZulu-Natal, Mpumulaga, and Gauteng provinces, HIV prevalence is still exhibiting an upward trend; HIV prevalence rose rapidly from 7.1% in 1990 to 36.5% in 2000. In other provinces, HIV-infection trends seem to be stabilizing at high rates, ranging from 11.2% to 27.9%. Results from the 2001 antenatal clinic sentinel surveillance survey were not readily available at the time of the writing of this report.

[HIV prevalence among sex workers tested in Natal increased from 50% in 1997 to 61% in 1998. Among male STD clinic patients tested in Johannesburg, HIV prevalence increased from 1% in 1988 to 19% 1994. Similarly, HIV prevalence increased among female STD patients from 2% in 1988 to 25% in 1994. In 1999, 11 million STD episodes were reported.

[The estimated number of adults and children living with HIV/AIDS on January 1, 2002, were:

| | | |
|---|---|---|
| Adults ages 15-49: | 4,700,000 | (rate: 20.1%) |
| Women ages 15-49: | 2,700,000 | |
| Children ages 0-15: | 250,000 | |

[An estimated 360,000 adults and children died of AIDS during 2001.

[At the end of 2001, an estimated 660,000 South African children under age 15 were living without one or both parents who had died of AIDS. (*End of update by the Editors*)]

## 11. Sexual Dysfunctions, Counseling, and Therapies

As mentioned several times earlier, particularly in Section 1, the sexual denial and repression maintained by the South African government and its censorship policies have severely limited the development of the facilities and properly trained personnel necessary if the average citizen is to have access to the diagnosis of sexual problems and dysfunctions, sexual counseling, and therapy. Broad-ranging government censorship of all books on sexuality, coupled with bans on vibrators and other sexual objects, the lack of sexual-education programs, and the absence of public discussion of sexuality issues severely affected the provision of sexuality counseling and therapy in the past.

Very little government support and public funds are available for research and education on sexuality issues. Without studies of sexuality among the indigenous populations of South Africa, sexual counseling and therapy is, of necessity, exercised by health professionals trained abroad using EuroAmerican models. Sexual counseling and therapy is available only to those who can pay private practitioners, or have access to the limited counseling available while they are attending the universities, colleges, technical colleges, and schools that currently fulfill only a peripheral role in primary prevention of the development of sexuality-related problems through research and consultancy services. Primary prevention services in the area of sexuality are meager, and campus sex counselors have to assume that hardly any students would be "unaffected" by sexuality-related problems. Only the degree to which students are affected by these problems will differ (Nicholas 1994a, 116-117).

## 12. Sex Research and Advanced Professional Education

The sexual behavior of blacks has been misrepresented to such a degree that an objective discussion is very difficult. The paucity of sociological and psychological studies is striking, with even the landmark studies of Kinsey and Masters and Johnson paying scant attention to the sexuality of black Americans. An important, but still limited, remedy to this lack has been undertaken by the authors of this chapter at the University of the Western Cape and other black institutions in South Africa.

## References and Suggested Readings

Abdool Karim, S. S., Q. Abdool Karim, E. Preston-Whyte, & N. Sakar. 1992. Reasons for lack of condom use among high school students. *South African Medical Journal*, 82:107-110.

Abler, R. M. & W. E. Sedlacek. 1989. Freshman sexual attitudes and behaviors over a 15-year period. *Journal of College Student Development*, 30:201-209.

Anon. 1995. Teens have their feet on the ground. *Sunday Times*, 14, 16.

Bowers, D. W. & V. A. Christophersen. 1977. University student cohabitation: A regional comparison of selected attitudes and behaviour. *Journal of Marriage and the Family*, 39:447-452.

Burman, S. 1992. The category of the illegitimate in South Africa. In: S. Burman & E. Preston-Whyte, eds., *Questionable issue: Illegitimacy in South Africa* (pp. 21-35). Cape Town: Oxford University Press.

Burman, S., & E. Preston-Whyte, eds. 1992. *Questionable issue: Illegitimacy in South Africa*. Cape Town: Oxford University Press.

Catlin, N., J. F., Keller, & J. W. Croake. 1976. Sexual history and behavior of unmarried cohabiting college couples. *College Student Journal*, 10:253-259.

Chapel, D. 1995 (January 8). Raunchy mag for swingers. *Sunday Times*, 12.

Chothia, F. 1993 (March 5). Storm over school sex education. *Weekly Main*, 5.

Cilliers, C. D. 1989. The role of the school in the Republic of South Africa in the prevention of AIDS—A situation analysis. *South African Journal of Education*, 1:1-6.

Cooper, C., R. Hamilton, H. Mashabela, S. Mackay, E. Sidiropoulos, C. Gordon-Brown, S. Murphy, & J. Frielinghaus. 1994. *Race relations survey 1993/1994*. Johannesburg: South African Institute of Race Relations.

Darling, C. A., & J. K. Davidson, Sr. 1986. Coitally active university students: Sexual behaviours, concerns and challenges. *Adolescence, 21*:403-419.

Darling, C. A., J. K. Davidson, & L. C. Passarello. 1992. The mystique of first intercourse among college youth: The role of partners. Contraceptive practices and psychological reactions. *Journal of Youth and Adolescence, 21*:97-117.

Daugherty, L. R., & J. M. Burger. 1984. The influence of parents, church, and peers on the sexual attitudes and behaviours of college students. *Archives of Sexual Behaviour, 13*: 351-358.

Department of Health. 1999. *South Africa: Demographic and health survey 1998.* A preliminary report. Department of Health. Pretoria.

Gebhard, P. H. 1977. The acquisition of basic sex information. *The Journal of Sex Research, 13*:13-21.

Gevisser, M. 1993 (April 8). Sex in the schoolroom—But it's safer. *Weekly Mail Education Supplement,* 1.

Gevisser, M., & E. Cameron, eds. 1994. *Defiant desire.* Johannesburg: Raven Press.

Hall, C. H. 1987. Sexual politics and resistance to law reform: A critique of the South African Law Commission Report on Women and Sexual Offenders in South Africa. Unpublished master's thesis, University of Cape Town, Cape Town, South Africa.

Havenga, A. M. 1985. *Women and sex offenders in South Africa.* Pretoria: Government Printers.

Houston, L. N. 1981. Romanticism and eroticism among black and white college students. *Adolescence, 17*:263-272.

Isaacs, G., & B. McKendrick. 1992. *Male homosexuality in South Africa—Identity formation, culture, and crisis.* Cape Town: Oxford University Press Southern Africa.

Kaats, G. R., & K. E. Davis. 1970. The dynamics of sexual behaviour of college students. *Journal of Marriage and the Family, 32*:390-399.

Kagan, J. 1989. *An Investigation into the sources of sexual information among pupils in standard nine and ten in a co-educational high school in Cape Town.* Unpublished master's thesis, University of Cape Town, Cape Town.

Keeling, R. P. 1991. Student health in the 1990's. *Chronicle of Higher Education, 37*:B1, B2.

Kenya Community Abroad. 2002 (January 31). *Dark knees tell all, says "virginity tester."* Kenyan Community Abroad (KCA), P.O. Box 5635, Washington, D.C. 20016-5635; info@kenyansabroad.org; http://www.kenyansabroad.org.

Knox, D., & K. Wilson. 1981. Dating behaviours of university students. *Family Relations, 30*:255-258.

Lachman, S. J. 1990. *The challenge of AIDS in the 1990's.* South Africa: Lennon Ltd. South Africa.

Loubser, W. 1994 (May 19). Seks en die standerd sesse [Sex and the standard sixes]. *Huisgenoot,* 18-20.

Masters, W. H., & V. E. Johnson. 1986. *Human sexual response.* Toronto: Bantam.

Monnig, H. V. 1983. *The Pedi.* Pretoria, South Africa: L. van Schaik.

Mosher, D. L. 1979. Sex guilt and sex myths in college men and women. *Journal of Sex Research, 15*:224-234.

Naidoo, C. 1994 (December 11). Keeping it all in the family. *Sunday Times,* 15.

Nicholas, L. J. 1990. *A profile of 1,886 UWC first year students: Career interests, guidance experiences, knowledge and attitudes toward AIDS and sexuality and religiosity.* An unpublished report: Centre for Student Counseling, University of the Western Cape.

Nicholas, L. J. 1991. *A profile of 2,113 UWC first year students: Career interests, guidance experiences, knowledge and attitudes toward AIDS and sexuality and religiosity.* An unpublished report: Centre for Student Counseling, University of the Western Cape.

Nicholas, L. J. 1992. *A profile of 1,558 UWC first year students: Career interests, guidance experiences, knowledge and attitudes toward AIDS and sexuality and religiosity.* An un-

published report: Centre for Student Counseling, University of the Western Cape.

Nicholas, L. J. 1993a. Intrafamilial communication about contraception: A survey of black South African freshmen. *International Journal for the Advancement of Counseling, 16*: 291-300.

Nicholas, L. J. 1993b. *A profile of 1,500 UWC first year students: Career interest, guidance experiences, knowledge and attitudes towards AIDS and sexuality and religiosity.* An unpublished report: Centre of Student Counseling, University of the Western Cape.

Nicholas, L. J. 1994a. *Sex counseling in educational settings.* Braamfontein: Skotaville Publishers.

Nicholas, L. J. 1994b. *A profile of 2,209 UWC first year students: Career interests, guidance experiences, knowledge and attitudes towards AIDS and sexuality and religiosity.* An unpublished report: Centre for Student Counseling, University of the Western Cape.

Nicholas, L. J., & K. Durrheim. 1994. *Religiosity, AIDS and sexuality knowledge, attitudes, beliefs and practices of black South African first-year university students.* An unpublished report: Centre for Student Counseling, University of the Western Cape.

Nicholas, L. J. & N. Orr. 1994. *Reliability of knowledge of AIDS scales in a sample of black first-year university students.* An unpublished report: Centre for Student Counseling, University of the Western Cape.

Nicholas, L., C. Tredoux, & P. Daniels. 1994. AIDS knowledge and attitudes towards homosexuals of black university students: 1990-1992. *Psychological Reports, 75*:819-823.

Oliver, L. 1987. *Sex and the South Africa woman.* Johannesburg: Lowry Publishers.

Preston-Whyte, E. M. 1995. Half-way there: Anthropology and intervention-oriented AIDS research in KwaZulu/Natal, South Africa. In: H. ten Brummelhuis & G. Herdt, ed., *Culture and sexual risk: Anthropological perspectives on AIDS.* Amsterdam: Gordon and Breach Science Publishers.

Preston-Whyte, E., & M. Zondi. 1992. African teenage pregnancy: Whose problem? In: S. Burman & E. Preston-Whyte, eds., *Questionable issue: Illegitimacy in South Africa* (pp. 226-246). Cape Town: Oxford University Press.

Robinson, I. E., & D. Jedlicka. 1982. Change in sexual attitudes and behaviour of college students from 1965 to 1980: A research note. *Journal of Marriage and the Family, 44*:237-241.

Rohrburg, J., & R. Jessor. 1975. Religiosity in youth: A personal and social control against deviant behaviour. *Journal of Personality, 43*:136-155.

SAIRR. 2001/2002. *Survey of Race Relations.* Braamfontein: SAIRR.

SAPA. 2003 (January 22). Hiding HIV could turn sex into rape. *Cape Times,* 1, 3.

St. Leger, C. 1994 (December 11). New boss to revamp AIDS campaign. *Sunday Times,* 3.

Sapire, K. E. 1988. Education in sexuality. *Nursing R.S.A., 3*: 19, 21, & 41.

Schoepf, B. G. 1995. Culture, sex research and AIDS prevention in Africa. In: H. ten Brummelhuis & G. Herdt, ed., *Culture and sexual risk: Anthropological perspectives on AIDS.* Amsterdam: Gordon and Breach Science Publishers.

Sidley, P. 1991 (December 20). Doing detective work on condoms. *Weekly Mail,* 19.

Shaikh, N., & T. Adendorff. 2000. *Department of Health. Provincial Administration: Western Cape. The Provincial and District HIV antenatal survey report.* Western Cape: PLP Printing.

Shishana, O., & L. Simbayi. 2002. *Nelson Mandela/HSRC study of HIV/AIDS South African National HIV prevalence, behavioural risks and mass media household survey 2002.* Pretoria Human Sciences Research Council.

Sorenson, R. C. 1973. *Adolescent sexuality in contemporary America.* New York: World Publishing.

Stander, K. 1988 (May 18). City's illegitimate birth rate 45 percent—MOH urges state action. *The Argus*, 1.

Statistics South Africa. 2002. *Causes of death in South Africa 1997-2001. Advanced release of recorded causes of death.* Pretoria: SSA.

Swarns, R. L. 2002 (February 5). A Bold Move on AIDS in South Africa. *The New York Times*, International Report, A10.

Swayer, C. 1994 (December 7). Censorship laws to be relaxed. *The Argus*, 1.

Thornton, A. 1990. The courtship process and adolescent sexuality. *Journal of Family Issues*, *11*:239-273.

Tshabalala-Msimang, M. E. 2000. *National HIV and syphilis sero-prevalence survey of women attending public antenatal clinics in South Africa.* Department of Health.

Underhill, G. 1995 (January 14). All quiet on the water front as pros lie low. *Weekend Argus*, 7.

Van Rooyen, J. C. W. 1987. *Censorship in South Africa.* Cape Town: Juta.

## PART 2:
## ANOTHER PERSPECTIVE

MERVYN BERNARD HURWITZ

## 1. Basic Sexological Premises

### A/B. Gender Roles and General Concepts of Sexuality and Love

The different ethnic groups have diverse concepts of gender roles. In the black traditional community, the male plays a dominant role. He is allowed more than one wife. When his wife is no longer able to bear children, he is allowed to find a younger, fertile wife to bear more children. This lifestyle is more prevalent in the rural areas. In the urban areas, the blacks are more Westernized and polygamy is less prevalent, with the male having a monogamous relationship with only one wife (Burman & Preston-Whyte 1992).

Traditionally, the black woman does not demand sex from her partner, nor does she make advances towards him. There is little foreplay, and once the male has been satisfied, there is little afterplay. However, recently, the urbanized black woman is becoming more demanding in her sexual relationship and the male is losing his secure dominant role. The women's liberation movement is gradually reaching the black urban woman. However, the man is still the traditional leader and plays a dominant role in decision making in the family, expecting his wife to be totally subservient (Monnig 1983).

Black males commonly become migrant laborers in the mines or in the city, leaving their wives in the rural areas to tend the farms and raise the children. The husband is usually the sole monetary supporter of the family. He returns to his rural home if there is illness or bereavement in the family, usually visiting only once or twice a year. He seldom allows his wife or family to visit him in the city.

## 2. Religious, Ethnic, and Gender Factors Affecting Sexuality

The South African community is made up of separate ethnic groups with different identities and affiliations and cannot be lumped together as one group. The white population is made up of two large groups, namely the Afrikaners (Boers) and the English-speaking people.

Afrikaners adhere to a strictly Calvinistic view. Sex is not taught at schools. Any discussion on sexuality is frowned upon and the topic is largely seen as taboo. In this male-dominated society, the woman has been assigned a secondary role. However, with the influence of the media and the gradual lifting of the censorship of sexually explicit information, the men are threatened by the changing role of women, who are becoming more sexually assertive. In a 1987 survey comparing English-speaking and Afrikaans-speaking white South Africans, Louise Olivier found that 72.8% of Afrikaans-speaking women and 69.2% of English-speaking women could discuss sexual matters with their mothers. Only 4.4% of women could discuss sexual matters with their fathers.

In the black communities, 6 million out of nearly 18 million people are affiliated to the Church of Zion or other independent Protestant churches. Many blacks still subscribe to ancestor worship and tribal ritual, despite the strong influence of the missionaries who have tried to inculcate a Christian monotheism and ethic.

Muslim and Hindu influences are found among the Asian minorities.

## 3. Knowledge and Education about Sexuality

### A. Government Policies and Programs

In the white population, sex education has been viewed as the parents' responsibility, with few health professionals becoming involved other than on a consultative basis.[1] Sometimes, sexual education is provided by the family doctor, who is approached when a young person becomes sexually active and wants counseling and instruction about the use of suitable contraception.

There is no formal sex education in either the white or black schools. Representation has been made to the Minister of Education in an effort to introduce sex education into the schools, but this has met with strong resistance. The Dutch Reformed Calvinistic approach indoctrinated by the church has been opposed to sex education in schools, and all discussion of sexuality is frowned upon. Private (nongovernment-controlled) schools do have sex-education classes. Lectures are given to pupils in the 11- to 17-year-old age group, usually by social workers and counselors at the Family Life Center, as well as by the author and other sex educators.

### B. Informal Sources of Sexual Knowledge

In 1992, television programs on sexuality were initiated, directed primarily at the youth. Panel discussions sponsored by the media have been held to look at sex education and to expose various topics of sexual interest.

However, there is very strict censorship in South Africa, and many of the sex books that are freely available overseas are banned in South Africa. There is thus a very limited number of books on sex education or explicit books on sex. Talk shows are becoming frequent on television, and phone-in shows are available on radio. There is, however, a move afoot to ban all these sources of sexual information.

The ritual passage for black girls in the traditional tribal situation is very secretive. In the Pedi tribe, Monnig reports that these rituals are conducted by the girl's mother or grandmother. The girl is told about menstruation and informed that she must avoid sex during this time. She receives detailed instruction on the work and duties of a woman, particularly in her relationship with a man, and is instructed on sexual matters. The young Pedi girls assist one another in stretching their own labia minora, which is said to ensure greater sexual gratification for men.

## 4. Autoerotic Behaviors and Patterns

There is no literature or data pertaining to autoerotic behavior and patterns in South African children, adolescents, or adults. "Blue movies" and autoerotic literature are banned. Pornographic programs and books are heavily censored. Studies of autoeroticism are discouraged by the church and schools. People returning from overseas with erotic literature have the publications confiscated at the airport and are liable to be punished.

In the English-speaking universities, some lectures and courses on sexuality have been introduced. Lectures in sexuality for medical students were introduced in the mid-1980s. Workshops on sexuality are given to doctors, nurses, social workers, and allied professionals to encourage them to feel more at ease with sexuality and to be able to discuss sexual problems with their patients.

## 5. Interpersonal Heterosexual Behaviors

### A. Children

Forty percent of South Africa's population is under 15 years of age. Children of preprimary school age often attend nursery schools or crèches where the sexes are mixed. They share common toilet facilities, are taught basic gender differences, and stereotypic gender-role models are reinforced. Both teachers and parents report that children play doctor-patient games and tend to explore one another. This is often a source of great anxiety to both parents and teachers.

In the black communities, there is overcrowding and a lack of privacy. The children often have to sleep in the same room as their parents, and many share a bed with parents or siblings. This early exposure to parental sexual activity sometimes causes anxiety and confusion that can affect their own sexual identity.

### B. Adolescents

*Puberty Rituals*

Pubertal rituals are carried out in many black tribes. Male circumcision in the black communities is common in both urban and rural areas and is seen as a prerequisite for manhood. The age of circumcision varies in different tribal groups from 9 to 22 years.[2] In the Xhosa tribe, for example, males are circumcised between the age of 18 and 22 years, in a ritual ceremony celebrated twice a year.[3] In most tribes, there is no anesthetic given for pain; the boy is simply given only a piece of wood to bite on. The youth is indoctrinated to believe that he has to endure pain to prove that he is fit to be called a "man."

Because of poor techniques and inexperienced or poorly trained traditional healers or *sangomas*, the complications of circumcision are sometimes serious, even functionally irreparable. Gangrene is not an infrequent complication following ritual circumcision.[4]

Courley and Kisner described 45 cases of youths who required hospitalization following ritual circumcision.[3] All 45 cases were septic on admission. In 5% of cases, the entire penis was necrotic; the mortality rate was 9%. Septicemia and dehydration are frequent causes of such mortality.

The chief cause of penile injury is a dressing that is too tight and applied for too long. The hemorrhage is controlled by applying leaves around the penile shaft and then binding the organ with a strip of sheepskin leather. A concerted effort is being made to educate the traditional healers in the use of commercial medicines and dressings rather than traditional leaves and sheepskin.[3]

Female circumcision is not carried out in South Africa, although some tribes, such as the Pedi, encourage the females at puberty to stretch the labia minora.

*Premarital Sexual Activities and Relationships*

Focusing on adolescent black children and teenagers, Preston-Whyte and Zondi found that both boys and girls admitted experiencing sex before their 12th or 13th year.[5] Some had experienced penetration before they reached physical maturity. By age 13, most had been sexually active, if not regularly, then at least on a number of occasions. Full penetration was the rule.

In a predominantly white South African survey, Olivier found that 30% of his respondents under age 17, 24 of 80,

were still virgins. In the colored community, Burman and Preston-Whyte (1992) found that 30.5% of all births occurred in teenagers, with 5% below the age of 16. Eighty-one percent of the teenage group had out-of-wedlock children.

There are no figures available on the number of teenagers who are involved in ongoing relationships while indulging in sexual activities. Peer pressure in the urban black community encourages sexual encounters that are often monitored by older teenagers.

The double standard is evident in the black communities. When a man's unmarried daughter becomes pregnant, he is enraged. Yet, when a son makes a girl pregnant, the father may be secretly and even overtly pleased. Among his peers, a boy who has many girlfriends, and who is known to have fathered a child or a number of children, is admired. His father often shares this attitude. The pressure is therefore towards, rather than away from, teenage sexual involvement. The relationship between a boy and girl who are "going together" is normally one that involves full intercourse (Burman & Preston-Whyte 1992).

### C. Adults

*Premarital Courtship, Dating, and Relationships*

The formal ritual of dating and courtship familiar to Western civilization is more prevalent in the white South African community, which tends to be more affluent and able to afford movies, discos, and weekends away on vacation. There are several singles clubs, discos, and bars catering to adolescents and young adults looking for dates or a "one night stand." With the incidence of sexually transmitted diseases, the educated and affluent groups are more inclined to be selective and less promiscuous in their relationships than their less-educated brothers and sisters from a lower socioeconomic class.

*Marriage and the Family*

Monogamy is more commonly accepted amongst the white group than the black group. Traditional black men who have not accepted the doctrine of Christianity are allowed to have more than one wife. In the rural setting, a man's wealth is assessed by the number of children and cattle he owns, and thus he may take a second wife. Cohabitation is common in the white society in nonreligious couples, but is frowned on by the church, particularly the strong Calvinistic elements of the Dutch Reformed Church. In the black traditional rural setting, marriage is not primarily concerned with legalizing sexual relations between two individuals, but rather with establishing paternity and giving the husband the right to sexual relations with his wife. In this value system, extramarital intercourse is possible and even socially accepted and provided for culturally (Monnig 1983).

Laws prohibiting interracial sex and marriage were repealed in 1985.

*Incidence of Oral and Anal Sex*

There are no figures available for the incidence of anal sex, fellatio, or cunnilingus. In my experience, anal intercourse is engaged in by a very small proportion of heterosexual couples. On the other hand, more than half the couples attending the Sexual Dysfunction Clinic at the Johannesburg Hospital reported engaging in cunnilingus and fellatio. Most men reported being happy to indulge in cunnilingus. Some women reported feeling uncomfortable with fellatio. In Olivier's 1987 survey, a surprising finding was that few women reported enjoying oral sex, only 9.2% in the 17- to 25-year age group and 5.9% in the over-age-25 cohort. From my personal experience in my private gynecological practice, I feel that these figures are low and that the overall figure is well over 30%.

## 6. Homoerotic, Homosexual, and Bisexual Behaviors

In Olivier's survey of 2,842 women, 89.7% were heterosexual, 0.3% were lesbian, and 2.5% were bisexual. Most of the women in this survey, 2,711 of 2,842, were white females. There is no legal status for lesbian or homosexual couples in the South African society. In 1992, homosexuality was more acceptable and less frowned upon than previously. Gay advice bureaus are available, but there is no legislation to protect the rights of homosexuals.

The incidence of homosexuality in the black population is low. This is borne out by the low incidence of HIV-positive homosexual black males (0.6%), compared to 31% of homosexual or bisexual white males.[6,7]

## 7. Gender Diversity and Transgender Issues

Transvestites, transgenderists, and transsexuals have no legal standing. There are very few centers available in South Africa for the treatment of these patients, and surgical operations are very rarely performed. At least two years of psychiatric treatment and evaluation are needed before any operative procedure is considered.

## 8. Significant Unconventional Sexual Behaviors

### A. Coercive Sex

*Sexual Abuse*

The Department of Health and Welfare keeps a social welfare register on all children who are abused. Legislation requires doctors, nurses, social workers, police officers, and members of the public to report cases of abuse. It would appear that sexual abuse is becoming more prevalent in all sectors of the community. This correlates with the escalating violence encountered throughout South Africa. Conviction for sexual abuse and rape carries a penalty of a lengthy prison sentence. In their study of teenage mothers, Burman and Preston-Whyte found that pregnancies occurred at a younger age among abused children than in the control group.

*Incest*

Incest is taboo in all groups in South Africa (Zulu report by Burman and Preston-Whyte; Pedi report by Monnig). If a pregnancy results from incest, a legal abortion may be performed.[8] There are no available statistics for the incidence of pedophilia, but it is a punishable offense.

*Sexual Harassment*

With the increase of feminism, more cases of sexual harassment are being reported in the workplace. South African men are known to be chauvinistic and to "put down" women both verbally and in terms of job opportunity. There is only recourse to the law in terms of discrimination and not in terms of harassment.

*Rape*

Rape cases are reported daily. However, in cases of family rape, they often are unreported. There is still a stigma attached to the rape victim and, despite attempts at educating the public, the rape victim is still often seen as inviting the sexual advances of the male. In black urban areas, two to three rapes are reported daily and many more are unreported. These rape cases are often committed by strangers or casual acquaintances.

### B. Prostitution

Prostitution is rife, particularly in the larger cities. Escort agencies provide a front for prostitution, which is illegal in South Africa. No figures are available of the number of practicing prostitutes or their activities. With the present high rate of unemployment, estimated at over 25% in the black community, prostitution is on the increase. As prostitution is illegal, there are no facilities for regular medical examinations of prostitutes to control STDs or other infections.

### C. Pornography and Erotica

As mentioned above in Sections 3B and 4, the Calvinist tradition has been very effective in maintaining severe restrictions on all pornographic and erotic material.

## 9. Contraception, Abortion, and Population Planning

### A. Contraception and Teenage Unmarried Pregnancies

Family-planning clinics are available in many areas and provide a free service. There is a reluctance among the black males to allow their partners to use contraception. Among the more-educated population, there is an attempt to limit the size of the family and to use some form of contraception.

Adolescent pregnancies are common in the black communities. Contraception is seldom used. The reasons given for failure to use contraception include cost, not admitting sexual activity, unplanned coitus, a belief that they are too young to become pregnant, fear of the effect of contraceptive methods, and subconsciously wanting to become pregnant.

The earlier the age of menarche, the earlier the first coitus occurs.[8] Van Coeverden found that when the menarche occurred before the age of 12, 56% of teenagers attending a family-planning clinic experienced coitus by the age of 15.[9] If menarche occurred after the age of 13, then 42% were sexually active by the age of 17.

There are no statistics available as to whether the sexually active teenagers have multiple partners or are involved in steady exclusive relationships. Personal observation suggests that promiscuity is common. Peer pressure often forces teenagers to have sexual contact in order to avoid being ostracized by their peer group. Unstable home and socioeconomic factors, as well as poor school attendance, boredom, drugs, and alcohol abuse, are some factors related to the early onset of coitus.

Premarital sexual relations vary considerably between the various racial groups in South Africa. Children raised in crowded ghetto conditions often lack parental control and have fewer recreational facilities to occupy their spare time and energy. Above all, for many black girls, there is very little to look forward to except childbirth.[5]

### B. Abortion

Although abortion was illegal in South Africa until late 1996, the Abortion and Sterilization Act of 1975 allowed for legal abortions under four well-defined circumstances:[8]

1. Where the continuation of a pregnancy poses a serious threat to the mother's physical and/or mental health;
2. Where a risk exists that the child will be seriously handicapped, physically or mentally;
3. In cases of rape or incest;
4. In cases of unlawful carnal intercourse with a woman who is permanently mentally handicapped.

A 1994 review covering a six-year period quotes the number of legal abortions in South Africa as being about 1,000 per annum and the registered number of instances where products of conception were found at surgery as being about 35,000 per annum.[10] The number of "back street abortions" performed annually is estimated at between 10,000 and 40,000. Many of the more-affluent patients travel overseas to countries where abortions are legal to have their pregnancies terminated. (See discussion of the new legislation adopted in November 1996, in Section 9C, Contraception, Abortion, and Population Planning, Abortion, of Part 1.)

## 10. Sexually Transmitted Diseases and HIV/AIDS

### A. Sexually Transmitted Diseases

Sexually transmitted diseases constitute a major public health problem in South Africa. It has been estimated that over one million patients seek treatment for sexually transmitted diseases each year at community clinics, and that more are seen at hospital outpatient departments and primary healthcare clinics. STDs in South Africa conform largely to Third World patterns. Pelvic inflammatory disease, mainly because of STDs, is the commonest reason for acute emergency admission to the gynecological wards and is the most common disease syndrome seen in gynecological outpatient departments.[11]

A survey in Alexandra township, a poor urban black township in Johannesburg, estimates that 20% of the population over the age of 15 is treated at least once a year for an STD.[6] A second study of patients seen at a university clinic in Alexandra township revealed that 10% of all patients seen were referred with an STD, 53% being men and 47% women.[7] Fifty-four percent of the patients were between the ages of 20 and 29. Most men presented with urethritis or an ulcer, while the women presented with pelvic inflammatory disease or a discharge.

Gonorrhea remains the most common cause of acute urethritis. Twenty percent of all cases also harbor chlamydia trachomatis, the commonest cause of nongonococcal urethritis (NGU).[11] The commonest organisms found in females with pelvic inflammatory disease are *Neisseria gonorrhoeae* in 65% of cases, *Mycoplasma hominis* in 53% of cases, and *Chlamydia trachomatis* in 5% of cases.

Mixed infections are common and anaerobic super-infections occur in 82% of cases.[11] Men are more likely to be repeat attendants for STD, and are more likely to report multiple sex partners. Professor Ron Ballard states that there are upwards of three million new cases of STDs each year in our population of 26 million.[12]

There are poor resources available for the treatment of STDs. Attempts are being made for a wide-ranging communication campaign to attempt to educate the population to reduce the number of sexual partners.

A major factor affecting the availability of contraception, abortion, and the diagnosis and treatment of STDs and HIV/AIDS is the state of the country's national healthcare system. In the January 1995 annual healthcare and education report, the South African bishops conference warned that the country's national healthcare system is close to collapse. The system, the report stated, is in a chaotic state because of poor coordination of services, inadequate resources, and injustice. Only 19% of South Africa's 41 million people have medical coverage through private systems. Public hospitals that offer inexpensive care to uninsured patients are crowded and understaffed. Health Minister Nkosazana Zuma initiated a study of a national health insurance plan that would provide universal coverage. This study includes examination of successful models from Kenya and Namibia that stress preventing illness by teaching healthy living habits through community health organizations.

### B. HIV/AIDS

In all of Africa, HIV infection is spread mainly through heterosexual intercourse.[13] Concomitant STDs, particularly genital ulcers, are implicated as cofactors in the transmission of the HIV virus.[14] The World Health Organization estimates that there are 5 million HIV-infected individuals in Africa. This epidemic has only recently reached South Africa, but there is every indication that the prevalence of HIV may reach alarming proportions in the future, and no field of medicine will remain unscathed.[15] It is estimated by the Department of National Health that there are currently 300,000 HIV-positive people in South Africa and 400 new cases per day.[16] The latest available statistics of AIDS in South Africa as of September 1992, total 27,389 confirmed cases.[17] However, AIDS is not a reportable disease in South Africa, and thus many cases are not recorded. (See Tables 24 and 25.)

A survey carried out at the Baragwanath Hospital, in Soweto, a black town adjoining Johannesburg, has revealed that between July 1988 and December 1990, 426 HIV-positive individuals were identified.[15] Eighty-five percent of these cases were traced to heterosexual transmission, 0.6% to homosexual contact, and 12.6% to perinatal maternal infection. In this study, a total of 111 HIV-positive women were diagnosed in the maternity units of Baragwanath Hospital, and 51 symptomatic children with perinatally acquired HIV infection were admitted to the pediatric wards.[18] Late 1994 data from the Baragwanath Hospital showed that 8% of patients in the prenatal clinic were HIV-positive. At the Johannesburg Hospital, 10% of the prenatal clients were HIV-positive; a similar incidence was reported in late 1994 by the Johannesburg City Council for the inner-city population that was HIV-positive. In 1994, the number of HIV-positive South Africans doubled in 12 months.

According to McIntyre, the rate of HIV-positive pregnant women in 1992 was 4/100, with the rate doubling every nine to 12 months.[19] As a result of these alarming statistics, an HIV clinic has been started in the maternity unit of Baragwanath Hospital. The most-recent figures show that at least two HIV-positive women give birth daily at the hospital; 200 HIV-positive women were identified in the first eight months of 1992.

The major brunt of the HIV epidemic in South Africa is expected to be borne by black heterosexual adults and by infants.[20] A total of 181 HIV-positive black adults were admitted to the medical wards of Baragwanath Hospital between August 1987 and December 1990. Equal numbers of both sexes were seen, of which 34% have died.

There are no statistics of lesbian HIV-positive women in South Africa. All age groups in both sexes are at risk of ac-

### Table 24

#### AIDS Risk (as of September 1992)

| AIDS Risk Category[16] | Percent of Total |
|---|---|
| Heterosexual | 50 |
| Homosexual/bisexual | 31 |
| Pediatric | 15 |
| Blood transfusion | 1.9 |
| Hemophiliacs | 1.4 |
| IV-drug users | 0.1 |

### Table 25

#### Percent of AIDS Cases[14] (as of September 1992)

| | Percentage of Cases by Race | Percentage of Nation's Population |
|---|---|---|
| Black | 62.4 | 68.3 |
| White | 33.2 | 17.1 |
| Colored (mixed race) | 3.7 | 11.0 |
| Asian | 0.4 | 3.2 |

quiring HIV infections.[21] Tuberculosis is the commonest infectious complication of AIDS in South Africa.[22]

In South Africa, the HIV virus is most commonly transmitted by sexual intercourse. Transmission of the virus from mother to child is the second commonest mode of spread in all African countries, including South Africa.[23] Homosexuality is relatively uncommon among black South Africans, but is a common form of transmission of the HIV virus in the white population. Homosexuality, however, does not play a major role in the pandemic spread of the HIV virus in any African country.[24]

In the African context, black promiscuous men are very reluctant to use condoms and complain about the cost and inconvenience of the use of condoms. Since status is equated to fertility, the use of condoms and contraception is frowned upon. Condoms cannot be prescribed in the Health Service, but they can be obtained free of charge from Family Planning Clinics. Doubts have been expressed about the advisability of media advertisements on the use of condoms in South Africa, prompted by pervading Calvinistic reticence (Lachman 1990). AIDS education is available in many black schools but is not permitted in state-controlled schools for predominantly white pupils. In the conservative Calvinistic white community, AIDS is seen as a problem experienced only among homosexuals or the black community.

In a survey of 122 black mothers in the Durban area, it was found that these mothers were at a high risk of acquiring AIDS.[24] Urban black mothers seldom discuss the risk of unprotected sex with their daughters, despite their knowledge of transmission modes and of ways to prevent HIV infection. Fifty percent of these mothers had children by the same consort, whereas 44% had more than one partner. Ninety-two percent of these mothers stated that they would like their partners to use condoms, yet all the mothers said that they had not experienced intercourse where their partners had used condoms.

In 1989, the Johannesburg City Health embarked on an AIDS-awareness campaign using messages placed on the outside of 30 city buses.[25] The role of health education is to provide the entire community with a means to prevent HIV infection. A toll-free dial and listening service is available to anyone who has access to a telephone. Callers can choose to hear this information in any of the eight major languages in South Africa.

In recognition of the seriousness of the AIDS problem, the Department of National Health and Population Development recently established an AIDS unit. The unit consists of a multidisciplinary team. There are AIDS clinics in all the major cities of South Africa but these are already insufficient for the needs of the community. Counseling HIV-positive patients embodies the principles of counseling and care for all patients who have an incurable disease. It is different in that no other medical condition carries the stigma, moral censure, and societal consequences that accompany AIDS.[26]

An April 1995 Update: Early results of a Department of Health survey showed that two out of 25 South Africans are HIV-positive. In 1995, an estimated 850,000 to one million South Africans were infected, with over 700 new cases every day. The infection rate in Kwazulu Natal is almost three times that of the rest of the country; the number of AIDS cases for the first quarter of 1995 was double that for the same period in 1994. An estimated 15% to 19% of the people in Natal were infected in April 1995. The least-infected regions of the country were the North West and Northern Cape. The epidemiological director cautioned that the extent of underreporting was not known.

In a July 1996 report at the 11th international conference on AIDS, South Africa had an estimated 1.8 million cases of HIV infection, second only to India's 3 million cases. In June 1996, Dr. Peter Piot, head of the United Nations Joint Program on HIV-AIDS, reported that 10% of the South African population is believed to be infected with HIV. In the province of Kwazulu Natal, the infection rate had reached 16% (Preston-Whyte 1995; Schoepf 1995). The rate was even higher in nearby Zambia and Zimbabwe, where 17% of the population lives with the virus. In South Africa's northern neighbor, Botswana, 18% of the people are infected. No one can explain this rapid rise in HIV infection in southern Africa, especially considering the fact that the infection reached South Africa later than it did other regions of Africa, and the efforts of the Mandela government in making AIDS prevention a national priority.

## 11. Sexual Dysfunctions, Counseling, and Therapies

### A. Concepts of Sexual Dysfunction

Any problem related to sexuality that may negatively affect either the male or the female, both as individuals or in a relationship, is viewed as a sexual dysfunction. In the male, the most common reasons for referral to the Sexual Dysfunction Clinic or to a sex therapist are premature ejaculation and loss of libido. Orgasmic dysfunction in the female and loss of libido are the most common sexual dysfunctions seen at the Sexual Dysfunction Clinic. In the black population, most males are worried about their performance, their ability to sustain an erection for an often-unrealistic length of time, or the inability to have intercourse up to 4 to 5 times a night.

### B. Availability of Diagnosis and Treatment

The root of many of the problems is basic ignorance. Thus, patients are given information about basic sexual anatomy and physiology. At the Sexual Dysfunction Clinic in Johannesburg, patients are preferably seen as couples by the team consisting of a gynecologist, social worker, and nurse. All patients are examined physically, and the female patients are given a complete pelvic exam. The partners are encouraged to participate in these physical examinations.

All males attending the Sexual Dysfunction Clinic at the Johannesburg Hospital are checked by Doppler flow for penile blood flow and penile blood pressure. Serum testosterone and prolactin levels are routinely carried out at the clinic on males with any form of sexual dysfunction. A urologist is available for consultation. Some couples or individuals prefer to be counseled privately and are seen by a single therapist in private practice who may be a gynecologist, urologist, psychiatrist, psychologist, social worker, or general practitioner.

Sex therapists in South Africa have been trained locally and often internationally. They attend international workshops and congresses. Sex therapists in South Africa come from many disciplines, all of which have an interest in the field of sexology.

## 12. Sex Research and Advanced Professional Education

There is very little research in the field of sexology in South Africa. There are no facilities to carry out major research programs. However, some individuals conduct sporadic research into various aspects of sexual dysfunction.[27,28] There are no available institutes or programs for research.

Medical students at the various medical schools receive lectures on sexual dysfunction as part of their medical curriculum. Students at the University of the Witwatersrand are encouraged to attend the Sexual Dysfunction Clinic at the Johannesburg Hospital. There are sexual dysfunction clinics at the Johannesburg Hospital, Groote Schuur Hospital in Cape Town, and the H. F. Verwoerd Hospital in Pretoria. There are no postgraduate facilities available for the advanced study of human sexuality.

The Sex Society of South Africa is in the process of being formed at press time. *The Medical Sex Journal of South Africa* is published quarterly by the South African Academy of Family Practice and Primary Care. The address of the editorial offices is: P.O. Box 23195, Joubert Park, Johannesburg, South Africa.

Additional information on sexuality is available from: Planned Parenthood Association of South Africa, Third Floor, Marlborough House, 60 Eloff Street, Johannesburg 2001, South Africa. Tel.: 27-11/331-2695.

## Conclusion

In the early 1990s, South Africa is faced with a major upheaval, both politically, socially, and economically. The uncertain political, social, and economic future of South Africa, faced with the transition from a white-dominated government to a multiracial or black government, poses many challenges for the country. Violence has become a way of life. Sexual abuse is common, as is murder, rape, and anarchy. The future of the medical and paramedical services is in a state of flux. It is not likely that the situation of sexology will improve significantly in the near future, simply because most of the nation's resources and the people's energies will, of necessity, be devoted to more pressing and urgent challenges, including the need to provide primary healthcare, food, housing, and basic necessities to the underprivileged masses.

## References and Suggested Readings

Burman, S., & E. Preston-Whyte, eds. 1992. *A questionable issue: Illegitimacy in South Africa*. Cape Town: Oxford University Press.

CIA. 2002 (January). *The world factbook 2002*. Washington, DC: Central Intelligence Agency. Available: http://www.cia.gov/cia/publications/factbook/index.html.

Lachman, S. J. 1990. *The challenge of AIDS in the 1990's: South Africa*. Lennon Ltd. South Africa.

Monnig, H. V. 1983. *The Pedi*. Pretoria, S. Africa: L. van Schaik.

Olivier, L. 1987. *Sex and the South Africa woman*. Johannesburg: Lowry Publishers.

Preston-Whyte, E. M. 1995. Half-way there: Anthropology and intervention-oriented AIDS research in KwaZulu/Natal, South Africa. In: H. ten Brummelhuis & G. Herdt, ed., *Culture and sexual risk: Anthropological perspectives on AIDS*. Amsterdam: Gordon and Breach Science Publishers.

Schoepf, B. G. 1995. Culture, sex research and AIDS prevention in Africa. In: H. ten Brummelhuis & G. Herdt, ed., *Culture and sexual risk: Anthropological perspectives on AIDS*. Amsterdam: Gordon and Breach Science Publishers.

UNAIDS. 2002. *Epidemiological fact sheets by country*. Geneva, Switzerland: Joint United Nations Programme on HIV/AIDS (UNAIDS/WHO). Available: http://www.unaids.org/hivaidsinfo/statistics/fact_sheets/index_en.htm.

## Endnotes

1. Van Coeverden, H. A., S. de Groot, & E. E. Greathead. 1991. Adolescent sexuality and contraception. *South Africa's Continuing Medical Education Monthly*, 9(11):1369-1379.
2. Venter, A. J. 1974 (December 13). Circumcision: The silent agony of becoming a man. *Personality Magazine*.
3. Cowley, I. P., & M. Kisner. 1970. Ritual circumcision (Umkhwethna) amongst the Xhosa of Ciskei. *British Journal Urology*, 66:318-321
4. Du Toit, D. F., & W. J. Villet. 1979. Gangrene of the penis after circumcision: Report of three cases. *South African Medical Journal*, 55(13):521-522.
5. Preston-Whyte, E., & M. Zondi. 1991. Adolescent sexuality and its implications for teenage pregnancy and AIDS.

*South Africa's Continuing Medical Education Monthly*, 9(11):1389-1394.
6. Frame, G., P. de L. G. M. Ferrinho, & I. D. Wilson. 1991. The care of patients with STD's: Review of previous research and a survey of general practitioners. *South African Family Practice*, 12:887-892.
7. Frame, G., P. de L. G. M. Ferrinho, & G. Phakathi. 1991. Patients with STD's at the Alexandra Health Centre and University Clinic. *South African Medical Journal*, 80(8):389-392.
8. Abortion and sterilization act no. 2, 1975. *Government Gazette*. No. 4608. March 12, 1975.
9. Van Coeverden, H. A., S. de Groot, & E. E. Greathead. 1987. The Cape Teenage Clinic. *South African Medical Journal*, 71(6):434-436.
10. Nash, E. S., J. H. Brink, F. C. V. Potocnik, & B. L. Dirks. 1992. South African psychiatrists' attitude to the present implementation of the Abortion and Sterilization Act of 1975. *South African Medical Journal*, 82(6):434-436.
11. Stevens J. 1990 (March). South African comment: Sexually transmitted disease. *Medicine International*, 72:5-7.
12. Ballard, R. (Professor, South Africa Institute for Medical Research). Personal communication.
13. Moodley, J., A. A. Hoosen, S. Naidoo, N. Nigil, & A. B. M. Klausman. 1992. HIV status and sexually transmitted pathogens in women attending a colposcopy clinic. *Southern African Journal of Epidemiology and Infection*, 7(1):24-26.
14. Piot, P., & M. Laga. 1989. Genital ulcers and other sexually transmitted diseases and the sexual transmission of HIV. *British Medical Journal*, 298:623-624.
15. Friedland, I. R., K. P. Klugman, A. S. Karstaedt, J. Patch, J. A. McIntyre, & C. A. Alwood. 1992. AIDS—The Baragwanath experience, Part 1. Epidemiology of HIV infection at Baragwanath Hospital 1988-1990. *South Africa Medical Journal*, 82(2):86-90.
16. Department of National Health and Population Development—AIDS Centre, SAIMR.
17. *Southern African Journal Epidemiology Infection*. 1992. 7(3):70.
18. Friedland, I. R., & J. A. McIntyre. 1992. AIDS—The Baragwanath experience, Part 2. HIV infection in pregnancy and childhood. *South Africa Medical Journal*, 82(2):90-94.
19. McIntyre, J. A. (Consultant Obstetrician, Baragwanath Hospital). Personal communication.
20. Schoub, B. D. 1990. The AIDS epidemic in South Africa—Perceptions and realities. *South Africa Medical Journal*, 77:607-609.
21. Karstaedt, A. S. 1992. AIDS—The Baragwanath experience, Part 3. HIV infection at Baragwanath Hospital. *South Africa Medical Journal*, 82(2):95-97.
22. Fleming, A. F. 1990. Opportunistic infections in AIDS in developed and developing countries. *Stevens Royal Society Tropical Medicine*, 84(1):1-6.
23. Schoub, B. D., et al. 1990. Considerations on the further expansion of the AIDS epidemic in South Africa. *South Africa Medical Journal*, 77:613-618.
24. Abdool Karim, Q., S. S. Abdool Karim, & J. Nkomokazi. 1991. Sexual behaviour and knowledge of AIDS among urban black mothers. *South Africa Medical Journal*, 80(7):340-343.
25. Evian, C. R., M. de Beer, M. Crewe, G. N. Padayachee, & H. S. Hurwitz. 1991 Evaluation of an AIDS awareness campaign using city buses in Johannesburg. *South Africa Medical Journal*, 80(7):343-346.
26. Allwood, C. W., L. R. Friedland, A. S. Karstaedt, & J. A. McIntyre. 1992. AIDS—The Baragwanath experience, Part 4. Counseling and ethical issues. *South Africa Medical Journal*, 82(2):98-101.
27. Hurwitz, M. B. 1989. Sexual dysfunction with infertility. *South Africa Medical Journal*, 76:58-62.
28. Hurwitz, M. B. 1992. Breast feeding and sexuality. *Medical Sex Journal South Africa*, in press.

# South Korea

## (*Taehan Min'guk*)

Hyung-Ki Choi, M.D., Ph.D., and Huso Yi, Ph.D. (cand.)*
with Ji-Kan Ryu, M.D., Koon Ho Rha, M.D., and
Woong Hee Lee, M.D.
*Redacted with additional information and updated as of
March 2003 by Huso Yi, Ph.D. (cand.), with additional
information by Yung-Chung Kim, Ki-Nam Chin,
Pilwha Chang, Whasoon Byun, and Jungim Hwang***

## Contents

## *Demographics and a Brief Historical Perspective*

### A. Demographics          ROBERT T. FRANCOEUR

The Republic of South Korea occupies the southern half of the Korean Peninsula in northeast Asia, with North Korea on its northern border, the Sea of Japan and Japan to the east, the East China Sea and China to the south, and the Yellow Sea and northern China to the west. With a total landmass of 38,023 square miles (98,480 km²), and a coastline of 1,500 miles (2,400 km), South Korea is slighter larger than the state of Indiana. The country is mountainous, with a rugged eastern coast. The western and southern coasts are deeply indented, with many islands and harbors. The climate is temperate, with heavier rainfall in summer than in winter.

In July 2002, South Korea had an estimated population of 48.3 million. (All data are from *The World Factbook 2002* (CIA 2002) unless otherwise stated.)

*Communications*: Professor Hyung-Ki Choi, M.D., Yongdong Severance Hospital, Department of Urology 146-92, Dogok-dong, Kangnam-ku, Seoul 135-270, Korea; urol3887@yumc.yonsei.ac.kr. Huso Yi, Ph.D. (cand.): Senior Research Associate, Institute for International Research on Youth at Risk, National Development and Research Institutes, Inc., 71 West 23rd Street, 8th Fl., New York, NY 10010 USA; huso.yi@ndri.org; *or*: Deputy Director, Korean Sexual Minority Culture and Rights Center, Inc., Samheung Bldg., 5th Fl., 256-2 Hangangno 2-ga, Yongsan-gu, Seoul, 140-871, Korea.

**Unless otherwise indicated at the beginning of a section or at the end of a paragraph, Hyung-Ki Choi, Ji-Kan Ryu, Koon Ho Rha, and Woong Hee Lee are the authors. In most sections, the material these authors supplied was redacted by Huso Yi and integrated with additional information. Additional comments are indicated in brackets as [. . . (*Huso Yi*)]. In the areas where the primary authors did not supply information, Huso Yi and others have summarized key studies to complete the picture. Written in 2000-2001, this chapter was updated in 2003 by Huso Yi.

(CIA 2002)

**Age Distribution and Sex Ratios**: *0-14 years*: 21.4% with 1.13 male(s) per female (sex ratio); *15-64 years*: 71% with 1.03 male(s) per female; *65 years and over*: 7.6% with 0.65 male(s) per female; *Total population sex ratio*: 1.01 male(s) to 1 female

**Life Expectancy at Birth**: *Total Population*: 74.88 years; *male*: 71.2 years; *female*: 78.95 years

**Urban/Rural Distribution**: 83% to 17%

**Ethnic Distribution**: Homogeneous, except for about 20,000 Chinese and 4,500 Chinese-Koreans

**Religious Distribution**: Christian: 49%; Buddhist: 47%; Confucianist: 3%; Shaminist and other: 1%***

**Birth Rate**: 14.55 births per 1,000 population. Family planning has been an important task since the 1960s. Korea's TFR decreased from 6.0 births per fertile woman in 1960 to 4.5 in 1970, 2.7 in 1980, 1.6 in 1990, 1.5 in 1998, and 1.7 in 2002.

**Death Rate**: 6.02 per 1,000 population

**Infant Mortality Rate**: 7.58 deaths per 1,000 live births

**Net Migration Rate**: 0 migrant(s) per 1,000 population

**Total Fertility Rate**: 1.72 children born per woman

**Population Growth Rate**: 0.85%

**HIV/AIDS** (1999 est.): *Adult prevalence*: 0.01%; *Persons living with HIV/AIDS*: 3,800; *Deaths*: < 180. (For additional details from www.UNAIDS.org, see end of Section 10B.)

**Literacy Rate** (*defined as those age 15 and over who can read and write*): 98% (*male*: 99.3%, *female*: 96.7%); Korean is the official language, but English is widely taught in the high schools. Education is free and compulsory from the 1st to 6th grades.

**Per Capita Gross Domestic Product** (*purchasing power parity*): $18.000 (2001 est.); *Inflation*: 4.3%; *Unemployment*: 3.9%; *Living below the poverty line*: 4% (2001 est.)

***Editors' Note*: The strong historical dimensions of this chapter and the recurring references to the historical and contemporary influence of Confucianism and its patriarchal views might seem to be unimportant, because 96% of Koreans are either Christian or Buddhist and only 3% identify with the Confucian/Neo-Confucian philosophy. However, Confucianism, and particularly Neo-Confucianism, continues to play a major role in Korean sexual culture.

## B. A Brief Historical Perspective

HYUNG-KI CHOI and COLLEAGUES
(Redacted by HUSO YI)

[*Comment 2001*: According to the *National History Compilation of the Republic of Korea* (NHCROK 2001), the beginning of Korea dates from 2333 B.C.E., when Tangun, a legendary figure born of the son of Heaven, married a woman from the bear-totem tribe and established the first kingdom, Chosun, literally meaning, "Land of the Morning Calm." Korea's early native culture was based on a warrior aristocracy, a shamanistic religion, and a subject class of rice cultivators. The ancient period was followed by the Three Kingdoms from 57 B.C.E. to 676 C.E.; the North-South Unified Shilla period (676 to 935 C.E.); and, starting as a province under the Shilla era, the Koryo dynasty from 913 to 1392 (the Koryo dynasty started as a province in 913 and governed the whole country in 935). (*End of comment by Huso Yi*)] In the Yi or Chosun dynasty (1392 to 1910), during which it was known as the Kingdom of Chosun, Korea was a staunch tributary ally of China during its Ming (1368-1644) and Ch'ing (1644-1911) dynasties. The Japanese, who invaded most of Korea in 1592, were finally expelled by combined Korean and Chinese forces in the late 17th century. This relationship with China brought a strong adherence to Buddhism and a government system modeled on Chinese bureaucracy. For the next 200 years, Korea was rigorously isolated from all non-Chinese foreign influence and was known as "the Hermit Kingdom."

Korea's isolation, and its status as a tributary of China, ended in 1874, when Japan imposed the Treaty of Kangwha to guarantee Japanese commercial access to Korea and other interests. The outcome of the Sino-Japanese war (1894-1895) recognized Korea's complete independence, but made the nation a protectorate of Japan. In 1910, Japan forcibly annexed Korea as the colony of Chosun. A harsh colonial policy was established to eradicate all Korean culture and make Korea an integral part of the Japanese empire. All Korean resistance was violently repressed, although resistance movements managed to survive in exile. During World War II, tens of thousands of Koreans were conscripted to work in Japan and in the Japanese-occupied territories. At the same time, thousands of Korean women were forced into "comfort services" for the Japanese military, a reality that was not dealt with publicly until 50 years later in the late 1990s.

Following Japan's surrender in 1945, Korea was arbitrarily divided into zones of Soviet and American occupation. The 38th parallel split the country geographically, economically, and politically into North and South. Korea's industrial and hydroelectric power was concentrated in the north, where careful Soviet plans established a communist government. In the agricultural south, American attempts to reunify the country under a republican government were inept. By 1948, when it was obvious that the country could not be united, the Republic of Korea was organized in the south, and the United States withdrew its occupation forces in June 1949. In June of 1950, Northern Korean troops invaded the south in an attempt to unify the country under a communist regime. Because it boycotted the United Nations Security Council debate on what response to make to the invasion, the Soviet Union could not veto the United Nations' decision to send troops to repel the invasion. Initially, American forces were successful in driving the communist forces back to the Chinese border. However, when Chinese troops entered the war, the tide reversed and the United Nations troops were driven south. Seoul, the capital, fell to the communists on January 4, 1951. Within two months, the communist forces were driven back to the 38th parallel, where the battle line stabilized despite intervals of fierce fighting. A truce was finally signed on July 27, 1953, with a demilitarized zone along the 38th parallel.

Postwar reconstruction of the south followed with major American support. Student demonstrations in 1960 forced the resignation of Korea's first president, Syngman Rhee. In May 1961, a military coup was established. The military government was given some democratic trappings in a 1972 referendum that allowed General Park to run for an unlimited series of six-year presidential terms. Following Park's assassination on October 26, 1979, by the government's chief of intelligence, General Chun Doo Hwan assumed power. Widespread violent political protests followed, although the nation's economy was making great strides, with modernization, industrialization, and a strong urban life. In 1986, South Korea achieved a favorable balance-of-payments ratio in its foreign trade.

Widespread demonstrations in mid-1987 led to new elections and a calmer political situation, although students called for greater efforts for reunification of the north and south, and protests of the large number of American troops continued. North-South talks in 1990 produced an agreement in principle on reunification in the near future. However, South Korea's interest in reunification became more cautious when North Korea faced a major widespread famine. The massive economic burdens West Germany encountered in helping East Germany become a part of a reunited Germany added to South Korea's growing hesitation over reunification. Establishment of diplomatic relations with China in 1992 was a clear signal that Korea will remain a major influence in the region. [*Comment 2001*: In addition, the Korean government began to build up good relationships with North Korea through the so-called "sunshine policy" of President Kim Dae-Jung, who was awarded a Nobel Peace Prize honoring his political efforts for democracy and reunification. (*End of comment by Huso Yi*)] [*Comment 2003*: In 2003, Roh Moo Hyun became the 16th President. Mr. Roh is a self-taught lawyer without a college education and acquired his liberal credentials by defending students and working-class workers involved in the democracy movement. He named his administration "Participatory Government" and swore to promote democracy and reformation. In his administration, female ministers were appointed, including Ms. Kang Gum-Sil at the age of 46 years old, who would head the male-dominated Justice Ministry for the first time. (*End of comment by Huso Yi*)]

## 1. Basic Sexological Premises

### A. Character of Gender Roles

HYUNG-KI CHOI and COLLEAGUES
(Redacted by HUSO YI)

[*Comment 2001*: The following examples of typical and popular Korean proverbs concerning women provide an insight into the position of women in Korean culture and the family:

> "If you don't beat your woman for three days, she becomes a fox."
> "If you listen to a woman's advice, the house comes to ruin; if you don't listen, the house comes to shame."
> "If a woman cries, no good luck for three years."
> "A woman's mouth is a cheap thing."
> "You can know in water 1,000 fathoms deep, but you can't know the mind of a woman."
> "When wood fire and a woman are stirred up, the outcome is a great misfortune."
> "Get slapped at the government office; come home and hit your woman."

"A bad wife is a grievance for 100 years; bad bean paste is a grievance for one year."

"The good-for-nothing daughter-in-law gets sick on the day of ancestral sacrifice."

"A son-in-law is a guest for 100 years; a daughter-in-law is an eating mouth 'til the day she dies." (*End of comment by Huso Yi*)]

Throughout Korean history, Korean women have been treated as second-class citizens regardless of their social and familial positions. In the social system, they have been limited to being bystanders in the main cultural systems, behind bureaucratic male dominance. Korean women have been the subjects of discriminations based on their role in marriage, their fertility, and their lack of a right to end their marriage in divorce, as well as their subordinate role in the public domain.

In the Koryo dynasty, monogamy was encouraged, and divorce and remarriage were widely practiced by both men and women. However, at the end of the Koryo dynasty, polygamy emerged. The Chosun dynasty (1392-1910) proclaimed monogamy and officially frowned on polygyny as a part of a social reformation policy, although powerful men were commonly allowed to have several wives. [*Comment 2001*: The Chosun dynasty reversed the entire previous marriage system by prohibiting women's remarriage, and furthermore, marriage between those of the same surname and family origin (Chung 1998). The law against remarriage was enforced in 1447 and lasted until 1894. The law against same-surname and family-origin marriage still exists in Korea. It will be discussed later. (*End of comment by Huso Yi*)] The conflicting system of polygyny and monogamy coexisted without much problem because of the lenient Neo-Confucian morals for males. Those who made the laws were not about to give up their privileged right. Nor were they about to improve the subordinate position of women. Women who openly opposed the practice of multiple wives were maltreated and humiliated. However, in 1899, near the end of Chosun dynasty, a formal protest against polygyny took place, headed by the newly organized woman's association. Their protest ended without any change, but it was a herald of an active organized women's movement in Korea.

Early marriage is another interesting feature of the Korean marriage heritage. Records of early marriage as far back as the Three Kingdom era (57 B.C.E. to 676 C.E.) document the practice of early marriage, which allowed children about 10 years old to be presented to a family as a bride or groom. The legal age for marriage in Chosun was 15 for boys and 14 for girls, with the exception of 12 years when a child had to assume responsibility for the family. At the time, the average legal age for marriage in other countries was 18 for men and 15 for women. It was generally believed that the risk of inappropriate sexual involvement increased if marriage was delayed, and so the legal age for marriage was lowered. The custom of early marriage continued well into the 20th century. In the 1991 national tax census, among 1,000 married couples, 10 men and 18 women married before the age of 5, 48 men and 132 women were married between ages 5 and 10, and 159 men and 488 women married between ages 10 and 15. In other words, 217, or one in five of the men, and 638, or nearly two thirds of the women, were married by age 15 (Chung 1998). These children had no choice in the commitment of marriage and parenthood. With no opportunity to reject or refuse their arranged partners, marriage was simply one's fate. Another surprising fact is that among 100 murderers in prison, 31 of the 47 female prisoners murdered their husbands (Chung 1998).

## B. Women of Korea: A Historical Overview

YUNG-CHUNG KIM (Summarized by HUSO YI)

*Women and Family*

As in other agrarian societies, the large patriarchal extended family was the basic organizational unit in Korea for many centuries, with relatively little change in its basic structure. The rule maintained in husband-wife relations the rigid distinction drawn in their roles. Whereas the man dominated in public affairs, the woman took full responsibility in the family. The wife was responsible for the education of the children, especially the girls, up to the age of marriage. There were no educational institutions for girls, and the mother assumed the role of teacher. Her influence was not limited to her daughters' upbringing. She was often honored and rewarded for her model behavior and contribution when her husband or sons were successful in public life.

The woman also took an active part in the family economy. She was expected to be an able and careful manager of family finances. In case the husband was disabled and could not support the family or was neglectful of his duties, the wife had to be able to use her skills to provide for the family. Also, one of the wife's functions in the family system was the performance of rituals in ancestor worship. Filial piety was the prime virtue by which family lineage was preserved, and ancestor worship was its salient feature.

In traditional Korea, it was customary for the ruler and *yangban* (rural ruling-class males) to keep several wives. There was a clear distinction between the primary spouse and the secondary wife/wives or concubines who were at his caprice. In contrast, the woman was subject to strict chastity. When the husband died, ideally the wife must remain chaste the rest of her life; this was the virtuous conduct expected of widows. However, there was less prejudice against remarriage for women in the Koryo period than during either the United Shilla period or the Chosun dynasty. Customs concerning marriage were basic features of the social structure. Because a person's social position was determined by bloodline and family background, a marriage violating or risking such established convention was neither desirable nor acceptable.

The marriage celebration was an expensive one. Such expensive and elaborate feasting and entertainment at weddings (and funerals) were responsible for the ruin of many of the less-affluent *yangban* in the later years of the Chosun dynasty. As the proverb goes: "If a family has three daughters, the pillars of the house will fall." So the marriage expenditures remained a grave social problem throughout the Chosun dynasty, and even today this is true to a great extent.

The position of a woman, on the whole, depended on the status of her father, husband, or son. Women of the ruling class, either by birth or by marriage, could enjoy the same privileges of comfort and honor as men of the same class. Hence, the conduct of women was governed by the rule of three obediences: obedience to the father in childhood, to the husband during marriage, and to the son in old age. The systematic subjugation of women in Korea started during the early reigns of the Chosun dynasty within the aristocratic milieu. The Confucian government started to enact various legal measures harshly discriminatory against women. Remarriage of widowed women was strictly forbidden by law. This prohibition was enforced by disqualifying the sons and grandsons of remarried women from taking the government-service examination.

Social status and rights were transmitted only from fathers to sons. Whereas chastity was thus being forced upon women, men were allowed to expel their wives on any of seven grounds, the so-called seven evils (*ch'ilgo chiak*): disobeying parents-in-law, bearing no son, committing adultery, jealousy, carrying a hereditary disease, talkative to a fault, and larceny. However, even in cases where the wife was guilty of one of these seven evils, the husband could not divorce her if she had served three years mourning for her husband's parents, if the man had gone from poverty to wealth since marrying, or if the wife had no family to depend upon when divorced.

Surprisingly, however, according to the stipulations in the new Confucian code, male and female offspring were both entitled to inherit the father's property. Although there were certain discrepancies between the law and its application, it is important to note that an equal right to property inheritance was recognized by the law, as it was during the Koryo period prior to the Chosun dynasty.

### Women "Professionals"

As pointed out earlier, because of firm adherence to the segregation of men and women, few women could engage in any form of activities outside the family compound. There were, however, some exceptions. Three special groups of women wielded considerable influence by performing certain public functions in traditional society. They were shamans, folk healers, and entertainers (*kisaeng*). The women who worked in these special jobs were, almost without exception, from lower-class families.

The mass culture of Korea since ancient times has been shamanistic in its basic character and tone. Records on female shamans first appeared during the early Shilla period. By that time, they had already outnumbered male shamans. The female shamans had three functions: as priests, as exorcists, and as diviners and fortunetellers.

The second group of women, the folk healers, were increasingly in demand during the Chosun dynasty. It was considered improper for a woman to be examined by a man even if he were a physician. When a woman healer was not available, women patients died because they refused to see male healers. It was, therefore, necessary for the government to train women in order for them to take care of female patients. Women healers could also have a law-enforcement role. When authorities needed to arrest a woman of the ruling class for some suspected crime, women healers from the lower class were called upon to act as policewomen.

The women entertainers (*kisaeng*) also belonged to the low social group. Because their occupation was to entertain men, they developed special talents and skills in poetry composition, singing, dancing, calligraphy, and painting. They were the few women who had free access to public events. For this reason, entertaining women most frequently appeared as heroines in ancient tales and novels. To romanticize the lives of the low-born women in these special cases would be wrong; however, compared to the secluded life of the court and *yangban* families, the lives of female shamans, healers, and *kisaeng* permitted them to have broader experiences and development of their talents.

### Women in the Modern Era

It is hardly accurate to speak of education for women during the Chosun dynasty. Education had barely developed even for the majority of men beyond the local village schools. Because of the new emphasis on Confucianism, and the government-service examination system, formal education facilities and curricula were expanded during the Yi dynasty. Needless to say, women were excluded from these schools.

Following the signing of treaties with Japan, the United States, and European nations in the 1880s, a modern system of schooling was introduced by government officials and leaders who traveled abroad, and by foreign missionaries who were to play a decisive role in women's education. To be exact, school education for girls began in 1886, when a Methodist missionary founded Ewha Haktang. In spite of persistent resistance by Confucian conservatives to women's education, various women's organizations, individuals, and government leaders founded many schools for women by the government by the turn of the 19th century. During the first decade of the 20th century, numerous women's societies were organized for various purposes, including modernization and Westernization.

In 1910, following Japan's victory over imperial Russia in the Russo-Japanese war (1904-1905), Japan annexed Korea. Education was the most important method for carrying on the Japanese colonial policy in Korea. Japan hoped to assimilate Korea culturally as well as politically and economically. The discriminatory policy was even more noticeable in women's education, which was perhaps the least concern of the government during this period. No institution of higher education was founded for women by the government. The colonial policy exploited Koreans more than ever through a military draft and forced labor. Women too, were either sent to factories, into forced labor, or as "comfort women" at army camps. Women leaders could not keep their positions unless they pledged loyalty and obedience to Japan.

During the Japanese colonization, on the other hand, women were politically active in the independence movement. In 1913, a teacher at a girl's school in Pyongyang (now located in North Korea) formed an underground organization. Some of the members organized an underground society called the Patriotic Women's League. Some churchwomen were active in support of the independence movement. They collected funds for resistance fighters and succeeded in sending the money to the government-in-exile in Shanghai. Among the various women's organizations that sprang up in the first quarter of the 20th century, the one that was most outstanding and had the most lasting effect was the Young Women's Christian Association (YWCA). Founded in 1922, this organization has continued, to the present, its activities that have helped promote women's status, social programs, participation, and volunteerism.

A review of the path of women through the centuries of Korean history reveals certain contrasting traits: on the one hand, a state of subjugation, and on the other, a state of self-reliance and full social participation. The differences between the modern era and the past are striking. Women's self-consciousness, buried deep in traditional society, was awakened with the coming of the enlightenment era. By the beginning of the 20th century, women were participating in the drive for political emancipation, social justice, and equal rights. Korean women were confident in their stride and bold in their ambitions as they stepped into the new age.

## C. Sociolegal Status of Males and Females

HUSO YI

After the establishment of the Republic of Korea in 1948, a new Constitution stated the equality of all, including women and children. Other equalities were spelled out in the sectors of politics, economics, general society, and culture, but in actuality, such equalities were not well maintained or protected. According to the annual report by the National Statistical Office (1999a), the majority of employed women are limited to part-time work, the opposite of the male employment pattern. The part-time jobs of women are usually low paying and involve blue-color-type work. In 1997, the average wage of women workers was only 59.9% of their male counterparts. As for participation in employed labor, the report indicates that in 1985, 72.3% of adult males were employed and 41.9% of the women. Twelve years later, in 1998, the data were 75.2% for men and 47.0% for women. However, when the labor participation is divided by marital status, the report indicates as follows:

1. The percentage of single women working in 1985 was 50.8%, which decreased to 46.0% in 1998.
2. The percentage of working single men increased from 43.5% in 1985 to 48.5% in 1998.
3. The percentage of married working women rose from 41.0% in 1985 to 47.3% in 1998.
4. The percentage of married working men has been relatively stable between 1985 and 1998 (86.8%), dropping slightly from a little above 86.8% between 1990 and 1997.

Therefore, unmarried women are the only group in which the participation rate has not increased since 1985.

Obviously, the labor participation rate of women has lagged far behind that of their male counterparts. Compared with statistics from developed countries, Korean women between ages 25 and 35 have an especially lower rate of labor participation. This is likely because of women in this age group being forced to choose their marital and childcare responsibilities over involvement in the workplace.

In terms of the educational status of women, as of 1995, women accounted for 34.8% of the total enrollment in high school and 13.1% of college and postgraduate educational attainment, compared to men, with 41.4% for high school and 25.6% for college and postgraduate enrollment. In addition, the serious gender imbalance in certain university departments continues to be a problem. The career consciousness of female students tends to be based on the division of societal gender roles. For example, in occupational choice, female students are accustomed to such traditional jobs as teaching and nursing, whereas male students prefer to become scientists and lawyers. In response to new educational opportunities, the average age of marriage has been pushed later, as the number of years women spend in school increases. In 1960, the average age at women's first marriage was 21.6 years old, whereas for men it was 25.4 years old, a difference of 3.8 years. In 1998, this increased to 26.2 years for women and 29.0 years for men, a difference of 2.8 years (National Statistical Office 1999a).

Meanwhile, after 1980, women began to use legal means to address and remove patriarchal structures and sex discrimination by new legislation, including the enactment of the Equal Employment Opportunity Act in 1987, the Mother-Child Welfare Act (supporting single mothers) in 1989, the Child Care Act (for support of working mothers) in 1991, and the 1993 Act Relating to Punishment of Sexual Violence and Protection of Victims, as well as the prevention of prostitution (for a review of current laws on Korean women, refer to Kim 1996). Another important issue in women's rights is the status and compensation of "comfort women" under Japanese colonialism (1910 to 1945). The Korean Council for Women Drafted into Military Sexual Slavery by Japan (2000), established in 1990, has made concerted efforts to solve the issue of comfort women and Japan's responsibilities for compensation. During World War II, women were sent to all combat areas and territories occupied by Japan. It is estimated that up to 200,000 women were drafted, of which approximately 80% were Korean women ranging from age 11 to 32.

Today, women's issues have become very important in national policy. Since 1994, the Korean Women's Development Institute (2000) has published *Women's Statistical Yearbook* in order to review and analyze the existing social statistics and indicators about the status of women in comprehensive and systemic ways. The women's social indicators system in the book is composed of 36 subareas, 98 detailed concerns, and 435 indicators under eight major categories: population, family/household, education, employment/economic activities, health, social welfare, social activities, and public safety. In February 1998, the Presidential Commission on Women's Affairs (2000), under the direct supervision of the President, was initiated to promote the status of women and expand women's participation in the public domain. Following Women's Affairs, another important step for women's rights has been taken by establishing the Ministry of Gender Inequality in January 2001. The ministry aims "to develop training and educational courses for women, to devise measures to prevent domestic and sexual violence and gender discrimination, and to provide appropriate services for victims" (Han 2002).

## D. Male Preference, Female Infanticide, and the Sex-Ratio Problem

HYUNG-KI CHOI and COLLEAGUES
(Redacted by HUSO YI)

The influence of Neo-Confucianism has been generally strong since the Chosun era, and it is linked with a male preference in offspring. During this era, the most legitimate method to have children was within a marriage, which was also designed as a joint commitment between two families to produce an heir for the husband's family. Contrary to Confucianism, the traditional Buddhist belief was that all human beings are just transient creatures, prone to be reborn in another life. This resulted in a certain unselfishness and less emphasis on male preference. However, in the Chosun dynasty, the long-term success of the family became the most important goal in marriage. In the eyes of parents, a son will provide economical and emotional supports after his parents' retirement. After their death, he will be in charge of funeral and memorial services. Only a male can head a Korean family. Without a son, a Korean family ceases to be a family, which was an utmost disgrace to parents and ancestors. As the importance of a son increased, his social position became more important. The son had priority in the parents' assets, and in case of the father's early demise, the son oftentimes assumed the role of father in the family.

This pattern of male preference changed social manners and it continues to this day in Korea. However, in 1962, the government introduced a family planning program as part of a powerful economic plan. It encouraged small families with fewer children. With the phenomenal economic growth, the concept of children has changed from a workforce resource to an investment, which requires much time and money. As the average length of education increased dramatically, this burden has also become more prominent. Thus, the small family has become the main pattern.

Widespread abortions have helped to preserve small families in case of unwanted pregnancies. Furthermore, with the advancement of modern reproductive medicine, such as chorionic villi sampling, amniocentesis, and ultrasound scans, the ascertainment of fetal sex has become possible, and small families with an existing male preference have resorted to so-called selective abortion or female infanticide. This has created a sex-ratio imbalance, with 113.4 males born in 1995 for every 100 female babies, much higher than the world average of 106 to 100. This imbalance has been particularly drastic for the third child, where the ratio was 179.4 males for every 100 females. This trend of female infanticide is slowing somewhat, with a ratio of

108.4 to 100 for the first child in 1997 and 134.0 to 100 for the third child (see Table 1).

According to a survey by the Korean Institute for Health and Social Welfare (1991), 71.2% of married women between ages 15 and 49 replied that a son is required in the marriage. This trend is more evident in older women with lower education. The reason for this male preference was family succession for 42.2% of the women, a sense of security for 34.2%, a balanced family for 16.8%, and economic security after retirement for 6.8% of the women surveyed. In a study of 260 married women in Seoul (Kim 1993), the preferred sex for a second child after a son was 52.8% for a daughter and 20.5% for another son. However, after an initial daughter, 83% wanted a son, and only 2.2% wanted a daughter. In a study of 1,546 married adults, 29.4% replied that a son is necessary, whereas 70.6% said a son is not a requirement (Chin et al. 1997). These results reveal an improving trend away from male preference compared to the 1991 survey. Still, the deep-seated preference continues for the next child to be a male, especially in families with daughters. Overall, the recent gender imbalance may be attributed to the easy societal acceptance of gender-selective abortion, a male-centered sexual culture in which the responsibility of contraceptive use primarily is attributed to women, and a deep-rooted patriarchal male preference (see Section 9, Contraception, Abortion, and Population Planning). [*Comment 2001*: In their study, as for the question of "why a son is necessary," 43.5% claimed that a son is needed for the family succession, 39.3% wanted a boy and a girl, 5.8% said "daughters will be taken to husband's family," and 5.8% "wanted to be respected by the parents of husband." (As noted in Section 1B, Basic Sexological Premises, Women of Korea: A Historical Overview, one of the seven evils for a wife is not bearing a son.) For those who needed a son for family succession, when they were asked, "who most claimed the need of a son," 54.3% said the husband himself, 35.5% said his parents, and only 6.9% said the wife.

[In the traditional idea of the Korean family system, it is said that when a woman gets married, she is no longer considered as a member of her family. This notion is indeed supported by the law of Head of Household. Thus, it should be noted that male preference is closely related to the family law that was initially established in the Chosun dynasty. First, when a woman marries, her name will be eliminated from her family register and transferred to her husband's family register. Not only ideologically, but also legally, married women are not members of their natal families. In addition, according to the law, married women cannot be the primary successor of the family inheritance. For example, when a husband, the first family head, is dead, the headship is inherited by his son or grandson. If a family does not have a male successor, the headship is taken by the family's unmarried daughter, not the wife. The wife is the third order for the headship. Even when a woman gets divorced, the headship still remains on the side of her ex-husband so that it is very difficult for women to head a family. In summary,

when a daughter is married, she is "taken" to her husband's family and then has no right for headship and inheritance unless the will specifies her inheritance. If a woman gets divorced, her name can be re-listed in her family register. It is extremely difficult for divorced women to win custody. Another case is the family without a son. After the daughter(s) leave by marriage and her/their father is dead, the headship passes to the mother. But the problem occurs after the mother is dead. Since there is no one to have headship in the family, the family becomes officially extinct (Kim 1992; Chang 1996). Active movements have been organized to correct the law/system of family headship. Critics claim that the law is unconstitutional and violates human rights. A coalition has submitted a petition to the United Nations and, as of mid-2001, was preparing for an appeal to the Supreme Court (Headquarter of the Family Headship Law Abolition 2000; Citizens for Abolition of the Family Headship (*Hoju*) System 2000).

[Such a legal system evokes bearing a son, "to be respected by the parents of husband." It is the most important obligation for married women to have a son. It is said, "A married woman should gift a son to her husband's parents." In that case, it is likely that son is regarded as a "property," as well as the source for family linkage survival. In the Chosun dynasty, if a married woman could not have a son, her husband would adopt a surrogate for a son. These days, it might be happening, but more frequently, women get abortions until they have a son. It is the fidelity and duty of married women to the husband's family. Once women "accomplish" this role, they are "accepted" and "respected."

[Selective abortion is not the only avenue to male preference. In Oriental medicine, there are treatments and pills for son-bearing. In a survey of 203 Oriental medical doctors by *Hankyere* (1996), 34% said that they learned in medical school about the treatment for son-bearing, whereas only 6% learned about the daughter-bearing treatment in school. Ninety percent of their patients asked for medications for son-bearing and 60% of the doctors prescribed it for them. Despite popular prescriptions and treatment, 45% of the doctors did not believe in their reliability and effectiveness. No clinical study has been reported about the medications. Another interesting finding was that 51% said that sex is determined when fertilization occurs and 49% said sex determination is later, around 3 months. It is believed in Oriental medicine that the third month of pregnancy is the time of sex determination, so that sex can be changed by treatment. (*End of comment by Huso Yi*)]

## E. General Concepts of Sexuality and Love

HUSO YI and KI-NAM CHIN

*Cultural Taboos*

Parallel with family succession in Confucian sexual values is "purity of kinship." "Purity of kinship" includes not only the prohibitions of interracial and interclass marriages, but also a third, particularly Korean, prohibition against marriage between persons with the same last names. [*Comment 2001*: In the legal system, this prohibition is quite complicated. For our purposes here, it is sufficient to note the system of Korean kinship. According the Committee of Korean Genealogy (2000), there are 254 surnames from 13 out of 14 Korean alphabets. The official report by the National Statistical Office (NSO 1985) revealed that, among 275 surnames, each of 44 surnames was reported by less than 100 people. As of the 1985

### Table 1

**Sex Rate at Birth by Birth Order (Males Born per 100 Females) by Year**

| Birth Order | 1971 | 1981 | 1985 | 1991 | 1993 | 1995 | 1997 | 1998 |
|---|---|---|---|---|---|---|---|---|
| Total | 109.0 | 107.2 | 109.5 | 112.4 | 115.3 | 113.2 | 108.3 | 110.2 |
| First | 108.1 | 106.3 | 106.0 | 105.7 | 106.5 | 105.8 | 105.1 | 106.0 |
| Second | 107.7 | 106.7 | 107.8 | 112.5 | 114.7 | 111.7 | 106.3 | 108.1 |
| Third | 109.7 | 107.1 | 129.2 | 179.5 | 202.6 | 177.5 | 133.6 | 118.8 |
| Fourth & Over | 110.1 | 112.9 | 146.8 | 194.7 | 237.9 | 205.4 | 155.4 | 155.2 |

population of 40,410,000 people, 5 surnames were reported by more than one million: 8,780,000 were owned by those who had the last name of Kim, 5,980,000 of Lee (or Yi or Rhee), 3,400,000 of Park, 1,910,000 of Choi (or Choy), and 1,780,000 of Chung (or Jung). (Note: there is no official romanization for Korean as in other languages, hence the alternate spellings.) Thus, 54% of the population had one of those five surnames. (The NSO recently finished another investigation in 2000, which was to be published in September 2001). It should be noted that the surname, however, is categorized by three criteria: 1. ancestor, 2. place of family origin, and 3. letter of surname (surname). For instance, although two Korean people have the same surname, they may have a different ancestor and/or place of family origin. Because the ancestor is hard to detect without genealogy, Koreans usually refer to two components, place of family origin and surname. In fact, no official classification for the place of family origin exists. Every genealogical archive shows different numbers. (According to the Committee of Genealogy, one archive reports 499 family origin places for Kim, whereas another notes 600, and others note 623. As for Lee (Yi, Rhee), in the census, only surname and origin is asked because of the incorrectness of the origin of ancestor.

[Korean genealogy started early in the Shilla dynasty, but only people of royal class could have their surnames. In the Koryo dynasty, ordinary people started to have surnames with the place of family origin. At the time, because they made their family origin based on the current living places, it is not unusual to have the same surnames regardless of the origin of the ancestor. Thus, in the early Chosun dynasty, people paid more attention to the place of family origin rather than the letter of surname when married. But, later in the mid-Chosun dynasty, marriage within the same surname and place of family origin was prohibited by the law, which has existed to now (Chung 1998). Today, the law enforces a prohibition of marriage within the same surname and place of family origin in the eighth degree. In a sense, a marriage within the same surname and family origin is constituted as incest, which therefore can violate the purity of kinship. Some family clans even prohibit marriage only within the same surname. The law has been criticized for a long time because of its unrealistic aspects. First, it has nothing to do with the matter of family purity or incest, unless it happens within blood relatives. Second, the place of family origin is not always correct, and furthermore, the fact that two have the same family origin does not tell the status of their kinship in all senses. For example, two peoples who have the same name and whose family came originally from the same city do not always indicate whether or not they are close relatives. Third, it is a reality that many who have same name and family origin get married, and, because of this fact, a specific period is granted for such married couples to get a marriage license. (*End of comment by Huso Yi*)]

Since the Chosun dynasty, these reproduction-oriented sexual norms have traditionally surrounded sexual acts with a total secrecy. This secrecy remains dominant, within marriage, in the family, and in public. [*Comment 2001*: However, this secrecy is no longer an absolute and universal factor inhibiting communications about any and all sexual issues in Korea today. Modern currents of sexual liberation, and global communications about sexual topics via the Internet and World Wide Web are reducing the traditional secrecy surrounding sexuality in Korean culture. As of the end of December, 2000, the Ministry of Information and Communication reported that the number of Korean Internet users topped 19 million (Korean Government Homepage 2000). Another study by NetValue also reported that Korean

Internet users spent 18.1 hours a month online, on average, more than any of the other 12 nations, including Hong Kong (the second at 12.1 hours/month), the U.S. (at 10.8 hours/month), and Singapore (at 9.9 hours/month) (*Korea Herald* 2001). It is not difficult to assume how much the Internet will have an impact upon the lives and sexuality of Koreans. (On the very same day, the Seoul District Prosecutor's Office launched an investigation into adult Internet sites and arrested six Internet adult-TV-station operators; the office announced that "we can no longer tolerate the Internet TV's overheated competition by broadcasting lots of lewd programs," and expanded the investigation to all 40 Internet adult-TV stations (Kim 2001) (*End of comment by Huso Yi*)]

Nevertheless, Confucian taboos continue to hinder institutional sexuality education programs, as well as discussions about sexuality within the family. Korean children grow up with a belief that ignorance of sex is good; they are still encouraged not to talk about sexuality. During childhood, they learn negative attitudes about sexuality, which during adolescence, because of their natural curiosity about sex, often turns into irresponsible sexual activities. [*Comment 2001*: In a nation-state study with 2,243 adolescents, 67.2% reported sexual violence in the middle/high school, and regarding the question of asking about potential sexual violence, 75.6% of the male adolescents and 23.9% of the females reported that they felt impulsive and had a terrible desire of experiencing "violent sexual activities" in middle/high school (Chung 1990). This negative view of sexuality is also related to the prevalence of verbal and physical sexual domestic violence in Korea (see Section 8, Significant Unconventional Sexual Behaviors) (*End of comment by Huso Yi*)]

### The Double Standard in Sexual Culture

The most outstanding aspect of sexual culture in male-dominant Confucianism is the different standards of sexual morality for men and women. Such ethical codes are formulated by stressing virginity for women. According to Confucianism, the woman is always placed lower than the man. The husband is compared to the sky and wife is depicted as the ground and, therefore, she is obedient to the husband (see *Woman's Four Book* by King Young-Jo, 1736/1987). [*Comment 2001*: *Woman's Four Book* was originally written by Chinese scholars. King Young-Jo imported and translated the book to correct the morals of women. In his introduction, he began with the metaphor, "Man is the sky and woman is the ground." Besides that dictum, many rules of obedience are described for women. For example, the title of the first chapter is, "The chapter of low and weak status," which implied women. The chapter begins: "The sky is high, the ground is low and *yang* is strong, *yin* is weak. The lowness and weakness is women's destiny. If the woman wants to be strong on her own, it violates the law of justice." (*End of comment by Huso Yi*)]

Under the ideology of the gender hierarchy, the moral superiority of the upper class and family purity, and the Chosun dynasty Constitution of 1485, women of the ruling class were prohibited from remarriage after the death of their husband. If a widow was recognized as a moral model, gracious grants were allowed for her entire family. By the end of Chosun era, the control of female virginity and fidelity had been firmly established, widely promoted by books about female domestic education. Contemporary Korean attitudes towards virginity are based on these historical events. To maintain the purity of one's family lineage, female virginity and sexual fidelity were and still are stressed for women, whereas men were and still are generously allowed the varieties of prostitution, polygyny, and other forms of sexual explorations.

*The Phallus-Centered Sexual Culture*

The male-dominant sexual culture of Korea has been very phallic oriented. Because the male sex is considered sexually superior to the female sex, sexual intercourse is not perceived of as a mutually intimate interpersonal relationship. Rather, it is perceived as a physiological or primitive event, a kind of tension release for the male. In this view, only the phallus is worth consideration. Thus, the entire Korean sexual culture exists for satisfying the male's sexual needs, downplaying the mental and intimate relationship between partners. Women are raised to passively play up to this male-dominant action, and those who are more obedient and passive are encouraged. Men, on the contrary, are portrayed and raised as strong, aggressive, and dominating figures, and this concept is carried into everyday sexual and marital relationships. Because this sexual discrimination is regarded as natural, intimate relationships between men and women are seriously distorted.

[*Comment 2001*: The Korean metaphoric/ideological description of the phallus-centered sexual culture that one finds in Korea has interesting ritual expressions in the traditional phallus-worship ceremonies of Japanese Shintoism and *lingam* and *yoni* worship in Hinduism (Gregersen 1994, 232, 355). In Korea, the phallus is literally called "male-root" and the vulva "female-root." Although many phallic stones were destroyed during Japan's colonization and the subsequent modernization, 840 stones and wooden objects have been discovered so far (Kim & Yoon 1997). Those that are made of wood are placed in the temple or hung on the ceiling of a household. (The size and shape of the wooden phalluses are just like modern sex toys). Oh (1997) analyzed 45 historical remains that are preserved for "sexual worship": 26 stones are categorized as being used in prayers for a son, 9 for protecting the village, 5 for preventing a women's promiscuity, 3 for family well-being, and 2 for cultivation. These stones convey a male preference. However, many vulva-shaped stones can be easily found next to phallic stones in a *ying-yang* context or separately. These vulval stones, as well as vulval fountains, are also worshiped, as are phallic stones. Vulval fountains are not only natural ones, but some that are designed on purpose. In order to be pregnant with a son, women not only pray in front of the stone, but also rub their genital areas on it. Many interesting worship ceremonies are still held all over the country. For instance, in a fishing village, fishermen have for hundreds of years carved wooden phalluses and offered them to a legendary virgin of the temple twice a year. It is believed that the virgin died in the ocean longing for sex, so the villagers believe that they should appease the virgin ghost in the ocean with wooden phalluses to avoid any misfortune and accidents. (*End of comment by Huso Yi*)]

## 2. Religious, Ethnic, and Gender Factors Affecting Sexuality

### A. Source and Character of Religious Values

HUSO YI

As already noted, Korea has developed and adopted several new religions that have molded its sexual values, family structure, concepts of love, and gender roles, both in public and the private space. The ancient shamanistic religion and warrior aristocracy encountered a new religious influence 2,000 years ago in Confucianism. Buddhism arrived in Korea around 400 C.E. and was actively persecuted for a hundred years. At the end of the Koryo era around 1400, Neo-Confucianism reversed the previous sex-positive attitudes in Buddhism. In the late 1700s, Catholicism arrived from Europe, followed a century later by Protestant-

ism. Today, 49% of South Koreans are Christians and 47% are Buddhists. Although only 3% of Koreans believe in Confucianism, it remains the basis of criminal law and sexual morals.

*Confucianism*          HYUNG-KI CHOI and COLLEAGUES
(Redacted by HUSO YI)

Confucianism was first introduced into Korea in the era of the Three Kingdom unification. The Unified Kingdom of Shilla was successful in blending the different lifestyles and cultures from the other two original kingdoms, and also was eager to accept the advanced cultures of mainland China. A new and unique cultural unification took place on the Korean peninsula, and one of the most important advancements was Confucianism. In this new era, the political idea of Confucianism, which stresses loyalty to authorities, was a convenient justification for the totalitarian rule of the kings. In the succeeding Koryo era, Confucianism continued to be the main ideological basis for the kingdom. Its beliefs were accepted as an efficient ideology supportive of the king and the ruling class. This is why, even though its official adherents are few in number in Korea, it has remained a major social influence. This practical social application is also the reason that Confucianism has flourished in the Far East.

Respected scholars were recruited to serve as high-ranking government officers, and all ceremonies and record keeping was modeled on the Confucian system. The government set up a learning center to sponsor further research and discussion of Confucianism. The kings and other nobles tried to practice the Confucian way of life in both their personal and public lives. One important aspect of Confucianism in the Koryo period 600 years ago is that it did not consider Buddhism as a hostile belief to Confucianism. The people of Koryo considered Buddhism as a personal religion for souls, and Confucianism as a bible for everyday human social lives. They respected both beliefs until the end of the Koryo era, when Buddhism became lavish and selfish. Orthodox followers of Confucianism then rejected Buddhism altogether, banning new recruits and halting financial support to the Buddhist temples. Confucianism was greatly appreciated by the reforming sect of the ruling class, which made it the official belief of the Chosun dynasty. It was the guideline of politics, society, and culture, encompassing all facets of everyday life. This marked the end of a thousand years of Buddhist public influence in Korean culture and the return of Confucianism in a Neo-Confucian form employing negativity against sexuality (Fellows 1979, 199-241; Noss & Noss 1990, 283-318).

Confucian belief regards the male as a positive being (*yang*) and the female as a negative counterpart (*ying*), based on the concept that the biological differences of the two sexes actually stem from a basic element of nature. Confucianism stresses the harmonious relationship of *yang* and *ying*, but *yang* is always more dominant than *ying* in every aspect. Thus, men are considered omnipotent compared to women, and male dominance and discrimination against women are justified. Furthermore, the Confucian way of life regards sex as an inevitable aspect needed to maintain the family and society, rather than an act of pleasure. Thus, in the Chosun era, sex was first considered as a reproductive process. The Chosun period is also known for its strict caste system, based on the Confucian theory that higher and ruling classes should be morally superior to the subjecting classes. Male preference and a double moral standard in sexual matters are only a few examples of this varied Confucian past (Fellows 1979, 199-241; Noss & Noss 1990, 283-318). [*Comment 2001*: In addition, it should be noted that these ideologies in Confucianism have been challenged by feminism since 1990, and are having an impact on changing the laws discriminating against the status of women and individuals' lifestyles (*End of comment by Huso Yi*)]

*Buddhism*          HYUNG-KI CHOI and COLLEAGUES

Buddhism was first introduced to Korea in the year 372 C.E. during the Three Kingdom period in which it was adopted and encouraged as the new faith by the royal court. Traditional shamanism and conservative nobles opposed Buddhism for 100 years after its initial introduction, but in all three Kingdoms, it was accepted by the sponsorship of royal endorsement. In the totalitarian kingdoms, Buddhism was a practical new faith helping to unify the common people. The people considered themselves subjects of both Buddha and the king, and this helped to unify the young kingdoms. The three kings and their royal courts gave generous contributions and slaves to the Buddhist temples to support cultivation of the land. Buddhism in this era was a tool to deepen the philosophical aspects of the people, and the monks were both scholars of learning and teachers (Fellows 1979, 129-194; Noss & Noss 1990, 157-231).

After the unification of the three kingdoms, Buddhism received more attention internationally by preaching abroad. However, the lavish construction of temples wasted resources, which became one of the reasons of the demise of the unified kingdom of Shilla. In the Koryo era, Buddhism still played a major role as the main religious belief of the kingdom. The monks of the Buddhist temples were exempt from military conscription and service, and even princes became monks in this era. This gave Buddhism a flavor of nobility, but toward the end of the Koryo dynasty, the powers of the Buddhist temples and monks became excessive, and power shifted back to Confucianism. During the Neo-Confucian Chosun period, the monks were subjected to harsh rules, including closure of major temples, seclusion in the mountains, forced labor, and heavy taxes. The social position of Buddhist monks was lowered substantially. Buddhism in this era shifted its base to the poor and unfortunate. Despite this oppression and decline in public image, 47% of Korean people still consider Buddhism as their faith. Buddhists in general are instructed to give up all desires, including those related to sex, and sexual activities are prohibited in many sects.

*Catholicism and Protestantism*

During the mid-Chosun dynasty at the end of the 17th century, a Korean scholar introduced a Catholic publication, marking the first recorded evidence of Christianity in Korea. Other books about Christianity followed and naturally became the subject of academic interest. Because Catholic belief differed so from the realistic beliefs of Confucianism, Catholic belief was initially considered similar to Buddhism, and so drew only academic attention and interest.

Towards the end of the 18th century, Christianity began to win over increasing numbers of the common people, mostly in the northern provinces near the Chinese border. Catholicism in Korea is unique in the fact that it was not initially introduced by priests, but rather through books imported by scholars and then self-propagated among the common people. Catholicism did not acknowledge the caste system, and thus was considered by the authorities as a threat to the society. Catholic worshipers also neglected the responsibility to conduct memorial services for one's ancestors, which was considered one of the most important elements in Koreans' everyday lives. Soon Catholicism was considered illegal and officially banned. Harsh punishments were given to the worshipers. The Chosun government also prohibited the importing of any Catholic book. Around 1801, some 300

Catholic worshipers, including a priest, were executed. A Korean informer notified the archbishop in Peking and called for a military demonstration by Western powers to stop this repression. This incident only aggravated the religious oppression of Catholics, and by 1839, three Western priests had been executed along with 80 more believers. However, Catholicism gained an underground popularity, so that by 1865, there were more than 23,000 Korean Catholics, with their own Catholic school.

The increasing popularity of Catholicism was in part attributed to the extremely corrupt period of the 19th-century Chosun. After the beginning of formal diplomatic relationships with France in 1887, freedom of religion was finally guaranteed in Chosun and an official Catholic Church was established in Seoul. Missionaries quickly set up Catholic parishes and became involved in publishing numerous books.

Protestantism was first introduced into Korea in 1884 by an American Presbyterian missionary named Dr. Horace N. Allen. In the next year, Dr. Horace G. Underwood (Presbyterian) and Rev. Henry G. Appenzeller (Methodist) arrived in Korea. They started by concentrating on offering practical knowledge on health, medicine, and general education to the poorer segments of the general public. Preaching followed. The Protestant belief of equality and freedom directly confronted traditional Confucianism, and became, as it spread, the foundation of a democratic movement. The Young Men's Christian Association (YMCA) was first established in 1903 in Korea and brought with it initiatives on reforming various aspects of everyday lives, including the prohibition of alcohol, abstinence from smoking, and equal rights. In 1915, the Chosun Christian College was founded, chiefly through the efforts of Dr. H. G. Underwood, the pioneering Protestant missionary who served as the Chosun Christian College's first president. During the Japanese occupation in the early 20th century, the Protestant churches and schools became a secret stronghold for the independence movement. It is no wonder that many of prominent leaders in this era were Protestants. Both Catholics and Protestants are currently actively involved in medicine, education, and various social movements. (As noted earlier, 49% of Koreans are Protestant or Catholic.)

## B. Character of Ethnic Values          HUSO YI

Korea is a very homogenous country in terms of ethnicity. Until recently, it was so and it is still rare for many Koreans to have close contact with other ethnic groups. Historically, when the neighboring countries, China and Japan, began to open their borders to Western culture in the late 19th century, Korea remained closed to trade with Western countries. Opening to trade with the West might lead to colonization by Japan or by Western nations, as happened with the British in Hong Kong and the Portuguese in Macau. Another reason for this policy of seclusion may be the size of Korea and its geographical location: a small country surrounded by China and Japan. The lack of contact with other cultures naturally restricted the acceptance of various sexual attitudes and behaviors from the outside. In recent years, the influence of globalization and the immigration of foreign laborers have challenged Korea's homogenous character and traditional isolation.

## 3. Knowledge and Education about Sexuality

### A. Historical Perspective

HYUNG-KI CHOI and COLLEAGUES

Unmarried young men and women in the Chosun dynasty received a very limited form of sexuality education, focused on how to achieve pregnancy and produce better descendants. The most important lesson was instruction on how to select the right time, as well as the best position and behaviors, for achieving pregnancy. When newlyweds started their honeymoon, the bride received a calendar with information about the fertile time. In many instances, husbands were also given this information. In some traditional extended families, married sons were not allowed to sleep in the same room with their wife unless the family patriarch approved, based on the wife's fertile period. Delivering a child was an important, often-sacred event in the Confucian Chosun family. Prenatal care was a mandatory obligation for pregnant couples and was dutifully accepted by all expectant parents. This prenatal care began even before conception and was the focus of sexuality education when taught in the elementary schools.

### B. Government Policies and Programs

HYUNG-KI CHOI and COLLEAGUES
(Redacted by HUSO YI)

The traditional silence of Korean society on sexuality issues and education has left its adolescents almost completely without guidance in dealing with the imported Western sexual cultures. This trend is accelerating with the fast pace of modernization, and the consequences can be observed in the increasing incidence of adolescent pregnancies, sexual abuse, and sexual crimes. The Planned Parenthood Federation of Korea (PPFK) started sexuality education in 1968. Since 1982, counseling centers for sexuality has been provided for adolescents in schools and industrial parks. Besides education and counseling, PPFK has published annual reports on counseling cases and educational projects to help understand adolescent sexuality.

In spite of such efforts and the obvious needs, formal sexuality education in schools has not been well established. What sexuality education exists in schools focuses solely on physical development and gender roles. For female students, the topics of menstruation, pregnancy, and virginity are the main content, whereas male students are taught about sexually transmitted disease and sexual activities. It is assumed that male students are sexually active but female students should not be. Research in the 1990s has noted the limitations and problems of the existing sexuality education in schools. For example, research by Lee (1996) reported that only 5.5% of students were satisfied with their school sexuality education program. [*Comment 2001*: In 1996, the Korean Government established the Korea Research Institute for Culture and Sexuality to develop effective sexuality education programs. Government policies, as stated in the Sex Education in the Adolescent Youth Protection Law, state that information and materials on homosexuality are illegal. The policies are based on homosexuals being sexually abstinent and denying themselves any sexual relationships, especially in adolescence. The policies also questioned whether homosexuality should be considered as a part of sexuality education program. (*End of comment by Huso Yi*)]

### C. Informal Sources of Sexual Knowledge

HYUNG-KI CHOI and COLLEAGUES
(Redacted by HUSO YI)

In the early 1990s, interest in sexual information increased enormously. Since then, books as well as other materials on sexuality have been produced. To meet academic interest, conferences on sexuality have been held and the mass media have taken up sexuality topics. In 1998, a public sexual education program was offered on television, and the instructor became a celebrity. It is now relatively easy to access information on sexuality.

In two studies by the Korean Research Institute on Sexuality and Culture (Kim et al. 1996, 1997), 37.1% of 1,976 male high school students reported that their primary source of sexual knowledge was adult materials and pornography. Fourteen percent of the males learned from their friends, whereas 37% of 3,134 female high school students obtained sexual knowledge from their peers, and 25.7% learned in school. The percentages were lower for students in the upper grades. These results show an increase in the influence of sexuality education programs in school. The study also tested sexual knowledge. Some examples of the kinds of questions asked include: "The hymen can tear during bicycle or horse riding," "The testis produces blood along with semen," "Kissing can induce fertilization in healthy couples," "Pregnancy stops periodic menstruation," "The sex of a fetus is determined at birth," "Douching immediately after intercourse prevents fertilization," "Condom use lowers risk of contacting STDs," and "Masturbation is not associated with transmission of AIDS." The mean score of the correct answers was 62 for female students and 65 for males. For the questions about STDs, the mean score was 53. The results reflected the current need for more effective sexuality education in Korean adolescents.

## 4. Autoerotic Behaviors and Patterns

### A. Children and Adolescents                HUSO YI

The Korean Research Institute of Sexuality and Culture (Kim et al. 1997) reported that 70% of female high school students agreed that "masturbation is natural to release sexual desire." In contrast with their positive attitudes, however, only 15.2% of the survey participants had experienced masturbation. For those who had masturbated, the frequency of masturbation was once a month (44.2%), two to four times per month (23.1%), and five to seven times per month (5%). With respect to self-reported feelings after masturbation, 35.6% felt guilty, 21.0% felt nothing, and 6.3% felt good. When asked about their response to a sexual urge, 41.9% "just endured," 10.5% exercised and/or engaged in favorite habits, 6.2% masturbated for relief, and 35.7% answered they had no experience of sexual urges. Meanwhile, 49.9% of male high school students reported masturbating, whereas 46.3% endured the sexual urge. There was a significant gender difference in masturbation.

### B. Adults                                    HUSO YI

Yoo, Oh, and Soh (1990) asked about parents' attitudes toward masturbation to see their relationship to their children's masturbation. In 75.2% of the parents showing positive attitudes toward their own masturbation, there was a linear trend by age: 77.8% in the parents in their 50s, 75.9% in their 40s, and 56.1% in their 30s. In terms of religious adherence, Buddhists were least positive about masturbation, 54.5%, compared with Protestants, 76.9%, and Catholics, 91.7%. In terms of negative views toward their own masturbation, more than 60% of the male and female respondents said, "It is against moral standards." The second reason showed a significant gender difference: 25.0% of the males answered, "It's harmful to sexual activity," whereas 12.5% of the females offered a religious reason, saying that "it evokes guilty feeling." Certainly, their attitude on masturbation was related to that of their children's masturbation. Those who feel good about their own masturbation showed positive attitudes toward their children's masturbation as well. Meanwhile, their reasons also revealed a significant gender difference. Half of the parents said children's masturbation is good because it shows "good evidence of physical development." But, in terms of gender difference, masturbation is a "unique method of resolution of sexual tension," answered by 13. 6% of the males and 33.3% of the females, a "relief of physical tension" by 4.5% of the males and 13.3% of the females, and a "relief of psychological tension" by 11.4% of the males and 2.2% of the females.

## 5. Interpersonal Heterosexual Behaviors

### A. Children

*Male Circumcision*

ROBERT T. FRANCOEUR and HUSO YI

In 1945, after World War II, very few South Koreans knew there was such a thing as a "naked penis," a penis with no foreskin. Male circumcision was practiced only within the tiny Jewish and Muslim enclaves. Nationwide, fewer than one in 1,000 South Korean boys were circumcised, and circumcision was equally unknown in neighboring China and Japan. In Asia, only the Filipinos embraced circumcision, or at least the Spanish version, which involves cutting a slit in the top of the foreskin rather that removing the foreskin altogether. Around the world, 50 years ago, only about 15% of boys were circumcised at birth or puberty. Only one "developed nation" stood out as a champion of circumcision and that was the United States, where 90% of newborn sons were circumcised. When American soldiers arrived in Korea to implement the United Nations trusteeship (1945-1948) and returned in even greater numbers to South Korea during the Korean War (1950-1953), South Koreans came to believe that practicing circumcision was "advanced and modern."

In the 1960s, South Koreans adopted circumcision with a passion, but also with some differences. Whereas Americans circumcise their sons soon after birth, South Korean physicians decided it was much healthier to circumcise their sons at puberty, when they were 12 years old and could understand the importance of leaving their childhood behind and becoming a man. Unlike most American circumcisers, who until recently used no anesthesia as they operated on the newborn boy, South Korean circumcisers use a local anesthesia. In the 1960s, Korean doctors and advice columnists launched a campaign in newspapers and magazines urging parents to have their adolescent sons circumcised during the long winter break before a boy enters middle school. Infections, the Korean doctors say, are much less likely if circumcision is done in the winter rather than in the summer.

Another reason Korean doctors cite in recommending circumcision is their claim that South Korean men have a gene that causes penile phimosis or "abundant foreskin." In their view, at least 90% of Korean men have "too much" foreskin. Strangely, there is no evidence of this alleged genotype for phimosis among South Koreans, where a 1971 study of men aged 19 to 31 entering military service found only 5% to be circumcised and fewer than 1% of uncircumcised men with phimosis (Jung 1971). The incidence of phimosis is similar to that in the rest of the world. At the same time, Kim, Lee, and Pang (1999) found that most physicians could not define phimosis, yet almost all of South Korean physicians recommend universal circumcision because they believe it eliminates tight foreskins and brings many benefits. Circumcision, they wrongly claim, makes for harder penises, eliminates the bad smell of the penis, reduces susceptibility to various sexually transmitted diseases, cures premature ejaculation, and prevents penile and cervical cancer. Finally, there is the irresistible claim that circumcision produces a definite "cure-all-aphrodisiac effect" in the penis.

Those who were not circumcised believed that they were "naturally circumcised." The common word for "natural circumcision" may be difficult to understand in other countries. But, it is a very popular Korean term, which refers to one of the following: 1. not having phimosis; 2. relatively short prepuce; 3. fully retractable when penis gets erected; and 4. the penis looks more or less the same when erect. Considering the same low rate of phimosis, the uncircumcised men also think circumcision is mandatory, but they feel "naturally circumcised" (Kim et al. 1999). The researchers noted, "nearly all textbooks, encyclopedias, and newspaper articles [in South Korea] essentially advocate universal or near-universal circumcision, and the debate is about when to be circumcised or to circumcise, rather than whether to be circumcised."

For unknown reasons deeply rooted in their ethos, South Korean doctors misinterpret the recent decrease in American parents circumcising their newborn sons—down to 59% in 1992—as recommending universal circumcision at about age 12, even though there is absolutely no evidence that American boys are now being circumcised at puberty. The doctors are also puzzled why such "advanced" countries as Japan and Denmark do not recommend universal circumcision. One advice columnist recently wrote that, "If a child feels different because he is not circumcised and his friends boast of having a superior penis because of circumcision, it is good to have him circumcised for psychological reasons." Today, at least 95% of South Korean boys entering middle school have been circumcised. For the other 5%, the question is not whether they should give up their foreskin, but when they should be circumcised. Korean boys simply take circumcision for granted. It is their right of passage to manhood.

### B. Adolescents

HUSO YI [*Updated 2003 by H. Yi*]

According to a study among female high school students (Kim et al. 1997), 44.4% had had heterosexual relationships. Of those who had not had vaginal intercourse, 47.8% reported that they just had not had the opportunity, 18.3% did not want to because "we are students," and 15.5% were not interested in the opposite gender. These results suggest that, if the opportunity offered itself, heterosexual relationships would be increased. With regard to a question about what sexual intimacies are permissible for unmarried adolescents, 44.7% regarded light kissing as permissible, 31.6% accepted holding hands, 19.7% regarded kissing and petting as acceptable, and only 1.4% found sexual intercourse acceptable. The results indicated that female students still wanted to keep their virginity although their attitudes toward sexuality became more open and liberal. In the study, 88.1% of the female students reported that virginity should be kept until marriage, whereas 65.7% of males favored premarital sexual activity. In their study, 91.7% had no coital experience, and only 7.5% had coital experiences. Among those who had coital experiences, 38.7% were coerced into having sex, 32.3% had sex "because of love," and 11.9% were raped. In the study of male students, of the 16.2% who had had coital experiences, 74.7% had had sex with a girlfriend, 34.1% had had intercourse with a woman they "happened to meet," and 16.6% had done so with prostitutes (Kim et al. 1996). A national sample of high school students indicated that the sexual intercourse rate among male students increased from 12% to 18% between 1988 and 1998, while female students' sexual intercourse rate increased from 3% to 8% between 1988 and 1997 (Han et al. 2001).

Most of adolescents held conservative views of sexual experiences. The study also noted a difference in contraceptive use between males and females; 20.4% of female students used contraceptive methods and 52.2% of males used them (Kim et al. 1996; Kim et al. 1997). The most frequent contraceptive method was condom use (37.5% of the females and 49.1% of the males). The next most frequent "contraceptive" method was withdrawal prior to ejaculation (33.3% of the females and 31.1% of the males). The low percentage of contraceptive usage may come from male partners' ignorance of condom use and/or the lack of opportunity (power) for that. Females have less opportunity to make decisions.

The Korean Sexuality Counseling Center (1997) for adolescents reported that most calls, 86.1%, were from boys. One in five boys, 20.6%, had questions about masturbation and 16.7% asked about sexual impulses. The callers were most curious about physical contacts with the other sex (50.2%), followed by pregnancy and delivery (17.4%). Boys tended to show self-centered, male-egoistic attitudes about the other sex, whereas girls focused on their responses and passive behaviors. The most frequent concern of high school girls, 31.6%, was boyfriends, followed by pregnancy, 12.4%, and abortion, 4.9%. This reflects passive attitudes about sex on the part of Korean females. The girls usually consulted with their friends, 44.5%, or with professional counselors, 33.6%. Parents and siblings were less frequently consulted, 12.2% and 4.1%, respectively. However, only 1.1% of girls considered their own schoolteachers as trustworthy consultants. A similar trend was seen with high school boys: 53.5% wanted to consult with their friends, but only a few were willing or wanted to share their sexual problems with parents (5.7%), siblings (5.1%), or teachers (1.5%). There is a substantial communication barrier between high school students and their parents and teachers, attributable to strong emotional barriers on both sides, which impede sincere discussion.

Youn's (1996) study with 849 adolescents revealed similar results that 9.8% of the female respondents had coital experiences while 22.9% of the males had it. However, the study revealed significant gender difference in sexual experiences. The male respondents reported the maximum number of sex partners, ranging between 25 and 40 partners, whereas the highest number for the females was 6. The average number of coital partners for the males steadily increased by grade, but the number of females' coital partners did not, as Table 2 shows. This may be because of the value of keeping virginity as a treasure to be maintained until marriage and a sort of sexual explosion in the first college year (grade 13). With respect to the question of practicing safer sex, 43% of the sexually active male adolescents had used contraceptive methods at least once, whereas 28% of the females had done so. But, only 7% of the respondents used contraceptives consistently.

## C. Adults
### Premarital Relations, Courtship, and Dating
HUSO YI

In 1991, the Women's Studies Center of Ewha Woman's University surveyed 352 male participants ranging in age from 20 to 40, which indicated that over 80% had had heterosexual experiences, and among those, 44.7% had their first sexual experiences with a female prostitute, 55.4% answered that prostitution should be allowed to prevent rape, and 25.6% were in favor of the legal regulation of prostitution (Chin et al. 1997).

A study of 1,596 married couples reported that 50.8% regarded premarital relations as negative and 36% as positive; 75% regarded extramarital affairs negatively and 13.2% as something positive (Chin et al. 1997). In their study, the responses of male and female participants showed significant differences. Females, and those who were younger, more educated, and had no religious affiliation, held more positive attitudes toward premarital and extramarital relations. An interesting factor was the participants' ambivalence. Around 80% were concerned about what they viewed as the current open and uncontrolled sexual culture. On the other hand, 61% agreed that Korea's sexual culture is repressed. The usual double moral standard, which is more permissive for males than for females, is more complicated in modern Korea, where premarital sexual experiences and sexual liberation are increasingly accepted, while at the same time, the traditional value of female virginity and sexual passivity is expected in a very patriarchal society. The result, obviously, is psychological stress more for women than for men.

### Sexual Behavior and Relationships of Single Adults
HUSO YI

As one might suspect from what has already been discussed, sexual behavior and relationships among Korean single adults are very limited because of negative attitudes toward premarital sexual relationships and the frequency of marriages arranged by parents or according to their socioeconomic status (Kendall 1996). Thus, it is likely that single adults do not feel a need for sexual relationships. Even though sexual liberation has influenced the sexual relationships of single adults, the value of female virginity is hard to be dismissed. In a study of single-adult sexual behaviors (Kim et al. 1998), around half of the male and female adults were in heterosexual relationships. But, being in relationships did not mean having sexual relationships: 52.9% of the male respondents had positive attitudes to sexual relationships, whereas 37.6% were opposed to that. In response to the question of "how one resolves a sexual urge" (multiple answers), 60% of males exercised, 52.1% masturbated, 38.3 used hobbies as a distraction, 37.0% held in their urge, 9.6% prayed, 11.7% claimed they never had a sexual urge, and 26.2% had sex. In the female group, 35.2% exercised, 8.1% masturbated, 33.8% engaged in hobbies, 21.8% repressed their urge, 3.7% had sex, and (surprisingly) 61.1% never had sexual urges. Such female repression of the sexual urge or self-reported asexuality can be related to the most frequent female sexual dysfunction, inhibited sexual orgasm (see Section 12, Sexual Dysfunctions, Counseling, and Therapies).

### Hymen Reconstruction and Plastic Surgery
HUSO YI

Hymen can be translated as "virgin-skin" in Korean. Despite the effort of educating Koreans about the meaning and function of the hymen, the existence of an intact hymen is still highly valued at marriage so that hymen reconstruction and plastic surgery is frequently popular. There was an interesting lawsuit case about the loss of a hymen. In 1994, a 40-year-old woman sued the Korean Medical Research Center because she was extremely psychologically distressed after she lost her hymen during a Pap

### Table 2

**Korean Adolescents Who Experienced Sexual Intercourse by Year in School**

| Grade | Males % | n / N | Females % | n / N | Combined % | n / N |
|---|---|---|---|---|---|---|
| 11 | 14.6 | 25 / 171 | 8.1 | 7 / 86 | 12.5 | 32 / 257 |
| 12 | 16.6 | 38 / 229 | 7.8 | 10 / 129 | 13.4 | 48 / 358 |
| 13 | 16.5 | 51 / 309 | 10.5 | 28 / 267 | 13.7 | 79 / 576 |
| 14 | 21.0 | 87 / 415 | 9.5 | 37 / 388 | 15.4 | 124 / 803 |
| 15 | 22.4 | 99 / 441 | 9.3 | 37 / 398 | 16.2 | 136 / 839 |
| 16 | 22.9 | 103 / 449 | 9.8 | 39 / 440 | 16.7 | 142 / 849 |

*Source:* Youn 1996

smear test. Even though the doctor claimed that the hymen is usually torn during the test (and can even be torn by exercise), the court said, "It is clear that the hymen is still recognized as a symbol of 'virginity' and keeping virginity is valued in society. It is admitted that she was distressed by the lost of her symbol of virginity, therefore the hospital must pay for compensation" (Park 1994). One Korean prenatal genetic clinic offers STD tests with hymen reconstructive surgery, so that women can be free from her "history" of past sexual experiences (http://www.yunlee.co.kr, in Korean). In addition, the vaginal-opening muscle (pubococcygeus muscle) tension surgery (called "beauty surgery") is also commonly provided after delivery or for middle-aged married women. These surgeries are not even approved by the Korean medical association (Seol 2000). Dr. Seol, one of the leading sex therapists, is strongly opposed to such surgeries, based as they are on myths (see Section 12, Sexual Dysfunctions, Counseling, and Therapies).

## *Marriage and Family: Structures and Patterns*
HYUNG-KI CHOI and COLLEAGUES
(Redacted by HUSO YI)

In 1948, when Korea initiated its own government, the law on monogamous marriage was enforced. According to the census, the crude marriage rate had not changed from 1975 (8.0) to 1997 (8.1). The average age at first marriage in 1987 was 27.3 for males and 24.5 for females, which was delayed to 28.7 and 25.9, respectively, in 1997. However, the crude divorce rate has increased significantly from 0.5 in 1975 to 2.0 in 1997. The number of divorces in 1998 was 124,000, an increase of 30% from 1997. It is calculated that one out of three Korean marriages today end in divorce (see Tables 3 and 4). The annual report also indicated that the most common cause of divorce was the extramarital affairs of husbands. Moon (1993) addressed the factors of dissatisfaction in sexual activities with spouse, husband dominance, lack of respect and affection, male-preferred sexual position, no foreplay, and absence of communication. The sexual activities of married couples were only initiated and led by the husband. It is hardly acceptable for wives to express their sexual interests because of the cultural value of male dominance in sexual relationships.

According to a survey with 1,200 housewives in 1996, 67.2% reported dissatisfaction with their sexual lives and 30.2% responded that their sexual lives were satisfactory (Kim 1996). Such a psychological distress of sexual dissatisfaction leads to the increase of extramarital sex and divorce. In recent years, the rate of divorce caused by adultery has been increasing by 15% annually.

## D. History and Structure of the Korean Family
*Patriarchy*   PILWHA CHANG (Summarized by HUSO YI)

The recently expanding discourses on sexuality and the enlarging diversity of lifestyles in contemporary Korean society might give an impression that the reign of traditional control over sexuality is loosening. However, "legitimate" sexual behavior has been, and still tends to be, limited to marital partners. Patriarchy has a vested interest in defining women's sexuality in a particular way. It has particular sexual scripts, which use sexuality as social control. Women and men's sexuality is treated differently. Women's sexuality has frequently been exploited and degraded and used to sell commodities, even to turn women themselves into commodities. This double standard works against women and in favor of men.

Korean history, from the 3rd century to the end of the 19th century, illustrates a gradual systematization of one of the most ideal types of patriarchy in the world. By the end of the 16th century, the state completed a patriarchal system by implementing Confucian ideology, with its gender hierarchy and sex segregation, through the gender division of labor and class divisions that upheld the patriarchal family in strict observance of patrilineage (rule of lineage, descent, or continuing family line from father to son), patrinymy (rule of continuing the surname of the father), and patrilocality (residential rule based on patrilineal locality). Women had to prove their worth as mothers, producing sons to continue the family line, and producing food and clothing, to survive in a woman-hostile environment. However strong and capable they might have been, Korean women were systematically denied activities outside the confines of the home, and their education was strictly prohibited.

Only in the national crisis at the end of the 19th century, when foreign powers threatened Korea's sovereignty, did some possibilities of cracking this rigidity arise. For about two centuries, some philosophical systems, among them Silhak and Tonghak, began to question the gender relations under new influences. [*Comment 2001*: Very briefly, Silhak can be compared to pragmatism and Tonghak can share its philosophy with a sort of socialism that claims the rights of lower-class people. (*End of comment by Huso Yi*)] However, it was only in a crisis situation when proper observation of traditional family rituals became difficult or impossible that such thoughts began to be heard and listened to. The national crisis created a space of critical reflection on the traditional ways of life. Within this space, reevaluation of the position of women began. Women's social participation had to be accepted, however reluctantly, as essential to national survival. The resulting discourse, however, focused on the national interests, and not on the value of education held for the personal development of women and their fuller participation in society.

In the last hundred years, Koreans have experienced crisis after crisis: the Japanese occupation, two World Wars, the division of the country into North and South, the Korean War, and the industrial war to join the world capitalist system. These crises prioritized efficiency and expediency, and justified sacrificing individual human rights for the sake of growth and stability. In this context, it was easy to brush aside women's claim for human rights as a luxury, and so the

| Table 3 |
|---|
| **Crude Marriage Rate and Crude Divorce Rate: 1975-1997** |

| Year | Total Marriage | Crude Marriage Rate | Total Divorce | Crude Divorce Rate |
|---|---|---|---|---|
| 1975 | 282,000 | 8.0 | 16,179 | 0.5 |
| 1985 | 375,253 | 9.2 | 38,429 | 0.9 |
| 1995 | 401,161 | 8.8 | 67,858 | 1.5 |
| 1996 | 389,319 | 8.5 | 79,733 | 1.7 |
| 1997 | 374,429 | 8.1 | 83,171 | 2.0 |

*Source*: National Statistical Office 1999b

| Table 4 |
|---|
| **Mean Age at First Marriage: 1987-1997** |

| Year | Male | Female |
|---|---|---|
| 1987 | 27.3 | 24.5 |
| 1990 | 27.9 | 24.9 |
| 1993 | 28.2 | 25.1 |
| 1996 | 28.6 | 25.7 |
| 1997 | 28.7 | 25.9 |

*Source*: National Statistical Office 1999b

tradition of utilizing women's instrumental values persisted. At the same time, such crises opened some windows of opportunity for women to participate in sociopolitical arenas. Also, it is true that the models of the "developed" world provided a stimulus for women's rights. Consequently, women's suffrage was included in the first modern Constitution in 1947, and primary education became compulsory for girls as well as boys. In the last few decades, Korea has managed to furnish the appearance of "modernity." Despite the appearance and some changes in patriarchal families, the underlying assumptions continue to be patriarchal, with the view that women's identity is only familial, guided by the "three obediences" to father, husband, and son, and without any independent public identity based on her own personal merit.

The marginal position of a daughter in her natal family rests in her future roles as wife and daughter-in-law in another household. Because of this, she was considered only as a temporary member of her natal family, her filial piety being transferred on marriage to her parents-in-law. Her duty of filial piety towards her own parents was not to bring shame and dishonor to her natal family by misbehaving in her new family. With marriage, a daughter had to break her ties with her natal home, "she who left the family and has become a stranger." Her parents told her that she now belonged to her husband's family where she had to persevere, however hard life might have been: "She ought never return to her old home but the ghost of her husband's home." It is another example of how married women are treated. In an old saying, once they are married, they have to finish their lives no matter what happens to them. Once married, a wife who committed any of seven evils could legitimately be divorced, and a divorce brought shame to her natal family. Because a wife could not be protected by her natal family, she had no alternative but to comply with the rules of her husband and his family to survive. In this environment, the sooner a wife made the transition, the easier it was for her in her new role. Physical distance from the natal family helped the process, hence the proverb: "Toilets and the wife's home are best kept at a distance."

Even if the environment of her husband's household was alien and hostile initially, the young wife can gradually establish her own position within the household by producing her own children, particularly sons. Producing the heir secures her status and her acceptance as a full member of her husband's family. Once a wife became the senior lady of the household, mother-in-law to her sons' wives, she had

achieved a measure of power. Many women must have softened the hardships by anticipating the day when they would enter the stage of being a mother-in-law. This is another dimension of intrafamily relationships that explains why having a son was, and still is, so much more important to a mother than having a daughter. As filial piety was the supreme principle, a mother's authority was respected, and through her sons she could enjoy a measure of social power.

However, although a mother possessed considerable power and influence within the family, her power did not extend beyond its boundary. A woman's power was based on the private relationship between mother and son, and, however strong an influence she may have on him, it could not extend beyond the scope of the village. As this power was derived from the son, and his power base lay in patriarchy, the mother's power could not and did not challenge the patriarchal system. Rather, the mother actively enforced patriarchal rules in their own interest. This is why, despite the existence of powerful women, the patriarchal system was not undermined or modified to improve the situation of women, nor to institutionalize the private nature of women's power publicly. Under this system, it is far easier for women to perceive other women as a threat to their livelihood and power than as allies to fight against the system.

### Problems of Today's Families and Its Direction of Change                    HUSO YI

There is little dispute that the family has been changing under the process of industrialization. Although this is widely acknowledged by empirical research and a broad range of data sets, the question still remains whether the external trends really confirm the change in the stereotyped ideology of the family, even with the notion that social procedures are now developing for basic functions other than the family. Besides, it is also necessary to notice that not all changes occur at an equal rate, nor do all segments of a society adjust equally to the changes taking place. Then, how much change has occurred in the Korean family and what are the implications of this change?

The decrease in average household size (from 5.2 in 1979 to 3.12 in 1995) may come from the increase in one-person households and non-family households because of the advance of the mean age of first marriage of women (from 21.5 in 1960 to 26.2 in 1998), the great flexibility in adapting to new ways of life, such as marriage, divorce, and remarriage, and more frequent family moving. Despite the changes in the physical organization of the family, traditional Confucian ethics, which stress patrilineage, filial piety, solidarity among brothers, and the importance of domestic harmony, are still pervasive in the Korean family. The unbalanced sex ratio of children, which has emerged as a serious social problem in Korea, shows a good case in point. In other words, the ideal of son preference is still pervasive as a main agent to support the male-centered norms and values of the patriarchal family. The findings from the 1981 Gallup survey of children and mothers (see Table 5) also shows that the traditional Korean concept of the family as a social institution to continue patrilineage is reflected in attitudes toward childrearing.

Despite the gradual changes in recent years, the idea that the role of homemaking belongs exclusively to women is still pervasive throughout Korean society. This has put great pressure on career women and forced them to perform dual roles. Women engaged in full-time homemaking, on the other hand, experience more social alienation and anxiety in the nuclear family life than in the traditional extended family life,

### Table 5

**Meaning of Giving Birth and Raising Children**

| | Mothers Only | | Both Parents | |
| --- | --- | --- | --- | --- |
| | Korea | U.S. | Korea | U.S. |
| To transmit my life to my child | 34.0 | 40.8 | 32.2 | 30.5 |
| To have a successful child who will further pursue my aspirations | 43.2 | 10.9 | 32.1 | 11.4 |
| To continue my family line/name | 48.3 | 23.1 | 68.2 | 28.4 |
| To contribute to a generation which will inherit the future society | 48.4 | 52.6 | 39.6 | 45.6 |
| To strengthen our family bond | 24.8 | 44.9 | 25.4 | 49.5 |
| To have security in my old age | 26.8 | 5.8 | 37.5 | 7.8 |
| To mature and enrich myself | 13.5 | 44.2 | 19.2 | 53.5 |
| Just to enjoy childbearing | 19.3 | 48.6 | 18.9 | 49.8 |
| To be recognized by society | 29.3 | 4.0 | 10.9 | 2.2 |
| To obtain additional work power in our family | 2.2 | 2.6 | 1.8 | 2.6 |

*Note*: Multiple answers may exceed 100%. *Source*: Chang 1998

which is increasingly more difficult to maintain in modern urban life. Full-time homemakers experience a serious conflict of role expectations and their own identities. Thus, although Korean families appear to be stable, in reality, they are increasingly at a crisis level of psychological dissolution.

### Sexuality and the Physically Disabled and Aged

HUSO YI

In a study about sexuality in 65 spinal-cord-injured males (Oh et al. 1990), 24 had problems with erections, 23 had difficulty in maintaining erections, and 24 were unable to ejaculate. During sexual intercourse, 41 had difficulty with erections, but the rest reported suffering from fears of not reaching orgasm, and fears of a passive response and rejection from partners. After the spinal-cord injury, about 80% of them said that their sexual and marital satisfaction had decreased. Although they were aware of sexual problems, only 5 had been in sex therapy because of a lack of facilities and accessibility.

The National Rehabilitation Center started a sexual rehabilitation clinic project in 1996. The clinic has provided sex therapy and counseling, couple sex therapy, group therapy, and erectile dysfunction therapy for more than 1,000 physically disabled people and their partners. The clinic also facilitates a place, called the "shelter for love," where physically disabled people and their partners can stay over to enjoy their sexual activities. Since 1998, the clinic staff has organized conferences about sexuality and disability. In 2000, Dr. B. S. Lee, a sexual rehabilitation specialist, published a small handbook, *Sexual Rehabilitation for the Spinal Cord Injured*. The book introduced the importance of sexuality in the physically disabled, cases reports about sex therapy for the foreign and Korean disabled, sexual concerns of the female and male disabled, medical treatment for erectile dysfunction, psychological issues on sexual rehabilitation, and marriage of the physically disabled. (For information: http://www.nrc.go.kr/eng/eindex.htm; contact: nrc1986@chollian.net.)

## 6. Homoerotic, Homosexual, and Bisexual Behaviors

### A. Historical Perspective

HUSO YI

The earliest Korean record of homosexuality may be from King Hyekong, the 36th king of the Shilla dynasty in *Samguk-Yusa* (a Three Kingdoms' story) written by Il Yeon in the 13th century. King Kyungduk did not have a son, but wanted one very badly because he needed an heir. He kept asking the messenger between God and man to go to God and ask for a son. God insisted that he was not destined to have a son, only daughters, yet the King was persistent. Finally, God let him have a son, but God put a female spirit in the son's body. King Hye-Kong was very feminine and liked only being around men all the time. He became the next king at the age of 8 in 765 C.E. because his father died early. However, he was killed at the age of 22 in April 780 by his subordinates because they could not accept his 'femininity.' Another story in *Samguk Yusa* is about Myojung, a very young Buddhist monk who lived during the reign of Wonsung (785-798 C.E.), the 38th king of the Shilla dynasty. It is said that he was loved and sought after by several male Shilla aristocrats, and even by a Chinese Emperor from the Tang dynasty (618-907 C.E.).

One of the best-known homosexual histories is the *Hwarang* or *Flower Boy*, the story of a homoerotic military elite, paralleling the Egyptian *mamluks*, the Japanese *samurai*, and the Theban Band of ancient Greece (Murray 2000). Prior to the introduction of Buddhism, ancient Korea maintained a transgendered shamanistic tradition, in which the *hwarang* seem to have been involved. With the transfer of religious legitimization to Buddhism, the code of the *hwarang* began to change from social and religious concerns to political and military programs. In the *Haedong-Kosung-Chon* [*Lives of Eminent Korean Monks*] written by the Buddhist Kakhun in 1215, the first criterion of the *hwarang* seems to have been appearance: "It was handsome youths who powdered their faces, wore ornamented dresses, and were respected as hwarang." After unification of the peninsula, ruled by the Three Kingdoms, in 676, the members of *hwarang* were rewarded with land and slaves.

In the Koryo dynasty, same-sex relationships, mostly between males, were very common among the ruling class. In a historical analysis of *Hallimbuilgok* by Seong, King Chungsun (1275-1325) maintained a long-term relationship with a *wonchung* (male lover), and King Kongmin (1325-1374) appointed at least five youths as "little-brother attendants" (*chajewhi*) as sexual partners. After the fall of the Koryo dynasty in 1392, the Chosun dynasty adopted Confucianism as a governing ideology in order to confirm their dynasty as totally different from the Koryo dynasty. Even though Confucianism had negative attitudes about same-sex relationships, there were still male-to-male relationships among the Buddhists and among the rural ruling class. Lesbian relationships were not treated with the same acceptance, as the palace chronicle from the Chosun dynasty reveals. King Sejong convened a meeting of his cabinet on October 24, 1436, to discuss the rumors that his daughter-in-law had been sleeping with her maidservant. These rumors had been somehow confirmed, so the ministers advised the king to strip his daughter-in-law of her noble status in order to preserve the honor and dignity of the royal family (Chung 1998).

Another historically known homosexual group was the *namsadang* in the Chosun dynasty (Murray 1992), which existed until it was broken up by force to extinguish the national culture under the colonization of Japan in the early 1910s. As a type of indigenous theater, the *namsadang* traveled around the country with various types of entertainment, including band music, song, masked dance, circus, and puppet plays. Reflecting the common peoples' harsh living conditions and their resentment toward the upper class, the *namsadang* was the voice of lower-class people. When boys, called *midong* (beautiful boys), first joined a troupe, they played the penetrated sex role and were probably male prostitutes for the rural ruling class (Leupp 1995). In this era, many members of the rural ruling class maintained boys for sexual purposes. Because same-sex relationships, however, were generally regarded as immoral in the eyes of Neo-Confucianism, the *namsadang* performers were treated as outcasts.

### B. Children and Adolescents

HUSO YI

As mentioned below, there is a law against informing adolescents about homosexuality and, in mental health settings, it is easy for lesbian and gay adolescents to be diagnosed as having either sexual maturation disorder, ego-dystonic orientation, or sexual relationship disorder. In fact, it is likely that mental health professionals will claim homosexual attraction is nothing but a phase of heterosexual development (Yi 2000). In another context, homosexuality may be diagnosed as either pseudo-homosexuality or true-homosexuality (Hong 1996; Lee 1993). Although no research on homosexuality among children and adolescents has been conducted, most research on adolescent sexuality asks questions about homosexual behaviors. Instead of considering homosexual behaviors as normal, these studies by the Korean Research Institute for Culture and Sexuality categorize homosexuality together with "sexual violence" (Lee et al. 1998), or asks females the question, "Have you ever fallen in love with a woman whom you consider as a man?" (Kim et al. 1997). Both studies found that around 13% of the female student respondents said they had had sexual relationships with the same gender.

## C. Adults

*Gender Roles, Courtship, and*          HUSO YI
*Relationship Patterns*

Before the emergence of gay identity in the mid-1990s, expressing homosexuality in Korea was somewhat easier than in the West, because the existence of homosexuality was denied at the same time there was a cultural tolerance for homophilic touch. Same-sex friends can hold hands together on the streets just like heterosexual couples. However, it might be inappropriate to see such same-sex friendships as homosexual relationships in the way that Western culture does (Shong & Icard 1996). One of cultural patterns related to homophilia is that when a husband's friend visits, his wife sleeps separately from her husband, who sleeps with his male friend. Also, because same-sex roommates before marriage are common, in fact, more acceptable than sharing with the opposite gender, living as a young "gay" couple is possible, and the neighbors hardly suspect them as lesbians or gay males (Yi 2000). But, because everyone's first role is to continue family linkage, lesbians and gay men are compelled to be married after a certain age. In addition, Christianity is certainly another hindrance for gay courtship, particularly because Korean Christianity is strongly fundamentalist (Martin & Berry 1998). These long-established cultural norms have been challenged by the gay community. Every issue of a gay magazine since 1997 reports the commitment ceremonies of lesbian and gay couples.

*Social Status of Lesbians, Gay Men, and Bisexuals*

HUSO YI [*Updated 2003 by H. Yi*]

The modern gay community can be traced from the 1960s as a form of subculture grown in *Nakwon* (paradise). From this culture, the decorous term for homosexuals began to be constructed: A derogatory term, *pogal* (the backward reading of the word *kalbo*, which refers to the most vulgar term for prostitute, and more generically meaning "promiscuous"), was created. In public, *tongsôngyônaeja* (men who only pursue sex with men) had been used to degrade homosexuals. Until the intense contact of Western gay culture, the word *homo* had been occasionally used by homosexuals themselves and later by heterosexuals as a term of insult. *Gay* had been also used, but referred to transsexuals, transvestites, or cross-dressers. Of those cultural codes, the most influential word is *iban* (other people), which has survived up to these days and represents homosexual identity, as does *gay*. The origin of *iban* is unknown, yet it is interpreted as contrasting to *ilban*, which means general people or default/first-class. An interesting response from political gay activists about the word was hesitation in using *iban*, because the word does not impose any positive meaning of pride. The concept of pride was never imagined until the 1990s, and then first conflicted with the very local term for homosexual, *iban*. Regardless, *iban* indicated a new consciousness of homosexuals as a social group, but then it was classified as the first blocked LGBT-related keyword for online gay interest groups on the largest Korean website as of May 2002.

In the 1970s, around 120 lesbians and gay men held a monthly social gathering at a Chinese restaurant. But, the social group did not survive to connect with the current gay community (Lee 1997). Today's gay movement emerged with Sappho, the first Korean lesbian group, organized by an American lesbian soldier. When she came to Korea in November 1991 to serve in the army and found no lesbian bars, she immediately realized that living as a lesbian was very difficult in Korea. Outside of meeting a few lesbians in a gay bar, there was no chance to meet with lesbians. She decided to organize a group for lesbians and placed an advertisement for her lesbian group in English newspapers. Eight foreign lesbians from the United States and Europe gathered together at the first meeting. The membership of Sappho changed often, because most of its members returned to their homes in the U.S., Canada, Belgium, Sweden, or Australia after two or three years in Korea. Sappho was still holding its small meetings in early 2001.

In the U.S., groups for lesbian and gay Korean-Americans were founded in New York (in December 1990) and in Los Angeles (in August 1993). A few members from these Korean-American groups had been in contact with Sappho and discussed forming Korean gay and lesbian rights groups and providing outreach and support to their various friends. In the meantime, a Korean-American gay man visited Korea and organized the first Korean gay and lesbian co-gendered group in December 1993. Unlike Sappho, this group was organized by Koreans, and is recognized as the first authentically Korean lesbian and gay men's support group.

Medicalization of homosexuality was first introduced in 1970 by a clinical case study, titled "Sexual Perversions in Korea" (Han 1970). On the basis of *Ying/Yang*, the research reporting of homosexual clients in the 1960s holds that the reason for the smaller number of homosexuals is that Koreans were sexually more mature than Westerners. By repetition of gender-related ideology and strategically importing the Western view of homosexuality as inversion, Korean psychiatry created a local stance and, even today, claims that, even though homosexuality is no longer seen as mental illness, it is still socially unacceptable and dysfunctional. Currently, the *Korean Standard Disease Classification*, adopted from WHO's *ICD-10*, classifies three categories: "Sexual Maturation Disorder," "Egodystonic Sexual Orientation," and "Sexual Relationship Disorder." However, inclusion of the words "normal heterosexuality" and "marriage" in the translation shows local homophobic motives created by a faxed culture of a psychopathological model of homosexuality. No affirmative mental health service is available. In the mental health setting, the *Korean Standard Disease Classification* (*KSDC*) states three "Psychological and Behavioral Disorders Associated with Sexual Development and Orientation" (http://www.nso.go.kr/stat/dis/e-diss.htm, in English):

- F 66.0 Sexual Maturation Disorder: The patient is suffering from uncertainty about his gender identity or sexual orientation, causing anxiety or depression. Most commonly this occurs in adolescents who are not certain whether they are homosexual, heterosexual or bisexual in orientation, or older married individuals who after a period of apparently normal heterosexuality, often within marriage, find themselves experiencing homosexual feelings.
- F 66.1 Egodystonic Sexual Orientation: The gender identity or sexual preference (either heterosexual, homosexual, bisexual, prepubertal or uncertain) is not in doubt but the individual wishes it were different because of associated psychological and behavioural disorders, and may seek treatment in order to change it.
- F 66.3 Sexual Relationship Disorder: The gender identity or sexual orientation (either hetero-, homo-, or bisexual) is responsible for difficulties in forming or maintaining a relationship with a sexual partner.

In the original text in *ICD-10*, F 66.0, Sexual Maturation Disorder, reads as follows:

> F 66.0 Sexual Maturation Disorder: The patient is suffering from uncertainty about his gender identity or sexual orientation, causing anxiety or depression. Most commonly this occurs in adolescents who are not certain whether they are homosexual, heterosexual or bisexual in orientation, or *individuals who, after a period of apparently stable sexual orientation (often with a longstanding relationship), find that their sexual orientation is changing.* (italics added)

In the *KSDC* version, the italicized phrase above has been replaced by: *older married individuals who after a period of apparently normal heterosexuality, often within marriage, find themselves experiencing homosexual feelings.*

Because there is no law protecting lesbians and gay males, Korea has no sodomy laws proscribing oral or anal intercourse, except a military law against homosexual relationships in the army. Meanwhile, in 2000, Korea passed the law of Youth Protection prohibiting distribution of materials that contain incest, animal sex, and homosexuality. The following are examples of institutional homophobia. Sodomy is also proscribed behavior for members of the military, and a general statute against anything contrary to sexual customs is enforced as criminal law. In 1997, the first Seoul Queer Film Festival was banned by the government, which declared it illegal on the grounds that all homosexual materials are obscene. Since 1998, the first gay magazine has been receiving a notice from the Korean Publication Ethics Committee warning that the publication consists of obscenity, therefore, it should not be distributed among youth. In 1999, a high school textbook portrayed gay men as AIDS disease carriers and sexual perverts. Increasing concerns over AIDS revealed the possibility of an anti-gay backlash. Even though AIDS organizations are supposedly fighting against the spread of AIDS, they are in fact fighting against the spread of homosexuals by promoting homophobia and conservative sexual morals.

In October 2000, when a famous actor, Mr. Hong, first came out as gay, his jobs vanished almost overnight. His gay presence as a victim, however, made the discourse of homosexuality in ordinary lives public and led to discriminatory policies. In 2001, the Seoul City Hall authorities ordered a two-month pay cut for a male firefighter for allegedly maintaining an inappropriate relationship with a male colleague, although neither of them identified as gay. Ironically, the distaste for homosexuality created an obsession with any perceived homophile relationships. People began to be afraid of personal touch with the same sex to avoid any suspicion of being homosexuals.

In July 2001, the Ministry of Information and Communications adopted an Internet content-rating system classifying gay and lesbian websites as "harmful media" that must be blocked on all public computer facilities accessible to youth (e.g., schools, public libraries, and Internet cafes). Homosexuality is classified under the category of "obscenity and perversion" in the *Criteria for Indecent Internet Sites*. The decision was based on the Korean government's Youth Protection Act of 1997, which classifies descriptions of "homosexual love" as "harmful to youth." The first case was enacted against the owner of the first and largest gay website in November 2001, with a notice that unless it was immediately marked as a 'harmful site,' and filtering software was installed to prevent youth access, he would be penalized approximately US$10,000 or two years' imprisonment. The first lawsuit was filed against the government, protesting the government's ban on the gay website as unconstitutional in January 2002, and the court decision was delivered in August 2002 stating that the Constitution of freedom is not applicable to homosexual distribution on the Internet.

## 7. Gender Diversity and Transgender Issues

### A. Sociolegal Status, Behaviors, and Treatment of Transvestite, Transgendered, and Transsexual Persons

HYUNG-KI CHOI and COLLEAGUES
(Redacted by HUSO YI) [*Updated 2003 by H. Yi*]

Until the mid-1980s, the care system for transgendered people was not well established in Korea because of little understanding of transsexualism and the negative attitude and prejudices of medical doctors. In desperation, many transsexual persons turned to non-licensed facilities for sex-reassignment surgery or self-injected hormones for partial physical transition. [*Comment 2001*: Yoo (1993) has noted that doctors' prejudices and ignorance of transgenderism/transsexualism result in a boundary between them and the patient. As a consequence, it is common that transgendered/transsexual people get more information from resources in Western countries, where the doctors learn about transsexualism from their clients. (*End of comment by Huso Yi*)] In 1989, Dr. Koo Sang-Hwan conducted the first sex-reassignment surgery for a male-to-female. As of late 2000, about 50 cases of sex-reassignment surgery have been reported. In 1990, the Korean Urology Association proposed 12 criteria for sex-reassignment surgery (SRS):

1. Accurate psychiatric diagnosis.
2. No success from long-term psychiatric treatment.
3. Establishment of psychosocial adjustment for the desired gender before SRS.
4. No other psychiatric illness or depression.
5. Sufficient period of hormone-replacement treatment with no side effects.
6. Over 21 years old and past puberty.
7. Physical appearance has to fit with the desired gender.
8. Family approval for SRS.
9. Agreement of spouse and/or family regarding infertility.
10. No drug and alcohol history.
11. No criminal record and no possibility for crime.
12. Under good medical supervision.

The transgendered (transsexual) patient has to meet all the above requirements and must get two recommendations from psychiatrists.

Even after the surgery, they cannot change their gender on any legal document. In 1990, the court rejected a male-to-female transsexual's petition stating, "Because the plastic surgery only made anatomical structures that look like those of the female artificially so that it does not change the chromosomal structure, he cannot be accepted as a female from our society's common sense and value." [*Comment 2003*: Added to that, the court ruled that "he cannot legally change his gender because he has no internal parts of the female body which are very important to the woman's role of giving birth. Thus, it is not appropriate in our society to change his gender." Since then, all of the cases of gender change have followed this court decision (Cho 1993). It is likely that gender in Korea is constituted by chromosome and familial "role." In the legal system, sex-reassignment surgery is regarded only as a part of plastic surgery and not a gender transition. However, since a male-to-female transgender entertainer gained a public recognition with her success as a model, actor, and singer, public awareness and attitude have widely changed. A number of literary works of fiction and nonfiction by transgendered people have been published. A clinic for sex-reassignment surgery has provided services for transgendered people. In November 2002, a law protecting transgendered persons' rights was submitted. The court approved a female-to-male transgender sex-change appeal in December 2002. More transgender people's sex-change petitions are expected in South Korea.

[Yet, the level of victimization of transgendered people in society is serious. In a case in which a male-to-female transsexual was raped, the judge said it was not rape, but a physical attack. The judge in this case also implied that the rape of a same-sex person could not be properly constituted as "rape," because such homosexual acts do not fit the sense of "sex." It is the court's stance that sex can only occur between the opposite sexes. (*End of comment by Huso Yi*)]

[*Update 2003*: In 1986, when a male transvestite approached Dr. Kim Seok Kwan, a plastic surgeon in Pusan, and asked if he could perform a sex-change operation, Kim told the man nobody knew anything about this operation in Korea, and that he could not help him. A few months later, a request from a second male transsexual sparked Kim's curiosity enough for him to start reading up on the subject. A short time later, Kim performed the first male-to-female sex change operation in South Korea.

[In the late 1980s, Kim's patients were overwhelmingly working class or poor—few could afford to travel abroad for the operation. (Kim still keeps the cost of his operations to $8,000 on average, while maintaining a lucrative practice in more traditional forms of plastic surgery.) For years, he performed the operations largely in obscurity, aware that news of his special skills was spreading by word of mouth among transvestites. Strong opposition came from the country's tradition-bound medical community, his wife, and his minister.

[By most estimates, South Koreans go under the knife for cosmetic alterations more than anyone else in Asia, with everything from eye and nose operations aimed at achieving a more Western look, to breast augmentations, calf remodeling, and hymen reconstruction among the most popular types of surgery. Some still object that sex-change operations are the ultimate expression of a plastic surgery culture in South Korea that has run amok.

[Kim also asked himself "whether it was right to change the gender of a patient, whether it was right to alter their most essential nature. I really hesitated." In the end, what persuaded him to continue was the realization that "gender surgery is performed to rescue people who are trapped in the wrong body. We are offering the possibility for normal lives to people whose minds and bodies don't match, and even the psychiatrists I consulted told me that this is their only hope."

[Returning to his practice in Pusan, after a year's training at the University of California at Davis, he found a long list of candidates desperate for the operation. In 1991, Kim's

first female-to-male surgery, which he also pioneered in Korea, caught the attention of the nation's news media. The brouhaha of screaming newspaper headlines and guest appearances on television programs eventually died down, but in the process, some of the taboo on public discussion of sexual issues and mores in Korea was lifted. But it took the emergence of one of his patients as a true superstar as a fixture in the Korean entertainment world to trigger a major cultural change in Korean sexual attitudes. Miss Ha Ri Su had lived most of her 28 years, unhappily, as a man, until in 2000, Dr. Kim transformed her into a ravishing transgender beauty. Today Koreans have embraced Miss Ha, knowing full well that this slinky, silky-haired singer, actor, comedienne, and model, armed with a 35-24-35 figure, was once a man. In a personal profile in *The New York Times*, Dr. Kim admitted, "Ha Ri Su was of great benefit to social awareness of this issue. I had no idea who she was, nor how important her example would become. She has encouraged other transgender patients, who have always had trouble holding jobs; for most of them, living in secret, working in bars or as prostitutes was the only thing they could do. Nowadays these people can live regular lives, as teachers, office workers or students" (French 2003). (*End of update by R. T. Francoeur*)]

## 8. Significant Unconventional Sexual Behaviors

**A. Coercive Sex**　　　HUSO YI [*Updated 2003 by H. Yi*]

It is very difficult to ascertain the actual frequency of sexual violence in Korea. According to the Korean Institute of Criminology (1998), the report rate for sexual assaults was estimated to be only 6.1% of actual incidents, whereas the rate in the advanced countries is around 30 to 40%. In 1998, the sexual violence counseling centers under the Ministry of Health and Welfare reported around 25,000 cases of sexual violence, which was twice the incidence in 1997. Of these cases, 33.5% involved rape; 21.9% involved physical sexual harassment, and the rest were about verbal sexual abuse. However, only 3.6% of the victims reported the incident to the police (Korean Institute for Health and Social Welfare 1999). The Korean Sexual Violence Relief Center (1999) reported that 95% of the victims are women (assaulters are mostly men) and 73% of the assaulters are acquaintances of their victims, who range in age from the teens to the 70s. Thirty percent of the victims are children under the age of 13, with 50% under the age of 19. Chang (2000) noted that sexual assaulters experienced no guilt for their behavior, believing that sexual violence may occur accidentally as an expression of a natural uncontrollable sexual urge of men. This conception leads men to look at rape as a kind of sexual act, rather than a crime infringing on a woman's body and personality. An interesting legal aspect in sexual violence is that current law does not allow a victim to file a suit against her father, leaving some incest victims with no means to their rights.

In a nationwide survey of gender roles and sexual violence funded by the United Nations Development Plan, Byun, Won, and Chung (2000) interviewed 542 men and 558 women ranging in age from 20 to 59 (see Table 6). Frotteurism, the forceful touching and rubbing of the genital area, particularly in the subway, is another sexual assault problem not included in Table 6.

**Table 6**

**Number (and Percentage) of Cases of Sexual Violence by Type of Offense and Age of the Victim**

| Age of Victim | Obscene Call | Penis Exposure | Sexual Misconduct | Attempted Rape | Rape | Others | Total |
|---|---|---|---|---|---|---|---|
| > 12 | | 1　(7.7) | 4　(17.4) | | | | 5　(7.1) |
| 13-18 | 3　(10.7) | 7　(53.8) | 1　(4.3) | 2 (100.0) | | 1　(25.0) | 14　(19.7) |
| 19-25 | 3　(10.7) | 5　(38.5) | 13　(56.5) | | 1 (100.0) | 2　(50.0) | 24　(33.8) |
| 26-35 | 9　(32.1) | | 3　(13.0) | | | 1　(25.0) | 13　(18.3) |
| 36 < | 13　(46.4) | | 2　(8.7) | | | | 15　(21.1) |
| Total | 28 (100.0) | 13 (100.0) | 23 (100.0) | 2 (100.0) | 1 (100.0) | 4 (100.0) | 71 (100.0) |

*Source*: Korean Women's Development Institute 2000a

In 1997, 128 males were arrested by the subway police for rubbing their genitals against women, and half of these sexual offenders were college graduates.

With the effort of the women's rights movements, Korea has achieved several legal enforcements, as noted earlier, to protect victims from sexual harassment. However, research on the public awareness of the anti-sexual violence laws showed that only 2.1% were familiar with the laws, 31.6% had some familiarity with them, 46.5% had heard of them, and 22.2% had never heard of them (Kim et al. 2000). Thus, it is necessary to implement an effective educational program to make the public aware of the sexual violence laws.

*Sexual Harassment*      HYUNG-KI CHOI and
            COLLEAGUES (Redacted by HUSO YI)
[*Comment 2001*: Cyber-sexual violence has become a major concern and issue in Korea. In July 2000, for example, a female middle-school student committed suicide after being harassed by Internet postings. In order to prevent sexual harassment on the Internet, the Ministry of Information and Communication established the Report Center of Cyber Sexual Violence in 2000 and has conducted a survey, which found that 58.9% of those surveyed had experienced cyber-sexual violence and 14.4% had witnessed it. Most cyber-sexual violence occurs in the chat rooms, bulletin boards, and email. The respondents were harassed by verbal abuse, pornographic pictures or movies, private videos (e.g., exposure of the body or sexual scenes), and suggestions of prostitution. (*End of comment by Huso Yi*)]

The issue of sexual harassment emerged when the Korean Women's Hotline opened in 1983. In the first survey of 700 married women, 42% reported that they had been hit by their husband at least once. Following up on the issue, the Hotline started to deal with the issues of kidnapping for prostitution and female sex workers. During this time, society began to pay attention to harassment against women. There were two important legal cases about sexual harassment. In 1986, Kwon In-Sook, a female college student, was interrogated by the police because of her democracy activism. During the interrogation, she was sexually harassed by the police. Later, with the help of an unprecedented 166 lawyers' arguments and human rights organizations, she was released. Another case dealt with rape. In 1988, when a woman was raped on her way home, she cut off the offender's tongue. However, she was sentenced to a year in prison. The case stimulated debates on rape and self-defense and the implication of women's self-defense. As a consequence, she was found innocent and acquitted. Confronted with societal situations such as these, the Korean Sexual Violence Relief Center was established in 1991.

*Rape*      HYUNG-KI CHOI and COLLEAGUES
            (Redacted by HUSO YI)
In one study, almost half (45.5%) of female high school students reported having been sexually harassed by being touched on the breast, hips, and genital areas and, among them, 99.3% had been harassed by their male friends (Kim et al. 1997). The victims' responses were: 70.8% tried to avoid the situation, 11.3% showed no resistance, 10.1% confronted the harasser with shouting, and only 0.8% looked for help. After being raped, 29.2% did nothing, 25.8% talked to friends, 14.6% told their mother, 2.2% reported the assault to the police, and 1.1% spoke to a teacher. Having no education about rape and a very low reporting rate does nothing to reduce the incidence of rape, and may well promote it. [*Comment 2001*: The law dealing with rape used to be categorized under the title "Crime Against Chastity." This divided the victims of rape into two groups, respectable women who deserve legal protection and those (fallen women) who do not. Therefore, it was irrelevant to the court decision whether or not the victim resisted. Also irrelevant was the victim's sexual history (Chang 2000). The myths of rape were still prevalent among males at that time: "Rape occurs because of men's uncontrollable sexual urge" (69.0%), "a sexy female's looks provoke rape" (93.9%), "the best prevention is women's caution" (66.2%), and "rape cannot occur if women persistently refuse" (52.6%) (Byun et al. 2000). (*End of comment by Huso Yi*)]

## B. Industrial Prostitution

WHASOON BYUN and JUNGIM HWANG
(Summarized by HUSO YI)

*Overview of Industrial Prostitution*

The entertainment industry in Korean society began to grow in the 1970s, based upon the material wealth of capitalism. Amidst a materialistic social environment, a great change occurred in the form of prostitution. Rather than being confined in certain districts, industrial prostitution began spreading rapidly as a form of secondary service available in new entertainment establishments that provided a primary service. Unlike traditional prostitution, industrial prostitution involves establishments centered mainly on the tertiary service industry, in which sex can be provided legally on the side. The tertiary service industry includes the restaurant and hotel/motel business, entertainment and cultural services, and individual and household services provided by individuals and by companies. The number of women employed in these businesses rose steadily from 21.2% in 1983, to 22.9% in 1986, and 23.3% in 1989. [*Comment 2001*: According to Our Society Research Center (1994), around 1.5 millions are engaged in the prostitution industry. That number was one fifth of the population aged 15 to 29 (6.2 million). Over 91% of the female prostitutes had run away from home, and more than 90% had experiences of incest and/or had been sexually abused by members of their family. (*End of comment by Huso Yi*)] These businesses hire women who then provide sex as an additional service paid for at the end by the consumer.

Establishments that incorporate "industrial prostitution" in their services include restaurants, singing-room (karaoke) salons, room salons (adults bars with private rooms served by escort women), ticket coffee shops, steambaths, (adult) barbershops, and massage parlors. According to data from the Ministry of Health and Welfare (1998), there were 40,123 so-called singing-room and room salons under the category of liquor parlors, about 3,000 steambaths, barbershops (under the category of sanitary parlors), and 535 massage parlors, bringing the total number of such establishments to 43,658. This is just the official count; the unofficial count is expected to be much higher than this. The prostitution at these facilities is called "second stops," and according to the specific type of establishment, sexual activities are conducted either at the same place or at another location. According to the Korea Anti-AIDS Federation's specialized analysis in 1997, 24.5% of the respondents experienced sex in singing-room salons and room salons. Other places were in the red-light district at 24%, massage parlors at 19.9%, barbershops at 17.2%, hotels and motels at 13.8%, and others at 0.6%. A survey by the Korean Research Institute on Sexuality and Culture (Kim et al. 1997) of female high school students' awareness of sex and factual findings showed 2.1% of the 773 respondents said they had part-time experience working at singing-room salons and room salons. Especially, with the economically hard times, dubbed "the IMF [International Monetary Fund] era," a number of women are likely to be lured into places where industrial prostitution is possible.

## Types of Facilities

1. Ticket Coffee Shop: In these shops, the customer pays for tickets sold by the hour and takes the woman out for sex. The money paid for the tickets make up for the woman's absent time from the coffee shop, whether the time is spent drinking wine, socializing, in prostitution, or other activities. When sex is provided as a service, the woman gets to keep that fee which is over and above the shop ticket.

2. Room Salon: Room salons and regular bars are allowed by law to hire female employees and hostesses. According to Article 6 of the eighth provision of the Food and Sanitation Law, a hostess refers to a woman, single or married, who drinks, sings, and dances with a customer to promote merrymaking. These women usually move to another place with the customer when he decides to engage in prostitution. Unlike women at ticket coffee shops, these women do not get paid for the time they lose at the shops, but go out for prostitution after reporting to their madams. The hostess gets to keep the money.

3. Singing-Room Salon: By law, it is illegal for singing-room salons to hire female employees. Although waitresses may be allowed, hiring a hostess is forbidden. Reality does not follow the law, and a lot of pubs have female hostesses catering to customers. The types of prostitution being conducted in these singing-room salons is identical to that at regular room salons, the only difference being that the hostesses have to report to the owner, not to the madams.

4. Barbershops, steambaths, and massage parlors: The female employees at barbershops, steambaths, and massage parlors provide shaving, massaging, and bathing services prior to prostitution. At barbershops, the female employees provide shaves and massages to the customers, and at steambaths, the women bathe the customers and provide massages, during which they incite sexual desires and then provide prostitution. At massage parlors, blind masseuses and female workers are employed, with the latter providing prostitution. When there were no female employees available, the blind women used to provide sex, but with the introduction of female employees, prostitution at massage parlors came into full swing. At most of these parlors, the cost for prostitution is included in the overall charge. The women take their share from the prostitution and the owners take the remainder. Prostitution is much more likely to occur in the barbershops, steambaths, and massage parlors than in the other facilities listed above.

Each facility has slightly different characteristics on the basis of its own type of services. But regardless of the type, prostitution is an important factor that maintains these facilities, where both the main service and prostitution are being conducted under the protection of the facility.

## Analysis of Industrial Prostitution

Many sociocultural, economic, and institutional factors draw women into industrial prostitution. From the perspective of sociocultural factors, a lot of women surveyed were exposed to the adult-entertainment industry at an early age because they had either run away from home or indulged in delinquency. They tended to run away because they did not want to study or because they were reared in an unfavorable home environment. More often than not, if the woman is a breadwinner for the family, albeit single or married, she usually selects the service industry after a divorce or separa-tion to make a living. The service industry is an easy way to make a lot of money in a short period of time. Women who choose this service industry may do so because they do not have much education, have no special skills, or do not want to work in a factory. Most of the women had experience working in a legitimate company before they turned to the prostitution service industry. But, they either failed or worked at low-paying jobs. Sometimes, they had no other choice but to quit their jobs to escape a hostile work environment in which a supervisor pressured them for sex. Meanwhile, with the nationwide economic crisis of the "IMF era," women have been observed moonlighting in the sex trade because they did not make enough money.

From the institutional perspective, all work facilities have health permits, but if a woman contracts venereal disease, she tends to it on her own. That is why a health permit becomes useless in solving the problem. Also, there are no social services that prostitutes can utilize, and they do not even look for them. The health permits are taken care of by the owner. Normally, establishments involved in industrial prostitution receive permits from the government. Therefore, the exploitation link is not as conspicuous as in the case of traditional prostitution. But despite that fact, many parts of the management structure are distributed among the women, those involved in the trade and related agencies, all of whom together collude in whatever corruption is needed.

[*Comment 2001*: In a report by the Seoul Metropolitan Police Agency, among 222 teenage female prostitutes,

- 67 (30.2%) were 16 years old, 48 (21.6%) were 18 years old, 38 (17.1%) were 15 years old, 35 (15.8%) were 17 years old, 26 (11.7%) were 14 years old, and 8 girls were under the age of 13.
- 47.3% of the girls attended school and the rest were suspended.
- 23 had been sentenced to probation.

As for 282 adult male partners,

- 123 (43.6%) were in their 30s, 115 (40.8%) were in their 20s, 36 (12.7%) were in their 40s, 5 (1.5%) were in their teen years, and 3 (1.1%) were over 50.
- 137 of them had been sentenced to prison and 145 were on probation.
- Half (53.5%) of the men met the women on the Internet, 62 (22.2%) met them through "telephone rooms," 38 (13.5%) met them by voicemail, 18 (6.4%) met them through friends, and 13 (4.6%) worked on the street (Report Center of Cyber Sexual Violence 2000). (Telephone rooms are telephone booths located in private spaces where someone can call another person to arrange for sex or call a sex worker for phone sex. Telephone calls in a private home can be easily traced and show up on the telephone bill, so Koreans are more likely to use the private telephone room. (*End of comment by Huso Yi*)]

**C. Pornography**    WHASOON BYUN and JUNGIM HWANG (Summarized by HUSO YI)

Historically, the earliest documented erotica can be found in the Koryo period (918-1392). Since the 17th century, erotica has been freely imported from China for the enjoyment of ordinary people. Compared to China and Japan, Korea was somewhat late in developing a taste for pornography because of the unique characteristics of conservatism in the Chosun dynasty. Later in the 18th century, erotica was created and produced by Koreans and widely distributed. However, the Korean erotica was not as explicit as much of that from China and Japan. After the industrialization of the 1970s, various kinds of pornography were developed as in other countries. Before the Internet was created, the main source for accessing pornography was at lodging houses and late-night coffee shops that served the role of adult theaters. Today, access to pornography has been much easier via Internet adult television, adult magazines, video purchases and rentals, and computer programs.

In a study of 1,976 male and 3,134 female high school students, 60.5% of the male students had seen all kinds of pornographic materials, such as magazines, adult videos, and computer-related materials, 28.1% had experience only with magazines, 27.4% only with adult videos, and 3.6% only with computer programs. Just under 2% had not seen any adult erotica. Meanwhile, 52.2% of the female students had never seen adult magazines, 36.3% no adult movies, and 93.9% no computer-related adult materials (Kim et al. 1997). Considering the lack of adequate sexuality education for Korean adolescents, the impact of their exposure to pornography remains to be studied. In 1997, for example, three 17-year-old male students and a 15-year-old female student recorded their sexual intercourse on videotape and sold it. The tape was spread nationwide. After conviction, one male was sentenced to six months in a juvenile prison, the other males were sentenced to work in social welfare, and the female student received two years of guidance. They said that they just wanted to make a tape like adults do.

## 9. Contraception, Abortion, and Population Planning

### A. Contraception

HYUNG-KI CHOI and COLLEAGUES

After 1961, when most active contraceptive programs were started, married women who practiced contraception increased from 44.2% in 1976 to 80.5% in 1997 (see Table 7). The most common method of contraception in 1976 was vasectomy, followed by the intrauterine device (IUD), oral pills, condoms, and fallopian tubal ligation. In 1988, the most common form became tubal ligation (37.2%). In 1997, the most common form of contraception was still tubal ligation (24.1%), followed by condoms, vasectomy, the IUD, and oral pills. The usage of the IUD and oral pill is considerably low in Korea.

### B. Teenage (Unmarried) Pregnancies

HUSO YI

As noted earlier, premarital sexual experience is still prohibited, and there is a strong denial of adolescents' sexual relationships. Besides, adolescent pregnancy and abortion are another serious problem. It is estimated that around one third of all abortions might be performed among unmarried adolescents (Youn 1995). However, no official report has been published on adolescent pregnancy and abortion. Given the fact that being a teenage mother is most undesirable, adolescents may have two choices, abortion or adoption: "Most adolescent mothers who carry their pregnancies to term surrender their babies to adoption agencies" (Youn 1996, 630). According to the Korean Ministry of Health and Welfare, the number of babies given up by adolescent mothers was 1,904 in 1993, 1,781 in 1994 (Youn 1995) and 1,802 in 1999 (Ministry of Health and Welfare, MOHW 2000) In summary, one third of the abortion cases were performed on pregnant teens and one third of the adopted babies were surrendered by teens (see Table 8).

### C. Abortion

HYUNG-KI CHOI and COLLEAGUES
(Redacted by HUSO YI)

In Korean law, an induced abortion, defined as the removing of a fetus before the 28th week of gestation, is allowed in cases of genetically inherited diseases, transmitted diseases, incest, rape, and those cases that may greatly harm maternal health. However, it has been used as a form of contraception in Korea, and the number of induced abortions runs between 1.5 to 2 million cases annually. There are 600,000 newborns in Korea each year, and the number of abortions is nearly three times the number of deliveries. The total number of abortions in Korea is the second highest in the world. One out of two married women has experienced an abortion. Eighty percent of abortions are done for gender-selection purposes, using an ultrasound scan to ascertain the gender, and then selectively aborting female fetuses. Those who seek abortions for reasons defined by the law account for only 20% of all abortions. Unmarried women have 18.5% of the induced abortions; 26.5% of these women were between ages 16 and 20. The overwhelming majority of women who had an abortion, 77.9% of married women and 71.3% of unmarried women, reported satisfaction with the results of the abortion. This reflects, perhaps, the fact that abortion has become commonplace in Korea (PPFK 1996).

### D. Cesarean Operations

HUSO YI

Korea's frequency of cesarean (c-) section delivery is the highest in the world. According to the National Health Insurance Corporation (NHIC), almost half (43%) of the Korean women who had a baby in 1999 delivered by the cesarean operation. The rate of increase has been surprisingly rapid: from 6.0% in 1985, to 13.3% in 1990, to 21.3% in 1995, and most recently, in 1999, to 43%.

By age-cohort group, 29.4% of mothers under 19 years old delivered by c-section, with 37.0% of mothers between ages 20 and 24, 40.7% between ages 25 and 29, 46.5% be-

### Table 7

**Contraceptive-Practice Rate of Married Women, Aged 15-44**

| Year | Total | Tubec-tomy | Vasec-tomy | IUD | Pills | Condom | Others |
|---|---|---|---|---|---|---|---|
| 1976 | 44.2% | 4.1% | 10.5% | 7.8% | 7.8% | 6.3% | 11.3% |
| 1979 | 54.5 | 14.5 | 9.6 | 7.2 | 7.2 | 5.2 | 12.1 |
| 1982 | 57.7 | 23.0 | 6.7 | 5.4 | 5.4 | 7.2 | 10.3 |
| 1985 | 70.4 | 31.6 | 7.4 | 4.3 | 4.3 | 7.2 | 11.0 |
| 1988 | 77.1 | 37.2 | 6.7 | 2.8 | 2.8 | 10.2 | 9.2 |
| 1991 | 79.4 | 35.3 | 9.0 | 3.0 | 3.0 | 10.2 | 9.9 |
| 1994 | 77.4 | 28.6 | 10.5 | 1.8 | 1.8 | 14.3 | 10.6 |
| 1997 | 80.5 | 24.1 | 13.2 | 1.8 | 1.8 | 15.1 | 13.6 |

*Source*: Korea Institute for Health and Social Affairs 1998

### Table 8

**Number of Adopted Children, 1995-1999**

| | Total | Domestic | Overseas |
|---|---|---|---|
| 1995 | 3,205 | 1,025 | 2,180 |
| 1996 | 3,309 | 1,229 | 2,080 |
| 1997 | 3,469 | 1,412 | 2,057 |
| 1998 | 3,675 | 1,426 | 2,249 |
| 1999 | (1,802)[a]/4,135 | (645)/1,726 | (1,157)/2,409 |

[a]Numbers in parentheses are the number of adopted children surrendered by adolescent mothers; the number following the / is the total number of adopted children.
*Source*: Ministry of Health and Welfare 2000: Child Health

tween 30 and 34, 58.4% between 35 and 39, and 68.7% over 40 years old (see the NHIC Web site: http://www.nhic.or.kr, in Korean).

The highest c-section frequency rate among hospitals was 75.6% of all deliveries. Even the lowest hospital rate (16.1%) exceeded the World Health Organization (WHO) recommendation of 10%. The 1999 rates for the United States was 20% and for Japan, 15%. A survey showed that 80% of the participants were recommended by doctors for cesareans without detailed benefits and risks (Kim 2000). The main reason of the highest rate comes from the insurance policy. Natural delivery costs about US$40 for outpatients and US$330 for inpatients, whereas the operation costs US$180 for outpatients and US$860 for inpatients. In addition, in cases of natural delivery, women need to be taken care of for at least 12 hours, but cesarean operations only take 40 minutes. Lawsuit cases regarding vaginal delivery accidents ranks the first. Thus, doctors prefer the high-profit and low-risk cesarean operation. The issue received public attention right after NHIC announced the annual report on cesarean operations in July of 2000. Since then, women's rights groups have worked to promote the "right of choice" for women's bodies, together with the issue of abortion.

## E. Population Programs

HYUNG-KI CHOI and COLLEAGUES

Family planning started in Korea in 1961 with the slogan of "Two children whether they are a boy or a girl." The population-increase rate has diminished from 2.32 in 1970 to 1.54 in 1980 to 1.02 in 1997. The total fertility rate has also decreased from 4.5 in 1970 to 2.8 in 1980 to 1.6 in 1997 (see Tables 9 and 10). Korea's population-increase rate and fertility rate decreased only after considerable effort. Although the trend and current rates are encouraging, this trend has not become solid. The reasons for this uncertainty

### Table 9

#### Natural Population Increase Rate

| Year | 1970 | 1980 | 1985 | 1990 | 1991 | 1992 | 1993 | 1994 | 1995 | 1996 | 1997 |
|------|------|------|------|------|------|------|------|------|------|------|------|
| Rate | 2.32 | 1.54 | 1.02 | 9.5 | 1.08 | 1.13 | 1.08 | 1.06 | 1.04 | 0.99 | 1.02 |

*Source*: National Statistical Office 1999b

### Table 10

#### Total Fertility Rate

| Year | 1970 | 1980 | 1985 | 1990 | 1991 | 1992 | 1993 | 1994 | 1995 | 1996 | 1997 |
|------|------|------|------|------|------|------|------|------|------|------|------|
| Rate | 4.5 | 2.8 | 1.7 | 1.6 | 1.7 | 1.8 | 1.7 | 1.7 | 1.7 | 1.6 | 1.6 |

*Source*: National Statistical Office 1999b

### Table 11

#### STD Screening Criteria and Required Frequency of Tests

| | Frequency of Tests | |
|---|---|---|
| | Serologic Test | STD Test |
| Waitresses and dancers at foreign amusement restaurants | Once every 3 months | Once a week |
| Waitresses and dancers at amusement restaurants | Once every 3 months | Once a month |
| Service girls at lodging houses/ love motels | Once every 6 months | Once every 6 months |
| Service Girls at massage rooms | Once every 3 months | Once every 3 months |

*Source*: Ministry of Health and Welfare 1999

are as follows: First, the strong preference toward boys is worsening the male-to-female ratio. Second, late deliveries for women in their later 30s are increasing. There are also significant increases in the reversal of tubal ligations and vasectomies. Third, there still exists a high rate of unwanted pregnancies, which corresponds to the high rate of induced abortion. Fourth, the number of emigrants has decreased considerably, but immigrants into Korea have increased recently. Fifth, the rapid decrease in the death ratio is producing significant increases in the adult and elderly populations.

## 10. Sexually Transmitted Diseases and HIV/AIDS

### A. Sexually Transmitted Diseases
*Incidence, Patterns, and Trends*

HYUNG-KI CHOI and COLLEAGUES

Korean law lists syphilis, gonorrhea, chlamydia, herpes, candida, chancre, cancroids, nongonococcal urethritis, and lymphogranuloma venereum as sexually transmitted diseases. The number of STDs steadily declined from 145,802 cases in 1985, to 121,585 in 1990, and to 120,320 in 1995, but it increased to 127,389 in 1996 and 134,726 in 1997. Beginning in 1984, a law mandated that those who are employed in situations with a high risk of STDs must have regular screenings. There are 324 centers designated to prevent, diagnose, and treat sexually transmitted diseases (see Table 11).

### B. HIV/AIDS
*Incidence, Patterns, and Trends*

HUSO YI [*Updated 2003 by H. Yi*]

The first report of an HIV-positive foreigner in Korea came in June 1985, followed by the first report of a Korean HIV-positive case (contracted abroad) in December 1985 (for review, see Oh & Choe 1999). The first AIDS patient was diagnosed in February 1987 following an unsafe transfusion in Kenya. As of the end of 1998, the total number of HIV-positive cases in Korea was 876 and the number of AIDS patients was 131 (see Table 12). The estimated number of HIV-positive cases as of the end of 2000 is around 5,000, most of them being in their 20s and 30s. According to a recent report by the National Institute of Health of South Korea (2002), as of September 2002, Korea had 1,888 HIV-positive cases; 277 new cases were reported in 2002. The annual-increase rate from 1994 to 1998 was 12.8%. In 1999, the increase was 44% compared to the previous five years. The reasons for this significant increase can be found in the increase in voluntary testing, increased awareness of HIV/AIDS prevention, and the need for HIV treatment. However, a 17.7% increase occurred from 1999 to 2000, with a 51.1% increase from 2000 to 2001 (see Table 12). The HIV infection rate in 2002 increased by 20% from the same period the previous year and, at the end of 2002, 400 new HIV cases were reported (CDCNPIN 2002, 2003).

Table 13 shows the epidemiology of HIV infection in Korea. Sexual contact accounted for 1,505 cases (97.2%): heterosexual contact for 1048 cases (67.7%), and homosexual for 457 (29.5%).

*Availability of Treatment, Prevention Programs, and Government Policies* HUSO YI

With the initial report of an HIV-positive case in 1985, the Korean government enacted a strict law to deal with this threat. Mandatory screening of all blood products was instituted in July 1985 and expanded in July 1987. According to the AIDS Prevention Law enacted in December 1987, mandatory HIV testing was required of certain groups at high risk: overseas sailors and those female workers at coffee shops, barbershops, amusement restaurants, lodging houses, and massage parlors (note Industrial Prostitution in Section 8, above). The latter group could not get working permission without HIV testing. The mandatory HIV-testing law stopped in June 1993. Yet, the programs provided by the law include informing the spouse and friends of HIV/AIDS-infected persons and close surveillance.

People with HIV are required to receive HIV-prevention training and counseling at local health centers, as well as to report to a government office when moving. The government provides medication for HIV/AIDS for free. The problem, however, is that these patients with HIV/AIDS first have to pay for medications at the hospital and then request reimbursement. Thus, if they do not have enough money for treatment in the first 3 months, they cannot get medication. With respect to the HIV test, voluntary tests rarely occurred because of the mandatory law for reporting. Only targeted groups in the sex industry get mandatory testing. The current policy does not consider the rights of people with HIV. Once notified that they are HIV-positive, they are listed under the permanent control of the government, so they cannot guarantee their privacy. It is reported that people with HIV suffer more from government surveillance than from illness and/or the fact of HIV infection. The AIDS-related law states that if people with HIV refuse to report regularly, government officers, designated by the state governor or the Ministry of Health department, can visit them in their living places without notification and take them to separate places for treatment. In case they refuse the officer's acts, they will be sentenced for one year in prison or a US$1,000 fine. People with HIV cannot work in the mandatory testing places. As shown, unlike those of developed countries, the AIDS-prevention law is primarily to enforce punishment and not to protect those with HIV, so that it certainly violates human rights (Chung 1999). In order to ensure their rights, actual name reporting at government offices, mandatory testing, separation for treatment, and excessive criminal law enforcement should be revised. Meanwhile, awareness about the importance of HIV testing may be different issue. A study reported that, among 507 college students, only 5 male students and 1 female student had taken the HIV test (Kang 1994).

[*Update 2002*: UNAIDS Epidemiological Assessment: The Republic of Korea has a low HIV-prevalence rate. By the end of June 2000, a cumulative total of 1,282 HIV cases including 197 AIDS cases had been reported. An estimated 4,000 HIV-infected individuals were living in the country at the end of 2001 (prevalence of 0.01% among people aged 15 to 49.) The great majority (96%) of HIV infections are estimated to be sexually transmitted, with 13% occurring among women. National seroprevalence surveys have identified only sporadic cases of HIV infection.

[The seroprevalence of syphilis is also very low (0.03% among blood donors). Gonococcal antimicrobial resistance is high; in 2000, penicillin resistance was 80% and quinolone (ciprofloxacin) resistance, 79.5%. Behavioral surveys in 2001 found that 26.8% of sex workers reported using condoms during all sexual contacts.

[The estimated number of adults and children living with HIV/AIDS on January 1, 2002, were:

| | | |
|---|---|---|
| Adults ages 15-49: | 4,000 | (rate: < 0.1%) |
| Women ages 15-49: | 960 | |
| Children ages 0-15: | < 100 | |

[An estimated 220 adults and children died of AIDS during 2001.

[At the end of 2001, an estimated 1,000 South Korean children under age 15 were living without one or both parents who had died of AIDS. (*End of update by the Editors*)]

## 11. Sexual Dysfunctions, Counseling, and Therapies

### A. Sexual Dysfunctions and Attitudes

HYUNG-KI CHOI and COLLEAGUES

Erectile dysfunction in males and inhibited female orgasm were the most frequently reported dysfunctions (Yoo et al. 1989). Male expectation anxiety and female orgasmic disorder were highly related to morality by repressing sexual desire. In terms of morality, it was also pointed out that masturbation and sexual fantasy were effective therapy for single adults, but little research had been done with married couples. In their study, more than 90% of the 120 married-couple respondents had sexual fantasies. With respect to the content of the sexual fantasies, the female showed more various content than those of the males: replacement of the partner (52.6% of males and 38.5% of females); unusual positions (21.1% of males and 13.2% of females); unusual sexual activity (15.8% of males and 3.8% of females); group-sex experiences (7.9% of males and 1.9% of females), and the use of sex toys (2.6% of males and 3.8% of females). The following things were

**Table 12**

**HIV/AIDS Cases in Korea, 1985-2002 (September)**

| | Total | 1985-93 | 1994 | 1995 | 1996 | 1997 | 1998 | 1999 | 2000 | 2001 | 2002 |
|---|---|---|---|---|---|---|---|---|---|---|---|
| HIV infected | 1,888 | 323 | 89 | 108 | 102 | 124 | 129 | 186 | 219 | 331 | 277 |
| Women | 221 | 34 | 11 | 19 | 12 | 17 | 18 | 26 | 25 | 35 | 24 |
| AIDS patients | 312 | 16 | 11 | 14 | 22 | 33 | 35 | 34 | 32 | 42 | 73 |
| AIDS deaths | 403 | 42 | 13 | 21 | 33 | 36 | 46 | 43 | 52 | 58 | 59 |

*Source*: Korean National Institute of Health 2002

**Table 13**

**Routes of HIV Infection in Korea, 1999**

| Route of Infection | Cases | Route of Infection | Cases |
|---|---|---|---|
| Sexual contact | | Blood products | 17 |
| Korean heterosexual | 339 | Maternal | 1 |
| Foreign heterosexual | 236 | Intravenous drug use | 0 |
| Homosexual | 191 | Others | 42 |
| Blood transfusion | | | |
| Domestic | 10 | Total | 876 |
| Abroad | 11 | | |

*Source*: Ministry of Health and Welfare 1999

only fantasized by the females: forced sexual encounters, sadistic imagery, observation of sexual activity, and sexual activities with animals. Thirty percent of the females gave no response. The findings suggested conflicts between the females' sexual desires and their activities, which results in sexual dysfunction.

### B. The Availability of Diagnosis and Treatment

HYUNG-KI CHOI and COLLEAGUES
(Redacted by HUSO YI)

[*Comment 2001*: Sex therapy was first offered by a few psychiatrists in the 1970s, and until the early 1980s, only partial analyses through case studies were available (Yoo et al. 1990). Later in the 1980s, as Korean society became more Westernized, the issue of sexual dysfunctions received attention. The first sex therapy clinic was established in April 1986 at Yonsei Medical Center. The clinic developed a Korean version of the *Self-Evaluation of Sexual Behavior & Gratification* (Lief 1981) and *DSFI: Derogatis Sexual Functioning Inventory* (Derogatis & Melisoratos 1979). These Korean translations were evaluated for reliability and validity and have been effective in sex-therapy settings (Lee et al. 1989). In a review of the 231 patients who visited the sex therapy clinic from its opening to April 1995, 75.8% were male and 24.2% were female. The most prevalent sexual disorders were male erectile dysfunction (40.1%), premature ejaculation (20.3%), and inhibited female orgasm (10.6%). Those who underwent sex therapy with their partners were 11.5% where the male had the problem and 20.0% where it was the female, which were significantly lower than those in Western countries (Yoo 1999) (*End of comment by Huso Yi*)]

Since the 1980s, there has been a rapid increase in the number of publications associated with sexual dysfunction and andrology. In the *Journal of Urology*, there were 13 papers published by Korean researchers and clinicians in 1983. This increased to 33 in 1988, and to 52 in 1993. In an effort to accommodate this increase, the *Korean Journal of Andrology* began publishing in 1989. *Andrology*, a textbook on sexual dysfunction and infertility, was authored by Hee-Young Lee, and in 1995, Sae-Chul Kim published *Diagnosis and Treatment of Male Sexual Dysfunction*. Hyung-Ki Choi also published the experiences of a sexual dysfunction clinic to further the knowledge of the general public.

Male sexual dysfunction includes a decrease in libido, erectile dysfunction, and ejaculatory abnormality. It is estimated that there are 1.2 million such patients in Korea. This number is ever increasing because of prolonged life expectancy, stress, and various traffic and industrial accidents. Since penile prosthesis implantation was introduced by Professor Hyung-Ki Choi and Sae-Chul Kim in Korea in 1983, some 800 cases were performed as of 1995. Professor Hee-Young Lee introduced triple pharmacologic agents for corporal injection in patients with erectile dysfunction, and vascular reconstruction for arteriogenic impotence was first performed in 1989. Sildenafil sulfate (Viagra) has been available to Korean patients since October 1999. In Korea, patients over 21 can purchase a monthly allowance of 8 sildenafil pills (Viagra) with written proof from a physician that they are free from any cardiovascular diseases.

No nationwide data on the clinical profiles of sexual dysfunctions are yet available in Korea. In 1998, Hyung-Ki Choi from Yonsei University reported the results of 2,000 consecutive patients visiting a sexual dysfunction clinic from September 1995 to March 1997. Patients in their 40s were most common at 29.4%, and unmarried patients comprised 11.5%. The most common complaint was erectile dysfunction with 61.8%, premature ejaculation with 15.0%, and those with both diseases at 11.7%; 40.4% of patients had a previous ex-perience of counseling or treatment with healthcare professionals, 70.3% being non-physician care. The most common associated diseases were diabetes (17.3%) and cardiovascular abnormality (13.8%). Medical treatment was offered in 64.7% of the patients, and among them, 21.5% gained erectile ability capable of intromission.

[*Comment 2001*: Another well-known sex therapy clinic is the Seoul-Cornell Clinic for Human Sexuality, with Dr. Hyun Uk Seol, who is a member of the Society for Scientific Study of Sexuality and was trained in sex therapy by Dr. Helen Singer Kaplan at Cornell Medical School in New York City. His clinic opened in 1995 and he has published a dozen books about sexuality from his own publisher, Sex-Academy. His sex therapy website (http://www.sex-academy.com; contact: seolhu@nuri.net) has good resources with online sex counseling. (*End of comment by Huso Yi*)]

### C. Therapist Training and Certification HUSO YI

There is no organization offering a certificate for sex therapy, nor is there any institutional training program for sex therapy in Korea. Usually, medical doctors, who are trained in psychiatry, obstetrics and gynecology, urology, andrology, and its related fields, practice sex therapy. In the medical school, the need for courses about sexuality has been discussed, but the problem remains as to which department should be responsible for the curricula (Hong et al. 1993). For sexuality counseling, several organizations, such as the Sexual Violence Relief Center, the Planned Parenthood Federation of Korea (PPFK), the Young Women's Christian Association (YWCA), and other social welfare organizations have developed their own programs on sexuality counselor certification, so that no official criteria or guidelines have yet been established.

## 12. Sex Research and Advanced Professional Education

### A. Graduate Programs and HUSO YI
### Sexological Research

The Korean Research Institute for Culture and Sexuality was founded in July 1996 under the supervision of the Planned Parenthood Federation of Korea with funding from the Korean government. The tasks of this Institute are to resolve the problems of male preference and the imbalance of sex-ratio at birth, prevent abortion by promoting contraceptive use, and establish effective sexuality education. The Institute has conducted not only nationwide studies about the issues of adolescent and adult sexuality, but also investigated sexuality education and counseling centers all over the country. The Institute has been very successful in developing resources for sexuality education, with more than 200 visual materials and a guidebook of sexuality education. Especially, the major achievement is that the Institute has offered training programs in sexuality education and counseling for the officers at local health centers, and school teachers since 1997. The training is composed of three courses. The trainees first attend lectures and a field study at a sexuality education center, and then attend 20 sessions of sexuality education and 50 sessions of a counseling internship. In the last course, they participate in the discussion of case studies, sexuality counseling supervision, and psychological testing. Those who pass the course receive the certificate of sexuality educator/counseling specialist (PPFK 2000). For information, see http://www.yline.re.kr; contact: sjoon@ppfk.re.kr.

The Korean Society of Human Sexuality (KSHS) was founded in 1988 and lasted until 1995. Composed mainly of scholars in medical science, KSHS also included social scientists, psychologists, relationship counselors, and other professionals. The Society published the *Journal of the Korean Society for Human Sexuality*, as well as held monthly colloquia on sexual issues and topics, such as sex therapy, sexuality and religion, sexuality education, sexual physiology, sex and art, transsexualism, homosexuality, psychosexual development, and so on. All abstracts of the journal (1989-1994) are available in English. Efforts were underway in 2001 to revive the organization.

In 1997, Ewha Woman's University* opened the Korean Women's Institute and offered women's studies courses at the undergraduate level. The Department of Women's Studies was established in the graduate school in 1982 and expanded to offer Ph.D. degrees in 1990. Through such achievements, Ewha Woman's University has led in the development of women's studies in Korea. The Asian Center for Women's Studies (ACWS) was established in May 1995 for the purpose of fostering an understanding of women's issues in Asia through extensive research, educational programs, and international exchanges (ACWS 2000). Since then, the ACWS has conducted the "Asian Women's Studies Curriculum Development Project" and English lectures/ workshops on "Women in Korea," held an international conference on women's studies, and published the *Asian Journal of Women's Studies*. For information, see http://home.ewha.ac.kr/~ewsadmin/www_page/eng/ (in English); contact: acwsewha@mm.ehwa.ac.kr.

The Korean Women's Development Institute (KWDI) is not focused mainly on sexological research itself, yet the KWDI, funded by Korean government, implements numerous research activities and projects in relation to gender and sexuality, with the Departments of Law and Politics, Education, Labor and Statistics, Family Health and Welfare, Social Culture, and Information Development. The Institute publishes an annual report comparing statistics for women and men, conducts research on sexual abuse, sexuality education, and prostitution, and produces visual materials on these topics (KWDI 1999). For information: http://kwdi.re.kr; contact: S4KWDI@unitel.or.kr.

[*Update 2003*: The Korean Sexual-Minority Culture and Rights Center (KSCRC), founded in August 2002, was the first interdisciplinary center for research, policy advocacy, education, cultural events, and publication in the LGBTQ community. KSCRC publishes a quarterly magazine and translations in sexuality and gender studies, as well as plans to conduct research about the lives of individuals who are sexual minorities. For information: http://kscrc.org/en/; contact: Huso Yi, kscrc-en@kscrc.org. (*End of update by H. Yi*)]

## B. Sexological Organization and Publications

HYUNG-KI CHOI and COLLEAGUES
In January 1982, at a World Health Organization meeting, the Korean Society of Andrology was formed with plans to publish a journal. The second meeting was held in September 1983. The interest in this new field of medicine was amplified by the first Korean implantation of a penile prosthesis in December 1983. The Korean Society enrolled as a member of the International Society of Andrology in 1985. The Asia-Pacific Society for Impotence Research (APSIR) was organized in November 1987 in Hong Kong,

and the founding delegates from Korea included Hyung-Ki Choi, first author of this chapter, Sae-Chul Kim, and Jun-Kyu Seo. Hyung-Ki Choi was elected president at this meeting for the second meeting of the Asia-Pacific Society for Impotence Research held in Seoul in November 1989, with 239 scientists and physicians attending. In June 1994, the Korean Society for Andrology held a meeting to update private physicians on erectile dysfunction.

## References and Suggested Readings

Asian Center for Women's Studies (ACWS). 2000. *Asian Center for Women's Studies: Activity report 1995-2000. 2* (in English). Seoul, Korea: Asian Center for Women's Studies, Ewha Woman's University.

Byun, W., & J. Hwang. 1999. A study of industrial prostitution. *Women's Studies Forum* [Korean Women's Development Institute], *15*:211-230.

Byun, W., Y. Won., & S. Chung. 2000. *Study of sexual consciousness and violence against women* (abstract in English). Seoul: Korean Women's Development Institute.

Centers for Disease Control and Prevention. National Prevention Information Network. 2002. *HIV infection rise by 20 percent* (Accession number 36194).

Centers for Disease Control and Prevention. National Prevention Information Network. 2003. *Report shows HIV cases top 2,000* (Accession number 36766).

Chang, P. 1998. Korean mothers, daughters, and wives. In: *Korean culture through women's eyes: Lectures in English* (in English). Seoul: Asian Center for Women's Studies, Ewha Woman's University.

Chang, P. 2000. Women and sexuality. In: *Women of Korea: Lectures in English* (in English). Seoul: Asian Center for Women's Studies, Ewha Woman's University.

Chang, S. B., Y. J. Lee, S. J. Park, E. I. Song, J. A. Suh, & Y. K. Oh. 1998. A study on college students' sexual behaviors. *Korea Research Institute for Culture and Sexuality Report* [Seoul], 98-03 (abstract in English).

Chang, Y. A. 1996. A study on reformation of the head of household law. *Korean Women's Development Institute Research Report*, 200-4. Seoul: KWDI.

Chin, K. N., Y. J. Lee, S. J. Park, E. I. Song, & S. R. Kim. 1997. A study of married adults' sexuality consciousness and attitudes. *Korea Research Institute for Culture and Sexuality Report* [Seoul], 97-01 (abstract in English).

Cho, D. H. 1993. Legal problems in operation for transsexualism. *Journal of Korean Society for Human Sexuality*, *4*(1): 16-20.

Choi, Y. A. 1996. *Reality and problems in sexual violence*. Presentation at 8th Symposium of Social-Ethics, Seoul.

Chung, D. C. 1990. A survey on sexual violence of adolescents at the urban area. *Journal of Korean Society of Human Sexuality*, *2*(1):33-62 (abstract in English).

Chung, H. M. 1999. *Criminal legal problems of AIDS and prevention strategy. Annual report, 98-12* (abstract in German). Seoul: Korean Institute of Criminology.

Chung, S. H. 1998. *Sexual customs in the Chosun Dynasty: The view of women and sexual culture*. Seoul: Garam Kihuk.

CIA. 2002 (January). *The world factbook 2002*. Washington, DC: Central Intelligence Agency. Available: http://www.cia.gov/cia/publications/factbook/index.html.

Citizens for Abolition of the Family Headship (*Hoju*) System. 2000. Available: http://antihoju.jinbo.net/(in Korean).

Committee of Korean Genealogy. 2000. Available: http://www.koreafamily.com (in Korean).

Derogatis, L. R., & N. Melisoratos. 1979. The DSFI: A multidimensional measure of sexual functions. *Journal of Sex and Marital Therapy*, *5*:244-281.

Fellows, W. J. 1979. *Religions east and west*. New York: Holt, Rinehart and Winston.

French, H. W. 2003 (June 21). Changing patients' sexes, and Korean mores. *The New York Times*, A4.

---

[*Comment 2001*: "Woman's" represents the university's founding with just one student; it further symbolizes its high respect for the individuality of Korea's wonderful women. Therefore, Ewha is not a "women's" university, but "Woman's university," keeping each woman's distinctive being intact in its name" (Quoted from the Ewha Woman's University website: http://www.ewha.ac.kr/ewhaeng/index.html). (*End of comment by Huso Yi*)]

Gregersen, E. 1994. *The world of human sexuality: Behaviors, customs and beliefs.* New York: Irvington Publishers.

Han, D. 1970. Sexual perversions in Korea. *Journal of Korean Neuropsychiatry, 9*(1):25-34.

Han, M. S. 2002. Minister's message. Ministry of gender inequality in Republic of Korea. Available in English: http://www.moge.go.kr/eng/index(eng).jsp.

Han, S., M. Kim-Choe, M. S. Lee, & S. H. Lee. 2001. Risk-taking behavior among high school students in South Korea. *Journal of Adolescence, 24*(4):571-574.

*Hankyere.* 1996 (September 19). Analysis about prevalence of 'son-bearing treatment' and its problem. *Hanhyere 21* [Seoul].

Headquarter of the Family Headship Law Abolition. 2000. Available: http://no-hoju.women21.or.kr/ (in Korean).

Hong, K. E. 1996. Sexual problems in adolescence. *Journal of Korean Medical Association, 39*(12):1514-1518.

Hong, K. E., D. Y. Cho, & H. C. Shin. 1993. Need of human sexuality course. *Journal of Korean Society for Human Sexuality, 4*(1):45-53.

Jung, K. M. 1971. A study on the foreskin and circumcision of the penis of Korean male. *Korean Journal of Public Health, 8*:369.

Kang, B. W. 1994. A study of the university students' consciousness about sex and AIDS. *Journal of Korean Society for Health Education, 11*(1):43-56.

Kendall, L. 1996. *Getting married in Korea.* Berkeley: University of California Press.

Kim, D. S., J. Y. Lee, & M. G. Pang. 1999. Male circumcision: A South Korean perspective. *British Journal of Urology International, 83,* Supplement; *1*:28-33.

Kim, D. S., & Y. S. Yoon. 1997. *Sexual stone of Korea.* Seoul: Blue Forrest Publisher.

Kim, E. 1992. Reformed family law and movement for reforming family law. *Korean Women's Development Institute research report,* 200-3 (in English). Seoul: KWDI.

Kim, E. 1996. The current laws on women in Korea. *Women's Studies Forum* [Korean Women's Development Institute, Seoul] (in English), *12*:33-49.

Kim, E., D. Yoon, & H. Park. 2000. *Acts on violence against women: Enforcement status and tasks* (abstract in English). Seoul: Korean Women's Development Institute.

Kim, H. J. 2001 (January 18). Prosecution to arrest Internet adult TV operators for showing porn. *Korea Herald* [Seoul] (available in English at http://www.koreaherald.co.kr/SITE/data/html_dir/2001/01/19/200101190034.asp).

Kim. H. W. 1996. *Effects of sexual satisfaction in marital adjustments.* Unpublished master's thesis, Seoul: Yonsei University.

Kim, J. H., Y. J. Lee, S. J. Park, E. I. Song, J. A. Suh, & Y. J. Oh. 1998. A study on unmarried working adults' sexuality consciousness and sexual behaviors. *Korea Research Institute for Culture and Sexuality Report* [Seoul], 98-104 (abstract in English).

Kim, J. R. 1993. *Study of male preference and reproductive health.* Unpublished master's thesis, Taegu: Kyemyung University.

Kim, S. W., Y. J. Lee, S. J. Park, S. R. Kim, & E. I. Song. 1997. *A study of high school girls' sexuality consciousness: Their sexual behaviors and problems of sexuality* (vol. 97, no. 102, abstract in English). Seoul: The Korea Research Institute for Culture and Sexuality.

Kim, S. W., D. J. Shin, I. S. Song, & S. J. Park. 1996. *A study of high school boys' sexuality consciousness.* Seoul: Korea Research Institute for Culture and Sexuality.

Kim, U. N. 2000. Protest to regain the right of delivery choice. *Sisa Journal* [Seoul], 561.

Kim, Y. C. 1976. *Women of Korea: A history from ancient times to 1945* (in English). Seoul: Ewha Woman's University Press.

King Y.-J. 1736. *Woman's four book* (trans. by J.-K. Kim in 1987). Seoul: Myung Moon Dang.

Korea Anti-AIDS Federation. 1997. *Annual report on AIDS specialized counseling.* Seoul: Korea Anti-AIDS Federation.

*Korea Herald.* 2001 (January 18). Koreans spend much time on Net. *Korea Herald* [Seoul] (available in English at http://www.koreaherald.co.kr/SITE/data/html_dir/2001/01/18/200101180033.asp).

Korean Council for Women Drafted into Military Sexual Slavery by Japan. 2000. Available at: http://witness.peacenet.or.kr/kindex.htm (in English).

Korean Government Homepage. 2000. Available: http://www.korea.net; for demographic information, see http://www.korea.net/menu/koreainfo/kitspeople.htm (in English).

Korea Institute for Health and Social Affairs. 1998. *National fertility and family health survey report.*

Korean Institute for Health and Social Welfare. 1991. *Sex preference for children and gender discrimination.* Seoul: Korean Institute for Health and Social Welfare.

Korean Institute for Health and Social Welfare. 1999. *Study of Korean sexual violence problems.* Seoul: Korean Institute for Health and Social Welfare.

Korean Institute of Criminology. 1998. *Investigation on sexual violence.* Seoul: Korean Institute of Criminology.

Korean Sexuality Counseling Center. 1997. *Sexuality counseling activity report.* Seoul: Planned Parenthood Federation of Korea.

Korean Sexual Violence Relief Center. 1999. Case report on sexual violence. *Nanumte* [*Sharing Place,* Seoul], 29.

Korean Women's Development Institute (KWDI). 1999. Korean women today. *KWDI Newsletter* [Seoul], 65 (in English).

Korean Women's Development Institute (KWDI). 2000a. *Study of sexual consciousness and violence against women.*

Korean Women's Development Institute (KWDI). 2000b. *Women's statistical yearbook* [women's social indicator information]. Available at: http://www.kwdi.re.kr (English).

Lee, B. S., & H. S. Chung. 2000. *Guidebook of sexual rehabilitation for the spinal cord injured.* Seoul: The National Rehabilitation Center.

Lee, C. 1996. *Study of Korean women's sexual attitudes.* Unpublished master's thesis, Pusan: Pusan University.

Lee, H. S. 1997. Birth of Korean gay community and its future. *Another World,* 5. Seoul: Kiri Kiri.

Lee, H. S., B. H. Oh, K. J. Yoo, M. S. Lee, & M. K. Kim. 1989. DSFI characteristics between normal and male sexual dysfunction. *Journal of Korean Society for Human Sexuality, 1*(1):83-93 (abstract in English).

Lee, J. S. 1993. Social aspects in transsexualism. *Journal of Korean Society for Human Sexuality, 4*(1):21-29 (abstract in English).

Lee, Y. J., S. R. Kim, & I. E. Song. 1998. A study of factors influenced to high school girl's experiences of having sex and attitudes on premarital intercourse. *Korea Research Institute for Culture and Sexuality Report* [Seoul], 98-102 (abstract in English).

Leupp, G. P. 1995. *Male colors: The construction of homosexuality in Tokugawa, Japan.* Berkeley: University of California Press.

Lief, H. I. 1981. *Sexual problem in medical practice: Sexual performance evaluation.* New York: American Medical Association.

Martin, F., & C. Berry. 1998. QueerNAsian on the Net: Syncretic sexualities in Taiwan and Korean cyberspaces. *Critical in Queeries, 2*(1):67-93.

Ministry of Health and Welfare (MOHW). 1998. *Statistical annual report.* Seoul: Ministry of Health and Welfare.

Ministry of Health and Welfare (MOHW). 1999. *Statistical annual report.* Seoul: Communicable Disease Control Division, Ministry of Health and Welfare.

Ministry of Health and Welfare (MOHW). 2000. *Statistical annual report.* Seoul: Ministry of Health and Welfare.

Moon, H. S. 1993. *Study of types about spousal relationships by marital and sexual satisfaction.* Unpublished doctoral dissertation, Seoul: Dongguk University.

Murray, S. 1992. *Oceanic homosexualities*. New York: Garland.

Murray, S. 2000. *Homosexualities*. Chicago: The University of Chicago Press.

National Statistical Office (NSO). 1985. *Census of surname and family origin*. Seoul: National Statistical Office.

National Statistical Office (NSO). 1998. *1997 annual report on the economically active population survey*. Seoul: National Statistical Office.

National Statistical Office (NSO). 1999a. *Annual report on the economically active population survey (1996-1999)*. Seoul: National Statistical Office.

National Statistical Office (NSO). 1999b. *Annual report on the vital statistics*. Seoul: National Statistical Office (available in English at http://www.nso.go.kr/eindex.html).

NHCROK. 2001. *National history compilation of the Republic of Korea*. Available: http://kuksa.nhcc.go.kr/english/index.html (in English).

Noss, D. S., & J. B. Noss. 1990. *A history of the world's religions*. New York: Macmillan.

Oh, B. H., K. J. Yoo, H. S. Lee, H. Y. Lee, & J. H. Moon. 1990. A study on the sexual behavior of spinal cord injured men. *Journal of Korean Society for Human Sexuality*, 2(1):92-105 (abstract in English).

Oh, C. S. 1997. History of son-wish-stone. In: D. S. Kim & Y. S. Yoon, *Sexual stone of Korea* (pp. 216-220). Seoul: Blue Forrest Publisher.

Our Society Research Center. 1994. *Sexuality and modern society*. Seoul: Blue Land Publisher.

Park, J. I. 1994 (August 25). Compensation for hymen lost: Not loss of virginity but a medical accident. *Chosun Daily* [Seoul].

Planned Parenthood Federation of Korea (PPFK). 1996. *Study of abortion cases in the major 20 hospitals*. Seoul: Planned Parenthood Federation of Korea.

Planned Parenthood Federation of Korea (PPFK). 2000. *The annual report of family health*. Seoul: Planned Parenthood Federation of Korea.

Presidential Commission on Women's Affairs. 2000. Available: http://www.pcwa.go.kr/w-en/home.htm (in English).

Report Center of Cyber Sexual Violence. 2000. *Survey about cyber sexual violence* (cited January 23, 2001; available: http://www.gender.co.kr, in Korean).

Seol, H. U. 2000. *Dr. Hyun Uk Seol's sexology Q&A volume 3*. Seoul: Sex-Academy.

Shong, S., & L. D. Icard. 1996. A Korean gay man in the United States: Toward a cultural context for social service practice. *Journal of Gay and Lesbian Social Services*, 5(2/3):115-137.

UNAIDS. 2002. *Epidemiological fact sheets by country*. Geneva, Switzerland: Joint United Nations Programme on HIV/AIDS (UNAIDS/WHO). Available: http://www.unaids.org/hivaidsinfo/statistics/fact_sheets/index_en.htm.

Yi, H. 1998. *History of homosexuality and gay movements in Korea*. Paper presented at the 5th Congress of Asian Sexology, Seoul.

Yi, H. 2000. *Coming out: 300 Q&A about gay and lesbian people* (trans. of E. Marcus's *Is it a choice?* with added Q&A about Korean gays). Seoul: Park Young-Yul Publisher.

Yoo, K. J. 1993. Psychiatric aspects in transsexualism. *Journal of Korean Society for Human Sexuality*, 4(1):5-11 (abstract in English).

Yoo, K. J., K. Namkoong, H. Y. Lee, H. S. Lee, B. H. Oh, & B. Y. Lee. 1990. Clinical study of patients who visited a sex clinic. *Journal of Korean Society for Human Sexuality*, 2(1):77-91 (abstract in English).

Yoo, K. J., B. H. Oh, H. S. Lee, M. K. Kim, & K. S. Yoon. 1989. Sexual fantasies in married couple. *Journal of Koran Society for Human Sexuality*, 1(1):71-82 (abstract in English).

Yoo, K. J., B. H. Oh, & E. H. Soh. 1990. Parents' attitude toward masturbation. *Journal of Korean Society for Human Sexuality*, 2(1):63-76 (abstract in English).

Youn, G. 1995 (March). Adolescent sexuality: A speculation on the abortion debate. *Jisung Paegee*, 27:122-125.

Youn, G. 1996. Sexual activities and attitudes of adolescent Koreans. *Archives of Sexual Behavior*, 25(6):629-643.

# Spain

## (*Reino de España*)

Jose Antonio Nieto, Ph.D. (coordinator), with
Jose Antonio Carrobles, Ph.D., Manuel Delgado Ruiz, Ph.D.,
Felix Lopez Sanchez, Ph.D., Virginia Maquieira D'Angelo, Ph.L.D.,
Josep-Vicent Marques, Ph.D., Bernardo Moreno Jimenez, Ph.D.,
Raquel Osborne Verdugo, Ph.D., Carmela Sanz Rueda, Ph.D.,
and Carmelo Vazquez Valverde, Ph.D.*

*Translated by*
Laura Berman, Ph.D., and Jose Nanin, M.A.
*Updates by Laura Berman, Ph.D., Jose Nanin, M.A.,
and the Editors*

## Contents

## Demographics and a Brief Historical Perspective

ROBERT T. FRANCOEUR

### A. Demographics

Spain, with Portugal to its west, occupies the Iberian peninsula in the southwest corner of Europe, south of France. With a total area of 194,896 square miles (504,778 km²), it is the size of the states of Arizona and Utah combined. Spain has a high, arid central plateau broken by mountain ranges and river valleys. The northwest is heavily watered, while the south has lowlands and a Mediterranean climate.

In July 2002, Spain had an estimated population of just over 40 million. (All data are from *The World Factbook 2002* (CIA 2002) unless otherwise stated.)

**Age Distribution and Sex Ratios**: *0-14 years*: 14.5% with 1.06 male(s) per female (sex ratio); *15-64 years*: 68.1% with 1.01 male(s) per female; *65 years and over*: 17.4% with 0.72 male(s) per female; *Total population sex ratio*: 0.96 male(s) to 1 female

**Life Expectancy at Birth**: *Total Population*: 79.08 years; *male*: 75.63 years; *female*: 82.76 years

**Urban/Rural Distribution**: 77% to 23%

**Ethnic Distribution**: A composite of Mediterranean and Nordic types

**Religious Distribution**: Roman Catholic: 94%, other: 6%

**Birth Rate**: 9.29 births per 1,000 population

**Death Rate**: 9.22 per 1,000 population

(CIA 2002)

**Infant Mortality Rate**: 4.85 deaths per 1,000 live births

**Net Migration Rate**: 0.87 migrant(s) per 1,000 population

**Total Fertility Rate**: 1.16 children born per woman

**Population Growth Rate**: 0.09%

**HIV/AIDS** (1999 est.): *Adult prevalence*: 0.58%; *Persons living with HIV/AIDS*: 120,000; *Deaths*: 2,000. (For additional details from www.UNAIDS.org, see end of Section 10B.)

**Literacy Rate** (*defined as those age 15 and over who can read and write*): 97%; education is free and compulsory from age 6 to 16

**Per Capita Gross Domestic Product** (*purchasing power parity*): $18,900 (2001 est.); *Inflation*: 3.8%; *Unemployment*: 13%

### B. A Brief Historical Perspective

Spain was settled by Iberians, Basques, and Celts, partly overrun by the Carthaginians from North Africa, and conquered by Rome about 200 B.C.E. In the 5th century of the Common Era, the Visigoths, who were then in power, adopted Christianity. By 711, an Islamic invasion from North Africa had displaced the Visigoths. Christian forces started a reconquest from the north that promoted a Spanish nationalism. The marriage of Ferdinand II of Aragon and Isabella I of Castile in 1491 led to the final expulsion of the Moors with the fall of Granada. The Spanish Inquisition, established in the 13th century, was infamous for its persecution and forced conversion of Jews and Muslims. The discovery of the New World by Columbus in 1492, the conquest of Mexico by Cortes, and of Peru by Pizarro marked the start of Spain's Colonial Empire. The Spanish Empire also included, at one time, the Netherlands, parts of Italy and Germany, the Philippines, Florida, and much of Central and South America. Cuba, Puerto Rico, and the Philippines were ceded in the Spanish-American War of 1898.

Spain's king was replaced by a dictatorship from 1923 until 1930, when the monarchy returned. A republic, declared in 1931, ended with a devastating three-year civil war (1936-1939) between the republicans and the military under General Francisco Franco. During World War II, Spain remained neutral, although favoring relations with the fascist countries. Franco set the stage for Prince Juan

Carlos to return as Spain's king after his death in 1975. Catalonia and the Basque country were granted self-rule and autonomy in 1980.

## 1. Basic Sexological Premises

### A. Character of Gender Roles

Stereotypes of masculinity and femininity have changed. Male heterosexism is still present in society, but it has not the strength it used to have. By the same token, women express their sexuality more openly. The extreme form of masculinity, *machismo*, no longer has societal approval. On the other hand, sexual purity of women no longer depends on the claim of virginity and chastity before marriage (see Section 5A/B, Interpersonal Heterosexual Behaviors, Children and Adolescents). Men and women are sexualized human beings. There is no longer room for the radical expressions of patriarchal heterosexism that used to depict women as desexualized persons without sexual needs. "Women must stay at home with a broken leg" is the English translation of the proverb, *La mujer en casa con la pata quabradaa*, that Spanish men traditionally cited to assign sexual passivity to the feminine gender role. Nowadays, this is a memory.

### B. Sociolegal Status of Males and Females

Politically speaking, adolescents are considered adults at age 18, when they can exercise the right to vote. However, responsibility for penal (criminal) acts is reached two years earlier, at age 16. Political and penal age are the same for males and females.

### C. General Concepts of Sexuality and Love

The Republic of 1931 recognized women's right to vote, their right to divorce, and, to a certain degree, the right to sexual liberty. With the triumph of Franco in 1939, affectionate and sexual relationships returned to the traditional model tied to the Catholic Church. Sex was considered wrong, love was eternal and only within marriage, and the moral double standard between the sexes reigned. Couples engaged in long courtships, men maintained extramarital relationships, and husbands claimed that they were defending their honor by nearly killing their wives who were presumed to have been adulterous. A very popular song expresses this love ideology: *Solamente Una Vez se Ama en la Vida* [*One Only Loves Once in Life*].

In the 1960s, tourism, the labor emigration to other European nations, and economic development introduced more-liberal customs to society. The automobile and student apartments facilitated sexual encounters without commitment. The contraceptive hormonal pill became available, despite the opposition of Franco's government. By the end of the 1960s, paternal authoritarianism had decreased, and women's presence in the labor and educational segments of society had become stronger.

The decade of the 1970s was a period of significant change. The feminist movement appeared, and couples began living together before marriage. Social pressure for sexual education appeared. A democratic free press was established. Legalized divorce recognized the right to love more than once in a lifetime.

The 1980s introduced changes of a different sort. Evidence of liberal sexual attitudes was widespread among intellectual and political activists, as expressed in the increase in premarital relationships, family planning, and voluntary interruption of pregnancy (abortion having been legalized, although with certain limits, as described in Section 9C, Contraception, Abortion, and Population Planning, Abortion. On the other hand, an economic recession, coupled with fatigue among the avant-garde minority, created more-conservative attitudes. These forces caused older children to delay leaving their homes of origin, and to reevaluate the institution of marriage.

This panorama of attitudes is pluralistic. It encompasses a measurable degree of sexual revolution, along with a rebirth of sensitive interaction (*Reivinicación de la ternura* [recognition of emotions, affections, and tenderness]). In recent years, it has become obvious that among many young couples, there is an unstable truce between women, who have changed a great deal after having become aware of the double standard, and men, who had changed little and still avoid home and childcare tasks. A theoretical rather than real egalitarianism of the sexes has prevailed and still dominates Spanish culture.

## 2. Religious, Ethnic, and Gender Factors Affecting Sexuality

### A. Source and Character of Religious Values

Although most of Spain's people are nominally Roman Catholic, the liturgical and moral orthodoxy of the Catholic Church are very weakly obeyed, except for some regions in the north. The majority of Spaniards do not accept or follow the Church's precepts regarding sexuality. Despite strict Catholic sexual expectations and the preaching on sexuality from pulpits and confessional boxes, popular and influential rituals and festivals have sexuality at their center. These celebrations are evidence of the paradoxical attitude of Spanish society to sexuality, especially that of the young. In other words, sexuality is celebrated. Maypoles, pigs, Christs, donkeys, bulls, Judas, the Carnival Kings, and similar allegories of hypergenitality and virility are keystones in Spanish Fiestas. In Spain, sexuality is an essential element and center of the festival domain.

However, in a typical paradox, the ritual reign of sexuality irreversibly leads to ceremonial destruction. Those same rituals that are centered on the metaphors of masculinity also recognize the fundamental role to which women must conform. Women are the *concitadoras* (who stir up emotions and feelings in men, stimulate them to action, and excite jealousy or hatred, interest or curiosity), as well as the watchful guardians (*vigilantes*) of their male opponents. This process of absorption is completed by converting the inappropriate sexual drives of male youth into social energy.

One has to consider the possibility that religion's cultural obsession for stimulating/repressing virility determines the expression of Spanish sexuality today. One consequence of this cultural conception of manliness as something basically extremely vulnerable, is the ambivalent tolerance of males who violate the sexual mores, as long as their noncompliance remains a private matter.

### B. Source and Character of Ethnic Values

The ethnic and religious values that serve as guidelines for the sexual behavior of the Spanish should not be perceived of as being homogeneous throughout this country. Different ethnic cultures and different social strata create contrasts, some, like the distinction between urban and rural, being more obvious than others. Keeping in mind this high level of variability, one can still identify a substratum base that determines sexual conduct and attitudes among the Spanish. This sexual ethos is characterized by a stress on (preference for) controlling the sexual conduct of the young, especially males, and mainly with the aim of guaranteeing the family procreation.

The cause of the anxiety the community associates with the sexual conduct of male youths has to deal with the strategy of socialization that they undergo. In traditional Spain, boys abandoned their childhood status to incorporate the life of an active young man as soon as they were considered mature enough, usually around age 16. In this phase, they were expected to gain sexual experience, generally by means of masturbation, visits to brothels, and sporadic contacts with relatives, especially with female members, such as female cousins and younger aunts. These traditional avenues for sexual initiation of adolescents have been recently replaced by the growing social acceptance of premarital relations.

The culture valued the sexual exploits of male youth and provided an abundance of opportunities, including community celebrations and public dances, which generally encouraged erotic relationships.

The social education of women in traditional Spanish society encouraged them to play their appropriate role in the social order. Women had the responsibility of taking advantage of the continual erotic stimulation and the hyper-value of masculinity that drives young men in order to attract them into the courting game that ends in marriage. Young women were expected to develop strategies that produced maximum enticement and minimal satisfaction, creating for the young male a desire that was never completely in accordance with the social mores. The woman embodied a game of approach-avoidance until just before or within marriage. A young woman's ability to employ her virginity as a bargaining tool makes the impatience and lack of sexual discipline of the male socially productive and profitable. The young male is caught in an extensive web of engagements associated with courtship that resolves itself by fully assimilating him into the institution of the family.

## 3. Knowledge and Education about Sexuality

### A. Government Policies and Programs for Sex Education

The Spanish government has not adopted or implemented any general plan to improve the knowledge and attitudes of Spanish people toward sexuality. Indirectly, one could support sexual education in provisions of the Spanish Constitution, under the educators' "liberty of class" (Article 20.1); children's rights according to the international agreement laws (Article 39); the rights of humans in general (Article 10.2); and the right to understand the full development of personality and the liberty of teaching (Article 27). In the *Official Bulletin of the State* (January 21, March 6, 1981), the government proposed addressing some minimal sexual issues in school, from preschool through secondary school, within the areas of "affectionate and social behavior" and/or the natural sciences.

In explaining Article 27 of the Constitution, *The Organic Law of the Right to Education* (1985) insisted on the freedom of teachers and the autonomy of school centers. This autonomy provides a margin of freedom that permits schools to introduce sexual education. The most ambitious proposal from the educational point of view was created by the Minister of Education in *LOGSE, The General Organic Law of the Educational System*, approved in 1991. This law explicitly defends and reiterates the necessity of sexual education within school at different grade levels.

This law appears positive because it formulates concrete objectives and supports a place in the curricula for education in sexual topics, because it promotes attitudes of gender equality and discourages discrimination between the sexes, and because it opts for an open curriculum that permits schools and professors to include sexual topics within the context of concrete programs. However, the authors also view this law as insufficient, because it does not clearly and systematically spell out the objectives and information contents for the different school levels.

In reality, the law contains only partial proposals. These programs treat sexuality horizontally, across all course content areas, instead of contextually and longitudinally within a concrete area of health or quality of life. Thus, sexual education is only provided in the basic course content areas and in schools with well-coordinated teams of professors who can adequately provide sexual education. However, adequate sexual education is impossible with this approach. If all teachers in the different disciplines are expected to include sexual education in their courses, they can appropriately address these issues only if they, meaning all teachers in the nation, are adequately educated in this area in addition to their main professional area. And this is impossible without massive funding for teacher education.

Although it seems progressive and favors renovation and freedom of teaching, the option of an open curriculum has limitations. Ideological premises, attitudes of fear, and simple lack of time or training prompts numerous educators to "forget" or avoid addressing sexual issues. In practice, sporadic "forgetfulness" is converted into habitual avoidance.

In summary, current Spanish legislation addresses sexual issues, provides some orientations on specific objectives, but does not guarantee that the education will be delivered. In practice, at least for the moment, there are only a few schools that provide systematic sexual education. It is only unique and isolated educators and groups based in innovative pedagogy that deal with this topic in a systematic fashion.

The most representative exception is in the Community of the Canary Islands, where the autonomous government has freed various educators of Harimaguada to form a group of sexuality educators who provide education in classrooms and systematically plan the delivery of sex education.

### B. Informal Sources of Sexual Knowledge

Recent publications on sexuality have been translated into Spanish and are currently available to the general public. There are also numerous publications by Spanish authors. Theater, television, and general communications frequently address the topic of sexuality and sexual issues.

From this point of view, freedom of speech and expression is high. Among the more outstanding examples of informal sexuality education is the state television chain TVE1, which offers a series of 30 programs on sexuality, *We Speak of Sex*, for an adult audience. This series has had a strong social resonance.

The Ministry of Health has carried out a campaign for prevention of unwanted pregnancy geared toward adolescents, stressing the slogan *Pontelo Ponselo*, or "Put it on. Put it on him"—referring to a condom. This campaign has had widespread acceptance. The same Ministry of Health has also published slides and pamphlets on sexuality that are of a reasonably good quality. Therefore, the Spanish society's informal sources of knowledge are equivalent to those of most European countries. But from the formal point of view, education is not widespread, and seems unlikely to become widespread in the foreseeable future.

[*Comment 1997*: Educators and researchers agree that one crucial informal source of knowledge about sexual issues for children is their parents. The authors of this chapter have discussed the importance and enormity of the changes that occurred with regard to social attitudes toward sexuality in Spain after Franco's death.

[While the rapid and radical shift in sexual norms had an impact on many facets of Spanish life, one of the most important was that of parent-child communications. Young people and their parents are suffering from a significant and atypical generation gap triggered by the political changes that occurred in Spain following Franco's death. The world in which the majority of young Spanish people are living today is tremendously different from that in which their parents grew into adults. Even those children who were born the year Franco died were only 18 in 1994. While the world around them promotes a newfound sexual freedom and liberal expression, the families in which they are being raised are based on the values of the ultratraditional model from Franco's dictatorship.

[How then must this affect the ability of parents and children to communicate about sexuality? The traditional value systems and gender-role expectations that governed the consciences of their parents' youth are in direct contrast with present-day powerful social and peer norms that encourage the sexual freedom of their children. The difference between the two sets of norms is clear when one imagines a parent who experienced adolescent dating with a mandatory chaperone or *duenna* confronting an adolescent son or daughter in a social climate in which peers are now likely to lose their virginity before the age of 18. In order for children to benefit from the wisdom and experience of their parents in Spain today, they must not only overcome a generation gap, but a generation crevice that began with the end of the Franco era and the weakening of Catholic-based social controls.

[Young people in Spain today have many choices to make about their sexuality. The next generation will not have it as difficult, because the distance between the social and sexual norms of this new generation of parents and the children they have will be much narrower than the current crevice. (*End of comment by L. Berman and J. Nanin*)]

## 4. Autoerotic Behaviors and Patterns

### A. Children and Adolescents

A national study on masturbation in children and young people found that 76.7% stated that they began masturbating between the ages of 10 to 15 years. Knowledge about masturbation came from conversations and readings (74.8% for males and 57.2% for women).

Studies carried out with 12- to 13-year-old elementary school students in *Education General Basica* (EGB) indicated that 87.74% of the girls and 38.42% of the boys had never masturbated. The numbers lessened when groups of 14- to 17-year-old high school students were studied from *Baccalaureate Unified Polyvalent* (BUP). In this study, 70.51% of the girls and 12.16% of the boys stated that they had never masturbated. All the data seem to indicate that the age of first masturbation differs notably between males and females. Almost three quarters of the boys, 71.4%, began masturbating between the ages of 10 and 12 years, while only 10% of the girls stated they have masturbated at that age. The percentages of adolescents masturbating clearly increases between 15 and 17 years.

The most-consistent masturbation frequency in children is once a month, with 25.7% of adolescents masturbating once a day. At this age, masturbation is commonly accompanied by feelings of blame, more in females (47.3%) than in males (44.3%), while the level of derived satisfaction is greater in males (60.3%) than in females (26.2%).

In university students, 19.1% of the males and 12.6% of the females report frequent masturbation. In a survey of university students, 90.8% of the males and 60.6% of the females reported that they have engaged in masturbatory behavior on some occasion.

### B. Adults

A national survey reported that 54.8% of adult men and 33.0% of adult women reported masturbation on some oc-

casion. In a study of stable couples, it appeared that 50.1% of the men and 23.5% of the women masturbated. Frequent masturbation is greater in men than in women: 7.14% of men masturbated almost daily and only 3.8% of the women masturbated that frequently.

While 100% of men masturbate in the final years of puberty (14 to 19 years) and in early adulthood (20 to 25 years), this percentage begins to diminish starting about age 25. In general, men indicated that the practice of masturbation diminished after having established a stable relationship. On the contrary, the percentage of women who masturbate begins to increase starting at 25 years and is greater during the ages of 30 to 39 years. The majority abandon this practice at about age 50.

The principal factors affecting masturbatory practice are religion and level in school: 67.5% of the nonbelieving subjects reported masturbation, while 24% of Catholics engaged in the behavior. The higher the level of schooling, the greater the rate of practice and frequency of masturbation. Less clear is the association of political orientation as associated with attitudes toward masturbation, although voters with a resolved conservative position tend to have a more-negative attitude on masturbation.

The content of sexual fantasies that accompany masturbation is varied. Among students, images of sexual relations with the opposite sex are predominant (84% of males and 49.0% of females). Fantasies containing homosexual behavior occur in 6.3% of men and in 5.3% of women. The factors or motives that commonly inspire masturbation include: thinking about opposite-sex people (66.4%), erotic stories about the opposite sex (56%), and fantasies about a sexual act and modifications of a sexual relation or pornographic movies (42.3%).

Masturbation may be preceded by feelings of frustration or depression: 15.9% of women and 8.3% of men reported depression or irritation; 8.2% of women and 13.1% of men reported situations of anxiety. The predominant feeling after masturbation is peacefulness (58.2%), while 10.1% experience feelings of blame and remorse. Masturbation continues to have negative connotations, with 12.2% considering it a symptom of sexual immaturity and 45.8% considering it an indication of sexual dissatisfaction. Only 8% considered it an egotistic act; 4.6% considered it sinful.

The masturbatory technique most commonly used is manual stimulation. Among men, 91.7% masturbate with manual stimulation of the penis; among women, 31.7% masturbate by stimulating the clitoris, 17.8% the vagina, and 4.3% the breasts.

## 5. Interpersonal Heterosexual Behaviors

### A/B. Children and Adolescents

*Premarital Sexual Activities and Relationships*

Heterosexual conduct in Spanish children and adolescents has greatly increased in recent years. Current data indicate that more than 54% of the women and 52.7% of the men have already had their first date at 13 years. During the period of adolescence, 55% of the girls and 66% of the boys have maintained affectionate relationships.

Clear differences are observed between boys and girls in sexual behavior. Among EGB (Basic General Education) students, 12 to 13 years, 55% of the males have kissed girls, in contrast to 24% of the girls who have kissed boys. Kisses involving the tongue is practiced less: 15% of the girls and 27% of the boys.

More-pronounced gender differences are reported with breast and genital stimulation. Breast stimulation through clothes was practiced by 14% of the girls and 39% of the boys. The difference in genital stimulation is even greater: 3.5% of girls and 33% of the boys. Data also indicate that males would rather stimulate their partner's genitals than allow themselves to be genitally stimulated; the opposite is true for girls. Genital contact without penetration is reported by 20% of the girls and 31% of the boys. In general, sexual behavior of the Spanish children and adolescents intensifies starting at 15 years in all sexual behaviors analyzed.

Attitudes regarding heterosexual relationships have changed most clearly since 1975, the year in which the *FOESSA Report* recognized the national level of intolerant attitudes among adolescents and young women (*a nivel nacional actitudes intolerantes frecuentmente asentadas entre los adolescentes y mujeres jóvenes*). Current data indicate that 46% of the girls and the 39% of the boys continue to consider virginity important, while 13% and 23%, respectively, report having engaged in coitus on some occasion. The national mean age for first genital intercourse is between 17 and 19 years, but this differs geographically, with the mean age dropping to 15 to 16 in the coastal regions. On the national level, 52% of young males and 37% of young females have maintained sexual relationships before 15 years.

Among those who have not had sexual relationships, the most important motives for maintaining virginity for women have been the fear of pregnancy (25%), the desire to remain virgins (17%), the lack of an opportunity (15%), and religious beliefs (13%). Among men, the most important motive is the lack of opportunity (56%). The data indicate that girls become sexually active within a couple (80%), while the boys engage in intercourse more within the frame of a friendship (48%). Among the motives mentioned for first sexual relations, the boys mention sexual desire (72%) and women mention love (52%). A majority of sexually active youths, 70%, experience some type of worry during sexual relationships. (See comment by L. Berman and J. Nanin at the end of Section 3B, Informal Sources of Sexual Knowledge.)

## C. Adults

### *Premarital Courtship, Dating, and Relationships*

For comments on the never-married, see Section 5A/B, Children and Adolescents, above.

In comparison to other European countries, the occurrence of cohabitation is low. Two percent of Spaniards are involved in a relationship in which time and space is shared but a marriage contract does not exist. On the whole, consensual unions of couples living together form an experimental and symbolic framework that breaks traditional boundaries of the Spanish family structure and forces the creation of different rules for cohabitation and interpersonal relationships.

### *Marriage and the Family*

The age at which adults marry has become clearly delayed in recent years. Various factors, including inflation in the cost of living, especially housing, the increased numbers of women in the work world and their greater sense of independence, the rise in juvenile unemployment and longer periods of education, and cultural indicators not easily quantified in percentages, such as the incidence of European patterns, all help to explain the delay of nuptials.

In 1986, the mean age for men's first marriage was 27.3 years; for women, it was 24.8. The decline in the number of births has been very important; the index of fecundity has decreased from 2.0 in 1970 to 1.4 in 1988. In 1991, 1.3 children were born per woman, well below the replacement level of 2.1.

The composition of the family structure has also suffered changes. The *familia troncal* (with several generations of the same family sharing the same dwelling), which was traditional in the rural environment, shows clear signs of retrogression. In the urban areas, the familiar typology of the nuclear family structure reflects changes including the delay of the age of marriage and an increase in marital breakups.

There has been a considerable increase in the number of women and men "singles," that is, celibates and divorced, who live alone without pair bonding. Reliable data do not exist to support conclusions around the forms of sexual expression and the satisfaction derived from sexuality for single individuals.

Between 1981 when divorce was legalized and 1988, the number of divorces continued to increase, except for slight decreases in 1983 and 1984. The 1986 rate of divorce was five for every 10,000 Spanish citizens.

Extramarital sexual relationships have been socially condemned, but with a distinct difference in treatment of men and women. A kind of tolerance (*pseudotolera-das*) existed for men who engaged in extramarital sex, while unfaithful women were socially ostracized. In traditional Spain, it was not infrequent in families of high economic standing to find a husband who, along with his wife, shared and maintained a separate living space with a *querida* (mistress). On the contrary, it was unthinkable for the wife to have a lover. Spanish culture clearly contains a sexism that favors sexual expression for men but not for women. As the autonomy and independence of the woman increases in Spanish society, inequalities in sexual extramarital relationships have been decreasing. Yet infidelity—a questionable term that needs to be reformed—is still more frequent in men than in women.

### *Incidence of Oral and Anal Sex*

No legal restriction exists for specific practices like fellatio and cunnilingus. Men perform cunnilingus more than women perform fellatio. The practice is recognized as less frequent in older men and women. It seems that fellatio and cunnilingus are more common in sporadic sexual relationships than in established long-term sexual relationships. There are also no legal restrictions on anal intercourse. However, it is exercised less than the above-mentioned practices.

### *Sexuality of the Disabled*

The sexuality of the mentally deficient and of the physically challenged until recently was generally considered marginal and was ignored. At the present time, it is addressed by public institutions. The Functional Unit of Sexual Rehabilitation and Assisted Reproduction at the National Hospital of Paraplegics of Toledo, specializing in spinal cord injuries, is a pioneer center where the sexuality of the physically challenged is central and considered a positive part of life. Private organizations also exist that are devoted to assisting and aiding the physically challenged in attaining open, expressive, and dignified sexual expression without taboos.

## 6. Homoerotic, Homosexual, and Bisexual Behaviors

### A. Male Homosexuality

Male homosexuality was not tolerated during the reign of Franco (1936-1975). Under Franco's *Ley de Peligrosidad Social*, the Law of Social Danger, "homosexuals," including lesbians (although these constitute a separate *terra ignota* camp), were considered a clear social danger. The political doctrine of this era was based on religious philosophy. In fact, national *catolicismo* was the political doctrine. Consequently, all attitudes and behaviors that were not in accordance with Catholic doctrines were not accepted. All kinds of stigmas were attached to homosexuals, including *grandes pecadores* (those who transgress religious principles) and *rojos* ("reds" [i.e., communists], citizens not in tune with the political ideals and, therefore, anti-Franquists). When homosexuals were recognized, it was not uncommon that they became the subjects of abuse, pejorative phrases, and physical attacks.

June 23, 1977, two years after Franco's death, was celebrated as "gay pride" day, an event with clear political connotations and denotations (*connotaciones y denotaciones políticas*). The public demonstration gave public recognition to homosexuality. Homosexuals ceased to be clandestine and began to call themselves, and be recognized as, gays. In 1978, coinciding with an epoch of transition from authoritarian to democratic rules, the Law of Social Danger was repealed. Homosexuality ceased to be legally persecuted. Socially, however, homophobia continues to exist.

More or less solid homosexual support groups soon appeared all over Spain with the clear and decided intention of defending the rights of homosexuals. With different degrees of activism, they have reached out to the public with manifestos, conferences, institutes, publicity, debates, a presence in the media, and other practices that have allowed them to impart knowledge and refuse any type of social discrimination.

The vindication of these groups and movements has customarily centered on gaining social rights of homosexual couples who live together, destruction of political files where homosexuality was an element of a suspicion, fighting against employment discrimination, rejecting the relevance of sexual orientation in cases of child custody, and promoting a sane public discourse that does not believe that heterosexuality is the only normal sexual expression.

There is no one homosexual model. As with heterosexual lifestyles, plural expression includes many different patterns of expression. Next to "effeminate" roles are those who express manifestations of "virility," whose ultimate end is to highlight in exaggerated form the dress, attitudes, and conducts that sustains the image of the "male." As for the places for homosexual encounters, these are typical of that found in other Western countries: train and bus stations, parks, specific streets and squares, discos and bars, saunas, and more.

## B. Lesbianism

Like other organized phenomena, the appearance of lesbianism in Spain is tied to feminism, which exploded in 1975 after the disappearance of Franquismo and the social effervescence (*efervescencia social*) that followed. After the initial push of the gay movement, which was more visible and organized, the first collective group of lesbians appeared in 1981, surging to almost 20 lesbian organizations all over Spain in 1990.

This surge, however, can be misleading. In reality, lesbian individuals and groups have had to fight a society in denial for the very limited time and visibility they have managed to gain in general. They have also great difficulty in creating organizations with enough weight to be heard.

Some lesbians have created their own collective spaces in order to meet and defend their identity and their rights. Some lesbian bars and discos exist in some cities, and magazines sporadically appear in an attempt to create a forum for education and support. As for sexual roles, this question is debated in interested circles, although no concrete posture has been accepted as respecting the values of all the groups and collectives. In this sense, one could say that a model does not exist for those who are living a lesbian lifestyle or are in a same-sex couple, where they are left to create their own pattern dictated by their own circumstances.

This absence of social visibility has its logical consequence in the legal domain.

The period of repression of homosexuality as *conducta de peligrosidad social*, socially dangerous behavior, is now in the past. However, the Spanish legal system has avoided dealing with the topic of the regulation of established gay and lesbian couples. This lack of regulation of the rights generated by living together is creating a significant form of discrimination vis-à-vis married heterosexual couples as well as cohabiting couples. This results in multiple forms of discrimination. For instance, the fear of loss of the custody of children can be traced to the invisibility of the lesbian's right to have a family. Not recognizing marriage or cohabitation creates a negative aftermath involving loss of pensions, inheritance rights, continuity in the lease of housing in case of death of one of the couple, and the exclusion of partners in Social Security. In all these difficulties, there is one exception: *Ley de Reproducción Asistida* [*The Law of Assisted Reproduction*], approved some years ago, "permits" the utilization of these techniques by women with no heterosexual partner. There have already been some cases publicized in the press.

Despite this one legal right, it can be affirmed that there is a legal void when it comes to defining the rights and respective responsibilities of homosexuals that can only be because of the exclusive legal attention to heterosexual relationships.

## 7. Gender Diversity and Transgender Issues

A clear term does not exist in Spanish that is equivalent to "transgenderism" in English. The conversion of gender identity and gender roles is included within the terms transsexuality, homosexuality, and transvestism. The differences that American sexologists pick up between the style of life of the transgenderist, who chronically crosscodes for gender behaviors and roles, and the transvestite, who only circumstantially and episodically dresses like the opposite sex, are nonexistent in Spain. For us, a transvestite is a person who reverses roles, dresses himself in clothing that does not correspond to his sex, regardless of whether this is permanent, chronic, episodic, or entertainment-related. The typical Spanish heterosexual confuses the transvestite with the homosexual, and the homophobic attitudes and responses that occur with regard to homosexuals are thus applicable in a gross mode to the transvestite.

From a political perspective, at the end of the 1970s, the transvestites worked together with homosexuals and contributed to the ascent and recognition of gay groups. Subsequently, their politics are changing to allow an image that is in alliance with the world of entertainment, transformation, and prostitution. The figure of the female impersonator is commercially marketed.

The first legal change of sex, endorsed by the Supreme Tribunal, occurred in 1979. In 1983, a modification of the Spanish Criminal Code decriminalized sex change by surgical intervention. At present, this surgery occurs in Madrid, Barcelona, and Zaragoza. Male-to-female sex change is more frequent than the reverse. However, some confusion, contradiction, and lack of uniformity exists, as evidenced by a variety of criteria and different decisions in the legal system.

Surgically effected change of sex is recognized by changing the birth name in the Civil Register. Sex-change surgery, even when registered, brings certain restrictions. They cannot, for instance, legally marry. Transsexuals are typically portrayed as having an "erratic," "exotic," "ambiguous" character, and by their "gender indetermination" in the media.

In 1987, the transsexuals organized, creating an organization to defend their rights. This association is recognized by the Ministry of the Interior.

## 8. Significant Unconventional Sexual Behaviors

### A. Coercive Sex
*Sexual Abuse of Children and Incest*

Since 1988, matters involving the sexual abuse of children in our country have been handled by the Ministry of Social Matters under the Direction of Legal Protection of the Minor (Dirección de Protección Jurídica del Menor); previously, this was done under the Ministry of Justice. The Royal Ordinance 791/1988 (July 20) created the Centro de Estudios del Menor (Center of Studies of the Minor).

The scientific treatment of this problem makes clear that frequent cases of sexual abuse with children exist, but few are documented. Those cases that become known usually coincide with some other criminal act that has come to the attention of the Center. The Center, in turn, registers the abuse with the police and security bodies of the state for criminal investigation. In the *Boletín Estadístico de Datos Técnicos* (*Statistical Bulletin of Technical Data*) of the Ministry of Social Matters, 1992, some relatives of 16-year-old minors were included with youngsters' antisocial behaviors (such as runaways, drug use, robberies, etc.). These biographies were on many occasions marked by child abuse, including sexual abuses. But, as already stated, documentation of these cases is difficult.

In 1991, 113 cases of "criminal" accusations of sexual abuse or rape were reported. In these and other cases of rape, incest, sexual aggression, or exhibitionism, the age of the victims is not specified in the Ministry of Interior data.

As with criminal reporting, the legal system has given most of its attention to child-abuse cases that involve protection of children, their education, and safe placement within the family environment. The effective criminal code, last reformed in 1983, includes various sections on child sexual abuse.

The legal classification of sexual crimes involves the age of the victim and the level of kinship or authority that exists between those implicated in the crime. At this writing, the initial draft of the Penal Code of 1992 is being debated. The draft is designed to provide treatment that is more in accord with the social reality, and picks up the circumstances that aggravate or attenuate criminal responsibility. Chapter V, Article 22, "of the circumstance of relationship/kinship," recognizes that if the wronged person is the spouse or a person tied to a permanent relationship, he or she can attenuate or aggravate the responsibility, according to the nature of the crime.

In describing "crimes against individual or personal freedom/integrity" (*delitos contra la libertad sexual*), Title VII highlights several levels of crime in terms of the age of the person against whom the crime is committed and the level of kinship, relationship, or superiority exercised in their relationship. When Parliament approves this new Penal Code, the state will be clearly responsible for minors, the helpless, and unprotected, who suffer the exploitation and sexual oppression from parents, family members, teachers, or strangers. Spanish public opinion is very sensitive about the sexual abuse of minors, because more and more publicity is given to such cases in the mass media, sociological studies, and the research of the Centro de Investigaciones Sociológicas (Center of Sociological Studies, or CIS).

The most recent survey on "Attitudes and Opinions of the Spanish Regarding Childhood" (1991) shows that 46% of the responding men and women over age 18 support changing the penal age, presently 16 years, to 18 years. Younger respondents, ages 18 to 25 years, and those who have voted to the political left clearly defend this posture. Over half of those surveyed, 52%, believe that the laws protecting children from parents or adults who exploit, abandon, or prostitute their children should be stricter. Spanish society is increasingly open to measures of support and care for children, including intervention by the public administrations to facilitate adoption and foster-home placement.

*Sexual Harassment (*Acoso Sexual*)*

In our usage, sexual harassment refers to a "behavior of a sexual character, not desired by the person to which it is directed." This includes not only aggression and rape, but also other behaviors, like verbal offenses, expressions, grimaces, unnecessary touching, and so on.

In spite of the many forms sexual harassment can take, central in this definition is the fact that the harassment is deliberate, the perpetrator is conscious of his or her actions and searches for trouble, and the fact that the harassment is imposed on an unwilling person.

While both men and women can be the object of sexual harassment, national and international data indicate that women suffer it most and, in this sense, it is an expression of the patriarchal society rooted in the inequality in gender relationships in both the labor world and in society in general. The first data on sexual harassment in the Spanish workforce came out of research on women from diverse labor sectors in the city of Madrid, carried out with the support of the Department of the Woman of a socialist union: Unión General de Trabajadores de Madrid (General Union of Workers of Madrid or U.G.T.).

In this study, sexual abuse and harassment are described in terms of a continuum, with five levels of intimidation and the negative aftermath in the psychological, physical, labor, and social order. In this research, 84% of the women had suffered some type of sexual harassment from companions as well as superiors through jokes, flattering remarks, and conversations containing sexual content (level 1); 55% had been objects of sexual harassment through nonverbal communication, without physical contact (level 2); 27% had suffered through strong verbal conduct and physical contact with sexual intention (levels 3 and 4); and 4% had suffered violent behavior to the point of coitus (level 5).

Older women are less subject to sexual harassment than younger women, with women ages 26 to 30 most at risk. In addition, women separated from their spouses, divorced women, and widows also suffer harassment with a greater frequency in all five types of harassment. According to this research and the women themselves, the civil status of women—divorced, widowed, or separated—allows the harasser to perceive them as "easy targets," because the male husband is legally invisible or nonexistent.

The strongest correlate for sexual aggression is the degree of vulnerability the woman has in her work position: the more insecure or vulnerable a woman is, the greater are her chances of being sexually harassed. Since harassment increases in relation to the power of males over females in any situation, the patriarchal hierarchy has been recognized as a central problem in the structural conditions of the Spanish workplace.

A sophisticated report by the (Communist) Union Labor Commissions shows that in a high percentage of the reported cases, the victims are women who are seeking employment, are pending contract renewal, or work in a masculine labor atmosphere. It is impossible to foresee a promising future if women continue to be discriminated against and insecure in their employment, and their work conditions remain inferior to those of males.

Until 1989, the legal system had no instruments that would allow reporting and remedying these practices. The 1989 Statute for Workers deals with the personal rights and dignity of workers and civil servants and the protection from verbal or physical offenses of a sexual nature.

Progressive lawyers have proposed expanding the Penal Code to include an article referring to sexual harassment under the heading of "crimes against individual or personal freedom/integrity" (*delitos contra la libertad sexual*). Nevertheless, in the first draft of the Penal Code of 1992, sexual harassment was not included as a distinct and separate crime. Joining forces, feminist and progressive judges have concluded that the current legal system framework is not sufficient to protect people who attempt to report situations of harassment, either within or outside of the workplace.

### Rape

In 1989, an important legislative reform was enacted in Spain as a result of a widespread opinion championed by feminist groups, progressive lawyers, the Institute of the Woman, and diverse sectors of the society. The 1989 Organic Law of the Proceedings of the Penal Code replaced the previous headings of "crimes against decency" (*delitos contra la honestidad*) with "crimes against individual or personal freedom/integrity" (*delitos contra la libertad sexual*). This eliminated from the Penal Code a 19th-century sexist conceptualization of sexuality and provided strong protection for the personal freedom and integrity of women.

Under the heading of sexual crimes are included rape (*violación*), sexual aggression and statutory rape (*estupro*), and abduction (*rapto*). According to this new gender-free code, rape is not limited to a man who sexually violates a woman through carnal access, vaginally, anally, or orally. It is to have carnal access with a person using strength or intimidation, or when the person is unconscious or deprived of mental capacity. Statutory rape involves carnal access with a person between 12 and 18 years of age. Abduction against the will of the person is considered more severe when the person is under the age of 12.

In the new Spanish legislation, one speaks of "people," not just "women," as victims of rape. This breaks the association between rape and a woman's virginity that was implied in the previous laws that dealt only with vaginal penetration.

However, court procedure still requires that the accusation should be made by the victim, or in cases of a minor or handicapped person, by the parent, legal guardian, or representative, or a member of the Fiscal Ministry. Although the victim may withdraw the accusation, the Fiscal Ministry continues with the official prosecution based on the victim's testimony.

In spite of certain advances in the reformed criminal code, diverse parties have pointed out that rape remains one of the less-reported crimes in spite of its graveness and high incidence. One fundamental reason behind this is the deeply embedded societal belief "that blames the victim for the crime committed against her and for the wide repercussions she will have subsequently in life" (*que tienden a acusar a la victima del propio delito que ha sido cometido contra ella y que tan amplias repercusiones tendra' posteriormente en su vida*).

Efforts in the legal system have been made to denounce this idea of victim precipitation, and the fact that stigmatization of women intensifies when the victims know their aggressor, since it is thought that there are other motives for their accusation. This is a particularly serious charge given that data provided by the Asociación de Asistencia a Mujeres Violadas in its 1990 annual report noted that 55% of the victims knew their aggressor. This association was created at the state level in 1986 to provide free legal and psychological services to women, to promote public campaigns in favor of reporting such crimes, and to protect the rights of the victim under the law. However, much remains to be done in order to guarantee the utmost assistance to violated women and improve the legal protection of the victim during all prosecution. Without these changes, rape will continue to be a frequent, but rarely prosecuted crime.

### [Domestic Violence

[*Update 1997*: In the late 1970s, when the dictatorship of Franco was overthrown and democracy returned to Spain, women began taking more jobs outside the home and thereby gained greater economic independence. This development brought inevitable challenges for the traditional *maschismo* values and began a long process of public education about the hidden secret of domestic violence. In 1996, police recorded 16,300 cases of domestic violence and battery. In 1997, 19,000 complaints were registered. The actual incidence, according to the Government's Institute for Women, is more like 200,000 cases.

[This issue came to national attention in late December of 1997 when a separated husband in southern Spain beat his 60-year-old wife of 40 years, threw her from a balcony at her home, doused her with gasoline, and burned her alive. Ms. Orantes had complained repeatedly to the authorities about her husband's violent behavior, and after they separated two years ago, a divorce court ruled that they should have joint custody of their home. She lived upstairs; he occupied the lower level. Then in early December, Ms. Orantes described on a regional television talk show nearly four decades of beatings during her marriage. Following her death, the interview was replayed several times, forcing both government and Church officials to acknowledge the problem and declare solutions would be forthcoming.

[The governing Popular Party and the leading opposition Socialist Party quickly filed separate motions in Parliament for stricter measures against domestic violence. In November, the Government announced that it was studying the creation of a separate division of prosecutors for domestic-violence cases, and the start of a media campaign about the problem. Since the killing of Ms. Orantes, Government ministers, judges, prosecutors, and associations representing divorced or separated Spaniards have spoken out against the violence, without a consensus on how to reduce the problem. The key will be "fighting *machismo* with a new mentality," said Archbishop Elias Yanes, president of the Episcopal Conference, the ruling body of the Roman Catholic Church in Spain. He warned that the Church might order "separation" in dangerous situations of domestic violence. Demonstrations in Madrid and other cities quickly followed, as the Prime Minister's spokesman took the unusual step to read aloud the toll-free number of the government's domestic violence hotline (*The New York Times* 1997). (*End of update by R. T. Francoeur*)]

## B. Prostitution

Prostitution is spread throughout the country in very diverse forms, involving street prostitution, housewives, students, junkies, illegal immigrants, and others. Sex workers also frequent bars, pubs, and clubs of all types, from the more sleazy to the most elegant. Escort services or agencies offer "company" for executives and businessmen. Massage services are also advertised in the press. In fact, all types of sexual services are offered by individuals or by organizations with many "employees" and a wide range of supplies.

Spain has had an abolitionist legislation since 1956 that supports the reformation of the prostitutes, the persecution of the pimps and go-betweens, and the deterrence of the clients. Prostitution is not monitored, *per se*, but the law criminalizes those who get some economical benefit from it.

In practice, sex workers have been harassed when caught in raids and/or when accused of other crimes not directly related to prostitution. The go-betweens, clients, and others, on the other hand, have been and are tolerated and only arrested when there is a scandal or someone is interested in revenge.

Nevertheless, in social debate of the first draft of the Penal Code, prostitution is completely depenalized, except in cases of minors and when coercion exists. If approved, procuring, pimping, and other activities associated with prostitution would no longer be crimes, and all forms of prostitution, including the bordellos, now forbidden, would be permitted.

Prostitution is tolerated because it is considered a necessary evil. That does not necessarily grant any freedom, and the prostitute is supposed to remain in an opaque area in which the activity is not seen or recognized, operating in the world of a hidden economy.

## C. Pornography and Erotica

During Franco's regime, pornography was completely prohibited. In recent years, sexually explicit magazines and films have appeared. After an early and short explosion of pornographic materials, prompted by the common belief that the masses were going to consume it voraciously, the situation soon settled down.

Pornographic magazines are sold at newspaper stands and in sex shops. X-rated films are shown in theaters with erotic publicity provided at the doors to entice customers inside. Sex shops increased in number, often near to areas of prostitution, where they display all types of erotic toys and devices. Some sex shops offer video booths and even live sex shows.

The onslaught of the video industry has seriously affected the market of porno theaters, many of which have closed because consumers prefer to rent a videotape and see it in their home. The many couples who now share this activity has shifted the market from the traditional consumer, the single male. Also, some regular television channels, not cable television, offer erotic movies at certain hours, not too late at night, which has also drawn customers away from the porno theaters.

Pornography no longer provokes major controversies in Spain; its "moderate" consumption passes through channels that are clearly defined and accepted.

## 9. Contraception, Abortion, and Population Planning

### A. Contraception

The data that exist on the use of contraceptives and abortion among Spanish youth is scarce, fragmentary, and rarely reliable. Nevertheless, what little data there are allow one to appreciate the fact that the use of contraceptives is very low, although it has been increasing in the last few years because of the problems of STDs and AIDS.

Current data show a linear increase in the use of contraceptives. Between ages 18 and 19, 10.9% regularly use some kind of contraceptive, 8.3% utilize effective contraceptives, and 2.6% ineffective methods. The percentage of regular contraceptive use increases to 54.3% for ages 25 to 29 years. Among 15-year-olds, 60% maintain or have been sexually active without using any method. In 1977, only 25% had utilized some effective method; in 1985 (the last year for which data are available), this percentage increased to 65.5%.

In 1985, 98.6% of the total number of women between ages 18 and 49 knew of at least one effective method of contraception. This reflects a clear improvement in comparison with 1975 when 10% of married women were not acquainted with any effective method. Today, the most utilized methods by women at risk for pregnancy, according to data of the National Survey of Fecundity are: the pill, 14%; IUD, 4.8%; condoms, 11%; rhythm method, 3.8%; and coitus interruptus, 13%. The best known method is the pill (97.6%) and the least known, the diaphragm (56.7%).

### B. Teenage Unmarried Pregnancies

The annual number of undesired pregnancies among 18- to 19-year-olds is 30,966; for those between ages 20 and 24, 190,839, of which 7.6% occurred in spite of contraceptive use.

In 1985, the last year for which official statistics exist, 29,586 children were born to adolescents under age 20; only 207 girls under age 15 gave birth, 0.04% of total births of that year.

In 1988, 14,124 women under age 24 years had IVE (*interrupción voluntaria de embarazo* [voluntary interruption of pregnancy]), 54.17% of the total number of abortions. What little data there are indicate an increase in minors giving birth, although, since 1985, that frequency seems to have stabilized. The high number of clandestine abortions among youths, because they cannot opt for IVE without the knowledge of their parents, results in unnecessary uterine perforations, hemorrhages, and infections. So, while maternal and neonatal morbidity and mortality may have diminished in Spain in recent years, adolescents are disproportionately represented in these statistics.

### C. Abortion

The law legalizing abortions was proclaimed on July 5, 1985, authorizing three types of abortions: eugenic abortion when the fetus is diagnosed with grave mental and/or physical problems; therapeutic abortion when the pregnancy is a threat to the mother's life or mental health; and ethical abortion in cases of rape or incest. An estimated total of 100,000 IVEs are performed annually in Spain, although the number of legal and recognized abortions is clearly much less. In 1990, 36,095 IVEs were performed and officially recorded in 86 different centers. This figure has been relatively stable for several years.

For a variety of reasons—religious, ethical, professional, and economic—the law legalizing abortion met great resistance in a medical profession that welcomed the right of conscience to refuse to perform abortions in official centers. The resistance is obvious in the data documenting that few legal abortions are practiced in public hospitals. Of these, 4.17% are performed to prevent physical harm to the mother; almost 100% of the abortions performed in private centers are performed for the mental health of the mother. Another pattern is that high-risk IVEs are usually performed in public facilities, while the private centers perform lower-risk IVEs.

At present, the government is studying the possibility of expanding the conditions for legal abortions, adding economic conditions as an acceptable cause for abortion, and allowing first trimester abortions on request. The latter option is advocated by the majority of Family Planning Centers and by progressive women's movements, despite strong legal difficulties.

### D. Population Control Efforts

Longstanding religious and political factors in Spain have hindered any attempt to justify the control of fecundity/fertility. The political changes that started in 1975 and the 1978 democratic constitution are changing the "old rules."

The new constitution partially legalized information about and sale of contraceptives. This same year, modification of the Penal Code enabled the government to create the Centers of Family Planning. At first, these centers were exclusively dependent on the state government. However, as such centers proliferated, more and more of them were funded by municipal governments and by private, nongovernmental associations.

In 1984, the National Plan of Centers of Family Planning was developed and linked with the Ministry of Health to facilitate programs dealing with contraceptive methods, STDs, and general material on sexual education, sterility, and fertility. At present, Spain has about 700 Centers of Family Planning, actively creating an awareness of the importance of fertility control by distributing sexual information and contraceptives.

## 10. Sexually Transmitted Diseases and HIV/AIDS

### A. Sexually Transmitted Diseases

The most reliable estimates on the epidemiology of sexually transmitted disease (STD) in Spain come from the obligatory registrations of the diseases. This registration (*Sistema de Información Sanitaria de las Enfermedades de Declaración Obligada*, or *SISEDO*, the *System of Sanitary Information on the Obligatory Declaration of the Illnesses*) is based on the weekly reports primary-care physicians make on a series of illnesses. However, as in other countries, only three diseases are reported: gonorrhea, syphilis, and HIV infection. Unfortunately, even with this limited requirement, an estimated 50% to 90% of actual cases go unreported. Since 1982, a laboratory in the Service of Bacteriology of the National Center of Viral Microbiology and Sanitary Immunology (CNMVVIS) has been analyzing the existence and specific characteristics of gonorrhea strains.

The number of gonorrhea and syphilis cases declined annually from 1985 to 1990, with 1,685 cases of syphilis and 13,702 of gonorrhea, 4.1 and 33.1 cases per 100,000 inhabitants, respectively, in 1990. The impact of AIDS and safer-sex practices is likely the main factor in this decline. Although a decline in STD cases has also been seen in other European countries, this tendency to decrease is not uniform. In Spain, the data document a decline for only six years, too brief a time to draw any conclusions other than that young people are more at risk, and both men and women are at risk. Among 16- to 25-year-olds, one finds more females than males infected. With syphilis and other STDs transmittable during childbirth, there is an increased risk of congenital STDs and possible serious repercussions for fertility in both sexes.

A few local or regional studies of STDs not reported to SISEDO are available, but nothing on a national level. With no uniform definitions and no standardized diagnostic methods, estimates on these STDs vary from study to study. Nevertheless, it is possible to say that chlamydia is a minor problem in Spain as compared to other European countries. But these figures should be considered with caution.

Spain does not have a significant tradition of clinics for STD treatment; patients usually seek treatment from general practitioners. In other countries, such as Italy, the situation is very similar, and efforts are being made to improve and structure national epidemiologic surveillance services for the cases of "second generation" STDs, e.g., chlamydia, genital herpes, and genital warts, among others.

### B. HIV/AIDS

Clinical criteria for AIDS cases in Spain follow those established by the Centers for Disease Control in the United States. According to the data available from the National AIDS Registry to the end of 1991, Spain's total of 11,555 cases, 288 cases per million inhabitants, puts the nation among the top in number of cases among countries in Europe. The largest increase in cases was produced between 1986 and 1988. At present, the effectiveness of initial preventive campaigns from public organizations seems to have produced a decrease in the number of new cases reported in recent years. The initial exponential pattern seems to be giving way to a linear pattern. Nevertheless, although the tendency for growth has slowed, the number of new cases continues to grow every year (Hart 1995).

In Spain, intravenous drug users (IVDUs) account for two out of three cases, 64%. A much smaller percentage, 16%, are homosexual or bisexual. Heterosexuals account for about 5% and their linear growth pattern is still not alarming. As of mid-1993, 341 cases of pediatric AIDS have been recorded, 80% of these children born to mothers at high risk. This pattern of etiology and distribution contrasts with the predominance of homosexual/bisexual transmission in North America, Western Europe, Australia, and New Zealand, and with the predominantly heterosexual transmission in parts of the Caribbean and sub-Saharan Africa.

Finally, at the end of 1991, 39% or 4,454 of the adolescent and adult HIV-positive persons had died, and 42% of the pediatric AIDS cases. The most frequent causes of death are opportunistic infections, 67%, and frequent bouts of extra-pulmonary tuberculosis, 18%. Several prevention programs from the central government are focusing on how to avoid infection, and indirectly, STDs, through safer-sexual practices, use of condoms, use of clean syringes, and so on (Hart 1995).

[*Update 2002*: UNAIDS Epidemiological Assessment: HIV prevalence and the epidemiological situation have been tested in a variety of unlinked anonymous surveys conducted in the 1990s on the national level and in seven regions and major urban areas. There were: a national 1995-1997 survey of sex workers who were tested in several STD clinics, a 1998 national unlinked anonymous survey of STD patients, a study of female prostitutes receiving STD care in Madrid, a 1988 study of prostitutes in Oviedo, both a national and a regional survey of intravenous drug users in Valencia, a 1987-1998 national survey of blood donors, and a 1995-1997 national survey of STD patients. Sources and summary data for the published results of these surveys are available at UNAIDS (2002).

[The estimated number of adults and children living with HIV/AIDS on January 1, 2002, were:

| | | |
|---|---|---|
| Adults ages 15-49: | 130,000 | (rate: 0.5%) |
| Women ages 15-49: | 26,000 | |
| Children ages 0-15: | 1,300 | |

[An estimated 2,300 adults and children died of AIDS during 2001.

[No estimate is available for the number of Spanish children who had lost one or both parents to AIDS and were under age 15 at the end of 2001. (*End of update by the Editors*)]

## 11. Sexual Dysfunctions, Counseling, and Therapies

### A. Concepts of Sexual Dysfunction

Sexual dysfunctions are mainly associated with problems in heterosexual relationships: mainly erectile dysfunction, early ejaculation, and loss of sexual desire in men, and inhibited sexual arousal and orgasm, painful intercourse, and loss of sexual desire in women. The primary characteristic that allows one to consider these dysfunctions as problems is the suffering and malaise they can cause for the people experiencing them.

In general, men and women with a sexual dysfunction are viewed with a certain condescension and tolerance, as patients or sick persons requiring medical assistance or sexological treatment. On the other hand, many Spanish people continue to view sexual dysfunctions in terms of pathological dysfunctions, such as rape, incest, pedophilia, child sexual abuse, exhibitionism, sadomasochism, fetishism, and so on.

## B. Availability of Diagnosis and Treatment

At the present time, Spain has a considerable and growing number and variety of centers and specialists who diagnose and treat sexual dysfunctions. Treatment can be sought at both public and private facilities, although, in general, private clinics continue to provide the best environment and treatment.

As for the specialists who treat these dysfunctions, they are, in order of importance, psychologists, psychiatrists, and urologists and gynecologists. A reasonable variety of technology and instruments are available for diagnostic use, mainly adapted from those developed in European countries, although Spain is beginning to develop technology, evaluation instruments, and treatment modalities specially adapted to the Spanish people.

As for the training of therapists, a variety of possibilities currently exist. Most training is available in seminars and courses of specialization, normally lasting some months, offered by graduate programs in psychology and medicine. These courses are usually sponsored and staffed by institutes, clinical centers, and sexological associations all over the country, although they tend to be more common in the provincial capitals, like Madrid or Barcelona.

At the university level, master's and doctoral level programs are available at the University of Salamanca and at the Universidad Nacional de Educacio a Distancia (UNED) in Madrid. These programs include instruction on the many aspects of sexological knowledge, as well as training in diagnostic evaluation, counseling, and the treatment of sexual dysfunctions.

## *12. Sex Research and Advanced Professional Education*

### A. Institutes and Programs for Research and Education

Sexuality research in the academic environment has been marginal and received little support. From the political transition of the late 1970s to the present, the academic gaps in this type of research have been paralleled by the proliferation of news of sexual attitudes and specific sexual practices in magazines and the daily press that is fragmentary, sensationalist, and endowed with little rigor.

The first survey of Spanish sexual behavior, *Encuesta Sobre el Sexo Masculino* [*Survey on the Masculine Sex*], was carried out in 1966 with 100 males. In 1972, Serrano Vicens published *La Sexualidad Femenina* [*Feminine Sexuality*], based on his clinical interviews of 1,417 women begun in the 1930s.

There are very few probing interviews, surveys, and empirical studies based on a quantitative methodology. Even surveys and empirical studies based on adolescents and university students are not representative because of the small size of the sample. However, studies have been conducted in Madrid, Valencia, Barcelona, Salamanca, León, Zaragoza, Pamplona, Oviedo, and other cities. Worth noting are the surveys conducted by Jose L. Zárraga (1987) and Malo de Molina, Valls Blanco, and Perez Gomez (1988). At the national level, under the auspices of the Master's in Human

Sexuality Program of the Universidad Nacional de Educacio a Distancia (UNED), a study of the sexuality of older males and females, is now under way.

Despite a glaring need, studies in sexuality are only recently appearing in Spanish universities. Specific courses in sexuality are being considered for inclusion in some programs at some universities. In 1991, a course in the psychology of sexuality was an elective in the undergraduate, Licenciatura (B.A.) program in psychology at the University of Salamanca. A Catedra in evolutionary psychology of sexuality was also introduced at the highest academic level. In the same year, the course in sexology at the School of Social Work of the University of Navarra was eliminated. A course in Sexual Anthropology was an elective in one of the UNED programs.

Various universities are currently planning to incorporate diverse viewpoints on sexuality into their Licenciatura programs. The Department of Psychology at the University of Salamanca offers a doctorate in sexology with an obvious psychological orientation. Since 1990, the Universidad Nacional de Educacio a Distancia (UNED) has offered a two-year multidisciplinary master's degree program with a clear sociocultural inclination leading to the diploma, Master in Human Sexuality. This is the first master's degree program in sexuality granted by a Spanish university. This program is sponsored and exists within the Department of Sociology.

Some private institutions, schools, associations, and clinical centers with diverse orientations outside of the university domain also offer programs in sexology: Espill Institute, Incisex, the Lambda Institute (now named Casa Lambda), and the Speculum Institute.

### B. Sexological Organizations

The offices of the Federacion Espagnola de Sociedades de Sexología are at: c. Valencians 6 Principla, Valencia 46002 Spain. Local or regional Sociedades de Sexología exist in many cities and provinces in Andalucia, Castilla y Leon, Cataluna, Galicia, Madrid, Malaga, Sevilla, and Valencia. Two regional organizations are:

Societat Catalan de Sexologia, Tren de Baix, 51 2o, 2o 08223 Teraessa, Barcelona, Spain. Tel.: 34-3/788-0277.

Sociedad Sexologica de Madrid, C/Barbieri, 3.3 dcha, Madrid 28004 Spain. Tel.: 24-1/522-25-10; Fax: 24-1/532-96-19.

About two dozen bulletins and small magazines dealing with sexual issues are published by local psychiatric and psychological organizations, educators, sexological societies, and feminist, lesbian, and gay-male support groups, in such cities as Barcelona, Bilbao, Madrid, Murcia, Pampolona, Rioja, and Salamanca.

There are well over 50 gay, lesbian, feminist, and HIV-positive/AIDS collectives and support groups in Spain. Among the cities with at least one such group are Albacete, Barcelona, Bilbao y Pamplona, Cordoba y Granada, Madrid, Murcia, Malaga, Palma de Mallorca, Salamanca, Santiago de Compostela, Sevilla, Valencia, and Zaragoza. The number of such groups fluctuates, as these local support groups appear and disappear quite often. Catholic or Christian gay groups are functioning in Barcelona, Madrid, and Malaga.

## *References and Suggested Readings*

*Boletín epidemiológico semanal.* Instituto de Salud Carlos III. Centro Nacional de Epidemiología. Ministerio de Sanidad y Consumo.

*Boletín estadistico de datos tecnicos* (*Statistical bulletin of technical data*). 1992. Madrid: Ministry of Social Matters.

Bosch, S., H. Vanaclocha, S. Guiral, C. Moya, I. Hernandez, & C. Alvarez Dardet. 1988. Programa de mejora de la calidad de la información epidemiológica en enfermedades de transmisión sexual. *Medicina Clínica, 90*:229-232.

Calle, M., C. Gonzalez, & J. Nuñez. 1988. *Discriminación y acoso sexual a la mujer en el trabajo*. Madrid: Largo Caballero.

Carrobles, J. A. 1990. *Biologia y psicofisiologia de la conducta sexual*. Madrid: Fundación Universidad-Empresa.

Carrobles, J. A., & A. Sanz Yaque. 1991. *Terapia sexual*. Madrid: Fundación Universidad-Empresa.

CIA. 2002 (January). *The world factbook 2002*. Washington, DC: Central Intelligence Agency. Available: http://www.cia.gov/cia/publications/factbook/index.html.

Delgado Perez, (with C. Ureña). 1992 (May). *La fecundidad de los adolescentes en el conjunto de España y en la comunidad autónoma de Madrid*. Madrid: Instituto de Demografía, CSIC.

Delgado y Otros, M., & J. A. Nieto, eds. 1991. *La sexualidad en la sociedad contemporanea lecturas antropologicas*. Madrid: Fundación Universidad-Empresa.

del Valle, T., & C. Sanz Rueda. 1991. *Genero y sexualidad*. Madrid: Fundación Universidad-Empresa.

Hart, A. 1995. Risky business? Men who buy heterosexual sex in Spain. In: H. ten Brummelhuis & G. Herdt, ed., *Culture and sexual risk: Anthropological perspectives on AIDS*. Amsterdam: Gordon and Breach Science Publishers.

Lopez Sanchez, F. 1990. *Educación sexual*. Madrid: Fundación Universidad-Empresa.

Malo de Molina, C., J. Mª Valls Blanco, & A. Perez Gomez. 1988. *La conducta sexual de los Españoles*. Madrid: Ediciónes B.

Marques, J. V., & R. Osborne. 1991. *Sexualidad y sexismo*. Madrid: Fundación Universidad-Empresa.

Moreno Jimenez, B. 1990. *La sexualidad humana: Estudio y perspectiva historica*. Madrid: Fundación Universidad-Empresa.

*The New York Times*. 1997 (December 26). Death of a wife in Spain brings outcry on domestic violence. *The New York Times* (International), p. A5.

Nieto, J. A. 1990. *Cultura y sociedad en las practicas sexuales*. Madrid: Fundación Universidad-Empresa.

Sanches, F. L. 1990. *Educación sexual*. Madrid: Fundación Universidad-Empresa.

Segura Benedicto, A., I. H. Aguado, & C. Alvarez-Dardet Diaz. 1991. *Epidemiologia y prevención de las enfermedades de transmisión sexual*. Madrid: Fundación Universidad-Empresa.

UNAIDS. 2002. *Epidemiological fact sheets by country*. Geneva, Switzerland: Joint United Nations Programme on HIV/AIDS (UNAIDS/WHO). Available: http://www.unaids.org/hivaidsinfo/statistics/fact_sheets/index_en.htm.

Usandizaga, J. A. 1990. *Bases anatomicas y fisiologicas de la sexualidad y de la reproducción humanas*. Madrid: Fundación Universidad-Empresa.

Zarraga. J. L. 1987. *La conducta sexual de los jóvenes Españoles*. Instituto de la Juventud.

# Sri Lanka
## (The Democratic Socialist Republic of Sri Lanka)

Victor C. de Munck, Ph.D.*
*Comments by Patricia Weerakoon, Ph.D.*

## Contents

## Demographics and a Brief Historical Perspective

ROBERT T. FRANCOEUR

### A. Demographics

Sri Lanka, formerly known as Ceylon, is a teardrop-shaped island about 18 miles (29 km) southeast of India in the Indian Ocean, between five and ten degrees north of the equator. It has a total area of 25,332 square miles (65,610 km²). Roughly the size of the state of West Virginia, Sri Lanka is 268 miles (432 km) along the north-south axis and 169 miles (272 km) at the island's widest point. The climate varies from a low mean temperature of about 60° F (16° C) in Nuwara Eliya, located in the central highlands, to a high of about 85° F (29° C) in Trincomalee on the eastern seaboard. Seasons are determined by the monsoon cycles rather than by temperature. The western portion of the island is wet and humid whereas the north and southeastern portions of the island are arid to semiarid. The northwest and southeast coasts receive 23.5 to 47 inches (60 to 120 cm) of rainfall per year, most of this coming during the winter monsoon between October and January. The southwest receives an average rainfall of 98.5 inches (250 cm), which is distributed throughout the year.

In July 2002, Sri Lanka had an estimated population of 19.58 million. (All data are from *The World Factbook 2002* (CIA 2002) unless otherwise stated.)

**Age Distribution and Sex Ratios**: *0-14 years*: 25.6% with 1.05 male(s) per female (sex ratio); *15-64 years*: 67.7% with 0.95 male(s) per female; *65 years and over*: 6.7% with 0.91 male(s) per female; *Total population sex ratio*: 0.97 male(s) to 1 female

**Life Expectancy at Birth**: *Total Population*: 72.35 years; *male*: 69.83 years; *female*: 75 years. Sri Lanka has an

*Communications: Victor C. de Munck, Ph.D., Department of Anthropology, State University of New York–New Paltz, New Paltz, New York, USA 12561; victor@bestweb.net. Updates: Patricia Weerakoon, Ph.D., Department of Biomedical Sciences, Faculty of Health Sciences, University of Sydney, P.O. Box 170, Lidcombe NSW 2141 Australia; P.Weerakoon@fhs.usyd.edu.au.*

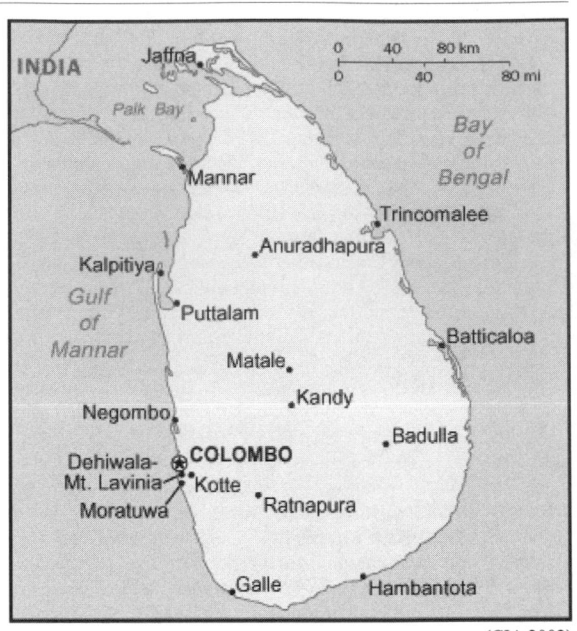

(CIA 2002)

extensive infrastructure of free state-run health services that support both traditional Aryuvedic and modern Western medical systems. There are more than 12,000 Aryuvedic doctors employed at health clinics throughout the country. In addition, there are approximately 500 hospitals, 4,000 doctors, and 10,000 nurses trained in Western medicine. In terms of medical care, literacy, and life expectancy, the quality of life in Sri Lanka is near that of a First World country even though it is a developing nation. The HDI (Human Development Index) aggregates measures of health, education, and standard-of-living indicators into a composite index. Comparatively, the United States has an HDI rank of .929, India a rank of .563, and Sri Lanka an HDI of .737, the highest in south Asia.

**Urban/Rural Distribution**: 22% to 77%

**Ethnic Distribution**: Sinhalese: 74%; Tamil: 18%; Moor: 7%; Burgher, Malay, and Vedda: 1%

**Religious Distribution**: Buddhist: 70%; Hindu: 15%; Christian: 8%; Muslim: 7% (1999 estimate)

**Birth Rate**: 16.36 births per 1,000 population

**Death Rate**: 6.45 per 1,000 population

**Infant Mortality Rate**: 15.65 deaths per 1,000 live births

**Net Migration Rate**: –1.39 migrant(s) per 1,000 population

**Total Fertility Rate**: 1.93 children born per woman

**Population Growth Rate**: 0.85%

**HIV/AIDS** (1999 est.): *Adult prevalence*: 0.07%; *Persons living with HIV/AIDS*: 7,500; *Deaths*: 490. (For additional details from www.UNAIDS.org, see end of Section 10B.)

**Literacy Rate** (*defined as those age 15 and over who can read and write*): 90.2% (*male*: 93.4%, *female*: 87.2%) (1995 est.). Education is free and compulsory from age 5 to 12. However, school dropout rates remain a problem and the median education level is estimated at five to nine years, with 40% of school-age children dropping out within nine years.

**Per Capita Gross Domestic Product** (*purchasing power parity*): $3,250 (2001 est.); *Inflation*: 14.2% (2001 est.); *Unemployment*: 7.7% (2001 est.); *Living below the poverty line*: 22% (1997 est.)

### B. A Brief Historical Perspective

The first literary reference to Sri Lanka is found in the Indian epic, the *Ramayana* written about 500 B.C.E. The epic tells the story of the Indian Prince Ram's 14-year exile from his homeland, Ayodhya. Accompanied by his wife, Sita, and his brother, Lakshman, the trio wandered through the north Indian forest. Ravenna, the demon king of Lanka, saw Sita and wanted her for his bride. Through magical treachery he abducted her and took her to the Island of Lanka. While she was there, she refused all his advances and was kept a prisoner. With the aid of Hanuman, the monkey-god, Ram went to do battle with Ravenna and eventually slew him. This epic has provided a mythohistorical basis for constructing a historiography of mutual enmity between Sri Lankan Tamils (of Indian origin) and the Sinhalese.

Unlike India, which has no tradition of historical writing, the Buddhist monks of Sri Lanka kept historical chronicles, the most famous of which is the *Mahavamsa* (the great dynasty or genealogy), written in the 6th century C.E. The *Mahavamsa* is a compilation of historical chapters, many of which center around the adventures of Vijaya, a Bengali prince who sailed to Sri Lanka in the 5th century B.C.E. and married the queen of the Vedas, Kuveni. Vijaya is acknowledged to be the primogeniture of the Sinhalese people.

Many of the other chapters in the *Mahavamsa* document the many Sinhalese Buddhist kings who rose up against Tamil conquerors. Aside from Vijaya, the central heroic figure in the *Mahavamsa* is King Duttugemunu, who, around 145 B.C.E., waged a 15-year war against the South Indian Tamil King Elara. Duttugemunu finally defeated Elara and is consequently considered a hero by the Sinhalese. The *Culavamsa* (or lesser dynasty) is a continuation of the *Mahavamsa*, and traces the history of Sri Lanka through the 18th century.

Both the *Mahavamsa* and *Culavamsa* were written by Buddhist monks whose main objective was to recount the glories of Buddhist kings who fought against Hindu kings. Contemporary popular accounts of the current civil war in Sri Lanka frequently cite the battle between the Tamil invader, Elara, and Duttugemunu, who is depicted as the defender of Buddhism and the freedom of the Sinhalese people, as the basis for the civil war that has been ongoing since 1982. But the actual history of Sri Lanka does not support this contention. In fact, according to Tambiah (1986), most of Sri Lankan history is marked with cordial and extensive trading relations between Tamils and Sinhalese, with only rare outbursts of interethnic violence. In fact, the last Sri Lankan king ruled from the highland city of Kandy and was of Tamil descent. In 1815, he signed a peace treaty with the British colonial government and abdicated his throne.

Sri Lanka does have a caste system, but unlike India, it is not rooted in religious scriptures. Though caste did, and to some extend still does, serve as a basis of Sri Lankan local and national-level social organization, it has always been identified with material socioeconomic differences rather than the purity-pollution ideology that is the key ideological component of the Indian caste system. Further, there are only about 20 castes in Sri Lanka and the dominant caste is the Goyigamas, a farmer caste. Goyigamas constitute about 50% of the Sinhalese population. Unlike India, which has a Brahmin caste and uncounted other castes and subcastes, there is no Brahmin population in Sri Lanka and thus, there is no Brahmanical hegemony over the 20-some caste systems in Sri Lanka.

In 1505, the Portuguese landed on the west coast of Sri Lanka. The Portuguese considered Sri Lanka an important site from which to maintain their dominance over Indian Ocean trade. At the onset of the Portuguese period, there were three independent kingdoms in Sri Lanka, a Tamil kingdom in the northern peninsula of Jaffna, a Sinhalese kingdom on the west coast in Kotte (near Colombo), and an-

other Sinhalese kingdom in Kandy in the central highlands. The Kandy and Kotte kingdoms had been at war, and the Portuguese allied themselves with the weak king of Kotte, building a fort in Colombo and eventually annexing the Kotte kingdom.

The Dutch became interested in wresting control of the western seaboard from the Portuguese, and allied themselves with the Kandyan king. After a long campaign, the combined Kandyan and Dutch forces finally defeated the Portuguese in 1656. The Dutch inflated the cost of their war efforts and presented the Kandyan king a bill that he could not repay. Through this strategy, they gained control over the Kotte and, eventually, Jaffna. The main mark that the Dutch left on Sri Lankan society is the codification of a legal system that included both indigenous and Dutch laws.

The Kandyan kings searched for allies to oust the Dutch from Sri Lanka and approached the British in the late 1700s. However, the British and Kandyans argued over the terms of their alliance, and the British managed to expel the Dutch relatively quickly with little assistance from the Kandyans. In 1815, with the aid of Sinhalese rebels, the British conquered Kandy and gained sovereignty over the entire island.

Sri Lanka was seen as a minor outpost in the British Empire until the British began to plant coffee and other plantation crops in the mid 1830s. As these crops became extremely profitable, Indian Tamils were recruited as cheap labor to work the coffee, and later, tea, coconut, and rubber plantations. After a leaf blight that decimated the coffee plant, tea became the dominant export crop. Tea plantations dominated the hillsides of Sri Lanka and required a permanent labor force, mostly of Indian Tamils. By 1911, there were 500,000 Indian Tamils (12% of the population) working in Sri Lanka.

On February 4, 1948, Sri Lanka became an independent nation, approximately six months after India, and largely as a residual result of India's fight for independence. The Sri Lankan government was organized as a Westminster-style parliamentary democracy. In 1956, partially because of a rise in jingoism and increasing ethnic strife, politicians from all parties began to "play the ethnic card." Sinhala was made the official and national language; Tamil was made an official but not the national language. The Sinhalese-controlled government began to allocate more and more development funds to Sinhalese areas and less to the Tamil north and east. The government supported colonization schemes of underdeveloped areas, primarily located in Tamil and Muslim states in the northeast. Thousands of poor Sinhalese families were recruited to apply for permits to settle in these newly colonized areas. Tamils and Muslims saw this as a government-sponsored "religious-ethnic invasion" designed to make them minorities in their own states.

Acceptance to a university was based on a merit system that was eventually replaced by a quota system. The merit system had benefited the Tamils, who made up a disproportionate number of the professional class. The quota system benefited the Sinhalese majority, who felt that the Tamils had been given an undue educational advantage by the divide-and-rule policies of the British.

The period of the 1950s to the 1980s was marked by a feeling of increasing disenfranchisement by the large Tamil minority and increasing acrimony between the two groups. In the 1970s, Tamils began to form into political factions that called for an independent Tamil state (called Eelam) in the north and east of the island. Initially, there were numerous subgroups, but by the early 1990s, only one viable group was left, the LTTE (the Liberation Tigers of Tamil Eelam), referred to in the media as the "Tigers." The LTTE was founded in 1972 by its current leader, Velupillai Prabhakaran.

In 1983, riots broke out throughout the country, but the most severe were in Colombo, where the Pettah district (the market center), controlled mostly by Tamils and Muslims, was looted and many buildings razed. After the outbreak of hostilities, several hundred thousand Tamil civilians fled the island. As of mid-1999, approximately 66,000 were housed in 133 refugee camps in south India, another 40,000 lived outside the Indian camps, and more than 200,000 Tamils had sought refuge in the West. Many fled to Germany and Canada, where they were granted political refugee status. These refugees are now the primary source of financial support for the LTTE. Besides the hundreds of dead from the rioting and the destruction of property, perhaps the biggest blow to the collective psyche of Tamils was the bombing and destruction of the Jaffna library, which housed extensive collections on Tamil culture. Tamils considered this intentional "culturocide" conducted by the Sinhalese government to be a deliberate attempt to expel Tamil culture and history from Sri Lanka.

As of 2001, the ongoing civil war had left an estimated 80,000 dead. Both sides have committed terrible atrocities against civilian populations. The LTTE has recruited young boys and girls, and Tamil "Tigers" wear a necklace with a cyanide pill, attached to it like an amulet, to swallow if they are ever captured by the enemy. The war continues despite the fact that the majority of the population on both sides seems to want peace. The LTTE demands an independent state in the northeastern portion of the country and the government, while willing to discuss federation or regional autonomy, utterly rejects the idea of dividing the island into two independent states. Most Tamils, particularly those living in the north and northeast, doubt that they can ever be incorporated into the nation-state of Sri Lanka as anything more than second-class citizens.

## 1. Basic Sexological Premises

### A. Character of Gender Roles

All researchers agree that Sri Lanka is a patriarchal country, however, the degree of patriarchy is in dispute. Many suggest that Sri Lanka is not nearly as patriarchal as other countries in South Asia; Anju Malhotra and Amy Ong Tsui write that, "in contrast to much of the rest of South Asia, Sri Lanka has a cultural heritage of relative gender equality in terms of later marriages, bilateral descent, daughter's value in the parental home, continued kin support following marriage and widespread access to education for women" (1999, 221). Since 1900 and probably earlier, Sri Lankans have practiced "late marriages" relative to India (de Silva, Stiles, & Gibbons 1993). In 1999, the mean marriage age for a Sri Lankan woman was 24.5 years of age and for a man it was 27.9 years of age.

Both Sri Lankans and researchers attribute the relative late age of marriage to difficulties in obtaining an adequate dowry for the bride. Brothers are expected to help contribute to the dowry fund and defer their marriages until all their sisters are married. Sisters are also expected to marry in order of their age. Once the family has accrued sufficient dowry funds for the first daughter, they must continue working to accrue a similar dowry for the next daughter. Dowry funds ideally consist of a house, rice paddy land, cash, jewelry, furniture, and other moveable goods. However, while the accumulation of a dowry fund is a family effort and may be a major factor in the late age of marriage, it does not explain why Sri Lankans should marry later than members of other South Asian nations where a dowry is also a prerequisite for most marriages.

What is unique to Sinhalese dowry practices is that they serve as a form of "pre-death" inheritance in which the dowry is legally transferred to the bride rather than to the groom's family (Tambiah 1973). McGilvray (1988) and de Munck (1996) also note that the dowry is legally transferred to the bride in Sri Lankan Tamil and Muslim communities, whereas in most of South Asia the dowry is transferred to the groom's family. In Sri Lanka, the bride retains legal control over the dowry but, on marriage, the groom acquires "proprietary" rights to the dowry funds. Malhotra and Tsui (1999) are correct in noting that relative to the rest of South Asia, there is greater gender equality in Sri Lanka, but part of that has to do with the wife's control over the dowry fund rather than the late marriages.

Nevertheless, nearly all researchers on gender roles in Sri Lanka have noted that patriarchal values pervade gender roles and relations in Sri Lanka. In a survey of 101 Sri Lankan Muslims and Sinhalese, all except one respondent said that it was "better to be born a man than a woman" (de Munck, n.d.). The main reason cited for this was that women are largely confined to the domestic compound while men control public spaces and places. Women often say that they are confined to the home like "frogs in a well." This phrase is common throughout South Asia as is evident by Patricia Jeffrey's (1979) book on gender in India, *Frogs in a Well*.

The ideal woman for Buddhists, Hindus, and Muslims is one who is obedient, modest, and hard working. She is seen predominantly in her role as mother rather than wife. In Sri Lanka, females, much more so than males, are evaluated according to a good-bad moral dichotomy. Any insinuation that a female has conducted herself immorally is enough to potentially ostracize her from the community and even her family (de Munck 1992; Hewammane & Brow 1999; Lynch 1999). Immoral behavior consists of suspicions of sexual immorality, flirting, cursing, disobedient behavior, drinking or smoking, and walking or being in places or areas where women should not be. Sri Lankans broadly conceive of national morality in terms of a rural-urban dichotomy, with traditional values (considered "good") upheld in the villages, and modern values, such as lack of sexual modesty by women (considered "bad"), associated with urban life.

The ideal man is seen in his roles as the breadwinner for his family and as involved in civic activities. Traditionally, a man was expected to make his living through farming and industry. After independence, work in the Sri Lankan civil service was (and remains) highly valued. In contemporary urban Sri Lanka, the ideal man should be educated and make his livelihood in a well-paid white-collar profession. An adult male should also strive to build a reputation as a civic leader through charitable public-service work. A man's reputation is gained through public works and, most importantly, through the collective reputation of his core female relatives (i.e., mother, wife, sister, and daughter). In this context, part of a man's moral duty (*dhamma*) is to serve as the moral guardian of his female relatives and to punish them for real or alleged violations. Economically, the ideal man should provide for his nuclear family and, if need be, his parents, brothers, and sisters. The ideal man provisions his family and also controls their behavior, particularly that of the family women.

### B. Sociolegal Status of Males and Females

The law treats males and females equally except that women are usually granted custody of the children in the case of divorce. Divorce is very uncommon in Sri Lanka, with an annual average rate of 0.25% (Seager & Olson 1986). Virginity at the time of marriage is extremely important for a woman, but not for a man. Traditionally, the wedding sheet was displayed to the public the morning after, but this practice has been discontinued except in very traditional homes or rural areas. Nonetheless, the bride is expected to be a virgin and if it is known that she is not, it is next to impossible for her to marry into a family of the same status as her own.

Sri Lanka has made great strides in erasing the educational gap between men and women. Among the elite, the education of women has been seen as a means to obtain a groom from a good family, and after marriage, these highly educated women often do not pursue a career.

This is changing, however, and although the younger and elder generations retain the same moral worldview, the major difference between mothers and daughters, as noted by Malhotra and Tsui, is that mothers see a career for a female as something that is determined by the economic needs of the family, whereas daughters view a career as a personal choice. In their sample, 83% of all daughters thought that a woman should continue to work after marriage and 52% thought that they should continue even after having children (1999, 237). The increase in females going on to the university has been dramatic, rising from 42% of the student population in 1989 to 52% in 1999. It should be noted, however, that only an estimated 1% of Sri Lankans have access to the university and that most women work in low-status, low-paying jobs as housemaids and day laborers, and in the plantation and agricultural sectors.

A growing number of women find employment in the garment factories in the Free Trade Zones. Many obtain employment as servants and maids in the Middle East, sending money back to their natal homes. These jobs are generally reserved for young unmarried women, whose sexual-moral reputations are tarnished because they are not under the surveillance and control of male relatives. Thus, when they return after one to five years of work, they are often unable to find a suitable marriage prospect (de Soysa 2001). It has been suggested that mechanization of agricultural work has forced unmarried women in particular to look for new forms of work. The female rate of unemployment is 22%, twice that of males.

[*Comment 2002*: Another important area where women's rights are only recently being addressed is the plantation sector. The plantation women collectively number about a million residents who live and work on estates. Most of these are descendents of Indian laborers brought in by the British.

[Writing on the issue of reproductive and sexual health in the plantation sector of Sri Lanka, Morrell (2002) comments on the high incidence of incest, teenage pregnancy, and promiscuity in the estate sector. Further, a recent newspaper article reports that 230,000 estate-sector children are employed as domestic aides (Farook 2002).

[Morrell (2002) has suggested that a concerted effort is needed to understand why moral standards have disintegrated, and to then set in motion a system of changes that would arrest this predicament of decay. He continues that, fortunately for the plantation families, Dr. Indira Hettiarachchi, Director of Health and Women's Programs of the Plantation Housing and Social Welfare Trust, has been doing just that and much more. This process is supported by the estate workers union, the Ceylon Workers Congress (CWC).

[This moral dilemma involves improving maternal and child health services within the environment of plantation privatization, which began in 1976. Morrell (2002), quoting Dr. N. Vidiyasagara's article in *The Journal of the College of Community Physicians of Sri Lanka* (Millennium Supplement 2001), notes that from 1972 to 1975, infant mortality in the estate sector was 100 per 1,000 births. By the year 2000, this had been successfully reduced to 15 per 1,000 births. Morrell attributes much of this to the activi-

ties of UNICEF, and grants-in-aid programs from countries such as the Netherlands and Norway. (*End of comment by P. Weerakoon*)]

## C. General Concepts of Sexuality and Love

Sexuality is considered a natural part of life. In a survey of 101 Sri Lankan males and females, 93% thought that women have a stronger libido or sexual drive than do men (de Munck, n.d.). Women's sexuality is considered dangerous and, for this reason, young women are not usually permitted to go out in public alone. They are typically accompanied by their mother or some elder, responsible female chaperone. Any occasion where a female is actually or suspected to be alone with a male is generally interpreted to be about sex.

Sri Lankan sexual foreplay is not very elaborate and does not involve kissing, which is considered unhygienic and disgusting. The missionary position is the most common for sexual intercourse, though it is also common for males to mount the female from the rear. The female-superior position is unusual except in the most Westernized families. Similarly, anal and oral sex are atypical and practiced mostly by very Westernized Sri Lankans. During sexual intercourse, a woman is expected to be the passive recipient and the man active. The duration of sex is not usually prolonged. Sri Lankans in general have a very Victorian attitude toward sex. Husbands and wives are not expected to engage in sexual intercourse when they are past 40 or 50 years old.

Traditionally, marriages were arranged and the preferred marriage partner was a cross-cousin (either the offspring of the mother's brother or the father's sister). Distant relatives of a marriageable age are also glossed as cross-cousins. Horoscopes of the prospective bride and bridegroom are compared to determine if they are psychologically compatible. The most important issue in arranged marriages is the negotiation over the dowry. The two families meet three or more times, often with village or religious leaders as mediators, to consider the dowry. The three key topics of these negotiations are, first, the determination of the respective status of each family; second, assertions about the virtues of the prospective groom and bride by their families; and third, the relative market value of the groom. The market value is determined by what the dowry rate is for prospective grooms from families of that particular socioeconomic status. If the groom has exceptional promise or character, the dowry is negotiated toward the upper limit of other members of that status niche. If the prospective bride has a good education and/or is known to be virtuous, modest, and obedient, then her family will negotiate a dowry for their benefit toward the lower limit. Both sides must first agree on the respective statuses of their families and these statuses must be perceived as being more or less equal. The prospective bride and groom both have "veto power" over their parents' selection of a mate. However, they must be circumspect in exercising this power and typically do so only if they find their parents' choice of a mate very disagreeable.

Elopement is also a common way for young adults to circumvent their parents' choice of mates, and elopement is a common and often-accepted practice in rural areas. Sorensen (1993) has estimated that approximately 50% of the marriages in the two communities she studied were a consequence of elopement. The girl's parents will often help with the elopement. The couple will go to another community to marry, usually returning to their original community after a "cooling off" period of a month or two and then setting up residence with or near to the supportive parents. The prospective groom's family typically is incensed over elopement marriages, as they have lost all leverage to obtain an equitable dowry. The bride's family will usually provide a small dowry so as not to tarnish their reputation. Very poor families, on occasion, encourage their attractive daughters to surreptitiously flirt with a boy from a well-to-do family. If a boy falls in love with a girl, he may insist that his parents arrange a marriage between them or threaten to elope or even commit suicide (de Munck 1996). All of these possible non-normative strategies eventuate in the absence of a dowry or a drastic reduction in its value.

[*Comment 2002*: Newspaper advertisements have long been a source of spouse selection in Sri Lanka. Traditionally, marriages were viewed as a contract between two families, rather than two individuals, and usually involved a third party called the "matchmaker" or "marriage broker." The role of this person was to find a suitable son-in-law or daughter-in-law for the parents. The selection was based on existing cultural norms, such as caste, religion, family background, wealth, beauty, character, and, specifically, the horoscope.

[Dissanayake (1982) writes of the role of the newspaper "marriage columns" as strengthening and legitimizing the traditional value systems in spouse selection. This is apparent when the advertisements are compared over the past decade since 1990. It can be seen that the main differences lie in the increased educational qualification of the females and the fact that many of the advertisements are for persons already residing outside of Sri Lanka or hoping to do so in the future. Below are some examples of advertisements from 1993 and 2002. Some of these would be extremely puzzling to a Westerner unaware of the crucial role of family, caste, and social structure, but the advertisements do reflect the blend of modernization and the importance of family structure. It also appears that the "marriage broker" is being replaced by "email."

• [From the *Sunday Observer*, May 1993:

*Looking for a bridegroom*: "Colombo-based Govi [*caste*] Buddhist parents of good social standing seek educated professional executive or businessman preferably non smoker, teetotaler [*does not take alcohol*] between 26-29 years, 5' 10" or taller; for their only daughter, 24 years, 5' 3" very attractive, well mannered. Dowry available. Send all details with horoscope."

*Looking for a bride*: "Catholic Karawa parents seek educated, simple, pretty girl below 28 years for son, senior mercantile executive, earning over Rs 30,000 monthly. Kuja in 7 [*horoscope*]. Write all details with horoscope."

• [From the *Sunday Observer*, August 2002:

*Looking for a bridegroom*: "Influential Sri Lankan parents Canadian Permanent Residents, mother Govi Buddhist, father Hindu Vellala [*caste*], seek for their 27 yr old eldest daughter 5' 3", mild mannered, gentle, well brought up with Sri Lankan cultural values, studied up to O/L in a leading Colombo Convent, presently reading for an Administration Degree in a Canadian University and employed in Canada, a suitable qualified partner with the same qualifications residing especially in U.S.A. or Canada graduated in Medicine, Law, Research Sciences or Allied Fields. Apply with full particulars and horoscope contact Email [*omitted*]."

*Looking for a bride*: "Well connected Australia based Sinhala / Buddhist family of very substantial means seek for their professionally qualified son, tall, handsome, 29 years, a suitable bride from similar background. Apply with all details and horoscope. Email [*omitted*]." (*End of comment by P. Weerakoon*)]

## 2. Religious, Ethnic, and Gender Factors Affecting Sexuality

### A. Source and Character of Religious Values

As a religiously pluralistic country, Sri Lankans do not have a single collective religious source or character. Buddhist and Hindu religious values center on the concepts of *dhamma* and *karma*. *Dhamma* refers to adhering to the teachings of the Buddha as they guide you to behave compassionately and properly in your everyday life; *karma* is a theory of causation that refers to how the transmigration of one's soul through a cycle of birth, death, and rebirth affects one's present-day situation. Life is thought to consist of suffering, which is based both on bad actions (*pau*) and false attachments (*maya*) to people, status, and the things that comprise this world. Through following the teachings of the Buddha, one can acquire good karma (*punya karma*) that not only minimizes suffering, but can even make life pleasurable. The following saying from the *Dhammapada*, the sayings and sermons of the Buddha, shows how good actions can lead to a good life: "If a man does what is good, let him do it again and again. Let him find pleasure therein. Blissful is the accumulation of good." (Cited in Holt 1998, 190).

"Doing good" for Sri Lankan Buddhists is guided by five precepts: 1. abstaining from destroying life; 2. abstinence from taking what is not yours—which includes not neglecting one's social responsibilities, as well as theft; 3. abstinence from fornication—which is taken to refer to any sexual misconduct; 4. abstinence from speaking falsely—which includes gossip and "ill-mannered utterances"; and 5. abstinence from intoxicating liquors, which are "the cause of sloth" (Obeyesekere 1968, 27).

Hindus and Buddhists share the same overall worldview. But there are some differences, particularly in the practice of their respective religious specialists. In Hinduism, celibacy for *swamis* or *yogis* is not absolute as it is for Buddhist *bhikkus* monks. In Hinduism, eroticism and sexual control are inextricably linked, so that control heightens eroticism, as is evident in the *Kama Sutra* and also in the images and stories of Krishna and Siva. (O'Flaherty 1973). Buddhist mythology, on the other hand, is devoid of sexual imagery. The Buddhist monk, as his Catholic counterpart, is celibate and sexless. The symbolic neutering of the Buddhist monk is signified by having his hair shorn at the time of his initiation and keeping it shorn thereafter (Obeyesekere 1981).

The Muslim worldview is very different. The Koran offers a view of heaven as a sensual and hedonistic paradise. This is evident in the following passage taken from the Koran: "He will regard them with robes of silk and the delights of paradise. Reclining upon soft couches where trees will spread their share around them, and fruits will hang in clusters over them. They shall be served with silver dishes, and beakers as large as goblets. . . . They shall dwell with bashful virgins whom neither men nor *jinn* [genie] will have touched before . . . virgins as fair as coral and rubies" (Koran 1956, 18-20, Sura 37, 40-45).

Sri Lankan Muslims typically conceive of heaven as a libidinous world devoid of cultural controls: sex, food, drink, and comforts are there for the asking. The Koranic heaven is one created for men. It is unclear as to the position of women in heaven, as only *Hourlis*, the "bashful virgins," are mentioned.

### B. Source and Character of Ethnic Values

Sri Lanka is an ethnically heterogeneous country. The dominant ethnic group is the Sinhalese, who comprise 74% of the population. The second largest ethnic group is the Tamils, who comprise 18% of the population. There are two important subdivisions among the Tamils. The majority of Tamils, known as Ceylon Tamils, are concentrated in Jaffna, the northernmost province, along the eastern seaboard, and in the capital of Colombo. Ceylon Tamils have been in Sri Lanka possibly as long as, or longer than, the Sinhalese, having migrated across the Palik Straits, an 18.6-mile (30-km) stretch of ocean that separates Sri Lanka from the tip of India. The second group of Tamils, known as Indian Tamils, were brought to Sri Lanka in the late 19th and early 20th century as plantation laborers and to mostly work on the tea plantations in the central highlands.

Sri Lankan Muslims or Moors, constitute the third major ethnic group and comprise 7% of the population. The Moors trace their descent back to Arab traders who came and stayed in Sri Lanka and married local Tamil or Sinhalese women. While both Tamils and Sinhalese historians and politicians have claimed that Moors are really a subbranch of their respective ethnic groups, Moors reject all such claims, asserting that they are the descendants of Arabic merchants who settled in Sri Lanka and eventually married Tamil or Sinhala women who had converted to Islam. Sri Lankan Moors view themselves as a separate ethnic group with distinctive social, religious, and cultural customs. Indeed, there are Moor families that claim descent to the Prophet Mohammed. Another 1% of Sri Lankans are Burghers (families of mixed Sri Lankan-European heritage), Malay (traders from Malaysia), and Vedas (tribal people).

These ethnic groups are mostly divided along religious and linguistic lines; the vast majority of Sinhalese are Buddhists and speak Sinhala, an Indo-Aryan language. The vast majority of Tamils are Hindus and speak Tamil, a Dravidian language. A small but significant number of Tamils and Sinhalese, about 7% of the population, converted to Christian denominations (primarily Roman Catholicism). All Moors and Malays are Muslims, and Burghers are Christians. The Vedas, presumed to be the original inhabitants of Sri Lanka, live in dwindling numbers in the south-central and eastern forests. The Vedas adhere to a local mixture of Buddhist and folk beliefs and customs; they are reputed to possess powerful forms of magic.

The principle of *purdah* is general to the South Asian subcontinent and was brought by Muslims from Central Asia who entered and eventually conquered most of the Indian subcontinent by the 17th century. *Purdah* is an Islamic custom that refers to the concealment of women and sexual segregation. All religious and ethnic communities in Sri Lanka practice it to varying degrees. Ethnic groups can be ranked in terms of the degree of adherence to the principle of *purdah* as follows, from strict to lenient: Muslims, Tamil (Hindus), Sinhalese (Buddhists), and Burghers (Christians).

Intercaste and interethnic marriages are legally sanctioned, but sociomorally sanctioned against. Intercaste or interethnic marriages are most likely to occur among the Westernized elite, where occupational status and Westernization have diminished the cultural force of ethnic and religious identities. Both intercaste and interethnic marriages are exceedingly rare and constitute less than 1% of all marriages. When they do occur, both sides of the family may ostracize the couple.

All ethnic groups in Sri Lanka are strongly against premarital and extramarital sex and view both acts as immoral. Not only the individual, but the entire family—and sometimes the community or ethnic group—is also held culpable for immoral sexual behavior. For this reason, pre- or extramarital sexual activity should always remain secret or private, for once it becomes public knowledge, foes can use this information to sully social as well as individual reputations.

## 3. Knowledge and Education about Sexuality

### A. Government Policies and Programs

There is no systematic sex education in Sri Lanka although efforts have been made to develop sex education classes since the late 1980s. Advanced biology or general science courses in high school do provide information on how sexual intercourse is performed, but any additional information is at the discretion of the teacher. Most Sri Lankans acquire their knowledge about sex from their peers and, occasionally, through movies and magazines. Parents are embarrassed to broach the topic of sex with their children, and children typically respond with a shudder of disgust when asked to consider their parent's sexuality. It is for these reasons that the government has been considering implementing sex education courses in public schools in recent years.

### B. Informal Sources of Sexual Knowledge

The primary informal sources of sexual knowledge are gossip, jokes, and stories told by peers. Most sexual knowledge is obtained through what James Scott (1991) referred to as "hidden transcripts," that is, stories or information disseminated in secret between friends. Because of the cramped sleeping quarters among the poor and in most rural homes, children have occasion to observe married adults in *flagrante delicto*. In this way, children obtain first- and second-hand information on sexual dimorphism and gendered sexual practices.

## 4. Autoerotic Behaviors and Patterns

Masturbation is considered unacceptable for girls, but is an acceptable practice for males. Most males learn about masturbation in their early teens, and it is not uncommon for boys to engage in male mutual masturbation, oral, and anal sex. It is also not considered abnormal for teenage males to practice interfemoral sex (one boy inserts his penis between the thighs of another boy), popularly called "cubbing." Among themselves, teenage boys will remark teasingly on the thighs of another boy, suggesting that these boys are potential partners for cubbing. While mutual masturbation and interfemoral sex are condoned as a "hidden transcript" of teenage male sexual life, such practices are expected to stop at the time of marriage. If they continue after marriage, peers will express strong disapproval, and may conjecture, pejoratively, that he is a homosexual.

## 5. Interpersonal Heterosexual Behaviors

### A. Children and Adolescents

Except in the Tamil areas, Sri Lankans typically do not construct walled domestic compounds. Rural Sinhalese homes are usually made with sun-baked brick, with tile or elephant grass for the roofing. The house compound is an open area that extends into a garden plot where manioc, banana, coconut, and vegetables are grown. Whenever possible, rice fields are adjacent to the homes, while the *chena* (or swidden) fields (where mainly maize, millet, sesame, and long beans are grown) are usually located in more remote areas of secondary scrub. In rural areas, the mud streets, footpaths, cultivation fields, scrublands, rivers, reservoirs, irrigation channels, forestlands, and garden compounds are places where children meet, work, and play. Parents are usually not overly concerned about the safety of their preadolescent children. Urban areas are, of course, much different. Homes in middle- to upper-class neighborhoods are usually protected by a fence or wall, and children are usually watched by parents or servants.

Rural children and adolescents have plenty of opportunities to meet and play away from the watchful, prying eyes of parents or other adults. Because most villages, except for those created through development projects, are comprised of dense and overlapping networks of kin, children tend to have great license to roam, and they are monitored very casually by the community as a whole. In the rural context, it is much easier for children and adolescents to experiment with sex. The frequency of sexual play by preadolescent children is hard to directly verify. Adults acknowledge that their adolescent children are "naturally" interested in sex and therefore they must be guarded, but there are no such concerns for preadolescent children.

Adolescent children are watched over by parents or guardians, but they are frequently given work, such as taking the goats or cattle to grazing lands, guarding the *chena* and paddy fields from birds and other predators, or fetching water or goods from a store. It is acknowledged by adults that when adolescents are engaged in such chores, they will flirt, display their genitals, and engage in sex play.

After menarche, parents severely limit the movement of their daughters and begin to consider prospective bridegrooms. A girl should be chaperoned by an adult if she is to go out in public, and she is to avoid all interactions with boys. The one exception to this rule is that girls are permitted to talk, and even flirt, with their male cross-cousins. For example, most rural Sri Lankans bathe at public wells or locations along a river or stream bank. Boys and girls will seek out public spots to bathe where a cross-cousin of the opposite sex is bathing, provided that there are other people present. The strictures of *purdah* are relaxed for adolescent cross-cousin interactions because of the preference for such marriages and the hope that one's child will not only agree to an arranged marriage with a cross-cousin, but will eagerly consent to the marriage. Social structure, cultural norms, and individual affections are intended to dovetail by relaxing the rules of *purdah* for cross-cousin interactions.

In urban areas, middle- and upper-class girls are expected to continue with their education. For such families, the goal of marrying their daughter to a cross-cousin has been replaced with the goal of marrying her to a doctor, lawyer, or engineer. Girls from middle- to upper-class families are encouraged to become proficient at English and English literature. The dowry transactions of the urban professional and elite differ substantially from that of the poor and rural peasants. In the former, the prospective groom is expected to bring socioeconomic prestige to the marriage, while the prospective bride brings nurturance, propriety, and high culture to the marriage. Of course, money, housing, and land are important components of the dowry transaction, but it is the prestige brought to the marriage by the prospective groom or bride that must first be settled and accepted by both families before the dowry negotiations over valued resources begins.

In urban areas, love affairs are not uncommon in high school. These are usually intensely romantic relationships and involve passing notes to one another, clandestine meetings often arranged with the help of friends, and handholding or kissing. They seldom lead to receptive-penetrative sex and seldom endure. Such romances are accepted and encouraged, and are even sources of prestige among high school or college peers, but they remain unacceptable to the parents of the lovers. The couple and their friends generally think of such romances as "young love" and do not expect them to lead to sexual intercourse. For urban females from Westernized families, kissing and handholding are daring but acceptable forms of premarital sex, but any form of receptive-penetrative sex, heavy petting, or oral sex is considered morally and socially wrong. However, the intensity of an idealized "young love" relationship can lead to tragedy if the relationship does not eventuate in marriage. The breakup of such adolescent love relationships has long been a leading cause of suicide in Sri Lanka.

## B. Adults

For a woman, all receptive-penetrative forms of sex should occur within the realm of marriage. While monogamy is both the law and the norm in Sri Lanka, Muslims are permitted to marry up to four wives, though they rarely do. Yalman (1967, 108-114) noted that polyandry and polygyny, though rare, were historically practiced among the Sinhalese, and he reported four cases of polyandry and two of polygyny at one of his fieldwork sites in 1956. At my rural fieldwork site, there was one polyandrous household. In both Yalman's and my own fieldwork case, the polyandrous marriages were not registered and were among poor rural farmers. Modern-day polygamy in Sri Lanka is a result of dire economic circumstances rather than a product of social norms.

Extramarital sex is extremely rare for wives in intact marriages, yet, it is not uncommon for husbands to visit brothels or seek out impoverished widowed or divorced women (usually those with children to support). In the area where I worked, such women were called "keeps" (using the English term) rather than "prostitutes" ("*ganika*" or "*vesi*"). In addition to money, a man would bring clothes, cooking utensils, and other gifts to his "keep" in return for sexual favors.

## 6. Homoerotic, Homosexual, and Bisexual Behaviors

Heterosexual sex is the only socially acceptable form of sex when someone is married. Homosexual sex is considered dirty and sinful; however, it is a common practice for unmarried males to engage in homoerotic and homosexual behaviors. These are not considered by the participants as homosexual acts, but as natural sexual outlets. Homosexual acts occurring between monks was documented in early Buddhist chronicles, where it was referred to as *pansalkeliya* ("temple game"). However, homosexuality is explicitly forbidden for monks.

In modern Sri Lanka, homosexual acts between men are illegal and are punishable by 12 years in jail, according to the 1883 penal code, sections 365 and 365a, which is still in effect. Lesbian sex is not acknowledged in the law. Until recently, the above discriminatory law had not been enforced, but the rise in "sex tourism," particularly of European homosexuals and pedophiliacs, has led the criminal system to apply this penal code more frequently, and consequently, there has been a dramatic rise in convictions (Fernando 2002).

Sherman de Rose, a gay activist in Sri Lanka, founded the first gay rights group called Companions on a Journey. With support from the Dutch government, the group bought a house in a wealthy section of Colombo and opened a meeting center for Sri Lankan gays, called the Drop-in Centre. The two primary missions of the center are to decriminalize homosexual acts and to increase AIDS awareness. In 2001, a second gay rights group was formed, primarily of young adults, and there has been an annual gay rights convention in Sri Lanka since 1998 as a result of growing gay rights activism. In a 1999 interview, de Rose noted that the law against homosexuality was being used to justify beatings and extortion of gays and lesbians by the police. He also noted that there is substantial evidence that men have been thrown out of their houses and fired from their jobs solely as a consequence of their sexual orientation.

Until recently, there has been no acknowledgement of lesbianism or gender-conflicted females in Sri Lanka. This is gradually changing and there are now two "lesbian awareness" groups in the Colombo area. The first Sri Lankan national lesbian convention was held in January 2000 with an estimated attendance of 150 people. According to one of the organizers, lesbians "are generally accepted if they are financially independent and come from upper-middle-class backgrounds." However, lesbianism is not accepted for women from lower socioeconomic backgrounds.

Rural women often come to the Colombo area in search of work at one of the many factories in Sri Lanka's Free Trade Zones. After they are hired, they live in nearby dormitories for a couple of years and then return home. The dormitories are popularly thought to be dens of lesbianism, prostitution, and casual sex, and on their return home, the women are often stigmatized and unable to marry, despite having saved money expressly for this purpose.

## 7. Gender Diversity and Transgender Issues

*Ponnaya* is derogatory slang for transvestites and very effeminate males. In male-to-male penetrative-receptive sex, such as interfemoral sex, *ponnayas* tend to take the passive role. There are an estimated 300 transvestite sex workers in Sri Lanka (Ratnapala 1999, 14). Transvestites are also said to find work as "makeup experts" or to work in bridal or fashion stores. Sri Lankan society does not condone public displays of gender switching or cross-dressing unless it is part of a village or religious ritual. Westernized mothers will frequently dress their young preschool-age boys in dresses, but this practice is discontinued when the boy enters school. In rural areas, boys and girls under the age of 5 or 6 usually just wear a t-shirt and no clothes from the waist down, except for a string that is intended to ward off the "evil eye" (*as wah*).

## 8. Significant Unconventional Sexual Behaviors

### A. Coercive Sex
*Rape*

Rape is defined by the penal code as sexual intercourse without the consent of the woman. If she is under 12 years of age, consent does not serve as a mitigating factor. Punishment for rape is up to 20 years in prison. The incidence of rape has increased every year from 1986, when it was 291, to 1996 (the last year for which data are available), when it was 716 (Fernando 2002). However, rape is notoriously underreported, as few women are willing to take the risks of humiliation and a prolonged difficult court case. If it becomes public knowledge that a woman was raped, there is a high probability that her family will be disgraced and will, in turn, cast her from the household. Chronic communal violence and interethnic hostilities have also led to higher incidences of rape across ethnic boundaries. In January 2002, for the first time, Sinhalese soldiers were brought to court for charges of raping a Tamil woman and were convicted. [*Comment 2002*: Female victims of sexual assault are most often admitted to a gynecological ward and first seen by a gynecologist. The women are most often deprived of a prompt and appropriate forensic examination because of the lack of facilities in most rural hospitals and the lack of knowledge of many of the attending doctors. In addition, the clinician may be reluctant to be involved in a criminal investigation. Most of the rape victims are also deprived of psychiatric help. (*End of comment by P. Weerakoon*)]

*Sexual Harassment*

Until 1995, sexual harassment was not considered a crime except if it included physical violence. Public sexual harassment, such as a male pressing up against a woman and simulating intercourse on a bus, pinching, or making lascivious remarks, are all referred to as "Eve teasing." These behaviors had become so prevalent that in 1995, the government added section 345 to the penal code, stipulating that all offenses that violated the modesty of a woman were now punishable by a jail sentence. Such behaviors included any form of sexual harassment at workplaces, during public transport, or at any other public place.

*Child Sexual Exploitation*

Sexual exploitation in Sri Lanka has been closely linked with the sex-tourist industry. In 2001, an organization called Protecting Environment and Children Everywhere (PEACE) was established with the goal of protecting Sri Lankan children from sexual exploitation. PEACE is affiliated with the End Child Prostitution in Asian Tourism campaign and supported through the United Nations. In 1980, it was estimated that there were 2,000 boys between the ages of 6 and 14 involved in prostitution (Seneviratne 1995, 10). Some of the boys are self-employed, but most are either sold into prostitution by their parents or lured by older boys, taxi drivers, hoteliers, or employees of hotels and guesthouses. Current estimates of the number of child sex workers are inconsistent, ranging from an estimated (and likely false) high of 30,000 to a low of 1,500 (Ratnapala 1999, 15). The latter figure seems to be the most accurate, as it is a result of extensive and careful study.

Young girls are also lured into prostitution. Abeyesekera (1991) offers a case study of a 15-year-old girl who had become separated from her family in Kandy and was abducted by a man who brought her to Colombo. There, she became a prostitute, and as her appearance declined, so did the conditions under which she worked. She was sold repeatedly, moving from one brothel or pimp to another until she was 60. Blind from a venereal disease, her left leg amputated, and part of a stable of beggars, she had, in effect, been a slave from childhood through the rest of her life.

[*Comment 2002*: Apart from the familial abuse common in every society, Sri Lanka appears to be particularly vulnerable to sexual exploitation. Sri Lanka is well known for its boy child pedophile activity, especially of 10- to 15-year-olds (Seneviratne 1996). One hundred fifty thousand mothers work in the Middle East as housemaids, leaving children more vulnerable to abuse from relatives and neighbors (Weeramunda 1996). One hundred thousand child domestics are at high risk of physical/sexual abuse from their employers, though further research is needed to confirm this. Boys at boarding school and other children in residential care, especially children with disabilities, are more likely to be vulnerable to sexual abuse from house parents (Weeramunda 1996). Street children needing food and shelter are probably at greater risk, though further research is needed to confirm this.

[Seneviratne (1996), in her book, *An Evil Under the Sun*, emphasized that, historically, children in Sri Lankan society have been much loved. She says that although prostitution has been in existence for hundreds of years, the sexual use of young children has only developed recently. "Boy prostitution has been available in cities by organized groups for locals, but organized prostitution of boys for foreign clients is a recent phenomena."

[Weeramunda (1996) conducted a survey with schoolchildren in three schools in Kalutara District situated near tourist hotels. Of those interviewed, 87 of the children (3%)

said they had had sexual relationships with tourists. Nearly two thirds of children being sexually exploited were male, 12% had their first sexual encounter at 10 years, and the majority were between 12 and 14 years old. None of the children saw the sexual encounters as a "*rakkshawa*" or job, and surprising to Weermunda, 80% attended school regularly and did not "play truant" or drop out of school.

[Miles (2000) assessed attitudes using a self-administered questionnaire with schoolchildren aged 13 to 17 years in four schools in a high-risk beach area of Sri Lanka (Moratuwa). He reports that 10% of children said they had done sexual things, 8% with other children their age, 5% with adults, and 6% with adults for money. He further reported that most children felt it was not acceptable for children to do sexual things with adults and appeared to be strongly against the damage they felt it could do to children and their communities. (*End of comment by P. Weerakoon*)]

### B. Adult Prostitution/Sex Workers

There is a long history of prostitution in Sri Lanka. A number of Buddhist Jataka tales, whose oral sources go back to 500 B.C.E., concern sex workers. A 13th-century text on social conditions speaks of "*vesya*" (prostitutes). Extraordinarily beautiful women could become socialized as courtesans (*ganika*) to serve the king. They would be trained in the "sixty-four womanly arts" and socialized to be cultured and provide sexual satisfaction to men of high rank.

Present-day Sri Lanka has a population of approximately 15,000 adult male and female sex workers (Ratnapala 1999, 71); the vast majority are in the Colombo area. Most of their clients are Sri Lankans, but tourists are the target clienteles that have spurred the rapid and extraordinary growth of the sex industry. For example, during my first visit to Sri Lanka in 1979, I saw no sex workers in Colombo. By 1982, they were not only present, but I was frequently hailed by pimps and male and female sex workers alike when walking along main streets in downtown Colombo.

There are an estimated 1,050 rural adult sex workers (Ratnapala 1999, 15). These sex workers mostly live in rural market towns, either in a hotel or rented house where they receive their clients. The clients are generally other villagers, town merchants, traders who are coming for the weekly market, and soldiers.

Ratnapala (1999, 84) estimated that the average sex worker has six clients per day, but barely makes sufficient money to meet their subsistence costs. Sex workers typically hail from very poor families. Only about 15% are educated up to the fifth year and mostly are married women, women who have a child out of wedlock, or who have been deserted by their husbands and are "single" but not able to marry. In a random sample of 100 female sex workers living at brothels, Ratnapala (1999, 10) found that 46 were married, 16 were deserted by their husbands, and the remainder (38) were single. Twenty-eight were between 18 and 25 years of age, 42 were between 26 and 30 years of age, and 30 were between 30 and 35 years of age. The majority of these sex workers did not voluntarily choose their profession, but were forced into it by dismal economic circumstances or were coerced into it, sometimes by their husbands.

## 9. Contraception, Abortion, and Population Planning

### A. Contraception

In a study of 500 Sinhalese Buddhist women in a southern town, Padma Karunaratne (1995) found that 17.4% of her sample used modern methods of contraception (i.e., the Pill, IUD, and condoms). Twelve-and-a-half percent of females opted for sterilization compared to only 0.8% of males; 21.8% used rhythm, 3.8% used withdrawal, and 2.6% used some other method of contraception. Thus, 58.8% of the adult female population used some form of contraception. However, the choice of when to use contraceptives differed substantially from that of Westerners. Women seldom chose to use any form of contraception prior to the birth of their first child. Only after the first child was born or the desired family size was reached did most women decide to adopt some form of birth control.

Husband and wife are typically too "*lajay*" ("shy") to discuss birth control methods. Aside from the Victorian cultural norms that inhibit couples from discussing contraception with each other, the three factors that most impede the use of birth control methods among married couples are:

1. neither men nor women are instructed in the way modern contraceptives work, so that they then use them improperly;
2. rumors about the harmful effects of a particular contraceptive may spread without impediment, as no one will know enough to refute them; and
3. most doctors at family planning clinics are males, and women are often too embarrassed to ask them about contraceptive options.

Better education about contraceptive use, and directing male or female patients to doctors of their own sex to discuss sensitive matters, would help increase the use of contraceptives.

### B. Abortion

Abortion is illegal in Sri Lanka unless the pregnancy threatens the life of the mother. Since 1970, members of Parliament have sought to pass amendments to liberalize the law on abortion, thus far to no avail.

It is impossible to obtain accurate figures on abortion rates in Sri Lanka, but in a 1997 newspaper article, Dr. Nafis Sadik estimated that 500 abortions were performed daily (*Catholic World News* 1997). Dr. Sriani Bansayake, Medical Director of Sri Lanka's Family Planning Association, estimated that, in 2001, between 765 and 1,000 abortions were performed daily. Since almost all of these abortions are carried out illegally, they are performed in unhygienic conditions with improper equipment and by untrained medical doctors. The women undergo agonizingly painful abortions that often lead to "death or serious injury" (Basnayake 2001). A study on reproductive health estimated that 12% of all maternal mortalities are a consequence of unsafe abortions (cited in *Saturday Magazine* 2002, 4).

In an article in a Sri Lankan newspaper magazine, Namini Wijedasa (2002) offered a description of an abortion clinic in a residential area of Colombo. The clinic was advertised as a maternity clinic run by a Western-trained medical doctor and his staff. The nurse is said to obtain only the first name of the patient, who gives her a "consultancy fee" of 200 rupees. The pregnant woman is told to come back the following day for a "womb wash." The fee for an abortion ranges between 5,000 to 15,000 rupees—a fee that is beyond the reach of the average Sri Lankan. As maternity/abortion clinics run by medical doctors are usually ignored by the police, well-to-do Sri Lankans do have abortion options denied poorer Sri Lankans, a point brought out by many Sri Lankan pro-choice activists. Professor Indralal de Silva, for instance, wrote: "When the rich need an abortion—whether it is illegal or not—they will have access to safe abortion[s]. . . . However, for the poor, the chance of having a safe abortion is still relatively less satisfactory" (Wijedasa 2002, 6).

## C. Family Planning

Modern-day Sri Lankans generally favor small families. This is reflected in the dramatic decline of the fertility rate from 5.3 children in 1980 to an estimated 1.9 in 2001. Much of this decline is because of the convergence of two modernizing processes: More married women are working and more women are receiving high school and college degrees. The societal image of women is gradually being reshaped from a traditional one, where to be a successful adult woman meant only to be a mother, to one where women choose to find their sense of identity in their occupation, as well as through their family.

Padma Karunaratne (1995) found that the increased "empowerment of women" in Sri Lanka has led to increased control over reproductive choices. Empowerment is reflected by the comparatively high levels of education Sri Lankan women enjoy, the deferred age of marriage, "egalitarian welfare measures adopted by successive governments" (Karunaratne 1995), and the new economic opportunities afforded by multinational companies locating factories in Sri Lankan Free Trade Zones and domestic work opportunities abroad (Gamburd 2001). In a study of 500 women in a southern rural town, Karunaratne noted that 90% had some formal schooling and lived within 5 miles (8 km) of a government-subsidized family health clinic. Even in this rural town, the vast majority of women had access to both public education and public health facilities.

A demographic and health survey conducted by UNESCO in 1993 showed that about 96% of adolescents between the ages of 15 and 19 had some knowledge of contraception. Family planning is an accepted and well-received practice in Sri Lanka, and recent studies indicate that adolescent populations have greater knowledge of modern contraceptive methods than do their elders (UNESCO Case Study–Sri Lanka 2002, 1, 6).

## 10. Sexually Transmitted Diseases and HIV/AIDS

### A. Sexually Transmitted Diseases

Syphilis, gonorrhea, and nongonococcal infections are the most common sexually transmitted infections. Studies indicate that 88% to 97% of Sri Lankan adolescents (depending on whether it is an urban or rural sample) are aware that infections could be sexually transmitted, but only between 47% and 52% knew that condom use could prevent the transmission of HIV (UNAIDS 2002).

### B. HIV/AIDS

No cases of HIV infection were found in testing for HIV/AIDS at an antenatal clinic in Colombo for 1990, 1993, 1995, and 1996 (UNAIDS 2002, 3). The Sri Lankan government estimated that by January 2001, there had been 89 deaths attributed to AIDS. Definite HIV-positive cases totaled 358, and 119 people had been diagnosed with AIDS. Because it is difficult to collect accurate statistics on a highly stigmatized disease, government officials believe that as many as 8,500 people may be infected with HIV (Samath 2001). United Nations projections estimate that by 2005, as many as 80,000 may be infected with HIV/AIDS, mostly because of the growth of the sex-tourist industry. It should also be noted that, at present, the Centers for Disease Control (1997, 1) does not consider HIV/AIDS to be of epidemic proportions in Sri Lanka: "The AIDS epidemic has yet to present overwhelming problems in Sri Lanka; AIDS cases are far less common there than they are in other Asian countries."

Almost all Sri Lankans are aware that condoms can prevent HIV/AIDS and other sexually transmitted diseases, but few use them because of the cultural emphasis on monogamy and the belief that condoms reduce sexual pleasure. In a 1997 study of condom use, 44.4% of males in Colombo and 26.3% of males in Matale, a rural area on the southern tip of Sri Lanka, reported using condoms in their "most recent intercourse of risk" (UNAIDS 2002, 9). Zero percent of the women reported using condoms. Sri Lankan females are unlikely to engage in what they perceive to be "risky sex"; thus, their sexual behaviors are confined to monogamous relations. The reason why more men in Colombo than Matale used a condom is a result of the general belief that HIV/AIDS was brought to Sri Lanka by tourists and is mostly confined to the sex-tourism industry. Sri Lankan males consider themselves more at risk with Colombo sex workers than with Matale sex workers, because the former are more likely to have had sex with a tourist.

[*Update 2002*: UNAIDS Epidemiological Assessment: The available HIV/AIDS data for Sri Lanka indicate that extensive spread of HIV had not occurred as of the year 2001. HIV testing among antenatal clinic attendees was conducted in the capital, Colombo, in 1990, 1993, 1995, and 1996. No evidence of HIV infection was detected. Outside Colombo, HIV testing of antenatal clinic women took place in various sites, including Anuradhapura, Badulla, Galle, Kandy, Kurunegala, and Ratnapura, at various times between 1990 and 1996. As in Colombo, no evidence of HIV infection was found among the antenatal clinic women tested at that time. Among sex workers tested in Colombo from 1990 through 1998, evidence of HIV infection was found in only one site, in 1993, where 0.2% of the sex workers tested were HIV-positive. Outside Colombo, sex workers were tested for HIV infection in Kandy, Anuradhapura, Galle, Kurunegala, Ratnapura, and Badulla between 1993 and 1998. Evidence of HIV infection was found in only one site, Kurunegaia, and only in 1995, where 0.5% of sex workers tested were HIV-positive.

[The best estimate of HIV prevalence in Sri Lanka, as of the end of 2001, is about 4,800. There are insufficient studies and data on the patterns and prevalence of HIV-risk behaviors in Sri Lanka to suggest that the potential for epidemic or more-extensive spread of HIV is very low. More systematic sentinel HIV surveillance needs to be developed, with primary emphasis on high-risk groups. In addition, baseline behavioral surveillance studies/surveys need to be implemented as soon as possible. Support for HIV/AIDS/STD programs needs to be expanded and focused on high-risk groups.

[The estimated number of adults and children living with HIV/AIDS on January 1, 2002, were:

| | | |
|---|---|---|
| Adults ages 15-49: | 4,800 | (rate: < 0.1%) |
| Women ages 15-49: | 1,400 | |
| Children ages 0-15: | 550 | |

[An estimated 250 adults and children died of AIDS during 2001.

[At the end of 2001, an estimated 2,000 Sri Lankan children under age 15 were living without one or both parents who had died of AIDS. (*End of update by the Editors*)]

## 11. Sexual Dysfunctions, Counseling, and Therapies

Since the 1980s, a number of nongovernmental organizations (NGOs) have been established to counsel women and children who are the victims of rape, sexual exploitation, violence, or harassment. In 1986, the Women's Development Centre was established to address issues such as rape and domestic violence. The Bar Association of Sri Lanka, the Sri Lankan Women Lawyers' Association, and various other organizations offer free legal aid to women and children. In addition to free legal aid, two associations—the Women's Development Centre and Women in Need—also provide free counseling services.

In Sri Lanka, as in most countries, HIV/AIDS evokes anger and contempt among the populace rather than compassion or understanding. Dr. Kamilaka Abyeratne, a 66-year-old female doctor who contracted AIDS through a blood transfusion, was the first Sri Lankan to go public with the disease. She has been instrumental in reducing the stigma associated with AIDS and also has worked to create AIDS-awareness programs. AIDSline is a telephone counseling service started in January 2000 by the Coalition for Care, Education, and Support Services (ACCESS). ACCESS is operated by trained volunteers and is open four hours a day from 4 p.m. to 8 p.m. AIDSline also provides free advice and guidance to callers seeking information on HIV/AIDS and other sexual matters. The service is available to both heterosexuals and homosexuals.

[*Comment 2002*: Reliable figures for the incidence and prevalence of sexual dysfunctions are not available for Sri Lanka. Sex therapy is usually offered by psychiatrists and psychologists attached to psychiatric units in larger hospitals. De Silva and Rodrigo (1995), working in a sexual dysfunction clinic run as a part of the psychiatric clinic in Kandy (hill country Sri Lanka), reported that the clients were almost exclusively male, largely complaining of erectile dysfunction and premature ejaculation. In their clinic, female problems were rare and usually referred by gynecologists. These were few and related to unconsummated marriages and dyspareunia. Other professionals working in the area, however, report a high proportion of couples presenting with unconsummated marriages (Weerakoon 1987), many of these being because of vaginismus. All of these women were virgins and most believed that first sexual intercourse was a very traumatic experience, always accompanied by bleeding, and often associated with significant genital trauma. This myth is common among young people in Sri Lanka.

[It is common in Sri Lanka for practitioners of Ayurvedic medicine and folk remedies to advertise their services and products (De Silva & Dissanayake 1989), with prominent advertisements in national language papers (Sinhalese and Tamil newspapers). These advertisements advertise treatment as well as imply causation for the conditions. Some of the lead lines in these advertisements translate as:

• Do you suffer from Impotence? Try our remedy today.
• Do you suffer from nocturnal emission?
• Are you losing precious semen with your urine?
• Instant (premature) ejaculation? Do not suffer any more.
• Sexual debility—there is a cure.

[The Ayurvedic remedies offered in this way are usually herbal preparations, both for oral ingestion and external application. The folk practitioners offer various "mystical" remedies. Many of the practitioners emphasize the supposed role of semen loss in the genesis of sexual "debility" and dysfunction, both in their advertisements and in their consultation. The "excessive" loss of semen, through masturbation, wet dreams (nocturnal emissions), spermatorrhoea (interpreted as cloudiness of the urine), and frequent coitus in youth and early adult life are claimed to cause many diseases and disabilities. These would include, in addition to erectile dysfunction and premature ejaculation, a whole range of other physical and mental symptoms. These beliefs, which are widespread, derive from the Ayurvedic theories of the composition and value of semen. The result is that many men present with serious concerns, often tinged with guilt about

their sexual desire and behavior. This syndrome has been reported in several Asian countries, e.g., the Dhat syndrome in India (Bhatia & Malik 1991).

[In Sri Lanka, the condition has been called the "Loss of Semen Syndrome." De Silva and Dissanayake (1989) assessed 28 consecutive males attending a sexual dysfunction clinic in Sri Lanka with such fears and symptoms. They reported that the four main groups of symptoms were:

• Physical symptoms, such as aches and pains, and/or mental symptoms, such as poor memory and concentration,
• Specific sexual dysfunctions,
• Anxiety about present or future sexual functioning (often associated with impending marriage and first sexual intercourse), and
• Direct complaints about the excessive loss of semen.

[They pointed out that many of the patients do not complain directly of a sexual problem; instead, they present with anxiety and depression or vague symptoms such as "general weakness," "sleep problems," and aches and pains—disclosing the sexual dysfunction in the course of a general history. (*End of comment by P. Weerakoon*)]

## 12. Sex Research and Advanced Professional Education

Recently, there has been an increase in research on sexology in Sri Lanka. Most of this research is concerned with medical, epidemiological, or sex exploitation and criminal issues. A number of studies were established and planned through the International Center for Research on Women. There have also been a number of studies that were a result of a collaborative effort between the University of Connecticut Health Center, the Institute for Community Research, in the United States, and the Center for Intersectoral Community Health Studies and the University of Peradeniya in Kandy, Sri Lanka. The Family Planning Association of Sri Lanka is also active in studying and disseminating information on sex education, effective contraception methods, safe-sex practices, pregnancy, delivery, and abortion. The Sri Lankan Ministry of Health, in collaboration with UNICEF, has initiated a multimedia campaign on HIV/AIDS. PEACE (Protecting Environment and Children Everywhere) is the main organization that does research and publicizes information on the sexual exploitation of children in Sri Lanka.

## References and Suggested Readings

Basnayake, S. 2001 (December 4). Abortions in Sri Lanka. Interview conducted by Manjari Peiris. *Daily Mirror.*

Bhatia, M. S., & S. C. Malik. 1991. Dhat syndrome: A useful diagnostic entity in Indian culture. *British Journal of Psychiatry, 159*:691-695.

Centers for Disease Control (CDC). 1997 (October 6). *Sri Lanka–Health: Economic cost of AIDS complacency.* CDC AIDS News Service.

CIA. 2002 (January). *The world factbook 2002.* Washington, DC: Central Intelligence Agency. Available: http://www.cia.gov/cia/publications/factbook/index.html.

de Munck, V. C. n.d. Patriarchy and cultural models of gender in Sri Lanka.

de Munck, V. C. 1992. The fallacy of the misplaced self. *Ethos, 20*(2):167-189.

de Munck, V. C. 1996. Love and marriage in a Sri Lankan Muslim community. *American Ethnologist, 23*(4):698-716.

De Silva, P., & S. A. W. Dissanayake. 1989. The loss of semen syndrome in Sri Lanka: A clinical study. *Sexual and Marital Therapy, 4*:195-204.

De Silva, P., & E. K. Rodrigo. 1995. Sex therapy in Sri Lanka–Development, problems and prospects. *International Review of Psychiatry, 7*:24-246.

De Silva, S., D. A. Stiles, & J. Gibbons. 1993. Sri Lanka. In: L. L. Adler, ed., *International handbook on gender roles* (pp. 358-373). Westport, CT: Greenwood Press.

de Soysa, N. 2001. The truth behind Sri Lanka's gender development statistics. *Third World Network*. Available: http://www.twnside.org.sg/title/2093.htm.

Dissanayake W. (1982) Newspapers as matchmakers–A Sri Lankan illustration. *Journal of Comparative Family Studies, 13*(1):97-108.

Farook A. H. M. 2002 (September 5). 23,000 estate children employed as domestic aides. *Daily News*. Available: http://origin.dailynews.lk/2002/09/05/new06.html.

Fernando, C. 2002. *Women and children as victims of crime: The Sri Lankan perspective.* Japan: Asian Crime Prevention Foundation. Available: http://www.acpf.org.

Gamburd, M. 2000. *The kitchen spoon's handle.* Ithaca, NY: Cornell University Press.

Gunasekera, P. C., & P. S. Wijesinghe. 1997. Female victims of sexual assault. *Ceylon Medical Journal, 42*:204-205.

Hewamanne, S., & J. Brown. 1999. "If they allow us we will fight": Strains of consciousness among women workers in the Katunayake Free Trade Zone. *Anthropology of Work Review, 19*:8-13.

Holt, C. J. 1998. The persistence of political Buddhism. In: T. Bartholomeusz & C. R. de Silva. *Buddhist fundamentalist and minority identities in Sri Lanka* (pp. 186-196). Albany: State University of New York Press.

Jayaweera, S. 1979. Aspects of the role and position of women. In: T. Fernando & R. N. Kearney, eds., *Modern Sri Lanka: A society in transition* (pp. 165-180). Syracuse, NY: Syracuse University Press.

Jayaweera, S. 1979. Education. In: T. Fernando & R. N. Kearney, eds., *Modern Sri Lanka: A society in transition* (pp.131-154). Syracuse, NY: Syracuse University Press.

Karunaratne, P. 1995. *Empowerment of women and reproductive choices: Is there a connection?* Paper presented at the Fifth Sri Lankan Conference. Durham: University of New Hampshire.

*Koran.* 1956. Trans. Marmadouke Pickthall. London: Penguin.

Lynch, C. 1999. Good girls or juki girls? *Anthropology of Work Review, 19*:18-22.

Lo Presti, L. 1999. Haven in Sri Lanka for gay men and women. Available: http://www.abc.net.au/ra/asiapac/archive/1999/jul/raap.htm.

*Mahavamsa or the great chronicle of Ceylon.* 1912. Trans. William Geiger. London: Oxford University Press.

Malhotra, A., & A. O. Tsui. 1999. Work and marriage: Mother-daughter similarities in Sri Lanka. *Journal of Comparative Family Studies, 30*(2):219-241.

McGilvray, D. 1988. Sex, repression, and Sanskritization in Sri Lanka. *Ethos, 16*:99-125.

Miles, G. M. 2000. Children don't do sex with adults for pleasure: Sri Lankan children's views on sex and sexual exploitation. *Child Abuse and Neglect, 24*(7):995-1003.

Morrell, S. A. 2002 (August 25). Incest, teenage pregnancies, sexual promiscuity: The plantation dilemma. *Sunday Observer.* Available: http://www.sundayobserver.lk/.

News/Gay, Lesbian Activities in Sri Lanka. 2002. Sri Lankan lesbians plan conference 1999. Available: http://www.geocities.com/srilankangay/news1.html.

Obeyesekere, G. 1968. Theodicy, sin and salvation in a sociology of Buddhism. In: E. R. Leach, ed., *Dialectic in practical religion* (pp. 7-40). Cambridge: Cambridge University Press.

Obeyesekere, G. 1981. *Medusa's hair.* Chicago: University of Chicago Press.

Ratnapala, N. 1999. *Sex workers in Sri Lanka.* Colombo, Sri Lanka: PEACE.

Sadik, N. 1997 (October 20). UN program seeks to cut Sri Lankan abortion rate with contraception. *Catholic World News.*

Samath, F. 2001. *Breaking the silence, bit by bit.* SHAAN online. Inter Press Service E-Zine. Available: http://www.ipsnews.net/hivaids/index.s.html.

Seager J., & A.Olson. 1986. *Women in the world: An international atlas.* New York: Simon & Schuster.

Seneviratne, M. 1995. *An evil under the sun: The sexual exploitation of children in Sri Lanka.* Colombo, Sri Lanka: PEACE.

*Sunday Observer,* Lake House Press. Associated Newspapers of Ceylon Limited.

United Nations. 1991. *The world's women: Trends and statistics 1970-1990.* New York.

UNAIDS. 2002. *Epidemiological fact sheets by country.* Geneva, Switzerland: Joint United Nations Programme on HIV/AIDS (UNAIDS/WHO). Available: http://www.unaids.org/hivaidsinfo/statistics/fact_sheets/index_en.htm.

UNESCO. 2002. *Case study–Sri Lanka demographic characteristics of adolescents.* Available: http://www.unescobkk.org/ips/arh-web/case_studies/srilanka/1.html.

Weerakoon, P. 1987 (March 25-29). The etiology of the unconsummated marriage–A study of 71 couples seen in a family therapy clinic. *Proceedings of the Centenary Congress.*

Weeramunda, A. J. 1996, Child prostitution: Extracts from a study in Kalutara. In: M. Senerawatne, ed., *The sexual exploitation of children in Sri Lanka* (pp. 40-46). Colombo, Sri Lanka: PEACE.

Wijedasa, N. 2002. Abortion: In the limelight again. *The Island, Saturday Magazine,* pp. 1-25.

Yalman, N. 1967. *Under the bo tree.* Berkeley: University of California Press.

# Sweden
## (*Konungariket Sverige*)

Jan E. Trost, Ph.D.,
with Mai-Briht Bergstrom-Walan, Ph.D.
*Updates by the Editors*

## Contents

## Demographics and a Brief Historical Perspective

ROBERT T. FRANCOEUR

### A. Demographics

On the Scandinavian Peninsula in northern Europe, Sweden is bordered by Norway on the west, Denmark on the south, and Finland on the east. One of the oldest democracies in the world, Sweden has lived in peace for 200 years. As titular head of a constitutional monarchy, the Swedish king has no power except to represent the country symbolically within Sweden and abroad.

Sweden's landmass of 173,732 square miles (449,964 km²), larger than the state of California, is mountainous along the northwest border. A quarter of the land is flat or rolling terrain, mainly in the central and southern areas where the largest cities are located.

In July 2002, Sweden had an estimated population of 8.88 million. (All data are from *The World Factbook 2002* (CIA 2002) unless otherwise stated.)

**Age Distribution and Sex Ratios**: *0-14 years*: 18% with 1.05 male(s) per female (sex ratio); *15-64 years*: 64.7% with 1.03 male(s) per female; *65 years and over*: 17.3% with 0.74 male(s) per female; *Total population sex ratio*: 0.98 male(s) to 1 female

**Life Expectancy at Birth**: *Total Population*: 79.84 years; *male*: 77.19 years; *female*: 82.64 years

**Urban/Rural Distribution**: 85% to 15%

**Ethnic Distribution**: Swedish: 89%; Finns: 2%; a small Sami minority, plus foreign-born or first-generation Yugoslavs, Danes, Norwegians, Greeks, and Turks

**Religious Distribution**: Lutheran: 87%; Roman Catholic, Orthodox, Baptist, Muslim, Jewish, and Buddhist minorities

---

*Communications*: Jan Trost, Ph.D., Uppsala University, Department of Sociology, P.O. Box 821, S-751 08 Uppsala, Sweden; jan.trost@soc.uu.se. Mai-Briht Bergstrom-Walan, Ph.D., Tysbergavagen 41, Stockholm, S-12241 Enskede, Sweden; maj.briht@pi.se.

(CIA 2002)

**Birth Rate**: 9.81 births per 1,000 population

**Death Rate**: 10.6 per 1,000 population

**Infant Mortality Rate**: 3.44 deaths per 1,000 live births

**Net Migration Rate**: 0.95 migrant(s) per 1,000 population

**Total Fertility Rate**: 1.54 children born per woman

**Population Growth Rate**: 0.02%

**HIV/AIDS** (1999 est.): *Adult prevalence*: 0.08%; *Persons living with HIV/AIDS*: 3,000; *Deaths*: < 100. (For additional details from www.UNAIDS.org, see end of Section 10B.)

**Literacy Rate** (*defined as those age 15 and over who can read and write*): 100%; education is free and compulsory from age 6 to 15

**Per Capita Gross Domestic Product** (*purchasing power parity*): $24,700 (2001 est.); *Inflation*: 2.7%; *Unemployment*: 3.9%; *Living below the poverty line*: NA

### B. A Brief Historical Perspective

The Swedes have lived in present-day Sweden for at least 5,000 years, longer than nearly any other European people. Nordic (Gothic) tribes from Sweden played a major role in the disintegration of the Roman Empire and helped create the first Russian state in the 19th century. The Swedes accepted Christianity in the 11th century and soon developed a strong centralized monarchy. In 1435, Sweden became the first European nation to develop a parliament with representatives from all segments of the population. Sweden threw off Danish rule, which began in 1397, in a 1521-1523 revolt led by Gustavus I. The Lutheran Church became the official state religion. For a time in the 17th century, Sweden was a major European power, controlling most of the Baltic seacoast. Following the Napoleonic wars, in which Sweden acquired Norway, Sweden maintained an armed neutrality in all later European wars.

## 1. Basic Sexological Premises

### A. Character of Gender Roles

Sweden has the reputation, especially among its own inhabitants, of being the leader in gender equity. Whether this is reality or not, the early strivings for equality—thinking of men and women as equal—started more than a century ago. Women's movements were in the vanguard of these early efforts. In the family and matrimonial law reform of 1920, no differentiation was made between the rights and responsibilities of men and women, husbands and wives. Unfortunately, while the law drew no difference between the genders, the reality of social consciousness and behavior did differentiate. Thus, efforts shifted to achieving gender equity. Today, Swedes are more prone to think of and work for the process of gender equity, the fair and reasonable treatment of both men and women.

Depending on one's perspective, Sweden has come close to, or is still far from, gender equity. If one takes a public or legal perspective, Sweden has come very far. Officially, women and men are treated equally and have the same rights and responsibilities. From a historical and cultural perspective, when compared with other European countries and those in the Middle East, Sweden is a real pioneer at the cutting edge. However, if we use the ideal of gender equity as the perspective and basis for evaluation, Sweden has a very long way to go. To illustrate: Sweden has led the way for other nations with a gender-neutral parental-leave law that provides almost full salary for up to a year for either parent of a new child. This means that the mother and the father can share this leave any way they want. They can split the paid leave any way they want, or either of them can take all the leave. The reality is far from gender equity. Quite a few new mothers take all the leave of absence from work; fathers never take the full leave. Very few fathers take more than a few weeks off, although their salary is fully paid during this leave. Officially, formally, there is full gender equity; in reality, Sweden is far from gender equity on this, and many other, issues. (*See also*: M. J. Intons-Peterson's (1988) comparative study of the gender concepts of Swedish and American youth and D. Meyer's 1989 study of *Sex and Power: The Rise of Women in America, Russia, Sweden and Italy*.)

### B. Sociolegal Status of Males and Females

For both females and males, the age of majority is 18 years. However, it is illegal to have sexual intercourse or engage in sexual (genital) touches with a person under the age of 15 years, regardless of whether the underage person is male or female, whether the couple is same- or opposite-gendered, and whether it is voluntary or involuntary. Sexual intercourse or contact is also prohibited by law under the age of 18 when the younger person is under the custody or supervision of the older person. Otherwise, the legal status and prohibitions, including sexual harassment and rape, are the same for all persons (Meyer 1989).

### C. General Concepts of Sexuality and Love

In general, the Swedes have a liberal and permissive attitude towards sexual relations and intercourse, although, as in all societies, some restrictions are commonly accepted. This is illustrated by a 1992 study on a representative sample of 729 Uppsala University students, aged 19 to 23. About 70% of both male and female respondents believed that it is acceptable for a 15-year-old girl to have sexual intercourse with a steady boyfriend; the same percentage approved of a 15-year-old boy having sex with his steady girlfriend. More than 90% of both male and female respondents did not approve of a 15-year-old girl having sexual intercourse with a casual partner. Only 40% of the males and 50% of the female respondents disapproved of a 15-year-old boy having sex with a casual partner. The double standard still colors what is acceptable, "even" in Sweden. It is stronger among males than among females, and this holds true even among the highly educated.

Almost all of those students disapproved of a married or cohabiting person having sexual intercourse with another person other than the spouse or cohabitation partner. In this regard, males and females did not apply a double standard and were equally restrictive in their views of "extra" sexual behavior by both men and women.

Generally speaking, females in this university sample were somewhat more restrictive or less permissive than males, but the differences are generally not significant.

## 2. Religious, Ethic, and Gender Factors Affecting Sexuality

### A/B. Source and Character of Religious and Ethnic Values

Almost 90% of Swedes are members of the state Lutheran Church. The remaining 10% are either atheists or belong to other churches, with slightly over 1% Roman Catholic and a scattering of other religious traditions, often stemming from significant immigrations. By international comparison, church attendance is very low. Annually, the 7.6 million members of the Lutheran Church attend less than 20 million services, less than three services per member per year. Stated in another way, less than 3% of the population on average attend church on any particular Sunday (*Statistical Yearbook of Sweden* 1993).

At the peak of the Viking culture around the year 1000, people in this part of the world subscribed to the Aesir (Asa) religious belief in a superior race of gods led by Odin. This Nordic religion, with its worship of Odin and Thor, the Aesirs (creators of mankind), and the Vanir (fertility deities linked with land and sea spirits and with dead ancestors), was more concerned with behavior than with doctrines and beliefs.

Around the year 1000 C.E., Christianity was introduced into Scandinavia, often with the threat to either convert to Christianity or to be decapitated. Subsequently, the kings in the various small Nordic kingdoms and their people subscribed to Christianity, at least officially. As occurred elsewhere with the imposition of Christian or other exogenous religions, this conversion did not bring a complete rejection of the early religious practices. In Iceland, for instance, the people accepted the new religion in the year 1000 C.E. only after Pope Sylvester II allowed them to keep their traditional religious customs of eating horse meat and practicing abortion/infanticide (Manniche 1989).

That Christianity's penetration of Scandinavia took centuries is evident in letters various Popes sent from Rome to their bishops, demanding that they make sure the Swedes follow the Christian rules for marrying and not use their traditional "pagan" rituals (Carlson 1965).

In 1527, King Gustavus Vasa decided that Sweden should abandon the Church of Rome and subscribe to the Reformation ideas of Martin Luther. At the time, King Vasa was at war and needed money. Luther maintained that the churches should not be decorated, and that the churches should not own a lot of property. This teaching suited King Vasa quite nicely. It allowed him to confiscate Church properties, gold, and other valuables, including copper bells, which he had turned into cannon to support his efforts to break away from the control of the Danish monarchy. Thirty-three years after King Vasa's death, the Swedish Parliament formally accepted his declaration of Lutheranism as the state religion at the "Uppsala Meeting" in 1593.

Today, the Swedish Lutheran Church is very liberal in action, but careful not to take formal stands in most sexual issues, such as premarital sex, cohabitation, and sex education. Like many other churches and congregations, the state church of Sweden is inclined to keep quiet on sexual issues to keep the few members they have.

## 3. Knowledge and Education about Sexuality

Carl von Linnaeus (1707-1778), a professor at Uppsala University, is internationally known for his botanical classification of all flowering plants, based on their sexual reproductive systems. A less known, but equally pioneering effort of Linnaeus (as he is more commonly known outside his homeland), was the lectures he gave his students on human sexuality. A few years ago, a manuscript was found, probably written by one of his students, Pehr Dubb, and rewritten by a young relative of Dubb's. In this manuscript, titled *Om Sättet Att Tilhopa Gå [On the Way to Be Together]*, Linnaeus shows a surprisingly great openness and support for sexual intercourse, considering he taught in the mid-18th century. Despite his accuracy in detailing the sexual anatomy of plants, Linnaeus had a somewhat limited, and inaccurate, knowledge of the human female's sexual organs.

### A. Government Policies and Programs

*School Programs*

During the 18th and early 19th centuries, venereal diseases flourished in Sweden. Starting in 1783, the government ordered its officials to distribute information about these diseases. An almanac published in 1814 provided a lot of information on venereal diseases without a moralistic overtone, and the straightforward message that the earlier the symptoms were taken seriously, the easier it was to treat a disease.

In 1897, the first female physician in Sweden, Karolina Widerstrom (1856-1949), started sex education in some of the schools for girls in Stockholm. She also published a pamphlet on education and sexual hygiene in 1906. Her perspective was astonishingly far ahead of the times. She claimed, for instance, that for their own health, women should be 20 years old before becoming a mother and the man 24 before becoming a father. She also added that the child had a right to be cared for, and that very young parents would find this hard to provide.

Widerstrom advocated sex education in schools and at home, in a natural environment where children could ask and get proper answers. She maintained that if physicians were the only ones providing sex education, then sex might be perceived as something special and strange, which it should not be.

In 1942, the Swedish Government decided it was preferable for pupils in regular schools to receive education on differences between men and women, and about sexual biology and hygiene. However, this was only a recommendation. Sex education did not become mandatory in all compulsory schools until 1956. Over the years, the content and form of the sexuality education program have been widely discussed. In the beginning, the education was mainly technical and biological in nature. This changed in the 1970s, as the emphasis shifted to education in sexuality, relationships, and living together. The curriculum became "softer" and more human.

Today, no one questions that there should be sexuality education in the compulsory schools. The amount of time devoted to this education and its content is very much up to the individual school, and the individual teacher. As elsewhere, some are good and some are even better.

Swedish sexuality education operates on four levels. In general, at the lowest level, education for pupils age 7 to 10 years deals with menstruation, intercourse, self-pleasuring, contraceptives, fertilization, pregnancy, and childbirth. The same topics are dealt with at higher levels, adjusted to the students' age and maturity. At the middle level, ages 10 to 13, added topics include the physical development at puberty, venereal diseases, homosexuality, exhibitionism, and pedophilia. On the upper level, ages 13 to 16, added topics include: petting, different views of sex roles, premarital relations, marriage and family including the views in some non-Christian cultures, abortion, pornography, prostitution, HIV/AIDS and "safer sex," and where to go for further information and advice. On the college level are included sexual desire, with its variations in the orientation and strength, falling in love, sexual problems and dysfunctions, ethical and religious viewpoints on contraception and abortion, societal support for the family (family law), sexual problems of certain immigrant groups, and the problem of world population.

A severe shortcoming is that teachers and physicians encounter almost no education and training in human sexuality within their professional curriculum. One would assume that they would receive this training, considering that they belong to professions that require education and training to teach and inform others.

Unfortunately, one has to admit that despite many years of effort on the part of some educators, the high-placed and idealistic goals set for sex education in the schools have not been reached, even if Sweden is ahead of most other countries.

*Youth Clinics*

In addition to sex education in the schools, Sweden has about 150 youth clinics. The first opened in the late 1960s mainly because of the many teenage abortions. Following a 1975 law allowing free abortions, the number of youth clinics increased significantly with a focus on preventing abortion by promoting contraceptive use. Other important tasks were to inform young people about STD, HIV, and AIDS prevention.

Youth clinics, headed by a midwife assisted by a gynecologist, psychologist, and social worker, deal with men and women under age 25, with most of the clients being female. The clinics provide one-on-one consultation. A great number of clients obtain contraceptive pills through these clinics. Clinic staff also participate in sex-education programs in the schools.

Some of the female clients are children of immigrant parents who have a more conservative attitude about the equality of the sexes and oppose premarital intercourse.

These situations pose new problems for the sex counselors. Resolving clashes between free Swedish sexual morality and other more-restrictive cultural codes is often difficult.

In some circles, both in Sweden and other countries, there was a fear that Sweden's liberal teenage sexuality and free abortion would increase teenage abortion. However, this did not happen. On the contrary, abortions decreased in the decade following enactment of the new law in 1975. This brought about international attention and was interpreted as a result of the Swedish school programs in sex education and the youth clinics. Many other countries then introduced sex education programs modeled on the Swedish approach.

## B. Informal Sources of Sexual Knowledge

As in other Western societies, mass media, print, broadcast, and videotaped, are important sources of information for Swedes of all ages. Friends seem to be very important for nonadults. Child pornography is the only pornography prohibited by law, but it is still available. In general, pornography seems to be an important educational resource for quite a few Swedes.

## 4. Autoerotic Behaviors and Patterns

In the Uppsala University study mentioned in Section 1C, above, about 15% of the males and the females said that to engage in self-pleasuring daily is abnormal. To me this indicates that very few find self-pleasuring abnormal unless it is done daily. As with much else in the field of sexuality, people do not talk about self-pleasuring, so little is really known about what they do and what they think.

In the Uppsala study, the median age for first self-pleasuring was about 13 for men and 14 for women. Almost none of the men had not engaged in self-pleasuring during the past year, while as many as 24% of the women had not self-pleasured in a year. Almost 70% of the men and about 25% of the women engaged in autoeroticism at least once a week.

## 5. Interpersonal Heterosexual Behaviors

### A. Children

No Swedish studies, either attitudinal nor behavioral, have been done on sexual exploration and sex-rehearsal play among children. These natural behaviors are probably more permitted today that half a century ago. But no one talked about this at that time, and very few talk about it now.

### B. Adolescents

There are no puberty rituals and never have been to my knowledge. One could argue that Christian confirmation is a sort of passage rite from childhood to adulthood, but given the current lack of church attendance, that seems fully irrelevant now. Quite a few adolescents have a number of periods of going steady and no one waits until marriage for first sexual intercourse. The median age for first sexual intercourse is around 15 years for both boys and girls (Lewin & Helmius 1983).

### C. Adults

*Premarital Courtship, Dating, and Relationships*

To begin, I want to emphasize the inadequacy and prejudicial tone of the term "premarital." The term presupposes the norm or model that everyone should marry, or at least that almost everyone should—and also that not to marry is deviant behavior, or to be more specific, deviant nonbehavior. As will be shown, that concept has not really been an issue in Sweden. Today, with all couples starting with nonmarital cohabitation, their behavior is not "premarital," but just something they do.

Eilert Sundt, a Norwegian minister and one of the first sociologists, studied people's behavior and norms in the mid-19th century. Among other phenomena, he found the system of night courting (*nattfrieri*). In the rural areas, with often long distances between homes, the young man courting a woman would stay overnight in the same bed with her, but he was not allowed to undress or be under the blankets. This way, young persons could get to know quite a few young persons of the other gender (Sundt 1855/1975). Another important system has been, and still is, the dance places, especially during summertime, where one can invite for a dance even a complete stranger.

I would say that in more-modern times, there is no courtship or dating system. People meet at dancing places, not as commonly as previously, and at bars, schools, college, work, or through friends. There is no Swedish term for what in America is labeled dating. It is even hard to find a similar concept in Swedish for what is denoted by the term *dating*.

The term *premarital* is somewhat odd. There is really no corresponding Swedish concept. Prior to the mid-1960s, the term was understandable, but no big issue. True, there were norms against premarital sex, but these were mainly ideal rather than behavioral norms, especially during the period of engagement.

During the 1950s and first half of the 1960s, the marriage rate in Sweden was historically at its peak. Suddenly, this rate started dropping rapidly. "Rapidly," in this context, means a decrease of about 50% in less than ten years. No other country has experienced such a rapid demographic change. The marriage rate continued its decline until the beginning of the 1980s (see Figure 1). This same tendency appears in remarriage statistics for men (Trost 1993a).

What happened in the mid-1960s? Nonmarital cohabitation "under marriage-like conditions" suddenly increased (see Figure 2). Cohabitation existed previously, but it was only a very marginal phenomenon (Trost 1979). The data shown in Figure 2 are probably understated, with the actual cohabitation rate more like 25% than 20%. Cohabitation quickly became a social institution, alongside the old social institution of marriage. One could argue that this change was superficial, and that the relationships are the same, independent of the formal marital status or its absence.

When arguing that there is no real change, only a demographic one, I would say that with the Swedish laws and traditions, the dyad constituting the marriage is the same as the dyad constituting the cohabiting couple. The emotional relationships are the same, the quarrels the same, the affection

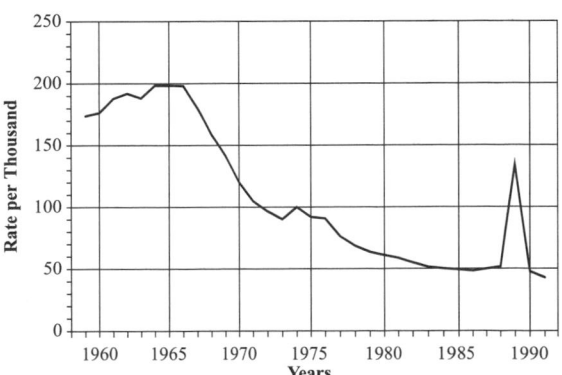

**Figure 1**

**Marriage Rates, Sweden, 1959-1991, First Marriages per 1,000 Not Married**

*Sources: Befolkningsförändringar*, different years

or lack of affection, housing subsidies, child allowance from society, just to mention a few elements, are all the same. The sole difference is the financial arrangements in case of separation/divorce and death of one of the spouses/cohabitants.

However, I would claim that the change here is in some of the norms surrounding marriage and cohabitation. Traditionally in Sweden, as elsewhere, four elements have been closely connected timewise: 1. the marriage ceremony, 2. moving in together, 3. having sexual intercourse together, and 4. having a first child about a year later.

As mentioned above, the norm against premarital sexual intercourse has never been more than an ideal norm in Sweden. Everyone has always known that Swedish couples had sex together before marriage, only usually no one talked about it. The social change that has occurred since the 1960s is that the four elements are now fully separated. Couples move in together without any ceremony, they have sex independent of the other three elements, and quite a few have children without being married. About half of all Swedish children are born to not-married mothers who are cohabiting with the fathers of the children.

This, in turn, means more than might be imagined at first sight. The social institution of the marriage ceremony has changed. Quite a few couples still marry, but the marriage does not move the couple from one situation to another; they are already living together. Today, Swedish couples do not marry and move in together at the same time; couples who marry have already cohabited as a couple. Some couples believe that a marriage ceremony will change their situation, but it changes nothing for them. For most couples, the marriage ceremony is a true ceremony, and still a sort of rite, not a passage rite but a confirmation rite. The marrying couple does not pass over to a different situation or stage, but rather confirms their relationship and its stability for themselves and for the surrounding social community.

Traditionally, prior to marriage, the couple would become engaged to be married. In Sweden, the engagement event was also a passage rite. The couple showed themselves and others that they were a serious couple. Engagement did not mean that they had decided when to marry, but just that they would marry some time in the future. Often relatives and friends would celebrate the engagement by attending a dinner party and giving the couple gifts for their future home.

Nowadays, quite a few cohabiting couples announce their engagement. However, I have never heard of any cou-

ple announcing their engagement before they started cohabiting. The Swedish term for engagement, *förlovning*, literally means a prepromise; the couple promise to marry each other. Today, for most Swedish couples, the term has no connection with marriage. For most couples, what happens is that when they mutually fall in love, they just move in together. After some time, months or years, if they are still cohabiting, they might announce their engagement, their intention to continue as a couple. Eventually, they might also marry, in which case, the marriage means about the same as the engagement, but is a little more serious.

Obviously, more studies are needed of these terms and concepts and their various meanings for people, both for those personally involved, and for the social community.

### Sexual Behavior and Single Adults

To my knowledge, no studies of single adults and their sexual behavior can be found in Sweden. What should be remembered, however, is that quite a few of those who are officially classified as singles, and even as living in a one-person household, very often are, one way or another, living in a dyadic relationship. Here I refer to those who are nonmaritally cohabiting, but who are classified, for a number of reasons, as living alone. I also refer to what is nowadays called LAT (living alone together), couples living apart in separate households, but still together as a couple. These dyadic relationships seem to be increasing gradually (Trost 1993b).

### Marriage and the Family

The marriage and family structure in Sweden has, as far as is known, always consisted of the nuclear family as an ideal base. Heterosexual couples have married, or the equivalent, and had children. Divorce was almost nonexistent by law, as well as in reality. The number of children averaged around 4.5 per couple. The extended family has never been a Swedish social institution. In rural areas, the son took over the farm after buying out his parents with a contract that gave them a small cottage and paid them in kind until they died. The fertility rate decreased during the last part of the 19th century and the first decades of the 20th century. For a long time, the ideal number of children in Sweden has been between two and three children. The real fertility rate has, for a couple of decades, fluctuated between a total fertility rate (TFR) of 1.6 and 2.1.

The new matrimonial law in effect since 1921 made divorce easier. The divorce rates started increasing during the first decade of the 20th century, and went on increasing until 1950, when they leveled off until 1966, when the rate again started to rise. The divorce rate has continued increasing, if analyzed carefully, until the last couple of years.

### Extradyadic Sex

Nothing is known about the prevalence or incidence of extradyadic sex among Swedes. The sole study where there is some relatively reliable data is from 1967 (*Om Sexuallivet i Sverige* 1969). In this study, about 4% of the married persons surveyed had had at least two sexual partners in the previous year, one of which had to be extradyadic. What changes have occurred in the past quarter century is not known. However, the attitudes toward extradyadic sex have not changed as far as we can see, with about 95% still negative toward it.

### Divorce and Remarriage

Most of those who separate or divorce from a cohabiting relationship soon start a new relationship, a remarriage, a recohabitation, or however one might label it. In 1800 and 1990, the proportion of marriages that were not first mar-

### Figure 2

**Cohabiting Women in Percentages of
All Couples (Married or Not), 1990**

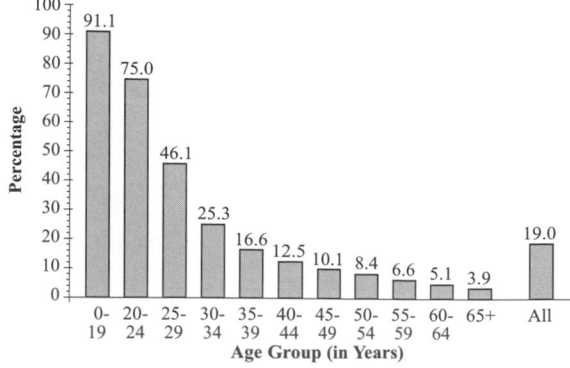

*Source: Folk—Och Bostadsräkningen 1990*

riages was approximately 25%. The important difference is that two centuries ago, all remarriages involved a widow or widower. Today, almost all remarriages follow a divorce, meaning that both former spouses are still alive to remarry. Between 1800 and 1990, there was a definite decrease in mortality rates and longer life expectancy, leaving fewer widowed seeking new mates. Heavy emigration at the end of the 19th century and the beginning of the 20th century also reduced the number of adults remarrying. At the same time, a rise in the divorce rate increased the number of second and subsequent marriages. In the end, the result has been a relatively stable 25% of all marriages involving second or subsequent remarriages (see Figure 3) (Zetterberg 2002).

Plural marriages (polygamy) are not legally recognized by law or in reality.

### Sexuality and the Physically Disabled and Aged

Sweden has pioneered in sex education for physically handicapped youth, and in training personnel working with them in institutions.

The first Nordic conference on sex and the handicapped was hosted by the Swedish Central Committee for Rehabilitation in Stockholm in 1969. An elected committee of five experts subsequently planned and provided both training for professionals in sexology and education for the disabled. This commission worked for the next ten years, arranging several seminars and courses, carrying on research, and publishing many reports and books about their work.

Students with physical handicaps get the same sex education as others in the Swedish schools. To help handicapped youths visualize love and sex between two disabled persons and between a handicapped and able-bodied person, an educational film/video, *Sex and the Handicapped*, was produced. It has been shown all over the world.

Between 1992 and 1994, a new project, Sexology and the Handicapped, was funded by the Swedish government to do research in the field and provide further training in sexology for personnel working with handicapped persons.

There are no studies on frequencies, occurrences, or varieties of sexual behaviors among the disabled or elderly. While the sexual needs of the disabled and older persons have received more attention in Sweden than in other countries, these phenomena are more often not talked about. There still is a prevailing public attitude that old people have left sex behind and that the disabled should be glad they are alive. Very ambitious attempts at changing this situation are being made by the Swedish association for the

disabled, which is raising the issues for both medical personnel and the disabled themselves.

### Incidence of Oral and Anal Sex

In the Uppsala study mentioned earlier, 10% of the 19- to 23-year-old male students, and almost 20% of the women, have had anal sex. In most cases, this appears to be an incidental or occasional experimentation rather than a reoccurring experience.

As for fellatio, about 20% of the young women and a third of the men have never experienced it. About 40% of the women and 30% of the men have practiced fellatio more often than monthly during the past year. The occurrence of cunnilingus shows a very similar picture.

As far as I know, there are no studies about Swedish attitudes about anal sex, fellatio, and cunnilingus—people just don't talk about these behaviors. There are no legal restrictions on what sexual outlets couples or individuals practice, as long as they are mutually voluntary and harmless.

## 6. Homoerotic, Homosexual, and Bisexual Behaviors

The state Lutheran Church keeps a low profile on homosexuality, as do most of the other churches and congregations. They are not in favor of varieties other than heterosexuality, and could be interpreted as being negative at least to homosexual behavior, if not to the homosexual inclination—to be homosexual does not mean to behave accordingly.

Almost no Swede would dare to say anything negative about homosexuality or same-gender couples in the mass media or otherwise more or less openly. But all homosexuals easily and often experience hidden and/or open discrimination. The law discriminated between same- and opposite-gender sexuality until the mid-1970s. It was, for instance, illegal for an adult man to have sex with a woman younger than 15 and with another man younger than 18. There was an unspoken presumption that adult women would not have sex with a boy younger than 15. Today, the law is clear in treating males and females equally, and not discriminating by age and gender between same- and opposite-gender relationships.

In Denmark, since October 1, 1989, same-gender couples can register their partnerships. This means that the laws applicable to married couples automatically apply also to these registered couples. Two differences remain. Same-gender couples cannot adopt a child jointly, and if one has a child, the partner cannot adopt the child and become its legal parent along with the natural parent. And there is no official, legal ceremony, or ritual attached to civil registration of same-gender relationships as there is in the marriage of opposite-gender couples. Norway adopted the same law on August 1, 1993. At the time of this writing, it appeared that Sweden would follow, enacting the same law during the United Nations Year of the Family in 1994.

The experience in Denmark is that relatively few same-gender couples have registered, a few hundred in all, the majority of whom being male couples. The law has not apparently changed the social attitudes in the general population.

However, in Sweden, since the mid-1960s, many homosexuals and their organizations have been arguing for the right to marry. Sweden was first in taking a step in that direction by putting cohabitation of same-gender couples on a par with cohabiting opposite-gender couples. The 1987 law provides that in the case of separating same- or opposite-gender couples, the partner most in need of the apartment or house has the right to remain in it, even if the lease, deed, or

### Figure 3

**Marriages Where Both Partners Were Never Married, Sweden, in Percentages**

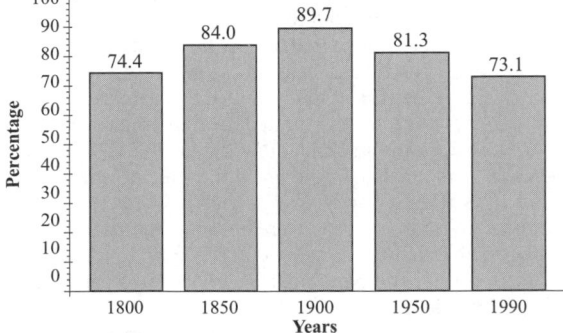

*Sources*: *Historisk Statistik* 1967, *Befolkningsrörelsen* 1990

title is written in the other cohabitant's name. The law also states that what the couple have accumulated for common usage in their household should be divided equally in case of death or separation, independent of which cohabitant actually paid for the item.

Riksförbundet för Sexuelit Likaberättigande (RFSL), founded in 1950, is a nonprofit organization working for gay and lesbian rights. A special HIV department in RFSL receives economic support from the government for their preventative measures.

## 7. Gender Diversity and Transgender Issues

Transvestites have no special legal status, but since neither they nor society looks on them as deviant or sick, there is and should be no treatment. Many transvestites are members of a chapter of Full Personality Expression (FPE), an international organization for cross-gendered persons. FPE holds monthly meetings and maintains an open house for members, as well as for other interested persons in Stockholm.

By law, transsexuals can and also, in practice, do change their sex, after following a standard course of long observation and treatment by psychiatrists. Following gender reassignment, all legal documents are changed to match the new sex. Estimates suggest that about half of those who sincerely want to change their sex follow through and are allowed to have the operation. Less than a dozen operations are performed annually in Sweden.

## 8. Significant Unconventional Sexual Behaviors

### A. Coercive Sex

*Sexual Abuse and Incest*

No one knows how frequent child sexual abuse or incest is. It occurs, and a certain number of cases are made known to the police. Of course, there are many more cases than those reported. However, in 1992, only 100 persons were sentenced for incest or for sexual activities with a minor. In the same year, 105 persons were sentenced for child sexual abuse and another 251 for having touched minors sexually.

The sentences for these crimes vary, with a maximum of four years imprisonment for incestuous abuse. Conviction for sexual touching of a minor can bring a sentence of up to one year's imprisonment. If these crimes are severe, the penalty can be up to eight years. These sentences are applied only if physical force or psychological coercion has not been used. If force has been used, the laws for rape are applied.

*Sexual Harassment*

In Sweden, as in so many other countries, sexual harassment is a new concept, even though the phenomenon is old. Studies made at universities indicate that between 10% and 25% of female students say they have been sexually harassed. Very few cases are reported. Businesses and schools have not developed any official policies to define and set policies for reporting sexual harassment. However, there is a growing awareness of sexual harassment issues among the people.

*Rape*

In Sweden, as elsewhere, most cases of rape are never reported and no one knows how frequent they are. It is known that among those rapes reported, most are perpetrated by a person known and trusted by the victim. In 1965, 1,565 cases of rape were reported to the police, and 203 perpetrators were sentenced to imprisonment.

The law differentiates between four types or degrees of rape or sexual assault. The most severe is what could be called flagrant rape or *grov våldtäki*, involving violence and dangerous use of physical force; conviction can bring four to ten years imprisonment. A second type of sexual assault is simple rape (*våldta-ki*), with the penalty ranging from two to six years imprisonment. Sexual force, or *sexuellt tvång*, is not defined as rape, although it involves forced sexual intercourse without the use of violence or threat of violence; the penalty can be up to four years in prison. Finally, there is sexual abuse, or *sexuellt utnyttjande*, in which the perpetrator abuses his or her position of power, authority, or guardianship.

### B. Prostitution

Prostitution is prevalent in the centers of the three largest Swedish cities: Stockholm, Gothenburg (Göteborg), and Malmo. Contacts with prostitutes can be made at bars all over the country, but these places are not directly linked with prostitution. Pimping is forbidden and conviction can result in up to four years imprisonment, up to six years if the case is severe. Very seldom is anyone reported for pimping, and almost never is anyone sentenced.

The police seldom ever take action against prostitutes and their customers, as so often occurs in some other countries. Sweden does not have as many influential moralists with double standards as are found in some other countries.

### C. Pornography and Erotica

The production, display, and sale of pornography are permitted unless children are involved in one way or another. Distasteful displays of pornography are not permitted, and involvement of a minor can bring a fine and maximum sentence of six months imprisonment. Very few cases are reported to the police for prosecution. Pornography and erotica are readily available at tobacconists, video stores, and many other places.

## 9. Contraception, Abortion, and Population Planning

### A. Contraception

Sex education, as mentioned above, has a long history in the compulsory schools. This is matched by the availability of, advertisement of, and information on condoms and other contraceptives. Vending machines for condoms can be found in hotels, bars, restaurants, and elsewhere, even at some bus stops on the street. All gas stations, groceries, supermarkets, and tobacconists openly sell condoms and often display them at the counter. Midwives and physicians prescribe contraceptive pills and fit IUDs. Male and female sterilization is free of charge upon request if the person is over age 25.

### B. Teenage Unmarried Pregnancies

It should be clear from the discussion of marriage and cohabitation rates above that almost no Swedish teenagers are married. This means that almost all pregnant teenage women are not married. Quite a few of them are cohabiting; how many is not known. About 3% of all children born in 1991 were born to mothers younger than 20. As is usually the case, it is not known how old the fathers were. Only about 15% of these mothers were married, thus less than a half percent of all children were born to a married teenage mother. The total fertility rate (TFR) for girls 15 to 19 years of age was 13.1, compared with a TFR of 154.1 for women 25 to 29 years of age.

In 1991, there were 3,564 children born to teenage mothers and 6,152 abortions performed on teenagers. Thus, about two thirds of the teenage pregnancies end with an induced abortion.

## C. Abortion

Prior to 1939, abortion was illegal in Sweden. In 1939, the law was changed to allow abortion under certain conditions and for specific reasons. Grounds for legal abortion were connected to the eugenic ideas popular in the Western world at that time. In Sweden, as elsewhere, there was an effort to keep the national stock pure and good. Gradually, the perspective changed, more grounds were added, and the law became more liberal. A 1975 law reform gives the woman the right to a legal abortion upon request until the end of the 18th week of gestation, without any costs to her.

Prior to the early 1970s, Sweden had an unknown number of illegal abortions and relatively few legal abortions. Estimates of illegally induced abortions during the 1950s range from 10,000 to 100,000 per year; about 5,000 legal abortion were done annually in this era. Now, illegal abortions are nonexistent because the cost of an abortion is covered by national health insurance, and no one other than the pregnant woman has to be involved in the decision, even if the pregnant woman is a minor.

In 1991, the total abortion rate (TAR) was 615.3 (see Figure 4). The specific age rates vary, although the younger the age group, the higher is the abortion rate for women who are older than 19 years. Since 1975, the TAR has been fairly stable. Since coital activities vary more among teenagers than among older women, the abortion data for teens need to be considered separately. For 15- to 17-year-olds, the abortion rate has decreased; for older teens, it has remained fairly stable over the years since 1975. The 1975 rates were approximately 16 per 1,000 girls age 15, 29 for girls age 16, and 33 for girls age 17; in 1991, these figures were 9, 17, and 21, respectively, with lows in all groups in 1983-85 of about 7, 12, and 18, and highs in 1988-90 of about 10, 19, and 25, respectively. For older teens, the 1975 rates were approximately 33 per 1,000 girls age 18 and 31 for girls age 19; in 1991, the rates were 28 and 33, respectively, with lows in 1983-85 of about 23 and 26, and highs in 1988-90 of about 31 and 34, respectively.

## D. Population Control Efforts

At the end of the 19th century, the fertility rate started on a decline that went on until the mid-1930s. By the mid-1930s, the birthrate was below replacement level, and some politicians and others were concerned about the risks of immigration overwhelming ethnic Swedes. During the 1940s, Sweden provided housing subsidies to poor households with minor children, government allowances for all mothers with a child under age 16, and other pronatal incentives. But even before these measures were enacted, the postwar baby boom came with its peak in 1946-1947.

When the fertility rate again came to a historic low in the 1960s and especially the 1970s, some politicians and demographers became emotionally concerned and involved. Discussions about new ways to make society more "child friendly" became popular. But the political decisions were hidden behind the mask of social welfare. Since the Nazis were defeated in 1945, very few Swedes have dared to admit being pronatalists.

In modern times, there have been no attempts to reduce the population, unless one counts the discussions about immigration policy as an issue in population growth.

## 10. Sexually Transmitted Diseases and HIV/AIDS

### A. Sexually Transmitted Diseases

*Incidence and Trends*

The previously most feared STD, syphilis, is now comparatively rare, dropping from 153 new cases in 1985 to 121 new cases reported in 1991. Gonorrhea has also decreased, from 5,389 new cases in 1985 to only 617 cases in 1991. Two thirds of these STDs occur in men.

In Sweden, chlamydia was not recognized until recently as an STD. After apparently peaking in 1990 at over 21,000 new cases, a decreasing trend seems to have arrived. Most cases of chlamydia occur in persons under age 30, with two thirds of reported cases detected in females.

Trichomonas, herpes, candida, condyloma, and other diseases are not classified as STDs, and reporting by treating physicians is not required. Thus, no data are available for these infections.

*Treatment and Prevention Efforts*

Treatment for all sexual infections is available free of charge or with only a nominal fee. Propaganda for condom use has traditionally been based on preventing unwanted pregnancies, contrary to the connection made in continental Europe and North America, where condom use has been promoted for prophylactic disease prevention. Swedish propaganda now includes prophylactic use.

Changes in the frequencies of the various STDs suggest a variety of factors. Decreases in gonorrhea and syphilis are connected both with more efficient treatment and increased education about condom use and about the risks of these diseases. The rise in chlamydia in the late 1980s is explained in part by the increased use of the contraceptive pill as an efficient protection against pregnancy and its lack of protection against STDs. The recent decrease in chlamydia is because of increased education and STD prevention.

### B. HIV/AIDS

*Incidence, Patterns, and Trends*

According to mid-1993 estimates, Sweden has between 3,000 and 4,000 persons with HIV infection. Each year 300 to 400 new cases have been reported. About 150 persons with HIV convert to full-blown AIDS, according to estimates from 1990 to the present. About 60% of the HIV-positive persons are between ages 25 and 39.

*Treatment, Prevention Programs, and Government Policies*

Distribution of free syringes and condoms, more-rigorous blood tests for blood donors and transfusions, and increased information and education on safer sex are being

### Figure 4

**Abortion Rates in Sweden, 1939-1992, per 1,000 Women Aged 15-44**

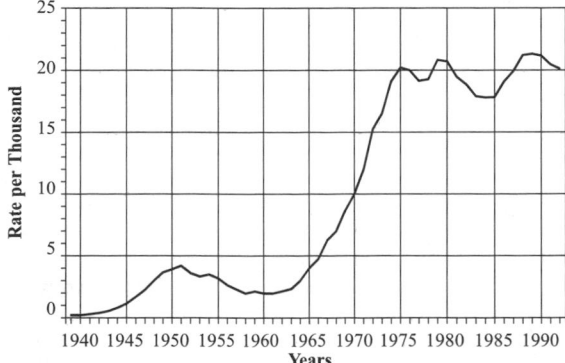

*Sources: Aborter,* various volumes

used to limit the spread of HIV and other sexually transmitted diseases. Local and national governments strongly support prevention, research, and treatment efforts, both to prevent further spread and to find a cure.

[*Update 2002*: UNAIDS Epidemiological Assessment: HIV testing is mandatory for blood donors, and systematic but voluntary for pregnant women, women having abortions, injecting drug users, STD patients, immigrants, refugees, and the deceased with autopsies. All diagnosed HIV infections are registered in the Swedish national HIV case-reporting system, using an identifying code. By mid-2001, a cumulative total of 5,523 cases of HIV infection has been notified since the beginning of the epidemic, approximately two thirds of which were in Stockholm. Among cases reported in 1997-1999, 48% were heterosexuals, 32% were homosexuals, and 8% were injecting drug users. Among heterosexual cases, 35% were diagnosed in persons originating from countries with a generalized HIV epidemic. Prevalence in pregnant women and STD patients is primarily generated through the national testing programs. Data on pregnant women revealed that the prevalence in Stockholm is four times higher than in the rest of the country. The incidence of syphilis has remained less than 2 per 100,000 since 1984.

[Data on prevalence among injecting drug users are available through a screening program of injecting drug users in the prison of Stockholm. In 1987, prevalence was 16% and 13% in 1988. Incidence was estimated around 0.9% in 1987 and 1.2% in 1988. When the HIV test was introduced in 1984, 300 injecting drug users in treatment in Stockholm were tested, resulting in a prevalence of 11%. Subsequent testing noted an incidence of 5% between 1984 and 1990, with seroconversion rates decreasing over time. As in most screening programs, persons known to be HIV infected are not retested. In the study on injecting drug users in prisons, those known positives not tested were added to both numerator and denominator; about 30% to 37% were not tested, and in addition, 15% to 25% refused to be tested. Those prevalence rates need, therefore, to be interpreted with caution. In the Stockholm area, it is estimated that there are 14,000 homosexuals, 3,000 to 4,000 drug abusers, and 9,000 immigrants from sub-Saharan Africa in the 15- to 64-year-old age group.

[The estimated number of adults and children living with HIV/AIDS on January 1, 2002, were:

| | |
|---|---|
| Adults ages 15-49: | 3,300 (rate: 0.1%) |
| Women ages 15-49: | 880 |
| Children ages 0-15: | < 100 |

[An estimated less than 100 adults and children died of AIDS during 2001.

[No estimate is available for the number of Swedish children who had lost one or both parents to AIDS and were under age 15 at the end of 2001.

[Adults in the *UNAIDS Fact Sheet* are defined as women and men aged 15 to 49. This age range covers people in their most sexually active years. While the risk of HIV infection obviously continues beyond the age of 50, this definition covers the vast majority of those who engage in substantial risk behaviors. (*End of update by the Editors*)]

## 11. Sexual Dysfunctions, Counseling, and Therapies

### A/B. Concepts of Sexual Dysfunction and Availability of Therapy

Swedish sex therapists, of which there are not many, work with both couples and individuals, using the techniques of the American pioneers William Masters and Virginia Johnson. Some therapists supplement this approach with the psychodynamic methods of Helen Singer Kaplan. The therapists are mostly licensed medical doctors or psychologists with postgraduate training in sex therapy in Sweden, Denmark, or the U.S.A.

Most couples seeking sex therapy are in their 30s and 40s and have had their problems even before they married. Sex therapy is generally short-term therapy, lasting between 10 and 20 hours. In many cases, a combination of sex therapy and psychotherapy is needed, because the sexual problem often has its roots in a deeper and broader personality dysfunction that goes back to childhood. Such cases require more intensive, long-term individual therapy.

Treatment is generally not covered by insurance, and most patients have to cover all costs themselves.

## 12. Sex Research and Advanced Professional Education

### A/B. Sexological Research and Postgraduate Education

The best known sexological research units can be found at various departments at Swedish universities: Gothenburg (Göteborg) University, Department of Psychology; Umeå University, Department of Rehabilitation; and Uppsala University, the Neurology and Sociology Departments.

Postcollege, graduate-level programs for the advanced study of human sexuality do not exist as programs. At the above-mentioned university departments, regular doctoral degrees are offered within the specialty of sexology.

### C. Important Sexological Organizations

The Swedish Sexological Association was established in 1980 with Jan Trost as its first president. At that time, the intention was to have an association consisting of members actively working in the scientific field of sexology in various disciplines. Subsequently, the association has changed to a professional organization whose members work clinically with matters related to sexuality, including physicians, psychologists, and contraception counselors.

The address for the Swedish Sexological Association is: c/o Lars-Gösta Dahlström, Göteborg University, Department of Psychology, P.O. Box 14158, S-400 20 Göteborg (Gothenburg), Sweden.

The Swedish Institute for Sexual Research is based in Stockholm. Director: Mai-Briht Bergstrom-Walan. Address: Tystbergavagen 41, S-111 44 Stockholm, Sweden.

Riksförbundet för Sexuell Upplysning (RFSU), founded in 1933, is a not-for-profit organization working for safe and liberal sex, safe in terms of preventing STDs, unwanted pregnancies, and sexual assaults of all kinds. The address for RFSU is: Rosenlundsgatan 13, S-104 62 Stockholm, Sweden; or: P.O. Box 17006, S-104 62 Stockholm, Sweden.

Riksförbundet för Sexuelit Likaberäattigande (RFSL), a gay and lesbian education and rights advocacy group, is based at: Stockholms Gay-hus. Sveavägen 57, S-104 30 Stockhom, Sweden; or: P.O. Box 350, S-101 24 Stockholm, Sweden.

In 1967, a government commission conducted a probability sample survey of about 2,000 men and women aged 18 to 60 years. The interviews, with 90% response, dealt with perception of sexual norms, attitudes, and behavior. Details were published by *Statens Offentliga Utredningar* (*SOU*) (Stockholm), 1969:2.

*Nordic Sexology* (*Nordisk Sexologi*) is published quarterly. Publisher's address: Soren Buss Jensen, M.D., Aalborg Psykiatriske Sygehus, Postboks 210, DK-9100 Aalborg, Denmark; or: Dansk Psykologisk Forlag, Hans Knudsens Plads 1 a. DK-2100 Copenhagen, Denmark.

## [13. Important Ethnic and Religious Minorities

ROBERT T. FRANCOEUR

[*Update 2002*: During the past 50 years, immigrants from 160 nations have transformed Sweden from an ethnically relatively homogeneous society into an intensely multiethnic one, according to Hans Lennart Zetterberg (2002), professor of social work at the University of Goteborg, Sweden. By the early 1990s, some 10% of the Swedish population was foreign born. In 2002, more than 1.3 million out of a population of nine million—15%—were immigrants or children of immigrants. Immigrants are drawn to Sweden in increasing numbers by the country's persistent labor shortage. They also take advantage of the country's liberal asylum policy, which grants refuge from the conflicts occurring in many of the Middle Eastern homelands.

[This change in Swedish life and culture has resulted in considerable cross-cultural tension and misunderstandings. According to Mansson (1993), this tension is most evident in love relationships, particularly when immigrant males from strongly patriarchal tribal cultures encounter egalitarian Swedish concepts of marriages based on love, the sexual rights and freedom of both men and women taken for granted in the prevailing Scandinavian sexual culture, and the open acceptance of premarital sex and cohabitation. As one commentator noted, "They aren't used to women being equal to men or nakedness being taken as natural instead of sexual or the idea that you can choose your own partner. They get scared and become defensive and much more fundamentalist than they would be at home." This cultural tension occurs within the context of important cultural patterns and processes that are reshaping the values, expectations, and lives of immigrant women and men, immigrant parents and their children, and the whole of Swedish culture.

[Nowhere has this been more evident than in the conflict of the tragic case of Fadime Sahindal, a 26-year-old Kurdish woman who became the victim of an "honor killing" by her father. Almost immediately after her death on January 21, 2002, Fadime became an international symbol and martyr for women's rights far beyond the borders of Sweden, and the focus of a new search for ways to protect immigrant women from patriarchal tribal values that allow "honor killing" by male relatives when a female relative brings "shame" on the clan or family by rejecting the patriarch's authority or an arranged marriage (Mojab & Hassanpour 2002; Williams 2002).

[Although Fadime's father, Rahmi Sahindal, came to Sweden from Turkey 20 years ago, he was still guided more by pressure from his Kurdish clansmen than by the rule of law or love for his daughter. In 1998, Fademi rejected a proposed marriage arranged by her father. When her father and brother threatened to kill her in 1998 for the "shame" she brought on the family, a Swedish lawmaker of Kurdish descent negotiated a compromise by which Fademi agreed to stay away from Uppsala where her parents lived. In return, her father promised not to stalk her outside their hometown while she was living in seclusion near Stockholm. Fademi continued her study for a sociology degree and became an outspoken advocate of the opportunities that Nordic immigration presented for women from fundamentalist backgrounds. In 2002, as she prepared to depart for Kenya to write her master's thesis, Fademi decided to visit her mother and sister in Uppsala to say farewell. According to friends, her sister is mentally disabled and suffered Fademi's long absence in sadness and confusion. When Fademi's father learned of her arrival in Uppsala, he showed up at the family home and shot Fademi in the head, killing her instantly.

[Following Fademi's murder, human rights activists warned that liberal European governments that continue to ignore the dangers of not integrating immigrant communities and dealing with conflicts in religious and cultural values, will do so at great peril. Dilsa Demirbag-Sten, a former government advisor on integration affairs whose Kurdish family came to Sweden from eastern Turkey when she was 7, has accused Swedish and other Scandinavian authorities of arrogance in their view that certain rights and freedoms accorded Nordic residents, such as gender equality and protection from forced marriage, are not necessarily applicable to immigrants. Swedish law, for example, allows girls from immigrant families to marry as young as 15, while marriage for Swedish citizens is not permitted until age 18. That *de facto* bow to immigrant cultural practice is expected to be legislated out of existence, as momentum gathers in a national campaign to prevent arranged and forced marriage. Currently, an estimated 30 to 40 young immigrant women in Sweden are hiding from male relatives who have vowed to kill them.

[At least 15% of Sweden's 9 million residents are non-Nordic and heavily concentrated in volatile ghettos of Somalis, Kurds, Bosnians, and dozens of other ethnic groups. There are towns and villages just outside of Stockholm and Uppsala where the entire population is foreign. This is the case in Botkyrka, a suburb only a 30-minute drive from central Stockholm where Fademi grew up. More than 80% of the 30,000 residents of Botkyrka are immigrants and refugees. Scandinavia's liberal values curry little favor in many of these settlements. Immigrants band together in these small towns and villages to protect their way of life. In such places, no Swedish is spoken, there is no Swedish television, and the people have no jobs that bring them in contact with Swedish people. A 1995 reform of laws on refugees and immigration worsened this situation by focusing training and jobs on the younger generation, causing strains within families between the older generation and their children, as well as between immigrants and Swedes.

[Fademi's death has led to support for a variety of policy changes to promote social integration. These include raising the minimum age for marriage to 18 for all women, advisory sessions for new arrivals on the vast differences in gender relations they will encounter and must respect, prohibition of head scarves or veils for girls under 16, and equal opportunity in all aspects of education. Parents from conservative religious backgrounds currently can opt to remove their children from sex education classes, swimming, and other coeducational sports, and fieldtrips.

[The significance of this and similar incidents of conflicting sexual and social values is clear, in the sense that, as birthrates in all the European countries continue to drop and shortages in the local labor pools increase, immigrants from less-economically developed countries will fill the vacuum and bring with them their highly patriarchal clan-based sexual mores. Cultural diversity is not the problem. The problem is to identify ways to improve tolerance and integration, rather than the isolating segregation of diverse cultural tradition to continue. Western cultural imperialism and hegemony will not solve the problem, because the information and energy flow in this situation is not one-way but a two-way road of cross-fertilization. (*End of update by R. T. Francoeur*)]

## References and Suggested Readings

Carlson, L. 1965. *Jag giver dig min dotter.* Stockholm: Nerenius & Santerus.

CIA. 2002 (January). *The world factbook 2002.* Washington, DC: Central Intelligence Agency. Available: http://www.cia.gov/cia/publications/factbook/index.html.

Intons-Peterson, M. J. 1988. *Gender concepts of Swedish and American youth*. New York: Lawrence Erlbaum Assoc.

Lewin, B. 1991. *Att Omplantera sexualieten*. Uppsala: Uppsala Universitet.

Lewin, B. 1987. *Att se sexualiteten: Om sexuell socialisation, Förhållnigssätt och sexuella erfarenheter bland människor med medfödda funktionshinder*. Uppsala: Uppsala Universitet.

Lewin B, & G. Helmius. 1983. *Ungdom och sexualitet*. Uppsala: Uppsala Universitet.

Manniche, E. 1989. *The family in Denmark*. Uppsala: Uppsala Universitet.

Månsson, S.-A. 1993. *Cultural conflict and the Swedish sexual myth: The male immigrant's encounter with Swedish sexual and cohabitation culture*. Westport, CT: Greenwood Publishers.

Meyer, D. 1989. *Sex and power: The rise of women in America, Russia, Sweden and Italy*. : Middletown, CT: Wesleyan University Press.

Mojab, S., & A. Hassanpour. 2002 (February 16). *In memory of Fadime Sahindal: Thoughts on the struggle against "honour killing"* (www.KurdistanObserver.com). Available: http://mywebpage.netscape.com/kurdistanobserve/17-2-02-opinion-in-memory-fadime-honor-killing.html.

Nordqvist, I., ed. 1972. *Life together: The situation of the handicapped*. Stockholm: Swedish Central Committee for Rehabilitation.

Nordqvist, I., ed. 1984. *Sexualitet, handikapp, terapi*. Stockholm: Handikappinstitutet.

*Om sexuallivet i Sverige*. 1969. Stockholm: Statens Offentliga Utredningar (SOU).

Rodman, H., & J. Trost. 1986. *The adolescent dilemma*. New York: Praeger.

*Statistical Yearbook of Sweden*. 1993.

Sundt, E. 1855/1975. *Om giftermaal i Norge*. Oslo: Gyldendal Norsk Förlag.

Trost, A.-C. 1982. *Abort och psykiska besvär*. Västerås: International Library.

Trost, J. 1979. *Unmarried cohabitation*. Västerås: International Library.

Trost, J. 1988. *Sexologisk ordbok*. Uppsala: Uppsala Universitet.

Trost, J. 1993a. *Familjen i Sverige [Family systems in Sweden]*. Stockholm: Liber. In press

Trost, J. 1993b. Family from a dyadic perspective. *Journal of Family Issues, 14*:92-104.

UNAIDS. 2002. *Epidemiological fact sheets by country*. Geneva, Switzerland: Joint United Nations Programme on HIV/AIDS (UNAIDS/WHO). Available: http://www.unaids.org/hivaidsinfo/statistics/fact_sheets/index_en.htm.

Williams, C. J. 2002 (March 7). Price of freedom, in blood: Case of Kurdish woman killed by her father for rejecting his authority illustrates Sweden's cultural double standards. *The Los Angeles Times*.

Zetterberg, H. L. 2002. *Sexual life in Sweden* (Trans. G. Fennell). New Brunswick, NJ: Transaction.

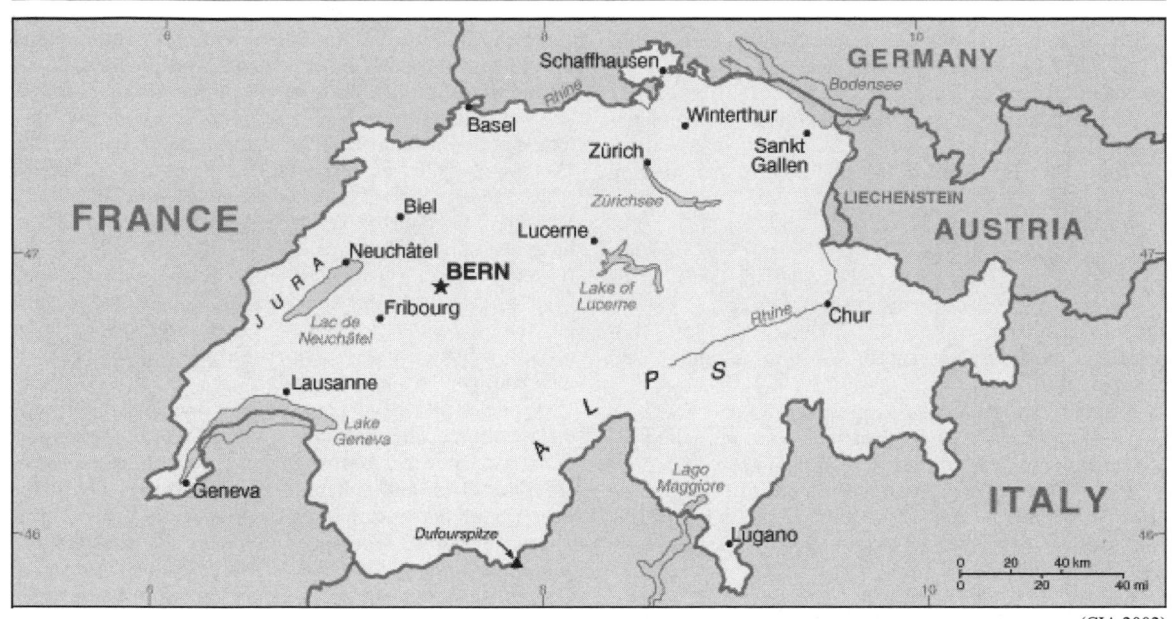

(CIA 2002)

# Switzerland
## (The Swiss Confederation)

Prof. Johannes Bitzer, M.D., Ph.D.,* Judith Adler, Ph.D.,
Prof. Dr. Udo Rauschfleisch Ph.D., Sibil Tschudin, M.D.,
Elizabeth Zemp, M.D., and Ulrike Kosta

## Contents

## *Demographics and a Brief Historical Perspective*

SIBIL TSCHUDIN

### A. Demographics

Switzerland is located in central Europe and spreads over an area of 15,942 square miles (41,290 km²), about twice the size of the state of New Jersey in the U.S. Most of the country is composed of a mountainous plateau bordered by the great bulk of the Alps in the south and by the Jura Mountains in the northwest. This long, relatively narrow plateau is crossed by the Aare River and contains the lakes of Neuchâtel and Zürich. The country's largest lakes—Geneva, Constance (Bodensee), and Maggiore—straddle the French, German-Austrian, and Italian borders, respectively. The Rhine, navigable from Basel to the North Sea, is the principal inland waterway. The strategically important alpine north-south communications are assured by numerous passes and by railroad tunnels, notably the Lötschberg, St. Gotthard, and Simplon. Switzerland consists of 26 federated states, of which 20 are called cantons and 6 are called half cantons. The cantons are Zürich, Bern, Lucerne, Uri, Schwyz, Glarus, Zug, Fribourg, Solothurn, Schaffhausen, Saint Gall, the Grisons (Graubünden), Aargau, Thurgau, Ticino, Vaud, Valais, Neuchâtel, Geneva, and Jura. Of the half cantons, Obwalden and Nidwalden together form Unterwalden, Basel-Land and Basel-Stadt form Basel, and Ausser-Rhoden and Inner-Rhoden form Appenzell. The capital of Switzerland is Berne.

German, French, and Italian are Switzerland's major and official languages; Romansh (a Rhaeto-Roman dialect spoken in parts of the Grisons) was designated a "semi-official" language in 1996, and entitled to federal funds to help promote its continued use. German dialects (Schwyzerdütsch) are spoken by about 65% of the inhabitants. French, spoken by about 20% of the population, predominates in the southwest; Italian, spoken by about 8%, is the language of Ticino, in the south. The few Romansh-speakers are in the southeast.

In December 2001, Switzerland had an estimated population of 7.3 million. The largest cities by population are Zürich (about 340,000), Basel (180,000), Geneva (170,000), Berne (130,000), and Lausanne (120,000). (All data are from the latest Swiss Census unless otherwise noted; data designated (*WFB*) are from *The World Factbook 2002*, CIA.)

**Age Distribution and Sex Ratios** (*WFB*): *0-14 years*: 16.8% with 1.05 male(s) per female (sex ratio); *15-64 years*: 67.7% with 1.03 male(s) per female; *65 years and over*: 15.5% with 0.69 male(s) per female; *Total population sex ratio*: 0.97 male(s) to 1 female

**Life Expectancy at Birth** (in 2000): *male*: 76.9 years; *female*: 82.6 years; (*WFB Total Population*: 79.86 years)

**Urban/Rural Distribution**: 85% to 15% (*WFB*)

**Ethnic Distribution**: German: 65%; French: 18%; Italian: 10%; Romansch: 1%; other: 6% (*WFB*)

**Religious Distribution**: Roman Catholic: 42%; Protestant: 35%; other Christian communities: 2%; Jewish: 0.2%; Islam: 4%; others: 1%; no religion: 11%

*Communications*: Prof. Johannes Bitzer, M.D., Ph.D. Leiter Gyn. Sozialmedizin und Psychosomatik Universitäts-Frauenklinik, Spitalstrasse 21, CH-4031 Basel, Switzerland; jbitzer@uhbs.ch.

**Birth Rate**: 10.1 births per 1,000 population; (*WFB* 9.84)

**Death Rate**: 8.4 per 1,000 population

**Infant Mortality Rate**: 3.2 deaths per 1,000 live births

**Net Migration Rate**: 2.01 migrant(s) per 1,000 population; (*WFB* 5.54)

**Total Fertility Rate**: 1.41 children born per woman; (*WFB* 1.73)

**Population Growth Rate**: 0.8%; (*WFB* 0.24%)

**HIV/AIDS**: *Total positive HIV tests (1985-2000)*: 25,007; *Persons with AIDS (1983-2000)*: 7,036; *Deaths*: 5,009. (*WFB* 1999 estimates: *Adult prevalence*: 0.46%; *Persons living with HIV/AIDS*: 17,000; *Deaths*: 150.) (For additional details from www.UNAIDS.org, see end of Section 10B.)

**Literacy Rate** (*defined as those age 15 and over who can read and write*): 99%; education is free and school attendance compulsory during 9 years, from age 7 to 16

**Per Capita Gross Domestic Product** (*purchasing power parity*): $28,600; *Inflation*: 1.5%; (*WFB* 2.4%); *Unemployment*: 3.8%; (*WFB* 5.3%); *Living below the poverty line*: NA

## B. A Brief Historical Perspective

In 58 B.C.E., the Helvetii who inhabited the area of Switzerland (called Helvetia in those times) were conquered by the Romans. In 1033, the territory was incorporated into the Holy Roman Empire. In the 1200s, Habsburg encroachments on the privileges of the three mountainous localities of Uri, Schwyz, and Unterwalden resulted in the conclusion of a defensive league among them in 1291. In the following centuries, the Swiss Confederation slowly added new cantons. In 1648, the Treaty of Westphalia gave Switzerland its independence from the Holy Roman Empire. French revolutionary troops occupied the country in 1798 and named it the Helvetic Republic, but Napoleon in 1803 restored its federal government. By 1815, the French- and Italian-speaking peoples of Switzerland had been granted political equality. In 1815, the Congress of Vienna guaranteed the neutrality and recognized the independence of Switzerland. In the revolutionary era of 1847, the Catholic cantons seceded and organized a separate union called the Sonderbund, but they were defeated and rejoined the federation. The victorious Radicals transformed the confederation into one federal state under a new constitution adopted in 1848 and recast in 1874, establishing a strong central government while giving significant control to each canton. National unity grew as the country prospered from its neutrality. Strict neutrality was its policy in both World Wars I and II. Geneva became the seat of the League of Nations (later the European headquarters of the United Nations) and of a number of international organizations. In September 2002, Switzerland became the 190th member of the UN.

Politically, Switzerland is a direct democracy. The referendum, as well as popular initiatives, are frequently employed to achieve political change. A council of states (two members from each canton, and one from each half canton) and a 200-member national council (whose members are directly elected every four years) together form the federal assembly. The chief executive, or federal council, is composed of seven members (elected for four years by the federal assembly) and includes the president of the confederation (elected by the federal assembly annually).

## 1. Basic Sexological Premises

ELIZABETH ZEMP and JOHANNES BITZER

## A. Character of Gender Roles

The people of Switzerland have had a longstanding history in which there was a strong traditional model, with men being economically responsible, involved in paid work and in public issues, and women being responsible for the family and education and limited to the private sector. This system was maintained by legislation and a social security system, both of which have economic qualities. From the 1960s and 1970s on, important changes have occurred, which modified and diminished the gender-role separation. Women were given the right to vote and to be elected to Parliament in 1971. This was decided in a plebiscite by the male population. Changes in gender roles have developed heterogeneously, with traditional family concepts prevailing more in rural areas, while in urban areas, the changing roles of women became more visible and equality between men and women was achieved.

While an increasing percentage of women have entered the workforce, the childcare situation still reflects traditional family role patterns. Daycare options for children, child-nurseries, and maternity and day schools, exist for only a small percentage of children under 14 years of age. There are regional differences with regard to this situation, with childcare options for only 2% of the children in the German-speaking part, 7% of the children in the French-speaking part, and 34% of the children in the Italian-speaking area of Switzerland. The Swiss school system has not yet adapted to the needs of employed women, with schedules changing from day to day and children expected to eat their lunches at home. Persisting traditional gender roles are still reflected in inequalities with regard to education, income, and participation in political boards. It is also reflected in the higher percentage of women with part-time employment. While the percentage of women in the workforce has consistently increased in the last four decades, only 53% of working women, and around 25% of women with children under age 15, work full-time.

## B. Sociolegal Status of Males and Females

Equal rights for women and men became part of the Swiss Constitution only in 1981. While some gender-specific differences persist in the law, such as those related to maternity and to military conscription (mandatory only for men), all others have been changed in the last decades. With regard to maternity and childcare, a 1945 plebiscite approved social security for maternity although the corresponding law was never enacted. Three related plebiscites were rejected in 1984, 1987, and 2001. Consequently, Switzerland still lacks a federal law concerning maternity policy. Since 1989, women may not be dismissed during pregnancy or the first 16 weeks after giving birth. Some cantonal laws regulate the duration and funding of maternity leaves, producing a wide range of practices among the administrative authorities. The Swiss social security system for the elderly is based on three pillars: a basic pension insurance, an occupational benefit plan, and private savings. Basic insurance was started in 1948, and is based on paid employment. Until 1997, women retired at age 62 and men at age 65. Thereafter, the age of retirement for women has risen to 64 years. As part of the ongoing revisions of the old-age and disability/invalid pension law, the government has proposed a flexible retirement age between 62 and 65 for men and women. Since 1994, women get credited to their account for each year of childcare. Widows with children are entitled to a pension, but widows without children must be at least 45 and have been married for at least 5 years.

Legal changes have also occurred with regard to domestic violence. Prior to 1992, the legal bases excluded rape that happened within marriage from being subject to litigation. In a 1992 revision, rape and sexual violence within marriage were redefined to be punishable, but only if the wife is denouncing it. The "Victims Help Law," enacted in 1993, regulates three areas designed to improve the position of victims of violence: counseling and treatment, support throughout the legal procedure and trial, and compensation claims for damages and reparations. This law obliges the cantons to provide counseling facilities, medical, psychological, social, material, and legal assistance. Although this law is not targeting primarily victims of sexual violence, it implies also an improvement for women who experienced sexual violence.

## C. General Concepts of Sexuality, Love, Marriage, and Family

The predominant concept in the institutionalized heterosexual relationship is that it should be based on love and last lifelong. In recent years, the diversity of this concept has increased considerably, with a shift to shorter, less-stable relations, with changing partnerships over the lifecycle. This shift is reflected in increases in the divorce rate, single households, and *single educating households*. There is also an increase in the acceptance of other forms of sexualities such as homosexuality and less stigmatization for transsexual individuals.

There is also an increasing trend for a separation of fertility and sexuality. The fertility rate is rather low, around 1.5 children per fertile woman. There is also a relatively high mean age at first marriage, 27.5 years for females and 29.8 years for males. Premarital sexuality is widespread and well accepted. It goes along with the easy availability of contraceptives and widespread sexual education in schools (see Sections 3 and 9 on these topics). Sexual activity is socially accepted also among the younger. This is reflected in the so-called "*Schutzalter*" or protection age, which is set at age 16. The legal marriage age is 18. Despite a relatively high percentage of sexually active teenagers, there is a low rate of unwanted consequences, especially teenage abortions (see also Section 9B, Contraception, Abortion, and Population Planning, Teenage (Unmarried) Pregnancies).

## 2. Religious, Ethnic, and Gender Factors Affecting Sexuality

ULRIKE KOSTA

According to the last census, 44% of the population in Switzerland is Roman Catholic, and 37% belong to the Protestant church. The number of Muslims has doubled since 1990 because of immigration from Kosovo, Bosnia-Herzegovina, and the Republic of Macedonia. With a population of 311,000, Muslims are the third-largest religious group in Switzerland (4.5% of the total population). The number of Greek Orthodox Church members has also increased greatly (133,000). There are also Jewish communities and Christ Catholic parishes.

The Protestant churches and the Roman Catholic Church have been losing a significant number of members for years. This trend continues and is linked to a process of secularization and changes in values. In the 1990s, the number of persons who indicated they did not belong to any church or religious group rose from 7.4% to 12% of the population.

The Protestant church in Switzerland is characterized by a variety of different regional churches. There are largely cantonal churches, which differ in their theological and organizational character and program.

An empirically conducted ecumenical study in the canton of Basel-Stadt from 1999 showed that more than two thirds of respondents described themselves as "religious in the broadest sense." There exists a great contrast between public (e.g., attending church services) and privately practiced forms of religiousness. Accordingly, religion is prac-

ticed primarily in a private setting. Christianity continues to be the determining form of religious faith. A study from 1984 stated a correlation between the religious engagement and the number of children married couples desired. Couples who are very much involved in religion want to have more children than other couples. The study showed no difference about the expected number of children between Catholic and Protestant couples.

Until the 1970s, the sexual morality of the Roman Catholic Church exercised considerable influence on the behavior and attitudes of its believers. The process of secularization has diminished this influence significantly. To this day, the Roman Catholic Church's sexual ethics are determined by the encyclicals of the popes and statements by the national Bishops' Conference. In its encyclicals and other official proclamations, the Roman Catholic Church puts marriage center-stage as the sole place of legitimate sexuality. It considers sexuality an expression of partnership, of human union, and assigns it the aims of personal encounter and procreation. It stresses the natural and central status of marriage and its sacramental character, and rejects all forms of artificial contraception (the pill was prohibited in the encyclical, *Humanae Vitae*, by Pope Paul VI in 1968). On the other hand, some Catholic authorities emphasize the individual responsibility and the quality of the relationship.

The Roman Catholic Church insists on absolute protection of nascent life and so proscribes abortion. According to their "Statement on the Blessing of Same-Sex Unions and the Ordination of Practicing Homosexuals," the Swiss bishops view marriage as an "integrating element of God's plan of creation," yet do not transfer this to partnerships between two homosexuals. The bishops also reject any discrimination of homosexuals. In brief, a deep tension exists between the official sexual morality of the Roman Catholic Church and the attitudes and behavior of the laity.

Like the Roman Catholic Church, the Protestant churches stress protection of marriage and the family. At the same time, they do not accord marriage the same sacramental and central character as the Roman Catholic Church. They also support strong protection of nascent life and reject the use of embryonic life for the purposes of acquiring stem cells, for instance. Switzerland's Protestant churches have also been at the center of years of intensive debate on the subject of homosexuality and same-sex unions.

Although religious values as applied to sexuality are still present in society, it is clear that their influence is diminishing and that sexual behavior is a decision for the individual.

## 3. Knowledge and Education about Sexuality

SIBIL TSCHUDIN

### A. Government Policies and Programs

At present, sexual education is listed as part of the compulsory school's syllabus. After the ninth school year, the basis for sex education is fragmentary and varies from canton to canton. Meanwhile, HIV-prevention education is compulsory. Although parents can veto their children's attendance in sexual education classes, the existence of a legal basis promotes sexual education. Still, the law does not guarantee its systematical realization.

Sexual education has been organized along two lines, the so-called "internal" model and the "external" model. The internal model is predominant in the German-speaking part of Switzerland and in the Ticino canton. Although theoretically responsible for the realization of sexual education, the cantonal offices just give a few pieces of advice to school headmasters and teachers and normally do not do any quality assessment. It therefore depends almost entirely on the teacher him- or herself how much emphasis is given to the topic. The teacher chooses the lesson content, as well as the number of classes she or he dedicates to sexual education. In the external model, sexual education is considered a special subject by offices and schools. Cantons and communities undertake the responsibility for its realization by engaging well-trained external experts. This procedure guarantees a qualitatively high standing and standardized education program, although only for a few lessons. The disadvantage of this model is the lack of sexual education's integration in everyday school life and the risk that the topic is totally delegated to the external expert by the teacher.

### Coexistence of Both Models

In some cantons with the internal model, external experts are additionally engaged quite systematically. The organization of sexual education and HIV prevention is not uniform all over the country on either the political or the administrative and practical level. This renders coordination more difficult and results in a lack of well-defined duties and responsibilities.

By a 1981 federal law, all cantons are obliged to establish an office for Planned Parenthood. The intention was mainly to guarantee adequate counseling in case of unwanted pregnancy, but these institutions also offer contraceptive counseling and sometimes even broader information concerning sexual health.

School health services make various offers for pupils, as, for example, a consultation hour on school grounds. These offers, however, vary from canton to canton. Zurich has a "*Fachstelle für Sexualpädagogik*," with a free sex consultation in person, by telephone, and via a website.

A recent study evaluated sexuality education programs and courses in Swiss schools. The researchers found there is an enormous heterogeneity between Switzerland's 26 federated states. Although the federal government has provided a legal basis for all schools to teach about HIV, the local implementation varies widely. It seems that on the obligatory school level, where students are age 7 to 16, the coverage of HIV/AIDS information is sufficient. At the higher school levels, much less time and effort are devoted to meeting this lifelong education need. In the German-speaking region, sexuality education seems to be less effective than in the French-speaking region. There is no basic sex education in the German-speaking part, which makes it more difficult for the teachers to approach AIDS as a subject.

### B. Informal Sources of Sexual Knowledge

Informal sources of sexual knowledge in Switzerland are magazines, telephone hotlines, and the Internet. *Bravo*, a German magazine for teenagers, is widely read in Switzerland. Durchblick has offered information about sex and contraception by experts (gynecologists) for over ten years, first as a telephone hotline, and nowadays mainly as an Internet forum.

## 4. Autoerotic Behaviors and Patterns
JUDITH ALDER and JOHANNES BITZER

### A. Children

In Switzerland, sex education and pedagogy for children generally only start in middle school (after 6th grade); the quantity and quality of sex education as described earlier, depends mostly on the teacher. Before that, sex education is done by parents, with wide differences in the ways parents talk about sexual matters to their children according to their social and religious background. In the past ten years, it can be observed, however, that more parents choose to explain to their children in more-concrete words what sexuality is and how children are created and born. Some children's books about reproduction have been published to help parents provide a child-concerned early sex education. Orientation about autoerotic behavior as part of a normal development process is done unsystematically by pediatricians and child therapists, but usually only if parents have questions about particular issues. There is so far no systematic survey about the autoerotic behavior of Swiss children.

Autoerotic behavior can be observed in young children by the way they touch, caress, massage, and scratch their genitals or rub themselves against, for example, a swing. Behavior like this is mostly done by coincidence, regular and planned masturbatory behavior at kindergarten age (1 to 6) being considered as abnormal. It depends mostly on the caregivers' reactions of whether they believe this behavior is normal but to be carried out in private, or if they view it as immoral and prohibited. Masturbatory behavior can be observed more in boys than in girls, which might be because of the visibility and reactivity of the genitals.

### B. Adolescents

No systematic surveys have been carried out on masturbation and other autoerotic behaviors in the general population of Swiss adolescents. There do exist a few Internet services and counseling centers for teenagers, which provide answers to questions about sexuality and family planning. The following information, therefore, cannot to be considered as completely representative for Swiss teenagers, since only interested adolescents contact these services. However, they reflect general observations.

In boys, masturbatory experiences are reported earlier than in girls, with boys starting to masturbate between the ages 11 to 14. Some myths about damaging effects of masturbation can still be encountered (e.g., "Frequent masturbation harms the spinal cord") in boys. In contrast to boys, who talk more openly about masturbatory experiences, girls tend to be more reluctant to talk about masturbation and generally start practicing it later (beginning about 14 years). The typical questions boys 13 to 15 years of age addressed to counselors concern anatomy and the size of the penis, breast stimulation, and masturbation. Girls mostly address questions about menstruation, the time of its onset, and the nature of orgasmic response. With increasing age, the focus of questions becomes very specific; i.e., premature ejaculation, STDs, and homosexuality, but also with a concern for knowledge about normal lovemaking and a worry about not wanting it enough.

### C. Adults

Questions about masturbation are not asked systematically in surveys about sexuality. The estimation about experience with masturbation in men lies between around 95%, with about 70% to 85% practicing masturbation on a more regular basis. Still fewer women have experiences with masturbation (50% to 70%). Questions addressed to counselors and physicians generally concern issues of the normality of masturbation parallel to a stable relationship, and sexual fantasies that are in combination with masturbation.

## 5. Interpersonal Heterosexual Behaviors
JUDITH ADLER

### A. Children

Interpersonal sexual behavior manifests around the time of kindergarten in Swiss children (ages 4 to 6). It is represented by a curious, inquiring, and exploratory behavior; boys and girls are interested in the look and size, sometimes the smell of each other's genitals. The inquiry, however, is mostly done in private, going to the toilet together, for example. Girls and boys then might touch or caress each other's genitals. The interests, however, at this age are still very wide, with some girls and boys not being interested at all.

Role-playing is of central importance for the definition of one's own sex, representing mostly stereotypes even in children with "modern" family structures (e.g., job sharing of parents). In indirect role-play (for example, when playing with dolls) as well as in direct role-play, sexual behavior can be observed when dolls, or boys and girls, respectively, lie on each other. However, children generally name behavior like that as playing "Tarzan" or anything else they know from television or computer games, without having the concept of lovemaking. Doctor's games are another form of interpersonal sexual behavior. Again, on one hand, the main drive is curiosity about differences in anatomy and not sexual excitement. On the other hand, this is a way to be pleasantly touched and tickled by children of the same age, on "neutral" parts of the body as well as the genitals. Caregivers' reactions, again, are of importance for the development of subsequent behavior.

## B. Adolescents

In 2003, about three quarters of 14-year-old girls had had some kind of interpersonal sexual contact. In boys, interpersonal sexual behavior starts a bit later, with about two thirds having had some experience by the age of 14. The first contacts are generally through kissing. Group games ("bottle game") are still a frequent way of making first experiences. Other rituals can be observed at parties in dancing games. While boys are more aware about possible sexual reaction, many girls are still surprised and insecure when they lubricate, and do not know it as a sign of sexual arousal. "Dating" often starts before the exchange of caresses and, in the beginning, seems to be more of a definition of a relationship. Dating—"going together"—starts as early as 10 or 11 years. Again, there are wide differences in heterosexual interests at the beginning of puberty.

The legal age for the protection of minors is set at 14 years for consensual sexual relationships. The age difference between the partners is considered as relevant. The age at first sexual intercourse has changed over the past 20 years, to a greater extent for boys than for girls. Boys seem to catch up with girls, with the latter still being somewhat earlier. Intercourse experiences are reported by around 10% of 14-year-olds, while two thirds of boys and girls report intercourse experience by age 17. The step from petting to intercourse, in general, is a small step, with a stronger emphasis on intercourse being done with the right person and is, therefore, a conscious choice and planned behavior.

Relationship changes are frequent in the teenage years and in the 20s, with the tendency to last longer after the age of 18 to 20. Sexual intercourse mostly is a firm part of romantic relationships after the age of 18.

## C. Adults

Sexual intercourse before marriage is very common and in most relationships the norm. Dating in general is very casual, young men asking women out as well as vice versa. There are no firm rules about dates or when it is acceptable to initiate sexual contact. Most couples live together for many years before getting married, some moving together when moving out from the parental home. Most young women and men in their 20s, however, choose to first live alone or in communities without bonding as a couple.

With women increasingly following professional careers and having longer education periods, the age at mar-riage and childbirth has risen significantly in the last ten years. In 2001, women were 28 and men 30.6 years on average when they got married (Bundesamt für Statistik, www.statistik.admin.ch). It was calculated that 58% of women and 53% of men under the age of 50 will get married over the course of time, if the rate of marriage in 2001 remains stable. While in 2001, almost 36,000 couples got married and 15,778 divorces were recorded—45.8% with children under age 18 years—the total population in 2001 was 7,261,210. The current statistics suggest a divorce rate of 38.5%, if the number of divorces remains stable over time. In the same year, 73,509 children were born, with 11.4% of mothers not married at the time of delivery. This number does not represent only the traditional single mother, since more and more couples choose not to get married when they start a family. The child/mother ratio in 2001 was 1.4:1.

In 1999, the Swiss people rejected implementation of a nationwide maternity insurance. This means that there is no obligation of salary payments for women who are on maternity leave. However, a 6-week maternity protection (time after birth where a woman cannot be expected to work) exists. Most governmental institutions and private enterprises, however, do provide 80% to 100% of the employee's salary during an 8- to 16-week period after birth. Also, for mothers who take unpaid maternity leave, there exists a one-year dismissal protection. Fathers do not have any paid parental leave in any institution. In all states, they have the right to one day off from work for the birth, and some states (e.g., Zürich), and some firms, offer a one- to two-week paternal leave after birth.

The interpersonal sexual behavior in the adult years has become more open minded in the past 20 years. Prevention of HIV has helped, to some degree, to open discussions about different sexual practices. Because no data are available on attitudes towards oral or anal practices for heterosexual couples, we rely on clinical observation. While anal sex is most common in gay couples, it is only occasionally used by heterosexual couples. While curiosity for many couples leads to a first tryout, women may experience it as painful and will not want to do it regularly. It is mostly women who will not be ready to try it at all, mostly because of shame feelings or fear of pain and partner reaction. The attitudes on oral sex are more alike in both sexes. Most couples do have experience with oral sex, and women, as men in general, experience it as pleasurable. Even though the attitude is more positive than with anal intercourse, oral sex is not practiced in every sexual contact.

Relationships in Switzerland, in general, are monogamously faithful. Even though most couples consider faithfulness as one of the most important premises of a functioning relationship, many couples experience at least one crisis because of an extramarital sexual contact during the course of time.

### Sexuality and the Physically Disabled and the Aged

In recent years, increasing efforts have been made to ameliorate the status of counseling and care for handicapped people regarding sexuality. At Nottwill, one of the large centers for paraplegics in Switzerland, courses are being offered for paraplegics and tetraplegics (quadriplegics) regarding sexuality and intimate relationships. In these courses, basic knowledge about the sexual behavior of males and females is taught, and the influence of the individual dysfunction analyzed. The focus of the courses lies in the development of new approaches to sexuality and sexual intimacy. The teaching includes communicative skills with partners, sensuality training, sensate focus, and so on. Information is also given about the use of new drugs for erection and orgasmic dysfunction (Viagra, Cialis, etc.). The courses are given in collaboration between urologists, gynecologists, psychologists, nurses, and social workers.

As far as the sexuality of the elderly is concerned, there are also activities in the larger cities of Switzerland in health education and adult educational programs. These programs are offered either by the universities or by other public teaching institutions. These activities are focused on giving information about the organic, endocrine, and psychosocial changes of aging, and in the development of an understanding of sexual needs and behavioral patterns of elderly people. In the institutions (*Alterspflegeheime*), there is a large variety regarding the openness and the active attitude of the caregivers with respect to the sexuality of the elderly.

## 6. Homoerotic, Homosexual, and Bisexual Behaviors

UDO RAUSCHFLEITSCH

There are no representative data about the number of lesbians, gays, and bisexuals in Switzerland. Since life for homosexuals and bisexuals is by far easier in the big cities, they usually prefer to leave the rural areas and live in the big cities. Here, as in several other countries, we can assume that about 7% to 9% of the men and about 5% to 7% of the women have a homosexual or bisexual orientation. These estimates include those individuals who have homosexual relationships, but have not come out as lesbian, gay, or bisexual.

Since there is quite an open atmosphere concerning homosexuality in Switzerland, it is not too difficult for young people today to have their coming out. Many of them have an early coming out at about 16 years. Difficulties occur only in traditional Roman Catholic or fundamentalist Protestant groups. But until now, there are no announcements at schools in Switzerland about coming-out groups for the young lesbians and gays, although these groups exist in the bigger cities. Information about homosexuality is rarely given at schools. Most of the young (and elder) people get this information by newspapers, radio, TV, and scientific or popular literature. Most of the mass media report positive information and criticize discrimination against lesbians, gays, and bisexuals.

Though there is quite an open, accepting atmosphere in Switzerland, we also find violence against lesbians, gays, and bisexuals. While lesbians are more often attacked by men living or working nearby (as van den Oort reports from Germany), gays are mostly victims of young men who beat and rob them in parks, public toilets, and other areas for anonymous sexual activities. The number of victims who file a report with the police is nowadays higher than it was in former times, when the victims feared (and really experienced) that they were not taken seriously and were blamed or even accused by the police. Even so, quite a number of violent deeds still go unreported, especially if the victims are men who fear to be known officially as being involved in same-sex activities (these victims are often married men). Concerning violence, it is necessary to take into consideration that the different forms of discrimination (verbal discrimination, discrimination in the job area, not having the same rights as heterosexual couples, etc.) are also violent acts, which hurt lesbians, gays, and bisexuals and leave scars in their personality. Professionals who work in the psychosocial field with counseling and psychotherapy have to know about these psychic injuries and their consequences (Rauchfleisch 2001; Rauchfleisch et al. 2002; Wiesendanger 2001).

Coming out is not an easy process even today, since the declaration of being lesbian, gay, or bisexual always includes the risk—or at least, the person who plans her or his coming out fears—that parents, friends, and colleagues at work may be shocked and may break with the homosexual or bisexual person. Moreover, at least in the past, the young lesbians and gays did not have models of other lesbians and gays who could give them a positive view of what it means to be lesbian or gay. This situation has changed during the last ten years, since today quite a lot of lesbians, gays, and bisexuals appear openly with their sexual orientation and their way of living.

Studies on the question of how many young people at which age have their coming out do not exist in Switzerland. But the data from other European countries and the United States lead to the conclusion that the coming out, also in Switzerland, nowadays is usually quite early, as mentioned above, at about the age of 16 years. This means that already during adolescence, lesbians and gays are sure about their same-sex orientation and look for and live a lifestyle according to this orientation.

But these statistical data of an early coming out do not mean that all gays and lesbians have their coming out already during adolescence. There are still women and men (especially bisexuals) who keep their same-sex orientation secret, and even live for some time in heterosexual relations, and have their coming out as same-sex oriented women and men in their 30s, 40s, or even 50s. Those people are in a special situation since they have emotional attachments and obligations to their spouses and children, which make their coming out more complicated than it is for people of younger age. These families especially often need professional counseling during the coming-out process, which is not only an individual step of the homosexual or bisexual person, but a step that all members of the family must undertake (Rauchfleisch 2001; Wiesendanger 2001). This counseling can be done in a few therapeutic sessions with the couple and/or with the whole family, as well as by couple therapy or by family therapy in the narrow sense. Unfortunately, there are not many therapists or centers where families with a lesbian mother or gay father can find professionals who are familiar with these problems. Because of this, the existing self-help groups for lesbian mothers and gay fathers fulfill an important function, since there they find sympathy, support, and advice in their, at times, difficult situation. There also exists a self-help group, Hetera, for wives of gay husbands, where they have the opportunity to talk about their disappointment, their grief, and their feelings of being cheated in different aspects during the time of their marriage.

Especially difficult is the situation for those lesbians, gays, and bisexuals who suffer from psychic illness. In Switzerland, as in many other European countries and in the United States, the majority of professionals nowadays have the opinion that same-sex orientation has nothing to do with psychic health or psychic disease, but that homosexuality as heterosexuality includes the whole range from psychic health to severe disturbance. It is this insight that there is no causal relationship between the sexual orientation and psychic health or disease that led the World Health Organization in 1991 to make the decision to cancel homosexuality as a diagnosis from the *ICD*.

But we know that there are interactions between psychic disturbances and same-sex orientation. On the one hand, we know from empirical studies that discrimination at work has a severe negative influence on the somatic and psychic well-being of a person (Schneeberger et al. 2002) and, as studies from other countries show, being lesbian, gay, or bisexual nowadays still means living in a special situation with specific burdens. Some symptoms (e.g., suicidal impulses, abuse of alcohol, and psychosomatic disturbances) can be understood as reactions to these stressful circumstances.

On the other hand, we must take into consideration that being resistant to stigmatization and offenses in everyday life needs a strong personality that is able to create coping strategies to handle these difficult situations. People who suffer from psychic illness (neuroses, personality disorders, or psychoses), per definition, do not have this strength and, because of this, have many more difficulties in handling the problems in the coming-out process. At times, patients with borderline personality disorders, in particular, use their same-sex orientation as an explanation for all the difficulties from which they suffer in everyday life (Rauchfleisch et al. 2002). It is important for therapists and counselors who work in the psychosocial field to know about these interactions between the same-sex orientation and the different psychic diseases.

There are not many professionals in Switzerland who are very experienced in this field. In the big cities, lesbian, gay, and bisexual therapists have formed groups where they discuss these problems. There is also a national Swiss organization called Medi-Gays, a group for lesbian, gay, and bisexual professionals in medicine and psychology.

Since the Roman Catholic Church as well as fundamentalist groups in the Protestant churches have a strong discriminative policy against homosexuality, lesbians and gays have founded the ecumenical group HuK (Homosexuelle und Kirche—Homosexuals and Church), which fights for acceptance of lesbian, gay, and bisexual Christians. In another group, ADAMIM, founded in the early 1990s, gay priests have found a place to share their experience in church, to draw the public's attention to their difficult situation in church, and to fight for their rights as being accepted members of their church.

There are also two large national organizations, one for lesbians, LOS (Lesbenorganisation Schweiz—Lesbian Organization Switzerland), and one for gays, Pink Cross, which work together when it is necessary to fight for the rights of lesbians and gays. There are also local homosexual groups in the big cities. Moreover, there are groups for lesbians, gays, and bisexuals who are working in different professions (e.g., in medical jobs or as teachers) and sections, formed by Pink Cross, and working for a better situation in church, in the working field, for legal rights, and so on.

Until now, there are only two cantons of Switzerland (Genf and Zürich) where lesbian and gay couples have the opportunity to legalize their partnership. A national law is in the works as of mid 2003, but it is not yet decided. As in other European countries that already have such a law, it will give same-sex couples the same rights as heterosexual (married) couples, but will not include the right for adoption, although long-term studies from other countries show that children who are brought up in lesbian or gay families do not differ from children who are brought up in heterosexual families, i.e., they do not show any specific pathology in their personality or behavior (Rauchfleisch 1997).

## 7. Gender Diversity and Transgender Issues

UDO RAUCHFLEITSCH

Switzerland at present has no special laws dealing with transsexuality. Though for many people, transsexuality is still something "strange" and "irritating," the acceptance of transgender persons in public has increased during the last 10 to 15 years. This leads to less discrimination and has made it easier for them to find a job and to live an "ordinary" life. Some get married in their new role (heterosexual preference), while others live in a lesbian (man-to-woman) or gay (woman-to man) relationship with a partner. This phenomenon shows that transsexuality is a dimension independent from sexual orientation.

There are some centers in Switzerland at the University Hospitals where specialists of surgery, endocrinology, psychiatry/clinical psychology, urology, and gynecology treat transgender/transsexual persons. The programs are adapted to the way of treatment that developed in other countries, especially in the United States. This modality requires at least one year of an ongoing psychotherapeutic accompaniment, a psychiatric expert opinion, one year of treatment with cross-gendered hormones, and then the operation. Medical insurance companies pay for the psychotherapeutic and medical treatment if a psychiatric expert opinion states that there is an indication for those interventions. But the insurance companies still refuse to pay for epilation and logopedic (voice) treatment before operation, though these interventions are important for a good integration of the transsexual person into the new gender role. After a sex-change operation, it is possible to change the first name in the personal status in all documents.

Experience with transgender/transsexual persons shows that within this group we find the whole range from psychic health to severe psychic disturbances. Severe psychopathology, especially schizophrenia, is a contraindication for treatment with cross-gendered hormones and surgery. Studies on long-term outcome show, in accordance with the international literature about transsexuality, that generally woman-to-man transsexuals have a better prognosis than man-to-woman transsexuals. Moreover, social integration is an important predictor for outcome (Wyler et al. 1979; Rauchfleisch et al. 1998). If the passing (fitting into the new gender role by the body structure) is good, it is easier for the person to be accepted in this role, while it is a more complicated situation for those with a poor passing. On the whole, passing for woman-to-man transgender persons is much better than for man-to-woman because of the strong consequences of the treatment with testosterone (especially breaking of the voice and growing of a beard). Those transsexual persons who have a solid professional education can often stay in their jobs and do not have great difficulties in social acceptance (family, friends, or public). Experiences with the psychotherapeutic accompaniment show that it is important and fruitful that this treatment is offered during the whole process, from the time before medical interventions until the operation, and even for some time afterwards. If there are spouses or children, it is important to integrate them, at least from time to time, into psychotherapy, or recommend them (especially children) for individual psychotherapy or counseling.

## 8. Significant Unconventional Sexual Behaviors

### A. Coercive Sexual Behaviors

*Child Sexual Abuse, Incest, and Pedosexuality (Pedophilia)*

As in many other countries, child sexual abuse is a crime with a high percentage of unreported cases, especially when it is an abuse in the sense of incest (done by the father or other close family member). This fact can be understood because of the closeness of the perpetrator to the victim. Often the victim does not dare to inform other people because of fears that they will not believe her or him, or the victim feels he or she is guilty for what happened; there might also be a loyalty conflict because the perpetrator is a person to whom the child is closely attached at the same time as the abuse is occurring, often causing total confusion about her or his own perception. Because of this emotional confusion and because of the feelings of shame and guilt, it can take many years until sex abuse is consciously recognized and reported to psychotherapists. Eighty to 90% of the victims are girls. The perpetrators are generally up to 90% men from all social levels. To fight sexual abuse of children, an emancipating education and a change of gender-specific power structures is demanded. In Switzerland, children and parents find help in various institutions and places for maltreated and abused children, by emergency telephone hotlines for children, in child-protection centers, and in psychiatric and psychological institutions for children and families.

*Pedosexuality*

We prefer this term instead of "pedophilia," which by "philia" conceals the aggressive dimension of these deeds. Pedosexuality focuses on the various dynamics and interactions between perpetrator and victim. Similar to incest are those cases where the perpetrator is a leader of Boy Scout groups, a clergyperson, a trainer of sport groups, and so on, who is quite close to the child. Most of the cases of pedosexuality belong to this group. In 2002, both worldwide and in Switzerland, pedosexuality became a public issue when pedosexual crimes committed by Roman Catholic priests decades earlier became a public scandal. It seems that not all these priests are men with pedosexual preferences, but instead chose to abuse children as the way of the lowest resistance ("*Weg des geringsten Widerstandes*"). Though the officials of the Roman Catholic Church, as usual in such cases, tried to talk of "singular cases" and denied any connection with the forced celibacy of priests, it is obvious that the structures and the sexual norms of the Roman Catholic Church are important factors and are directly (causally) related to these pedosexual acts of priests.

In other, far fewer cases of pedosexuality, the victim does not know the perpetrator who tries to get into contact with the child and abuses it.

*Sexual Harassment*

As in other European countries and in the United States, many women are victims of sexual harassment at their workplace. A study conducted in 1993 (Ducret & Fehlmann) reported that 72% of the women surveyed indicated that they had experienced sexual advances by men against their will or were victims of sexual insults at least once and usually more often. Those affected are more often single women, frequently in insecure positions, with a low self-esteem, and in a professional situation of great dependence and in jobs dominated by men. The perpetrators are "ordinary" men, frequently married, fathers of children, and mostly more than 10 years at the present workplace. As shown by this and other studies, sexual harassment has a very bad influence, not only on the victims (feelings of shame and helplessness, sleeping disorders, anxiety, depression, and disturbances in personal relationships), but also on the working place (lower efficiency of work, bad climate at the place of work, and leaving the job).

A law (*Eidgenössisches Gleichstellungsgesetz*, Arts. 3 and 4), enacted in 1996, declared sexual harassment punishable and obliged the employer to inform the employees about this law and to deal effectively with complaints. Until now, information events were undertaken in many public and private workshops, and in some cantons. Also both Protestant and Roman Catholic authorities have published information about sexual harassment and, as public and private institutions, have identified persons of confidence who, in case of sexual harassment, help women to clarify their situation, intervene at the workplace of the women, and support them if they want to start a legal procedure.

## 9. Contraception, Abortion, and Population Planning

SIBIL TSCHUDIN

### A. Contraception

In the first half of the 20th century, contraception was mainly limited to the use of natural family planning methods such as the one Knaus Ogino devised. The response to questions about family planning was strongly—and might still be slightly—influenced by social factors and religion. That means that contraceptives were more accepted and used in Protestant regions than in Catholic ones, more in cities than in rural regions, and more by better-educated persons than by people of lower social status. With the introduction of the pill on the Swiss market in the early 1960s and the development of more-convenient IUDs, as well as in consequence of the women's emancipation movement, the demand for and use of effective contraceptives has changed drastically. Nowadays, its use is widely accepted. Birth control is still mainly left to women. After the detection of HIV/AIDS, and certainly because of information and large advertising campaigns during the last decade, the awareness of this problem and the acceptance of condom use has grown considerably.

In a survey carried out in 1996, a representative sample of 1,000 women between ages 15 to 45 were asked about the actual contraceptive method they used. The results showed a predominance of oral contraceptives (OC) by 31%, followed by condoms (17%), IUD (6%), tubal ligation (6%), vasectomy (5%), natural family planning methods (5%), coitus interruptus (2%), and depot-injections, diaphragm, and spermicides (1% each). Twenty-two percent indicated they used no contraceptive at all. Of this 22%, 18% were pregnant or intended to get pregnant; the remaining 4% would have been upset by an unwanted pregnancy. Young women (age group 20 to 25 years) use the pill in an even higher percentage of about 50%. Contraceptives are not covered by health insurance and must be paid for by the consumers themselves. This is an important factor that limits their use, especially by the young, people with low income, and asylum-seeking immigrants. Whereas condoms can be purchased easily in drugstores and supermarkets, the pill can only be bought in pharmacies on prescription.

### B. Teenage (Unmarried) Pregnancies

In comparison with some other European countries, the pregnancy and birthrate of teenagers (age 15 to 19 years) is relatively low. In 1998, 3.9 per 1,000 teenagers gave birth to a child in Switzerland, while the rates in 1997 for the U.K., Sweden, and Netherlands were 30.1, 7.2, and 4.3 per 1,000, respectively. The estimated abortion rate for teenagers in Switzerland was 6.1 per 1,000 in 1998, indicating that three of five teenage pregnancies end by artificial abortion. The estimated pregnancy rate for the age group of 15 to 19 years is about 10 per 1,000. Teenagers can make the decision on their own, and if they fear that it could be seriously harmful to them if their parents were informed about the unwanted pregnancy, their wish for secrecy will be taken into account. Single mothers are given an assistance or guardianship for their children only if they are not of age or express a need for assistance. Various institutions offer help to the young mother, if there is not sufficient support by the teenager's parents and family.

### C. Abortion

In the 19th century, legislation concerning artificial abortion was a responsibility and duty of the cantons. From 1893 to 1938, nationwide regulation of this issue within the federal penalty legislation was discussed and a federal law was worked out. In 1942, it came into force and reduced the more liberal management of abortion in some cantons to medical indication. That meant abortion was only legal if severe danger for the pregnant woman's life or health was feared. Otherwise, abortion was illegal and punished by prison or fine. The new legal limitation did not lead to a reduction of the number of legal abortions (about 15,000 per year in those times). But the following decades and the changing and more and more liberal attitude of Swiss people towards abortion led to a reduction in illegal abortions at first, and after the introduction of the pill, to a reduction of legal abortions as well. In the 1960s and 1970s, a so-called "abortion tourism" (mainly from Catholic and conservative cantons to more-liberal ones) was common, and the women often were made to feel guilty when seeking help in case of unwanted pregnancy. In the 1980s and 1990s, the law was interpreted very liberally. Unofficially, women were now allowed to decide themselves, and their decision was legitimated by the physician's expertise attesting to the risk of psychological sequelae if the woman were forced to keep the unwanted pregnancy. Since 1988, no woman has been punished by law for illegal abortion.

In 1971, Swiss women finally got their right to vote. Soon afterwards, an initiative to exempt abortion from punishment was launched, and then withdrawn in favor of the so-called "*Fristenregelung*" (time-limited permission that means legalization of abortion on demand of the pregnant woman within the first 12 weeks of pregnancy). In 1977, however, this law and a later law enlarged to a social indication were barely rejected by a plebiscite. Before the paragraphs concerning abortion in the penal code could be revised, a federal law charging the cantons to establish a center for planned parenthood offering counseling for free was launched in 1981 and put into operation in 1994. After years of debates and discussions, the second initiative to introduce the "*Fristenregelung*" was clearly accepted by more than 70% by plebiscite in 2002. This act legalized the practice of most cantons during the preceding two decades, and put an end to the varying, and therefore unjust, handling by the cantons. Abortion is now legal on demand of the woman when executed during the first 12 weeks of pregnancy.

The methods used are medical abortion by *mifepristone* and *misoprostol* until 49 days of pregnancy, and vacuum aspiration and curettage until 12 weeks of gestation. Medical abortion can only be offered by a physician, who can execute a curettage in case of failure of the method. The operation can be carried out in public hospitals, normally under general or epidural anesthesia, or in private practice, usually executed under local anesthesia. Private clinics generally refuse to carry out artificial abortions.

In any case, the following prerequisites must be met:

• Written demand of the pregnant woman;
• Pregnancy under a maximum of 12 weeks of gestation;
• Counseling concerning risks, complications, and possible sequelae by the physician performing a medical or surgical abortion;
• Counseling of adolescents under the age of 16 years in a specialized office;
• All abortions must be reported anonymously to the responsible health authority; and
• Beyond 12 weeks of gestation, abortion can be performed if there is a medical reason. This reason must be more severe the more the pregnancy is advanced. During the second trimester, abortion because of psychosocial or psychiatric reasons is exceptional. Most abortions at this state of pregnancy are executed on demand of the woman or couple after detection of severe fetal

malformations or chromosomal aberrations. Up to 14 weeks of pregnancy, a vacuum aspiration is the method used; afterwards, abortion is induced by *mifepristone* and *misoprostol*, occasionally followed by a curettage because of incomplete release of the placenta. The costs of any abortion procedures in the above-mentioned contexts are carried by the obligatory health assurance.

## 10. Sexually Transmitted Diseases and HIV/AIDS

JOHANNES BITZER

### A. Sexually Transmitted Diseases

Since the 1920s, there has been a political effort to control sexually transmitted diseases by reporting cases to state institutions. Registered prostitutes are legally required to be examined at regular intervals for venereal diseases.

#### The Legal Framework

In 1999, a modification regarding the reporting of sexually transmitted diseases was established in Switzerland. The new legal dispositions abolished the necessity for the physicians to report classic infections like gonorrhea, chlamydia, syphilis, and chancroid. In addition, the new law interrupted the automatic registration performed by the laboratories of *Treponema pallidum*. These new regulations seem to be appropriate regarding the assessment of infections. The new regulation says the following: Obligatory declaration refers to HIV and AIDS, laboratory declaration refers to HIV-positive tests, gonorrhea, chlamydia trachomatis, and hepatitis B and C. In addition, the following infections have to be declared (reported) by physicians: HIV, AIDS, and hepatitis B and C.

#### The Epidemiology

The incidence of the different infections is changing. Gonorrhea has diminished and syphilis seems to be increasing.

There are very few specialized STD clinics, because these are usually integrated into the dermatological department of university hospitals. Thus, patients with STDs are usually seen either in practices of general practitioners, gynecologists, or urologists, or at the outpatient departments of the dermatology, gynecology, and urology units. There are, however, specialized HIV clinics, which are usually directed by infectiologists (internal medicine). Several dermatological outpatient departments in Switzerland have decided to survey other STDs. Their list includes: orchitis in men, rectitis, cervicitis, chlamydia, gonorrhea, syphilis, chancroid, genital herpes, genital condylomata, pelvic inflammatory disease, and *Trichomonas*. Unfortunately, the data gathered by the six outpatient university departments are not representative for the Swiss population.

For the general population, there is a declaration system called *Sentinella*. Between 150 and 250 general practitioners are cooperating on a voluntary basis to report infectious diseases. Since 1995, 30 gynecologists have been included.

In 1998, gynecologists have participated in a prevalence study on chlamydia in women under 35 years of age. From this study, it has been extrapolated that the numbers given by the laboratories represent only 5% of the total reservoir of chlamydia infections of women between 20 to 35 years. It is therefore estimated that chlamydia infections have spread out in Switzerland, with 2,400 infection cases in 2000. This means, that chlamydia is the most prevalent sexual STD infection in Switzerland. Compared with AIDS, the detection and tracing of other STDs is not optimal. This provides a reason for reconsideration, especially regarding the resurgence of classical STDs in all European countries.

The laboratory reports do not permit an in-depth epidemiological analysis. On one hand, the available data are incomplete, and on the other hand, they do not mention the total number of tests. This makes it impossible to ascertain whether an increase in positive test results is because of an increase in infections or to an increase in the number of tests.

## B. HIV/AIDS

*Overview*

HIV- and AIDS-prevention programs are quite widespread in Switzerland. Two major organizations are involved in public education and programs.

The AIDS Hilfe Schweiz, l'Aide Suisse contre le SIDA (aids@aids.ch) is a private association founded in 1985 and financed by Bundesamt für Gesundheit (BAG—the Federal Administration of Health). This organization has 21 cantonal and regional subcenters. The secretariat of the organization, based in Zurich (Konradstrasse 20, 8005 Zurich; case postale 1118, 8031 Zurich), develops specially tailored programs for HIV prevention especially for homosexual and bisexual men, female and male sex workers, drug consumers, and young people. This secretariat also coordinates the action of the other centers, which are financed by the cantons. The local or cantonal centers' services include medical information, legal advice, personal counseling, networking, and group formation.

A second regular information service is the SIDA Infodoc Swiss (www.infodoc-gf.ch). This organization is responsible for the collection of bibliographic information. SIDA Infothek publishes regularly a journal called *Aids Infothek*, which comments on the actual issues and also reviews recent publications.

The general approach in family planning consultations is to provide counsel for prevention of unwanted pregnancy in combination with protection against sexually transmitted diseases, especially HIV. This is accomplished by promoting the use of condoms. Tests can be made anonymously and free of charge at the Aidshilfe institutions. Testing is also available at the outpatient departments.

HIV-infected persons are obliged by law to inform their sexual partners about the risk. On the other hand, HIV-positive prostitutes are not obliged to inform their clients. Clients of sex workers are responsible for protecting themselves.

Partner tracing is not obligatory, nor are possibly infected persons obliged to be tested for HIV. HIV testing can be only performed with the informed consent of the person. Testing by institutions and hospitals for protection of medical personal without informed consent of the patients is not allowed. The general policy is to encourage people to get tested, but all the efforts are dealt with on a voluntary basis because coercion is thought to push people into isolation and anonymity that prevent them from collaborating with the health system. Infected persons are strongly encouraged to inform their partners. They are advised about the legal consequences of infecting another person in the presence of knowledge of one's own infection. Further obligations are not regulated by law.

*HIV Prevention Programs*

For the past 14 years, since 1989, the Institute for Social and Preventive Medicine of the University of Lausanne has performed various studies regarding the global strategy of prevention of HIV infections. Global evaluation surveys, as well as specific studies in specific populations, have been performed. The last report on the global evaluation of 1996 to 1998 shows the following results:

- Public awareness of the need for ongoing HIV prevention and consciousness of risk-reduction behavior remain at a high level. The results of HIV-prevention education are steady and persistent. There is no diminution of preventive behavior in recent years and the number of new infections has continuously declined. It can be seen that there is no longer a major difference in the different regions of Switzerland, and preexisting differences between cities and rural areas and between different groups of education have diminished. There is also general agreement that the confederation has to continue health education on this issue to make it part of normal life.

- A major element of HIV prevention is a solidarity, which manifests itself on the level of solidarity with affected persons, solidarity with the manifestly ill persons, especially regarding their jobs and their insurance, and solidarity with other countries affected by the infection.

- A special program for women's health and prevention of AIDS was set up between 1994 and 1998, making it possible to form groups of experts in reproductive and sexual health to integrate women's health into gender-sensitive programs and activities at universities and hospitals.

- There is, however, still a lack of uniformity between the different cantons in Switzerland. Another study has focused on the sexuality and sexual behavioral of HIV-positive persons (published in 1998). The infected persons suffer from various psycho-effective problems, like diminution of self-esteem, fear of being rejected, the difficulties of maintaining protected intercourse, the denial of the disease, the deterioration of physical well-being, and the questioning and doubts about maternity or paternity.

- From this study, it was concluded that, besides the medical care, more intensive psychological care is necessary. Furthermore, health personal should be informed about the special emotional needs of HIV-positive persons.

Another study of the needs of HIV-positive persons found that the quality of information and of counseling is too heterogeneous across the country. There are no guidelines regarding information-giving and patient education. Moralizing continues. The insurance companies do not pay for artificial insemination for HIV-positive males who want a child, but without the risk of infecting their partner with unprotected intercourse. Psychological support during pregnancy is insufficient. There is a need for continuous education for obstetricians and midwifes. There are still too many tests performed without informed consent.

Finally, a third study has evaluated sexual education at schools. As in other areas, this study showed an enormous heterogeneity between the different regions. Although there is a legal basis for all schools to teach about HIV, the practice is very different. It seems that on the obligatory school level, the coverage of the subject is sufficient, whereas at the higher school levels, it is much less. In the German-speaking region, sexuality education seems to be less effective than in the French-speaking region. There is no basic sex education in the German-speaking part, which makes it more difficult for the teachers to approach AIDS as a subject.

[*Update 2002*: UNAIDS Epidemiological Assessment: By the end of 2001, a cumulative total of 25,637 cases of HIV infection was reported in the country. The number of newly diagnosed AIDS cases has declined since 1995. This development is associated with improved therapy (highly active antiretroviral therapies, HAART). Injecting drug users and men who have sex with men each contributed approximately 25% to the reported AIDS cases in 2000 and 2001. The proportion of cases in the heterosexual transmission group had been steadily increasing until 1999, and seems to have stabilized since then at around 45%. As a result, the proportion of cases in women has also increased over the years to over 30%.

[The number of death reports for persons with AIDS increased until 1994 and has since declined. In 1999, approximately 120 persons with HIV or AIDS were reported to have died. This number is less than 20% of the number reported for the peak year 1994. Death reports are not complete for 2000 and 2001, but it is estimated that the decline in AIDS-related mortality is continuing, although at a slower rate.

[The number of newly diagnosed HIV infections has also been declining in Switzerland between 1992 and 1999 to 2000 and appears to be stabilizing. Heterosexual contacts have been the dominant transmission route since 1990 (over a third of all newly diagnosed HIV infections, over 50% since 1997). Men who have sex with men make up approximately 25%, and injecting drug users approximately 15% of reported positive HIV tests in 2000 and 2001. Among heterosexually infected cases, the proportion of cases with nationalities from countries with a generalized epidemic is increasing, although the absolute number of cases in this group has been more or less stable in the second half of the last decade.

[The estimated number of adults and children living with HIV/AIDS on January 1, 2002, were:

| | | |
|---|---|---|
| Adults ages 15-49: | 19,000 | (rate: 0.1%) |
| Women ages 15-49: | 6,000 | |
| Children ages 0-15: | 300 | |

[An estimated less than 100 adults and children died of AIDS during 2001.

[No estimate is available for the number of Swiss children who had lost one or both parents to AIDS and were under age 15 at the end of 2001. (*End of update by the Editors*)]

## 11. Sexual Dysfunctions, Counseling, and Therapies

JUDITH ALDER

The definition of sexual dysfunction followed in Switzerland is in agreement with the international classifications of mental disorders *ICD-10*, chapter F52 (sexual dysfunction not in relation to a medical factor), and *DSM-IV* (sexual and gender identity disorders). However, in the general population, there is a lack of definition of what "normal sexual behavior" is. This is particularly true in the lack of public knowledge about what is the "normal" range of frequency for sexual activity and what types of sexual behavior are considered within the "normal" range. In general, a sexual dysfunction is diagnosed only after a longer period of its persistence and not shortly after the development.

An impairment of sexual behavior/response that has the following features is understood as sexual dysfunction:

• Disorder of sexual drive or satisfaction;
• Lack of the physiological reaction needed for satisfactory sexual interaction;
• Inability to experience and control orgasm; or
• Painful intercourse.

A recent Swiss survey of sexual dysfunction in women shows that lack of libido is the most-often-named sexual problem (41%), followed by orgasmic disorders (19%), dyspareunia (painful intercourse) (12%), vaginal spasms (10%), sexual aversion (8%), and excitement disorder (1%) (Buddeberg et al. 1994). In men, the most frequent sexual

dysfunction is erectile dysfunction (41.7%), followed by early ejaculation (30.6%), lack of libido (9.7%), painful intercourse (2.8%), and sexual aversion and delayed ejaculation (both 1.4%) (Buddeberg et al. 1994). In general, sexual dysfunction certainly is not something people talk about when they are confronted with it. Even women during menopause rarely have an exchange about the changes and problems in sexuality they experience during these years.

### Availability of Diagnosis and Treatment

People with sexual problems generally consult first their family physician or gynecologist. Many patients who do not mention the problem to their doctor will not receive treatment for a long time. Questions about sexual functioning are still not part of a routine history taking. Only a few men would consult a urologist in the first place; they generally wait until their general practitioner physician refers them. If the problem is recognized, diagnosis by physicians generally is mostly adequate. However, if the problem is related to addictive behavior or medication, it may not be assessed carefully enough. Sexual problems in the first place are still looked upon from a somatic perspective and more so for men than for women. Only if a medical treatment is unsuccessful will the patient be referred for specialized counseling. However, there is a clear shortage of therapists who have special skills in sexual counseling, and it is generally rather difficult to find therapy places for patients with a sexual dysfunction. There are only a few centers in the larger cities that offer special counseling and therapy for sexual dysfunction. And these generally have waiting lists.

### Training and Certification of Therapists

A recent study assessed knowledge of and sensitivity to the sexual side effects of antidepressants in general practitioners and psychiatrists (Kunz et al. 1998). The response rate (12.5%) of the contacted physicians was very low, demonstrating at least partly the lack of relevance that healthcare providers give to sexual matters in counseling for other psychological problems. Only one half of physicians responding judged their competence in sexual medicine as fair or good. Differences in sexual history taking were observed between general practitioners and psychiatrists, the latter addressing more frequently sexual medicine-related questions. The results emphasize the importance of knowledge and competence in sexual medicine for general practitioners and psychiatrists, both showing interest in continuing education on this topic. Diagnosis and treatment of sexual dysfunction is part of most curricula in psychology and—later on—psychotherapy specialization. These curricula include sexual dysfunction as one part of the training among the other mental disorders. There are only a few private institutes, Zentrum für Agogik and Höhere Fachschule Luzern being two, which offer a specialization course in sexology and sexual counseling. However, there is no official regulation or certification for those providing sexual counseling in Switzerland.

## 12. Sex Research and Advanced Professional Education

JOHANNES BITZER

There is no Swiss professorial society for sexological research and sexology. There are, however, different professional associations that deal with sexual issues. These include the Swiss Society for Psychosocial and Psychosomatic Medicine, especially the Division of Psychosomatic Obstetrics and Gynecology; the Swiss Society for Fertility, Sterility, and Family Planning; the Swiss Society of Urology; and the Swiss Society of Gynecology and Obstetrics. In recent years, efforts have been made to integrate sexology in the curricula for training medical students. Until now, there is not yet a specific training program, which could be compared to other training programs designed to teach certain skills (*Fertigkeitsausweise*).

In 1998, a collaboration between the institutes of Basel, Zurich, and Lausanne for social and preventive medicine made a survey analyzing 140 publications regarding reproductive and sexual health: 23% of the publications were routine statistics, 12% repetitive studies, 61% isolated studies, and 5% ongoing studies. The largest amount of studies, 40%, concentrated on STDs and HIV, followed by unwanted pregnancies 33%, contraception 29%, sex education 14%, sexual behavior 8%, deliveries 8%, and violence 6%. This analysis showed that there is a lack of epidemiological data regarding the country as a nation in almost all areas, including unwanted pregnancies, STDs, violence, contraceptive behavior, and so on.

A quite-positive development can be found in the recent and current research projects undertaken by several research groups in Switzerland:

- The Institutes of Social and Preventive Medicine in Switzerland are focused on epidemiological research.
- The Institute in Zürich (Schmid, Gutzwiler) has done major research projects on sexual and reproductive health of the Swiss population. Furthermore, they have made surveys regarding sexual behavior especially in the older age group. Another focus of research of this group is HIV and AIDS prevention.
- The Institute in Lausanne (Dubois-Arber, Spencer) performed several evaluation studies on HIV/AIDS prevention, unwanted pregnancies, and teenager sexuality. Another focus of their research is violence and especially sexual violence. (Hofner et al.).
- Another publication was made in 2001 by the Institute of Social and Preventive Medicine of Lausanne. The study focused on the sexual health of the canton Waadt. The study focused mainly on postcoital contraception and a knowledge of contraceptive methods.
- The Institute in Basel (E. Zemp, U. Ackermann-Liebrich) is focusing especially on women's health issues. This includes research on family planning services, maternity care, mammography, etc.
- Research on teenager health was extended by P. A. Michaud and F. Narring.
- Several research projects on violence and especially sexual violence have been performed by different research groups (Godenzi, Felber, Gilloz).
- Research on contraception and sexuality is being performed by various university groups (J. Bitzer et al., M. Bianchi-Demicheli, etc.).
- The group of C. Buddeberg at the Zürich Institute of Psychosocial Medicine has published on several issues: Sexual counseling skills, and sexual behavior of elder females and males (M. Schmid-Mast, C. Buddeberg, F. Gutzwiller).
- The group of Johannes Bitzer at the Division of Social medicine and Psychosomatic Gynecology has done research on sexual dysfunction, counseling, and adolescent and perimenopausal sexuality.
- Another important institution is the Professor Willi Pasini Institute of Sexology at the psychiatric university hospital of Geneva. The work is now continued by Dr. Dominique Chatton, a psychiatrist.
- Several groups have done prevalence studies on STDs (Feuz et al., Lauper).
- One of the most important areas of research in Switzerland is the study of sexual and reproductive health per-

formed by Karen Klaue and Brenda Spencer with the collaboration of Hugues Balthasar. This study was financed by the Office Fédéral de la Santé Publique, Berne, and was carried out at the Institut Universitaire de Médecine Sociale et Préventive, Lausanne. The background of the study is the important political initiative, called Postulate of Genner of June 2000, which demands that the government produce a survey on the report how the sexual health of the Swiss population could be improved. The study was performed from the December 1, 2001, to June 3, 2002. One of the major objectives of the study was the integration in coordination of different services and programs like mother and child healthcare, family planning, and AIDS help, prevention, and protection, with a special focus on groups like teenagers, men, and women apart from their role as mothers.

- Gender studies have also become an important part of the research and academic activities in Switzerland. The approach is multidisciplinary and includes the sensitivities and nuances of researchers in different disciplines like medicine, social signs, linguistics, history, and so on, to include in their research gender-specific questions and what is called gender mainstreaming.
- A competence center for gender studies was founded in 1998 in Zurich. In Lausanne, there is a chair for gender studies. There is a Swiss society for women and gender research, founded in 1996.

There is no official specifically sexological journal devoted to publication of sexological research. Research results are usually published in German or English journals.

## References and Suggested Readings

Abelin, T., N. Bachmann, B. Bisig, et al. 2000. *Enquête suisse sur la santé 1997: Canton du Valais.* Sion: Etat du Valais: Département de la Santé, des Affaires Sociales et de l'Énergie.

Ackermann-Liebrich, U., E. Zemp Stutz, E. Martin-Diener, et al. 1996. *Women's health profile Switzerland.* Basel: Institute for Social and Preventive Medicine.

Addor, V., C. Ferron, F. Narring, et al. 1997. Interruptions de grossesse dans und canton suisse de 1990 à 1993: Implications pour la surveillance épidémiologique. *Rev. Epidemiol Sante Publique,* 45(474):82.

Aide Suisse contre le SIDA (ASS). 1997. *Etre soi-même: Brochure à l'intention des jeunes gays, bis et lesbiennes et leur entourage.* Zurich: Aide Suisse contre le SIDA (ASS).

Aide Suisse contre le SIDA (ASS). 1998. *Les homosexuels et le SIDA: La recherche d'une solution; Rapport sur la situation en Suisse.* Zurich: Aide Suisse contre le SIDA (ASS).

BAG Bulletin. 2002 (July). *HIV und AIDS in der schweiz: Statistik bis ende Juni 2002; BAG Bulletin,* 31(29).

Bianchi-Demicheli, F., E. Perrin, F. Lüdicke, et al. 2001. Contraception and sexuality after termination of pregnancy: A comparison between Lugano and Geneva. *Swiss Med Wkly,* 131(35-36):515-520.

Birrer, A., T. Bodmer, U. Bollag, et al. 2000. *Le système de déclaration sentinelle en Suisse.* Berne: Office Fédéral de la Santé Publique.

Bruhin, E., M. Werner, T. Abel, et al. 2001. *Lifestyle and HIV prevention: Patterns of sexual risk and their determinants: A project on basic research and prevention development based on the concept of health relevant lifestyles.* Bern: Swiss National Science Foundation.

Cavaleri, A., M. Verwey, E. Konigs, et al. 1996. *Evaluation de la stratégie de prévention du SIDA en Suisse, phase 69, 1993-1995. Prévention du SIDA auprès des prostituées étrangères: Le Projet Barfüsserfrauen.* Lausanne: Institut Universitaire de Médecine Sociale et Préventive. (Cah Rech Doc IUMSP, no. 120.8).

CIA. 2002 (January). *The world factbook 2002*. Washington, DC: Central Intelligence Agency. Available: http://www .cia.gov/cia/publications/factbook/index.html

Coda, P., M. J. Glardon, & M. Schmid. 1998. *Santé sexuelle et reproductive en Suisse: Étude préparatoire avec recensement des études, publications et statistiques*. Basel: Institute für Sozial- und Präventivmedizin.

Couturier, E., N. Dupin, M. Janier, et al. 2001. *Résurgence de la syhilis en France, 2000-2001*. BEH 2001:(36-36).

Dubois-Arber, F., A. Jeannin, G. Meystre-Agustoni, et al. 1993. *Evaluation de la stratégie de prévention du SIDA en Suisse sur mandat de l'Office Fédéral de la Santé Publöique: Quatrième rapport de synthése 1991-1992*. Lausanne: Institut Universitaire de Médecine Sociale et Préventive. (Cah Rech Doc IUMSP, no 82).

Dubois-Arber, F., A. Jeannin, G. Meystre-Agustoni, et al. 1996. *Evaluation de la stratégie de prévention du SIDA en Suisse sur mandat de l'Office Fédéral de la Santé Publique: Cinquième rapport de synthèse 1993-1995*. Lausanne: Institut Universitaire de Médicine Sociale et Préventive.

Dubois-Arber, F., A. Jeannin, B. Spencer, et al. 1999. *Evaluation de la straégie de prévention du SIDA en Suisse: Sicième rapport de synthèse 1996-1998*. Lausanne: Institut Universitaire de Médecine Sociale et Préventive.

Dubois-Arber, F., A. Jeannin, & B. Spencer. 1999. Long term global evaluation of a national AIDS prevention strategy: The case of Switzerland. *AIDS 1999, 13*:2571-2582.

Dubois-Arber, F., P. Lehmann, D. Hausser, et al. 1989. *Evaluation des campagnes de prévention du SIDA en Suisse: Deuxième rapport de synthèse*. Lausanne: Institut Universitaire de Médecine Sociale et Préventive. (Cah Rech Doc IUMSP, no 39).

Ducret, V., & Ch. Fehlmann. 1993. *Sexuelle belästigung am arbeitsplatz. Worüber frauen schweigen. Untersuchung in Genf. Eidg. Büro für die gleichstellung von frau und mann (Hg.)*. Bern: Eidg. Druck- und Materialzentrale.

Ernst, M. L., M. Haour-Knipe, & B. Spencer. 1998. *Evaluation des aktionsprogrammes gesundheit von frauen: Schwerpunkt HIV-prävention 1994-1997. Evaluation of the women's health: HIV prevention programme 1994-1997*. Lausanne: Institut Universitaire de Médecine Sociale et Préventive. (*Raisons de Santé*, 22).

Felber, P. 2001. *Groupe de travail 'violence domestique,' Centre Suisse de Prévention de la Criminalité. Campagne violence domestique 2002-2003*. Neuchâtel: Centre Suisse de Prévention de la Criminalité.

Fenton, K., J. Giesecke, & F. Hamers. 2001. Europe-wide surveillance for sexually transmitted infections: A timely and appropriate intervention. *Euro Surveillance, 6*(5):69-70.

Feuz, M. 2002. Les infections sexuellement transmissibles en Suisse: Historique du système de déclaration, situation actuelle et perspectives. *Infothèque SIDA, 14*(1):11-13.

Gilloz, L., J. De Puy, & V. Ducret. 1997. *Domination et violence envers la femme dans le couple*. Lausanne: Editions Payot.

Godenzi, A., & G. Müller. 2002. *Première étude de longue durée sur la résolution non violente des conflits au sein de la famille: Communiqué de presse*. Berne: Fonds National Suisse; 2002. (*PNR 40, Violence au quotidien et criminalité organisée*).

Hausser, D., P. Lehmann, F. Dubois-Arber, et al. 1987. *Evaluation des campagnes de prévention contre le SIDA en Suisse sur mandat de l'OFSP (Rapport de synthèse)*. Lausanne: Institut Universitaire de Médecine Sociale et Préventive. (Cah Rech Doc IUMSP, no 23).

Hausser, D., E. Zimmermann, & F. Dubois-Arber. 1991. *Evaluation de la stratégie de prévention due SIDA en Suisse. 3ème rapport de synthèse 1989-1990*. Lausanne: Institut Universitaire de Médecine Sociale et Préventive. (Cah Rech Doc IUMSP, no 52).

Hofner, M. C. 2000. *Formation VIH/SIDA 1989-1999: Rapport final contrat no 6057. Unité de prévention, Ed.* Lausanne: Institut Universitaire de Médecine Sociale et Préventive.

Hofner, M. C., & S. Siggen. 2001. *Violence conjugale dans le canton de Vaud: Recherche réparatoire réalisée sur mandat du Bureau de l'Égalité entre les Femmes et les Hommes du Canton de Vaud*. Lausanne: Institut Universitaire de Médicine Sociale et Préventive/UP; Bureau de l'Égalité entre les Femmes et les Hommes, Vaud.

*Infoplease.com: Encyclopedia–Switzerland*: Geography, history, government.

Intégrité Sexuelle et Violence contre les Femmes, Commission Fédéreale pour les Questions Féminines, ed. *Histoire de l'égalité en Suisse de 1848 à 2000: Femmes, pouvoir, histoire* (pp. 1-12). 2001. Berne: CFQF.

Kantonale und Spitalstatistiken. 2001 (January). In: *Schwangerschaftsabbruch in der Schweiz–Eine neuregelung ist notwendig: Ja zur fristenregelung; Arbeitsgruppe "Schwangerschaftsabbruch."*

Kennzahlen Volkszählung, Bundesamt für Statistik, 2002.

Kunz, R., A. Leuthold, & C. Buddeberg. 1998. Sexuelle dysfunktionen unter antidepressiva: Ergebnisse einer ärztebefragung. *Schweiz Rundschau Med (PRAXIS), 18*(87):610-616.

*Loi fédérale sur la lutte contre les maladies transmissibles de l'homme (loi sur les épidémies) du 18 décembre 1970 (état le 27 novembre 2001)*. 2001. Berne: Chancellerie Fédérale.

Meystre-Aqustoni, G., R. Thomas, M. Häusermann, et al. 1998. *La sexualité des personnes vivant avec le VIH/SIDA*. Lausanne: Institut Universitaire de Médecine Sociale et Préventive. (*Raisons de Santé*, 17).

Narring, F., P. A. Michaud, H. Wydler, et al. 1997. Sexualité des adolescents et SIDA: Processus et négociations autoukr des relations sexuelles et du choix de la contraception. Lausanne: Institut Universitaire de Médecine Sociale et Préventive. (*Raisons de Santé*, 24).

Narring, F., A. Tschumper, P. A. Michaud, et al. 1994. *La santé des adolescents en Suisse: Rapport d'une enquête national sur la santé et les styles de vie des 15-20 ans*. Lausanne: Institut Universitaire de Médecine Sociale et Préventive; 1994. (Cah Rech Doc IUMSP, 113a).

Paget, J., V. Batter, & M. Zwahlen. 1999. The Swiss Network of Dermatology Policlinics HIV prevalence study: Rationale, characteristics and results (1990-1996). *Soz- Präventivmed, 44*(1):7.

Paget, J., E. Rundler, & R. Zbinden. 2000. The prevalence of genital chlamydial infection among women consulting their gynecologist in Switzerland: The sentinelle chlamydia prevalence study. Swiss Surveillance Network of Sentinel Gynecologists. In: *Sentinella 1998: Rapport annuel du système de déclaration Sentinella en Suisse*. Berne: Office Fédéral de la Santé Publique.

Raeber, P. A., & J. L. Zurcher. 2002. *Epidémiologie: Suivre les épidémies et les germes à la trace: Loi sur les épidémies*. Feuille Info/OFSP (1.2):1-2.

Rapp, R. 2002 (January). Die gesetzliche regelung des schwangerschaftsabbruchs in der Schweiz. In: *Dokumentation der Weiterbildungstagung* [Zürich].

Rauchfleisch, U. 1997. *Alternative familienformen. Eineltern, gleichgeschlechtliche paare, hausmänner*. Göttingen: Vandenhoeck & Ruprecht.

Rauchfleisch, U. 2001. *Schwule. Lesben. Bisexuelle. Lebensweisen, Vorurteile, Einsichten. 3. Aufl*. Göttingen: Vandenhoeck & Ruprecht.

Rauchfleisch, U., J. Frossard, G. Waser, K. Wiesendanger, & W. Roth. 2002. *Gleich und doch anders. Psychotherapie und beratung von lesben, schwulen, bisexuellen und ihren angehörigen*. Stuttgart: Klett-Cotta.

Rauchfleisch, U., D. Barth, & R. Battegay. 1998. Resultate einer langzeitkatamnese von transsexuellen. *Nervenarzt, 69*, 799-805.

*Repräsentativ-befragung von 1000 frauen im alter von 15-45 jahren, GfS Forschungsinstitut*. 1996 (May).

Schmid Mast, M., & T. Bucher. 1999. Sexuell aktiv ins alter. *Unimagazin: Die Zeitschrift der Universität Zürich*, (1):1-5.

Schmid Mast, M., R. Hornung, F. Gutzwiller, et al. 2002. Sexualität in der Zweiten. *Lebenshälfte Gynäkol Geburtshilfliche Rundsch*, *40*:13-19.

Schneeberger, A., U. Rauchfleisch, & R. Battegay. 2002: Psychosomatische folgen und begleitphänomene der diskriminierung am arbeitsplatz bei homosexuellen menschen Schweiz. *Arch. Neurol. Psychiat.*, *153*:137-143.

So-Barazetti, B., M. J. Glardon, E. Palasthy, et al. 1996. *Projekt "Ressources en santé sexuelle accessibles partout": Bestandesaufnahme und bedarfserhebung bei familienplanungsstellen und Aids-Hilfen in der Schweiz*. Savigny: Schweizerische Vereinigung für Familienplanung und Sexualerziehung.

Somaini, B., W. Twisselmann, T. Ferber, et al. 1999. *VIH et SIDA: Programme national 1999 à 2003*. Berne: OFSP (Office Fédéral de la Santé Publique).

Spencer, B., et al. *Politiques et pratiques cantonales en matière de prévention VIH/SIDA et education sexuelle à l'école*. In: *Raison de Santé* 66.

Statistik Schweiz Eckdaten. 2003. *Bundesamt für statistik*.

Thomas, R., M. Haour-Knipe, P. Huynh Do, et al. 2001. *Die bedürfnisse der menschen mit HIV/AIDS in der Schweiz: Kurzfassung*. Lausanne: Institut Universitaire de Médecine Sociale et Préventive.

Tschumper, A., F. Narring, C. Meier, et al. 1998. Sexual victimization in adolescent girls (age 15-20 years) enrolled in post-mandatory schools or professional training programmes in Switzerland. *Acta Paediatr*, 87:212-217.

UNAIDS. 2002. *Epidemiological fact sheets by country*. Geneva, Switzerland: Joint United Nations Programme on HIV/AIDS (UNAIDS/WHO). Available: http://www.unaids.org/hivaidsinfo/statistics/fact_sheets/index_en.htm.

Université de Genève, Formation Continue Universitaire. 2002. *Certificat de formation continue en sexologie clinique*. Available: http://www.unige.ch/formcont/. (Accessed June 10, 2002).

Von Türk, A., V. Addor, A. Jeannin, et al. 2001. *Etat de santé de la population vaudoise, 2001. Cahier thématique 4, Santé sexuelle et procréative: Troisième rapport pour la Commission Cantonale de Prévention*. Lausanne: Service de la Santé Publique; 2001. Available: http://www.sanimedia.ch.

Wiesendanger, K. 2001. *Schwule und lesben in psychotherapie, seelsorge und beratung*. Göttingen: Vandenhoeck & Ruprecht.

Wyler, J., R. Battegay, S. Krupp, M. Rist, & U. Rauchfleisch. 1979. Der transsexualismus und dessen therapie. *Schweiz. Arch. Neurol. Psychiat.*, *124*:43-58.

Zemp, E., P. Coda, M. J. Glardon, & M. Schmid. 1999. *Travaux de conceptualisation pour la promotion de la santé des femmes*. Bâle: Institut de Médecine Sociale et Préventive.

# Tanzania
## (The United Republic of Tanzania)

Philip Setel, Eleuther Mwageni,
Namsifu Mndeme, and Yusuf Hemed*
*Additional comments by Beldina Opiyo-Omolo, B.Sc.***

## Contents

## Demographics and a Brief Historical Perspective

PHILIP SETEL

### A. Demographics

The United Republic of Tanzania is situated on the mainland of the East Coast of Africa and includes the Islands of Zanzibar and Pemba, separated from the mainland by a 25-mile-wide (40-km) channel. The country is one of the largest in Eastern Africa, with an area of about 364,900 square miles (945,000 square kilometers), about twice the size of the state of California in the United States. Tanzania shares borders with Kenya and Uganda to the north, Rwanda and Burundi to the northwest, Zaire to the west, Zambia to the southwest, and Malawi and Mozambique to the south.

*Communications*: Philip Setel, Project Director, Adult Morbidity and Mortality Project (AMMP-2), Ministry of Health, P.O. Box 65243, Dar es Salaam, Tanzania; setel.ammp@twiga.com. Eleuther Mwageni, Namsifu Mndeme, and Yusuf Hemed: ammp.dar@twiga .com (shared email). *Comments*: Beldina Opiyo-Omolo, B.Sc., Department of Health, East Stroudsburg University of Pennsylvania, East Stroudsburg, PA 18301 USA; bopiyo@yahoo.com.

**Editors' Note*: We would call the reader's attention to a simple but crucial sentence in the Brief Historical Perspective, where the authors note that "Tanzania is one of the poorest countries in the world, with a per capita gross domestic product (GDP) of US$220." (Five years earlier, in 1997, the GDP was $700.) Since 1990, Tanzania's economic condition has steadily worsened, stressed by a near 3% annual population growth. Between 1993 and 1996, close to a half million Rwandan Hutu fled into Tanzania to escape ethnic strife with the Tutsi. In the 1990s, the nation's infrastructure and access to medical services and commodities, well-established in the 1970s, collapsed. In the midst of the deteriorating situation, Philip Setel, Project Director, Adult Morbidity and Mortality Project in the Ministry of Health, recognized the importance of this *International Encyclopedia* and organized a team to research and write this chapter on their country. Unfortunately, deteriorating meager resources and more-urgent health priorities, including over 800,000 AIDS orphans, made it impossible for them to provide information on all the topics in our standard outline. We thank them for their sincere effort and the insights they provide that are not available elsewhere.

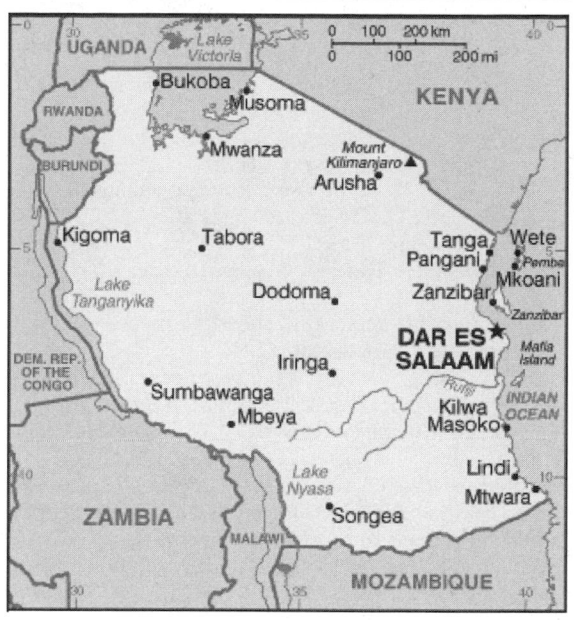

(CIA 2002)

Tanzania has a diverse topography. The narrow coastline lies less than 200 meters (655 ft.) above sea level. Most of the country is a plateau with an altitude of more than 1,000 meters (3,280 ft.) above sea level. The landscape rises towards the south to reach about 3,000 meters (9,840 ft.) above sea level in the Southern Highlands. Further north, the altitude reaches over 5,000 meters (16,400 ft.) in the Northern Highlands of Tanzania. Mount Kilimanjaro, the highest point in Africa, is 5,895 meters (19,340 ft.) above sea level. Tanzania contains three of Africa's best-known lakes: Victoria in the north, Tanganyika in the west, and Nyasa in the south. The highlands of Tanzania are the most fertile areas in the country, and have a denser population than other parts of the country. Tanzania's climate is reflected in the variations in altitude. The coastal area has high temperatures of about 30° C (86° F) and receives long rains between February and May and short rains during the October to December period. The plateau is subject to high temperatures during the day and is relatively cool at night. This area has a low rainfall and experiences long dry spells between May and October. The highlands as well as the western part of the country have high rainfall, especially between February and April.

In July 2002, Tanzania had an estimated population of just over 37 million. The estimates presented below explicitly take into account the effects of excess mortality because of AIDS. This can result in lower life expectancy, higher infant mortality and death rates, lower population and growth rates, and changes in the distribution of population by age and sex than would otherwise be expected. (All data are from *The World Factbook 2002* (CIA 2002) unless otherwise stated.)

**Age Distribution and Sex Ratios**: *0-14 years*: 44.6% with 1.01 male(s) per female (sex ratio); *15-64 years*: 52.5% with 0.98 male(s) per female; *65 years and over*: 2.9% with 0.83 male(s) per female; *Total population sex ratio*: 0.99 male(s) to 1 female

**Life Expectancy at Birth**: *Total Population*: 51.98 years; *male*: 51.04 years; *female*: 52.95 years

**Urban/Rural Distribution**: 25% to 75%. In 2001, Dar es Saalam, the capital, had an estimated population of about 1.4 million and Mwanza about 225,000.

**Ethnic Distribution**: Mainland: native African 99% (of which 95% are Bantu consisting of more than 130 tribes);

other 1% (consisting of Asian, European, and Arab). Zanzibar: Arab, native African, and mixed Arab.

**Religious Distribution**: Mainland: Christian: 45%; Muslim: 35%; indigenous beliefs: 30%. Zanzibar: more than 99% Muslim. Tanzanians often affiliate with both indigenous and Western religious beliefs.

**Birth Rate**: 39.12 births per 1,000 population

**Death Rate**: 13.02 per 1,000 population

**Infant Mortality Rate**: 77.85 deaths per 1,000 live births

**Net Migration Rate**: –0.08 migrant(s) per 1,000 population

**Total Fertility Rate**: 1.33 children born per woman

**Population Growth Rate**: 2.6%

**HIV/AIDS** (1999 est.): *Adult prevalence*: 8.09%; *Persons living with HIV/AIDS*: 1.3 million; *Deaths*: 140,000. (For additional details from www.UNAIDS.org, see end of Section 10B.)

**Literacy Rate** (*defined as those age 15 and over who can read and write*): 67.8% (*male*: 79.4%, *female*: 56.8%). Education is free and compulsory between ages 7 and 14. Swahili and English are the official languages of Tanzania, though the majority of people continue to use the language of their ethnic group.

**Per Capita Gross Domestic Product** (*purchasing power parity*): $610 (2001 est.); *Inflation*: 5%; *Unemployment*: NA; *Living below the poverty line*: 51.1% (1991 est.)

Some basic demographic indicators for the country are presented in Table 1. Population growth in Tanzania, as in most African countries, is largely influenced by fertility and mortality rates, particularly deaths because of HIV/AIDS. As shown in Table 1, the total fertility rate is high, but showed a significant decline in the 1990s.

## B. A Brief Historical Perspective and Cultural Setting

The original inhabitants of Tanzania were probably hunter/gatherers of the Khoisan-speaking peoples. The remnants of these are the Sandawe and Hadzapi minorities found in central Tanzania. During the first millennium, Bantu-speaking people occupied and settled most of what is now Tanzania. The Nilotic people migrating from the Sudan and the Semi-Cushitic who settled in the northern plains of the country followed later.

Tanzanian contacts with people from outside the African continent began around 700 C.E., when Arab traders visited the East African coast. Portuguese explorers reached the coastal area around 1500 and dominated trade up to the 17th century, when the Arabs from Oman displaced them. The fluorescence of coastal trade and society gave rise to the Swahili language about 1,200 years ago. Swahili has become a *lingua franca* from south Somalia, to Kenya, Uganda, the Democratic Republic of Congo, the Comoros, and North Mozambique. Following the partition of Africa by the colonialists, Tanganyika became a colony of Germany, together with Rwanda and Burundi. After World War I, Tanganyika was taken over by British colonialists as a protectorate. Tanganyika attained its independence in 1961 after about 77 years of colonial rule. Zanzibar was under the dominance of the Oman Arabs until 1890, when it came under the British colonial rule. In 1964, Zanzibar became independent. In the same year, Tanganyika and Zanzibar united to form a United Republic of Tanzania.

Tanzania is one of the poorest countries in the world, with a per capita gross domestic product (GDP) of US$220 (Population Reference Bureau

2000). The country has a mixed economy, with agriculture, mining, and tourism contributing the largest shares. Economic performance and trends in Tanzania have not been favorable since attaining independence in 1961. During the 1960s, the GDP was estimated to be growing at an annual rate of 6%. There was a growth decline of GDP to about 4% during the 1970s, and a further decline to less than 2% growth during the 1980s (The Planning Commission 1992).

Several internal and external factors have contributed to the dismal economic situation, especially during the late 1970s and mid 1980s. Internally, the economy was mismanaged and there were many policy failures. An annual population growth rate of about 3% during this period was another contributing factor (The Planning Commission 1992). Population growth put additional pressure on economic and social conditions, especially in terms of provision of social services and access to basic commodities. The existence and the quality of a good health infrastructure, for example, which was established in the early 1970s, deteriorated, and services collapsed because of lack of drugs and medical supplies.

Externally, the Tanzanian economy was affected by the deterioration of the country's major exports (sisal, coffee, and tea) on the world market and the oil crisis of the 1970s. Between 1978 and 1979, the country also considerably depleted its economic resources in the war against Uganda, which toppled President Idi Amin. Finally, there was a tremendous decline in external assistance as the country's external debt burden increased because of some of the factors just mentioned. The combined effects of these factors were devastating to the living standards of the population.

The economic growth rate has started to show some signs of recovery as a result of economic reforms. GDP grew 3% in 1994 and 3.9% in 1995 (Bureau of Statistics and Macro International 1997). This growth rate was still lower than the targeted 5% envisaged by the 1995-1998 Economic Recovery Programmes.

## 1. Basic Sexological Premises, and 2. Religious, Ethnic, and Gender Factors Affecting Sexuality

### A. Character of Gender Roles

Gender roles are shaped within the social structure. There is, however, a diversity of tribal societies often with distinct gender roles in Tanzania. In most of Tanzania, gender roles reflect the dominance of men over women. Customs tend to discriminate against women and men have an upper hand in the ownership and control of resources of pro-

### Table 1

### Selected Demographic Indicators, Tanzania 1967-1997

| Indicator | 1967 | 1978 | 1988 | 2000 | 2002 |
|---|---|---|---|---|---|
| Population (millions) | 12.3 | 17.5 | 23.2 | 35.3 | 37 |
| Density (pop. per km²) | 14.0 | 20.0 | 26.0 | 37.4 | — |
| Percent urban | 6.4 | 13.8 | 18.3 | 20.0 | 25 |
| Crude birthrate | 47.0 | 49.0 | 46.0 | 42.0 | 39 |
| Crude death rate | 24.4 | 19.0 | 15.0 | 13.0 | 13 |
| Total fertility rate | 6.6 | 6.9 | 6.5 | 5.6 | 1.33 |
| Infant mortality rate (per 1,000 live births) | 155.0 | 137.0 | 115.0 | 99.0 | 78 |
| Under-5 mortality rate per 1,000 | — | — | — | 143.0 | — |
| Life expectancy at birth | 41.0 | 44.0 | 48.0 | 53.0 | 52 |
| Household size | 4.4 | 4.9 | 5.2 | — | — |

*Source*: Bureau of Statistics 1989; Ngallaba et al. 1993; Population Reference Bureau 2000

duction and distribution (such as land, livestock, tools, and children) as well as in decision making. There is a strong sexual division of labor, especially in the domestic sphere, which is associated with women.

### B. Sociolegal Status of Males and Females

The social and family structures of Tanzania's many ethnic groups influence the ideological, cultural values and norms including sexuality. Traditionally, the social structure has been based on two kinship patterns, the patrilineal and matrilineal systems. In patrilineal systems, inheritance and power is vested with the husband's clan, based on the father-son relationship. In matrilineal societies, the status of children is established through their mother's clan. A woman's brother, though, has power and authority over the children of his sister and they normally inherit through him. In other words, contrary to the patrilineal system, in the matrilineal system, ties are not established between mother and daughters but between the mother's brother and her children. An estimated 80% of the Tanzania's ethnic groups are patrilineal (TGNP & SARDC-WIDSAA 1997). Matrilineal societies, historically more prevalent in coastal areas, declined in the 19th and 20th centuries.

### C. General Concepts of Sexuality and Love

Sexuality is rooted in social reproduction (Setel 1999) and is part of the social structure as stated earlier. Traditionally, in many societies, the issue of sexuality was considered secretive and the domain of adults. Sexual knowledge and education was part and parcel of initiation into adulthood for both males and females. Sexual life in Tanzania is widely considered to have three major roles: reproduction, expansion of kinship, and physical pleasure (Mbunda 1991). Sexual pleasure required expertise and the appropriate social context. Different ethnic groups had different ways of achieving sexual excitement. These included use of amulets, massage, caresses, fondling, wearing beads, waist, and belly dancing. However, sexual pleasure had to occur in a socially accepted context like marriage. Other kinds of sexual activity, such as adultery, homosexuality, child abuse, incest, and rape, were unacceptable, as they violated the social order.

Sexuality is also associated with physical and social development within the communities' social-control framework. There was a clear code of "dos and don'ts" at different stages of physical development. Members of the community are expected to observe certain norms before puberty, at puberty, and at marriage (see norms in Sections 5A, Interpersonal Heterosexual Behaviors, Children, 5B, Adolescents, and 5C, Adults). Those who conform are rewarded and those who do not are punished. For example, among the Zaramo, brides who were not virgins on their wedding day were ridiculed and were regarded as a disgrace to their family members; the marriage could be dissolved on such occasions (Mbunda 1991). Likewise, among the traditional Meru and other groups that follow the age-set system (Maasai, for example), it was considered to be incest for a man to have a sexual affair or to marry any woman other than a woman of his own age set (Haram 1999). This is because these daughters were considered as their categorical daughters. Most of these norms were not only monitored by the family, but also by the community, including neighbors, elders, and clan members.

These norms were imparted from one generation to another through socialization, a process whereby the youngest members of the community were prepared to live in the world of adults, reflecting the norms and values of the specific society. This socialization process took a variety of forms from one society to another, although at the lowest level, it involved the family as an institution and the community at the highest level. On both levels, socialization was done separately for girls and boys. At the family level, boys were socialized at the father's fireplace school and girls by mothers in the kitchen school (Mbunda 1991). While boys were trained to be "men" (outside looking, open minded, and making decisions), girls were trained for their role of housewife and mother.

At the community level, socialization was achieved through initiation ceremonies. These were meant to transmit knowledge and values concerning procreation, mores, sexual skills, and good manners. Initiation ceremonies were offered once boys and girls had attained puberty. As stated earlier, boys and girls were separated for these rites. Boys' initiation is called (in Kiswahili) *jando* and that for girls *unyago* (Ntukula 1994). Among the Zaramo, for example, the *jando* curriculum for boys included good manners, bravery, the secrets of life, marriage, death, the responsibilities a man has to carry, and the customs and taboos to be observed. Girls were taught about male physiology, sexual intercourse, pregnancy, childbirth, and responsibilities of a good wife and mother in their *unyago* 'schools.' (Mbunda 1991). In some societies, circumcision (of both males and females) culminated the initiation ceremony.

### 3. Knowledge and Education about Sexuality

BELDINA OPIYO-OMOLO

### A. Formal Sources of Sexual Knowledge

See the preceding paragraph.

[*Comment 2003*: In Tanzania, puberty is a culturally marked period of the lifecycle in which young men and women learn about their social responsibilities, including knowledge about sexual behavior and reproduction as adults in their communities through initiation rites, or passage to adulthood.

### [B. Informal Sources of Sexual Knowledge

[Although sex education was an important component of puberty rituals for Tanzanian adolescents, in the past, such rituals were not common to all Tanzanian settings. The Shinyanga Region of west central Tanzania is a case in point. Knowledge about sexuality was not necessarily acquired through structured rituals of initiation. Young girls learned about their bodies and about the reproductive cycle in an informal, non-uniform way. For example, mothers would give some instruction on sexual techniques to daughters who were about to get married on how to satisfy their husbands, thus preventing them from wandering off elsewhere to find pleasure. Other informal networks of information available to young girls included discussion with each other, and practical experience gained through interactions with young men who visited the huts where the girls slept late at night. The girls slept in what was called *Maji*, outer rooms for grandparents where girls slept on their own. (*End of comment by B. Opiyo-Omolo*)]

### 4. Autoerotic Behaviors and Patterns

For attitudes toward masturbation and its practice by children, adolescents, and adult men and women, see Sections 5A, Children, and 5B, Adolescents, below.

### 5. Interpersonal Heterosexual Behaviors

#### A. Children

The following list indicates specific sexual behaviors that are acceptable as normal before puberty by different tribal cultures. This is not a comprehensive list because attitudinal information is only available for a few behaviors in the many tribal traditions in Tanzania.

- Playing with one's own genitals: Chagga
- Singing & dancing love songs: Chagga, Fipa, Nyakusa, Sukuma, Zaramo
- Touching or fondling and sucking mother's breasts: Chagga, Gogo, Makonde, Makonde Malaba, Maasai, Nyakyusa, Nyaturu Sukuma, Zaramo
- Playing father/mother games: Chagga, Fipa, Makonde, Makonde Malaba, Maasai, Nyakyusa, Nyaturu Sukuma, Zaramo
- Fondling and kissing: Chagga, Makonde, Makonde Malaba
- Masturbation: Fipa
- Interest in sexually exciting stories and games: Fipa, Nyaturu
- Interest in one's own genitals or buttocks: looking or touching: Gogo, Maasai, Nyaturu, Zaramo
- Enjoying genitals being touched during washing: Gogo, Zaramo
- Causing penis or clitoris to become erect: Gogo, Makonde, Makonde Malaba, Sukuma
- Interest in opposite sex: Maasai
- Lovemaking and sexual intercourse: age 7 to 14: Maasai (*Source*: Mbunda 1991)

Sexual behaviors that are unacceptable for children before they enter puberty; again this is not a comprehensive list.

- Sexual intercourse: Chagga, Fipa, Gogo, Makonde, Makonde Malaba, Maasai, Nyaturu, Sukuma, Zaramo
- Overindulgence in private masturbation: Fipa, Makonde, Makonde Malaba
- Interest in watching animals mate: Gogo, Makonde, Makonde Malaba, Nyakyusa, Nyaturu
- Watching people mating: Zaramo
- Public masturbation: Makonde, Sukuma
- Prostitution: Makonde
- Sodomy: Maasai
- Bestiality: Maasai
- Rape: Maasai
- Incest: Maasai
- Preoccupation with one's own genitals: Nyakyusa, Nyaturu, Zaramo
- Association with the other sex: Nyakyusa
- Touching anothers' genitals: Zaramo (*Source*: Mbunda 1991)

## B. Adolescents

The onset of puberty brings major changes in what behaviors the various cultures of Tanzania consider acceptable for adolescents. Acceptable behaviors include:

- Interest in the other sex: Chagga, Fipa, Gogo, Makonde, Makonde Malaba, Maasai, Nyakyusa, Nyaturtu, Zaramo
- Private masturbation: Chagga, Fipa, Gogo, Nyakyusa, Nyaturtu, Sukuma, Zaramo
- Interest in sex-related stories, songs, and dancing: Chagga, Fipa, Gogo, Makonde, Makonde Malaba, Nyakyusa, Sukuma, Zaramo
- Female or male circumcision: Chagga, Gogo, Maasai, Nyaturu, Zaramo
- Interest in sex ornaments, e.g., beads: Chagga, Zaramo
- Interest in sexual development: Fipa, Gogo, Nyakyusa, Nyaturu, Zaramo
- Interest in learning lovemaking techniques: Fipa, Zaramo
- Playing father and mother: Gogo
- Sexual intercourse with several partners: Maasai
- Sexual fantasies: Gogo, Nyakyusa

- Enlargement of clitoris: Nyakyusa
- Interest in male activities: Nyaturu
- Playing *chagulaga* ("Choose the one you love"), a premarital sex-for-fun game often played after evening dances, where a boy runs after a girl, usually one with whom some kind of understanding has been established: Sukuma (*Source*: Mbunda 1991)

Sexual practices unacceptable for adolescents after the onset of puberty include:

- Public masturbation: Chagga, Makonde, Makonde Malaba, Nyakyusa, Nyaturu, Zaramo
- Interest in watching animals mate: Chagga, Fipa, Gogo, Nyakyusa, Sukuma
- Sexual intercourse: Chagga, Fipa, Gogo, Makonde, Makonde Malaba, Nyakyusa, Nyaturu, Sukuma, Zaramo
- Courtship: Makonde, Makonde Malaba, Nyakyusa
- Sodomy: Makonde, Makonde Malaba, Maasai, Nyakyusa
- Bestiality: Makonde, Makonde Malaba, Maasai
- Rape: Makonde, Maasai
- Incest: Makonde, Maasai
- Child abuse: Makonde, Makonde Malaba
- Lesbianism: Maasai, Nyakyusa
- Close association with the other sex: Nyakyusa, Nyaturu (*Source*: Mbunda 1991)

*Male Circumcision.* See Section 5B above.

*Female Circumcision.* The government of Tanzania has made female circumcision (genital mutilation) illegal and a punishable offense. Although it has been illegal for some time, female circumcision was traditionally and still is practiced secretly in several regions of Tanzania as an initiation ritual of preparing youth for womanhood. The justifications for female circumcision are varied. It is argued that female circumcision trained a woman to overcome the pains, and thus prepared her to bear the pains of child labor and birth (Haram 1999). It is also reported that female circumcision in some ethnic groups of Tanzania was practiced as a measure to control the sexuality of women (Mbunda 1994; Haram 1999). It is assumed that circumcision reduces the woman's sexual urge and thus makes her faithful to her partner (Mbunda 1991; Haram 1999).

Data on the levels and patterns of female circumcision in Tanzania have been documented by the 1996 DHS (Bureau of Statistics & Macro International 1997). Nationwide, about 18% of Tanzanian women have undergone circumcision, mainly in eight out of 25 regions in the country. The regions with the highest incidence are: Arusha 81.4%; Dodoma 67.4%; Mara 43.7%; Kilimanjaro 36.9%; Iringa 27%; Singida 25.4%; Tanga 25.1%; and Morogoro 20.2%.

Clitoridectomy and excision are the major types of circumcision in the country. The majority of women are circumcised between ages 6 to 20 years. Circumcision is more likely to be practiced by those living in the rural areas than their urban counterparts. As in many other parts of sub-Saharan Africa, traditional practitioners perform circumcision. These are normally elderly women who have experience in the practice.

The unhygienic condition through which female circumcision is conducted is creating serious health risks among women. Political leaders, religious organizations, and other nongovernmental agencies (NGOs) have campaigned against the practice, but without success. This is because, as stated previously, the practice is done secretly. Sometimes the victims and the practitioners are either hidden or shielded. Perhaps sensitization of the adults, the main promoters, and examination of the cultural factors underlying the practice can help.

## C. Adults

Patterns of sexual values and relations in Tanzania have changed following the influence of colonialism and imperialism since the beginning of the 19th century. However, local or "customary" norms and patterns are still practiced in many rural areas. The coming of colonialism led to the introduction of a cash economy based especially on plantation agriculture. This led to labor migration from labor-exporting areas to the plantations and mines. The process had an impact in both areas. The male labor migration led to a deficit of men in labor-exporting areas and a surplus of men in the cash-economy areas. Rural migration, urbanization, and formal education are other factors that have led to social change in traditions. As a result, family composition, structure, and functions have also changed, as they have in similar ways in much of the rest of sub-Saharan Africa. Extended family and kinship structures are changing to a more nuclear model. Parental authority is weakening, intermarriages among Tanzanian ethic groups are on the increase, and an increasing number of people remain unmarried or are attached to temporary relationships. For example, in the past, conjugal relations were formalized with negotiations between parents and relatives of the couples (taking care of the parents' of the couples interests). Nowadays, it is not uncommon to find that such negotiations involve the partners concerned.

### The Ideal Spouse

The characteristics of the ideal husband and wife vary with different cultures within Tanzania. Some examples of ideal characteristics for husbands follow with no indication of ranking:

- Sexually virile and attractive: Chagga, Fipa, Gogo, Makonde, Nyakyusa, Nyaturu, Sukuma, Zaramo
- Graduate of puberty initiation: Chagga, Gogo, Makonde, Makonde Malaba, Zaramo
- Circumcised: Chagga, Gogo, Maasai, Nyaturu
- Uncircumcised: Nyakyusa
- Hard working and productive: Chagga, Fipa, Makonde, Maasai, Zaramo
- Able to support the family financially: Chagga, Fipa, Gogo, Nyakyusa, Nyaturu, Sukuma
- Healthy and strong: Chagga, Makonde, Makonde Malaba
- Loyal to family, clan, and in-laws: Chagga, Fipa, Gogo, Makonde, Makonde Malaba, Masai, Nyakyusa, Nyaturu, Sukuma, Zaramo
- Affectionate to wife and children: Chagga, Fipa, Gogo, Makonde, Makonde Malaba, Nyakyusa, Nyaturu, Sukuma, Zaramo
- Sexually stimulating and appealing: Fipa, Makonde, Makonde Malaba, Maasai, Nyakyusa, Sukuma, Nyaturu, Zaramo
- Rich in cows or cattle: Gogo, Maasai
- Courageous in war: Nyakyusa
- Cooperative and helpful to in-laws: Nyaturu (*Source*: Mbunda 1991)

The characteristics valued in a wife are as follows (not ranked):

- Sexually energetic and attractive: Chagga, Gogo, Makonde, Makonde Malaba, Maasai, Sukuma Nyakyusa, Nyaturu, Zaramo
- Enlarged clitoris: Nyakyusa
- Able to bear many children: Chagga, Fipa, Gogo, Makonde, Maasai, Nyakyusa, Nyaturu, Sukuma, Zaramo
- Able to care for family: Chagga, Fipa, Gogo, Makonde, Maasai, Nyakyusa, Nyaturu, Sukuma, Makonde Malaba
- Loyal and affectionate to husband and children: Chagga, Fipa, Gogo, Makonde, Maasai, Nyakyusa, Nyaturu, Sukuma, Zaramo, Makonde Malaba
- Affectionate to clan and in-laws: Chagga, Fipa, Makonde, Makonde Malaba, Maasai, Nyaturu, Nyakyusa, Sukuma, Zaramo
- Expert at lovemaking and sexual intercourse: Fipa, Gogo, Makonde, Makonde Malaba, Nyakyusa
- Good housewife and cook: Gogo, Makonde, Nyakyusa
- Able to get along with husband's other wives: Gogo
- Hard working: Makonde, Makonde Malaba, Nyaturu, Sukuma, Zaramo
- Well-educated sexually: Maasai
- Circumcised: Nyaturu
- Graduate of puberty initiation: Zaramo (*Source*: Mbunda 1991)

### Marital Norms and Values

Just as puberty marks the transition from childhood to adolescence and a new set of behavioral values, both acceptable and unacceptable, so marriage is marked by a new set of behavioral values. Among the norms acceptable for married persons are:

- Courtship: Chagga, Fipa, Gogo, Nyakyusa, Nyaturu, Sukuma, Zaramo
- Wedding: Chagga, Fipa, Gogo, Nyakyusa, Sukuma, Zaramo
- Sexual intercourse: Chagga, Fipa, Gogo, Makonde, Makonde Malaba, Nyakyusa, Nyaturu, Zaramo
- Masturbation: Chagga, Makonde, Makonde Malaba
- Polygamy: Chagga, Fipa, Gogo, Makonde, Makonde Malaba, Nyakyusa, Nyaturu, Zaramo
- Secret liaisons for barren couples: Gogo
- Fondling: Makonde, Makonde Malaba
- Sex-related stories and dances: Makonde, Makonde Malaba
- Sexual intercourse with spouse only: Masai
- Pregnancy and childbirth: Chagga, Fipa, Gogo, Makonde, Makonde-Malaba, Masai, Sukuma, Nyakyusa, Nyaturu, Zaramo
- Playing *chagulaga*: Sukuma (*Source*: Mbunda 1991)

Unacceptable sexual behaviors for married persons include:

- Adultery: Chagga, Fipa, Makonde, Makonde Malaba, Maasai, Nyakyusa, Nyaturu, Sukuma, Zaramo. As noted later in Section 9, Contraception, Abortion, and Population Planning, available data indicate that between 14% and 26% of Tanzanian men are involved in extramarital relationships (Weinstein et al 1995; Mwageni 1996).
- Sodomy: Chagga, Fipa, Makonde, Makonde Malaba, Maasai, Nyakyusa, Nyaturu, Sukuma, Zaramo
- Child abuse: Chagga, Maasai, Nyakyusa, Sukuma
- Rape: Chagga, Gogo, Makonde, Makonde Malaba, Maasai, Nyaturu, Sukuma, Zaramo
- Prostitution: Chagga, Fipa, Makonde, Nyaturu, Sukuma, Zaramo
- Abortion: Chagga, Fipa, Gogo, Makonde, Makonde Malaba, Nyakyusa, Zaramo
- Incest: Chagga, Fipa, Makonde, Makonde Malaba, Maasai, Nyaturu, Sukuma, Zaramo
- Bestiality: Fipa, Maasai, Nyakyusa, Nyaturu, Sukuma, Zaramo
- Masturbation: Fipa
- Lesbianism: Makonde, Makonde Malaba, Maasai, Nyakyusa
- Polyandry: Nyakyusa (*Source*: Mbunda 1991)

[*"Dry Sex" or "Wet Sex"*

[*Comment 2001*: As noted earlier in the Nigeria and Kenya chapters, sexual relations in subequatorial Africa are male-dominated, with the male initiating coitus and dictating its style and pace. Female response and satisfaction are not considered important. Coitus usually takes place with no foreplay. The male-above position is standard, and marital coitus is for procreation, not for pleasure. Women in many African cultures do not even know what female orgasm is, and may have never experienced it. In describing mating customs in the chapter on Ghana, Augustine Ankoma reports that penile-vaginal penetrative sex with little foreplay is the normal sexual style. Although among the well-educated youth, some forms of foreplay are gaining a foothold, fellatio and cunnilingus are abhorrent. Genital manipulation is hardly accepted and traditionally women feel shy to touch the penis, and most men are not interested in having their genitals manipulated.

[These male-oriented cultural values underlie what is appropriately termed "dry sex," a common practice throughout sub-Saharan Africa. The "dry sex" mating behavior fits comfortably with the male distaste for vaginal secretions, foreplay, and disinterest in female sexual arousal and orgasm. In this setting, males quickly reach orgasm and their satisfaction. Women experience painful intercourse, with no arousal and no orgasm.

[In many African cultures, women prepare themselves to pleasure their husbands with a dry vagina by mixing the powdered stem and leaf of the *Mugugudhu* tree with water, wrapped in a bit of nylon stocking and inserted into the vagina 10 to 15 minutes before intercourse. Other women use *Mutendo wegudo*, soil mixed with baboon urine, which they obtain from traditional healers, Still others use detergents, salt, cotton, or shredded newspaper. These swell the vaginal tissue, make it hot, and dry it out. The women admit that sexual intercourse is "very painful, but our African husbands enjoy sex with a dry vagina" (Schoofs 2000).

[The inevitable results of "dry sex" include increased friction, vaginal lacerations, suppression of the vagina's natural bacteria, and torn condoms (when these are used). All these consequences increase a woman's risk of STD and HIV infections. Fortunately, the tradition of "dry sex" is waning among the educated urban young, but any change in this traditional mating behavior is also resisted because of rejection of Western gender roles (Stellwaggon 2001).

["Dry sex" is a well-established and more or less wide spread practice in various subequatorial African cultures. It is common in Southern Africa, particularly in Zimbabwe, Zambia, Malawi, some parts of Nigeria, some parts of Uganda, in Southern Sudan, and even in Kenya and Botswana. The only difference is in what these women use for drying up their vaginas.

[In the northwest part of Tanzania and neighboring regions, "wet sex" is widely known and practiced. "Wet sex" consists of foreplay where there is intense stimulation by the male partner on the woman's labia and clitoral regions. This stimulation results in copious production of secretions (thought to come from Bartholin's glands). People talk about it openly, sometimes mixed with a sense of humor and intertribe jokes. Some researchers have blamed this practice for the high incidence and prevalence of HIV and STDs. The implications of this kind of information for action plans (resource inputs and sociocultural issues) are enormous. Now that these behaviors have been brought into public attention, a well thought-out survey that is representative of different segments of the populations becomes essential for an effective public health policy (Tanzania, personal communication 2003).

[In March 2003, when the editor of *CCIES* inquired whether "dry sex" was observed in Botswana, Dr. Ian Taylor replied; "'Dry sex' is common in Botswana as well and leads to vaginal tears and lesions which help spread HIV/AIDS, it is true." (*End of comment by B. Opiyo-Omolo*)]

## 6. Homoerotic, Homosexual, and Bisexual Behaviors

[*Comment 2003*: In Tanzania, male homosexuality is illegal under the penal code inherited from the British. The law in Tanzania criminalizes gays. Male homosexual acts are punishable by up to 14 years, even though in practice, the law is rarely enforced, because it is difficult to obtain any proof that someone is a homosexual. In Swahili, there is traditionally no word for *male homosexual*. However, recently a word has been coined: *Msenge*, a Swahili word for "passive" or "femme" gay man. There is also a term for *lesbian*: *Msagaji*, literally, "one who grinds." The verb for lesbian lovemaking, *Sagana* means "grind together." In Tanzania, lesbians are even less visible than gay men. (*End of comment by B. Opiyo-Omolo*)]

## 7. Gender Diversity and Transgender Issues

Not reported.

## 8. Significant Unconventional Sexual Behaviors

As noted earlier, the purpose of sexual relations was traditionally viewed as having three functions: reproduction, expansion of kinship, and pleasure. It was also reported that some unconventional sexual relations that were harshly dealt with were sanctioned within a specific social context. However, sexual life, like political, religious, cultural, and social life, continues to change, and new forms of sexual behavior, some of which could be called "unconventional," are emerging, as described in detail in the following sections.

### A. Coercive Sexual Behaviors

The penal code recognizes various sexual offenses. These offenses include forced marriage, sexual assault, and procurement of women or girls for the purpose of prostitution (The Centre for Reproductive Law and Policy 1997. In Tanzania, child sexual abuse and rape are punishable by imprisonment for life.

*Child Sexual Abuse, Rape, and Sexual Harassment*

Reported sexual abuse of young girls is on the increase in Tanzania. In 1995, about 756 child sexual abuse cases were reported (TAMWA undated). In 1997, of the 129 reported incidences of sexual abuse, 63% were in Dar es Salaam and 8% were in Mbeya (LHRC 1997). The victims of sexual abuse are as young as nine months old while the assailants are adults mainly in their 20s or 30s, but a few are as old as 50 years (LHRC 1997). The majority of the cases, however, are not reported because of social stigma, fear, ignorance, and cumbersome legal procedures. The increase in reported sexual abuse cases could easily be because of a rise in the consciousness of women's rights and an increased willingness to use official judicial channels to deal with such matters.

In the case of child sexual abuse, the assailant usually seduces the victim with sweets or other gifts and later abuses the child. In other incidences, the assailants are individuals trusted by mothers to take temporary care of their children while they perform other duties nearby or are a distance away doing some errand. Others are simply ambushed on their way home or to school. Sexual abuse is not limited only to girls, but also involves boys. While sexual abuse for boys involves anal penetration, for girls it is both anal and vaginal penetration. The assailants are sometimes known to the victims and in others cases they are not.

The reasons for the increase of sexual abuse to children are not exactly known. It is argued that some adults are seeking to have sexual relations with young people thought to be free of HIV (Rajani & Kudreti 1995). Certain groups of people appear to be more vulnerable to sexual abuse than others. For example, girls, street children, the disabled, and children that are not biologically related to the family are more likely to be abused than others. Sexual abuse in such situations is made in exchange of protection offered by the assailants. Abuse to children is also caused by inability of the assailant to approach mature women. Sometimes abuse is associated with superstition; success in business is believed to be associated with having sexual relations with certain special groups of people. Usually, a traditional fortuneteller gives such advice. For example, LHRC (1997) reported that in November 1996, one assailant, assisted by his wife, abused a 9-year-old girl in one of the gold-mining areas of Tanzania dominated by small-scale miners. In other incidences, assailants claim to have irresistible sexual drive (LHRC 1997).

Reported incidences of rape increased from 81 in 1990 to 365 in 1993. It is noted that rape cases increased from 497 in 1991 to 736 in 1992, while sexual assaults increased from 8 in 1992 to 37 in 1993 (TGNP & SARDC-WIDSAA 1997).

Between 1990 and 1992, no cases of sexual harassment were recorded in Tanzania. This does not mean they were no such incidences, but, as argued earlier, people did not report such incidents. However, by 1995, 74 cases were reported (TAMWA undated). These included touches on the buttocks or breasts. Protection against sexual harassment in the working place is found in the Security of Employment Act, although the definition of harassment is not provided. Although police are responsible for arresting the accused once any offense is reported, most cases go unreported and no one is arrested.

## B. Prostitution

Prostitution is translated in Kiswahili as *umalaya* and the prostitute as *Malaya*. *Umalaya* is used to refer to the sex life of an individual considered to be promiscuous or loose in sexual relations. Prostitution is mainly urban-based and usually refers to women; in the traditional African culture, promiscuous or "loose" men are not considered as prostitutes. Traditionally, men were free to take as many sexual partners as they liked or could afford. In the 1970s and 1980s, women practicing *umalaya* were known to be from certain ethnic groups. However, currently this is not the case, as it involves many Tanzanian ethnic groups. There are no real brothels, pimps, or touts in Tanzania. Most of the *Malaya* women are working for themselves.

There are several forms of prostitution. The "classical" *Malaya* women operate indoors. They stay inside their rooms and wait for men to visit them. These women have sex with any number of men who visit them for an agreed charge. Apart from providing her customers with sexual services, such a woman can offer other services to a regular partner, like food, bath water, and breakfast, in case a man spends a night in the house. In most cases, it is the customer who pays for most of these expenses. Although this form of prostitution ensures security from police arrests, it does not allow women to control who should come to them.

Another form of prostitution involves barmaids, guesthouse workers, and promiscuous married women. These types of women have their own residences like the classical *Malaya*; however, they may or may not invite their clientele to their places. Promiscuous married women mainly prefer guesthouses or the residence of the customer, while for the other categories of women, in addition to these two places, a customer may rent a separate room. In these types of sexual relationships, a woman has several boyfriends who may provide shelter or money for food and clothing in exchange for sexual pleasure (Setel 1999).

A new form of *umalaya* has emerged in Tanzania in the late 1990s, nicknamed *Uchangu Doa* (the person is nicknamed *Changu Doa* or *CD*. The name comes from a species of fish from the Indian Ocean. These fish are small in size, abundant, easy to fish, and cheaper compared to other species. The species is also known as *janja* (literally meaning clever in a cunning way, deceitful, or crafty). These features of the fish describe why the name *Changu Doa* was adopted to label this type of sexual behavior. *CDs* are young women in their teens and 20s, who usually earn their living by having multiple sexual partners. This type of sexual behavior is normally urban-based. *CDs* use different tactics to attract their customers. The tactics include positioning themselves in very strategic locations like street junctions or near famous pubs, tourist hotels, casinos, nightclubs, and other dark spots. They dress scantly in order attract the attention of their customers. The *CDs* "uniforms" include tights, see-through materials, miniskirts, and colorful materials. *CDs* are often assertive with their customers by calling, signaling, or revealing their most "valuable" body parts if need be. Many *CDs* acquire their training and tactics from peer groups, as well as from reading and watching pornographic magazines or films.

The *CDs* practice their operations during nights. Their "day" begins at around 9 p.m. Quitting time is largely influenced by their success in being picked by a customer, but is seldom later than 3 to 4 a.m. The main customers of the *CDs* are normally people who are seemingly rich, such as government officials and foreigners, especially the whites, tourists, and businessmen. Most of these people have money, yet do not have time to look around for women in order to satisfy their sexual desires.

Payment for services is negotiable and depends on the duration of the service, the economic and social status of the customer, status of the urban area, the location where the *CD* was encountered, time of the night, and education level of the *CD*. The longer the duration of services, the higher the price. *CDs* operate in large or well-known urban areas like Dar es Salaam, Arusha, or Dodoma. Those encountered near tourist hotels, city centers, and nightclubs or casinos are likely to be more expensive than elsewhere. Foreigners and wealthy customers are likely to be charged more than others. At times, a foreigner may even be required to pay in foreign currency. Likewise, *CDs* picked in the early hours of their operation may charge more than those picked in the late hours of the "day." Educated *CDs* have a better bargaining power and thus may be more expensive than those less educated.

Though *CDs* are mainly operating in urban areas, there are elements of this type of sexual behavior in rural areas, especially in small towns. In the rural areas, while *CDs* linger near bars and guesthouses, they are, however, not as aggressive as those found in large urban areas.

Rural women who have migrated to the city, and poor urban women, dominate the prostitution sector. Increased economic hardships, unemployment, and commercialization of goods as well as services, have contributed to the increase in prostitution. It can be argued that women engage in different forms of prostitution for economic motives as a means to secure resources that are owned and monopolized by men. Through such sexual relations, women use men as patrons to secure employment, cover for illicit business, advance their economic aspirations, purchase land, meet their material needs, and obtain cash to make their ends meet (White 1990). In a way, such relations provide social and economic security among the women concerned. To some women, though, different forms of prostitution are practiced so as to maximize their sexual desires. The male partners, however, are after sexual pleasure, and having many sexual partners may be a symbol of virility as well as economic status. There is a feeling that a man who has several female partners has resources to do so and is thus wealthy.

Prostitution is illegal in Tanzania. Thus, such individuals are from time to time rounded up by police and the locations known to house prostitutes are raided. However, the victims of these raids are always females, as the male partners and patrons are left untouched.

### C. Pornography and Erotica

[*Comment 2003*: Pornography is illegal in Tanzania. However, with greater access to technology and increasing Internet usage, Tanzania's antipornography laws are becoming more difficult to enforce. In June 2001, Tanzanian President Benjamin Mkapa announced that his government would be cracking down on pornography, particularly on the Internet.

[At a 2002 meeting of the UN committee on the Rights of the Child in Geneva, Switzerland, the committee raised concerns about the large and reportedly increasing number of child victims of commercial sex exploitation and sex tourism in Tanzania, including pornography. Under Tanzania Sexual Offenses Act of 1998, people found guilty of sexual exploitation of children, including child pornography, can face long jail terms.

[Despite all these, Tanzania still lacks the resources to put its antipornography policies into practice. The body charged with policing the Internet, the Tanzania Communication Commission (TCC), will have to find a way of stretching resources if it is to control the problem. (*End of comment by B. Opiyo-Omolo*)]

### D. Other Unconventional Sexual Behaviors

There are occasional reported cases of males having carnal knowledge with animals (donkeys, goats, and birds, mostly ducks). This behavior is associated with superstition. The few cases reported involved men working in mining areas. It is thought by some individuals that having sexual relations with animals may increase their luck.

## 9. Contraception, Abortion, and Population Planning

### A. Contraception

*Contraceptive Knowledge*

Large-scale reliable data on contraception in Tanzania has been available since 1993 following the introduction of the Demographic and Health Surveys (DHS) and the Tanzania Reproductive and Child Health Survey (TRCHS). According to TRCHS, as many as 93% of Tanzanians are aware of contraception (National Bureau of Statistics & Macro International 2000). Knowledge of modern methods is higher than it is of the traditional contraceptives, with 92% of the people aware of modern methods compared with 62% aware of traditional contraceptives. The most popular modern methods are the pill, IUD, male condom, injectables, and female sterilization, while withdrawal and periodic abstinence are the best known among the traditional ones. Men are more likely than women to be aware of the methods (92.8% vs.

90.9%). Among the currently married, men and women are more knowledgeable than sexually active unmarried men and women: 97.1% and 95.3% versus 96.1% and 91.6%, respectively.

Knowledge of modern contraceptive methods is higher among Tanzanian men and women who are: aged 20 to 34; living in urban areas; those with primary education or higher; monogamous men; those with one to three children; those who have not experienced child death; and skilled workers (Mwageni 1996; Bureau of Statistics & Macro International 1997). There are also regional variations in terms of awareness of the methods, with higher levels in Dar es Salaam, the coast, and the Lindi, Tabora, and Mbeya regions than in the rest of the country. (Compare with contraceptive use described below.)

*Contraceptive Use*

Rates of contraceptive use are inconsistent with awareness of the methods. Overall, 29.3% of men are more likely to use the methods than women (22.3%). Modern methods are more used than the traditional ones. The most popular methods are condoms, the calendar or rhythm method, pill, and injection. The discrepancy between knowledge and use calls for more promotion of family planning activities in Tanzania (National Bureau of Statistics & Macro International 2000).

The difference in use of methods between men and women needs more attention. It seems there is underreporting or exaggeration of some methods by men and women, respectively. Examination of variations in reporting usage of two methods, namely condom and withdrawal, may shed more light on this aspect (see Table 2). These two methods have been chosen because both partners have to be aware of their use. Under normal circumstances, if reporting is correct, very little difference would be expected between men and women. According to Table 2, concordance in reporting is more likely to occur with withdrawal than with the condom.

More unmarried women than married women use contraceptives, 33% compared with 25.4% (National Bureau of Statistics & Macro International 2000). However, among men, the opposite is the case (37% of husbands compared with 31% of single men). Several plausible reasons can be offered for this pattern. Firstly, it appears that the unmarried women are concerned about premarital childbearing. Secondly, a reasonable proportion of married men may have extramarital sexual relations with these single women, and use methods such as condoms both for family planning and for protection against STDs. Available data indicate that be-

### Table 2

**Male-Female Variation in the Use of Condoms and Withdrawal in Tanzania (in Percentages)**

| Category | Condom | | | Withdrawal | | |
|---|---|---|---|---|---|---|
| | Men | Women | Difference | Men | Women | Difference |
| Tanzania (Total) | 7.3 | 1.3 | 6.0 | 2.4 | 1.9 | 0.5 |
| Mainland Tanzania | 7.5 | 1.3 | 6.2 | 2.4 | 1.9 | 0.5 |
| Total urban | 15.2 | 3.5 | 11.7 | 1.3 | 1.1 | 0.2 |
| Dar es Salaam | 16.9 | 4.4 | 12.5 | 1.1 | 1.5 | −0.4 |
| Other urban | 14.4 | 3.1 | 11.3 | 1.3 | 0.9 | 0.4 |
| Total rural | 5.2 | 0.7 | 4.5 | 2.8 | 2.2 | 0.6 |
| Currently married | 16.1 | 6.5 | 9.6 | 19.2 | 11.5 | 7.7 |
| Sexually active single | 35.2 | 18.4 | 16.8 | 11.5 | 8.1 | 3.4 |

*Source*: Compiled from Tanzania DHS 1996

tween 14% and 26% of men are involved in extramarital relationships in Tanzania (Weinstein et al. 1995; Mwageni 1996. Thirdly, it is possible that unmarried women are concerned with the costs of taking care of the children. Fourthly, this group of women may consist of students, who by law are not allowed to marry or bear children.

Data also reveal regional variation in the use of methods, with Kilimanjaro 38%), Dar es Salaam (30%), and the Coast regions (27%) leading in contraceptive use among women, while Rukwa (53%), Mbeya (39%), Singida (37%), Kigoma (33%), Dar es Salaam (32%) and Coastal regions (31%) are prominent for men using contraceptives (Bureau of Statistics & Macro International 1997). Furthermore, contraceptive use is higher for Tanzanian men and women who are: between age 30 to 40 years, living in urban areas, with secondary education or higher, with three to five living children, those with no experience of dead children, and highly skilled workers (Muvandi & Simbamwaka 1996; Mwageni 1996; Bureau of Statistics & Macro International 1997).

### Trends in Contraceptive Knowledge and Use

Nationwide trends in Tanzania reveal an increase over time in awareness and use of both modern and traditional contraceptive methods. In 1991, for example, knowledge of modern and traditional contraceptive methods was 72% and 44%, respectively. By 1999, these levels had increased to 91% and 58% (National Bureau of Statistics & Macro International 2000). Use of modern contraceptive methods among women in 1991 was 10%; by 1999, this level had increased to 22% (National Bureau of Statistics & Macro International 2000).

### Attitudes Towards Family Planning

Attitudes towards family planning are an important aspect in effective use of contraceptive methods. Several methods can be used to ascertain attitudes towards family planning, including surveys of approval, intention to use methods in the future, and acceptability of media messages on family planning.

Available data reveal that among the married, about 48% approve of family planning methods (Bureau of Statistics & Macro International 1997). Surprisingly, women (78%) are more likely than men (51%) to approve of family planning, although the level of knowledge and use is higher for men than for women. Otherwise, approval is likely to be higher among the educated and urban residents compared to other categories. In terms of differences between couples, approval is higher when the wife is older in age, where couples have age differences of less than four years, and where both the husband and wife are educated than the other way around. Further findings reveal that individuals with no religion and the unmarried are unlikely to approve of family planning (Muvandi & Simbamwaka 1996).

The intention to use family planning in the future is considerably high among both males and females than current actual use, although it is higher for the men than for the women. The majority of men and women accept the dissemination of family planning messages and information through media channels, especially radio and television (Bureau of Statistics & Macro International 1997).

### B. Teenage (Unmarried) Pregnancies

Teenage pregnancy is not an uncommon phenomenon in Tanzania. According to available data, the youngest age at which girls become sexually active in the country is 11 years (Mpangile, Leshabari & Kihwele 1993). About 26% of women in the country begin childbearing during their teen years, between 15 and 19 years of age (Bureau of Statistics & Macro International 1997). As reported earlier,

there are cases where girls had their first pregnancy at age 13 (Rugumyamheto et al. 1994; Tumbo-Masabo 1994; Mwageni 1998). Teenage pregnancy is more common among girls with no education (40%), as well as rural residents (27%), than among educated or urban residents (Bureau of Statistics & Macro International 1997).

Studies conducted in Tanzania reveal that the men responsible for adolescent pregnancies are heterogeneous. It is noted that the partner's age ranged between 16 to 52, the majority of them being over age 45 (Mpangile, Leshabari & Kihwele 1993). In another study, the partners of teenage mothers were noted to be of different social status, including the jobless, fellow students, mechanics, drivers, teachers, and managers (Mwageni 1998).

Teenage pregnancy is influenced by several factors. As noted, premarital sex was rare in the past because of earlier mean age of marriage, more parental control, as well as strong social sanctions. These conditions are no longer effective nowadays. Lack of communication between parents and children is another plausible factor. Ignorance among teenagers of the woman's physiological changes also contributes to teenage pregnancy. In a study of 40 teenage mothers in Dar es Salaam and Kigoma, Tumbo-Masabo (1994) noted that many of them learned about the relationship between menarche and conception after they had conceived. Such girls had also little knowledge of the process of labor and childbirth. One can argue that many teenage pregnancies happen because of ignorance of the consequences of sexual behavior.

Legal measures to control teenage pregnancy in Tanzania are complicated by contradictions within the existing laws. According to the Marriage Act, a man can marry upon attaining 18 years of age, and a woman at age 15. However, the Penal Code also states that "any person may marry or permit the marriage of a girl under the age of 12 years in accordance with the custom of the tribe or religion." At the same time, the law states that "any person who carnally knows any girl under age of 14 years is guilty of a felony and is liable to imprisonment for life, with or without corporal punishment."

### C. Abortion

Induced abortion is illegal in Tanzania except when performed to save the mother's life. However, there is widespread practice of illegal induced abortion. [*Comment 2003*: In Tanzania, young girls who find themselves pregnant are expelled from school, a stark reality that is seen as instrumental to a young girl's decision to abort. (*End of comment by B. Opiyo-Omolo*)] Using a sample of 300 respondents among women who were admitted to a hospital in Dar es Salaam, a study found that 34% of them had practiced illegal abortion (Justeen, Kapiga & Asten 1992). In another study again done in Dar es Salaam, about 35% of the respondents interviewed had admitted intentionally terminating their pregnancies (Mpangile, Leshabari & Kihwele 1993). These estimates of abortion could be on the low side, because many abortions are conducted secretly and never reported. Either the male partner or a relative—mother, sister, or aunt, or the victim herself—facilitates the connection to the abortionist, including payment. The abortionists consist mainly of health workers or sometimes quacks. Places where abortions are conducted are numerous, including health facilities, hospitals, health centers, dispensaries, ordinary bedrooms, and occasionally in a simple room.

Induced abortion is more a problem of the young, unmarried, those with primary education, those who have lived in the city for six years or more, and those who know little about modern or traditional methods of family planning. The main reasons leading to abortion decisions include: inability to take care of an additional child, accidental pregnancy, inadequate birth spacing, and because the woman concerned was a student and feared expulsion (Mpangile, Leshabari & Kihwele 1993). Stambach (1996), in a study conducted in Machame, contends that there is a feeling among the residents that abortion rates are higher among secondary school students than other categories. This is because students want to avoid having their educational aspirations terminated. Stambach (1996) also asserts that some, especially older persons, associate higher rates of abortion among schoolgirls to the abandoning of traditional norms like female circumcision.

### D. Population Planning

The population policy of Tanzania provides the framework within which population planning is undertaken. Tanzania, like many other African countries, moved gradually from a position of implicit population policies in the 1970s to a position where active steps were taken towards the formulation of explicit policies in the mid-1980s. Early implicit population policies in Tanzania followed the country's policy of socialism and rural development introduced in 1967. As a result, several measures related to population policy were taken. These included: a spatial population distribution policy, which relocated, dislocated, and scattered rural families and the urban unemployed into planned settlements. Another policy was the growth pole policy, which was designed to promote an industrial dispersion away from the capital city (Dar es Salaam to ten other regional towns), and the Human Resource Deployment Act, which aimed at discouraging rural-to-urban migration.

Tanzania officially formulated a National Population Policy in 1992. The major objective of Tanzania's population policy is to "reinforce national development through developing available resources in order to improve the quality of life of the people" (Planning Commission 1992). The emphasis of this population policy is "on regulating population growth rate, enhancing population quality and improving the health and welfare of women and children" (Planning Commission 1992). Other concerns set forth in the policy include establishing information education and communication (IEC) systems that disseminate knowledge and information about use of services related to family planning, and making family planning means or services easily accessible. The policy also focuses on preparing young unmarried people to become responsible parents after their marriage through provision of family life education. The policy underscores the importance of educating the public on the benefits of women marrying after age 18 years. Taken together, the policy is really concerned with regulating population growth in Tanzania.

In 1959, long before the launching of the national population policy, the Family Planning Association of Tanzania (UMATI) began efforts to regulate reproductive behavior in Tanzania. During the early years, UMATI's services were urban-based (Ministry of Health 1989). As UMATI expanded, services were further extended to several other regions in the country. UMATI now has branches in all the regions, and several districts, as well as some villages of Tanzania.

The efforts of UMATI to introduce family planning (FP) in the early post-independence period were not well received by many people. The attitudes of many, including some party, government, and religious leaders, were negative. As in most parts of Africa, FP services in Tanzania were seen by many as designed by outsiders to control Tanzania's population. During the early post-independence period, the majority of African countries, including Tanzania, did not consider population growth as a problem. This was partly because of the feeling that there were few people, while resources were plenty. In addition, the economies of many countries by then could cope well with the small population size.

However, as population growth slowly began to put pressure on resources, changes began to be implemented in many African countries. In the case of Tanzania, in 1974, FP services began to be provided officially in all government health facilities (Ministry of Health 1989). UMATI was officially recognized and given the responsibility of procuring and distributing contraceptives in all maternal and child health (MCH) clinics established in almost all health institutions. Following these developments, the Ministry of Health began to involve itself in expanding and improving the quality of FP services in the country. In 1989, the Ministry of Health developed and launched the National Family Planning Programme for the years 1989 to 1993.

The program set out national goals, targets, and strategies for achieving FP services in Tanzania. The broad objective of the program was to raise the contraceptive acceptance rate in the country from 7% to 25% by 1993. In 1999, however, only 16% of women used modern contraceptives (National Bureau of Statistics & Macro International 2000). Other specific objectives were: improvement of the quality and accessibility of FP services; improvement in the general health of mothers and children; and raising awareness and demand of FP services in the country (Ministry of Health 1989).

## 10. Sexually Transmitted Diseases and HIV/AIDS

### A. Sexually Transmitted Diseases

STDs other than HIV/AIDS are common and have been identified as important factors in HIV transmission. It is estimated that an average of 2,372 cases of STDs were reported per month in 1995 and, in total, there were about 28,463 STD cases in 1995 (Bureau of Statistics & Macro International 1997). More females than males are infected with STDs, 58% and 42%, respectively. These findings however, do not tell the true picture among men, since women are more frequent users of health facilities than men. Among the most common STDs in Tanzania, apart from HIV/AIDS, are discharge from the penis, gonorrhea, penile sores/ulcers, and syphilis (Bureau Statistics & Macro International 1997). According to the Department of Health Services, sexually active persons aged 20 to 39, formerly married, urban residents, those without education, and those with complete primary education are more likely to be infected with an STD than other groups (Bureau Statistics & Macro International 1997). Policies that affect prevention of STDs are similar to those of HIV/AIDS as stated in Section 10B, below.

### B. HIV/AIDS

[*Update 2002*: UNAIDS Epidemiological Assessment: Tanzania is made up of mainland Tanzania and the island of Zanzibar. HIV information among antenatal clinic attendees has been available from mainland Tanzania since the mid-1980s. Mbeya district produced more consistently better quality of data on HIV prevalence among antenatal clinic attendees than any other district. The prevalence in Mbeya shows a fluctuation of HIV-infection rates ranging from 23% to 24% in 1998, to 29.5% in 1999, and 21.6% in 2000. In Moshi district, another district outside the major urban area, HIV prevalence was 20% in 1998 and 16.6% in 2000. No antenatal clinic surveillance survey was conducted in 2001. Implementation of a 2002 antenatal clinic sentinel surveillance survey has begun and results will be available later in 2003.

[Serial population-based surveys conducted in the Kagera region of mainland Tanzania showed a decline in HIV-1 prevalence from 24.2% in 1987 to 18.3% in 1993 in Bukoba town. HIV prevalence among women aged 15-24 years in Bukoba town declined from 27.6% in 1987 to 11.2% in 1993. For rural Bukoba, there was a decline in HIV prevalence from 10% in 1987 to 6.8% in 1996. A marked decline in HIV prevalence was also recorded among young women aged 15-24 years, from 9.7% in 1987 to 3.1% in 1996.

[In Zanzibar, fluctuating HIV-prevalence rates have been observed among antenatal clinic attendees, with rates lower than those observed in mainland Tanzania. HIV prevalence increased from 0.3% in 1987 to 3.8% in 1995, and then to 0.6% in 1996, 11.4% in 1997, and 0.7% in both 1999 and 2000. A population-based HIV serosurvey was to be conducted in 2002 to validate the magnitude of HIV infection in Zanzibar.

[Information on HIV prevalence among sex workers in Dar es Salaam has been available since the mid-1980s. HIV prevalence among sex workers tested increased from 29% in 1986 to 50% in 1993. Outside of Dar es Salaam, HIV information on sex workers is available from Kilimanjaro, Arusha, Moshi, Tanga, Dodoma, and Singida in 1988. In Zanzibar, HIV prevalence among STD clinic patients tested increased from 5% in 1992 to 28% in 1993.

[The estimated number of adults and children living with HIV/AIDS on January 1, 2002, were:

| | | |
|---|---|---|
| Adults ages 15-49: | 1,300,000 | (rate: 7.8%) |
| Women ages 15-49: | 750,000 | |
| Children ages 0-15: | 170,000 | |

[An estimated 140,000 adults and children died of AIDS during 2001.

[At the end of 2001, an estimated 810,000 Tanzanian children under age 15 were living without one or both parents who had died of AIDS. (*End of update by the Editors*)]

## 11. Sexual Dysfunctions, Counseling, and Therapies

[*Comment 2003*: The most obvious sexual disorder is sterility. A barren woman is always in despair. The desire for children makes impotence in men even more disgraceful and pitiful. A childless couple is scorned and despised. The source of childlessness is usually attributed to the wife rather than the husband. Although family planning centers and general hospitals may provide some advice and counseling, professional therapy is almost nonexistent. (*End of comment by B. Opiyo-Omolo*)]

## 12. Sex Research and Advanced Professional Education

Not reported.

## A Brief Conclusion

Although this is, as explained in the Editor's opening Note, a partial report with no information on some important aspects of sexual attitudes and behavior in Tanzania, the authors and Editor hope that enough information is provided for the reader to form a clear picture of sexuality in Tanzania.

## References and Suggested Readings

Bureau of Statistics and Macro International.1997. *Tanzania demographic and health survey 1996*. Calverton, MD, USA: Bureau of Statistics and Macro International, Inc.

Bureau of Statistics.1989. *1988 population census: Preliminary report*. Dar es Salaam: Ministry of Finance, Economic Affairs and Planning.

CIA. 2002 (January). *The world factbook 2002*. Washington, DC: Central Intelligence Agency. Available: http://www.cia.gov/cia/publications/factbook/index.html

Haram, L. 1999. *Women out of sight, modern women in gendered worlds: The case of the Meru of Northern Tanzania* [Thesis submitted in partial fulfillment of requirements for the degree of Doctorem Rerum Politicarum]. University of Bergen.

Justeen, A., S. H. Kapiga, & H. A. G. A. van Asten. 1992. Abortions in a hospital setting: Hidden realities in Dar-es-Salaam, Tanzania. *Studies in Family Planning*, 23(5):325-329.

Legal and Human Rights Centre.1997. *Human rights report 1, Extent of child abuse: A newspapers survey. January 1996-June 1997*. Dar es Salaam: Author.

Liljeström, R., P. Masanja, C. P. B. Mkai, & Z. Tumbo-Masabo. 1994. The pubescent girl–Past and present. In: Z. Tumbo-Masabo & R. Liljeström, eds., *Chelewa, Chelewa: The dilemma of teenage girls*. The Scandinavian Institute of African Studies.

Mbunda, D. 1991. *Traditional sex education in Tanzania: A study of 12 ethnic groups*. New York: The Margaret Sanger Center.

Ministry of Health and Social Welfare. 1989. *The National Family Planning Programme: Plan of operations, 1989-1993*. Dar es Salaam: Author.

Mpangile, G. S, T. Leshabari, & D. J. Kihwele. 1993 (November). Factors associated with induced abortion in public hospitals in Dar-es-Salaam, Tanzania. *Reproductive Health Matters*, 2:21-31.

Mwageni, E. A. 1996. *Determinants of contraceptive behaviour among men in Tanzania* [Thesis for the degree of Doctor of Philosophy in Applied Population Research]. University of Exeter.

Mwageni, E. A .1998. *Final evaluation report of the Mbeya Teenage Mother's Centre*. Family Planning Association of Tanzania, UMATI, and ICCO.

National Bureau of Statistics, Tanzania, and Macro International, Inc. 2000. *Tanzania reproductive and child health survey 1999*. Calverton, MD: National Bureau of Statistics and Macro International Inc.

Ngallaba, S. A., S. H. Kapiga, I. Ruyobya, & J. T. Boerma. 1993. *Tanzania demographic and health survey 1991/1992*. Bureau of Statistics, Planning Commission, Dar es Salaam and Institute for Resource Development, Maryland.

Ntukula, M. 1994. The initiation rite. In: Z. Tumbo-Masabo & R. Liljeström, eds., *Chelewa, Chelewa: The dilemma of teenage girls*. The Scandinavian Institute of African Studies.

Population Planning Unit, Bureau of Statistics, and National Family Planning Programme. 1995. *Population and development in Tanzania*, Dar es Salaam: Authors.

Population Reference Bureau. 2000. *World population data sheet*. Washington: Author.

Rajani, R., & M. Kudrati. 1995. The varieties of sexual experience of the street children of Mwanza, Tanzania. In: S. Zeidenstein & K. Moore, eds., *Learning about sexuality: A practical beginning*. New York: The Population Council, International Women's Health Coalition.

Rugumyamheto, A., V. Kainamula, & J. Mziray. 1994. In: Z. Tumbo-Masabo & R. Liljeström, eds., *Chelewa, Chelewa: The dilemma of teenage girls*. The Scandinavian Institute of African Studies.

Setel, P. W. 1999. *A plague of paradoxes: AIDS, culture, and demography in Northern Tanzania*. Chicago and London: The University of Chicago Press.

Schoofs, M. 2000. AIDS: The agony of Africa. *The Village Voice* [New York]. A Pulitzer Prize-winning 8-part series. Available: www.villagevoice.com/specials/africa/.

Stambach, A. 1996. *Kutoa Mimba: Debates about schoolgirl abortion in Northern Tanzania*. A paper presented at IUSSP conference in Trivandrum, India.

Stillwaggon, E. 2001 (May 21). AIDS and poverty in Africa. *The Nation*, 2-25.

Tanzania. 2003 (March-May). Personal communications between Yusuf Hemed and R. T. Francoeur.

Tanzania Gender Networking Programme and SAREC-WIDSAA. 1997. *Beyond inequalities: Women in Tanzania*. Dar es Salaam and Harare: TGNP/SARDC.

The Centre for Reproductive Law and Policy. 1997. *Women of the world: Laws and policies affecting their reproductive lives*. New York: Anglophone Africa.

Tumbo-Masabo, Z. 1994. Too little too late. In: Z. Tumbo-Masabo & R. Liljeström, eds., *Chelewa, Chelewa: The di-lemma of teenage girls*. The Scandinavian Institute of African Studies.

UNAIDS. 2002. *Epidemiological fact sheets by country*. Geneva, Switzerland: Joint United Nations Programme on HIV/AIDS (UNAIDS/WHO). Available: http://www.unaids.org/hivaidsinfo/statistics/fact_sheets/index_en.htm.

Weinstein, K. I., S. Ngallaba, A. R. Cross, & F. M. Mburu. 1995. *Tanzania knowledge, attitudes and practices survey 1994*. Dar es Salaam, Tanzania: Bureau of Statistics, Planning Commission, and Calverton, MD: Macro International Inc.

White, L. 1990. *The comforts of home: Prostitution in colonial Nairobi*. Chicago: The University of Chicago Press.

# Thailand
## (*Prathet Thai*)

Kittiwut Jod Taywaditep, Ph.D., Eli Coleman, Ph.D.,
and Pacharin Dumronggittigule, M.Sc.
*Updates by K. J. Taywaditep, Ryan Bishop, Ph.D., and
Lillian S. Robinson, Ph.D.*

## Contents

### *Demographics and a Brief Historical Perspective*
ROBERT T. FRANCOEUR

#### A. Demographics

Thailand, formerly known as Siam, is a kingdom located in Southeast Asia. The total area of Thailand is 198,450 square miles (514,000 km$^2$). The capital, Bangkok, situated in the central region, is also the largest city, with a population of 7.8 million. Thailand is bordered on the north and west by Myanmar (formerly Burma), on the north and east across the Mekong River by Laos, on the southeast by Kampuchea (Cambodia), and on the south by Malaysia.

In July 2002, Thailand had an estimated population of 62.3 million. (All data are from *The World Factbook 2002* (CIA 2002) unless otherwise stated.)

**Age Distribution and Sex Ratios**: *0-14 years*: 23.3% with 1.04 male(s) per female (sex ratio); *15-64 years*: 69.9% with 0.97 male(s) per female; *65 years and over*: 6.8% with 0.78 male(s) per female; *Total population sex ratio*: 0.97 male(s) to 1 female

**Life Expectancy at Birth**: *Total Population*: 69.18 years; *male*: 66 years; *female*: 72.51 years

**Urban/Rural Distribution**: 20% to 80%

**Ethnic Distribution**: Thai: 75%; Chinese: 14%; other: 11%

**Religious Distribution**: Buddhism: 95%; Muslin: 3.8%; Christianity: 0.5%; Hinduism: 0.1%; other: 0.6% (1991 est.)

**Birth Rate**: 16.39 births per 1,000 population

**Death Rate**: 7.55 per 1,000 population

**Infant Mortality Rate**: 29.5 deaths per 1,000 live births

**Net Migration Rate**: 0 migrant(s) per 1,000 population

*Communications*: Kittiwut Taywaditep, M.D., 3550 North Lake Shore Dr., Apt 1402, Chicago, IL 60657 USA; U21815@uic.edu. Eli Coleman, Ph.D., Program in Human Sexuality, University of Minnesota Medical School, 1300 South Second Street, Minneapolis, MN 55454 USA; colem001@tc.umn.edu.

(CIA 2002)

**Total Fertility Rate**: 1.86 children born per woman

**Population Growth Rate**: 0.88%

**HIV/AIDS** (1999 est.): *Adult prevalence*: 2.15%; *Persons living with HIV/AIDS*: 755,000; *Deaths*: 66,000. (For additional details from www.UNAIDS.org, see end of Section 10B.)

**Literacy Rate** (*defined as those age 15 and over who can read and write*): 93.8% (*male*: 96%, *female*: 91.6%), with 96% attending six years of compulsory education. The chief language of Thailand is Thai, one of the 40 or so languages in the Tai family found in Thailand, Laos, North Vietnam, and parts of China (Crystal 1987). Among a number of languages previously spoken in this region, the Thai language or Siamese Tai became the language of administration and prestige in the late 12th century, with its script invented in 1283 (Wyatt 1984). Today, the regional dialects are also spoken in Thailand, as well as Lao, Chinese, and Malay. English is taught in schools and colleges and is also used in academia, commerce, and government.

**Per Capita Gross Domestic Product** (*purchasing power parity*): $6,600 (2001 est.); *Inflation*: 1.6%; *Unem-*

*ployment*: 3.9%; *Living below the poverty line*: 12.5% (1998 est.)

## B. A Brief Historical Perspective

Historians have hypothesized that Thai (or "Tai") people began migrating from southern China to the central portion of the Indochinese peninsula in the 6th century. Over the centuries, the Thai identity has emerged from the interaction between these Tai people, later immigrants, and the indigenous inhabitants of this region, namely the Mon and Khmer (Wyatt 1984). Following the Burmese destruction of their previous Ayudhya kingdom in 1767, the Thai people rose from the ruins with an astonishing vigor. The kingdom of Siam was reconstituted within a few years by combining other principalities and kingdoms (e.g., Chiangmai and Khorat), thereby expanding its territories to include a number of distinct civilizations and peoples in the Indochinese region. The new capital, Bangkok, was established on the bank of the Chaophraya River in 1782, with walls and buildings built from thousands of boatloads of bricks taken from the ruins of Ayudhya. In the new city of shining monasteries and a new royal palace, with bustling canals crisscrossing the city instead of roads, the intermingling of classes, cultures, and ethnicities in the early Bangkok Empire has been vividly depicted by David Wyatt:

> [The] princes and officials constructed homes along the network of canals radiating eastward from the palace and Chinese and Indian merchants built their shops and warehouses along the river to the south. . . . [Outside the main walls of the city,] . . . the Chams attached to the army; there are a group of Malays who manned naval vessels, clustered around an Islamic house of worship; north of the city, [there was] a settlement of Roman Catholics descended from Portuguese and Japanese Christians. (1984, 146)

Thailand has been independent during most of its history, except for a few relatively brief periods of occupation by Burma or the Japanese military. This long-term independence has allowed for a very distinct blend of cultures to thrive over many centuries. Thailand is also the only country in Southeast Asia never taken over by a European power, thanks in part to King Chulalongkorn and his son, King Mongkut, who modernized the country and signed trade agreements with both Britain and France in the late 19th century and early 20th century. The kingdom's name was changed from Siam to Thailand in 1939 during a politically tumultuous time. Reflecting the nationalistic attempt to revise the country's ethnic identity, the new name had a linguistic kinship with Thai-speaking peoples in the periphery of the kingdom, therefore downplaying the powers of the central Siamese people and the Chinese, who began to gain economic significance (Wyatt 1984).

The absolute monarchy transferred power to the politicians and the military in a bloodless revolution in 1932, although the monarchy is still held in very high regard in the present Thai society. Thailand considers itself a democratic nation; however, corruption, multiple coups, and the tremendous influence of the military in politics have led journalists to ridicule the nation's democratic system as "half-democracy." After the mid-1992 bloody uprising against the military's longstanding influence in the House of Representatives, the role of the military in politics has been under scrutiny more than ever.

## C. Thai Language, Sex Research, and Resources

*The Thai Language*

In this chapter, romanization of Thai words is adapted from the Thai Royal Academy's system, with the goal of ap-

proximating the original pronunciation (without the intonation) while maintaining the readability of the text for readers unfamiliar with the transliteration system. In general, the spelling of Sanskrit-, Pali-, or English-derived vocabulary prefers the reflection of its Thai pronunciation over the etymological origin. Aspirated consonants *p*, *t*, and *k* are represented by *ph*, *th*, and *kh*. For example, *phii* is pronounced "pee," not "fee," and the *th*, as in *kathoey*, is pronounced as the *t* in the words "to" or "ten," not as the *th* in "than" or "think." Proper nouns are represented in romanization with an initial capital letter. Romanization of personal names follows the individual's preference or the spelling in English-language print, and ranks or degrees are, with few exceptions, omitted. In order to facilitate literature searches on an international level, papers and quotations by Thai authors are referred to by their last names, not first names as is common in Thailand.

*Gender/Sexuality Studies*

Systematic studies of gender and sexuality in Thailand are relatively new. Mostly spurred by the HIV epidemic, the majority of data on sexual behavior was collected in the early 1990s in response to the public health demands. Although considerable data have been generated, critics have pointed out that synthesis on a conceptual level is still needed. Also missing is the documentation of the ancient sexuality in this region, which would have provided a historiographic insight into the dynamics of the Thai sexuality over time. Exchange of findings and discourse among researchers are also hindered to a certain degree by the less-established avenues for publication and presentation. Many papers appear only in local academic bulletins or conferences, whereas others are published in international journals.

*Resources*

In writing this chapter, we relied primarily on two sources: the published papers and presentations, which provided most of the reviewed empirical data, and the analysis and interpretation of the cultural phenomena in Thailand. Although our analysis of some Thai social constructions and themes (e.g., gender roles and sexual norms) may not represent a consensus, we nevertheless try to present the converged opinions among researchers and observers whom we have worked with over the years. Finally, it is important to bear in mind that what is known about gender and sexuality in Thailand is changing rapidly, and this review summarizes formal and informal observations in Thai society up until early 1997. [*Update 2003*: In *Woman, Man, Bangkok: Love, Sex, and Popular Culture in Thailand*, Scot Barmé (2002) has created a vibrant cultural history of early modern Thailand, with focuses on conflicts and controversies, such as the status of women, gender relations, polygamy, class antagonisms, and the emergence of a commercial mass culture. (*End of update by R. T. Francoeur*)]

## 1. Basic Sexological Premises

### A. The Ideal Gender Images: *Kulasatrii* and *Chaai Chaatrii*

*The Ideal Thai Woman*

There is not much question that Thailand is a male-dominated, patriarchal society, as political and corporate leadership has always been in the hands of men. On the other hand, the power of Thai women, especially in rural societies, lies in their domestic role as the mother-nurturer (see Keyes 1985; and the discussion in Section 2A, Religious and Ethnic Factors Affecting Sexuality, Religious Factors). Women in Thailand look up to the role of motherhood as an ideal. A woman's status changes to adulthood at the point of her childbirth, after which she is recognized semiformally as *mae* or "mother" (Keyes 1984; Pyne 1994). In fact, the preparation for this "mother" title takes place informally much earlier, as young girls or unmarried women are often titled *mae* with an endearing or humorous tone. Thai men refer to the female gender with a sense of reverence as "the gender of mothers" (*phayt mae*), acknowledging women's burden in childbearing and parenting responsibilities. The ultimate insult for Thai men is *yet mae*, which literally translates to "motherfucker" in English, indicating the utmost respect that mothers have in Thai culture.

Regarding the nurturer role, women's specialization in economic-type occupations illustrates their powerful role in providing for the well-being of their families. Women's dedication to nurturance is evident in the expression that a good woman "wakes up earlier and goes to sleep later than her husband." The variety and extent of women's nurturing responsibilities are superbly illustrated in two studies in two vastly different contexts: Penny Van Esterik (1982) depicts the household and religious responsibilities of well-to-do women in western central Thailand; Susanne Thorbek (1988) details the endless household duties of the slum-dwelling women in Khlong Toey, Bangkok. Since the economic climate changed in the 1960s and 1970s, women have accounted for almost half, and sometimes more than half, of the large number of rural Thais who migrate to the cities in order to augment the family income (Keyes 1984). Today, women account for 80% of the total employment in the ten largest export industries and 45% of the manufacturing workforce (data cited in Pyne 1994). Over the years, Thai women have made significant contributions in the arts, education, and commerce. With higher education, women have also risen to leadership positions in the middle class. The "glass ceiling" exists for women in the academic and corporate settings, as evident in the fact that, although there are many women in high positions, the topmost position of an organization still belongs to a man. Nevertheless, aside from the obvious underrepresentation in areas such as the military, law enforcement, and religion, the status of women in Thailand is perhaps higher than other countries in Asia with the exception of Singapore. For more-extensive discussions on the gender division of labor, as well as the impact of the rapid socioeconomic changes in recent decades, the reader is referred to the work by Kirsch (1982) and Hnin Hnin Pyne (1994).

The mother-nurturer role is also idealized in the female code of social and sexual conduct. Historically, the Thai tradition has defined a *kulasatrii* ("virtuous woman") as proficient and sophisticated in household duties; graceful, pleasant, yet unassuming in her appearance and social manners; and conservative in her sexuality. These features bear striking similarities to the traditional "feminine mystique" in other cultures, which has come under the criticism of the Western feminist movement. However, the concept of *kulasatrii* has not been overtly discussed in terms of gender inequality or subordination in Thailand. There has been little dialogue devoted to whether the *kulasatrii* role has been restrictive or unjust to Thai women. On the contrary, most contemporary Thai women wholeheartedly endorse the *kulasatrii* notion without resentment, regarding it as a sign of dignity and honor, a sense of cultural identity in which they can take pride. In school, girls are taught what it means to be a *kulasatrii*, while celebrity figures constantly praise its value in the media. As more and more contemporary women work outside of their homes, the ideal image of a *kulasatrii* remains a goal for which a woman must strive, while simultaneously attempting to fulfill new responsibilities necessitated by the changing society.

### The Ideal Thai Man

There are two ideal male images available for Thai men. Corresponding to the Buddha's biography, Thai men face the recluse/householder or monastic/secular dichotomy (P. Van Esterik 1982). The monastic-recluse image, personified by the Buddha's life, is the *Sangha*. Through monastic discipline and practice of the *dharma*, monks not only eschew worldly attachments, but also their sexuality and male gender characteristics. On the other hand, the secular male image is represented by the notion of *chaai chaatrii*, which is an embodiment of the typical masculine features also found in other cultures: authority, courage, self-assurance, physical and emotional strengths, and sexual prowess. Various expressions for manhood and manliness reflect an image of a vigorous and muscular warrior: *chaai chaat tha-haan* (referring to the soldier), *chaai ok saam sok* (the muscular chest), *chaai chaat acha-nai* (the stallion's stamina and perhaps muscularity), and *chaai cha-kan* (strength and vigor). In older men, these youth-typical physical features are de-emphasized as other characteristics become more salient, such as bravery, wisdom, and power (in either political, social, or metaphysical spheres). Nurturance is another ideal dimension in men, as exemplified in the image of a prestigious older man, *pho liang*, who earns respect from his community from his resourcefulness and generous contributions. Traditionally, powerful men and politicians in Thai society have always been expected to exhibit this nurturing trait, perhaps modeled after the paternalism of the Siamese kings since the beginning of the kingdom (Kirsch 1985).

The masculine attributes in the *chaai chaatrii* image have found behavioral expression in the image of a *nug layng*. Translated to a midway between "playboy" and "gangster" in English, the term portrays a powerful man of action who works hard and plays equally hard, is supportive of his friends, fierce to his foes, and also a great womanizer (Thorbek 1988). Although popularized and personified by the Prime Minister, Sarit Thanarat, in the late 1950s and early 1960s, the image was hardly a new social construction of the male image. Like Sarit's political ideology, which "exaggerated traditional values and institutions, buttressing social and political hierarchy at the expense of egalitarianism and even human rights" (Wyatt 1984, 285), his *nug layng* image was simply a paragon of the traditional Thai male role. Sarit excelled in this role in both politics and private life. While known for his emphasis on cleanliness and orderliness and his harsh measures against crimes, Sarit was also notorious for the number of mistresses he kept, which was somewhere between 50 and 200 (Thorbek 1984). Certainly Sarit was not alone in this interpretation of manliness. Over the years, the secular image of Thai men had drifted even further away into the realm of worldly activities and became the antithesis of the *Sangha*. Manliness has become associated with almost every behavior considered by the Thai culture as vices: smoking, drinking, gambling, womanizing, commercial sex, minor wives, public brawls, petty crimes, and corruption, and the list goes on.

Despite such undesirable associations, the code of masculinity has maintained its prestige in Thai society for a long time. Its prestige has only recently been challenged after one of the male vices—commercial sex—was implicated for the spread of HIV. In part, the Theravada view that ordination is always an option for men (see Section 2, Religious and Ethnic Factors Affecting Sexuality, below) could probably account for the longstanding tolerance toward male vices. Further, the ultimate financial control in the households has usually been in the men's hands, therefore, allowing them to foot the expenses from these vices. Another mechanism also helps prevent any violation of the male role prescriptions: Secular men who do not participate in these male vices are often labeled by other men with a number of emasculating terms, such as "not a genuine man," a *kathoey* (see Section 7, Gender Diversity and Transgender Issues), or *naa tua mia* ("the female face"). The male image's drift away from the religious ideal is best illustrated in the use of the term *tid*. Abbreviated from the Pali term *pandit* and once granted to a layman who had passed through the monkhood and held knowledge of the Buddhist teachings, *tid* has become a term of derision for "a clumsy [man] who is a tyro in the ways of worldly life" (Sathian Kosed, in Rajadhon 1961, 69).

Despite the rigidity of Thai gender-role manifestations, it is interesting to note that Thai people perceive transience in gender identity. In Buddhist philosophy, the notion of individual "personality" is false, because a being differs upon each incarnation (Kirsch 1982). Gender differs in every life, with social position, fortune or misfortune, mental and physical dispositions, life events, and even the species (human, animal, ghost, or deity) and location of rebirth (strata of heavens or hells), all of which depend on the being's fund of merit accumulated through committing good deeds in past lives. In the Thai interpretation, women are commonly seen as lower on the hierarchy of merit because they cannot be ordained. Khin Thitsa (1980, cited in Thorbek 1988, 84) observed that according to the Theravada view, "a being is born as a woman because of bad *karma* or lack of sufficient good merit."

In Susanne Thorbek's study (1988, 97), a woman illustrates her frustration with being a woman: In a minor domestic crisis, she shouts, "Oh, it's my evil fate to have been born a woman!" Somewhat more reservedly, a pious young woman in Penny Van Esterik's study (1982), also admitted her desire to be reborn as a male in order to become a monk. Yet, another more "worldly" woman, seemingly satisfied with her female gender and hoping to be reborn as a deity of the sensuous heavens, argued that those who desired a specific gender upon rebirth would be born of indeterminate sex. Even within a lifespan, men's transitions between the *Sangha* and the laity demonstrates the transient nature of gender as the two masculine gender roles are abruptly switched. As serious as they are in observing the gender codes, Thai men and women accept gender identities as important yet temporary. Even those in frustration learn to think life will be "better off the next time around," especially as long as they do not question the inequity of their sometimes arduous, yet transient, states.

[*Comment 2003*: Some observers claim that Thai gender roles are astoundingly malleable and that Thai men and women are able to effortlessly slide up and down the sex/gender continuum (e.g., Morris 1994, 2000). That observation strikes me as false. In my experience, growing to manhood in Thailand and living more recently in Chicago, I would maintain that Thai men and women are no more rigid, nor less rigid, in their gender roles and identities than their Western counterparts. Morris may have misread Thai men's soft and unassuming social demeanor as feminine, whereas in the Thai gender code, gentleness is not viewed as conflicting with ideal masculinity. Morris may also have observed contemporary Thai women being independent and masculine-appearing, but the same observations can be made by foreigners about American women wearing pants and short hair. Critics have objected to the methodology used to arrive at the conclusion about Thai gender fluidity (such as Morris' observation), suggesting that the observers relied heavily on anecdotal reports by secondary sources.

[I wonder if the propagation of the idea that Thais' gender roles are so different and "exotic" might have been fueled somewhat by the orientalist fantasy. My own observations as a native of Thailand do not concur at all with Morris' conclusions. I would add, however, that the Thai people's conceptualization of gender and other attributes of the self are not fixed from one lifetime to another, in accordance with the idea of reincarnation. However, there is little convincing evidence that within one person's lifetime, Thai people are fluid and malleable in regards to their gender roles (Jackson 1997; Morris 1994, 2000; Nanda 2000). (*End of comment by K. J. Taywaditep*)]

[*Comment 2003*: In the late 19th century, the women of Siam were already challenging the traditional patriarchal value system and setting the stage of today's seeming sudden revolution in gender roles and attitudes. *Narirom*, a fortnightly magazine, first appeared in 1888, while *Maekasin Watthana*, produced by the Watthana School for Girls, appeared in 1892. The following quote from an October 14, 1914, article in *Satri Niphon* [*Women's Writing*], one of Siam's earliest women's magazines, is indicative of the rich history of feminist and gender debates at the roots of contemporary Thai cultural history:

> [In] the past, Siamese women were like dolls kept in a cupboard . . . cut off from the outside world. They were strictly controlled and not allowed to go anywhere. . . . Nowadays the position of women is greatly improved however, they are coping out of the dark (Quoted by Barmé 2002, 17).

(For details on protofeminist discourses in early-20th-century Siam, see: Barmé 2002, 17-42). (*End of comment by R. T. Francoeur*)]

## B. Romance, Love, and Marriage

Most cultures glorify and idolize romance between men and women, and Thai people are no exception. Themes of quests for eternal love and the consequences of passion—ecstasy, aspirations, heartbreaks, jealously, elopements, and deaths—abound in the Thai folklore, literature, and music. Borrowed from the *karma* concept, people explain an unexpected, overwhelming infatuation in metaphysical terms: They were meant for each other because of destiny (*bu-phay vassana*) or they had made merit together in previous lives.

In the Thai vocabulary, there are specific words for "love," "lust," "infatuation," "love at first sight," "sexual desire," and so on. In particular, the words *khuaam ruk* (love) and *khuaam khrai* (lust) are distinct, although they are sometimes used together as *ruk-khrai* to connote affectionate relationships. As will be evident later in the chapter, premarital sex outside the commercial-sex context is forbidden, and the distinction between love and lust are inculcated in young people to deter them from premarital sex within a romantic relationship. In such warnings, love is usually idealized as pure, noble, and epitomized by patience, responsibility, and maturity, whereas lust embodies the qualities opposite to these virtues. The Third Buddhist Precept—to refrain from sexual misconduct, mostly understood to refer to adultery, rape, sexual abuse of children, and careless sexual activities that result in the sorrow of others—is often used as a reference for the danger and demerit of lust. It is noteworthy that in the Buddhist philosophy, both love and lust are worldly attachments, leading to suffering. Lust, however, is deemed more harmful because it violates the Third Precept. In the Thai society, where people make distinctions between "ideal Buddhism" (i.e., as in the supreme Buddhist philosophy) and "practical Buddhism" (i.e., for the laity, guided by the Five Precepts), it is easy to see why love is socially accepted and lust is not.

Because of the social acceptance of love, various expressions of romance are found in everyday life and art forms.

The English-derived term "romantic" has been widely used in Thai to connote an intimate and private ambience for a couple, often without a sexual undertone, such as "romantic" restaurant, music, or sentiment. Women, prohibited from sexual expression unless married (see below), account for a majority of the consumers of popular literature and television drama in which young women's love lives are portrayed. These contemporary romantic tales are enormously popular, as is evident in their multiple republications and repeated television and film adaptations. Embedded in these love tales are the cultural scripts on love, romance, and marriage; these scripts reflect the corresponding constructions in the Thai culture at large, as well as provide models for the newer generations of audiences. A certain Western ethos is abundant in these novels, many of which are adaptations from the classics by Jane Austen, and Charlotte and Emily Bronte, for example. However, the ethos, particularly the Victorian values for women and the chivalrous demeanor for men, seems congruent with the Thai conceptualizations of gender and heterosexual relationships, and therefore is not seen by contemporary Thais as foreign. Emphasis on women's virtues, such as the *kulasatrii* code, chastity, patience, and honesty, can be found across a variety of backgrounds and scenarios. The barriers the heroines face symbolize the obstructions Thai women encounter in fulfilling their love, for example, jealous and manipulative women in villain roles (the "bad girl" stereotype, see Section 5A, Interpersonal Heterosexual Behaviors, Adolescent Sexual Behavior), parental objections, and men's exploitation and sexual discrimination. Cultural and class differences are also significant challenges, ranging from the relationship between a northern woman and a military officer from Bangkok in *Sao Khruea Faa* (which resembles *Madam Butterfly*), to the interracial love between a Thai woman and a Japanese soldier during World War II in *Khuu Kam*, to the intergenerational love between a young woman and a rich and handsome "playboy" many years older in *Salakjit*.

In urban areas, shopping malls, coffee shops, school activities, and, to a lesser extent, nightclubs and discotheques provide places for young people to meet. In rural Thailand, Buddhist temples (*wat*) are instrumental in bringing men and women together during the services, temple fairs, and fundraising ceremonies, where the atmosphere of *sanuk* (fun and enjoyment) predominates (Thorbek 1988). Young women often appear at the *wat* in their best outfits and hairstyles, and the idiomatic expression that a young woman is attractive enough "to go to the *wat*" highlights the social function of temples in rural Thailand (Sathian Kosed, in Rajadhon 1961). Young women also take a keen interest in the young monks who, at the end of the Lenten retreat, will leave the monkhood to become "ripe" laymen, ready for marriage and settling down (P. Van Esterik 1982). Flirtation between men and women is allowed, and although women are somewhat restricted by the *kulasatrii* notion, in numerous age-old courting songs, women are quite bold in making allusions to sex or outright marriage propositions (Keyes 1984). However, women's candor about romance and sex is still minimal compared to that of men, and it is even more disapproved for middle- and upper-class women. Kirsch (1984) has speculated that young women in the villages may appear to be deeply concerned with love, marriage, and family because they are striving to fulfill the traditional images of women as "mother-nurturer" in rural environments in which alternative options are severely limited.

In contrast with the passionate nature of courting, the ethos of marriage and parenting emphasizes more the practical and grounded values, such as mutual support, trust, and emotional commitment. In the contemporary Thai image of

an ideal marriage, the husband and wife live together in a harmonious, mutually respectful relationship, with the expectation on provision and security weighted towards the man, and the domestic responsibilities towards the woman. A traditional Thai expression compares a married couple to an elephant, with the husband as the two front legs and the wife as the hind ones. In an ideal couple, decision making is the man's responsibility and the woman's role is to be supportive and cooperative. A traditional *kulasatrii* shows deference to her husband, as he is the master of the household. In a hierarchical society such as Thailand, where people diligently make obeisance to persons of a higher status, this meant that some women in ancient times showed their husbands an extreme courtesy, which today would be reserved for the elders, teachers, or monks.

In the past few decades, lower- and middle-class women have increasingly worked outside of the homes while continuing to be in charge of the household chores and childcare. Men, however, have not been expected much to adopt the household responsibilities; it is still quite uncommon to expect married men to take on the same extent of responsibilities as their wives in cooking, cleaning, and parenting. In middle-class families, the women's double responsibility is usually helped by live-in parent(s) or, if they can afford it, maids. In families with lesser means and no live-in parents, the burden on the women can be significant and often becomes a commonly cited cause of sexual disinterest and marital discord (Dumronggittigule, Sombathmai, Taywaditep, & Mandel 1995).

In fact, the divorce rate in Thailand has been growing steadily, paralleling an increase in economic autonomy for women. Divorce and remarrying are not uncommon, although there is a small but palpable degree of stigma, especially among the urban middle-class Thais. We will present further discussions about the tradition of marriage, family settlement, and the dynamics within a married couple in Section 5B, Interpersonal Heterosexual Behaviors, below.

## C. A Double Standard for Sexuality and Gender Stereotypes

One of the most consistent findings from sex research in Thailand is that minor wives and commercial sex are common sexual outlets for men of all ages, social standings, and marital statuses. This tolerance of married men's extramarital sex is merely a part of the larger double standard regarding sexual practices, which mandates different rules for men and for women. As confirmed by studies on childrearing practices, Thai parents train girls more strictly than boys in the behaviors that are part of the gender roles (Archavanitkul & Havanon 1990). Girls are taught that a good woman remains a virgin until marriage and continues to be emotionally and sexually faithful to her husband afterwards. As adolescents, Thai fathers are known for being particularly protective and possessive of their daughters, exercising great control over their friendships with other teenage boys (Thorbek 1988). For boys, however, sexual abandon is accepted or even encouraged. As Sukanya Hantrakul (1983, quoted in Kaime-Atterhog, Ard-Am, & Sethaput 1994) notes: "Culturally, Thai society flatters men for their promiscuity. . . . Women's magazines always advise women to tolerate the situation and accommodate themselves to it."

This double standard in sexual practices may have culminated in an undercurrent of tension between the genders, which, although not readily observable, has been felt and noted by many (e.g., Jackson 1989). Some mistrust and suspicion between the genders can be seen in the negative stereotypes men hold for women, and vice versa. For example, women are stereotyped as emotionally volatile and needy, and they are often manipulative; a Thai proverb notes that the typical Thai woman, while maintaining the *kulasatrii* appearance, possesses "one hundred wagons full of stratagems." Conversely, many women believe that men are often unreliable, unable to have an emotional commitment, inefficient in household management and parenting, and constantly driven by their sexual urges. Many women believe that while men get emotional support and recreation from their male peers, relationships with women exist mostly to fulfill the men's sexual desires, as well as the societal expectations on the men to have a family. However, the men's sexual desires are often perceived as insatiable, with an immature, uncontrollable character like a child's craving—yet "naturally" and "instinctually" driven in a way that can hardly be limited to their spouses. As men continue to search for sexual gratification from commercial sex and minor wives, women unwillingly come to terms with the men's extramarital escapades.

The myth that men's sexual desires are boundless and immutable is quite pervasive (see more discussion in Section 8A, Significant Unconventional Sexual Behaviors, Coercive Sex). It is common to hear Thai women voice their concern about being raped. When activists demanded that commercial sex be eradicated, respectable men and women have publicly expressed the concern that "good women" would be endangered. Similarly, before HIV became a widespread concern in the Thai society, married women sometimes encouraged their husbands to visit sex workers, in part so they could be relieved of the obligation to serve their husband's sexual demands, and possibly to prevent the husband's worse crime of having a stable, emotionally committed relationship with a minor wife. These examples may reflect Thai women's helplessness regarding the men's presumably uncontrollable sexual drive, and consequently, their strategies to protect themselves and preserve their marriages. More recent surveys (see Section 5B, Interpersonal Heterosexual Behaviors, Adult Sexual Behavior) have found that married women in the HIV epidemic face an even more difficult dilemma as they realize that they are at risk for HIV infection from their husbands' use of commercial sex. Encouraging the husband to have a minor wife as an alternative is still a painful decision for a woman to make.

### D. Gender in Everyday Life: Social Manners, the Touch Taboo, Female Pollution, and Gender Segregation

In general, Thai people are noted for their tender, friendly, and graceful ways of social and public behavior. Despite the clear masculine code of conduct, Thai men display less of the overt "masculine" behavior than men in many other cultures. Since the 1940s, urban middle- and upper-class men have adopted the Western chivalrous and "gentlemanly" social manners of "honoring" women, such as opening doors for women, and the "ladies first" etiquette. In addition, nurturance, as stated above, is a quality expected in Thai men, even among those in the position of power (see Kirsch 1985). Therefore, Thai men are often known for their polite, sweet, and caring gestures, as well as their respect for others. Women are expected to be all of these and more: the code of *kulasatrii* contains numerous guidance and taboos for the "proper woman." Thus, the Thai gender-coded rules of conduct seem to place more demands on women than on men, as reflected in an oft-quoted phrase from a poem that "It is hard to be born a woman." The famous male poet who immortalized this phrase, Soonthon Phuu, in fact wrote "but being a man is actually many times more difficult" as a retort to this phrase, but somehow the complete quote never became as popular.

Although urban Thais have adopted Western clothing styles since the early 1940s, formal social situations, such as the workplace, school, and university, still demand that trousers are strictly for men, and skirts or dresses are for women. Because motorcycles are one of the most popular means of transportation in urban Thailand, women who work in offices and female students struggle every day in their dresses while commuting to and from work. As a passenger, women must sit facing the side of the motorcycle to avoid an unseemly sitting position, compromising their balance and safety in so doing. Perhaps it is small, everyday things like this that best illustrates how the life of a *kulasatrii* is not any easier today than it was in Soonthon Phuu's time 200 years ago.

In ancient Thailand, acquiring an expertise in certain exclusive areas, such as occultism or martial arts, was seen metaphorically as endowing the apprentice with the mentor spirits, known as *mii khruu* or "under mentorship." Among the numerous rules of conduct for the learned men, some suggest a belief that men are superior to women, and others indicate some anxiety and animosity surrounding sex and the female anatomy. For example, some learned men must refrain from having sex with a woman. Many men were also prohibited from socializing with women (occasionally including the sister or mother) or their mentor spirits might be weakened by the "weaker sex." Certain parts of the female body, such as genitalia, buttocks, or menstrual blood, and anything that contacts these body parts, such as sarongs, were considered sacrilegious and harmful to the learned men. Folklore anecdotes portray a vicious sabotage done by a piece of fabric from a woman's sarong, and a learned man who lost his powers because he had unwittingly walked underneath an elevated house where a woman was physically above him.

Over the years, despite the decline of occultism and superstition, these folk beliefs remain even in those who are not learned men themselves. Tied into the still-popular fatalism (*duang*), many men today believe their destiny can be jeopardized (*choak suay* or "bad luck") by circumstances such as walking under a row of laundry containing women's skirts or underwear, or engaging in cunnilingus. Men are also told not to have sex with a menstruating woman or they might become seriously ill (Fuller, Edwards, Sermsri, & Vorakitphokatorn 1993). Even men who are not superstitious keep away from these situations to protect the integrity of their "manhood" or to avoid social disgrace. Even women themselves observe the behavioral restrictions which flow from this idea of symbolic female pollution. A woman who wears a Buddhist amulet is advised to step out of her sarong instead of pulling it over her head, and sarongs are often separated from men's wear or upper garments in laundry (Manderson 1992).

Examples of gender segregation abound in Thai society. One of the 227 monastic rules of the monks dictates that in addition to being celibate, monks are not to have any physical contact with women. Women, including the monks' family members, are precluded from certain activities in religious ceremonies to prevent any possibility of ritual purity violation, even accidental contact such as a slight brush of hands. Interestingly, this practice can also be seen in the way modern, urbane gentlemen act toward women: A proper gentleman does not touch a woman in casual circumstances. If he transgresses this social etiquette, an apology is in order. To Thai people, this decorum is impelled by two remarkably different, yet compatible cultural imperatives: firstly, the chivalrous, gentlemanly manners of "honoring" women adopted from the West, and secondly, the animistic belief which prohibits men from touching an unmarried woman to prevent an offense to her guardian spirits (*phii puu yaa*). However, one can also discern the prevailing myth of men's boundless sexual desires behind this touch taboo. A man's touching of a woman is assumed to have a sexual intention unless otherwise explained. Gender segregation can also be seen on a more formal, institutionalized level. Thai people are socialized to mingle mostly with members of the same gender from a young age. Single-sex schools are very common. In colleges, all dormitories are men- or women-only, with strict rules prohibiting visitations from the other gender, even the students' family members.

Given the foregoing discussion about the touch taboo and gender segregation, it should come as no surprise that open physical expression of affection between men and women is deemed socially inappropriate in the Thai society. Until very recently, a (presumably unmarried) young couple would be frowned upon if they walked hand-in-hand affectionately in public. Conservatives openly condemn the influence of Western culture and the media on younger Thais' public behavior toward the other gender. In contrast, public expressions of affection among members of the same gender are quite common. As pointed out by Jackson (1989), Westerners often misinterpret such displays of same-gender affection as an expression of homoeroticism, or misconstrue it as a lack of homophobia among the Thai people. In fact, this same-gender physical intimacy is not viewed in any sexual way by Thai men or women. It is something similar to the sports camaraderie among Western men or casual affection among Western women, and not associated with either homosexuality or an absence of homophobia. Contrary to the Westerners' misperceptions, anti-homosexual attitudes exist in Thai society as they do elsewhere in the world (see Section 6, Homoerotic, Homosexual, and Bisexual Behaviors).

In summary, we have outlined a number of key belief systems that underlie the gender construction in Thai society: the Theravada gender roles, folk myths and animistic beliefs, and traditional class-relevant ideals, among others. Although diversified in origins, these belief systems share common elements which enable their assembly into a coherent cultural structure. To illustrate, men in general are allowed greater latitude in their sexual and moral conduct, perhaps because religious salvation awaits them as a viable option; the myth of masculinity which associates maleness with vices and sexual freedom, therefore, finds a corresponding solution in the Theravada role for men. Similarly, a consistent dictum about women can be found across these diverse belief systems. A woman's virtue is based on the degree to which she excels in promoting the well-being of religion and family, and it also depends upon her sexual conduct with men. A woman's moral status, therefore, is always relational and conditional. She is either higher or lower than men because of what she does (and does not do) with men. This idea is consistent with the Theravada role for women, the *kulasatrii* code of the female ideal, and a number of practices couched as ways to protect women from men's exploits.

It is noteworthy that the cultural construction determines whether or not a new practice or idea from another cultural origin will "fit" into the prevailing coherent structure. The relatively Western chivalrous manners, for example, have been assimilated into the Thai culture because they correspond to the indigenous notion that women are "noble" yet "weaker," thus needing honoring treatment and protection. The relatively recent rise of commercial sex in Thailand may be an adoption of capitalism, but Thai people have always been familiar in Buddhist tales with prototype women who commoditize sex in dire straits (Keyes 1984). The popularity of female meditation teachers in the 1970s in Bangkok was a unique phenomenon (J. Van Esterik 1982), but the

acceptance seemed to rest upon the perception that these lay teachers, like *mae chii*, would never pursue political or monastic goals. Some Thais did not even see the female meditation teachers as women, because these women did not fit conventional female images. Western feminism has been met with objection as being too radical, unrealistic, or culturally inappropriate, probably because the feminist manifestos do not find much corresponding agenda in the Thai gender construction. While the Thai society is undergoing rapid changes, the fundamental gender construction remains, and it determines which new influences will be selected and which will be discarded. Whatever the result of the transformation may be, the key in predicting the future of gender relations in Thailand lies in unraveling the gender constructions of the past and the present.

## 2. Religious, Ethnic, and Gender Factors Affecting Sexuality

### A. Religious Factors

*Buddhism, the Dominant Religious Factor*

The main and official religion of Thailand is Theravada Buddhism, with more than 90% of the population following this tradition. The profound influences of Buddhism on gender and sexuality in Thailand are intertwined with Hinduist practice, local animistic beliefs, and popular demonology from ancient times. The predominant animistic belief system involves *phii*, or the spirits, either of ancestral origin or those residing in natural objects. The spirits can inflict illnesses and misfortune upon individuals for deviant conduct, or, on the contrary, they can provide protection, healing, and bring about fortune for those who follow ethics and placate the spirits. In addition, about 4% of the population are Muslim, mostly living in the southern part of Thailand. Christianity has become steadily more popular, and over a century of work by the missionaries can be seen in many schools which offer good education to Thai children without seeking to convert them.

The tolerant philosophy of Buddhism and the constitutional guarantees of religious freedom have provided a fertile ground for adoption and admixing new religious beliefs with traditional beliefs. In the Thai eyes, the superstition and metaphysics in animism, demonology, and Hinduist cosmology are not at odds with the Buddhist cosmology depicted in the Buddhist canon and religious folk tales. These strands of belief systems maintain peaceful coexistence, and many Thais follow some of these practices to a certain degree during different parts of their lives.

Although the guidelines to achieve *nirvana* are offered, Buddhism emphasizes to the laity "the middle way" and the importance of avoiding extremism. This pragmatic approach is also seen in the domain of sexuality. Despite the deprecation of sexuality in the ideal Buddhism, celibacy is likely to be pertinent only to the monastic lifestyle, while diverse sexual expression has been tolerated among the lay followers, especially the men for whom sexual, military, and social prowess has always been extolled (Cabezón 1993). The Five Precepts are guidelines for lay Buddhists "for a socially-just life, free of exploitation of oneself and others." Again, pragmatism prevails: All of the Precepts are not rigidly expected in most lay Buddhists in Thailand (as well as in other Buddhist cultures) except for the elderly or extraordinarily pious laypersons (Cabezón 1993).

The Third Buddhist Precept specifically addresses human sexuality: Refrain from sexual misconduct or "wrong doing in sexual matters." Although being open to various interpretations, depending on the different contexts, malfeasance is usually considered by Thai people to mean adultery, rape, sexual abuse of children, and careless sexual activities that result in the sorrow of others (Allyn 1991). Premarital sex, prostitution, masturbation, cross-gendered behavior, and homosexuality, on the other hand, are not explicitly mentioned. Any objection to some of these sexual phenomena is perhaps grounded in other non-Buddhist beliefs, such as classism, animism, or Western medical theories. In subsequent sections, we will present further discussions on the Buddhist attitudes toward homosexuality (Section 6, Homoerotic, Homosexual, and Bisexual Behaviors) and commercial sex (Section 8B, Significant Unconventional Sexual Behaviors, Prostitution).

### Gender Roles in Theravada Buddhism and Their Implications

Many ideal images for men and women are found in religious folk tales, which the monks read or retell during sermons (*thetsana*). These sermons, although rarely translated from the Buddhist canon (*Tripitaka* or *Phra Trai-pidok* in Thai), are taken by most Thais as the authentic teachings of the Buddha (Keyes 1984). Similarly, other ritual traditions, folk operas, and local legends contain gender-relevant images in the depiction of men and women's lives, both sovereign and common, showing their sins and merits through their actions and relationships, all of which purportedly convey Buddhist messages. Thereby, the Theravada worldview, both authentic and interpreted through the Thai eyes, has exerted enormous influences on the gender construction in Thailand.

With a firm belief in *karma* and reincarnation, Thai people are concerned with accumulating merit in everyday life in order to attain an enhanced status in rebirth rather than striving for *nirvana* (Kirsch 1982). Earning merit and an enhanced rebirth status are depicted in the story of Prince Vessantara (or *Phra Vessandon* in Thai pronunciation), who is reborn in his next life as the historic Buddha because of his unconditional generosity expressed by giving away his valuables, including his wealth, children, and wife. In real life, men and women "make merit," and the Theravada culture prescribes different ways for this quest. The ideal "merit making" for men is through ordination in the *Sangha* (order of monks, or in Thai, *Phra Song*). Women, on the other hand, are not allowed to be ordained. Although the order of *Bhikkhuni* (the female equivalent to the *Sangha* monks) was established by the Buddha with some reluctance, the practice disappeared from Sri Lanka and India after several centuries and never existed in Southeast Asia (Keyes 1984; P. Van Esterik 1982). Today, laywomen can intensify their Buddhist practice by becoming *mae chii* (often erroneously translated to "nun"). These are lay female ascetics who shave their heads and wear white robes. Although *mae chii* abstain from worldly pleasures and sexuality, the laity consider giving alms to *mae chii* a lesser merit-making activity than alms given to the monks. Hence, these women usually depend on themselves and/or on their relatives for the necessities of life. Obviously, *mae chii* are not as highly regarded as monks, and indeed many *mae chii* are even perceived negatively (P. Van Esterik 1982).

The fact that the Buddhist religious roles for women are underdeveloped has led Kirsch (1985) to comment that women in Theravada societies are "religiously disadvantaged." Conventionally, the exclusion of women from monastic roles has been rationalized by the view that women are less ready than men to attain the Buddhist salvation because of their deeper enmeshment in worldly matters. Instead, women's greatest contribution to Buddhism lies in their secular role through enabling the religious pursuit for the men in their lives. Hence, the role for women in religion is characterized by the mother-nurturer image: Women support and provide for Buddhism by way of "giving" young men to the *Sangha*, and "nurturing" the religion by alms giving (Keyes 1984). The ways in which Thai women constantly support Buddhist institutions and contribute to various spiritual functions in their communities have been well illustrated in Penny Van Esterik's work (1982).

This mother-nurturer image is also prominent in the Thai women's secular pursuits. Women are expected to provide for the well-being of their husbands, children, and parents. As pointed out by Kirsch (1985), this historical mother-nurturer role has had a self-perpetuating effect on the exclusion of women from monastic roles. Because women are barred from the monastic position, and because the weight of filial and family obligations falls more on women than on men, women are doubly locked in the same secular mother-nurturer role with no other options. They, therefore, are indeed enmeshed in worldly matters, and their redemption lies in the actions of the men in their lives.

Two important religious texts illustrate this condition. In the tale of Prince Vessantara, his wife, Queen Maddi, is praised because of her unconditional support of his generosity. In *Anisong Buat* ("Blessings of Ordination"), a woman with no merit is saved from hell because she had allowed her son to be ordained as a monk (Keyes 1984). In reality, the mother-nurturer image entails a certain life path for women, as noted by Kirsch (1985, 319): "Under typical circumstances young women could expect to remain rooted in village life, eventually snaring a husband, having children, and 'replacing' their mothers."

Men, as seen in the depiction of Prince Vessantara and the young son with religious aspirations in the "Blessings of Ordination," are afforded autonomy, as well as geographic and social mobility, to pursue both religious and secular goals, therefore "affirming" the conventional wisdom that men are more ready than women to give up attachments.

Undoubtedly, these differential role prescriptions for men and women have led to a clear division of labor along gender lines. Thai women's role of mother and their routine merit-making activities necessitate their specialization in economic-entrepreneurial activities, such as small-scale trading, productive activities in the field, and craft work at home. Thai men, encouraged by the logistic freedom, prefer political-bureaucratic activities, particularly those in government service (Kirsch 1982). The connection between monastic institutions and polity has always been salient to Thai people (see Kirsch 1982; J. Van Esterik 1982), therefore, positions in bureaucracy and politics represent a man's ideal pursuit should he choose to excel in the secular role. In the 19th century, more Thai men began to strive for secular success when the Buddhist reformation in Thailand demanded more intensified discipline in monks; this coincided with an expansion of government occupations that resulted from a bureaucratic system reorganization in the 1890s (Kirsch 1982).

Becoming a temporary member of the monkhood has long been seen in Thailand as a rite of passage which demarcates Thai men's transformation from "raw" to "ripe," or from immature men to scholars or wise men (*bundit*, from Pali *pandit*). In Sathian Kosed's *Popular Buddhism in Thailand* (published in Rajadhon 1961), young Buddhist men, upon turning 20 years old, are expected to become a monk for the period of about three months during the Buddhist Lenten period. Because the merit from ordination of a married man will be transferred to his wife (and because she must consent to his ordination), parents are understandably anxious to see that their sons are ordained before they get married. Traditionally, a "raw" unordained adult man would be seen as uneducated and, therefore, not a suitable man to be a husband or son-in-law. The man's girlfriend or fiancée, therefore, delights in his temporary monkhood as it should enhance her parents' approval of him. She often sees this as a sign of relationship commitment, and promises to wait patiently for the day he leaves his monkhood at the end of the Lenten period. In Thai society today, this practice of ordination has changed and is less significant, as men are more involved in secular education or occupied by their employment. Statistics show that today, members of the *Sangha* account for a smaller percent of the male population than in earlier times (Keyes 1984). As early as the late 1940s, when Sathian Kosed wrote *Popular Buddhism in Thailand*, there were already some signs of weakening customs around the Buddhist ordination.

Many other phenomena related to gender and sexuality in Thailand today can be traced to the Theravada worldview. As will be more evident in subsequent discussions, the Thai culture exhibits a double standard, which gives men a greater latitude to express their sexuality and other "deviant" behaviors (e.g., drinking, gambling, and extramarital sex). Keyes (1984) has pointed out that whereas women are seen as inherently close to the Buddha's teachings about sufferings, men require the discipline of ordination in order to achieve this insight, for they tend to digress from the Buddhist Precepts. With Keyes' notion in mind, we can speculate that Thai men perceive that demeritorious behaviors can be amended through their eventual ordination. Up to 70% of all men in central Thailand become monks on a temporary basis (J. Van Esterik 1982). Other adult males renounce "worldly" living to be ordained to the *Sangha*, living a midlife or old age "robed in yellow" as is commonly said in Thai. With such redemptive options, Thai men may feel little need to suppress their passions and vices. These attachments are, after all, easy to give up and are insubstantial compared to the salvation available to them in their twilight years.

On the contrary, women's lack of access to direct religious salvation makes them work harder to maintain virtuous lives, which means refraining from and disapproving of sexual indulgences, in order to keep their demerit to a minimum. With no access to formal Buddhist scholastic activities, it is unlikely that women would be able to discern which virtues and sins were defined by the Theravada values and which by the local gender construction (see discussion of *kulasatrii* in Section 1A, Basic Sexological Premises, Ideal Gender Images). Further, because women believe that their strongest merit is to be a mother of a son who is ordained, the pressure on women to marry and have a family is heightened. They must do everything to enhance their likelihood of marriage, perhaps including adherence to the ideal female images no matter how difficult. Viewed this way, both men and women in Thai society strongly endorse a double standard regarding gender and sexuality, albeit for different reasons.

*Key Beliefs in the Thai Constructions of Gender and Sexuality*

Before we proceed to other topics, it may be helpful to summarize the key strands of worldviews which will be apparent in subsequent discussions of gender and sexuality in Thailand. The most important influences are religious belief systems. Not only do the Five Buddhist Precepts constitute the ethical guidelines for laypeople, the Theravada gender images have been passed on to the society through sermons, folk tales and operas, and rituals. Animistic and Hinduist beliefs are embedded in the Thai consciousness through these folk tales, as is evident in metaphysical cosmology and entities, angels and ghosts, heavens and hells.

Other influences can also be identified in contemporary Thai society. For example, the consumerist and capitalist ideology is evident in commercial sex and pornography industries. More recently added to the mix is the newer generation's perception of sexuality in contemporary Europe, North America, and Japan, often interpreted as "modern," liberal, or hedonistic. Another school of thought present in the educated, urban middle class is the Western medical models of diseases and deviance, as well as psychological theories of sexuality; the Thai translations for "the subconscious," "latent," or "ego" are not uncommon in the conversation among the educated. Among other members of the same social strata, one can also discern the rise of contemporaneous Western ideological and political movements, such as feminism, women's studies, and the gay/lesbian identity. In a similar vein, the humanistic approach to understanding sexuality has become more visible in recent years, although it is often mislabeled as "modern," "Western," or "radical." Unfortunately, the humanistic movement may suffer from such misrepresentations in the present cultural climate, in which Thai tradition is seen as threatened by Western influences, and many Thai intellectuals are paying lip service to the conservation of traditional Thai identity.

## B. Ethnic Differences and Social Structure

Today, there are four regions of Thailand with distinct cultures: the north, the northeast, the central area, and the south. Although regional and cultural differences exist, there is a strong national identity, and the central Thai language is taught and understood throughout the country. This is enhanced by a well-developed mass media and communications system, a good telephone service, and a reliable transportation system servicing all parts of the country. The only exception to this is the hill tribe people in the mountainous regions that surround northern Thailand. The hill tribe people migrated south from China and have remained relatively separate and distinct. However, as the government cracks down on the growing of poppies (for opium and heroin production) and deforestation, the hill tribe people have been moving into the lowlands of Thailand or, through better roads and transportation, commute regularly into the lowland cities for work. Hill tribe people have maintained their own languages, cultures, and customs in the past several centuries. More details on the lives of hill tribe populations can be found in the books edited by Nancy Eberhardt (1988) and McKinnon and Bhruksasri (1983).

Other cultural differences also exist. The stratification of upper, middle, and lower classes is mostly based on the past social hierarchy (*sakdi na*) and the family's financial powers. This social stratification is no longer enforced by contemporary law, but its presence is recognized by most Thais. There is also a distinction between urban and rural Thais. Constituting a majority of the Thai population, people in the rural villages of Thailand have led more-simple lives rooted in rich traditions, with less interference from international cultures or capitalism. Urban Thailand, on the other hand, has gained its cultural richness from the diverse social classes, ethnicities, and international cultures. The rural/urban division is still highly salient to most Thais, even though the differences have become gradually smaller because of the media, improved communication and transportation, and the migration of rural Thais to find work in big cities. Among other changes, gender and sexuality in rural villagers today have been greatly adulterated by the urban cultural images through the ubiquitous popular media (Keyes 1984).

In addition, there is also an ethnic division between the Thais and the 10% of the population who are of Chinese descent. Mostly excluded from the upper echelons of nobility, Sino-Thai people have gained power and status through commerce. The ethnic Chinese in Thailand have managed to blend well into the urban middle-class communities with particularly great contributions in commerce and, more recently, the sciences, while still maintaining their traditional heritage through customs and Confucian family values. Despite the longstanding tradition of classes, social mobility is common, and the ethnic Chinese stand as examples of "rags-to-riches" possibilities (Kirsch 1982). Racial prejudice exists on a subtle level, but has never resulted in overt segregation or violence, even during the anti-Chinese nationalistic government in 1939. Readers who are interested in the lives of Chinese and Sino-Thai peoples in Thailand are referred to the work of Anne Maxwell Hill (1988) and William Skinner (1957).

It is important to bear in mind these cultural, regional, and ethnic differences, because they significantly limit generalizations about the sexual attitudes and values in Thailand. In this chapter, a majority of the research data on sexual attitudes and behavior has been derived from samples of lower- and middle-class ethnic Thais. Most empirical studies have been conducted in urban cities, such as Bangkok and Chiang-mai, although data from the rural villages of the north and the northeast account for a considerable portion of our review. In addition, Thailand's rapid economic progress in recent decades has had a dramatic impact on every level of sociocultural structures. Likewise, the nature of gender and sexuality in Thai society is undergoing rapid transformations. As a result, the great degree of flux and heterogeneity in Thai society demands that we pay great attention to the contexts in our attempt to understand gender and sexuality in Thailand.

## 3. Knowledge and Education about Sexuality

Like parents in many other cultures, most Thai parents do not educate their children about sexuality, and when children ask about sex, they are likely to avoid answering or they provide incorrect information. Since parents are unlikely to display affection in front of their children, role-modeling of affection between the genders is usually derived not from parents, but from literature or the media. Men are more likely to discuss sex with other men, especially when they are socializing and drinking with each other. Women also prefer to discuss sex and their marital issues with their same-gender peers (Thorbek 1988). Sexual communication between a married couple has received much attention among Thai sex and AIDS researchers recently, but data are still scarce (see Section 5B, Interpersonal Heterosexual Behaviors, Adult Sexual Behavior).

Sexual matters are not typically discussed in a serious fashion in the Thai society. When sex is mentioned, it is often in the context of playful banter or humor. Playful joking about sex with striking curiosity and candor is not uncommon. For example, a newlywed couple would be teased lightheartedly and openly: "Did you have fun last night? Was last night happy? How many times?" (Allyn 1991). As in many cultures, Thai people have an extensive sexual vocabulary (see Allyn 1991). For every colloquialism that Thai people find offensive or obscene, there are a number of euphemistic equivalents. Euphemistic substitutes are made by way of symbolic animals or objects (e.g., "dragon" or "dove" for penis, "oyster" for vagina, and "eggs" for testicles); children's language (e.g., "little kid" or "Mr. That" for penis); extreme obscurity (e.g., "said activity" for having sex, "using mouth" for oral sex, and "Miss Body" for prostitute); literary references (e.g., "Lord of the world" for penis); or medical terms (e.g., "birth canal" for vagina).

With such a variety of alternative terms, Thai people feel that sexual matters in everyday conversation should be tastefully alluded to in moderate amounts, with an artful choice of words, timing, and comic sensibility. Thai people do have a strict sense of social appropriateness surrounding such humor, especially in the presence of elders or women. Discussions about sex are uncomfortable when they are excessively crude or straightforward, overly solemn or intellectual, and socially inappropriate. Such discomfort is reflected in the Thai words which are equivalent to "one-track mind," "dirty mind," "lewd," "sex-obsessed," "sex-crazed," or "nympho" in English, with a variety of nuances ranging from playful to pathologizing to disapproving. Such attitudes have been one of the barriers for sexuality education; rather than objecting to content of sexuality education *per se*, adults and educators feel embarrassed by discussions about sex that seem too intellectual and straightforward.

Sexuality education was introduced in Thai schools in 1978. Although the curriculum has been revised over the years, it has been limited to reproductive issues and sexually transmitted diseases (STDs). As in many other countries, sexuality education in Thailand has been rarely taught in a comprehensive manner. Embedded in the contexts of health education and biology, attention to sociocultural contexts was more an exception than a rule. Although family planning and population control is practiced by most Thais, contraception is not emphasized in school. Instead, a typical Thai gains this knowledge from family planning media campaigns, clinics, and physicians.

Dusitsin (1995) has expressed concerns that Thai people can no longer rely on learning about sex from sexual humor, which contains alarming amounts of sexual myths and misinformation. Dusitsin's proposal of a Program for the Promotion of Sexual Health (see Sections 12, Sexual Dysfunctions, Counseling, and Therapies, and 13, Research and Advanced Education) gives a priority to developing curricula for sexuality education for both students and non-student populations. Other Thai researchers and experts have voiced the same philosophy and have called for more comprehensive curricula, with greater coverage of psychosocial issues, such as a discourse on gender, homophobia, and sexual commercialism. They have also urged that sexuality education must have its own identity and objectives clearly distinguished from the highly visible AIDS-prevention campaigns, in order to avoid the constricted scope and sex-negative attitudes. Others have also enthusiastically supported the idea of covering non-student populations, who usually have limited access to services and education.

## 4. Autoerotic Behaviors and Patterns

Very few of the sex surveys conducted in the wake of the HIV epidemic have reported any data about the incidence of masturbation, let alone discussed the attitudes and behaviors surrounding this behavior. This may be because of the fact that masturbation, like most other sexual matters, is somewhat a taboo subject in Thailand, and has been ignored perhaps because it does not have a direct bearing on the public-health agenda.

One study did examine adolescent autoerotic attitudes and behaviors (Chompootaweep, Yamarat, Poomsuwan, & Dusitsin 1991). Many more male students (42%) than female students (6%) reported having masturbated. The modal age of first masturbatory experience was 13 years. Adolescents were likely to maintain negative attitudes about masturbation, viewing it as "unnatural," or citing myths about masturbation, such as a belief that it causes sexually transmitted diseases. The gender difference found in the rates of reported masturbation is striking, although it is also typical of other domains in sexual surveys in Thailand. Within the same socioeconomic stratum, Thai men always report having much more sexual interest and experience than Thai women. Young women, in particular, might be uncomfortable with the idea of masturbation because it is an acknowledgment of sexual curiosity, which is deemed inappropriate and shameful for women (Ford & Kittisuksathit 1994).

Data on the masturbatory experiences of adults are also scarce. In one study of army conscripts in northern Thailand, 89% of the men (age 21) reported having masturbated (Nopkesorn, Sungkarom, & Sornlum 1991). There is little or no formal information on adults' attitudes about masturbation, but the myths held by adults are likely to be different from those of adolescents. One common myth among male adults is that men are endowed with a finite number of orgasms, thus it is advisable to indulge in masturbation in moderation.

Perhaps the general attitudes of Thai people regarding masturbation can be inferred from the terms used to describe the act. The formal Thai terminology for masturbation, *sumrej khuam khrai duay tua eng*, which simply means "to consummate sexual desire by yourself," has replaced a former technical term *atta-kaam-kiriya*, which means "sexual act with oneself." The tone of these rather clinical and inconvenient terms is neutral, strictly free of judgment or implications about health consequences. There is really no clear discussion about masturbation, either positive or negative, in the Third Buddhist Precept or in animistic practice. Therefore, any disapproval of masturbation in the Thai society is likely to be a result of the general anxiety surrounding sexual indulgences, or perhaps from the Western anachronism introduced to the Thai thinking by way of past medical education.

Most Thais, however, prefer the playful vernacular *chak wow*, meaning to "fly a kite." The term compares male masturbation to the hand action of flying a kite, a popular Thai pastime. An even more euphemistic term for male masturbation is *pai sa-naam luang*, which means "to go to the grand field," referring to the very popular park area near the royal palace in Bangkok where people fly kites. For women, the slang term *tok bed* is used, meaning "to use a fishing pole." These playful and euphemistic expressions reflect the acknowledgment that masturbation occurs for both men and women, and yet some discomfort prevents a straightforward verbal expression.

## 5. Interpersonal Heterosexual Behaviors

### A. Adolescent Sexual Behavior

Numerous studies up to the mid-1990s have shown that about half of Thai men have sexual intercourse before they are 18 years old, and that most of them have their first experience with a commercial sex worker (e.g., Sittitrai, Phanuphak, Barry, & Brown 1992; Udomratn & Tungphaisal 1990). Justified as a way of preserving the virtue of "good women," Thai adolescents seek premarital sexual experience from commercial sex workers. Prior to the HIV epidemic, there was virtually no stigma attached to this practice. Sex with a sex worker has often been considered a rite of passage and an accepted manner of learning about sex for young men. Some Thai fathers were known to pay sex workers to have sex with their sons as a way of giving their youngsters some sex education or acknowledging their adulthood. In primarily male colleges, senior students welcomed freshmen, most of whom had no prior sexual experience, by accompanying them to the local brothel or bars/cafes which offer commercial sex. In the contemporary Thai society where increasingly fewer men are interested in the *Sangha*, the young men's use of sexual intercourse as a rite of passage seems like a symbolic commentary on how the male image has drifted further away from the monastic role in the direction of worldliness.

Thai male adolescents eagerly look forward to their first intercourse and, as its slang term (*khuen khruu*) roughly implies, a learning process with someone sexually experienced. For many young Thai men, this practice continues beyond their first sexual experience, and commercial sex becomes a bachelor's recreation. In fact, the phrase *pai thiow*, meaning "to go out for fun," is a euphemism for a visit to the brothel. Going to a brothel with friends is a social as well as a sexual experience, often occurring after an evening of drinking or social gathering. Young men who do not seem interested in joining their peers at a brothel are sometimes teased for being homosexual (Ford & Kittisuksathit 1994). This pattern of sexual behavior in young Thai men will be confirmed by more findings reviewed in the section on the premarital sex of adults (see Section 5B, Interpersonal Heterosexual Behaviors, Adult Sexual Behavior).

On the other hand, young women are supposed to be virgins until they are married. Sex is thus not a recreational option for unmarried women as it is for men. Violation of this rule occurs in the cases of prostitutes and "carefree women." A "carefree woman," or an unmarried woman who seeks sexual pleasure from casual partners, is stereotyped as shallow, emotionally disturbed, and self-destructive. She presumably has lost her virginity because she was amoral, careless, gullible, or blindly following the Western code of sexual behavior. Needless to say, sex before marriage for women is the key criterion that distinguishes a "bad woman" from a "good woman." Female sex workers are subject to the same stereotype, but perhaps to a lesser degree, possibly because they are perceived to be forced into commercial sex by poverty. In addition, the *kulasatrii* notion mostly pertains to the upper and middle classes (Pyne 1994), and thus has less to do with the lower-class origin of most sex workers. Despite such class difference, the *kulasatrii* status is much like the Buddhist concept of merit in that it is based on the person's conduct, not on the social standing *per se*, and it is subject to decline for any transgression. Inasmuch as social mobility and merit accumulation are afforded everyone in Thailand (although perhaps not with equal ease), every woman, every *kulasatrii* can fall from grace if her conduct is compromised. Therefore, gender segregation, the stringent rules of *kulasatrii*, and strict parental supervision all are useful mechanisms for maintaining the virtue of "good" women.

In keeping with the value on women's virginity, the Thai culture prescribes that romantic relationships between young men and women must be without sex. In general, young people in Thailand today choose their own romantic partner, although parents exercise sanctions on their choice and limit their premarital sexual interaction (Ford & Kittisuksathit 1994). As a man and a woman enter a purely romantic premarital relationship, they are known as being each other's *fan*, an originally English term used in Thai with a different connotation. When in a relationship, many young women start to act as if they are practicing the traditional gender script of husband and wife (without the sex) by adopting a more submissive and deferential role with their *fan*. Even under such a nonsexual premise, many young Thai lovers are still very reluctant to reveal that they have a *fan* to parents or adults for fear of disapproval. In the conservative middle-class ethic, romantic interest is inappropriate for adolescents because they cannot support themselves. Many young lovers simply refer to their *fan* as a male or a female friend. This reluctance to disclose romantic relationships remains in many married adults, who refer to a spouse as a *fan* even after years of marriage.

In an exceptional study of adolescence, Chompootaweep et al. (1991) randomly surveyed secondary-level schools in Bangkok and collected questionnaires from 4,337 students (mean age = 14.7) and 454 teachers. Both male and female students reported that the best age to develop a romantic relationship was 18 to 20 years of age, in contrast to the ages 21 to 25, which their teachers thought was the appropriate age to start romantic relationships. This demonstrates the intergenerational difference in attitude toward adolescent romantic relationships; Thai teachers, like Thai parents, see romance between adolescents as precocious and inappropriate. Fifty-five percent of the male students subscribed to the idea that men should have some sexual experience before getting married, while only 24% of the female students thought this was appropriate for men. Among the teachers, 74% of the male teachers and 58% of the female teachers endorsed men's premarital sexual experience. A double standard was clearly illustrated, as only 15% of both male and female participants endorsed premarital sex for women. In terms of sexual behavior, 12% of the male students and only 1% of the female students reported having had intercourse.

These observations have been further confirmed in another excellent study (Ford & Kittisuksathit 1994) which we have cited throughout this chapter. In this study, qualitative data were obtained from focus groups with young factory workers (ages 15 to 24) whose socioeconomic status was more representative of the general Thai youth populations than high-school or college samples. Sexual desire was perceived by both young men and women to be a male attribute. The young men openly expressed their sexual feelings and experiences; the young women felt ashamed of their sexual curiosity and thought women should wait until they were older and married before they found out about sex. In the minds of the young men, sexual intercourse seemed like an adventure, a gain, a forceful act, or an act of satisfying one's greed. Some slang terms used by the young men for sexual intercourse can be roughly translated to "taking," "earning," "playing," "grinding," "gobbling," and "poking the yolk." On the contrary, sexual intercourse was seen by the young women as a loss of their body/self (*sia tua*), and women who have lost their virginity were seen as "impure," "soiled," or "tarnished." In addition, there is a belief that a forbidden sexual experience can predispose a young woman to becoming sexually out of control, (*jai taek*), especially if the liaison ends with the man deserting her. Such a woman might turn into a "carefree woman" or even a prostitute (Thorbek 1988).

In addition to demonstrating a double standard among Thai adolescents, Chompootaweep et al. (1991) also found that the gender and sexual attitudes of Thais in the same urban environment differed as a function of their ages. The young factory workers in Ford and Kittisuksathit's study (1994) pointedly articulated this sense of being in the midst of social transformation. Repeatedly referring to "[things are] different today," these adolescents were acutely aware of their living in a period in which sexual constructions were rapidly changing from the clear prescriptions of the "traditional" norms to the more amorphous and perplexing "modern" ways.

## B. Adult Sexual Behavior

### Premarital and Adult Sexual Experience

The *Survey of Partner Relations and HIV Infection* (Sittitrai et al., 1992; referred to hereafter as "the *Partner Relations Survey*") is a large population-based study that examined sexual attitudes and behaviors among 2,801 men and women. Currently married men reported an average of 30.2 premarital sexual partners. Never-married men reported an average of 14.3 premarital sexual partners. The picture was completely different for women, who reported

little or no premarital sexual experiences, with means of 0.03 and 0.01 premarital sexual partners for married women and never-married women, respectively. This gender difference again reflects a double standard on premarital sex for men and women. Although the extent of reporting biases could not be determined, as in most sex surveys, the social-desirability biases could have influenced men to overreport and/or women to underreport their premarital sexual experiences. The biases, if there were any, did indeed reflect the double standard that promotes premarital sex in men and discourages it in women.

Many researchers have studied Thai military conscripts in order to describe the sexual behaviors of the general populations of young Thai men. Thai men ages 20 to 22, who are not in higher education, are inducted to the Royal Thai Army by lottery; randomly selected samples, therefore, provide an excellent representation of men in the lower socioeconomic strata of Thai society (Beyrer, Eiumtrakul, Celentano, Nelson, Ruckphaopunt, & Khamboonruang 1995). In a study of conscripts from northern Thailand in 1990 and 1991 (Nopkesorn et al. 1991), 97% of these 21-year-old men reported having had sexual intercourse, with about 54% reporting having the first intercourse before the age of 16. The first sexual intercourse for 74% of the men was with a female sex worker, compared to 12% with a lover, and 8% with a girlfriend. A majority of men, 90%, had had sex with a female sex worker, mostly starting between the ages of 15 to 18. By the age of 16, about half of the sample had had their first visit to a female sex worker.

Until AIDS became a widespread anxiety in the mid-1990s, commercial sex had been the primary sexual outlet for Thai bachelors, justified as a means of protecting virtuous Thai women from premarital sex. For Thai male adults, the use of commercial sex continues in the same way as it began in adolescence (see Section 5A, Interpersonal Heterosexual Behaviors, Adolescent Sexual Behavior), only with less economic restriction. Taking care of men's sexual needs by offering services from a sex worker is considered part of hospitality in many business dealings. Upon arrival in a new city, traveling men or male tourists often make a point of visiting local brothels or erotic massage parlors as local attractions.

This picture may, however, be changing with a new generation of Thais because of several factors. Young women have been found to be more likely to engage in premarital sexual activity than the previous generations. Western culture, as perceived and interpreted through the Thai eyes, has been implicated in this change over the last few decades. More recently, it has also been attributed to the men's heightened fear of HIV. As prevention campaigns have publicized high rates of HIV infection among female sex workers, Thai men have become more wary of visiting professional sex workers. For example, a decrease in the use of commercial sex workers among the northern Thai conscripts, for example, has been documented over the few years prior to 1996 (Nelson et al. 1996).

In response to the worries about AIDS and commercial sex, Thai men have turned to a number of other ways of fulfilling their sexual desires. While many Thai men have become less sexually active, others, especially those in the urban middle-class settings, have been paying for sex with nonprofessional sex workers who are not in the sex establishments. Others turn to the big-city singles or nightlife scenes for casual sex with pickup partners. Finally, there is a growing number of men who have sex with their girlfriends in the context of a committed romantic relationship. Helped by the anonymity of big cities and the widely available contraceptive methods, there are increasing number of cohabiting couples, much to the chagrin of conservatives who are concerned with the virtue of Thai women. Although this phenomenon has been consistently observed in recent studies (e.g., Nelson et al. 1996), many researchers feel that there is much resistance from the Thai public, who are not quite ready to formally approve of these unmarried sexual couples.

Thai women, not unlike those in many other cultures, take risks in having sexual experience. In addition to concerns about pregnancy and health, they face the risks of stigmatization for losing their virginity outside a marriage. As many sex workers have reported, because an unmarried woman's virtue is eminently tied to her virginity, a woman who has lost her virginity has nothing to lose in choosing the path of commercial sex (Thorbek 1988). Other women keep their premarital sexual experience a secret, although the psychological repercussions may continue. A small number of women who are neither secretive nor disturbed by their premarital sex are suspected to have had a "bad influence" from Western culture, or are pathologized as sensation-seeking, promiscuous, or morally corrupt (see the "bad girl" stereotype in Section 5A, Interpersonal Heterosexual Behaviors, Adolescent Sexual Behavior). The expressions which characterize women who seek sexual gratification with little restraint are *jai ngaai* ("feeble mind/heart"), and *jai taek* ("broken mind/heart"), suggesting that the women are morally corrupt or out of control. Together, the nonprofessional women who exchange sex for money and the "carefree" single women in the urban nightlife and singles scenes are categorized as *ying ruk sanuk*, or "fun-loving women," or the slang *kai long*, or "stray chicken." These "depraved" women are seen as "only good for sex but not suitable for being the mother of your children."

In spite of the blame on Western influence, the image of "bad" women who seek sexual pleasures is not new. Kirsch (1985) has observed that in the 19th century, King Mongkut characterized "spinsters and divorcees" as "artful women" who viewed monks as "fattened hogs" (i.e., potential husbands); monks exposed to such women's seduction "are likely to be driven crazy by their new found love" (p. 311). Similarly, Penny Van Esterik (1982) has found that some lay villagers were suspicious of *mae chii* (female ascetics) who lived near the temples in which monks resided. She further cites a story recorded by Attagara about a woman who dressed up as a *mae chii* and seduced a local abbot who was so ashamed of his weakness that he held his breath and died. A line in the *Jataka* tales (tales about the Buddha's past lives) says that "Women desire rich lovers like cows seeking new pastures" (p. 76). These illustrations suggest that women who did not fit the model of motherhood, like unmarried women, divorcées, or *mae chii*, might have always been viewed with suspicion, with a projection of the male-typical boundless and uncontrollable sexual desires on to them.

In addition to the well-known "bad woman" stereotype and the *kulasatrii* ideal, there is yet another type of women in the Thai consciousness, namely the widows. (Although this word in Thai can also refer to divorced women, this discussion pertains only to women whose husbands are deceased). Mostly of middle- and lower-class social strata, many widows seem to be less bound by the conservatism of a *kulasatrii*, yet they are not stigmatized as depraved. Because a widow presumably has had sexual experience in her prior marriage, virginity no longer is an issue of virtue for her. Therefore, she can seek sexual pleasure without severe social stigma, given that, of course, scandals such as affairs with married men or pregnancy out of wedlock are avoided. With the exception of female sex workers, widows seem to be the only women in Thai society "allowed" to have sex outside of marriage. In literature, jokes, and popular song lyrics, widows are portrayed as temptresses: straightfor-

ward about their sexual interest—often toward younger men—witty and flirtatious, exuberantly sensual and seductive, and well versed in their sexual practices. To many heterosexual male adolescents, an idealized fantasy of their first sexual experience is an encounter with such a woman who is sexually disinhibited, yet not a sex worker. The Thai culture seems to have an alternative for a woman to be sexually active with fewer reservations, but she needs to have lost a husband who had introduced her to the joy of sex.

## Marriage and Family Dynamics

Choice of a marriage mate is usually based on the individual's preference. Thai women have greater power in their spouse selection than do Chinese-Thai women in Thailand (Pyne 1994). Elopements are also, however, well known, indicating the power of parental objection (Kirsch 1982). A married couple may reside for a time with the wife's family, but their ideal residence is an independent nuclear household. In extended families, the strong matrilineal ties generally entail men's moving into the woman's family. Well-known exceptions to this custom exist, especially among the ethnic Chinese in Thailand as exemplified in the work with Yunnanese families by Hill (1988). With the couple establishing an independent household in the wife's family compound, both usually continue to work the land owned by the wife's parents, with the son-in-law's labor construed as a form of brideprice. Despite such a matrilocal pattern of postnuptial residence, authority is passed down through the men in the family, and the son-in-law eventually becomes the head of the household (Pyne 1994).

Women maintain strong connections with their mothers, even when migration and poverty make contacts difficult (Thorbek 1982). Women working in cities often send money to their families upcountry, visit them annually, and most return to the villages when their target income is achieved (Pyne 1994) or when their employment or marriage ends.

A traditional Thai marriage is symbolized by tying the bride and groom's wrists with holy string during a ceremony at which the family and community are present (Pyne 1994). A women changes her surname to her husband's upon marriage and her title changes from *naangsao* ("Miss") to *naang* ("Missus"). In addition to the informal gender-neutral *fan*, a variety of terms for husband and wife exist for use in different contexts, ranging from the playful and frank (*phua* for husband, and *mia* for wife) to the formal and polite (*saamii* for husband, and *phan-ya* for wife). There is a slight discomfort with the frank terms for husband and wife, and most Thai people see the formal, legal, slightly detached terms as more civilized and polite. The importance of the couple's image as parents can be seen in the endearing terms for husband and wife, *pho baan* and *mae baan* (father and mother of the home). In fact, the birth of the first child is a critical event for a traditional Thai couple, as it denotes the union and symbolizes a stable relationship (Pyne 1994). Although a preference for having sons has been documented elsewhere (e.g., P. Van Esterik 1982), and it is particularly strong in the Chinese-Thai families, both sons and daughters are valued for different reasons. While the son's potential ordination in the *Sangha* can accumulate merit for the parents (Rajadhon 1961), a daughter is viewed as being reliable and dependable, especially for the care of parents in old age (Pyne 1994). Data from the *Demographic and Health Survey* (cited in Pyne 1994) indicate that half of all married women (ages 15 to 49) intend to have two children, and 80% want two or three.

The nurturing responsibilities of contemporary Thai women are undeniable in the statistics of women who work outside of their homes, as well as the proportions of women among migrants and the workforce (see Pyne 1994). Employers consider female workers to be hard working, enthusiastic, loyal, patient, and attentive to detail. Interestingly, centuries ago, the same qualities in Thai women did not escape the eyes of foreign observers. In the 17th century, Simon La Loubère (1693, quoted in Kirsch 1982, 16) noted on his visit to Siam: "how lazy the ordinary life of the Siamese [commoner] is . . . he does almost nothing but continue sitting or lying, playing, smoking, and sleeping." In contrast, he observed that the Siamese women "plow the land, they sell and buy in the cities"; and "The women . . . are always busy . . . trafficking in the bazaars, doing the light work in the fields and marketing." Similarly, a Chinese visitor to Siam during the Ming dynasty observed that "when there are affairs to be settled [in Siam,] they are settled by women. In determination and judgment the women really surpass the men" (Kirsch 1988, 27).

In Thai households today, men are typically the main source of income in a married couple. Major decisions of allocating resources thus remain in the hands of the men, whereas the women often manage the finances on a day-to-day basis (Pyne 1994; Thorbek 1988). In general, women are often more organized and economical than their husbands. Many women spend much energy trying to keep their husbands' vices in check with varying degrees of success. Thai women also engage in small homegrown businesses, such as vegetable gardening, market-vendor trading, and fabric weaving, if the family earning from the men is not adequate. Nevertheless, these earning women seem to spend most of their own incomes on the necessities of the family and often give sums of money to their mothers (Thorbek 1988). Similarly, a majority of women in commercial sex businesses send their income to parents, siblings, and other relatives in their native villages (Wawer, Podhisita, Kanungsukkasem, Pramualratana, & McNamara 1996). Thai women take their "nurturer" role seriously and few things can deter them from their mission.

## Incidence of Vaginal, Oral, and Anal Sex

Data on the incidence of vaginal, oral, and anal sex among Thai people have been provided by the large-scale *Partner Relations Survey* (Sittitrai et al. 1992). Among sexually experienced participants, vaginal intercourse was by far the most frequent sexual behavior, reported by 99.9% of the male and 99.8% of the female participants. Other sexual behaviors, however, are much more rare: Performing oral intercourse (presumably on the other gender) was reported by only 0.7% of the male and 13% of the female participants. Receiving oral sex was reported by 21% of the male participants and no data were available for the female participants' experience of receiving oral sex. Receptive anal intercourse was experienced by 0.9% of the male and 2% of the female participants. Insertive anal intercourse was experienced by 4% of the male participants.

The striking rarity of the non-genitogenital sexual acts, especially cunnilingus, among Thai people illustrates some sociocultural constructions that play important roles in the Thai sexuality. Even if reporting biases were operating in these findings, the reluctance toward having or reporting oral sex may suggest some aversion to certain body parts, especially the vagina or anus. As previously mentioned, Thai men's anxiety about losing dignity or masculinity from performing oral sex on a woman might have been a cultural residue from occultism and superstition of the past (see previous discussion on *mii khruu* in Section 1D, Basic Sexological Premises, Gender in Everyday Life). In addition to this superstitious reasoning, Thais also apply the concepts of social hierarchy and dignity to body parts: Certain parts of the body, such as the head or the face, are associated with personal

honor or integrity, whereas other "inferior" parts, such as the legs, feet, anus, and the female reproductive organs, are associated with impurity and baseness. This belief is still extremely common in Thai society, even among those who are not particularly superstitious. In the updated belief of body hierarchy, the impurity of inferior body parts is associated with germs or crudeness, while violation is framed as poor hygiene or lack of social etiquette.

In social interactions, the body hierarchy prohibits some behaviors, such as raising one's lower extremities high in the presence of others or touching an older person's head with one's hand (or even worse, with one's foot). In sexual situations, this belief also prevents certain sexual acts. Viewed in this cultural context, one can understand Thai people's repulsion toward oral or anal sex, as well as other sexual acts, such as oral-anal sex or foot fetishism. In these acts, "lowering" a highly guarded body part (e.g., a man's face or head) to contact an organ of a much lower order (e.g., feet or a woman's genitals) can cause damage to the man's personal integrity and dignity. Many Thais today openly disapprove of these sexual acts as deviant, unnatural, or unsanitary, while others are excited by the lack of inhibition they find in Western erotica.

Perhaps because of the lack of direct public health implications, very few studies have generated data on the sexual behavior within married couples. In a 1981 study, a majority of married Thai women (ages 17 to 65) randomly sampled in Bangkok reported low sexual desire or enjoyment after the birth of their children (Bussaratid, Na Ranong, Boonyaprakob, & Sitasuwan 1981). Frequency of sexual intercourse was once a week or less in 49% of the women. Only 24% reported having orgasm with every intercourse; women 35 years or older reported fewer experiences of orgasm. In another study of female outpatients in 1975, the mean frequency of intercourse was 2.3 per week (Pongthai, Sakornratanakul, & Chaturachinda 1980). Another study examined the sexual behavior in pregnant women ages 17 to 44 in Bangkok and found that sexual abstention increased as pregnancy progressed, ranging from 4% of the women in the first trimester to 56% of the women in the third trimester (Aribarg, Aribarg, Rakiti, & Harnroongroj 1982). The most common reasons for abstinence and decreased frequency of sex were fear of fetal injury (reported by 30% of the women), and somatic symptoms of pregnancy (22%). A number of the pregnant women also abstained from sex to protect their fetuses from STD, as 13% of the women knew that their husbands had had extramarital sex.

Unfortunately, most of the available data on the sexual behavior within Thai couples are from research conducted prior to 1982. The paucity of more-recent findings points to the need for more research. Information in this area will afford us a better understanding of extramarital sex, sexual dysfunctions, heterosexual transmission of HIV and sexually transmitted diseases, and marital satisfaction and discord.

## Extramarital Sex

Perhaps extramarital sexual practices in Thailand are best illustrated by the findings from the *Partner Relations Survey* by Werasit Sittitrai and his colleagues (1992). They found that 31% of urban male participants and 12% of rural male participants—17% overall—reported having had sex outside their relationship in the previous 12 months. The data from women were quite different: only 1% of the urban female participants and 0.7% of the rural female participants—0.9% overall—reported sex outside their relationship in the previous 12 months. The remarkable gender difference in extramarital sex in these findings will be more extensively discussed below.

Despite the historical acceptance, male polygamy is no longer legally or socially acceptable in the contemporary Thai society. However, the tradition continues in modern days in a more secretive fashion. Whereas a "virtuous woman" or *kulasatrii* (see traditional female gender role in Section 1, Basic Sexological Premises) must remain faithful to her husband, there were no equivalent rules in history mandating fidelity in the "virtuous man." In fact, upper-class Thai men were historically known to maintain mansions with a co-residence of multiple wives and their children. Among the royalty and courtiers in the past, wives were classified as principal, secondary, and slave (Pyne 1994). Today, the tradition of "minor wives" still remains, but the practice is different from that of the past. Also, because of the expense involved, minor wives are mostly limited to the wealthy men, although Thorbek (1988) has also documented the practice in men of lower socioeconomic strata. [*Comment 2003*: Barmé (2002, 157-178) has provided a history of Thai polygyny in the 20th century, tracing its variations and cultural response in government and public debates, cartoons, cinema, and pop media, from pre-modern Siam to modern Thai culture. (*End of comment by R. T. Francoeur*)]

Euphemistically called having a "little home," the practice of keeping a minor wife usually occurs today in secrecy from the "primary wife," and minor wives rarely share the home with the man and his family as in the old days. While almost all married women today object to this practice, and indeed for many it has been grounds for divorce, other women learn to cope with their anger and emotional betrayal. Minor wives are viewed with contempt by the Thai society along the lines of being amoral women or home breakers. They do not achieve social or legal recognition as a spouse. A Thai phrase "drinking water from underneath someone else's elbow" illustrates the humiliation and powerlessness of a minor wife, often used to deter young women from considering a relationship with a married male suitor.

Frustrated with the husband's infidelity, potential or real, some married women have been taught by older women and sex journalists to break out of the conservative sexual norms of a *kulasatrii* by adopting the dual role of "a *kulasatrii* outside the bedroom, and a prostitute inside." Extramarital sex for a married woman is, however, not a viable option. In a seminar with participants from rural villages in northern Thailand, men told Pacharin Dumronggittigule and her colleagues (personal communication 1995) that if a woman had more sexual desire than her husband could satisfy, she should "hit her feet with a hammer," indicating their belief that the use of drastic means was needed to suppress women's sexual desires. In a folk-tale epic, *Khun Chaang, Khun Phaen*, the heroine, Wanthong, was persecuted for being torn between her relationships with the two male protagonists. Although women today are not persecuted, as was Wanthong, her tragic fate reflects the society's clear prohibitive rule against women's emotional and sexual infidelity.

Whereas minor wives are the secret sexual indulgence for wealthy men, sex with commercial sex workers is widely accepted by almost all male adults, regardless of age, socioeconomic class, or marital status. After marriage, Thai men seem be monogamous with their wives for a period of time, although the duration of this monogamy has not been investigated. A great number, however, resume their use of commercial sex, often in the context of all-male, "husbands' night out" socialization with their peers.

Dumronggittigule and her colleagues (1995) examined the married men's use of commercial sex by conducting focus groups with married villagers in northern Thailand. They found that the cultural processes behind this phenomenon were different from the processes for the Thai bachelors.

Thai men visit commercial sex workers after socializing with male friends, a pattern established since the start of their experience with commercial sex. For married men's gatherings, women are not necessarily precluded from the social gatherings, as the meals are often prepared by women, but excessive alcohol consumption and gambling repel women from further participation. Married men reported that their sexual desires are enhanced because of the alcohol and the sex talk among the men. Married women, on the contrary, reported that after a long day of work outside and inside the home, they were not sexually thrilled by their husbands' drunken manners and alcohol smells, and many refused to have sex. Other couples reportedly avoided this conflict by having an a priori agreement that the husbands could take their sexual desire elsewhere.

Moreover, the villagers reported other common causes of diminished sexual attraction within the couple. Women reported that the strenuous work inside and outside the home caused them to be exhausted, irritable, and uninterested in sex, and their husband's drinking and gambling with male friends did not help. Men, on the other hand, commented on their wife's homely appearance, angry temperament, and sexual unresponsiveness, all of which made them turn to drinking, gambling, and commercial sex as recreation. As this spiral of blame and self-defense continued, conflicts and resentment grew. Following what they had seen in other couples, many women decided that consenting to their husband's use of commercial sex could relieve this dilemma. Thus, the use of commercial sex by married men is often consented to or known by their wives. For both men and women, the husband's extramarital sex is not a cause of marital conflicts, but an attempted solution designed to preserve their marriage.

Married women, therefore, do not simply consent to their husband's use of commercial sex because "Thai people have permissive attitudes toward men's extramarital sex," as is often quoted. In the same study cited above, Dumronggittigule and colleagues (1995) used anonymous questionnaires to collect data from 170 married couples in the villages. They found feelings of frustration, worry, and helplessness among the women who believed their husbands had regular sex with sex workers. Almost all the married women objected to their husband visiting sex workers. Ninety-one percent of these women had asked their husband to refrain from such behavior, but 47% of the women believed their husbands would visit or had visited sex workers. Although they felt vulnerable to HIV infection, these married women still did not think that their husband would respond to their fears. Instead, these women would rather protect themselves from HIV by having protected sex with their husbands; 83% reported they would be willing to have their husbands use condoms with them. The women's interest in self-protection, however, might not lead to an actual prevention; most couples had never used condoms with each other and were unlikely to change upon the women's requests.

### Alcohol Use and Sexual Behavior

The use of alcohol is a regular part of Thai culture and tradition despite the prohibition in the Buddhist Fifth Precept. Many male adolescents in northern Thailand begin drinking commercially produced whiskey or village-prepared liquor at the age of 14 or 15. They will often drink alcohol with a few friends and go as a small group to have sex with sex workers (van Landingham et al. 1993). Adolescent girls will often start drinking at the age of 17 or 18. They are more likely to drink when there are parties as part of a celebration. Drinking and sex in combination is a common way for adolescents to be sexual with one another (Nopkesorn, Sweat,

Kaensing, & Teppa 1993). Thai men often report that alcohol makes them "horny," although using condoms is usually more difficult in an intoxicated state. Data confirm that alcohol use does interfere with the use of condoms in the commercial sex settings (Mastro & Limpakarnjanarat 1995).

## 6. Homoerotic, Homosexual, and Bisexual Behaviors

### A. Attitudes Toward Homosexuality in Buddhism and Thai Society

Although homosexual behavior in Thailand is assumed to be quite common, little formal research has been done. Most of the available data pertain to men, and there is a paucity of information regarding women. There has been a general reluctance, as with other Asian cultures, to openly discuss or scientifically study homosexual behaviors. In a large 1990 population-based survey (Sittitrai et al. 1992), extremely low rates of male homosexual behavior were reported; the authors cautioned that, because of societal attitudes, these estimates were probably too low and reflected the research participants' underreporting of homoerotic and homosexual experiences (the prevalence of same-gender sexual behavior will be further reviewed below).

The attitudes toward homosexuality are quite complex: On the one hand, the behavior is clearly stigmatized, and on the other, tolerated. Probably the manner in which it is expressed is a more critical variable for social acceptance. In the culture in which men's sexual desires are exaggerated, it is understandable that men might, from time to time, hypothetically engage in sexual behavior with other men for pragmatic purposes (e.g., when women are not available or when they need money). Women may face stronger negative sanction than men. Again, a double standard regarding general sexuality may be at play here. Homosexual behavior for women is less tolerated, probably because virtuous women express their sexuality only with their husbands.

Overall, most contemporary Thais view heterosexuality as the norm; homosexuality is seen as a deviance or an unnatural act, often resulting from one's bad *karma* or the lack of merit in past lives. To the more superstitious Thais, homosexual acts, which are an aberration from "how nature intends," are punishable by animistic powers. Contemporary Thais still express their disapproval of homosexuality by saying, often blithely, that "lightning will strike" those who engage in sex with a person of the same gender. The educated Thais understand homosexuality in terms of mental problems or illness. Many think homosexuality is caused by problems in upbringing or parental characteristics (e.g., a domineering mother and a passive father), while others also attribute it to the child's oversocialization with the opposite gender, e.g., a boy spending too much time with his aunts, sisters, or female peers, or not having a father around as a male role model. This pathology model of homosexuality most likely originated in the Western psychiatric theories of sexuality which dominated Western medicine and psychology until the 1960s and 1970s. Many Thai physicians and psychologists still subscribe to these antiquated theories and remain impervious to new research findings or the American Psychiatric Association's declassification of homosexuality as a mental illness in 1974.

Buddhism is mostly silent on the topic of homosexuality. Despite some ambivalence toward homosexuality in many Buddhist cultures, Cabezón (1993) notes Buddhism only condemns homosexuality more for being an instance of sexuality rather than its same-gender sex. "The principal question for Buddhism has not been one of heterosexuality versus homosexuality, but one of sexuality versus celibacy" (p. 82).

Cabezón further notes that, as far as the laity are concerned, homosexuality is rarely mentioned as a transgression of the Third Precept in Buddhist texts and oral commentaries.

References to homosexuality have been found in the Buddhist canon and the *Jataka*, the stories of the Buddha's previous lives. Leonard Zwilling has noted that only in the *Vinaya*, the monastic discipline which forms one of the three sections of the Buddhist canon, is there mention of same-gender attraction and effeminacy in men. These instances were, according to Zwilling, "derogated much to the same degree as comparable heterosexual acts" (quoted in Cabezón 1993, 88). As for other sections of the Buddhist canon, John Garret Jones (cited in Cabezón 1993) has concluded that there is an implicit affirmation from the silence regarding homosexuality, and the silence is certainly not because of the lack of material.

Whereas the canon is silent about homosexuality, the *Jataka* literature, in which the previously mentioned tale of Prince Vessantara is embedded, is replete with sentiments about same-gender affection. One example can be found in the eloquent past-life stories of the Buddha and his disciple and attendant, Ananda. In one scenario, the Buddha and Ananda are depicted as two deer who "always went about together . . . ruminating and cuddling together, very happy, head to head, nozzle to nozzle, horn to horn." In another story, a serpent king who falls in love with Ananda "encircled the ascetic with snakes folds, and embraced him, with his great hood upon his head; and there he lay a little, till his affection was satisfied" (Jones 1979, quoted in Cabezón 1993, 89). These examples are but a few of many instances which articulate same-gender affection in the context of friendships between men in the *Jatakas*. Considering the enormous number of warnings about the dangers of heterosexual relationships, Cabezón argues that the absence of warning about same-gender relationship is remarkable. It suggests that the attitude toward homosexuality in the Indian *Jataka* texts is one of acceptance, and occasionally even a eulogy, of these feelings.

Allyn (1991) cites yet another Buddhist story, possibly a folk version, told on Thai radio about a male disciple who had fallen in love with the Buddha. The disciple expresses admiration for the Buddha's beauty. The Buddha responded to these acts of admiration by a gentle reminder of the body's impermanence, a likely response for a female admirer as well. Taken together with the analysis of the canon and the *Jataka* tales, this story illustrates Buddhism's neutral position on the issue of homosexuality. Nevertheless, it should be noted that some negative attitudes can be found in the Buddhist practice today. For example, some Thai people have heard that a man who acknowledges his homosexuality will be denied Buddhist ordination, although such instances may have been very rare or never enforced.

In contrast to the neutral position of Buddhism, anti-homosexual attitudes are quite common among Thai people. Chompootaweep and colleagues (1991) found that 75% of both male and female adolescents reported negative attitudes toward homosexuality. In addition to these disapproving attitudes, Thai people who have sex with the same gender also have other important considerations when they make sexual and relationship decisions. Thais are concerned about matters which would cause an individual or family to lose face, and maintaining relationships with their family is of an extreme importance. To reveal one's homosexual orientation to one's parents would, in a sense, violate the Third Precept of Buddhism, and this has caused many Thai gays and lesbians to hide their homosexuality from their parents for fear of causing them sorrow (Allyn 1991). On the other hand, what an individual does in privacy is less of a concern. Thus, a person's homosexual sex, *per se*, may be easier for his or her family than other more visible features, such as long-term same-gender relationships (Jackson 1989) or coming out as an openly gay or lesbian person.

The fact that same-gender sex is less stigmatized than the public disclosure of this behavior deserves some discussion. Same-gender sexual experience does not necessarily carry the assumption of homosexuality or a homosexual identity in Thailand (Sittitrai, Brown, & Virulak 1991). There are no laws prohibiting homosexual behavior (Jackson 1989). On the other hand, the social pressure to be in conformity with the expectations of family and culture is extremely intense. Indeed, these sanctions may have a stronger effect than religious or legal sanctions. A public statement of homosexual identity would violate two important values of Thai culture: harmony—not to confront disagreements or conflicts—and the great value placed upon preservation of family units and preserving lineage through marriage and procreation. Allyn (1991) also contends that the anti-homosexual attitudes in the Thai society are primarily the discrimination against the feminine *kathoey* (see Section 7, Gender Diversity and Transgender Issues) who, according to stereotype, display overt and loud gender-atypical social manners.

## B. Social Constructions of Sexual Orientation in Thailand

The labels homosexual, bisexual, and heterosexual are Western constructs and do not exactly fit the traditional social constructions in Thailand. Assuming a gay or bisexual identity is also a new, if not foreign, concept; for example, there is no translation or the equivalent Thai word for "gay," and as of 1996, the construct "sexual orientation" had not been translated even for academic use. In the past few decades, Thai people have increasingly used the English words "gay" and "lesbian" in both the mainstream and academic contexts. The terms "homo" and "homosexual" are also used. Conventionally, the most widely used term for "homosexual" was an extremely obscure euphemism *len phuean*, roughly translated as "playing with friends." Another popular usage employs a literary analogy, *mai paa deow kan*, meaning "trees in the same forest" (Allyn 1991). The now-rare term *lakka-phayt*, roughly translated to "sexual perversion" in English, was sometimes used to describe homosexuality within the medical context, therefore illustrating the past influence of Western psychiatry.

The technical terms "heterosexual" and "homosexual" were transliterated into Thai 20 or 30 years ago for academic purposes. The term for "heterosexual" was *rug taang phayt*, meaning "loving the different gender" and the term for "homosexual" was *rug ruam phayt*, meaning "loving the same gender." This might indicate that the Thai construct of loving another is inseparable from eroticizing another. By the same logic, bisexuality was subsequently translated to *rug song phayt*, meaning "loving two genders." However, the directly borrowed term "bisexual" and its shortened derivative, *bai*, are more popular and have been part of the Thai sexual vocabulary of late.

More recently, with influences from Western cultures, the concepts of homosexuality and sexual orientation have infiltrated the Thai thinking. These concepts quickly became popularized and transformed to fit the indigenous constructs (see also Section 7, Gender Diversity and Transgender Issues, for the discussion of the indigenous concept of *kathoey*). In the following discussions, the Thai social constructions of homosexuality in men and women will be examined separately to maximize clarity. We realize that this approach has its own shortcomings, as male and female

homosexualities in most cultures are, conceptually and politically speaking, not discrete entities. However, much more has been written about male homosexuality in Thailand, and a discourse to conceptually bridge the parallel phenomena in men and women has yet to be made. There is still little evidence that the discussion about this construct in one gender can be generalized to the other.

## C. Homosexuality in Men

A small number of studies have attempted to find the prevalence of homosexual behavior in men. In a population-based study (Sittitrai et al. 1992), only 3.1% of the men reported having had sex with men and women, and 0.2% reported it with men exclusively. The authors of the study speculated that these statistics were an underestimation because of underreporting. Cohorts of military conscripts, comprised of men mostly age 21 from lower socioeconomic populations, have also shown varying rates of male-male sexual experience. Among the 1990 conscripts from northern Thailand (Nopkesorn et al. 1991), 26% reported having had sex with a man, 15% reported past anal intercourse with a man, and 12% reported sexual arousal in response to male nudes. In the 1992 conscripts from northern Thailand (Nopkesorn, Sweat et al. 1993), 14% reported having had at least one instance of insertive anal sex with a *kathoey* in their lifetimes, 3% with non-*kathoey* men, and 3% reported having had receptive anal sex. In another study of 2,047 military conscripts from northern Thailand (Beyrer, et al. 1995), 134 men (7%) reported having had sex with men; most of these men were also more likely to have higher numbers of female sexual partners than other men who had sex with women exclusively.

In Thai society today, men who have sex with men are either *gay king* or *gay queen*: A *gay king* is a man who plays the insertive role in sex, whereas a *gay queen* takes a passive and receptive role in sex (Allyn 1991). Versatility in sexual behavior is obviously not a traditional construct, and the gender dichotomy pervades the Thai conceptualization of sex between men. Gender dimorphism also necessitates that the society views homosexuality in reference to the fundamental genders of male and female. Also, cross-gendered manners and behavior are seen as indicating the essence of homosexuality in a person (other terms for male homosexuality related to cross-gendered behaviors will be discussed in Section 7, Gender Diversity and Transgender Issues). *Gay queens* are assumed to have feminine characteristics, and are therefore, "true homosexuals." On the other hand, *gay kings*, stereotyped as male-acting and male-appearing, are seen as less likely to be "permanently" homosexual. Thai people think that *gay kings* are simply heterosexual men going through a phrase of sexual experimentation with other men. *Gay kings* are also variously referred to as "100% male" (*phuu-chaai roi poe-sen*) and "a complete man" (*phuu-chaai tem tua*) (Jackson 1989), which reflects the belief that the insertive homosexual sex act does not jeopardize one's masculinity. The idea that *gay kings* are confused or adventurous heterosexuals can be seen in many Thai movies and fiction about gay relationships with a tragic ending, when the *gay king* hero leaves a devastated *gay queen* to marry a woman. Moreover, the Thai myth of men's boundless sexuality states that "a real man" (i.e., real heterosexual) can derive sexual pleasure from anyone, regardless of gender. The playful term for bisexual men, *suea bai* (meaning "bisexual tiger") connotes this admiration of bisexual men's sexual vigor (Allyn 1991). Bisexual behavior, therefore, is seen as an attribute of *gay kings*, bisexual men, and "indiscriminate" heterosexual men alike.

Actual data on sexual behavior confirm the fluidity of sex between men in Thailand as implied by the classification above. For example, military conscripts who reported same-gender sexual behavior were more likely to be married, have girlfriends, and visit female sex partners more often than their counterparts who have had sex with women exclusively (Beyrer et al. 1995). Northeastern men recruited through the social network of men who had sex with men demonstrated equally complicated behaviors. Their reported sex acts covered a whole gamut of insertive and receptive intercourse, both oral and anal; their sexual partners included both genders of commercial sex workers, casual partners, and lovers (Sittitrai, Brown, & Sakondhavat 1993).

Primary affectional and sexual relationships between men are quite common, although these relationships are not akin to the Western concept of the gay couple. These relationships may be of very short duration, without much long-term commitment, and without much social or familial recognition. There are distinct problems maintaining homosexual relationships. First, because long-term relationships by nature end up being more public, they invite more public scrutiny and negative sanction. Second, the same-sex relationships would interfere with what the heterosexist norm expects of a man: to get married to a woman and have children. Finally, there are no models for same-sex relationships within Thai culture. The only role models would come from *farang* (Westerners), but their codes of conduct would not necessarily work in the Thai culture. This lack of role models and solutions for the Thai male couples has caused much jealousy and conflicts around infidelity, creating many heartaches and failed relationships (Jackson 1989). For many other couples, however, male romantic and sexual relationships adhere closely to the heterosexual model of sex roles: in fact, a *gay king* almost always pairs with a *gay queen*, and Thais find it difficult to comprehend if two *gay kings* or two *gay queens* would settle down together. Following the traditional Thai heterosexual relationship which prescribes monogamy in the women and sexual freedom in the men, *gay kings* also have a tendency to seek out sexual pleasures outside their relationship with a *gay queen*.

In reaching "gay men," *gay kings*, *gay queens*, and *kathoey* for HIV prevention, there is an effort in Thai society to organize and empower these individuals. This attempt follows HIV-prevention strategies from Western cultures. Local activists and international agencies in Thailand are fostering an adoption of the gay-identity concept to identify, reach, and empower men who have sex with men, in an effort to prevent the spread of HIV among them and their partners, both male and female. There remains an ethical question regarding the cultural imperialism of the West, which is imposing Western-constructed identities on a culture which has maintained different constructs of sexual orientation and sexual behavior. Examination of Thai and other cultures which have diverse constructs of sexual orientation has challenged the universality of categories of sexual orientation adopted by the West. This has forced HIV-prevention campaigns in the West to employ strategies which take into account the fact that not all segments of society identify themselves as gay, straight, or bisexual. One example of such attempts is to identify the population of interest based on their sexual behavior (e.g., "men who have sex with men" or "men who have sex with both men and women"), instead of selecting them by their "risk group" or "gay" or "bisexual" self-identity. Hopefully, the cultural exchange will lead to greater understanding of homosexuality and the promotion of sexual health among those individuals who engage in same-gender sex in any society (Coleman 1996).

Regarding the gay identity in Thailand, there has been a rapid development since the mid-1980s of a gay identity with a Thai twist. Meanwhile, gay enterprising and political activities began to thrive in Bangkok and other big cities. Until the late 1980s, the only regular media coverage on homosexuality was an advice column in the widely popular tabloid *Plaek* ("Strange") titled *Chiiwit Sao Chao Gay* ("The Sad Lives of Gays") in which Go Paaknaam, a straight-identified columnist, published letters about sexual and relationship problems from men who have sex with men (Allyn 1991). In contrast to the previous coverage which tended to be rare and eccentric, in recent years Thailand has seen a proliferation of magazines in the format of erotica for gay men. In addition to erotica, these publications also provide an avenue for men to meet through personal advertisements, as well as the new forum for exchanging social and political views. More social networks have been formed, often composed of previously isolated gay men, many of whom do not have access to or participate in the thriving gay bar scenes in big cities. A more solidified yet multifaceted gay identity has slowly evolved as Thai men participate in the discourse on their sexuality through these publications. In the meantime, Thai mainstream media, especially newspaper and magazines, have increased accurate representations of gay life, as well as progressive treatises on homosexuality, although sensationalistic coverage is still common.

In addition, entertainment businesses for gay men have flourished in big cities. A variety of gay restaurants and pubs have been opened, with and without *deg off* ("off-boys," or male sex workers), providing places for leisure, sex, and socialization. Bangkok sports one of the world's most famous gay saunas (bathhouses). Men in these surroundings are motivated not only by a bit of the Thai *sanuk* (fun, pleasure, and enjoyment), but also the camaraderie and the search for a relationship partner (Allyn 1991). These new developments represent a remarkable difference in how men who have sex with men meet one another today; in the past, these encounters were non-public, secretive and often involved commercial sex workers. Instead, the thriving of Bangkok gay scenes allows men who have sex with men to have more continuity between their sexual activities, their social life, and their sexual identity. As Allyn notes: "Love stories were being made here, most of them bittersweet ones. Gay Thai men have perhaps added the key ingredient to the development of a gay identity: love" (p. 157). Allyn further notes that, "Over the past two decades, superficial aspects of Western, particularly American gay culture, have been imported to a certain degree but, as the kingdom traditionally has done, by adaptation, not adoption" (p. 158).

One example of such an adaptation is the recent concept of *kulagay* invented by the Thai gay media, although it is still not widely in use. As in *kulasatrii*, *kula* being "virtuous" or "decent," a *kulagay* is a virtuous Thai gay man who adheres to traditional Thai values, contributes to society, and rejects the Thai stereotypes of the *kathoey* and promiscuity (Allyn 1991). The invention of the *kulagay* identity reflects the movement's attempt to assimilate homosexuality into the social fabric of Thai society by way of deference to the traditional values.

In 1981, a "gay rights" organization called Chaai Chawb Chaai (men liking men) was established, but was disbanded shortly thereafter because there was no evidence of discrimination (Allyn 1991). In 1989, two organizations were formed in response to the HIV epidemic: Fraternity for AIDS Cessation in Thailand (FACT), and Gay Entrepreneurs Association of Thailand (GEAT). GEAT is made up of Bangkok bar owners and is concerned with issues of business. After great success from their educational theater group, the White Line, FACT also developed a subsidiary group called FACT Friends, which began weekly support groups for the many Thai gay men who were tired of the commercial gay scene.

By 1991, FACT was awarded international grants and transformed from a grassroots volunteer organization to a foundation with a formal structure (Allyn 1991).

Despite the many developments of a gay identity in Thailand, the average Thai gay man lives his gay life separately from the other parts of his life. Allyn (1991) speculates that this way of life is sufficient for many, as many Thai gay men have expressed satisfaction. Allyn further suggests that Thai people are trained since childhood to accept their lot in life. Similar to the way the perceived transience of gender helps many Thai women to accept their role (see Section 1, Basic Sexological Premises), Thai gay men perhaps think that their sexual orientation is only one of the many sufferings a being faces in different incarnations. Therefore, a private sex life and the constraint of being a "model Thai" may not be fraught with as much psychological pain as his Western counterparts might experience. To date, there is no evidence that gay men in Thailand are more psychologically distressed than heterosexual men.

### D. Homosexuality in Women

There is an extreme paucity of information on women who have sex with women. Adopted several decades ago, the term "lesbian" is now recognized by most Thai people as describing love or sex between women, along with its derivatives *ael bii* (Thai acronym for "L.B.") and *bian*, which could be used pejoratively or euphemistically. Also, a rather vulgar slang *tii ching*, or "playing [small, paired] cymbals," compares two vaginas in lesbian sex with a pair of opposing, identical concave musical instruments. In the past decade, other terms for lesbianism have come into vogue. Paralleling the *gay king-gay queen* dichotomy in male homosexuality, lesbians are categorized into *thom* (derived from "tomboy") and *dii* (short for "lady"), mostly based on their social manners and appearances. The *thom* women, with the masculine appearance, are assumed to have a dominant role in the relationship. Women who are *dii*, on the other hand, are feminine looking and passive in gender role. Because of the extreme popularity of these terms, most Thais now refer to lesbianism (female homosexuality) as "women being *thom-dii*."

Thai people are quite confused by the feminine *dii* women because they are indistinguishable from the typical Thai women in their social manners. Most Thais speculate that *dii* women will eventually grow out of their phase of experimentation or confusion, and commit to a relationship with a man (much as they think of the *gay king* men). On the other hand, the masculine *thom* women are seen by Thais as women who want to be a man, much as feminine homosexual men are assumed to want to be a woman. Androgynous behavior in women, although not traditionally praised, has been relatively tolerated in adolescents. Popular fiction has portrayed a number of female protagonists who have "tomboy" demeanor: bold, assertive, and boyishly naughty, while nonchalant and unaware of their feminine attractiveness hidden inside. Nevertheless, these characters are unmistakably heterosexual, as there is never any depiction of homoeroticism or lesbian character in the lives of these tomboys. As a rule, these young heroines always outgrow their tomboy phase as they are transformed into a "fully grown woman" by their first love with a man whom they marry at the end of the story.

Prior to the late 1980s, Thai people in general seemed to show little awareness of the existence of love and sex between women. In the 1980s, a tabloid ran an advice column for lesbians, *Go Sa Yaang*, by a straight man, Go Paaknaam, following the popularity of his column for gay men (Allyn 1991). Yet, lesbian women never had erotic publications or enterprises as these businesses began to flourish for gay

men. However, sex and love between women started to come into public attention in the late 1980s and early 1990s. As more and more young women have shown up in public looking like pairs of a *thom* and a *dii*, displaying public intimacy slightly beyond the usual confines of peer manners, the media have called it an epidemic of *thom-dii-ism*. Much anxiety and concerns have been expressed by parents and the media regarding this increased visibility of lesbianism. Many conservatives search for a cause of lesbianism in the modern or Western values, claiming that women today are taught to strive for power and autonomy. For these conservatives, women are attracted to other women because they have become more like men. Others have blamed androgynous women in the Thai pop culture for modeling gender-atypical behavior and, in turn, inducing lesbian interests among the adoring young fans.

Sensationalistic media and conservatives aside, women who love (and have sex with) women have recently emerged in Thai society with an agenda to forge ahead with a Thai lesbian identity in their own right. Anjaree is a new organization for Thai lesbian women which came into public attention in 1992. The name of the organization comes from merging two words, *anya* and *jaree*, to denote "a different path" (Otaganonta 1995). Aside from publishing a newsletter, *Anjaree Sarn*, the organization also played a key role in setting up the Asian Lesbian Network, which hosted its first meeting in 1990 in Bangkok. This initiative earned Anjaree the Filipa de Sausa Award, presented by the International Gay and Lesbian Rights Commission based in New York, which is given to individuals and groups that take initiatives to promote the rights of sexual minorities. One of the group's founders states in a *Bangkok Post* interview:

> I don't think people need to identify themselves as heterosexuals or homosexuals. American society places much importance on defining oneself as this or that, but in Thailand, sexual orientation has never been a major part of self identity. But we are aware of the obstacles that Thai lesbians face. That's why we have to assert ourselves in this way. Still there is no need for us to identify ourselves only as lesbians. (Otaganonta 1995, 36)

As evident in the discussions about homosexuality in men and women above, Western constructions of homosexuality have had inevitable influences in the ways contemporary Thais understand sex and love between people of the same gender. The Thai vocabulary for homosexuality, lesbian, gay, *gay king*, *gay queen*, *thom*, *dii*, all had their origin in the English language. Alternative to the simplistic notion that Thai people are emulating Western sexuality, we argue that Thai people might have found that their indigenous constructions could no longer explain or fit their observations of sexual phenomena. In an attempt to find satisfactory explanations, Thai people have found plausible frameworks in the Western paradigm of sexual orientation and homosexuality which complements their indigenous construction. In the following section, we turn to a review of the *kathoey*, which was possibly the only indigenous social construction of non-heterosexuality in Thailand before the arrival of the Western paradigm.

### 7. Gender Diversity and Transgender Issues

As noted in the previous section, traditional Thai sexuality did not reflect clear distinctions between homosexuality, bisexuality, and heterosexuality as explicitly drawn by Western cultures. Rather, the most salient of all sexual distinctions is the bipolarity of gender: A person is either a man or a woman. Based on these two fundamental male and female genders, the *kathoey* exists as another gender identity in the Thai society. Roughly equivalent to the English term "hermaphrodite," *kathoey* (pronounced "ka-toey") has been defined as a "person or animal of which the sex is indeterminate" in the Thai-English dictionary (McFarland 1982). Despite such a medical connotation, *kathoey* has been used, at least in the last several decades, to describe a biologically male person who has sex with men, therefore covering a gamut of male homosexualities.

The use of the term *kathoey* to describe male homosexualities, however, has slowly given way to the more contemporary *gay* and its derivatives. Today, *kathoey* mostly refers to men who have feminine social behaviors, without much specific reference to their biological gender or sexual behavior. Being associated with feminine characters and other stereotypes (see below), the term is considered derogatory by Thai gay men today, many of whom adamantly distinguish themselves from *kathoey*. Other derogatory slang words, applied to both gay men and *kathoey*, are *tut* and *tutsii* (the latter from the title of an American movie, *Tootsie*, starring cross-dressed Dustin Hoffman), which, because their pronunciations are close to the derogatory Thai word for "ass," suggest anal intercourse (Jackson 1997; Nanda 2000).

As implied in the usage today, a *kathoey* is a man who sees himself more as a woman and often dresses, to varying degrees, as a women, and is likely to have sex with men. Some take estrogens and progesterone to facilitate breast development and other body transformations. A few will undergo surgical sex-reassignment surgery. This surgery is well known and available in Thailand, although it is extremely expensive by Thai standards. In Western conceptualization, the *kathoey* may be considered either effeminate homosexual men, transvestites, or pre- or post-operative transsexuals, none of which is readily applicable to the traditional construction of sexuality in Thailand. Thai people mainly see the *kathoey* as either the "third gender," or a combination of the male and female genders. Alternatively, they are also seen as a female gender, but of the "other" variety, as reflected in a synonym *ying praphayt song*, meaning "women of the second kind."

These understandings of the *kathoey* suggest that Thai people have traditionally tried to make sense of this phenomenon in fundamental male-female terms. As a result, the Thai interpretations of the *kathoey* have been within the confines of the gender bipolarity. Nevertheless, the *kathoey* have been a well-known category in the sexual and gender typology of the Thai culture. Children and adults can often identify at least one *kathoey* in every village or school. Despite their subtle "outcast" status, the village *kathoey* are often given duties in local festivities and ceremonies, mostly in female-typical roles such as floral arrangements or food preparation. The *kathoey* seem to have adopted the "nurturer" role prescribed to Theravada women, and ideas of female pollution (e.g., the touch taboo and fear of menstruation) are extended to the *kathoey* as well. Social discrimination varies in degrees, ranging from hostile animosity to stereotypic assumptions. Some of the assumptions are based on the idea that the *kathoey* are unnatural, a result of poor *karma* from past lives; other assumptions are typical of generalizations about women as a whole.

To illustrate the stereotype, the Thai cinema and contemporary literature usually dramatize the *kathoey* as highly histrionic in gestures, emotionally unstable, subject to men's abandonment, and thus leading lives of bitterness, loneliness, suicides, or promiscuity. Although there are plenty of *kathoey* who hold other professions, stereotype predicates that many *kathoey* become street sex workers or small-time criminals, and others become beauticians, fashion designers,

hairdressers, florists, artists, or entertainers (Allyn 1991). A few comedians and media personalities have been publicly known for their *kathoey* sensibilities and camp humor, while other *kathoey* celebrities have caused public sensations by their flamboyance or eccentricities. Many *kathoey* have healthy long-term relationships with men, although Jackson (1989) has noted the stereotype of *kathoey* providing financial support to young men with whom they are in a romantic relationship. This "kept boy" tradition is an interesting reverse of the minor wife tradition in straight men. Stereotype notwithstanding, the image of *kathoey* as a resourceful member of the community and a benefactor of young men is remarkably more positive than the Western images that most cross-gendered individuals are street transsexuals who live marginalized lives in the underworld of drugs and prostitution. In Thailand, *kathoey* find each other or married women for social support and, despite a degree of discrimination from the new gay-identified men, they are well accepted into the contemporary gay scenes.

Because for most Thais, the concepts of gay and *kathoey* are not clearly distinguished from one another, the stereotypic features of the *kathoey* are thought to be also attributes of gay men, particular *gay queens*. Some Thai men who have sex with men alternately refer to themselves as gay for political reasons, and *kathoey* for self-deprecating humor. These images of the *kathoey* (and to a lesser degree, "gay men") in the Thai society bare striking similarities to the stereotyped lives of gay men and drag queens in Western societies before the gay liberation movement in the late 1960s and early 1970s. Interestingly, the American play, *The Boys in the Band* by Mart Crowley, was translated to the Thai context in the late 1980s and became an immensely popular show. The appreciation that the mainstream audience had for the images of *kathoey* and gay men—as individuals struggling with societal pressure and self-hatred—sums up the overall social climate toward homosexuality today: characterized by sympathy, fascination, and curiosity, yet riddled with ambivalence and stereotyping.

Another cross-gendered phenomenon is found primarily in women in the cults of the ancestral spirits (*phii*) in northern Thailand (see also Manderson 1992). Members of the *phii* cults believe that ancestral guardian spirits are passed on matrilineally to young women in order to maintain health, harmony, and well-being in the family. Certain women, by becoming "possessed" by the *phii*, serve as mediums for the spirits, and they are called *maa khii*. In their annual ritual, these women, and sometimes children, are possessed by their ancestral spirits and perform dances, which include displays of wild and rude behaviors (e.g., drinking, smoking Thai cigars, and shouting expletives and insults), as well as stereotypically masculine behaviors (e.g., wearing men's clothes and flirting and dancing with young women). However, because of their revered role as *maa khii*, many of these women are held in high esteem. Outside these rituals and performances, these women, most of whom are married to a man and hold respectable roles (e.g., healers and midwives) in their village community, return to their everyday behavior typical of the female gender. Although most of these women do not remember the specific events during the trance, they are well aware of the male characters they take on during the dances. In an interesting twist of role, these women hold positions of power, in contrast to the general patriarchal Thai society and the male domination in Buddhism.

While most *maa khii* are women, a noticeable minority are male, and many are also *kathoey*. We have observed that the *maa khii* who are *kathoey* also enjoy a more-revered place in the community, overcoming some of the ordinary stigma they would otherwise experience. During the spiritual dance (*fawn phii*), the mediums who are *kathoey*, like their female counterparts, exhibit male-stereotypical behavior remarkably different from their own manners during ordinary circumstances.

## 8. Significant Unconventional Sexual Behaviors

### A. Coercive Sex

As discussed earlier in Section 1B, Basic Sexological Premises, Romance, Love, and Marriage, the Third Precept of Buddhism professes to refrain from sexual misconduct, mostly understood to refer to adultery, rape, sexual abuse of children, and careless sexual activities that result in the harm to others. Rape is a criminal offense but the law is rarely enforced. However, rape crime reports are abundant in mainstream and tabloid journalism, often written in a sensational and graphic style which seems designed to titillate the reader. No data exist regarding the extent of the problem. In a study of northern Thai men conscripted to the army in 1990 (Nopkesorn et al. 1991), 5% of the 21-year-old men reported having forced or coerced a woman for sex. The incidence of incest is not known. These matters are rarely discussed or reported.

Young men in Ford and Kittisuksathit's focus groups (1994) made references to the use of violence in order to force women to acquiesce to intercourse. They rationalized that coercion occurred when their sexual desire was provoked by women beyond self-control, and it was mostly directed to women in casual encounters not their *fans*. Numerous folk music and literature provide a cultural script for courtship and sexual persuasion, as apparent in this study. Men see that intercourse involves prior steps of cunning moves, social pressuring, and physical advances, whereas women see intercourse in terms of "submission" or "surrender." Aside from the cultural script, men perhaps generalize from their own experiences of erotic stimulation and ejaculation to the larger patterns of male sexuality. They, therefore, perceive that sexual arousal in men, once initiated, takes its own course and is not subject to control, as characterized by the term *naa meued*, or a state of "black-out" from lust.

Social support for women who have been raped or victimized by incest is not widely available. Consistent with the men's rationalization that they are provoked beyond control, a woman is sometimes viewed as provoking rape because of her appearance (e.g., wearing a provocative dress) or her social behavior (e.g., drinking or frequenting potentially unsafe places). Consequently, Thai parents teach their girls not to dress improperly, and not to go alone to unfamiliar places in order to avoid being raped, as if rape is a price one pays for violating the code of *kulasatrii*. Others, following the cultural script of courtship and sex, see rape as an obscure area, where men's coercion and women's surrendering cannot be clearly differentiated. Women who have been raped or experienced incest in Thailand are socially stigmatized based on these attitudes, in addition to the perception that the woman is flawed because she has been "violated." Understandably, women or their families rarely report these incidents.

### B. Prostitution—Commercial Sex

Although the topic of commercial sex appears under the general section of unconventional behaviors, it should be noted that this phenomenon is not considered unconventional in Thailand. However, the topic deserves a focus separate from the general patterns of sexuality as already covered in the sections on adolescent and adult sexual behaviors (Sections 5A and 5B, Interpersonal Heterosexual Behaviors, Adolescent Sexual Behavior and Adult Sexual Behavior). In our discussion of this topic, we use the more value-neutral terms, such as "sex worker" and "commercial sex," while reserving the terms "prostitute" and "prostitution" for the contexts which require expression of sociocultural values.

### History and Current Situations of Commercial Sex in Thailand

Among Thai people, there is a general attitude that prostitution has always been, and will always be, a part of the social fabric of Thailand. This attitude is primarily rationalized by the prevailing myth that men have a greater sexual desire than women. The endorsement of prostitution does not come from men only; a majority of Thai women, especially of the upper and middle classes, readily agree with this logic. In college-level sexuality education courses, female students openly say that prostitution exists to protect "good women" from being raped. Married women from northern Thai rural villages talk in focus groups about their preference for their husbands to seek out sex workers (given a condom is used) rather than taking on a minor wife. Reflecting the general societal attitudes, the married women believe that prostitution is a practical solution for married men whose greater sexual demand cannot be met by their wives (Dumronggittigule et al. 1995).

Thailand is well known throughout the world for its highly organized and diverse commercial sex businesses. Many tourists visit Thailand for this special interest, although many others are obviously drawn by the culture and nature of Thailand, as well as the charming hospitality of Thai people. Tourism caters to men seeking sex in Thailand, and this aspect, which most Thais are not proud of, has been openly acknowledged and advertised. Through the assistance of tour guides or hotel services, commercial sex is available to any male tourist as it is for Thai men. Even outside of Thailand, a large number of Thai sex workers have been working in European countries and Japan since the 1980s; an estimate of 70,000 Thai women are working in commercial sex in Japan alone (Hornblower 1993).

Since the abolition of slavery in 1905, brothels have proliferated steadily and eventually became commonplace throughout the country. The sex industry proliferated during the Vietnam War in the 1960s and 1970s. As military bases of the United States of America were built up in Thailand, many women were induced into the entertainment and sex businesses for American servicemen. When the war ended in 1976, tourism began to grow and has become the largest source of foreign income. Meanwhile, commercial sex became an inevitable part of the tourist attraction (Limanonda 1993).

Prostitution became technically illegal in 1960 from the United Nations' pressure (Brinkmann 1992). In 1966, the Entertainment Places Act led to a plethora of new businesses which served as fronts for commercial sex, such as erotic massage parlors, bars, nightclubs, coffee shops, and barber shops (Manderson 1992). Ironically, although prostitution is illegal, these sex businesses often have government or police officials among their owners. In other cases, these officials are paid by the establishment owners to avoid enforcing the law (Brinkmann 1992). Subsequent attempts from the Thai government to eradicate prostitution have occurred over the years, most notably in 1981 and 1982, but all have been quickly abandoned (Rojanapithayakorn & Hanenberg 1996). Instead, the Thai government has focused on controlling sexually transmitted diseases (STDs) among sex workers using the police authorities and the structure of public-health services (see below).

The number of commercial sex workers in Thailand was estimated to be around 500,000 to 700,000 in 1980 (Thepanom Muangman, Public Health Faculty, Mahidol University;

cited in Keyes 1984). The clientele of these sex workers have been estimated to be about 80% Thai (data cited in Manderson 1992). Most sex workers in rural and urban areas work in establishments such as brothels, restaurants, bars, or erotic massage parlors, all of which are under the management of men. "Direct" sex workers, or those who have sex with their clients on the premises, such as in brothels or erotic cafes, usually charge lower fees and, therefore, are popular among working-class and younger men. "Indirect" sex workers work under the premise of selling other services, such as massage or dancing, with the option to have sex with clients who offer to *off* them (or take them out) for an additional sum or fee. The fee for "direct" sex workers varies from 50 baht (US$2.00) to 500 baht (US$20.00), while that of "indirect" sex workers varies from 500 baht (US$20.00) to several thousands of baht (Weniger et al. 1991).

The demographic and socioeconomic characteristics of female sex workers have been reported in a study of 800 female sex workers from two provinces, one in the north and another in the south (van Griensven, Limanonda, et al. 1995). Only 1% of the women reported that they were younger than 16 years of age, and 11% reported starting working in commercial sex before the age of 16. The national origin was Thai for 85% of the women, with 8% Burmese and 1% Chinese, and 6% from a northern hill tribe. Most of the women, 80%, were from rural areas, while 89% had moved directly from their village of origin to an urban area primarily to work as sex workers. Most had low levels of education: 87% completed less than seven grades of school and 25% could not read or write.

## [The Complexity of Thai Commercial Sex

RYAN BISHOP and LILLIAN S. ROBINSON

[*Comment 2003*: Commercial sex in Thailand provides a complex set of complementary and conflicting intra- and international forces, systems, and trajectories, constituting what might be called a political economy of desire in the second half of the 20th century and beyond, but relying upon a much longer institutional, intellectual, and representational tradition.

[For commercial sex within the kingdom catering to Thai nationals, there is an equally complex set of practices in play, including regional and racial typologies and hierarchies. The indigenous sex industry is clearly much larger than the international sex industry in terms of bodies serving and serviced, although not in terms of revenue generated or circulated.

[Some commentators, including Truong (1990), Hill (1993), and Brock and Thistlethwaite (1996) maintain that Buddhism plays a large role in perpetuating male dominance in Thai culture, thus making it easier for a sex industry to develop and subjugate women. But virtually all of the world's major religions, especially the three Jerusalemic monotheistic ones, include patriarchal power structures that do not necessarily lead to the establishment of prostitution as a major industry, and few other Buddhist societies have developed this industry to the extent that Thailand has. Further, despite allegations to the contrary, Therevada Buddhism as practiced and institutionalized in Thailand explicitly prohibits the practice of prostitution.

[We argue that international sex tourism in Thailand is a complex industry that brings together Cold War geopolitical strategies, international banks, alienated, if comparatively privileged workers from around the globe, and sex workers in girlie bars to constitute the linchpin of a $5-billion-a-year industry. The discussion that follows, drawn from our fieldwork in Thailand, concentrates solely on the emergence of international sex tourism to Thailand, which has become a synecdoche for prostitution itself in interna-

tional consciousness (Bishop & Robinson 1998, 1999a, 1999b, 2002a, 2002b).

[Sex tourism to Thailand arose in a context informed by the availability in the First World of paid and in some cases lengthy holiday time and, because of the promotion of mass tourism, the growing affordability of foreign travel for those with a modest amount of discretionary income. Unlike sex tourism sites in Africa and the Caribbean, where sun, sand, and, in the former case, safaris preceded sex in the chronology of seductive sibilants, in Thailand the sex preceded the tourism. Building upon the vast sex industry serving a local clientele, there emerged a parallel set of institutions tailored to the needs and desires of U.S. and other foreign servicemen present during the Vietnam War period. These included men stationed at the enormous American airbases in Thailand itself, as well as the thousands who were rotated in each week from the combat zone for R&R, rest and recreation. Providing for the needs of troops in the country and those on leave from the front naturally entailed offering accommodations, food and drink, souvenirs of all sorts, and nonsexual entertainment facilities along with sex, all of which assumed significant weight within the Thai economy.

[The establishment in 1967 of U.S. government contracts with Thailand, along with several other sites, to provide R&R for the leisure time of foreign troops clearly brings together key notions of labor, masculinity, and sexuality. There is, after all, no job traditionally reserved to men that is more structured around the body, in its existential dimension, than the military, nor any in whose performance notions of masculinity and male sexuality are more openly deployed to manipulate the men doing the job. From the commonplace that army service will "make a man" of the boy joining up, through training by means of gendered and sexualized insults to the structures of command and compliance, the military relies on a definition of the person-gendered male. For this reason, when the combat soldier's perquisites on the job include opportunities for sexual release in the form of camp followers, military brothels, sanctioned rape, or leaves spent in tolerated red-light districts, that release is understood as an integral part of his functioning on the job.

[In Thailand during the Indochina (Vietnam) War, a new sexual institution, the go-go or dance bar, sprang up to supplement traditional bordellos, massage parlors, sexual exhibitions, and "pickup" bars. These dance bars, which have become permanent fixtures in the commercial sex zones of Bangkok and the beach resorts, were modeled, superficially at least, on similar establishments in North America—featuring the same strobe lights, 30-year-old rock music, dancers on display, and promise of sexual encounters. The chief difference is that, instead of one or two dancers on platforms suspended overhead, the Thai bars feature dozens of dancers on a stage, performing with the crotch at eye level, and virtually no female customers. So, instead of the sexual opportunities being consensual arrangements between customers, it is the dancers who also offer that form of entertainment. The Sexual Revolution enacted in late-1960s America is thus parodied—or exposed—in its Bangkok offshoots.

[Typically, there are so many entertainers working on any given night, that each can dance for only a couple of cuts on the tape before being cycled offstage. The message is about sexual abundance. It is while onstage, wearing a button with her identifying number, that a performer is likeliest to catch the eye of a potential customer, who can order her from the waitress along with his beer. When this happens, she steps down and joins him, and he orders a "lady drink" (nonalcoholic) for her. They will fool around for a while, joking and touching, before coming to an agreement to have sex in a room onsite or at a hotel. If such an agreement is reached, the man pays the bar a fine for taking away a dancer, the amount he pays her directly being understood as a tip. If their relationship is limited to a drink or two, she will rejoin the dancers waiting to go back on stage. The dancer gets some credit for having drinks bought for her, and is expected to go out with customers a minimum of twice a week.

[What happens sexually in these encounters tends to be fairly vanilla or mainstream vaginal and oral sex, with the exotic making its appearance in the erotic chiefly through the customers' sense of abundance and availability, as well as the comparatively low cost of sexual services. What Thai sex workers have to offer the foreign customer is a sense of readiness—indeed, eagerness—to serve sexually, assuring acceptance without the necessity of engaging anything in the transaction but cash, and without the possibility of rejection.

[As our use of the present tense suggests, the girlie bars survived the war that brought them into being. This is because, like the World War II military aircraft factories, they too were converted to civilian use. In 1971, while the Vietnam War continued to rage, Robert McNamara, President of the World Bank and, by no means incidentally, U.S. Secretary of Defense when the R&R contracts were signed, led a World Bank mission to Thailand. When highly placed officials in the Kingdom's governmental and financial classes expressed concern about what would happen to their country's economy once the foreign troops were gone, McNamara assigned a team of World Bank development experts to the problem, and their report, issued in 1975 as the last Americans left Vietnam, recommended that Thailand's path to economic development be through the establishment of a mass-tourism industry.

[That the recommended mass tourism would necessarily build on the infrastructure set up to entertain the troops—an infrastructure itself dependent on commercial sex—went without saying. Although the industry has grown enormously, with tourism replacing rice-export as the country's largest source of foreign exchange by the mid-1980s, the continuity is still apparent, as military R&R contracts were replaced by corporate ones covering oil-industry workers in all-male Middle Eastern environments, and corporate-incentive travel complemented appeals to individual men traveling on their own seeking sexual fulfillment through the commercial transaction. The customers' relation to the larger structures that institutionalize their sexuality parallels Thai peasant girls' need for an adequate livelihood and to create the political economy of desire that characterizes commercial sex in Thailand today. (*End of comment by R. Bishop and L. S. Robinson*)]

## Government Surveillance of Commercial Sex Workers

A system of monitoring sex workers has been in place because the government has long implicated them for the spread of STDs (Rojanapithayakorn & Hanenberg 1996). Most "direct" sex workers in Thailand are under the STD monitoring system, which the Department of Communicable Disease Control (DCDC) has adapted over a period of 40 years. There are hundreds of government STD/AIDS clinics all over Thailand, each keeping a logbook of its local commercial sex establishments. The logbook contains location of the businesses, and it is frequently updated with the help of STD patients who show up for services. The officers semiannually visit these establishments to assess the numbers of sex workers and other changes; their enumeration of establishments has been reported regularly since 1971.

In 1990, the Sentinel Surveillance reported that each sex worker had an average of two customers per night, with the mean of 2.6 for direct sex workers, and 1.4 for indirect sex workers (unpublished data, cited in Rojanapithayakorn & Hanenberg 1996). In 1994, the compiled lists of commercial sex establishments showed 37 different kinds of sex businesses, mostly concentrated in Bangkok and provincial towns. The report also showed there were on average 67 commercial sex establishments in most provinces, with an average of 663 female sex workers per province. The total number of sex workers who worked in listed establishments was approximately 67,000 in 1994. These numbers reflect sex workers who are under the surveillance system by the government.

Vithayasai and Vithayasai (1990) provided the first evidence that by 1988, HIV was already spreading among female sex workers and their customers in northern Thailand. Many other studies have consistently shown that female sex workers in the north have disproportionately higher rates of HIV infection than those in other parts of Thailand; brothel-based female sex workers were found to have an HIV incidence of 20 seroconversions per 100 person-years of follow-up (cited in Mastro & Limpakarnjanarat 1995). In 1994, the national median prevalence of HIV infection was 27% among brothel-based commercial sex workers (Division of Epidemiology, Thai Ministry of Public Health; data cited in Mastro & Limpakarnjanarat 1995).

Female sex workers have many barriers to having protected sex with their clients, for example, clients' insistence on not using condoms (Pramualratana, Podhisita, et al. 1993), lack of negotiation strategies (Brinkmann 1992), clients' healthy and attractive appearance and the sex workers' trust in "regular" acquainted clients (Wawer et al. 1996), and alcohol use by either the client or the sex workers (Mastro & Limpakarnjanarat 1995). However, this picture has changed dramatically by the mid-1990s, as the government's nationwide 100 Percent Condom Program came into effect. Whereas the 1989 survey of sex workers found that 14% of their sex acts were with a condom, the rate increased to over 90% in December 1994 (Rojanapithayakorn & Hanenberg 1996; see more discussion in Section 10B, HIV/AIDS).

### Male Commercial Sex Workers

The number of male sex workers in Thailand has been estimated to be approximately 5,000 to 8,000 (Brinkmann 1992), a number much smaller than the estimates of female sex workers. Although there are very few studies on male sex workers, a study has provided a glimpse of the demographics and sexual behavior of men who work in gay bars with commercial sex (Sittitrai, Phanuphak, et al. 1989). Many of these men, referred to in Thai as "business boys," stated that their primary sexual attraction was for women. They reported that their sexual behavior outside of the bars was predominately heterosexual and many had sex with female sex workers for sexual pleasure. Similar findings were found in the study of male commercial sex workers in northern Thailand: 58% of them described themselves as preferring female partners outside of work, and 14% of all men were married (Kunawararak et al. 1995).

At the beginning of the 1990s, male sex workers' HIV seroprevalence remained comparatively low compared to the alarmingly high rates in female sex workers, and this was hypothesized to be because of the male sex workers' use of condoms from early on in the HIV epidemic. However, recent findings can no longer sustain this optimism. In a recent study (Kunawararak et al. 1995) in which male sex workers were followed prospectively from 1989 to 1994, their HIV prevalence increased from 1.4% to 20%, with an overall incidence of 11.9 per 100 person-years, a rate considerably higher than those found in any other groups of Thai men.

Most sex workers in Thailand enter the commercial sex business in their late teens or early 20s, and many others in their early teens. The phenomenon of children in commercial sex will be the focus of the following section. However, it is important to note that much of the discussion about the sociocultural factors that lead young women and men into the sex industry will be applicable to both child, adolescent, and adult sex workers as well.

### Child Sex Workers

Much to the embarrassment of the Thai officials and activists alike, commercial sex involving children has become a tourist draw to Thailand. The HIV pandemic has fueled the demand of a great number of customers for younger sex workers because of their perceived likelihood of being free of HIV infection and other STDs. In many brothels, children as young as 10 and 11 are promoted by managers as "fresh" and "healthy," and the price is prorated accordingly. In contrast to this myth, child sex workers are reported to have very high HIV seroprevalence, above 50% according to Hiew (1992). New evidence suggests that women who start as sex workers at a young age might be more susceptible to HIV infection than those who start later, even after controlling for the effects from the work duration (van Griensven et al. 1995).

Children proven to be virgins are especially sought after by Chinese and Middle Eastern clients. There is an ancient Chinese myth that "deflowering" a virgin girl will revitalize the sexual potency of an old man and make him prosper in business (O'Grady 1992). Others are sexually attracted to children and adolescents because of their youthful qualities. Because child sex workers are accessible in Thailand, the country has become a tourist destination for those who believe in these myths, as well as pedophiles and ephebophiles around the world. In their own countries, they could be imprisoned, castrated, or killed for being caught having sex with a child. In Thailand, however, their sexual behaviors go unnoticed and only cost them some money.

In theory, sex with children is illegal in Thailand, but the law has rarely been enforced. More-recent external and internal pressures on the exploitation of children in commercial sex have led to some changes, but to what extent is unknown (see below). These pressures also have made it difficult to estimate the number of child sex workers in Thailand, as they are "going underground" (Boonchalaksi & Guest 1994). The estimates have ranged from 30,000 to 40,000 proposed by the Thai Red Cross and Sittitrai and Brown (1991), to 800,000 suggested by the Center for the Protection of Children's Rights. Estimates have been calculated based upon the ratio of child to adult sex workers, with children making up 20 to 40% of all the sex workers in Thailand. The most-scientific report available to us has estimated the prevalence of child sex workers to be 36,000 (Guest 1994). This number comprises 1.7% of the female population who are below the age of 18.

The buying and selling of child sex workers in Thailand is a lucrative business, as it is elsewhere in Asia (*End Child Prostitution in Asian Tourism*, ECPAT, 1992, cited in Kaime-Atterhog, Ard-Am, and Sethaput 1994). Girls and boys (albeit mostly girls) are brought into Thailand from the hill tribe areas, Myanmar (Burma), China, Kampuchea (Cambodia), and Laos (Friends of Women Foundation 1992). In addition, they are also bought from rural Thailand for as high as US$8,000 (Serrill 1993) and brought to the cities and larger tourist locations. Farmers under greater economic pressures have been forced to make many sacrifices, including sending

their children to work in the cities in order to send money home (Srisang 1990). These farmer parents are not always aware that their children are to become sex workers. In other cases, the entry into the sex industry does not happen until after an initial period of working in other low-paying jobs.

The business of finding job placements in the cities for rural children is not a new phenomenon. However, the growth of this business, and its connection to the sex industry, have been boosted by the socioeconomic shift in recent decades, and now it can be found in most parts of the country. As Thailand is moving toward the status of a newly industrialized country (NIC), most of the rapid economic development is concentrated in urbanization and industrialization. Although all socioeconomic strata have enjoyed their share of the country's economic boom, income inequalities have widened and poverty persists (Pyne 1994). Wealth is concentrated in the cities, while the rural poor are becoming more and more landless, and profits from their domestic businesses in rural areas are diminishing. Poverty, combined with the women's obligation to provide for their parents, and the lack of job opportunities for unskilled laborers, create an enormous pressure that has forced many Thai women to consider the sex industry as an occupation.

While many children and young women have been bought, most available data suggest that the process is not involuntary or forced. Hantrakul (1988, quoted in Manderson 1992) has pointed out that, "More and more prostitutes . . . have shown their strong determination in stepping in the profession. Sex is harnessed to an economic end. Men are seen as targets, a source of income" (p. 467). Data from van Griensven et al. (1995) support this notion: When asked how they entered commercial sex, 58% of the female sex workers said it was their own decision, and 37% said a friend or relative had advised them. Only 3% reported that they were either sold by their parents or recruited by an agent or employer. A number of the women, 14%, also had one or more sisters in commercial sex. Poverty was the most common reason for entering the profession, reported by 58% of the women.

After years of living through the sociocultural changes that have put more strains on rural women, being a sex worker to support one's family has become an acceptable value in several communities in the north. Some children go into this business without reservation and with full parental permission and support. Many of these girls return home with honor, marry, and repeat the cycle by sending their own daughters into the sex business when they come of age (Phongpaichit 1982; Limanonda 1993). This phenomenon is also true of some of the hill tribe villagers. Almost all sex workers are clear about their desire to quit working in the sex industry once their goals of income are met, and many would return to their native villages to marry and take care of their parents. Upon reintegration into the village, women who have worked as sex workers may be subject to condemnation, but it is usually based not on their prostitution, but on their having sex outside of marriage (Manderson 1992). This offense, however, can be amended by their active accumulation of merit, such as caretaking of parents and helping local charities. In any case, many women have already been recognized by family and the community for their previous remittances during the years of work in the city, as their financial contributions are already evident in the family's house, motorcycle, and even donations to the local temple. Although the cults of ancestral spirits (*phii puu yaa*) frown upon women's premarital sex, the act of kinship loyalty and filial piety is considered adequate to propitiate the spirits. In fact, when commercial sex agents recruit women from the villages, they frequently offer some "customary payments" to the family and the ancestral spirits much like a brideprice. With an income up to 25 times the median income of women in factories and clerical jobs (Phongpaichit 1982), sex workers can easily redress their sexual misdemeanors by their generous support of kinship.

Nonetheless, other evidence suggests that many children and families are deceived by the brokers, and that the children are led to believe they will go to the cities to work as domestic servants or waiters/waitresses, only to find themselves forced into commercial sex. Sometimes, coercion takes the form of financial threats rather than physical confinement of the women. Many women must continue working to earn the sum of money for which their families are indebted to the commercial sex agents. For example, 31% of the female sex workers in van Griensven's study (1995) reported they were in debt to their employer. Worse cases are seen in women in commercial sex businesses in foreign countries. In a 1993 article in *Time* magazine, Hornblower (1993) reported that numerous Thai women are working in Japan as "virtual indentured sex slaves" in bars controlled by Japanese gangsters. These women, mostly from rural villages of Thailand, are usually sold by Thai brokers for an average of US$14,000 each, and then resold to the clubs by Japanese brokers for about US$30,000. The women are obligated and threatened to work under hostile circumstances to earn this sum of money, but very few can.

The recent concern about child sex workers in Thailand seems to have been fueled by the awareness of the HIV pandemic and the growing anguish about child victimization around the world. Initially, the pressure for a governmental policy towards child sex workers came from foreign sources, with the pressure more recently internalized. When the government of Prime Minister Chuan Leekpai took office in 1992, he promised to eliminate child sex workers during his term of office. Impressive work has been done by the Task Force to End Child Exploitation in Thailand, a coalition of 24 government and private agencies dedicated to exposing European links of child sex trade in Thailand (Serrill 1993). Brothels in Thailand known to employ children were raided and closed, and the events were highly publicized in Thai newspapers (Kaime-Atterhog et al. 1994). However, data are still lacking regarding the extent of success in reducing the child sex trade. Although some reports have mentioned the age restriction that sex workers must be at least 18 years old (e.g., Kunawararak et al. 1995), statistics still show a small number of female sex workers under 15 years old in brothels (e.g., van Griensven et al. 1995).

### Sociocultural Factors Behind the Entry to Commercial Sex

One consistent finding across many studies of female and child sex workers is that a large number come from the northern provinces of Thailand (Redd Barna 1989; Archavanitkul & Havanon 1990; van Griensven et al. 1995; Wawer et al. 1996). It has been theorized that these young women are especially in demand because of the long-held admiration for their lighter skin compared to their counterparts in the northeast or the south of the country. Others have theorized that working in the sex business is a tradition long present in the north. Formerly part of the kingdom of Lanna, this part of the country was more often at war with other kingdoms and had a history of being colonized. It was the custom to use women from the area to placate the occupying forces through the offering of sex services (Skrobanek 1988).

In addition to these perspectives, others have offered hypotheses that take into account sociocultural factors that are not unique to northern Thailand and are thus applicable to the general Thai culture as well. Lenore Manderson (1992),

for example, eloquently argues that commercial sex, much like Buddhist monasteries, provides alternatives for both men and women to step out of their ordinary cultural roles. For men, the alternative is in the sexual realm; commercial sex provides a sexual outlet for the unmarried men and a way for married men to step temporarily outside their marriage while avoiding a divorce. For young women, she argues, the process of leaving behind (temporarily) their kinship as well as their "normal sexuality" (i.e., sex with affectional ties) gives women an alternative option to become self-sufficient. By supporting themselves and their family through the commoditization of sex, these young women achieve a degree of autonomy without having to enter the role of "mother" or marriage. Traditionally, *mae chii* undergo a similar process of abandoning attachments (in their case, worldly and sexual pleasures) in order to achieve autonomy in the spiritual realm. In a society in which women are expected to be mother or wife, female sex workers and *mae chii* reject both roles in the way they use (or do not use) their bodies and sexuality.

Other scholars, such as Khin Thitsa, Thomas Kirsch, and Charles Keyes, have looked even deeper into the Theravada gender construction for the cultural explanation of commercial sex. Keyes (1984) acknowledges that prostitutes have never been stigmatized in Buddhist societies, because the women still have the opportunity to alter their behavior at some time; prostitutes and courtesans were indeed among the alms of women in early Buddhist society. Despite such tolerance in the Buddhist society, he suggests that the rise of commercial sex in contemporary Thailand has more to do with the emergence the new images of men and women, which are associated with sex without any tempering moral irony found in traditional popular Buddhism. According to Keyes, the decision to enter commercial sex in Thailand today is the women's "participation in the increasingly materialistic culture of Thailand" (p. 236), probably driven by the "secularized image of woman as sex object" (p. 236). A number of scholars and activists have made similar comments. The growth of commercial sex in Thai society cannot be explained by the traditional gender roles in Buddhism; quite the opposite, it thrives on the increasingly consumerist and materialistic nature of the contemporary Thai culture.

On the other hand, Kirsch (1985) argues that women's choice of entering commercial sex is not necessarily at odds with the range of "ideal" female images in Buddhism. In particular, the Buddhist-sanctioned mother-nurturer image of women has found a new expression in the new sociocultural context, where young rural women have expanded their means of providing for the family to a new arena, "in towns, cities, the nation, and beyond" (p. 313).

### C. Pornography and Erotica

The popularity of pornography and erotica in contemporary Thailand cannot be denied, although we were not able to identify formal data on its extent and variety. Erotic magazines and videotapes, most of which are designed for the male customer, are available in street markets, newsstands, and video stores. Imports and unauthorized copies of foreign (mostly American, European, and Japanese) erotica are easily available and popular. Thai-produced erotica tends to be more suggestive and less explicit than the XXX-rated erotica produced in the West. Heterosexual erotica has a greater market, but same-sex erotica is also available.

By exploring the production and consumption of pornographic and erotic materials in Thailand, we can better understand Thai people's attitudes toward this topic, as well as the underlying social constructions of gender and sexuality. While there is no equivalent of the term "pornography," the nonjudgmental colloquialism is the suffix *po*, ("nude") added to the format of the medium (e.g., books, magazines, pictures, movies, and dances); hence *phaap po* is a nude picture. The more judgmental suffix *laa-mok* ("obscene") is also used, especially by the press to convey journalistic technicality or even an air of morality. Sex videos are also called *nang ek*, or "X movies," although censorship in Thailand does not use the nominal rating system used in the United States. There is also a tongue-in-cheek distinction of *po tae mai plueay*, or "nude but not naked," implying the more discreet depiction of the unclothed bodies.

Although none of these terms indicates the gender of the customers or users, Thai people generally see that pornography is chiefly men's indulgence, consistent with the idea that vices and sex are men's recreation.

Depictions of nude female bodies or women in swimsuits on calendars are not an uncommon sight in male-dominated settings, such as bars, construction sites, warehouses, and auto shops. Caucasian and Japanese models are also as popular as Thai models. In fact, until a few decades ago when domestic production of pornography was prohibited by poor technology and strict laws, Thai men relied on pirated copies of Western porn and imported magazines, such as *Playboy*. Hence, the last few generations of Thai men have been exposed to Western sexuality primarily through pornography from Europe and North America. Because these materials portray sexual practices with the variety and explicitness unprecedented in the Thai media, Thai people who are acquainted with Western pornography have come to associate Westerners with sexual disinhibition and hedonism.

Prior to the popularity of videotapes, imported and pirated, Western erotica was available in the underground market in the formats of print, 8-millimeter film, and photographic slides. Illegal prints of Western hardcore pornography, known as *nangsue pok khao*, or "white-cover publication" were produced by small, obscure publishers, and surreptitiously sold in bookstores, by mail order, or by solicitors in public areas. Nationally distributed magazines on display at newsstands and bookstores have burgeoned since the late 1970s. Following the format of American publications such as *Playboy*, these magazines, such as *Man*—among the earliest of its genre—print glossy photographs of Thai female models, and feature regular as well as erotic columns. The proliferation of gay men's erotic magazines followed in the mid-1980s.

The legal status of these magazines, straight and gay, is somewhat ambiguous. While sometimes up to 20 or 30 different publications compete on the newsstands for years, the police have also made numerous raids on publishers and bookstores that carry these so-called "obscene" magazines. Such raids often follow a moral surge in politics or an administrative reform in the police department. Similar arrests have been made with the video rental stores that carry pornographic films. Interestingly, grounds for objection to these pornographic materials have never been based on the material's unauthorized status or even the exploitation of women. As known by all the customers and providers of pornography in Thailand, the disapproval is because of the "sex and obscenities" involved. In news coverage of these raids, officials commonly espouse Buddhist moral messages about sexual stoicism and, less often, the degradation of the *kulasatrii* image. Thai censorship of films has also been stricter on sexual matters than on violence, even when the sex or body exposure appears in nonexploitative contexts. In formality and the law, the Thai society is more sex-negative than what its sex industry has led most outsiders to believe.

The depiction of the Thai female models in Thai erotic magazines for heterosexual men is perhaps an embodiment of the modern, urban "bad girl" image. Although many of them are indeed recruited from the commercial sex scenes in Bangkok, the glossy images and the accompanying biographies suggest that the models are single, educated, and middle-class adventurous women who do these poses on a one-time-only basis. To the reader, these women might as well be *kulasatrii* elsewhere, but here they let their hair down in front of the camera and become modern, beautiful, and sensual women who are in touch with their sexuality. Neither are these models the ordinary "carefree" women available in the one-night-stand scenes; their model-quality appearance is more than what the reader could expect in those environments. Hence, these models represent a high-end variant of carefree women, characterized by their overwhelming sexual magnetism, an excellent match indeed for men and their boundless sexual desires. A few famous models in the erotica industry have gone on to fashion, music, and acting in television or film with great success.

The image of these celebrity erotica models can be juxtaposed, like the other side of the coin, with that of the beauty-pageant winners, such as Miss Thailand, who also frequently become media celebrities. Both images are of Thai women who achieve success and fame because of their appearance. Pageant contestants and winners always take great pains to extol the virtues of Thai women in their public statements, and many openly object to the pageant's swimsuit display requirement. Pageant winners invariably stress their "nurturer" ideology by speaking of helping children, the elderly, and the disabled. In contrast, erotica models send off an air of iconoclastic indifference in their seductive, hedonistic, and "I don't care" statements. Interestingly, women's indifferent and autonomous attitudes, along the lines of "I am who I am" or "I don't give a damn," have become fashionable and used in numerous poetry and song lyrics by female pop stars. This image, however, is not a new image for women in Thai society, because the "bad women" image has always been around. Nevertheless, the tough "I-am-who-I-am" statements are urban women's announcement of their moral independence, setting them in contrast with the conventional perceptions that women in the sex industry and "carefree" women are fooled into their positions, and that women in general are helpless abiders of societal values. As more and more contemporary women are becoming dissatisfied with the traditional role or the victim stereotype, these iconoclastic sentiments seem refreshing: Adopting the role opposite to a *kulasatrii* by choice is an act of liberation.

Thailand is also famous for its sex shows in the go-go nightclubs (*baa a-go-go*), most notoriously in the red-light districts of Patpong, Pattaya, and Chiangmai. Approaching these performances of dances, sexual tricks, and intercourse as cultural texts, Lenore Manderson (1992) has examined the continuity which links these public sex shows with the disempowerment of women, prostitution, and the Thai social constructions of sex and gender. Although the extreme explicitness and violent themes in these shows undeniably reflect misogyny and subordination of women, she also notices that the themes reflect what Thai people understand about the sexuality of Thai men and of the Westerners in the audience. These acts are what the sex industry thinks will captivate the (mostly) male clientele. The themes thus represent not the everyday sexuality, but the erotic possibilities on the edge of male libidinal fantasy, their "wildest dreams."

Salient in the imageries designed to excite, thrill, or even shock the male customers is the ruleless, "anything goes" atmosphere. Disinhibition pervades the bars in which customers have quick access to sex on the premises. The unpredictable, even improbable, performances, including genital manipulation of objects or snakes, and sex between women, all affirm a polysexual theme. Another theme designed to excite is the extreme objectification of women as sex objects for sale. Sex workers are numbered for customers' selection, and their nakedness (or uniform bar costume) enhances their anonymity. Finally, there is a theme of satire in which men are insulted and parodied for their fear of the female genitalia, the widespread touch taboo and gender segregation are overturned, and the Thai gender-power hierarchy toppled. Naked women dance on a raised platform, literally placing men under the female genitalia (Manderson 1992).

## 9. Contraception, Abortion, and Population Planning

### A. Contraception and Population Control

Thailand is extremely proud of its relatively high rates of contraceptive use and successful population control. Birthrates have been declining over the years. In 1995, the Institute for Population and Social Research at Mahidol University reported that the natural growth rate was about 1%. The fertility rates have also decreased significantly in the last few decades, from six births per woman in the 1960s to two births per woman in the late 1980s (cited in Pyne 1994).

The contraceptive prevalence rates have increased dramatically in the last two decades, from 15% to 68% among married women (cited in Pyne 1994). Contraceptive methods are readily available and utilized (Sittitrai et al. 1992). Common methods of contraception in Thailand include hormone pills and injections, intrauterine devices (IUDs), vaginal inserts, rhythm, condoms, withdrawal, vasectomy, and female tubal ligation. For women, the contraceptive hormonal pill is by far the more-preferred method. However, the most-prevalent method today is female sterilization, followed by the pill, while the least-popular method is the condom (cited in Pyne 1994).

The success of contraception in Thailand has been invariably linked to Mechai Viravaidya, the man *Time* magazine called "a champion of condoms, a pusher of the Pill, a voice for vasectomies." ("The Good News," *Time* 1989). Launched by Viravaidya in 1974, the private nonprofit organization, Population and Community Development Association (PDA), has tackled overpopulation by promoting family planning and distributing birth control devices. The PDA proactively places temporary birth control clinics where people gather, in bus terminals, village fairs, and buffalo markets. At these unconventional sites, they dispense condoms and the pill; free IUDs and vasectomies are even offered on special occasions. Playful but persuasive jingles promoting family planning punctuate music and soap operas on the radio, reaching every household in Thailand. Helped by his humor, creativity, and charisma, the success of the PDA and Viravaidya can be seen in the growing financial support from the government. Moreover, Thai people now use the term *mechai* as a slang term for condoms.

In the *Partner Relations Survey* (Sittitrai et al. 1992), the research participants reported that condoms were readily available. Considerable proportions of the participants reported having used them some time in their lifetimes: 52% of the men, 22% of the women, or 35% overall. Attitudes toward condoms were not especially surprising. Most men feared a lack of pleasure or diminished sexual performance with the use of the condom, and couples found using condoms threatening to the trust in their relationship.

Recently, the heightened HIV awareness and the government-sanctioned 100 Percent Condom Program have significantly increased the use of condoms, especially in the context of commercial sex (see also Sections 8B, Significant Unconventional Sexual Behaviors, Prostitution, and 10B, HIV/AIDS). Although the government received condoms from foreign donors before 1990, all condoms provided to sex workers since 1990 have been bought by the country's own funds (Rojanapithayakorn & Hanenberg 1996). In 1990, the government distributed about 6.5 million condoms; in 1992, they spent US$2.2 million to buy and distribute 55.9 million condoms. Commercial sex workers receive as many free condoms as they require from government STD clinics and outreach workers. On the national level, the recent increase in condom use has been documented to relate in time and magnitude with the overall decline of STDs and HIV incidence.

### B. Abortion

Abortion is illegal in Thailand except when performed for medical reasons. Most Thais are strongly anti-abortion, mainly because of the First Precept of Buddhism which prohibits killing of living beings. In general, "living beings" are interpreted as people, animals, and sometimes small creatures, but most Thais also see this Precept as pertaining to the aborting of a fetus as well. Again, premarital or extramarital sex is frowned upon and there is little sympathy for the woman who becomes pregnant out of wedlock. She is most likely to be viewed as at fault for becoming pregnant, because only women (not men) can control their sexual desire. Thus, abortion has often been associated with a lack of morals and virtue on the woman's part.

In Ford and Kittisuksathit's study (1994), the young women who worked in factories were well aware of the dilemma of premarital pregnancy in the lives of their friends or siblings. Most expressed great concerns about unwanted, premarital pregnancy, which is a clear indicator of "sinful behavior" they have committed. In discussing the consequences of sex, women mostly talked about the feared premarital pregnancy, with allusions to "baby dumping," infanticide, and abortion, whereas young men focused on issues of STD and HIV. Most women expressed the hope that their partner would care for and marry them, and the child could be kept. Other young women clearly insisted that they would seek an abortion because they were emotionally and financially not ready for having a child. The blame for unwanted pregnancy, as expressed by both the young men and women, was placed on the woman for "allowing" intercourse to occur.

Apart from the social stigma, there are other important reasons behind Thai women's decision to have abortion. Pregnancy presents a grave problem for women in low-paying jobs in which employers have little tolerance of absenteeism (Pyne 1994). Having a child in urban environments is expensive, and, because few companies offer support for maternal and childcare, a woman risks losing her employment because of the additional task of parenting. For rural women who migrate to work in the cities, losing their jobs means jeopardizing their only source of income on which they and their family upcountry depend.

In curious contrast to the prevailing anti-abortion attitudes, abortion is not rare in practice. Illegal abortion clinics, many of which are run by nonprofessional women, offer traditional but unsafe techniques of abortion, such as forceful massage or injecting chemicals into the uterus. Thorbek (1988) has documented experiences of women who had undergone such traumatic procedures and the adverse health consequences. A more-pragmatic approach has been developed in recent years, thereby allowing women to have safe, confidential abortion operations in many urban clinics. In these clinics, medically trained professionals use standard medical procedures, such as suction, to remove the fetus. Never advertising openly, these urban clinics rely on word of mouth to draw clients, and fairly large fees are charged. To date, there has not been a Thai-equivalent of the Western movement that has gained recognition of a women's right to choose to have an abortion.

## 10. Sexually Transmitted Diseases and HIV/AIDS

### A. Sexually Transmitted Diseases

Thailand reports high rates of sexually transmitted diseases (STDs). In the *Partner Relations Survey* (Sittitrai et al. 1992), the lifetime prevalence rates of STDs were 49% among urban men and 33% among rural men, or 38% overall. Much lower proportions of women reported a history of STDs: 11% in urban women and 9% in rural women, or 10% overall. Gonorrhea and nongonococcal urethritis (NGU) were the most common STDs in male participants, whereas chlamydia and urethritis were the most common in female participants. Knowledge about STD prevention and treatment was inadequate, especially in the face of the HIV pandemic. Data from military conscripts have confirmed the linkage between STDs and HIV infection. In these young men from lower socioeconomic backgrounds, HIV infection was strongly associated with a history of STDs (Nelson et al. 1996), particularly a positive serology for syphilis, a history of gonorrhea, syphilis, genital herpes, genital warts, and genital ulcers (Beyrer et al. 1995).

Almost all STD cases in Thailand could be traced to commercial sex. In a 1989 report, 96% of male clients at government STD clinics attributed their infection to having had sex with a sex worker (cited in Rojanapithayakorn & Hanenberg 1996). The government STD clinics carry out the Ministry of Public Health's sentinel surveillance (previously described in Section 8B, Significant Unconventional Sexual Behaviors, Prostitution) and have notably provided STD-related services to the general population and medical examinations to sex workers for at least 20 years. Although sex workers are encouraged to have a weekly examination, records show that they visited government STD clinics only once every seven weeks in 1994. Male sex workers have been also included in sentinel surveillance since 1989 (Kunawararak et al. 1995). In addition, these clinics trace the partners of individuals with STD. The male clients are asked to name the establishments from which they might have contracted STD, and outreach workers are then dispatched for further tests or scheduling treatment for the sex workers. The government STD clinics also have good collaboration with the police offices, allowing enforcement against uncooperative establishments.

### B. HIV/AIDS

HIV was first detected in Thailand in 1984 (Limsuwan, Kanapa & Siristonapun 1986). The government was slow to respond to the pandemic and its entry into Thailand. Economic pressures created by the need for tourist dollars and the early low numbers of actual AIDS cases slowed the government's response to the pandemic (Sricharatchanya 1987).

This slow response caught Thai governmental officials and healthcare providers unprepared for the rapid explosion of new cases of HIV infection and AIDS. Infection rates remained quite low through 1987, mostly affecting men who had sex with men. Then, there was a rapid increase in seroprevalence among injecting drug users (IDUs). In 1988, 86% of known seropositive cases were among IDUs, 4% were men who had sex with men, and 2% were heterosexual women. By 1990, another shift had oc-

curred and shortly thereafter, female sex workers showed extremely high seroprevalence rates. This phase of the pandemic was first detected in northern Thailand in 1989 (Limanonda, Tirasawat, & Chongvatana 1993; Vithayasai & Vithayasai 1990). As injecting drug use was shown to be very rare among sex workers, heterosexual intercourse was then identified as a potentially effective mode of HIV transmission in Thailand. In 1991, the HIV seroprevalence among urban brothel sex workers in a northern province rose to 49% (Ministry of Public Health 1991). Because many Thai men have unprotected sex inside and outside of their marriage, high rates of HIV infection were soon detected not only in sex workers, but also in their clients, pregnant women, and newborns. The 1994 national median prevalence rates of HIV infection were 8.5% among men attending STD clinics, and 1.8% among women attending prenatal clinics (Division of Epidemiology, Thai Ministry of Public Health; data cited in Mastro & Limpakarnjanarat 1995).

A series of studies have focused on the men newly conscripted to the military in order to infer the extent of HIV infection among Thai men at large. Prior to 1993, the HIV-seroprevalence rates in these northern conscripts ranged between 10% and 13% (Beyrer et al. 1995; Nelson et al. 1996), considerably higher than the rates among conscripts from other parts of the country. Some unique sexual patterns of the young men in northern Thailand have been linked to their greater risk of HIV infection. When compared to men from other provinces, upper-northern young men were more likely to have initiated sexual activity at a younger age—before age of 16—to have had their first experience with a female sex worker, to have had more-frequent sexual contacts with sex workers, and to have reported a history of STDs (Nopkesorn, Mastro et al. 1993; Nopkesorn, Sweat et al. 1993).

Estimates have indicated that the number of persons living with HIV totals several hundreds of thousands (Division of Epidemiology, MOPH 1984-1993). The forecast is grim in terms of further HIV infection and its socioeconomic impact on the entire country (Sittitrai et al. 1992). However, by the mid-1990s, there has been some good news of behavioral change and decreasing new cases of HIV infection. Paralleling the success of the mass advertising campaign and the 100 Percent Condom Program, condom use in commercial sex increased from 14% of the sex acts in 1989 to 90% of the sex acts in 1994 (Rojanapithayakorn & Hanenberg 1996). As the government distributed massive amounts of condoms to commercial sex establishments all over the country, the incidence of STDs correspondingly decreased by over 85%. Meanwhile, the HIV seroprevalence among the military conscripts from northern Thailand declined from 10.4% in 1991 to 6.7% in 1995 (Nelson et al. 1996). New conscripts have greater proportions of men who never had sex with sex workers, and greater proportions of men who never had STDs.

Initiated in 1989 on a small-scale basis, the widely successful 100 Percent Condom Program was later adopted nationwide, with participation from every province in Thailand by April 1992 (Rojanapithayakorn & Hanenberg 1996). The program promotes condom use by sex workers and their clients without exception. Sex workers are instructed to withhold service and refund the fee upon the client's refusal to use a condom. The program utilizes the preexisting structures of the police and the Ministry of Public Health's STD surveillance system to enforce compliance from commercial sex establishments. STDs, monitored by the hundreds of government STD clinics around the country, are used as a marker of noncompliance with the program. When the source of STD is traced to a noncompliant establishment, temporary or indefinite closure of the business by the police is warranted. With the cooperation from every sex establishment, customers quickly learn that they cannot go elsewhere to find a sex worker who would allow unprotected sex, and the commercial sex establishments understand that they are not losing clients to competitors.

[*Update 2002*: UNAIDS Epidemiological Assessment: Thailand was the first country in Asia to document HIV epidemics among injection drug users and female sex workers and their clients. After a brief period of denial, the country organized a national program, supervised from the highest levels of government, to respond to the epidemic.

[Thailand has a comprehensive HIV Sentinel Surveillance (HSS) system, started in 14 provinces in 1989 and expanded to all 76 provinces by 1990. The system includes blood donors, antenatal clinic attendees, injection drug users, male STD clinic patients, and both direct (brothel-based) and indirect (massage parlors and others) female sex workers. HIV data on injection drug users have been supplemented by separate serosurveys.

[Surveillance data indicate that HIV prevalence peaked among female sex workers and their clients in the mid-1990s and has since been slowly decreasing. In Bangkok, 1% of injection drug users were HIV-positive in late 1987, increasing to 30% by the end of 1998; since then, HIV prevalence among injection drug users tested has remained between 20% and 50% both in and outside Bangkok. As of the end of 2001, an estimated 1.79% of the population aged 15 to 49 years was infected with HIV.

[HIV/AIDS is monitored and projected by the Thai Working Group on HIV/AIDS Projection. Estimates developed in 2000 indicate that approximately 2% of men and 1% of women are living with HIV; infection levels among adult males will remain above 1.5% until the end of 2006. Until the end of 2006, over 50,000 will die annually from AIDS-related causes; over 90% of these deaths will occur in people aged 20 to 44.

[Recognizing that most HIV transmissions were occurring through commercial sex, efforts focused on reducing the number of males visiting female sex workers and on promoting condom use in all commercial and casual sexual contacts. These efforts substantially changed levels of risk behavior. The percentage of adult men visiting female sex workers has fallen from almost 25% of the population to roughly 10%, and condom use when visiting sex workers has become the norm. The success of Thailand's "100 percent condom program" has not had much effect on the slow but steady transmission of HIV from infected male clients of female sex workers or from infected male injection drug users to their regular sex partners. There has also been limited success in reducing HIV prevalence among the injection drug user population. At present, 670,000 are living with HIV/AIDS; close to 30,000 new infections occur each year. The Ministry of Public Health budget for HIV decreased following the crisis in 1997; many of the international donors who left Thailand during the economic boom years have not returned.

[The estimated number of adults and children living with HIV/AIDS on January 1, 2002, were:

| | | |
|---|---|---|
| Adults ages 15-49: | 650,000 | (rate: 1.8%) |
| Women ages 15-49: | 220,000 | |
| Children ages 0-15: | 21,000 | |

[An estimated 55,000 adults and children died of AIDS during 2001.

[At the end of 2001, an estimated 290,000 Thai children under age 15 were living without one or both parents who had died of AIDS. (*End of update by the Editors*)]

## 11. Sexual Dysfunctions, Counseling, and Therapies

Within Thai psychiatry and psychology, there has not been much focus on the treatment of sexual dysfunctions or disorders. There is recognition of some sexual dysfunctions, but it is mostly limited to male erectile or ejaculatory problems. Vernacular expressions exist for these male sexual dysfunctions, suggesting Thai people's familiarity with these phenomena. For example, *kaam tai daan* means "sexual unresponsiveness" in men or women. There are a few terms for male erectile dysfunction: the playful *nokkhao mai kha*⁷ ("the dove doesn't coo") and the more cruel *makhuea phao* ("roasted eggplant"; Allyn 1991). Another slang, *mai soo* ("not up for a fight"), suggests an injury on the man's male pride for not being able to enter a "battle" with prowess. Premature ejaculation is referred to with a playful yet humiliating analogy *nokkra-jok mai than kin naam*, or "faster than a sparrow can sip water."

The incidence of various sexual dysfunctions have not yet been investigated. However, in the past two or three decades, many sex columns have appeared in the mainstream newspapers and magazines, offering advice and counsel in rather sexually explicit, but technical, detail. These are most often written by physicians who claim expertise in treating sexual problems and disorders. Other columnists in women's fashion and housekeeping magazines present themselves as older, experienced women who offer sage advice to younger ones about sex and relationships. The concepts of "squeeze technique" or "start-stop" techniques have been introduced to the typical middle-class Thai through these extremely popular advice columns.

A more systematic and academic effort to establish therapeutic services for sexual dysfunctions is underway. In the proposal for a multi-component interdisciplinary Program for the Promotion of Sexual Health (to be housed within the Chulalongkorn University in Bangkok), Nikorn Dusitsin (1995) included a counseling clinic and hotline counseling as one of the program's main components. Responding to the need for more sex counselors and educators, the program also contains workshops and courses aimed at training intermediate-level educators, including social workers, teachers, and military personnel, in order to provide sexuality counseling and education. Dusitin proposed a problem-based, participatory format for the curricula of these intensive workshops. The content of the curriculum was proposed to combine physiology, psychology, and sociocultural contexts.

## 12. Sex Research and Advanced Professional Education

In a review of the history of sex research in Thailand, Chanya Sethaput (1995) noted the remarkable changes in methodologies and scope of sex research before and after the HIV epidemic in Thailand. These differences lent themselves to a pragmatic classification of pre- and post-AIDS eras of Thai sex research. She noted that only a handful of sex surveys were conducted before the HIV epidemic started in Thailand in 1984. In the pre-AIDS era, she identified the earliest study in 1962 in which the focus was on attitudes towards dating and marriage. In fact, most of the pre-AIDS research was concerned with the attitudes and knowledge in premarital sex, extramarital sex, cohabitation of unmarried couples, sexually transmitted diseases, and abortion. Sampled mostly from the educated, urban populations, such as college or high-school students, these early studies found gender differences in the attitudes of men and women, confirming the existence of a double standard in the sexual domain. Assessment of sexual behaviors was more of an exception than a rule. Early findings on sexual knowledge among Thai people had been used in the design of a curriculum for sexuality education, which was later enforced by the Ministry of Education in schools across the country.

An abundance of studies have emerged after the first cases of AIDS were identified in Thailand about 1984. Driven by a public-health agenda, the post-AIDS sex research expanded its objectives to include more-diverse questions (Sethaput 1995). Initially focused on "high-risk groups" such as sex workers and "gay" men, the populations of interest subsequently expanded to the customers of commercial sex (college students, soldiers, fishermen, truck drivers, and construction and factory workers), spouses and partners of men who visited sex workers, and other "vulnerable" groups, such as adolescents, and pregnant women. Present samples are no longer limited to convenience samples in urban cities or colleges, but include also rural villages, housing projects for the poor, and work sites, for example. Face-to-face interviews, which previously would have been difficult or unacceptable, have become a more-common assessment method, along with focus-group discussions and other qualitative techniques. Sexual behaviors have become more prominent in the researchers' inquiry, as questionnaires and interview schedules have become increasingly candid and explicit, with a newfound assumption that respondents are more open about sexuality. Previously ignored topics have become main research questions, for example, AIDS knowledge, attitudes toward condoms, masturbation, and same-gender attraction and homosexuality. New research questions have also attempted to identify vulnerability factors to HIV-risk behavior. Guided by the theory of reasoned behavior and the health-belief model, this entails the assessments of psychological variables and individual differences.

Sethaput (1995) briefly reviewed findings, which have formed the basis of the current understanding of sexuality in Thailand. The following findings are now widely known and accepted:

- most populations have a saturation of knowledge regarding HIV transmission,
- extramarital and premarital sexual practices are common in men,
- married women are often well aware of their husbands' use of commercial sex,
- there is a double standard regarding gender and sexual expressions for men and women, and
- the discovery of new, evolving sexual patterns, such as the formation of a sexual network among unmarried men and women in urban settings.

This accrued fund of knowledge from cumulative research has also formed the foundation of our review in this chapter.

A recent publication on *General Sex Education* by Wasikasin, Aimpradit, et al. (1994) represents a renewed and integrative energy in sexology and research in Thailand (1994). This work, published by the Thammasat University, Bangkok, was written by two social workers, two physicians, and a lawyer. As a textbook, it offers an unprecedented integration of disciplines, and its attention to psychosocial contexts is far from the sole emphasis on reproductive biology common in earlier publications.

To date, there is no training in sexological research *per se*. Most researchers in the area of HIV/AIDS have received training from Western institutions, or have applied their basic training in other areas of research to sexual topics. There are a few notable sexologists, for example, Dr. Suwattana Aribarg at the Chulalongkorn University in Bangkok. Dr. Aribarg and her husband give lectures in human sexuality to medical students and she provides counseling through the Chulalongkorn Psychiatric Clinic. Other sex researchers in various institutes and universities in Thailand have also put forth their efforts to the academic and public attention, and many have gradually received greater national and international recognition over the years.

In late 1995, the Mahidol University Institute for Population and Social Research organized an important seminar on sex research. Charged with enthusiasm, the event brought together key sex researchers in Thailand and their body of knowledge, symbolizing a renaissance of sex research in Thailand. Fongkaew (1995), for example, delineated basic paradigms and constructs commonly used in sex research, and cautioned Thai sex researchers to be aware of their own assumptions and values. Some researchers challenged fellow researchers to theorize and problematize data on sexuality and gender, pushing toward the formation of a theoretical model that could capture the sexual complexities in Thailand. Other researchers urged that investigations must be led by pragmatic implications; much data are still needed for the advancement of social issues, for example, the improvement of the status of women and increasing social acceptance of gays and lesbians. Key ingredients for effective interventions are yet to be identified, especially the often overlooked "positive factors" which might protect individuals from behavioral or attitudinal problems. Finally, there was a consensus that researchers should take a more-assertive role in making specific recommendations based on the findings from their research.

As of 1995, advanced education in human sexuality was not available in Thailand, and most Thai scholars still needed to study abroad. In the aforementioned seminar on sex research in Thailand, Dusitsin (1995) stated that the training of new sexological researchers was one of the priorities of his proposed Program for the Promotion of Sexual Health. Through the efforts of the Asian Federation of Sexology and the World Association for Sexology, increasing numbers of Thai sexologists have been identified. The first sexological organization in Thailand, the Sexology Society, was formed in May, 1995. The organization, chaired by Dr. Nikorn Dusitsin, is located at the Institute of Health Research, Chulalongkorn University, in Bangkok.

## Summary

Sexuality in Thailand, like the country's peaceful yet interesting coexistence of peoples and cultures, is a convergence of values and practices resulting from admixing of cultures over the centuries. In recent years, these sexual attitudes and behaviors have undergone enormous changes influenced by the rapid economic growth, urbanization, exposure to Western cultures, and, most recently, the HIV epidemic. While economic growth has afforded the country more-effective population control and improved public health services, certain strata of the society have suffered from socioeconomic pressures. The growth of tourism, combined with the indigenous attitudes toward sexuality, commercial sex, and homosexuality, have provided fertile grounds for the commercial sex industry to flourish in Thailand despite its illegal status. Exploitation of children for commercial sex purposes, and the high rates of HIV infection among sex workers and the population at large, are some of the many problems that have followed. The rise of HIV infection has caused Thai people to question and challenge many sexual norms and practices, most notably the men's rite-of-passage practice of having the first sexual intercourse with a female sex worker.

Although well known for their general tolerance and harmony, the lack of conflicts or hostility in the Thai society does not necessarily indicate that Thai people always maintain embracing attitudes about gender inequality, homosexuality, abortion, or sexuality in general. The Third Buddhist Precept clearly prohibits sex that causes sorrow in others, such as irresponsible and exploitative sex, adultery, sexual coercion, and abuse. Other phenomena, such as masturbation, prostitution, subordination of women, and homosexuality, remain uncertain. Most of the current attitudes about these practices can be traced to non-Buddhist sources. Today, these non-Buddhist beliefs are primarily a blend between indigenous concepts (e.g., class structures, animism, and gender codes) and Western ideologies (e.g., capitalism and medical and psychological theories of sexuality).

Thailand is noted for being a male-dominated patriarchal society, and the gender roles and expectations for Thai men and women differ accordingly. Despite the fact that many Thai men in the past had households with many wives, polygamy is no longer socially or legally acceptable. Mutual monogamy as well as emotional commitment constitute today's ideal marriage. Traditionally, men and women in Thai society depend on each other for the fulfillment of both religious and secular goals, as well as their needs for love and passion. Despite such reciprocal needs, the existence of power differential is clear, and it may have been affirmed by the gender hierarchy sanctioned by Theravada Buddhism. Passion, courtship, romance, and love between men and women are glorified, and the love-inspired sentiments in Thai literature and music can rival the jubilance and pathos in any other culture.

Nonetheless, an uneasy tension between the genders is evident in the way Thai men and women view one another, especially in the areas of intimacy, trust, and sexuality. A double standard for men and women still exists in the practices of premarital and extramarital sex. Manliness, or *chaai chaatrii*, has become increasingly associated with various vices, especially the search for sexual gratification. A man is encouraged to seek sexual pleasure as recreation, and sex with commercial sex workers represents an acceptable and "responsible" behavior to fulfill the sexual desires of single and married men. On the other hand, the dichotomous stereotype of the good-woman/bad-woman exists: a "good" woman, personified in the image of a *kulasatrii*, is expected to be a virgin when she marries and to remain monogamous with her husband; otherwise she is categorized as "bad." Men and women are socialized to maintain distance from the opposite gender. Newer generations of Thai people are finding that the clear-cut traditional gender constructions can no longer explain their evolving, amorphous forms of gender relations.

In the traditional household, Thai women have always excelled at their mother-nurturer role. Outside the household context, women have made tremendous contributions, especially in the areas of the arts, business, and academia. Women are still a long way from achieving equal recognition in the political and religious hierarchies. Today, Thai women struggle with modern realities in the workforce while simultaneously striving toward the positive, if difficult, ideal of a *kulasatrii*.

Another area that has received recent attention is male and female homosexual behaviors. Same-gender sexual behavior was traditionally recognized as associated with the gender-nonconformity among the *kathoey*, who were seen as a "third gender." Indigenously, the *kathoey* were relatively tolerated and often held some special social roles in the community. Previously an undiscussed topic, the Thai vocabulary managed without a word for homosexuality by using a euphemism such as "trees in the same forest" until the past few decades. More recently, the words "gay" and "lesbian" have been adopted from English, illustrating the search for vocabularies to represent types of homosexualities, which had existed without labels. Homophobia, stereotypes, and misconceptions about homosexuality are common, especially among the middle class who have learned antiquated Western psychiatric theories. On the other hand, gay businesses and the sex industry have grown to significant visibility. Meanwhile, a few advocate groups have emerged to advance their agenda and formulate new social identities for gays and lesbians in Thailand.

Sexological research in Thailand is at an exciting stage. Prompted by the HIV/AIDS epidemic and the controversies regarding the commercial sex industry, large amounts of data have been collected on sexual behaviors and attitudes. Descriptive studies on sexual practices and norms have offered valuable insights into the sexuality of Thai people, although much more data are needed, especially in certain areas not directly associated with public health (e.g., abortion, rape, and incest). Still in its infancy stage, sex therapies and counseling in Thailand are starting to adopt Western psychology, and the providers could learn much more from further research to help customize their services to fit the unique features of the Thai sexuality. Care must be taken when Western models or assumptions are applied to Thai sexual phenomena. Characterized by interwoven traditions over centuries, the people of Thailand defy such simplification, as their constructions of gender and sexuality continue on an evolving course that is as mystifying as it is enlightening.

## References and Suggested Readings

Allyn, E. 1991. *Trees in the same forest: The men of Thailand revisited*. San Francisco: Bua Luang Publishing.

Archavanitkul, K., & N. Havanon. 1990. *Situation, opportunities and problems encountered by young girls in Thai society*. Research report funded by Terre des Hommes, Bangkok, Thailand.

Aribarg, A., S. Aribarg, W. Rakiti, & S. Harnroongroj. 1982. Sexual behavior during pregnancy. *Journal of Psychiatric Association Thailand*, 27:147-160.

Barmé, S. 2002. *Woman, man, Bangkok. Love, sex and popular culture in Thailand*. Lanham, MD: Rowman & Littlefield Publishers.

Beyrer, C., S. Eiumtrakul, D. D. Celentano, K. E. Nelson, S. Ruckphaopunt, & C. Khamboonruang. 1995. Same-sex behavior, sexually transmitted diseases and HIV risks among young northern Thai men. *AIDS*, 9:171-176.

Bishop, R., & L. S. Robinson. 1998. *Night market: Sexual cultures and the Thai economic miracle*. New York & London: Routledge.

Bishop, R., & L. S. Robinson. 1999a. In the night market: Tourism, sex, and commerce in contemporary Thailand. *Women's Studies Quarterly*, 27:32-46.

Bishop, R., & L. S. Robinson. 1999b. Genealogies of exotic desire: The Thai night market in the Western imagination. In: P. Jackson & N. Cook, eds., *Gender and sexuality in modern Thailand* (pp. 191-205). Chiang Mai: Silkworm Press.

Bishop, R., & L. S. Robinson. 2002a. How my dick spent its summer vacation: Sex tourism and the commerce of global communication. *Genders*, 35. Available: http://www.genders.org.

Bishop, R., & L. S. Robinson. 2002b. Traveller's tails: Sex diaries of tourists returning from Thailand (pp. 13-23). In: S. Thorbek & B. Pattanaik, eds., *Transnational prostitution: Changing global patterns*. London: Zed Books.

Boonchalaksi, W., & P. Guest. 1994. *Prostitution in Thailand*. Salaya, Phutthamonthon Nakhon Pathom, Thailand: The Institute for Population and Social Research, Mahidol University.

Brinkman, U. K. 1992. *Features of the AIDS epidemic in Thailand*. Department of Population and International Health: Working Paper Series, No. 3.

Brock, R. N., & S. B. Thistlethwaite. 1996. *Casting stones: Prostitution and liberation in Asia and the United States.* Minnesota: Fortress Press.

Bussaratid, S., S. Na Ranong, V. Boonyaprakob, & C. Sitasuwan. 1981. Sexual behavior in married Thai females. *Siriraj Hospital Gazette, 33:*84-90.

Cabezón, J. E. 1993. Homosexuality and Buddhism. In: A. Swidler, ed., *Homosexuality and world religions.* Valley Forge, PA: Trinity Press International.

Chompootaweep, S., K. Yamarat, P. Poomsuwan, & N. Dusitsin. 1991. A Study of reproductive health in adolescence of secondary school students and teachers in Bangkok. *Thai Journal of Health Research, 5*(2).

CIA. 2002 (January). *The world factbook 2002.* Washington, DC: Central Intelligence Agency. Available: http://www.cia.gov/cia/publications/factbook/index.html.

Coleman, E. 1996. Importing and exporting constructs of homosexuality. *Sexuality and human bonding: Proceedings of the XII World Congress of Sexology.* Amsterdam: Elsevier.

Crystal, D. 1987. *The Cambridge encyclopedia of language.* New York: Cambridge University Press.

Dusitsin, N. 1995. Program for the promotion of sexual health. In: A. Chamratrithirong, chairperson, *Directions in research on sexual behavior in Thailand.* Seminar conducted at the meeting of the Mahidol University Institute for Population and Social Research, Bangkok, Thailand.

Division of Epidemiology. 1984-1993. *Statistics on reported cases of AIDS, ARC and HIV seropositives.* Thailand: Office of the Permanent Secretary of Ministry of Public Health.

Dumronggittigule, P., S. Sombathmai, K. Taywaditep, & J. Mandel. 1995 (September). *HIV Prevention strategies among northern Thai married couples: A study from the village.* Paper presented at the Third Conference on AIDS in Asia and the Pacific, Chiangmai, Thailand.

Eberhardt, N., ed. 1988. *Gender, power, and the construction of the moral order: Studies from the Thai periphery* (Monograph 4). University of Wisconsin-Madison, Center for Southeast Asian Studies.

Fongkaew, W. 1995. Gender roles and sexuality in Thai sex research. In: A. Chamratrithirong, chairperson, *Directions in research on sexual behavior in Thailand.* Seminar conducted at the meeting of the Mahidol University Institute for Population and Social Research, Bangkok, Thailand.

Ford, N. J., & S. Kittisuksathit. 1994. Destinations unknown: The gender construction and changing nature of the sexual expressions of Thai youth. *AIDS Care, 6:*517-531.

Friends of Women Foundation. 1992 (June). *Newsletter, 3:*1.

Fuller, T. D., J. N. Edwards, S. Sermsri, & S. Vorakitphokatorn. 1993. Gender and health: Some Asian evidence. *Journal of Health and Social Behavior, 34:*252-271.

Guest, P. 1994. Guesstimating the unestimateable: The number of child prostitutes in Thailand. In: O. Ard-am & C. Sethaput, eds., *Child prostitution in Thailand: A documentary analysis and estimation on the number of child prostitutes* (pp. 73-98). Bangkok, Thailand: Institute for Population and Social Research, Mahidol University.

Havanon, N., A. Bennett, & J. Knodel. 1992 (June). *Sexual networking in a provincial Thai setting* (AIDS Prevention Monograph Series Paper No. 1). Bangkok: G. M. Press Printing Service Co, Ltd.

Hiew, C. 1992. *Child prostitutes as victims of tourism in children in prostitution: Victims of tourism in Asia.* Bangkok, Thailand: ECPAT.

Hill, A. M. 1988. Women without talents are virtuous. In: N. Eberhardt, ed., *Gender, power, and the construction of the moral order: Studies from the Thai periphery* (Monograph 4). University of Wisconsin-Madison, Center for Southeast Asian Studies.

Hornblower, M. 1993 (June 21). The skin trade. *Time,* 44-52.

Jackson, P. A. 1989. *Male homosexuality in Thailand: An interpretation of contemporary Thai sources.* Elmhurst, NY: Global Academic Publishers.

Jackson, P. A. 1997. Kathoey gays man: The historical emergences of gay male identity in Thailand. In: L. Manderson & M. Jolly, ed., *Sites of desire: Economics of pleasure: Sexualities in Asia and the Pacific* (pp. 166-190). Chicago, IL: University of Chicago.

Kaime-Atterhog, W., O. Ard-Am, & C. Sethaput. 1994. Child prostitution in Thailand: A documentary assessment. In: O. Ard-am & C. Sethaput, eds., *Child prostitution in Thailand: A documentary analysis and estimation on the number of child prostitutes* (pp. 37-71). Bangkok, Thailand: Institute for Population and Social Research, Mahidol University.

Keyes, C. F. 1984. Mother or mistress but never a monk: Buddhist notions of female gender in rural Thailand. *American Ethnologist, 11:*223-241.

Kirsch, T. 1982. Buddhism, sex-roles, and the Thai economy. In: P. Van Esterik, ed., *Women of Southeast Asia* (Occasional Paper No. 9). DeKalb: Northern Illinois University, Center for Southeast Asian Studies.

Kirsch, A. T. 1985. Text and context: Buddhist sex roles/culture of gender revisited. *American Ethnologist, 12:*302-320.

Kunawararak, P. C. Beyrer, C. Natpratan, W. Feng, D. D. Celentano, M. de Boer, K. E. Nelson, & C. Khamboonruang. 1995. The epidemiology of HIV and syphilis among male commercial sex workers in northern Thailand. *AIDS, 9.*

Limanonda, B. 1993. *Female commercial sex workers and AIDS: Perspectives from Thai rural communities.* Paper presented at the 5th International Conference on Thai Studies—SOAS at Centre of South East Asian Studies, School of Oriental and African Studies (SOAS), University of London, London, England, July 5-10.

Limanonda, B., P. Tirasawat, & N. Chongvatana. 1993. *The demographic and behavioral study of female commercial sex workers in Thailand* (Publication No. 207/36). Bangkok: Institute of Population Studies, Chulalongkorn University.

Limsuwan, A., S. Kanapa, & Y. Siristonapun. 1986. Acquired immune deficiency syndrome in Thailand: A report of two cases. *Journal of the Medical Association of Thailand, 69:* 164-169.

Manderson, L. 1992. Public sex performances in Patpong and explorations of the edges of imagination. *Journal of Sex Research, 29:*451-475.

McFarland, G. B. 1982. *Thai-English dictionary.* Stanford, CA: Stanford University Press.

McKinnon, J., & W. Bhruksasri, eds. 1983. *Highlanders of Thailand.* Kuala Lumper: Oxford University Press.

Ministry of Public Health. 1991. *Sentinel surveillance of HIV infection.* Bangkok, Thailand: Ministry of Public Health.

Morris, R. 1994. Three sexes and four sexualities: Redressing the discourses on gender and sexuality in contemporary Thailand. *Positions* [Durham, NC: Duke University Press], *2*(1):15-43.

Morris, R. 2000. *In the place of origins: Modernity and its mediums in Northern Thailand (Body, commodity, text).* Durham, NC: Duke University Press.

Nanda, S. 2000. *Gender diversity: Cross-cultural variations* (chap. 5: Transgendered males in Thailand and the Philippines, pp.72-83). Prospect Heights, IL: Waveland Press.

Nelson, K. E., D. D. Celentano, S. Eiumtrakul, D. R. Hoover, C. Beyrer, S. Suprasert, S. Kuntolbutra, & C. Khamboonruang. 1996. Changes in sexual behavior and a decline in HIV infection among young men in Thailand. *New England Journal of Medicine, 335:*297-303.

Nopkesorn, T., T. D. Mastro, S. Sangkharomya, M. Sweat, P. Singharaj, K. Limpakarnjanarat, H. Gayle, & B. Weniger. 1993. HIV-1 infection in young men in northern Thailand. *AIDS, 7:*1233-1239.

Nopkesorn, T., S. Sungkarom, & R. Sornlum. 1991. *HIV prevalence and sexual behaviors among Thai men aged 21 in northern Thailand* (Research Report No. 3. Program on AIDS). Bangkok: The Thai Red Cross Society.

Nopkesorn, T., M. D. Sweat, S. Kaensing, & T. Teppa. 1993. *Sexual behavior for HIV-infection in young men in Payao*

(Research Report No. 6. Program on AIDS). Bangkok: The Thai Red Cross Society.

O'Grady, R. 1992. *The child and the tourist: The story behind the escalation of child prostitution in Asia.* Bangkok, Thailand: The Campaign to End Child Prostitution in Asian Tourism.

Otaganonta, W. 1995 (June 21). Women who love women. *Bangkok Post,* 29, 36.

Phongpaichit, P. 1982. *From peasant girls to Bangkok masseuses.* Geneva, Switzerland: International Labour Office.

Pongthai, S., P. Sakornratanakul, & K. Chaturachinda. 1980. Marriage and sexual activity. *Journal of Medical Association Thailand,* 63:11-14.

Pramualratana, A., C. Podhisita, U. Kanungsukkasem, M. J. Wawer, & R. McNamara. 1993. *The social context of condom use in low-priced brothels in Thailand: A qualitative analysis.* Paper presented at the 3rd National AIDS Seminar, Bangkok, Thailand.

Pyne, H. H. 1994. Reproductive experiences and needs of Thai women: Where has development taken us? In: G. Sen & R. C. Snow, eds., *Power and decision: The social control of reproduction.* Boston: Harvard University Press.

Rajadhon, A. 1961. Popular Buddhism in Thailand. In: W. J. Gedney, ed./trans., *Life and ritual in old Siam: Three studies of Thai life and customs.* New Haven, CT: Human Relations Area Files Press. (Original work published 1948, 1949).

Redd Barna. 1989. *The sexual exploitation of children in developing countries.* Redd Barna, Norway.

Rojanapithayakorn, W., & R. Hanenberg. 1996. The 100 percent condom program in Thailand. *AIDS,* 10:1-7.

Serrill, M. S. 1993 (June 21). Defiling the children. *Time,* 52.

Sethaput, C. 1995. A historical review of research on sexuality in Thailand. In: A. Chamratrithirong, chairperson, *Directions in research on sexual behavior in Thailand.* Seminar conducted at the meeting of the Mahidol University Institute for Population and Social Research, Bangkok, Thailand.

Sittitrai, W., T. Brown, & C. Sakondhavat. 1993. Levels of HIV risk behaviour and AIDS knowledge in Thai men having sex with men. *AIDS Care,* 5:261-271.

Sittitrai, W., T. Brown, & S. Virulak. 1991. Patterns of bisexuality in Thailand. In: R. Tielman, M. Carballo, & A. Hendriks, eds., *Bisexuality and HIV/AIDS.* Buffalo, NY: Prometheus Books.

Sittitrai, W., P. Phanuphak, J. Barry, & T. Brown. 1992. *Thai sexual behavior and risk of HIV infection: A report of the 1990 survey of partner relations and risk of HIV infection in Thailand.* Bangkok, Thailand: Program on AIDS. Thai Red Cross Society and Institute of Population Studies, Chulalongkorn University.

Sittitrai, W., P. Phanuphak, N. Satirakorn, E. E. Wee, & R. E. Roddy. 1989. *Demographics and sexual practices of male*

bar *workers in Bangkok.* Fifth International Conference on AIDS, June 4-9, Abstract no. M.D.P. 19.

Skinner, W. G. 1957. *Chinese society in Thailand: An analytical history.* Ithaca, NY: Cornell University Press.

Skrobanek, S. undated. *Strategies against prostitution: The case of Thailand.* Bangkok, Thailand: Foundation for Women.

Sricharatchanya, P. 1987 (November 5). Scare stories spur Thailand into action. *Far Eastern Economic Review,* 52.

Srisang, S. S. 1990. Tourism and child prostitution in Thailand. In: *Caught in modern slavery: Tourism and child prostitution in Asia* (pp. 37-46). Bangkok, Thailand: The Ecumenical Coalition on Third World Tourism.

*Time.* 1989 (January 2). The good news: Thailand controls a baby boom, 50.

Thorbek, S. 1987. *Voices from the city: Women of Bangkok.* London: Zed Books.

Udomratn, P., & S. Tungphaisal. 1990. Sexual behavior in Thai society. *Journal of Psychiatric Association Thailand,* 35: 115-127.

UNAIDS. 2002. *Epidemiological fact sheets by country.* Geneva, Switzerland: Joint United Nations Programme on HIV/ AIDS (UNAIDS/WHO). Available: http://www.unaids.org/ hivaidsinfo/statistics/fact_sheets/index_en.htm.

Van Esterik, J. 1982. Women meditation teachers in Thailand. In: P. Van Esterik, ed., *Women of Southeast Asia* (Occasional Paper No. 9). DeKalb: Northern Illinois University, Center for Southeast Asian Studies.

van Griensven, G. J. P., B. Limanonda, N. Chongwatana, P. Tirasawat, & R. A. Coutinho. 1995. Socioeconomic and demographic characteristics and HIV-1 infection among female commercial sex workers in Thailand. *AIDS Care,* 7: 557-565.

van Landingham, M., S. Suprasert, W. Sittitrai, & C. Vaddhanaphuti. 1993. Sexual activity among never-married men in northern Thailand. *Demography,* 30(3).

Vithayasai, V., & P. Vithayasai. 1990. An analysis of HIV infection rates in northern Thailand. *Thai AIDS Journal,* 2:99-108.

Wasikasin, W., N. Aimpradit, S. Kiatinan, P. Likhitlersuang, & S. Boonchalearmwipat. 1994. *General sex education.* Bangkok, Thailand: Thammasat University.

Wawer, M. J., C. Podhisita, U. Kanungsukkasem, A. Pramualratana, & R. McNamara. 1996. Origins and working conditions of female sex workers in urban Thailand: Consequences of social context for HIV transmission. *Social Sciences and Medicine,* 42:453-462.

Weniger, B. G., K. Limpakarnjanarat, K. Ungchusak, S. Thanprasertsuk, K. Choopanya, S. Vanichseni, T. Uneklabh, P. Thongcharoen, & C. Wasi. 1991. The epidemiology of HIV infection and AIDS in Thailand. *AIDS,* 5(Suppl. 2), s71-s85.

Wyatt, D. K. 1984. *Thailand: A short history.* New Haven, CT: Yale University Press.

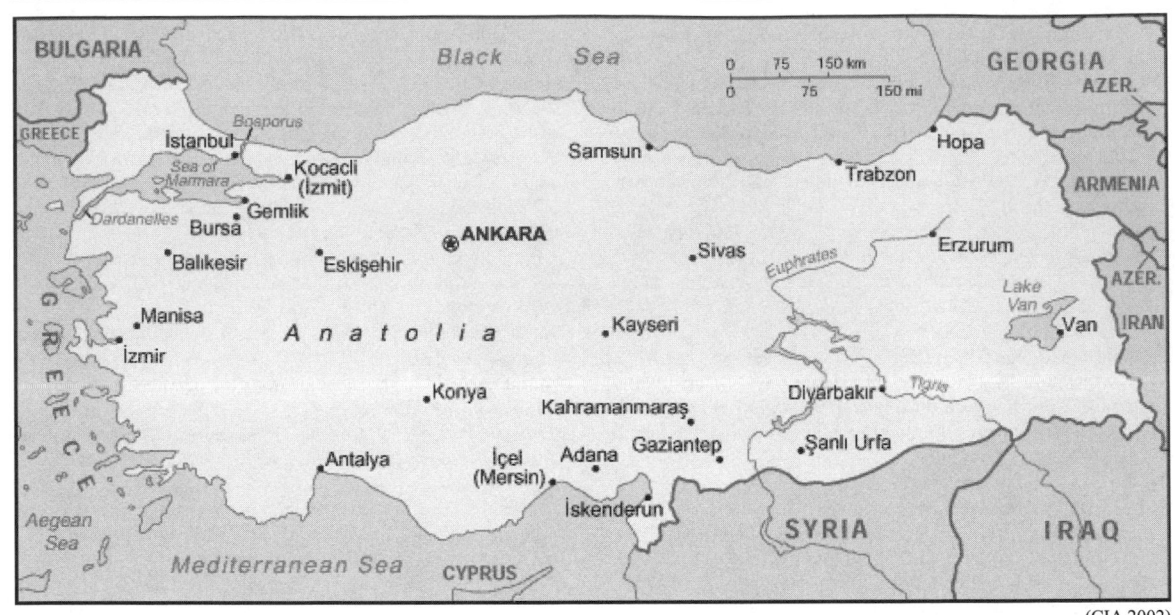

# Turkey
## (*Türkiye Cumhuriyeti*)
## (The Republic of Turkey)

Hamdullah Aydın, M.D., and Zeynep Gülçat, Ph.D.*
*Rewritten and updated in 2003 by H. Aydın and Z. Gülçat*

## Contents

## *Demographics and a Brief Historical Perspective*
### HAMDULLAH AYDIN and ZEYNEP GÜLÇAT

### A. Demographics

Turkey is located at the intersection of two continents, with the small region of Thrace and the ancient city of Istanbul in Europe, and the larger part of the country, Anatolia, in Asia Minor. Turkey is twice the size of the state of California,

with an area of 301,380 square miles (780,580 km²). Anatolia (Asia Minor or Asiatic Turkey) is surrounded by the Black Sea, the Aegean Sea, and the Mediterranean. An inland sea, the Marmara, separates Anatolia from Thrace to the northwest. Turkey has 4,470 miles (7,200 km) of coastline. Rectangular in shape, Turkey stretches 972 miles (1,565 km) east to west, and 404 miles (650 km) north to south. Its neighbors are Greece and Bulgaria to the west, Georgia and Armenia on the northeast, Nakhitchevan and Iran to the east, and Iraq and Syria on the south. Central Anatolia and the eastern regions are typically hot and dry during the summer and cold and rainy during winter. The coastline along the north, west, and south of Turkey has a milder climate throughout the year.

Turkey's agricultural production is, on the whole, self-sufficient, while the natural resources, although rich, are not fully utilized at present. A radical transition toward industrial development has occurred in Turkey's economy, which was mainly based on agriculture in the past. State intervention in the economy has gradually diminished since the 1980s, and at present, the economy relies on free market rules. Turkey possesses a wealth of historical sites with rich potential for summer as well as winter tourism. Many ancient cultures of Anatolia, including the Mesopotamian, Sumerian, and Hittite, constitute Turkey's basic cultural heritage. An Islamic culture is woven into this background.

In 2000, Turkey had an estimated population of 67.8 million (State Institute of Statistics, SIS). [*Update 2002*: In July 2002, the estimated population was 67.3 million [*WFB*]. (Data were provided by the authors from Turkish sources; the editors added some alternate data given in parentheses with *WFB* in brackets from *The World Factbook 2002* (CIA 2002).)

[**Age Distribution and Sex Ratios**: *0-14 years*: 30.9% (27.8% with 1.04 male(s) per female sex ratio [*WFB*]); *15-64 years*: 63.4% (65.9% with 1.03 male(s) per female [*WFB*]); *65 years and over*: 5.7% (6.3% with 0.85 male(s) per female [*WFB*]); *Total population sex ratio*: 1.02 male(s) to 1 female [*WFB*]. More than half of Turkey's population are under age 24.

[**Life Expectancy at Birth**: *Total Population*: 71.52 years [*WFB*]; *male*: 70.8 (69.15 [*WFB*]) years; *female*: 75.9 (74.01 [*WFB*]) years

[**Urban/Rural Distribution**: 71% to 29% [*WFB*]. Ankara, the capital of Turkey, with 2.8 million people, is in the center of Anatolia. Turkey's largest city, Istanbul, has a

*Communications*: Hamdullah Aydın, M.D., Professor of Psychiatry, Director of Psychiatry Department, Gulhane Military Medical Academy and Faculty of Medicine, GATA, 06018, Ankara, Turkey; hAydın@gata.edu.tr. Zeynep Gülçat, Ph.D., Clinical Psychologist, Department of Psychiatry, Gulhane Military Medical Academy and Faculty of Medicine, GATA, 06018, Ankara, Turkey; zeygul@superonline.com.

population of 9.5 million. Located in the northwest, along the shores of the Bosphorus River, the point where East and West meet, Istanbul and its environs are the most densely populated, urbanized, and developed part of the country. The city is a center of trade, large and small-scale industry, as well as a center of arts and historical places.

[**Ethnic Distribution** [*WFB est.*]: Turkish: 80%; Kurdish: 20%. The authors wish to emphasize that there are a number of ethnic groups in Turkey, but their percentage in the population is not known. The same is true for religion (below): Their percentage in the population is not known also. The Turkish State is based on secularity and nationality. Each person who holds a Turkish identity card is considered as a Turkish citizen, no matter which ethnic origin he or she is from or which religious belief he or she holds.

[**Religious Distribution** [*WFB est.*]: Muslim: 99.8% (mostly Sunni); other: 0.2% (Christian and Jewish)

[**Birth Rate**: 20.9 births per 1,000 population and declining; (17.95 [*WFB*])

[**Death Rate**: 5.27 per 1,000 population; (5.95 [*WFB*])

[**Infant Mortality Rate**: 35.8 deaths per 1,000 live births; (45.77 [*WFB*])

[**Net Migration Rate**: 0 migrant(s) per 1,000 [*WFB*]

[**Total Fertility Rate**: 2.5 children born per woman; (2.12 [*WFB*]); *Mean Family Size*: 4.75 people

[**Population Growth Rate**: 1.57%; (1.24% [*WFB*])

[**HIV/AIDS** (1999 est. [*WFB*]): *Adult prevalence*: 0.01%; *Persons living with HIV/AIDS*: NA; *Deaths*: NA. (For additional details from www.UNAIDS.org, see Section 10B.)

[**Literacy Rate** (*defined as those age 15 and over who can read and write*): 82% (85%; *male*: 94%, *female*: 77% [*WFB*]); 95% attendance for free and compulsory school between ages 6 and 14

[**Per Capita Gross Domestic Product** (*purchasing power parity*): $6,700 (2001 est. [*WFB*]) (1997 government est.); *Inflation*: 69%; *Unemployment*: 10.6% plus underemployment of 5.6%; *Living below the poverty line*: NA [*WFB*]. (*End of update by Robert T. Francoeur*)] After consecutive economic crises that Turkey faced during the last few years, per capita income dropped to about $3,000 in early 2002. Following the elections and the establishment of the new government in late 2002, per capita GDP has shown an inclination to increase.

Turkey, like many countries, has experienced a huge population shift in the past 50 years. The percentage of the population living in cities had doubled in 35 years, from 25% in 1950 to 53% in 1985. In 2000, it was nearly 70%. Istanbul is one of the most densely populated cities in Europe, with 9.5 million inhabitants. Ankara, the capital, has 2.8 million. This dramatic population shift can almost entirely be attributed to the massive departure of people from the rural areas of central, eastern, and southeastern regions of Anatolia. The population shift facilitated changes in the family structure from the patriarchal to the nuclear model. The rapid transformation and urbanization also created difficulties in religious, moral, and sociocultural adaptation. Housing problems in urban areas induced migrants into building shanty houses called *gecekondu* ("built overnight") in the vicinity of big cities. These *gecekondu* are lacking in municipal services and facilities. As a result, a whole new subculture has emerged with its own lifestyle, bringing with it many social and economic problems. *Gecekondu* families are employed in small-scale or marginal jobs. Although they have now become permanent and essential factors in the urban economy, they are not yet fully integrated into the urban culture because of their low education levels, limited income, and cultural differences reflecting both "tradition" and "modernity."

Another important social phenomenon has been the out-migration of labor from the rural parts of Turkey to the countries of Western Europe, beginning in the early 1960s. It is estimated that two to three million Turkish workers currently reside in Western European countries. The so-called "second generation" born in these countries are subject to identity problems. They call themselves "European Turks," while they are labeled as *Almancılar* (Germaners) in Turkey. A considerable number of workers have migrated back to Turkey in the last decade, bringing back Western values, which probably have affected male and female roles, as well as relations between men and women. The response to this process depends on many factors, including environmental support, family background, and individual characteristics. It remains to be seen how this out-migration and back-migration will affect the overall sexual attitudes and behavior in Turkey.

Thus, as Kağıtçıbaşı (1982a) has noted, Turkish society presents a highly complex, heterogeneous picture, with diverse backgrounds differentiating along social class, rural-urban, and regional development dimensions. From the historical point of view, various cultural influences, which include the nomadic-Turkish, ancient Anatolian, Islamic-Middle Eastern, Mediterranean, and contemporary Western attitudes and values have shaped and are still shaping Turkish society today.

## B. A Brief Historical Perspective

The ancient inhabitants of present-day Turkey were among the world's first agriculturalists. The Hittite, an Indo-European people, created an empire in central Anatolia over 4,000 years ago and controlled much of what is modern-day Turkey for a thousand years. Phrygian and Lydian cultures also flourished in Anatolia. The rise of Greek civilization, with city-states like Troy on the coast of Anatolia and expansion of the Assyrian Empire led to the collapse of the Hittite about 900 B.C.E.

In the early centuries, among the ancient Turkish tribes in central Asia, both sexes were considered as equals, where men and women took equal share of responsibility in affairs of the country, although there had been a dominance of patriarchal or matriarchal families in different Turkish tribes throughout history. Records of ancient Turkish families revealed that monogamy was the basic model, although some tribes were polygynous. Also, in some tribes, marital union became valid only after the birth of the first child (Tezcan 1998). There are also records indicating that there was an annual tradition of freedom in terms of social and sexual interaction, which could be an ancient model of some contemporary carnivals or Mardi Gras in the West.

In the 6th century B.C.E., Anatolia, except for some city-states on the Aegean coast, was incorporated into the Persian Empire. Alexander the Great conquered the area, but it returned to Persian rule when his empire collapsed around 300 B.C.E. By the end of the 1st century of the Common Era, Thrace and Anatolia were incorporated into the Roman Empire. Constantine the Great founded the city of Constantinople on the site of ancient Byzantium in 330 as the Empire's eastern capital. Following the decline of the Roman Empire in the west, Constantinople became the capital of the independent Eastern Roman (Byzantine) Empire in the 7th century and retained this role for a thousand years. Repeated attacks by Islamic forces were fought off in the 7th and 8th centuries, but the empire lost control of central Anatolia to the Seljuk Turks. The 13th-century Mongol invasions left Anatolia mainly untouched, but they weakened both Byzantine and Seljuk power. In 1453, the Byzantine Empire fell to the Ottoman Turks, led by Fatih Sultan Mehmet (the Conqueror). The Ottomans established a vast empire that lasted until the end of World War I.

After embracing the Muslim religion, the social life of Turkish women became restricted and they lost most of the rights of their ancestors. In the six centuries of Islamic influence and Ottoman control prior to the 20th century, discrimination between the sexes grew and women were forced to live as a separate group. The harem life was introduced and in the 15th century, the palace of the sultan was divided into *Harem* (women's section) and *Selamlık* (men's section). Soon, harem life and polygyny became customary throughout the state. According to the Islamic family laws adopted by the Ottomans, women could not choose their husband, marriages were arranged by the older members of the family. A woman was not supposed to be seen by her husband before or during the marriage ceremony, and could easily be divorced by her husband, who alone could decide to do so.

Towards the end of the 19th century, with the penetration of Western ideas into Ottoman society, women were allowed some education, and their status began to improve. Turkey's Independence War under the leadership of Mustafa Kemal Atatürk resulted in the fall of the sultanate and abolishment of the religious authority and spiritual leadership of the caliphate. Thus, the religiously based system of the Ottoman Empire was ended. The Turkish Republic was declared in 1923 and a sudden break was made with old values and concepts. Secularism, Statism, Nationalism, Reformism, Populism, and Republicanism were declared as the ideologies of the new state. Turkish civil law was accepted in 1926, triggering a wave of rapid change in social life throughout the country. Polygyny was ended and religious marriages were rendered legally (but not always socially) invalid. Women gained equal rights with men, including the rights of inheritance, divorce, and owning property. In 1934, Turkey was among the first nations to give women the political rights to vote and hold elected office. At the beginning, however, these radical changes could not be assimilated equally in all parts of the country. Thus, for example, polygyny can still be seen today in the less-developed regions of Turkey, though it is rare. Many uneducated women are still not aware of their civil rights. Also, for many women, legal rights may have little practical value if social and economic pressures do not allow them to use these rights.

In summary, with the declaration of the Turkish Republic and the adoption of Western values and lifestyle in the first quarter of the 20th century, a sudden break has occurred in the community. Such an abrupt change affected concepts and experiences in sexuality in contradictory ways in the community, which had a rich and complex background. While liberating women and mitigating segregation between male and female roles, it has, at the same time, created gaps between generations and social structures that were, and still are, in the process of integration.

## 1. Basic Sexological Premises

### A. Character of Gender Roles

*The Effects of Social Change*

At the beginning of the 20th century, a movement against Ottoman marriage customs concerned with the plight of Turkish women began. The protesters were mostly upper and middle-class men who were allowed by Islamic rules to marry up to four wives, supplemented by concubines, repudiate them at will, and exercise strict control over their mobility outside the household. These protesters were against arranged marriages; they desired educated wives with whom they could have intellectual, as well as emotional communication, and a social life where the sexes could mingle freely (Kandiyoti 1995).

In this period, the Turkish nationalist movement also introduced new elements into the debate between Western ideologies and Islam. The ideologues of the Turkish nationalism asserted that ancient Turkish customs in Central Asia involved total equality between conjugal partners in a monogamous and democratic family. In 1917, the Family Code was accepted, and represented the first intervention of the central state into the family, which had previously been under the control of the religious authorities. With the establishment of the Turkish Republic in 1923, a major break had taken place, and the caliphate was abolished. The new constitution was based on secularism, and measures were taken to heighten Turkey's national consciousness in place of an Islamic identification. Revolutionary changes in the new state included the romanization of the alphabet, the new dress code, and an interpretation of Turkish history stressing its pre-Islamic cultural heritage. Laws were enacted for compulsory and standard primary education throughout the country. The state and the parents of children were made responsible for the education of each child. The modern woman of the Turkish Republic experienced a kind of metamorphosis, becoming a prominent figure, dressed in the Western style in a school or military uniform, and wearing evening dresses in ballroom dances. In the male-oriented society where son-preference was the main attitude, Mustafa Kemal Atatürk, the founder of the Turkish Republic, set a new tone by adopting daughters. Highly trained professional women started working in the republican offices. However, as members of a strictly segregated society in which male honor was dependent on the behavior of their womenfolk, women could only enter the public arena by emphasizing their respectability and nonavailability as sexual objects (Kandiyoti 1995).

Initially, these changes affected only a small urban layer. The spread of schooling and health services throughout the country proceeded gradually. Marriage alliances remained firmly under the control of local communities and followed customary practices, which were now denounced as 'traditional' or even 'backward' by the enlightened technocrats of the Republic. Turkey was assumed to be moving from tradition to modernity, and the idealized model of the 'modern' nuclear family involved companionate marriage, role-sharing between spouses, and child orientation. The ideology of the modern nuclear family was a radical departure from the pressures and control of older kin characteristic of Muslim societies. However, Kağıtçıbaşı (1982b) argued that the "modern" Turkish family was not based on the autonomy of its members, which modernization theory implied, and that emotional interdependence between family members persisted. Ayata (1988) commented that tradition and modernity are being lived concretely in Turkish households as a literal "split" between the styles of consumption, formal dress, and conduct displayed in the guest room, and those adopted in the intimate inner space of the rest of the house, which is a place of informality and closeness.

Social change is almost an everyday matter for people in Turkey. Technological innovation and a new monetary economic base for agriculture, land fragmentation and shifts in income distribution, the growth of industry, cultural diffusion, education, and the mass media have all helped precipitate this social change, along with internal and international migration. This unceasing mobility has caused people to change and adopt themselves into a more "modern" lifestyle in terms of contemporary paradigms and technology. As a result of this adaptation process, perhaps Turkish people have learned to realize their potential capabilities more rapidly. However, these changes probably could not be assimilated in the same rate/speed in all parts, resulting in a kind of splitting between layers of the Turkish society.

The Turkish State, through family legislation and the inclusion of women in the definition of full citizenship, has brought about a decrease in the legitimacy of patriarchy. On the other hand, discriminatory practices in many areas, such as employment, education, and social welfare have not ended, and women's basic role as caretaker within the family has not changed substantially. Meanwhile, women's monetary contributions have become necessary for the survival of households leading to some conflict in the sexual division of labor within the family.

### Family, Kinship, and Community

In traditional Turkey, members of a whole village are often related to each other through marriages and blood relations. Thus, kinship forms the basis of social relations in the rural setting. Brothers and nephews stand together in disputes and are called upon for help, support, defense, or even revenge.

With economic change, out-migration from the village occurred and accordingly, the pattern of daily contact, mutual services, and solidarity has been weakening. Still, in times of need and crisis, family and kin are called upon for help. Whenever the husband has to leave the village for long periods to work in the city or abroad, he may leave his wife with his parents, as she is accepted as a member of her husband's core family when she marries. When this is not possible, other kin take over this function. Similarly, kinship ties are functional in shared agricultural work, constructing housing, childcare, and so on, and this function continues even in the urban *gecekondu* context.

If, as a result of migration, kinship bonds weaken, and the neighborhood assumes greater importance as a support system, because public services are still insufficient in rural areas. Thus, as family extends into kin, so kinship extends into neighborhood and community in terms of networks of bonds involving duties, responsibilities, common concerns, support, and help.

It appears that male power is more prominent in lower-class families, where males have less resources in terms of income and occupation than in the middle classes. Kuyaş (1982) found that middle-class women perceive mutuality or sharing between spouses and think this is how it should be, whereas lower-class women perceive almost total male control, but again feel this is how it should be.

Despite the overwhelming prevalence of nuclear family residences, "extended" families and wider kinship ties have not decreased in importance in the city.

### Sex Roles

Although Turkey is in the process of rapid social change, it can safely be claimed that the general family pattern is predominantly patriarchal. While there are powerful crosscurrents acting both to reinforce and to mitigate male dominance in different contexts, the second-class status of women in the Middle East still prevails in Turkey. Clearly defined sex roles, division of labor, and separate social networks both help the women endure the status difference and yet, at the same time, serve to reinforce and perpetuate this difference. Supportive same-sex friendship/kinship networks further contribute to this separation (Kağıtçıbaşı 1982a).

The concept of honor, referring to the sexual modesty of a woman, implies that men control the sexuality of women. Honor is largely dependent on others' evaluations, and an insult to honor results in disputes, fights, or even blood feuds. The ties among the family members, kin, and community are so close that sometimes the honor of a whole village or community is affected by the honor of one man.

Özgür and Sunar (1982), who examined the problem of homicide in Turkey, attributed the high rates of homicide to a traditional system of norms that condone and require a violent response to violations of personal honor. Male homicide was found to stem from more normatively approved motives, such as self-defense, property defense, or honor, whereas a greater proportion of female homicides stemmed from domestic quarrels, jealousy, and similar motives.

Within the family, young women are controlled and their status is low. The young bride, in particular, is expected to serve all adults within the patrilocal household. Once she bears a son, however, her status improves, especially when the son grows up and brings in a bride and the cycle thus repeats itself. Hence, every woman in the traditional rural society prefers a son as a child; if she does not bear one, her marriage may be threatened (Kağıtçıbaşı 1982a).

The preference for sons does not only depend on an economic basis. The son, especially the eldest one, is responsible for all women in the family, including his mother in the absence of his father. In contrast to the central role of the son in the patrilocal family, a daughter leaves the household to get married when she reaches an age to be "useful." However, Kıray (1976) noted the changing value placed on daughters, who now often replace sons as the "dependable" child.

In the traditional Turkish family, the mother's relationship to her son is intimate and affectionate, in contrast with that of the father who is authoritative and distant. In some conservative groups, the father is such an authority figure that his son cannot even talk to his own wife or show affection to his own children in the presence of his father. In fact, the mother often protects the son from the father's disciplinary acts. The mother-son relationship is generally stronger than the husband-wife relationship in the traditional family, where any public show of affection between spouses is disapproved. A man does not even talk about his wife in the company of others, and if he has to, often he uses the word "family" to mean "wife." Communication and role sharing between spouses is limited, sex roles well differentiated and non-overlapping. Males are the decision makers in the family.

### Status of Women as Laborers and Professionals

The effect of introducing modern technology into agriculture and the resultant economic-structural change for rural woman has been a general reduction in her workload. With farm mechanization and the monopoly of such farming by men, women's farming decreased. With the introduction of ready-made goods, such as clothing and food, women's domestic chores have also decreased. This change has been considered to have a positive effect on women's well-being, relieving them from some of their heavy burdens. However, it can also be claimed that decreased workload has alienated women from production and has stressed their reproductive role (Kağıtçıbaşı 1982a).

In some areas, with the participation of men in factory work, an opposite outcome of economic-structural change has taken place, with women again being disadvantaged, as they are completely tied down in agricultural and domestic work and do not have access to education and mobility. Most "unskilled" women in rural Turkey are engaged in the production of handicrafts, such as embroidery and carpet-making, which is also considered a part of women's duties and responsibilities for her home. Years before they marry, young girls and their mothers begin preparing *çehiz* (handmade carpets, rugs, quilts, tablecloths, and scarves), which will be needed when they establish their own homes. These handicrafts constitute a major part of the folk arts, and during the past few decades, they have become a source of income for the households because they have gained monetary value as well.

Women's work in the rural economy is often not considered "work," for it is, rather, a total lifestyle. It is not differentiated as to locality or time. Different types of work may be done in the same place and at the same time, such as food production, housework, and childcare. Neither does it involve specialization or formal training.

Underestimation of women's work also derives from social values, which assign the provider role to men. In the idealized image of the affluent family, the woman does not have to work, an image that is especially prevalent in urban and small-town culture and that is spreading among *gecekondu* dwellers and villagers, who emulate townspeople (Kağıtçıbaşı 1982a).

Kandiyoti (1982) noted that urban Turkish women do not in any way challenge the male role. Lower-class urban women may retreat into domesticity, or if they have to work, it is considered unimportant or temporary. In the case of lower- and middle-class women, subordination is reflected in their very limited access to the outside world. In the case of professional women, husbands are still reluctant to take over roles traditionally accepted as belonging to women, such as taking care of children or sharing housework.

In rural areas, a negative relationship pertains between socioeconomic development and women's labor participation. Özbay (1982) pointed to the fact that women's labor-force participation is decreasing, though it is still high; and women's literacy is increasing, though it is still low. In urban areas, on the other hand, the substantial percentage of professional, highly educated, highly skilled women is notable in view of the low overall female education and skills in Turkey. The overall figures show that the proportion of working women has been declining in Turkey. According to the 1997 figures of the State Institute of Statistics (SIS), women's labor-force participation was 34.7% in 1990, 31.4% in 1992, and 25.2% in 1997 (Aydın 1998).

Erkut (1982) addressed the fact that, "despite the low levels of educational attainment for women in general, substantial numbers of Turkish women obtain professional degrees and practice in what are considered to be male-dominated occupations in the West." She explained that this has happened as women have been able to pursue professional careers without posing a threat to the male sex role and its privileged status. Highly educated women have had access to the support and services of other women, from the extended family and kin or from among the less advantaged, so that their professional roles have not had to hinge upon their husbands' help in carrying out their domestic chores. Men have thus enjoyed the enhanced family prestige and income provided by career women, without themselves changing their status or incurring more work. Erkut (1982) pointed out that men are the real beneficiaries of "the rise of a few women made possible by the exploitation of many." Thus, positive attitudes toward professional education of elite women exist side by side with negative attitudes toward women's universal education deriving from traditional culture.

*Fertility and the Value of Children*

As a result of high fertility rates in the past, the population of Turkey is young. Government policy changed from a pronatalist to an antinatalist one during the 1960s, and accordingly, fertility rates started to decline.

In the village setting, the child is socialized not only in a family, but also in a kinship-community system characterized by mutual obligations. Expectations from the child, accordingly, are not only individual and familial, but communal as well. In the face-to-face interpersonal relations of the small community, everybody is a "significant other," and no one can be ignored; thus, other-directed behavior tendencies develop from childhood on.

Kağıtçıbaşı (1982b) noted that with development, and especially with education, the perceived economic value of children decreases, but their perceived psychological value increases, at least in relative terms. When the economic value of children is high, the number of children increases, whereas when a low economic value is coupled with a high psychological value, the result is lowered fertility. Thus, the value of children forms an explanatory link, at the individual level, between the level of development and fertility rates. The economic value of children goes hand in hand with son preference, as sons are more dependable sources of economic benefits, especially in old age. This is of key importance in the sociocultural economic context, where patriarchal traditions are strong and institutional support of the elderly is lacking. The dependent, inferior status of the uneducated woman is crucial in this context. It is apparent in the widespread male decision making and the low levels of communication and role sharing between spouses. It is an inherent part of a general pattern of interdependent relationships, appearing first as dependency of the child on the parents and then as the reversal of this relationship. Socioeconomic development, and especially women's education and professionalization, are the key precipitators of change in this pattern.

The traditional Turkish way of adopting a child, which was also prevalent during the Ottoman Empire, is significant in some aspects. Wealthy traditional families usually adopt a child who is in economic or social need. Moreover, it is usually a girl, which seems to reflect the inclination to protect the weak. The child, called an *evlatlık*, is sometimes of an age when she (or he) is well aware that she is adopted and has a different status in the family. The *evlatlık* is well-cared for, is educated like other children, and is provided for, until she marries. On the other hand, she is expected to help with the housework, which constitutes her different role in the household. This traditional practice, which, partly because of economic and social changes, is on the decline, may be considered as an informal social-support system to protect the child where state supports are lacking. The *evlatlık* tradition does not exclude the more contemporary legal adoption system. Couples who wish to legally adopt a child must meet specific strict rules and usually have to wait for long periods. The couples (on the whole, those without children) usually prefer to adopt a newborn child, probably because they wish the child to think that she (or he) is their biological offspring.

Another type of adoption is seen in infertile couples in traditional Turkish communities in which one child of a relative (who is usually a brother or sister of one of the spouses) is adopted. The purpose of choosing a close relative's child seems to be related to the wish to keep the family ties together.

## B. Sociolegal Status of Males and Females

Today, civil marriage is generally practiced with or without an additional religious ceremony. However, the practice of religious marriage alone has not disappeared. Polygyny was prohibited in 1926 with the acceptance of the Civil Code. Nevertheless, it is still possible to see it in some regions, although it is rare and was not very common even before 1926.

According to the Constitution of the Republic of Turkey, citizens cannot be discriminated against on the basis of their gender, and all individuals have personal, inviolable, nontransferable, vested basic rights and liberties. In spite of this legal foundation for equality between the sexes, there were articles in laws that contradicted this principle. For example, according to the Civil Code, the husband was the head of the marital union and was in charge of the choice of residence. The Civil Code stated that husband spoke for and represented the marital union; the woman only had the right to represent the union for the permanent needs of the house (Ergöçmen 1997). The latest changes in the Civil Code were made in 2001, which discarded some regulations that held inequalities between men and women. One of the changes, for example, which was made in 1997, is the legislation concerning the wife's taking her husband's family name. Another important change involves the regulation of equal sharing between husband and wife of the property that was obtained during marriage in case of divorce.

Equality between the sexes was introduced in the legal structure through the reforms implemented following the declaration of the Republic, and opportunities were provided for effective participation of women in public life. One of the most important steps in this respect was recognizing women's right to vote and hold elected office as early as 1934. In spite of this relatively early access to participation in the political decision-making process, women in Turkey have limited political involvement in terms of representation in the Parliament.

Even though under the civil code women have inheritance rights equal to men's, in some rural areas women still get either nothing or much less than what men get, and inheritance issues are resolved informally within the family or the village. This practice is, however, on the decline and equal sharing is the rule for urban people.

On the other hand, there are two types of regulations with regard to women in the labor force. The first set of regulations prevents women from undertaking dangerous work, while the second set relates to protective measures regarding maternal activities of women.

Since the foundation of the Turkish Republic in 1923, the basic principles in education have been the universality of services and the equality of opportunities. There are also principles like coeducation and the right of all to education. Primary education, which had been five years, but was recently raised to eight years after long debates in the Parliament, is compulsory for every Turkish child, and is free in public schools. At present, debates between politicians, and in public continue as to whether compulsory education should be raised to 12 years.

Almost all boys and girls attend primary education, although the dropout rate at later stages of education is higher for girls. For instance, whereas 91% of boys and 87% of girls attended primary school in the 1994-1995 academic year, 78% of boys continued on to secondary school while only 53% of the girls continued into secondary schools. Women, thus, still lag behind men in literacy and level of education (Ergöçmen 1997).

The legal age of marriage, which had been 15 for females and 17 for males until recently, was raised to 18 for both sexes. To secure the family unit is both a part of the main Turkish traditional approach and the official policy of the state. Thus, for example, if both the husband and the wife are government employees appointed in different cities, they have the right to demand to be employed in the same town to maintain the family union. In 1989, the State Department of Family Research was established as an independent branch under the Prime Ministry to develop national policies for the maintenance and welfare of the Turkish family.

In the past, punishment for *zina* (adultery) for women constituted the husband's right to divorce her, while the woman was also sentenced to imprisonment. For men, adultery was not punished as severely. Recent regulations in the civil code abolished this inequality, and adultery is currently not considered a criminal act for either men or women.

On the other hand, adultery is severely punished by religious tradition or by some radical groups in the society. In Islam, a woman who commits the crime of adultery (which has to be witnessed by four adult Muslim males to be considered as evidence for adultery) is supposed to be stoned to death, whereas no such strict punishment exists for adulter-

ous men. Interestingly, there had been no recorded case of punishment for adultery during the whole history of the Ottoman Empire, which implies that religious rules were less harshly practiced during the Ottoman reign.

The civil law of Turkey accepts the absolute divorce of couples. Moreover, a legal separation period for the married couple is also possible before absolute divorce. Turkish divorce law has been revised as a result of changes in social life, and the new regulations of 1988 made attaining a divorce much easier. For example, at present, a three-year period of separation is sufficient to grant a divorce, even if one of the spouses disagrees.

Divorce rates showed an increase in 1988 because of the enactment of the new law, but have stabilized and remained constant during subsequent years. The most commonly cited cause of divorce is incompatibility between spouses, with willful desertion and adultery following (SIS 1995). As far as women are concerned, the causes of divorce are adultery (81.3%), intrafamilial violence (65.5%), and alcoholism (59%).

## C. General Concepts of Sexuality and Love

Reflections of the Oedipal theme can be traced in the Anatolian culture and folklore. The colloquial Turkish language and Turkish slang is full of examples of male sexual aggression toward women or threats of castration directed toward men. In rural Turkey, the custom of firing guns during the wedding ceremony, sometimes with fatal consequences, can also be regarded as an example of the Oedipal theme.

Physical contact between same-sex people is common in Turkey. It is socially acceptable for women and men to embrace, kiss, and hold hand-in-hand with same-sex friends or relatives in public. However, physical closeness and any show of affection between the sexes in public are generally not condoned even between husband and wife.

In Turkish folklore and legends (such as those of Yusuf and Züleyha, Ferhat and Şirin, Kerem and Aslı, and Leyla and Mecnun) the main theme is longing for the loved one. Love and passion, almost devoid of bodily senses and sexuality, is experienced as a search for the mystical, a way to reach God. Ancient Turkish verses, tales, and music reflect the mystical quality of love. In traditional Turkish arts, such as carpetmaking, which is usually woven by women, decorations and ornaments carry messages for the loved one.

Turkish melodrama represents the woman by her changing status in society as well as by the split in her identity. Films present prudent, poor, but highly talented women who are exploited in the patriarchal household and become very famous and rich by the help of a man who is financially and socially in a higher position. However, fame and fortune do not help her to form a stable identity; she is abused again, because she cannot attain the idealized love and security she has aspired to.

With few exceptions, Turkish media serve to accentuate traditional gender roles. İmamoğlu (1996), in her review of newspapers, noted that whether representing leftist, rightist, or liberal viewpoints in the political spectrum, Turkish newspapers share the ideology of perpetuating gender stereotypes in a subtle but consistent way. She concludes that, similar to Western newspapers, women seem to be defined in terms of their relationship to men. Women's maternal and marital roles and sex-object images are emphasized, while their femininity is defined from a male perspective.

In summary, it is not easy to reach a conclusion regarding the basic concepts of sexuality, love, and sexual attitudes of the society. Besides the media, which carry Western values into the very homes of the most isolated, reflections of many ancient cultures and civilizations can also be found alongside

Islamic, Arabic, and Persian influences. These can be traced in Turkish legends and folk tales, sharing common themes with Middle Eastern and Mediterranean cultures.

## 2. Religious, Ethnic, and Gender Factors Affecting Sexuality

### A. Source and Character of Religious Values

Turkey is a secular state according to the Constitution. Although the community is predominantly Muslim, mostly Sunni, with a considerable part belonging the Alevi tradition, Turkish people are unique in their mild interpretation of Islam. A number of varieties of Islamic interpretation exist side by side, as well as non-Muslim groups. In the past decade, radical religious movements in the Middle East have found supporters in Turkey, and these fundamentalist groups had exerted pressure in favor of a return to *şeriat* (laws according to the Koran). Their political party was closed down in early 1998, their activities being against the Constitution. Another political party with a much milder religious discourse was successful in the November 2002 elections, and a new government was established. The Turkish Constitution is based on secularity, not permitting any religious ideology to control the political system.

Contemporary interpreters of the Koran believe in the equality of males and females, although some fundamentalists refrain from any other interpretation of the Koran, even mildly deviating from the original. On the other hand, the effects of Islamic tradition on many sexual behavior patterns of Turkish men and women can be discerned, except for the educated urban minority. Significant differences probably exist in the sexual attitudes or behavior of people from rural and urban areas. In terms of sexual behavior, Turkey manifests a very complex picture, as the Turkish cultural mosaic is made up of many different value systems. There are insufficient data to support a conclusion. As Tekeli (1995) said, along with ancient Turkish traditions and Islamic influences, elements of secular Western culture, atheistic socialism, and various regional cultures interact with each other to create an extremely rich and complex whole. This mix gives Turkish citizens their distinctive, more liberal characteristic.

Early in the Ottoman reign, the presence of two witnesses who testified to the decision of the woman and the man (or their representatives) was a sufficient condition to form a marital bond. Marriages were not officially recorded until the establishment of the Turkish Republic. The marital union was basically a contract between two partners. Thus, no official approval was considered necessary. Later, this ceremony took place in the presence of an *imam*, a religious leader, and this practice was called *imam nikahı*, a religious marriage.

On the other hand, the religious marital union could easily be broken if the husband alone so desired. This marital arrangement rested on the absolute fidelity of the woman, while permitting the man sexual freedom. The woman could not divorce her husband and marry again under any circumstance, except when her husband divorced her. The most she could do was to leave home if her husband brought in a new wife.

According to Islamic rules, a man can marry again as soon as he divorces his wife, whereas a woman has to wait for at least three months if she wishes to marry another because of possible pregnancy from former husband. However, if the man divorces his wife more than twice, he cannot marry her again; an exception arises if the woman marries another man and is divorced by him. This is called *hülle*, and has, in a way, a protective function for women. In modern Turkey, which generally interprets Islam in a very mild manner, it is not seen. A kind of Islamic marriage contract called *mut'a*, which is valid for a short period of time or under certain conditions, is also very rare in Turkey, although in some fundamentalist religious groups, it is sometimes resorted to, presumably with the purpose of justifying sexual involvement.

*Mehir* (a kind of dowry), which involves paying an amount to the bride's parents, has been known from ancient times, probably originating in the process of transition to the patriarchal social order, when women began to be regarded as commodities with a price that could be paid for. Starting with the early years of Islam, it took the form of a payment made directly to the woman for her security. Thus, while the woman was withdrawn from social life and productivity, some means of security was provided for her. This practice, which could be regarded as "progressive" centuries ago, is maintained today as a tradition. Today, in rural areas mostly, it prevails as *başlık* (brideprice or dowry), an amount of money paid by the groom or his family to the girl's parents. *Başlık* is an indication of social and economic power for both sides. This practice is declining with urbanization and nuclearization of the family.

Another practice, although rare, seen in Turkey, as in many other predominantly Islamic countries, is polygamous marriages. Only 1.6% of all married women are or once were, in religion-based polygynous marriages according to a nationwide survey in 1988 (HIPS 1989a). Thus, it is obvious that polygynous marriages are not widespread. However, there are some variations by rural/urban, geographical, socioeconomic, and sociocultural characteristics. For example, polygynous marriages are more widespread in the east, in rural areas, and among those who have no education.

Contemporary authorities of Islam in Turkey do not regard polygamy as a valid norm of religion in modern times, and most approve only of monogamy. In spite of this, again, most men and women prefer a religious ceremony in addition to the official marriage, as it is accepted rather as a declaration of the marital union before God and society. On the other hand, while religious marriages are socially recognized, they have no legal standing. Surveys imply that the prevalence of such marriages is of a sizable magnitude. Among all marital unions in Turkey, 8.3% are based only on religious ceremonies, whereas 80.5% of the officially married couples have chosen to have both a civil and a religious ceremony (HIPS 1989b). Since marital unions based only on religious ceremonies are not legally recognized, the partners are deprived of their institutional rights within the family, such as inheritance, or parental rights on the education of their children. Whereas 4% of urban women live in religious unions, three times as many do so in rural areas.

More legendary than real, in Islam, a man who intended to marry was supposed to present the bride with the amount of gold which equaled her body weight. Thus, heavier women were more precious in the past, when religious marriages were the only form of marital union. A man could marry four wives, but had to treat them all equally.

### B. Character of Ethnic Values

The family, as a valued social system, has always been important for Turkish people. According to the traditions of ancient Turkish states, such as Hun Turks and Göktürks, which served to keep the family secure and united, men would marry their stepmother or their brother's wife if their husbands died.

Since the acceptance of Islam, religious and ethnic factors have become so mingled with each other through the centuries, that it is not always possible to distinguish their separate effects on sexual attitudes and behavior. Although a variety of ethnic groups exist in Turkey, they are not recognized by the state, which accepts each person as a Turkish citizen, regardless of ethnicity. Statistical data are not available for these groups as separate entities.

If the agrarian society and its values are taken as the core society or as a reference point, modifications in outlooks and ways of life can probably be better understood: The family system in the small agricultural community is generally assumed to be patriarchal with close kin and family relations. On the other hand, surveys have shown that the majority of families are nuclear and probably have always been.

Kağıtçıbaşı (1982a) noted that the extended family has been an ideal, especially in rural areas, which involves expectations of living in old age with the adult son's family and being supported by him. Underlying this ideal is, on the one hand, economic necessity, mainly, lack of institutional support or other means of old-age security, resulting in dependence on children and a consequently high value put on children's loyalty to the parents and the family. On the other hand, idealization of the extended family is partly the continuation of a tradition or a sign of longing for the past, as well as a sort of status aspiration. In the past, generally, rural patriarchal extended families have been the rich families, which could afford to keep all the family members under the same roof, as they had large land holdings to live on. Consequently, in the eyes of the poor peasant, the extended family has been identified with wealth, thus symbolizing an ideal.

According to Kağıtçıbaşı (1982a), the dynamic nature of the family underwent modifications in the face of changing socioeconomic conditions in Turkey. A typical pattern of change through the lifecycle of the rural family involves, first, the newly married couple living with the husband's parents (the patriarchal extended family) as a valued pattern, and, because of economic necessities, moving out as the young man gains more income and autonomy (the nuclear family), and then later on, the aged parent(s) moving in again for protection in old age (the transient extended family).

Even when conjugal families live in separate households, the functions of an extended family are served by them, in that they are called upon to provide material support when needed, forming what might be called the "functionally extended family." Thus, close family ties extending into kinship relations serve an important function of security in times of crises and conflicts, which are often faced by the families undergoing change in both the rural and the marginal urban context (Kağıtçıbaşı 1982a).

The spatial proximity of the separate family and kin households, even in the cities, symbolizes and may even strengthen the close mutual bonds of family and kin. Mutual support within the family is the rule. Thus, for example, older brothers are expected to finance younger siblings' education and be available for assistance for their parents in old age. Family relations are mostly patriarchal, with men having authority over their wives and children. Young brides in rural areas often have to live within their husband's family, which can cause many interpersonal and role problems between her and the in-laws. This "extended family" holds, at least, three generations in the same household, with grandparents having authority over the family income and childcare. After the bride gives birth to a child, particularly if it is a son, she ascends to a higher status in the family.

Endogamous marriage—marriage within one's own religious, ethnic, or kinship group—which is still commonly practiced in some regions, has various social functions, such as maintaining local cohesiveness, control over land, and protection of the family from "strangers." Twenty-one percent of marriages were found to be consanguineous. It increases to 31% in the east and decreases to 13% in western Turkey. Educational level of women seems to be an important determinant. The percentage of consanguineous marriages drops with women's increased education (HIPS 1989b).

Marriage in the rural context appears to assume more of a social than an individual or conjugal character, as a means of maintaining economic and social ties. It is especially instrumental in strengthening existing kinship relations or extending them outside the village to similar ethnic groups or in forming neighborhood and territorial ties, and in increasing the number of relatives and friends who are potential sources of aid. Thus, arranged marriages are common in rural parts of Turkey and not rare in small towns or even cities.

Related to the social function of marriage, a tradition called *kız isteme* ("asking for" the girl) involves asking the girl's parents' permission for her to marry. The elderly, respectable members of the boy's family pay a visit to ask for the permission of her parents to *kız alma* ("taking" the girl). In other words, they ask for the permission of the girl's family for the young couple to get married. The girl and the boy may or may not know each other; may not even have met each other before the visit. That is, they themselves may have decided to get married, or the marriage may be arranged by their parents, in which case the girl is usually "selected" by the boy's mother or other female kin for her beauty, her wealth, her parents' social status, or other qualities valued by the community. The boy's parents should bring special presents for the *kız isteme* occasion, such as flowers and sweets, which may also show variations according to regional custom. *Kız isteme* has been modified throughout the modernization process and may vary in different socioeconomic subcultures. In transitional families, for example, who mostly live in small towns and *gecekondu* areas, parents bargain on the household needs of the young couple. Sometimes the process may take months until the families agree.

Abduction and elopement still exist in the peasant culture, although not condoned. Only 1.3% of marriages in 1989 involved elopement. The responses to such action range from tolerance to strong disapproval and even vengeance and strife between the families involved. It is also seen as a breach of the proper standards for formal marriage and the financial contract, namely, the dowry.

Weddings are important in the social life of Turkish people. Mothers, especially in the traditional context, prepare themselves and their daughters or sons for their wedding ceremony, and their marriage in general, almost before the child is born! During the marriage ceremony, relatives bring the newlyweds presents, such as household needs, or jewelry and gold, if wealthy. These presents are accepted to belong to the woman and constitute a kind of security for her. If, later, it has to be exchanged for money, her husband is obliged to ask her permission. Valuable presents given during the engagement period are to be returned if the engagement is broken.

In arranged marriages, the man is not supposed to see the bride until the wedding night. After the wedding ceremonies, the husband presents his wife a gold coin as a gift in exchange for seeing her in person. This is called *yüz görümlülüğü* (a "price" for seeing the bride's face).

Another traditional practice, the dowry, has functions such as the economic gains it brings to the family in exchange for the loss of labor of the girl, or, providing security for the wife if her husband dies. However, if the man is unable to pay the dowry, abduction may provide a solution. Another function of the dowry is providing support for the wife in case of divorce; yet divorce is quite rare in rural Turkey, as it is not condoned and is resorted to only under extreme conditions. Since endogamy is more prevalent in rural Turkey, or, at least because people are tied in close kinship bonds with patriarchal, authoritarian relations, individual acts such as divorce are limited. One socially acceptable reason for divorce may be evidence, or even suspicions, about fidelity.

Some personal and social conditions, such as infertility or failure to give birth to a son, may lead the man to another marital union. In this case, he usually does not leave his first wife if she does not intend to divorce him. He behaves as a responsible husband for both women.

In summary, it can be said that, although some groups organize their life according to Islam, it cannot be generalized to the whole community. Ancient Turkish influences and Anatolian civilizations constitute the main background, while Islamic and Western effects are woven into this pattern. Traditional institutions, such as marriage and kinship relations, serve both individual and social functions. Such "ceremonial" patterns help people perceive themselves both as individuals and as a part of the Turkish community.

## 3. Knowledge and Education about Sexuality

### A. Government Policies and Programs

The Turkish State, as well as the "elite" or "intellectual" men and women in Turkey have always been concerned about "sexual education in the society" since the establishment of the Turkish Republic. What they did, for example, was to translate the Western classics into the Turkish language and, thereby, in a subtle and indirect way, introduce the Turkish society to Western ideologies, among which is the more "liberal" approach to sexuality. Along this line of thought, Mustafa Kemal Atatürk founded the first music school in the 1920s in Ankara, which gave education in Western classical music and instruments, and which later became the first conservatory of music in modern Turkey.

At present, sexual education is formally or informally given on different levels, depending on the age, education, socioeconomic status, and the needs of groups. One example of the more "formal" efforts for sexual education is the "parenting" schools, which were started about a decade ago. Also, about 15 years ago, the Turkish Family Planning Association organized a workshop on sexual education and therapeutic intervention in sexual disorders in Ankara for professionals such as urologists, psychiatrists, and clinical psychologists working in the area.

During the last 20 years, sexual education has been a topic of debate in professional circles in Turkey. Previously, even in medical schools, sexual education was limited to courses on the anatomy and physiology of the sexual organs. Recently, in medical schools and in some psychology undergraduate and graduate programs, human sexuality, sexual functions, and dysfunction have become a part of the curriculum.

In the past, in elementary education and high schools, there were no formal sexual education programs. In primary education, biology courses included information only about reproduction in various life forms, including humans. While it remains to be decided on which level sexual education programs should be given, a preliminary "trial" sexual education program in some chosen primary schools was started nearly five years ago. The "trial" program mainly consists of basic information about the anatomy and physiology of both sexes, including information about intra-uterine development and childbirth. The courses are taught by trained lecturers to girls and boys separately, who can ask questions and discuss the topics during lessons.

In a study on the sexual attitudes of adolescents by Başgül (1997), 12- to 15-year-old students reported that sexual education should be included in the curriculum. In another study, which included 13,000 female high school students, it was found that 75% had some information on

sexuality, including contraceptive methods and sexually transmitted diseases, although, on the whole, the level of sexual knowledge was limited in this group (Vicdan 1993).

In the 1999-2000 academic year, a project for 'sexual education' in primary and secondary schools was put into practice by the Ministry of National Education. The program covers topics such as physical growth, development, and maturation, male and female reproductive systems, adolescence, sexuality and sexual identity, contraception, and sexually transmitted diseases (Milli Eğitim Bakanlığı 2000). Attempts to integrate sexual education programs into primary education continue, and although still not a formal part of the curricula, are given on a "trial" basis in some schools in 2003.

To summarize, as a state policy, attempts have started to integrate sexual education into formal school curricula, and Turkish students, on the whole, seem to be emotionally ready and willing to receive such education. On another line of sexual education, a number of nongovernmental organizations, among which is the Family Planning Association and various other associations, provide educational programs on family planning and contraceptive methods in rural and *gecekondu* areas.

### B. Informal Sources of Sexual Knowledge

A conservative and "reserved" attitude in discussing sexual matters with children is apparent in Turkish families. Moreover, parents may not possess the knowledge about how and what kind of information or experience they should share with their children. On the other hand, some parents with little or no formal education probably lack even the basic information in sexuality. Thus, most teens in Turkey obtain information about sex and sexuality from popular publications, or share experiences and information with each other. For some, fear and anxiety about sexuality stemming from tales about, for example, "the first night" experience, prevail, and some girls expect great pain or to have excessive bleeding during intercourse. Many young boys, and even men worry about the size of their sexual organ or their performance, or whether they will be able to "satisfy" their partner.

Various studies indicate that the main sources of sexual information are peers and publications for adolescents. A study by Ekşi (1982) revealed that for 15%, the source of sexual knowledge was the family, for 35% peers, for 20% the media, for 8% the school, and for 12% other sources. One quarter of adolescents reported that they had no information about sexual matters before puberty. Negative feelings toward changes in puberty were much more prominent in girls. On the other hand, 7% of college students reported that the most important problem for them was sex and sexuality, among various psychosocial problems. In another study, adolescents' same-sex peer group was found to be the main source of information about sexuality, followed by the mother for girls and the father for boys. Within same-sex peer groups, sex was a frequent subject of talk among friends. Younger members learned about sex in these intimate groups. The media was again another important source of sexual information for both male and female students (Başgül 1997).

In rural communities, the elders traditionally supply the adolescents with information about sexuality. Adolescents also learned by watching the copulation of animals, before popular magazines, TV programs, video films, and, recently, DVD became a part of most households, even in isolated rural communities.

From the religious point of view, parents are responsible to provide information for their children. Every adolescent is personally responsible for his (or her) own thoughts and behavior regarding religion, and on reaching puberty, is obliged to follow Islamic rules as a proper Muslim, performing the rituals of Islamic belief. One of the rituals is called *abdest*, which involves bathing parts of the body in a predetermined order before praying and after any type of sexual activity, whether intentional or spontaneous. Parents have to teach their children to *take abdest* whenever they have a "wet dream." This is called *şeytan aldatması* (deception or misleading of the devil). Parents' traditional approach to pubertal or prepubertal children, which is also apart of religious education, has been carried over generations throughout centuries in history. On the biological basis, it implies that a "wet dream" or nocturnal ejaculation is not provoked by erotic stimuli alone, and sexual content in dreams may occur without any experience or information about sexuality.

Another religion-based attitude is the responsibility of elder family members to provide sexual information to the bride and the groom before marriage. The *sağdıç* (best man) talks to the groom, giving information before the wedding, while the *yenge* (chaperon), a female family member, informs the bride about sexual issues.

In summary, while there are no clear state policies to regulate formal sexual education, in rural communities at least, the traditional Turkish family system supplies some information about sex and sexuality to children and adolescents.

## 4. Autoerotic Behaviors and Patterns

A large-scale survey on autoerotic activity in Turkey does not exist. Studies in student populations showed that, for 50%, the main sexual activity was masturbation (Çok et al. 1998). In Erkmen et al.'s (1990) study, 11.5% of female and 87.2% of male university students reported to have masturbated, while 21.0% of females and 26.0% of males reported that they considered masturbation as "unhealthy." Similarly, Ekşi (1990) reported that, male students regarded masturbation as "distressing," particularly if fathers were less educated. Taken together, these studies imply that while autoerotic activity is not rare among adolescents and young adults in Turkey, it is, nevertheless, a source of distress. Even among the highly educated, masturbation is not always regarded as an acceptable sexual outlet.

Clinical observations and self-report studies with sexually dysfunctional patients in Turkey show that masturbation is more commonly reported by males, while sexual fantasies and autoerotic activities are rarely reported by Turkish females. However, these observations rest on clinical samples and may not reflect patterns of sexual behavior in the "normal" population. Attempts to study sexual attitudes and behavior of the Turkish population are hindered by reluctance in responding to questionnaires, and so on, because sexuality is considered as a taboo by the larger part of the community.

Regarding religion and its practice, masturbation is regarded as a kind of "sin" by many Muslims. Although there appears to be no written rule in the Koran that prohibits it, most people who refrain from autoerotic activities believe that such behavior is sinful.

## 5. Interpersonal Heterosexual Behaviors

### A. Children

According to Islam, puberty is a stage when a child is ready to take on some adult responsibilities. As a part of this, while adolescent girls are expected to behave and dress as mature women, every male child should be circumcised before he reaches puberty. In the traditional context, *sünnet* (circumcision) is usually performed by a *sünnetçi*, always a male, trained and experienced in circumcision, but without a medical degree. During the operation, which usually takes place at home, the *kirve* (a close friend or relative, always a

male) holds the child, apparently to soothe him if he is scared, and the *sünnetçi* conducts the operation, usually without anesthesia if performed in the traditional way.

Great importance is attached to the *sünnet* ritual traditionally. The ceremony involved in *sünnet* is called *düğün* (wedding), carrying the implication that it is regarded as a step toward manhood. A special feast is prepared, and the child is dressed in a white gown and a cap adorned with decorations. Following the *sünnet*, he is laid down with prayers in a decorated bed, and guests bring in presents while being offered food and sherbet.

*Sünnet* is a religious rule, although many people believe that it is also a requirement for healthy sexuality, both in the medical and functional sense. Because of this, if the child is born in a hospital, many parents now prefer *sünnet* to take place in the hospital setting.

Although circumcision is an obligation for males according to the Islamic rules, it is also seen in many pre-Islamic cultures and religious practices. The age of circumcision in Islam varies from birth to adolescence, while Turkish boys are mostly circumcised between 3 and 6 years (Öztürk 1963). As is well known, this period is regarded as a critical stage in psychosexual development, and circumcision at this age might be risky for later development. Öztürk (1963), who studied this phenomenon in Turkish males, found no evidence to support the hypothesis that circumcision at an early age (or during the phallic stage) might have a negative effect later.

### B. Adolescents

The primary and secondary sexual characteristics of Turkish boys develop at roughly the same age as Europeans, whereas the rate of physical development for girls is closer to the Mediterranean region, where puberty begins at an earlier age. Along with the development of secondary sex characteristics, menarche and first nocturnal ejaculation are accepted as an indication to begin sexual education in the traditional sense.

During the Ottoman Empire, private teachers educated young girls in special subjects, such as music, literature, and the arts, while boys attended public schools, which also provided religious education. After the establishment of the Turkish Republic, a revolutionary project in the educational system was put into practice, and during the 1960s, sexual segregation in schools was totally abolished.

Studies indicate that, about half of unmarried male college students report having experienced sexual intercourse, whereas the percentage drops to between 4% to 19% for college girls (Çok et al. 1998; Ekşi 1990). This big difference probably reflects males' experiences with prostitutes. Overall, 66.2% of male and 8.5% of female university students reported premarital sexual intercourse (Erkmen et al. 1990).

### C. Adults

*Marriage*

About 92% of Turkish citizens marry to establish a family. In rural communities, the age of marriage is quite low, although it is expected that a young man complete military service before he can support a family, or indeed, to be regarded as a "man." For urban men and women, because of longer time spent in education, the age of marriage is higher.

Marriages are highly concentrated in the 15 to 24 years for females, and 20 to 29 years for males. Medical screening is obligatory for men and women before marriage, according to the law enacted in 1930. As a preventive measure, the aim was to recognize and cure those with contagious diseases. The law was passed in the period between the two World Wars, when serious economic and social problems had to be overcome. At that time, one of the main concerns of the newly established Turkish Republic was to prevent epidemics of tuberculosis, syphilis, malaria, and others.

In the social sphere, *hamams* (Turkish baths) had been a major locus of social interaction until modern facilities supplied hot water to houses. There were, and still are, separate sections or days for men and women in *hamams*. Children of both sexes are accepted into the women's section. In the past, women went to *hamams* with their female friends and kin and spent long hours bathing, chatting, gossiping, singing, dancing, and sharing the food they prepared for this occasion. Older women looked for young girls whom they could choose as wives for their sons. And, there used to be tales about young girls getting pregnant in baths while sitting on the marble seats, presumably from men who sat in the same place to take a bath during men's hours!

*Hamams* are still a social factor in traditional Turkish life. They are still popular for some sections of the community, especially for the lower socioeconomic groups in cities, or in small towns with no hot water supplies in houses. Interestingly, *hamams* are also popular in the high society in Turkey, probably as an eccentric activity, universally common for people with very high income.

### Weddings, Virginity, Potency, and Childbirth

Traditional wedding ceremonies in Anatolia last for four to seven days. The ceremony starts with music, played on local instruments. A flag is hung over the groom's house as an announcement of the wedding, and guests are accepted. Men and women entertain themselves separately until the *gerdek* (first night of the wedding). Some traditional activities common during the ceremonies are: *hamam* (Turkish bath), lasting for hours during which food is served, and *kına gecesi* ("henna night"), during which the hands of the bride and groom are colored with henna. Guests sing and dance and are served food and drinks. On the wedding day proper, a group of men and women take the bride from her home. She rides on horseback to the groom's house with the crowd, while everyone is singing and dancing. When the bride enters the house, coins (or gold, if wealthy) are spread over her. The groom's friends punch him before the newlyweds are left by themselves, representing rejection as a bachelor. The ceremonies end with prayers.

As a symbol of passing from virginity to womanhood, a lock of the bride's hair is cut on the day after the wedding. Magical practices, such as holding a mirror to the bride's face, and spilling water as the bride leaves her home, are believed to facilitate the her "adaptation" to marriage.

Virginity is still a treasured value for women in most parts of Turkey. Even educated young people who flirt reserve sexual intercourse until wedding. In traditional regions, parents or older members of the family wait outside the couples' room, to see whether intercourse has taken place. Traditionally, a blood stain on the bed sheet caused by the perforation of the hymen should be displayed to the waiting family, and is taken as proof of chastity on the part of the woman, as well as the honor of the man who has successfully performed the sexual act. Psychiatrists or gynecologists sometimes observe that it is a source of great pressure on the couple. The bride is expected to have no sexual experience, and, for many young men also, the first night of marriage is the first time he experiences intercourse. There are many cases of erection or intromission difficulties (i.e., erectile dysfunction and vaginismus) that can be attributed to the embarrassing and stressful events on the wedding night, plus, a general lack of sexual knowledge. Tragic consequences may ensue if the bride is not a virgin, or, if it is a case of a penetrable hymen often mistaken for previous loss of virginity. However, it is not unheard of that the newly weds show their families red paint or some other blood to escape the embarrassment.

Sexual potency and fertility have been important aspects of sexual identity of the Turkish male throughout history. Thus, methods to enhance potency and fertility, such as *kuvvet macunu* (herbal pastes) and potions were invented, and selected food recommended. Pastes and potions are still prepared today and handed out freely in some regions on special feasts. The preparations may take days, and large amounts of herbs are boiled in huge pots during the festivals. These annual ceremonies are local organizations, led by townsmen dressed in traditional costumes. As a part of the ceremonies, *kuvvet macunu* are handed out with prayers. They are believed to protect the user from diseases, make him sexually potent, and promote the health of children born that year.

After childbirth, the *lohusa* period is the 40 days during which it is believed that both the mother and the child require special care. The mother is usually confined to bed in the first ten days. A special bed, adorned with ornaments is prepared for her. She puts on her best traditional dress and jewelry, accepting guests in her bed during the first ten days. She is fed with sweets and dishes believed to make her physically stronger and to "increase her milk." Guests bring presents such as gold coins or clothes for the child. Prayers are said and guests are offered *lohusa şerbeti* (a special sweet sherbet). After the ten-day period, if her health permits, she gets up, but does not leave the house. She is helped by her female kin for her personal and the child's care, and for her responsibilities in the house. In the *lohusa* period, the woman is restricted in her sexual activities also.

### Divorce and Widowhood

The crude divorce rate of Turkey, less than one in 1,000 marriages per year, is low, compared to divorce rates in many other countries. Reasons for this could be the strong religious and family ties, and the traditional nature of Turkish society. However, it should be noted that official figures do not reflect the divorces among religious marriages. (See also earlier comments about divorce in Section 2B, Religious and Ethnic Factors Affecting Sexuality, Character of Ethnic Values).

In Turkey, 49% of all divorces occur in the first five years of marriage, and 45% occur in childless couples, an indication that children help to keep the continuity of marriages (SIS 1995). In other words, not having children may be considered as a social implication and probably a reason for divorce.

Levine (1982), who investigated the nature of divorce in Turkey, considered divorce as a "barometer of social change," "a struggle against conservatism," and "an act of female emancipation." Reviewing national divorce statistics, he noted that divorce is associated more with urbanism and urban occupations, with a higher level of development, with changing women's roles, with developed agriculture rather than with full-scale industry, and with being barely literate (especially among women). Thus, it is the people "caught in the middle of economic and structural change" who are most vulnerable to divorce, as they are subject to the most stress. In effect, the urban poor who are dislocated and economically vulnerable are more likely to get divorced. Levine views the patriarchal family as a hindrance to individual autonomy and initiative, in which the needs of the family hold primacy over those of individual members. In these families, divorce can be seen as a liberating act, although it brings with it serious problems of readjustment, especially for the woman, in a society which does not condone it.

By tradition, in the east and in southeast Turkey especially, if the husband died, it used to be the duty of one of his brothers to marry the widow. This was functional in providing security for the woman and her children, but is very rare at present.

## 6. Homoerotic, Homosexual, and Bisexual Behaviors

### A. Children and Adolescents

Case histories of psychiatric patients sometimes reveal homoerotic activity during childhood, although systematic research in Turkey for this period is not available. On the other hand, a number of retrospective self-report studies with late adolescent male homosexuals and transsexuals imply that, in both groups, the first sexual experience occurs at an early age. Most transsexuals and about one third of homosexuals reported that they had their first sexual experience before age 12 (Gülçat et al. 1988; İnci 1993), which appears to be quite early compared to the general population. These studies also showed that sexual intercourse was mostly initiated by the subjects themselves, that is, without being forced, which seems particularly to be the case for transsexuals. Most homosexuals and transsexuals came from families with more than three children, had pathological relations with parents, and traumatic childhood experiences, such as the loss of one or both parents, or physical and/or sexual abuse.

Based on the MMPI results of subjects in the 20- to 25-year-old age group, Battal et al. (1989) argued that transsexuals were characterized by the existence of early infantile conflicts and fixations, while homosexuals showed pathological resolutions for identification processes. Comparing homosexuals and transsexuals, İnci (1993) found that self-esteem and self-image of homosexuals were lower than that of transsexuals in the late adolescent group. Anxiety, depression, and oversensitivity were also characteristic of homosexuals, while suicide attempts seemed to be common in both groups.

### B. Adults

*Same Sex Behavior Versus Homosexual Identity*

Turkish males who play the "active" role in homosexual relations are not socially regarded as homosexuals in the Turkish culture. The active homosexual role is more likely to be assumed as a variety of sexuality experienced by a heterosexual male. That is, homosexuality is rather restricted in meaning, and covers almost exclusively effeminacy and the "passive" homosexual role. This attitude is even apparent in some legal and official practices of establishments like the armed forces. Homosexuals are not accepted in the army, and if such acts are witnessed during the military service, which is compulsory for every Turkish male citizen, the effeminate, passive partner is sent for medical evaluation, and discharged from the army if diagnosed.

Little is known about lesbians in the present-day Turkey. Legends about females who lived and fought like brigands are still told, without their sexual orientation being directly mentioned or alluded to. It can be claimed that there is no observable negative attitude in the society as far as lesbianism is concerned.

## 7. Gender Diversity and Transgender Issues

Sex-reassignment operations are occasionally performed in Turkey. In recent years, debates centering on ethical issues about the incompleteness of medical and/or psychological evaluation processes took place in the media. It is legally accepted that transsexuals obtain an identity in accordance with their acquired sex; they can change their name with a court order and they can officially marry.

It can be claimed that there is a double standard concerning attitudes toward male homosexuals and transsexuals in Turkey. On the one hand, they are alienated, ridiculed, and even persecuted by the society in general, and by the police, as they are regarded as a threat to social values. On the other hand, they are also condoned, especially those in the show business, who usually publicly claim that "God had willed them to be" as they are. Although very rare, female-to-male sex-reassignment operations are performed in Turkey.

## 8. Significant Unconventional Sexual Behaviors

### A. Coercive Sex

*Child Sexual Abuse and Incest*

Statistical data about child sexual abuse is almost nonexistent in Turkey. During the last decade, several initiatives were started to prevent child sexual abuse with the support of international organizations. Several associations, such as Çocuk İhmali ve İstismarını Önleme Derneği (The Association for the Prevention of Child Neglect and Abuse), were founded to help abused children and to conduct studies (TC Hükümeti ve UNICEF 1991).

Although no statistical data are available, child sexual abuse does not seem to be rare in Turkey. Occasional news in the media indicate that child sexual abuse, including incest, occurs. However, such acts are not condoned, and child molesters, whether homosexual or heterosexual, are strongly disapproved of in the community. Indeed, prisoners convicted of such acts are alienated or even killed by other prisoners. For this reason, child molesters are usually kept in separate cells.

Among cases of child abuse, sexual abuse seems to be the most frequent type. It is estimated that child sexual abuse is involved in approximately 50% of all kinds of child abuse, including unreported and unregistered cases. According to forensic medical records, 350 to 400 cases of child sexual abuse are documented each year. These figures are not conclusive though, because Turkish society is sensitive in sexual matters, and a considerable proportion of cases may not even come to the attention of legal authorities, because families are concerned about the protection of children and the honor of the family from publicity. On the other hand, because scandalous news sells, the media may also be exaggerating the news and figures to increase their sales (Kozcu 1991).

Child sexual abuse rehabilitation services have been established in a number of university and state hospitals in Turkey. Victims of abuse are generally referred to these centers by legal authorities.

Although incest is defined in all cultures, the boundaries of definition may vary. The Turkish culture does not consider sexual relations and marriage between, for instance, cousins, as incestuous. Thus, it is not uncommon for daughters and sons of brothers and sisters to marry. In fact, arranged marriages, especially in the eastern parts of Turkey, are often preferred, if it also serves to keep the unity of land and power.

*Other Unconventional Sexual Outlets*

There are no recorded cases, although it is claimed that males occasionally use animals (such as sheep) for sexual outlets in rural areas. Especially in isolated villages, where acceptable sexual outlets for unmarried adolescents are lacking, intercourse with animals should probably not be viewed as perversion.

### B. Prostitution

Commercial sex is legal in Turkey, and registered prostitutes are under periodic medical control. Illegal prostitution also exists, which stems mostly from immigrants from neighboring countries. Many unregistered prostitutes constitute a threat for public health, because they are not subject to routine medical checkups. Because of this, in metropolitan areas, STD appears to spread rapidly.

Prostitutes may be playing a special role for adolescent males in their first sexual intercourse. An older male kin may facilitate the adolescent's first experience by offering to take the boy to a prostitute, who is usually informed beforehand.

### C. Pornography and Erotica

Many publications on sexuality can be found in bookstores and newsstands. A number of popular magazines publish articles on sexuality frequently, which mostly focus on enhancing sexual satisfaction. Serious publications on sexuality, including an encyclopedia and books on sexuality for children and adolescents, are available in many bookstores.

Although there is no strict control over them, pornographic publications are not distributed freely in Turkey. Selling and purchasing them under the age of 18 is illegal. In one 1990 study by Erkmen et al., 26% of women and 48% of men reported that pornographic material should be freely published. On the other hand, many organizations have campaigns against pornography, with the aim of protecting children and moral values.

## 9. Contraception, Abortion, and Population Planning

### A. Contraception

The shift from a pronatalist to an antinatalist policy during the 1960s influenced contraceptive use by the introduction of modern methods to the public. In the early 1960s, only one fifth of Turkish women used some method of contraception. Traditional methods were more common then. The Family Planning Project was implemented by the end of the 1960s. The proportion of users was 38% in 1978, increased to 51% in 1983, and to 64% in 1988. By 1988, modern methods accounted for almost half of all contraceptive use, which shows significant changes in contraceptive methods (Hancıoğlu 1997). In general, Turkish women believe that lactation prevents pregnancy, and many breastfeed their children.

Almost all women (99.1%) between 15 and 49 have some idea about contraceptive methods, and 62.6% currently use some method of contraception. The most common is the IUD (18.8%), followed by condoms (6.6%) and contraceptive pills (4.9%). Regional differences in terms of contraceptive use are very high. In the east, 42% use a contraceptive, whereas in the west, the proportion is 72% (HIPS 1989a).

Among the reasons of *not* using contraceptives, the most common one is health concerns related to the method. Other reasons are husbands' opposition, lack of knowledge, difficulty in availability, and religious beliefs (HIPS 1989a).

The preferred method of contraception for Turkish males seems to be withdrawal. More than one quarter of sexually active males report using the withdrawal method, while 6.6% use condoms and 1.0% refrain from intercourse during the ovulation period (HIPS 1989a).

There is a strong positive correlation between education and the use of modern contraceptives such as the pill, the diaphragm, and IUDs. In urban areas, the main source of obtaining IUDs is doctors in private practice, whereas in rural parts, women obtain IUDs from Health Centers (HIPS 1989a).

The majority of college students claim that they would refrain from unsafe sexual activities that might expose them to AIDS, and most are willing to use condoms during sex (Çok et al. 2001). The media has played an important role in campaigns for condom use in the prevention of HIV/AIDS, which has also promoted indirectly their usefulness as a contraceptive.

There are also some interesting traditional methods of contraception in Turkey. These include swallowing herbal preparations made from local plants or vegetable skins, and homemade or readymade materials, such as soap inserted into the vagina. There is also a local belief that if the woman is able to pass a kitten over the saddle of a horse while riding, she will be protected from pregnancy!

### B. Teenage (Unmarried) Pregnancies

In 1995, the State Department of Social Services started a project for teenage mothers. Although statistical data are not yet available, unmarried teenage pregnancies are probably quite rare in Turkey. Since pregnancy out of wedlock is traumatic for both parties involved, if it occurs, the incident is probably covered up. Generally, these cases are not referred to state hospitals, where the signed consent of a parent is required before any medical measure is taken. Those who can afford to do so seek abortion in some private offices. In small towns or villages, where the risk of scandal is high, or where private services are not available, traditional methods of abortion are resorted to. On the other hand, pregnancy in the married adolescent presents a more common problem for Turkey, because the age of marriage is quite low, especially in rural areas. In 1991-1992, 4% of all pregnancies were to teenagers. These pregnancies are usually unplanned, and antenatal followup is lacking. Risks of pregnancy increase with low education and with younger age of the mother where symptoms may not be understood and spontaneous abortions may occur. However, if the pregnant adolescent is living in the traditional household with the family, there is a good chance that she will be well cared for, even if medical care may not be sought.

### C. Abortion

Until 1983, induced abortion in Turkey was prohibited except for eugenic reasons or when the woman's life was threatened by pregnancy. In May 1983, the law on population planning was liberalized to provide abortion in a legal and safe manner. At present, women may obtain an abortion on request up to the 10th week of pregnancy for medical or social reasons.

In 1988, 23.6% of all pregnancies were terminated by induced abortion, 8.2% by spontaneous miscarriages, and 1% by stillbirths (HIPS 1989b). The number of abortions induced for legal and medical indications was 15,571, while there were 49,655 abortions for unspecified causes, with 121 deaths in 1995.

Traditional methods of abortion, such as pushing sticks or long feathers into the uterus are probably still occasionally resorted to in rural areas. To induce abortion, some women take herbal preparations, such as boiled onions or aspirin, to trigger bleeding in the uterus. Carrying heavy loads or heavy massage on the lower back are some other traditional methods to induce abortion.

### D. Population Programs

Following the loss of males during the War of Independence (1918-1924), a shortage of manpower and a high mortality rate led the State toward a pronatalist policy to promote population growth until the mid 1960s. As a part of this policy, the government provided financial support for each child. During the late 1950s, public opinion began to change, and the adverse effects of rapid population growth were gradually accepted. An antinatalist population planning law was enacted in 1965, legalizing contraception and promoting avoidance of unwanted pregnancies by public education.

Illegal abortion under unhealthy conditions was a cause behind high maternal mortality rates until 1983. The population planning law was revised, and abortions up to the

10th week of pregnancy and voluntary surgical contraception were legalized, while midwives were permitted to insert IUDs (Hancıoğlu 1997). In 1996, mother and child health and family planning centers throughout Turkey were increased to 274, while the number of units giving exclusively family planning services was 532.

## 10. Sexually Transmitted Diseases and HIV/AIDS

### A. Sexually Transmitted Diseases

Among STDs, syphilis is one that is compulsory to be reported to the Ministry of Health. Because of its high incidence, a concentrated syphilis control program was started in 1925, and was carried out in the regions where it was widespread. The medical staff included control committees composed of a bacteriologist as a laboratory director, medical specialists, and specially trained health personnel.

Statistical data about syphilis cases are reported by the health control committees in the provincial directorates and by venereal disease dispensaries in certain cities. The patients are obliged to seek treatment at least once a week. The cases are recorded and sent to the Ministry of Health monthly. The registered syphilis patients were 3,841 in 2000. Out of this number, 3,416 were previously registered, 3,313 were still in the treatment program, and 443 were completely cured; 11 of these patients died (SIS 2001).

Information on syphilis and other sexually transmitted diseases was an important part of the curricula of medical schools in the past when they were widespread. Each case of syphilis has been followed up until treatment is completed. It does not constitute a major health problem now; its prevalence rate has decreased from 7.1 per 100,000 to 5.1 in the 10 years between 1987 and 1997.

*Incidence, Patterns, and Trends of STD*

The Ministry of Health declared that the number of cases with gonococcal infections was 1,071 and cases of hepatitis B was 2,435 in 1996. Out of 3,267 prostitutes screened in 1997, 1,136 were infected with gonorrhea, 36 with syphilis, and 27 with hepatitis. Only a small percentage of college students reported gonorrhea (1.3%) and hepatitis B (3%), whereas none reported having a history of syphilis (Çok et al. 1998).

*Availability of Treatment and Prevention Efforts*

There are 12 venereal disease dispensaries in Turkey, in addition to services for sexually transmitted diseases in most public hospitals. The Ministry of Health has organized courses and conferences, and prepared brochures and booklets for the public and professionals, in accordance with the World Health Organization for the control, prevention, and care of STD and HIV infections.

### B. HIV/AIDS

The number of diagnosed HIV/AIDS cases was 753 by the end of 1997 in a population of about 63 million in Turkey. Regarding the 1997 Turkish HIV/AIDS statistics, the Ministry of Health stated that 84.6% of HIV/AIDS cases were Turkish citizens, while 15.4% were foreigners; 9% of the HIV cases were infected by homosexual contact, 11.2% by intravenous injections, 6.4% by blood transfusions, 44.2% by heterosexual contact, 0.9% by infected mothers, and 28.3% by unknown causes.

Because of low public awareness of HIV/AIDS, the prevalence of commercial sex, the lack of educational campaigns, immigration patterns, tourism, and returning workers from Europe, HIV/AIDS is considered as a potentially serious health problem in Turkey.

Çok et al. (2000) reported that, while the majority of college students were aware of the disease, 30% stated they did not discuss HIV/AIDS with anyone. Students learned about AIDS from a variety of sources, including the media, booklets, and peers. Only a small percentage of the students obtained information from health professionals, family members, or at school. The study also revealed that Turkish students had a moderate level of knowledge about the transmission, symptoms, and prevention of HIV/AIDS. The majority believed that they were not at risk for getting AIDS or that the risk was very low. Six percent stated that AIDS did not concern them. About half of the students stated that they would avoid people with AIDS, whereas 23% were willing to open their houses to anyone with AIDS.

The figures for HIV/AIDS cases, covering a period of 10 years, are given in Table 1 (SIS 2001).

[*Update 2002*: UNAIDS Epidemiological Assessment: By mid 2001, a cumulative total of 1,245 cases of HIV had been reported, transmitted primarily through sexual contact and injection drug use. HIV testing is mandatory for blood donors, prostitutes, and military conscripts abroad. All diagnosed HIV infections are reported in a national HIV case-reporting system. The numbers of cases diagnosed among injection drug users are small. Universal assessment testing (UAT) surveys have been conducted in injection drug users and STD patients in Istanbul in 1992 and 1995.

[The estimated number of adults and children living with HIV/AIDS on January 1, 2002, were:

| | |
|---|---|
| Adults ages 15-49: | 3,700 (rate: 0.1%) |
| Women ages 15-49: | NA |
| Children ages 0-15: | NA |

[No estimate is available for the number of adults and children who died of AIDS during 2001.

[No estimate is available for the number of Turkish children who had lost one or both parents to AIDS and were under age 15 at the end of 2001. (*End of update by the Editors*)]

## 11. Sexual Dysfunctions, Counseling, and Therapies

### A. Concepts of Sexual Dysfunction

Because children are socially regarded as a natural consequence of marriage in Turkey, there is a strong expectation of a child almost immediately after marriage. Indeed, most young men and women expect to have a child in a short time after they marry. In cases of unconsummated marriage, the young couple faces an additional burden in explaining to others the reasons for not having a child. Thus, the majority of these couples seek sex therapy to make conception possible.

In childless couples, the blame is usually attributed to the wife. In such cases, couples often seek help from traditional healers who supply the couple with charms, prayers or sacred objects as a remedy for infertility or sexual dysfunction. Visits to *türbe* (tombs of holy persons) are another traditional way to deal with various social and health problems, especially for women. During the *türbe* visit, the usual practice is to pray for the spirit of the holy person, and to ask for his or her help. Sometimes pieces of rags or col-

**Table 1**

**Cases of HIV/AIDS in Turkey, 1991-2000**

| | 1991 | 1992 | 1993 | 1994 | 1995 | 1996 | 1997 | 1998 | 1999 | 2000 |
|---|---|---|---|---|---|---|---|---|---|---|
| Total | 38 | 64 | 74 | 86 | 91 | 119 | 143 | 109 | 119 | 158 |
| Cases | 17 | 28 | 29 | 34 | 34 | 37 | 38 | 29 | 28 | 46 |
| Carriers | 21 | 36 | 45 | 52 | 57 | 82 | 105 | 80 | 91 | 112 |

ored strings are tied to the branches of trees around the *türbe* or just left over the tombs. While unmarried women may pray for husbands, childless women pray for a child.

Sexual dysfunction is most commonly perceived as a failure of men in Turkish society. Sex therapists usually have difficulty in getting in contact with wives, even as a part of therapy. It is considered socially inappropriate for a woman to have a sexual problem, because she is not even expected to desire sex. On the other hand, sometimes men resist participating in sex therapy if they think the problem belongs exclusively to the wife.

Various magical practices are still met in some parts of Turkey, as a remedy for almost each problem a person can face, among which are sexual problems, childbearing, or infertility. One such practice is a vow or a promise to God that if the woman can give birth to a son, his hair shall not be cut, he will be dressed as a girl, and sacrifices made each year until his 7th birthday (Soylu et al. 1997).

Traditionally, sexual dysfunction and infertility, along with many other health problems and diseases, have been explained by folkloric beliefs, some of them based in Islam, and others apparently unrelated to religion. There are still many people who believe that erectile dysfunction, vaginismus, or lack of sexual desire are consequences of evil forces, such as *büyü*, or magical procedures conducted by those who mean to destroy the happiness of the couple. In other cases, the supposed cause is the *nazar*, or the evil eye, or the *djins*, spirits described in the Koran, which sometimes reveal themselves to human beings. One example of such a *djin* is *alkarısı*, a witch-woman who visits those who have just given birth to a child. *Alkarısı* is believed to inflict a disease called *albasması*, characterized by the woman seeing everything in red, turning hot, getting cramps, and choking.

If the cause of the sexual dysfunction or infertility is attributed to magical forces, treatment is usually sought from traditional healers called *hoca*, *medyum*, *falcı*, and so on, rather than medical doctors. Although prohibited by law, such paramedical healers provide their clients with preventive or curative measures, such as charms, prayers, and specific rituals. Doctors or psychologists have observed that many young couples with sexual problems, while claiming that they do not believe in supernatural phenomena, were pressed to seek a solution from traditional healers.

A study of patients at a primary healthcare unit revealed that one in 13 patients had a symptom of sexual dysfunction during the previous month, and one in 20 had a sexual dysfunction sometime in the past. Lack of sexual desire was the most prevalent symptom, occurring in 3.9% of all patients (Sağduyu et al. 1997).

In a survey by Sağduyu et al. (1997), which included patients in the 15- to 65-year age group referred to a primary healthcare unit, 32.1% refused to participate in a study related to sexuality, 11.8% reported having no sexual experiences, while 92.8% of males and 54.0% of females valued sexuality positively. Negative feelings about sexuality were prominent in the older age group. Among patients with sexual dysfunction, 25% of females and 5% of males suffered from lack of sexual desire.

Kayır (1990) reported that among women with sexual dysfunction, vaginismus was diagnosed in 52%, low sexual desire in 25%, anorgasmia in 15%, and painful intercourse (dyspareunia) in 2%. Among male sexual dysfunction patients, 48% experienced erectile dysfunction, 20% had premature ejaculation, 5% had low sexual desire, and 2% experienced inhibited ejaculation, while 22% had more than one sexual dysfunction. Özkan (1981) reported similar findings in a psychiatric population, with 49% of male patients having erectile dysfunction. He found that 52.9% complained of premature ejaculation, whereas 35.5% of female psychiatric patients complained of dyspareunia, 53.3% of vaginismus, 66.6% of anorgasmia, 60% of lack of sexual arousal, and 84.4% of low sexual desire.

The figures and clinical observations imply that vaginismus is seen relatively frequently in Turkey, compared to Western countries. Five to 10% of patients with sexual dysfunction suffer from vaginismus. Many of these can be traced back to lack of sexual education and conservative attitudes, which, in turn, lead women to see sexual intercourse as an activity to be feared and avoided. During the evaluation process, it is observed that the majority of sexually dysfunctional couples' problems are initially related to mild or moderate vaginismus-like complaints, which, on further interview, turn out not to be true vaginismus cases. Rather, the vaginismus-like symptoms are the result of the wife consciously or otherwise taking over the sexual problem (or, in other words, she assumes the blame for her husband's lack of desire or erectile problem). Thus, the problem becomes more complicated, where tactful and original approaches on the part of the therapist may be needed.

## B. Availability of Diagnosis and Treatment

Centers for sexual dysfunction in university-associated hospitals have been established in Turkey during the past 20 years. In these units, patients are fully screened upon admission. The screening covers psychological and physical examinations. Methods such as Doppler ultrasonography and endocrinologic and neurologic examinations are available in most centers. In some sexual dysfunction units, more-detailed examinations, such as neurophysiological and neuropsychological evaluations, and nocturnal penile tumescence (NPT) can be made if necessary.

Kayır (1995) argued that the improvement in diagnostic and therapeutic services has encouraged people with sexual dysfunction to refer to centers, while perhaps also leading to the idea that each sexual problem is an illness that can be treated by doctors.

Treatment is available according to the etiology of the sexual problem and the specific needs of the patient. The first step in therapy consists of providing basic information about sex and sexuality if the therapist decides that the couple lacks sexual knowledge. The information may range from basic anatomy and physiology of male and female sex organs, to the concept of marriage and marital relationship, according to the needs of the couple. Sometimes, especially with couples who come from low sociocultural backgrounds, this approach proves to be sufficient in solving the problem and no further therapy may be needed.

Couples therapy, based on Masters and Johnson's techniques, is the main approach if both partners are willing to attend therapy sessions, whether the etiology is psychological and/or organic. Group therapies for men and women with similar sexual problems are also available in some centers. In spite of the availability of a variety of therapy techniques, traditional values may sometimes hinder persons with sexual problems from taking part in therapeutic attempts to solve problems that prevail in the sexual area.

Many couples who seek treatment for their sexual problem are not highly motivated for sex therapy, because they expect the therapist to almost magically "cure" the problem by a simple intervention, such as by prescribing a drug (Sungur 1998).

Generally, professional help is not sought when the couple is first faced with a sexual problem, especially if it is a case of female sexual dysfunction. The typical Turkish couple at first communicates the problem to their families and tries to tackle the problem within the family's own resources, such as by taking the advice of the more experienced members, or to seek solutions with the help of traditional healers. In some cases, suggestions, reassurance, and parapsychological approaches work and the presenting problem is solved. In many cases, as expected, the difficulties persist and the marital relationship is threatened. The couple and families begin to split and blame each other. Usually, it is only then that the couple is referred for sex therapy. The delay and the introduction of other variables, such as the couple's blaming attitude and the families' concern, and even intrusion are factors which make the therapeutic process more difficult and complicated. The sexual problem of the couple can easily become a problem of the whole family, including the parents, siblings, and even relatives, which places an additional burden on patients and therapists. When incomplete sexual knowledge, erroneous expectations, lack of sexual experience, fears, and false beliefs are added to the picture, therapists are faced with multifaceted problems which they have to deal with, even though the couple is initially referred with a sexual dysfunction problem. Thus, the therapy proceeds on several levels at the same time, which may range from a teaching process to marital counseling and even to an insight-oriented approach. Thus, as Sungur (1994) has pointed out, formal training in sex therapy in Turkey is not sufficient for sex therapists, who must also have experience in handling marital problems, as well as giving special attention to cultural factors which may necessitate modifications in treatment programs.

In some cases with organic etiology, a psychotherapeutic approach is also utilized to help the adaptation of the patients before or after organic interventions. Penile prosthesis is the most common method for male organic sexual dysfunction. A penile revascularization operation is made for some patients.

Sildenafil (Viagra) became very popular in Turkey as soon as it was marketed. It was approved by the Ministry of Health and became available in the market in May 1999. Although strict regulations on the prescription were imposed in the beginning, these were shortly changed, and specialists, such as urologists, cardiologists, psychiatrists, and endocrinologists can now freely prescribe the medication.

## 12. Sex Research and Advanced Professional Education

Two main lines of sexual research can be delineated in Turkey: The first consists of surveys in the student population which mainly cover sexual attitudes, knowledge, and experience. Some of these studies have been reviewed elsewhere in this chapter. The second sexual research area is the clinical population, mainly, those who are referred with sexual problems. A series of studies have focused on psychological factors involved in sexual dysfunction: Işıklı (1993) found that sexually dysfunctional couples' problems in the relationship accumulated around emotions, cognition, and communications.

Bozkurt (1996) found that patients with psychogenic erectile problems were significantly more anxious and depressed when compared to organic patients. In the psychogenic impotence group, who were referred to the Psychiatry Clinic of Gülhane Military Medical Academy, 19.4% had mood disorders, 5.6% had anxiety disorders, and 22.2% had mixed mood and anxiety disorders. In the organically impotent group, no pathology in the mood and anxiety disorders spectrum was found.

The MMPI profiles of psychogenic erectile dysfunctional subjects had more similarity with neurotics than with normal controls. The personality characteristics of the psychogenic groups, revealed by the MMPI, suggested that, while there was no problem with the sexual role, depressive tendencies with difficulty in implementing activities, and an inclination to introversion could be expected (Aydın 1991).

Özgen et al.'s (1993) study indicated that organic causes more commonly underlie sexual dysfunction in the older age group, whereas psychological factors predominated in younger patients. If a dysfunction appeared in one area of sexuality, it tended to spread to other areas, causing problems in experiencing sexuality. As a result, it was claimed that the person's perception of and being in the sexual sphere were distorted.

Beyond clinical samples, in a recent population survey on the prevalence of erectile dysfunction, in a sample comprised of 1982 males, 64.3% who were over 40 years of age reported some degree of erectile dysfunction (35.7% minimal; 23% moderate; and 5.6% complete). The prevalence of erectile dysfunction increased with age, with diabetes, and with cardiovascular and prostatic disease (Akkuş et al. 1999). Gülçat (1995) found that 30% of nonclinical male subjects had some kind of mild to moderate degrees of problems related to sexual functioning. While these findings are in accordance with surveys in Western countries, it also implies the need for further studies in the area of sexuality and sexual problems in Turkey.

Advanced education in sexual dysfunction, evaluation methods, and treatment have been offered in some University Hospitals for nearly 20 years. There has been a growing interest and data accumulation in studies on sexuality in the last two decades. Since 1988, congresses and symposia are organized on issues in sexual dysfunction and treatment. The main aim has been to adopt a multidisciplinary approach in which psychiatrists, psychologists, urologists, and gynecologists work together in the assessment and treatment of sexual disorders. In late 1999, the Sexual Education, Treatment, and Research Association was founded to integrate the studies of various disciplines, prepare educational programs for the layman as well as for professionals, conduct research, and set ethical standards in the patient-therapist relationship.

The Turkish Family Planning Association, located at 73/1, Ataç-2 Sokak, 06420 Kocatepe, Ankara, Turkey, is the main organization dealing with sexuality issues, family planning, and sexual health. The website of the association is www.ada.net.tr/tapd; email: tapd@ada.net.tr).

## A Final Remark—February 2003

Social change involving modifications in social structure, attitudes, beliefs, and norms is rapidly altering the Turkish society. Shifts in the demographic composition of rural and urban areas, industrial growth, and related changes in the economy and social structure precipitate modifications in family structure, functions, and dynamics, as well as in traditional male and female roles.

Globalization is one of the most important factors that force people to reorganize their lives according to modern and even postmodern paradigms. Turkish society has a rich cultural accumulation, which gave the chance for the majority of Turkish people to go through this shift without any serious consequences.

Thus, the Turkish panorama of sexuality reveals that traditional and modern attitudes coexist side by side, and this fact, while constituting a fertile ground for social, interpersonal, and intrapsychic conflicts, also adds to the richness of the Turkish culture.

In the global sense, it can be claimed that the traditionally "reserved" Turkish society has become more comfortable in personally or publicly discussing sexual matters in recents decades. It is apparent in the frequency of sexually related material that appear in the press and other media. It can also be observed by the increasing number of people with sexual problems who seek help from health professionals, which can also be related to the increasing level of knowledge and experience of the latter in dealing with such problems.

In the general frame of Turkish State policies, rapid changes toward modernization, or, in many ways, toward Westernization in social life and relations occur continuously. In this respect, during the last years, and also a part of Turkey's integration process into the European Union, some changes in the legislation in the Civil Code were enacted, which improved the regulations regarding the equality of civil rights of men and women. (The latest changes in the Civil Code were mentioned in Section 1, Basic Sexological Premises.)

In this process of modernization, or namely, Westernization, some communities, among which are ethnic groups, women' organizations, and gay unions, have been voicing their demands more freely. Various organizations of Turkish women are becoming more active in securing and 'updating' women's rights in the last decades. Gay unions now claim their right not to be treated as 'queers,' but to be accepted as "normal" or ordinary members of the society. Some ethnic and religious groups have also been more accepted by the Turkish society in general.

## References and Suggested Readings

Akkuş, E., A. Kadıoğlu, A. Esen, Ş. Doran, A. Ergen, H. Akbulut, M. Sungur, K. Anafarta, T. Yılmaz, E. Eker, & H. Hattat. 1999. Prevalence of erectile dysfunction in Turkey. Unpublished data.

Ayata, S. 1988. Statü yarışması ve salon kullanımı [Status competition and utilization of the guest room]. *Toplum ve Bilim*, *42*:5-25.

Aydın, H. 1991. Psikojen empotansta kişilik yapısının araştırılması [A study on the personality structure in patients with psychogenic impotency] *GATA Bülteni*, *33*:187-194.

Aydın, O. 1998 (October). *Çalışma yaşamında kadın işçilerin korunması* [*Protective measures for women laborers*]. Paper presented at the Symposium on Legal Regulations for Women Laborers (Ministry of Social Security), Ankara.

Başgül, F. U. 1997. *12-15 yaş grubu ergenlerin cinsel eğitim konusundaki görüşleri* [*Opinions of adolescents in the 12-15 age group on sexual education*]. Unpublished thesis at Ankara Üniversitesi Sosyal Bilimler Enstitüsü, Ankara.

Battal, S., H. Aydın, & Z. Gülçat. 1989. Cinsel kimlik ve cinsel davranış bozukluklarında kişilik özellikleri [Personality characteristics in gender identity and sexual behavior disorders]. *GATA Bülteni*, *31*:651-660.

Bozkurt, A., H. Aydın, & H. Işıklı. 1999. *Psychopathology in male sexual dysfunction*. Presented at XI World Congress of Psychiatry, Hamburg/Germany (abstracts book, vol. II, p. 23).

Bozkurt, A. 1996. *Erkek cinsel işlev bozukluklarında psikopatolojinin araştırılması* [*A study on psychopathology in male sexual dysfunctions*]. Unpublished dissertation, GATA, Ankara.

Brooks, G. 1995. *Nine parts of desire: The hidden world of Islamic women*. New York: Anchor Books/Doubleday.

CIA. 2002 (January). *The world factbook 2002*. Washington, DC: Central Intelligence Agency. Available: http://www .cia.gov/cia/publications/factbook/index.html.

Çok, F. 2000 (April/May). Reflections on an adolescent sexuality education program in Turkey. *SIECUS Report*, *28*(4):6-8.

Çok, F., L. Gray, & H. Ersever. 2001. Turkish university students' sexual behaviour, knowledge and perceptions on HIV/AIDS. *Culture, Health and Sexuality*, *3*(1):81-99.

Çok, F., H. Ersever, & L. A. Gray. 1998. Bir grup üniversite öğrencisinde cinsel davranış [Sexual behavior in a group of university students]. *HIV/AIDS*, *1*:23-29.

DIE. 2001. *Türkiye istatistik yıllığı* [*SIS, Statistical yearbook of Turkey*]. Ankara: Devlet İstatistik Enstitüsü Matbaası [State Institute of Statistics, Printing Division].

Ekşi, A. 1982. *Gençlerimiz ve sorunları* [*Turkish teenagers and their problems*]. İstanbul: Istanbul University Publications, #2790.

Ekşi, A. 1990. *Çocuk, genç, anababalar* [*Children, teenagers, parents*]. Istanbul : Bilgi Publications.

Ergöçmen, B. A. 1997. Women's status and fertility in Turkey. In: Hacettepe University, Institute of Population Studies (HIPS) and Macro International Inc. (MI), *Fertility trends, women's status and reproductive expectations in Turkey: Results of further analysis of the 1993 Turkish demographic and health survey*. Calverton, MD: HIPS MI.

Erkmen, H., N. Dilbaz, G. Seber, C. Kaptanoğlu, & D. Tekin. 1990. Sexual attitudes of Turkish university students. *Journal of Sex Education & Therapy*, *16*:251-261.

Erkut, S. 1982. Dualism in values toward education of Turkish women. In: Ç. Kağıtçıbaşı, ed., *Sex roles, family and community in Turkey* (Turkish studies 3). Bloomington, IN: Indiana University Press.

Gülçat, Z. 1995. *Cinsel işlev bozukluklarından empotansın psikolojik boyutları üzerine bir araştırma* [*A study on the psychological aspects of impotence*]. Unpublished dissertation, University of Ankara.

Gülçat, Z., H. Aydın, S. Battal, & K. Aydınalp. 1988. *Transseksüel ve homoseksüeller üzerine psikososyal bir çalışma* [*A psychosocial study on transsexuals and homosexuals*]. Proceedings of papers presented at the 24th National Congress of Psychiatry and Neurological Sciences in Ankara (pp. 638-649).

Hacettepe University Institute of Population Studies (HIPS). 1989a. *1988 Turkish fertility and health survey*. Ankara: HIPS.

Hacettepe University Institute of Population Studies (HIPS). 1989b. *1983 Turkish population and health survey*. Ankara: HIPS.

Hancıoğlu, A. 1997. Fertility trends in Turkey: 1978-1993. In: Hacettepe University, Institute of Population Studies (HIPS) and Macro International Inc. (MI), *Fertility trends, women's status and reproductive expectations in Turkey: Results of further analysis of the 1993 Turkish demographic and health survey*. Calverton, MD: HIPS MI.

Işıklı, H. 1993. *Cinsel fonksiyon bozukluklarında eş ilişkilerinin değerlendirilmesi* [*Evaluation of marital relationship in sexually dysfunctional couples*]. Unpublished dissertation, GATA, Ankara.

İmamoğlu, O. 1996. The perpetuation of gender stereotypes through the media: The case of Turkish newspapers. In: N. Dacovic, D. Derman, & K. Ross, eds., *Gender and media*. Ankara: Med-Campus Project # A 126 Publications, Mediation.

İnci, Y. 1993. *Homoseksüel ve transseksüellerde kendilik kavramı* [*Self concept in homosexuals and transsexuals*]. Unpublished dissertation, GATA, Ankara.

Kağıtçıbaşı, Ç. 1982a. Introduction. In: Ç. Kağıtçıbaşı, ed., *Sex roles, family and community in Turkey* (Turkish studies 3). Bloomington, IN: Indiana University Press.

Kağıtçıbaşı, Ç. 1982b. Sex roles, value of children and fertility. In: Ç. Kağıtçıbaşı, ed., *Sex roles, family and community in Turkey* (Turkish studies 3). Bloomington, IN: Indiana University Press.

Kandiyoti, D. 1982. Urban change and women's roles in Turkey: An overview and evaluation. In: Ç. Kağıtçıbaşı, ed., *Sex roles, family and community in Turkey* (Turkish studies 3). Bloomington, IN: Indiana University Press.

Kandiyoti, D. 1995. Patterns of patriarchy: Notes for an analysis of male dominance in Turkish society. In: Ş. Tekeli, ed., Women in modern Turkish society: A reader. London and New Jersey: Zed Books.

Kayır, A., P. Geyran, R. Tükel, & A. Kızıltuğ. 1990. *Cinsel sorunlarda başvuru özellikleri ve tedavi seçimi* [*Patient referrals and treatment choice in sexual problems*]. Paper presented at 26th National Psychiatry Congress, Turkey.

Kayır, A. 1995. Women and their sexual problems in Turkey. In: Ş. Tekeli, ed., *Women in modern Turkish society: A reader.* London and New Jersey: Zed Books.

Kıray, M. 1976. The new role of mothers: Changing intra-familial relationships in a small town in Turkey. In: J. G. Peristiany, ed., *Mediterranean family structures.* London: Cambridge University Press.

Kozcu, Ş. 1991. Çocuk istismarı ve ihmali aile yazıları III [Child abuse and neglect III]. *TC Başbakanlık Aile Araştırma Kurumu Başkanlığı.* Ankara: MN Ofset.

Kuyaş, N. 1982. Female labor power relations in the urban Turkish family. In: Ç. Kağıtçıbaşı, ed., *Sex roles, family and community in Turkey* (Turkish studies 3). Bloomington, IN: Indiana University Press.

Levine, N. 1982. Social change and family crisis: The nature of Turkish divorce. In: Ç. Kağıtçıbaşı, ed., *Sex roles, family and community in Turkey* (Turkish studies 3). Bloomington, IN: Indiana University Press.

Ministry of Health (Republic of Turkey). 1996. *Health statistics 1995* (Publication no. 579). Ankara: Ministry of Health.

Milli Eğitim Bakanlığı (Ministry of National Education). 2000. *Ergenlik döneminde değişim* [*Changes during adolescence*]. Ankara: MEB.

Özbay, F. 1982. Women's education in rural Turkey. In: Ç. Kağıtçıbaşı, ed., *Sex roles, family and community in Turkey* (Turkish studies 3). Bloomington, IN: Indiana University Press.

Özgren, F., Z. Gülçat, A. Özşahin, H. Aydın, & H. Işıklı. 1993. Erkek cinsel fonksiyon bozukluklarında sorun alanları üzerine bir araştırma [A study on problem areas in male sexual dysfunctions]. *GATA Bülteni, 35*:701-710.

Özgür, S., & D. Sunar. 1982. Social psychological patterns of homicide in Turkey: A comparison of male and female convicted murders. In: Ç. Kağıtçıbaşı, ed., *Sex roles, family and community in Turkey* (Turkish studies 3). Bloomington, IN: Indiana University Press.

Özkan, İ. 1981. *Psikiyatriye başvuran 1242 hasta arasından seçilen "cinsel sorunlu 100 denek" in genel değerlendirmesi* [*General evaluation on the 100 subjects with sexual problems which are selected among the 1242 patients who are referred to psychiatry clinic*]. Unpublished dissertation, Ankara Üniversitesi Psıkıyatri Kürsüsü, Ankara.

Öztürk, O. 1963. Psychological effects of circumcision practised in Turkey. *Turkish Journal of Pediatrics, 5*:66-74.

Sağduyu, A., M. Rezaki, G. M. Rezaki, I. Kaplan, & G. Özgen. 1997. Sağlık ocağına başvuran hastalarda cinsel sorunlar [Sexual problems in patients at a primary health care clinic]. *Türk Psikiyatri Dergisi, 8*(2):102-109.

Soylu, L. M., L. Tamam, & A. Avcı. 1997. Bir adağın cinsel kimlik ve işlevlere olası etkileri: Bir olgu sunumu [Possible influence of a vow on gender identity and sexual function: A case report), *3 P, 5*(2):146-149.

SIS (State Institute of Statistics, Prime Ministry, Republic of Turkey). 1995. *Divorce Statistics—1993.* Ankara: SIS.

Sungur, M. Z. 1994. Evaluation of couples referred to a sexual dysfunction unit and prognostic factors in sexual and marital therapy. *Sex and Marital Therapy, 9*:251-265.

Sungur, M. Z. 1998. Difficulties encountered during the assessment and treatment of sexual dysfunction—A Turkish perspective. *Sex and Marital Therapy, 13*:71-81.

TC Hükümeti ve UNICEF (The Government of Turkish Republic and UNICEF). 1991.*Türkiye'de anne ve çocukların durum analizi* [*Analysis of the state of mothers and children in Turkey*]. Ankara: Yeniçağ Matbaası.

Tekeli, Ş. 1995. Introduction: Women in Turkey in the 1980s. In: Ş. Tekeli, ed., *Women in modern Turkish society: A reader.* London and New Jersey: Zed Books.

Tezcan, M. 1998. İslam öncesi ve sonrası eski Türk ailesinin sosoyokültürel nitelikleri [Sociocultural characteristics of pre-Islamic and Islamic Turkish family]. *Türk Dünyası, 15*:12-23.

UNAIDS. 2002. *Epidemiological fact sheets by country.* Geneva, Switzerland: Joint United Nations Programme on HIV/AIDS (UNAIDS/WHO). Available: http://www.unaids.org/hivaidsinfo/statistics/fact_sheets/index_en.htm.

Vicdan, K. 1993. *Ülkemizde adolesanların demografik ve epidemiyolojik özellikleri: Mevcut problemler ve çözüm önerileri* [*Demographic and epidemiologic characteristics of Turkish adolescents: Problems and proposals*]. Unpublished dissertation. Ankara: Dr. Zekai Tahir Burak Kadın Hastanesi.

Yüksel, Ş., A. Kayır, A. Sarımurat, R. Tükel, & H. Sabuncu. 1988. *Marital relationship in women with and without sexual dysfunction.* Paper presented at the 3rd World Congress on Behavior Therapy, Edinborough, Scotland.

## Editors' Suggested Readings

Badran, M. 1995. *Feminists, Islam, and nation: Gender and the making of modern Egypt.* Princeton, NJ: Princeton University Press.

Beck, L. G., & N. Keddie, eds. 1978. *Women in the Muslim world.* Cambridge, MA: Harvard University Press.

Fernea, E. W. 1998. *In search of feminism: One woman's global journey* (Turkey, pp. 200-239). New York: Doubleday.

Janssen, Th. 2003. Transvestites and transexuals in Turkey. In: A. Schmitt & J. Sofer, eds., *Sexuality and eroticism among males in Moslem societies.* New York: Harrington Park Press (Haworth Press).

Mernissi, F. 1993. *Islam and democracy: Fear of the modern world.* Reading, MA: Addison-Wesley.

Murray, S. O. 1997a. Homosexuality among slave elites in Ottoman Turkey. In: S. O. Murray & W. Roscoe, eds., *Islamic homosexualities: Culture, history, and literature.* New York/London: New York University Press.

Murray, S. O. 1997b. The will not to know: Islamic accommodations of male homosexuality. In: S. O. Murray & W. Roscoe, eds., *Islamic homosexualities: Culture, history, and literature.* New York/London: New York University Press.

Murray, S. O. 1997c. Woman-woman love in Islamic societies. In: S. O. Murray & W. Roscoe, eds., *Islamic homosexualities: Culture, history, and literature.* New York/London: New York University Press.

Murray, S. O., & W. Roscoe, eds. 1997. *Islamic homosexualities: Culture, history, and literature.* New York/London: New York University Press.

Naipaul, V. S. 1998. *Beyond belief: Islamic excursions among the converted peoples.* New York: Random House.

Necef, M. U. 2003. Turkey on the brink of modernity. In: A. Schmitt & J. Sofer, eds., *Sexuality and eroticism among males in Moslem societies.* New York: Harrington Park Press (Haworth Press).

Parrinder, G. 1980. *Sex in the world's great religions.* Don Mills, Ontario, Canada: General Publishing Company.

Sofer, J. 2003. The dawn of a gay movement in Turkey. In: A, Schmitt & J. Sofer, eds., *Sexuality and eroticism among males in Moslem societies.* New York: Harrington Park Press (Haworth Press).

Zilfi, M. C. 1997. *Women in the Ottoman Empire: Middle Eastern women in the early modern era.* New York and Cologne: Leiden Brill.

(CIA 2002)

# Ukraine

## (*Ukrayina*)

Tamara V. Hovorun, Ph.D., and
Borys M. Vornyk, Ph.D. (Medicine)
*Rewritten and updated in 2003 by*
*T. V. Hovorun and B. M. Vornyk*

## Contents

## *Demographics and a Brief Historical Perspective*

### A. Demographics          ROBERT T. FRANCOEUR

Located in southeastern Europe, Ukraine is bordered on the north by Belarusia, by the Russian Federation on the northeast and east, by Moldova and Romania on the southwest, and by Hungary, Poland, and the Slovak Republic on the west. It shares a Black Sea border with Turkey. Ukraine's territory is 233,090 square miles (603,700 km²),

slightly smaller than Texas, or as large as France and Denmark combined.

According to the last all-Ukrainian census (2001), Ukraine had an estimated population of 48.457 million, 53.7% females and 46.3% males. (Unless otherwise indicated by *AUC* (all-Ukrainian census), all data are from *The World Factbook 2002* (CIA 2002).)

**Age Distribution and Sex Ratios**: *0-14 years*: 16.8% with 1.04 male(s) per female (sex ratio); *AUC* (1999): 0-16 years: 19.4%; *15-64 years*: 68.7% with 0.91 male(s) per female; *AUC* (1999): Working age: 57.2%; *65 years and over*: 14.5% with 0.5 male(s) per female; *AUC* (1999): Above working age: 23.4%; *Total population sex ratio*: 0.86 male(s) to 1 female; *AUC* (2000) *Total*: 67.9 years; *male*: 62.4 years; *female*: 73.6 years

**Life Expectancy at Birth**: *Total Population*: 66.33 years; *male*: 60.86 years; *female*: 72.06 years

**Urban/Rural Distribution**: 67.2% to 32.8%

**Ethnic Distribution**: Ukrainian: 73%; Russian: 22%; Jewish: 0.2%; other: 4%

**Religious Distribution**: Ukrainian Orthodox–Moscow Patriarchate, Ukrainian Orthodox–Kiev Patriarchate, Ukrainian Autocephalous Orthodox, Ukrainian Catholic (Uniate), Protestant, Jewish

**Birth Rate**: 9.59 births per 1,000 population; *AUC* (2001): 7.7 births per 1,000 population

**Death Rate**: 16.4 per 1,000 population; *AUC* (2001): 15.2 per 1,000 population

**Infant Mortality Rate**: 21.14 deaths per 1,000 live births; *AUC*: 10.57 during 9 months in 2002

**Net Migration Rate**: –0.42 migrant(s) per 1,000 population

**Total Fertility Rate**: 1.32 children born per woman

**Population Growth Rate**: –0.72%; *AUC* (2001): –0.75%

**HIV/AIDS** (1999 est.): *Adult prevalence*: 0.96%; *Persons living with HIV/AIDS*: 240,000; *Deaths*: 4,000. (For additional details from www.UNAIDS.org, see end of Section 10B.)

**Literacy Rate** (*defined as those age 15 and over who can read and write*): 98% (*male*: 100%, *female*: 97%) (1989 est.); education is free and compulsory from age 7 to 15

**Per Capita Gross Domestic Product** (*purchasing power parity*): $4,200 (2001 est.); *Inflation*: 12%; *Unemployment*: 3.6% officially registered, with large numbers

*Communications*: Prof. Tamara Hovorun, Drahomanov National Pedagogical University, Vul. Pirohova, 9, Kyiv, 01601 Ukraine; dhovorun@imbg.org.ua. Prof. Borys Vornyk, P.O. Box 274, Kyiv, 01034 Ukraine; vornik@ukr.net *or* vornik@un.kiev.ua.

of unregistered and underemployed workers (November 2001); *Living below the poverty line*: 29%

## B. A Brief Historical Perspective

TAMARA HOVORUN and BORYS VORNYK

For most people, Ukraine was unknown as a country until recent times, although it has a very ancient and rich history and a highly developed national identity and culture. Its relative obscurity is because of the fact that Ukraine has been an independent free nation for only eight years in this century. Although the Ukrainians gave the world the first example of a democratic constitution and republic under the Cossacks in the 1500s and 1600s, and never waged war against any other country, they continually had to resist numerous invasions by neighboring nations. For almost 300 years prior to 1917, part or all of Ukraine was a colonial part of Czarist Russia. At the turn of the last century, Austria-Hungary controlled part of Ukraine within its empire. Ukraine was an independent nation for three years from the end of World War I in 1918 until it was taken over by the Russian Communists in 1921. Seventy years as part of the Soviet Union under Moscow followed, with independence and freedom regained with the collapse of the Soviet Union in 1991. The national flag of Ukraine has the most-peaceful colors: the upper half blue as a symbol of a cloudless sky or birth-giving water and the lower half yellow as a symbol of ripe wheat or the sun. Its modern state insignia, the Triad (*Tryzub*) can be traced back to Kyiv Rus. The interpretation of its meaning is multisemantic. Some suggest that it symbolizes the triangular unity of creation, the universe, spirit, wisdom, and will as the source of individual and national development. (For additional historical and ethnic perspectives, see Section 2A, Religious, Ethnic, and Gender Factors Affecting Sexuality, Character of Ethnic Values, below.)

## 1. Basic Sexological Premises

### A. The Character of Gender Roles

In order to draw connections between contemporary problems and historical setting attention must be paid to the main feature in gender relationships that distinguishes Ukraine from Russia and from the other former Soviet states. This is the high status of Ukrainian women as mother, sister, and wife. Throughout history, Ukraine had not been characterized by the traditional patriarchal family structure that existed, for example, in Russia; gender roles in Ukraine contrast sharply with female dependency and submissiveness. There was no male-domination marriage relationships, and Ukrainian women held high positions in both family and community settings. This was in part because of sociocultural circumstances. Throughout the several different periods of sexual culture development in Ukraine, sex and gender behavior grew from beliefs in ancient pagan cultures that valued the feelings, sensations, desires, and pleasures of sexual intercourse. Intimacy was considered to be harmonious with nature and male-female relationships.

The origin of Ukraine, the Kyiv Rus, was governed by a highly educated woman, Queen Olga (reign 946-966), who began the country's conversion to Christianity. There are also many historical witnesses of the gender-equality norms in later times, particularly during the rule of the grand dukes of Kyiv in the 11th century. The marital agreement, for example, was based on mutual desires of both the male and the female to establish a family. Mutual respect for male and female was the norm, as well as respect for responsibilities in housekeeping and childrearing. In Ukrainian customs, tradition, mythology, and folklore, it is hard to find accounts of either physical or mental abuse of women, or inequalities in family relationships between husband and wife.

In many Ukrainian regions, the woman selected her spouse and often initiated the marriage relationship. Later, especially during the period of the Cossack Republic during the 16th and 17th centuries, the women educated the children, organized the communities, and maintained their own organizations of social activity while men were away on military service. According to the numerous historical evidences, there was no wide gap between the observed behavior patterns of men and women. The roles of Ukrainian women and men in the family and the social continuum were mutually inclusive.

Traditional Ukrainian culture reflects no rigid stereotypical perceptions of gender roles. Though labor activities were gender-specific, neither male nor female tasks were considered superior. Similarly, the concepts of masculinity and femininity were not characterized by rigid boundaries and were mutually permeable. The self was seen as individualized and not tied to a particular gender scheme. Ukrainian folklore reflects the notion that an individual is shaped more by situational influences than by certain gender-specific predispositions. Thus, a strong woman and a sensitive man were not seen as deviant, but rather as products of specific life circumstances. Such democratic receptions on gender roles are remarkable, given the dominance of patriarchal models in many other cultural systems.

Leopold von Sacher-Masoch (1999), who got to know Galician Ukrainians in terms of identity, wrote the following:

> The Polish woman wants to give orders, while the Ukrainian one wants to be free. While the Polish woman rules over her husband, the Russian one wants to submit to him, just like the German one, and the Ukrainian woman demands equality with him. At any opportunity her unrestrainable Cossack spirit goes ablaze, recognizing no master and no servant. Between the Don and the Carpathians live the natural born democrats; neither Byzantine emperor, nor the Vikings, nor any Polish king or Russian tzar have broken their spirit, have suppressed their consciousness. They are always ready to trade the flow for a spear, they live in small republican communities as equal among equals; for the Eastern Slavs, they are the sprouts of the future, the sprouts of freedom.

Sadly, 300 years of Russian oppression, and especially 70 years of Soviet governance, have greatly affected family and gender development in Ukraine.

Ukraine scores on the Gender Development Index (GDI, *Ukraine Human Development Report* 2002), which measures the degree of disparities between the status of men and women, reflects an equality in the workplace that is greater than in many countries. In fact, in 1997 and 1998, the Ukrainian GDI scores were especially equal to the human development index, indicating a high level of gender equality. However, further progress in the area of gender equality is needed.

The development of gender issues in the Soviet period was characterized by a lot of contradictory tendencies. On the one hand, all women and men received equal access to education and professional activity. And this has had notable effects on the formation of gender dimensions. Thus, at the beginning of the 1940s, women held 39% of the jobs in the workplace and 53% in 1990, in comparison to 32% in Western Europe. In the public sector, women still continue to be the main labor in heavy and dangerous jobs that jeopardize their reproductive health. Women perform 45% of trade and care-providing services, constitute 82% of employed workers in public nourishment, in healthcare 81%, in public education 75%, and in culture 73%.

The ratio of women and men graduating from the university is 45% to 35%. The prevalence of women shows up in the total number of specialists with college and university degrees. Thus, women constitute 58% of engineers, 67% of physicians, 87% of economists, 89% of bookkeepers, 91% of librarians, 45% of agrarians, and 45% of scientists. Despite unprecedented rates of educational levels, the status of women in the government and politics is very low, only about 6%. There is no woman minister in contemporary Ukrainian Government. Even in those spheres of the economy, where women hold 80% to 90% of the jobs as in manufacturing, the share of women at the level of state power is about 5.1%. There are no women among the heads of regional (*oblast*) administrations and there is usually only a handful among the heads of district administrators.

The number of women in decision-making positions is very small—the Ukrainian Parliament has been traditionally dominated by men. Though women make up more than a half of Ukraine's population, they account for only 7% of the Verkhovna Rada's deputies. In Soviet times, there were institutionalized quotas at all the levels of positions—not less than 30% of administrative seats were reserved for women. Now, the inclusion of women in state power, in politics, defense, finances, and entrepreneurship affairs is not adequate to the gender ratio.

Although the Constitution of Ukraine proclaims the rights of men and women are equal, a lot of things still need to be done in order to alter the mass consciousness.

In many ways, the Ukrainian society has remained sexist because gender differences were emphasized in many spheres. It imposed separateness between women and men in traditional responsibilities for child and family care. Even in the secondary school curriculum, a course in "home servicing" is only for girls and assumed different experiences for boys and girls with wide-ranging consequences. It supported women's attachment to the family and their concern with cooking, caring, and nurturing, while autonomy and public involvement were expected of men.

Women remained socially dependent because society maintains a lot of prejudice against women occupying high positions, especially in the social structure. Only a small number of the 27% of women holding doctorates, and the 11% of women with doctorates in the sciences, have received academic grants, prestigious positions, or social recognition as politicians. Instead of the state developing support industries to lighten the burden in housekeeping, men and women engaged in an endless and fruitless discussion of which gender is/was the stronger.

Social, economic, and political inefficiency—we are still discussing whether Ukrainian society should recognize private property—has left almost no opportunities for effective problem solving, training in management skills, persistence, and competitiveness. Lack of autonomy, self-sufficiency, pursuit of self-interest, and competence have contributed very much to the demasculinization of the male population in Ukraine. Males are at greater risk healthwise than women. The mortality rate is an example, especially for those aged 35 to 39, which is more than three times higher for men than for women. Men are more likely to experience premature death. Tuberculosis and HIV infections, which are considered in Ukraine as epidemics, are mainly found estimated among men. The male suicide rate is 50% higher than that of women. Men have the highest smoking rates as well as drug and alcohol use involving criminal activity. Also contributing to men's mortality are job-transition-related stress and unhealthy lifestyles. Examples of sexism are quite obvious in the male population, when women retain custody of children and do not support men's involvement in family life.

Finally, in the society where there was a lack of responsibility and respect for personality, both genders were losing such human characteristics as being cooperative, warm, sympathetic, loving, creative, and altruistic in relationships, sensitive to others, and intelligent in communications.

Although the Constitution of Ukraine proclaims equal rights for both sexes, a lot of things still need to be done in order to overcome gender differences in social and family status for men and women. A broad media campaign is still going in order to ensure that the best things for her are still to be found in children-church-kitchen and for him to be masculine in earning money, drinking alcohol, and so on. The slogan of gender equality, which became very popular in recent years among some NGO democratic organizations, does not correspond to the social processes in the country. Ukrainian society is not yet ready to accept a woman as a parliamentarian and men as care-providers. The gender problem is not the provision of equal access for men and women to education, health protection, or economic resources, but in raising the mass consciousness on equalitarian ideas. On one hand, Ukraine needs to take measures that will give women greater equality with men in terms of political power. On the other hand, women will not be elected unless they start to conduct election campaigns for themselves.

## B. General Concepts and Constructions of Sexuality and Love

The sexuality of Ukrainians is strongly influenced by gender factors such as the high authority of women in family settings. Boys and girls in adolescence were given a great freedom in heterosexual communication, in interactions during dating nights (*vetchornytsi*), but without engaging in premarital intercourse. Even though Ukraine was a colony of Russia, there was *not* a landowner's serfdom right for the first conjugal night (*jus primae nocte*).

The Ukrainian ethnosexology has been described in marriage customs and traditions, as well as in the contents of erotic folklore—love songs, proverbs, proverbial phrases, or riddles. So-called obscene songs are widely represented in ethnology studies conducted by Ivan Franco, Pavlo Chubinsky, Phedir Vovk, Mychailo Maksymovych, and others. Ethnologic studies have uncovered in Ukrainian folklore considerable information on sexual techniques, interactions, and building the sexual relationship. They also emphasize the representation of sexuality as a harmonious part of human existence, equally esteemed by both sexes. Sexual desire is seen as a harmonic part of human life and is often paralleled to various natural phenomena.

Historical research shows that the emotional side, love and communication of the partners, plays a major part in the sexual expression of Ukrainians. Sexual behavior is considered to be natural for lovers, which in turn is based on a loving attachment and a mutual agreement as an important part of the relationship's development. In central Ukraine, the roles that males and females play in sexual relations is more equal or blessed by woman's initiative than in western parts of the country, which is more characterized by Puritanic values. Traditional Ukrainian culture is characterized by self-disclosure in intimate communication, which contributes to dating, going steady, and getting engaged.

The general trend in erotic folklore is expressed in jokes about partners making love, keeping sex alive, mutual desire in order to avoid rejection, equal roles of husband and wife interested in sex, a vulnerability of engaging in extramarital sex, men and women receiving intimate satisfaction, and keeping a sexual appetite, not only in young age, but in the older years. Ukrainian folklore emphasizes the essential role of sexuality for maintaining physical and psychological well-being. Notably, sexuality is presented as equally important to both men and women and is often portrayed as an object of preoccupation for both sexes; women's natural clothing, emphasizing and at times revealing their physique, testifies to the value placed on sexual attraction.

During the Soviet period in Ukraine, human sexuality was a taboo subject as far as the mass media, scientific investigation, and education were concerned. After the 1920s, the only legitimate function of sexuality was reproduction. The emphasis on sex education for adults was exclusively focused on information about the reproductive systems and on social and moral control of sexual behavior. The information that was communicated in sex education focused on physiology and commitment, while avoiding discussion of values, trust, intimacy, self-awareness, and concern for others.

Society is always a kind of external support for personal development and self-conception providing values and orientation for sexual behavior. The image of sexual behavior was always negative. Sex was considered a "bad" part of one's personality that was in disharmony with the "good" part that involved strict conscious control and abstinence. This viewpoint grew out of the prevailing negative attitude toward personal freedom and intimacy, self-respect, and personal responsibility. It is apparent that the totalitarian Soviet society could not help children understand the changes of their bodies and emotions, or teach them responsible decision making. Even in the mid-1980s, when schools recognized the necessity of sex education and faced the task of informing teenagers about love and intimacy, the compulsory course in ethics and psychology of the family did not include any information about sexual activity. It was a sexless course about sexless behavior. The same situation exists in contemporary Ukrainian society in general.

Although Ukrainian society has become more permissive sexually in recent years, it still does not provide adequate values for human sexuality. With the breakdown of the Soviet regime, sexuality became one of the most important symbols of social and cultural liberation. Widespread public silence and ignorance about sex in former years has been replaced by everyday representations in commerce and movies. Television programs and filmmakers exploit sex, but still present it as a part of personality that is hardly related to the self-ideal and is quite dissonant with accepted family gender roles. Public display of the bodies of young women as available sexual objects for men, and sexual intercourse as something far from personal relationships in advertising and the mass media perpetuate the distances between men and women as social beings and between sex and the family.

Ethnicity, culture, national customs, and traditions help create models of gender behavior, develop respect for values, and develop some interpersonal skills. Sexual competence involves many personality qualities and activities that should be taught to children as they develop. Family-oriented customs and traditions that help gender-socialization processes, such as marriage, housekeeping, and parenthood, have almost been destroyed in most regions of Ukraine because of the Soviet ideal of creating a new society without ethnicity and religion. The incidence of divorce and child abuse and neglect documented in the Ukraine reflects this influence. The incidence of divorce and abuse is two-and-a-half times higher in the eastern part of the Ukraine, where traditional values were more quickly lost, than in the western regions that retained many of their traditions after they were joined to the Ukraine during the 1940s. In the west, teenage girls and boys are quite knowledgeable about housekeeping, bringing up children, and the proper treatment of relatives, because they are involved in sophisticated and living traditions that are maintained by their families.

For three generations, the Ukrainians have grown up in a system which neglected personal dignity and expressions of respect. The social system as well as family communications were mostly oriented to punishment rather than to the encouragement of self-worth. Another evidence of this distortion can be found in the language people use to address each other in public places. In the Ukraine, there are proper words for addressing a person as a sexual human being, as there are in America or other countries, such as miss, missus, lady, sir, mister, gentlemen, and so on. As a result of the Soviet imposition of the word "comrade," referring to persons who share political ideas in common, the salutations *panni* and *pan*, "respectful woman or man," were almost totally eliminated from usage. Today, Ukrainians address a person mostly by their gender identity "woman" or "girl" for females, and "man," "young man," or "guy" for males. So, the social and sexual identity of the individual oppose each other. Such greetings are mutual and cause no offense or embarrassment to anyone. The fact that most Ukrainians consider these sexual definitions of the self as a normal social greeting does not mean that it is unimportant to the sexual culture. Those Ukrainians who allow themselves to be defined by belonging to a particular sex are those who were raised with a lack of respect for individual personality.

## 2. Religious, Ethnic, and Gender Factors Affecting Sexuality

### A. Character of Ethnic Values

Ukrainians have developed as an ethnic group over a period of at least three to four thousand years. Scientists distinguish several periods in the development of Ukrainian religious values. At the beginning of the 20th century, scientists found the first archeological evidence of an ancient settlement and culture on the territory of Ukraine. These have been dated back to 4500 to 2000 before the Common Era and the birth of Christ. The culture was named Trypil'ska, after the name of the village Trypillja near Kyiv (Kiev) where the first signs of this ancient culture were discovered. Similarities in gender roles and behaviors between this ancient culture and elements of the modern Ukrainian culture make this discovery particularly significant. The people of the Trypil'ska culture were agricultural, living in small and large families in separate two-story buildings usually situated in circles near rivers. The largest of these ancient towns discovered recently in Dnipro region is five times larger than the well-known Babylon. The most wonderful of the remains of this civilization unearthed were ceramic figures of different women and the special places or shrines in houses where these were placed. All of the figures showed obvious evidence of a connection with religious beliefs, specifically a Mother cult and worship to the female. These figures have pronounced sexual signs and even such details as fatness and hairdos. The principal role of a woman in Trypil'ska culture was connected with a highly developed agricultural cult in which the female symbolized fertility and the Goddess Earth. It all gave a woman the right to be a priestess and a head of the family.

From the 7th to the 3rd centuries B.C.E., Indo-European Scythian tribes controlled the Ukrainian steppes.

The period from 500 to 900 C.E. is the time of the Slavic tribes and Slavic community development as a separate ethnic population. Slavic tribes began migrating from the northwest into what is now Russia in the 5th century. The division of the ancient Slavs into various tribes began in the 2nd to 4th centuries when the Goth and Huns forced them to split. In the south, they eventually formed the tribes of the Polianians, Siverianians, Derelianians, and so on. Some of these tribes were united in Kyivan Rus by the spread of Christianity from Byzantium (Constantinople) in the 10th and 11th centuries; Volodymyr the Saint was converted in 988.

Western historians give greater importance than do Ukranian historians to the role of Scandinavian chieftains, Norsemen or Vikings, in the 9th century. A common western view claims that the Viking Rurik founded the first Russian dynasty in 862 in Novgorod—hence the distinction between Novgorod and Kyivan Rus, and the possible origin of the term *Russian*. Ukranian scholars trace the origin of the term *Rus* to the common root of many Ukrainian rivers, Ros', Rosavitsa, Rosava, and so on, where Slavic tribes settled. Hence, the Slavs were called Rusychi or Rusyny, and Rus is the synonym of Ukraine but not Russia. Ukrainian historians note that Rus existed long before the arrival of the Norsemen and that the word Russia referring to a nation does not occur until Peter the Great.

The Moguls overran the country in the 13th century, destroying Kyiv in 1240. Kyiv was freed from Mogul conquest after 80 years in 1320, when the Lithuanian Duke Gedimin (ca. 1275-ca. 1340) together with Rus dukes and their military troops fought the Moguls in three battles, the last and largest held by the river Irpin' near Kyiv. After that victory, the Lithuanians ruled the country with the help of Rus Dukes. In 1386, when the Lithuanian Kingdom united with Poland, Rus, according to the convention, received a separate government, which was called Het'man. As time passed, Poland extended its power over Ukraine. In addition, while the 11th-century grand dukes of Kyian Rus held such centralized power as existed, most of the sons of the Kyivan Rurikovechi Dynasty ruled in Novgorod.

From the 13th to the 16th centuries, Kyiv was under the influence of Poland and Western Europe, with the 1500s and 1600s being the time of the Cossack Republic. In 1547, Ivan the Terrible formally proclaimed himself the first czar of the Rus, and Russia the true successor of the fallen Roman and Byzantine Empires. In 1654, Ukraine asked the czar of Muscovy for protection against Poland and signed the treaty of Pereyasav, which recognized the suzerainty of Moscow. The Cossacks under Chemelnytsky may have wanted a full defensive partnership such as now exists between Canada and the United States. Moscow, however, interpreted the treaty as an invitation to take over Kyiv. Peter the Great (1682-1725) extended Moscow's domain, and in 1721, founded the Russian Empire, which included Ukraine.

As described by Veles (Rehbinder 1993), the Slavic culture was pagan, based on the worship of the numerous gods of the Great Mother Nature. The unity of female and male substances was considered a kind of magical activity for enriching the fertility of the Earth. Even today, the Ukrainians sing some seasonal songs (*koljadky, tsedrivky*), which are a kind of communication and dialogue of the individual with nature—animals, plants, sun, moon, and wind. A summer holiday of love, Kupala, has persisted from ancient times down to the present. In this ancient context, sexual intercourse was viewed as a relationship, the attachment feeling to the partner.

Nestor the Chronicler (ca. 1056-1114) supplemented and continued the primary Rus chronicles in *Povist Vremennykh Lit* (*A Tale of Bygone Years* 1990). A monk in the Kyivan Cave Monastery and the most educated man of his time, Nestor described the differences in sex and gender behavior between the tribes: "Polyany—Slavs who lived in the central regions of what is now modern Ukraine—maintain their parents' traditions, peaceful and obedient, and their marriage customs." The neighboring Derevljany "lived like animals, killed each other . . . and there was no marriage customs other than kidnapping the young women." Nestor the Chronicler

also condemned another neighboring culture, where the people "had vulgar, disgraceful words and used them in the presence of parents and women. And they did not know about marriage, but cavorted between villages. The men traveled around, playing, dancing, and singing all kinds of devil songs, stealing wives for themselves—women they found agreeable—and having two or three wives." His view was ceratinly colored by his perspective as a Kyivan monk. The Derevljany had killed Ihor, the husband of Queen Olga (ca. 890-969), who in turn wiped out several of their towns.

The prominent feature of the ancient Slavic psychology was love-living, life-loving, and a tenderness and joyful mood. When Nestor the Chronicler wrote about Ihor's campaign, he described the feelings of attachment and emotional evolvement of the ancient Slavs. Later on, when Kyivan (Kievan) Rus reached its heyday in the reign of Grand Prince Jaroslav the Wise (1019-1054), the Church, which represented Christianity, could not eliminate this sensitive character of pagan culture. Christianity, with its cult of emotionless asceticism and abstinence, could not overcome the cheerful character of folk traditions, and either tried to adopt and incorporate some of them into religious holidays or to prohibit them altogether. Thus the Christian tradition began its long coexistence with ancient ethnic values. (See Section 1 in the chapter on Russia for further elaboration on this coexistence.)

## B. Sources and Character of Religious Values

Three quarters of the Ukrainian people are Eastern Orthodox, 13.5% Ukrainian Catholic or Uniate, 2.3% Jewish, and 8.2% Baptist, Mennonite, Protestant, and Muslim.

From the 8th century, Ukraine was also known as Rus. In 988, the rulers and people of Kyiv adopted Christianity. During the reign of Prince Oleg, Kyiv was referred to as the "mother of Rus cities," which explains the particular importance given to the development of Christianity in this region. As a result of a jurisdictional division between church and secular power, matrimonial and family cases fell within the Church's competence and domain. Legislation of the norms of matrimonial law dates from the second half of the 11th century. As recorded in the legislative code of Prince Jaroslav the Wise, and later in other books, the new legal code incorporated the centuries-old experience of eastern Slavic social life.

The Church assumed an exclusive right to register marriages and insisted on rooting out pagan traditions. For example, marriage without a religious ceremony was considered to be void. In its views of marriage and family life, the Church was guided by the norms of Christian morality. The Church sought to incorporate into the mass consciousness ideas of the sanctity and inviolability of marriage and conjugal fidelity.

Men and women who were related up to the sixth generation were forbidden to marry. In addition, children from one family could not marry the brothers or sisters in another unrelated family. These restrictions were obviously adopted from Byzantine law, but were less strictly enforced. In Kyivan Rus, men married when they were 15 years old, while women married between ages 13 and 14. The Church forbade marriage of Christians with non-Christians. Engagement usually involved mutual consent and was followed by a festive dinner. Cheese was an obligatory dish shared by the bride and groom; the ritual of cutting cheese and bread meant that agreement had been reached. A lack of virginity in either partner was not an obstacle to marriage. There was a law that proclaimed the woman-slave free if she was tempted into intercourse and gave birth to a child. In case an unmarried woman gave birth to a child, she had to live in some church facility and was socially culpable. It was forbidden to have two spouses. Divorce was allowed only in exceptional cases and only after a court trial. A wife's adultery could be a serious reason for divorce; not so with a husband's adultery. After divorce, a husband had to pay his former wife a large financial compensation.

The Church in Kyivan Rus controlled norms of sexual behavior. First of all, it was forbidden to have any sexual relations between relatives and even relatives-in-law. Any intercourse outside the marital union was considered sinful, even when totally secret. Considerable attention was paid to any sexually deviant behavior. Thus, punishment for zoophilia was recorded in the statutes of Kyivan Rus. Childbearing was protected, and the Church took care of pregnant women and helped them. Anyone associated with an abortion or attempted abortion was guilty of a serious crime.

Within a marriage, and in society in general, there was a moral responsibility to respect all persons, regardless of gender, in Kyivan Rus. Thus, in the *Edification to Children* by Volodymyr Monomach (1052-1125), one finds a great appreciation of the individual: "Protect widows, do not let the powerful ruin anyone. . . . Let your eyes look down but your soul aspire to height. . . . Love your wife, but don't let her control you" (1991).

The ancient and cheerful ethnic culture, coupled with moral Christian demands, helped to produce gender behavior patterns based on mutual respect of men and women, feelings of connection and attachment to each other, and the capacity to appreciate the romantic love as well as erotic sensations (Chubyns'kyj 1994). For the Ukrainian couple, intimacy was characterized by affection, consent, and long-lasting commitment. The psychology of love is widely described in Ukrainian songs, which are considered the best in the world and expressive of the national character (Shlemkevych 1992). The respect for women was so appreciated among the Ukrainians that Mirza-Avakjants wrote in 1920 that "the modern woman of every country could envy the position of Ukrainian woman in the sixteenth and seventeenth." More than a century and a half of Cossack Republic strengthened the independent women's position in family life and made this a national characteristic.

## 3. Knowledge and Education about Sexuality

The sexual health of young Ukrainians is a real problem. There is a considerable gap between young people's sexual activity and their level of sociopsychological and moral responsibility. The main problem in Ukraine is a lack of information for adolescents about sexuality, family planning, safer sex, and so on. Although several National Programs for Family Planning have been developed during the period of independence, there is still no compulsory sex education. Sexuality and related issues continue to be regarded by teachers and parents as prohibited. Only in recent years have some efforts been undertaken in order to develop sex education in a curriculum of the discipline "Healthy Education" (technically referred to as *valeology*).

The main idea is to supply all children from preschool to college with a compulsory sex education program that provides adequate knowledge of the emotional, psychological, and physical aspects of gender and sexual behavior. In addition, this program includes discussions of self-understanding, intimacy, family life, values, attitudes, orientations, and skills concerning the behavior and relationships of both genders.

Teachers, psychologists, and sexologists are collaborating in developing a program to provide information about human sexuality, including discussions of human reproduction, pregnancy, childbirth, sexual responses, contraception, abortion, and sexually transmitted diseases. They are conscious that the most important value for children of postcommunist society is to develop the ability to understand and respect the individual . That is the reason the context of valeology leads children to question, "Where did I come from?" "What do I want to be?" and "Who am I?" The development of self-reflecting capacity with regard to gender and sexual behavior is emphasized at every age level.

To a large degree, sex and gender behavior begins in the home. At various stages, children should receive knowledge about sex and reproduction from their parents. Thus, the new program initiated efforts to encourage family-based sexuality education. A substantial gap, however, exists between the knowledge provided by the family and the average child's curiosity needs. This gap makes clear the need for child- and parent-oriented knowledge that revives national family customs and traditions.

The society is interested in exploring the social influences, especially television, which create the sexual environments in which children are growing up. Ukrainian mass media, however, are preoccupied with non-family-oriented commerce and movies. Still, many scientists have begun to collaborate with the mass media, especially television, to prepare sexually oriented programs for adolescents, teenagers, and their parents.

Sex education has been an important part of some national programs, in particular, the National Family Planning Program 1995-2000, the National Program "Reproductive Health 2001-2005," and both the National AIDS Prevention Program 2001-2003 and the National AIDS Prevention Program 2003-2008—now in preparation. Some international agencies, such as UNFPA, UNAIDS, UNICEF, DTID, and others are major donors of developing educational programs on safe sexual behavior among children and youth. (See section 5A, Interpersonal Heterosexual Behaviors, Children, for more details on the sexual knowledge of children and their sources of such information.)

## 4. Autoerotic Behaviors and Patterns

Ukrainian folk beliefs, proverbs, parables, and humorous refrains condemn autoerotic behavior and ridicule it as unnatural and abusive for the potential marital partner. This widespread opinion contributes very much to the contemporary Ukrainian negative attitude towards autoerotic behaviors.

### A. Children and Adolescents

There is a lot of misunderstanding and fear among adults concerning children's autoeroticism. As the young child starts to explore his or her genitals, a strong punishment usually follows when adults detect this natural curiosity. Thus, from early childhood, the deliberate manipulation of genitals is mostly prohibited by the family and social environment. Most children do not receive any information about their genitals as the source of pleasure and good feelings. Parents usually worry about the occurrence of masturbation, that this initial sexual experience is immediately suppressed whenever discovered.

Normally, the second period of interest in exploration of one's own body appears at puberty. The practice of masturbation considerably increases during these years and occurs alone or with other children in pairs or small groups. There are a lot of myths among the people about the harmful results of masturbation. Some boys believe it will impair or make intercourse impossible in the future, or result in mental retardation. Similarly, many physicians commonly consider adolescent masturbation to be harmful when it becomes a dominant concern, the focus for leisure activity, or a source of strong feelings of guilt. There is, however, some shift among healthcare professionals to accept adolescent masturbation as a normal activity. Still, most parents try to restrict teenager masturbation. In comparison to the Western experience in sex education, autosexuality during childhood is considered by most Ukrainians not as a pleasurable kind of sexual expression, but as a hindrance to sexual pleasure. This may be partly connected with the former imposition of ideas about sex as shameful, and not a useful human activity for the socialist society.

For children who are being raised in orphanages outside a family, the opening of the sexual sensations generated in the genital areas usually becomes a habit. Thus, masturbation provides an easy way for self-soothing, reducing tension, and calming down for many boys and girls. Children raised in an emotionally deprived environment frequently seek consolation in their own bodies.

## B. Adults

Autoerotic satisfaction among adults is widespread. It often occurs as a part of intercourse for sexual stimulation. Adults who are not in some sexual relationships are very often engaged in self-stimulation. Masturbation is also engaged in, despite moral and social prohibitions, as a way for releasing sexual excitement and tension.

Modern sexological clinics and sex shops sell devices for genital massage to stimulate an orgasm. The most usable by women, and rather popular for sexual self-pleasuring, are vibrators and dildoes for clitoral and vaginal stimulation. Among men, the most enjoyable are active devices that substitute for intercourse.

## 5. Interpersonal Heterosexual Behaviors

The complexity of interactions between the former ideological system and indigenous Ukrainian traditions has resulted in many areas of tension and confusion in sexual behavior and gender identity.

## A. Children

### Sexual Knowledge and Attitudes

Juvenile sexual behavior is a kind of a mirror of the social problems and their influence on the development of gender consciousness.

Findings indicate that more than 70% of children ages 6 to 8 could not identify the right words for the sexual parts of the body for either the same or opposite sex. Those who could give some kind of explanation used many crude words and felt embarrassed and shy. More than 75% of the children did not understand the meaning of "birth control". Less than 20% of those that age knew from where a baby comes, and only 30% of those who did know received this knowledge from parents or another adult relative. Only 15% of the children could explain the intimate behavior in connection with human feelings of love, friendship, and the desire to have a baby.

Children's awareness of their own body was extremely narrow. About half of the children considered the sexual parts of the body as places of the most bad feelings and experienced shame in being naked or seeing an adult naked. The shame of body exposure is even greater in children from small towns and villages. The rather prudish approach to nudity and bodily functions has greatly affected the sexual behavior of children. In observing some paintings with nude bodies, most elementary school children express their confusion by laughing, chattering, and showing some kind of ignorance.

### Gender Images

There is a lot of confusion about gender roles among our youth. Children understand that the roles of male and female in family and social life are becoming more interchangeable, although the mass media follow the traditional divisions and propagate gender stereotypes; even school textbooks are mostly oriented on gender division of household functions. That's why children assume a contradictory model of gender behavior and interaction within the family and society. Though boys and girls seek an equally high social position within the society, that achievement requires a wide spectrum of habits, skills, and knowledge. But even today, the family orients the children to fulfill the traditional roles. The husband-father fulfills instrumental roles and deals with problems of the outside environment, and the wife-mother handles the relational and upbringing nurture functions and deals with problems of emotions and attitudes. Both of these roles are becoming very important for gender socialization and gender identification despite one's sexual identity.

## B. Adolescents

### Attitudes Toward Nudity and Body Functions

The ambivalence toward nudity, bodily functions, personal hygiene, and patterns of sexual behavior, combined with the lack of proper sexual education, increases during adolescence and has an impact on sexual and gender self-perception. We asked 12- to 13-year-old boys and girls questions concerning their knowledge of the main physiological changes in bodily functions during adolescence. More than 70% of the boys demonstrated poor understanding of the indicators of growing up as a man or a woman. Although many adolescents have seen many movies with sexual themes, only a third of them had ever discussed sexual topics with a relative or teacher. Most boys were extremely shy when explaining the function of a condom or the origin of a baby. More than 60% used the pronoun "it" rather than the terms penis, vagina, breast, and uterus. (See Igor Kon's comments on similar issues in Section 1B, Basic Sexological Premises, Sociolegal Status of Males and Females, in the chapter on Russia.)

In comparison to boys, 70% of the girls interviewed had discussed the topic of male and female body maturation at puberty with their mothers, grandmothers, or elder sisters. The topic of bodily functions, however, remained uncomfortable for girls to discuss. More than 60% of the girls replied to the questions, "Are you glad to be growing up as a woman?" and "What feelings do you experience during your period?" that it would be better without the menstruation cycle, pubic hair, or breast development, that it made them feel dirty, sick, or bad.

Their reaction might be more positive if they did not have difficulties and anxiety connected with school toilet facilities. Is it partly connected with pain or feeling unwell? The interviews revealed that menstrual periods make them more serious (heavy) because of hygiene problems and the embarrassment before classmates, boys, and teachers of physical education. Many Ukrainians continue to experience emotional problems as they get older, because of the social taboos surrounding menstruation and the social embarrassment of talking about the subject.

Ukrainian adolescent boys experienced the same discomfort answering the questions "What do you know about menstruation?" and "What do you know about erections and pollution?"

Was the sexual knowledge expanded substantially throughout the adolescent years? Most of the children obtained good information about the reproductive system from school lessons on biology. But, most adolescents of both sexes still showed a poor understanding of the questions concerning sexual behavior and sexual feelings. Such questions as "What is AIDS?" "How does one protect him/herself from contracting AIDS?" "Can a condom prevent pregnancy or transmitted diseases?" "Is masturbation harmful to ones health?" "Can a child in adolescent age become a father or a mother?" and "What do you know about using birth control?" embarrassed the adolescents. In talking about sexual subjects, most adolescents could not find appropriate words for the sexual organs.

These findings suggested that children viewed these topics regarding body functions, intercourse, and relationships to be shameful aspects of their personality. The adolescent sex vocabulary of most boys and girls was full of vulgar ("dirty") words. Most Ukrainian adolescents consider clothing as an important expression of masculine or feminine behavior, and regard it as an important factor in their personality and physical beauty.

When assessing the problems of gender self-consciousness in teenagers in Ukraine, we see a growing gap between the lack of sexual knowledge and sexual experience, the practice of gender behavior, and moral/psychological maturity.

*Satisfaction with Parental Lifestyles*

Observing the wealth of the West, combined with the poverty of their native country, has had an impact on gender self-consciousness and sex orientations of youth. Ukraine is rearing a third generation of children who are strongly dissatisfied with their parents' family and social life. Fathers and especially mothers with double duties are rarely viewed as role models.

*Sexarche and Teenage Pregnancy*

There is a growing tendency for Ukrainian youth to become involved in sexual intercourse at an earlier age. According to studies conducted in large industrial cities among the students at professional high schools, more than 50% of the women and 80% of the men have engaged in sexual activity before age 17.5. In 1980, the average age of first sexual experience was 19 years for men and 20 for women. According to survey data, more than 50% of teenagers are sexually active with at least three partners before the age of 20. For most of teenagers, sex exists as a curiosity that may involve a kind of commitment, but not love and passionate feelings. Most sexually active teenagers do not protect themselves from an unwanted pregnancy, because sexual knowledge, including information about contraceptives, remains low and comes mainly through interaction with peers. (For more information, see Section 9, Contraception, Abortion, and Population Planning.)

Ukrainian teenagers usually plan their nearest future with the creation of their own families, as the median age for marriage is now 19 to 21 years for females and 21 to 23 for males. Ukrainian teenagers usually do not consider economic and psychological maturity as necessary conditions for getting married. More than 80% of teenagers who get married consider themselves very dependent on their parents and family for financial support, for help with housing, and assistance in taking care of their children. A lack of privacy and opportunity for experiencing premarital sexual relationships lead teenagers to consider their sexual (physical) maturity sufficient basis for marriage. That is why about 45% of young couples are divorced within the first year of their marriage.

As evidence of the separateness between the sexual sphere and personality itself in mass consciousness, we might consider the content of the sex vocabulary of Ukrainians. The Ukrainian youth have adopted a lot of abusive words from the Russian sexual vocabulary that express bondage of women, rape, and humiliation of the people engaging in sexual intercourse. This is partly a result of the authoritarian society that encouraged cruel attitudes toward women and a misconception of male behavior.

## C. Adults

*Premarital Sexual Relationships,
Dating, and Courtship*

In the late 1960s, premarital sex in men's consciousness was a taboo for both the fiancé and fiancée, as the bride should be a virgin until marriage. The ethic of premarital virginity during dating was a major theme in sex education and mass media. To abstain from sex meant to escape from being betrayed by the groom or from potential pregnancy. The statistics of those years reveal the increasing quantity of unmarried mothers and forced weddings. In recent decades, the situation has changed considerably. Today, most teenagers and adults consider sex before marriage rather acceptable, and thus, premarital sex relations are widespread.

The initial selection of a potential mate usually occurs among a reference group—college mates, colleagues at work, or a common-interest community that brings together people with similar values, educational, or cultural levels. The length of courtship for young couples is usually about 12 to 18 months between meeting and marriage, with dating two to three times a week. In various strata of people, dating activity takes different forms. Dating is mostly oriented toward dancing, visiting friends, parties, cinemas, bars, and cafeterias.

The discovery of one other person in a romantic relationship is followed by the wedding arrangements initiated mostly by the man. The choice of a mate is determined by the young people themselves as it was in ancient Ukraine, although the parents usually have to confirm the engagement. The final ceremony of marriage depends on religious, ethnic, and cultural level, and social group.

In Soviet times, a lot of Communist symbols were included in the wedding process—a ritual of laying flowers at the local Lenin monument, special greetings, and promises. Wedding ceremonies in a church were prohibited and couples who had religious weddings were often prosecuted by the authorities. Nowadays, the wedding ceremony has become more relaxed, but it is still formalized. In the countryside, people keep traditions of a large wedding celebration with almost all villagers invited as guests. A lot of fun, music, singing of celebration songs, dancing, treating, and role playing characterize such family holiday. Usually, any large wedding celebration is very expensive for parents, who have to carry the burden of wedding debts sometimes after the young have divorced.

A few years ago, some registry offices started to propose that couples use a relationship contract to define some problems of their future family life. These contracts usually do not include any legal documentation and are used as a moral obligation that helps the bride to clear up some unexpected areas of marital interaction.

*Sexual Behavior and Relationships of Single Adults*

The number of single Ukrainians is increasing significantly, especially among highly educated people—teachers, physicians, engineers, and business owners. Psychologists trace this phenomenon to increasing levels of personal aspirations and expectations of potential partners of the opposite sex. The single trend is occurring in every age group and for both sexes.

It is difficult to tell with any accuracy how many persons remain single because of unrealistic expectations of a significant other, immaturity in emotional responses and communications, or egocentrism. Singles include adults who have never been married and divorced women with children. Most of them are lonely and have many problems in maintaining a relationship with a person of the opposite sex. Most places of entertainment cater to teenagers for meetings with mates. Because of the lack of privacy in their own flat or available rooms in hotels, it becomes embarrassing and hard for a single person to get together and be intimate with a partner.

During the last two decades, some marriage bureaus, consultation family centers, and radio programs have started providing matrimonial services, advertising in order to introduce the partners and help with dating. There are obvious proposals in some newspapers for dating that serve sexual purposes.

### Marriage and Family

Despite an increasing number of singles, most Ukrainians live in families. In 2003, Ukraine legislated the new Family Code, which determined the basics of marriage, spouses' property rights, parents' and children's rights and duties, as well as those of adopters and adopted, and so on. New clauses in the Code have been introduced dealing with the process and responsibility of engagement, the guarantee of rights for supporting a parent or caregiver for a disabled child, setting a contract for married life and the terms for its validity, the child's right for a proper upbringing by the parents or relatives, parental duties before and after childbirth, and so on. In Ukraine, the minimum age for marriage is 17 years for women and 18 for men. The marriage can be dissolved by mutual consent of the spouses. The divorce is equally available to both men and women. The husband is required to provide the maintenance of children until they are 18 years old. Custody of children, maintenance, and property must be decided before the couple divorce.

The main stream in developing marriage and family during the transition period involves replacing the patriarchal model of family functioning and shifting to a self-sufficient model. The phenomenon of increasing numbers of street children—about 53,000 children are in out-of-home care across the country—has been promoted in part by destructive tendencies during transition. A growing number of infants are abandoned soon after birth. Most of these infants receive institutional care. Thus, in 1991, the rate of children (aged 0 to 3) in infant homes was 153.4 per 100,000 population. In 2000, this increased to 308.5 per 100,000. Some children receive care in foster families, which are starting to develop in Ukraine in the adoption system. The recent transition period has also caused a rise in the age of first marriage. Thus, in 1997, the average age of first marriage for women was 21.6 years and for men 23.5. In 2000, it rose to 22.8 and 25.3, correspondingly. As a result, the Ukrainian family produces fewer children, with an increase in the share of nonmarital births from 11.9% of total live births to 17.3% in 2001.

The typical family in Ukraine is a nuclear family. This kind of family started to increase from the 1930s after the dissolution of the extended family pattern. Shifts in family structure were mostly triggered by increasing urbanization. Millions of young people were induced to migrate to urban industrial regions in search for employment, education, and occupational mobility. In 1920, 20% of Ukrainians lived in city areas; by 1980, this percentage had more than tripled. This process has increased labor participation rates for women and decreased the size of the nuclear family. More than half of all Ukrainian families are one-child families.

The nuclear family has increased the demands for equal sharing of responsibilities and household roles between the spouses, as well as raised the intrafamily factors like emotional support, shared values, sexual satisfaction, common income distribution, attention and expression, mutual assistance, and moral protection.

### Divorce and Remarriage

The increasing divorce rates are a reflection of the diminished dependence of spouses on each other and the desire of obtaining a legal marital dissolution rather than remaining in a harmful relationship.

The incidence of divorce has increased rapidly since the 1960s. The failure of a marriage usually stems from a multiplicity of factors. A marital relationship breaks down as the result of failure of spousal and parental roles. Marriage failures then correlate with such factors as early marriage, addiction to alcohol, material and financial needs, and lack of interpersonal communication. The incidence of marriage failure is still growing. The general rate of divorce in Ukraine per 100 marriages in 1990 was about 39.9, in 1991 40.7, in 1995 45.9, in 1990 51.0, and in 2000 71.9 per 1,000. The rate of children (age 0 to 17) involved in divorce per 1,000 population was 12.9 in 1991 and 13.0 in 2000. According to statistics, Ukrainian men seldom want to divorce; the initiative usually comes from women. There is a great difference in the divorce rates for urban and rural citizens, 5.5 per 1,000 compared with 1.9 per 1,000 in rural areas. Surveys indicate that about 75% of divorced men remarry within five years and only half of divorced women within 10 to 15 years after their divorce. In the case of remarriage, the rights of all children of every spouse are protected as stepchildren.

### Cohabitation

In the past 25 years, as the marriage rate slowly declined, the number of unmarried cohabiting couples quadrupled. Cohabitation among Ukrainians is called "to live on trust." The estimated rate of cohabitation is about 17% among all couples, and it has been increasing during the past decade, especially among the young generation. The process of mate selection has passed from the state and relatives' control to personal choice. In Ukraine, there is no special law regulating cohabitation, but legislation does offer some protection for the rights and responsibilities of cohabiting partners, and their children, who are protected as though the couple were married. While the legal system provides some rights for persons who cohabit for some period of time, these rights are much less than those of married couples.

### D. Persons with Physical Disabilities, and Older Persons

Unfortunately, most individuals with disabilities are cut off from the active contacts with the social environment. The services for any social assistance, education, welfare, and transportation facilities are almost totally absent, as they were in former Soviet times when the needs of this population were mostly ignored by society and treated as a family concern. Privacy and independence are vital for the physically handicapped. Even in large cities, it is hard to find the convenient access and passages across the streets, as well as a lot of other facilities for the disabled. These necessities affect the development of sexuality very much because of the personal isolation. Only specialized sanatoriums offer places for temporary relationships of individuals with special needs. In Ukraine today, there are about 60 disabled persons per 1,000 under 60 years of age.

Only recently has the Ukrainian society begun to recognize the abused fate of the physically handicapped, and to break their isolation by improving the conditions of their existence by providing for common interests—sports, education, hobbies, and therapy—and by slowly increasing their access to social allowances.

The Ukrainian society also needs to overcome a rather strict and condemnatory attitude toward any sexual activity by older people or public acknowledgment of same. In comparison to Western contemporaries, Ukrainian women over 40 years old usually consider themselves too old for any sexual intimacy, and thus stop taking care of their own appearance and sexual attractiveness.

## E. Incidence of Oral and Anal Sex

Traditionally, in Ukraine, sex is an extremely personal and very private matter. Moral, emotional, gender, and age factors influence attitudes toward anal sex and its enjoyment. While anal sex holds a great attraction for male homosexuals, and heterosexual couples may engage in anal sex for the enjoyment of one or both partners, there are no special studies undertaken to discover the frequency of anal sex. What data are available usually comes from sexological clinics. According to this data, more than 30% of males have had an experience with anal sex, either with a woman or with a man, prior to age 30 years. In jails, anal sex is usually engaged in as a temporary substitute for heterosexuality, or for maintenance of power.

Oral sex is rather popular for both heterosexual and homosexual couples. It is also very often practiced by adolescents as a part of youth subculture which is largely propagated by mass media, especially by commercials. Cunnilingus is mostly a part of couple foreplay during lovemaking in order to stimulate female orgasm. It is used in many cases by men with sexual dysfunctions. Fellatio is much more widespread as a kind of foreplay for intercourse, or as a separate sexual activity. Fellatio technique involving partial penis penetration into the woman's mouth or penis licking or sucking or kissing are very popular among the lovers of all ages, but mostly among teenagers and persons under age 30.

## 6. Homoerotic, Homosexual, and Bisexual Behaviors

Historically, gender and sexual behavior in Ukraine were strongly influenced by the Christian tradition, which restricted any manifestation of sexuality and considered homosexual orientation as a great sin.

The concept of a homosexual identity as same-sex attractions and sexual behavior has some historical evidence in Ukrainian history. Tolerance towards homosexuality can be traced to the Cossack Republic (1500s to 1600s), where liberation and personal freedom had become the key notions of social activity. Later, during the period of Russian oppression, there was evidence of a homosexual underground for men. The development of lesbian networks is a modern-day phenomenon.

Ukraine, as well as the other states of the former Soviet Union, was and still remains a very heterosexist society with strict gender stereotyping. All social institutions and social opinion place considerable pressure on gay men and lesbian women. Most individuals with a same-sex orientation kept their sexual drives and orientation deeply hidden.

The democratic processes in the newly independent Ukraine gave the opportunity for the people to share the discovery of their sexual-orientation and gender-identity problems within sympathetic communities and support groups, in the mass media, and with specialists—physicians, sexologists, and psychologists. However, most Ukrainians still consider homosexual behavior as abnormal and socially unacceptable and reject both male and female homosexuality.

This is partly because of the rigid manifestation of cultural heterosexism, as well to a reminiscence of Soviet mass psychology and nontolerance to another one.

## A. Children

Because information on sexology and psychology of gender was prohibited in former Soviet Ukraine, little is known about the early experiences of those who today identity themselves as gay or lesbian. No national research on developmental sexuality in childhood was conducted.

In an ideological system that denies any non-heterosexual form of behavior, children with the same-sex orientation encounter a lot of discrimination and even violence. Atypical gender behavior during childhood is usually ridiculed within the society and results in being rejected by parents, relatives, or teachers as not adjusted to the male or female social role. In early childhood, the measurement of gender-role behavior includes easily observable facts, as preference for same play interests, toys, sex peers, dressing, and so on.

The behavior markers of gender identity emerge in Ukrainian children typically between ages 2 and 5 years. At puberty, a child's sexual interests and desires normally emerge. In many features, lesbian, gay, and bisexual youths are similar to other children. However, a pervasive heterosexism of the social environment at home and school causes young gay men or lesbians to experience their cross-gender feelings and behavior in isolation from the significant others. Because of the inner conflict stirred by social and family rejection, they must hide their sexual attraction from others at the very time they are becoming aware of it. Growing up with forbidden and unacceptable sexual attractions influences personality development, often resulting in a negative image of the self as a homosexual female or male.

The initial recognition of same-sex attraction usually becomes evident at puberty and adolescence. Discovery of one's orientation often leads to some sexual activity involving persons of the same sex, starting with simple touching, kissing, petting, stroking the genitals, oral-genital contact, and more rarely, anal intercourse.

Although attendance at a professional high school or summer camp provides wide opportunity for teenage sexual experimentation, and many adolescents have even more homosexual than heterosexual encounters, they are not considered as really gay or lesbian behaviors. The capacity to respond sexually to a person of the same gender in the teenage years is considered being bisexual rather than homosexual. Many teenagers who identity themselves as homosexual in fact are bisexual. Many such Ukrainian youths try to change their sexual orientation by different kinds of therapies. These usually are not successful in reaching the desired goal.

A predominant sexual attraction to persons of the same gender with a constitutional lack of attraction to members of the opposite gender in late teenage years signals the development of a homosexual orientation.

## B. Adults

*Gender Roles, Courtship, and Relationship Patterns*

In the Ukrainian society, where intimacy and relationships have been focused primarily on heterosexual patterns of behavior, the sexual minority groups try to develop their own language for communicating with similarly minded peers about courtship and discovering sexual roles for future intercourse. The image of the self as a homosexual female or male is mostly dependent on the success of lifelong intimacy with a partner and on the opportunity for the self-extension in experiencing the feelings of sexual attractiveness, physical fitness, and good looks. In a traditionally hostile society, coming out as a homosexual poses great problems. The inability to define one's self in terms of social and private activities thus becomes a common characteristic of adults with gender dysphoria.

Many lesbian women and gay men are modeling their relationships on heterosexual behavior forms and communication. A lifelong monogamous commitment is often a desirable model of homosexual relationship. The partners share household and home labor in accordance with active (masculine) and passive (feminine) roles in sexual intercourse. There are a lot of jealous feelings in the attitudes towards each other, passionate love, and sympathy. Many homosexual adults develop their sexual and romantic relationships much as heterosexual couples do, but with the significant difference of fear for manifesting that love and attachment in a hostile environment. In contrast to gay men, many lesbian couples have made parenting an important part of their life. But because homosexual relationships are usually hidden, long-term monogamous homosexual couples are rare in Ukraine.

Despite the hostile social environment, homosexual adults elaborate some elements in dressing, gestures, and behavior that signal a homosexual orientation to knowledgeable observers. Still, even in metropolitan Kyiv, homosexual persons meet each other in covert ways and endure some period for tentative exploration before overtly connecting. Usually there are some places in cities and towns where homosexual individuals can meet each other. In such public places, including sections of certain parks, certain bars, and steam baths, homosexual persons can safely meet, interact, and relate to each other.

In former Soviet times, disclosure or discovery of homosexual orientation meant destruction, ostracism in the workplace and family, forced hospital treatment, and even prison. Lesbians and gays today are as diverse as the society to which they belong. They differ widely in both educational level and economic status. Depending on their social status, they may either conceal their sexual orientation or be open about it. They may have multiple partners or prefer one. Feelings of unhappiness because of the lack of a mate, feelings of alienation, a minimum of understanding regarding their situation, stressful life experiences, anxiety, depression, and substance abuse are common difficulties in the private lives of homosexual persons in Ukraine.

### Social Status

The social attitude regarding homosexual persons in the former Soviet Ukraine was determined by Statute N121 in the criminal code, which supported penalties for the male homosexuality, as well as for the homosexual seduction of children, teenagers, and adults, and punishment for homosexual rape. Female homosexuality was not noted as criminal in that law.

In postliberation Ukraine, researchers and clinicians studying the patterns and quantity of homosexual, lesbian, and bisexual behavior have rejected the Soviet diagnosis of homosexuality as deviant and a mental illness and now make use of the Western paradigms, statistics, and assessment measures, particularly those of the American, Alfred Kinsey, and his colleagues.

This dramatic shift, coupled with the beginning of the democratic process in Ukraine, has given impetus for homosexuals to "come out from the closet." Today, Ukrainians can openly visit a consulting center to meet a sexologist or psychologist to discuss some private problems concerning lesbian or gay orientation or activity. Today, lesbian women and gay men are becoming more open about their sexual identities, social processes in which developmental changes

affect their life. One can easily find many advertisements in the erotic newspapers placed by homosexuals of both sexes seeking a partner. There have also been some recent efforts to organize a gay liberation movement. In May 1995, the First Ukrainian International Congress of Homosexuals and Lesbians, which called itself Two Colors, was held in Kyiv. The association was organized to serve the social, political, and cultural needs of the gay and lesbian population by promoting a positive image for homosexual status in society. In comparison to Western gay liberation movements, Ukrainian lesbians and gays are not separate in their social needs; they are one in their efforts to promote common ideas.

In the late 1990s, the first Ukrainian magazine for gays began publication. Called *One of Us*, it explores different intimate and social factors that are important in the gay lifestyle for men trying to create their non-heterosexual identities in community life.

Although homosexuals in post-socialist Ukraine are not relegated to a deviant status, there is still a lot of prejudice against gay and lesbian persons, and many individuals oriented toward same-sex sexuality keep their attitudes hidden. This is partly because of the rigid manifestation of cultural heterosexism, as well to a reminiscence of Soviet mass psychology of nonreconciliation and nontolerance of anyone who does not fit the majority model. Homophobic tendencies among Ukrainians were and are mostly connected with gay men but not lesbians. This is in part because of a fear for the younger generation being molested, seduced, or infected by HIV. But another factor is an ancient blame for men's abstinence from heterosexual intercourse causing a decrease in childbirth, threatening the future of the nation.

### The Ukrainian Homosexual Culture

The basic demographic characteristics and size of the homosexual population in Ukraine remains a subject of debate. Little is yet known about the relationships of homosexual couples, as well as about the functioning and life course of families with lesbian and gay adults.

As mentioned, most homosexual women and men try to remain invisible. The dominance of exclusively heterosexual orientations in Ukrainian society presses homosexuals to hide their drives and attitudes. One result of this hostile environment is the number of men and women who pose as transsexuals to obtain sex-change surgery in order to change their sex into their passports and thus obtain the opportunity for a legal relationship with a partner of the desired sex. Ukrainian scientists have suggested the significant importance of social factors in the origin of such orientation because of the high valuation by the Soviet system for manifestation of masculine features and of masculine traits expressed by women. Thus lesbian women are more independent, dominant, unconventional, and self-sufficient than most Ukrainian heterosexual women.

The patterns of a sexual partnership among gays and lesbians are significantly influenced by the sexist society with strict polarization of gender roles in housekeeping, raising the children, and in the social sphere. What limited statistics are available suggest that only about 1.5% of gay male couples achieve a stable, long-lasting relationship of more than five years; 2.7% have relationships that last three years, while about 7% have relationships that last a year or so. Lesbians and gays have occasional sexual encounters for anonymous short-time enjoyment; some have sex in pairs or in groups. Some homosexual couples emphasize social needs rather than pure sexual contacts.

Homosexual as well as bisexual relationships satisfy many social, sexual, and emotional needs—many homosexual couples enjoy common professional interests, shared lifestyle, cognitive satisfaction, and cooperation, although their welfare in Ukrainian society is generally not so high. Although there are many different challenges in gay and lesbian experiences, including communications and intimacy, the main widespread problems involve a special need for a positive self-redefinition, coming out as a part of personality development and interpersonal growth, and social activity and well-being as an affirmation of the personality. Ukrainian society needs to provide a social environment in which gay and lesbian persons can feel that their sexual orientation is not pathological or immoral.

## 7. Gender Diversity and Transgender Issues

The beginning of the democratic processes in Ukraine allowed the problems of people with gender conflicts to surface. Because of this, Ukrainian society faces some new questions about the status of such individuals in postsocialist society and the ways in which they interact with the public, family, and friends.

Ukrainian scientists consider that the cases of gender dysphoria, in which a person rejects his or her biological sex and requests surgery and the gender identity of the opposite sex, occurs in about 1 out of every 30,000 to 50,000 persons.

During the Soviet rule, the only center that provided medical treatment and sex-change surgery for transsexuals was in Moscow. In the late 1980s, when legal and medical procedures for altering sex were for the first time performed in Kyiv, female-to-male transsexuals outnumbered male-to-female transsexuals seven to one. In Western countries, the proportion is about equal or favors male-to-female by about three to one. The reasons for this sharp difference might be social-learning experience and the prevailing status of men in Soviet society.

A government commission for transsexualism has recently been organized in Kyiv to deal with individuals with gender dysphoria. The chairman is Professor Borys Vornyk (Address: 8 Smolenska vul., Kyiv 02057). Its members include qualified transgendered "alienist" persons, surgeons, sexologists, psychologists, and lawyers. The clinical and psychological strategy for managing sex change and identity cases is based on the best of foreign experience and practice. The procedure of personality evaluation before undergoing sex reassignment are based on preliminary criteria: originally over age 21, but since 1995, over age 25; having no children under age 18; no criminal offenses; a consistent gender disorder not connected with psychosis—absence of mental diseases or psychosis; a long-standing (from early childhood age), irreversible, cross-gender identification with positive self-conception, physical appearance, and demeanor as a member of the opposite sex, and a strong identity with the opposite sex; and referral to "nuclear" transsexual by a psychiatrist and psychologist based on at least one year of psychotherapy—a stable ego conception; economic and residence stability—minimum problems in self-support; sexual satisfaction of self and the partner, if involved; a positive relationship with family; adequate psychological support; and an adequate understanding of the hazards of the operation.

The commission considers the importance of family diagnosis in an evaluation of gender identity, as the transsexuals will meet a lot of psychological problems involving military registration and alienation from and nonacceptance by society.

Many people react negatively to the phenomena of transsexualism and transvestism because these contradict traditional gender behavior and assumptions.

A transvestite's social and family situation is usually very difficult, because the lack of privacy in everyday life does not allow him to have the opportunity to dress even partially as a member of the opposite sex. The cases of male-to-female cross-dressing are usually connected with a hyperfeminine expression. The lack of community and nonavailability of public places for mixing with others as a woman restrict the options for cross-dressing.

Cases of berdachism and other atypical sexual identities are extremely rare in Ukraine and exist mostly as rumors rather than as clinical or scientific studies.

## 8. Significant Unconventional Sexual Behaviors

The incidence of socially unaccepted kinds of sexual behaviors are increasing rapidly as the process of political and economic transition affects the whole culture and everyone in it.

### A. Coercive Sexual Behavior

*Child Sexual Abuse, Incest, and Pedophilia*

Any kind of child molestation has always been condemned in Ukrainian society, and Ukrainian folk traditions consider any sexual abuse of children as the most heinous of crimes.

Known cases of sexual abuse are mostly connected with girls assaulted between 3 and 7 or 8 years old. More than half of the offenders are close friends or neighbors of the parents. More than half the victims have been killed by the seducers after the pedophilic acts because of the fear for criminal responsibility and punishment. The penalty for sex molestation is the same as for the rape of minors or incest; Statute 117 of the criminal code mentions the penalty from three to 15 years in jail and even death. Most of the perpetrators of this crime are men 20 to 30 years old.

More often than not, cases of pedophilia are not connected with penetration. only with genital foundling or handling. The children involved in such sex games with adults are about equally male or female.

The frequency of pedophilia in our country is sometimes connected with homeless girls and boys who run away from home to escape from parents and are in turn victimized by adult male strangers in return for some food, money, reward, and temporary shelter. Usually, they do not report their offenders and keep the sexual experience secret from parents and others. Cases of incest are a rather rarely reported form of child sexual abuse. Accounts of sex between a parent and child are more frequent than are officially reported. Sexual relations between a mother and son or a father/stepfather and daughter are seldom discovered or reported. Very few scientific statistics and little information are available about sexual relations between brothers and sisters. The recent development of sexual consultation centers with psychoanalytic services will help in obtaining data on the incestuous involvement of children in Ukraine.

*Sexual Harassment*

[*Editors' Note*: In this section, the Ukrainian authors adopt a broader and less specific definition of sexual harassment than is common in Western usage.]

Violations of personal boundaries, a basic element in the administrative-commanding system of the former Soviet Ukraine, made sexual harassment an everyday normative behavior in official and informal relations. Fear of the authority that was taught by the Soviets fostered a tolerant attitude towards sexual harassment as a usual and expected behavior of authorities and subordinate persons. Although Statute 119 in the Ukrainian criminal code deals with a penalty for forcing a woman to engage in sex, no incidents of such violations were ever reported or registered.

Sexual harassment behavior is widespread, especially among youths. Sexual remarks, jokes, explicit conversation about having sex, as well as such behavior as following, staring, leering, and taunting are regarded by both men and women as inoffensive and even just larking. Such behavior is mostly considered to be an acceptable way of getting acquainted in public places, and as normal masculine communication in mixed-gender interactions.

According to a survey conducted in different regions of Ukraine, one in seven students in secondary school and college has been subject of undesirable contact, and one in six students is confronted with sexual harassment. The incidence of teenager sexual harassment is strongly determined by the type of child educational institution. Girls become the object of sexual harassment much more often than boys. Every third girl has experienced sexual harassment, every fifth girl has experienced undesirable touch, and one in ten has been the subject of sexual abuse as a strong traumatic experience. Sexual harassment is accepted as an inevitable in receiving a prestigious job. Young women also have more chances to be an object of sexual harassment in the job market. There are many economic factors that contribute to sexual violence against women.

*Sexual Assault and Rape*

The incidence of rape is growing very quickly. Stranger rape accounts for about 94% of all reported rape cases; 67% involve group or gang rape; 13% result in serious physical harm. According to the criminal statistics for the Kyiv region, most of the reported perpetrators were under age 20. Most of the victims are under the age of 18. Most of the rapists did not have a previous criminal record and used alcohol.

**B. Prostitution**

The danger of prosecution does not limit the offers of sexual services in return for financial gain. Historically in the Ukrainian community, there was always a negative attitude toward women who had sexual relations with men outside marriage. But starting at least in the early 1970s, the attitude towards prostitution, especially among youth and middle-aged adults, has shifted to be very permissive. Prostitution is spreading among young women and girls as young as 10 to 15 years old. Poverty and transition-related issues, such as unemployment, have increased the need to earn money on the streets. These young girls are the victims of drug and alcohol abuse, poor diets, venereal diseases, and sexual abuse. Another phenomenon linked with prostitution is trafficking in persons. Many women and some men, discouraged by job opportunities at home, look for a work abroad. In many cases, Ukrainian migrants are being engaged in prostitution, becoming the victim of exploitation and violence.

Ukraine is considered to be a major source of young girls and women sold into international commercial sex markets, especially in the Middle East and Balkans. As the result of being trafficked, a lot of women have found themselves trapped in slavery dependence and had to solve their problems by sexual servicing.

**C. Pornography and Erotica**

A Project of Law prohibiting the production and distribution of pornography, and the formation of the Presidential commission on obscenity were still being discussed in the Ukrainian Parliament as of mid-1995.

Although Ukrainian society has become more permissive sexually, it does not provide adequate values of human sexual activity. With the breakdown of the Soviet regime, sexuality became one of the most important symbols of social and cultural liberation. Widespread public ignorance about sex in former years has been replaced by everyday representations in commerce and movies. Television programs and filmmakers have exploited sex; the display of the bodies of young women as available sexual objects are not only on cinema screens, but in advertising, on posters, photographs, and drawings. After 70 years of repression, Ukraine has a large market for pornographic products. Television programs portray and revel in various types of sexual experience, and frank expressions of nudity with erotic excitement are displayed in public places for everybody.

The public discussion of the harmful role of pornography for grownup sexual expectations and values makes it clear that, under the slogans of democracy, new businessmen are exploiting sex roles, promoting the image of a happy life associated with sexual pleasure, drinking, smoking, and male control of the opposite sex.

Newly opened sex shops and the appearance of such newspapers as *Pan Plus Pani* and the sex magazine *Lel'* have broken all previous taboos on sexual subjects, recognizing the sexual culture and providing sexual education for different age groups. Artistic eroticism has started to recover from years of repression, producing pictures, stories, and theater plays in the best national traditions, based on gender equality in relationships, personal freedom and dignity, Ukrainian humor, and the pursuit of a full-blooded life.

## 9. Contraception, Abortion, and Population Planning

**A. Attitudes, Education, Availability, and Usage of Contraceptives**

The maintenance of an appropriate population level is vital to the survival of any society, but especially for Ukraine after the Soviet takeover. During the famines deliberately created by Soviet policy in 1920 and especially 1933, six million Ukrainian peasants from the central, east, and south regions died from artificial hunger or were removed from their native land to Siberia and the Far East. The devastation of World War II also reduced Ukraine's population significantly.

From the middle of 1979, the Ukraine birthrate started to drop rapidly; since the end of 1980, the birthrate has remained below the replacement rate. Although the former Soviet authorities tried to encourage families to have more children in order to get a larger labor force, their efforts did not reverse the trend. By the end of 1960, most Ukrainian women had to combine parenthood with professional work because of economic needs and the necessity of guaranteeing family income.

As a consequence, Ukraine is characterized by the rapidly increasing proportion of older persons. In 1960, there was one person of pension age for every 11.5 nonpension persons. Today the ratio is one in every six. And the birthrate continues to decline. Under such circumstances, the social and economic situation has had a great impact on the family: We have an increase of single persons of marriageable age, and a high proportion of divorce and one-parent families (the number of one-parent families in 2002 constituted 14.0% of all families).

Historically, most Ukrainian families did not limit the number of their children, nor did religious doctrine permit use of contraception. However, sexual intercourse was forbidden during major religious festivals. And most women knew about medicinal herbs that could be used to prevent pregnancy or induce a miscarriage. In the 11th century, the daughter of King Jaroslav Mudryj Jevpraksija wrote the first book on the medical use of herbs, describing their use in preventing or terminating pregnancy. The average Ukrainian family was large, with the women sometimes having more than ten childbirths and five to nine surviving children.

The involvement of Ukrainian women in the labor force in 1930 and in 1950 reduced the number of childbirths and increased the number of induced abortions, even though from 1936 to 1955, abortion was forbidden by Soviet law. In the end, economic factors enabled the government to give impetus to a family planning policy and promote the development of contraception. Nevertheless, from the late 1960s to the present, Ukraine remains at the head of countries where abortion is the main form of birth control.

Induced abortion is not a method of contraception, but one of family planning. In 1998, 45 pregnancies out of 100 ended in abortion. The number of abortions has been decreasing in recent years (see Table 1).

Overall, the number of abortions among women of reproductive age in 1998 was as follows: ages 18 to 34, 79.1%; ages 35 to 49, 18.3%; ages 15 to 17, 2.6%; and under age 14, 0.05%. In recent years, the situation has improved. There has been no increase in the number of abortions among girls under the age of 14 and teenagers aged 15 to 17. Among girls aged 10 to 14 years who interrupted their pregnancy, the number having an abortion increased from 47.4% to 94.0%. This was promoted by the creation of a network of family planning centers and work with girls who have already become pregnant.

Since sex-education programs were focused on adults, the sexual behavior of youths was not regarded as important for family planning. In the context of such policies, the incidence of teenage pregnancy started to rise. A second reason for the failure of the government program to promote contraception was the fact that the sex-education programs were focused mostly on women in gynecological clinics, and not on all women of childbearing age. This policy ignored the family as a unit of a man and a woman and the male's responsibility in family planning. With this policy, husbands simply assumed that the wife would take responsibility for contraception, which they sometimes, but not always, did.

But the major factor was that the most effective birth-control methods, such as oral contraceptives and hormonal implants, were not recommended by the physicians, and remained unpopular among both adults and teenagers. In addition to the strong prejudice against the hormonal contraceptive pills, another factor in their nonuse is their high cost in Ukraine.

From 1994 on, tubal ligation for the female and male vasectomy have been increasingly chosen by Ukrainian couples who do not want any more children or who prefer to remain childless.

In general, Ukraine needs a greater availability of contraception and improved sex information in order to reduce the increasing numbers of unwanted pregnancies.

### B. Teenage Pregnancies

Teenage pregnancy is often a motivation for establishing a marriage relationship. According to one survey, unmarried pregnancy occurred among 83% of young couples under 20 years old; most of them considered the childbirth undesirable. The decision to have an abortion or to keep a child is made by the young woman with additional agreement of parents or relatives when the girl is under 16 or 17 years old. There are no special schools or classes for pregnant teenagers. Usually, the relatives take the responsibility for a newborn baby. The destiny of such babies is often unhappy when a young mother gives her child up for adoption or to an orphanage. During recent decades, the population of the rejected babies in an orphanage has increased many times in comparison to the number of the orphaned children in Ukraine after World War II. The high rate of adolescent pregnancy demonstrates that Ukraine needs to improve its school and community sex-education programs and to provide free or low-cost contraceptive services to all teenagers who need them.

### C. Abortion

Abortions have been legal in Ukraine since 1955. They are available to any woman after the age of 18 years and are mostly free of charge—the state pays the medical expenses of low-income women. The abortion is usually done at a special clinic or gynecology department up to 12 weeks after the last menstrual period. Although abortions usually are medically safe, many factors affect the women after an operation: anxiety, depression, and complications in reproductive function.

In Ukraine, abortion is the main cause of infertility. More than 200,000 cases of inflammatory diseases of the fallopian tubes and ovaries are recorded annually, of which 130,000 are first occurrences among women aged 18 years. Among teenagers aged 15 to 17 years, about 10% have inflammatory diseases of the reproductive system. Twenty-six women died in 1998 as a result of an abortion, for a rate of 0.05 deaths per 1,000 abortions. Seven deaths occurred as a result of an abortion that was not performed in a medical establishment.

The percentage of miscarriages out of the total number of pregnancies also increased as a result of abortions. In 1998, the percentage increased by 1.8 times in comparison to 1990. About 60% of stillbirths are premature births, and from 50% to 70% are first births. There has been a growing antiabortion movement in Ukraine, especially among some religious denominations, scientists, teachers, and some social organizations. These groups emphasize that a woman should take responsibility either for preventing pregnancy or for giving the life to a new baby because of the right to life of the unborn fetus.

### D. Efforts to Regulate Population Growth

With regard to the demographic situation, the Ukrainian government considers the improvement of living standards for all women, but especially for young couples, as a measure of fertility, womanhood, and parenthood. For this purpose, the Committee of Women's Affairs, the Children, and the Population was organized in April 1995 by the cabinet of the ministers of Ukraine. The committee started to develop family-planning policy and different social programs to permit the women and the families to promote their well-being, their health, and parenthood.

Since Ukraine became an independent state, a series of strategic national programs have been adopted. Among them: a Long-Term Program on Improvement of the Status of Women, Family, Protection of Maternity, and Childhood;

### Table 1

### Abortion Rates in Ukraine for Selected Years

| Year | Abortions per 100 pregnancies | Abortions per 100 deliveries |
|------|------|------|
| 1991 | 60.1 | 145 (est.) |
| 1995 | 59.2 | 119 |
| 1998 | 54.4 | 106 |
| 2000 | 55.0 | — |
| 2001 | 48.1 | 92 |

*Source*: Data of the Ministry of Health of Ukraine

a National Program on Family Planning, and a National Program "Children of Ukraine." In 1997, the National Plan of Action for 1997-2000 "on the improvement of status of women and their role in society" was approved. The National Program of Family Planning has the following strategic objectives:

- Form regional institutions for family planning;
- Prepare medical and educational personnel to work on family planning;
- Meet the population's contraception needs;
- Prevent undesired pregnancies; and
- Create an infrastructure for infertility treatment.

## 10. Sexually Transmitted Diseases and HIV/AIDS

### A. Sexually Transmitted Diseases

The history of the medical treatment of sexually related diseases in the 19th century was connected with such scientists as J. Zelenev. J. Popov, B. Zadoroznij, and J. Mavrov. In Czarist Russia, around 1850, it was estimated that about 10% of all reported illnesses involved venereal diseases. Syphilis and gonorrhea were found mostly in the large industrial centers like Kyiv, Kharkiv, Odesa, and Mykolajiv. In 1901, *The Journal of Skin and Venereal Diseases* was founded in Charkiv; it carried articles describing the symptoms of common sexually transmitted diseases and their complications.

World War I and the October 1917 Revolution led to widespread sexual promiscuity and increasing cases of venereal diseases. In 1920 in Ukraine, special dispensaries for treating STDs were organized in all large cities. This helped to slow the spread of these infections. World War II created a huge new public health problem, which lasted until 1950. In comparison to other former Soviet republics, Ukraine was characterized by the lowest level of STDs, because of the sanitary preventive measures.

### Incidence, Patterns, and Trends

After the dissolution of the U.S.S.R., social factors such as large-scale migrations, the ease of reproducing erotic and pornographic videos and their availability, changes in the economic situation, and the double moral standard have influenced the recent outburst of venereal diseases. In Ukraine, as in other countries, the teenaged population appears hardest hit by the STD epidemic. Venereal diseases are increasing in epidemic proportions among teenagers because of lack of knowledge, early sexual experience, multiple sexual partners, and a high level of sexual activity.

In the past five years, syphilis cases among 14-year-old boys has increased about 400%, and for 15- to 17-year-olds by about 800%. Among teenage girls, syphilis has increased by about 500%. Venereal diseases such as gonorrhea and syphilis are now the chief sexually related diseases in Ukraine. The incidence of gonorrhea and syphilis began to climb in 1992. In 1995, 208.5 new cases were reported per 100,000 population. In 1996, the rate was 226.5, declining to 144.8 in 2000. Among 15- to 19-year-old girls and 12- to 14-year-olds, an epidemic has become a national pandemic. There has been an unprecedented increase in the incidence of syphilis among women. The indicator rose from 6.2 cases per 100,000 in 1990 to 134.8 in 1998, which naturally has created a favorable environment for the spread of HIV infection. Females and males between the ages of 17 and 27 are most at risk of infection, and they account for the majority of all STD cases reported. In the past five years, the common infections, like syphilis, gonorrhea, herpes, and chlamydia, have increased about 300% in adult females and by 400% in adult males. This continuing increase in the incidence of STDs is creating urgent social problems.

### Availability of Treatment and Prevention Efforts

In Ukraine today, there is a system of STD control, and appropriate healthcare is available throughout the country for people of all ages, in the rural areas as well as in the cities and large metropolitan areas. Everyone can obtain free and confidential routine medical testing and care. It is obligatory for all the personnel of medicine, nutrition, and provision services to be tested periodically for STDs and HIV, since the best way to fight the epidemic process is to block it. Some clinics provide resident treatment, and some dispensaries provide outpatient care with pre- and post-test counseling. All services are free, with the patient paying only for medication when they can afford it. Besides medical services, these clinics provide free printed contraception and HIV/AIDS information.

The program for high-risk youth includes testing and follow-up care. Special venereal departments provide a wide range of medical services, all free and confidential. The only requirement for the patient is to identify all the partners, so they can be tested and referred to medical services in case treatment is needed. Some venereal clinics offer extensive treatment for individuals addicted to drugs or alcohol, or to a person whose behavior put him or her at risk for being infected.

Ukrainian physicians prepare special information for adolescents aged 14 to 18 in order to give them the facts they need to protect themselves from STDs. But this work is insufficient in the area of mass media, especially television, and in educational programs in the schools, where some are still embarrassed when speaking of "sexually transmissible." A sexually enlightened society is not afraid to influence the consciousness and attitudes of the masses with an honest voice.

According to a UNAIDS report for 2002, the incidence of syphilis cases increased dramatically from less than 10 cases per 100,000 in 1990 to 118 per 100,000 in 1995; in some regions this rate reached 220 per 100,000. Over 60,000 new syphilis cases were reported in 1995 alone. Gonorrhea has been underreported.

### B. HIV/AIDS

The epidemiology of HIV and AIDS infection in Ukraine demonstrates worrisome trends.

### Incidence, Patterns, and Trends

The epidemic of HIV/AIDS in Ukraine has progressed in two stages: The first phase started in 1987 when the first six cases of HIV infection were registered among Ukrainian citizens. Until 1994, annually about 40 HIV-infected people were registered. Geographically, the cases of infection concerned large industrial cities and the spreading speed was quite slow. The main way of infection transmission was heterosexual. The number of HIV-positive Ukrainians during that period was 183. The second stage started in 1995 when the two first cases of HIV infection among intravenous drug users (IDUs) were found in Mykolajiv. Since that time, the rate of infected IDUs has been growing rapidly. By January 1, 2002, there were 43,600 HIV/AIDS IDU cases.

Starting from 1998, consecutive substantial reduction in the rate of HIV-registered cases can be explained not by the slowing down of the epidemic, but by the adoption in 1998 of a new law "About HIV/AIDS Prevention and Social Defense of Population." In accord with the United Nations Declaration, that law initiated the use of HIV-testing on a volunteer basis.

In 1997, HIV/AIDS infection reached all regions of the country. By the end of 2000, the eastern and southern regions of Ukraine were most affected by the epidemic. The Odessa, Dnipropetrovsk, and Donetsk regions contained 60% of the entire HIV-positive population of Ukraine.

The explosive character of the HIV/AIDS epidemic in Ukraine is connected with the dramatic growing of the number of IDUs, the peculiarities of intravenous drug use, the late initiation of prophylactic work inside the IDU group, and the lack of attention to such work by the official authorities and establishments.

The period between 1990 and 2000 was characterized by a sharp increase in drug dependency. In 1990, narcotic services were monitoring 22,466 individuals, while by the beginning of 2001, there were 75,489 clients. The experts estimate that the real number of drug users can be five to ten times higher. Nearly 95% of the registered drug users are actually IDUs.

The rates of the HIV/AIDS-epidemic spread in Ukraine are the highest in the Central and Eastern Europe. During the recent years, the number of people registered as ill or dead from AIDS has increased dramatically.

The maximum loss from AIDS among males in the age group 30-to-34 years was 29%, while in females, this was true for 26% of the age group 25-to-29 years. The data of AIDS rates and deaths from AIDS are lower than actual rates because of insufficient levels of medical diagnostics; 84% of all individuals who died from AIDS were only diagnosed with AIDS when they were in the terminal stage of the disease or after they had died.

The epidemiological situation in Ukraine becomes even worse: The number of people who donate their blood while being HIV-infected is getting larger (from 0.06% in 1997 to 0.07% in 2000); as are those who have other sexually transmitted diseases (from 0.5% to 0.71%); those with multiple sexual partners (from 0.55% to 1.02%); and pregnant women (from 0.09% to 0.17%). Among European countries, Ukraine is the leader in the level of HIV-infected blood donors, as well as in the speed of the epidemic's spread, in the Central and Eastern Europe.

The trends of the epidemic development remain vague because of lack of adequate information. We can assume the beginning of the dangerous tendency of the epidemic to transfer to the "main" groups of the population. This assumption is supported by the fact that the rate of individuals infected by sexual activity through sexual ways, and not through intravenous drug use or transfusion, is getting larger. The rate of those infected through intravenous drug use in 1997 constituted 83%; in 1998, 77%; in 1999, 65%; and only 62% in 2000. But between 1997 and 2000, the percentage of pregnant women who were infected through sexual relations grew from 66% to 75%.

*Availability of Treatment and Prevention Programs*

The first national program for HIV/AIDS prevention was adopted in February 1992 and ran through 1994. Now the fourth one is running out, and the next has been developed for years 2004-2006. All plans were developed by a national committee against AIDS and are supported by a number of organizations: the Ministry of Public Health, the Ministry of Economics, the Social Defense Ministry, and the Department for Family and Youth. The general lines of the programs include promotion of condom use, an educational project, mass media action, and providing healthcare clinics.

The general goal is to slow down the epidemic of HIV and save thousands of lives. Medical aspects of the program are designed to reduce or eliminate the risk of getting HIV. The health workers have set themselves an ambitious goal:

mass awareness and understanding of how sexual intercourse can be made safer to reduce the risk of getting HIV. Another effort is to supply the population with condoms; approximately 150 million condoms will be provided annually for the needs of the Ukrainian population. The medical campaign against AIDS also requires testing donated blood and blood products by checking two million blood samples annually on a voluntary basis. Testing is compulsory for pregnant and some categories of the population.

Special attention will be given to laboratory testing for HIV-infection. More then 170 institutions will make four million tests a year, using clinical tests produced by the American firm Abbott and the French firm Sanofi Diagnostic Pasteur. The state will also promote development of a national industry for transfusion blood screening. The program also contains measures for healthcare of laboratory and hospital personnel in order to reduce the risk of their becoming infected.

The development of AIDS service organizations requires special training programs for responding without fear to the needs of all HIV-infected people who require medical or psychological help. Already, clinics in regional centers serve people with HIV or AIDS. Usually, they offer confidential medical services, pre- and post-test counseling, meals, housing and rental assistance, and complete medical evaluations. Again, all such services are free and confidential. The national program includes research studies of the viral causes of AIDS, the development of new diagnostic and treatment methods, and the search for an AIDS vaccine.

The main program direction is on promoting AIDS awareness among the population. A mass media effort on radio and television and in the newspapers should be effective in raising the knowledge about AIDS, especially how everyone can gain some protection. The information-educational work is focused on separating the scientific facts from the myths and providing information about the connection between sexual intercourse, oral and anal sex, and HIV transmission. High-risk groups will receive special attention, for example, prevention of mother-to-child HIV/AIDS transmission.

In November 2000, the President of Ukraine issued a decree, "About Urgent Steps to Prevent HIV/AIDS Spread." In order to fulfill this decree, the Government created a committee, which is responsible for inventing and monitoring strategic programs; coordinating central and peripheral executive authorities; and keeping the President, the Parliament, and the international public informed about the state of anti-epidemic measures.

Because of this Decree, the number of centers for AIDS prophylactics and control is getting larger. By November 2001, there were 27 such centers, seven of them had inpatient departments. Meanwhile, the National Program "Reproductive Health 2001-2005" (passed by Presidential Decree) and the HIV/AIDS Prophylactics Program of 2001-2003 (passed by Decree of the Cabinet of Ministers) have assumed governmental control over the epidemiological situation, medical examination on a voluntary basis together with after-test counseling, and regular and complete informing of the public about HIV/AIDS.

The main obstacle to realization of the governmental program lies in absence of its adequate regulation, monitoring, and effectiveness examination. The Program is missing the chapters about estimated results, effectiveness, criteria, and evaluation of fulfilled projects. The coordination of actions between different Ministries, departments, and specialized governmental institutions is a separate difficult question. Governmental programs on HIV/AIDS prevention assume counseling services for the public. But the realization of the corresponding measures still remains in the initial stage.

The effectiveness of the existing counseling services is not sufficient, particularly for teenagers, youth, and especially for those groups who are at high risk for HIV-infection.

The most difficult obstacles on the way to effective counseling are:

- insufficient training of the specialists who deal with HIV/AIDS prevention and high-risk groups;
- lack of knowledge among children and youth about governmental establishments that give counseling services on HIV/AIDS;
- negative attitudes towards HIV-positive individuals on the part of both society and medical staff; and
- absence of control over the quality of counseling services as for HIV/AIDS.

[*Update 2002*: UNAIDS Epidemiological Assessment: By the end of 2001, a cumulative total of 39,752 cases of HIV infection had been reported to the National Health Authorities. Until 1991, HIV/AIDS surveillance was organized mostly through mandatory screening in subgroups of the population, together with contact tracing. Testing policies changed in 1991 with the introduction of anonymous voluntary testing. Testing remained compulsory for sex workers, IDUs, STD patients, blood donors and "other populations based on epidemiological considerations." In reality, few changes occurred; voluntary, anonymous, and free testing was less than 5% of all testing done in 1996. Diagnosed HIV infections that have been officially investigated are reported nationally with the name of the individual.

[In early 1995, HIV started to spread very rapidly among IDUs. The number of diagnosed infections increased from 398 cases for the whole period 1987 to 1994, to 1,490 in 1995, 5,400 in 1996, and a total of 23,315 in 1997 to 1999. These figures represent only officially registered cases and therefore underestimate the number of diagnosed cases. Highest rates of reported HIV infections were initially found in the region of Odessa and Nykolayev, but cases are now reported from all 27 regions of the country. Increases in HIV prevalence were also seen among STD patients and blood donors.

[Prevalence is mostly estimated from the screening programs. Sentinel surveillance is being implemented in IDUs in Odessa. Data on the relatively low HIV spread among homosexuals should be interpreted with caution in the context of a society where, until 1991, homosexuality was illegal and punishable. The diffusion of the epidemic through heterosexual contact is difficult to assess. Proportions of HIV-positive tests among pregnant women in Odessa and Nykolayev have reached levels similar to those of Western European cities. However, because the mode of transmission is not available in most cases, it is not possible to determine to what extent pregnant women have been infected through IDU or other means.

[The estimated number of adults and children living with HIV/AIDS on January 1, 2002, were:

| | | |
|---|---|---|
| Adults ages 15-49: | 250,000 | (rate: 1.0%) |
| Women ages 15-49: | 76,000 | |
| Children ages 0-15: | NA | |

[An estimated 11,000 adults and children died of AIDS during 2001.

[No estimate is available for the number of Ukrainian children who had lost one or both parents to AIDS and were under age 15 at the end of 2001. (*End of update by the Editors*)]

## 11. Sexual Dysfunctions, Counseling, and Therapies

### A. Concepts of Sexual Dysfunction

A network of sexological consulting centers started to appear in Ukraine in 1965. It was a time when the first Scientific Research Institute of Kidney and Urinogenital Diseases started to function. There was a lab of endocrinology, which in 1972 was renamed the department of sexopathology, with two laboratories, endocrinology and spermatology. In 1974, the department was redesignated the Ukrainian Scientific Counseling and Organizational Methodical Center of Sexopathology and Andrology. The inspiration for its development belonged to Ivan Junda (1924-1994)—the honored scientist, State prize-winner, doctor of medical sciences, and professor. The main direction of his research was the etiology, pathogenesis, clinical symptoms, and methods of sexual dysfunction, treatment, men's infertility, and its prophylactics.

From the time of the Chernobyl catastrophe, the main direction of the research has been the occurrence of erectile dysfunction, urinary tract diseases in the territory of radiation dissemination, risk factors in the development of men's barrenness and women's infertility, and new methods of treatment of sexological and preventative measures for andrological diseases.

In 1992, the Ministry of Health renamed the department the Department of Sexology and Andrology. The head of the department is Honored Physician of Ukraine, Doctor of Medical Sciences, Professor Ihor Horpinchenko. The main direction of the research and treatment has been generative and copulative function in survivors of the Chernobyl catastrophe, an approbation of nontraditional treatment methods, and development of surgical methods for vascular forms of erectile dysfunctions. Special attention is paid to the research of the prevalence of some dysfunctions and infertility of nucleosides. The sexological investigation of such patients has led to development of tactics for their rehabilitation.

### B. The Availability of Diagnosis and Treatment

Ukraine was the first of the former Soviet republics where the system of regional counseling centers was created. Since the beginning of the 1990s, every large city in Ukraine has had its family or sexology consultation centers where sexologists and psychologists have begun to work together. Medical examination of the individual or couple is accompanied by psychological testing. This cooperation became more widespread with the creation in 1997 of Family Planning Centers.

Many women and men are seeking help at these centers, be it guidance, information, or reassurance. The number of sexological problems are considerable, but most are connected with the individual psychological culture. The diagnostic services of the consultation centers focus on the communications abilities and relationships between wife and husband or lovers, and the psychology of human sexual response. The latter is not limited to coitus, but extends to all the pleasurable and negative sensations associated with any sexuoerotic contact.

The treatment part of the counseling deals with couple guidance and relationship problems, and on teaching interpersonal skills that can be applied in their everyday interactions as a couple. The program, usually a combination of traditional psychotherapy with behavioral-oriented therapy, is aimed at personal growth of the patient(s), and sexual healing, using dialogue, role playing, and group therapy. Constant efforts are made to help the patient(s) develop a warm and well-functioning relationship.

Most counseling services are free of charge and confidential. There are some nongovernmental family consultation services, available for those who can afford them.

## C. Therapist Training and Certification

There is no special licensing for sexologists at the Ukrainian universities. Mostly, sexologists by profession are those who hold the position of urologists (about 50%), psychiatrists (about 40%), and endocrinologists (about 10%), all with the education of a physician. Nevertheless, in 1988, a new physician speciality as sexologist was introduced by an order passed by Ministry of Health. In 1992, an order from the Ministry of Health regarding improvement of serological services stimulated development of medical-psychological and andrological counseling centers, as well as the Ukrainian Center of Sexopathology and Andrology at the Institute of Urology and Nephrology of the Academy of Medical Sciences. The Academic Director is Prof. O. Vozianov and the Center's Head is Prof. I. Horpinchenko. Since 1997, each regional (*oblast*) center has a department of medical-psychological family counseling, which is functioning under the guidance of regional head sexopathologist. Mostly, they deal with andrology diseases and infertility problems and are free of charge.

Sexological or family consultation centers are staffed primarily by physician-sexologists and by psychologists. Medical sexology as a discipline for physicians is taught by gynecologists, psychiatrists in graduate courses at the medical universities in Kyiv, Odesa, Dnipropetrovs'k, and other cities, and in postgraduate courses at the Chair of Sexology and Medical Psychology, the Ukrainian Medical Postgraduate Academy (Kharkiv). Psychological problems in sexology are studied at the Teachers Training Universities in graduate courses, and in the candidate and doctoral program at the Institute of Psychology. The Ministry of Public Health of Ukraine, the Ministry of Education, the State Universities, and their scientific boards establish the criteria for programs, coursework, and requirements for education and certification in fields involved in diagnosis and treatment of sexual dysfunctions.

## 12. Sex Research and Advanced Professional Education

### A. Institutes and Programs for Sexological Research

Several government agencies are involved in and support sexological research. These include some divisions of the Ministry of Public Health of Ukraine and Ministry of Science and Education of Ukraine, Academy of Pedagogical Sciences, and Academy of Medical Sciences.

Institute of Urology and Nephrology: Professor Olexandr Vozianov, director. Department of Sexopathology, Androgyny, and Sexology Clinic: Professor Ihor Horpinchenko, chairperson. Address: 9a, Kotsubinskyj vul., Kyiv 04053; tel.: 38-044-216-5054; fax 38-044-244-6862. Research includes: the sexology and andrology of aging; the Chernobil catastrophe and changes in the reproductive function; development of objective diagnostic methods for sexual dysfunctions; investigation of the pathospermia factors in infertility couples; and biochemical aspects of erectile dysfunction.

Kyiv Research Institute of Clinical and Experimental Surgery: Professor Valerej Saenko, director. Address: 30 Herojiv Sevastopolia vul., Kyiv 04180; tel.: 38-044-483-1374; fax 38-044-483-5219. Research includes: improvement and development of body surgery corrections of transsexual persons; diagnosis and treatment of the vascular impotence; and endoorthopedic prosthetic appliances.

Kyiv Medical Postgraduate Academy, the section of Parenatology of Child Obstetrics and Gynecology: Professor Zoreslava Shkiriak-Nyzhnyk, chairperson. Address: 8 Manujil'skoho vul., Kyiv 04050; tel.: 380-44-213-6271; fax 380-44-213-6271, chislow@public.ua.net. Research includes: family and female reproductive health; sexual enlightment; sexual morality; and bioethics.

Kyiv Research Sexology and Andrology Center: Head: Holotsvan Olena, Ph.D. Address: 8 Smolenska vul., Kyiv 04057; tel.: 380-044-228-0103; fax 380-44-543-8421. Research includes: adult sexual dysfunction; male and female infertility; personal disharmonies in sexual relationship; social and biological factors in transsexuality and homosexuality; hospital investigation and the treatment of sexual diseases (prostatitis, urethritis, epidermitis, etc.); and treatment of gender identity disorders and conditions.

Ukrainian Postgraduate Academy (Kharkiv). The Chair of Sexology and Medical Psychology: Professor Valentyn Kryshtal'. Address: 81/85 Myronositska vul. Charkiv 310023; tel.: 38-057-245-1056. Research includes: gender dysphoria; sexual identity disorders; prophylactics of sexual dysfunctions; VCT counseling; matrimonial disharmonies; causes as well as medical and psychological methods for the evaluation of dysfunctional couples; marital therapy and treatment programs.

Other major institutes with programs for sexology and gender-related research are governed by the Ministry of Science and Education and Academy of Pedagogical Sciences.

National Pedagogical M. Dragomanov University, Institute of Psychology and Pedagogy. Address: 9 Pyrohova vul., Kyiv; tel.: 380-044-216-3007; fax 380-44-224-2251. Research includes: techniques for teaching human sexuality courses; childhood sexual development and behavior; and comparisons of gender behavior in cross-cultural investigations.

Ukrainian Academy of Pedagogical Sciences, H. Kostjuk Institute of Psychology, Prof. P. Chamata's Laboratory of the Psychology of Personality: Professor Myroslav Boryshevskiy, chairperson. Address: 2 Pan'kivs'ka vul., Kyiv 01033; tel.: 380-44- 244-3320; fax 380-44-244-1963. Research includes: development of gender self-consciousness in childhood and adolescence; parental roles in developing child sexuality; and development of sex-education programs for children and teenagers.

V. Hnatjuk Ternopil Pedagogical University, Institute of Psychology. Head of the Institute: Professor Volodymyr Kravets; tel.: 380-353-3-1297. Research program manager: Dotsent Oksana Kikinezhadi. Address: 2 Maksyma Kryvonosa vul., Ternopil, 46027; tel.: 380-35-222-1587; email: okikinezhd@tspu.edu.ua. Research includes: gender socialization; psychosexual development; and sexual education.

### B. Graduate Programs and the Advanced Study of Human Sexuality

According to the basic college education, there are a variety of postgraduate advanced courses of study available in Ukraine. Some of these are listed here with their focus, sponsoring agency, and address.

Master's degree programs in human sexuality: Ministry of Public Health of Ukraine, Ukrainian Postgraduate Academy. The chair of sexology and medical psychology: Professor Valentyn Kryshtal'. Address: 81/85 Myronositska vul., Kharkiv 310023; tel.: 380-57-245-1056.

Graduate courses in sexology for the physicians' advanced training; doctorate programs in sexuality and family studies: Ministry of Public Health of Ukraine. Address: Kyiv Research Institute of Urology and Nephrology, 9 a In. Kotsubinskiy vul., Kyiv 252053; fax: 380-44-244-6862.

Postgraduate courses on sexual behavior for an academic degree in developmental psychology: Mychailo Drahomanov National Pedagogical University, Address: 9 Pyrohova vul, Kyiv 01601; fax: 380-44-224-2251.

### C. Ukrainian Sexological Journals

Four sexological journals are published in Ukraine:

*The Journal of Sexology and Andrology.* Address: Editor, 9 a Kotsubynskoho vul., Kyiv 04053; fax: 380-44-244-6862.

*All-Ukrainian Scientific-Practical Journal: Man's Health.* Edited by Kyiv State Department of the Ministry of Public Health, Institute of Urology and Nephrology Academy of Medical Sciences. Address: 53 Hlybochitskaja vul., Kyiv, 04050; tel.: 380-44-23784; tcl./fax: 380-44-243-3533; email: elenaprofessional@svitonline.com.

*Scientific Medical Journal: Dermatology, Cosmetology, Sexopathology.* Established in 1997, and edited by Dnipropetrovsk State Medical Academy, Sexual Health Center. Address: 3a, Artema vul., Dnipropetrovsk, 49001; tel.: 380-562-44-0562; fax: 380-567-44-3140.

*The Journal of Sexopathology and Andrology.* Address: Borys Vornyk, Ph.D., editor, 8 Smolenska vul., Kyiv 02057; fax: 380-44-456-2203. (A semi-annual publication).

Two important popular mass-media publications in Ukraine deal with sexuality:

*Lel'.* Editor: S. Chyrkov. Address: 38-44 Dehtjarivs'ka vul., Kyiv 04119; tel.: 380-44-211-0268; 213-3220; email: lel@torba.com. (A quarterly Ukrainian erotic magazine).

*Family Medical-Social Problems* (a quarterly journal) Editor: V. Chajka. Address: Panfilova Prospect 3, Donetsk 83114; tel.: 380-622-58-4366.

### D. Major Sexological Organizations

The Ukrainian Society of Sexologists. Address: 9 a In. Kotsubinskiy vul., Kyiv 04053; tel.: 380-044-216-5054; fax 380-44-244-6862. This national professional organization includes physicians, psychologists, and teachers of secondary high schools, colleges, and graduate schools who unite their efforts in a scientific research and applied work on human sexuality.

The European-Asian Association of Sexologists. Address: P.O. Box 274., Kyiv 01034; tel.: 380-44-455-0280; email: eaas@ukr.net. This is an international organization of sexologists from former Soviet republics and of professionals from abroad. Its annual meetings in sexual science are usually held in September in Kyiv, the capital of Ukraine.

Ukrainian Family Planning Association. Address: Pr. Pobedy 30, apt. 32 Kyiv, 03055; tel.: 380-44-236-6540; fax: 380-44-236-9704; email: ufpa@semja.kiev.ua.

## 14. Ethnic Minorities

Ukraine is motherland to more than 130 ethnic groups. Bulgarians, Serbs, and Poles have been settled in Ukrainian territory since the 18th century, Moldavians since the 16th century, gypsies since the 15th century, and Jews since the 14th century. Most of these ethnic minorities identify themselves with some nation in the world, but some of them, like the Budjak Gaguasers and Tavrida Tartars, have developed as an ethnic group within Ukraine, and thus consider themselves a native minority population.

### A. The Tartars

In the 1940s, all Tartars, descendants of various Mogul and Turkish tribes, were forced to leave their homes in Ukraine. Today, those who survived Stalin's genocide policies are trying to return to the Crimea and Tavrida steppes.

According to the all-Ukrainian census in 2001, 248,200 Tatars were registered, which is 5.3 times higher than in 1989. In the Crimea, there are 243,400 Tatars, 12% of the population, which is 6.3 times higher than in 1989.

The Tartar family, as any family, is a system for social control and inculcating cultural behavior patterns for all its members. Before their forced eviction, the Tartars lived mostly in extended families. These family communities included two or more brothers with their wives, married children, and grandchildren. Such kin constituted an independent economic and social group, which remained a primary vehicle for preserving and transferring customs and traditions.

Most Tartar families today are nuclear, although the authority of males, especially older males, is maintained as a tradition. In all family settings, the superiority of males is considered normal and natural. Marriage is prohibited within seven generations of blood kinship. Tartar sexual culture is more permissive for men, whether young or old; women are held to much stricter standards. The wife's devotion to her husband is very much appreciated and expected, as well as the obedience of all women to their father, brothers, and male relatives by marriage. The family is viewed as a social, religious, and moral unity, based on the wife's efforts to support her husband and maintain a positive psychological climate among the relatives. That is why developing honesty and innocence is the main focus in raising girls. The Tartars have different rituals to protect virginity, and its public manifestation indicates the important role virginity plays in the appreciation of marital intimacy. It is taboo for bridegrooms to admit sexual competence before their wedding.

In modern Tartar wedding celebrations, a lot of ethnic prescriptions are maintained. The women's and men's communities are located in different rooms. Newlyweds are expected to show the groom's relatives the signs of the bride's virginity by the time of marriage. The young wife puts a red kerchief on her head, while her husband wears a red ribbon-belt around his waist as a symbol of sexual innocence. Red strings link the generations, as well as brothers, sisters, and relatives by marriage. All play special roles during the wedding ceremony and try to help the young couple as they settle into married and family life. According to ethnic beliefs, sexual feelings and private matters should be subject to human reason and the stability of marital relationships. Some traditional presents for newlyweds symbolize the support of the family: a wedding candle to make life light and clear, and a round meat pie (*kobete*) to symbolize good health and children.

### B. Koreans

Koreans as an ethnic minority came to Ukraine mostly after World War II. In families where one spouse is Korean and the other non-Korean, national customs are much more carefully maintained when the wife is Korean than when the husband is Korean and his wife non-Korean. Korean gender behavior is determined by the commandments of *Conphutsy* [Confucian?] ideals of great respect for ancestors, harmony within the marital unit and society, strict subordination of the younger to their elders, and the high authority of the father and male relatives.

Korean marriage is considered not only the unity of husband and wife, but of two families or kinships. Although the dominant position of the male is preserved in all family matters, the Korean woman does not change her last name after marriage. Thus, many Korean families in Ukraine have doubled names with two surnames. The Korean minority has adjusted to Ukrainian holidays but try to preserve their national festivals. One of the more important of these is the commemorative feast in which every person celebrates in him- or herself the past, the present, and the future of parentage.

An appreciation of the growing personality and the older generation is at the core of most Korean family holidays. Among these is the celebration of a hundred days after the baby's birth. The belief is that if a hundred guests share in the banquet that day, the child will live a happy and long life. When a baby is 1 year old, he or she may foretell his or her future destiny. For that purpose, the parents place some different toys before the child. If the baby chooses the money, it will be successful in business in the future; if a book is chosen, the future adult will be lucky in science and intellectual pursuits, and so on.

Since Korean marriage is considered to be a union of two kinships, special gender behavior patterns are honored during the wedding ceremony. The bride and groom stand face-to-face, bow to each other, ritually clean the hands, exchange goblets of wine, and drink from the cup. Usually, Korean families remember and commemorate four times a year at least four generations of their ancestors who are known by name and profession.

The sexual attitudes and customs of Tartar and Korean ethnic minorities in Ukraine, like any ethnic minority in any country, are continually undergoing change and adapting, being influenced by the majority culture and, at the same time, more or less influencing and changing that majority culture.

## *References and Suggested Readings\**

*A tale of bygone years.* 1982. Kyiv: Rainbow (in Ukrainian).

*Adolescent reproductive and sexual health in Ukraine* (situational analysis). 1999, Kyiv: MOH, UNFPA (in Ukrainian and English).

*Bandurka: Ukrainian obscene songs.* 1995. Kyiv: Dnipro, The Basis (in Russian).

Bogdushkin N., & M. Andreev. 1995. The problem of the young pregnancy and childbirth. *Kharkov Medical Journal,* 1.

Bohachevsla-Khomjak, M. 1995. *By white on the white* (women in Ukrainian public life 1884-1939). Kyiv: Lybid' (in Ukrainian).

Boryshevskyj, M. 1990. *Psychologichni pytannia statevoho vyhovannia uchniv* [*The psychological questions of sex nurturing the pupils*]. Kyiv: Edition Radjanska Shkola (in Ukrainian).

Boryshevskyj, M. 1992. *Stateve vychovannya* [*The sex nurturing*]. Kyiv: Encyclopedia of the Mother and Child. Edition Ukrainian encyclopedia after Bazhana (in Ukrainian).

Chubyns'kiy, P. 1994. Shameless songs. *Lel,* 6(17).

Chugunov, V. *The system of sexology. Vol. 1. The sexology of our country in XIX-XX cc.*

Chujko, L. 1994. The tendencies of family development. *Economic reforms in Ukraine.* SINTO.

CIA. 2002 (January). *The world factbook 2002.* Washington, DC: Central Intelligence Agency. Available: http://www.cia.gov/cia/publications/factbook/index.html.

*For a teacher about the psychology and pedagogy of child sexual development: Scientific-methodical text-book.* 1996. Kyiv: Institute of the Content and Methods of Education (in Ukrainian).

*Gender analysis of Ukrainian society.* 1999. Kyiv: PFUN (in Ukrainian).

Gorpinchenko, I. 1991. *Herontologicheskaya seksopatologija* [*Herontology sexopatology*]. Kyiv: Edition Zdorovja (in Russian).

Gorpinchenko, I. 1991. *Otkrovenno o sokrovennom* [*Sincerely about innermost*]. Kyiv: Edition Zdorovja (in Russian).

Govorun, T., & O. Shargana. 1990. *Bat'kam pro stateve vychovannya ditej* [*For parents about sexual education of the children*]. Kyiv: Edition Radjanska Shkola (in Ukrainian).

*Historical-theoretical research.* 2001. Kharkiv (in Ukrainian).

Horpinchenko, I., L. Imshenetskaja, M. Bojko, et al. 1996. *Clinical sexology and andrology.* Kyiv: The Health (in Ukrainian).

Horpinchenko, I. 1991. *Herontological [Gerontological] sexology.* Kyiv: The Health (in Russian).

Horpinchenko, I., L. Imshenetskaja, M. Bojko, et al. 1997. *Sexology and andrology.* Kyiv: Abrys (in Russian).

Hovorun, T., & O. Shargan. 1990. *For parents about children sexual education.* Kyiv: Soviet School (in Ukrainian).

Hovorun, T., & O. Kikinezhdi. 1999. *Gender and sexuality: Psychological aspects* (Textbook). Ternopil: Educational Book-Bohdan (in Ukrainian).

Janiw, W. 1993. *Grundrisse zur geschichte der Ukrainischen ethopsychologie.* Munchen: Ukrainischef Freif Universitat (in German and Ukrainian).

Jul'ko A. 1994. *Spravochnik po seksologiji* [*Reference book on sexology, sexopathology, and andrology*]. Kyiv: Edition Zdorovja (in Russian).

Junda, I., & L. Junda. 1990. *Social-psychological and medical-biological basis of family life* (Textbook). Kyiv: High School (in Russian).

Junda, I. 1981. *Male's genital diseases.* Kyiv: The Health (in Russian).

Junda, I. 1987. *Prostitutes.* Kyiv: The Health (in Russian).

Kacharian, G., & A. Kacharian. 1994. *Psychotherapy of sexual dysfunctions in marital conflicts.* Moscow: The Medicine (in Russian).

Kozulia, O. 1993. *Women in the history of Ukraine.* Kyiv: Ukrainian Center of Spirit Culture (in Ukrainian).

Kravets, V. 1997. *The activity of school's psychologist in pupils' education about marriage.* Ternopil: Pedagogical University (in Ukrainian).

Kravets, V. 2000. *The theory and practice of pupil's education about marriage.* Kyiv: Kyiv's Trugh (in Ukrainian).

Kryshtal, V., et al. 1990. *Seksualnaja garmonija supruzeskoj pary* [*Sexual harmony in marital couples*]. Charkov: Edition Interbook (in Russian).

Kryshtal, V., & B. Gulman. 1997. *Sexology. Vol. 1, Normal sexology.* Kharkiv: Academy of Sexological Research (in Russian).

Kryshtal, V., & B. Gulman. 1997. *Sexology. Vol. 2, Clinical sexology. Part 1. The general sexopathology.* Kharkiv: Academy of Sexological Research (in Russian).

Kryshtal, V., & B. Gulman. 1998. *Sexology. Vol. 3, Clinical sexology of men.* Kharkiv: Academy of Sexological Research (in Russian).

Kryshtal, V., & B. Gulman. 1998. *Sexology. Vol. 4, Clinical sexology of women.* Kharkiv: Academy of Sexological Research (in Russian).

Kyrylenko, S., T. Govorun, et al. 1995. *Problemy simejnoho ta statevoho vychovannya* [*The problems of the family and sexual upbringings*]. Kyiv: Vydavnytstvo Vyschych Uchbovych Zakladiv (in Ukrainian).

Mirza Avakjants, N. 1920. *Ukrainian woman in XVI-XVIIc.* Poltava: Private printing.

Monomach, V. 1991. The edification of children. In: V. Rychka, ed., *Behind the chronicler lines.* Kyiv: Soviet School.

Nestor the Chronicler. 1990. The song of Ihor's campaign. In: *A tale of bygone years.* Kyiv: Soviet Writer.

Paraschuk, J. 1994. *Besplodije v supruzestve* [*Infertility in conjugality*]. Charkov: Edition Zdorovja (in Russian).

Rehbinder, B. 1993. *Veles book: The life and religion of ancient Slavonic.* Kyiv: Photovideoservis.

---

*\*Editors' Note*: Because of differences in transliterating certain Ukrainian characters and the anglicizing of names since this chapter was first written, names spelled with *G* or *H* in English appear alphabetically as the authors originally spelled them. For example, the first author of this section, T. V. Hovorun, originally appeared in volume 3 of the *IES* as "Govorun."

Ryzhko, P. 1995. Venereal diseases. *Charkov Medical Journal*, 1.

Shkiriak-Nyzhnyk, Z. 2001. *The school of reproductive health: Respect yourself.* Kyiv: Foundation of Social Workers (in Ukrainian).

Shkiriak-Nyzhnyk, Z., & A. Nepochatova-Kurashkevich. 1990. *Seksualna kultura simejnych vidnosyn [Sexual culture in marriage relationship].* Kyiv: The Knowledge of Ukrainian Society Republic (in Ukrainian).

Tomenko, M. 2002. *The theory of Ukrainian love.* Kyiv: International Tourism (in Ukrainian).

Tsvid, A. 1998. *Sin's mystery. Philosophical erotic poems.* Kyiv: Khreschatyk (in Ukrainian).

*Ukraine human development report.* 2002. Kyiv: UNDP.

*Ukrainian soul.* 1992. Kyiv: Phenix (in Ukrainian).

UNAIDS. 2002. *Epidemiological fact sheets by country.* Geneva, Switzerland: Joint United Nations Programme on HIV/AIDS (UNAIDS/WHO). Available: http://www.unaids.org/hivaidsinfo/statistics/fact_sheets/index_en.htm.

Unda, I., & L. Imshenetskaya. 1990. *Besplodie v supruzestve [Infertility in conjugality].* Kyiv: Edition Zdorovja (in Russian).

Unda, I., & L. Unda. 1990. *Sotsial'no-psichologicheskije e medico-biologicheskije osnovy simejnoj zhyzni [Social-psychological and medical-biological basis of the marital life].* Kyiv: Edition Vyscha Shkola (in Russian).

von Sacher-Masoch, L. [Leopold fon Zakher-Mazokh]. 1999. Women's images from Galicia. In: *Ivan Herasym Vybrani tvory—L'viv: Litopys.*

Vornyk, B. 1998. *Gender identity disorders.* Kyiv: The Family (in Russian).

Vornyk, B. 1999. *Sexologia dlja vsech [Sexology for all].* Kyiv: ABK-Press (in Russian).

Vornyk, B., & O. Holotsvan, et al. 1999. *Safe behavior (The informational textbook for teenagers).* Kyiv: The Family (in Ukrainian).

Vornyk, B., V. Kolomiets, & K. Talalayev. 2001. *Prevention of sexual abuse.* Kyiv (in Russian).

Vovk, Ph. 1995. *Ukrainian studies in ethnography and anthropology.* Kyiv: The Art (in Ukrainian).

Vozianov, O., I. Gorpinchenko, et al. 1995. *Clinichna seksologija e andrologija [Clinical sexology and andrology].* Kyiv: Edition Zdorovja (in Ukrainian).

Zabuzhko, O. 1996. *Field studies of Ukrainian sex.* Kyiv: Zhoda (in Ukrainian).

Zhyla, V., & J. Kushniruk. 1990. *Garmonija e discharmonija intimnoj Zhyzni [Harmony and disharmony of the intimacy life].* Kyiv: Edition Zdorovja (in Russian).

# United Kingdom of Great Britain and Northern Ireland

Kevan R. Wylie, M.B., Ch.B., M.Med.Sc., M.R.C.Psych., D.S.M.,* chapter coordinator and contributor, with Anthony Bains, B.A., Tina Ball, Ph.D., Patricia Barnes, M.A., CQSW, BASMT (Accred.), Rohan Collier, Ph.D., Jane Craig, M.B., MRCP (UK), Linda Delaney, L.L.B., M.Jur., Julia Field, B.A., Danya Glaser, MBBS, D.Ch., FRCPsych., Peter Greenhouse, M.A., MRCOG, MFFP, Mary Griffin, M.B., M.Sc., MFFP, Margot Huish, B.A., BASMT (Accred.), Anne M. Johnson, M.A., M.Sc., M.D., MRCGP, FFPAM, George Kinghorn, M.D., FRCP, Helen Mott, B.A. (Hons.), Paula Nicolson, Ph.D., Jane Read, B.A. (Hons.), UKCP, Fran Reader, FRCOG, MFFP, BASMT (Accred.), Gwyneth Sampson, DPM, MRCPsych., Peter Selman, DPSA, Ph.D., José von Bühler, R.M.N., Dip.H.S., Jane Wadsworth, B.Sc., M.Sc., Kaye Wellings, M.A., M.Sc., and Stephen Whittle, Ph.D.
*Extensive updates and some sections rewritten by the original authors as noted in the text*

## Contents

## *Demographics and a Brief Historical Perspective*

### A. Demographics

ROBERT T. FRANCOEUR

The United Kingdom, composed of England, Wales, Scotland, and Northern Ireland, faces the northwestern edge of Europe. The British Isles, with 94,525 square miles (244,820 km²) is about the size of New York State. The English Channel separates the British Isles from France on the south, Belgium, the Netherlands, Denmark, and the southern tip of Norway to the east. To the west, across the Irish Sea, is the Republic of Ireland. In 1920, the British Parliament divided Northern Ireland from Southern Ireland and gave each its own parliament and government. A few years later, when Ireland became a dominion and then an inde-

(CIA 2002)

pendent republic, six of the nine counties of Ulster in the northeast corner of the country chose to remain a part of the United Kingdom. The Crown Colony of Hong Kong and Asia is now part of the People's Republic of China (see separate chapter on Hong Kong). There was devolution to a Scottish Parliament in 1999. The formation of a multiparty Northern Ireland assembly was initiated in 1999, although it was temporarily suspended in early 2000.

Geographically and culturally, the main island of the British Isles has three regional entities, England, Scotland, and Wales. The Principality of Wales in western Britain has an area of 8,019 square miles (20,769 km²) and a population of about three million. After early Anglo-Saxon invaders drove the Celtic people into the mountains of Wales, these people, who became known as Welsh ("foreign"), developed their own distinct nationality. English is the dominant language, with less than 20% of the people of Wales speaking both English and Welsh; some 32,000 speak only Welsh. The former kingdom of Scotland occupies the northern third of the main British island. The central lowlands, a belt approxi-

---

*Communications*: Kevin R. Wylie, M.B., Whiteley Wood Clinic, Woofindin Road, Sheffield S10 3TL England, United Kingdom; k.r.wylie@sheffield.ac.uk.

mately 60 miles (96.5 km) wide stretching from the Firth of Clyde to the Firth of Forth, divides the farming region of the Southern Uplands from the granite Highlands in the north. About three quarters of Scotland's five million people live in the Lowlands, concentrating in the industrial center of Glasgow (population: three quarters of a million) and the capital, Edinburgh (population: half a million). The Hebrides, Orkney, and Shetland Islands are also part of Scotland. England, the heart of the United Kingdom, has a population of close to 50 million people. London, the capital, has a population of about seven million; Birmingham, the second largest city, has a population of about a million.

The United Kingdom of Great Britain also includes the Channel Islands, the Isle of Man, Gibraltar (between Spain and Africa), the British West Indies and Bermuda in the Caribbean, the Falkland Islands and dependencies in the South Atlantic, and Pitcairn Island in the Pacific Ocean. This chapter focuses on the sexuality in England, Wales, and Scotland.

In July 2002, the United Kingdom had an estimated population of 60 million. (All data are from *The World Factbook 2002* (CIA 2002) unless otherwise stated.)

**Age Distribution and Sex Ratios**: *0-14 years*: 18.7% with 1.05 male(s) per female (sex ratio); *15-64 years*: 65.5% with 1.02 male(s) per female; *65 years and over*: 15.8% with 0.72 male(s) per female; *Total population sex ratio*: 0.97 male(s) to 1 female

**Life Expectancy at Birth**: *Total Population*: 77.99 years; *male*: 75.29 years; *female*: 80.84 years

**Urban/Rural Distribution**: 89% to 11%

**Ethnic Distribution**: English: 81.5%; Scottish: 9.6%; Irish: 2.4%; Welsh: 1.9%; Ulster: 1.8%; West Indian, Indian, Pakistani, and other: 2.8%

**Religious Distribution**: Anglican: 27 million; Roman Catholic: 9 million; Muslim: 1 million; Presbyterian: 800,000; Methodist: 760,000; Sikh: 400,000; Hindu: 350,000; Jewish: 300,000

**Birth Rate**: 11.34 births per 1,000 population

**Death Rate**: 10.3 per 1,000 population

**Infant Mortality Rate**: 5.45 deaths per 1,000 live births

**Net Migration Rate**: 1.06 migrant(s) per 1,000 population

**Total Fertility Rate**: 1.73 children born per woman

**Population Growth Rate**: 0.21%

**HIV/AIDS** (1999 est.): *Adult prevalence*: 0.11%; *Persons living with HIV/AIDS*: 31,000; *Deaths*: 450. (For additional details from www.UNAIDS.org, see end of Section 10B.)

**Literacy Rate** (*defined as those age 15 and over who can read and write*): 100%; education is compulsory from age 5 to 16

**Per Capita Gross Domestic Product** (*purchasing power parity*): $24,700 (2001 est.); *Inflation*: 1.8%; *Unemployment*: 5.1%; *Living below the poverty line*: 17%

**B. A Brief Historical Perspective**   KEVAN R. WYLIE

Until about 10,000 years ago, Britain was connected to the European continent by a land bridge that made it convenient for peoples to migrate back and forth. With the end of the last great Ice Age, and the slow but inevitable melting of the ice masses that covered Europe and North America, the sea level gradually rose, separating the continent from the British Isles with the English Channel. Despite the new obstacle, people continued migrating, as the Celts did to the isles some 2,500 to 3,000 years ago. This Celtic influence can still be found in the language and culture of the Welsh and Gaelic (Irish) enclaves. England became part of the Roman Empire in 43 of the Common Era. The Roman legions withdrew in 410. In subsequent centuries, particularly the

8th through 11th centuries, waves of Germanic Jutes, Angles, and Saxons competed with Danish invaders for control of the island. In 1066, Duke William led the Norman conquest of Britain, bringing continental feudalism and the French language, essential elements in later English culture.

In 1215, the nobles forced King John to sign the Magna Carta, guaranteeing the rights of the people and the rule of law, and setting the stage for the development of a parliamentary system of government. Defeat in the Hundred Years War with France (1338-1453) was followed by a long civil war, the War of the Roses (1455-1485). While European countries were racked by wars, English culture and a strong economy flourished under the powerful Tudor monarchy and a long period of domestic peace. Establishment of the Church of England in 1534 under the monarch separated England's religious institutions from the authority of Rome. Under Queen Elizabeth I, England became a major naval power, with colonies in the Americas. Britain's trade throughout Europe and the Orient also expanded. Scotland became part of England in 1603 when James VI of Scotland became James I of England. A struggle between Parliament and the Stuart kings, a bloody civil war (1642-1649), and establishment of a republic under the Puritans, ended with the restoration of the monarchy in 1688. The sovereignty of Parliament was confirmed in the "Glorious Revolution" of 1688 and a Bill of Rights in 1689.

The 18th century in England was distinguished by a strengthening of the parliamentary system and technical and entrepreneurial innovations that produced the Industrial Revolution. England lost its colonies in the American Revolution, expanded its empire with growing colonies in Canada and India, and strengthened its position as a leading world power. The 19th century was marked by extension of the vote in 1832 and 1867, formation of trade unions, development of universal public education, the spread of industrialization and urbanization, and, under Queen Victoria (1837-1901), the addition of large parts of Africa and Asia to the empire.

Britain suffered huge casualties and economic dislocations as a result of World Wars I and II. Although industrial growth returned after the wars, Britain lost its leadership role to other nations. Ireland became an independent republic in 1921, but the Irish question has persisted. In recent years, the socialized medicine, social security support systems have posed increasing questions for the government and people.

## 1. Basic Sexological Premises

PAULA NICOLSON [*Rewritten and updated in late 2001 by P. Nicolson*]

### A. Character of Gender Roles

Gender roles in the United Kingdom have been influenced both by social class, which has ensured the maintenance of gender segregation, particularly among the upper and working classes, and fluctuating demographic, political, and cultural changes over the past 80 years, which have stimulated shifts in traditional patterns. For example, during World War II, women were employed in manufacturing, commerce, and agriculture, accompanied by good state provision of daycare for children. However, following the demobilization of the male population in the 1950s, there was a political emphasis on 'pronatalism' in order to replenish the population and to free up employment possibilities for men. Therefore, women's responsibility for the mental and *physical* health of their families was encouraged, which meant a return to traditional gender lifestyles.

Although since the mid 1980s there has been a clear political commitment to seeing men and women as equal, a division of labor remains in the home, which spills over into the workplace. This distinguishes men's and women's behavior and expectations along traditional stereotypical lines: Men are seen as powerful, rational, and "naturally" the breadwinners, and women are seen as dependent, emotional, and "naturally" suited to the domestic sphere.

Feminist influence, hand in hand with high levels of male unemployment since the early 1980s among all social classes, has meant that many men have taken greater responsibility and interest in childcare than previously. The resulting image of the "new man" in touch with his emotions, with nurturing skills, remains a contestable one, however.

Increased educational opportunities have enabled women to enter professional life, a process that has increased since the 1970s, although few women rise above middle-management level.

During the 1990s, biological essentialist explanations of gender roles have emerged as a "backlash." Darwinist natural selection theory, embraced by evolutionary psychology and sociobiology, has been enthusiastically taken up by the conservative forces within the academic community and the British media. They espouse the view that there are natural, irrefutable, and irreversible reasons why women are better suited to childcare than men. Also, women are less suited by their "natures" to reach the top of their professions. Women are "naturally" averse to the risk-taking and aggressive behaviors appropriate to high-powered work. These are the predominant explanations of gender-role differences as we enter the 21st century.

## B. Sociolegal Status of Males and Females

Males and females officially have equal status in the United Kingdom in terms of human rights, but there remain certain sociopolitical distinctions. For instance, many women receive reduced unemployment benefits and pensions because they have not had to pay full contributions during their working lives and have had career breaks. However, women are entitled to a retirement pension at the age of 60, while the retirement age for men remains 65. This is currently the subject of political debate and statutory changes.

The legal age of consent for heterosexual women and men is 16. It is only recently that the age of consent for homosexual men was reduced from 21 to 18. The ban on homosexuals of both sexes in the armed services was lifted at the end of 1999.

The age of heterosexual consent means that it remains illegal for doctors to prescribe contraceptives to women and men under the age of 16 without parental consent, a contentious issue, which remains unresolved. The Labour Government elected in 1997 pledged to cut teenage pregnancies. However, recent evidence suggests that teenage girls do not wish to take oral contraception on a regular basis because of the well publicized "health scares." Many consider an abortion to be safer.

Certain legal judgments have demonstrated inequalities in attitudes towards women and men. For instance, some adolescent and older men found guilty of rape have received relatively light punishments; in some rape cases, women have been portrayed as guilty of "contributory negligence"; men who have killed their female partners because they "nagged" or were unfaithful were given light sentences or had the murder charge changed to manslaughter; conversely, women who killed male partners after years of violent physical and sexual abuse have been found guilty of murder and given long-term prison sentences. This is indicative of the underlying ideology that favors male domestic authority and the traditional view of the male sex drive as dominant.

Lone mothers are frequently portrayed by politicians as irresponsible, and their entitlement to state benefits questioned. This was counterbalanced to some extent by the creation of the controversial Child Support Agency, which pursued absent fathers for maintenance. Recent developments, however, have encouraged single parents to work outside the home, and benefits have been withdrawn from those who resist.

## C. General Concepts of Sexuality and Love

The majority of the population in the United Kingdom are able to choose their sexual partners on the basis of attraction and love. This, however, does not apply among some minority ethnic groups, nor to social-class groups where a socially suitable marriage is encouraged.

Since the late 1960s, there has been an increased liberalization of attitudes towards sexuality. The age of first heterosexual intercourse for women has come down from a median age of 21 for those born in the 1930s and 1940s, to 17 for those born between 1966 and 1975. The gap between the age of first intercourse for women and men has decreased over the past 50 years, and for the current generation of young people, it is virtually the same for both sexes. A sizeable minority of both sexes is sexually active before the age of 16. A high proportion of sexually active 16-year-olds do not use contraception (Wellings et al. 1994).

The category 'homosexual' is no longer seen as discrete and exclusive, with more people changing sexual orientation over the course of their life (Dancey 1994). However, it remains the case that heterosexuality is taken as the norm, and sexual satisfaction is understood to be orgasm for both partners during intercourse (Nicolson 1993). There has been an increase in the availability of practitioners, and the willingness of couples and individuals to seek psychosexual counseling when they fail to achieve sexual satisfaction. The availability of Viagra has influenced the debate on sexual satisfaction, and declarations that a female version will soon be on the market have been welcomed as an antidote to anorgasmia in women.

Serial monogamy rather than lifetime marriage remains the norm in the U.K. as in the U.S.A., with fewer people getting married and as many as one-in-two marriages ending in divorce.

## 2. Religious, Ethnic, and Gender Factors Affecting Sexuality

JOSÉ VON BÜHLER

### A. Sources and Character of Religious Values

Since the 1950s, Britain has become increasingly a pluralistic country in terms of cultures, ethnicity, and religion. Hinduism mixes with Roman Catholicism, Islam with Judaism, and Methodism with Buddhism. Some of these religions are almost inseparable from their social fabric, culture, and ethnic grouping. Others offer a moral and spiritual framework separate from ethnic practices. The common denominator in the existence of this pluralism is that, apart from the establishment franchise of Anglicanism, which in reality makes it the "state religion," all religious bodies in the United Kingdom are equal under the law of the land. This equality confers certain rights and privileges in respect of education, worship, social welfare, and democratic political rights.

However, the multifaceted character implied in interdenominationality in many instances is generally not understood by the public at large, or even the members of the various groups. Philosophically and socially, there is frequently a disconnection that does not allow for cross-fertilization of ideas. Nor does it allow for comparative analysis of the positive approach to sexual concepts and even sexual activities in many religions when their scriptures are properly understood! In this climate, it is easy for fundamentalists of every denomination to represent human sexuality in the religious/spiritual content as negative and somehow taboo. This tension was noted in a 1992 report from the Sex Education Forum, an umbrella body for several religious and secular organizations concerned with providing and supporting sex education for young people. The report, *An Enquiry into Sex Education: Report of a Survey of LEA Support and Monitoring of School Sex Education* (Thompson & Scott 1992), clearly identified "anxieties concerning ethnicity and religious issues to be a significant barrier to the effective provision of sex education." Indirectly, the report confirmed that the distance between religious legal equality and ethnic, social, and moral framework patterns and concepts is rather unequal among the various religious and ethnic groups in the United Kingdom.

Prior to the 1950s, the religious influences forming sexual constructs came almost exclusively from "the official church" of England, and "unofficially" from the other Christian denominations. In recent decades, the picture has become more complex. Since midcentury, the Church of England's approach to social morality and sexuality has fluctuated between two poles, the traditionalists and the modernists, or the "permission givers" and the "orthodox moral directors." With the national religious scene resembling the circular approach of the politicians to sexual knowledge and attitudes, the sociosexual control and influence appears to bounce back and forth between church and state according to a mutually cooperative formula. In many cases, however, liberal attitudes have triumphed, as evidenced by the Church's acceptance of divorce, homosexuality, and contraception. In other cases, the traditionalists have retained a firm moral control. This doctrinal "pendulum" is confusing for the majority of the population who are not experts at moral and theological niceties and subtleties. The people themselves are part of the system of confusion: While expecting clear and definite moral messages from both establishment and Church, they reserve the right to judge the validity of those messages, even when they are biblically based.

With quiet, behind-the-curtains efficiency, the Roman Catholic Church has been influential in shaping national morality and sexuality. Its most authoritarian pronouncements about homosexuality and abortion have been tempered by professions of love for the individual while condemning same-gender sexual activity. To the democratic soul of the British people, Roman Catholic moral doctrine appears autocratic and dictatorial, even while it provides a secure, unchangeable frame of reference that is not answerable to cultural and ethnic differences, a characteristic attractive to the orderly British. Other Christian denominations, such as Methodism and the evangelical Protestant churches, swing between permission and condemnation. Methodists, for instance, accept that sexual learning should present the biologically functional principles and, at the same time, should be equally aware of human relationships and their influence in the happiness of the individual.

Whatever the sexual-moral code of the many Christian traditions in Britain, the individual appears to have the final word in moral choices, as long as these choices are based on "fairness" and "not hurting other people." Nonetheless, it appears that religious beliefs are still a major influence on sexual attitudes and values. In this regard, for instance, the findings of the research study, *Sexual Attitudes and Life Styles* (Johnson, Wadsworth, Wellings, & Field 1994), regarding first sexual intercourse are rather revealing:

Respondents belonging to the Church of England or other Christian Churches (excluding the Roman Catholic Church) were less likely to experience sexual intercourse before the age of 16, and those from non-Christian religions even less likely to do so. More surprisingly perhaps, given the position of the Roman Catholic Church on sexual behaviour, those reporting Roman Catholic affiliation are no less likely than those reporting other affiliations to report intercourse before the age of 16, and if anything slightly more so.

Notice that this applies exclusively to first sexual intercourse and not to other sexual intimacies.

In the ever-swinging pendulum of action and counteraction, an example of final-choice control is that of the decision made recently by members of the Church of England regarding homosexuality. Whereas the moral traditionalists within the hierarchy of the Church have tried to reverse the acceptance of gay priests, priest advocates of homosexual rights have topped the polls in the Southward and London dioceses in elections for the Church of England's General Synod, the "church's parliament."

Nonetheless, Christianity no longer has total influencing control over the sexual morality of the British people. The pluralistic and interdenominational society in existence in Britain has seen to that. The influence of Islam, for instance, is evident in national moral pronouncements because of the increasing number of adherents to the faith and its sexual moral code. In common with Catholicism, Islamic sexual and moral teachings transcend ethnicity and culture. Human sexuality is not a taboo subject, but must be dealt with in the context of the family with an open mind and in a way enriching to the individual's developmental and religious perspectives.

The influence of Hinduism and its sexual-moral code on the general population has not been as public. Hinduism is a pragmatic religion, and perhaps because of this pragmatism, issues of sex and sexual activities and practices are rarely discussed. Traditionally, there is an association between religion, erotica, and the highly culturally priced art of love, but in modern culture, one suspects that this connection is the domain of the "literati" and quite foreign to the contemporary Hindu family. Judaism teaches that sexual pleasure is an integral part of the marital/sexual relationship. In its positive view of sexual relations, the principle of pleasure and sharing mutual happiness by a physical relationship is validated.

[*Update 2001*: The dawn of the 21st century brought with it, contrary to liberal expectations, a much greater reentrenchment of the ecclesiastical negative status in terms of sexual freedoms. The axis of dialogue and understanding moved considerably to the right. Within the Anglican Church, the sense of fear about individualistic decisionmaking was significantly expressed in some of the pronouncements of individual bishops. These pronouncements traveled uncomfortably between narrow lines. The Anglican Church, or at least one of its Bishops, apparently chastised married couples who did not respond to the extraordinary insistence of the churches in the procreative model for the "selfishness" of not having children. The whole episode, as is often the case in modern times, became the domain of all the spin-doctors, albeit of the theological variety, and in doing so, lost all of its potential strength for change.

[The Roman Catholic Church seemed to forget, at least temporarily, its focus on the sins of the flesh in favor of a partial examination of conscience in the matters of violence, cruelty, and persecution of others by Church members in the past. In what I believe to be one of the most personally brave and spiritually significant gestures of any Pope in history, John Paul II knelt and expressed his sorrow for past injustices of the Roman Catholic Church in a special penitential on Sunday, March 12, 2000. The reaction by friend and foe was mixed, precisely because of the partial condition of the expression of sorrow. The apology was about the past. The apology was further diluted by considering that historical activities, however much in error, cannot be judged with the same measuring rods of the present. George Monbiot in *The Guardian* (March 9, 2000) made the comment, in discussing Cardinal Biffi's "medievalist" approach, that "those who believe in absurdities will commit atrocities." The Papal apology recognized, directly or indirectly, that the belief in the exclusive goodness of one religion might have led to the atrocities leading to the apology, that perhaps, in the past, the Church believed in absurdities and committed atrocities. In the light of history and future revision, might it not be possible that the Roman Catholic Church might acknowledge an absurdly fundamental antipathy towards sexuality and its scientific and humanistic study? Might it not be possible that the Church's undoubtedly rich and full contribution to the healthy study of sexual processes and their spiritual value might lead to a further apology? An apology this time in terms of all those, regardless of sexual orientation, whose sexuality is denied or condemned without the compassion of, at least, analysis of the life journey of that individual?

[The impact of the millennial developments, either from Rome or Canterbury, as it affects the British, is still to be seen. There is no doubt that new avenues for dialogue, criticism, expressed resentments, and outright dismissal of the religious developments will exist. We must wait to see if what appears to be the fear of the religious establishment about secularization are realized. History has a proven record for reinventing the wheel, and spirituality can be reinvented too. In the midst of this confusion, sexology in England has a unique opportunity to restructure its approach in relation to its preparedness to encounter spirituality ecumenically. (*End of update by J. von Bühler*)]

## B. Character of Ethnic Values

As suggested above, ethnicity plays an important part in the development of sexual and moral values, sometimes in connection with and sometimes apart from its religious connections. Four major cultural and ethnic components constitute the United Kingdom, the Irish, Scottish, Welsh, and the English themselves. Even within these groups, geographical position and class are influential. It is interesting to see that, although the various Christian denominations have adherents in every area of the British Isles, the ethnic groupings are numerically visible in the denomination of choice geographically. The Scottish have a tradition of Calvinism and Presbyterianism, the Northern Irish of Orange Protestantism, the Welsh of Chapel Christianity and Methodism, and the English as loyal but convenient subjects of Anglicanism in the tenets of the Church of England. This is, of course, a simplification of the religious/ethnic distribution, but it gives an idea of the association between ethnic values, religious tradition, and the influence of moral-theological principles on sexual values, and the acceptance or denial of sexual behavior. In this mixing pot of cultures, colors, religions, and nationalities, the views are almost infinite, and the British public has an almost inexhaustible amount of choices, although the majority of them are still of the prohibitive (sex-negative) kind. Yet, despite the many ethnic and religious prohibitions of sex, the British show an almost universal acceptance of sex before marriage, teenage sexuality, and the public discussion of topics, such as homosexuality, that were avoided not too long ago.

The British, according to Johnson et al. (1994), view sex outside a regular relationship as wrong, monogamy is upheld more by women than men, women show a greater tolerance of homosexuality than men, and, in general, there appears to be an attitudinal trait for permissiveness. In the United Kingdom today, moral, religious, and ethnic influences on sexual attitudes, values, and behavior are no longer a case of *Roma locuta est, causa finita est* ("Rome has spoken, the argument is closed"), but more one of *Vox Populi* ("the voice of the people") with spiritual insurances.

## 3. Knowledge and Education about Sexuality

JOSÉ VON BÜHLER and PATRICIA BARNES

### A. Government Policies and Programs

Historically, there has been a reluctance to legislate in the area of sex education in England and Wales. The government has taken formal responsibility for this only in recent years, prior to that issuing general "guidelines" on the general content and moral code. The actual responsibility for the delivery of sex education was undertaken by independent voluntary agencies. Prior to World War II, the focus was on social hygiene, public health, and personal morality, addressing predominantly issues of sexually transmitted disease and unplanned pregnancy.

In the postwar years, educational philosophy and research adopted a sociological perspective and centered on the family. A partnership developed between educational and health establishments, and slowly the form and content of sex education became more concerned with the general well-being of the individual.

In 1968, the government provided funding to the newly formed Health Education Authority and the voluntary agencies, particularly the Family Planning Association (F.P.A.) and National Marriage Guidance Council (N.M.G.C.), to train teachers and provide resources for sex education. Although the political agenda was predominantly preventative in terms of public health, developments in sociological and psychological thinking were woven into educational efforts. These Personal and Social Educational Programmes (PSE) inevitably had a heterosexual and reproductive orientation. The medical and nursing professions began to teach from a "humanistic" platform, but it would be some time before a clear definition of humanistic principles in the discussion and delivery of sex education existed. The union of social trends and public policy brought about the beginning of social awareness of a sexuality in which the individual's personal growth mattered and sexual concepts started moving away from the purely biological.

The late 1970s and early 1980s saw the public face of feminism, antiracism, and gay liberation. The impact on local government and education was in the form of legislation on equal opportunities and antiracist policies. Despite a growing social need and awareness, a formal educational curriculum in sexuality for secondary, higher, and professional education did not exist. Some medical schools experimented, not without problems, with seminars and study days. They were influenced by a growing number of professional counselors and sex therapists, pioneers in the principles of particularity and personal entitlements in the field of sexual development. The Local Education Authorities, for example, were responsible for providing sexual curriculum guidance to schools, but the government did not involve itself in the growing revisionist consensus developing between education, health, and voluntary agencies, which put the person at the center of this consensus.

The political ethos of the 1980s concentrated on a dramatic return to a "new moral framework," which in essence represented a return to Victorian values. The role and function of the local education authorities and F.P.A. were inherently discredited. The responsibility for sex education in secondary schools (11- to 18-year-olds) suddenly transferred to the individual school governing bodies (H.M.S.O. 1987). The requirement was that sex education should be delivered within a moral framework, and that parents had to be consulted about the curricular nature. In 1987, the Department for Education issued guidelines and specific directives to school governors on the teaching of so-called controversial subjects, such as HIV, AIDS, and homosexuality. The guidelines and directives conveyed a clear public message that sex education was viewed by the government as inherently controversial. This message caused a fundamental dilemma between the needs of pupils and the requirements of the system. This dilemma was also present between the health needs in an age in which sexual awareness became part of a larger social picture and the apparent reluctance of responsible government bodies to accept sex education in its wider context of human sexuality.

At this time, there was politically little to be done regarding sex education in colleges, universities, and medical and nursing education. The academic input in these areas was neither of an official nature nor sufficiently effective to present a case for socially individualistic approaches. In many ways, this was supportive of the political status quo. The legislative disinterest in the activities of higher and professional education in the field of human sexuality and the dedicated work of individuals allowed universities and medical schools to design and deliver functional and integrative programs in human sexuality. Thankfully, these educational programs provided the United Kingdom with practitioners, teachers, and researchers in the field of sexuality since the mid-1980s. At the same time, voluntary agencies became repositories of the considerable body of knowledge and skills in the education and therapeutic interventions in human sexuality. It is difficult to understand today how such dichotomies could exist hand in hand with the World Health Organization's definition of sexual health. That definition clearly affirms the primacy of a "social and personal ethic." It also affirms the need for "freedom from fear, shame, guilt, false beliefs and other psychological factors inhibiting sexual response and impairing sexual relationships." University, medical, and professional education and the therapeutic professions tried to synthesize the issues of education and health, particularity by establishing working and investigative groups. The advantage of these groups was that many of their members were experts in the field of human sexuality.

In 1988, Section 28 of the Local Government Act was enacted to prohibit the Local Education Authorities from "promoting homosexuality." Much confusion ensued. In reality, this clause only applied to the Local Education Authorities' activities and not to educational processes in the classroom. However, this act firmly reestablished the religious/moral influence on sex education.

Also in 1988, a National Curriculum in education was introduced. This differentiated between the "core" or mandatory subjects of mathematics, English, and science that had specific curricula to cover at different key stages and the "noncore" subjects. Sex education was a "noncore" item. In the interest of public health, however, the reproductive and disease components were included in the core science curriculum, and therefore were obligatory to teach.

In 1990, the National Curriculum Council published *Curriculum Guidance 5: Health Education*, which recommended that the nine health education themes (of which sex education was one) should be coordinated across the curriculum. Four key stages representing age bands were identified to assist delivery of appropriate information in a developmental manner. However, many revisions in both guidance and legislation occurred subsequently with particular reference to the sex education component.

Advised by counselors and sexual and marital psychotherapists, the medical and nursing professions perceived sex education as important in their own clinical effectiveness in the treatment of sexual dysfunction. Some medical schools and nursing colleges established their own sexual health curriculum, but once more, the teaching input focused primarily on the organic and health content of sexuality. The integrative delivery of the subject, supposedly suited to increase knowledge and change attitudes both in higher and professional education (von Bühler & Tamblin 1995), depended on the clinical and scientific expertise of a few professionals, who, in many cases, had to fight against long-held concepts and prejudices. This situation led to an educational lottery with little academic cohesion and, of course, the unavoidable controversy between the purely medical and the more-eclectic approach.

Health economics and a realistic awareness of social needs obliged the government to produce the *Health of the Nation* document in 1992, identifying key areas for intervention. Among the goals listed were the reduction of pregnancies of girls aged 13 to 15 by 50%, from 9.5 per 1,000 girls in 1989 to no more than 4.8 per 1,000 girls by the year 2000. England has the highest rate of teenage pregnancies among western European countries. In the document, school sex education was seen as a central means by which the pregnancy targets might be achieved.

Meanwhile, an amendment to the Education Act of 1993 was passed without debate in Parliament (effective from September 1994). This required:

1. all secondary schools to have a sex education policy that includes teaching on HIV/AIDS and sexually transmitted disease,
2. biological aspects of sexual behavior to be taught in the science curriculum, and
3. a parental right to withdraw children from all or part of the nonscience sex education.

The implications of these amendments are daunting, both in terms of the individual and society. There is much evidence to suggest that the majority of parents do not have the skills or desire to be responsible for the sex education of their children (Allen 1987). More often than not, the needs of girls are understood and addressed more effectively than those of the boys or groups of people with special needs.

The recent authoritative study by Wellings, Field, Johnson, and Wadsworth (1994), *Sexual Behaviour in Britain: The National Survey of Attitudes and Lifestyles*, examined trends in age at first sexual intercourse, and these trends show that during the past four decades, the median age at first heterosexual intercourse has fallen from 21 years to 17 years for women and from 20 to 17 for men. The proportion of respondents reporting sexual intercourse before the age of 16 has increased from fewer than 1% in women aged 55 and over, to nearly one in five of those in their teens. (*Note*: This study has also been published as Johnson et al. 1994, *Sexual Attitudes and Lifestyles*.)

The people of the United Kingdom need to ask what are the real risks for sexually active children and young people? What are the implications for children who receive either none or fragmented and perhaps unreliable sex education? Human sexual activity is associated with increasing levels of risk and disease, unplanned pregnancy, and marital relationship breakdown. The health and sex education of the British government are far too vulnerable to the swings of political and moral pressures. Adolescent sexuality and sexual activity are realities. Effective sex education should offer adequate information, enable the development of communication and social skills, and provide opportunities to explore attitudes, values, and beliefs in a pluralistic society. The balance of these three elements is crucial if sexual issues for the individual and the nation are to be tackled realistically.

[*Update 2001*: The General Election of 1997 appeared to have brought a wind of sexual education fresh air. The Blair Government wanted to modernize Britain and, what better vehicle of modernization than to overhaul the education system? Part of that overhaul was to address the evidently comatose life of Section 28 of the Local Government Act. Britain has never been clear about the social position of this legal clause. Does it deal with fundamental homosexual issues, with human rights issues, or with purely educational curricular issues? Does it deal with the responsibilities of local councils or moral boundaries for teaching? Whatever the reason behind its enactment during the Thatcher administration, its re-presentation for repeal to the House of Lords has been fraught with political danger for the present-day authorities. Similar attempts to sexual modernization, such as the reduction of the age of consent to 16 in parity with heterosexual usage for homosexual acts, met with a barrage of loudly expressed prejudice by the right tendency in the establishment. Neither those for repeal nor those against repeal have been able to present a research-validated argument, perhaps sending a clear message for sexology to address scientifically issues of everyday importance, of humanistic importance. The opponents of the repeal of Section 28 have expansively used the word "promotion" of homosexuality in the national debate. This has needed a strong voice advocating the "promotion" of health and knowledge of those being educated, as well as the obligation of education authorities to protect those being educated against man's inhumanity to man. Unfortunately, such a voice has not usually been provided by sexology, but by voluntary pressure groups.

[Significantly, the drive against change comes strongly from the newly devolved Scotland, where an alliance of commerce, politic, and religion demands the recognition by the rest of the country to acknowledge the devolved political muscle.

[On Thursday, March 16, 2000, England awoke to an announcement by the Education Secretary: There would be new rules on sex education via an amendment to the Learning Skills Bill. The amendment supposedly gives legal backing to teaching that describes "marriage and permanent relationships as key building blocks of community and society." The morning newspapers commented that the announcement was a "bid to defuse the row over Clause 28 [Section 28] of the Local Government Act, which forbids the 'promotion' of homosexuality." One evening paper published a column titled, "Pupils may not be taught that marriage is best." The journalists appear as confused as the Education Secretary in the issue of the academic administration of a good, positive, nonpartisan sexual education.

[It appears that the change will be slow in the ability of politicians in the United Kingdom to enact intelligent legislation in favor of a comprehensive sexual education curriculum. (*End of update by J. von Bühler*)]

## B. Informal Sources of Sexual Knowledge

In common with most Western European countries, the media plays an important and increasingly more acceptable role in popular sex education. British television frequently uses specialists in human sexuality and human relationships in research and program presentation. Sex programs are scientifically based in some instances, and in others positive learning occurs through humor and candid discussion of issues. These programs are pluralist. Likewise, radio has increased its importance and credible influence in sex educa-

tion. Magazines for all ages are available, usually with literary articles of sexual relevance. In 1993, a new educational resource emerged: that of the Sex Education Video in which sexually explicit images are used to teach, for instance, the nature of orgasm and the importance of masturbation. Accustomed to total censorship of more-explicit material, the British public still has to pass judgment on these "educational videos."

Professional and voluntary agencies independent of the government frequently publish books or guides on sexuality covering all aspects of sexual function and meaning, from infertility to menopause, from the realities of being gay to the psychodynamics of marriage. Of course, the newspapers are a good fountain of information reporting on sexual matters, particularly after these have been debated in Parliament. Unfortunately, not all newspapers are married to the truth scientifically or philosophically. The theater, cinema, music, and advertising images are also part of the informal sex education movement. Finally, the United Kingdom is rich in voluntary and professional organizations dealing with sexual and relationship issues whose members are active in teaching and bringing to the notice of the general public the importance of sexual knowledge in ownership of their sexuality.

## 4. Autoerotic Behaviors and Patterns

MARGOT HUISH

The *Shorter Oxford Dictionary* cites the derivation of the word *masturbate* from the Latin root *manus* (hand) and *stuprare* (to defile) and defines "to masturbate" as "to practice self abuse," with the added definition of "abuse or revilement of oneself, self-pollution." Colloquial and slang forms of the word continue to be used as terms of abuse and derision. However, there are many rich colloquial words and phrases for masturbation, such as "the five knuckle shuffle," "playing the one-eyed piccolo," and "tossing the caber," which graphically describe male rather than female activity. Sex therapists often find that clients express discomfort with the word *masturbation* and all that it implies. The impression is that clients will use *masturbate* to describe autoerotic behavior, but will frequently use other forms of expression to describe similar mutual activity in their relationship. This perhaps reinforces the notion that sole masturbation is considered undesirable, whereas mutual or shared masturbation is more acceptable.

Historically, attitudes regarding masturbation have been negative and condemnatory. Masturbation has been seen both as a sin and as a sickness in the teachings of Judaism and Christianity. Not until the end of the 19th century was there a shift from the belief that masturbation was the cause of insanity to the suggestion that it was the cause of neurosis and neurasthenia. David S. G. Kay (1992) comments that:

> Following World War I, the major focus shifted from the purely medical to the psychological and to psychiatric analysis of masturbation.... Between the two world wars, medical professionals began to perceive masturbation as a harmless sexual behaviour.... The Psychoanalytic Society reinforced a conviction that masturbation was not the cause of medical or psychiatric disorders. Recidivistically, various preachers and educators continued to reinforce the Judeo-Christian sex ethic with their condemnation of masturbation ... [while] psychologists and psychiatrists began to research the relationship between anxiety, guilt and masturbation, since the guilt and anxiety related to masturbation were considered emotionally damaging when transmitted by the family, religion, medicine, law and education.

The impression gathered informally from seven United Kingdom sex therapists is that a high percentage of clients and their partners regard self-masturbation as embarrassing, while others view it as an undesirable practice, cloaked in secrecy and creating feelings of shame and guilt. These negative views appear to have been replicated by respondents involved in the question design work for the survey of *Sexual Attitudes and Lifestyles in the United Kingdom* (1990/1991) (Wellings 1994). Questions on masturbation were reluctantly excluded because the discussion on masturbatory practice had met with distaste and embarrassment. The view of masturbation as a sexually separate, secret, and dark activity may be reinforced in some people's minds when they read national newspaper reports of occasional accidental deaths resulting from unusual autocrotic practices, such as autoasphyxiation and various extreme forms of bondage.

Despite, or perhaps because of, the Victorian legacy of repression and negative attitudes towards masturbation, the activity is frequently mentioned in some comedy programs on United Kingdom television and radio. However, the subject has also been presented with a refreshingly positive image in television and video sex education programs. This reflects the therapeutic value of masturbation as held by professionals within the psychosexual counseling and therapy practices, which reinforces its "normality" and status as a pleasurable sexual expression in its own right. It is perhaps also reflective of the need to encourage safer sex in the age of HIV and AIDS. Therapists have noticed how clients have responded to the "permission giving" aspects of the recent programs when they discuss masturbation. However, within the multicultural mix in the United Kingdom, there are many who associate masturbation, and especially ejaculation, with illness, fatigue, anxiety, mental illness, and loss of power. The more "open" attitude towards masturbation is reflected in radio phone-in programs and in magazines, especially those geared towards the young.

In a recent sex survey in *More!* magazine, completed by over 3,000 females aged between 16 and 25 years, 33% said they never masturbated, 33% did so rarely, 15% masturbated once a week, and 14% did so more than once weekly. Forty-four percent of the respondents used fantasies during masturbation, but surprisingly, only 11% reported masturbation as the best way to reach orgasm—oral sex and penetrative sex scored higher at 41% and 28%, respectively.

In an unpublished study, Sevda Zeki reported that out of 20 women aged 65 to 74 years, and 20 aged 75 to 91 years, more-permissive attitudes towards sex had significant statistical relationships with higher reported amounts of masturbation and orgasms in masturbation. A higher level of composite knowledge had a significant relationship with higher reported amounts of masturbation, while women who knew the role of the clitoris in achieving orgasm were more likely to masturbate than those who did not understand clitoral function. Women who had the most-permissive attitudes towards women masturbating in their later years were more likely to report that they themselves masturbated.

Sex therapists confirm that sexual knowledge, education, and permissiveness are significant in all age groups when considering views, attitudes, and experience of sex in general and masturbation in particular. The impression given by sex therapy clients during history taking is that a small number of male clients report self-masturbation between ages 4 and 10, but the highest percentage recall starting masturbation between 10 and 14 years. Female clients report starting to masturbate anywhere between 10 and 25 years, but far greater numbers are concentrated at 15 years and upwards, with an impression that a significant number of women have never chosen self-masturbation as a way of expressing their sexuality. It is also the impression that male partners are less likely to expect their female partners to self-masturbate, while these same female partners expect that their husbands/boyfriends do masturbate in secret, especially when there is a sexual dysfunction that precludes or limits the opportunity for penetrative sex. Clients, especially female clients, in individual therapy sessions often admit to self-masturbation, but do not wish their partners to know this information. Therapists report a greater acceptance of masturbation among single clients, and point out that there are many people with physical and learning disabilities for whom masturbation may be the only outlet for the expression of sexual feelings.

Project SIGMA, the first British in-depth study of sex, gay men, and AIDS, surveyed 1,083 gay and bisexual men over a four-year period between 1987 and 1991. Self-masturbation was reported during their lifetime by 99.5% of men, while 90% reported doing so within the previous month (average 17 times). The percentages by age group of those engaging in self-masturbation during the previous month were: under age 21, 86%; 21 to 30, 92%; 31 to 40, 94%; and 40-plus, 81%. As David S. G. Kay (1992) states:

> Although the high incidence of masturbation is useful information for encouraging its acceptance by clients, the ability of masturbation to produce orgasm has more therapeutic importance. Masturbation has been used in the treatment of erectile failure, premature and retarded ejaculation, general sexual dysfunction, and primary and secondary orgasmic dysfunction. . . . There appear to be no rational arguments for regarding masturbation as undesirable as a private form of sexual activity.

[*Update 2001*: The last two years prior to March 2000 saw an increase in U.K. television airtime given to shows with a sexual content, whether educational, informative, comedy, news, specialist subject area, or soft pornography. While the subject of masturbation does crop up on these programs, it has found a regular forum in some late-evening light-entertainment hosted shows in front of live audiences. One show host has frequently and openly discussed various aspects of masturbatory practice with members of his audience, has shown Internet images of masturbation, and on one occasion, discussed the potential merits of a tongue-shaped vibrator with a female guest who is a Member of Parliament. Some magazines also appear to be more forthcoming about mentioning masturbation. *More* magazine, which focuses on a readership from age 19 to 27 years, published a supplement in April 1999 called "Back to Basic Bonking Guide," featuring a step-by-step master class in masturbation and education called "know your bits." In mid-2000, this magazine ran an article featuring men and masturbation. During 1999, *More* encouraged readers to send in their most embarrassing sex questions, one of which was concerned with potential health problems following the use of inserting various fruits during masturbation. While there has always been a U.K. market for masturbatory devices though sex shops and mail-order catalogues, masturbation seems to have finally arrived in the mainstream of U.K. acceptability, now that the National Family Planning Association has produced a "Sexwares" catalogue of vibrators for men and women. (*End of update by M. Huish*)]

## 5. Interpersonal Heterosexual Behaviors

### A/B. Children and Adolescents   DANYA GLASER

Little research has been conducted on the sexual behavior of children and adolescents in the United Kingdom. Findings from one study of children in different preschool settings show that many children are curious about each others' genitalia, expressing this curiosity by looking at and touching each other. The extent to which such exploratory behavior has mature sexual meaning is unclear. A smaller proportion of preschool children enact sexual intercourse, usually by lying on top one another while fully dressed. It is likely that such behavior is imitative of adult behavior based on prior observation. These behaviors do not generally give rise to adult concerns unless the children appear preoccupied by genitally oriented activity or the behavior is coercive towards other children.

Oral-genital contact appears to be very rare, as are attempts to insert fingers or objects into another child's vagina or anus. Coercive, preoccupied, or very explicitly imitative behavior is associated with previous significant and inappropriate exposure to adult sexual activity, or sexual abuse of the child.

## C. Adults     JANE WADSWORTH, ANNE M. JOHNSON, KAYE WELLINGS, and JULIA FIELD

*The National Survey of Sexual Attitudes and Lifestyles*

In 1990 and 1991, Wadsworth, Johnson, Wellings, and Field undertook a large population survey in Great Britain, *The National Survey of Sexual Attitudes and Lifestyles* (Johnson et al. 1992, 1994; Wellings et al. 1994). A key aim of this survey was to provide information for models to predict the epidemic of HIV using data on partnerships and activity, but in addition, this study provided valuable information about sexual behavior in the United Kingdom, as well as specific information of practical use in the planning of sexual health services—genitourinary medicine clinics, family planning, and sex education—and healthpromotion strategy.

The national study involved interviews of a random sample of 18,876 men and women aged 16 to 59. The responses were obtained partly through a face-to-face interview and partly from a booklet, which was completed by the respondent and sealed in an envelope out of sight of the interviewer to ensure complete confidentiality. Questions were asked about first sexual experiences, sex education, contraception, fertility, numbers and sex of partners, frequency of sexual intercourse, prevalence of different sexual practices, and, for men, contact with prostitutes. Other topics included attitudes towards sexual behavior and AIDS, family of origin and current family circumstances, educational achievements, and employment. The full methodology has been published (Johnson et al. 1994; Wadsworth et al. 1993). Among the more important findings were the following:

*1. Age at First Heterosexual Intercourse (Sexarche).* The median age at first intercourse for men and women now in their 50s was 20, while for those under 20, it was 17, a decline of three years over three decades. An increase among young people in intercourse under the age of 16—in Britain the age of legal consent for women—is closely associated with this change. Seven percent of men and 1% of women now in their 50s first had intercourse before they became 16, while 28% of the men and 19% of the women aged 16 to 19 had done so.

*2. Number of Partners of the Opposite Sex.* The numbers of heterosexual partners reported in different time intervals are shown in Table 1. Very similar proportions of both men and women had no partners in the previous year, in the last five years, or ever. Three quarters of men and women had only one partner in the previous year, while half the men and two thirds of the women had one partner in the previous five years. However, men were more likely to report large numbers of partners than women.

The number of partners was strongly related to age and marital status. Twenty percent of young people, aged 16 to 24, reported no partners in the previous five years, but they were twice as likely as those aged 25 to 34 to report ten or more partners. In contrast, over 80% of those aged 45 to 59 had one partner in the previous five years. Married people were less likely to have had more than one partner in the previous year (5% of men and 2% of women) than single people (28% of men and 18% of women).

Those who were cohabiting (by their own description as living with a partner of the opposite sex to whom they were not married) were less likely to have had only one partner than those who were married (15% of men and 8% of women had more than one partner in the last year). Multivariate analysis showed that age and marital status were most strongly associated with numbers of partners, but first intercourse before age 16 was also positively associated with numbers of partners.

*3. Frequency of Sexual Intercourse.* The median frequency of intercourse was three times during the preceding four weeks. But this varied with age as well as with the length and status of the current relationship. Among married or cohabiting people aged 16 to 24, the median frequency was seven times in the previous four weeks. Multivariate analysis showed that in addition to age and marital status, frequency of intercourse was inversely related to the duration of the current relationship, but positively associated with numbers of partners in the last five years.

*4. Sexual Practices.* For the majority of respondents, sexual intercourse involved vaginal intercourse. Oral sex (fellatio and/or cunnilingus), anal sex, and nonpenetrative sex were less commonly practiced (see Table 2). Younger people were more likely to report sexual practices other than vaginal intercourse, as were those in long-term relationships.

Those who had more than one partner in the previous year were also more likely to report oral, anal, and nonpenetrative sex than those who had one partner. Oral sex and nonpenetrative sex have become more commonly prac-

## Table 1

### Number of Partners of the Opposite Sex in Different Time Intervals (in Percentages)

| Time Interval | Number of Partners | Male (n = 8,047) | Female (n = 10,059) |
|---|---|---|---|
| Ever | 0 | 6.8 | 5.9 |
| | 1 | 20.9 | 39.1 |
| | 2 | 10.7 | 17.0 |
| | 3-4 | 18.6 | 18.4 |
| | 5-9 | 19.5 | 13.2 |
| | 10+ | 24.5 | 6.8 |
| In the past 5 years | 0 | 8.9 | 9.3 |
| | 1 | 56.4 | 67.1 |
| | 2 | 10.1 | 11.3 |
| | 3-4 | 12.2 | 8.2 |
| | 5-9 | 8.1 | 3.7 |
| | 10+ | 4.8 | 0.2 |
| In the past year | 0 | 13.3 | 14.2 |
| | 1 | 72.5 | 78.6 |
| | 2 | 8.4 | 4.9 |
| | 3-4 | 4.1 | 1.8 |
| | 5+ | 1.8 | 0.1 |

Percentages approximated from the authors' bar graph (adapted from Johnson, Wadsworth, Wellings, and Fields 1994, 115).

ticed among respondents who became sexually active in recent decades compared with those who became sexually active in the 1950s and 1960s, but no such trend is shown for anal sex.

*5. Sexual Diversity.* Sexual experience with a partner of the same sex at some time in their lives was reported by 3.6% of the men and 1.8% of women. These proportions appear not to have changed with successive generations, but there are pronounced geographical variations, particularly among men. In the previous five years, 1.4% of the men had had a male partner in Great Britain as a whole. In greater London, however, this proportion was 4.6%, just over three times as many.

Considering only those who have ever had a homosexual partnership (see Table 3), only 9% of men and 5% of women have been exclusively homosexual throughout their life. In the last year, 19% of the men had male partners, 62% had female partners, and 10% had both male and female partners. Similar patterns were found for women respondents, but a slightly higher proportion had exclusively male partners.

*6. Attitudes to Sexual Behavior.* Data on attitudes towards sexuality showed that people in Great Britain have a strong commitment to monogamy, with marked toleration of premarital sex. Fewer than 10% of respondents believed that sex before marriage is wrong, but 80% of respondents felt that sex outside marriage is wrong.

Commitment to a regular ("steady") relationship was valued almost as highly as marriage, particularly among women. Homosexual relationships were considered to be wrong by almost 60% of women and 70% of men. Attitudes towards sexuality varied considerably with experience. For example, fewer than 50% of the men who have experienced sex outside marriage considered adultery to be wrong, compared with 80% of the men who had not had this experience.

These data show considerable diversity of sexual behavior in the general population of the United Kingdom. The majority have faithful relationships with one partner ("se-rial monogamy"), even if during their lifetime the majority of British men and women have had more than one partner.

Frequency of sexual intercourse is strongly related to the duration of the relationship, as well as to the respondent's age. Vaginal intercourse is the most popular form of having sex, and experience of anal intercourse is reported by only about one in 20 respondents, slightly more by men than women. Greater diversity in sexual practices is more likely among those who report more partners.

Patterns of homosexual behavior show geographical variations, with a markedly increased prevalence in central London. More than half of those of either sex who have ever had a partner of the same sex have had one or more partners of the opposite sex also. There have been changes in heterosexual behavior across the generations, particularly in the age of first sexual intercourse and the increase in those who have experienced sexual intercourse before the age of 16.

The pattern of partnerships clearly shows that people in Great Britain have larger numbers of partners when they are young and if they have not settled into a committed relationship. Men have more partners than women and nearly a quarter of men reported ten or more partners. There are, however, some differences between couples who are married and those who are living together without being married. In particular, the data suggest that extra relationships are more likely among those who are cohabiting than among married couples.

[*Update 2003*: As mentioned earlier in this section on adult heterosexual behavior, Wadsworth, Johnson, Wellings, and Field undertook a large population survey in Great Britain in 1990 and 1991, *The National Survey of Sexual Attitudes and Lifestyles* (Johnson et al. 1992, 1994; Wellings et al. 1994). In 2001, Johnson et al. published the results of a second *National Survey of Sexual Attitudes and Lifestyles*, conducted in the late 1990s. These two surveys have resulted in new and more-robust estimates of the distribution of sexual behavior within the population of the United Kingdom. The 1990-1991 survey and a comparison between findings in the two surveys provide evidence of increased reporting of a range of sexual behaviors within the population. The authors recognize that the magnitude of measured change is likely to be a combination of both actual changes in behaviors, along with increasing willingness to report previously socially censored behaviors, such as tolerance of homosexuality and casual partnerships.

[Some differences merit consideration. Just over three quarters of men and women report more than one lifetime partner, although the number reporting at least 10 lifetime partners is substantially lower in women (19.4%) than in men (34.6%). These numbers decline with increasing age for both genders, although the survey is limited to men and women 16 to 44 years of age. Nearly a third of men and just over a fifth of women had formed new heterosexual or homosexual relationships in the previous year, ranging from a mean of 2.04 new relationships among single men aged 25 to 34 years to 0.05 new relationships among married women aged 35 to 44 years. New partner acquisition is highest among the single or previously married. The authors estimate that 14.6% of men and 9% of women had concurrent partnerships at some time in the past year, although, again, the prevalence declined with increasing age. More than twice as many men as women reported new sexual partners outside the U.K. in the past five years.

[Overall, according to the authors' review, the number of single, separated, divorced, and widowed individuals remained unchanged over the decade. However, the number of people reporting cohabitation rose from 9.6% in 1990 to

### Table 2

**Prevalence of Different Sexual Practices in the Previous Year (in Percentages)**

|                        | Men (*n* =7,870) | Women (*n* = 9,786) |
|------------------------|:----------------:|:-------------------:|
| Vaginal intercourse    | 85.6             | 84.7                |
| Cunnilingus/fellatio   | 62.6             | 56.6                |
| Nonpenetrative sex     | 65.6             | 60.5                |
| Anal sex               | 6.9              | 6.1                 |

Percentages approximated from the authors' bar graph (adapted from Johnson, Wadsworth, Wellings, and Fields 1994, 164).

### Table 3

**Sex of the Partners of Respondents Who Ever Had a Homosexual Relationship**

| Time Interval |       | Exclusively Male | Exclusively Female | Male & Female | No Partners |
|---------------|-------|:----------------:|:------------------:|:-------------:|:-----------:|
| Ever          | Men   | 10.0%            | 0.0%               | 90.0%         | 0.0%        |
|               | Women | 0.0              | 5.0                | 95.0          | 0.0         |
| Last 5 years  | Men   | 16.8             | 56.2               | 22.0          | 5.0         |
|               | Women | 58.0             | 9.0                | 27.0          | 6.0         |
| Last year     | Men   | 20.0             | 61.0               | 9.0           | 10.0        |
|               | Women | 66.0             | 11.0               | 9.0           | 14.0        |

Percentages approximated from the authors' bar graph (adapted from Johnson, Wadsworth, Wellings, and Fields 1994, 210).

17.3% in 2000. During the same period, the number reported as married dropped from 51.5% in 1990 to 42% in 2000. First sex with a new partner took place within one month of meeting their most recent sexual partner for 56.5% of all men, compared with 42.8% of all women. Cohabitation is associated with a higher rate of partner change. The authors suggest that the proportion of the population reporting two or more sexual partners in the past year and inconsistent condom use in the past month is an indicator that unsafe sex has increased significantly among both men and women between the two surveys. The proportion of the population who regarded themselves as at-risk of HIV/AIDS remained low (4.5% of men and 2.9% of women).

[Looking at heterosexual practices, the proportion reporting vaginal intercourse in the previous month has varied very little over the past decade, whereas there has been an increase in oral-genital contact in the previous year for both genders and a considerably increased practice of anal sex in the previous year for both men and women. There was also an increase in reported homosexual partnerships, at any time and in the previous five years, among both women and men (Johnson, Mercer, Erens et al. 2001). (*End of update by K. R. Wylie*)]

### D. Sex and Persons with Disabilities   TINA BALL

Historically, the whole area of sexuality for people with disabilities has been seen as problematic and negative within the United Kingdom. Fears of "moral degeneracy" and eugenic theories led to the mass segregation of people with learning disabilities in institutions throughout most of the 20th century (Burns 1993). People with physical disabilities have often been seen as asexual (Williams 1993). The sexual and relationship difficulties of people with acquired cognitive impairments (and their partners) have been particularly unmentionable and even unthinkable.

At present, there are several strands contributing to changes in this picture. Some people continue to believe that sexuality should not be considered for those with disabilities. Some parents of young people with congenital disabilities often express fears and anxieties as their children begin to express sexual interests and wish they could stay as "holy innocents." However, the growing self-advocacy movements and the political movements of people with disabilities have ensured that disabled people's own voices have been heard asserting their sexual natures and needs. An example of this would be the way in which the leadership of the Association to Aid the Sexual and Personal Relationships of People with a Disability (formerly SPOD) has been taken over by people with disabilities.

Professionals have developed a range of sex education approaches and packages for persons with disabilities. Typical of these materials are those designed for people with learning disabilities (Craft 1991; McCarthy & Thompson 1992). Involving parents in these educational initiatives has been shown to be very valuable (Craft & Crosby 1991). Another example is the sex education materials created by people with learning disabilities for their own use (People First 1993).

The incidence of sexual problems is probably higher among people with all kinds of disabilities than it is in the general population. Negative attitudes towards people with disabilities lead to restricted opportunities for the development of sexual relationships; at the same time, an impaired or negative self-image can inhibit healthy sexual functioning. Some kinds of physical disabilities directly cause sexual problems, e.g., spinal cord injuries and multiple sclerosis. The growth in importance of physical treatments for erectile dysfunction, in particular, appears to be leading to a

much more active approach to the assessment and treatment of such difficulties in specialist services, with many employing nurses and other healthcare professionals to work with persons who have sexual problems linked with or resulting from their disabilities. There remains much room for improvement in this area. The awareness and understanding of the impact of particular disabling conditions on women's sexual functioning and relationships remains less well understood and has certainly received less attention in the literature (Williams 1993).

Sexual dysfunction in people with learning disabilities has also received little attention. Studies have indicated a high level of negative experiences of sex, including dyspareunia in women with learning disabilities (e.g., McCarthy 1993). There is undoubtedly a higher than average incidence of sexual abuse of both women and men with learning disabilities (Turk & Brown 1993). The law recognizes this vulnerability and there are specific laws designed to protect people with learning disabilities from sexual exploitation (Gunn 1991). The complexity of the legal situation at times deters staff members who are working with people with learning disabilities from offering appropriate support and education, especially if they are already uneasy with sexual issues. Several local authorities, health authorities, and voluntary agencies have designed policy statements on sexuality in an attempt to provide clear guidelines for care staff and other professionals (e.g., East Sussex 1992; Hertfordshire County Council 1989). There are also increasing moves to work to prevent and treat sexual abuse in people with learning disabilities (Craft 1993).

### E. Incidence of Oral Sex and Anal Sex

KEVAN R. WYLIE

The *National Survey of Sexual Attitudes and Lifestyles* (1994) revealed that oral sex was a common experience, although less so than vaginal intercourse and nonpenetrative sex. Experience of cunnilingus was slightly greater for both men (72.9%) and women (66.2%) than fellatio (69.4% of men and 64.0% of women). Overall experience of oral sex was reported by 75.2% of men and 69.2% of women. More than 80% reported practicing both forms of oral sex in the previous year, and it was usually practiced alongside vaginal intercourse.

Anal intercourse was practiced by less than 7% of all men and women, although a higher percentage of men had experience with it (13.9% of men and 12.9% of women). It was rarely practiced in isolation from other sexual activities. At the time of the survey, legal restrictions made such a practice an offense, which has subsequently been changed. (See also Section 8C, Significant Unconventional Sexual Behaviors, on rape.)

[*Update 2001*: The United Kingdom sociosexual investigations of gay men and AIDS (Project SIGMA) was used to analyze the extent to which acts of anal intercourse are distributed among gay men (Coxon & McMannus 2000). Most individuals (60%) who engage in anal intercourse do so only once or twice a month, but there is also a long tail of the sample who engage in this activity much more, with one tenth of the individuals performing half of the total acts of anal intercourse. The factors which most affected rates in concentration of risk behavior included relationship status, HIV-negative status, and concordant/disconcordant partner status. Highest-risk anal intercourse is primarily in the relatively infrequent acts of a relatively large number of gay men (rather than in the very frequent acts of a few), and it is this which is likely to lead to more-rapid diffusion of infection and ultimately higher levels of infected individuals. (*End of update by K. R. Wylie*)]

## 6. *Homoerotic, Homosexual, and Bisexual Behaviors*

ANTHONY BAINES

Heterosexism, the assumption that everyone is heterosexual and the subsequent discrimination against same-sex desire and attraction in men and women, is a significant cultural ideology in the United Kingdom. Sexual diversity in all its manifestations is not encouraged legally, socially, or politically.

The legal situation for lesbians and gay men in the United Kingdom is not a positive one. There are no laws to protect lesbians and gay men from discrimination. Male homosexuality was only partially decriminalized in 1967, for those men over the age of 21, with the stipulation that it would occur in private and with no more than two persons present. The age of consent for sex between men has since been reduced to age 18 (The Criminal Justice and Public Order Act 1994), but this is still two years above that for heterosexuals. Significantly, legislation has never stipulated an age of consent for lesbians, because of the invisibility of, and public refusal to accept, lesbian sexuality.

Other examples of discrimination against lesbians and gay men include their being banned from the Armed Forces and being ineligible for marriage under British law. A piece of legislation in the late 1980s also legitimized prejudice and discrimination against homosexuals. Section 28 added a new Section 2A to the Local Government Act of 1986, which states that a local authority shall not "intentionally promote homosexuality or publish material with the intention of promoting homosexuality." It would appear that such legislation is supported to a significant extent by social attitudes. Wellings et al. (1994) reported that 70.2% of men and 57.9% of the women surveyed believe that sex between two men is always or mostly wrong.

The experience of institutionalized or personal homophobia and heterosexism can affect the self-esteem of lesbians, gay men, and bisexuals, with implications for their emotional and mental well-being. In the face of such marginalization and stigmatization, the process of "coming out"—informing people of one's homosexuality or bisexuality and thus challenging preconceptions of heterosexuality—can be incredibly empowering. Acknowledging one's own sexual identity, informing those who share one's surroundings, and meeting people who share one's sexual identity to gain support and solidarity can be a major step on the road to healthy self-acceptance for many lesbians, gay men, and bisexuals.

In spite of the oppressive culture towards lesbians, gay men, and bisexuals—or perhaps because of this—strong, diverse lesbian, gay, and bisexual communities have developed, predominantly in the larger cities of the United Kingdom, such as London, Manchester, and Edinburgh. There are networks across the United Kingdom, reaching into the more rural areas, to provide a range of services to lesbians, gay men, and bisexuals, including telephone helplines, counseling, and social groups. There are also numerous lobbying groups from all shades of the political spectrum, working for lesbian, gay, and bisexual rights.

The emergence of HIV and its devastating impact on gay communities has led to a huge community response, with many of the United Kingdom's major national and local voluntary groups being set up by gay men.

Lesbians, gay men, and bisexuals meet each other in a variety of settings, and through various means, at pubs and cafés, saunas, social groups, parties, parks, and other "cruising areas," as well as through personal advertisements in a variety of publications. Most of the United Kingdom's larger cities and towns have a commercial gay scene and some semblance of a visible lesbian, gay, and bisexual community. The media has also been used to exchange information and promote this sense of community. There are national and local lesbian and gay newspapers, magazines, radio programs, and film festivals. The mainstream-quality media also often run stories and features from a lesbian and gay perspective. Lesbian and gay film seasons and programs have also been screened on television.

The growing confidence among lesbian, gay, and bisexual communities has also been illustrated by the increasing number and scale of festivals and parades around the United Kingdom, where lesbians, gay men, and bisexuals have come together, building and promoting a sense of community. In 1995, the annual Lesbian, Gay, and Bisexual Pride Festival in London attracted approximately 200,000 people.

The lesbian, gay, and bisexual communities of the United Kingdom are diverse, with same-sex desire cutting across age, class, ethnicity, religion, culture, ability, and health status. This is illustrated by the plethora of support and interest groups that have emerged to address these concerns.

[*Update 2003*: There have been some changes in the legal, social, and political lives of lesbians and gay men in the U.K. since the original United Kingdom chapter was written in 1996.

[The European Court recently ruled that the ban on lesbians and gay men serving in the Armed Forces is unlawful. As of 2002, the U.K. Forces were reviewing their employment policies in light of this. In relation to immigration rules, same-sex couples can apply to stay in the U.K. if the foreign partner is living in the country legally, and the relationship has existed for at least two years. However, the age of consent for gay men remains at 18 (two years above that for heterosexuals) despite attempts by the Labour Government to reduce it to 16. This should change within the life of the current Parliament. Section 28 also remains on the statute books despite promises of repeal.

[Rather more positively, developments in HIV treatments have raised optimism among people affected by HIV, particularly gay and bisexual men, who have been one of the communities most affected by the epidemic. Combination therapy has reduced levels of illness in people with HIV and enabled some people to return to work. (*End of update by A. Baines*)]

[*Update 2003*: In December 2002, Barbara Roche, U.K. minister for social exclusion and equalities, announced that gay men, lesbians, and bisexuals would be granted many of the same rights as married couples in Britain, though not the legal status of marriage itself, under government plans to officially recognize civil same-sex partnerships. The partnerships would give homosexual and bisexual couples property and inheritance rights and grant each person the status of next-of-kin to the other. According to Roche, the proposals would end situations where homosexuals were refused hospital visits to partners or excluded from funerals.

[Arguing that there was now an "extremely strong case" for giving legal recognition to gay unions, she said, "I do think society has moved on, and I think that we recognize that there are very many people in gay relationships who are in very loving relationships—indeed they may have been very long enduring relationships—but their partnership has no recognition in law."

[Detailed legislation will not be worked out at least until early 2004, and even then, the proposals would not amount to "gay marriages." However, same-sex couples would be free to arrange their own private ceremonies to mark the event.

[The opposition Conservatives, who have frequently seen their traditional and liberal wings fall out over gay rights and "family values" issues, came out in support. "Whilst we attach a huge importance to the institution of marriage, we do recognize that gay couples suffer from some serious particular grievances," the party's shadow home secretary, Oliver Letwin, said. The third-party Liberal Democrats said the proposals were "welcome but long overdue. Couples of any sex must be made equal before the law."

[In leading up to this legislation, homosexuality was legalized in 1967; the age of consent for gay men was cut to 18 from 21 in 1994, and then to 16 in 2000; in 2001, the mayor of London set up the first register for gay couples, and in November 2002, gay couples gained the same legal right as heterosexual couples to adopt (Hoge 2002).

[While the government debates the issue of civil rights of gay couples, an ongoing, often emotional debate has heated up in the Church of England over the ordination of homosexual clergy, with warnings from the Archbishop of Canterbury, Dr. George Carey, that this issue could provoke a schism. Unexpectedly, a triad of events, in the U.K., Canadian and American branches of the Anglican Church, provoked extensive and emotional public debate of what had been an "in-house" issue.

[In October 2002, news reports confirmed that Canon Gene Robinson, who left his wife and children to move in with his male lover, was almost certain to stand for election as the next bishop of New Hampshire in the United States. In June 2003, Canon Robinson was elected bishop of New Hampshire on the second ballot. In July, following heated debate and refutation of allegations of "inappropriate behavior," the bishops, clergy, and lay delegates at the late-July 2003 General Convention of the national Episcopal Church in the U.S.A. ratified Canon Robinson's election as bishop of New Hampshire by a two-thirds majority.

[Meanwhile, in Vancouver, British Colombia (Canada), Bishop Michael Ingham announced that he would be the first bishop in the Anglican Communion to bless same-sex unions. In a strongly negative response, the bishops representing 38 million Anglicans in Africa and Asia said that Ingham's decision represented "a defining moment in which the clear choice has to be made between remaining a communion or disintegrating into a federation of churches (Kraus 2003).

[In June, while the Canadian and American debates fueled extensive media coverage, the Reverend Jeffrey John was nominated as the new bishop of Reading, south of London. John confirmed his nomination in a *Times of London* interview, and also the fact that he is homosexual and in a 27-year relationship with a fellow clergyman. He added that the relationship has been platonic for years—in keeping with church policy opposing homosexual acts by clergy members. Despite his celibate life, Jeffrey John was pressed to withdraw his candidacy after a private meeting with the new Archbishop of Canterbury, Rowan Williams, that lasted hours. (*End of update by R. T. Francoeur*)]

## 7. Gender Diversity and Transgender Issues

STEPHEN WHITTLE and GWYNETH A. SAMPSON
*[Rewritten and updated in late 2001
by S. Whittle and G. A. Sampson]*

Transvestism and transsexualism are moderately visible phenomena in United Kingdom society in the 21st century. However, this is a recent state of affairs, visibility having grown considerably in the 1990s. The reasons for this are manifold, despite the fact that there is still little legal recognition of the new gender status of a person who has undergone sex-reassignment treatment.

Male transvestism has long been a feature of the theater from the late medieval period when cross-dressing males provided the female characters for the stage. Cross dressing, or drag as it is referred to, as a stage act remains popular, with artists such as Danny la Rue and, more recently, Lily Savage gaining a national popularity. Female cross-dressing has not had such prominence, the writer Radclyffe Hall and the entertainer Vesta Tilly being notable exceptions in the 1920s and 1930s.

However, transvestism has remained a peripheral activity, with little social acceptance on a more personal level. Since the organization of the Beaumont Society in the late 1960s, which was originally founded to provide advice and safe social meeting venues for heterosexual transvestites, there has been a gradual proliferation of similar groups. There now exist a variety of organizations and settings throughout the country where men may cross dress in discrete venues. The development of "gay village" areas in the late 1980s and 1990s in many major cities also provided other locales, such as public houses and clubs where heterosexual and homosexual transvestites may meet and socialize. There is also a large underground network of "contact magazines," which allow homosexual and bisexual transvestites to make sexual contacts. It is difficult to estimate the total numbers of transvestites in the United Kingdom, as there has been little, if any, work to extrapolate figures.

There is little social acknowledgement of female cross dressing, it being seen to belong to some radical lesbians and "butch dykes" and a subgrouping of lesbian culture. However, the U.K.'s first "drag king" club, Naïve, opened in London, and several temporary venues now exist where events such as "drag king" competitions take place.

Transsexual people are a much more visible feature of British society, having gained considerable media interest. Newspapers, women's magazines, and television have regular features concerning transsexualism. Nonetheless, the individual transsexual person may be, in fact, far more hidden than this media interest otherwise portrays. The first recorded transsexual surgery in Britain was performed in 1944 by Sir Harold Gilles, an eminent plastic surgeon, on Michael Dillon, a (female-to-male) transsexual man. Since then, several thousand transsexual people have gained sex-reassignment surgery in the U.K. or abroad. Again, little work has been done to count the total number of transsexual people, but estimates based upon the numbers who have attended recognized Gender Identity Clinics, those who have joined self-help organizations, and those who have gained media attention, put the figures at around 10,000 to 15,000 transsexuals in the United Kingdom (McMullen & Whittle 1995). Several have published highly regarded autobiographical accounts, most notably racing-car driver Roberta Cowell (1954), the Mt. Everest climber and *Times* journalist Jan Morris (1974), and models April Ashley (1982) and Caroline Cossey (Tula) (1991). In recent years, there have appeared autobiographies from (female-to-male) transsexual men, including journalist Paul Hewitt (1995), Raymond Thompson, (1995) and Mark Rees (1996).

The first formal Gender Identity Clinic was set up by psychiatrist John Randell at Charing Cross Hospital in London in the early 1970s. Specifically catering to the needs of transsexual people, this clinic remains at the forefront of psychiatric and surgical services in this field. Currently, it has as its Head of Research, Richard Green, former president of the Harry Benjamin International Gender Dysphoria Association, which provides an academic and medical research base for those working in the field. There are several other clinics throughout the country, as well as a small clinic catering to the needs of transsexual adolescents and their families at the Portman Clinic in London.

The current legal position for transsexual people was embodied in the common-law decision in the case of *Corbett v Corbett* (1970, 2 All E.R., 33-48). In this case, the marriage between a male-to-female postsurgical-reassignment transsexual woman and a male partner was declared to be void. It was held that, for the purposes of marriage, a transsexual person would always be of their original sex designation at birth. It has also been held that the birth certificate records in the United Kingdom are a record of historical fact and, hence, are unalterable unless there was a substantial mistake at the time of registration. As a result, though, transsexual people, on one level, seem to be accommodated by the U.K. law, in that most of their personal documentation can be altered to show their new gender grouping and their new name; their birth certificate records, which are used as a form of identification for many purposes, will still show their old status and name, and they cannot marry a member of the opposite gender (i.e., same-sex) grouping. This means that for all legal purposes, they remain a member of their natal sex grouping. The iniquities that result from this, not only in terms of personal privacy, but also inadequate protection in employment legislation, have meant that transsexuals in the United Kingdom have taken the government to the European Court of Human Rights on several occasions. The case of *Rees v UK* (1987, 9 E.H.R.R. 56) led to a compromise solution whereby passports may now record the new name and gender status of the transsexual person on production of a sworn declaration of name change and a doctor's letter to the effect that the gender change undergone is permanent. Similarly, driving licenses will now record the new gender role, as can all other documents apart from the birth certificate.

However, transsexual people have not been satisfied with this solution and have continued to plead their cause to the government through the campaigning group, Press for Change (PFC). Press for Change provides legal advice and encourages parliamentary lobbying. Currently (2000), PFC is supporting cases concerning an issue of pension rights, which has been referred to the European High Court of Justice; a request for the declaration of validity of a transsexual person's marriage before the High Court; many employment cases; and cases involving several other areas of the law.

There are numerous self-help organizations for transsexual people, and many join these, albeit often only in their initial stages of transition. The largest are: the Gender Trust, which predominately caters to male-to-female transsexual women, and the FTM Network, which caters to female-to-male transsexual men. At any one time, both of these organizations have almost 2,000 members between them. Transsexualism is becoming increasingly socially accepted in the United Kingdom, with transsexual people finally succeeding in retaining or obtaining high-status job positions, including positions in education and local government, and high-profile positions in the entertainment industry.

In May 1999, the Home Secretary, Jack Straw, announced the creation of a Government Inter-Departmental Working Group with the following terms of reference:

to consider, with particular reference to birth certificates, the need for appropriate legal measures to address the problems experienced by transsexual people, having due regard to scientific and societal developments, and measures undertaken in other countries to deal with this issue.

The report was published in April 2000, and the Working Group identified three options for future consideration by the government of the United Kingdom:

1. to leave the current situation unchanged;
2. to issue birth certificates showing the new name and, possibly, sex; and
3. to grant full legal recognition of the acquired sex, subject to certain criteria and procedures.

The report indicates that the first two of these options would be unlikely to resolve the problems that transsexual people face because of their current lack of appropriate legal status. As such, the report indicates that the U.K. government would only meet its obligations under Human Rights legislation if they granted full recognition of the transsexual person's acquired sex. It must now only be a matter of time before transsexual people obtain full legal recognition of their new status alongside their increased social acceptance.

## 8. Significant Unconventional Sexual Behaviors

KEVAN R. WYLIE

### A. Child Sexual Abuse, Incest, and Pedophilia

Any form of sexual contact between adults and children evokes an emotive reaction. Sexual abuse of young children, intrafamilial sexual abuse (usually incestuous), and extrafamilial (usually pedophilia) are all offenses in the United Kingdom. Increasing awareness of child sexual abuse (CSA) has ensured a more-sympathetic approach to dealing with victims. It is accepted that sexual abuse is a traumatic event for most children, and for some, that it is followed by a post-traumatic stress reaction. The advantages and limitations in applying therapy to such a framework in the United Kingdom have been described by Jehu (1991).

There is evidence of an increased number of proceedings against offenders over the last decade, but it remains unclear whether this is a real increase in the number of offenses or improved methods of securing evidence for prosecution. While real or reporting patterns may have changed through the influences of feminism, media attention, academic acceptance, and public sensitization to such crimes, it is probably the case that "old attitudes die hard." There have been cases in the United Kingdom in which public opinion has turned surprisingly against those reporting child sexual abuse (the Cleveland affair, Orkney ritual abuse, and Rochdale Satanic abuse cases).

Police, social services, educational, and health services are now duty-bound to inform each other when cases of alleged abuse occur. Regional units within the United Kingdom have facilities to record interview sessions on video of children being asked open questions about the alleged abuse. Recent changes brought about by the Criminal Justice Act (1994) allow the use of video disclosure of abuse to a social worker for presentation in court. Video links within the court allow questioning of the minor in a room separate from the court to avoid the minor's facing the offender directly. Social workers have a statutory duty to be involved with families when children are placed on the "At Risk" register and must act on the balance of probability. The police, on the other hand, must establish beyond reasonable doubt that an offense has occurred. Offenders are charged with indecent assault. Inappropriate touching and the circumstances of the event are pivotal in deciding to embark with criminal proceedings. Corroborative statements, whenever possible, and medical evidence are often vital. There is however, no time limit for bringing such offenses to court.

There is currently debate in the United Kingdom regarding the reality of "false memory syndrome," with cases of abuse being alleged up to 20 years or later than the alleged offenses took place. There are reports in the United Kingdom of men in their 60s and 70s being given short custodial sentences for offenses of sexual abuse or incest that occurred many years previously.

In 1994, prosecution of around 2,000 cases of indecent assault on females under 16 years of age were initiated and around 65% of those charged were found guilty. Only half of these were given custodial sentences. The punishment can be ten years imprisonment. It has been argued by Fisher and Howells (1993) that significant social-skill deficits occur in some sex offenders. Where these exist, the deficit is in the cognitive component of social competence. Sex offenders often have major difficulties in establishing and maintaining longer-term intimate relationships, with factors likely to include empathy deficits and inappropriate culturally induced expectations concerning sexual relationships. A recent article presented opinion as to whether a sexual offender should be allowed castration where there is a history of persistent sexual abuse (Alexander et al. 1993).

In law, incest is the act of intercourse by a man with a woman he knows to be his daughter, granddaughter, sister (or half sister), or mother. Three quarters of the cases reported involve father-daughter incest. Incest implies consent—although this is no defense—and is differentiated from unlawful sexual intercourse with a girl under the age of 13 or 16. All are offenses under the Sexual Offences Act 1956. The punishment for incest is seven years custodial sentence, unless the girl is under 13. If this is the case (effectively constituting rape), the punishment is life imprisonment. The number of persons proceeded against on the offense of incest are a small proportion of those charged with child sexual abuse.

The incidence of pedophilia is unknown in the United Kingdom. A small central unit exists to investigate this area, and while the offense is abhorred, limited resources are available to seek out actively and investigate crimes being committed by pedophiles. Several lobby groups now exist to promote awareness of the existence of this problem and the need for active targeting of police time towards preventing the continuation of such practices. Further, to date no national register exists to identify individuals when changing residence. It is not normally the case that such offenders are offered therapy unless supervised probation is ordered. (See also Section 8E below for information on child pornography.)

[*Update 2001*: In July 2000, the Home Office released a summary report and recommendations to reform the law on sex offenses: *Setting the Boundaries*. This is a consultation document. As a matter of public policy, the age of legal consent is recommended to remain at 16 years of age. With regard to specific offenses against children, the law should state that below the age of 13, a child cannot effectively consent to sexual activity. A recommendation of an offense of adult (over 18) sexual abuse of a child (under 16) is recommended, which would cover all sexual behavior that was wrong because it involved a child, and would compliment other serious nonconsensual offenses, such as rape, sexual assault by penetration, and sexual assault. It is recommended there should be no time limit on prosecution for the new offense of adult sexual activity with a child. An offense of the persistent sexual abuse of a child reflecting a course of conviction should be reintroduced. There is some recognition that children sexually abuse other children and that sentencing decisions should reflect specialist assessment of risk and potential for longer-term offending and include treatment options. The concept of familial sexual abuse for the modern family is suggested. (*End of update by K. R. Wylie*)]

## B. Sexual Harassment

HELEN MOTT and ROHAN COLLIER
[*Rewritten and updated in late 2001
by H. Mott and R. Collier*]

### Incidence

Sexual harassment is a widespread problem in British society. What marks it as an unconventional behavior, therefore, is not a question of rarity, but the fact that it is recognized as wrongful conduct under the law, particularly in the workplace (see below). Its roots in patriarchal society mean that, for the most part, it is women who suffer most from sexual harassment inflicted by men, although the concept has been extended to cover alternative permutations. While sexual harassment, as an exercise in gendered power relations, can be seen to affect women in all walks of life (cf. Wise & Stanley 1997), in general usage, the term is understood to refer primarily to the experience of women in the workplace.

There are as many definitions of sexual harassment as there are theoretical approaches to it, although most contain the common elements of citing conduct based on sex or of a sexual nature that is unwelcome or offensive, and/or detrimental to the interests of the recipient. The emphasis on the recipient creates a tension between objective and subjective standards, so that although the term *sexual harassment* is common currency, the people's ideas about what constitutes it can vary widely. Thus, a National Opinion Polls survey in 1991 found that one in six women said they had experienced sexual harassment, but when they were asked whether they had experienced certain kinds of (unwanted sexual) behavior that offended them, the figure rose to one in three (Collier 1995). The results of this survey, and others like it, suggest that people may be reluctant to label the full range of potentially sexually harassing behaviors as harassment *per se*.

The likelihood of a formal complaint being made to the authorities in the case of sexual harassment also appears to be low. Davidson & Earnshaw (1991) found that 65% of personnel directors in their study believed that between 70% and 100% of cases were never reported to them. This supports North American research (e.g., Livingston 1982, which claims that only 2.5% of harassment victims took any official action). For reasons such as these, it is, therefore, very difficult to attempt to quantify the incidence of sexual harassment. Recent surveys in Britain seem to show that, on average, between 30% and 50% of women claim to have experienced sexual harassment at work (Alfred Marks 1991; Industrial Society 1993; London Buses Ltd. 1991; Mott & Condor 1995), although in certain occupations, such as the police force, the figure has been as high as 90% (Her Majesty's Inspectorate of Constabulary 1993). The scale of the problem suggests that it is ill advised to concentrate upon the likely psychological profile of the harasser (or indeed the recipient). While individual factors may be relevant to individual cases, it is clear that sexual harassment is essentially a social problem.

### Legal Penalties

As noted above, it is rare for complaints to reach any level of authority and it is, therefore, rarer still for the legal system to become formally involved. Sexual harassment cases in Britain can be brought within the ambit of several laws. Presently, most cases are dealt with by the Industrial Tribunal under the Sex Discrimination Act (1975). This act, which is applicable to all institutions, makes it unlawful to discriminate by treating a woman less favorably on the grounds of her sex. It also makes it unlawful to victimize a woman who has complained of sexual harassment, to promise or withhold benefits in exchange for sexual favors, or to subject her to detriment. All of these elements of the Sex Discrimination Act can be relevant to sexual harassment in the workplace, and are applicable to men as well as women, although the scarcity of recorded cases successfully brought by men tends to suggest that this application is more theoretical than practical. Generally, both the individual harasser and the relevant organization will be jointly liable, unless the organization can prove that it has taken reasonable steps to prevent sexual harassment. Complainants can expect to receive monetary compensation (for which there is no upper limit) for financial loss, medical expenses, and damages, such as injury to feelings. Tribunals may also require that the organization take steps to prevent harassment happening again, or to transfer the harasser within the organization. Cases can also be brought to the Industrial Tribunal under the Employment Protection (Consolidation) Act (1978) when a person has been an employee of the relevant organization for at least two years full-time. Victims of harassment might claim constructive dismissal if they were in fact obliged to resign, or unfair dismissal if, as a direct or indirect consequence of being sexually harassed, they were dismissed from work. The Tribunal can rule for the reinstatement, re-engagement, or compensation of the injured party (subject to certain financial limits).

The number of cases involving sexual harassment brought to the Industrial Tribunal in Britain under the Sex Discrimination Act has been steadily increasing since 1986. There has been concern that the requirement under the Act to prove disparate treatment of the sexes prevents some cases from being adequately addressed. The aim of the Tribunal is to uphold the rights of the victim, and thereby, to provide a remedy, such as compensation. This can certainly penalize the perpetrator by the award of damages, but there is no power to punish. For these reasons, legal commentators such as Dine & Watt (1995) have called for more victims of harassment to take their cases to the civil or criminal courts, a practice which was rare, given that victims needed to mould their experiences to existing law, e.g., suing for breach of contract; trespass to the person (civil courts); or assault or false imprisonment (criminal courts).

In 1991, the EC issued a Code of Practice concerning sexual harassment following a Recommendation asking member states to promote awareness of the unacceptable nature of sexual harassment. This Code points out that sexual harassment is a form of sex discrimination and is, therefore, unlawful under the Equal Treatment Directive (1976). The Code also provides for the inclusion of harassment on the grounds of sexuality (in addition to gender) as sexual harassment. In addition, the Code recommends that organizations provide a clear policy prohibiting sexual harassment in the workplace and guaranteeing prompt and efficient action in the event of harassment. This Code of Practice strengthened the hand of those seeking to challenge the prevalence of sexual harassment in the workplace.

In 1997, a new law, the Protection from Harassment Act, came into force. The intention behind the Act was primarily to deal effectively with stalkers, although all types of harassment are theoretically covered. The Act states that a person must not pursue a course of conduct, which a reasonable person should know would amount to the harassment of another. It is necessary for two incidents constituting harassment to have occurred. The Act gives powers to both the criminal and the civil courts. Harassment is now an arrestable criminal offense carrying a maximum of six months in prison and/or a fine of up to £5,000. Should the offender have caused fear of violence, the offense carries up to 5 years' imprisonment and unlimited fine. The Court may also issue a Restraining Order upon the offender. A victim of harassment may also bring a civil claim under the Act, and may be awarded damages (including damages for anxiety), and may be granted an injunction against the perpetrator, the violation of which would constitute a criminal offense.

## Social Response

The category of behavior, which we now call sexual harassment, has a very long history, although its naming has only come into being very recently. Sexual harassment as a concept came to Britain from North America in the late 1970s and early 1980s with the publication of Farley's (1978) and MacKinnon's (1979) highly influential texts. These texts, however, were academic, and it is only much more recently that "sexual harassment" has passed into the wider domain, so that since the late 1980s, it has been a topic for public discussion and debate. Since that time, there has been coverage in the press of successful Industrial Tribunal cases, and the subject has been addressed as a storyline in the two most popular television soap operas. In the year running from May 1993 to 1994, no less than 90 articles in *The (London) Times* newspaper discussed sexual harassment.

Women are now much more aware of their rights, and have higher expectations in terms of how they are treated at work than in the past. However, a recent study (Mott & Condor 1995) revealed that women continue to find it difficult to confront sexual harassment, as dominant workplace ideologies that legitimize unsolicited sexual behavior and mitigate against confrontation, remain. It is also clear that the pervasive and everyday nature of much sexual harassment (especially in the form of sexual remarks and joking) in many workplaces makes it unrealistic to expect an immediate changeover to zero tolerance.

Results from many studies have shown that sexual harassment can have a devastating effect for victims, both in terms of their performance at work and their personal well-being. Eighty-six percent of harassment victims in the COHSE (1991) study reported an adverse effect on emotional well-being, while 33% said that their quality of work deteriorated. Despite this, and despite the potential risks of litigation, the response of many organizations and trade unions to the problem has not been adequate. In the study mentioned above, over half the employees who complained of harassment felt that their complaints had not been dealt with adequately, and 10% found that they (rather than the harasser) had effectively been punished by being transferred to another job or department. An Industrial Society Survey (1993) found that 60% of British employers had no sexual harassment policy in place.

## C. Rape                               KEVAN R. WYLIE

In England and Wales, rape is defined as sexual intercourse with a woman without her consent. This must involve penile penetration "to the slightest degree" of the vagina. Emission is not necessary for the act to constitute rape. Penetration of the anus constitutes "buggery," and penetration of the mouth constitutes "gross indecency" or "indecent assault." Attitudes towards rape have changed over the last couple of decades, with women feeling more able to report cases to the police. There was a twofold increase in the proportion of rapes committed by "intimates" (30% of all rapes by 1985) and in the number of rapes taking place indoors, particularly in the home of the victim, which had similarly doubled (30% of all rapes by 1985).

Police forces now have dedicated nonpolice-station units where persons alleging rape are counseled. These units often resemble living dwellings rather than the institutional nature of the police station. Within the units are video interview rooms and a medical suite. Premises and facilities of victim examination suites are reviewed by Lewington and Rogers (1995). Should the victim be willing to make a formal statement, attempts to trace the offender take place to allow for questioning of the suspect. It remains the case that victims of rape experience anonymity during court proceedings, while the offender is not offered such protection.

Victims are offered support by Rape Crisis and Victim Support units. Cohn (1990) found that the incidence of rape, as well as assault, burglary, collective violence, and domestic violence, increased with ambient temperature, at least up to about 85° Fahrenheit (29° C), and concluded that, in general, the most violent crimes against persons occurred linearly with increasing ambient temperature, while property crimes did not strongly relate to temperature changes.

The issue of "date rape" has started to make an impression in the United Kingdom, although it does not constitute a specific offense as such. The issue of stranger rape has been construed by some as "clumsy seduction." Marital rape is now accepted as an offense.

Rape is an offense under the Sexual Offences Act 1956 and there has been a threefold increase in the number of cases in which proceedings have started in the courts in England and Wales over the last decade. Of the 1,625 cases proceeded against in 1994, just under a quarter were found guilty and sentenced. Almost all of these cases were punished with immediate custodial sentences, which is normally life imprisonment. Sentencing has shown a general trend towards an increased length of custodial sentence passed. In sentencing, judges are less likely to regard prior consensual contact as a valid reason for passing noncustodial sentences on convicted rapists (Lloyd 1991).

A number of male partners of rape victims remain seriously troubled many months after the rape (Bateman & Mendelssohn 1989) and have become profoundly worried about their identity as men, shunning their male friends, avoiding sexual contact with their partner, and withdrawing from regular social interaction. They may require intensive psychoanalytic therapy to begin to understand what it means for them that their partner has been raped.

In a review of sexual offenders, rapists were found more likely to report having a current female partner and to have experienced consenting heterosexual intercourse with an adult, than were nonincest offenders against male children. However, no evidence emerged that rapists and nonincest offenders against female children differed significantly in this respect (Bownes 1993). Using the GRIMS and GRISS questionnaires, the investigation found evidence of marital and relationship difficulties and sexual problems among all offense categories of those sentenced for sexual offenses as being substantially higher than those among the general population. A prevalence of 62% for marital/relationship dysfunction among offenders who had a current relationship with an adult female partner, and a prevalence of 57% for sexual dysfunction amongst offenders who had experienced heterosexual intercourse with an adult, were reported. Treatment programs need to address these elements.

Until recently, buggery with a male under the age of 21, or with a woman or with an animal, led on conviction to punishment with life imprisonment. However, when Section 143 of the Criminal Justice and Public Order Act 1994 came into force on November 3, 1994, the amended Section 12 of the Sexual Offences Act 1956 (The Acts of Buggery) in effect legalized anal intercourse for consenting couples over 18 years of age, be they gay or heterosexual. About 10% of cases are thought to be heterosexual and, unless force accompanies the act, these cases rarely proceed to court. Where anal intercourse occurred as a result of sexual assault, this amendment would obviously not apply.

While Mezey and King (1989) had difficulty in getting victims to cooperate with an interview for their research project on male rape, their results indicated that failure to report to the police was a problem. Most of the assailants and subjects were homosexual or bisexual, and only a few cases conformed to the stereotype of sudden unprovoked attack by complete strangers in a public place. The assault had considerable impact on the subjects' sexual identity. It was concluded that these findings suggest that male victims' immediate and long-term responses were similar to those described by female rape victims.

A study by Hickson et al. (1994) reported the prevalence of nonconsensual sex amongst homosexually active men as 27.6%, of which 3.9% involved female assailants. A third of the men had been forced into sexual activity, usually anal intercourse, by men with whom they had previously had consensual sexual activity. These results supported the belief that male rape is not usually committed by men identified as heterosexual.

The majority of those persons found guilty of buggery were given immediate custodial sentences. Around 40% were found guilty of the 379 cases in which proceedings took place in 1994.

What is commendable is the high detection rate by the United Kingdom police of sexual offenses that are reported as having been committed, particularly for rape, unlawful sexual intercourse with girls under 16, incest, and buggery. There are less-successful detection rates with indecent assault on females aged 16 years and over, when compared to the offenses of indecent assault on females under 16 years of age, with a similar but less marked pattern seen with indecent assault on a male in both age groups. The "clear-up" rates for sex crimes are generally considered to be substantially higher than those for other crimes. There are, of course, an unestimatable number of sex crimes never reaching the police.

[*Update 2001*: A Government consultation paper detailing law changes, giving better protection for victims of child sex abuse and rape, went into effect in the summer of 2000. A sexual offenses review group is currently advising the Government. In 1999 to 2000, rape and other sex crimes rose overall by 4.5%, with a 10% rise in rape of women and a 19% rise in rape of males. Experts believe part of this, especially the male rape figures, is also because of more reporting of the crime. Increasing numbers of the accused are friends or ex-boyfriends of the victims, indicating a greater willingness to report date or acquaintance rapes—notoriously the most difficult type to prove in court.

> The above mentioned Home Office document setting the boundaries (for consultation) recommends the offence of rape should be retained as penile penetration without consent and extend it to include oral penetration. This should be defined as penetration of the anus, mouth or genitalia to the slightest extent and for the avoidance of doubt, surgically reconstructed male or female genitalia should be included in the definition in law. ("Attacks and Sex Crime Up as Robberies Soar," *Daily Mail* newspaper, July 18, 2000)

[A new offense of sexual assault by penetration should be introduced for all other penetration without consent. Consent should be defined in law as "free agreement." A non-exhaustive list of examples is given within the draft documentation. (*End of update by K. R. Wylie*)]

## D. Prostitution                                    KEVAN R. WYLIE

It has been estimated that in major cities in the United Kingdom outside of London, between 800 and 1,000 women work as prostitutes at any one time. An excess of 10,000 male clients use such services in any one city. Paying for sex remains a stigmatized behavior, although 6.8% of men reported paying for sex with a woman at some time and 1.8% had done so within the last five years (Wellings et al. 1994). Recent experience was most common in the age group of men aged 25 to 44, although prevalence of ever paying for sex was five times more common in the older age group (10.3% vs. 2.1%). It was most common in widowed, separated, and divorced men within the last five years, and the men were more likely to be from social classes I and II (possibly away from home on business). A history of a homosexual partner (at any time) was associated with specifically raised odds of commercial sex contact (possibly some bisexual men).

The prostitute population is not stable. Women enter and leave, depending upon life circumstances. The risk of HIV through sexual services is very low, and the risk of contracting HIV is much greater through the use of drug injecting. It has been argued that if a sexual act is consensual and does not harm others, it should be acceptable to repeal the laws prohibiting soliciting. By doing so, it would free street workingwomen from harassment, and reduce police and court time of those who are attempting to uphold a law that does little to abolish the "trade" (Carr 1995). The *National Vice Squad Survey* (Benson & Matthews 1995) found that one third of police vice squads want brothels to be legalized.

Prostitution can constitute one of several offenses. These include "curb crawling" (approaching a prostitute and being a "nuisance") and soliciting under the Sexual Offences Act 1985, behaving in an indecent manner in a public place under the Vagrancy Act 1824, loitering or soliciting for the purposes of prostitution under the Street Offences Act 1959, and procurement of persons for immoral purposes under the Sexual Offences Acts 1956 and 1967. Women offer sexual services to men within several settings. Such services are usually offered within the so-called red light areas of a town or city. Establishments offering saunas and massage parlors are usually a cover for offering such services. These can range from masturbation of the man ("hand relief") and oral sex to intercourse (usually with the insistence of using a condom).

Establishments known as brothels exist, usually a house with several rooms being used by women offering sexual services. Such brothels are usually run by a "madam." The equivalent on the street are girls working for a "pimp." Both the provider and organizer, as well as the user, can be charged with one or more of the above offenses. The policy of many police forces in the United Kingdom would be to caution a prostitute on a couple of occasions and advise her of support services to try and help her move away from using such activity as the route for financial gain. Often such persons need assistance in severing the link with their "pimp," to whom they may be in debt or exploited through addiction to drugs. Many of the punishments carry short custodial sentences as an option, although the vast majority are dealt with by fine. The average fine for curb crawlers in 1995 was £110. The exceptions are conviction of living on the earnings of prostitution or exercising control over a prostitute, where a custodial sentence is much commoner. However, cases cannot be brought on the uncorroborated word of a prostitute or solely on police evidence.

Soliciting by a man is an offense usually dealt with by the courts by a fine, if indicted. There is increasing awareness of male prostitution, particularly in the capital city. Such men are called "call boys" and many offer their services to visiting businessmen in hotels. This is an area where detection by the police is very low. Low levels of reporting occur and usually the police are only aware as a con-

sequence of robbery or associated assault. Of the 124 cases proceeded against in 1994, 89 were found guilty.

It is generally felt that the tolerance towards prostitution in England and Wales is fairly high, provided that such occurs in private. Much of the action of the police is in an attempt to appease complaining residents. An interesting development in the United Kingdom has been the call by the Inland Revenue for disclosure of such income by prostitutes for payment of Income Tax.

In mid-1996, the Government-controlled telephone company, British Telecom, joined Westminster, London's largest borough, in a crackdown on prostitutes who paste sexually explicit business cards advertising their services on the 700 bright red phone kiosks available to the public on the streets. After using computers to locate the offending prostitutes, telephone inspectors notify them they have one week to cease their postings. If the postings continue, the telephone company blocks their incoming calls. In announcing their effort, authorities said their objection "is not with prostitution as such, but with the people who illegally litter and deface the city's streets with this offensive and often pornographic advertising material." School teachers had complained that schoolchildren have been found collecting and trading the cards, many of which are illustrated.

In early 1996, British Telecom and Westminster sanitation teams, starting as early as 6 A.M. each day, removed 150,000 cards a week, 1.1 million such cards in an eight-week period; an estimated seven million cards are removed in a year. "Vice-carders," mostly young men hired by a half dozen prostitutes to post their cards, follow the sanitation teams, creating a no-win situation.

In 1991, the last time Westminster officials tried a similar scheme, Oftel, the Government telecommunications-regulating authority, said that blocking incoming calls was a violation of advertisers' rights. Before the current campaign, British Telecom changed its contract for all its customers, stipulating that they cannot advertise their telephone number in public phone kiosks. Whatever the success this effort has in controlling this advertising, it will not stop prostitutes from advertising their sexual services. Prostitution is legal in Britain, and so sex workers will continue advertising in other outlets, such as community newspapers. (See the discussion of *pikku bira* in Section 8B of the chapter on Japan.)

[*Update 2001*: A redefinition of terms such as *prostitution* was part of the U.K. government consultation paper to change the sex laws in Britain. The document, *Setting the Boundaries*, suggests consideration be given to the regulation of soliciting by men for the purposes of prostitution under Section 1 of the Street Offences Act 1959 on the same basis as soliciting by women. It also recommended that a specific trafficking offense with powers to trace assets overseas be introduced. Offenses regarding commercial sexual exploitation of children will be listed. It also recommended a new offense for the sexual exploitation of adults to include an offense for anybody in England and Wales who recruits people for sex work anywhere in the world. (*End of update by K. R. Wylie*)]

**E. Pornography and Erotica**   KEVAN R. WYLIE

There has been a general relaxation within England and Wales over erotica and nudity when displayed within newspapers and on television. There has been a trend away from the "page 3" bare-breasted girl in the tabloid press, in part fueled by complaints from feminists, but also because of increased availability of such material elsewhere. Hard pornography cannot be shown on British television, nor can scenes of an erect penis or bondage. Among European nations, only Ireland appears stricter than the United Kingdom, with no nudity or pubic hair permitted.

Despite such liberalism, there remains tight enforcement against many forms of pornographic material. Possession of adult pornography does not in itself constitute an offense. However, possessing obscene material for gain, whether that be to lend, publish, or display, would constitute an offense under the Obscene Publications Act 1959/1964. The law explicitly forbids pornography involving minors and extends to taking indecent photographs of children (Protection of Children Act 1978). The sentence on conviction is three years imprisonment. Possession of photographs of child pornography carries punishment usually by fine (but six months custodial sentence is possible), and associated investigation may ensue for possible child sexual abuse and of pedophilia. A proactive measure against pedophilia exists whereby photographic developers are requested to inform the police when they notice suspicious photographs of young children. The increasing incidence of transfer of pornographic material using personal computers over the Internet has led to rising concern. However a group, Parents Against Injustice (PAIN), campaigns against overzealous misinterpretation of innocent family photographs of children bathing, running in the garden naked, or being bounced on grandfather's knee. The fact is that photographs can be very subjective.

Many book classics were banned under the Obscene Publications Act, and the infamous 1960 obscenity trial prevented copies of *Lady Chatterley's Lover* and *Queen Mab*, first published in 1829, from home ownership. Daniel Defoe was one of the earliest English authors to include superpermissive parent figures, incestuous relationships, and lower-class characters who were all sexually uninhibited, passionate, and with responsive female characters. The links between poverty and exploitation and between sexual attitudes and cultural practice have been noted many times over. However, pornography has certainly moved more from the "peep shows" and cinemas to the home, with the increasing numbers of videotapes displaying such material.

Pornographic videotapes are now obtainable through mail order, both within the United Kingdom and from Europe. Self-help videos, like *The Lover's Guide*, had sold 1.3 million copies by late 1995. Although explicit, they are considered educational and have a license. The importation of obscene pornography, however, constitutes a criminal offense, although it is acknowledged that it occurs in considerable volume, given relaxed cross-country border controls within Europe. Political action was taken in 1993 to prevent satellite programming of pornographic material from Red Hot Dutch into the United Kingdom. This involved making it an offense to sell "smart cards" or advertise and publish information about the service. A similar course of action was taken in 1995 to ban the Swedish channel TV Erotica. The 1990 Broadcasting Act forbids programs that might "seriously impair the physical, mental or moral development of minors."

The United Kingdom now has three subscription-pay-TV adult soft-porn channels, Adult Channel, Television X, and Playboy TV, all of which operate in a scrambled form at nighttime. There are approximately 100,000 subscribers. The Church of England and Methodist Church have sold their shares in the BSkyB company because of this new venture.

[*Update 2001*: Recent court rulings have introduced a "Restricted 18" or R18 certification for explicit-sexual-act videotapes which are on sale only in the U.K. through official sex shops. In 2000, the High Court ruled that "extremely explicit" videos could go on sale in licensed sex shops, and dismissed a challenge by the British Board of Film Classification against the decision of its own Video Appeals Committee (VAC). The VAC was established by Parliament in 1984 to rule on appeals from firms that feel they have been harshly treated by the British Board of Film Classification. The Home Secretary (Home Office) responded by stating that ways of protection of children from exposure to sexually explicit material was under consideration. The British Board of Film Classification Guidelines reads as follows:

'R18'—TO BE SUPPLIED ONLY IN LICENSED SEX SHOPS TO PERSONS OF NOT LESS THAN 18 YEARS

The 'R18' category is a special and legally restricted classification for videos where the focus is mainly on real sexual activity and the purpose is primarily to induce sexual arousal. Such videos may be supplied to adults only in licensed sex shops, of which there are only about 60 in the UK. 'R18' videos may not be supplied by mail order.

The sex scenes in all 'R18' videos must be non-violent and between consenting adults. They must also be legal, both in the acts portrayed and in the degree of explicitness shown. There are no limits on length and strength apart from those of the criminal law. Group sex is allowed and, insofar as the law permits, there is parity as between homosexual and heterosexual sex.

Erections may be shown, as may a broader range of mild fetish material, but no threats of humiliation or realistic depictions of pain are permitted.

There must be no clear sight of penetration, oral, vaginal or anal, or of masturbation.

Ejaculation must not be shown.

Context may justify exceptions.

[(*End of update by K. R. Wylie*)]

## 9. Contraception, Abortion, and Population Planning

### A. Contraception Attitudes and Use

FRAN READER [*Rewritten and updated in late 2001 by F. Reader*]

Contraception is widely accepted, although there remains considerable variance between knowledge about and actual use of contraception. There is a constant trend towards a more open discussion about contraception and sexuality that has been accelerated by the arrival of HIV and AIDS.

The Education Reform Act of 1988 places a statutory responsibility on schools to provide a broad and balanced curriculum that "promotes a spiritual, moral, cultural, mental, and physical development of pupils at the school and in society," and which "prepares pupils for the opportunities, responsibilities, and experiences of adult life." This philosophy forms the basis of Personal and Social Education (PSE), which is a theme running throughout a child's life at school. Sex education is part of the wider topic of health education. Health education is not a mandatory foundation subject, but it is expected to be a theme that is incorporated across the whole curriculum. School governors have the responsibility to decide whether and/or what sex education should be taught. Parents have the right to withdraw their children from the PSE aspect of sex education, but not from the biological science aspects of the National Curriculum, which provide information about human sexual behavior and sexually transmitted infections, including HIV and AIDS. In Scotland, there is no legislation regarding the teaching of sex education in schools. Each Local Authority decides or delegates the decision to the individual school, and the curriculum guidelines define sexuality and relationships as an important area of health education. In Northern Ireland, heath education is given as one of six mandatory cross-curricula themes in the Education Reform Order of 1989. Sex education is not specifically mentioned, but it is widely expected to form a major component of health education.

The age of consent for heterosexual sexual activity is 16 in England, Wales, and Scotland, and 17 in Northern Ireland. Doctors may prescribe contraception to those under 16 years old. The present legislation in England and Wales follows the House of Lords Ruling in the Gillick case of 1985. In that case, the Lords ruled that "a girl under 16 of sufficient understanding and intelligence may have the legal capacity to give valid consent to contraceptive advice and treatment including necessary medical examination." In Scotland, the Age of Legal Capacity Act came into force in September 1991, bringing Scotland in line with England and Wales. In Northern Ireland, a similar legal situation exists, except the age of consent for medical advice is 17.

In 1993, the Conservative Government launched a *Health of the Nation* initiative. Sexual Health was one of the key sections, with one of the targets being to halve the rate of unplanned pregnancy in under-18-year-olds by the year 2000. This did not happen. The present New Labour Government has therefore established a Teenage Pregnancy Unit to research the reasons for unplanned teenage pregnancy and establish strategies that will tackle the problem effectively. This forms part of a wider Government initiative to address the causes of social exclusion. A Sexual Health Strategy document was anticipated in the autumn of 2000.

Since 1974, all contraceptive advice provided by the National Health Services, and all prescribed supplies, were made available free of charge, irrespective of age and marital status. In the United Kingdom, most contraceptive services are provided by either general practitioners (GPs) or by Community and Hospital Clinics. Community and Hospital Family Planning Clinics have always been able to supply condoms free of charge. This has not been available to GPs, although some medical practices now offer this service. Government policy supports the dual provision and choice to maximize the use of services; however, there has been a marked reduction in the number of Community Family Planning Clinics with a shift to GP providers. Since 1990, new contractual arrangements were introduced for GPs that affected their fees and allowances, encouraging a greater emphasis on Health Promotion. This system has continued to shift contraceptive care to general practice. The Community Family Planning Clinics have, therefore, looked to complement GP services, and specifically target teenagers and vulnerable groups that may have problems in accessing care from GPs.

Community Clinics, backed up by specialist contraceptive clinics in hospitals, also tend to provide a wider range of contraceptive methods than are available from GPs. Snowdens' research in 1985 showed that only 55% of the women using Family Planning Clinics were prescribed the pill as opposed to 84% of GP patients. This trend has continued. Community Clinics, therefore, remain a service of choice for those women wishing to use the less-common methods of contraception, and they remain the main source of training for physicians and nurses.

Contraception is now recognized as a part of core training for all GPs, obstetricians and gynecologists, and specialists in genitourinary medicine. Specialists in the field undergo training with the Faculty of Family Planning and Reproductive Health Care, which is part of the Royal College of Obstetricians and Gynaecologists. Initial training is recognized as

the Diploma of the Faculty of Family Planning (DFFP) and the specialist training as Membership (MFFP). The Faculty also aims to maintain standards for various skills by awarding letters of competence to practitioners who have completed training in techniques of fitting intrauterine devices or implants. The Faculty has also introduced a process of five-year recertification for all its certificates.

Since the *Health of the Nation* initiative, there has been an increasing shift to integrate the community and hospital contraceptive services with community and hospital services for sexually transmitted infections (STIs/STDs). Doctors and nurses initially trained in one or the other discipline are entering into programs of combined training, or at least improving their appreciation and understanding of the other discipline. The integration of family planning and sexual health is providing a "one stop shop" approach to the management of all potential problems arising from sexual activity. It is now common practice to be advised to use contraception to prevent unplanned pregnancy backed up by either the male or female condom for the prevention of sexually transmitted infections.

Contraceptive methods currently available in the United Kingdom are combination oral contraception, progesterone-only pills, long-acting injectable progestogens, a three-year etonogestrel implant, an intrauterine system with Levonorgestrel (IUS), copper intrauterine devices (IUD), including GyneFix, male and female condoms, diaphragms and cervical caps, natural family planning, including Persona, and male and female sterilization. The 1997 statistics for Great Britain show that the combined oral contraceptive pill is still the most common method of contraception used by women under 30. In total, it is used by 26% of women between the ages of 16 and 49. Conversely, sterilization is the most common method used over the age of 30, with male and female sterilization being equally represented. In total, 21% of 16- to 49-year-olds use sterilization as their method. Condom usage has increased in recent years, and with this, there has been a decrease in the use of oral contraceptives. The use of combined oral contraception always fluctuates, tending to fall after media-publicized concern about safety. In October 1995, the Committee on Safety of Medicines (CSM) raised concern about pills containing the progestogens, desogestrel and gestodene, and an increased risk of venous thrombosis. As with similar pill scares in the past, this generated a fall in the uptake of the combined pill, and may have been responsible for the rise in the abortion rate seen across all age groups.

Methods of contraception introduced over the past 10 years include the female condom (Femidom), introduced in 1992. So far, this method has not caught on, and the male condom maintains dominance as the most popular barrier method. The five-year capsule Levonorgestrel implant (Norplant) was introduced in 1993 and withdrawn in 1999, to be replaced by a single rod etonogestrel implant (Implanon). An intrauterine system (IUS) with Levonorgestrel (Mirena) was introduced into the United Kingdom in 1995 and now has a five-year license. This new method has been widely accepted in the United Kingdom, particularly for the management of contraception in older women as an alternative to female sterilization. The Personal Contraceptive System for the electronic prediction of the fertile phase (Persona) was introduced in 1996. It is not available on the NHS and has not proved to be as successful as was anticipated. It is mostly used by women looking to space pregnancies. In 1998, the fixed, frameless, and flexible intrauterine device (GyneFix) was introduced. A training program is underway to teach doctors the new fitting technique. The copper IUD, Gyne T 380, with a 10-year license, became unavailable in the U.K.

at the end of 1999 following its withdrawal by the manufacturer for commercial reasons. This was considered a retrograde step by family planning specialists in the U.K., who saw this device as the gold standard IUD. It is hoped that a similar device will be reintroduced, but in the meantime, the introduction of the Nova T 380 IUD has been welcomed as an alternative, although it only has a 5-year license at present, and is currently not available to GPs on their drug tariff.

Emergency contraception with both the hormonal and IUD method are widely available within the United Kingdom through general practitioners, community clinics, sexually transmitted disease (STD) clinics, and accident and emergency departments. In 2000, the progesterone-only emergency contraceptive (POEC) method was licensed and marketed as Levonelle 2. The concept of advance-prescribing of POEC is gaining favor, and there is an expectation that it will become an over-the-counter (OTC) medicine in the near future.

## B. Teenage (Unmarried) Pregnancy

MARY GRIFFIN

United Kingdom data specifically relating to unmarried teenagers are scarce. Official statistics have been collected by separate organizations in England and Wales, Scotland, and Northern Ireland, but uniform data have not been gathered for the three groupings. The information given in this section is mainly for England and Wales, with a little, where available, on Scotland and Northern Ireland.

The trend in the United Kingdom is increasingly towards teenage mothers not marrying (Family Planning Association 1994). Some prefer to cohabit with their partner, since there is little stigma attached to this, although many maintain a single-parent lifestyle. Indeed, it can be advantageous for teenagers not to marry in terms of welfare benefits and housing, although cohabiting teenage mothers do have the highest rate of reported homelessness (18%), according to recent research from the *National Child Development Survey* (Joseph Rowntree Foundation 1995). The trend away from marriage is reflected in the outcome of conceptions in England and Wales for 1992 for all women under 20, the total number being 93,000, of which 8,300 were conceptions inside marriage. Of the 84,700 conceptions outside of marriage, 37% were legally aborted, 58% led to maternity outside of marriage, and only 5% to maternity inside marriage (OPCS 1992). Looking at live births for 16- to 19-year-olds in England and Wales, in 1983, 56.3% were registered outside of marriage, but this had increased to 87.8% by 1993 (OPCS). In Scotland, for the 15-to-19 age group, the percentages rose from 54.5% in 1984 to 89.3% in 1994 (General Register Office for Scotland). Even in Northern Ireland, which tends to be more conservative and a few years behind social trends on the mainland, single parents are no longer a rarity and are increasingly accepted without social stigma.

While 16 years is legally the lowest age for marriage in the United Kingdom, parental consent is required up to the age of 18 in England, Wales, and Northern Ireland, but not in Scotland. In the first three regions, written consent of both parents is required, even if they are estranged, so that some teenagers wishing to marry may not be able to do so before the birth of the baby if this legal requirement cannot be fulfilled.

Looking at trends over the last two decades, the introduction of free contraception in 1974 led to a decline in teenage pregnancy rates. In 1973, the total conception rate per 1,000 teenagers in England and Wales was 9.2 for 13- to 15-year-olds (and therefore unmarried) and 75.2 for 15- to 19-year-olds (marital status unspecified). Ten years later,

the rates were 8.3 and 56.0, respectively, of which just over half were terminated for the 13-to-15 age group and a third for the 15-to-19 age group. Thereafter, rates increased until a peak in 1990 (10.1 for the 13-to-15 group, with half legally terminated, and 69.0 for the 15- to 19-year-olds, with just under a third terminated) (OPCS). The peak came a year later in Scotland, but there was no particular trend in Northern Ireland.

Several factors probably contributed to this phenomenon. Firstly, the Gillick case, which eventually concluded in 1985 in favor of young people's rights, caused a great deal of confusion over teenagers' access to confidential help and advice, and anxieties still persist (Wareham & Drummond 1994), despite the joint statement referred to by Mrs. Gillick in a letter to the *British Medical Journal* (Gillick 1994). Secondly, the onset of economic recession led to a decline in young people's job opportunities. A third contributory factor was cuts in family planning clinics, thereby restricting access to services (Brook Advisory Centres 1995). The Government's concern over the rise in teenage pregnancies led to teenage sexual health being identified as one of the key areas targeted for action in their policy document, *Health of the Nation* (Department of Health 1992)—a specific aim being to reduce the 1989 conception rate in under-16-year-olds by at least 50% by the year 2000. Rates are already falling again and teenagers are far less likely to have a baby today than 25 years ago.

In England and Wales, the total conception rate per 1,000 for 13- to 15-year-olds in 1993 was 8.1 (with 50% legally terminated) and for 15- to 19-year-olds, 59.6 with just over one third terminated. In Northern Ireland, the total number of live births to under-15-year-olds for 1990 to 1993 inclusive ranged between 4 to 7, but rose to 11 in 1994. Total live births to 15- to 19-year-olds (marital status unspecified) rose to 1,856 in 1992, but has since fallen to 1,486 in 1994 (General Register Office for Northern Ireland). Since Northern Ireland is not as liberal towards abortion as the other three countries, some pregnant teenagers go to the larger cities on the mainland to obtain abortions. Legally, the situation with regard to abortion in Northern Ireland is a very gray area, and those involved in women's health and welfare agencies are aware that doctors there are increasingly prepared to widen grounds for justifying therapeutic abortion in the interests of a teenager's physical or mental health. This trend may be reflected in the statistics, though official figures for terminations were unavailable because of the legal situation.

With regard to the social background of young parents, longitudinal data from the *National Child Development Survey* show that half the teenage mothers who were single when their babies were born went on to cohabit with or marry the father. The study found no significant differences in childhood factors between young parents whose babies were born within marriage and those who were single or cohabiting when they gave birth. The data also suggested that the predisposition to have a child when young was independent of any thoughts about marriage, cohabitation, or single parenthood. Sixty-seven percent of those married at the time of conception had planned the pregnancy, compared with 26% of those cohabiting, 17% who married during pregnancy, and 8% who had no live-in relationship before birth (summarized by Joseph Rowntree Foundation 1995).

Despite the expansion of services and increased provision of information for teenagers in the United Kingdom since *Health of the Nation*, it seems that risk-taking behavior, failure to anticipate risk, lack of knowledge, and errors in the use of contraception are still major causes of unwanted teenage pregnancies (Lo et al. 1994; Pearson et al. 1995; Wareham & Drummond 1994).

[*Summary and Update 2001*: Within Western Europe, the United Kingdom has the highest rate of teenage births. However, data specifically relating to unmarried teenagers are scarce. As noted above, the trend in the U.K. is increasing toward teenage mothers not marrying (Family Planning Association 1994). Some prefer to cohabit with their partner. Many maintain a single-parent lifestyle, although there is still stigma attached to this. Indeed, it can be advantageous for teenagers not to marry in terms of welfare benefits and housing, although cohabiting teenage mothers have the highest rate of reported homelessness, with 18% recorded in the *National Child Development Survey* (Joseph Rowntree Foundation 1995). Even in Northern Ireland, which tends to be more conservative and a few years behind social trends on the mainland, single parents are no longer a rarity and are increasingly accepted without social stigma. While 16 years is legally the lowest age for marriage in the United Kingdom, parental consent is required up to the age of 18 in England, Wales, and Northern Ireland, but not in Scotland. In the first three regions, written consent of both parents is required, even if they are estranged, so that some teenagers wishing to marry may not be able to do so before the birth of their baby if this legal requirement cannot be fulfilled.

[Looking at trends over the last three decades, the introduction of free contraception in 1974 led to a decline in the pregnancy rate. In 1973, the total conception rate per 1,000 teenagers in England and Wales was 9.2 for 13- to 15-year-olds (and therefore unmarried), and 75.2 for 15- to 19-year-olds (marital status unspecified). Ten years later, the rates were 8.3 and 56.0, respectively, all of which, just over half, were terminated for the 13-to-15 age group and a third for the 15-to-19 age group. Thereafter, rates increased until a peak in 1990 (OPCS). Several factors probably contributed to this phenomenon. First, the Gillick case, which eventually concluded in 1985 in favor of young people's rights, caused a great deal of confusion and anger over teenagers' access to confidential help and advice, and anxieties still persist despite the joint statement referred to by Mrs. Gillick in a letter to the *British Medical Journal* (Gillick 1994). Second, the onset of economic recession led to a decline in young people's job opportunities. A third contributory factor was cuts in family planning clinics, thereby restricting access to services (Brook Advisory Centres 1995).

[With regard to abortion, since Northern Ireland is not as liberal as the other three countries, some pregnant teenagers go to the larger cities on the mainland to obtain abortions. Legally, the situation with regard to abortion in Northern Ireland is a very grey area, and those involved in women's health and welfare agencies are aware that doctors are increasingly prepared to widen grounds for justifying therapeutic abortion in the interests of a teenager's physical or mental health. This trend may be reflected in the statistics, though official figures for terminations were unavailable because of the legal situation. Currently in England, just over half of all teenage pregnancies are terminated, and this ratio has changed little since the mid 1970s. Over a third of conceptions to women in their 20s are terminated, with the figure rising (ONS1998). Pregnant teenagers are one-and-a-half times more likely than women in their 20s to have an abortion at 13 weeks or later (ONS 1997).

[The government's concern over the rise in teenage pregnancies through the 1980s led to teenage sexual health being identified as one of the key areas targeted for action in their policy document, *Health of the Nation* (Department of Health 1992). A specific aim of the new policy was to reduce the 1989 conception rate in under-16-year-olds by at least 50% by the year 2000. However, the target was not met and U.K. rates have stuck at around 25 live births per 1,000 women aged 15 to 19. Rates for Scotland, Northern Ireland, and England have tended to be similar, but Wales has a higher rate, as have certain areas in England.

[The following information is mainly for England, and based on the Report in 1999 of the Social Exclusion Unit (SEU) on Teenage Pregnancy (Cm 4342), in response to a remit from the Prime Minister to develop an integrated strategy to reduce rates of teenage parenthood and propose solutions to combat the risk of social exclusion for vulnerable teenage parents and their children. The newly developed administrations for Scotland, Wales, and Northern Ireland, and their Government Offices, are also considering what action set out in the Report could be applied in the light of the particular circumstances present in each country.

[The report highlighted the following facts:

- There are nearly 90,000 conceptions a year to teenagers, of which approximately 7,700 are to under-16-year-olds and 2,200 to girls aged 14 or under, with 56,000 conceptions resulting in live births. However, more than two thirds of girls under 16 do not have sex, and most reach their 20s without getting pregnant.
- Teenage parenthood is more common in areas of deprivation and poverty and for those with poor educational attainment, but even in the most prosperous areas, teenage births are higher than in some comparable European countries.
- Half of those sexually active at the time they are 16 do not use contraception for the first time, and for a significant group, sex is forced or unwanted.
- Half of under-16s and more than a third of 16- and 17-year-olds opt for abortion if they get pregnant. This totals just over 15,000 abortions a year for girls under age 18.
- Ninety percent of teenage mothers have babies outside marriage (20 years ago, it was around 40%).
- Fifty percent of relationships started in the teenage years break down.
- The death rate for the babies of teenage mothers is 60% higher than those of older mothers, and these babies are more likely to be of low birthweight, have childhood accidents, and be admitted to the hospital.
- The daughters of teenage mothers have a higher chance of becoming teenage mothers themselves.

[Although the Social Exclusion Unit (SEU) on Teenage Pregnancy could not identify a single explanation for the U.K.'s relative failure to reduce teenage birthrates, they drew attention to three important factors: namely low expectations of young people disadvantaged in childhood and with little prospect of a job; ignorance about contraception, what to expect in relationships, and what it means to be a parent; and "mixed messages," with one part of the adult world bombarding teenagers with explicit messages that sexual activity is the norm and another part that is embarrassed by any mention of sex and more often silent about it, hoping that if sex is not talked about, it won't happen. In studying the phenomenon of social exclusion, the Unit identified certain risk factors for teenage parenthood—namely poverty, children who had been in foster care, children of teenage mothers, those with educational problems or not continuing in education after 16, those who had been sexually abused in childhood, mental health problems, and crime. It has been estimated that 24% of the 11,000 prisoners in Young Offenders Institutions are fathers (HMIP 1977). The unit suggests that multiple risk factors may explain the overrepresentation of some ethnic minorities among teenage parents. Information from the *Labour Force Surveys* (1985-1995), the *Fourth National Survey of Ethnic Minorities* (1994), and the *Health and Lifestyle Surveys* (1994) show that four groups in particular—Bangladeshis, Africans, Caribbeans, and Pakistanis—are all at substantially greater risk of teenage parenthood than the national average. The Unit's analysis highlighted two main goals—reducing the rate of teenage conceptions, with a specific aim of halving the rate of conceptions among under-18-year-olds by the year 2010, and getting more teenage parents into education, training, or employment to reduce their risk of long-term social exclusion. The action plan for achieving these goals is quoted below:

- A national campaign involving government media, the voluntary sector, and others to improve understanding and change behavior.
- Collaborative action with new mechanisms to coordinate action at both the national and local levels and ensure that the strategy is on track (until now, there has not been an agency or individual prepared to take responsibility for tackling the problem as a whole).
- Better prevention of the causes of teenage pregnancy, including better education in and out of school, access to contraception, and targeting of at-risk groups, with a new focus on reaching young men . . ., who have often been overlooked in past attempts to tackle this issue.
- Better support for pregnant teenagers and teenage parents, with a new focus on returning to education with childcare to help, working to a position where no under-18 single parent is put in a lone tenancy, and pilot programs around the country providing intensive support for parents and child.

[The report recommends the implementation of a 10-year program to improve the climate in which young people prepare for adulthood and the support for teenage parents and their children. Funding some £60 million over the following three years is envisaged. A new unit in the Department of Health to coordinate the work has been set up. However, despite the expansion of services and increased provision of information for teenagers in the U.K. since *Health of the Nation*, recent studies, such as *Effective Health Care—Preventing and Reducing Adverse Effects for Unintended Teenage Pregnancies* (1997), and *Teenage Mothers—Decisions and Outcomes* (1998), indicate that risk-taking behavior, failure to anticipate risk, lack of knowledge, and errors in the use of contraception, remain major causes of unwanted pregnancies. It remains to be seen whether the changes called for in the *Report*—"fewer unwanted pregnancies, fewer children brought up in poverty, and successive generations of children and young people having better chances for the future" are achievable. (*End of update by M. Griffin*)]

[*Update 2003*: In an attempt to reduce the high rates of teenage pregnancy, the U.K. Departments of Health and Education have backed Exeter University in training teachers to discuss various pre-sex "stopping points" with teenagers under age 16 and encouraging them to discover "levels of intimacy," including holding hands and oral sex, instead of full sexual intercourse. Early in 2003, more than 100,000 children were taking the course at one in every 30 secondary schools.

[Critics of the course, called "A Pause," objected that the program has no framework for talking about responsibility or the emotional side of relationships and, in effect, implicitly supports underage sexual activity and excites the sexual interest of children.

[Opponents of the program expressed hope that the Sexual Offenses Bill, then going through the House of Lords, would lead to the course being banned. A provision in the Bill would make it an offense for anyone to "arrange or facilitate the commission of a child sex offence" (Owen 2003). (*End of update by R. T. Francoeur*)]

## C. Abortion     JANE READ and LINDA DELANEY

### Legal Status and Availability

Until 1967, most pregnancies could not lawfully be terminated by abortion. The Offences Against the Person Act of 1861 specifically criminalized both successful and unsuccessful abortion attempts by those who assisted women and by pregnant women themselves (curiously, the former, but not the latter, could be convicted, even if there was found to be no pregnancy). However, as prosecutions under the 1861 Act had to establish that the accused acted "unlawfully," it became possible to defend a criminal charge by showing that the abortion was carried out in the honest belief, based on reasonable grounds and adequate knowledge, that the continuance of the pregnancy would turn the woman into "a physical or mental wreck"; this was the outcome of the famous case of R. vs. Bourne (1939-1KB 687), brought after an eminent surgeon performed an abortion on a 14-year-old who had been raped and whose mental well-being was said to have been gravely threatened by the resulting pregnancy.

In 1967, Parliament provided statutory defenses by passing the Abortion Act. Substantially amended by the Human Fertilization and Embryology Act of 1990, the Abortion Act of 1967 permits abortion on liberal therapeutic and eugenic grounds if two registered medical practitioners—one would suffice in an emergency—certify the existence of such a ground, and the abortion is carried out by a registered medical practitioner. In brief, the amended law allows abortion when it is performed to prevent grave permanent injury to the mental or physical health of the woman, or risk to her life, or the birth of a "seriously handicapped" child. For these three situations, there is no time limit; in other cases, the limit is the end of the 24th week of pregnancy.

An important change in the 1967 Act resulting from enactment of the Human Fertility and Embryology Act 1990 is the severance of the link that applied previously with the Infant Life (Preservation) Act 1929. The effect of this has been, paradoxically, a slight liberalization of the Abortion Act as it was between 1967 and 1990. Prior to 1990, women could not, under any circumstance, have their pregnancy terminated after the 28th week of pregnancy, since, under the Infant Life (Preservation) Act of 1929, this was considered to be the point at which a fetus became viable. Although Clause (a) (given below) states a limit of 24 weeks of pregnancy, there is no mention of a time limit for the other three clauses. In effect, the situation in England and Wales is that abortion is rarely done after 22 weeks of pregnancy. Essentially, any woman who is considering a decision to terminate her pregnancy, whether as a result of her social, economic, personal, family, or medical circumstances, must have the consent of two medical practitioners before the abortion may be performed.

The clauses in the Abortion Act 1967, as amended by the HFE Act 1990, under which she can do this and to which the two doctors must conform are as follows:

1. that the pregnancy has not exceeded its 24th week and that the continuance of the pregnancy would involve risk to the life of the pregnant woman, or of injury to the physical or mental health of the pregnant woman or any existing children of her family, greater than if the pregnancy were terminated; or

2. that the termination is necessary to prevent grave permanent injury to the physical or mental health of the pregnant woman; or

3. that the continuance of the pregnancy would involve risk to the life of the pregnant woman, greater than if the pregnancy were terminated; or

4. that there is a substantial risk that if the child were born it would suffer from such physical or mental abnormalities as to be seriously handicapped. (The Abortion Act 1967 as amended, HMSO)

Thus, it is clear that the procedures for a woman to have a legal termination of her pregnancy are grounded not only in the medical aspects, but are based on the need to adhere to the law of abortion. When a woman presents for consideration of an abortion, therefore, she is entering a legal process.

There is no requirement on the part of Health Authorities to provide abortion services, and abortion provision is not consistent across the country. In some areas, the service may be relatively available through the Health Service, and in other areas, there will be little provision, and women will either have to pay for a legal termination in the private sector or nonprofit charity sector, as well as possibly having to travel some distance to get to a private clinic.

### Social Attitudes Toward Abortion

There is evidence that attitudes toward abortion and provision of abortion have liberalized over the past 10 to 15 years. In a fact sheet on the legal and ethical issues surrounding abortion, the Family Planning Association quotes the *British Social Attitudes Survey*, in which it was shown that the number of United Kingdom people who felt abortion should be allowed when a woman's health was endangered increased from 87% in 1983 to 95% in 1989. This trend was consistent when other questions, such as the economic situation of the woman and her family, and the woman's own choice, were considered (FPA *Factsheet 6B* 1992, 4).

This trend is also reflected in the medical profession. "A national survey of consultant gynecologists in 1989 found that 73% believed that a woman should have the right to choose abortion" (Paintin 1992, 968). This same survey, carried out by Savage and Francome, also showed that 87% of gynecologists at the Royal College of Obstetricians and Gynaecologists had been right to oppose one of the more recent changes to the Abortion Act, the Alton Bill. There seems to be a general understanding that people feel that the current system works quite well.

### Incidence

The latest available figures (Office of Population Census and Surveys *Monitor* April 11, 1995) show that during 1993, a total of 168,711 abortions were performed in England and Wales, 2% fewer than in 1992, when the total was 172,063. The 1992 total figure included both the resident and nonresident figures, with 160,495 resident women obtaining abortions and the remainder being accounted for mainly by Irish women seeking an abortion abroad, since it is not legal in the Republic of Ireland. The 1992 TOP (terminations of pregnancy) rate for residents of the United Kingdom was 12.51 per 1,000 women.

The reason most frequently cited by women seeking an abortion was risk of injury to the physical and mental health of the pregnant woman. The main provider was the National Health Service. Section 4 of the Abortion Act of 1967 affords legal protection to healthcare workers who refuse to participate in abortion on grounds of conscience. Prospective fathers, on the other hand, were, in *Paton vs. Trustees of*

*BPAC* (1979—QB 276), denied the right to intervene to prevent an abortion.

There has been little change in the proportion of women seeking abortion since the introduction of the 1967 Abortion Act. In a 1992 article in the *British Medical Journal*, David Paintin, then a Research Fellow at St. Mary's Hospital, London, observed that: "The lack of change in the proportion of pregnancies ending in legal abortion suggests that the behavior factors that lead to unwanted conception and abortion are intrinsic to our society and that easy availability is not a primary factor in the decision concerning abortion" (Paintin 1992, 967). This is an important point, since those who oppose abortion seem to believe that should abortion become more "freely" available, there would be a marked increase in the number of women who choose legal abortion, and that any "loosening" of the restrictions that pertain to abortion in England and Wales should therefore be opposed. In England and Wales, in 1991, the vast majority of legal abortions—88%—were performed before the 13th week of pregnancy (Family Planning Association *Factsheet 6A* 1994, Table 6, 7).

## D. Population Planning Programs and Policies

PETER SELMAN

"No population policy please, we're British!" (Coleman & Salt 1992).

Despite the fact that birthrates in the United Kingdom have been falling since the late 19th century, and the fertility rate has dropped below replacement level (namely, a Net Reproduction Rate below 1.00), between 1927 and 1943 and since 1973, the population of the United Kingdom has grown steadily, with a reduction in size evident only in the late 1970s, when the population fell from 55,922,000 in 1974-1975 to 55,835,000 in 1978-1979. Since then, the population has increased steadily to 58 million in 1992. Experts project the population of the United Kingdom will surpass 62 million by the year 2031, after which a steady decline is expected, with the population returning to the 1992 level by the year 2061 (OPCS 1994).

The initial fall in the birthrate occurred, as in most countries, without any government pressure and in the face of opposition to birth control. In England and Wales, the period total fertility rate fell from 4.8 in the 1870s to a low point of 1.72 in 1933 (OPCS 1987). It was at this stage that we find the first signs of concern over population decline, as birthrates fell to below replacement level, and differences in fertility became apparent as middle-class groups married late and had few children while lower-working-class people had a substantially higher fertility. This led to concern about the quality of the population and to the development of the eugenics movement. A number of publications warned of the dangers of depopulation (Charles 1936; Glass 1936; Hogben 1938), a national decline (Reddawa 1939), "race suicide" (McCleary 1943), and a rejection of parenthood (Titmuss 1942). Charles (1938) projected the British population for 1995 at 20 million, a little more than a third of the actual population today.

In 1944, a Royal Commission on Population was set up to consider whether Britain was indeed facing a population decline and whether measures should be taken "in the national interest" to influence future trends. The Royal Commission reported in June 1949, soon after the 1947 crude birthrate was announced as 20.5, the highest figure since the end of World War I, and the net reproduction rate (NRR) had risen to 1.21. The commission saw this as a temporary aberration and projected a long-term decline in population. The Commission did not, however, recommend any counter action and no official population policy followed. Others were less sanguine (McCleary 1943; Titmuss 1942); in the same year, Eva Hubback (1947) projected the 1999 British population at 34 million.

No one predicted that within a decade the birthrate would be rising sharply to the highest level since the end of World War I (Holmans 1963). Nor was there any expectation that migration would play a role in boosting population growth: "The Royal Commission never dreamt that 2.5 million colored immigrants and their descendants would be living in Britain just thirty years after their report" (Coleman & Salt 1992). Restrictions on Commonwealth immigration were introduced in the early 1960s and have since been maintained by both political parties. However, these policies are more because of racist concerns than to any fear of excess population. Nevertheless, it is important to note that, without such immigration and the consequent births to immigrants and their descendants, Britain's population would by now most certainly be in decline.

By 1964, the crude birthrate had risen to 18.5 and the total fertility rate to 2.93 (0PCS 1987), and in 1965 the General Register Office projected a population for England and Wales in 2001 of over 66 million. This led to new concerns about overpopulation. In 1971, a Population Panel was appointed following the publication in that year of a *White Paper* responding to a report from the House of Commons Select Committee on Science and Technology on the Population of the United Kingdom, which had concluded that "the government must act to prevent the consequences of population growth becoming intolerable for the every day conditions of life."

The *Report of the Population Panel* was published in March 1973, by which time the birthrate had fallen substantially and the net reproduction rate was once again below 1.00. It concluded that the population of Great Britain would "almost certainly rise from 54 million in 1971 to around 64 million in the course of the first decade of the next century . . . [and to] over 80 million around the middle of the next century." If, however, fertility were to fall rapidly, population could decline to 40 million by 2050, and there would be "profound changes in the age structure" with serious social consequences. Reviewing the implications of anticipated growth, the Panel concluded that "there is no reason to suppose that 64 million (by the beginning of the 20th century) would be in any way intolerable or disastrous," but that "to absorb a further 20 million by 2051 could be much more intractable" so that "a slower rate of increase . . . is clearly preferable." Less attention was paid to the possibility of a population decline, other than to state that "if there were to be a fall in fertility which led . . . to an excess of deaths over births, this should not be a cause of public concern."

No explicit population policy was recommended, although the Government was advised to extend family planning services and inform people about the fact of the population problem. The panel was less happy about persuading people of the advantages of smaller families and opposed fiscal and other disincentives to having children. By 1977, the crude birthrate had fallen to 11.5 and the total fertility rate to 1.66, the lowest levels since records began, and any further measures to discourage parenthood were viewed as inappropriate.

Since then, the crude birthrate has risen again and has remained steady between 13 and 14 since 1985. In 1990, the total fertility was 1.8, below replacement level, but high in comparison with other European countries such as Italy (1.29) and Spain

(1.3). The population is, nevertheless, projected to grow until the second quarter of the 21st century (OPCS 1994). Concern is expressed over the implications of an aging population (Johnson & Falkingham 1992), but there is no overt policy to increase fertility, and recently, more concern has been focused on rising divorce rates, the decline in marriage, and the associated increase in childbearing outside marriage, especially among teenagers (Selman 1996).

Despite two substantial reports on population, the United Kingdom has never developed a population policy, which is probably just as well, given the wrong assumptions each report made about the future. Whether this will continue to be the case in the 21st century, if a significant population decline occurs alongside a more rapidly aging population, remains to be seen.

## 10. Sexually Transmitted Diseases and HIV/AIDS

### A. Sexually Transmitted Diseases

PETER GREENHOUSE

*Incidence, Patterns, and Trends*

The United Kingdom's unique network of specialist clinics (see Treatment and Prevention, below) collect detailed statistics for the Department of Health (HMSO 1995/16), which reflect trends in sexually transmitted diseases (STD) with a high degree of accuracy. These statistics give a better indication of the true incidence of STD in the United Kingdom than those of most other countries, because of the relative low proportion of infections treated outside the National Health Service (NHS). It is estimated that over 95% of the epidemic STDs, namely, syphilis and gonorrhea, are managed at the NHS clinics. The proportion is somewhat less for the more endemic diseases—chlamydia, genital herpes, and genital warts—because of their covert nature, with the proportion for chlamydia being recently reduced by a belated surge of interest among gynecologists, contraceptive-care professionals, and general practice physicians. The majority of HIV care is also organized from the NHS clinics (see Section 10B, HIV/AIDS, below).

Control of syphilis and gonorrhea has been particularly successful in the United Kingdom (see Table 4). There are fewer cases of infectious syphilis per year in men in England (194 cases in 1994) than there are clinics in the United Kingdom, 230. The figure for women was roughly half the male figure, 110 cases in 1994. Twenty percent of the male cases were acquired through homosexual contact. The median age for new cases of syphilis is higher than for other STDs, 33 for men and 28 for women. Syphilis has become an imported disease, having been virtually eliminated as a congenital infection, with only one infection reported in 700,000 live births in 1993.

The pattern of gonorrhea cases during the 1900s (see Table 4) can act as a surrogate marker for other sexual activity, closely reflecting changes caused by demographics, war, travel, contraceptive practice, and sexual mores (Greenhouse 1994). The gonorrhea pattern can also illuminate these

#### Table 4

#### Incidence of Gonorrhea and Syphilis, England, 1918 to 1994

| Disease | Number of New Cases in Selected Years (in Thousands of Cases) | | | | | | | | | | |
|---|---|---|---|---|---|---|---|---|---|---|---|
| | 1918 | 1920 | 1922 | 1930 | 1940 | 1946 | 1955 | 1964 | 1977 | 1987 | 1994 |
| Gonorrhea | 17.4 | 37.9 | 27.9 | 40.5 | 26.3 | 47.4 | 17.4 | 37.9 | 58.7 | 24.5 | 11.6 |
| Syphilis | 26.8 | 42.1 | 24.2 | 18.9 | 11.4 | 24.2 | 5.0 | 3.8 | 4.2 | 1.8 | 1.3 |

Percentages approximated from the authors' line graph.

social trends. The post-World War II decline in gonorrhea cases was because of the arrival of penicillin and the reactionary morality of the 1950s. This was followed by a tremendous rise in the 1960s, as the baby boomers reached adolescence, sexual behavior gradually changed, and contraception increased. The maximum incidence of gonorrhea occurred in 1976, with 58,725 cases, in conjunction with the all-time peak in prescriptions for the oral contraceptive pill. Starting in 1986, the incidence of gonorrhea dropped by 50% in two years following the public HIV-education campaign directed at the heterosexual population. There is now less gonorrhea in the United Kingdom than at any time since record keeping began. The current rate is around one sixth that of 20 years ago. Statistics for 1994 record 11,574 cases, with an overall rate of 37 per 100,000 population aged 15 to 64 (HMSO 1995/16). However, the rate varies considerably with age and sex; the highest incidence occurred in women aged 16 to 19 years, and increased from 95 cases to 123 per 100,000 between 1993 and 1994 (HMSO 1995/16; *Communicable Disease Report* 1995, 62-63). Detailed information on geographic distribution, antibiotic-resistant strains, and location of acquisition is also published (*Communicable Disease Report* 1995, 62-63).

*Chlamydia trachomatis*, the principal preventable cause of pelvic inflammatory disease, infertility, and ectopic pregnancy, is the commonest curable STD in the United Kingdom. All isolation rates for chlamydia substantially underestimate its true incidence, since screening tests are, at best, 75 to 80% sensitive, and most infected men and women show no symptoms. The cases identified at NHS STD clinics represent only the tip of the iceberg. The differential age and sex rates for chlamydia (*Communicable Disease Report* 1995, 122-123) are similar in distribution to those of gonorrhea (*Communicable Disease Report* 1995, 62-63), herpes and warts (*Communicable Disease Report* 1995, 186-187), and representative of all STDs combined, with the highest rates in adolescent women, and a late lower peak in male cases. The peak incidence of 360 cases per 100,000 women aged 16 to 19 years—four times more than in men of the same age—should be compared with observed rates from 9.5% to 23% in studies of women of this age who are having an abortion. No significant differences were found in the chlamydial isolation rates (of around 10%) in women attending clinics for either contraception, abortion, or STD (Radcliffe 1993), although, even nowadays, most women are not routinely screened in the contraception clinics. Chlamydia and nonspecific genital infection rose steadily until 1986, peaking at 157,792 cases, and has shown a slight decline since then, despite improved diagnostic techniques.

At least 85% of all pelvic inflammatory disease (PID) is sexually acquired, a minimum of 75% because of chlamydia. Around 10% of pelvic inflammatory disease is treated in a hospital. The massive drop in gonorrhea in the United Kingdom in 1986 to 1988 was not matched by a significant drop in hospital cases of acute salpingitis. A similar phenomenon in 1970-1977 in Sweden alerted Westrom (1988) to the true etiology of salpingitis, and appropriate diagnosis, treatment, contact tracing, and education was initiated. In both countries, salpingitis incidence had doubled between 1965 and 1974. From 1978 to 1983, salpingitis admissions were halved in Sweden (Westrom 1988), but increased by 50% from 1975 to 1984 in Britain, which almost two decades later has yet to introduce a similar salpingitis-prevention campaign. Contact-tracing studies indicate very high infection rates of over 70% in male partners of women with salpingitis, the vast majority of whom are asymptomatic.

There has been a continuing long-term upward trend in first-attack incidence of both genital herpes and genital warts, full details of which have been published (*Communicable Disease Report* 1995, 186-187). Herpes is more common in women, increasing from 32 to 98 per 100,000 between 1981 and 1994. Seroepidemiological studies in the United Kingdom show that around 90% of men and women aged 25 to 34 have antibodies to both herpes viruses (HSV 1 and 2), of which about one third are HSV 1. Up to 50% of oral lesions have been found to harbor HSV 1. Thus, although oral and genital herpes infection is ubiquitous, relatively few individuals suffer overt symptoms, and many will have acquired oral infection in childhood. This information is of considerable value in diffusing the stress of a first-episode attack acquired sexually.

Full details of the minor STDs are also available from published statistics (HMSO 1995/16). Long-term trends in total attendance for all diagnoses shows a continuous increase to a current high of 671,281 in 1993. Records show an increasing proportion of clinic attendees are female, from one seventh in 1950 to one quarter in 1960 and one third in 1970. Now, 51% of all attendees are women, with some clinics up two thirds, depending on the extent of contraceptive and other sexual health services provided. These trends are set to continue as the clinical workload comes closer to reflecting the gross disparity in STD morbidity suffered by women.

*Treatment and Prevention*

Thanks to exceptional, far-sighted public-health legislation, the United Kingdom has had specialist clinics offering free and entirely confidential STD advice and treatment in every major town since 1917. Accessible care is available to all regardless of nationality or domicile. Voluntary contact tracing and treatment of partners is facilitated by health advisers, without the intrusion of coercive legislation. The United Kingdom is the only country where Venereology (currently known as Genito-Urinary Medicine) developed as a distinct medical specialty in its own right (Waugh 1990), rather than as a minor adjunct to other fields, such as dermatology in Europe, or infectious diseases and public health in the United States. Consequently, Britain has a well-trained, academically based specialist body, whose numbers have doubled in the last decade as the result of substantial government investment in improved premises, equipment, and expanded support staff. The specialty coordinates clinical care and epidemiologic research, and can implement rapid and consistent responses to changing public-health priorities in the control of STD, having been ideally placed to take the lead in caring for HIV (see Section 10B, below). The advantage of this approach is evidenced by the relatively low prevalence of HIV and other STDs compared to most countries other than Scandinavia (see Incidence, Patterns, and Trends above).

An important disadvantage is that other specialists are poorly trained or are unaware of STD, and are unlikely to be able to broach the subject (Clarke 1995) without either embarrassment or moralism. (This holds the greatest potential for damage in women's heathcare.) Not only are most genitourinary physicians untrained in gynecology, most gynecologists and family planning specialists were, until recently, ignorant of the significance of covert STD in their patients. This resulted in considerable morbidity from uterine instrumentation during abortion or IUD insertion, and multiple recurrences of salpingitis because of reinfection from untreated partners, leading to increased chronic dyspareunia, ectopic pregnancy, and infertility.

Despite governmental interference in school sex education policy (see Section 3A), there have been substantial advances in the general level of education on HIV and, to a lesser extent, on contraception, aided by the government's

*Health of the Nation* initiative on sexual health. Education on conventional STD, however, has been almost entirely neglected. Sexual health education is usually delivered by those without specific knowledge or experience of STD care. Thus, the public as a whole, including health professionals, remain largely ignorant in this area. In the recent international survey on STD awareness for the American Social Health Association (Clarke 1995), the United Kingdom compared poorly against five other countries. Only 1% of Britons had heard of chlamydia, and 75% said that their doctors would not talk about sex or STD. This ignorance, combined with the traditional British attitude of prurience and prudishness about sex, creates the societal taboo of STD. This stigma, causing guilt, shame, and blame, is based on misinformation, fear, and an automatic presumption of infidelity, which is often erroneous because of the very asymptomatic nature of most STDs that causes them to be endemic. This major pitfall results in substantial psychosexual trauma that plagues work in all fields of sexology.

A simple solution will be found in the increasing integration of sexual health promotion with clinical service provision. Teaching that most STDs produce no symptoms, can be present for many years, are acquired from partners who are likewise unaware, and may, therefore, have been present before the current relationship, should do much to destigmatize the subject. Furthermore, a national consensus of specialists in public health, family planning, genitourinary medicine, and health education has recently promoted a concise definition of sexual health: "the enjoyment of sexual activity of one's choice without causing or suffering physical or mental harm" (Greenhouse 1994). This same consensus agreed that these specialties should progressively converge to provide services for contraception, abortion, STD/HIV, sexual assault, psychosexual care, and health promotion under the banner of sexual health clinics (Greenhouse 1994). Broadening the scope of these services allows access to more appropriately coordinated care "under one roof." This is essential for the youngest in the most vulnerable situations, and may persuade people to attend a clinic to check that they are healthy rather than waiting until they are ill. With careful education input, this should improve public understanding, reduce stigma, prevent iatrogenic morbidity, and achieve even more-effective control of STD in clinical situations where they would previously have gone undetected.

## B. HIV/AIDS   JANE CRAIG and GEORGE KINGHORN
*[Rewritten and updated in late 2001*
*by J. Craig and G. Kinghorn]*

Based on anonymous seroprevalence data, there were, in 2001, an estimated total of 30,000 people living with HIV in the United Kingdom, a third of them undiagnosed. Newly diagnosed HIV infections appear to be increasing to over 2,900 in 1999. Antiretroviral therapy is delaying the onset of AIDS and deaths in many of those who are treated; deaths fell by two thirds between 1995 and 1991. As a result, the number of individuals living with HIV is increasing, from 16,891 in 1998 to 19,179 in 1999. Nevertheless, the prevalence still remains lower than in many European countries.

By the end of March 2000, a total of 41,174 HIV-infected individuals had been diagnosed and reported in the U.K. since 1984. Of these, 7,198 (17%) were female. A cumulative total of 16,995 (2,113, or 12% of which were female) cases of AIDS have been reported and 11,793 (69%) are known to have died. A further 1,753 HIV-infected individuals have died without AIDS being reported. A total of 967 HIV infections and 411 AIDS cases in children aged less than 15 years at diagnosis have been reported by the end of March 2000. Most were infected by maternal transmission.

London and its surrounds have reported 62% of all HIV infections and AIDS cases in the U.K. to date. Scotland reports 7% of all U.K. HIV infections and 6% of AIDS cases.

Within the U.K., sexual intercourse between men remains the major route of infection for people who have been diagnosed as having HIV. The number of infections being diagnosed where sex between men and women is the route of infection has risen steadily, so that newly diagnosed cases infected by heterosexual exposure exceeded those transmitted by sex between men in 1999. The majority of these, however, are attributed to heterosexual exposure while in areas of higher prevalence, usually sub-Saharan Africa, rather than other exposure categories, such as partners of injecting drug users. Injecting drug use has made a relatively small contribution to the HIV epidemic in the U.K., except in Scotland, where it has been responsible for more of the diagnosed infections than sex between men.

In England, Wales, and Northern Ireland, the proportion of reported HIV infections attributable to sex between men has fallen from 92% in 1985 to 46% in 1999. The proportion attributed to injecting drug use has remained fairly static over the same period (5% in 1985, and 3% in 1999), but the proportion of reported HIV infections attributed to heterosexual exposure has risen from 3% to 49%.

In Scotland, the trend is somewhat different, in that the proportion of reported HIV infections attributed to sex between men has risen from 9% in 1985 to 39% in 1999. The proportion of incident HIV infections attributed to heterosexual exposure has also risen, from 2% to 50% over the same period. Those attributable to injecting drug use have fallen from 90% to 11%. This may reflect the efforts of locally targeted prevention programs amongst drug users.

For U.K. residents, medical care and treatments are provided free of charge under the National Health Service. Genitourinary medicine (GUM) clinics offer a voluntary, open-access, confidential HIV-testing service nationwide and are the major providers for HIV treatment and care. There are ongoing anonymous unlinked HIV-seroprevalence studies at selected sites, including attendees at GUM clinics and women attending antenatal clinics. Since 1999, it has been recommended that all pregnant women throughout England should be offered HIV testing, and targets for the proportions of pregnant women accepting testing have been set. In the first half of 1999, 71% of HIV-infected pregnant women in inner London had been diagnosed by the time they gave birth. This is substantially higher than in previous years. However, elsewhere in the U.K., a majority of infected pregnant women still remain undiagnosed. This places their neonates at risk of vertical transmission, which is now largely preventable with combination antiretroviral treatment, cesarean-section delivery, and avoidance of breastfeeding. All blood donors have been tested for HIV since 1985. There have been no reports of HIV transmissions in the U.K. since the introduction of heat treatment of blood products.

The gay community has become well organized and motivated with self-initiated prevention and education campaigns. There are also numerous patient-interest and support groups. Initiatives, such as outreach work among targeted groups rather than didactic healthcare messages, seem to be more successful, and many have accepted safer-sex practices. There is also recent evidence that suggests that transmission is less common from those who have learned of their infection from voluntary testing programs, as compared with those who choose to remain ignorant of their HIV status. Nevertheless, maintenance of lifelong safer sexual practice often proves difficult for those whose prognosis has vastly improved since the advent of successful combination antiretroviral treatments. Continuing support and dialogue about the sexual health needs of HIV-positive patients is essential.

National needle and syringe-exchange programs have been operational since 1990 and have contributed to reduced transmission from the use of equipment shared by injecting drug users, although in closed communities, such as prisons, the potential for HIV spread by this route still persists. Although sexual health no longer has the key health-priority status originally set in England in 1992, a new national Sexual Health and HIV strategy is now being formulated, and a final report was due in 2001. This should help to increase better coordination and collaboration between local sexual health service providers, and increase the involvement of primary care in screening and management of sexually transmitted infections and HIV.

School sex education remains a controversial topic. Opponents often claim that such lessons reduce the age of first sexual activity. At present, attendance at sex education classes is voluntary and parents have the right to withdraw their children. However, sex education programs have been shown to be effective in delaying the onset and frequency of sexual activity, and may also result in an increased use of contraception, in particular, condoms. Effective programs seem to be those focusing on reducing specific risk behaviors, combined with opportunities to improve personal development and communication skills. This has obvious implications for the provision of school-based sex education in the future.

Overall, there is a greater awareness of HIV infection, but risk recognition remains an issue for many, as is reflected by the increasing number of heterosexual infections acquired from those parts of the world with explosive rates of HIV. Increasing rates of sexually transmitted infections among HIV-positive individuals is a concern because of the associated increased risk of HIV transmission. It also suggests increasing unsafe sexual practices. Prevention programs need to target such groups, as well as continuing their efforts amongst other high-risk communities.

[*Update 2002*: UNAIDS Epidemiological Assessment: By mid-2001, the country reported a cumulative total of 46,131 cases of HIV infection. Risk of HIV acquisition in the U.K. is highest for gay men. Two thirds of the U.K. burden is in London. High levels of risk behavior are present among young heterosexuals.

[There are improved survival rates, as well as a decline in numbers of deaths and new AIDS cases with the availability of antiretroviral therapies. There is rising prevalence of diagnoses of infections requiring care and treatment, a 13% increase in prevalence of diagnosed HIV infection between 1997 and 1998. From 1999 onwards, there have been more diagnoses of heterosexually acquired HIV infection; 64% of HIV diagnoses heterosexually acquired were probably acquired in sub-Saharan Africa. There has been increased sharing of injection equipment and rising hepatitis B cases among injection drug users, but so far, HIV infection rates in injection drug users remain low. In addition, there have been increases in other STDs, especially gonorrhea, chlamydia, and genital warts. Changes in HIV infection worldwide, especially in South Asia, have the potential to have an impact on the U.K. because of high immigration rates.

[Testing is mandatory for blood donors, and voluntary otherwise. All detected HIV-infected cases are reported in a national database, using an identifying code. Continuous universal assessment testing (UAT) surveys have been conducted among newborns since 1988 in the Thames region (in the southeast of England including London), Oxford, and four other regions since 1993. UAT surveys have been carried out among pregnant women since 1990 in selected centers of England and Wales, using sera collected for rubella screening during antenatal visits. In both studies, the prevalence increased steadily in London. In parallel, UAT surveys of women having abortions found a twofold higher prevalence (4.6 to 7.8 per 1,000) compared to that found among women attending antenatal centers. The majority of HIV-infected women originate from high-prevalence countries and have mostly been infected heterosexuality. In Scotland, continuous UAT of newborns indicates that prevalence was substantially higher in Edinburgh (up to 2.5 per 1,000) and Dundee (up to 2.8 per 1,000) than in the rest of Scotland (less than 0.2 per 1,000), including in Glasgow (less than 0.3 per 1,000). However, prevalence has decreased significantly in Edinburgh (from 2.5 in 1990 to 0.8 in 1994; $p < 0.05$), while no clear trend could be detected in other parts of Scotland. UAT surveys have been conducted also in STD patients and injection drug users in treatment centers. A prevalence survey of all patients seen for care within the year is carried out annually; this shows rising prevalence.

[The estimated number of adults and children living with HIV/AIDS on January 1, 2002, were:

| | |
|---|---|
| Adults ages 15-49: | 34,000 (rate: 0.1%) |
| Women ages 15-49: | 7,400 |
| Children ages 0-15: | 550 |

[An estimated 460 adults and children died of AIDS during 2001.

[No estimate is available for the number of British children who had lost one or both parents to AIDS and were under age 15 at the end of 2001. (*End of update by the Editors*)]

## 11. Sexual Dysfunctions, Counseling, and Therapies

KEVAN R. WYLIE

### A. Concepts of Sexual Dysfunction

British society appears to be having a reemergence of sexual awareness. After a very conservative attitude towards sex in the first half of the 20th century, there was an awakening in the 1960s alongside the increased use of illicit drugs, the emergence of rock and roll, and a "free" society. The permissive society continued into the 1970s and early 1980s, until, like many other countries, the fear of AIDS changed the sexual behavior of many in the mid-1980s. Out of this has grown a more-cautious approach to sexual encounters with others and a reemergence of encouraging more satisfying sexual relationships within a monogamous relationship.

There is wider access to articles and books on sexual fulfillment, and awareness of dysfunction has increased, primarily as a result of articles in the popular press and lifestyle magazines. There is some evidence that there has been a reversal of the age of the first sexual experience of teenagers, and there has been an increase in patients requesting help over the wide spectrum of sexual dysfunction. One area where this has become particularly evident is male erectile disorder, for which a proliferation of treatment centers, both within the health service and in the private sector, has developed. A recent attempt to define sexual dysfunction is "the persistent impairment of the normal patterns of sexual interest or response."

### B. The Availability of Diagnosis and Treatment

[*Rewritten and updated in late 2001 by K. R. Wylie*]

Within the United Kingdom, all patients are entitled to free consultation under the National Health Service. The planning and availability of sexual dysfunction clinics varies widely from area to area. Traditionally, these have been within family planning clinics, and have gradually been extended by interested clinicians within gynecology, psychiatry/psychosexual, and genitourinary clinics. The Family Planning Association Service has been traditionally run by doctors, although there has been a gradual introduction of nursing and psychology staff into these and other treatment clinics. Seminars held by Drs. Balint and Main in the 1960s and 1970s developed the concept of psychosexual medicine and emphasized the importance of using the physical (vaginal) examination in the management of female sexual problems. In the 1980s, patients with male erectile disorder started to be seen within urology, rather than psychosexual clinics, although in the 1990s, it is becoming generally agreed that, because around half of these cases are of a psychological nature and a proportion have both organic and psychological components, there is a need for either dual clinics or access to either. There is an interesting awareness of the need to consider cultural factors in sexual dysfunction, and this is particularly important for various clinic groups.

A non-Health Service organization offering treatment for sexual dysfunction is available from Relate (formerly Marriage Guidance). Paul Brown, a psychologist, showed in 1974 that psychodynamically trained counselors were able to focus specifically on sexual dysfunctions using behavioral approaches. This organization has a network of specially trained sex therapists who have training in relationship work. This service is not provided free, but clients are charged nominal sums according to their income, typically £20.00 to £30.00 per session. Other agencies include the Catholic Marriage Advisory Council and the Jewish Marriage Council. Private facilities for diagnosis and treatment of sexual disorders do exist, but are primarily around major cities or areas where no NHS provision is easily accessible.

Treatment approaches include the traditional medical approach using medication, intracavernous injections, VCDs, and so on. Psychotherapeutic treatments are usually based on the behavioral model proposed by William Masters and Virginia Johnson, although increasingly with cognitive and systemic strategies incorporated. Some workers continue to use a dynamic model of working with patients. Increasingly, couple therapy is adopted incorporating both relationship and sexual therapy. Surrogacy services are available from the Birmingham clinic run by Martin Cole.

Specialist services for transsexualism and gender dysphoria exist, with assessment for treatment and surgery available at several centers in the U.K. These are primarily Charring Cross Hospital in London, and the gender-dysphoria services in Sheffield, Leicester, Nottingham, Leeds, and Glasgow. Surgery is confined to specialist centers, namely London, Brighton, Leicester, and Rhyl.

In a wider context, the funding from the government for marriage support was subject to review by Sir Graham Hart for the Lord Chancellor's Department, and a report was issued in 1999. In summary, fewer people now get married in the U.K. (around 75% now marry by the age of 50 compared to 95% in the 1960s), and marriage is much more likely to be deferred and preceded by a period of cohabitation. Divorce now occurs about seven times more often than in the 1960s, with about four in ten marriages likely to end in divorce. The United Kingdom Government through the Lord Chancellor's Department, until the year 2000, provided three million pounds sterling to marriage support in various agencies. The total allocation of funds will increase to five million in 2002-2003, covering both strategic funding of bodies with a significant national loan and research and developmental grants. Marriage-support services in the United Kingdom are provided by Relate (formerly known as the National Marriage Guidance Council), the London Marriage Guidance Council

(ex-part of the former National Marriage Guidance Council), Catholic Marriage Care, Jewish Marriage Care, Tavistock Marital Studies Institute, Family Welfare Association, and One Plus One. In addition to these seven major agencies, there are numerous other smaller bodies, which provide counseling for couples or individuals in marital difficulties.

In England and Wales, the main responsibilities for marriage, relationships, and sexual problems can be subdivided into the Lord Chancellor's Department, which includes funding of marriage-support services and deals with divorce law and private law and Children Act proceedings, and the Department of Health, which is involved with a variety of areas, including family planning, family health services, and hospital services, as well as Public Law Children Act proceedings. The Department for Education and Employment also handles a variety of areas, including personal and social education in schools. The Home Office is involved with substantive marriage law and a coordinating role on family policy and the Department of Social Security for state benefits and the Child Support Agency.

## C. Therapist Training and Certification

As of 1996, there was no central certification body within the United Kingdom. The main association is the British Association for Sexual and Marital Therapists (BASMT), which was formed in 1974. This organization approves certain training courses and provides an accreditation process for which individuals can apply. The majority of new therapists will complete an approved course and a further 200 hours of supervised work, alongside fulfilling other criteria (first detailed in 1992) before accreditation. The approved training courses are listed in Section 12. The address for BASMT is P.O. Box 62, Sheffield, S10 3TL United Kingdom.

Since 1997, a group of BASMT members (The Committee for European Affairs) has met as an approved task force for the European Federation of Sexology. The goals are to establish a consensus within Europe as to what precisely constitutes a multidisciplinary profession of sexology, and subsequently, to devise European Codes of Ethics and Practice for those defining themselves as sexologists; they also seek to define European standards of training and to draw up a European register of accredited practitioners within given subspecialities of sexology.

Medical practitioners may become members of BASMT. Alternatively, they may follow a training course of seminars run by the Institute of Psychosexual Medicine (IPM) and are subsequently examined to become members of the institute. Members are recognized as competent to receive referrals. A diploma recognizes the skills of those who have been training for two years, but do not wish to make the treatment of sexual problems a specialist field. Contact: IPM, 11 Chandos Street, Cavendish Square, London, W1M 9DE United Kingdom.

The Diploma in Sexual Medicine (DSM) is awarded to doctors who can produce evidence of training and experience, as well as successfully passing written and oral examinations in the fields of sexual medicine. Areas in which the above must be demonstrated are gynecology, sexual medicine, and the physical and psychological aspects of assessing and treating sexual problems. Details are available from the Institute of Obstetrics and Gynaecology, Queen Charlotte's Hospital, Goldhawk Road, London, W6 0XG United Kingdom.

The Royal Medical Colleges do not offer training or accreditation in sexual dysfunction, but membership does reflect postgraduate training and examination to an advanced level within a given speciality. Three relevant colleges are:

Royal College of Obstetrics and Gynaecology, 27 Sussex Place, Regents Park, London, NW1 4RG United Kingdom—The Faculty of Family Planning and Reproductive

Health Care (RCOG) have a particular interest in the field of psychosexual medicine.

Royal College of Surgeons of England, 35-43 Lincoln's Inn Fields, London, WC2A 3PN United Kingdom.

Royal College of Psychiatrists, 17 Belgrave Square, London, SW1X 8PG United Kingdom.

[*Update 2001*: The British Association for Sexual and Marital Therapy became known as the British Association for Sexual and Relationship Therapy, effective May 1999. The Committee for European Affairs was renamed the Committee for the International Sexological Societies (CISS). This Committee has been influential in encouraging the development of a multidisciplinary profession of sexology and European codes of ethics and practice for those defining themselves as sexologists. CISS continues to work towards defining European standards of training, with the ultimate aim of drawing up a European register of accredited practitioners within given subspecialties of sexology. (*End of update by K. R. Wylie*)]

## 12. Sex Research and Advanced Professional Education

KEVAN R. WYLIE [*Rewritten and updated in late 2001 by K. R. Wylie*]

### A. Institutes and Programs for Sexological Research

The support and financial availability for research within the United Kingdom remains limited. Several sexological research units exist, including the MRC unit in Edinburgh, the Institute of Psychiatry, and teams in Oxford, Sheffield, and Southampton. There remain many political pressures to frustrate sexological research, with the government declining to finance the United Kingdom National Survey of Sexual Attitudes in Lifestyle in 1989. Political influence is also exerted on education with the Health Education Authority shelving a *Pocket Guide to Sex* after the government attacked its colloquial frankness.

### B. Programs for the Advanced Study of Human Sexuality

Sex education is now compulsory in state secondary schools as a result of the 1993 Education Act, although reference to nonbiological behavior has been removed from the national science curriculum. Guidance on sex and relationship education in schools was reissued in 2000 (DFEE) "to take account of the revised National Curriculum, published in September 1999, the need for guidance arising out of the new Personal, Social and Health Education (PSHE) framework and the Social Exclusion Unit report on teenage pregnancy."

The training in human sexuality in the United Kingdom Medical Schools for medical undergraduates has been reviewed by Reader (1994). Education and training in human sexuality, including postgraduate training, has been considered by Griffin (1995).

Postgraduate training exists for various professions. These courses are usually attended by both medical graduates, as well as workers from other healthcare disciplines. As courses expand to the master's level, the qualifications required for entry into these courses become more stringent. These courses are classified as either a course approved or nonapproved by the British Association for Sexual and Relationship Therapy (BASRT). The BASRT approved courses are:

Diploma in Psychosexual Therapy (Marriage Guidance), Herbert Gray College, Little Church Street, Rugby CV21 3AP United Kingdom.

Master of Science degree; Post Graduate diploma and Post Graduate certificate in the Theory and Practice of Psychotherapy for Sexual Dysfunction, The Porterbrook Clinic, 75 Osborne Road, Nether Edge, Sheffield S11 9BF United Kingdom.

Diploma in Psychosexual Health Care, Department of Psychiatry, Withington Hospital, Didsbury, Manchester M20 8LR United Kingdom.

Master of Science degree in Human Sexuality, Human Sexuality Unit, 3rd Floor Lanesborough Wing, St. George's Hospital Medical School, Cranmer Terrace, London SW17 0RE United Kingdom.

Master of Science degree in Therapy with Couples, The Registry, Institute of Psychiatry, De Crespigny Park, Denmark Hill, London SE5 8AF United Kingdom.

Certificate in Psychosexual Counselling and Therapy, South East Hants Health Authority, c/o Myrtle Cottage, Selbourne, Nr Alton, Hants GU34 3LB United Kingdom.

The Master of Science degree in Human Sexuality and Relationship Psychotherapy offered by East Berkshire College has not been approved.

### C. Sexological Journals and Periodicals

The major sexological journals in the United Kingdom are:

*Sexual and Relationship Therapy.* Editor: Kevan R. Wylie, Porterbrook Clinic, 75 Osborne Road, Nether Edge, Sheffield S11 9BF United Kingdom (published four times a year from 1996) http://www.tandf.co.uk/journals.

*The International Journal for Impotence Research.* Editors: William L. Furlow and Gorm Wagner Smith-Gordon and Company Ltd., Number 1, 16 Gunter Grove, London SW10 0UJ United Kingdom (published quarterly).

*British Journal of Family Planning.* Editor: Fran Reader, RGOG, 27 Sussex Place, Regent's Park, London NW1 4RG United Kingdom.

*The Institute of Psychosexual Medicine Journal.* Editors: Dr. H. Montford and Dr. R. Skrine, c/o 11 Chandos Street, London, United Kingdom (published three times a year).

*The British Journal of Sexual Medicine.* Editor: Paul Woolley, Hayward Medical Communications Ltd., 44 Earlham Street, Covent Garden, London WC2H 9LA, United Kingdom (currently suspended).

*Journal of Sexual Health.* Editor: Dr. Alan Riley, MAP Publishing, Sussex Court, 10 Station Road, Chertsey, Surrey KT16 8BE United Kingdom (no longer published).

*Perversions: The International Journal of Gay and Lesbian Studies.* Editors: Neil McKenna and Linda Semple, BM Perversions, London WC1N 3XX United Kingdom (published three times a year).

*The Journal of Gender Studies.* Editors: Jenny Wolmark and Jenny Hockey, University of Humberside, Ing Lemine Avenue, Hill HU6 7RX United Kingdom (published twice a year).

*The Journal of Sexualities.* Editor: Ken Plummer, University of Essex, Colchester, U.K. (published by Sage Publications four times a year).

### D. Important National and Regional Sexological Organizations

Organizations dealing with sexuality include the following:

SIMSED, Bredon House, 321 Tettenhall Road, Wolverhampton WV6 0JZ United Kingdom.

British Association for Sexual and Relationship Therapy (BASRT), P.O. Box 13686, London SW20 9ZH United Kingdom.

Family Planning Association, 27-35 Mortimer Street, London W1N 7RJ United Kingdom; tel.: 44-71-636-7866; fax: 44-71-436-328.

Marie Stopes U.K., 6 Grafton Mews, London W1P 5LF United Kingdom; tel.: 44-71-382-2494; fax: 44-71-388-1885.

Sex Education Forum and National Children's Bureau, 8 Walkley Street, London C1V 7QE United Kingdom; tel.: 44-71-278-9441; fax: 44-71-278-9512.

Institute of Psychosexual Medicine, 11 Chandos Street, Cavendish Square, London W1M 9DE United Kingdom.

British Society for Psychosomatic Obstetrics, Gynaecology and Andrology, 11 Chelmsford Square, London NW10 3AP United Kingdom.

Marce Society (Mental illness related to childrearing), c/o Dr. T. Friedman, Liaison Psychiatry Service, Leicester General Hospital, Gwendoeln Road, Leicester LE5 4PW United Kingdom.

Tavistock Marital Studies Institute, The Tavistock Centre, 120 Belsize Lane, London NW3 5BN United Kingdom.

Institute for Sex Education and Research, 40 School Road, Moseley, Birmingham B13 9SN United Kingdom.

Relate, Herbert Gray College, Little Church Street, Rugby CV21 3AP United Kingdom.

## 13. Significant Differences in Sexual Attitudes and Behaviors among Ethnic Minorities

KEVAN R. WYLIE

It is well acknowledged that sexual function and behavior is affected by both social and cultural influence. Until recently, there has been a trend towards trying to fit patients into existing services without considering development of new therapist skills to meet a patient's individual cultural needs. Specific skills for counseling clients of different cultures have only recently been developed. The approach proposed by d'Ardenne and Mahtani (1989) has been practiced based on using an essentially client-centered and non-hierarchical model. The use of English language and nonverbal communication, as well as bilingualism and the use of interpreters, are important factors to consider. Within their text, there is a large resource list of organizations in the United Kingdom that may help therapists develop cultural knowledge in a certain field.

Clulow (1993) has considered ethnic and religious differences in couple relationships. The presentation of ethnic minorities to sexual dysfunction clinics poses particular problems to clinicians in addition to the cultural issues mentioned above. There are high expectations that physical remedies will be available (Ghosh et al. 1985). An excellent review of presentation of sexual problems within different cultures, clinical assessment, and their management has recently been presented by Bhugra and De Silva (1993). As newer medications become recognized as having potentially beneficial applications in sexual dysfunction, the clinician may have a further armamentarium towards helping some patients within this group.

The issue of HIV, sexuality, and ethnic minorities, particularly Afro-Caribbeans, is an area where there is increasing interest in the United Kingdom.

### [Black and Ethnic Minority Groups

DINESH BHUGRA

[*Update 2001*: Cultural and social factors are well known to influence attitudes towards sex, the purpose of sex (whether it is seen as a pleasurable or procreative activity), and the type of sexual activity. Therapists need to be aware of social and cultural attitudes, taboos, and expectations arising from within the specific culture. The therapist must use strategies that are culturally appropriate and acceptable to the patients. The issues of family, the role of marriage within the relationship, and expectations from the female within a set of expected gender roles need to be part of any assessment. A non-hierarchical and client-centered approach is the way forward. The use of family or the partner as an interpreter must be avoided wherever possible.

[Differences in religious attitudes to sex and procreation will influence couple and sexual therapy. Often patients present with unrealistic expectations, such as seeking physical treatments and not using psychological approaches, because of the lack of privacy and social taboos. Under these circumstances, the therapists must be prepared to modify their approach by using a combination of strategies (see Bhugra & de Silva 1993, 2000). The role of newer therapeutic modalities, such as sildenafil (Viagra) are bound to increase demand, and expectations will change further. Homosexual orientation may well be seen as extremely negative in some cultures. It is likely that certain paraphilias may well be less or more prevalent in some cultures. The attitudes towards HIV and AIDS and preventive strategies will vary, and therapists in the U.K. need to be aware of heterogeneity and cultural differences.

[In the U.K., black and ethnic minority groups form around 6% of the population. They are not seen very frequently in sexual dysfunction clinics. It is possible that South Asians will use visiting alternative health practitioners and herbal medicines. The data on such usage are not available. For African and African-Caribbean populations, the data from sexual dysfunction clinics are even sparser. Johnson et al. demonstrated in a community survey that sexual practices do differ across ethnic groups, as do same-sex experiences and attitudes to one-night stands, abortions, and same-sex experiences. For any service, planning providers must take into account the composition of local communities. (*End of update by D. Bhugra*)]

## References and Suggested Readings

Alexander, M., J. Gunn, P. A. G. Cook, P. J. Taylor, & J. Finch. 1993. Should a sexual offender be allowed castration? *British Medical Journal*, 307:790-793.

Alfred Marks Bureau. 1991. *Sexual harassment in the office: A quantitative report on client attitudes and experience*. Richmond-upon-Thames: Adsearch.

Allen, I. 1987. Education in sex and personal relationships. Reprinted in Special Edition on Sex Education, *Sexual and Marital Therapy*, 9(2), 1994.

Allen, I., & Bourke. 1998. *Teenage mothers: Decisions and outcomes*. Policy Studies Institute.

American Psychiatric Association. 1994. *Diagnostic and statistical manual of mental disorders, 4th ed.* Washington, DC: American Psychiatric Association.

Bateman, A., & E. F. Mendelssohn. 1989. Sexual offences: Help for the forgotten victims. *Sexual and Marital Therapy*, 4:5-10.

Benson, C., & R. Matthews. 1995. *The national vice squad survey*. London: Middlesex University.

Berthoud, et al. 1985-1995. *Analysis of labour force surveys*. Institute of Social and Economic Research, Essex University.

Bhugra, D., & P. De Silva. 1993. Cross-cultural aspects of sexual dysfunction. *International Review of Psychiatry*, 5:245-254.

Bhugra, D., & P. de Silva. 2000. Cross cultural aspects of couple therapy. *Sexual and Relationship Therapy*, 15:183-192.

Bownes, I. T. 1993. Sexual and relationship dysfunction in sexual offenders. *Sexual and Marital Therapy*, 8:157-165.

Brook Advisory Centres. August 1995. *Teenage pregnancy—Key facts*. London.

Burns, J. 1993. Sexuality, sexual problems, and people with learning difficulties. In: J. Ussher & C. Baker, eds., *Psychological perspectives on sexual problems*. London: Routledge.

Carr, S. V. 1995. The health of women working in the sex industry—A moral and ethical perspective. *Sexual and Marital Therapy*, 10:201-213.

Central Policy Review Staff. 1973. *Report of the Population Panel. Cmnd. 5258*. London: HMSO.

Charles, E. 1936. *The menace of under-population*. London: Watts & Co.

Charles, E. 1938. Present trends of fertility and mortality. In: L. Hogben, *Political arithmetic*. London: Allen & Unwym.

CIA. 2002 (January). *The world factbook 2002*. Washington, DC: Central Intelligence Agency. Available: http://www.cia.gov/cia/publications/factbook/index.html.

Clarke, P. June 1995. *Awareness of sexually transmitted diseases: An international survey*. Presented at 19th International Congress of Chemotherapy, Montreal, Canada.

Clulow, C. 1993. Marriage across frontiers: National ethnic and religious differences in partnership. *Sexual and Marital Therapy*, 8:81-87.

Coleman, D., & J. Salt. 1992. *The British population: Patterns, trends, processes*. Oxford: Oxford University Press.

Collier, R. 1995. *Combating sexual harassment in the workplace*. Buckingham: Open University Press.

Communicable Disease Report. 1995. *Sexually transmitted diseases quarterly report: Genital infection with chlamydia trachomatis in England and Wales*. London: HMSO, 5:122-123.

Communicable Disease Report. 1995. *Sexually transmitted diseases quarterly report: Genital warts and genital herpes simplex virus infections in England and Wales*. London: HMSO, 5:186-187.

Communicable Disease Report. 1995. *Sexually transmitted diseases quarterly report: Gonorrhea in England and Wales*. London: HMSO, 5:62-63.

Confederation of Health Service Employees (COHSE). 1991. *An abuse of power: Sexual harassment in the National Health Service*. Banstead, Surrey: COHSE.

Cossey, C. 1991. *My story*. London: Faber and Faber.

Cowell, R. 1954. *Roberta Cowell's story*. Surrey: Windmill Press.

Coxon, A. P. M., & T. J. McManus. 2000. How many account for how much? Concentration of high-risk sexual behaviour amongst gay men. *Journal of Sex Research*, 37:1-7.

Craft, A. 1991. *Living your life: A sex education and personal development programme for care workers with people with learning disabilities*. Wisbech, Cambs: Learning Development Aids.

Craft, A. 1993. *It could never happen here! The prevention and treatment of sexual abuse of adults with learning disabilities in residential settings*. Chesterfield and Nottingham: Association for Residential Care, National Association for the Protection from Sexual Abuse of Adults and Children with Learning Disabilities.

Craft, A., & M. Craft. 1988. *Sex and the mentally handicapped* (rev. ed.). London: Routledge.

Craft, A., & J. Crosby. 1991. *Parental involvement in the sex education of students with severe learning difficulties: A handbook*. Nottingham: Department of Mental Handicap, University of Nottingham Medical School.

d'Ardenne, P., & A. Mahtani. 1989. *Transcultural counseling in action*. London: Sage Publications.

Dancey, C. 1994. Sexual orientation in women. In: P. Choi & P. Nicolson, eds., *Female sexuality: Psychology, biology and social context*. Hemel Hempstead: Harvester Wheatsheaf.

Davidson, M. J., & S. Earnshaw. 1991. Policies, practices and attitudes towards sexual harassment in UK organizations. *Women in Management Review and Abstracts*, 6:15-21.

Davies, P. M., F. C. I. Hickson, P. Weatherburn, & A. J. Hunt. 1993. *Sex, Gay men and AIDS*. London: The Falmer Press, The Taylor & Francis Group.

Department of Health. 1992. *The health of the nation: A strategy for health in England*. London: HMSO.

Department of Health. 1995. Sexually transmitted diseases. England 1994. *Statistical Bulletin 16*. London: HMSO.

Dine, J., & B. Watt. 1995. Sexual harassment: Moving away from discrimination. *The Modern Law Review*, 58:343-363.

East Sussex County Council. 1992. *Personal relationships and sexuality: Guidelines for careers working with people with learning disabilities*. Brighton: East Sussex County Council.

Effective Health Care. 1997. *Preventing and reducing the adverse effects of unintended teenage pregnancies* [National Health Services Centre for Reviews and Dissemination, University of York], 3(1).

Fallowell, D., & A. Ashley. 1982. *April Ashley's odyssey*. London: Jonathan Cape Ltd.

Family Planning Association (FBA). 1994 (March). *Abortion: Statistical trends. Factsheet 6A*. London.

Family Planning Association (FBA). 1994 (May). *Abortion: Legal and ethical issues. Factsheet 6B*. London.

Family Planning Association (FBA). 1994 (October). *Factsheet 5A: Teenage pregnancies*. London.

Farley, L. 1978. *Sexual shakedown: The sexual harassment of women on the job*. New York: McGraw-Hill.

Fisher, D., & L. L. K. Howells. 1993. Social relationships and sexual offenders. *Sexual and Marital Therapy*, 8:123-136.

General Register Office (Northern Ireland). *Annual reports 1990-1994. (Abstract 12)*. Belfast: GRO(NI).

General Register Office (Scotland). *Annual reports 1984 and 1994*. Edinburgh: GRO(S).

Ghosh, G., M. Dubble, & A. Ingram. 1985. *Treating patients of Asian origin presenting in the United Kingdom with sexual dysfunction*. Paper presented at the Seventh World Congress of Sexology, New Delhi, India.

Gillick, V. 1994. Letter. Confidentiality, contraception and young people. *British Medical Journal*, 308:342-343.

Glass, D. V. 1963. *The struggle for population*. Oxford: Oxford University Press.

Greenhouse, P. 1994. A sexual health service under one roof. In: J. Pillaye, ed., *Sexual health promotion in genitourinary medicine clinics* (Chapter 3). London: Health Education Authority.

Griffin, M. 1995. Education and training in human sexuality. *International Review of Psychiatry*, 7:275-284.

Gunn, M. 1991. *Sex and the law: A brief guide for staff working with people with learning difficulties*. London: Family Planning Association.

H.M.S.O. 1987. *Guidance on sex education 11/87*. London: Department of Education and Science.

H.M.S.O. 1988. *Circular 12/88. Local government act 1988*. London: Department of the Environment.

H.M.S.O. 1988. *Education reform act*. London: Department of Education and Science.

H.M.S.O. 1992. *Health of a nation: A strategy for health in England*. London: Department of Health.

H.M.S.O. 1993. *Education act*. London: Department of Education and Science.

Health Education Authority. 1993/1994. *Analysis of health education and lifestyle surveys*. London: Health Education Authority.

Health Service Circular. 1999. *Reducing mother to baby transmission of HIV* (HSC 1999/183). London: National Health Service Executive.

Her Majesty's Inspectorate of Constabulary. (1993). *Equal opportunities in the police service*. London: Her Majesty's Inspectorate of Constabulary.

Hertfordshire County Council. 1989. *Departmental policies and guidelines for staff on the sexual and personal relationships of people with a mental handicap*. Hertford: Hertfordshire County Council Social Services Department.

Hewitt, P., & J. Warren. 1995. *A self made man*. London: Headline Books.

Hicken, I. ed. 1994. *Sexual health education and training*. Milton Keynes, England: The English National Board for Nursing Midwifery and Health Visiting, Learning Materials Design.

Hogben, L., ed. 1938. *Political arithmetic*. London: Allen & Unwin.

Hoge, W. 2002 (December 7). Britain announces proposal for same-sex partnerships. *The New York Times*, A8.

Holmans, A. E. 1963. Current population trends in Britain. *Scottish Journal of Political Economy, 1*:31-56.

Home Office: Report of the Interdepartmental Working Group on Transsexual People, 2000. London: Home Office. Available: http://www.homeoffice.gov.uk/ccpd/wptrans.pdf.

Hubback, E. M. 1947. *The population of Britain*. London: Penguin Books.

*ICD-10. Classification of Mental & Behavioural Disorders. Clinical Descriptions and Diagnostic Guidelines*. 1992. World Health Organization.

Industrial Society. 1993. *No offense? Sexual harassment, how it happens and how to beat it*. London: Industrial Society.

Jehu, D. 1991. Post traumatic stress reactions among adults molested as children. *Sexual and Marital Therapy, 6*:227-243.

Johnson, A. M., C. H. Mercer, B. Erens, et al. 2001. Sexual behaviour in Britain: Partnerships, practices and HIV risk behaviour. *Lancet, 358*:1835-1842.

Johnson, A. M., J. Wadsworth, K. Wellings, S. Bradshaw, & J. Field. 1992. Sexual lifestyles and HIV risks. *Nature, 306*: 410-412.

Johnson, A. M., J. Wadsworth, K. Wellings, & J. Field. 1994. *Sexual attitudes and lifestyles*. Oxford, United Kingdom: Blackwell Scientific Publications Ltd.

Johnson, P., & J. Falkingham. 1992. *Aging and social welfare*. London: Sage.

Joseph Rowntree Foundation. 1995 (July). Findings: Social backgrounds and post-birth experiences of young parents. *Social Policy Research*, 80.

Kay, D. S. G. 1992. Masturbation and mental health—Uses and abuses. *Sexual and Marital Therapy (Journal of the British Association for Sexual and Marital Therapy), 7*(1).

Kirby, D. 1995. Sex and HIV/AIDS education in schools. *British Medical Journal, 311*:403.

Kitzinger, C. 1994. Anti-lesbian harassment. In: C. Brant & Y-L. Too, eds. *Rethinking sexual harassment*. London: Pluto Press.

Komonchack, J., M. Collins, & D. A. Lane, eds. 1990. *The new dictionary of theology*. Dublin: Gill and Macmillan Ltd.

Kraus, C. 2003 (July 5). In blessing gay unions, bishop courts a schism. *The New York Times*, A4.

Lewington, F. R., & D. J. Rogers. 1995. Forensic services for victims of sexual abuse and assault. *Sexual and Marital Therapy, 10*:215-229.

Livingston, J. A. 1982. Responses to sexual harassment on the job: Legal, organizational, and individual actions. *Journal of Social Issues, 38*:5-22.

Lloyd, C. 1991. The offense: Changes in the pattern and nature of sex offenses. *Criminal Behaviour and Mental Health, 1*: 115-122.

Lo, S. V., S. Kaul, R. Kaul, S. Cooling, & J. P. Calvert. 1994. Teenage pregnancy—Contraceptive use and non-use. *British Journal of Family Planning, 20*:79-83.

London Buses Ltd. 1991. *Report on a sexual harassment survey undertaken at three LBL workplaces*. London: London Buses Ltd.

MacKinnon, C. 1979. *Sexual harassment of working women: A case of sex discrimination*. New Haven, CT: Yale University Press.

McCarthy, M. 1993. Sexual experiences of women with learning difficulties in long-stay hospitals. *Sexuality and Disability, 11*(4):277-285.

McCarthy, M., & D. Thompson. 1993. *Sex and the 3R's: Rights, responsibilities, and risks. A sex education resource package for people with learning difficulties*. Brighton: Pavilion.

McCleary, G. F. 1942. *Race suicide*. London: Allen & Unwln.

McMullen, M., & S. Whittle. 1995. *Transvestites, transsexuals and the law*. Belper: Beaumont Trust.

Mezey, G., & M. King. 1989. The effects of sexual assault on men: A survey of 22 victims. *Psychological Medicine, 19*: 205-209.

Miller, D. 1995. *Some of my best friends are gay*. Tyneside: MESMAC.

Miller, E., P. A. Waight, R. S. Tedder, et al. 1995. Incidence of HIV infection in homosexual men in London, 1988-94. *British Medical Journal, 311*:545.

Morris, J. 1974. *Conundrum*. London: Coronet Books.

Mott, H., & S. Condor. 1995. *Putting us in our place: Secretaries and sexual harassment*. Paper presented to the British Psychological Society Social Section Conference, College of Ripon and York St. John, University of York, September 14.

National Education Curriculum Council. 1990. *Curriculum guidance 5*. York: National Curriculum Council.

Nicolson, P. 1993. Why women refer themselves for sex therapy. In: J. M. Ussher & C. D. Baker, eds., *Psychological perspectives on sexual problems*. London: Routledge.

Office of National Statistics (ONS). 1997. *Abortion statistics series*.

Office of National Statistics (ONS). 1998. *Analysis of abortion and birth statistics*.

Office of Population Census and Surveys. 1987. *Birth statistics: Historical series of statistics from registration of births in England and Wales 1837-1983* (Series FM1, no. 13). London: HMSO.

Office of Population Census and Surveys (OPCS). *Monitor-FM1 and birth statistics series for 1992 and 1993*. London: HMSO.

Office of Population Census and Surveys. 1994. *1992-based national population projections* (Series PP2, no. 19). London: HMSO.

Office of Population Census and Surveys. 1994. *Monitor. AB94/1*. London: Government Statistical Service.

Owen, G. 2003 (February 21). Government urges under-16s to experiment with oral sex. *The London Times*. Available: http://www.timesonline.co.uk/article/0,,2-585546,00.html.

Paintin, D. October 24, 1992. *British Medical Journal, 305*: 967-968.

Pearson, V. A. H., M. R. Owen, D. R. Phillips, D. J. Pereira Gray, & M. N. Marshall. 1995. Family planning services in Devon, U.K.: Awareness, experience and attitudes of pregnant teenagers. *British Journal of Family Planning, 21*:45-49.

People First. 1993. *Everything you ever wanted to know about safer sex . . . But nobody bothered to tell you*. London: People First.

P.H.L.S. AIDS Centre. 1995. Communicable Disease Surveillance Centre and Scottish Centre for Infection and Environmental Health. *Communicable Disease Report, 5*:183.

P.H.L.S. AIDS Centre. 1995 (June). Communicable Disease Surveillance Centre and Scottish Centre for Infection and Environmental Health. Unpublished "AIDS/HIV Quarterly Surveillance Tables, No. 28."

P.H.L.S., AIDS and STD Centre–Communicable Disease Surveillance Centre, and Scottish Centre for Infection & Environmental Health. *Communicable disease report 2000, 10*(13):123-124.

P.H.L.S., MDS and STD Centre–Communicable Disease Surveillance Centre, and Scottish Centre for Infection & Environmental Health. Unpublished "Quarterly Surveillance Tables No. 46, May 2000."

Policy Studies Institute. 1994. *Fourth national survey of ethnic minorities*.

Radcliffe, K. W., et al. 1993. A comparison of sexual behavior and risk behavior for HIV infection between women in three clinical settings. *Genitourinary Medicine, 69*:441-445.

Read, J. 1995. *Counseling for fertility problems*. London: Sage Publications.

Reader, F. C. 1994. Training in human sexuality in United Kingdom medical schools. *Sexual and Marital Therapy, 9*: 193-200.

Reddaway, W. B. 1939. *The economics of a declining population*. London: Allen & Unwin.

Rees, M. 1996. *Royal Commission on Population. Report.* Cmnd. 7956. London: HMSO.

*Report of the Population Panel*. 1973. *Cmnd 5258*. London: HMSO.

Report of the Social Exclusion Unit. 1999. *Teenage pregnancy*. Cm 4342. The Stationery Office.

Savage, W., & C. Francome. 1989. *Lancet, ii*:1323-1324.

Secretary of State for Health. 1992. *The health of the nation: A strategy for health in England*. London: H.M.S.O.

Selman, P. 1996. Teenage pregnancy in the 1960s and 1980s. In: J. Millar & H. Jones, *The politics of the family*. London: Avebury.

Snaith, P., A. Butler, J. Donnelly, & D. Bromham. 1994. A regional gender reassignment service. *Psychiatric Bulletin, 18*:753-756.

Sweat, M., S. Gregorich, G. Sangiwa, et al. 2000. Cost-effectiveness of voluntary HIV-1 counselling and testing in reducing sexual transmission of HIV-1 in Kenya and Tanzania. *Lancet, 356*:113-121.

*Thematic review of young prisoners by HM Chief Inspector of Prisons for England and Wales*. 1997. Her Majesty's Inspector of Prisons (HMIP).

Thompson, R., & K. Sewell. 1995. *What took you so long?* Harmondsbury: Penguin.

Thomson, R., & L. Scott. 1992. *An enquiry into sex education: "Report of a survey of LEA support and monitoring of school sex education."* London: National Children's Bureau.

Titmuss, R. 1942. *Parents revolt: A study of the declining birth rate in acquisitive societies*. London: Secker & Warburg.

Turk, V., & H. Brown. 1993. The sexual abuse of adults with learning disabilities: Results of a two-year incidence survey. *Mental Handicap Research, 6*:193-216.

UNAIDS. 2002. *Epidemiological fact sheets by country*. Geneva, Switzerland: Joint United Nations Programme on HIV/AIDS (UNAIDS/WHO). Available: http://www.unaids.org/hivaidsinfo/statistics/fact_sheets/index_en.htm.

von Bühler, J., & L. Tamblin. 1995. *Sexual knowledge and attitudes of students attending an integrative human sexuality and relationship psychotherapy programme*. Research paper presented at the XIIth World Congress of Sexology, Yokohama, Japan.

Wadsworth, J., J. Field, A. M. Johnson, S. Bradshaw, & K. Wellings. 1993. Methodology of the National Survey of Sexual Attitudes and Lifestyles. *Journal of the Royal Statistics Society* (Series A), *156*:407-421.

Walker, P. A., J. C. Berger, R. Green, D. R. Laub, et al. 1985. Standards of care, the hormonal and surgical reassignment of gender dysphoric persons. *Archives of Sexual Behaviour, 14*:79-90.

Wareham, V., & N. Drummond. 1994. Contraception use among teenagers seeking abortion—A survey from Grampian. *British Journal of Family Planning, 20*:76-78.

Watson, H. 1994. Red herrings and mystifications. In: C. Brant & Y-H Too, eds. *Rethinking sexual harassment*. London: Pluto Press.

Waugh, M. A. 1990. History of clinical developments in sexually transmitted diseases. In: K. K. Holmes, et al., eds., *Sexually transmitted diseases* (2nd ed., chap. 1). New York: McGraw-Hill.

Wellings, K., J. Field, A. M. Johnson, & J. Wadsworth. 1994. *Sexual behaviour in Britain: The National Survey of Attitudes and Lifestyles*. Harmondsworth: Penguin.

Westrom, L. 1988. Decrease in incidence of women treated in hospitals for acute salpingitis in Sweden. *Genitourinary Medicine, 64*:59-64.

Whittle, S. 2000. *The transgender debate: The crisis surrounding gender identity*. South Street Press, Reading, UK: Garnet Publishing Limited.

Williams, C. 1993. Sexuality and disability. In: J. Ussher & C. Baker, eds., *Psychological perspectives on sexual problems*. London: Routledge.

Wise, S., & L. Stanley. 1987. *Georgie Porgie: Sexual harassment in everyday life*. London: Pandora Press.

Zeki, S. 1992. Unpublished dissertation for the Master of Science in Clinical Psychology, University College, London.

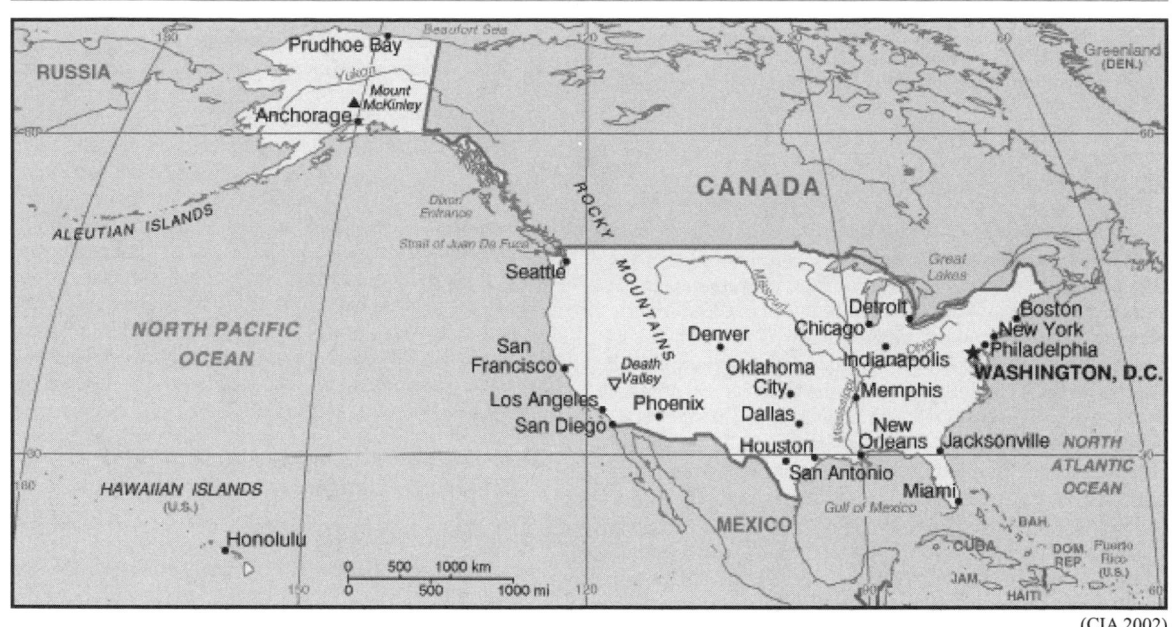

(CIA 2002)

# United States of America

David L. Weis, Ph.D., and Patricia Barthalow Koch, Ph.D., editors and contributors, with other contributions by Diane Baker, M.A.; Ph.D.; Sandy Bargainnier, Ed.D.; Sarah C. Conklin, Ph.D.; Martha Cornog, M.A., M.S.; Richard Cross, M.D.; Marilyn Fithian, Ph.D.; Jeannie Forrest, M.A.; Andrew D. Forsythe, M.S.; Robert T. Francoeur, Ph.D., A.C.S.; Barbara Garris, M.A.; Patricia Goodson, Ph.D.; William E. Hartmann, Ph.D.; Robert O. Hawkins, Jr., Ph.D.; Linda L. Hendrixson, Ph.D.; Barrie J. Highby, Ph.D.; Ariadne (Ari) Kane, Ed.D.; Sharon E. King, M.S.Ed.; Robert Morgan Lawrence, D.C.; Brenda Love; Charlene L. Muehlenhard, Ph.D.; Raymond J. Noonan, Ph.D.; Miguel A. Pérez, Ph.D.; Timothy Perper, Ph.D.; Helda L. Pinzón-Pérez, Ph.D.; Carol Queen, Ph.D.; Herbert P. Samuels, Ph.D.; Julian Slowinski, Psy.D.; William Stackhouse, Ph.D.; William R. Stayton, Th.D.; and Mitchell S. Tepper, M.P.H.*

*Updates coordinated by Raymond J. Noonan, Ph.D., and Robert T. Francoeur, Ph.D., with comments and updates by Mark O. Bigler L.C.S.W., Ph.D., Walter Bockting, Ph.D., Peggy Clarke, M.P.H., Sarah C. Conklin, Ph.D., Al Cooper, Ph.D., Martha Cornog, M.A., M.S., Susan Dudley, Ph.D.,*

*Warren Farrell, Ph.D., James R. Fleckenstein, Robert T. Francoeur, Ph.D., Patricia Goodson, Ph.D., Erica Goodstone, Ph.D., Karen Allyn Gordon, M.P.H., Ph.D. (cand.), Eric Griffin-Shelley, Ph.D., Robert W. Hatfield, Ph.D., Loraine Hutchins, Ph.D., Michael Hyde, M.F.A., Ph.D. (cand.), Ariadne (Ari) Kane, Ed.D., Patricia Barthalow Koch, Ph.D., John Money, Ph.D., Charlene L. Muehlenhard, Ph.D., Raymond J. Noonan, Ph.D., Miguel A. Pérez, Ph.D., Helda L. Pinzón-Pérez, Ph.D., William Prendergast, Ph.D., Ruth Rubenstein, Ph.D., Herbert P. Samuels, Ph.D., William Taverner, M.A., David L. Weis, Ph.D., C. Christine Wheeler, Ph.D., and Walter L. Williams, Ph.D.***

## Contents

*Communications*: Robert T. Francoeur, Ph.D., 4310 Cleveland Lane, Rockaway, NJ 07866-5811 USA; rtfrancoeu@aol.com. Raymond J. Noonan, Ph.D., Health and Physical Education Department, Fashion Institute of Technology of the State University of New York, 27th Street and 7th Avenue, New York, NY 10001 USA; 212-217-7460; rjnoonan@SexQuest.com. David L. Weis, Ph.D., Bowling Green State University, Family and Consumer Science, Bowling Green, OH 43403-0001 USA; weis@bgnet.bgsu.edu. Patricia Barthalow Koch, Ph.D., Pennsylvania State University, 304 East Henderson Bldg., University Park, PA 16802 USA; p34@psu.edu.

**In addition to the above sexologists who authored specific sections of this chapter, the authors and general editor are grateful to other colleagues who served as special consultants: Mark O. Bigler, L.C.S.W., Ph.D.; Bonnie Bullough, R.N.; Vern L. Bullough, R.N., Ph.D.; Sandra S. Cole, Ph.D.; Carol A. Darling, Ph.D.; J. Kenneth Davidson, Ph.D.; Clive Davis, Ph.D.; Karen Komisky-Brash, M.A.; Barbara Van Oss Marin, Ph.D.; Ted McIlvenna, Th.D, Ph.D.; Gina Ogden, Ph.D.; Paul Okami, Ph.D.; Letitia Anne Peplau, Ph.D.; and Stephanie Wadell, M.A. Although these colleagues generously contributed resource materials and their expertise for sections of the chapter, the authors and general editor accept full responsibility for the final integration of the material presented in this chapter.

## Demographics and a Brief Historical Perspective

ROBERT T. FRANCOEUR

### A. Demographics

The United States is located in the southern part of the North American continent. Its mainland is south of Canada and north of Mexico and the Caribbean Sea, Cuba, Puerto Rico, and other Caribbean island nations. The North Atlantic and North Pacific Oceans border the mainland on the east and west. The United States is the third-largest country by size, after Russia and Canada, and by population, after China and India. In comparing landmass, the U.S. is about half the size of Russia, three-tenths the size of Africa, about half the size of South America, slightly larger than China, and about two and a half times the size of Western Europe. The state of Alaska lies off Canada's northwestern border, and the islands of Hawaii are 2,090 miles (3,360 km) southwest of San Francisco in the North Pacific.

The mainland climate is mostly temperate, but it is tropical in Florida and Hawaii, arctic in Alaska, semiarid in the Great Plains west of the Mississippi River, and arid in the Great Basin of the southwest.

In July 2002, the United States had an estimated population of 280.5 million. (All data are from *The World Factbook 2002* (CIA 2002) unless otherwise stated.)

**Age Distribution and Sex Ratios**: *0-14 years*: 21% with 1.05 male(s) per female (sex ratio); *15-64 years*: 66.4% with 0.98 male(s) per female; *65 years and over*: 12.6% with 0.72 male(s) per female; *Total population sex ratio*: 0.96 male(s) to 1 female

**Life Expectancy at Birth**: *Total Population*: 77.4 years; *male*: 74.5 years; *female*: 80.2 years

**Urban/Rural Distribution**: 76% to 24%

**Ethnic Distribution**: White: 77.1%; black: 12.9%; Asian: 4.2%; Amerindian and Alaska native: 1.5%; native Hawaiian and other Pacific islander: 0.3%; other: 4% (2000). *Note*: A separate listing for Hispanic is not included because the U.S. Census Bureau considers Hispanic to mean a person of Latin American descent (especially of Cuban, Mexican, or Puerto Rican origin) living in the U.S. who may be of any race or ethnic group (white, black, Asian, etc.). In January 2003, the Census Bureau announced that the Hispanic population had jumped to roughly 37 million. For the first time, Hispanics nosed past blacks (with 36.2 million) as the largest minority group in the United States.

**Religious Distribution**: Protestant: 56%; Roman Catholic: 28%; Jewish: 2%; other: 4%; none: 10%

**Birth Rate**: 14.1 births per 1,000 population

**Death Rate**: 8.7 per 1,000 population

**Infant Mortality Rate**: 6.69 deaths per 1,000 live births

**Net Migration Rate**: 3.5 migrant(s) per 1,000 population

**Total Fertility Rate**: 6.8 children born per woman

**Population Growth Rate**: 2.07%

**HIV/AIDS** (1999 est.): *Adult prevalence*: 0.61%; *Persons living with HIV/AIDS*: 850,000; *Deaths*: 20,000. (For additional details from www.UNAIDS.org, see end of Section 10B.)

**Literacy Rate** (*defined as those age 15 and over who can read and write*): 97%; education is free and compulsory from age 6 to 17

**Per Capita Gross Domestic Product** (*purchasing power parity*): $36,300; *Inflation*: 2.8%; *Unemployment*: 5%; *Living below the poverty line*: 12.7% (2001 est.)

### B. A Brief Historical Perspective

Britain's American colonies broke with the mother country in 1776 and were recognized as the new nation of the United States of America following the Treaty of Paris in 1783. During the 19th and 20th centuries, 37 new states were added to the original 13 as the nation expanded across the North American continent and acquired a number of overseas possessions: Cuba, the Panama Canal Zone, the Philippines, and Hawaii and Alaska. The two most traumatic experiences in the nation's history were the Civil War (1861-1865) and the Great Depression of the 1930s. Buoyed by victories in World Wars I and II and the end of the Cold War in 1991, the U.S. remains the world's most powerful nation. The economy has been marked by steady growth, low unemployment and inflation, and rapid advances in technology.

### C. Demographic Challenges and a Sketch of Diversity, Change, and Social Conflict

DAVID L. WEIS

*Demographic Challenges*

In one sense, great diversity is virtually guaranteed by the sheer size of the United States. The U.S.A. is a union of 50 participating states. It is one of the larger nations in the world, with the 48 contiguous states spanning more than 3,000 miles (4,800 km) across the North American continent, from its eastern shores on the Atlantic Ocean to its western shores on the Pacific Ocean, and more than 2,000 miles (3,200 km) from its northern border with Canada to its southern border with Mexico and the Gulf of Mexico. In addition, the state of Alaska, itself a large landmass covering thousands of square miles in the northwest corner of North America, and the state of Hawaii, a collection of islands in the mid-Pacific Ocean, are part of the union.

The United States has a population of more than 280 million racially and ethnically heterogeneous people (Wilkinson 1987; CIA 2002). A majority, about 190 million are white descendants of immigrants from the European continent, with sizable groups from Great Britain, Ireland, Italy, Germany, and Poland. The last decade of the 20th century marked a major shift in the ethnic balance of the U.S. Between 1990 and 2002, white Americans whose ancestors came from Europe dropped from 80.1% to 75.1%. African-Americans, most of whose ancestors were brought to North America as slaves before the 20th century, dropped from second to third place, from 12.1% to 12.3%. Hispanics moved from third place at 9.0% in 1990 to second place in 2002 at 12.5% (see Section 2B, Religious, Ethnic, and Gender Factors Affecting Sexuality, Racial, Ethnic, and Gender Perspectives, U.S. Latinos and Sexual Health in 2003). Their ancestors emigrated from such places as Mexico, Puerto Rico, Cuba, Haiti, and the Dominican Republic, as well as other Central and South American nations. Hispanics represent the fastest-growing minority group in the U.S. There are also more than two million Native Americans—Eskimos, Aleuts, and those mistakenly at one time called Indians—whose ancestors have occupied North America for thousands of years, and whose residence within the boundaries of what is now the U.S.A. predates all of the other groups mentioned.

Another group experiencing rapid growth in recent decades is Asian-Americans; there are now more than three million residents of Asian heritage. Substantial populations of Japanese and Chinese immigrants have been in the U.S.A. since the 19th century. More recently, there has been an increase from such nations as India, Vietnam, Korea, the Philippines, Cambodia, Indonesia, and Pakistan. Finally, there are smaller groups of immigrants from virtually every nation, with growing numbers of Muslims in recent decades. The size of the various nonwhite minority groups has been increasing in the last 30 years, both in terms of real numbers and as a percentage of the total U.S. population (Wilkinson 1987; *World Almanac 1993*).

It is fair to conclude that the U.S.A. is generally a nation of former immigrants. Moreover, one continuing feature of American history has been the successive immigration of different groups at different points in time (Wells 1985).

Approximately two thirds of the population lives within 100 miles (160 km) of one of the coastal shorelines. Most of the largest metropolitan areas lie within these coastal areas, and it is worth noting that most sexologists in the U.S.A. also reside in these same areas.

The United States is somewhat unique among the world's economies in that it is simultaneously one of the largest agricultural producers, as well as one of the largest industrialized nations, exporting manufactured goods and technology to the rest of the world. Historically, the northeast and upper midwest have been the principal industrial centers, and the southeast and the central Great Plains have been the agricultural centers.

One of the economically richest nations in the world, America, nevertheless, has an estimated 500,000 to 600,000 individuals and 125,000 to 150,000 families homeless on any night. Overall, 15% of Americans—30% of the poor—are without health insurance. Infant-mortality rates and life-expectancy rates vary widely, depending on socioeconomic status and residence in urban, suburban, or rural settings. Fifty-two million American married couples are paralleled by 2.8 million unmarried households and close to 8 million single-parent families.

In summarizing aspects of sexuality in America, it is helpful to keep in mind that the United States of the 21st century will look profoundly different from the nation described in this chapter. Four major trends for the future have been detailed in *Population Profile of the United States* (1995), published by the U.S. Census Bureau.

- The average life expectancy for an American in 1900 was 47 years. An American born in 1970 had a life expectancy of 70.8 years. This rose to 76 years in 1993 and is projected to reach 82.6 years by 2050.
- The median age of Americans is currently 34; early in the 21st century, it will be 39. There are currently 33 million Americans over 65; this number will more than double to 80 million in 2050.
- America's ethnic minorities will continue to grow far more quickly than the majority white population, because of immigration and higher birthrates. In 1994, for the first time, more Hispanics than whites were added to the population. If current trends hold, the percentage of white Americans will decline from 73.7% in 1995 to 52.5% in 2050.
- In 1994, 24% of all children under age 18 (18.6 million) lived with a single parent, double the percent in 1970. Of these single parents, 36% had never been married, up 50% from 1985. Meanwhile, the number of unmarried cohabiting couples increased 700% in the past decade.

There is also great diversity in religious affiliation in the United States (Marciano 1987; see Section 2A). To a considerable degree, the choice of religious denomination is directly related to the ethnic patterns previously described. The overwhelming majority of Americans represent the Judeo-Christian heritage, but that statement is potentially misleading. Within the Judeo-Christian heritage, there are substantial populations of Roman Catholics, mainstream Protestants (Lutheran, Methodist, Baptist, Episcopalian, and others), and a growing number of fundamentalist Christians. There is no great uniformity in religious practice or

sexual mores shared by these various groups. In addition, there is a relatively small percentage of Americans who are Jewish and range from ultra-orthodox to conservative, reformed, and liberal. In recent decades, as immigration from Asia has increased, there has been a corresponding growth in the Muslim and Hindu faiths.

Several trends related to the practice of religion in the U.S.A. have become a source of recent social concern. These trends include: the declining attendance at the traditional Protestant and Catholic churches in what has been labeled the growing "secularization" of American culture; the "religious revivalism" reflected by the growth of fundamentalist churches; the growth of religious cults (e.g., Hare Krishna and the Unification Church); the growing power of the conservative Christian Coalition; and the emergence of the "Electronic Church" (religious broadcasting) (Marciano 1987). Throughout the history of this nation, diversity of religious beliefs and the separation of church and state have been central elements in conflicts over sexual morality.

The subcultures and peoples of the United States are as varied, diverse, and complex as any other large nation. The unique feature of sexuality in the United States is that we have far more information and data on American sexual attitudes, values, and behaviors than is available for any other country.

## A Sketch of Recent Diversity, Change, and Social Conflict

A few examples will illustrate some of the issues that have been affected by this complex of influences.

[*Update 1998*: The dominant news story in the U.S. through much of 1998 concerned the alleged extramarital sexual practices of President Bill Clinton. Stories about Clinton's sexual experiences with a number of women routinely surfaced throughout his presidential term. Certainly, no American president has ever been subjected to as much speculation about extramarital sex while still in office. As early as his first presidential campaign in 1992, Gennifer Flowers alleged that she had had a long-term affair with Clinton while he had been governor of Arkansas. Clinton initially denied her specific allegations. He did admit in a televised interview that he and his wife had had extramarital experiences, claiming that he and his wife had resolved their marital problems. Later, after his election, he admitted to an affair with Flowers. In 1994, Paula Jones, a former Arkansas state employee, revealed at a press conference sponsored by a fundamentalist Christian group that she believed Clinton had sexually harassed her in 1991 while he was governor. Later that year, Jones filed a civil suit charging the President with sexual harassment. Jones claimed that Clinton invited her to his hotel room (using a state trooper as an intermediary), exposed himself, and asked her to perform fellatio (Isikoff & Thomas 1997; Taylor 1997). The U.S. Supreme Court ruled unanimously in 1997 that the suit could proceed while Clinton was still in office (Isikoff & Thomas 1997).

[Enter Kenneth Starr. Starr, a Republican judge, had been appointed as a special prosecutor early in the Clinton presidency to investigate possible improprieties in an Arkansas business deal involving the Clintons that had come to be known as the Whitewater investigation. By November 1996, having spent three years and roughly $30 million and failing to generate credible evidence of wrongdoing by the Clintons, Starr's investigators began questioning women who may have had sexual encounters with Clinton (Isikoff & Fineman 1997). With the Supreme Court ruling that the Jones lawsuit could proceed, Jones's lawyers also began a search for women who could testify that they had been approached by the President while working for him. Members of the American press followed leads along the same lines. By early 1997, these separate lines of inquiry led all three groups to Linda Tripp, Monica Lewinsky, and Kathleen Willey.

[Kathleen Willey, a former volunteer in the White House social office, was initially called to testify in the Jones case. She made charges that Clinton had kissed and fondled her in the White House Oval Office in 1993 when she met with him there seeking a full-time job. Upon leaving Clinton's office, Willey saw Linda Tripp in the hallway. According to Tripp's affidavit, Willey had left that meeting looking disheveled and told her that the President had made sexual overtures toward her. Clinton's attorney, Robert Bennett, called the charges a lie and attacked Tripp (Fineman & Breslau 1998; Isikoff & Thomas 1998). Tripp claimed that Willey had been pleased and "joyful" about the experience. Willey later claimed that she was distraught and upset by the incident. However, a friend of Willey's claimed that Willey had instructed her to lie about being distraught over the incident. According to the friend, Willey had not been upset (Isikoff 1997). The Willey allegations did not become public until a *60 Minutes* television interview in March 1998. Clinton denied the charges.

[In January 1998, President Clinton and Monica Lewinsky each signed affidavits in the Paula Jones case that they had never had sexual relations with each other. However, throughout 1997, Lewinsky had told a friend of hers on numerous occasions that she had been having an affair with the President. The friend was Linda Tripp. Believing that she would be called to testify about what Lewinsky had told her and fearing that she would be attacked by Clinton's defense team, Tripp began taping her phone calls with Lewinsky. A week after the Lewinsky affidavit denying any sexual involvement with Clinton, Tripp approached Kenneth Starr's investigators with her story. They proceeded to wire her for subsequent conversations with Monica Lewinsky. Roughly a week later, the story hit the headlines that Clinton may have had an affair with Lewinsky, that he may have perjured himself in the Jones case by denying it, that there was taped evidence of Lewinsky telling a friend about the affair, and that Clinton and his associates may have obstructed justice by urging Lewinsky to lie under oath (Fineman & Breslau 1998; Isikoff & Thomas 1998). There seemed to be little else in the news besides this ongoing saga.

[As we went to press, it was not yet clear how these allegations would turn out. On April 1, 1998, the suit by Paula Jones was thrown out of court. The federal judge in the case ruled that Clinton had not committed a crime of either sexual assault or sexual harassment, even if Jones's claims were factual. Two thirds of American adults had indicated months earlier that they did not believe the Jones incident constituted sexual harassment (Isikoff & Thomas 1997).

[In an ironic twist, President Clinton's approval ratings increased to their highest levels ever in the months after the Lewinsky story became national news. There was considerable speculation in the press about what this meant. It seemed clear that the majority of the American public did not want to see Clinton removed from office for the charges that had surfaced thus far. Many interpreted the polls as indicating that most Americans believed that a person's sex life—even the President's—is a private matter and should not be subjected to public investigation, unless it was specifically criminal itself. The message from the American public seemed to be, "Stay out of our bedrooms."

[Another ironic consequence of these collected stories was that, at least for the time being, discourse about sexuality had never been freer or more open. Americans in general and the American media routinely discussed the President's sex life, extramarital sex, oral sex, and the like. As a culture,

we seemed to be talking about sex more than ever. (*End of update by D. L. Weis*)]

[*Update 2003*: As we went to press in 1998 with *Sexuality in America*, the single volume of the U.S. chapter taken from volume 3 of *The International Encyclopedia of Sexuality*, it was not yet clear how the allegations about President Clinton having sex with Monica Lewinski and other women would fall out. At first, Clinton denied those charges, waggling his finger at television cameras as he claimed that he had never had sex with "that woman." Of course, we know now that Clinton and Lewinsky did have oral sex together (apparently, she performed oral sex on him, but he did *not* return the favor). The U.S. House of Representatives voted—in an overwhelmingly partisan display—to impeach him, and the U.S. Senate ultimately voted *not* to convict Mr. Clinton. The entire episode left many Americans and people around the world wondering what this all meant. Our concern here is with what it tells us about American sexuality and our themes of change, conflict, and diversity.

[First, we should mention that at no point did a majority of American citizens favor ousting Mr. Clinton from office over this affair. Roughly two thirds of the American public continued to support his presidency. The Republican party pursued impeachment on the assumption that, when Americans finally learned what Mr. Clinton had done, they would want him removed from office. That never happened. Roughly one third did respond that way, but only one third. In fact, numerous polls indicated that a majority of Americans were more likely to condemn Congress for impeaching Clinton than to have believed that he should be removed from office (Schell 1999). Social disapproval was the punishment for those who were seen as trying to get Clinton. Popularity ratings for Congress, Linda Tripp, and Ken Starr sank below 10% (Leland 1998/1999). Most social observers believed that this represented a shift from what would have occurred in the past, say if the extramarital sexual adventures of Presidents Kennedy, Eisenhower, and Franklin Roosevelt had become widely known. It is not an exaggeration to suggest that this is what allowed him to finish his term in office.

[A second consequence of the Bill Clinton sex scandal would be that sexual discourse is now even more open in America. According to John Leland (1998/1999), this open discourse about sex, including the Clinton scandal, oral sex, Viagra, and so on, is the principal distinguishing characteristic of the present culture. To this, we can add that the episode has made social conservatives even more determined to reverse what they see as the moral decay of American society.

[Third, there is the issue of what we might call the Bill Clinton definition of sex, stemming from his frequently reshown claim that he had not had sex with Monica Lewinsky. There are now several studies of what Americans think "sex" is. Sanders and Reinisch (1999) asked 599 midwestern college students in 1991 if they believed that various acts constituted "having sex." Roughly 60% indicated that they believed engaging in oral sex did *not* constitute having sex. In addition, nearly 20% indicated that anal sex was also *not* having sex. By the way, the editor of the *Journal of the American Medical Association* was fired shortly after publishing this study (Cowley & Springen 1999). Hawkins and a research group (2002) completed a study of 311 7th- to 12th-grade students in rural Arkansas (Clinton's home state). The students were asked to indicate what the words "abstinent" and "sexual activity" mean. The responses demonstrate a general lack of consensus about what these terms mean. Many of these young people, but not all, believed sex is intercourse. Similarly, abstinence was widely seen as abstaining from intercourse. Remez (2000) reported that "many" adolescents engage in oral sex without having intercourse and that "many" do *not* regard this as sexual activity. This view is also common in the Baptist (which Clinton is) tradition. One Baptist minister described the behavior as disgusting, but insisted that it did *not* constitute having sex (Woodward 1998). Thus, many Americans do, in fact, appear to share the view that oral sex is *not* having sex. Clearly, there is great opportunity for sex education in America—even today.

[Finally, we would like to note that the 2000 presidential election in the U.S.A. also demonstrates our general themes of change, conflict, and diversity. The polls from 1998 through 2000 strongly suggest that Mr. Clinton would have been re-elected if he could have run. True, those same polls indicate that one third of Americans would have bitterly opposed him. The actual election results, with Gore and Bush drawing almost exactly 50% of the vote, demonstrates that the cultural war between competing factions (which we discuss throughout this American chapter) is about as great as it has ever been. This has played out as a regular theme of the George W. Bush administration.

[There were, of course, other examples of change, conflict, and diversity besides the Clinton affair, which we mentioned in *Sexuality in America* in 1998 and our original chapter in 1997. (*End of update by D. L. Weis*)]

- In late 1993, *Private Parts* by radio disc-jockey Howard Stern (1993), the inventor of "Shock Rock" radio, was published. Stern's radio shows had had a large audience across the U.S.A. for more than a decade. He had been strongly condemned by some for the sexual explicitness of his shows and criticized by others for the sexist nature of those same shows. On several occasions, his shows had been investigated by the Federal Communications Commission (FCC). *Private Parts*, a lurid account of Stern's shows and his sexual fantasies, was roundly criticized. However, it also became the bestselling book in the U.S. in 1993 (Adler 1994). By 1998, Stern had a nationally syndicated television show in addition to his nationally syndicated radio show. *Private Parts* was released as a movie in 1997 to critical acclaim and huge audiences. A compact disc of the soundtrack to the movie was also a national hit in 1997.

- Dr. Joycelyn Elders was fired in late 1994 as the Surgeon General of the United States for saying that children perhaps should be taught in school about masturbation. Elders, who was called the "Condom Queen" by conservatives in the United States, had become what the press described as a "political liability" to President Bill Clinton for expressing her views on controversial social issues, such as abortion, condom education for youth, and drug legalization (Cohn 1994). However, her firing was a direct reaction to comments she made about including masturbation as a part of sex-education programs for children. Elders made her comments on December 1, 1994, in an address to a World AIDS Day conference in New York City. In response to a question from the audience about her views on masturbation, Elders said, "I think that is something that is a part of human sexuality, and it's a part of something that perhaps should be taught. But we've not even taught our children the very basics." She added, "I feel that we have tried ignorance for a very long time, and it's time we try education" (Hunt 1994). In announcing her dismissal, the Clinton administration pointedly indicated that the President disagreed with her views.

- By the middle of the 1990s, seven physicians and clinical staff members had been killed by anti-abortion activists. Over 80% of abortion providers in the U.S.A. have been picketed, and many have experienced other forms of harassment, including bomb and death threats, blockades, invasion of facilities, destruction of property, and assaults on patients and staff. The most recent tactic adopted by abortion opponents is to locate women who have had a bad experience with an abortion in order to persuade them to file a malpractice suit against the physician who performed the abortion.

- The term "sexual harassment" did not appear in American culture until around 1975. In the years since, there has been a tremendous growth in research on the problem and growing social conflict over its prevalence and definition. As late as 1991, when Anita Hill testified against Supreme Court nominee Clarence Thomas, only 29% of Americans believed her claims (Solomon & Miller 1994). Yet, the number of women filing claims doubled in the 1990s, and the U.S. Supreme Court ruled in 1993 that harassment could be determined if a worker demonstrated that the workplace environment was "hostile" or "abusive" to a "reasonable person" (Kaplan 1993). Workers would no longer have to demonstrate that severe psychological injury had occurred as a consequence. Similar controversies over definitions, prevalence, and credibility of claims have emerged with the issues of incest, child sexual abuse, and date or acquaintance rape.

- In June 1997, the Southern Baptist Convention, the nation's second-largest religious denomination, called for a boycott of Walt Disney Company stores and theme parks to protest its "anti-Christian and anti-family trend" in extending health benefits to the same-sex partners of employees. The Baptists declared that such policies constituted an overly permissive stance toward homosexuality (Morganthau 1997). Gay activists were outraged by the decision, regarding it as mean-spirited.

- In April 1997, Ellen DeGeneres, star of the sitcom, "Ellen," publicly announced that she was gay. On April 30 of the same year, her television character also came out of the closet, making Ellen the first leading lesbian in an American sitcom (Marin & Miller 1997). By early 1998, the ABC network canceled the show because of sagging ratings, a problem that had begun before the television "coming out."

- Some years ago, the Iowa state legislature passed a bill outlawing nude dancing in establishments that serve alcohol. The activity moved to "juice bars." In 1997, the legislature decided to make nude dancing illegal in any establishment holding a sales-tax permit, except businesses devoted primarily to the arts. As a result, the Southern Comfort Free Theater for the Performing Arts opened in Mount Joy, Iowa. Patrons are asked for "donations" and are described as "students." In a similar story in Orlando, Florida, a ban on nude dancing has been circumvented by the establishment of "gentlemen's clubs," where patrons pay membership dues (*Newsweek* 1997).

- After decades of explicitly banning homosexuals from the military, President Clinton proposed ending the ban shortly after he assumed office in 1992. The policy put into place, popularly known as "Don't ask, don't tell," was one in which the military agreed that they would stop asking recruits to report their sexual orientation. However, gays and lesbians can only serve in the armed forces if they keep their orientation private (*Newsweek* 1993, 6). By mid-1998, the Servicemembers Legal Defense Network reported that violations of the policy not to ask, pursue, or harass homosexuals had soared from 443 violations in 1996 to 563 violations in 1997. Reported cases of physical and verbal harassment of gay servicemembers rose 38% from 1996 to 1997, while cases of illegal asking by military authorities increased by 39%. In 1996, an airman at Hickham Air Force Base had his life sentence for forcible sodomy reduced to 20 months in return for outing 17 other allegedly gay servicemen. All the accused airmen were discharged, while the rapist served less than a year.

- There is a growing wave of censorship being engineered by grassroots far-right organizations targeting, in particular, sexuality education textbooks and programs in local school districts throughout the country. Fear of personal attacks, disruption, controversy, and costly lawsuits have resulted in more teachers, administrators, and school boards yielding to the demands of vocal minority groups. In more than a third of documented incidents, challenged materials and programs were either removed, canceled, or replaced with abstinence-only material or curricula (Sedway 1992). In 1996, the U.S. Congress overwhelmingly passed the Communications Decency Act (CDA), a bill intended to regulate "indecent" and "patently offensive" speech on the Internet, which included information on abortion. In mid-1996, a three-judge federal panel in Philadelphia declared unconstitutional major parts of the new law. Even as the judges described attempts to regulate content on the Internet as a "profoundly repugnant" affront to the First Amendment's guarantee of free speech, the government planned an appeal to the U.S. Supreme Court. Both the Senate and House of Representatives had overwhelmingly passed the CDA, and the President signed into law the bill that included it (Levy 1997). The law was finally ruled unconstitutional by the Supreme Court on June 27, 1997, although various government efforts continue to try to circumvent the decision (Noonan 1998).

- In the mid-1990s, a broad-based evangelical-revivalist movement, modeled in part on the Million Man March, which brought hundreds of thousands of African-American men to Washington, packed athletic stadiums across the country with men confessing their failures as husbands and fathers, and promising with great emotion to fulfill their Christian duties as men, husbands, fathers, and the heads of their families. The Promise Keepers, like the Million Men Marches, were criticized and denounced by feminists and others for their alleged devotion to traditional patriarchal and sexist values.

- In mid-1995, Norma Leah McCorvey, the Jane Roe at the epicenter of the 1973 *Roe v. Wade* Supreme Court decision legalizing abortion, announced she had quit her work at a Dallas, Texas, abortion clinic, had been baptized in a swimming pool by a minister of Operation Rescue, a national anti-abortion group, and would be working at the Operation Rescue office next door to the abortion clinic. Although there is "immense symbolic importance" in McCorvey's announcement, it is odd that the born-again-Christian Operation Rescue group would embrace her so enthusiastically, given her declarations that she still believes "a woman has a right to have an abortion, a safe and legal abortion, in the first trimester" of pregnancy, and that she would continue living with her lesbian partner and working for lesbian rights (Verhovek 1995). In mid-1996, abortion again emerged as a major election issue when Robert Dole, the Republican Party candidate for president, called for a statement of tolerance in the Republican platform, a move vehemently opposed by conservative Republicans.

- In 1996, with the state of Hawaii on the verge of granting legal status to same-sex unions, several states moved quickly to enact laws banning the legal recognition of such unions, despite the Constitutional requirement that all states reciprocally recognize the legal acts of other states. In June 1996, a House Judiciary Committee passed a bill that would absolve individual states from recognizing same-sex marriages if legalized in another state. The bill would also bar Federal recognition of such marriages in procedures involving taxes, pensions, and other benefits. Despite emotional debate in Congress, the measure cleared both the U.S. House of Representatives and the Senate. Although the President signed the bill into law, this debate remained a lightning-rod issue (Schmitt 1996).

[*Update 2003*: A few fairly obvious events in the news since 1998 are worth mentioning here to bring our central theme of change, conflict, and diversity up to the present.

- [In early 1998, Pfizer Pharmaceutical began marketing a drug for erectile dysfunction. Viagra quickly became the fastest and largest-selling pharmaceutical in world history (Watson 1998). Sales were helped when Bob Dole, an unsuccessful Republican presidential candidate, appeared in television advertisements for Viagra with his appreciative wife, Elizabeth Dole. (See details on the use of Viagra by R. Hatfield in Section 11B, Sexual Dysfunctions, Counseling, and Therapies, Current Status.)

- [On October 6, 1998, Aaron McKinney and Russell Henderson, a pair of high school dropouts, met Matthew Shepard, a slightly built gay University of Wyoming college student, at a bar in Laramie. Posing as gay men cruising, they lured Shepard into their truck. They robbed and beat him, leaving him tied spread-eagled to a fence post. He was discovered 18 hours later, but died within days of complications from the experience, including six skull fractures. The two were charged with first-degree murder. Later, there was some conflict between civil-rights crusaders, who wanted to use the incident to pass hate-crime legislation and conservative Christian groups, who claimed the story demonstrated the growing homosexual immorality of American life (Miller 1998; Hammer 1999). I remember some demonstrating their hatred at the Shepard funeral. Twenty-one Americans were murdered in 1998 because they were gay or lesbian (Alter 1998). The Matt Shepard story was turned into a Home Box Office (HBO) documentary in 2003.

- [In recent years, the American Catholic Church has been rocked by a continuing scandal over priests sexually abusing children. Much of the controversy has centered on dioceses along the eastern seaboard, although it has involved parishes across the country. Boston serves as a good example. Cardinal Bernard Law became embroiled in controversy over the handling of sexual abuse cases against priests that extended back before he came to Boston in 1984. The Rev. John J. Geoghan, convicted of sexually molesting a boy, was moved from parish to parish by the Boston Archdiocese for 30 years, even though the Church knew about his "problem." Lawyers in the case estimate that there may, in fact, have been as many as 130 victims of this particular priest. The Cardinal apologized many times and paid out more than $10 million to victims, but he also provided little information about any of this to the public. The Church had reversed its policy of withholding information from legal authorities and turned over records concerning 70 priests from over the last 40 years. As of 2002, there were 86 separate civil suits against the Boston Archdiocese pending (Clemerson et al. 2002; Miller et al. 2002; Woodward 2002). The National Conference of Catholic Bishops estimates that the Church has paid out more than $800 million to settle cases since the 1980s (Miller et al. 2002). Eventually, Cardinal Law did resign. The issue of exactly how the Church should respond to this crisis and how it ought to modify policy on these questions are still unresolved. Perhaps this is the greatest challenge ever facing the American Catholic Church. Its continuing vitality as a mainstream religion is at stake. (See details by W. Prendergast in Section 8A, Significant Unconventional Sexual Behaviors, Coercive Sex.)

- [One of the hottest trends in American television in the late 1990s and early 21st century has been the appearance of sexually pointed (though not explicit) programs, like "Sex in the City," "Oz," and "The Sopranos," on cable television. The open portrayal of sex and violence in these premium cable shows would never be permitted on network television, even today. HBO is the leader in this trend. They do not have enough subscribers nationwide to pull high ratings by themselves, but they are hurting the networks. Moreover, they are pushing the envelope. On the whole, these shows are smarter, edgier, franker, better written, and better acted than the typical network programming. They also march boldly into territory where the networks fear to go. These shows appeal to female viewers, who make up 40% of the audience (Hamilton & Brown 1999; Vineberg 2001).

- [In June 2003, the U.S. Supreme Court ruled that laws which specifically criminalize homosexual behavior are unconstitutional, opening the door to a range of legal possibilities I have never seen in my lifetime. Less than a week later, U.S. Senate Majority Leader, Bill Frisk (R-Tenn.) announced that he would support a proposed constitutional amendment that would ban all gay marriages (sponsored May 21 by Marilyn Musgrave (R-Colo.) among others) (Mann 2003), opening the door to visions of legal battles that will continue for decades. (*End of update by D. L. Weis*)]

Each of the above events in the late 1990s and early 21st century serves as an intriguing indicator of the state of sexuality in the United States, and each also reveals much about the interaction of politics and sexual issues as we approached the end of the 20th century. They demonstrate that, despite the immense social changes that have occurred during the 20th century, strong elements of religious fundamentalism and conservatism remain active within the culture. In fact, a full explanation of sexuality in the United States requires an understanding of the diverse sexual, social, and political ideologies characterizing the culture and the ongoing conflict between various groups over those ideologies.

In this respect, there is a rather schizophrenic character to sexuality in the United States. On the one hand, the U.S.A. is a country with a multibillion-dollar-a-year erotica/pornography business; a mass-media system where movies, television, books, magazines, and popular music are saturated with sexually titillating content alongside serious educational material; a high rate of premarital sex (nearly 90% by the 1990s); one of the most active and open gay-rights movements in the world; and a continuing public fascination with unusual sexual practices, extramarital sex, and gender-orientation issues, including, most recently, bisexuality.

On the other hand, federal, state, and local governments have invested heavily in recent years in prosecuting businesses for obscenity, allowed discriminatory practices based on sexual orientation, largely failed to implement comprehensive sexuality-education programs in the schools, and refused to support accessibility to contraceptives for adolescents. The consequences of these failures include one of the highest teenage-pregnancy and abortion rates in the world and increasing incidents of gay-bashing that reflect the prevalence of homonegative and homophobic attitudes in the U.S.A.

These examples illustrate one of the major themes in this chapter: the changing nature of sexuality in the U.S.A. throughout the 20th century. Although accounts of changing sexual norms and practices are frequently portrayed as occurring in a linear process, we would suggest that the more-typical pattern is one reflected by ongoing conflicts between competing groups over sexual ideology and practice. Each of the examples cited is an illustration of how those conflicts are currently manifested in the social and political arenas in the U.S.A.

A focus on the conflict between groups with contrasting ideologies and agendas over sexual issues will be a second theme of this chapter. This process of changing sexual attitudes, practices, and policies in an atmosphere that approaches "civil war" is a reflection of the tremendous diversity within American culture. In many respects, the widespread conflict over sexual issues is a direct outcome of the diversity of groups holding a vested interest in the outcomes of these conflicts, with some groups seeking to impose their beliefs on everyone.

The diversity of these groups will be the third major theme of the chapter. One example that will be apparent throughout this chapter is the question of gender. There is growing evidence that men and women in the U.S.A. tend to hold different sexual attitudes and ideologies, to exhibit different patterns of sexual behavior, and to pursue different sexual lifestyles—frequently at odds with each other (Oliver & Hyde 1993). In some ways, it may even be useful to view male and female perspectives as stemming from distinct gender cultures. In reviewing sexuality in the U.S.A., we will frequently attempt to assess how change occurs in a context of conflict between diverse social groups.

## 1. Basic Sexological Premises

DAVID L. WEIS

This overall theme of social change occurring in a process of conflict between diverse groups is woven throughout the history of the United States itself. There are at least two ways in which a study of history is important to an understanding of contemporary sexological premises and sexual patterns in the U.S.A. First, there is a specific history of sexual norms and customs changing over time. To the extent that sexual attitudes and practices are shared by the members of a social group or population in a particular time period, they can be viewed as social institutions. Unfortunately, it is exceedingly difficult to describe such sexual institutions in the U.S.A. prior to the 20th century, because there are few reliable empirical datasets available for that period. To a large extent, we have to rely on records of what people said about their own or others' sexual attitudes and practices, and such statements may be suspect. Still, it seems reasonable to suggest that current sexual norms and customs have been shaped, at least in part, by earlier patterns.

In addition, there is a second way in which the general social history of the U.S.A. is important to understanding changing sexual institutions. Sexuality, like other social institutions, does not operate in a vacuum. It is related to and influenced by other social institutions, such as the economy, government, marriage and the family, religion, and education, as well as social patterns such as age distributions and gender ratios. As we will discuss in Section 2, Religious, Ethnic, and Gender Factors Affecting Sexuality, a good deal of research evidence indicates that such social institutions are often related to various sexual variables. Researchers have not consistently tested these associations, but the point is a crucial one theoretically for explaining the dynamics of sexual processes in a culture as large and diverse as the U.S.A.

## A. From Colonial Times to the Industrial Revolution

In 1776, at the time of the War for American Independence, the U.S.A. became a nation of 13 states located along the shore of the Atlantic Ocean. Most of the inhabitants of the former British colonies were of English descent, and they tended to be Protestant. Although the first Africans had been brought to America as indentured servants as early as 1620, the practice of slavery quickly evolved. By the time of independence, an active slave trade involving hundreds of thousands of Africans and Caribbeans was well established. Of course, the Africans and Caribbeans brought their own customs with them, although they were frequently prevented from practicing them. West of the 13 original states, the remainder of the North American continent within the area now constituting the nation was inhabited by several million Native Americans representing hundreds of tribes, each with its own set of customs.

At its birth, the U.S.A. was essentially an agrarian society. More than 90% of the population were farmers. There were few cities with as many as 5,000 residents. Boston was the largest city with 16,000, and New York was the second largest with 13,000 (Reiss 1980). The Industrial Revolution had yet to begin. Few men, and virtually no women, were employed outside the family home. Although it has become common to think of the 20th-century pattern of role specialization, with the man serving as the family provider and the woman as the housekeeper and childcare provider, as the traditional American pattern, it did not characterize this early-American agrarian family. Family tasks tended to be performed out of necessity, with both men and women making direct and important contributions to the economic welfare of their families. Sexual norms and practices in early America arose in this social context.

The images of early-American sexuality in folklore are those of antihedonistic Puritanism and sexually repressed Victorianism. In popular culture, these terms have come to be associated with sexual prudishness. This view is oversimplistic and potentially misleading. Recent scholars (D'Emilio & Freedman 1988; Robinson 1976; Seidman 1991) tend to agree that sexuality was valued by the 18th-century Puritans and 19th-century Victorians within the context of marriage. To the Puritans, marriage was viewed as a spiritual union, and one that tended to emphasize the duties associated with commitment to that union. Marriage involved mutual affection and respect, and the couple was viewed as a primary social unit. Spouses were expected to fulfill reciprocal duties. One of these was sexual expression. No marriage was considered complete unless it was consummated sexually. The Puritans accepted erotic pleasure, as long as it promoted the mutual comfort and affection of the conjugal pair. The reciprocal duties of marital sexuality were justified, because they were seen as preventing individuals from becoming preoccupied with carnal desires and the temptation to practice improper sex outside of marriage (Seidman 1991). Of course, one of the principal functions of marital sex was reproduction. Pleasure alone did not justify sexual union. Instead, the regulation of sexual behavior reinforced the primacy of marital reproductive sex and the need for children (D'Emilio & Freedman 1988).

Within this context, it is certainly true that the early English settlers tried to regulate nonmarital forms of sexual ex-

pression. However, even this point can be exaggerated. Reiss (1980) has noted that Americans have always had a courtship system where individuals were free to select partners of their own choice. To some extent, this may have been because of necessities imposed by immigration to frontier territories, but it also was a consequence of the freedom settlers had from the institutions of social control found in Europe. Elsewhere, Reiss (1960, 1967) has maintained that such autonomy in courtship is associated with greater premarital sexual permissiveness.

In this regard, it is interesting to note that the settlers in New England developed the practice of bundling as a form of courtship. In colonial New England, settlers faced harsh winters. They commonly faced fuel shortages, and mechanized transportation forms had yet to be developed. Single men would travel miles to visit the home of an eligible female. Typically, they would spend the night before returning home the next day. Few New England homes of the period had multiple rooms for housing a guest, and few could heat the house for an entire 24-hour day. At night, the woman's family would bundle the man and the woman separately in blankets, and they would spend the night together talking to each other as they shared the same bed. It is worth noting that the practice of bundling was restricted to winters. Reiss (1980) has argued that the implicit understanding that the couple would avoid a sexual encounter was not always honored. In fact, a study of marriages in Groton, Massachusetts, from 1761 to 1775 found that one third of the women were pregnant at the time of their weddings (cited in Reiss 1980). This system was acceptable because betrothals were rarely broken at the time and because it served to produce the marital unions the Puritans valued so highly. Eventually, bundling was replaced by visits in the sitting parlors of 19th-century homes and by the practice of dating outside parental supervision in the 20th century (Reiss 1980).

Around 1800, the Industrial Revolution began changing this world, albeit gradually. In the two centuries since, virtually every aspect of American life has been transformed. The 19th century was marked by social turmoil, a frontier mentality open to radical change, and a resulting patchquilt of conflicting trends and values. Among the events that left their mark on American culture in the 19th century were the following:

- The century started with 16 states and ended with 45 states; the 1803 Louisiana Purchase doubled the country's size. Victory in the War of 1812 with England and a war with Mexico also added territory.
- A Victorian ethic dominated the country. Preachers and health advocates, like Sylvester Graham and John Kellogg, promoted a fear of sexual excesses, such as sex before age 30 or more than once in three years, and a paranoia about the dangers of masturbation.
- Despite a dominant conservative trend and three major economic depressions, small religious groups pioneered a variety of marital and communal lifestyles, and had an influence far beyond their tiny numbers. The Perfectionist Methodists of the Oneida Community (1831-1881) endorsed women's rights and group marriage; the Church of Latter-Day Saints (Mormons) practiced polygyny; Protestant Hutterites celebrated the communal life; and the Shakers and Harmony Community promoted a celibate lifestyle.
- In 1837, the first colleges for women opened.
- In 1848, the first women's rights convention was held in Seneca Falls, New York.
- A midcentury California gold rush and completion of the transcontinental railroad opened the west to an explosive

growth. San Francisco, for example, doubled its population from 400 to 810 between 1847 and 1857; four years later, its population was 25,000. A major shortage of women led to importing thousands of women from Mexico, Chile, China, and the Pacific islands, with widespread prostitution.

- In 1861-1865, a devastating Civil War led to the abolition of slavery, as well as to new opportunities for employment, such as secretaries using the new mass-produced typewriters, and nurses using the skills they developed when they took care of the wounded in the Civil War.
- In 1869, the Territory of Wyoming gave women the vote.
- In 1873, the Comstock Law prohibited mailing obscene literature, including information about marital sex and contraception; it was finally declared unconstitutional a century later.
- In the latter part of the 1800s, a few thousand Americans were part of an influential "free love" movement, which advocated sexual freedom for women, the separation of sex and reproduction, the intellectual equality of women and men, self-health and knowledge of one's own body and its functions, and women's right to the vote, to enjoy sex, and to obtain a divorce.

Pankhurst and Houseknecht (1983) have identified five major trends that they maintain began to change and shape the modern institutions of marriage and the family in the 19th century and continued to have an impact on American culture in the 20th century. The author of this section suggests that they have had a similar influence on sexual institutions. These trends are:

1. Industrialization, with its consequent process of urbanization and the eventual emergence of suburbs surrounding metropolitan areas;
2. A shift in the family from an economic-producing unit to that of a consumer;
3. The entry of men, and later of women, into the paid labor force;
4. The elongation and expansion of formal education, especially among women and minorities; and
5. Technological change.

We do not have the space to explore fully the impact of each of these trends. However, relevant effects would include increased lifespans, decreased maternal and infant mortality at childbirth, the development of effective contraceptives, the emergence of a consumer culture that allows families to purchase most of their goods and services, the creation of labor-saving household technologies, increased leisure time, the development of modern forms of transportation, especially automobiles and airplanes, an increasing divorce rate, the increasing entry of wives and mothers into the labor force, decreasing birthrates and family size, increasing rates of single-parent families and cohabitation, increasing percentages of adults living alone, and increasing proportions of married couples with no children currently living at home (Coontz 1992). Many of these changes have resulted in greater personal autonomy for individuals. As Reiss (1960, 1967) has argued, such autonomy may be a major factor underlying several changes in sexuality throughout American history.

It should be stressed that these changes have not necessarily been linear or consistent throughout the period of the Industrial Revolution. Many began to emerge in the 19th century but accelerated and became mainstream patterns only in the 20th century. For example, as late as 1900, a majority of Americans were still farmers. The 1920 census was the first to show a majority of the population living in towns and cities. By 1980, only 4% of Americans still lived on farms (Reiss 1980). Similarly, women began entering the labor force in the early 19th century. However, it was not until 1975 that one half of married women were employed. By 1990, 70% of married women between the ages of 25 and 44 were employed (Coontz 1992). Yet another example is provided by the divorce rate. It had been gradually increasing for decades. That rate doubled between 1965 and 1975, and for the first time, couples with children began divorcing in sizable numbers at that time (Coontz 1992; Reiss 1980; Seidman 1991).

Seidman (1991) has described the principal change in American sexuality during the 19th century as the "sexualization of love." It could also be described as a shift to companionate marriage. Marriage came to be defined less as an institutional arrangement of reciprocal duties, and more as a personal relationship between the spouses. The modern concept of love as a form of companionship, intimacy, and sharing came to be seen as the primary justification for marriage. As this process continued, the erotic longings between the partners, and the sexual pleasures shared by them, became inseparable from the qualities that defined love and marriage. By the early part of the 20th century, the desires and pleasures associated with sex came to be seen as a chief motivation and sustaining force in love and marriage (Seidman 1991). This view has come to be so dominant in the contemporary U.S.A. that few Americans today can envision any other basis for marriage.

D'Emilio and Freedman (1988) have argued that what they call the liberal sexual ethic described in the previous paragraph has been the attempt to promote this view of the erotic as the peak experience of marriage while limiting its expression elsewhere. However, as this view became the dominant American sexual ideology of the 20th century, it also served to legitimate the erotic aspects of sexuality itself (Seidman 1991). Eventually, groups emerged which have sought to value sex for its inherent pleasure and expressive qualities, as well as for its value as a form of self-expression. In effect, as the view that sexual gratification was a critical part of happiness for married persons became the dominant sexual ideology of 20th-century America, then it was only a matter of time until some groups began to question how it could be restricted only to married persons (D'Emilio & Freedman 1988).

## B. The 20th Century

The social turmoil and the pace of social change that marked the 19th century accelerated exponentially in the 20th century. American culture in the 20th century became increasingly complicated and changed by often-unanticipated developments in technology, communications, and medicine. Among the events that have been identified as significant in 20th-century United States are the following:

- In the early 1900s, Sigmund Freud and Havelock Ellis helped trigger the emergence of a more-positive approach to sexuality, especially in recognizing the normal sexuality of women and children, and the need for sex education.
- In 1916, spurred by Havelock Ellis, Margaret Sanger, a New York nurse, launched a crusade to educate poor and immigrant women about contraception, and established the first Planned Parenthood clinics.
- World War I brought women out of their Victorian homes into the war effort and work in the factories; shorter skirts and hairstyles were viewed as patriotic fashion and gave women more freedom. American soldiers encountered the more-relaxed sexual mores of France and Europe.

- The "Roarin' Twenties" were marked by the invention of cellulose sanitary napkins, the mobility of Henry Ford's affordable automobiles, new leisure and affluence, the advent of movies with female vamp stars and irresistible sex idols, and the appearance of the "Charleston," the "flapper," and cheek-to-cheek, body-clutching dancing.
- From 1929 to 1941, the Great Depression brought a return to sexual conservatism.
- World War II opened new opportunities for women, both at home and in the military support. Interracial marriages set the stage for revoking miscegenation laws later in 1967.
- In the 1940s, the advent of antibiotics brought cures for some sexually transmitted diseases.
- In 1948 and 1953, Alfred Kinsey and colleagues published *Sexual Behavior in the Human Male* and *Sexual Behavior in the Human Female*. They brought sexual topics into widespread public discussion.
- In the 1950s, Elvis Presley became the first major rock 'n' roll star; television became a major influence on young Americans. Senator Joseph McCarthy portrayed sex education as part of a Communist plot to take over the U.S. Coed dormitories appeared on college campuses and bikini swimsuits swept the nation. Motels became popular, providing comfort for vacationing Americans, as well as for Americans seeking privacy for sexual relations.
- In 1953, the first issue of *Playboy* magazine was published.
- In 1957, the Supreme Court decision in *Roth v. U.S.* set new criteria for obscenity that opened the door to the works of D. H. Lawrence and Henry Miller, and other classic erotic works.
- In the 1950s and 1960s, the beatniks, hippies, flower children, and drug culture emerged.
- In the early 1960s, the hormonal contraceptive pill became available.
- In 1961, Illinois adopted the first "consenting adult" law decriminalizing sexual behavior between consenting adults.
- In 1963, Betty Friedan's *Feminine Mystique* was published, giving voice to the modern feminist movement.
- In 1968, William Masters and Virginia Johnson published *Human Sexual Response*.
- Following the 1969 Stonewall Inn Riot in Greenwich Village, New York City, homosexuals rebelled against police harassment, and launched the gay-rights and gay-pride movement.
- In the 1970s, television talk shows popularized discussions of alternative lifestyles, triggered by the publication of Nena and George O'Neill's *Open Marriage* in 1972.
- In 1970, the White House Commission on Pornography and Obscenity found no real harm in sexually explicit material. President Richard Nixon refused to issue the report.
- In 1972, the first openly gay male was ordained to the ministry of a major Christian church.
- In 1973, the U.S. Supreme Court legalized abortion.
- In the 1980s, openly gay legislators appeared in federal and state governments, and in professional sports.
- In 1983, AIDS was recognized, leading to a new advocacy for sex education in the schools and general public.
- In the late 1980s, conservative Christian activists, including the Moral Majority, the Christian Coalition, Focus on the Family, and similar organizations, emerged as politically and socially powerful groups.

These and other events too numerous to list, let alone analyze here, both contributed to and reflect the tension between the two ideologies mentioned above—one viewing sex as legitimate only in marriage, but as a necessary component of marital happiness, and the other viewing sex as a valid and important experience in its own right. The attempt to reconcile them can be seen as an underlying dynamic for many sexual practices and changes in the 20th century. These broad-based trends include:

1. The emergence in the 1920s of dating and in the 1940s of "going steady" as courtship forms (Reiss 1980);
2. The rising percentage of young people having premarital sexual experiences (D'Emilio & Freedman 1988; Kinsey et al. 1948, 1953; Reiss 1980; Seidman 1991);
3. The greater equality between the genders (D'Emilio & Freedman 1988; Reiss 1980; Seidman 1991);
4. The eroticization of the female, including a decline in the double standard and an increased focus on female sexual satisfaction (D'Emilio & Freedman 1988; Seidman 1991);
5. The emergence of professions devoted to sexuality—research, education, and therapy;
6. The expansion of marital sexuality, including increases in frequency, satisfaction, and variation in behavior (Hunt 1974);
7. The emergence of a homosexual identity and subculture, including a gay-rights movement (D'Emilio & Freedman 1988; Seidman 1991);
8. The passage of consenting-adult laws;
9. The commercialization of sex, by which we mean the appearance of an "industry" providing sexual goods and services (D'Emilio & Freedman 1988; Seidman 1991).

Reactions to these trends, and the continuing tension between the two major ideologies we have outlined above, lie at the very heart of the ongoing conflicts over sexual issues today. Robinson (1976) has characterized this conflict as a battle between 19th-century romanticism and what he calls sexual modernism. Romanticism affirmed the essential worth of the erotic, but only within the context of an intense interpersonal relationship transformed by a spiritual and physical union. Modernism reaffirms this romantic ideal, but also transforms it by acknowledging the value of "an innocent physical need" (p. 194). Although the modernist is glad to be rid of Victorian repression and anticipates the promise of a greater sexual freedom, there is a concomitant fear of a future of emotional emptiness.

Reiss (1981) has characterized this as a conflict between what he calls the traditional-romantic and modern-naturalistic ideologies. He maintains that this distinction can be used to explain current conflicts over such issues as abortion, gender roles and differences, pornography, definitions of sexual exploitation, concepts of sexual normality, and even accounts of sexual history itself. This perspective is useful in interpreting mass-media claims about sexuality in the U.S.A. Thus, Lyons (1983), reporting for *The New York Times*, proclaimed that the "sexual revolution" was over by the 1980s and that America was experiencing a return to traditional values and lifestyles. To support his argument, he claimed that there was a recent decrease in the number of sex partners and a shift away from indiscriminate, casual sexual behavior (Lyons 1983). In contrast, Walsh (1993), writing for *Utne Reader*, proclaimed that the 1990s have been characterized by a renewed sexual revolution (second-wavers), with pioneering new philosophies and techniques employing technology (latex, computer imaging, computer networks, virtual-reality sex, phone sex, cathode rays, and group safe sex) to achieve sensual pleasure in a safe way.

From 1970 to 1990, as these social processes continued, Americans witnessed: 1. a decrease in the marriage rate;

2. an increase in the divorce rate; 3. an increase in the birthrate for unmarried mothers (although the overall adolescent birthrate decreased); 4. an increase in single-parent families; and 5. an increase in married couples without children at home (Ahlburg & DeVita 1992).

## [C. The 21st Century
[*Sexuality and Terrorism in the United States*

RAYMOND J. NOONAN

[*Update 2003*: On September 11, 2001, terrorists, in a spectacular, well-planned, and coordinated attack, struck the United States by flying hijacked jumbo jets into the Twin Towers of the World Trade Center in New York City and the Pentagon in Washington, D.C., with another jet apparently bound for another Washington landmark being brought down in a field in western Pennsylvania. Although it has been minimally highlighted, sexuality factors may well have been among the root causes of the attack, and, it would appear, other terrorist activities worldwide. In addition, little has been written about the impact that these attacks, as well as the subsequent "war on terrorism" or the military actions in Afghanistan and Iraq, may have had on the sexuality of Americans in the aftermath. Indeed, using the *human sexuality complex* (Noonan 1998b) as a theoretical framework, i.e., looking at our sexuality as a complex ecological system in a holistic environment, one would surmise that these events, like other outside factors, such as economic, political, and other social factors, of necessity, have had—and would have to have—an impact. Certainly, they have triggered responses that will be felt in the sexual sphere, as well as other aspects of American life, as we advance through the 21st century.

[Terrorism is a relatively simple set of destructive behaviors with a complex set of motivations. The possibility that terrorism might be ultimately rooted in sexual motivations often receives a look of incredulous bemusement. Yet, it should be apparent that sexuality factors, including profoundly different views of the roles and essence of men and women and their relative power in personal relationships and society, the value of premarital virginity and its relationship to marriage as an economic institution benefiting the extended family versus marriage and relationships as expressions of love and personal autonomy, and the conflict in demarcating masculinity and femininity arising from same-sex relationships and the globalization of American popular culture, have the capacity to provide the fuel for the intensity of the clash between civilizations that has come to define international terrorism.

[These are especially salient when religion, with its precepts and notions of purity and impurity so deeply linked to sex and the dualistic split between the body and mind/spirit, is considered. It is easier to understand territorial, political, and economic motivations—or even ancient interethnic rivalries—whereas the religious motivations, such as the Islamic fundamentalism ascribed to the 9/11 terrorists, seem incongruous with the way most Americans view religion and the efforts needed to impose it and its sexual and gender ethic on everyone. The sole exception in the United States seems to be the Christian-fundamentalist anti-abortion terrorists who attack abortion clinics and sometimes kill clinic workers, albeit on a much smaller scale than the worldwide attacks of the Islamic extremists. Still, abortion terrorists have helped to restrict access to legal abortions in hospitals, as well as to providers in many U.S. states (Baird-Windle & Bader 2001). The difference between the two groups may signify a difference between the worldviews of the monolithic entity known as Western Civilization and some of the other non-Western cultures, which will be discussed later.

[Norman Doidge (2001), a research psychiatrist and psychoanalyst who teaches at Columbia University and the University of Toronto, summarized the various news reports that several of the September 11 terrorists had visited prostitutes and lap dancers in the days prior to the attacks and noted suggestions that various commentators have made about their possible motivation for frequently behaving in ways contrary to their expressed piousness: For example, they may have been using sex as an anxiety reliever prior to their suicide missions or as a confirmation of their belief that they were protecting Islam from the sexual licentiousness that they ascribed to Western cultures, in particular to that of the United States, which would then "justify" the murders in their own minds. In contrast, Doidge suggested that their behavior "reveals the ambivalent sexual undercurrent that is part of Islamic extremism with its view of woman as sin-evoking temptress, best appreciated either totally veiled, or totally unveiled." In summarizing other terrorists with similar contradictions, he wrote further:

But fanatics throughout history have had a markedly hypocritical attitude toward sex. Most fanatical sects have an obsession with sexual purity, alongside extraordinary lapses of restraint. Most divide the world into the pure and the impure, the sacred and the profane, clean and unclean, pure ascetic man and female temptress. . . . Fanatical leaders frequently demand their members subordinate all desires to the cause. . . .

Islamic extremism doesn't master sexuality—it exploits it by linking it to politics. In order to train Islamic suicide bombers, teenage boys are isolated from television and any outside influence when they are at the height of their sexual drive, playing on the Koranic promise to "martyrs" that, within moments of their death, they will be greeted by the 72 houris of heaven—virgins with whom they will have sex for eternity. Sex in this earthly world is devalued, but the promise of sex in the world to come is used to heat up the imaginations of these isolated, inexperienced loners. . . .

Such cults frustrate everyday erotic longing for other people, so that the devotees will turn that longing toward the cult leader and the cause. Becoming overheated "lovers of the cause," they, like lovers everywhere, become willing to sacrifice for their beloved. At the same time, their leaders manipulate the guilt followers feel about sexual desire, saying, "If you still have sexual feelings, you obviously are not devoted enough, and must sacrifice more."

People who deny themselves erotic outlets soon see any normal expression of eros as the devil incarnate. . . .

[It is known that sexual activity can have an ameliorative effect on suicidal ideation and depression, preventing many suicides (Planned Parenthood Federation of America 2003). It may also have the same effect on some forms of violence. Individuals who have a positive attitude toward sex, *per se*, tend not to be terrorists. However, in wars of liberation, it is known that when they are successful, there often follows a period of unrestrained sexual activities, although it may not last if the leadership turns out to be generally repressive of sexuality, as occurred in Russia following the October 1917 Revolution, as noted in the chapter on Ukraine in this volume. This sexual freedom can be attributed to the fact that sexuality often symbolizes personal liberation for many people, particularly if they have lived under sexually repressive social systems.

[Suppression of the sexual impulse allows the power of sex to be subverted for destructive political ends, as in the case of current Muslim and Christian extremists, although it can be used for "positive" purposes, as the channeling of religious fervor for some clerics (cf. George Orwell's *1984*). Thus, combined with other factors, such as the fact that it has been almost a century since Muslim colonial aspirations, which peaked with the Ottoman Empire, were dismantled at the end of World War I, ending centuries of dominance and Arab Islamic control over vast areas of Europe, Africa, and Asia. Yet, little if anything is said about the fact that, like the European Christian colonialists of the past, the Arab Muslim colonialists of the past conquered many more lands, imposing Islam on the inhabitants. (This silence may be attributable to the anti-Western sentiments that are currently fashionable in some American circles, as well as often well-meaning efforts to promote multiculturalism and diversity.) Indeed, as noted by Wolfgang Giegerich (a Jungian psychologist, in Fraim 2002), Islam was once the leading intellectual force in the world, although it has had little to offer the world for centuries. This has resulted in a sense of inferiority and shame that few Westerners can feel, which may account for the level of desperation seen in the terrorist attacks here and abroad.

[In his essay, "Islamic Terrorism," Giegerich (in Fraim 2002) has noted that, of the world's great religions, Islam is the only one that does not have a significant tradition of self-reflection—one in which basic premises and human-behavioral imperatives are evaluated in light of social and other advances in civilization. In fact, Giegerich advances the theory that it is a temporal clash and not a clash of civilizations that exists, one in which Islamic thought is stuck in the Middle Ages. Thus, he believes the West must look to its own past to understand their anger in order to find solutions. Thus, one can readily imagine how sexuality factors, as very powerful modern images projected through American popular culture, are fueling the terrorists' aggression (see the section on Sexuality and American Popular Culture at the end of this chapter).

[It is clear that one major factor in the sexual revolution in the West that has been increasingly adopted by younger people all over the world as they are exposed to Western ideals is the central importance of love and intimacy as a foundation for marriage and other sexual relationships. This is in sharp contrast to the centrality of marriage as an economic community and family institution, for example, in Islam today and most other religious traditions in both the East and West in the past if not still today. Thus, unsanctioned sexual relations threaten the power politics of traditional patriarchal societies, as younger people assume this aspect of control over their own lives.

[Another probable overlooked sex-related factor in terrorism is the Malthusian principle of population growth and its effects on the ecological psychosocial environment (Malthus 1798). Historically, programs aimed at increasing population growth have been promoted to fill the ranks of warriors, taxpayers, menial laborers, and religious adherents, to which, today, has been added consumer markets. This is in addition to the intrapsychological pressures some people feel to prove their masculinity or femininity to themselves and others by having babies.

[One of the most important sequelae of the terrorist attacks in the U.S. has been the reassertion both of male heroism and its closely allied cousin, the conservative political agenda. Much of this resurgence has as much to do with the traditional male role as protector—reinvigorated as a result of the attacks—as it probably has to do with the reaction to both the misandrist and heterophobic undercurrents that can be found in contemporary American culture, which are fueled largely by those who wish to exploit them for their own personal and political agendas on both the left and the right. Thus, we can probably expect to see a gender shift toward the expression of more-traditional masculine posturing, which has been clearly evident in the post-9/11 world in the United States. Indeed, much was made of the exaggerated images of President George W. Bush's genital region (reminiscent of the codpieces used to enhance the "manhood" of the aristocracy in the 15th and 16th centuries), when he descended from the cockpit of a fighter jet and crossed the deck of an aircraft carrier after the war in Iraq (Goldstein 2003). Research is needed to ascertain the impact that these new gender realities will have on American sexuality.

[*Effects of Terrorism and War on the Sexuality of Americans.* It is well known that war can have a significant impact on birthrates in the immediate areas of armed conflict (declining during a war and increasing immediately following it), as noted by the authors on the chapters on Croatia and Israel in this volume, although research on the concomitant effects on sexual behavior, *per se*, are rare, if nonexistent. Certainly, the post-World War II baby boom has been partially attributed to the impact of men returning from military service. The impact of terrorist bombings, being that they are typically more sporadic and uncertain and are directed against civilian populations, is also likely to have had an effect where they have occurred as they have had in Israel. Similar effects of the tensions of the Cold War appear not to have had an effect, although it has been conjectured that the potential nuclear threat may have encouraged early sexual experimentation in the sexual revolution of the 1960s and 1970s, combined with the introduction of the oral contraceptive pill, following the stifling 1950s. Still, even unarmed conflict can have an impact on sexuality, as noted in the chapter on Russia in this volume, where, following the collapse of Communism and the ensuing severe economic crisis, the birth and marriage rates fell sharply, as well as life expectancies, and divorce rates increased. Even population migration caused by wars can result in cross-cultural conflicts in the new lands, often surrounding sexual issues, as noted in the chapter on Sweden in this volume. In addition, the incidence of sexually transmitted diseases can increase, as noted in the chapter on Ukraine. Indeed, even wide-area events like the historic blackout of August 2003 affecting New York and several other northeastern states and parts of Canada, suggesting vulnerabilities to less-violent forms of terrorism, brought reminiscences of increased birthrates following past regional blackouts.

[The heightened levels of security also can have an effect. There is a fine line between reasonable security procedures and the enhanced anxiety generated by exaggerated security measures. In addition to keeping vigilant about one's surroundings, such measures keep gloom-and-doom scenarios fresh in people's minds, with the enhanced anxiety that can have an impact on intimate relationships. To be sure, terrorist attacks remain a dangerous reality and probable source of anxiety in the U.S. and worldwide. Post-traumatic stress disorder has been documented in New York City, where it was the most prevalent following the terrorist attacks, as well as in the rest of the U.S. It is likely to continue for some time, given that political and business leaders appear committed to not rebuilding the Twin Towers (Noonan 2002). Certainly, the terrorists were more aware of the symbolic value of the Towers than our leaders are. Surely, also, the Malthusian effects noted above are part of the overemphasis being placed on 9/11 memorials at the World Trade Center site, which is also working against the restoration efforts, which could accelerate the healing process. Stress is well known to disrupt sexual functioning as well as creates other strains on intimate relationships.

[Comments about the new awareness of the importance of family and personal relationships, in contrast to work and other concerns, were made in the immediate aftermath of the attacks on the United States. However, this was largely anecdotal, and may have amounted to a blip in actual practice that is beginning to shift again. Further research is needed to clarify these changes, although whether sufficient previous data are available for comparison is uncertain.

[Americans appear to be deeply ambivalent about the leadership role in world affairs it has had roughly since World War II. The September 11 attacks may, thus, signify a turning point in American world (and domestic) consciousness, with a retreat from leadership roles in any domain (clearly evident in the failure to recognize the symbolic importance of rebuilding the Twin Towers), with the possible exception of computer technology. And this failure to lead is reflected in some areas of the sexual arena as well, as can be seen throughout this chapter. The much-touted "American Century" of the 1900s (mostly the second half), may have been our historical apogee, with the ebb and flow of dominant nations and empires about to shift. The United States has certainly lost its illusion of moral authority in the eyes of much of the world (if not in the eyes of its own people), as fundamental corruptions in the legal, political, and economic systems become more apparent—this despite the fact that much of how these American systems operate more closely approach the ideals that free peoples value than those of many other countries. Sexuality factors—including ostensibly "liberal" attitudes and behaviors, are not the predominant reason for this decline in American moral authority, although it is cited as such by some critics, both inside and outside our country—further justifying oppressive political and sexual agendas that have yet to be seen.

[Terrorism and AIDS notwithstanding, we in the West, and Americans in particular, continue to live in a significantly less-risky era than our ancestors. As a result, women as well as men have enjoyed this relatively risk-free environment for decades, perhaps contributing to the increased devaluation of men because their traditional role as protector has been diminished. Yet, it appears that fanatical Islamic fundamentalists are intent on world domination, in a way similar to that for which fundamentalist Christians also strive. The early Arab Muslims seemed to be the Eastern equivalents of the Western colonialists of Europe. The contrast in methods of achieving it appears to be the difference between a series of conquests up to the Ottoman Empire, which fell after World War I, on the one hand, and the evangelical missionaries that have continued to thrive in many areas throughout the world. It remains to be seen to what extent the extensive out-migration of Islam to the West is, in effect, a silent evangelical push to reestablish the dominance of Islam, following the generally bloodless approach of the Christians, or is simply a search for religious freedom and the promise of a better life that is still America. In the meantime, *Cherchez le sexe* to determine the level of intensity with which terrorists will act to impose their visions on others. (*End of update by R. J. Noonan*)]

## 2. Religious, Ethnic, and Gender Factors Affecting Sexuality

Social scientists have demonstrated an association between human behavior and such social factors as religion, race, gender, social class, and education. This is as true of sexuality as of other forms of behavior. Although sexuality researchers have not always incorporated a recognition of this principle in their designs and analyses, there is still abundant evidence that sexual practices in the U.S.A. are strongly related to social factors. In this section, we examine several examples. First, we review the general influence of the Judeo-Christian heritage in the U.S.A. and describe the sexual culture of a particular religious group within this tradition, the Church of Jesus Christ of Latter-Day Saints (Mormons). Next, we see a brief discussion of reemerging spirituality-sexuality movements. Then we review the sexual customs of two of the largest minority groups in the U.S.A., African-Americans and Hispanic-Americans, followed by a look at Native American sexuality. Finally, we review the emergence of feminist ideology in the U.S.A., a view constructed around the concept of gender, which is contrasted with a look at emerging men's perspectives on sex and gender and a review of the concept of heterophobia in American life. These reviews are by no means exhaustive or complete, but should serve to illustrate both the diversity of social groups within the U.S.A. and the influence that membership in such groups exerts on sexual customs and practices.

## A. Sources and Character of Religious Values

*General Character and Ramifications of American Religious Perspectives on Sexuality*

ROBERT T. FRANCOEUR and TIMOTHY PERPER

Sexual science in America is a mid- to late-20th-century discipline. By contrast, Western religious thought about love, sexuality, marriage, the social and familial roles of men and women, and the emotions and behavioral patterns associated with courtship, pair bonding, conception, and birth have textual bases in the Jewish *Pentatuch* and other biblical writings. In pre-Christian Hellenic thought, the first great document of sexology is Plato's *Symposium* (ca. 400 B.C.E.). Because Judaic and Hellenic thought have strongly influenced the sexual views of Christianity and all of Western culture, one must acknowledge that the theological, religious, and secular writings that permeate American conceptions of sexuality are embedded in this 3,500-year-old matrix that gives sexuality its place in life (and unique meanings). This section will explore the sources and character of religious values in the U.S.A. and their impact on sexual attitudes, behaviors, and policies.

*Religious Groups in the U.S.A.* Statistically, Americans are 61% Protestant—21% Baptist, 12% Methodist, 8% Lutheran, 4% Presbyterian, 3% Episcopalian, and 13% other Protestant groups, including the Church of Latter-Day Saints (see the second major subsection below for a more in-depth discussion of the sexual doctrines and practices of this religious group), Seventh-Day Adventists, Jehovah's Witnesses, Christian Scientists, and others. Roman and Eastern-rite Catholics account for 25% of Americans, Jews 2%, 5% other religious groups, and 7% are not affiliated with any church. Therefore, the two largest denominations in the U.S.A. are the Roman Catholic Church with a membership of over 50 million and Southern Baptist Conventions with between 10 and 15 million members (Greeley 1992). There are also 2.5 million Muslims in the U.S.A.

Because Americans tend to cluster geographically according to both their religious and ethnic heritages, local communities can be much more strongly affected by a small but highly concentrated religious or ethnic tradition than the above percentages might suggest at first sight. With recent public debate focusing on sexual morality (e.g., contraception, abortion, and homosexuality), a paradoxical realignment has occurred, with liberal Roman Catholics, mainstream Protestant churches, and liberal and reformed Jews lining up on one side of these issues, and conservative (Vatican) Roman Catholics, fundamentalist Protestants, including the televangelists and Southern Baptists, Orthodox Jews, and fundamentalist Muslims on the other side.

*A Basic Conflict Between Two Worldviews.* American religious institutions on the national level, their local religious communities, and individual members are caught in a pervasive tension between the security of traditional unchanging values and the imperative need to adapt perennial religious and moral values to a radically new and rapidly changing environment. This tension permeates every religious group in the United States today, threatening schism and religious "civil war" (Francoeur 1994).

At one end of the spectrum are fundamentalist, evangelical, charismatic factions that accept as word-for-word truth the writings of the Bible as the word of God, and advocate the establishment of the United States as a Christian nation. For them, living under God's rule would be evidenced by the man firmly established as the head of each family in the U.S.A. and the woman in her God-given role as submissive wife and bearer of children for the Kingdom of Heaven. Similar fundamentalist strains in the United States are apparent among ultra-orthodox Jews and radical Muslims (LeHaye & LeHaye 1976; Marty & Appleby 1992, 1993, 1994; Penner & Penner 1981; Wheat & Wheat 1981). These embody an absolutist/natural law/fixed worldview.

On the conservative side, books about sexuality written by married couples dominate the market and sell millions of copies without ever being noticed by the mainstream publishing industry. *Intended for Pleasure* (Wheat & Wheat 1981) and *The Gift of Sex* (Penner & Penner 1981)—the latter couple having been trained by Masters and Johnson—provide detailed information on birth control and express deep appreciation of sex as a gift to be enjoyed in marriage. Tim and Beverly LeHaye's *The Act of Marriage* celebrates marital sexual pleasure, but disapproves of homosexuality and some sexual fantasy. All books in this category stress mutual pleasuring and the importance of female enjoyment of marital sex.

At the other end of the spectrum are various mainstream Protestants, Catholics, Jews, and Muslims who accept a processual/evolutionary worldview (Fox 1983, 1988; Curran & McCormick 1993; Heyward 1989; Kosnick et al. 1977; Nelson 1978, 1983, 1992; Nelson & Longfellow 1994; Ranke-Heinemann 1990; Spong 1988; Thayer 1987; Timmerman 1986) rather than the fixed fundamentalist worldview. In this processual worldview, the sacred divinely revealed texts are respected as

> the record of the response to the word of God addressed to the Church throughout centuries of changing social, historical, and cultural traditions. The Faithful responded with the realities of their particular situation, guided by the direction of previous revelation, but not captive to it. (Thayer et al. 1987)

The most creative and substantive analysis of the evolution and variations in biblical sexual ethics over time is William Countryman's *Dirt, Greed, and Sex: Sexual Ethics in the New Testament and Their Implications for Today.* (For a full annotated list of sexuality texts, see Cornog & Perper 1995.)

The tension between the values and morals derived from fixed worldviews and those derived from processual worldviews is evident in official church debates about sexual morality and is also experienced by church members as they struggle to find their way through the confusion resulting from these two views. But it also affects the lives of secular Americans with no connection with a church, mosque, or synagogue, because the religious debate over sexual values permeates all levels of American society, and no one can es-

cape the impact of this debate and conflict on politics, legislation, and social policies. Table 1 is an attempt to describe in a nondefinitive way the two divergent sets of values derived from the processual and fixed worldviews. Table 2 lists some religious traditions in both the fixed and processual worldviews in the major religions around the world.

Modern America is a ferment of discourse and debate concerning relationships between sexuality and religion. This occurs on the local and personal level among church members, as well as on the administrative level among the church leadership. The vast majority of local church debates are not reported in the popular press. These debates center on the interpretations of revelation, religious truths, and the nature and place of sexuality within a particular absolutist/natural law/fixed worldview or processual/evolutionary worldview. From time to time, denominational leaders and assemblies issue authoritative statements in denominational position or workstudy papers. These formal statements are designed to answer questions of sexual morality and set church policy. However, contradictory majority and minority positions rooted in the opposing fixed and processual worldviews accomplish little beyond stirring heated debate and deferring the problem to further committee study (Francoeur 1987, 1994).

However, there is often a great difference between official church doctrine and its worldview and the views and practices of its members. For example, the most erotophilic religion in America may be grassroots Roman Catholicism as expressed and lived by the laity. Many rank-and-file American Catholics express great and amused doubt and scorn for the sexual pronouncements of the Vatican (Greeley 1995). Peter Gardella (1985) has made a strong case for the thesis that Christianity has, in fact, given America an ethic of sexual pleasure.

*The Conservative Christian Coalition.* Among the major forces in the American religious scene that affect public sexual mores is the conservative Christian Coalition. Among the fundamentalist Christians, one finds an extraordinary heterogeneity. There exists a large and virtually unstudied mixture of Pentecostal, fundamentalist, and evangelical/charismatic churches whose preachers expound on sexuality, marriage, family, and morality. Their opinions are diverse, and poorly known or understood by those outside their domain, especially sexologists. Two examples illustrate this: A religious pamphlet published by the Rose of Sharon Press in Tennessee, the buckle of the so-called Bible Belt in the U.S.A., extols the clitoris as the "cradle of love," and the Reverend Timothy LeHaye reminds his followers that God indeed created the delights of oral sex for married couples (only) to enjoy. No statistical data exist concerning these groups, and we know nothing about sexual behavior among individuals within these churches.

The current strength of the power of the American religious right is evident in the wide-reaching branches of Pat Robertson's political machine, the Christian Coalition, and the "electronic churches," including Robertson's cable television Christian Broadcasting Network (CBN), with annual revenues of $140 million (Roberts & Cohen 1995). A parallel conservative culture is James Dobson's multimedia empire, Focus on the Family, which includes ten radio shows, 11 magazines (including speciality publications for doctors, teachers, and single parents), bestselling books, filmstrips, and videos of all kinds, curriculum guides, church-bulletin fillers, and sermon outlines faxed to thousands of pastors every week. The popularity of Dobson's first book, *Dare to Discipline*—with more than 2 million copies sold in 1977—inspired his formation of Focus on the Family,

## Table 1

## A Cognitive and Normative Continuum of Sexual Values Derived from Two Distinct Worldviews, Fixed and Process, Within the Christian Tradition

| | Christian Religions Type A | Christian Religions Type B |
|---|---|---|
| Basic vision | *Cosmos*—a finished universe | *Cosmogenesis*—an evolving universe |
| Typology | The universe, humankind is created perfect and complete in the beginning. | The universe, humankind is incomplete and not yet fully formed. |
| | Theological understanding of humans emphasizes Adam. | Theological emphasis has shifted to Christ (The Adam) at the end of time. |
| Origin of evil | Evil results from primeval 'fall' of a perfect couple who introduce moral and physical evil into a paradisical world. | Evil is a natural part of a finite creation, growth, and the birth pains involved in our groping as imperfect humans struggling for the fullness of creation. |
| Solution to the problem of evil | Redemption by identification with the crucified Savior. Asceticism, mortification. | Identification with the Adam, the resurrected but still fully human transfigured Christ. Re-creation, growth. |
| Authority system | Patriarchal and sexist. Male-dominated and ruled. Autocratic hierarchy controls power and all decisions; clergy vs. laity. | Egalitarian—'In his kingdom there is neither male nor female, freeman or slave, Jew or Roman.' |
| Concept of truth | Emphasis on one true Church as sole possessor of all truth. | Recognition that other churches and religions possess different perspectives of truth, with some elements of revelation clearer in them than in the "one true Church." |
| Biblical orientation | Fundamentalist, evangelical, word-for-word, black-and-white clarity. Revelation has ended. | Emphasizes continuing revelation and reincarnation of perennial truths and values as humans participate in the creation process. |
| Liturgical focus | Redemption and Good Friday, Purgatory, Supernatural. | Easter and the creation challenge of incarnation. Epiphany of numinous cosmos. |
| Social structure | Gender roles clearly assigned with high definition of proper roles for men and women. | There being neither male nor female in Christ, gender roles are flexible, including women priests and ministers. |
| Goal | Supernatural transcendence of nature. | Unveiling, Revelation of divine in all. |
| Ecological morality | Humans are stewards of the earth, given dominion by God over all creation. | Emphasis on personal responsibility in a continuing creation/incarnation. |
| Self-image | Carefully limited; isolationist, exclusive, Isaias's 'remnant.' Sects. | Inclusive, ecumenical, catalytic leader among equals. |
| Human morality | Emphasis on laws and conformity of actions to these laws. | Emphasis on persons and their interrelationships. We create the human of the future and the future of humanity. |
| Sexual morality | The 'monster in the groins' that must be restrained. | A positive, natural, creative energy in our being as sexual (embodied) persons "Knowing" (*yadah*), Communion. |
| | Justified in marriage for procreation. | An essential element in our personality in all relationships. |
| | Genital reductionism. | Diffused, degenitalized sensual embodiment. |
| | Heterosexual/monogamous. | "Polymorphic perversity," "paneroticism." |
| | Noncoital sex is unnatural, disordered. | Noncoital sex can express the incarnation of Christian love. |
| | Contraceptive love is unnatural and disordered. | Contraception can be just as creative and life-serving as reproductive love. |
| | Monolithic—celibate or reproductive marital sexuality. | Pluralistic—sexual persons must learn to incarnate *chesed/agape* with *eros* in all their relationships, primary and secondary, genital and nongenital, intimate, and passionate. |
| Energy conception | Competitive. | Synergistic. |
| | Consumerist. | Conservationist. |
| | Technology-driven and obsessed. | Concerned with appropriate technologies. |

**Table 2**

**A Spectrum of Ethical Systems with Typical Adherents in
Different Religious Traditions**

This table is an attempt to visualize the range of sexual moralities in different religious traditions and relate them in terms of their basic worldviews. There is often more agreement between different Jews, Protestants, and Catholics at one or the other end of the spectrum, than there is between Protestants, or Catholics, or Jews who disagree in their worldviews. Protestants in the covenant tradition, for instance, have more in common with liberal Catholics who disagree with the Vatican's opposition to such practices as contraception, masturbation, premarital sex, abortion, divorce, and homosexuality, than they do with their fellow Protestants who are members of the fundamentalist Christian Coalition, Eagle Forum, or Focus on the Family.

| Tradition Source | A Spectrum or Continuum | |
| --- | --- | --- |
| | Fixed Philosophy of Nature | Process Philosophy of Nature |
| Roman Catholic tradition | Act-oriented natural law/divine law order ethics expressed in formal Vatican pronouncements | A person-oriented, evolving ethics expressed by many contemporary theologians and the 1977 Catholic Theological Society of America study of human sexuality. |
| Protestant nominalism | Fundamentalism based on a literal interpretation of the Bible, as endorsed by the Moral Majority and the religious New Right: Seventh-Day Adventists, Jehovah's Witnesses, and Church of Latter-Day Saints | An ethic based on the covenant announced between Jesus and humans—examples in the 1970 United Presbyterian workstudy document on Sexuality and the Human Community, Unitarian/Universalists, and the Society of Friends (Quakers) |
| Humanism | Stoicism and epicurean asceticism | Situation ethics, e.g., the 1976 American Humanist Association's "A New Bill of Sexual Rights and Responsibilities" |
| Judaism | Orthodox and Hasidic concern for strict observation of the Torah and Talmudic prescriptions | Liberal and reformed application of moral principles to today's situations |
| Islam | Orthodox; observance of female seclusion (*purdah*) and wearing of the veil (*chador*); ritual purifications associated with sexual activities | Secular; more or less adoption of Western gender equality; flexible/lax observance of sex-associated purification rituals |

While Eastern religions may, in some cases, fit in with this dualism of worldviews, the ascetic traditions of the East are positive traditions and lack the negativism towards sexuality that permeates the history of Christian asceticism and celibacy. Eastern asceticism is seen as a positive balance to the Eastern's embrace of sexuality as both a natural pleasure to be greatly enjoyed and a path to the divine union. Also, the relationship with the dichotomous *weltanschauungs* evident in Western traditions needs to be explored and explicated.

| Tradition | Fixed Philosophy of Nature | Process Philosophy of Nature |
| --- | --- | --- |
| Hinduism | Ascetic tradition of monks with world-denying sexual abstinence; yoga; ritual taboos and purification rites associated with sexual activities | Sacramental view of sex with worship of male *lingam* and female *yoni*; the *Kama Sutra* |
| Buddhism | Ascetic tradition of monks with sexual abstinence | Tantric traditions in which sexual relations are a path to divine union |

which now has an annual budget of $100 million and a staff of 1,300 workers who answer more than 250,000 telephone calls and letters a month (Roberts & Cohen 1995).

In the late 1980s, Protestant fundamentalist televangelists from the South were reaching millions of listeners. Their influence was weakened by several major sex scandals, but they continue to play a major role in the anti-abortion movement and are part of the Christian Coalition. In the same era, the National Conference of Catholic Bishops tried to establish a cable television network to bring the Catholic faith to the masses. Where they failed, a determined Catholic fundamentalist-charismatic, Mother Angelica, from Mobile, Alabama, succeeded with the Eternal Word Network, which brings ultraconservative interpretations of Catholic sexual and social morality to devoted listeners 24 hours a day.

In the southern states, on the east and west coasts, and in the populous midwest states are several hundred "mega-churches," which draw upwards of 5,000 to 20,000 faithful every week to each church. Congregations seated in upholstered theater seats are inspired by the style of a professional theater with a large choir, orchestra, large screens displaying hymn verses for congregational singing, interpretive dance, Bible lessons with soft-rock concerts, and morality plays that rival anything on music television (MTV). These mega-churches are usually huge glass and steel shopping-mall-like complexes with large theater-stage sanctuaries, scores of meeting and classrooms for a variety of activities, including aerobics, multimedia Bible classes, counseling centers, and even bowling alleys, accompanied by acres of parking space. Sermons delivered by skilled "teaching pastors" include such topics as: how to find joy in a violent world, create a "happy day" each week, find rhythm between work and rest, handle teenage children, and discipline one's mind to a biblical perspective. Youth, in particular, are attracted to the instant intimacy of this large-group, Disney-World environment. Weekly contributions from 15,000 members at one mega-church averaged $228,000, giving the church an annual budget of almost $12 million (Roberts & Cohen 1995). With the mainstream small local churches suffering a steady decline in attendance and contributions, many of the more-traditional pastors are turning to the mega-churches for pastoral retraining. Thus, the mega-churches are establishing smaller, local congregations. It appears that the way these churches deal with sexual issues may have a major impact on American sexuality because of the large memberships they are attracting.

*Emergence of a Sex-Positive Individual-Based Value System.* Diotima of Mantinea, Socrates' instructress in the art of love in the *Symposium*, explained that the god Eros provides an avenue or way by which human beings reach upward to the Divine—a view modern classical scholars chauvinistically attribute to Socrates and call the "Erotic Ascent." Historically, Diotima's argument became the basis of the later Christian idea that God is Love. In Eurocentric Christianity, the first great flowering of Eros came between 1050 C.E. and 1200 C.E., when Ovid's *The Art of Love* reached Europe from Arab-Spanish sources. The synthesis of sexuality and spirituality quickly assumed major status as a popular doctrine expressed in the music of the troubadours of "courtly love."

Its most ardent opponents were the faculty of the medieval universities led by Thomas Aquinas, who developed a full and coherent alternative to the theology of the Platonic Erotic Ascent in the 13th century. The Thomistic synthesis, with its denunciation of the Erotic Ascent and analysis of the essence and goals of human sexuality in terms of a "natural law," became the official Catholic view. This synthesis is the basis on which the modern magisterium and hierarchy of the Roman Catholic Church grounds its absolute condemnation of contraception, abortion, and the practice of homosexuality. By contrast, Protestantism has been much more accepting of sexuality and sexual pleasure, and more flexible with and accommodating to such issues as divorce, contraception, abortion, masturbation, premarital sex, and even homosexuality.

However, it was not the theory of Thomistic Aristotelianism that ultimately superseded late-medieval and Renaissance beliefs in Eros. These dwindled as Europe staggered under waves of the Black Death, which ultimately killed one quarter of Europe's population; the Crusades, during which 22,000 people were killed in the Provençal city of Bezier alone; endless local wars among nobles, kings, and petty brigands where the peasants were invariably victimized; Turkish invasions; the epidemic of syphilis in 1493; peasant uprisings in Germany and England in the 1300s and 1400s; and the Inquisition, that specifically targeted women as its victims.

Protestant reformers, from Luther through Calvin, Knox, and Zwingli, not only rejected the "natural law" approach to sexual morality, but extended, strengthened, and normalized the nuclear family and the blessing of marital sex. This type of marriage was a valuable social institution for assuring the distribution of new wealth from father to son. For example, in northern European merchant families, it replaced the older, southern European models of inheritance by name, and social status by membership in a "house" (e.g., the "house of the Medici"), with this type of lineage system.

An important characteristic of the Renaissance was appreciation and acceptance of individual control of one's own life. Thus, the late 1500s and early 1600s saw a new struggle of the young to wrest control over their love affairs and marriages from their parents and families. Shakespeare's *Romeo and Juliet* epitomizes what was to become the central issue of the modern-American religious debate

about sexuality and spirituality. Who is to control the sexuality of the young? Older and more powerful individuals, who have vested interests in the outcome of youthful sexuality; celibate church leaders still convinced of the unchangeable patriarchal sexual values expressed in the Genesis story of creation; or young people, who claim for themselves the right to find the right mates and express their erotic passion in a way that, for them, brings sexuality and transcendence together?

Of growing significance in the 1990s in the U.S.A. is the question of the sacred nature of Eros. Among the liberal religious bestsellers pioneering a new synthesis of sexuality and spirituality are: *Human Sexuality: New Directions in American Catholic Thought* (Kosnick et al. 1977), which was sponsored by the Catholic Theological Society of America, but was condemned by the Vatican; *Original Blessing* (1983) and *The Coming of the Cosmic Christ* (1988) by the Dominican, Matthew Fox (censured and expelled from his community by the Vatican); sociologist and erotic-novel author, Father Andrew Greeley's *Sex: The Catholic Experience* (1995); lesbian theologian, Carter Heyward's 1989 *Touching Our Strength: The Erotic as Power and the Love of God*; Presbyterian seminary professor, James Nelson's books *Embodiment* (1978), *Between Two Gardens: Reflections on Sexuality and Religious Experience* (1983), and *Body Theology* (1992); James Nelson and Sandra Longfellow's anthology on *Sexuality and the Sacred* (1994); William Phipps' *Recovering Biblical Sensuousness* (1975); Catholic-feminist theologian, Joan Timmerman's *The Mardi Gras Syndrome: Rethinking Christian Sexuality* (1986); and Episcopalian Bishop John Shelly Spong's 1988 *Living in Sin? A Bishop Rethinks Human Sexuality*. In addition, some Christians have turned to Eastern religions, particularly in the Tantric and Taoist traditions, to seek the nexus between sexuality and spirituality (Francoeur 1992).

*Current and Future Religious Debate.* During the 1980s, the most virulently debated issue was abortion. In 1994, between U.S. Supreme Court decisions and violence and murder by extreme anti-abortionists, support for anti-abortion stands stalled. For the majority of Americans, abortion appeared to fade as the central moral dilemma and joined the list of unresolved moral issues that includes war, drugs, crime, capital punishment, discrimination, and related social ills. Certain far-right religious leaders, who still have a devoted and vocal following and claim to speak for Christ, even conceded reluctantly that they could not win their war against abortion, and seemed to refocus their crusade on homosexuality and "the danger of homosexual rights" as their mobilizing issue.

However, with the mid-1995 success of the Republicans' conservative hundred-day Contract with America, the Christian Coalition announced its own Contract with the American Family. Two-dozen legislative proposals were introduced into Congress, including an unprecedented attempt to ban and criminalize some now-legal abortions. A bill to reinstate a ban on abortions at American military hospitals overseas was passed. Other proposed bills would ban family planning programs from including abortion counseling for low-income women and adolescents; refuse funding to institutions that favor requiring obstetric/gynecology programs to provide training in abortion procedures; overturn an executive order lifting a ban against using foreign-aid money for abortion counseling or referrals; end or restrict support for agencies, including the United Nations, that offer family planning programs with abortions funded by private money; limit federal Medicaid money for abortions to situations where the woman's life is threatened and ban it in cases of incest or rape; ban fetal-tissue research; ban clinical testing of RU-486; restore a ban on counseling women about abortion at clinics that receive any federal money; and prohibit the federal employee's health benefit plan from covering abortion. The ultimate goal is to make all abortions under all circumstances a crime.

The list of controversial sexual issues that are religiously debated with little hope of being resolved in the near future includes:

1. Individual sexual choice: Who should be in control of one's sexuality? Should it be church leaders or people themselves, who claim the right to express their sexuality with those of their own choosing in ways that would bring them mutual pleasure, eroticism, and spirituality?
2. Contraception: Should minors have access to contraception? Should condoms be distributed in the schools? Does education about contraception and sexual behaviors outside of marriage promote "promiscuity"? Should people be free to choose the best method of contraception for themselves without religious restriction?
3. Abortion: Should women have control of their own reproductive faculty? Is the embryo/fetus a person with inalienable rights at the moment of conception or does fetal personhood develop over the nine months of gestation? When do fetal rights transcend those of pregnant women, if at all?
4. Nonmarital sexuality: Can sex outside marriage be morally acceptable? If so, under what circumstances? How can it be reconciled with traditional Judeo-Christian morality that limits sexual expression to the marital union?
5. Sexual orientation: Are homosexuality and bisexuality natural and normal states of being? Should sexually active gays, lesbians, and bisexuals be welcomed into church membership? Should they be ordained into the ministry? Should variation in orientation be presented in sex-education curricula as normal, moral, and socially acceptable?
6. Masturbation: Is self-loving and autoeroticism a natural, normal, and morally acceptable expression of human sexuality? (See the first item in Section B of American Demographics at the beginning of this chapter for an illustration of the impact this issue has had on American politics.)

The American religious, and consequent social and political debates over each of these issues are not likely to be resolved in the near future. The dichotomy of the two worldviews is too deeply embedded in the American culture to allow for a quick resolution. The more likely prognosis is for continued, tension-filled confrontations within churches, denominations, and political/legislative arenas throughout the United States.

The Religious Right's social and political agenda deeply divides American society. Although 40% of Americans express concern about the Democrats' ties to radical liberal groups, 39% are worried by Republican ties to conservative special-interest groups like the Religious Right, the Family Research Council, Focus on the Family, Eagle Forum, and the Christian Coalition (Roberts & Cohen 1995). These results reflect the continuing diversity of worldviews within the Judeo-Christian tradition. They also indicate that these religious differences not only result in contrasting sexual ideologies, but also have an important impact on political processes in the U.S.A. more broadly. As such, religion continues to be a major American social influence.

## Church of Jesus Christ of Latter-Day Saints

JEANNIE FORREST

*Mormon Origins and Polygyny.* One example of a particular religious group within the general Judeo-Christian heritage is provided by the Church of Jesus Christ of Latter-Day Saints (LDS), which is the fastest-growing religion in the world today. The over seven million members are known colloquially as the Mormons. They base their belief system on the Bible and additional scriptures, most significantly the *Book of Mormon*, which is understood to be a record of God's dealings with an ancient population of the American continent. The Mormons believe this book came from gold plates revealed to the church founder, Joseph Smith, in Ontario County, New York, in 1823. The church was officially organized in 1829.

The early Mormons were persecuted because their founder claimed the Bible had not been translated properly, that all other religions were false, that religious leaders did not have God's authority—the priesthood—to act in God's name, and finally that the practice of polygyny was a part of the divine plan. There was also the political reality that the tightknit Mormon communities exercised considerable local power. Interestingly, the term "polygamy" as used in LDS church history and old doctrine means the "condition or practice of having more than one spouse." A more-accurate definition of the Mormon practice of that century lies in the word "polygyny," meaning having more than one wife at one time. The role of polygyny in the church is a source of some embarrassment to mainstream modern-day Mormons, who may discuss the practice somewhat wryly as a revelation designed to build the church population at a time when they literally had to forge new communities under hardship. After several attempts to settle in an area and build a sectarian community, the Mormon pioneers ultimately settled in the Salt Lake City area of Utah, where the church is now headquartered.

Modern Mormon doctrine does not include the practice of polygyny. Church prophet and leader, Wilfred Woodruff, officially eliminated polygyny from doctrine in the *Manifesto of 1890* (Ludlow 1992). This proclamation against plural marriage ended a decade of hardship and persecution against the church members, particularly by the Republican Party that had as part of its platform elimination of the "immoral practice of multiple wives." While mainstream Mormons are not held accountable for not practicing plural marriage, they still must "suffer the curse of monogamy." Today, small fundamentalist splinter groups still practice polygyny, despite state laws against it and lack of official church acknowledgment. Even before the church abandoned its practice of plural marriage, only a small fraction of Mormon men, between 3 and 15%, had more than one wife (Murstein 1974, 350-364).

Perhaps the persecution faced by the early members of the LDS regarding their marital patterns has contributed to a unique and paradoxical tension around sexuality. On one hand, there is nothing more sacred than sex within the bounds of church-sanctioned marriage. On the other hand, rarely is there found a modern-American subculture more prohibitive and repressive about sexuality.

*Salvation and Sex.* To further understand this tension, one needs a basic understanding of the Mormon Plan of Salvation. Before birth, the Mormons believe, the soul is alive as an intelligence in a spirit world. During this preexistence, a variety of situations are possible, including acts of valor that would allow the soul to be born into a family of Mormons where opportunities for service abound. At birth, the soul passes through a veil of forgetfulness where all memory of the preexistence is lost (Church of Jesus Christ of Latter-Day Saints 1989; Moses 3:5, 7; Abraham 3:21-23, 35, 38; Talmage 1977).

During life on this earth, individuals face choices throughout the course of their lives that determine in which of three kingdoms they will spend eternity. The highest kingdom, the Celestial Kingdom, is reserved for those Latter-Day Saints who meet all the requirements of doctrine, one of the most important of which is marriage to another Saint in special temple rites. The exaltation and eternal life in the highest degree of the Celestial Kingdom are achieved only by faithful Mormons through the achievement and building of an eternal marriage, discussed later. (Other good people can only hope to reach the Terrestrial Kingdom, a kind of heaven on earth, while unrepented adulterers, practicing homosexuals, murderers, and other sinners are limited to the Telestial Kingdom, which some describe as a Mormon version of the Christian hell.)

[*Comment 1997*: According to Mormon tradition, "hell" is not a place, but rather a state of mind. Those who do not achieve the highest degree of glory (the Celestial Kingdom) will recognize the reward they might have had and live out their eternities with the knowledge of this lost potential. However, the Telestial Kingdom, though typically described in less-than-positive terms, is not generally thought of as the fire and brimstone of the traditional Christian hell. In fact, one prominent Mormon Church leader described the Telestial Kingdom as follows: ". . . all who receive any one of these orders of glory are at last saved, and upon them Satan will finally have no claim. Even the telestial glory 'surpasses all understanding; And no man knows it except him to whom God has revealed it'" (Talmage 1977, 92-93). (*End of comment by M. O. Bigler*)]

In Mormon belief, one's marital status is decisive for the life hereafter. Without marriage, one can only become a servant angel ministering to those who are far more worthy of glory, the truly married. But most of those who have married on earth are married for *time only* (until death), and not truly married unless they have their marriage sealed in the temple. In heaven, those who are married only for this life will be single, no better than bachelors and spinsters. (In the Mormon view of heaven, one can enjoy all the pleasures of sex, food, and other sensual delights.) Those who are married by a prophet in the temple are sealed to each other and married *for time and eternity*. Couples in a sealed marriage will remain married for eternity, and enjoy reigning in separate kingdoms. It is also possible to marry for eternity and not for time. Thus a kindly man may marry a spinster for eternity but not for time, leaving her to her celibate lifestyle here, but destined for all the delights of the Celestial Kingdom as his mate in eternity (Murstein 1974, 350-362).

*Gender Roles*. As with all societies, gender roles among Mormons are scripted very early in life. The LDS church plays a distinct role in gender definition and scripting. Church activities segregate children at around the age of 12: boys are guided into vigorous endeavors, such as scouting and outdoor gamesmanship, whereas girls learn household activities and crafts.

[*Comment 1997*: To clarify Forrest's comment above, it is important to note that Mormon adolescents frequently participate in mixed-gender activities. Although young men and young women generally meet separately as a part of the official church youth program (known variously as Mutual Improvement Association (M.I.A.), Mutual, and Young Men's/Young Women's Program), males and females come together for Sunday School and the Mormon worship service known as Sacrament Meeting. In addition, LDS seminar-ies—religious study programs for high-school-age teens (grades 9 through 12) that operate in virtually every location around the world where congregations of Mormons are found—are always conducted with male and female students meeting together. Furthermore, Mormon youth regularly attend church-sponsored dances and participate together in community activities, including school proms, holiday celebrations, and cultural events. Young Mormon women and men are encouraged to interact, though care is usually taken to provide chaperons or to direct young people into activities where the possibility of sexual contact is limited (e.g., Mormon youths are strongly encouraged by their church leaders and parents to date in groups and to establish curfews that will not keep them out past midnight). (*End of comment by M. O. Bigler*)]

It is not unusual for a preadolescent girl to have an LDS-designed poster on her bedroom wall urging her to remain "temple worthy," or reminding her of gospel precepts that will keep her safe from worldly situations. For example, one poster is of a young girl looking into a mirror in whose reflection is a vision of herself as a young woman in a bridal scene with a handsome man. The caption says, "looking forward to a temple marriage." Young men are also urged to bridle their carnal urges. Masturbation is expressly forbidden, and moral cleanliness, a requirement for any temple ceremony, essentially equates to abstaining from sexual activity before marriage.

[*Comment 1997*: In Mormon practice, "moral cleanliness" at its most basic level is understood as abstaining from sexual activity before marriage and remaining faithful to one's spouse. It is not at all equated with celibacy, as the author has implied. A pamphlet for youth, recently published by the church, makes this position clear: "Our Heavenly Father has counseled that sexual intimacy should be reserved for his children within the bonds of marriage. . . . Because sexual intimacy is so sacred, the Lord requires self-control and purity before marriage as well as full fidelity after marriage" (Church of Jesus Christ of Latter-Day Saints 1990, 14-15). (*End of comment by M. O. Bigler*)]

Gender roles become even more firmly established during transitions into adulthood. Church officials clearly define the position, duties, and destiny of women in the divine plan. Women are to be "copartners with God in bringing his spirit children into the world" (Tanner 1973); this is generally understood metaphorically without any sexual connotation. Rather than focus on the erotic element of this distinction (having babies does require first having sexual intercourse), the LDS leaders instead urge women to stay home in order to love and care for children to ensure a generation of Mormons who learn about their "duty as citizens and what they must do to return to their Heavenly Father." Women are regarded as sacred vessels, with important roles not only in childbearing, but also as positive influences on men's lives. A "general authority" in the church, Hugh B. Brown, suggests that "women are more willing to make sacrifices than are men, more patient in suffering, and more earnest in prayer" (Relief Society 1965). Women in the Mormon community are indeed known for their good works. The Relief Society is the oldest women's group in the United States and is remarkably active with community support of all kinds.

[*Comment 1997*: Most Mormons, female and male alike, continue to hold traditional views concerning gender and gender roles. In general, Mormon women today still view motherhood and caregiving as fundamental traits of a "righteous" woman. However, it is also fair to say that the beliefs of church officials and the broader membership regarding gender roles have liberalized somewhat since President Hugh B. Brown's statement in 1965. For example, in a recent general conference of the church, Chieko N. Okazaki, First Counselor in the Relief Society General Presidency, urged LDS women to obtain an education and career training:

> Each year it becomes increasingly important for women to improve their abilities to take care of themselves and their children economically, if circumstances should require.... If anything, [the counsel of Elder Howard W. Hunter] has become even more relevant in the almost twenty years that have passed as the national economy has made it increasingly difficult for one wage to support a family, as more mothers are left alone to raise their children, and as more women spend lengthy portions of their lives single. He is telling all of us to use the oar of study to prepare ourselves professionally for worthy and rewarding activities, including paid employment. (Okazaki 1994) (*End of comment by M. O. Bigler*)]

LDS men have a clearly defined role as well. Men bear the responsibility and the privilege of the Priesthood, which is a spiritual calling and connection to God specifically not given to women. An exception to this is found in LDS mission work, where young women on evangelical missions for the church have a type of "priesthood calling" on a temporary basis, lasting only for the duration of the mission.

[*Comment 1997*: Throughout the church's history, Mormon women have served missions for the church. Today, young women (typically in their early 20s) are embarking on proselytizing and church service missions in ever-increasing numbers. Although Mormon men are encouraged much more strongly than are women to go on missions, teaching and preaching are not restricted to priesthood holders (males) in the church today. In fact, the priesthood is not a prerequisite for participation in most church positions, all of which are filled by lay members. Nevertheless, church leadership at its highest levels, both locally and generally, remains a function of the priesthood (male members). (*End of comment by M. O. Bigler*)]

Through the priesthood, God governs all things. Priesthood power is considered a vital source of eternal strength and energy, a responsibility delegated to men for the well-being of mankind. Holding the priesthood means having authority to act as God's authorized agent, which includes some church organizational duties. The right of worthy priesthood holders is to preside over their descendants through all ages, achieving its highest function in the family. As the presiding priesthood holder in the home, decisions relating to discipline often fall to the man, and the role of providing for the household is ultimately his, in spite of the presence of more employed Mormon women. Giving righteous advice, loving family members, and the laying-on-of-hands for healing purposes are all rights of the man of the house.

[*Comment 1997*: In the ideal Mormon household, discipline, family decisions, and the day-to-day management of the home are seen as a shared responsibility between a unified husband and wife. Although Mormon fathers have been designated the presiding authority in the family (once again a function of the priesthood), it is the mother who is typically responsible for managing the home and children. However, male church members are counseled against the misuse of their designation as leader in the home, and men have been encouraged by the prophet and president of the church himself to share in parenting and home management:

> A man who holds the priesthood accepts his wife as a partner in the leadership of the home and family with full knowledge of and full participation in all decisions relating thereto.... You share, as a loving partner, the care of the children. Help her to manage and keep up your home.

Help teach, train, and discipline your children. (Hunter 1994, 5-7) (*End of comment by M. O. Bigler*)]

*Body Theology.* The Mormon doctrine about the body is worth noting since it creates another element of sexual tension. In many Christian religions, the body is considered simply a vessel housing the spirit/soul for the duration of life. For the Mormons, the body itself is highly revered and serves an eternal function. At the point of resurrection, the body of an individual is returned to "perfection," ridding it of all the faults and defects of this life. A Mormon friend of mine often queries, "Just whose version of perfection will I get in Eternity? I have a list of modifications right here."

One indication of the importance of the body is manifested by the wearing of "garments." During the Temple marriage, a couple is given special "garments" to wear. This special underwear (manufactured by the Mormon church) is designed to serve as a reminder of the sanctity of the covenants made in the temple and to protect the body from harm. A quiet Mormon joke about the garments refers to them as "Mormon contraceptives," since they must be worn next to the skin at all times and are notoriously unsexy in appearance. Women wear their foundation garments, such as brassieres and slips, over the Mormon garments. Because of the design of the garments, only modest clothing can be worn. However, the modern garments are much more relaxed and functional than traditional ones. The old versions are still available, with the tops extending just below the elbows and the bottoms below the knee, but most younger Mormon women opt for the cap sleeve and midthigh cotton versions for comfort and more choice in clothing.

[*Comment 1997*: Mormon garments (which are worn by both women and men) serve as a constant reminder of sacred covenants made in temple ceremonies. Mormons also believe that these undergarments help protect the wearer against physical and spiritual harm. In addition, the design of the underclothing encourages the wearing of modest clothing. Although temple garments are to be worn day and night under normal circumstances, church members are not required by either doctrine or dictum to keep their underclothing on during activities such as bathing or while participating in sporting events. Nor are faithful Mormons required to wear their garments during sexual activity. (*End of comment by M. O. Bigler*)]

*Adolescent Dating.* Adolescent dating rituals are very similar to those of other conservative American cultural groups. As LDS children grow older, the church plays more of a role in their lives, interweaving doctrinal and social activities. The transitions through church steps for adolescents are made in tandem with all their church peers. For instance, at 8 years old, children reach the "age of understanding" and are baptized into the church. Many of their peers are also taking this step, which takes on social significance in the form of family gatherings and informal parties. Later, dating is encouraged in group settings around church activities, since this context is most likely to encourage an interfaith marriage. Teens are often told, "if you don't date outside, you won't fall in love outside, and you won't marry outside the faith."

[*Comment 1997*: Dating among Mormon teens is not restricted solely to church activities, although local congregations do often sponsor teen-oriented events, such as dances, firesides (discussions of religious topics especially relevant to teens), and cultural activities (plays, concerts, art exhibits, etc.). While dating outside of the church is not strictly forbidden, it is, as the author states, discouraged by church leaders and parents in an effort to reduce the chances that a member will marry outside of the church. Families of particularly staunch members are likely to view the marriage of a child to someone from outside of the church as a lamentable and perhaps even shameful event. Although Mormons who are married to nonmembers are not excluded from church activity or normal religious practice, one's relationship to the church is undoubtedly affected by the "part-member" status of the family. (*End of comment by M. O. Bigler*)]

At Brigham Young University, a Mormon-owned and op-erated institution in Provo, Utah, approximately 45 miles (72 km) south of Salt Lake City, a subculture of dating reigns. Known to be an ideal place for Mormon youth to find a same-faith marriage partner, it is also a hotbed of sexual explora-tion. Mormon coeds fine-tune their "NCMOS," (pronounced "nick-moes"), which is an acronym for "noncommittal make-out sessions." These sexual forays include "every-thing but intercourse": extensive kissing, petting, and "dry humping" (rubbing bodies) is common, but touching of the genitals is typically off-bounds, as is penetration of any kind.

[*Comment 1997*: Brigham Young University, the oldest private university west of the Mississippi River, boasts a student body of more than 30,000, comprised almost en-tirely of young Mormons who come from every state in the country and many nations outside of the United States. The amount and types of sexual activities that the author reports occur among BYU students are not all that atypical of young college students in general. However, given the strict code of sexual conduct that Mormons have for themselves, even nongenital sex play and sexual activity short of inter-course give BYU the appearance of a "hotbed of sexual ex-ploration." At the same time, such activity also suggests that young Mormons have healthy sexual appetites, and perhaps are not as peculiar as it may first appear when com-pared to their peers on other American campuses. (*End of comment by M. O. Bigler*)]

*Marriage, Sex, and the Celestial Kingdom*. In order to ac-cess the Celestial Kingdom, a couple must marry in the tem-ple. These temple rites seal the two partners together not just for life, but for all eternity. When a couple is in the Celestial Kingdom together, they can enjoy the full experience of their resurrected and eternally perfect bodies. The purpose of the sealed marriage is primarily to ensure the eternal con-nection between partners, allowing them to procreate and populate their own worlds (eternal procreation). An essen-tial precept, "As man is, so God once was; as God is, so man can become," guides heterosexual couples through life with the promise that they, as the God they worship has done, will become creators of their own world (Murstein 1974).

Although not formally prohibited, birth control is re-garded with clear reservation by church members, since large families are viewed favorably. Women who leave the Mormon church often refer, "with tongue in cheek," to their loss of opportunity to bear children during the afterlife. One woman commented, "At least I know I won't be barefoot and pregnant through time and eternity."

[*Comment 1997*: While birth control is regarded with reservation by many church members and authorities, vari-ous forms of contraception are commonly practiced, even by active, faithful members. Today, the decision to use birth control is left to the discretion of the couple. (*End of com-ment by M. O. Bigler*)]

The gender roles established early in the life of the cou-ple are metaphorically established again during the mar-riage ceremony. The order of the Plan of Salvation is clearly outlined during the ceremony, as is the order of the house-hold that symbolically supports the Divine Order when it is in accord with the Plan of Salvation. An interesting element of the temple marriage is the giving of a name to the bride, known only to her husband. This name is for the use of the husband in calling his wife to him in the afterlife. She does not have access to his secret name—the calling of partners in eternity is purely a masculine prerogative. The giving of the name to the bride is kept secret from outsiders, as is much of the rest of the ceremony, which is closed to all those without special church endowments. Mormon church wed-dings are different from typical American weddings in that only worthy LDS family members and friends are allowed into the temple to observe the ceremony itself. If a family member is an inactive church member or a nonmember, they will be excluded from the wedding ceremony, joining the party outside the temple or at the reception.

In the face of the lack of sexuality education, the first act of sexual intercourse for a good Mormon is likely to be ill-informed. One contemporary of mine recalls her first sexual experience, which took place after an LDS temple mar-riage: "We were both virgins, and it literally took us several weeks to consummate the marriage by having intercourse. We had been raised to believe sex was a sacred thing, so we just sat in bed, prayerfully, kissing gently and waiting for something to happen. Obviously, something finally did, but I was dreadfully disappointed. It not only didn't feel sacred, it didn't even feel good." This particular couple did not seek therapy for support or education, relying instead on the Holy Spirit, a decision common among LDS couples.

Because the church operates with a lay ministry, the lo-cal bishop has an enormous influence on how issues of sexu-ality are handled. In most instances in which married cou-ples face difficulty with sexual relations or general marital dissatisfaction, the bishop is the first and most likely source of comfort and counsel. Often the bishop is just a kindly in-tentioned neighbor with limited or no training. Many times, his response is based on his own experience, attitudes, aver-sions, and parental training. Some extremely compassion-ate bishops give forgiving responses to an individual who has erred sexually. Some bishops advise specifically against such behaviors as oral or anal sex. Others, repulsed by the vulgarity of even discussing the topic of sexuality, take ref-uge in esoteric spiritual or academic language or avoid the topic altogether. Still others may be open-minded and sug-gest that either the lay ministry has an extremely limited role in the bedroom of other folks or advise liberal mea-sures, such as doing whatever works best for the couple in-volved. If marriage counseling is clearly needed, a referral may be made by the bishop to the LDS Social Services or to an LDS therapist, who can give professional advice with an empathy for the doctrinal requirements. In sharp contrast, other bishops respond with an injunction to leave the fel-lowship if someone has premarital intercourse, commits adultery, or engages in homosexual relations, all of which are forbidden by church doctrine.

[*Comment 1997*: Problems that result from limited sexu-ality education coupled with well intentioned but poorly trained lay clergy are compounded for Mormons by a dearth of LDS therapists and other mental-health professionals who have specific training and experience in the area of sexuality. (*End of comment by M. O. Bigler*)]

Divorce is discouraged, but not uncommon. The divorce rate in the state of Utah, in spite of a predominantly LDS population, matches those of many states. Even marriages sealed in the temple are now relatively easy to unseal. Re-marriage from a doctrinal standpoint is difficult to compre-hend in light of the eternal marriage concept, but temple di-vorces will officially separate the couple for the purposes of the Celestial Kingdom.

[*Comment 1997*: If a temple divorce has been granted, a second marriage can be sealed in a Mormon temple. Mar-riages that take place outside of the temple are officially recognized by the church as legal and valid, with the understanding that these unions will not carry on into the eternities. (*End of comment by M. O. Bigler*)]

*The Mormon Family.* An ideal Mormon family works together, putting the sense of "family" first, honoring the doctrine that families will endure throughout eternity. It is a rare LDS home that lacks some visible reminder of this doctrine in an embroidered or otherwise handcrafted item proclaiming, "Families are Forever." The cultural value placed on family as a priority distinctly impacts those who choose not to have children, making those couples at least the object of social curiosity, if not censure.

Utah, the Mormon Mecca, is culturally oriented toward family because of the LDS church influence. Exemplifying this is Enid Waldholtz, the Republican congresswoman elected to office in 1994 from Utah, who is only the second member of Congress to bear a child while in office. This choice on the part of LDS Congresswoman Waldholtz clearly cemented her popularity among her Mormon constituents. She made a clear statement about her support for family life by meeting one of the most basic expectations of a Mormon couple with this childbirth.

*Sex Education.* Children are taught about sexuality more by implicit measures than direct and overt messages. Sexual exploration at a very early age is treated with quiet but firm repression. Mormon adults often describe their sense of guilt at their developing sexuality, often beginning at a very early age. These ideas are often disseminated by parents during "morality lessons," which might include the suggestion of singing hymns if "impure thoughts" enter one's mind, or using affirmative reminders that one's primary objective is to reach the Celestial Kingdom, which demands the purity of the body temple. "Impure thoughts" are usually not specifically defined, but are so pervasively assumed to be sexually related that many Mormon adults still claim to equate words such as "purity" and "morality" with specific sexual connotations.

In spite of the importance placed on having babies in a married state, very little formal education is done regarding sexuality and pregnancy. Countless times after I have made a simple junior- or high-school presentation on HIV prevention, students have lined up to ask me other "related" questions, often regarding basic body functioning, for example, "I haven't started my period. . . . How do I know if I'm pregnant? . . . Can I get pregnant from kissing?"

[*Comment 1997*: Mormon families are counseled by their leaders to hold a weekly Family Home Evening each Monday night. This is a specially designated time during the week for the family to join together to study religious topics, enjoy activities outside of the home, or address important family issues. Family Home Evening, as it has been outlined, provides LDS families with a perfect opportunity to provide sexuality education in the home within the framework of the family's own value system. After observing this practice among Mormon families, Dr. Ruth Westheimer and her colleague Louis Lieberman noted:

In particular, we have been impressed by the manner in which the Church of Jesus Christ of Latter-day Saints (the Mormons) has approached the difficult task of teaching moral and ethical precepts in the area of sexuality. If Jews, Italians, Chinese, and Japanese, among other groups, may be said to be child-centered societies, the Mormons must be said to be family-centered, par excellence. There appears to be a structured, systematic, integrated and total approach to morality through the family. Thus, sexual morality is taught as part of a system and way of life that fo-

cuses on the goal of eternal or celestial marriage. The church reaches out to the family through many media: songs, family meetings, family resource books, television, videos, etc., to provide the Mormon perspective on all aspects of sexuality for all family members. (Westheimer & Lieberman 1988, 109)

[Unfortunately, all too often, Mormon families fail to take advantage of this valuable resource, and miss an obvious opportunity to educate their children about matters related to human sexuality. (*End of comment by M. O. Bigler*)]

Many couples marry with limited information even about the act of intercourse. If they have been properly parented in the faith, they will have been protected from exposure to sexual or "perverted" images. A Mormon church leader, Dallin Oakes, in a speech at Brigham Young University, said "We are surrounded by the promotional literature of illicit sexual relations on the printed page and on the screen. For your own good, avoid it." He added, "Pornographic or erotic stories and pictures are worse than filthy or polluted food. The body has defenses to rid itself of unwholesome food, but the brain won't vomit back filth."

Biological information about menstruation is disseminated clinically. Some women recall this clinical information as imbued with a sense of shame, in which menstruation is described as a sickness or something one does not discuss in polite company. For example, I dated a Mormon man who was so unfamiliar with menstrual issues and women's bodies—in spite of having several sisters—that he did not know what the purpose of a tampon was or how it functioned.

*Abortion.* Abortion is considered a most venal sin. Since Mormon doctrine regards the bearing of children as an opportunity to bring "spirit" children into an earthly form, abortion is not only considered murder, but in addition, a denial of a body for a predestined soul.

*Gay Culture.* Both the San Francisco and New York gay cultures take special note of the Brigham Young University gay underground, famous for its size and covert scope. Many of the returning missionaries come back to BYU to find a mate and resolve the same-sex desires often stirred on the two-year LDS mission strongly encouraged by the Church with strictly enforced male-only companionship.* Sometimes that resolution does not come easily. Support groups for Mormon homosexuals in the Provo and Salt Lake area around BYU give voice to the pain of these men. Lesbians face the same dilemma, since they are surrounded by the cultural pressure to marry and have families.

The divine mandate of heterosexual marriage regards homosexuality as a repudiation of the gift and giver of life. Thus, homosexuality is regarded as a direct violation of God's plan, which is that men should cleave to women. Sexual relations between any nonmarried persons is considered sinful and homosexuality falls into this category. According

---

[*A note on LDS missionary services: Mormon men are strongly encouraged (*not* required) to serve a two-year mission at the age of 19. Formal sanctions are not imposed on those males who choose not to go on a mission. However, in a strong Mormon family or LDS community, social sanctions can be quite severe. The status of "Returned Missionary" is a valuable asset to a young man's marriage potential. In contrast, the decision not to serve a mission—or worse yet, leaving on a mission and returning home early—often brings shame to both the young man and his family. Mormon women, on the other hand, can choose to go on an 18-month mission at the age of 21. However, the expectation of service is not nearly as great for females as it is for males, and the decision not to go, particularly if a young woman opts to get married instead, results in few, if any, negative repercussions. (*End of comment by M. O. Bigler*)]

to Dallin Oaks, one of the church apostles, "Eternal laws that pertain to chastity before marriage and personal purity within marriage apply to all sexual behavior. However, marriage is not doctrinal therapy for homosexual relationships" (Ludlow 1992). Since so much of the restored gospel hinges upon the legally and temple-wedded heterosexual couple, practicing homosexuals are excommunicated.

Often the feelings of a gay person meet responses of incredulity on the part of parents and church leaders. One parent counseled his son not to act on his "supposed" same-gender feelings, "to date young women seriously, to wait and see" (Schow et al. 1991). Because homosexual couples cannot reproduce, this parent urged his son to "choose otherwise." The church offers "counseling to those who are troubled by homosexual thoughts and actions" in order that they might become acceptable to God. Repentance is offered in these circumstances. "Homosexuality and like practices are deep sins; they can be cured; they can be forgiven" (*Church News* 1978). In order to remain a Mormon in good standing, homosexuals must remain celibate and refrain from all same-gender eroticism. Acceptance is not advocated at any level.

[*Comment 1997*: The current Mormon position on homosexuality can be described as one of limited tolerance. Because sexual activity is reserved for marriage, and same-sex relationships are not recognized by most legal bodies or by the church, homosexual activity is therefore forbidden. As the author correctly notes, to continue to be a Mormon in good standing, homosexual men and women must remain celibate and refrain from all same-sex sexual activity. The church's position officially allows for individuals who are sexually attracted to members of the same gender to remain fully involved in church activities, so long as there is no sexual activity. This stance, though still extremely restrictive, is quite a departure from past policy and practice when virtually any indication of same-sex attraction could be used as grounds for excommunication. However, despite the apparent shift in thinking toward greater acceptance, it remains difficult, if not impossible, for members who feel a same-sex attraction to continue to actively practice Mormonism. Unfortunately, homophobia is often a more-powerful emotion for many church members than the New Testament challenge to "Love thy neighbor as thyself." Frequently, this homophobia is internalized and, despite Ludlow's declaration that "marriage is not doctrinal therapy for homosexual relationships," many gay, lesbian, and bisexual Mormons follow the traditional course that has been set for them by getting married and starting a family. Some carry on with a heterosexual life and take the secret of homosexuality to the grave. Others find their true sexual feelings too powerful to deny and may have clandestine same-sex relationships or seek out friendly advice, often from a bishop or other church authority. For those who acknowledge same-sex attraction, reparative or reorientation therapy is a common recommendation. These programs have demonstrated little lasting success in changing sexual orientation. Participation in reparative or reorientation therapy is often experienced as the ultimate failure, since the promise of change is directly linked to the sincerity and worthiness of one's efforts.

[Change-orientated therapy, therefore, is commonly the final step for many gay, lesbian, and bisexual Mormons before leaving the church or being asked to leave. In the end, homosexual Mormons are often left with a choice between their church and their sexuality. Because the two are diametrically opposed, there is little room for compromise. (*End of comment by M. O. Bigler*)]

*Summary.* The Mormon culture is distinct in many ways. Known for hard work, loyal families, and abstinence from alcohol and tobacco, the Mormons are steadfast in their maintenance of traditional family values. Sexually conservative and repressive, Mormon doctrines may be the ideal for people disillusioned with or anxious about the liberalization of sexual attitudes and practices occurring in the United States in recent decades. According to the 1995 United States census, Utah—with a 70% Mormon population—ranks first in fertility and last in teen pregnancy. The Mormons, long considered remarkable for their nearly anachronistic traditional values, may actually be on the cutting edge of the Christian Right's abstinence- and morality-based vision of American family life.

## [Spirituality-Sexuality Movements

LORAINE HUTCHINS

[*Editors' Note*: The basic sexological premises that underlie American sexual attitudes, values, and behavior are derived from the 2,000-year-old Greco-Roman philosophies of the Stoics, Zoroastrians, Platonic and Neoplatonic dualists, and many popular Gnostics. If anything can be said about these philosophies, which the early Christians adopted, it is that they were and are clearly anti-pleasure, anti-sex and anti-woman. This is radically true of all Euro-American cultures, but especially true of American culture, because of the sex-negative values the poorer immigrants and Puritans brought with them to the colonies. With its ongoing incarnational mission, Christianity should have, but did not develop a sex-positive integration of sex and spirit. One consequence of the resulting pervasive religious repression of sex that emerged early in the sexual revolution of the 1960s was the development of grassroots, at times spontaneous-combustion efforts to rejoin and integrate sexuality and spirituality. Factors in this phenomenon include the flowering of women's liberation, the advent of the "pill," the breakdown of religious and social condemnations of premarital sex, gay/lesbian/bi/trans liberation, and a growing interest in the more sex-and-pleasure-positive philosophies of Taoism and Tantra (Francoeur 1992).]

[*Update 2003*: We could say the impulse to integrate sexuality and spirituality is at the erotic core of creation. The need to reintegrate them began when the customs of people who revered the Earth were smashed apart by dominators.

[Seeds to the emerging spirituality-sexuality movement are found in the ancient Eastern ways of Taoism and Tantra and the sexual liberation movements of the 1960s and 1970s. By the 1980s, the teachings of Baghwan Shree Rajneesh (Osho) (1977) and his many students, such as Margo Anand (1991), gave new life to practices that would heal the split between sexuality and spirituality. It is no coincidence that this erotic-spiritual awakening bloomed in the face of AIDS. The increasing visibility and leadership of women and sexual minorities also profoundly changed the face of this movement to reintegrate sex and spirit. Among the more visible are sexologists Annie Sprinkle and Joseph Kramer, who teach sacred erotic massage and sacred intimacy mentoring in ways that bridge the gaps between women and men, gays and straights. In 1997, Deborah Taj Anapol convened a national Celebration of Eros, a Conference on Sacred Sexuality, bringing together for the first time, teachers from Tantric, Taoist, Sufi, Buddhist, Jewish, Pagan, Wiccan, Occult, Native American, and Afro-Caribbean traditions. The blossoming of groups and training programs continues to grow every year.

[The U.S. spirituality-sexuality movement sparks most intensely in retreat centers and gathering places, such as Shalom Mountain (Livingston Manor, NY), Omega Institute (Rhinebeck, NY), Harbin Hot Springs (Middletown, CA), Wildwood (Guerneville, CA), Kirkridge (Bangor, PA),

Burning Man (Black Rock City, NV), the Body Sacred (Livingston Manor, NY), Esalen (Big Sur, CA), Dawn Manor (Livingston Manor), Short Mountain (Radical Faery Center, Liberty, TN), Ramblewood (Darlington, MD), Sacred Connections (various locations in CA), and American Ridge (a campsite outside Seattle, WA). Integration of different views and approaches occurs in state parks at summer festivals, in the special temple rooms of sex-workers redefining their own erotic ministries, in covens meeting down side roads, in church halls, on shores, and in meadows.

[Among the more influential resources are the following—listed alphabetically: Margo Anand's *The Art of Sexual Ecstasy: The Path of Sacred Sexuality for Western Lovers*; Bodhi Avinasha and Sunyata Sarasswati's *The Jewel and the Lotus: The Tantric Path to Higher Consciousness*; Georg Fuerstein's *Enlightened Sexuality: Essays on Body-Positive Spirituality*; Donald Kraig's *Sex Magick: Sacred Erotic Spirituality*; Miranda Shaw's *Passionate Enlightenment: Women in Tantric Buddhism*; and Kenneth Ray Stubbs' *Women of the Light: The New Sacred Prostitute*. Jenny Wade's *Transcendent Sex* presents ordinary women's and men's accounts of transcendent sex experiences (without drugs and Tantra) connecting heart, genitals, soul, and spirit. Each of these practitioners/teachers represents a different aspect of the emerging "sacred sexualities" movement in the U.S. The Quodoshka website, http://www.spiritualsexuality.com, is maintained by teachers trained by Harley Swift Deer and presents a very influential strain not represented in the books listed here.

[The network of modern spirituality-sexuality integration is being created at all these places, through the stories participants tell, the practices taught privately, on websites, and in chat groups. Knowledge of this reintegration lives in the doing and in being. Every time we use our spines as breath-flutes, all our organs are instruments of praise. We are just beginning to create communities that reclaim and celebrate these ancient ways of healing the broken vessel of our world, of teaching each other how to reweave the roots and impulses that make us whole. (*End of update by L. Hutchins*)]

## B. Racial, Ethnic, and Gender Perspectives

In addition to the religious factor, two other social factors continue to exert considerable influence on American sexual ideologies and practices, race/ethnicity and gender. In this section, we examine the sexual customs of two of the largest racial and ethnic minority groups in the U.S.A., African-Americans and Latino-Americans, followed by a look at Native Americans. Next, we examine the effects of feminism and feminist perspectives on sexuality in America and sexological research, and the emerging perspectives of men on these issues. Finally, we look at the concept of heterophobia.

### *African-American Sexuality* HERBERT SAMUELS

The term African-American is widely and often carelessly used to suggest or imply that the more than 30 million African-Americans constitute some kind of homogeneous community or culture. This is both contrary to reality and dangerous, as the term properly includes a rich diversity of very different, and often distinct subcultures, each with its own set of sexual values, attitudes, and behavioral patterns. Included under the rainbow umbrella of African-Americans are urban African-Americans in the northeast, ranging from Boston south to Washington, D.C., African-Americans in Los Angeles on the West Coast, and African-Americans in urban centers in the southern states. Rural African-Americans are often quite different from urban African-Americans, even in nearby metropolitan centers. Socioeconomic

and educational differences add to the diversity of African-American subcultures. This perspective is essential to avoid overgeneralizations about the observations provided here.

*Historical Perspective.* A review of the past record reveals that many white Americans have regarded the majority of African-Americans as representing the sexual instinct in its raw state. This belief that African-American sexual behavior is somehow more sordid and crude than the sexual behavior of white Americans is by no means a new concept. Reports dating from the mid-16th century depict the sexual behavior of Africans as bestial. The same descriptions were later applied to the Africans brought to the New World by the slave trade.

Moreover, the folk view of the sexuality of blacks is often hard to distinguish from what appears in the scientific literature. In the guise of science, some investigators have presented such conclusions as: 1. African-American men and women are guided by "bestial instinct" (DeRachewiltz 1964; Jacobus 1937; Purchas 1905); 2. the black man is more animalistic in bed (DeRachewiltz 1964; Jacobus 1937; Purchas 1905); 3. the black man's penis is larger than the penis of the white man (DeRachewiltz 1964; Edwardes & Masters 1963; Jacobus 1937); 4. the black man is a sexual superman whose potency and virility is greater than the white man's (DeRachewiltz 1964; Jacobus 1937; Jefferson 1954); 5. the black man's reproductive capacity is colossal (Jacobus 1937); 6. black men are obsessed with the idea of having sex with white women (Edwardes & Masters 1963; Fanon 1967); 7. all black women want to sleep with anyone who comes along (DeRachewiltz 1964; Jacobus 1937; Rogers 1967); and 8. black women respond instantly and enthusiastically to all sexual advances (DeRachewiltz 1964; Jacobus 1937). Blacks have also been characterized as holding more-permissive attitudes regarding extramarital affairs (Bell 1968; Christensen & Johnson 1978; Houston 1981; Reiss 1964, 1967; Roebuck & McGee 1977; Staples 1978). This simplistic notion may well misrepresent the complexity of African-American sexual values. According to Robert Staples (1986, 258),

Blacks have traditionally had a more naturalistic attitude toward human sexuality, seeing it as the normal expression of sexual attraction between men and women. Even in African societies, sexual conduct was not the result of some divine guidance by God or other deities. It was secularly regulated and encompassed the tolerance of a wide range of sexual attitudes and behaviors. Sexual deviance, where so defined, was not an act against God's will but a violation of community standards.

*Gender, Gender Role, Sex, Love, and Marriage.* Gender and gender roles are culturally defined constructs that determine the boundaries of acceptable and unacceptable behavior for men and women. These notions are often based on stereotypes—a fixed, oversimplified, and extremely distorted idea about a group of people. In the general American culture, the traditional stereotyped female is gentle, kind, dependent, passive, and submissive. The traditional stereotyped male is tough, brutal, independent, aggressive, and intractable. Any deviation from one's expected gender role may be met with skepticism about one's psychological health. For example, the traditional view of the black male—as it relates to gender-role identification—is that he has been emasculated by the experience of slavery and is suffering from gender-identity problems because of absent or inadequate male role models. Moreover, because of these two problems, he has a more-feminine gender identity than white males (Grier & Cobbs 1968; Glazer & Moynihan 1964; Pettigrew 1964;

Wilkinson & Taylor 1977). Grier and Cobbs (1968, 59) suggest that:

> For the black man in this country, it is not so much a matter of acquiring manhood as it is a struggle to feel it is his own. Whereas the white man regards his manhood as an ordained right, the black man is engaged in a never ending battle for its possession. For the black man, attaining any portion of manhood is an active process. He must penetrate barriers and overcome opposition in order to assume a masculine posture. For the innermost psychological obstacles to manhood are never so formidable as the impediments woven into American society.

Pettigrew (1964) supported the notion that black males are more feminine than white males because of certain responses to items in the masculinity-femininity scale on the *Minnesota Multiphasic Personality Inventory* (*MMPI*). Two items that Pettigrew noted were the statements, "I would like to be a singer" and "I think I feel more intensely than most people do." Black males responded more positively to these statements than did white males. This pattern was interpreted to mean that black males are more feminine than white males. Pettigrew based his conclusion regarding the black male's gender identity on two studies. One study included a sample of Alabama convicts; the other was a group of veterans with tuberculosis! As Pleck (1981) notes, these are hardly representative samples.

In contrast to the emasculated, feminine, black male hypothesis, Hershey (1978) argues that black males have a stronger masculine identity than white males. In her study of sex-role identities and sex-role stereotyping, the black men's mean masculinity score was significantly higher than the mean masculinity score of the white men in her sample.

To the extent that African-American males have been emasculated by gender-role stereotyping, African-American females have been defeminized by gender-role stereotyping. The so-called black matriarchy has been historically blamed for the deterioration of the black family, because black women have greater participation in family decision making in a society where male control is the "normal rule." Because white stereotyped norms are violated, African-American women are seen as being domineering. By virtue of the historical legacy of slavery and discrimination against African-American men, African-American women were in the labor market, received education, and supported their families.

According to Staples,

> Sex relations have a different nature and meaning to black people. Their sexual expression derives from the emphasis in the black culture on feeling, of releasing the natural functions of the body without artificiality or mechanical movements. In some circles this is called "soul" and may be found among peoples of African descent throughout the world. (Cited by Francoeur 1991, 90-92)

In a practical sense, this means that black men do not moderate their enthusiasm for sex relations as white men do. They do not have a history of suppressing the sexual expression of the majority of their women while singling out a segment of the female population for premarital and extramarital adventures (Staples 1977, 141-42).

The major problem with such studies is that few have questioned the stereotyped assumptions regarding gender-role socialization upon which their conclusions are based.

*Views and Practices of Sex Education.* Black males and females are socialized very early into heterosexual relations by their culture and extended-family system. The less-stringent age and gender-role orientations that are evident in the black community exposes children at an early age to a more permissive sexual ethos. Many African-Americans perceive sex as a natural function; thus, children are not hidden from discussions of a sexual nature.

Academically, many sexuality or family life education programs employ the Health Belief Model, not only as a way to predict sexual behavior, but to facilitate behavior change. This model has certain assumptions that are based on Euro-American social norms. These norms may not be consistent with the beliefs and values of many African-Americans. Mays and Cochran (1990) correctly maintain that such attitude-behavior models

> assume that people are motivated to pursue rational courses of action. They further assume that people have the resources necessary to proceed directly with these rational decisions. . . . Black Americans confront an environment in which much of their surrounding milieu is beyond their personal control. Models of human behavior that emphasize individualistic, direct, and rational behavioral decisions overlook the fact that many blacks do not have personal control over traditional categories of resources—for example, money, education, and mobility.

For many African-Americans, educational models that place emphasis on social norms and the extent of commitment to social responsibilities, rather than those that value individualistic rational reasoning, may be better predictors of future behavior.

*Masturbation.* Most studies indicate that African-American men and women masturbate less than do white men and women. In a recent national study, *The Social Organization of Sexuality* (Laumann et al. 1994), one third of white men and 56% of white women reported that they had not masturbated at all in the past year. However, black men were almost twice as likely to report that they had not masturbated at all during the past year, and about 68% of black women reported that they did not masturbate in the past year. However, those African-Americans who do masturbate demonstrate the same childhood, adolescent, and adult patterns as their white counterparts. Blacks may not acknowledge that they masturbate as readily as whites, because of the belief that admitting that one masturbates means one is unable to find a sex partner.

*Children and Sex.* African-American children, according to Staples (1972), are socialized very early into heterosexual relations by their culture and extended-family system. This socialization pattern exposes them at an early age to a more permissive sexual ethos. Thus, African-American children may have a knowledge of sexual intercourse, masturbation, condom usage, and other sexual practices at a younger age.

*Adolescents and Sex.* Compared to white teenagers, African-American teenagers begin coitus about two years earlier, on the average, and are more likely to progress directly from light petting to sexual intercourse (Brooks-Gunn & Furstenburg 1989). Consequently, African-American females may be at greater risk of pregnancy.

Black men start dating earlier, are more likely to have a romantic involvement in high school, have the most liberal sexual attitudes, and are most inclined to have nonmarital sex without commitment (Broderick 1965; Larson et al. 1976; Johnson & Johnson 1978). (See Section 5B for additional data comparing black and white adolescent sexual patterns.)

*Adults.* In the aftermath of the Civil War, blacks married in record numbers because, under the inhumane institution of slavery, legal marriage had been denied to them. Three out of four black adults were living in intact nuclear families by the early part of the 20th century, and the overwhelming majority of black children were born to parents who were legally married. Today, an African-American child has but a one-in-five chance of being raised by two parents (Chideya et al. 1993). Out-of-wedlock births have risen since the 1960s, particularly among African-Americans. Two out of three first births to African-American women under the age of 35 are now out of wedlock.

Traditionally, women in American society have tended to marry men in their own social class or to "marry up" to a higher socioeconomic group. This pattern has been substantially disrupted among African-Americans, largely because of a distorted gender ratio among blacks. This imbalance in the proportion of males and females of marriageable age has been present for several decades, but has become exacerbated in recent years. By the 1990s, there were roughly 50 adult African-American women for every 42 African-American men, largely because of abnormally high rates of black-male mortality and incarceration (Staples & Johnson 1993). Because the proportion of African-American women who attend college and earn degrees is much higher than the rate for men, this problem is even more severe for higher-status women. As a result, increasing numbers of black women are remaining single or marrying partners from lower-status groups (i.e., less education and/or income). There is no evidence that large groups of black women are choosing to marry outside their race (Staples & Johnson 1993).

Joseph Scott (1976) has argued that these social conditions are largely responsible for the emergence of a pattern he calls "mansharing." Mansharing is a lifestyle where a number of African-American women, each of whom typically maintains her own separate residence, "share" a man for intimate relationships. Typically, he splits time living with each of the women. Scott (1976) argued that mansharing represented the appearance of a new, polygamous family form in the African-American community. However, we want to stress that this does not mean that black women like or prefer this lifestyle. Cazenave (1979) has noted that lifestyles can sometimes be imposed by external social constraints. There is some evidence (Allen & Agbasegbe 1980) that most black women do not approve of mansharing as a lifestyle, but feel they have reduced options in an environment with few eligible male partners. Scott concluded that:

> Until there is some way to correct the sex ratio imbalance and until blacks control the economic and welfare institutions in such a way to stop the breaking up of black monogamous relationships we cannot be too harsh on black men and women who find some satisfactory adjustments in sharing themselves and their economic resources in a new, at least for this society, family form which meets their most basic needs. (Scott 1976, 80)

*Homosexuality and Bisexuality.* Attitudes within the African-American community reflect those in the majority culture. According to Staples (1981), homosexuality may be tolerated in the black community but will not be approved openly. Bell and Weinberg (1978), in their study of homosexuality, found that black male homosexuals tended to be younger than their white counterparts, had less education, and were employed at a lower occupational level. Moreover, black male gays more often expressed the belief that their homosexuality and homosexual contacts had helped more than hurt their careers.

Compared to black gay males, black lesbians had fewer transient sexual partners. Most reported that the majority of their sexual encounters were with women for whom they cared emotionally.

*Coercive Sex and Pornography.* The incidence of rape among African-Americans has been subject to some controversy. According to the Department of Health and Human Services, 683,000 adult women were raped in 1990. By contrast, the National Victim Center estimated that there were 130,236 rapes in 1990 and 207,610 in 1991. Although earlier reports indicated that African-American women were more likely to be sexually assaulted than white women, newer studies do not find any statistically significant difference between African-American and white samples. The historical notion that most rapists are black men is totally without merit; indeed, most rapists and their victims are members of the same race or ethnic group.

There is an important difference between the attitudes of those whites who support the antipornography movement in the United States and the lack of interest this issue stirs among African-Americans. For African-Americans, as Robert Staples (1986, 258) argues, issues of poverty, education, job opportunities, and teenage pregnancy are far more pressing concerns than the crusade against pornography.

> Rather than seeing the depiction of heterosexual intercourse or nudity as an inherent debasement of women as a fringe group as [white religious conservatives and] feminists claim, the black community would see women as having equal rights to the enjoyment of sexual stimuli. It is nothing more than a continuation of the white male's traditional double standard and paternalism to regard erotica as existing only for male pleasure and women only as sexual objects. Since that double standard has never attracted many American blacks, the claim that women are exploited by exhibiting their nude bodies or engaging in heterosexual intercourse lacks credibility. After all, it was the white missionaries who forced African women to regard their quasi-nude bodies as sinful and placed them in clothes. This probably accounts for the rather conspicuous absence of black women in the feminist fight against porn.

*Contraception and Abortion.* Since the early 1970s, many in the African-American community have viewed contraceptive use as a form of genocide advocated by whites. Thus, control over reproduction has had political and social implications.

The majority of women having abortions are white. Although 12% of the population is of African-American ancestry, black women constitute approximately 31% of the women who seek abortions. There is a history of forced sterilization against African-Americans, which many perceive as a form of genocide similar to contraception.

*STDs and HIV/AIDS.* In 1932, the United States Public Health Service recruited 600 African-American men from Tuskegee, Alabama, to participate in an experiment involving untreated syphilis. The aim of this study was to determine if there were any racial differences in the development of syphilis. The Tuskegee participants were never informed that they had syphilis. This wanton disregard for human life allowed the disease to spread to the sexual partners of these men, as well as their offspring. This experiment continued until 1972! The repercussions from the "Tuskegee Experiment" still resonate strongly through African-American communities, and have a negative impact on HIV/AIDS prevention programs.

HIV was the eighth-leading cause of death for all Americans in 1990, but it was the sixth-leading cause of death for African-Americans. It is the leading cause of death for African-American men between the ages of 35 and 44, and the second-leading cause of death for black men and women between 25 and 35. Again this raises the specter of genocide among many members of the African-American community, in that many believe that the virus was man-made!

[*Update 2003*: The HIV/AIDS epidemic continues to be a major health crisis facing the African-American community. Although African-Americans make up only about 12% of the U.S. population, they accounted for half of the new HIV infections reported in the United States in 2001. And many new infections occur among young African-Americans. According to the CDC:

- African-American men accounted for 43% of new HIV cases reported among men in 2001.
- 32% of African-American men who have sex with men were found to be infected with HIV in a recent multi-city study of men ages 23 to 29 years, compared to 14% of Latinos and 7% of whites in the study.
- While information on recent HIV infection is limited, data reported to CDC through 2001 suggest that the leading cause of HIV infection among African-American men is sexual contact with other men, followed by injection drug use and heterosexual contact.
- African-American women accounted for nearly 64% of HIV-1 cases reported among women in 2001.
- The rate of HIV infection among African-American women, ages 20 to 44, in 25 states with HIV reporting before 1994, was 80.1 per 100,000 population from 1994 to 1998—four times higher than the rates among Latinas of the same age, and more than 16 times higher than the rates among white women.
- The latest data available on recent HIV infection suggest that the leading cause of HIV infection among African-American women is heterosexual contact, followed by injection drug use.

[(CDC 2001; Lee & Fleming 2001; Valleroy 1998, 2000). (See discussion of "Brothers on the Down Low" in Section 6B, Homoerotic, Homosexual, and Bisexual Behaviors, Adults, Health Issues). (*End of update by H. Samuels*)]

*Sexual Dysfunction.* The stereotyped notions about the sexual experiences of African-Americans not only influence the attitudes that whites may have about African-Americans, but also affect the way in which African-Americans perceive themselves. For example, the willingness of an African-American male who is experiencing difficulty in maintaining an erection or ejaculatory control to seek help may be dependent on how closely he identifies with the myth of the "super potent" black man. Any man may feel embarrassment about a sexual problem, but for the African-American male, the embarrassment that he may feel is compounded by the images of the myth.

For clinicians, an awareness of this historical legacy is essential to the treatment process. A key component in the treatment of many sexual problems is the use of self-pleasuring exercises. These exercises are an effective method for a person to learn more about his or her own sex responses. Many African-Americans have negative feelings about masturbation that may infringe on the treatment process. First, changing these negative feelings may take more time than is typical for other clients. Second, African-Americans who do masturbate may be more reluctant to discuss this issue because, for many, admitting that they masturbate indicates that they cannot find a sexual partner.

[*The Interaction of Gender and Race*
PATRICIA BARTHALOW KOCH
[*Update 1998*: *Sexuality and African-American Women.* Gender and race have traditionally been defined and operationalized as fixed biological categories into which people could neatly be sorted. However, many scholars now consider gender and race as social constructions, based on social and political influences, rather than on biological characteristics (Irvine 1995; Simon 1996). Additionally, many research studies have confounded socioeconomic status with race. Shortcomings often encountered in sexuality research include the lack of historical context, cultural insensitivity, and generalizations or assumptions about gender (Burgess 1994). Various aspects of African-American women's sexuality are quintessential examples of the salience and interaction of gender and race upon sexuality in the United States. African-American women's sexual attitudes, values, behaviors, and relationships have been shaped by their gender and racial heritage, including the historical experience of slavery and continued marginalization in American society (Staples & Johnson 1993).

[To the extent that African-American males have been "emasculated" by gender-role stereotyping, as described by Samuels above, African-American females have often been "defeminized" by this same process. By virtue of the historical legacy of slavery and continuing discrimination against African-American men in the labor force and other aspects of "mainstream" American society, e.g., housing and education, African-American women have always needed to be in the labor force to support their families (Anderson 1996). This economic necessity has contributed to the myth of the "black matriarchy," which has then been blamed for the deterioration of the black family. African-American women have been described as domineering authoritarians who drive away their husbands and destroy their sons' ability to perform effectively as productive adults. These "castrating matriarchs" and "lazy black men" have been chided as the "cause" of poverty among African-American families, avoiding any search for causes in a political and economic system that provided African-Americans with few opportunities to successfully support intact families (Anderson 1996; Staples & Johnson 1993).

[In essence, there tends to be more-egalitarian gender roles and fluidity among African-Americans than among Anglo-Americans (Broman 1991; Farley & Allen 1987). White stereotypic norms seem to be violated when black women have greater participation in family decision-making than has been present within a dominant Anglo society where male control is more the "rule." Therefore, according to Burgess (1994), African-American women are seen as domineering. African-American women have most often been portrayed in some combination of four primary images: 1. as highly maternal, family-oriented, and self-sacrificing "Mammies" or "Aunt Jemimas"; 2. as threatening and argumentative "Sapphires"; 3. as seductive, sexually irresponsible, promiscuous "Jezebels"; and 4. as ignorant, lazy, greedy, breeding "Welfare Mothers" (Collins 1990; Weitz 1993; West 1995).

[In reality, African-American women must play dual roles. They are pressured to be more androgynous or masculine in order to make it in the work world, since they are often more successful at gaining employment than are African-American men. Yet, they also often try to maintain traditional female gender roles, especially that of mothering, to sustain relationships within their domestic networks (Binion 1990). As a hedge against failure, poor black men may limit their affective and economic commitments to family, approaching marriage and fatherhood ambivalently (Anderson 1996). Black women often want to be supportive of their men, yet sometimes find the men's behavior to be distancing, oppressive, or abusive (Lorde 1984). Lorde has noted that female-headed households in the black community do not always occur by default. She and others contend that black women are less likely to accept oppressive conditions in their marriages than white women, and, therefore, are much more likely to leave abusive unions with males. African-American women often develop matrifocal kin networks in which female family members, e.g., grandmothers and aunts, share the family and childcare responsibilities. Compared to their Anglo-American counterparts, African-American women are less likely to marry, more likely to be divorced or separated, and less likely to remarry (Anderson 1990).

[Regarding specific sexual behaviors, black men and women appear to engage in cunnilingus and fellatio less often than their white peers (Belcastro 1985; Hunt 1974; Laumann et al. 1994). A lack of foreplay is a grievance often expressed by married black women (Staples 1981), although black women report a higher frequency of intercourse per week than white women (Fisher 1980). Concerning such differences, Staples (1972, 9) suggests that:

> Unlike many white women who see sexual relations as primarily an activity designed to give men pleasure, black women expect their sexual partners to try and sexually satisfy them, and criticize him if he doesn't. Sex is not necessarily something that is done to them. . . . Also in contrast to many white women, the black woman tends to be open within the peer group about her sexual experiences. . . . [This] allows black women to develop standards of sexual conduct to which males must address themselves.

[Rape and sexual assault have a unique history for African-American women because of the sexual exploitation of slaves for over 250 years before the American Civil War (Getman 1984). Throughout America's history, sexual assault on African-American women has been perceived and treated with less concern than for Anglo-American women (Wyatt 1992). For example, by 1660 in the American South, there were laws supporting sex between black women and white men in order to insure that interracial children would be slaves owned by the white slave masters. However, sex between a black man and white woman was severely punished with the alleged black "assailant" being castrated or sentenced to death, usually by lynching. Yet, there were no penalties for the rape of black women by white men. The stereotype that black women are "oversexed" by nature and, thus, cannot be rape victims, still exists in America today (Getman 1984). When both a rape victim and defendant are black, there is less likelihood of conviction compared to both victim and defendant being white (LaFree, Ruskin, & Visher 1985). Because of this and discriminatory police practices toward other crimes in the black community, black victims may feel less support and are, therefore, less likely to report being raped (Wyatt, Newcomb, & Notgrass 1990). Hooks (1990) has emphasized that sexism and racism are "interlocking systems of domination that maintain each other." (*End of update by P. B. Koch*)]

## U.S. Latinos and Sexual Health

MIGUEL A. PÉREZ and HELDA L. PINZÓN-PÉREZ
[*Rewritten and updated in September 2002 by M. A. Pérez and H. L. Pinzón-Pérez*]
[*Demographics.* Latinos* in the United States are a heterogeneous group comprised of Mexicans, Puerto Ricans, Cubans, Central Americans, and South Americans. Like most other ethnic/racial groups residing in the United States, La-

tinos exist in a distinct social environment, have developed a unique culture, and are often disfranchised from mainstream society. The heterogeneity of the Latino population residing in the U.S. can be observed in each group's unique culture, beliefs, language, socioeconomic background, family name, racial ascription, and culinary preferences (Castex 1994; Neale 1989; Williams 1989). Further evidence of the heterogeneity can be found in the 2000 U.S. Census, which found that 9 out of 10 Latinos reported racial/ethnic classifications other than Hispanic on the census forms. Two characteristics have been found to unify Latinos in the U.S.: having ancestors in a Latin American country, excluding Brazil, and having one or more family members who speak or were fluent in the Spanish language.

[Latinos are one of, if not the fastest-growing population groups in the U.S. According to census data, in the last decade, the U.S. Latino population growth has been twice that of the general population (U.S. Census Bureau [USCB] 2000). As Table 3 shows, over 12% of the U.S. population is classified as being of Hispanic or Latino descent; this figure is expected to increase to 21% by the year 2050. Although Latinos can be found in almost every state, two states, Texas and California, account for over 50% of all Hispanics in the United States (USCB 2002).

[Several factors have been identified as contributors to this high population growth, among them, high fertility rates, high levels of immigration to the United States, and the relatively young population (Brindis 1992, USCB 2002). Among Latinos, persons of Mexican origin form the largest population group, accounting for approximately 59% of the Latino population in the U.S.; Puerto Ricans place at a distant second, with approximately 10% of the population. The last decade has seen a marked increased in populations from Central and South America, which now account for approximately 3.5% of the total U.S. Latino population (USBC 2002).

[Overall, U.S. Latinos are a relatively young population, with a median age of 25.9 years compared to 35.3 years for non-Latinos. While 26% of non-Latinos are below the age of 18, 35% of Hispanics are found in that age group (USBC 2002). Among U.S. ethnic groups, only Native Americans have a younger population. Table 4 shows the mean age for each of the Latino groups in the U.S. (USCB 2002).

**Table 3**

**U.S. Population Distribution 1990-2000**

|  | 1990 | 2002 |
|---|---|---|
| Whites | 80.3% | 75.1% |
| African-Americans | 12.1 | 12.3 |
| Hispanics/Latinos | 9.0 | 12.5 |
| Asian/Pacific Islander | 2.9 | 3.7 |
| Native Americans | 1.1 | 1.1 |
| Others | 3.9 | 5.5 |

*Source*: U.S. Census Bureau 2002

**Table 4**

**Mean Ages for Latino Groups in the U.S.**

| Latino Group | Mean Age |
|---|---|
| Mexicans | 24.2 |
| Puerto Ricans | 27.3 |
| Central Americans | 29.2 |
| South Americans | 33.1 |
| Cubans | 40.7 |

*Source*: U.S. Census Bureau 2002

---

*The terms "Latino"" and "Hispanic" are used interchangeably in this section to describe a heterogeneous group of people representing a kaleidoscope of experiences, educational attainment, acculturation levels, and citizenship status. The term "Latina" pertains specifically to Hispanic women.

[While the following material describes relevant sexological concepts among Latinos in the U.S., it cannot report all sexual-related knowledge and practices among this rapidly increasing heterogeneous population group. The following paragraphs, however, will highlight relevant sexological issues and hopefully dispel some of the stereotypes related to Latino sexuality. Comparisons presented here represent general data for Latinos; thus, the reader needs to keep in mind that there are differences among first-generation and other-generation Latinos, by age group, by economic level, and by acculturation level. The truth is that the variety of sexual practices and patterns among Latinos in the United States, and for that matter in Latin America, are only surpassed by the limits of human imagination.

[*Family Issues*. The majority of Latinos in the U.S. do not define their *familia* (family) in terms of the traditional nuclear-family concept accepted by mainstream America. It is, therefore, not uncommon for Latinos to reside in multigenerational households with members of their extended family (Alberda & Tilly 1992; Garcia 1993). This arrangement permits the division of labor, sharing of economic and domestic responsibilities, and most importantly, allows extended family members to participate in the rearing of children (Kutsche 1983; Leaper-Campbell 1996). The strong identification with the extended family explains the *apegamiento* (unity) traditionally ascribed to Latinos, highlights an individual's willingness to place the *familia*'s need before his or her own, and elucidates the role grandparents, as well as uncles and aunts, play in shaping Latinos' earlier views on sexuality (Brindis 1997).

[The Latino culture has been erroneously depicted as being patriarchal in nature. This impression, carefully maintained through the male's role as the family's representative before society, hides the decision-making role Latinas have in the family unit. In fact, Latinas are the base of the family structure, are the primary caregivers in the home, and have important nonpublic and nonverbal authority within the family (de la Vega 1990). In short, Latinas maintain the equilibrium and smoothness of family relationships. Similarly, realities associated with immigration have increased the number of Latina heads of household who support and maintain their families, in many cases without the direct intervention of any males.

[On the other hand, Latinas in their caregiving role, traditionally tend to pay more attention to the family's needs than their own. This expectation is most often noted in young women taking care of older relatives, while their male counterparts seek to forge their own future, albeit not too far from the family unit. Furthermore, traditional Latino families may also discourage young Latinas to pursue higher education and, instead, may seek to prepare them for marriage.

[Along with family orientation, Latinos often show the closely related concept of *simpatía*. The latter refers to Latinos' willingness to go along with items that may not be understood or that they may disagree with. Szapocznik (1995) has suggested that familism and *simpatía* may now be liabilities for Latinos in the United States, particularly for gay men who attempt to conceal their true HIV-status from their families and friends.

[Several authors (de la Vega 1990; Lifshitz 1990; Fennelly 1988) have emphasized the importance of recognizing the differences in family and cultural expectations regarding sexual behavior for females and males in the Latino culture. The acknowledgment of these differences assists in the understanding of the complexity of sexuality-related issues within this population group. This is particu-

larly true as we view Latinos in the U.S. through the prism of acculturation.

[*Sexological Concepts: Acculturation and Sexual Practices*. Among Latinos, sexual matters are considered to be private affairs not to be discussed in public. Therefore, it is not surprising that some Latinos have little understanding of their bodies, the sexual response cycle, and may still view sexuality exclusively within the context of procreation.

[Sexuality is an important life element among Latinos and is as complex as the heterogeneity of the population group. Latino sexuality is not limited or circumscribed to coital activity, but it is rather expressed through a variety of life attitudes which reinforce male and female sexual identities and roles. Sexual tones are evident in music, art, and dress codes, which emphasize the role of sexuality while avoiding offending community etiquette and expectations. *Coquetería* (to be discussed later) and *modestia* are opposing forces that characterize a woman's ability to openly pursue her sexuality while maintaining clearly delineated boundaries. In the United States, sexual patterns are not only affected by culture, but also by the individual's degree of acculturation and assimilation (Spector 1991).

[Acculturation and education also play a pivotal role in the acceptance of new expressions of sexuality. In a 1990 study, Marín, Marín, and Juárez found that Latinas with higher levels of acculturation reported more multiple sexual partners than those with lower acculturation levels. The same study found that less-acculturated males were more likely to carry condoms and report fewer sexual partners. A follow-up study found that less-acculturated Latinas were less likely to carry condoms and experienced higher levels of sexual discomfort (Marín, Gomez, & Hearst 1993). More-acculturated and educated Latinas are also more likely to adopt a leading role during heterosexual activities. Acculturation notwithstanding, sexuality continues to be a taboo topic for many Latinos, particularly for older, Spanish-speaking Latinos.

[Until the advent of the AIDS epidemic, few researchers had systematically documented sexual practices and knowledge among Latinos. Inappropriate application of methodological tools, language difficulties, and cultural insensitivity have all been identified as barriers to data collection among U.S. Latinos (Ford & Norris 1991). The lack of data about Latinos has been further exacerbated by the lack of identification of Latinos as a specific population group, particularly in large federally funded studies.

[*Sexual Stereotypes*. It is perhaps significant that general knowledge of Latino sexuality is denoted more by stereotypes than factual information. De la Vega (1990) concluded that numerous myths and stereotypes are found among Latinos, as within any group of individuals. It is important that these subtle cultural forms of differentiation not be missed by North American service providers, as they may be the nuances that allow for the development of educational strategies that will effectively reach the Latino population.

[Perhaps the most widely accepted stereotype for Latino males is that of the proverbially promiscuous "Don Juan." This eternally charming individual is known for his ability to sexually conquer and satisfy a large number of females. "Don Juan" characterizes the expectation that Latino men acquire sexual knowledge as a result of their early onset of sexual activity (Blasini-Caceres & Cook 1997).

[A second stereotype deals with the submissive, passive, and docile feminine nature of Latinas in sexuality matters. Traditional cultural expectations dictate that a woman refrain from sexual activity until marriage, thereby, limiting her ability to acquire knowledge. The submissive nature of Latinas is highly contrasted with the expectation that they be erotic, creative, and pleasing in sexuality-related matters. This dichotomy is evident in the seemingly contradicting popular advice provided to young Latinas by elder relatives that they need to be a "*señora en la casa, una dama en la mesa, y una puta en la cama*" (a lady in the house and a whore in bed).

[A third stereotype among Latino males is that they are always ready and willing to engage in sexual activity. This stereotype may lead to the conclusion that, on the whole, Latino males are more likely to force their sexual needs on unwilling partners. This stereotype does not seem to be supported in the professional literature. Finally, anecdotal and empirical evidence seem to suggest differing expectations based on acculturation levels. In fact, more-conservative norms may be found among more-educated Latinos.

[*Gender and Gender Roles*. Worth and Rodriguez (1987) reported that despite the fact some Latinos in the United States have nontraditional lifestyles, they continue to adhere to traditional gender roles. Fennelly (1992) reported on cultural double standards and suggested that, whereas males are encouraged to develop strong self-reliant identities and explore their sexuality, females are taught the value of *etiqueta*, or proper and expected forms of feminine sexual behavior. These, sometimes-conflicting cultural norms contribute to what has been called the "cult of virginity" (Garcia 1980).

[This "cult of virginity" has its roots in the Catholic Church's teachings and is seen as a sign of purity for women. The basic premise of virginity until marriage has been found to decrease a number of sexual health problems, such as unplanned pregnancies, and to decrease the number of STDs. The primary problem with this concept, at least as practiced among Latinos, is that it is not applied equally to both genders. The literature suggests that these double standards result in either females postponing sexual activities, underreporting of sexual contacts (Taggart 1992), and in some cases, denial of other sexual behaviors, such as anal sex, which are engaged in to preserve the "cult of virginity" basic premises. This, however, does not prevent sexual innuendo from taking place.

[*Coquetería* is a term used to describe a group of female behaviors aimed at reinforcing sexual attraction. Some of these behaviors include the use of sexually appealing clothing, the adoption of manners that stimulate sexual attraction, and the use of verbiage that indicate sexual interest. Latinas are not the only ones to discreetly express their sexual or personal interests. *Piropos* are statements generally expressed by men that include a sexual connotation within the context of respect and value for females. Cultural sexual standards are also denoted in language which arbitrarily classifies females as either suitable for marriage, *novias*, or those who can be pursued for sexual conquests, *amantes* (Alexander 1992; Carballo-Diéguez 1989). This dichotomy of sexual and gender roles may explain the reason sexual discussions seldom take place among spouses, since *esposas* (wives) are expected to possess little knowledge about their own sexuality, and even less about their spouse's. It has been suggested that, in some cases, the only Latinas totally in charge of their own sexuality are commercial sex workers, as they can be less constricted to express and fully explore their sexuality.

[De la Vega (1990) suggested that sexual double standards are based on the erroneous belief that males are less able than females to control themselves sexually. It is believed that women exercise greater control over their sexual impulses, while males appear to be guided by their instincts. In this context, male infidelity is more easily tolerated than

female infidelity. Research indicates that Latinos who have poor sexual communication skills engage in extramarital affairs more often than those who have fewer difficulties communicating with their sexual partners. A 1994 study found that infidelity rates were higher among those who attended church infrequently than regular church attenders (Choi, Catalnia, & Docini 1994).

[*Machismo and* Marianismo. *Machismo* has been described as a strong force in most Latino communities, which encourages males to be sexually dominant and the primary providers for their families; it stresses male physical aggression, high risk-taking, breaking rules, and casual, uninvolved sexual relations (de la Vega 1990). In contrast, *Marianismo* refers to Latino cultural expectations that include the spiritual and moral superiority of women, and encourage Latinas to be virginal, seductive, privately wise, publicly humble, fragile, and yet, provide the glue that holds the family together. It has been argued that while these standards lead to womanizing, they also foster the tenet among males that they are responsible for their family's welfare. Low education and acculturation have been found to correlate with stronger *machismo* views among Latinos in the U.S.

[*Sexual Education*. The AIDS epidemic has spearheaded an emphasis on the need to investigate sexuality education and communication patterns among Latinos in the United States. Family bonds, moral values, *machismo*, *Marianismo*, *etiqueta*, as well as profound religious beliefs, combine to prevent U.S. Latinos from openly discussing sexuality with family members. In some cases, just saying sexual words in front of family members may be difficult for some Latinos (Medina 1987). The secrecy surrounding sexuality prevents Latinos from receiving adequate, if any, information about sexuality, contraceptives, and HIV/AIDS and other STDs (Amaro 1991; Carrier & Bolton 1991; Mays & Cochran 1988). In 1992, only 67% of Latinos said they had communicated with their children about AIDS, as compared to 77% of European-Americans and 74% of African-Americans (Schoenborn, Marsh, & Hardy 1994).

[In traditional Latino families, sexuality education may come from extended family members rather than nuclear-family members. Aunts, uncles, and grandparents may assume the role of sexuality educators for younger generations. For instance, Marín, Marín, and Juárez (1990) reported that Latinos were less willing than non-Hispanics to discuss certain sexual topics (i.e., drug use and sex) with an older family member.

[In a study of first-generation immigrant adolescents employed in agriculture, Pérez and Pinzón (1997) found that Latino parents failed to adequately educate their children about sexuality-related matters. However, not all Latino parents hesitate to address sexuality-related issues with their offspring. Some researchers have found that 57 % of Latino parents do communicate with their children about sexuality. In those cases, home-based sexuality education is the primary responsibility of the mother (Biddlecom & Hardy 1991; Dawson & Hardy 1989).

[Latino heterogeneity is further supported by Durant (1990) who reported that Mexican-American females where less likely than non-Latinas to have communicated with their parents about contraception, sex, and pregnancy. Dawson (1990) found that Mexican-Americans were less likely to broach these topics with their children (50%) than were Puerto Ricans (74%) and other Latinos (64%). In those instances where parents educate their children about sexuality, the responsibility most often lies with the mother. Romo, Lefkowitz, and Sigman (2002) found that maternal messages, self-disclosure, and a nonjudgmental attitude played a key role in interactive conversations with their adolescents

[The data suggest that some Latino parents rely on the schools and, in some cases, mass media to educate their children about sexuality-related issues. In a 1994 study, Schoenborn, Marsh, and Hardy found that 46% of Latinos had received AIDS information through radio public service announcements (PSAs), compared to 36% of European-Americans and 44% of African-Americans.

[An additional 14% of Latinos said they had received information through store displays or brochures, compared to 7% of European-Americans and 12% of African-Americans. Marín, Marín, and Juárez (1990) concluded that this lack of sexual education may contribute to higher rates of childbearing among Latinos. This is among the greatest paradoxes encountered among Latinos, since research suggests that home-based sexuality education plays a key role in decreasing pregnancy rates among Latino adolescents (Brindis 1997) and increasing condom use (Moran & Corley 1991).

[*Contraception.* Throughout Latin America, the number of children in a household assists in establishing a male's role in the community. A large number of children, especially among low-income populations, are sometimes necessary for economic survival; the more hands available for work, the greater the family's income. It is, therefore, not surprising that contraceptive methods are skeptically viewed by some Latinos.

[Religion, condom use during first sexual experience (Marín, Marín, & Juárez 1990), sexual orientation (Rotheram-Borus et al. 1994), education, and income (Fennelly 1992) have been identified as being involved with attitudes and likelihood of using contraceptives among Latinos in the U.S. In a survey of urban adolescents, Sonestein, Pleck, and Ku (1989) found that Latino males have more-negative attitudes towards condom use than their non-Hispanic counterparts. In a study of 131 bisexual youths in New York City, Rotheram-Borus and colleagues (1994) found that males were more likely to use condoms with a male than with a female sexual partner.

[Contraceptive use is further compounded by the fact that contraception among Latinos is primarily the responsibility of the woman, who may not have the ability to promote safer-sex practices, including the use of barrier methods, with their sexual partners (Mikawa 1992; Norris & Ford 1992; Marín, Marín, & Juárez 1990). Latino women were less likely to use condoms if their sexual partners opposed condom use than were Latinas whose partners did not oppose them or voiced no opinion. Males' unwillingness to utilize condoms may place their partners at risk for unwanted pregnancies and sexually transmitted diseases. Other studies have found that Latino males are less likely to use condoms with their spouses, or other primary partners, than with other sexual partners (Pérez & Fennelly 1996; Sandoval et al. 1995). Jemmott, Jemmott, and Villarruel (2002) found that Latino college students were more likely to use condoms if they perceived partner and/or peer approval and perceived themselves capable of using the condoms. Similarly, condom use among Latinas has been related to their partners' willingness to use condoms and women's fears about their partners having multiple sexual partners (Flaskerud, Uman, Lara, Romero, & Taka 1996).

[The couple's acculturation and assimilation level, their adherence to Catholic Church doctrine, and their desire for large or small families also play a key role in their decision to use contraceptives (Marín, Marín, & Juárez 1990). The data indicate that more and more Latino men tend to share the decision on whether or not to use contraceptives with their sexual partners.

[*Adolescents and Sexuality.* Latino youths in the United States balance conflicting messages from two cultures regarding their sexuality (Brindis 1992). While the dominant culture appears to promote high levels of nonmarital sexual activities, Latino youths, particularly females, must also deal with the more conservative Latino cultural norms towards sexuality and the "cult of virginity."

[Studies investigating sexual behaviors among Latino adolescents have yielded mixed results. Brindis (1992) found that coital activity rates for Latino youth fall somewhere between that of African-Americans and European-Americans. In contrast to self-reports of lower sexual-activity levels among Latino youth, a national survey found no differences among the proportion of Latino and non-Latino Anglo-American young men who engaged in sexual activities before age 13 (4% and 3%, respectively) (Sonestein, Pleck, & Ku 1991). Similarly, Forrest and Sing (1990) found that among never-married females 15 to 19, 49% of Latinas reported being sexually active compared to 52% of European-Americans and 61% of African-Americans. Differences, however, have been found based on attitudes towards premarital sex (Ginson & Kempf 1990; Padilla & Baird 1991). The data suggest that among adolescents, Latino males tend to engage in sexual intercourse at an earlier age than do females (13 and 15 years of age, respectively). In cross-cultural comparisons, Latino adolescents have been found to have higher sexual risk-taking behaviors (i.e., unprotected sex) than their non-Latino counterparts (Brindis, Wolfe, McCater, Ball, et al. 1995). Brindis (1997) concluded that "acculturation is a key variable influencing adolescent attitudes, behavior, and knowledge about reproduction and contraception" (p. 8).

[Some very conservative families see teenage pregnancy, and in some cases, pregnancy before marriage, as a "failure." These views are expressed in the often-used phrase *fracazó la muchacha.* It is important to clarify that this "failure" does not represent a rejection of the newborn, but rather the woman's limitation to pursue educational goals, employment opportunities, and her possibilities for marriage. National data show that in the 1990s, the birthrate among Latina females age 15 to 19 has decreased by 12% compared to 19% for non-Hispanic whites (Moore et al. 2001).

[One of the pivotal stages in a Latino woman's life is the *quinceañera* celebration—an event that is analogous to the traditional "sweet sixteen" observed in North America. The *quinceañera* party marks a woman's transition to adulthood, including accessibility for marriage and childbearing. During this joyous time, the female is formally introduced to society and is recognized as having achieved full womanhood.

[Educational level and formal instruction play a role in parental willingness to discuss and educate their adolescent offspring about sexuality. Those with more education have been found to be more willing to educate their children about sexuality-related issues.

[*Adults and Sexuality.* There is a dearth of data related to the frequency and sexual preferences, masturbatory frequency and techniques, use of pornography, and sexual dysfunctions among Latinos in the United States. Latino males are more likely than non-Hispanic whites and African-Americans to indicate a greater level of physical satisfaction with their partner during the last 12 months in primary relationships (51%, 47%, and 43%, respectively). Conversely, Latinas are less likely (39%) than non-Hispanic whites

(40%) and African-Americans (44%) to report the same level of satisfaction with their sexual partners (Laumann et al. 1994). Not surprisingly, 96% of Latino men reported always or usually having an orgasm with their partners during the year preceding the *National Health and Social Life Survey* (*NHSLS*), compared to 68% of Latinas.

[Sexual discussions among Latino men tend to occur within same-gender groups while they are under the influence of alcohol, with sex-industry workers, and in the context of jokes (Carrier & Magaña 1991; de la Vega 1990; Hu & Keller 1989). In a national survey of sexual behaviors, Billy, Tanfer, Grady, and Klepinger (1992) found that Latino men reported a median of 6.1 sexual partners over a lifetime as compared to 8.0 for African-Americans and 6.4 for non-Latino white males. The same study found that Latinos were more likely than non-Latinos to report four or more sexual partners in the last 18 months. In a survey of over 1,500 Latinos, Marín, Gomez, and Hearst (1993) found that 60% of single Latino males reported multiple sexual partners in the previous 12 months.

[Although dialogs about sexual issues are often avoided, Latinos have other more socially acceptable forms to express their sensuality and sexual desire. Some of these mediums include music, dance, art, and poetry. Research indicates that Latino males learn about their sexuality through practical experience rather than through sexual education. Anecdotes suggest that it is not uncommon for young Latinos to lose their virginity through an experience with a sex-industry worker, usually encouraged by older relatives, in what could be termed a "sexual rite of passage."

[Data from the *NHSLS* show that Latino males are more likely to engage in masturbation at least once a week than females (24.4% and 4.7%, respectively). The disparity in rates may indicate that Latinas are less likely to acknowledge engaging in this non-acceptable social behavior as perceived by the traditional Latino culture.

[Data from the *NHSLS* show that Latinos, including women, are less likely than non-Hispanic whites, and more likely than African-Americans to report engaging in fellatio and cunnilingus. Latino males are more likely than females to report that they have performed oral sex (70.7% and 59.7%, respectively). Similarly, Latino males are also more likely than Latinas to report receiving oral sex (72.3% and 63.7%, respectively). Table 5 shows common sexual dysfunction problems by ethnic group in the United States.

[*Pregnancy.* Researchers have identified acculturation level, parental communication, low education, language, and country of origin as a determinant for pregnancy among Latino women (Durant 1990). Given the cultural significance of motherhood, it is not surprising that in the United States, Latinas experience more per-capita births than their non-Latina counterparts. In 1990, the average number of children per Latino family was 3.76 compared to 3.43 for African-Americans and 3.11 for European-Americans (USDC 1991).

Data from the 2000 census show that Latinas had an average of 2.5 births compared to 1.8 for non-Hispanic whites and Asian Pacific Islander women (USBC 2001). Brindis (1997) has suggested that the higher number of children among Latinas may be a residual effect of an intrinsic belief that developed among immigrants based on economic needs and high mortality rates in their countries of origin.

[Garcia (1980) suggested that motherhood serves to secure an identity for the Latino woman. In a 1991 survey, Segura found that the meaning of motherhood among Latinas differed, depending on their country of birth. In his study, Segura surveyed Mexican-born women and American-born Chicanas; the findings indicate that while Mexican-born women viewed motherhood as all-encompassing, Chicanas gave greater meaning to childrearing. Among Latinas, Puerto Rican females have the highest rate of pregnancies. Among Mexican women, those born in Mexico experience more pregnancies than those born in the U.S. (Aneshensel, Becerra, Fiedler, & Schuler 1990). Darabi and Ortiz (1987) concluded that "one plausible explanation of these findings could be that Mexican-origin women marry at very early ages" (p. 27). Further differences were reported by Fennelly (1992), who found birthrates among Latino adolescent females ranging from a high of 21% among Mexican-Americans to a low of 6% among Cuban mothers. Fennelly-Darabi and Ortiz (1987) reported that Latino women were more likely than non-Latino women to have a second birth shortly after the first, and were less likely to have positive attitudes towards abortions.

[Despite higher birthrates than other ethnic groups, lower socioeconomic backgrounds, and fewer prenatal visits to physicians, Latinas as a group have fewer low-birthweight babies. This finding has confused experts who would expect the opposite to be true based on socioeconomic factors. Several explanations have been offered, such as better nutrition in the form of complete proteins, less use of alcohol and other psychoactive drugs during pregnancy, and increased family support during the months preceding childbirth. Other researchers have attempted to link higher birthweights with religiosity and spirituality of Latinas in the United States (Magaña & Clark 1995).

[Latinas in the U.S. have also been found to have among the lowest abortion rates. In a study by Kaplan, Stewart, and Crane (2001), only 7.5% of the Latinas aged 14 to 24 had ever had an induced abortion.

[*Marriage.* Marriage is highly valued among Latino groups; however, in some cases, no difference is made between legal unions and long-term cohabitation. Fennelly-Darabi, Kandiah, and Ortiz (1989) reported that it is not possible to determine the number of couples in informal unions. In a later study, Landale and Fennelly (1992) reported that while the number of nonmarital unions has decreased on the island of Puerto Rico, they have greatly increased among Puerto Ricans living on the U.S. mainland.

## Table 5

### Sexual Dysfunctions by Ethnicity

| | Whites | | African-Americans | | Latinos | | Asians | |
|---|---|---|---|---|---|---|---|---|
| | Males | Females | Males | Females | Males | Females | Males | Females |
| Lack interest in sex | 14 | 29 | 19 | 44 | 13 | 30 | 24 | 42 |
| Unable to achieve orgasm | 7 | 24 | 9 | 32 | 9 | 22 | 19 | 34 |
| Sex not pleasurable | 7 | 21 | 16 | 32 | 8 | 20 | 9 | 23 |
| Erection problems | 10 | N/A | 13 | N/A | 5 | N/A | 12 | N/A |
| Lubrication problems | N/A | 22 | N/A | 15 | N/A | 12 | N/A | 17 |

*Source*: Laumann, Paik, and Rosen 1999

[According to the Census Bureau, in 1990 in the U.S., Latino marriage rates (62.3%) were almost the same as non-Latino whites (64%) and were higher than that of African-Americans (46.3%). By 1999, Census data showed a 68% marriage rate among Latinos, compared to 82% for non-Hispanic whites (USCB 1999).

[On the other hand, data of the National Council of la Raza indicate that "The number of Hispanic single parents has increased at a faster rate than Black or White female-headed families" (1993, 12). According to Brison and Casper (1998), 42% of Latino children are born to a single parent, compared to 58% of African-American children and 25% of non-Hispanic white children. Data from the 1999 *Current Population Survey* showed that Latino families were more likely than non-Latino whites to be headed by a female head of household without a spouse. Puerto Ricans were found in that study to be more likely to have a female head of household (see Table 6). According to the U.S. Census Bureau, in 1991, 60% of Latino families with a female head of household with children under 18 lived under the poverty line (USBC 1993).

[Fennelly, Kandiah, and Ortiz (1989, 96) argued that "A woman's marital status at the time she bears a child is important because of the implications for her later fertility, and for her own and her children's economic and social status." The social and legal implications of out-of-wedlock births have then been used to explain the reasons why there are more premarital pregnancies than premarital births in the Latino culture. It has been a time-honored tradition among some Latinos to marry while the woman is pregnant, in order to provide a stable and legal union for the newborn.

[*Rape.* According to the U.S. Department of Justice, Bureau of Justice Statistics (2002), 750,000 Hispanic persons age 12 or older were victims of rape, sexual assault, aggravated assault, and simple assault during 2001. That figure represents an increase from 2000, when about 690,470 Hispanics were victims of rapes, sexual assaults, robberies, and aggravated and simple assaults. While federal statistics show low levels of sexual assault among Latinas, some researchers (Sorenson & Siegel 1992) have speculated that these low incidence rates are primarily because of underreporting by Latinas.

[Research findings seem to suggest that acculturation and gender, not culture, are key determinants of attitudes towards forcible sexual activities. In a study of attitudes towards date rape among college students, Fischer (1987) found that Latino students held more-traditional gender roles and had a more-positive attitude towards forcible intercourse under certain circumstances. These included spending a lot of money on the woman, the length of time they had dated, the female "leading" the man on, and the female's previous sexual history. Acculturation and gender were also found to play a role in the views of college students towards forcible sexual encounters. According to Fischer (1987),

"Bicultural and bilingual Hispanic women are less rejecting of forcible rape than assimilated Hispanic and majority women are, while Hispanic males, regardless of degree of acculturation, are less rejecting of forcible date rape than are majority males" (p. 99).

[Lefley and colleagues (1993) reported that Latinos not only had different definitions of sexual coercion, but also were more likely to blame the victim than were their Anglo-American counterparts. A review of the literature did not support the notion of espousal rape. Males under the influence of alcohol may force their spouses to engage in sexual activities. Forcible sexual intercourse may not be perceived as a violation of a female's body if it happens within the context of marriage. As a result, espousal-rape reports among Latinos in the U.S. are more likely to occur among the acculturated, assimilated second generation, and those with higher educational levels.

[*Same-Gender Sexual Activities.* In a study of African-American, Latino, Asian/Eurasian, and Caucasian gay adolescent males, Newman and Muzzonigro (1993) found that traditional families were less accepting of homosexuality than low-traditional families. Bonilla and Porter (1990) found that Latinos did not differ significantly from their African-American and white counterparts on attitudes toward homosexuality; however, they were less tolerant in their perceptions of civil liberties. This lack of acceptance may force males to hide their sexual orientation or to pursue heterosexual lifestyles (i.e., marriage) while secretly engaging in same-gender sexual activities.

[Family acceptance is only part of the equation explaining Latino views toward same-gender sexual activities. Same-gender sex has different meanings and connotations for Latinos than for the non-Latino population in the United States. As a general rule, same-gender relationships are heavily stigmatized among Latinos, even among highly acculturated groups (Fischer 1987). Homosexuality is not a topic easily discussed among males (Pérez & Fennelly 1996).

[Magaña and Carrier (1991) suggested that it is not totally uncommon for Latino males to turn to "effeminate" males to satisfy their sexual needs under certain conditions. They identified lack of a female sexual partner and/or lack the economic resources to visit a sex worker as an acceptable reason for male-male sexual activities. Same-gender sexual behaviors are also more likely to appear while under the influence of alcohol. Same-gender sexual activity perceptions are also affected by Latino cultural norms. Latinos do not necessarily classify the penile inserter during male-male anal sex as homosexual (Amaro 1991; Carrier 1976). As a result, Latino males engaging in same-gender sexual activities may not perceive themselves, or be perceived as, "homosexual" or "bisexual," as long as they play the appropriate dominant sexual role—a role which tends to mirror that of the male in a heterosexual couple (CDC 1993). Carrier (1976) reported that unlike their American "gay" counterparts, Mexican males engaging in same-gender sex prefer anal intercourse over fellatio or other forms of sexual gratification. Also, in contrast to their Anglo-American counterparts, Latino males are more likely to assume only the passive or receptive role during same-gender encounters. Ross, Paulsen, and Stalstrom (1988) concluded that it is not the sexual act itself, but rather the cross-gender behavior which gets labeled and heavily stigmatized among Latinos.

[The lack of identification with the homosexual community may explain the inability of Latino men who engage in sex with other men to identify or respond to educational programs targeting homosexuals. But, most importantly, it

#### Table 6

#### Family Households by Hispanic Origin

| | Married Couple | Male Householder —no spouse present | Female Householder —no spouse present |
|---|---|---|---|
| Mexican | 70% | 9% | 21% |
| Puerto Rican | 57 | 6 | 37 |
| Cuban | 79 | 4 | 17 |
| Central & South American | 67 | 10 | 24 |

*Source*: USCB 1999

emphasizes the need for researchers to concentrate more on behaviors than labels when studying sexual interactions (Alcalay et al. 1990; Carrier & Magaña 1991). The labeling-versus-behavior distinction is important in light of the fact that 45% of AIDS cases among Latinos are the result of same-gender sex, and that an additional 7% of AIDS cases are related to same-gender sex with intravenous drug users (CDC 1994). (For additional discussion of HIV/AIDS and Latinos, see section 10B, Sexually Transmitted Diseases and HIV/AIDS, below.)

[Acculturation plays a major role in Latino participation in same-gender sexual activity. According to Greene (1994), same-gender male sexual activity may be prompted by the "Cult of Virginity," since a Latino male may not be able to find a female sexual partner.

[In the Latino culture, female-female sexual activity is even more stigmatized than male-to-male sexual activity. This rejection can be explained by what Trujillo (1991) labeled a threat to the traditional male dominance. The lack of acceptance may also be explained by the fact that female-to-female sexual contact dispels the myth of Latinas being submissive and not well versed in sexuality-related matters.

[*Bisexuality.* De la Vega (1990) discussed three bisexual patterns among Latino men in the United States. The first type he labeled the closeted, self-identified, homosexual Latino. He described this type as a male with homosexual tendencies, but who lives a heterosexual lifestyle. The second type discussed by de la Vega, is the closeted, latent-homosexual Latino; this type is characterized by a male who describes himself as a heterosexual, but who engages in same-gender sex while under the influence of mind-altering substances, primarily alcohol. Finally, de la Vega described the "super-macho" heterosexual Latino. This man allows himself to have sexual contacts with other males, since he considers them to be "pseudo-females." This last type of male will not admit, even to himself, that he may express homosexual tendencies.

[*Summary.* Latinos in the United States represent a wide range of educational attainment, socioeconomic levels, and skin color. Sexual practices and knowledge among this population have been found to be heavily influenced by strict cultural norms largely shaped by the Catholic Church. However, the data suggest that Latino sexual norms and behaviors are as varied as the heterogeneous groups they represent. Further research is needed to properly investigate sexual attitudes and behaviors among the individual groups. (*End of update by M. A. Pérez and H. L. Pinzón-Pérez*]

## [American Indian (Native American) Sexuality

WALTER L. WILLIAMS
[*Update 2003*: While the aboriginal cultures of North America were extremely diverse, many Native American religions place a high value on the freedom of each person to follow the dictates of his or her own individual spirit guardian. This focus on individual freedom is exemplified by their accepting attitude toward people's sexual drives. They value sex as a gift from the spirit world, to be freely enjoyed from youth to old age. With this positive view of sex, erotic behaviors are not viewed as "sinful," but rather as expressions of each individual's spirit. With the exception of rape, which is condemned as a violation of a non-consenting person's right to their own sexual inclinations, sex is seen as something to be celebrated rather than denied.

[With this view, among traditionalist Native Americans, sexual exploration is seen as normal for people from early childhood, and traditionalist adults are more likely to view children's erotic expression with amusement rather than alarm. Children are given great freedom, and their wishes are respected by adults. If a child freely agrees to engage in sex play with another child or with an adult, there is no concept that they are "below the age of consent."

[When a child reaches puberty, a ceremony is common to mark the transition from childhood to adulthood. After puberty, a person is considered an adult and can marry and have children if they choose. While personal attractions and intimate relations are common between spouses, the most important role of marriage in Native American traditional cultures is as an economic arrangement.

[Marriage provides the complementary contributions of both husbands and wives. In aboriginal times, the role of the husband was twofold: He was expected to bring in meat through hunting and also to serve as a warrior to protect the community from outside attack. The wife, likewise, had two major roles: to bring in plant foods (either by gathering wild plants or cultivating domestic plants in farming communities), and to produce children. In hunting-gathering bands and tribes, producing children was an integral part of economic survival. As the parents became elders, they depended upon children to take care of them in their old age. Females' unique ability to give birth and to nurse the young with their breast milk was valued equally to men's warrior roles.

[In fact, the danger of a woman dying during childbirth was as great as the danger faced by warriors at war. Women were honored for subjecting themselves to the danger of childbirth, just as men were honored for subjecting themselves to the danger of warfare. Both warriors and mothers were given social status, as they sacrificed themselves for the good of the band or the tribe. A woman's status was based upon her position as a mother rather than her position as a wife. In matrilineal tribes, even unmarried women who became mothers had high status, and she could live with her female and male relatives in a woman-centered kinship system.

[Marriage, however, was institutionalized primarily for the economic contributions that these close intimate bonds produced. People survived not as husband-wife pairs, but as members of a larger extended-family kinship grouping. Bringing an unrelated person into the household as a new spouse added another person to the economic unit of the extended family. The new spouse's family was considered as in-laws, who might become an additional resource during times of scarcity. Thus, the function of a large extended kinship system was to provide a wide network of persons to whom one could turn during times of need.

[Husbands and wives had sexual intercourse to produce children, but sex was not considered to be limited to its reproductive role. While Christian ideologues have asserted that "the only purpose of sex is reproduction," Native American views do not limit sex to this function. Sex is most importantly seen as a reflection of two people's close intimate bonding and love for each other.

[Another purpose of sex is to cement close intimate relationships between friends. Friendship is considered to be extremely important in Native communities, much more so than in Western culture. Friendships exist between husbands and wives, of course, but close intimate bonds between same-sex friends are also equally valued. Since close relationships between two male "blood brothers" or two close female friends are encouraged by society, these friendships might provide the cover for a sexual relationship. Sex might or might not be involved, but sexual involvement is a reflection of the friendship. Ironically, because friends can freely show emotion to each other, there is little social recognition of private sexual behavior between friends. Their sexual activities are considered to be a private matter between friends.

[The dual system of marriage (promoting close relationships between different genders) and friendship (promoting close same-gender relationships) functioned in aboriginal times to keep band and tribal societies unified. Because sex was an integral part of human relationships, it was viewed positively as an important social force that tied individuals together in wide webs of interpersonal relations. For aboriginal Native American cultures, then, the role of sex in promoting close interpersonal ties was just as important as its reproductive function.

[Among Indian people, homosexual relationships have often existed within the context of close friendships, both between two men and between two women. But in indigenous times, marriage was another matter. Marriage was an economic union of a masculine hunter and a feminine plant provider. This division of labor by gender was not absolute, since food preparation, domestic work, childcare duties, and craftwork varied by culture and even by individual preference. Such activities were often shared by both spouses. Nevertheless, a major purpose of marriage was to provide both meat and plant foods for the survival of the extended family and the rearing of the next generation.

[With marriage partners complementing each other's economic roles, it is not surprising that marriage between two masculine men, or two feminine women, was traditionally frowned upon. A marriage between two hunters or two plant providers would not make sense in terms of economic survival. People needed both meat and plants to survive. Nevertheless, rather than prohibit same-sex marriages altogether, many indigenous Native American cultures recognized homosexual marriages when one partner took on an alternative gender role. Thus, an androgynous or feminine male was expected to marry a masculine man, while a masculine female most likely took a woman as a wife. It was expected that a feminine male would prefer to do women's work, while a masculine female was often noted as a hunter.

[With this cross-labor expectation for transgendered individuals, the mixed-gender nature of marriage could be preserved, while still allowing those persons with same-sex inclinations to fulfill their erotic desires.

[In many aboriginal tribes, the feminine male or masculine female had a special honored role. Because they were seen as uniting the spirit of a man and the spirit of a woman, some indigenous languages referred to these transgendered persons as "two-spirit people." Early French explorers called them "berdache," adapting a Persian word *bardaj*, meaning a close intimate friend of the same sex with whom one had a homosexual relationship. These androgynous roles were seen by native societies as being different and distinct from the regular roles of men and women. Some anthropologists suggest that this pattern is "gender-mixing," while others call it a transgender or alternative gender role. The important point is that Native values allowed for more than two gender options.

[In the concepts of spirituality in many Native shamanistic religions, the person who was different from the average person was thought to have been created that way by the spirits. Two-spirit persons were respected because their "spirit" (i.e., what Westerners refer to as a person's basic character) was more important than their biological sex in determining their social identity. In fact, two-spirit persons were considered to be "exceptional" rather than "abnormal."

[Early European explorers often reported their amazement that many North American Indian tribes respected two-spirit persons as spiritually gifted. Since women had high status in most aboriginal cultures, and the spirit of women was as highly regarded as the spirit of men, a person who combined the spirits of both was seen as having an extraordinary spirituality. Such sacred people were often honored with special ceremonial roles in religious ceremonies, and they were often known as healers and shamans. They had the advantage of seeing things from both the masculine and the feminine perspectives, and so were respected as seers and prophets. Two-spirit people were known as creative persons who worked hard to help their extended family and their community. They often served as healers, artists, performers, and teachers of the young.

[Having such high social and religious status, the sexual behaviors of two-spirit people were also considered sacred. They usually engaged in sex with a person of the same sex, but this was not seen as a homosexual relationship. Instead, it was conceived as a "heterogender" relationship. The distinct gender role of the two-spirit person, reflecting their transgendered spirit, was more important than the physical sex of their body. Thus, the masculine husband of a male two-spirit, or the feminine wife of a female two-spirit, were not considered homosexual. Because the spouse conformed to the standard gender role for their sex, they were considered as a man or a woman, nothing more and nothing less. The fact that their spouse was of the same biological sex was not the defining factor. Therefore, indigenous Native American cultures did not define people by dividing them into two sexual orientations, "heterosexual" or "homosexual." People were defined primarily by their gender role, as reflected in their labor preferences, dress, and personality.

[The fluidity of gender roles and the ease of ending a marriage meant that a person could be married to a two-spirit person of the same sex, but could later marry heterosexually with no change in identity or social status. Or, in the case of Plains tribes where plural wives were common, a masculine man might have a male two-spirit wife in addition to his female wives.

[Native Americans were not the only world cultures to give high veneration to the sacredness of transgendered persons and same-sex marriages. Similar traditions of alternative gender roles that were associated with same-sex erotic behaviors were known in ancient cultures of Asia, Oceania, Africa, and the Middle East. Especially, similar religious traditions exist among the native peoples of Siberia. Since the ancestors of Native Americans migrated from Siberia over 20,000 years ago, this evidence suggests that two-spirit traditions are quite ancient.

[Just as in the case with Native Americans, the expansionist imperialism of homophobic European cultures after 1492 marked the beginning of a new era of attack on transgenderism and same-sex love. The early Spanish conquistadors and Catholic priests killed and tortured two-spirit persons, whom they labeled "sodomites." By the early 20th century, both United States government officials and Christian missionaries were forcing two-spirit people to change their dress and behavior to conform to standard gender roles, and refused to recognize their same-sex marriages.

[Even heterosexual marriages changed drastically among Native Americans under United States domination. The Christian conception of marriage involving only one man and one woman forced men who had plural wives to choose one woman and abandon all of their other wives. Large extended families were largely broken up in favor of nuclear marriage. Marriages that were once easily ended by either spouse were forced to continue, unless the husband and wife went through an expensive and emotionally draining legal divorce process. As a result, many unhappy spouses continued to stay married. Without the protection of her other adult relatives living in the same household, which in matrilineal societies had served to protect women from an angry husband's wrath, domestic violence increased dramatically among 20th-century Indians. Plagued by poverty, alcoholism, and powerlessness, some Native men took out their frustrations on their wives and children. Because of the pervasive influence of missionaries on Indian reservations, many Indians converted to Christianity and absorbed repressive Western attitudes toward sex.

[Despite this deterioration in family relations and traditional sexual freedom, the most astounding fact of life for contemporary American Indians is the revival of traditional Native American religions and values. With this revitalization in recent decades, a new respect for two-spirit people— and a new determination to continue Native attitudes toward sex—has reasserted itself. Native American sexuality has not succumbed to the Western onslaught, but instead has started influencing mainstream American attitudes toward a more accepting and celebratory approach to sex. As among the aboriginal Americans, modern Americans of the 21st century are beginning to see sex as a gift from the spirit world, to be appreciated and enjoyed widely. (*End of update by W. L. Williams*)]

## Feminism and Sexuality in the United States
### PATRICIA BARTHALOW KOCH

*A Brief History of the Feminist Movements.* Earlier in this section, we discussed groups that illustrate ways in which religion and race or ethnicity operate as social factors defining subcultures within the U.S.A. and influence sexuality. Gender can be regarded in a similar manner. Here, we now consider feminist perspectives as reflections of a distinct social group or subculture.

Feminism is defined and implemented in various ways by different people. In its broadest interpretation, feminism represents advocacy for women's interests; in a stricter definition, it is the "theory of the political, social, and economic equality of the sexes" (LeGates 1995, 494). Although the terms "feminism" and "feminist" are only about a hundred years old, advocates for women's interests have been active for centuries throughout the world. As Robin Morgan (1984, 5) wrote in *Sisterhood Is Global*, "An indigenous feminism has been present in every culture in the world and in every period of history since the suppression of women began." Throughout history, women have protested, individually and collectively, against a range of injustices—often as part of other social movements in which gender equality was not the focus of the activity and women were not organized to take action on behalf of their gender.

However, stress on the ideologies of liberty, equality, and emancipation of men in the 18th-century political revolutions in Britain, France, and the United States laid the groundwork for these ideologies to be championed in women's lives also. In addition, the Industrial Revolution of the 19th century provided educational and economic opportunities supportive of a feminist movement in many societies.

Actual women's movements, or organized and sustained activities for gender equality supported by a relatively large number of people over a period of years, have occurred since the mid-1800s in many countries throughout the world. The United States, as well as most European societies, experienced extensive women's movements in the closing decades of the 19th century, with another wave of feminism occurring in the 1960s.

The beginning of an organized women's movement in the United States has been traced to the Seneca Falls Convention of 1848 where a Declaration of Principles called for gender equality (Chefetz & Dworkin 1986). Issues addressed included women's legal rights to property, children,

and to their own earnings; equal educational and employment opportunities; the changing of negative feminine stereotypes; and increased opportunities for women to improve their physical fitness and health. These early feminists also addressed more-explicit sexual issues, including the abolition of the sexual double standard of expecting men to be "promiscuous" and women to be "pure"; equality between sexual partners; and the right of married women to refuse sexual activity with their husbands. Yet, although feminist ideology was well developed during these pre-Civil War years, the progressive feminist leaders had few followers. "In the 19th and early 20th centuries the United States was not ready for a mass movement which questioned the entire gender role and sex stratification systems" (Chefetz & Dworkin 1986, 112).

Only when the issues were narrowed to focus upon women's right to vote did the movement gain mass following. By 1917, about two million women were members of the National American Woman Suffrage Association, and millions more were supporters of the women's suffrage campaign (Kraditor 1965). The reasons for supporting a woman's right to vote, however, were varied. For some, it was an issue of basic human rights and gender equality. Many others, who believed in gender-role differentiation, supported suffrage on the basis that women would bring higher moral standards into governmental decisions. This more-conservative perspective dominated the movement. After achieving the right to vote in 1920 with the passage of the 19th Amendment to the U.S. Constitution, this first wave of feminism dissipated.

A second wave of feminism developed within the United States, as well as worldwide, in the 1960s. At this time, many women were finding that, while their participation in educational institutions and the labor force was increasing, their political, legal, economic, and social status was not improving. This American feminist movement came on the heels of the black civil rights movement, which had already focused attention on the immorality of discrimination and legitimized mass protest and activism as methods for achieving equality (Freeman 1995). The contemporary women's movement was organized around many interrelated issues, including: legal equality; control over one's own body, including abortion rights; elimination of discrimination based on gender, race, ethnicity, and sexual orientation; securing more political power; and the ending of institutional and social roadblocks to professional and personal achievement. By the mid-1970s, this issue became a mass movement, with over half of American women supporting many of its principles and demands (Chefetz & Dworkin 1986).

The second women's movement had two origins, from two different strata of society, with different styles, values, and forms of organization (Freeman 1995). Although the members of both branches were predominantly white, middle-class, and college-educated, there was a generation gap between them. The younger branch was comprised of a vast array of local, decentralized, grassroots groups that concentrated on a small number or only one issue, rather than the entire movement. Members tended to adjure hierarchical structure and the traditional political system. Some of the activities in which they engaged included: running consciousness-raising groups; providing educational conferences and literature; establishing woman-supporting services (bookstores, health clinics, rape crisis centers, and battered-women shelters); and organizing public-awareness campaigns and marches. This branch was responsible for infusing the movement with new issues, strategies, and techniques for social change. Many of its projects became institutionalized within

American society (e.g., rape crisis centers) through government funding and entrepreneurship.

These feminists also took their particular perspectives into other arenas, including the pro-choice, environmental, and antinuclear movements. They also had an impact on academia, establishing women's centers and women's studies departments, programs, and courses on campuses throughout the country. By the early 1980s, there were over 300 women's studies programs and 30,000 courses in colleges and universities, and a national professional association, the National Women's Studies Association (Boxer 1982). Many periodicals devoted exclusively to scholarship on women or gender were begun; Searing (1987) listed 94 such journals.

The second branch of the women's movement was the older, more-traditional division that formed top-down national organizations with officers and boards of directors, and often paid staffs and memberships. Most of these organizations sought support through contributions, foundations, or government contracts to conduct research and services. Some of these feminist organizations included: the Women's Legal Defense Fund, the Center for Women's Policy Studies, the Feminist Majority Foundation, and the National Coalition Against Domestic Violence, with other previously established groups taking on a more-feminist agenda, such as the National Federation of Business and Professional Women and the American Association of University Women.

The National Organization for Women (NOW), an action organization devoted to women's rights, was the primary feminist group to develop a mass membership. NOW focused its attention at the national level to become politically powerful. One of its major campaigns was the passage of an Equal Rights Amendment (ERA) to the U.S. Constitution guaranteeing legal equality for women. The ERA was endorsed by the U.S. Congress and sent to the states for ratification in 1972. In 1978, over 100,000 people marched in Washington D.C. in support of the Equal Rights Amendment. But the ERA and feminism were to meet with strong opposition from well-organized conservative and right-wing political and religious groups that depicted feminist goals as "an attack on the family and the American way of life" (Freeman 1995, 525). Stop-ERA campaigns were adeptly organized by these politically savvy groups and, by 1982, the ERA had failed to pass within the allotted timeframe by seven votes in three states.

Yet, it cannot be said that the feminist movement failed. Many states passed equal rights amendments of their own, and many discriminatory federal, state, and local laws were changed with the Supreme Court unanimously ruling in favor of interpreting constitutional law to provide equal opportunity for women. In addition, a powerful women's health movement had been spawned, and efforts for reproductive freedom, including abortion rights, would be continued to combat anti-abortion groups throughout the 1980s and 1990s. As Freeman (1995, 528) concluded: "The real revolution of the contemporary women's movement is that the vast majority of the [United States] public no longer questions the right of any woman, married or unmarried, with or without children to work for wages to achieve her fullest potential."

Although feminists agree there are still many strides to be made in achieving the goals of legal, economic, political, and social equality for women in the United States, they are often divided over philosophy, goals, and strategies for achieving equality in these areas. Feminism is not a monolithic ideology. There is "not a single interpretation on what feminism means but a variety of feminisms representing diverse ideas and perspectives radiating out from a core set of assumptions regarding the elimination of women's secondary status in society" (Pollis 1988, 86-87).

*Feminism and Sexuality.* Sexuality has always been a critical issue to feminists, because they see the norms regarding "proper" and "normal" sexual behavior as functioning to socialize and suppress women's expression and behavior in an effort to control female fertility as socioeconomic and political assets (Tiefer 1995). "The personal is political," the feminist rallying cry, applies particularly to sexuality, which is often the most personal, hidden, suppressed, and guilt-ridden aspect of women's lives. MacKinnon (1982, 515) captures this essence well in the analogy that: "Sexuality is to feminism what work is to Marxism: that which is most one's own, yet most taken away."

Although women are now being seen as sexual beings in their own right, not simply as reproducers or sexual property, Tiefer (1995, 115) describes how women's sexual equality is still constrained by many factors, including:

> Persistent socioeconomic inequality that makes women dependent on men and therefore sexually subordinate; unequal laws such as those regarding age of sexual consent and rights in same-sex relationships; lack of secure reproductive rights; poor self-image or a narrow window of confidence because of ideals of female attractiveness; ignorance of woman-centered erotic techniques, social norms about partner choice; and traumatic scars from sexual abuse.

In general, feminists believe that both women's and men's sexuality is socially constructed and must be examined within its social context (McCormick 1994). Gender-role socialization is viewed as a very powerful process creating unequal power relationships and stereotypic expectations for appropriate sexual feelings and behaviors of women and men. Male gender-role socialization based on male political, social, and economic dominance is likely to result in male sexual control, aggression, and difficulties with intimacy. On the other hand, female gender-role socialization based on political, social, and economic oppression of women is likely to result in disinterest and dissatisfaction with sex, as well as passivity and victimization. Feminists question the assumption of a binary gender system and challenge traditional concepts of masculinity and femininity (Irvine 1990). They politicize sexuality by examining the impact that power inequalities between men and women have on sexual expression.

Although most feminists may agree upon the relevance of socialization and context in the creation of male and female sexuality, they may vehemently disagree about the nature of sexual oppression and the strategies for its elimination (McCormick 1994). This has resulted in the emergence of two major feminist camps: radical feminists and liberal feminists.

As described by McCormick (1994, 211), radical feminists have polarized male and female sexuality—often demonizing men and idealizing women in this process. They view women as victims who must be protected. They use evidence showing girls and women as the predominant victims and boys and men as the perpetrators of rape, sexual harassment, prostitution, domestic violence, and childhood sexual abuse to support their views.

Radical feminists are vehemently opposed to pornography, "likening erotic images and literature to an instruction manual by which men are taught how to bind, batter, torture, and humiliate women" (McCormick 1994, 211). They have spearheaded many efforts to censor pornographic/erotic materials, often joining with right-wing organizations in these efforts. Another goal of radical feminists is the elimination of prostitution, which they view as trafficking in women's bodies. They believe that all women in the sex trades are being victimized.

Because of these beliefs, radical feminists are criticized as treating women as children who are incapable of giving true consent to their choice of sexual activities. In response, these feminists argue that it is our sociopolitical system that treats women as second class and has robbed them of the equality needed for consensual sexual expression. Until this system is changed, true consent from women is not possible. In fact, orthodox radical feminists do not recognize the possibility of consensual heterosexuality, finding little difference between conventional heterosexual intercourse and rape, viewing both acts as representing male supremacy (McCormick 1994, 211). Radical feminists are accused of advocating "politically correct sex" by idealizing monogamous, egalitarian, lesbian sex and celibacy, and rejecting any other forms of consensual relationships or activity.

On the other hand, liberal feminists defend women's rights to sexual pleasure and autonomy. They believe that, if women are viewed only as victims, they are stripped of their adult autonomy and their potential to secure joyous and empowering sexual pleasure and relationships on their own behalf (McCormick 1994, 211). These feminists do not view all erotic material as harmful and believe in women's right to create their own erotic material. They differentiate between the depictions of forced sex in pornography and actual violence against women. Although not always pleased with all types of pornographic material, they believe in the right of free speech and choice, and acknowledge that censorship efforts could never eliminate all pornographic material anyway. In addition, who is to decide what is pornographic and what is erotic? Regarding prostitution, they view sex work as a legitimate occupational choice for some, and acknowledge the tremendous range of experience with sex work primarily based on social class.

Liberal feminism dominated the first phase of the women's movement of the 1960s. The emphasis was on women's empowerment to achieve professional and personal, including sexual, potentials. The expansion of sexual possibilities was explored, with pleasure being emphasized. The strategies of consciousness-raising, education, and female-centered care were used to help eliminate sexual shame and passivity, with women being encouraged to discover and develop new sexual realities for themselves (Tiefer 1995, 115). However, beginning in the 1970s, the pendulum began to swing away from an emphasis on the power of self-definition towards the agendas of the radical feminists who emphasized issues of sexual violence against women, including rape, incest, battery, and harassment. Thus, during this current feminist movement, much more time and emphasis has been devoted to women's sexual victimization, danger, and repression than to women's sexual equality, pleasure, and relationship enhancement.

Today, many in the general public, professionals, and even sexologists fail to distinguish between differences within feminism. They are most aware of and react primarily to the radical-feminist ideologies and strategies. Thus, feminism has become stereotyped by the extreme positions of the radicals and seems to have lost much of its overt mass support, with many trying to distance themselves from these extreme positions. For example, it is not unusual to hear someone today say, "I believe in women's rights but I'm not a feminist."

*Feminist Critiques of and Contributions to Sexology.* Feminist sexology is the scholarly study of sexuality that is of, by, and for women's interests. Employing diverse epistemolo-

gies, methods, and sources of data, feminist scholars examine women's sexual experiences and the cultural frame that constructs sexuality. They challenge the assumptions that sexuality is an eternal essence, arguing "that a kiss is not a kiss and a sigh is not a sigh and a heterosexual is not a heterosexual and an orgasm is not an orgasm in any transhistorical, transcultural way" (Tiefer 1995, 597). These theories and approaches have resulted in an enormous body of work during the last two decades reexamining theories, methods, and paradigms of gender and sexuality, and contributing to social change (Vance & Pollis 1990).

During this time, feminists and others have challenged the preeminence and validity of traditional science, particularly as it has been applied to human beings and their behaviors. They have argued that traditional science, rather than being objective and value-free, takes place in a particular cultural context (one that is often sexist and heterosexist), which thus becomes incorporated into research, education, or therapy (McCormick 1994). For example, research on unintended and adolescent pregnancy is focused almost exclusively on females, reflecting a double standard requiring women to be the sexual gatekeepers while relieving men of such responsibilities.

Another example comes from therapy. Numerous studies have determined that relationship factors, including intimacy, nongenital stimulation, affection, and communication, are better predictors of women's sexual satisfaction than frequency of intercourse or orgasm. Nevertheless, the dominant therapeutic paradigm, as enforced by the *Diagnostic and Statistical Manual of Mental Disorders*, uses physiologically based genital performance during heterosexual intercourse as the standard for determining women's sexual dysfunctions (Tiefer 1995).

Feminist scholarship uses the following principles in overcoming the deficits in understanding of women's experiences, gender and gender asymmetry, and sexuality:

1. Acknowledgment of the pervasive influence of gender in all aspects of social life, including the practice of science;
2. A multifaceted challenge to the normative canons of science, especially the tenet of objectivity, which splits subject from object, and theory from practice;
3. Advocacy of consciousness raising as a research strategy that elevates and legitimates experience as a valid way of knowing, essential to uncovering meaning structures and diversity among individuals;
4. Conceptualization of gender as a social category, constructed and maintained through the gender-attribution process, and as a social structure;
5. Emphasis on the heterogeneity of experience and the central importance of language, community, culture, and historical context in constituting the individual; and
6. Commitment to engage in research that is based on women's experience and is likely to empower them to eliminate sexism and contribute to societal change (Pollis 1986, 88).

Sexology has been criticized for being reticent to integrate feminist perspectives and scholarship into its establishment for fear of being perceived as unscientific and radical (Irvine 1990). However, in recent years, feminist perspectives have become more visible in the scholarly journals, conferences, and among the membership and leadership of professional sexological organizations. Future goals for feminist sexologists include more attention to understanding the intersections of race, class, and culture within gender, and making the results of their work more usable.

[*The Emergence of Men's Perspectives on Sexuality*

WARREN FARRELL

[*Update 2003*: In the 1950s, both sexes were defined by roles. In the early 2000s, men are still defined largely by roles; women define themselves. (The following discussion is based on the author's *The Myth of Male Power*, Farrell 1993/2001). As the women's movement has helped women develop options and no men's movement of any consequence has done the same for men, we have entered the Era of the Multi-Option Woman and the No-Option Man. Thus, in the U.S., our daughters now have the option to join the armed services, but our sons have no option but to register for the draft.

[The Era of the Multi-Option Woman and the No-Option Man extends itself to the sexual arena (see also: Bly 1990; Cassell 1993; Farrell 1999; Goldberg 1977; Gurian 1977; Halpern 1994; Jeffers 1989; Kipnis 1991; La Framboise 1996; Lyndon 1992; Lynch 1999; Philpot 1997; Simon 1995):

- Young women now have the *option* of asking a man out on a date; young men have the *expectation*.
- Young women now have the *option* of taking sexual initiatives (e.g., being the first to kiss); young men have the *expectation*.
- On a date, young women now have the *option* to pay; young men have the *expectation*.
- Parents are more likely to let their children watch a man using a gun to kill than to watch a man using his penis to have sex (see also Fekete 1994). In essence, we say sex is dirty, then we tell our sons it is their responsibility to initiate the dirt. We expect the boy to do this before he understands either sex or girls. This leaves most boys feeling morally inferior to most girls—having to compensate for their inequality by buying drinks, dinners, and diamonds.
- Girls and boys today often hang out in groups before they date. The politics of turning a group friendship into a one-on-one sexual encounter can be even more daunting than asking out a girl one barely knows. Why? It hurts more to be rejected by someone we know in front of a group than by someone we do not know.
- We have developed a birth control pill for women, but no pill for men. For more than a decade, the ability to do this technologically has been within five to seven years of achievement, but the politics have prevented it (see Farrell 2001 for sections on reproduction and abortion; see also Money 1988/1990).
- If a man and woman have sex, the woman can abort or sue for support; he has no rights to learn about the abortion and no right to avoid paying child support.
- If the result of sex is a child raised by a mother and father, she is 135 times more likely to have left the workplace to raise the child than is he, and therefore, should there be a divorce, she is able to claim that the child should be raised primarily by her to create stability. Under these circumstances, should the father wish 50% involvement after divorce, he can expect to pay more than $100,000 to fight for it—and still be unlikely to get it.
- If men were to articulate their potential rights in the areas of sex, reproduction, and parenting, they might be called Men's ABC Rights:
  - Men's A right relates to Abortion—to an equal say in whether a fetus he would be responsible to support if it became a child, should in fact become a child; or conversely, an opportunity to legally agree to support the child emotionally and financially completely by himself in exchange for the woman not aborting the child.
  - Men's B right relates to Birth Control—the right to a male birth control pill being made a national priority

so men can both relieve women of the primary responsibility for contraception, and have equal rights to the convenience of a pill.
  - Men's C right relates to Caring—men's equal right to stay at home and care for the child during marriage, and to care for it equally should there be a divorce.
- When women marry someone they meet in the workplace, it is usually a man above them at work who took the initiative—also the most frequent form of sexual harassment. When it works, it is called courtship. When it does not work, it is called harassment (see also Symons 1981). If the courtship continues, it is called a marriage, with the woman's picture in the paper; if it breaks up, it is called a lawsuit, with the man's picture in the paper. Many men, then, walk a fine line between being a candidate for husband and a candidate for harasser.
- In the workplace, if a woman caresses a man on the rear, he is likely to say, "thank you"; if a man caresses a woman on her rear, she is likely to say "sue you." Women's preference is the law; a man who exercises his preference is an outlaw.
- Several top universities, such as Berkeley, Harvard, and Swarthmore, already allow a woman who is drunk to claim the next morning that she was raped, even if she said "yes" the evening before! Many men feel a top university that does not ask women to take responsibility for the choice of getting drunk neglects to prepare women for the responsibility of leadership in business or politics. They feel it would be like a law that excused drunken driving with the rationalization that if a person had too much to drink, they are not responsible (see also Roiphe 1993).

[Many men feel the feminist movement has persuaded the public that men had the power, and that men used women to serve men's sexual needs at the expense of women's. The average heterosexual male, though, desires sex a lot more than he has it. It is in his interest to have women be more sexual, not less; to wear fewer clothes, not have faces covered by veils; to have sex without children, not have children and be deprived of sex. From his perspective, women are to sex what the OPEC nations are to oil: the more they keep it in short supply, the more power they have.

[A more accurate view than the feminist perspective of the gender politics of sex, according to many of these men—in organizations such as the National Coalition of Free Men—is best discussed in books like *The Myth of Male Power*. *The Myth of Male Power* explains how sexual harassment and date rape legislation both hold only the man responsible for the traditional male role of taking the direct sexual initiatives; neither holds the woman responsible for the traditional female role of taking indirect sexual initiatives. The following serve as some examples (see also Gelles & Straus 1988).

[*Sex in the Workplace.* For example, *Cosmopolitan*, which has been the bestselling magazine to single women during the entire women's movement—and still is—features articles instructing women how to take indirect sexual initiatives. Thus, a real article titled, "How to Catch a Man at Work," tells her (and I'm quoting *Cosmo* here), "As you pass his desk, drop a pile of papers or a purse, then stoop down to gather them up. He'll help. Lean close to him, put your hand on his shoulder to steady your balance. . . ." Or, "Immediately after you meet him, touch him in some way, even if it's to pick imaginary lint off his jacket." Or, "Brush up against him in the elevator." Or "If you have good legs, wear a very tight, short skirt and high heels. Bend over with your back to a man (to pick up something or look in a file drawer)." Of course, it's hard for a man to say, "Your honor, I initiated because she picked imaginary lint off my jacket."

[The problem with indirect initiatives is when the wrong man approaches the woman who has leaned over the file drawer in her tight, short skirt; suddenly, an environment she's helped to create feels hostile. But only he becomes vulnerable to a lawsuit.

[Is it possible there is something deeper—maybe unconscious—going on here? First, sexual harassment lawsuits can sometimes be the latest way of making men have to overcome barriers to be sexual with women in an era when the birth control pill had reduced those barriers (see also Symons 1981). Second, prior to divorces becoming popular, women had their source of income guaranteed for a lifetime. Once divorces became acceptable, though, feminists began to demand that the government become a substitute husband (Gilder 1987)—thus, the EEOC's decision number 84-1 allows complaining to a girlfriend at work to be "sufficient to support a finding of harassment" (Pollak 1991). That used to be called gossip. Now it's called evidence.

[In one decade, then, women had gotten more protection against offensive jokes in the workplace than men had gotten in centuries against being killed in the workplace. For example, one construction worker dies every workday hour—yet in the U.S., we have six fish-and-game inspectors for each workplace inspector (see also Kimbrell 1995). The plea for female protection is ironic, since feminists were the first group to decry how protective legislation discriminated against women by not allowing women to be hired in certain positions. The protection desired is from men's methods of sexualizing the work environment, not women's. For example:

[*Miniskirts-Without-Repercussions.* The miniskirt, long nails, nail polish, and indirect initiatives were historically designed to catch a man, lead to marriage, and therefore, in the past, to the end of a woman's involvement in the workplace. These indirect initiatives, therefore, unconsciously signal to a man that this woman wants an end to her involvement in the workplace (see also Cassell 1993). Feminists, though, have not asked the government to make laws against this form of sexualizing the workplace.

[*"Dirty" Jokes*: Feminists often claim that dirty jokes are the male method of intimidating women. In fact, men tell dirty jokes to peers in order to bond, not intimidate. When a male boss tells a dirty joke, it's often his unconscious way of getting his staff to not take him so seriously and, therefore, not be intimidated (see also Fekete 1994; Roiphe 1993).

[*Hazing Versus Harassment.* Historically, men knew that if a man was preoccupied with his vulnerability, he couldn't protect. So a short guy will be hazed with jokes like, "Which is higher, your IQ or your size?" All novices were hazed before they could be accepted as part of the team. Men test men before men trust men. From a man's unconscious perspective, *if a woman isn't being hazed, she's not being tested and therefore, she's not being trusted.*

[*Better Solutions Than Current Workplace Sex Regulations.* How would many men want to deal with sexual contact in the workplace?

[Step one: Resocializing women to share responsibility for taking sexual initiatives, rather than just blaming men when they do it wrong. Men will be our sexual harassers as long as men are our initiators.

[Step two: Changing "sexual harassment" seminars to "sexual contact in the workplace" seminars in which men can also discuss the effect of the *Cosmo*-type indirect initiatives.

[Step three: If a woman feels sexually harassed, encourage her to tell the man directly. Most men want to please women, not anger women.

[*The Politics of Date Rape.* A date obviously does not imply permission to be sexual, which, therefore, allows the possibility of date rape. From both sexes' perspective, date rape is not only a legitimate issue, but a serious one, because when a woman is raped by a man she is dating, her ability to trust is raped even more than when she's raped by a stranger (whom she had no expectation of trusting). Every time a woman experiences a date rape, every man is also hurt—because every man in that woman's life will be less trusted and have more to prove than he otherwise would (see also Roiphe 1993).

[The problem is the politics of date rape. The word "rape" has become to sexual politics since the 1980s what the word "communism" became to American politics in the 1940s and 1950s: When the mere accusation can result in the assumption of guilt, it is a setup for false accusations to be levied at any enemy. When this exists in an atmosphere in which famous people like Marilyn French (author of *The Women's Room*) can say, "All men are rapists and that's all they are" (Jennes 1983), without protest, and a Vassar College Assistant Dean of Students can be quoted in *Time* magazine saying, "Men who are unjustly accused of rape can sometimes gain from the experience" (attributed to Vassar College Assistant Dean of Student Life, Catherine Comins, in Gibbs 1991),[1] without protest, then men have become the new communists.

[The flaw is that none of this holds women responsible for their part in the male-female dance. Yet, 25 million women in the U.S. read an average of 20 romance novels per month, often featuring the formula of a working woman who is approached by a successful man, the woman resisting, the man overcoming her resistance, and the woman getting "swept away" (see also Cassell 1993). The book titles that sell best to women are titles like Danielle Steele's *Sweet Savage Love*, in which the heroine marries her rapist and rejects the man who saves her; they do not include titles like *He Stopped When I Said No.*

[Twenty-five million women is five times the number of readers of *Playboy* and *Penthouse* combined. The solution to the politics of date rape must include recognizing that his overcoming her resistance may be her fantasy at least as much as his. It also includes thinking of men not as the political enemy, but as our sons. For example, imagine your son dating a woman from Vassar who feels that a man could gain from being falsely accused of rape. When your son comes home for the holidays and tells you he might be spending next semester in prison—where he will be considered "fresh meat" by the prisoners—do you tell him, "Don't worry, boys who are unjustly accused of rape can sometimes gain from the experience"? Do you feel good about paying taxpayer dollars to support colleges that subject your son to random acts of imprisonment because he wasn't born as your daughter? Now suppose your son entered the armed services rather than college, how would you feel about the U.S. Air Force study that was kept quiet because it discovered that 60% of the rape accusations turned out to be false—not unfounded, but false?[2] (see also Lynch 1997).

---

[1] I called Catherine Comins and then faxed a letter to her at Vassar to be certain she was not misquoted. She did not respond.

[2] Written correspondence to me from Charles P. McDowell, Ph.D., M.P.A., M.L.S., Supervisory Special Agent of the U.S. Air Force Office of Special Investigations, March 20, 1992. This is based on an Air Force study of 556 rape allegations.

[So the big question is: How do we make dating the most positive experience possible for both our daughters and our sons? Do we do that by criminalization, or by resocialization? Thus far, we've focused on criminalization—and the criminalization has been focused on criminalizing only the male role.

[One reason we have focused on criminalization is our acceptance of the belief that rape is a manifestation of male political and economic power. In fact, any given black man is three times as likely as a white man to be reported as a rapist. Do blacks suddenly have more political and economic power? Maybe rape does not derive from power, but rather from powerlessness.

[To check this out, we must challenge the current belief that rape has nothing to do with sexual attraction—it is just an act of violence, and that this is "proven" by the fact that women of every age are raped. In fact, being at the age of greatest sexual attraction makes the chances of being raped at least 8,400% greater than being raped at an age over 50 years old. That is, when a woman is between ages 16 and 19, her chances of being raped are 84 in 20,000; when she is between 50 and 64, her chances are less than one in 20,000 (USBJS 1987). Sexual attraction, then, does have something to do with who is raped.

[If rape were just an act of violence, then it should not be distinguished from any other violent crime. Other violent crimes are not distinguished by the body parts involved. If they were, "assault to the head" is a crime deserving greater punishment than rape, unless feminists are saying that a woman's vagina is more important than a woman's head.

[We hear that date rape is always a crime, never a misunderstanding. Yet, anyone who works with both sexes knows it is possible for a woman to go back to a man's room, tell him she doesn't want to have intercourse, mean it, start kissing, willingly have intercourse, and then wish she had not in the morning. How? Kissing is like eating potato chips. Before we know it, we've gone farther than we said we would, and in the morning we regret it. But that doesn't mean Lay's raped us. Date rape can be a crime, a misunderstanding, or buyer's remorse (see also Farrell 1986).

[*Solutions to Date Rape and Stranger Rape.* Since men rape, is it not really the man's role that needs changing?

[The problem is both sexes' roles: It is both sexes' roles together which create the following four factors that make rape a predictable possible outgrowth of male-female relationships in most cultures (see also Kammer 1994; Levin 1988).

1. Boys' "addiction" to sex with girls being reinforced, even as girls' sexual caution is reinforced (through pregnancy, herpes, and AIDS, for example). The consequence? An increase in the gap between male demand and female supply.
2. Saying "sex is dirty" and "boys, initiate the dirt." The consequence? Boys being the mistrusted sex.
3. Because boys are mistrusted more, they're rejected more; and because they want more sex than the girls do, they're rejected still more. The consequence? Rather than take rejections personally, a boy learns to turn a woman into a sex object—it hurts him less to be rejected by an object.
4. Being objectified makes her feel alienated and being rejected makes him feel hurt, angry, and powerless. When rejection and sexual identity go hand in hand, we sow the seeds of violence—especially among boys who have no source of power. His violence and objectifying reinforce the starting assumptions: Sex is dirty and dangerous, and men can't be trusted. This power-

lessness is reinforced by "The Male Date Rape Catch-22:" society telling men to be the salespersons of sex, then putting only men in jail if they sell well.

[Some feminists are now expanding the definitions of rape to "unwanted sexual activity." Yet, the *Journal of Sex Research* reported the findings that 63% of the men and 46% of the women said they had experienced unwanted intercourse (Muehlenhard & Cook 1988). (For example, a man sometimes fears intercourse when he feels a woman will read into it more of a commitment than he wants.) By feminist definitions of rape as unwanted sex or unwanted intercourse, most men have been raped—and that's how rape begins to look like an epidemic. It is also how rape gets trivialized.

[*In Conclusion.* To go from the old "male pursue/female resist" to the feminist "male pursue/female sue" is not progress, but just the latest method of getting men to jump through brand-new hoops for the same old sex.

[Men will be our rapists as long as men are our initiators. Men will rape as long as the four factors leading to rape are part of our two-sex socialization. The solution lies in updating the dance—in women and men sharing responsibilities for the direct initiative-taking and paying for dates—in communication, not litigation or criminalization.

[Sexual harassment and date rape are perfect metaphors for some of the most important challenges of the 21st century: the challenge to the stereotype of "innocent woman/guilty man"; the challenge to keep male-female sexual contact flexible and fluid rather than petrified and paralyzed; the challenge to respond to sexual nuance more with communication and less with legislation—understanding that communication at least responds to nuance with nuance, while legislation responds to nuance with rigidity; and the challenge to our genetic heritage of protecting women—and therefore infantilizing women.

[If we really want to protect people from being hurt, we would have to make laws against love, and against marriage, automobiles, and gossip. The only way we can prevent people from being hurt is to prevent them from living. If we desire to protect men from hurt, we would have to outlaw women's sexual rejection of men.

[The answers we develop cannot emerge from feminism-in-isolation, but from both sexes helping each other reweave the tapestry that has been passed from one generation to the next over the centuries for purposes that were functional then, but dysfunctional now (see also Sommers 1994; Steele 1990). Only then will we make a transition from a woman's movement *versus* a men's movement to a gender transition movement—from gender war to gender love.

[Additional resources on the Web are available at: American Coalition for Fathers and Children: www.acfc.org; Children's Rights Council: www.vix.com.crc; Everyman: www.everyman.org; Independent Women's Forum: www.iwf.org; National Coalition of Free Men: www.ncfm.org; National Congress for Fathers & Children: www.ncfc.org; and Dr. Warren Farrell: www.warrenfarrell.com. (*End of update by W. Farrell*)]

[*Heterophobia: The Evolution of an Idea*

RAYMOND J. NOONAN

[*Update 2003*: The term *heterophobia* is, perhaps, only about two decades old—a much shorter period than its more familiar sibling, *homophobia*, which *Webster's Ninth New Collegiate Dictionary* dates to 1958. Still, the value of heterophobia as a concept appears to be largely unrecognized among many, if not most, American sexologists today as sexual science and philosophy advances into the new millennium. Is heterophobia just another example of the me-too victimology that continues to grow and flourish in contemporary America? Or is there more to it from which students of sexology and the general public can learn?

[*Webster's* defines *homophobia* simply as the "irrational fear of homosexuality or homosexuals" (p. 578); the term *heterophobia*, however, does not appear at all. It does appear in Francoeur, Perper, & Cornog's 1995 *Complete Dictionary of Sexology*, where they define it similarly as a fear of heterosexuals, although they do not use the "irrational" component. *Heterophobia* also appears among the myriad other terms for various phobias in some of the comprehensive lists of phobias published on the World Wide Web. In a non-sex-related context, it has also been defined as a fear of things different (such as other cultures).

[*Heterophobia* appeared for the first time in the 1982 book, *The Anatomy of Freedom*, by the well-known feminist, Robin Morgan. In the sexological literature, *heterophobia* first seems to have appeared in print in a 1990 chapter by Edward W. Eichel in the controversial book *Kinsey, Sex and Fraud*, in which he devoted the chapter to the "new" concept of "heterophobia," although I recall having heard and thought about it in the early 1980s. Eichel defined it similarly to Francoeur et al.'s definition in their *Dictionary*. In 1996, Raymond J. Noonan, this author, discussed the term in one of his chapters in the book, *Does Anyone Still Remember When Sex Was Fun?* in which he equated it more with the general antisexualism of American culture. He broadened the definition and used it more as a synonym for this generalized sex-negativity that has crystallized around heterosexual behavior—particularly against heterosexual males—and especially against heterosexual intercourse (see Noonan, 1996b, 1997, 1998a). In that book, he also introduced the concept of "internalized heterophobia." Later, he suggested that homophobia was, in fact, partially enabled and empowered by heterophobia, as the significant impetus for the hostility is probably more often from the "sexual" root of *homosexual* than on the "homo" prefix, which incites only slightly more, overall. Still, some of the fuel for heterophobia may also be rooted in the current misandrist sentiments that have become more prevalent in some quarters of American society in recent years. Misandry, of course, may or may not be in reaction to misogyny, which appears to have become somewhat less prevalent.

[In late 1998, however, *heterophobia* appeared for the first time in the title of a book—the first comprehensive treatment of the subject by anyone inside or outside of sexology. In *Heterophobia: Sexual Harassment and the Future of Feminism*, Daphne Patai tied the concept to what she called the Sexual Harassment Industry (SHI), which was being used, she argued, to separate men and women for often personal or political gain or self-interest. She defined *heterophobia* as the "fear of, and antagonism toward, the Other—in the present context men in general—and toward heterosexuality in particular" (p. 5). She went on to document how this hostility, which "is not limited to the lunatic feminist fringe where it originated in the late 1960s" (p. 14), was being implemented by the expansion of sexual harassment indoctrination sessions and laws.

[More recently, it is interesting to note that Meignant, et al., the authors of the entry on France in this volume of the *Continuum Complete International Encyclopedia of Sexuality*, have selected *heterophobia* as the term to describe their conception of a heterosexuality-heterophobia scale, positing that it is heterophobia that is the opposite of heterosexuality and not homosexuality at the other end of Kinsey's continuum. Their model includes a separate homosex-

uality-homophobia scale conceived as opposites as well. I would be more inclined to consider as more accurate a heterophobia-heterophilia scale, as well as a homophobia-homophilia scale, based solely on the traditional contrast inherent in the meanings of the Greek roots. Also, most sexologists consider Kinsey's scale to be a continuum, and not a description of opposites. In addition, as heterosexuality, bisexuality, and homosexuality have begun to be seen as multidimensional, Kinsey's scale has been increasingly applied to each dimension, resulting in a non-integer composite score, not necessarily congruent across all dimensions.

[Thus, the term is confusing for many people for several reasons. On the one hand, some look at it as just another of the many me-too social constructions that have arisen in the pseudoscience of victimology in recent decades. (Many of us recall John Money's 1995 criticism of the ascendancy of victimology and its negative impact on sexual science, which is recommended reading for insights into the history of the problem.) Others look at the parallelism between heterophobia and homophobia, and suggest that the former trivializes the latter. Yet, heterophobia may be one of the root contributors in the etiology of homophobia, as noted earlier. For others, it is merely a curiosity or parallel-construction word game. But for others still, it is part of both the recognition and politicization of heterosexuals' cultural interests in contrast to those of gays—particularly where those interests are perceived to clash.

[Indeed, the last sense parallels the use of *homophobia* as a political epithet to stigmatize those who are opposed to gay lifestyles regardless of their reasons—suggesting that religious or moral opposition, for example, is based on mental illness. Increasingly, some writers have argued for a more-descriptive term, such as *homonegativity*, that does not rely on quasi-scientific ambiguity based on an etymological relationship with the psychological concept of phobia. Its heterosexual counterpart would then be *heteronegativity*. Both may be conceptualized as *internalized* as well.

[As such, recognition of the impact of heterophobia on sexual health, research, and education in American culture is on the cutting edge of contemporary sexology. In effect, heterophobia has become an unacknowledged—and often unmentionable—force that influences public policy, as well as sexual science, and, in silent alliance with conservative religious and other social forces, determines how sexual issues as a whole are studied or not studied—as well as how sexual lives are lived by women and men and their relationships together—in contemporary American society. (*End of update by R. J. Noonan*)]

### General Summary of Social Factors

PATRICIA BARTHALOW KOCH

This discussion of social factors influencing sexuality in the U.S.A. has selectively focused on religion, race/ethnicity, and gender. Essentially, we have taken the view that such social variables exert influence largely through membership in corresponding social groups. Our review examined the general tradition of the Judeo-Christian heritage of the U.S.A., membership in the Mormon church and the re-emergence of "sacred sexuality," African-American, Latino, and Native American minority groups, identification with feminist and men's perspectives, and heterophobia as specific examples.

We recognize that this approach omits other important social factors, such as education, social class, and size of city of residence. Our purpose has not been to provide an exhaustive review of all pertinent social groups within the U.S.A. Rather, we wished to demonstrate the abundant evidence that a full understanding of sexuality in American culture eventually will require a recognition of the diverse social groups that reside in this nation. As we proceed to examine what sexuality researchers have learned about specific forms of sexual attitudes and behavior, the authors will report, where possible, the results of research which documents an association between sexuality and social variables.

Unfortunately, a recognition of these associations has not always been incorporated into investigations of sexual practices. For example, much of the existing research has been conducted with predominantly white, middle-class, college-educated populations. Researchers have frequently failed to adequately describe the demographic characteristics of their samples, and they have often failed to test possible correlations with social variables. One consequence is that American sexual scientists have yet to develop a full understanding of the very diversity of social groups we have tried to describe. Closing such gaps in our knowledge remains one of the principle tasks of sexual science in the United States.

## 3. Knowledge and Education about Sexuality

PATRICIA BARTHALOW KOCH

According to the National Coalition to Support Sexuality Education,

Sexuality education is a lifelong process of acquiring information and forming attitudes, beliefs, and values about identity, relationships, and intimacy. It encompasses sexual development, reproductive health, interpersonal relationships, affection, intimacy, body image, and gender roles [among other topics]. Sexuality education seeks to assist children [people] in understanding a positive view of sexuality, provide them with information and skills about taking care of their sexual health, and help them to acquire skills to make decisions now and in the future. (SIECUS 1992)

### A. A Brief History of American Sexuality Education

Sexuality education in the United States has always been marked by tension between maintaining the status quo of the "acceptable" expression of individual sexuality, and change as precipitated by the economic, social, and political events of the time. The major loci for sexuality education have shifted from the family and the community (in earlier times being more influenced by religion, and in modern times, by consumerism and the media), to schools. Much of the education has been developed by and targeted towards middle-class whites. As will be described in more detail, the two major movements to formalize sexuality education in the United States were spearheaded for the advancement of either "social protection" or "social justice." Throughout history, the goals, content, and methodologies of sexuality education in these two movements have often been in opposition to one another.

According to D'Emilio and Freedman (1988), young people in colonial America learned about sexuality through two primary mechanisms. In these agrarian communities, observation of sexual activity among animals was common. Observation of sexual activity among adults was also common, since families lived in small, often-unpartitioned dwellings, where it was not unusual for adults and children to sleep together. Second, more formal moral instruction about the role of sexuality in people's lives came from parents and clergy, with lawmakers endorsing the religious doctrines. The major message was that sexual activity ought to be limited to marriage and aimed at procreation. However, within the marital relationship, both the man and

woman were entitled to experience pleasure during the procreative act.

Ministers throughout the colonies invoked biblical injunctions against extramarital and nonprocreative sexual acts, while colonial statutes in both New England and the Chesapeake area outlawed fornication, rape, sodomy, adultery, and sometimes incest, prescribing corporal or capital punishment, fines, and in some cases, banishment for sexual transgressors. Together, these moral authorities attempted to socialize youth to channel sexual desires toward marriage (D'Emilio & Freedmen 1988, 18).

A small minority of colonists also were exposed to a limited number of gynecological and medical-advice texts from London. These underscored the primary goal of sexuality as reproduction, with pleasure only to be associated with this goal.

After the War for American Independence, small autonomous rural communities gave way to more-commercialized areas, and church and state regulation of morality began to decline. Individual responsibility and choice became more emphasized. Thus, instruction on sexuality changed from community (external) control to individual (internal) control. For example, between the 1830s and 1870s, information about contraceptive devices and abortion techniques circulated widely through printed matter (pamphlets, circulars, and books) and lectures. However, peer education was the primary source of sexuality education, with more-"educated" people, especially women, passing along their knowledge to friends and family members.

Increasing secularization and the rise of the medical profession spawned a health-reform movement in the 1830s that emphasized a quest for physical, as well as spiritual, perfection. With advances in publishing and literacy, a prolific sexual-advice literature, written by doctors and health reformers of both genders, emerged. The central message was that, for bodily well-being (as well as economic success), men and women had to control and channel their sexual desires toward procreative, marital relations. "Properly channeled, experts claimed, sexual relations promised to contribute to individual health, marital intimacy, and even spiritual joy" (D'Emilio & Freedman 1988, 72). The popularity of these materials demonstrated Americans' need for and interest in sexuality education. Much of the self-help and medical-advice literature directed at men emphasized the dangers of masturbation. Women were taught that they had less sexual passion than men, and their role was to help men to control their sexual drives. In other words, a standard of female "purity" was the major theme of the sexuality education of the time.

Two studies of women's sexuality conducted in the early 1900s provide insight into the sources of sexual information for women during the 19th century. Katharine B. Davis (1929) studied 1,000 women (three quarters born before 1890) and Dr. Clelia Mosher (1980) surveyed 45 women (four fifths born between 1850 and 1880). Over 40% of the women in Davis' study and half in Mosher's reported that they received less-than-adequate instruction about sex before marriage. Those who indicated that they had received some sexual information identified Alice Stockham's advice manual, *Tokology*, about pregnancy, childbirth, and childrearing as their chief source.

In the later 19th century, a combined health and social-reform movement developed that attempted to control the content of and access to sexuality education. Middle-class reformers organized voluntary associations, such as the Women's Christian Temperance Union (WCTU), to address issues, including prostitution and obscenity. The social-purity movement in the late 19th century added the demand for female equality and a single sexual standard to the earlier moral-reform movements. The WCTU spearheaded a sex-education campaign through the White Cross to help men resist sexual temptation. Social-purity leaders authored marital advice books that recognized women's sexual desires and stressed that women could enjoy intercourse only if they really wanted it. Women's rights and social-purity advocates issued the first formal call for sex education in America. They argued that women should teach children about sex: "Show your sons and daughters the sanctities and the terrors of this awful power of sex, its capacities to bless or curse its owner" (D'Emilio & Freedman 1988, 155). They demanded a public discourse of sexuality that emphasized love and reproductive responsibility rather than lust.

An example of the restricted character of sexuality education at the time was the enactment of the 1873 "Comstock Law" for the "Suppression of Trade in, and Circulation of Obscene Literature and Articles of Immoral Use." This revision of the federal postal law forbade the mailing of information or advertisements about contraception and abortion, as well as any material about sexuality. The Comstock Law was in effect until being overturned by a federal appeals court in 1936 in a decision about contraception: *United States v. Dow Package*.

Yet, the turn of the 19th century ushered in a more "progressive" era fueled by industrial capitalism. Progressive reform provoked by the middle class called upon government and social institutions, including schools, to intervene in social and economic issues, such as sex education. One of the major movements for sex education was the social-hygiene movement spearheaded by Dr. Prince Morrow to prevent the spread of syphilis and gonorrhea. In 1905, he formed the Society of Sanitary and Moral Prophylaxis in New York City, later renamed the American Social Hygiene Association. This society was joined by the WCTU, YMCA, state boards of health, and the National Education Association in an "unrelenting campaign of education to wipe out the ignorance and the prejudices that allowed venereal diseases to infect the nation" (D'Emilio & Freedman 1988, 205). They held public meetings and conferences, published and distributed written materials, and endorsed sex education in the public schools. While insisting on frank and open discussions of sexual-health matters, they promulgated the traditional emphasis of sexuality in marriage for reproductive purposes and the avoidance of erotic temptation (like masturbation). More-conservative Americans considered such openness to be offensive. Former-President Howard Taft described sex education as "full of danger if carried on in general public schools" (D'Emilio & Freedman 1988, 207). Others considered this type of education to be too restrictive. For example, Maurice Bigelow, Professor of Biology at Columbia University Teachers' College, objected to the terms "sex" and "reproduction" being used synonymously. Not until after 1920 would these activists see any progress towards the goal of having some basic sex (reproductive) instruction integrated into any school curriculum.

The early 1900s found American minds being expanded by the writings of Sigmund Freud and Havelock Ellis, among others. These psychologists helped popularize the notion of sexuality as a marker of self-identity and a force permeating one's life, which, if repressed, risks negative consequences. In addition, socialist and feminist ideologies and the industrial economy created an environment fertile for the demand of birth-control information and services. These events spearheaded the second major movement for sexuality education, which was based on social-justice issues, particularly for women and the poor.

In 1912, Margaret Sanger began a series of articles on female sexuality for a New York newspaper, which was confiscated by postal officials for violating the Comstock antiobscenity law. Later, to challenge the constitutionality of this law, she published her own magazine, *The Woman Rebel*, filled with information about birth control. She was charged with nine counts of violating the law, with a penalty of 45 years in prison, after writing and distributing a pamphlet, *Family Limitation*. To avoid prosecution, she fled to Europe; but in her absence, efforts mounted to distribute birth-control information. By early 1915, activists had distributed over 100,000 copies of *Family Limitation*, and a movement for community sexuality education was solidified. Public sentiment in favor of the right to such information was so strong that charges were dropped against Sanger when she returned to America. Community education about and access to birth control, particularly for middle-class women, began to become accepted, if not expected, as a matter of public health, as well as an issue of female equality (social justice).

Premarital experience became a more-common form of sexuality education among the white middle-class, beginning in the 1920s and accelerating as youth became more autonomous from their families (through automobiles, attendance at college, participation in more leisure activities like movies, and war experiences). Dating, necking, and petting among young peers became a norm. "Where adults might see flagrantly loose behavior, young people themselves had constructed a set of norms that regulated their activity while allowing the accumulation of experience and sexual learning" (D'Emilio & Freedman 1988, 261).

Courses on marriage and the family and (sexual) hygiene were being introduced into the college curriculum. Marriage manuals began to emphasize sexual expression and pleasure, rather than sexual control and reproduction, with more-explicit instructions as to how to achieve satisfying sexual relationships (such as "foreplay" and "simultaneous orgasm"). By the end of the 1930s, many marriage manuals were focusing on sexual "techniques." In addition, scientific reports, such as *Sexual Behavior in the Human Male* by Alfred Kinsey and his associates (1948) and the corresponding *Sexual Behavior in the Human Female* (1953), were major popular works primarily read by the middle class. These books provided sexuality education about the types and frequencies of various sexual expressions among white Americans to more than a quarter of a million people. They also are considered landmarks in sexuality education:

> What they [Americans] have learned and will learn may have a tremendous effect on the future social history of mankind. For they [Kinsey and colleagues] are presenting facts. They are revealing not what should be, but what is. For the first time, data on human sex behavior is entirely separated from questions of philosophy, moral values, and social customs. (D'Emilio & Freedman 1988, 286)

As scientific information on sexuality became readily available to the American public, more-explicit presentation of sexual material in printed and audiovisual media became possible through the courts' decisions narrowing the definition of obscenity. The proliferation of such sexually explicit materials was encouraged by the expansion of the consumer-oriented economy. For example, advertising was developing into a major industry beginning in the 1920s. Sex was used to sell everything from cars to toothpaste. Gender-role education, in particular, was an indirect outcome of the advertising media. A "paperback revolution" began in 1939, placing affordable materials, such as "romance novels," in drugstores and newsstands all over the country.

In December 1953, Hugh Hefner published the first issue of *Playboy*, whose trademark was a female "Playmate of the Month" displayed in a glossy nude centerfold. The early *Playboy* philosophy suggested males should "enjoy the pleasures the female has to offer without becoming emotionally involved" (D'Emilio & Freedman 1988, 302). By the end of the 1950s, *Playboy* had a circulation of one million, with the readership peaking at six million by the early 1970s. Many a man identified *Playboy* as his first, and perhaps most influential, source of sex education.

By the 1970s, sex manuals had taken the place of marital advice manuals. Popular books, like the 1972 *Joy of Sex* by Dr. Alex Comfort, encouraged sexual experimentation by illustrating sexual techniques. Sexual references became even more prolific in the mainstream media. For example, the ratio of sexual references per page tripled between 1950 and 1980 in magazines, including *Reader's Digest*, *Time*, and *Newsweek*. In addition, Masters and Johnson's groundbreaking book, *Human Sexual Response*, emphasizing that women's sexual desires and responses were equal to those of men, was published in 1966. The media were influencing Americans—female and male, married and single—to consider sexual pleasure as a legitimate, necessary component of their lives.

Yet, even with the explicit and abundant presentation of sexuality in the popular media, parents were still not likely to provide sexuality education to their children, nor were the schools.

In 1964, a lawyer, a sociologist, a clergyman, a family life educator, a public health educator, and a physician came together to form the Sexuality Information and Education Council of the United States (SIECUS). SIECUS is a non-profit voluntary health organization with the aim to help people understand, appreciate, and use their sexuality in a responsible and informed manner. Dr. Mary Calderone was a co-founder and the first executive director. SIECUS soon became known all over the country as a source of information on human sexuality and sex education.

This private initiative for sexuality education was followed by a governmental one in 1966 when the Office of Education of the federal Department of Health, Education, and Welfare announced its newly developed policy supporting

> family life and sex education as an integral part of the curriculum from preschool to college and adult levels; it will support training for teachers . . . it will aid programs designed to help parents . . . it will support research and development in all aspects of family life and sex education. (Haffner 1989, 1)

In 1967, a membership organization, first called the American Association of Sex Educators and Counselors, was formed to bring together professionals from all disciplines who were teaching and counseling about human sexuality. The organization later expanded to include therapists, and is known today as the American Association of Sex Educators, Counselors, and Therapists (AASECT). Opposition to sexuality education from conservative political and religious groups grew quickly. In 1968, the Christian Crusade published, "Is the Schoolhouse the Proper Place to Teach Raw Sex?" and the John Birch Society was calling sex education a "Communist plot." In response, over 150 public leaders joined the National Committee for Responsible Family Life and Sex Education.

In 1970, Maryland became the first state to mandate family-life and human-development education at all levels in their public schools. However, the new "purity" movement by conservatives was under way, coordinating over 300 organizations throughout the country to oppose sex education in the public schools. Several states passed antisexuality-education mandates, with Louisiana barring sex education altogether in 1968. By the late 1970s, only half-a-dozen states had mandated sex education into their schools, and implementation in the local classrooms was limited.

In 1972, AASECT began developing training standards and competency criteria for certification of sexuality educators, counselors, and therapists. A list of the professionals who have become certified in these three areas is provided in a published register so that other professionals and consumers can locate people who are trained. (Currently, this list identifies over 1,000 certified professionals.) AASECT also has developed a code of ethics for professionals working in these fields.

In 1979, the federal government through the Department of Health, Education, and Welfare conducted a national analysis of sex-education programs in the United States. The researchers calculated that less than 10% of all students were receiving instruction about sexuality in their high schools. The report's overall conclusion stated:

> Comprehensive programs must include far more than discussions of reproduction. They should cover other topics such as contraception, numerous sexual activities, the emotional and social aspects of sexual activity, values clarification, and decision-making and communication skills. In addition to being concerned with the imparting of knowledge, they should also focus on the clarifying of values, the raising of self-esteem, and the developing of personal and social skills. These tasks clearly require that sex education topics be covered in many courses in many grades. (Kirby, Atter, & Scales 1979, 1)

When AIDS burst upon the scene in the 1980s, education with the goal of "social protection" from this deadly disease was targeted for inclusion in public-school curricula. In a relatively short time, most states came to require, or at least recommend, that AIDS education be included in school curricula. The number of states mandating or recommending AIDS education surpassed those mandating or recommending sexuality education. Money and other resources were being infused into AIDS-education initiatives. For example, in 1987-88, 80% of the $6.3 million spent nationwide on sexuality education went specifically to AIDS-education efforts. Today, policies and curricula addressing AIDS tend to be much more specific and detailed than those dealing with other aspects of sexuality education, including pregnancy prevention. This may lead to students receiving a narrow and negative view of human sexuality (e.g., "sex kills!").

Throughout this time, SIECUS remained committed to comprehensive sexuality education, as emphasized in its mission statement: "SIECUS affirms that sexuality is a natural and healthy part of living and advocates the right of individuals to make responsible sexual choices. SIECUS develops, collects, and disseminates information and promotes comprehensive education about sexuality" (Haffner 1989, 4). In 1989, SIECUS convened a national colloquium on the future of sexuality education, "Sex Education 2000," to which 65 national organizations sent representatives. The mission was to assure that all children and youth receive comprehensive sexuality education by the year 2000. Thirteen specific goals for the year 2000 were set forth as follows:

1. Sexuality education will be viewed as a community-wide responsibility.
2. All parents will receive assistance in providing sexuality education for their child(ren).

3. All schools will provide sexuality education for children and youth.
4. All religious institutions serving youth will provide sexuality education.
5. All national youth-serving agencies will implement sexuality education programs and policies.
6. The media will assume a more proactive role in sexuality education.
7. Federal policies and programs will support sexuality education.
8. Each state will have policies for school-based sexuality education and assure that mandates are implemented on a local level.
9. Guidelines, materials, strategies, and support for sexuality education will be available at the community level.
10. All teachers and group leaders providing sexuality education to youth will receive appropriate training.
11. Methodologies will be developed to evaluate sexuality education programs.
12. Broad support for sexuality education will be activated.
13. In order to realize the overall goal of comprehensive sexuality education for all children and youth, SIECUS calls upon national organizations to join together as a national coalition to support sexuality education (SIECUS 1990).

To aid in the attainment of the third goal of providing comprehensive sexuality education in the schools, a national Task Force with SIECUS's leadership published *Guidelines for Comprehensive Sexuality Education, Kindergarten Through 12th Grade* in 1991. These guidelines, based on six key concepts, provide a framework to create new sexuality-education programs or improve existing ones. The guidelines are based on values related to human sexuality that reflect the beliefs of most communities in a pluralistic society. They represent a starting point for curriculum development at the local level. Currently, another Task Force is working on ways to help providers of preschool education incorporate the beginnings of comprehensive sexuality education into their programs. In 1994, SIECUS also launched an international initiative in order to disseminate information on comprehensive sexuality education to the international community and to aid in the development of specific international efforts in this area.

Yet, in light of progress that has been made, challenges to sexuality programs from conservative organizations have become more frequent, more organized, and more successful than ever before (Sedway 1992). These nationally organized groups, including Eagle Forum, Focus on the Family, American Family Association, and Citizens for Excellence in Education, target local school programs that do not conform to their specific ideology. They attempt to control what others can read or learn, not just in sexuality education (which now is the major target), but in all areas of public education, including science (with the teaching of creationism), history, and literature (with censorship of many classics in children's literature). Although these groups represent a minority of parents in a school district, through well-organized national support, they often effectively use a variety of intimidating tactics to prevent the establishment of sexuality-education programs altogether or establish abstinence-only ones. Their tactics include personal attacks on persons supporting comprehensive sexuality education, threatening and sometimes pursuing costly litigation against school districts, and flooding school boards with misinformation, among other strategies. The greater impact of this anti-sexuality-education campaign on education, in general, and American society, overall, has been poignantly described:

> In another sense, the continuing series of attacks aimed at public education must be viewed in the context of the larger battle—what has come to be known as a "Cultural Civil War"—over free expression. Motion pictures, television programs, fine art, music lyrics, and even political speech have all come under assault in recent years from many of the same religious right leaders behind attacks on school programs. In the vast majority of cases, in the schools and out, challengers generally seek the same remedy, i.e., to restrict what others can see, hear, or read. At stake in attacks on schoolbooks and programs is students' exposure to a broad spectrum of ideas in the classroom—in essence, their freedom to learn. And when the freedom to learn is threatened in sexuality education, students are denied information that can save their lives. (Sedway 1992, 13-14)

## B. Current Status of Sexuality Education
### Youth-Serving Agencies

National youth-serving agencies (YSAs) in the United States provide sexuality education to over two million youths each year. Over the past two decades, YSAs began developing such programs, primarily in response to the problems of adolescent pregnancy and HIV/AIDS.

> Second only to schools in the number of youth they serve, youth-serving agencies are excellent providers of sexuality education programs, both because they work with large numbers of youth, including many underserved youth, and because they provide an environment that is informal and conducive to creative and experiential learning. Some YSAs reach youth who have dropped out of school. Others reach youth who have not received sexuality education programs in their schools. The people who work at YSAs often build close relationships with the youth in their programs which allows for better communication and more effective educational efforts. (Dietz 1989/1990, 16)

For example, the American Red Cross reaches over one million youth each year in the U.S. with their "AIDS Prevention Program," "Black Youth Project," and "AIDS Prevention Program for Hispanic Youth and Families." The Boys Clubs of America has developed a substance abuse/pregnancy prevention program, called "Smart Moves." The Girls Clubs of America has a primary commitment to providing health promotion, sexuality education, and pregnancy-prevention services to its members and reaches over 200,000 youth each year. The Girl Scouts of the U.S.A. developed a curriculum, "Decision for Your Life: Preventing Teenage Pregnancy," that focuses on the consequences of teen parenthood and the development of communication, decision-making, assertiveness, and values-clarification skills. The March of Dimes Birth Defects Foundation developed the "Project Alpha" sexuality-education program that explores teenage pregnancy from the male perspective and helps young men learn how to take more responsibility. The National Network of Runaway and Youth Services has developed an HIV/AIDS education program for high-risk youth, called "Safe Choices." The program provides training for staff at runaway shelters, residential treatment facilities, detention facilities, group homes, street outreach programs, hotlines, foster-family programs, and other agencies that serve high-risk youth.

In addition to the national efforts of YSAs, many local affiliates have designed their own programs to meet the needs of their local communities in culturally sensitive ways. For example, the National 4-H Council estimates that most state extension offices have developed their own programs to reduce teenage pregnancy in their areas.

## Table 7

### State Requirements for Sexuality, STD, and HIV/AIDS Education in Primary and Secondary Schools

**Sexuality Education—Required from Kindergarten Through Senior High School**

Alabama, Arkansas, Delaware, District of Columbia, Florida, Georgia, Illinois, Iowa, Kansas, Maryland, Minnesota, Nevada, New Jersey, New Mexico, North Carolina, Rhode Island, Tennessee, Vermont, Virginia, and West Virginia

**Sexuality Education—Required for Grades 5 or 6 Through Senior High School**

South Carolina, Texas, and Utah

**Sexuality Education—Not Required**

Alaska, Arizona, California, Colorado, Connecticut, Hawaii, Idaho, Indiana, Kentucky, Louisiana, Maine, Massachusetts, Michigan, Mississippi, Missouri, Montana, Nebraska, New Hampshire, New York, North Dakota, Ohio, Oklahoma, Oregon, Pennsylvania, South Dakota, Washington, Wisconsin, and Wyoming

**STD/HIV/AIDS Education—Required from Kindergarten Through Senior High School**

Alabama, Arizona, Arkansas, Connecticut, Delaware, District of Columbia, Florida, Georgia, Idaho, Indiana, Iowa, Kansas, Michigan, Minnesota, Missouri, Nevada, NewHampshire, New Jersey, New Mexico, New York, North Carolina, Ohio, Oregon, Pennsylvania, Rhode Island,[1] Tennessee,[2] Vermont, Virginia, Washington, and Wisconsin

**STD/HIV/AIDS Education—Required Grades 5 or 6 Through Senior High School**

California, Illinois, Maryland, Oklahoma, South Carolina, Texas, Utah,[3] and WestVirginia

**STD/HIV/AIDS Education—Not Required**

Alaska, Colorado, Hawaii, Kentucky, Louisiana,[4] Maine, Massachusetts, Mississippi, Montana, Nebraska, North Dakota, South Dakota, and Wyoming

[1] Instruction in sexuality and HIV/AIDS is required at least once a year in all grades.

[2] Instruction in sexuality and HIV/AIDS is required only in counties with more than 19.5 pregnancies per 1,000 females aged 15 to 17. Only one county did not meet this standard.

[3] HIV/AIDS education is required from 3rd to 12th grades.

[4] Louisiana law prohibits sex education before the 7th grade, and in New Orleans, before the 3rd grade.

*Source*: *Sexuality Education in America: A State-by-State Review* (NARAL/The NARAL Foundation 1995).

## Schools

More than 85% of the American public approve of sexuality education being provided in the schools, compared with 76% in 1975 and 69% in 1965 (Kenney, Guardado, & Brown 1989). Today, roughly 60% of teenagers receive at least some sex education in their schools, although only a third receive a somewhat "comprehensive" program.

Each state can mandate or require that sexuality education and/or AIDS education be provided in the local school districts. Short of mandating such educational programs, states may simply recommend that the school districts within their boundaries offer education on sexuality, in general, and/or more-specific AIDS education. In 1992, 17 states had mandated sexuality education and 30 more recommended it; see Table 7 (Haffner 1992). In addition, 34 states had mandated AIDS education, while 14 more recommended it. Only four states (Massachusetts, Mississippi, South Dakota, and Wyoming) had no position on sexuality education within their schools, whereas Ohio, Wyoming, and Tennessee had no position on AIDS education. In 1995, NARAL and the NARAL Foundation (1995) issued a detailed state-by-state review of sexuality education in America with selected details of legislative action in 1994 and 1995.

Although the majority of states either mandate or recommend sexuality and AIDS education, this does not guarantee that local school districts are implementing the suggested curricula. Inconsistencies in and lack of implementation of these curricula result from: absence of provisions for mandate enforcement, lax regulations regarding compliance, diversity in program objectives, restrictions on course content, lack of provisions for teacher training, and insufficient evaluation.

In 1988, SIECUS conducted a project to examine and evaluate the recommended state sexuality and AIDS-education curricula (di Mauro 1989-90). Of the 23 state curricula that they evaluated for sexuality education, only 22%

were deemed to be accurate. Although most curricula stated that human sexuality is natural and positive, there was a lack of any content in the curricula to support this concept. Most focused on the negative consequences of sexual interaction, and little attention was paid to the psychosocial dimensions of sexuality, such as gender identification and roles, sexual functioning and satisfaction, or values and ethics. Only one half of the curricula provided thorough information about birth control.

In an evaluation of the 34 state-recommended AIDS-education curricula, 32% were found to be accurate in basic concepts and presentation. The majority (85%) emphasized abstinence and "just say no" skills, whereas only 9% covered safer sex as a preventive practice. Thorough information about condoms was provided in less than 10% of the curricula. There was no mention of homosexuality in over one third of the curricula. In 38%, homosexuals were identified as the "cause of AIDS." The Utah curriculum was especially negative and restrictive:

> Utah's teachers are not free to discuss the "intricacies of intercourse, sexual stimulation, erotic behavior"; the acceptance of or advocacy of homosexuality as a desirable or acceptable sexual adjustment or lifestyle; the advocacy or encouragement of contraceptive methods or devices by unmarried minors; and the acceptance or advocacy of "free sex," promiscuity, or the so-called "new morality." This section of their curriculum is replete with warnings of legal violations for instructors crossing prohibition lines; their guidelines indicate that with parental consent it is possible to discuss condom use at any grade level, but without it, such discussions are Class B misdemeanors. (di Mauro 1989-90, 6; see also the discussion of Mormon sexuality in Section 2A.)

Currently, a broad focus on sexuality education is being supplanted by a narrow focus on AIDS education. Sexuality and AIDS education are being treated independently with separate curricula and teacher training. The report concluded that: "What is needed [for each state] is a comprehensive sexuality education or family-life education curriculum with an extensive AIDS education component that contextualizes preventive information within a positive, life-affirming approach to human sexuality" (di Mauro 1989-90, 6).

Yet, recommended curriculum content cannot automatically be equated with what is actually being taught in the classroom. To determine what is being taught, a study of public school teachers in five specialty areas (health education, biology, home economics, physical education, and school nursing) in grades 7 through 12 was conducted (Forrest & Silverman 1989). It was estimated that, nationwide, 50,000 public school teachers were providing some type of sexuality education in grades 7 through 12 in 1987-88, representing 45% of the teachers employed in those areas. Roughly 38.7 hours of sex education were being offered in grades 7 through 12, with 5.0 hours devoted to birth control and 5.9 hours covering STDs.

The teachers cited the encouragement of abstinence as one of their primary goals. The messages that they most want to give included: responsibility regarding sexual relationships and parenthood, the importance of abstinence and ways of resisting pressures to become sexually active, and information on AIDS and other STDs. The teachers agreed that sexuality education belongs in the schools and that students should be taught to examine and develop their own values about sexual behaviors. They reported that there is often a gap between what should be taught, and when and what actually is allowed to be taught. The largest gap concerned sources of birth-control methods; 97% of the teachers believed they should be allowed to provide information to students about where they could access birth control, but this was allowed in less than half of their schools. In fact, one quarter of the teachers were permitted to discuss birth control with students only when they are asked a student-initiated question. In addition, over 90% of the teachers believed that their students should be taught about homosexuality and abortion, topics that are often restricted by school districts. In addition, the teachers believed that the wide range of sexuality topics should be addressed with students no later than 7th or 8th grade; however, this is not usually done until 10th through 12th grades, if at all.

The teachers described many barriers to implementing quality sexuality education in their classrooms. The major problem that they identified was opposition or lack of support from parents, the community, or school administrators. They also felt that they lacked appropriate materials because of the difficulties in getting current relevant materials approved for use. They also encountered student-related barriers, such as discomfort, lack of basic knowledge of anatomy and physiology, and misinformation, poor attitudes, and a lack of values and morals reflecting favorable attitudes toward teen pregnancy. Teachers also lacked enough time and training to teach the material effectively. Almost none of them were certified as sexuality or family-life educators by the American Association of Sex Educators, Counselors, and Therapists or the National Council on Family Relations. The level of the teachers' own knowledge on sexual topics was questionable, and some experienced personal conflicts in dealing with certain issues. The authors concluded that:

Perhaps the most important step toward improved sex education would be increased, clear support of the teachers. One form this support should take is the development of curricula that provide teachers with constructive, planned ways to raise and deal with the topics on their students'

minds, since the data indicate that students will often raise topics even if they are not in the curriculum. Greater support should also help increase the availability of high-quality instructional materials and on-going education and information for teachers. Adequate teaching materials and support for teaching in earlier grades the topics students want to know about might help solve the problem of student inattention and negative reactions, to say nothing of helping with the problems of teenage pregnancy and the spread of AIDS and other STDs. (Forrest & Silverman 1989, 72)

Yet, in recent years, well-organized conservative organizations throughout the United States have been promoting the adoption of their own abstinence-only curricula in the public schools. Since 1985, the Illinois Committee on the Status of Women has received $1.7 million in state and federal funds to promote such a curriculum, called *Sex Respect*. They have been successful in having *Sex Respect* adopted in over 1,600 school systems, even though this curriculum is designed to proselytize a particular conservative sexual-value system. The *Sex Respect* curriculum has been criticized because it:

(1) substitutes biased opinion for fact; (2) conveys insufficient and inaccurate information; (3) relies on scare tactics; (4) ignores realities of life for many students; (5) reinforces gender stereotypes; (6) lacks respect for cultural and economic differences; (7) presents one side of controversial issues; (8) fails to meaningfully involve parents; [and] (9) is marketed using inadequate evaluations. (Trudell & Whatley 1991, 125)

Careful scientific evaluation of over 40 sexuality- and AIDS-education curricula commissioned separately by the Centers for Disease Control and the World Health Organization resulted in the following conclusions:

1. Comprehensive sexuality and HIV/AIDS-education programs do not hasten the onset of intercourse nor increase the number of partners or frequency of intercourse.
2. Skill-based programs can delay the onset of sexual intercourse and increase the use of contraception, condoms, and other safer-sex practices among sexually experienced youth.
3. Programs that promote both the postponement of sexual intercourse and safer-sex practices are more effective than abstinence-only programs, like *Sex Respect* (Haffner 1994).

[*Abstinence-Only Sexuality Education*

PATRICIA BARTHALOW KOCH
[*Update 1998*: Under the 1996 Welfare Reform Law, funds were made available to the states to establish programs that have as their "exclusive purpose" the "promotion of abstinence-only education." Funding of $50 million a year is guaranteed for these programs for the next five years. To qualify for a federal grant, a state abstinence-only program must teach:

1. The social, psychological, and health gains to be realized by abstaining from sexual activity;
2. Abstinence from sexual activity outside marriage as the expected standard for all school-age children;
3. Abstinence from sexual activity is the only certain way to avoid out-of-wedlock pregnancy, STDs, and other associated health problems;
4. A mutually faithful monogamous relationship in the context of marriage is the expected standard of human sexuality;

5. Sexual activity outside of the context of marriage is likely to have harmful psychological and physical effects;

6. Bearing children out-of-wedlock is likely to have harmful consequences for the child, the child's parents, and society;

7. How to reject sexual advances, and how alcohol and drug use increase vulnerability to sexual advances; and

8. The importance of attaining self-sufficiency before engaging in sexual activity.

[All 50 states have submitted abstinence-only education proposals; many of them are school-based. Yet, national and worldwide research have found abstinence-only programs to be considerably less effective, if effective at all, when compared with comprehensive sexuality education programs, in preventing unintended pregnancy and STDs among youth (Brick & Roffman 1993; Nelson 1996). Yet, no federal funding is forthcoming to support comprehensive sexuality education.

[It is safe to predict that the trend of increasing sexual experience among adolescents will continue, and that young people will not respond favorably to these abstinence-only programs. Perhaps when the general public realizes the ineffectiveness of these programs, greater support for and expansion of more comprehensive sexuality education will result. (*End of update by P. B. Koch*)]

## C. Informal Sources of Sexual Knowledge

Researchers over the past 50 years have consistently found that adolescents identify peers, particularly of their same gender, as their primary source of sexuality education, followed by various types of media, including print and visual media. Parents and schools are usually identified as significantly less-influential sources.

### Peers as a Sexual Information Source

Males seem to be more dependent on peers for their sexuality education than are females. One problematic aspect of receiving sexuality education informally from peers is that the information they provide is often inaccurate. However, when peers are formally trained to provide sexuality education, such as on the high school or college level, they are very effective in providing information and encouraging the development of positive attitudes towards responsible and healthy sexual expression. Thus, the peer model is being used more widely in school and community sexuality-education programs.

### The Media

The various media are pervasive and influential sources of sexuality education in American culture. Media have been identified by adolescents and college students as being more influential than their families in the development of their sexual attitudes and behaviors. As to television, the radio, and movies, adolescents spend more time being entertained by the media than any other activity, perhaps with the exception of sleeping (Haffner & Kelly 1987).

Television, in particular, has been identified as the most influential source of sexual messages in American society, even though sexual behavior is not explicitly depicted. Yet, in an analysis of the sexual content of prime-time television programming, about 20,000 scenes of suggested sexual intercourse and other behaviors, and sexual comments and innuendos were documented in one year (Haffner & Kelly 1987). These portrayals of sexual interaction are six times more likely to happen in an extramarital, rather than a marital, relationship. In soap operas, 94% of the sexual encounters happen between people who are not married to one another. Minority groups are extremely underrepresented on TV, with gay and lesbian characters nearly nonexistent.

In the United States, by the time a child graduates from high school, she or he will have spent more time watching TV than being in a formal classroom setting. There is conflicting evidence as to the impact media portrayals have on youth's developing sexuality (Haffner & Kelly 1987). Gender-role stereotyping is a pervasive aspect of television programming, with children who watch more TV demonstrating more stereotypic gender-role behaviors than those who watch less. Some studies have linked young people's television-viewing habits, including the watching of music videos, to the likelihood that they would engage in sexual intercourse, while others have not supported this relationship. Yet, there is no denying that TV serves as a sexuality educator. Adolescents report that TV is equally or more encouraging about engaging in sexual intercourse than are their friends, and those that have high TV-viewing habits are likely to be dissatisfied about remaining virgins. In addition, those who believe that TV accurately portrays sexual experiences are more likely to be dissatisfied with their own.

Soap operas are one of the most popular television genres. Depictions of sexual behaviors are common. Yet, television censors still establish rules, such as not showing unbuttoning clothes or the characters at the moment of "penetration." Unfortunately, very few references to or depictions of safer sex are part of television programs. As the National Academy of Sciences concluded, the media provide "young people with lots of clues about how to be sexy, but . . . little information about how to be sexually responsible" (Haffner & Kelly 1987, 9).

Sexuality has become a focal point of some newer types of television programming. Sexual topics, such as teenage pregnancy, incest, or AIDS, are often the subject matter of made-for-TV movies and "after-school specials." In addition, the "sexually unconventional," such as transvestites, sex addicts, or bigamists, are often the guests of television talk shows, such as Donahue, Oprah, and Geraldo. Some critics believe that this diversity has encouraged viewers to become more tolerant and open, whereas others believe it has done the opposite, reinforcing negative and hostile attitudes. Among adolescents and young adults, music videos have become one of the most popular forms of television entertainment. Yet, context studies of these music videos indicate that women tend to be treated as "sex objects." Madonna is one exception, depicting a powerful image of female sexuality.

The motto that "Sex Sells" has been generously applied to television advertising. Television uses sexual innuendos and images to sell almost every product from toothpaste to automobiles. The most sexually explicit commercials are generally those for jeans, beer, and perfumes. Paradoxically, commercials and public service announcements for birth control methods are banned from television. Those for "feminine hygiene" products and the prevention of sexually transmissible diseases, including AIDS, are quite restricted.

Subscriber cable television offers more sexually oriented programming, such as the *Playboy Channel*, than does network TV. However, the *Exxxtacy Channel* was forced out of business because of numerous government obscenity prosecutions. Virtual-reality technology is being developed to allow cable subscribers to use goggles, gloves, and body sensors to enjoy their own virtual sexual reality.

Filmmaking is a huge business and American films are marketed worldwide. Movies have been reported as one of the leading sources of sexual information for adolescent Anglo-American, Latino, and Native American males (Davis & Harris 1982). Films are given greater license to depict sexual behavior explicitly than on television; however, they are still censored. In fact, films, such as *Basic Instinct*, have more explicit sex in their uncut versions that are marketed abroad than the "cut" versions that are marketed domestically. Female nudity has become acceptable, whereas male frontal nudity is still censored. Sexual behaviors other than heterosexual intercourse tend to be missing from most films.

Videocassettes and videocassette recorders (VCRs) have revolutionized the viewing habits of Americans. Two hundred million X-rated videocassettes were rented in the U.S. in 1989. One study of college students determined that males viewed about six hours and females two hours of sexually explicit material on their VCRs a month (Strong & DeVault 1994).

Another very popular form of media, directed at females, is the romance novel, comprising 40% of all paperback book sales in the U.S. Romance novels are believed to both reflect and create the sexual fantasies and desires of their female American audience. The basic formula of this form of media is: "Female meets devastating man, sparks fly, lovers meld, lovers are torn apart, get back together, resolve their problems, and commit themselves, usually, to marriage" (Strong & DeVault 1994, 22).

Sexual language is disguised by euphemisms. For example, the male penis is referred to as a "love muscle" and the female vagina as a "temple of love." Yet, romance novels are filled with sensuality, sexuality, and passion, with some people considering them softcore pornography.

Young males in the U.S. tend to learn about sexuality through more-explicit magazines, such as *Playboy* and *Penthouse*. *Playboy* is one of the most popular magazines worldwide, selling about 10 million issues monthly. Half of college men, but much fewer women, report that pornography has been a source of information for them regarding sexual behaviors (Duncan & Nicholson 1991).

Finally, with increased public access to computer technology, sexuality education is now being offered through the computer-based superhighway. This represents the "wave of the future" and is thoroughly discussed later in this chapter.

*Parents as a Source of Sexual Information*

It is widely believed that parents should be the primary sexuality educators of their children. They certainly provide a great deal of indirect sexuality education to their children through the ways that they display affection, react to nudity and bodies, and interact with people of different genders and orientations—as well as the attitudes they express (or the lack of expression) towards a myriad of sexual topics.

However, most parents in the United States provide little direct sexuality education to their children, even though the majority of children express the desire to be able to talk to their parents about sexuality. Studies of American adolescents consistently find that up to three quarters state that they have not discussed sexuality with their parents (Hass 1979; Sorenson 1973). Parents have expressed the following as barriers to discussing sexuality with their children: anxiety over giving misinformation or inappropriate information for the developmental level of their children; lack of skills in communicating about sexuality, since very few parents ever had role models on how to handle such discussions; and fear that discussing sexuality with their children will actually encourage them to become involved in sexual relationships.

When sexuality education occurs in the home, the mother is generally the parent who handles such discussions with both daughters and sons. Studies do indicate that, when parents talk to their children about sexuality, the children are more likely to wait to become involved in sexual behaviors until they are older, than those children who have not talked with their parents (Shah & Zelnick 1981). Further, when par-

ent-educated teens do engage in sexual intercourse, they are more likely to use an effective means of birth control consistently and to have fewer sexual partners. In addition, high family sexual communication seems to be related to similarity in sexual attitudes between parents and their children.

Recognizing the importance of having parents involved in their children's sexuality education, efforts are being made to prepare parents to become better sexuality educators. Sexuality-education programs for parents are offered separate from, and in conjunction with, children's programs in some schools, and through some community and religious organizations. The goals of these programs include developing parents' communication skills so that they can become more "askable," increasing their knowledge about various aspects of sexuality, and exploring their attitudes and values surrounding these issues. For example, the National Congress of Parents and Teachers' Associations (PTA) has created programs and publications on aspects of sexuality and HIV/AIDS prevention for use by local affiliates.

It is clear that we must continue to strive to reach all Americans with positive and comprehensive sexuality education through all of our available informal and formal channels. It is also imperative that sound qualitative and quantitative research methodologies be used to ascertain the impact of differing sexuality education strategies and sources on the diverse groups of people—e.g., gender, age, orientation, race, and ethnicity—in the United States.

## [D. Sexuality Education 2003 Update

WILLIAM TAVERNER

[*Update 2003*: In 1996, the United States Congress authorized, and President Bill Clinton approved, approximately $100 million in annual spending for "abstinence-until-marriage" education programs. These programs attempt to establish "sexual abstinence" as the social standard for American teens and, in fact, for any unmarried American. Programs in states that accept these federal funds are prohibited from teaching the effectiveness of other methods of contraception and prevention from sexually transmitted infections. To the contrary, such programs often overstate the failure of these effective methods since the programs are not required to be based upon medically accurate research.

[There is currently no evidence that "abstinence-only" education programs are effective in reducing teen sexual activity, sexually transmitted infections, pregnancy, or in yielding any measurable outcome in the health of teens. There is, however, ample research that illustrates the characteristics of sexuality education programs that are effective. According to *The National Campaign to Prevent Teen Pregnancy Report* (Kirby 2001), the most effective sex and HIV education programs share 10 common characteristics. These curricula and programs:

1. Focus on reducing one or more sexual behaviors that lead to unintended pregnancy or HIV/STD infection.
2. Are based on theoretical approaches that have been demonstrated to influence other health-related behavior and identify specific important sexual antecedents to be targeted.
3. Deliver and consistently reinforce a clear message about abstaining from sexual activity and/or using condoms or other forms of contraception. This appears to be one of the most important characteristics that distinguish effective from ineffective programs.
4. Provide basic, accurate information about the risks of teen sexual activity and about ways to avoid intercourse or use methods of protection against pregnancy and STDs.

## Table 8

### Principles for Sexuality Education

**1. YOUNG PEOPLE NEED AND DESERVE RESPECT.** This respect includes an appreciation for the difficulty and confusion of the teen years and a recognition of the constellation of factors that has contributed to the problems teens face. It means treating them as intelligent and capable of making changes in their lives.

**2. TEENS NEED TO BE ACCEPTED WHERE THEY ARE.** This means listening and hearing what young people have to say, though we as adults might disagree. In general, we are much better off helping teens explore the possible pitfalls of their attitudes rather than moralistically telling them what they ought to believe.

**3. TEENS LEARN AS MUCH OR MORE FROM EACH OTHER AS FROM ADULTS.** Often, if we let young people talk, allow them to respond to each other's questions and comments and ask for their advice, they feel empowered and take responsibility for their own learning. It is much more powerful for a peer to challenge another teen's attitude than for an adult to do so.

**4. EXPLICIT INFORMATION AND COMMUNICATION ABOUT SEXUALITY IS ESSENTIAL.** For most of their lives young people have gotten the message that sex is hidden, mysterious and something you should not talk about in a serious and honest way. Limiting what teens can talk about and using vague terminology perpetuates the "secrecy" of sex.

**5. A POSITIVE APPROACH TO SEXUALITY EDUCATION IS THE BEST APPROACH.** This means moving beyond talking about the dangers of sex and acknowledging in a balanced way the pleasures of sex. It means associating things open, playful, and humorous with sexuality rather than only things grave and serious. It means offering a model of what it is to be sexually healthy rather than focusing on what is sexually unhealthy.

**6. YOUNG PEOPLE HAVE A FUNDAMENTAL RIGHT TO SEXUALITY EDUCATION.** They have a right to know about their own bodies and how they function. They have a right to know about the sexual changes that are occurring now and that will continue throughout their lifetimes. They have the right to have their many questions answered. People who have explored their own values and attitudes and have accurate information are in the best position to make healthy decisions about their sexual lives.

**7. GENDER EQUALITY AND GREATER FLEXIBILITY IN SEX-ROLE BEHAVIOR LET ALL YOUNG PEOPLE REACH THEIR FULL POTENTIAL.** We strongly advocate the right of every young person, whether male or female, to achieve her/his full human potential. Strict adherence to traditional gender-role behavior limits people's choices and restricts their potential. Flexible gender-role behavior is fundamental to personal and sexual health in all its dimensions.

**8. ALL SEXUAL ORIENTATIONS AND GENDER IDENTITIES MUST BE ACKNOWLEDGED.** We must recognize the reality that some adolescents are, or think they may be lesbian, gay, bisexual, or transgender. It is important to create an environment that recognizes the needs of these often isolated and invisible youth. Teaching frankly about sexual orientation also benefits heterosexual youth because it allays fears about same-sex feelings that many of them experience.

**9. SEX IS MORE THAN SEXUAL INTERCOURSE.** This means teaching young people that there are many ways to be sexual with a partner besides intercourse and most of these behaviors are safer and healthier than intercourse. The word "sex" often has a vague meaning. When talking about intercourse, the word "intercourse" is used.

Reprinted with permission from S. Brown and B. Taverner (2001), *Streetwise to Sex-Wise: Sexuality Education for High-Risk Youth.* Copyright © 2001 Planned Parenthood of Greater Northern New Jersey.

---

5. Include activities that address social pressures that influence sexual behavior.
6. Provide examples of and practice with communication, negotiation, and refusal skills.
7. Employ teaching methods designed to involve participants and have them personalize the information.
8. Incorporate behavioral goals, teaching methods, and materials that are appropriate to the age, sexual experience, and culture of the students.
9. Last a sufficient length of time (i.e., more than a few hours).
10. Select teachers or peer leaders who believe in the program and then provide them with adequate training (Reprinted with permission; Kirby 2001).

[Later in 2001, the U.S. Surgeon General released a report detailing the necessity for a comprehensive approach to sexuality education. Citing the alarmingly high rates of sexually transmitted infections and unplanned pregnancies among Americans, Surgeon General David Satcher indicated that the United States needs to provide "evidence-based intervention models" for education, including accurate information about contraception and prevention of sexually transmitted infections (Satcher 2001).

[Americans overwhelmingly echoed their support for comprehensive sexuality education. Over 80% of Americans support education that teaches abstinence, pregnancy, and prevention from sexually transmitted infections (Dailard 2001). Polling by the Kaiser Family Foundation found even greater support among American parents. Ninety percent of parents want schools to teach their children about birth control (Kaiser 2000) and 85% want their children to learn about condoms (Kaiser 2000). Lost in the picture are teens who become sexually active, often without having the knowledge or skills to prevent pregnancy or infection. Sexual activity among young Americans often precedes sexuality education. Almost half of teen males, for example, report having had intercourse before learning how to say no to sex in school (Daillard 2001).

[Despite the lack of research for abstinence-only education, the calls for comprehensive sexuality education among parents and experts, and the reality of teen sexual activity, President George W. Bush's 2003 budget actually increased funding for abstinence-only education by $85 million (White House, February 2002).

[*Who Does the Real Sex Ed?*

[Table 8 lists the key philosophical principles for sexuality education developed by the Center for Family Life Education (CFLE), part of Planned Parenthood of Greater Northern New Jersey. CFLE publishes many of the education manuals used by sexuality educators inside and outside of the organization, and in many other parts of the world. The organization is an affiliate of the national Planned Parenthood. With a current staff of 820 sexuality educators and 700 volunteers working in 127 affiliates nationwide, Planned Parenthood has provided over 1.5 million sexuality education programs, making it the largest network of sexuality educators in the country. Planned Parenthood educators have an impact on Americans of all ages, and on a substantial range of topics, including abstinence, contraception, safer sex, sexual harassment, sexual orientation, and more.

[Other major organizations that support and advocate for comprehensive sexuality education include Advocates for Youth, the American Association of Sex Educators, Counselors, and Therapists, the National Campaign to Prevent Teen Pregnancy, the Network for Family Life Education, and the Sexuality Information and Education Council of the United States (SIECUS). The SIECUS website, http://www.siecus.org, has a list of the nearly 150 national service and professional organizations that are a part of the National Coalition to Support Sexuality Education).

[Inside the classroom, many "sexuality educators" have a limited amount of time to actually teach about sexuality; 71% of sexuality educators acknowledged that they spend less than a quarter of their time teaching sexuality education, and the majority identify "health" as their main subject area (Kaiser 2000). The time classroom educators do spend on sexuality tends to focus on abstinence, much more so than they did 20 years ago (Darroch 2000). Today, 33% of U.S. school districts have no specific policy on sexuality education, 57% promote abstinence as either the *only* option, or as the *preferred* option, leaving only 10% of school districts that teach abstinence as one option in a broader education program (Landry 1999). Classroom teachers may be feeling the impact of political restrictions on what they can and cannot say. More than 9 in 10 teachers believe students should be taught about contraception, but many feel restricted from doing so Darroch 2000). In other subjects, teachers report a considerable gap between what they *think* young people need to learn and what they actually teach. Almost 80% of school educators think that students should learn about sexual orientation, but just over half spend any time teaching about it. And, almost 90% think students should learn facts about abortion, but 30% fewer actually spend time teaching about this controversial subject.

[The picture becomes even more interesting when one asks young people what *they think* is being taught in the classroom. When teachers and students are asked about what subjects were or were not covered in sexuality education, they report very differently. For example, 95% of teachers report having taught their students "how to deal with the pressure to have sex," but only 79% percent of students report having learned this; 86% of teachers say they taught students how to get tested for HIV and other STDs, but only 69% of students say they were taught this. And, while 78% of teachers said they taught about what to do when "you or a friend has been sexually assaulted," only 59% of students say this information was given to them (Kaiser 2000). Clearly, there is a disconnect between what teachers say they are teaching and what students say they are learning.

[The gap widens when one examines what American parents want their children to learn, versus what their children report having actually learned in the classroom. Strikingly, 97% of parents want their children to learn "how to talk with their parents," but only 62% of students report having learned this; 76% of parents want their children to learn about sexual orientation, but only 41% of students say this is taught. (See Table 9 for an excerpted summary of the

gap between parental expectations and the reality that their children report.)

[When students are asked what subjects they need *more* information about, over half say that they need to know what to do in the case of rape or sexual assault and more information about HIV and other STDs. Moreover, 40% say they need to learn skills for talking to a partner about birth control and STDs, and how to deal with the emotional consequences of being sexually active. Evidently, learning about abstinence is not enough. (*End of update by W. Taverner*)]

## 4. Autoerotic Behaviors and Patterns

ROBERT T. FRANCOEUR*

### A. Research Weaknesses and Challenges

Five weaknesses or shortcomings and three challenges can be identified in the current research on autoerotic attitudes and behavior patterns in the U.S.A. The weaknesses are:

1. the virtual absence of recent data on noncollege men and women, especially married women and men;
2. the small sample sizes in available research;
3. a problem with the representativeness of the samples;
4. very limited or no data on African-Americans, Latinos, and other ethnic/racial groups; and
5. a limited use of theory as a driving force in the development of research questions.

The challenges include:

1. finding available research funds;
2. overcoming the negative views in academia toward sex research in general, and especially for research on masturbation; and
3. disseminating the findings to the "consumer" to relieve the guilt feelings that many persons experience as a result of their masturbation practices.

### B. Children and Adolescents

In 1985, Mary Calderone, M.D., a pioneer of American sexology and cofounder of the Sexuality Information and Education Council of the United States, documented the presence of a functioning erectile reflex in a 17-week-old male fetus. Considering the homologies of the male and female genital systems, it is logical to assume that females also develop the capacity for cyclical vaginal lubrication while still in the womb. In a 1940 study of boys three to 20 weeks old, seven of nine infants had erections from five to 40 times a day. Seven-month-old girls have been observed experiencing what to all appearances can only be judged to

**Table 9**

**The Gap Between What Parents Want and Schools Teach**

| Selected Topics | What parents want sex ed to teach | What students say is taught |
|---|---|---|
| What to do if raped | 97% | 59% |
| How to talk with parents | 97 | 62 |
| How to use and where to get birth control | 84 | 59 |
| Abortion | 79 | 61 |
| Sexual orientation/ homosexuality | 76 | 41 |

*Source*: Kaiser Family Foundation 2000. *Sex Education in America: A View from Inside the Nation's Classrooms.*

*With input from J. Kenneth Davidson, Sr.

be a reflexive orgasm induced by rubbing or putting pressure on their genitals.

The natural reflexes that result in fetal and infant erections and vaginal lubrication are very much like the knee jerk and other reflexes, except that they are accompanied by smiles and cooing that clearly suggest the infant is enjoying something quite pleasurable (Martinson 1990, 1995). Sooner or later, most children learn the pleasures of stimulating their genitals. Once that connection is made, the threat of punishment and sin may not be enough to keep a child from masturbating. Generally, American adults are very uncomfortable with masturbation by infants and children. There are exceptions, of course, as for instance, the practice of indigenous Hawaiian adult caregivers masturbating or fellating infants to calm them at night.

Most children seem to forget their early masturbation experiences. Two thirds of the males in Kinsey's study reported hearing about masturbation from other boys in their prepubescent or early adolescent years before they tried it themselves. Fewer than one in three males reported they rediscovered masturbation entirely on their own. Two out of three females in Kinsey's sample learned about masturbation by accident, sometimes not until after they were married. Some women reported they had masturbated for some time before they realized what they were doing.

In the 1940s, Kinsey and his associates reported that close to 90% of males and about 50% of females masturbated by the midteens. Studies in the 1980s show an increase in these numbers, with a fair estimate that today nearly three quarters of girls masturbate by adolescence and another 10% or so wait until their 20s. About 80% of adolescent girls and 90% of adolescent boys masturbate with frequencies ranging from once a week to about daily (Hass & Hass 1993, 151, 285).

## C. Adults

Race and ethnicity, religion, educational level, and sexual education appear to be important variables that affect the incidence of masturbation. African-Americans engage in masturbation less often than whites and are more negative about it. Very little is known about Latino masturbation attitudes and practices. We are not aware of any studies on masturbation among other major groups, such as Asians and Native Americans. Religion is a key variable, especially given the continuing condemnation of masturbation by the Roman Catholic Church. Granted many Catholics engage in masturbation, but on a continuum, they are more likely to experience guilt feelings than Protestants or Jews. Likewise, persons from fundamentalist-Protestant backgrounds are more likely to have negative attitudes toward masturbation than liberal Protestants. Kinsey and many subsequent researchers have found that, as education level increases, especially among women, the acceptance and approval of masturbation as a sexual outlet increases. Finally, experience with sex education is an important variable (Heiby & Becker 1980). Persons who have had sex education appear to hold more-tolerant attitudes.

Data indicate that about 72% of young husbands masturbate an average of about twice a month. About 68% of young wives do so, with an average frequency of slightly less than once a month (Hunt 1974, 86). According to data reported by Edward Brecher in *Love, Sex and Aging* (1984), women in their 50s, 60s, and 70s reported a consistent masturbation frequency of 0.6 to 0.7 times a week. In their 50s, men reported masturbating 1.2 times a week, with a decline to 0.8 times a week in their 60s, and 0.7 times a week over age 70.

The incidence of masturbation has continued to increase in recent years among both college and postcollege women. During the 1980s, between 46% and 69% of college women in several surveys reported masturbating. In the 1990s, other surveys have found 45% to 78%. Postcollege women also became more accepting of masturbation as they received psychological permission, instruction, and support in learning about their own bodies. In fact, in self-reports of masturbation, a majority of postcollege-age, college-educated women indicated this was a sexual outlet. In a large-scale sample of college-educated women, without regard to marital status, frequency of masturbation was 7.1 times per month. By contrast, high-school-educated, married women engaged in masturbation only 3.7 times per month (Davidson & Darling 1993).

Not all women feel comfortable with masturbation. Among college women, 30% reported "shame" as a major reason for not engaging in this outlet. Other research indicates that only about half of college women believe that masturbation is a "healthy practice." Even with the apparent increasing incidence of masturbation, considerable data exist that suggest negative feelings toward the practice still deter many college women from choosing this source of sexual fulfillment. And, of those who do engage in masturbation, they do so much less frequently than men, 3.3 times a month for college women compared with 4.8 times for college men (Davidson & Darling 1993).

In general, women are more likely than men to report guilt feelings about their masturbation. Further, substantial evidence suggests that such guilt feelings may interfere with the physiological and/or psychological sexual satisfaction derived from masturbation. In fact, the presence of masturbatory guilt has various implications for female sexuality. Such guilt feelings have been found to inhibit the use of the diaphragm, which necessitates touching the genitals for insertion (Byrne & Fisher 1983). Presumably, this would also affect use of other vaginally inserted contraceptives. Women with high levels of masturbatory guilt experience more emotional trauma after contracting an STD, and exhibit greater fear about telling their sex partner about being infected, than women with low masturbatory guilt. Masturbatory guilt may also inhibit women from experiencing high levels of arousal during foreplay as a prelude to having vaginal intercourse.

One indication of changing attitudes of women toward self-loving is the publication of *Sex for One: The Joy of Selfloving*, by Betty Dodson (1988), and her subsequent appearance on television talk shows. At the same time, the swift dismissal of the U.S. Surgeon General for daring to suggest that masturbation might be mentioned as part of safer-sex education for children indicates that a prevailing negative societal attitude toward masturbation continues.

## [D. Research Update     WALTER BOCKTING

[*Update 2003*: New findings of studies on masturbation in the U.S. are consistent with recent European studies (Dekker & Schmidt 2002; Kontula & Haavio-Mannila 2002) in challenging the belief that masturbation is a substitute for sex with a partner. According to Kinsey's "hydraulic" theory of sexuality (Laumann et al. 1994, 133), each individual has a given sex drive that can be measured by his or her total sexual outlet; when sex with a partner is less frequent, masturbation becomes the alternative sexual outlet to reach orgasm. However, results from the U.S. *National Health and Social Life Survey* (Laumann et al. 1994) and two recent studies among U.S. college students (Pinkerton, Bogart, Cecil, & Abramson 2002; Zamboni & Crawford 2002) found no such relationship between partner sex and masturbation. Rather, findings indicated that people who have regular sex partners, live with their sex partners, or are married, are more likely to masturbate than people without sexual partners or who live alone (Michael, Gagnon, Laumann, & Kolata 1994).

[A number of demographic factors have been shown to influence the prevalence and frequency of masturbation. Men are more likely to masturbate than women (63% versus 37% reported masturbating in the last year) and to masturbate more frequently (Laumann et al. 1994; Pinkerton et al. 2002). In terms of age, younger (18-24) and older (50-59) men and women are less likely to masturbate. Rather than being a function of biological age in and of itself, this may be because of the prevailing social attitudes and norms during adolescence when masturbation habits are formed (Kontula & Haavio-Mannila 2002; Pinkerton et al. 2002). The more-conservative attitudes toward masturbation and sexuality in the United States might also explain why the increase in young women's masturbation found in Europe (Dekker & Schmidt 2002) has not yet been observed in America. In terms of education, the higher educated are more likely to masturbate and do so more frequently. Finally, black men and women are less likely to report masturbating than white men and women, however, those black women who did report masturbating were doing so more frequently than white women (Laumann et al. 1994).

[The most common reasons for masturbation reported by Americans are: 1. to relieve sexual tension (73% for men and 63% for women); 2. physical pleasure (40% for men and 42% for women); 3. partner unavailable (32% for both genders); 4. to relax (26% of men and 32% of women); 5. to go to sleep (16% for men and 12% for women); 6. partner doesn't want sex (16% for men and 6% for women); 7. boredom (11% of men and 5% of women); and 8. fear of AIDS/STD (7% for men and 5% for women). Fifty-four percent of men and 47% of women felt guilty after masturbation (Laumann et al. 1994).

[The taboo associated with masturbation (Bullough 2002) and the stigma associated with the study of masturbation (Coleman 2002) has left this safer-sex practice virtually unexplored in HIV-prevention research. To fill this gap, Robinson and colleagues (2002) examined the relationship between masturbation and HIV risk among low-income African-American women. The majority (62%) had experience with masturbation, over a third (36%) reported recent masturbation, and a few (13%) reported more than occasional feelings of guilt. Women who masturbated were more likely to report having multiple sexual partners, being in a nonmonogamous relationship, and engaging in high-risk sexual behavior. Thus, while masturbation is very safe sex, the women who reported masturbating were more (not less) likely to be at risk for HIV infection or transmission. Consistent with these findings, a study among U.S. college students found that women who masturbate more often had a greater number of lifetime sexual partners, and women who started masturbating at an earlier age were at higher risk for HIV (Pinkerton et al. 2002).

[Together, these findings indicate that masturbation is indeed not a substitute for those who are sexually deprived, but an activity that stimulates and is stimulated by other sexual behavior (Michael et al. 2002, 165). Sexual attitudes and social norms seem to influence the practice and experience of masturbation. Although many of the misconceptions about masturbation have faded because of an increased understanding of human sexuality (Bullough 2002), much about the role of masturbation in sexual development and sexual health remains to be discovered. (*End of update by W. Bockting*)]

[*Current Cultural Observations*    MARTHA CORNOG
[*Comment 2003*: Cultural involvement with masturbation has expanded considerably in the United States over the last few decades. Use of sex toys and sex aids has be-

come more common and a subject for research (Blank & Whidden 2000; Davis, Blank, Lin, & Bonillas 1996; Elliott & Brantley 1997, 28-29; Maines 1998). While public discourse has evoked many of the old taboos—we recall the chastisement of Paul "Pee-Wee Herman" Reubens, charged with masturbating in a dark theater, and Dr. Joycelyn Elders, dismissed as Surgeon General for suggesting schools mention masturbation as part of sex education—the topic has become a reliable vehicle for humor in film, television, and stand-up comedy (Cornog 2003, 285-291).

[Certainly, the market for sexually arousing materials ("pornography") has expanded in print, video, and now on the Net (Lane 2000). Since many people use these materials during masturbation, we know one thing, at least: There's a whole lot of masturbating going on. Elliott and Brantley (1997, 28) reported that 67% of the male college students in their sample used a "pornographic magazine" to masturbate, and 13% of female students did so.

[Group masturbation, which has probably flourished underground for centuries and is mentioned in connection with boys' "circle jerks" as early as the 1700s, has become somewhat accepted as an adult activity with the growth of semipublic "jacks" clubs in the U.S. and also internationally (Cornog 2002). On a lesser scale, far more people probably share masturbation with each other than ever before, especially through telephone sex and cybersex.

[A long-neglected area has been publishing. Only a dozen books about masturbation appeared in the U.S. from 1960 to 1990. But 18 have come out since 1990, five in the last three years. American culture seems to be evolving towards seeing masturbation as a fascinating subject, as real sex with its own unique pleasures, and as an activity to share with someone you love as well as enjoy alone. (*End of comment by M. Cornog*)]

## 5. Interpersonal Heterosexual Behaviors

**A. Childhood Sexuality**        DAVID L. WEIS*

Within American culture, childhood sexuality remains an area that has been largely unexplored by researchers. Childhood is widely seen as a period of asexual innocence. Strong taboos continue concerning childhood eroticism, and childhood sexual expression and learning are still divisive social issues. This general ambience of anxiety associated with the sexuality of children is probably understandable, given the general history of sexuality in the U.S.A., with its focus on adult dyadic sex within committed intimate relationships and its opposition to other sexual expressions. This ambience remains, despite the fact that nearly a century has passed since Freud introduced his theory of psychosexual stages with an emphasis placed on the sexual character of childhood development. This reluctance to accept childhood sexuality is somewhat ironic, because Freudian theory, with its concepts of psychosexual stages (oral, anal, phallic, and latency), penis envy, the Oedipus/Electra complexes, repression, and the unconscious, has been immensely popular in the United States throughout much of the 20th century. Yet, the general American public has been able to ignore the prominence given to childhood sexual development by Freudian theorists and to maintain its central belief that childhood is and ought to be devoid of sexuality.

Perhaps no area reviewed in this section has been the subject of less scientific research than this topic of childhood sexuality. To some extent, the paucity of research has been because of general social concerns about the ethical implications of studying children or assumptions about the

---

*With input from Paul Okami.

possible harm to children that would result if they were to be included in sexuality research. Researchers have frequently had difficulty gaining the permission of legal guardians to ask children questions about their knowledge of sexuality. In this atmosphere, it would be exceedingly difficult to get permission to ask children about their sexual behavior. One consequence of this general social concern has been that most of the relevant research has been confined to asking adults or college students to report retrospectively about events that occurred in their childhood. There are rather clear and obvious limitations to this approach.

On the other hand, we should recognize that many American scientists themselves have been unwilling to study the sexuality of children. A recent review, *Sexuality Research in the United States: An Assessment of the Social and Behavioral Sciences* (di Mauro 1995), is notable for the fact that it never mentions childhood sexuality. It might be interesting to determine the extent to which American researchers accept the premise that scientific explorations of sexuality might be harmful to children. For example, the field of child development, a sizable branch of American psychology, has largely ignored the issue of sexuality in their work (Maccoby & Martin 1983; Mussen 1983). An examination of standard developmental texts or reviews of the child-development research literature is striking for its omission of sexuality. Significant bodies of child-development research in such important areas as language acquisition, cognition, communication, social behavior, parent-child interaction, attachment (Allgeier & Allgeier 1988), parenting styles, and child compliance have emerged with scant attention to the possible sexual elements of these areas, or to the ways in which these areas might be related to sexual development (Mussen 1983). As just one example, Piaget never investigated the issue of children's sexual cognition, and there has been little subsequent research exploring the application of his theoretical model to sexual development. Similarly, the emergence of family systems theory has also largely ignored the sexuality of children—except to explain the occurrence of incest.

At the same time, it is just as true that sexuality researchers have largely ignored the work of child developmentalists and other scientific disciplines in their own work. They have speculated about how theories of psychoanalysis, social learning, cognition, attribution, social exchange, and symbolic interactionism might be applied to the sexuality of children or to the process of sexual development, but they have rarely tested such assertions empirically (see Allgeier & Allgeier 1988 and Martinson 1976 for examples). Moreover, sex researchers have largely failed to examine how the various processes studied by developmentalists relate to sexuality.

A third domain of this fractured American approach to child development is the fairly recent emergence of professional fields devoted solely to the issue of child sexual abuse. We present a review of child sexual abuse itself later in this chapter (see second subsection in Section 8A, Significant Unconventional Sexual Behaviors, Coercive Sex). Here, we wish to make the point that professional groups—e.g., social workers and family therapists devoted to the treatment of victims of child sexual abuse—have emerged, largely since the 1970s, with a corresponding body of work devoted to that concern. After having been largely neglected for much of the 20th century, the treatment of child sexual abuse has become a sizable "industry" in recent years. Unfortunately, much of the work that has been done within this perspective has failed to consider existing data on normative childhood sexuality (Okami 1992, 1995). For example, it is frequently asserted that child sexual abuse has the negative consequence of "sexualizing" the child's world. We do not mean to claim that

child sexual abuse is either harmless or nonexistent. However, the notion that a "sexualized" childhood is a tragic outcome of sexual abuse rests on the American premise that childhood should be devoid of sexuality. It assumes that childhood should not be sexual. From this perspective, the concept of child sexual abuse has been extended to include family nudity—a point certain to shock naturists in many countries around the world—parents bathing with their children, "excessive" displays of physical affection (such as kissing and hugging), and even children of the same age engaging in sex play (Okami 1992, 1995). Thus, we seem to have come full circle. Many professionals have come to accept the premise that childhood ought to be an innocent period, free of sexuality. The fact that this view ignores much of the existing data seems to have had little impact on either the American public or many professionals working with children.

### Childhood Sexual Development and Expression

In reviewing the process of child sexual development and the phenomenon of child eroticism, it is crucial to consider the meanings that children attach to their experience. There is a tendency to interpret childhood experiences in terms of the meanings that adults have learned to attach to similar events. This ignores the reality that young children almost certainly do not assign the same meanings to "sexual" events as adults. They have yet to conceptualize a system of experiences, attitudes, and motives that adults label as "sexual" (Allgeier & Allgeier 1988; Gagnon & Simon 1973; Martinson 1976). A good example is provided by the case of childhood "masturbation." Young children often discover that "playing" with their genitals is a pleasurable experience. However, this may well not be the same as "masturbating." Masturbation, as adults understand that term, is a set of behaviors defined as "sexual" because they are recognized as producing "sexual arousal" and typically having orgasm or "sexual climax" as a goal. Young children have yet to construct this complex set of meanings. They know little more than that the experience is pleasurable; it feels good. In fact, it would be useful to see research that examines the process by which children eventually learn to label such self-pleasuring as a specifically sexual behavior called masturbation.

From this perspective, sexual development is, to a considerable extent, a process characterized by the gradual construction of a system of sexual meanings. Gagnon and Simon (1973) have provided a theoretical model of sexual scripting that examines how these meanings are assembled in a series of stages through social interaction with various socialization agents. In their discussion of the model, Gagnon and Simon stressed their intention that it would serve as an organizing framework for future research on the process of sexual development. Although we believe that the model does provide a potentially fruitful framework for thinking about the process of sexual development, and despite the fact that more than 20 years have passed since its original presentation, there is nearly as great a need for research of this type today as when they formulated the model.

One component of the model proposed by Gagnon and Simon (1973) was the concept of assemblies, by which they meant to convey their view that sexual development is actively constructed by humans rather than merely being an organic process. Among the major assemblies they identified were:

1. the emergence of a specific gender identity,
2. the learning of a sense of modesty,
3. the acquisition of a sexual vocabulary,
4. the internalization of mass-media messages about sexuality,
5. the learning of specific acts defined as sexual,

6. the learning of gender, family, and sexual roles,
7. the learning of the mechanisms and process of sexual arousal,
8. the development of sexual fantasies and imagery,
9. the development of a sexual value system,
10. the emergence of a sexual orientation, and
11. the adoption of an adult sexual lifestyle.

Gagnon and Simon maintained that these assemblies were constructed through interactions with a variety of socialization agents, such as parents and family members, same-sex peers, cross-sex peers, and the mass media. To this list, we would suggest adding the church, the school, the neighborhood/community, and boyfriends/girlfriends as potentially important socialization agents. For Gagnon and Simon, the task for researchers was to examine and identify the associations between the activities of various socialization agents and the corresponding construction of specific sexual assemblies. Although a fair amount of research has been conducted on such associations among adolescents (see the following section), sadly there remains relatively little research along these lines for younger children. As such, we will not present a detailed discussion of the activities of each socialization agent here.

Lacking space to review each of the assemblies, we have had to be selective and have chosen to focus on the more explicitly erotic dimensions. However, we do wish to note that each is ultimately important to a full understanding of sexual development, and it is likely that each of these assemblies is related to the others. Although we do not have space to review the research on the development of gender roles and gender identity, it appears that most American children have formed a stable gender identity by the age of 2 or 3 (Maccoby & Martin 1983; Money & Ehrhardt 1972). It also seems likely that, as children acquire sexual information and experience, they filter what they learn in terms of what is appropriate for males and females. Since norms for male and female behavior, both sexual and nonsexual, tend to differ, this filtering process seems likely to lead to differences in the content of and processes of male and female sexual development.

On the other hand, we would caution the reader to resist the temptation to conclude that gender differences in sexuality are invariably large, or that they apply to all dimensions of sexuality. Recent reviews of existing research indicate that many aspects of sexuality are not characterized by male-female differences and that many differences are small in magnitude (Oliver & Hyde 1993). Ultimately, the issue is a matter for empirical investigation. Unfortunately, there has been relatively little empirical research attempting to link gender-role development (of which there has been a great deal of research in the last 30 years) with the processes of more overtly sexual development.

*Childhood Sexual Eroticism and Expression.* Martinson (1976) has drawn a distinction between what he calls reflexive and eroticized sexual experiences. Reflexive experience is pleasurable and may be a result of learning contingencies, but eroticized experience is characterized by self-conscious awareness and labeling of behavior as sexual. As a general guideline, younger and less-experienced children would seem more likely to react to sexual stimuli in a reflexive manner; older and more-experienced children are more likely to have learned erotic meanings and to define similar behaviors as "sexual." However, there has been virtually no research detailing the process in which this transition occurs or identifying the factors associated with it.

*Sexual Capacity and Autoerotic Play.* It has been clear for several decades that infants are capable of reflexive sexual responses from birth. Male infants are capable of erections, and female infants are capable of vaginal lubrication (Allgeier & Allgeier 1988; Halverson 1940). Lewis (1965) observed pelvic thrusting movements in infants as early as 8 months of age. Generally, these events appear to be reactions to spontaneous stimuli, such as touching or brushing of the genitals. However, the Kinsey research group (1953) did report several cases of infants less than 1 year of age who had been observed purposely stimulating their own genitals. In their cross-cultural survey, Ford and Beach (1951) reported that, in cultures with a permissive norm, both boys and girls progress from absent-minded fingering of their genitals in the first year of life to systematic masturbation by the age of 6 to 8.

With few exceptions, most research on childhood sexual experiences has asked adolescents or adults to describe events in their past. Males participating in such studies commonly report memories of what they call "their first pleasurable erection" at such ages as 6 and 9 (Martinson 1976), although, as we have just seen, studies of infants themselves document the occurrence of erections from birth. Kinsey and his associates (1953) did report that almost all boys could have orgasms without ejaculation three to five years before puberty, and more than one half could reach orgasm by age 3 or 4. Comparable data for females have not been presented. In addition, both boys and girls between the ages of 6 and 10 have reported becoming sexually aroused by thinking about sexual events (Langfeldt 1979).

Much has been made in the U.S.A. of the fact that sexual arousal in boys is readily visible (erections). A number of authors have argued that this increases the probability that young boys will "discover" their penis and are, thus, more likely to stimulate their own genitals than are girls. This idea has become part of the folklore of American culture. We know of no evidence that substantiates this idea. In fact, Galenson and Roiphe (1980) report that there are no gender differences in autoerotic play during the first year of life.

American culture does not encourage such childhood sex play and actively seeks to restrict it. In a study in the 1950s, only 2% of mothers reported that they were "permissive" about their own children's sex play (Sears, Maccoby, & Levin 1957). It is also interesting to note that the researchers in this study did not provide a response category that allowed mothers to indicate they "supported" or "encouraged" sex play. Martinson (1973) found this pattern extended well into the 1970s. In a later investigation of parental views toward masturbation, Gagnon (1985) found that the majority (86%) of this sample believed that their preadolescent children had masturbated. However, only 60% of the parents thought that this was acceptable, and only one third wanted their children to have a positive attitude about masturbation.

*Sex Play with Other Children.* The capacity to interact with another person in an eroticized manner and to experience sexual feelings, either homosexual or heterosexual, is clearly present by the age of 5 to 6. Langfeldt (1979) did observe both mounting and presenting behaviors in boys and girls at 2 years of age. He also observed that prepubertal boys who engaged in sex play with other children typically displayed penile erections during sex play. Ford and Beach (1951) found that children in cultures, unlike the U.S.A., who are able to observe adult sexual relations will engage in copulatory behaviors as early as 6 or 7 years of age. Moreover, in some cultures, adults actively instruct children in the techniques or practice of sexual relations (Ford & Beach 1951; Reiss 1986). This cross-cultural evidence appears to have had little impact on the way in which most Americans, including many sexuality professionals, think about childhood sociosexual interactions.

Again, most of the research in the U.S.A. has been based on recall data from adolescents or adults. Our impressions of childhood sexual interactions are biased toward periods that such older respondents can remember. A number of studies have examined the frequency of childhood sexual behaviors (Broderick 1965, 1966; Broderick & Fowler 1961; Goldman & Goldman 1982; Kinsey et al. 1948, 1953; Martinson 1973, 1976; Ramsey 1943). Taken together, these studies demonstrate that many American children develop and maintain an erotic interest in the other or same sex, and begin experiencing a wide range of sexual behaviors as early as age 5 to 6. It is not uncommon for Americans to report that they remember "playing doctor" or similar games that provide opportunities for observing and touching the genitals of other children, undressing other children, or displaying their own genitals to others. Many American children also acquire experience with kissing and deep kissing (what Americans call French kissing). In fact, generations of American children have played institutionalized kissing games, such as "spin the bottle" and "post office." These studies also provide evidence that at least some American children experience sexual fondling, oral sex, anal sex, and intercourse prior to puberty. Many of these behaviors are experienced in either heterosexual or homosexual combinations or both.

We have purposely avoided reporting the specific frequencies of the childhood sociosexual experiences in these studies because each possesses severe limitations with respect to generalizability. Most have had small samples drawn from a narrow segment of the total population in a specific geographic region. As early as the 1960s, researchers found evidence of racial and community differences in the rate of such behaviors (Broderick 1965, 1966; Broderick & Fowler 1961). In addition, most have used volunteer samples with respondents who were trying to recall events that had occurred ten or more years earlier. Moreover, these studies were conducted over a period of five decades, during which there would seem to be great potential for changes. Comparisons among these studies are virtually impossible. As a result, we would have little confidence in the specific accuracy of frequency estimates.

A review of a few of these studies illustrates this point. Interviewing a group of boys in a midwestern city in the early 1940s, Ramsey (1943) found that 85% had masturbated prior to age 13, one third had engaged in homosexual play, two thirds had engaged in heterosexual play, and one third had attempted or completed intercourse. The Kinsey group (1948), using a broader sample of adults, reported that 45% had masturbated by age 13, 30% had engaged in homosexual play, 40% had engaged in heterosexual play, and 20% had attempted intercourse. For girls, the Kinsey group (1953) reported that roughly 20% had masturbated prior to age 13, roughly one third had engaged in both heterosexual and homosexual play, and 17% had attempted intercourse. They also reported an actual decline in sexual behaviors after age 10 (Kinsey et al. 1948). The large differences between the Ramsey and Kinsey findings could be because of sample size, differences in geographic region or size of the city, differences in the time period of data collection, or differences in the age range of the samples. Here, it is interesting to note that the Kinsey group (1948) also interviewed a small sample of boys. Roughly 70% reported some form of child sex play, a figure that is much closer to Ramsey's findings. In the larger Kinsey sample, only 57% of adult males and 48% of adult females reported memories of childhood sex play, usually between the ages of 8 to 13 (Kinsey et al. 1948, 1953). It would seem possible, then, that studies with adult samples recalling their childhood experiences might well yield lower estimates than studies of children themselves.

John Money (1976) and Money and Ehrhardt (1972) argue that childhood sex play with other children is a necessary and valuable form of rehearsal and preparation for later adult sexual behavior. He has also suggested that such sex play may occur as part of a developmental stage in childhood. Certainly, this phenomenon has been observed in other primate species, such as the chimpanzee (DeWaal 1982). However, Kilpatrick (1986, 1987) found no differences in various ages of adult sexual functioning between persons who had childhood sexual experiences with other children and those who did not. Given the complexity of the model of sexual assemblies we have presented here, it is not surprising that the effects are not that simple.

*Sibling Incest.* We discuss incest and child sexual abuse more fully in Section 8A, Significant Unconventional Sexual Behaviors, on coercive sex. Here, we merely wish to note that, in one of the few studies of sibling incest with a nonclinical sample, Finkelhor (1980) found that 15% of female and 10% of male college students reported having a sexual experience with a brother or sister. Approximately 40% of these students had been under the age of 8 at the time of the sexual activity, and roughly 50% had been between the ages of 8 and 12. Three quarters of the experiences had been heterosexual. Some type of force had been used in one quarter of the experiences. The most common sexual activities were touching and fondling of the genitals. Only 12% of the students had ever told anyone about these sexual activities with a brother or a sister. Interestingly, most of the students reported that they did not have either strong positive or negative feelings about these experiences. Positive reactions were reported by 30%, and another 30% reported negative reactions. Positive reactions were associated with consensual activities (no force had been used) and an age difference of four or fewer years. For males, there were no correlations between prior sibling experiences and current sexual activity. Among females, those who had had sibling sexual experiences were more likely to be currently sexually active. Those women who had positive sibling experiences after age 9 had significantly higher sexual self-esteem, whereas those who had sexual experiences before age 9 with a sibling more than four years older had lower self-esteem.

*Sexual Contacts with Adults.* A recent national survey (Laumann et al. 1994) found that 12% of men and 17% of women reported they had been sexually touched by an older person while they were children. The offender was typically not a stranger, but a family friend or a relative, a finding that is comparable to more-limited samples. We present a more complete review of sexual contacts with adults later in Section 8A, Significant Unconventional Sexual Behaviors, Coercive Sex, on child sexual abuse and incest. Relatively few studies of adult-child sexual contacts have been conducted with nonclinical samples. In general, they indicate that children experience a wide range of reactions, from highly negative or traumatic to highly positive, to such contacts in both the short term and long term (Kilpatrick 1986, 1987; Nelson 1986; Farrell 1990). Moreover, there do not appear to be any simple or direct correlations between such childhood experiences and later measures of adult sexual functioning. In her study of incest, Nelson (1986) found no correlation between affective outcomes and type of erotic activity, sexual orientation, or consanguinity. Kilpatrick (1986) did find that the use of force or abuse was significantly related to impaired adult sexual functioning in several areas.

*Same-Sex Childhood Experiences.* Our discussion to this point has not focused exclusively on heterosexual experience, but it is certainly fair to say that investigations of heterosexual child sex play have dominated existing research. One study of 4- to 14-year-old children found that more than one half of boys and one third of girls reported at least one homosexual experience (Elias & Gebhard 1969). Masturbation, touching of the genitals, and exhibition were the most common activities, although there were also some reports of oral and anal contacts. The fact that children have had such a homosexual experience does not appear to be related to adult sexual orientation (Bell, Weinberg, & Hammersmith 1981; Van Wyk & Geist 1984).

Storms (1981) has hypothesized that such experiences may be related to adult sexual orientation as a function of sexual maturation. He suggests that persons who become sexually mature during the period of homosocial networks (discussed below) may be more likely to romanticize and eroticize these childhood homosexual experiences and, thus, develop a later preference for sexual partners of the same gender. In effect, when sexual maturation, goal-directed masturbation, homosexual explorations, and eroticized fantasies are paired before heterosexual socialization occurs (typically at about age 13), they are more likely to lead to a homosexual orientation later. As far as we know, Storms's ideas have never been directly tested through research.

*Childhood Social Networks.* During middle childhood (roughly ages 6 to 12), both boys and girls in the U.S.A. tend to form networks of same-sex friends. A pattern of gender segregation, where boys and girls have separate friends and play groups, is central to the daily life of middle childhood. This pattern of homosocial networks is readily observable at elementary schools across the U.S.A. Girls and boys tend to cluster at school into separated, same-sex groups. At lunchtime, they frequently sit at separate "girls' tables" and "boys' tables." On the playground, space and activities tend to be gendered. After school, children tend to associate and play in gender-segregated groupings. In fact, this pattern of gender separation may be more pronounced in middle childhood in the U.S.A. than the more-publicized racial segregation.

It should be acknowledged that these homosocial networks are not characterized by a total separation of the genders. There are some opportunities for heterosocial interactions and play, and children do vary with respect to the extent in which they associate with the other sex. As just one obvious example, some girls, who are known as "tomboys," spend considerable time associating with boys. Still, to a large extent, the worlds of boys and girls in middle childhood in the U.S.A. are separated.

Maltz and Borker (1983) have suggested that these homosocial networks can be viewed as distinct male and female cultures. As cultures, each has its own set of patterns, norms, and rules of discourse. Boys tend to play in groups that are arranged in a hierarchy. They stress a norm of achievement ("doing") and emphasize competitive, physical activities. Conflict is overt and is often resolved directly through physical fighting. Differentiation between boys is made directly in terms of power and status within the group. Since boys belong to more than one such group, and because group memberships do change over time, each boy has an opportunity to occupy a range of positions within these hierarchies. Boys' groups also tend to be inclusive. New members are easily accommodated, even if they must begin their membership in a lower-status position. Courage and testing limits are prime values of boys' groups, and breaking rules is a valued form of bonding. In examining how these patterns influence male communication, Maltz and Borker (1983) report that males are more likely to interrupt others, they are more likely to ignore the previous statement made by another speaker, they are more likely to

resist an interruption, and they are more likely to directly challenge statements by others.

Girls tend to associate in smaller groups or friendship pairs. Girls, for example, tend to be highly invested in establishing and maintaining a "best friend" relationship. They stress a norm of cooperation ("sharing") and pursue activities that emphasize "working together" and "being nice." They frequently play games that involve "taking turns." Friendship is seen as requiring intimacy, equality, mutual commitment, and cooperation. However, girls' groups also tend to be exclusive. Membership is carefully reserved for those who have demonstrated they are good friends. Conflict tends to be covert, and it is highly disruptive, leading to a pattern of shifting alliances among associates. Differentiation between girls is not made in terms of power, but rather in relative closeness. Girls are more likely to affirm the value of rules, especially if they are seen as serving group cohesion or making things fair. Girls may break rules, but their gender group does not provide the intense encouragement and support for this behavior seen among boys. Maltz and Borker (1983) note that girls are more likely to ask questions to facilitate conversation, they are more likely to take turns talking, they are more likely to encourage others to speak, and they are more likely to feel quietly victimized when they have been interrupted.

These largely segregated gender networks in middle childhood serve as the contexts for learning about adolescent and adult sexual patterns, as well as for other areas of social life. There is, of course, a certain irony to the fact that homosocial networks serve as a principal learning context for heterosexuality in a culture with such strong taboos against homosexuality as the U.S.A. In fact, Martinson (1973) has argued that these gender networks and this period serve as the settings for a fair amount of homosexual exploration and activity. In one sense, it is almost certainly true that some homosexual activity results from these patterns of social organization. However, this assertion is largely undocumented, and we are not aware of any studies that compare the level of homosexual activity in cultures with homosocial networks with cultures having some other form of childhood networks.

Thorne and Luria (1986) have used this concept of gendered cultures to examine the process of sexual learning in middle childhood. They found that "talking dirty" is a common format for the rule-breaking that characterizes boys' groups. They noted that talking dirty serves to define boys as apart from adults, and that boys get visibly excited while engaging in such talk. Boys also often share pornography with each other and take great care to avoid detection and confiscation by adults. These processes provide knowledge about what is sexually arousing, and they also create a hidden, forbidden, and arousing world shared with other boys, apart from adults and girls. Miller and Simon (1981) have argued that the importance attached to rule violations creates a sense of excitement and fervor about sexual activity and accomplishment.

One other feature of boys' groups is that they serve as a setting for learning both homoeroticism and homophobia. Boys learn to engage in what Thorne and Luria call "fag talk." That is, they learn to insult other boys by calling them names, like "faggot" and "queer." Eventually, they learn that homosexuality is disapproved by the male peer group. Boys at age 5 to 6 can be observed touching each other frequently. By age 11 to 12, touching is less frequent and reduced to ritual gestures like poking each other. On the other hand, much of the time spent with other boys is spent talking about sex. This serves to maintain a high level of arousal within the group. Moreover, the sanctioning of rule-breaking leads to some homosexual experimentation that is kept hidden from the group. Homosexual experiences may become one more form of breaking the rules and one more feature of the secret, forbidden world of sexuality.

In contrast, girls are more likely to focus on their own and their friends' physical appearance. They monitor one another's emotions. They share secrets and become mutually vulnerable through self-disclosure. They have giggling sessions with their friends, with sex often being the source of amusement. Their talks with other girls tend to focus less on physical activities and more on relationships and romance. They also plot together how to get particular boys and girls together in a relationship.

These sexual patterns are largely consistent with the norms of the respective gender cultures. Males tend to focus on physical activities; females on cooperation and sharing. They are also quite consistent with patterns that will become firmly established in adolescent sociosexual patterns. Thus, male and female peer groups become the launching pads for heterosexual coupling as boys and girls begin to "go together." Finally, they serve to heighten the romantic/erotic component of interactions with the other gender.

[*Puberty and Menarche*    ROBERT T. FRANCOEUR
[*Update 1998*: A puzzling phenomenon has been noted in new data regarding the onset of female puberty in the United States (see Table 10). According to a 1997 study of 17,000 girls ages 3 through 12 seen in 65 pediatric practices around the country, American girls are reaching puberty earlier than previously believed. Nearly half of African-American and 15% of white girls are beginning to develop sexually by age 8 (Herman-Giddens 1997). The average age of menstruation for white girls has been unchanged for 45 years. For black girls—about 9.6% of the 17,000 girls in the study—the average age of menarche is about four months younger than it was 30 years ago, when poor nutrition and poverty, which can delay puberty, afflicted more blacks.

[Preliminary comparisons of these data with puberty onset and menarche data from a variety of other countries indicate that the age of menarche is roughly similar around the world, while the onset of puberty is about two years earlier in the United States than it is in other countries.

[The study raises questions about whether environmental estrogens, chemicals that mimic the female hormone estrogen, are inducing earlier puberty among some girls. Environmental estrogens occur from the breakdown of chemicals in products ranging from pesticides to plastic wrap. Natural estrogen is used in some hair products, including pomades marketed to blacks. Research is needed to ascertain whether and to what extent natural and environmental estrogen may be affecting sexual development.

[As the study's lead author, Marcia Herman-Giddens of the University of North Carolina at Chapel Hill, noted, the new data also suggest that sex education should begin sooner than is current practice. "I don't think parents, teachers, or society in general have been really thinking of chil-

dren that young having to deal with puberty." (*End of update by R. T. Francoeur*)]

### Professional and Social Issues of Childhood Sexuality

As we stated at the beginning of this section and as should be apparent from the review of sex education in the U.S.A., there are a number of issues concerning childhood sexuality that have been controversial for decades. Moreover, several new issues have become points of social conflict in recent years. We can only briefly mention four here.

*The Oedipus and Electra Complexes.* The Goldmans' (1982) multinational study of children and sexual learning, including a sizable American sample, raises questions about these complexes. Freud's thesis about castration anxiety and its resolution (typically by the age of 5) would presumably require some awareness of genital differences between males and females, unless one wishes to interpret Freud's terminology strictly as metaphorical. In the Goldman study, the majority of English-speaking children did not understand these differences until they were 7 to 9 years old. Interestingly, a majority of the Swedish children could accurately describe these differences by the age of 5.

*Is There a Latency Period?* The notion of a latency period, roughly from ages 6 to 11, has had great appeal in American culture. This may be because of the impression that the homosocial networks of middle childhood reflect a lack of sexual interest, and to the fact that many Americans prefer to believe that childhood is a period of sexual innocence. Freud (1938) originally proposed in 1905 that middle childhood is characterized by relative sexual disinterest and inactivity, something like a dormant period. Freud also maintained that latency was more pronounced among boys than girls. The review above should certainly dispel the notion that childhood, at any point, is essentially characterized by sexual disinterest.

In addition, Broderick (1965, 1966) not only provided evidence of active sex play during middle childhood, but also demonstrated that most children indicate they wish to marry as an adult, and that most of these children are actively involved in a process of increasing heterosocial interaction and love involvements during childhood. A majority said they had had a boyfriend or girlfriend and had been in love, and 32% had dated by age 13. If anything, we would expect that the age norms for many of these behaviors have actually decreased since that time. Interestingly, those children who indicated that they did not wish to marry eventually were substantially less likely to report any of these activities.

*Parental Nudity.* Experts have disagreed over the years as to the impact of parental nudity on children (Okami 1995). Some have argued that childhood exposure to parental/adult nudity is potentially traumatic—largely because of the large size of adult organs. Others have insisted that strong taboos on family nudity may lead to a view that the body is unacceptable or shameful. This group has argued that a relaxed attitude toward nudity can help children develop positive feelings about sexuality. Similar concerns have been expressed about the primal scene and sleeping in the parental bed. In a survey of 500 psychiatrists, 48% indicated that they believe that children who witness their parents engaging in intercourse do suffer psychological effects (Pankhurst 1979). American experts appear to overlook the fact that most families throughout the world sleep in one-room dwellings. In one study of these issues, Lewis and Janda (1988) asked 200 college students to report their

### Table 10

### The Onset of Puberty in American Girls

| | Breast and Pubic Hair Development | | | Average Age of Menarche |
|---|---|---|---|---|
| | By Age 8 | By Age 7 | By Age 3 | |
| African-American girls | 48.3% | 27.2% | 3% | 12.16 years |
| White girls | 14.7% | 6.7% | 1% | 12.88 years |

childhood experiences. Exposure to parental nudity for ages zero to 5 and 6 to 11 was generally unrelated to a series of measures of adult sexual adjustment. Sleeping in the parental bed yielded several small, but significant correlations. Persons who had slept in their parents' bed as children had higher self-esteem, greater comfort about sexuality, reduced sexual guilt and anxiety, greater frequency of sex, greater comfort with affection, and a higher acceptance of casual sex as college students.

Okami (1995) reviewed the literature in these same three areas. His review provides a thorough summary of clinical opinions in each area, as well as an assessment of the empirical evidence. Despite the growing number of clinical professionals who label such acts as sexual abuse, there is virtually no empirical evidence of harm. In fact, the only variable found to be associated with harm is cosleeping, which has been found to be associated with sleep disturbances. However, Okami notes that these sleep disturbances may well have preceded and precipitated the cosleeping, rather than vice versa.

*Female Genital Cutting.* In December 1996, the Centers for Disease Control and Prevention (CDC) estimated that more than 150,000 women and girls of African origin or ancestry in the United States were at risk in 1995 of being subjected to genital cutting or had already been cut. This estimate was based on 1990 Census Bureau data gathered before the recent increase in refugees and immigrants from the 28 countries that span Africa's midsection where female genital cutting varies widely in prevalence and severity (Dugger 1996ab). A second source cites a different estimate from the CDC using data on how much circumcision is practiced in immigrants' homelands and, making assumptions about sex and age, that about 270,00 African females in the United States were circumcised in their home country or are at risk here (Hamm 1996).

In 1996, Congress adopted a dual strategy to combat the practice here. In April 1996, Congress passed a bill requiring the Immigration and Naturalization Service to inform new arrivals of U.S. laws against genital cutting. It also mandated the Department of Health and Human Services to educate immigrants about the harm of genital cutting and to educate medical professionals about treating circumcised women. A law, which went into effect March 29, 1997, also criminalizes the practice, making it punishable by up to five years in prison and a fine of up to $250,000 for individuals and $500,000 for organizations such as hospitals. Enforcement of the law, however, is problematic for several reasons. First, no one is sure how the law will apply to those immigrants who take their daughters out of the country for the rite. Second, doctors who spot cases of genital mutilation are reluctant to report it for fear of breaking up tight-knit families. Also, when the wounds are healed, it is impossible to ascertain whether the rite was performed here or before arrival in the United States. Finally, there is the secretiveness surrounding this rite of passage, which many African cultures consider essential, and also the hidden nature of the wounds and scars. Sierra Leoneans, for instance, who consider genital cutting part of an elaborate, highly secret initiation rite, view questions about it as a profound invasion of their privacy (Dugger 1996ab).

A government prevention program focuses on educating both old and recent immigrants in how to survive and assimilate in American society while maintaining their own culture and religion. To this purpose, the U.S. Department of Health and Human Services has organized meetings with advocates for refugees and nonprofit groups that work closely with Africans to develop strategies for combating

this practice. Muslim religious leaders, for instance, are invited to explain that the Koran does not require this practice. However, lack of a specific budget hampers this effort.

In one attempt to ameliorate this clash of cultural values, doctors at Harborview Medical Center in Seattle, Washington, persuaded Somali mothers to be satisfied with nicking the clitoral hood without removing any tissue. The ritual usually involves removing the clitoris and sewing the labia closed. The compromise was abandoned in December of 1996 when the hospital was inundated with hundreds of complaints, led by a group of feminists, protesting even this compromise, even though the nicking of the clitoral hood has no short- or long-term negative consequences. The massive objection to this compromise raises serious questions of ethnocentrism on the part of the Americans who protested it. It seems somewhat ironic that such complaints would be made in a culture where we routinely circumcise penises. Although some maintained that the compromise of nicking may violate the letter of the law, it remains to be seen what kind of solution will be achieved in this matter (Dugger 1996b).

*Child Pornography.* It is widely believed, and the Federal Bureau of Investigation (FBI) perpetuates the notion, that child pornography is pervasive and increasing. Several state and federal laws have been enacted in the last 20 years to combat this perceived social problem. The mere possession of a photograph of a naked child has been criminalized in some states. Yet, it is virtually impossible to find any commercial child pornography in the U.S.A. In fact, most of the materials seized by the FBI are private photographs of naked children—with no adults appearing in the photos and no sexual behaviors depicted (Klein 1994; Stanley 1989). Efforts to raid child-pornography businesses have routinely failed to seize any child pornography. FBI sting operations may well have arisen from the corresponding frustrations of government agencies to find any child pornography. One recent legend now circulating is the claim that the U.S. government is now the largest producer of child pornography in the world. This claim is unsubstantiated as far as we know, but, again, it reflects the anxiety of American culture over the sexuality of its children.

[*Childhood Sexuality, 1997 to 2003*    DAVID L. WEIS

[*Update 2003*: Since the publication of the original edition of the *International Encyclopedia* in 1997 and the single volume, *Sexuality in America: Understanding Our Sexual Values and Behaviors*, in 1998, the focus of writings about childhood sexuality has continued to be placed on child sexual abuse (CSA). Much of this research still continues with the assumption that early sexual experience in childhood will almost certainly be harmful (Loeb et al. 2002). Yet, meta-analyses of child sexual abuse using college samples have shown only small effects, if any. Survivors of child sexual abuse have been found to have slightly lower scores on various measures of personality adjustment. However, these findings were not significant when family environment was also assessed. Finally, males have reported different kinds of child sexual abuse experiences than females (Leonard & Follette 2002; Loeb et al. 2002; Rind, Bauserman, & Tromovitch 1998).

[One of the few voices crying in the wind against the onslaught of abstinence-only education and the characterization of childhood sex as pathological or as high-risk behavior is Judith Levine (2002). She calls this the "politics of fear." Levine actually argues that children should be taught that most expressions of sexuality are normal and healthy. She cautions that the recent trend is potentially harmful and may lead to greater anxiety about sex and greater life-long social problems. She maintains that we need to teach our children how to experience sexual pleasure in a safe way.

[At the same time, other researchers (Alexander 2003) are beginning to explore such areas as the possible link between sex differences in the brain and male-female toy preferences, gender recognition in infancy, and other behaviors. (*End of update by D. L. Weis*)]

## B. Adolescent Sexuality DAVID L. WEIS

*Courtship, Dating, and Premarital Sex*

In stark contrast to the relative inattention given to childhood sexuality in the U.S.A., Americans have been fascinated by the sexual behavior of adolescents throughout the 20th century. One is tempted to describe the interest as an obsession. Perhaps no area of sexuality has received as much scrutiny, by both the general public and professionals, as the sexual practices of American teenagers. There have been literally hundreds of scientific studies attempting to determine the rate of adolescent premarital coitus, as well as other aspects of adolescent sexuality. The easy availability of populations to study is only one of the more-obvious reasons for this extensive research.

Since more than 90% of Americans ultimately do marry, investigations of adolescent sexual development and premarital sexual practices largely overlap. General trends have been well documented, compared to other areas of sexuality. Given the vast scope of this research, we can review only the highlights here. (For more extensive reviews of research on adolescent and premarital sexuality, see Cannon & Long 1971; Clayton & Bokemeier 1980; and Miller & Moore 1990.)

The issue of premarital sexuality and virginity has been a focus of considerable social conflict and concern throughout the 20th century, and remains so to this day. Beginning in the early years of that century, a large literature documents the continuing concern of American adults about the increasing number of teenagers who have experienced sexual intercourse prior to marriage. Interestingly, each successive birth cohort of American adults in that century has been concerned about the tendency of their offspring to exceed their own rate of premarital coitus.

Much of the professional literature has reflected these same concerns. Through much of the 20th century, the tone of most professional writings has been moralistic. Adults in the U.S.A., including most sexuality researchers, have tended to view adolescent premarital sexual intercourse, premarital sex, as a deviant behavior, as a violation of existing social norms, and as a growing social problem (Spanier 1975). Research has tended to parallel this perspective by emphasizing the costs or negative consequences of adolescent sexuality, such as sexually transmitted disease (venereal disease), "illegitimate" pregnancy, and loss of reputation (Reiss 1960). This tone may have shifted to a less-judgmental, more-analytic perspective in the 1960s and 1970s (Clayton & Bokemeier 1980). However, with the emergence of AIDS and the rise of out-of-wedlock pregnancies in the early 1980s, the general tone has reverted in recent years, with studies of "risk-taking" behavior, "at-risk" youth, and portrayals of adolescent sexuality as a form of delinquency (Miller & Moore 1990).

*Trends in Adolescent Sexuality*

Despite these adult concerns, it would be fair to suggest that premarital virginity has largely disappeared in the U.S.A., both as a reality and as a social ideal. As we enter the 21st century, the overwhelming majority of Americans now have sexual intercourse prior to marriage, and they begin at younger ages than in the past. "Love" has largely re-placed marital status as the most valued criteria for evaluating sexual experience (Reiss 1960, 1967, 1980). Virtually all Americans believe that intimate relationships (like marriage) should be based on love, that love justifies sexual activity, and that sex with love is a more-fulfilling human experience. This view has not only been used to justify premarital sexual activity between loving partners, but has also become a criterion for evaluating marital sexuality itself and justifying a pattern of divorce and remarriage.

*Premarital Sexual Behavior.* These trends may not be quite as dramatic as most Americans imagine. A study of marriages in Groton, Massachusetts, from 1761 to 1775 found that one third of the women were pregnant at the time of their weddings (cited in Reiss 1980), demonstrating that premarital sex was already fairly common in the colonial period (see discussion of bundling in Section 1A, Basic Sexological Premises). Several early sexuality surveys also document that premarital sex occurred among some groups prior to the 20th century. Terman (1938) compared groups who were born in different cohorts around the beginning of the 20th century. Of those born before 1890, 50% of the men and only 13% of the women had premarital coitus. Two thirds of the men who had premarital sex did so with someone other than their future spouse, whereas two thirds of the women who had premarital sex did so only with their future spouse. For those born after 1900, two thirds of the men and nearly half of the women had premarital sex. The relative percentage having premarital sex with their fiancés also increased. Fully half of the men and 47% of the women had sexual relations with their fiancé(e)s prior to marriage.

The Kinsey team (1953) found that one quarter of the women born before 1900 reported they had premarital sex, whereas one half of those born after 1900 said they had premarital sex. Like the Terman study, the major change was an increase in the percentage of women born after 1900 who had premarital sex with their fiancés. The Kinsey study also indicated that the period of most-rapid change was from 1918 to 1930—the "Roaring Twenties." Burgess and Wallin (1953) reported similar findings for a birth cohort born between 1910 and 1919. These studies indicated that roughly two thirds of the men born after 1900 had premarital sex. The Kinsey studies also found that there had been comparable increases in female masturbation and petting behavior as well.

It is important to note that the growth of premarital sex in the first half of the 20th century occurred primarily within the context of ongoing, intimate relationships. It appears that the percentage of males and females having premarital sex remained fairly stable through the 1950s and early 1960s. In a study of college students during the 1950s, Ehrmann (1959) found rates similar to the Kinsey figures cited above. Ehrmann found that males tended to have greater sexual experience with females from a social class lower than their own, but they tended to marry women from their own social class. Males who were "going steady" were the least likely to be having intercourse. In contrast, females who were "going steady" were the most likely to be having intercourse. In a study comparing college students in Scandinavia, Indiana, and Utah (predominantly Mormon), Christensen (1962) and Christensen and Carpenter (1962) found that rates of premarital sex vary by the norms of the culture and that guilt is most likely to occur when premarital sex is discrepant with those norms.

A second wave of increases in premarital sex seems to have occurred in the period from 1965 to 1980. A number of studies of college students through this period indicated increasing percentages of males and females having premarital coitus (Bauman & Wilson 1974; Bell & Chaskes 1968;

Christensen & Gregg 1970; Robinson, King, & Balswick 1972; Simon, Berger, & Gagnon 1972; Vener & Stewart 1974). For example, Bauman and Wilson (1974) found that, for men, the rate having premarital sex increased from 56% in 1968 to 73% in 1972. For women, the increase was from 46% to 73%. There was no significant change in the number of sexual partners for either gender. Several of these studies indicate that the increases were still moderate by 1970 (Bell & Chaskes 1968; Simon et al. 1972). In an unusual study of male college students attending an eastern university in the 1940s, 1960s, and 1970s, Finger (1975) found that 45% had premarital sex in 1943-44, 62% in 1967-68, and 75% in 1969-73.

Subsequent studies have indicated that this pattern of increasing premarital sex characterized American youth in general. In a study of urban samples in the mid-1970s, Udry, Bauman, and Morris (1975) found that 45% of white teenage women had intercourse by age 20, and 80% of black women did. Roughly 10% of whites had premarital sex by age 15 and 20% of blacks did. Zelnik and Kantner found similar percentages in their studies in 1971 and 1976 (Udry, Bauman, & Morris 1975; Zelnik, Kantner, & Ford 1981).

Reports of increasing sexual activity among adolescents have not been limited to coitus. A number of researchers have reported similar increases in the rate of heavy petting (manual caressing of the genitals) through the late 1960s and 1970s (Clayton & Bokemeier 1980; Vener & Stewart 1974). There have also been reports of increasing levels of oral sex among adolescents (Haas 1979; Newcomer & Udry 1985). In some studies, teenage girls have been more likely to have participated in oral sex than intercourse, and between 16% to 25% of teens who have never had intercourse have had oral sex (Newcomer & Udry 1985). Weis (1983) has noted that this group may be involved in a transition from virginity to nonvirginity, at least among whites.

Perhaps the single best indicator of the trends occurring from 1965 to 1980 is the series of studies by Zelnik and Kantner in 1971, 1976, and 1979 (Zelnik et al. 1981). These studies, known as the *National Surveys of Young Women*, investigated the sexual histories of 15- to 19-year-old women. The 1971 and 1976 studies were full national probability studies while the 1979 study focused on women living in metropolitan areas. The Zelnik and Kantner research shows a dramatic rise in sexual activity for both black and white women from 1971 to 1976. The pattern of increases continued for white women through 1979, but premarital sex rates for black women remained stable from 1976 to 1979. Among metropolitan women, premarital sex rose from 30.4% in 1971 to 49.8% in 1979. For blacks, the rate moved from 53.7% in 1971 to 66.3% in 1976, and was 66.2% in 1979. The 1979 study also showed that 70% of males had premarital sexual intercourse; the figure for black men was 75% (Zelnik & Shah 1983; Zelnik et al. 1983).

In a review of these trends, Hofferth, Kahn, and Baldwin (1987) noted that females in the 1980s became sexually active at younger ages and that fewer teenagers married. As a result, the rate of premarital sex increased. The proportion of women at risk of premarital pregnancy increased dramatically from 1965 to the 1980s. The out-of-wedlock pregnancy rate among teenagers increased for both blacks and whites from 1971 to 1976. This trend continued for whites through 1982, but remained level for blacks after 1976. Finally, they noted that, for women born between 1938 and 1940, 33.3% had premarital sex by age 20. For women born between 1953 and 1955, the figure was 65.5%.

Despite recent claims in some quarters of a return to chastity and abstinence in the late 1980s and 1990s (McCleary 1992), there is no evidence of a decline in premarital sexual

behavior. National data from 1988 indicate that one quarter of females have premarital sexual intercourse by age 15; 60% do so by age 19. About one third of United States males have premarital sexual intercourse by age 15, and 86% by age 19 (Miller & Moore 1990). In fact, a random telephone survey of 100 students attending a midwestern state university in 1994 found that 92% had had sexual intercourse; only 8% said they were still virgins. Nearly two thirds (63%) said that they had participated in what the survey described as a "one-night stand." With respect to their most recent sexual intercourse, 42% reported using something to "protect" themselves. Of these, 84% reported using condoms; 16% said they used the pill (Turco 1994). If anything, the trends that have been well established throughout the 20th century appear to be continuing. Given the continuation of patterns that have been frequently cited as leading to increasing rates of premarital sex, such as industrialization, rapid transportation, dating, and "going steady," we would not expect a reversal in what is now a century-long trend.

[*Premarital Sex Before Age 15*

ROBERT T. FRANCOEUR

[*Update 2003*: In the 1990s, about 20% of adolescents had had sexual intercourse before their 15th birthday—and one in seven of the sexually experienced 14-year-old girls had been pregnant, according to an analysis by the National Campaign to Prevent Teen Pregnancy (NCPTP). Based on seven studies conducted in the late 1990s—three federally financed surveys of young people by the *National Survey of Family Growth*, the *National Longitudinal Survey of Adolescent Health*, and the *National Longitudinal Survey of Youth*—and four smaller data sets, the NCPTP analysis provides a comprehensive look at the sexual activities of 12- to 14-year-olds, a group often overlooked in discussions of adolescent sexuality.

[A variety of more-recent surveys indicate that teens are increasingly delaying their sexual initiation. Recent federal data, for instance, indicate that the birthrate for girls 14 and younger declined 43% from 1991 to 2001, while the decline for older teenagers was 27%. And according to an Alan Guttmacher Institute report, the pregnancy rate for 12- to 14-year-olds dropped 40% from 1990 to 1999.

[On the danger side, only about a third of parents of sexually experienced 14-year-olds knew that their child was having sex. While most parents said they had spoken to their young adolescent children about sex, far fewer teenagers remembered having any such conversations with their parents.

[The analysis found that young teens had plenty of opportunity to engage in sex:

- About half of the 14-year-olds had attended a party with no adult supervision;
- about a quarter of the 12- to 14-years-olds had dated or had a romantic relationship with someone at least two years older—the greater the age difference, the more likely the relationship would include sexual intercourse;
- in one study, 4 in 10 of the sexually active young people had had sex in the 18 months preceding the survey; and
- half of the sexually active had engaged in intercourse more than twice in the last year.

[Adding to the risk of pregnancy and sexually transmitted diseases are other high-risk behaviors engaged in by young nonvirgins (see Table 11).

[The fact that half to three-quarters of the experienced 12- to 14-year-olds said they had used contraception the first time they had sex indicates their first intercourse was not unexpected (Lewin 2003) (*End of update by R. T. Francoeur*)]

*Premarital Sexual Attitudes (Permissiveness).* There has also been a substantial number of studies examining the attitudes of Americans toward premarital sex, although systematic research in this area began later than research on premarital sexual behavior. Reiss (1960) used the term "permissiveness" to describe the extent to which the attitudes of an individual or a social group approved premarital sex in various circumstances. In general, research has found that premarital sex attitudes have become progressively more permissive throughout the 20th century, roughly parallel to the increases in premarital sexual behavior (Bell & Chaskes 1970; Cannon & Long 1971; Christensen & Gregg 1970; Clayton & Bokemeier 1980; Glenn & Weaver 1979; Vener & Stewart 1974). Reiss (1967) developed what has come to be called Autonomy Theory to explain this process. According to Reiss, premarital sexual permissiveness will increase in cultures where the adolescent system of courtship becomes autonomous with respect to adult institutions of social control, such as the church, parents, and the school. This appears to have happened in the U.S.A. and most other industrialized nations in the 20th century.

By far, the biggest change has been the growth of a standard that Reiss (1960, 1967, 1980) called "permissiveness with affection," in which premarital sex is seen as acceptable for couples who have mutually affectionate relationships. This standard has grown in popularity in the U.S.A. as the double standard—the view that premarital sex is acceptable for males but not for females—has declined (Clayton & Bokemeier 1980; Reiss 1967, 1980). By 1980, a majority of adults as well as young people in the U.S.A. believed that premarital sex is appropriate for couples involved together in a serious relationship (Glenn & Weaver 1979). Moreover, although there has been a historical tendency for males to be more permissive about premarital sex than females, these gender differences have been diminishing in recent decades (Clayton & Bokemeier 1980).

## Circumstances of Adolescent Sexual Experiences

Most research on adolescent sexuality has tended to focus on whether or not teenagers or college students have had premarital sexual intercourse. Although this allows us to provide reasonable estimates of the percentages of Americans who have had premarital sex in various time periods and to track trends in the rate of virginity and nonvirginity, this same focus has frequently led researchers to ignore the circumstances in which adolescent sexuality occurs (Miller & Moore 1990). As a consequence, we cannot be as confident about the trends in several related areas, and many questions about the specific nature of adolescent sexual experiences and relationships remain to be explored.

*First Intercourse.* A good example of this lack of perspective is provided by the evidence concerning age at first intercourse. The available research indicates that the average age of first intercourse has been declining since 1970. It seems likely that this trend extends back prior to 1970, but the paucity of relevant data from earlier time periods makes such a conclusion highly tentative. As late as that year, only

**Table 11**

**Risky Behaviors Associated with Early Sexual Experience**

| Risk Behavior | Virgins | Nonvirgins |
|---|---|---|
| Drinking regularly | 3% | 18% |
| Smoking regularly | 8 | 29 |
| Have used marijuana | 10 | 43 |

about one quarter of the males and 7% of the females who attended college had intercourse prior to age 18 (Simon et al. 1972). In the Zelnik and Kantner studies, the average age for females dropped from 16.5 in 1971 to 16.2 in 1976 (Zelnik et al. 1981). By 1979, the average age of first intercourse for women was 16.2; for males, it was 15.7. Blacks of both genders tended to experience sexarche at slightly younger ages than whites. Females had first partners who were nearly three years older, whereas males had first partners who were about one year older than they (Zelnik & Shah 1983).

In a study of college females in the 1980s, Weis (1983) found the average age of sexarche to be 16.2. A later study of college students found that the average age was 16.5 (Sprecher, Barbee, & Schwartz 1995). It should be noted, however, that persons who attend college may well be more likely to postpone sexual activity. It is conceivable that a trend of declining age at first intercourse is still occurring among populations that do not attend college, and it is possible that teenagers in the 1990s (who have yet to reach the age of college) may also be having intercourse at younger ages.

Intercourse appears to be, at least among whites, the culmination of a sequence of increasing and expanding experiences with kissing, petting, and possibly oral sex (Spanier 1975; Weis 1983). There is some evidence that women who have rehearsed these noncoital activities extensively, and thus gradually learned the processes of sexual interaction, are more likely to report positive reactions to their first intercourse (Weis 1983). Weis (1983) found that there is great variation as to when people go through these stages and how quickly.

Most authors have stressed the negative aspects of first intercourse for females by citing the finding that females are significantly more likely to report negative affective reactions to their first intercourse than males (Koch 1988; Sprecher et al. 1995). However, the available data strongly suggest that the differences between males and females may not be large in magnitude. It is clear that females report a wide range of affect, from strongly positive to strongly negative (Koch 1988; Schwartz 1993; Weis 1983), but it is also clear that many males report experiencing negative reactions as well. In a study of college students, the males were more likely to report experiencing high levels of anxiety, the females were less likely to report experiencing high levels of subjective pleasure, while sizable numbers of both genders reported experiencing guilt (Sprecher et al. 1995). Positive reactions to first intercourse have been found to be related to prior experience with noncoital sexual activities, having an orgasm in that first intercourse encounter, descriptions of the partner as gentle and caring (for females), involvement with the first partner for more than one month prior to first intercourse, continued involvement with the partner following the first intercourse, and situational factors, such as the consumption of alcohol (Schwartz 1993; Sprecher et al. 1995; Weis 1983). Several researchers have reported that age is associated with affective reactions, but Weis (1983) found that age was not as strongly or directly related as the level of prior noncoital experience. Schwartz (1993) also reported that Scandinavian teenagers were more likely to report positive reactions than a group of American adolescents.

Over the past three decades, a convergence of male and female premarital sex behavior has been identified, with females reporting less emotional attachment to their first coital partners than in the past (Hopkins 1977; Kallen & Stephenson 1982; Koch 1988). Yet, there is still a significant difference between the genders, with males reporting more casual relationships and females more intimate relationships with their first partners (Koch 1988).

In the only national study of first intercourse, Zelnik and Shah (1983) found that more than 60% of the females were "going with" or engaged to their first partner. Another third described their first partner as a friend. Roughly a third of the males described their first partner as a friend, and 40% were "going with" or engaged to their first partner. The males were twice as likely to have their first intercourse with someone they had just met, although few males or females did this (Zelnik & Shah 1983).

Relationship factors have been reported to be associated with affective reactions to the first intercourse. However, the precise nature of this association remains unclear. There is some evidence that involvement with a partner for longer than one month, and continuing involvement following the first intercourse, are associated with positive affective reactions (Sprecher et al. 1995). There is some evidence that females who are "going with" or engaged to their first partner are more likely to experience positive affect (Weis 1983). However, Weis (1983) also found that attributions that the first partner was caring, considerate, and gentle were more strongly related to affective reactions. Moreover, many women who were "going with" or engaged to their first partner, nonetheless, described their partners as uncaring and inconsiderate. It should be noted that each of these studies found so few participants who were married at the time of their first intercourse that no analyses could be done for that relationship category. For example, not one woman in the Weis (1983) study was married at the time of her first intercourse.

Adolescents appear to have many reasons for becoming involved in premarital sexual behavior. Motivations most frequently mentioned by a group of college women for becoming involved in their first intercourse experience included (rank-ordered by declining frequency): love-caring, partner pressure, curiosity, both wanted to, alcohol or other drugs, and sexual arousal (Koch 1988). The comparable rank-ordering of motivations by a group of college men included: both wanted to, curiosity, love-caring, sexual arousal, to "get laid," and alcohol/drug use. Women were four times more likely to report partner pressure than men, whereas men were seven times as likely to say they were looking to "get laid" and twice as likely to report sexual arousal as a motivation for sexarche (Koch 1988).

Most American teenagers describe their first intercourse as an "unplanned, spontaneous" event. Only 17% of the females and one quarter of the males in a national study said they had planned their first intercourse (Zelnik & Shah 1983). In the same study, less than one half of the males and females used a contraceptive. Those who had their first intercourse at age 18 or older were more likely to use a contraceptive. White women were more likely to have used some form of contraception, but black women were more likely to use a medically prescribed method. Women who described their first intercourse as planned were more likely to have used a contraceptive—fully three quarters of these women did. However, more than two thirds of these women relied on their partners to use a condom or withdrawal. Black women were more likely to use a contraceptive themselves, rather than rely on their partner.

Finally, various aspects of sexarche have been found to be significantly related to later sexual functioning among college students (Koch 1988). Women who had experienced first coitus at an earlier age had less difficulty reaching orgasm during later sexual interactions than did women who had sexarche at a later age. Men with earlier sexarche had less difficulty in keeping an erection during later sexual in-

teractions than men who had been older at sexarche. Also, women who had reported negative reactions to their first intercourse were subsequently more likely than those who felt more positively to experience: lack of sexual interest, sexual repulsion, inability to reach orgasm, or genital discomfort, pain, or vaginal spasms. Men who reacted negatively to their first intercourse were more likely to ejaculate too quickly during later sexual experiences than men who had positive reactions. Both men and women were more likely to experience subsequent sexual functioning concerns when they were pressured by a close partner to engage in intercourse for the first time.

*Number of Premarital Sexual Partners.* It is difficult to provide good estimates on the number of premarital sex partners prior to 1950, simply because researchers failed to ask such a question. On the other hand, it does seem clear that the increase in the percentage of American women who reported they had ever had premarital sex after 1900 was primarily because of an increase in the percentage of women who reported they had premarital sex only with their fiancé (Kinsey et al. 1953; Terman 1938). In contrast, there is abundant evidence of a significant increase in the number of premarital sex coital partners for females from the late 1960s through the late 1980s (Cannon & Long 1971; Clayton & Bokemeier 1980; Miller & Moore 1990; Vener & Stewart 1974; Zelnik et al. 1983). This finding is, however, potentially misleading. A close inspection of the results of pertinent studies reveals that most of the increase is explained by a shift from zero to one partner and from one to two partners. There were no increases in the percentage with seven or more partners.

Among males, there is some evidence that adolescent boys of recent decades are less likely to use the services of a prostitute than in the past (Cannon & Long 1971). In a unique study of males attending the same eastern university from the 1940s through the 1970s, Finger (1975) actually reported a decline in the number of premarital sex partners with a corresponding increase in the frequency of sexual relations. This was primarily because of an increase in the percentage of men who had premarital sex only with their girlfriends. Finger also reported a decline in the percentage of males reporting they ever had a homosexual experience. However, among those who had a homosexual experience, the frequency of such encounters had increased.

Although there appears to be consistent evidence that there have been significant increases in the number of premarital sex partners throughout the 20th century, at least for females, it should be stressed that, as late as 1990, the majority of American teens had had zero or one premarital sex partner. Only 4% of white females, 6% of black females, 11% of white males, and 23% of black males reported six or more partners (Miller & Moore 1990). Thus, the widely held idea that large percentages of American adolescents are now "promiscuous" is greatly exaggerated.

*Rates of Teen Pregnancy and Birth.* In an examination of how the trends we have been reviewing are related to trends in adolescent pregnancy and birth, it is important to bear in mind that, as late as 1965, several states in the U.S.A. prohibited the sale of contraceptives to *married* couples. Such laws banning the sale of contraceptives to teenagers and/or single persons were common until 1977 (see Section 9A on contraception). Details on out-of-wedlock births, contraception, and abortion are presented later. Here, we want to note that the birthrate among unmarried women has been increasing since 1965, with a notable surge in the rate during the 1980s (Baldwin 1980; Forrest & Fordyce 1988; Miller & Moore 1990). Throughout this period, the percentage of unmarried, adolescent women exposed to the risk of pregnancy has been increasing. One principal reason for this is, of course, the increasing percentage of unmarried persons having premarital sex in the U.S. (Forrest & Fordyce 1988). (See also Section 9B, Contraception, Abortion, and Population Planning, Childbirth and Single Women.)

However, there are several interesting twists among these trends, many of which do not fit with the conventional wisdom in the U.S.A. First, much of the increase since 1980 is attributable to women 20 years of age or older. In fact, the adolescent birthrate has actually been declining since the early 1970s (Baldwin 1980; Forrest & Fordyce 1988). Second, the overall birthrate for adolescent women increased through the late 1940s and 1950s, remained stable in the 1960s, increased in the early 1970s, and has been declining since (Baldwin 1980). The misperception, widespread through the U.S.A., that teen-pregnancy rates have been rising is largely because of two factors: 1. the increasing number of such pregnancies, but not the rate, when the children of the baby-boomer generation began having children, and 2. the fact that, as the average age at first marriage has been increasing, adolescent pregnancies are more likely to occur with unmarried women (Baldwin 1980; Miller & Moore 1990). Finally, the perception that adolescent pregnancy has become a recent social problem has emerged as the out-of-wedlock birthrate has increased more dramatically among white women in the last two decades (Baldwin 1980; Miller & Moore 1990).

*Contraceptive Use.* To most Americans, an increase in the rate of adolescent pregnancy (widely assumed, though not true) would seem to be an inevitable result of increases in premarital sexual activity. However, research in many European countries demonstrates that high rates of adolescent sexual activity can be associated with low rates of adolescent pregnancy, when contraceptives are used widely, consistently, and effectively (Jones et al. 1985). There seems little doubt that the U.S.A. has one of the highest adolescent-pregnancy rates among developed nations, largely because of inconsistent contraceptive use (Forrest & Fordyce 1988; Miller & Moore 1990).

It appears that roughly one half of adolescent women use no contraceptive during their first intercourse (Miller & Moore 1990), and most of the women reporting the use of some contraceptive during their first intercourse note that their partner used a condom (Weis 1983). Moreover, most adolescent girls who seek contraceptive services have been having sexual intercourse for some time, many for more than a year before they seek services (Miller & Moore 1990; Settlage, Baroff, & Cooper 1973). After this delay, it appears that roughly two thirds of American teenagers now use some form of contraceptive (Miller & Moore 1990).

Although these figures certainly indicate that large numbers of American youths continue to experience sexual intercourse with no contraceptive protection, they nonetheless represent an increase in contraceptive use over the last several decades. Research in the early 1970s indicated that two thirds to three quarters of American teens rarely or never used contraceptives (Sorensen 1973; Zelnik et al. 1981). Forrest and Fordyce (1988) report that overall use of medically sound contraceptives remained stable through the 1980s. Of those women age 20 or less who sought family-planning services in 1980, nearly three quarters used the pill. By 1990, this had dropped to 52%. In 1980, 14% had used no contraceptive at all (Eckard 1982).

By 1990, Peterson (1995) reported that 31.5% of 15- to 19-year-old women consistently used some form of contraceptive; 24.3% of 15- to 17-year-olds did so, as did 41.2% of 18- and 19-year-olds. This behavior appears to be unrelated to social class (Settlage et al. 1973). Among women of childbearing age (15 to 44), Peterson (1995) found that 52.2% of Hispanic, 60.5% of white non-Hispanic, and 58.7% of black non-Hispanic women reported using some form of contraceptive (see Table 17 in Section 9A under Current Contraceptive Behavior).

Despite the popularity of the idea that adolescent pregnancy is a result of poor sexual knowledge, knowledge of one's sexuality or birth control has not been shown to be a strong predictor of contraceptive behavior among teenagers (Byrne & Fisher 1983). No relationship was found between contraceptive use and early sex education by family, or a congruence between attitudes and behavior. Reiss, Banwart, and Foreman (1975), however, reported that contraceptive use among teenagers is correlated with endorsement of sexual choice (permissiveness), self-confidence about desirability, and involvement in an intimate relationship.

*Explanations of Adolescent Sexuality*

Of course, researchers are not content to provide descriptions of social trends. Instead, they seek to provide theoretically useful explanations of the factors underlying those trends. The essence of scientific analysis is the identification and testing of potential correlates of those trends. There have been thousands of studies of adolescent sexuality testing possible correlates. We cannot review them all here. We will, however, briefly identify several different approaches that have been used to explain the trends we have described above. We have tried to select perspectives that have enjoyed some popularity among sexuality professionals at some point. We have also tried to include explanatory models that represent the diversity of professional opinions about adolescent sexuality.

*Changes in Social Institutions.* By far, the most common approach to explaining the growing acceptance of premarital sex within American culture and the increasing tendency of adolescents to have premarital sex has been a sociological perspective that locates these trends as part of a series of social changes occurring in response to industrialization and urbanization. (Much of this explanation was presented in Section 1, Basic Sexological Premises, where we reviewed the sexual history of the U.S.A.) As patterns of residence and community relations changed in the late 19th and early 20th centuries, changes began to occur in most social institutions. These included changes in male-female roles, a lengthening of the period of formal education, and the emergence of new forms of heterosexual courtship (Ehrmann 1964; Reiss 1967, 1976). One example of the complex web of social changes that have occurred in the last century is the increasing average age of first marriage (Surra 1990). In one century, the average age at first marriage has shifted from the late teens to the mid-20s. Combined with the earlier age at which American adolescents reach puberty, this has led to a much longer period between physical maturation and marriage, thus, greatly expanding the probability that sexual activity will occur prior to marriage.

As social institutions changed in response to the growing industrial character of American society and the increasingly urban pattern of residence, new forms of adolescent courtship emerged. The custom of dating appeared in the 1920s following World War I, and the practice of "going steady" emerged in the 1940s following World War II (Reiss 1980). By the 1990s, the practice of "going together" has become so universally common that few American young people can conceive of other courtship forms. Dating provided a forum for adolescents to pursue male-female relationships independent of adult supervision and control. The appearance of modern transportation, such as the automobile, and the development of urban recreational businesses allowed adolescents to interact with each other away from home. Increasingly, decisions about appropriate sexual behavior were made by adolescents themselves. The practice of "going steady" placed adolescents into a relationship with many of the features of marriage. Steady relationships were defined as monogamous and exclusive with respect to sexuality and intimacy. As such, they carried high potential for intimacy, commitment, and feelings of love. Together, the increased independence and greater potential for intimacy led to increased rates of premarital sexual behavior (D'Emilio & Freedman 1988; Kinsey et al. 1948, 1953; Seidman 1991). There is evidence that this general pattern has occurred in other countries as a consequence of industrialization as well (Jones et al. 1985).

Reiss (1960, 1967) developed the Autonomy Theory of Premarital Permissiveness, mentioned earlier, to explain the association between social institutions and premarital sexual permissiveness. Essentially, Reiss maintained that, as adolescent courtship institutions (dating and going steady) become independent of adult institutions of social control (parental supervision, the schools, and the church), the level of premarital permissiveness in a culture increases. There has been considerable research testing the specific propositions of the theory since Reiss proposed it (Cannon & Long 1971; Clayton & Bokemeier 1980; Miller & Moore 1990). Generally, research from this perspective has tended to presume that premarital sex has become normative within American culture.

*Sources of Sexual Information and Sexual Knowledge.* Several other explanations of premarital sexual behavior have been more likely to view it as a social problem and more likely to focus on the individual character of premarital sex attitudes and behavior. One of the more popular and enduring ideas within American culture about adolescent sexual activity is the belief that sexual behavior and pregnancy risk are influenced by knowledge about sexuality and its consequences. In fact, advocates of sex education in the schools have argued for more than a century that American teens typically possess inadequate and inaccurate sexual knowledge. Some have maintained that sex education could solve such social problems as out-of-wedlock pregnancy and sexually transmitted disease by providing thorough and accurate information about sexuality. Embedded in these assertions is an underlying presumption that sexual decision-making and behavior are primarily cognitive processes. Operating from this perspective, there have been dozens of studies of the sources of sexual information for children and adolescents in the U.S.A. Generally, these studies have found that young people in the U.S.A. are more likely to receive sexual information from their peers or the mass media than from adult sources, such as parents or the school (Spanier 1975; Wilson 1994). These studies have been used to conclude that peers are a poor source of sexual information, and that such inaccurate information leads directly to unwanted pregnancies and disease. We should note here that few studies of sexual information have sought to demonstrate a correlation between source of information and sexual decisions or outcomes. That connection has typically been assumed. (See also Section 3, which deals with formal and informal sources of sexual knowledge and education.)

However, in a national probability study of American college students, Spanier (1975, 1978) found no differences in premarital sexual behavior between those students who had ever had a sex-education course and those who had not—regardless of who taught the course, when it was offered, or what material was included. Moreover, a number of studies have found a weak correlation between sexual

knowledge and sexual behavior or contraceptive use (Byrne & Fisher 1983). More generally, researchers have consistently found a low correlation between knowledge level and a variety of health-related behaviors, such as smoking, drug use, and eating patterns (Kirby 1985).

*Cognitive Development.* A somewhat similar focus on cognitive processes has been the basis for an argument that adolescents typically lack a sufficient level of cognitive development required for effective sexual decisions. A number of authors have argued that adolescence is characterized by a cognitive level that is inconsistent with sound sexual decision-making and contraceptive use (Cobliner 1974; Cvetkovich, Grote, Bjorseth, & Sarkissian 1975). Within this perspective, it has become common to describe adolescents as having an unreal sense of infallibility that leads them to underestimate the actual risks of sexual experience (Miller & Moore 1990).

Although references to the works of Jean Piaget have been common in this realm, actual empirical tests of a correlation between Piaget's stages of cognitive development and sexual decisions remain to be conducted. Moreover, this explanation has failed to incorporate the cross-cultural evidence that adolescents in many other nations establish high rates of sexual frequency, maintain consistent contraceptive use, and experience low rates of adolescent pregnancy (Jones et al. 1985).

*Interaction of Hormonal and Social Determinants.* Udry (1990) has attempted to examine how pubertal development, hormones, and social processes may interact to affect the sexual behavior of adolescents. Hormonal studies seem to indicate that androgenic hormones at puberty directly contribute to explaining sexual motivation and noncoital sexual behaviors in Caucasian male and female adolescents (Udry & Billy 1987; Udry et al. 1985, 1986). Because of the differing social encouragement versus constraints for young white males and females, initiation of coitus seems to be strongly hormone dependent for males, whereas for females it seems to be strongly influenced by a wide variety of social sources with no identifiable hormone predictors. The interaction of hormonal and social determinants is unclear for African-American youth and does not fit the models for white youth that emphasize the importance of sociocultural context on sexual behavior.

*Delinquency Models.* Perhaps the zenith of models which regard adolescent sexuality as a social problem is the emergence of frameworks that explicitly define adolescent sexual behavior as a form of juvenile delinquency (Jessor & Jessor 1977; Miller & Moore 1990). Vener and Stewart (1974) reported that sexual behavior by 15- and 16-year-olds was correlated with the use of cigarettes, alcohol, and illicit drugs, and with less approval for traditional institutions like the police, the school, and religion.

In a subsequent study using this perspective, Jessor and Jessor (1977) conceptualized sexual behavior as a "problem behavior" if it occurred prior to age-appropriate norms. In other words, intercourse was characterized as deviant and delinquent if it occurred prior to the mean age (roughly 17 years of age at the time of the study). Jessor and Jessor found that such early sexual behavior was correlated with other "problem behaviors" such as alcohol use, illicit-drug consumption, and political protest. They concluded that these associations demonstrated that adolescents tend to exhibit multiple forms of delinquency.

By the 1990s, Miller and Moore (1990) reported that a number of studies have found that "early" sexual behavior is associated with a variety of "criminal" behaviors such as those described above. Some authors have overlooked the fact that these studies have found this association with delinquent behaviors only for early sexual behavior and have tended to characterize all adolescent sexual behavior as delinquent. These studies do suggest the possibility that developmental issues may be relevant to these findings.

*Sexual Affect.* A different approach has been taken by a group of researchers interested in examining the role of affective reactions to sexual stimulation, both as a factor that may influence sexual decisions and behavior and as an outcome of sexual experience. Sorensen (1973) reported that 71% of teenagers agreed with the view that using the birth-control pill indicates that a girl is planning to have sex. This has been offered as evidence that adolescents are unwilling or unable to accept responsibility for contraceptive use, and thus lack cognitive development. However, affective theorists would argue that it is just as likely that sexual guilt, fear, or embarrassment prevent such a decision.

In the early 1960s, Christensen (1962) conceptualized sexual guilt as a variable response to sexual experience. He found that adolescents are more likely to report experiencing guilt in cultures with restrictive premarital sex norms. He called this a value-behavior discrepancy. Schwartz (1973) found that persons with high sex guilt retain less information in a birth-control lecture, especially when aroused by a sexually stimulating condition. In the Schwartz study, females retained more information than males across all conditions.

Donn Byrne and his associates have maintained that individuals can be placed on a continuum ranging from erotophilic, reacting to sexual stimuli with strongly positive emotions, to erotophobic, reacting to sexual stimuli with strongly negative emotions. Erotophobic persons have been shown to be less likely to seek contraceptive information, to have lower levels of contraceptive knowledge, and to be less likely to purchase contraceptives or use those contraceptive methods that require them to touch themselves (Byrne & Fisher 1983; Goldfarb, Gerrard, Gibbons, & Plante 1988). However, they are no less likely to retain information about contraceptives, even though they become more sexually aroused by a lecture (Goldfarb et al. 1988).

There is a need for much future research on the association between adolescent sexuality and affective variables. However, the studies just mentioned suggest that affective variables may prove to be a fruitful way of explaining adolescent sexual behavior and its consequences. This approach seems particularly suited to examining the variety of ways that adolescents behave and the diverse consequences of such behavior.

*Reference Group.* Yet another approach to explaining adolescent sexuality has been the attempt to identify persons or groups who have influenced teenagers. Perhaps the most developed theoretical perspective of this type is known as Reference Group Theory. There is some evidence that, as adolescents progress from age 12 to 16, they shift their primary reference-group identification from their parents to their peers. Peer orientation has been shown to be related to sexual intercourse. Moreover, association with peers who are seen as approving premarital sex is correlated with premarital sexual permissiveness and premarital sexual behavior (Cannon & Long 1971; Clayton & Bokemeier 1980; Floyd & South 1972; Reiss 1967; Teevan 1972). Similarly, Fisher (1986) found that the correlation between the attitudes of teenagers and their parents decreased as adolescence progressed. However, females who cited their mothers as their major source of sexual information were less likely to engage in intercourse and more likely to use contraceptives when they did.

These results should not be interpreted to mean that parents or families do not or cannot exert influence on the sexuality of adolescents. There have been relatively few scientific studies of the influence of differing parental styles and the premarital sexual behavior of children. One study (Miller, McCoy, Olson, & Wallace 1986) found that adolescents were least likely to have premarital sex or to approve of premarital sex when their parents were moderately strict. Teenagers who described their parents as very strict or not at all strict were more likely to have had premarital sex. This correlation also held when parents were asked to describe the rules they set for their children. There is some evidence that the age of a mother's first intercourse is related to the age of her daughter's first intercourse (Miller & Moore 1990). Miller and Moore (1990) also showed that girls from single-parent families tend to have sex at younger ages.

Thus, there appears to be two conflicting sets of empirical findings. One set of studies finds evidence that adolescent sexuality is most strongly related to peer influences, especially as age increases. Another set of studies provides evidence that families and parents can exert influence in various ways. Obviously, important questions remain to be resolved.

*Rehearsal.* A more direct perspective views adolescent sexuality as a developmental process, in which intercourse is seen as the culmination of a sequence of progressively sexual behaviors (Miller & Moore 1990; Simon et al. 1972; Weis 1983). Adolescents appear to move through a series of stages, from kissing to petting of the female's breasts to genital petting to intercourse. There is evidence that, among white adolescents, this pattern is strongly consistent. White adolescents appear to take an average of two years to move through this sequence (Miller & Moore 1990; Weis 1983). In contrast, blacks appear to move through the stages more quickly, and there is greater variability in the actual sequence of behaviors (Miller & Moore 1990). Within this perspective, each subsequent sexual behavior can be viewed as a rehearsal for the next behavior in the sequence.

Not only is there evidence that adolescent sexual experience is acquired in a process that produces an escalating and expanding repertoire of sexual behaviors, but dating and "going steady" appear to serve as the key social contexts in which this process occurs (Clayton & Bokemeier 1980; Reiss 1967; Spanier 1975). The age of onset of dating and the frequency of dating appear to be major factors in the emergence of sexual behavior (Spanier 1975). In fact, adolescent experiences with intimate relationships (dating and "going steady") and the sequencing of sexual behaviors have been shown to be more influential in predicting premarital sexual intercourse than general social background variables, parental conservatism or liberalism, or religiosity (Herold & Goodwin 1981; Spanier 1975).

As dating frequency and noncoital experiences increase, exposure to eroticism, sexual knowledge, and interest in sex are all likely to increase concomitantly. Male behavior appears to be more strongly related to the sequencing of behaviors. In contrast, female behavior seems to be more a result of involvement in affectionate relationships. Increased dating interaction and frequency increase sexual intimacy, since opportunities and desire increase. This process is likely to overshadow the influence of prior religious, parental, or peer influences. Thus, adolescent courtship provides the context for the general process of sexual interaction. As Reiss (1967, 1980) has noted, such adolescent courtship also serves as a rehearsal experience for adult patterns of intimate involvement. It is also possible that such adolescent rehearsal experiences are a more powerful and direct explanation of adolescent sexual behavior (Spanier 1975; Weis 1983).

*Multivariate Causal Models.* An important trend in American research on adolescent sexuality has been the growing recognition that several of the factors reviewed here will eventually need to be included in a sound theory of adolescent sexual development and expression. Reiss (1967) was one of the first to test competing hypotheses in an attempt to identify the strongest predictors of premarital sexual permissiveness. Since then, a number of researchers have used multivariate techniques to examine the relative strength of premarital sex correlates (Byrne & Fisher 1983; Christopher & Cate 1988; DeLamater & MacCorquodale 1979; Herold & Goodwin 1981; Reiss et al. 1975; Udry 1990; Udry, Tolbert, & Morris 1986; Weis 1983).

A few examples should illustrate the potential usefulness of this multivariate approach. Herold and Goodwin (1981) found that the best predictors of the transition from virginity to nonvirginity for females were perceived peer experience with premarital sex, involvement in a steady, "committed" relationship, and religiosity. In contrast, parental education, grade-point average, sex education, and dating frequency failed to enter the multivariate equation.

Udry and his associates (1990; Udry et al. 1986) have investigated the relative influence of hormonal and social variables in explaining adolescent sexual behavior. Several studies demonstrate that androgenic hormones present at puberty directly contribute to the sexual motivation and precoital sexual behavior of white males. For white males, the initiation of coitus seems to be strongly related to androgen levels. Female initiation of coitus seems, on the other hand, to be strongly related to a series of social variables, but not to any hormonal predictors. Udry has argued that these results reflect the differing social encouragement versus constraints placed on males and females respectively. Interestingly, the behavior of African-American youth does not appear to fit with these same explanations, so that the exact interaction between social factors and hormonal variables remains unclear.

### Adolescent Sexual Relationships:
### The Neglected Research

Before moving to the issue of adult heterosexuality, we wish to make a few comments about the nature of intimacy in adolescent sexual relationships and the process of relationship formation. Most of the research on adolescent sexuality reviewed here has tended to focus on the specifically and explicitly sexual elements of such experiences and to ignore the broader relational aspects. In one sense, this is understandable, given the fact that Americans have generally viewed adolescent sexuality, especially its premarital forms, as a social problem. Consistent with this perspective, Americans have tended to deny the possibility that any genuine intimacy occurs in sexual experiences involving adolescents. This is unfortunate in at least two respects. First, it tends to ignore the fact that most adolescent sexual encounters in the U.S.A. occur within the context of what the participants define as a meaningful, intimate relationship. It also ignores the reality that sexual expression within loving, intimate relationships (rather than marital status) has become the dominant attitudinal standard for Americans of all ages. Second, the tendency to ignore the relational character of adolescent sexuality means that researchers have tended to overlook the reality that patterns of sexual and intimate interactions are largely learned within the context of adolescent experiences, and these are likely to be extended well into adulthood. Thus, the failure to investigate these larger relational questions probably impairs our ability to fully understand adult intimate relationships as well. This is not meant to denigrate other forms of sexual expression or

to deny that other forms of expression do occur, both in adolescence and later. Rather, it is to suggest that one strong characteristic of American sexuality is the tendency to associate love and sexuality. Any attempt to understand or explain American sexual expression must acknowledge that it generally occurs within the context of ongoing, intimate relationships. This is as true for adolescents as for adults.

The separation of sexuality and relational concerns is well reflected by the emergence of two independent bodies of research within the American academy. On the one hand, there is a well-established field of research on the formation of adolescent intimate relationships, dating and courtship, and mate selection. This tradition extends back to the 1920s and has largely been explored by family sociologists. Social exchange theory has become the dominant perspective in this tradition in recent decades. Surra (1990) provides an excellent review of such research through the 1980s. However, this tradition has largely failed to consider sexuality as an issue in courtship and mate selection, although it ought to be apparent that sexual dynamics and processes are key components of adolescent attraction, dating, courtship, and mate selection. Sexuality carries the potential both for increasing intimacy between teenagers or young adults and for creating intense relationship conflict and, possibly, termination. Yet, Surra's (1990) review is notable precisely for the fact that there is not one single citation of a study including sexuality variables. This is not an indictment of Surra *per se*. Her goal was to review the field of mate selection as it stood at the beginning of the 1990s. Her assessment serves to document that researchers in this area continue to ignore the role of sexuality in adolescent relationship processes after seven decades of empirical research.

This tendency to ignore sexuality within the courtship process is unfortunate, because of the growing evidence that one of the major influences on premarital sexual behavior is the intimate relationship in which most adolescent sexual activity occurs. Being involved in a loving and caring relationship increases the probability of a decision to engage in intercourse (Christopher & Cate 1985) and contributes to sustained activity once it begins (DeLamater & MasCorquodale 1979; Peplau, Rubin, & Hill 1977). In fact, most adolescent sexual experiences in the U.S.A., especially for females, occur within the context of an ongoing intimate relationship. It does appear, however, that as the general rates of premarital sex have increased and as the average age of first intercourse have declined throughout the 20th century, intercourse has tended to occur at earlier stages in a relationship (Bell & Chaskes 1970; Christensen & Carpenter 1962; Christensen & Gregg 1970). With respect to attitudes, Americans are more likely to approve of premarital sex in the context of a relationship. This permissiveness-with-affection-and/or-commitment standard has increasingly become the norm for both adults and young people (Christensen & Carpenter 1962; Christensen & Gregg 1970; Reiss 1960, 1967).

A second body of research examining the formation of sexual relationships has begun to emerge in recent decades. Much of this work has been done by biologists or evolutionary social psychologists and extends a model of mammalian mating first presented by Beach (1976). We discuss it here because it also reflects the separation of the sexual and intimate domains of relationships, and because much of the pertinent human research has been done with samples of college students. Essentially, this body of work forms the foundation for what might be called female selection theory.

The traditional view had always been that males are the aggressors and initiators of sexual involvement. From this perspective, females were seen as sexual "gatekeepers."

Their role supposedly was to regulate male access by accepting or rejecting male advances (Perper 1985; Perper & Weis 1987). Beginning with Beach (1976), a growing number of researchers have provided evidence that this traditional view is highly flawed. Instead, females select desirable partners and initiate sexual interaction by proceptively signaling selected males (Fisher 1992; Givens 1978; Moore 1985; Moore & Butler 1989; Perper 1985; Perper & Weis 1987). Males, in turn, respond to these proceptive signals. Moore (1985; Moore & Butler 1989) has demonstrated that, not only do women use such signaling, but that men are more likely to "approach" women who do. Perper (1985; Perper & Weis 1987) has provided evidence that American women employ a variety of complex strategies to arouse male interest and response. Finally, Jesser (1978) has provided some evidence that males are just as likely to accept direct initiations from women as they are to respond to more-covert strategies, although females tend to believe that men are "turned off" by female sexual assertiveness.

This new line of research raises fundamental questions about the roles of males and females in the formation and maintenance of sexual relationships—for both adolescents and adults. It indicates a need for research that is focused on the dynamics within and the processes of sexual relationships themselves. As just one example, Christopher and Cate (1988) found that, early in a relationship, the level of conflict was positively related to a greater likelihood of intercourse. As the relationship progressed, love and relationship satisfaction eventually became significant predictors of sexual involvement. In the case of adolescence, we need to move beyond "social bookkeeping," counting the number of American teenagers who have premarital sex, to examine what actually happens in their relationships with each other.

*[Adolescent Sexuality; 1998 to 2003* DAVID L. WEIS
[One of the most popular and controversial areas of sex research in the U.S.A. continues to be adolescent sexual behavior. As a general guide, we can suggest there is growing recognition that social context, interpersonal relationships, and physical development all have an influence on whether sexual intercourse occurs, at what age, and with what outcomes or consequences. Susan Newcomer (2002) has provided a useful summary of recent research. She notes that 1. boys tend to begin having intercourse earlier than girls, 2. youth who reach puberty earlier tend to have intercourse earlier, 3. African-American youth tend to have intercourse earlier than either Hispanic or white youth, 4. youth from poor households tend to have intercourse earlier, 5. youth who have intercourse for the first time before the median age are less likely to use protection against disease or pregnancy, 6. girls tend to have male partners for intercourse who are slightly older than the girl (this is true of marriage, as well), and 7. condom use by adolescents has increased in the last decade. She also notes that, while it is popular to blame the media for the sexual adventuring of youth, there are no scientifically sound studies which demonstrate that consumption of sexually explicit media has any effect on sexual behavior. I would like to stress that Newcomer's comments apply only to sexual intercourse specifically.

[Much has been made, in some quarters, of a decline in the percentage of sexually active high school students in recent years (Centers for Disease Control 2002). By 2001, the percentage of high school students who have had sexual intercourse dropped by about 6% to slightly below 50%. The drop was more pronounced for black teens. Still, 55% of 11th graders in a recent study in Toledo, Ohio, reported having had intercourse. One third said they had intercourse with a friend. The rate would have been higher if questions about oral sex had been included (Stepp 2003). A recent poll by *The New York Times* found that 20% of American teens do have sexual intercourse by age 15. Most of these sexually active 12- to 14-year-olds were using contraceptives. About one third of their parents knew they were having intercourse. Data in the report came from the *National Survey of Family Growth*, the *National Longitudinal Survey of Adolescent Health*, and the *National Longitudinal Survey of Youth* (Lewin 2003). So, reports of a possible decrease should be interpreted with caution.

[In fact, this point needs to be considered in the light of two additional findings. One is the evidence that American teens may only be postponing the onset of intercourse (which has mistakenly come to be described as sexual debut), catching up to the levels of the late 1980s by age 21 (CDC 2002). Here, it is worth noting that there have been no published studies documenting any such decline among college students. The other is the fact that this constant focus on sexual intercourse as the only sexual behavior of interest actually serves to distort adolescent sexual development, a point I made two decades ago (Weis 1985). Teens engage in a wide variety of noncoital sexual behaviors before they have intercourse. Moreover, the constant focus on intercourse, to the exclusion of other sexual behaviors, may actually have hidden one of the major trends in adolescent sexuality of the last decade. This has been the tremendous growth of oral sex as a practice in its own right (Paul & Hayes 2002). Thus, the rate of American adolescents engaging in sexual behaviors leading to the orgasm of one or both partners has actually increased in the last 15 years. About one third of 15- to 17-year-olds and two thirds of the 18- to 24-year-olds in a recent Kaiser Foundation study reported they had oral sex (Hoff & Greene 2000). The reality is that there is a major development in adolescent sexual practices that does not involve intercourse.

[Finally, the focus on the percentage of teens having (or not having) intercourse has served to obscure two additional trends of the last decade. Contraceptive behavior increased and pregnancy rates decreased among high school students in the 1990s (Meschke, Bartholomae & Zentall 2000). The U.S.A. now has the lowest teenage pregnancy rate in more than a half century.

[To highlight the political nature of this area, we can point to a recent Heritage Foundation report in June 2003 using Add Health datasets (age 14 to 17), but not citing any prior refereed studies nor reporting any actual statistical analyses. They claimed that teenagers who have sexual intercourse are more likely to report suffering from depression and to attempt suicide than abstinent teens (Rector, Johnson, & Noyes 2003).

[There have been a few other recent indicators with relevance to adolescent sexuality. A 2000 report of a series of national surveys of teenagers, parents, teachers, and school principals by the Kaiser Family Foundation provides impressive evidence that strides have been made in providing American youth a comprehensive sex education in schools. In contrast to 50 years ago, virtually all American public schools now offer some form of sex education. By far, the most common approach is to provide a comprehensive perspective that includes information about contraceptives, sexually transmitted diseases, and basic anatomy and physiology, in addition to recommendations to remain abstinent. Less than one half of the programs provided any information about homosexuality or how to discuss sex with a partner. About one third of principals described their programs as abstinence-only (Hoff & Greene 2000). Even for advocates of comprehensive sex education, I would maintain that this represents important gains since 1970 (when I entered the field). Kirby (2002) has also noted that involvement in education is associated with lower pregnancy rates and lower sexual risk-taking, that sex education programs are not associated with increases in sexual behavior, but are associated with increased contraceptive and condom use.

[One way of reading recent studies is that teens who believe sexual activity is appropriate and acceptable are, in fact, more likely to engage in sexual behavior, particularly if they have opportunities (Gillmore, Archibald, Morrison, Wilsdon, Wells, Hoppe, Naliom, & Murowchick 2002; Whitbeck, Yoder, Hoyt, & Conger 1999). It does appear that about 80% of American youth do now have sexual intercourse by age 19 (Singh & Darroch 1999).

[There have been some important recent developments in the field of sexuality research. We have begun to finally see an expansion of research on teenagers beyond the standard WASP populations (Moore & Chase-Lansdale 2001; O'Sullivan & Meyer-Bahlburg 2003; Raffaelli & Green 2003). There even has been some expansion of the creativity of hypotheses tested and explanations investigated (Levin, Xu, & Bartkowski 2002). Using *National Longitudinal Study of Adolescent Health* data, Levin and his associates found that there are two predictable peaks of coital debut during each year. One is a summer peak, not associated with involvement in a romantic relationship. The other is a holiday peak, occurring in December and associated with involvement in a romantic relationship, especially for girls.

[*The Context of Sexual Relationships and Courtship: Hanging Out, Hooking Up, and Buddy Sex*. In the original edition of the *Encyclopedia*, I asserted that researchers have largely ignored the relationship context surrounding adolescent sexuality and that most adolescent sexual experiences occurred within intimate relationships. At one time, there was a good understanding that adolescent males and females went through a fairly predictable sexual and courtship sequence. Bailey (1989) has summarized this well. Couples met, were attracted, began dating, went steady, and eventually became engaged and were married. At some time in this sequence, they became sexually involved as well. Through the course of the 20th century, the stage where sexual intercourse began started moving to earlier points in the sequence. As late as the 1960s, sexual experimentation tended to take place during the college years. This courtship system can be traced as far back as the 1920s and flourished through the 1950s and 1960s, extending into the 1980s (Bailey 1989). The pattern of going steady or going together (exclusive intimate relationships) seems to have remained popular well into the 1980s. However, questions can and should be raised about the extent to which this system even exists today.

[Nearly two decades ago, Carol Cassell (1984) used the term, "swept away," to describe what she maintained was a chief sexual fantasy (script) for women in America. She argued that young women were socialized to pair sexual excitement with passion, to wrap sexual desire in a cloak of romance. This is the stuff of song, movies, books, and magazines. It is the very core of the entire romance industry. According to Cassell, the swept away script allowed women to deny responsibility for their own sexual decisions and activity. The strategy allowed young women to gain sexual experience in a society that was still uncomfortable with female sexuality. However, it now seems appropriate to question whether the concept of being swept away is still relevant in 2003, and if so, for whom?

[In fact, there has been relatively little research on dating and courtship for decades. Several recent publications call our understanding of this 20th-century concept of courtship into question (Glenn & Marquardt 2001; Hall 2003; Harris 2003; Stepp 2003). Each of these authors indicates that young people today tend to "hang out" in small groups, because "there is nothing to do" (Hall 2003). Quite often, this happens in house parties accompanied by drinking where people "hook up" with whomever. Hooking up is intentionally vague and may be used to refer to kissing, petting, oral sex, or intercourse. One can never be certain about its precise meaning (Glenn & Marquardt 2001; Hall 2003). Few young people consider oral sex to be sex at all (the Bill Clinton standard), and intimate relationships are widely seen as a great responsibility. Apparently, hooking up is seen as easier (Hall 2003).

[Despite the prominence of this hanging out script, most college women today still appear to hold marriage as a major life goal. Women outnumber men on college campuses. In 1997, there were 79 male college students for every 100 female students. Male-female relationships are now either characterized by a high degree of commitment (exclusivity) or very little (nonexclusive friendship). Hooking up is widely seen as a "sex without commitment" interaction. College men rarely ask women for dates. Only about 50% of college women report they have been asked for as many as six dates during their four years of college. Coed dorms are the most common place to meet partners and to hang out. The culture of courtship has largely become the culture of hook ups (Glenn & Marquardt 2001).

[Within this culture, it appears that many young people today may make a distinction between casual sex and relationship sex, and may have both. Casual sex may occur with friends, or with friends from different groups of friends, what Stepp (2003) called "buddy sex." Young women, in particular, now appear to believe that they have every right to enjoy sex in whatever form they choose—à la *Ally McBeal* or *Sex in the City* (Glenn & Marquardt 2001; Stepp 2003; Webb 2002). As a result, much teen sex may no longer be connected to the courtship system, especially since dating implies exclusivity for most young people today. There no longer appears to be any concept of dating around. Dating implies serious involvement.

[In one of the few actual studies of these patterns, Glenn and Marquardt (2001) reported that college women whose parents were divorced were more willing and more likely to hook up, although they were also more eager to marry early. Given that the current generation of adolescents and young adults has grown up against the background of a high divorce rate, and given that the median age of first marriage is now in the late 20s, it makes sense that new forms of male-female relationships would be emerging. Glenn and Marquardt (2001) have raised questions about whether this pattern of hooking up with "buddy sex," a "sex friend," or a "friend with privilege" provides adequate preparation and training for marriage. One could just as easily ask if the traditional courtship script provides adequate training for the realities of contemporary intimate relationships.

[At the same time, I would like to suggest that these informal and unstructured forms of sexual interaction are not as new or unique as one might think. At least as far back as the 1960s, hippies (the Haight-Ashbury scene is just one example) began experimenting with new forms of male-female pair bonding. Libby (1977) described a script for "getting together" as a substitute for the practice of dating. "Getting together" was defined as an unstructured activity that allowed men and women to sexually interact without the formal protocols of dating or the expectations of exclusive intimacy. Rather, sexual interaction might be seen as friendship or mutual pleasure. Thus, such scripts have existed within American culture for some time. In any event, there is great need for more research in this general area. Given the immense changes in sexual practices and intimate relationships among adults in the last century, it only makes sense that adolescent practices will also change. (*End of update by D. L. Weis*)]

## C. Adult Heterosexuality
DAVID L. WEIS

*The National Health and Social Life Survey*

Strangely, there has been considerably more research on the sexual conduct of American adolescents than of adults, and much of the existing research on adults has tended to focus on sexual "problems" such as extramarital sex (ES) and sexual dysfunction (see Section 12 on sex dysfunctions and therapies). There has been little research on the patterns of sexual interactions within nonclinical marital relationships. This is striking, precisely because of the fact that marriage is the most widely accepted setting for sexual relations in the U.S.A. and because more than 90% of Americans do marry. Taken together, the preponderance of research on adolescent sexuality, extramarital sex, and dysfunction indicates the tendency of American sexuality professionals to focus on sexual behaviors that have been defined as social problems, rather than on "normal" sexuality.

In October 1994, a national survey of adult sexual practices was released with great media fanfare (Laumann, Gagnon, Michael, & Michaels 1994). The survey, titled the *National Health and Social Life Survey* (*NHSLS*), randomly sampled 3,432 persons, aged 18 to 50. It was touted as the most comprehensive American sex survey ever, and the first national study of adult sexuality. However, Reiss (1995) has noted that this claim is misleading, as there have been more than a dozen national surveys of a more-limited scope. Given our interest in reviewing the nature of American sexuality research, it is interesting to note that the survey was originally planned and approved as a government-sponsored project. Funding was denied for this project and a similar study of teens (the Udry study) when conservatives in the U.S. Congress objected to the studies. Conservatives argued that the government should not use taxpayer money to study private matters like oral sex—clearly rejecting the significance of the health concerns involved. The researchers found private funding instead. Also interesting is the fact that conservatives hailed the findings when the study was released (Peterson 1994).

There is little doubt that the *NHSLS* is the most comprehensive study of adult sexuality to date, with literally hundreds of variables assessed. Among the key findings are the following:

- Most Americans report that they are satisfied with their sex life—even those who rarely have sex. Among married persons, 87% reported they were satisfied with their sex life.
- For the entire sample, 30% of men and 26% of women have sex two or three times a week; 36% of men and 37% of women have sex a few times a month; and 27% of men and 30% of women have sex a few times a year. Married persons have sex more often than single people, and persons who are cohabiting have sex more often than marrieds.
- Approximately 80% of married women and 65% of married men have never had extramarital sex. The majority of those who are cohabiting also have never "cheated." The group most likely to have extradyadic sex is unmarried men, aged 42 to 51, who have lived with a woman for three years or less (32%).

- There has been a slight increase in the number of lifetime sexual partners, largely because people now have intercourse earlier, marry later, and are more likely to get divorced.
- Among marrieds, 94% had sex only with their spouse in the last year; 75% of cohabiting persons had sex only with their partner in the last year. About 80% of American adults have had either one or no sexual partners in the last year. Only 3% have had five or more partners in the last year. About 50% of men and 30% of women have had five or more partners since age 18.
- Most Americans have a fairly limited sexual "menu" of activities. Roughly 80% of both men and women reported that sexual intercourse is very appealing; only 50% of men and 33% of women find receiving oral sex appealing; 37% of men and 19% of women describe giving oral sex as appealing. About 25% of both men and women have tried anal sex at least once.
- People who already have an active sex life with a current sexual partner are more likely to masturbate. Among married people, 57% of husbands and 37% of wives have masturbated in the last year.
- About 2.8% of men and 1.4% of women identified themselves as homosexual or bisexual. Only 9% of men and 4% of women reported ever having a homosexual experience. These rates are considerably higher in the 12 largest U.S. cities.
- Most heterosexuals are not at risk of contracting AIDS, because they are not part of social networks with high risk.

The *NHSLS* has sparked considerable controversy among sexuality professionals. Questions have been raised, primarily about the legitimacy of the prevalence estimates for such behaviors as number of sexual partners, homosexual experience, and extramarital sex. In general, the *NHSLS* estimates tend to be lower than those found in most prior sex research—including prior national studies (Billy, Tanfer, Grady, & Klepinger 1993). It should be noted that the *NHSLS* estimates are remarkably similar to findings in a series of studies conducted by the National Opinion Research Center using similar national probability samples (Davis & Smith 1994; Greeley et al. 1990; Smith 1990, 1991). These national samples have been carefully constructed to be representative of gender, age, race, education, marital status, size of city of residence, and religion in the U.S.A. The *NHSLS* did obtain a 79% response rate, probably because participants were financially reimbursed. Few prior studies have had comparable response rates, and few have reimbursed participants. Questions about how this had an impact on the results are a legitimate matter for future research.

In a review of the *NHSLS*, Reiss (1995) credits the study for its comprehensiveness, the richness of the data generated, the theoretical nature of the investigation, and the high quality of the sampling techniques. However, he also raises several questions that may influence the validity of the findings. Here, we will focus on a few of the more serious. One concerns the fact that 21% of the respondents were interviewed with someone else present during the interview. As Reiss notes, a person with an intimate partner or a family member present may well have answered questions differently for obvious reasons. For example, only 5% of persons interviewed with another person present reported that they had two or more sexual partners in the last year. In contrast, 17% of those interviewed with no one else present reported two or more partners in the last year. This is a sizable difference, and it raises questions about the validity of responses to many questions in the survey. Similarly, the *NHSLS* asked respondents to report the number of sexual partners they have had since age 18. Most previous studies asked respondents to report their lifetime number of sexual partners. Here, one half of the sample did have sexual relations prior to age 18. This reduced estimates for lifetime number of partners. The *NHSLS* reported a median number of six sexual partners for men and two for women. Reiss notes that these estimates are lower than comparable studies (Billy et al. 1993), and that this reported gender difference cannot possibly be true in the real world.

To this critique, we can add that it is possible that prevalence estimates have been inflated by the volunteer bias of most sex research. There are unexamined questions about the effects of volunteer bias and response rates. Paul Gebhard (1993), a member of the original Kinsey research team, has argued that estimates of lifetime prevalence rates for homosexual behavior have been remarkably similar when adjusted for sampling weaknesses. Gebhard also criticized the NORC and *NHSLS* studies for failing to use trained sex researchers to conduct their interviews, and for their own sampling flaws that overrepresented rural populations. In fairness, it is appropriate to note that several of the volunteer samples overrepresent urban populations, and there is evidence that urban-rural differences in sexual attitudes remain substantial (Weis & Jurich 1985). Finally, although there is a general consensus that persons who agree to participate in sex research are more permissive and more sexually experienced, two recent studies strongly suggest that persons who decline to answer particular items in a sex survey are attempting to hide behavior in which they have engaged (Wiederman 1993; Wiederman, Weis, & Allgeier 1994).

Although these questions will require considerable future research to resolve, it should be acknowledged that the *NHSLS* is a major contribution to the field of sex research in the U.S.A. It is a landmark study with important new information about the sexual practices of the vast and diverse American adult population, and it will set the parameters for questions yet to be explored. Finally, it provides important data on each of the topics we will explore further in this section.

*Sexuality and Single Adults*

Practically every American spends at least a portion of his or her adult life unmarried. At any one point in time, more than 20% of the U.S. population is single, and this percentage has been increasing for several decades (Francoeur 1991; Shostak 1987). The chief reasons for this are the greater tendency to postpone marriage (median age is now in the late 20s), the increasing divorce rate (5 per 1,000 by the 1980s and fairly stable thereafter), and the increasing rate of cohabitation (which tripled since 1960), both as an alternative to marriage and as a form of courtship prior to marriage (Glick 1984; Norton & Moorman 1987; Shostak 1987). Glick (1984) has speculated that the prolongation of formal education, the increasing acceptability of premarital sexuality, the growing independence of women, and the earlier mortality of males may also be factors promoting the growth of singlehood.

Actually, the single adult population contains three groups who may share little in common: Those who have never married, those who have divorced, and those who are widowed. Persons within each group may or may not have chosen to be single, and they may or may not intend to remain single. Also, persons in each group may be living alone, may be living with roommates who are not intimate or sexual partners, or may be cohabiting with an intimate partner. By 1980, it was estimated that close to 2% of the adult U.S. population was cohabiting (Glick & Norton 1977;

Yllo 1978). Of course, some single persons are gay or lesbian, although they are not typically included in estimates of cohabitation, even when they live with their partners.

It should be stressed that the population of single adults is a fluid one. The U.S.A. has high rates of marriage, divorce, and remarriage (Glick 1984; Norton & Moorman 1987). Most of those who are classified as having never married at any one point will eventually marry. This is especially true for the growing group who have remained unmarried well past the age of 20. Approximately three quarters of women who get divorced, and more men, eventually remarry (Glick 1984; Norton & Moorman 1987). Thus, the composition of the single population is always shifting as some marry and others divorce or are widowed. We are not aware of any research examining the impact of this shifting character on the sexual lifestyles of single persons. Some singles become involved in intimate relationships that lead to cohabitation or marriage, although we know little about whether these processes are similar to adolescent courtship. For those singles who are not involved in an ongoing intimate relationship, it is possible that finding sexual partners can be problematic.

It is popularly believed that being single in adulthood has become more acceptable in the United States today. There is, however, some evidence that married couples continue to associate primarily with other couples. Certainly, it is more acceptable to be sexually active while single today. Singles have greater social and sexual freedom than ever before to pursue a variety of lifestyles. In fact, the labeling of a category of "single adults" may serve to obscure the fact that the range of sexual and intimate lifestyle options is just as wide as for married persons.

Despite the large number of single adults in the U.S., there has been virtually no research on the sexual practices or attitudes of these groups. The *NHSLS* (Laumann et al. 1994) did distinguish between "single" and cohabiting respondents, an important distinction. As we discussed earlier, the *NHSLS* did find that "single" persons had sex less frequently than married persons, and that cohabiting persons had sex more often than married persons.

[*Cohabitation* ROBERT T. FRANCOEUR
[*Update 2003*: America is still a society devoted to marriage, with 55.4 million married couples accounting for 52% of the households. But the 1990 and 2000 censuses show that the number of unmarried couples rose from 3.2 million in 1990 to 5.5 million in 2000, a very significant 72% increase. The change clearly indicates continuing changes in mores and more-fluid living arrangements. The change is also alarming to conservatives and President Bush, who want to amend the tax laws that penalize married couples, and also promote welfare rules they believe will encourage marriage and family unity.

[The census of 2000 was the first to ask questions about same-sex households, so the same-sex statistics are difficult to interpret. Gay activists claimed their numbers were "dramatically underestimates," but this could be because of differences in the 1990 and 2000 censuses, and the reluctance of gays to admit their household status on the first such census to ask about same-sex households. Same-sex couples tend to gravitate to the larger cities, especially if they live in the west or midwest.

- California is home to one in eight of the nation's unmarried partners. Alaska is second, with 12%, and Maine, Vermont, and Nevada third, with 11% (see Tables 12 and 13).
- California also has 16% of the nation's same-sex couples, 54% of which are male. Utah had the fewest same-sex couples, 4%, followed by Alabama at 5%.

• Opposite-sex unmarried couples are 12 years younger than their married counterparts, perhaps because Americans are marrying later in life.

• The average age of unmarried-partner households was 37 years for men and 35 for women. Husbands averaged 49 years and wives 47 years. Single-sex couples were mostly in their 40s (Marquis 2003). (*End of update by R. T. Francoeur*)]

*The Never Married.* We know of no research that has focused on the population of never-married adults who are not cohabiting. Of course, this group does include persons in their early 20s who have yet to marry. A portion of that group is included in many of the studies of premarital sexuality, although that group is not isolated for separate analysis. There is virtually no scientific information on how never-married persons find or meet sexual partners, establish sexual encounters, or maintain sexual relationships.

### Table 12

**Unmarried-Couple Households by State, as a Percentage of All Couple Households**

| Percent | States |
|---------|--------|
| 9.1% | National Average |
| Over 11% | Alaska, Maine, New Hampshire, New Mexico, Nevada, Vermont, and Washington, DC |
| 9.1% to 11.0% | Arizona, California, Colorado, Delaware, Hawaii, Louisiana, Maryland, New York, Oregon, Washington |
| 8.0% to 5.2% | Georgia, Illinois, Iowa, Minnesota, Mississippi, Missouri, Montana, New Jersey, North Carolina, Pennsylvania, South Carolina, South Dakota, Virginia, West Virginia, Wyoming |
| 5.2% to 8.0% | Alabama, Arkansas, Connecticut, Florida, Idaho, Indiana, Kansas, Kentucky, Massachusetts, Michigan, Nebraska, North Dakota, Ohio, Oklahoma, Rhode Island, Tennessee, Texas, Utah, Wisconsin |

*Source*: U.S. Census Bureau

### Table 13

**Unmarried-Couple Households by Race and Ethnicity, as a Percentage of All Couple Households**

| | Same-Sex Partners | Opposite-Sex Partners | Total Unmarried Couples |
|---|---|---|---|
| Total | 1.0% | 8.1% | 9.1% |
| **Race** | | | |
| White | 0.9 | 7.3 | 8.2 |
| Black or African-American | 1.4 | 15.5 | 16.9 |
| American Indian/Alaskan Native | 1.3 | 16.0 | 17.4 |
| Asian alone | 0.7 | 4.0 | 4.7 |
| Hawaiian/Other Pacific Islander | 1.4 | 10.8 | 12.3 |
| Some other race | 1.2 | 12.4 | 13.6 |
| Two or more races | 1.6 | 12.1 | 13.7 |
| **Ethnicity** | | | |
| Hispanic or Latino (of any race) | 1.3 | 10.9 | 12.2 |
| Non-Hispanic white | 0.9 | 7.2 | 8.1 |

*Source*: U.S. Census Bureau. Percentages may not add up to 100% because of rounding.

[*Marriage and Child Support Efforts. Update 2003*: Early in 2003, as part of his "faith-based initiative," President Bush used an executive order to bypass a reluctant Congress and authorize $2.2 million in grants to 12 states and a variety of religious, nonprofit, and tribal organizations to advance the nation's child support enforcement system and promote marriage. Bush's assurance that no government money "will be used to directly support inherently religious activities" has not satisfied skeptics, who are concerned some of the grants may violate the constitutional separation of church and state.

[According to the commissioner of the Office of Child Support Enforcement, "These are grants to government and community organizations, including faith-based organizations, that want to try interesting new program approaches to improve the child support program and financial well being of children," Heller said. A spokesperson for one grant recipient described her group as "a nonprofit organization of inter-religious clergy, mental health professionals and individuals dedicated to reducing the divorce rate and birth to unmarried parents through education." The group, which advocates marriage, is not a religious organization, but it does train clergy and counselors to help engaged and wedded couples. "People go to churches. Seventy-five percent of people who get married get married at churches so that's where our customers are." Another grant to an agency in Alabama was aimed at strengthening marriage, by helping poor, ethnically diverse single parents learn marital skills, improve their employment prospects, and increase child support payments (McDonough 2003). (*End of update by R. T. Francoeur*)]

*Divorced (Postmarital Sex)*. Divorce has increased in the U.S.A. dramatically throughout the 20th century (Berscheid 1983). The rate has leveled since 1980 (*Current Population Reports* 1985; Glick 1984; Norton & Moorman 1987; Shostak 1987). Of the roughly 40% of the American population that gets divorced, about 70% eventually remarry, often within a few years (Glick 1984; Norton & Moorman 1987).

Again, there has been little research on this group. It appears that about 80% of women, and nearly all men, remain sexually active following a divorce (Gebhard 1968; Hunt 1974). Most persons have sex with a new partner within the first year following a divorce (Hunt 1974). In the 1970s, Hunt (1974) reported that divorced women averaged four sexual partners a year, and had a higher frequency of orgasm in their postmarital sex than they had in their marriage. Men averaged nearly eight partners a year.

Again, there has been little research on the process by which divorced persons form or maintain sexual relationships. However, it is fair to suggest that, as the title of an American novel and corresponding movie implies, most divorced persons find that they must "start over." After a period of marriage, they find themselves in the position of dating and courting again. Some have anecdotally reported that they find this anxiety-provoking, whereas others find it exhilarating.

*Widowed*. This process of "starting over" may be relevant to those persons who are widowed as well. Our review of the research literature identified only one study of the sexual practices of widowed persons. Nearly three decades ago, Gebhard (1968) reported that widowed persons were less likely to have sexual experiences than divorced persons. Francoeur (1991) has suggested that this may be in part because of a sense of loyalty to the former spouse or to perceived and real pressure from kin members.

### Marital Sex

By far, the most common adult sexual lifestyle in the U.S.A. is legal marriage, and marriage is the context for the overwhelming majority of sexual experiences in the country. In fact, marriage is the only context in which sexuality is universally approved. Despite this, researchers have investigated marital sexuality less than nonmarital forms of sexual expression. Greenblat (1983) has suggested that sex within marriage is more likely to be the object of jokes than of scientific investigation. Strong and DeVault (1994) report that only nine of 553 articles on sexuality that appeared in scholarly journals between 1987 and 1992 were devoted to marital sexuality.

This pattern of research is somewhat odd in light of the widespread belief that effective sexual functioning is indispensable to a good marriage (Frank & Anderson 1979). In this regard, it is striking that much of the research conducted on couples has utilized clients in sex therapy. Here we review works on nonclinical samples.

*Sexual Frequency and Practices.* Most of the research on sexual relations within marriage has assessed the frequency of sexual relations. Many of these studies have also examined how that frequency is related to marital satisfaction. Americans seem to be fascinated with comparing their own frequency to other couples. Until recently, this research was based on volunteer samples, which typically were also quite small.

Perhaps the first sex survey ever conducted in the U.S.A. was done by Clelia Duel Mosher (1980), who investigated the sexual practices and attitudes of 45 women between 1890 and 1920. Most of these women reported that they found sex to be pleasurable and believed that it was "necessary" for both men and women. The women who were interviewed before 1900 were less likely to describe sex as important or enjoyable, and they were less likely to associate sex with the expression of love. The Mosher survey documents the first signs of a shift to a post-Victorian culture.

In a study of more than a thousand men and women, Dickinson and Bean (1932) reported that sexual dissatisfaction was more important in explaining marital difficulties than disputes over work, money, and children. Davis (1929) drew similar conclusions in her study of 2,200 women. Sexual satisfaction within marriage had clearly become a norm in the U.S.A. by the early 20th century. Somewhat later, Hamilton (1948) interviewed 100 married men and women and concluded that an unsatisfactory sex life is the principal cause of marital dysfunction. Without addressing the validity of that particular claim, the Hamilton data do demonstrate that, in the small sample surveyed in the 1930s and 1940s, sex was considered to be an important part of a marriage.

The Kinsey group (1953) reported that married couples in the 1940s had sex an average of two times a week in the early years of marriage, declining to about once a week after ten years of marriage. By comparing those born before 1900 and those born after 1900, they found that the frequency of marital coitus had remained the same. However, virtually every other aspect of marital sex had changed. Couples born after 1900 engaged in more and longer foreplay, used more coital positions, were more likely to have oral sex, were more likely to use French (deep) kissing and manual caressing of genitals, and had sex more often naked.

More-recent studies have tended to fit two patterns. Small samples with volunteers have found a general average of three to four times a week in early marriage with a decline to twice a week in later years. However, studies with national samples have tended to get lower figures more like Kinsey's (Bell & Bell 1972; Blumstein & Schwartz 1983; Call, Sprecher, & Schwartz 1995; Hite 1976, 1983; Hunt 1974; Sarrel & Sarrel 1980; Tavris & Sadd 1974; Trussell & Westoff 1980; Udry 1980; Westoff 1974). Interestingly, married women tend to report lower frequencies than married men (Call et al. 1996).

A few researchers have asked respondents to report their ideal or preferred frequency. Hite (1976) found that one third of married women would like to have sex at least daily, another third wanted it two to five times a week, and a final third less often.

*1. Changes Throughout Marriage.* The evidence of a decrease over time or length of marriage is strong and consistent (Blumstein & Schwartz 1983; Edwards & Booth 1976; Greeley 1991; Hunt 1974; Kinsey et al. 1953; Michael et al. 1994; Trussell & Westoff 1980; Westoff 1980). Longitudinal studies of the same couples over time have also documented this pattern (James 1981; Udry 1980), as have retrospective studies of couples looking back over the course of their marriage (Greenblat 1983).

In a national study of the 1988 *National Survey of Families and Households* (Call et al. 1995), frequency decreases over the length of marriage were correlated with biological aging, diminished health, and habituation. In a multivariate analysis, age was most strongly related to frequency, followed by marital happiness, and factors that reduce the opportunity for sex (such as pregnancy and small children). Couples who had not cohabited prior to marriage and who were still in their first marriage had less-frequent sex than cohabiters, married persons who had cohabited prior to marriage, and those who were in their second or later marriage.

These findings are largely consistent with prior research. Decreasing frequency of marital sex has been found to relate to age-related reductions in the biological capacity for sex, including declines in male motivation and physical ability, declines in women's testosterone levels, and increases in illness (Greenblat 1983; Hengeveld 1991; James 1983; Udry, Deven, & Coleman 1982). Negative social attitudes about sex and the elderly may also lead some to believe that their interest and capacity should decline (Masters & Johnson 1970; Riportella-Muller 1989). However, these aging factors do not explain the decline in frequency that occurs within the first several years of marriage (Jasso 1985; Kahn & Udry 1986). James (1981) found that the coital rate dropped by one half during the first year of marriage. Some have suggested that there is a honeymoon effect early in the marriage. As the honeymoon period ends, habituation occurs and frequency declines (Blumstein & Schwartz 1983; Doddridge, Schumm, & Berger 1987). Habituation may be seen as a decreased interest in sex that occurs with the increased accessibility of a regular sexual partner and the routine predictability of behavior with that partner over time (Call et al. 1995).

Other reasons that have been cited as influencing a decrease in frequency include fatigue, work demands, childcare, and management of complex schedules (Michael et al. 1994).

*2. Effects of Children.* A few comments on the effects of children are worth special note. There is some evidence that sexual frequency declines by the third trimester of pregnancy—prior to the actual birth of a child (Kumar, Brant, & Robson 1981). The birth of a child introduces parental roles into the marital relationship. The child increases fatigue, reduces time alone together for the couple, and decreases time in situations that are conducive to sexual encounters (Blumstein & Schwartz 1983; Doddridge et al. 1987; Greenblat 1983).

*3. Association with Sexual and Marital Satisfaction.* A majority of Americans report that they are satisfied with their marital sex life (Hunt 1974; Lauman et al. 1994). In general, researchers have not found frequency to be related to sexual or marital satisfaction (Blumstein & Schwartz 1983; Frank, Anderson, & Rubinstein 1978). However, there is evidence that the congruence between ideal and actual frequency is related (Frank & Anderson 1979). There is some evidence that sexual problems are likely to occur fairly early in a marriage (Brayshaw 1962; Murphy et al. 1980).

Some studies have found social factors associated with relationship satisfaction. Rainwater (1964) found, in a study of couples in poverty in four different cultures, that lower-class couples were more likely to have highly gender-segregated role relationships (traditional gender roles); they were less likely to have close sexual relationships, and the wife was not likely to view sex with her husband as gratifying.

Several studies have found that sexual satisfaction is related to both sexual and nonsexual aspects of the marriage. The Kinsey group (1953) found that divorce was related to decreases in the wife's orgasm rate. Hunt (1974) reported a strong correlation between marital closeness and sexual satisfaction. He found that the most important predictor was the extent to which couples share similar sexual desire. Thornton (1977) found that couples who spend more time having sex than they do fighting tend to have happier marriages. Sarrel and Sarrel (1980) found that couples who talk with each other about sex often, who rate their communication about sex as good, where the wife likes oral sex, and where the man believes the women's movement has been good for women tend to have more satisfying sexual relationships.

Hite (1976) asked women to identify what aspect of their marital sex gave them the greatest satisfaction. Responses given by 20% or more included closeness, orgasm, coitus, and foreplay. In response to what they liked least, more than 10% said oral or anal sex, lack of orgasm, the "messiness" following sex, excessive or rough foreplay, and the routine nature of their activities.

In the *Redbook* magazine surveys (Tavris & Sadd 1975; Tavris 1978), marital satisfaction did not decline with length of marriage or age. The majority reported enjoying oral sex. Most respondents believed that good communication is an important ingredient of marital and sexual happiness. The most common complaint was that they had sex too infrequently. For women, religiosity was related to a happier sex life and marital satisfaction.

In an unusual study of 100 mostly white and well-educated couples who were happily married (selected because none had ever had extramarital sex or been in therapy), Frank and Anderson (1979) found that 85% described themselves as sexually satisfied. One half of the wives reported they had difficulty becoming aroused or reaching orgasm. Roughly 10% of the husbands reported they had experienced erectile difficulties. One third of the couples expressed complaints about such things as anxiety, too little foreplay, and low sexual desire. There was no correlation between sexual dysfunctions and marital satisfaction, but complaints by the wife were associated with reduced marital happiness.

*4. Unexplored Issues.* This review of research on marital sexuality serves to confirm the narrow range of the questions researchers have investigated. We know little about the dynamics of sexual relationships in marriage—about the ways couples interact sexually, about how they transact or negotiate sexual encounters, or about how they initiate and terminate encounters. Little is known about how sexuality in marriage is affected by power dynamics between the couple. There has been little study of sexual coercion in marriage. Perhaps it is time to end the focus on counting episodes and begin to examine what happens within marital sexual relationships.

*Extramarital Sexual Relationships.* Researchers have been studying extramarital sex for decades, although the range of the questions they have examined has been fairly narrow. (For more-thorough reviews of extramarital sex research and nonexclusive lifestyles, see Macklin 1980; Thompson 1983; Weis 1983.)

*1. Extramarital Sex Attitudes.* One focus of concern has been the degree of normative consensus reflected by extramarital sex attitudes. A series of national surveys indicate that extramarital sex has consistently been disapproved by 75% to 85% of the adult American population (Glenn & Weaver 1979; Greeley, Michael, & Smith 1990; Reiss, Anderson, & Sponaugle 1980; Weis & Jurich 1985). Weis and Jurich (1985) found that nearly one third of residents in the 12 largest cities found extramarital sex acceptable, the only locations in the U.S.A. where as many as 20% approved. In small towns and rural areas, fewer than 10% approved. The norm of sexual exclusivity within marriage is so widespread in American culture that few question it.

Approval of extramarital sex has been found to be related to 1. being male, 2. young age, 3. being nonwhite, 4. living in a large city, 5. high levels of education, 6. low religiosity, and 7. being unmarried (Glenn & Weaver 1979; Reiss et al. 1980; Weis & Jurich 1985; Weis & Slosnerick 1981). Although a number of researchers have reported that approval of extramarital sex is related to lower levels of marital happiness, Weis and Jurich (1985) found that marital happiness was less strongly related to extramarital sex attitudes than several of these other variables.

*2. Extramarital Sex Incidence/Prevalence.* A second major concern of researchers has been the attempt to establish estimates of the prevalence and/or incidence of extramarital sexual behavior. Generally, this has taken the form of asking respondents to indicate whether or not they have ever had extramarital sex. Authors have regularly claimed that roughly one half of married persons in the U.S.A. have had at least one extramarital sex experience, citing the Kinsey research (1948, 1953) as the basis for this claim. Although the point is often ignored, the Kinsey team actually found that 33% of husbands and 26% of wives reported having extramarital sex. Because of suspicions of underreporting, they raised the estimate for male—but not female—extramarital sex to 50%. Several researchers have reported that the figures for husbands have remained "fairly stable" since then, but that the rate for wives has increased to approximately that of husbands (Blumstein & Schwartz 1983; Hunt 1974; Levin 1975). Researchers have reported lifetime prevalence rates from as low as 20% (Johnson 1970) to nearly 75% (Hite 1981).

Several recent studies by the National Opinion Research Center (NORC) (Smith 1990, 1991; Greeley et al. 1990) have found that only 2% to 3% of American married men and women have extramarital sex each year. Further, they reported that 65% of wives and 30% of husbands have the same number of lifetime sexual partners as spouses. According to these researchers, the increases in premarital sex and cohabitation, the rising rate of divorce, and the later age at first marriage that have characterized the last 40 years have resulted in less sexual exclusivity among the unmarried, but no such trend has occurred among married persons in the U.S.A. The Greeley group concluded that Americans are overwhelmingly "monogamous" [sic] and that rates of extramarital sex have been overestimated by previous researchers. *The National Health and Social Life Survey* (Laumann et al. 1994), also conducted by the NORC, found that only 35% of men and 20% of women reported ever having extramarital sex, and 94% had sex only with their spouse in the last year.

As we have already discussed, making comparisons between the results of the NORC national probability samples and previous studies is most difficult. Most previous studies have reported lifetime prevalence rates. The NORC studies have generally reported annual incidence rates. It seems likely that the conditions surrounding the collection of data and the greater representation of rural respondents in the NORC studies led to low estimates. On the other hand, the volunteer nature of most previous studies and their greater inclusion of urban respondents may well have led to high estimates. For the time being, we must conclude that questions about the incidence and prevalence of extramarital sex in the U.S.A. remain largely unanswered.

*3. Marital Happiness.* The third major focus of extramarital sex research has been the attempt to demonstrate an association between extramarital sexual behavior and marital happiness/satisfaction. By far, this has been the most frequently tested hypothesis. As a consequence, there has been little research exploring the circumstances or conditions surrounding extramarital sexual behavior itself or testing alternative hypotheses. A number of researchers have found that extramarital sexual behavior is significantly related to lower levels of marital happiness (Bell et al. 1975; Edwards & Booth 1976; Glass & Wright 1977, 1985; Prins, Buunk, & Van Yperen 1993; Saunders & Edwards 1984). Lower marital happiness has also been found to be related to extramarital sex attitudes (Reiss et al. 1980; Weis & Jurich 1985).

However, the association may not be as strong as these findings imply. The research by Glass and Wright (1977, 1985) suggests that the actual association between extramarital sex and marital happiness may be quite complex. In their earlier study, Glass and Wright (1977) found that husbands who had extramarital sex in the early years of marriage did have lower marital satisfaction. However, there were no differences in marital satisfaction between husbands who had never had extramarital sex and those who began extramarital sex later in their marriages. Interestingly, exactly the reverse was true for wives. There were no differences in marital satisfaction between wives who had never had extramarital sex and those who began it early in their marriages. Yet, wives who began their extramarital sex experiences later in marriage did have significantly lower marital satisfaction. In their later study, Glass and Wright (1985) found that extramarital sex was related to lower marital happiness only for wives. They concluded that male extramarital sex is likely to be more strongly associated with individual factors, rather than marital issues.

The Glass and Wright studies represent a level of complexity that has rarely been seen in extramarital sex research. Few studies have examined the possibility that marital happiness might relate to different types of extramarital sex experiences. As just one example, we can take the case of consensual extramarital sex. In one of the few comparisons of couples who had made an agreement to include extramarital sex in their marriage with couples who did not have this agreement and had a sexually exclusive relationship, there were no significant differences in marital stability, marital happiness, or level of jealousy (Rubin & Adams 1986). Similarly, Gilmartin (1978) found no differences in marital happiness between a group of couples who participated in swinging and a control group of nonswinging couples.

Moreover, Albert Ellis (1969) has made the obvious point, substantiated by all the studies cited here, that some people who have extramarital sex also report high marital satisfaction. In fact, although the two variables have been consistently found to be significantly related, the proportion of extramarital sex variance explained by marital quality variables has tended to be rather small. This may be in part because of the tendency to dichotomize extramarital sex into "ever versus never" categories, thus ignoring the diversity of extramarital sex types. This treatment of extramarital sex as a simplistic construct that uniformly reflects poor marital dynamics may reduce our ability to establish better explanations of extramarital sex. For example, Weis and Jurich (1985) did report that extramarital sex attitudes and marital happiness were significantly related in a series of national probability samples, but they also found that marital happiness was more weakly related to extramarital sex attitudes than several background variables.

*4. Exploring the Diversity of Extramarital Sex Experience.* This failure to recognize the diversity of extramarital sexual experience may be the single greatest obstacle to the development of sound research and theory. Extramarital sex experiences are, in fact, a class of relationship types, every bit as complex as other relationship forms. With few exceptions, American researchers have failed to recognize the historical and cross-cultural evidence that male and female extramarital sexual behavior is universal, despite the strong normative traditions and sanctions against it. They have also largely ignored the cross-cultural evidence that amply demonstrates a wide variety of extramarital sex patterns and normative responses to it (Buss 1994; Fisher 1992; Ford & Beach 1951; Frayser 1985; Murdock 1949).

*5. Specific Aspects of Extramarital Sex.* Ultimately, a full understanding of extramarital sex will require more-thorough investigation of the myriad ways in which extramarital sexual experiences vary. Several factors require additional research. These include:

- *Specific Sexual Behaviors Involved.* Extramarital sex can range from flirting, kissing, and petting to intercourse (Glass & Wright 1985; Hurlbert 1992; Kinsey et al. 1948, 1953).
- *Specific Relationship Behaviors Involved.* Extramarital sexual relationships vary from those in which sexual interaction is nearly the sum total of the relationship to those where sexuality is a minimal component (Hurlbert 1992; Richardson 1985; Thompson 1983, 1984).
- *Number of Extramarital Sex Partners.* In general, the scant evidence available suggests that most Americans have a small number of extramarital sex partners (Bell et al. 1975; Greeley et al. 1990; Kinsey et al. 1953; Pietropinto & Simenauer 1977).
- *Length of Extramarital Sex Relationship.* It appears that most, but certainly not all, extramarital sexual relationships are of relatively short duration and entail less than ten actual sexual encounters, with some evidence that females tend to be involved for longer periods (Bell et al. 1975; Gagnon 1977; Hall 1987; Hunt 1974; Hurlbert 1992; Kinsey et al. 1953; Pietropinto & Simenauer 1977).
- *Level of Involvement.* Extramarital sex ranges from single sexual encounters in which partners know little of each other to highly intimate affairs with characteristics that are quite similar to intimate marriages.
- *Consensual Versus Secretive.* Although most extramarital sex is secretive or clandestine (Gagnon 1977; Hunt 1974), it is important to recognize that some spouses do

know about their partner's extramarital sex activities and expressly agree to permit extramarital sex (see section below on alternatives to traditional marriage) (Blumstein & Schwartz 1983; Thompson 1983; Weis 1983).

- *Motives and Meanings.* There are dozens of motives for extramarital sex. Weis and Slosnerick (1981) demonstrated that a distinction between individual motives (such as adventure, variety, romance, or pleasure) and marital motives (such as revenge against a spouse, marital hostility, marital sex problems, or as an alternative marriage form) was useful in explaining differences in extramarital sex attitudes.
- *Bisexual/Homosexual.* Extramarital sex has usually been assumed to be heterosexual, but there is evidence that at least some extramarital sex is homosexual (D. Dixon 1985; J. K. Dixon 1984).

*6. Gender Issues.* Before discussing theoretical factors for extramarital sex, we want to note that the available evidence strongly suggests that researchers explore the possibility of separate predictive models for men and women. There is evidence that men are more likely to have extramarital sex than women and to have more numerous extramarital sexual encounters (Buss 1994; Glass & Wright 1985), more likely to report extramarital sexual relationships with limited involvement (Glass & Wright 1985; Spanier & Margolis 1983), and tend to have more partners (Buss 1994; Thompson 1983). Men and women may also experience different outcomes. There is some evidence that women are more likely to report experiencing guilt as a result of extramarital sex (Spanier & Margolis 1983). It is possible that women, as a group, are more likely to be motivated to engage in extramarital sexual activities by marital factors and may be more likely to seek intimacy as a primary goal in extramarital sex (Reibstein & Richards 1993). Several studies have found that marital variables are more strongly related to extramarital sex for women than for men (Glass & Wright 1985; Saunders & Edwards 1984). All of these findings indicate that the extramarital sex experiences of men and women may differ substantially.

*7. Building Theoretical Models.* Edwards and Booth (1976) have argued that the context of marital interaction is more important than background factors in explaining the process leading to extramarital sexual involvement. However, Weis and Slosnerick (1981) have maintained that individuals enter marriage with internalized scripts for sex, love, and marriage. Ultimately, the scripts of married persons stem from an interaction of marital dynamics and background factors. Each of these, in turn, is likely to be influenced by one's position within the social structure.

As just noted, there is evidence of a significant correlation between marital happiness and both dichotomous measures of extramarital sex experience and extramarital sex attitudes, although this association has not always been a strong or robust one. In a study of extramarital sex attitudes (approval), Weis and Slosnerick (1981) isolated two orthogonal factors of justifications for extramarital sex. One was a set of motivations for extramarital sex that mentioned aspects of the marital relationship. The other was a set of individual motives for extramarital sex. Both factors were significantly related to approval of extramarital sex, but the individual motivations were more strongly related than the marital motivations.

These findings suggest two possible paths for future research that seeks to elaborate the complex nature of the association between extramarital sex and marital satisfaction. One is to contrast the types of extramarital sexual experiences that persons with individual versus marital motivations tend to have and to explore how these relate to marital satisfaction and, perhaps, to outcomes of extramarital sexual relationships. The other is to separate happily and unhappily married persons and to investigate the types of extramarital sex experiences and outcomes for each group. It seems reasonable to expect that the two groups might well pursue different kinds of extramarital sexual experiences under different circumstances, with different outcomes.

A second theoretical factor may be background variables. A number of researchers have reported that premarital sexual attitudes and behavior are related to extramarital sexual attitudes and behavior, several arguing that it is the best predictor of extramarital sexual involvement (Bukstel et al. 1978; Christensen 1962, 1973; Glenn & Weaver 1979; Medora & Burton 1981; Reiss et al. 1980; Singh et al. 1976; Thompson 1983; Weis & Jurich 1985; Weis & Slosnerick 1981). Extramarital sex variables have been found to correlate with premarital sexual permissiveness, number of premarital sexual partners, and early premarital sexual experience (low age). Weis and Jurich (1985) found premarital sexual permissiveness was the strongest and most consistent predictor of extramarital sex attitudes in a series of regression analyses with national probability samples throughout the 1970s.

Several questions remain to be explored. Do these findings suggest that there is something particular about premarital sexual interactions with partners that is associated with extramarital sex, or are measures of premarital sex merely indicative of a broader interest in and history of sexual pleasure in various forms? Which of these will prove to be more useful in explaining various types of extramarital sex activities? For example, Joan Dixon (1984) found that female swingers tend to have early and continuing histories of heterosexual involvement, but that they also tend to have early and continuing histories of masturbation and high current sexual frequencies with partners. Gilmartin (1978) also found that swingers tend to have early heterosexual experiences and high sexual frequencies with their spouses. One might conceivably argue that such persons like sex, and extramarital sex is an extension of a broader orientation to pleasure.

A third factor has been suggested by Cazenave (1979), who has criticized work in the area of alternative lifestyles for its emphasis on ideological preference and its failure to explore how structural variables (such as age, gender, and race) may impose external constraints. In fact, there is evidence that extramarital sexual behavior and extramarital sexual permissiveness (attitudes) are related to 1. young age, 2. being nonwhite, 3. low education for behavior and high education for attitudes, 4. low religiosity, and 5. residence in a large city (Fisher 1992; Greeley et al. 1990; Smith 1990, 1991). Several of these associations may, in fact, be quite complex. For example, the Kinsey group (1948, 1953) found that blue-collar males tend to have extramarital sex in their 20s and their behavior diminishes by their 40s. White-collar males with college educations tended to have little extramarital sex in their 20s. This rate gradually increased to an average of once a week by age 50. In contrast, female extramarital sex peaked in the late 30s and early 40s. Finally, there is a need for research that explores the role of such American social trends as the increasing age at first marriage, the growing divorce rate, the unbalanced gender ratio, and greater mobility and travel in extramarital sexual behavior.

*8. Unexplored Issues.* There has been little research to this point on the process of extramarital sexual relationships. For example, there has been little investigation of how opportunities for extramarital sexual involvement occur in a culture with strong prohibitions against extramarital sex.

Cross-sex friendships and interactions have been frequently cited as creating the opportunity for extramarital sex (Johnson 1970; Saunders & Edwards 1984; Weis & Slosnerick 1981), although this has not been empirically tested. The matter is somewhat complicated by the evidence that friendships outside of marriage are associated with higher levels of marital satisfaction (Weis & Slosnerick 1981). Wellman (1985, 1992) has documented how the friendship networks of men have shifted from public spaces (bars, cafés, and clubs) to private homes. This has led to a narrowing of the concept of friendship to emotional support and companionship. Husbands' and wives' networks are now both based in private, domestic space, and many wives actively maintain their husbands' ties to friends and kin. Men get much of their emotional support from women, as well as men, and women get almost all of their support from women. Wellman argues that marriage may impose constraints on men's ability to spend time and be intimate with other men or women. Whether this is related to extramarital sex remains to be explored.

Similarly, little is known about the outcomes of extramarital sexual involvement. Generally, it is assumed that extramarital sexual relationships are short in duration, exploitive in character, and tragic in outcome. For example, it is generally assumed that extramarital sex and cross-sex friendships will be a source of jealousy in a marriage. Although there is a growing body of evidence about jealousy, little research has specifically investigated jealousy in the context of extramarital sex (Bringle 1991; Bringle & Boebinger 1990; Buunk 1981, 1982; Denfeld 1974; Jenks 1985).

*Alternatives to Traditional Marriage.* Although most extramarital sex is secretive, some couples do pursue lifestyles that permit extramarital sex (Blumstein & Schwartz 1983; Thompson 1983; Weis 1983). There is some evidence that consensual extramarital sex is unrelated to marital satisfaction (Gilmartin 1978; Ramey 1976; Rubin & Adams 1986; Wachowiak & Bragg 1980), suggesting there might be different outcomes for the consensual and nonconsensual forms of extramarital sex.

A number of models for consensual extramarital sex have been proposed, particularly during the 1970s. These include swinging (recreational and shared extramarital sex) (Bartell 1971; Gilmartin 1978; Jenks 1985), comarital sex (Smith & Smith 1974), open marriage (O'Neill & O'Neill 1972), intimate friendship networks (extramarital sex within a context of friendship) (Francoeur & Francoeur 1974; Ramey 1976), and group marriage (Constantine & Constantine 1973; Rimmer 1966). Certainly, there are differences among these various nonexclusive lifestyles. We do not have the space to review fully the distinctions among them here (see Libby & Whitehurst 1977; Weis 1983; see also next section on Polyamory and Alternative Non-Monogamy). What unites them for the discussion here is that they all represent a consensual agreement to allow multilateral sexual involvement. As such, extramarital sex is assigned a different set of meanings from betrayal.

Consensual agreements can vary in terms of the degree of sexual involvement desired, the degree of intimate involvement desired, the degree of openness with the spouse, and the amount of time spent with the extramarital sex partner (Sprenkle & Weis 1978). Buunk (1980) studied the strategies couples employ in establishing ground rules for sexually open marriages. The five most common were: 1. primary value placed on maintaining the marriage, 2. limiting the intensity of extramarital sexual involvements, 3. keeping the spouse fully informed of extramarital sexual relationships, 4. approving extramarital sex only if it involves mate

exchange, and 5. tolerating extramarital sex if it is invisible to the spouse. It would be useful to see research on the association between the types of strategies employed and outcomes of extramarital sex.

Interestingly, husbands tend to initiate swinging (Bartell 1971; Weis 1983). There is some evidence that most couples swing for a few years, rather than pursuing it for a lifetime (Weis 1983). Dropouts from swinging report problems with jealousy, guilt, emotional attachment, and perceived threat to the marriage (Denfeld 1974). As far as we know, there have been no studies comparing dropouts and those who enjoy and continue swinging.

The Constantine study (1973) is virtually the only source of data on group marriage in contemporary America. They report that the typical relationship includes four adults. Most enter a group with their spouses, and if the group dissolves, most of the original pair bonds survive. In fact, the original pair bonds retain some primacy after the formation of the group, and this may be a factor working against the success of the group. Jealousy between male partners appears to be a common problem.

Studies of marital models that permit extramarital sex have tended to employ small, volunteer samples with no control or contrast groups for comparison. There is no basis for a firm estimate of the incidence or prevalence of such alternative lifestyles, although Blumstein and Schwartz (1983) suggested that as many as one of seven marriages in the U.S.A. may have some agreement allowing extramarital sex. Despite the vast attention given to these alternative lifestyles in the 1970s, and despite the more recent claims that Americans are "returning to traditional models of monogamous marriage," there is no scientific basis for concluding that these patterns increased in popularity earlier or that they have become less common in the 1980s and 1990s.

*[Polyamory and Alternative Non-Monogamy*

JAMES R. FLECKENSTEIN

[*Update 2003*: The term "polyamory" was coined in 1990 by neopagan leader Morning Glory Zell (1990) to describe a lifestyle that embraces multiple, simultaneous, openly conducted, romantic relationships which generally, but not always, expressly include a sexual component. The word is a combination of Latin and Greek roots for "many loves."

[Polyamory takes many forms, the most frequently encountered variants being:

- Open Relationships—A clearly defined group (generally two) of adults who expressly agree that their relationship will be *open*, (i.e., nonexclusive) in the romantic/emotional and, generally also, sexual dimensions. These agreements are seldom entirely open-ended. Much more often, these agreements incorporate a variety of boundaries and constraints, including restrictions concerning the primacy of the original relationship, gender of the other partner(s), degree of permissible emotional involvement, permissible sexual practices/activities, and so on (O'Neill & O'Neill 1972; Francoeur & Francoeur 1974).
- Group Marriage (*aka* triad, quad, etc.)—A clearly defined group of at least three adults who expressly agree to consider each member of the group to be "married" to every other member of the group. Such relationships may be open (i.e., members may have sexual and/or romantic/emotional relationships with others outside the group) or closed (also known as *polyfidelitous*) in which no such relationships are permitted outside the group (Constantine & Constantine 1973).

• Intimate Network—A clearly defined group of adults, partnered in various configurations or nominally single, whose members expressly agree to form a network, within which friendships may include a romantic/emotional and/or sexual component. These networks may also be open or closed (Ramey 1976).

[It should be noted that polyamory represents an *approach* to intimate relationships, rather than merely a particular practice. Therefore, it is possible for an unpartnered person, or a person presently celibate, nevertheless to accurately describe him- or herself as being polyamorous in philosophy and approach to relationships.

[Further, unlike its "sibling" swinging, polyamorous relating is expressly open to the full range of romantic/emotional connection, is not couple-centered, and philosophically at least, tends to de-emphasize the sexual dimension in favor of the emotional/romantic dimension. It also differs in that polyamory generally embraces the concept of an alternative family structure, seeking to replace the extended and expanded families of the past with a new form of "intentional family," whereas swinging centers exclusively on the sexual/friendship needs of adults.

[Though some authors (e.g., Walston 2001) trace the genesis of polyamory to the Free Love movements and communal living experiments of the 19th century, this treatment will concern itself only with its 20th-century emergence as a distinct relationship option.

[*1. Early Research—1960s and 1970s.* The relationship approach that would ultimately become identified as polyamory first emerged in the research literature as a subset of swinging or comarital sexuality, described by Symonds (1968) as "utopian swingers," as contrasted to "recreational swingers." The main observed difference was that utopian swingers embraced a sexually nonexclusive lifestyle as but one aspect of a larger unconventional and nonconformist worldview, whereas recreational swingers' only area of significant deviance was their nonexclusive sexuality. (See also Denfield & Gordon (1970), Bartell (1971), Gilmartin (1974, 1978), and Jenks (1985)). Varni (1971) characterized essentially this same subgroup of swingers as "communal" in his five-part segmentation, reflecting this group's ties to the various communal-living experiments of the 1960s, though his "interpersonal" swinger category also would describe the behavior of a significant portion of today's polyamorists.

[Smith and Smith (1973) drew the distinction between the "recreational" and "utopian" subcultures more clearly, based on the two groups' very different approaches to reconciling what they *prefer* versus what they will *accept*. Many contemporary polyamorists explicitly reject swinging, and the most oft-stated public reason remains that pinpointed by Smith and Smith for their "utopians" three decades ago— that they desire a total relationship, and find sexual nonexclusivity alone insufficient or unfulfilling.

[Seminal research on polyamory included studies of "group marriage" and "intimate networks." The preeminent researchers of group marriage were Larry and Joan Constantine (1971), whose 1973 book, *Group Marriage: A Study of Contemporary Multilateral Marriage*, represented the consummation of years of research. The Constantines created the term "multilateral marriage" to describe the object of their studies. They defined a multilateral marriage as "one in which three or more people each consider themselves to have a primary relationship with at least two other individuals in the group."

[The Constantines were virtually alone in examining the effects on children being raised by adults who practice nontraditional intimate relationships. Their 1976 work, *Trea-*

*sures of the Island: Children in Alternative Families*, reviewed and summarized their own and others' research that demonstrated conclusively the falsity of the oft-repeated assertion that being raised in nontraditional families is invariably detrimental to children. (Decades of subsequent research on children raised in gay and lesbian households, who are subject to the same canard, have further refuted that notion. It nevertheless retains wide public acceptance.)

[The concept of intimate networks, a term first used by Farson et al. in 1969, was explored to the fullest by James W. Ramey in several papers (1972, 1975), and ultimately a book (1976). Ramey (1972) described relationship networks he called "intimate friendships," defined as "an otherwise traditional friendship in which sexual intimacy is considered appropriate behavior." Ramey placed intimate friendships at the approximate midpoint on a continuum of sexually nonexclusive relationship options, ranging from beginning swinging to group marriage.

[The term *SOM/R*, for Sexually Open Marriage or Sexually Open Relationship, was used by Knapp and Whitehurst in 1975, referring to their earlier independent studies of such relationships. Unlike many of their contemporaries, their research (Knapp 1974, 1975; Whitehurst 1974) focused on what today would be identified as polyamorous relationships, inasmuch as the subjects, though partnered, nevertheless engaged *individually* in independent relationships and sexuality, as contrasted to the couples *as couples* model that characterizes swinging.

[*2. Early Popular Influences.* The bestselling 1972 book, *Open Marriage*, by Nena and George O'Neill is widely credited with being a major turning point for widespread mainstream public interest in new forms of egalitarian, growth-focused marital relationships. Though the O'Neills touched on sexual nonexclusivity only as an adjunct to their main premises, the term "open marriage" has come to mean "*sexually* open marriage." The O'Neills were not opposed to sexual openness; rather, they took a neutral stance (O'Neill & O'Neill 1972, 254). Their model of nonpossessive, mutually supportive, self-actualizing relationships nevertheless became a key prototype for polyamory.

[Popular fiction also heavily influenced the development of polyamory in the United States. The fictional works of authors Robert Rimmer (*The Harrad Experiment* (1966), *Proposition 31* (1968)) and Robert Heinlein (*Stranger in a Strange Land* (1961), *The Moon Is a Harsh Mistress* (1966), *Time Enough for Love* (1973)) introduced a variety of models of sexually nonexclusive, egalitarian, love/affection-based relationships. As is so often the case with radical commentary on entrenched social institutions, these models were safely embedded in fictional milieus so as to diminish their perceived threat to prevailing cultural norms. Anapol (1997) credits *Stranger* and *Harrad* as being responsible for polyamory "taking shape as a mass movement."

[Other critical influences in the popular press were Roy and Roy's (1967) *Honest Sex*, Mazur's (1973) *The New Intimacy: Open Ended Marriage and Alternative Lifestyles*, Francoeur and Francoeur's (1974) *Hot and Cool Sex: Cultures in Conflict*, and Ellis' (1972) *The Civilized Couple's Guide to Extramarital Adventure: The Book to Read Before You Begin That Affair*, among others.

[*3. The Influence of 20th-Century Communal Experiments.* The 1960s and 1970s experiments with communal-living arrangements also contributed to the culture of polyamory. Though communes varied widely in the degree of sexual nonexclusivity that was openly practiced or tacitly allowed, for many, sexual openness proved a source of contention, and in some cases, was *the* factor leading to the dissolution of the commune. Nevertheless, the culture of generalized nonpossessiveness, extended intimacy, and rejection of social norms that existed in most communal-living experiments fostered an environment where the *ideal* of sexual nonexclusivity, if not the *practice*, took firm root.

[Several terms in wide use in the polyamory movement today originated in the Kerista commune in San Francisco, which lasted for approximately 20 years (1971-1991). The most frequently heard of these is the term *compersion*, which is defined as the opposite of jealousy, the pleasurable feeling one gets at seeing or contemplating a loved one enjoying love or having another pleasurable experience, including a sexual one. Kerista also claims credit for the term *polyfidelity* (Furchgot 1993), which describes their version of sexually open relationships in which each person in a group (called a Best Friend Identity Cluster) was expected to be relationally nonpreferential with respect to every other opposite-sex member of the group, including sexually. The term as commonly used today no longer connotes such a rigid nonpreferentiality, but rather a relationship structure in which the participants, whatever their number, agree to be sexually intimate only with other members of the group. It no longer assumes perfect symmetrical equality of these relationships, nor does it expressly embrace a purely heterosexual norm.

[*4. Retrenchment in the Era of AIDS.* In the 1980s, the advent of the AIDS crisis allowed all nonexclusive sexuality to be portrayed as inordinately dangerous, and possibly fatal. Simultaneously, a general public swing toward politicosocial conservatism during the Reagan and G. H. W. Bush administrations reinforced social opprobrium for nontraditional intimate relationships. As a consequence, research into SOMs/SORs virtually ceased. While the gay, lesbian, bisexual, and transgendered movement was galvanized by the crisis, and consequently made grudging progress throughout the 1980s, all other forms on nontraditional relationships were effectively driven underground.

[One bright spot in an otherwise bleak research landscape is Blumstein and Schwartz' 1983 *American Couples: Money, Work, Sex.* This exhaustive analysis of data provided by over 6,000 couples—heterosexual, gay, and lesbian—while not statistically representative of the entire U.S. population, nevertheless provided valuable insights into the attitudes of key demographic groups within society. One significant finding was that among their sample population, 15% of married couples, 28% of heterosexual cohabiting couples, 29% of lesbian couples, and 65% of gay male couples had explicit agreements for SOMs/SORs (Blumstein & Schwartz 1983, 585). Unfortunately, their data do not describe the exact nature of the SOM/SOR agreements; these, therefore, could encompass polyamory, swinging, or other variants of SOM/SOR behavior.

[*5. The 1990s' Renaissance.* Polyamory, now with its own distinct name, reemerged in the 1990s, fueled by the ever-increasing reach of the Internet/World Wide Web and by the generally more liberal social climate that accompanied the Clinton administration. It had clearly detached itself from the swinging movement, developing its own set of norms which focused on individual growth, strict equality between the genders, high investment in communications, openness to all sexual orientations, and a broad acceptance of a variety of relationship configurations.

[The emergent polyamory community was heavily influenced by several divergent communities from whose ranks many of its practitioners were drawn. Chief among these were the more sexually liberal elements of the neopagan movement, such as the Zells; the science-fiction fandom community, who were in the process of rediscovering Heinlein and a number of other science fiction/fantasy au-

thors who were incorporating polyamorous themes into their fiction, such as Marion Zimmer Bradley, Marge Piercy, Ursula K. LeGuin, S. M. Stirling, and Laurell K. Hamilton; and significant segments of the bisexual movement, which, while struggling for acceptance within both the homosexual and heterosexual communities, also sought to find a philosophical "home" where they would be more easily accepted and where any nonsexually exclusive practices would be treated with respect. Many of the early leaders in what would become the polyamory movement were also influenced by, or led, efforts to reintegrate sexuality with both traditional and nontraditional forms of spirituality, exemplified by the creation of The Body Sacred in 1993 (organized by Deborah Anapol, the Rev. Jerry Jud, Rustum Roy, and others) and various earlier "sex and spirit" retreat experiences.

[Two leaders of the contemporary polyamory movement emerged in the early 1990s: Deborah Anapol and Ryam Nearing. The two collaborated briefly in the mid-1990s, but shortly separated to pursue their different visions of the polyamorous ideal. Nearing actually began her "public" advocacy in the mid 1980s, with the 1984 publication of her book, *The Polyfidelity Primer.* Nearing freely accepts, but generally does not emphasize, SOMs/SORs, favoring the polyfidelitous model. She also emphasizes the familial aspects of the polyamorous relationship, including enhanced parenting. Anapol's *Polyamory: Love Without Limits*, originally was published in 1992, and a new edition was released in 1997. Anapol's vision ultimately led her more in the direction of the "sacred sexuality" movement. Both appear to incorporate polyamory into a wider worldview that emphasizes environmental stewardship, interpersonal connectedness, non-creedal spirituality, antimaterialism, and a strong sense of intentional-community building.

[One possibly unanticipated consequence of the two most visible leaders of the contemporary polyamory movement placing polyamory in this context was to further entrench in the minds of some contemporary observers (e.g., Gould 2000) the 1970s' image of polyamory as a marginal, idealistic, "counterculture" phenomenon. This effect was amplified by the counterculture rhetoric and "progressive" political leanings frequently displayed by many authors of popular treatments of polyamory throughout the 1990s (e.g., West 1996; Easton & Liszt 1997; Munson & Stelboum 1999).

[One exception was Perper, Cornog, and Francoeur's *Sex, Love and Marriage in the 21st Century* (1999). The vignettes in this book, which focused on clergy and laypersons' approaches to nonmonogamy, demonstrated that polyamory could and did represent a considered response by a growing number of more-mainstream, nonradical adults to the increasingly painful dysfunctions and limitations of contemporary monogamous marriage, and that a polyamorous SOM/SOR could be compatible with a variety of different philosophies, spiritual paths, and worldviews.

[Throughout the 1990s, the polyamory movement gained momentum and visibility. By the close of the decade, such mainstream publications as *Time* magazine were beginning to treat polyamory somewhat evenhandedly (Cloud 1999).

[*6. The New Millennium.* The turn of the century saw mainstream U.S. media, such as *Elle* magazine, the *Montel Williams Show*, and the *John Walsh Show* offering treatments of polyamory that eschewed the sensationalist approach that characterized most previous media coverage. In 2002, the *Oxford English Dictionary* decided to include *polyamory*, though the definition adopted focuses only on the consensual nonexclusive-sexuality aspect of the practice, unfortunately further blurring the boundaries between polyamory and traditional swinging in the public mind.

[The Web-inspired grassroots nature of the polyamory movement in the United States cannot be overemphasized. An online search in February 2003 of the popular Yahoo Groups online email lists revealed no fewer than 323 groups with a purported connection to polyamory. One website accessed at the same time listed contact information for 92 local and/or regional polyamory support or social groups in the United States.

[*7. Conclusion.* As it developed, polyamory grew farther and farther from its supposed point of origin in the couple-centered swinging milieu. In hindsight, it has become obvious that polyamory was always a parallel development, an equal sibling of swinging, not a descendent or variant. Both movements were born of the radical gender realignment occasioned by World War II, delayed briefly by the socially conservative retrenchment of the 1950s, and emerged as distinct entities in the 1960s and 1970s, midwived by the advent of readily accessible birth control, changing public attitudes about premarital sexuality, and a growing awareness of women's rights in general and, specifically, their right to enjoy the same sexual freedoms as men had accessed for millennia.

[While many who practice polyamory do adhere to Symonds' and Varni's stereotype regarding its incorporation into a particular (utopian) worldview, strong anecdotal evidence suggests that there exists today a wide diversity of backgrounds, attitudes, and beliefs among polyamorists. Research into the true demographics and sociographics of polyamorists suffers from the same challenges facing research into other practices widely viewed as "deviant"—most practitioners are invisible, safely "closeted," and only the more extreme practitioners or those with "less to lose" are readily available for study.

[As polyamory continues to emerge as a discrete relationship form, more research will be needed to develop a clearer picture of its actual incidence and frequency, the variations in form, and the demographic and sociographic characteristics of its practitioners. (*End of update by J. R. Fleckenstein*)]

### Sexuality and People with Physical and Developmental Disabilities    MITCHELL S. TEPPER

*Government Policies Affecting Sexuality and Disability.* Over the past 20 years, pivotal legislation has been enacted in the United States that enables people with disabilities to gain their rightful place as equal members of American society. These changes have been led by spirited people with disabilities and their advocates. The Rehabilitation Act of 1973, the 1975 Education for All Handicapped Children Act (Public Law 94-142), and the Americans with Disabilities Act passed in 1990 have all added opportunities for inclusion and integration into the community for people of all abilities. With inclusion and integration have come greater opportunities for social interaction and sexual expression. The same spirit that has raised disability-rights issues to a national priority is now demanding that people with disabilities be recognized as sexual beings with a right to sexual education, sexual healthcare, and sexual expression afforded under the law.

Demands for the sexual rights of people with disabilities have resulted in a resurgence of research interest in the area of sexuality and disability in the 1990s. Notably, the National Center for Medical Rehabilitation Research (NCMRR) of the National Institute of Child Health and Human Development under the National Institutes of Health has identified sexuality as a priority issue that has an impact on the quality of life of people with disabilities. It subsequently issued a Request for Applications on Reproductive Function in Peo-

ple with Physical Disabilities in February of 1992. The purpose of the request was to develop new knowledge in the areas of reproductive physiology, anatomy, and behavior that are common to people with disabilities, with the goal of restoring, improving, or enhancing reproductive function lost as a consequence of injury, disease, or congenital disorder. The request for applications included a specific objective to characterize the effect of impairments of sexual function on psychosocial adaptation, emotional state, and establishment of intimate relationships. Special focus was placed on research with women and minorities who have disabilities. NCMRR has funded six studies on sexuality and disability over the last three years. Two of the studies were with women who have spinal cord injury, and a third was a study of women with a variety of disabilities.

*Consumers with Disabilities Leading the Way.* Research, education, and advocacy efforts in the area of sexuality and disability are being led by people with disabilities (consumers). A review of the most recent annotated bibliography on sexuality and disability published by the Sexuality Information and Education Council of the United States (SIECUS 1995) reveals a growing number of books, newsletters, special issues of publications, and curricula on sexuality and disability written by people with disabilities. In addition, national consumer-based organizations, like the National Spinal Cord Injury Association, the National Multiple Sclerosis Foundation, and the Arthritis Foundation, are beginning to publish self-help brochures on the specific effects of particular disabilities on sexuality. Most recently, self-help groups have been appearing on the Internet, computer bulletin-board services, and commercial computer services like America Online.

*Healthcare Professionals Involved in Sexuality and Disability.* In addition to the work by people with disabilities and nonprofessional advocates, healthcare professionals are also taking an increased interest in sexuality and disability. The American Association of Physical Medicine and Rehabilitation has a Sexuality Task Force; the American Association of Sexuality Educators, Counselors, and Therapists has a special-interest group that focuses on educating medical and allied help professionals in the area of sexuality and disability; the Society for the Scientific Study of Sexuality includes presentations and workshops in the area of sexuality and disability for its members; and Planned Parenthood agencies around the country have increased education and services in the area of sexual healthcare to people with disabilities. More rehabilitation hospitals are including "privacy" rooms to give patients an opportunity to experiment sexually while still in the hospital, and many are adding specialty programs in the area of fertility and erectile function for men, obstetric and gynecological care for women, and parenting for both men and women with disabilities.

*Portrayals of Sexuality and Disability in the Popular Media.* The portrayal of people with disabilities as sexual beings has improved over time in the popular media. Movies that include a focus on the sexuality and relationships of people with disabilities, such as *Forest Gump, Passion Fish, Water Dance, Regarding Henry, My Left Foot, Children of a Lesser God,* and *Born on the Fourth of July,* have dealt with the issue of sexuality and disability with varying degrees of sensitivity, and have enjoyed success at both the box office and in video stores. TV shows have also included people with disabilities and sexuality themes. One show, *LA Law,* where one of the stars portrayed a person with a developmental disability who had a sexual relationship with another person with a developmental disability, was honored by the Coalition of Sexuality and Disability for the positive portrayal of sexuality and disability in the media. There has also been an increase in TV commercials that include people with disabilities in relationships or with children. Popular magazines ranging from *Bride* to *Penthouse* and *Playboy* are also beginning to include feature articles on sexuality and disability. Efforts to portray people with disabilities as part of everyday life in the media are slowly helping to explode the myth that people with disabilities are asexual.

*Problems, Controversies, and Hurdles.* Two of the most serious sexual problems facing people with disabilities are 1. the high rate of sexual abuse, exploitation, and unwanted sexual activity, especially among women with physical disabilities and all people with developmental disabilities, and 2. the risk of STDs, including HIV, among people with cognitive impairments who are sexually active. Two leading areas of controversy are 1. the issue of what constitutes informed consent for sexual activity in people with serious cognitive impairments, and 2. the area of reproductive rights, eugenics, abortion, and prenatal testing for disabilities. As far as hurdles, there is still a need for greater access to information and educational material that affirms the sexuality of people of all abilities, including people with early- and late-onset disabilities, physical, sensory, and mental disabilities, and disabilities that hinder learning. Despite the positive current trends in sexuality and disability, we still have a long way to go in increasing the number of sexuality education and training programs for teachers, healthcare workers, and family members to help them understand and support the normal sexual development and behavior of persons with disabilities. A goal is that all social agencies and healthcare delivery systems develop policies and procedures that will insure sexual-health services and benefits are provided on an equal basis to all persons without discrimination because of disability.

*Sexuality and Older Persons* ROBERT T. FRANCOEUR

In 1860, over half of the American population was under 20 years of age and only 13% over age 45. In 1990, less than a third were under age 20, and 21% were over age 45. The so-called Baby Boomers born between 1945 and 1965 are now in their middle years. With the birthrate less than 15 per 1,000, America has become a graying society.

Although Americans over age 50 are the fastest-growing segment of our population, research on their lifestyles and patterns of intimacy has been almost exclusively limited to studies of the chronically ill, the socially isolated, and the poor. Edward Brecher (1984) was one of the first to study older healthy Americans. His sample of 4,246 persons between ages 40 and 92 was largely white and affluent, although he did include a low-income group. His overall conclusion was that the sexual interests and activities of older persons are the best-kept secrets in America. Although there is a common belief that the elderly are no longer interested in sexual intimacy, older persons were just as affected as young people by the social turmoil and changing attitudes of the 1960s and 1970s.

Brecher found that healthy, older person today are "enormously different from the older person of 40 or 50 years ago," and very much interested in intimacy and sexual relations. Not one of Brecher's 4,246 respondents was sexually inactive, although masturbation was the

most common sexual outlet. Forty-four percent rated their sexual satisfaction as most enjoyable; less than 1% rated their sexual activity as not enjoyable (see Table 14). Poor health was a major determinant in hindering older persons from maintaining an active sexual life.

About half of these couples reported engaging in oral-genital sex and did not limit their sexual activities to nighttime. Most of the men and women were usually orgasmic. About one in 15 had participated in group sex after age 50. One in five couples had engaged in extramarital sex; 1% of couples had a mutually accepted "open marriage." Forty percent of older single women reported a relationship with a married man. A third thought it was acceptable for an older man or woman to have a much younger lover.

In another study of healthy, upper-middle-class men and women, ages 80 to 102 living in residential retirement communities, 14% of the men and 29% of the women were still married. Sexual touching and caressing, followed by masturbation and then intercourse were the most common sexual activities. Of these outlets, only touching and caressing declined with age, a decline more evident in men than in women. Those who had been sexually active earlier in life tended to remain sexually active in their 80s and 90s, although the frequency of sexual intercourse was sometimes limited by their current physical health and by social circumstances, including the lack of an available partner (Bretschneider & McCoy 1988).

*The Starr-Weiner Report on Sex and Sexuality in the Mature Years* (1981) examined the sexual lives and attitudes of 800 persons, aged 60 to 91, from four regions of the country. When the sexual activities of these 60- to 90-year-olds were compared with the 40-year-olds Kinsey studied 35 years earlier, there was no significant decline when opportunities for sexual activity existed. "Sex remains pretty much the same unless some outside event intrudes, such as a health problem, the loss of a spouse, impotence, or boredom." A reliable predictor of the sexually active life of older persons is their acceptance or rejection of the social stereotype of the dependent, sickly older person. Older persons who maintain an active participation in life in general tend to be more sexually active in their later years.

Starr and Weiner also identified two major problems with no easy remedy. First is the tendency for older men to become asexual when they encounter an occasional erec-

**Table 14**

**Sexual Activity among 4,246 Americans, Ages 45 to 92, in the Brecher 1984 Survey**

| | Age Group | | |
|---|---|---|---|
| | 50s | 60s | 70+ |
| **Women** | | | |
| Orgasms while asleep or awakening | 26% | 24% | 17% |
| Women who masturbate | 47% | 37% | 33% |
| Masturbation frequency for women who masturbate | 0.7/week | 0.6/week | 0.7/week |
| Wives having sex with husband | 88% | 76% | 65% |
| Frequency of marital sex | 1.3/week | 1.0/week | 0.7/week |
| **Men** | | | |
| Orgasms while asleep or awakening | 25% | 21% | 17% |
| Men who masturbate | 66% | 50% | 43% |
| Masturbation frequency for men who masturbate | 1.2/week | 0.8/week | 0.7/week |
| Men having sex with wife | 87% | 78% | 59% |
| Frequency of marital sex | 1.3/week | 1.0/week | 0.6/week |

tion or orgasmic problem. Instead of exploring noncoital pleasuring, many older men simply give up all interest in sex. The second problem is the ever-growing number of older women who are without sexual partners and, thus, deprived, against their will, of sexual intimacy and pleasure. (See Section 6B below on sexuality among older homosexual men and women.)

### A Closing Comment

Throughout this section, we have noted the tendency of sexuality researchers in the U.S.A. to focus on the incidence and/or frequency of sexual behaviors in various lifestyles. There has been little corresponding research on the process of sexual relationships or the dynamics within them. This is precisely the same point we made in summarizing the section on adolescent sexuality. Suffice it to say that American researchers need to move beyond asking how many people "do it" and how often they "do it" to more fully investigate the contexts surrounding adult sexual lifestyles, and to identify the social, psychological, and biological factors associated with sexual practice.

[*Update 2003*: Compared with research on childhood and adolescent sexuality, there has been considerably less research on the sexual practices of adults. Some important studies (Smith 1991; Gagnon, Giami, Michaels, & de Colomby 2001) have been completed in recent years. Although it did not get much attention at the time, Smith (1989) did report that roughly 20% of adult Americans did not have a sexual partner in the last year. In a study comparing different sexual-orientation groups, Horowitz and his associates (2001) reported the same finding. There has been little research on this group that is not having sex. The study by Gagnon and his associates (2001) is one of the first to ever compare national surveys from two countries. Compared to stereotypes, they found that French adults tended to be more monogamous and to exhibit fewer male-female differences. Interestingly, older American women were more likely than others to report no sexual partners. (See summary by T. Perper in the chapter on France, Section 5A, Interpersonal Heterosexual Behaviors, A French/U.S. Comparison, in this volume).

[Research on adult populations does appear to be becoming more sophisticated. Using national data, Liu (2003) found that the quality of marital sex does decline slightly and gradually with length of marriage. Wives were less satisfied with marital sex than husbands. In a series of studies (Byers 2001; Lawrance & Byers 1995), we have seen growing evidence that marital sex is well explained by social exchange variables. Exchange variables have been linked to relationship satisfaction, sexual satisfaction, sexual communication, and sexual functioning itself for both sexes (Weis 1998). (*End of update by D. L. Weis*)]

## 6. Homoerotic, Homosexual, and Bisexual Behaviors

To this point, we have examined the general sociohistorical context of sexuality in the U.S.A. and reviewed evidence concerning what may be called mainstream sexual behaviors, in the sense that a majority of Americans engage in these activities. Our review of autoerotic behaviors and the development of heterosexual patterns throughout the lifecycle may be seen in this light. We did occasionally mention less-common patterns. For example, the review of childhood sexuality did note that homosexual activities do occur in childhood, and research that examined the development of homosexual behavior was briefly discussed. However, the focus of the chapter so far has clearly been on mainstream, and essentially heterosexual, patterns.

Our review will now shift to an examination of a variety of sexual patterns that are less common, as this has also been a prime concern of sexuality professionals in the U.S.A. We hope that the reader will note that many of the general themes we have stressed so far—change and diversity, for example—are applicable to these patterns as well. In reviewing heterosexual lifestyle patterns, we stressed that researchers have tended to focus on the incidence or frequency of sexual behaviors and less likely to investigate relationship dynamics or theoretical explanations of behavior. These same trends also tend to characterize the study of less-conventional sexual behavior.

### A. Children and Adolescents

ROBERT HAWKINS and WILLIAM STACKHOUSE

Although research on childhood sexual activity in the United States is limited, what little we know (and can remember on a personal level) indicates that a great deal of same-gender sex play takes place among children, usually of an exploratory nature. Occasionally, a lesbian, gay, or bisexual adult will recall such childhood activity as being different from exploratory activity with someone of the other gender, and therefore indicative of an early awareness of orientation. But it appears that, for the majority of people, childhood sexual play, while it includes same-gender activity, has little implication for adult orientation.

Some research shows a relationship for males between cross-gender behavior as a child (known as "sissy" behavior) and homoeroticism as an adult, but that relationship has not been shown to be causal and may be more a result of the patriarchal homophobic character of the culture than any innate biological characteristic of the child. This is more apparent when one compares the research on females who engage in cross-gender-role behavior as a child (known as "tomboy" behavior), wherein the same relationship is not present. Even the labels for the person engaging in cross-gender-role behavior carry different connotations in the culture. For a boy, being called "sissy" is considerably more detrimental to healthy development than is being called "tomboy" for a girl (Green 1987).

When the American child is developing a lesbian, gay, or bisexual identity, the heterosexism and homophobia of the culture dictates that this is not an acceptable orientation, and it becomes difficult at best for the child to develop into an adolescent or adult with a positive self-image. Lesbian and gay youth, particularly those from small communities, seldom receive support from their peers or from the sex education and family life courses in their school. Books that could be supportive, such as Leslea Newman's *Heather Has Two Mommies* (1989) or *Gloria Goes to Gay Pride* (1991), are usually banned from school curricula or simply not considered appropriate for children, even though they were written specifically for all children to read. Counselors and teachers generally assume that all of their students are heterosexually oriented, even though some students in any school will have a same-gender orientation.

As children grow into adolescents and attempt to deal constructively with the tensions and uncertainties of adolescence, gay, lesbian, and bisexual teenagers have to confront the question of the gender of the person to whom they find themselves sexually attracted. Do they surrender to peer and cultural pressure and date only members of the other gender? Do they tell a best friend of their orientation and risk losing that friend or being ostracized or physically attacked? Should they get sexually involved with someone of the other gender to attempt to prove that they really are "straight"? Just what do they do when they find themselves sexually attracted to someone of the same gender? Fortunately, the number and quality of resources that lesbian and gay teens can use are increasing, both on national and local levels. During the late 1980s and early 1990s, many books, pamphlets, and other resources have been published, providing practical guidelines and insights into what lesbian and gay youth should know about dating, living together, and coping in a hostile world.

However, the resources that are available for them are usually available only through homophile groups and a few commercial bookstores, and are generally not available through school libraries or other youth agencies. For example, the Boy Scouts organization has been explicitly noninclusive for both homosexual youth members and adult leaders. In rare cases, such as in New York City, a special high school has been established for gay and lesbian youth who are unable to cope with the discrimination that they face in a regular school setting. This discrimination comes from other students, as well as teachers, administrators, and counselors, making it difficult for these students to obtain an education.

Although this discrimination is still rampant in elementary and secondary schools, it is lessening somewhat in colleges and universities. Most American public and large private colleges and universities recognize and fund student organizations such as a Gay and Lesbian Alliance (GALA) or a Lesbian and Gay Organization (LAGO). Several chapters of gay fraternities and lesbian sororities have been organized. However, even where such organizations exist, many lesbian and gay collegians avoid them or keep their membership quiet. Even at religiously based institutions of higher education, there are differences with respect to the acceptance of these organizations. As late as 1995, one university, the Roman Catholic-affiliated Notre Dame, refused to allow any homophile organizations, and even denied the availability of counseling-center-sponsored group-support activities for lesbians, gays, and bisexuals. At the same time, a large Jewish orthodox-affiliated university, Yeshiva, provides numerous opportunities and funding for gay and lesbian organizations at both the graduate and undergraduate levels.

Even though information on issues confronting lesbian, gay, and bisexual adolescents may be available in printed form, the difficulty in gaining access to such materials, the anti-homoeroticism that is rampant in the media, the negative stereotypes that are still being touted as representative of all who are homoerotic, and the silence on ambieroticism or bisexuality all combine to make life unnecessarily difficult for the adolescent lesbian, gay, or bisexual person in this country. One result is that almost one third of adolescent suicides are related to the issue of homoeroticism. The data on attempted suicide among adolescents are also informative. About 10% of heterosexual male and female adolescents attempt suicide, while twice as many lesbian adolescents and three to four times as many gay adolescents attempt suicide (Youth Suicide National Center Report 1989). The lack of support and acceptance of these young people is undoubtedly a factor in this difference.

## B. Adults

ROBERT HAWKINS and WILLIAM STACKHOUSE
*Research on Gender Orientation*
The question of gender orientation and the definition of orientation is complex and confusing for both sexuality researchers and the layperson alike. Several researchers have concluded, after extensive study, that there is no clinical description that can be applied to the label "homosexual"— that there is virtually no single phenomenon that can be labeled "homosexuality" and then described in clinical terms. Yet, some theorists have suggested models to define and categorize. When researchers then indicate that they are using a specific model, usually there is no internal consistency.

Take, for example, the Kinsey continuum of orientation. After interviewing 5,300 men and 5,940 women in the 1940s, Kinsey and associates developed a continuous scale based on the ratio of sexual fantasies and physical contacts with one's own gender and with the other gender. Along this continuum are seven points, labeled from 0 to 6, with a "Kinsey 0" being a person whose behavior and fantasies have always involved persons of the other gender, and a "Kinsey 6" being a person whose behavior and fantasies have always involved persons of their own gender.

Even where researchers have indicated their use of the Kinsey scale, the actual definitions of research subjects have varied significantly from the original and also varied from study to study. In some instances, fantasy data are not available and consequently not considered; in other instances, behavior alone is the criteria for being placed in a "Kinsey" category, with no recognition of the difference in subjective experience of the sexual activity. In other studies, subjects are placed on the continuum solely according to the gender of the partner with whom they are living.

There are other models available that begin to reflect some of the complexities of gender orientation. Moses and Hawkins (1982, 1986) indicated that the minimum data necessary for identifying orientation in subjects were an assessment of the gender of emotional relationship partners, the gender of sexual attraction partners, and the gender of partners in sexual fantasy content, and that all three of these should be considered from a past and a present perspective, implying that, although orientation may be consistent throughout one's life, it is not necessarily so. It is seen as a potentially dynamic characteristic.

An even more complex model was developed by Fred Klein, a physician and gender-orientation researcher. Klein indicated that an assessment of orientation needed to consider seven criteria over three time periods, resulting in a Sexual Orientations Grid of 21 cells. The criteria are: 1. sexual attraction; 2. sexual behavior; 3. sexual fantasies; 4. emotional/affectional relationship preference; 5. social relationship preference; 6. lifestyle; and 7. self-identification, with each of these criteria being assessed over three time periods: the past, the present, and the future ideal. This was the first model to present the notion that one's self-label might be an important facet of one's orientation, and the time factor was an acknowledgment of the potentially dynamic character of orientation. Research subjects can rate themselves on these criteria using a three-by-seven grid and the Kinsey ratings, summing the ratings, and then dividing by 21 to produce a position on a scale identified popularly as "The Kinsey Scale" (Klein 1978; Klein, Sepekoff, & Wolf 1985). Although the initial response to Klein's model was that it was more comprehensive and realistic, its complexities have kept most researchers from using or disseminating it widely. It has thus remained unfamiliar to many.

### Developmental Biological Insights

Several studies in the past decade have attempted to identify biological determinants for adult homoeroticism from a heterosexist theoretical base, in which heterosexual behavior is viewed as the basic, natural human behavior, and anything else is deviant. There is usually little recognition of definitional complexity or the possibility of precursors rather than determinants. Subjects are typically placed in the dichotomous classification so prevalent in the culture—that one is either gay or straight, homosexual or heterosexual—with no recognition of the Kinsey continuum, and especially no recognition of Klein's model. Researchers have purported to examine twins, siblings, adopted children, and brains of people who are homosexual and those who are not.

For example, Simon LeVay (1991) reported finding a portion of the hypothalamus that was smaller in homosexual men than in heterosexual men and was equal in size to that portion in heterosexual women. There were no lesbian brains identified as such in this study. The "finding" was quickly seized by the popular media and soon became what is called "common knowledge." There were many problems with the study, but these were generally ignored, even in the scientific press. The definitional problem, whereby subjects were classified according to whether they were known to be gay or not (obviously all subjects were no longer living, so no information could be garnered from the subjects), has been ignored. The size of the sample (19 men previously identified as gay, 16 men identified as not known to be gay and, therefore, heterosexual; one man known to be identified as bisexual and included in the study as such; and six women, all classified as heterosexual) has also generally been ignored. The fact that the size of another part of the hypothalamus in the women's brains did not coincide with other research on women's brains was ignored in discussions, and the possibility that what was found may have had something to do with body build and general physical characteristics rather than directly with sexual orientation was also never discussed. The overly simplistic design was convenient, because including even a few of the other variables, such as body build or sexual history, would mean that the sample size would have to be considerably larger to enable any conclusions to be drawn.

Dean Hamer and his research team (1993) have reported the discovery of a genetic region, the Xq28 region on the X chromosome, that is claimed to be associated with male homosexuality in about three quarters of gay men and inherited on the maternal side of the family. Similar research on lesbian women does not show similar findings. There is also no attempt in all of this research to explain the "exceptions" that are reported. If there is a "gay" gene, then why is it that all men who are gay do not show it? Most biologically focused studies suffer from similar problems, first with the issue of definition, then with the exclusion or nonsimilarity of research on women who are attracted to women, and finally with assumptions, conclusions, and discussions of results that assume the "natural" state of the human being is exclusively heterosexual.

Although the question of a biological basis for homoeroticism has, in recent years, seen increased interest and attention, such research consistently does not consider the complexities of orientation, such as emotional attraction, behavior, and other criteria that constitute sexual orientation in Klein's model. Most of the classification methods for identifying orientation of subjects in these studies are overly simplified. Although there may be biological precursors to orientation, no well-designed, appropriately controlled study has been done to support that conclusion.

One positive side effect of the popular interpretation of research into possible biological roots of homoerotic orientation has been in easing the acceptance of gay and lesbian persons by some churches. One can paraphrase a common response among some mainstream Protestant church people and leaders: "If homosexual orientations are not a freely chosen preference but in some way rooted in prenatal genetic, hormonal, and/or neural templates, then God and nature made them this way, and we and the church must accept that reality."

## Bisexuality Research

The research on bisexuality or ambieroticism is even more scant. It is very difficult to do research on bisexuality if one cannot define it, and there is no simple, dichotomous cultural model as is available with research on homosexu-

ality. In a 1994 book, *Dual Attraction*, Weinberg, Williams, and Pryor report that using the Kinsey scale with sexual behaviors, sexual feeling, and romantic feelings, they identified five different types of bisexuals in their study of 435 men and 338 women:

1. The Pure Type, scoring at least 3 on all criteria;
2. The Mid Type, scoring 3 on one criteria and 2 to 4 on the other two;
3. The Heterosexual-Leaning Type, scoring 0-2 on each of the three criteria;
4. The Homosexual-Leaning Type, scoring 4 to 6 on each dimension; and
5. The Varied Type, whose scores did not fit any of the first four categories or types.

Additionally, it is only in the recent past that models for development of a bisexual identity have been proposed, and further research into ambieroticism, such as was begun by Fred Klein, has moved very slowly. The heterosexist nature of the culture, combined with the indigenous psychological and sociological perspectives of many researchers, has precluded the acceptance of a somewhat radical notion that the basic state of the human sexual orientation is ambierotic and mutable, with exclusive heterosexual or exclusive homosexual behavior being equally deviant from the biological norm. Further research on bisexuality appears to be moving in that direction. (See Section C below for more on bisexuality.)

## Incidence

In much of the public discussion of homoeroticism, there is a preoccupation with the general question, "How many are there?" The answer to this question carries political and economic implications, and there is a need to understand the extent of the economic power and political power that this group wields. For example, is the culture required, in policy decisions, to provide for this group, or is it such a small number that policymakers are not required to respond to identified needs of this population? Commerce is in a strategic position to profit from this population, and economically driven decisions in the marketplace are taking these numbers into serious account. For example, in 1994, advertisements focusing directly on lesbian women and gay men as consumers were introduced in popular television and print media, and more mainstream commercial advertisements were being placed in homoerotically focused magazines, such as *The Advocate*, and in programs for fundraising benefits for homoerotic communities.

Another area where numbers are considered in policy decisions is the increasing recognition and development of domestic-partner benefits, such as health insurance and death benefits. This began in the early 1990s when some employers became aware that lesbians, gay men, and bisexuals comprise enough of the workforce to have an effect on productivity and efficiency, and that accommodating their needs is beneficial to the company so that it can have and keep well-qualified people.

Ignoring the basic fact that there is no definition of what "a homosexual" or "a bisexual" person is, until the mid-1990s, the most-often-cited figure for incidence of homosexuality came from the research of Kinsey and associates carried out in the 1940s. These data have been used to estimate the number of homoerotic people in the population without any indication of the simplistic nature of the definition. The commonly cited figure that 10% of American men are homosexual is a combination of Kinsey's finding that 4% of his sample were exclusively homosexual (Kinsey 6) and 6% were predominantly homosexual (Kinsey 5) (Kinsey et al. 1948). His data on homosexual activity in women indicated approximately 9% were either exclusively or predominantly homosexual (Kinsey 5 or 6) (Kinsey et al. 1953).

Laumann et al. (1994) found that almost 3% of their subjects were homosexual. Although these two sets of figures may, at first, seem at odds, the 1994 figure had a 1% error rate, and the Kinsey figure for exclusive homosexuality was 4%, so the two major studies do not differ greatly. There were some other problems with the 1994 study, such as the use of females as interviewers and the tendency of males in this culture to deny homosexual activity, even in anonymous questionnaires, but especially in face-to-face contact with anyone else; however, even with those design problems, the numbers are similar (Schmalz 1993).

*Clinical View*

In 1973, the American Psychiatric Association removed homosexuality from the *Diagnostic and Statistical Manual of Mental Disorders*. This was a major turning point, both in the United States and worldwide, in the clinical acceptance of homosexuality. Homosexuality was no longer to be viewed as an illness. The impact within psychology and psychiatry was profound and has influenced many aspects of society. The basis for this change was the scientific conclusion that, among individuals who were not in clinical treatment, it was impossible to distinguish heterosexual and homosexual persons. Evelyn Hooker first arrived at this conclusion in 1957 with the first controlled study to include a comparison on a nonclinical sample of heterosexual and homosexual men.

Since then, research designs employing the principle that such nonclinical participants exist have resulted in many studies confirming that, in itself, homosexuality is not an illness. The illness model of homosexuality that had existed as the basis for so much discrimination is no longer supported by the psychiatric and psychological establishments. In 1973, the *Comprehensive Textbook of Psychiatry* was revised to state: "many homosexuals, both male and female, function responsibly and honorably, often in positions of high trust, and live emotionally stable, mature, and well adjusted lives, psychodynamically indistinguishable from well-adjusted heterosexuals, except for their alternative sexual preferences."

This has led clinicians to change their point of reference regarding homosexuals, from a pathological frame to a counseling frame, from looking at persons as sick to looking at how persons may maximize their human potential in society. Since then, many studies and books have examined aspects of the development of gay men and lesbian women, looking at identity development (social, sexual, and psychological), family issues, relationship issues, work and career development, and other dimensions of identity and lifestyle. There now exists a large body of American literature, in both the professional and general press aimed at maximizing the health and wholeness of gay men and lesbians.

Still, gay and lesbian individuals often have difficulty with their own self-acceptance and the process of deciding just how to live as gay or lesbian persons. Mental-health professionals who specialize in working with gay and lesbian clients offer individual and group counseling throughout the U.S.A. Various organizations also routinely offer support groups for a wide range of concerns. In addition, counseling is now available to the family members and friends of gay and lesbian persons who have difficulty in accepting the homosexuality of their loved ones.

*Legal Issues*

In examining the legal status of lesbians, gays, and bisexuals, one needs a rudimentary understanding of the legal system in the United States. There are levels of jurisdiction throughout the country; each jurisdiction, from local villages, to city, county, state, and the federal governments, has its own legal codes. In addition, the military has its own legal code. The issue of rights for lesbians and gays has been raised at all levels of jurisdiction. Supposedly, all of these laws are subject to the provisions of the Constitution of the United States, which provides consistency. Each state has its own state constitution, which is also to be consistent with the federal Constitution, as are the governing documents of cities and local communities.

Generally, lesbian women and gay men have no protection against discrimination based on orientation or the perception of orientation, and in 1995, only nine states had laws including sexual orientation as a minority protected from discrimination. Historically, attempts to obtain protection have followed the patterns of other oppressed groups in the United States. First, there were attempts to gain protection against discrimination in public accommodations and employment. More recently, this has expanded to include equal treatment with regard to employment-related benefits accorded to married heterosexual relationships. Examples include the benefits accrued to persons by their legally married status (as of 1995 same-gender partners are not allowed to marry legally in any state in the U.S.), as well as benefits in relation to parental status (such as adoption or custody issues), and bereavement leave with respect to family members.

Opposition to these attempts to expand discrimination protection either takes the stance that homosexual activity is immoral and, therefore, not deserving of consideration for equal protection, or suggests that lesbian women and gay men are seeking "special treatment." There is even an argument put forth that suggests that lesbian women and gay men are not an oppressed minority and should not be treated as such. Where legal protections have been instituted, it has usually been based on the need for equal treatment.

In the past decade, some local jurisdictions have passed laws recognizing the civil rights of same-gender couple relationships and of homoerotic individuals. Similarly, many corporations, of all sizes, have granted gay and lesbian couples the same benefits as heterosexual couples. For example, in Dallas, Texas, a major corporation threatened not to locate a new corporate facility in that city if the corporation's policy on domestic-partnership benefits for same-gendered couples was declared illegal by virtue of the city's discriminatory laws. The economic impact of this decision caused the city government to rescind the law.

In May 1993, a court case highlighted a conflict between the antidiscrimination clause in the Constitution of the State of Hawaii and that state's ban on the recognition of same-gender unions. The state's Supreme Court asked the state to prove its "compelling interest" for continuing the discrimination or to end it. Lawyers generally admit that it will be very difficult to prove a "compelling interest," and if it cannot be done, the state will be forced to grant legal recognition of same-gender partnerships. Currently, all 50 states grant reciprocal recognition of the legality of heterosexual marriage, but if Hawaii legalizes homosexual marriages, the other 49 states will have to decide whether to continue that reciprocity. In early 1995, several states sought to pass legislation that would limit their reciprocity to heterosexual marriage in the event that Hawaii recognized same-gender marriages (Rotello 1996; Eskridge 1996; Sullivan 1996).

Lesbians and gays are also treated differently with respect to serving in the United States armed forces. For many years, they were specifically excluded in official policy, yet were differentially managed in individual cases. For example, when the war in Kuwait broke out, some lesbians and gays who were scheduled for separation from the service were required to serve until the end of the conflict. In another instance, an enlisted man, Perry Watkins, repeatedly told the military that he was gay, but they kept reenlisting him until someone finally decided that he should be separated from the service, and the legal process to do so was instituted (Shilts 1993).

In 1994, the military instituted a policy called "Don't ask, don't tell," in which recruits were no longer to be asked if they had "homosexual tendencies," but were also forbidden from telling anyone if they were homoerotic. Prior to this, the official policy being enforced was one in which activity was not a requirement for dismissal; simply acknowledging one's homoerotic orientation was enough to cause separation from the service. For example, Joseph Stephan, a midshipman at the United States Naval Academy, was only three months from graduation when he was asked if he was a homosexual. He indicated that he was, but never was asked, nor did he ever acknowledge any homosexual activity. He was separated from the navy and was denied his bachelor's degree from the Naval Academy (Rotello 1996; Eskridge 1996; Shilts 1993; Sullivan 1996).

Lesbians and gays have to pay special attention to wills, as biological families have successfully contested wills that left nothing to the blood relatives and everything to the person's life partner. This situation has led to the development of agencies and books focusing specifically on estate planning for lesbian and gay couples and individuals.

The legal issues for bisexuals generally focus on that part of their lives that includes someone of the same gender, so it is the homoerotic aspect of their ambieroticism that suffers from the lack of legal protection. Additionally, there is no legal option for triangular relationships that provides legitimacy, so if a bisexual person has a primary relationship simultaneously with a man and a woman, that relationship cannot be legitimized as a marriage.

### [The End of Anti-Sodomy Laws

ROBERT T. FRANCOEUR

[*Update 2003*: On July 25, 2003, after months of public media debate, the U.S. Supreme Court struck down a Texas law banning sexual relationships between gay men, ruling in *Lawrence v. Texas 02-102* that the law was an unconstitutional violation of their privacy. The 6-3 ruling of the Court reversed its 1986 ruling on *Bowers v. Hardwick* that supported state laws punishing homosexuals for engaging in what such laws historically called "deviant or unnatural sex." Laws forbidding homosexual sex, once universal, now are rare. Those on the books are rarely enforced, but underpin other kinds of discrimination.

[Justice Kennedy, writing the majority statement, argued that the two Texas plaintiffs "are entitled to respect for their private lives. The state cannot demean their existence or control their destiny by making their private sexual conduct a crime." Speaking for the minority, Justice Scalia took the unusual step of reading his dissent from the bench, concluding that "The court has largely signed on to the so-called homosexual agenda." Adding that he has "nothing against homosexuals," Scalia warned that "The court has taken sides in the culture war" that will lead to approval of gay marriages.

[This case began in 1998, when a neighbor with a grudge faked a distress call to police, telling them that a man was "going crazy" in the apartment next to his. Police went to the apartment, pushed open the door and found the two men having anal sex. After their conviction on a misdemeanor charge of committing an unnatural sex act, the plaintiffs were each fined $200 and spent a night in jail.

[Forty years ago, all 50 states had an anti-sodomy law. In 37 states, the statutes have been repealed by lawmakers or blocked by state courts. Of the 13 remaining states, four—Texas, Kansas, Oklahoma, and Missouri—prohibit oral and anal sex between same-sex couples. The other nine states ban consensual sodomy for everyone, homosexual or heterosexual, married or not: Alabama, Florida, Idaho, Louisiana, Mississippi, North Carolina, South Carolina, Utah, and Virginia. All these laws apparently are invalidated by this Supreme Court ruling.

[The Supreme Court was widely criticized 17 years ago when it upheld a similar anti-sodomy law in Georgia. A long list of legal and medical groups joined gay rights and human rights supporters in backing the Texas men. Many friend-of-the-court briefs argued that times have changed since 1986, and that the court should catch up. Conservative politicians and church leaders were enraged by the Court's decision. Pat Robertson, a former presidential candidate, announced a prayer crusade for the demise of three conservative justices who contributed to the majority of six.

[Texas defended its sodomy law as in keeping with the state's interest in protecting marriage and childrearing. Homosexual sodomy, the state argued in legal papers "has nothing to do with marriage or conception or parenthood and it is not on a par with these sacred choices." Texas lawyers urged the Court to draw a constitutional line "at the threshold of the marital bedroom" (Associated Press June 26, 2003). (*End of update by R. T. Francoeur*)]

### Religious Issues

With the removal of homosexuality from the category of mental illness in 1973, the major foundation for legal discrimination against homosexuality was removed. As a result, religious intolerance of homosexuality, which had always been present, took on a more significant role in the debate on homosexuality within American social and political dialogue. Those who believe homosexuality to be immoral on religious grounds have since become more vocal in their quest to have their particular moral positions on homosexuality and other religious and moral issues inserted into the nation's laws (see also Section 2 on religious factors).

At the same time as Americans witnessed the radical change in the clinical view of homosexuality and the emergence of the gay-liberation movement, religious bodies in the U.S. were challenged on their stances with regard to homosexuality. Within Christian and Jewish sects, the debate generally has centered on the interpretation of sacred Biblical texts (Boswell 1980; Countryman 1988; Curran 1993; Francoeur in Gramick & Furey 1988; Gold 1992; Kosnick et al. 1977; Helminiak 1994; McNeill 1976; Presbyterian Church 1991; Thayer et al. 1987). The central locus of the debate is concerned with certain Old Testament texts, particularly the story of Sodom and Gomorrah, and the New Testament comments of the Apostle Paul in 1 Corinthians 6: 9 and I Timothy 1:9-10 (Helminiak 1994), which appear to condemn homosexuality. In actuality, the debate is waged on the basis of how ancient texts are interpreted and used for modern guidance. Many "fundamentalist" and traditional sects accept the ancient texts for their literal meaning and condemn all homosexual expression (Presbyterian Church, Part 2 1991). These sects, however, generally do not address the extent to which they completely ignore many other Biblical texts and do not use them for modern guidance. Other, liberal, bodies interpret the ancient texts in their historical context in the light of current biological and psychological knowledge about the origins and nature of homosexual and other orientations. These bodies, particularly liberal reformed—and to some extent conservative—Judaism, the

Episcopal Church, and the United Church of Christ, frequently welcome homosexual men and women to membership, and even to the ministry (Heyward 1989; Presbyterian Church 1991; Thayer 1987). Within the Catholic Church in America, there is a quite-visible split that, on the grassroots level, constitutes a silent schism on the issue of homosexuality. On the pastoral level, many, perhaps a majority of the clergy, accept the tolerant and liberal position expressed by the Catholic Theological Society of America (Kosnick et al. 1977), and quietly ignore the dogmatic condemnation of homosexuality by the Vatican (Curran 1993; Francoeur in Gramick & Furey 1988; McNeill 1976).

Among American religious bodies, the major continuing issues regarding homosexuality center on welcome, support, and affirmation of members within congregations and on the presence of openly gay and lesbian persons in religious leadership. Recently, support for gay and lesbian members has often led to performing "holy unions" for gay and lesbian partners. Given that the legal option of marriage has not been available, religious bodies have been the logical place for couples to seek such recognition and support. Many congregations have offered these services to both their members and to gay and lesbian persons in their communities. Although there are gays and lesbians in leadership in some religious bodies, they are few, and often do not receive the support of predominantly heterosexual congregations. The one religious place where gay and lesbian persons have found a guaranteed welcome has been in the special ministries that exist for gay and lesbian persons. This includes a variety of individual denominations and individual congregations with a special outreach to gay and lesbian persons.

### Social Issues

The growing visibility of homosexuals in American society and the scrutiny of the press probing the private lives of public figures have led some politicians to acknowledge publicly their homoerotic orientation. In 1980, Robert E. Bauman, a leading conservative Republican Congressman from Maryland, lost his bid for reelection after revealing his homoerotic orientation. About the same time, Congressman Gerry E. Studds from Massachusetts revealed his homoeroticism and he served in the House of Representatives until 1996. Elaine Noble was the first openly lesbian legislator in the state of Massachusetts. On the federal level, Representative Barney Frank, also from Massachusetts, disclosed his homoerotic orientation in 1987, and also continues to serve. In 1994, President Bill Clinton named Roberta Achtenberg as his highest-ranking lesbian appointee, and she was confirmed by the Congress as assistant secretary for fair housing and equal opportunity in the Department of Housing and Urban Development. In 1995, she announced that she was leaving that post to run for mayor of San Francisco.

Thanks to the political and educational activism of a wide variety of gay and lesbian individuals and groups, American society is becoming increasingly sensitized to the prevailing discrimination of heterosexism and homophobia. On the negative side, there has been an apparent increase in violence against people perceived to be homosexual. Studies have indicated increases in the reporting of violent crimes that are based on the perceived homosexuality of the victim, and students have reported witnessing harassment of students and teachers thought to be homosexual. In some instances, the growing hostility is purported to be linked with fear and anxiety about AIDS, but lesbian and gay leaders suggest that this is simply a convenient new excuse to further hate and discrimination. Lesbians, gays, and bisexuals see themselves as the last large minority that is not legally protected from discrimination, and thus, as a group, they fulfill

the need of some people to find scapegoats for whatever social ills occur. The other negative aspect of this increased visibility is that it causes the opposition to become aggressive. Observing the progress made by lesbians and gays in attempting to obtain equal rights, those opposed have taken a proactive approach in attempting to limit the rights and opportunities for lesbians and gays to enjoy a full and unrestricted life. This has taken many forms, including the development and dissemination of a video filled with partial truths and false information designed to arouse fear of and hatred toward homoerotic individuals and groups. There have also been referendums on ballots to deny homosexuals equal protection. While some of these have been passed in several jurisdictions, some of them have subsequently been declared unconstitutional by state and federal courts. That has not deterred others from developing similar referendums. In September 1996, Congress voted to deny Federal benefits to married people of the same sex and to permit states to ignore such marriages sanctioned in other states. A separate bill that would have banned for the first time discrimination against homosexuals in the workplace was defeated by a single vote.

On the positive side, openly gay or lesbian people have been elected to almost every level of government, with the exception of the executive branch of the state and federal governments (governors and the president and vice president). Voters in several jurisdictions have enacted legislation to protect the civil rights of lesbians and gays. The amount of literature and published research on lesbian and gay issues has increased exponentially in recent years, and the arts have moved to include lesbian, gay, and bisexual subjects in other than classically stereotypic and tragic roles. Research and commentary regarding gay, lesbian, and bisexual issues in the academic disciplines has become acceptable, and the result has been a concomitant exponential increase in published works in all the academic disciplines. There are even a few departments in universities specifically devoted to studies of lesbian, gay, and bisexual issues. In all the arts and literature, there are more and more instances of openly lesbian and gay themes, stories, and characters. And there are more openly gay, lesbian, and bisexual people in professional and amateur sports (such as Martina Navratalova in tennis, and Greg Louganis, the Olympic multiple-gold-medal diver), and in commerce (billionaire David Geffan).

Some people who are known privately but widely to be lesbian or gay are challenged by the gay and lesbian communities to be open. On occasion, they are "outed," that is, they are publicly announced to be lesbian or gay. Whether this is appropriate and ethical, given the extent of the homophobia in the culture, is a question. Originally, this practice was instituted only in cases where a person was widely known to be homoerotic and was not only keeping that information secret, but also was engaging in antihomosexual activity, such as gay public officials supporting antigay, antilesbian legislation. It later developed into a more-general application of "outing," which many have questioned and challenged.

One of the major problems for lesbian, gay, and bisexual adolescents is the lack of positive role models available in the homophobic, heterosexist culture. This lack contributes to the lowered self-esteem of lesbian and gay youth. The increased visibility of lesbian women and gay men throughout all levels of the society means that younger lesbians and gays are able to see others of identical orientation who have succeeded in whatever their chosen career. This has a positive effect on ego and the development of self-image.

### Family Issues

Gay and lesbian people have been at the forefront of defining operative, nontraditional, nonbiological family concepts. Although this may have grown from the difficulties of association with biological families and the impracticality of the "heterosexual husband-wife with children" relationship model, it has resulted in the active development and maintenance of alternative family structures of great depth and commitment that have subsequently provided an alternative model for the heterosexual society. This includes not only nonmarital couples and their children, but also committed longstanding friendship circles that constitute a chosen extended family, a set of associations often with stronger bonds than those that may exist through the unchosen avenue of blood relatives.

The depth and extent of these intentional relationships have become dramatically evident in the caring provided to those within such networks in the HIV/AIDS epidemic. The depth and extent of this caring has provided incontrovertible evidence of the wholesomeness and loving nature of these associations, and has significantly challenged the remainder of society.

The social, familial, and internalized heterosexist homophobia sometimes creates a situation in which the lesbian or gay man sees heterosexual marriage as the only public option for life. They may or may not include secret homosexual activity while married. With the increased visibility of lesbians, gays, and bisexuals, this pattern of behavior is less likely to occur without conscious awareness and dissonance on the part of both marital partners. Sometimes, but rarely, the only way a gay man or lesbian can cope successfully with the social pressures is to find a homoerotic person of the other gender to agree to a "marriage of convenience," in which they might live as roommates and have separate sexual lives.

Some lesbians and gay men choose to have children. Women have the option of childbearing through the medically established procedure of donor insemination available in this country, or they can, and sometimes do, seek and find a man who will biologically impregnate them. Men obviously do not have this option. Therefore, the issues for lesbians who want a child are different from those for a gay man who wants one. In keeping with the resourcefulness and creativity of many lesbians and gay men, there are many patterns that have been developed to achieve biological parenthood.

Support organizations for the heterosexual relatives of homoerotic individuals have formed and become available. Most notable is the organization Parents and Friends of Lesbians and Gays (PFLAG), with headquarters in Washington, D.C., and groups throughout the United States. Where there are lesbian and gay community centers, usually one finds programs for children of lesbian and gay parents, such as the Center Kids, a program at the Lesbian and Gay Community Center in New York City. These centers also usually have support groups and education sessions for the biological families of lesbians and gays, as well as for the chosen families.

### Health Issues

American lesbian women and gay men have many of the same health issues as their heteroerotic counterparts, but there are some issues that are unique, including the fact that the assumption of heterosexuality for individuals in the culture in general continues into the sphere of the healthcare consumer. When the healthcare professional is taking a history and asks, "Are you married or single or divorced?" there is little room for the lesbian or gay individual to indicate that she or he is in a long-term relationship with another person. And if the person is bisexually active, the answer to that question could be very misleading to the professional who should be concerned with whatever may have an impact the patient's health.

Lesbian women and gay men also have to interact with hospitals and other healthcare facilities that often do not recognize the rights of a nonmarital partner to determine the course of treatment or to visit in an intensive-care unit unless they have obtained either a power of attorney or have officially been designated as a "healthcare proxy."

Although lesbians have the lowest rates of sexually transmitted diseases of any orientation group, they also have some special concerns that would not apply to heteroerotic women, but would apply to bisexual women. Those issues are related to the fact that this person is sexually active with another woman. There is some debate concerning whether lesbians who are not sexually active with a man should have a Pap smear as often as a woman who is sexually active with a man. Additionally, if a patient tells the healthcare professional that she is a lesbian, the assumption is then made that she is not being sexually active with a man. This assumption should always be checked, because it is not necessarily true. A comprehensive sex history is needed to avoid incorrect assumptions, but is seldom done.

Gay men, on the other hand, have a high rate of sexually transmitted diseases. Prior to the 1980s, there was no major push for these men to wear condoms to prevent STDs, because most of the diseases could be cured by medical intervention. However, with the advent of HIV/AIDS, that situation changed, and the increased use of condoms in this population has significantly decreased the incidence of other STDs. The high frequency of sexual activity in many gay men means that their healthcare needs include concerns for the many diseases that can be transmitted sexually—and a comprehensive sex history is mandatory if the professional is to provide appropriate healthcare.

In the early 1980s, what we now know as AIDS was called GRID, Gay Related Immunodeficiency Disease, and it was believed that gay men were the only people who had it. While that has changed, the largest percentage of cases of AIDS in the United States continues to be among gay men, and part of gay-male identity is now referenced to HIV status, i.e., whether he is HIV-positive or HIV-negative. There is some concern about the effect that this has on one's psychological health, with some people questioning the acceptance of that reference to "Gay Related" when the infectious potential of HIV is not influenced by a person's sexual orientation.

Additionally, gay men have been likened in a psychological manner to Vietnam veterans, in that both have experienced the death of many people with whom close bonds had been established. There has been a suggestion that many gay men, particularly in the regions of the country that are hardest hit by the HIV/AIDS epidemic, are suffering from posttraumatic stress disorder and are in need of psychological treatment. Those lesbians who are very involved in the care of and are friends of HIV-positive gay men, are also experiencing trauma associated with multiple bereavement.

Another group that is receiving little attention in this epidemic are those gay men who are HIV negative, who have lost partners to AIDS, and who are having to deal with survivor guilt and associated issues. Many of these men must also cope with the very strong feelings of pleasure that were associated with sexual activity before HIV became a threat. These men are at great risk for HIV infection; yet, in the mid-1990s, the public-health focus has turned to women and children at risk, generally ignoring gay men.

[*Brothers on the Down Low. Update 2003*: "On the Down Low" or "DL," refers to men who identify themselves as heterosexual but engage in sexual activities with other men. This behavior has long been known to exist in all races, but appears to be more common among African-American men than white men. The DL, a relatively new term, is maintained by the perception among many African-American men that if their double life were known, they would be shamed, stigmatized, and ostracized from the black community, which provides a safe haven from a racist society.

[The total number of black men on the "Down Low" is difficult to estimate. But according to the Centers for Disease Control in Atlanta, approximately 25% of black HIV-positive men who had sex with men consider themselves heterosexual. Experts are concerned that men involved in these secret sexual relationships are fueling the rising incidence of HIV among women (Denizet-Lewis 2003; King & Harris 2004). (*End of update by H. Samuels*)]

### Homosexuality in the Later Years

Very little is known about sexuality and aging among the estimated 3.5 million American men and women over age 60 who are homosexual. For gay men and lesbians, aging can create unique conflicts and problems. The death of a partner in a long-term relationship may bring out homophobic reactions among family members that lead these relatives to ignore the bereaved partner or contest a will and estate. Gay men and lesbians who decide to acknowledge their orientation after years of passing as heterosexual face the possibility of quite different outcomes when loved ones, children, and grandchildren, learn of their relative's sexual orientation. Gay men, who are fearful that their orientation will be discovered as it becomes evident they are not going to marry, may adopt a loner life with relatively little sexual and social intimacy. Lesbian couples have to cope with two female incomes, which would usually be lower than most dual-career gay male or heterosexual couples (Friend 1987).

By necessity, gay men and lesbians develop skills in coping and crisis management, which give them an advantage in the aging process. More-flexible gender roles may allow older homosexuals to take aging more in stride and develop ways of taking care of themselves that seem comfortable and appropriate. "These skills may not be developed to the same degree among heterosexual men or women, who may be used to having or expecting a wife or husband to look after them" (Friend 1987, 311). Gay people tend to plan ahead for their own independence and security, whereas heterosexuals are more likely to assume that their children will take care of them in their old age. Homosexual men and women have significantly more close friends who serve as a "surrogate family" than do heterosexuals. In larger urban areas, organizations like Senior Action in a Gay Environment (SAGE) provide a variety of social and support services for older homosexuals.

### Gay Men, Lesbian Women, and Bisexuals—Comparisons

Because gay men are socialized as males and generally perceive themselves as males, their socialization process is somewhat different from that of lesbian women, who are socialized as females and generally perceive themselves as being female. This means that, from a general perspective, just as there are differences in male and female socialization, there are differences between lesbians and gay men, as well as differences among them. For example, in general analyses of gay and lesbian relationships, one difference often noted between the two is the role of sexual activity and sexual exclusivity. Generally, lesbian relationships are sexually exclusive and gay male relationships are not. This appears to be especially true of long-term relationships, and can be explained by the differences in socialization of women and men around sexual activity issues.

When gay men and lesbian women join together to form groups working toward a common goal, sometimes there are issues of power differentials and attitudes toward sexual activity that prevent the original goals from being reached by dividing the group along gender lines. Again, this can be explained by the differential socialization process.

It was not until the late 1980s that people identified as bisexual were welcomed into what were previously lesbian and gay organizations, and they are still viewed with caution in many circles. Bisexuals are sometimes accused by heterosexual people of being gay or lesbian and are labeled homophobic and fake by some homoerotic people. There are few bisexual support groups, most of them in large cities. The United States is only just beginning to attempt to understand the bisexual phenomenon.

## C. Bisexuality

CAROL QUEEN with ROBERT MORGAN LAWRENCE

The ambivalence about bisexuality is reflected in the history of the concept. For several years after the terms *homosexuality* and *heterosexuality* were coined in the late 1800s, bisexuality was largely ignored by the physicians and sex researchers who had newly medicalized sex. Sigmund Freud, with his theory of sexual development borrowed from Darwinian evolutionary models, helped to change that. By the 1920s, when Wilhelm Stekel wrote *Bi-Sexual Love*, the erotic capacity to desire both males and females could be envisioned as universal, if likely to be outgrown by adulthood. Havelock Ellis, by contrast, viewed bisexuality as a distinct sexual-orientation category, comparable to both homo- and heterosexuality.

Alfred Kinsey (1948, 1953) conceptualized bisexuality not in evolutionary terms, as the Freudians tended to do, but in simple behavioral terms. In his sexual-orientation scale, bisexuality was represented on a continuum between exclusive heterosexuality (the 0 end of Kinsey's scale) and exclusive homosexuality (at 6), with a Kinsey 3 equally attracted to or having had sexual experience with males and females.

Since most humans experience their erotic desires and relationships in a social context, many (perhaps most) bisexuals have more sexual experience with one or the other gender, depending upon whether their social affiliations tend to be mostly heterosexual or homosexual. Indeed, researchers have noted that many people who have displayed "bisexual" behavior over the lifespan—that is, people who have had sexual experience with both males and females—tend to identify sexually according to the gender of their current partner (Blumstein & Schwartz 1983). This is reported as especially true of women. When the current partner is female, women are more likely to identify themselves as lesbian, and when the current partner is male, as heterosexual. Factors such as political or social affiliation can also lead an individual to—or away from—a bisexual identity.

One common stereotype about bisexuals suggests a person is not "really" bisexual unless he or she is a Kinsey 3. This is related to the presumption that the individual is "really" homosexual but hiding behind a heterosexual relationship. The notion that all, or most, people are "really" homosexual or heterosexual has been termed "monosexuality." Monosexuals are individuals who desire members of only one gender, whereas bisexuals desire both. The term was apparently first used to describe hetero- and homosexuals by Stekel (1922). Today, this term has gained new currency in the American bisexual community as bisexuals seek to understand and combat the sources of stereotyping and social opprobrium they term "biphobia" (Hutchins & Kaahumanu 1991). Expressions of biphobia encompass caustic dismissals, such as Bergler's (1956) "Nobody can dance at two different weddings at the same time"; difficult relations between bisexual women and some lesbians (Weise 1992); and media-fed concerns that bisexual men are "spreading AIDS" into the heterosexual population. (The latter concern ignores the possibility that bisexual men can be as responsible about safe-sex practices as anyone else, that heterosexuals may also contract HIV from other heterosexuals, and that bisexual men may choose to live monogamous lives with female—or male—partners.)

Until recently, American bisexuals had few sources of support for their sexuality unless they derived it from the gay community—which has been far from uniformly supportive. In fact, it should be noted that many gays deny the reality and/or possibility of bisexuality. In the 1970s, a few support groups for bisexuals were formed; the best known of these was San Francisco's Bisexual Center. By the late 1980s, groups and organizations had emerged that aimed specifically to develop a supportive bisexual community; at the time of this writing, these are extensively networked and are producing their own publications and conferences.

Because of insufficient support, the influence of negative and alienating stereotypes, and the apparent fact that many bisexuals have lived as lesbians, gay men, or heterosexuals, it has been difficult to estimate what percentage of the population is, or has been, bisexual. It is probable that many more people have bisexual histories than would answer affirmatively to a survey researcher asking "Are you bisexual?" Too, many researchers have conflated or collapsed homosexuality and bisexuality (for a recent example, see Laumann et al. 1994), a further indication that many still consider one a variant of the other.

To stress the multidimensional nature of sexuality, Fred Klein (1985) developed his Sexual Orientation Grid, which expands Kinsey's concept of the continuum. He considers not only experience and desire, but also dreams, fantasies, social networks, relationships, ideal sexual orientation, and other variables. Additionally, Klein breaks the scale into temporal units (adolescence; early adulthood; present) so it can better reflect changes in behavior and sexual identity over the lifespan. Coleman (1987) has also developed a scale that takes factors like these into account and that serves as a clinical interview tool. Researchers using these scales, as well as Kinsey's, find that, although some display continuity of sexual identity over the lifespan, other individuals change identity over time. Many rate themselves near the middle of the Kinsey scale when asked their ideal, but report their relationships fall closer to one or the other end.

That behavior and identity are not fixed (and are sometimes not even consonant) is of special interest and relevance to researchers of bisexuality. The differences between homosexual and heterosexual may be less important and intriguing than those between monosexual and bisexual. Why, for example, is a prospective partner's gender of primary importance to some (monosexuals) and not to others (many bisexuals)? Other researchers note that bisexuality assumes different forms in different cultures, subcultures, and individuals. Klein (1978) suggests four primary types: 1. sequential (in which an individual will alternately partner or engage in sex with only men, then only women); 2. concurrent (in which an individual partners or engages in sex with both genders during the same period of time); 3. historical (bisexual behavior in an individual's past, especially adolescence); and 4. transitional (through which a heterosexual moves toward homosexuality or a homosexual moves toward heterosexuality).

Other American researchers have concentrated not on the taxonomy of bisexuality, but on the development and adjustment of bisexuals in day-to-day life. Some of this research has been incidental to studies done on gay and lesbian or heterosexual populations; other researchers have looked at self-identified bisexual populations. Just as estimates on the percentage of bisexuals in the population are inconclusive, so is information about what percentage of people who have a history of sexual experience with both genders defines themselves as bisexual. What differentiates those who do from those who do not is still a matter of speculation, although research into the formation of bisexual identity suggests that, at least for them, identity formation is more open-ended than linear.

A common monosexual accusation is that bisexuals are "confused." Although this may be descriptive of some bisexuals before they find the label with which to self-identify, and some may also experience ongoing distress or uncertainty because of the dearth of societal validation (Weinberg & Williams 1994), some research has indicated that self-identified bisexuals are high in self-esteem, self-confidence, and independence of social norms (Rubenstein 1982; Twining 1983).

Much more attention has been given to bisexuals, especially males, who are heterosexually married than to those whose primary relationships are homosexual. These marriages are most successful when the partners communicate openly, the spouse is aware and accepting of the bisexual partner's sexuality, and both partners are committed to the relationship. Especially as the bisexual community brings self-identified bisexual people together, more bisexuals are choosing to partner with other bisexuals. These relationships may be monogamous, open, polyamorous, or—much more rarely—triadic.

Bisexuals bringing issues related to their sexual identities into therapy may seek help in interpreting their attractions to both genders; other issues are isolation and alienation, fears about coming out or about nonvoluntary disclosure of their sexuality, and relationship concerns.

What bisexual community spokespeople call "bisexual invisibility" hinders many individuals from easily resolving their concerns about adopting a non-normative sexual identity. Many do not know about the existence of a community of peers. While some individuals move towards a bisexual identity after considering themselves heterosexual, others have previously been gay- or lesbian-identified. As such, diversity in the bisexual community is broad, and will undoubtedly become broader as more people gain access to its institutions.

## D. Orientations: A 2003 Update and Commentary
DAVID L. WEIS

[*Update 2003*: In March 2000, the state of Vermont enacted a law granting legal recognition to same-sex unions. Some of Vermont's 250 town and city clerks vowed to defy the law and not grant civil unions. The Catholic Bishop of Vermont called for religious Americans to pray and work for a constitutional amendment that would bar civil unions. Opponents of the new law quickly introduced a "Defense of Marriage" bill to ban same-sex unions and marriages. Within months, 33 states had enacted laws banning same-sex marriages and the U.S. Congress passed a law allowing individual states not to recognize the civil unions or marriage of a same-sex couple from another state.

[Despite the growing disputes, this legal breakthrough set the stage for an even more giddy time in the summer of 2003 for advocates of human rights for GLBT (gay, lesbian, bisexual, and transgender) people.

- Three of the seven provinces in Canada made gay marriage legal, when a federal court ruled that provincial bans on gay unions or marriages violate Canada's constitution.

- In July 2003, the Supreme Court of the United States ruled that sodomy laws banning homosexual behavior are unconstitutional. The ruling enraged conservatives (see Legal Issues in Section 6B, Adults, above).

- The hippest television show in the summer season, "Queer Eye for the Straight Guy," was Bravo/NBC's "hilarious reality show in which five gay connoisseurs of fashion, grooming, interior design, food and culture rebuild a clueless hetero from the ground up" (Gordon & Sigesmund 2002; Wilson 2003).

- The Vatican released an instruction declaring that "Laws in favour of homosexual unions are contrary to right reason [and a] grave detriment to the common good. . . . The Catholic law-maker has a moral duty to express his opposition clearly and publicly and vote against it. To vote in favour of a law so harmful to the common good is gravely immoral."

[The next day, President Bush equated gay marriage with "sin" and said he would support an amendment to the U.S. Constitution that would ban gay marriages.

- After 70 years of advising brides how to walk down the aisle and celebrate their wedding, a full-page article in *Bride's* magazine discussed recent developments in same-sex ceremonies. Gay and lesbian couples told why they want their friends and community to recognize their unions publicly. The article also offered advice on how to be a good guest at a gay union or wedding.

- By the summer of 2003, many of the nations newspapers, *The New York Times*, *St. Louis Post-Dispatch*, *Charlotte North Carolina Observer*, and *Boston Globe* among them, were publishing announcements of same-sex commitments in their wedding pages.

- In July, the nation's attention was focused on public debate at the National Convention of the Episcopal Church in the U.S. where bishops, clergy, and laity passionately debated whether or not to confirm the election of Rev. Canon V. Gene Robinson as Bishop of the Diocese of New Hampshire. Robinson had been selected from dozens of candidates, even though he acknowledged being in a relationship with another man for 14 years. The day before the convention was scheduled to vote, there was a delay, when allegations emerged that Robinson had engaged in "inappropriate touches" with another man and was connected to a pornographic website. When neither allegation was substantiated, Robinson was confirmed as the first openly homosexual Bishop in the Anglican Communion. The possibility of a schism heated up, as conservative American Episcopalians aligned themselves with African and Asian bishops who also strongly opposed the election and confirmation of a homosexual. The Archbishop of Canterbury quickly called for a meeting of top officials in October to find a way to avoid a schism among the 2.3 million members in the U.S. and the 70 million in the worldwide Anglican Communion.

- Following the vote confirming Canon Robinson as Bishop of New Hampshire, tensions and anxieties were very obvious, with everyone at the Minneapolis Convention wanting to avoid a global schism in the Church of England. Further conflict seemed inevitable, since discussion and a vote on whether or not to give full church approval to gay unions and appoint a commission to write a ritual for gay unions to include in the *Book of Common Prayer*. In a sensitive and delicate compromise, the Convention acknowledged that "differences exist" among the bishops about whether such blessings should be allowed, but the Convention "recogniz(ed) that local faith communities are operating within the bounds of our common life as they explore and experience liturgies celebrating and blessing same-sex unions." The compromise effectively left the decision of blessing gay unions up to the local pastor and bishop.

- Some credible scientific evidence was announced that the likelihood of acquiring the HIV virus through oral sex is negligible (Page-Shafer et al. 2002).

- In the midst of the media blitz over homosexual issues and breakthroughs, a New Jersey survey revealed that likely voters in that state favored granting legal recognition of gay/lesbian marriages by 55% to 41% and legal recognition of gay/lesbian unions by 69% to 26%. The New Jersey courts were expected to rule shortly on whether the state would recognize gay unions.

[In the summer of 2003, television brought all of these events to the attention of families watching the evening news, evening after evening, across the nation and around the world. Even small local newspapers felt compelled to report these events, often in front-page headlines, and with commentary, pro or con, on the likely social consequences of these events. What happened in the summer of 2003 was not a series of isolated events that transpired behind the closed doors of one church, one magazine, one television network, or in a 2.7-minute newsbite, sandwiched between news from Iraq or North Korea. The debates over a gay bishop and a same-sex ritual affected not just a large mainstream church in the U.S. They affected the Anglican communities in Asia, Africa, Europe, and North America. The media saturation reports of these events had some impact on the consciousness of all Americans: They influenced the subconscious attitudes and awareness of basic sexual issues. More or less, these same events were also affected by the civil recognition of gay marriages in Belgium and the Netherlands, and the acceptance of gay unions in Canada and its provinces, France, Germany, some jurisdictions in Spain, and the Scandinavian countries.

[I cannot remember such a series of encouraging events in North America in my lifetime. Celebration seems appropriate. On the other hand, this will certainly unify the social forces opposing these changes to renew their battle. There still is support in the U.S. Congress for the Defense of Marriage Act (Casert 2003). Only days after the sodomy ruling, congressional Republicans and President George W. Bush announced their intention to pass legislation that would ban homosexual marriage in the U.S. (Mann 2003). I suspect the issue will increase the polarity already rampant in American politics. However, I do not believe it will stop the now century-long trend toward greater sexual freedom for adults.

[All of this has also served to remind me just how little we know about GLBT persons, lifestyles, and issues. In the last decade, there has been increasing recognition of the need to study how GLBT people are related to quality of life, health, and mental health (Bailey 1999; Cochran 2001). Some of this may depend on how these groups are defined. For example, Cochran, Sullivan, and Mays (2003) found that, for both males and females, groups of homosexual and bisexual persons (combined) were more likely to experience a wide range of mental health difficulties (depression, suicide attempts, etc.) than persons who were heterosexual only. In a study of a national sample in the Netherlands, researchers found that a combined group of homosexual and bisexual men, but not women, experienced a lower quality of life than heterosexual-only men. Persons with lower quality of life were also found to have lower self-esteem and more external locus of control (Sandfort, de Graaf, & Bijl

2003). In contrast, Horowitz, Weis, and Laflin (2001) found few quality-of-life, social-background, or health-behavior differences among separate groups of heterosexual, homosexual, bisexual, and asexual respondents in a national study of the U.S.A. Since research in this area is still in its infancy, we have much to learn before resolving these apparently contradictory findings.

[Serious scientific questions also remain about how stable GLBT identities are, versus their susceptibility to change over the course of the lifecycle. Recently, Diamond (2003a) conducted a study of women who identified themselves as lesbian and/or bisexual at the beginning of a five-year study. Over a quarter of the women relinquished that identity during the period of the study. Interestingly, the women did not report that their pattern of attraction to same-sex persons had changed. Rather, their interpretations of what this meant had changed. Half of them decided they were heterosexual and half gave up all identity labels. Findings such as this suggest that sexual orientation may be more flexible than most previous models have maintained.

[Finally, perhaps the time has come for sexual scientists to begin a debate as to whether the very concept of sexual orientation is a useful one. Certainly, there is growing recognition of the complexities of experience and identity embedded within the labels of GLBT. The penultimate example of this complexity may well be the model of sexual orientation proposed by Klein, Sepekoff, and Wolf (1985). They maintained that orientation could vary along seven dimensions (such as behavior, fantasy, attraction, relationships, etc.) in any of three different time periods, creating 21 different cells or types of orientation. To say this would make research difficult is an understatement. In a review of the literature, Diamond (2003b) recently described evidence that orientation toward romantic partners and sexual desire are independent. All of this makes me wonder if the characterization of people as GLBT serves to help us or hinder us from greater understanding.

[Personally, I have found myself becoming fond of the label "men who have sex with men," a construct that is common in research on HIV. Of course, there are also "women who have sex with women." There are two reasons I like this terminology. First, it is relatively explicit about just who is and is not included in the group—people who behaviorally engage in sexual activity with members of their own gender and/or sex. Second, it promotes the idea that not everyone who engages in such behavior is the same in other respects. Getting *everyone* to understand this point strikes me as a good goal for sexual scientists as we begin the 21st century. (*End of update by D. L. Weis*)]

## 7. Gender Diversity and Transgender Issues

### [A. Intersexuality and the Politics of Difference

ROBERT T. FRANCOEUR

[*Update 1997*: On March 12, 1993, the "Op-Ed" page of *The New York Times* carried a full-page reflection on "How Many Sexes Are There?" The March/April issue of *The Sciences*, published by the New York Academy of Sciences, featured an article on "The Five Sexes: Why Male and Female Are Not Enough." These articles, by biologist Anne Fausto-Sterling, are evidence of a trend in changing definitions of gender roles over the past decade that is echoed in the appearance in 1995 of *Hermaphrodites with Attitudes*, a newsletter published by cross-gendered persons who endorse Fausto-Sterling's call for the medical profession to recognize gender diversity and cease using surgery and gender reassignment to force true hermaphrodites ("herms"),

female pseudohermaphrodites ("ferms"), and male pseudohermaphrodites ("merms") into the dichotomous mold of male or female. (*End of update by R. T. Francoeur*)]

[*Update 1998*: In the past ten years, female impersonators, transvestites, and other gender-bending images have become popular subjects of television talk shows and prime-time television "magazines" like *Prime Time Live* and *60 Minutes*. Major films have made cross-dressing and transvestite issues a common theme—to mention a few: *La Cage Aux Folles* and its remake *The Bird Cage*; *Yentl* (with Barbra Streisand); *Victor/Victoria* (with Julie Andrews); *Tootsie* (with Dustin Hoffman); *Mrs. Doubtfire* (with Robin Williams); *M Butterfly*; *Adventures of Priscilla, Queen of the Desert*; *Glen or Glenda*; *Farewell My Concubine*; *Just Like a Woman*; *Different for Girls*; *The Sheltering Sky* (with Debra Winger); *Bull Durham* (featuring a rookie pitcher who wears a garter belt under his uniform); *Love Compassion and Valor*; and *To Wong Foo, Thanks for Everything, Julie Newmar* (featuring Wesley Snipes, John Leguizamos, and Patrick Swayze). RuPaul, a stunning six-foot-seven African-American drag queen has gained national recognition as a model for GLAM Lipstick and as a popular television talk show host and radio disk jockey. Rudolph Giuliani, the former mayor of New York, appeared comically at several public events in drag. Dennis Rodman, Chicago Bulls professional basketball player, has also appeared in drag several times, including once dressed as a bride. Female impersonation, cross-dressing, and transvestism seem to be "in vogue camp."

[In 1992, the polymorphous San Francisco culture saw the birth of Transgender Nation, an energetic transgender political movement, developed out of Queer Nation, a post-gay/lesbian group, which sought to transcend gender-identity politics. Transgender Nation made news when some members were arrested for protesting the psychiatric labeling of transsexuality as a mental illness at the American Psychiatric meeting. About the same time, openly transsexual scholars, including Susan Stryker and Sandy Stone, became visible in academic positions at leading universities.

[Whether this broad spectrum of transgendered persons becomes significant in the long term of American sexual culture is not at present clear, but its synchronicity with the recent emergence of a very small but potentially important activist group of transgendered persons is worth investigation. In 1993, Cheryl Chase founded the Intersex Society of North America. ISNA's immediate goal was to "create a community of intersex people who could provide each other with peer support to deal with their shame, stigma, grief, and rage, as well as with practical issues such as how to obtain old medical records or how to locate a sympathetic psychotherapist or endocrinologist." According to Chase,

ISNA's longer-term and more fundamental goal, however, is to change the way intersex infants are treated. We advocate that surgery not be performed on ambiguous genitals unless there is a medical reason (such as blocked or painful urination) and that parents be given the conceptual tools and emotional support to accept their children's physical differences. While it is fascinating to think about the potential development of new genders or subject positions grounded in forms of embodiment that fall outside the familiar male/female dichotomy, we recognize that the two-sex/gender model is currently hegemonic and, therefore, advocate that children be raised either as boys or girls according to which designation seems likely to offer the child the greatest future sense of comfort. Advocating gender assignment without resorting to normalizing surgery is a radical position given that it requires the willful disruption of the assumed concordance between body shape and gender category. However, this is the only position that prevents irreversible physical damage to the intersex person's body, that preserves the intersex person's agency regarding their own flesh, and that recognizes genital sensation and erotic functioning to be at least as important as reproductive capacity. If an intersex child or adult decides to change gender or to undergo surgical or hormonal alteration of his/her body, that decision should also be fully respected and facilitated. The key point is that intersex subjects should not be violated for the comfort and convenience of others (Chase 1998).

[ISNA has publicized its message and activist agenda with an astute and effective use of the media, including: Public Broadcast Radio and Television; publications like *The New York Times*, *New York Post*, *Mademoiselle* (February 1998), *Rolling Stone* (December 11, 1997); a special issue of *Chrysalis* (published by AEGIS, the American Educational Gender Information Service); a newsletter titled *Hermaphrodites with Attitude*; dialogues and protest demonstrations at medical meetings; and articles in professional journals, such as *Urology Times* and *Archives of Pediatric and Adolescent Medicine*.

[Of particular interest is the use ISNA has made of the Internet to connect and cooperate with other groups, including: the Turner Syndrome Society, Androgen Insensitivity (AIS) Support Group, Klinefelter's Syndrome (K.S.) & Associates, the Ambiguous Genital Support Network, Hermaphrodite Education and Listening Post (HELP), the Gay and Lesbian Medical Association, the Workgroup on Violence in Pediatrics and Gynecology, the Genital Mutilation Survivors' Support Network (organized by German intersexuals), and Hijra Nippon (organized by activist intersexuals in Japan). (*End of update by R. T. Francoeur*)]

[*Update 2003*: In the early 1990s, Cheryl Chase used the Internet and World Wide Web very effectively to organize an advocacy group to change the standard medical practice of performing genital surgery on newborns with ambiguous or intersex genitals. When Chase retired as the director of the Intersex Society of North America (ISNA) in early 2003, ISNA had persuaded many pediatricians to postpone genital surgery on infants unless the condition was life-threatening. With new leadership, ISNA is pursuing its goal of systematic change in medical practice to end shame, secrecy, and unwanted genital surgeries for people born with an anatomy that someone decided does not meet the medical criteria for a standard male or female. In ten brief years, ISNA has achieved its goal of persuading the medical community to use a model of care that is patient-centered, rather than concealment-centered (www.isna.org). Among the recommendations ISNA is pressing with physicians are the following:

- An intersex or hermaphrodite person is an individual (of any age) born with ambiguous genitals. Intersexuality needs to be considered as a problem of stigma and trauma, not as a gender problem.
- The distress of parents must not be treated by surgery on the child.
- Professional mental healthcare is an essential for both the intersex persons and the family.
- Honest, complete disclosure is good medicine.
- All children should be assigned as boy or girl, without early surgery.

[From the 1950s into the 1970s, it became standard medical procedure to treat newborns with ambiguous genitals with cosmetic surgery designed to bring their genitals into conformity with what was then considered the norm for

male or female. Based on what was known (or assumed at the time), psychologists believed infants were born with a "blank slate," so to speak, and grew into their gender as a male or female. It was then also assumed that when a child was born with ambiguous genitals, cosmetic surgery and strict rearing for the appropriate gender was the best way to produce a normal boy or girl. Over the next 30 years, these assumptions were increasingly challenged in a very controversial and emotionally charged case known in the clinical literature and the popular media as "the John/Joan case."

[It started in Winnipeg, Canada, on August 22, 1965, when a teenage mother gave birth to identical twin boys, Bruce and Brian. When the infants were 7 months old, the mother told her doctor that the boys cried when urinating. The doctor told the parents that the boys' foreskins were too tight and he prescribed circumcision. On April 27, 1966, in a tragic accident, the physician performing the circumcision with an electric cauterizing knife caused a severe injury to Bruce's penis and testes. After a few days, the penis dried up and fell off, leaving only a stub. Eventually, after desperate attempts to find someone who could help them deal with the problem, the parents were recommended to Johns Hopkins Hospital where John Money was a world-renowned expert on psychosexual development. Money had been pioneering treatment of adult transsexuals using a sex-change operation. At age 17 months, the decision was made to surgically turn "John" into a girl and raise her as "Joan." The testes were removed so they would not produce male secondary sex characteristics. Estrogen replacement and vaginal surgery in the adolescent years would complete the work of gender reassignment.

[Early reports suggested a perfectly normal gender-identity development for the reassigned girl (Money & Tucker 1975, 91-99). However, in a 1979 report on British television, Williams and Smith reported that "Joan" experienced considerable difficulty in adjusting to her female gender role. Then in her teens, they reported she was displaying symptoms that made them "suspicious that she will ever make the adjustment as a woman." Finally, after years of detective work to find out what actually happened to Brian after his father finally told him the whole story, Milton Diamond, a sexologist at the University of Hawaii School of Medicine, published a report in the *Archives of Pediatric and Adolescent Medicine* (Diamond & Sigmundson 1997). David had reasserted his male gender and had had reconstructive surgery to recreate male anatomy. He had married and was enjoying being an adoptive father. A sensational story in *Rolling Stone* and a book titled *As Nature Made Him: The Boy Who Was Raised as a Girl* (Colapinto 2000) followed, with television appearances on Oprah, ABC, *Dateline*, the BBC, *60 Minutes*, and more.

[In 2003, we know much of David's story, from his infancy as Bruce to the surgical accident, his childhood and teen years as "Joan," and his current life as David. But there is also much we have yet to learn about this tragic and complex story. One thing we do know, however: There are aspects of our gender that are encoded in the neural pathways of our brain before birth. And this encoding is irreversible. Cheryl Chase and the intersex members of ISNA have used David's story and their own stories as persons born with ambiguous genitals to establish a new medical treatment based on the rights of an "intersex" child not to be subjected to genital surgery until they can make their own decision how they want their condition to be treated. (*End of update by R. T. Francoeur*)]

[*Update 1998*: It is estimated that one in 100 infants are born with some anomaly in sex differentiation, and about one in 2,000 newborns are different enough to make their gender assignment as "boy" or "girl" problematic. Thus, the members of ISNA would appear to have minuscule potential for achieving their goal of persuading society to accept a "politics of difference" with recognition and valuing of other-gendered persons. A minority as small as ISNA would seem to have little chance of successfully challenging the prevailing medical paradigm of immediate surgical intervention to remedy sexual ambiguity (Coleman 1991). However, as medical ethicist Karen Lebacqz (1997) has observed,

> The politics of difference has emerged out of the self-identification of groups that may be minorities in society but that are large enough to become a political force. . . . [T]he advent of new technologies such as the Internet may facilitate the process, as individuals who are widely scattered geographically can find each other and form connections and agendas.

[Only the future will tell whether American society is at a watershed where reconstructions of societal and individual responses to gender are possible. Whether the mass media and Internet are powerful enough to enable American culture to replace its all-prevailing gender dichotomy with a "politics of difference," similar in some respects to the valuing of "third-gendered persons" in other cultures, remains to be seen. (*End of update by R. T. Francoeur*)]

## B. Cross-Gender: Overview, Issues, and Persons

ARIADNE (ARI) KANE [*Rewritten and updated in June 2003 by A. Kane*]

*An Indigenous View*

American society, with its cultural diversity, has long assumed that one's gender perception, role, and presentation are all a function of biological anatomy, as visually ascertained at birth. This biocentric viewpoint served as the basis for looking at sexual and gender variations for both sexologists and therapists. Until the mid-1970s, many sexual and gender options were seen and diagnosed as deviations from the male/female anatomical/medical model. Gender options, as style modes of clothing and accouterment, gender shifts, and transsexualism were viewed as dis-eases [sic] of the psyche. Those who chose such options were considered "gender-conflicted" and were treated on the basis of known medical or psychological modalities (Pauly 1994).

Factors contributing to the current trend of changing gender roles include the rise and powerful articulation of feminism among both women and men; the knowledge explosion in molecular biology, specifically genetics and endocrinology; artistic diversity in both the visual arts and music with their individual styles and presentations (with cinema, television, and music increasingly dealing with gender and cross-gender issues); the emergence of an articulate, vocative, and visible gay-lesbian-cross-gender "community"; and the influence of computer technology and its application in almost all sectors of American life. The impact of these factors on the daily lives of Americans—how they think, how they feel both about themselves as well as society, and how they act and present themselves to each other—has been awesome.

[From this social context, there is an incentive to challenge the biocentric notions about perceptions and gender roles as derivative of the dimorphic nature of *Homo sapiens*, i.e., two sexes implies only two gender forms. This challenge to gender rigidity, in roles and presentations, is seen in many areas of American social and economic life. Women as bus drivers and heavy-equipment operators and men as nurses and secretaries represent only one aspect of the varied paradigm shift occurring in America in the nature of gender identity and its concomitant behaviors. Instead of a binary

### Table 15

### The Transgender Phenomenon: A Flow Chart

| Group A | |
|---|---|
| Bigenderist | A person who can comfortably express him- or herself in either a conventional or nontraditional gender role |
| Transgenderist | A person who wants to live permanently in an alternative gender-role form, either traditionally or unconventionally |
| Androgyne | A person who desires to blend traditional gender-role behaviors (e.g., many rock stars—David Bowie, Mick Jagger) |
| Gender Bender | A person who engages in dissonant gender-role presentations and behaviors (female or male dressed in conventional modes with moustaches or beards) |
| **Group B** | |
| Masculine Impressionist | Females who perform on stage as men |
| Femme Impressionist | Males who perform on stage as well known women singers or comics |
| Cross-Dresser | Males or females who desire/choose to wear an item or items of apparel or accessories or use enhancers (makeup) typically worn or used by the other gender category |
| Transvestite | Historically, an adult male who wears an item or items of feminine apparel and accessories to create an image of a woman/girl. Some adult females have also been known to wear items of masculine apparel to create an image of a man/boy |
| Drag King | Any female who presents a complete visual masculine image in various social/public settings |
| Drag Queen | Any male who presents a complete visual feminine image in various social/public settings |
| **Group C** | |
| Transsexual | Males or females who have chosen a preferred gender role (transgenderist) and wants biologic congruity with that gender-role preference. This process involves an appropriate sex hormonal therapy, cosmetic, surgical, and sex reassignment |
| Intersexual | Individuals who are diagnosed as having ambiguous biologic genitalia are labeled intersexed or hermaphrodites |

model for sex and gender, there is a need for a new model consisting of several distinct biologic sexes (see Fausto-Sterling) with concomitant gender forms (see Table 15). One needs a model of two or more sexes and many genders. Here, a sociocentric view of gender, in which one can think of gender in terms of three basic parameters: perception (Jungian constructs of *anima/animus*), social role (cuing, interactions, and gender-role inventories), and presentation (modes of presenting one's self, for whom, when, motivations, etc.). Thus, the gender of a person is seen as a composite of these three parameters in dynamic equilibrium, time-dependent and ever-changing, over the lifespan.

[In addition to the sociocentric view of gender, there are other models that focus away from gender-conflict issues toward other facets of gender diversity. These include concepts like the "gender rainbow" paradigm suggested by gender counselors Leah Cahan Schaefer and C. Christine Wheeler, June Reinisch's concept of "gender flavors," and James Weinrich's model of "gender landscapes" (see Francoeur 1991, 100-101). In each of these models, gender-conflict issues are broadened to include gender explorations and gender clarifications. For the cross-gender person, these models provide alternative avenues in their search for personal growth in a tolerant and more nurturant society. For the healthcare professional, the sociocentric model of gender and selected use of the above concepts provide a realistic basis for studying CD/CG (cross dressing/cross gender) behavior. It is also a more sensitive approach to the issues and problems of gender expression in a multicultural American society.

Traditionally, the terms "transvestite" (TV) and "transsexual" (TS) have been used to label individuals, mostly males, who wear apparel usually associated with the other sex, or who want to cross a gender boundary and seek anatomical congruity with the other sex. These terms are too inclusive and stigmatize the person, who may be on a gender exploration, or who sees personal gender expression as only one piece in their total personality matrix. To deal with this limitation, the following new glossary has been proposed, with the terms serving as "mileposts" on the road to gender "happiness:"

- A "cross-dresser" (CD) is a person, male or female, who wears an item or items of apparel usually worn by the other gender; it is a descriptor of behavior and includes previously used terms like TV (transvestite), FI (female impersonator), and DQ (drag queen).
- "Cross-gender" (CG) refers to a person, male or female, who desires to cross and explore a gender role different from typical gender roles associated with their biologic sex. It can also be used as a behavior descriptor.
- A "transsexual" (TS) is a person, male or female, who has chosen a preferred gender role and wants anatomical congruity with that gender-role preference. This can be accomplished by an appropriate sex-hormone-therapy program and genital-reconstruction surgery (GRS). *Note*: For a male-to-female (MTF) TS, this is known as vaginoplasty; for the female-to-male (FTM) TS, it is known as phalloplasty. Sex-reassignment surgery (SRS) is an outmoded phrase, replaced by GRS.
- "New Women/New Men" refer to persons, male or female, who have transited to a preferred gender role, i.e., transgenderist, and have had genital-reconstruction surgery.
- The "CD/CG/TS paraculture" refers to the community of people, males and females, whose general behavior patterns include a major component of gender-diverse activity.

The term "transgender" indicates that a person is crossing gender boundaries usually associated with traditional gender traits of one or the other sex. Transgender, transgendered, and transgenderist are also used to indicate transcending—rising above—traditional gender forms and expressions, a usage that has gained popularity both within the paraculture, as well as in the healthcare and academic professions.

### A Clinical View

The term "transsexualism" was coined by D. O. Cauldwell, an American sexologist, and popularized by Harry Benjamin in the 1950s and 1960s. Research on this phenomenon was facilitated in 1980 when the concepts of transsexualism and gender disorders were recognized in the American Psychiatric Association's *Diagnostic and Statistical Manual III*. In 1988, transsexualism was defined by the *DSM-III-R* as having the following diagnostic criteria:

1. persistent discomfort and sense of inappropriateness about one's assigned sex;
2. persistent preoccupation for at least two years with getting rid of one's primary and secondary sex characteristics and acquiring the sex characteristics of the other sex; and
3. having reached puberty (otherwise, the diagnosis would be childhood gender identity disorder).

*DSM-IV* has replaced the term "transsexual" with the generic term "gender identity disorder."

Transsexualism is estimated to affect at least 1 in 50,000 individuals over the age of 15 years, with a 1:1 male-to-female ratio. The greater visibility of male-to-female transsexuals may reflect a more-negative bias toward male homosexuality or a lack of available female-to-male treatment in a society. Whatever the real incidence, this disorder carries more social significance and impact than the actual prevalence might suggest because of the questions raised for anyone who watches and listens to transsexuals (and transvestites) in their frequent appearances on television talk shows (Pauly 1994, 591).

An individual's perception of his or her own body, and the way she or he feels about these perceptions, are important in the clinical diagnosis of gender disorders. In 1975, Lindgren and Pauly introduced a Body Image Scale, a 30-item list of body parts, for which the individual is asked to rate her or his feelings on a five-point scale ranging from (1) very satisfied to (5) very dissatisfied. This scale is useful in following the progress and evaluating the success of genital-reconstruction surgery (GRS).

Evaluating the outcome of genital-reconstruction surgery is complicated and difficult. The most recent evaluation leaves little question that the vast majority of post-operative transsexuals claim satisfaction and would pursue the same course if they had to do it again. Post-operative satisfaction ranged from 71.4% to 87.8% for post-operative male-to-female transsexuals, with only 8.1% to 10.3% expressing dissatisfaction. Among female-to-male transsexuals surveyed, 80.7% to 89.5% were satisfied with their outcome, compared with only 6.0% to 9.7% who are not satisfied. The difference between male-to-female and female-to-male satisfaction was not statistically significant (Pauly 1994, 597).

The publicity that followed the American Christine Jorgenson's sex-change surgery in Denmark in 1953, led to widespread public and professional discussion, and ultimately a distinction between transsexualism and transvestism. Harry Benjamin developed a three-point scale of transvestism, with transsexuals viewed as an extreme form of transvestism; he later came to regard the two as different entities.

The variety of cross-dressers includes fetishistic females and males who cross-dress for erotic arousal and those who enjoy cross-dressing to express their feminine or masculine personas; it includes individuals who cross-dress and live full-time in the other gender role, and those who cross-dress only occasionally and/or partially, with the whole range between these two ends of the spectrum.

In the 1960s, Virginia (Charles) Prince, a Los Angeles transvestite, began publishing *Transvestia*, a magazine for heterosexual cross-dressers. Encouraged by the response, Prince organized a "sorority without sisters," the Society for the Second Self or Tri-Ess (SSS), with chapters in several major cities. As a result of her worldwide travels, lectures, and television appearances, research on transvestism increased significantly because of the availability of research subjects.

As the cross-gender movement grew and became more visible, dissident and new voices appeared. At present, there are a variety of support groups for cross-dressers; some accept only heterosexual or homosexual and bisexual members, while others are not concerned with orientation. Some CD groups include transsexuals, others do not. In addition, there is a small industry, including "tall or big girl" fashion shops and mail-order catalogs, that cater to the clothing and other needs of cross-gendered persons.

### Current Status of American CD/CG Paraculture

It is apparent that many more American males and females are openly cross-dressing than at any other time in the last 100 years. The motivations for this activity are quite varied, ranging from female- or male-impersonation (FI, MI) as "Miss Coquette" or "Mr. Baggypants" at a Halloween party, to lip-synching performances at FI and MI reviews (i.e., "La Cage aux Folles" or Mr. Elvis Presley look-alike shows), to femme expressions in daily activities such as work or socializing. While it appears less obvious, there are many more females who cross-dress with the intent of expressing some part of their masculine persona (*animus*).

In the last decade, there has been a dramatic increase in the number of social contact groups, both for males who cross-dress and want social contact with others of similar persuasion in a secure setting, and for females who want to explore more fully the dimensions of their masculinity. Both female and male adolescents are cross-dressing to reflect feelings of their favorite musical stars, e.g., k.d. lang, RuPaul, Boy George, Melissa Etheridge, Michael Jackson, or the Erasure or Indigo Girls rock groups. (It should be noted that several of these performers are also known to be gay or lesbian, perhaps creating some public confusion about the association between cross-dressing and sexual orientation.) There are also young people who show some affinity for atypical gender-role expression. These may be early phases of mixing aspects of traditional gender norms with explorations of the limits of gender duality, that may benefit from appropriate professional help.

One segment of this paraculture is definitely exploring gender options with the aim of resolving gender conflict. Such conflicts may not be limited to the intrapsychic, but extend into resolving tensions between the rights of individual expression and the norms of conventional gender roles and presentations. When the desire to "shift" gender is experienced, there is a need for professional help in understanding the motivation for the gender shift and to develop a program that will clarify some of the important questions that individuals may have to address in pursuing such a choice. Such a program of gender exploration or gender shift may involve the use of hormones and also the decision to have genital-reconstruction surgery. Some of these people label themselves transgenderists, in the sense noted above, and can fully develop and express an alternate gender role and lifestyle. Some may be satisfied with this shift and not want to pursue sex-reassignment surgery. For others, after living full-time for one-and-a-half to two years in the preferred gender role, the decision is to complete the shift with surgery, in which case, the label "transsexual" is appropriate.

Currently, more and more people are challenging the binary gender forms and want to explore other gender options. If surgery is not the ultimate objective, these individuals may choose to blend traits and become more androgy-nous or gynandrous, expressing a feminine-masculine or masculine-feminine gender role. This segment of the paraculture is also receiving some attention.

As for legal issues involving CD/CG behaviors, most states do not have statutes that specifically prohibit the practice of CD/CG presentation in public. However, there may be some local ordinances that restrict this behavior in their jurisdiction. If tested in the judicial system, such laws would probably be ruled unconstitutional. Obtaining a legal change of name is not a problem in most areas of the country, and should be accompanied by some form of public notice for creditors, usually in the classified section of a local newspaper. Change of birth certificate may pose some problems; again, each state has its own guidelines.

With regard to genital-reconstruction surgery, a medical group created a set of guidelines for the preoperative transsexual about 1980. *Standards of Care* details guidelines for the client, the healthcare counselor/therapist, and the surgeon for handling the process of gender shift prior to surgery. These guidelines have been reviewed and updated to reflect cultural and professional changes in society. This document is available from any of the organizations listed at the end of this section. Few, if any medical-insurance plans pay for this surgery, which for a male-to-female runs about $10,000 to $15,000. In recent years, several reputable gender clinics have discontinued providing this surgery.

For healthcare professionals, sex educators, counselors, therapists, physicians, nurses, and sexologists, there are two major programs available to update one's knowledge about gender or to facilitate change in attitudes about gender issues. Segments in the standard Sexual Attitudes Reassessment (SAR) Workshop focus on CD/CG behaviors and lifestyles. In the Gender Attitude Reassessment Program (GARP), the focus is on all aspects of gender and its diversity; 10 to 15 units deal with specific topics in the phenomenon of gender. Both of these programs are given at national professional meetings and in continuing education programs at major universities and mental health centers in the United States.

Within the paraculture structures, there are several programs for CD/TG/TS/AN Americans. Two of the oldest and "personal-growth-oriented" are Fantasia Fair and Be All. Fantasia Fair, founded 28 years ago, provides a living/learning experience for adult male cross-dressers who want to explore the many dimensions of their femme persona in a tolerant open community. Fantasia events, often held at Provincetown on Cape Cod, Massachusetts, emphasize personal growth in all aspects of their programming. Be All, an offshoot of Fantasia Fair, focuses on the practical and social aspects of femme persona development. It is usually held in a motel/inn near a major city and is sponsored by a regional group of social contact organizations.

Organizations providing information on gender issues include:

Educational Institute for Sex and Gender Diversity (EISGD), 126 Western Avenue, #246, Augusta, ME 04330 (USA); email: infoisgd@aol.com

Harry Benjamin International Gender Dysphoria Association (HBIGDA), 1300 South 2nd St., Suite 180, Minneapolis, MN 55454; email: hbgda@famprac.umn.com.

I.C.T.L.E.P., Inc., 5707 Firenza St., Houston, TX 77035-5515.

The Society for the Second Self (Tri-Ess), 8880 Bellaire (B2pmb 104), Houston, TX 77036; email: info@tri-ess.org.

International Foundation for Gender Education (IFGE), P.O. Box 540229, Waltham, MA 02454-0229; www.ifge.org.

A comprehensive list of current transgender education and support groups can be found on the Web via Yahoo! Directory > Transgendered > Organization, and via Yahoo! Directory > Society and Culture > Cultures and Groups > Transgendered > Organizations. (*End of update by A. Kane*)]

## [C. A Second View of Gender Diversity

C. CHRISTINE WHEELER

[*Conceptualizations: Gender—Its Experience and Expression, Then and Now*

[*Update 2003*: In the past decade, in the U.S., gender has become one of the most hotly debated issues in a dozen areas, including:

- medicine,
- physiological dilemmas,
- endocrine syndromes and effects in neuroscience,
- the politics of clinical diagnosis,
- psychological/psychiatric and management or treatment considerations,
- cultural tolerance or intolerance,
- social policies and their influence in legal systems and the law,
- religions, and
- individual rights and our concepts of freedom and expression.

[Conceptualizations of gender, sex, and sexuality have dramatically shifted from a traditional dualistic binary paradigm to new confrontations of gender bending, blending, and activism for diversity. The cultural and scientific challenges that are raised by the mere existence of transgender and transsexual individuals have forced simplistic ideas to explosion and exploration. Public disclosures (autobiographic and personal profiles in the mass media, and controversies, continue to educate the American people about gender conceptualizations and to foster passionate discussion about the meaning of male and female—still further challenging our understandings of gender. In the U.S., the lens of gender, in all its refractions, most recently has dramatically shifted in focus from a perspective or picture of pathology to one of sexual health and wellness.

[In both research and medicine, the gender identity-development-disorder's debate centers primarily on whether gender as a condition (Gender Identity Disorders, GID) should be considered a disorder or removed from the *Diagnostic and Statistical Manual* (*DSM*) of the American Psychiatric Association (APA) and declared a normal variant, in analogy to the 1973 decision of the APA on homosexuality. The intersex controversy focuses on the assignment of gender and related issues of psychosocial and medical management, particularly with newborns. The GID debate extends to intersexuality, because if intersex people have significant gender-identity problems, *DSM-IV* classifies them as GID Not Otherwise Specified (GIDNOS), which implies a mental-disorder status. The powerful emergence of the Female-to-Male (FTM) movement illuminates controversy in departures from traditional concepts of gender identity and diversity, and its influences within the transgender culture, healthcare, and public policy. The conflict in our judicial system has to do with historical concepts that create an impenetrable barrier of social policy enshrined as law. But that's now (Wheeler 2001, 2003; Wheeler & Schaefer 1997).

[*Historical Influences*

[What was then? What was it like a few decades back, 30 to 40 years ago, in the beginning? Well, in a nutshell, there was little awareness, and few people interested or involved. In an historical snapshot, here's what was for American scientists to consider:

- Descriptions of gender-variant identities date back to classic Greek writings.
- The first specific reference in the medical literature was Friedreich in 1830.
- Current vaginoplasty dates from the late 19th century and Robert Abbe's pioneering use of skin grafts for construction.
- The surgical precursor to the current rectosigmoid vaginoplasty was reported in 1904 (Baldwin/Ann.Surg.)
- Bogoras, a Russian surgeon, first used the tubed abdominal flap for phallic reconstruction in 1936.
- Throughout the early and middle 20th century, various behavioral scientists contributed to the descriptive literature.

[By the late 1940s, pioneering endocrinologist and world-acclaimed "Father of Transsexualism," Harry Benjamin, M.D., working in New York City, became the first proponent of hormone therapy, presented his first paper at the New York Academy of Medicine in 1954, authored the first definitive text on gender conditions, and popularized the theory of Gender Identity Disorders as a real medical entity (Wheeler 1999). Ultimately, the initial success of Christine Jorgenson's highly publicized surgery abroad, combined with the efforts of Dr. Benjamin and others, led to the formation of the first gender-identity clinic at Johns Hopkins in 1963 with John Money, Ph.D.

[By the early 1970s, Dr. Jorges Burou of Casablanca, Morocco, and Dr. Stanley Beiber of Trinidad, Colorado, had reported on over 1,000 successful postoperative surgical procedures. At that time, surgical nomenclature had already shifted from "sex change" to "gender confirmation" and was well on its way to genital-restructuring surgical lingo. And, of course, Richard Green, M.D., J.D., was already following his "kids" expressing cross-gender concerns—a group of young people with GID, for the earliest longitudinal study of sexual identity development in children.

[However, physicians, along with academics, healthcare providers, and public policymakers, were reluctant to "join" others who were interested (Wheeler & Schaefer 1984a). They feared the consequences. That was then and that is now today, as well. A major exception, of course, was Dr. Harry Benjamin. His thanks and appreciation, however, were demonstrated by *no* New York City hospital wishing to accept him into their physician roster or on their board. But Benjamin's knowledge, his intuition, and his genius about what was right and most acceptably "human" kept him going in a gender-protective direction, even without the support or approval of his mainstream colleagues right into the 1980s.

[In fact, the scenario used to go something like this: People would get hormones and surgery by going to a doctor's office and saying "I want!" and the doctor would say "yes" or "no." That's all. No evaluating, no education, no support, no consequences, no interpretations, no lawsuits, no nothing! (Gemme & Wheeler 1977). Then the atmosphere changed. And then what happened was Dr. Harry Benjamin interviewed a transgendered person. Dr. Wardell Pomeroy, Alfred Kinsey's colleague, followed suit. Eventually, Paul Walker, Ph.D., Alice Webb, Donald Laub, M.D., and others joined Benjamin and Pomeroy to form the Harry Benjamin International Gender Dysphoria Association, which then developed and published the *Standards of Care*. Other factors leading to the current status were "The Letters" written by clinicians in support of hormones and genital surgery, clinical evaluations, the activism, and the involvement of lawyers (Pomeroy, Flax, Wheeler 1982; Wheeler 1993).

[Today, many clients are taking control of their own management and deciding not to take the option of genital surgery (Wheeler 2003; Wheeler & Schaefer 1984b)—more arguing, more confusion, and *more* satisfied people because they have more options, and more and better care! (Wheeler & Schaefer 1999). As a noted research sociologist explains, one of the best ways to understand the rules of society is to study those that break the rules (Devor 2003).

[By the mid 1990s, the refinement of endocrinology in manipulating sex hormones, and public acceptance of plastic reconstructive surgeries to alter secondary sex characteristics to alleviate psychological distress fortified further acceptance for thousands of people to alter their gender expression and presentation. Body phenotype surgeries became routine for maxillofacial, genital, breast, and scalp reconfiguration to allow trans individuals greater satisfaction, with their bodies being more congruent with their gender and sex identities.

[*Current Status of American Trans People*

[Today, the variety, diversity, and varied trajectories of thousands of people expressing gender change, with or without transitions, in the United States each year, has become super popular—the focus of talk shows, much controversy, the center of new documentaries, legislation, and change in advocacy, and the emergence of consumer-driven groups. Gender is so compelling in America today because everything about sex and sexuality is both known yet paradoxical. Variation in expression of switching gender has always been linked with cultural taboos—even today, people associate gender with sex.

[Today, in contrast with the silence of the first half of the 1900s, these debates are conducted in many diverse media, such as pamphlets, newsletter, websites, Internet lists and chat rooms, videos, newspaper reports, meeting presentations, college and even some senior high school courses, and scientific publications. Debates today focus on three major clusters of issues: gender feeling/expression/experience, gender-confirming procedures and surgery, and information management.

[The popularization of transgenderism in the news has included:

- Art and Entertainment Network's 2003 release of the acclaimed *Role Reversal* (Wheeler 2003b),
- ABC's *Boy or Girl? When Doctors Choose a Child's Sex*,
- Intersex Society of North American's *Hermaphrodites Speak*,
- Arts and Entertainment Network's *Investigative Reports: Transgender Revolution*,
- *Multiple Genders: Mind and Body in Conflict*,
- *XXXY*,
- *You Don't Know Dick: Courageous Hearts of Transsexual Men*,
- *A Change of Gender*, and
- London's Richochette Television production, *History of the Sex Change*.

And, of course, there was the 2002 publication of the U.S. Surgeon General's report, *A Call To Action*, describing the nation's sexual health crisis and calling for:

- respectful dialogue among people with divergent opinions,
- acceptance of the diversity of sexualities, and
- thoughtful implementation of a range of programs.

Despite the debates stirred by the Surgeon General's *Call to Action*, the fact that this document was released is in itself an important positive step. (Ironically, paradoxically, another former U.S. Surgeon General was transgendered.)

[Further evidence of gender-related changes in the United States include: the city of San Francisco offering municipal employees sex-change treatment as part of their medical benefits plan, Florida transsexual Michael Kantaras winning custody of his two children, and *Teen People* magazine highlighting an article on transgendered teens on its May 2003 cover. It seems as though a new autobiography from a trans person is being promoted every other month, further increasing public awareness and attitudes, primarily in positive directions.

[In the winds of the times, prevailing policies, the critics, and their questions have all changed. Biological determinists, social constructionists, and activists alike contribute to solving the puzzle and the larger picture of what it means to be human.

[What has changed is our society and our scientific knowledge. We have witnessed a shift from 19th- and 20th-century thinking based on the assumption that one's biological sex, and the gender assignment made at birth because of it, will be followed by a gender/sexual identity, role behavior, sexual orientation, courtship and love, sexual functioning, and psychological health that falls in line, more or less, with societal expectations.

[For centuries, the definitive criterion of one's "true sex" was external genitality. In the late 19th and early 20th centuries, gonadal histology, and the sex chromosomes (for intersex) were added to the basic criteria. But each of these defining criteria can be ambiguous and may be discrepant from one another.

[The history of science teaches us that we see only a limited piece of the legendary mosaic. Many grasp a kernel of truth, but the entire entity eludes us because it is always much more than the parts we have our hands on, Further, many thinkers contend that there are far more "mistakes of society" than "mistakes of nature."

[Today, society's definitions of gender roles are changing, even as transgender individuals encounter more tolerance, enjoy the benefits of some legal protection, and exercise greater autonomy in medical decision-making. These changes influence the life experiences of gender-variant people (GID), along with the evaluation of long-term outcome, and the need to be considered in any revision of psychosocial and medical management. Planned policy changes should be informed by empirical data and followed by assessments of long-term outcome of new approaches. Guidelines should never be left to individuals. They should be arrived at by multidisciplinary committees of appropriate specialists with opportunities for input from others working in the specific area and individual patients or consumers themselves.

[And so the debates continue with passion, determination, and questions. While the progress that *has* been made in the present time (the now) is admirable, there is still too much prejudice—both among the workers in the field and among trans people themselves. It all has to do with *how* we look at each other and what we see!

[If Dr. Harry Benjamin were alive today, what would he say? In his 100 years, he answered this question often enough: "I'm not here to promote any particular operation or treatment. I'm here to try to promote scientific objectivity, open-mindedness and a bit of compassion." To which, Dr. Leah Cahan Schaefer and I would add "and a lot of compassion and love!" (Schaefer & Wheeler 1997; Wheeler 1988).

[*The Varieties of Operational Definitions*

[In keeping with our changing conceptualizations of sex, gender, and transgender, our operational terms and definitions have likewise changed. Sometimes the changes have been superficial, sometimes radical, even in the few years since Ari Kane composed his preceding "Indigenous Clinician's View of the Current (1995) Status of American CD/CG Paraculture." The basic terminology current in 2003 includes:

- *Sex*: social status based on genital appearance—a person may be female, male, intersexed, or hermaphrodite;
- *Intersexed* or *hermaphrodite*: social status assigned to a person having sex characteristics of both females and males;
- *Gender*: social status based on convincing performance of femininity or masculinity—persons may be girls or women, boys or men, or transgendered;
- *Transgendered*: persons who feel they do not fit well as either women or men, may be neither gender, both genders, or a gender different than what their sex would normally dictate. Such a person may appear ambiguously gendered to others, and may change their gender and live unnoticed as another gender; may also be known as a *cross-dresser* or *transvestite*, as well as *female impersonator, drag queen, androgyne* (one who presents both or neither gender), *fetishist*, and *autogynophile*;
- *Transsexed (Transsexual)*: persons designated as one sex and gender at birth, but identify themselves, and may even live, as another gender and another sex; many use various social, hormonal, and surgical techniques to sufficiently alter both their gender presentations and sex statuses to more completely express their feelings; today, many *trans people* identify as *trans women* (male to female, or *MTF*) and *trans men* (female to male, or *FTM*);
- *Gender or Transgender Community*: in the U.S. today, this collective group or loose association of people includes both those individuals expressing gender diversity or variance (sometimes known as consumers), as well as non-gender-diverse people and healthcare providers;
- *Gender Identity Disorder*: incongruence between the physical anatomic sex (phenotype) and gender identity, i.e., self-identification as male or female;
- *Gender Dysphoria*: the experience of gender incongruence; and
- *Sexual Identity*: basic personality feature with three overlapping component parts: (a) gender (core morphologic) identity, a basic awareness of being male or female, both, or neither; (b) observable gender role, expression of culturally typical feminine or masculine behavior; and (c) sexual orientation, or in brief, sex-partner attraction (same, both, opposite, none, or all stimuli—i.e., homo-, bi-, hetero-, or ambisexual).

[Many in the U.S. prefer the above tripartite operational definition of the last term "sexual identity" to other gender terminology, which varies worldwide. The most extreme form of experience and expression, in which a person needs to adapt their phenotype with hormones and surgeries for congruence with their gender identity, is called *transsexualism*. The complexities and definitions of the transsexual condition have been well articulated by Milton Diamond (2003, *Transgender Tapestry*, in press) in a chapter appropriately titled, "What's in a Name? Some Terms Used in the Discussion of Sex and Gender."

### [*Etiology of Adult Transsexualism*

[There are no reliable statistics of trans people, but an educated, reasonable estimate would be between 2% and 5% of the general population, comparable to the most recent estimates of homosexuality. Numbers of transsexual people in the population are considerably smaller and difficult to estimate because many never present to clinics or request hormones through practitioners (hormones are easily acquired over the Internet without medical monitoring), and many others reject maxillofacial and genital surgery. The sex ratio of transsexual people presenting for genital surgery in the U.S. has shifted from 1:1 during the late 1960s to almost 2:1 male to female currently. It is estimated that fewer than approximately 1 in 20,000 is transsexual in the U.S.

[Transsexualism can be considered a neuro-developmental condition of the brain. Several sexually dimorphic nuclei have been found in the hypothalamic area of the brain (Allen & Gorski 1990; Swaab et al. 2001). In human males, by early adulthood, the volume of the sexually dimorphic limbic nucleus (BSTc) is almost twice as large as in females and its number of neurons is almost double ($p < 0.006$) (Zhou et al. 1995; Kruijver et al. 2000; Chung et al. 2002). Further, in transsexualism this nucleus has a sex-reversed structure. In 42 human brains examined, the BSTc had a structure concordant with the psychological identification as male or female, inferring BSTc is an important part of a sexually dimorphic neural circuit, and that it is involved in the development of gender identity (Kruijver et al. 2000). Findings were independent of sexual orientation and exogenous sex-hormone use.

[Brain sexual differentiation begins during fetal development, continues after birth (Kawata 1995; Swaab et al. 2001), and is significantly influenced by hormones (although the exact mechanism is not fully understood) at several critical periods of dimorphic development when gender identity is established—initially fetal, again around birth, and postnatal. Genetic influences may contribute to an altered hormone influence in critical early brain development (Landen 1999; Coolidge et al. 2002). Similarly, medication and environmental influences (Diamond et al. 1996; Whitten et al. 2002), and stress or trauma to the mother during pregnancy may be contributing factors (Ward et al. 2002; Swaab et al. 2002).

[Development of gender identity is usually consistent with phenotype, with small numbers of children experiencing incongruence. Adult gender-incongruent outcomes cannot be predicted with certainty. In a minority of children, regardless of phenotypical socialization and nurture, gender incongruence will persist into adulthood and manifest as transsexualism (Green 1987; Ekins 1997; Prosser 1998; Di Ceglie 2000; Ekins & King 2001; Bates 2001).

[Etiologically, an innate biological predisposition is supported by a sex-reversed BSTc in trans people, along with other studies, one example of which, indicates a higher than average correlation with left-handedness (Green & Young 2001). There is no evidence that nurturing and socialization contradictory to phenotype is causal, nor that nurture entirely consistent with phenotype can prevent it (Diamond 1996). Neither contrary socialization nor psychological or psychiatric treatments alone overcome gender conditions (Green 1999). Histories from those with anomalies of genitalia provide evidence that gender identity may resolve independently of genital configuration, even when that appearance and the assigned identity are enhanced by medical and social interventions (Imperato-McGinley 1979; Rosler & Kohn 1983; Diamond 1997; Diamond and Sigmundson 1997; Kipnis & Diamond 1998; Reiner 1999; Reiner 2000).

[Etiology and causality of gender conditions are highly complex and involve multiple factors, requiring careful diagnostic process, based largely on self-assessment, facilitated by a specialist professional. By contrast to the United States, the United Kingdom's government—and consequently the healthcare system or medical model—does not recognize transsexualism in diagnostic descriptions of a "mental illness" (See Lord Chancellor's Department—government policy concerning transsexual people at: www.lcd .gov.uk/constitution/transsex/policy.htm).

[In the U.S., many transsexual people benefit from hormones and various surgeries realigning phenotype with gender identity, coupled with well-integrated psychosocial interventions to support the person in living and working in their social role. Treatments vary and need to be tailored to individual needs and circumstances.

### [A Clinical View: Standard of Care

[The standard of care in evaluating an individual for any gender condition involves interviewing the patient and obtaining information from family members, friends, previous pertinent medical treatments, and other sources, if possible, with the patient's consent. Diagnostic evaluation clinically focuses primarily on psychosexual and social development, psychiatric history, and current mental status (Wheeler 1992, 1993, 1997, 2003). No specialized tests exist that can assist with differential diagnosis. Additionally, the presence of comorbid diagnoses[1] need to be assessed. As my colleagues and I have written in the chapter "Gender Identity Disorders" in *Treatment of Psychiatric Disorders* (Vol. 2), edited by Glen O. Gabbard, M.D., and published by the American Psychiatric Association (Schaefer, Wheeler, Futterweit 1995), "Although histories of psychiatric treatments for substance abuse, adjustment disorders, serious suicidal thoughts, and depression are not uncommon in gender dysphoric patients, there is no evidence of a frequent occurrence of comorbidity, making comparison with estimates in the general population meaningless. Many of these disorders are defense mechanisms against the frustration, psychological pain, anxiety, and discrimination stemming from patients' inability to live safely and comfortably in society with their condition or in their desired gender roles."

[A clinical picture emerges when a person's concerns and uncertainties, distress, and questions about their gender identity continue and they remain feeling conflicted.[2] Gender-conflicted or dissatisfied people are diagnosed as suffering from a gender-identity disorder when they meet specified criteria in one of two official diagnostic sources—*Diagnostic and Statistical Manual of Mental Disorders—Fourth Edition* (*DSM-IV*) or the *International Classification of Diseases-10* (*ICD-10*). For example, *DSM-IV* 302.85 Gender Identity Disorder (GID) in adolescents or adults diagnostic criteria includes: a strong and persistent cross-gender identification;[3] and persistent discomfort with one's sex, or sense of inappropriateness in the gender role of that sex[4]; absence of physical intersex condition; and disturbance causes clinically significant distress or impairment in social, occupational, or other important areas of functioning.

[While a clinician can help a person to understand their symptoms and dilemmas as a gender condition, most people seeking help for Gender Identity Disorders come self-diagnosed in that they bring their diagnosis to the clinician. In diagnostics and treatment, there are many patients seeking treatments, both psychotherapeutic and endocrinological, for *social*—rather than genital—sex reassignment.

[Further, the Harry Benjamin International Gender Dysphoria Association's *Standards of Care* (original document 1977, revised publications 1978, 1979, 1980, 1981, 1985, 1990, 2001) articulate professional consensus about the psychiatric, psychological, medical, and surgical management of GID. Clinicians use these guidelines to understand the range of assistance needed for gender patients. There are five elements of clinical work: diagnostic assessment, psychotherapy, real-life experience, hormonal therapy, and surgical therapy. People with gender distress, and others (i.e., families, employers, and social institutions) may use the *Standards of Care* to better understand treatment possibilities and professional thinking. Treatment goals include learning a prolonged personal comfort with one's gender identity and expression to maximize overall psychological well-being and self-fulfillment (Schaefer & Wheeler 2003). The *Standards of Care* are intended to provide flexible directions for treatment of GID (Wheeler 2003). Clinical departures from these guidelines are appropriate in light of a patient's unique social, psychological, or anatomical needs, as well as the development of an experienced professional's method of handling a common situation, or specifically because of a research protocol. Such departures should be recognized, explained to the patient, and documented, both for legal protection and for short- and long-term results.

[As my colleagues and I further point out in our medical treatment chapter for gender identity disorders (Schaefer, Wheeler, & Futterweit 1995), "one option not open to patients is the option to do *nothing* about their gender condition, because such an attitude can only have disastrous consequences. Suppression and repression causes depression and are always immobilizing and sometimes fatal. Sadly, suicide attempts are not unknown for those who live their lives immersed in feelings of helplessness and hopelessness. To ignore totally one's gender or one's inner awareness of it—a fundamental aspect of the human personality—is, in and of itself, a form of gender suicide."

[*Outcome Studies for Sex-Reassignment Surgery.* Comprehensive reviews of follow-up studies on post-genitally operated individuals (Lawrence 2003; Phäfflin & Junge 1992, 1998; Wheeler & Schaefer 1997b) primarily reflect no regret and identify dissatisfaction associated with unsatisfactory physical and functional results of the surgery. Age at surgery, previous marriage or parenthood, sexual orientation, and compliance with minimal eligibility requirements for sex-reassignment surgery (with the HBIGDA's *Standards of Care*) are not associated with outcomes. There is an emerging consensus that a person's self-reported satisfaction or regret is more meaningful than previously thought criteria, such as employment, choice of sexual partners, or utilization of healthcare services (Carroll 1999; Green & Fleming 1990; Kuiper & Cohen-Kettenis 1988; Snaith, Tarsh, & Reid 1993). (*End of update by C. C. Wheeler*)]

---

[1]Axis I psychiatric symptoms, as anxiety disorders, dissociation, schizophrenia, mood, and other psychotic disorders (e.g., paranoia), plus Axis II personality disorders, as borderline, avoidant, narcissistic, obsessive-compulsive, etc.

[2]Emotional struggles are known clinically as: gender issues, a gender problem, a gender concern, gender distress, gender dysphoria, gender-identity problem, cross-dressing, transvestism, transgenderism, or transsexualism. They are expressed throughout one's lifetime—from childhood into old age—in various degrees of dissatisfaction with sexual anatomy, gender body charac-

teristics, gender roles, gender identity, as well as the perceptions of others.

[3]Symptoms may include a stated desire to be, frequent passing as, desire to live or be treated as, or the conviction that one has the typical feelings and reactions of, the other sex.

[4]Symptoms may include a preoccupation with getting rid of primary and secondary sex characteristics (e.g., request for hormones, surgery, or other procedures to physically alter sexual characteristics to simulate the other sex) or belief that he or she was born the wrong sex.

## *8. Significant Unconventional Sexual Behaviors*

DAVID L. WEIS

In this section, we consider a group of "other" sexual behaviors. These include sexual coercion (rape, sexual harassment, and child sexual abuse), prostitution, pornography, paraphilias, and fetishes. As a general rule, Americans tend to view heterosexual relations between consenting adults in an ongoing relationship, such as marriage, as the norm. It is true that such sexual relations are the modal pattern in the U.S.A. (Laumann et al. 1994), as is true of every culture. However, the earlier reviews of extramarital sex, alternative lifestyles, homosexuality, and bisexuality all serve to illustrate that sizable percentages of Americans engage in sexual behavior that departs from this assumed norm. American sexologists have struggled for some time to develop acceptable terminology to describe other sexual practices. The concept of sexual orientation has allowed us to view homosexuality and bisexuality as variations in orientation. Similarly, the concepts of gender transposition and gender diversity have provided terminology for examining cross-gender behaviors.

Typically, nonmarital sexual practices have been labeled as sexual deviance or sexual variance. There are, however, at least two problems with such terms. First, no matter what the proper sociological conceptualization, these terms inevitably convey a sense of pathology, dysfunction, or abnormality to behaviors which are situationally defined. For example, consider the act of exhibitionism, exposing one's genitals to another. When practiced in the streets, the act is defined as a crime and is quite rare. When practiced in certain business establishments, the practitioner is paid for the act and clients pay to see it; and when practiced in the privacy of one's home with an intimate partner, it is seen as normal and healthy sexual interaction. Second, some of these behaviors are, in fact, quite common. Muehlenhard reviews evidence that shows many women are victims of sexual coercion. Several recent surveys provide evidence that nearly one quarter of Americans view pornographic videotapes each year (Davis 1990; Laumann et al. 1994). It appears that relatively small percentages of Americans participate in any one of the various fetish groups reviewed below. However, taken together and added to the forms of nonmarital sexual expression we have already reviewed, it seems clear that rather large percentages of Americans do participate in some "other" form of sexual practice.

## A. Coercive Sex

### *Sexual Assault and Rape*

CHARLENE L. MUEHLENHARD and BARRIE J. HIGHBY
[*Updated by C. L. Muehlenhard*]

*Basic Concepts.* The conceptualization of rape and the treatment of rapists and rape victims in the United States have changed substantially since the 1970s, largely because of the work of feminists. The situation is complex, however; there are many perspectives on these issues. Even the terminology related to rape is at issue. Some people use the term *sexual assault* instead of *rape* to emphasize the violent nature of the act and to place greater emphasis on the behavior of the perpetrator; recent reforms in the criminal codes of some states no longer speak of rape, but of varying degrees of sexual assault (Estrich 1987; Koss 1993a). Others, however, prefer to retain the term *rape* "to signify the outrage of this crime" (Koss 1993a, 199). Some regard rape as different and more serious than assault and contend that "to label rape as a form of assault . . . may obscure its unique indignity" (Estrich 1987, 81). There is no clear consensus in

the law, the popular media, research literature, or feminist writings. We will use the term *rape*.

Similarly, some people use the term *rape survivor* instead of *rape victim*. Each term has advantages. The term *victim* highlights the harm that rape causes. The term *survivor* has more optimistic connotations and, thus, may empower someone who has been raped; it also highlights similarities between people who have survived rape and people who have survived other life-threatening events. The term *survivor*, however, may perpetuate the stereotype that only rapes that are life-threatening—that is, that involve a great deal of extrinsic violence—are worthy of being regarded as "real rape." Thus, we will use the term *rape victim*.

*Definitions.* Rape can generally be defined as one person's forcing another to engage in nonconsensual sex. This general definition, however, leaves many questions unanswered (Muehlenhard et al. 1992b). What behaviors count as sex? Whom do these definitions cover? What counts as force? What counts as consent? In the United States, thinking about each of these questions has changed since the 1970s, and controversy remains.

Defining rape is complicated by the fact that there are many types of definitions. In the legal domain, the federal government and all 50 states each have their own definition. Legal definitions are written by legislatures, which are composed primarily of men; thus, these definitions are likely to be written from men's perspectives (Estrich 1987). The definitions held by the general public are influenced by the law, the media, folk wisdom, jokes, and so forth. Some researchers base their definitions on legal definitions, which makes them subject to the same biases as legal definitions; others make conscious decisions to deviate from legal definitions, which they find biased or inadequate. Finally, there are political definitions, written by activists wanting to make various political points. For example, MacKinnon (1987, 82) wrote,

> Politically, I call it rape whenever a woman has sex and feels violated. You might think that's too broad. I'm not talking about sending all of you men to jail for that. I'm talking about attempting to change the nature of the relations between women and men by having women ask ourselves, "Did I feel violated?"

Persons who regard legal definitions as the most valid criticize such political definitions as being too broad (e.g., Farrell 1993). Based on the assumption that language is power, however, political activists have resisted the status quo by challenging widely held definitions and encouraging people to think about the assumptions behind these definitions.

Prior to the 1970s, definitions of rape often included only penile-vaginal sexual intercourse. This definition has been criticized as too phallocentric, promoting the ideas that an act must involve a man's penis and must have the potential for reproduction to count as "real sex" (Muehlenhard et al. 1992b; Rotkin 1972/1986). Currently, most definitions of rape use a broader conceptualization of sex, including many kinds of sexual penetration (e.g., penile-vaginal intercourse, fellatio, cunnilingus, anal intercourse, or penetration of the genitals or rectum by an object). Some definitions are even broader, including behaviors such as touching someone's genitals, breasts, or buttocks (Estrich 1987; Koss 1993a).

Another contentious question involves whom these definitions cover. If rape is defined as forced penile-vaginal intercourse, then by definition, an act of rape must involve a woman and a man; this definition would exclude coercive sex between two individuals of the same gender. Definitions that are limited to situations in which the perpetrator penetrates the victim exclude situations in which a woman forces a man to engage in penile-vaginal intercourse, because such situations would involve the victim penetrating the perpetrator (Koss 1993a). Some definitions of rape include only the experiences of adolescents and adults (e.g., Koss et al. 1987), whereas others also include the experiences of children (e.g., Russell 1984).

Prior to the 1970s, rape laws in the U.S. included a "marital exclusion," exempting husbands from being charged with raping their wives. By the mid-1990s, this marital exclusion had been removed from the laws of all 50 states, as well as from federal law (X 1994). In some states, however, laws still define rape between spouses more narrowly than rape between nonspouses, giving married women less legal protection than unmarried women. Furthermore, some state laws still treat rape less seriously if it occurs between two people who have previously engaged in consensual sex (X 1994).

Yet another contentious question involves what counts as force. Most definitions include physical force and threats of physical force. Many also include sex with someone who is unable to consent because of being intoxicated, asleep, or otherwise unable to consent. There is disagreement, however, regarding how intoxicated one needs to be, whether the alcohol or drugs need to be administered to the victim by the perpetrator, what happens if both persons are intoxicated, and so forth. This is particularly relevant in cases of date or acquaintance rape (Muehlenhard et al. 1992b).

Even regarding threats of physical force, there is disagreement about how direct such threats need to be. For example, in some court cases, appellate judges have written that a woman's acquiescing to sex with a man because she is afraid that he will harm her (e.g., because he has harmed her in the past, or because they are in an isolated location and he is behaving in a way she regards as threatening) is not sufficient to define the incident as rape. Instead, as Estrich commented, these judges interpreted the law to mean that a woman should not cry and give in; she should fight like a "real man" (1987, 65).

*Conceptualizations of Rape and Rapists.* Prior to the changes initiated by feminists in the 1970s, rape was commonly conceptualized as a sexual act in which a man responded to a woman's sexual provocations. Rapists were often assumed to be either black men who raped white women or else men who were lower class or crazy and who were provoked by women who dressed or behaved too provocatively (Davis 1981; Donat & D'Emilio 1992; Gise & Paddison 1988; LaFree 1982; Mio & Foster 1991). Amir (1971, 273), for example, discussed "victim precipitated rape," which he conceptualized as rape incited by female victims who spoke, dressed, or behaved too provocatively (e.g., who went to a man's residence or who attended "a picnic where alcohol is present"). MacDonald (1971, 311) wrote that

the woman who accepts a ride home from a stranger, picks up a hitchhiker, sunbathes alone or works in the garden in a two-piece bathing suit which exposes rather than conceals her anatomy invites rape. The woman who by immodest dress, suggestive remarks or behavior flaunts her sexuality should not be surprised if she is attacked sexually. These ladies are referred to as "rape bait" by police officers.

Female victims were often thought to have desired or enjoyed the experience (Gise & Paddison 1988; Griffin 1971; Mio & Foster 1991; Muehlenhard et al. 1992a). For example, Wille (1961, 19) wrote about the typical rape victim's "unconscious desires to be the victim of a sexual as-

sault." Husbands, in effect, "owned" their wives and were entitled to their sexuality; thus, the concept of marital rape was nonexistent (Clark & Lewis 1977; Donat & D'Emilio 1992). Sexual acts that occurred between acquaintances or on dates were often assumed to be sexual encounters that the woman had let get out of hand (e.g., Amir 1971).

In the 1970s, feminist writers began to conceptualize rape as violence (e.g., Brownmiller 1975; Griffin 1971). In a classic article, Griffin (1971, 312) wrote that

rape is an act of aggression in which the victim is denied her self-determination. It is an act of violence which, if not actually followed by beatings or murder, nevertheless always carries with it the threat of death. And finally, rape is a form of mass terrorism, for the victims of rape are chosen indiscriminately.

Griffin also emphasized that the fear of rape limits women's freedom, and as such, rape functions as do other forms of violence. Conceptualizing rape as violence has numerous advantages: acknowledging the serious consequences of rape; highlighting the similarities between the effects of rape and the effects of other kinds of violence; taking the emphasis of rape prevention off restricting women's sexual behavior; and acknowledging that rape affects all women, even those who have not actually been raped, by instilling fear and, thus, restricting women's freedom.

Currently, in the United States, it is common to hear people say, "Rape isn't sex; it's violence." Nevertheless, many writers, including both feminist political activists and researchers, have found value in conceptualizing rape as having elements of sex as well as violence (Muehlenhard et al. 1996). Feminists have discussed similarities between rape and other sexual situations which may also be coercive:

So long as we say that [rape involves] *abuses of violence, not sex,* we fail to criticize what has been made of sex, what has been done to us through sex, because we leave the line between rape and intercourse . . . right where it is. (MacKinnon 1987, 87, emphasis in original)

Our understanding of rapists has been enhanced by investigating both the sexual and the violent aspects of their behavior and attitudes. Rapists are more likely than nonrapists to become sexually aroused by depictions of sexual violence, as well as to feel hostile toward women, to accept rape myths and violence against women, and to view heterosexual relationships as adversarial. They drink more heavily and are more likely to have drinking problems, which may serve as a release or an excuse for sexually violent behavior. They are also more likely to have witnessed parental abuse or to have been physically or sexually abused in their childhoods. They begin having sexual experiences, either consensual or nonconsensual, earlier than nonrapists (Berkowitz 1992; Burt 1991; Koss & Dinero 1988; Finkelhor & Yllo 1985; Malamuth 1986; Russell 1982/1990).

[*Update 2003*: Recent research has supported and extended knowledge about sexually aggressive men. Analyzing a sample of U.S. college men, Abbey et al. (2001) found that 33% reported engaging in some form of sexual assault. Compared with other men, those who had engaged in sexual assault had more-hostile attitudes toward women, were more accepting of verbally pressuring a woman to have sex, described their friends as more approving of forced sex, and had greater expectancies that alcohol increased men's sex drive. There were also differences in their descriptions of their consensual sexual experiences: Compared with other men, the sexually assaultive men reported having had sex at a younger age, having had more partners, and drinking more prior to sex. Numerous other studies have also found high levels of alcohol use among sexually aggressive men (Testa 2002).

[A meta-analysis by Murnen et al. (2002) found support linking men's sexual aggression to their masculine ideology. The two largest effect sizes were for Malamuth's construct of "hostile masculinity" (which includes a desire to dominate and control women and a distrustful, defensive, and insecure orientation toward women; Malamuth et al. 1991), and for Mosher's construct of "hypermasculinity" (in which men regard violence as manly, consider danger to be exciting, and have calloused attitudes toward women; Mosher & Sirkin 1984). (*End of update by C. L. Muehlenhard*)]

Research has also dispelled myths about rape. Rapists represent all ethnic groups and social classes (Russell 1984, 1990), and the overwhelming majority of rapes occur between acquaintances (Kilpatrick et al. 1987; Koss et al. 1988; Russell 1984) and between members of the same race or ethnicity (Amir 1971; O'Brien 1987). Research shows that men can be raped and women can be rapists (Brand & Kidd 1986; Muehlenhard 1998; Muehlenhard & Cook 1988; Sarrel & Masters 1982; Struckman-Johnson et al. 2003; Waterman et al. 1989). Still, because rape and the fear of rape affects women more than men, and because of the differences in how women's and men's sexuality is conceptualized in the United States, some claim it would be a mistake to treat rape as a gender-neutral phenomenon (MacKinnon 1990; Rush 1990). Finally, "thanks to the feminist movement, no one any longer defends the dangerous claim that rape is a sexually arousing or sought-after experience on the part of the victim" (Palmer 1988, 514).

*Prevalence.* How prevalent is rape? Estimates of prevalence depend not only on how rape is defined, but also on the methodology used. Conducting interviews in the presence of family members yields lower prevalence estimates than conducting interviews in private or using anonymous surveys, which is understandable given that many rape victims do not tell their families about having been raped, and some rape victims have been raped by family members (Koss 1993a; Koss et al. 1988; Russell 1984). Asking respondents if they have been "raped" yields lower prevalence estimates than asking if they have had an experience that meets the researchers' definition of rape, because many rape victims do not label their experience as "rape" (Kahn & Andreoli Mathie 2000; Peterson & Muehlenhard 2003). Asking respondents a single question about their experiences generally yields lower estimates than does asking multiple questions, perhaps because asking only one such question fails to elicit memories of rapes that may have occurred in numerous contexts (e.g., with strangers, casual acquaintances, dates, or family members, obtained by force or threats of force or when the victim was unable to consent, and so forth; Koss 1993a). [(*Updates added by C. L. Muehlenhard, 2003*)]

Until recently, statistical reports on the prevalence of rape published by the U.S. government were inadequate: The *Uniform Crime Reports*, published by the Federal Bureau of Investigation (FBI 1993), include only rapes that were reported to the police—a small minority of all rapes (Russell 1984). The *National Crime Victimization Surveys* (*NCVS*), conducted by the government's Bureau of Justice Statistics (BJS), also have serious methodological flaws (BJS 1993; Koss 1992; Russell 1984). [*Update 2003*: Some of these flaws have subsequently been addressed (e.g., in the past, *NCVS* reports concluded that rape was rare, despite the fact that respondents had been asked no questions about rape; see Russell 1984). Other flaws remain, however (e.g., the interviews are not necessarily confidential, and family members and others are sometimes present during the interviews; Tjaden & Thoennes 2000).

[Recently, the National Violence Against Women (NVAW) Survey, cosponsored by the National Institute of Justice and the Centers for Disease Control and Prevention, has corrected many of these problems (Tjaden & Thoennes 2000). The data from this national telephone survey came from 8,000 women and 8,000 men, selected from the 50 U.S. states and the District of Columbia by random-digit dialing. The NVAW included questions about forcible rape, physical assault, and stalking. Rape was defined as "forced vaginal, oral, and anal sex" (Tjaden & Thoennes 2000, 13). Respondents were asked multiple questions about experiences they had had that met the researchers' definition of rape. Respondents were asked about both completed and attempted rape (in this summary of the NVAW data, the term *rape* refers to both completed and attempted rape).

[NVAW results showed that of the women surveyed, 17.6% reported having been raped (14.8% reported completed rape and an additional 2.8% reported attempted rape). Of the men surveyed, 3.0% reported having been raped (2.1% reported completed rape and an additional 0.9% reported attempted rape). Many of the rape victims reported being raped more than once (Tjaden & Thoennes 2000).

[Among those who reported being raped, 21.6% of the women and 48.0% of the men experienced their first rape before age 12, and 32.4% of the women and 23.0% of the men experienced their first rape between ages 12 and 17. Therefore, 54.0% of the female rape victims and 71.0% of the male rape victims experienced their first rape when they were children or adolescents. Among all respondents, 9.6% of the women and 0.9% of the men reported having been raped as adults (Tjaden & Thoennes 2000).

[In the NVAW Survey, more American Indian/Alaska Native women (34.1%) than white women (17.7%), African-American women (18.8%), and mixed-race women (24.4%) reported having been raped. More non-Hispanic women (18.4%) than Hispanic women (14.6%) reported having been raped. (Statistical comparisons among racial and ethnic groups did not include men or Asian/Pacific Islander women because of limitations with the data.)

[Consistent with previous findings, the NVAW Survey revealed that women are especially at risk from current and former intimate partners; 7.7% of the women and 0.3% of the men in the sample reported having been raped by a current or former intimate partner (spouse, cohabiting partner, boyfriend/girlfriend, or date). The rape victims were asked about their most recent rape: Among the female rape victims, 61.9% were raped by a current or former intimate partner; 6.5% were raped by a relative; 21.3% were raped by another acquaintance; and 16.7% were raped by a stranger. (Data for male rape victims were insufficient to calculate reliable percentages.) (*End of update by C. L. Muehlenhard*)]

*Consequences for Rape Victims.* Research in the U.S. on the consequences of rape has improved dramatically in the past several decades. Prior to the 1970s, studies of rape victims consisted of occasional case studies of victims who sought psychotherapy, a biased sample because most rape victims do not seek therapy, and those who do are likely to be atypical (e.g., to be in greater distress, to be of higher socioeconomic status, etc.). The next generation of studies involved assessing rape victims who reported the rapes to police or emergency-room personnel; this practice allowed longitudinal assessment of the aftermath of rape, but the samples were still biased because most rapes are never reported. Currently, the consequences of rape are often studied by surveying random samples of people; this practice allows comparisons of rape victims with nonvictims, regardless of whether the rape victims had reported the rapes to authorities or had labeled their experiences as rape. Some researchers even conduct prospective studies, in which members of a high-risk group (e.g., first-year college students) are assessed annually; if someone in the sample is raped during the time span of the study, their pre- and postrape adjustment can be compared (e.g., Humphrey & White 2000).

Research shows that most rape victims experience psychological, physical, and sexual problems after being raped. It is important to remember, however, that not all rape victims experience all of these consequences; some experience many consequences, whereas others experience relatively few consequences.

The psychological consequences of rape can include depression; fear; anxiety; anger; problems with self-esteem and social adjustment; feeling betrayed, humiliated, or guilty; and experiencing problems with trust (Lystad 1982; Muehlenhard et al. 1991; Resick 1993; Resick & Nishith 1997). Recently, some of these psychological consequences have been conceptualized as post-traumatic stress disorder (PTSD) (American Psychiatric Association 1994). This symptom constellation includes reexperiencing the rape (such as in dreams or flashbacks), feeling numb and avoiding reminders of the rape, and experiencing hyperarousal (such as insomnia, difficulty concentrating, outbursts of anger, or an exaggerated startle response; see Herman 1992; Resnick et al. 1993).

[*Update 2003*: Although it is likely that being raped causes these psychological problems, it is possible that in some cases these psychological problems increase individuals' vulnerability to rape. For example, in a longitudinal study of college women's experiences with sexual coercion, women who reported being verbally sexually coerced *during* the semester had lower self-esteem scores than did other women *at the beginning* of the semester, suggesting that low self-esteem left the women vulnerable to verbal sexual coercion (Jones & Muehlenhard 1994). Thus, research that finds differences between rape victims and nonvictims must be interpreted cautiously. (*End of update by C. L. Muehlenhard*)]

Sexual problems resulting from rape can include avoidance of sex, decreased sexual satisfaction, sexual dysfunctions, and flashbacks to the rape during sex (Kilpatrick et al. 1987; Lystad 1982; Warshaw 1988). Some rape victims engage in sex indiscriminately in ways that they do not feel good about, perhaps because the rape made them feel devalued, as if "they now have nothing left that's worth protecting" (Warshaw 1988, 74).

[*Update 2003*: Paradoxically, one consequence of sexual victimization seems to be further sexual victimization. Numerous studies have shown evidence that women who experienced child sexual abuse are more likely than others to be sexually victimized as adolescents or adults (see Muehlenhard et al. 1998 for a review). Some studies have also found this for men (Brenner & Muehlenhard 1995). NVAW data replicated this pattern: Among women who reported having been raped before age 18, 18.3% reported having been raped again as an adult; among women who did not report having been raped before age 18, only 8.7% reported having been raped as an adult (Tjaden & Thoennes 2000). In a longitudinal study of U.S. college women, Humphrey and White (2000) found that sexual victimization during childhood (before age 14) predicted an increased risk of sexual victimization as an adolescent (from age 14 until the beginning of the college); in turn, sexual victimization during adolescence predicted an increased risk of sexual victimization during college. As with studies comparing the psychological

characteristics of rape victims and nonvictims, studies comparing the subsequent victimization rates of these groups must also be interpreted cautiously: It could be the case that earlier victimization increases the risk of later victimization, but it could also be the case that personality, family, or environmental factors increase some individuals' risk as a child, as an adolescent, and as an adult.

[Numerous studies suggest that being raped leads to behavior changes. For example, as mentioned above, after being raped, some rape victims avoid sex, and others engage in sex indiscriminately. Brener et al. (1999) found that women who had been raped were significantly more likely than other women to engage in numerous health-risk behaviors. Analyzing data from a nationally representative sample of U.S. college students, they found that 20% of the women and 4% of the men reported having been raped, defined as having been forced to engage in sexual intercourse against their will. Multivariate analyses, controlling for age, parents' education, race, and sorority membership, found that women who had been raped were more likely than other women to report having thought seriously about suicide during the prior year; fighting physically with a boyfriend or spouse during the prior year; smoking cigarettes, drinking heavily, driving after drinking alcohol, and using marijuana during the prior month; having had two or more sexual partners during the prior three months; having used alcohol or drugs during their last sexual intercourse; and having had sexual intercourse before age 15. It could be the case that being raped increases the likelihood that women will engage in these health-risk behaviors; however, it could also be the case that engaging in these behaviors increases women's vulnerability to rape or that other factors increase the likelihood of these behaviors and of rape. (*End of update by C. L. Muehlenhard*)]

The physical consequences of rape can include physical injuries (including injuries from weapons or fists, as well as vaginal or anal injuries), sexually transmitted diseases, pregnancy, reproductive problems causing infertility, and psychosomatic problems (Koss 1993b; Resick 1993; Resick & Nishith 1997; Warshaw 1988).

[*Update 2003*: In the NVAW study (Tjaden & Thoennes 2000), among those who reported having been raped as an adult (age 18 and older), 31.5% of the female rape victims and 16.1% of the male rape victims reported having been physically injured during their most recent rape. These injuries ranged from bruises and sore muscles to broken bones, chipped teeth, and knife wounds. Of the women injured during a rape, 35.6% reported receiving medical treatment for their injuries. (*End of update by C. L. Muehlenhard*)]

Divulging the rape to someone else may result in various problems: feeling embarrassed or uncomfortable; reliving aspects of the experience; being disbelieved or blamed; and being questioned about one's behavior and dress, which might lead victims to feel as if they are "on trial," and needing to prove their innocence to others. When rape victims report the rape to the police, their report may be disbelieved or trivialized, although police attitudes and sensitivity have improved during the last several decades. Should the case go to trial, recent "rape shield laws" generally prohibit defense attorneys from inquiring about the victim's sexual past; nevertheless, defense attorneys typically try to discredit victims (Allison & Wrightsman 1993; Estrich 1987; Gelles 1977; Griffin 1971; Roth & Lebowitz 1988).

Contrary to stereotypes, acquaintance or date rape is as traumatic as stranger rape. Victims of acquaintance rape are as likely as victims of stranger rape to experience depression, anxiety, problems with relationships, problems with sex, and thoughts of suicide (Koss et al. 1988). Women who are raped by acquaintances they had trusted may doubt their ability to evaluate the character of others and may be reluctant to trust others. Women raped by acquaintances are less likely than women raped by strangers to be believed and supported by others. If the victim and rapist have mutual friends, the friends may be reluctant to believe that a friend of theirs could be a rapist; they may thus be reluctant to take the victim's side against the perpetrator, and the victim may feel unsupported. If the rapist goes to the same school, workplace, or social functions as the victim, the victim may feel uncomfortable and withdraw from these activities (Kilpatrick et al. 1987; Koss et al. 1988; Russell 1982/1990; Stacy et al. 1992; Warshaw 1988).

[*Update 2003*: NVAW data (Tjaden & Thoennes 2000) revealed that rape by current or former intimate partners was especially dangerous for women: 36.2% of women raped by intimates, compared with 23.6% of women raped by nonintimates, were physically injured. In a multivariate analysis, in which other explanatory variables were held constant, women raped by intimates were 2.2 times more likely to be injured than women raped by nonintimates. (*End of update by C. L. Muehlenhard*)]

People raped by their spouses or cohabiting partners may experience consequences that other rape victims do not experience. Whereas stranger rape is typically a one-time occurrence, the rape of wives and other partners is likely to occur repeatedly and may last for years (Russell 1982/1990). Many also experience other forms of domestic violence. Victims raped by a spouse or cohabiting partner must decide either to live with the perpetrator and risk subsequent rapes or to divorce or separate, which requires many lifestyle adjustments, and which does not guarantee that they will not be raped by their ex-spouse or ex-partner (Koss et al. 1988; Lystad 1982; Russell 1982/1990). The consequences may also extend to children living in the household (Mio & Foster 1991). Children may be aware of the problem and may even witness the rapes. They may fear the parent or stepparent who is the perpetrator and may develop negative views of sex and relationships.

Boys and men who have been raped experience many of the same consequences that girls and women do, although being a male victim may result in additional consequences that female victims do not encounter. Being forced into submission is incongruous with the male sex-role stereotype that espouses control and dominance. Males raped by females often confront beliefs that they must have desired and enjoyed the act and that male victims are less traumatized than are female victims. Males raped by other males, regardless of their sexual orientation, often confront homophobic attitudes. Males also confront the myth—held by others and sometimes by the victims themselves—that if they had an erection, they must have wanted sex (Groth & Burgess 1980; Russell 1984; Sarrel & Masters 1982; Smith et al. 1988; Warshaw 1988).

Lesbian and gay rape victims may encounter difficulty in attempting to obtain services from crisis-intervention and social-service centers, as many of these agencies are not prepared to serve lesbian and gay clients (Renzetti 1996; Waterman et al. 1989). Obtaining services may require that gay or lesbian rape victims "come out," revealing their sexual orientation and risking possible discrimination, possibly even losing their jobs, housing, or children should others find out (legal protection of lesbians and gays in the United States varies from city to city and state to state; in most of the U.S., there is no such protection). If rape occurs in a lesbian or gay relationship in which the perpetrator is the biological parent of the children, if the victimized partner leaves the relationship, she or he will probably have to leave the children with the perpetrator. Furthermore, the gay and lesbian community is often tight-knit, so lesbian or gay rape victims may be reluctant to tell mutual friends or to participate in the community's social functions (Grover 1990; Muehlenhard et al. 1991).

*Punishment of Rapists.* The typical punishment for rapists is no penalty, given that most rapes are not reported to the police (Koss et al. 1988; Russell 1984). Even those that are reported rarely result in arrest and conviction (Allison & Wrightsman 1993). Among those who are convicted of rape, punishment varies from merely being placed on parole to life in prison.

Until the 1970s, the penalty for rape included the death penalty; 89% of the men executed for rape in the United States from 1930 to 1967 were African-American (Estrich 1987, 107). In 1977, the U.S. Supreme Court found the death penalty for rape to be unconstitutional (*Coker v. Georgia*, 433 U.S. 584, 1977; see Estrich 1987). Studies of actual sentences given to convicted rapists reveal that the harshest penalties for rape are still imposed on African-American men convicted of raping white women (Estrich 1987; LaFree 1980). There is also a bias against convicting affluent, successful men and men who rape women they know or who rape women who do not conform to cultural expectations of how a "good woman" should behave (Estrich 1987; LaFree et al. 1985).

*Prevention.* Prior to the 1970s, rape prevention was generally regarded as women's responsibility. Because rape was regarded as an act of sex incited by provocative women, rape prevention consisted largely of expecting women to restrict their behavior (expecting women not to talk or dress provocatively, not to go out at night, etc.).

Currently, a variety of prevention strategies are common in the U.S. (Muehlenhard et al. 1992a). Some people still urge women to restrict their behavior, and research shows that women do indeed restrict their behavior because of the fear of rape: Women report avoiding going outside alone at night, not talking to strangers, wearing bulky clothing, having unlisted phone numbers, and so on (Gordon & Riger 1989; Hickman & Muehlenhard 1997). These precautions limit women's freedom and diminish women's quality of life. [*Update 2003*: Furthermore, this approach focuses on stranger rape; paradoxically, although stranger rape accounts for a minority of all rapes (Tjaden & Thoennes 2000), women fear stranger rape more than acquaintance rape and take more precautions to avoid stranger rape than acquaintance rape (Hickman & Muehlenhard 1997; Pain 1997; Poirier & Muehlenhard 2000). (*End of update by C. L. Muehlenhard*)]

There are other prevention strategies that are not predicated on women's restricting their behavior. For instance, many universities have installed extra lighting and emergency telephones (often marked by blue lights) to help women feel safer. These strategies are aimed primarily at preventing stranger rape, however, and will not help women who are raped indoors by husbands, partners, dates, or other acquaintances. To address these problems, many universities have initiated lectures and workshops presented to college dormitory residents, fraternities, sororities, and athletic groups; some high schools and even junior high schools have also initiated such programs, although they sometimes meet resistance from parents and school boards (Donat & D'Emilio 1992). There is evidence that such programs can lead to attitude change (Jones & Muehlenhard 1990), although the effectiveness of these strategies in actually preventing rape is unknown.

Some women take self-defense classes. For example, Model Mugging programs teach women self-defense strategies that utilize women's physical strengths, such as lower-body strength (Allison & Wrightsman 1993). Research shows that active-resistance strategies (e.g., physically fighting, screaming, and running away) are generally more effective than the passive-resistance strategies (e.g., pleading, crying, reasoning, or doing nothing), and active strategies do not increase the risk of physical harm (Bart & O'Brien 1984; Ullman 1997; Ullman & Knight 1992; Zoucha-Jensen & Coyne 1993). Unfortunately, no strategy is effective all of the time or for all people, and even experiencing an attempted rape can be traumatic. Furthermore, many feminist theorists have argued that, because most rapists are men, it is unfair to place the burden of rape prevention on women (Berkowitz 1992; Koss 1993b).

The most important strategies for preventing rape involve working for broader social change: changing men's and women's attitudes about rape, sex, and gender roles; working toward gender equality; discouraging violence as a problem-solving technique; and emphasizing that coercive sex in any context, whether with a stranger or acquaintance, is never acceptable.

[*Sexual Rape in the Military* ROBERT T. FRANCOEUR
[*Update 2003*: In the early 1990s, Americans became very aware of "sexual harassment" when several women charged Senator Bob Packwood with sexual harassment; when, in Congressional hearings to confirm Clarence Thomas as an associate justice of the U.S. Supreme Court, Anita Hill claimed that she had been a victim of repeated sexual harassment by Thomas; and when women officers attending the annual Tailhook Convention of the U.S. Navy made public charges of sexual harassment and assault against male officers. Three admirals were issued letters of censure, but as one woman officer later reported, "not a single Naval officer who took part in Tailhook got anything more than a slap on the wrist."

[The Tailhook scandal eventually left the headlines, but it erupted again in 2003 at the Air Force Academy in Colorado Springs, when women cadets took their charges to the press and television news reporters, finally forcing a Congressional hearing and three independent military investigations of the top command at the Academy. With close to 800 women in the 4,200-member Cadet Corp, the command admitted to processing 56 cases of rape in the previous 10 years, and expelling only eight male cadets and court marshalling only one cadet, who was acquitted. As one female cadet commented: 'They tell you to expect getting raped, and if it doesn't happen to you, you're one of the rare ones. They say if you want a chance to stay here, if you want to graduate, you don't tell. You just deal with it."

[Attempts of the Pentagon to deal with the emerging scandal failed in mid 2003 when the General appointed in 1991 to solve the problem was forced to resign along with the four top officers in March 2003. Congressional hearings and three independent military investigations were initiated, with reports that rapists had routinely used the General's disciplinary crackdown on minor infractions as a shield to intimidate victims and thwart their efforts to seek prosecution. In effect, the commander set a tone to blame the victim, which in turn discouraged women cadets from lodging formal complaints for fear of retribution against themselves or classmates who could serve as witnesses. It was soon documented that claims of sexual assault were rarely investigated or seldom severely punished.

[In August 2003, the Air Force general counsel issued a report based on her five-month investigation that substantiated many of claims made in a 1996 report to the Air Force, the inspector general, and the Senate Armed Services Committee. Air Force records showed at least 30 sexual assaults were reported to Academy officials since the report was given to the Air Force Chief of Staff in 1996 and passed on in 2000 to the Senate Armed Forces committee. The 2003 report confirmed allegations that were known to the highest-level officials in the Pentagon and Congress, namely that:

- The Air Force Academy maintained "a culture of silence and intimidation" that stigmatized women who came forward. This culture, filtered down from the highest levels of command, placed the institution and peers above personal integrity.
- The reporting consisted of a fractured composite of agencies, functioning separately, but there was no formal program to help victims.
- No one had ultimate responsibility for investigating and dealing with incidents.
- Sixteen cases of assault spanning several years included one woman so traumatized she slept with a weapon; another woman raped at the Academy's prep school, who was so ostracized for reporting the attack, she didn't report a subsequent gang rape; another who suffered a cut vagina in an attack but didn't report it until she experienced "noticeable" blood loss; and others who were left to "suffer silently in shame."
- The school "reflects institutional/cultural dysfunction" that officials should confront.

[On August 28, the office of the Department of Defense inspector general released the results of a survey of female cadets that showed that the problem in the Air Force Academy has been much more common than originally suspected, with 12%, one-in-six female cadets, reporting being raped or the victim of an attempted rape. Since 10% of the female cadets declined to answer the survey, the inspector general concluded that the true extent of the problem is probably much higher than 12% (Janofsky 2003; Moss 2003; Schemo 2003a, 2003b; Zubeck 2003). (*End of update by R. T. Francoeur*)]

## Child Sexual Abuse and Incest

DIANE BAKER and SHARON E. KING
Knowledge of child sexual abuse (CSA) has undergone cycles of awareness and suppression, as both professionals and the general public have struggled to come to terms with its existence since child sexual abuse first gained widespread attention in the 1890s, when Freud proposed that it was at the root of hysterical neurosis. Although modern clinical work tends to confirm the link between child sexual abuse and various neuroses, Freud quietly abandoned his early belief in response to the strong opposition from Victorian attitudes of that era. Linking neuroses with repressed childhood sexual conflict, Freud's Oedipal and Electra complexes, was revolutionary, but at least much more acceptable than admitting the reality and prevalence of child sexual abuse.

During the past 20 years, child sexual abuse has received renewed attention from American clinicians, researchers, and the general public. Recently, child sexual abuse has been the focus of a substantial amount of American research that has, in turn, led to broader recognition of the initial and long-term problems associated with child sexual abuse.

*Definitions.* The definition presented by the National Center on Child Abuse and Neglect is "Contact and interactions between a child and an adult when the child is being used for the sexual stimulation of the perpetrator or another person." This definition is problematic, however, in that it leaves key terms open to question. For example, in considering who is a child, researchers have employed cutoff ages anywhere between 12 and 17 years for victims of child sexual abuse. In deciding who is an adult, some researchers have required perpetrators to be at least 16 years of age; others have required age differences between victim and perpetrator of five years or ten years; still others have not required any age difference at all if force or coercion was used. In determining what is sexual stimulation, some authors include noncontact experiences, such as exhibitionism or propositioning, whereas others require manual contact, and still others, genital contact. In a 1987 study designed to determine the effect of varying the operational definition of child sexual abuse on its prevalence, the percentage of college men identified as victims ranged from 24% to 4% based on how restrictive the criteria used were. The parameters defining child sexual abuse, therefore, will have strong implications for how widespread a problem society considers it.

A second major issue is determining, in the absence of physical injury, what has been damaged. This issue is complicated by a consistently identified minority of victims who report such experiences as having been positive. Some authors have pointed to this subset and wondered whether the abuse was against the individual or societal values, and further, whether in defining child sexual abuse, consideration should be given to the victim's view of the experience as negative or positive. Yet, a victim's view of a child sexual abuse experience as positive does not preclude the possibility that it was a harmful or damaging one.

A cogent argument against using the victim's assessment of the experience as positive or negative in defining abuse is that the inequalities of knowledge, sophistication, and power inherent in any child-adult relationship prevent the child from giving informed consent to engage in sexual behavior. From this perspective, it is the emotional and intellectual immaturity of the child that causes the developmentally inappropriate exposure to adult sexuality to be harmful and abusive.

These issues of definition influence the composition of the groups studied by researchers and, thereby, the results obtained. As yet, there has been no completely satisfactory way to define child sexual abuse to ensure that the research results are relevant and helpful to the greatest number of people. Currently, the most widely used set of criteria for defining child sexual abuse are contact experiences between a child aged 12 or younger with an individual five or more years older, or between a child aged 13 to 16 with an individual ten or more years older. These criteria emphasize the differences in developmental maturity between the victim and perpetrator, while minimizing the inclusion of age-appropriate sexual exploration between peers as sexual abuse.

*Prevalence of Child Sexual Abuse.* Accurate estimates of the prevalence of child sexual abuse in either the general population or clinical populations have been difficult to obtain, in part because of the differences in operational definitions discussed above, in part to the sensitive nature of the topic, and in part to differing methods of assessment (e.g., questionnaire, face-to-face interview, or telephone interview). Estimates of the percentage of adult women who have experienced child sexual abuse vary from 6% to 62% and of adult men from 3% to 31%. In general, percentages are higher among clinical samples than among community-based samples. Additionally, more people disclose abuse histories when information is gathered via an interview rather than by questionnaire, when specific questions about childhood sexual experiences are asked, and when such

terms as "sexual abuse" and "molestation" are avoided (see also Prendergast 1993).

More confidence can be placed in the accuracy of prevalence rates when the samples used are large, random, and community-based. In a 1990 random sample of over 2,000 adults across the United States, 27% of women and 16% of men reported having experienced such abuse as children. In other large-scale studies, about 25% of women and 17% of college men have been identified as having histories of child sexual abuse. The majority of child sexual abuse cases are perpetrated by a nonrelative, generally an acquaintance or family friend; about 30% of girls are abused by a relative (with about 4% involving father-daughter incest), whereas about 10% of boys are abused by a relative. Finally, the prevalence of child sexual abuse does not seem to vary with social class or ethnicity (Hunter 1990).

*Theories Explaining Child Sexual Abuse.* Upon hearing of child sexual abuse, people generally react strongly, wondering how such abuse could occur. Originally, professionals held a simplistic view of child sexual abuse, considering it to be the result of the isolated actions of a depraved and flawed perpetrator. In the past several decades, however, two more-complicated theories of child sexual abuse have dominated the field.

Family systems theory posits that families function as integrated systems and that irregularities in the system are displayed through symptomatic behavior in one or more family members. From this perspective, the occurrence of incest reflects a distortion in the family system, specifically in the marital subsystem, that is being expressed through a parent's (usually the father's) sexual behavior with a child. This model proposes, then, that child sexual abuse occurs as a misguided attempt to cope with problems in the family. Treatment, therefore, involves recognition of the underlying problems and the institution of changes by all family members rather than through removal of the perpetrator.

Although less simplistic than earlier proposals, this model has been criticized for seeming to blame the victims for the abuse and by removing responsibility from the perpetrator. Additionally, the model is relevant only to incest, which is a relatively small fraction of the child sexual abuse cases.

In order to address these concerns, Finkelhor proposed a four-factor model of child sexual abuse incorporating some aspects of the family systems' perspective, but shifting responsibility for the abuse back to the perpetrator. He conceptualized child sexual abuse as resulting from an interaction between environmental circumstances and the personality of the perpetrator, rather than simply as inherent in the perpetrator or in the family system.

In this model, four preconditions must be met for child sexual abuse to occur. First, the offender must have some motivation to abuse sexually; thus, child sexual abuse satisfies some emotional or sexual need in the perpetrator that is not readily satisfied in other ways. Second, the offender must overcome his or her inhibitions against child sexual abuse. Inhibitions may be overcome in a variety of ways, such as substance use, rationalization, the influence of stressors, or personality factors (e.g., impulsivity). Third, environmental impediments to the abuse must be removed; the offender must have private access to a child. Therefore, she or he may target children who are without consistent adult supervision or obtain employment that provides contact with children. Fourth, the offender capitalizes on the lowered resistance of the child; children who are insecure, needy, uneducated about sexuality, and/or have a trusting relationship with the offender have lowered resistance.

These children are less likely to be assertive in refusing abusive overtures or to disclose immediately that the abuse took place. All of these factors, working in concert, allow child sexual abuse to occur.

Some people remain uncomfortable with the third and fourth preconditions of this model, because they appear to place some responsibility for the child sexual abuse outside the perpetrator and onto the child and his or her non-offending parent(s). Finkelhor stresses, however, that without the first and second preconditions, qualities, and behaviors of the offender alone, child sexual abuse would never occur. These preconditions place responsibility for the act squarely with the perpetrator.

*Who Is at Risk for Child Sexual Abuse?* The environmental circumstances in which boys are sexually abused versus those in which girls are sexually abused differ in some important ways. Some of these differences were highlighted by Tzeng and Schwarzin (1987), who compared the demographic characteristics of boys and girls in over 15,000 substantiated cases of sexual abuse in Illinois. They found that girls who had been sexually abused tended to live in homes that did not differ from those of the general population in the numbers and kinds of parents/caretakers present, whereas boys who had been sexually abused were significantly more likely to come from single-parent homes and/or from families with either new or many children/dependents. On the other hand, the girls' families tended to display significantly more dysfunction, and caretakers were more physically and/or mentally impaired than caretakers in the boys' families. These results are similar to those of Finkelhor, who found the risk of child sexual abuse among girls increased approximately twofold when a mother was absent from the home. These findings point to an increased risk of sexual abuse when parents are absent, impaired, or overworked (see also Prendergast 1993).

Some differences in the perpetrators of abuse of boys versus girls have also been identified. Tzeng and Schwarzin (1987) and others reported that sexual abuse of boys is more likely to be perpetrated by a stranger, whereas abuse of girls is more likely to be perpetrated by a relative. Further, when boys are abused by a relative, these relatives are more likely to be within five years of age of the boys, whereas relatives who abuse girls are more likely to be ten or more years older than the girls. Although the vast majority of perpetrators of both boys and girls are men, boys are more likely to be abused by women than are girls (17% versus 2%). Thus, for boys, child sexual abuse experiences tend to occur outside the home and to be perpetrated by a nonfamily member or, if inside the home and perpetrated by a relative, the relative is less likely to be a parent-figure or to have adult status. Girls are more likely to be abused within the home by a relative ten or more years older. Risk to girls is increased by sevenfold for girls with a stepfather. A general consensus among researchers is that more boys are somewhat more likely to experience severe abuse (actual intercourse) than are girls.

These differences suggest that boys and girls may be experiencing child sexual abuse situations that require differing coping skills. Girls may, more typically, need to adjust to the notion that an adult in a position of trust has been abusive, and boys may, more typically, need to adjust to the notion that the world outside the home is not safe and may need to react to a more-severe physical experience. It should be stressed that all of these differences are generalizations, and there is substantial overlap in the nature of the child sexual abuse experiences of boys and girls.

*Initial Effects of Child Sexual Abuse.* Although researchers have identified a wide array of problems occurring among children who have been sexually abused, most have failed to find any substantial differences in symptomatology between male and female victims. When studying these initial effects, researchers have recently begun to divide subjects into three groups based on their stage of development: preschool (ages 3 to 6), school age (ages 7 to 12), and adolescent (ages 13 to 17). By using these groupings, the presence and frequency of various behaviors and symptoms can be compared to those considered developmentally appropriate for the stage.

Among both preschool boys and girls, the most frequent behavioral symptom associated with child sexual abuse experiences is an increase in sexualized behaviors (Beitchman et al. 1991). This increase has been noted in a number of studies using a variety of methodologies, including chart review, parent rating, observed play with anatomically correct dolls, and human-figure drawing. However, the prevalence of this behavior varies widely depending on the context, from 10% of the sample in the case of human-figure drawing to 90% of the sample in play with anatomically correct dolls; still, this finding is among the most robust in the literature. [*Comment 1997*: These studies do not make comparisons to groups of "normal" children and their rate of sexual behavior. (*End of comment by D. L. Weis*)]

Emotionally, preschool children are likely to respond to sexual abuse with anxiety, signs of post-traumatic stress (e.g., nightmares, vigilance, or bed wetting), and depression (Kendall-Tackett et al. 1993). These children are also likely to exhibit greater immaturity than nonabused controls, showing increases in both dependency and impulsivity relative to physically abused and nonabused age peers.

Among school-age children, researchers have focused on behavioral problems that interfere with academic and social success. Sexually abused children have been assessed by their teachers as significantly less able than their nonabused peers to learn in the school environment. This difficulty may be a function of the wide range of behavioral and emotional problems they display. For example, approximately half of the school-age girls with histories of child sexual abuse show high levels of immaturity and aggression (Kendall-Tacketts et al. 1993). Similarly, both parents and teachers rated sexually abused children as more emotionally disturbed and neurotic than their classmates, displaying both depression and a wide range of fears (Beitchman et al. 1991; Browne & Finkelhor 1986; Kendall-Tackett et al. 1993). Additionally, like preschool children, the sexually abused school-age boys and girls display clear-cut increases in sexualized behaviors, including such problems as excessive and inappropriate masturbation and sexual aggression (Browne & Finkelhor 1986; Kendall-Tackett et al. 1993). All of these symptoms would be expected to lead to problems in school for children, regardless of their intelligence.

A somewhat different presentation has been observed among adolescents with a history of sexual abuse. Although acting-out behaviors, such as running away, substance use, and sexual promiscuity were more common in these adolescents than their nonabused peers, they were less common than among clinical groups of adolescents (Beitchman et al. 1991). The predominant finding among sexually abused adolescents is an increase in depressive symptomatology, such as low self-esteem and suicidal ideation. This depression may be expressed through self-injurious behaviors, as exhibited by more than two thirds of sexually abused adolescents (Kendall-Tackett et al. 1993), or through suicide attempts made by a third of these adolescents in a clinical sample.

Although there is an extensive list of symptoms and problems associated with the initial effects of sexual abuse, it should be noted that not all children display such effects.

Indeed, 20% to 40% of sexually abused children have been found to be asymptomatic at the time of initial assessment (Kendall-Tackett et al. 1993). Unfortunately, some of these children have become symptomatic by the time of later assessments. There is fairly consistent evidence that from a third to a half of sexually abused children show improvement in symptom presentation 12 to 18 months after the abuse, although another quarter to a third show deterioration in function.

*Long-Term Effects of Child Sexual Abuse.* Although the long-term effects of child sexual abuse experiences have been studied in both men and women, the majority of the work has been done with women. Reviews of this research have been conducted by Browne and Finkelhor (1986) and Beitchman et al. (1992). The results vary somewhat, depending on whether the samples were community-based or clinically based; still, there is substantial overlap across the two populations.

In both clinical and community-based surveys of women with histories of child sexual abuse, the most common long-term effect is depression. Depression is particularly striking among the community-based samples of victims, in which significantly more women with a history of child sexual abuse report both more-severe and more-frequent episodes of depression compared to those without such experiences. Almost one in five college women reporting a history of child sexual abuse had been hospitalized for depression compared to one in 25 women who had not been abused. In a community-based study of the Los Angeles area, researchers found that a history of child sexual abuse was associated with a fourfold increase in the lifetime prevalence rate for major depression among women. Other prominent depression-related symptoms include problems with self-esteem, which appear to intensify as time elapses from the abuse, and an increased risk for self-injurious or destructive behaviors (Browne & Finkelhor 1986).

Increases in problems with anxiety occur among some women with sexual abuse histories. Problems with anxiety are more prominent among clinical samples than community samples (Beitchman et al. 1992; Brown & Finkelhor 1986). Anxiety seems to be particularly prevalent among women sexually abused by a family member and in cases in which force was used during the abuse.

Relationship difficulties are more common among women with histories of child sexual abuse compared to nonabused women. Abused women are more likely to fear intimacy and to have sexual dysfunctions, particularly when the abuse was more severe and/or was perpetrated by a father or stepfather (Beitchman et al. 1992). A history of child sexual abuse in women is also associated with an increased risk of further revictimization in the forms of rape and domestic violence.

Much less research has been conducted on the long-term effects of sexual abuse in men; much of the information available has been based on clinical case studies or extrapolated from studies with some adult male victims, but in which the majority of the subjects were women. Therefore, conclusions are much more tentative. Several community-based surveys found that men who reported child sexual abuse experiences exhibited a higher rate of psychopathology (e.g., depression, anxiety, or symptoms of post-traumatic stress) than those who did not report such experiences. Men who have been sexually abused have reported significant problems with poor self-esteem and self-concept. Men may respond to such feelings by self-medicating with alcohol and drugs, as indicated by the large degree of substance abuse and dependence among male victims; sexually abused women, on the other hand, report greater levels of depression and anxiety.

Clinicians suggest that intense anger, sexual dysfunction, problems with intimacy, gender-identity confusion, and substance abuse are prominent symptoms for males with a history of child sexual abuse seeking therapy. Additionally, disclosure of sexual abuse is particularly difficult for men. Issues related to disclosure include fears of not being believed (particularly if the perpetrator was female), fears others will consider them homosexual, concerns that they are homosexual because they have been abused by a man, and issues related to masculine identity.

*Correlates of More-Severe Effects.* Although the preceding paragraphs present a grim picture of the aftereffects of child sexual abuse, not all individuals suffer such severe effects. In fact, in a given sample of abuse survivors, a quarter to a third of the individuals can be expected to appear symptom-free on the chosen assessment instruments (Kendall-Tackett et al. 1993). About one third of these asymptomatic individuals may become symptomatic at later assessments. Still, these differences in outcome have led researchers to examine variables associated with more-severe effects.

One variable consistently associated with more-severe effects is the use of force (Beitchman et al. 1992; Browne & Finkelhor 1986; Kendall-Tackett et al. 1993). This finding has been most robust in studies of the initial effects of child sexual abuse among children (Kendall-Tackett et al. 1993). A number of researchers also have identified an association between the use of force and victims' reports of the degree of trauma experienced among adult survivors as well (Beitchman et. al. 1992; Browne & Finkelhor 1986). There is also some evidence that family-background variables, such as high levels of conflict and low levels of support, are related to more-severe effects. The situation is further complicated in that, for some individuals, the use of force has been associated with a decrease in self-blame, thereby reducing the severity of effects.

The relationship of the perpetrator to the victim has also been examined. Among children, the initial effects of abuse are more severe when the perpetrator has a closer relationship to the child (Kendall-Tackett et al. 1993). The situation is less clear for the long-term effects among adults. In general, whether the perpetrator was a family member has little impact on later outcome among adults (Beitchman et al. 1992; Browne & Finkelhor 1986) with one important caveat: Trauma and psychopathology effects are more severe if the abuse was perpetrated by a father or stepfather (Beitchman et al. 1992; Browne & Finkelhor 1986). This difference may represent a greater degree of family dysfunction and a more significant breach of trust when a father perpetrated the abuse (Beitchman et al. 1992). The lack of a general effect of intrafamilial versus extrafamilial abuse among adults may be a reflection that it was the quality of the relationship with the abuser (i.e., how much he was trusted) that influenced outcome rather than whether he was a relative. Finkelhor has extended this notion by proposing that the important variable is the degree to which the child was seduced and persuaded by the perpetrator, whether or not the child had a prior relationship with the perpetrator.

A third major variable examined to determine its relationship to long-term effects has been the duration of the abuse. This variable has been difficult to assess for a number of reasons. First, the criterion for child sexual abuse of long duration varies among researchers, from abuse that occurred for more than six months to abuse that occurred for more than five years. Second, as noted by Beitchman et al. (1992), researchers have tended to use very different measures, some assessing a subjective sense of harm, and others assessing a more objective degree of psychopathology. There is some evidence, however, that child sexual abuse of longer duration leads to an increase in psychopathology in community-based samples. The two major reviewers of long-term effects of child sexual abuse (Beitchman et al. 1992; Browne & Finkelhor 1986) have both concluded that more research must be conducted before firm conclusions can be drawn, whereas reviewers of initial effects have suggested that longer duration is associated with a worse outcome (Kendall-Tackett et al. 1993).

The severity of the child sexual abuse experience has also been examined in relation to psychopathology and harm in adulthood; here again, the results are mixed. There is general agreement that increased trauma and maladjustment are associated with contact abuse versus noncontact abuse, both initially and in the long term. Further, abuse involving genital contact, whether manual, oral, or invasive, is associated with more-serious outcomes than kissing or clothed contact. Researchers differ, however, in whether invasive contact as compared to manual contact is associated with increased trauma in the long term. Initially, invasive contact is associated with a worse outcome (Kendall-Tackett et al. 1993). Further research is necessary to determine the long-term effects of invasive contact.

One nonabuse-related variable, family support, has also been consistently identified as contributing significantly to both the initial and long-term effects of child sexual abuse. Kendall-Tackett et al. (1993) reviewed three studies examining the relationship of maternal support to symptom outcome in children who had been sexually abused. All three studies concluded that children whose mothers were low in support exhibited worse outcomes following the abuse. This conclusion was supported by the findings of other researchers who examined long-term coping among college women with histories of child sexual abuse.

*Theories about the Nature of the Effects.* Researchers have cataloged a multitude of symptoms associated with child sexual abuse that therapists have, in turn, attempted to address in treatment. Therapeutic treatment of any type is greatly facilitated by a theory or framework to organize and to approach symptoms. Many clinicians note that it is an impaired trust in self and others that underlies many of the symptoms associated with child sexual abuse.

This difficulty with trust has led some researchers and therapists to conceptualize the symptoms associated with child sexual abuse as a function of post-traumatic stress disorder (PTSD). This disorder encompasses some of the more-troubling symptoms experienced by sexual abuse survivors, such as depression, nightmares, and affective numbing. All of the PTSD conceptualizations of sexual abuse incorporate the idea that exposure to the abuse is experienced by the victim as overwhelming, because of intense fear and/or to extreme violations of beliefs about the way the world operates. When confronted with the abuse then, the child is unable to cope, given his or her current level of internal resources, and so must distort cognitions and/or affect in an effort to adjust to the experience. These distortions are, then, the basis for the symptoms that appear following the abuse.

However, there are some limitations to the application of PTSD to sexual abuse symptomatology. Among the most compelling of these limitations is the fact that the symptoms of PTSD do not encompass all of the problems associated with child sexual abuse. Also, many survivors do not meet the criteria for PTSD. In one group of survivors, only 10% could be diagnosed with PTSD at the time of the survey, and

only 36% could have ever been diagnosed with the disorder. Clearly, more work is needed in the conceptualization of the symptoms associated with a history of child sexual abuse.

Toward this end, Finkelhor has proposed a theory of child sexual abuse symptomatology, the Traumagenic Dynamics Model of Child Sexual Abuse (TD), which attempts to address the empirical findings more fully. The TD model emphasizes that the trauma associated with child sexual abuse may be because of the stress of the ongoing nature of the abuse situation, rather than an isolated event that is overwhelming and far removed from usual human experience (as described by the PTSD criteria in the *Diagnostic and Statistical Manual III Revised* (*DSM III-R*). This differentiation does not suggest that one type of trauma is more harmful than another; it simply highlights a qualitative difference in events that may lead to different coping responses and/or symptomatology.

The TD model includes four dynamics that occur to varying degrees in any child sexual abuse situation and that are postulated to contribute to the symptoms identified in the research literature. These dynamics include: (a) Traumatic Sexualization, which occurs when the child is taught distortions about his or her sexuality, and may lead to the increase in sexual dysfunctions observed among adult survivors; (b) Betrayal, which occurs in two ways, either when the child finds that an adult she or he trusted has hurt him or her or when the child discloses the abuse to an adult who refuses to believe or help the child. Finkelhor characterized the increased depression and revictimization seen among survivors as a result of the lost trust and unmet dependency needs. It can also lead to increased anger and hostility as a mechanism of keeping others at a distance; (c) Powerlessness, which occurs in a variety of ways in the child sexual abuse situation, for example, when the child finds himself or herself incapable of physically warding off the perpetrator. Powerlessness is further manifest when the child is unable to extricate himself or herself from the abuse situation or unable to do so in a satisfactory way (e.g., without being removed from the home). This powerlessness dynamic leads to anxiety and fear in adult survivors as well as a decreased coping ability; (d) Stigmatization, which occurs either directly through the labeling of the child by others as bad or dirty following disclosure of the abuse or indirectly through the sneaking behavior of the perpetrator and the admonitions that the abuse be kept secret. Stigmatization may be associated with the low self-esteem and the self-destructive behaviors, such as substance abuse and suicide attempts, observed among survivors.

However the effects are conceptualized, recent evidence has demonstrated that child sexual abuse is prevalent and commonly results in harmful effects. Finkelhor and others have attempted to make sense of a confusing array of symptoms presented by many, but not all victims of child sexual abuse. More-sophisticated research designs (e.g., involving structural equation modeling) are required before the relationship between various experiences of child sexual abuse and outcomes become more clear.

*Clergy Sexual Abuse*          SHARON E. KING

In the past ten years, sexual abuse of minors by clergy has become a major public scandal and crisis for all the churches, although the public attention is often focused on the Catholic clergy because of their requirement of celibacy. Until recently, charges of sexual abuse by clergy were treated as an internal problem within Church jurisdiction and not reported to police. The main issue for Church officials was to control damage to their institution's image. That silence exploded with national media coverage of the case of James Porter, a Massachusetts priest, who victimized, often sadistically, over 200 minors in several states between 1960 and 1972, and a similar case in Louisiana. Media coverage triggered a flood of new charges of abuse. Ten of 97 priests in a southwestern diocese, nine of 110 in a midwestern diocese, seven of 91 in a southern diocese, and 15 of 220 and 40 of 279 in the eastern United States were charged in civil and criminal suits. In December 1993, 12 of 44 priests in a California minor seminary were charged with having been sexually active with 11- to 17-year-old boys between 1964 and 1987. Between 1984 and 1994, an estimated 5,000 survivors reported their abuse to Church authorities. By early 1995, over 600 cases were pending (Sipe 1995, 26-28). Meanwhile, the Catholic dioceses of Sante Fe and Chicago admitted being in danger of bankruptcy; between 1984 and 1994, Catholic officials admitted to paying out over a half billion dollars in damages to survivors (Rossetti 1991).

Sipe (1995, 26-27) estimates that, at any one time, 6% of Catholic clergy are sexually involved with minors; the situation does not appear to be as serious in Protestant and Jewish circles. One third of the cases of abuse by priests can be classified as true pedophiles, with a three-to-one preference for boys. Two thirds of the abusive priests are involved with adolescents with a more even gender distribution. Four times as many priests are involved with adult women as with minors.

"The crisis of image has been compounded by church authorities who were slow, defensive, and even duplicitous in their public response as abuse by clergy became public and other indications of trouble mounted" (Sipe 1995, 8). Even as late as 1992, fully two thirds of the American Catholic bishops were confused or unconvinced that there is a problem of sexual abuse by the clergy, although even the Pope has acknowledged the crisis.

Civil authorities have responded by extending the statutes of limitations on reporting such abuse. New laws in all states require any professional to report suspected sexual abuse of a minor; in many states, any person is required to report suspected abuse. However, such laws are often vague in defining "reasonable suspicion."

The year 1990 was a watershed as confused Church authorities began losing their damage-control efforts to the rising tide of victims' voices expressed in civil and criminal lawsuits against priests, dioceses, and religious orders. Support groups for survivors spread across the nation: Victims of Clergy Abuse LINKUP, Survivors Connections, American Coalition for Abused Awareness, and Survivors Network of Those Abused by Priests (SNAP).

In 1992, the Catholic Archdiocese of Chicago adopted a model plan for processing allegations of clergy abuse; unfortunately, it remains incompletely and unevenly implemented. In 1993, St. John's (Benedictine) Abbey and University in Collegeville, Minnesota, established an ecumenical Interfaith Institute to study this problem.

How survivors are treated by a religious community varies greatly, and survivors should be reminded that, when they set out to seek legal action against anyone, the course may be extremely difficult. Far too often, survivors feel that they are revictimized by a system that protects the abuser, rather than one that is sensitive to the trauma of the victim.

*[Clergy Sexual Abuse—A 2003 Update*

WILLIAM PRENDERGAST

*[Update 2003*: In discussing the present, media-sustained uproar over sexual molestation by religious personnel, which first came to the attention of investigative reporters in the 1980s, the twofold emphasis has been on Catholic priests and cases of molestation of children. The problem of clerical abuse is far greater and includes religious personnel from all religions: Catholic priests and brothers, Protestant ministers of many denominations, Jewish rabbis, and recently, Muslim imams. It also encompasses the sexual molestation of adult women and men, the fathering of children who are then abandoned, and even drug-involved sexual molestation.

[An extremely important element found in a majority of these cases is a religious one. Quite often the molester informs the victim that God has given him permission to use the body of the victim in any way he pleases and, secondly, that God will protect him from all harm should the victim tell his parents, the police, and so on. The element of "threat(s)" made by these molesters includes personal threats to the victim, as well as threats against his or her family members and religious threats ("God will punish you if you tell!"). Since this group of molesters, like the pedophile or hebophile groups in other molestations, carefully chooses inadequate, timid, easily impressed, and passive types to molest, these pronouncements are believed and contribute to long-lasting guilt in the victims that is especially difficult to treat. Parents and other adults in their close-to-idolization of religious personnel contribute to the damage done to these victims by not believing anything the victim reports, proving the "protection" dictate of the offender. For all of the above reasons, a very high percentage of victims of molestation by clerical abusers never tell anyone of their experience(s).

[As early as the mid-1960s, psychologists were already treating both priests and their victims, but none of the victims at that time was willing to be exposed by reporting. Many abused in childhood or adolescence only began to confront their abuse years later when they were adults, often married and successful in business. All of them were badly traumatized by their molestations (some of which lasted for years!) and their lives were a confused shamble of problems and failures (Prendergast 1996, 2003; Sipe 1995, 1999).

[Several times in the 1970s and 1980s, reports in the media, including pioneering investigations by the *National Catholic Reporter*, focused on allegations of sexual abuse by clergy in Boston, Rhode Island, and Louisiana. Bishops in these dioceses managed to ignore the allegations, often transferring the priests from parish to parish without informing the pastor in the new parish of the potential for continued abuse. Finally, in 2002, investigative reporters for the *Boston Globe* documented a massive coverup by Church authorities that forced the Vatican and the Pope to recognize the scandal, and forced the resignation of Bernard Law, the Cardinal Archbishop of Boston, and of other bishops in Florida, Milwaukee, and Phoenix, The media took the lead in publishing these reports on their front pages in large, bold figures. In reality, these molestations have been going on for hundreds of years and have been kept secret and protected by the superiors involved in their denominations. While an improvement has recently occurred, much of the same secrecy and protection continues in the form of transferring accused personnel from one place to another without informing the supervisors at the new assignment of the accusations made. In cases today, many of these cases are hidden from the congregations, go unreported to the authorities, and never reach the light of day (Cozzens 2002; Sipe 1995, 1999).

[The Catholic Church, at the present time, is the primary focus of these investigations. In late 2002 and early 2003, the Archdiocese of Boston, Massachusetts, was a major press focus. Cardinal Law, its appointed leader, followed traditional methods in dealing with accusations against priests and transferred them to other assignments. What made Boston so striking an example of the problem was the outrage and public denouncement by the lay Catholics, the public, law officials, and even the priests under Cardinal Law's jurisdiction. In a historic "first," the Boston priests sent a petition demanding Law's replacement. In late 2002, Law quietly flew to the Vatican and received permission to resign his post.

[As of early 2003, there were more than 400 pending lawsuits in Boston, with subpoenas for depositions in the Cardinal's handling of these cases. There is a real possibility that the Boston Archdiocese and several other dioceses will have to file bankruptcy because of the staggering amounts demanded by these lawsuits.

[An extensive *New York Times* survey of documented cases of sexual abuse by priests through December 21, 2002, turned up the following findings:

• By the end of 2002, 1,200 priests in 161 of the 177 Latin Rite dioceses in the U.S. were accused of sexual abuse.
• By mid-2003, six bishops and archbishops had been forced to resign because of their involvement in sexual abuse or their complicity in reassigning known sexual abusers.
• Nationwide, 1.8% of all priests ordained from 1955 to 2001 have been charged with abuse.
• Eighty percent of the accused priests were accused of molesting boys. For laypeople accused, 80% of the victims are girls.
• Over half of the accused priests, 57%, were involved only with teenagers; the remaining 43% were accused of molesting children 12 years or younger (Goodstein 2003).
• Most priests accused were ordained between the mid-1950s and the 1970s, a period of great upheaval in the Church, when the Vatican II Council "opened the windows of the church to the world."
• The number of priests accused of abuse declined sharply by the 1990s. Some claim the decline is because of the victims' very slow recognition of their trauma and their delay in reporting the abuse for years.

[In attempting to find a solution to the problem and greatly concerned about the hundreds and even thousands of millions of dollars being awarded in lawsuits, the Catholic Bishops made this subject the focus of their annual meeting in Dallas on June 13-15, 2002. After debates, arguments, and many disagreements, the group came up with a proposed charter for the protection of children (not adults) that was sent to the Vatican in Rome for consideration. The Charter basically contained 13 Articles, as follows:

1. It bars priests who commit sexual abuse from any parish work and all public ministry in the future, and recommends to the Vatican that they be laicized.
2. Any priest who has sexually abused minors more than once in the past will be recommended for laicization.
3. A priest who abused only once in the past will be governed by strict rules determining if he can be returned to ministry after treatment. Victims will have a say in the process.
4. It allows bishops, acting on the advice of an advisory board composed mainly of laypeople (Diocesan Response Team) to decide whether to remove (laicize) abusive clergy from the priesthood.
5. It requires bishops to report all allegations of abuse of minors to civil authorities.
6. It says bishops should no longer make confidentiality agreements in settlement of civil lawsuits over sex abuse unless the victim insists.

7. It requires background checks for all diocesan and parish workers who have contact with children.
8. It requires bishops to provide an "accurate and complete" description of a priest's personnel record if the cleric seeks to transfer to another diocese.
9. It creates a commission to research how the U.S. Church has responded to sex abuse by priests.
10. It creates a national Office of Child and Youth Protection in the U.S. The Conference of Catholic Bishops is to implement "safe environment" programs and take other actions to protect children from abuse.
11. It creates a review board, including parents, to work with the Child Protection Office to annually examine how the bishops are responding to abuse.
12. It has dioceses establish an immediate outreach program to support victims of priestly sexual abuse (*The Sunday Star Ledger* 2002).

[Problems emerged immediately, especially with the second and third articles, which appeared to allow at least one molestation to go unpunished. The Articles were signed by a majority of the Bishops (249 to 2) and forwarded to Rome for Vatican approval. There were many doubts that the Vatican would accept the Dallas recommendations.

[On October 29-30, 2002, the Vatican decision came. Changes were made and, in essence, the Vatican would not accept this tougher policy (U.S. Conference of Catholic Bishops 2002). The following changes were made:

1. The deletion of the reporting requirement was the biggest surprise. Bishops "should comply with all applicable civil laws," said the Vatican. This meant that only about half of the states would be reporting.
2. Priests accused of misconduct would not be removed from functioning as priests until "a preliminary investigation in harmony with canon law is completed."
3. The Vatican insisted that: "all appropriate steps shall be taken to *protect* the reputation of the accused during the investigation." In this circumstance, the parish would not be informed that its priest is under suspicion of sexually abusing children.
4. The new charter also reduces the role and input of diocesan review boards made up of laypeople. The priests could appeal any penalty in secret Church courts run by clerics.
5. The new norms eliminated the requirement to keep victims apprised of the status of the case against a priest.
6. The most problematic change was the apparent elimination of the zero-tolerance provision. The Vatican reinstated the statue of limitations. This requires a victim to report his or her abuse within 10 years of turning 18, or by age 28. There is continued debate over this requirement (Goodstein 2002).

[The Bishops, however, concluded that their document "remained essentially intact" and that their promise to protect children remained strong.

[One thing that must be stated in all of this is that priests do not become sex molesters and perverts, but perverts and sex molesters become priests. The importance of this factor lies in the fact that it makes it possible to perform prescreening testing by qualified sexologists and sex therapists in order to identify potential problems and make recommendations regarding suitability or treatment to the referring agency (the Bishops). This would eliminate 75% to 80% of the pedophiles and hebophiles from the priesthood and prevent damaging young, impressionable children and adolescents.

[A second factor that must be addressed is the common confusion regarding homosexuality and these pedophilic molestations. There is no connection! Mature adult homosexuals are not interested in children or adolescents. Here again, these molesters were already pedophiles or hebophiles *prior* to becoming priests. Continuing cases of homosexual behavior and molestation in the seminaries confirms this hypothesis. Again, the urgent need for qualified screening and testing prior to acceptance, and even during training, becomes a paramount prevention need (Prendergast 1996, 2003).

[In July 2003, as this *Encyclopedia* went to press, the attorney general for the State of Massachusetts released his report of a 16-month investigation of the Roman Catholic Archdiocese of Boston that involved 30,000 pages of Church documents and 100 hours of grand jury testimony. According to this 76-page official report, 789 children were known to have been sexually abused by 250 priests and other church workers in the Roman Catholic Archdiocese of Boston between 1940 and the present. However, the attorney general clearly stated that he had "absolutely no doubt that the number [of abusers] is far greater." No criminal charges would be filed against Church authorities, because the laws in effect at the time did not require clergy to report suspected cases of sexual abuse of minors. However, civil charges are likely to be filed by the victims, in suits that could easily force individual Church entities into bankruptcy. Summing up this report, the attorney general blamed the scandal on "a massive, inexcusable failure of leadership by the Archdiocese of Boston" and on "an institutional culture" of secrecy that prompted Church leaders to protect the Church and "sacrifice the children for many, many years." (*End of update by W. Prendergast*)]

[*Comment 2003*: A factor that appears not to have been publicly recognized is the fact that a significant number of Catholics have strong internal conflicts surrounding sexuality, probably as a result of their Catholic indoctrination. This is especially true, it seems, for boys who might feel some attraction for males as they approach and enter adolescence. Thus, although a majority might enter the priesthood because of true spiritual involvement with Catholicism, it appears that a certain number of boys do so in an attempt to resolve these conflicts between their internalized Catholic beliefs and their troubling sexuality. This is based on the belief, promoted by Catholic theology like many other theologies, that spiritual devotion will negate the "temptations of the flesh," a totally unrealistic and untrue belief rooted in the antisexualism of both Catholic and other religious and cultural belief systems. Hence, we find some observers arguing for allowing priests to marry, which continues to not be an option for the Church. (It is interesting to note further, that one major factor for why priests were originally forbidden to marry was not because of any spiritual basis, but because the Church wanted to stem the flow of the large sums of money as inheritances that went to the wives of priests and bishops when they died, which otherwise would have remained with the Church.) Thus, the task of reforming the Church's attitudes toward sexuality as a whole remains a complex issue that could be accelerated by the current sexual-abuse crisis involving priests. Nevertheless, it is important to point out that the vast majority of priests do *not* sexually molest anyone, although they still often teach many of the sexually unhealthy doctrines of the Church. (*End of comment by R. J. Noonan*)]

*Satanic Ritual Abuse*                    SHARON E. KING
"Satanic" ritual abuse is another area of recent concern. As the 1989 report by the ritual abuse task force by the Los Angeles County Commission for Women shows, it is a controversial area that requires careful and serious attention. Books and groups dealing with cult and ritual abuse continue to expose this alarming and controversial topic. Unfortunately, it often takes on the atmosphere of a circus and witchhunt. There is no scientific evidence that this type of child sexual abuse is widespread or common.

*Recovered Memories and False Memory Syndrome*
DIANE BAKER and SHARON E. KING
Of great concern recently are a number of cases involving children in daycare centers reporting that they were sexually abused by their caretakers. Although some investigations have led to convictions, other cases have been found to lack any substance at all. In one case, a middle-aged male retracted his charge that a prominent Catholic cardinal archbishop had sexually abused him when he was in the seminary, claiming that his lawyer had probably prompted or influenced his "recovered memory" of being abused.

Concern over false reporting is not limited to young children. Teachers all over the country report that they no longer touch their students as they once did. Hugging a child, allowing a young child to sit on one's lap, or being alone in a room with a child are just some of the things that teachers must now monitor. Cases in which children have projected sexual abuse that was happening at home onto a teacher, and the false reporting of sexual abuse by a teacher in order to get back at the teacher are now issues that mental-health workers and the legal system must unravel in some of the more unusual cases placed before the courts.

Better questioning of young victims by mental-health and legal workers is one area that continues to improve. As with any inquiry, it has become evident that the invitation to tell what happened cannot, in any way, be colored by suggestive questioning on the part of the interviewer.

Increasing numbers of adult women and men have begun to disclose incidents of sexual abuse that happened to them when they were children. Their sexual abuse occurred during a time when it was not safe for children to disclose such information and when the support systems of the state and therapeutic communities were not in place.

In some incidents where adults disclose what happened to them as children, they have always known what happened to them, but they have never before spoken out or sought help. In some instances, however, adults report "remembering" or retrieving lost memories of childhood sexual abuse. Remembering and dealing with unresolved issues of childhood sexual abuse can often explain to a victim how and why his or her life has been affected by the abuse. Weight problems, depression, sleep disturbances, intimacy and sexual disorders, unexplained fears, compulsive behaviors, self-esteem issues, and psychosomatic disorders are just a few of the symptoms that can be resolved when an adult finally confronts the repressed and unresolved trauma of childhood sexual abuse.

In a response to their own daughter's accusation of being sexually abused by her father, the Freyds' of Philadelphia started an organization that examines the False Memory Syndrome. Dr. Pamela Freyd and her husband have been most public in their denial of their daughter's accusations, basing their response on a belief that her "memories" were suggested by her therapist. After a period of silence on her part, Dr. Jennifer Freyd publicly countered her parents' denial of what happened to her, citing her mother's public debate as yet another example of her intrusiveness. Whatever the struggle between the members of the Freyd family, this small organization has brought forth a concern about the authenticity and reliability of retrieved memories.

*Sexual Harassment*       ROBERT T. FRANCOEUR

Public awareness of sexual harassment is also a recent phenomenon in American culture, even though sexual discrimination was prohibited by federal law over 30 years ago by Title VII of the 1964 Civil Rights Act. In 1979, Stanford University Law School professor Catharine MacKinnon broadly defined sexual harassment as "the unwanted imposition of sexual requirements in the context of a relationship of unequal power." More-recent definitions include unwanted sexual advances, touches, and actions between peers and coworkers. Sexual harassment can also occur when a subordinate offers sexual favors in return for a promotion, better evaluation, or grade.

A 1976 *Redbook* magazine survey reported that 88% of the more than 9,000 women responding reported having experienced overt sexual harassment and regarded it as a serious work-related problem. A 1988 *Men's Health* survey reported 57% of the magazine's male readers stated they had been sexually propositioned at work, and 58% admitted they had at least occasional sexual fantasies about coworkers.

In a broad survey of over 20,000 federal government workers, 42% of the women and 15% of the men reported having been sexually harassed at work in the preceding two years. Most of the harassers, 78%, were male. Both women and men victims reported that the harassment had negative effects on their emotional and physical condition, their ability to work with others on the job, and their feelings about work. Women were considerably more likely than men to have been harassed by a supervisor, 37% versus 14% (Levinson et al. 1988).

A random-sample survey of undergraduate women at the Berkeley campus of the University of California found that 30% had received unwanted sexual attention from at least one male instructor during their undergraduate years. Examples of harassment included: verbal advances and explicit sexual propositions; invitations to date or to one's apartment; touches, kisses, and fondling; leering or standing too close; writing emotional letters; being too helpful; and offering grades in exchange for sexual favors (see Table 16).

It took over 15 years for the government to identify the sexual-harassment implications of the 1964 Civil Rights Act, and even longer for business corporations to understand the law. In a 1981 *Redbook-Harvard Business Review* survey, 63% of the top-level managers and 52% of middle managers believed that "the amount of sexual harassment at work is greatly exaggerated." Although the amount of sexual harassment in the workplace has probably decreased because of the growing awareness of its risks, *Working Woman* reported that at least some business managers believe that "More than 95% of our complaints have merit" (Gutek 1985).

Although most research on sexual harassment has focused on its occurrence in the workplace and academia, sexual harassment has also been studied in the relationship between psychologists or psychotherapists and their clients, and between physicians and other healthcare workers and their patients.

In 1991, televised hearings of Supreme Court nominee Clarence Thomas and Anita Hill captured the nation's attention and sparked considerable debate and a growing awareness of sexual harassment. About the same time, the United States Navy became the focus of congressional investigations and media headlines when close to 100 male pilots and officers at an annual Tailhook convention were charged with blatant examples of sexual harassment. Sexual harassment was also the subject of *Disclosure*, a popular and powerful 1994 film dealing with a female executive sexually harassing a male employee. As a result, practically every American corporation, professional organization, and educational institution has been forced to develop and adopt a statement defining the nature of sexual harassment and its policies for responding to it.

The "interim guidelines" issued by the Equal Employment Opportunity Commission in 1980, established that "unwelcome sexual advances, requests for sexual favors, and other verbal or physical conduct of a sexual nature constitute sexual harassment" when

1. submission to such conduct is made either explicitly or implicitly a term or condition of an individual's employment,
2. submission to or rejection of such conduct by an individual is used as the basis for employment decisions affecting such individual, or when
3. such conduct has the purpose or effect of substantially interfering with an individual's work performance or creating an intimidating, hostile, or offensive working environment.

In 1985, sociologist Barbara Gutek explained the occurrence of sexual harassment in the workplace in terms of a gender-role spillover model. She defined a work role as "a set of shared expectations about behavior in a job," and a gender role as "a set of shared expectations about the behavior of women and men." Gender-role spillover occurs when gender roles are carried into the workplace, often in inappropriate ways, for example, when the woman in a work group is expected to make coffee or take notes at the meeting. Despite many attitudinal changes in American society, women are still often seen as subservient and sex objects. When these aspects of gender roles spill over into the workplace, sexual harassment can easily occur, despite its negative effects on the employees and organization (Gutek 1985, 17).

*[False Accusations of Sexual Harassment and Rape*
           RAYMOND J. NOONAN

[*Comment 2003*: Troubling news reports occasionally surface about false accusations of both rape and sexual harassment, as well as child sexual abuse, domestic violence, and other sexual assaults, that threaten to undermine the effectiveness of efforts to prevent these crimes. At the same time, false reports can destroy the lives and livelihoods of those falsely accused in ways similar to the victims of actual occurrences of these crimes. At one level, it trivializes the experiences of true victims and makes it more difficult for some of them to come forward. Yet, false accusations are typically not taken as seriously by many people, including the legal system, the media, and the general public, much as awareness of the true crimes were often brushed aside in the past. Statistics from Canada suggest that at least 5% of rape allegations are untrue; other reports from the U.S. suggest levels of false accusations as high as 50% or more. Little re-

**Table 16**

**Varieties of Sexual Harassment in the Workplace**

| Type of Harassment | % of Males Reporting | % of Females Reporting |
|---|---|---|
| Uninvited sexual attention | 20 | 50 |
| Touching | 16 | 45 |
| Suggestive invitations, talk, and joking | 15 | 42 |
| Harassed by same sex | 12 | 7 |

Based on De Witt 1991; U.S. Merit Systems Board 1981, 1988; and other sources.

search is being done, generally, on why they occur or what the true incidence is, although some information can be obtained at some men's rights websites. Financial and political gain, personal revenge, morning-after regrets, and ammunition in divorce and custody battles appear to be some of the motivations. Nevertheless, it is likely that the levels are currently underestimated, with the problems associated with them affecting both men, women, families, and children, although the brunt of false accusations are typically directed at men. Young (1999), Patai (1998), and others have begun to document these hidden statistics, including the near-equal levels of domestic abuse by both men and women against each other. Certainly, these are issues that need further investigation to find out the true extent of the problems and ways to combat them—at the same time that effective measures are sought to stop the true instances of sex crimes and to help victims on both sides of the coin. *(End of comment by R. J. Noonan)]*

## B. Prostitution/Sex Workers

ROBERT T. FRANCOEUR and PATRICIA BARTHALOW KOCH

*Historical Perspective*

In the American colonies and early days of the United States, prostitution did not thrive in the sparse rural population. Despite a shortage of women, there were still women on the financial fringe in the small cities—recent immigrants and unattached, single women with few skills—for whom prostitution provided a way of survival and, at times, a way to find a husband or other male supporter. Female servants, apprentices, and slaves were not allowed to marry—a custom that encouraged prostitution. In contrast, indentured male servants were apprentices and could earn money to support themselves and their families, although they received no salary. Until the end of the American Civil War, African and Caribbean women brought to the United States in the slave trade were frequently and regularly exploited sexually by their owners (Barry 1984).

In the 19th century, the Industrial Revolution in New England and the Middle Atlantic cities precipitated a massive influx of women from rural areas and from abroad looking for work and other opportunities. For example, women preferred the freedom that textile-mill work gave them to the tightly regulated life of a domestic servant, even though the wages were lower. There was little, if any, social life available after work hours for these single persons living apart from their families. Since they often shared a boarding house room with six to eight women, sometimes sleeping three to a bed, they frequently found their only relief at the local tavern. With men moving to the western frontier and a surplus of women, some women turned to prostitution for escape or affection. Too often they found that only sex work offered them a living wage (D'Emilio & Freedman 1988).

Throughout the mid-1800s, waves of immigration created a surplus of males who left their wives and families in Europe. In each new wave of immigration, some of the unattached immigrant women turned to prostitution in an effort to survive; some were already involved in "the trade." Males far outnumbered women in the western frontier towns and mining camps. Thousands of women were imported from Mexico, Chile, Peru, the South Pacific, and China to work in the flourishing brothels. After the Civil War, American cities followed the European practice of segregating prostitutes to certain areas of the city, which came to be known as "red-light" districts, and requiring them to register or be licensed. Regular physical examinations were required of all sex workers.

Between 1880 and 1920, prostitution was commonplace and legal. Since few prostitutes bothered to register, licens-

ing was not effective in controlling disease. Police supervision only spawned crime and corruption via bribes for protection or "looking the other way." In 1910, Congress passed the Mann Act, which forbade the transportation of women across state lines for "immoral" purposes. In the decade before World War I, the Social Hygiene Movement, Women's Christian Temperance Union, Young Men's Christian Association, and other "purity" organizations worked for the criminalization of prostitution. By the end of World War I, these efforts were successful in ending politicians' tolerance of prostitution. "Legal brothels were destroyed and prostitutes were dispersed from stable homes in red-light districts to the city at large where they were less likely to be self-employed or work for other women and more likely to be controlled by exploitive men including pimps, gangsters, slum landlords, unscrupulous club owners, and corrupt politicians" (McCormick 1994, 91).

Currently, prostitution is illegal in all states except Nevada, where a 1971 court decision allowed counties with a sparse population the discretion of legalizing and licensing prostitution. State legal codes forbid making money from the provision of sexual services, including prostitution, keeping a brothel, and pandering, procuring, transporting, or detaining women for "immoral" purposes. Patronizing a prostitute is illegal in some states; a convicted offender may face a fine of $500 or more and a year or more in jail. In some states, pimps may be sentenced to 10 to 20 years in jail and fined $2,000 or more.

*The Spectrum of Sex Workers and Their Clients*

Sex workers vary greatly in status, income, and working conditions, as well as in the services they offer—oral sex being the most common sexual practice offered. The vast majority of sex workers are females with male customers. Most prostitutes view their work as temporary, often on a part-time basis to supplement their traditionally female, poorly paid employment, and to support themselves and their families (McCormick 1994). The average prostitute's career lasts five years, since youthful attractiveness is valued by customers. The sexual orientation of female sex workers reflects that of the larger population, and includes heterosexual, lesbian, and bisexual women. While sex workers are predominantly female, the "managers," at all levels, are predominantly male. Pimps—those who live off the earnings of a sex worker—often exploit the workers' romantic feelings, emotional needs, or fear of violence, and often come from disenfranchised groups themselves.

On the one hand, many believe that females turn to prostitution because of dysfunctional families and individual psychopathology. The belief that female prostitutes are more likely than other women to be depressed, alienated, emotionally volatile, or engage in criminal activities and excessive use of alcohol and street drugs are often based on small, specialized samples (McCormick 1994). Research is also inconclusive as to the proportion of sex workers who abuse alcohol and other drugs. At least one study has indicated that call girls were as well adjusted as a control group of nonsex-worker peers who were matched for age and educational level (McCormick 1994). Yet, for many juveniles, sexual and physical abuse seems to be related, at least indirectly, to their becoming involved with prostitution.

On the other hand, economic survival, not psychopathology, may be the most important contributing factor to engaging in prostitution. Poor and disadvantaged women may engage in sex work because it is the best-paying or only job available. More-advantaged women may also engage in sex work because of the often unparalleled economic rewards, coupled with the flexibility in working hours, and the sense of control over clients. Although non-commercial sex is described as more satisfying by most sex workers, many report achieving satisfaction and orgasm though their work (Savitz & Rosen 1988).

On the lowest rung of female and male sex workers are those who solicit on the street; above them are those working in bars and hotel lobbies. Their limited overhead is matched by their low fees. Streetworkers, usually from the lower socioeconomic class or runaway teenagers, face high risks of violence, robbery, and exploitation, as well as drug addiction, STDs, and HIV infections. Approximately 35% of streetwalkers have been physically abused and 30 to 70% raped while on the job (Delacoste & Alexander 1987). In addition, because of their visibility, streetworkers are the most vulnerable to harassment and arrest by law enforcement agents. While 10% to 20% of sex workers are streetwalkers, they constitute 90% of sex-worker arrests. Prostitution is the only crime in America in which the majority of offenders are female. In dealing with prostitutes, the courts often become a "revolving door system," with the sex worker posting bail and back on the street shortly after being arrested. Paradoxically, she is often fined, making it financially important for her to turn again to sex work to survive.

Government estimates suggest that half of the five million teenagers who run away from their homes each year spend at least some time as sex workers. Poor self-images, rejection by peers, few friends, unsupervised homes, and emotional, if not sexual, abuse in the home make them susceptible to the lure of big-city glamour where their survival needs force them to find work on the streets.

Houses of prostitution are less common today than they were in the past. The famous houses of the Storyville area of New Orleans or San Francisco's Barbary Coast were often very luxurious, and women both lived and worked in the same brothel for many years. Because of legal problems, most brothels today are rundown and in disrepair. If tolerated by the local police, they may be better maintained. In many places, regular, "go-go," and "topless" bars and massage parlors double as "fast-service" brothels. Brothels sometimes advertise their services in "underground" newspapers or in the "free press."

Escorts and call girls are at the upper level of sex workers. Young, slender, attractive, middle- and upper-class white women command the highest fees and the best working conditions among sex workers. Call girls typically see a small number of regular, scheduled clients. For them, sex work provides a much higher income than they would earn in almost any other profession, plus better control over their working hours.

The typical customer of a female sex worker, a "john," appears indistinguishable from the average American male. They are often involved in sexual relationships with another woman and report that they purchase sex by choice—perhaps for the adventurous, dangerous, or forbidden aspects of sex with a prostitute. Some frequent prostitutes because their usual sexual partners are unwilling to participate in certain sexual behaviors (like oral or anal sex). Other men frequent prostitutes because they have difficulty in establishing an ongoing sexual relationship because of lack of opportunity or physical or emotional barriers.

Most heterosexual male prostitutes are not street hustlers, but have steady customers or relationships that are ongoing and similar to those of a high-priced call girl. Their clients are often wealthy older women. Much more common are males who sell their sexual services to other males. In fact, most male prostitutes identify themselves as homosexual or bisexual. In large cities, gay male prostitutes cruise gay bars, gay bathhouses, public toilets, bus and train stations, and other areas known to local clients.

Sex work also includes a variety of erotic entertainment jobs, including erotic dancing, live pornography or "peep shows," and acting in pornographic films and videos. Female burlesque shows have long been part of the American scene. However, the professional burlesque queens of the past have been replaced by amateur, poorly paid "table dancers." Feminists Barbara Ehrenreich, Gloria Hass, and Elizabeth Jacobs (1987) maintain that male go-go dancers play a role in advancing the rights of women and in breaking down patriarchal biases, because their female viewers treat them as sex objects and reduce their phallic power to impotence within bikini shorts.

The incidence of HIV infection and AIDS varies among sex workers and is increased by IV-drug use, untreated STDs, and unsafe-sex practices. In general, it is high among female and gay male sex workers on the street, and lowest among high-priced call girls and heterosexual male prostitutes.

## Economic Factors

In the early 1990s, there were an estimated 450,000 female prostitutes working in the United States, a profession lacking job security and fringe benefits, such as health insurance and social security. Most working outside the high-class escort services do not pay taxes. Nor are taxes paid on any of the monies that are exchanged in the underground economy associated with prostitution, such as: the monies that pass between prostitutes and their pimps; the hotel, motel, massage parlor, or bar owners and clerks; or the recruiters like cab drivers and doormen who make prostitution possible.

A 1985 survey of the cost of enforcing antiprostitution laws in the 16 largest cities of the U.S. estimated police enforcement costs at $53,155,688, court costs at $35,627,496, and correction costs at $31,770,211, for a total 1985 cost of $119,553,395. In 1985, Dallas, Texas, police made only 2,665 arrests for the 15,000 violent crimes reported. They made 7,280 prostitution arrests at a cost of over $10 million and almost 800,000 hours of police work. In 1986, Boston, Cleveland, and Houston police arrested twice as many people for prostitution as they did for all homicides, rapes, robberies, and assaults combined. Meanwhile, 90% of perpetrators of violent crimes evaded arrest. Between 1976 and 1985, violent crimes in the 16 largest cities rose by 32% while arrests for violent crimes rose only 3.7%, and arrests for robbery and homicide actually dropped by 15%. Equally important, the 16 largest cities continue to spend more on enforcing prostitution laws than they do on either education or public welfare (Pearl 1987).

Working in pairs, police spend an average of 21 hours to obtain a solicitation, make an arrest, transport the prostitute to the detention center, process her papers, write up a report, and testify in court. Undercover police cruising the street looking to get a solicitation need frequent changes of disguises and rented cars. Making an arrest of a call girl is even more difficult, requiring greater expense for false identification and credit cards, hotel room, luggage, and other paraphernalia to convince the call girl this is a legitimate customer and not a policeman. The hotel room is usually wiretapped and the solicitation videotaped.

Arrests of prostitutes working in massage parlors present their own difficulties. It usually takes half an hour for an undercover policeman to undress, shower, and get into the massage before an illegal service is offered. For a while, Houston police ran their own parlor. When that was declared entrapment by the courts, teams of 10 undercover officers began working existing modeling studios as customers. "Ten officers at a time, at $60 each, with no guarantee that we'd get solicited. . . . We could spend $3000 or $4000 and not make a case" (Pearl 1987).

### Current and Future Status

Historically, sex workers have been blamed for the spread of sexually transmissible diseases (STDs). However, recent research has indicated that sex workers are much more likely to practice safer sex than the "average teenager" (McCormick 1994). While prostitutes are being blamed for transmitting HIV to their clients, data from the Centers for Disease Control indicate that only a small proportion of persons with AIDS contracted HIV from a prostitute. However, rates of HIV infection are quite high—up to 80%—among sex workers who also use intravenous drugs. Unfortunately, sex workers are usually at higher risk of contracting an STD, including HIV, from their lovers with whom they do not use a condom than from their clients with whom they use a condom.

Today in the United States, religious and political conservatives and radical feminists continue to oppose prostitution through such groups as WHISPER (Women Hurt in Systems of Prostitution Engaged in Revolt), an organization devoted to rescuing women and children from sex work. On the other hand, sex workers have begun to organize and advocate better working conditions and treatment through such groups as COYOTE (Call Off Your Old Tired Ethics), Scapegoat, and U.S. PROStitutes. These groups lobby for the decriminalization and legalization of prostitution, inform the public about the realities of prostitution, and offer various services to sex workers. In addition, liberal feminists inside and outside of the sex industry have founded the International Committee for Prostitutes' Rights (ICPR) in order to preserve their rights to life, liberty, and security.

In spite of continued economic inequities in the United States, some observers believe prostitution will decline because of the availability of effective contraceptives, a continued liberalization of sexual attitudes and divorce, a decline in the double standard in employment and sexual expression between the genders, and the risk of AIDS. In the Kinsey study of male sexuality in the late 1940s, 69% of white males reported having had at least one experience with a prostitute. The recent national study of 18- to 59-year-olds, *Sex in America*, found that only 16% of the men ever paid for sex (Gagnon, Laumann, & Kolata 1994). Yet, it seems that prostitution will continue to exist in some form or another. Although some people support the decriminalization of sexual activity between consenting adults, whether or not money is exchanged, this is not likely to happen in the United States.

## C. Pornography and Erotica

ROBERT T. FRANCOEUR

### The Legal Context

A landmark legal definition of obscenity was established by the Supreme Court in the 1957 *Roth v. the United States* decision. For a book, movie, magazine, or picture to be legally obscene,

- the dominant theme of the work, as a whole, must appeal to a prurient interest in sex;
- the work must be patently offensive by contemporary community standards; and
- the work must be devoid of serious literary, artistic, political, or scientific value.

This ruling permitted the publication in the U.S.A., for the first time, of such works as D. H. Lawrence's *Lady Chatterley's Lover*, James Joyce's *Ulysses*, and works by Henry Miller. However, this definition left the meaning of the term "community standards" unclear.

In the 1973 *Miller v. the United States* decision, the Supreme Court attempted to tighten the restrictions on obscene material by requiring that defenders of an alleged obscene work prove that it has "serious literary, artistic, or scientific merit." Despite this clarification, the courts still faced the near-impossible task of determining what has "literary, artistic, or scientific merit," who represents the "average community member," and what the "community" is. In 1987, the Supreme Court attempted to refine the *Roth* and *Miller* decisions by saying "a reasonable person," not "an ordinary member of the community," could decide whether some allegedly obscene material has any serious literary, artistic, political, or scientific value. Justice Potter Stewart further confused the situation when he remarked that "You know it when you see it."

In 1969, the Supreme Court ruled that private possession of obscene material was not a crime and is not subject to legal regulation. However, federal laws continue to prohibit obscene material from being broadcast on radio and television, mailed, imported, or carried across state lines. In recent years, pornographic material of any kind involving underaged children has been the target of repeated federal "sting" operations, raising issues of police entrapment.

### Research Models

For at least two decades, there has been often-heated debate among the public, among feminists groups, and among scientists regarding the social and psychological impact of pornography, particularly materials that link sex with the objectification of women and with violence. A psychological research theory, the catharsis model, assumes that pornography and other sexually explicit materials provide a "safety valve" in a sexually repressive society. This model views pornography and other sexually explicit materials as "not so good, perhaps disgusting, but still useful" in diverting tensions that otherwise might trigger aggressive antisocial behavior. A different hypothesis suggests an imitation model in which sexually explicit books, pictures, and movies provide powerful role models that can, by conditioning and scripting, promote antisocial, sexually aggressive behavior. A third model of pornography addresses the personal and societal uses of pornography in different cultures, as a product designed as an alternative source of sexual arousal gratification and a way of enhancing masturbation. There are also models of pornography based on communication, Marxist, psychoanalytic, feminist, and religious theories (Francoeur 1991, 637).

### Commission Studies

A 1970 White House Commission funded research by experts in the field and concluded that neither hardcore nor softcore pornography leads to antisocial behavior and recommended that all obscenity laws except those protecting minors be abolished. The majority of the commission concluded that pornography provides a useful safety valve in an otherwise sexually repressive culture. President Richard Nixon refused to officially accept the commission's report.

A 1986 investigation by then-Attorney General Edwin Meese did not sponsor any new research and took a different approach in reaching its conclusion. This commission reexamined the alleged connection between pornography and child abuse, incest, and rape by inviting anyone interested in speaking to the issue. The commission was widely criticized for having a preset agenda, for appointing biased commission members, and for relying on "the totality of evidence," which gave equal weight to the testimony of fundamentalist ministers, police officers, antipornography activists, and putative victims of pornography. This allowed the commission to conclude there is a "proven" causal connection between violent pornography and sexual assaults. This commission concluded that there is a causal connection between viewing sexually explicit materials, especially violent pornography, and the commission of rape and other sexual assaults. The commission recommended stricter penalties to regulate the pornography traffic, enactment of laws to keep hardcore pornography off home cable television and home telephone services, more vigorous prosecution of obscenity cases, and encouraged private citizens to use protests and boycotts to discourage the marketing of pornography. Among the many criticisms of the Meese Commission, Robert Staples, a black sociologist, pointed out that in the black community, pornography is a trivial issue. It is "a peculiar kind of white man's problem," because blacks see the depiction of heterosexual intercourse and nudity, not as a sexist debasement of women, but as a celebration of the equal rights of women and men to enjoy sexual stimuli and pleasure (Nobile & Nadler 1986).

Concurrent with the *Meese Commission Report*, the 1986 *Report of the U.S. Surgeon General* concluded that we still know little about the patterns of use or the power of attitudes in precipitating sexually aggressive behavior. Much research is still needed in order to demonstrate that the present knowledge of laboratory studies has significant real-world implications for predicting behavior. This report did not call for censorship, boycotts, and other tactics advocated by the Meese Commission. Rather, it recommended development of "street-based, innovative approaches" to educate the public about the different types of sexually explicit material and their possible effects.

*Local Efforts at Regulation*

In 1985, Andrea Dworkin, Catherine MacKinnon, and Women Against Pornography joined forces with local citizens' groups in Minneapolis, Minnesota, and Long Island, New York, to promote a new kind of pornography legislation. Using a civil rights argument, the proposed legislation stated that

> Pornography is sex discrimination. [Where it exists, it poses] a substantial threat to the health, safety, peace, welfare, and equality of citizens in the community . . . . Pornography is a systematic practice of exploitation and subordination based on sex that differentially harms women. The harm of pornography includes dehumanization, sexual exploitation, forced sex, forced prostitution, physical injury, and social and sexual terrorism and inferiority presented as entertainment.

The proposed legislation would have made producing, selling, or exhibiting pornography an act of sex discrimination. Women forced to participate in pornographic films, exposed by force of circumstances to view pornography in any place of employment, education, home, or public place, or assaulted by a male inspired by pornography could sue in civil court for damages based on sex discrimination. The American Civil Liberties Union (ACLU), Feminist Anti-Censorship Taskforce (FACT), and others challenged this kind of legislation. After considerable nationwide debate about civil rights, sex discrimination, and the constitutional right to free speech, these legislative efforts were abandoned.

*Contemporary Aspects*

The availability of sexually explicit, X-rated videocassette rentals and sales has become a major factor in American home entertainment. In the past decade, feminist softcore pornography or erotica has made its mark in the popular media by portraying women as persons who enjoy sexual pleasure as much as men. This material appears in the pages of such mainstream women's magazines as *Cosmopolitan*. It is promoted by sex boutiques, with names like Eve's Garden, Adam and Eve, and Good Vibrations, catering to women. Another growing phenomenon is a variation on the Tupperware and Mary Kay Cosmetics home parties that bring women the opportunity to examine and, of course, purchase sex toys, love lotions, and lingerie in the privacy of their homes, surrounded by other women with whom they are friends. Exotic lingerie is also available in specialty stores in major shopping malls and by mail order from Victoria's Secret and Frederick's of Hollywood. Since 1992, Feminists for Free Expression, opposed to censorship and supported by such notables as Betty Friedan, Erica Jong, and Nancy Friday, has countered the efforts of some feminists to suppress pornography with an alternative view for the feminist community.

Erotic romance novels have become an acceptable form of softcore pornography for women. Far outselling gothic novels, science fiction, self-help, and other books aimed at women, erotic romances often center around a traditional rape myth, a story in which the woman is at first unwilling, but finally yields in a sensual rapture to a man. In nonsexual characteristics, women who read erotic romantic novels are very much like women who do not. However, they appear to enjoy sex more and have a richer sexual fantasy life (Coles & Shamp 1984; Lawrence & Herold 1988).

Researchers and theorists, both feminist and nonfeminist, have almost completely ignored the existence of gay pornography. Lesbian pornography tends towards two extremes, about evenly divided in popularity, with little middle ground. Small independent presses publish softcore pornography or erotica. Erotica on audiocassettes are very popular among lesbians. On the other side is a hardcore lesbian literature with a strong SM character that makes some feminists uncomfortable. *On Our Backs*, a tabloid magazine, is the largest publication of this type. *Eidos*, another tabloid, carries numerous ads for lesbians who desire bondage and dominance or sadomasochistic relations.

Considerably more pornography designed for homosexual men is available. Most of this genre is hardcore pornography with an emphasis on leather, SM, and younger males. At the same time, gay videos have pioneered in eroticizing the condom, nonoxynol-9, and safer-sex practices.

Dial-a-porn, or telephone sex, is a multimillion-dollar-a-year business producing massive profits for telephone companies and the companies providing phone-in services. In one year, dial-in services, including dial-a-porn, earned Pacific Bell $24.5 million and the phone-in companies $47.2 million. Because of constitutional concerns, the Public Utilities Commission and Federal Communications Commission (FCC) do not allow telephone companies to censor telephone messages or to discriminate among dial-for-a-message 1-900 services on the basis of content. Telephone companies cannot legally deny telephone lines to adults willing to pay the bill, although at least one court has ruled that it is not unlawful discrimination for a telephone company to refuse to provide services for dial-a-porn services. The FCC does require dial-a-porn services to screen out calls by minors by supplying their customers with special access numbers or having them pay by credit card. Concerned parents may pay a one-time fee to block all phones in a residence from access to dial-a-porn.

## D. Paraphilias and Unusual Sexual Practices

BRENDA LOVE

In 1990, a Los Angeles man named Jeff Vilencia formed a group called Squish Productions. Through magazine articles, television appearances, and radio interviews, Vilencia had attracted more than 300 members to his group by 1995, all of whom shared the fetish of becoming aroused by the sight of others stepping on small living things such as snails and insects.

Although the fetish shared by Vilencia and his fellow members in Squish Productions may seem—and may in fact be—novel, paraphilias are nothing new. Paraphilias and fetishes have most likely been in existence in the U.S. for as long as there have been inhabitants on the Western continents. Although while a few immigrants may have brought sexual preferences, such as autoerotic asphyxiation, sadomasochism (SM), foot fetishes, and bestiality with them, other paraphilias have unquestionably developed here. In the world of paraphilias and fetishes, there is always something new. And thanks to increased awareness of and access to information about unorthodox sexual practices and their practitioners, interest in paraphilias appears to be growing in the United States.

### Definitions

"Fetish," as defined for the American health professional by the *Diagnostic and Statistical Manual of Mental Disorders III* (*DSM III*), "is the use of nonliving objects (fetishes) as a repeatedly preferred or exclusive method of achieving sexual excitement." Such objects "tend to be articles of clothing, such as female undergarments, shoes, and boots, or, more rarely, parts of the human body, such as hair or nails" (American Psychiatric Association 1980).

The manual also states that the fetish object "is often associated with someone with whom the individual was intimately involved during childhood, most often a caretaker.... Usually the disorder begins by adolescence, although the fetish may have been endowed with special significance earlier, in childhood. Once established, the disorder tends to be chronic" (American Psychiatric Association 1980).

"Paraphilias," on the other hand, are defined by *DSM III* as recurrent, fixed, compulsive, sexually motivated thoughts or actions by a personally or socially maladjusted individual that interfere with the individual's capacity for reciprocal affection. It is important to note that a paraphilia is not merely an activity that may appear strange or disgusting to an observer; rather, the activity or compulsion must meet all of the above criteria to be considered a problem requiring therapy.

It is also important to note in the area of paraphilias that many patients mention their unusual sexual interest simply to receive validation. The therapist can do much for the mental health of a patient by mentioning a support group or club for people with the interest, or by giving the patient the clinical name for the practice, stressing that the term *paraphilia* only applies when the above *DSM III* criteria apply. This can be followed by therapy to improve the person's self-esteem, communication, and social skills. The confession of activities involving minors or nonconsensual activities, however, of course requires immediate intervention by health professionals.

### Background on Fetishes and Paraphilias in the U.S.A.

Fetishes change according to current fashions and customs. A hundred years ago, fetishists were aroused by such things as handkerchiefs, gloves, black rubber aprons, garters, corsets, enemas, seeing females wring the necks of chickens, or whipping horses. Today many of these stimuli have been replaced by pantyhose, high heels, tennis shoes, cigarettes, escalators, latex, or phone sex.

In addition, today's technology adds to the variety of ways a fetishist can pursue his or her predilection. In the past, one had either to create one's own drawings, or hope to catch a glimpse of an arousing person, object, or situation. Today, the fetishist has access to television, photographs, Internet newsgroups, clubs, videos, and magazines. Membership in fetish groups has increased during the last decade. And as computer technology has decreased the cost of publishing, groups or individuals have been increasingly able to print their own sex magazines, books, and newsletters, thereby avoiding the censorship imposed by mainstream publications.

At the same time, even the more straitlaced mainstream media have helped to increase the information available about fetishes and paraphilias. Unfortunately, many national television talk shows have "cashed in" on fetishes and victims of sexual trauma by sensationalizing their lives, rather than trying to educate the public. Hollywood also sensationalizes the issue, portraying erotic asphyxia, lust murder, sadomasochism, and nipple piercing. An example of the media's exploitation and sensationalization of unusual sex practices was the hundreds of hours of air time devoted to keeping the public informed of the status of John Wayne Bobbit, the circumstances leading to his castration at the hands of his wife, the subsequent surgical reattachment of his penis, and his appearance in an X-rated video.

Perhaps the most important development in the growth of interest in paraphilias and fetishes has been the Internet, the worldwide computer network through which up to 500,000 "lurkers" a month enter the "alt.sex" newsgroups. Users of these newsgroups, which offer uncensored forums devoted to a wide variety of sexual interests, can exchange or download photos and information, including what would normally be considered illegal in the United States, with other Internet users.

While the Internet has played an increasing role in the lives of fetishists in recent years, it would not be correct to attribute the growing popularity of fetishism and other unorthodox forms of sexuality to the Internet alone, as those in Washington who seek to censor the Internet seem to believe. The role of the Internet is more modest according to Robin Roberts, an Internet guru in California and founder of Backdrop, one of America's oldest fantasy and bondage clubs. Established in 1965, Backdrop promoted itself with discreet ads in the *Berkeley Barb* with post office boxes or mail-drop services as the method of contact. Today, Backdrop has about 5,700 members, but Roberts does not attribute the club's growth to exposure on the Internet.

Roberts explains that Internet lurkers rarely participate in dialog and tend not to join sex clubs. They are typically readers of *Forum* magazine or "Letters to the Editor" columns. For those users who do participate in sex online, computers provide anonymity, and a way to explore taboos in a safe, nonthreatening environment. Roberts does note, however, that for those who are active participants in computer sex, rather than just lurkers, the Internet provides 24-hour access to other users, an equal chance to express one's opinions, and an unlimited number of fantasies. At the same time, Roberts does not feel computer sex will replace fetish clubs, because of the simple fact that electronic mail does not provide touch, intonation of the voice, nuances of speech, or visual impressions.

### The Growing Popularity of Fetishes and Paraphilias

Not everyone who accesses information about paraphilias and fetishes through these new technological avenues is a fetishist. Many are among the growing number of experimenters who, even though they do not have a fetish, will join groups or purchase sex toys and SM paraphernalia.

Such experimentation seems to be on the increase; a 1994 survey conducted in two San Francisco sex boutiques indicated that approximately 55% of their customers had at least experimented with SM (Love 1994).

Ann Grogan, owner of San Francisco's Romantasy boutique, has seen an increase in such experimentation among the customers who frequent her sex-accessory establishment, one of two operating in San Francisco in 1995 geared toward women customers.

"Gender play is becoming more and more popular among customers of all ages, primarily ages 30-50 years," Grogan says. "Couples now buy matching corsets and wrist restraints." During the last five years, females in increasing numbers have shown an interest in transgender play, assuming the dominant role in the sexual relationship. Many men are also expressing an interest in anal sexuality, measured in part by the purchase of dildoes and harnesses to be used on men by the women. And a growing number of recently divorced female customers in their 50s have shown a curiosity about safe sex and pleasuring themselves.

Grogan can also testify to the increasing influence of the Internet:

The latest trend seems to be the appearance of couples who have met on the Internet. They appear together at Romantasy after only one or two meetings, because in previous communications they have gotten far beyond the awkward preliminary dialog about each other's sexual preferences and have jumped into a willingness to act out each other's fantasies. Meeting on the Internet seems to be a "fast track to intimacy." (Grogan 1995)

Ted McIlvenna, president of the Institute for the Advanced Study of Human Sexuality, expects that interest and participation in paraphilias and fetishes will continue to grow. "In the next five years," McIlvenna believes,

we will see a group of people seeking information and support groups for their sex interests which, in the past, people have considered excessive or compulsive. This is not an evil path; instead it is remedial sex education. Because of the massive number of people involved—in the U.S. the estimate is forty million people—I have labeled this the "sexual accessories movement." Mental health professionals, including sexual health professionals, must monitor and study but leave this movement alone; their sexuality belongs to them. We can expect people to buy more, join more, and experiment more, and we can only hope that out of this will emerge societal control methods that will enable people to have better and more fulfilling sex lives. (McIlvenna 1995)

Given the recent and anticipated growth of many of the fetish clubs described below, it is important to ask about what causes paraphilias. Although there has been much scientific interest in this question, science has not yet discovered the etiology of fetishes or "paraphilic lovemaps," according to John Money (1988), the leading expert on paraphilias. It does appear, however, that, as is the case with substance abuse and addiction, a small percentage of the population seems more predisposed toward the development of paraphilias, often because of childhood trauma. Money says,

The retrospective biographies of adolescent and adult paraphiles point to the years of childhood sexual rehearsal play as the vulnerable developmental period. . . . The harsh truth is that as a society we do not want our children to be lustfully normal. If they are timorous enough to be discovered engaging their lust in normal sexual rehearsal play or in masturbation, they become, in countless numbers, the victims of humiliation and abusive violence. (Money 1988)

Money has explained how these early traumas can lead to paraphilias:

They [adults who subject sexually curious children to abuse] do not know that what they destroy, or vandalize, is the incorporation of lust into the normal development of the lovemap. The expression of lust is diverted or detoured from its normal route. Thus, to illustrate: those adults who humiliate and punish a small boy for strutting around with an erected penis, boasting to the girls who watch him, do not know that they are thereby exposing the boy to risk of developing a lovemap of paraphilic exhibitionism. (Money 1988)

### Fetish and Paraphilia Clubs

The United States is probably home to more fetish clubs than any other country. As Brenda Love (1992) wrote in *The Encyclopedia of Unusual Sex Practices*, which catalogs over 700 sexual practices,

international advertising is fairly inexpensive and computerized printing of newsletters has made it simpler to form clubs. People with fetishes as obscure as large penises, big balls, hairy bodies, mud wrestlers, shaving, cigars, used condoms, genital modification, and throwing pies have been able to find others with similar interests willing to form clubs.

Sadomasochist (SM) clubs are probably the most prevalent type of fetish clubs in the U.S.A. today, although very few of the members could be defined as having a true SM fetish or paraphilia.

SM has become an umbrella term for many sexual activities, and because of its accouterments and role-playing, people wanting to experiment with or improve their sexuality join these groups. "It was only in the late fifteenth century that the first unambiguous case report of SM was reported, and then as a medical curiosity rather than a problem" (H. Ellis 1936a). William Simon has eloquently described the allure of SM:

The sadomasochistic script plays upon the potential absolutism of hierarchy, not merely to experience hierarchy with the relief accompanying the elimination of its ambiguities but to experience the dangerous emotions that invariably accompany acknowledgment of its exercise, the rage and fear of rage in both the other and ourselves. (Simon 1994)

Charles Moser (1988) estimates that approximately 10% of the adult population are SM practitioners. This estimate is based on Kinsey's report that approximately 50% reported some erotic response to being bitten (Kinsey 1953). However, there is no direct empirical evidence verifying this estimate. Moser divides SM behaviors

into two types, physical and psychological. . . . Physical behaviors may be further subdivided into the following categories: bondage, physical discipline, intense stimulation, sensory deprivation, and body alteration. . . . Psychological pain is induced by feelings of humiliation, degradation, uncertainty, apprehension, powerlessness, anxiety, and fear. . . . Both physical and psychological behaviors are devised to emphasize the transfer of power from the submissive to the dominant partner. SM practitioners often report it is this consensual exchange of power that is erotic to them and the pain is just a method of achieving this power exchange. (Moser 1988)

Moser lists the common types of clinical problems presented by SM practitioners to their therapists as: "1) Am I normal? 2) Can you make these desires go away? 3) SM is destroying our relationship; 4) I cannot lead this double life anymore; 5) I cannot find a partner; and 6) Is it violence or SM?" (Moser 1988). All but the last question are also the concern of most fetishists.

Foot-fetish club members have a more focused interest than do SM practitioners. Weinberg et al. (1994) conducted a survey of 262 members of a gay foot-fetishist group called the Foot Fraternity that had approximately 1,000 members in 1990, but had grown to over 4,000 by 1995. These sexologists also compared the ratio of self-masturbation during sexual encounters to that of oral-genital activity and to anal intercourse. Fetishists tended to masturbate to orgasm while engaging in foot play rather than experiencing orgasm as a result of some type of penetrative sex with a partner. Furthermore, the researchers discovered that 76% responded that they masturbated themselves to orgasm frequently, whereas 48.1% performed oral-genital activity, and only 9.55% performed anal intercourse.

Weinberg et al. (1994) reported that their research highlighted the psychological importance a support group or club has for fetishists.

> Despite the lack of a widespread fetish subculture, the Foot Fraternity itself can be considered an embryonic subculture. Almost 70 percent of the respondents said membership in the Foot Fraternity allowed them to pursue their fetish interests more easily. Some 66 percent said membership increased their interest in feet and footwear, and over 40 percent said that they learned new ways of expressing their sexuality. Thus, the organization helped to sustain, as well as expand, its members' unconventional sexual interest. Almost 70 percent said the Foot Fraternity got them to correspond with others with similar interests, 50 percent that it got them to meet others with similar interests, and 40 percent that this led them to engage in foot play with another member. Finally, over 40 percent said that membership in the Foot Fraternity helped remove confusion about their interest in feet and footwear and almost 60 percent that it increased their self-acceptance. (Weinberg et al. 1994)

These statistics regarding benefits of membership can most likely be applied to other sexual interest groups as well.

Doug Gaines, founder of this Cleveland-based club, estimates that 15% of the U.S. population has a foot or related fetish, an opinion based on the fact that he has received 80,000 requests for club information. He promotes the group in magazines, radio interviews, and a foot-fetish Internet newsgroup.

Interestingly, Gaines seconded the findings of researchers on the genesis of fetishes by identifying childhood experiences, such as being tickled, riding on the foot of a parent ("playing horsey"), or seeing a parent's foot immediately prior to being picked up and nurtured, as predominant memories of most of his members. The Foot Fraternity offers a newsletter, glossy magazine, and videos of men modeling their feet. The selection of photos is determined by a detailed membership questionnaire which asks what type of shoe, sock, or foot the new member finds erotic.

The activities in which foot enthusiasts participate include masturbation while looking at photos of feet, slipping off a partner's shoes in order to smell the stockings and foot, or placing oneself underneath the foot in a submissive posture. The foot is massaged and licked completely (toes, between toes, bottom, etc.). SM dominance and submission scenes, for example, where a partner takes on the role of a policeman and the fetishist must kiss his boot to get out of being given a traffic ticket, are popular.

Another common scene consists of acting out the roles of principal and student. Foot fetishists rarely use pain in their dominance/submission; rather, these scenes simply serve as an excuse for foot worship. A few foot fetishists attend auctions where they are able to purchase shoes once belonging to their favorite sports figures or movie stars hoping that the "scent" of the person remains in the shoe.

Squish Productions, mentioned earlier, can also be viewed as a foot-fetish club. Unlike the Foot Fraternity, Squish has yet to be the subject of any in-depth survey by sexologists. Even so, the genesis of the Squish fetish appears to be similar to that found in other fetishes, as evidenced by Squish founder Jeff Vilencia's recollections of his childhood. Identifying what he considers to be his childhood trigger point in the development of his fetish, Vilencia recalled that, as the younger of two children, he was the "victim" of an older sister who enjoyed kicking and stepping on him. Upon reaching puberty, he discovered feeling aroused when seeing females step on bugs. The bug apparently only serves as a projection of himself, because his fantasy involves taking the bug's place under the woman's foot.

Cross-dressing and other forms of transgender activity are found in many countries. The new *DSM IV* no longer lists this activity as a paraphilia, but rather as "gender dysphoria." Clubs such as ETVC in San Francisco have an extensive library for members, social outings, support-group hotline, newsletter, makeup classes, and lingerie modeling. Membership in ETVC increased from 329 in 1988 to a total of 433 in 1995.

Another group, Texas Tea Party, sponsors an annual party that, after eight years of existence, drew about 400 people in 1995. Estimates on the percentage of the population who have ever cross-dressed range from 1.5 to 10%. Groups attract new members with newspaper and magazine advertisements, appearances on television and radio, magazine articles on the subject, and by staffing a booth at the annual San Francisco Lesbian and Gay Freedom Day Parade and Celebration.

A recent survey of 942 transgenderists by Linda and Cynthia Phillips indicates that most members experienced cross-dressing in puberty, although one member did not begin cross-dressing until the age of 72. The average transgenderist did not seek out a transgender club until his early 40s. Sexual arousal while cross-dressing is also more common during adolescence, and appears to diminish as the boy grows older. Therefore, an adult male transgenderist dresses to feel "feminine," whereas an underwear fetishist uses the lingerie for sexual arousal. (Females who cross-dress do not tend to experience arousal while cross-dressing) (Phillips 1994).

No one knows how many cross-dressers or clubs exist in the U.S., but it is known that many people purchase special-interest cross-dressing magazines. One of these, *Tapestry*, had a 1995 quarterly distribution of 10,000 issues compared to 2,000 five years earlier. And a fairly new magazine, *Transformation*, had an international distribution of 50,000 in 1995.

Infantilism is fairly unique to the U.S. and growing in popularity. Its practitioners take on the persona of infants or young children. They may wear diapers under their business suits, drink from a baby bottle, use an assortment of toys and baby furniture, and, if they have a partner, they may participate by reading bedtime stories, diapering, spanking, or using other forms of affection or punishment.

One practitioner, who asked to be identified only as Tommy, is the founder of Diaper Pail Friends. Inside his home in a prestigious San Francisco suburb, a visitor will find an adult-sized high chair, bibs, and numerous baby bottles in the kitchen. Downstairs, Tommy's bedroom features a large crib with a view of the Bay area, a collection of adult-sized baby clothes, and a trail of toys leading to a train set that fills the center of an adjacent room.

Diaper Pail Friends is about 15 years old, and grew from about 1,000 members in 1990 to more than 3,000 in 1995. Most of the members discovered the group through articles in magazines or books, television talk shows, or an Internet newsgroup. The club publishes a newsletter, short stories, videos, and distributes adult-sized baby paraphernalia.

A group of sexologists conducted an extensive survey of the Diaper Pail Friends, but had not yet published their findings as of 1995. Tommy, however, concluded from an informal survey of the group's members that

> Even a casual review of infantilists in the DPF Rosters show that there are tremendous differences between one infantilist and another. In fact, there would seem to be as many personal, individual variations as there are people. Nevertheless, certain patterns do seem to become evident, patterns that seem to encompass a very large percentage of the environmental and inborn factors that are involved with the creation of Infantilism in human personality. These patterns are [in order of prevalence] (1) deficient early nurturing, (2) rejection of Softness, (3) childhood sexual abuse [primarily in female members], and (4) bed wetting. Every infantilist probably has one or more of these patterns in their history, and each infantilist combines them in varying degrees. The variations are limitless. (Tommy 1992)

A Chicago-based national acrotomophile club (people aroused by seeing amputees) has a membership of about 300. They sponsor an annual conference during the first week of June and have spawned local chapters that also hold meetings. Quarterly pamphlets are sent to members and a couple of Internet newsgroups exist. New membership is not aggressively recruited, but the number of self-identified acrotomophiles has increased since the 1989 publication of Grant Riddle's book, *Amputees and Devotees*, which examines the psychological basis of this phenomenon.

According to Riddle, many "devotees" are aware of this preference as a child, but there seems to be a wide variety of reasons for its development. One of these is being overly criticized by parents and wishing to be like a handicapped neighbor, assuming this would relieve some of the pressure. Another cause is being taught that sex is dirty, and from there, having to rationalize that if one cares for someone handicapped, one can justifiably ask for sex in return. Activities of acrotomophiles include having a healthy partner pretend to limp or use crutches; most acrotomophiles, however, content themselves with viewing photos (mostly of clothed females) or possibly catching a glimpse of an amputee on the street (Riddle 1989).

Autoerotic asphyxia (self-strangulation) seems originally to have been carried to Europe by French Foreign Legionnaires returning from war in Indochina (Michaldimitrakis 1986). Erotic asphyxia involves using a pillow, gag, gas mask, latex or leather hood, plastic bag, or other object to block oxygen intake. It may also involve strangulation by a partner's hands, or with a scarf or Velcro blood-pressure cuff. Corseting of the waist is another less obvious method of impeding oxygen intake.

This practice takes the lives of an estimated 250 to 1,000 Americans each year. It is believed that many more people experiment with asphyxia safely alone and/or with a partner, but because this act carries great legal liability if things go wrong, it is impossible to estimate the number of people who engage in it. During the early 1990s, a Seattle man made an effort, through workshops and lectures, to teach safety techniques to practitioners. Although he found many interested parties, he had to limit his public appearances and advice because of legal concerns.

Although there is little information available about the asphyxiphile's childhood, John Money has described one case in his book, *Breathless Orgasm*. This subject recalled first becoming interested in asphyxia when his childhood sweetheart drowned. He began by thinking of her drowning experience and soon discovered he was becoming aroused by visualizing her nude body under water and thinking about her suffocating (Money et al. 1991).

Another asphixiphile, who related his experience to the audience at a San Francisco lecture on the subject, described being raised as a Jehovah's Witness and taught that masturbation was a sin. This did not deter him from engaging in masturbation, but rather made it much more exciting, because he felt he could be "struck by lightning." After giving up his religious practice in his late teens, he immediately discovered that masturbation lost its intensity. He then found that by putting himself in a life-or-death situation, i.e., asphyxia, he could recover this lost intensity.

Most data on asphyxiphiles have been collected from the death scene of the victims. Ray Blanchard and Stephen J. Hucker have collected a vast data bank of coroner's reports and other materials on the subject. In their study of 117 incidents, they discovered that older men

> were more likely to have been simultaneously engaged in bondage or transvestitism, suggesting elaboration of the masturbatory ritual over time. The greatest degree of transvestitism was associated with intermediate rather than high levels of bondage, suggesting that response competition from bondage may limit asphyxiators' involvement in a third paraphilia like transvestitism. (Blanchard et al. 1991).

Sexual asphyxia is rarely depicted in print media, but has been shown in a few films, such as the 1993 movie, *The Rising Sun*, and also in the 1976 French-Japanese movie, *In the Realm of the Senses*.

Chubby Chasers, a San Francisco club of men attracted to the obese, almost doubled in membership between 1990 and 1995 and grew to include 50 different international groups. This club was involved on the Internet early and recruited many of its members there. This club also staffs a booth at the annual San Francisco Lesbian and Gay Freedom Day Parade. Membership in the organization includes a newsletter and invitation to many social activities. Many, but not all, "chasers" had a parent or close relative who was very obese, and recall having a preference for "chubbies" when they were as young as 4 or 5. For those with this interest, there are full-color commercial magazines depicting obese nude females, sometimes with a slender male partner, available in adult book stores.

There are a number of food fetishists or "piesexuals," a word coined by a well-known pie enthusiast, Mike Brown, who began his affair with pies at age 13. Mr. Brown produces pie videos and also hosts annual "bring your own pie" throwing parties, where couples undress and hit each other with pies. There is an Internet newsgroup and also several clubs catering to this interest. *Splosh* magazine, although not sexual, features attractive females smeared with an assortment of food and mud, another messy fetish.

Other more obscure fetish/paraphilia organizations include WES (We Enjoy Shaving) of Reno, Nevada; the Wisconsin STEAM journal for agoraphiles, who enjoy engaging in sex in public; and Hot Ash, a New York club for people aroused by partners who smoke. Hot Ash publishes a newsletter and sells videos for those with this interest.

New York is also the home of a vampire sex club whose members make small cuts on others and rub or lick the blood off. Blood sports are also common among some SM practitioners in the forms of caning, cutting, or piercing. San Francisco had coprophilia (feces) and urophilia (urine) clubs before the AIDS epidemic. Some of the newest groups include Fire Play, whose members drip hot wax on their partners, rub lit cigarettes on their bodies, and/or use chemical irritants. Some with this interest rub a small part of the body with diluted alcohol and ignite it.

In another new paraphilic activity, some men catch bees and use them to sting the penis. The venom not only doubles the size of the penis for a few days, but also seems to bring about a change in the neural system that enhances the arousal stage.

The foregoing are but a few of the many unorthodox sexual practices now being pursued in the United States. Many more exist, and new ones are being invented all the time. And thanks to technology, including the Internet, advances in the quality and availability of home-based desktop publishing, and the rise of sensationalist television talk shows, interest and participation in these activities is on the increase.

In the coming years, the continuing growth of fetish/paraphilia sex groups will require therapists to learn to make clear determinations among people who experiment with various activities, those who self-report to have a fetish but five years later become bored with it, and the few clinically defined paraphiles who truly need some type of intervention or treatment.

## 9. Contraception, Abortion, and Population Planning

PATRICIA BARTHALOW KOCH

[*Comment 1997*: In the final sections of this review of sexuality in American culture, we consider several areas which are concerned with health and/or technology. The areas of contraception, abortion, and sexually transmitted disease each have rather obvious health implications, but each is also influenced by growing medical technology and illustrates a relationship between sexual conduct and technological advances. We would note that the question of effective social policy in each of these areas remains a matter of considerable social conflict within the U.S.A. The identification and treatment of sexual "dysfunctions" reflect these same concerns. In fact, the growing recognition that various sexual conditions can be diagnosed and treated, and the growing public acceptance of the legitimacy of such treatment, may be one of the more profound, if subtle, changes in American sexuality in the last century. In no small way, this process has served to fuel the growth of an array of sexual professions, with a corresponding need to provide graduate education for such professionals and the emergence of professional organizations. We provide a brief review of each of these professional developments. Finally, we close with a series of reviews on American popular culture, each enabled to some degree by technological developments, which both reflect and influence sexual information and communication about American sexuality. Some mention of this was already made earlier in the section on fetishes and paraphilias (see Section 8D, Significant Unconventional Sexual Behaviors). As always seems to be the case with sexual issues within the U.S.A., they all have generated a fair amount of political activity and social conflict. (*End of comment by D. L. Weis*)]

## A. Contraception

PATRICIA BARTHALOW KOCH

*A Brief History*

"The struggle for reproductive self-determination is one of the oldest projects of humanity; one of our earliest collective attempts to alter the biological limits of our existence" (Gordon 1976, 403). Throughout U.S. history, as elsewhere, many have been desperate to learn safe and effective ways to prevent conception and induce abortion, while others have believed artificial contraception is unacceptable because it interferes with the course of nature.

Brodie (1994) conducted a historical analysis of efforts for reproductive control in colonial and 19th-century America. New England fertility rates in colonial times were higher than those in most of Europe. Colonists had little real ability, and perhaps little will, to intervene in their reproduction. It has been estimated that one third of the brides of this time were pregnant. Although the Puritans viewed marriage with children as the highest form of life, the prevalence of premarital pregnancy was not viewed as a threat to this value, because virtually all such pregnancies led to marriage (Reiss 1980).

On the other hand, Native Americans seemed to possess knowledge and cultural practices—breastfeeding, periodic abstinence, abortion, and infanticide—specific to their particular tribes, enabling them to maintain small families. Fertility among the African and Caribbean women brought as slaves varied widely, depending on the region of the United States—in some places, fecundity reaching human capacity and in other places, fertility rates decreasing. According to Brodie (1994, 53): "Fecundity assured slave women that they were valuable to the master and offered some hope against being sold. Yet preventing the birth of new slaves for the master could be a form of resistance to slavery."

The three most common forms of birth control during this time were coitus interruptus (withdrawal), breastfeeding, and abortion. The effectiveness of breastfeeding in preventing another pregnancy depended on how long the woman breastfed, on when her menstruation resumed after childbirth, and on how long and how often the infant suckled. However, by the 19th century, the option of bottle-feeding infants was becoming more available and popular.

Abortion methods included violent exercises, uterine insertions, and the use of drugs. These methods may have been no more dangerous than the pregnancy and childbirth complications of the time, but it has been suggested that these methods were also a common cause of death for women. American folk medicine was evolving from the knowledge and indigenous practices of the Native Americans, European settlers, and African/Caribbean slaves. Many abortifacients were made from plants, such as pennyroyal, tansy, aloe, cohash, and squaw root. Such "remedies" were often passed down through family Bibles and cookbooks. Over 1,500 medical almanacs, many containing herbal remedies to "bring on a woman's courses," were circulated before the American Revolution. Yet there was little public discussion of birth control and no laws or statutes governing information or practice.

Brodie documents that reproductive control during most of the 19th century in America was neither rare nor taboo. Information was available about withdrawal, douching (the "water cure"), rhythm (although the information was not very accurate), condoms, spermicides, abortion-inducing drugs, and early varieties of the diaphragm. When other contraceptive options were available, couples seemed to prefer them over withdrawal; sexual abstinence was not one of the chief means of controlling birthrates. Abortion was not illegal until "quickening" (movement of the fetus).

Beginning in the 1830s, reproductive control became a commercial enterprise in the expanding American market economy. Douches and syringes, vaginal sponges, condoms, diaphragms (or "womb veils"), cervical caps, and pessaries (intravaginal and intrauterine devices) began to be widely advertised through a burgeoning literature on the subjects of sexuality and reproductive control, euphemistically called "feminine hygiene." Education through this means was made possible by the technological improvements in printing and the increased basic literacy of the American public.

The self-help literature instructed readers on how to make contraceptive and abortion agents at home from products readily available in the household or garden. Douching was the most frequent method for reproductive control used by middle- and upper-class women. The invention of the vulcanization process for rubber by Goodyear in the 1840s enabled condoms to be made more cheaply. In addition, the appearance of the mail-order catalog allowed the public to "shop" for contraceptive devices confidentially.

The birthrate of white native-born married women was reduced almost by half between 1800 and 1900, coinciding with the major social upheaval of industrialization and urbanization. Many American couples wanted fewer children and greater spacing between them. This became possible with the evolving availability of information about and access to more-effective contraceptive techniques.

By the mid-1800s, the abortion rate among the white middle class increased sharply with greater access to diverse sources of information about abortion, abortion drugs and instruments, and persons offering abortion services. There was little outcry about abortion being "immoral" until the American Medical Association launched a campaign to curb it at mid century. Historians have debated whether the new opposition to abortion by male physicians was more because of the threat of competition from female midwives or to a concern about the dangers of unsafe abortion.

As reproductive control became commercialized after 1850, and as some women became increasingly able to assert a degree of independent control over their fertility through contraception and abortion, the deep ambivalences with which many Americans regarded such changes came increasingly into play. In the second half of the 19th century, diverse groups emerged to try to restore

American "social purity," and one of the issues they focused on was restricting sexual freedom and control of reproduction. . . . All branches of government were their allies; their goals were won through enactments of federal and state legislation and sustained by judicial decisions that criminalized contraception and abortion, both of which had in earlier decades been legal. (Brodie 1994, 253)

Laws began to alter 200 years of American custom and public policy towards contraception and abortion. Federal and state laws made it a felony to mail products or information about contraception and abortion. Such materials were then labeled "obscene." In 1873, Congress passed "The Act for the Suppression of Trade in, and Circulation of Obscene Literature and Articles of Immoral Use," which tightened the loopholes on interstate trade and importation of birth-control materials from abroad. This law was better known as the Comstock Law, named after Anthony Comstock, a leading "social purity" proponent and crusader against "obscenity." Comstock was even appointed a special agent of the U.S. Post Office and allowed to inspect and seize such "illegal" material until his death in 1915.

The combined force of the social purity legions and of overwhelming public acquiescence overrode a generation of commercialization and growing public discourse and drove reproductive control, if not totally back underground, at least into a netherworld of back-fence gossip and back-alley abortion. (Brodie 1994, 288)

The Comstock Law would stand until a federal appeals court would overturn its anticontraceptive provisions in 1936 (*United States v. One Package*) on the grounds that the weight of authority of the medical world concerning the safety and reliability of contraception was not available when the law was originally passed. (The anti-obscenity provisions of the Comstock Law remained intact for several more decades.)

What is referred to as "the birth-control movement" was begun in the United States shortly before World War I, primarily by socialists and sexual liberals as both a political and moral issue. Margaret Sanger's leadership, in the early 1900s, was responsible for gaining support from mainstream America and centralizing the cause through her American Birth Control League. Sanger attributed her indomitable dedication to making birth-control information and methods available to American women, particularly of the working class, to her nursing experiences with poor women during which they would beg her to tell them the "secrets" of the rich for limiting children.

In 1915, she began publishing *Woman Rebel*, a monthly magazine advocating birth control. She was indicted for violating the Comstock Law, but the case was dropped and she continued dispensing birth-control information through lectures and publications. In 1916, she was arrested again for opening the first birth-control clinic in the United States in a poor slum in Brooklyn, New York. She served 30 days in jail; however, the testimonials of her poor birth-control clients at the trial helped to fuel the birth-control movement.

Gordon (1976) documents the birth-control movement throughout the 20th century in the United States. In the early 1920s, most doctors were opposed to contraception. However, through the efforts of Margaret Sanger and Dr. Robert Latou Dickenson, contraception was scientifically studied and became accepted as a health issue, not simply a moral one. Clergy, particularly of the Protestant and Jewish faiths, also began to view contraceptive choice as an individual moral decision when it affected the health of a family. To this day, however, the Catholic Church has remained staunch in its opposition to "artificial birth control." Yet, this opposition has not deterred Catholic women in the United States from using birth-control methods as frequently as women of other or no faiths.

The Great Depression of the 1930s forced many more Americans into accepting and practicing birth-control measures. Social workers, based on their interactions with many poor and struggling families, became proponents in support of better education about, and access to, birth control for all women, not just the middle class and wealthy. The manufacturing of condoms became a large industry. In the 1930s, with the formation of the American Birth Control League, over 300 clinics throughout the United States were providing contraceptive information and services; this increased to more than 800 clinics by 1942.

Yet, despite the fact that a 1937 poll indicated that 79% of American women supported the use of birth control, those who did not have access to private doctors were limited in their access to birth-control information and devices. However, judges, doctors, government officials, entrepreneurs, and others were beginning to respond to grassroots pressure. For example, in 1927, the American Medical Association officially recognized birth control as part of medical practice. In 1942, Planned Parenthood Federation of America

(PPFA) was founded with a commitment to helping women better plan family size and child spacing. PPFA was greatly responsible for making birth control more accessible to women of various backgrounds, particularly those of lower socioeconomic levels, throughout the United States.

### Development of the Oral Contraceptive Pill and IUD

During the 1950s, research was progressing in the United States that would transform contraceptive technology and practice worldwide. Asbell (1995) details the biography of the "drug that changed the world." The quest for a female contraceptive that could be "swallowed like an aspirin" began when Margaret Sanger and Katherine McCormick, a wealthy American woman dedicated to the birth-control movement, enlisted Gregory Pincus, an accomplished reproductive scientist, to develop a contraceptive pill. Applying the basic research findings of others, particularly Russel Marker, who produced a chemical imitation of progesterone from the roots of Mexican yam trees, Pincus developed just such a pill combining synthetic estrogen and progesterone.

With the help of John Rock, a noted Harvard gynecologist and researcher, the oral contraceptive was initially given to 50 Massachusetts volunteers, and then field tested with approximately 200 women in Puerto Rico in 1956, where it was believed opposition to such a drug would be less than in the United States. However, the pill was heartily condemned by the Catholic Church, leaving Puerto Rican women to face the dilemma of choosing to be in the trials (and committing a mortal sin) or bearing more children that they could not adequately support. In addition, the standards for informed consent for research subjects were not as strict as they are today, so that participants in these trials were not thoroughly informed as to the experimental procedures being used and the potential risks involved (which were generally unknown).

In 1957, the pill was first approved by the Food and Drug Administration (FDA) for treatment of menstrual disorders. At this time, it was observed that many women who had never before experienced menstrual disorders suddenly developed this problem and sought treatment with the pill. By 1960, the pill was formally approved by the FDA as a contraceptive following double-blind clinical trials with 897 Puerto Rican women. Such a procedure would well be considered ethically questionable today.

The pill was extremely attractive to many potential users because of its convenience and efficacy. Women now had the option of engaging in intercourse with minimal threat of pregnancy. This method separated the act of coitus from the action taken to restrict fertility (ingestion of the pill). In addition, the woman was in sole charge of this method of birth control and did not need any cooperation from her male partner. Many believed this innovation in birth control was responsible for a "sexual revolution" in which women were to become more "sexually active," displaying patterns of sexual attitudes and behaviors more like men, although there is little scientific evidence to support this claim. As Ira Reiss explained the evolutionary changes taking place in American sexual expression:

> Sexual standards and behavior seem more closely related to social structure and cultural and religious values than to the availability of contraceptive techniques . . . [increased premarital sexuality] was promoted by a courtship system that had been evolving for a hundred years in the United States permitting young people to choose their own marriage partners, and which therefore encouraged choice of when as well as with whom to share sex. (Asbell 1995, 201)

By 1967, the Population Council estimated that 6.5 million women were using the birth-control pill in the U.S., while 6.3 million women were using it in other parts of the world. Some were concerned as to whether millions of women were serving as guinea pigs in a massive experiment, since careful large-scale studies of its safety had not been conducted before it was marketed (Seaman 1969). Disturbing side effects, including deep-vein thrombosis, heart disease and attacks, elevated blood pressure, strokes, gallbladder disease, liver tumors, and depression, were being reported. In the first few years of use in the U.S., more than 100 court claims were filed against its manufacturer. Some countries, including Norway and the Soviet Union, banned the pill. Some American women mobilized to create a women's health movement, spearheaded by the National Women's Health Network, to help the public become better informed about the benefits and risks of pill use, as well as other medical procedures and drugs. Yet, accurate information about the benefits and risks of pill use was often unavailable, difficult to access, and distorted and sensationalized. In the 1970s, pill sales dropped 20%.

Twenty-five years later, oral contraception has become one of the most extensively studied medications ever prescribed. Today, pills with less than 50 micrograms of estrogen are associated with a significantly lower risk of serious negative effects and are as effective in preventing pregnancy as the higher-dose pills of the past (Hatcher et al. 1994).

The intrauterine device (IUD) also became popular in the United States as the "perfect" alternative to the pill because of its effectiveness and convenience. However, the Dalkon Shield, which was marketed from 1971 to 1975, was implicated in a number of cases of pelvic inflammatory disease and spontaneous septic abortions resulting in the deaths of at least 20 women. In 1974, the Shield was taken off the U.S. market, although it was still distributed abroad. Currently, there are only two IUDs for sale in the United States, the TCu-380A (ParaGard) and the Progesterone T device (Progestasert).

### Government Policy and Legal Issues

While research was expanding birth-control options, the 1950s and 1960s saw the development and implementation of federal policies supporting population control programs designed to deal with overpopulation throughout the world. Birth control was offered as a "tool" for economic development to Third World countries. The 1960 budget of $2 million for family-planning programs grew to $250 million in 1972 (Asbell 1995). However, American goals were often in conflict with the cultural beliefs of the people in various countries. Reproductive options cannot be separated from the economic options and social mores of a culture.

Governmental policies on birth control were also changing at home. In 1964, President Lyndon B. Johnson, over strong political opposition, provided federal funds to support birth-control clinics for the American poor. These efforts were continued by President Richard M. Nixon, who in 1970 declared "a new national goal: adequate family-planning services within the next five years for all those who want them but cannot afford them" (Asbell 1995).

Important legal changes were also occurring in the U.S. during this time. In 1965, the Supreme Court decided, in *Griswold v. Connecticut*, that laws prohibiting the sale of contraceptives to married couples violated a constitutional "right of privacy." Writing the majority opinion, Justice William O. Douglas declared:

> we deal with a right of privacy older than the Bill of Rights—older than our political parties, older than our

school system. Marriage is a coming together for better or worse, hopefully enduring and intimate to the degree of being sacred. (Asbell 1995, 241)

The court asked, "Would we allow the police to search the sacred precincts of marital bedrooms for telltale signs of the use of contraceptives?" The judges responded, "The very idea is repulsive to the notions of privacy surrounding the marital relationship."

In 1972, the Supreme Court extended this "right to privacy" for contraceptive use to unmarried people (*Eisenstadt v. Baird*) on the basis that a legal prohibition would violate the equal protection clause of the 14th Amendment. A 1977 Supreme Court decision (*Carey v. Population Services*) struck down laws prohibiting the sale of contraception to minors, the selling of contraception by others besides pharmacists, and advertisements for or displays of contraceptives.

### Recent Developments in Birth Control

More-recent developments in contraceptive technology receive tougher scrutiny than in the past before winning FDA approval. For example, Norplant was developed by the international nonprofit Population Council, which began clinical trials including half a million women in 46 countries, not including the U.S.

However, Norplant was not approved for use in the United States by the Food and Drug Administration (FDA) until 1990. This approval was opposed by the National Women's Health Network because the long-term safety of Norplant had not been established. Wyeth-Ayerst, the U.S. distributor, is required by law to report any unusual events associated with Norplant use to the FDA, while an internationally coordinated surveillance of Norplant use and its effects is being conducted by the World Health Organization and others in eight developing countries. Currently, a class-action suit is being formulated by a group of Norplant users in the U.S., primarily because of the difficulties they experienced in having the Norplant rods removed. Such complications are a serious impediment keeping American pharmaceutical companies from researching and developing new contraceptives.

Depro-Provera (Depo-medroxyprogesterone acetate or DMPA) is the most commonly employed injectable progestin used in over 90 countries worldwide. However, it was not approved for use in the U.S. by the FDA until 1992. Women's health activists, organized by the National Women's Health Network, had opposed its approval in the absence of more long-term studies of its safety.

In 1993, the FDA approved the first female condom, called Reality, for over-the-counter sale in the United States. The female condom, or vaginal pouch, is a polyurethane lubricated sheath that lines the vagina and partially covers the perineum. Although the method failure rate of the female condom (5%) is similar to that of the male condom (3%), it has a higher failure rate with typical use (21%) than does the male condom (12%) (Hatcher et al. 1994). This may reflect the "newness" of this female method and inexperience with its use. Yet, in a study of 360 women using female condoms, only 2 discontinued its use.

Although a combination of RU-486 (mifespristone) and prostaglandin has been tested in over a dozen countries, particularly in France, it has generated controversy in the U.S. and was only approved for use here in 1996. Because RU-486, when combined with a prostaglandin, is an effective early abortifacient, its use has been opposed by anti-abortion proponents, even for research purposes or its potential use in the treatment of breast cancer, Cushing's syndrome, endometriosis, and brain tumors. Because it was so politically controversial, RU-486 had not been expected to be ap-

proved for any use in the United States, which turned out not to be the case.

What is the future for the development of new birth-control methods in the United States? Contraceptive-vaccine researchers acknowledge that a new form of birth control for men is badly needed. Yet, it is believed that immunizing men against their own sperm would risk destroying the testes. However, researchers in the U.S. are talking with the FDA to test a vaccine with women that induces the woman's immune system to attack sperm. Previously, such vaccines have been tested on mice, rabbits, and baboons with an effectiveness rate of 75 to 80%.

In the past, Federal agencies have shied away from supporting such work because "right-to-lifer" advocates view such a vaccine as abortive and, therefore, unacceptable. In addition to the possibility of medical liability, American pharmaceutical companies are unlikely to market such a vaccine because of the protests and boycotts that "right-to-life" groups threaten to organize. Because of the threat of boycotts from adversarial groups and lawsuits from persons claiming to be harmed by new contraceptive technologies, only one American company remains active in contraceptive research and development. In the late 1960s, nine American drug companies were competing to find new and better birth-control methods.

### Current Contraceptive Behavior

Between 1988 and 1990, the proportion of women in the United States, from the age of 15 to 44, who had never had vaginal-penile intercourse declined from 12% to 9%. (Data used in this section are based on the 1982 and 1988 *National Survey of Family Growth* (*NSFG*) and the 1990 *NSFG Telephone Reinterview*) (Peterson 1995). The proportion of 15- to 44-year-olds who were at risk for unintended pregnancy but were not contracepting increased from 7% to 12%. This increase was most pronounced among 15- to 44-year-olds (8% to 22%), never-married women (11% to 20%), and non-Hispanic white women (5% to 11%).

In 1990, 34.5 million women, or 59% of those aged 15 to 44, in the United States were using some type of contraception—with almost three quarters (70.7%) of married women using contraception; see Table 17. There is little difference in contraceptive use based on religious background between Catholic, Protestant, and Jewish women. The leading methods used by contraceptors were female sterilization (29.5%), the contraceptive pill (28.5%), and the male condom (17.7%). (Information on the use of three newer methods—Norplant, the female condom, and Depo-Provera—was not available at the time of the surveys). Overall, the use of female and male sterilization, the condom, and periodic abstinence had increased from 1988, whereas the use of the pill, IUD, and diaphragm had decreased.

Female sterilization is most widely used among older and less-educated women who have completed their childbearing, with over one half (52.0%) of female contraceptors age 40 to 44 having been sterilized. Anglo-American women are much more likely to have male partners with a vasectomy (15.5%) than are African-American women (1.3%). The aging of the baby-boom generation in the United States portends a continued rise in female sterilization rates throughout the next decade and a rise in vasectomies among the better educated.

The increased use of the condom was most pronounced among young (aged 15 to 44), African-American, never-married, childless, or less-educated women, and those living below the poverty level. For example, condom use among never-married women tripled between 1982 and 1990 (4% to 13%). The percentage of adolescents using

## Table 17

**Number of Women 15-44 Years of Age, Percent Using Any Method of Contraception, and Percent Distribution of Contraceptors by Method, According to Age, Race and Origin, and Marital Status, 1988 and 1990**

| Age, Race, and Marital Status | Number of Women Using a Method (in Thousands) | Percent Using Any Method | Female Sterilization | Male Sterilization | Pill | IUD | Diaphragm | Condom | Periodic Abstinence[1] | Other |
|---|---|---|---|---|---|---|---|---|---|---|
| **1990[2]** | | | | | | | | | | |
| All women | 34,516 | 59.3 | 29.5 | 12.6 | 28.5 | 1.4 | 2.8 | 17.7 | 2.7 | 4.8 |
| **Age** | | | | | | | | | | |
| 15-19 | 2,623 | 31 5 | 0.0 | 0.0 | 52.0 | 0.0 | 0.0 | 44.0 | 1.0 | 3.0 |
| 15-17 | 1,165 | 24.3 | 0.0 | 0.0 | 41.1 | 0.0 | 0.0 | 51.9 | 2.2 | 4.7 |
| 18-19 | 1,458 | 41.2 | 0.0 | 0.0 | 60.7 | 0.0 | 0.0 | 37 6 | 0.0 | 1.7 |
| 20-24 | 5,065 | 55.3 | 8.0 | 1.8 | 55.4 | 0.8 | 0.6 | 25.3 | 2.8 | 5.3 |
| 25-29 | 6,385 | 60.0 | 17.4 | 5.0 | 47.3 | 0.4 | 2.3 | 19.0 | 2.7 | 5.9 |
| 30-34 | 7,344 | 66.2 | 32.7 | 13.0 | 23.9 | 0.9 | 4.7 | 15.9 | 3.5 | 5.4 |
| 35-39 | 7,138 | 70.6 | 44.2 | 19.8 | 10.6 | 3.3 | 3.3 | 10.3 | 3.4 | 5.2 |
| 40-44 | 5,962 | 66.9 | 52.0 | 26.5 | 2.2 | 1.8 | 3.8 | 9.2 | 1.6 | 2.9 |
| **Race and Origin** | | | | | | | | | | |
| Hispanic | 2,856 | 52.2 | 33.1 | 6.4 | 31.4 | 1.9 | 1.5 | 17.1 | 3.7 | 5.1 |
| White non-Hispanic | 25,928 | 60.5 | 27.3 | 15.5 | 28.5 | 1.3 | 3.0 | 17.0 | 2.7 | 4.7 |
| Black non-Hispanic | 4,412 | 58.7 | 41.0 | 1.3 | 28.5 | 1.4 | 1.6 | 19.4 | 1.2 | 5.6 |
| **Marital Status** | | | | | | | | | | |
| Currently married | 21,608 | 70.7 | 33.5 | 33.5 | 19.2 | 20.6 | 1.4 | 14.0 | 3.5 | 3.8 |
| Divorced, separated, widowed | 4,026 | 57.3 | 52.1 | 2.8 | 22.4 | 2.5 | 0.9 | 9.7 | 0.6 | 9.0 |
| Never married | 8,882 | 43.0 | 9.6 | 1.1 | 50.5 | 0.8 | 0.6 | 30.1 | 1.8 | 5.5 |
| **1988** | | | | | | | | | | |
| All women | 34,912 | 60.3 | 27.5 | 11.7 | 30.7 | 2.0 | 5.7 | 14.6 | 2.3 | 5.4 |
| **Age** | | | | | | | | | | |
| 15-19 | 2,950 | 32.1 | 1.5 | 0.2 | 58.8 | 0.0 | 1.0 | 32.8 | 0.8 | 4.8 |
| 15-17 | 1,076 | 19.9 | 0.0 | 0.0 | 53.3 | 0.0 | 0.7 | 40.4 | 0.9 | 4.7 |
| 18-19 | 1,874 | 49.6 | 2.4 | 0.4 | 61.9 | 0.0 | 1.2 | 28.4 | 0.8 | 4.9 |
| 20-24 | 5,550 | 59.0 | 4.6 | 1.8 | 68.2 | 0.3 | 3.7 | 14.5 | 1.7 | 5.2 |
| 25-29 | 6,967 | 64.5 | 17.0 | 6.0 | 44.5 | 1.3 | 5.5 | 15.6 | 2.4 | 7.6 |
| 30-34 | 7,437 | 68.0 | 32.5 | 14.0 | 21.5 | 2.9 | 8.9 | 12.0 | 2.7 | 5.5 |
| 35-39 | 6,726 | 70.2 | 44.9 | 19.7 | 5.2 | 2.7 | 7.7 | 11.8 | 3.0 | 5.1 |
| 40-44 | 5,282 | 66.0 | 51.1 | 22.2 | 3.2 | 3.7 | 3.9 | 10.5 | 2.2 | 3.2 |
| **Race and Origin** | | | | | | | | | | |
| Hispanic | 2,799 | 50.4 | 31.7 | 4.3 | 33.4 | 5.0 | 2.4 | 13.6 | 2.5 | 7.1 |
| White non-Hispanic | 25,799 | 62.9 | 25.6 | 14.3 | 29.5 | 1.5 | 6.6 | 15.2 | 2.3 | 5.0 |
| Black non-Hispanic | 4,208 | 56.8 | 37.8 | 0.9 | 38.1 | 3.2 | 2.0 | 10.1 | 2.1 | 5.9 |
| **Marital Status** | | | | | | | | | | |
| Currently married | 21,657 | 74.3 | 31.4 | 17.3 | 20.4 | 2.0 | 6.2 | 14.3 | 2.8 | 5.6 |
| Divorced, separated, widowed | 4,429 | 57.6 | 50.7 | 3.6 | 25.3 | 3.6 | 5.3 | 5.9 | 1.9 | 3.8 |
| Never married | 8,826 | 41.9 | 6.4 | 1.8 | 59.0 | 1.3 | 4.9 | 19.6 | 1.3 | 5.7 |

[1]Includes natural family planning and other types of periodic abstinence.

[2]Percentages for 1990 were calculated excluding cases for whom contraceptive status was not ascertained. Overall, contraceptive status was not ascertained for 0.3% of U.S. women in 1990.

*Source*: Peterson, L. S. (1995, February). "Contraceptive Use in the United States: 1982-1990." From *Vital and Health Statistics. Advanced Data No. 260*, Hyattsville, MD: National Center for Health Statistics.

condoms rose from 33% to 44% between 1988 and 1990. Almost all contracepting teenagers used either the pill (52%) or condom (44%) in 1990. However, it must be kept in mind that only 56% of condom users report using them consistently every time they have intercourse.

The use of contraception at first intercourse by adolescents has increased significantly since the early 1980s. For example, during 1980-1982, 53% of unmarried women aged 15 to 19 used contraception during their first intercourse experience. By 1988-1990, this percentage rose to 71%, mainly attributable to rising condom use (from 28% to 55%). The increase in condom use was particularly striking among Hispanic teens, with a threefold increase from 1980 to 1990 (17% to 58%).

Table 18 depicts the latest estimates of pregnancy prevention with typical use (indicating user failure) and perfect use (indicating method failure) among the contraceptive methods currently available in the United States (Hatcher et al. 1994). The most effective methods are Norplant, the oral contraceptive pill, male and female sterilization, Depo-Provera, and IUDs.

[*A Contraceptive Revolution?* WILLIAM TAVERNER
[*Update 2003*: In the seven years since Patricia Barthalow Koch prepared the above status report, major advances have been made in the availability of new contraceptive methods in the United States. From 2001 to 2002 alone, the U.S. Food and Drug Administration (FDA) approved six new contraceptive methods. Some have celebrated the new options as indicative of a "contraceptive revolution"; others have questioned how "new" the methods really are. Andrea Tone, for instance, comments that, rather than being truly innovative, many of the "new" methods are little more than repackaging of old technologies (Tone 2002-2003). For example, the widely advertised contraceptive patch uses the same fundamental hormonal technology as "the pill," "the shot," or any other mode of entry to the body.

[New methods introduced to the American public since 1997 include:

- *Essure*, a new type of female sterilization without incision. A "micro-insert" is placed in each fallopian tube, facilitating local tissue growth that serves as a barrier (Conceptus).
- *Lea's Shield*, a cup-shaped cervical cap designed to cover the cervix without being held in place by the cervix (U.S. Food & Drug Administration).
- *Lunelle*, a monthly hormonal shot, and an alternative to Depo Provera, an injection given every three months (Hatcher et al. 2003).
- *Male polyurethane condoms* became commercially available in 1997 (Brick & Taverner 2001). Two male polyurethane condoms are marketed in the United States, Avanti by Durex and Supra by Trojan, providing a condom alternative for people with latex allergies.
- *Mirena*, a hormonal intrauterine device effective for 10 years (Hatcher et al. 2003).
- *NuvaRing*, a hormonal vaginal ring, inserted in the vagina for three weeks, and removed the week of menstruation (Hatcher et al. 2003).
- *Ortho Evra*, a transdermal hormonal patch usually worn on the lower abdomen or buttocks for one week, for each of three weeks, and not worn the week of menstruation (Hatcher et al. 2003).

[*Comings and Goings.* Other notable changes in contraceptive availability during the last several years involve the contraceptive sponge, implants, and spermicides. In 1995, the contraceptive sponge was removed from the market when the manufacturer decided to stop production, rather than make government-ordered changes to the manufacturing plant. The sponge regained popularity when an episode of the television sitcom, *Seinfeld*, featured a character who dealt with the impending loss of her favorite method by hoarding many boxes of the sponge, and then determining whether each potential sexual partner was "sponge-worthy." In 1998, a pharmaceutical company purchased the rights to the sponge and anticipated FDA approval some time in 2003.

[Norplant, a six-rod hormonal implant system, was sold in the United States from 1991 until 2000. The method was FDA-approved for five years, but is possibly effective for up to seven years (Hatcher et al. 2003). Although Norplant is not available to new users, some women continue to use their previously implanted method; other women look forward to the

### Table 18

**Percentage of Women Experiencing a Birth Control Failure During the First Year of Typical Use and the First Year of Perfect Use and the Percentage Continuing Use at the End of the First Year**

| Method | % of Women Experiencing an Accidental Pregnancy Within the First Year of Use | | % of Women Continuing Use at One Year |
|---|---|---|---|
| | Typical Use | Perfect Use | |
| Chance | 85 | 85 | |
| Spermicide | 21 | 6 | 43 |
| Periodic Abstinence | 20 | | 67 |
| Calendar | | 9 | |
| Ovulation Method | | 3 | |
| Sympto-Thermal | | 2 | |
| Post-Ovulation | | 1 | |
| Withdrawal | 19 | 4 | |
| Cap (with spermicide) | | | |
| Parous Women | 36 | 24 | 45 |
| Nulliparous Women | 18 | 9 | 58 |
| Sponge | | | |
| Parous Women | 36 | 20 | 45 |
| Nulliparous Women | 18 | 9 | 58 |
| Diaphragm (with spermicide) | 18 | 6 | 58 |
| Condom | | | |
| Female (Reality) | 21 | 5 | 56 |
| Male | 12 | 3 | 63 |
| Pill | 3 | | |
| Progestin Only | | 0.5 | N.A. |
| Combined | | 0.1 | N.A. |
| IUD | | | |
| Progesterone T | 2.0 | 1.5 | 81 |
| Copper T 380A | 0.8 | 0.6 | 78 |
| Depo-Provera | 0.3 | 0.3 | 70 |
| Norplant (6 Capsules) | 0.09 | 0.09 | 85 |
| Female Sterilization | 0.4 | 0.4 | 100 |
| Male Sterilization | 0.15 | 0.10 | 100 |

*Source*: Hatcher et al. (1994, 13)

eventual marketing and availability of Jadelle, a two-rod implant system that received FDA approval in 1996 (Schwartz & Gabelnick 2002), and Implanon, a single implant effective for three years and currently available in several European countries (Hatcher et al. 2003).

[Research on nonoxynol-9, a spermicide found in contraceptive film, foam, jelly, sponges, and suppositories, has had many United States health organizations rethinking the extent to which they endorse such products. While nonoxynol-9 products continue to work with moderately high effectiveness as contraceptive methods, they may also exacerbate individuals' risk of HIV infection. Nonoxynol-9 may irritate the vaginal walls, causing lesions that could facilitate the transmission of HIV (Schwartz & Gabelnick 2002).

[Research has also clarified the effectiveness of coitus interruptus (withdrawal), a method whose failure has been traditionally overstated by American educators. Tests of its effectiveness show that it has a "perfect use" failure rate of 4% and a typical use failure rate of 27% (Hatcher et al. 2003). Still, its efficacy remains highly user-dependent, as effectiveness relies on the male's ability to predict ejaculation and withdraw in time.

[*For Emergency Use Only.* New forms of emergency contraception became available in the late 1990s, including the "Yuzpe Regimen" and "Plan B," a progestin-only method. Although they are sometimes confused with abortifacients, all methods of emergency contraception actually prevent pregnancy before it begins, and will not disturb an implanted pregnancy (Hatcher et al. 2003; Brick & Taverner 2003). Plan B is more effective and has fewer side effects (Brick & Taverner 2003). For several years, it was recommended that use of emergency contraception begin within 72 hours of unprotected vaginal intercourse; in 2002, the period was extended to 120 hours. However, the earlier the regimen is begun, the more effective it is. Recognizing that timing is of the essence, and that increased access to emergency contraception could greatly reduce the number of unplanned pregnancies every year, five states have enacted laws permitting the dispensing of emergency contraception without a prescription. These states include Alaska, California, Hawaii, New Mexico, and Washington (Alan Guttmacher Institute 2003). The 45 other American states still require a woman to visit a doctor or reproductive health center before emergency contraception may be dispensed.

[*A New Gag Rule.* Despite all the reliable, safe contraceptive methods available for sexually active teens, the United States government has championed abstinence as the contraceptive method of choice since 1996. Federal funding in excess of $100 million supports "abstinence-only" education programs that forbid any discussion of the effectiveness of other methods. No research has indicated that such programs are effective in reducing teen sexual activity, or delaying the initiation of sexual intercourse (Kirby 2001). Nevertheless, in government-funded abstinence-only programs, American educators are unable to provide basic contraceptive information to teens, at least three quarters of whom have had intercourse by their late teens (Alan Guttmacher Institute 2002). Perhaps consequently, U.S. teens continue to experience pregnancy, birth, and abortion at rates much higher than most other industrialized nations (Moss 2003; Singh & Darroch 2000), despite similar levels of sexual activity between U.S. teens and teens in other developed nations.

[*Limited Coverage.* Half of American health insurance companies do not cover any reversible methods of contraception. Plans that do cover contraceptive methods often do not cover all FDA-approved options. Twenty states require insurance companies to provide full contraceptive coverage, but 10 of these states allow employers offering health insurance not to offer contraceptive coverage for religious reasons. The other 30 states have no laws requiring that contraceptives be covered by insurers (Planned Parenthood Federation).

[*Who Is Using What?* Sixty million American women are in their reproductive years, age 15 to 44. Sixty-four percent of these women practice some method of contraception. Among women of reproductive age who use contraception, 61% use reversible methods, such as oral contraception and condoms, while the remaining 39% rely on male and female sterilization. Half of American women aged 40 to 44 have been sterilized, and an additional 20% have a partner who has had a vasectomy (Alan Guttmacher Institute 1999).

[Among younger Americans, condoms are becoming increasingly popular for their *first* act of intercourse. More than two thirds of teens use a condom at first intercourse; however, condom use fades among both men and women as they become older (Alan Guttmacher Institute 2002). By their late 20s, almost half of men and women rely on female methods (Alan Guttmacher Institute *Facts in Brief* 1999). Among teen females and women in their 20s, the most popular contraceptive method is the pill (Alan Guttmacher Institute 1999).

[Perhaps because of the political climate described earlier, the mindset of protection against *both* unplanned pregnancy *and* sexually transmitted infections has not caught on in the United States as it has in other developed nations. A "trade-off" is evident in American contraceptive decision-making, where individuals decide to focus exclusively on one aspect of protection, but not on both (Ott et al. 2002; Taverner 2003). Consequently, one in four sexually active U.S. teens has a sexually transmitted infection (STI/STD), and scores of millions of Americans are infected with a viral STI (SIECUS; CDC). (*End of update by W. Taverner*)]

## B. Childbirth and Single Women

PATRICIA BARTHALOW KOCH

Each year, one million American teenage girls become pregnant, a per-thousand rate twice that of Canada, England, and Sweden, and ten times that of the Netherlands. A similar disproportionately high rate is reported for teenage abortions (Jones et al. 1986).

The birthrate for unmarried American women has surged since 1980, with the rate for white women nearly doubling, and the rate for teenagers dropping from 53% of the unwed births in 1973, to 41% in 1980, and 30% in 1992. One out of every four American babies in 1992 was born to an unmarried woman. The unwed birthrate rose sharply for women 20 years and older. The highest rates were among women ages 20 to 24 (68.5 births per 1,000), followed by 18- and 19-year olds (67.3 per 1,000) and 25- to 29-year-olds (56.5 per 1,000). Overall, according to a 1995 report from the National Center for Health Statistics, the unmarried birthrate rose 54% between 1980 and 1992, from 29.4 births per 1,000 unmarried women ages 15 to 44 in 1980 to 45.2 births per 1,000 in both 1991 and 1992 (Holmes 1996a).

In 1970, the birthrate for unmarried black women was seven times the rate for white women, and four times the rate for white women in 1980. Since 1980, the white unmarried birthrate has risen by 94% while the rate for blacks rose only 7%. By 1992, the birthrate for single black women was just 2.5 times the rate for white women. In 1992, the out-of-wedlock birthrates were 95.3 for Hispanic women, 86.5 for black women, and 35.2 for white women (Holmes 1996a).

Commenting on the social implications of these statistics, Charles F. Westoff, a Princeton University demographer, said they "reflect the declining significance of marriage as a social obligation or a social necessity for reproduction." Poorly educated, low-income teenage mothers and their children are overwhelmingly likely to experience long-term negative consequences of early childbearing as single parents (Associated Press News Release, June 7, 1995). A 1996 study, sponsored by the charitable Robin Hood Foundation, estimated the public cost of unwed teenage pregnancy at $7 billion. The study looked at the consequences for teenage mothers, their children, and the fathers of the babies, compared with people from the same social background when pregnancy was delayed until the woman was 20 or 21. The breakdown of annual costs included $2.2 billion in welfare and food-stamp benefits, $1.5 billion in medical-care costs, $900 million in increased foster-care expenses, $1 billion for additional prison construction, and $1.3 billion in lost tax revenue from the reduced productivity of teenage women who bear children (Holmes 1996a).

At the present rate, something like 50% or more of America's children will spend at least part of their childhood in a single-parent family. About half of this number will be the result of divorce or separation; the rest will be born to a mother who has never been married (Luker 1996).

In any given year, roughly 12% of American infants are born to teenage mothers. However, the vast majority of these teenage mothers are 18 or 19 years old, and thus only technically teenagers. American teenagers have been producing children at about the same rate for most of the 20th century. Fewer than a third of all single mothers are teenagers, even when we include the 18- to 19-year-olds. And this proportion is declining. What is different in recent decades is that increasing numbers of teenage mothers are unmarried when they give birth. In 1970, only 30% of teenage mothers had never been married; by 1995, 70% of teenage mothers had never been married (Luker 1996).

While there is no good reason to suppose that the teenage birthrate is going up in any significant way—it was, in fact, higher in the 1950s—one must admit that the rate of single parenting is going up. In 1947, virtually all single mothers were widows, or living apart from their mate after separation or divorce. In 1947, fewer than one in 100 had never been married. Today, overall, never-married single mothers account for one in three, and the percentage is rising. The number of single teenage mothers is going up at a rapid rate, but so is the number of single mothers at every age.

These data suggest that we are participants in, or at least witness to, an important shift in the nature of American family life that is echoing throughout the industrialized world. According to Luker (1996), the last years of the 20th century may turn out to be the beginning of a time when the very notions of childrearing on the one hand and family life on the other are increasingly disconnected. While the rate of out-of-wedlock births is clearly on the way up, the rate of marriage may be declining, and the age of first marriage is clearly being delayed. In 1995, 60% of American families were headed by a single parent, half of them never-married. Luker (1996) suggests two possible outcomes. The present situation may prove to be only a temporary deviation from a stable pattern of long standing. Or it may mark the first hesitant appearance of an important new pattern.

If the latter interpretation turns out to have substance, one can ask why this is happening. Luker cites several influential shifts in social attitudes and behavior. First, "illegitimacy" has lost its moral sting. Second, many women are realizing that they do not need to put up with the abuse, domination, and other burdens they associate with married life. This has special resonance for women in poverty, who ask why they should live with a male who is unreliable and has

no skills or job. Third, although welfare benefits are declining throughout the industrialized world, teenage pregnancies are on the rise regardless of the level of welfare benefits. Finally, the vast majority of teenage pregnancies are unintended and not linked with the availability of welfare aid.

So long as teenagers are sexually active, the most effective way to reduce the incidence of childbearing is to assure that they have access to contraception before the fact, and abortion, if needed, after the fact. The many Americans who oppose sexuality and contraceptive education in the schools, distribution of contraceptives in schools, and abortion can only hope that someone discovers a way to reduce teenage sexual activity itself. That seems unlikely, given the decreasing age of puberty among American youth, the declining age of first sexual intercourse, and the clear trend to delay marriage well into the 20s or even 30s. Admonitions to "Just say 'No'" are scarcely going to suffice as a workable national policy. In analyzing the politics of teenage pregnancy and single mothers in the United States, Kristin Luker (1996) concluded that:

> Americans have every right to be concerned about early childbearing and to place the issue high on the national agenda. But they should think of it as a *measure*, not a cause, of poverty and other social ills. A teenager who has a baby usually adds but a slight burden to her life, which is already profoundly disadvantaged. . . . Early childbearing may make a bad situation worse, but the real causes of poverty lie elsewhere.

*[Factors in a Falling Birth Rate*

ROBERT T. FRANCOEUR

[*Update 2003*: America's birthrate fell to a record low in 2002 as teenagers and women in their prime childbearing years had fewer babies, according to June 25, 2003, statistics from the Health and Human Services Department. The birthrate was 13.9 per 1,000 people in 2002, compared with 14.1 for 2001. This most recent figure is the lowest in government records that go back to the turn of the 20th century. A major factor in the decline has been the reduction in births by teenagers; other factors in this decline include the aging of the population, the fact that women in their prime childbearing years have been choosing to have fewer children, and the fact that, as the population ages, there are fewer women in their 20s and 30s.

[However, the percentages of premature and low-birthweight babies continued to rise, as they did throughout the last decade of the 20th century. Twelve percent of births in 2002 were premature, compared with 11.9% in 2001. In addition, 7.8% were listed as low-birthweight, the highest level in 30 years. These increases came despite greater access to prenatal care. In 2002, 83.8% of women began receiving care in the first trimester of pregnancy, compared with 83.4% in 2001 and 75.8% in 1990. The birthrate for unmarried women declined, but this group still accounted for more than one third of all births. (*End of update by R. T. Francoeur*)]

**[C. Condom Distribution in the Schools**

ROBERT T. FRANCOEUR

[*Update 1998*: Seventy-two percent of American high school seniors, on average, have engaged in sexual intercourse, although the percentage is higher for teenagers in large cities and their suburbs. At the same time, American teenagers have the highest rate of teenage pregnancy and abortion in North America and Europe. They are also rapidly becoming the highest risk group for HIV/AIDS infection in the United States. American parents, educators, and healthcare professionals are consequently struggling to decide on ways to deal with this reality. Typical of the conflicted, schizophrenic American approach to sexual issues, religious conservatives call for teaching abstinence-only education and saying nothing about contraceptives and other ways of reducing the risk of contracting sexually transmissible diseases and HIV infections. At the same time, others advocate educating and counseling: "You don't have to be sexually active, but if you are, this is what you can do to protect yourself." However, the problem is so serious in New York, Baltimore, Chicago, Los Angeles, San Francisco, Philadelphia, Miami, and other large cities, that school boards in these cities now allow school nurses and school-based health clinics to distribute free condoms to students, usually without requiring parental notification or permission (Guttmacher 1997; Richardson 1997).

[Typical of the opposition is Dr. Alma Rose George, president of the National Medical Association, who opposes schools giving condoms to teens without their parents knowing about it: "When you give condoms out to teens, you are promoting sexual activity. It's saying that it's all right. We shouldn't make it so easy for them." Faye Wattleton, former president of the Planned Parenthood Federation of America, approves of schools distributing condoms, and maintains that "mandatory parental consent would be counterproductive and meaningless." Some critics claim that condom distribution programs are inherently racist and a form of genocide because the decisions are mostly made by a white majority for predominantly black schools.

[Recently, a study comparing the sexual activity and condom use of 7,000 students in New York City high schools, and 4,000 similar high school students in Chicago, supported the effectiveness of school condom distribution (Guttmacher 1997). The New York schools combined HIV/AIDS education with free condoms, while the Chicago schools had similar HIV/AIDS education but no condom distribution. In both cities, 60% of the students were sexually active regardless of whether or not their schools distributed condoms. However, students in schools that distributed condoms were significantly more likely to have used a condom in their last intercourse than teens in schools that did not distribute condoms. Regardless of the data available on the ineffectiveness of abstinence-only education and the effectiveness of condom distribution, this debate will continue. (*End of update by R. T. Francoeur*)]

## D. Abortion            PATRICIA BARTHALOW KOCH

In America today, it seems that two camps are at war over the abortion issue. "Pro-choice" supporters advocate the right of the individual woman to decide whether or not to continue a pregnancy. They contend that the rights of a woman must take precedence over the "assumed" rights of a fertilized human egg or fetus. They believe that a woman can never be free unless she has reproductive control over her own body. Pro-choice advocates in the United States include various Protestant and Jewish organizations, Catholics for Free Choice, Planned Parenthood, the National Organization for Women (NOW), National Abortion Rights Action League (NARAL), and the American Civil Liberties Union (ACLU), among others.

Anti-abortion groups have politically identified themselves as "pro-life" supporters of "the right to life" for the unborn. This coalition involves such constituents as Eastern Orthodox, charismatic and conservative Roman Catholics, fundamentalist Protestants, and Orthodox Jews in influential groups like Operation Rescue, Focus on the Family, and the Christian Coalition. These groups use various methods

in order to prevent women from being able to have abortions, including, in some cases, personal intimidation of abortion providers and clients and political action.

The basic motivation of the protection of human life of those in the anti-abortion movement has, however, been questioned. For example, an analysis of the voting records of U.S. senators who are anti-abortion advocates indicates that they had the lowest scores on votes for family-support issues, bills for school-lunch programs, and for aid to the elderly (Prescott & Wallace 1978).

*[Abortion—The 25th Anniversary of the Roe v. Wade Decision*   PATRICIA BARTHALOW KOCH

[*Update 1998*: A 1998 report on the status of abortion rights in the United States documents that there are more obstacles today for women seeking their constitutional right to abortion than ever before since the Supreme Court's *Roe v. Wade* decision in 1973 (NARAL 1998). The report documents the increasing risk of unintended pregnancy, with concomitant increasing difficulties in obtaining abortions, resulting in increased risks to women's health and well-being. The factors contributing to this include increased anti-abortion legislation enacted at the state and federal levels, an acute shortage of medical providers being trained in abortion procedures in medical schools, a parallel shortage of medical providers willing to contend with constant harassment from anti-choice activists, lack of sexuality education, and denial of insurance coverage for contraception. As Chief Justice William Renquist stated in the Supreme Court's *Planned Parenthood v. Casey* decision, "Roe continues to exist but only in the way a storefront on a western movie exists: a mere facade to give the illusion of reality" (*Planned Parenthood of Southeastern PA v. Casey* 1992).

[In 1998, states were enforcing an unprecedented number of abortion restrictions, including: mandatory waiting periods, Medicaid funding bans, parental notification and consent laws, bans on the use of public facilities for abortion, prohibitions on the participation of public employees in providing abortion services, bans on actual abortion procedures (e.g., "partial-birth" abortions), and prohibitions on the use of public funds to counsel women about or provide referrals for abortion services. In 1998, for example, 17 states were enforcing three or more abortion restrictions, a 467% increase from 1992. Over half the states enacted some restriction on access to abortion in 1997. An anti-abortion bill introduced into a state legislature in 1997 was more than twice as likely to be enacted than in 1996. Efforts to ban "partial-birth" or "late-term" abortions dominated legislative debate at both the federal and state levels in 1997. This resulted in 16 states banning this rare procedure and the U.S. Congress passing a bill to ban it. The bill was not signed by President Clinton, because it contained no provision to protect the mother's health or life.

[There is also diminishing access to abortion providers because of increased harassment and violence by anti-abortion groups and a shortage of physicians trained and willing to provide abortion services. Between 1982 and 1992, the number of abortion providers nationwide decreased by 18%. Many residency programs have eliminated abortion instruction from the curriculum altogether or have relegated it to an elective course. Currently, there are no abortion providers in 84% of the counties in the United States. The American Medical Association has concluded that the shortage of abortion providers has "the potential to threaten the safety of induced abortion" (AMA 1992).

[Private insurance companies, often with the blessing of state legislatures, are cutting back on coverage for contraceptive services. Almost half—49%—of the typical large insurance plans exclude coverage for prescription contraception, although for women this often constitutes their major medication expenses. Illinois, North Dakota, and Texas have even enacted state legislation allowing healthcare institutions or insurers to refuse to provide or counsel patients for healthcare services that violate their "organizational conscience," including family planning, infertility services, vasectomy, female sterilization, and abortion procedures.

[These increasing obstacles to obtaining legal abortions demonstrate the successes of the anti-abortion groups, particularly in electing supporters into state and federal legislatures. It seems likely that the trend to erode access to abortion services will continue, at least in the short term. (*End of update by P. B. Koch*)]

*A Brief Legal History*   PATRICIA BARTHALOW KOCH

As documented by Brodie (1994), early American common law accepted abortion up until "quickening" (movement of the fetus). Not until the early 1800s did individual states begin to outlaw abortion at any stage of pregnancy. By 1880, most abortions were illegal in the United States, except those "necessary to save the life of the woman." However, since the right and practice of early abortion had already taken root in American society, abortionists openly continued to practice with public support and little legal enforcement. In the 1890s, doctors estimated that there were approximately two million abortions performed each year in the U.S. (Brodie 1994).

Before 1970, legal abortion was not available in the United States (Gordon 1976). In the 1950s, about one million illegal abortions were performed a year, with more than 1,000 women dying each year as a result. Three quarters of the women who died from abortions in 1969 were women of color. Middle- and upper-class women, often with difficulty and great expense, could get "therapeutic abortions" from private physicians. By 1966, four fifths of all abortions were estimated to be for married women, and the ratio of legal to illegal abortions was one to 110.

In 1970, New York State passed legislation that allowed abortion on demand through the 24th week if it was done in a medical facility by a physician. However, on January 22, 1973, the U.S. Supreme Court decided a landmark case on abortion—*Roe v. Wade*. The Court stated the "right of privacy . . . founded in the Fourteenth Amendment's concept of personal liberty . . . is broad enough to encompass a woman's decision whether or not to terminate her pregnancy" (Tribe 1992). The major points of this decision were:

1. An abortion decision and procedure must be left up to the pregnant woman and her physician during the first trimester of pregnancy.
2. In the second trimester, the state may choose to regulate the abortion procedure in order to promote its interest in the health of the pregnant woman.
3. Once viability occurs, the state may promote its interest in the potentiality of human life by regulating and even prohibiting abortion except when judged medically necessary for the preservation of the health or life of the pregnant woman.

Although induced abortion is the most commonly performed surgical procedure in the United States, various restrictions continue to be placed upon the accessibility of abortion for certain groups of women. For example, in 1976, the Hyde Amendment, implemented through the United States Congress, prohibited federal Medicaid funds from being used to pay for abortions for women with low incomes. This is believed to contribute to the fact that low-income women of color are more likely to have second-trimester abortions, rather than first-trimester ones, since it takes time for them to save enough money for the procedure.

In addition, the Supreme Court has upheld various state laws that have been instituted to restrict abortions. In 1989, a Missouri law prohibiting the use of "public facilities" and "public employees" from being used to perform or assist abortions not necessary to save the life of the pregnant woman was upheld (*Webster v. Reproductive Health Services*). The court also upheld one of the strictest parental notification laws in the country in 1990 (*Hodgson v. Minnesota*). This law required notification of both of a minor's parents before she could have an abortion, even if she had never lived with them. Along with this restriction came a "waiting period" provision. A court decision in *Rust v. Sullivan* (1991) upheld a "gag rule" that prohibited counselors and physicians in federally funded family-planning clinics from providing information and making referrals about abortion. In 1992, the court upheld many restrictions set forth in a Pennsylvania law (*Planned Parenthood v. Casey*). These restrictions included requiring physicians to provide women seeking abortions with pro-childbirth information, followed by a 24-hour "waiting period," and parental notification for minors (Tribe 1992).

Nineteen years after the *Roe* decision, the *Casey* decision demonstrated that the Supreme Court was divided more sharply than ever over abortion. While a minority of justices wanted to overturn the *Roe* decision outright, the majority did not allow a complete ban of abortion. However, by enacting the "undue burden" standard, they did lower the standard by which abortion laws are to be judged unconstitutional. This standard places the burden of proof on those challenging an abortion restriction to establish that it is a "substantial obstacle" to their constitutional rights.

The various state laws now restricting abortion are particularly burdensome for younger and poorer women, and open the way for the creation of increasing obstacles to women's access to abortion. Currently, only 13 states provide funding for poor women for abortions, and 35 states enforce parent-notification/consent laws for minors seeking abortions. At the same time, the Supreme Court has upheld the right to abortion in many cases.

The recent murders of physicians and staff at abortion clinics, arson and bombing of abortion clinics, and the blocking of abortion clinics by anti-abortion protesters have contributed to women's difficulty in receiving this still-legal medical procedure. Over 80% of all abortion providers have been picketed, and many have experienced other forms of harassment, including bomb threats, blockades, invasions of facilities, property destruction, assault of staff and patients, and death threats.

In 1988, Operation Rescue, the term adopted by anti-abortion groups, brought thousands of protesters to Atlanta to blockade the abortion clinics. Using an 1871 statute enacted to protect African-Americans from the Ku Klux Klan, the federal courts invoked injunctions against the protesters. However, in 1993, this decision was overturned, leading to Operation Rescue blockades of abortion clinics in ten more U.S. cities. The federal government moved to apply the Racketeer Influenced and Corrupt Organization (RICO) Act against such blockades on the grounds that it was a form of extortion and part of a nationwide conspiracy. This application of the RICO Act was upheld unanimously by the Supreme Court in 1994. Despite this protection, there has nevertheless been a serious decline in the number of facilities and physicians willing to perform abortions.

## Current Abortion Practice

PATRICIA BARTHALOW KOCH

Legally induced abortion has become the most commonly performed surgical procedure in the United States. In 1988, 6 million pregnancies and 1.5 million legal abortions were reported. One in five women (21%) of women of reproductive age have had an abortion (Hatcher et al. 1994). If current abortion rates continue, nearly half of all American women will have at least one abortion during their lifetime.

Women having abortions in the United States come from every background and walk of life (Koch 1995). Abortion rates are highest among 18- to 19-year-old women, with almost 60% being less than 25 years old. One in eight (12%) are minors, aged 17 or younger. Of these minors, over 98% are unmarried and in school or college, with fewer than one tenth having had any previous children.

The vast majority (80%) of adult women having abortions are separated, divorced, or never married, with 20% currently married. One third of American women seeking abortions are poor. Almost half are currently mothers, with most of them already having two or more children. Half of the women seeking abortions were using a form of birth control during the month in which they conceived. About one third of abortion clients are employed, one third attend public school or college, and the other third are unemployed. The majority of women (69%) getting abortions are Anglo-American. Latinas are 60% more likely than Anglos to terminate an unintended pregnancy, but are less likely to do so than are African-American women.

Women with a more-liberal religious or humanist commitment are four times more likely to get an abortion than those adhering to conservative religious beliefs, according to Alan Guttmacher Institute surveys in 1991 and 1996. Catholic women are just as likely as other women to get abortions. Catholic women, who constitute 31% of the female population, had 31% of the abortions in 1996. In 1991, one sixth of abortion clients in the U.S. were born-again or evangelical Christians (Alan Guttmacher Institute 1991). In a similar 1996 survey, evangelical or born-again Christians, who account for almost half the American population, had 18% of the abortions.

Women give multiple reasons for their decision to have an abortion, the most important reasons being financial inability to support the child and inability to handle all the responsibilities of parenting. Three quarters of abortion clients believe that having a baby would interfere with work, school, or their other family responsibilities. Over half are concerned about being single parents and believe that the relationship with the father will be ending soon. Adolescent women, in particular, usually believe that they are not mature enough to have a child. One fifth of the women seeking an abortion are concerned that either the fetus or they, themselves, have a serious health problem which necessitates an abortion. One in 100 abortion clients are rape or incest survivors. Most abortion clients (70%) want to have children in the future.

Half of the abortions in the U.S. are performed before the eighth week of gestation and five out of six are performed before the 13th week (Hatcher et al. 1994). The safest and easiest time for the procedure is within the first three months. Most (97%) women receiving abortions during this time have no complications or postabortion complaints. Vacuum curettage is the most widely used abortion procedure in the United States, accounting for 97% of abortions in 1989. Intra-amniotic infusion is the rarest form of abortion performed, accounting for only 1% of abortions in 1989.

The weight of research evidence indicates that legal abortion, particularly in the first trimester, does not create short or long-term physical or psychological risks for women, including impairment of future fertility (Russo & Zierk 1992). In 1985, the maternal death rate for legal abortions was 0.5 per 100,000 for suction methods, 4.0 for induced labor, and one in 10,000 for childbirth (Hatcher et al. 1994).

## Attitudes Toward Abortion

PATRICIA BARTHALOW KOCH

The National Opinion Research Center has been documenting attitudes toward abortion since 1972 (Smith 1996). Throughout this time period, public support for abortion under various circumstances has increased (see Table 19). The vast majority of Americans approve of abortion if a pregnancy seriously endangers the health of the mother, if the fetus has a serious defect, or if the pregnancy resulted from a rape or incest. Approximately half of the American public approves of abortion if the woman does not want to marry the father or if the parents cannot afford a child or do not want any more children. Close to half of Americans approve of abortion if the woman wants it for any reason. Level of education has the strongest effect on people's attitudes, with college-educated people being significantly more approving than those who are less educated. Catholics, fundamentalist Protestants, and Mormons who have a strong religious commitment are the most likely to disapprove of abortion. Anglo-Americans are somewhat more approving than African-Americans; men and adults under 30 are slightly more approving than women and adults over 65. In general, approval of legal abortion and the right of women to control their reproductive ability is associated with a broad commitment to basic civil liberties.

America is at a crossroads in terms of protecting the access of all women to abortion (Tribe 1992, 6). (See comments on efforts of the Christian Coalition to enact laws that restrict and limit access to abortion and abortion informa-

### Table 19

**Percentage of U.S.A. Adults Approving of Legal Abortion for Various Reasons (*Updated to 2000*)**

| Reason for Abortion | 1972 | 1980 | 1990 | 1994 | 1996 | 1998 | 2000 |
|---|---|---|---|---|---|---|---|
| Pregnancy poses serious health danger for woman | 86.9% | 90.1% | 91.8% | 90.6% | 91.6% | 87.9% | 88.5% |
| Strong chance of serious defect of fetus | 78.6 | 83.1 | 81.2 | 82.3 | 81.8 | 78.6 | 78.7 |
| Pregnancy resulted from rape | 79.1 | 83.4 | 84.8 | 83.6 | 84.3 | 80.1 | 80.6 |
| Parent(s) low income—cannot afford a child | 48.8 | 51.7 | 48.1 | 50.4 | 46.6 | 44.3 | 42.2 |
| Unmarried woman who does not want to marry father | 43.5 | 48.4 | 45.3 | 47.6 | 44.9 | 42.3 | 39.1 |
| Married woman who does not want more children | 39.7 | 47.1 | 45.1 | 48.3 | 46.7 | 42.3 | 40.7 |
| Woman wants an abortion for any reason | NA* | 41.1 | 43.4 | 46.3 | 45.0 | 40.9 | 39.9 |

*NA = Not asked

*Source*: *General Social Surveys*. Chicago: National Opinion Research Center (NORC).

tion in Section 2A, Religious, Ethnic, and Gender Factors Affecting Sexuality, Sources and Character of Religious Values). The era of absolute judicial protection of legal abortion rights that began with the Supreme Court's 1973 decision in *Roe v. Wade* ended with that Court's 1989 decision upholding certain state regulations of abortion in the case of *Webster v. Reproductive Health Services*. Thus, a woman's right to decide whether to terminate a pregnancy was placed in the arena of rough-and-tumble politics, subject to regulation, and possibly even prohibition, by federal and state elected representatives. The range of abortion rights that many Americans have taken for granted are now in jeopardy. Even as the public agenda is stretched to address such new questions as the right to die, the use of aborted fetal tissue in treating disease, and the ethics and legal consequences of reproductive technologies, no issue threatens to divide Americans politically in quite as powerful a way as the abortion issue still does.

[*Abortion Update 2003*          SUSAN DUDLEY
[*Update 2003*: Social conflict about abortion in the United States remains passionate on both sides, and is played out on several fronts: by both peaceful and violent demonstrators at public rallies and at abortion-clinic entrances, by politicians and their supporters in the state and federal legislatures, and by lawyers and advocates in the courts.

[The true motivation of anti-abortion activists who claim that their concern is protection of human life has been further questioned by correlational research that suggests that states with the most-restrictive laws and regulations on abortion tend to have fewer safeguards for maternal and infant health and safety than states where abortion laws are less restrictive (Schroedel 2000).

[When mainstream medical associations take a position on abortion, it is usually with the recognition that the provision of legal and medically safe abortion is a public health necessity that prevents the mortality and morbidity that invariably accompany illegal black-market abortion practices.

[Several of the more prominent advocacy organizations on both sides of the abortion debate have changed their names in recent years. The National Abortion Rights Action League (NARAL) became the National Abortion and Reproductive Rights Action League, and then more recently changed its name to NARAL Prochoice America. Operation Rescue also uses the name Operation Save America.

[The incidence of illegal and violent action taken by anti-abortion protestors has been high. Since 1977, the National Abortion Federation has documented at least 7 murders, 17 attempted murders, 353 death threats, 3 kidnappings, 41 bombings, 570 bomb threats, 166 arsons, 372 clinic invasions, 100 butyric acid attacks, receipt of 545 anthrax threat letters, 123 cases of assault and battery, 71 burglaries, 444 stalking incidents, and 686 clinic blockades.

[Enactment of the federal Freedom of Access to Clinic Entrances (FACE) Act in 1994 has helped to curb the incidence of illegal anti-abortion activities in recent years. This law forbids the use of "force, threat of force or physical obstruction" to prevent someone from providing or receiving reproductive health services. Nevertheless, 56% of clinics experienced anti-abortion harassment in 2000 (Henshaw & Finer 2001).

[The U.S. Supreme Court has issued several important rulings in response to challenges against laws passed to ban specific abortion procedures or to limit the availability of abortion in the U.S. For example, *Stenberg v Carhart* in 2000 resulted in overturning abortion-procedure bans that had been enacted in a number of states. In the same year, *Hill v Colorado* established that protestors coming closer

than eight feet from clinic patrons could be found guilty of harassment. In 2003, *Planned Parenthood v American Coalition of Life Advocates* asserted that protestors are not free to make threats against the life and safety of abortion providers or their patients.

[In 2003, 17 states provide some funding for poor women for abortion, and 32 states enforce parent-notification/consent laws for minors seeking abortions (Alan Guttmacher Institute 2003).

[In 2000, 1.31 million abortions took place in the U.S., and it remains one of the most common procedures. Mifepristone was approved for induction of medical abortion in the U.S. in 2000, and approximately 6% of women who had abortions that year opted for this method instead of surgical abortions (Finer & Henshaw 2003).

[Each year, 2 out of every 100 women of reproductive age have an abortion, and 48% of them have had at least one previous abortion (Alan Guttmacher Institute 2003). At the current rate, it is estimated that 43% of American women will have an abortion in their lifetimes.

[Fifty-two percent of U.S. women who get abortions each year are younger than 25. Teenagers account for 19% of all abortions, and women 20 to 24 account for the other 33% (Alan Guttmacher Institute 2003).

[Fifty-four percent of women having abortions report that they used a contraceptive method during the month they became pregnant, and 8% report that they have never used a birth-control method (Alan Guttmacher Institute 2003).

[Unintended pregnancies are more than 3 times as likely to be terminated by abortion by black women and 2½ times as likely by Hispanic women as by white women in America (Alan Guttmacher Institute 2003).

[Also in 2003, application of RICO (organized racketeering) statutes in the prosecution of illegal anti-abortion activities was limited in a ruling on *Scheidler v. National Organization for Women*. (*End of update by S. Dudley*)]

[*Update 2003*: In early February 2003, President Bush announced a commitment of $15 billion over the next five years to fight AIDS in the 15 African and Caribbean nations with the highest rates of AIDS infection. This allocation immediately raised the question of how distribution of the money could be managed without violating the so-called Mexico City policy barring American foreign aid to groups that consider abortion to be a valid family-planning option. One of the President's first acts in office in 2000 was to reinstate this ban, which was first imposed by President Ronald Reagan and later suspended by the Clinton administration.

[Faced with a clash between two goals—disseminating the AIDS money widely and holding to the anti-abortion position, the President adopted a compromise that would allow groups to receive the money to fight AIDS through the State Department's foreign assistance program as long as none of the money went to any family-planning activities that encourage or perform abortions.

[The policy would allow an organization that conducted family-planning activities that included abortion in one country to qualify for the AIDS money in another country. It would prohibit sending the money to an organization that ran integrated health clinics that included both AIDS treatment and abortion or abortion counseling, but would allow it if the AIDS treatment program and the family-planning activities were conducted and financed completely separately.

[Some groups that work on health and family-planning issues in poor countries said the administration's policy was likely to prove too restrictive by forcing them to choose between providing a full range of health services, including family planning, and taking the AIDS treatment money from the United States. (*End of update by R. T. Francoeur*)]

[*Update 2003*: The first indication of the social and medical impact of the legalization of mifepristone (RU-486) came in mid-January 2003 from an Alan Guttmacher Institute report. In a survey of American women ages 15 to 44 in the first six months of 2001, Finer and Henshaw reported that the U.S. abortion rate was continuing to decline and had reached its lowest point since the 1970s, 21.3 abortions per 1,000 women ages 15 to 44. The number of providers also declined in the first half of 2001. However, physicians used mifepristone to perform more than 37,000 nonsurgical abortions, about 6% of all abortions induced in the first six months after the controversial drug became available to American women. (*End of update by R. T. Francoeur*)]

## [E. Other Reproductive and Sexual Health Issues

[*Infertility and Assisted Pregnancy*

ROBERT T. FRANCOEUR

[*Update 1998*: America's romance with assisted reproductive technology began a hundred years ago when J. Marion Sims made 55 attempts at "ethereal copulation," as artificial insemination with donor semen (AID) was then known. His success rate at Jefferson Medical School in Philadelphia was only 4%, because insemination was performed just before or after menstruation, which was wrongly believed at the time to be a woman's most fertile period. In 1960, Bunge and Sherman experimented with artificial insemination using frozen donor semen at the State University of Iowa, whereas Behrman and associates at the University of Michigan reported 29 successful pregnancies using frozen semen. By 1974, America had 28 private and public sperm banks, with approximately 20,000 pregnancies a year from artificial insemination, double the mid-1960s' rate (Francoeur 1977).

[In 1981, reproductive specialists at Eastern Virginia Medical Center produced American's first *in-vitro* fertilized (IVF) baby, three years after the world's first IVF baby in Cambridge, England. Some American feminists organized a Feminist International Network on the Reproductive Technologies to protest "female slavery and exploitation by male infertility specialists and patriarchal husbands" (Ardetti, Klein, & Minder 1984).

[Other forms of assisted reproductive technology have followed, including embryo transplants, surrogate motherhood, embryo lavage for harvesting ova from donors, epididymal aspiration of sperm, and microinsemination of ova with single sperm. Social complications quickly followed. The court fight of Mary Beth Whitehead, a New Jersey surrogate mother, to retain custody of "Baby M," whom she had contracted to carry for an infertile couple, made national news. In the aftermath, several states outlawed surrogate-mother contracts and prohibited payment. In 1990, when a divorcing couple fought over custody of seven frozen embryos remaining from fertility treatments, the court declared the frozen embryos "human life from the moment of conception," and awarded custody to the mother (Holmes, Hoskins, & Gross 1981; Corea 1985). The 1990s have witnessed a flood of new technologies, including insertion of sperm and zygotes into the fallopian tube (GIFT and ZIFT), postmenopausal pregnancies, and frozen eggs.

[Three major psychological, social, and ethical controversies have emerged from these technologies. The first involves "designer and discount designer embryos." Several American infertility clinics now offer infertile couples the option of paying $20,000 or more to select donor sperm and egg from a select list of designer donors. After IVF, several designer zygotes are implanted in the adoptive woman's uterus. If any embryos are left in cryogenic storage after a successful pregnancy, they may be sold at a discount to other infertile couples.

[The high risk of multiple births is a second issue. England, Australia, and most European countries have laws prohibiting transfer of more than two or three embryos in each pregnancy attempt. These clinics have a success rate about 20% lower than American clinics, which are not subject to any limit on the number of embryos they transfer. American clinics typically transfer four or five embryos per attempt, but some clinics transfer as many as ten. The result is a high risk of multiple pregnancies that are themselves dangerous to both mother and offspring. In a survey of 281 American infertility clinics in 1995, 37% of all births were multiple births, contrasted with 2% in the general population. Woman under age 35 experienced a 17% pregnancy rate and a 3% multiple-pregnancy risk when two embryos were transferred. Transfer of four embryos gave a 34% pregnancy rate, but a multiple-pregnancy risk of 15%. Transferring more than four embryos does not improve the fertility rate, but it does increase the multiple births. In 1997, infertility treatment resulted in the survival of the McCaughey septuplets, the world's second set of surviving septuplets, the first being in Saudi Arabia.

[Some clinics transfer multiple embryos in the hope of raising their fertility rate, in order to attract more clients. A clinic that reduces the risk of multiple pregnancy faces a lower fertility rate and may not survive in the competition for clients. The present practice is not pleasant for infertile couples who have to decide whether to let a multiple pregnancy go to full term and risk losing all or some of the offspring, or to resort to "selective reduction," which aborts several of the multiple embryos early in pregnancy. Selective reduction improves the survival of the one or two remaining embryos, but it may also trigger a miscarriage of all the embryos.

[Finally, there is the issue of payment for donor eggs. When egg donation was first introduced, donors were paid a few hundred dollars. More recently, the standard fee has been $2,500. In early 1998, a major New Jersey hospital offered donors $5,000, because their clients were being forced to wait up to a year for an egg. The shortage of donor eggs has brought private egg brokers into the market, with some brokers offering $35,000 for a suitable donor. (*End of update by R. T. Francoeur*)]

## 10. Sexually Transmitted Diseases and HIV/AIDS

## A. Sexually Transmitted Diseases

ROBERT T. FRANCOEUR

It is impossible to obtain reliable statistics about the incidence of STDs, because American physicians are only required by law to report cases of HIV and syphilis to the Centers for Disease Control and Prevention (CDC). Public clinics keep fairly reliable statistics, but many private physicians record syphilis and other STDs as urinary infections and do not report them to the CDC. A second, equally important factor leading to the lack of data is the number of persons infected with various STDs who are without symptoms and do not know they are infectious. This "silent epidemic" includes most males infected with candidiasis, 10% of males and 60 to 80% of females infected with chlamydia, 5 to 20% of males and up to 80% of females with gonorrhea, and many males and females with hemophilus, NGU, and trichomonas infections.

In 1995, the nation's three most commonly reported infections were sexually transmitted, according to statistics from the federal Centers for Disease Control and Prevention released in October 1996. Chlamydia, tracked for the first time in 1995, topped the list with 477,638 cases. Gonorrhea, the most commonly reported infectious disease in 1994 with 418,068 cases dropped to second in 1995 with 392,848 cases. AIDS dropped from second place in 1994 (78,279 cases) to third place in 1995 (71,547 cases). In 1995, five sexually transmitted diseases, chlamydia, gonorrhea, AIDS, syphilis, and hepatitis B, accounted for 87% of the total number of infectious cases caused by the top ten maladies. Chlamydia was more commonly reported among women, striking 383,956 in 1995; gonorrhea and AIDS were more common with men, with 203,563 and 58,007 cases, respectively.

The latest data suggest that the national incidence of gonorrhea and syphilis has continued to decline (U.S. Department of Health and Human Services 1994). Reported cases of gonorrhea peaked at a million cases in 1978 and declined to about 700,000 cases in 1990. With a realistic estimate suggesting two million new cases annually, gonorrhea is one of the most commonly encountered STDs, especially among the young. About 50,000 new cases of syphilis are reported annually; an estimated 125,000 new cases occur annually. Syphilis is primarily an adult disease, mostly concentrated in larger cities, and one of the least common STDs. The incidence of syphilis rose sharply between the late 1980s and the early 1990s, and then continued its more long-term decline. Congenital syphilis rates have decreased in parallel to declining rates of syphilis among women. Infants most at risk were born to unmarried, African-American women who receive little or no prenatal care. Syphilis and gonorrhea have consistently been more common in the southern states. Reasons for this are not well understood, but may include differences in racial and ethnic distribution of the population, poverty, and the availability and quality of healthcare services.

Chlamydia is the most prevalent bacterial STD in the United States, with four million adults and possibly 10% of all college students infected. It is more common in higher socioeconomic groups and among university students. Prevention and control programs were begun in 1994, and are a high priority because of the potential impact on pelvic inflammatory disease (PID) and its sequelae, infertility and ectopic pregnancy. Twenty to 40% of women infected with chlamydia develop PID. Many states have implemented reporting procedures and begun collecting case data for chlamydia.

Three million new cases of trichomonas are reported annually, but probably another six million harbor the protozoan without symptoms. Fifteen million Americans have had at least one bout of genital herpes. About a million new cases of genital warts are reported annually.

STD rates continue to be much higher for African-Americans and other minorities than for white Americans, sixtyfold higher for blacks and fivefold higher for Latinos. About 81% of the total reported cases of gonorrhea occur among African-Americans, with the risk for 15- to 19-year-old blacks more than twentyfold higher than for white adolescents. Similarly, the general gonorrhea rate is fortyfold higher for blacks and threefold higher for Latinos than it is for white Americans. There are no known biologic reasons to explain these differences. Rather, race and ethnicity in the United States are risk markers that correlate with poverty, access to quality healthcare, healthcare-seeking behavior, illicit drug use, and living in communities with a high prevalence of STDs.

[*Recent Developments* PATRICIA BARTHALOW KOCH
[*Update 1998*: In 1997, a Committee on Prevention and Control of Sexually Transmitted Diseases issued an important analysis of the epidemiology of STDs (except for HIV) and effectiveness of public health strategies to prevent and control them in the United States (Eng & Butler 1997).

[The Committee, sponsored by the Institute of Medicine, an adviser to the federal government, concluded that STDs are hidden epidemics of enormous health and economic consequence in the United States. The incidence rates of curable STDs in the United States are the highest in the developed world, with rates that are 50 to 100 times higher than other industrialized nations. For example, the reported incidence of gonorrhea in 1995 was 150 cases per 100,000 persons in the United States versus three cases per 100,000 in Sweden. STDs continue to have a disproportionate impact on women, infants, young people, and racial/ethnic minorities. The estimated overall costs from STDs in the United States was nearly $17 billion in 1994.

[Updates concerning the epidemiology and consequences of STDs in the United States are provided by the Centers for Disease Control and Prevention (CDC 1998). Chlamydia (an estimated 4,000,000 new cases each year) and gonorrhea (800,000 new cases each year) are a major cause of pelvic inflammatory disease (PID). Among American women with PID, 20% will become infertile, and 9% will have an ectopic pregnancy, which is the leading cause of first-trimester pregnancy-related deaths in American women. The ectopic pregnancy rate could be reduced by as much as 50% with early detection and treatment of STDs. In addition, fetal or neonatal death occurs in up to 40% of pregnant women who have untreated syphilis. There are an estimated 101,000 new cases of syphilis each year, with 3,400 infants born with congenital syphilis.

[Genital herpes may now be the most common STD in the United States, with perhaps more than 45 million Americans, including 18% of whites and 46% of blacks, carrying the herpes virus. Despite an emphasis on safe sex to prevent HIV/AIDS, the Centers for Disease Control reported that genital herpes had increased fivefold since the late 1970s among white teenagers and doubled among whites in their 20s. In all, about one in five Americans is infected with genital herpes. There are an estimated 200,000 to 500,000 new symptomatic cases each year. In addition, it is likely that more than 24 million Americans are infected with human papilloma virus (HPV), with an estimated 500,000 to a million new infections each year. Sexually transmitted HPV is the most important risk factor for cervical cancer, which was responsible for about 5,000 deaths in 1995.

[To deal with this silent epidemic in the United States, the Institute of Medicine Committee made a strong advocacy statement in support of establishing an effective national system for STD prevention. To accomplish this, four major strategies were recommended for implementation by public- and private-sector policymakers at the local, state, and national levels:

1. Overcome barriers to adoption of healthy sexual behaviors, particularly through a nationally organized mass-media campaign;
2. Develop strong leadership, strengthen investment, and improve information systems for STD prevention;
3. Design and implement essential STD-related services in innovative ways for adolescents and underserved populations; and
4. Ensure access to and quality of essential clinical services for STDs.

[The report concluded that the veil of enforced secrecy about sexual health must be lifted, public awareness raised, and bold national leadership must come from the highest levels in order to overcome the public health shame of STD epidemics. However, it is unlikely that these recommendations will be put into action, and Americans will needlessly continue to suffer the physical, emotional, social, and financial consequences of these preventable diseases. (*End of update by P. B. Koch*)]

[*Update 2002*: For the first time in over a decade, the Centers for Disease Control reported an increase in cases of syphilis, largely because of outbreaks among gay and bisexual men in several U.S. cities. After dropping every year since 1990, the syphilis rate increased from 2.1 cases per 100,000 people in 2000 to 2.2 cases per 100,000 in 2001. Syphilis among women actually dropped 17.6% in 2001. More than two thirds of the new syphilis patients were men. Between 1997 and 2001, syphilis outbreaks erupted in New York City, Seattle, Chicago, San Francisco, and Miami, with a major contribution from men having sex with men (Yee 2002). (*End of update by R. T. Francoeur*)]

[*Status as of 2003*          KAREN ALLYN GORDON

[*Update 2003*: While obtaining accurate and current data on sexually transmitted diseases (STD) and sexually transmitted infections (STI) in the United States is difficult, the availability of public health data has greatly improved over the last decade because of changes in case identification, expanded reporting, surveillance systems, and epidemiological investigations. For some diseases, such as chlamydia, increased cases may be attributed to increased screening efforts and better identification through use of more-sensitive screening tests. Underestimating and reporting of STDs may also be influenced by reluctance to seek treatment in a public clinic, lack of reporting from private practitioners, access to quality services, fear of discrimination, cost, stigma, and stresses of daily life. Much remains to be investigated beyond clinical concerns in terms of the social level of infection and disease patterns in geographic regions and population subgroups as identified by age, race, ethnicity, socioeconomic level, and sexual-practice patterns.

[More is known about the trends of some STDs because of long-term surveillance. Over a 40-year period, 1950 to 2000, data are available on syphilis, gonorrhea, and chancroid through reporting by state health departments. Hepatitis B was added as of 1970 and chlamydia as of 1990. As of 2000, all 50 states and the District of Columbia require reporting of chlamydia cases to the Centers for Disease Control and Prevention (CDC).

[For nationally notifiable diseases for 2002, virus-based conditions include human immunodeficiency virus (HIV infection), acquired immunodeficiency syndrome (AIDS), and hepatitis B, while bacterial conditions include gonorrhea, chlamydia, and syphilis.

[In all, about 25 diseases or infections occur from or are associated with sexual intercourse, for which only estimated data on incidence and prevalence are available on herpes, human papilloma virus (HPV), trichomoniasis, and bacterial vaginosis. The rates for notifiable STDs for 2000 exceed the national health objectives proposed in *Healthy People 2010*.

[Among the most common STDs in the United States, trends show a decline in cases of gonorrhea from 445.10 per 100,00 in 1980 to 128.3 per 100,00 in 2001, as well as syphilis from 20.34 of primary and secondary cases per 100,00 in 1990 to 2.1 cases of primary and secondary cases in 2001. Outbreaks in certain geographic areas and among men who have sex with men, for example, reflect the persistence of the disease and difficulty in eradication (Fox et al. 2001). During 2001, a 2% increase (2.17 cases per 100,000) reflected a 15.4% increase among men, but a 17.7% decrease among women, across all ethnic and racial groups. Rates are disproportionately high in certain cities or geographic regions such as the South. Chancroid reflected a decline from 0.3 cases per 100,000 in 1980 to 0.01 cases per 100,000 in 2001.

[By comparison, *Chlamydia trachomatis* (a notifiable disease in 1995) increased from 190.42 cases per 100,000 in 1990 to 278.3 cases per 100,000 in 2001. Regional data suggest that declines in prevalence of chlamydia may be related to increased use of screening programs through family planning clinics.

[In 2000, rates of chlamydia and gonorrhea were higher for female 15- to 19-year-olds and in male 20- to 24-year-olds. In 2001, the rate for females was 435.19 cases per 100,000. Disproportionately higher rates of chlamydia occurred among blacks and American Indian and Alaskan Natives, showing a similar pattern for gonorrhea and syphilis, both primary and secondary.

[Estimates of human papilloma virus prevalence suggest that up to 20 million people are infected, with the prevalence of HPV-16 being at least twice as high among women as among men. Based on data from the *National Health and Examination Survey* (*NHANES*) of 1999, estimated prevalence of herpes in the general U.S. population ages 14 to 49 was 19%, suggesting an increase in prevalence among teens over the last two decades.

[Consequences of STDs place women at risk for more-serious medical complications. Pelvic inflammatory disease (PID) is a serious consequence associated with gonorrhea and chlamydia, which can lead to infertility, chronic pelvic pain, and ectopic pregnancy. The consequences of reactivation or reinfection of certain types of HPV, with its increased risk for dysplasia and cervical cancer in women, make this an especially serious STD. Herpes, hepatitis B, and HIV infection can be passed from an infected woman to a fetus or infant.

[In the United States, state and federally funded programs for reporting, control, and prevention underscore the need for heightened awareness of the magnitude of epidemics associated with sexual activity. Despite the decline of STDs such as syphilis, the patterns of increase of HIV in selected subpopulations and viral STDs, such as genital herpes and HPV across all socioeconomic levels and among teens, call for new behavioral surveillance and relevant interventions related to sexual practices and relationships (Cates et al. 1999; CDC 2000, 2001, 2002, 2003; Gross 2003; National Center for Health Statistics 2002). (*End of update by K. A. Gordon*)]

[*Human Papilloma Virus and Cervical Cancer*

PEGGY CLARKE

[*Update 2003*: Worldwide, cervical cancer is the second most common cancer in women. In the United States, cervical cancer accounts for over 12,000 new cases and over 4,400 deaths each year. Detected early, this cancer is preventable in virtually all cases. In recent years, the direct link between cervical cancer and human papilloma virus (HPV), which is a sexually acquired infection, has been confirmed.

[There are over 70 different strains of HPV, only a small number of which are linked to cervical cancer. Other strains, of significantly lower health risk and non-cancer causing, can appear as visible genital warts. As many as 20 million Americans may be infected with one or several strains of HPV, some of which pass out of the body undetected. Most HPV infections are transient and the majority of those infected are unaware of the infection and shed the virus with no ill effects. In most cases, the HPV virus is harmless and carries no symptoms; however, an HPV infection that causes changes in the cervical cells can, if left untreated, lead to cervical cancer.

[While anyone who has ever been sexually active may have acquired an HPV infection, only rare cases will lead to cervical cancer. However, cervical cancer is fully preventable, if early pre-cancerous cells can be detected and treated early. The PAP test detects changes in the cervix, showing that a person may be at risk for cervical cancer. This test involves collecting a small sample of cells from the cervix, with subsequent examination under a microscope for the presence of abnormal cells.

[In addition to the PAP test, there now exists a test to detect the presence of specific cancer-related types of HPV. This test is performed by collecting cells from the cervix and is then sent to a lab for evaluation. Testing for HPV infection, in combination with a PAP test, has been approved for routine screening of women who are 30 years and older. (The combination test is called DNA with PAP test.) A negative test result means the patient has little or no risk of having cervical cancer, providing added confidence in the screening for infection. A positive test result indicates the presence of cancer-related HPV. A positive HPV test result with a normal PAP result does not mean the patient has or will develop cervical cancer; however, following screening guidelines, the positive result indicates the need for close medical monitoring. (*End of update by P. Clarke*)]

## B. HIV/AIDS

*A National Perspective, 1997*  ANDREW D. FORSYTH

In a single decade, human immunodeficiency virus (HIV), the agent that causes acquired immunodeficiency syndrome (AIDS), has become one of the greatest threats to public health in the United States. By 1992, AIDS surpassed heart disease, cancer, suicide, and homicide to become the leading cause of death among men between ages 25 and 54 (CDC 1993a). Similarly, AIDS became the fourth leading cause of death among women between ages 25 to 44 in 1992 and the eighth leading cause of death among all United States citizens. Over one million people are estimated to be infected with HIV in the United States—approximately 1 in 250—and over 441,528 cases of AIDS have been diagnosed, 62% of which have already resulted in death (CDC 1994a).

Trends suggest that AIDS will continue to have a significant impact in the United States in coming years. Throughout the 1980s and early 1990s, there was a steady increase in the number of documented AIDS cases. However, between 1993 and 1994, the number of AIDS cases reported to public health departments nationwide dramatically increased because of the implementation of an expanded surveillance definition of AIDS, which included cases of severe immunosuppression manifesting in earlier stages of HIV infection. Although the number of AIDS cases declined in 1994 relative to the previous year, it still represents a considerable increase over cases reported in 1992 (CDC 1995a).

Consistent with previous years, the most severely affected segment of the U.S. population in 1994 was men who have sex with men. Although men constitute 82% of all AIDS cases reported among adults and adolescents (13 years or older), men who have sex with men represent the single largest at-risk group, constituting 44% of all nonpediatric AIDS cases (CDC 1994a). Young men who have sex with men (between ages 20 and 24) constitute a particularly salient at-risk group for HIV infection, representing 60% of AIDS cases among all men of that same age. In contrast, 53% of all men with AIDS occur in men who have sex with men.

Even so, the number of AIDS cases reported among men who have sex with men decreased by 1.1% for the second consecutive year in 1992, suggesting that infection rates among this segment of the population may be leveling off (CDC 1993a). The same cannot be said for heterosexual men who inject drugs and men who inject drugs and have sex with men; they represent the second and third largest at-risk groups among men, explaining 24% and 6% of AIDS cases, respectively (CDC 1994b). Newly reported AIDS cases for these groups continue to increase sharply. Although only 4% of all men diagnosed with AIDS by 1994 were infected via sexual contact with an infected woman, they had the largest proportionate increase in AIDS cases among all men in recent years (CDC 1994a).

The proportion of AIDS cases reported among women has more than doubled since the mid-1980s (CDC 1994b). In 1994, 58,448 cumulative cases of AIDS were documented among women, comprising 13% of all adults and adolescents (13 years or older) diagnosed with AIDS in the United States (CDC 1994a). Although they represent a minority of all AIDS cases, the incidence of AIDS among women has increased more rapidly than have rates for men, with over 24% of all cases of AIDS among women reported in the last year alone (CDC 1994b). The impact of the CDC's implementation of the expanded case definition for AIDS is particularly salient for incidence rates among women: In 1994, 59% of cases of women with AIDS were reported based on the revised surveillance definitions. Correspondingly, the incidence of AIDS opportunistic illness (AIDS-OI) has increased more rapidly among women than it has for men. Overall, the modes of HIV transmission for women also differ considerably from those for men: Women are most likely to be infected via intravenous drug use (41%) or sex with infected men (38%). Although 19% of women with AIDS reported no risk of exposure to HIV, follow-up data from local public health departments suggested an inverse trend. Most of those with previously unidentified risk exposure were infected via heterosexual contact (66%) or intravenous drug use (27%) (CDC 1994b).

Because women of childbearing age (i.e., 15 to 44 years old) represent 84% of AIDS cases among women, perinatal transmission of HIV presents itself as a serious problem (CDC 1994b). In comparison with the statistics for HIV transmission for all women cited above, the most frequently reported modes of HIV transmission for seropositive new mothers were by heterosexual contact with infected male partners (36%) and injection drug use (30%) (CDC 1994a). However, it is often impossible to separate these two avenues of infection, because women may be having sex with of an infected male while also using IV drugs, both before and during pregnancy. According to recent trends, approximately 7,000 HIV-infected women gave birth to infants in the United States in 1993; about 30% of these infants may have contracted HIV perinatally (Gwinn et al. 1991). In 1994, 1,017 cases of AIDS were documented among children less than 13 years of age, an increase of 8% from 1993. In 92% of these cases, children contracted HIV perinatally (CDC 1994a). Demographically, there were no apparent differences in perinatal transmission rates between boys and girls; however, most newly reported cases of pediatric AIDS occurred among African-American (62%) and Hispanic (23%) children (CDC 1995a). By December 1994, a cumulative total of 6,209 AIDS cases were documented among children 13 years or younger (CDC 1994a).

In any discussion of incidence, etiology, and the avenues of infection for HIV/AIDS, the official CDC statistics are quite misleading, especially when comparing figures for different years. The clinical definition of the AIDS syndrome has been expanded several times, making the incidence seem comparatively lower in earlier years. In addition, the CDC has not been consistent in studying modes of infection, especially for women. The intake interview questions asked of men and women seeking HIV testing have changed significantly over the years; they also differ significantly for men and women, with several possible avenues of infection left out in the questions for women. In the 1980s, being born in a developing country could be listed as an avenue for men and women testing HIV-positive; women, but not men, were asked if they had had sex with a person from a developing nation. Also, the criteria for assignment to the "unidentified risk" category has changed back and forth, which in turn raises or lowers the number of infected individuals in other categories.

Clearly, adolescents and young adults are at-risk for HIV infection as well, although modes of transmission for them vary considerably. In 1994, there was a cumulative total of 1,965 cases of AIDS among adolescents between ages 13 and 19 years (CDC 1994a). For this age group, males represented 66% of AIDS cases and most frequently contracted HIV through receipt of infected blood products (44%), through sex with men (32%), or through injection drug use (7%). In contrast, females between the ages of 13 and 19 most frequently contracted HIV through sexual contact with infected men (52%) or injection drug use (18%); 22% of these young women failed to identify an exposure category. For young adults between the ages of 20 and 24, men represented 77% of AIDS cases, most of whom contracted HIV through sex with men (63%), injection drug use (13%), or sex with men and injection drug use (11%). Young women in this group were most likely to be infected with HIV through sexual contact with infected men (50%) or injection drug use (33%). Another 14% of women in this age group failed to identify an exposure category, although it is possible that the most frequent mode of transmission for them and their younger peers parallels that of older women who initially failed to report an exposure category, most of whom were infected via sexual contact with infected men (CDC 1994a).

The impact of the AIDS epidemic has been especially devastating in communities of color in the United States, largely because of a number of socioeconomic factors that disproportionately affect racial and ethnic minorities (CDC 1993b). Although they represent only 21% of the population, racial and ethnic minorities presently constitute 47% of cumulative AIDS cases among adult and adolescent men, 76% of cases among adult and adolescent women, and 81% of all pediatric AIDS cases (CDC 1994a). In 1994, African-Americans and Hispanics alone represented 58% of the 80,691 reported AIDS cases for that year, and they had the highest rates of infection per 100,000 people (100.8 and 51.0, respectively). In contrast, Asian/Pacific Islanders and American Indians/Alaska Natives comprised 577 (0.007%) and 227 (0.003%) of AIDS cases, respectively, reported in 1994 and had the lowest rates of infection per 100,000 people (6.4 and 12.0%, respectively). Whites comprised 33,193 (41%) of AIDS cases reported in 1994 and had the third highest infection rate per 100,000 people (17.2%).

The disproportionate effects of AIDS on racial minorities in the U.S. are most salient among women and children. In 1994, infection rates among African-American and Hispanic adult and adolescent women (i.e., 13 years and older) were 16.5 and 6.8 times higher than were rates for white women of the same ages, respectively (CDC 1994a). Likewise, infection rates among African-American and Hispanic children (i.e., less than 13 years old) were 21 and 7.5 times higher than were rates for white children, respectively. Although racial and ethnic status do not themselves confer risk for HIV/AIDS, a number of sociocultural factors

inherent to many communities of color increase the risk of HIV infection, including chronic underemployment, poverty, lack of access to health-education services, and inadequate healthcare (CDC 1993b).

Clearly, AIDS has quickly emerged as a leading threat to public health facing United States citizens. Although there appear to be trends indicating that the impact of AIDS is leveling off in some risk groups (e.g., men who have sex with men), it is increasing steadily in others (e.g., African-American and Hispanic women and children). Furthermore, it is possible that additional segments of the population are currently "at risk" for HIV infection, including the severely mentally ill, older adults, and women who have sex with women. AIDS cases among them may constitute a third wave in the AIDS epidemic.

Because there is no cure for AIDS, behavioral change that reduces risk of exposure to HIV (e.g., unprotected sex and sharing of needles while injecting drugs) is paramount. Interventions focusing on AIDS education, self-protective behavioral change, and utilization of existing medical and testing services together represent the most promising course of action in the prevention of HIV infection and AIDS in the United States.

The clinical definition of AIDS has been revised twice by the Centers for Disease Control, first in 1987 and then in 1993, when new female symptoms for invasive cervical (stage 4) and other disease were added, along with a revision in the T4 (helper) cell count. These redefinitions need to be considered when interpreting statistics on the rates of AIDS infection.

Confidential testing for HIV status is available nationwide, with a free or sliding-scale fee and counselors available to assist in informing partners of HIV-positive persons. Several states have won the right to test all prospective employees for HIV and share this information with related agencies. The American Civil Liberties Union has won a court decision denying mandatory testing. Legal and ethical challenges posed by HIV/AIDS are far-reaching, and it may be another decade before consistent, reasonable, and effective guidelines emerge.

Although African-Americans constitute 12% of the population, they represent 27% of the reported AIDS cases (CDC 1992), these infections being more because of heterosexual intercourse and IV-drug use than to gay and bisexual men. Hispanics are also overrepresented, with 16% of reported cases. Consequently, there is an urgent need for development of the education and prevention programs in the African-American and Latino communities.

College students pose a particular problem. Changes in college-student behaviors between 1982 and 1988 were not encouraging. In a comparison of student behavior among 363 unmarried students in 1982 (when the term AIDS was coined and few articles were published on the subject) and 273 students in 1988, the number of students having intercourse, the number of partners, and the lifetime incidence of intercourse all increased. In 1988, 72% of men and 83% of women had received oral sex, and 69% of males and 76% of females had given oral sex; 14 and 17%, respectively, had engaged in anal sex. Twenty percent of males and 12% of females in 1988 had four or more partners. Students with multiple or casual partners were less likely to use condoms; there also was no increase in condom use from the first to the most recent intercourse (Bishop & Lipsitz 1991).

Despite the need and proven effectiveness of sterile needle-exchange programs for IV-drug users and the free distribution of condoms in high schools, both programs have met considerable opposition from conservative groups and the religious right. At the same time, the need for safer-sex education for all segments of the population has allowed educators to make considerable progress in general sexuality education that might not have been possible if AIDS did not pose such a major public health problem.

## [*Emerging Trends Prior to 2000*

PATRICIA BARTHALOW KOCH

[*Update 1998*: A major development in the course of the AIDS epidemic in the United States was heralded in 1996. For the first time, there was a marked decrease in deaths among people with AIDS (PWAs)—12% less during the first two quarters of 1996 as compared to 1995 (CDC 1996). This decline in deaths is likely because of two factors:

1. The slowing of the epidemic overall, in part because of the effectiveness of prevention efforts, with an increase in people diagnosed with AIDS of only 2% in 1995; and
2. Improved treatments, including the use of protease inhibitors, which lengthen the lifespan of PWAs.

[Yet, it must be noted that AIDS deaths are not declining among all groups. For example, deaths declined among men by 15% but increased among women by 3%. Deaths declined among men who have sex with men by 18%, among injecting-drug users by 6%, but increased among people contracting AIDS through heterosexual contact by 3%. The death rate is also not decreasing equally among various racial/ethnic groups. Declines were greater among whites (21%) than among Hispanics (10%) or blacks (2%).

[The cumulative number of AIDS cases reported to the CDC through June 30, 1997, was 612,078. Adult and adolescent cases totaled 604,176, with 511,934 (85%) cases in males and 92,242 (15%) cases in females. An additional 7,902 cases were reported in children under age 13. Racial/ethnic minorities continued to be disproportionately affected by AIDS, as illustrated by the breakdown of AIDS cases by race/ethnicity: white, not Hispanic—279,072 (46%); black, not Hispanic—216,980 (36%); Hispanic—109,252 (18%); Asian/Pacific Islander—4,370 (7%); American Indian/Alaskan Native—1,677 (3%).

[With the increasing number of people living with HIV and AIDS, additional resources will be needed for services, treatment, and care. A major breakthrough in the treatment of HIV disease has been the use of "drug cocktail" therapy, which combines the use of multiple drugs, usually a protease inhibitor with one or two reverse transcriptase inhibitors. Research has shown that this combination-drug therapy can dramatically prolong survival and slow disease progression in people with advanced AIDS, as well as holding the virus for many months below minimum detectable blood levels (Smart 1996). In fact, AIDS deaths in the United States declined 44% between 1996 and 1997. As of mid-1998, the long-term effectiveness of these treatments is unknown, with concern over the development of resistance leading to more virulent strains of HIV. Also, the expense of these drugs (approximately $20,000 or more per year) prohibits large segments of HIV-infected people, often from minority groups, from receiving treatment. Prevention efforts must still be emphasized, since they remain the best and most cost-effective strategies for containing HIV and saving lives. (*End of update by P. B. Koch*)]

[*Update 2002*: UNAIDS Epidemiological Assessment: The current status of the epidemic and recent trends in the U.S. include the following:

• Women account for an increasing proportion of people with HIV and AIDS, but men still account for the largest proportion.

• Racial/ethnic disparities among people with HIV and AIDS continue to increase. Among men with AIDS recently diagnosed, 62% were non-Hispanic black or Hispanic; among women, 81% were non-Hispanic black or Hispanic.

• The impact of HIV among adolescents and young adults (ages 13 to 24 years) is not apparent from AIDS case surveillance data alone. In 25 states with HIV reporting, adolescents and young adults accounted for 13% of recent HIV diagnoses compared with 3% of AIDS diagnoses. HIV surveillance data suggest steady HIV transmission among people in this age group.

• HIV surveillance data indicate an epidemic with higher proportions of women, blacks, and heterosexually acquired infections than indicated by AIDS case data alone.

• Male-to-male sexual contact, still the predominant mode of HIV exposure, accounted for 41% of all recent AIDS diagnoses, and 54% of cases recently diagnosed among men.

• The proportion of AIDS cases attributed to heterosexual contact has continued to increase, and accounted for 22% of recently diagnosed cases (11% of cases among men, and 59% of cases among women).

• Injection drug use accounted for 30% of all recently diagnosed AIDS cases (27% of cases among men, and 38% of cases among women).

• Perinatally acquired AIDS has declined significantly, primarily because of the use of zidovudine to prevent HIV transmission.

• Regional trends: In all regions of the United States, most AIDS cases, cumulative and recent, have been diagnosed among persons from larger metropolitan areas. In each region, rates (cases reported per 100,000 population) were highest in the large metropolitan areas, intermediate in smaller metropolitan areas, and lowest in rural areas. Large metropolitan-area rates were highest in the Northeast; smaller metropolitan-area rates were highest in the Northeast and South; and rural-area rates were highest in the South.

[The estimated number of adults and children living with HIV/AIDS on January 1, 2002, were:

| | |
|---|---|
| Adults ages 15-49: | 890,000 (rate: 0.6%) |
| Women ages 15-49: | 180,000 |
| Children ages 0-15: | 10,000 |

[An estimated 15,000 adults and children died of AIDS during 2001.

[No estimate is available for the number of American children who had lost one or both parents to AIDS and were under age 15 at the end of 2001. (*End of update by the Editors*)]

## [*A 2003 HIV/AIDS Update*    ROBERT T. FRANCOEUR

[*Update 2003*: In 2002, for the first time in a decade, the number of newly diagnosed cases of AIDS rose in the United States, a disturbing turnaround that health officials warn reflects growing complacency about the dangers of HIV.

[For gays and bisexual men, HIV diagnoses rose for the third straight year. HIV diagnoses among gay and bisexual men rose 7.1% in 2002 in 25 states with long-standing HIV reporting procedures, according to the Centers for Disease Control and Prevention. The number represented an increase of nearly 18% since 1999, disturbing because the number of newly diagnosed HIV cases per year fell steadily throughout the 1990s, even among gay men. For the country as a whole, the CDC reported 42,136 AIDS diagnoses in 2002, a 2.2% increase from the previous year, and the first rise since 1993.

[The increase in HIV cases can be blamed on a younger generation that does not remember the devastation of the AIDS epidemic, lack of concern because of the advent of life-extending AIDS-treatment drugs, and burnout from years of safe-sex warnings. Other reasons for the increase include persons at risk are not diagnosed early enough and pass the infection to others before they know they have HIV, and the difficulty of HIV+ persons adhering to complex HIV drug regimens. There were 16,371 AIDS deaths in 2002—a 5.9% decline from 2001.

[These statistics indicate the need for more prevention efforts aimed at gay and bisexual men. One strategy announced by the CDC involves providing money to community groups in large cities that have had outbreaks of sexually transmitted diseases, such as syphilis and AIDS (July 29, 2003: http://www.cdc.gov). (*End of update by R. T. Francoeur*)]

## [HIV/AIDS among Latinos and Latinas

MIGUEL A. PÉREZ and HELDA L. PINZÓN-PÉREZ
[*Update 2003*: According to the CDC, the proportional distribution of AIDS cases in the United States has shifted among U.S. ethnic groups. Gender, cultural factors, perceptions of HIV/AIDS and/or stigma associated with AIDS, perceptions of the quality and availability of services, among other factors, have a tremendous impact on behaviors that put Latinos at risk for infection.

[While the rates have decreased among whites, the number of cases among Latinos has increased accordingly. In 1996, Latinos accounted for 17.3% of all male AIDS cases in the United States; that figured had increased to 19% by 2000 (CDC 1996; CDC 2002). As of June 1998, Latino men accounted for 18%, and Latinas 20%, of the cumulative AIDS cases, respectively (CDC 1998). Table 20 shows the proportion of AIDS cases among ethnic groups in the U.S. and contrasts that to the proportion of the population they represent.

[Latinos in their reproductive years seem to be at a great risk for HIV infection. In addition to the known risk factors for HIV infection (see Table 21), risk factors for Latinos include poverty, lack of access to healthcare, sexual roles, and socioeconomic factors (Blasini-Caceres & Cook 1997; Keeling 1993).

[The data show an increase in the number of HIV and AIDS cases among Latinas in the United States. A comparison by gender and ethnicity is found in Table 22. In fact, intravenous drug use and sexual contact with men seem to be the primary transmission modes for Latino women (Blasini-Caceres & Cook 1997). Weeks and colleagues (1995) concluded that, although the number of heterosexual cases is increasing among Latinas, the number of AIDS-prevention programs geared towards them continues to be inadequate.

[Among Latinos, Puerto Ricans have the highest incidence of HIV infection. Puerto Ricans also have the fourth-highest rate in the nation (NCLR 1992). According to the Centers for Disease Control and Prevention (1993), up to 70% of AIDS cases are related to intravenous drug use in Puerto Rico.

[Studies among Latinos have yielded different results in regard to awareness about HIV/AIDS. Dawson (1990) reported that 41% of Latinos said they had some knowledge about AIDS, compared to 39% for African-Americans and 48% for European-Americans. However, less than half (48%) of Latinos understood the connection between HIV and AIDS, compared to 69% among European-Americans. These figures did not vary greatly two years later, when Schoenborn, Marsh, and Hardy (1994) reported that 40% of Latinos, 47% of European-Americans, and 39% of African-Americans had "some" knowledge about AIDS. In a study of Latinos, Miller, Guarnaccia, and Fasina (2002) found lower knowledge levels about AIDS among individuals with lower acculturation levels and whose primary language was Spanish. The same study found that Latinos were knowledgeable about general facts and about transmission modes.

[Latinos are less likely than other ethnic groups to accurately identify HIV-transmission modes. Alcalay, Sniderman, Mitchell, and Griffin (1990) found that Latinos were more likely (36%) than European-Americans (15%) to believe they could get AIDS from blood donations. The same study found that Latinos were more likely than non-Latinos to believe that HIV transmission could occur through casual contact (e.g., hugging or from water fountains). Dawson (1990) found that 7% of Latinos believed it was "very likely" they could become infected with HIV by eating at a restaurant where the cook had AIDS, compared to 5% of European-American respondents. The researchers also found that 19% of Latinos believed they could catch AIDS from an unclean public toilet, whereas only 8% of the European-American respondents and 10% of African-Americans believed this to be an exposure category. In 2002, Miller, Guarnaccia, and Fasina found that Latinos could correctly identify transmission modes regardless of acculturation level.

[Knowledge about AIDS seems to be related to language preference among some Latinos. Research indicates that Spanish-speaking Latinos are more likely than bilingual Latinos to believe AIDS is spread through casual contact (Hu

### Table 20

**2000 AIDS Cases in the U.S. by Population Group**

| | Percentage of AIDS Cases | Percentage of Estimated Population |
|---|---|---|
| Whites | 32% | 71% |
| African-Americans | 47 | 12 |
| Hispanics/Latinos | 19 | 13 |
| Asian-Americans | 1 | 4 |
| Native Americans | < 1 | 1 |

*Source*: CDC 2002

### Table 21

**Adult Male AIDS Cases by Exposure Category**

| | White Non-Hispanic | Black Non-Hispanic | Hispanic |
|---|---|---|---|
| Men who have sex with men (MSM) | 68% | 27% | 35% |
| Injection drug use (IDU) | 12 | 36 | 36 |
| MSM and IDU | 8 | 6 | 5 |
| Heterosexual contact | 5 | 16 | 13 |
| Other/Not identified | 7 | 16 | 11 |

*Source*: CDC 2002

### Table 22

**2000 AIDS Cases in the U.S. by Gender**

| | Female | Male |
|---|---|---|
| Whites | 1,895 | 11,466 |
| African-Americans | 6,545 | 13,218 |
| Hispanics/Latinos | 1,855 | 6,285 |
| Asian-Americans | 77 | 300 |
| Native Americans | 68 | 135 |

*Source*: CDC 2002

& Keller 1989). Another survey found that 24.1% of Spanish-speaking Latinos answered positively to the question, "Do you believe that one can catch AIDS from shaking hands with someone who has AIDS?" in comparison to 1.7% of English-speaking Latinos (Alcalay, Sniderman, Mitchell, & Griffin 1990).

[Hu and Keller (1989) found that, despite their lesser knowledge about AIDS, Spanish-speaking Latinos reported a higher interest in learning about AIDS (88%) than English-speaking groups (83%). Pérez and Fennelly (1996) found that Latino farm workers are willing to learn about AIDS, even though their reluctance to discuss sex has not decreased. One might expect that lower levels of knowledge about HIV/AIDS among Latinos in the United States would lead to more discrimination towards persons with AIDS. Instead, Alcalay et al. (1990) found no differences between Latinos and non-Hispanics in their likelihood to support AIDS victims' rights. (*End of update by M. A. Pérez and H. L. Pinzón-Pérez*)]

## C. HIV/AIDS: Five Specific Emerging Issues
LINDA L. HENDRIXSON

*AIDS as a Family Dilemma*

As the AIDS pandemic continues through its second decade in the United States, unforeseen issues have emerged as important considerations in attempts to meet the needs of people living with AIDS (PLWAs).

What began as a disease syndrome affecting individuals has become a problem which confronts whole families in America. Researchers, health providers, and policymakers have had to re-work their approaches to take into account the impact that AIDS has on family members, both immediate and extended. Our definition of "family" has undergone much change throughout this pandemic. As we consider the people who care for PLWAs, and those who care about them, family has come to be defined much more broadly than before. The family of origin has been replaced or extended to include non-blood-related friends, lovers, AIDS buddies, and others who provide emotional and instrumental support.

For many PLWAs, estrangement from birth families is a way-of-life. AIDS exacerbates those earlier problems. Others become estranged after their diagnosis is discovered. Families who have not disclosed the illness of their family member live with fear of ostracism and discrimination. If an AIDS diagnosis is kept secret within the family, social isolation becomes a continuing problem. Family pressures escalate if children are involved, especially if those children are infected. The financial strain of caring for adults and/or children with AIDS can be considerable. Finding competent doctors is an additional serious challenge throughout the country. Medical costs, health insurance, adequate healthcare, and social support, caregiving, child custody, disclosure, stigma, discrimination, loss, and grieving are among the troubling issues facing families and others living with AIDS (Macklin 1989).

*Emerging Populations and Changing Locales*

AIDS is no longer found in what were originally perceived to be the only affected American AIDS populations—white, middle-class gay men and minority intravenous drug users in the inner cities (Voeller 1991; Wiener 1991). AIDS is now found in:

- people who live in rural locations;
- middle- and upper-class women, many of whom do not misuse drugs or alcohol;
- women who have only vaginal sex with men;
- women who have rectal sex with men, but do not report this behavior;

- women who have received contaminated donor semen;
- women who have had oral sex with other women;
- middle- and upper-class men;
- men who have only vaginal sex with women, and do not have sex with other men;
- black, Hispanic, and Asian gay and bisexual men;
- teenagers who have been sexually abused as children;
- people who use drugs, such as heroin, but do not use needles;
- athletes who use contaminated needles while injecting illegal steroids;
- women with blood-clotting disorders;
- people who have received contaminated organ transplants and other body tissues;
- senior citizens; and
- babies who nurse from infected mothers.

There is no longer a statistically precise AIDS profile or pattern. To a great extent, epidemiological categories have become meaningless.

The spread of AIDS to rural and small-town locations is worth noting. Most people still equate AIDS with major urban areas, and, true, the numbers of cases are highest there. However, the pandemic has diffused from urban epicenters, past suburbia, and into small, rural enclaves in the U.S. (Cleveland & Davenport 1989) The spread of AIDS in Africa along truck routes, as men seek sex away from home, is not unlike the spread of AIDS along major highways in the U.S., as people travel in and out of metropolitan AIDS epicenters. The government is paying little attention to rural AIDS in America; it is the least understood and least researched part of our national epidemic, with numbers of infected rising dramatically.

Limited research shows that some PLWAs who left their rural birthplaces for life in the city, are now returning to their rural families to be cared for. But many PLWAs who grew up in cities are leaving their urban birthplaces and moving to the country where they believe it is healthier for them, mentally and physically. This is especially true for recovering addicts whose city friends have died of AIDS, and who hope to escape a similar fate.

Besides the "in-migration" of people with AIDS to rural locations, there are many indigenous people in small towns who are infected as well. The numbers of cases of HIV/AIDS is increasing rapidly in rural America, where social services are inadequate, medical care is generally poor, and community denial is a reality. Federal and state monies continue to be channeled to inner-city agencies, leaving rural and small-town providers with scant resources to ease increasing caseloads (Hendrixson 1996).

*Complexion of the Pandemic*

The face of AIDS is changing in other ways, as well. There is now a considerable number of infected people who have outlived medical predictions about their morbidity and mortality. These are divided into two groups: asymptomatic non-progressors, and long-term survivors. Both groups test HIV-antibody-positive, indicating past infection with human immunodeficiency virus.

Despite being HIV-antibody-positive, the first group shows no other laboratory or clinical symptoms of HIV disease. The second group has experienced immune suppression and some opportunistic infections, and is diagnosed as having AIDS, but continues to live beyond its expected lifespan (Laurence 1994). In addition, there are others who are inexplicably uncharacteristic:

- people who have been diagnosed with AIDS, but who do not test HIV-antibody-positive, meaning that there is no indication of previous exposure to the virus, despite their illnesses;

- people who have "retro-converted" from testing HIV-antibody-positive to now testing HIV-antibody-negative; and
- people who are repeatedly exposed to HIV through sex or contaminated blood and who do not become infected.

Scientists have no explanation for these anomalies. Little research has been done on people who do not fit the accustomed pattern physicians look for. Yet, the very fact that they challenge medical expectations is a clue that they hold answers that may help thousands of others in this country.

In many ways, some new drug treatments have helped infected people forestall serious illnesses, turning AIDS into more of a chronic than an acute-illness syndrome. Yet many PLWAs have renounced AZT and other toxic antiretroviral drugs, because of their serious side effects. Increasing numbers of patients are embracing alternative therapies—physical, mental, and spiritual—rather than taking potent AIDS drugs. Others are combining the best of conventional and unconventional medicine in their own self-styled treatment plans. The new protease inhibitors offer much promise, but it is too early to know what side effects they may produce. The bottom line is that AIDS no longer automatically equates with death ("The End of AIDS" 1996).

### HIV-Positive Children Coming of Age

As life is extended, more and more children born with the virus are moving through late childhood and early adolescence in relatively good physical health. New challenges await them and their families. Some children may know they are infected with HIV; others may not. They continue to grow socially, with sexual feelings beginning to emerge. How do we help them fit in with their uninfected peers? How do we teach them about their sexuality? How do we prepare them for dating situations? What do we say when they speak of marriage hopes? How do we teach them about safer sex? What new approaches in HIV/AIDS education should health teachers consider as these children enter their classes? Parents, teachers, and youth leaders are wrestling with new questions that were unanticipated ten years ago when we believed that HIV-antibody-positive children would not live much beyond toddlerhood.

### New Paradigms, New Theories

At least one revolutionary theory about AIDS is gaining prominence, as a cure for the syndrome continues to elude us. Dr. Peter Duesberg, a cancer geneticist, virologist, and molecular biologist at the University of California-Berkeley, and a member of the elite National Academy of Sciences, along with other well-established scientists, has challenged the standard medical and scientific HIV hypothesis. He maintains that AIDS researchers have never definitively proven that HIV alone causes AIDS. He theorizes that HIV cannot be the sole cause of such a complex cascade of physiological events as the complete suppression of the entire human immune system, eventually leading to fatal opportunistic infections and conditions such as cancer and dementia.

Duesberg, one of the first scientists to discover retroviruses, the family of viruses to which HIV belongs, contends that HIV is a benign "carrier" retrovirus which a healthy immune system inactivates as it would any intruder. HIV antibodies result from this normal defense response. Being HIV-antibody-positive only means that a person's immune system is working properly. It does not mean that the person will develop AIDS.

Duesberg and others believe that the serious immune suppression which manifests as severely lowered T-cell counts and opportunistic infections that may become fatal,

can result from one or more of the following factors, all of which are immune-suppressive:

- continuous, long-term misuse of legal and illegal recreational drugs, including sexual aphrodisiacs such as nitrite inhalants, used by men to facilitate rectal sex with other men;
- over-use of prescription drugs, including antibiotics, antivirals, and anti-parasitics, often taken for repeated sexually transmitted infections;
- toxic effects of AZT and other antiretroviral drugs, which are intended to interfere with cell DNA replication ("DNA chain terminators"), and, therefore, kill *all* body cells without discrimination;
- malnutrition, which often accompanies long-term illicit drug and alcohol use; or
- untreated sexual diseases and other recurring illnesses, which also suppress immunity.

One or a combination of these factors eventually brings on the potentially fatal condition which the CDC arbitrarily calls "AIDS."

Duesberg points to the number of people with AIDS who do not test HIV-antibody-positive, as well as those who are HIV-antibody-positive but are not symptomatic. He questions why scientists are not interested in studying these people who defy the accepted AIDS dogma. Duesberg's efforts to have his research papers published by the mainstream American scientific press, to present his views at scientific AIDS conferences, and to be awarded funding to do additional AIDS research have met with virtual failure in this country.

Duesberg (1996) has been shut out by the powerful medical/scientific establishment which pretends to be open to new ideas and theories, but which, he maintains, is chained to the HIV-equals-AIDS hypothesis. He presented his challenge in a 1996 book titled *Inventing the AIDS Virus*.

### Conclusion

In the 15th year of the AIDS pandemic, we have no cure and no vaccine for this disease. Thousands have died in our country, most of them young people. Thousands more have died in other countries. New advances in drug treatments and alternative/holistic modalities have helped some American PLWAs, but many families continue to silently mourn the death of their loved ones. The stigma of AIDS is ever-present; the fear continues. Yet, compassion and love have emerged, as well, as caring people reach out to help those who are suffering. AIDS appears to have "dug in" for the long term while science looks for answers. In the meanwhile, we need to ask two questions. First, as scientists search for the truth of AIDS, are they asking the right questions? Second, as the disease shifts from its former pattern of early, premature death to a more manageable long-term chronic illness, are we meeting the needs of all the people infected and affected by this disease—PLWAs, their families, and their loved ones?

## D. The Impact of AIDS on Our Perception of Sexuality    RAYMOND J. NOONAN

Little has been written on the impact that AIDS has had and continues to have on our collective sensibilities about sexuality and our innate needs to express aspects of our sexual selves. Research has been sparse, if nonexistent, on the various meanings ascribed—both by professionals in the sexual sciences and members of the general public—to either sexuality itself or to the disease complex of AIDS.

Professionals in any field often serve to support and maintain the various cultural norms of any given society.

As such, with the exception of the safety-valve role of those who might be referred to as the "loyal opposition," rarely are there expressions of sentiments or ideas that seriously challenge widely held beliefs and assumptions. Within the various disciplines encompassing the sexual sciences, the struggling theory, for example, that HIV may not be the direct cause of AIDS (see previous section), is one of the few examples of such reassessments. Among the popular press, nevertheless, various accounts have sporadically appeared with critical appraisals of either our general or specific approaches to current AIDS perspectives, including Farber (1993, 1993ab), Fumento (1990), Patton (1990), and others.

### Current Trends

It cannot be denied that AIDS is a serious, debilitating, and potentially deadly disease. Yet, the American response to it has often been one in which the reality of the disease, as well as myths promoted as facts, have been appropriated to further some related or unrelated political aim. Metaphorical allusions are often used to discuss the issue, not to impart factual information about or to motivate persons to AIDS prevention, but to further a political agenda or even to attack some political group(s) perceived as adversaries. Such political goals and targets have included:

- claims that AIDS is God's punishment for sexual impropriety made by some homophobic religious leaders and others;
- instituting and promoting sex education by supporters;
- the promotion of male contraceptive responsibility by some health and sexuality professionals;
- AIDS used as a scare tactic to discourage sexual activity, particularly among the young, by some parents and others;
- providing the "scientific" reason for postponing sexual activity, being more selective about who one's sexual partners are, and reducing the number of sexual partners, by some educational, political, and health authorities;
- the promotion of monogamy and abstinence;
- the promotion of community and solidarity among compatriots, from gays to fundamentalist Christians, who perceive they are under attack;
- the use of AIDS to promote anti-male, anti-white, and/or anti-Western attitudes; and
- the advocacy of some noncoital sex practices to communicate covert negative (heterophobic) views of heterosexuality and penile-vaginal intercourse (see Noonan 1996, 182-185).

For most sexologists and sexuality educators, the co-opting of the issues of protection and responsibility, especially for young people, reflects the intrinsically good part of human nature that seeks to find the "silver lining" in the dark cloud of HIV/AIDS. Although these political goals and targets probably do not apply to all people who are concerned about HIV/AIDS, these philosophies have had a more profound effect on overall public and professional approaches to sexuality and related issues than the number of their supporters would suggest. Some examples follow.

Although it is well known that anal intercourse offers the most effective way for HIV to be transmitted sexually, and that vaginal-penile intercourse is far less risky, rarely have investigators asked those whose infections are suspected to have been heterosexually transmitted, particularly women, whether and how often they engaged in anal intercourse. Instead, heterosexually transmitted HIV infections are assumed to be vaginally transmitted, although this is generally unlikely on the individual scale, and not likely to result

in an HIV epidemic in the heterosexual population (Brody 1995; National Research Council 1993).

Concentrating only on the condom for both contraception and STD/AIDS prevention ignores the effectiveness of spermicidal agents with nonoxynol-9 in the prevention of pregnancy and infection as a reasonable alternative for couples who object to condom use (North 1990) (see Table 18 in Section 9A on contraception). It also ignores the negative impact condoms have on sexual intimacy for some couples (Juran 1995).

In addition, our terminology with respect to AIDS has had a profound impact on our perception of sexuality. For example, the well-known slogan, "When you sleep with someone, you are having sex with everyone she or he has slept with for the last x-number of years," is believed to be literally true by many people. The effectiveness of this slogan is seriously undermined when questions are raised about the kind of statistical and/or epidemiological evidence available to support this statement. To many, such slogans imply a view of sexuality that denigrates *all* sexual experiences, no matter how valid or valuable they are or have been. The "epidemic" of AIDS is another phrase that many, if not most, people believe to be literally true. They fail to realize that the word is being used in its metaphorical sense, with its emotional connotations being more important than its literal truth. The same can be said for the statement, "Everyone is equally at risk for AIDS." Granted this statement is true, but only in the trivial sense that we are all, as mortal human beings, prone to sickness and death. The fact that ethnic and racial minorities in the U.S. are disproportionately represented in the AIDS and HIV-positive statistics (CDC 1996) should dispel that myth completely. Brandt (1988) has insightfully analyzed the notion of AIDS-as-metaphor:

> At a moment when the dangers of promiscuous sex are being emphasized, it suggests that every *single* sexual encounter is a promiscuous encounter. . . . As anonymous sex is being questioned, this metaphor suggests that no matter how well known a partner may be, the relationship is *anonymous*. Finally, the metaphor implies to heterosexuals that if they are having sex with their partner's (heterosexual) partners, they are in fact engaging in homosexual acts. In this view, every sexual act becomes a homosexual encounter. (p. 77, emphasis in original)

In fact, our very use of the terms "safe" or "safer sex" implies that all sex is dangerous, when in fact it usually is not (Noonan 1996a).

It is typical within American culture to ignore the chronic problems that result from the general American uncomfortableness with sexuality and sexual pleasure. In terms of responding to the health issues surrounding AIDS, Americans have two choices:

1. We can continue to respond as we have to other sexual issues, by spotlighting them and ignoring the broader issues of sane healthy sexuality, which includes the celebration of sexual intimacy and pleasure. This narrow panic response is typical of American culture and its dealing with such issues as teenage pregnancy, child sexual abuse, satanic ritual practices, sexual "promiscuity," the "threats" to heterosexual marriage and the family posed by recognition of same-sex marriages, and the "epidemics" of herpes and heterosexual AIDS; or

2. We can respond to the AIDS crisis within the context of positive broad-based accommodation to radical changes in American sexual behavior and relation-

ships. This broad-based, sex-positive approach could well include: the availability of comprehensive, more affordable, and more reliable sexual-health and STD evaluations for men, comparable to the regularly scheduled gynecological exams generally encouraged for women; the development of effective alternatives to the condom, including the availability of effective male contraceptives that are separated from the sexual act of intercourse, easy to use, and reliable; making birth control as automatic for men as the pill has been for women (ideally, they would also work to prevent STDs); the expansion of research to make all contraceptives safe for both women and men; the elimination of fear as a method to induce the suppression of sexual behavior; and sex-positive encouragement for making affirmative intentional decisions to have sex, in addition to the "traditional" support for deciding not to do so (Noonan 1996a).

At this time, it remains unclear whether the American response to AIDS will follow its customary pattern of initial panic in the mass media, followed by a benign neglect and silence prompted by our traditional discomfort with sex-positive values, or whether this country will, at long last, confront the issue of AIDS, and deal with it in the broader context of a safe, sane, and healthy celebration of sexuality.

## 11. Sexual Dysfunctions, Counseling, and Therapies

### A. Brief History of American Sexual Therapy

WILLIAM HARTMAN and MARILYN FITHIAN

The scientific study of sexual dysfunctions and the development of therapeutic modalities in the United States started with Robert Latou Dickinson (1861-1950). Born and educated in Germany and Switzerland, he earned his medical degree in New York and began collecting sex histories from his patients in 1890. In the course of his practice, he gathered 5,200 case histories of female patients—married and single, lesbian and heterosexual—and published extensively on sexual problems of women (Brecher 1979; Dickinson & Beam 1931, 1934; Dickinson & Person 1925).

The turn-of-the-century popularity of Sigmund Freud's psychoanalysis strongly influenced early American sexual therapy. Although its popularity has faded significantly, the psychoanalytic model is still practiced or integrated with other modalities by some therapists working with sexual problems. The 1948 and 1953 Alfred Kinsey studies brought an increased awareness of human sexuality as a subject of scientific investigation that could include the treatment of sexual disorders as part of psychiatry and medicine. The pioneering work of Joseph Wolpe and Arnold Lazarus (1966) in adapting behavioral therapy, shifted sexual therapy away from the analytical and medical model, as therapists began to view dysfunctional sexual behavior as the result of learned responses that can be modified.

William Masters and Virginia Johnson began their epoch-making study of the anatomy and physiology of human sexual response in 1964. Their initial research with 312 males and 382 females, published as *Human Sexual Response* (1966), remains the keystone of modern sex therapy, not just in the United States, but anywhere sex therapy is studied or practiced. *Human Sexual Inadequacy* followed in 1970. Masters and Johnson used a male-female dual-therapy team, and a brief, intensive, reeducation process that involved behavior-oriented exercises like sensate focus. It appeared to be highly successful because they worked with a select population of healthy people in basically solid relationships. After their success with relatively simple cases,

they and other therapists began to encounter more difficult cases, which could not be solved with the original behavioral approach.

In the early 1970s, Joseph LoPiccolo advocated the use of additional approaches designed to reduce anxiety within the behavioral therapy model suggested by Masters and Johnson (LoPiccolo & LoPiccolo 1978; LoPiccolo & Lobitz 1973; Lobitz & LoPiccolo 1972). LoPiccolo's (1978) analysis of the theoretical basis for sexual therapy identified seven major underlying elements in every sex therapy model: 1. mutual responsibility, 2. information, education, and permission giving, 3. attitude change, 4. anxiety reduction, 5. communication and feedback, 6. intervention in destructive sex roles, lifestyles, and family interaction, and 7. prescribing changes in sex therapy.

John Gagnon and William Simon (1973) stressed the importance of addressing social scripting in sex therapy. Harold Lief, a physician and family therapist, pointed out the importance of nonsexual interpersonal issues and communications problems as factors in sexual difficulties. Lief (1963, 1965) also advocated incorporating the principles of marital therapy into sex therapy. As therapists began to integrate other modes of psychotherapy, such as cognitive, gestalt, and imagery therapies, it soon became apparent that there was no single "official" form of sex therapy. In addition, some sex therapists became sensitive to the impact and influence of ethnic values on some sexual problems (McGoldrick et al. 1982).

Helen Singer Kaplan, a psychiatrist at Cornell University College of Medicine, made an important and profound contribution to sex therapy when she blended traditional concepts from psychotherapy and psychoanalysis with cognitive psychology and behavioral therapy. Kaplan's *New Sex Therapy* (1974) explored the role of such important therapeutic issues as resistance, repression, and unconscious motivations in sex therapy. This new approach focused not only on altering behavior with techniques like the sensate-focus exercises, but also with exploring and modifying covert or unconscious thought patterns and motivations that may underlie a sexual difficulty (Kaplan 1974, 1979, 1983).

Specific areas of sexual therapy have been developed, including Lonnie Barbach's (1980) and Betty Dodson's (1987) independent work with nonorgasmic women, Bernard Apfelbaum and Dean Dauw's use of surrogates in their work with single persons, William Hartman and Marilyn Fithian's (1972) integration of films, body imagery, and body work with dysfunctional couples, and Bernie Zilbergeld's (1978, 1992) focus on male sexual health and problems.

There have been no major innovative treatments developed in sex therapy programs in recent years, although new refinements continue to occur. Some would comment that one does not have to reinvent the wheel when the results are good, but the early success rates have declined as the presenting problems have become more complicated and difficult to treat. Nevertheless, self-reported success rates from reputable sex therapy clinics run between 80% and 92%. However, critical reviews of sex therapy treatment models emphasize the paucity of scientific data in determining the effectiveness of such programs.

Today, few professionals who counsel clients with sexual difficulties see themselves as pure sex therapists. More and more, the term "sex therapy" refers to a focus of intervention, rather than to a distinctive and exclusive technique. Individual psychologists, psychotherapists, marriage counselors, and family therapists may be more or less skilled in providing counseling and applying therapeutic modalities appropriate to specific sexual problems, but each tends to apply those interventions and techniques with which they are more comfortable. The American Association of Sex Educators, Counselors, and Therapists and the American Board of Sexology each examine and certify treatment professionals' knowledge of human sexual functioning as well as their skills in treating sexual dysfunctions. Board-certified therapists, counselors, and physicians are likely to be a more reliable treatment resource.

Informal support groups also provide opportunities for dealing with sexual problems and difficulties. Many hospitals and service organizations provide workshops and support groups for patients recovering from heart attacks, and persons with diabetes, emphysema, multiple sclerosis, cystic fibrosis, arthritis, and other chronic diseases. These support groups usually include both patients and their partners.

## B. Current Status 2003

JULIAN SLOWINSKI, WILLIAM R. STAYTON, and ROBERT W. HATFIELD [*Updated August 2003 by R. W. Hatfield*]

Recently, American sex therapy has incorporated important advances in medicine and pharmacology. More-precise knowledge and techniques now allow a therapist to develop a hormone profile for a patient, monitor nocturnal penile tumescence, and check penile and vaginal blood flow. With patients now more likely to report negative side effects of medications on their sexual responses, physicians have developed strategies for altering the course of medication. New surgical methods improve penile blood supply. Moreover, prosthetics, vacuum devices, oral medications, and other aids, like injections, urethral suppositories, and electrical devices to stimulate erection, have been developed.

Breakthroughs are also occurring in female sex research with direct implications for sex therapy. Examples include the efforts of sex-affirming women to redefine sexual satisfaction in women's terms and to expand our appreciation of the spectrum of erotic/sexual responses beyond the phallic/coital (Ogden 1995), Joanne Loulan's (1984) exploration of lesbian sexual archetypes, sexual responses of women with a spinal cord injury, the effects on women's libido of homeopathics to increase the bioavailability of testosterone, and work combining testosterone with estrogen replacement to increase both sexual desire and pleasure in perimenopausal women. One sidelight in this exciting female sex research is that the old methods of sensate focus and pleasuring exercises are still working successfully. For example, the self-help materials are still very useful in working with preorgasmic women. The traditional sensate-focus exercises are still effective in working with desire and orgasm issues, painful intercourse, and vaginal spasms.

More good news are the trends in treating male sexual dysfunction today. For the motivated and cooperative male, there is treatment for virtually every dysfunction. In addition to the ever-helpful sensate-focus exercises, we have medications for increasing desire and arousal, such as yohimbe, a bark extract of the African tree yohimbe, and a combination of green oat and palmetto-grass extract. These are available through a physician's prescription, at health food stores, or through mail-order catalogs. As of mid-1995, there is enthusiastic anecdotal feedback from individual therapists who are using yohimbe and oat extract with their clients; but what is anxiously awaited—and needed—in this area are the results of controlled clinical studies to document the actual therapeutic effects, if any.

The vacuum pump for erections has been much improved with automatic monitoring of blood flow. With some clients, penile injections produce remarkable results. Monoxydyl and nitroglycerin are being used as topical preparations, as are prostaglandin E1 suppositories inserted into the urethral meatus. Taken alone, these medications are seldom effective in the long term. Without therapy, the person will often misuse or stop using the medication or method. However, when sex therapy is added, the success rate increases dramatically, because both the relationship and the dysfunction are being treated.

[*Update 2003*: Unquestionably, the 1998 introduction of Viagra (sildenafil citrate) oral pharmacological treatment for erectile dysfunction by the Pfizer Corporation heralded the greatest public focus on sexual dysfunctions since the 1965 Masters and Johnson publication of *Human Sexual Response*. Public awareness of this new drug came so suddenly that just one year after its introduction, the Viagra name was added to the *Oxford English Dictionary*. By 2002, over 20 million men (and a few women) had been prescribed more than one billion tablets retailing for $6.00 or more per tablet. Pfizer reported 2002 sales of Viagra at $1.7 billion. Just a few years earlier, Pfizer had projected that sales would be $4.5 billion (Simons 2003). Although the medication is reported to be effective for as high as 70% of the men who try it, it appears that the human intricacies of sexual response and sexual relationships were not accounted for by the drug companies. Many men experiencing problems with erection did not suddenly become expert lovers or experience increased pleasure in their relationships with Viagra alone. In 2003, three additional drug company giants entered the market to compete with Pfizer. Bayer and GlaxoSmithKline are co-marketing Levitra (vardenafil HCL), with the Eli Lilly company due to introduce their entry (in late 2003 or early 2004) into the erectile-dysfunction-medication market with a drug called Cialis (tadalafil). TAP Pharmaceuticals will be introducing Uprima (apomorphine), also in 2003 or 2004. Five years of Viagra marketing (over $100 million per year), and the anticipated expenditure of many hundreds of millions of additional dollars by Pfizer's new competition, will certainly bring with it added sex information and misinformation, symptom relief and frustration, and other ambivalent reactions to drug effects and side-effects.

[When an effective treatment for a male sexual dysfunction is discovered, it is invariably applied to women. The success of the vacuum device on erectile dysfunction has led to a female clitoral suction device called the Eros Clitoral Pump. Adequate research to determine the true effectiveness of this device has yet to be published. Human studies of attempts to treat female sexual dysfunctions with Viagra have not been encouraging, but given the relative financial success of Viagra, some drug companies are hoping for another breakthrough medication, this time for female sexual problems. (*End of update by R. W. Hatfield*)]

### Problems

Several problems currently impede the delivery of sex therapy to clients. Primary among these is the state of flux in the insurance industry (third-party payers) with the shift toward managed care, health maintenance organizations, and provider networks. The availability of third-party payment makes it much more feasible for patients to avail themselves of sex therapy. The insurance industry has changed the entire healthcare-provider field by creating the impression that therapists, like others in the medical field, are not to be trusted to know how long therapy should last, or what methods should be used to treat psychodynamic problems. This has created the image that all psychological problems can be treated by brief therapy within a predetermined number of sessions or merely with medications. The insurance industry has also made confidentiality problematic, because clients must sign away some rights to confidentiality in order to receive mental-health coverage, although the 2003 federal HIPAA regulations regarding patient records improved this situation somewhat. Increasingly, insurance plans refuse to pay for sex therapy. This has prompted many therapists to give a diagnosis that is acceptable to the plan, but not necessarily the most accurate diagnosis.

Secondly, the rise of the religious right appears to have had a negative impact on sex therapy in America. Although there has been no general decline in premarital sex in America, the "abstinence-only until marriage" ethic can be a considerable barrier to normal adolescent sexual rehearsal explorations for some people, and may well result in an increased likelihood of dysfunction when newlywed couples confront their sexuality and sexual functioning on the wedding night. Masters and Johnson, as well as several other researchers, have discovered that a high level of religious orthodoxy is significantly related to greater incidence of sexual dysfunction. Two responses are likely: The individuals and/or couple may become so stressed that it is difficult for them to function naturally within the permitted circumstances, or they may rebel even before marriage and get involved in promiscuous and/or risky practices.

A third concern is a growing challenge as to whether sex therapy is even a separate discipline. There are those who believe that sex therapy needs to be subsumed under psychology, marriage and family therapy, social work, or psychiatry. The fact is that few of these disciplines have educational or training programs that teach about the healthy aspects of sex and sexuality or the creative treatment of sexual problems.

Finally, the amount of money and effort given to research on female sexuality significantly lags behind research on male sexuality (di Mauro 1995).

Because humans are born sexual but not lovers, sex therapy is increasingly seen as including good sex education, good medicine, and good psychotherapy/counseling. In the last ten years, sex therapy has added important concerns related to gender-identity dysphoria, sexual (gender) orientations, and lifestyle issues.

[*The Field of Sex Therapy* ROBERT W. HATFIELD

[*Update 2003*: One might expect that the decades following the 1970 birth of sex therapy as a profession would be characterized by ever-improving research into treatment methods, expansion of graduate programs designed to train sex therapists, and an increasing number of highly trained sex therapists available to those individuals and couples suffering from sexual problems and dysfunctions. The reality in the new millennium is much the opposite. There are only half as many board-certified sex therapists in 2003 than there were in the mid-1980s, and while recent surveys indicate that the actual prevalence of sexual disorders in the U.S. is probably higher than we ever previously believed, the number of medical schools and helping-professions graduate schools that provide basic sexuality education and training in the treatment of sexual dysfunctions is significantly fewer than in the 1980s.

[Today, those professionals available to the person or couple who seeks help come from a fragmented collection of specialties that rarely communicate with each other. That's not the way it began.

[A few noble professional organizations in the field of sexology were created over the past 45 years to be multidisciplinary groups of highly trained physicians, psychotherapists, social scientists, biologists, and many others who began to share their unique perspectives and knowledge to further the growth of the field. However, in 2003, while there are a larger number of sexology professional groups than ever before, most are increasingly specialized, and almost all report fewer members each year.

[It seems counterintuitive that sex therapy as a field of study and as a profession is today in such disarray. There is no single explanation for the current situation. Knowledgeable scientists and clinicians have observed that useful theory regarding normal sexual functioning never coalesced; that early treatment methods avoided the complexity of the human sexual experience and focused almost exclusively on symptom elimination; that shifting corporate structures and vacillating national economies that could not or would not deal effectively with healthcare led to a rigid managedcare system that quickly limited or eliminated services such as counseling or therapy directed at intimate relationship issues; and, most recently, the rapid medicalization of the field of treating sexual problems by prescribing simple pharmacological or biomechanical interventions that appear to be much more economical.

[It is expected that the trends away from health-insurance support of sex therapy and the growth of the number of new sex drugs and devices will continue. The only signs that sex therapy may get a second wind of fresh research and new treatment methods while addressing its theory deficiencies is a very recent trend where several of the professional organizations are beginning to communicate and even collaborate with each other. The number of researchers, academicians, and clinicians who have true expertise in some area(s) of sexology is very small. It is fairly obvious to most expert observers that the field is much too small to survive the layers of fragmentation that have occurred over the past few decades. (*End of update by R. W. Hatfield*)]

## Psychotropic Drugs

JULIAN SLOWINSKI, WILLIAM R. STAYTON, and ROBERT W. HATFIELD

[*Update 2003*: Antidepressants, antianxiety, and antipanic medications are being used in conjunction with psychotherapy in treating desire-, excitement-, and orgasmphase problems, as well as paraphilic obsessive-compulsive behaviors (Coleman 2002). Studies are demonstrating that the most commonly prescribed category of antidepressant medications, SSRIs, can be useful in treating specific sexual disorders. A side effect of SSRIs, such as Zoloft, Paxil, and Prozac, is a predictable increase in the latency time for ejaculation by 3 to 5 minutes. While this can be an unwanted and frustrating side effect for some men, it has been beneficial for others who present with problems of ejaculatory control (early ejaculation). For women, SSRIs may have the similar unwanted side effect of increasing the latency to orgasm. Both genders who experience this medication side effect as unwanted can become frustrated in their sexual interactions, with frustration and distraction causing a loss of arousal or desire leading to the possibility of an iatrogenic sexual dysfunction. Behavioral sex therapy techniques to treat premature ejaculation are generally highly successful, but studies have shown that for those men who do not respond to these interventions, a relatively low dose of an SSRI medication is usually therapeutic. Interestingly, a majority of these medicated men maintained good ejaculatory control following a brief (2- to 3-month) use of the SSRI. For the others, discontinuation of the medication resulted in a return of the premature-ejaculation symptoms. This finding suggests the possible presence in some men of high levels of performance anxiety, relationship problems, or a constitutional tendency towards difficulty with ejaculation control.

[There have been encouraging findings (Coleman 2002) with the use of a variety of psychoactive medications in the treatment of certain types of compulsive sexual behaviors (CSB). A significant number of CSB patients have realized near or complete relief from sexual obsessions and compulsions when taking certain medications. The most frequently prescribed and studied of these are the SSRI medications. Since these same medications have been found to often be effective for other types of obsessive-compulsive disorders, it is hypothesized that the neurotransmitter serotonin is associated with the symptoms.

[An unfortunate side effect of SSRIs is the frequent complaint by patients of some loss of sexual desire. Certain formulations of the SSRI medications have been found to be more likely to cause unwanted sexual side effects than others. It seems that whenever a new SSRI has been approved for sale by the FDA, the drug company makes strong claims that their antidepressant causes fewer sexual side effects than the competition. Actual clinical experience with the new medication often does not support the corporate claims. Sometimes, changing from one SSRI formulation to another may result in a reduction or relief from a side effect, but in other cases, careful clinical experimentation with dosage, time of day medication is taken, or other medication-management efforts can have a beneficial effect. As previously stated, if the medication has the effect of merely slowing down typical sexual responsiveness, the patient may become overly frustrated and begin to avoid interactions. Also, because the possibility of sexual side effects with these types of medications are commonly known among the general public, there is a significant likelihood of an expectancy effect, where any perceived change in responsiveness is exaggerated by worry or anxiety that the medication is causing problems. This is unfortunate, since it is known that effective treatment of depression, anxiety, and obsessive-compulsive symptoms can result in a return to normal or near-normal libido. A great deal more high-quality research is needed to help us understand the complex interactions of medications and the biopsychosocial aspects of human sexual functioning. On the pharmacopoeia's horizon is the possibility of clinically useful true aphrodisiac drugs. Although such a class of medication would almost certainly be misused and abused, it could also offer relief to many who suffer from desire or arousal dysfunctions. (*End of update by R. W. Hatfield*)]

## Vulvodynia, a Newly Identified Syndrome

JULIAN SLOWINSKI

One of the new challenges facing American sex therapists and gynecologists today is the occurrence in many women of a painful burning sensation in the vulvar and vaginal area. This condition, recently named vulvodynia, or burning vulva syndrome, is a form of vestibulitis that can have a number of causes, from microorganisms that cause dermatosis to inflammation of the vestibular glands. The presenting complaint of these women is burning and painful intercourse. Some women develop secondary vaginismus. Discomfort varies from constant pain to localized spots highly sensitive to touch. In many cases, the psychological and relationship consequences are grave. Many women become depressed as a result and frustrated by attempts at treatment.

Current treatment includes topical preparations, laser surgery to ablate affected areas, dietary restrictions, and referral to a physical therapist to realign pelvic structure and reduce pressure on the spinal nerves serving the genital area. Some affected women have sought relief with acupuncture. Therapy may be enhanced by focusing on the effects of the condition on the sexual functioning of the patient, her relationship with her partner, and her self-image. Pain-reduction techniques, including self-hypnosis, have

proven valuable in some cases. Low doses of an antidepressant, including some SSRIs, may reduce the pain.

There is much work to be done in the treatment of vulvodynia, including making the public aware of this condition and educating physicians in the role that sex therapists can play in supporting these women and their partners.

## The Medicalization of Sex Therapy

JULIAN SLOWINSKI, WILLIAM R. STAYTON, and ROBERT W. HATFIELD [*Updated August 2003 by R. W. Hatfield*]

There is an increasing medicalization in sex therapy today. Although this may at first seem to benefit many patients—and it does—there is a concern among sex therapists that many conditions will be summarily treated through medications by primary physicians, with a corresponding failure to address the dynamic and interpersonal aspects of the patient. In short, there is a danger of incomplete evaluation of the patient's status if only the medical aspects are considered and the therapist is left out of the process. In the ideal situation, the sex therapist and physician would collaborate on the treatment plan, using medication as indicated.

[*Update 2003*: Even though Viagra sales have been substantial, they are less than half of the expected sales. It is apparent that Pfizer and their newly arriving corporate competitors from Bayer/GSK, TAP Pharmaceutical Products, and Eli Lilly see this failure by Pfizer to meet market expectations primarily as a mere marketing problem to be solved (Simons 2003).

[Cursory diagnosis and the simple prescription of sexual-response-enhancing drugs such as Viagra may be adequate for some individuals who are experiencing only or primarily an acute medical problem. Five years of clinical experience with Viagra is revealing that this approach is likely to be inadequate or even destructive when sexual dysfunction is associated with more-complex human factors, such as guilt, shame, fear, trauma, and significant relationship dysfunction. On a personal level, large numbers of couples and individuals are discovering the simple truth that healthy and pleasurable relationships are more complicated than erections and lubrication. Sadly, many who gain or regain physiological erectile functioning discover that emotional and relationship problems remain, and they end up feeling more hopeless about themselves or their relationship than they did before taking the medication. It is obvious that many of these people eventually give up, unaware that their problems and solutions to the problems could not be found at any pharmacy.

[Current trends are not encouraging. There has been little useful information making its way to the general public regarding truths about the utility of medications for sexual functioning. There is every indication that corporate interests among drug companies will increase the flood of advertising that simplistically asserts that their product will solve the problem. Hundreds of millions of dollars a year are and will be spent to convince physicians and the general public of this. The public does not want to hear that humans are complicated, and science has always been woefully inadequate in publicizing their complex findings in a useful manner. What some call corporate greed appears to cause some large drug companies nowadays to grossly distort or exaggerate the benefits and lack of harm of their prescription medications until the FDA eventually steps in. Lately, it has been observed that corporations that produce prescription and nonprescription sex pills have begun to invent fictitious diagnostic categories, such as "Female Sexual Dysfunction," and then claim that their product effectively treats, or even cures the problem.

[Additionally, there is an exploding trend, with the apparent discovery by a large number of smaller companies, that the FDA takes little or no notice if the product is not a prescription drug and is marketed in small print as a food product. Anyone who reads their email knows that there seems to be an endless number of companies that tout that their vitamin-herbal-mineral product will enlarge your breasts, penis, or scrotum, or greatly enhance your erections, lubrication, desire, staying power, and overall sexual performance and enjoyment. Billions of dollars are being made by mainstream and back-alley businesses on the sexual unhappiness, misunderstanding, ignorance, and suffering of a significant proportion of our population. We are in an unfortunate moment in history in which diagnosis and treatment decisions are removed from the expertise of science and medicine, and replaced by the corporate decisions of healthcare insurance providers and drug companies. There is no encouraging indication of hope on the horizon that any person, institution, professional organization, business, or government agency can or will step forward to protect and educate us. Fortunately, this is not true in all world cultures, but in most essential ways, the United States remains with two feet firmly mired in the dark ages on issues of human sexuality and sexual health. And unfortunately, unique aspects of our culture make solutions to these problems much more complex than the problems themselves. Known and needed changes in the areas of religiosity, education, business, childrearing, and government are likely to occur at a painfully slow pace. (*End of update by R. W. Hatfield*)]

[*Incidence Rates*     PATRICIA BARTHALOW KOCH

[*Update 1998*: Although it is extremely difficult to ascertain accurately the occurrence of the various sexual disorders and dysfunctions in the United States, research on various clinical and community samples has provided a glimpse as to their prevalence (Spector & Carey 1990). Sexual desire problems are the most common complaint seen in sex therapy in the United States, with affected men outnumbering women. It is also the most common sexual complaint of lesbian couples (Nichols 1989). Community studies indicate that 16% to 34% of the population experiences inhibited sexual desire. Between 11% and 48% of the female population may experience arousal-phase disorder, whereas 4% to 9% of males report this disorder. Erectile disorder is the most common complaint of men, and inhibited orgasm is the most common complaint of women seeking sex therapy in the United States. It is estimated that 5% to 10% of women in the general population experiences persistent or recurrent inhibited orgasm. On the other hand, inhibited orgasm is one of the least common dysfunctions among American males (1% to 10%). It seems to be a more common difficulty among gay men than among heterosexual men, however. The most common dysfunction of heterosexual men is rapid ejaculation, with 36% to 38% reporting persistent or recurrent rapid ejaculation. Dyspareunia is much more common in women than men, with 8% to 23% of women experiencing genital pain. Yet, few lesbian women report this difficulty. Over 100 diseases and disorders of the urogenital system have been linked with painful intercourse. (*End of update by P. B. Koch*)]

[*Culturally Appropriate Counseling and Therapy*
PATRICIA BARTHALOW KOCH
[*Update 1998*: Minority women and men in the United States experience the entire range of sexual problems and dysfunctions as those experienced by Anglo-Americans (Wyatt et al. 1978). However, most of the research has been conducted with samples of white, middle-class clients. This

has left a critical need for research regarding the effectiveness of various sex counseling and therapy techniques among males and females from various racial/ethnic groups (Christensen 1988).

[A primary issue is that most minority clients do not have the confidence in or financial resources for professional help and are most likely to turn to extended family or close friends—if anyone—with a sexual concern. Discussion of most sexual matters may be considered too intimate or shameful to discuss with anyone but a long-trusted confidante. People from minority groups may also have experienced prejudicial treatment from professionals in the dominant group that has led them to have mistrust, hostility, or expectations that their problem will not be understood. Thus, they usually come into contact with professionals only in a crisis when seeking help for legal, financial, reproductive, gynecological, or other medical problems, rather than for relationship or mental health issues.

[Professional helpers are overwhelmingly drawn from the white middle class and generally are middle-aged, and well educated (Atkinson et al. 1983). Their personal attitudes, values, and behaviors usually represent those of the dominant, more privileged culture. Unfortunately, the training of most sex counselors and therapists has not provided opportunities to become aware of and informed about the effects of gender, race/ethnicity, and class on their treatment of minority clients. Language barriers can be seriously problematic. Even when English is the primary language of therapist and client, an Anglo-American ethnocentrism may result in: misunderstanding, misdiagnosing, and/or mistreating a minority client's problem; trying to control aspects of the client's sexuality or fertility rather than helping him or her to make personally satisfying and culturally sensitive choices; or ignoring sources of help and support from within the client's culture (Christensen 1988; McGoldrick, Pearce, & Giordano 1982). The therapist may need to focus, not just on the individual, but also on the institutions and sexist/racist policies that may be affecting the client adversely (systemically induced dysfunction). (*End of update by P. B. Koch*)]

[*Sexuality of Menopausal Women*

PATRICIA BARTHALOW KOCH
[*Update 1998*: As America's baby boomers experience mid-life and older age, the sexual concerns of peri- and postmenopausal women have gained greater attention. Older women have been increasingly discussing sexual issues, along with their other health concerns (such as hot flashes, osteoporosis, and heart disease), with their physicians, and are turning to sex counselors and therapists for help. Some of the chief complaints experienced by mid-life heterosexual women are decreased sexual desire, decreased frequency and intensity of orgasm, and decreased frequency of sexual behaviors with a partner, although some women experience heightened sexual response and satisfaction during this time (Mansfield, Voda, & Koch 1995). Interestingly, mid-life lesbian women report less decline in sexual functioning and satisfaction than do their heterosexual peers (Cole 1988).

[Hormone replacement therapy (HRT) has been widely touted as a "miracle" drug to help women fight the "estrogen deficiency disease" of menopause and maintain their youth (e.g., smoother skin and elimination of hot flashes) and health (e.g., decreased risk of heart disease, osteoporosis, and perhaps Alzheimer's disease). However, others have addressed the naturalness of menopause and raised questions as to the actual and relative health risks involved with the use of HRT (such as increased breast cancer) (Love 1997). Regarding sexual functioning, estrogen seems to be important in maintaining vaginal lubrication and perhaps vaginal vasocongestion, whereas testosterone seems to be important for the pleasurable sensations associated with sexual arousal (Anderson 1991). There are also natural ways to replace estrogen, such as a diet high in soy-based foods, and vaginal dryness may be reduced with a vaginal lubricant, such as K-Y jelly.

[It should not be assumed that sexual concerns of mid-life women are always related to hormonal menopausal changes, since various research studies have found no connection, or only a weak link, between sexual functioning and menopausal status (Mansfield, Voda, & Koch 1995). Growing older in our culture also creates difficulties for women, such as perceived loss of attractiveness and value, that can affect self-esteem and sexuality. Continued or new difficulties in an ongoing sexual relationship can precipitate sexual concerns. As women reach mid-life, they may become more assertive about having their needs met, rather than fulfilling the more traditional gender roles and male phallocentric definitions of sexual satisfaction (Ehrenreich, Hass, & Jacobs 1987, 153; Ogden 1995). Indeed, a partner's ill health or declining sexual responsiveness may also affect the couple's sexual relationship. Thus, in diagnosing and treating a mid-life woman's sexual concerns, physiological, psychological, relational, and sociocultural factors should all be considered (Mansfield & Koch 1997). (*End of update by P. B. Koch*)]

[*Male Erectile Problems*     ROBERT T. FRANCOEUR

[*Update 1998*: Throughout recorded history, impotence or erectile dysfunction (ED) has been a major concern of men, and the curing of this sexual dysfunction one of medicine's shadiest niches, populated by hundreds of bizarre remedies ranging from ground rhinoceros horns, boar gall, and tiger-penis soup to mail-ordered electrified jockstraps and a never-ending offer of magical pills containing no more than common vitamins and herbs.

[In 1966, inflatable and flexible penile implants were introduced, followed by surgery to boost penile arterial flow in 1973. In 1982, the Food and Drug Administration approved a vacuum pump that pulls blood into the penis by creating a vacuum around a sheathed penis. In the same year, a milestone demonstration by Giles Brindley, a British physician, opened a new door to a major medical breakthrough in the treatment of erectile dysfunction. On-stage at a medical conference in Las Vegas, Brindley demonstrated the result of injecting the penis with papaverine, a drug that lowers blood pressure. Several penile injection therapies were soon being tested and welcomed by patients, including: alprostadil; "cocktails" of papaverine, phentolamine, and prostaglandin E1; and phentolamine combined with the protein VIP. Urethral suppositories containing alprostadil were approved by the FDA in 1997. In 1998, pills containing sildenafil, apomorphine, and phentolamine were in various stages of testing and FDA approval (Stipp & Whitaker 1998).

[In December 1992, the National Institutes of Health convened a Consensus Development Conference to address the issue of male erectile dysfunction (National Institutes of Health 1992). Specific issues investigated included:

1. The prevalence and clinical, psychological, and social impact of erectile dysfunction;
2. The risk factors for erectile dysfunction and how they might be used in preventing its development;
3. The need for and appropriate diagnostic assessment and evaluation of patients with erectile dysfunction;
4. The efficacies and risks of behavioral, pharmacological, surgical, and other treatments for erectile dysfunction;

5. Strategies for improving public and professional awareness and knowledge of erectile dysfunction; and
6. Future directions for research in prevention, diagnosis, and management of erectile dysfunction.

Among their findings, the panel concluded that:

1. The term "erectile dysfunction" should replace the term "impotence";
2. The likelihood of erectile dysfunction increases with age, but is not an inevitable consequence of aging;
3. Embarrassment of patients and reluctance of both patients and healthcare providers to discuss sexual matters candidly contribute to underdiagnosis of erectile dysfunction;
4. Many cases of erectile dysfunction can be successfully managed with appropriately selected therapy;
5. The diagnosis and treatment of erectile dysfunction must be specific and responsive to the individual patient's needs, and compliance as well as the desires and expectations of both the patient and partner are important considerations in selecting appropriate therapy;
6. Education of healthcare providers and the public on aspects of human sexuality, sexual dysfunction, and the availability of successful treatments is essential; and
7. Erectile dysfunction is an important public health problem, deserving increased support for basic science investigation and applied research.

[In the early 1980s, an estimated 10 million Americans suffered from erectile dysfunction. In 1987, a federally funded survey, the Massachusetts Male Aging Study led by Boston University urologist Irwin Goldstein, provided evidence for NIH to triple the early estimate of erectile dysfunction to 30 million Americans.

[*Update 2003*: Pharmaceutical companies concerned about their public images and the stockholders' focus on the bottom line resulted in caution about entering this area, despite the enormous profit potential. That reticence quickly ended in April 1998 with the successful introduction of Viagra by the Pfizer Corporation. Today, several other major pharmaceutical companies are rushing to find and market "sex cures." While citizens can be hopeful that the drug companies will be more ethical than the shaman and snake-oil salesmen of the past and present, the state of corporate ethics as we move into the new millennium does not promote optimism.

[When Pfizer Pharmaceutical released the first erection pill in 1998, the initial demand by men—and women—for this prescription medication far exceeded the expected market. For many weeks after Viagra's release, television programs, newspapers, and magazines were filled with discussions of the erection pill, of other possible modes of delivery including a transdermal gel, and the use of this medication by both men and women. While early reports and discussions focused on the "miracle of better loving through chemistry," it quickly shifted to broader psychological and relationship repercussions, both beneficial and harmful, for both men and women who have lived with impotence for some time. Health insurance companies quickly moved to limit their coverage of the medication, leaving potential users wondering about the cost of $6 to $10 per pill and their ability to pay. At the same time, questions are being asked how the insurance companies can justify paying for the erection pill while they refuse to pay for the cost of the birth control pill and mammograms. Sex therapists, like Leonore Tiefer, have warned that the erection pill is yet another example of the tendency of Americans to medicalize sex and seek "magic bullet" therapy:

The primary disadvantage of medicalization is that it denies, obscures, and ignores the social causes. . . . [T]he spotlight directed on "the erection" within current medical practice isolates and diminishes the man even as it offers succor for his insecurity and loss of self-esteem. Erections are presented as understandable and manipulable in and of themselves, unhooked from person, script, or relationship (Tiefer 1995, 155, 167).

[Perhaps the early cautions and criticisms have been at least partially supported. By 2003, Viagra sales have been disappointing, with Pfizer realizing less than half the sales that they expected (Simons 2003).

[One beneficial effect of Viagra has been that discussion of men's problems with erections entered the public domain, where men can more openly admit their dysfunction and a desire to try the new medication. Similarly, their partners now feel freer to talk about the topic. This public discussion of erectile problems, like the open discussion of oral sex that followed allegations of sexual impropriety against President Clinton, may have a salubrious effect on American sexual life (Kaschak & Tiefer, 2001; Kleinplatz, 2001). (*End of update by R. T. Francoeur, with R. W. Hatfield*)]

## [C. Holistic and Touch Therapies

ERICA GOODSTONE

[*Update 2003*: In contrast to the increased medicalization of sex therapy in contemporary practice is the expanding use of various touch therapies and other holistic therapeutic modalities. These therapies typically seek to integrate the mind and the body and to focus on the person as a whole, with benefits that can extend to the relationship and other aspects of life.

[Touch has always been an integral part of sex therapy as originally created by Masters and Johnson (1970), i.e., touch between the two sexual partners as homework assignments, not usually in the office and not between the sex therapist and client. Typically, homework assignments involve only a few types of touch: sensate focus, touching and stroking erogenous body parts (including penis, vagina, and breast stimulation) as part of foreplay, and oral-genital stimulation, as well as specific techniques for specific dysfunctions, such as the stop/start and squeeze techniques for premature ejaculation, and vaginal stimulation or insertion of dilators to alleviate dyspareunia and vaginismus.

[Touch affects more than just sexual performance. Gentle and nurturing touch can resurrect desire and eliminate sexual dysfunctions by alleviating physical aches and pains, relaxing the body so that blood flow can increase, and calming the spectator mind. Touch therapy that does not involve sensual or sexual stimulation can actually open the door to sensual awareness, emotional expression, positive thinking, and, ultimately, more pleasurable and satisfying intimate love relationships.

[Studies of touch-therapy methods (massage therapy, acupuncture, acupressure, craniosacral therapy, reflexology, Therapeutic Touch, etc.) and body-psychotherapy modalities (bioenergetic analysis, Rubenfeld synergy, hakomi, etc.) have shown promising and impressive improvements in the functioning of clients suffering from physical and emotional illnesses, post-traumatic stress disorder, sexual abuse issues, and even sexual dysfunctions (see, e.g., http:// www.umi.com/hp/Products/Dissertations.html; http://www .amtamassage.org/publications/enhancing-health.htm#8; http://www.acupuncture.com; http://www.eabp.org; http:// www.usabp.org).

[Dr. Tiffany Field's Touch Research Institute at Jackson Memorial Hospital in Miami, Florida, and Dr. John Upledger's Healthplex Center in Palm Beach Gardens, Florida, have amassed an impressive amount of data in studies of the benefits of their particular modalities, massage therapy and craniosacral therapy, respectively (http:// www.miami.edu / touch-research/; http://www.upledger.com/ therapies/cst.htm). Numerous studies, some conducted by the National Center for Complementary and Alternative Medicine of the National Institutes of Health (http://www .nlm.nih.gov/nccam/camonpubmed.html), have shown the healing benefits of massage, acupuncture, and acupressure. Many doctoral dissertations and other studies have focused on the benefits of Therapeutic Touch, a method developed by Dr. Delores Krieger, a nurse educator at New York University in New York City (http://www.therapeutic-touch.org; http://www.phact.org/e/tt/). Further research is needed to determine the effectiveness and benefits of the various modalities with respect to sexuality and sexual dysfunctions.

[The following simplified categorization of touch and holistic therapies indicates the enormous, largely untapped resources available to therapists and clients in the field of sex therapy.

[*Traditional Massage, Swedish Massage, and Massage Therapy*

[Massage is probably the best known, most thoroughly researched, and one of the few licensed methods of touch therapy in this country. Carefully draping the client's body with a sheet and towels, the therapist typically utilizes oils and creams, as well as herbal and aromatic essences, music, soft lighting, and basic massage strokes directly on the client's skin. The goal is usually to alleviate muscular tension, improve circulation, eliminate painful nerve constrictions, treat acute and chronic soft-tissue injuries and problems, and relieve stress by relaxing the mind and body.

[*Contemporary Western Massage and Bodywork*

[Expanding upon the practice of traditional massage therapy, these methods may include the use of water, ice, heat, chair massage, onsite massage, medical massage, sports massage, pregnancy massage, infant massage, and more recently, animal massage.

[*Structural, Functional, Movement, and Alignment Therapies*

[These methods of touch therapy (e.g., Alexander Technique, Feldenkrais, and Myofascial Release) utilize techniques to improve body alignment, organ functioning, flexibility of movement, hormonal balance, and integration of the body as a holographic system. These methods may involve actual re-sculpting of the connective tissue, improved flow of cerebral spinal fluid, lymph drainage, realignment of subluxated vertebrae, trigger-point release, or simply guiding the body to move in an easier, more fluid, and graceful manner.

[*Asian Bodywork*

[These methods of touch therapy (e.g., Acupuncture, Acupressure, Chi Gong, and Thai Massage) originated in different parts of Asia and are mostly derived from Traditional Chinese Medicine Theory. This ancient theory describes the health of the body in terms of the five basic elements (fire, water, earth, metal, and wood) and the functioning of the 12 pairs of primary meridians and the eight extraordinary meridians, lines of energy flowing in specific patterns throughout the body. Stimulating points along the meridians using finger, hand, foot, knee, or elbow pressure, and in some cases, fine needles, the goal is to release restrictions in the flow of energy (or *chi*) throughout the body.

[*Energetic Bodywork*

[These methods of touch therapy (e.g., Polarity Therapy, Reiki, and Chakra Healing) focus on the energetic fields within and surrounding the body. These methods range from direct contact on the skin, to indirect contact an inch to a foot or more above the body, to distant indirect contact from another room, another city, or anywhere on the planet. Training may be simple to complex, requiring anywhere from one weekend of basic training, to several years of ongoing instruction, to a secretive initiation process open to only a select number of students.

[*Somatic and Expressive Arts Therapies*

[These methods include body-centered therapies that may or may not involve actual touch. Through movement, dance, sports, yoga postures, martial arts, dramatic performances, artistic expression, and visualization, as well as through hands-on touch, the body may allow us to express emotions and feel sensations that have previously been unavailable to our conscious minds. Some practitioners are trained artists, some have received training in one or more body-therapy methods, while others are graduates of accredited academic programs.

[*Body Psychotherapy*

[The common element of all body-psychotherapy methods (e.g., Rubenfeld Synergy, Bioenergetic Analysis, Core Energetics, and Reichian Therapy) is the focus on body awareness and the judicious use of touch during the psychotherapeutic session. The touch may vary from very gentle and respectful of the client's needs to more-forceful touch focused on breaking through defenses and body armoring. A body-psychotherapy session may include guided imagery, focused breathing, role playing, movement, expressive arts, as well as emotional release work. Body psychotherapists are trained and certified in both psychotherapy and body-therapy methods or in specific body-psychotherapy modalities.

[Current sex therapists may choose to study a particular body-therapy modality and enroll in a training program to learn how to use touch therapy in combination with their counseling and therapy techniques—and then apply this knowledge and understanding to the practice of sex therapy. Without any additional training, however, sex therapists can employ the services of qualified, certified, and/or licensed body-therapy practitioners as an adjunctive and associative practice with some of their clients.

[Further information can be obtained at the Center for Loving Touch website, http://www.sexualreawakening .com. Here you will find links to many of the major body-therapy and body-psychotherapy organizations, including the U.S. Association for Body Psychotherapy. (*End of update by E. Goodstone*)]

## D. Education and Certification of Sex Therapists

JULIAN SLOWINSKI and WILLIAM R. STAYTON

Since American sex educators, counselors, and therapists are not licensed by any government agency, reputable professionals in the field operate under one of several traditional professional licenses as part of their practice as a physician, psychologist, psychoanalyst, social worker, marriage and family counselor, or pastoral counselor.

The American Association of Sex Educators, Counselors, and Therapists (AASECT) does offer its own certification for sex educators, counselors, and therapists following successful completion of specified training programs that include supervised practice. Continuing education credits are required for renewal of this certification.

## E. Sex Surrogates: The Continuing Controversy

RAYMOND J. NOONAN [*Updated by R. J. Noonan*]

Three decades after Masters and Johnson pioneered modern sex therapy, the use of sexual partner surrogates, despite a long history of controversy, continues, largely because it has been found by some professionals to be an effective therapeutic modality in certain circumstances for persons without partners and for specially challenged persons with physical limitations. Still, as Dauw (1988) has noted, little in-depth research has been conducted about surrogates, their effectiveness, or their appropriateness in working with specific sexual dysfunctions. Misconceptions about surrogates are widespread (Apfelbaum 1984), in part, because of a common confusion between the roles of sex surrogates and prostitutes, based on the potential for intimate sexual interaction and the surrogate being paid for her or his work. Roberts (1981) has suggested that "the most common misconception" is of the surrogate as "an elitist type of prostitute." In addition, some authors have commented on the effects of media accounts of sex surrogates, which have tended to focus on the bizarre, the sensational, and even the untrue (Braun 1975; Lily 1977).

The distinction commonly noted between surrogates and prostitutes usually relies on the intent of the sexual interaction: the prostitute's intent being immediate gratification localized on genital pleasure, whereas the surrogate's intent is long-term therapeutic reeducation and reorientation of inadequate capabilities of functioning or relating sexually (Brown 1981; Jacobs et al. 1975; Roberts 1981). In 1970, Masters and Johnson noted that ". . . so much more is needed and demanded from a substitute partner than effectiveness of purely physical sexual performance that to use prostitutes would have been at best clinically unsuccessful and at worst psychologically disastrous."

[*Update 2003*: IPSA, the International Professional Surrogates Association (http://members.aol.com/Ipsa1/home .html), remains the organization most involved with surrogate partner therapy, primarily training new surrogates and educating the public and professionals about its potential benefits (Vaughan 2004). (*End of update by R. J. Noonan*)] In describing the therapeutic process, IPSA (n.d.) wrote,

> A surrogate partner is a member of a three-way therapeutic team consisting of therapist, client and surrogate partner. The surrogate participates, as a partner to the client, in experiential exercises designed to build the client's skills in the areas of physical and emotional intimacy. This partner work includes exercises in communication, relaxation, sensual and sexual touching and social skills training.

Others, including Allen (1978), Apfelbaum (1977, 1984), Brown (1981), Dauw (1988), Masters and Johnson (1970), Roberts (1981), Symonds (1973), Williams (1978), and Wolfe (1978) have described, either briefly or in part, typical surrogate sessions or alternative models. According to Jacobs, et al. (1975): "The usual therapeutic approach is slow and thorough. Exercises are graduated and concentrate on body awareness, relaxation and sensual/sexual experiences that are primarily non-genital." Where appropriate, the surrogate also teaches "vital social skills and traditional courtship patterns which finally include sexual interaction." However, none of these writers gave a perspective of the relative amount of time or importance that each aspect of the surrogate therapy session or program places on the entire process. Such a perspective would give a clearer understanding of the true functions of a sex surrogate that would allow the integration of the use of surrogate therapy into a useful theoretical perspective relative to clinical sexology, as well as to normative sexual functioning.

The use of sex surrogates was introduced by Masters and Johnson (1970) as a way to treat single men who did not have partners available to participate in their couple-oriented sex-therapy program. As the practice evolved, surrogates some-times specialized in working with specific populations, such as single heterosexual or homosexual men, with couples as a coach, or with people with physical disabilities.

Today, the use of surrogates remains controversial with complex legal, moral, ethical, professional, and clinical im-plications. [*Update 2003*: As of mid-2003, surrogate partner therapy, when performed under the supervision of a li-censed therapist, is completely legal throughout the U.S. (Vaughan 2004). (*End of update by R. J. Noonan*)] Although Masters and Johnson eventually abandoned the practice (Redlich 1977), the use of professional sex surrogates has been ethically permissible as part of the sex therapist's ar-mamentarium, according to the American Association of Sex Educators, Counselors, and Therapists (AASECT 1978, 1987). Still, a recent version of AASECT's (1993) *Code of Ethics* ceased to mention the use of surrogates ex-plicitly. Instead, the 1993 code merely stated that a member of AASECT should not make a "referral to an unqualified or incompetent person" (p. 14), which would presumably refer to surrogates, among others.

In their 1987 *Code of Ethics*, however, and in at least one earlier version, AASECT addressed the issue of surrogates directly, and promulgated the parameters for their ethical use, including the understanding that the surrogate is not a sex therapist or psychotherapist, and that the therapist must protect the dignity and welfare of both the client and the sur-rogate. In addition, it outlined how issues of confidentiality and consent should be addressed. In many ways, this docu-ment is similar in putting the client's welfare first to the *Code of Ethics* espoused by the International Professional Surrogates Association (IPSA 1989). Among IPSA's strict requirements for members are the necessity that surrogates practice only within the context of the therapeutic triangle consisting of the client, surrogate, and supervising thera-pist, that the relationship with the client always be within the context of the therapy, that the surrogate recognize and act in accordance with the boundaries and limitations of her competence, and that the surrogate be responsible for all precautions against pregnancy and disease. Confidentiality and continuing-education requirements are also among the 17 items listed in the code, although the surrogate's primary role as a cotherapist or substitute partner in any given therapeutic situation is left open to agreement between the therapist and surrogate.

In 1997, there were estimated to be fewer than 200 sur-rogates worldwide, according to Vena Blanchard, president of IPSA (personal communication, March 15, 1997), with maybe 100 practicing in the U.S.A. [*Update 2003*: As of mid-2003, Blanchard estimated that there were fewer than 100 practicing surrogates in the country (Vaughan 2004). (*End of update by R. J. Noonan*)] These numbers are down by about two thirds from the 300 estimated to be practicing in the U.S. in 1983-1984 (Noonan 1995/1984), a time when the number of surrogates peaked. However, the downward trend of the subsequent decade, caused primarily by fears surrounding AIDS, has been showing signs of reversing since the mid-1990s, according to Blanchard, who pointed to the number of new surrogates being trained and request-ing training by IPSA. Still, according to Blanchard, only a few urban areas, primarily on the two coasts (mostly in Cal-ifornia), have surrogates working, with most of the country not being served.

Noonan (1995/1984) surveyed 54 sex surrogates who were part of a surrogates' networking mailing list represent-ing about 65 to 70% of all known legitimate trained surro-gates in 1983-1984. The 54 surrogate respondents repre-sented about 36% of the 150 estimated known surrogates, who were estimated to be approximately one half of all sur-rogates practicing in the U.S. at the time. In addition to de-mographic data, the instrument asked respondents to esti-mate the percentage of time they spent in each of seven ac-tivities with clients. The data gathered seemed to support strongly the hypothesis that sex surrogates provide more than sexual service for their clients, spending about 87% of their professional time doing nonsexual activities. In addi-tion to functioning as a sexual intimate, Noonan found that the surrogate functions as educator, counselor, and cothera-pist, providing sex education, sex counseling, social-skills education, coping-skills counseling, emotional support, sensuality and relaxation education and coaching, and self-awareness education. The results indicated that a majority of time is spent outside of the sexual realm, suggesting fur-ther that surrogate therapy employs a more holistic method-ological approach than previous writings, both professional and lay, would seem to indicate. Clearly, the sex surrogate functions far beyond the realm of the prostitute.

Specifically, Noonan's (1995/1984) results showed that the surrogate spends much of her or his time talking with the client, with approximately 34% of the time spent giving sex-ual information, as well as reassurance and support. Almost one half of the surrogate's time (48.5%) is spent in experien-tial exercises involving the body nonsexually, with the ma-jority of that time devoted to teaching the client basically how to feel—how to be aware of what is coming in through the senses. Combining the two averages, we find that the sur-rogate typically spends 82.5% of the therapeutic time en-hancing the cognitive, emotional, and sensual worlds of the client. Only after this foundation is developed does the surro-gate spend almost 13% of the time focusing on erotic activi-ties, including sexual intercourse, cunnilingus, and fellatio, and teaching sexual techniques. The remaining 4.5% focuses on social skills in public settings, clearly the least important aspect of what the surrogate deals with.

Finally, a profile emerged of the "average" sex surrogate in 1983-1984: she is a white female, in her late 30s/early 40s, and not very religious. She is one way or another single with 1.4 children, college-educated, lives in California, has been practicing as a surrogate for four years three months, and sees 27 clients per year. Finally, she is a heterosexual who does not need to concern herself or her partner with chemical or mechanical methods of contraception, because she has been sterilized (Noonan 1995/1984). It is interesting to note that among the 54 respondents, six of the surrogates had earned doctorates, with the average being a bachelor's de-gree plus some advanced study, indicating the atypically high level of educational achievement in this group.

### Present and Future Issues

Surrogate therapy has no doubt changed somewhat over the past two decades for various reasons. These changes need to be elucidated, documented, and incorporated into our collective knowledge about normative sexuality and how to address the various problems we have created or maintained around its expression.

Since 1983, the impact of AIDS has become a deep con-cern of both surrogates and therapists. Exactly how it has af-fected the work of surrogates remains to be studied. Cer-tainly in the years immediately following Noonan's (1995/1984) study of the functions of sex surrogates, many surro-gates, who in retrospect were not particularly at risk for HIV infection, stopped practicing or modified their practice as surrogates out of fear. Many therapists also stopped referring clients to surrogates out of fear of legal liability. As the reality of HIV infection has become better known, surrogates, who are mostly female working with heterosexual males, are continuing to help clients function better sexually while promoting responsible sexual behavior at all levels. [*Update 2003*: A recent report indicated that some surrogates began to focus on integrating safer sex and condom use into the therapy to help clients more effectively deal with the new reality, which continues today (Vaughan 2004). In addition, given the current emphasis on pharmacological treatment of some sexual dysfunctions, it remains to be seen what kind of impact this will have on surrogate therapy, especially in light of the fact that such dysfunctions are likely to increase with the greying of America. (*End of update by R. J. Noonan*)] Little or no research exists that has investigated how gay male surrogates, who worked mostly with gay male clients in the 1980s, have changed their practice.

Since the 1980s, women have become more aware of how surrogates might help them effectively deal with various sexual dysfunctions. Some female clients will ask their therapists, or seek out therapists who are open to the possibility, to find a male surrogate with whom they might work. Largely because of the sexual double standard that continues to operate in many, if not most, therapists, however, most clients of surrogates continue to be male. The degree to which women have begun to work with surrogates to solve their sexual problems, or who consider it a viable option, are questions that require additional research. In addition, the differences that may exist in the design of the therapy program itself and how a female client might work with a surrogate, as compared to how males work with surrogates, is also a topic open to research. It appears that heterosexual male surrogates remain today the rarest of sex surrogates, as in the early 1980s.

Despite these research needs, the population of surrogates is likely to remain resistant to study, both because of the legal ambiguities often involved with their practice and the fact that the use of surrogates retains a relatively high visibility in public consciousness, although surrogates themselves are usually quite invisible. Because they are a small group, they will be difficult to study with any reasonable assurances of confidentiality.

The most troubling aspect of research on sex surrogates may be the indication, yet to be verified by any research, that there are probably many more surrogates working with clients and therapists in the United States, who are independently trained by varying standards by the therapists with whom they may be working, and who are both isolated from other surrogates and from researchers. This leaves them unaware of the most recent knowledge and advances in the field, because rarely are therapists trained in working with surrogates. It also deprives us of the knowledge gained from experience that these "hidden" surrogates may have learned.

## 12. Sex Research and Advanced Professional Education

**A. A Research Assessment** ROBERT T. FRANCOEUR

The United States has a long tradition and unequaled wealth of sexological research. The survey work of Alfred Kinsey and his colleagues in the 1940s and 1950s and the clinical/therapeutic research of William Masters and Virginia Johnson are but tips of the iceberg, referred to and cited in almost any discussion of sexological research anywhere in the world (Brecher 1979; Bullough 1994; Pomeroy 1972).

Sexological research in the United States today is vital to the management of many social and public health problems. Each year, one million teenage girls become pregnant, a per-thousand-rate twice that of Canada, England, and Sweden, and ten times that of the Netherlands; the disproportion is similar for teenage abortions (Jones et al. 1986). The nation spends $25 billion on families begun by teenagers for social, health, and welfare services. One million Americans are HIV-positive and almost one quarter of a million have died of AIDS. Yet only one in ten American children receives sexuality education that includes information about HIV/AIDS transmission and prevention. One in five adolescent girls in grades 8 through 11 is subject to sexual harassment, while three quarters of girls under age 14 who have had sexual relations have been raped. These and other public health problems are well documented and increasingly understood in the context of poverty, family trauma, ethnic discrimination, lack of educational opportunities, and inadequate health services. However, there is little recognition of the need for sexological research to deal effectively with these problems. Congress has several times refused or withdrawn funding for well-designed and important surveys because of pressure from conservative minorities (di Mauro 1995).

In 1995, the Sexuality Research Assessment Project of the Social Science Research Council (605 Third Avenue, 17th Floor. New York, New York 10158) published a comprehensive review of *Sexuality Research in the United States: An Assessment of the Social and Behavioral Sciences* (di Mauro 1995). This report identified and described major gaps and needs in American sexological research. There is a serious lack of a framework for the analysis of sexual behaviors in the context of society and culture. This framework is needed to examine how sexual socialization occurs in families, schools, the media, and peer groups, and to address the complex perspectives of different situations, populations, and cultural communities. Areas of need identified by the project include: gender, HIV/AIDS, adolescent sexuality, sexual orientation, sexual coercion, and research methodology. Three major barriers hindering sexuality research are 1. the lack of comprehensive research training in sexuality, 2. inadequate mechanisms and efforts to disseminate research findings to policymakers, advocates, practitioners, and program representatives in diverse communities who need this information, and 3. the lack of federal, private-sector, and academic funding for research.

[*Gender Differences in Sex Research*

RAYMOND J. NOONAN

[*Update 2003*: A perplexing problem that has repeatedly emerged in sex surveys of men and women regarding their sexual attitudes and behavior is the differing levels of sexual activities that each sex tends to report. Males tend to report higher levels of various sexual activities with greater sexual permissiveness than do females, which tends to reflect cultural gender-role expectations. This has led to such anomalies as heterosexual men reporting more sexual partners than heterosexual women do, which one would expect to be statistically equivalent. Thus, the limitations of self-reports become a salient question affecting the validity of any results, as well as public policy based on them. One possible explanation suggested that men overreported their sexual partners, activities, and so on, and women underreported them to accommodate society's double standard.

Alexander and Fisher (2003) sought to shed some light on this question through the imaginative use of a research technique called the "bogus pipeline," in which they asked men and women questions in written surveys about their sexual attitudes and behaviors under the false belief that their truthfulness could be detected (in this case, by being attached to a polygraph that was actually non-functioning). Results were compared with those of two groups, one in which the testing was anonymous (but without the belief that truthfulness was detectable), and one in which there was the possibility that someone might see the answers (the "exposure threat").

Although the results were not as clear as expected, they indicated that under the exposure-threat conditions, answers reflecting traditional sex differences with respect to sexual behaviors were more likely, whereas when they thought their truthfulness could be detected, the women's and men's responses were more similar. In fact, the responses of the women were generally more exaggerated than the men's, meaning their sexual activity was greater than normally found in surveys, which was attributed to the fact that women have greater expectations to respond and be perceived in socially appropriate ways (Alexander & Fisher 2003). Thus, women and men may be more similar than different, and further research needs to clarify these findings, as well as have them applied to future research on sexual behaviors. (*End of update by R. J. Noonan*)]

## B. Advanced Sexological Institutes, Organizations, and Publications

MARTHA CORNOG and ROBERT T. FRANCOEUR
[*Rewritten and updated in August 2003 by M. Cornog and R. T. Francoeur*)]

### Advanced Sexuality Education and Institutes

The longest-established American sexological research institution is the Kinsey Institute for Research in Sex, Gender, and Reproduction, based at the University of Indiana, Bloomington, Indiana (http://www.kinseyinstitute.org). Another major, younger institution is the Institute for the Advanced Study of Human Sexuality (IASHS; address: 1525 Franklin Street, San Francisco, CA 94109, http://www.iashs.edu), which has its own degree program—see below. Two additional key organizations focus strongly on sexual research and public policy: the Sexuality Information and Education Council of the U.S. (SIECUS; address: 130 West 42nd Street, Suite 350, New York, NY 10036, http://www.siecus.org), and the Planned Parenthood Federation of America (PPFA; address of headquarters: 434 West 33rd Street, New York, NY 10001, http://www.ppfa.org).

The libraries of the Kinsey Institute and the IASHS both have extensive collections on sexuality, including research, policy, and erotica. The SIECUS and PPFA libraries also have significant holdings, as does California State University at Northridge (CSUN) with its Vern and Bonnie Bullough Collection on Human Sexuality. A more complete selection of libraries specializing in sexuality topics, including homosexuality, may be found via the index to the *Directory of Special Libraries and Information Centers* (Gale Research).

A number of U.S. universities grant degrees with majors or concentrations in sexology and/or sex education, counseling, and therapy. Extensive listings of all types of educational programs of all types is available from the Society for the Scientific Study of Sexuality (http://www.sexscience.org; click on "Resources" and then on "Educational Opportunities"), and at the Kinsey Institute website (http://www.kinseyinstitute.org).

- *The Alfred Kinsey Institute for Research in Sex, Gender, and Reproduction* and the University of Indiana in Bloomington offer an undergraduate individualized major in human sexuality, a doctoral minor in human sexuality through the Kinsey Institute, and a doctoral minor and undergraduate interdisciplinary major in Gender Studies.

- *The Institute for the Advanced Study of Human Sexuality*, now in its 27th year, offers five graduate degree programs and five certificate programs for those wishing academic and professional training in human sexuality, specifically for persons who intend to make the field of human sexuality a major focus in their professional careers. On-site and distance learning courses are scheduled so as to accommodate the busy professional. The Institute is home of the most comprehensive sexological library in the world, the result of more than 27 years of archival research and efforts to obtain the rights for the reproduction of film and other materials for student use. The library system contains more than 75,000 books, 150,000 magazines, journals, and pamphlets, 50,000 videotapes, 200,000 films, and more than 900,000 photographs and slides. The Institute's degree programs and certificate programs have been approved and registered by the California Bureau for Private Postsecondary and Vocational Education (BPPVE). For further information, contact: http://www.iashs.edu or 415-928-1133.

- *California State University in Northridge* offers an interdisciplinary minor in Human Sexuality through the College of Social and Behavioral Sciences. CSUN is also the base for the College of Social and Behavioral Sciences' Center for Sex Research (http://www.csun.edu/~sr2022/) and the extensive Vern and Bonnie Bullough Library Collection on Human Sexuality. Contact: Coordinator, Dept. of Family Environmental Sciences, 18111 Nordhoff St., Northridge, CA 91330.

- *University of Minnesota Program in Human Sexuality*, the only American graduate program with an endowed chair in Human Sexuality, and the Department of Family Practice and Community Health offer educational opportunities in medical school education, academic courses, continuing education, Sexual Attitude Reassessment (SAR), and a post-doctoral clinical/research fellowship. Contact: http://www.med.umn.edu/fp/phs/phspostd.htm.

- *Columbia University School of Public Health*, New York, NY, offers a Sexuality and Health track, an interdepartmental program, jointly created and delivered by the Departments of Population and Family Health and of Sociomedical Sciences, leading to a master in public health (M.P.H.) degree.

- *San Francisco State University* (San Francisco, CA), offers an undergraduate minor and a master of arts degree in Human Sexuality Studies in the Human Sexuality Studies Program, to provide students with knowledge about processes and variations in sexual cultures, sexual identity and gender-role formation, and the social, cultural, historical, and ethical foundations of sexuality, intimate relationships, and sexual health. Contact: SFSU, Human Sexuality Studies Program, 1600 Holloway Avenue, San Francisco, CA 94132; tel.; 415-405-3570; http://www.sfsu.edu/~bulletin/current/programs/humsexst.htm.

- *Widener University's Center for Education, School of Human Service Professions*, in Chester, PA, offers master's and doctoral programs in Human Sexuality Education. The program continues the tradition of the graduate program at the University of Pennsylvania (where it operated the past 20 years). Clergy, educators, counselors, and others who wish to become certified sex educators, to do counseling or therapy, to get advanced training, or to engage in sex research may apply. Contact: Program Coordinator, Human Sexuality Education, 987 Old Eagle School Road, Ste. 719, Wayne, PA 19087; tel.: 610-971-0700; William.R.Stayton@widener.edu.

- *The American Academy of Clinical Sexologists* (AACS), headed by Dr. William Granzig at Maimonides University in North Miami Beach, Florida, offers mental health counselors, clinical social workers, marriage and family counselors, and psychologists a two-semester program leading to certification in sex therapy, and a doctoral degree program in clinical sexology. For those who wish to practice sex therapy, a program of continuing education in certain sexological subjects, which, when certain other requirements are met, qualify a graduate student for state certification as a sex therapist. Students may also qualify for a doctor of philosophy degree in Clinical Sexology by combining the two semesters of certification study with an additional four semesters of study and completion of a doctoral dissertation. Contact: http://www.esextherapy.com; tel.: 407-645-1641. For the program on Long Island, NY, contact: womentc@aol.com.

- *Universite du Quebec au Montreal* (UQAM), in Montreal, Quebec, Canada, offers North America's undergraduate and master's-level degrees in *Sexologie*. The program has over 25 full-time faculty in a wide range of disciplines. All instruction is in French.
- *University of Guelph* (Guelph, Ontario, Canada) offers graduate programs, summer course workshops, and an annual institute through the Department of Family Relations and Applied Nutrition.

In the late 1960s, several American medical schools introduced programs in human sexuality into their curricula for training physicians. These programs reached their zenith in the early 1980s. By the late 1980s, many of them were under fire from newly appointed conservative administrators and threatened with cutbacks and elimination. Indications suggest a significant decline in sexuality training for physicians and other healthcare professionals, but the picture is not clear, because no one has studied the situation nationwide. (See Richard Cross' comments in Section C below.)

Two East Coast institutes are focused on the interconnection of sexuality and religion:

- Religious Institute on Sexual Morality, Justice, and Healing, 304 Main Avenue, #335, Norwalk, CT 06851; tel.: 203-840-1148; http://www.religiousinstitute.org.
- Center for Sexuality and Religion, 987 Old Eagle School Road, Suite 719, Wayne, PA 19087; tel.: 610-995-0341; http://www.ctrsr.org.

### Sexological Organizations

There are three major American sexological membership organizations:

- The American Association of Sex Educators, Counselors, and Therapists (AASECT). Founded in 1967; currently around 1,500 members. Address: P.O. Box 5488, Richmond, VA 23220; http://www.aasect.org .
- The Society for the Scientific Study of Sexuality (SSSS). Founded in 1957; currently around 1,000 members. Address: P.O. Box 416, Allentown, PA 18105; http://www.sexscience.org .
- The Society for Sex Therapy and Research (SSTAR). Founded in 1974; currently about 200 members. Address: 409 12th Street NW, P.O. Box 96920, Washington, DC 20090; http://www.sstarnet.org .

Several dozen other groups exist for various types of professionals concerned with sex-related issues. Typical among these are: the Association for the Behavioral Treatment of Sexual Abusers, the Association of Nurses in AIDS Care, the National Council on Family Relations, the Society for the Philosophy of Sex and Love, and the Society for the Psychological Study of Lesbian, Gay, and Bisexual Issues.

At least 100 U.S. advocacy and common-interest organizations deal in one way or another with advocacy for gay and lesbian viewpoints or provide a vehicle for the gay and lesbian practitioners of a profession or hobby to socialize or work together. Among the largest and most comprehensive are the Lambda Legal Defense and Education Fund, the National Gay and Lesbian Task Force, and Parents, Families, and Friends of Lesbians and Gays, each with 15,000 or more member/contributors and budgets in the millions of dollars. Typical of smaller special-interest groups are: Federal Lesbians and Gays (federal government workers), Gay and Lesbian Medical Association, Good Gay Poets, International Association of Gay and Lesbian Martial Artists, International Gay and Lesbian Travel Association, and Lesbian and Gay Bands of America.

Similar organizations exist in America for many sexual viewpoints and behaviors other than homosexuality—and for sexual matters perceived as problems. An all-too-brief sampling from the 40th edition of the *Encyclopedia of Associations* (the *EoA*, from Gale Research Publications) includes: Adult Video Association (pro-pornography/erotica), Americans for Decency, American Sunbathing Association (nudism), DC Feminists Against Pornography, Eagle Forum, Focus on the Family, Impotents Anonymous, National Association of People with AIDS, North American Swing Club Association and the Lifestyles Organization (both recreational nonmonogamy), Renaissance Transgender Association, Sex Worker Foundation for Art, Culture, and Education, Sexaholics Anonymous, Society for the Second Self (Tri-Ess, for transvestites), and Women Exploited by Abortion. Browse the *EoA* index under subjects like "sex," "AIDS," and so on, for more organizations.

Other, often-small special-interest groups may not be listed in the *EoA* but can be located by scanning sex-related websites and publications like *The Black Book*, edited by Bill Brent and Lori Selke (Black Books, http://www.blackbooks.com). Such groups include DPF (Diaper Pail Friends: infantilism and nepiophilia, http://www.dpf.com), the National Association of Rubberists (rubber or latex fetish, http://www.rubberist.net), and the Society of Janus (sadomasochism, http://www.soj.com).

### Sexological Journals and Publications

U.S.-published professional journals that focus on sexuality-related research and commentary include: *Archives of Sexual Behavior, Annual Review of Sex Research, Electronic Journal of Human Sexuality, Journal of Bisexuality, Journal of Child Sexual Abuse, Journal of Gay and Lesbian Psychotherapy, Journal of the Gay and Lesbian Medical Association, Journal of Gender Studies, Journal of the History of Sexuality, Journal of Homosexuality, Journal of Lesbian Studies, Journal of Marriage and Family, Journal of Psychology and Human Sexuality, Journal of Sex and Marital Therapy, Journal of Sex Research, Journal of Sex and Aggression, Marriage and Family Review, Journal of the History of Sexuality, Maledicta* (language), *Sexuality and Culture, Sexuality and Disability*, and *SIECUS Report*. This is not an exhaustive list; consult periodical directories at a public or university library for other titles.

For identifying U.S. national and local gay and lesbian newspapers and magazines, consult the most recent annual edition of *Gayellow Pages* (Renaissance House). A less comprehensive and less frequent, but quite useful sister guide to small sex-topic periodicals, as well as organizations and vendors, is *The Black Book*, noted above. Large periodical directories may also list some of these publications. (*End of update by M. Cornog and R. T. Francoeur*)]

## [C. International Sexuality Description Project

ROBERT T. FRANCOEUR

[*Update 2003*: The editors of the four-volume *International Encyclopedia of Sexuality* (1997, 2000) and this 2003 in-depth report on 62 countries, the *Continuum Complete International Encyclopedia of Sexuality*, welcome the appearance of an important complementary project, the International Sexuality Description Project. The following summary is based on information supplied by David P. Schmitt.

[ISDP is an anonymous survey study designed to assess sexual attitudes and behaviors across a large number of cultures (Schmitt et al. 2003). Founded by David P. Schmitt of Bradley University in 2000, the ISDP includes a network of psychologists, biologists, sociologists, and other social scientists from 56 nations. In total, more than 100 research scholars took part in the ISDP and administered an anonymous sex survey to 100 men and 100 women, typically college students in their country. The ISDP survey was translated from English into 30 languages using a translation/back-translation procedure and was eventually administered to a total sample of over 17,000 people. The ISDP survey included measures of romantic attachment styles, global self-esteem, the "Big Five" personality traits, short-term mating desires, human mate-poaching behaviors, sociosexuality, and the "Sexy Seven" measure of human sexuality (Schmitt & Buss 2000).

[In its first report (Schmitt et al. 2003), ISDP addressed the hypothesis of evolutionary psychologists that men and women possess both long-term and short-term mating strategies, with men's short-term strategies differentially rooted in the desire for sexual variety. The ISPD survey results supported the existence of culturally universal sex differences in the desire for sexual variety.

[A second report focused "on adult romantic attachment, specifically gender differences in the 'dismissing' form of adult romantic attachment. Dismissing romantic attachment orientations are indicated by an avoidance of close personal relationship and the tendency to prevent romantic disappointment by maintaining a sense of relational independence and emotional distance." This article critically evaluates whether men are universally more dismissing than women (Schmitt & Buss 2003).

[A follow-up study, the ISDP-2, is currently underway and will include samples from more than 60 cultures. In this new study, they have included measures of impression management, sex-role ideology, sexual aggression, domestic violence, HIV/AIDS knowledge, and HIV/AIDS risk behavior. The founding director of the ISDP, David P. Schmitt, may be contacted at dps@bradley.edu. (*End of update by R. T. Francoeur*)]

## D. Sexuality Education of Physicians and Clergy

*Medical School Sexuality Education*

RICHARD J. CROSS

Medical schools have always taught certain aspects of sexuality, e.g., the anatomy of the male and female sex organs, the menstrual cycle, basic obstetrics, and some psychology and psychiatry. That picture began to change about 30 years ago when Harold I. Lief (1963, 1965), a psychiatrist at Tulane University Medical School in Louisiana, wrote articles pointing out that most Americans regarded physicians as authorities on human sexuality, that the field of sexology was changing fast, and that only three medical schools in the country were even trying to teach modern sexology. The situation gradually improved, and when Harold Lief and Richard J. Cross, a physician who had introduced sexology education at the Robert Wood Johnson Medical School at Rutgers University in New Jersey, sent a questionnaire to all medical schools in the U.S. and Canada in 1980, they found only three schools that said they did not teach sexuality. However, they did not publish their results because of the poor response rate and apparent unreliability of self-serving responses from medical school administrators. It was clear, however, that the improvement was limited; part of the change reported was because of different interpretations of the questionnaire and differing definitions of "sexuality." No one knows just what is being taught in the different medical schools today.

Part of the problem is that medical schools have traditionally defined education as the acquisition of factual information and certain skills by students. In the field of sexuality education, affective learning is also important. The greatest shortcoming of most practicing physicians is their discomfort. Since early childhood, they have been taught that sex is a private subject and that it is impolite and/or improper to talk about it. Physicians, who have not learned to confront and overcome their discomfort in talking about sex, transmit to their patients nonverbal, and sometimes verbal, messages that they do not want to hear about sexual problems. Their patients, who are often equally uncomfortable, cooperate by not raising any sexual issues. The result, too often, is "a conspiracy of silence," in which sexual issues that sometimes have a great impact on health never get discussed.

A number of medical schools have instituted courses or short programs in sexuality that emphasize attitudes, values, and feelings, rather than the memorization of factual information. These courses make extensive use of sexually explicit, educational films and videos and panels of people who are willing and able to talk about their personal sexual experiences. Following each large-group session, the students break into smaller groups who meet with facilitators to process what they have heard and seen with an emphasis on their personal feelings and reactions. Such programs seem to give medical students a better understanding of their own sexuality, a greater tolerance for unusual sexual attitudes they may encounter in their patients, and greater comfort in dealing with and discussing sexual issues.

Unfortunately, these programs rarely elicit enthusiastic support from the medical school faculties, who, after all, have been selected for their expertise in analyzing scientific data. Time is jealously guarded in the medical school curriculum. Money has always been a concern in higher education, but money gets tighter year-by-year, and small groups are expensive to organize and run. Many sexuality programs in medical schools are elective, which is sad, because the students who need these courses most are often the least likely to register for them.

Despite 30 years of improved sexuality education, most American doctors still do an inadequate job of helping patients with sexual problems. Comprehensive courses seem to help, but in the current conservative political and economic climate, it seems unlikely that they will be greatly expanded in the near future. In fact, there are indications that some programs are in danger of being cut back. There is, on the other hand, a small but growing move in the Association of American Medical Colleges to go beyond stuffing facts into students by dealing with attitudes and feelings in the medical school curricula. If this takes hold, sexuality courses may lead the way. Time alone will tell.

*Sexuality Education for Clergy in Theological Schools and Seminaries*

PATRICIA GOODSON and SARAH C. CONKLIN

*History.* Protestantism has historically enjoyed the status of dominant religion in this country, but democracy, with its emphasis on religious freedom and pluralism, has nourished the establishment of countless religious groups. Because these groups are numerous, and the education of their leadership varies considerably, a discussion of clergy training in sexuality requires qualification.

The main focus here will be on the seminaries and students included in the studies conducted by Conklin (1995) and Goodson (1996). Denominationally, the emphasis in these studies was mainly on Protestant and Roman Catholic clergy, although Jewish seminary faculty members were interviewed for the study by Conklin. By including both conservative and liberal schools and denominations, the largest religious groups are represented, but the samples are neither random nor the results generalizable.

Seminaries and theological schools are defined here as institutions of higher education accredited by the Association of Theological Schools (ATS). They offer post-baccalaureate degrees leading to ordination and licensure of pastors, priests, ministers, rabbis, chaplains, and pastoral counselors (categories broadly referred to as clergy).

Traditionally, clergy students have been characterized as young, white, and male, but this profile is slowly changing. First, it is becoming an older population composed of more part-time and second-career students. Second, diversity in both ethnicity and gender is increasing. In a comparison of motivations, women were more inclined to report entering seminary to discover "ways to best serve Christ in the church and the world" or "personal spiritual growth and faith development" rather than "preparing to be a parish minister," which was the overwhelmingly reported motivation for men entering seminary (Aleshire in Hunter 1990, 1265). In terms of sexuality education, seminary students are now perceived as being "more diverse in attitudes, more willing to share personal experiences, and more open about sexual orientation" than in previous generations (Conklin 1995, 231).

Conflict over whether seminary education accents professional training or personal formation may be a factor accounting for the apparent lack of emphasis on sexuality content (Kelsey 1993). As the percentage of female students has increased, greater awareness and sensitivity about the negative sexual experiences of women has been accompanied by curricular changes. As clinical settings for counseling practice have been included in most seminary curricula, less emphasis has been placed on foundational education (languages, such as Latin, Greek, and Hebrew, are less often required), but issues of training remain problematic, especially concerning sexuality education.

The scientific literature contains abundant evidence of the positive role that clergy may have in health promotion generally and in sexual health promotion, specifically. One study affirmed, for instance, that nearly half of all referrals made by clergy to mental-health professionals "involved marriage and family problems" (Weaver 1995, 133).

Recently, however, this supportive role has come into question as trust in clergy generally has been undermined by the misconduct of a few. Fortune (1991) contends that omission of sexuality components in professional training misses an intervention opportunity for clergy students to explore ethical boundary issues concerning what appropriate sexual conduct consists of prior to entering the profession. Such evidence clearly points to the appropriateness of marriage, family, and sexuality content in clergy training, but such content seems lacking or is limited by various internal and external restrictions.

*Prevalence.* When seminary course offerings were surveyed in the early 1980s, only a small number of courses included the term *sex* or *sexuality* in their title or description (McCann-Winter 1983). It might be assumed that sexual content is included in courses not so named, but this low prevalence still indicates that sexuality content is not prevalent in most clergy training programs.

A review of literature on training in pastoral counseling cites one study in which 50 to 80% of the sampled clergy thought their training in pastoral counseling was inadequate and did not equip them to deal with marital counseling issues (Weaver 1995). A study by Allen and Cole (1975) comparing samples of Protestant seminary students in 1962 and 1971 found that the students in the more recent sample did not perceive themselves as better trained in family-planning issues than those students in 1962. A recent study by Goodson (1996) documented that 82% of the Protestant seminary students surveyed declared having had zero hours of training in family planning in their seminaries, and 66% expressed desire for more training on this topic.

When seminary faculty members who include some aspect of sexuality in their courses were interviewed (Conklin 1995), they indicated that they did not identify themselves as sexuality educators, and they expressed anxiety about how their teaching of sexuality content would be viewed by others. Yet, they expressed optimism and hope, because sexuality content and courses are sought and positively evaluated by students, even though not required. There is eagerness and enthusiasm by students, congregants, and clergy to have sexuality issues addressed openly and to move in the direction of health, justice, and wholeness.

*Content.* Profound changes have occurred in the past four decades regarding sexuality education in seminaries. Resources which were once viewed as advantageous are now seen as outdated. More use is being made of commercial films, literature, and case studies. Printed materials with sexuality content have vastly increased in both quantity and quality. The Sexual Attitude Reassessment (SAR) model, providing intense and condensed exposure to a range of explicit materials, panels, and speakers interspersed with small-group processing, is still viewed with both affirmation as effective and with suspicion as risky (Rosser et al. 1995).

Increased awareness of the pervasiveness of negative outcomes related to sexuality has provided the impetus for continuing-education requirements, mandatory screening of various sorts, development of training programs, trainers, centers, and professional counselors, therapists, and consultants focusing on prevention of various kinds of violations. An understanding of sexuality based upon the content of sexual relationships, rather than the form of sexual acts, is described as a paradigmatic change now underway.

In the Conklin study (1995), sexual orientation and related terms were included, either as central concerns or peripherally, in all but one of the 39 interviews with seminary faculty. Prevention of harm seemed a more common goal than promotion of sexual health, and resources, language, and experiences for classroom use which focus on positive aspects of sexuality seem to be lacking. Examples of content frequently mentioned in the interviews included sexual violence, such as rape, abuse, and incest, sexual harassment and misconduct, sexually transmitted diseases, and sexual compulsivity. Content having religious connections included ordination, celibacy, incarnation, sexual theology, and sacrament.

*Support and Resistance.* While the need for professional sexuality education within seminaries has been documented in a few studies, and Conklin's qualitative assessment has indicated strong faculty support for teaching sexuality content, some resistance is still expected. Limitations may arise from diverse sources, such as denominational executives and curriculum committees, seminary reward and assignment systems for faculty, financial restrictions, and students' reluctance to deal with sexual issues or be in value conflict with their institution or instructor's teaching.

Goodson's survey (1996) of the attitudes of Protestant seminary students toward family planning identified 4.5% of conservative students, as compared to 0.9% of non-conservative students (*p* < .05), espousing unfavorable views of family planning, and potentially opposing its teaching in seminary. With this same sample, when analyzing a statistical model to predict intention to promote family planning in their future careers, the variable "attitudes toward sexuality" emerged as a strong mediator of the relationship between the variables "religious beliefs" and "attitudes toward family planning." While "religious beliefs" exhibited a correlation of 0.81 with the "attitudes toward sexuality" variable, conservative students had, on average, more-negative views of sexuality when compared to their non-conservative counterparts. The difference was statistically large: 1.04 standard deviation units, and significant at the 0.001 level of probability.

*Resources and Intervention Needs.* Given these findings, it is clear that religious beliefs need to be considered when selecting resources and planning interventions. At present, it seems broad-based support for sexuality education comes from insurers encouraging risk-reduction measures to prevent actionable behaviors which could lead to claims or litigation. Some administrative encouragement of faculty efforts has been reported, especially in response to student pressure or suggestions from peers or superiors. However, this support seems to be far outweighed by administrative indifference or caution, although perceived hostility has decreased.

A high standard has been set by faculty members who have taught and written about sexuality. Impetus to do more, not less, seems dominant, especially among faculty. However, no one has clearly articulated as a unified plan of action what there should be more of in this area. There is, however, some openness toward planning and development rather than a rigid adherence to an already conceived plan or model. A current resource encouraging the development of plans or models is the Center for Sexuality and Religion in Wayne, Pennsylvania.

As we see it, a two-pronged approach to sexuality education is needed, in which promotion of assets and prevention of deficits are both necessary (Conklin 1995). Clearly, the main assets of Protestant and Catholic churches include their nurturing, caring, and supportive environments, as well as maintenance of centers for dissemination of knowledge and training of their leaders. Nevertheless, such training has been characterized as deficient, and the need to plan, implement, and evaluate appropriate sexuality programs is notorious. The outcomes of a successful two-pronged intervention, which balances emphasis on both sexual health and sexual harm, may be worth pursuing, if we consider the important role clergy and churches have had, and may continue to have, in promoting the health and well-being of people in this country.

[*Update 2003*: Reports of clergy sexual misconduct in the media have reinforced the belief that theological education must actively seek to professionally train male and female clergy and ministers to competently and responsibly care for and minister to the well-being of individuals (including their sexual health). In order to provide this preparation, theological schools may need to revise and implement curricula to address sexuality-training needs. The authors developed and administered an assessment of sexuality education currently offered in American seminaries and theological schools. The instrument included a measure of institutional readiness to begin or share sexuality-related experiences (Conklin 2001). Surveys went to all 183 institutions in the U.S. accredited at the time by the Association of Theological Schools (ATS). Thirty-seven percent (*N* = 69 schools) responded. Questions addressed both developmental and educational experiences contributing to formation (personal development) as well as professional academic preparation for leadership roles in ministry.

[Results varied from 85% reporting current curricular efforts in which the sexuality content is embedded, to 47% saying they offered courses in which the sexuality content "stands alone," to 12% citing previous noncurricular events (workshops, convocations, or spiritual direction) in which the sexuality content was embedded. When *all* questions were counted, those concerning noncurricular efforts and previously offered courses, as well as current curricular efforts, the frequency of responses was equally split between those who did offer sexuality-related courses, content, or experiences and those who did not. An implication to be drawn from this finding is that about the same number of schools report doing nothing regarding teaching of sexuality as report doing something. But one needs to remember that two thirds of the 183 seminaries did not respond. The content and duration of *what* the theological schools *are* doing still needs to be investigated. Also, the attitudes of clergy toward pastoral counseling, and their training regarding sexuality issues, are questions needing further research (Goodson 2002). Although many schools express willingness to implement and share sexuality-education efforts and some clergy report feeling competent to counsel regarding sexuality issues, much more needs to be done. (*End of update by S. C. Conklin & P. Goodson*)]

## [Sexuality and American Popular Culture

RAYMOND J. NOONAN

[*Update 2003*: Popular culture encompasses the cultural artifacts and practices of the masses. And it is through American popular culture that we have exported our sexual ideology to the world, which may, in part, have provided the fuel that energizes religious fundamentalist fanatics to commit terrorist acts (see discussion on Sexuality and Terrorism in the United States in Section 1, Basic Sexological Premises). Indeed, it is usually these images from American popular culture that most ordinary people think of when they think of Americans and who we are. It is typically young and brash, and it lives in the present with only fleeting recognition of the past or the future. It encompasses literature and the visual arts, theater and the cinema, and music. It also embraces fashion and the media. In the last 30 years, it has begun to have a history, which is continually being written, and, indeed, a philosophy.

[In that respect, it is much like the history of previous decades, in which Hollywood movies exported American culture to Europe and the rest of the world, similar to, although more efficiently than the rest of the world exported their cultural artifacts to the United States. Marshall McLuhan (1964) might have explained it as a natural extension of the impact of the new medium—motion pictures—that involved the viewer through the two most-immediate senses, sight and sound, more deeply than the written word. Of course, it occurred even much earlier, more slowly again and sporadic, this time over centuries or so, when the East and West met in the days when the great sailing ships opened new horizons. The influence on sexual practices in Japan, for example, can be seen in their erotic art of the 1800s, as these cultures began to show the influence of contact with Western cultures, for better or worse (Kronhausen & Kronhausen 1970ab).

[Thus, much of popular culture is enabled by technology. It has been noted that almost every technological innovation is soon used for sexual expression (Noonan 1998c). It was true of Gutenberg's printing press in the 1400s and the camera in the 1800s. It was true more recently of the videocassette recorder (VCR) and video camera, and later, cable television; and it is true today of the DVD and the Internet and World Wide Web. All facilitated the sharing of sexual ideologies and experiences.

[As a result, we had a rich erotic literature develop that was rather cheaply and easily disseminated, both into and out of the country, extending the erotic "writing of harlots" that has evolved little through the ages. After all, there are only a finite (though extensive) number of ways our anatomy can fit together that is satisfying for most people. The banned writings of D. H. Lawrence, Henry Miller, and many others are just part of a long tradition that has largely become assimilated into everyday literature, film, and television. Advertising especially capitalizes on the erotic impulse to sell practically anything. Thus, the groundbreaking work of Lawrence and others of the genre have entered a baroque period, where the art is refined, but not much of it is cutting-edge or often even exemplary. Much of it is stylized and predictable, and, when it is good, it touches a chord in many readers or viewers as "real." That is often the demarcation between gratuitous sex in the media and pornography, on the one hand, and sex that could be a part of one's ordinary life—that is part of one's own storyline, good or bad, on the other.

[Thus, the following sections highlight several contemporary topics that are continuing to have a profound impact on American sexual culture in our everyday lives. The first is the ubiquitous Internet, originated by the U.S. Defense Advanced Research Projects Agency (DARPA) and driven by Cold-War fears of nuclear war that eventually became a means of communication for scientists. It was finally released for commercial use in the mid-1990s, at which time development advanced rapidly, often driven by sex-related entrepreneurs, especially those seeking the best and most-profitable ways of delivering explicit sexual images to a vast, worldwide market (see Noonan 1998c). The first article appeared in volume 3 of the first edition of the *International Encyclopedia of Sexuality*, when the Internet boom was still new. The second article updates that one, and focuses on contemporary online sexual activities and the diverse uses that sexologists and the general public have made of the medium as its sophistication and use have spread in the intervening years. In addition, it looks at some of the problems, such as compulsive Internet sexual behaviors, and their implications for sex-related therapies.

[The third article looks at the cutting-edge on the literary front: gay and lesbian literature. It might be said that this genre is at the stage that sexually oriented literature depicting the diverse lifestyles of heterosexuals was decades ago, when society broke the bonds of postal regulations and other laws prohibiting the sale and distribution of authors who have since become classics in erotica, if not American and English literature. As noted above, such depictions have become commonplace in literature, film, and television, with little extraordinarily novel. Gay and lesbian literature, on the other hand, being relatively recently released from similar, if not somewhat greater prohibitions, is poised to break new ground and to produce future classics. Indeed, new courses in gay and lesbian literature are being written and offered more frequently in colleges across the nation.

[The fourth article delves into sexually explicit lyrics in popular music, offering a look at the historical antecedents,

often hidden, that have been a part of the folk and even classical tradition for at least two centuries. Thus, critics, whose contemporary uproar in the United States over sexually explicit words and concepts in rap and hip-hop and other popular genres continues to make headlines, need look no further than Cole Porter and the psychedelic music of the 1960s for sexual content in the musical lyrics of our nearest previous generations.

[The final article takes a sociological look at fashion in America and the reciprocal influence that it has on a generation's sexuality and how their sexuality, in turn, along with current events, influences the fashions of the day. It, too, looks at the historical antecedents of how contemporary fashion, widely recognized by sexologists as accentuating the secondary sex characteristics of both males and females to make them more attractive to potential friends, lovers, or spouses, has changed through the ages. Thus, fashion reflects the images of attractiveness that define each generation and its social context within then-current definitions of gender and the place of each in the social hierarchy and the cultural sphere. (*End of update by R. J. Noonan*)]

## A Door to the Future: Sexuality on the Information Superhighway

*Sexuality and the Internet* SANDRA BARGAINNIER

People interested in sexual topics have always been quick to explore a new mode of communication—from graffiti on a prehistoric cave wall, movable type, photography, and radio, to video cameras, VCRs, and videocassette rentals and sales—as a way around the censorship society uses to regulate and limit the dissemination of sexual information. The most recent new mode of communication, the computer-based "information superhighway," the Internet or simply "the Net," is no exception. From its birth, the Net has raised images of erotica, pornography, and cybersex available in the privacy of one's home. The Net does provide sexuality information for the general "online" public, but it can also provide a wealth of reliable information for sex researchers, sex educators, and sex therapists. However, the use of the Net to access sexuality information has also brought the inevitable sequel of society's effort to regulate this new avenue of sex information.

The Internet is not a physical or tangible entity, but rather a giant network which interconnects innumerable smaller groups of linked computer networks. In early 1995, the global network of the Internet had 2 million Internet hosts; in late 1995-1996, 5 million hosts; and in early 1996, 9.5 million hosts. This is expected to double to 20 million hosts sometime in 1997. However, the number of Internet hosts is misleading, because many hosts limit access of their users with firewalls and other electronic barriers.

Gateways to a variety of electronic messaging services allow Internet users to communicate with over 15 million educational, commercial, government, military, and other types of users throughout the worldwide matrix of computer networks that exchange mail or news. These rapidly developing, and constantly changing, network information and retrieval tools are transforming the way people learn, interact, and relate. These networks provide users with easy access to documents, sounds, images, and other file-system data; library catalog and user-directory data; weather, geography, and physical-science data; and other types of information (Schwartz & Quarterman 1993). Professional journals, papers, conferences, courses, and dialogues are increasingly delivered electronically.

Although the federal government initiated the Internet during the "Cold War" as a way to send top-secret information quickly and securely, no government or group controls or is in charge of the Internet today. The Internet depends on the continuing cooperation of all the interconnected networks (Butler 1994). Because there is no proprietary control, anyone can send email (electronic mail), start a newsgroup, develop a listserv, download files, and/or have their own World Wide Web (WWW) home page or Web site. This freedom has opened the cyberspace doors to the sexuality arena.

For sexuality professionals, the opportunities in cyberspace are limitless. Email is just one of many functions. This one-on-one mode of electronic communication allows colleagues to communicate and collaborate in their research worldwide, pursue new leads quickly, test new ideas and hypotheses immediately, and build networks of like-minded colleagues. Whole documents can be attached to email, sent electronically around the globe, and downloaded by the recipients almost instantly. Both time and money can be saved by editing online and bypassing postal delays and costs.

Many American university professors communicate with their students by email. Lessons, syllabi, and homework are passed back and forth with email. Email can also provide the shy or quiet students in a class another venue for participation.

Listserv mailing lists are similar to email, but instead of communicating with only one other person, communication takes place among many. Many Americans of all ages subscribe to a mailing list and use it as a good place to debate issues, share professional ideas, and try out new concepts with others. Subscribers automatically receive correspondence from others who belong to the list. It is like reading everyone's email about a particular topic. Hundreds of listservs exist, including those that address rape, gay and bisexual issues, feminist theory, women's health, AIDS, addictions, survivors of incest, and advocacy, to name a few.

In addition to sending email to individuals or to a mailing list, Americans are increasingly meeting people and sharing interests through newsgroups. Like listservs, newsgroups are open discussions and exchanges on particular topics. Users, however, need not subscribe to the discussion mailing list in advance, but can instead access the database at any time (Butler 1994). One must access a special program called a newsreader to retrieve messages/discussions from a newsgroup. A local site may have many newsgroups or a few.

Newsgroups are as diverse as the individuals posting on them. Usenet newsgroups are arranged in a hierarchical order, with their names describing their area of interest. The major hierarchies are talk, alt, biz, soc, news, rec, sci, comp, and misc. Some examples of newsgroups in the field of sexuality are: sci.med.aids, talk.abortion, soc.women, soc.men, soc.bi, alt.sex, alt.transgendered, alt.sexual.abuse.recovery, and alt.politics.homosexuality. This hierarchy and system of naming help the user decide which groups may be of interest.

Many groups provide informative discussions and support. Other groups are often magnets for "flamers" (those who insult) or people posing as someone else (i.e., a young adult male posing online as a lesbian). One benefit of the newsgroup is that anyone can read the articles/discussions but not participate. These voyeurs are called "lurkers." This may be a safe starting point for a few months until one has an understanding of the group, their history, and past discussions. "Newbies" (newcomers to groups) are often flamed if they ask neophyte questions in some newsgroups. Reading a newsgroup's "FAQ" (frequently asked questions) page prior to inquiring online is one way newbies can avoid being flamed for naive or inappropriate inquiries.

In addition to transmitting messages that can be read or accessed later, Internet users can also engage in an immediate dialogue (called "chat") in "real time" with other users. Real-time communication allows one-to-one communica-

tion, and "Internet Relay Chat" (IRC) allows two or more people to type messages to each other that almost immediately appear on the other's computer screen. IRC is analogous to a telephone party line. In addition, most commercial online services have their own chat systems allowing members to converse. An example of a chat system is the Human Sexuality Forum on CompuServe, a proprietary online network that also offers members access to the Internet.

In addition to email, newsgroups, listservs, and chats, one can access information by transferring files from one computer to another with FTP (file transfer protocol). One important aspect of FTP is that it allows files to be transferred between computers of completely dissimilar types. It also provides public file sharing (*The Internet Unleashed*, 1994). These files may contain text, pictures, sound, or computer programs.

Another method of connecting with remote locations is through Telnet. Telnet allows the user to "log in" on a remote machine in real time. For example, a student can use Telnet to connect to a remote library to access the library's online card catalog.

American sexuality professionals now communicate, collaborate, and discuss issues with colleagues around the globe. They can also access information from around the world. Two of the more common methods for accessing information are Gopher and the World Wide Web (WWW). A user can collect data, read conference proceedings, tap into libraries, and even search for jobs online.

Gopher guides an individual's search through the resources available on a remote computer. It is menu driven and easy to use. Most American colleges and universities have a local Gopher menu. Gopher can also be accessed through most commercial online services. Gopher allows users to access information from various locations. The National Institute for Health, the Centers for Disease Control and Prevention, and the National Library of Medicine are just a few examples of sites that are accessible via Gopher.

Most information sites that can be reached through Gopher can also be accessed via the World Wide Web. The "Web" uses a "hypertext" formatting language called hypertext markup language (HTML). Programs called Web browsers that "browse" the Web can display HTML documents containing text, images, sound, animation, and moving video. Any HTML document can include links to other types of information or resources. These hypertext links allow information to be accessed and organized in very flexible ways, and allow people to locate and efficiently view related information, even if the information is stored on numerous computers all around the world.

Many organizations now have "home pages" on the Web. The homepage typically serves as a table of contents for the site, and provides links to other similar sites. Some websites that may be of interest to the sexuality professional are: the Society for the Scientific Study of Sexuality (SSSS) [http://www.sexscience.org]; the Kinsey Institute [http://www.kinseyinstitute.org]; the Sexuality Information and Education Council of the United States (SIECUS) [http://www.siecus.org/]; the Queer Resources Directory [http://www.qrd.org/qrd/]; and Tstar [http://travesti.geophys.mcgill.ca/~tstar/]. TStar provides resources and information for the transgendered community. The TStar home page is also a gateway to other resources on the Web, such as the Lesbian, Gay, Transgendered Alliance, and the Gay, Bi-Sexual, Lesbian, and Transgender Information from the United Kingdom. [*Editors' Note: The SexQuest Web Index for Sexual Health* provides links to many of the best sexuality research, education, and therapy sites on the Web: http://www.SexQuest.com/SexQuest.html.]

Sex researchers, educators, and therapists can use email, listservs, newsgroups, and the World Wide Web for updated information and resources. Sexuality professionals can also use the Internet as a new frontier for sex research. Approximately 200 active Usenet newsgroups deal with sex and variations of some sexual theme (Tamosaitis 1995). Very few have researched who these newsgroup users are, what sexuality knowledge they possess, what sexual attitudes they hold, or in which types of behavior they engage.

In the fall of 1994, a modified version of the Kinsey Institute Sex Knowledge Test was distributed to 4,000 users online (Tamosaitis 1995). The results showed that over 83% were male, white, highly educated, single, middle- to upper-class, and not afraid of technology. The majority were in their 20s and 30s and predominantly bicoastal, with 63% living either on the West or East coasts. The survey demonstrated that both the sexually oriented and general online user group respondents are more knowledgeable about women's sexuality issues than they are about comparable men's issues when compared to the general offline population polled (Tamosaitis 1995). This study, the first of its kind, could provide the impetus for further online research. Of the 20 most popular Usenet newsgroup forums, half are on sex-related topics (Lewis 1995).

Several universities are also concerned about sexually explicit material and are limiting or prohibiting access to certain newsgroups. In November 1994, Carnegie Mellon University moved to eliminate all sexually oriented Usenet newsgroups from its computers. Stanford, Penn State, Iowa State and other universities have also attempted to limit access (Tamosaitis 1995).

## Legal Challenges to Free Speech on the Internet

BARBARA GARRIS

Politically, any mention of sexuality in international cyberspace, from the most benign to the most perverse, is currently under scrutiny in the Supreme Court. In June 1995, Senator James Exon offered the Communications Decency Act of 1995 as an amendment to the Telecommunications Act of 1996, which was then included in the Telecom Act as Title 5, Section 507. The Communications Decency Act (CDA) expands regulations on obscene and indecent material to minors which would be transmitted to them through the telephone lines by way of the worldwide Internet, or any other online service (Italiano 1996; Lewis 1995; Lohn 1996).

The bill included, in a very subtle unthreatening way, elements of the old Comstock Act of 1873, which, in the past, made it a crime to send material on birth control and abortion through the postal service (Schwartz 1996a). This archaic act, inserted by Representative Henry J. Hyde, a longtime abortion foe, remains on the legislative books today as 18 U.S.C. Sec. 1462. Elements of the Comstock Act prohibiting dissemination of contraceptive information and the sale of contraceptives to married and single women had been declared unconstitutional in various decisions, the last two in 1966 and 1972. However, the prohibition against providing information about abortion remains on the books to the present. In the new Communications Decency Act, the maximum fine for providing information about abortion has been raised from $5,000 to $250,000 for anyone convicted of knowingly transmitting any "obscene, lewd, lascivious, filthy, or indecent" communications on the nation's telecommunications networks including the Internet. Meanwhile, other legislators sponsored legislation, the Comstock Clean-up Act of 1996, to repeal completely the remnants of the Comstock Act.

The Telecommunications Act of 1996 was signed by President Clinton on February 8, 1996. Although the President signed the bill into law, he immediately issued a disclaimer, saying that

> I do object to the provision in the Act concerning the transmission of abortion related speech and information. . . . The Department of Justice has advised me of its longstanding policy that this and related abortion provisions in current law are unconstitutional and will not be enforced because they violate the First Amendment [protecting freedom of speech].

The CDA was included in the Telecommunications Act supposedly to squelch online pornography and make the World Wide Web and the Internet, as well as other online services, "safe" for children. But the wording crafted by Internet-illiterate congressmen was so vague and overly broad that even the most innocent use of health-related information could result in a $250,000 fine and two years in prison. Free-speech activists, spearheaded by the American Civil Liberties Union, Electronic Freedom Foundation, American Library Association, and many others, were appalled and filed suit to keep at bay any prosecution and punishment for this alleged online crime until the case can be heard by the United States Supreme Court.

Suit was immediately filed by the American Library Association and the Citizen's Internet Empowerment Coalition in the United States District Court for the Eastern District of Pennsylvania seeking a preliminary injunction against the CDA on the constitutional grounds of the right to free speech. "Plaintiffs include various organizations and individuals who, inter alia, are associated with the computer and/or communications industries, or who publish or post materials on the Internet, or belong to various citizen groups." The case was heard before Judge Sloviter, Chief Judge, United States Court of Appeals for the Third Circuit, and Judges Buckwalter and Dalzell, Judges for the Eastern District of Pennsylvania.

An injunction was granted on June 11, 1996, after all three judges had schooled themselves with hands-on experience with the Internet. The basis for the injunction was threefold:

1. That whatever previous decisions had been handed down limiting indecent expression on other media (such as cable television and radio) could not be applied to cyberspace,
2. Control over pornography aimed at children rested with the parents and schools, not with the government nor with online services transmitting the offensive material, and
3. There was no technological way available to the Internet of checking the age of Internet users, except the use of credit card numbers, to access hardcore pornography.

All three judges saw the CDA as patently unconstitutional and asked the Supreme Court for a final ruling (EPIC 1996; McCullaugh 1996; *The New York Times* 1996; Quinttner 1996; Schwartz 1996b).

On July 1, 1996, the U.S. Department of Justice officially filed an appeal. In its September 30, 1996, edition, *HotWired* magazine reported that the U.S. Department of Justice was stalling for time, and the U.S. Supreme Court granted them an extra month to submit filings. The case was supposed to have been heard in the Supreme Court in October 1996, but no new hearing date had been published as of November 1996. As of March 1997, the CDA was going to the Supreme Court, with a decision expected in June.

Judge Dalzell's opinion sums up the ongoing debate over sex on the Internet:

True it is that many find some of the speech on the Internet to be offensive, and amid the din of cyberspace many hear discordant voices that they regard as indecent. The absence of governmental regulation of Internet content has unquestionably produced a kind of chaos, but as one of plaintiffs' experts put it with such resonance at the hearing: "What achieved success was the very chaos that the Internet is. The strength of the Internet is that chaos."

Just as the strength of the Internet is chaos, so the strength of our liberty depends upon the chaos and cacophony of the unfettered speech the First Amendment protects.

For these reasons, I without hesitation hold that the CDA is unconstitutional on its face.

Since the filing of this case, three other state cases have been brought to court. A New York City case, filed April 30, 1996, by Joe Shea, a reporter for the *American Reporter*, sought to overturn the CDA, claiming that the law limits freedom of speech for the press. On July 29, 1996, the court ruled in favor of Shea. This case is expected to be folded into the primary case brought to the Supreme Court by the American Civil Liberties Union (ACLU) et al. suit mentioned above. At the same time, journalism professor Bill Loving of the University of Oklahoma filed suit against the university charging that it blocked access on April 1, 1996, to a newsgroup, "alt.sex," after the university received complaints from a fundamentalist religious organization. Loving claimed that restricting students' access to the Internet is a violation of their First Amendment rights. (As of late 1996, he was awaiting the University's response.) Finally, effective July 1, 1996, the Georgia State General Assembly passed a law providing criminal sanctions against anyone falsely identifying themselves on the Internet. A suit (*ACLU of Georgia et al. vs. Miller et al.*), seeking a preliminary injunction against the Georgia statue, was filed September 24, 1996, by the ACLU, Electronic Frontiers Georgia, Georgia State Representative Mitchell Kaye, and others. As of late 1996, the hearing had not been held.

*Summing Up*                    SANDRA BARGAINNIER

What is considered sexually explicit? Are safe-sex guidelines considered sexually explicit? Obviously, this type of law could disband the educational and informative sex-related Internet resources and the sex-related newsgroups.

Another concern associated with the Internet is the loss of community in the real world and the formation of online communities. Opponents believe that people are not honest about who they are in cyberspace, which is a fantasy land. Proponents say that virtual communities provide a place for support, information, and understanding. Many feel that gender, race, age, orientation, and physical appearance are not apparent in cyberspace unless a person wants to make such characteristics public. People with physical disabilities or less-than-glamorous appearances find that virtual communities treat them as they always wanted to be treated—as thinkers and transmitters of ideas and feelings, not just an able body or a face (Rheingold 1995). Many young people can be part of a community for the first time in their life by interacting with an online community. An online community might, for example, provide a teenage lesbian who feels alienated at school and home with a sense of self-worth and understanding.

Not since the invention of television has a technology changed how a nation and a world spend their time, gather information, and communicate, as has the Internet. Sexuality professionals and the public have the capacity to access tremendous amounts of sexual information, some of it valid and educational, some of it entertaining, and some that oth-

ers might label "obscene." But who is to judge? Sexuality professionals need to get involved before others judge what is deemed acceptable sexuality information. The Internet will also serve as a new frontier for sex research, sex education, sex information, collaboration, and communication (Tamosaitis 1995).

## [Online Sexual Activity

AL COOPER and ERIC GRIFFIN-SHELLEY

[*Update 2003*: The Internet is a key element in the Information Age in the United States, as well as worldwide, in which "rapid and far reaching technological advances are revolutionizing the ways in which people relate, communicate, and live their daily lives" (Jerome, DeLeone, Folen, Earles, & Gedney 2000). Sexuality is an integral part of these phenomena such that Online Sexual Activity (OSA) has been dubbed the "next sexual revolution" (Cooper & Griffin-Shelley 2002).

[The search engine *Google* now examines over three billion Web pages (Google 2003), up from one billion less than three years ago (Inktomi 2000). Sex is the most searched-for topic on the Net (CIOL 2001). The 172 million Americans online represent over half of the U.S. population (Neilsen NetRatings 2003), and worldwide there are 605 million Net users (Nua 2003). Twenty to 33% of people use the Net for online sexual activity (Cooper, Delmonico, & Burg 2000; Egan 2000).

[As with any human activity, Internet use has advantages, e.g., opening a previously inaccessible market, and disadvantages, e.g., identity theft. It stands to reason, then, that the same is true for Internet activities involving sexuality (Cooper, Scherer, Boies & Gordon 1999; Barak & King 2000). This chapter will provide a brief overview of these important and evolving issues. The speed of this revolution, and the intensity of its impact, are because of the "Triple A Engine" of accessibility (anytime, anywhere), affordability (a quick and easy local phone call), and anonymity (the perception that your identity is hidden) (Cooper, Scherer, Boies, & Gordon 1999). In addition, Internet activity can have a "disinhibiting" effect (Suler 2001), i.e., allowing people to engage in sexual activities that they might not otherwise have done. A geometrically expanding literature (Griffin-Shelley 2003) and research base (Noonan 2001) substantiate the power of this revolution.

## [*Definitions*

[For research and clinical work to proceed with a scientific foundation, one of the first steps is the development of a common agreed-upon nosology. Cooper and Griffin-Shelley (2002) have proposed this set of definitions:

[*Online Sexual Activity* (OSA) is defined as use of the Internet for any activity (including text, audio, and graphic files) that involves sexuality, whether for purposes of recreation, entertainment, exploration, support, education, commerce, efforts to attain and secure sexual or romantic partners, and so on.

[*Cybersex* is a subcategory of OSA, and can be defined as using the medium of the Internet to engage in sexually gratifying activities, such as, looking at pictures, engaging in sexual chat, exchanging explicit sexual images or emails, "*cybering*" (i.e., sharing fantasies over the Internet which involve being sexual together while one or both people masturbate), and so on.

[*Online Sexual Problems* (OSP) includes the full range of difficulties that people can have because of engaging in OSA. Such difficulties include negative financial, legal, occupational, relational, and/or personal repercussions from OSA. The "problem" may range from a single incident to a pattern of excessive involvement. The consequences may involve feelings of guilt, loss of a job/relationship, STDs, and so on.

[Finally, *Online Sexual Compulsivity* (OSC) is a subtype of OSP and refers to excessive OSA behaviors that interfere with the work, social, and/or recreational dimensions of the person's life. In addition, there are indications of a "loss of control" of the ability to regulate the activity and/or to minimize adverse consequences (Cooper 1998; Cooper 2000; Griffiths 2001; Delmonico, Griffin, & Carnes 2002).

## [*Sexual Education and Information*

[Clearly, anonymously accessible and affordable information on human sexuality available worldwide at any time is a sex educator's dream. These dreams are becoming reality through the efforts of professional organizations such as the American Association of Sex Educators, Counselors, and Therapists (www.aasect.org) and businesses such as www.bettersex.com or www.sex-centre.com (Bay-Cheng 2001). As with any health topic, the quality of information varies widely from the most empirically based and up-to-date to the most biased and misinformed, so consumers need to proceed with caution having a "buyer beware" attitude (Barak & Fisher 2001).

[People appear more comfortable obtaining information on sexuality via the Internet because of the "Triple A" and the accompanying capacity to reduce shame and inhibition (Millner & Kiser 2002). Online "sexperts" offer news, answers to frequently asked questions (FAQs) (Ochs & Binik 2000), education, e.g., the "Sexploration" columns of www.MSNBC.com, and individual consultation. Sexual education efforts are international in scope, e.g., Lunin, Karizanskaya, Melikhova, Light, & Brandt-Sorheim (1997) report on efforts in Russia. Although beyond the scope of this article, online therapy for relationships and sexual issues is expanding, although many legal, ethical, and professional concerns remain to be resolved.

[Research on the reasons people engage in online sexual activity is in the early stages (Cooper, Scherer, Boies, & Gordon 1999; Cooper, Griffin-Shelley, Delmonico, & Mathy 2001). Cooper, Scherer, Boies, and Gordon (1999) found that for the 9,265 respondents in their study, most used adult websites, sex chat, and other sexual activities as "casual recreation"; 91.7 % spent less than 11 hours per week on online sexual activity and 46.6% spent less than 1 hour per week. Eighty-four percent of men and 80% of women were satisfied with their online sexual activity, and 87% reported never feeling guilt or ashamed. Most people (81.6%) of the second large scale study (*n* = 7,037) indicated that their online sexual activity served as a "distraction." Just under a third used online sexual activity for education (31.7%) and to cope with stress (29.9%) (Cooper, Griffin-Shelley, Delmonico, & Mathy 2001). Other reasons for online sexual activity included meeting people online for face-to-face (f2f) dating, socializing, engaging in sexual activities that the person would not do in real time, getting support for sexual concerns, and purchasing sexual materials.

[Gender has appeared to be an important variable in the early research in terms of Internet sexuality (Cooper, Scherer, Bois, & Gordon 1999; Cooper, Delmonico, & Burg 2000; Goodson, McCormick, & Evans 2001; Leiblum & Doring 2002). Women tend to be less involved in online sexual activity and prefer interactive media, i.e., chat rooms to more-voyeuristic activities like viewing pictures. Of note, recent research in Sweden (Cooper, Månsson, Daneback, Tikkanen, & Ross 2003) indicated that more-sophisticated research designs might significantly increase the percentage of women who participate in this type of research. Leiblum

and Doring (2002) and Podlas (2000) suggest cyberspace may be the leading edge of a continuing frontier for women's sexual liberation.

## [*Sexually Disenfranchised and Alternative Communities*

[Lesbian, gay, bisexual, and transgendered youth have appeared to suffer delayed development because of the intense hatred, discrimination, shame, and humiliation that the dominant culture expresses towards them. For example, most put off "coming out," and even their own understanding and acceptance, until they leave home for college or the city where there is more freedom, acceptance, and respect for their orientation. The Internet is changing that by giving sexually disenfranchised adolescents information, role models, peers, and opportunities for interaction unheard of even at the end of the 20th century (Burke 2000; Ross & Kauth 2002). These teens and other sexual minorities no longer have to live in shame, fear, and isolation (McKenna 2001). They can learn the "how tos" of sex through informative websites, pictures, and videos. They can connect with other people like themselves in online discussion groups, email lists, chat rooms, and instant messaging (Plymire & Forman 2000; Ross & Kauth 2002). They can find people and places to "hook up" to explore their sexual preference without having to go to bars, bathhouses, or bathrooms, or other clandestine rendezvous spots.

[Men who have sex with men are finding new vistas on the Net, but not without risks such as transmission of STDs (Bull, McFarlane, & Reitmeijer, 2001; Benotsch, Kalichman, & Cage, 2001; Elford, Bolding, & Sherr, 2001; Ross, & Kauth, 2002). At the same time, the Internet may offer new ways to prevent problems related to sexual activity (Bull & McFarlane, 2000; Bull, McFarlane, & King, 2001; Hospers, Harternick, Van Den Hoek, & Veenstra, 2002;). The Net can also be a vehicle for support and health information for those already suffering from STDs and HIV/AIDS (Reeves, 2001; Kalichman, Benotsch, Weinhardt, Austin, & Luke, 2002; Kalichman, Weinhardt, Benotsch, DiFonzo, Luke & Austin, 2002),

[Of course, the broadening of opportunities and freedom are not limited to sexual minorities. Any person or group may find love and sexual expression via the Net. Those who feel they are unattractive can establish relationships based more on their communication skills than their physical appearance. Support and connections have created the possibility of alternative cyber communities for sexual minorities and those with disabilities (Pendergass, Nosek, & Holcomb 2001; Tepper & Owens 2002). Elderly people who want to continue to be emotionally and sexually active are making connections and finding new vistas open to them from all over the world.

[People with atypical sexual interests and illegal preoccupations can find new arenas via the Net (Galbreath, Berlin, & Sawyer 2002; Kim & Bailey 1997). People, particularly men, are experimenting with a seemingly endless series of sexual variations, from voyeuristic interests (including pictures and video files from "spy cams") to exhibitionistic sites where those with their own "webcams" offer free or paid glimpses into their lives (Waskul 2002). The dominant/submissive lifestyle and sadomasochism are well represented and often link online and face-to-face ("f2f") experiences for those seeking them (Palandri & Green 2000). People with fetishes, from bestiality to trampling and even pedophilia (Durkin & Bryant 1999), are there for those looking for community (Galbreath, Berlin, & Sawyer 2002). Despite preliminary research indicating that much of this activity is beneficial, or at least benign, there is enough that is not (Cooper, Galbreath, Becker, & Griffin-Shelley 2003) that policymakers and legislators, as well as the general public, have expressed concern and inquired about how to control and regulate this global phenomena.

### [Online Relationships

[The impact of the Net on courtship and sexual relationships is only beginning to be the subject of empirical studies despite the increasing numbers of people who are using it for these purposes (Cooper, Scherer, & Marcus 2002). Success stories and disasters are regularly heard on the news, in consultation rooms, and, of course, across the Internet. Clearly, opportunities for meeting romantic and sexual partners have increased because of the Net, and online dating services, such as match.com and eharmony, are experiencing rapid growth and increased acceptance (Levine 2000). Proximity, physical appearance, and similarity do not play the role they do in face-to-face encounters (Cooper & Sportolari 1997), and the disinhibiting effect of Internet communication (Suler 2001) may lead to quicker and deeper connections between people.

[One of the early problems reported by clinicians was "Internet infidelity" (Shaw 1997; Young, Griffin-Shelley, Cooper, O'Mara, & Buchanan 2000). Some assert that the lack of actual contact negated the reality of the "affair," while others point out that partners reported that the feelings of violation and betrayal were similar to what they experienced when the infidelity involved face-to-face sexual contact (Schneider 2002).

[It may be possible to deceive and defraud people more easily in cyberspace than in real time. Stories abound of people who have found their "true love" online (Seiden 2001), as well as accounts of people discovering that the person they were connecting to lied about their gender, age, appearance, or life circumstances (Cornwell & Lundgren 2001). As the research about what makes for a good long-term relationship (Gottman 1994) becomes clearer and the instruments to measure those traits become more robust, this powerful medium may ultimately be proven to be better at helping a person to choose a life-mate than doing it "the old fashioned way," i.e., without the benefit of computer-assisted technology. At the same time, because of the increased likelihood of fantasy and projection being a larger part of online relationships, users will need to be cautious and aware that there may be a greater chance of reenacting traumatic and unsuccessful relationships in this venue (Schwartz & Southern 2000). Younger people who have "grown up with the Net" will find it an increasingly integral part of their romantic and sexual lives (Cooper, Månsson, Daneback, Tikkanen, & Ross 2003). Finally, as people become more sophisticated about life in cyberspace and online relationships, and more of the "facts" are known and disseminated, the chances will increase that more good and less harm will be the result.

### [Online Sexual Problems/Online Sexual Compulsivity

[While the majority of online sexual activity has not led to problems, it does for some (Griffiths 2000; Putnam 2000; Stein, Black, Shapira, & Spitzer 2001). Research suggests that as many as a quarter of male Internet users indicate some level of difficulty associated with online sexual activity. Cooper, Scherer, Bois, and Gordon (1999) and Cooper, Griffin-Shelley, Delmonico, and Mathy (2001) indicated that 8% of users report Online Sexual Problems (OSP). Cooper, Delmonico, and Burg (2000) identified 1% of their sample as having Online Sexual Compulsivity (OSC). In addition, this research supports what clinical practice reports, i.e., that some people (perhaps 15%) are "at risk" for online

sexual problems, even when they do not have a prior history of acting out sexually (Cooper, Delmonico, & Burg 2000).

[Young people are not the only populations that can blossom or suffer as a result of their online romantic and sexual activity. Shy, lonely, and vulnerable adults (separated, divorced, or isolated), as well as those in a host of other "minority" categories (including the disabled or mentally ill) can find both happiness and harm via the Internet. Most adults are naïve about, or unaware of, the specific vulnerabilities of this medium, and are susceptible to victimization online via deception, romantic role-play, fraud, and exploitation.

[There are also secondary victims of people who have online sexual problems, i.e., people who suffer consequences because of the OSP person's Internet activities (Schneider 2000; Schneider 2002). For example, a wife and her children were left to survive on their own when their husband/father was caught in a police sting of people exchanging child pornography. Likewise, the congregation in a local synagogue was abandoned when their rabbi was abruptly fired after repeated incidents with online sexual activity.

[The implications for clinical practice include requiring expanded knowledge of behavioral problems that are new (e.g., cyber-affairs), expansions of existing disorders (e.g., cyber exhibitionism), and additional unhealthy opportunities for those with longstanding problems (e.g., pedophilia online) (Cooper & McLoughlin 2001). Some clinicians see the need for providing online education and/or counseling around sexual issues (Newman 1997; Graugaard & Winter 1998), as well as simply encouraging clients to use the Net as a resource and support network (Putnam 2000; Kalichman, Benotsch, Weinhardt, Austin, & Luke 2002). Noonan (1998c) has suggested terminology, *self-defined lovemap-inappropriate sexual arousal* (SDLISA), to describe the kinds of unexpected responses that some individuals may have from viewing gay or pedophilic (or other paraphilic) images that are not congruent with their identified lovemap. Such responses might be more significant today because of the ease with which such images might be encountered on the Internet, either by accident or curiosity or otherwise, and should be investigated.

[Treatment for online sexual problems and online sexual compulsivity is usually multi-modal, including individual, group, and couples therapies, as well as encouragement to obtain a medication evaluation when appropriate (Cooper & Marcus 2003; Orzack & Ross 2000; Putnam & Maheu 2000; Schneider and Weiss 2001; Delmonico, Griffin, & Carnes 2002; Griffin, Moriarty, & Delmonico 2001).

### [Children, Adolescents, College Students, and Young Adults

[Children and adolescents are growing up with the Internet as part of their lives (Longo, Brown, & Orcutt 2002). From school research projects to chatting with friends, young people in America are increasingly familiar with the Internet's power for self-help and self-harm. As with other groups, the Net opens up unheard-of opportunities, e.g., friends around the world, and terrifying dangers, i.e., pedophiles posing as peers. Parents, teachers, legislators, and police are struggling to keep up and encourage healthy online activity while protecting this obviously vulnerable population (Finkelhor, Mitchell, & Wolak 2000). Nevertheless, Noonan (1998c) has noted how the notion of sexual predators online has been greatly exaggerated, particularly in comparison to the much greater risk of harm documented in many offline contexts, e.g., risk of intrafamily sexual abuse.

[Children, obviously, need more help and supervision than teenagers. Resources are emerging (Flowers-Coulson, Kushner, & Bankowski 2000; Hagley, Pearson, Carne 2002; Longo et. al. 2002) to assist caregivers around Internet use. The first suggestion, as always, is to talk to children and teens. We know that most parents have difficulty talking to children and adolescents about sexuality. The Internet offers opportunities for sex education unparalleled a few years ago (e.g., www.siecus.org; www.plannedparenthood.org), including those for sexual minorities (e.g., www.youthresource.org for gay, lesbian, bisexual, and transgendered youth). In addition, there are safe places to ask questions from premier health professionals filling in the gaps where parents and sex educators leave off (Mayo Clinic 2000). Adolescence is a time of identity development, experimentation, and education (Goodson, McCormick, & Evans 2000a; Goodson, McCormick, & Evans 2000b; Roffman, Shannon, & Dwyer 1997; Shpritz 1997; Zillman 2000). The online environment offers teens a new and broader stage to "try on" differing personas, ages, and even sexual orientations (Longo, Brown, & Orcutt 2002).

[Unwanted exposure to sexual material or activity can be troubling and may even be traumatic, especially for children and youth who are not developmentally ready to handle more-adult sexual activity. Accidental encounters can happen through misspelling a URL, using a search engine without blocking software, or intrusive and sexually suggestive emails ("spam"). Purveyors of sexual materials and pedophiles may also be much more aggressive in the fairly anonymous world of cyberspace (Mitchell, Finkelhor, & Wolak 2001).

[Children and adolescents are also "at risk" for online sexual problems, online sexual compulsivity, and Internet addiction (Young 1998). Few empirical data currently exist about this area, but we know from offline life that children and teens can be sexual victimizers as well as victims. As children get older, they, obviously, are more capable of engaging in paraphilic behaviors, as well as sexually stalking, harassing, and assaulting others on- and offline. If children or teenagers meet online contacts in real time, they may also be at higher risk for transmission of STDs and HIV/AIDS (Cooper, Scherer, Bois, & Gordon 1999; McFarlane, Bull, & Rietmeijer 2002), although paradoxically, the Internet may also have unrivaled potential to help with STD prevention and safer sex efforts (Keller, Labelle, Karimi, & Gupta 2002).

[*Ethics and Regulation: Work Environments, Legal Considerations*

[The newness of the Internet makes ethical guidelines for behavior and regulation an evolving landscape (Plant & Donahey 2002). As individuals and groups encounter difficulties, guidelines and policies are being developed. This is happening in businesses, online service provider organizations, schools and universities, and private and governmental agencies. These responses include identifying problematic material and behaviors, as well as defining appropriate responses and restrictions (Cooper, Golden, & Kent-Ferraro 2002). The rapidly increasing usage of the Internet from the workplace has provided a brand new avenue for the availability, spread, and distribution of sexually related material and its consumption by employees with jobs that require them to go online everyday (Cooper, McLoughlin, Reich, & Kent-Ferraro 2002). In fact, approximately 50% of all Internet users use accounts that are financed by their employers, and in one study, almost 20% of the 40,000 surveyed adults reported engaging in online sexual activity while at work (Cooper, Scherer, and Mathy 2001). This corroborates data from other sources, which report that adult-content sites are the fourth most visited category while at work (Goldberg 1998), and that 70% of all adult-content traffic occurs during the 9-to-5 workday (Carnes 2001). The implications of this phenomenon are potentially huge and of growing concern to clinical and organizational psychologists, as well as employers (Cooper, Safir, Rosenmann, Scherr, & McLoughlin, in press).

[Law enforcement at all levels, as well as policymakers and legislators are struggling to respond to new forms of sexual violence via the Net. These challenging scenarios include online harassment (Biber, Doverspike, Baznik, Cober, & Ritter 2002; McGarth & Casey 2002), cyber stalking (Deirmenjian 1999), cyper "peeping " or voyeurism/exhibitionism (Waskul 2002), rape websites (Gossett & Byne 2002), child seduction (Quayle & Taylor 2001), cybersex with minors (Jaffee & Sharma 2001), adult sex shops and pornography (Fisher & Barak 2000), child pornography (McCabe 2000; Burke, Sowerbutts, Blundell, & Sherry 2002), male violence (Cunneen & Stubbs 2000), and online pedophilia (Durkin 1997; Durkin & Bryant1999). At the same time, other groups are concerned that control of the Internet is going too far, and thus, they are organizing to advocate for freedom and liberty in cyberspace, e.g., www.peacefire.org, which promotes computer programs capable of circumventing blocking software.

[*The Future of Internet Sexuality*

[The future involves harnessing the power of the Internet to improve sexual relationships (Cooper, Scherer, & Marcus 2002). In part, this means refining the research methodology (Binik 2001; Cooper, Scherer, & Mathy 2001; Ochs, Mah, & Binik 2002) and gaining access to more data in order to better understand this geometrically expanding phenomena (Cooper, Månsson, Daneback, Tikkanen, & Ross 2003; Mustanski 2001; Noonan 1998c, 2001). It is also true that the "Triple A" provides an opportunity for better, more honest, and more accurate information on all aspects of sexuality, including: sexual preference (Renaud, Rouleau, Granger, Barasetti, & Bouchard 2002), orientation (Sell 1997), sexual disenfranchised populations (Appleby 2001; Quartaro & Spier 2002; Ross & Kauth 2002; Rhodes DiClemente, Cecil, Hergenrather,& Yee 2002), the function and impact of explicit sexual stimuli (McCabe 2000; Mehta 2001; Fisher & Barak 2001), and various other atypical sexual practices and behaviors (Ochs, Mah, & Binik 2002). Also, as the Internet facilitates and makes research on sexuality easier, more will become known about the lesser-known sexual practices in various countries and communities around the globe. Already, Internet-based studies are emerging from Israel (Barak & Safir 1997), Sweden (Cooper, Månsson, Daneback, Tikkanen, & Ross 2003; Tikkanen & Ross 2000), and China (Wang & Ross 2002). If the science of sexuality is to become an increasingly recognized and respected field, then the more empirical data that can be gathered on every facet of it, the better.

[In addition to having a future, Net sexuality has existed long enough to have a past (Noonan 1998c; Stern 2001; Stern & Handel 2001). It is increasingly clear that the Internet has much to offer, both in terms of benefits, as well as some highly problematic areas, in relation to human sexuality. With more research to guide and expand the empirical knowledge base, increased attention to resources and training for clinicians and sex educators around these issues, and a more mature and sophisticated understanding of the online world, the impact of the Internet could help the world to move towards the more empowered and enhanced relationship with sexuality that most of us seek. (*End of update by A. Cooper and E. Griffin-Shelley*)]

## [Gay and Lesbian Literature in the United States: The Politics of Inclusion/Exclusion

MICHAEL HYDE

[*Update 2003*: The difficulty in dealing with the notion of gay and lesbian literature in the United States is having to identify what is meant by "gay and lesbian literature," whether it be the literature produced by gays and lesbians, a literature that describes gay or lesbian experience or showcases gay and lesbian characters, or, more appropriately, some nonspecific amalgam of both. A great deal of what might actually be described as "gay or lesbian literature" has been written by authors who are neither lesbian nor gay, and just as equally, what might be—but never is—labeled as "heterosexual literature" finds its origins in lesbian and gay writers.

[This idea of a particularly gay and lesbian literature, as distinct from some other literature, is a uniquely American one as well as an increasingly dated one. The cordoning off of gay and lesbian literature from a mainstream literature arose for two reasons: from homophobia, on the one hand, and on the other, from the push of a minority culture to know and define itself. Prior to the Stonewall Uprising in 1969, literature explicitly centering on the experiences of gays and lesbians was largely an underground literature, considered subversive and part of a counterculture, produced and sold almost exclusively by lesbian and gay publishers and booksellers. Some crossover into mainstream American literature did exist, however—James Baldwin's *Giovanni's Room*, Gore Vidal's *The City and the Pillar*, or Ann Bannon's *Odd Girl Out* or *Women in the Shadows*—prior to the 1970s, but such crossovers were much more the exceptions than the rule. Other writers dealt with the pressure to conform to a mainstream literature through the use of literary masks or personae that transformed stories of same-sex desire into more widely acceptable works of heterosexual desire. In Willa Cather's 1918 novel, *My Antonia*, for example, her first-person narrator identifies himself clearly as male, but as Cather's novel evolves, the narrator fails in so many traditionally masculine roles that he becomes more of a mouthpiece for Cather's own feelings of same-sex longing and affection than a fully evolved heterosexual male character (Faderman 1995).

[The Stonewall Uprising in 1969 marks what is considered by many to be the beginning of the gay civil rights movement, and subsequently, publishing witnessed a surge of gay and lesbian writing, primarily because of the heightened visibility of the gay and lesbian community. Not surprisingly, then, gay and lesbian literature post-Stonewall acquired a profound and important connection to a political movement. Lesbian and gay writers became more and more aware of the potential within themselves—whether desired or not—to become voices for and, to some degree, responsible to, a larger community.

[During the 1970s, some of the most influential literary works were notable for their frankness in rendering the experience of gays and lesbians, particularly the sexual experience of gays and lesbians. Perhaps two of the most resonant and enduring fictions were Andrew Holleran's *Dancer from the Dance* and Larry Kramer's *Faggots*, clear descendents of John Rechy's *City of Night* from 1963, a fictional investigation of gay male prostitution. Both *Faggots* and *Dancer from the Dance*, published in 1978, highlighted fast-paced geographies of Manhattan nightclubs and Fire Island affluence, engaging issues of alcoholism, drug abuse, and promiscuity as reflective of a particularly gay lifestyle. Kramer's *Faggots* had been intended as a satire of the life the novel described, but many readers engaged the work, not as social critique,

but as purely descriptive of gay life. Although both of these works sold well, to both gay and straight audiences, the works were also harshly criticized (both within and outside the gay community), as the novels seemed not only to glorify unlawful behavior and promiscuity, but also suggested a gay identity that was linked primarily to such behavior.

[Rita Mae Brown's *Rubyfruit Jungle* in 1973 proved to be an equally groundbreaking and unapologetic celebration of lesbian sex and sexuality. Very little writing throughout the 1970s actually examined themes of growing up lesbian or gay. *Rubyfruit Jungle* offered a previously underrepresented look at a girl's coming of age—emotionally, physically, intellectually, and sexually—as she moves from her Southern roots, in love with the head cheerleader, to a series of comedic sexual adventures. Prior to the 1970s, lesbian characters in more-mainstream fiction were relegated to two types—largely the *femme fatale* or the medical oddity (Faderman 1995); Brown's central character signaled a sharp change in the types of roles lesbians might occupy in fiction.

[While the gay and lesbian community drew strength from this shared sense of "difference," minority politics also creates a tension in its assertion of "sameness" to the majority—in this case, heterosexual—culture. The stories of Armistead Maupin, first appearing in the *San Francisco Chronicle* in 1976 and later collected in *Tales of the City*, evolved a world in which gay and straight characters coexisted with equal weight, the stories shifting tonally from the comic to the touching, and to a degree, shrugging off expectations of how minority characters should behave in fiction. Often, characters representative of any minority group (sexual, racial, or ethnic) have been expected to behave as positive role models for their community, but the genius of Maupin's *Tales of the City* lay in his willingness to let his characters behave with all the positive and negative traits of their everyday human counterparts. As gay and lesbian literature started to reflect more and more the verisimilitude of lived life, gay and lesbian characters, less and less, would need to exhibit saintly behavior to be allowed a place in fiction.

[Gay and lesbian poetry during the 1970s concerned itself largely with identity politics, although themes of sexual endeavors and homosexual affections were likewise characteristic. Allen Ginsberg, made famous by his poetic treatise *Howl* (1955), continued his use of the literary medium as a forum for public shock and protest, writing about sexual desire in ways both celebratory and shocking, in *Mind Breaths* (1978). Richard Howard's *Two Part Inventions* (1974) imagined poetic dialogues between historical and literary personae, in one exemplary case divining a conversation between gay literary giants, Walt Whitman and Oscar Wilde, placing homosexuality within a larger literary-historical context.

[Throughout the 1970s, the lesbian rights movement aligned forcibly with the feminist movement, producing some of the most powerful poetry in American literature. So much of lesbian feminist poetry during the 1970s and into the 1980s worked to articulate the desires and concerns—as well the epistemological stance—of the lesbian and feminist movements, building on groundbreaking ideas from such radical idealists as Andrea Dworkin, whose *Woman Hating: A Radical Look at Sexuality* (1974) revolutionized thinking about the roles of gender and sexuality in America. Lesbian feminist poets like Adrienne Rich (*Diving into the Wreck*, 1973; *Twenty-One Love Poems*, 1977) and Marge Piercy (*The High Cost of Living*, 1978) pushed for a redefined sense of womanhood that was all inclusive and empowering, and the poetic voice became one of protest and deep sensitivity where goals of feminists and lesbians could unite in the push for change (Bennett 1995). Adrienne Rich's notion of a "lesbian continuum"—along which all women could situate themselves in terms of their affection for fellow women—greatly influenced the work of lesbian feminists, theorists, and writers throughout much of the following decade.

[In the 1980s, lesbian writing continued mainly to be a vehicle for voicing social concerns and identity politics. Audre Lorde, a black lesbian feminist, emerged as a powerful voice with *Zami: A New Spelling of My Name* in 1982 and, in 1984, with *Sister Outsider,* a collection of influential essays concerning race, gender, sexuality, and identity in America. Lorde's writing, although forceful and unapologetic, exhibited a profound grace and sensitivity to peoples of all racial, gender, and sexuality orientations, and her firm belief in the connection of her own lesbian sexuality and black heritage as one linked identity, assisted in unifying efforts for change within both minority communities. Chicana writers, Gloria Anzaldúa and Cherríe Moraga, dissatisfied with what they viewed as the backseat role of non-whites in the feminist movement, compiled *This Bridge Called My Back: Writings by Radical Women of Color* (1981), which articulated the challenges of simultaneously occupying two minority positions (racial and sexual) in America. Writer and cultural theorist, Sarah Schulman, notable for her risky and experimental styles, examined the relationship between aesthetics, politics, and identity. In *The Sophie Horowitz Story* (1984), for example, a lesbian reporter trails feminist bank robbers, and Schulman's novel jabs at the essentially misogynist tendencies in the detective-novel genre. In her challenging of traditional narrative forms, Schulman examines the role of art in shaping politics and social change, encouraging her readers to question *meaning* and how meaning is derived. During the latter half of the 1980s, the detective genre became a popular medium for lesbian writers in general, evidenced by Katherine Forrest's *Murder at the Nightwood Bar* in 1987 or Mary Wings' *She Came Too Late* in 1987 and *She Came in a Flash* in 1988 (Summers 1995).

[Much of gay fiction during the early 1980s followed in a new form of *bildungsroman*: the "coming out" story. As gay and lesbian communities moved toward a renewed sense of solidarity, "coming out" stories allowed their own writers the possibility of self-expression and self-healing and afforded their gay and lesbian readers the knowledge that they were not alone in feeling the stresses of a minority culture. Edmund White's *A Boy's Own Story* in 1982, a semi-autobiographical fiction, epitomized the subgenre, following an adolescent's coming of age and of sexual identity in the American Midwest. Remarkable for its emotional openness and frank description of sexual encounters, *A Boy's Own Story* reached both gay and straight readers. Randal Kenan's *A Visitation of Spirits* (1989), set in the American South, followed in a similar vein, treating themes of race and homophobia, as a family comes to terms with a son's sexual identity. In the way that White's Midwestern landscape shows the power of geography on identity, Kenan's *A Visitation of Spirits* takes a virtually unprecedented look at the intersection of race and homosexuality within a particularly volatile Southern landscape, with consequences remarkably divergent from the geographies of suburban and urban luxury and escapist indulgence characteristic in the fiction a decade before.

[Historically, gay and lesbian communities have been joined under the same aegis of homosexuality, often without taking into account the effect of gender on this singular label of homosexuality and how distinctly lesbian and gay communities do emerge, one from the other. In the latter half of the 1980s, as lesbian writing focused on gender politics and gay justice, gay male writing centered more and more on the sudden AIDS crisis that seemed so endemic to the culture of gay men living at that time. Paul Monette's *Borrowed Time: An AIDS Memoir* (1988) was written after the death of his lover to AIDS and proved to be one of the most powerful books ever written concerning the experience of AIDS and its aftermath of personal loss. Andrew Holleran's *Ground Zero* (1988), David Feinberg's *Eighty-Sixed* (1989), and James Purdy's *Garments the Living Wear* (1989) all touched on the epidemic that so affected and began to describe gay communities throughout the late 1980s. Journalist Randy Shilts' book, *And the Band Played On: Politics, People and the AIDS Epidemic* (1987), detailed the effects—both small and large, personal and bureaucratic—leading to the spread of AIDS throughout the United States and the devastation, in the wake of the religious-conservative backlash, felt supremely within the gay community.

[The subject of AIDS continued to be a topic of gay writing throughout the 1990s. Playwright Tony Kushner's work brought the crisis to both heterosexual and homosexual theater audiences. Kushner's *Angels in America: A Gay Fantasia on National Themes* existed in two sections, *Part 1: Millennium Approaches* (1992) and *Part II: Perestroika* (1993), and showcased main characters infected with AIDS. The play worked to characterize the state of America not only in terms of sexual identity, but racial and ethnic as well. *Part 1: Millennium Approaches* appeared on Broadway in 1993 and won the Pulitzer Prize for drama that year. In some sense, the medium of theater first showed the signs of gay-subject or gay-themed work reaching a large audience in a formidable way. Jonathan Larson's widely popular and critically successful musical, *Rent*, which appeared on Broadway in 1996, likewise featured gay personages, one of whom dies of AIDS. Larson, himself, was not gay, but his work underscored a heterosexual concern for the AIDS epidemic that had been so widely regarded as a gay disease, and also announced an emergence of a "gay literature" into a more mainstream venue.

[Until the beginning of the 1990s, lesbian literature had functioned primarily as a polemical literature, advancing a politics and an agenda as opposed to attempting appeal to a wider, non-lesbian readership (Faderman 1995). Throughout the 1990s, however, literary works appeared that posited a lesbian identity as only one facet of an individual's identity, in a way making the lesbian agenda appear gentler and closer to mainstream. Jenifer Levin's *The Sea of Light* (1993), Paula Martinac's *Home Movies* (1993), Carol Anshaw's *Aquamarine* (1992) and *Seven Moves* (1996), and Blanche McCrary Boyd's *The Revolution of Little Girls* (1992) offered glimpses of lesbian characters not bound fully by lesbian communities, but integral to and incorporated into a more everyday America. Dorothy Allison's *Bastard Out of Carolina* (1992), a finalist for the National Book Award, fictionalized the author's own harsh experience growing up lesbian in the South, and garnered both critical and popular success.

[One work of gay literature to have had perhaps the biggest reach throughout mainstream America was Michael Cunningham's *The Hours* (1998), a novel inspired by Virginia Woolf's *Mrs. Dalloway. The Hours* imagines the lives of three separate women—Virginia Woolf being one of these—interweaving the three stories into a singular narrative movement. *The Hours* spent weeks on *The New York Times* Bestsellers List, was awarded both the 1999 Pulitzer Prize and PEN/Faulkner Award, and was adapted into a recent film of the same name, starring Nicole Kidman, Meryl Streep, and Julianne Moore.

[The popularity and success of *The Hours*, perhaps, signals the disappearance of a gay and lesbian literature as separate from some otherwise "mainstream" literature, and hints at a future of assimilation, in which "homosexuality" will not be placed in opposition to a "normalcy." To a certain degree, media and advertising have allowed a greater visibility and viability of the gay and lesbian communities that help to afford their literature a place with booksellers (Shulman 1998; Arnold 2003). However, a clear distinction seems to exist between a literature that shows gay and lesbians as affectionate, which is permissible, while a literature showing gays and lesbians as sexual or desirous, is not. In 1997, for example, David Leavitt's novella, *The Term Paper Artist*, was pulled from publication in *Esquire*, after chiefs at the magazine feared advertisers would be offended by Leavitt's descriptions of man-to-man oral sex; the censorship of Leavitt's piece caused long-time *Esquire* literary editor, Will Blythe, to resign in protest of the magazine's decision.

[As gay and lesbian literature moves to become more mainstreamed, opinions differ on whether this will be a good or bad thing. Those reluctant to the mainstreaming of a gay and lesbian literature—and of gay and lesbian culture in general—fear that certain stories and certain voices might falter to homogenization. Publishing trends, however, reveal that new commercial markets have been opening up for gay and lesbian writers, not just in terms of literary fiction and poetry, but also in terms of the genre fictions (e.g., detective, romance, and horror) geared toward gay readers (Arnold 2001). Such growth and evolution seems promising, not only for gay writers and readers, but also for the roles they might play and occupy within the larger culture of the United States. (*End of update by M. Hyde*)]

## [Varied Sentiments: The Expression of Sexuality in Music    RAYMOND J. NOONAN

[*Update 2003*: It has been said that each generation thinks it invented sex, that it was the first to discover one of life's most magnificent treasures. Perhaps nowhere is this more evident than in the musical record of each generation's contribution to the lyrics of its age. What is important to a generation—and to a society—can be found embedded in the lyrics of its popular songs. One way to evaluate the validity of sentiments expressed in the music is to observe how often people choose to listen to it in their free time—and like sex, enjoying music is a most popular pastime. And by far, one of the most prevalent themes found throughout this repertory, past and present, is that of romantic love—and, if one looks deeper, the celebration (as well as sometimes the denigration) of sexuality—in all its permutations. For most people, their relationships are what provide meaning to life. Music, the mirror of life, reflects the best and worst of life back to us, from anger and sexism to the profoundest love and eroticism.

[Studies of the arts with predominantly sexual themes—sometimes called the "erotic arts"—has a long, if sometimes not wholly respected, history, with treatises on sex in literature, the performing arts (e.g., film, video, theater, and performance), and the visual arts (e.g., painting, drawing, photography, and sculpture) being the best represented in both the academic and popular literature. All of these lend themselves to the printed page by affording the author and reader the benefit of photographs and film stills as illustrations of the text. Music, however, has not lent itself as effectively to books and journals, or any of the traditional print media. In printed form, music notation requires some skill to interpret and some musical talent and training to even approach an understanding of how the piece is supposed to sound, or sometimes even to discern what verse follows another. Furthermore, the printed notation of most modern (popular) music only provides a bare-bones outline of the words, melody, rhythm, and accompaniment of any particular song. The "arrangement" chosen by the artists, as well as the individuals' or groups' own innate voices and styles, then create the distinctions that separate one version of the

song from another. Just as the printing press revolutionized the collection and dissemination of knowledge, and engravings and photographs made it possible to illustrate a text with a picture worth a thousand words, so, too, are advances in multimedia computer technology revolutionizing the future of all literature by allowing us to create texts that can be viewed on electronic screens accompanied by both high quality images *and* sound. Thus, we are beginning to see hypertext "books" on compact disk (CD), digital versatile disk (DVD), and on the Internet illustrated with examples derived from moving video pictures as well as "snapshots" of digitally recorded or "sampled" sounds taken from diverse sources. Histories of music are coming alive.

[What follows is a review of various musical genres and the way principally American songwriters have addressed or portrayed sexuality in their lyrics. It will proceed largely from where other writers have left off. Of necessity, the review cannot be comprehensive because our musical heritage—even what currently exists in recordings—is so extensive. We will, however, review the highlights of what Cray (1969) called the "Erotic Muse," the myriad ways in which sexuality has appeared in our musical literature, with an emphasis on the music of the United States and the English-speaking Western world during the last 200 years. We will elucidate the sentiments expressed and, to some extent, their meanings within their time and culture. We will not delve deeply, since this has been done elsewhere as noted below, into the sexual aspects of music purely as sound and rhythm, or as a motivator, subtext, or accompaniment to movement or dance or lovemaking.

### [*Historical Antecedents*

[As a subject for serious writing, either academic or journalistic, the profoundly important and eternal interrelationship of sexuality and music has had relatively little written about it in the past few decades. The sole exceptions have surrounded publicity about attempts by small but vocal self-styled censors within government and a few private parents' groups to promulgate "studies" which "prove" the harm to children, women, and others that sexually explicit lyrics in popular music—dubbed "porn rock" by critics—has caused. This reflects, in general, both a deep ignorance of the long connection of sexuality and music and an almost universally inadequate comprehensive sexuality education program or critical-thinking component of most education. It is exacerbated by an official predisposition to conceptualize sexuality primarily in terms of its sometimes problematic aspects accompanied by largely hypocritical moral pretexts, and to focus on useless, superficial, or oppressive "solutions."

[By the early 1960s, few scholars with training in the sexual sciences had explored the topic of sex and music. Of those outside of sexology who did, the most important studies were by musicologists interested in tracing the lineage of popular folk songs from the traditional music that had been passed from generation to generation of the common people through oral transmission. While a large part of this oral tradition in English probably has been lost, much of it was collected by folklorists in England and America during the folklore revival of the 1800s (and during the two centuries previous in England and other countries) and stored hidden in various libraries across the world. What music scholars discovered was that many of the original songs from which the folk songs were derived embodied sexual situations described with explicit imagery. These songs, when finally written down, were then passed on to posterity only after they had been revised or obliterated to conform to the "moral" expectations of the educational, religious, and political leaders of each era. The importance of these discoveries will be discussed shortly. The reader is referred to Cray (1969) and Reeves (1965) for a more complete history of the process that occurred and the mechanisms that probably took place. Oscar Brand (1962), himself a scholar and folksinger, writing on the modern American folk song revival in the 1960s, discussed a similar process, though with some differences, that occurred during the ascendancy of folk music at that time, and its impact on today's music.

[Bridging this interest in folklore with sexology is *The Horn Book* by Gershon Legman (1964), by far the most important study of eroticism in folklore and folk song that has ever appeared in the English language. A former bibliographer for Alfred Kinsey, Legman, an erudite scholar with a breadth and depth of knowledge of erotic folklore equalled by none, looked at and evaluated the written record of erotic literature and music that had been amassed by collectors of erotica during the past 500 years, the sum of which appears to have been largely unknown by other scholars. His work clearly elucidates the role that sexuality has played in the history of music in all cultures in all times and should provide scholars with a foundation upon which any research or discussion of sexuality and music henceforth will be based.

[The earliest consideration of the topic in the sexological literature was written before 1910 by Havelock Ellis (1936b) in his opus, *Studies in the Psychology of Sex*, in which he discussed the influence and effects of music on animals and man and the roles he believed it played in arousing sexual attraction within the framework of Darwin's model of natural selection. Among general surveys of sexual science that have appeared more recently, the most extensive review of sexuality in the music of the Western world was an article by MacDougald (1973) in *The Encyclopedia of Sexual Behavior*, edited by Albert Ellis and Albert Abarbanel (1973). Laemmel (1976) also briefly covered the topic in his overview of sexuality in the arts in the mostly psychiatrically oriented volume edited by Sadock, Kaplan, and Freedman (1976). Webb (1975) provides the most comprehensive perspectives on all the erotic arts, including insightful sections devoted to popular music and musical theatre, in which he highlighted some of the developments in musical eroticism that had also occurred through the 1960s. MacDougald (1973) noted that, by the time he wrote his article in 1961, only eight scientific studies, none of them definitive, existed about the interrelationship of music, "the most expressive and least tangible of the arts," and sex. In his survey, he discussed the transition from religious to secular music and the rise of the classical tradition in which woman would become a vital part of a previously all-male world. He also considered some of the popular forms of music up to the 1950s, including Latin American, modern, and jazz dancing, and some of the popular singers of the 1940s and early 1950s.

[Rock 'n' roll, which originally appealed primarily to the young—and which became so problematic for so many adults since its inception because of its inherent sexual overtones—was in its infancy, and so was not treated at all by MacDougald (1973). So, too, were two of the antecedents of rock music—folk music and the blues—not covered, because so many of these songs, as noted above, were suppressed and hidden from view. Then, too, traditional demarcations of culture into "high" and "low," as well as generational biases, may have played a part, in which certain forms of culture were not deemed worthy of scholarly consideration. Webb's (1975) observations on rock 'n' roll and the blues, as well as the musical theater using a rock format, were more salient, because he wrote his analysis from a perspective that benefitted from its occurring during a phase of the latest sexual revolution that overlapped almost two

thirds of the two decades of rock history at the time he wrote it. Laemmel (1976), on the other hand, devoted only several superficial paragraphs to the subject. Nashville-style and other country music had not yet fully developed or matured into the form we know it today, and so was not considered by any of these writers. The profound revelations in folk music noted above also seems to have been unknown to them.

[The Ellis and Abarbanel (1973) volume, however, did include an article on sexual dynamics in dance in which Nikolais (1973) traced the role of sexuality in and on modern dance from Isadora Duncan onward, including psychological interpretations of art by Freud and Jung and their application to dance; another article by Goodman (1973) discussed social dancing, where the dance was shown to symbolize the erotic interactions of men and women in a mutually enlightening, socially acceptable way that allowed them to move together or withdraw gracefully as they so chose. (This is reminiscent of D. H. Lawrence's (1936/ 1953) reference to Romeo's statement, "To me, dancing is just making love to music," to which Lawrence responded, "To the music one should dance, and dancing, dance.")

[MacDougald (1973) traced the historical connection of sexuality and music by noting that many musical instruments originated as representations of the genitalia whose primary use was to celebrate the functions of sex and/or fertility by early peoples. For example, in the Pacific islands, Africa, and Asia, some early drums were shaped as, and represented, the vulva and were played with a drumstick representing a phallus. The flute also has been historically identified as a symbolic penis. MacDougald (1973) wrote,

Although this symbolic identification might seem naive to us, it has had great significance in many sexual manifestations—circumcision, menstruation, ceremonies, dances, rituals, etc.—around the world. In a number of European languages the word "flute" has definite sexual connotations, cf. the English expressions "the living flute," "the silent flute," "the one-eyed flute," etc. as in "The Cupid" (1736) Farmer:

> The flute is good that's made of wood
> And is, I own, the neatest;
> Yet none the less I must confess
> The *silent flute's* the sweetest. (p. 747)

[A similar symbolism continued into the 17th-century classical baroque period in Europe, during which a number of "love instruments" that symbolically connected Eros and music came into wide use, including the *viola d'amore*, the *oboe d'amore*, and the *clarinette d'amour*. Even in the 20th century and since, the manner in which some rock and blues musicians play their instruments suggests a strong connection to their erotic origins.

[While the intent of much of the music prior to the Middle Ages was purposely sexual, medieval music took on a specifically nonworldly religious tone under the Roman Catholic Church. After the Dark Ages, however, secular interests began to signal the emergence of the Renaissance that would begin in a few centuries. Sexual love would prove to be a stong impetus toward that artistic and intellectual revival and began to make its appearance in music, as well as the other arts.

[Ballads and lyrical songs about love apparently were the first nonreligious songs written, appearing in Europe during the 12th and 13th centuries in Provence in the south of France. The poet-musicians who wrote them were called *troubadours* and were usually members of the nobility, often knights, and sometimes commoners. Their music and poetry, which were devoted to chivalrous love, later spread to the north of France where *trouvères* imitated the new movement. From Provence, also, the love poetry and music of the *troubadours* spread to Italy and, more importantly, to Germany, where the *minnesingers* developed their own narrative style, being less formal and less distant than their French counterparts (Apel 1969).

[Out of the writings of the *troubadours* and *minnesingers* of this era came a bold new concept that would give people a glimpse of some future era: a view of woman as active and passive, in MacDougald's (1973) words, "a feminine creature to be loved and to love." This is perhaps the most important development in the secular musical celebration of the vernacular of Europe, and it stood in stark contrast to the Catholic religious music that had dominated the continent for a millennium. This movement eventually evolved into the 16th-century classical tradition of the Renaissance, during which madrigals were composed in which woman and love were mere abstractions. MacDougald (1973) wrote,

[... D]uring the Dark Ages Christianity effectively stifled the composition of secular "emotional" music, resulting in a thousand long years in which virtually no love songs, certainly one of the fundamental urges of the human heart, were composed! Although the musical dictatorship of the Church was ironclad for centuries, it could not restrain the natural inherent desire of man to sing of nonchurchly things. (p. 748)

[Thus, secularity began to merge with sacred music, paralleling, but lagging centuries behind, the gains realized during the emergence of the *troubadours* and those who followed their spirit. It is interesting to note that, in the classical tradition, there is a distinction between the art song (created with serious artistic intent by accomplished musicians) and the folk song (arising in the vernacular of the common people by untrained musicians). It could be said that the folk (i.e., popular) songs of the day that arose from the people were analogous to the vulgate of the Catholic Church, that is, both were in general circulation and both were for the masses (cf. *vulgar*, of the common people). In that sense, it can be seen how all nonclassical music might be considered vulgar (or, by extension, obscene, following the modern corruption of the word). Thus, we see a similar pattern during the 16th through the 20th centuries, particularly with regard to the folk and blues songs that arose from ordinary people in their day-to-day lives, that contrasted with unofficially or officially sanctioned popular music that avoided, but did not always completely destroy, the emotionality derived from sexual eroticism. The second millennium would finally end with a rich literature of songs specifically confronting and affirming our sexual heritage on a variety of levels. The reason for the love song's primacy in this new secular order are seen quite clearly by Legman (1964):

Erotic poetry, especially in the form of song, is extremely ancient. It was considered by the Greeks to be a special form of the poetic art, with its own muse, Erato—she with the lyre—indicating the intimate relation to music. This relation is always sensed, as to erotic poetry in particular, and is clearly admitted by the repressive religious objection to all music other than that used in worship, and even there with the prohibition of certain too 'sensual' instruments and 'lascivious' modes.... The only other forms of poetry thought worthy of muses by the Greeks were lyric and heroic poetry (that is to say, songs and ballads, but on themes other than erotic), and these were understood to be derivative. They could hardly have preceded love poetry, or rather love song, which is, after all, not unique to the

human species or even to the mammalian order. The love-calls and sexual displays of any number of male animals and birds, even insects . . . imply a long pre-history of erotic song and erotic dance, as integral parts of the sexual approach of living creatures, long preceding the appearance of human life on earth. (p. 408)

[By the turn of the 17th century, a new form of musical expression was being developed in Italy in the classical tradition (but with additional roots in the folk tradition, as Legman (1964) notes)—the opera—that was to continue the trend of introducing woman, not as a symbol, but as a human being with a host of human characteristics, good and bad, into European music. The reader is referred to MacDougald (1973) who has summarized these developments in detail with numerous examples from the operatic repertoire. I will note simply that he attributes chiefly to Mozart the transition of woman from being nonexistent as an active, motivating force at the end of 16th century to being an integral and vital part of the classical operatic tradition by the end of the 18th century. Laemmel (1976) states further that the overture to Mozart's *Don Giovanni*, which immortalized the Don Juan theme, "initiated the romantic movement in music by dramatizing the eternal battle between the sexes." Sexuality, love, and sensuality would reach a pinnacle in classical music in the 19th and early 20th centuries with operatic and symphonic works, some performed with the eroticism underscored in ballet, by Wagner (*Tristan und Isolde*, 1865), Bizet (*Carmen*, 1875), Rimsky-Korsakov (*Scheherazade*, 1888), Debussy (*Prélude á l'Après-midi d'un Faun*, 1892-1894), Stravinsky (*Le Sacre du Printemps*, 1913), Ravel (*Bolero*, 1928), Shostakovich (*Lady Macbeth of Mtsensk*, 1934), and others.

[An illustration of the response of the media provides some insight into the impact that one of these operas had when it was performed. "Shostakovich is without a doubt the foremost composer of pornographic music in the field of art," said one critic in 1955 (MacDougald 1973) in reference to the sexual imagery of *Lady Macbeth of Mtsensk*, while the Soviet *Pravda* criticized how, in it, "'Love' is smeared all over the opera in the most vulgar manner" (Gillespie 1968). Legman (1964) notes further how popular dances, such as the "Bunny Hug," the "Turkey Trot," the "Tango," the "Shimmy," the "Twist," and others since the 16th century, all evoked religious and moral opposition when they first appeared. People today are seldom aware of how ubiquitous self-styled 'defenders of the public morality' have been, and that virtually every new form of music and dance was criticized on those grounds throughout history with varying degrees of success in their suppression.

[In the first decade of the 20th century, an important form of vocal and instrumental music indigenous to America was introduced by Jelly Roll Morton called "the blues." Soon afterward, "jazz" appeared as the background music in the brothels of New Orleans, co-evolving with the blues from ragtime, minstrel-show music, and early brass and string bands (Abel 1969; Webb 1975). Laemmel (1976) notes the erotic roots of jazz, the first major artform to be born in America, and suggests the name's derivation from *jass*, a sexual term in a Creole dialect for the Congo dances. By the middle of the 20th century, this new type of music, more overtly sensual, was having a significant impact on musical expression. The rhythm of swing by such artists as Louis Armstrong, Benny Goodman, Duke Ellington, Gene Krupa, and Lionel Hampton had solidified "the beat" as a necessary component of popular music and jazz. Because rhythm is an inherent component of sexual activity, rhythm in music is considered an aspect that cannot be divorced from its sensual and sexual overtones and their relationship to dance. This period was also the time when the voices of popular stars like Peggy Lee, Sarah Vaughan, and Lena Horne evoked sexual feelings in their audiences, as did the voice of one of the first teen idols, Frank Sinatra. MacDougald (1973), presumably reflecting his own generation's attitudes toward the music of his youth, describes one of the most important composers of that period, whose lyrics boldly and uniquely expressed specifically sexual themes:

> When the subject of sex and popular music arises, one automatically thinks of that genius, Cole Porter, whose *oeuvre* is a kind of musical erotikon, to use an apt word. The lyrics that Porter writes are admittedly the "sexiest" of any writer and it is contended that he likewise composes "sexy music." It is undeniable that his songs . . . do possess a haunting appeal that induces an erotic mood.

[Porter's songs, indeed, have a universal appeal—perhaps because of their eroticism and positive affirmation of the power of love—that has helped his music survive into the rock era. His songs continue to be recorded by contemporary artists of all musical persuasions, the 1990 collection of Porter songs, *Red, Hot & Blue*—recorded by various artists both as a tribute to Porter, who had to hide his homosexuality to practice professionally, and as a means of benefiting AIDS research and relief—being a noteworthy example. As such, one could call Porter the first modern songwriter in the contemporary popular song idiom. He was the muse whose musical influence most directly presaged the range of sexual ideas expressed in the lyrics of music popular in the closing decades of the 20th century to the present.

[Describing Porter's lyrics as "sexy" also introduces three of the predominant underlying questions usually asked about sexuality in musical lyrics, one's answers to each betraying a different philosophical stance in the continuing debate on the topic: How does the vocabulary a songwriter uses influence the response to the music—both by the intended audience and by would-be censors? What is the purpose of sexuality in music today and is it necessary for song lyrics to depict only "acceptable" behavior and feelings? and Is it a legitimate function of songs to excite or seduce, i.e., to "turn on" the listener by creating an erotic mood?

[At the same time that Porter's songs would enjoy wide popularity, "race music" would, by the 1950s, be limited to black venues and audiences. This genre would often be more sensual and sexually direct than their white counterparts. Nevertheless, these songs would soon be introduced to white audiences, as various singers in the 1950s, especially Elvis Presley, began adapting ("covering") what became known as rhythm and blues, which is sometimes still used synonymously for much of this early black-inspired rock 'n' roll. Still, these covers were typically more suggestive than direct.

[Simultaneous important developments would emerge in the 1960s, a renaissance decade in American popular music. At the dawn of the decade, black performers with artistic roots in rhythm and blues would lay the groundwork for what would later be known as soul music. Groups such as the Supremes, the Temptations, and others exemplified the so-called "Motown sound," while the Ronettes, the Exciters, and others pioneered the innovative recording techniques of Phil Spector's "wall of sound." The dominant sentiment expressed in much of this music was that of teenage love with only the mildest hint of sexuality, *per se*. In the meantime, the Beatles ushered in a new era in popular music, a revolution which quickly influenced and reflected the growing "youth culture," which, with the new sexual revolution, the civil-rights movement, worldwide student pro-

tests, and the new psychedelic-drug era, spawned a host of American and British rock groups. They, too, were influenced by rhythm and blues. Finally, by the end of the decade, the folk revival began, which was more heavily influenced by the social movements mentioned above, with Bob Dylan, Joan Baez, and others, especially Dylan, paving new paths, which would later merge with rock as folk-rock, probably the first of rock music's eclectic penchant for fusing with other musical styles. In 1969, Dylan experimented further with country music in *Nashville Skyline*, which contained the well-known specifically sexual song, *Lay Lady Lay*. Country songs by both male and female artists would, in the 1970s and beyond, also focus on sexual themes, including premarital sex, adultery, divorce, and other topics, such as Loretta Lynn's celebratory song, *The Pill*.

[Popular songs with sexually explicit lyrics would remain mostly invisible until rap music became widely popular in the 1990s. Similar developments occurred among largely white audiences with heavy metal and other minor genres of rock music. Rap music is rightly considered the most significant American musical innovation since jazz. Arising from the urban-ghetto experience of young blacks, rap has antecedents in both African-American rhythm and blues (R&B), the immediate predecessor if not the actual beginning of rock 'n' roll) and the "talking blues" of early American folk music, both of which became more widely popularized in the 1960s as noted above. Additional roots derive from the Caribbean as well as the Negro spirituals of the black slave experience. Rap is itself not a single genre, but has been broken into various "topical" areas, such as hip hop, as well as along geographical lines, i.e., New York City versus Los Angeles. Widely popularized across both black and white audiences in the United States, as well as other races and internationally, during the 1980s, rap, since the 1990s, is heard on radio and television and in the movies. As one might expect, based on our previous discussion of sexual expression in song lyrics, sexuality has come to play an integral part of rap lyrics.

[The most controversial form of rap, not surprisingly, therefore, are those songs which express sexual ideas—or more precisely, those that use unconventional "street" language to express these ideas—in their lyrics. The group which, in its early years, most typified this genre, variously known as "explicit" or "dirty" rap, was 2 Live Crew, a rap group based in Miami, Florida, in the 1980s. In fact, 2 Live Crew would go on to relive, in a sense, the path followed by Lenny Bruce through arrests and the courts in his groundbreaking comedy bits, which similarly used street language and sex, as well as satirical jabs at religion and politics, in the 1950s and 1960s, paving the way for today's standup comedians. Of particular significance is a word that they used and other performers continue to use today, the expletive *fuck* and its various derivatives, which, although it has its obvious sexual meaning, is more often used to signify camaraderie and shared generational experiences—an important aspect of the music of youth—as well as a host of other nonsexual meanings. Still, sex is where these words derive their power. Numerous other black artists would further develop the rap idiom with explicitly sexual themes or language, along with a few white artists, most notably, Eminem.

[*Sexual Themes in Popular Song Lyrics*

[Musical lyrics could be a goldmine to sexologists, as well as to any student of human nature who takes the time to listen to their content and context. While many say that the beat, with its "primitive" cadence suggesting sexual rhythms, is the prime motivation behind many forms of today's popular music, the lyrics—perhaps more so than the instrumental parts of the songs—embody the wide range of expression we conceptualize as sexual. In contemporary Western culture, the music and the beat provide the background for our sexual, social, and private lives—even our work lives—especially for the young, but also increasingly for the rest of us. Indeed, it has been so for people of all ages in all cultures in many parts of their lives throughout the centuries. Yet, it is the lyrics on which many adults focus today—particularly those intended for young audiences—because of their often sexual content. MacDougald (1973) has noted that one of the problems in examining the relationship of sex to music is the confounding nature of "association," that which imparts meaning to a song without its necessarily being explicitly sexual. Thus, a title suggesting romanticism, or even the situation in which a song is experienced, will color one's perception of the erotic attributes of a song or its effects on any particular listener. Noonan (1998b) has also noted how one's own personal successes and failures in intimate relationships can have a similar impact on one's perception of sexuality in other sociopolitical contexts.

[While the underlying eroticism of early rock 'n' roll was subject to criticism since its beginnings in the 1950s, (it is well known by now that the very term *rock 'n'roll* is a euphemism for sexual intercourse), the lyrics tended more to suggest sexual situations than to describe or depict them directly. As rock has matured, this has become less so. As the "baby boomers" got older, their music began to reflect more of the issues they considered important—and sexuality at the beginning of the current sexual revolution which began in the 1960s and continues to evolve—was a most important part of life. Not that suggestion has been any less represented on the contemporary music scene, but our perception of it has changed. What appears to offend many people today, at least ostensibly, is the explicit slang that has become apparently more prevalent than in the past. Part of this perception has arisen from the fact that, while the use of this language has probably not increased in daily life during the rock era, the airing of the language via the public airwaves, both on radio and television, has increased as restrictions by government agencies like the U.S. Federal Communications Commission (FCC) have gradually eased. This has been attributed, at least in part, to the rise of cable television networks (as well as video rental stores) which allow viewers a greater choice of viewing options—and viewers have tended to choose the more "adult" options, i.e., those that reflect the language and situations that make up their world or their dreams. Indeed, given the choice of an "edited-for-television" film and its uncut version, most will choose the original—and broadcast stations make a point of noting with much fanfare when a particular film is being shown for the first time "in its entirety" within its broadcast area. Others have noted how versions of popular theatrical films are sometimes released in two versions: an R-rated (restricted) American version and a complete version (with more sex) for Europe, South America, and other areas in the world.

[Simultaneously, both broadcast and cable television networks, most notably Music Television (MTV), began exploiting a new artform, the music video—a powerful marketing tool for selling recordings that was discovered in the early 1980s—which became increasingly popular. While their kinetic energy was ideally suited to the young and to the medium, music videos have greatly influenced many other forms of commercial fare, especially television advertising, as well as live theater and film, with music videos even aimed at adult audiences appearing in large numbers with its own music network, VH1, as well as networks aimed at various ethnic audiences (e.g., Black Entertainment Television, BET, and the various flavors of MTV). A discussion of the sexual content of the visual part of music

videos is beyond the scope of this article, but suffice it to say that music videos have generated at least as much concern for the shallow and stereotypical ways in which they depict sexuality and the sex roles of men and women as for the presumed sexual messages they promote. Some have even argued that music videos and the recordings they represent are promoting sexual activity among those who would not otherwise tend to be sexual. While few professionals seem to have refuted the illogical argument that sex needs to be promoted, that argument has been used with great emotional force in the suppression of both sexually explicit—and sexually implicit ("suggestive")—lyrics over the last two centuries. (*End of update by R. J. Noonan*)]

## [Seduction of Fashion: A Sociological Perspective

RUTH P. RUBINSTEIN

[*Update 2003*: The seven deadly sins were guidelines for behavior instituted by Judeo-Christian authorities as central to an orderly social life (Lyman 1978). The importance of each of these cultural constructs depended upon the political context of a particular period. Throughout the history of Western society, however, expectations and behavior were gender specific, where men were expected to work and women were expected to follow. Moving up the social-class structure and employment outside the home as avenues of getting away from family authority were usually closed to women. They depended upon the men in their family. To attract a man, a woman had to stand out. Fashionable attire evolved around arousing male/female interest and entailed the violation of two of the seven deadly sins—the sin of lust and the sin of pride.

### [*The Sin of Lust*

[Women's fashions sought to arouse male interest in two distinct ways: It demonstrated her family's wealth and encouraged male lust. Clothes that hug the body, expose the body, and use a variety of color and ornament, Church fathers decreed, distracts male attention from spirituality. Hence, women should refrain and focus on modest attire. In the Church's first 500 years, women were exhorted to renounce male dress and to cover their heads as a sign of subservience to men (I Cor. 11:4-10; I Cor. 14:34-35; I Tim. 2: 11-15; Reuther 1974).

[Lust was the longest recognized, best known, and always a part of the seven deadly sins, observed sociologist Sanford Lyman (1978). He notes that marriage is a link, not only to the wedded couple, but also to families, lineages, and status groups. For this reason, sexual expression is an objective of societal control mechanisms (Lyman 1978, 92).

[St. Augustine had observed that the male organ activates itself independent of desire. It is independent of a male's will, responsibility, and control. It was only after Adam and Eve sinned did they recognize that they were naked—that they were stripped "from the grace that prevented the bodily nakedness from causing them embarrassment." Thereafter, all mankind was afflicted with what Augustine referred to as "the insubordination of the flesh." This insubordination resulted in a sense of shame (Lyman 1978, 55).

[Augustine's lust-shame theory accounted for the near-universal covering of male genitalia. The liberation of lust from human will accounted for the origins of the injunction for female modesty, the requirement for privacy during sexual intercourse, and the grudging necessity for marriage (Lyman 1978, 56-58).

### [*The Sin of Pride*

[Theologians and social commentators locate the sin of pride in men and argue that men adorning themselves indicates pride. According to Allanus de Insulis, the evil in the sin of pride is that the prideful man is removed from sacred and communal constraints. He divorces himself from its kind, disregards his associates, separating himself from those who can restrain him. It is a person with a haughty ego. The human frame itself is pressed into service in behalf of arrogance (Lyman 1978, 141).

[Gregory the Great argued that pride entails arrogance that emanates from within the person, where the male favors himself in his thought. He silently utters his own praises and uses attire to glorify himself (Lyman 1978, 136). Georg Simmel relates male pride to the wearing of adornment. He suggests that adornment "intensifies and enlarges the impression of the personality by operating as a sort of radiation emanating from it" (Lyman 1978, 142). "The personality is more when it radiates" (Lyman 1978, 143).

[The phenomenon of fashion began as an expression of male pride. It emerged in the court of the Duke of Burgundy, Philip the Bold, in the late 14th century. For a great feast at Amiens he appeared in a voluminous black-velvet overcoat with long wide sleeves (*houppelande*), the left sleeve of which was decorated with roses worked in gold, sapphires, rubies, and pearls (Kemper 1977, 77). Philip's successors— John the Fearless, Philip the Good, and Charles the Bold— continued to emphasize clothes that reshape the body and emphasize sartorial splendor (Kemper 1977, 77).

[In the collection of her Majesty, the Queen of England, there is a painting called "The Field of the Cloth of Gold" (ca. 1520, anonymous). It portrays Henry VIII and his entourage of 5,000 winding their way to the Castle of Guiness where the French King Francis I had his headquarters. Henry VIII is portrayed in the outfit depicted in the painting made famous by Holbein the Younger. The king's distinctive style consists of broad shoulders, barrel-chest, and a prominent codpiece wearing the Renaissance style of slashing. The style entails the simultaneous display of several layers and colors of fabric, giving the impression that the outfit is bejeweled.

[The meeting between Henry VIII of England and Francis I of France was an extravagant event that relied on dress and courtly procession to persuade the courts and noble guests of the power of each of the rulers. Called "The Field of the Cloth of Gold," the meeting lasted 20 days, during which the kings visited, dined, jousted, and "excelled in theatrical acts of courtesy and friendship," observed Phyllis Mack (1987, 59). As in other such occasions, this one, too, had spectators, some of which were prostitutes who traditionally followed the troops.

[Although ceremonial robes alter very slowly and are less likely to be affected by fashion changes, they are nevertheless an important source of male pride. In the French court, they made their last impressive appearance at the assembly of all estates called by Louis XVI on May 5, 1789. Men of the nobility wore "magnificent gold—embroidered court dress and hats with flowing plumes" (Batterberry & Batterberry 1977, 192). Until the French Revolution, much of male attire was designed to reflect a man's access to wealth, prestige, and power.

[American social critic, economist Thorstein Veblen, identified the motivation underlying the pursuit of fanciful attire by men. In *The Theory of the Leisure Class* (1899), he argued that that it was not sufficient to have possession of power and wealth; such ownership must be put on evidence—hence, fashionable attire. Fashionable attire consisted of three essential elements: sumptuous fabrics indicating wealth, garments designed in the latest style, i.e., indicating being in the know; and in a style that informs that so attired, the individual could not possibly engage in physical labor (Veblen 1899, 33-80).

Male members of the aristocracy were also portrayed with armor, swords, gold chains, and jewels.

[Initially, only the husbands' appearance mattered. But with the increase in wealth, the manner in which wives and children were attired began to matter. To support his claim, a man's dependents had to dress according to his rank. Veblen (1899, 120-121) characterized the clothing of wives and children as vicarious consumption.

[Male attire was seductive in the sense that it suggested that a man who is well dressed or fashionably attired had access to resources that women need. He could secure appropriate clothes, a roof over their heads, and obtain food for her and their potential children.

*[Lust and Pride*

[Renaissance dress and Cavalier styles are two fashions where male attire committed both sins, the sin of lust and the sin of pride. Prior to the Renaissance, for over a thousand years, male attire in Europe consisted of a robe (tunic) long or short and a loose-fitting belt. The body and its contours were concealed. In the second half of the 14th century in Italy, older men continued to wear the long robe, but young well-to-do men adopted a style that violated the norm of modesty by adopting sexy and prideful appearance. Male dress hugged the body, exposed the body, and used a variety of color and ornament—the Church's definition of seductiveness.

[*Renaissance Dress.* Renaissance male dress consisted of a short jacket cut tightly to the body reaching the upper thigh. The sleeves were close fitting and buttoned from the elbow to the wrist. The upper part of the sleeve was tailored in such a way that made it possible to move the arm freely. The short outfit exposed the legs, which were covered in skintight hose. Each leg was cut separately and fastened to the inside of the jacket with corded laces somewhat like shoestrings. Calling further attention to the body was the use of two contrasting colors, where the color used on the left leg and left arm matched the right side of the jacket. The right leg and arm matched the left side.

[The hose, which were two separate articles, were supposed to overlap at the top, but often did not. Bending down often meant exposing the buttocks and "what is inside." This led to much criticism. Around 1370, the two pieces together were sewn in the rear, leaving an opening in the front, which was then covered by a separate triangle of cloth. This addition was transformed into a codpiece—an article of dress celebrating male virility. Renaissance style of dress was modified and worn throughout the Western world.

[The inspiration for the new style was the Greco-Roman tradition that celebrated the virtue of the naked body (Hollander 1978, 83-85). An early version of the décolleté can be found in the Snake Goddess of Crete; clinging or transparent draped garments that covered, yet showed off the body, making the female body even more alluring, can be found in the sculptures of the Parthenon.

[*Cavalier Fashion.* Associated with the Dutch, the Cavalier fashion was international in scope. It was worn by King Henry IV of France and King Charles I of England. It was a playful fashion (Batterberry & Batterberry 1977, 132, 138-139). The wire and padding that gave male dress its structure and stiffness were eliminated. The ruff had become smaller and then softer. The dress consisted of a doublet (jacket) where some of its buttons were left unbuttoned. The breeches were left drooping, and the hose allowed to fall untidily around the shoe tops. There was also a big moustache, playful ribbons, sashes, bows, and a flamboyant felt hat sitting precariously on the wearer's head. The image conveyed the message that there were few barriers to male-female interaction (Kybalova, Herbenova, & Lamarova 1968, 177, 180, 183).

[*Design Approaches to Fashion*

[In his book, *The Psychology of Clothes*, psychologist J. C. Flugel (1966) observed that there are three different orientations to the development of a style. One is where the body itself is of little interest. A profusion of garments are hung on the body. Maximum gorgeousness is achieved by piling one luxurious garment over another in a way that leads to interesting variations in line, and a profusion of glorious colors. Royal robes are an example of this style (Flugel 1966, 156). Layering of fabric was used in the 17th-century portraiture of the nobility by Velasquez, Rubens, and Van Dyck to achieve a sense of sumptuous "nonchalance" appropriate to noble sitters, as Hollander (1978) observes.

[A second orientation is the desire to show the attractive features of the body better. Clothes are used to frame the body. The third orientation involves rendering the body more alluring by using "transparencies and half-concealments" (Flugel 1966, 157). These are garments that reveal the form of the body and give it an additional grace. Flugel (1966, 160) explained that a new female fashion, a period's desired appearance, can also evolve by emphasizing a new part of the body, or a feature, by treating it as reflecting the spirit of the period. The body part or feature displayed is rendered as "seductively alluring" as a special center of "erotic charm." In the Middle Ages, for example, the corset was used "to make the breasts inconspicuous." As the ascetic trend of the Middle Ages diminished, the breasts were brought out of hiding and female fashion focused on the abdomen. Women were portrayed as if pregnant. They also adopted the gait and carriage distinctive of pregnancy. Flugel called this theory "the shifting erogenous zones theory of fashion." With each new fashion, there is a change in emphasis. The focus is transferred from one part of the body to another. Unfamiliar, the image generates interest. A new erogenous zone had been thus created.

[Another source of fashion was the style of dress adopted by a king's mistress—a woman who had successfully attracted and kept a king's attention. Her style became a source of fashion. Madame de Pompadour, the mistress of King Louis XV of France perfected and popularized the robe á la Française to such an extent that it "practically became the French national costume" (Batterberry & Batterberry 1977, 161-165; Kemper 1977, 105-106).

[With little chance for respectable employment, women had to depend on the men in the families for survival. Women until the 1980s had little opportunity to acquire wealth, prestige, and power. Over the centuries, Western European women developed styles of appearance that enabled them to capture male attention. They enhanced their physical appeal, yet remained within the bounds of modesty. Where these images were successful and enabled the woman to attract the attention of the man she wanted, her style was adopted by other women; it became the fashion, and the image became integrated into the vocabulary of images existing in Western culture. Three such images have been identified: adopting elements of male dress, creating an image of harmony, and the glamorous look. These styles are integrated into the vocabulary of images generally available in Western society. In the United States, they were popularized by actresses and fashion designers who searched for a costume to convey the image of a character on the stage, in movies, and in personal appearances.

[A new seductive image was offered by the art and literature of the 1950s. Ballet had acquired new importance after World War II, and designer Clair McCardle offered the ballerina look for everyday attire. The style emphasized long limbs, flat-chestedness, ballet slippers, and hair swept back to reveal a long delicate neck. Embodying these qualities was actress Audrey Hepburn, a former ballet student. She was chosen to play the role of an inexperienced teenager falling in love with a sophisticated older male. She appeared in about 12 movies of the same theme, and in each she conveyed the essence and vulnerability of a new bloom (Rubinstein 2001, 139-150).

[Cultural fascination with adolescent sexuality was reflected in the success of *Lolita*, the novel by Vladimir Nabokov (1954), which was initially banned. Also conveying vulnerability was the partiality of teen and young adult women for their older brother's or father's shirt, jacket, or coat. Overwhelming in size, these garments made the young women look smaller and in need of adult care. The vulnerable teenager was decreed seductive in the December 1968 issue of *GQ* magazine. A panel of 30 men psychologists, sociologists, and members of the editorial staff believed it to be one of the basic images American men would enjoy (*GQ* 1968). This cultural atmosphere helped to legitimate a liaison between an older mature male and a romantic teenager. Each of the seductive images emerges in a specific socioemotional context, each with its own impact on the interaction.

[*Male Attire: Rationality and Self-Restraint*

[With the spread of the puritanical ethos in England in the 19th century, male fashion in England ceased. Calvinism's strong aversion to the ostentation and etiquette of the courts, as well as to all the luxury and extravagance, were replaced by a demand for thrift (Harvey 1995). A new fashion of sobriety and modesty for both men and women appeared. Male attire became form-following rather than form-fitting, and in "funereal" somber black. It reflected the puritanical ethos for thrift. According to the German sociologist Rene Konig, a man' suit today is "fundamentally a direct descendant of the puritan dress, a political demonstration against the ostentation of the court" (Konig 1973, 117). Lively colors, the scintillating velvet, and silk fabrics that characterized the clothing of the nobility today can be found in Roman Catholic countries.

[It is a common phenomenon that men in uniforms look seductive. The sizing standards developed during the Civil War made it possible for ready-to-wear military uniforms to reflect rationality and self-restraint. The uniform conveyed to women that, in addition to physical prowess, the soldier was upright and dependable.

[The male suit has continued to offer middle-class women a sense of security. To convey prowess, hip-hop male outfits often include massive gold jewelry around the neck. The fingers are ornamented with heavy rings or with tatoos on each of the fingers.

[Despite positive reviews by the industry, the enterprise of American menswear designer John Bartlett failed, when his artistically designed collection used a variety of colors and was body-hugging, i.e., seductive in the Church's definition. The male puritanical ethos allows veering only in the direction of affirming social identities.

[*Spirit of the Period*

[A specific sociocultural context and the attire of celebrities were also a source of seductive images. The aesthetic that characterized the flapper was that of youthfulness (Flugel 1966, 161-162). Visually, the flapper of the 1920 conveyed intensity, energy, and volatility (Sage 1926, 216). Social critics described its impact as leading to a revolution of "morals and manners." The flapper bobbed her hair, and her dresses were tight, straight, and short, with a low waist usually placed about the hips. Her chest was flattened, her waist was hidden, and her legs were kept in plain view. Moreover, women frequented the saloons and drank with men, swearing and smoking. They also used contraceptives (Yellis 1969, 46-47).

[The birthrate declined during the Depression of the 1930s, when the fashionable style came from Paris. It was long, lean, and plunging in the back. After World War II, it became patriotic to have children, and Dior's 1947 "New Look" was transformed into the "pregnant look" and "the sack" look. These styles concealed the pregnancy. The art of dress gave in to the miniskirt in the 1960s. The miniskirt is youthful in feeling and allowed freedom of movement.

[The 1980s—the era characterized by the pursuit of wealth and conspicuous consumption—was an era of too many stretch limousines, too many yachts off Newport Beach, and too many fur coats in Aspen (Phillips 1990). To better convey the image of success, American businessmen flew to England to buy 'bespoke' suits—a dark suit made to order by English tailors. The realm of black had continued to spread. Moreover, the tailoring industry in England shifted emphasis from the ostentatious, body-hugging attire the dandies wore, to a form-following suit in dark funereal color announcing self-restraint. President Reagan, on the other hand, also had a custom-made suit, but he had his made in Los Angeles, the movie capital. It was made from specially woven yarn in earth-tone colors. Being an actor, he was aware that a color of cloth that complements one's skin tone enhances appearance and encourages affective response.

[Production of women's fashions in France emanated from the need to provide skilled women with work. The revolutions of the 19th century had disrupted the economy and left many women unemployed and their children hungry. According to Charles Frederick Worth, Empress Eugenie couturier, the king had asked him to create a new fashion with each new season. Everything his wife wore was immediately copied, first by the upper class and then it filtered to the lower classes. To make sure that members of the upper class did spend their money on new clothes, he instituted the practice that those wishing to appear before him must be dressed in the latest fashion. France became the center of fashion.

[In the United States of the 1960s and 1970s, informality and youthfulness characterized female fashion. Fashion in the Reagan White House (in the 1980s) had become increasingly form-fitting, slinky, and slithering, accentuating female curves, and expensive. It was based on what Flugel described as "the interplay of concealment and half transparencies." Exposed backs, low necklines, side and front slits, and the pouf were expected to create sexual allure (Rubinstein 2001, 299). Nancy Reagan's delight in clothes, balanced for color and ornament, extravagant and luxurious, was consistently reported in the news. The fashion reflected the spirit of the 1980s—glorification of capitalism, free markets, and finance (Cannon 1990). In 1985, looking rich was very important. Television programs focused on the real and imagined lives of wealthy people, such as *Lifestyles of the Rich and Famous*, *Dallas*, and *Dynasty*, which were enormously popular with the American public.

[The fashion during the Clinton presidency was for the young. There were skirts that looked like flimsy silk half-slips, shoes styled like bedroom slippers, body-hugging pants made of snakeskins and with wild-animal prints. Harking back to the Garden of Eden and the jungle, this fashion suggested sexual temptation and danger.

[Soon after George W. Bush assumed the presidency, snakeskin pants, bags, and jackets disappeared. The young continue to wear their low-riding pants (where the naval is exposed). Also exposed are the feet. Flip-flops, footwear traditionally worn around the swimming pool to prevent slipping or on the beach as protection from the hot sand, had become fashionable and were called "toe cleavage" by Guy Trebay of *The New York Times* (June 17, 2003). Flip-flops are the simplest of all footwear—two scraps of leather or cloth. With little structure, they are the cheapest to produce and most affordable, but offer the foot little support. Clothes, too, offered little support. Schoolgirls' jumpers, miniskirts, and tops were offered in bold color combinations, or a prairie skirt with a nipped Victorian jacket, tattered jeans with rosebud-striped silk jacket, and a denim dress dripping with cowry or puka shells worn for good luck by indigenous groups. Spring/Summer 2003 outfits could be asymmetrically hemmed, spliced, or bisected, *The New York Times* accurately predicted (September 22, 2002). The jewelry in fashion consisted of two styles, one with earrings worn close to the ear, the other dangling downward, as if the wearer hoped to reach the forces underlying the universe for nurturing, support, and protection.

[*American Popular Culture.* Hip-hop attire increases the size of the individual and says, "I am here, you can't ignore me." The trendy jeans have strategically placed faux-faded stripes that direct the observer's gaze towards the genitals. The young know the look they want and they search for it. Finding the right style was about "being yourself."

[The essence of pride and lust are also conjured in fantasy images. These images reflect what societal gatekeepers think women want from men and what they think men want from women.

[*What Women Want from Men.* In the figure of Superman, the bespectacled mild-mannered newspaper reporter, Clark Kent, was invulnerable to the forces of evil once he changed into a Superman costume. He saved women and destroyed criminals. He, however, was unable to connect to his beloved Lois Lane (Kimmel 1996, 211-212). Another fantasy hero was the cynical, dangerous, hard-boiled detective—a central character in film noir. He was depicted as a man who made the world safe for women and children. He was sexually alluring, but unavailable for marriage (Savage 1998). Perhaps the most famous reflection on what men want from women was a statement made by the actor Humphrey Bogart in June 1945, "I'm tough and intend to stay that way."

[*What Men Want from Women.* The "bombshell" and the "pinup" were two distinct images that men had created. The term *bombshell* first emerged in the 1930s during the Depression. The name referred to big-bosomed women who worked outside the home and were economically and socially emancipated (E. T. May 1988). Images of pinup girls accompanied men through the depth of the Depression, the battlefields of World War II, and the war in Korea. *Esquire Magazine* viewed female sexuality as an inspiration to American fighting men. Artist Alberto Vargas and George Petty were commissioned to depict images of ideal females that came to be known as "pinup girls." The images consisted of curvaceous young women in skintight short shorts. Among those posing were famous actresses: Marilyn Monroe, Betty Grable, and Rita Hayworth. Military men used pinups to adorn their vehicles, noses of bombers, and anything else they could (Christian 1998).

[In conclusion, the dichotomies of Male/Female and Lust/Pride established by Christianity were intellectual constructs that became 'a taken for granted' social reality. They underlie the organization of society, patterns of interaction and social life congruent with these social constructs. For some, these social distinctions may have been false, resulting in the closing of the possibility of patterns of interaction and expressions of emotion that enhanced societal development and personal growth. The direction that American fashion takes as we enter the new world concerned with international strife and war is likely to reflect these new realities in much the same way. (*End of update by R. P. Rubinstein, in memory of Paul Shapiro, Ph.D.*)]

## [Concluding Remarks

### [Change, Diversity, and Conflict: Points and Counterpoints
DAVID L. WEIS

[*Update 1998*: In the beginning of this chapter, we identified the assessment of how change occurs in a context of conflict between diverse social groups as a major theme in our analysis of sexual behaviors and values in the United States. Subsequent pages are rich in details relating to this theme. The reader is encouraged to savor the entire chapter and digest all of these details. However, we would like to conclude by recapitulating and integrating some of the major points related to this theme.

### [Change

[Over a quarter of a billion Americans, representing a wide variety of ethnic, racial, and religious traditions, continue to struggle with the interface of science, technology, and society in all domains of life, nowhere less or more intimately than in our sexual behaviors and values. Recent computerized technology has enabled us to produce, access, and consume more information than has ever been possible in the history of the world. As we noted elsewhere, professionals and the public can now turn to the Internet, rather than to more traditional sources, to obtain sexual information, receive counseling, and even interact sexually. This provides many redundant opportunities. For example, persons who have felt alienated and isolated from the sexual "mainstream," such as the physically disabled and transgendered, have found information, support, and a new medium for self-expression on the Net. Yet, the use of this technology is not without conflict. The war over censorship versus freedom of speech and self-expression, waged with other print and broadcast media, is continuing with renewed fervor as state-of-the-art technology tests the limits of access to sexual information and sexually explicit dialogues and materials.

[As we have seen in every aspect of our sexuality examined in these pages, numerous changes are taking place in Americans' collective and individual sexual lives. As Weis described in "Demographic Challenges" at the beginning of the chapter, various factors are having an impact on the experience of sexuality: the changing racial/ethnic fabric; the "graying" of America; and more-varied lifestyle patterns (e.g., increases in wives/mothers working outside of the home and in the number of cohabiting couples, and a growing disconnection between childrearing and married life).

[Yet, the public representation and institutionalized values of American sexuality are often not keeping pace with the realities of people's private lives. For example, it is well documented that television, considered the most influential medium in American life, continues to present stereotypical views of gender roles, which do not reflect the realities of people's personal, family, sexual, and work lives. As Weis noted in Section 8 on unconventional sexual behaviors, while heterosexual marriage is the modal pattern for sexual relations in the United States, sizable percentages of Americans depart from this assumed norm to engage in nonmarital sexual expressions, including premarital, extramarital, same-gender, and unconventional sexual behaviors and relationships. Contrary to the goals of most public policies and programs dealing with adolescent sexuality, the

facts demonstrate that "premarital virginity" has largely disappeared in the United States.

[Because change is actually a constant within people's sexual lives on both the individual and societal levels, research must focus more on the process and dynamics of sexuality rather than simply recording "social bookkeeping." More-varied and complex qualitative and quantitative research methodologies and analyses must be applied to the study of human sexuality.

### [Diversity

[The theme of diversity is woven throughout every thread of sexual life within the United States. Our country is known for being a "salad bowl" of diversity with a continuous struggle to achieve its promise of human rights—no matter one's gender, racial/ethnic background, socioeconomic status, religious persuasion, or physical characteristics.

[Much of our public and scholarly discourse about sexuality still relies heavily on simplistic, often dichotomous, categorizations for complex phenomena, such as gender, race, ethnicity, and sexual orientation. However, the sexologists who contributed to this book have tried to expose perspectives and research supporting the complexity of personal characteristics as they interface with sexual expression. Although this was not always possible, since scholarly research and information about diversity and sexuality tend to be limited, it is important to note the many aspects of diversity that are treated in some detail. The complexity of gender (Section 7) is evident in the paradigms of the "gender rainbow" (Leah Schaefer and Constance Wheeler), "gender flavors" (June Reinisch), "gender landscapes" (James Weinrich), and the identification of five sexes (Anne Fausto-Sterling). Samuels, and Pérez and Pinzón-Pérez (Section 2B) emphasize the varied characteristics and cultures of those labeled "African-Americans" or "Latinos," and the effects of these upon individuals' sexuality. Koch (Section 2B) dispels the myth of "the feminist" representing a monolithic ideology. Francoeur and Perper (Section 2A) explore the varieties and complexities of fixed and processual religious groups, a diversity highlighted by Forrest's (Section 2A) discussion of the sexual values found among members of the Church of Jesus Christ of Latter-Day Saints, or Mormons. The work of Kinsey, Klein, Weinberg, Williams, Pryor, and Moses and Hawkins, among many others, illuminates the diversity among homosexually and bisexually oriented people (Section 6). In discussing adult heterosexualities, Weis (Section 5) describes the varieties of sexual expression and relationships among married and nonmarried individuals. Francoeur and Koch (Section 8B) describe the diversity among sex workers, while Love (Section 8D) points out that the United States has more fetish clubs than any other country in the world, and discusses some common and unique fetishes. These are but a few examples of how every aspect of sexuality is reflective of and affected by diversity. It is obvious that a major challenge to American thinking about sexuality requires that we stop viewing sexuality in simplistic terms of male or female, black or white, gay or straight, marital or nonmarital, or normal or abnormal.

[We still have great strides to make in closing the gaps in our knowledge and understanding of how sexuality is affected by and reflective of diversity. The majority of past and current research does not conceptualize or operationalize many personal and social variables as multidimensional (e.g., gender, race, and sexual orientation)—when they are addressed at all. Koch's 1997 study of the 12 quantitative research articles published in *The Journal of Sex Research* in 1996 reveals, for example, that the race/ethnicity of the subjects is not reported in two thirds of the studies. For the other third of the studies, no statistical analyses are presented to examine similarities or differences, based on race/ethnicity, in the sexual topics being examined. Similarly, in half of the 12 quantitative studies, the sexual orientation of the subjects was not reported. In the one study that identified the subjects' sexual orientation, no analyses of similarities or differences, based on sexual orientation, was conducted on the independent variables under study. None of the research examined the interaction among variables such as gender, race/ethnicity, and sexual orientation. As we have repeatedly seen throughout this book, these interactions are paramount for an accurate and realistic understanding of human sexuality. The sexual experiences of Anglo-American heterosexual men often differ from those of Anglo-American heterosexual women, which also differ from those of Anglo-American gay men, which also differ from those of African-American gay men, which also differ from those of African-American lesbians, which also differ from those of Latina lesbians, and so on. Our research sensibilities and methodologies must become more sensitive and sophisticated if we are to truly advance sexual science, education, therapy, and policy.

[Without adequate research, and sometimes even with it, people rely on stereotypes to form personal opinions and public policy. Too often these stereotypes lead to adverse judgments or prejudices. These prejudices then influence individual and collective actions, resulting in discrimination against underrepresented groups. This text was filled with examples of discrimination affecting people's sexual relationships, sexual health, and sexual rights. For example, women of lower socioeconomic status in the U.S.A. have much more restricted access to legalized abortion services than do women of higher economic status. Individuals from marginalized groups are disproportionately affected by sexually transmissible diseases, including HIV disease, because of poverty and poorer education and healthcare. Gay men and lesbian women are the last large minority group in the U.S.A. that generally has no legal protections against discrimination. They are subjected to discrimination in all areas of their lives: housing, employment, healthcare, relationship and family formation, and military service, as well as being targets of gay bashing and other hate crimes. Sexual scientists, researchers, educators, and other professionals, as well as citizens at large, must take action to stop ignorance and prejudicial attitudes from continuing to shape public policy, resulting in harm to people's health and well-being.

## [Conflict

[With the advancements in science and technology, the diverse groups in our society have not been able to keep abreast by implementing concomitant social progress. It seems that the more things change, the more they stay the same. As described in the section on "Contraception, Abortion, and Population Planning," abortion, especially until "quickening," was widely practiced throughout the history of the United States until the second half of the 19th century. At that time, various factions of "social purity" groups banded together with branches of government to restrict sexual freedoms and control reproduction. Laws, including the "Comstock Law," began to alter 200 years of American custom and public policy towards contraception and abortion. The anticontraceptive provisions of the Comstock Law were enforced until 1936, when finally a federal appeals court overturned them based on the medical authorities who supported the safety and reliability of contraception.

[Following are examples that illustrate the "point" and "counterpoint" of sexual conflicts in the United States.

## [Points

- Today, we are experiencing a well-organized and often successful resurgence of the social purity movement, which is restricting sexuality education, sexual health, sexual research, and many sexual freedoms. For example, there are currently more barriers to U.S. women's access to abortion than since the Supreme Court's 1973 *Roe v. Wade* decision. The moral issues of groups of religious and political conservatives are more influential in determining legislated public policy than the well-researched and documented public health concerns surrounding non-access to legalized abortion. New "Comstock laws" are being enacted that once again restrict access to birth control information and services, even though the weight of the authority of the medical world supports their safety, reliability, and necessity.
- Federal funding of abstinence-only education is another example of policy and practice being driven by special interest groups' concern with moral issues rather than by knowledge gained through experience and research. Abstinence-only education has been shown, both nationally and worldwide, to be less effective in preventing unintended pregnancy and sexually transmissible disease risk than more-comprehensive forms of sexuality education. Yet, some effective sexuality education programs are being replaced throughout the country with the less-than-effective abstinence-only ones. At the same time that a nationwide study of puberty documents that half of America's black girls and one in five white girls has begun puberty by age 8 (the 3rd grade), school boards, administrators, and parents are abandoning sexuality education or postponing it until junior or senior high school, even in states with sex education mandates.
- In addition, our knowledge of normative sexual development throughout the lifespan, particularly in childhood and adolescence, is severely hampered by lack of funding and other barriers established by conservative "social purity" groups that wield power through federal, state, and local governments. Funding for sexuality research by well-respected scientists, like Udry and Laumann, has been blocked, despite the fact that such research is critical to expanding our basic knowledge of sexual development, practices, and relationships, as well as reducing sexual health risks, including HIV disease.

## [Counterpoints

- Despite long-term opposition of some groups to contraception and abortion—the Comstock Laws, arrests of Margaret Sanger for distributing birth control, opposition of the Popes to "artificial" birth control, and the recent successes of the "pro-life" movement to restrict access to abortion—the general trend over the course of the 20th century has been a greater ability of women and couples to control their fertility and greater use of a variety of family planning practices.
- Despite a century of efforts by various adult groups to limit adolescent premarital sexual behavior, the clear trend of the 20th century has been increasing percentages of adolescents engaging in premarital sexual practices at progressively earlier ages. By the 1990s, fewer than 10% of American youth are virgins on their wedding day. Attitudes have also become progressively more permissive.
- Despite the efforts of some groups to restrict the availability of sexual information and to block sex education

in the schools (again, a century-long effort), the general trend has been toward more sex education in the schools and greater availability of information through a number of sources, particularly various media. Nevertheless, conservative members of the Senate and House of Representatives did pass a bill limiting sexual information on the Internet; however, the Supreme Court ruled the law unconstitutional.

- Although many sexual issues remain controversial, discourse about sex has become freer and more open. More people talk about sex in public settings and discuss a wider variety of sexual practices than in the past. For example, public discussions of homosexuality are much more common now; and everyone seems to be talking about oral sex in the wake of the sexual allegations against former President Clinton. There is also more sexual content on American television, both on the networks and cable; in movies, including in the theaters and on videocassettes; in all forms of printed material, such as general-circulation and sexually explicit magazines; and in all forms of popular music, from heavy metal and rap to country music.

- Homosexuality has become increasingly visible. The "coming out" of Ellen in a television sitcom series of that name is one example of this greater visibility. In addition to Ellen, there are more gay characters being portrayed on American television and in movies than ever before. There is also a growing availability of gay-related fiction. Disney and other corporations have begun to extend job benefits to gay couples, although conservative groups threatened to boycott Disney because of this. Hawaii is considering some kind of legal recognition of homosexual unions or marriage, although other states have stated that they will refuse to legally recognize such unions. Even the U.S. Supreme Court has ruled that same-gender sexual harassment does exist. However, gays still have not been granted full equality in the U.S. and face continuing challenges to their civil rights.

- Finally, the rising age at marriage and the growing divorce rate throughout the 20th century have increased the relative percentage of unmarried adults, at any one time, who are pursuing various nonmarital lifestyles and relationships. There seems to be greater awareness of this trend and acceptance of this trend in adult sexual expression.

[Some of the obstacles we face in better understanding American sexual values and behavior originate and work within the scientific community itself. Scientists from various disciplines must learn to work together in a more collaborative fashion to examine the various contributing factors and outcomes of specific sexual development, health, and educational issues. Competition between biological, psychological, and sociocultural research perspectives and practices needs to be minimized and a more holistic biopsychosocial perspective adopted.

[As we begin the 21st century, the historical theme of sexuality being embedded in change, occurring within a context of conflict among diverse social groups in the United States, will certainly continue. The spheres of influence of various social groups will ebb and flow with changing demographics and social consciousness. The dimensions of change will be directly affected by the speed and direction of technological development. As in the past, persons with fixed-world ideological views will continue to try to impede social progress in adapting to change and diversity. Yet, on balance, the trend throughout American history has been towards liberalization in sexual attitudes and behaviors. It is

our belief that education, research, and human rights will continue to be critically needed guideposts in the determination of sexual values, practices, policies, and programs in the United States in the future. (*End of update by D. L. Weis*)]

## [An American "Call to Action" to Promote Sexual Health and Responsible Sexual Behavior

ROBERT T. FRANCOEUR and RAYMOND J. NOONAN, with CHRISTIAN J. THRASHER.

[*Update 2003*: About 60 experts in various facets of sexuality in America worked with us and with David L. Weis and Patricia Barthalow Koch, our knowledgeable coeditors on this chapter, to develop this extensive examination of sexuality in the United States. We cannot speak for our contributors. We also decided not to speak for ourselves as editors. But we want to have a brief statement and summary to bring the many pieces of this American mosaic together.

[We could find no better working statement to express the underlying message of this survey of American sexual attitudes and behaviors than the "Call to Action" issued in 2001 by David Satcher, M.D., Ph.D., the 16th Surgeon General of the United States. In the last year of his appointment by President Bill Clinton as Surgeon General, Dr. Satcher committed himself and the U.S. Department of Health and Human Services to community-based research studies that linked together the sexual health of Americans with responsible sexual behavior. In 2001, as he left office and President George W. Bush entered the White House, Dr. Satcher's *Surgeon General's Call to Action to Promote Sexual Health and Responsible Sexual Behavior* was released. The *Call to Action* was developed through a collaborative process. Its content was based on the strongest science ascertained with broad input from a diverse spectrum of health professionals, academics, policymakers, parents, teachers, clergy, social service workers, and social movement representatives. The *Call to Action* utilized public and private platforms to raise awareness about health problems related to human sexuality and their effects on all Americans, especially the economically disadvantaged, racial and ethnic minorities, persons with different sexual identities and orientations, disabled persons, and adolescents, as well as persons of all ages and backgrounds.

[The overall goal of the *Call to Action* was, and is, to open up and facilitate a mature, respectful, honest, and thoughtful discussion about sexuality. As a country, Americans must understand that sexuality encompasses more than sexual behavior, sometimes referred to as the "-uality" of sexuality. Sexuality has many aspects beyond the physical ones that we are saturated with everyday in this country. Sexuality is a fundamental part of human life.

[With Ford Foundation support, Dr. Satcher and the National Center for Primary Care at Morehouse School of Medicine in Atlanta, Georgia, are working to develop a strategy for improving sexual health, as well as increasing public discourse about human sexuality in the United States using The *Call to Action* as a framework. A National Advisory Committee has been formed with leaders from many different disciplines within the field of sexuality to guide these domestic efforts in furthering the *Call to Action*.

[Sexuality is an integral part of human life. It carries the awesome potential to create new life. It can foster intimacy and bonding as well as shared pleasure in relationships. Yet, it can have negative aspects, including sexually transmitted infections, HIV/AIDS, unintended pregnancy, and coercive or violent behavior. These result from America's inability to deal appropriately with human sexuality, an inability we share with many other nations of the world. All individuals and communities share important responsibilities for sexual health. These include assurance of access to culturally and developmentally appropriate comprehensive sexuality education and sexual and reproductive healthcare and counseling; the need to make informed sexual and reproductive choices; the need for respect for diversity; and freedom from stigmatization and violence on the basis of gender, race, ethnicity, religion, or sexual orientation.

[In the words of Dr. David Satcher,

Finding common ground might not be easy, but it is possible. The process leading to this *Call to Action* has already shown that persons with very different views can come together and discuss difficult issues and find broad areas of agreement. Approaches and solutions might be complex, but we do have evidence of success. We need to appreciate the diversity of our culture, engage in mature, thoughtful and respectful discussion, be informed by the science that is available to us, and invest in continued research. This is a call to action. Americans cannot remain complacent. Doing nothing is unacceptable. Our efforts will not only have an impact on the current health status of our citizens; they will lay a foundation for a healthier society in the future.
*(End of update by R. T. Francoeur and R. J. Noonan)*]

## [Epilogue: A Transcultural Inventory of Courtship and Mating

JOHN MONEY*

[*Editors' Note*: John Money, Ph.D., is considered by many sexologists as the most important theoretical sexologist of the 20th century, offering many insights and connections across the many disciplines that make up sexology and sexosophy, the philosophical underpinnings of sexual beliefs and practices. While reading his contribution, consider how the many aspects of sexuality covered in this chapter might fit together as a unified whole within the rubric of Money's characterizations. Given that the United States is a multicultural nation derived from many other nations, these concepts can help to explain the origins of the various attitudes, beliefs, and behaviors described in this chapter, which did not develop overnight. It will be more difficult, however, to resolve some of the conflicts that might have been predicted by his synthesis, yet it might ultimately help to resolve some of the conflicts by providing better understanding of the commonalities that exist among all Americans, as well as among all human beings; thus, they can be applied to all of the countries in this *Encyclopedia*. Of primary importance, perhaps, is that Money's synthesis includes the importance of both the mind and the body together, hence his well-known criticism of the false dichotomy of pure essentialist and social-constructionist adherents. Although some of his theses remain controversial, perhaps his synthesis, together with our "Call to Action" in the previous section, might help us to sort out those attributes that are culturally dysfunctional in the modern world, eventually leading to a sane sexual society that benefits everyone.

## [Evolutionary Derobotization

[*Update 2003*: Around the world, people who share a common heritage include in that heritage explanations and legends, among others, of creation, life in the hereafter, and procreation. The action patterns of courtship and mating exist synchronously as maps in the brain and its nervous system and in the mind. They are robotic in apes and in monkeys and

*Supported by the National Institute of Child Health and Human Development, Department of Health and Human Services, Grant #R25-HD00325-46.

even more so in four-legged mammals than they are in our own human species. Robotism of an action pattern of courtship and mating means that it is highly replicative or stereotyped from one occasion to the next and from one partner to another. By contrast, a nonrobotic action pattern of courtship and mating is developmentally more subject to individual idiosyncracy and to community doctrine. The term, *lovemap* (Money 1986, 1999), is the overall term that I coined for the concept of the action pattern of courtship and mating, the wide diversity and underlying universals of which can be found in the pages of this chapter and throughout the *Encyclopedia*. The lovemap includes ideation, imagery, and practices, i.e., the way we form our ideas and imagery relating to sex and the way we develop our behavioral practices.

[In the absence of replicable experimental evolutionary data, one must be satisfied with conjecture. It is my conjecture that derobotization of the prototypic human lovemap was part of a more widespread derobotization of action patterns once phylogenically mapped in the human brain; and that derobotization was the price to pay, so to speak, for the evolutionary emancipation of the human language map (speechmap) from a robotic system of hoots and howls into a system of syntactical reasoning, symbolic logic, and mathematical calculation.

## [Ten Constants of Sexual Doctrines

[Doctrines of courtship and mating differ from one community to another, to a greater or lesser degree, on the basis of ten constants: progeny, age, morphology, gender, pedigree, caste or class, number, duration, privacy, and accessories. The annotations that follows apply predominantly, though not exclusively, to the doctrine of sexuality in Christendom.

[*1. Progeny*: Singly or severally, the action patterns of human courtship and mating are both recreational and procreational. As a species, we have, however, been bioengineered to procreate dieciously, that is by the union of male and female, and not parthenogenically. Diecious procreation is the pivotal constant around which devolve the other constants of our courtship and mating doctrine. Until very recent times, failure to procreate was considered grounds for annulment of a marriage and was attributed to barrenness of the female, not to sterility or impotence of the male partner. Arguments about contraception is a recent phenomenon. For most of human history, predictably effective contraception did not exist. Having progeny implies also the provision of family and community care of the offspring.

[*2. Age*: Procreatively, it makes sense that age matching should prevail over age mismatching in social doctrines of courtship and mating. In the system of arranged marriages, however, an infant or child may be betrothed to an adult partner, but without copulation until the age of maturity. The age of the end of childhood may be arbitrarily legislated to extend from the onset to the end of adolescence. Thus, a young adult man or woman who has sex with, say, a 17-year-old may be charged in one culture with sexual child abuse. At the older extreme of the age scale, in another culture, an adult of 60 who has sex with a 25-year-old may be envied or ridiculed, but not accused of sexual abuse. In the juvenile years, age-matched sexual rehearsal play that is positively endorsed in the ideology of one society is prohibited and abusively penalized in another.

[*3. Morphology*: Chronological age and morphological age are not necessarily in perfect agreement. When they disagree, morphological age is given precedence. Take the example of a pubertally precocious boy who, by age 6 has the mature morphological development, although short in stature, of advanced teenage. He is misconstrued by strangers as a socially retarded teenager, not a socially advanced juvenile. Conversely, a morphologically retarded hypopituitary-dwarfed girl aged 19 is misconstrued as a prepubertal child presenting herself as a young adult woman. In uncounted ways, our morphology is also our destiny.

[*4. Gender*: As members of a diecious species, we come to expect of our fellow human beings that their morphology and appearance will be concordant with the action patterns of their courtship and mating. Historically and transculturally, however, there are examples of communities that have not only tolerated, but idealized male/female bipotentiality—the other sex for procreation and the same sex for playfulness. Homosexuality and heterosexuality in ideation, imagery, and practice, may be concurrent, or they may occur sequentially. Each may be fixated and may exclude the other, but exclusive homosexuality has not occurred with a sufficiently high incidence to slow the population explosion of the human species. Contemporary technology that permits ascertainment of the sex of a fetus and its abortion only if it is female has already changed the sex ratio at birth in some parts of the world in favor of an excess of boys. For them, subsequently, there are too few age-matched females for traditional family formation. People with a fixation on sex reassignment nowadays call themselves transgendered (not transvestite or transsexual as formerly). Diagnostically, they are classified as having a gender-identity disorder whereas, more accurately, they have primarily a body-image disorder.

[*5. Pedigree*: Human beings are designed phylogenically to live in troops and to be troop bonded. To the extent that they are members of the same family of birth, they share genes in common. Alternatively, they may be totemic kin by assignment. Either way, if a couple has the correct totemic pedigree relationship, they may be obliged to procreate and, if not, forbidden to do so. Thus, whereas first-cousin marriages may be the ideal in one culture, they may be prohibited as incest in another. Keeping track of the totemic pedigree of an entire community may have constituted a major deployment of the human intellect in ancient times, as it continues to do among Aboriginal elders of Australia's Arnhem Land today (Money et al. 1970).

[*6. Caste and class*: Our primate heritage dictates not only that we are a troop-bonding species, but also a species that recognizes a hierarchy of authority and leadership within the troop. Thus, a community's code of courtship and mating specifies matching of procreating couples on the criteria of caste, class, title, race, religion, language, wealth, or some other special criterion. A partnership that is legally miscegenation and an abomination in one community may be idealized or romanticized as a source of power and privilege in another.

[*7. Number*: As well as being troopbonders, human beings are pairbonders. The action pattern of neonatal nutritional bonding are, in part, prototypes of those that will later come into play as action patterns of procreative pair bonding. At its most intense, this kind of bonding is known as limerence or as being lovesmitten or lovestruck. Limerence is typically for one partner at a time, but there may be more than one partner, if not concurrently then sequentially; and partners may be either matched or mismatched on the criterion of social class, caste, age, or fidelity.

[*8. Duration*: Single or multiple partnerships each may be either transient or long-lasting. As is the case in some bird species, monogamous fidelity that appears to be lifelong, may actually apply to lifelong pairing for parenthood (nest building, incubation, and feeding of the young, season after season), and not with respect to copulation. The proof lies in DNA testing of each generation. A doctrine that specifies monogamy as the ideal may persecute nonconformists, or it may tolerate separation and divorce, or turn a blind eye to an affair—a system within a system. Duration covers any length of time, from a hurried lunchtime assignation to the anonymity of a one-night stand, to a "seven-year-itch" marriage, or to a love affair in limerent perpetuity. The youngest age for the onset of a long-lasting love affair (Money 1997, 122) is as early as age 8, if not earlier. Worldwide, juvenile sexual rehearsal play is condemned more often than it is condoned or imbedded in social doctrines of sexuality. Illegitimate grandparenthood is an economic issue as well as an issue of morality.

[*9. Privacy*: One arrives naked on this planet, and it takes not weeks or months, but years of exposure to the sexual taboo to develop a full sense of shame or guilt about exposing the naked sex organs and their action patterns. A taboo imposes a negative sanction on an action pattern normally manifested in the course of human development, for example, the taboo on eating certain foods, on talking to members of certain kinship groups, or offending ancestral spirits. The taboo on sex is particularly effective, as it is nonlethal, but is subject to some degree of on/off regulation. Its function in society, when instilled at a very young age, is that thenceforth, the very threat of its sanctions calls forth obedience. Thus a taboo is a political weapon. Its presence is a temptation to some to rebel against it, which is precisely what happened in the 1960s and 1970s, the era of the sexual revolution in Western civilization. We still live in the era of the counterrevolution. The privacy rule is total when it applies to any public manifestation of courtship and mating, including kissing. Not only genital eroticism, but also genital exposure for a gynecological examination may be subject to taboo. In the electronic or print media, depiction of the genitalia and their action patterns may be prosecuted as obscene and pornographic. Indeed, pornography may be defined as that which is explicitly seen or heard in public when a doctrine's privacy rule regarding sexual pairing is disregarded. By the same token, multipartnered sex, as in group-sex parties, is outlawed, except for the infrequent celebration of ceremonial carnivals or bacchanals. Under conditions of severely crowded family living, the scarcity of auditory and visual privacy interferes with intimacy in courtship and mating. Likewise, the scarcity of privacy interferes with diagnostic and prognostic observation and recording of data at first hand in couples with a complaint of sexual malfunction. The privacy rule skews data on the prevalence of genital adornment by piercing, tattoo, or scarification—and likewise data on genital mutilation as a sequel to clitoral or penile circumcision.

[*10. Accessories*: Copulatory toys include vibrators, dildos, butt plugs, cock rings or straps, and various paraphernalia specific to selective paraphilic lovemaps, notably those in the category of sadomasochism or of bondage and discipline. The copulatory accessory that is by no means a toy, however, but a pregnancy planner or preventer, is the contraceptive device or substance. Contraceptives range from the condom and the intrauterine device (IUD), to the hormonal Pill or patch. In the public forum, contraception arouses the same strong passions as do abortion and sterilization as methods of replacing procreational sex with recreational sex. There is no accessory, either medicinal or mechanical, that offers complete prophylaxis against the lethal human immunodeficiency virus (HIV), which is the agent of acquired immune deficiency syndrome (AIDS). As of the year 2003, HIV faced a challenge for lethality, namely the corona virus that is the agent of severe acute respiratory syndrome (SARS). SARS may be spread by, *inter alia*, sexual contact, whereas

HIV is spread predominantly by that route. Other sexually transmitted diseases (STD), though of great individual and public heath concern, are not inexorably deadly.

**[Phylism Theory**

[There are no passes or failures generated by the ten constants of a doctrine of courtship and mating, for they do not constitute a test but rather an agenda. They are applicable to the systematic gathering and inventorying of data pertaining to the sexual ideation, imagery, and practice of a single individual or of an entire community. A doctrine's propositions may be highly consistent with one another or chaotically inconsistent and contradictory. A doctrine, no matter how self-contradictory, must first be recorded nonjudgmentally before judgment can be passed.

[The ten constants have their origin in logical analysis of such philosophical antitheses as are represented in teleological versus mechanistic, hereditary versus acquired, organic versus intrapsychic, or nature versus nurture. My own position on all of these antitheses is that each of the pair needs the other, without which there is a void. The contribution of each needs to be established, not by proclamation, but empirically, step by laborious step. The bits and pieces of the building blocks of the ten constants of ideation, imagery, and practices of human sexuality I like to call *phylisms*. That means they belong to all of us collectively and phylogenically as members of our species—for example, the transcendental experience of orgasmic climax. The metaphorical buildings made from phylismic building blocks are ontogenic. They embody individual history, which may or may not be shared by other people.

[Phylism theory is an outgrowth of imprinting theory: At a critical or sensitive stage of development, there is a threefold confluence of an innate recognition mechanism, an innate releasing mechanism, and an innate response mechanism. The classic example is that of a newly hatched duckling that recognizes a moving squat-shaped thing (usually, of course, the mother duck), which in turn triggers an innate releasing mechanism, which in turn releases the actual response of following the squat-shaped moving thing. The long-term outcome is that following the moving thing, even if it is a waddling human being, becomes fixated (think native language) for a prolonged period of time (see below under paraphilias).

*[Phylisms of Courtship*

[Remnants of our robotic past can be observed when two people are mutually attracted and make a move on each other. Whether in an urban club or park, or in a tribal rainforest, the action patterns are similar regardless of individual, ontogenic embellishments. Much abbreviated, they are as follows (based on Givens 1983; Perper 1985; Eibl-Eibelsfelt 1985; Money 1998, Ch. 1): eye contact, stare, blush, gaze averted, eyelids droop, gaze again, squint, smile, vocal animation, breathiness, louder voice, silly laughter, mutual rotation, move closer, wet lips, adjust clothing to uncover skin, inadvertent touch, mirror gestures, synchronize movements, hold hands, pat, embrace, kiss and fondle with accelerated heartrate and breathing, sweating, genital secretions, dry mouth, and butterflies in the stomach. Although not inevitable, copulation ensues.

[The courtship responses of men and women are not identical but complementary to one another, as they are in the act of procreative copulation. Women on the whole are more dependent on contractative (touch) than on visual stimuli for the arousal and maintenance of erotic responsivity. Contractation applies to tactile or dactylic (fingering and fondling) senses. Women are not erotically unresponsive to the visual image of sexuality nor are men unresponsive to contrectative stimuli. The difference between men and women is not absolute, but a matter of proportion. Men are aroused at a distance not by smell, as is typical in other mammalian species, but by what the eyes see. From an evolutionary perspective, it may well be that human male eroticism is a spinoff from bipedal locomotion. Derobotized, we meet one another eye to eye, vertically, in a sexual encounter, whereas four-legged mammals meet one another horizontally, rump end to snout end, in a robotized sexual encounter. Thus, bipedal locomotion may have been an evolutionary forerunner of derobotization of both the lovemap and the speechmap (see above) in us human beings.

[The male-female difference in the ratio of visual to contrectative sexuality is entrenched in the doctrine of sexual orthodoxy in Christendom. Since we live in the era of the globalization of goods and services, our sexual doctrine becomes globalized also. Thus, the sexuality of tribal peoples in remote places becomes observed and recorded by people whose own doctrines are Westernized and judgmental. Observers condemn and neglect that which they study while they are studying it. Until the very recent past, for example, official ethnology did not accept the idea that falling in love was scientifically suitable for study in tribal peoples.

[It is commonly avowed that contrectative sexuality is superior to concupiscent sexuality. The former, it is claimed, is more romantic and spiritual, and ostensibly less carnal and animalistic than concupiscent sexuality (Money 2003). It is love, not lust. Too much or too little of either type, however, can give cause for clinical concern. It can give cause also for political concern by reason of linking politically correct sexuality to romantic sex and to women only. Politically incorrect sexuality is linked to carnal sex and to men only.

*[Sambian Orthodoxy*

[A prime example of a doctrine of sexuality before exposure to the doctrine of Christendom is that of the Sambia people of Papua New Guinea studied by Gilbert Herdt (1981, 1987; see summary in Section 13 of the chapter on Papua New Guinea in this volume). This was not a sex-negative doctrine, but it was linked to abusive indoctrination in boyhood in preparation for intertribal killing to qualify for manhood. In a Sambia farming hamlet, when a cohort of prepubertal boys in the mid-juvenile age group were separated from the perceived dangers of the influence of females, they lived, ate, and slept together in the long house, a kind of male dormitory. They were ready for the first stage of their initiation into manhood. Its ceremonial beginning lasted several days and nights and can be summed up as brutal ceremonial hazing and brainwashing, including food, water, and sleep deprivation, nose piercing, and being hauled naked across the shoulders of a male sponsor along an avenue of older males armed with whips for lashing them. The mystery of the secret ceremony of sucking the flute consisted of enforced sucking of the penis of an older, unmarried youth in the men's house. It was the duty of the older boy (or boys) to supply the younger ones with enough "men's milk" to ensure that they would be able to develop pubertally. When the younger boys became old enough to make men's milk themselves, then it was their duty to have it sucked out by still younger ones.

[The mystery of what happened in the men's house must be kept secret from all females and uninitiated males. Looking at or talking to females, even one's mother, was strictly forbidden. At around age 20, the tribal age of marriage, the tribal elders found a suitable bride in a neighboring hamlet. The candidate for marriage had to prove his worthiness by participating in an intertribal war party, and returning home with the body of a slain enemy. Initiation was final and complete when the first child was born.

[Some men raised up in this system fell in love with their wives, though some did not. A few had evaded the men's milk ritual as often as possible, but none had become exclusively gay in the Western sense.

[Women talked only to women about their sexuality, so that, in the absence of a woman ethnologist, data are lacking. After World War II, Australian governmental patrols suppressed the indigenous sexual orthodoxy in favor of the orthodoxy of Christendom.

## [Malleability: The Paraphilias

[During its critical formative stage as a personalized lovemap in the individual, or as a shared doctrine in the community, human sexuality is self-evidently malleable to some degree. That does not by any means signify that sexuality is infinitely malleable regardless of chronology. Nonetheless, it is an all-but-universal axiom in Western culture that sexuality is forever malleable and subject to voluntary control. Sexuality that proves to be unmalleable is at risk of being classified as lawbreaking and maybe a crime. It is subject to chastisement, punishment, deprivation, torture, and in some instances, the death penalty.

[Only a small cadre of biomedical scientists engage in a truly scientific search for causal explanations of human sexuality and its aberrations, which is nowhere more clear than in the case of the paraphilias, legally known as the perversions. Paraphilias often give the impression of being as idiosyncratic and contrived as the plot of a novel or screenplay and, therefore, easily altered. That puts the cart before the horse insofar as an author may well have drawn on his or her own uniquely paraphilic disposition for the theme of his or her art. Thus, the novels of the Marquis de Sade gave his name to sadism, the paraphilia, and those of Leopold von Sacher-Masoch gave his name to masochism.

[It is a remarkable feature of the paraphilias that no two people have a paraphilia which is an exact replica, the one of the other. It is the theme that they share, not the precise details. It is also remarkable that, despite idiosyncratic variations, the paraphilias can be cataloged as exemplifying seven major themes or stratagems. These stratagems are trickeries whereby neither love nor lust is forfeited, but both are saved by being separated or dissociated, often with one partner for love and another for lust.

[The origin of the paraphilic stratagems is probably before recorded history, and they probably embody extremely ancient paradigms of wisdom (so ancient that they are called paleodigms; Money 1989). They now survive in the legends and myths of folk wisdom—for example, the folk wisdom that sacrifice leads to expiation of guilt. Listed by name only, the seven grand stratagems of the paraphilias are as follows: sacrifice and expiation; marauding and predation; mercantilism and venality; fetishism and talismanism; stigmatism and eligibility; protectorship and rescue; and solicitation and allure (see Money 1997, 252; 1999, 125).

[At one extreme, paraphilias may be rated as inordinately fixated and life threatening. At the other extreme, by contrast, they are ludic (playful) and erotically enhancing.

[The transcultural record is incomplete as is also the historical record, so that the comparative occurrence and prevalence of the paraphilias in time and place is not known. One likely possibility is that the paraphilias are specifically an offshoot of Christendom's dark side. They represent a slowly progressive evolutionary accommodation to the austerity of Christendom's doctrine of sexuality for procreation only. In other words, the social evolution of

paraphilic sexuality is taking place under our very noses and we are not perceiving what is happening.

[The majority of the paraphilias are not named in *DSM-IV-TR* (APA 2000) except as "Not Otherwise Specified." For many of these, there was no scientific name until the book *Lovemaps* was published (Money 1986). Earlier, they had been named, if at all, only in street slang, or in the criminal justice vocabulary of lawbreaking, or in the ecclesiastical vocabulary of heresy. Their recognition as sexological syndromes began in tabloids and pictorials where individuals could search for and maybe correspond with others similar to themselves. Then, at the end of the 20th century, came the great invention of the Internet on which people with the same paraphilia could find and communicate with one another. On the Internet, unknown paraphilias became known and compared, and little-known paraphilias became more prevalent than had previously been suspected, women's paraphilias included. It remains to be seen whether or not the Internet confirms that women's paraphilias are more contractative than men's, and men's more visual than contractative.

[It would be scientifically foolish to expect the human genome to be phylogenetically coded for a fetish for nylon pantyhose, since nylon is a 20th-century invention. However, it would not be foolish to propose that the erotic feel of human skin might be transposed on an ontogenetic basis to nylon, and that the erotic feel of nylon could thenceforth become fixated, if not indefinitely, then for an extended period of time (think native language again). The paraphilias are, indeed, strongly resistant to change. However, over the years of a lifetime, a paraphilia may spontaneously metamorphose or undergo remission (Lehne & Money 2000, 2003).

## [Doctrinal and Sexual Orthodoxy

[In human sexuality, doctrinal orthodoxy is under the control of those who have the power to enforce it by way of laws, taboos, prohibitions, and punishments. The information provided, in the United States and country-by-country, in this *International Encyclopedia* allows a scholar to trace the global range and dispersal of Christendom's doctrine of sexual orthodoxy. In other cultures in the United States, as well as in other countries, information about the history and current status of Muslim, Confucian, Buddhist, Hindu, animist, and Shinto religious influences provides similar insights into doctrinal orthodoxy in non-Christian cultures. Given the rapid pace of globalization and cultural interactions, neither doctrinal nor sexual orthodoxy are static doctrines. Both are actively in the process of evolving. (*End of update by J. Money*)]

## *References and Suggested Readings*

Abbey, A., P. McAuslan, T. Zawacki, A. M. Clinton, & P. O. Buck. 2001. Attitudinal, experiential, and situational predictors of sexual assault perpetration. *Journal of Interpersonal Violence*, 16:784-807.

Adler, J. 1994 (January 10). Farewell, year of the creep. *Newsweek*, 59.

Ahlburg, D. A., & C. J. DeVita. 1992. New realities of the American family. *Population Bulletin, 47*(2).

Alan Guttmacher Institute. 1991. *Abortion in the United States: Facts in brief.* New York: Author.

Alan Guttmacher Institute 1999. *Facts in brief: Contraceptive use.* New York: Author.

Alan Guttmacher Institute. 2002. *Facts in brief: Sexual and reproductive health: Women and men.* New York: Author.

Alan Guttmacher Institute. 2003 (July). *Induced abortion: Facts in brief.* Alan Guttmacher Institute. Available: www.agi-usa.org/pubs/fb_induced_abortion.html.

Alan Guttmacher Institute. 2003 (July). *State policies in brief: Access to emergency contraception.* New York: Author.

Alberda, R., & C. Tilly. 1992. All in the family: Family types, access to income, and family income policies. *Policy Studies Journal, 20*(3):388-404.

Alcalay, R., P. M. Sniderman, J. Mitchell, & R. Griffin. 1990. Ethnic differences in knowledge of AIDS transmission and attitudes among gays and people with AIDS. *International Quarterly of Community Health Education, 10*(3):213-222.

Alcorn, R. C. 1990. *Is rescuing right? Breaking the law to save the unborn.* Downers Grove, IL: InterVarsity Press.

Alexander, J. M. 1992 (April). Meeting changing STD counseling needs: A glossary of contemporary Mexican sexual terms. Prepared for the *Resource Book* of the Third Annual New Orleans HIV/AIDS Conference for Primary Health Care Providers.

Alexander, M. G., & T. D. Fisher. 2003 (February). Truth and consequences: Using the bogus pipeline to examine sex differences in self-reported sexuality. *Journal of Sex Research, 40*(1):27-35.

Allen, J. E., & L. P. Cole. 1975. Clergy skills in family-planning education and counseling. *Journal of Religion and Health, 14*(3):198-205.

Allen, L. S., & R. A. Gorski. 1990. Sex difference in the bed nucleus of the stria terminalis of the human brain. *Journal of Comparative Neurology, 302*:697-706.

Allen, N. 1978 (June). Sex therapy and the single woman. *Forum,* 44-48.

Allen, W. R., & B. A. Agbasegbe. 1980. A comment on Scott's 'Black polygamous family formation.' *Alternative Lifestyles, 3*:375-381.

Allgeier, A. R., & E. R. Allgeier. 1988. *Sexual interactions* (2nd ed.). Lexington, MA: D. C. Heath.

Allison, D. 1993. *Bastard out of Carolina.* New York: Plume.

Allison, J. A., & L. S. Wrightsman. 1993. *Rape: The misunderstood crime.* Newbury Park, CA: Sage Publications.

Alter, J. 1998 (October 26). Trickle down hate. *Newsweek, 132*: 44.

Altman, L. K. 1997 (February 28). U.S. reporting sharp decrease in AIDS deaths. *The New York Times,* A1, A24.

Amaro, I. 1991. *Hispanic sexual behavior: Implications for research and HIV prevention.* Washington, DC: National Coalition of Hispanic Health and Human Services Organizations.

American Association of Sex Educators, Counselors, and Therapists (AASECT). 1978 (March, rev.). *AASECT code of ethics.* Washington, DC: Author.

American Association of Sex Educators, Counselors, and Therapists (AASECT). 1987. *AASECT code of ethics.* Washington, DC: Author.

American Medical Association. 1992. Induced termination of pregnancy before and after *Roe v. Wade. Journal of the American Medical Association, 268*(22):3237.

American Psychiatric Association. 1980. *Diagnostic and statistical manual of mental disorders III (DSM III)* (3rd ed. 302.81, p. 268). Washington, DC: American Psychiatric Association.

American Psychiatric Association. 1994. *Diagnostic and statistical manual of mental disorders* (4th ed.). Washington, DC: American Psychiatric Association.

American Psychiatric Association. 2000. *Diagnostic and statistical manual of mental disorders* (4th ed., text rev.) (*DSM-IV-TR*). Washington, DC: American Psychiatric Press.

Amir, M. 1971. *Patterns in forcible rape.* Chicago: University of Chicago Press.

Anand, M. 1991. *The art of sexual ecstasy: The path of sacred sexuality for Western lovers.* New York: J.P. Tarcher.

Anapol, D. M. 1997. *Polyamory: The new love without limits: Secrets of sustainable intimate relationships.* San Rafael, CA: IntiNet Resource Center.

Anderson, K. 1996. *Changing woman: A history of racial ethnic women in modern America.* New York: Oxford Press.

Anderson, P. B., D. de Mauro, & R. J. Noonan, eds. 1996. *Does anyone still remember when sex was fun? Positive sexuality in the age of AIDS* (3rd ed.). Dubuque, IA: Kendall/Hunt Publishing Co.

Aneshensel, C. S., R. M. Becerra, E. P. Fiedler, & R. H. Schuler. 1990. Onset of fertility related events during adolescence: A prospective comparison of Mexican American and non-Hispanic white females. *American Journal of Public Health, 80*(8):959-963.

Annon, J. S. 1974. *The behavioral treatment of sexual problems. Volume 1: Brief therapy.* Honolulu, HI: Kapiolani Health Services.

Ansen, D. 1994 (April 18). Boy meets girl meets boy. *Newsweek,* 60.

Anshaw, C. 1997. *Aquamarine.* Boston: Mariner Books.

Anshaw, C. 1997. *Seven moves.* Boston: Mariner Books.

Anzaldúa, G., & C. Moraga, eds. 1983. *This bridge called my back: Writing by radical women of color.* New York: Women of Color Press.

Apel, W. 1969. *Harvard dictionary of music* (2nd ed., rev.). Cambridge: Belknap Press of Harvard University Press.

Apfelbaum, B. 1977. The myth of the surrogate. *Journal of Sex Research, 13* (4):238-249.

Apfelbaum, B. 1984. The ego-analytic approach to individual body-work sex therapy: Five case examples. *Journal of Sex Research, 20*(1):44-70.

Appelby, G. A. 2001. Interviewing working-class gay men over the Internet. *Journal of Gay & Lesbian Social Services: Issues in Practice, Policy & Research, 12*:133-151.

Arditti, R., E. D. Klein, & S. Minden. 1984. *Test-tube women: What future for motherhood?* London: Pandora Press.

Arnold, M. 2001 (May 10). Transition time for gay works. *The New York Times.*

Arnold, M. 2003 (February 27). A new phase for gay books. *The New York Times.* (Retrieved March 28, 2003). http://www.nytimes.com/2003/02/07/books/27BOOK.html.

Asbell, B. 1995. *The pill: A biography of the drug that changed the world.* New York: Random House.

Atkinson, D. R., G. Morten, & D. W. Sue. 1993. *Counseling American minorities: A cross cultural perspective* (2nd ed.). Dubuque, IA: William C. Brown Company.

Atwater, L. 1982. *The extramarital connection: Sex, intimacy, and identity.* New York: Irvington.

Avinasha, B., & S. Sarasswati. 1987. *The jewel and the lotus: The Tantric path to higher consciousness.* Taos, NM: Kriya Jyoti Tantra Society.

Bailey, B. 1989. *From front porch to back seat: Courtship in 20th century America.* Baltimore: Johns Hopkins University Press.

Bailey, J. M. 1999. Homosexuality and mental illness. *Archives of General Psychiatry, 56*:883-884.

Baird-Windle, P., & E. J. Bader. 2001. *Targets of hatred: Anti-abortion terrorism.* New York: Palgrave.

Baldwin, J. 1956. *Giovanni's room.* New York: Dial Press.

Baldwin, W. 1980. The fertility of young adolescents. *Journal of Adolescent Health Care, 1*:54-59.

Bannon, A. 1975. *Odd girl out.* New York: Arno Press.

Bannon, A. 2002. *Women in the shadows.* San Francisco: Cleis Press.

Barak, A., & W. A. Fisher. 2001. Toward an Internet-driven, theoretically-based innovative approach to sex education. *The Journal of Sex Research, 38*(4):324-332.

Barak, A., & W. A. Ficher. 2002. The future of Internet sexuality. In: A. Cooper, ed., *Sex and the Internet: A guidebook for clinicians.* New York: Brunner-Routledge.

Barak, A., W. A. Fisher, S. Belfry, & D. R. Lashambe. 1999. Sex, guys, and cyberspace: Effects of Internet pornography and individual differences on men's attitudes toward women. *Journal of Psychology and Human Sexuality, 11*: 63-92.

Barak, A., & S. A. King. 2000. The two faces of the Internet: Introduction to the special issue on the Internet and sexuality. *CyberPsychology and Behavior, 3*(4):517-520.

Barak, A., & M. P. Safir. 1997. Sex and the Internet: An Israeli perspective. *Journal of Sex Education and Therapy*, 22: 67-73.

Barbach, L. 1980. *Women discover orgasm: A therapist's guide to a new treatment approach*. New York: Free Press.

Barry, K. 1984. *Female sexual slavery*. New York: New York University Press.

Bart, P. B., & P. H. O'Brien. 1985. Stopping rape: Effective avoidance strategies. *Signs*, 10:83-101.

Bartell, G. D. 1971. *Group sex: A scientist's eyewitness report on the American way of swinging*. New York: Wyden.

Bates D. J. 2002. *Locating the transsexual narrative in the gendered landscape*. New Zealand: University of Waikato.

Batterberry, M., & A. Batterberry. (1977). *Fashion: The mirror of history*. New York: Greenwich House.

Bauman, K. E., & R. R. Wilson. 1974 Sexual behavior of unmarried university students in 1968 and 1972. *Journal of Sex Research*, 10:327-333.

Bay-Cheng, L. Y. 2001. SexEd.Com: Values and norms in Web-based sexuality education. *Journal of Sex Research*, 38:241-251.

Beach, R. A. 1976. Sexual attractivity, proceptivity and receptivity in female mammals. *Hormones and Behavior*, 7: 105-138.

Beitchman, J. H., et al. 1992. A review of the long-term effects of child sexual abuse. *Child Abuse and Neglect*, 16:101-118.

Beitchman, J. H., K. Zucker, J. Hood, G. DaCosta, & D. Akman. 1991. A review of the short-term effects of childhood sexual abuse. *Child Abuse and Neglect*, 15:537-556.

Belcastro, P. A. 1985. Sexual behavior differences between black and white students. *Journal of Sex Research*, 21:56-67.

Bell, A. P., & M. Weinberg. 1978. *Homosexualities: A study of diversity among men and women*. New York: Simon and Schuster.

Bell, A. P., M. S. Weinberg, & S. K. Hammersmith. 1981. *Sexual preference: Its development in men and women*. Bloomington, IN: Indiana University Press.

Bell, A. P. 1968 (October). *Black sexuality: Fact and fancy*. Paper presented to Focus: Black American Series, Indiana University, Bloomington, IN.

Bell, R. R., & P. I. Bell. 1972 (December). Sexual satisfaction among married women. *Medical Aspects of Human Sexuality*, 136-144.

Bell, R. R., S. Turner, & L. Rosen. 1975. A multivariate analysis of female extramarital coitus. *Journal of Marriage and the Family*, 37(2):375-384.

Bell, R., & J. B. Chaskes. 1968. Premarital sexual experience among coeds, 1958 and 1968. *Journal of Marriage and the Family*, 30:81-84.

Bennett, P. 1995. Lesbian poetry in the United States, 1890-1990: A brief overview. In: G. E. Haggerty & B. Zimmerman, eds., *Professions of desire: Lesbian and gay studies in literature* (pp. 98-110). New York: Modern Language Association.

Benotsch, E., S. Kalichman, & M. Cage. 2001. Men who have met sex partners via the Internet: Prevalence, predictors, and implications for HIV prevention. *Archives of Sexual Behavior*, 31(2):177-183.

Berger, R. J., P. Seales, & C. E. Cottle. 1991. *Pornography*. New York: Praeger.

Bergler, E. 1956. *Homosexuality: Disease or way of life*. New York: Collier.

Berkowitz, A. 1992. College men as perpetrators of acquaintance rape and sexual assault: A review of recent research. *Journal of American College Health*, 40:175-181.

Bernstein, A. C., & P. A. Cowan. 1975. Children's concepts of how people get babies. *Child Development*, 46:77-91.

Berscheid, E. 1983. Emotion. In: H. H. Kelley, et al., eds., *Close relationships* (pp. 110-168). New York: W.H. Freeman and Co.

Biale, D. 1992. *Eros and the Jews: From Biblical Israel to contemporary American*. New York: Basic Books.

Biber, J. K., D. Doverspike, D. Baznik, A. Cober, & B. A. Ritter. 2002. Sexual harassment in online communications: Effects of gender and discourse medium. *CyberPsychology & Behavior*, 5:33-42.

Biddlecom, A. E., & A. M. Hardy. 1991. AIDS knowledge and attitudes of Hispanic Americans: United States, 1990. *Advance data. Number 207*. Washington, DC: U.S. Department of Health and Human Services.

Billy, J. O. G., K. Tanfer, W. R. Grady, & D. H. Klepinger. 1992. Sexual behavior of men in the United States. *Family Planning Perspectives*, 25(2):52-60.

Binik, Y. M. 2001. Sexuality and the Internet: Lots of hyp(otheses), only a little data. *Journal of Sex Research*, 38:281-293.

Binion, V. J. 1990. Psychological androgyny: A black female perspective. *Sex Roles*, 22(7/8):487-507.

Bishop, P. D., & A. Lipsitz. 1991. Sexual behavior among college students in the AIDS era: A comparative study. *Journal of Psychology and Human Sexuality*, 4:467-476.

Blanchard, R., & S. J. Hucker. 1991 (September). Age, transvestism, bondage, and concurrent paraphilic activities in 117 fatal cases of autoerotic asphyxia. *British Journal of Psychiatry*, 159:371-377.

Blank, J., with A. Whidden. 2000. *Good vibrations: The new complete guide to vibrators* (4th ed.). San Francisco: Down There Press.

Blasini-Caceres, L., & A. B. Cook. 1997. *Hispanic/Latina women and AIDS: A critical perspective* (Working paper #36). East Lansing, MI: The Julian Samora Research Institute, Michigan State University.

Blumstein, P., & P. Schwartz. 1983. *American couples*. New York: William Morrow.

Bly, R. 1990. *Iron John*. New York: Addison-Wesley.

Bolin, A. 1988. *In search of Eve: Transsexual rites of passage*. South Hadley, MA: Bergin and Garvey Publishers.

Bonilla, L., & J. Porter. 1990. A comparison of Latino, black, and non-Hispanic white attitudes toward homosexuality. *Hispanic Journal of Behavioral Sciences*, 12(4):437-452.

Boswell, J. 1980. *Christianity, social tolerance, and homosexuality*. Chicago: University of Chicago Press.

Boswell, J. 1994. *Same-sex unions in premodern Europe*. New York: Villard Books.

Boyd, B. M. 1992. *The revolution of little girls*. New York: Vintage Books.

Brand, O., ed. 1960. *Bawdy songs and backroom ballads*. New York: Grove Press.

Brand, O. 1962. *The ballad mongers: Rise of the modern folk song*. New York: Funk & Wagnalls.

Brand, P. A., & A. H. Kidd. 1986. Frequency of physical aggression in heterosexual and female homosexual dyads. *Psychological Reports*, 59:1307-1313.

Brandt, A. M. 1988 (Autumn). AIDS and metaphor. *Social Research*, 55(3):430. Cited in M. Fumento, 1990, *The myth of heterosexual AIDS*. New York: Basic Books.

Braun, S., ed. 1975. *Catalog of sexual consciousness* (pp. 135-137). New York: Grove Press.

Brayshaw, A. J. 1962. Middle-aged marriage: Idealism, realism, and the search for meaning. *Marriage and Family Living*, 24:358-364.

Brecher, E. M. 1979. *The sex researchers*. San Francisco: Specific Press.

Brecher, E. M., & the Editors of Consumer Reports Books. 1984. *Love, sex, and aging: A Consumer Union report*. Boston: Little, Brown.

Brener, N. D., P. M. McMahon, C. W. Warren, & K. A. Douglas. 1999. Forced sexual intercourse and associated health-risk behaviors among female college students in the United States. *Journal of Consulting and Clinical Psychology*, 67:252-259.

Brenner, L. M., & C. L. Muehlenhard. 1995 (November). *When sexually abused boys and girls grow up: Will girls be revictimized while boys become perpetrators?* Paper presented at the annual meeting of the Society for the Scientific Study of Sexuality, San Francisco.

Bretschneider, J. G., & N. L. McCoy. 1988. Sexual interest and behavior in healthy 80- to 101-year-olds. *Archives of Sexual Behavior, 17*(2):109-129.

Brett, G. H. 1993. Networked information retrieval tools in the academic environment: Towards a cybernetic library. *Internet Research, 3*(3):26-36.

Brick, P., & D. M. Roffman. 1993 (November). 'Abstinence, no buts' is simplistic. *Educational Leadership, 51*:90-92.

Brick, P., & B. Taverner. 2001.Contraception in perspective: A history of birth control. In: *Positive images: Teaching abstinence, contraception, and sexual health.* Morristown, NJ: Planned Parenthood of Greater Northern New Jersey.

Brick, P., & B. Taverner. 2003. The importance of timing: Knowing the difference between emergency contraception and mifepristone. In: P. Brick & B. Taverner, ed., *Educating about abortion.* Morristown, NJ: Planned Parenthood of Greater Northern New Jersey.

Brindis, C. 1992. Adolescent pregnancy prevention for Hispanic youth: The role of schools, families, and communities. *Journal of School Health, 62*(7):345-351.

Brindis, C. 1997. Adolescent pregnancy prevention for Hispanic Youth. *The Prevention Researcher, 4*(1):8-10.

Brindis, C., A. L. Wolfe, V. McCater, & S. Ball. 1995. The association between immigrant status and risk-behavior patterns in Latino adolescents. *Journal of Adolescent Health, 17*(2): 99-105.

Bringle, R. G. 1991. Psychosocial aspects of jealousy: A transactional model. In: P. Salovey, ed., *The psychology of jealousy and envy* (pp. 103-131). New York: Guilford Press.

Bringle, R. G., & K. L. G. Boebinger. 1990. Jealousy and the 'third' person in the love triangle. *Journal of Social and Personal Relationships, 7*:119-133.

Brison, K., & L. M. Casper. 1998. Household and family characteristics, March 1977. *Current Population Reports* (Series P20-509). Washington, DC: Government Printing Office.

Broderick, C. B. 1965. Social heterosexual development among urban Negroes and whites. *Journal of Marriage and the Family, 27*(2):200-203.

Broderick, C. B. 1966a. Socio-sexual development in a suburban community. *Journal of Sex Research, 2*:1-24.

Broderick, C. B. 1966b. Sexual behavior among pre-adolescents. *Journal of Social Issues, 22*:6-21.

Broderick, C. B., & S. E. Fowler. 1961. New patterns of relationships between the sexes among preadolescents. *Marriage and Family Living, 23*:27-30.

Brodie, J. F. 1994. *Contraception and abortion in nineteenth-century America.* Ithaca, NY: Cornell University Press.

Brody, S. 1995. Lack of evidence for transmission of human immunodeficiency virus through vaginal intercourse. *Archives of Sexual Behavior, 24*(4):383-393.

Broman, C. L. 1991. Gender, work-family roles and psychological well-being of blacks. *Journal of Marriage and Family, 53*:509-520.

Brooks-Gunn, J., & F. F. Furstenberg. 1989. Adolescent sexual behavior. *American Psychologist, 44*:249-259.

Brown, D. A. 1981. An interview with a sex surrogate. In: D. A. Brown & C. Chary, eds., *Sexuality in America* (pp. 301-317). Ann Arbor, MI: Greenfield Books.

Brown, R. M. 1983. *Rubyfruit jungle.* New York: Bantam Books.

Browne, A., & D. Finkelhor. 1986. Impact of child sexual abuse: A review of research. *Psychological Bulletin, 99*:66-77.

Brownmiller, S. 1975. *Against our will: Men, women, and rape.* New York: Bantam.

Bukstel, L. H., G. D. Roeder, P. R. Kilmann, J. Laughlin, & W. M. Sotile. 1978. Projected extramarital sexual involvement in unmarried college students. *Journal of Marriage and the Family, 40*:337-340.

Bull, S. S., & M. McFarlane. 2000. Soliciting sex on the Internet: What are the risks for sexually transmitted diseases and HIV? *Sexually Transmitted Diseases, 27*:545-550.

Bull, S. S., M. McFarlane, & D. King. 2001. Barriers to STD/HIV prevention on the Internet. *Health Education Research, 16*:661-670.

Bull, S. S., M. McFarlane, & C. Rietmeijer. 2001. HIV and sexually transmitted infection risk behaviors among men seeking sex with men on-line. *American Journal of Public Health, 9*:988-989.

Bullough, V. L. 1994. *Science in the bedroom: A history of sex research.* New York: Basic Books.

Bullough, V. L. 2002. Masturbation: A historical overview. *Journal of Psychology & Human Sexuality, 14*(2/3):17-34.

Bullough, V. L., & B. Bullough. 1987. *Women and prostitution: A social history.* Buffalo, NY: Prometheus Press.

Bullough, V. L., & B. Bullough. 1992. *Annotated bibliography of prostitution, 1970-1992.* New York: Garland.

Bullough, V. L., & B. Bullough. 1993. *Cross-dressing, sex, and gender.* Philadelphia: University of Pennsylvania Press.

Bullough, V. L., & B. Bullough. 1994a. Prostitution. In: V. L. Bullough & B. Bullough, eds., *Human sexuality: An encyclopedia.* New York: Garland Publishing.

Bullough, V. L., & B. Bullough. 1994b. Cross-dressing. In: V. L. Bullough & B. Bullough, eds., *Human sexuality: An encyclopedia* (pp. 156-160). New York: Garland Publishing.

Bureau of Justice Statistics. 1993. *Sourcebook of criminal justice statistics–1992.* Washington, DC: U.S. Government Printing Office.

Burgess, E. W., & P. Wallin. 1953. *Engagement and marriage.* Philadelphia: Lippincott.

Burke, A., S. Sowerbutts, B. Blundell, & M. Sherry. 2002. Child pornography and the Internet: Policing and treatment issues. *Psychiatry, Psychology and Law, 9*:79-84.

Burke, S. K. 2000. In search of lesbian community in an electronic world. *CyberPsychology & Behavior, 3*(4):591-604.

Burt, M. R. 1991. Rape Myths and Acquaintance Rape. In: A. Parrot & L. Bechhofer, eds., *Acquaintance rape: The hidden crime.* New York: Wiley.

Buss, D. M. 1994. *The evolution of desire: Strategies of human mating.* New York: Basic Books.

Butler, M. 1994. *How to use the Internet.* Emeryville. CA: Ziff & Davis Press.

Butterfield, F. 2003 (July 24). 789 children abused by priests since 1940, Massachusetts says. *Boston Globe.*

Buunk, B. 1980. Sexually open marriages: Ground rules for countering potential threats to marriage. *Alternative Lifestyles, 3*:312-328.

Buunk, B. 1981. Jealousy in sexually open marriages. *Alternative Lifestyles, 4*:357-372.

Buunk, B. 1982. Strategies of jealousy: styles of coping with extramarital involvement of the spouse. *Family Relations, 31*:13-18.

Byrne, D., & W. A. Fisher, eds. 1983. *Adolescents, sex, and contraception.* Hillsdale, NJ: Erlbaum.

Califia, P. 1997. *Sex changes: The politics of transgenderism.* San Francisco, CA: Cleis Press.

Call, V., S. Sprecher, & P. Schwartz. 1995. The incidence and frequency of marital sex in a national sample. *Journal of Marriage and the Family, 57*:639-652.

Cannon, K. L., & R. Long. 1971. Premarital sexual behavior in the sixties. *Journal of Marriage and the Family, 33*:36-49.

Cannon, L. 1990. *President Reagan: The role of a lifetime.* New York: Simon and Schuster.

Carballo-Diéguez, A. 1989. Hispanic culture, gay male culture, and AIDS: Counseling implications. *Journal of Counseling and Development, 68*:26-30.

Carnes, P., ed., D. L. Delmonico, E. Griffin, & J. Moriarty. 2001. *In the shadows of the Net: Breaking free of compulsive online behavior.* Center City, MN: Hazelden Educational Materials.

Carrier, J. M. 1976. Cultural factors affecting urban Mexican male homosexual behavior. *Archives of Sexual Behavior, 5*(2):103-124.

Carrier, J. M., & J. R. Magaña. 1991. Use of ethnosexual data on men of Mexican origin for HIV/AIDS prevention programs. *Journal of Sex Research, 28*(2):189-202.

Carrier, J. M., & R. Bolton. 1987. Anthropological perspectives on sexuality and HIV prevention. *Annual Review of Sex Research, 2*:49-75.

Carroll R. A, 1999. Outcomes of treatment for gender dysphoria. *Journal of Sex Education and Therapy, 24*:128-136.

Casert, R. 2003 (January 31). *Belgium now 2nd nation to approve gay marriage.* Associated Press News Service.

Cassell, C. 1993. *The tender bargaining.* Los Angeles: Lowell.

Castex, G. M. 1994. Providing services to Hispanic/Latino populations: Profiles in diversity. *Social Work, 39*(3):288-296.

Cates, W., et al. 1999. Estimates of the incidence and prevalence of sexually transmitted diseases in the United States. *Sexually Transmitted Disease, 26*(supplement):S2-S7.

Cather, W. 1987. *My Antonia.* New York: Chelsea House Publishers.

Cazenave, N. A. 1979. Social structure and personal choice: Effects on intimacy, marriage and the family alternative lifestyle research. *Alternative Lifestyles, 2*:331-358.

Cazenave, N. A. 1981. Black men in America: The quest for manhood. In: H. P. McAdoo, ed., *Black families* (pp. 176-185). Beverly Hills: Sage.

Centers for Disease Control (CDC). 1992. HIV infection, syphilis, tuberculosis, screening among migrant farm workers–Florida 1992. *Morbidity and Mortality Weekly Report, 41*(39):723-725.

Centers for Disease Control (CDC). 1993a. The scope of the HIV/AIDS epidemic in the United States. *Fact sheet. (Publication no. D-534).* Rockville, MD: CDC National AIDS Clearinghouse.

Centers for Disease Control (CDC). 1993b. HIV/AIDS and race/ethnicity. *Fact sheet. (Publication no. D-293).* Rockville, MD: CDC National AIDS Clearinghouse.

Centers for Disease Control (CDC). 1993c (August). Study of non-identifying gay men. *HIV/AIDS Prevention Newsletter, 4*(2):6-7.

Centers for Disease Control (CDC). 1994a. *HIV/AIDS surveillance report, 6*(2):1-39.

Centers for Disease Control (CDC). 1994b. *HIV/AIDS surveillance report. Year-end edition, 6*:11.

Centers for Disease Control (CDC). 1994c. Women and HIV/AIDS. *Fact sheet. (Publication no. D-290).* Rockville, MD: CDC National AIDS Clearinghouse.

Centers for Disease Control (CDC). 1995a. Update: Acquired immunodeficiency syndrome–United States, 1994. *Morbidity and Mortality Weekly Report, 44*(4):64-67.

Centers for Disease Control (CDC). 1995b. Update: AIDS among women. *Morbidity and Mortality Weekly Report, 44*(5):81-84.

Centers for Disease Control and Prevention (CDC). 1996. *HIV/AIDS surveillance report, Year-end 1995 edition, 7*(2):1-18.

Centers for Disease Control and Prevention (CDC). 1996. *1996 HIV/AIDS trends provide evidence of success in HIV prevention and treatment.* Available: http://www.cdc.gov/od/oc/medialpressrel/aids-dl.htm.

Centers for Disease Control and Prevention (CDC). 1998. The challenge of STD prevention in the United States. Available: http://www.cdc.gov/nchstp/dstd/STD_Prevention_in_the_United_States.htm.

Centers for Disease Control and Prevention (CDC). 2000. *Tracking the hidden epidemics: Trends in STDs in the United States.* Atlanta, GA: U.S. Department of Health and Human Services, Author. Available: www.cdc.gov/nchstp/dstd/Stats_Trends/Trends2000.pdf.

Centers for Disease Control and Prevention (CDC). 2001. HIV 2001: Incidence among young men who have sex with men–Seven U.S. cities, 1994-2000. *Morbidity and Mortality Weekly Report–MMWR, 50*:440-444.

Centers for Disease Control and Prevention (CDC). 2001. *HIV/AIDS surveillance report, 13*(2).

Centers for Disease Control and Prevention (CDC). 2001. Summary of notifiable diseases, United States, 2001. *Morbidity and Mortality Weekly Report–MMWR, 50*:53.

Centers for Disease Control and Prevention (CDC). 2002. *HIV/AIDS surveillance report.* Available: http://www.cdc.gov/hiv/stats/hasrsupp.htm. Accessed 8/15/02.

Centers for Disease Control and Prevention (CDC). 2002 (October). *Sexually transmitted disease surveillance 2001 supplement, chlamydia prevalence monitoring project.* Available: www.cdc.gov/std/Chlamydia2001/.

Centers for Disease Control and Prevention (CDC). 2002. Summary of notifiable diseases, United States, 2000. *Morbidity and Mortality Weekly Report–MMWR, 49*:53.

Centers for Disease Control and Prevention (CDC). 2003. AIDS cases in adolescents and adults, by age–United States, 1994-2000. *HIV/AIDS Surveillance Supplemental Report, 9*(1):1-25.

Centers for Disease Control & Prevention (CDC). 2003. *Fact sheets* [on STDs]. Available: www.cdc.gov.

Centers for Disease Control and Prevention (CDC). 2003 (March 31). *HIV/AIDS surveillance report.* Data reported through December 2001. National Center for HIV, STD, and TB Prevention, Divisions of HIV/AIDS Prevention. Available: www.cdc.gov/hiv/stats.htm.

Chase, C. 1998 (April). Hermaphrodites with attitude: Mapping the emergence of intersex political activism. *Gay and Lesbian Quarterly, 4*(2):189-211.

Chefetz, J. S., & A. G. Dworkin. 1986. *Female revolt: Women's movements in the world and historical perspective.* New Jersey: Rowman & Allanheld.

Chideya, F., et al. 1993 (August 30). Endangered family. *Newsweek,* 17-27.

Choi, K. H., J. A. Catania, & M. Dolcini. 1994. Extramarital sex and HIV risk behavior among U.S. adults: Results from the national AIDS behavior survey. *American Journal of Public Health, 84*(12):2003-2007.

Christensen, C. P. 1988. Issues in sex therapy with ethnic and racial minority women. *Women and Therapy, 7*(2l3):187-205.

Christensen, F. M. 1990. *Pornography: The other side.* New York: Praeger.

Christensen, H. T. 1962a. Value-behavior discrepancies regarding premarital coitus in three Western cultures. *American Sociological Review, 27*:66-74.

Christensen, H. T. 1962b. A cross-cultural comparison of attitudes toward marital infidelity. *International Journal of Comparative Sociology, 3*:124-137.

Christensen, H. T. 1973. Attitudes toward infidelity: A nine-culture sampling of university student opinion. *Journal of Comparative Family Studies, 4*:197-214.

Christensen, H. T., & C. F. Gregg. 1970 (November). Changing sex norms in America and Scandinavia. *Journal of Marriage and the Family,* 616-627.

Christensen, H. T., & G. R. Carpenter. 1962. Timing patterns in the development of sexual intimacy: An attitudinal report on three modern Western societies. *Marriage and Family Living, 24*:30-35.

Christensen, H., & L. Johnson. 1978. Premarital coitus and the southern black: A comparative view. *Journal of Marriage and the Family, 40*:721-732.

Christian, S. 1998 (November 25). University trove of pinups is admired by all sorts, even some feminists. *The New York Times,* B3.

Christopher, F. S., & R. M. Cate. 1985. Premarital sexual pathways and relationship development. *Journal of Social and Personal Relationships, 2*:271-288.

Christopher, F. S., & R. M. Cate. 1988. Premarital sexual involvement: A developmental investigation of relational correlates. *Adolescence, 23*:793-803.

Chung W. C. J., G. J. De Vries, & D. Swaab. 2002. Sex differentiation of the bed nucleus of the stria terminalis in humans may extend into adulthood. *Journal Neuroscience, 22*(3): 1027-1033.

*Church News.* 1978 (December 16, Vol. 6). Salt Lake City, UT: Church of Jesus Christ of the Latter-Day Saints Publication.

Church of Jesus Christ of Latter-Day Saints. 1989. *Pearl of great price.* Salt Lake City, UT: Author.

Church of Jesus Christ of Latter-Day Saints. 1990. *For the strength of youth.* Salt Lake City, UT: Author.

CIA. 2002 (January). *The world factbook 2002.* Washington, DC: Central Intelligence Agency. Available: http://www.cia.gov/cia/publications/factbook/index.html.

*CIOL.* Retrieved February 8, 2003. http://www.ciol.com/content/news/repts/101021611.asp.

Clark, L., & D. J. Lewis. 1977. *Rape: The price of coercive sexuality.* Toronto: Women's Press.

Claude, P. 1993. Providing culturally sensitive health care to Hispanic clients. *Nurse Practitioner, 18*(12):40-51

Clayton, R. R., & J. L. Bokemeier. 1980. Premarital sex in the seventies. *Journal of Marriage and the Family, 42*:759-776.

Clemerson, L., S. Smalley, B. Braiker, & R. B. Kaiser. 2002 (February 25). Faith in our fathers? *Newsweek, 139*:24.

Cleveland, P. H., & J. Davenport. 1989 (Summer). AIDS: A growing problem for rural communities. *Human Services in the Rural Environment, 13*(1):23-29.

Cloud, J. 1999 (November 15). Henry and Mary and Janet. *Time* Magazine.

Clunis, D. M., & G. D. Green. 1988. *Lesbian couples.* Seattle, Washington: Seal Press.

Cobliner, W. G. 1974. Pregnancy in the single adolescent girl: The role of cognitive functions. *Journal of Youth and Adolescence, 3*:17-29.

Cochran, S. D. 2001. Emerging issues in research on lesbians' and gay men's mental health: Does sexual orientation really matter? *American Psychologist, 56*:931-947.

Cochran, S. D., J. G. Sullivan, & V. M. Mays. 2003. Prevalence of mental disorders, psychological distress, and mental services use among lesbian, gay, and bisexual adults in the United States. *Journal of Consulting Clinical Psychology, 71*:53-61.

Cohn, B. 1994 (December 19). Goodbye to the 'condom queen.' *Newsweek,* 26-27.

Colapinto, J. 2000. *As nature made him: The boy who was raised as a girl.* New York: Harper Collins.

Cole, E. 1988. Sex at menopause: Each in her own way. *Women and Therapy, 7*:159-168.

Coleman, E. 1987. Assessment of sexual orientation. *Journal of Homosexuality, 14*(1/2):9-24.

Coleman, E. 1991. Compulsive sexual behavior: New concepts and treatments. *Journal of Psychology and Human Sexuality, 4*(2):37-52.

Coleman, E., ed. 1991. *John Money: A tribute.* New York: Haworth Press. Also published as vol. 4, no. 2 of the *Journal of Psychology and Human Sexuality.*

Coleman, E. 2002. Masturbation as a means of achieving sexual health. *Journal of Psychology & Human Sexuality, 14*(2/3):5-16.

Coleman, E. 2002 (May). *Plenary presentation.* Midcontinent & Eastern Region Conference of the Society for the Scientific Study of Sexuality, Big Rapids, MI.

Coles, C. D., & M. J. Shamp. 1984. Some sexual, personality, and demographic characteristics of women readers of erotic romances. *Archives of Sexual Behavior, 13*:187-209.

Collins, P. H. 1990. *Black feminist thought: Knowledge, consciousness, and the politics of empowerment.* Boston: Unwin Hyman.

*Conceptus, What is Essure?* Available: www.essure.com.

Conklin, S. C. 1995. *Sexuality education of clergy in seminaries and theological schools: Perceptions of faculty advocates regarding curriculum implications.* Unpublished doctoral dissertation. University of Pennsylvania, Philadelphia.

Conklin, S. C. 2001. Seminary sexuality education survey: Current efforts, perceived need and readiness. *Journal of Sex Education & Therapy, 26*(4):301-309.

Constantine, L. L. 1973. *Group marriage: A study of contemporary multilateral marriage.* New York: Macmillan.

Constantine, L. L. & J. M. Constantine. 1971. *Report on ongoing research in group marriage.* Presentation at January meeting, Society for the Scientific Study of Sex, New York.

Constantine, L. L. & J. M. Constantine. 1976. *Treasures of the island: Children in alternative families.* Beverly Hills, CA: Sage Publications.

Coolidge, F. L., L. L. Theda, & S. E. Young. 2002. The heritability of gender identity disorder in a child and adolescent sample. *Behavior Genetics, 32*:251-257.

Coontz, S. 1992. *The way we never were: American families and the nostalgia trap.* New York: Harper Collins Basic Books.

Cooper, A. 1998. Sexuality and the Internet: Surfing into the New Millennium. *CyberPsychology and Behavior, 1*(2):187-194

Cooper, A. 2000. Cybersex and sexual compulsivity: The dark side of the force. *Sexual Addiction & Compulsivity, 7*(1-3):1-3.

Cooper, A., ed. 2002. *Sex and the Internet: A guidebook for clinicians.* New York: Brunner-Routledge.

Cooper, A., S. Boies, M. Maheu, & D. Greenfield. 1999. Sexuality and the Internet: The next sexual revolution. In: F. Muscarella & L. Szuchman, eds., *The psychological science of sexuality: A research based approach.* New York: Wiley Press.

Cooper, A., D. Delmonico, & R. Burg. 2000. Cybersex users, abusers, and compulsives: New findings and implications. *Sexual Addiction and Compulsivity: Journal of Treatment and Prevention, 7*(1-2):5-30.

Cooper, A., N. Galbreath, M. A. Becker, & E. Griffin-Shelley. 2003. Sex on the Internet: Furthering our understanding of men with online sexual problems. (Submitted for publication to *Psychology of Addictive Behaviors*).

Cooper, A., G. Golden, & J. Kent-Ferraro. 2002. Online sexual behaviors in the workplace: How can human resource departments and employee assistance programs respond effectively? *Sexual Addiction and Compulsivity, 9*:149-165.

Cooper, A., & E. Griffin-Shelley. 2002. Introduction. The Internet: The next sexual revolution. In: A. Cooper, ed., *Sex and the Internet: A guidebook for clinicians.* New York: Brunner-Routledge.

Cooper, A., E. Griffin-Shelley, D. L. Delmonico, & R. M. Mathy. 2001. Online sexual problems: Assessment and predictive variables. *Sexual Addiction and Compulsivity: The Journal of Treatment and Prevention, 8*(3-4):267-286.

Cooper, A., & Marcus, D. 2003. Men Who Lose Control of their Sexual Behavior. In: Levine, S., ed., *Handbook of clinical sexuality for mental health professionals.*

Cooper, A., S. A. Månsson, K. Daneback, R. Tikkanen, & M. W. Ross. 2003. Predicting the future of Internet sex: Online sexual activities in Sweden. *Sexual and Relationship Therapy, 16*(4):321-328.

Cooper, A., & I. P. McLoughlin. 2001. What clinicians need to know about Internet sexuality. *Sexual & Relationship Therapy, 16*:321-327.

Cooper, A., I. McLoughlin, P. Reich, & J. Kent-Ferraro. 2002. Virtual sexuality in the workplace: A wake-up call for clinicians, employers and employees. In: A. Cooper, ed., *Sex and the Internet: A guidebook for clinicians.* New York: Brunner-Routledge.

Cooper, A., J. Morahan-Martin, R. M. Mathy, & M. Maheu. 2002. Toward an increased understanding of user demographics in online sexual activities. *Journal of Sex & Marital Therapy, 28*:105-129.

Cooper, A., M. Safir, A. Rosenman, T. Scherr, I. McLoughlin. In press. Workplace worries: A preliminary look at online sexual activities at the office. *Professional Psychology.*

Cooper, A., C. Scherer, S. C. Boies, & B. Gordon. 1999. Sexuality on the Internet: From sexual exploration to pathological expression. *Professional Psychology: Research and Practice, 30*(2):154-164.

Cooper, A., C. Scherer, & D. Marcus. 2002. Harnessing the power of the Internet to improve sexual relationships. In: A. Cooper, ed., *Sex and the Internet: A guidebook for clinicians*. New York: Brunner-Routledge.

Cooper, A., C. Scherer, & R. M. Mathy. 2001. Overcoming methodological concerns in the investigating of online sexual activities. *CyberPsychology & Behavior, 4*(4):437-447.

Cooper, A., & L. Sportolari. 1997. Romance and cyberspace: Understanding online attraction, *Journal of Sex Education and Therapy, 22*(1):1-12.

Corea, G. 1985. *The mother machine: Reproductive technologies from artificial insemination to artificial wombs*. New York: Harper & Row.

Cornog, M. 1994. Appendix on sexological research. In: V. L. Bullough & B. Bullough, eds., *Human sexuality: An encyclopedia* (pp 607-617). New York: Garland Publishing.

Cornog, M. 2002. Group masturbation among young and old(er): A summary with questions. *Journal of Sex Education & Therapy, 26*:340-346.

Cornog, M. 2003. *The big book of masturbation: From angst to zeal*. San Francisco: Down There Press.

Cornog, M., & T. Perper. 1996. *For sex education, see librarian*. New York: Greenwood Press.

Cornwell, B., & D. C. Lundgren. 2001. Love on the Internet: Involvement and misrepresentation in romantic relationships in cyberspace vs. realspace. *Computers in Human Behavior, 1*:197-211.

Countryman, L. W. 1988. *Dirt, greed and sex: Sexual ethics in the New Testament and their implications for today*. Philadelphia: Fortress Press.

Cowley, G., & K. Springen. 1999 (January 25). A second opinion on sex. *Newsweek, 133*:28.

Cozzens, D. 2002. *Sacred silence: Denial and the crisis in the Church*. Collegeville, MN: Liturgical Press.

Cray, E., ed. 1969. *The erotic muse*. New York: Pyramid Special Books.

Cunneen, C., & J. Stubbs. 2000. Male violence, male fantasy and the commodification of women through the Internet. *Interactive Review of Victimology, 7*:5-28.

Cunningham, M. 1998. *The hours*. New York: Farrar, Straus, Giroux.

Curran, C. E., & R. A. McCormick, eds. 1993. *Dialogue about Catholic sexual teaching*. Mahwah, NJ: Paulist Press.

Current Population Reports. 1985. *Marital status and living arrangements, March, 1984*. United States Department of Commerce, Bureau of the Census.

Dailard, C. 2001 (February). Sex education: Politicians, parents, teachers and teens. *Guttmacher report on public policy*.

Darabi, K. F., & V. Ortiz. 1987. Childbearing among young Latino women in the United States. *American Journal of Public Health, 77*(1):25-28.

Darroch, J. E., et al. 2000. Changing emphases in sexuality education in U.S. public secondary schools, 1988-1999. *Family Planning Perspectives, 32*(5):204-211, 265.

Dauw, D. C. 1988. Evaluating the effectiveness of the SECS' surrogate-assisted sex therapy model. *Journal of Sex Research, 24*:269-275.

Davidson, J. K., & C. Anderson Darling. 1993. Masturbatory guilt and sexual responsiveness among post-college-age women: Sexual satisfaction revisited. *Journal of Sex and Marital Therapy, 19*(4):289-300.

Davis, A. Y. 1981. *Women, race and class*. New York: Vintage Books.

Davis, C. M., J. Blank, H.-Y. Lin, & C. Bonillas. 1996. Characteristics of vibrator use among women. *Journal of Sex Research, 33*:313-320.

Davis, D. 1999 (August 25-31). Phallus rising: Or the prisoner of joy. *New York Press, 12*(34):1, 14.

Davis, J. A. 1990. *General social surveys, 1972-1990: Cumulative codebook*. Chicago: National Opinion Research Center, University of Chicago.

Davis, J. A., & T. W. Smith. 1994. *General social surveys, 1979-1994: Cumulative codebook*. Chicago: National Opinion Research Center.

Davis, K. B. 1929. *Factors in the sex life of twenty-two hundred women*. New York: Harper and Row.

Davis, S. M., & M. B. Harris. 1982. Sexual knowledge, sexual interest, and sources of sexual information of rural and urban adolescents from three cultures. *Adolescence, 17*:471-492.

Dawson, D. A. 1990. AIDS knowledge and attitudes for January-March 1990. Provisional data from the national health interview survey. *Advanced data from vital and health statistics. Number 193*. Hyattsville, MD: National Center for Health Statistics.

Dawson, D. A., & A. M. Hardy. 1989. *AIDS knowledge and attitudes of Hispanic Americans. Provisional data from the 1988 national health interview survey. Advanced data from vital and health statistics. Number 166*. Hyattsville, MD: National Center for Health Statistics.

Dekker, A., & G. Schmidt. 2002. Patterns of masturbatory behavior: Changes between the sixties and the nineties. *Journal of Psychology & Human Sexuality, 14*(2/3):35-48.

de la Cancela, V. 1989. Minority AIDS prevention: Moving beyond cultural perspectives towards sociopolitical empowerment. *AIDS Education and Prevention, 1*(2):141-153.

de la Vega, E. 1990. Considerations for reaching the Latino population with sexuality and HIV/AIDS information and education. *SIECUS Report, 18*(3).

Deirmenjian, J. M. 1999. Stalking in cyberspace. *Journal American Academic Psychiatry Law, 27*:407-413.

Delacoste, F., & P. Alexander. 1987. *Sex work: Writings by women in the sex industry*. Pittsburgh, PA: Cleis Press.

DeLamater, J. D., & P. MacCorquodale. 1979. *Premarital sexuality: Attitudes, relationships, behavior*. Madison, WI: University of Wisconsin Press.

Delmonico, D. L., E. Griffin, & P. J. Carnes. 2002. Treating online compulsive sexual behavior: When cybersex is the drug of choice. In: A. Cooper, ed., *Sex and the Internet: A guidebook for clinicians*. New York: Brunner-Routledge.

D'Emilio, J., & E. B. Freedman. 1988. *Intimate matters: A history of sexuality in America*. New York: Harper and Row.

Denfeld, D. 1974. Dropouts from swinging. *Family Coordinator, 23*:45-59.

Denfeld, D., & M. Gordon. 1970. The sociology of mate swapping: Or, the family that swings together clings together. *Journal of Sex Research, 6*(2):85-100.

Denizet-Lewis, B. 2003 (August 3). Double lives on the down low. *The New York Times (Sunday) Magazine*.

DeRachewitz, B. 1964. *Black Eros: Sexual customs of Africa from prehistory to the present day*. New York: Lyle Stuart.

DeWaal, F. 1982. *Chimpanzee politics: Power and sex among apes*. New York: Harper Colophon Books.

DeWitt, K. 1991 (October 13). As harassment plays, many U.S. employees live it. *The New York Times*, 24.

Diamond, L. M. 2003a. Was it a phase? Young women's relinquishment of lesbian/bisexual identities over a 5-year period. *Journal of Personality & Social Psychology, 84*:352-364.

Diamond, L. M. 2003b. What does sexual orientation orient? A biobehavioral model distinguishing romantic love and sexual desire. *Psychological Review, 110*:173-193.

Diamond, M. T. 1996. Self-testing among transsexuals: A check on sexual identity, *Journal of Psychology & Human Sexuality, 8*(3):61-82.

Diamond, M. T. 1997. Sexual identity and sexual orientation in children with traumatized or ambiguous genitalia. *Journal of Sex Research, 34*(2):199-222.

Diamond, M., T. Binstock, & J. V. Kohl. 1996. From fertilization to adult sexual behavior: Nonhormonal influences on sexual behavior. *Hormones & Behavior, 30*:333-353.

Diamond, M. T., & H. K. Sigmundson. 1997. Sex reassignment at birth. Long term review and clinical implications. *Archives of Pediatrics & Adolescent Medicine, 151*:298-304.

Diaz, R. M. 1998. *Latino gay men and HIV: Culture, sexuality, and risk behavior.* New York: Routledge.

Di Ceglie, D. 2000. Gender identity disorder in young people. *Advances Psychiatric Treatment,* 6:458-466.

Dickinson, R. L., & H. H. Pierson. 1925. The average sex life of American women. *Journal of the American Medical Association,* 85:1113-1117.

Dickinson, R. L., & L. Bean. 1931/1932. *A thousand marriages: A medical study of sex adjustment.* Baltimore: Williams & Wilkins.

Dickinson, R. L., & L. Bean. 1934. *The single woman.* Baltimore: Williams and Wilkins.

Dietz, P. 1989/1990 (December/January). Youth-serving agencies as effective providers of sexuality education. *SIECUS Report, 18*:16-20.

di Mauro, D. 1989/1990 (December/January). Sexuality education 1990: A review of state sexuality and AIDS education curricula. *SIECUS Report, 18*:1-9.

di Mauro, D. 1995. *Sexuality research in the United States: An assessment of the social and behavioral sciences.* New York: Social Sciences Research Council.

Dixon, D. 1985. Perceived sexual satisfaction and marital happiness of bisexual and heterosexual swinging husbands. Special issue: Bisexualities: Theory and research. *Journal of Homosexuality, 11*(1-2):209-222.

Dixon, J. K. 1984. The commencement of bisexual activity in swinging married women over age 30. *Journal of Sex Research, 20*:71-90.

Docter, R. F. 1988. *Transvestites and transsexuals: Toward a theory of cross-gender behavior.* New York: Plenum Press.

Doddridge, R., W. Schumm, & M. Berger. 1987. Factors related to decline in preferred frequency of sexual intercourse among young couples. *Psychological Reports, 60*:391-395.

Dodson, B. 1987. *Sex for one: The joy of selfloving.* New York: Harmony Books. Published in 1974 and 1983 under the titles of *Selflove and orgasm* and *Liberating masturbation.*

Doidge, N. 2001. (November 8). *The terrorists and their last-night temptresses.* Available: http://www.jewishworldreview.com/cols/doidge110801.asp.

Donat, P. L. N., & J. D'Emilio. 1992. A feminist redefinition of rape and sexual assault: Historical foundations and change. *Journal of Social Issues, 48*(1):9-22.

Donnerstein, E., D. Linz, & S. Penrod. 1987. *The question of pornography: Research findings and policy implications.* New York: The Free Press.

Duberman, M., M. Vicinus, & G. Chauncey, eds. 1989. *Hidden from history: Reclaiming the gay and lesbian past.* New York: New American Library.

Duesberg, P. H. 1996. *Inventing the AIDS virus.* Washington, DC: Regnery Press.

Dugger, C. W. 1996a (December 28). Tug of taboos: African genital rite vs. U.S. law. *The New York Times,* 1, 9.

Dugger, C. W. 1996b (October 12). New law bans genital cutting in United States. *The New York Times,* 1, 28.

Duncan, D. F., & T. Nicholson. 1991. Pornography as a source of sex information for students at a southeastern state university. *Psychological Reports, 68*:802.

Durant, R. 1990. Sexual behaviors among Hispanic female adolescents in the U.S. *Pediatrics, 85*(6):1051-1058.

Durkin, K. F. 1997. Misuse of the Internet by pedophiles: Implications for law enforcement and probation practice. *Federal Probation, 61*(3):14-18.

Durkin, K. F., & C. D. Bryant. 1999. Propagandizing pederasty: A thematic analysis of the on-line exculpatory accounts of unrepentant pedophiles. *Deviant Behavior, 20*:103-127.

Dworkin, A. 1974. *Woman hating: A radical look at sexuality.* New York: Dutton.

Easton, D., & C. A. Liszt. 1998. *The ethical slut: A guide to infinite sexual possibilities.* San Francisco: Greenery Press.

Eckard, E. 1982. *Contraceptive use patterns, prior source, and pregnancy history of female family planning patients: United States, 1980.* Washington, DC: United States Department of Health and Human Services, Public Health Service, Vital Statistics, No. 82.

Edwardes, A., & R. E. L. Masters. 1963. *The cradle of erotica: A study of Afro-Asian sexual expression and an analysis of erotic freedom in social relationships.* New York: The Julian Press.

Edwards, J. N., & A. Booth. 1976. Sexual behavior in and out of marriage: An assessment of correlates. *Journal of Marriage and the Family, 38*(1):73-81.

Egan, J. 2000 (December 10). Lonely gay teen seeking same. *The New York Times,* 112-127.

Ehrenreich, B., G. Hass, & E. Jacobs. 1987. *Remaking love: The feminization of sex.* New York: Doubleday/Anchor.

Ehrmann, W. W. 1959. *Premarital dating behavior.* New York: Holt, Rinehart and Winston.

Ehrmann, W. W. 1964. Marital and nonmarital sexual behavior. In: H. T. Christensen, ed., *Handbook of marriage and the family* (pp. 585-622). Chicago: Rand McNally.

Eibl-Eibesfeldt, I. 1989. *Human ethology.* New York: Aldine de Gruyter.

Eichel, E. W. 1990. Heterophobia: The Kinsey agenda in sex education. In: J. A. Reisman, & E. W. Eichel, *Kinsey, sex and fraud: An indoctrination of a people* (pp. 117-137). Lafayette, LA: Lochinvar-Huntington House Publication.

Ekins, R. 1997. *Male femaling.* London, New York, Routledge.

Ekins, R., & D. King. 2001. Telling body transgendered stories. In: F. Haynes & T. McKenna, eds., *Unseen genders: Beyond the binaries.* New York: Peter Lang.

Elias, J., & P. Gebhard. 1969. Sexuality and sexual learning in childhood. *Phi Delta Kappan, 50*:401-405.

Elford, J., G. Bolding, & L. Sherr. 2001. Seeking sex on the Internet and sexual risk behaviour among gay men using London gyms. *AIDS, 15*:1409-1415.

Elliott, L., & C. Brantley. 1997. *Sex on campus: The naked truth about the real sex lives of college students.* New York: Random House.

Ellis, A. 1969. Healthy and disturbed reasons for having extramarital relations. In: G. Neubeck, ed., *Extramarital relations* (pp. 153-161). Englewood Cliffs, NJ: Prentice-Hall.

Ellis, A. 1972. *The civilized couple's guide to extramarital adventure: The book to read before you begin that affair.* New York: P.H. Wyden.

Ellis, A., & Abarbanel, A., eds. 1973. *The encyclopedia of sexual behavior.* New York: Jason Aronson.

Ellis, H. 1936a. *Love and pain, Studies in the psychology of sex. Vol. 1* (originally published 1903). New York: Random House.

Ellis, H. 1936b. Sexual selection in man: Hearing. *Studies in the psychology of sex* (vol. 1, part 3). New York: Random House.

Eng, T. R., & W. T. Butler. 1997. *The hidden epidemic: Confronting sexually transmitted diseases.* Washington, D.C.: National Academy Press.

EPIC (online) 1996 (September 30). *CDA ruled unconstitutional.*

Eskridge, W. N. 1996. *The case for same-sex marriage.* New York: Free Press.

Estrich, S. 1987. *Real rape.* Cambridge, MA: Harvard University Press.

Faderman, L. 1991. *Odd girls and twilight lovers.* New York: Columbia University Press.

Faderman, L. 1995. What is lesbian literature? Forming a historical canon. In: G. E. Haggerty & B. Zimmerman, eds., *Professions of desire: Lesbian and gay studies in literature* (pp. 49-59). New York: Modern Language Association.

Fanon, F. 1967. *Black skin, white mask.* New York: Grove Press.

Farber, C. 1993 (March). Out of Africa. *Spin,* 60-63, 86-87.

Farber, C. 1993a (April). Out of Africa: Part Two. *Spin,* 74-77, 106-107.

Farber, C. 1993b (April). Sex in the '90s. *Spin*, 15.

Farley, R., & W. R. Allen. 1987. *The color line and the quality of life in America.* New York: Russell Sage Foundation.

Farrell, W. 1986/1988. *Why men are the way they are.* New York: McGraw-Hill; Putnam-Berkley.

Farrell, W. 1990. The last taboo?: The complexities of incest and female sexuality. In: M. Perry, ed., *Handbook of sexology: Volume 7: Childhood and adolescent sexology.* New York: Elsevier.

Farrell, W. 1993/2001. *The myth of male power: Why men are the disposable sex.* New York: Simon & Schuster; Putnam-Berkley.

Farrell, W. 1999. *Women can't hear what men don't say.* New York: Tarcher/Putnam/Penguin.

Farrell, W. 2001. *Father and child reunion.* New York: Tarcher/Putnam/Penguin.

Farson, R. E., P. M. Hauser, H. Stroup, & A. J. Weiner. 1969. *The future of the family.* New York: Family Service Association of America.

Federal Bureau of Investigation. 1993. *Uniform crime reports for the United States 1992.* Washington, DC: U.S. Government Printing Office.

Feinberg, D. 1989. *Eighty-sixed.* New York: Viking Press.

Fekete, J. 1994. *Moral panic.* Montreal: Robert Davies Publishing.

Fennelly, K. 1988. *El embarazo precoz: Childbearing among Hispanic teenagers in the United States.* New York: Columbia University, School of Public Health.

Fennelly, K. 1992. Sexual activity and childbearing among Hispanic adolescents in the United States. In: R. Lerner, et al., eds., *Early adolescence: Perspectives on research, policy and intervention.* Hillsdale, NJ: Eldbaum Press.

Fennelly, K., V. Kandiah, & V. Ortiz. 1989. The cross-cultural study of fertility among Hispanic adolescents in the Americas. *Studies in Family Planning*, 20(2):96-101.

Fennelly-Darabi, K., & V. Ortiz. 1987. Childbearing among young Latino women in the United States. *American Journal of Public Health*, 77(1):25-28.

Fine, M., & A. Asch, eds. 1988. *Women with disabilities: Essays in psychology, culture, and politics.* Philadelphia: Temple University Press.

Fineman, H., & K. Breslau. 1998 (February 2). Sex, lies and the President. *Newsweek*, 20-29.

Finer, L. B., & S. K. Henshaw. 2003. Abortion incidence and services in the United States in 2000. *Perspectives Sexual & Reproductive Health*, 35:6-15.

Finger, F. W. 1975. Changes in sex practices and beliefs of male college students over 30 years. *Journal of Sex Research*, 11:304-317.

Finkelhor, D. 1980. Sex among siblings: A survey on prevalence, variety, and effects. *Archives of Sexual Behavior*, 9:171-194.

Finkelhor, D., K. J. Mitchell, & J. Wolak. 2000. *Online victimization: A report on the nation's youth.* National Center for Missing and Exploited Children. Available: http://www.missingkids.com/html/index_search.html.

Finkelhor, D., & K. Yllo. 1985. *License to rape: Sexual abuse of wives.* New York: Free Press.

Fischer, G. J. 1987. Hispanic and majority student attitudes towards forcible date rape as a function of differences in attitudes towards women. *Sex Roles*, 17(2):93-101.

Fisher, H. E. 1992. *Anatomy of love: The natural history of monogamy, adultery, and divorce.* New York: Norton.

Fisher, T. D. 1986. An exploratory study of parent-child communication about sex and the sexual attitudes of early, middle, and late adolescents. *Journal of Genetic Psychology*, 147:543-557.

Fisher, W. A., & A. Barak. 2000. Online sex shops: Phenomenological, psychological, and ideological perspectives on Internet sexuality. *CyberPsychology & Behavior*, 3(4):575-589.

Fisher, W. A., & A. Barak. 2001. Internet pornography: A social psychological perspective on Internet sexuality. *Journal of Sex Research*, 38:312-323.

Flaskerud, J. H., G. Uman, R. Lara, L. Romero, & K. Taka. 1996. Sexual practices, attitudes, and knowledge related to HIV transmission in low income Los Angeles Hispanic women. *Journal of Sex Research*, 33(4):343-353.

Flowers-Coulson, P. A., M. A. Kushner, & S. Bankowski. 2000. The information is out there, but is anyone getting it? Adolescent misconceptions about sexuality education and reproductive health and the use of the Internet to get answers. *Journal of Sex Education & Therapy*, 25:178-188.

Floyd, H. H. Jr., & D. R. South. 1972. Dilemma of youth: The choice of parents or peers as a frame of reference for behavior. *Journal of Marriage and the Family*, 34:627-634.

Flugel, J. C. 1966. *The psychology of clothes.* London: The Hogan Press.

Ford, C. S., & F. A. Beach. 1951. *Patterns of sexual behavior.* New York: Harper and Brothers.

Ford, K., & A. Norris. 1991. Methodological considerations for survey research on sexual behavior: Urban African American and Hispanic youth. *Journal of Sex Research*, 28(4):539-555.

Ford, K., & A. E. Norris. 1993. Urban Hispanic adolescents and young adults: Relationship of acculturation to sexual behavior. *Journal of Sex Research*, 30(4):316-323.

Forrest, J. D., & R. R. Fordyce. 1988. U.S. women's contraceptive attitudes and practices: How have they changed in the 1980s? *Family Planning Perspectives*, 20(3):112-118.

Forrest, J. D., & J. Silverman. 1989. What public school teachers teach about preventing pregnancy, AIDS and sexually transmitted diseases. *Family Planning Perspectives*, 21:65-72.

Forrest, J. D., & S. Singh. 1990. The sexual and reproductive behavior of American women, 1982-1988. *Family Planning Perspectives*, 22(5):206-214.

Forrest, K. 1987. *Murder at the Nightwood Bar.* Tallahassee, FL: NAIAD Press.

Fortune, M. M. 1991. *Is nothing sacred? When sex invades the pastoral relationship.* San Francisco: Harper.

Fox, K. K., C. del Rio, K. K. Holmes, et al. 2001. Gonorrhea in the HIV era: A reversal of trends among men who have sex with men. *American Journal of Public Health*, 91:959-964.

Fox, M. 1983. *Original blessing.* Sante Fe, New Mexico: Bear and Company.

Fox, M. 1988. *The coming of the cosmic Christ: The healing of mother earth and the birth of a global renaissance.* San Francisco: Harper and Row.

Fox, R. 1995. A history of bisexuality research. In: A. D'Augelli & C. Patterson, eds., *Lesbian, gay and bisexual identities over the lifespan.* New York: Oxford University Press.

Fraim, J. 2002. A new extraversion in analytical psychology? Jungian reflections on September 11: A global nightmare [L. Zoja & D. Williams (Daimon Verlag 2002)] [book review]. *CG Jung Page.* Available: http://www.cgjungpage.org/911fraimreview.html.

Francoeur, A. K., & R. T. Francoeur. 1974. *Hot and cool sex: Cultures in conflict.* New York: Harcourt, Brace, Jovanovich.

Francoeur, R. T. 1977. *Utopian motherhood: New trends in human reproduction* (3rd ed.). Cranbury, NJ: A.S. Barnes/Perpetua Books.

Francoeur, R. T. 1987. Human sexuality. In: M. B. Sussman & S. K. Steinmetz, eds., *Handbook of marriage and the family.* New York: Plenum Press.

Francoeur, R. T. 1988. Two different worlds, two different moralities. In: J. Gramick & P. Furey, eds., *The Vatican and homosexuality.* New York, NY: Crossroads.

Francoeur, R. T. 1990. Current religious doctrines of sexual and erotic development in childhood. In: M. Perry, ed., *Handbook of sexology: Volume 7: Childhood and adolescent sexology.* New York: Elsevier.

Francoeur, R. T. 1991a. *Becoming a sexual person* (2nd ed.). New York: Macmillan.

Francoeur, R. T. 1991b. *Taking sides: Clashing views on controversial issues in human sexuality* (3rd ed.). Guilford, CT: Dushkin Publishing Group.

Francoeur, R. T. 1992a. The religious repression of Eros. In: D. Steinberg, ed., *The erotic impulse: Honoring the sensual self.* New York: J.R. Tarcher.

Francoeur, R. T. 1992b. (April/May). Sexuality and spirituality: The relevance of Eastern traditions. *SIECUS Report, 20*(4):1-8.

Francoeur, R. T. 1994. Religion and sexuality. In: V. L. Bullough & B. Bullough, eds., *Human sexuality: An encyclopedia* (pp. 514-520). New York: Garland.

Francoeur, R. T., M. Cornog, & T. Perper (eds.). 1999. *Sex, love and marriage in the 21st century: The next sexual revolution.* San Jose, CA: toExcel.

Francoeur, R. T., T. Perper, & M. Cornog. 1995. *The complete dictionary of sexuality.* New York: Continuum.

Frank, E., & C. Anderson. 1979 (July/August). Sex and the happily married. *The Sciences*, 10-13.

Frank, E., C. Anderson, & D. Rubinstein. 1978. Frequency of sexual dysfunction in 'normal' couples. *New England Journal of Medicine, 299*:111-115.

Frayser, S. 1985. *Varieties of sexual experience: An anthropological perspective on human Sexuality.* New Haven, CT: HRAF Press.

Freeman, J. 1995. From suffrage to women's liberation: Feminism in twentieth-century America. In: J. Freeman, ed., *Women: A feminist perspective.* Mountain View, CA: Mayfield.

Freud, S. 1938. Three contributions to the theory of sex. In: A. A. Brill, ed., *The basic writings of Sigmund Freud* (originally published in 1905). New York: The Modern Library.

Friend. R. A. 1987. The individual and social psychology of aging: Clinical implications for lesbians and gay men. *Journal of Homosexuality, 14*(1-2):307-331.

Fuerstein, G. 1992. *Enlightened sexuality: Essays on body-positive spirituality.* Ithaca, NY: Crossing Press.

Fumento, M. 1990. *The myth of heterosexual AIDS.* New York: Basic Books [A New Republic Book].

Furchgot, E. 1993 (Spring/Summer). What happened to Kerista? *Communities Journal*, 80/81.

Gagnon, J. H. 1977. *Human sexualities.* New York: Scott, Foresman.

Gagnon, J. H. 1985. Attitudes and responses of parents to preadolescent masturbation. *Archives of Sexual Behavior, 14*:451-466.

Gagnon, J. H., & W. Simon. 1973. *Sexual conduct: The social sources of human sexuality.* Chicago: Aldine.

Gaines, D. 1995 (June 30). *Founder of the foot fraternity.* Interview with Brenda Love. San Francisco.

Galbreath, N., F. Berlin, & Sawyer. 2002. Paraphilias and the Internet. In: A. Cooper, ed., *Sex and the Internet: A guidebook for clinicians.* New York: Brunner-Routledge.

Galenson, E. 1990. Observation of early infantile sexual and erotic development. In: M. Perry, ed., *Handbook of sexology: Volume 7: Childhood and adolescent sexology.* New York: Elsevier.

Galenson, E., & H. Roiphe. 1980. Some suggested revisions concerning early female development. In: M. Kirkpatrick, ed., *Women's sexual development: Exploration of inner space* (pp. 83-105). New York: Plenum.

Garcia, C. 1993. What do we mean by extended family? A closer look at Hispanic multigenerational families. *Journal of Cross Cultural Gerontology, 8*(2):137-146.

Garcia, F. 1980. The cult of virginity. In: *Program on teaching and learning: Conference on the educational and occupational needs of Hispanic women* (pp. 65-73). Washington, DC: National Institute of Education.

Gardella, P. 1985. *Innocent ecstasy: How Christianity gave America an ethic of sexual pleasure.* New York: Oxford University Press.

Gebhard, P. H. 1968. Postmarital coitus among widows and divorcees. In: P. Bohannan, ed., *Divorce and after* (pp. 81-96). New York: Doubleday.

Gebhard, P. H. 1993 (September/October). Kinsey's famous figures. *Indiana Alumni Magazine*, 64.

Gelles, R. J. 1977. Power, sex, and violence: The case of marital rape. *Family Coordinator, 26*:339-347.

Gelles, R. J., & M. A. Straus. 1988. *Intimate violence.* New York: Simon & Schuster.

Gemme, R., & C. C. Wheeler, eds. 1977. *Progress in sexology.* New York, NY: Plenum Publishing Corp.

Getman, K. 1984. Sexual control in the slaveholding South: The implementation and maintenance of a racial caste system. *Harvard Women's Law Review, 7*:115-53.

Gibbs, N. 1991 (June 3). When is it rape? *Time*, 52.

Gibson, J. W., & J. Kempf. 1990. Attitudinal predictors of sexual activity in Hispanic adolescent females. *Journal of Adolescent Research, 5*(4):414-430.

Gilder, G. 1987. *Men and marriage.* Gretna, LA: Pelican.

Giles, J., & C. S. Lee. 1994 (August 15). There's nothing like a dame. *Newsweek*, 69.

Gillespie, J. 1968. *The musical experience.* Belmont, CA: Wadworth.

Gilmartin, B. G. 1974. Sexual deviance and social networks: A study of social, family, and marital interaction patterns among co-marital sex participants. In: J. R. Smith & L. G. Smith, eds., *Beyond monogamy: Recent studies of sexual alternatives in marriage.* Baltimore: John Hopkins University.

Gilmartin, B. G. 1978. *The Gilmartin report.* Secaucus, NJ: Citadel.

Ginsberg, A. 1978. *Mindbreaths.* San Francisco: City Light Books.

Ginsberg, A. 1995. *Howl.* New York: HarperPerennial.

Gise, L. H., & P. Paddison. 1988. Rape, sexual abuse, and its victims. *Psychiatric Clinics of North America, 11*:629-648.

Givens, D. 1978. The nonverbal basis of attraction: Flirtation, courtship, and seduction. *Psychiatry, 41*:346-359.

Givens, D. B. 1983. *Love signals: How to attract a mate.* New York: Crown.

Glass, S. P., & T. L. Wright. 1977. The relationship of extramarital sex, length of marriage and sex differences on marital satisfaction and romanticism: Athanasiou's data reanalyzed. *Journal of Marriage and the Family, 39*:691-703.

Glass, S. P., & T. L. Wright. 1985. Sex differences in type of extramarital involvement and marital dissatisfaction. *Sex Roles, 12*:1101-1120.

Glazer, N., & D. P. Moynihan. 1964. *Beyond the melting pot: The Negroes, Puerto Ricans, Jews, Otawoams, Italians, and Irish of New York City.* Cambridge, MA: MIT Press.

Glenn, N., & E. Marquardt. 2001. *Hooking up, hanging out and hoping for Mr. Right: College women on mating and dating today.* New York: Institute for American Values. Available: www.AmericanValues.org.

Glenn, N. D., & C. N. Weaver. 1979. Attitudes toward premarital, extramarital, and homosexual relations in the U.S. in the 1970s. *Journal of Sex Research, 15*:108-118.

Glick, P. C. 1984. Marriage, divorce, and living arrangements: Prospective changes. *Journal of Family Issues, 5*:7-26.

Glick, P. C., & A. Norton. 1977. *Marrying, divorcing, and living together in the U.S. today.* Washington, DC: Population Reference Bureau.

Gold, Rabbi M. 1992. *Does God belong in the bedroom?* Philadelphia: The Jewish Publication Society.

Goldberg, H. 1977. *The hazards of being male.* New York: Signet.

Goldfarb, L., M. Gerrarc, F. X. Gibbons, & T. Plante. 1988. Attitudes toward sex, arousal, and the retention of contraceptive information. *Journal of Personality and Social Psychology, 55*:634-641.

Goldman, R. J., & J. G. D. Goldman. 1982. *Children's sexual thinking.* Boston: Routledge & Kegan Paul.

Goldstein, R. 2002 (May 21-27). Bush's basket: Why the President had to show his balls. *Village Voice, 48*(22):48.

Goodman, D. 1973. Dancing, social. In: A. Ellis & A. Abarbanel, eds., *The encyclopedia of sexual behavior* (pp. 746-756). New York: Jason Aronson.

Goodson, P. 1996. *Protestant seminary students' views of family planning and intention to promote family planning through education.* Unpublished doctoral dissertation. The University of Texas at Austin, TX.

Goodson, P. 2002. Predictors of intention to promote family planning: A survey of Protestant seminarians in the United States. *Health Education & Behavior, 29*(5):521-541.

Goodson, P., D. McCormick, & A. Evans. 2000a. Sex and the Internet: A survey instrument to assess college students' behavior and attitudes. *CyberPsychology & Behavior, 3*(2): 129-149.

Goodson, P., D. McCormick, & A. Evans. 2000b. Sex on the Internet: College students' emotional arousal when viewing sexually explicit materials on-line. *Journal of Sex Education & Therapy, 25*:252-260.

Goodson, P., D. McCormick, & A. Evans. 2001. Searching for sexually explicit materials on the Internet: An exploratory study of college students' behavior and attitudes. *Archives of Sexual Behavior, 30*:101-118.

Goodstein, L. 2003 (January 12). Trail of pain in Church crisis leads to nearly every diocese. *The New York Times*, A1, A20.

*Google.* Retrieved May 6, 2003. http://www.google.com/.

Gordon, D., & B. J. Sigesmund. 2003 (August 11). Queen for a day. *Newsweek*, 50-51.

Gordon, L. 1976. *Woman's body, woman's right: A social history of birth control in America.* New York: Penguin.

Gordon, M. T., & S. Riger. 1989. *The female fear.* New York: Free Press.

Gossett, J. L., & S. Byrne. 2002. "Click Here": A content analysis of Internet rape sites. *Gender & Society, 16*:689-709.

Gottman, J. 1994. *Why marriages succeed or fail.* New York: Simon and Schuster.

*GQ.* 1968 (December). Entire issue.

Gould, T. 2000. *The lifestyle: A look at the erotic rites of swingers.* Toronto: Firefly Books, Ltd.

Graugaard, C., & G. Winther. 1998. Sex counselling on the Internet–A year with www.lyst.dk. *Scandinavian Journal of Sexology, 1*:201-204.

Greeley, A. 1995. *Sex: The Catholic experience.* Allen, TX: Thomas More Press.

Greeley, A. M. 1991. *Faithful attraction: Discovering intimacy, love, and fidelity in American marriage.* New York: Doherty.

Greeley, A. M., R. T. Michael, & T. W. Smith. 1990. Americans and their sexual partners. *Society, 27*(5):36-42.

Green, R. 1987. *The "sissy boy syndrome" and the development of homosexuality.* New Haven, CT: Yale University Press.

Green, R. 1999. Cited in *Bellinger v Bellinger*, Ct of Appeal, para 32 July 17th (Judgement, 2001) TLR 22-11-2000.

Green, R., & D. T. Fleming. 1990. Transsexual surgery follow-up: Status in the 1990s. *Annual Review of Sex Research, 1*: 163-174.

Green, R., & R. Young. 2001. Hand preference, sexual preference, and transsexualism. *Archives of Sexual Behavior, 30*: 565-574.

Greenblat, C. S. 1983. The salience of sexuality in the early years of marriage. *Journal of Marriage and the Family, 45*: 289-299.

Greene, B. 1994. Ethnic-minority lesbians and gay men: Mental health and treatment issues. *Journal of Consulting & Clinical Psychology, 62*:243-251.

Grier, W., & W. Cobbs. 1968. *Black rage.* New York: Basic Books.

Griffin, E., J. Moriarty, & D. L. Delmonico. 2001. *Cybersex unhooked: A workbook for breaking free of compulsive online sexual behavior.* Center City, MN: Hazelden Educational Materials.

Griffin, S. 1971. Rape: The all-American crime. *Ramparts, 10*: 26-35.

Griffin-Shelley, E. 2003. The Internet and sexuality: A literature review–1983-2002. *Sexual and Relationship Therapy Journal*, (in press).

Griffit, W. 1985 (September). *Some prosocial effects of exposure to consensual erotica.* Paper presented at annual meeting of the Society for the Scientific Study of Sex, San Diego, CA.

Griffiths, M. 2000. Excessive Internet use: Implications for sexual behavior. *Cyberpsychology & Behavior, 3*(4):537-552.

Griffiths, M. 2001. Sex on the Internet: Observations and implications for Internet sex addiction. *Journal of Sex Research, 38*:333-342.

Grogan, A. 1995 (July 5). Owner of Romantasy Boutique. Interview with Brenda Love. San Francisco.

Groth, A. N., & A. W. Burgess. 1980. Male rape: Offenders and victims. *American Journal of Psychiatry, 137*:806-810.

Gross, M. 2003. The second wave will drown us. *American Journal of Public Health, 93*:872-881.

Grover, J. 1990. Is lesbian battering the same as straight battering? Children from violent lesbian homes. Battered lesbians are battered women. In: *Confronting lesbian battering: A manual for the battered women's movement* (pp. 41-46). St. Paul, MN: Minnesota Coalition for Battered Women.

Gurian, M. 1976/1977. *The wonder of boys.* New York: Nash Publishing Corp.; New York: Signet.

Gutek, B. A. 1985. *Sex and the workplace.* San Francisco, CA: Jossey-Bass.

Guttmacher, S., et al. 1997 (September). Condom availability in New York City public high schools: Relationships to condom use and sexual behavior. *American Journal of Public Health, 87*(9):1427-1433.

Gwinn, M., M. Pappaioanou, J. R. George, et al. 1991. Prevalence of HIV infection in childbearing women in the United States. *Journal of the American Medical Association, 265*(13):1704-1708.

Haffner, D. W. 1989 (March/April). SIECUS: 25 years of commitment to sexual health and education. *SIECUS Report, 17*:1-6.

Haffner, D. W. 1992 (February/March). 1992 report card on the States: Sexual rights in America. *SIECUS Report, 20*:1-7.

Haffner, D. W. 1994 (August/September). The good news about sexuality education. *SIECUS Report*, 17-18.

Haffner, D. W., & M. Kelly. 1987 (March/April). Adolescent sexuality in the media. *SIECUS Report*, 9-12.

Hagley, M., H. Pearson, & C. Carne. 2002. Sexual health advice centre. *International Journal of Adolescent Medicine & Health, 14*:125-130.

Hahn, H., & R. Stout. 1994. *The Internet yellow page.* Berkeley, CA: Osborne McGraw-Hill.

Hall, A. 2003 (May). The mating habits of the suburban high school teenager. *Boston Magazine.* Available: http://www.bostonmagazine.com/ArticleDisplay.php?id-242.

Hall, T. 1987 (June 1). Infidelity and women: Shifting patterns. *The New York Times.*

Halpern, H. 1994. *Finally getting it right.* New York: Bantam.

Halverson, H. M. 1940. Genital and sphincter behavior of the male infant. *Journal of Genetic Psychology, 56*:95-136.

Hamer, D., S. Hu, V. Magnuson, N. Hu, & A. Pattatucci. 1993. A linkage between DNA markers on the X chromosome and male sexual orientation. *Science, 261*:321-327.

Hamilton, G. V. 1948. *A research in marriage.* New York: Lear Publications.

Hamilton, K., & C. Brown. 1999 (June 21). They're havin' a heat wave. *Newsweek*, 133.

Hamm, L. M. (Associated Press). 1996 (November 4). Not just Africa: Female circumcision even happens in U.S. *New Jersey On-Line–Newark Star Ledger's Electronic Edition.*

Hammer, J. 1999 (November 8). The "gay panic" defense. *Newsweek, 134*:40.

Harris, M. 2003 (March 3). Casual sex rampant among Canadian teens: Educators rapped for not providing enough information on relationships. Available: www.Canada.com.

Hartman, W. E., & M. A. Fithian. 1972. *Treatment of sexual dysfunction: A bio-psycho-social approach.* Long Beach, CA: Center for Marital and Sexual Studies.

Harvey, J. 1995. *Men in black*. Chicago: The University of Chicago Press.

Haseltine, F. P., S. S. Cole, & D. B. Gray, eds. 1993. *Reproductive issues for persons with physical disabilities*. Baltimore: Paul H. Brookes Publishing Co.

Hass, A. 1979. *Teenage sexuality*. New York: Macmillan.

Hass, K., & A. Hass. 1993. *Understanding sexuality*. St. Louis: Mosby.

Hatcher, R. A., A. L. Nelson, M. Zieman, et al. 2003. *A pocket guide to managing contraception*. Tiger, GA: Bridging the Gap Foundation.

Hatcher, R., J. Trussell, F. Stewart, G. Stewart, D. Kowal, F. Guest, W. Cates, Jr., & M. Pokicar. 1994. *Contraceptive technology* (16th rev. ed.). New York: Irvington.

Hawkins, G., & F. E. Zimring. *Pornography in a free society*. Cambridge: Cambridge University Press.

Hawkins, M. J., M. Davis, C. Eady, S. Rausch, J. Donnelly, & M. Young. 2002. Meanings of abstinence and sexual activity for rural youth. *American Journal of Health Education, 33*:140-145.

Heiby, E., & J. D. Becker. 1980. Effect of filmed modeling on the self-reported frequency of masturbation. *Archives of Sexual Behavior, 9*(2):115-120.

Helminiak, D. A. 1994. *What the Bible really says about homosexuality*. San Francisco: Alamo Press.

Hendrixson, L. L. 1996. *The psychosocial and psychosexual impact of HIV/AIDS on rural women: A qualitative study*. Unpublished doctoral dissertation, New York University.

Hengeveld, M. W. 1991. Erectile disorders: A psychological review. In: U. Jonas, W. F. Thon, & C. G. Stief, eds., *Erectile dysfunction* (pp. 207-235). Berlin: Springer-Verlag.

Henshaw, S. K., & L. B. Finer. 2003. The accessibility of abortion services in the United States, 2001. *Perspectives Sexual Reproductive Health, 35*:16-24.

Herdt, G. H. 1981. *Guardians of the flute: Idioms of masculinity*. New York: McGraw-Hill.

Herdt, G. H. 1987. *The Sambia: Ritual and gender in New Guinea*. New York: Holt, Rinehart and Winston.

Herman, J. L. 1992. *Trauma and recovery*. New York: Basic Books.

Herman-Giddens, M. E. 1997 (April). Secondary sexual characteristics and menses in young girls seen in office practice: A study from the Pediatric Research in Office Settings Network. *Pediatrics, 99*(44):505-12.

Herold, E. S., & M. S. Goodwin. 1981. Adamant virgins, potential nonvirgins and nonvirgins. *Journal of Sex Research, 17*: 97-113.

Hershey, M. 1978. Racial differences in sex-role identities and sex stereotyping: Evidence against a common assumption. *Social Science Quarterly, 58*:584-596.

Heyward, C. 1989. *Touching our strength: The erotic as power and the love of God*. San Francisco: HarperSanFrancisco.

Hickman, S. E., & C. L. Muehlenhard. 1997. College women's fears and precautionary behaviors relating to acquaintance rape and stranger rape. *Psychology of Women Quarterly, 21*: 527-547.

Hite, S. 1976. *The Hite report*. New York: Dell.

Hite, S. 1983. *The Hite report on male sexuality*. New York: Knopf.

Hofferth, S. L., J. R. Kahn, & W. Baldwin. 1987. Premarital sexual activity among U.S. teenage women over the past three decades. *Family Planning Perspectives, 19*(2):46-53.

Hollander, A. 1978. *Seeing through clothes*. New York: Viking.

Holleran, A. 1988. *Dancer from the dance*. New York: Morrow.

Holleran, A. 1988. *Ground zero*. New York: Morrow.

Holmes, H. B., B. B. Hoskins, & M. Gross, eds. 1981. *The custom-made child? Women-centered perspectives*. Clifton, NJ: Humana Press.

Holmes, S. A. 1996a (June 13). Public cost of teen-age pregnancy is put at $7 billion this year. *The New York Times*, A19.

Holmes, S. A. 1996b (October 5). U.S. reports drop in rate of births to unwed women. *The New York Times*, 1, 9.

Holzman, H., & S. Pines. 1982. Buying sex: The phenomenology of being a john. *Deviant Behavior, 4*:89-116.

Hooker, E. E. A. 1957. The adjustment of the male overt homosexual. *Journal of Projective Techniques, 21*:17-31.

Hooks, B. 1990. *Yearning: race, gender, and cultural politics*. Boston: South End Press.

Hopkins, J. 1977. Sexual behavior in adolescence. *Journal of Social Issues, 33*:67-85.

Horowitz, S. M., D. L. Weis, & M. T. Laflin. 2001. Differences between sexual orientation behavior groups and social background, quality of life, and health behaviors. *Journal of Sex Research, 38*:205-218.

Hospers, H. J., P. Harterink, K. Van Den Hoek, & J. Veenstra. 2002. Chatters on the Internet: A special target group for HIV prevention. *AIDS Care, 14*:539-544.

Houston, L. 1981. Romanticism and eroticism among black and white college students. *Adolescence, 16*:263-272.

Howard, R. 1974. *Two-part inventions*. New York: Atheneum.

Hu, D. J., & R. Keller. 1989. Communicating AIDS information to Hispanics: The importance of language in media preference. *American Journal of Preventive Medicine, 54*: 196-200.

Humphrey, J. A., & J. W. White. 2000. Women's vulnerability to sexual assault from adolescence to young adulthood. *Journal of Adolescent Health, 27*:419-424.

Hunt, M. 1974. *Sexual behavior in the 1970s*. Chicago: Playboy Press.

Hunt, T. 1994 (December 10). Clinton fires surgeon general (AP News Service). *Bowling Green Sentinel Tribune*, 3.

Hunter, H. W. 1995. *Being a righteous husband and father*. Salt Lake City, UT: Church of Jesus Christ of Latter-Day Saints.

Hunter, M. 1990. *The sexually abused male*. Lexington, MA: Lexington Books.

Hunter, R. J., ed. 1990. *Dictionary of pastoral care and counseling*. Nashville, TN: Abingdon Press.

Hurlbert, D. F. 1992. Factors influencing a woman's decision to end an extramarital sexual relationship. *Journal of Sex and Marital Therapy, 18*(2):104-113.

Hutchins, L., & L. Kaahumanu, eds. 1991. *By any other name: Bisexual people speak out*. Boston: Alyson.

Imperato-McGinley, J., R. E. Peterson, T. Gautier, & E. Sturia. 1979. Male pseudohermaphroditism secondary to 5 alpha-reductase deficiency–A model for the role of androgens in both the development of the male phenotype and the evolution of a male gender identity. *Journal of Steroid Biochemistry, 11*(1B):637-645.

Inktomi. 2000. *Web surpasses one billion documents*. http://www.inktomi.com/new/press/2000/billion.html.

International Professional Surrogates Association (IPSA). 1989 (June). *Code of ethics* [Brochure]. Los Angeles: Author.

International Professional Surrogates Association (IPSA). n.d. General information about IPSA and surrogates. *Surrogate partner therapy* [Brochure]. Los Angeles: Author.

*The Internet unleashed*. 1994. Indianapolis, IN: SAMS Publishing.

Investigative Staff of the *Boston Globe*. 2002. *Betrayal: The crisis in the Catholic Church*. Boston: Little, Brown & Co.

Irvine, J. 1990. *Disorders of desire: Sex and gender in modern American sexology*. Philadelphia: Temple University Press.

Irvine, J. 1995. *Sexuality education across cultures: Working with differences*. San Francisco: Jossey-Bass.

Isikoff, M. 1997 (August 11). A twist in Jones v. Clinton. *Newsweek*, 30-31.

Isikoff, M., & H. Fineman. 1997 (July 7). A Starr-crossed probe? *Newsweek*, 31.

Isikoff, M., & E. Thomas. 1997 (June 8). I want him to admit what he did. *Newsweek*, 30-38.

Isikoff, M., & E. Thomas. 1998 (February 2). Clinton and the intern. *Newsweek*, 30-46.

Itialiano, L. 1996 (March). Communications decency act: Threat to cyber space? Or much ado about nothing? *NJ Online*.

Jacobs, M., L. A. Thompson, & P. Truxaw. 1975. The use of sexual surrogates in counseling. *The Counseling Psychologist, 5*(1):73-77.

Jacobus, X. 1937. *Untrodden fields of anthropology.* New York: Falstaff Press.

Jaffe, M. E., & K. K. Sharma. 2001. Cybersex with minors: Forensic implications. *Journal of Forensic Sciences, 46*:1397-1402.

James, W. H. 1981. The honeymoon effect on marital coitus. *Journal of Sex Research, 17*:114-123.

James, W. H. 1983. Decline in coital rates with spouses' ages and duration of marriage. *Journal of Bioscience, 15*:83-87.

Janofsky, M. 2003 (March 16). Women recount life of sexual ordeals and rage as cadets. *The New York Times*, A1, A22.

Jasso, G. 1985. Marital coital frequency and the passage of time: Estimating the separate effects of spouses' ages and marital duration, birth and marriage cohorts, and period influences. *American Sociological Review, 50*:224-241.

Jeffers, S. 1989. *Opening our hearts to men.* New York: Ballantine Books.

Jefferson, T. 1954. *Notes on the state of Virginia.* Chapel Hill, NC: University of North Carolina Press.

Jemmott, L. S., J. B. Jemmott, & A. M. Villarruel. 2002. Predicting intentions and condom use among Latino college students. *Journal of Assoc. Nurses AIDS Care, 13*(2):59-69.

Jenks, R. J. 1985a. A comparative study of swingers and nonswingers: Attitudes and beliefs. *Lifestyles, 8*(1):5-20.

Jenks, R. J. 1985b. Swinging: A test of two theories and a proposed new model. *Archives of Sexual Behavior, 14*:517-527.

Jennes, G. 1983 (February 20). Out of the pages. *People.*

Jerome, L. W., P. H. DeLeon, L. C. James, R. Folen, J. Earles, & J. J. Gedney. 2000. The coming of age of telecommunication in psychological research and practice. *American Psychologist, 55*(4):407-421.

Jesser, C. J. 1978. Male responses to direct verbal sexual initiatives of females. *Journal of Sex Research, 14*:118-128.

Jessor, S. L., R. Jessor. 1977. *Problem behavior and psychosocial development: A longitudinal study of youth.* New York: Academic Press.

Johnson, L. B. 1978. Sexual behavior of southern blacks. In: R. Staples, ed., *The black family: Essays and studies.* Belmont, CA: Wadsworth Press.

Johnson, L. B. 1986. Religion and sexuality: A comparison of black and white college students in three regions of the U.S. Unpublished manuscript.

Johnson, R. E. 1970. Some correlates of extramarital coitus. *Journal of Marriage and the Family, 32*:449-456.

Jones, E., J. Forrest, N. Goldman, S. Henshaw, R. Lincoln, J. Rossoff, C. Westoff, & D. Wulf. 1985. Teenage pregnancy in developed countries: Determinants and policy implications. *Family Planning Perspectives, 17*:53-63.

Jones, E. F., et al. 1986. *Teenage pregnancy in industrialized countries.* New Haven, CT: Yale University Press.

Jones, J., & C. L. Muehlenhard. 1990 (November). *Using education to prevent rape on college campuses.* Presented at the annual meeting of the Society for the Scientific Study of Sex, Minneapolis, MN.

Jones, J. M., & C. L. Muehlenhard. 1994 (August). *The consequences of men's use of verbal and physical sexual coercion on women.* Poster presented at the meeting of the American Psychological Association, Los Angeles.

*Joseph Smith's testimony.* Salt Lake City: Church of Jesus Christ of the Latter-Day Saints Publication.

Juran, S. 1995. The 90's: gender differences in AIDS-related sexual concerns and behaviors, condom use and subjective condom experience. *Journal of Psychology & Human Sexuality, 7*(3):39-59.

Kahn, A. S., & V. Andreoli Mathie. 2000. Understanding the unacknowledged rape victim. In: C. B. Travis & J. W. White, eds., *Sexuality, society, and feminism* (pp. 377-403). Washington, DC: American Psychological Association.

Kahn, J. R., & J. R. Udry. 1986. Marital coital frequency: Unnoticed outliers and unspecified interactions lead to erroneous conclusions. *American Sociological Review, 51*:734-737.

Kaiser Family Foundation. 2000. *Sex education in America: A view from inside the nation's classrooms.* Menlo Park, CA: Author.

Kalichman, S. C., E. G. Benotsch, L. S. Weinhardt, J. Austin, & W. Luke. 2002. Internet use among people living with HIV/AIDS: Association of health information, health behaviors, and health status. *AIDS Education and Prevention, 14*:51-61.

Kalichman, S. C., L. Weinhardt, E. Benotsch, K. DiFonzo, W. Luke, & J. Austin. 2002. Internet access and Internet use for health information among people living with HIV-AIDS. *Patient Education and Counseling, 46*:109-116.

Kallen, D., & J. Stephenson. 1982. Talking about sex revisited. *Journal of Youth and Adolescence, 11*:11-23.

Kammer, J. 1994. *Good will toward men.* New York: St. Martin's Press.

Kaplan, C. P., P. I. Erickson, S. L. Stewart, & L. A. Crane. 2001. Young Latinas and abortion: The role of cultural factors, reproductive behavior, and alternative roles to motherhood. *Health Care Women International, 22*(7):667-689.

Kaplan, D. A. 1993 (November 22). Take down the girlie calendars. *Newsweek*, p. 34.

Kaplan, H. S. 1979. *Disorders of sexual desire and other new concepts and techniques in sex therapy.* New York: Brunner/Mazel.

Kaplan, H. S. 1983. *The evaluation of sexual disorders: psychological and medical aspects.* New York: Brunner/Mazel.

Kaplan, H. S. 1974. *The new sex therapy: Active treatment of sexual dysfunctions.* New York: Brunner/Mazel.

Kaschak, E., & L. Tiefer, eds. 2001. *A new view of women's sexual problems.* New York: Haworth Press.

Kawata, M. 1995. Roles of steroid hormones and their receptors in structural organization in the nervous system. *Neuroscience Research, 24*:1-46.

Keller, S. H., H. Labelle, N. Karimi, & S. Gupta. 2002. STD/HIV prevention for teenagers: A look at the Internet universe. *Journal of Sex Education & Therapy, 22*:341-353.

Kelsey, D. H. 1993. *Between Athens and Berlin: The theological education debate.* Grand Rapids, MI: Eerdmans.

Kemper, R. H. 1977. *A history of costume.* New York: Newsweek Books.

Kenan, R. 1989. *A visitation of spirits.* New York: Vintage Books.

Kendall-Tackett, K., L. A. Williams, & D. Finkelhor. 1993. Impact of sexual abuse on children: A review and synthesis of recent empirical studies. *Psychological Bulletin, 113*:164-180.

Kenney, A., S. Guardado, & L. Brown. 1989. Sex education and AIDS education in the schools: What states and large school districts are doing. *Family Planning Perspectives, 21*:56-64.

Kilpatrick, A. C. 1986. Some correlates of women's childhood sexual experiences: A retrospective survey. *Journal of Sex Research, 22*:221-242.

Kilpatrick, A. C. 1987. Childhood sexual experiences: Problems and issues in studying long-range effects. *Journal of Sex Research, 23*:173-196.

Kilpatrick, D. G., C. L. Best, B. E. Saunders, & L. J. Veronen. 1987. Rape in marriage and in dating relationships: How bad is it for mental health? *Annals of the New York Academy of Sciences, 528*:335-344.

Kim, P. Y., & M. Bailey. 1997. Sidestreets on the information highway: Paraphilias and sexual variations on the Internet. *Journal of Sex Education & Therapy, 22*:35-43.

Kimbrell, A. 1995. *The masculine mystique.* New York: Ballantine Books.

Kimmel, M. 1996. *Manhood in America.* New York: Free Press.

King, J. L., & E. L. Harris. 2004 (Febuary, in press). *On the down low: A journey into the lives of "straight" black men who sleep with men.*

Kinsey, A. C., W. Pomeroy, & C. Martin. 1948. *Sexual behavior in the human male.* Philadelphia: Saunders.

Kinsey, A. C., W. Pomeroy, C. Martin, & P. Gebhard. 1953. *Sexual behavior in the human female.* Philadelphia: Saunders.

Kipnis, A. R. 1991. *Knights without armor.* Los Angeles: Tarcher.

Kipnis, K., & M. T. Diamond. 1998. Pediatric ethics and the surgical assignment of sex. *Journal of Clinical Ethics, 9*(4): 398-410.

Kirby, D. 1985. Sexuality education: A more realistic view of its effects. *Journal of School Health, 55*(10):421-424.

Kirby, D. 2001. *Emerging answers: Research findings on programs to reduce teen pregnancy.* Washington, DC: National Campaign to Prevent Teen Pregnancy. (Reprinted with permission).

Kirby, D., J. Atter, & P. Scales. 1979. *An analysis of U.S. sex education programs and evaluation methods: Executive summary.* Atlanta, GA: U.S. Department of Health, Education, and Welfare.

Kirkendall, L. A., & I. G. McBride. 1990. Preadolescent and adolescent imagery and sexual fantasies: Beliefs and experiences. In: M. Perry, ed., *Handbook of sexology: Volume 7: Childhood and adolescent sexology.* New York: Elsevier.

Klein, F. 1978. *The bisexual option: A concept of one hundred percent intimacy.* New York: Arbor House.

Klein, F., B. Sepekoff, & T. J. Wolf. 1985. Sexual orientation: A multi-variable dynamic process. *Journal of Homosexuality, 11*(1/2):35-50.

Klein, M. 1994. Response to the FBI–The rest of the 'child porn' story. *AASECT Newsletter.*

Kleinplatz, P. J., ed. 2001. *New directions in sex therapy: Innovations and alternatives.* Philadelphia: Brunner Routledge.

Knapp, J. J. 1975. Some non-monogamous marriage styles and related attitudes and practices of marriage counselors. *Family Coordinator, 24*:505-514.

Knapp, J. J. 1974. *Co-marital sex and marriage counseling: Sexually open marriages and related attitudes and practices of marriage counselors.* Doctoral Dissertation, University of Florida.

Knapp, J. J., & R. N. Whitehurst. 1975. Sexually open marriage and relationships: Issues and prospects. In: R. Libby & R. N. Whitehurst, ed., 1977, *Marriage and alternatives.* New York: Scott, Foresman and Co.

Koch, P. B. 1988. The relationship of first sexual intercourse to later sexual functioning concerns of adolescents. *Journal of Adolescent Research, 3*:345-352.

Koch, P. B. 1995. *Exploring our sexuality: An interactive text.* Dubuque, IA: Kendall/Hunt.

Koch, P. B. 1997. *The international encyclopedia of sexuality.* Plenary presented at the Annual Conference of the Midcontinent Region of the Society for the Scientific Study of Sexuality, Chicago, IL.

Konig, R. 1973. *A la mode: On the social psychology of fashion.* New York: Seabury Press.

Kontula, O., & E. Haavio-Mannila. 2002. Masturbation in a generational perspective. *Journal of Psychology & Human Sexuality, 14*(2/3):49-84.

Kosnick, A., W. Carroll, A. Cunningham, R. Modras, & J. Schulte. 1977. *Human sexuality: New directions in American Catholic thought.* New York: Paulist Press.

Koss, M. P. 1992. The underdetection of rape: Methodological choices influence incidence estimates. *Journal of Social Issues, 48*(1):61-75.

Koss, M. P. 1993a. Detecting the scope of rape: A review of prevalence research methods. *Journal of Interpersonal Violence, 8*:198-222.

Koss, M. P. 1993b. Rape: Scope, impact, interventions, and public policy responses. *American Psychologist, 48*:1062-1069.

Koss, M. P., & T. E. Dinero. 1988. Predictors of sexual aggression among a national sample of male college students. In: R. A. Prentky & V. L. Quinsey, eds., *Human sexual aggression: Current perspectives* (pp. 133-147). New York: New York Academy of Sciences.

Koss, M. P., T. E. Dinero, C. A. Seibel, & S. L. Cox. 1988. Stranger and acquaintance rape: Are there differences in the victim's experience? *Psychology of Women Quarterly, 12*: 1-24.

Koss, M. P., C. A. Gidycz, & N. Wisniewski. 1987. The scope of rape: Incidence and prevalence of sexual aggression and victimization in a national sample of higher education students. *Journal of Consulting and Clinical Psychology, 55*: 162-170.

Kraditor, A. 1965. *The ideas of the women's suffrage movement.* New York: Columbia University Press.

Kraig, D. 1999. *Sex magick: Sacred erotic spirituality.* St. Paul, MN: Llewellyn Publ.

Kramer, L. 1994. *Faggots.* New York: Penguin.

Krivacska, J. J. 1990. Child sexual abuse and its prevention. In: M. Perry, ed., *Handbook of sexology: Volume 7: Childhood and adolescent sexology.* New York: Elsevier.

Kronhausen, P., & Kronhausen, E., eds. 1970a. *Erotic art.* New York: Grove Press.

Kronhausen, P., & Kronhausen, E., eds. 1970b. *Erotic art 2.* New York: Grove Press.

Kruijver, F. P. M., J.-N. Zhou, C. W. Pool, et al. 2000. Male to female transsexuals have female neuron numbers in a limbic nucleus. *Journal of Clinical Endocrinology & Metabolism, 85*(5):2034-2041.

Kuiper, A. J., & P. Cohen-Kettenis. 1988. Sex reassignment surgery: A study of 141 Dutch transsexuals. *Archives of Sexual Behavior, 17*:439-457.

Kushner, T. 1993. *Angels in America: A gay fantasia on national themes.* New York: Theatre Communications Group.

Kutsche, P. 1983. Household and family in Hispanic northern New Mexico. *Journal of Comparative Family Studies, 14*(2): 151-165.

Kybalova, L., O. Herbenova, & M. Lamarova. 1968. *The pictorial encyclopedia of fashion.* New York: Crown Publishing.

Laemmel, K. 1976. Sex and the arts. In: B. J. Sadock, H. I. Kaplan, & A. M. Freedman, eds., *The sexual experience.* Boston: Williams & Wilkins.

LaFramboise, D. 1996. *The princess at the window.* New York: Penguin Books.

LaFree, G. D. 1982. Male power and female victimization: Toward a theory of interracial rape. *American Journal of Sociology, 88*:311-328.

LaFree, G. D., B. F. Reskin, & C. A. Visher. 1985. Jurors' responses to victims' behavior and legal issues in sexual assault trials. *Social Problems, 32*:389-407.

Landen, M. 1999 (in press). *Transsexualism, epidemiology, phenomenology, aetiology, regret after surgery, and public attitudes.* Sweden: Institute of Clinical Neuroscience, Goteborg University.

Landry, D. J., L. Kaeser, & C. L. Richards. 1999. Abstinence promotion and the provision of information about contraception in public school district sexuality education polices. *Family Planning Perspectives, 31*(6):280-286.

Lane, F. S. 2000. *Obscene profits: The entrepreneurs of pornography in the cyber age.* New York: Routledge.

Langfeldt, T. 1979. Processes in sexual development. In: M. Cook & G. Wilson, eds., *Love and attraction.* Oxford: Pergamon Press.

Larson, D. L., E. A. Spreitzer, & E. E. Snyder. 1976. Social factors in the frequency of romantic involvement among adolescents. *Adolescences, II:7-12.*

Larson, J. 1997. *Rent.* New York: Rob Weisbach Books.

Laumann, E. O., J. H. Gagnon, R. T. Michael, & S. Michaels. 1994. *The social organization of sexuality: Sexual practices in the United States.* Chicago: University of Chicago Press.

Laumann, E. O., A. Paik, & R. C. Rosen. 1999. Sexual dysfunction in the United States: Prevalence and predictors. *Journal of the American Medical Association, 281*:537-544.

Laurence, J. 1994 (March/April). Long-term survival versus nonprogression. *The AIDS Reader, 4*(2):39-40, 71.

Laver, J. 1960. *Viyella*. Nottingham, England: William Hollins.

Lawrence, A. 2003. Factors associated with satisfaction or regret following male-to-female sex reassignment surgery. *Archives of Sexual Behavior, 32*:299-315.

Lawrence, D. H. 1936/1953. Making love to music. In: D. H. Lawrence, *Sex, literature and censorship* (H. T. Moore, ed., pp. 40-46). New York: Twayne Publishers.

Lawrence, K., & E. S. Herold. 1988. Women's attitudes toward and experience with sexually explicit materials. *Journal of Sex Research, 24*:161-169.

Lawrence, R. J. 1989. *The poisoning of Eros: Sexual values in conflict.* New York: Augustine Moore Press.

Leaper-Campbell, V. D. 1996. Predictors of Mexican American mothers' and fathers' attitudes toward gender equality. Hispanic. *Journal of Behavioral Sciences, 18*:343-355.

Leavitt, D. 1997. The term paper artist. In: D. Leavitt, *Arkansas: Three novellas*. Boston: Houghton Mifflin.

Lebacqz, K. 1997. Difference or defect? Intersexuality and the politics of difference. *The Annual. Society of Christian Ethics, 17*:213-229.

Lee, L., & P. Fleming. 2001. Trends in HIV diagnoses among women in the United States, 1994-1998. *Journal of the American Medical Association, 56*(3):9499.

Lefley, H. P., C. S. Scott, M. Llabre, & D. Hicks. 1993. Cultural beliefs about rape and victims' response in three ethnic groups. *American Journal of Orthopsychiatry, 63*(4):623-632.

LeGates, M. 1995. Feminists before feminism: Origins and varieties of women's protests in Europe and North America before the twentieth century. In: J. Freeman, ed., *Women: A feminist perspective*. Mountain View, CA: Mayfield.

Legman, G. 1964. *The horn book: Studies in erotic folklore and bibliography*. New Hyde Park, NY: University Books.

LeHaye, T., & B. LeHaye. 1976. *The act of marriage: The beauty of sexual love*. Grand Rapids, MI: Zondervan.

Lehne, G., & J. Money. 2000. The first case of paraphilia treated with Depo-Provera: Forty-year outcome. *Journal of Sex Education and Therapy, 25*:213-220.

Lehne, G., & J. Money. 2003. Multiplex versus multiple taxonomy of paraphilia: Case example. *Sexual Abuse: A Journal of Research and Treatment, 15*:61-72.

Leiblum, S. R., & L. A. Pervin, eds. 1980. *Principles and practice of sex therapy*. New York: Guilford Press.

Leiblum, S. R., & R. C. Rosen, eds. 1988. *Sexual desire disorders*. New York: Guilford Press.

Leland, J. 1998/1999 (December 28/January 4). Let's talk about sex. *Newsweek, 132/133*:62.

LeVay, S. 1991. A difference in hypothalamic structure between heterosexual and homosexual men. *Science, 253*: 1034-1037.

Levin, J. 1994. *The sea of light*. New York: Plume.

Levin, M. 1988. *Feminism & freedom*. New Brunswick, NJ: Transaction.

Levin, R. J. 1975 (October). The Redbook report on premarital and extramarital sex. *Redbook*, 38-44; 190-192.

Levine, D. 2000. Virtual attraction: What rocks your boat. *CyberPsychology & Behavior, 3*(4):565-573.

Levinson, D. R., M. L. Johnson, & D. M. Devaney. 1988. *Sexual harassment in the federal government: An update*. Washington, DC: U.S. Merit Systems Protection Board.

Levy, S. 1997 (March 31). U.S. v. the Internet. *Newsweek*, 77-79.

Lewin, T. 2003 (May 20). 1 in 5 teenagers has sex before 15, study finds. *The New York Times*, A18.

Lewis, P. H. 1995 (March 26). Cybersex stays hot, despite a plan for cooling it off. *The New York Times News Service* (on-line).

Lewis, R. J., & L. H. Janda. 1988. The relationship between adult sexual adjustment and childhood experiences regarding exposure to nudity, sleeping in the parental bed, and parental attitudes toward sexuality. *Archives of Sexual Behavior, 17*:349-362.

Lewis, W. C. 1965. Coital movements in the first year of life. *International Journal of Psychoanalysis, 46*:372-374.

Libby, R. W., & R. N. Whitehurst, eds. 1977. *Marriage and alternatives: Exploring intimate relationships*. Glenview, IL: Scott-Foresman.

Lieblum, S., & N. Doring. 2002. Internet sexuality: Known risks and fresh chances for women. In: A. Cooper, ed., *Sex and the Internet: A guidebook for clinicians*. New York: Brunner-Routledge.

Lief, H. I. 1963. What medical schools teach about sex. *Bulletin of the Tulane University Medical Faculty, 22*:161-168.

Lief, H. I. 1965. Sex education of medical students and doctors. *Pacific Medical Surgery, 73*:52-58.

Lifshitz, A. 1990. Critical cultural barriers that bar meeting the needs of Latinas. *SIECUS Report, 18*(3):16-17.

Lily, T. 1977 (March). Sexual surrogate: Notes of a therapist. *SIECUS Report*, 12-13.

Lobitz, W. C., & J. LoPiccolo. New methods in the behavioral treatment of sexual dysfunction. *Journal of Behavior Therapy and Experimental Psychiatry, 3*(4):265-271.

Lohr, S. 1996 (June 13). A complex medium that will be hard to regulate. *The New York Times*.

Longo, R., S. Brown, & D. Orcutt. 2002. Effects of Internet sexuality on children and adolescents. In: A. Cooper, ed., *Sex and the Internet: A guidebook for clinicians*. New York: Brunner-Routledge.

LoPiccolo, J., & W. C. Lobitz. 1973. Behavior therapy of sexual dysfunction. In: L. A. Hammerlynck, L. C. Handy, & E. J. Mash, eds., *Behavior change: Methodology, concepts and practice*. Champaign, IL: Research Press.

LoPiccolo, J., & L. LoPiccolo, eds. 1978. *Handbook of sex therapy*. New York: Plenum Press.

Lorch, D. 1996 (February 1). Quinceañera: A girl grows up. *The New York Times*, C1, C4.

Lorde, A. 1982. *Zami: A new spelling of my name*. Trumansburg, NY: Crossing Press.

Lorde. A. 1984. *Sister outsider: Essays and speeches*. Trumansburg, NY: Crossing Press.

Loulan, J. 1984. *Lesbian sex*. San Francisco: Spinsters/Aunt Lute.

Love, B. 1992. *The encyclopedia of unusual sex practices*. New York: Barricade Books.

Love, B. 1994. Interviews and surveys of 200 adult book store customers and analysis of same, 1994. In: *A longitudinal study of sexuality*. San Francisco: The Institute for the Advanced Study of Sexuality.

Love, S. 1997. *Dr. Susan Love's hormone book*. New York: Random House.

Ludlow, D. H., ed. 1992. *The encyclopedia of Mormonism*. New York: McMillan Publishing Co.

Luker, K. 1996. *Dubious conceptions: The politics of teenage pregnancy*. Cambridge, MA: Harvard University Press.

Lunin, I., J. Karizanskaya, L. Melikhova, L. Light, & P. Brandt-Sorheim. 1997. Use the Internet for sex education in Russia. *Journal of Sex Education and Therapy, 22*:74-78.

Lyman, S. M. 1978. *The seven deadly sins: Society and evil*. New York: St. Martin's Press.

Lynch, F. R. 1997. *The diversity machine*. New York: Free Press.

Lyndon, N. 1992. *No more sex war: The failures of feminism*. London: Sinclair-Stevenson.

Lyons, R. D. 1983 (October 4). Sex in America: Conservative attitudes prevail. *The New York Times*.

Lystad, M. H. 1982. Sexual abuse in the home: A review of the literature. *International Journal of Family Psychiatry, 3*:3-31.

Maccoby, E. E., & J. A. Martin. 1983. Socialization in the context of the family: Parent-child interaction. In: P. H. Mussen, ed., *Handbook of child psychology: Volume 4* (4th ed., pp. 1-101). New York: J. Wiley.

MacDonald, J. M. 1971. *Rape offenders and their victims.* Springfield, IL: Thomas.

MacDougald, Jr., D. 1973. Music and sex. In: A. Ellis & A. Abarbanel, eds., *The encyclopedia of sexual behavior* (pp. 746-756). New York: Jason Aronson.

Mack, P. 1987. Political rhetoric and poetic meaning in Renaissance culture: Clement Marot and the field of the cloth of gold. In: P. Mack & M. C. Jacobs, eds., *Politics and culture in early modern Europe* (p. 59). Cambridge: Cambridge University Press.

MacKinnon, C. 1982. Marxism, method, and the state: An agenda for theory. *Signs, 7*:515-544.

MacKinnon, C. A. 1987. *Feminism unmodified: Discourses on life and law.* Cambridge, MA: Harvard University Press.

MacKinnon, C. A. 1990. Liberalism and the death of feminism. In: D. Leidholdt & J. G. Raymond, eds., *The sexual liberals and the attack on feminism* (pp. 3-13). New York: Pergamon.

Macklin, E. D. 1980. Nontraditional family forms: A decade of research. *Journal of Marriage and the Family, 42*:905-920

Macklin, E. D., ed. 1989. *AIDS and families: Report of the AIDS Task Force. Groves Conference on Marriage and the Family.* Binghamton, NY: Harrington Park Press.

Magaña, A., & N. M. Clark. 1995. Examining a paradox: Does religiosity contribute to positive birth outcomes in Mexican American populations? *Health Education Quarterly, 22*(1): 96-109.

Maines, R. P. 1998. *The technology of orgasm: "Hysteria," the vibrator, and women's sexual satisfaction.* Baltimore: Johns Hopkins University Press.

Malamuth, N. M. 1986. Predictors of naturalistic sexual aggression. *Journal of Personality and Social Psychology, 50*: 953-962.

Malamuth, N. M., R. J. Sockloskie, M. P. Koss, & J. S. Tanaka. 1991. Characteristics of aggressors against women: Testing a model using a national sample of college students. *Journal of Consulting and Clinical Psychology, 59*:670-681.

Malin, M. H. 1987 (June 14-20). *A preliminary report of a case of necrophilia.* Paper presented at the Eighth World Congress for Sexology, Heidelberg.

Malthus, T. (1798). An essay on the principle of population. Available: http://www.faculty.rsu.edu/~felwell/Theorists/Malthus/essay2.htm.

Maltz, D. N., & R. A. Borker. 1983. A cultural approach to male-female miscommunication. In: J. J. Gumperz, ed., *Language and social identity* (pp. 195-216). New York: Cambridge University Press.

Mann, W. C. 2003 (June 30). Senate leader supports idea of banning gay marriages. *Sentinel-Tribune* (Associated Press), 6.

Mansfield, P. K., & P. B. Koch. 1997. Enhancing your sexual response. *Menopause Management, 6*(2):25.

Mansfield, P. K., A. M. Voda, & P. B. Koch. 1995. Predictors of sexual response changes in heterosexual midlife women. *Health Values, 19*(1):10-20.

Marciano, T. D. 1987. Families and religion. In: M. B. Sussman & S. K. Steinmetz, eds., *Handbook of marriage and the family* (pp. 285-316). New York: Plenum Press.

Marcus, I. M., & J. F. Francis, eds. 1975. *Masturbation from infancy to senescence.* New York: International Universities Press.

Marín, B. V., C. A. Gomez, & N. Hearst. 1993. Multiple heterosexual partners and condom use among Hispanics and non-Hispanic whites. *Family Planning Perspectives, 25*:170-174.

Marín, B. V., G. Marín, & R. Juárez. 1990. Differences between Hispanics and non-Hispanics in willingness to provide AIDS prevention advice. *Hispanic Journal of Behavioral Sciences, 12*(2):153-164.

Marin, R., & S. Miller. 1997 (April 14). Ellen steps out. *Newsweek*, 65-67.

Marquis, C. 2003 (March 13). Total of unmarried couples surged in 2000 U.S. Census. *The New York Times*, A22.

Marsh, M., & W. Ronner. 1996. *The empty cradle: Infertility in America from colonial times to the present.* Baltimore: Johns Hopkins University Press.

Martinac, P. 1993. *Home movies.* Seattle, WA: Seal Press.

Martinson, F. M. 1973. *Infant and child sexuality: A Sociological Perspective.* St. Peter, MN: The Book Mark.

Martinson, F. M. 1976. Eroticism in infancy and childhood. *Journal of Sex Research, 12*:251-262.

Martinson, F. M. 1990. Current legal status of the erotic and sexual rights of children. In: M. Perry, ed., *Handbook of sexology: Volume 7: Childhood and adolescent sexology.* New York: Elsevier.

Martinson, F. M. 1995. *The sexual life of children.* Westport, CT: Greenwood Press.

Marty, M. E., & R. S. Appleby, eds. 1992. *Fundamentalisms observed, Volume 1.* Chicago: University of Chicago Press.

Marty, M. E., & R. S. Appleby, eds. 1993. *Fundamentalism and society, Volume 2.* Chicago: University of Chicago Press.

Marty, M. E., & R. S. Appleby, eds. 1993. *Fundamentalism and the state, Volume 3.* Chicago: University of Chicago Press.

Marty, M. E., & R. S. Appleby, eds. 1994. *Accounting for fundamentalism, Volume 4.* Chicago: University of Chicago Press.

Masters, W. H., & V. E. Johnson. 1966. *Human sexual response.* Boston: MA: Little Brown.

Masters, W. H., & V. E. Johnson. 1970. *Human sexual inadequacy.* Boston, MA: Little Brown.

Maupin, A. 1996. *Tales of the city.* New York: HarperCollins.

May, E. T. 1988. *Homeward bound: American families in the Cold War era* (pp. 62-63). New York: Basic Books.

Mayo Clinic. 2000 (July 24). *Discussing "birds and bees."* Retrieved July 24, 2000. www.mayohealth.org/mayo/990/htm.kids.htm.

Mays, V. M., & S. D. Cochran. 1988. Issues in the perception of AIDS risk and risk reduction by black and Hispanic/Latino women. *American Psychologist, 43*(11):949-957.

Mays, V. M., & S. D. Cochran. 1990. Methodological issues in the assessment and prediction of AIDS risk-related sexual behaviors among black Americans. In: B. Voeller, J. M. Reinisch, & G. M. Gottlieb, eds., *AIDS and sex: An integrated biomedical and biobehavioral approach.* New York: Oxford University Press.

Mazur, R. 1973/2002. *The new intimacy: Open ended marriage and alternative lifestyles.* Boston: Beacon Press; Lincoln NE: iUniverse.

McCabe, K. 2000. Child pornography and the Internet. *Social Science Computer Review, 18*:73-76.

McCann, J., & M. K. Biaggio. 1989. Sexual satisfaction in marriage as a function of life meaning. *Archives of Sexual Behavior, 18*:59-72.

McCann-Winter, E. J. S. 1983. *Clergy education about homosexuality: An outcomes analysis of knowledge, attitudes, and counseling behaviors.* Unpublished doctoral dissertation, University of Pennsylvania, Philadelphia.

McCleary, K. 1992 (May). The chastity revolution. *Reader's Digest*, 69-71.

McCormick, N. B. 1994a. Feminism and sexology. In: V. L. Bullough & B. Bullough, eds., *Human sexuality: An encyclopedia* (pp. 208-212). New York: Garland Publishing, Inc.

McCormick, N. B. 1994b. *Sexual salvation: Affirming women's sexual rights and pleasures.* Westport, CT: Praeger.

McCullagh, D. 1996 (August 20). CDA update. *The Netizen* (On-line).

McDonough, S. 2003 (January 2). U.S. awards marriage grants to 12 states. Associated Press Online. Available: http://www.washingtonpost.com/wp-dyn/articles/A3802-2003Jan2.html; Health and Human Services Department: http://www.hhs.gov.

McFarlane, M., S. S. Bull, & C. A. Rietmeijer. 2002. Young adults on the Internet: Risk behaviors for sexually transmitted diseases and HIV. *Journal of Adolescent Health, 31*:11-16.

McGarth, M. G., & E. Casey. 2002. Forensic psychiatry and the Internet: Practical perspectives on sexual predators and obsessional harassers in cyberspace. *Journal of the American Academy of Psychiatry and the Law, 30*:81-94.

McGoldrick, M., J. K. Pearce, & J. Giordano, eds. 1982. *Ethnicity and family therapy*. New York: Guilford Press.

McIlvenna, T. 1995 (July 3). Telephone interview with Brenda Love, Palo Alto, California.

McKenna, K. Y. A. 2001. Demarginalizing the sexual shelf. *Journal of Sex Research, 3*:302-312.

McLuhan, M. (1964). Understanding media: The extensions of man. New York: McGraw-Hill.

McNeil, J. 1976. *The Church and the homosexual*. Kansas City, Missouri: Sheed Andrews and McMeel.

McWhirter, D., & A. Mattison. 1984. *The male couple: How relationships develop*. Englewood Cliffs, NJ: Prentice-Hall.

Medina, C. 1987. Latino culture and sex education. *SIECUS Report, 15*(3):1-4.

Medora, N., & M. Burton. 1981. Extramarital sexual attitudes and norms of an undergraduate student population. *Adolescence, 16*:251-262.

Mehta, M. D. 2001. Pornography in Usenet: A study of 9800 randomly selected images. *CyberPsychology & Behavior, 4*(6):695-703.

Michael, R. T., J. H. Gagnon, E. O. Laumann, & G. Kolata. 1994. *Sex in America: A definitive survey*. Boston: Little, Brown.

Michaldimitrakis, M. 1986. Accidental death during intercourse by males. *American Journal of Forensic Medicine and Pathology, 7*:74.

Mikawa, J. K., et al. Cultural practices of Hispanics: Implications for the prevention of AIDS. *Hispanic Journal of Behavioral Sciences, 14*(4):421-433.

Miller, B. C., J. K. McCoy, T. D. Olson, & C. M. Wallace. 1986. Parental discipline and control attempts in relation to adolescent sexual attitudes and behavior. *Journal of Marriage and the Family, 48*:503-512.

Miller, B. C., & K. A. Moore. 1990. Adolescent sexual behavior, pregnancy, and parenting: Research through the 1980s. *Journal of Marriage and the Family, 52*:1025-1044.

Miller, J. E., P. Guarnaccia, & A. Fasina. 2002. AIDS knowledge among Latinos: The roles of language, culture, and socioeconomic status. *Journal of Immigrant Health, 4*(2):63-72.

Miller, L., D. France, L. Clemerson, S. Smalley, M. Carmichael, & J. Scelfo. 2002 (March 4). Sins of the fathers. *Newsweek,* 139.

Miller, M. 1998 (December 21). The final days and nights of a gay martyr. *Newsweek,* 132.

Miller, P. Y., & W. Simon. 1981. The development of sexuality in adolescence. In: J. Adelson, ed., *Handbook of adolescent psychology* (pp. 383-407). New York: J. Wiley.

Millner, V. S., & J. D. Kiser. 2002. Sexual information and Internet resources. *Family Journal: Counseling & Therapy for Couples & Families, 10*:234- 239.

Mio, J. S., & J. D. Foster. 1991. The effects of rape upon victims and families: Implications for a comprehensive family therapy. *American Journal of Family Therapy, 19*:147-159.

Mississippi State University Libraries. 2003. *Politically correct fashion*. Available: http://library.msstate.edu/exhibits/fashion/Polcor.asp.

Mitchell, K. J., D. Finkelhor, & J. Wolak. 2001. Risk factors for and impact of online sexual solicitation of youth. *Journal of the American Medical Association, 285*:3011-3014.

Monette, P. 1988. *Borrowed time: An AIDS memoir*. San Diego, CA: Harcourt Brace Jovanovich.

Money, J. 1976. Childhood: The last frontier in sex research. *The Sciences, 16*:12-27.

Money, J. 1985. *The destroying angel*. Buffalo, NY: Prometheus Press.

Money, J. 1986. *Lovemaps: Clinical concepts of sexual/erotic health and pathology, paraphilia, and gender transposition in childhood, adolescence, and maturity*. New York: Irvington.

Money, J. 1986/1994. *Lovemaps: Sexual/erotic health and pathology, paraphilia, and gender transposition in childhood, adolescence, and maturity* Buffalo, NY: Prometheus.

Money, J. 1988/1990. *Gay, straight, and in-between: The sexology of erotic orientation*. New York: Oxford University Press.

Money, J. 1989. Paleodigms and paleodigmatics: A new theoretical construct applicable to Munchausen's syndrome by proxy, child-abuse dwarfism, paraphilias, anorexia nervosa, and other syndromes. *American Journal of Psychotherapy, 43*:15-24.

Money, J. 1995. *Gendermaps: Social constructionism, feminism, and sexosophical history*. New York: Continuum.

Money, J. 1997. *Principles of developmental sexology*. New York: Continuum.

Money, J. 1998. *Sin, science, and the sex police: Essays on sexology and sexosophy*. Amherst, NY: Prometheus Books.

Money, J. 1999. *The lovemap guidebook: A definitive statement*. New York: Continuum.

Money, J. 2003 (In press). Human sexuality: Romantic and concupiscent. *Journal of Psychology and Human Sexuality, 15*.

Money, J., J. E. Cawte, G. N. Bianchi, & B. Nurcombe. 1970. Sex training and traditions in Arnhem Land. *British Journal of Medical Psychology, 43*:383-399.

Money, J., & A. A. Ehrhardt. 1972. *Man & woman, boy & girl*. Baltimore: Johns Hopkins University Press.

Money, J., & R. W. Keyes. 1993. *The armed robbery orgasm*. Amhearst, NY: Prometheus Books.

Money, J., & M. Lamacz. 1989. *Vandalized lovemaps: Paraphilic outcome of seven cases in pediatric sexology*. Buffalo, NY: Prometheus Press.

Money, J., G. Wainwright, & D. Hingsburger. 1991. *The breathless orgasm: A lovemap biography of asphyxiophilia*. Buffalo, NY: Prometheus Books.

Moore, K., A. Papillo, S. Williams, J. Jager, & F. Jones. 2001. *Facts at a glance*. Washington, DC: Child Trends Inc.

Moore, M. M. 1985. Nonverbal courtship patterns in women: Context and consequences. *Ethology and Sociobiology, 6*: 201-212.

Moore, M. M., & D. L. Butler. 1989. Predictive aspects of nonverbal courtship behavior in women. *Semiotica, 76*:205-215.

Moran, J. R., & M. D. Corley. 1991. Source of sexual information and sexual attitudes and behaviors of Anglo and Hispanic adolescent males. *Adolescence, 26*(104):857-864.

Morgan, R. 1982. *The anatomy of freedom: Feminism, physics, and global politics*. Garden City, NY: Anchor Press/Doubleday.

Morgan, R. 1984. *Sisterhood is global*. Garden City, NY: Anchor Press.

Morganthau, T. 1997 (June 30). Baptists vs. Mickey. *Newsweek,* 51.

Moser, C. 1988. *Sadomasochism: The sexually unusual guide to understanding and helping*. New York: Harrington Park Press.

Moses, A., & R. Hawkins, Jr. 1982/1986. *Counseling lesbian women and gay men: A life-issues approach*. Englewood Cliffs, NJ: Paramount Publishing.

Mosher, C. D. 1980. *The Mosher survey: Sexual attitudes of forty-five Victorian women* (J. Mahood & K. Wenburg, eds.). New York: Arno Press.

Mosher, D. L. 1994. Pornography. In: V. L. Bullough & B. Bullough, eds., *Human sexuality: An encyclopedia*. New York: Garland Publishing.

Mosher, D. L., & M. Sirkin. 1984. Measuring a macho personality constellation. *Journal of Research in Personality, 18*: 150-163.

Moss, M. 2003 (March 26). General's crackdown faulted in rapes. *The New York Times,* A10.

Moss, T. 2003 (January). Adolescent pregnancy and childbearing in the United States. *Advocates for Youth fact sheet*.

Muehlenhard, C. L. 1998. The importance and danger of studying sexually aggressive women. In: P. B. Anderson & C. Struckman-Johnson, eds., *Sexually aggressive women: Current perspectives and controversies* (pp. 19-48). New York: Guilford.

Muehlenhard, C. L., & S. W. Cook. 1988. Men's self-reports of unwanted sexual activity. *Journal of Sex Research*, 24:58-72.

Muehlenhard, C. L., S. Danoff-Burg, & I. G. Powch. 1996. Is rape sex or violence? Conceptual issues and implications. In: D. M. Buss & N. Malamuth, eds., *Sex, power, conflict: Evolutionary and feminist perspectives*. New York: Oxford University Press.

Muehlenhard, C. L., M. F. Goggins, J. M. Jones, & A. T. Satterfield. 1991. Sexual violence and coercion in close relationships. In: K. McKinney & S. Sprecher, eds., *Sexuality in close relationships*. Hillsdale, NJ: Lawrence Erlbaum Associates.

Muehlenhard, C. L., P. A. Harney, & J. M. Jones. 1992. From victim-precipitated rape to date rape: How far have we come? *Annual Review of Sex Research*, 3:219-253.

Muehlenhard, C. L., B. J. Highby, R. S. Lee, T. S. Bryan, & W. A. Dodrill. 1998. The sexual revictimization of women and men sexually abused as children: A review of the literature. *Annual Review of Sex Research*, 9:1-47.

Muehlenhard, C. L., I. G. Powch, J. L. Phelps, & L. M. Giusti. 1992. Definitions of rape: Scientific and political implications. *Journal of Social Issues*, 48(1):23-44.

Munson, M., & J. P. Stelboum, eds. 1999. *The lesbian polyamory reader: Open relationships, non-monogamy, and casual sex*. New York: Haworth Press.

Murdock, G. P. 1949. *Social structure*. New York: Macmillan.

Murnen, S. K., C. Wright, & G. Kaluzny. 2002. If "boys will be boys," then girls will be victims? A meta-analytic review of the research that relates masculine ideology to sexual aggression. *Sex Roles*, 46:359-375.

Murphy, G. J., W. W. Hudson, & P. L. Cheung. 1980. Marital and sexual discord among older couples. *Social Work Research and Abstracts*, 16:11-16.

Murry, V. M. 1995. An Ecological analysis of pregnancy resolution decisions among African American and Hispanic adolescent females. *Youth and Society*, 26(3):325-360.

Murstein, B. I. 1974. *Love, sex, and marriage through the ages*. New York: Springer.

Mussen, P. H., ed. 1983. *Handbook of child psychology: Volume 1, History, theory, and methods* (4th ed.). New York: J. Wiley.

Mustanski, B. S. 2001. Getting wired: Exploiting the Internet for the collection of valid sexuality data. *Journal of Sex Research*, 38:292-302.

NARAL. 1995. *Sexuality education in America: A state-by-state review*. Washington, DC: NARAL and the NARAL Foundation.

National Abortion Rights Action League (NARAL) 1998. *A state-by-state review of abortion and reproductive rights: Who decides?* Washington, D.C.: NARAL.

National Center for Health Statistics. 2002. *Health, United States, 2002*. Available: www.cdc.gov/nchs/hus.htm.

National Council of la Raza. 1992 (February). *State of Hispanic America 1991: An overview*. Washington, DC: National Council of la Raza.

National Council of la Raza. 1993. *State of Hispanic America: Toward a Latino anti-poverty agenda*. Washington, DC: National Council of la Raza.

National Institutes of Health Consensus Development Conference Statement. 1992 (December 7-9). Impotence. NIH consensus statement (No. 91), *Impotence*, 10(4):1-31.

National Opinion Research Center (NORC). *General Social Surveys, 1998-2002*. Available: www.icpsr.umich.edu/gss.

National Research Council. Panel on Monitoring the Social Impact of the AIDS Epidemic. 1993. *The social impact of AIDS in the United States*. Washington, DC: National Academy Press.

Neale, T. H. 1989. *Hispanic heritage in the U.S.: Tradition, achievement, and aspiration. CRS report for Congress 89-532 Gov. Congressional Research Service*. Washington, DC: The Library of Congress.

Nelson, J. B. 1978. *Embodiment*. Minneapolis: Augsburg Publishing House.

Nelson, J. B. 1983. *Between two gardens: Reflections on sexuality and religious experience*. New York: Pilgrim Press.

Nelson, J. A. 1986. Incest: Self-report findings from a nonclinical sample. *Journal of Sex Research*, 22:463-477.

Nelson, J. B. 1992. *Body theology*. Louisville, Kentucky: Westminster/John Knox.

Nelson, J. B., & S. P. Longfellow, eds. 1994. *Sexuality and the sacred: Sources for theological reflection*. Louisville, KY: Westminster/John Knox Press.

Nelson, K. L. 1996 (August/September). The conflict over sexuality education: Interviews with participants on both sides of the debate. *SIECUS Report*, 12-16.

*NetGuide*. 1995 (April). Millions hooked on the Net, p. 139.

Nettl, B. 1973. *Folk and traditional music of the Western continents* (2nd ed.). Englewood Cliffs, NJ: Prentice-Hall.

Newcomer, S. F., & J. R. Udry. 1985. Oral sex in an adolescent population. *Archives of Sexual Behavior*, 14:41-46.

Newman, B. 1997. The use of online services to encourage exploration of ego-dystonic sexual interests. *Journal of Sex Education and Therapy*, 22:45-48.

Newman, B. S., & P. G. Muzzonigro. 1993. The effects of traditional family values on the coming out process of gay male adolescents. *Adolescence*, 28(109):213-226.

Newman, L. 1989. *Heather has two mommies*. Northampton, MA: In Other Words Publishers.

Newman, L. 1991. *Gloria goes to gay pride*. Boston: Alyson Publications.

*Newsweek*. 1996 (December 2). The end of AIDS, 64-73.

*Newsweek*. 1997 (June 30). Nude fight. 8.

*The New York Times*. 1996 (June 13). Panel of three judges turns back federal law intended to regulate decency on Internet.

*Newsweek*. 1993 (August 2). A cheeky protest, 6.

*Newsweek*. 1993 (August 2). Aspin on gays in the military, 4.

*Newsweek*. 1994 (March 14). Was it real or memories? 54-55.

Nichols, M. 1989. Sex therapy with lesbians, gay men, and bisexuals. In: S. R. Leiblum & R. C. Rosen, eds., *Principles and practice of sex therapy* (2nd ed.). New York: Guilford.

*Nielson Netratings*. Retrieved February 8, 2003. http://www.nielsen-netratings.com/hot_off_the_net.jsp.

Nikolais, A. 1973. Dance, sexual dynamics in contemporary. In: A. Ellis & A. Abarbanel, eds., *The encyclopedia of sexual behavior* (pp. 746-756). New York: Jason Aronson.

Nobile, P., & E. Nadler. 1986. *United States of America vs. sex*. New York: Minotaur Press.

Noonan, R. J. 1995/1984. *Sex surrogates: A clarification of their functions* (Master's thesis, New York University). Available at: http://www.SexQuest.com/surrogat.htm. New York: SexQuest/The Sex Institute.

Noonan, R. J. 1996a. New directions, new hope for sexuality: On the cutting edge of Sane Sex. In: P. B. Anderson, D. de Mauro, & R. J. Noonan, eds., *Does anyone still remember when sex was fun? Positive sexuality in the age of AIDS* (3rd ed.; pp. 144-221). Dubuque, IA: Kendall/Hunt Publishing Co.

Noonan, R. J. 1996b. Survival strategies for lovers in the 1990s. In: P. B. Anderson, D. de Mauro, & R. J. Noonan, eds., *Does anyone still remember when sex was fun? Positive sexuality in the age of AIDS* (3rd ed.; pp. 1-12). Dubuque, IA: Kendall/Hunt Publishing Co.

Noonan, R. J. 1997. The impact of AIDS on our perception of sexuality. In: R. T. Francoeur, ed., *International Encyclopedia of Sexuality* (Vol. 3, pp. 1622-1625). New York: Continuum.

Noonan, R. J. 1998a. The impact of AIDS on our perception of sexuality. In: R. T. Francoeur, ed., *Sexuality in America:*

*Understanding our sexual values and behavior* (pp. 248-251). New York: Continuum.

Noonan, R. J. 1998b. *A philosophical inquiry into the role of sexology in space life sciences research and human factors considerations for extended spaceflight.* Doctoral dissertation, New York University (UMI publication number 9832759).

Noonan, R. J. 1998c. The psychology of sex: A mirror from the Internet. In: J. Gackenbach, ed., *Psychology and the Internet: Intrapersonal, interpersonal and transpersonal implications* (pp. 143-168). New York: Academic Press.

Noonan, R. J. 1998d (November). The social construction of sexual harassment and heterophobia. In: R. J. Noonan, chair, *Alt.sex.conference II: A follow-up symposium on controversial unaddressed issues.* Symposium conducted during the 1998 Joint Annual Meeting of the Society for the Scientific Study of Sexuality (SSSS) and the American Association of Sex Educators, Counselors, and Therapists (AASECT), November 13, 1998, Los Angeles, CA.

Noonan, R. J. 1999 (November). *Heterophobia: The evolution of an idea.* Workshop presented at the 1999 Joint Annual Meeting of the Society for the Scientific Study of Sexuality (SSSS) and the American Association of Sex Educators, Counselors, and Therapists (AASECT), November 6, 1999, St. Louis, MO.

Noonan, R. J. 2001. Web resources for sex researchers: The state of the art, now and in the future. *Journal of Sex Research,* 38:348-352.

Noonan, R. J. 2002 (September 11). *Let us forget: The Twin Towers and Bin Laden's New York.* Available: http://www.paragraphics.com/September11/RJNforget.html.

Norris, A. E., & K. Ford. 1992. Beliefs about condoms and accessibility of condom intentions in Hispanic and African American youth. *Hispanic Journal of Behavioral Science,* 14(3):373-382.

North, B. J. 1990. Effectiveness of vaginal contraceptives in prevention of sexually transmitted diseases. In: N. J. Alexander, H. L. Gabelnick, & J. M. Spieler, eds., *Heterosexual transmission of AIDS: Proceedings of the Second Contraceptive Research and Development (CONRAD) Program International Workshop, held in Norfolk, VA, February 1-3, 1989* (pp. 273-290). New York: Wiley-Liss.

Norton, A. J., & J. E. Moorman. 1987. Current trends in marriage and divorce among American women. *Journal of Marriage and the Family,* 49:3-14.

*Nua.* Retrieved May 6, 2003. http://www.nua.ie/surveys/how_many_online/index.html

O'Brien, R. M. 1987. The interracial nature of violent crimes: A reexamination. *American Journal of Sociology,* 92:817-835.

Ochs, E. P. P., & Y. M. Binik. 2000. A sex-expert system on the Internet: Fact or fantasy. *CyberPsychology & Behavior, 3:* 617-629.

Ochs, E. P., K. Mah, & Y. M. Binik. 2002. Obtaining data about human sexual functioning from the Internet. In: A. Cooper, ed., *Sex and the Internet: A guidebook for clinicians.* New York: Brunner-Routledge.

Ogden, G. 1995. *Women who love sex.* New York: Pocket Books.

Okami, P. 1992. Child perpetrators of sexual abuse: The emergence of a problematic deviant category. *Journal of Sex Research,* 29:109-130.

Okami, P. 1995. Childhood exposure to parental nudity, parent-child co-sleeping, and 'primal scenes:' A review of clinical opinion and empirical evidence. *Journal of Sex Research,* 32:51-64.

Okazaki, C. N. 1994 (November). Rowing your boat. *Ensign,* 24(11):92-94.

Oliver, M. B., & J. S. Hyde. 1993. Gender differences in sexuality: A meta-analysis. *Psychological Bulletin, 114:*29-51.

O'Neill, N., & G. O'Neill. 1972. *Open marriage: A new lifestyle for couples.* New York: M. Evans.

Orzack, M. H., & C. J. Ross. 2000. Should virtual sex be treated like other sexual addictions? *Sexual Addiction and Compulsivity: Journal of Treatment and Prevention,* 7(1-2):113-126.

Ott, M. A. et al. 2002 (January/February). The trade-off between hormonal contraceptives and condoms among adolescents. *Family Planning Perspectives.*

Padilla, A. M., & T. L. Barids. 1991. Mexican-American adolescent sexuality and sexual knowledge: An exploratory study. *Hispanic Journal of Behavioral Sciences,* 13(1):95-104.

Page-Shafer, K., C. H. Shiboski, D. H. Osmond, et al. 2002. Risk of HIV infection attributable to oral sex among men who have sex with men and in the population of men who have sex with men. *AIDS,* 16(17):2350-2352.

Pain, R. 1997. Whither women's tear? Perceptions of sexual violence in public and private space. *International Review of Victimology,* 4:297-312.

Palandri, M., & L. Green. 2000. Image management in a bondage, discipline, sadomasochist subculture: A cyber-ethnographic study. *CyberPsychology & Behavior,* 3:631-641.

Palmer, C. T. 1988. Twelve reasons why rape is not sexually motivated: A skeptical examination. *Journal of Sex Research,* 25:512-530.

Palmer, P. 1993. *Contemporary lesbian writing: Dreams, desire, difference.* Philadelphia: Open University Press.

Paluszny, M. 1979. Current thinking on children's sexuality. *Medical Aspects of Human Sexuality, 13:*120-121.

Pankhurst, J., & S. K. Houseknecht. 1983. The family, politics, and religion in the 1980s. *Journal of Family Issues,* 4:5-34.

Patai, D. 1996. The feminist turn against men. *Partisan Review/ 4, 63*(3):580-594.

Patai, D. 1998. *Heterophobia: Sexual harassment and the future of feminism.* Lantham, MD: Rowman & Littlefield Publishers.

Patai, D., & Koertge, N. 1994. *Professing feminism: Cautionary tales from the strange world of women's studies.* New York: Basic Books.

Patton, C. 1990. *Inventing AIDS.* New York: Routledge.

Pauly, I. B. 1994. Transsexualism. In: V. L. Bullough & B. Bullough, eds., *Human sexuality: An encyclopedia* (pp. 590-598). New York: Garland Publishing.

Pauly, I., & T. Lindgren. 1976. Body image and gender identity. *Journal of Homosexuality,* 2:133-142.

Pearl, J. 1987. The highest paying customers: America's cities and the costs of prostitution control. *Hastings Law Journal, 38:*769-800.

Pendergrass, S., M. A. Nosek, & J. D. Holcomb. 2001. Design and evaluation of an Internet site to educate women with disabilities on reproductive health care. *Sexuality & Disability,* 19:71-83.

Penner, C., & J. Penner. 1981. *The gift of sex: A guide to sexual fulfillment.* Dallas: Word.

Peplau, L. A., Z. Rubin, & C. T. Hill. 1977. Sexual intimacy in dating relationships. *Journal of Social Issues,* 33:86-109.

Pérez, M. A., & K. Fennelly. 1996. Risk factors for HIV and AIDS among Latino farmworkers in Pennsylvania. In: S. I. Mishra, P. F. Conner & R. F. Magaña, eds., *AIDS crossing borders: The spread of HIV among migrant Latinos* (pp. 137-155). Boulder, CO: Westview Press.

Pérez, M. A., & H. L. Pinzón. 1997. Sexual communication patterns among Latino adolescent farm workers: A case study. *American Journal of Health Studies,* 13(2):74-83.

Perper, T. 1985. *Sex signals: The biology of love.* Philadelphia: ISI Press.

Perper, T., & D. L. Weis. 1987. Proceptive and rejective strategies of U.S. and Canadian college women. *Journal of Sex Research,* 23:455-480.

Peterson, K. S. 1994 (October 7). Turns out we are 'sexually conventional.' *USA Today,* 1-2A.

Peterson, L. S. 1995 (February). Contraceptive use in the United States: 1982-90. *Advance data, No. 260.* Hyattsville,

MD: Centers for Disease Control, U.S. Department of Health and Human Services.

Peterson, Z. D., & C. L. Muehlenhard. 2003. *Was it rape? The function of women's rape myth acceptance and definitions of sex in labeling their own experiences.* Manuscript submitted for publication.

Pettigrew, T. 1964. *A profile of the Negro American.* Princeton, NJ: Van Nostrand.

Phäfflin, F. 1992. Regrets after sex reassignment surgery. *Journal of the Psychology of Human Sexuality, 5:*69-85.

Phäfflin, F., & A. Junge. 1998. Sex reassignment: Thirty years of international follow-up studies after sex reassignment surgery: A comprehensive review 1961-1991. (Retrieved September 16, 2001, from http://www.symposion.com/ijt/pfaefflin/1000.htm.)

Phillips, K. P. 1990. *The politics of rich and poor: Wealth and the American electorate in the Reagan aftermath.* New York: Random House.

Phillips, L., & C. Phillips. 1994. *Survey of transgenderists.* Bulverde, TX 78163: P.O. Box 17.

Philpot, C. L., G. R. Brooks, D.-D. Lusterman, & R. L. Nutt. 1997. *Bridging separate gender worlds.* Washington, DC: American Psychological Association.

Phipps, W. E. 1975. *Recovering biblical sensuousness.* Philadelphia: Westminster Press.

Piercy, M. 1977. *The high cost of living.* New York: HarperCollins.

Pietropinto, A., & J. Simenauer. 1977. *Beyond the male myth: A nationwide survey.* New York: New American Library.

Pinkerton, S. D., L. M. Bogart, H. Cecil, et al. 2002. Factors associated with masturbation in a collegiate sample. *Journal of Psychology & Human Sexuality, 14*(2/3):103-122.

Planned Parenthood Federation of America. 2003 (April). *The health benefits of sexual expression* (White paper). New York: Katherine Dexter McCormick Library, Author, in cooperation with the Society for the Scientific Study of Sexuality.

*Planned Parenthood Federation of America's "Fair Access to Contraception Project."* n.d. Available: www.covermypills .org.

*Planned Parenthood of Southeastern Pennsylvania v. Casey,* 505 U.S. 833, 954 (1992) (C. J. Rehnquist, dissenting and concurring in part).

Plant, S. M., & K. M. Donahey. 2002. Sexuality and the Internet: Ethics and regulation. In: A. Cooper, ed., *Sex and the Internet: A guidebook for clinicians.* New York: Brunner-Routledge.

Pleck, J. 1981. *The myth of masculinity.* Cambridge, MA: MIT Press.

Plymire, D. C., & P. J. Forman. 2000. Breaking the silence: Lesbian fans, the Internet, and the sexual politics of women's sport. *International Journal of Sexuality & Gender Studies, 5:*141-153.

Podlas, K. 2000. Mistresses of their domain: How female entrepreneurs in cyberporn are initiating a gender power shift. *CyberPsychology & Behavior, 3*(5):847-854.

Poirier, J., & C. L. Muehlenhard. 2000 (November). *Feeling more vulnerable to stranger rape while knowing that acquaintance rape is more common: Exploring the paradox.* Paper presented at the annual meeting of the Society for the Scientific Study of Sexuality, Orlando, FL.

Pollak, R. 1991 (November 11). Presumed innocent? *The Nation, 253*(16):593.

Pomeroy, W. B. 1972. *Dr. Kinsey and the Institute for Sex Research.* New York: Harper and Row.

Pomeroy, W. B., C. C. Flax, & C. C. Wheeler. 1982. *Taking a sex history.* New York: The Free Press.

Prendergast, W. E. 1991. *Treating sex offenders in correctional institutions and outpatient clinics: A guide to clinical practice.* Binghamton, NY: Haworth Press.

Prendergast, W. E. 1993. *The merry-go-round of sexual abuse: Identifying and treating survivors.* Binghamton, NY: Haworth Press.

Prendergast, W. E. 1996. *Sexual abuse of children and adolescents.* New York: Continuum.

Prendergast, W. E. 2003. *Treating sex offenders: A guide to clinical practice with adults, clerics, children and adolescents.* New York: Haworth Press.

Prescott, J. W., & D. Wallace. 1978 (July-August). Abortion and the 'right-to-life.' *The Humanist,* 18-24.

Prins, K. S., B. P. Buunk, & N. W. VanYperen. 1993. Equity, normative disapproval and extramarital relationships. *Journal of Social and Personal Relationships, 10:*39-53.

Prosser, J. 1998. *Second skins: The body narratives of transsexuality.* New York: Columbia University Press.

Purchas, S. 1905. *Haklutus posthumus, or Purchas his pilgrimes: Contayning a history of the world in sea voyages and land travells by Englishmen and others.* Glascow, Scotland: J. Maclehose and Sons.

Purdy, J. 1989. *Garments the living wear.* San Francisco: City Lights.

Putnam, D. E. 2000. Initiation and maintenance of online sexual compulsivity: Implication for assessment and treatment. *CyberPsychology & Behavior, 3:*553- 564.

Putnam, D. E., & M. M. Maheu. 2000. Online sexual addiction and compulsivity: Integrating Web resources and behavioral telehealth in treatment. *Sexual Addiction and Compulsivity: Journal of Treatment and Prevention, 7*(1-2):91-112.

Quinttner, J. 1996 (June 24). Free speech for the Net. *Time Magazine, 147*(26).

Quartaro, G. K., & T. E. Spier. 2002. We'd like to ask you some questions, but we have to find you first: An Internet-based study of lesbian clients in therapy with lesbian feminist therapists. *Journal of Technology in Human Services, 19*(2/3): 109-118.

Quayle, E., & M. Taylor. 2001. Child seduction and self-representation on the Internet. *CyberPsychology & Behavior, 4*(5):597-608.

Rainwater, L. 1964. Marital sexuality in four cultures of poverty. *Journal of Marriage and the Family, 26:*457-466.

Rajneesh, B. S. (Osho). 1977. *Tantra spirituality and sex.* Rainbow Bridge.

Ramey, J. W. 1972. Emerging patterns of innovative marriage behavior. *Family Coordinator, 21:*435-456.

Ramey, J. W. 1975 (October). Intimate groups and networks: Frequent consequence of sexually open marriage. *Family Coordinator,* 515-530.

Ramey, J. W. 1976. *Intimate friendships.* Englewood Cliffs, NJ: Prentice-Hall.

Ramsey, G. V. 1943. The sexual development of boys. *American Journal of Psychology, 56:*217-233.

Ranke-Heinemann, U. 1990. *Eunuchs for the kingdom of Heaven: Women, sexuality, and the Catholic Church.* New York: Doubleday.

Rechy, J. 1963. *City of night.* New York: Grove Press.

Rector, R. E., K. A. Johnson, & L. R. Noyes. 2003 (June 2). Sexually active teenagers are more likely to be depressed and to attempt suicide. Washington, DC: Heritage Foundation.

Redlich, F. 1977. The ethics of sex therapy. In: W. H. Masters, V. E. Johnson, & R. C. Kolodny, eds., *Ethical issues in sex therapy and research.* Boston: Little, Brown and Company.

Reeves, J., ed. 1965. *The idiom of the people: English traditional verse edited with an introduction and notes from the manuscripts of Cecil J. Sharp.* New York: Norton.

Reeves, P. M. 2001. How individuals coping with HIV/AIDS use the Internet. *Health Education Research, 16:*709-719.

Reibstein, J. A., & M. Richards. 1993. *Sexual arrangements: Marriage and the temptation of infidelity.* New York: Scribner.

Reichelt, P. A., & H. H. Werley. 1975. Contraception, abortion and venereal disease: Teenagers' knowledge and the effect of education. *Family Planning Perspectives, 7*(2):83-88.

Reiner, W. G. 2000 (September 29). *Division of Pediatric Urology, Johns Hopkins Medical Institutions, at NYU Child Study Center Grand Rounds Summary: The genesis of gender identity in the male: Prenatal androgen effects on gender identity and gender role.*

Reiner, W. G. 1999. Assignment of sex in neonates with ambiguous genitalia. *Current Opinions Pediatrics, 11*(4):363-365.

Reiss, I. 1960. *Premarital sexual standards in America.* New York: Free Press.

Reiss, I. 1964. Premarital sexual permissiveness among Negroes and whites. *American Sociological Review, 29*:688-698.

Reiss, I. 1967. *The social context of premarital sexual permissiveness.* New York: Holt, Rinehart and Winston.

Reiss, I. L. 1976/1980. *Family systems in America* (2nd ed./3rd ed.). New York: Holt, Rinehart and Winston.

Reiss, I. 1981. Some observations on ideology and sexuality in America. *Journal of Marriage and the Family, 43*(2):271-283.

Reiss, I. L. 1986. *Journey into sexuality: An exploratory voyage.* Englewood Cliffs, NJ: Prentice-Hall.

Reiss, I. L. 1995. Is this the definitive sexual survey? Review of E. O. Laumann, J. H. Gagnon, R. T. Michael, & S. Michaels, The social organization of sexuality: Sexual practices in the united states. *Journal of Sex Research, 32*:77-85.

Reiss, I. L., R. E. Anderson, & G. C. Sponaugle. 1980. A multivariate model of the determinants of extramarital sexual permissiveness. *Journal of Marriage and the Family, 42*:395-411.

Reiss, I. L., A. Banwart, & H. Foreman. 1975. Premarital contraceptive usage: A study and some theoretical explorations. *Journal of Marriage and the Family, 37*:619-630.

*Relief Society Conference,* 1965 (September 29). Salt Lake City: Church of Jesus Christ of the Latter-Day Saints Publication.

Remez, L. 2000. Special report–Oral sex among adolescents: Is it sex or is it abstinence? *Family Planning Perspectives, 32*: 298-304.

Renaud, P., J. L. Rouleau, L. Granger, I. Baresetti, & S. Bouchard. 2002. Measuring sexual preferences in virtual reality: A pilot study. *CyberPsychology & Behavior, 5*(1):1-9.

Renzetti, C. M. 1996. The poverty of services for battered lesbians. In: C. M. Renzetti & C. H. Miley, eds., *Violence in gay and lesbian domestic partnerships* (pp. 61-68). New York: Harrington Park Press.

Resick, P. A. 1993. The psychological impact of rape. *Journal of Interpersonal Violence, 8*:223-255.

Resick, P. A., & P. Nishith. 1997. Sexual assault. In: R. C. Davis, A. J. Lurigio, & W. G. Skogan, eds., *Victims of crime* (2nd ed., pp. 27-52). Thousand Oaks, CA: Sage Publications.

Resnick, H. S., D. G. Kilpatrick, B. S. Dansky, B. E. Saunders, & C. L. Best. 1993. Prevalence of civilian trauma and posttraumatic stress disorder in a representative national sample of women. *Journal of Consulting and Clinical Psychology, 61*:984-991.

Reuther, R. R., ed. 1974. *Religion and sexism: Images of women in Jewish and Christian traditions.* New York: Simon and Schuster.

Rheingold, H. 1995 (March/April). The virtual community. *Utne Reader, 68*:61-64.

Rhodes, S. D., R. J. DiClemente, H. Cecil, K. C. Hergenrather, & L. J. Yee. 2002. Risk among men who have sex with men in the United States: A comparison of an Internet sample and a conventional outreach sample. *AIDS Education & Prevention, 14*:41-50.

Rich, A. 1973. *Diving into the wreck.* New York: Norton.

Rich, A. 1978. Twenty-one love poems. In: A. Rich, *The dream of a common language: Poems, 1974-1977* (pp. 25-36). New York: Norton.

Richardson, L. W. 1985. *The new other woman: Contemporary single women in affairs with married men.* New York: Free Press.

Richardson, D., ed. 1996. *Theorising heterosexuality: Telling it straight.* Buckingham (England)/Philadelphia: Open University Press.

Richardson, L. 1997 (October 16). When sex is just a matter of fact: To high school students, free condoms seem normal, not debatable. *The New York Times,* B1, B6.

Riddle, G. 1989. *Amputees and devotees.* Sunnyvale, CA: Halcyon Press.

Rimmer, R. H. 1966. *The Harrad experiment.* New York: Bantam.

Riportella-Muller, R. 1989. Sexuality in the elderly: A review. In: K. McKinney & S. Sprecher, eds., *Human sexuality: The societal and interpersonal context* (pp. 210-236). Norwood, NJ: Ablex.

Roberts, B. 1981. Surrogate partners and their use in sex therapy. In: D. A. Brown & C. Chary, eds., *Sexuality in America* (pp. 283-300). Ann Arbor, MI: Greenfield Books.

Roberts, S. V., & G. Cohen. 1995 (April 24). The religious right: Church meets state; On God's green earth; The heavy hitter. *U.S. News and World Report,* 26-39.

Robinson, B. E., W. O. Bockting, & T. Harrell. 2002. Masturbation and sexual health: An exploratory study of low income African American women. *Journal of Psychology & Human Sexuality, 14*(2/3):85-102.

Robinson, I. E., K. King, & J. O. Balswick. 1972. The premarital sexual revolution among college females. *Family Coordinator, 21*:189-194.

Robinson, P. 1976. *The modernization of sex.* New York: Harper and Row.

Roebuck, J., & M. McGee. 1977. Attitudes toward premarital sex and sexual behavior among black high school girls. *Journal of Sex Research, 13*:104-114.

Roffman, D. M., D. Shannon, & C. Dwyer. 1997. Adolescents, sexual health, and the Internet: Possibilities, prospects, and the challenges for educators. *Journal of Sex Education and Therapy, 22*:49-55.

Rogers, J. A. 1967. *Sex and race: Negro-Caucasian mixing in all ages and all lands* (9th ed.). New York: J. A. Rogers.

Roiphe, K. 1993. *The morning after: Sex, fear and feminism on campus.* Boston: Little, Brown & Company.

Romo, L. F., E. S. Lefkowitz, M. Sigman, & K. Terry. 2002. A longitudinal study of maternal messages about dating and sexuality and their influence on Latino adolescents. *Journal of Adolescent Health, 31*(1):59-69.

Rosen, R. C., & J. G. Beck. 1988. *Patterns of sexual arousal: Psychophysiological processes and clinical applications.* New York: Guilford Press.

Rosler, A., & G. Kohn. 1983. Male pseudohermaphroditism due to 17B-hydroxysteroid dehydrogenase deficiency studies on the natural history of the defect and the effect of androgens on the gender role. *Journal of Steroid Biochemistry, 19*(1):663-674.

Ross, M. W., & M. R. Kauth. 2002. Men who have sex with men and the Internet: Emerging clinical issues and their management. In: A. Cooper, ed., *Sex and the Internet: A guidebook for clinicians.* New York: Brunner-Routledge.

Ross, M. W., J. A. Paulsen, & O. W. Stalstrom. 1988. Homosexuality and mental health: A cross-cultural review. *Journal of Homosexuality, 15*(1):131-152.

Rosser, B. R. S., S. M. Dwyer, E. Coleman, M. Miner, M. Metz, B. Robinson, & W. O. Bockting. 1995. Using sexually explicit material in sex education: An eighteen year comparative analysis. *Journal of Sex Education and Therapy, 21*(2): 118-128.

Rossetti, S. J. 1991. *Slayer of the soul: Child sexual abuse and the Catholic Church.* Mystic, CT: Twenty-Third Publications.

Rotello, G. 1996 (June 24). To have and to hold: The case for gay marriage. *The Nation,* 11-18.

Roth, S., & L. Lebowitz. 1988. The experience of sexual trauma. *Journal of Traumatic Stress, 1*:79-107.

Rotheram-Borus, M. J., M. Rosario, et al. 1994. Sexual and substance use acts of gay and bisexual male adolescents in New York City. *Journal of Sex Research, 31*(1):47-57.

Rotkin, K. 1986. The phallacy of our sexual norm. In: S. Bem, ed., *Psychology of sex roles* (pp. 384-391). Acton, MA:

Copley Publishing. (Reprinted from *RT: A Journal of Radical Therapy*, 1972, 3.)

Roy, R., & D. Roy. 1969. *Honest sex: A sexual ethic by and for concerned Christians*. New York: New American Library.

Rubenstein, M. 1982. *An in-depth study of bisexuality and its relationship to self-esteem*. Unpublished doctoral dissertation, The Institute for Advanced Study of Human Sexuality, San Francisco.

Rubin, A. M., & J. R. Adams. 1986. Outcomes of sexually open marriages. *Journal of Sex Research*, *22*:311-319.

Rubinstein, R. P. 2001. *Dress codes: Meanings and messages in American culture*. Boulder, CO: Westview Press.

Rush, F. 1990. The many faces of backlash. In: D. Leidholdt & J. Raymond, eds., *The sexual liberals and the attack on feminism* (pp. 165-174). New York: Pergamon.

Russell, D. E. H. 1990. *Rape in marriage* (rev. ed.; originally published in 1982). Bloomington: Indiana University Press.

Russell, D. E. H. 1984. *Sexual exploitation: Rape, child sexual abuse, and workplace harassment*. Newbury Park, CA: Sage.

Russo, N., & K. Zierk. 1992. Abortion, childbearing, and women's well-being. *Professional Psychology: Research and Practice*, *23*:269.

Sadock, B. J., H. I. Kaplan, & A. M. Freedman, eds. 1976. *The sexual experience*. Boston: Williams & Wilkins.

Sage, E. 1926. *A study of costume*. New York: Charles Scribner and Sons.

Samuels, H. P. 1994. Race, sex, and myths: Images of African-American men and women. In: V. L. Bullough & B. Bullough, eds., *Human sexuality: An encyclopedia*. New York: Garland Press.

Samuels, H. P. 1995. Sexology, sexosophy, and African-American sexuality: Implications for sex therapy and sexuality education. *SIECUS Report*, *23*:3.

Sanders, S. A., & J. Machover Reinisch. 1999. Would you say you 'had sex' if . . .? *Journal of the American Medical Association*, *281*:275-277.

Sandfort, T. G. M., R. de Graaf, & R. V. Bijl. 2003. Same-sex sexuality and quality of life: Findings from the Netherlands Mental Health Survey and Incidence Study. *Archives of Sexual Behavior*, *32*:15-22.

Sandoval, A., R. Duran, L. O'Donnel, & C. R. O'Donnell. 1995. Barriers to condom use in primary and nonprimary relationships among Hispanic STD clinic patients. *Hispanic Journal of Behavioral Sciences*, *17*(3):385-397.

Sarrel, P. M, & W. H. Masters. 1982. Sexual molestation of men by women. *Archives of Sexual Behavior*, *11*:117-231.

Sarrel, P., & L. Sarrel. 1980 (October) and 1981 (February). The Redbook report on sexual relationships, Parts 1 and 2. *Redbook*, 73-60, 140-145.

Satcher, D. 2001. *The Surgeon General's call to action to promote sexual health and responsible sexual behavior*. Washington, DC: Office of the Surgeon General. Available: http://www.surgeongeneral.gov/library.

Saunders, J. M., & J. M. Edwards. 1984. Extramarital sexuality: A predictive model of permissive attitudes. *Journal of Marriage and Family*, *46*:825-835.

Savage, Jr., W. W. 1998. *Comics, cowboys, and jungle queens*. Hanover, NH: Wesleyan University Press.

Savitz, L., & L. Rosen. 1988. The sexuality of prostitutes: Sexual enjoyment reported by 'streetwalkers.' *Journal of Sex Research*, *24*:200-208.

Schaefer, L. C., & C. C. Wheeler. 1997. *Reflections: Harry Benjamin, the persistent pioneer 1885-1986*. In XV Harry Benjamin International Gender Dysphoria Association Symposium, The State of Our Art and the State of Our Science, Vancouver Hospital, Centre for Sexuality, Gender Identity and Reproductive Health, Vancouver, BC: Bristol Myers-Squibb/Wyeth-Ayerst.

Schaefer, L. C., & C. C. Wheeler. 2003 (In press). Guilt in cross gender identity conditions: Presentations and treatment. In: J. Drescher, ed., *Journal of Gay & Lesbian Psychotherapy*.

Schaefer, L. C., C. C. Wheeler, & W. Futterweit. 1995, Gender identity disorders (Transsexualism). In: P. O. Gebbard, ed., *Treatment of psychiatric disorders* (2nd ed.), Washington, DC: American Psychiatric Press.

Schell, J. 1999 (February 22). Sextuple jeopardy. *Nation*, *268*: 8.

Schemo, D. J. 2003a (March 26). Four top officers at Air Force Academy are replaced in wake of rape scandal. *The New York Times*, A10.

Schemo, D. J. 2003b (August 29). Rate of rape at Academy is put at 12% in survey. *The New York Times*, A12.

Schmalz, J. 1993 (April 16). Survey stirs debate on number of gay men in U.S. *The New York Times*, 20.

Schmitt, D. P., L. Alcalay, J. Allik, L. Ault, I. Austers, K. L. Bennett, G. Bianchi, F. Boholst, M. A. Borg Cunen, J. Braeckman, E. G. Brainerd Jr., L. G. A. Caral, G. Caron, M. M. Casullo, M. Cunningham, I. Daibo, C. De Backer, E. De Souza, R. Diaz-Loving, G. Diniz, K. Durkin, M. Echegaray, E. Eremsoy, H. A. Euler, R. Falzon, M. L. Fisher, D. Foley, D. P. Fry, S. Fry, M. A. Ghayur, D. L. Golden, K. Grammar, L. Grimaldi, J. Halberstadt, D. Herrera, J. Hertel, H. Hoffman, Z. Hradilekova, J. Hudek-Kene-evi, J. Jaafar, M. Jankauskaite, H. Kabangu-Stahel, I. Kardum, B. Khoury, H. Kwon, K. Laidra, A. Laireiter, D. Lakerveld, A. Lampart, M. Lauri, M. Lavallée, S. Lee, L. C. Leung, K. D. Locke, V. Locke, I. Luksik, I. Magaisa, J. Marcinkeviciene, A. Mata, R. Mata, B. McCarthy, M. E. Mills, J. Moreira, S. Moreira, M. Moya, M. Munyea, P. Noller, A. Opre, A. Panayiotou, N. Petrovic, K. Poels, M Popper, M. Poulimenou, V. P'yatokha, M. Raymond, U. Reips, S. E. Reneau, S. Rivera-Aragon, W. C. Rowatt, W. Ruch, V. S. Rus, M. P. Safir, S. Salas, F. Sambataro, K. N. Sandnabba, M. K. Schulmeyer, A. Schütz, T. Scrimali, T. K. Shackelford, P. R. Shaver, F. Sichona, F. Simonetti, T. Sineshaw, R. Sookdew, T. Speelman, S. Spyrou, H. C. Sümer, N. Sümer, M. Supekova, T. Szlendak, R. Taylor, B. Timmermans, W. Tooke, I. Tsaousis, F. S. K., Tungaraza, G. Vandermassen, T. Vanhoomissen, F. Van Overwalle, I. Vanwesenbeek, P. L. Vasey, J. Verissimo, M. Voracek, W. W. N. Wan, T. Wang, P. Weiss, A. Wijaya, L. Woertment, G. Youn, & A. Zupaneie. (2003). Universal sex differences in the desire for sexual variety: Tests from 52 nations, 6 continents, and 13 islands. *Journal of Personality and Social Psychology*, *85*(1):85-104.

Schmitt, D. P., & D. M. Buss. 2000. Sexual dimensions of person description: Beyond or subsumed by the Big Five? *Journal of Research Personality*. *34*:141-177.

Schmitt, E. 1996 (June 13). Panel passes bill to let states refuse to recognize gay marriage. *The New York Times*, A15.

Schneider, J. P. 2000. A qualitative study of cybersex participants: Gender differences, recovery issues, and implications for therapists. *Sexual Addiction & Compulsivity, 7*: 249-278.

Schneider, J. 2002. The new 'elephant in the living room': Effects of compulsive cybersex behaviors on the spouse. In: A. Cooper, ed., *Sex and the Internet: A guidebook for clinicians*. New York: Brunner-Routledge.

Schneider, J., & R. Weiss. 2001. *Cybersex exposed: Recognizing the obsession*. Center City, MN: Hazelden Educational Materials.

Schoenborn, C. A., S. L. Marsh, & A. M. Hardy. 1994 (February). AIDS knowledge and attitudes for 1992: Data from the national health interview survey. *Advance data from Vital and Health Statistics #243. National Center for Health Statistics*. Hyattsville, MD: Government Printing Office.

Schroedel, J. R. 2000. *Is the fetus a person? A comparison of policies across the fifty states*. Ithaca, NY: Cornell University Press.

Schulman, S. 1984. *The Sophie Horowitz story*. Tallahassee, FL: Naiad Press.

Schulman, S. 1998. *Stage struck: Theater, AIDS, and the marketing of gay America*. Durham, NC: Duke University Press.

Schwartz, I. 1993. Affective reactions of American and Swedish women to their first premarital coitus: A cross-cultural comparison. *Journal of Sex Research, 30*:18-26.

Schwartz, J. 1996a (February 9). Abortion provision stirs online furor. *Washington Post* (On-line).

Schwartz, J. 1996b (June 13). Court upholds free speech on Internet, blocks decency law. *Washington Post* (On-line).

Schwartz, J. L., & H. L. Gabelnick. 2002 (November/December). Current contraceptive research, *Perspectives in Sexual and Reproductive Health, 34*(6).

Schwartz, M. F., & J. S. Quarterman. 1993. The changing global Internet service infrastructure. *Internet Research, 3*(1):8-25.

Schwartz, M. F., & S. Southern. 2000. Compulsive cybersex: The new tea room. Sexual *Addiction and Compulsivity: Journal of Treatment and Prevention, 7*(1-2):127-144.

Schwartz, S. 1973. Effects of sex guilt and sexual arousal on the retention of birth control information. *Journal of Consulting and Clinical Psychology, 41*:61-64.

Scott, J. W. 1976. Polygamy: A futuristic family arrangement for African-Americans. *Black Books Bulletin,* 4.

Scott, J. W. 1986. From teenage parenthood to polygamy: Case studies in black polygamous family formation. *Western Journal of Black Studies, 10*(4):172-179.

Schow, R., W. Schow, & M. Raynes. 1991. *Peculiar people: Mormons and same-sex orientation.* Salt Lake City, UT: Signature Books.

Seaman, B. 1969. *The doctor's case against the pill.* New York: Peter H. Wyden.

Sears, R. R., E. E. Maccoby, & H. Levin. 1957. Patterns of child rearing. Evanston, IL: Row, Peterson.

Sebok, A. J. 2002 (April 22). Child abuse as mass tort?: How the Catholic Church's scandal may play out in court. Available: http://writ.corporate.findlaw.com/sebok/20020422.htm.

Sedway, M. 1992 (February/March). Far right takes aim at sexuality education. *SIECUS Report, 20*(3):13-19.

Segura, D. A. 1991. Ambivalence or continuity? Motherhood and employment among Chicanas and Mexican immigrant women workers. *Aztlan, 20*(2):150.

Seiden, H. M. 2001. Creating passion: An Internet love story. *Journal of Applied Psychoanalytic Studies, 3*:187-195.

Seidman, S. 1991. *Romantic longings: Love in America, 1830-1980.* New York: Routledge.

Sell, R. L. 1997. Research and the Internet: An e-mail survey of sexual orientation. *American Journal of Public Health, 87*: 297.

Settlage, D., S. Fordney, S. Baroff, & D. Cooper. 1973. Sexual experience of younger teenage girls seeking contraceptive assistance for the first time. *Family Planning Perspectives, 5*:223-226.

Shapiro, L. 1994 (January 24). They're daddy's little girls. *Newsweek,* 66.

Shah, R., & M. Zelnick. 1981. Parent and peer influence on sexual behavior, contraceptive use, and pregnancy experience of young women. *Journal of Marriage and the Family, 43*: 339-348.

Sharp, C. J. 1907/1965. *English folk songs: Some conclusions.* (London). Cited in: J. Reeves, ed., *The idiom of the people: English traditional verse edited with an introduction and notes from the manuscripts of Cecil J. Sharp.* New York: Norton.

Shaw, J. 1997. Treatment rationale for Internet infidelity. *Journal of Sex Education and Therapy, 22*:29-34.

Shaw, M. 1994. *Passionate enlightenment: Women in Tantric Buddhism.* Princeton, NJ: Princeton University Press.

Sherwin, B. B. 1991. The psychoendocrinology of aging and female sexuality. *Annual Review of Sex Research, 2*:181-198.

Shilts, R. 1987. *And the band played on: Politics, people, and the AIDS epidemic.* New York: St. Martin's Press.

Shilts, R. 1993. *Conduct unbecoming: Gays and lesbians in the U.S. military.* New York: St. Martin's Press.

Shostak, A. B. 1987. Singlehood. In: M. B. Sussman & S. K. Steinmetz, eds., *Handbook of marriage and the family* (pp. 355-368). New York: Plenum.

Shpritz, D. 1997. One teenager's search for sexual health on the Net. *Journal of Sex Education and Therapy, 22*:56-57.

SIECUS. 1990. *Sex education 2000. A call to action.* New York: SIECUS.

SIECUS. 1991. *Comprehensive sexuality education, kindergarten-12th grade.* New York: SIECUS.

SIECUS (Sex Information and Education Council of the U.S.). 2003. *SIECUS fact sheet: The truth about STDs.* Available: http://www.siecus.org.

*SIECUS Fact Sheet #2* (on comprehensive sexuality education). 1992. National Coalition to Support Sexuality Education.

Simon, R. J., ed. 1995. *Neither victim nor enemy.* Lanham, MD: University Press of America/Women's Freedom Network.

Simon, W. 1993. *Postmodern sexualities.* London: Rutledge.

Simon, W. 1994. Deviance as history: The future of perversion. *Archives of Sexual Behavior, 23*(1):16.

Simon, W., A. S. Berger, & J. H. Gagnon. 1972. Beyond anxiety and fantasy: The coital experiences of college youth. *Journal of Youth and Adolescence, 1*:203-222.

Simons, J. 2003 (June 9). Taking on Viagra. *Fortune Magazine, 147*:11.

Singh, B. K., B. L. Walton, & J. J. Williams. 1976. Extramarital sexual permissiveness: Conditions and contingencies. *Journal of Marriage and the Family, 38*:701-712.

Singh, S., & J. E. Darroch. 2000. Adolescent pregnancy and childbearing: Levels and trends in developed countries. *Family Planning Perspectives, 32*(1).

Sipe, A. R. 1995. *Sex, priests, and power: Anatomy of a crisis.* New York: Brunner/Mazel.

Sipe, A. R. 1999. The problem of prevention in clergy sexual abuse. In: *Bless me Father for I have sinned.* Westport CT: Praeger.

Slowinski, J. W. 1994. Religious influence on sexual attitudes and functioning. In: V. L. Bullough & B. Bullough, eds., *Human sexuality: An encyclopedia* (pp. 520-522). New York: Garland.

Smart, T. 1996 (February). Protease inhibitors come of age. *Newsletter of Experimental AIDS Therapies, 10*(2):1.

Smedes, L. B. 1994. *Sex for Christians: The limits and liberties of sexual living* (rev. ed.). Grand Rapids, MI: William B. Erdsman.

Smith, L. G., & J. R. Smith. 1973. Co-marital sex: The incorporation of extramarital sex into the marriage relationship. In: J. Money & J. Zubin, eds., *Critical issues in contemporary sexual behavior.* Baltimore: Johns Hopkins Press.

Smith, L. G., & J. R. Smith. 1974. Co-marital sex: The incorporation of extramarital sex into the marriage relationship. In: J. R. Smith & L. G. Smith, eds., *Beyond monogamy* (pp. 84-102). Baltimore: Johns Hopkins Press.

Smith, R. E., C. J. Pine, & M. E. Hawley. 1988. Social cognitions about adult male victims of female sexual assault. *Journal of Sex Research, 24*:101-112.

Smith, T. W. 1987 (August). *Unpublished data from 1972-1987 general social surveys* Chicago: National Opinion Research Center.

Smith, T. W. 1990 (February). *Adult sexual behavior in 1989: Number of partners, frequency, and risk.* Paper presented at the annual meeting of the American Association for the Advancement of Science, New Orleans, LA.

Smith, T. W. 1991. Adult sexual behavior in 1989: Number of partners, frequency of intercourse and risk of AIDS. *Family Planning Perspectives, 23*(3):102-107.

Smith, T. W. 1996 (December). *Unpublished data from 1972-1994. General social surveys.* Chicago: National Opinion Research Center.

Snaith, P., M. J. Tarsh, & R. Reid. 1993. Sex reassignment surgery: A study of 141 Dutch transsexuals. *British Journal of Psychiatry, 162*:681-685.

Solomon, J., & S. Miller. 1994 (September 12). 'Hero' or 'harasser'? *Newsweek*, 48-50.

Solomon, H., J. Man, J. Gill, & G. Jackson. 2002. Viagra on the Internet: Unsafe sexual practice. *International Journal of Clinical Practice*, 56:403-404.

Sommers, C. H. 1994. *Who stole feminism?* New York: Simon & Schuster.

Sonestein, F. L., J. H. Pleck, & L. C. Ku. 1991. Levels of sexual activity among adolescent males in the United States. *Family Planning Perspectives*, 23(4):162-167.

Sorensen, R. C. 1973. *Adolescent sexuality in contemporary America*. New York: World.

Sorenson, S. V., & J. M. Siegel. 1992. Gender ethnicity and sexual assault: Findings from a Los Angeles study. *Journal of Social Issues*, 48(1):93-104.

Spaccarelli, S. 1994. Stress, appraisal, and coping in child sexual abuse: A theoretical and empirical review. *Psychological Bulletin*, 116:340-362.

Spanier, G. B. 1975. Sexualization and premarital sexual behavior. *Family Coordinator*, 24:33-41.

Spanier, G. B. 1976. Formal and informal sex education as determinants of premarital sexual behavior. *Archives of Sexual Behavior*, 5:39-67.

Spanier, G. B. 1978. Sex education and premarital sexual behavior among American college students. *Adolescence*, 8: 659-674.

Spanier, G. B., & R. L. Margolis. 1983. Marital separation and extramarital sexual behavior. *Journal of Sex Research*, 19: 23-48.

Spector, I., & M. Carey. 1990. Incidence and prevalence of the sexual dysfunctions: A critical review of the empirical literature. *Archives of Sexual Behavior*, 19:389-408.

Spector, R. E., ed. 1991. *Cultural diversity in health and illness*. Norwalk, CA: Appleton and Lange.

Spong, J. S. 1988. *Living in sin? A bishop rethinks human sexuality*. San Francisco: HarperSanFrancisco.

Sprecher, S., A. Barbee, & P. Schwartz. 1995. 'Was it good for you, too?': Gender differences in first sexual intercourse experiences. *Journal of Sex Research*, 32:3-15.

Sprenkle, D. H., & D. L. Weis. 1978. Extramarital sexuality: Implications for marital therapists. *Journal of Sex and Marital Therapy*, 4:279-291.

Stacy, R. D., M. Prisbell, & K. Tollefsrud. 1992. A comparison of attitudes among college students toward sexual violence committed by strangers and by acquaintances: A research report. *Journal of Sex Education and Therapy*, 18:257-263.

Stan, A. M. 1995. *Debating sexual correctness*. New York: Dell Publishing.

Stanley, L. A. 1989. The child porn myth. *Cardozo Arts and Entertainment Law Journal*, 7:295-358.

Staples, R. 1972. Research on black sexuality: Its implications for family life, sex education and public policy. *The Family Coordinator*, 21:183-188.

Staples, R. 1974. Black sexuality. In: M. Calderone, ed., *Sexuality and human values* (pp. 62-70). New York: Association Press.

Staples, R. 1977. The myth of the impotent black males. In: D. Y. Wilkinson & R. L. Taylor, eds., *The black male in America*. Chicago: Nelson-Hall.

Staples, R., ed. 1978. *The black family: Essays and studies*. Belmont, CA: Wadsworth Publishing Co.

Staples, R. 1981. *The world of black singles: Changing patterns of male/female relations*. Westport: CT: Greenwood Press.

Staples, R. 1982. *Black masculinity: The black male's role in American society*. San Francisco: The Black Scholar Press.

Staples, R. 1986. The black response. In: R. T. Francoeur, ed., *Taking sides: Clashing views on controversial issues in human sexuality*. Guilford, CT: Dushkin Publishing.

Staples, R., & L. Boulin Johnson. 1993. *Black families at the crossroads: Challenges and prospects*. San Francisco: Jossey-Bass.

*The Sunday Star Ledger*. 2002 (June 16). Newark, NJ.

Starr, B. D., & M. Bakur Weiner. 1981. *The Starr-Weiner report on sex and sexuality in the mature years*. Briarcliff Manor, NY: Stein and Day.

Steele, B. 1990. *The feminist takeover*. Gaithersburg, MD: Human Life International.

Stein, D. J., D. W. Black, N. A. Shapira, & R. L. Spitzer. 2001. Hypersexual disorder and preoccupation with Internet pornography. *American Journal of Psychiatry*, 158:1590-1594.

Steinfeld, P. 2003 (August 16). A divided Episcopal Church? Yes indeed, a study says, but in ways perhaps unexpected. *The New York Times*, A9.

Stekel, W. 1922. *Bi-Sexual love*. New York: Emerson Books.

Stepp, L. S. 2003 (January 28). What's love got to do with it? "Buddysex" and the new dating culture. *Washington Post*. Available: http://www.chicagotribune.com/features/lifesty/chi-030128epbuddysex,1,1185691.story.

Stern, H. 1993. *Private parts*. New York: Simon and Schuster.

Stern, S. E. 2001. Sexuality and mass media: The historical context of psychology's reaction to sexuality on the Internet. *Journal of Sex Research*, 38:283-292.

Stern, S. E., & A. D. Handel. 2001. Sexuality and mass media: The historical context of psychology's reaction to sexuality on the Internet. *Journal of Sex Research*, 38:283-291.

Stevenson, R. W. 2003 (February 15). Bush eases ban on AIDS money to pro-abortion groups abroad. *The New York Times*, A5.

Stine, G. J. 1995. *AIDS update: 1994-1995*. Englewood Cliffs, NJ: Prentice-Hall.

Stipp, D., & R. Whitaker. 1998 (March 16). The selling of impotence. *Fortune*, 137(5):115-24.

Storms, M. D. 1981. A theory of erotic orientation development. *Psychological Review*, 88:340-353.

Strong, B., & C. DeVault. 1994. *Human sexuality*. Mountain View, CA: Mayfield.

Struckman-Johnson, C., D. Struckman-Johnson, & P. B. Anderson. 2003. Tactics of sexual coercion: When men and women won't take no for an answer. *Journal of Sex Research*, 40:76-86.

Stubbs, K. R. 1994. *Women of the light: The new sacred prostitute*. Larkspur, CA: Secret Garden Press.

Suler, J. 2001. *The online disinhibition effect*. http://www.rider.edu/users/suler/psycyber/disinhibit.htm.

Sullivan, A. 1996. *Virtually normal: An argument about homosexuality*. New York: Knopf.

Summers, C. J., ed. 1995. *The gay and lesbian literary heritage*. New York: Henry Holt.

Surra, C. A. 1990. Research and theory on mate selection and premarital relationships in the 1980s. *Journal of Marriage and the Family*, 52:844-865.

Swaab, D. F., W. C. J. Chung, F. P. M. Kruijver, et al. 2001. Structural and functional differences in the human hypothalamus. *Hormones & Behavior*, 40:93-98.

Swaab, D. F., W. C. J. Chung, F. P. M. Kruijver, et al. 2002 (In press). Sex differences in the human hypothalamus in the different stages of human life. *Neurobiology of Aging*.

Symonds, C. 1968. *Pilot study of the peripheral behavior of sexual mate swappers*. Master's thesis, University of California, Riverside.

Symonds, C. 1973 (September). Sex surrogates. *Penthouse Forum*. Quoted in S. Braun, ed., 1975, *Catalog of sexual consciousness* (p. 137). New York: Grove Press.

Symons, D. 1981. *The evolution of human sexuality*. New York: Oxford University Press.

Szapocznik, J. 1995. Research on disclosure of HIV status: Cultural evolution finds an ally in science. *Health Psychology*, 14(1):4-5.

Taggart, J. M. 1992. Gender segregation and cultural constructions of sexuality in two Hispanic societies. *American Ethnologist*, 19:75-96.

Talmage, J. E. 1977. *A study of the articles of faith*. Salt Lake City, UT: Church of Jesus Christ of Latter-Day Saints.

Tamosaitis, N. 1995. *Net.sex.* Emeryville, CA: Ziff-Davis Press.

Tangri, S., M. R. Burt, & L. B. Johnson. 1982. Sexual harassment at work: Three explanatory models. *Journal of Social Issues, 38*(4):33-54.

Tanner, N. E. 1973. *The role of womanhood.* Salt Lake City: Church of Jesus Christ of the Latter-Day Saints Publication.

Taverner, B. 2003 (February/March). All together now: Combining pregnancy and STI prevention programs. *SIECUS Report, 21*(3).

Tavris, C. 1978 (February). 40,000 Men tell about their sexual behavior, their fantasies, their ideal women, and their wives. *Redbook,* 111-113, 178-181.

Tavris, C., & S. Sadd. 1975. *The Redbook report on female sexuality.* New York: Delacorte.

Taylor, S. 1997 (June 9). The facts of the matter. *Newsweek,* 39.

Teevan, J. J., Jr. 1972. Reference groups and premarital sexual behavior. *Journal of Marriage and the Family, 34*:283-291.

Tepper, M. S., & A. Owens. 2002. Access to pleasure: Onramp to specific information on disability, illness, and other expected changes throughout the lifespan. In: A. Cooper, ed., *Sex and the Internet: A guidebook for clinicians.* New York: Brunner-Routledge.

Terman, L. M. 1938. *Psychological factors in marital happiness.* New York: McGraw-Hill.

Testa, M. 2002. The impact of men's alcohol consumption on perpetration of sexual aggression. *Clinical Psychology Review, 22*:1239-1263.

Thayer, N. S. T., et al. 1987 (March). Report of the task force on changing patterns of sexuality and family life. *The Voice.* Newark, NJ: Episcopal Diocese of Northern New Jersey.

Thompson, A. P. 1983. Extramarital sex: A review of the research literature. *Journal of Sex Research, 19*:1-22.

Thompson, A. P. 1984. Emotional and sexual components of extramarital relations. *Journal of Marriage and the Family, 46*:35-42.

Thorne, B., & Z. Luria. 1986. Sexuality and gender in children's daily worlds. *Social Problems,* 33(3):176-190.

Thornton, B. 1977. Toward a linear prediction model of marital happiness. *Personality and Social Psychology Bulletin, 3*: 674-676.

Tiefer, L. 1995. *Sex is not a natural act and other essays.* San Francisco: Westview.

Tikkanen, R., & M. W. Ross. 2000. Looking for sexual compatibility: Experiences among Swedish men in visiting Internet gay chat rooms. *CyberPsychology & Behavior, 3*(4):605-616.

*Time Magazine.* 1995 (Spring). Special issue: Welcome to cyberspace.

Timmerman, J. 1986. *The Mardi Gras syndrome: Rethinking Christian sexuality.* New York: CrossRoads.

Tjaden , P., & N. Thoennes. 2000. *Full report of the prevalence, incidence, and consequences of violence against women* (NCJ 183781). Washington, DC: U.S. Department of Justice.

Tommy. 1992. A theory on infantilism. Reprint available from DPF, 38 Miller Avenue, Suite 127, Mill Valley, CA 94941.

Tone, A. 2002/2003 (December/January). The contraceptive conundrum, *SIECUS Report, 31*(2).

Toner, R. 2003 (July 25). Opposition to gay marriage is declining, study finds. *The New York Times,* A16.

Tribe, L. H. 1992. *Abortion: The clash of absolutes.* New York: W. W. Norton.

Trudell, B., & M. Whatley. 1991. Sex respect: A problematic public school sexuality curriculum. *Journal of Sex Education and Therapy, 17*:125-140.

Trujillo, C. 1991. *Chicana lesbians: The girls our mothers warned us about.* Berkeley, CA: Third Woman Press.

Trussell, J., & C. Westoff. 1980. Contraceptive practice and trends in coital frequency. *Family Planning Perspectives, 12*: 246-249.

Turco, S. A. 1994 (September 22). Students admit sexual activity. *BG News, 80*(22):1, 5.

Twining, A. 1983. *Bisexual women: Identity in adult development.* Unpublished doctoral dissertation, Boston University School of Education.

Tzeng, O. C. S., & H. J. Schwarzin. 1987. Gender and race differences in child sexual abuse correlates. *International Journal of Intercultural Relation, 14*:135-161.

Udry, J. R. 1980. Changes in the frequency of marital intercourse from panel data. *Archives of Sexual Behavior, 9*:319-325.

Udry, J. R. 1990. Hormonal and social determinants of adolescent sexual initiation. In: J. Bancroft & J. M. Reinisch, eds., *Adolescence and puberty* (pp. 70-87). New York: Oxford Press.

Udry, J. R., K. E. Bauman, & N. M. Morris. 1975. Changes in premarital coital experience of recent decade of birth cohorts of urban American women. *Journal of Marriage and the Family, 37*:783-787.

Udry, J. R., F. R. Deven, & S. J. Coleman. 1982. A cross-national comparison of the relative influence of male and female age on the frequency of marital intercourse. *Journal of Biosocial Science, 14*:1-6.

Udry, J. R., L. M. Tolbert, & N. M. Morris. 1986. Biosocial foundations for adolescent female sexuality. *Demography, 23*:217-230.

Ullman, S. E. 1997. Review and critique of empirical studies of rape avoidance. *Criminal Justice and Behavior, 24*:177-204.

Ullman, S. E., & R. A. Knight. 1992. Fighting back: Women's resistance to rape. *Journal of Interpersonal Violence, 7*: 31-43.

UNAIDS. 2002. *Epidemiological fact sheets by country.* Geneva, Switzerland: Joint United Nations Programme on HIV/AIDS (UNAIDS/WHO). Available: http://www.unaids.org/hivaidsinfo/statistics/fact_sheets/index_en.htm.

United Presbyterian Church in the U.S.A. General Assembly Special Committee on Human Sexuality. 1991. *Part 1: Keeping body and soul together: Sexuality, spirituality, and social justice. Part 2: Minority report of the special committee on human sexuality* (Report to the 203rd General Assembly). Baltimore: Presbyterian Church (U.S.A.).

U.S. Bureau of the Census. 1993. *Hispanic Americans today. Current population reports, P23-183.* Washington, DC: Government Printing Office.

U.S. Census Bureau. 1999. *Family composition. Current population survey.* Washington, DC: Government Printing Office.

U.S. Census Bureau. 2001. *Fertility of American women: June 2000.* Available: http://www.census.gov/prod/2001pubs/p20-543rv.pdf. Accessed 9/20/02.

U.S. Census Bureau. 2002. *Population estimates.* Available: http://eire.census.gov/popest/estimates.php. Accessed 9/20/2002.

U.S. Conference of Catholic Bishops. 2002. Available: http://www.nccbuscc.org.

U.S. Department of Commerce. 1991. *Statistical abstract of the United States 1991. 111th edition. Bureau of the Census.* Washington, DC: Government Printing Office.

U.S. Department of Health and Human Services. 1994 (December). *Sexually transmitted disease surveillance 1993.* Atlanta, GA: Public Health Service, Centers for Disease Control and Prevention.

U.S. Department of Justice. 2002. *Victim characteristics.* Available: http://www.ojp.usdoj.gov/bjs/cvict_v.htm. Accessed 9/21/02.

U.S. Food and Drug Administration. n.d. *Lea's shield–P010043: Summary of safety and effectiveness data.* Available: www.fda.gov.

*U.S. News and World Report.* 1995 (April 24). The religious right: Church meets state, 26-39.

Valleroy, V., D. MacKellar, J. Karon, R. Janssen, et al. 1998. HIV infection in disadvantaged out-of-school youth: Prevalence for U.S. Job Corps entrants, 1990 through 1996. *Journal of Acquired Immune Deficiency Syndrome, 19*:6773.

Valleroy, V., D. MacKellar, J. Karon, et al. 2000. HIV prevalence and associated risks in young men who have sex with men. *Journal of the American Medical Association, 284*(2): 198-204.

Vance, C. S., & C. A. Pollis. 1990. Introduction: A special issue on feminist perspectives on sexuality. *Journal of Sex Research, 27*:1-5.

Van Wyk, P. H., & C. S. Geist. 1984. Psychosexual development of heterosexual, bisexual, and homosexual behavior. *Archives of Sexual Behavior, 13:505-544.*

Varni, C. 1971. An exploratory study of spouse swapping. *Pacific Sociology Review, 15*(4).

Vaughan, D. 2004 (January, in press). Compassionate counseling: A look at surrogate partner therapy [working title]. *Penthouse Forum.*

Veblen, T. 1899/1960. *The theory of the leisure class.* New York: Mentor Books.

Vener, A. M., & C. S. Stewart. 1974. Adolescent sexual behavior in middle America revisited: 1970-1973. *Journal of Marriage and the Family, 36*:728-735.

Verhovek, S. H. 1995 (August 12). New twist for a landmark case: Roe v. Wade becomes Roe v. Roe. *The New York Times,* 1, 9.

Vidal, G. 1965. *The city and the pillar.* New York: Dutton.

Vineberg, S. 2001 (July 22). The courage to aim both high and low. *The New York Times.*

Voeller, B. 1991. AIDS and heterosexual anal intercourse. *Archives of Sexual Behavior, 20*(3):233-276.

Wachowiak. C., & H. Bragg. 1980. Open marriage and marital adjustment. *Journal of Marriage and the Family, 42*(1):57-62.

Wade, J. 2004. *Transcendent sex.* New York: Simon & Schuster.

Walsh, J. 1993 (July/August). The new sexual revolution: Liberation at last? or the same old mess? *Utne Reader,* No. *58:* 59-65.

Walston, J. 2001. *The polyamory movement.* Unpublished paper presented at Indiana University Southeast.

Wang, Q., & M. W. Ross. 2002. Differences between chat room and e-mail sampling approaches in Chinese men who have sex with men. *AIDS Education & Prevention, 14*:361-366.

Ward, O. B., I. L. Ward, J. H. Denning, et al. 2002. Postparturitional testosterone surge in male offspring of rats stressed and/or fed ethanol during late pregnancy. *Hormones & Behavior, 41*:229-235.

Warshaw, R. 1988. *I never called it rape.* New York: Harper & Row.

Waskul, D. D. 2002. The naked self: Being a body in televideo cybersex. *Symbolic Interaction, 25*:199-227.

Waterman, C. K., L. J. Dawson, & M. J. Bologna. 1989. Sexual coercion in gay male and lesbian relationships: Predictors and implications for support services. *Journal of Sex Research, 26*:118-124.

Watson, R. 1998 (June 22). The globe is gaga for Viagra. *Newsweek,* 131.

Weaver, A. J. 1995. Has there been a failure to prepare and support parish-based clergy in their role as front-line community mental health workers: A review. *Journal of Pastoral Care, 49*(2):129-147.

Webb, A. I. 2002 (September 16-23). Dangerous liaisons: Japan's casual "sex friends" risk more than broken hearts. *NewsweekInternational/MSNBC.*

Webb, P. 1975. *The erotic arts.* Boston: New York Graphic Society.

Weeks, M. R., J. J. Schensul, S. S. Williams, M. Singer, & M. Grier. 1995. AIDS prevention for African-American and Latina women: Building culturally and gender-appropriate interventions. *AIDS Education and Prevention, 7*(3):251-264.

Weinberg, M., & C. J. Williams. 1994. *Dual attraction.* New York: Oxford University Press.

Weinberg, M. S., C. J. Williams, & C. Calham. 1994. Homosexual foot fetishism. *Archives of Sexual Behavior, 23*(6): 611-626.

Weinrich, J. D. 1997. Storage bedfellows: Homosexuality, gay liberation, and the Internet. *Journal of Sex Education and Therapy, 22*:58-66.

Weis, D. L. 1983. Affective reactions of women to their initial experience of coitus. *Journal of Sex Research, 19*:209-237.

Weis, D. L. 1983. Open marriage and multilateral relationships: The emergence of nonexclusive models of the marital relationship. In: E. D. Macklin & R. H. Rubin, eds., *Contemporary families and alternative lifestyles: Handbook on research and theory* (pp. 194-216). Beverly Hills, CA: Sage.

Weis, D. L., & J. Jurich. 1985. Size of community of residence as a predictor of attitudes toward extramarital sexual relations. *Journal of Marriage and the Family, 47*(1):173-179.

Weis, D. L., & M. Slosnerick. 1981. Attitudes toward sexual and nonsexual extramarital involvement among a sample of college students. *Journal of Marriage and the Family, 43:* 349-358.

Weise, E. R., ed. 1992. *Closer to home: Bisexuality and feminism.* Seattle, WA: Seal Press.

Weitz, R., & L. Gordon. 1993. Images of black women among Anglo college students. *Sex Roles, 28*(1/2):19-34.

Wellman, B. 1992. Men in network: Private communities, domestic friendships. In: P. M. Nardi, ed., *Men's friendships* (pp. 74-114). Newbury Park, CA: Sage.

Wellman, B. 1985. Domestic work, paid work and net work. In: S. W. Duck & D. Perlman, eds., *Understanding personal relationships* (pp. 159-191). Newbury Park, CA: Sage.

Wells, R. V. 1985. *Uncle Sam's family: Issues and perspectives on American demographic history.* Albany, NY: State University of New York Press.

West, C. M. 1995. Mammy, Sapphire, and Jezebel: Historical images of black women and their implications for psychotherapy. *Psychotherapy, 32*(3):458-66.

West, C. 1996. *Lesbian polyfidelity.* San Francisco: Booklegger Publishing.

Westheimer, R., & L. Lieberman. 1988. *Sex and morality: Who is teaching our sex standards?* Boston, MA: Harcourt, Brace, Jovanovich.

Westoff, C. 1974. Coital frequency and contraception. *Family Planning Perspectives, 6*:136-141.

Wheat, E., & G. Wheat. 1981. *Intended for pleasure* (rev. ed.) Grand Rapids, MI: Fleming H. Revell/Baker Book House.

Wheeler, C. C. 1988. Memorial for Harry Benjamin. *Archives of Sexual Behavior. 17*(1):28-31.

Wheeler, C. C. 1993 (October 21-24). Adapting the Kinsey sex history interview as intake assessment for diagnostic criteria and evaluation of gender dysphoric patients. Panel: *DSM III & IV/Standards of care: Diagnostic considerations.* XIII International Symposium–Gender Dysphoria: Advances in Treatment. The Harry Benjamin International Gender Dysphoria Association, Inc., New York City.

Wheeler, C. C. 1999 (August 17-21). Harry Benjamin, M.D.: A legacy of persisting influences from the persistent pioneer. Panel: *Remembering Harry Benjamin: Reflections on the pioneer in understanding and helping transsexuals.* XVI The Harry Benjamin International Gender Dysphoria Association Symposium, London, England.

Wheeler, C. C. 2001. *Gender identity disorders: Then and now, history panel.* XVII The Harry Benjamin International Gender Dysphoria Association Symposium.

Wheeler, C. C. 2003a. *Role reversal.* For Arts & Entertainment Television Networks, On-air Consultant Psychotherapist.

Wheeler, C. C. 2003b (In press). The Harry Benjamin International Gender Dysphoria Association's current *Standards of care for gender identity disorders* (6th ver.): Myths and controversial issues. In: J. Drescher, ed., *Journal of Gay and Lesbian Psychotherapy.*

Wheeler, C. C., & L. C. Schaefer. 1984a. The nonsurgery true transsexual (Benjamin's Category IV): A theoretical rationale. In: H. I. Lief & Z. Hoch, eds., *International research in sexology* (Sexual medicine, vol. I). New York: Praeger.

Wheeler, C. C., & L. C. Schaefer. 1984b. The true transsexual and life-style options. In: Z. Hoch, ed., *Sexual behavior.* London: Plenum Publishing Corp.

Wheeler, C. C., & L. C. Schaefer. 1997 (August 8-10). *Holistic psychotherapy treatment model, Clinical treatment of gender identity conditions, The Hero's Journey.* Workshop, The 3rd Annual All Female-To-Male Conference, Boston.

Wheeler, C. C., & L. C. Schaefer. 1997 (September 10-13). *The unspoken truths of genital surgery outcomes.* XV The Harry Benjamin International Gender Dysphoria Association Symposium, Vancouver, British Columbia, Canada.

Wheeler, C. C., & L. C. Schaefer. 1999 (August 17-21). *Anatomy of gender relationships: Can this "marriage" be saved?* XVI The Harry Benjamin International Gender Dysphoria Association Symposium, London, England.

Wheeler, D. L. 1995 (April 7). A birth-control vaccine. *The Chronicle of Higher Education, 41*(A8):9 & 15.

White, E. 1982. *A boy's own story.* New York: Dutton.

White House Press Release. 2002 (February). *Working toward independence: Encourage abstinence and prevent teen pregnancy.* Available: www.whitehouse.gov.

Whitehurst, R. N. 1974. *Open marriage: Problems and prospects.* Paper presented at the annual meeting of the National Council on Family Relations, St. Louis, October, 1974.

Whitley, M. P., & S. B. Poulsen. 1975. Assertiveness and sexual satisfaction in employed professional women. *Journal of Marriage and the Family, 37*:573-581.

Whitten, P. L., H. B. Patisaul & L. J. Young. 2002. Neurobehavioral actions of coumestrol and related isoflavonoids in rodents. *Neurotoxicology Teratology. 24*:47-54.

Wiederman, M. W. 1993. Demographic and sexual characteristics of nonrespondents to sexual experience items in a national survey. *Journal of Sex Research, 30*:27-35.

Wiederman, M. W., D. L. Weis, & E. R. Allgeier. 1994. The effect of question preface on response rates to a telephone survey of sexual experience. *Archives of Sexual Behavior, 23*: 203-215.

Wiener, L. S. 1991 (September). Women and human immunodeficiency virus: A historical and personal psychosocial perspective. *Social Work, 36*(5):375-378.

Wilkinson, D. 1987. Ethnicity. In: M. B. Sussman & S. K. Steinmetz, eds., *Handbook of marriage and the family* (pp. 183-210). New York: Plenum Press.

Wilkinson, D. Y., & R. L. Taylor. 1977. *The black male in America.* Chicago: Nelson-Hall.

Wilkinson, S., & Kitzinger C., eds. 1993. *Heterosexuality: A feminism and psychology reader.* London/Newbury Park, CA: Sage Publications.

Wille, W. S. 1961. Case study of a rapist: An analysis of the causation of criminal behavior. *Journal of Social Therapy, 7*:10-21.

Williams, J. D. 1989. *U.S. Hispanics: A demographic profile. CRS report for Congress 89-460 Gov. Congressional Research Service.* Washington, DC: The Library of Congress.

Williams, M. H. 1978. Individual sex therapy. In: J. LoPiccolo & L. LoPiccolo, eds., *Handbook of sex therapy* (pp. 477-483). New York: Plenum Press.

Williams, W. L. 1992. *The spirit and the flesh: Sexual diversity in American Indian culture.* Boston: Beacon Press.

Wilson, C. 2003 (August 4). Gay taste? Here's straight talk. *USA Today.*

Wings, M. 1986. *She came too late.* Los Angeles, CA: Alyson Publications.

Wings, M. 2001. *She came in a flash.* Los Angeles, CA: Alyson Publications.

Wolfe, L. 1978. The question of surrogates in sex therapy. In: J. LoPiccolo & L. LoPiccolo, eds., *Handbook of sex therapy* (pp. 491-497). New York: Plenum Press.

Wolpe, J., & A. A. Lazarus. 1966. *Behavior therapy techniques.* New York: Pergamon Press.

Woodward, K. L. 1998 (November 2). Sex, sin and salvation. *Newsweek, 132*:37.

Woodward, K. L. 2002 (March 4). Bing Crosby had it right. *Newsweek, 139*:53.

Woolf, V. 1928. *Mrs. Dalloway.* New York: Modern Library.

*World almanac and book of facts, 1993.* New York: World Almanac, Pharos Books.

*World almanac and book of facts, 1996.* New York: World Almanac, Pharos Books.

Worth, D., & R. Rodriquez. 1987 (January/February). Latina women and AIDS. *SIECUS Report, 25*(3):5-7.

Wyatt, G. E. 1992. The sociocultural context of African American and white American women's rape. *Journal of Social Issues, 48*(1):77-91.

Wyatt, G. E., M. Newcomb, & C. Notgrass. 1990. Internal and external mediators of women's rape experiences. *Psychology of Women Quarterly, 14*:153-76.

Wyatt, G. E., & G. J. Powell, eds. 1988. *Lasting effects of child sexual abuse.* London: Sage Publications.

X, L. 1994. A brief series of anecdotes about the backlash experienced by those of us working on marital and date rape. *Journal of Sex Research, 31*:141-143.

Yee, D. 2002 (October 31). *Syphilis on the rise after dropping during 1990s.* Associated Press Online.

Yellis, K. A. 1969. Prosperity's child: Some thoughts on the flapper. *American Quarterly, 21*(1):44-64.

Yllo, K. A. 1978. Nonmarital cohabitation: Beyond the college campus. *Alternative Lifestyles, 1*:37-54.

Young, C. 1999. *Ceasefire! Why women and men must join forces to achieve true equality.* New York: Free Press.

Young, K. S. 1998. *Caught in the Net.* New York: John Wiley & Sons.

Young, K. S., E. Griffin-Shelley, A. Cooper, J. O'Mara, & J. Buchanan. 2000. Online infidelity: A new dimension in couple relationships with implications for evaluation and treatment. *Sexual Addiction & Compulsivity, 7*(1-2):59-74.

Zamboni, B. D., & I. Crawford. 2002. Using masturbation in sex therapy: Relationships between masturbation, sexual desire, and sexual fantasy. *Journal of Psychology & Human Sexuality, 14*(2/3):123-141.

Zell, M. G. 1990. A bouquet of lovers: Strategies for responsible open relationships. *Green Egg 89*, Beltane.

Zelnik, M., J. F. Kantner, & K. Ford. 1981. *Sex and pregnancy in adolescence.* Beverly Hills, CA: Sage.

Zelnik, M., & F. K. Shah. 1983. First intercourse among young Americans. *Family Planning Perspectives, 15*(2):64-70.

Zhou, J.-N., M. A. Hofman, L. J. G. Gooren, & D. F. Swaab. 1995. A sex difference in the human brain and its relation to transsexuality. *Nature, 378*:68-70.

Zilbergeld, B. 1978. *Male sexuality: A guide to sexual fulfillment.* Boston, MA: Little Brown.

Zilbergeld, B. 1992. *The new male sexuality.* New York: Bantam Books.

Zillmann, D. 2000. Influence of unrestrained access of erotica on adolescents' and young adults' dispositions toward sexuality. *Journal of Adolescent Health, 27*:41-44.

Zoucha-Jensen, J. M., & A. Coyne. 1993. The effects of resistance strategies on rape. *American Journal of Public Health, 83*:1633-1634.

Zubeck, P. 2003 (August 24). Air Force and Congress knew about sexual assaults, report shows. *Newark [New Jersey] Star-Ledger*, 4.

# Vietnam
## (*Công Hoa Xa Hôi Chú Nghia Viêt Nam*)
## (Socialist Republic of Vietnam)

Jakob Pastoetter, Ph.D.*
*Updates by J. Pastoetter*

## Contents

## *Demographics and a Brief Historical Perspective*

ROBERT T. FRANCOEUR

### A. Demographics

Vietnam is the second largest country in Southeast Asia after Indonesia. With 127,240 square miles (329,560 km²), it is twice the size of the state of Arizona, slightly larger than Malaysia (including East Malaysia), and about 15% smaller than Japan. Vietnam is bordered on the north by China, on the east by the Gulf of Tonkin and the South China Sea, and on the west by Cambodia, Laos, and the Gulf of Thailand. The country extends some 1,000 miles (1,600 km) from north to south. Its widest east-to-west point is 370 miles (600 km), whereas in some places it is only 30 miles (50 km) wide. The capital, Hanoi (2.194 million), is situated in the northern region, while the largest city, Ho Chi Minh City (4.392 million), the former Saigon, is in the south.

In July 2002, Vietnam had an estimated population of 81 million, up from only 47 million in 1975. (All data are from *The World Factbook 2002* (CIA 2002) unless otherwise stated.)

**Age Distribution and Sex Ratios**: *0-14 years*: 31.6% with 1.07 male(s) per female (sex ratio); *15-64 years*: 62.9% with 0.96 male(s) per female; *65 years and over*: 5.5% with 0.65 male(s) per female; *Total population sex ratio*: 0.97 male(s) to 1 female. Almost 80% of Vietnamese are under age 40.

**Life Expectancy at Birth**: *Total Population*: 69.86 years; *male*: 67.4 years; *female*: 72.5 years

**Urban/Rural Distribution**: 19% to 81%. The rural population is concentrated in the two main rice-growing deltas: the Red River in the north and the Mekong in the

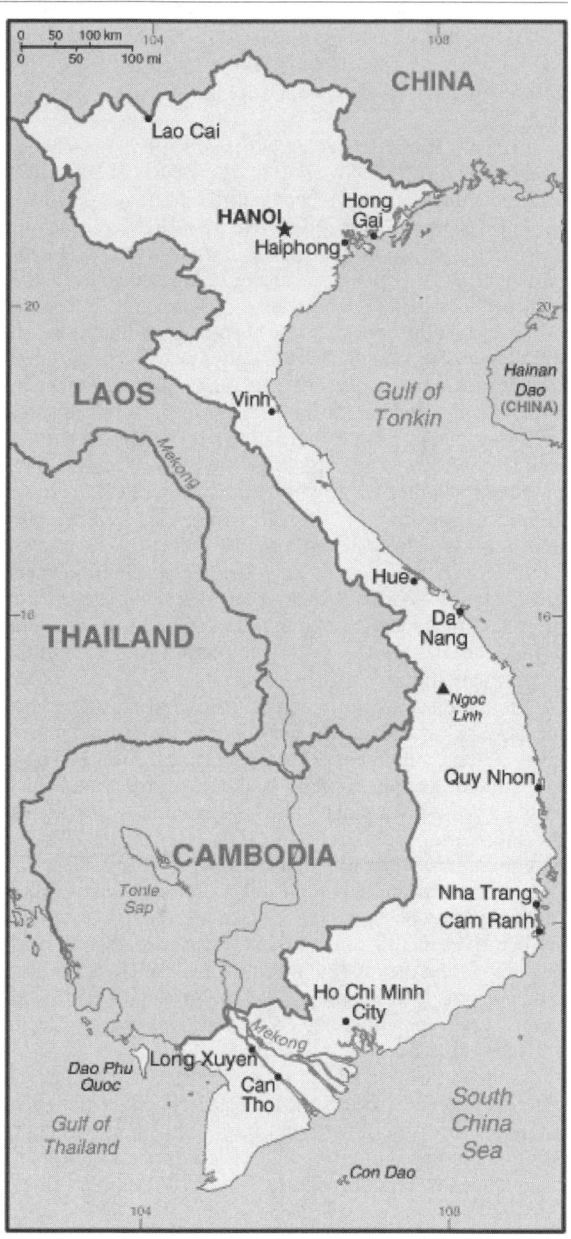

(CIA 2002)

south. In the Red River Delta (excluding Hanoi), population density averages 1,170 per square kilometer (0.4 mi²), and in Thai Binh it rises to 1,230 per square kilometer (0.4 mi²), among the highest rural densities in the world. The Mekong Delta, which is over twice as large as the Red River Delta, has a far lower population density at 400 per square kilometer (0.4 mi²) and is the source of the rice surpluses that Vietnam exports.

**Ethnic Distribution**: Vietnamese: 85% to 90%; Chinese, Hmong, Thai, Chm and mountain group minorities.

**Religious Distribution**: Buddhist, Hoa Hao, Cao Dai, Christian (predominantly Roman Catholic and some Protestant), indigenous beliefs, and Muslim

**Birth Rate**: 20.89 births per 1,000 population

**Death Rate**: 6.14 per 1,000 population

**Infant Mortality Rate**: 29.34 deaths per 1,000 live births

**Net Migration Rate**: –0.47 migrant(s) per 1,000 population

**Total Fertility Rate**: 2.44 children born per woman

**Population Growth Rate**: 1.43%

*Communications*: Jakob Pastoetter, Ph.D., Eichborndamm 38 D-13403, Berlin, Germany; jmpastoetter@compuserve.de.

**HIV/AIDS** (1999 est.): *Adult prevalence*: 0.24%; *Persons living with HIV/AIDS*: 100,000; *Deaths*: 2,500. (For additional details from www.UNAIDS.org, see end of Section 10B.)

**Literacy Rate** (*defined as those age 15 and over who can read and write*): 93.7% (*male*: 96.5%, *female*: 91.2%) (1995 est.); education is free and compulsory from age 6 to 11

**Per Capita Gross Domestic Product** (*purchasing power parity*): $2,100 (2001 est.); *Inflation*: –0.3%; *Unemployment*: 25% (1995 est.); *Living below the poverty line*: 37% (1998 est.)

Traditionally, education has been of great importance to the Vietnamese, and the State has always set aside a significant portion of its budget for education. Although access to higher levels of education has been limited, the introduction of near-universal primary education has produced a high literacy rate. According to the 1999 World Bank figures, 83% of the population over 15 years old was literate. [*Comment 2001*: The meaning of "literate" is not specified, whether this means able to write one's name, or able to read a newspaper. (*End of comment by R. T. Francoeur*)] In rural areas, the education system has been nearly as well developed as in urban areas, particularly in the north: 87% of the rural population was literate in 1989 compared with 95% of the urban population.

Vietnam has a good record in providing healthcare, as measured by such indicators as life expectancy, infant mortality, and the number of doctors per citizen. After 1954, the government set up a public-health infrastructure, which reached down to hamlet level. This system was extended to the south after reunification in 1976. In the late 1980s, a combination of reform factors, budgetary constraints, the decision to shift more responsibility for healthcare financing to the provinces, the reduced social role of agricultural cooperatives in 1988, and the introduction of fees in 1989, began to affect the quality of healthcare. By 1996, the government was devoting only 1% of the gross domestic product to health spending, and 85% of all spending on health services came from private sources.

Vietnam has one of the most complex ethnolinguistic patterns in Asia. About 50 different ethnic minorities make up more than 10% of the population, while approximately 87% of the population is ethnic Vietnamese (Kinh). The Vietnamese were significantly Sinicized during a millennium of Chinese rule. Vietnamese, one of the Mon-Khmer languages of the Austro-Asiatic language family, exhibits strong Chinese influence. Diverse cultural traditions, geographic variations, and historical events have created distinct traditional regions within the country. The general topographic dichotomy of highland and lowland regions also has ethnolinguistic significance: The lowlands generally have been occupied by ethnic Vietnamese, while the highlands have been home to numerous smaller ethnic groups that differ culturally and linguistically from the Vietnamese. The highland peoples can be divided into the northern ethnic groups, with affinities to peoples in southern China, and the southern highland populations, with ties to the Mon-Khmer and Austronesian peoples of Cambodia, Indonesia, and elsewhere in Southeast Asia (see Section 13, Sexual Attitudes and Behaviors among Ethnic Minorities).

A north-south variation also evolved among the ethnic Vietnamese as they expanded southward from the Red River Delta along the coastal plain and into the Mekong River Delta. The Vietnamese themselves have long made a distinction between the northern region, with Hanoi as its cultural center, the central region, with the traditional royal capital of Hue, and the southern region, with Saigon (Ho Chi Minh City) as its urban center. The French also divided Vietnam into three parts: the northern Tonkin, the central Annam, and Cochinchina in the south. Official efforts to move families from the densely populated areas to the "new economic zones" in the Central Highlands have tended to marginalize the minority groups living there, in addition to causing ecological stress.

The once sizeable overseas Chinese community, which was largely concentrated in the south, was depleted after many decided to leave the country as "boat people" when the government closed down private businesses in 1978. The 1989 census counted 962,000 Chinese, barely changed from the 949,000 recorded in the 1979 census. But as elsewhere in Southeast Asia, the Chinese minority wields great influence in the economy. Ho Chi Minh City alone is estimated to have about half a million Cantonese-speaking ethnic Chinese residents.

Vietnamese is the official language. Although the Vietnamese language is distinct, it nevertheless can be described as a fusion of Mon-Khmer, Tai, and Chinese elements. The minorities have languages of their own, and the Constitution guarantees their right to use these languages before the courts. English is gaining popularity as a second language, whereas many people still speak French, Russian, and German. In the early 17th century, Catholic missionaries introduced *chu quôc ngu* ("national written language") using an adapted form of the Western alphabet. The four letters, *f*, *j*, *w*, and *z*, are omitted, and accents are added. The resultant *chu quôc ngu* was made popular by the French and has been used officially since 1918. In Vietnamese, quite a few words are spelled in the same way. Differences in meaning result through pronunciation: e.g., *ca* (to sing), *cà* (eggplant), and *cá* (fish).

The names of the authors, researchers, institutions, titles of books, and locations occurring in this chapter are written in the form in which they were used in the international research literature. In order to facilitate literature searches, Vietnamese authors are referred to in exactly the writing of their names in the quoted articles and books. To avoid confusion for the non-Vietnamese users of the *International Encyclopedia of Sexuality*, who might not know what the family, middle, and first names are, we also did not alter the order of the three parts of the names, but used the form we found.

## B. A Brief Historical Perspective

The two most characteristic features of Vietnam's history are the country's struggle against foreign occupation and intervention, which has been going on for a good part of the last 2,000 years, and the ability of the Vietnamese people to learn from their occupants and finally overcome the foreign rule. The invaders were mostly, but not exclusively the Han Chinese, who ruled Vietnam for over 1,000 years from 111 B.C.E. to the 15th century. The Chinese were also in power during the wars between the Monguls and the Cham state, from 1428 to 1672, when Le Loi expelled the Chinese and was crowned emperor. In the middle of the 19th century, the French began intervening in the country's affairs on a large scale. Within ten years of seizing Saigon, they had taken control of the whole country, which they governed as a colony and incorporated into French Indochina in spite of resistance from the Vietnamese.

After 1940, when France surrendered to Germany in World War II, the Vichy government had to accept the presence of Japanese troops in Vietnam, although the Vichy government continued to govern the colony. During this period, Ho Chi Minh founded the Viet Minh, a nationalist liberation movement inspired by communist ideals, whose aim was to free Vietnam from foreign rule. A few months before the Japanese were defeated and finally surrendered to the Allied forces in September 1945, the Viet Minh took direct control from the French, and Ho Chi Minh declared the Democratic Republic of Vietnam independent on 2 September 1945.

After the end of World War II, the French deployed a substantial number of troops and fought the Viet Minh, led again by Ho Chi Minh, in order to regain control over Vietnam. The French were defeated decisively in 1954 at Dien Bien Phu and were forced to withdraw after they had dominated Vietnam for almost 100 years. However, the Viet Minh controlled only the northern part of Vietnam. The establishment of a second government, led by Ngo Dinh Diem in Saigon, led to the separation of the country into North and South Vietnam along the 17th parallel, the latter backed by the United States. Under the influence of the Korean War and the so-called domino theory, the United States gave South Vietnam political and military support against North Vietnamese attempts to take over the south. The United States' involvement gradually grew from a few advisers to hundreds of thousands of ground troops to fight the National Liberation Front, otherwise known as Viet Cong. Nevertheless, the Viet Cong and the North Vietnamese prevailed. In 1973, the United States signed a treaty with North Vietnam that provided for withdrawal of all American ground troops and aimed at restoring peace. After the American withdrawal, the government of South Vietnam crumbled rapidly and the North took control in 1975, ending a war that had lasted nearly 30 years. In July 1976, the nation was reunited, and the Socialist Republic of Vietnam was established.

Important events since the reunification of the country include a border war with China in 1979 and Vietnam's invasion of Cambodia the year before. Vietnam finally withdrew its troops from Cambodia in 1989. Perhaps the key feature, though, was the country's economic deterioration and its dire position by the mid 1980s. The breakthrough came at the end of 1986 with the introduction of the *doi moi*, or renovation policy. The aim was to move from a centrally planned to a market economy while still retaining the socialist political structure. The introduction of the new foreign investment law in December 1987, allowing and encouraging foreign investment, was a major step from which all the current excitement in the international business community has stemmed. Parallels have been drawn to China's experience. Such has been the rapidity and the strength of the process, that the near-total withdrawal of Soviet aid in 1991 and the collapse of the COMECON trading bloc, which should in theory have cut away the great majority of Vietnam's trade, had little effect.

There is now far greater openness towards foreign countries in general, and improved relations with other Southeast Asian and Western nations in particular. Vietnam became a full member of the Association of Southeast Asian Nations (ASEAN) at the meeting in Brunei in July 1995. Full diplomatic relations with the United States were reestablished in July 1995, some 20 years after the fall of Saigon.

Nevertheless, Vietnam is in desperate need of foreign investors. Over the last six years, the inflow of foreign capital dwindled from US$3 billion to little more than US$500 million since Vietnam lost its privileged position as favorite of Western investors because of the multiple domestic and external trading restrictions and widespread corruption. Many foreign investors have left the country in frustration, according to the *Neue Züricher Zeitung* (7/14/2000). The situation might change as a result of normalization of trade relations between the U.S. and Vietnam in 2000, which opened the Vietnamese market for American investors in such important key sectors as telecommunications and financial services. Still, Vietnam is one of the world's poorest countries. Its average per capita gross domestic product is estimated to be about US$150 per year; the statutory minimum wage is US$35 per month in Ho Chi Minh City and Hanoi and US$30 elsewhere for local employees employed by foreign invested enterprises. The economic reforms during the last few years have permitted some people to fare better in the private sector, but overall living standards still remain low. Viewed in this light, it is evident that, even with an inflation rate decreased from almost 400% in 1988 to 17% in 1995, it will be many years before Vietnam comes close to reaching the financial strength attributed to some of its Asian neighbors—especially since the growth rate for 1999 dwindled to 3% from an official estimate of 5.8% in 1998.

Real household income per head rose by 5% in 1995 and 4.2% in 1996. The percentage of people living in poverty (as defined by the World Bank) has fallen from almost 55% in 1992 to less than 30% by 1998. The poorest quintile of the population does not appear to have fared so well. Between 1994 and 1996, its income per head rose by just 0.5% annually, far less than the annual growth of 6.8% experienced by the top quintile.

Official figures obtained by Reuters show less than 600,000 foreign tourists visited Vietnam in 1998, down from 690,000 the previous year, a drop the government blamed on Asia's economic crisis. Hanoi lumps tourist figures with total arrivals, including business and official visitors, ending up with a figure of 1.5 million in 1998, down from 1.7 million in 1997. Its goal in 2000 was two million total visitors, compared with nearby Thailand, which expected to attract 8.2 million tourists during the same period.

## 1. Basic Sexological Premises

*Author's Note*: Because of the specific difficulties of doing sex research in a communist and Neo-Confucian country like Vietnam, we could not do field research on our own, and instead had to rely on the published papers and books about Vietnam. The challenge we faced in preparing this chapter was confirmed early on by Professor Frank Proschan, an expert on Vietnamese culture at the Folklore Institute at Indiana University (Bloomington), who told us that no Vietnamese scholar would be able to write such a chapter, because the Vietnamese have just started walking the path of independent science after many years of Confucian and communist censorship. The Vietnamese resources we subsequently found and incorporated into this chapter supported this thesis. Because the resources came from many different fields of research—history, medicine, ethnology, anthropology, sociology, religious studies, sexology, and sociology—we thought it best to leave them as much unchanged as possible to prevent misinterpretation (compare Gammeltoft 1999). At the same time, we also tried to make the text as readable as possible, without too many direct quotations or heavy use of indirect speech. Nevertheless, the chapter should be transparent enough to track all the sources down to find more in-depth information if necessary.

What information we have on contemporary sexuality in Vietnam had to be gleaned on the one hand from the Vietnamese and international anthropological and ethnological literature, as well as AIDS, STD, and family planning research (compare Sections 9, Contraception, Abortion, and Population Planning, and 10, Sexually Transmitted Diseases and HIV/AIDS). On the other hand, there exists the domestic social science research, which is focused mainly on "gender and development," and more recently on the nature of the Vietnamese family. For the French period, the late 1800s and the first half of the 20th century, we used mainly the works of Jacobus X. (1898, writing as "A French

Army-Surgeon") and Annick Guénel (1997). For the Vietnam War period, a major resource was *Saigon After Dark* by Philip Marnais (1967). We emphasize that neither Jacobus X. nor Philip Marnais are acknowledged anthropologists or ethnologists. Although their writings are quite sensationalistic and written from the point of view of a so-called ethnoerotologist and an American journalist, respectively, the facts they provide are regarded as reliable, even if they reveal more about the colonial fantasies and fears connected with "alien" sexuality, than they do about the perception and feelings of the native Vietnamese. Last but not least, Professor Frank Proschan of Indiana University, an expert on Vietnamese culture at the Folklore Institute, provided us not only with his own findings, but also books and articles about other subjects only available in Vietnam. We cannot stress the fact enough that without him we would not have been able to include reliable information about the Vietnamese homosexual culture. Additional information, as well as confirmation, was acquired by interviewing Vietnamese students at Indiana University and the Kinsey Institute and author Robert Taylor (1997), who served as an officer in the U.S. Army during the Vietnam War.

## A. Character of Gender Roles

### Reality and Fantasy

The character of Vietnamese gender roles reflects the over 2,000-year influence of Confucianism, which is still the most important single influence on gender roles. Vietnamese women were comparably less degraded by the "three submissions" (to father, husband, and eldest son) and the four virtues (skill with her hands, an agreeable appearance, prudence in speech, and exemplary conduct) than women in China (see Section 2, Religious, Ethnic, and Gender Factors Affecting Sexuality). Gender roles in Vietnam are changing rapidly, though with different speeds in different social layers. Although men are still more visible in society, it is not necessarily a sign of their also having more power. Far from a clear picture, the one sure statement is that Vietnamese gender roles are loaded with contradictions.

There is still a continuity of Vietnamese ideas of the power of women within the household ("the general of the interior"), and the way in which state socialism splits men and women. For example, the Peasant Union represents men and the Women's Union only women, thereby encouraging a popular public view that women are not farmers and need not be directly involved in economic change, although up to 80% of the field work is done by them. Also, the psychological dimensions of male-female relationships within the family and community are unrepresented and unidentified in the State bureaucracy, and new contradictions begin to emerge between the power of women in the family and culture and their empowerment by the state. As Wazir Jahan Karim observed in 1995, "This seems to be a repeat of a typical Southeast Asian model of change and development: that women continue to experience contradictory statements of their usefulness and power, and that the public view usually contradicts the popular."

Unlike the prevalence of male domination in neighboring cultures, the earliest legend about the founding of Vietnam claims equality among the spouses. The mythic founders of Vietnam were a couple, Au Co, the wife, and Lac Long Quan, the husband. The husband was a dragon, suited to live on the coastal plains; the wife was a fairy who wanted to live in the mountains. As they agreed to part, 50 sons followed their mother and governed the northern part of Vietnam, while 50 sons followed their father and reigned over the kingdom bordering the South China Sea. Before separating, they pledged mutual respect and aid in time of crisis.

Vietnamese folklore, female Buddhas, goddesses, and proverbs seem to show that Vietnamese women have some influence in society. Goddesses commonly presided over the cultivation of rice and other food crops. Streets and districts are named after female cult heroes, such as the Trung sisters (40 C.E.), who led a revolt of independence, and Trieu Thi Trinh, who took up a similar warrior role in the 3rd century. She is described as nine feet tall, with three-foot-long breasts and a voice like a temple bell, able to eat a bushel of rice and walk 1,500 miles (2,400 km) in a single day. Vietnamese nationalists have also resurrected the poetry of Ho Xuan Huong, a female poet who was critical of gender inequality more than 50 years before French colonization.

[*Update 2003*: In a recent analysis of "Romantic Love and Gender Hegemony in Vietnam," Alexander Soucy (2000) argues that the government of the Socialist Republic of Vietnam has not been very successful in its effort to achieve gender equality. While the government has rejected the patriarchal Confucian dictates of the three submissions and four virtues of women, young Vietnamese women continue to be subservient to men. In Soucy's view, the ideal of romantic love, as disseminated through the popular mass media, is a new form reinforcing old structures of gender hegemony (Soucy 2000). (*End of update by J. Pastoetter*)]

### Gender and Economic Control

Nearly all the country's market stalls today are run by women. Though they are more often small merchants, it is interesting that the richest private capitalist in Vietnam today is also a woman. Not only do women form the overwhelming majority of all active merchants in the country, they constitute the majority of the customers as well. As O'Harrow (1995) points out, in spite of the male role of provider, which is implicit in the Confucian paradigm, Vietnamese mothers raise their daughters to understand, if not explicitly, then by example, that they should always have their own money and cannot depend on men.

The most commonly acquired commodity for this kind of female protective investment is jewelry, preferably in unalloyed gold or with recognizable gems. Young girls quietly watch their mother's elaborate systems of boxes, jars, purses, hidden floor boards, and furtive containers of every kind and dimension, never opened in the father's presence. They observe and learn. The extraordinary interest Vietnamese women appear to take in jewelry is commonly misunderstood by outsiders as simple vanity. But in fact, the precious contents are considered the mother's property and will stay with her should she leave.

### Relationships Between (Married) Women and Men

According to O'Harrow (1995), the polite term for a wife is *noi tro* ("interior helper"), the common, not-so-polite epithet is *Noi Ttoung* or "general of the interior." The women of Ha Dong, in particular, have a reputation for being fierce spouses that has gained them the nickname of *Su Tu Ha Dong* or "Ha Dong Lionesses." It is said about their husbands that they belong to a very ancient club, the *Hoi So Vo* or "Society of Men Who Fear Their Wives." Folk humor aside, it is a strategy to survive that motivates women to gain control of the family finances. Because the wife is, in fact, the backbone of the family, many families get into deep trouble or even break up when the wife/mother dies. The social system in Southeast Asia is based on a system of moral debts and balances. The relationship between (married) women and men is not one between two individuals, but between two life projects which depend on one another. Break one side away and the whole system crumbles.

Contrary to Western notions, where feelings of guilt support freedom before marriage but faithfulness afterwards, in societies where shame and the notion of virgin marriage is operative, extramarital affairs outnumber premarital ones. If a Vietnamese woman takes a lover and can keep the fact secret and so avoid shame, she can maintain an upper hand. The man, on the other hand, while much less bound by problems of public shame for having a girlfriend, is more likely to be worried about surrendering self-control and so losing his face. As O'Harrow (1995) points out, Vietnamese women seldom have male friends, *per se*, because they have very few social mechanisms for dealing with men on an equal footing. Men are always patrons or clients, fathers, sons, husbands, or lovers. A wife deals with her husband with the same mechanisms that a mother uses to deal with her son, and a lover is usually treated as a daughter treats her father. So one can understand why tales of female sexual insatiability also attach to the Ha Dong lioness myth: It is the woman who controls the man, and he is the one who loses face.

## Relationships Between (Unmarried) Women and Men

It seems that at least in the urban centers of Vietnam, women are behaving in quite the same way as in the Western world: They have boyfriends and have sexual intercourse with them, but they are still anxious to pretend that the current boyfriend is the first and only one. Over 95% of the 279 unmarried women in the Hanoi sample of Bélanger and Hong (1998) had a boyfriend at the time of the survey, and they defined a boyfriend as a male friend with whom they had a committed relationship, and in most cases, a person with whom they had sexual intercourse. Once dating was initiated, one third of the women had had their first sexual experience in less than a year. After a year, two thirds had had sexual intercourse. The average duration between the two events was about 15 months. Most of the women did not engage in sex unless they knew their boyfriend for some time. Nevertheless, all the women but one said that their boyfriend took the initiative to engage in sexual relations. It was also not possible for them to introduce the subject of birth control, or to reveal that they had boyfriends before him. The women were afraid that, if they revealed their previous experiences to their current boyfriends, they might lose his respect and thus damage the relationship. They may obtain an abortion if they do not want to marry him (at least at the moment).

## Proper Work for Women

According to the Confucian cultural norms, women in pre-revolutionary Vietnam were supposed to have little or no authority in any sphere—political, economic, educational, or familial. There were no women in the "council of notables" that governed the village, nor were they part of the village political community that met in the communal hall. Because a woman was always incorporated within a family and subject to male authority within the family, a woman's economic management and enterprise was always subject to male control and therefore not "real" authority.

Under Communist rule a new social role for women in the countryside has opened up: *co giao*, "Miss Teacher," who teaches her pupils norms and behaviors, which may conflict with those of the parents. Vietnamese studies cite with approval cases where rural students admonish their parents on the grounds that "Miss Teacher would not like it," "it" being, for example, not boiling water before drinking, or quarreling. However, women's present leading role in primary-level education, as well as in health, is conceptualized as an extension of women's traditional role in the family: teaching children and caring for the sick.

As Pelzer White (1987) further points out, women are seen as making good cooperative accountants only as an extension of their traditional role as the keeper of the household budget. On the other hand, young men would never be allowed to train for careers as caretakers of very young children and infants. Only during the war was there a policy, expressed in a 1967 law, to promote women to leading positions in the countryside. The percentage of women acting as cooperative chairmen and other management posts shot up. After demobilization, however, the roles changed again. Even today, women face hostility from their husbands, and especially from their mother-in-laws, if they have higher status jobs.

## The "New" Vietnamese Middle-Class Woman

As Fahey (1998) observed, over the past ten years, Vietnam has witnessed a dramatic change in the images of women. The globalization process has drawn many urban women into the commercial sphere, as consumers of products as well as models with which to advertise products.

Nevertheless, the images of the women visible in the streets remain contradictory. The communist ideal for women was equality with men, to be achieved through the demise of private property and women's domestic role. Interestingly, women were also highly praised by the Communist Party as freedom fighters and war heroes; however, they are underrepresented in the political hierarchy. Female members of the National Assembly and of the Vietnamese Communist Central Committee do exist, but they represent an infinitesimal portion of the whole, and exercise almost no real decision-making power. The Politburo has never had a female member, and the female representation in the National Assembly began to decline immediately after the war, from 27% in 1976, to 22% in 1981, and to 18% in 1987 (Fahey 1998). By 1992, the proportion had increased only marginally, but it was expected to decline as the quota that required proportional female representation of 18% was eliminated before the last election. Such data suggest that the recent changes in women's position may have less to do with economic renovation as such, and more to do with restoration of certain aspects of pre-war gender practices. However, as Vietnamese women told Fahey (1998), they regard the decline in representation as irrelevant, because the National Assembly is losing authority and ambitious women can use their time more productively in private enterprise.

On the other hand, Vietnamese women are flooded with more and more Western images of how up-to-date women live. Beauty contests, fashion clubs, and magazines exert the strongest influence. Fahey (1998) reported that fashion clubs appeared in the early 1990s, with members including fashion designers, models, and companies eager to establish a fashion industry. The first modeling agency, CATD, begun by a young overseas Vietnamese woman, was licensed in Vietnam in 1995. Vietnam now has two locally produced fashion magazines: one for women in general (*Thoi Trang*) and the other for younger women (*Thoi Trang Tre*). Another magazine called *Thoi Trang Dien Anh* [*Movie Fashion*] reproduces sections from international fashion magazines, including French and American fashions, and appears to be more popular in the South. These magazines also have small sections for men, perhaps indicating that the commercialization of beauty is not entirely limited to women. Most newspapers now have a women's section that covers topics from how to pluck eyebrows to Japanese-sponsored parades.

A popular activity for middle-class women, especially those with substantial independent incomes, is attending the gym before work. The membership fee is about US$10 per month or 5 to 10% of these women's monthly income.

Interviews with these women reveal that they attend them both for social interaction and to improve their body shape. Although they are conscious of maintaining a shapely body, and coyly admit this, they inevitably refer to both inner and outer beauty when asked open-ended questions about the definition of a beautiful woman.

*The Male Gender Image*

Proschan (1998) observed that traditional Vietnamese society was strongly shaped by Neo-Confucian conceptions and practices of ancestral veneration and filial responsibility (*hieu*):

> A man's most important duty is to reproduce a male child to carry on the ancestral line: "The Annamite* loathes dying without being assured of male dependants. One can say that there exists a veritable obligation, of the religious or at least mystical order, to give birth as early as possible to the cult's heir" (Khèrian 1937, 29). Ethnologist Nguyen Van Huyen noted in 1939 that "male celibacy is always in complete disfavor. It continues to be considered as an act of filial impiety," with bachelors prohibited from participating in certain family and village rituals (Nguyen Van Huyen 1944/1939, 41). The tenacity of this traditional stricture is evident from current census data: of Vietnamese males over the age of 40, barely 1% has never married (Vietnam Population Census 1989).

That Vietnamese men are as imbued with the work ethic as are the women can be attested to by any observer of the economic activity of the Vietnamese refugee communities in the West, where Vietnamese men commonly hold two or sometimes three jobs at a time to support their families. But the popular notion persists, commonly abetted by male authors, such as the 19th-century libertine and poet, Tran Te Xoung (1890), that the height of machismo is not some Mediterranean predilection to physical abuse of women, but rather a gentlemanly idleness at their expense: "Drink and gamble 'til you're in over your head, but even if you are out of money, your kid's mother is still out there selling her wares."

It is interesting to note that during the Vietnam War, men envied the American soldiers. Vietnamese men have little or no body hair, but hairiness is regarded as a strong symbol of masculinity. It seems to have put men into a state of constant humiliation to watch hairy GIs being admired by Vietnamese women. The body image of men was changing a lot in the 1990s. The bodybuilding industry began to boom. Today, street posters of bodybuilders, often with Western faces, advertise gymnasiums; national competitions are held; and magazines are available for those who wish to know more. The body shape acquired by bodybuilders is significantly different from that of the majority of Vietnamese men, and there appears to be no precedent for such a practice. As to how Vietnamese men will be able to deal with this strong influence, and how it will change their attitudes toward their bodies are important questions.

**B. Sociolegal Status of Males and Females**

*Children and Adolescents*

Over 100 years ago, Jacobus X. (1898), whose observations as "A French Army-Surgeon" are regarded as quite reliable "although embed with racist and colonialist attitudes of superiority" (Proschan letter 2000), observed that children were breastfed until they were 3 or 4 years old if a boy; and even longer if it was a girl. When the Vietnamese child could

---

*Annamite(s) is the term used for the Vietnamese during the periods of the Kingdom and French Protectorate.

walk alone, he was allowed to run free, almost or quite naked, or roll in the dust, or wallow in the mire. After he was 12, he wore a ragged pair of pants and an old coat, the cast-off garments of his father, and then went to work, minding the buffaloes, helping his parents cultivate the rice field, or steering the sampan or junk. Children born to concubines had the same rights as the children of the legitimate wife. There was no distinction between "natural" and "adulterine" children in Cochin China. Girls and boys mingled promiscuously, "with the result that might be expected. That is why it is rare to find an Annamite girl, of more than ten years of age, a virgin." But that was 100 years ago.

*Adults*

Although the Vietnamese adopted the Confucian principle of male superiority, they still granted women some rights. Except for some restrictions concerning properties reserved for ancestor worship, daughters shared in the inheritance of parental properties on the same basis as their brothers. Divorced women and widows who remarried after their husband's death remained the owners of properties acquired during their marriage (*Le Code*, Codex Juris, Articles 388, 374, 375, 376; Nguyen & Ta 1987).

The full and complete equality of Vietnamese women was enshrined in the first Constitution of the Democratic Republic of Vietnam of 1946: "Women enjoy equal rights with men in all spheres." The 1980 Constitution guarantees equal rights for men and women in all respects, although a resolution passed by the Council of Ministers in December 1984 highlighted problems involved in promoting female status. Women are still a minority at the executive level. On the other hand, Vietnam has an official matriarchal heritage.

**C. General Concepts of Sexuality and Love**

Grammar makes clear how important marriage is in Vietnamese society. Proschan (1998) provides this example: "When Vietnamese ask one another about their marital status they do not ask 'Are you married?' but 'Have you married yet?' A proper response is not a yes-or-no answer but the answer 'Already' or 'Not yet'." Although the minimum legal age at marriage is 18 years for women, postponing marriage until age 22 is strongly recommended. Up to and through the French Colonial period, Vietnamese women were not regarded as nubile until about their 16th or 17th year. However, according to the *Ly-Ky* [*The Book of Rites*], girls might marry after 14 years and men at 16. Any marriages prior to those ages were not accepted.

According to Proschan (1998), if men feared that marriage might complicate their lives, they tried to find a girl who did not see in them as the focus of her desires and demands. In fact, many Vietnamese men believed that women were perfectly satisfied with something like a companionate marriage, which involved sufficient ardor to produce offspring, but was not complicated by passionate desire. A hundred years earlier, Jacobus X. (1898) confirmed this rather unromantic view of marriage:

> Marriage is for the Annamite a question of business and the procreation of descendants, rather than of sentimental love. On her side, the woman has not generally a very great affection for her husband, but concentrates all her love on her children.

Proschan (1998) writes that before colonial and revolutionary legal reforms made monogamy the only acceptable form of marriage, polygamy (specifically, polygyny) had been equally legitimate. When polygyny lost its legal sanction, it nevertheless continued outside the law, and women in polygynous relationships lost the protections and rights that the older legal codes had afforded their pre-decessors—i.e., those of second wives or concubines. In-dications are that extramarital heterosexual relations were frequent enough among married men that most people—male or female—assumed that they were the norm. There were numerous available partners—female or male—for men whose wives "fail[ed] to provide proper attention and stimulation" (Khuat Thu Hong 1998), as one researcher characterized the common rationale.

## 2. Religious, Ethnic, and Gender Factors Affecting Sexuality

### A. Source and Character of Religious Values

*Religious and Social Factors Present in Vietnam*

The traditional Vietnamese religion includes elements of Hinduism and all three Chinese religions: Mahayana Buddhism, Daoism, and Confucianism. Although Confu-cianism (i.e., Neo-Confucianism in its rather value-conser-vative form) is without doubt the most influential and deeply rooted of these influences, to say that the Vietnam-ese are "Confucian" is to oversimplify their social and per-sonal realities. The most widespread feature of Vietnamese Confucianism is the cult of ancestors, practiced in individ-ual households and clan temples. As such, it is strongly tied to folk religion.

There is also a wide variety of Buddhist sects, sects be-longing to the "new" religions of Cadoaism and Hoa Hao, and the Protestant and Roman Catholic Churches. The num-ber of Christian adherents in 1991 constituted an estimated 7% of the total population: 180,000 Protestants and five million Roman Catholics. The Catholic Church has been active in Vietnam since the 17th century, and since 1933 has been led mainly by Vietnamese priests. The number of Muslims is estimated at 50,000.

While the Vietnamese government guarantees freedom of religion, other factors influencing (and changing) the character of social values can be observed in communist ideology and Western ideas. The latter, first introduced dur-ing the French occupation followed by the Vietnam War, has been given fresh impetus since 1986 through *doi moi* economic reforms.

*Ancestor Worship*

Ancestor worship, which originated with Confucian-ism, holds that the soul of the dead person does disappear from sight but stays around to look after the family. Emper-ors and kings built imperial temples where they worshipped the late emperors whose achievements and exploits were re-corded on ancestral tablets and steles. Wealthy people have their family temples for the whole family to worship their ancestors. Poor people, who have no temple of their own, set up an altar in the best part of their home to show grati-tude and respect for their ancestors. Because of the war, which produced a serious shortage of dwelling places, most houses are now too small, and very few family temples or permanent ancestors' altars can be set up.

It is the responsibility of the eldest son to take care of the various anniversaries during the year. For this, he receives income from a number of rice fields or land as a hereditary state. The eldest son records the ancestor's date of death in a family register.

On the day of the anniversary, the chief of the family, properly attired, stands solemnly before the altar, with three sticks of incense in his hands, held to the level of his fore-head, and says the pseudonym, the real name, and the date of death, and invites the ancestor to the feast. At the same time, he will pray to the dead to protect the members of his family. Various dishes have to be prepared for display be-fore the altar on each ancestor's anniversary.

Nowadays, probably 70% of the Vietnamese are follow-ers of ancestor worship.

*Buddhism*

The origins of Buddhism in Vietnam can be traced to the 2nd century. For the Buddhist, life is seen as a vast sea of suf-fering. Wisdom lies in the suppression of desires: desires for life, happiness, riches, power, and so on, which are believed to be the roots of human suffering. The very essence of Bud-dhism is the Law of Karma, which states that man is reincar-nated and rewarded in the next life for his good deeds in this life, and punished for his bad ones. The present existence is conditioned by earlier existence and will condition those to follow. Desire must first be overcome; a pure heart is neces-sary to break the chains binding man to his earthly existence.

In 1920, an organized movement for the restoration of Buddhism began throughout the country. Starting in 1931, Associations of Buddhist Studies were established in the South, the Center, and North Vietnam. Many translations of both Greater and Lesser Vehicle Buddhist Texts were distrib-uted. Finally, after many assemblies of monks and National Delegate Congresses, the Buddhist Institute for the Propaga-tion of the Faith, the *Viean Houa Naio*, was established.

The most important Buddhist sect is Cadoaism. For-mally inaugurated in 1926, this syncretic religion is based on spiritualist séances with a predominantly ethical content, but sometimes with political overtones. Several other sects exist, like the Tien Thien and the Tay Ninh. It is estimated that these Buddhist sects have two million adherents. An-other influential sect is Hoa Hao. Founded in 1939, it has one and a half million adherents.

Through Buddhist-nun monasteries, Buddhism exerted a strong influence for the equality of men and women. Al-though the monasteries were skeptically regarded by the Confucianist elite—one of the common defamations being that the nuns were involved in lesbian sexual practices—Buddhism gave women another role model besides that of wife and mother. This was especially true for elderly wid-ows who were entering Buddhist orders. On the other hand, their influence on the priesthood seems to be difficult to detect.

*Daoism*

Vietnamese Daoism, derived from the doctrine of Lao Tzu, is based essentially on the participation of man in the universal order. This order depends on the equilibrium of the two elements Yin and Yang, which represent the constant du-ality of nature: rest and motion, liquid and solid, light and darkness, concentration and expansion, and material and spiritual. The material world being imbued with these two principles, the Daoist believes that whoever is able to act ac-cording to these principles could become the master of the world. This belief, in turn, has promoted a kind of mysticism, reflected in the magical practices of certain sorcerers who claim to possess the secret of the universe.

The Daoist refrains from troubling the natural order of things; on the contrary, he conforms to it in every circum-stance. He considers the taking of initiatives to be a waste of time and energy. In respecting the basic Daoist doctrines of passivity and absence of care, he avoids the active life. These doctrines, which were adopted by many Confucian scholars as well, are summed up in the Daoist maxim: "Do nothing and everything will be accomplished simultaneously." The supreme divinity of Daoism is the Emperor of Jade. With his ministers of Death and Birth, he controls the destiny of men. The cult is replete with incantations, charms, and amulets, which once were made for prosperous trade, with the sorcerers intervening in every possible occasion in life.

In the context of sexuality, *yang* is identified with semen or seminal essence (*jing, yin*), which is why Daoists are encouraged to have intercourse often, but without ejaculating. The aim is to build up *jing* but retain *yang* through not ejaculating, but at the same time enabling the woman to reach orgasm and give off her *yin* essence, which additionally strengthens the man. Another Daoist practice is to get a young man and woman together and to gather up their sexual secretions and swallow them—a practice that is believed to prolong life for the Daoist. Jacobus X. (1898) reported that it was still very common at the end of the 1800s, although he did put it strongly as a "strange freak of eroticism":

> The old Celadon is accompanied by a servant or strong coolie, who copulates with a woman in his presence, and then retires . . . When once the agent is retired, well and duly paid, the old debauchee is left alone with the woman, who is still resting upon the field of battle. Then the man approaches, and eagerly receives in *bucca sua*, the liquid which runs *ex vulva feminae*.

## Confucianism

Confucianism, a generic Western term, is a *Weltanschauung*, i.e., a social ethic, a political ideology, a scholarly tradition, and a way of life, but it is not an organized religion. Chinese governors introduced Confucianism to Vietnam from 939 to 1407. The doctrine of Confucius is set forth in four classical texts and in five canonical books. By rigid rules, it determines the attitude that every man in society should adopt to guide his relationships as an individual with his superiors, with his wife and friends, and with his inferiors. The philosophy suggests a moral code, which advocates the Middle Way for the worthy man's behavior. According to Mencius, the most distinguished disciple of Confucius, man is inherently good. To preserve his goodness, he needs to check his passions. The wise man improves himself through study; he knows himself and is the master of his passions.

There are four rules for a man to achieve self-perfection: to cultivate himself, to run his family, to rule the country, and pacify the world. The three important sets of social interaction are between king and citizen, between father and son (*hieu*—filial piety or responsibility), and between husband and wife. Five cardinal virtues have to be achieved in order to become a man of virtue: humanity, equity, urbanity, intelligence, and honesty. As for the woman, Confucius teaches four virtues: skill with her hands, agreeable appearance, prudence in speech, and exemplary conduct, and three submissions or obediences: to the father until she is married, to the husband after she leaves her parents' house, and to the eldest son when her husband dies. Interestingly, the real order as seen by most Vietnamese, and also by the French, is a different one: the Vietnamese woman was inferior to her father but just about equal to her husband, provisionally superior to her minor brothers, and always superior to her sons.

In sexual matters, Confucianism is quite "puritanic." A "good" young girl is not only expected to keep her virginity until she gets married and to get married only once in her life, she is not supposed to make herself attractive, even to her own husband. Confucianism does not consider sexual activity as wrong, but love and tenderness are treated with mistrust, and physical displays of them are considered at least questionable. This rule applies not only to showing affection in public, but also to its display in the privacy of the home. As early as in the 17th century, male and female poets protested against it.

## "Popular Religion"

As Thien Do (1997) showed, there exists also a very specific Vietnamese "popular religion" characterized by the propitiation of spirits and deities of a certain typology:

1. The tutelary or guardian spirits, either originally worshipped by the villagers or historically instituted by Vietnamese or Chinese rulers. They include the nation-founding patriarch, past male and female heroes, and able ministers;
2. The nature spirits of the grottos, rocks, and trees, and rivers and oceans;
3. Immortals (*tien*) and holy sages (*thanh*), in the Daoist tradition, together with Lady Lieu Hanh and her affiliates, including the Mandarin Snakes and the Five Tigers (Agents), forming the *chu vi* (divine ensemble) in the belief systems of sorcerers and mediums;
4. Deities of Cham and Khmer origin, such as Po Yan Inu Nagar, the Whale Spirit, and the Neak Ta (Ong Ta); and
5. Consecrated to a lesser extent are founding patriarchs of the arts and crafts (including the martial arts), the domestic deities, marginal demonic spirits, and lonely ghosts.

The places of veneration and features of spiritual practices are divided between the village communal house or *dinh*, where local participants emulate the court elite in Daoist-Confucian formats, the private Buddhist-Daoist temple or *chua*, where a three-religion pattern of Chinese origin has been practiced and modified to suit Vietnamese adherents, the trance mediumship, with the special importance of the Earth God and of female deities, and finally the practice of self-cultivation, mainly practiced by Daoists (*ong dao*).

Of importance for gender images is the fact that many of the Vietnamese deities were thought of as female and sometimes even worshipped exclusively by women. This behavior has not stopped with communism or *doi moi*. Since the late 1980s, village pagodas have undergone a frenzy of refurbishment. As Stephanie Fahey (1998) reports, in a pagoda in a village near Hanoi, a local woman pharmacist of 200 years ago is revered for the birth of the prosperous traditional craft of pharmaceutical production, and a temple on West Lake features Ba Chua Lieu, supposedly a princess who developed a prosperous silk industry. The young, as well as the prosperous, patronize these pagodas to implore the appropriate female deities with such different petitions as economic success and the birth of a son. It seems that with the demise of the Communist moral code, the Vietnamese are searching their past for more-traditional values.

Among the religions in Vietnam, the "Popular Religion" seems to be the most liberal in sexual aspects. Khuat Thu Hong (1998) presents dozens of examples that show this liberal attitude from ancient times to the present. Lingam and yoni worship is the most obvious. But there is also the worship of the god No Nuong (*No* meaning a bamboo phallus, and *Nuong*, a vulva, made of a spathe from an areca tree). This worship centers on the ritual striking together of these genital symbols by the village head and deputy village head, while the young boys and girls called out, *tung tung, dap* (onomatopoeia of a drumbeat in Vietnamese) according to the beat. There is also the game of grabbing eels from a jar: In this game, each team of a young man and a woman observed the following rule: While trying to catch the eel in the jar, neither the young man nor the woman could look into the jar, and the young man had to keep one hand on the young women's breast. At the same time, a committee of judges closely watched, along with fellow villagers who called out and teased them.

*Communism*

Communist ideology expects all men to behave according to the principles of a "new society" founded on a Marxist-Leninist base. Regarding gender issues, it implies equality of men and women. Because Engels depicted traditional childrearing practices as the main impediment for achieving gender equality, communist societies tended to socialize childcare and education to enable women to work for the society as men do. The institutions of marriage and the family were considered to be the key to the reproduction of social inequality, because the practices that evolve within these institutions obviously preserved the underlying system of private property and its inheritance. Thus, communist thought was suspicious of devotion to family and treated this as "unsocialist" in a man, especially a Party member. In its first two decades, the Communist government in Vietnam made specific efforts to destroy all Confucian traces in Vietnamese society. To break the strong ties binding members of Vietnamese families that had been molded by Confucian principles, the Communists even encouraged betrayal among family members. Over the years, the anti-Confucian policy has changed Vietnamese family structure considerably. The government has acquired most of the authority and influence attributed to Confucian scholars, especially regarding questions of sexual morality and behavior.

Interestingly, communist gender ideas changed dramatically during the war with the South and after the reunification. The typical functionary now clearly resembled the ideal authoritarian Confucian gentlemen. Women are supposed to care for the family and especially the husband. The few state-honored female revolutionists and freedom fighters fell into oblivion.

At the same time, it was the Communist government that set up the Central Committee for Mother and Infant Welfare in 1971. The committee's responsibility was to guide and unify the organization of *crèches* (day nurseries). About one third of all children were raised in such facilities. Further support was given to women to separate themselves from domestic duties according to the 1980 State Constitution, Article 63, requiring the state and society to ensure the development of maternity homes, *crèches*, kindergartens, community dining halls, and other social amenities to create favorable conditions for women to work, study, and rest. Even men were asked to share household tasks. But these efforts remained rather at cultural and ideological levels. Vietnamese Communists were keen to maintain the family as a social, but not necessarily an economic unit. For that reason, they argued that it was necessary for women to handle both employment and domestic duties.

Communism brought improvement for women by reducing early forced marriages, publicly condemning wife-beating, providing free childcare, and recognizing the economic value of housework. Legislation, together with women's prolonged contribution to the war effort, assisted in dismantling the absolute authority of the Confucian "three submissions." But with *doi moi*, it seems that the Communist Party has withdrawn from social engineering. Membership figures indicate that the Party is losing women's support, with a drop in membership from 34% women in 1960 to only 16% today. Most women enjoy the rediscovered freedom of wearing nice and individual clothes and putting on makeup. In the heydays of Communist rule, these fashions were badly received, as this newspaper excerpt shows:

You young people, I know you need make-up to be beautiful . . . but you should also keep the Vietnamese manner; simplicity, purity and wholesomeness are beauty. It is advisable not to imitate the alien "styles" imported from the European capitalist counties, and you see, these styles could really reflect only the lowly liking and crazy, carefree and pessimistic moods. A girl living in such a wholesome social situation as you are in now is advised not to wear such a queer and carefree hairstyle. And such thin, tight and revealing clothes as you are wearing now, in our North, all the decent, cultured women have never cared to wear. (*Vietnamese Woman* No. 293, May 1972, 6)

*War and the Influence of Western Civilization*

In the northern areas controlled by the non-Communist side prior to 1975, the authorities did not carry out a policy systematically hostile to Confucianism. But disruption of the old social framework because of war, which forced people to abandon their villages for urban areas, as well as the impact of new living conditions and broader contact with Western civilization, also loosened traditional family ties. Children became more independent from their parents and the former strict obedience to the elders diminished.

Since 1986, the same changes were occurring in the Socialist Republic of Vietnam because of the influence of the official policy of a free-market economy. The ideals of consuming and having fun through buying goods are especially attractive to the younger generation, which is also the vast majority of the Vietnamese, 80% of whom are under 40 years of age. Pelzer White (1993) concluded that the beauty contests and calendars now sanctioned by the Communist state as a signal to the international business community that Vietnam is open for business, also convey a visual message supporting social change.

## B. Character of Ethnic Values

*The Concept of "Phuc Duc"*

The single most specific Vietnamese concept that exerts influence on the gender roles of men and women seems to be the concept of *phuc duc* or "merit-virtue," a kind of karma concept. It refers to the merit that, in a former life, oneself and/or an ancestor acquired through virtuous deeds that is then passed on to succeeding generations, and the merit that a member of the present generation passes to future generations as yet unborn. It is "quantifiable," as in "a lot of *phuc duc*."

Based on the manner in which one lives one's life, it can be an evil force (*vo phuc*) as well as a benevolent one. It is considered influential over a span of five generations. Thus, the nature of one's *phuc duc*, together with the horoscope and geomancy, which reads the composition of *am* (*yin*) and *dong* (*yang*) in the earth, determines the course of life. The individual can exert only a limited personal influence. The definition of what is regarded as a virtuous life follows the Buddhist-Confucian code. The specific Vietnamese interpretation goes back at least to the 15th century and can be found in the poem, *Gia Huan Ca*. It is interesting to note that the primary determinant is not the act itself, but the motivation beneath the act.

Slote (1998) presented an example of how *phuc duc* works with *Kieu*, the hero in the epic poem, *Kim Van Kieu*:

She is a girl of particular charm, beauty, accomplishment, and morality, who sells herself as a minor wife to an unscrupulous scholar in order to redeem her father who has been beset by ill fortune. The scholar, a man devoid of virtue, turns out to be the husband of the madame of a brothel and Kieu is forced into prostitution. Under these circumstances, Kieu's sacrificial act brings much *phuc duc*. On the other hand, were she to have become a prostitute for profit alone, she would have been condemned, her family would have suffered, and future generations would have borne the penalties. In a parallel sense Kieu's misfortune inasmuch as her life had been thoroughly virtuous, could be ascribed to bad *phuc duc* visited upon her because of transgressions of some ancestor.

Coupled with the nature of the motivation that serves to precipitate the act is the issue of sacrifice. An act that is performed easily brings far less reward than an equivalent action that is difficult and involves suffering. Since it was very difficult to bear the life in a brothel for Kieu, she was finally reunited with the man she loved, to whom she had originally been betrothed.

Based on the belief that "merit virtue is caused by the maternal," women can create destiny. Deserving women of good conduct bring felicity to their descendants, just as tragedy, poverty, and other incidents of bad fortune can be blamed on one's wife, mother, or grandmother. So important was (and still is) this concept, that although the wealth and status of a bride's family matters, it is secondary to her *phuc duc*. A poor but virtuous woman of good heritage and blessed at birth by the heavens, who would increase the family's fortune and ultimate destiny, would be a most desirable bride. And when a marriage is arranged between a poor but virtuous girl and the son of a wealthy family, the girl's family also usually benefits. To a great extent, *phuc duc* has been influential in making the class system less stringent than in other cultures.

With the responsibility of acquiring *phuc duc*, a double standard has been created: Men, if they chose, were relatively free to act in ways that are scarcely designed to build *phuc duc*. Examples are gambling, cheating, and whoring. On the other hand, there were also the elderly men referred to as living saints, a position that carried great esteem because it contributes to the building of *phuc duc* for the family. As Slote (1998) observed, the very concept of *phuc duc* may lead to manipulation, because it can be used as a metaphor in the service of many emotions: hostility, competitiveness, defiance, self-sacrifice, guilt, and control. It is also a justification when all else fails, when the children misbehave, or when one is beset by misfortune.

### Astrology and the Influence of the "Thay Boi"

Another very strong influence on sexual behavior is the belief that the specific constellation of stars at the time of one's birth can reveal one's destiny. The *thay boi* (the mostly female fortune teller) is the first resource to consult if something goes wrong. A good example of *thay boi* influence is the following statement of a 30-year-old transvestite (Bao, Long, & Taylor 1998, 20):

In my childhood when my father was alive, he forced me to wear shorts, but I did not and he fought me. My mother resorted to the fortune teller and knew that was my fate. It means that she must have such a child, no one expected that. My father who was a government officer felt shy and did not agree and said "the male should be male and the female should be female." My mother could not stand it and said to my father you could not fight me any more. If you fight him I will leave. She said to my father you can not prevent him from that and finally he accepted me. I have always been like this when I was growing up. All my relatives did not accept me. I think that is my fate. What problems I suffer because I can't wear male clothes. I only wanted to be a girl.

One might suggest that the astrologer seems to be as important for Vietnamese society as sex therapists, psychologists, and marriage counselors are for Western societies. Even today, nearly two thirds of the couples in the south and (because of the stronger influence of communism in the north) a smaller part in the north have their horoscopes

matched before marriage (Goodkind 1996). Since geomancy is believed to reveal if the location of one's house is the reason for quarreling in the family or even for sterility, asking a geomancer is also regarded as helpful. According to Young (1998), the third precise way to measure the energy believed to cause change in the fortune of any individual is to study the shape of the person's face. Although it cannot be changed by reading the face of others, one gains intimate knowledge about them.

### Alteration of the Genitals

Khuat Thu Hong (1998) mentions that some men, especially male prostitutes, are undergoing the surgery of "putting pellets" (small, metal balls—usually two or three at a time, but some men have as many as nine or ten) or "swords" (the sword-like plastic pieces are punched through the penis) into their penis. The men argue that the altered penis creates special pleasure for women.

## 3. Knowledge and Education about Sexuality

Although Vietnam can be regarded as a fairly liberal society when it comes to sexual behavior, talking or writing about sexuality is a totally different matter. Vietnam never produced sex education books like the Indian *Kama Sutra* or the Chinese and Japanese pillow books. Most young people get married without the least elementary knowledge, as a collection of interviews in Khuat Thu Hong's (1998) book shows:

On our wedding night, neither of us knew anything—meaning that we slept together as friends. We even tried to do something, but we didn't know what we were doing (born 1959).

On my wedding day, I didn't understand why when we slept with another, one person laid atop another. . . . I thought we were only supposed to lie side by side (born 1957).

After 1950, a few books on sexuality and sex education were published. Most prominent was Dr. Nguyen Manh Bong's book, *What Lovers Should Know*, published by Huong Son Publishers in Hanoi 1949. Similar publications appeared in the south of Vietnam during the succeeding years. In 1970, one Saigon newspaper ran a column called "Replying to Your Questions on Sexuality," which was written by two psychologists. In the North, prior to *doi moi*, there were almost no publications on sexuality. In the 1970s, the sole publication on sex education was *Girl's Hygiene*, which included quite sketchy information on female sexual organs, menstruation, and how to maintain personal hygiene. In 1988, David Reuben's book, *Answering Those Questions You Don't Dare Ask*, was translated from English and attracted much attention, but was banned from official circulation until 1989. Other books were translated from German, including Rudolf Neubert's *Marital Relations*, published in 1989. In 1991, David Elia and Genevieve Doucet's book, *1000 Questions and Answers About Women and Their Bodies*, was translated from French and published in Vietnam.

In recent years, many books by Vietnamese on sex and sexuality have begun to appear in bookstores. Ho Ngoc Dai's 1991 book, *Chuyen Ay* [*That Conversation*], which talked about sexuality within a philosophical and psychological framework, drew much attention. Books based on scientific knowledge are more common and include Doan Van Thong's book, *Nhung Thac Mac Tham kin Cua Ban Tre* [*The Secret Questions of Young Friends*] published by Tien

Giang Publishers in 1991, and Minh Phuong's book, *Hoi Dap ve Gioi Tinh va Tinh Duc* [*Questions and Answers about Sex and Sexuality*], edited by Dr. Le Van Tri, published by Medical Publishers in 1995. Psychologist Dr. Pham Con Son has also written about love, sexuality, marriage, and family in books such as *Nhung Thu Dich Cua Hanh Phuc Lua Doi* [*The Foes of a Couple's Happiness*], published by Dong Thap Publishers in 1996. The Research Center for Gender, Family, and Environmental Development is the first social science research institute to begin writing books on sex and sexuality, including Dr. Dao Xuan Dung's book, *Gia Duc Tinh Duc* [*Sex Education*], published in 1996 by Youth Publishing House. In addition, there are series of other books written by local and foreign authors mainly from Russia, the Czech Republic, and Poland (Khuat Thu Hong 1998).

As Gammeltoft (1999) points out, many aspects of everyday life in Vietnam are politicized through governmental mass education and mass mobilization campaigns. In fields as diverse as diet, marriage, religion, and pregnancy, there are politically right and wrong answers to any question, and everyone knows precisely what is politically correct and socially desirable and what is not. This is particularly true for family planning issues, which have been given a very high priority on the government agenda since the late 1980s. There are efforts to educate people about sexual issues, as may be exemplified by this report:

> One morning at the shrimp factory I watched as 700 women in identical white smocks cleaned the shrimp. Suddenly their work was interrupted—all had to stand and watch a video on AIDS prevention. Some cases had appeared in town, a manager told me. That night the scenes were the same in boomtown Nam Can. AIDS is just another risk of frontier living. (*National Geographic* February 1993, 35)

Sex education has been limited because of Vietnam's traditional bias against the public mention of anything sexual. Although this situation may seem similar to other countries, in Vietnam much of the opposition to "sex education" comes from administrators and teachers, of whom many are reportedly too embarrassed to discuss intimate sexual matters with the students. Faced with an increasing HIV-infection rate and an abortion rate thought to be among the highest in the world, Hanoi health officials opened the city's first sex education café in November 1999. The café fills a void in sex education, as the subject is not taught in schools, and many parents admit they are too embarrassed to raise the issue with teenage children who are becoming increasingly sexually active. The idea for the Hanoi café stemmed from a study that detailed how young people spend their time. It is also modeled on a similar initiative in Ho Chi Minh City. The café offers a place where young people can spend time talking with their friends and freely ask for information about sex and AIDS. Although the café will not distribute condoms, a female physician specializing in reproductive health, and an HIV/AIDS counselor are on hand to answer questions. On average, about 50 customers, ages 16 to 24, have visited the café on a daily basis (Watkin, *South China Morning Post* December 20, 1999).

In 2000, a pilot project sponsored by the United Nations Fund for Population Activities was started that allows high schools in eight of Vietnam's 61 provinces to offer advice on obtaining contraceptives at government clinics and pharmacies. Three thousand pharmacists in five provinces are being trained to provide customers with better information on contraceptives, and state-run radio airs a weekly show answering youths' sex-related queries (Cohen, *Far Eastern Economic Review*, 6/29).

As far as homosexuality is concerned, only in the last three years has a grassroots group emerged with the aim of reducing the spread of HIV/AIDS among gay and bisexual men in Ho Chi Minh City. The Nguyen Friendship Society consists of about 50 volunteers who prepare and print leaflets about sex education to be handed out to patrons in bars and clubs.

## 4. Autoerotic Behaviors and Patterns

No information about autoerotic practices exists except for the French period. According to Jacobus X. (1898), masturbation occurred very often: "Nearly all the boys practice masturbation from the age of fourteen or fifteen years," but it seemed to him that it was practiced only by males:

> This, no doubt, results from the ease with which the girl or woman can satisfy her natural desires; moreover, the great frequency of the "flowers" [an STD, probably gonorrhea] must help to limit this special form of vice. I never met but two cases, and both of these were the mistresses of Europeans (Jacobus X. 1898).

## 5. Interpersonal Heterosexual Behaviors

### A. Talking About Sexuality

The Vietnamese prefer a flowery, euphemistic vocabulary when they speak about sexuality. For example, a man having sexual desires might say, "I am going to buy a tree." Food is also heavily connected with sexual activity. Words like "crisp, sticky, spicy" are used to describe food as well as women and are frequent in erotic fantasies. Many dishes are identified with female figures or organs: The white rice flour cake is the image of a virgin; the pulpy interior of a breadfruit with its sticky juice is associated with the vagina; the eating of a rice flour pancake is similar to the defloration rite; the sucking of the honey flambéed banana and the scooping of water in the rice field are symbols of having sex. As in many Asian countries, this type of language helps people to speak about sexual matters without using the terms that would embarrass them.

### B. Sexual Behaviors

*Kissing and Sex Positions*

In traditional Vietnam, kissing in the "Western" sense was forbidden. Instead, nose sniffing or rubbing, comparable with Inuit customs, was practiced. The preferred position for sexual intercourse among the Vietnamese was both partners lying face-to-face, side-by-side, or the rear-entry position. The reason for these preferences, Jacobus X. (1898) suggests, is the structure of the Vietnamese bed, which is made of bamboo slats. In the missionary position, which he calls *la position de l'amour classique*, a man would scrape the skin off his knees.

*Premarital Relations, Courtship, and Dating*

The information one can gather about the beliefs and practices of young people regarding premarital relations and the role of sexuality are quite contradictory and are evidence that sex research is still underdeveloped in Vietnam. For example, the Departments of Psychology and Sociology of Hanoi University conducted research in 1992 on the sexual relations of university and high school students in Hanoi (Hoang Ba Thinh 1992). About 72.4% of female students in their fourth year of university had sexual relations, with only 17.6% having had one (usually their first) partner, whereas the others had between two and four partners. Yet, after graduating, only 8.2% of respondents had married one of these partners. Among those female students who had boyfriends, it was quite common for them to live together in the dormitories. An early 1990s survey by CARE (Cooperative for American Relief Everywhere) found that just over half of Vietnamese men had had two or more sexual partners in the previous two weeks (Franklin 1993).

In a recent survey, only 34% of students in Ho Chi Minh City responded that they found premarital sex "acceptable." Although not considered high by international standards, the statistic was shocking to most Vietnamese. A socially more acceptable figure was that only 10.3% of men and 1.4% of women had had sexual intercourse before their marriage, and 57.5% said they did not plan to have sex before marriage, whereas only 14.7% replied that they did plan to have sex before marriage (Chittick 1997).

O'Harrow (1995) reports that premarital intercourse is quite common in Vietnamese villages, but also that there is still an obligation on the man's part to marry the girl he has deflowered, and she reminds him of this fact in the strongest possible terms. Young couples in Hanoi, even married couples, face great difficulty in finding a place for private encounters. The evening stroller through the city's lakeside public parks must step carefully to avoid interrupting lovers hard at work.

### Marriage and Family

In the past, Vietnamese marriages were arranged through matrimonial agents (*mai-dongs*) who brought the two families together and arranged the question of the wedding portion (brideprice). Interestingly, the woman did not bring any marriage portion, and it was the groom who paid for the wedding presents, brought to the common lot his fortune of rice fields and cattle, and often had to pay money to the wife's family. In return, his compensation was comparatively small: a tobacco jar, for example, a box for betel nuts, or a cigarette case. The wedding ceremony was quite simple: The future husband and wife met, mutually offered themselves to each other, and chewed betel nut together. Though Confucian tradition permits the husband to take lesser wives (theoretically to be chosen for him by the first wife), economic realities (and relatively innocuous modern laws) would force him to be content with one at a time. O'Harrow (1995) reports also that to give a woman a piece of fine jewelry in the Vietnamese tradition is to help confirm her independence as a human being, and for a mother to hand over a piece of her jewelry to her daughter is a universally understood gesture, for which the subtext is "may this protect you from misery." Nowadays, divorce is increasingly easy to obtain.

### Adultery

A quite questionable story found in different sources dating back to the 19th century is that a woman found guilty of adultery would be thrown to a specially trained elephant, which in turn threw her into the air with his trunk and trampled her to death when she landed. Quite telling is the gusto with which this story was spread by European authors.

The early *Annamite Code* contained the following article: "An adulteress shall receive ninety blows of the rattan upon her buttocks, and her husband may afterwards marry her to another, or sell her if he pleases, or keep her in his house." Jacobus X. (1898) quotes *Le Code*: "Shop men who commit adultery with the wife of their master shall be treated as servitors or slaves, and punished by strangulation."

As O'Harrow (1995) shows, moral values in Vietnamese society are enforced by constraints of shame rather than guilt. A Vietnamese woman can cheat (in the Western sense) on her husband without regret, as long as it is not known. The following saying illustrates the point: "Flirtations with desire, I wore a wedding ring for protection; I lost my wedding ring, but my desire remains." Vietnamese men, in their turn, know the "rules of the game" and have less of a tendency than women to brag publicly about their conquests.

It seems that the younger generation in particular, which grew up during *doi moi*, tends to excuse adultery. Unhappiness in marriage, being sexually unfulfilled, or just being attracted by another person are now regarded as legitimate reasons to have sexual contact with another person other than one's partner (Khuat Thu Hong 1998).

According to Fahey (1998), middle-class urban women often confide during informal interviews that their husbands have a mistress or entertain several girlfriends. Because women are still responsible for family finances and the welfare of children, it is common for them to have secret savings as a buffer against their husband's indiscretions with other women.

### Incidence of Oral and Anal Sex

Jacobus X. (1898) described oral sex as a way to avoid infection with a venereal disease. Apparently, it is not a very successful method, as he later writes: "I have found eruptions, ulcerations, and the scars of chancres, on the lips and tongue of the unhappy victims of this form of debauchery. When once they are affected, they in turn help to spread the syphilitic virus, by a law of reciprocity which it would be very difficult to repress." This was confirmed by the French surgeon Joyeux (1930).

Anal sex seems to have been far more common as a homosexual practice than among heterosexual couples. Jacobus X. (1898) suggests that it was a phenomenon that only occurred between prostitutes and their customers: "The woman is old when she takes to sodomy, which she does rather from economic motives, on account of the money it brings, than from natural taste."

## 6. Homoerotic, Homosexual, and Bisexual Behaviors

### A. Contemporary Practices

In Vietnam, there has historically been relatively little male homosexuality, although a few of the emperors of the 16th and 17th centuries did maintain male concubines. In present-day Vietnam, homosexuality is still regarded as being a foreign problem, and, as in other socialist countries, there is a lack of official research on homosexual behavior. In fact, homosexuality is quite a common sexual behavior. It may well be that the Communist state is reluctant to recognize its existence. As long as it is not practiced "openly," state officials will not interfere. This is evident in the 1998 case of a lesbian couple who married in public. Because of the public ceremony, Vietnamese authorities were forced to act, even though they did not know how to deal with the couple:

> Two women were wed in Vinh Long province (about 70 kilometers from Ho Chi Minh City). Hundreds of people, including friends, family members and a number of curious onlookers attended the ceremony on Saturday to celebrate the marriage of a 30-year-old woman to another woman aged about 20. Local authorities did not know how to react to the marriage (*Lao Dong* [Newspaper] March 8, 1998).

Two months later, the government reacted:

> Government officials have broken up the country's first known lesbian marriage and extracted a promise from the lovers they will never live together. Twenty officials from various Communist Party groups met the couple for three hours at their home in the Mekong Delta town of Vinh

Long. They were acting on instructions of the Justice Ministry in Hanoi "to put an end to the marriage," the *Thanh Nien* newspaper reported. It is unclear what kind of persuasion was used to get the couple's agreement or what punishment they could face if they change their minds, but they signed a document promising not to live together, the justice official said. "They would have had no trouble with their relationship if they had not chosen to have a public wedding," a member of the provincial justice department said. The issue was raised at the most recent session of the National Assembly during debate on amendments to the law. There were many other homosexual women living together in the province but Hong Kim Huong, 30, and Cao Tien Duyen, 23, were the only ones who were married publicly, he said. He said the wedding was an unwelcome challenge to traditional sensibilities and public morality but added: "As long as they don't wed publicly they are left in peace." (Reuters May 23, 1998).

In 1997, the same newspaper launched a virulent critique of a marriage between two men in Ho Chi Minh City. The apparently lavish ceremony held in a big Saigon hotel provoked an avalanche of protests from residents. Other homosexual marriages have taken place in Vietnam in discrete ceremonies, but homosexuality remains taboo in the country, although it is not officially illegal.

Vietnam's first gay wedding took place in Ho Chi Minh City. The two men celebrated their union at a local restaurant with over one hundred guests. Some authorities, however, were not in the mood to congratulate the grooms. "It should be publicly condemned," said Nguyen Thi Thuong, vice-director of the city's state-run Consulting Center for Love, Marriage and Families. "Public opinion does not support this." The police are reported as saying that no laws exist which would enable them to punish the happy couple. The honeymooners could not be reached for comment (Reuters April 7, 1997).

Sexual encounters between male adolescents may be facilitated by socially sanctioned close physical contacts considered "normal" between males, such as holding hands and resting or sleeping close together in the same bed. As far as the prevailing sexual activities, mutual masturbation and fellatio, are concerned, there does not appear to be any strongly developed sense of playing a masculine or feminine sexual role of the kind as is often found in other societies where anal intercourse is more prevalent and the ultimate objective of homosexual encounters.

Proschan (1998) has reported that although "gay" might be the only English word some of his informants had known, they had embraced it as their own and imbued it with meanings that diverge from those of English-speakers elsewhere:

Vietnamese men today are fashioning diverse ways of living as men-who-love-men, drawing variously on endogenous traditions and identities as well as exogenous concepts and practices, combining and recombining them, and at the same time contesting both cultural conventions that would condemn homosexuality as incompatible with filial piety and metropolitan notions that would insist there is only one way to be authentically gay.

## B. Homosexuality Under French Rule

Jacobus X. (1898) interpreted homosexuality as a questionable behavior resulting from the Chinese cultural influence, and a sign of decadence that disappeared after the French influence gained influence. If it was practiced by the French, he claimed, it was only to escape the dangers of

syphilitic female prostitutes. Interestingly, he does not discuss the interdependency between male prostitution and homosexuality. According to him, the customers in this era were Chinese and French, and the prostitutes Annamite boys:

It is only the nays and the boys who come in direct and permanent contact with the Europeans. Nay signifies "basket." The nays are children of from seven to fifteen years, who are provided with round baskets. They are found on the quays, in the market, and in front of the shops, waiting for a customer to make a purchase of any kind. . . . It is from these baskets that the class of boys is recruited. These latter are from fifteen to twenty-five years of age [acting as valet]. . . . When once he [the nay with his basket in which he carries the goods] gets to your house, if he should suspect that you have depraved tastes, he will soon offer you his services: "Captain" (everybody was a captain in 1860) "me much know chewchew banana," and if the client appeared to hesitate, "Me know ablic." That is sabir (patois). The nay and the boy are generally, to use the Tardieu's expression, "suckers of the dart." . . . Whilst the European lies at full length on a long chair, or on his bed, the boy—kneeling or stooping—*inguina osculatur, sugit, emissumque semen in bucca recipit, usque ad ultimam guttam* [a kiss between the thighs, rise, ejaculate in the mouth of recipient, even to the ultimate].

Although by preference a "sucker of the dart," the nay, or the boy, will not refuse sodomy, but he is not enthusiastic about it. It is not any moral reason which stops him, for he is above prejudices of that sort. It is simply the disproportion, which exists between the anus of a lad of ten or twelve years, and the penis of an adult European, for two nays have no objection to committing the act with one another. (Jacobus X. 1898)

## C. Homosexuality During the Vietnam War

*Lesbianism*

According to Marnais (1967), who describes in detail male and female homosexuality, lesbianism could be found at all levels of society during the Vietnam War. There were three bars catering exclusively to lesbians, and lesbian marriages were also not uncommon in Saigon, obviously tolerated by a society that referred to such couples as "friends." He interpreted lesbianism in Saigon as particularly rife among the city's prostitutes. The so-called "bull dyke" lesbian did not exist, but there was a role division between the "Sugar Mommy" and the young girl who lived at her expense. In the late 1960s, the *Saigon Daily* news reported a case about a major lesbian "call-girl" operation catering mainly to wealthy female tourists from the West and to jaded Saigon society women. The organization was disbanded when there was proof of the involvement of girls under 15.

*Male Homosexuality*

During the Vietnam War, much of Saigon's organized homosexual activity revolved around the city's "gay" bars. According to Marnais (1967), there were a total of 18 such establishments in existence during the late 1960s. Many of the customers could be found among middle-aged Saigon businessmen and teenage students. Only a small minority displayed the slightest effeminate trait. There were also homosexual steambaths, nightclubs, and coffee shops, and young boys, impoverished and orphaned by the war, sold themselves openly on street corners to passersby. There were at least four "call-boy" operations, catering mainly to wealthy Chinese businessmen and foreign (primarily French) residents. For American soldiers, it was risky to be involved in homosexual activity, because the army did not tolerate it, and suspected homosexuals were immediately given a dishonorable discharge (Taylor 1997).

The only hint that the long years of living in the jungle and tunnels of the Ho Chi Minh Trail left traces in the specific sexual preferences of the Viet Cong can be found in the reports of journalists. According to Scholl-Latour (2000), most of the Viet Cong were so uninterested in women when Saigon finally fell that the female prostitutes did not appeal to them. But it seems far more probable that it was the strict discipline of the Viet Cong that prevented them from "fraternizing" with prostitutes.

### D. Homosexuality and Vietnamese Law

Proschan (Aronson 1999; "Frank" 2000) writes that neither homosexual identity nor behaviors had ever been explicitly illegal in Vietnam. The ancient legal codes of the Le Dynasty (1428-1787) and the Nguyen Dynasty (1802-1945) detailed the penalties for crimes such as heterosexual rape, assault, adultery, and incest, but left homosexuality unmentioned. The only provisions in the codes that might refer to deviant sexuality were the prohibition against "men who wear weird or sorceress garments" (*Le Code*, Article 640; Nguyen & Ta 1987), and a prohibition of castration and self-castration (*Le Code*, Article 305; *Nguyen Code*, Article 344). Both provisions were not found in earlier Chinese codes. On the few occasions when homosexual activities seem to have been punished, they had been treated as rape or as adultery (disregarding the fact that both partners were the same sex, and concentrating instead on the fact that one or both were married to other partners). Vietnamese legal codes had always been strongly influenced by the Chinese codes of the same eras. In 1740, when the Ching Dynasty in China elaborated for the first time in Chinese history punishment for sodomy between consenting adults, the Vietnamese did not follow suit, once again omitting any such prohibitions in the *Nguyen Code* that was promulgated soon after. Nor did the French colonials institute explicit prohibitions against sodomy or pederasty in their colonies, because under the *Code Napoléon*, these acts did not fall under the purview of the legal system.

Although homosexuality or sodomy was not specifically referred to anywhere in modern Vietnamese criminal law, "sex buying and selling in any form" was prohibited, as were more-general and vague crimes such as "undermining public morality." In the latest Law on Marriage and Family (1986), no article mentioned the State attitude or any guidelines for public opinion about homosexual behavior. The Penal Code did not mention homosexuality either in its articles on incest, rape, prostitution, sexual assault, or child marriage. But Vietnamese authorities could find legal basis for punishing homosexual behavior if they chose, because crimes such as "undermining public morality" could be used (as similar crimes of "public indecency" or "soliciting" are in the U.S.) to prosecute homosexuality.

### E. Language and Homosexuality

The Vietnamese use more than one expression for the Western neologism *homosexuality*, although all have the same underlying meaning of "half man and half woman." For example, *Dong Tinh Luyen Ai* is a literal translation via Chinese of "homosexuality," which dates back to 1869. Its entry date into the Vietnamese language is not very clear. It did not appear in Dao Duy Anh's *Han Viet Tu Dien* of 1931, but it did appear in his *Phap Viet Tu Dien* of 1936, and might have had limited currency in the journalistic vocabulary of the 1930s.

The concept of homosexuality only came into greater use with the introduction of Western psychology and sexology in so-called hygiene manuals in the 1950s and 1960s. *Ai Nam Ai Nu* is the closest descriptive approximation to what is meant ontologically and behaviorally by the Western term *homosexuality*, though, if one takes *Ai* as a verb, the term comes closer to "bisexual" behavior. It did not come into use before the 1940s. Another variation on this term, which is more common in the biological and medical vocabulary, is *Ban Nam Ban Nu*. *Pe De*, for the French *pederaste*, is probably the most common byword for a gay person in Vietnam. It is urban in origin and can be dated to the French usage of the word. From the Chinese is borrowed *Ke Gian*, which is mostly used to depict anal intercourse, being thus is not limited to same-sex practice ("Vinh N." 1999).

### F. Sex Tourism

As publications like *The Men of Viet Nam: A Travel Guide to Gay Viet Nam* and websites like www.utopia asia.com suggest, foreign homosexual sex tourism is on the rise. Many Western visitors, who are called "Rice Queens," leave behind everything they know about safe sex practices when they come to Vietnam. According to an estimate of the Nguyen Friendship Society, one third of Vietnamese men who have sex with foreigners do not use a condom, and may have never used a condom before.

## 7. Gender Diversity and Transgender Issues

Bao, Long, & Taylor (1998) report that a transgendered person in Vietnam is mainly a "man" who wears female clothes and presents himself as a female. *Bong cai* is the common term in the south and is translated literally as "female shadow," whereas *dong co* is the common term in the north and is translated as "woman goes into a trance," revealing its origin from the shamanistic tradition: The male *ong dong* or the female *ba dong* are shamanic mediums who incarnate a pantheon of spirits, both male and female, during the course of a *len dong* performance in one of the fortuneteller's temples. They take on, in succession, the costume and comportment of the numerous spirits invoked, in what can be a daylong show of elaborate costumery. It seems that Vietnamese transgendered males only have sex with men, never with women or with other transgendered persons. Transgendered males refer to one another as "sisters" (*chi em*).

There are quite a few transvestites in Saigon who are trying to earn a living through prostitution. They look for customers in certain nightclubs and bars, as well as on the streets. Being a transvestite seems not to be something that is displayed in public, and the search for customers is done in an aggressive though feminine way.

Jacobus X. (1898) mentions transvestitism in connection with prostitution during the French period of Vietnam:

> I cannot, however, pass over in silence, one eccentric form of the *lusus amoris*. The Chinese actors who play the women's parts, come in their costumes [to the brothel], and assume the character of a modest virgin, afraid of losing her virginity, a refinement of vice which is much appreciated. In the presence of a number of old men, not very particular, the scenes of the first night of wedded life are represented without any shame.

Commenting on transvestite singers and transvestite striptease in the homosexual nightclubs of Saigon catering to male homosexual transvestites during the Vietnamese-American War, Marnais (1967) reported that transvestite prostitutes would congregate daily on the terrace of the Continental Hotel in Saigon. They were reported to have disappeared from view after the Communist takeover of

South Vietnam in 1975, but recent reports from the informants of Carrier, Nguyen, and Su (1997) returning from Saigon show that male transvestites can be seen on the streets once again, and some are again earning their income as prostitutes.

They may also make a living by joining a lottery team (*lo to*), often during adolescence, as singers. "Lottery team" refers to a mobile lottery team, who sell tickets and then spin for a prize at that establishment. The teams use singing to advertise (Bao, Long, & Taylor 1998).

## 8. Significant Unconventional Sexual Behaviors

### A. Coercive Sex

Coercive sex is prohibited in Vietnam. Article 112 of the Vietnamese Penal Code says:

1. Any person who uses force or any other means to have sexual intercourse with another person against his will shall be sentenced to imprisonment from 1 to 5 years. Any person who commits rape of a minor aged from 13 upward or a girl to whom he has the responsibility to give care and education or to provide medical treatment shall be sentenced to imprisonment from 2 to 7 years.

2. Any person who commits a crime in one of the following cases shall be sentenced to imprisonment from 5 to 15 years:
   a. Organized rape or rape that does serious harm to the victim's health
   b. Rape of many persons or creation of serious harms to the victim's health
   c. Relapse into former crime with more severity.

3. Any person who commits a crime which causes the death or the suicide of the victim or commits a crime in a specially serious circumstance shall be sentenced to imprisonment from 12 to 20 years, to life imprisonment or to death penalty.

4. Any cases of having sex with a child aged under 13 shall be regarded as committing a rape and the person in question shall be sentenced to imprisonment from 7 to 15 years. Any person who commits a crime belonging to one of the cases stipulated in items 2 and 3 of this article shall be sentenced to imprisonment from 12 to 20 years, to life imprisonment or to death penalty.

### Child Sexual Abuse and Pedophilia

Incestuous relations and child marriages, as well as early marriages, are prohibited by the Penal Code in Articles 112, 146, and 145. Although reliable statistical data are not available, it seems quite certain that the number of juvenile prostitutes has increased rather quickly in recent years. Based on the ratio of age range of prostitutes provided by the Nam Ha province, it is known that among 164 prostitutes, 17.6% of them are in the 13-to-16-year age group and 19.5% are in the 16-to-18-year age group. Together, there are 37.4% in the 13-to-19-year age group. Another research document on prostitution in Ho Chi Minh City shows that in 1989, juvenile prostitutes accounted for 2.1% of the total number of prostitutes; in 1990, the rate was 5.2%, and in 1995, it was as high as 15% (Hoang Ba & Pham Kim Ngoc 1996). The United Nations Children's Fund (UNICEF) had a 1995 estimate that there were 40,000 child sex workers throughout Vietnam.

Jacobus X. (1898) records a variety of proverbial sayings common in French-dominated Vietnam of the 19th century: "For a girl to be still a virgin at ten years old, she must have neither brothers nor fathers." The same author reports on pedophilia:

... whilst he is a *nay* [a boy who is carrying a "basket" for a customer], he has not usually reached the age of puberty. As may easily be imagined, these poor little wretches fall into the hands of "active" pederasts, who are not remarkable for gentleness and kindness, and who brutally assuage their lewd passions without caring what may be the result. I have often found, in these unfortunate *nays*, marks of attempts that have been committed almost by violence, the fact being that a lad not yet arrived at puberty, and frail and weak, is incapable of making any serious resistance to brutal attempts at sodomy on the part of an adult European or Asiatic. (Jacobus X. 1898)

During the Vietnam War, sex with children and incestuous sex was frequently connected with prostitution. Marnais (1967) reported that it was possible to watch live sex shows with teenage twins and also hire them for sex. In a Saigon brothel called the "Doll House," over 50 girls, none older than 12, served the clients for sadomasochistic games. In the "House of Pain," very young girls got injections of heroin to make them physically and psychologically dependent.

### Rape

There exist few statistics about sexual abuse, and they are not very reliable. It is, for instance, quite questionable when Hoang Ba and Pham Kim Ngoc (1996) state that before the 1990s, only 400 cases of rape of women and children had occurred in the whole country in one year:

From January 1993 to July 1995, 1,685 cases of rape (324 cases being of children) occurred. Compared with the years prior to 1990, cases of child raping only accounted for 4 to 6% of the total, but in the past three years, this rate has increased. Concretely speaking, in 1993 rapes of children accounted for 14.6%, in 1994 16.6% and in the first months of 1995, the rate reached as high as 30%. The victims were young girls in the age group 10-13 but there were also cases of raping little girls aged only 4-5. In Ho Chi Minh City in 1994, 55 rapes of children occurred out of a total of 107 cases. 43 of them were under 13 (Hoang Ba & Pham Kim Ngoc 1996).

### Incest

As O'Harrow (1995) remarked, the vocative system of the Vietnamese language is largely devoid of pronouns and uses, relying instead on static kinship terms. Thus, in Vietnamese, a husband and wife enjoy a fictive incest. The husband speaks to his wife using the same terms he has always used towards his real younger sisters, referring to himself as "older brother" (*anh*) and calling his wife "little sister" (*em*). Also, a very peculiar incest taboo is found in Vietnam: It is forbidden for a Buddhist student to marry the widow of his teacher (Gregersen 1996). The traditional punishment for incest was strangulation of the offender.

### B. Prostitution

#### Prostitution in the Pre-Colonial Era

Jacobus X. (1898) reported that prostitution was very common during the 19th century. He distinguished between the Annamite "Bamboo," the Chinese brothel, and the "Flower Boats," the Annamite "Daylight Whore" and the Annamite "Mistress of the European." These girls were either sold by their poor parents or even kidnapped by professional girl traders. It seems that the Annamite "Bamboo" was the brothel for the natives and the lower social layers of the French colonials. The prostitutes were Vietnamese girls who had to wait for customers in bamboo huts, hence the name. The infection rate with STDs was high, and the standard of hygiene quite low. Jacobus X. (1898) mentioned black lacquered teeth (a Chinese fashion) and hairless pubes as ethnic peculiarities. The girls had to sell themselves for very little money, and most of the money went to the pimp.

He also described the style of living of Chinese prostitutes, who first came from Singapore. They resided in big houses and waited on the verandas for clients. An elder women acted as "mama." On the first floor were a lot of Chinese beds with dark-colored mosquito curtains to conceal the couples. For waiting opium-smokers, there would be a pipe. Although few of the girls smoked, they were instructed in preparing the pipes. The owners of the brothels and flower boats, which are houseboats in the channels, worked without license, and were free to carry on their trade. However, they had to put up with the extortion of the Mandarins. Under the most trivial presumption of harboring criminals, their inhabitants might be mercilessly driven out. Interestingly, the Chinese prostitutes had a chance to become a concubine of a man of reputation, and then rise to a more honored position. The houses of prostitution of Cholon were almost exclusively reserved for the Chinese and resembled the "society houses" in Europe. They were quite luxurious, with salons, divans, sofas, mirrors, and pictures.

Besides these brothels, there also existed the so-called "Daylight Whore" and the system of the mistress. Apparently, the first was formerly in the bamboo but left because of her age. She also had a *souteneur,* who protected her from the police officers. They lingered in the streets and around restaurants, waiting to contact some possible client. After the initial contact was made, they followed the client to his house, ready to suggest sodomy and the kneeling instead of the horizontal position.

The mistress of the European was often bought directly from the parents "for some 20 piasters," a young girl of 15 or 16, selected from those whose fate it would ultimately be to be sent to the "bamboo." It was quite common, though, to take the mistress of some friend or colleague who was leaving the colony, and thus get a woman "who has had some training, requires no outfit, and understands a little French." To prevent the mistress from "going wrong," Jacobus X. (1898) suggested setting his own Annamite boy over her as bodyguard.

### Official French Policy Towards Prostitution

According to Troung (1990) who quoted the report of the Commission of Enquiry of the League of Nations (1933), French colonial policy adhered to the International Convention for the Suppression of the White Slave Traffic of 1910, but did not accede to the International Convention for the Suppression of the Traffic in Women and Children of 1921. The general policy pursued by the French government in Indochina was regulation, i.e., control through registration and supervision of brothels and women who were already prostitutes, and safeguarding women and girls from being induced by force or deceit into prostitution. The control of prostitution was entrusted to municipal and provincial authorities. The age of consent for registered prostitution was established at 18 years for Asians and 21 years for Europeans. The police registered a prostitute if she was found soliciting in the streets or if a person complained of having been "contaminated" by her. In 1926, about 24 licensed brothels paid taxes every month to the Hanoi city administration in addition to the hotels and lodging houses that secretly harbored prostitution. In 1935, H. Virgitti, mayor of Hanoi, disclosed that there were about 4,000 people working in the sex industry, not including geishas and dancers (Khuat Thu Hong 1998).

It is interesting to note that traffic in women was considered by the French colonial administration a problem solely connected with Asian traditions and customs. The 1929 report of the police prosecutor at the Court of Appeal in Saigon cited the following example of this quite hypocritical attitude towards the Vietnamese and the belief in the colonial authorities' own superiority:

> It may be that the supervision exercised, the severe sentences by the courts and the administrative measures taken against foreign Asiatics sentenced for offences of this nature, have warned delinquent people against the consequences of this shameful commerce; it may be that the mental attitude modified through French influence and through contact with our civilization, so respectful of the rights of women and children, has brought about an almost complete change of the native customs (Commission of Enquiry of the League of Nations 1933, 218).

The French believed that licensed brothels were a far more humane and civilized treatment of prostitutes who were assumed to have entered the profession deliberately, even though the conditions were quite unbearable because of extreme exploitation. Medical officers sometimes sent girls to hospital not because of venereal diseases, but because they were in a state of "very great exhaustion, having been obliged by the keepers of the house to receive an excessive number of customers" (Commission of Enquiry of the League of Nations 1933, 217).

As in other colonies, Vietnam had a double standard. The few white prostitutes possessed certain rights; they could, for example, institute legal procedures against *souteneurs* of French nationality, and the men were invariably punished and expelled (Commission of Enquiry of the League of Nations 1933, 215-217). Because of the ideas of the Social Purity movement, prostitution was regarded as evil. Because the aim was not to analyze the social and economic reasons for prostitution, prostitutes became criminalized, in contrast to their customers.

The French also used *Bordels Mobile de Campagne,* huge trailer trucks converted into mobile field brothels with ten women to each truck. The *Bordels Mobile* traveled to every fighting front. When on leave in Hanoi or Saigon, the French soldiers preferred non-military-organized establishments.

### Vietnam War Period

According to Khuat Thu Hong (1998), archive materials indicate that in 1954 in Hanoi alone, there were around 12,000 professional prostitutes working in 45 brothels and 55 cabaret houses of whom over 6,000 were licensed. After 1954, in northern Vietnam, prostitution was theoretically eliminated. Article 202 of the Criminal Code states that any sheltering, enticement, or inducement of prostitutes is an illegal act, and punishment will vary by degree of violation. Yet, every year, about 300 to 400 persons were discovered working in this trade.

Between 1959 and 1962, organized prostitution in the South was almost totally crushed by Madame Nhu, who closed down every brothel and heavily fined the owners. This changed after the Ngo Dinh Diem regime was overthrown in 1963. During the late 1960s, about 32 establishments in Saigon were houses of prostitution, ranging from modest apartments to elegant three-story establishments. A good deal of the sex business was in the hands of the Vietnamese underworld, like the "Yellow Pang Society." In the French as well as in the American period, the "Flower Boats" or sampans plied their trade. They were frequently family operations, with the daughter(s) working as prostitute(s) while the brothers pimped on dry land. Some of the larger junks, however, were professionally run, often by the Saigon underworld. Prior to 1975, statistics from the Ministry of Society of the Saigon government reported about 200,000 professional prostitutes. In Saigon alone in 1968, there were about 10,000 professional prostitutes. By 1974, the figure had reached 100,000.

During the Vietnam War, one million soldiers from the United States were stationed throughout Southeast Asia. Most of these host countries signed agreements to provide their services as "Rest and Recreation" centers for United States military and aid personnel. Their presence contributed to the proliferation of commercial sexual intercourse. Although the U.S. Army was not officially involved in providing sex workers to cover itself against congressional reaction at home, it is known that some of the brothels kept by the Vietnamese Government and the ARVIN (Army of Vietnam) were exclusively reserved for GIs. The first military brothel opened in 1966 in Pleiku in the central highlands. According to Marnais (1967), it was to be the model for other "recreation centers," including several within the Saigon area:

The Pleiku brothel has twenty rooms, whitewashed and pleasantly furnished. The girls are all carefully selected on the basis of good looks, personality and knowledge of English. (U.S. Army Intelligence also runs a security check on each girl to make sure she is not a Viet Cong agent out to pick up useful information from her trusting bedmates.) The girls are closely supervised by a matron under contract to the Pleiku Administrative Council. An American GI pays 300 piastres ($2.50) for a ticket, allowing him up to three hours with any given girl. (Twosomes and other exotic sexual ménages are out.) Between 100 and 300 GIs visit the house each day, passing through a sandbagged guard post where they are required to show their ticket and have it stamped by a Vietnamese soldier. Fifteen percent of the girl's earnings are deducted to pay for expenses at the center, but a hard-working and a popular prostitute can earn between 8000 to 15,000 piastres ($66 to $125) a month, a good salary in today's Vietnam.

The main reason for the U.S. Army to provide those establishments was the alarmingly high venereal disease rate among U.S. enlisted men. However, most of the soldiers preferred to look for prostitutes themselves in bars catering to GIs.

A prostitute earned as much as $180 per month. The average government civil servant earned roughly $30 a month, and even cabinet ministers and Assembly members had fixed salaries of $120. A special form of prostitution was the "mistress," i.e., a paid steady girlfriend. GIs considered this a "safer" alternative to the brothels and bar girls. There existed rumors about an incurable strain of syphilis, called "Black Clap," and Viet Cong girls who were able to put razor blades into their vaginas to castrate or even kill clients (Gulzow & Mitchell 1980). The latter rumor is without doubt a reflection of the ability of some trained girls to use their vaginas to smoke cigarettes, shoot arrows, or to put razor blades or other sharp materials in them without getting hurt.

While under French rule, marriages of French soldiers and Vietnamese women were prohibited. American soldiers, on the other hand, could marry. A U.S. Army study of 64 GIs who had filed applications to marry Vietnamese girls between June 1964 and November 1966 concluded that a high proportion of GIs who married Vietnamese women were divorced, sexually inhibited, fearful of American women, or disenchanted with some aspects of American life (Marnais 1967).

## The Present

After the Viet Cong occupation of Saigon, the new government tried to eliminate prostitution by closing brothels and sending prostitutes to work or to so-called reeducation centers. Between 1975 and 1985, 14,304 prostitutes in Ho Chi Minh City were sent to those centers. The Government claimed that prostitution was eradicated in the South by 1985. But as Stephanie Fahey (1998) remarked: "In a country where the Communist Party attempted to eradicate prostitution and pornography, prostitutes are now found in almost every bar, restaurant and hotel whether private or state-owned." According to statistics from the Department of Criminal Police, Ministry of the Interior, in the first six months of 1990, Vietnam had 40,000 prostitutes and 1,000 brothels. By the first six months of 1993, there were 200,000 prostitutes and 2,000 brothels. A report prepared by SCF (Save the Children Fund) in 1995 estimated that there were 149 brothels in Ho Chi Minh City alone. Many of the establishments are, officially, bars selling beer to Vietnamese clients. According to one recent unofficial estimate (Khuat Thu Hong 1998), there may be half a million sex workers in all of Vietnam, not including the increasing number of male prostitutes in the southern provinces and the big northern cities. Government Resolutions 53, 87, and 88, passed in 1994 and 1995, strengthen management over cultural activities and monitor the struggle against the so-called social evils, including prostitution, gambling, and drug use.

The reasons for women to become sex workers remain the same as during the Vietnam War and in other developing countries where there are few opportunities in rural areas and low wages in the jobs open for uneducated girls. Poverty is not the sole reason pushing women into prostitution. Family conflicts and their feeling of hopelessness about their husbands or boyfriends are also important reasons. The women interviewed by Cooper and Hanson (1998) stated that they were much better off now than in their villages. Although prostitution is illegal in Vietnam, because of economic problems, it is again becoming the booming business it was during the Vietnam War. But tourists report that because of corruption, the interpretation of the law is quite broad. Some of the girls who are looking for customers and are talking to tourists are agent provocateurs for corrupt policemen who force the foreigner to pay large sums to "avoid an incident." On the other hand, there are also police actions to clean up streets and districts with known prostitution, as Cooper and Hanson (1998) were told by a madam.

Prostitutes can be found on the street, sometimes with a pimp in the background, in massage parlors, and nightclubs. Two types of social networks are most common in the sex workers: peer and friend relations. They often work together in groups of two to five at a site, and this site remains fixed for a number of prostitutes for an extended period of time, from several months to a year or two. Many prostitutes are organized in groups for protection, or they may become friends. As a result of these social groupings, newcomers may be bullied by older prostitutes. They often make friends with a man who is referred to as their "boyfriend" (*bo ruot*). He may be a familiar client or a man who lives with the prostitute in a hired room and can protect her during work. Prostitutes have sexual relations with clients, boyfriends, and husbands. The average number of sexual contacts of the ten prostitutes interviewed by Bao, Long, and Taylor (1998) was 23 per month, some having 40 or 50.

## Clients of Prostitutes

Clients of sex workers are called *Khach lang choi* in Vietnamese. According to the study by Bao, Long, and Taylor (1998), all social classes, with the exception of farmers, can be found among them: workers, truck drivers, students, engineers, married, and unmarried men. The clients often start off going to a *beer hug bar* or restaurant to drink beer where they end up negotiating sex with one of the beer hug girls. Or they drink beer or alcohol first at one place and then go to another place to seek sex.

As in other developing countries, sex tourism is a growing business. Although reliable statistics are not available, such indicators as websites with advice for international tourists show a tremendous increase of travelers interested in sex, especially because Vietnam wrongly has the reputation of being "safer" with regard to STDs and AIDS than other countries in Southeast Asia. Because by law, Vietnamese citizens are prohibited from going into a hotel room of a tourist unless they are registered guests, prostitutes and customers meet at small Vietnamese-owned mini-hotels that cater to the locals and tolerate prostitution.

*Healthcare*

Since the early 1990s, the New Zealand Prostitutes Collective has worked together with the Save the Children Fund in providing peer-training workshops for sex workers. According to the SCF official report of 1995:

> Peer educators and peer counselors serve as credible and impactful disseminators of preventive/protective knowledge and behavior skills, and as positively reinforcing role models and change agents in the referent target populations (including sex workers). (p. 4)

On the street, an outreach worker reported to Cooper and Hanson (1998) that there is at the start always some mistrust when they try to bring women for an STD checkup, but with developing relationships, the women are glad that someone looks after them.

*Sexual Slavery*

According to Article 115 of the Penal Code, any person who buys and sells women shall be sentenced to imprisonment from 5 to 7 years. Any person who engages in this kind of behavior with an organization, takes the woman abroad, buys or sells many women, or relapses into this crime shall be sentenced to 5 to 20 years in prison.

According to news in the *South China Morning Post* (July 29, 1999), domestic sexual slavery is increasing, with an estimated 20% of Vietnam's commercial sex workers held in brothels against their will. In Vietnam, women can be sold to brothels for two million dong (HK$1,120), but according to the Ministry of Labor, brothels in Taiwan and China pay up to US$7,000 (HK$54,250) for young Vietnamese women. Therefore, it is no wonder that Vietnam is becoming an important source of women destined for sexual slavery in Hong Kong, Macao, and Southeast Asia. Many victims are lured into marriages with foreigners and migrate with their new husbands before being sold to brothels.

**C. Pornography and Erotica**

Jacobus X. (1898) reported that in the second half of the 19th century, Chinese merchants were famous for selling Chinese and Japanese phalli (dildos) and the colored albums of Chinese erotica. At first, the merchants had quite a bad reputation, but this changed gradually, with the merchants becoming esteemed for their business.

During the Vietnam War, the main sources for pornographic photographs were the black market moneychangers who always had some pictures to sell to GIs. The Tu Do Street was the main center to purchase pornographic material, according to Marnais (1967). During the early 1960s, the only pornographic pictures and books available in the city were imports from Hong Kong and Bangkok, where little cartoon folios, pornographic poems, and photographs were turned out by the hundreds of thousands. By 1967, with the influx of GIs, the market had grown, and a group of

domestic entrepreneurs has sprung up to take advantage of it. Pornographic paperbacks, featuring young Vietnamese girls and boys sold along the "Rue Cat," were printed on Saigon's presses.

The "blue" movie houses were located on the same street in little rooms above shops or bars, and the locations fluctuated frequently to keep the authorities away. The windows were painted black or covered with heavy curtains. The movies usually showed a young woman waking up in her small room, taking off her few clothes, starting to masturbate with some kind of dildo or fruit, and ending with a male or female visitor to her room having intercourse with her. As in the 1960s, they were usually short 16-mm films, mostly in black and white and without sound; some were more expensively produced in color, some with threesomes or bestiality. In the background of the rooms were prostitutes waiting for potential customers, most of whom were Westerners. Prostitutes also used pornographic pictures and movies to get their clients "in the mood." European pornographic films existed for homosexuals. Although pornography is forbidden today, according to Stephanie Fahey (1998), government research institutes are known to import pornographic magazines for resale.

## 9. Contraception, Abortion, and Population Planning

**A. Vietnam's Family Planning Policy**

The Vietnamese family planning program has its roots in the early 1960s, when some contraceptive methods became available in both the southern and northern regions on a limited basis. Beginning in 1962 in the northern province, the government planning policy was directed to reducing the rate of population growth, and the use of certain relatively permanent contraceptive methods, such as the IUD, was promoted. Until the 1970s, however, a governmental policy was not formally implemented. The family planning program in the southern province began in the late 1960s, largely in response to concern over maternal and infant mortality and the increasing number of illegal abortions. In the mid-1970s, the Government of the Republic of South Vietnam stated that family planning had been adopted as an official policy, but inadequate medical facilities made it impossible to implement an effective family planning program.

The Committee for Population and Family Planning (CPFP) was established during the early 1980s, and a one- or two-child policy was formally initiated in late 1988. At about the same time, Vietnam introduced comprehensive free-market reforms, which increased the effectiveness of the population program. The program included an extensive media campaign, free provision of contraceptive services and devices, and the creation of incentives and disincentives to encourage compliance. With a government target to reduce the total fertility rate to 3.0 births per woman by the year 2000, the fertility rate had already fallen to 3.1 by 1994. The sharp drop in Vietnam's fertility over the past several years, which has attracted global attention, can be linked to the general context of how family planning is delivered—including penalties for family planning violation, and to the widespread use of modern contraceptive methods and abortion. The intrauterine device (IUD) is by far the most popular contraceptive method, followed by traditional methods (withdrawal, "rhythm," and breastfeeding), increasing use of the condom, and the pill a distant last place.

**B. Increasing Condom Use**

The condom was rarely used in Vietnam until recently, but both knowledge and use of the condom have increased significantly over the past ten years. Among married women aged 15 to 49, knowledge of the condom rose from 45% in 1988 to 76% in 1994, and the use of the condom more than tripled from 1% in 1988 to 4% in 1994. The predominant contraceptive method, however, has been the IUD: In 1988, 33% of the respondents relied on the IUD (with neither a decrease nor increase in 1994). But the IUD is nevertheless known and feared for its side effects: heavy bleeding, infection of the ovaries, and severe abdominal pains, as well as very likely infection of the cervix, ectopic pregnancies, and a low effectiveness rate in general (Goodkind & Anh 1997). As Gammeltoft (1999) was told by a woman: "You know, in the old days, heaven decided how many children one would have. Today we have the IUD, so heaven still decides." One reason for failure and health problems may be that for a long time, the only IUDs available were used IUDs from Communist East Block countries. Some health providers also complain that the IUDs, which today are imported from the U.S., are too large for the uteruses of Vietnamese women. Most improbable seems to be the opinion of Women's Union cadres that "it is a disease of the mind," and that women simply blame all their troubles in life on the IUD.

According to Goodkind (1997), primary reliance on the IUD and abortion is typical of former Marxist states, which have tended to discourage supply-based methods, thus reflecting an indifference to consumer choice and an inability to afford these methods, or to keep tight reins on their distribution and use. Within Asia, Vietnam is distinguished by having the highest levels of IUD and abortion use in the region, perhaps partly because policymakers see this strategy as the most effective way to meet current fertility targets.

One reason for the rise in condom use is the increased availability of the product because of free-market reforms introduced in the mid-1980s. In combination with family planning promotion in the late 1980s, these reforms allowed for two channels of condom distribution: through the public health sector and sales through private pharmacies and family-owned roadside stalls. There are drawbacks, however, to obtaining condoms through public-sector centers, namely, the necessity to travel some distance to reach a center, the need to register one's name to receive supplies, and the necessity to use whatever brand of condom is being offered. But because condoms are offered free of charge, a growing number of condom users seems to prefer going through the private sector. In recent years, the growth of social marketing programs has increased the number of brands available and also competition, which has kept prices low.

The condom is more popular than the pill, both for spacing births and for preventing them. One reason for the greater popularity of the condom may be its greater compatibility with traditional methods, such as withdrawal. Data from the 1994 national Vietnam Inter-Censal Demographic Survey (VICDS), being both an inter-census demographic survey and a family planning survey, indicated that 31% of married women of reproductive age who switched from the condom to another method did prefer one or both traditional methods, rhythm or withdrawal, compared with only 24% of those women who switched from the pill. Given the high prevalence of traditional-method use in Vietnam—22% in 1994—these attitudinal dynamics seem to favor use of the condom over the pill. As Goodkind (1997) pointed out, the preference for condoms cannot be fully accounted for only by conventional explanations like the lesser compatibility of the pill with traditional methods, monetary concerns, or problems in pill supplies. In addition to these reasons, one might speculate that the national family planning leaders discouraged pill use, because they were skeptical that rural women could use it effectively. Also, the IUD and sterilization, even abortion, are being looked at much more favorably, because they re-

flect the socialist legacy of de-emphasizing consumer choice and ensuring compliance with the one- or two-child policy. Goodkind argued that enduring cultural factors, including its Confucian heritage, may also contribute to a preference for condoms over the pill. Vietnam exhibits the same family-formation characteristics as many other Confucian societies in East Asia: patrilineal family organization, son preference, lunar birth timing, and high rates of abortion. Preference of the condom may stem from traditional Chinese medical beliefs, which are intertwined with Confucian, Buddhist, and Daoist religious philosophies. These beliefs often emphasize the importance of maintaining a balance of natural body rhythms. The pill may thus be perceived as interfering with the menstrual cycle and disturbing the proper balance between "hot and cold" food intake.

## C. Socioeconomic Characteristics and Contraceptive Methods

The condom is the only method with a higher preference among urban users and among those with higher levels of educational and occupational status. In 1994, 10% of urban residents used condoms, compared with 4% of rural residents. However, women of all occupational statuses and educational levels overwhelmingly prefer the IUD and traditional methods, with the pill coming in a distant last place.

Goodkind (1997) suggested that because Vietnam is currently developing very rapidly, its population is becoming better educated, more affluent, and more urbanized. Economic reforms have contributed to a rising standard of living as well as to a growing disparity between rich and poor. These conditions have also increased the numbers of commercial sex workers and their patrons. Because of these social and demographic developments, one can expect the use of condoms to increase both for pregnancy and STD prevention outside marriage.

According to a recent but undated United Nations study, 40% of Vietnamese married men have had extramarital sex. Another survey conducted in 1993 showed that 69% of homosexual men and 38% of urban heterosexual men used condoms during their sexual encounters. Half of sex workers had not used a condom during their most recent sexual encounters (Goodkind 1997).

The decision to use condoms is partly a question of government efforts to improve knowledge and awareness of HIV and other STDs and how to prevent them. There are influential political groups, however, who assume that condoms encourage people to engage in premarital or extramarital sex; these groups object to the discussion and distribution of condoms. Others, like the Vietnam Women's Union, hold a more pragmatic view. They have recently prepared a publication about AIDS prevention that is targeted to young people.

Condom use will very likely continue to increase because:

- Family-size desires are still declining;
- Economic reforms and increased personal income have made condoms more accessible;
- Condoms are suitable to use with traditional methods;
- Current social mobility and migratory patterns are redistributing more Vietnamese into better educated, wealthier social groups; and
- Recent increases in adolescent and extramarital sexual activity, coupled with a growing concern over STD/AIDS prevention.

## D. The 1994 Vietnam Inter-Censal Demographic Survey (VICDS)

North Vietnam was among the first countries in the developing world to adopt an official policy to reduce population growth. Following reunification, policies to reduce population growth received increasing political attention from the national government. In January 1993, the Communist Party Central Committee identified population growth as contributing to a wide range of social, economic, and ecological problems. A resolution endorsed the recommendation that each family should have only one or two children, so that fertility could be lowered and population stabilization achieved. In June 1993, the prime minister approved the "Population and Family Planning Strategy to the Year 2000," a comprehensive plan to guide the implementation of the resolution.

The 1994 Vietnam Inter-Censal Demographic Survey (VICDS) was conducted from April through June 1994 in a nationwide effort to obtain information about fertility, investigate the prior trend of fertility decline, and determine whether the decline is likely to continue. (An intercensal survey is a national survey conducted to obtain information not gathered in the regular national censuses.) Results revealed a substantial change over recent years in reproductive attitudes and behavior. Fertility has continued to decline to a level not far above three children per woman. Compared with the late 1980s, contraceptive knowledge has broadened and contraceptive use has increased. Stated family-size preferences have shifted noticeably downward. The findings also confirmed that urban women are characterized by far lower fertility than rural women, that the Red River Delta (which includes Hanoi) followed by the Southeast (Ho Chi Minh City) show the lowest fertility levels, and that the Central Highlands show the highest fertility rates. Finally, the survey documented that there is an inverse association between fertility levels and educational attainment: The fertility rate for each successively higher educational grouping is lower than for the previous grouping.

### E. Knowledge of Contraceptive Methods

By 1988, 94% of all married Vietnamese women were familiar with at least some methods of contraception, including at least one modern method; 90% of the married women were familiar with the IUD (Goodkind 1997). By 1994, a marked increase in familiarity with specific methods, both modern and traditional, was evident. About 75% of the women surveyed indicated awareness of the condom and both male and female sterilization, whereas 68% said they had heard about the pill. Reported contraceptive use was substantial and, according to the VICDS (1994), continued to increase between 1988 and 1994. About 73% of married women reported ever having practiced some form of contraception, compared with 60% in 1988. In 1997, according to the most recent Demographic and Health Survey of Vietnam (VN-DHS II), more than 84% of currently married women aged 15 to 49 have ever used a contraceptive method. The contraceptive prevalence rate (CPR) is 75%, and 56% of ever-married women are currently using a modern method. The total CPR is up by 10% over the level of the 1994 survey, and the use of modern methods rose by 12%, with traditional-method use falling by about 2% owing to less-frequent use of periodic abstinence. Compared with the 1988 DHS NCPFP, Vietnam Demographic and Health Survey, 1988 (Hanoie 1990), and 1994 VICDS, the contraceptive mix has not changed very much. About half of the reported increase was attributed to use of modern methods and half to increased use of traditional methods. As far as the "method mix" is concerned, two features stand out: the dominance of the IUD among modern methods, and the relatively high share of traditional methods. Current use of oral contraceptives is still very low, being used by 2% of married women.

### F. Abortion

In North Vietnam, since 1962, abortion on request (with the husband's consent) was available during the first trimester of pregnancy and was usually performed by vacuum curettage. Because of the 1933 decree enforcing a French law prohibiting abortion and the use of contraception in the Republic of South Vietnam, abortions could be performed only for narrowly interpreted indications. Between the late 1960s and the early 1970s, family planning clinics offered services only to women with at least five living children. Even when family planning clinics were later expanded to include women with one living child, a marriage or cohabitation certificate was required to obtain an abortion.

Abortion on request has been available in North Vietnam since at least 1971, and in the entire country since its unification in 1975. The Law on the Protection of Public Health (June 30, 1989) states that "women shall be entitled to have an abortion if they so desire." According to Decision No. 162 of the Council of Ministers in January 1989, the State will supply, free of charge, birth-control devices and public-health services, including induced abortion, to eligible persons that register to practice family planning. As mentioned earlier, it is typical of former Marxist states to primarily rely on abortion, together with the IUD, for population control. Henceforth, all possible grounds for abortion are permitted, as long as the abortion is performed by a physician.

The proportion of single women among all women seeking abortion has increased to 20 to 30% in 1995 (compared with 7% in 1991), suggesting an increase in premarital sexual activity. Attitudes toward informal dating have become more tolerant, especially in urban areas. The availability of Western videos, TV programs, and other media have brought specific images of sex and romance to young people, and these are slowly changing the norms of acceptable behavior in Vietnamese culture.

According to the United Nations, Vietnam had 59 abortions per 1,000 women in 1987, 71 per 1,000 in 1988, and 70 per 1,000 in 1989. The Alan Guttmacher Institute reported in 1998 that Vietnam had the highest abortion rate of any nation in 1996, with 83 abortions per 1,000 women between the ages of 15 and 44. This number covers only abortions performed at state clinics; and when private clinics are included, the abortion rate was 111 per 1,000 women, or a total of roughly two million abortions. In 1999, the state-run media reported that the abortion rate in Hanoi continues to rise. In the first six months of 1999, 33,215 abortions were performed at Hanoi city hospitals, a 3% increase over the previous year, and nearly double the number of reported births. Although the government does not espouse abortion as a preferred family planning method, the procedure is heavily subsidized by the government, and many published family-planning campaigns still list abortion as a method of birth control after IUDs, condoms, and the pill, according to the *Deutsche Presse-Agentur* (7/1999).

## 10. Sexually Transmitted Diseases and HIV/AIDS

### A. Sexually Transmitted Diseases

There is no information on venereal diseases in the early days of what is now Vietnam, although some descriptions of Sino-Annamese medicine suggest that this "scholarly" medicine did already know a distinction between the early and late symptoms of syphilis. Altogether, the frequencies of STDs were apparently only high in those regions that had a close contact with Europeans. Figures for the early French period are also difficult to obtain. The first French colonial physicians were largely concerned with malaria and dysentery, since these were responsible for decimating the troops. However, as rates of morbidity for sexually transmitted diseases (STDs) in the colonial army increased to one in ten in 1887, the French colony of 1890 reached first place, along with Madagascar, in all reports on venereal diseases. The situation did not improve at the beginning of the 20th century. Between 1903 and 1911, morbidity attributed to syphilis increased among the French troops to account for 23 to 40 hospital admissions per 1,000 men. In a division stationed in Tonkin, the medical officer noted that in 1902, venereal diseases accounted for 8.4% of total morbidity (508 admissions), of which 1.1% were for syphilis, 3.7% for gonorrhea, and 3.5% for chancroid and its complications. In 1904, out of 607 admissions, the total percentage of venereal diseases went up to 19.1%, with percentages for each of the three conditions at 3.7%, 9.7%, and 5.7%, respectively. For the medical officer, the spectacular rise coincided with the 1901-1902 expedition to China, which had mobilized contingents from Tonkin (Guénel 1997).

According to Assistance Médicale d'Indochine, founded in 1904, STDs became the second most common reason for hospitalization after malaria in the 1910s. The first statistics regarding STDs in the Vietnamese population are available through the maternity hospital in Cholon: During the first quarter of 1927, out of 2,500 births, 40% of the children had congenital syphilis. Guénel (1997) suggests this accounted for a large part of the perinatal mortality of 38%. In the North, at Hanoi, one in four children was estimated to die of syphilis during the first year. But one has to keep in mind that even in 1930, not more than 10% of the population in the big cities was accessing the services of the Assistance Médicale, and hardly any of the rural population did. All over Indochina, 92% of the prostitutes were infected with STDs compared with 10% in France.

Although hospital admissions because of syphilis infections decreased slightly during the 1930s, from 61% in 1930 to 21% in 1938, gonorrhea increased from 49% in 1930 to 70% in 1938. The two Indochina wars reactivated the problem of infected servicemen: Between 1945 and 1954, 12% of the 1.6 million men (700,000 of whom were Indochinese) were suffering from one of the four STDs then diagnosed. In 1975, the South Vietnamese government estimated that 10% of the population, or one million people, were infected, compared with a paltry 350 STD-infected American soldiers in 1963 (Greenberg 1972). In North Vietnam, as well as later in the unified country, the existence of venereal diseases was denied.

According to the WHO (1993), in 1991, gonorrhea still accounted for the highest percentage among STDs with 11 cases per 100,000 inhabitants. The Ho Chi Minh City Dermato-Venereology Institute, reorganized in 1975, reported a certain stabilization of STDs since 1985, representing, on average, 10% of all consultations (13,700 in 1993 for STDs alone), with a still marked prevalence of syphilis and gonorrhea, 25% and 17%, respectively, of STDs in 1993, according to Guénel (1997). The National Institute situated in Hanoi assesses the prevalence of syphilis at 10,000 cases per annum. But as Guénel points out, the incidence of STDs in Vietnam elude national statistics, much more so than in industrialized countries.

## B. HIV/AIDS

Epidemiological and laboratory data indicate that epidemic spread of the HIV virus, the cause of AIDS, did not occur in any large human population until the mid- to late 1970s. During the early to mid-1980s, extensive spread was documented for sub-Saharan Africa, the industrialized Western countries of North America, Europe, and Oceania, and many countries of Latin America, including the Caribbean. Although a few HIV infections and AIDS cases were detected in Asia during that period, there was no evidence of an epidemic spread, leading to speculation that AIDS would not become a major global health problem. Since the late 1980s, however, when explosive epidemics of HIV were documented in several South and Southeast Asian countries, the general complacency about AIDS has given way to alarm over the virus's potentially devastating impact on individual lives, as well as on the economies of the region.

In Vietnam, the first AIDS case was identified in 1990. It is safe to say that the epidemic will continue to spread, although the prevalence and distribution of AIDS, as well as the future of other STDs, such as syphilis and gonorrhea, will vary widely among Asian countries. Countries with low STD-prevalence rates should not expect to have high rates of HIV and AIDS, but countries and populations with high STD rates are at high risk of developing high HIV/AIDS rates in the future, the reason being that syphilis and other STDs are spread through the same routes as HIV.

A study conducted by Franklin on HIV/AIDS in late 1993 found that 54% of the men interviewed in cafés, restaurants, nightclubs, parks, and the streets where sex was sold or where dates for sex could be made, had had two or more sexual partners in the previous two weeks (as cited by Goodkind 1997). Within three years, from 1996 to 1999, the number of reported HIV cases doubled. By late 1999, approximately 15,800 Vietnamese were reported HIV-positive, and approximately 1,500 had died of AIDS. The actual number of infections, however, could be ten times that number. Most cases go undetected because HIV testing is only done selectively. The actual number of people infected with HIV by the end of 1999 was expected to exceed 129,000. Vietnam's biggest city, Ho Chi Minh City, claimed the highest number with 2,600 cases. The disease is expected to have an especially harmful effect, not only on individual lives, but also on the economy, because 50% of those infected are between 15 and 24 years old.

HIV cases among Vietnam's prison inmates have tripled since 1998, now comprising one fifth of all infections in the country, according to a government newspaper. A total of 22,161 inmates had tested HIV-positive as of July 20, 1999, with 3,621 AIDS cases and 1,895 inmate deaths from AIDS since the first case detection in 1990. A National AIDS Committee official said that the actual number of HIV infections in Vietnam's prisons could be 10 times higher. Infected inmates remain in the general prison population until they develop AIDS, when they are transferred to the prison's clinic. Hoping to curb the spread of the virus, the Ministry of Public Security launched an HIV/AIDS-awareness campaign in prisons and correctional institutions in 1999 (Associated Press 7/28/99).

The Vietnamese government has launched nationwide campaigns to raise people's awareness. Using mass media and other avenues, the campaigns are designed to provide Vietnamese students and 90% of people between ages 15 and 50 with general knowledge of the epidemic and how to protect themselves. However, cultural taboos have proven to be a hindrance to tackling the issue. An estimated 200,000 intravenous drug users and 100,000 prostitutes are blamed for the spread of AIDS.

[*Update 2002*: UNAIDS Epidemiological Assessment: After the first HIV case was reported in Vietnam in 1990, the number of reported HIV infections and AIDS cases grew rapidly in all provinces. The total of reported HIV infections had reached 43,410 by December 2001. An estimated 130,000 people were living with HIV/AIDS at the end of 2001.

[In 2000, HIV prevalence was highest among injecting drug users (24%). Although data on HIV/STD risk behavior are not included in routine HIV surveillance, behavioral surveys of injecting drug users indicate that 28% share equipment. Sexual transmission of HIV has increased among female sex workers; the prevalence rate increased from 0.6% in 1994 to 3.5% in 2000. In 2000, while the majority of reported HIV infections occurred among injecting drug users (63% of cumulative numbers), estimates of HIV/AIDS indicate that the majority of HIV infections are sexually transmitted (81%).

[Available data from point prevalence studies suggest that there is a major burden of STDs, and particularly syphilis, among sex workers. There is a lower, but still significant, STD prevalence among women, including pregnant women. Quinolone resistance is emerging (56.7% for first-generation Quinolone and 42.7% for second-generation Quinolone). Gonococcal resistance to penicillin is also important (47%).

[The estimated number of adults and children living with HIV/AIDS on January 1, 2002, were:

| | | |
|---|---|---|
| Adults ages 15-49: | 130,000 | (rate: 0.3%) |
| Women ages 15-49: | 35,000 | |
| Children ages 0-15: | 2,500 | |

[An estimated 6,600 adults and children died of AIDS during 2001.

[At the end of 2001, an estimated 22,000 Vietnamese children under age 15 were living without one or both parents who had died of AIDS. (*End of update by the Editors*)]

[*HIV/AIDS, 2001-2003*

[*Update 2003*: In mid 2001, Vietnam's Ministry of Health AIDS Committee reported positive HIV test results for 37,111 people, but admitted the actual number of HIV carriers in the country might have exceeded 137,000. The committee estimated that the actual number of HIV-positive citizens could reach 197,000 by 2005, with increases of 12,000 to 18,000 per year over the next five years. The number of Vietnamese with AIDS increased by 24.1% in 2001, while AIDS-related deaths rose by 22%. To prevent an increase in cases, the Vietnamese government allocated $4.2 million to buy HIV test kits, ensure safe blood transfusions, and raise public awareness. Ho Chi Minh City ranked first among the nation's 61 cities and provinces for HIV infection, with 7,690 cases reported. Illegal drug users accounted for 65% of the reported HIV-positive population, while nearly 25% of all IV-drug users in Vietnam in 2001 were HIV-positive. At the same time, 20% of the prostitutes tested HIV-positive, up eightfold since 1994. Between 1994 and 2001, HIV infection rose tenfold among pregnant women and tripled among tuberculosis patients.

[Dr. Laurent Zessler, a UNAIDS representative in Hanoi, said that the AIDS epidemic could easily become "extremely serious" in Vietnam, adding that he does not feel the Vietnamese government is "acknowledging the full magnitude of the problem." Zessler said that schools should offer more HIV-prevention education and the government should increase access to condoms, especially among sex workers. Condoms should be made available at bars, clubs, and brothels, he said, adding that condoms are currently only available in family planning and health clinics. "It's really a political and organizational issue. We have the condoms here. They are quite cheap. But the decision has not been made to make them more available" (Mozes, Reuters Health January 2, 2002).

[In mid February 2003, Vietnam Vice President Truong My Hoa announced that the country needs to "take a more active approach" in its HIV/AIDS treatment and prevention efforts, according to *Vietnam News*. She said that the "current breathtaking spread" of the disease has "damaged" the health of many citizens and affected the country's socioeconomic growth. Truong called for the country's AIDS Standing Bureau and Health Ministry to offer "more effective" solutions to help establish a national AIDS-prevention strategy by 2010. According to a Ministry of Health report, the number of new HIV cases in Vietnam in 2002 was almost 16,000, up 28% from 2001 (Xinhua News Agency February 19, 2003). According to a February 18, 2003, report by *Agence France-Presse*, Vietnam Ministry of Health officials announced that the ministry would make Lamzidivir, a combination of the antiretroviral drugs lamivudine and zidovudine, available to local health centers at a low cost. HIV-positive pregnant women and healthcare workers will receive the drug free of charge, but the drug will be available to others for $900 per year. The drugs will be produced by the Vietnamese drug maker, MST Trading. A spokesperson for the pharmaceutical company said it has been manufacturing Lamzidivir for an "unnamed" South Korean firm to export to South Africa. (*End of update by J. Pastoetter*)]

## 11. Sexual Dysfunctions, Counseling, and Therapies

As O'Harrow (1995) pointed out, Vietnamese men tend to think of lovemaking in almost medical terms, concerned about the maintenance of their potency, psychological as well as physical. The main "sex therapy" for impotence is Chinese medicine. On the side of women, giving birth only to daughters is still regarded as the only noteworthy female "sexual dysfunction." But she can rely on her confidante, the soothsayer, fortuneteller, or *thay boi*. The *thay boi* is nearly always herself female, and although men also come to learn the future from her, the majority of her clients are women, with whom she maintains a semi-psychic relationship. The ability to be of help depends on the *thay boi*'s combined knowledge of and sensitivity to the predictable psychological concerns of her women clients, the range going from faithless husbands to vicious mother-in-laws, prying sister-in-laws, and rebellious children. She controls the commonly accepted cultural signs and knows the symbols that are needed to interpret these phenomena in a manner acceptable to her clients. The fortuneteller is the only credible yet disinterested female confidante available to Vietnamese women suffering psychological pain.

## 12. Sex Research and Advanced Professional Education

### A. The Nature of Vietnamese Sex Research and Resources

According to Fahey (1998), very little social science research of any sort—in the Western meaning of the word—has been conducted in the country after the reunification of Vietnam in 1976. The Communist Party's approach to social issues has been prescriptive rather than analytic. It was not until the mid-1980s that social research centers were established. Most contemporary Vietnamese research on women's issues is generated through these centers, including the Center for Research on Gender in Hanoi and the Center for Scientific Study of Women and the Family in Ho Chi Minh City. As Fahey (1998) further observes, the Women's Union and women's branches of organizations like the Vietnam General Confederation of Labor have a much longer history, with the responsibility of lobbying for women's rights and conflict resolution. Although they have generated some information on women's position, more recently they have been co-opted by international organizations for the administration of aid and have lost much of their lobbying role. At the same time, the Women's Union, a national organization of over 11 million members and 7,000 employees, has shifted from an organization responsible for protecting women's rights to an implementation agency for programs of immunization, family planning, credit, and nutrition education for international funding organizations.

Fahey (1998) points out that, for political reasons, the social science research by Vietnamese scholars largely plays down the importance of divisions other than those stemming from Confucianism or the cult of the ancestors cutting across the nature of the family-like class and regional differences. Research is concentrated rather on politically relevant issues, like female employment, access to birth control, and prostitution and other so-called "social evils," like drug addiction, alcoholism, and gambling. Concerns with no immediate policy relevance, such as the commodification of women, have hardly been considered as yet. But in 1996, a very interesting survey was conducted by the Hanoi Institute of Sociology in cooperation with the Population Council to gain understanding of the participants' views toward sexuality and sexual activity, including differences across the pre-*doi moi* and *doi moi*-era generation (Khuat Thu Hong 1998).

## B. Institutes for Sexological Research

There is no independent institute for sexological research in Vietnam. The main Vietnamese organizations involved in sexological research are strictly regulated by the government and its ministries. The more-recent research projects were conducted by the Research Center of Gender, Family and Environment in Development (CGFED) and by the Center for Women and Family Studies (CWFS). The Institute of Sociology and the Institute of Educational Psychology of Hanoi University are leading in surveys dealing with sexual-related topics. The Committee for Population and Family Planning (CPFP) and the Women's Union, as well as the Youth Union of Vietnam, both in Hanoi, have also conducted some sexological research. There is also the Vietnam Family Planning Association (VINAFPA). The Population Council Hanoi supports these institutions and single researchers, as well as conducts its own studies. The Population Council assists the Vietnamese government in testing reproductive-health interventions and incorporating them into current maternal and child health and family planning policies, programs, and research.

The reproductive-health-program objectives are to develop intervention research and training and to provide research results to individuals at all levels in the public and private sectors. The current agenda addresses a broad range of reproductive concerns, including youth reproductive health, male involvement, reproductive tract infections (RTIs), sexuality, violence, and sexual harassment. The Save the Children Fund (SCF) is very active in conducting studies about child prostitution.

## [*Sexual Attitudes and Behaviors among Ethnic Minorities*

[*Update 2002*: About 10% of the population of Vietnam belongs either to the Chinese, the Cham, or the Montagnards (hill tribes). Especially since the Reunification in 1976, but also in the 150 years since the colonization, first the French and then Vietnamese nationalists worked for the assimilation of these ethnic groups. These efforts, in combination with the devastating effects of the Vietnam War, led to a near extinction of cultural specifics. Many Chinese fled the country as boat people. In the process, the Cham lost most of their customs and were discouraged from using their ethnic lan-

guage. Eighty-five percent of the Montagnard villages were destroyed. Between 200,000 and 220,000 of the estimated one million Montagnards had died. The Vietnamese government resettled large numbers of Vietnamese in upland "economic zones," and the hill tribes were forced to move into newly erected cities. Meanwhile, one fourth of the central highlands had been deforested between 1975 and 1985. The Vietnamese Vice Minister of Culture summed up the direction of future policy when he proclaimed in 1976: "It is necessary to eradicate all the outmoded customs . . . while gradually bringing the new culture to each ethnic minority. The state has the duty to bring new, progressive culture to these people . . . in order to build a new culture with socialist objectives and Vietnamese national characteristics." As a result, nothing is known about the fate of the Cham and Montagnard minorities in recent years. There are some indications that they are disappearing.

[The following summary is based on the most recent reports, which were made several decades ago by Lebar, Hickey, and Musgrave (1964), the Cultural Information Analysis Center (1966), Mole (1970), and Hickey (1982ab). One has to keep in mind that the latter two were research projects done for the United States Army. The Army hoped to get a better understanding of these minorities in order to motivate and use them in the war against North Vietnam.

## [A. Cham

[The Chams remaining in Vietnam are descendants of the ancient kingdom of Champa. They are located mainly along the south central coast of Vietnam and speak a language of the Malayo-Polynesian stock. Around 1960, there were 45,000 in all of South Vietnam. The sexual behavior of the Cham was strongly influenced by Hinduism and later by Islam, but they have retained some beliefs and practices of both traditions. Parents permitted their daughters great freedom of choice in marriage. The girl's parents made the overtures in asking the boy in marriage. Among the non-Muslim Chams, there was no marriage ritual. When marriage was agreed upon, the boy went to live in the compound of the girl's family. A feast was held, and the boy presented the girl with gold or silver as a symbol of the marriage. Among the well-to-do, this gift may have been larger, including much silver, or several buffaloes. Muslim marriages, however, did entail a ritual. Imams acted as witnesses, and the parents had a role in the ritual. The girl's parents asked the groom if he accepted their daughter in marriage, and he was expected to respond positively. A large feast followed. The boy had to live in the girl's family. For those few who could afford it, polygyny was allowed, though seldom practiced. The consent of the first wife was necessary. Divorce was generally demanded by the woman, who got the house as well as two thirds of the common property.

## [B. Montagnards

[Around 60 different tribes dwelled in the wooded hills of the southern portion of the Annam Cordillera. Geographically, this area has come to be known as the Vietnamese Central Highlands. The French gave these tribes the collective name "Montagnards." They speak languages of the Mon-Khmer or Malayo-Polynesian linguistic stocks and physically resemble Cambodians, Malays, and Indonesians. Although divided into nearly 40 distinct ethnic groups, Montagnard characteristics have historically set them apart from the Cham and Vietnamese. According to Lebar, Hickey, and Musgrave (1964), the Montagnard tribes of North Vietnam were the Black Tai, Khua, Laqua, Lati, May, Muong, Nhang, Pa-y, Red Tai, Ruc, Sach, Tho, T'ou Lao, Trung-cha, and White Tai. In South Vietnam were found the

Bahnar, Bih, Bout, Bru, Cao, Chams, Chrau, Churu, Cua, Duane, Halang, Hre, Hroy, Jarai, Jeh, Kalo, Katu, Kayong, Kil, Krung, Lang Ya, Lat, Laya, Loven, Ma, Menam, Mnong, Monom, Noang, Noar, Nop, Pacoh, Phuong, Pru, Raglai, Rai, Rengao, Rhadé Rein, Saran, Seeding, Sop, Sre, Stieng, and Tring. These tribes had further subgroups.

[Men and women seem to have occupied positions of near equality in most Montagnard tribes, although only men could become elders. The health of the adults may be described as good, because they had survived in spite of a high infant-mortality rate, exposure to many endemic diseases, and malnutrition. Village sanitation and the tribesmen's personal hygiene practices were rudimentary. Some tribes, such as the Jeh, held the belief that cleanliness angers the spirits. Mite-borne typhus and venereal diseases were associated with poor sanitation and inadequate sexual hygiene. Malaria was very common.

[As Mole (1970) reported, the family structure varied greatly from tribe to tribe. In some tribes, parents chose marriage partners for their children based upon alliances or economic factors. Others allowed the male to choose his own bride(s) with the encouragement and economic support of the clan. A few tribes were so structured that the girl or her mother made the choice of a groom. The newly married couple might reside with the parents of the groom (patrilocal) in an extended-family longhouse or in a single-unit house in the groom's family village (neolocal). They might live in the same family village as the bride's family in a single-family house or with the bride's extended-family longhouse (matrilocal). In rare cases, the newly married couple established their home in a new community or in one unrelated to the parents of either groom or bride.

[Some tribes required dowries of the husband, others, dowries of the wife, whereas some had no required payments. Marriage arrangements usually required the services of an intermediary in order to save "face" and act as a buffer when marriage-price bargaining became serious. When the marriage ceremony occurred, it was surrounded with prescribed rituals that had to be followed for the villagers to consider the marriage properly begun.

[When children were born, their name was determined by whether the family was patrilineal or matrilineal. Customs pertaining to divorce were so varied that specific statements required reference to a particular tribe in order to have factual relevance. The same goes for the rules about what had to be done after the death of one's husband or wife. For example, among the Upland Cham Group of the Jarai, when a wife died, her unmarried sister had to marry the widower. If there were no unmarried sisters, the widower returned to his maternal longhouse, while his children remained at their mother's longhouse. With the Rhadé, if a husband died, one of his younger brothers was expected to take the widow as his wife. If the eligible brothers were already married, one of them might take the widow as a second wife, although this was not obligatory. It was taboo for a man to marry the widow of his younger brother.

[Reflecting a negative attitude towards the genitals is the widely practiced custom of shielding a newborn child from the influence of evil spirits by giving him or her names like "pig," "naughty," or the names of sex organs. Because male babies were more highly prized, yet had a higher death rate, they were often given girls' names and dressed in girls' clothing to fool the spirits.

[In most tribes, children of both sexes were brought up together until puberty began. Puberty rites included the filing of the teeth, because long teeth were regarded as animal, or as by most tribes, filed down and lacquered teeth were regarded as enhancing the male's and/or female's sex appeal. Premari-

tal sexual relations were mostly discouraged by fines and the knowledge that any village misfortune, such as the sudden death of some animal, was to be blamed upon the guilty lovers. The fine had to be paid to both the village and their parents, mainly as compensation for not consulting them. The couple was also required to marry. On the other hand, among the Jarai, unmarried young people who were not engaged might freely indulge in sexual relations as long as they did not have them with any member of their family.

[Marriage and adultery were regarded quite similarly by the different tribes. They greatly respected marriage, so harmonious relationships between husband and wife were prized. The traditional tribal laws regarding adultery reflected the binding nature of wedlock. However, adultery, a deviation from the marriage pattern, was a frequent cause of family discord. If a married woman committed adultery and had a child, the Bahnar considered her husband the father. If a married man had a child by an unmarried girl, he paid her a fine; if he asked the girl to become his wife of second rank and she refused, he owed her nothing. Theoretically, once the fine had been paid, the normal life of the family went on as before. In actuality, the Bahnar could be very jealous, and adultery could produce antagonism among the persons involved.

[The Hre regarded adultery even more seriously as a violation requiring village intervention to punish the guilty. The penalties for adultery were one buffalo or five copper pots; if one adulterer was unmarried, it was only one pig. Since brother-sister incest was believed not only to bring misfortune to the guilty party, but also disaster to the village, sacrifices imploring the pardon of the spirits were required, and the property of the parents of the guilty pair was confiscated and divided among their relatives. The offenders had to publicly apologize to the village, eat from a trough used by pigs, and were banished from the village.

[Roots and herbs for use as abortive preparations were known by all the tribes, though it depended upon the village policy if they were more or less in use. Generally, it was thought as acceptable to kill ill or deformed infants after the birth. (*End of update by J. Pastoetter*)]

## Summary

Vietnam is a country with a long and complex history and cultural traditions that vary a good deal in the different regions. We hope this heterogeneous character is clear in our chapter. As in other Southeast Asian countries, Vietnamese society is in rapid transformation because of the enormous influx of "modern" thinking as presented by commercials, international women's and men's magazines, and the introduction of Western economic system rules. The Vietnamese people are trying to find, at least in privacy, some stability and security, especially for the traditional values of the national ethic system of Confucianism. From a sexological viewpoint, this is, literally, a deadly mixture. It involves a tension between sexual hedonism and the perception of sex as something to buy or sell on one side, and the customs and traditions demanding a strict separation between sexual pleasures and ordinary life on the other side. Talking about sexuality, be it in public or in intimate partnership, is a Vietnamese taboo. This makes for an ideal breeding ground for AIDS and other STDs. But it also means that a neutral and unprejudiced approach to sexual habits is hardly possible, not just for the people, but also for the state representatives and researchers. Foreign researchers, in particular, are not seen as neutral and nonjudgmental, but as outsiders. The perceived threat of the etic (outside) researcher calls into play the most important rule of Confucianism, "save face."

Our chapter is a direct result of this cultural rule, and it is not accidental that most of the historic and culturally relevant materials we drew on reflect a strong subjective coloring. This material was gathered by foreigners, who reported (and often exaggerated) only what was interesting from their etic viewpoint, with little objectivity and considerable sensational flavoring to create French or American public interest in their books. Unfortunately, we have no other resources. Sex research in Vietnam is still, even today, only legitimate if it serves public health issues like STD and AIDS research, family planning and abortion-related issues, or elimination of the victimization of women and children. Even then, it is difficult to decide which survey results are accurate and which are only politically correct. Gammeltoft (1999) reports this problem most insistently, and our experience with Vietnamese students and Vietnamese research confirmed this. To all these difficulties, one has to add that Vietnam is a nation with many different regional traditions. Without substantial funding and government cooperation, sexological field research in Vietnam will not be possible. Sexological research in Vietnam still awaits the arrival of a Vietnamese "Kinsey," much as sexological research was not possible in China until Dalin Liu obtained government cooperation and support for a Kinsey-like nationwide survey of 20,000 Chinese men and women (see M. P. Lau's summary of Dalin Liu's research in the chapter on China in this volume).

A long ignored but promising approach to Vietnamese sexuality might be a survey of U.S. Vietnam War veterans. Unfortunately, the U.S. Army did not care enough about the Vietnamese people or their own soldiers to gather data on what was going on in thousands of brothels and in the provinces during the war. Insights and perspectives provided by Robert Taylor (1997) suggest that this kind of retrospective research would still be possible in the U.S.A., as well as in Vietnam. It would be extremely useful to have data regarding how the military and civil societies deal with sexuality under the circumstances of war.

Vietnam won the war against the United States 25 years ago, but now it seems the U.S.A. will win the cultural war. At least, such is the perception of many people in Vietnam and the United States. This is only partly true, and then mainly for the young people. As for effective countermeasures against the rising tide of AIDS and other STDs, and more so for a healthy and even joyful sexuality, neither traditional Vietnamese values nor American pop culture offers any solutions for these challenges. In fact, they may make effective solutions more difficult. What Vietnam needs is an extended understanding of its own sexual heritage, neutral scientific sex surveys, and a broad public embracing of sex education. With these, Vietnam should be able to win the war against sexual ignorance.

## Acknowledgments

The author wishes to acknowledge the staff and Library of the Archive of Sexology, Berlin, especially its Director, Prof. Dr. Erwin Haeberle, for assistance and use of its holdings, and the staff and Library of Indiana University, Bloomington, and of the Kinsey Institute for Research in Sex, Gender, and Reproduction for assistance and use of their libraries and collections. The author also thanks Professor Frank Proschan, an expert on Vietnamese culture at the Folklore Institute at Indiana University (Bloomington).

## References and Suggested Readings*

Aronson, J. 1999. Homosex in Hanoi? In: W. L. Leap, ed., *Sex, the public sphere, and public sex. Public sex/Gay space* (pp. 203-221). New York: Columbia University Press.

Bao, V. N., L. D. Long, & Y. Taylor. 1998 (November). *"Suffered lives": Assessment of social and behavioral practices for HIV/AIDS prevention in Can Tho*. A report prepared for Family Health International and the National AIDS Committee. The Population Council, Vietnam Office.

Bélanger, D., & T. H. Khuat. 1998 (June). Young single women using abortion in Hanoi, Viet Nam. *Asia-Pacific Population Journal, 13*(2):3-26. (Bangkok, Thailand).

Carrier, J., B. Nguyen, & S. Su. 1997. Sexual relations between migrating populations (Vietnamese with Mexican and Anglo) and HIV/STD infections in southern California. In: G. Herdt, ed., *Sexual cultures and migration in the era of AIDS: Anthropological and demographic perspectives* (pp. 225-250). Oxford: Clarendon Press.

Chittick, J. B. 1997. *The threat of HIV/AIDS on Viet Nam's youth: Meeting the challenge of prevention* (A report on the 1996 Viet Nam Youth Union Conference with additional commentary on the Government's approach to the teen AIDS epidemic in 1997). Boston: (Unpublished).

CIA. 2002 (January). *The world factbook 2002*. Washington, DC: Central Intelligence Agency. Available: http://www.cia.gov/cia/publications/factbook/index.html.

Commission of Enquiry of the League of Nations, 1933.

Cooper, M., & J. Hanson. 1998. Where there are no tourists . . . yet: A visit to the slum brothels in Ho Chi Minh City, Vietnam. In: M. Oppermann, ed., *Sex tourism and prostitution: Aspects of leisure, recreation, and work* (pp. 144-152). New York: Cognizant Communication.

Cultural Information Analysis Center, American University. 1966. *Minority groups in the Republic of Vietnam*. Washington, DC: Headquarters, Dept. of the Army.

Do, T. 1997. Popular Religion in contemporary southern Vietnam: A personal approach. *Sojourn, 12*(1):64-91.

Fahey, S. 1998. Vietnam's women in the Renovation Era. In: K. Sen & M. Stivens, eds., *Gender and power in affluent Asia* (pp. 222-249). London/New York: Routledge.

"Frank." 2000. *On the legality of homosexuality in Vietnam*. Available: http://www.utopia-asia.com/vietterm.htm (The VN-GBLF E-Mail Forum).

Franklin, B. 1993. *The risk of AIDS in Vietnam* (Monograph Series 1). Hanoi: Care International in Vietnam.

Gammeltoft, T. 1999. *Women's bodies, women's worries. Health and family planning in a Vietnamese rural community*. Richmond, VA: Curzon Press.

Goodkind, D. 1994 (November/December). Abortion in Vietnam: Measurements, puzzles, and concerns (Pt. 1). *Studies in Family Planning, 25*(6):342-352.

Goodkind, D. M. 1995 (March). Vietnam's one-or-two-child policy in action. *Population and Development Review, 21*(1): 85-111, 217-218, 220.

Goodkind, D. 1996. State agendas, local sentiments: Vietnamese wedding practices amidst socialist transformations. *Social Forces, 75*(2):717-742.

Goodkind, D. 1997 (Spring). The Vietnamese double marriage squeeze. *International Migration Review, 31*(1):108-27.

Goodkind, D., & P. T. Anh. 1997 (December). Reasons for rising condom use in Vietnam. *International Family Planning Perspectives, 23*(4):173-178.

Greenberg, J. H. 1972. Venereal disease in the armed forces. *Medical Clinics of North America, 56*(5):1087-1100.

Gregersen, E. 1996. *The world of human sexuality*. New York: Irvington Publishers.

Guénel, A. 1997. Sexually transmitted diseases in Vietnam and Cambodia since the French Colonial Period. In: M. Lewis,

---

*Non-Vietnamese scholars follow no standardized format for listing the author(s). The common practice of adding a comma after the first or second name leaves the reader without a clue as to which of the three names is the family name. Citations here follow the format used in our sources.

S. Bamber, & M. Waugh, eds., *Sex, disease, and society. A comparative history of sexually transmitted diseases and HIV/AIDS in Asia and the Pacific* (pp. 139-153). Westport, CT/London: Greenwood Press.

Gulzow, M. & C. Mitchell. 1980 (October). "Vagina dentate" and "incurable venereal disease" legends from the Vietnam war. *Western Folklore*. 39:306-316.

Hickey, G. C. 1982a. *Sons of the mountains: Ethnohistory of the Vietnamese Central Highlands to 1954*. New Haven, CT: Yale University Press.

Hickey, G. C. 1982b. *Free in the forest: Ethnohistory of the Vietnamese Central Highlands, 1954-1976*. New Haven, CT: Yale University Press.

Hoang Ba Thinh. 1992. *Œsai Lech Trong Quan He Tinh Cam Khac Gioi Trong Sinh Vien: Bieu Hien, Nguyen Nhan Va Kien Nghi. Ky Yeu Hoi Thao Khoa Hoc "Doi Moi Cac Chinh Sach Xa Hoi Nham Khac Phuc Te Nam Xa Hoi Trong Dieu Kien Kinh Te Thi Truong."* Bo Noi Vu [Hanoi University].

Hoang, B. T. 1999. *Sexual exploitation of children*. Hanoi: The Gioi Publishers.

Hoang, B. & P. K. Ngoc. 1996. Teen-age sexuality in Vietnam. *Vietnam Social Sciences*, 6(56):57-69.

Joyeux, B. 1930. *Le péril vénérien et la prostitution a Hanoi*. Hanoi: Imprimerie d'Extrême-Orient.

Karim, W. J. 1995. Bilaterism and gender in Southeast Asia. In: W. J. Karim, ed., *"Male" and "female" in developing Southeast Asia* (pp. 35-74). Oxford/Washington, DC: Berg Publishers.

Khuat Thu Hong. 1998. *Study on sexuality in Vietnam: The known and unknown issues* (South & East Asia Regional Working Papers No. 11). Hanoi: Population Council.

Lebar, F. M., G. C. Hickey, & J. K. Musgrave. 1964. *Ethnic groups of mainland Southeast Asia*. New Haven, CT: Human Relations Area Files Press.

Mackay, J. 2000. *The Penguin atlas of human sexual behavior. Sexuality and sexual practice around the world*. New York/London: Penguin Group.

Marnais, P. 1967. *Saigon after dark*. New York: MacFadden-Bartell.

Mole, R. L. 1970. *The Montagnards of South Vietnam: A study of nine tribes*. Rutland Vermont: C. E. Tuttle Co.

Nguyen Huu Minh. 1997 (June). Age at first marriage in Viet Nam: Patterns and determinants. *Asia-Pacific Population Journal*, 12(2):49-74.

Nguyen Ngoc Huy & Ta Van Tai. 1987. *Le Code: Law in traditional Vietnam: A comparative Sino-Vietnamese legal study with historical-juridical analysis and annotations*. Athens, OH: Ohio University Press.

O'Harrow, S. 1995. Vietnamese women and Confucianism: Creating spaces from patriarchy. In: W. J. Karim, ed., *"Male" and "female" in developing Southeast Asia* (pp. 161-180). Oxford/Washington, DC: Berg Publishers.

Pelzer White, C. 1987. State, culture and gender: Continuity and change in women's position in rural Vietnam. In: H. Afshar, ed., *Women, state, and ideology: Studies from Africa and Asia* (pp. 226-234). Albany: State University of New York Press.

Proschan, F. 1998. *Filial piety and non-procreative male-to-male sex among Vietnamese*. Unpublished paper presented at the Annual meeting of the American Anthropological Association.

Proschan, F. 1999. *"Syphilis, opiomania, and pederasty": Colonial constructions of Vietnamese (and French) genders, sexualities, and social diseases*. Unpublished article.

Scholl-Latour, P. 2000. *Der tod im reisfeld. Dreißig jahre krieg in Indochina*. Muenchen, Germany: DTV.

Slote, W. H., & G. A. DeVos, eds. 1998. *Confucianism and the family*. Albany, NY: State University of New York Press.

Soucy, A. 2000. Romantic love and gender hegemony in Vietnam. In: S. Blackburn, ed., *Love, sex and power: Women in Southeast Asia*. Clayton, Australia: Monash Asia Institute.

Taylor, R. 1997. *The innocent*. Santa Barbara, CA: Fithian Press.

Truong, T. D. 1990. *Sex, money, and morality: Prostitution and tourism in Southeast Asia*. London: Atlantic Highlands; New York: Zed Books.

UNAIDS. 2002. *Epidemiological fact sheets by country*. Geneva, Switzerland: Joint United Nations Programme on HIV/AIDS (UNAIDS/WHO). Available: http://www.unaids.org/hivaidsinfo/statistics/fact_sheets/index_en.htm.

"Vinh N." 1999. *Vietnamese terms for homosexuality*. Available: http://www.utopia-asia.com/vietterm.htm (The VN-GBLF E-Mail Forum).

WHO (World Health Organization), Western Pacific Regional Office. 1993. *Le SIDA dans la région du Pacifique occidental*. Manila: WHO.

Wijeyewardene, G., ed. 1990. *Ethnic groups across national boundaries in mainland Southeast Asia*. Singapore: Institute of Southeast Asian Studies.

X., Jacobus [as "A French Army-Surgeon"]. 1898. *Untrodden Fields of Anthropology by a French Army Surgeon; Observations on the Esoteric Manners and Customs of Semi-Civilized Peoples; Being a Record of Thirty Years Experience in Asia, Africa, America and Oceania* (Two volumes). Paris: Librairie de Médicine, Folklore et Anthropologie. [Second, enlarged English edition of *L'Amour aux colonies*, 1893; a facsimile edition was published by Robert F. Krieger Publishing Company, Huntington, NY, in 1972].

Young, S. B. 1998. The Orthodox Chinese Confucian social paradigm versus Vietnamese individualism (pp. 137-161). In: W. H. Slote & G. A. DeVos, eds., *Confucianism and the family*. Albany, NY: State University of New York Press.

# Last-Minute Developments

*Added by the Editors
after the manuscript had been typeset*

## Contents

## *Argentina*

### 6. Homoerotic, Homosexual, and Bisexual Behaviors

*Gay Unions*                    SOPHIA KAMENETZKY

[*Update 2003*: July 26, 2003: Buenos Aires, the capital city of Argentina, is the first city in Latin America to recognize civil unions for same-sex individuals. The new law applies only to city employees, and provides only a few basic rights. Despite these limits, observers see the action as a major legal breakthrough to the nationwide recognition of civil unions of same-sex couples. Medical and social rights of a city employee are extended to the employee's partner. Employees can ask for a leave to take care of a sick partner. They can jointly apply for loans and have the right to continue receiving state pensions in case of a partner's death. However, the rights to inherit at a partner's death and to adopt children have not been recognized.

The law was passed by the state legislature in December 2002, and in May, the city issued its normative regulations. Soon afterward, special public registries were opening where couples could inscribe their union, independently of their sex. This means that heterosexual partners who decide not to marry can register to benefit from the same limited rights given to homosexual couples. Partners, who have reached the age of majority, can register by presenting at least two witnesses to certify that the two have been living together in the city of Buenos Aires for at least one year, and that they are single or divorced. Civil unions terminate by either death or marriage of a partner. A partner can also annul the union by making a presentation to the Public Registry and certifying that he has given notice of his decision to the other party.

As expected, the Catholic and Evangelical Churches were enraged by the recognition of same-sex civil unions, noting that the New Testament says that homosexuality is "one of the most horrendous perversions." Despite the reli-gious opposition, in mid-2003, Mexico, Brazil, and Chile appeared ready to join Argentina in ratification of similar laws recognizing same-sex civil unions.

## *Australia*

### 10. Sexually Transmitted Diseases and HIV/AIDS

*Lesbian Sexual Health Risks*   RAYMOND J. NOONAN

[*Update 2003*: Research findings from Sydney, Australia, published in the journal *Sexually Transmitted Infections* indicate that lesbians are just as likely to get sexually transmitted diseases as their heterosexual counterparts, in contrast to previous assumptions that they are at low risk for these diseases. In addition, they are far more likely to be drug users and to have had sex with homosexual men, making them almost eight times more likely to be infected with hepatitis C. Based on a study of 2,800 women at the Sydney Sexual Health Centre, doctors found that bacterial vaginosis was more prevalent in "women who had sex with other women," while herpes and genital warts were common in both groups, with gonorrhea and chlamydia rates low and similar. BBC News (2000) quoted the researchers as saying, "a woman's sexual identity is not an accurate predictor of behaviour, with a high proportion of 'lesbian' women reporting sex with (often high risk) men." In fact, they reported that women who had sex with women were more than three times more likely to report having had sex with a homosexual or bisexual man, with almost one in ten of these women having had more than 50 male sex partners.

While it remains true that women who have sex with *only* women are at low risk for STDs, this research suggests that medical personnel should adopt the same approach often used in taking sex histories from men who have sex with men, i.e., eschewing labels and asking self-identified lesbian women whether they also have sex with men, in order to get a more-accurate assessment of risk.

BBC News (2003) also reported on a recent study from the United States that lesbians have a higher risk of heart disease and are generally more overweight than other women, further suggesting that health education messages targeted specifically to lesbian women need to be developed. The report noted that lesbians are more likely to be unconcerned about their weight, perhaps, quoting researchers, because "weight control is often perceived as a conventionally feminine behaviour," which might necessitate "a strategy that de-emphasises traditional feminine values."

*References*

BBC News. 2000 (October 23). Health: Lesbians have 'same risk of sex diseases.' Available: http://news.bbc.co.uk/1/hi/health/986898.stm.
BBC News. 2003 (September 13). Health: Lesbians 'have higher heart disease risk.' Available: http://news.bbc.co.uk/1/hi/health/3100702.stm.

## *Canada*

### 6. Homoerotic, Homosexual, and Bisexual Behaviors

*Gay Marriage Legislation*      MICHAEL BARRETT

[*Update 2003*: In June 2003, the Ontario Province Court of Appeals ruled in favor of a same-sex couples' right to marry. The judgment was not conditional and the judge gave approval to issue marriage licenses to same-sex couples in Ontario with the release of the decision. At the national level, the federal government said that it would not appeal the ruling—the federal government mandates marriage laws while the provinces enact them. This means that legislation will now be brought forward to recognize same-sex marriage. The intent appears to be to do so in a way that will not compromise the rights of religious groups who choose not to marry same-sex couples on religious grounds. Nine provinces said at the time that they would support legislation that recognized same-sex unions. Alberta said that it would use the "notwithstanding" clause of the Constitution to block the legislation.

Earlier, in May of 2003, the British Columbia Court of Appeals had amended common law in a way that recognized same-sex unions, i.e., marriage was defined as the union of "two persons to the exclusion of all others." Implementation of the decision had been suspended until July 2004, but the subsequent ruling in Ontario led the B.C. Court of Appeals to lift that suspension in July 2003 on the basis that the provinces would otherwise be unequal in their handling of the issue.

In the wake of these provincial court decisions, the federal government is now faced with determining how the Canadian Constitution can be interpreted in terms of the rights of religious institutions to refuse to marry same-sex couples and in terms of federal and provincial responsibilities with respect to marriage (Krauss 2003abc).

*References*
Krauss, C. 2003a (June 18). Canadian leaders decide to propose a same-sex marriage law. *The New York Times*, A1, A8.
Krauss, C. 2003b (June 19). Gay marriage plan: Sign of sweeping social change in Canada. *The New York Times*, A8.
Krauss, C. 2003c (July 5). In blessing gay unions, bishop courts a schism. *The New York Times*, A4.

## 8. Significant Unconventional Sexual Behaviors

*Sexual Abuse and the Churches*    JULIE FRASER
[*Update 2003*: March 2003: Sexual abuse in Canada has also received attention in the past decade when accusations of abuse, alleged and proven, have increasingly been leveled at religious institutions and at members of those institutions. Catholic, Anglican, and United Churches, to name a few, have been associated with sexual abuse scandals, the financial and legal ramifications of which have threatened their livelihood and brought them into legal arguments with the Canadian Government.

A great many of these lawsuits pertain to abuse that happened at church-run schools. In many cases, although not all, these were schools for Native Canadian children. According to Sebok (2002), the Canadian Government took over the education of Native Canadian children in 1883 and relied heavily on Catholic, Methodist, Anglican, and Presbyterian churches. The Canadian experience with boarding schools for native children came to an end in mid-1980 and is now considered a political and cultural tragedy. It was not until the late 1990s that the victims began to sue individually for sexual abuse suffered while attending these schools.

The number of cases is too numerous to report; however, some of the more important legal issues will be highlighted. One legal focus has been the relative responsibility of the Government versus the churches. For example, in *FSM v. Clarke*, 11 W.W.R. 301 (B.S.S.C. 1999), a pupil at a residential school between 1969 and 1976 alleged that a dormitory supervisor sexually assaulted him and other pupils. He sued the Anglican Church and the Government of Canada. In this case, the court found the Anglican Church 60% responsible, and the Canadian government 40% responsible (Sebok 2002). Subsequent to this, other cases followed pertaining to incidences of sexual abuse happening as much as 50 years prior. In *M. M. v. Roman Catholic Church of Canada*, 180 D.L.R. (4") 737 (Man. Q.B. 1999), for example, a 70-year-old woman who had attended a school between 1930 and 1942 alleged not only sexual abuse, but also that the Church "strove to deprive the plaintiff of her culture and way of life."

While the survivors of the abuse deal with the psychological trauma, the churches deal with the negative publicity, as well as the potentially crippling financial burden associated with litigation. As of 2002, there were approximately 9,000 outstanding residential school lawsuits. The Anglican Church estimates that the combined liability for the government and the churches might reach $1 billion (Canadian). One western Anglican diocese has ceased to operate under the weight of individual lawsuits.

## *India*

## 5. Interpersonal Heterosexual Behaviors

*"Assisted" Arranged Marriages*

ROBERT T. FRANCOEUR
[*Update 2003*: Although traditional arranged marriages are still the norm in India, the practice is evolving in response to the spread of romantic love among the middle class in the larger cities of India. A second stimulus for change is occurring within the clannish, tight-knit Indian expatriate communities in Britain, as second- and third-generation children adapt the nature of the arrangement to life in the U.K. (Francoeur 1982, 66; Alvarez 2003).

In traditional Indian arranged marriages, selecting the best spouse for a son or daughter has been the exclusive responsibility of parents and grandparents, and particularly the "Aunt Bijis," as Muslims call their matchmakers. Parents and Aunt Bijis rely on recommendations from other family members and friends, and on "matrimonials" placed in the appropriate Indian newspaper, in India, the U.K., the U.S.A., or any other place with a large immigrant Indian population.

Typical matrimonials, like the two below, describe the age, physical appearance, education, and caste of the son or daughter:

> Parents invite correspondence from a tall, handsome, professional, or educated businessman for their 27-year-old, 5' 5", very handsome, fair complexion, homely [domestic-skilled] daughter with green card and M.B.B.S from a prestigious institution in India.

> Physician father Brahmin invites correspondence from presentable, charming, and homely Gujarati girls for his U.S. citizen son, 29, 5' 8", 145, vegetarian, M.S. (computer eng). Send biodata with recent photographs (returnable). (Francoeur 1991, 37)

Twenty years ago, in Bombay, India's most cosmopolitan city, the revolutionary idea of romantic love that swept the U.S. a hundred years earlier was adopted by some middle-class youths from what they saw at the cinema. But in Bombay, as well as elsewhere in India, it is not easy for young people to meet without the supervision of some family member. A young woman talking with a man in the museum coffee shop or dancing in one of the discotheques runs the risk of ruining her reputation and chances for a decent marriage. An Indian woman at an American college will be very careful not to compromise her prospects back home by letting her parents know she has dated a foreigner. In 1990, only 5% of college students in India met without the introduction being arranged by their parents.

Modifications in the traditional arranged marriage began to appear as early as the 1960s, when a couple brought together by their parents would have an initial meeting before their extended families and then met alone several times, either with family members in another room or at a restaurant, before delivering a verdict. In the 21st century, couples meet in public venues without the family encounter first.

But the problem has been how to make that first connection. In Bombay and other large cities in the 1980s, the owners of large halls solved this problem by sponsoring a Saturday evening for young people. Young women are admitted free while the young men pay a small admission fee for the privilege of going on stage to describe themselves and the kind of woman they are looking for in more detail than a "matrimonial" permits. After presenting himself, the young man wanders through the hall, hoping some young woman will slip him her name and address or phone number, so they can explore their mutual interests. If they connect, then the parents can be brought into the picture to take over the formal arrangements (Francoeur 1982, 66).

In the 21st century, young Indian natives and expatriates are pushing the cultural boundaries.

There is a boom in Asian marriage websites, chat rooms, Internet personal advertisements and even South Asian versions of speed dating, the latest phenomenon to hit the Indian community in London, with men and women meeting each other for just three minutes at restaurants and bars before moving on to the next potential mate.

One young professional Indian woman in London turned to Asian speed dating—with her mother's blessing—after 10 unsuccessful introductions. She described these formal introductions as awkward, drawn-out affairs in which the young man, his mother, and several other relatives came over to meet her family. She wore her best Indian outfit, a sari or elegant Indian pants and top, and sat quietly, despite her normal chattiness. When called upon, she poured tea, and then talked briefly to her potential mate in a side room.

In an "assisted arranged marriage," the abiding principles behind an arranged marriage still remain strong on the assumption that lust and romantic love do not make a lasting marriage, and when it comes to weigh similar backgrounds and compatibility, family knows best. But parents and elders, eager to avoid alienating their children, making them miserable, or seeing them go unmarried, have shown considerable flexibility. The arrangement is becoming more fluid, a bit more open, a nice compromise (Alvarez 2003).

### References

Alvarez, L. 2003 (June 22). Arranged marriages get a little rearranging. *The New York Times*, International Section, A3.

Francoeur, R. T. 1982. *Becoming a sexual person* (1st ed.). New York: John Wiley & Son.

Francoeur, R. T. 1991. *Becoming a sexual person* (2nd ed.). New York: Macmillan Publishing.

## Indonesia

### 7. Gender Diversity and Transgender Issues

*New Roles for Transvestites*   ROBERT T. FRANCOEUR

[*Update 2003*: Public records of transvestites taking prominent roles in Indonesian culture date from a 14th-century ruler, Hayam Wuruk, who is described in court annals as dressing as a woman in front of his ministers and using a woman's name. Later, after the arrival of Islam, men often played the role of women in the village dance dramas of East Java, and they still do. The first president of independent Indonesia, Sukarno, writes proudly in his memoirs of playing female roles when he was a young man, putting powder on his face and rouge on his lips, and stuffing "two sweet breads" in his blouse. "With this addition to my shapely figure, everybody said I looked absolutely beautiful," he reported. "After the show I pulled the breads out of my blouse and ate them."

Under the autocratic rule of Sukarno's successor, General Suharto, transvestites have won some rights. Known as *waria*—a combination of *wanita* (woman) and *pria* (man), transvestites are still sometimes rounded up and detained by the police if they are suspected of working as prostitutes. However, this varies, because in some cities they court business openly in what amounts to a late-night transvestite parade down the main thoroughfares looking for clients. In major cities, particularly on the Java, local governments provide training programs for transvestites who want to run beauty salons, become hairstylists, or run a wedding business providing brides with gowns, décor, and makeup, all in one package.

In the larger cities, the government hires older *waria* to help young *waria* learn a trade so they can become independent and not need to earn a living in prostitution. On Indonesian television, transvestites are regular hosts on comedy shows and appear as characters in a popular puppet show. In 1977, when sex-change operations were still relatively unusual in the West, government television showed a movie called *I Am Vivian*. Based on a true story, it showed how an Indonesian boy who felt more like a girl was finally accepted by his family as a transvestite. In one of the more striking scenes, a doctor advises Vivian to have a sex-change operation. The movie ends with her in a white wedding gown, complete with veil, being carried by the groom to the bridal suite. In modern Indonesia, sex-change operations are out of vogue. Some transvestites dress as a modest Muslim woman with a *jilbab*, the traditional head covering, but change to male garb when they go to the mosque to pray.

But Merlyn Sopjan, a 30-year old *waria* interviewed by Jane Perlez (2003) for a *New York Times* International report, is typical of the "new" Indonesian *waria*:

For two years, Merlyn Sopjan lived with her boyfriend. Using his name, she became Mrs. Nanang. She was known in the neighborhood as his wife, and tucked his photo into her wallet. She was admired for her feminine looks: with liquid eyes and pancake makeup, she has the allure of a model. . . . The women on the block knew, she said, that under her demure clothes and despite her "wiggling" walk, she was physically a man. "I lived in his house and I was part of the community," she said, showing off a snapshot of herself with Mr. Nanang as they posed as a couple in casual clothes, her arm on his shoulder.

Now Merlyn and others like her are trying to create roles for themselves beyond their long tolerated positions as television stars, entertainers and beauticians, moving even into the political arena. Last month Merlyn tried to register as a candidate for mayor in Malang, the town in East Java near here where she is now finishing her civil engineering thesis at the university. Her application was denied by city officials on the ground that she missed the filing deadline by five minutes. It was not an explicit rejection on the basis of gender, though Merlyn suspects that had something to do with it. The rejection received sympathetic press coverage, with reporters asking why a "waria" should not have the same rights as anyone else. "I want waria to have a role in government," Merlyn said. "That's my mission."

(See the comments on *hijra* and their recent attempts to run for government office in India in Section 7, Gender Diversity and Transgender Issues, in the chapter on India.)

### Reference

Perlez, J. 2003 (July 24). For these transvestites, still more role changes. *The New York Times*, A4.

## Japan

### 5. Interpersonal Heterosexual Behaviors

*New Dating Behavior*                    ROBERT T. FRANCOEUR

[*Update 2003*: In the decades between the end of World War II and 1990, Japan moved from defeat to become a major industrialized nation. Social historians have only begun to identify, examine, and analyze the various political, economic, and cultural interactions that opened the Japanese people to outside influences in those years. During the years of prosperity, new generations of Japanese boys and girls grew up in a world of high expectations they would make it through the competition of higher education, find a reliable, lifelong job, marry a suitable partner in a marriage arranged by their parents, and begin their own family. In this world, the traditional rituals of courtship were still functional and supportive of the transition from child to young adult.

Prosperity allowed many of Japan's youth to vacation abroad during school breaks where they encountered Canadian, American, Australian, and other Western youth with very different courtship patterns. Although this undoubtedly meant some changes in gender roles, courtship, dating, and family, before the "economic bubble" collapsed in the 1990s, most university and high school graduates got jobs in a highly structured world that set their path through courtship and dating to marriage. In the 1990s, jobs for youth dried up and what remained were temporary jobs on the fringes of a depressed economy. In the process, with more free time and decreasing parental supervision, the younger generation began forming their own social groups, which, like their jobs, became part-time, low-stress, and temporary. Traditional expectations of financial security, independence, and marriage remain, but they are on hold. In the process, dating behavior has changed significantly.

Or so two surveys suggest (Webb 2002).

The first study, conducted by social scientists at the University of California, San Francisco, and Hiroshima University Medical School, surveyed 602 teens, ages 15 to 19, in the Shibuya section of Tokyo. A similar survey involved 16-year-olds in two rural prefectures. These surveys suggest that the traditional family-chaperoned courtship has given way to youth-controlled, part-time, low-stress, no-commitment, temporary relationships. "To many young Japanese people, everything about sex is casual," Masako Ono-Kihara, a public-health expert at Hiroshima University School of Medicine, observed. "Girls now share their boyfriends like they'd share chips. Everyone's hand is in the bag."

In a pattern reminiscent of American sexual relations after the advent of the contraceptive pill and before AIDS, 43% of the boys and girls in the Tokyo survey said they keep five or more *sekusutomo* or "sex friends" at a time. In the rural survey, 20% of boys and 18% of girls said they have at least five "sex friends" in a "circle of friends" who keep in touch by mobile phone. It is not unusual, according to the survey findings, to be a member of several social circles of friends, and to engage in sex with two or more in each circle. (See the update on "buddy sex" in Section 5B, Interpersonal Heterosexual Behaviors, Adolescent Sexuality, in the United States chapter).

Although the young Japanese assume their *sekusutomo* relations are very low risk because Japan has a very low rate of HIV infection and they are not having sex with prostitutes or foreigners, new studies show a significant rise in the incidence of STD infections among young Japanese. According to the Ministry of Health, STDs rose by 21% among Japa-

nese men under 24, and by 14% for women in same age group between 1998 and 2000 (the latest figures available). Condoms are seldom used by "sex friends"—condom sales have dropped 25% in the past decade. The abortion rate nearly doubled between 1999 and 2002 to 13 per 1,000. But that hardly compares with the American rate of 51 per 1,000.

To cope with these new health issues, the Ministry of Education has outlined a broad sex-education curriculum for high schools. However, since the program is optional and many school administrators are afraid of offending parents when answering questions about why this new program is needed, efforts to deal with the new dating patterns so far have not been effective.

*Reference*

Webb, A. I. 2002 (September 16). Dangerous liaisons: Japan's casual 'friends' risk more than broken hearts. *Newsweek MSNBC* Web archives. *Newsweek International* 2002 (September 9).

### 1. Basic Sexological Premises

*Gender Inequality in the Workplace*

ROBERT T. FRANCOEUR

[*Update 2003*: Japan has been struggling since 1990 to pull itself out of a very painful and persistent economic slump that has had a negative impact on society in many ways, including courtship and premarital sex (see entry on New Dating Behavior, above). Many experts have concluded that expanding the role and status of women in the professional workforce could provide a far bigger stimulus to recovery than any scheme tried so far, including huge public-works projects to bailouts of failing companies.

In 2003, the World Economic Forum ranked Japan 69th among the 75 member nations in empowering its women. While 40% of Japanese women work outside the home, they hold only about 9% of managerial positions, compared with about 45% in the United States (see Table 1). At the same time, women's wages are about 65% of those of their male counterparts, one of the largest gaps in the industrial world. According to many labor economists, Japan is effectively fighting with one hand tied behind its back when it shunts women off the corporate ladder. "Japan has gone as far as it can go with a social model that consists of men filling all of the economic, management and political roles," Eiko Shinotsuka, the first woman to serve on the board of the Bank of Japan, told *The New York Times*, "We've never had such a long economic crisis as this one, though, and people are beginning to recognize that the place of women in our society is an important factor."

Japanese corporations follow a strict protocol that hires men almost exclusively for career positions open to ad-

---

#### Table 1

#### A Comparison of Japanese, European, and American Professional Women

|         | All Workers | Managerial Workers | Civil Service Workers General | Civil Service Workers Managerial | National Parliament & Congress |
|---------|-------------|--------------------|-------------------------------|----------------------------------|--------------------------------|
| Japan   | 41.0%       | 8.9%               | 20.2%                         | 1.4%                             | 7.3%                           |
| U.S.A.  | 46.6        | 46.0               | 49.3                          | 23.1                             | 14.3                           |
| Sweden  | 48.0        | 30.5               | 43.0                          | 51.0                             | 45.3                           |
| Britain | 44.9        | 30.0               | 49.1                          | 17.2                             | 17.9                           |
| Germany | 44.0        | 26.9               | 39.0                          | 9.5                              | 32.2                           |

*Source*: Cabinet Office of Japan; International Labor Organization; Inter-Parliamentary Union.

vancement, while short-term work, clerical jobs, and serving tea are reserved for the "Office Ladies," O.L.s. In July of 2003, the Ministry of Economy pointed out that the profit margin in companies where women make up 40% to 50% of the staff were double the profit margin of companies where women account for 10% or less.

There is growing concern in some circles about the persistent failure of employers to provide flex time for working mothers, daycare centers, and pregnancy leaves, and provide women employees with the opportunity to advance their professional careers. Japan has practically no facilities for nursery schools and daycare. The Ministry of Education, for example, provides one public nursery school with a capacity of 20 children for the 38,000 government employees who work in Kasumigaseki, central Tokyo's administrative district. One good point is that this nursery school stays open until 10 p.m. Along with the persistent economic slump, experts are worried by the projections of a population decline that could produce huge labor shortages in the next half-century and possibly even economic collapse.

Still, the government resists putting any pressure of corporations to expand women's place in the economy. A government advisory panel has recommended that the public and private sectors aim to have at least 30% of managerial positions filled by women by 2020. There is even talk of the government adopting an affirmative action policy. At the same time, supporters of women's rights have been told by a former Prime Minister that the main reason for Japan's falling birthrate is the over-education of its women. Meanwhile, a top aide for the Prime Minister was recently quoted as saying that often women who are raped deserve it, while a legislator from the governing party said, approvingly, that the men who carried out such acts are virile and "good specimens."

Summing up the problem, one successful woman manager told *The New York Times*, "Men are really intimidated by professional women in Japan. But this is still a society where even when it looks like a woman has some authority, the men usually manage to stay on top."

*Reference*
French, H. W. 2003 (July 25). Japan's neglected resource: Female workers. *The New York Times*, A3.

## Morocco

### 1. Basic Sexological Premises
*Character of Gender Roles* ROBERT T. FRANCOEUR
[*Update 2003*: In the gender-segregated culture of Morocco and the Magribi (North African), reproduction is still a very important aspect of sex, more important than eroticism. In the Magribi value system, women's main social capital is their bodies. A woman's virginity is all-important—a deflowered woman is a used, secondhand object. This apartheid, the social segregation of males and females by the veil, by exclusion from public life, and seclusion in the *harim*, according to De Martino (1992, 25, 28), makes woman

a mysterious, almost unattainable, often idealized object. Simultaneously she is desired and feared precisely because she is unknown. Even where the separation is less rigorous (at work, on the beach) rarely is heterosexual "love made." If at all, petting, masturbation, and sodomy are practiced. The vagina is excluded as a holy, forbidden part of the female body. Woman is the prime target of the desire (and fantasies) of the Moroccan. The diverting to the ass, just to release tensions, is something different from "homosexuality" as understood in the West. . . . The

cardinal point of Islamic sexuality is not the general practice of sodomy, but the despising of women (De Martino 1992, 28).

On the other side, today everywhere in Morocco, personal prestige and power are revered. Men seem to be entrapped by an excessive adoration of virility, identification with the father, hero worship, a cult of force and domination, contempt of everything weak, and distain and fear of women (De Martino 1992, 25).

### 3. Knowledge and Education about Sexuality
*Sexuality Education* ROBERT T. FRANCOEUR
[*Update 2003*: In the home, any mention of sexuality or intimate matters is taboo, *haram*, holy, forbidden, protected. It would embarrass both parties. Because parents would not discuss sexual matters with a son or daughter, they are left to get their sex education from their peers. Sexuality then is seen as something not belonging to the family, something "outside," and therefore suspect, shameful, and bad (Eppink 1992, 33).

### 4. Autoerotic Behaviors and Patterns
*Masturbation* ROBERT T. FRANCOEUR
[*Update 2003*: According to Eppink,

Masturbation as a possibility for sexual fulfillment is strongly repudiated and least valued, because it lacks an object [to be penetrated]. This has to do with the value attached to intromission and ejaculation.

In the Western middle-class frame of reference, sexuality is highly related to eroticism and love. This is by no means the case in all cultures and in all times. Vanggaard describes types of aggressive sexuality in cultures of pre-Christian Europe: The sexual act of the active man is intended to make the object passive, to submit him [*sic*]. This seems to be true for North Africa as well. Masturbating—not submitting some other person—is not manly; therefore "*kaffat*/masturbator" is a term of abuse.

Nevertheless (fitting the pattern of group security) boys often masturbate together, outside or in a room, or at the movies where it is quite common. This is done touching each other, but it is not normal to look at each other's penis and to talk about it.

Masturbation is one of the most delicate topics to talk about. Often it is claimed that it is not necessary, "because there are so many other possibilities." (Eppink 1992, 35)

### 5. Interpersonal Heterosexual Behaviors
*Adolescent Sexual Behavior* ROBERT T. FRANCOEUR
[*Update 2003*: Boys under age 9 develop a protective all-male peer group with whom they hang out. They walk hand-in-hand, share jokes, complement each other on their manly looks, and exchange "friendship letters," which some view as a kind of homoerotic same-sex love letters. Between ages 9 and 17, a boy becomes a *zamel*, the recipient of anal sex with cousins, teachers, and neighbors, either out of necessity because he is forced into it, by intimidation, by seduction, or by the offer of presents or money. At age 15 or 16, a *zamel* loses his admirers or he starts refusing their advances. He becomes a "man," meaning that now he becomes the active partner in anal sex with younger boys and actively courts girls. Youths, who continue as recipients of anal intercourse, are ridiculed as *hassas*. Some *hassases* become "swishing faggots," "drag queens" who create their own little subculture, appearing as women:

an image of an image, the imitation of the image the *Magribi* has of a woman, distant, separated, idealized, and despised all at the same time. Finally, in their mature years, there is the great mass of men who like to fuck—girls, *hassases*, married women, boys, tourists, and prostitutes alike. (De Martino 1992)

As they mature sexually, Moroccan boys can masturbate, accept passive anal contact with another male, or try to have active anal contact with another male, a female, or an animal, or have heterosexual vaginal intercourse. In these options, the highest value is attached to the last possibility and the lowest to the first possibility. But regardless of the sexual expression, the emphasis in sexual contacts is not on friendship or romantic love, but on penetration and ejaculation. Penetration is a manifestation of male power, so sex is essentially penetration and quick ejaculation. This does not mean that affection is never felt; but romantic love does not predominate in a sexual relationship, nor in marriage. Kissing and oral-genital contact are not customary. Foreplay and petting—like masturbation—are viewed as inferior, and such behavior is often labeled as "weak" or "strange" (De Martino 1992, 28); Eppink 1992, 36-37).

### References

De Martino, G. 1992. An Italian in Morocco. In: A. Schmitt & J. Sofer, eds., *Sexuality and eroticism among males in Moslem societies*. New York: Harrington Park Press (Haworth Press).

Eppink, A. 1992. Moroccan boys and sex. In: A. Schmitt & J. Sofer, eds., *Sexuality and eroticism among males in Moslem societies*. New York: Harrington Park Press (Haworth Press).

# Nepal

## 5. Interpersonal Heterosexual Behaviors

*New Courtship Rituals*      ROBERT T. FRANCOEUR

[*Update 2003*: Until recently, young Nepalese in a small village 100 miles (160 km) southwest of Katmandu were guided as they entered the adult world by centuries-old social customs and traditions. But that world has been changing, according to anthropologist Laura M. Ahearn, who has spent 15 years in a village she calls Junigau. It is still three-hours walk from Junigau to Tansen, the district center, but electricity reached into Junigau in 1996 and that means television and CD players will soon arrive. The traditional ways of Junigau, like those of every other rural village today, are vulnerable to the influences of the world outside.

In recent years, every aspect of Junigau's social fabric has been changed, even the deepest-rooted customs, from kinships and their role in every aspect of village life to the basic definitions of love, courtship, and marriage. Modern music and the popular Hindi romance films shown at the Tansen theater send a message about the importance of education, literacy, and modern lifestyles and values. Many young Junigau women attend college in Tansen. For young men, a career as a Gurkha soldier with the British or Indian armies is much more attractive than the hard labor of a subsistence farmer, the traditional economic base of Junigau. As a Gurkha soldier, a young man trades long tours of duty away from home for financial independence from his elders.

For centuries, Nepalese have viewed marriage as a joining of two families, with the selection of who married whom decided by the elders largely on the basis of complicated kinship and caste relationships. Marriages between certain types of cousins, for example, are highly desirable, while marriage to "the wrong type of cousin," is definitely taboo and frowned upon. Becoming espoused to someone from a caste below the Magars, who make up bulk of Junigau's residents, is out of the question.

In traditional Junigau arranged marriages, husband and wife sometimes speak for the first time on their wedding day. It is not uncommon, in Ahearn's observations, for a bride to wail plaintively throughout the marriage ceremony, and for the stunned groom to perform his part of the rituals, including the symbolic ritual defloration, with grim resignation.

After the marriage, the bride moves in with her husband's family and her status as the newest daughter-in-law in the kinship hits rock bottom. The heaviest labor, the hardest chores are her lot, along with the custom of washing her husband's feet every morning and then drinking the wash water. (Some women, influenced by the world outside the valley, no longer wash their husband's feet.)

Between 1963 and 1983, 73% of all first marriages in Junigau were arranged, with elopements accounting for only 15%. Ten years later, in 1993, 35% of all first marriages were elopements and arranged marriages dropped to 54%. Since 1993, 9 out of 10 marriages have been elopements. According to Ahearn, elopements are showing a similar increase in other Nepalese villages.

Since dating is still taboo and meetings between young men and women are frowned on, the young people manage their selection and courtship with florid, exuberant, extremely romantic love letters. But before the couple makes any contact, both are likely to check one another out, with furtive inquiries among acquaintances, or tentative feeler letters.

Nepal being a very patriarchal culture, it is the young man who begins the correspondence. But first he must recruit a responsible messenger—often a younger sibling or young relative who is sworn to secrecy, to deliver his declarations of undying love to the woman he has chosen.

The love letters, in English or Hindi, often refer to well-known figures, designed to impress the recipient. "Love is the sort of thing that anyone can feel—even a great man of the world like Hitler loved Eva, they say." Or, "And Napoleon, who with bravery conquered the 'world,' united it, and took it forward, was astounded when he saw one particular widow." These letters employ a very Nepalese, non-Western notion of romance and love. As Ahearn explains, in the Nepalese culture, love is very serious from the start and inextricably entwined with economic development, progress, and appearing educated and modern. Love equals "life success."

For a young woman, the path of romance is considerably more tricky than for her suitor. Answering a suitor's letter all but commits her to marrying him, even though she may only slightly know him or doesn't know him at all. If the courtship letters become public knowledge and she does not marry her correspondent, she will be disgraced, her courtship life over.

Both men and women put great effort into the crafting of these letters. "It's a distinctive genre," said Ahearn, "very different from spoken Nepali and from written Nepali." How-to books are available in Tansen and Katmandu, but more often, the correspondents share tips on what to say and not say with friends.

If the correspondence goes well, a wedding plan is agreed upon. The couple elopes, and when they return, a Brahman priest performs a brief ceremony at the house of the groom's family if his parents agree. If the marriage goes against caste or kinship taboos, the bride's parents may refuse to accept the couple. More often, the bride's parents come to accept the union, inviting her back to their house for a feast, and allowing her to "visit when she wishes."

Few older villagers are happy with their children choosing a spouse out of love. Like Tevye in *The Fiddler on the Roof* bemoaning his daughter's choice of a young revolutionary she loves over the wealthy butcher in his 60s tha

Tevye chose for her, many Junigau parents yearn for the old days when they had more control of their children. The freedom to choose one's own mate upsets the centuries-old stable hierarchies that once determined who repaired the roof and who comes to family celebrations. Change who controls the choice of mate, change how males and females relate, and everything in the society is affected.

*References*

Ahearn, L. M. 2001. *Invitations to love: Literacy, love letters and social change in Nepal.* Ann Arbor MI: University of Michigan.

Goode, E. 1999 (February 9). Arranged marriage gives way to courtship by mail. *The New York Times,* A3.

## Nigeria
### 8. Significant Unconventional Sexual Behaviors
*Update on Sexual Rights and* Sharia
*Death Penalties*          ROBERT T. FRANCOEUR
[*Update 2003*: Addendum to Section 8D, Female Genital Mutilation and Other Harmful Practices: On August 27, 2003, an Associated Press release described the tearful appearance of 32-year-old Amina Lawal in a northern Nigerian Islamic appeals court to plead for her life. Divorced in 1999, Ms. Lawal was convicted in March 2002 of having sex outside marriage, two years after her divorce. The *Sharia* judges ordered that Ms. Lawal be buried up to her neck in sand and stoned. However, execution was delayed during her appeals and to allow her daughter, to be weaned. One of Ms. Lawal's lawyer contended that, under some interpretations of *Sharia*, babies can remain in gestation in their mother's womb for up to five years, making it possible under Islam that her former husband could have fathered the child. The judges said they would announce their ruling on her appeal September 25, 2003.

*Reference*

Associated Press. 2003 (August 28). Nigerian woman facing death sentence seeks leniency. *The New York Times,* A13.

## Norway
### 1. Basic Sexological Premises
*Gender Equality Affirmative Action*
                    ROBERT T. FRANCOEUR
[*Update 2003*: In mid 2003, despite strong vocal opposition from the nation's business community and organizations, Norway's Parliament is expected to pass legislation soon that will force an estimated 600 of the nation's largest businesses to increase the number of women on their corporate boards from the current 8.4% to 40% by July 2005, with penalties applied in 2007. Most corporate boards average six members who are among the nation's recently wealthy, and frequently hold a seat on a dozen or more corporate boards. Norway passed an Equal Status Act in 1979 requiring that 40% of the boards of local and state governments be women. In 1981, Norway had its first woman prime minister. By 1986, women held 44% of the Cabinet posts, a presence that has remained steady for 17 years.

Sweden is preparing to follow Norway's example with the threat of legal action if the boards of publicly listed companies do not increase the number of women on their boards from the present 8% to 25% by 2004. By contrast, in 2001, women held 12.4% of all board seats in Fortune 1,000 companies.

*Reference*

Alvarez, L. 2003 (July 14). Norway is set to compel boardrooms to let more women in. *The New York Times,* A3.

## Philippines
### 10. Sexually Transmitted Diseases and HIV/AIDS
*An HIV/AIDS Paradox*        ROBERT T. FRANCOEUR
[*Update 2003*: Prevailing public-health wisdom says that very low condom use should result in a high incidence of HIV infections and AIDS. In a paradox no one has yet explained, the Philippines has both a very low rate of condom use and, simultaneously, a very low rate of HIV infection. On the other hand, worldwide, encouraging regular condom use is an important element in HIV/AIDS-prevention efforts.

The reality is that, in 2003, only about 10,000 Filipinos were believed to be HIV-positive in a total population of 84.5 million. No one suggests underreporting as an explanation for this paradox.

Factors that one would expect to produce high rates of HIV and AIDS:

- More than half all Filipinos are of reproductive age and sexually active.
- The culture places a strong emphasis on large families.
- Only 23% of sexually active young men say they have ever used a condom.
- Only 4% say they use condoms regularly.
- Very porous borders allow uncontrolled immigration.
- A very conservative and politically powerful Catholic Church makes recommending or even mentioning condoms highly ill-advised.
- Only two out of five sex workers say they use condoms regularly. Most cannot afford condoms, or the antiviral drugs when they are infected.
- Eight-and-a-half million Filipinos who work overseas are potential carriers of disease whenever they visit home.
- The government has no AIDS-awareness program.
- The government restricts the campaigns of independent family-planning groups and NGOs, limiting their promotion of condom use.

The factors might offset the above high-risk factors, but experts are skeptical that the risk-reducing factors below, alone or in combination, might explain the low rate of HIV and AIDS. Which leads many experts to suggest that the low rate of HIV/AIDS is just a lucky-chance combination of the factors below, and that a real epidemic explosion might occur any time.

- A low ratio of customers to sex workers. The average Filipina commercial sex worker averages about four customers per week, significantly fewer clients than their counterparts in other countries, according to a 2003 government survey.
- Other studies suggest that a relatively low proportion of men frequent sex workers.
- The small number of intravenous drug users.
- Low rates of ulcerated sexually transmitted diseases, syphilis and herpes in particular. Breaks in the skin surface facilitate HIV infection.
- Most men here are circumcised—some speculate this could be a factor in preventing or reducing infection that would then reduce the risk of HIV.
- Anal sex appears to be less common than in other countries.

In January of 2003, government figures showed that just 1,810 people had tested positive for HIV. The United Nations office on AIDS estimates that the actual number may be closer to 9,400, still an extraordinarily low rate of about 0.01%. In Vietnam, which has a population the same size as the Philippines, and where the HIV epidemic is still thought to be in its early stages, 130,000 people are already HIV-infected, compared with 9,400 Filipinos with HIV/AIDS. Costa Rica has about the same number of people with HIV and AIDS as does the Philippines, but Costa Rica has only 3.8 million people, not 84.5 million people (Mydans 2003).

*Reference*

Mydans, S. 2003 (April 2). Low rate of AIDS virus in Philippines is a puzzle. *The New York Times*, A12.

## Russia

### 9. Contraception, Abortion, and Population Planning

*New Abortion Laws*      ROBERT T. FRANCOEUR

[*Update 2003*: On August 11, 2003, Russia increased its restrictions on abortion for the first time since 1936 when the Soviet Union lifted a ban on abortion imposed by Stalin. Abortion is still legal and with no limits in the first 12 weeks of pregnancy; but the new restrictions appear to reflect the first stirrings of a wider debate over the morality of abortion, the effect repeated abortions are having on women's health, and on the demographic future of Russia.

With contraceptives of any kind unaffordable and more frequently simply unavailable under the Communists, abortion was the common and widely accepted means of birth control, giving Russia one of the highest abortion rates in the world. With the collapse of the Soviet Union came increased availability of contraceptives and a substantial decline in abortions, from a high of 4.6 million in 1988 to 1.7 million in 2002. Apparently, conservative lawmakers are hoping to reduce the number of abortions further with government-imposed restrictions on what has effectively been free and virtually unlimited access to abortion. (See Igor Kohn's comments on the alliance of Communist politicians and hierarchy of the Russian Orthodox Church and their crusade against sexual education and pornography, in Section 3A, Knowledge and Education about Sexuality, and Section 8C, Significant Unconventional Sexual Behaviors, Pornography and Erotica, in the chapter on Russia.)

Before the new restrictions, effective August 11, women could receive an abortion between the 12th and 22nd weeks of their pregnancies by citing one of 13 special circumstances, called "social indicators," including divorce, poverty, unemployment, or poor housing. The government's decision has reduced the number to four: rape, imprisonment, the death or severe disability of the husband, or a court ruling stripping a woman of her parental rights. Being a single mother or a refugee is no longer reason enough to abort a pregnancy after the 12th week.

Under the new law, pregnancies can still be aborted after 12 weeks on medical grounds, including severe disabilities of the fetus or a threat to the mother's life. Although the public's reaction to the new limitations was "strikingly subdued," some lawmakers and leaders of the Russian Orthodox Church welcomed the change and vowed to continue fighting for greater restrictions through new legislation. That threat is causing growing concern among some doctors and in the Russia Family Planning Association that a woman's right to an abortion could soon be curtailed.

Aleksandr C. Chuyev, a member of the lower house of Parliament, who introduced legislation earlier in 2003 to ban all abortions after the 12th week and then took part in negotiations with the Ministry of Health to draft the new restrictions, announced that the new law was "a first step." Churyev welcomed the restrictions, characterizing them as a compromise. He announced plans to sponsor a new bill later in 2003 that would give a human fetus the same rights as a child.

The nascent antiabortion debate is influenced by the resurgence of religion and the growing influence of the Russian Orthodox Church after 70 years of official atheism under Soviet rule. Russia's demographic crisis is also a factor, as politicians look for ways to reverse the declining population trend. Russia has a total fertility rate of 1.3 children per fertile woman, and a negative 0.33% population growth rate. Although the abortion rate has declined significantly in the past 15 years, there are still nearly 13 abortions for every 10 live births in Russia. Few appear ready to call for an outright ban on abortions, even within the church, but the voices against abortion are growing.

Anatoly A. Korsunsky, the Health Ministry's chief of maternity and childhood health, said in an interview that the new restrictions had been carefully weighed, taking into account the risks repeated abortions carry for a woman's health. Abortions in the later stages of pregnancy and repeated abortions, which are common in Russia, pose the greatest risks to fertility and health generally. In 2002, 40,000 of Russia's 1.7 million abortions were carried out under one of the 13 indicators allowing mid- and late-term abortions. Korsunsky claimed that limiting the circumstances under which these late abortions would be allowed was not intended to force women to continue with unwanted pregnancies, but rather to encourage them to avoid abortions in the first place through traditional family planning and birth control.

The list of 13 social indicators had been in place since they were adopted in 1987. Opponents of reducing the indicators from 13 to 4 opposed the new limits as unnecessary to reduce the number of abortions, given the steady decline that has already occurred.

*Reference*

Myers, S. L. 2003 (August 24). After decades, Russia narrows grounds for abortions. *The New York Times*, A-3

## Sweden

### 8. Significant Unconventional Sexual Behaviors

*Prostitution*     JAN TROST and ROBERT T. FRANCOEUR

[*Update 2003*: Prior to January 1, 1999, prostitution was tolerated in Sweden. Prevalent in Stockholm, Gothenburg, and Malmo, pimping was illegal, but seldom reported, and very seldom was anyone sentenced to prison for pimping. At the same time, the police seldom if ever took action against prostitutes or their customers.

Despite this reality, the Swedish government had long given priority to combating prostitution and human trafficking for sexual purposes. Increasingly, prostitution has been viewed as a form of male violence against women and children, a significant social problem, and a major obstacle to gender equality, so long as men could buy, sell, and exploit women and children by prostituting them.

Since January 1, 1999, when the Act Prohibiting the Purchase of Sexual Services became effective, Sweden has defined prostitution as a gross violation of a woman's integrity. Purchasing or attempting to purchase sexual services is officially a criminal offense punishable by fines or up to six months imprisonment. Women and children who are victims of prostitution and trafficking are considered the weaker party and the victims of exploitation by the procurers and buyers. Under a new law, they do not run any legal risk. "By adopting these measures Sweden has given notice to the world that it regards prostitution as a serious form of oppression of women, and that efforts must be made to combat it" (Ministry of Industry, Employment and Communication 2003). Under the Act Prohibiting the Purchase of Sexual Services, adopted in 1998, a person who obtains casual sexual services in exchange for payment shall be sentenced—unless otherwise subject to more severe penal code punishment—to a fine and six months imprisonment, whether the services are purchased on the street, in brothels or massage parlors, from escort services, or any similar circumstance.

In the four years since enforcement of the new Act began, there has been a dramatic drop in the number of women in street prostitution, according to police and social services. The number of men who buy sexual services and recruit women into prostitution has also fallen. At the same time, public approval of this strict law has risen from 76% in 1999 to 81% in 2002. Opposition to the law dropped from 15% to 14%.

Sweden's current Penal Code provides a maximum penalty of up to four years for anyone convicted of promoting or encouraging or improperly exploiting for commercial purposes casual sexual relations for payment.

According to the International Organization of Migration, at least half a million women are sold annually to local prostitution markets in Europe. According to the National Criminal Investigation Department, between 200 and 500 women arrive in Sweden every year as victims of trafficking. Most of them come from the Baltic, former Soviet Union, and Eastern European countries, after being recruited with bogus offers of work.

In the Campaign Against Prostitution and Trafficking of Women in Sweden, women brought into the country for casual sexual purposes are not subject to being returned to their homeland. They are provided with temporary residence permits and lodging while they testify in court proceedings against their accused procurers and exploiters. In some cases, they are granted permanent residence in Sweden under the terms of the Aliens Act on humanitarian grounds.

Sweden's national campaign is

focused on different measures directed towards buyers and potential buyers of prostituted women and children, mostly girls in Sweden, as well as towards those men who travel to other countries for the specific purpose of buying and exploiting prostituted women and children. The campaign [has] also highlighted, with the long-term objective to ameliorate, the circumstances and conditions that those women and children who are, or who have been, victims of prostitution and trafficking live under (Ministry of Industry 2003).

*Reference*
Ministry of Industry, Employment and Communication. 2003 (April). *Fact sheet: Prostitution and trafficking in women.* Available: http://naring.regeringen.se/pressinfo/faktablad/PDF/N3036.pdf

## *Turkey*

## 6. Homoerotic, Homosexual, and Bisexual Behaviors

*Same-Sex Behavior*

MEHMET ENIS ODMEN and ROBERT T. FRANCOEUR
[*Update 2003*: One of the most sensitive and controversial issues in intercultural discussions arises when one discussant is part of the Western Judeo-Christian cultures and the other person is non-Western—African, Asian, and Islamic/Middle Eastern—and when the topic is the sexual activity between persons of the same sex. The question is not just one of terminology and labeling either the behavior or the person, because it does often involve quite different views of what same-sex behavior connotes when associated with self- or other-identification. Does a male having sex with another male mean that person is what Western people

commonly term a "homosexual," a person who self-identifies and is identified by others as having a "homosexual identity?" Does this equation make this male somehow *essentially* different from a person who identifies himself as being "a heterosexual."

As we wrote in *The Complete Dictionary of Sexology* (Francoeur 1995):

Before the mid-19th century, the term "homosexual" did not exist. It was coined in 1869 by a Hungarian physician, Karoly Maria Benkert, writing under the pseudonym Kertbeny. Kertbeny's intention was to create a value-neutral expression to replace value-laden words like "pederaster," "sodomite," "bugger," "catamite," and "ganymede." Similar intentions underlay the use of "urning" by Ulrichs in 1862 and "inversion" popularized by Havelock Ellis in the early 20th century, although used earlier. These labels had the advantage of openly disavowing the pejorative meanings of terms like "sodomite" but none of these terms are successful in expressing the rainbow complexities of self-identity.

One problem is that *homosexual* can be an adjective or a noun. As an adjective in the sentence "Mutual penile masturbation by two men is a homosexual act," the word *homosexual* indicates the basic concept of sexual activity between people of the same sex. But it leaves unclear what acts are and are not to be called homosexual. If a man kisses another man when greeting him in a gay bar, is that a "homosexual kiss"? The usage here varies immensely and many would say "Yes" or "No" depending on whether or not the men self-identified themselves as "gay."

Use of the word "homosexual" as a noun referring to a person who engages in a certain act or experiences a certain emotional state of sexual attraction or limerence (qv) with a person of the same gender. Few concepts are as difficult to define, or to defend once defined, as the assertion that someone "is" a homosexual. If, at age 15, a woman engaged in erotic caresses with another woman, "is" she a homosexual? A question such as this poses three crucial problems in defining homosexuality and, by extension, heterosexuality as well. (1) Labelling someone "a homosexual" in his or her entirety because of a possibly small portion of their overall life and existence is using a part to define the whole. (2) It is an arbitrary term that is not subject to defensible definition: how many homosexual acts constitute a person "a homosexual." (3) It also represents a dangerous philosophical essentialism to speak of a person as "being" a homosexual or heterosexual because in so doing we impute to that person's essential nature a certain quality or characteristic when it is still questionable what human nature really is. (Francoeur 1995, 281)

All of which is an essential prelude to our discussion of some participant-observer comments about sexual behavior offered by three Western males who identify as homosexual or gay with personal experiences with same-sex behavior in Turkey. The comments that follow are from brief chapters by Janssen, Necef, and Sofer in *Sexuality and Eroticism among Males in Moslem Societies*, edited by Arno Schmitt and Jehoeda Sofer (1992). This discussion is particularly relevant in light of similar observations of same-sex behaviors in Section 6, Homoerotic, Homosexual, and Bisexual Behaviors, in the chapter on Iran and Herb Samuels' brief report on "Down Low African-Americans" in Section 6B, Homoerotic, Homosexual, and Bisexual Behaviors, Adults, Health Issues, in the United States chapter. In the simplest terms, African-American men on the "Down Low" who sleep with men are "heterosexual."

In the rural areas of Turkey, Morocco, Egypt, Iran, Turkey, and other cultures where patriarchal tribal societies prevail, there is little room for the development of *personal individuality*. Almost everything is predetermined in the rural society. In rural cultures, one thinks of one's self and others think of that person in relation to other people and groups, not in terms of a person's sexual behavior. He is the son of a father and a mother. In Turkey, he addresses his father and mother as *baba* and *anne* (or *ana*) all his life. It would be inconceivable for a Turk to call his (or her) parents by their given names. Turks are also expected to add the words *abi* or *abla* to the names of their older brothers and sisters to show respect. Parents seldom leave room for initiative. A parent asking a child which ice cream it wants is very exceptional. To put it bluntly: A Turkish boy grows up under the wings of his elder family members, marries the woman recommended by them, works industriously for his family, fights fanatically for his cause, and dies bravely for his country and flag (Janssen 1992; Necef 1992; Sofer).

But, in the bustling metropolitan urban life of Istanbul's 8.5 million people, surrounded by the 7 million inhabitants of Cairo or Tehran, or even the 3 million people in Casablanca or Ankara, a "city man" can develop a concept of self-identity or self-identified ego similar to that found in gay communities in Europe and North America. In big cities, one can find a homosexual subculture with discotheques, bars, beaches, and so on. Compared with the West, or even with Greece, homosexual self-identity is still underdeveloped. In spite of all this, the role and self-identity of "homosexual" does exist in the big cities at least. For individuals to develop the role and identity of "a homosexual" and for society to recognize this self-identification—to accept it in whatever manner—requires a certain social climate. The big cities with less rigid control by family and neighbors—a certain anonymity—less personal dependence, more reliance on impersonal society (social security instead of family or patron), and more privacy offer this climate.

One typical aspect of the Turkish scene is the importance of role-playing: some men acting or dressing up like women and others underlining their masculinity. It is still *ibne* and *kulampara* rather than "gays" and "straights." Transvestism plays a much larger social role in Turkey and southern Europe than in the north or the U.S.A. This seems to be the result of relations between the sexes. Turkish men and women almost live in two different worlds. The homosexuals are just aping a different side of the "normal" world.

The word *homosexual* entered the Turkish vocabulary by translations from European languages, first as *homoseksüel*. During the Turkification of the language after the foundation of the republic in 1923, the word *elcinşel* (equal-sexual) was coined, but this did not fit the roles and identities in Turkey, and confusion arose.

The existing roles for sexual relations between men were *ibne* and *kulampara*. An *ibne* is an effeminate man who plays the passive or recipient role in anal intercourse. He does not marry, because he is thought to be impotent. An *ibne* can be a transvestite, earning his living by dancing, singing, or prostituting himself. To be an *ibne* is the worst thing a Turkish man can be, for two reasons. First, because he accepts anal intercourse "like a woman" and second because he moves and speaks in an unmanly manner.

Given these views, it may come as a surprise that the most popular (male) singers in Turkey are transvestites (*ibneler*). Turks explain their admiration for these artists by pointing to their artistic talent and to the fact that nearly all artists are crazy and strange. All these singers interpret heterosexual love songs (though in some cases the sex of the loved one is unclear). They also even act in films playing the role of a straight lover.

The other role is played by the *kulampara* ("having to do with boys"). A *kulampara* is over age 16 and nearly always married. Like all Turkish men, he is expected to marry after military service at the latest. But because of the brideprice still required in rural Turkey, some poor peasants marry later.

In contrast to *ibne*, the *kulampara* does not constitute a special type of man, a "homosexual" or "gay man" in the Western sense. Any married man "too full of lust" or separated too long from his wife looks for prostitutes, mistresses, animals (dogs and donkeys), or an *ibne*. Nobody would consider himself as "abnormal," "perverse, "sinful," let alone "homosexual" for having anal sex with an *ibne*. Behavior does not dictate self-identity. To have anal intercourse with an *ibne* is an enjoyment open to all men. Any man could be seduced by an *ibne*.

Conversations with Turkish men show that sexual play with other men plays a rather important role in young men's sex life, especially in rural areas. While still young, playing the passive (recipient) role in anal sex apparently does not disturb them unduly. After marriage, most men are exclusively heterosexual.

## References

Francoeur, R. T., ed. 1995. *The complete dictionary of sexology* (New expanded ed.). New York: Continuum International.

Janssen, T. 1992. Transvestites and transsexuals in Turkey. In: A. Schmitt & J. Sofer, eds., *Sexuality and eroticism among males in Moslem societies*. New York: Harrington Park Press (Haworth Press).

Necef, M. U. 1992. Turkey on the brink of modernity. In: A. Schmitt & J. Sofer, eds., *Sexuality and eroticism among males in Moslem societies*. New York: Harrington Park Press (Haworth Press).

Sofer, J. 1992. The dawn of a gay movement in Turkey. In: A. Schmitt & J. Sofer, eds., *Sexuality and eroticism among males in Moslem societies*. New York: Harrington Park Press (Haworth Press).

# Global Trends: Some Final Impressions

## from *The Continuum Complete International Encyclopedia of Sexuality*

*Robert T. Francoeur, Ph.D., and*
*Raymond J. Noonan, Ph.D.*

O ur role as editors of *The Continuum Complete International Encyclopedia of Sexuality* (*CCIES*) has been carefully limited to recruiting scholars who could report with some authority about the sexual attitudes, values, and behavioral patterns of a particular country or some particular aspect. We provided them with our standard content outline, and left them free to write. We then copyedited their manuscript without altering in any way their thoughts, although we did seek clarification when necessary and encouraged them to fill in any gaps we found. In the case of chapters in volumes 1 to 3 published in 1997 and volume 4 published in 2001, we invited the original authors and some new authorities to update these chapters. Sometimes, we sought—or inadvertently found—scholars with alternative perspectives or interpretations who broadened an entry with commentary. As editors, our role has been that of a catalyst—to facilitate bringing together those with the broadest possible perspectives to enrich the product.

At the same time, as we read and reread these chapters and exchanged communications with the authors, we could not help but be impressed by some similar developments in different countries, some common threads of changing attitudes and behavioral patterns. Sometimes, we found these similarities in survey results or commentaries by the authors or updaters. At other times, a specific seemingly minor local event reported first in the local media caught worldwide attention, signaling what might become a cultural turning point. Whether we were impressed by a general broad-based trend, like the plummeting birthrates around the world, or one of the local events noted below, they all seem to suggest that, today, at the dawn of the 21st century, the human race is engaged in the biggest sexual revolution in at least 5,000 years. It will be far more radical in its consequences than the geographically limited revolutions of the Roarin' Twenties and the 1960s-1970s, although each had a progressively greater impact through the dissemination of American popular culture through the media. Unlike those revolutions, which at first mainly affected North America and Europe, this new revolution is stirring in large and small, rich and poor, agrarian and industrial nations all around the world. Fueled by television and the print media, by economics and technology, by medical and reproductive advances, and by the Internet, it is racing along in Europe and North America. But it is also sprouting all over Africa, Latin America, and Asia, where it is shaking up traditional views of sex, the way men and women relate, our patterns of sexual intimacy, as well as the way we bond, marry, and create families.

Our work on these reports on 62 countries and places—one quarter of all the nations in the world, including China, India, Japan, and key countries in Europe, the Americas, and Africa—has left us convinced that this new sexual revolution is being led less often by males who have dominated civilizations worldwide for the past several thousand years, but by women, who are taking a more-public stance for more gender equality—and sometimes to gain dominance. For thousands of years, males largely have created and controlled the technological advances that triggered all the minor Euro-American sexual revolutions of the past. Five to eight thousand years ago, men restructured the whole of human society and male-female relationships, when our ancestors discovered agriculture, domesticated animals, invented the wheel, smelted bronze for tools and weapons, and created alphabets to record their history, laws, trade agreements, and treaties. When men built the first cities in the Middle East, Egypt, and the Indus Valley, they created a new lifestyle: Men held most of the power and women became the subordinate sex relegated to the private world of babymaker and homemaker. The equality men and women had enjoyed in earlier, nomadic hunter-gather societies disappeared in the male-controlled world of ancient city life. In this urban hierarchy, women had three faces, the *Trevia* of virgin maiden, wife/mother, and whore. A good woman's value depended on her premarital virginity, her marital fidelity, her production of male heirs, and catering to men's needs.

Over the centuries, men invented ever faster, easier, and cheaper ways to communicate and travel. Males drove the medical technologies that improved our health and more than doubled human life expectancy in a brief century. Male-driven science and technology gave many of us the increasing leisure, mobility, and affluence essential for the occasional minor sexual revolutions that have come our way. Forty years ago, male scientists, urged on by Margaret Sanger, developed antibiotics to control sexual diseases and the contraceptive technologies that have given women, for the first time in human history, the freedom to enjoy sex without the fear of an unwanted pregnancy.

Obviously, our years of work on *CCIES* have left us with some controversial conclusions, with which our readers may or may not agree. This is not the place to debate the validity of our observations. We will only suggest some reasons for them. Only the future will confirm or refute our observations and forecasts. And so we conclude *CCIES* with some highlights encountered along the way. Agree or disagree. Add or reject. We invite our readers to join us in looking to the future.

We begin with a brief look at economics, education, and gender—with Japan in the east, Scandinavia in the west, and the Middle East and North Africa in-between. In 2003, as noted in our chapter on Last-Minute Developments, Japan ranked 69th out of 75 member nations of the World Economic Forum for its record of empowering women. While 40% of Japanese women are employed outside the home, only 9% hold managerial positions. In Scandinavia, women hold slightly less than a third of the managerial positions, but less than 10% of the positions on corporate boards. In 2003, Norway passed a law requiring corporations to raise the percentage of female board members from the then 9% to 40% by 2007, or face stiff penalties. Sweden, with 30% female corporate board members, was planning to follow Norway's example. (In the U.S., women hold 46% of the board memberships.) In 2003, the first woman to serve on the board of the Bank of Japan warned that "Japan has gone as far as it can with a social model that consists of men filling all of the economic, management and political roles."

At the same time, the World Bank was pointing out a similar tension with warnings that women remain a "huge, untapped" economic resource in the Middle East and North Africa, where more women workers are needed to transform economies that must depend increasingly on private-sector exports to compete worldwide. Despite the fact that women make up half the 325 million people in these regions, and in some countries as many as 63% of university students, they comprise only 32% of the labor force, according to the World Bank report on "Gender and Development in the Middle East and North Africa: Women in the Public Sphere." According to the World Bank's vice president for the Middle East and North Africa, "No country can raise the standard of living and improve the well-being of its people without the participation of half of its population. Experience in other countries has shown over and over again that women are important actors in development."

In the 19 countries of the Middle East and North Africa, women's workforce participation is "lower than would be expected on the basis of the region's fertility rates, education levels and the age structure of the female population," the World Bank report found. It is less than half the 74% rate in the Asia and Pacific region, with their successful exporting countries, where women have played a pivotal role in emerging industries. With improved health and education, one of every three women in the Middle East is 30 years old or younger. But these younger women are likely to face greater obstacles in finding a job and playing an active public role in their societies than their contemporaries elsewhere. There are far-reaching economic and social consequences when men who find their self-image in being the breadwinner for the family discourage women from employment outside the home. Middle East and North African countries have the highest proportion of dependents to wage earners in the world. Each wage earner in these regions supports more than two nonworking dependents, a problem that cannot be counteracted even by lowering unemployment rates.

Along with the gender differences in employment, one needs to consider, also, the growing gender differences in education. These educational differences were highlighted in the annual survey of educational policy issued by the Organization for Economic Cooperation and Development, which concluded that young women are steadily moving ahead of their male peers in educational achievement and aspiration. "In most OECD countries, young women are now more likely than young men to obtain first degrees from university-level institutions. Only in Japan, Switzerland and Turkey is the proportion of young men obtaining their first university-level degrees significantly higher for young men than for young women." On average, females now make up more than two-thirds of the graduates in the humanities, arts, education and health studies. In mathematics and computer science they account for less than a third, and in engineering about a quarter. According to the report at age 15, girls were better readers than boys in every one of the 43 countries that took part of the 2000 study. In about half of these countries, boys were ahead in mathematics. As a consequence, in most OECD countries, females expressed higher expectations for their future occupations than males.

These higher expectations are an important factor in our future. It has meaning for young men and women in Japan, the Middle East, North Africa, and the West. In Japan, for instance, young women are increasingly expressing their anger with chauvinist and nonproductive males. "I would like to get married, but I don't want to lower my living standard" is a typical position of young Japanese businesswomen who live with their parents and frequently travel abroad. The number of unmarried men and women over age 39 has doubled in 20 years. Japan's birthrate is 1.4 children per childbearing woman and shriveling like a dried prune.

With these observations in mind, we can move on to briefer mentions of our other observations:

- Continued rapid globalization and technological development will escalate anxieties, tensions, and open conflicts for people and societies rooted in fundamentalist, traditional, agrarian, patriarchal value systems, as television, the Internet, and daily physical contact exposes them to the more-permissive, gender-equal, and individualistic values of industrial and postindustrial Western societies. The currents of enculturation are already working in both directions, with both agrarian and industrial societies caught in the maelstrom of rapid change.

- In Iran, a very fundamentalist Islamic country ruled by very conservative religious leaders determined to keep women in their place, are encountering repeated opposition from the younger college-educated generation, including the daughters of leading moderate government officials. With Revolutionary Guard everywhere, one would hardly expect teenage "infidel" girls in high tops, tank shirts, bare midriffs, and jeans to risk arrest by hanging out on city streets. Where did these rebellious teenagers pick up their "satanic" fashions and the courage to wear them in public? Answer: By 1994, a quarter of a million Iranians were watching popular Western television programs beamed down from satellites to low-tech dish antennae and decoders hidden in their apartments and shared with neighbors, despite threats by the Ministry of Culture and Islamic Guidance.

- In Africa, where nearly 70% of the world's HIV-infected people live, most new victims are women infected by their husbands who are accustomed to having a "homewife" and one or more "traveling-wives" for company while they're away at work. With a burgeoning feminist movement pushing to transform these sexual politics, the AIDS crisis is forcing African men to listen to their women, and that empowers women. Women in Kenya have enlisted the aid of Anglican Church leaders to reduce and eliminate "sexual access" to widows who are "inherited" by a male relative of the deceased husband. Although not easily, and with resistance from some feminists, new laws and healthy alternative rituals are being adopted to replace female genital mutilation.

- In Latin America, Peruvian women have enthusiastically endorsed a government campaign to make contraception available to all women, especially the poor. In a nation where 90% of the people are Catholic and many rural women have 10 or more children, Peru's women are ignoring the Pope's ban on contraception and asserting their right to control their own sexual and reproductive lives.

- In Islamic northern Nigeria and in Pakistan, several young women who claimed they were raped—and named their assailants—have triggered international human rights protests when the media publicized that they were tried and convicted of fornication and sentenced to death by stoning. Islamic law requires four adult males be present to witness the rape in order to prove it had taken place.

- Worldwide, the media reported increasing challenges to the traditional marriage arranged by parents or family: In Upsala, Sweden, in 2002, the "honor killing" of 26-year-old Fademi Sahindal by her father, when this Kurdish woman announced she would marry her Swedish lover, provoked international outrage.

- In May 2003, India's television and print media propelled Nisha Sharma, a 21-year-old computer student, to Hindi stardom as a "New Age woman and role model" for the nation's young women. Ms. Sharma called off her wedding after the groom's family demanded a dowry of $25,000 in addition to the gifts already received from the bride's family. Ms. Sharma reported the groom to the police, who put him in jail pending formal charges that he and his mother had violated India's laws against dowries.

- In Thailand, pioneering single women are choosing to buck social and family traditions by living on their own when they cannot find a nonchauvinist husband. Many of them are even having a child by a lover who lives on his own.
- In Algeria, Muslim women are turning to personal ads to find mates of their own choice, despite strong family disapproval and censorship by fundamentalist Islamic men.
- There is a growing tradition of financially established single Italian men, "mammoni," to continue living with their parents into their 30s, 40s, and beyond, instead of marrying and moving out on their own. This, plus a birthrate below 1.1 child per fertile woman, are radically changing the traditional Italian extended family. Italian

husbands and Catholic bishops complain that the Italian women are not listening to them anymore. So many Italian women, married and unmarried, are using the pill and having abortions, that Italy now has the lowest birthrate of any nation in the world.

- China has been widely condemned for its one-child-per-family policy, forced abortions, and female infanticide. But because these policies have also created a serious surplus of males, young Chinese women are enjoying an unexpected change in bargaining power and choice in picking the best possible husband.
- Meanwhile, an unmarried Polish woman begged a doctor for an illegal abortion and created a national movement to legalize abortion when her ex-lover reported her and the doctor "to teach her a lesson."
- In Ireland, a 14-year-old girl who tried to go to England for an abortion forced the government to allow at least some abortions. With one in six Irish marriages ending in separation and 75,000 broken marriages, President

---

## In Memoriam

# Dr. David Lee Weis

**friend, colleague, teacher, and sexologist,**
**who died of diabetes complications at age 52 on September 5, 2003**

David Weis was a major contributor and coeditor of the United States chapter in *IES* (volume 3; 1997), the 1998 updated *Sexuality in America: Understanding Our Sexual Values and Behaviors*, and in the 2003 U.S.A. update in the present expanded single-volume *Continuum Complete International Encyclopedia of Sexuality*.

In late August, when David emailed us the last of his major summaries and updates for *CCIES*, we called to thank him for his usual lucid and penetrating summaries. We were delighted with his contribution, and he was happy with our delight. Two weeks later, we were formatting and integrating his contributions when a family friend called with news of his totally unexpected death. We will miss him as a friend and as a colleague. Our field will be diminished by his loss.

David was professor of family and consumer sciences at Bowling Green State University, where he was well known for his keen intellect as well as his sense of humor, "bubbling forth with ideas and stories to share with colleagues and students alike." "As brilliant and committed as Dave's professional contributions have been," one of his students observed, "he always extended generous support of us newcomers with humility and genuine interest. The world is less bright without his warmth and wit."

Besides coordinating the contributions of three dozen other American sexologists for the original U.S.A. chapter, Dave provided his own major summaries of the latest research on childhood, adolescent, and adult sexual behavior. His history of "Change, Conflict, and Diversity" in the U.S.A. chapter provided an organizing theme for that chapter/volume.

David was, in the words of Ira Reiss, one of America's leading sexologists and sociologists, "a talented thinker and researcher who contributed much to the sociological analysis of sexuality." Not long after joining the Society for the Scientific Study of Sexuality, Dave won the prestigious Hugo G. Beigel Research Award for outstanding article of the year in the *Journal of Sex Research*. The Beigel Award was given to Dave in 1984 for a research paper on affective reactions of women to their initial experience of coitus. In 1998, Dave edited a special issue of the *Journal of Sex Research* on Theory in the Study of Sexuality.

As Candace Blake Weis, his wife, knew better that we, "He loved intellectual challenge, and he had a great knack for having a different perception than most people. He loved his students. He would have active discussions in the classroom, sometimes about sensitive and controversial subjects, and there were lively discussions."

A Toledo, Ohio, native who grew up in the Cleveland area, David received his bachelor's degree in health and physical education from Bowling Green State University (BGSU) in 1973, a master's degree in family studies from Purdue University in 1976, and a Ph.D. from Purdue in 1979. After seven years teaching at Rutgers University in New Jersey, he returned to teach at BGSU. In 2001, David was named as one of BGSU's 25 most-accomplished graduates.

We dedicate this edition of the *Continuum Complete International Encyclopedia of Sexuality*, in which David played a major role, to his memory, with our sympathy to his wife, Candace Blake Weis, his daughter, Rebecca Weis, and his parents and two brothers and two sisters.

We will miss him.

ROBERT T. FRANCOEUR, TIMOTHY PERPER, MARTHA CORNOG,
RAYMOND J. NOONAN, and the other members of the *CCIES* team

Mary Robinson pressed for a referendum to lift the constitutional ban on divorce and allow women some relief in alimony and child support.

- Fifty thousand women attended the Fourth World Conference on Women in Beijing. Women from many nations eloquently claimed the right to control their sexual and reproductive lives, equal inheritance rights, access to credit, and freedom from violence. In the end, the women of Africa, led by Namibians, forged a compromise that blocked the Vatican's proposal to excise the words "sexual freedom" from a particular document. As one observer commented, "It's shocking to find African countries more progressive than others."
- There is a continued shift away from a procreative morality and motivation for sex to a relationship- and pleasure-based morality.
- Increasing popularity of hormonal contraception, the morning-after pill, condoms, and new contraceptives are facilitating the shift to lower fertility rates, lower teen-pregnancy rates, and increasing rates of nonmarital sex, especially for women. In both developing and industrial/postindustrial societies, women are increasingly taking responsibility for preventing unwanted pregnancies, and for initiating a nonmarital relationship.
- Increasing years between puberty and the age of marriage make premarital sexual abstinence increasingly more difficult and unlikely.
- A continued increase in life expectancy and erosion of the sexual double standard are making men and women equally as likely to experiment with extramarital sex and to divorce and remarry or remain single. Men and women continue to experiment with extramarital relations earlier, more often, and with more partners than in the past.
- In Finland, the popularity of both marriage and cohabitation are declining. Two national surveys, in 1972 and 1993, show that the fastest-growing lifestyle is LAT, couples "living alone together" (in a sexual relationship). In these same surveys, LATs report being much happier with their personal and intimate lives than married or unmarried cohabiting couples. Similar trends have been reported in Germany and elsewhere.
- There is increasing recognition of the rights and needs of sexual minorities, the elderly, and those who are disabled or handicapped. The "graying" of Europe and America is paralleled by developing nations like Iran and Costa Rica with a third or more of their population 14 years old or younger.
- There is a spreading recognition and acceptance of protected sexual relations and the promotion of protected sex, as the shift from agrarian to urban life continues.
- There is growing social, legal, and religious acceptance of homosexual, bisexual, transgendered, and gender-variant persons.

Conclusive evidence of a global sexual revolution underway and led primarily by women? Certainly not, if taken individually. But we will leave it to our readers to judge the cumulative weight of these and other developments found in the *CCIES*.

Around the world, women are demanding and getting countless, often unnoticed social changes that, taken together, create an irresistible tidal wave no one can long escape. Around the world, the ways in which women and men relate are shifting gradually toward a new gender equality that will inevitably also change our marital relationships and family structures. The spread of manufacturing and technological development has brought women in many developing nations a growing financial and psychological independence that in many small but important ways helps them take increasing control of their own lives and set their own goals.

Obviously, societies do not change overnight. Patriarchy is not going to disappear overnight, and perhaps not in the foreseeable future, but just maybe, an irresistible tide is shifting, away from male dominance toward a growing equality of the sexes. At least, that is our hope.

To be sure, many men are participating with women in effecting many of these changes. At the same time, many men—and women—are noting the excesses that have been accumulating in at least the United States, which we are also exporting to the rest of the world in our popular culture. The best example is that of sexual harassment, which has become grossly misused and distorted from the original problem. And there are other indications that when women get power, they are just as likely to abuse it as men. The United States is no longer a patriarchal society, if it ever was. Yet, many Americans believe it still is, because sexual politics have transformed it through its use as a metaphor to a perceived reality—and that is not helpful in achieving our goals.

Thus, we need to avoid the simplistic traps that remain all too common. The human sexuality complex exists in an environment that has multiple forces that act on it—in much the same way that it influences them reciprocally. Politics remains an undeniable obstacle to real progress on a global level while it simultaneously provides the means for redressing the inequities of the past. Yet, solutions that merely shift the inequities to men are not a long-term solution; they just exacerbate the crises. Solutions that demonize men's sexuality while extolling women's sexuality are doing the same. This is the sexual counterrevolution noted by John Money in the epilogue to the United States chapter that is currently underway in this country. And that is counterproductive as a long-term strategy.

For real lasting change to occur that benefits both sexes requires a joint effort of both women and men working together for the common good. The current situation of social groups working toward and promoting only their own self-interests and empowerment needs to change on a global level so that sex enriches the lives of everyone.

# Contributors and Acknowledgments

## The Editors

**ROBERT T. FRANCOEUR, M.A., M.S., Ph.D.** Trained in embryology, evolution, theology, and the humanities, Dr. Francoeur's main work has been to synthesize and integrate the findings of primary sexological researchers. He is the author of 22 books, contributor to 78 textbooks, handbooks, and encyclopedias, author of 58 technical papers on various aspects of sexuality, and editor-in-chief of *The Complete Dictionary of Sexology* (1991, 1995). A Fellow of the Society for the Scientific Study of Sexuality, he is professor emeritus of human sexuality at Fairleigh Dickinson University, Madison, New Jersey, USA. In 2003, Dr. Francoeur joined the National Advisory Council for implementation of the former U.S. Surgeon General David Satcher's *Call to Action to Promote Sexual Health and Responsible Sexual Behavior 2001*. 4310 Cleveland Lane, Rockaway NJ 07866-5811 USA; rtfrancoeu@aol.com

**RAYMOND J. NOONAN, Ph.D.**, is an assistant professor of human sexuality and health education, and chairperson of the Health and Physical Education Department at the Fashion Institute of Technology of the State University of New York (FIT-SUNY) in Manhattan. Dr. Noonan has written and presented on sexuality in the environment of space, sexuality and the Internet, philosophy and sex, heterophobia and sex negativity in American culture, and sexual expression in musical lyrics. He was coeditor of *Does Anyone Still Remember When Sex Was Fun? Positive Sexuality in the Age of AIDS* (3rd ed., 1996). He also produces SexQuest.com, providing educational consulting in human sexuality and educational content for the World Wide Web. Health and Physical Education Department, FIT-SUNY, 27th Street and 7th Avenue, New York, NY 10001 USA; 212-217-7460; rjnoonan@SexQuest.com

## Associate Editors

**Africa**: BELDINA OPIYO-OMOLO, B.Sc., is a graduate student in the Master of Public Health program at East Stroudsburg University in Pennsylvania, USA, and a member of the Luo people of Kenya. Ms. Opiyo-Omolo provided extensive network connections with Africans dealing with sexuality and contributed major updates and comments on Kenya, Nigeria, Ghana, Tanzania, and other subequatorial African nations. bopiyo@yahoo.com

**Europe**: JAKOB PASTOETTER, Ph.D., is former Deputy Director of the Magnus Hirschfeld Archive for Sexology at Humboldt University (Berlin), and a member of the Governing Board of the German Society for Social Scientific Sexuality Research, Dr. Pastoetter authored the chapter on Vietnam, updated the chapter on Germany, and personally recruited several key European and African chapters for the *Continuum Complete International Encyclopedia of Sexuality* (*CCIES*). Duenzelbach 10, 82272 Moorenweis, Germany; jmpastoetter@compuserve.de

**Latin America**: LUCIANE RAIBIN, M.S. A native of Brazil, Raibin earned a B.S. and M.S. degree in biology at Fairleigh Dickinson University, Madison, New Jersey, while studying human sexuality with the *IES/CCIES* Editor. As associate editor, she facilitated correspondence with contributors in Colombia, Cuba, and other Latin American countries, provided updates for Brazil, and assisted with translations.

315 South Avenue, Garwood, NJ 07027 USA; L.Raibin@hotmail.com

**Information Resources**: TIMOTHY PERPER, Ph.D. Besides writing the Preface for *IES/CCIES* and a major discussion on Japanese *manga* for *CCIES*, Dr. Perper provided invaluable advice and helpful discussion on sensitive issues. Dr. Perper is author of *Sex Signals: The Biology of Love*, coeditor of *The Complete Dictionary of Sexology*, and coauthor with his wife, Martha Cornog, of several major texts on sexuality. 717 Pemberton, Philadelphia, PA 19147 USA; perpcorn@dca.net

**Information Resources**: MARTHA CORNOG, M.A., M.S., is a linguist and librarian. Ms. Cornog was a reliable source of advice and information for *IES* and *CCIES*. She is coauthor with her husband, Timothy Perper, of the award-winning *For Sex Information: See Librarian*, coeditor of *The Complete Dictionary of Sexology*, and editor of *The Big Book of Masturbation from Angst to Zeal*. 717 Pemberton, Philadelphia, PA 19147 USA; perpcorn@dca.net

## Authors of Individual Chapters

**Preface:**

TIMOTHY PERPER, Ph.D. is a Philadelphia-based independent sex researcher and writer, behavioral biologist, expert on human courtship and flirtation behaviors, author of *Sex Signals: The Biology of Love* (1985), coauthor of *For Sex Education, See Librarian* (1996), author of numerous professional articles on human sexual behavior, an elected fellow of the American Anthropological Association, and coauthor of a *Sexuality and Culture* monograph, *Eroticism for the Masses: Japanese Manga Comics and their Assimilation into the U.S.* 717 Pemberton, Philadelphia, PA 19147; perpcorn@dca.net

**Introduction:**

IRA L. REISS, Ph.D. Professor of sociology at the University of Minnesota, Dr. Reiss is former president of the International Academy of Sex Research, the National Council on Family Relations, and the Society for the Scientific Study of Sex, recipient of the 1990 Kinsey Award for Distinguished Scientific Achievement, and author of eleven books and more than a hundred professional articles. His latest books are *Journey into Sexuality: An Exploratory Voyage*, *An End to Shame: Shaping Our Next Sexual Revolution*, and *Solving Sexual Crises: Rape, AIDS, Child Sexual Abuse, Teen Pregnancy*. 5932 Medicine Lake Road, Minneapolis, MN 55422 USA; reiss001@atlas.socsci.umn.edu

**Argentina:**

SOPHIA KAMENETZKY, M.D. A native of Argentina, Dr. Kamenetzky has dedicated herself to increasing the sexual knowledge of women and organizing sexual education courses. Postgraduate studies in France and study visits to African, Asian, and Latin American countries provided her with an understanding of the roles and problems of women in different societies. Former medical advisor and director of public relations with Latin American Universities for the Population Information Program (at George Washington University, Washington, DC), she facilitates seminars on sexuality and the role of emotions in the health of the immune system. P.O. Box 352530, Palm Coast, FL 32135-2530 USA; mkamen@aol.com

**Australia:**

ROSEMARY COATES, Ph.D. Inaugural president and Honorary Life Member for the Western Australia Sexology Society, Dr. Coates is an associate professor of physiotherapy in the Division of Health Sciences at Curtin University, Western Australia, and vice-president of the Family Planning Association of Western Australia. She is author of *Sexual Awareness Manual, Teacher's Survival Manual*, and comparative studies of sexual knowledge, attitudes, and behavior among college-aged people. Curtin University, Shelby Street, Shenton Park, Western Australia 6008, Australia; icoatesr@info.curtin.edu.au

*Updates*: TONY WILLMETT, R.E., M.A., Ph.D., a member of the Faculty of Education, Australian Catholic University National and consultant in the area of human relationships education, he is author of *Catholic Schools Australian Landscapes: Resources for Creating Distinctive Catholic Schools* and *Relationships and Sexuality*. School of Religious Education, Australian Catholic University National, McAuley at Banyo Campus, P.O. Box 456, Virginia. Queensland 4014, Australia; t.willmett@mcauley.acu.edu.au

## Austria:

DR. ROTRAUD PERNER, L.L.D. Founder and director of the Training Program for Sexual and Social Life Counselors (GAMED), Vienna Academy for Holistic Medicine, and director of the training program for sexual and social counselors at the Verein fuer Prophylaktisches Gesundheitsarbeit (Association for Prophylactic Health Work), Linz, Dr. Perner holds diplomas in psychoanalysis and systematic sexual therapy plus five other psychotherapeutic-related diplomas. She is currently first chairperson of the Austrian Society for Sexology and a member of the University of Vienna Department of Education. 8633 Weichselboden 20, Stmk. 1013 Wien, Postfach 23, Austria; rotraud.a.perner@chello.at

*Updates*: LINDA BRAILOVE KNEUCKER, a family and sexual counselor activist for the rights of children and the reduction of child sexual abuse, provided translation, redaction, and updates for the Austrian chapter. kneucker@magnet.at. RAOUL KNEUCKER, retired science administrator of the Austrian federal government, now works on a new program for public understanding of science. Raoul.Kneucker@gmx.at. MARTIN VORACEK, Ph.D., M.Sc. Univ.-Klinik für Tiefenpsychologie und Psychotherapie AKH/Währinger Gürtel 18-20, A-1090 Wien, Austria. martin.voracek@chello.at

## Bahrain:

JULANNE McCARTHY, M.A., M.S.N., holds a Master's degree in anthropology from Indiana University (Bloomington campus), and a Master's degree in adult health nursing (University of Illinois-Urbana). After nine years working in a Bahrain hospital, she researched and wrote the Bahrain chapter with insights and observations provided by twenty Bahraini professionals and eight expatriates in a variety of disciplines, as well as with anecdotal insights from personal contacts and local popular print media.

## Botswana:

GODISANG MOOKODI is a lecturer in the Development, Gender, and Families in the Department of Sociology, University of Botswana.

OLEOSI NTSHEBE is a postgraduate student at the University of Botswana, conducting research on the sexual health of the Basarwa.

IAN TAYLOR, Ph.D., is a lecturer in African politics in the Department of Political and Administrative Studies, University of Botswana. Department of Political & Administrative Studies. University of Botswana, Private Bag 00705, Gaborone, Botswana; tayloric@mopipi.ub.bw

## Brazil:

SÉRGIO LUIZ GONÇALVES DE FREITAS, M.D. President of Associação Brasileira de Sexologia (AB-SEX), Scientific Director of the Sociedade Brasileira de Estudos da Impotencia Sexual, Dr. Freitas has also organized three National Sexological Conferences in Brazil and the First Pan-American Congress of Sexology in 1986. A gynecologist and surgeon, he has served 22 years in the National Institute of Public Health (INSS), where he founded the Department of Sexology in 1986 and *The Journal of Sexology*. Associação Brasileira de Sexologia, Rua Tamandare 693-Conj 77 01525-001, São Paulo, SP, Brazil.

LOURENÇO STÉLIO REGA, M.Th. Professor Rega's research interest is in the anthropological perspectives of sexual ethics. Author of *Perspectiva Crista do Sexo* (1990) and *Libertação e Sexualidade, uma Abalise* (1991), he is a professor of sexual and medical ethics and Dean of the Baptist Theological Faculty of São Paulo.

ELÍ FERNANDES DE OLIVEIRA. Eli Fernandes combines his theological and psychological training as a counselor working with couples, children, and homosexuals. He is president of the São Paulo Baptist Convention and pastor of the Baptist Church of Liberty in São Paulo.

*Updates*: LUCIANE RAIBIN, M.S., and RAYMOND J. NOONAN, Ph.D. (see listings above, Associate Editors and Editor), and Dra. SANDRA ALMEIDA, who is a Brazilian lawyer and women's rights advocate currently living in New York.

## Bulgaria:

MICHAIL ALEXANDROV OKOLIYSKI, Ph.D. With a doctorate in rehabilitation science (from Humboldt University, Berlin), Dr. Okoliyski helped organize and presented at a wide variety of European and Bulgarian conferences and programs. His main interests include AIDS prevention and epidemiology in Bulgaria, gathering data on Bulgarian sexual behavior, and prostitution and sex tourism in Bulgaria. In 1994, he cofounded the Human Sexuality Research Foundation. National Center of Public Health, Sophia, Bulgaria; mental@mbox.cit.bg.

PETKO VELICHKOV, M.D., has done some research and mostly clinical work in sexuality, offering postgraduate training for medical specialists and an elective/optional course for medical students in the field of human sexuality. In 1994, Dr. Velichkov cofounded the Human Sexuality Research Foundation in Sofia; he has been the Foundation's executive director since then. Human Sexuality Research Foundation, 16, Kosta Lulchev Str. bl. 244, Sofia 11113, Bulgaria; sexology@acad.bg; www.sexology.bol.bg

## Canada:

MICHAEL BARRETT, Ph.D. Professor of zoology at the University of Toronto in Ontario, Canada, Dr. Barrett is Chairperson of SIECCAN, the Sex Information and Education Council of Canada, and the author of *Population and Canada*. He has also published studies on sexual experience, birth control usage, sex education, and abortion in Canada. University of Toronto, Zoology Department, 25 Harboard Street, Toronto, ON, M5S 3G5, Canada; barrett@zoo.utoronto.ca

ALAN KING, Ph.D., is director of the Social Policy Evaluation Group at Queen's University, Kingston, Ontario, Canada.

JOSEPH LEVY, Ph.D., is a professor in the Department of Sexology at the University of Quebec at Montreal and a leading expert on sexuality among the French-speaking peoples of the Quebec Province. Levy.joseph_josy@uqam.ca

ELEANOR MATICKA-TYNDALE, Ph.D., is a member of the Department of Sociology and Anthropology at the University of Windsor in Ontario, Canada.

ALEX MCKAY, Ph.D., is Research Coordinator for the Sex Information and Education Council of Canada.

JULIE FRASER, Ph.D., is a postdoctoral Fellow in Social Justice and Sexual Health at the University of Windsor, Ontario, Canada; fraser1@uwindsor.ca

## China:

FANG-FU RUAN. A physician and medical historian, Dr. Fang-fu Ruan taught at the Beijing Medical University until 1985. Editor and major author of *Xingzhishi Shiuce* [*Guide to Sexuality*] (1985) prepared for the People's Republic of China, he has also written *Sex in China: Studies in Sexology in Chinese Culture* (1991). He has also published on sex education, transsexualism, sexual repression, and gender orientations in China in professional journals. A visiting professor at several American universities, Dr. Ruan is chairperson of the department of Oriental Studies at the Institute for the Advanced Study of Human Sexuality in San Francisco, and professor and Dean of Instruction at the Academy of Chinese Culture and Health Sciences in Oakland, California. P.O. Box 70571, Oakland, CA 94612-0571 USA; *or* 1130 3rd Ave., Apt 903; Oakland, CA 94606 USA; ruanff@yahoo.com

M. P. LAU, M.D. A psychiatrist, Dr. Lau lived in Hong Kong for 30 years before moving to Canada, where he has lived for the past three decades while maintaining close ties with colleagues in China. The author of a major analysis, included in this *Encyclopedia* chapter, of the nationwide survey conducted in China by Professor Liu Dalin, Dr. Lau teaches in the Department of Psychiatry at the University of Toronto in Ontario, Canada, and is an active member of the Culture, Community, and Health Program at Toronto's Clarke Institute of Psychiatry, 164 Nipigon Ave., Willowdale, Ont. M2M 2W4 Canada; kay_ewok@hotmail.com

## Colombia:

JOSÉ MANUEL GONZÁLEZ Ph.D., is director of *Revista Latinoamericana de Sexologia*, Graduate Director for Sexual Education (Simón Bolivar University) and Director of the González Clinique in Barranquilla, Colombia. With his doctorate from the University of Habana (Cuba) in 2000, he is the author of *Educacion de la Sexualidad* (Barranquilla: Club del Libro, 1994). Apartao Aereo 1190, Barranquilla, Colombia; jmgonzalez@playnet.net.co

RUBÉN ARDILA, Ph.D., a practicing psychologist, is director of the *Revista Latinoamericana de Psicologia*, president of the Fundacion para el Avance de la Psicologia, a professor and researcher at the National University of Colombia, and author of various books on human behavior

PEDRO GUERRERO, M.D., a psychiatrist and sexual therapist, is director of the National Project of Sexual Education in the Colombian National Ministry of Education. He is the author of various books on human sexuality.

GLORIA PENAGOS, M.D., a gynecologist and sexual educator, teaches and does research at the University of Antioquia. She is also a member of the board of directors of the Colombian Society of Sexologists.

BERNARD USECHE, Ph.D., is a psychologist, sexual therapist, director of the graduate program in sexual education at the University of Caldas, and author of various investigations and books about human sexuality.

## Costa Rica:

ANNA ARROBA earned a M.A. degree in anthropology and is working on her doctorate. She is currently director of Association de Mujeres en Salud (AMES), a NGO women's service agency in Costa Rica, and teaches at the University of Costa Rica. Her short article on "A New View of Women's Sexuality: The Case of Costa Rica" in Kaschak and Tiefer's *A New View of Women's Sexual Problems* (2001), led to her chapter in *CCIES*. She is currently working on *The History and Politics of the Body*, a historical and anthropological

perspective on the negative ways women's bodies have been defamed and controlled. Apt 538-2050, San Pedro Montes de Oca, Costa Rica. aarroba@cariari.ucr.ac.cr *or* ames@racsa.co.cr

Research assistance by LAURA FUENTES BELGRAVE, B.A., currently working on a master's degree in sociology.

## Croatia:

ALEKSANDAR ŠTULHOFER, Ph.D., associate professor of sociology at the University of Zagreb, introduced the first university-level course on human sexuality in Croatia in 1996. He has written extensively on adolescent sexuality, sex education, female sexuality, and sexual dysfunctions. His latest book is *Trafficking in Women and Children for Sexual Exploitation* (2001). He was the host of *Intimate Conversations*, a radio sex-counseling show (Family Radio, 2000-2001), and is currently author/host of a public TV show (*Shape of Things*), which frequently covers sexuality topics. University of Zagreb, Sociology Department, Faculty of Philosophy, I. Lucica 3, 10,000 Zagreb, Croatia; astulhof@ffzg.hr

GORDAN BOSANAC. A physicist at the R. Boskovic Institute, he also teaches a course on culture, technology, and communications at the Peace Studies in Zagreb.

GORDANA BULJAN-FLANDER, Ph.D., is a psychologist/psychotherapist at Psychotrauma Center, Children's Hospital Zagreb, since 1981, coordinator, educator, and supervisor on the Prevention and Intervention in the Field of Child Abuse project, and head of the hotline for abused and neglected children. She also provides clinical training for the Department of Psychology and Medical School for Nurses (University of Zagreb), and lectures at postgraduate studies in domestic violence at the Police Academy.

VLASTA HIRŠL-HEĆEJ, M.D., M.A., is consultant epidemiologist, the Head of the Department of Reproductive Health, and Chief of the Division of Epidemiology and Health Statistics in Children's Hospital Zagreb, University of Zagreb Medical School. She has published over 30 scientific and professional papers on health problems of children and adolescents, reproductive health and family planning in Croatia, sexual behavior, and sex education. In the past decade, she has authored several publications for Croatian adolescents about responsible sexuality.

PETRA HOBLAJ is young researcher at the Institute for Social Research (IDIZ, Zagreb) with research interest in the history of school-based sex education initiatives in Croatia.

IVANKA IVKANEC, B.A., works as an expert adviser with the Museum of Ethnology in Zagreb, where she has organized 18 exhibitions, two of which explored sexual mores and relevant folk traditions in Croatia. Her work has been the inspiration for a documentary TV sequel titled *Folk Intimacy*.

ANA KARLOVIĆ is a psychologist, co-coordinator of the NGO *Brave Phone*, a hotline for abused and neglected children. She is a member of the multidisciplinary team in Psychotrauma Center, which offers counseling and individual and group therapy of abused and/or neglected children and families with related problems, and the author of several brochures and leaflets on child abuse and neglect.

ALEKSANDRA KORAĆ, Ph.D., assistant professor of family law at the Faculty of Law, University of Zagreb, is a member of the working committee of the Ministry of Labor and Social Welfare for the Proposal of the Family Act (enacted in 1999), a member of the working committee of the Ministry of Health for the proposal of the laws concerning human procreation (assisted procreation, abortion, sterilization, and educational measurements), and a member of the working group of the Government of the Republic of Croatia for the implementation of the European Convention for the Protection of Human Rights and Fundamental Freedoms (1996-1998).

MAJA MAMULA, M.A., has been coordinator of the Women's Center Against Sexual Violence, a counselor, trainer, and supervisor of women's groups and SOS lines, and a representative of governmental institutions on the issues of sexual violence against women. Presently, she lectures on women, violence, and security at the Center for Women's Studies and on the psychology of sexuality at the Croatian Studies, University of Zagreb. She has authored several brochures and manuals on issues of violence against women.

JADRANKA MIMICA is clinical psychologist at UNAIDS Focal Point for Croatia. Her particular interests are in the area of behavioral studies, as well as in facilitating social mobilization to decrease risks associated with drug use and unsafe sexual practices.

ŽELJKO MRKŠIĆ studied sociology and works as a publisher and NGO activist.

SANJA SAGASTA, a graduate student at the University of Zagreb, Department of Croatian Language and Literature, is a poet and cofounder of numerous lesbian projects and initiatives in Croatia.

HRVOJE TILJAK, M.D., Ph.D., trained in general practice/family medicine at the University of Zagreb and University of Antwerp (Belgium), lectures at the Department of Family Medicine, University of Zagreb Medical School. In 1996, he was one of the organizers of the continuing medical education course *Sexual Problems in Family Practice*, the first of its kind at the University of Zagreb Medical School.

## Cuba:

MARIELA CASTRO ESPÍN, B.Ed., M.Sc., is director of Cuba's National Center of Sex Education (CENESEX), chairwoman of the Cuban Multidisciplinary Society for the Study of Sexuality, director of the magazine *Sexología y Sociedad*, and a member of CENESEX's Scientific Board. President of the 16th World Congress of Sexology, Havana, April 2003, she is also assistant professor at the Pedagogic University of Havana, associate professor at the Medical University of Havana (1999), president of Sexology and Sexual Education Chair, president of the Sociedad Cubana Multidisciplinaria de Estudios de la Sexualidad, and author of several books, educational programs, and scientific articles in national and international magazines. CENESEX—Centro Nacional de Education Sexual, Calle 10 #46 esq. 21, Vedado, Ciudad de la Habana, Cuba; cenesex@infomed.sld.cu

MARÍA DOLORES CÓRDOVA LLORCA, Ph.D., is a permanent professor of the National School of Public Health and the National Center of Sexual Education (CENESEX), secretary of the Scientific Council of CENESEX, vice-director of CENESEX, and vice president of Sexology and Sexual Education. She has taught and been an advisor at universities in Spain, Brazil, Bolivia, Ecuador, México, and Perú, and is the author of different articles published in national and international magazines. Subdirectora de Investigationes, CENESEX, Calle 10 #46 esq. 21, Vedado, Ciudad de la Habana, Cuba; cenesex@infomed.sld.cu

Other contributors to the Cuba chapter are: ALICIA GÓNZALEZ HERNÁNDEZ, Ph.D. (Pedagogy, ISPEJV); BEATRIZ CASTELLANOS SIMONS, Ph.D. (Pedagogy); NATIVIDAD GUERRERO BORREGO, Ph.D. (Psychology, Head of the Center for Youth Studies, CESJ); EDDY ABREU GUERRA, Ph.D. (Psychology, CENESEX); BEATRIZ TORRES RODRÍGUEZ, Ph.D. (Psychology, CENESEX); CARIDAD T. GARCÍA ÁLVAREZ, M.Sci. (Social research, INEN); ADA ALFONSO RODRÍGUEZ, Dra. Med., M.Sc. (Sexual pedagogy, CENESEX); MARICEL REBOLLAR SÁNCHEZ, M.Sc. (Education); OSCAR DÍAZ NORIEGA, Dr. Med., M.Sc. (Sexual pedagogy); JORGE RENATO IBARRA GUITART, Dr. Hist. Sci. (Assistant Researcher, Institute of Cuban History); SONIA JIMÉNEZ BERRIOS, Lic. (Journalist, sociologist, and assistant researcher, Center for Psychological and Sociological Research of the Ministry of Science, Technology, and the Environment); GLORIA MARÍA ANTONIA TORRES CUERTO, Dra. (Pedagogy, Director of School Health of the Ministry of Education); DAIMELIS MONZÓN WAT (Psychologist); JORGE PELÁEZ MENDOZA, Dr. Med. (Second degree specialist, Chairman of the National Commission on Infantile and Juvenile Gynecology of the Mother Child Division, Ministry of Public Health); MAYRA RODRÍGUEZ LAUZERIQUE, M.Sc. (Sexuality, CENESEX); OFELIA BRAVO FERNÁNDEZ, M.Sc. (Sexuality, CENESEX); LAUREN BARDISA ESCURRA, Dr. Med.; MIGUEL SOSA MARÍN, Dr. Med. (Cuban Society for Family Development, SOCUDEF); ROSAIDA OCHOA SOTO, Dr. Med. (National Center for Prevention and Control of STI and HIV-AIDS); LEONARDO CHACÓN ASUSTA (Psychologist); and MIRHA CUCCO GARCÍA, Dra. (Director of the "Marie Langera" Community Center, Madrid, Spain).

## Cyprus, Greek:

GEORGE JOHN GEORGIOU, Ph.D., the only certified sexologist on the island of Cyprus, is director of the Natural Therapy Center in Larnaca. Educated at Oxford (U.K.) and Surrey (U.K.) in clinical psychology, he earned a doctorate in clinical sexology from the Institute for the Advanced Study of Human Sexuality in San Francisco, with extensive training in homeopathic medicine in London. He is also a Fellow of the American Academy of Clinical Sexologists, and a Diplomate of the American Board of Sexology and Sex Therapists. He was the main researcher for two WHO studies, on HIV/AIDS and on drugs. Other research has dealt with sex and religion, herbal medicine, and nutrition. He is the author of a 1995 book in Greek on *Premature Ejaculation*. P.O. Box 42008, 6530 Larnaca, Cyprus; drgeorge@svscom.net

ALEXANDER F. MODINOS, B.Arch., A.R.I.B.A., is cofounder and president of the Gay Liberation Movement of Cyprus, founder and member of the AIDS Solidarity Movement of Cyprus, and contact person for Cyprus to the European Council of AIDS Service Organizations (EUROCASO).

LAURA PAPANTONIOU, M.S. (epidemiology), M.D., is Senior Medical Officer, Department of Medical and Public Health Services, the Ministry of Health (Nicosia), editor of *Health for All*, a public service journal published by the Ministry of Health. She is the focal point for women's affairs in the Ministry. plaura@cytanet.com.cy

NICOS PERISTIANIS, Ph.D. (hon.), is executive dean of Intercollege and president of the Cyprus Sociological Association. With graduate studies in the U.K. and U.S., his main research interests are in the sociology of social change, social institutions, and ethnic and cultural identity. nicosp@Intercol.edu

NATHALIEL PAPAGEORGIOU, a career police officer with more than 35 years field experience, is Assistant Chief of Police (Support Services) in Nicosia. criminaldept@cytanet.com.cy

## Cyprus, Turkish:

SERIN KELÂMI, B.Sci. (hons., psychology), was born and raised in Cyprus, and later lived in Berlin, Germany, with her late husband, Alpay, for 27 years (1965-1992). Since the death of her husband in 1992, she moved to London, and is currently working as a relationship counselor. 27 Albert Road, London N 22 7AQ, United Kingdom; skelami@aol.com

KEMAL BOLAYIR, M.D., is a medical doctor and associate professor of urology in Lefkosa, Northern Cyprus. He is the initiator and organizer of eight International Urological Symposia in Northern Cyprus (1982-1994). He presented dozens of lectures in national and international urology and andrology meetings and is the author of 40 publications in medical journals in Turkish and English. Post Office Box 597, Lefkosa, Mersin, Turkey; kbolayin@superonline.com

## The Czech Republic:

JAROSLAV ZVERINA, M.D., is director of the Institute of Sexology and a member of the First Medical Faculty at Charles University, Prague, Czechoslovakia. President of the Sexological Society of Prague and a member of the Executive Committee of the European Federation of Sexology, Dr. Zernina has authored *Advice for Intimate Life* (1991) and *Medical Sexology* (1992), both in Czech. His research focuses on the behavioral and biological aspects of sexology and reproductive medicine, mainly andrology. He has published in *Archives of Sexual Behavior* and authored a chapter on "Sexuelle Teaktionen auf Optische Stimuli bei Frauen" in *Prakitische Sexualmedizin*, edited by W. Eicher (Weisbaden, 1988). Institute for Sexology, Karlos nam. 32, 128-21 Prague, Czech Republic; jaroslav.zverina@lf1.cuni.cz

*Translation*: ANTON ROS, M.D., a native of the Czech Republic and physician in Wintersville, Ohio, and LYNNE ROS, a former student of the editor of this *Encyclopedia*, with extensive experience in the healthcare professions, provided translation and clarification of difficult sections in Dr. Zverina's manuscript.

## Denmark:

CHRISTIAN GRAUGAARD, M.D., Ph.D., senior researcher at the University of Copenhagen, has written extensively on sexuality and the history of sexology

LENE FALGAARD EPLOV, M.D., Ph.D. Currently training to become a psychiatrist, Dr. Eplov has done extensive research on the sexual behavior of Danes.

ANNAMARIA GIRALDI, M.D., Ph.D., chairman of the scientific committee of the International Society for the Study of Women's Sexual Health and associate editor at the *International Journal of Impotence Research*, has done extensive research on male and female sexual function.

ELLIDS KRISTENSEN, M.D. Trained as a psychiatrist and a specialist in clinical sexology, he is chief physician at the Clinic of Scxology in Copenhagen.

BO MØHL is chief psychologist at the Psychiatric Clinic, Rigshospitalet, and has written extensively on sexology, health psychology, and clinical psychology.

ELSE MUNCK, M.D. Trained as a child and adolescent psychiatrist, Dr. Munck is also a psychoanalytical psychotherapist and a specialist in clinical sexology, and chief physician at the Centre of Forensic Psychiatry, Nordvang Hospital, Copenhagen.

ANNETTE FUGLSANG OWENS, M.D., Ph.D., is founder and director of the Charlottesville Sexual Health & Wellness Clinic, Virginia, USA.

HANNE RISØR, M.D. Trained as a sexologist and a specialist in general medicine, she is chairperson of the Danish Family Planning Association and active in the International Planned Parenthood Federation (IPPF) for two decades.

GERD WINTHER was a social worker and sexologist affiliated with the Clinic of Sexology from 1972 to 1996, when she established a private sexological practice in Copenhagen.

## Egypt:

BAHIRA SHERIF, Ph.D. A cultural anthropologist with fieldwork in Egypt, Dr. Sherif is an assistant professor of Individual and Family Studies at the University of Delaware.

After earning a B.A. degree from Yale University and a Ph.D. at the University of Pennsylvania, she focused her research on ethnically diverse families, Islam, gender issues in the Middle East, intergenerational relations, and women's employment. Her publications include "Islamic Families in America: Diversity and Uniformity in the Family Experience" for Harriette Pipes' *Family Ethnicity: Strength in Diversity* (1999), "Treat your Elders with Respect and Kindness: The Islamic Model." in *Aging in Africa: Colonial and Post-Colonial Representation* (1999), and "Understanding the Rights of Women: The Egyptian Example," in *Women's Rights in an International Perspective* (L. Walters, ed., 1999). Dept. of Individual and Family Studies, University of Delaware, DE 19711 USA; bsherif@udel.ed

Update by HUSSEIN GHANEM, M.D., Professor of Andrology, Sexology & STDs. Cairo University hmghanem@hotmail.com

## Estonia:

ELINA HAAVIO-MANNILA, Ph.D. and OSMO KONTULA, Ph.D. See Finland below.

KAI HALDRE, M.D., a graduate of Tartu University, Estonia, has worked as a gynecologist at Tallinn Pelgulinna Maternity Hospital, and served as an executive director of the Estonian Family Planning Association (member of IPPF) from its establishment in 1994 to 2001. He established a FPA Sexual Health Clinic where he currently works. He is also working on a Ph.D. at Tartu University, researching "Reproductive health and behavior of adolescence girls in Estonia." He is a founding member of the Estonian Academic Society for Sexology. Sexual Health Clinic, Suur-Ameerika 18A, Tallinn 10122 Estonia; kai.haldre@kliinikum.ee *or* kaihaldre@hotmail.com

## Finland:

ELINA HAAVIO-MANNILA, Ph.D., is coauthor with Osmo Kontula of *Suomalainen Seksi: Tietoa Suomalaisten Sukupuolielämän Muutoksesta* [*Finnish Sex: Information of Changes in Sexual Life in Finland*] (1993-1994), *Tyopaikan Rakkausuhteet* [*Love Relations in the Work Place*] (1987), and *Unfinished Democracy: Women in Nordic Politics* (1985). With Osmo Kontulo, she was responsible for national sociological surveys of sexual life in Finland. She is currently professor of sociology at the University of Helsinki, vice president of the Finish Sociological Association (Westermarck Society), board member of the European Sociological Association Steering Group, and vice chairperson of the Finish Academy of Science and Letters. Sociology Dept. Box 18 (Unioninkatu 35), FIN-00014, University of Helsinki, Helsinki, Finland; elina.haavio-mannila@helsinki.fi

OSMO KONTULA, Ph.D. As research director of Docent at the Department of Public Health, the University of Helsinki, Dr. Kontula had directed two national surveys of sexual life in Finland. He is coeditor, with Elina Haavio-Mannila, of *Finnish Sex: Information of Changes in Sexual Life in Finland*) (1993). Since 1986, Dr. Kontula has authored or coauthored about 25 books on sexology, drug use, and the health impacts of economic recession. Population Research Institute (Vaestontutkimuslaitos), P.O. Box 849 (Iso Roobertinkatu 20-22A), FIN 00101 Helsinki, Finland; osmo.kontula@vaestoliitto.fi *or* kontula@cc.helsinki.fi

## France:

MICHEL MEIGNANT, M.D. A University of Paris graduate, Dr. Meignant is President of the French Federation for Psychotherapy (FFdP), Past President and Advisory Committee member of European Association for Psychotherapy. He received a Masters of Human Sexuality from the Institute for Advanced Study of Human Sexuality,

San Francisco, and studied at the Masters and Johnson Reproduction Biology Research Foundation. He directed the French translation and wrote a preface for Helen Singer Kaplan's book on *The New Sex Therapy* and for Masters and Johnson's *Homosexuality in Perspective*. 2 bis rue Scheffer F-75116 Paris, France; meignant@wanadoo.fr

CHARLES GELLMAN, M.D. Neurologist, psychiatrist, gestalt-therapist, and sexotherapist, Charles Gellman is also Président de l'Ecole Parisienne de Gestalt, former Président de la Société Française de Sexologie Clinique (1974-1996), and a member of the Conseil d'Administration de le Société Française de Sexologie Clinique, SFSC (Paris). His most recent publications include *Le Coaching, l'Art du Contact*, and *Le Contact Sexuel*. 103 av. Charles de Gaulle, 92200 Neuilly sur Seine, France; gestalt@wanadoo.fr

ROBERT GELLMAN, M.D. Psychiatre des Hôpitaux, Chef de service au groupe hospitalier Paris-Maison-Blanche, Directeur d'Enseignement au Diplôme Universitaire de Sexologie de l'Université Paris; Président de l'Ecole Française de Sexologie; and Vice-président et membre fondateur de l'Association des Sexologues Cliniciens Francophones.

CLAIRE GELLMAN-BARROUX, a psychologist and psychoanalyst, is vice president of the French School of Sexology and the Sexologie et de l'Association Inter-Hospitalo Universitaire de Sexologie. She is the former president and founding member of the Association des Sexologues Cliniciens Francophones, and former secretary of the World Association of Sexology.

PIERRE DALENS, M.D. A physician and psychoanalyst, Dr. Dalens is an honorary member of the Société Française de Sexologie Clinique, the Institut International de Sexoanalyse and secretary general of the Institut. Dr. Dalens is president and cofounder of the Associations de Recherche en Sexualité du Sud Ouest de la France (A.R.S.S.O.) and the l'Institut Psychorelationnel Européen (I.P.R.E.), and a Diplomate of Sexologie Clinique. 25, Avenue de l'Entre Deux Mers, 33370 Fargues Saint Hilaire (Près Bordeaux), France; pierre.dalens@wanadoo.fr

LAURENT MALTERRE, is an honorary member of the Société Française de Sexologie Clinique, member of the French Federation of Psychotherapy, president of the Association Gender: Troubles de la Genralité, Transsexualisme, Prise en Charge Thérapeutique et Recherché, cofounding member of the Association de Recherche en Sexualité du Sud Ouest de la France (A.R.S.S.O.), and diplomate of Sexologie Clinique de la S.F.S.C. 74, Rue des Gravilliers, 75003 Paris, France; laurentmalterre@hotmail.com

FRANCE PARAMELLE is a neuropsychiatric sexologist and psychoanalyst, specializing in criminality, the sociocultural factors influencing human sexual behavior, and female homosexuality. france.Paramelle@wanadoo.fr

Translation by GENEVIEVE PARENT, B.A., M.A., a double graduate of the Sexology Program at the University of Quebec in Montreal. She has held several positions as a sexuality teacher, clinical sexologist, psychotherapist, and certified sexual abuse counselor. Genevieve_parent@hotmail.com

### French Polynesia:

ANNE BOLIN, Ph.D., professor of Anthropology in the Department of Sociology and Anthropology at Elon University, North Carolina, and recipient of the Elon University Distinguished Scholar Award for 2001, her research areas include women and gender, the body, human sexuality, sports ethnography, and bodybuilding. Her book, *In Search of Eve: Transsexual Rites of Passage* (Bergin and Garvey), received a *Choice* Magazine Award for an Outstanding Academic Book for 1988-89. Her most recent book is *Athletic Intruders: Women, Culture and Exercise* (2003). Her cur-

rent research is with competitive women bodybuilders for a book titled *Elegant Ironworkers: Beauties and Beasts in Bodybuilding*. She is an active and successful competitor in amateur women's bodybuilding. Elon University, Sociology Dept., Nox 2115, Elon College, North Carolina 27244 USA (*or* 1223 Franklin Street, Burlington, NC 27215 USA; Anne.Bolin@elon.edu

### Germany:

RUEDIGER LAUTMANN, Ph.D. Professor of Sociology and Sociology of Law at the University of Breman, Dr. Lautmann has published widely on the social controls of sexual behavior in Germany since the Nazi period. Universitat Bremen, FB 8, GW 2, B 1460, 28334 Bremen, Germany; LautmannHH@aol.com

KURT STARKE, Ph.D. Dr. Starke, a sociologist and political scientist, has served for 20 years as Department Head, Head of Research in Sexology, and Vice-Director of the Central Institute of Youth Research in Leipzig Hauptstr. 6 A, 04774 Zeuckritz, Germany; kurt@starke.I.uunet.de

*Updates*: JAKOB PASTOETTER, Ph.D. (See under Vietnam.) HARTMUT A. G. BOSINSKI, M.D., is a physician and psychotherapist in Sexual Medicine, with special interests in forensic sexology, gender-identity disorders, and sexual dysfunctions. A member of the Board of Directors of the German Academy for Sexual Medicine, he is Head of the Division of Sexual Medicine, Christian-Albrechts-University, Kiel, Germany; hagbosi@sexmed.uni-kiel.de

### Ghana:

AUGUSTINE K. ANKOMAH, Ph.D. A graduate of the University of Ghana, the University of Ife, Nigeria, and the Institute of Population Studies, the University of Exeter (U.K.), he has taught sociology at the University of Cape Coast in Ghana. His research has focused on the sexual behavior of young women in Ghana and its implications for AIDS, family planning service provision, contraceptive use, and reproductive health as they relate to sexual behavior and HIV infection. He is currently comparing sociocultural determinants of induced abortion in Kenya, Peru, and the Philippines.

*Updates*: Beldina Opiyo-Omolo, B.Sc. (See listing under Associate Editor for Africa.)

### Greece:

DIMOSTHENIS AGRAFIOTIS, Ph.D. A sociologist, Dr. Agrafiotis teaches and conducts sexological research at the Athens School of Public Health. He also works with the Collaborating Center for the Global Program on AIDS and the Sociology of AIDS of the World Health Organization.

ELIZABETH IOANNIDI-KAPOLOU, Ph.D., a sociologist-researcher in the Department of Sociology, the National School of Public Health (Athens), researches sexual behavior mainly related to HIV risk in a cross-national perspective, women's sexuality and reproductive health, social exclusion, and migrant and refugee integration. Department of Sociology, National School of Public Health, 196 Alexandras Ave., Athens 115-21 Greece; ioanel@otenet.gr

PANGIOTA MANDI, Ph.D. Dr. Mandi, a sociologist, teaches and conducts sexological research at the Athens School of Public Health. She also works with the Collaborating Center for the Global Program on AIDS and the Sociology of AIDS of the World Health Organization.

### Hong Kong:

EMIL MAN-LUN NG, M.D., is a professor in the Department of Psychiatry at the University of Hong Kong, vice-president of the Hong Kong Sex Education Association and served as President of the Fourteenth World Congress of

Sexology (Hong Kong, August 1999). A member of the Royal College of Psychiatrists (U.K.) since 1976, he is a Fellow of the Hong Kong College of Psychiatrists, the Royal College of Psychiatrists (U.K.), the American College of Sexologists, and the Royal Australian and New Zealand College of Psychiatrists. His main areas of research are Chinese sexual attitudes and culture, and sex education and therapy for the Chinese. He is coeditor of *A Dictionary of Sexology*, coeditor of *Practical Sexual Medicine*, and coeditor with E. Haeberle of the English-language edition, *Sexual Behavior in Modern China: Report of the Nationwide Survey of 20,000 Men and Women* (1997). Queen Mary Hospital, University of Hong Kong, Psychiatry Dept., Hong Kong; nml@i.am

JOYCE L. C. MA, Ph.D., is a senior lecturer/associate professor in the Department of Social Work at the Chinese University of Hong Kong, a faculty member of Family Studies, Hong Kong, a branch of Family Studies, New York, and a social work member of the Gender Identity Team, Sex Clinic, Department of Psychiatry, the University of Hong Kong. Focusing her clinical and research interests on couple and family therapy, she has published two dozen journal papers and contributed chapters to eleven books. joycelai@cuhk.edu.hk

## Iceland:

SÓLEY S. BENDER, R.N., B.S.N., M.S., coordinator/main author of the Iceland chapter, is assistant professor of nursing at the University of Iceland. She has chaired a working group of the Icelandic Association for Sexual and Reproductive Health, developing a sex education curriculum for young people 16 to 20 years old. As a nurse specialist for the Icelandic Association for Sexual and Reproductive Health, she coordinates sexual and reproductive counseling for young people and does educational and counseling work. A doctoral candidate at the Department of Medicine at the University of Iceland, she has edited, coauthored, and authored several articles and major reports on the sexual and reproductive health of Iceland's young people. Dept. of Nursing, University of Iceland, Eirberg, Eiriksgotu 34, 101 Reykjavik, Iceland; ssb@rhi.hi.is

GUDRÚN JÓNSDÓTTIR, Ph.D, a retired professor of social work, researches sexual violence against women and children, and studies incest survivors' experiences of abuse in Iceland and Britain. gsisi@isl.is

SIGRÚN JÚLÍUSDÓTTIR, Ph.D. Professor and Chief of Social Work Education at the University of Iceland, Dr. Juliusdottir is a member of the American Family Therapy Academy, the Swedish Association of Supervisors, and the Icelandic Association of Sexology. Her main area of research is family matters, intimate interaction, and divorce issues. sigjul@rhi.hi.is

THORVALDUR KRISTINSSON is a leading figure in the Icelandic gay movement and presently the chairman of Samtökin '78, the Lesbian and Gay Association of Iceland.

## India:

JAYAJI K. NATH, M.D., is the director of the National Institute for Research in Sex Education, Counseling, and Therapy (NIRSECT-India). A fellow of the Indian Academy of Juvenile and Adolescent Gynaecology and Obstetrics and the International Council of Sex Education and Parenthood of the American University, Dr. Nath is also a consultant on Sexual Medicine at the Mahatma Gandhi Mission Hospital in Bombay.

VISHWARATH R. NAYAR is the founder-director of the National Institute for Research in Sex Education, Counseling, and Therapy (NIRSECT-India), and organizer of two national sexological conferences in India. With J. K.

Nath, he is working on a training curriculum for sexuality teachers in India.

*Comments*: KAREN PECHILIS-PRENTISS, Ph.D., professor of religion at Drew University, does fieldwork and researches gender roles and women in India. Drew University, Religion Department, Madison, New Jersey 07940 USA; kpechili@drew.edu. APARNA KADARI, B.A., M.B.A. Born and raised Hindu in Hyderabad, southern India, Ms. Kadari has traveled all over India. Fluent in Hindi, Urdu, Telugu, and English, she has lectured in the Editor's Sexualities and Cultures graduate course at Fairleigh Dickinson University. aparnakadari@yahoo.com

## Indonesia:

RAMSEY ELKHOLY, Ph.D., has focused his research on hunter-gatherers with an emphasis on Sumatran groups, their sociality and environmental perceptions. His report on the Orang-Rimba indigenous forest people of Indonesia, "Hunter-Gatherers, Native Ecologies and Human Sociality," appeared in the *Journal of the Royal Anthropological Institute* (U.K.). 105 Fifth Avenue, Apt. #6E, New York, NY 10003 USA; relkholy@hotmail.com

WIMPIE PANGKAHILA, M.D., a Lecturer in the Medical School and secretary of the Study Group on Human Reproduction of Udayana University (Bali, Indonesia), is also chairperson of the Indonesian Society of Andrology in Bali. Specializing in infertility, adolescent sexuality, and sexual dysfunctions, he is author of *What You Should Know about Sex* (1981), *About the Sexual Problem in the Family* (1988), *Discussing Sexual Problems in the Family* (1991), *We and Sex* (1991), and *Some Sexual Problems in the Female* (1991). JL By Pass Ngurah Rai 84, Sanur Denpaser, 80228 Bali, Indonesia; wim@denpasar.wasantara.net.id

## Iran:

PAULA DREW, Ph.D., a British-born cultural anthropologist, held consecutive tenured positions at the University of Tabriz in northern Iran and the National University of Tehran for fourteen years between 1964 and the fall of the Shah in 1978. In these universities, she taught Iranian women French, German, English, and Psychology in Persian. For three years, she served as academic and personal advisor to female students in the humanities. She also ran a clinic for mothers and babies in an Iranian oasis community for almost ten years. Fieldnote observations formed the basis for her doctoral dissertation, "Arranging Marriages in Iran." 122 High Street, Randolph, New Jersey 07869 USA; Spid@nac.net

## Ireland:

THOMAS PHELIM KELLY, M.B. A physician and medical coordinator for Family Planning Services in Dublin, Dr. Kelly also has a private practice as a psychosexual therapist.

Comments by HARRY A. WALSH, Ph.D. Born and raised in Ireland, Dr. Walsh is a Catholic priest, and the executive director of The Institute for Child and Adolescent Sexual Health in Monticello, Minnesota. 1201 Golf Course Rd. #1207, Monticello, Minnesota 55362 USA; dialeat@msn.com

## Israel:

RONNY A. SHTARKSHALL, Ph.D., is a professor in the Department of Social Medicine, the Hebrew University and Hadassah, Braun School of Public Health and Community Medicine, in Jerusalem. A member of the Board of Directors for the Israeli Family Planning Association, he is coauthor of *Avoiding AIDS: Preventing AIDS While Preserving Sex and Youth, Sexuality and Relations Between the*

*Sexes: A Facilitator's Handbook*, and program modules, published by the Israeli Ministry of Education and Culture (1987). His current interests are the sexual attitudes and behaviors of adolescents, and sex, sexuality, and relationships in a national Israeli sample. 15 Yasmin St. (Box 1116), Mevasseret-Zion, Israel 90805; ronys@M.D.2.huji.ac.il

MINAH ZEMACH, Ph.D. A native of Israel, with a doctorate degree in psychology from Yale University, she is the director and senior researcher at the Dachaf Research Institute in Tel Aviv (since 1979). An expert in developing surveys and making population analyses and predictions for social, political, and commercial purposes, she coauthored a chapter on "Surveys" in *Research Methods in Social Sciences* and *Zug O Peret (Odds or Even)*, an analysis of relationships among Israeli couples.

## Italy:

BRUNO P. F. WANROOIJ, Ph.D., is professor of history and social sciences at Syracuse University in Italy and at Georgetown University in the USA. He is the author of *Storia del Pudore: La Questione Sessuale in Italia (1860-1940)*, "Italy: Sexuality, Morality, and Public Authority in Italy," "Universalismo versus Cosmopolitismo. I Cattolici Italiani e Hollywood," "Back to the Future: Gender, Morality and Modernization in Twentieth Century Italy," "Impariamo ad Amare," and *L'Avvio della Consulenza Matrimoniale in Italia (1948-1975)*. Syracuse University in Italy Program, Humanities Dept. Piazza Savonarola, 15, 50132 Firenze, Italy; bpwanroo@syr.fl.it *or* wanrooij@mail.dada.it

## Japan:

YOSHIRO HATANO, Ph.D. (University of Oregon, USA), is professor at Tokyo Gakugei University. He has also been a board member and director of the Japanese Association for Sex Education, an advisory committee member of W.A.S. (the World Association of Sexology), secretary general of W.A.S. and Organizing Committee for the Twelfth World Congress of Sexology, vice president of the Asian Federation of Sexology. Kyushuu University of Health and Welfare, Yoshino-cho, Nobeoka City, Miyazaki Prefecture, Japan (code 882-8508); yhatano@phoenix.ac.jp

TSUGUO SHIMAZAKI is a graduate of Waseda University and a journalist/staff member of Shogakukan Press, Tokyo. He serves as secretary general and a board member and director of the Japanese Association for Sex Education, and deputy secretary general of the Twelfth World Congress of Sexology (W.C.S.) Organizing Committee. He has been a visiting professor at Chiba University and adjunct professor at Roanoke College (USA). Nikon Information Center for Sexology (NICS), Hobunkan Bldg. 6F, 3-11-4, Kanda Jinbo-cho, Chiyoda-ku, Tokyo 101-0051 Japan; nics@mail.at-m.or.jp

Lengthy analysis of *manga* by TIMOTHY PERPER, Ph.D., and MARTHA CORNOG, M.S., M.A. (See listing for Perper under Preface; for Cornog under Associate Editors.) perpcorn@dca.net

*Updates*: YOSHIMI KAJI, M.A., a 1993 graduate of the New York University Human Sexuality Program, Kaji was a staff researcher for several years at the Japanese Association for Sex Education. Recently, she began working with families and friends of lesbians and gays in Japan. 2-5-10-1505 Shirogane, Minato-ku, Tokyo 108-0072 Japan; ykaji@crocus.ocn.ne.jp

## Kenya:

NORBERT BROCKMAN. Associate professor of politics and AASECT-certified sex educator, Dr. Brockman teaches at St. Mary's University in San Antonio, where he focuses his research on African studies and political psychology, and the relationship between power and sexual behavior, professional incest, and power and sex roles in the women's and men's movements. He has taught in Kenya and worked at the Amani Counselling Centre in Nairobi.

*Updates*: BELDINA OPIYO-OMOLO, B.Sc. (see listing under Associate Editors), and PAUL MWANGI KARIUKI, Ph.D., a native of Kenya, a Roman Catholic priest, and doctoral student in psychology at Duquenne University in Pittsburgh, Pennsylvania.

## Mexico:

EUSEBIO RUBIO, M.D. Dr. Rubio is founder of Asociacion Mexicana para la Salud Sexual A.C., Mexico City, Mexico, a nonprofit organization that provides low-cost medical and psychological help to low-income persons and training in sex therapy for professionals. He also conducts research projects at AMSSAC and is active in the World Association for Sexology. Pestaluzzi 1204 705, Colonia del Valle, Mexico D.F. 03100 Mexico; eusebio@internet.com.mx *or* Eusebio@mail.internet.com.mx

## Morocco:

ABDERRAZAK MOUSSAÏD, M.D., founded the Moroccan Society of Sexology. A medical doctor at the University of Casablanca, specializing in psychosomatic medicine and sexology, he is a Díplome-inter-universitaire de sexologie from the Faculté de Médicine de Paris XIII-Boigny. 38, Boulevard Rahal El Meskini 20 000, Casablanca, Morocco.

NADIA KADIRI, M.D., is a psychiatrist in the University Psychiatric Center in Casablanca and a member of the Scientific Committee on the Moroccan Society of Sexology. Centre Psychiatrique Universitaire, Rue Tarik Ib Ziad, Casablanca, Morocco; psych@casanet.net.ma *or* nadiakadiri@yahoo.com

ABDELKRIM TIRRAF, M.D., is a specialist in male erectile problems, sterility, and sexual maladies. Dr. Tirraf is a Diplomé in andrology from the Université de Paris and a member of the Moroccan Society of Sexology.

## Nepal:

ELIZABETH SCHROEDER, M.S.W. An adjunct professor of Human Sexuality and Health Counseling at Montclair State University, she is pursuing a doctorate in Human Sexuality Education at Widener University. A sexuality trainer and consultant who has provided trainings throughout the U.S., she has developed adult peer educator and teacher training programs on sexuality and reproductive health in Kathmandu, Nepal. 45 Essex Avenue, 2nd Floor, Montclair, NJ 07042 USA; ElizSchroe@aol.com

## The Netherlands:

JELTO J. DRENTH, M.D. President and chairman of the Dutch Society for Sexology, Dr. Drenth, is a member of the Sexology Department of the Rutgers Foundation and Consultation Bureau for Contraceptive and Sexological Advice in The Hague, Netherlands. Visserstraat 39, 712 CS Groningen, The Netherlands; *or* Nederlandse Vereniging voor Seksuologie, P.O. Box 40551, 2504 LN The Hague, The Netherlands; jvla@smps.azm.nl

A. KOOS SLOB, M.D. Dr. Slob is Senior Scientist and professor of pathophysiology of sexuality in the Department of Endocrinology and Reproduction, the Faculty of Medicine, Erasmus University, Rotterdam. Editor-in-chief of the *Dutch Journal of Sexology*, Dr. Slob was the first recipient of the "Van EM.D.e Boas-Van Ussel" Award (1987) from the Dutch Society for Sexology. He also holds the special chair for Physiology and Pathophysiology of Sexuality, the Trustfund, Erasmus University. Erasmus University,

Faculty of Medicine, (P.O. Box 1738), 3011 HT Rotterdam, Netherlands; slob@endov.fgg.eur.nl

## Nigeria:

UWEM EDIMO ESIET, M.D., M.P.H., a public health physician, has served on the task force on producing the National Guidelines for Sexuality Education in Nigeria and on the committee responsible for producing the Sexuality Education Curriculum for Nigerian schools. A leading commentator on sexuality in Nigeria, he is cofounder, chapter coordinator, and medical director of Action Health Incorporated (AHI) in Lagos, one of Nigeria's largest and most effective NGOs working for adolescent reproductive health. In 1996, AHI coordinated the first Nigerian National Conference on Adolescent Reproductive Health, and successfully lobbied the Nigerian Ministry of Education to approve the integration of sexuality education into the Nigerian secondary school curriculum. Action Health Inc., Plot 54 Somorin Street, Ifako-Gbagada, P.O. 803, Yaba, Lagos, Nigeria; ahi@linkserve.com.ng

NIKE ESIET, B.Sc., M.H.P. (Harvard), a journalist, and former public relations officer for Society for Women and AIDS, Nigeria Chapter (SWAAN), Mrs. Esiet is project director and cofounder of Lagos-based Action Health Incorporated (AHI), working for adolescent reproductive health. Her work has been supported by a three-year "social entrepreneur" fellowship from the U.S.-based Ashoka: Innovators for the Public and support from the MacArthur Foundation. nikeoesiet@linkserve.com.ng

CHRISTINE OLUFUNKE ADEBAJO, Ph.D., is Deputy General Secretary of the National Association of Nigerian Nurses and Midwives (NANNM), president of the Federation of Female Nurses and Midwives of Nigeria (FENAM), and vice president of Nigeria's National Council for Population Activities. She has authored two books on female circumcision and strategies for its eradication.

IBIRONKE AKINSETE Professor Akinsete is President of the Society for Women and AIDS in Africa, Nigerian Chapter (SWAAN).

MAIRO VICTORIA BELLO is Project Director/Coordinator for the Adolescent Health and Information Project in Tarauni, Kano, Nigeria. An officer of Women for Independence, Self-Sufficiency, and Economic Advancement (WISSEA), her research focuses on adolescent sexuality and socialization, sexual violence and abuse, and women's health and reproductive track infections.

RAKIYA BOOTH, M.B.B.S., is director of primary healthcare services of the Christian Health Association of Nigeria in Jos, specializing in STD and AIDS education.

IMO I. ESIET, Esq., B.Sc. (Hons), L.L.B. (Hons), B.L., is a member of the Nigerian Bar Association and a counselor and legal advisor involved in women's rights.

MRS. FOYIN OYEBOLA is program officer at the Planned Parenthood Federation of Nigeria National Headquarters in Lagos, and a member of the Campaign Against Unwanted Pregnancy in Lagos.

BILKISU YUSUF, a journalist, media administrator, and social activist, has contributed to several books, with chapters on such topics as "Challenges of the Muslim Women," "Hausa Fulani Women: The State of the Struggle," "Challenges Facing Muslim Women in Secular States," and "The Impact of Islam and Culture on Marriage Age in Hausa Society."

*Updates*: Beldina Opiyo-Omolo, B.Sc. (See listing under Associate Editors.)

## Norway:

ELSA ALMÅS, is a specialist in clinical psychology, president of both the Norwegian Society for Clinical Sexology and the Nordic Association for Clinical Sexology, a member of the Harry Benjamin International Gender Dysphoria Association, and a member of the Resource and Reference Group for Sexual Dysfunctions in Norway. She authored *Den Skjulte Lyst* [*The Hidden Desire*] and with Esben Esther Pirelli Benestad, coauthored *Sexologi i Praksis* [*Sexology in Practice*]. Grimstad MPAT-Institute, Storgaten 42, 4876 Grimstad, Norway; elsa.almas@sexologi.com

ESBEN ESTHER PIRELLI BENESTAD, M.D., a general practitioner (University of Oslo) and family therapist in private practice, is a board-member of the Norwegian Society for Clinical Sexology, a member of the Harry Benjamin International Gender Dysphoria Association and the Nordic Group for Developing Sexological Education and Authorization. Benedtad's main research and clinical work is in general health service, family and sex therapy, psychotherapy, education and supervision in sexology, public sex education and counseling in gender issues. Grimstad MPAT-Institute, Storgaten 42, 4876 Grimstad, Norway. esben.benestad@sexologi.com or esther.pirelli@sexologi.com

## Outer Space and Antarctica:

RAYMOND J. NOONAN, Ph.D. Since 1987, Dr. Noonan has presented his ideas and research on the need for sex research in space at numerous conferences, including those of the Aerospace Medical Association (AsMA), the Society for the Scientific Study of Sexuality (SSSS), the National Space Society (NSS), and the American Association of Sex Educators, Counselors, and Therapists (AASECT). A recent article, "Sexuality and Space: Theoretical Considerations for Extended Spaceflight," is under review by the AsMA journal, *Aviation, Space, and Environmental Medicine*. Sex in space was the subject of his doctoral dissertation in 1998 in the Human Sexuality Program at New York University. His look at Antarctica derived from its use in research as a space analog environment. His fuller biographical sketch appears under Editors at the beginning of this section.

## Papua New Guinea:

SHIRLEY OLIVER-MILLER. As Senior Program Officer II, Margaret Sanger Center International, Planned Parenthood of New York City, since 1980, Shirley Oliver-Miller has been responsible for managing government and nongovernment projects, and developing and implementing program strategies around reproductive and sexual health issues. She has worked in 37 countries, developing programs for government and nongovernmental agencies around population health. Author of a dozen training manuals, she has trained thousands of professionals, with support from the United States Agency for International Development (USAID), United Nations Funds for Population Activities (UNFPA), and the World Health Organization (WHO). shirley.oliver-miller@ppnyc.org

Updates by EDGAR GREGERSON, Ph.D. Professor of anthropology at Queens College and the Graduate Center of the City University of New York, he is a Fellow of the Royal Anthropological Institute and the American Anthropological Association. His masterwork is *The World of Human Sexuality: Behaviors, Customs and Beliefs*. 302 West 12th St., New York, NY 10014 USA; eagqc@qcvaxa.acc.qc.edu

## The Philippines:

JOSE FLORANTE J. LEYSON, M.S., M.D., F.A.C.S., is director of the Sexual Dysfunction Center, Spinal Cord Injury Service, Dept. of Veterans Affairs, New Jersey Health Care Systems. He edited *Sexual Rehabilitation of the Spinal-Cord-Injured Patient* and is recipient of the 1986 Filipino Physician of the Year Award from the Department of Veterans Affairs. 6 Ranney Road, Long Valley, NJ 07853 USA.

## Poland:

ANNA SIERZPOWSKA-KETNER, M.D., Ph.D. A psychiatrist and sexologist, Dr. Sierzpowska-Ketner is senior lecturer/consultant forensic expert in sexology in the Department of Sexology at the Postgraduate Medical Education Center, vice-president of the Polish Sexological Society, and secretary of the Sexological Section of the Polish Medical Association. Specializing in sexual dysfunctions, paraphilias, sexual fantasies, sex offenders, and their victims, Dr. Sierzposka-Ketner is also coauthor of an *Encyclopedia of Sexology*. Polish Sexological Society, Sex Research Department, ul. Marymoncka 34, 01-813 Warsaw, Poland. (*Correspondence*: ul. Londynska 12m 31, 03-921 Warsaw, Poland)

## Portugal:

NUNO NODIN is a counsellor at the Associação para o Planeamento Familiar (Portuguese Family Planning Association) and the Sexualidade em Linha (telephone help-line for adolescents), both in Lisboa (Lisbon). He also teaches at the Instituto Superior de Psicologia Aplicada, Lisboa. Trained in sexuality and counseling with the Associação para o Planeamento da Família and in the psychological and social aspects of AIDS with the Instituto Superior de Psicologia Aplicada, his main areas of interest are sexuality education, sexual and reproductive health, psychotherapy, and counseling: R. Conselheiro Lopo Vaz, 24, 1° Dto., 1800-142 Lisboa, Portugal. nunonodin@mail.teleweb.pt

ANA MARGARIDA OURÔ, a clinical psychologist in a military rest home for adult men with severe disabilities, her clinical and research interests include women's psychology, rape and battered women, domestic violence, handicaps, and disability. Among her publications are a study of the psychology of pregnant HIV-positive women (2000), and "The Womb Is Satisfied, the Eyes Are Not: Social Support in Adolescents Who Carried Their Pregnancy to Term and Women Who Interrupted Their Pregnancy."

SARA MOREIRA is a sex education counselor at the Portuguese Family Planning Association and a counselor at Sexualidade em Linha (telephone help-line for adolescents). Her main work has been in youth counseling at the Family Planning Association and Sexuality help-line; peer-education youth training in sexuality projects; the Family Planning Association Project on Child and Adolescent Sexual Abuse; and the Family Planning Association cooperation project with Portuguese-speaking countries. Rua D. António Caetano de Sousa, 3, 2° Dto.,1500 Lisboa, Portugal. sara_moreira@sapo.pt

## Puerto Rico (The United States of America)

LUIS MONTESINOS, Ph.D. Dr. Montesinos is an assistant professor at Montclair State College in New Jersey, where he teaches undergraduate and graduate courses in human sexuality, health psychology, and behavioral modification. Psychology Department, Montclair State University, Upper Montclair, NJ 07043 USA.

JUAN PRECIADO, Ph.D. Dr. Preciado, an associate professor in the Department of Urban and Community health at Hostos Community College of the City University of New York, has given numerous presentations on sexual health and cultural issues in Europe and Latin America. His research interests are in health education. quetzalo1@aol.com

*Updates*: FELIX M. VELÁZQUEZ-SOTO, M.S., is a professor of biology, chairman of Health, Occupational Safety and Environmental Protection, and certified sex educator at the University of Puerto Rico in Cayey. 205 Antonio R. Barceló Avenue, Cayey, Puerto Rico 00736 USA; f_velazquez1@hotmail.com. GLORIVEE ROSARIO-PÉREZ, Ph.D,, is associate professor of microbiology and immunology, and Coordinator of University Sex Education Symposia, University of Puerto Rico (Medical Science Campus). University of Puerto Rico at Cayey, Biology Department, 205 Antonio R. Barceló Avenue, Cayey, Puerto Rico 00736 USA; glorivee@hotmail.com

## Russia:

IGOR S. KON, Ph.D. Dr. Kon, sociologist, psychologist, and anthropologist, has been Chief Researcher at the Institute for Ethnography and Anthropology, the Russian Academy of Sciences, since 1974. A member of the Russian Academy of Education, Dr. Kon is also A. D. White Professor-at-Large at Cornell University (1990-1995), a member of the International Academy of Sex Research, and a member of the Polish Sexological Academy. In addition to over 300 professional articles, he has authored *Introduction to Sexology*, published in Hungarian, German, Ukrainian, Estonian, Chinese, and in Russian after being banned for ten years. Among his numerous other books are *Taste of the Forbidden Fruit, Sex and the Soviet Society*, and *The Sexual Revolution in Russia*. Between 1985 and the present, he held short-term lecture appointments at universities of Stanford all over the world. Vavilova Str., 48-372, Moscow, Russia 117333; igor_kon@mail.ru *or* igor_kon@yahoo.com

## South Africa:

MERVYN BERNARD HURWITZ, M.D. A Diplomat and Fellow of the South African College of Gynaecologists and Fellow of the Royal College of Obstetricians and Gynaecologists, Dr. Hurwitz was Head of the Sexual Dysfunction Clinic at Johannesburg Hospital in South Africa, and Lecturer and Examiner in the Department of Obstetrics & Gynecology, University of Witwatersrand, Johannesburg. A member of the editorial board of the *Medical Sex Journal of South Africa*, Dr. Hurwitz is the author of *Educating the Doctor and Patient in Human Sexuality* (1986), *Sex and the Disabled* (1987), and *Breast Feeding and Sexuality* (1992). 127 Lakeside Court, Lake Village, Arkansas 71638-5012 USA; hurwitz@cei.net

LIONEL JOHN NICHOLAS, Ph.D. Dr. Nicholas is senior psychologist and senior lecturer at the University of the Western Cape, Bellville, South Africa, and an adjunct professor at the Institute for the Advanced Study of Human Sexuality in San Francisco. Since 1990, he has conducted an annual survey of sexual experience, attitudes, and AIDS knowledge among black South African first-year university students. 49 Arthur's Seat Mansions, Beach Road, Sea Point 8001, Cape Town, South Africa; lnicholas@uwc.ac.za

PRISCILLA SANDRA DANIELS, M.S. Ms. Daniels is senior lecturer and departmental chairperson of human ecology and dietetics, as well as Vice-Dean of the Faculty of Community and Health Sciences at the University of the Western Cape in Bellville, South Africa. With research interests in sexuality, family and women's issues, she is coauthor of chapters on "Sexual Harassment and Rape in Educational Settings," "Sexual Attitudes and Behaviours of University Students," and "Sex in South Africa" in *Sex Counseling in University Settings*.

Updates by Beldina Opiyo-Omolo, B.Sc. (See Associate Editor listing.)

## South Korea:

DR. HYUNG-KI CHOI, M.D. Director of the Sex Clinic at Yonsei Medical Center and the president of the Asian Federation of Sexology, Dr. Choi is one of the founders of the Asia-Pacific Society for Impotence Research (APSIR) and served the president for the APSIR. He is one of the leading scholars and therapists of the world in sexual impotence. Yongdong Severance Hospital, Dept of Urology, 146-92,

Dogok-dong, Kangnam-ku, Seoul 135-270, South Korea; urol3887@yumc.yonsei.ac.kr

MR. HUSO YI, a doctoral candidate in the Program in Human Sexuality, New York University, and Senior Research Associate at the National Development and Research Institute, his main interests are the global/cross-cultural aspects of sexual identity, health, and inequality. He was a cofounding member for the first gay student activist organization in Korea. Since 1995, he has worked for the rights of sexual minorities in Korea, given a number of presentations about East Asian gay and bisexual men, co-authored articles, and reviewed books on homosexuality. 18 First Place, #2, Brooklyn, NY 11231 USA; huso.yi@ ndri.org, *or* hy236@nyu.edu

DR. YUNG-CHUNG KIM was a professor of history and Dean of the Graduate School at Ewha Women's University. From 1977 to 1983, she served as the Director of the Korean Women's Institute. In the mid 1980s, she was President of the Korean Women's Development Institute. Currently, she is on the United Nations Committee for the Convention on the Elimination of All Forms of Discrimination Against Women.

DR. PILWHA CHANG has played a key role in the development of Women's Studies and is affiliated with various women's organizations. She was the Commissioner for the Presidential Commission of Women's Affairs in 1998 and founded the Asian Center for Women's Studies in 1995. She has been a professor of the Department of Women's Studies, Graduate School of Ewha University from 1984 to the present.

DR. WHASON BYUN is the director of Family, Health, and Welfare Division of the Korean Women's Development Institute (KWDI) and lecturer on Women's Policy at Seong-Sin Women's University. Her publications include articles on women's and family issues.

## Spain:

JOSE ANTONIO NIETO, Ph.D. (Chapter Coordinator) Since receiving his doctorate from the New School for Social Research in New York, Dr. Nieto has specialized in the anthropology of sexuality. Currently Head Professor and Director of the Human Sexuality Program at the Universidad Nacional de Educacio a Distancia, he has authored *Cultura y Sociedad en las Practicas Sexuale, La Sexualidad en la Sociedad Contemporanea, Lecturas Antropologicas*, and *Sexualidad y Deseo: Critica Antropologica de la Cultura*. Among his research interests are sexual behavior and HIV infections in Europe. Travesia de Tellez, 2, Escl. 1a-2o-A, Madrid, 28007 Spain; janieto@sr.uned.es

JOSE ANTONIO CARROBLES, Ph.D. Dr. Carrobles is full professor and director of the Department of Biological Psychology and Health at the Universidad Autonoma in Madrid, and professor of sexology and sexual therapy in the Master's Program in Human Sexuality at the Universidad Nacional de Educacio a Distancia in Madrid. His interests focus on sexual dysfunctions, sexual differences, sex therapy and the psychology of health.

MANUEL DELGADO RUIZ, Ph.D. Dr. Delgado Ruiz is professor of anthropology at the University of Barcelona and the Master's Program in Human Sexuality at the Universidad Nacional de Educacio a Distancia in Madrid.

FELIX LOPEZ SANCHEZ, Ph.D. A professor of Psychology of Sexuality and Director of the Sexology Doctoral Program at the University of Salamanca, Dr. Sanchez is also a professor in the Master's Program in Human Sexuality at the Universidad Nacional de Educacio a Distancia in Madrid and Director of the Center for Sexual Documentation in Salamanca. His publications include *Principios Basicos*

*de Educacion Sexual, Educacion Sexual en la Adolescencia, Para Comprender la Sexualidad*, and *Educacion Aexual en el Aula*.

VIRGINA MAQUIEIRA D'ANGELO, Ph.D. Dr. Maquieira D'Angelo is professor in the Department of Sociology and Social Anthropology at the Universidad Autonoma de Madrid, and a professor in the Master's Program in Human Sexuality at the Universidad Nacional de Educacio a Distancia in Madrid. A member of the Consejo del Instituto Universitario de Estudio de la Mujer and an International Editor for *Gender and Society*, she is also editor of *Mujer y Hombres en la Formacion del Pensamiento Occidental* and coeditor of *Violencia y Sociedad Patriarcal*.

JOSEP-VICENT MARQUES, Ph.D. Dr. Marques is professor in the Department of Sociology and Social Anthropology at the University of Valencia, and a professor in the Master's Program in Human Sexuality at the Universidad Nacional de Educacio a Distancia.

FERNANDO MORENO JIMINEZ, Ph.D., studied sexology at the Interdisciplinary Institute of Ciencias Sexologicas at Louvain, Belgium. He is professor of biological psychology and health at the Universidad Autonoma in Madrid and a professor in the Master's Program in Human Sexuality at the Universidad Nacional de Educacio a Distancia.

RAQUEL OSBORNE VERDUGO, Ph.D., is professor of sociology at the Universidad Nacional de Educacio a Distancia and in the Master's Program in Human Sexuality at the same university. Her publications include *Las Prostitutes, Las Mujeres en la Encrucijada de la Sexualidad*, and *Sexualidad y Sexismo*.

CARMELA SANZ RUEDA, Ph.D., is professor in the Department of Social Psychology at the Universidad Complutense in Madrid, and a professor in the Master's Program in Human Sexuality at the Universidad Nacional de Educacio a Distancia. A founding member of the Instituto de Investigaciones Feministas de la Universidad Complutense, she has authored *La Comunicacion Interpersonal en el Matrimonio: El Punto de Vista de la Mujer, Nuevas Perspectivas sobre la Mujer*, and *Genero y Sexualidad*.

CARMELO VASQUEZ VALVERDE, Ph.D. Dr. Vasquez Valverde is professor of psychology at the Universidad Complutense in Madrid and a professor in the Master's Program in Human Sexuality at the Universidad Nacional de Educacio a Distancia.

## Sri Lanka:

VICTOR C. De MUNCK, Ph.D., is a cognitive and cross-cultural anthropologist, interested in the variable and universal features of conceptions of the self and romantic love, and cultural model theory. He has recently published a monograph, *Culture, Self and Meaning*, and a number of cross-cultural studies on romantic love and gender, Lithuanian ethnography, and a comparative study of cultural models of romantic love and sexual choices in the United States and Russia. Department of Anthropology, State University of New York–New Paltz, New Paltz, NY 12561 USA; victor@bestweb.net

Comments by PATRICIA WEERAKOON, Ph.D., a native of Sri Lanka, she is currently a sexual/marital counselor and sexuality educator with the Medical Faculty of the University of Sydney (Australia). A lecturer in Biomedical Sciences, Dr. Weerakoon is a sexuality educator and researcher with special interest in sexuality and sexual health as relevant to health professional practice, and E-learning School of Biomedical Sciences. The University of Sydney, P.O. Box 170, Lidcombe, NSW 1825, Australia; P.Weerakoon@ cchs.usyd.edu.au

## Sweden:

JAN TROST, Ph.D. Professor of Sociology at Sweden's Uppsala University, Dr. Trost has served on the editorial staffs of numerous professional publications including *Nordisk Sexologi*, *Journal of Marriage and the Family*, and *Alternative Lifestyles*, and as an expert on the revision of Family Law for the Swedish Government. He has edited seven books, including *The Family in Change*, and authored or coauthored 11 books, including *To Cohabit and to Marry: Facts and Foibles*. Uppsala University, Department of Sociology, P.O. Box 821, S-751 08 Uppsala, Sweden; jan.trost@soc.uu.se

MAI-BRIHT BERGSTROM-WALAN, Ph.D. A psychologist, Dr. Berstrom-Walan is founder and director of the Swedish Institute for Sexual Research, a Diplomate of Sexology, and certified Sex Therapist. She organized the 1976 International Symposium of Sex Education and Therapy in Stockholm and served as Vice-President of the European Federation of Sexology. A registered midwife, she has authored several books on sex education and films, including *The Swedish Hite Report*. Tysbergavagen 41, Stockholm S-12241 Enskede, Sweden; maj.briht@pi.se

## Switzerland:

PROFESSOR JOHANNES BITZER is head of the division of psychosomatic obstetrics and gynecology in psychosocial medicine at the Department of Obstetrics and Gynecology, University Hospital Basle. A gynecologist and psychotherapist, Professor Bitzer's research interests include family planning, menopause, sexology, somatoform disorders, and teaching of psychosomatic obstetrics and gynecology.

DR. SIBIL TSCHUDIN. MD. An obstetrician and gynecologist, Dr. Taschudin is Senior Lecturer in the division of psychosomatic obstetrics and gynecology, Department of Obstetrics and Gynecology at the University of Basle. Her main fields of research are in adolescent gynecology, contraception, and sexology.

DR. JUDITH ALDER is a psychologist in the division of psychosomatic obstetrics and gynecology in psychosocial medicine. Her main research interests are in psychooncology, education, and body-image changes.

DR. ELISABETH ZEMP, Ph.D., is based in the Institute of Preventive and Social Medicine, University of Basle. Her main research focuses on women's health, the epidemiology of women's health, HIV, cancer, therapeutic abortion, and other issues.

PROFESSOR UDO RAUCHFLEISCH is a psychologist and former head psychologist of the Department of Psychiatry outpatient department. Professor Rauchfleisch is a leading researcher in a variety of fields in psychology and psychiatry: dissocial behavior, homosexuality, transsexualism, personality disorders, diagnostic classification and procedures in psychology and psychiatry, test psychology, and others.

KOSTKA ULRIKE is a theologian in the Division of medical ethics in medicine. His main interest is in the ethics of reproductive medicine.

## Tanzania:

PHILIP SETEL, Ph.D., is Project Director of the Adult Morbidity and Mortality Project of the Tanzanian Ministry of Health and a Reader in Health Transition Studies and Principal Research Associate at the University of Newcastle upon Tyne. He has written extensively on AIDS, sexuality, fertility, and gender in Tanzania and Papua New Guinea. His 1999 book, *A Plague of Paradoxes: AIDS, Culture, and Demography in Northern Tanzania* (University of

Chicago Press) was one of the first extended case studies of AIDS in Africa. Project Director, Adult Morbidity and Mortality Project (AMMP), Tanzanian Ministry of Health, P.O. Box 65243, Dar es Salaam, Tanzania; setel.ammp@twiga.com

YUSUSF HEMED, M.D., a District Medical Officer, Regional Medical Officer, and Consultant Gynaecologist/Obstetrician, Dr. Hemed was Director of Hospital Services Ministry of Health, Tanzania, before becoming the Deputy Project Director of the Adult Morbidity and Mortality Project of the Tanzanian Ministry of Health. He has been involved extensively with Reproductive Health work in Tanzania and recently designed the National Monitoring and Evaluation Framework for the Multisectoral Response to the HIV/AIDS epidemic in Tanzania. hemed@cats-net.com

ELEUTHER MWAGENI, Ph.D., is Senior Lecturer in Demography and Population Studies in the Development Studies Institute, Sokoine University of Agriculture, Morogor, Tanzania. In addition to teaching demography and population studies to graduate and undergraduate students, he has been extensively involved in evaluating programs for teenage mothers and youth centers, the Family Planning Association of Tanzania, and collecting demographic and health-status data for the Ministry of Health. mwageni@suanet.ac.tz, mwageni@hotmail.com, *or* emwageni@yahoo .co.uk

*Comments*: BELDINA OPIYO-OMOLO, B.Sc. (See Associate Editor listing.)

## Thailand:

KITTIWUT JOD TAYWADITEP, Ph.D., grew up in northern Thailand. After he graduated from the medical school at the Chiang Mai University, he became involved in HIV/AIDS education, prevention, counseling, and research on human sexuality and HIV-risk. His work in Thailand was funded by the Center for AIDS Prevention Studies at the University of California, San Francisco. He received a doctoral degree in clinical psychology from the University of Illinois at Chicago (UIC). His work in Chicago has focused on gender, sexuality, prejudice, GLBT psychology, and HIV-risk prevention. He currently works as a staff psychologist at the Counseling Center at UIC. University of Illinois at Chicago, Counseling Center (MC 333), 2010 SSB 1200 W. Harrison, Chicago IL 60607 USA; kittiwut@uic.edu

PACHARIN DUMMRONGGITTIGULE, M.S. has been an instructor in biology at Payap University, Thailand, since 1986. She has been the principle investigator on a HIV-prevention project among married couples in northern Thai villages, and is a Senior Program Officer at the Thailand Research Fund in Bangkok.

ELI COLEMAN, Ph.D. Director and professor in the Program in Human Sexuality at the University of Minnesota Medical School, he is a past president and Fellow of the Society for the Scientific Study of Sexuality, secretary of the World Association for Sexology, and editor of the *Journal of Psychology of Human Sexuality*. A key organizer in the World Association for Sexology, he has many publications to his credit and has done field research in sexology in Thailand. Human Sexuality Program, University of Minnesota, 1300 South Second Street, Minneapolis MN 55454 USA; colem001@tc.umn.edu

Comments by RYAN BISHOP, Ph.D., associate professor of English and American Studies at the National University of Singapore and coauthor of *Night Market: Sexual Cultures and the Thai Economic Miracle* and several other works on commercial sex in Thailand. Department of English, National University of Singapore, AS5, Singapore 117570; llrb@nus.edu.sg. LILLIAN S. ROBINSON, Ph.D., Coauthor of *Night Market: Sexual Cultures and the Thai*

*Economic Miracle*, Dr. Robinsone is Professor of Women's Studies and Principal of the Simone de Beauvoir Institute at Montreal's Concordia University. Simone de Beauvoir Institute, Concordia University, 1455 de Maisonneuve Boulevard West-MU 201, Montreal, QC H3G 1M8 Canada; robinson@vax2.concordia.ca

## Turkey:

HAMDULLAH AYDIN, M.D., is professor of psychiatry at the Gulhane Military Medical Academy and Faculty of Medicine in Ankara. Following postdoctoral study and research at Baylor College of Medicine in Houston, Texas (1983-1984), much of his clinical work and education focuses on sexual dysfunctions, neuropsychology, and neurophysiology. Among his recent professional articles (in Turkish) are *Sexuality and Sexual Function* and *Psychopharmacological Treatment in Sexual Dysfunctions*. S. Adem Yavuz Sok 9/11, 06440 Kizilay, Ankara, Turkey; haydin@gata.edu.tr

ZEYNEP GÜLÇAT, Ph.D., is currently a clinical psychologist at the Gulhane Military Medical Academy and Faculty of Medicine in Ankara, Turkey. Her main interest is in sexual dysfunctions and neuropsychology. Among her recent professional publications (in Turkish) are *A Study on the Psychology of Impotence, Paraphilias and Incest*, and *Sexual Identity and Sexual Orientation Disorder*. Fevzi Çakmak Sok, 41/A-5, 06440 Kizilay, Ankara, Turkey; zeygul@superonline.com

## Ukraine:

TAMARA HOVORUN (GOVORUN), Ph.D., is chair of the psychology department, assistant professor, and postdoctoral researcher at the Ukrainian Pedagogical University in Kiev, Ukraine. She is also the head of the psychological department of Kiev's Research Sexology and Andrology Center, a member of the Ukrainian Psychologists' Society, and chairman of Sexual Education in the Ukrainian Sexologists Society. Her research in sex education, psychosexual development, and psychotherapy of sexual disorders has led to many publications. Psychology Chair, Ukrainian Pedagogical University, 9 Pirogova Street, Kijiv 252030 Ukraine *or* 4/2 Solomjanska str. Apart. 111, Kijiv 252110 Ukraine; dhovorun@imbg.org.ua

BORYS M. VORNIK, Ph.D. Dr. Vornik is director of Kiev's Research Sexology and Andrology Center, vice-president of the All-Union Sexologists' Association (Ukraine), and chief of the Ukranian Commission for Transsexual Persons. P.O. Box 274, Kiev, 34 Ukraine 252034. vornik@un.kiev.ua

## United Kingdom:

KEVAN R. WYLIE, M.B., Ch.B., M.Med.Sc., M.R.C. Psych., D.S.M., coordinated and authored several sections for the U.K. chapter. He is a consultant psychiatrist at the Whiteley Wood Clinic and specialist in sexual medicine at the Clinic, Community Mental Health Care Directorate in Sheffield. A recent publication is *Physical Treatments of Sexual Dysfunction* in the Royal College of Psychiatry Monograph Series. In addition to recruiting and coordinating the specialists who created chapter, Dr. Wylie authored Section 5C5 on heterosexual behaviors, Section 8 on significant unconventional sexual behaviors, Section 12 on sexual dysfunctions and therapies, and Section 13 on advanced education, research and sexological organizations. Whiteley Wood Clinic, Woofindin Road, Sheffield S10 3TL England, UK; mail@kevanwylie.co.uk *or* k.r.wylie@sheffield.ac.uk

ANTHONY BAINS, B.A., is a gay men's community worker at the Centre for HIV and Sexual Health in Sheffield. His interests include HIV prevention in gay and bisexual men. (Section 6 on homosexual, lesbian and bisexual issues.) Sheffield Centre for HIV & Sexual Health, 22 Collegiate Crescent, Sheffield S10 2BA UK.

TINA BALL, Ph.D., is a consultant clinical psychologist in learning disabilities, she also works as a member of the clinical team at the Porterbrook Clinic, a National Health Service for sexual and relationship difficulties. A specialist working with people with disabilities and sexual problems, she authored Section 5D on sexuality and persons with disabilities. Porterbrook Clinic, c/o Whiteley Wood Clinic, Woofindin Road, Sheffield S10 3TL UK.

PATRICIA BARNES, M.A., C.Q.S.W., BASMT(Accred.), UKCP registered psychotherapist, is director and clinician of the sex and marital therapy clinic, at the Psychiatric and Psychological Consultant Service in London. Editor of a 1994 special issue of the journal of the British Association for Sex and Marital Therapy on sex education, she also coauthored *Woman's Guide to Loving Sex*. (Coauthored Section 3 on sexual knowledge and education.) British Association for Sex & Marital Therapy, 7 Grange Park Place, Thruston Rd., Wimbledon, London SW20 0EE UK.

ROHAN COLLIER, Ph.D., principal women's advisor at the London Borough of Hendon, specializes in issues of sexual harassment and domestic violence. (Section 8B on sexual harassment.) 1 Old Palace Lane, Richmond Surrey, England 7W9 1PG UK.

JANE CRAIG, M.B., Ch.B., MRCP (UK), is registrar in genitourinary medicine at the Royal Hallamshire Hospital (Sheffield), where she manages the clinical aspects of genital herpes and HIV/AIDS. (Coauthored Section 10 on HIV/AIDS.) c/o Department of Genitourinary Medicine, Royal Hallamshire Hospital, Glossof Road, Sheffield, S10 2JF UK.

LINDA DELANY, L.L.B., M.Jur., Solicitor, is a senior lecturer in the School of Law at Manchester Metropolitan University, where her interests focus of legal issues of healthcare. (Section 9C on abortion.) All Saints Oxford Road, Manchester, UK.

JULIA FIELD, B.A., is one of four authors of *Sexual Behaviour in Britain: The National Survey of Attitudes and Lifestyles* (1994). She coauthored Section 5C on interpersonal heterosexual adult behavior. Social and Community Planning Research, 35 Northampton Square, London EC1V 0AX UK.

DANYA GLASER, MBBS, D.CH., FRCPsych, is a consultant child and adolescent psychiatrist working with the victims of child sexual and emotional abuse. Her publications include coauthoring *Child Sexual Abuse* (1993), as well as authoring section 5A/B on heterosexual behavior of children and adolescents. Dept. of Psychological Medicine, Great Ormond Street Hospital for Children, London WC1N 3JH UK.

PETER GREENHOUSE, M.A., MRCOG, MFFP, a consultant in sexual health at Ipswich Hospital, where he develops and integrates sexual health education with holistic clinical care, particularly in the management of sexually transmitted diseases. (Section 10 on sexually transmitted diseases.) Department of Sexual Health, Ipswich Hospital, Ipswich IP4 5PD UK.

MARY GRIFFIN, M.B., M.Sc., MFFP, is joint academic coordinator in the diploma program in couple relationship and sexual dysfunction at London's Institute of Psychiatry, and clinical assistant in the Sexual Therapy Clinic at the Maudsley Hospital. (Section 9B on teenage pregnancy.) Room 56, O.P.D., Maudsley Hospital, Denmark Hill, London SE5 8AZ UK.

MARGOT HUISH, B.A., BASMT (Accred.), holds a diploma in human sexuality from St. George's Hospital Medical School, the University of London, where she is a course tutor and a sexual relationship therapist at Barnet General Hospital. (Section 4 on autoerotic behaviors and patterns.) 96 Hadley Road, New Barnet Herts EN5 5QR UK.

ANNE M. JOHNSON, M.A., M.Sc., M.D., is a staff member of the Academic Department of Genito-urinary Medicine, Mortimer Market Centre, in London and one of the four coauthors of *Sexual Behaviour in Britain: The National Survey of Attitudes and Lifestyles* (1994). (Section 5 on Interpersonal Heterosexual Adult Behavior.) Academic Department of Genitourinary Medicine, Mortimer Market Centre, off Capper Street, London WC1E 6AU UK.

GEORGE KINGHORN, M.D. FRCP, is clinical director for communicable diseases in the Central Sheffield University Hospitals, chairman of the Royal College of Physicians Genitourinary Medicine Committee, and has published widely, particularly on genital ulcer diseases, the control of sexually transmitted diseases, and the treatment of HIV infection and AIDS. (Section 11 on HIV/AIDS.) c/o Department of Genitourinary Medicine, Royal Hallamshire Hospital, Glossof Road, Sheffield, S10 2JF UK.

HELEN MOTT, B.A. (Hons.) (social psychology) is a doctoral student in psychology at Lancaster University, specializing in sexual harassment. (Section 8B on sexual harassment.) 82 Pembroke Road, Clifton, Bristol BS8 3EG UK.

PAULA NICOLSON, Ph.D., lectures in health psychology in the Department of Psychiatry, the Centre for Health and Related Research at Sheffield University. Chair elect of the British Psychological Society's Psychology of Women Section, she coauthored *Applied Psychology for Social Workers* (1990), and coedited *The Psychology of Women's Health and Health Care* (1992) and *Female Sexuality* (1994). (Section 2 on ethnic and religious influences.) Dept. of Psychiatry, Sheffield Centre for Health & Related Research, Regent Court, 30 Regent Street, Sheffield S14 DA UK.

JANE READ, B.A.(Hons.), a UKCP registered psychotherapist accredited by the British Association for Sexual and Marital Therapy, holds Diplomas in counseling and in human sexuality. Her publications include *Counseling for Fertility Problems* (1995) and a 1995 article on "Female Sexual Dysfunction" in the *International Review of Psychiatry*. (Section 9C on abortion.) 16 Hatfield Road, Chiswick, London W4 1AF UK.

FRAN READER, FRCOG, MFFP, BASMT (Accred.), is a consultant in family planning and reproductive health in the Reproductive and Sexual Health Care Centre at Ipswich Hospital, NHS Trust, Ipswich, Suffolk. (Section 9A on contraception.) Old Rectory, 100 Seckford Street, Woodbridge, Suffock 1P12 4LZ UK.

GWYNETH SAMPSON, DPM, MRCPsych., is an honorary lecturer at the University of Sheffield and a consultant psychiatrist at the Porterbrook Clinic in Sheffield. (Section 7 on gender diversity.)

PETER SELMAN, Ph.D., DPSA, senior lecturer and head of the department of social policy at the University of Newcastle upon Tyne, has published extensively on family planning services, population studies, demographic analysis, and comparative social policy. In addition to books on *Society and Fertility* (1979) and *Family Planning* (1987), he authored Section 9D on population planning.

JOSÉ M. A. HERBERT-PARDO VON BÜHLER, R.M.N., CPN, Dip.H.S., is a specialist in Human Sexuality and Relationship Psychotherapy, Cardinal Clinic, Bishops Lodge, Oakley Green, Berkshire. Author of *Human Sexuality and Relationship Psychotherapy*, he also coauthored section 3 on sexual knowledge and education.

JANE WADSWORTH, B.Sc., M.Sc., a staff member at the Department of Epidemiology and Public Health, St. Mary's Hospital Medical School, London. She is also coauthor of *Sexual Behaviour in Britain: The National Survey of Attitudes and Lifestyles* (1994). (Section 5 on Interpersonal Heterosexual Adult Behavior.)

KAYE WELLINGS, M.A., M.Sc., works in the AIDS Public Education in Europe department at the London School of Hygiene and Tropical Medicine. She is one of the four authors of *Sexual Behaviour in Britain: The National Survey of Attitudes and Lifestyles* (1994). (Section 5 on Interpersonal Heterosexual Adult Behavior). AIDS Public Education in Europe, London School of Hygiene and Tropical Medicine, Keppel Street, London WC1E 7HT UK.

STEPHEN WHITTLE, Ph.D., M.A., L.L.B., is a lecturer in law at the School of Law, Manchester Metropolitan University, where he specializes in issues of gender, sex, sexuality, and the law. Vice-president of Press for Change, he coauthored Section 7 on gender diversity. School of Law, Manchester Metropolitan University, Hathersage Rd., Manchester M13 0JA UK.

## The United States of America:

DAVID L. WEIS. Ph.D., coeditor, is currently a professor of human development and family studies at Bowling Green State University in Ohio. A member of and officer for the National Council on Family Relations, the Society for the Scientific Study of Sexuality, and the International Network on Personal Relationships, he also served as an associate editor for the *Journal of Sex Research*. Weis has published numerous research articles in professional journals in such areas as adolescent sexuality, marital exclusivity, marital and sexual belief systems, sexual interaction processes, peer education programming, and has conducted workshops in these areas, as well as in interpersonal communications, intimacy, flirtation behavior, dual-career marriages, and black families. Weis received the Hugo Beigel Award for Outstanding Sexuality Research for his study of the emotional reactions to first intercourse. (Introduction; Section 1, Basic Sexological Premises; and Section 5, Interpersonal Heterosexual Behaviors.) Bowling Green State University, Family and Consumer Science, Bowling Green, OH 43403-0001 USA; weis@bgnet.bgsu.edu

PATRICIA BARTHALOW KOCH, Ph.D., coeditor of the United States of America chapter, is an associate professor of biobehavioral health and health education at Pennsylvania State University. She earned a master's degree in the Program in Human Sexuality, Marriage, and Family Life Education at New York University and studied in Japan and Sweden. Her doctorate is in health education from Pennsylvania State University, specializing in sexuality education, sexual health issues, human development, and counseling. She has many publications, including a textbook, *Exploring Our Sexuality: An Interactive Text* (Kendall/Hunt). (Section 3, Sexuality Knowledge and Education; and Section 9, Contraception and Abortion.) Pennsylvania State University, 304 East Henderson Bldg., University Park, PA 16802 USA; p34@psu.edu

*Biographical Sketches: Section Authors/Updaters:*

Most of the following contributors are active members of the Society for the Scientific Study of Sexuality, and several have held national or regional offices in the Society.

DIANE E. BAKER is completing her doctoral dissertation on child sexual abuse in the Psychology Department at Syracuse University, Syracuse, New York. (Section 8A, Incest and Child Sexual Abuse.)

SUSAN BARGAINNIER, Ed.D., is an assistant professor at the State University of New York in Oswego, specializing in wellness promotion. (A Door to the Future: Sexuality on the Information Superhighway.)

MARK O. BIGLER, Ph.D., is a lifelong member of the Church of Jesus Christ of the Latter-Day Saints, a graduate of New York University's doctoral program in human sexuality, and director of community education programs at the Utah AIDS Foundation. (Section 2A, Sexuality and the Church of Jesus Christ of the Latter-Day Saints.)

WALTER BOCKTING, Ph.D., an Assistant Professor at the Program in Human Sexuality, Department of Family Practice and Community Health, University of Minnesota Medical School, he is editor of *Masturbation as a Means of Achieving Sexual Health* (2003). (Section 4B, Autoeroticism.)

PEGGY CLARKE, M.P.H., is former president of the American Social Health Association and former assistant commissioner for AIDS Program Services of the New York City Department of Health. She currently teaches health education at Fashion Institute of Technology (State University of New York) in Manhattan. (Section 10A, HPV and Cervical Cancer)

SARAH C. CONKLIN, Ph.D., earned an M.A. degree in guidance and counseling from the University of St. Thomas, an M.A. in theology from United Theological Seminary of the Twin Cities (Minneapolis-St. Paul), and a Ph.D. in human sexuality education from the University of Pennsylvania. She is currently an assistant professor of health and sexuality education at the University of Wyoming (Laramie). (Section 12, Clergy Education).

AL COOPER, Ph.D., director of the San Jose Marital and Sexuality Centre, edited the first professional book on *Sex and the Internet: A Guidebook for Clinicians* (Brunner-Routledge, 2003). alcooper@myinternetcity.com. (Online Sexual Activity.)

MARTHA CORNOG, M.A., M.S. (See listing above for Associate Editors.) (Section 4, Autoeroticism, and Section 12, Sexuality Research and Advanced Education.)

RICHARD CROSS, M.D., pioneered medical school sexuality education while he was a professor at the Robert Wood Johnson School of Medicine at Rutgers University, New Brunswick, NJ. (Section 12E, Medical School Education.)

SUSAN DUDLEY, Ph.D., has been involved with reproductive issues throughout her career: from basic physiological research on reproduction, to an NIH-sponsored faculty appointment in the Department of Obstetrics and Gynecology at Pennsylvania State University Medical School, and as Deputy Director at the National Abortion Federation (NAF) from 1998 to 2003. (Section 9C, Abortion.)

WARREN FARRELL, Ph.D., the author of *Why Men Are the Way They Are*, *The Myth of Male Power*, and *Women Can't Hear What Men Don't Say*, has taught at the School of Medicine at the University of California in San Diego, as well as in psychology, women's studies, sociology, and political science. He is a former Board Member of N.O.W. in NYC, an American Board of Sexology Certified Sex Therapist, and frequent keynoter at sexuality conferences. www.warrenfarrell.com; warren@warrenfarrell.com (Section 2B, Emerging Men's Perspectives on Sexuality.)

MARILYN A. FITHIAN, Ph.D., is cofounder of the Center for Marital and Sexual Studies, Long Beach, California, and coauthor of *Treatment of Sexual Dysfunction*, *Any Man Can*, and other works. (Section 12, Sexual Dysfunctions and Therapies.)

JAMES R. FLECKENSTEIN is President and CEO of the Institute for 21st Century Relationships, a charitable education and research organization dedicated to fostering and supporting complete freedom of relationship choice among consenting adults. (Section 5C, Polyamory.)

JEANNIE FORREST, M.Ed., worked for seven years as a family educator with the Church of the Latter-Day Saints and was married to a Mormon. She earned an M.Ed. degree in health education in the Human Sexuality Program at New York University. (Section 2A, Sexuality and the Church of Jesus Christ of the Latter-Day Saints.)

ANDREW D. FORSYTH is a fourth-year graduate student in clinical psychology in the Department of Psychology at Syracuse University whose interests include the assessment of high-risk sexual behaviors among at-risk groups. (Section 10: HIV/AIDS.)

ROBERT T. FRANCOEUR, Ph.D. (See listing under Editors.) (Sections 2, Religious Values, 4, Autoerotic Behavior, 5, Sexuality and Older Persons, 8, Sexual Harassment, Prostitution, and Pornography, 10, STDs, 12, Research Assessment, and Conclusion: "Call to Action.")

BARBARA GARRIS, M.A., earned a bachelor's degree in anthropology and sociology at Mountclair State University and did graduate studies at New York University in women's studies. She worked for AT&T. (Legal Challenges to Free Speech on the Internet.)

PATRICIA GOODSON, Ph.D. After a master's degree in philosophy of education from the Pontificia Universidade Catolica de Campinas, Brazil, and an M.A. in general theological studies (Covenant Theological Seminary, St. Louis, MO), she completed her doctorate in health education at the University of Texas (Austin). She is currently an assistant professor in health at the University of Texas (San Antonio). (Section 12: Clergy Education.)

ERICA GOODSTONE, Ph.D., received her doctorate in human sexuality, marriage, and family living at New York University. Former Science and Research Chair and board member (U.S. Association for Body Psychotherapy), Chair and Professor/Health & Physical Education (FIT/SUNY), Dr. Goodstone is a certified sex therapist, licensed and board-certified marriage and family therapist, and massage and bodywork therapist. DrErica@sexualreawakening.com. (Section 11C, Holistic and Touch Therapies.)

KAREN ALLYN GORDON, M.P.H., Ph.D. (cand.), a researcher, teacher, and administrator in public health and health education for over 25 years in nonprofit and university health settings, focuses her work on sexuality education, personal health promotion, substance-use prevention, implementation of U.S. national health objectives, and teacher training. She currently teaches at Fashion Institute of Technology/SUNY and the College of New Jersey. (Section 10A, STDs.)

ERIC GRIFFIN-SHELLEY, Ph.D., a licensed psychologist in private practice (Lafayette Hill, PA), specializes in sexual addiction treatment. He has authored *Sex and Love: Addiction Treatment and Recovery* (1991) and edited *Adolescent Sex and Love Addicts* (1994). Ericgs1@aol.com. (Online Sexual Activity.)

WILLIAM E. HARTMAN, Ph.D., recently deceased, was cofounder of the Center for Marital and Sexual Studies, Long Beach, California, and coauthor of *Treatment of Sexual Dysfunction*, *Any Man Can*, and other works. (Section 12, Sexual Dysfunctions and Therapies.)

ROBERT W. HATFIELD, Ph.D., is an adjunct professor of psychology at the University of Cincinnati (Ohio) and associate director of the university's Psychological Services Center. A board-certified sexual counselor and therapist, Dr. Hatfield is particularly interested in the therapeutic effects of touch (somatosensory stimulation). (Section 11, Sexual Dysfunction)

ROBERT HAWKINS, Ph.D., former associate dean of the School of Allied Health Professions at the Health Sciences Center of the State University of New York at Stony Brook, is also coauthor of *Counseling Lesbian Women and Gay Men: A Life-Issues Approach*. (Section 6, Homosexual and Lesbian Issues.)

LINDA L. HENDRIXSON, Ph.D., focused her doctoral dissertation for the human sexuality program at New York University on issues of HIV-positive women in rural northwestern New Jersey. She has taught at various New Jersey and Pennsylvania universities and published on issues related to sexuality and health education. (Section 10B, Emerging Issues in HIV/AIDS)

BARRIE J. HIGHBY, Ph.D., is a clinical psychologist in the U.S. Air Force at the Ramstein Air Force Base in Germany. She completed her Ph.D. in Psychology at the University of Kansas in 2001. Her research was on perceptions of the causes and prevention of rape. (Section 8A, Sexual Coercion and Rape.)

LORAINE HUTCHINS, Ph.D., a sexologist and sex coach in Washington, DC, she has researched contemporary forms of sacred sexualities in the U.S., and coedited the groundbreaking anthology *Bi Any Other Name: Bisexual People Speak Out*. Her latest research, a book on *Harlots and Healers*, examines the emerging professions of sex coaching, sacred intimacy, and sexological bodywork. lorainehutchins@starpower.net (Section 2A, Spirituality and Sexuality Movements.)

MICHAEL HYDE, M.F.A., Ph.D. (cand.), is completing doctoral work at New York University and has conducted social research concerning the intersection of gay identity and public aesthetics. His dissertation examines the prescriptive use of literature during the last century as a moralizing agent in American education and homosexual culture. He teaches writing, short fiction, and gay and lesbian literature at Fashion Institute of Technology/SUNY in Manhattan. (Gay and Lesbian Literature)

ARIADNE (ARI) KANE, Ed.D., is a nationally known gender specialist, author, and educator, as well as a diplomat of the American Board of Sexology. (Section 7, Gender Diversity and Transgender Issues.)

SHARON KING, M.S.Ed., graduated from the Human Sexuality Program at the University of Pennsylvania where she completed all but her dissertation for the doctorate. Her specialty is survivor therapy. (Section 8A, Child Sexual Abuse and Incest.)

JOHN MONEY, Ph.D., is professor emeritus of pediatrics and of medical psychology at the Johns Hopkins School of Medicine. Among the many national and international honors he has received are the Harry Benjamin Distinguished Scholar Award, the Masters and Johnson Award, and a special award from the National Institute of Child Health and Human Development on the occasion of its 25th anniversary. Author of numerous seminal and pioneering works on gender and psychosexual development, his major works include: *The Adam Principle: Genes, Genitals, Hormones, & Gender*; *The Principles of Developmental Sexology*; *Vandalized Lovemaps*; *Venuses Penuses*; *Gay, Straight and Inbetween*; *Lovemaps*; and *The Destroying Angel*. (Epilogue.)

ROBERT MORGAN LAWRENCE, D.C., is on the Board of Advisors of San Francisco Sex Information. He lectures extensively about sexuality and health. (Section 6B, Bisexuality.)

BRENDA LOVE is author of the *Encyclopedia of Unusual Sex* and has worked at the Institute for the Advanced Study of Human Sexuality in San Francisco. (Section 8D, Paraphilic Behaviors.)

CHARLENE L. MUEHLENHARD, Ph.D., is an associate professor of psychology and women's studies at the University of Kansas. Her research focuses on rape and other forms of sexual coercion, as well as on communication and miscommunication about sex. (Section 8A, Sexual Coercion and Rape.)

RAYMOND J. NOONAN, Ph.D. (See listing under Editors and the chapter on Outer Space and Antarctica.) (Sections 1C, Sex and Terrorism, 2B, Heterophobia, 8A, Clergy Sexual Abuse, and False Accusations of Sexual Harassment and Rape, 10B, Impact of AIDS on Our Perception of Sex, 11E, Sex Surrogates, 12A, Gender Differences in Sex Research, Sex in American Popular Culture and in Music Lyrics, and Conclusion: "Call to Action.")

MIGUEL A. PERÉZ, Ph.D., teaches kinesiology at the Fresno campus of the California State University, where he also pursues an interest in sexuality. (Section 2B, Latino Sexuality.)

TIMOTHY PERPER, Ph.D. (See listing under Associate Editors, and Preface.) (Section 2A, Religious Values and Sexuality.)

HELDA L. PINZÓN-PERÉZ, Ph.D., is a Colombian-born nurse with wide experience in public health. A professor at Pennsylvania State University, her research interest include Latino/a health issues, community health, and Latino/a adolescent health. (Section 2B, Latino Sexuality.)

WILLIAM E. PRENDERGAST, Ph.D., a clinical psychologist at the New Jersey State, Adult Diagnostic and Treatment Center for sex offenders for 30 years, is the author of the *Merry-Go-Round of Sexual Abuse: Identifying and Treating Survivors, Sexual Abuse of Children and Adolescents*, and *Treating Sex Offenders in Correctional Institutions and Outpatient Clinics*. (Section 8A, Clergy Sexual Abuse.)

CAROL QUEEN has written extensively on bisexuality and other topics related to sexual diversity, including *Exhibitionism for the Shy: Show Off, Dress Up, and Talk Hot* (1995). She is a cultural sexologist in the doctorate program at the Institute for Advanced Study of Human Sexuality. (Section 6B, Bisexuality.)

RUTH P. RUBINSTEIN, Ph.D., is an associate professor of sociology at the Fashion Institute of Technology/State University of New York in Manhattan. Her research and publications have mostly been on the phenomenon of fashion, including "Color, Circumcision, Tattoos and Scars," in *Psychology of Fashion*, and *Dress Codes and Messages in American Culture*. (Seduction of Fashion.)

HERBERT P. SAMUELS, Ph.D., is associate professor of natural and applied sciences at the City University of New York/Laguardia Community College. (Section 2B, African-American Sexuality.)

JULIAN SLOWINSKI, Psy.D., is a marital and sex therapist at Pennsylvania Hospital and faculty member at the University of Pennsylvania School of Medicine, Department of Psychiatry. (Section 11, Sexual Dysfunctions and Therapies.)

WILLIAM STACKHOUSE, Ph.D., is director of the HIV Prevention Program for the Bureau of HIV Program Services at the New York City Department of Health, and adjunct assistant professor in the Graduate Department of Applied Psychology at New York University. (Section 6, Male Homosexuality and Lesbianism.)

WILLIAM R. STAYTON, Th.D., is assistant professor of psychiatry and human behavior at Jefferson Medical College and adjunct professor in the Human Sexuality Program at Widener University (Pennsylvania) (Section 11 Sexual Dysfunctions and Therapies.)

WILLIAM TAVERNER, M.A., education director for Planned Parenthood Association of Greater Northern New Jersey, editor of *Taking Sides: Clashing Views on Controversial Issues in Human Sexuality*, and coauthor of *Positive Images: Teaching Abstinence, Contraception, and Sexua Health Educating about Abortion*, and *Streetwise to Sex-Wise: Sexuality Education for High-Risk Youth*. (Section 3 Sexuality Education, and Section 9A, Contraception.)

MITCHELL S. TEPPER, M.P.H., Ph.D., has specialized in sexuality and disabilities and received his doctorate at the University of Pennsylvania, Program in Human Sexuality. (Section 5D, Sexuality and People with Disabilities.)

C. CHRISTINE WHEELER, Ph.D., is past president of the Harry Benjamin International Gender Dysphoria Association, and a prolific speaker and writer on gender diversity, counseling, and therapy. (Section 7C, Gender Diversity.)

WALTER L. WILLIAMS, Ph.D., an ethnohistorian, professor of Anthropology, History, and Gender Studies at the University of Southern California, and author of the international award-winner, *The Spirit and the Flesh: Sexual Diversity in American Indian Culture*, and other important ethnographic studies. (Section 2B, Native American Sexuality.)

## Vietnam:

JAKOB PASTÖTTER, M.A., Ph.D. Deputy Director of the Magnus Hirschfeld Archive for Sexology at Humboldt University (Berlin) for several years, Dr. Pastoetter is a member of the Governing Board of DGSS (German Society for Social Scientific Sexuality Research), book review editor for *Sexuality and Culture*, and European Associate Editor for *CCIES*. A 1998-2000 Visiting Scholar at the Kinsey Institute for Research in Sex, Gender, and Reproduction, his doctorate is in human ontogenetics (Humboldt University, Berlin). His most recent publication is an article on "Pornography as Academic Field of Research" ["Pornographie als Akademisches Forschungsfeld"] in *Sexualmedizin* (September, 2000, *22*:247-250). Duenzelbach 10, 82272 Moorenweis, Germany. jmpastoetter@compuserve.de

## *Acknowledgments from Robert T. Francoeur, Editor*

First and foremost, I must acknowledge the crucial role of the 280 colleagues who were so convinced of the importance of this project that they took time in their busy professional lives to write on the 62 countries and places that are now in this volume. I thank each one of them for their generous dedication, the time and energy they gave to this "labor of love."

In 1995, Jack Heidenry, a dear friend of 40 some years, stepped in with an invitation to publish the first three volumes with Continuum International the same week my initial publisher refused to publish a multivolume *Encyclopedia*.

In 1996, Dr. Ray Noonan stepped into his labor with *IES* at a critical time in our early production when we needed a copyeditor and graphic design person knowledgeable in sexology. His invaluable services merited promotion to associate editor for *IES-4*, and as editor for the present volume. *CCIES* would not be if not for his calm, unflappable, and methodical creativity and skills in editing, design, and typography.

Another friend and colleague, Dr. Eli Coleman, director of the Program in Human Sexuality at the University of Minnesota Medical School, must be mentioned. Around 1995, Eli, Kittiwut Jod Taywaditep, and Pacharin Dumronggittigule produced a fascinating insider/outsider picture of sexuality in Thailand for *IES-3*. Just before *IES 1-3* went to the printer, Eli, then Secretary General of the World Association for Sexology, diplomatically facilitated WAS endorsement of *IES* as "an important and significant contribution to our understanding and appreciation of the rich diversity of human sexual attitudes, values, and behavior around the world."

The addition of several new associate editors made the challenge of creating *CCIES* a good bit smoother, so I must thank them: Luciane Raibin for her patient work as my communications bridge with our Latino and Portuguese contributors; Beldina Opiyo-Omolo, a native of Kenya and graduate student in public health administration at Stroudsburg State University, for her research and communications with a half-dozen African nations; Jakob Pastoetter, whom I met at the Kinsey Institute in time to prepare an *IES-4* chapter on Vietnam, who then joined *CCIES* as an associate editor. In the last months before publication of *CCIES*, Jakob managed to recruit a dozen enthusiastic experts to write chapters on Botswana, Denmark, Bulgaria, and Switzerland.

Time and time again, Martha Cornog and Timothy Perper, associate editors for information resources, drew on their many years of varied editorial and library experience to advise me on major content and editorial decisions. They always came through just when I needed them most.

Evander Lomke, our Senior Editor at Continuum for *IES-4* and *CCIES*, could not have been more supportive and helpful in guiding us through the intricacies of creating and publishing what started as a 400-page single volume dealing with 20 countries and ended as a unique sexological reference and resource.

Finally, we are pleased to thank UNAIDS HIV/AIDS Information and Data, www.UNAIDS.org, for granting permission to reprint their brief country-by-country Assessment of Epidemiological Situation. The assessments provided in this volume were current as of January 1, 2003, and the latest available at press time. Readers of *CCIES* are referred to the regularly updated assessments and complete information available on the Internet at www.UNAIDS.org.

# An International Directory of Sexological Organizations, Associations, and Institutes

## By Region and by Country

*Compiled by Robert T. Francoeur, Ph.D.*

Information for this International Directory was compiled from a variety of resources. Our primary resource was, of course, the authors of Section 12 in the 62 countries and places of *The Continuum Complete International Encyclopedia of Sexuality*. In addition, the Editor is happy to acknowledge the generous cooperation of Smita Palmar, at the Sexuality Information and Education Council of the U.S. (SIECUS), Mac Edwards, editor of the *SIECUS Report*, Dr. Eli Coleman, past president of the World Association of Sexology (WAS), and Howard Ruppel, Jr., Chancellor and Academic Dean of the Institute for the Advanced Study of Human Sexuality (San Francisco).

This directory covers close to 300 regional and national sexological organizations in 70 countries.

## Regional Sexological Organizations

### AFRICAN REGION:

**Center for African Family Studies**
P.O. Box 60054
Nairobi, Kenya
Tel.: 254-2/448618-20

**International Planned Parenthood Federation (IPPF)–Africa Region**
P.O. Box 30234
Nairobi, Kenya
Tel.: 254-2/720280; Fax: 254-2/726596

**International Planned Parenthood Federation (IPPF)–Sub-Region for Central & West Africa**
B.P. 4101, Lome, Togo
Tel.: 228/210716; Fax: 228/215140

**United Nations Family Planning Association (UNFPA)–South Africa**
Construction House, Fifth Floor
110 Takawira St., P.O. Box 4775
Harare, Zimbabwe
Tel.: 263-4/738793; Fax: 263-4/738792

### ASIAN, SOUTH PACIFIC, and AUSTRALIAN REGION:

**Asian Federation for Sexology (AFS)**
Dr. M.L. Ng, Chairman, Department of Psychiatry
University of Hong Kong, Queen Mary Hospital
Pokfulam Road, Hong Kong
Tel.: 852/855-4486; Fax: 852/855-1345
Email: HRMCNML@hkucc.hku.hk

**European-Asian Association of Sexologists (EAAS)**
P.O. Box 274
Kiev, 252034 Ukraine
Tel.: 380-44/446-1346; Fax: 380-44/228-0103

**International Planned Parenthood Federation (IPPF)–East and Southeast Asia Office**
246 Jalan Ampang
50450 Kuala Lumpur, Malaysia
Tel.: 60-3/456-6122; Fax: 60-3/456-6386

**United Nations Family Planning Association (UNFPA)–East and Southeast Asia Region Office**
Population Education Clearinghouse
United Nations Building
Rajdammnern Avenue
Bangkok 10200 Thailand
Tel.: 66-2/391-0577; Fax: 66-2/391-0866

**United Nations Family Planning Association (UNFPA)–South Pacific Region**
G.P.O. Box 14500
Suva, Fiji
Tel.: 679/31-2865; Fax: 679/30-4877

**United Nations Family Planning Association (UNFPA)–East and Southeast Asia Region Office**
Population Education Clearing House
United Nations Building
Rajdammnern Ave.
Bangkok 10200 Thailand
Tel.: 66-2/391-0577; Fax: 66-2/391-0866

### EUROPE and the MIDDLE EAST REGION

**European Federation of Sexology (EFS)**
Universitaire Maurice Clalumeau
55 Boulevard de la Cluse
CH-1205 Geneva, Switzerland
Tel.: 41-22/347-3031; Fax: 41-22/320-9286

**European-Asian Association of Sexologists (EAAS)**
P.O. Box 274
Kiev, 252034 Ukraine
Tel.: 380-44/446-1346; Fax: 380-44/228-0103

**International Planned Parenthood Federation (IPPF)–Arab World Region**
2 Place Virgile
Norte Dame
1082 Tunis, Tunisia
Tel.: 216-1/894-173; Fax: 216-1/789-934

**United Nations Family Planning Association (UNFPA)–Arab States and Europe**
P.O. Box 830824
Amman 11183 Jordan
Tel.: 962-6/817040; Fax: 962-6/816580

**World Health Organization (WHO)–European Region**
Scherfigsvej 8, DK-2100
Copenhagen, Denmark 10130
Tel.: 45/39-171717; Fax: 45/39-171818
Email: postmaster@who.dk; Web: www.who.dk

### WESTERN HEMISPHERE— the AMERICAS:

**International Planned Parenthood Federation–Western Hemisphere Region (IPPF/WHR)**
(Latin and South America, including the Caribbean)
902 Broadway, Tenth Floor
New York, NY 10010 USA
Tel.: 212/995-8800; Fax: 212/995-8853
Email: info@ippf.org; Web: www.ippf.org

## Sexological Organizations: Alphabetical by Country

### ARGENTINA

**Asociacion Argentina de Sexologia y Educacion Sexual (AASES)**
Cuba 2243-9°A
Buenos Aires, 1428 Argentina
Tel.: 54-1/782-1614; Fax: 54-1/812-2770

**Centro de Educacion, Terapia e Investigacion en Sexualidad (CETIS)**
Darregueyra 2247–Dto "B"
1425 Capital Federal
Buenos Aires, Argentina
Tel.: 54-1/773-4141; Fax: 54-1/777-3459

**Circulo Argentino de Sexologia**
Callao 1178, 7 B
Buenos Aires, 1425 Argentine

**Sociedad Argentina de Sexualidad Humana**
Dr. León Guimdim, Director
Darragueira 2247, P.B. "B"
1425 Buenos Aires, Argentina

# AUSTRALIA

**Australian Association of Sex Educators, Counselors, and Therapists (AASERT)**
P.O. Box 346
Lane Cove, NSW, 2066 Australia
Tel.: 61-2/427-1292
*Also*: 21 Carr Street
Coogee, New South Wales 2034 Australia

**Family Planning Australia, Inc.**
Lua Building, Suite 3, First Floor
39 Geils C, P.O. Box 9026
Deakin, ACT 26000 Australia
Tel.: 61-6/282-5298; Fax: 61-6/285-1244

**Family Planning Victoria**
266-272 Church Street
Richmond 3121 Australia
Tel.: 61-3/429-1868

**Western Australian Sexology Society**
c/FPA 70 Roe Street
Northbridge, Western Australia 6000 Australia

# AUSTRIA

**Austrian Planned Parenthood Society (Österreichisches Gesellschaft für Familienplanung, ÖGF)**
Bastiengasse 36-38
A-1180 Vienna, Austria

**Austrian Society for Research in Sexology. (Österreichische Gesellschaft für Sexualforschung ÖGS)**
Postfach 23
A-1013 Vienna, Austria

**Austrian Institute for Family Research (Österreichisches Institut für Familienforschung, ÖIF)**
Gonzagagasse 19
A-1010 Vienna, Austria

# BAHRAIN

**Bahrain Family Planning Association**
Al-Qufool, Bahrain
Tel: 0973-232233, 256622; Fax: 0973-276408

**Al-Farsi Library–College of Health Sciences**
P.O. Box 12, Ministry of Health
Al Sulmaniya, Bahrain
Tel: 0973 255555 ext. 5202; Fax: 0973 252569; Telex: 8511 HEALTH BN

# BELGIUM

**Federation Belge Pour le Planning Familial et l'Education Sexuelle (FFBPFLES)**
Rue de la Tulipe, 34
B-1050 Brussels, Belgium
Tel.: 32-2/502-8203; Fax: 32-2/502-5613

# BELARUS

**Institute Republicain de l'Ecole Superieure**
Prof. Anatoly Makarov
Moskovskaja Str. 15
220001 Minsk, Belarus
Fax: 375 172271736
Email: root@study.minsk.by

# BELIZE

**Belize Family Life Association**
127 Barracks Road
P.O. Box 529
Belize City, Belize

# BOLIVIA

**Asociacion Boliviana de Educacion Sexual**
Cas Correo 8158
La Paz, Bolivia

**Centro de Investigaciones Sociales**
Edificio Alborado Pico 11-1105
Box 6931, Correo Central
La Paz, Bolivia
Tel.: 591-2/352931

# BOTSWANA

**Botswana Family Welfare Association**
Private Bag 00100
Gaborone. Botswana
Tel.: 267/300489; Fax: 267/301222

# BRAZIL

**Brazilian Association of Sexology (Associação Brasieira de Sexologia–AB-SEX)**
Rua Tamandare 693-Conj. 31
São Paulo, SP, Brazil
*Also*: Dr. Sergie Luiz G. de Freitas, M.D., President
Rua Tamandare, 693, Conj. 77
01525-001 São Paulo, SP, Brazil

**Centro de Sexolgia de Brasilia**
SHIS-QI-19, Conjunto 10, Casa 6
Brasilia, DF, Brazil
Tel.: 55-61/366-4393; Fax: 55-61/366-3504

**Grupo Transas do Corpo Acoes Educativas em Saude e Sexualidade (GTC/AESS)**
Av. Anhanguera, No. 5674
Sala 1304-Centro
74039-900 Goiania-Go, Brazil
Tel./Fax: 55-62/223-3817
Email: gtcaess@ax.apc.org

**Grupo de Trabalho e Pesquisa em Orientação Sexual (GTPOS)**
Rua Monte Aprazivel, 143
Vila Nova Conceicão, CEP
04513-030 São Paulo, SP, Brazil
Tel.: 55-11/822-8249; Fax: 55-11/822-2174

**Brazilian Society for Human Sexuality (Sociedade Brasileira de Sexualidade Humana)**
Rua Amancio Moro
77 Alto da Gloria Curitiba
Parana, 80030 Brazil
*Also*: Av. N.S. Copacabana, 1072, s. 703
22020-001 Rio de Janeiro, RJ, Brazil
Tel.: 55-41/264-3424

**Sociedade Brasileira de Sexolgia**
Praca Serzedelo Correia 15, Apt. 703
Copacabana, Rio de Janeiro, 22040 Brazil
Tel.: 55-21/236-6413

**Brazilian Sexual Impotency Research Society (Sociedade Brasileira de Pesquisa sobre Impotencia Sexual)**
Roberto Tullii, M.D., Dir.
Alameda Gabriel Monteiro da Silva, 1719
01441-000 São Paulo, SP, Brazil

**Brazilian Sexual Education Association. (Associacão Brasileira de Educacão Sexual)**
Alameda Itu, 859, Apto 61
01421-000 São Paulo, SP, Brazil

**Sexology Nucleus of Rio de Janeiro (Nucleo de Sexologia do Rio de Janeiro–NUDES)**
Av Copacabana, 1018, Grupo 1109
22060-000 Rio de Janeiro, RJ, Brazil

**National Sexology Commission of the Brazilian
Federation of the Societies of Gynecology and
Obstetrics (Comission Nacional de Sexologia da
Federacão Brasileira das Sociadades de
Ginecologia e Obstetricia–FEBRASGO)**
Edf. Venancio 2000, Bloco 50, Sala 137
70302-000 Brasilia, DF, Brazil
**Paranaense Commission of Sexology (Comissal
Paranaense de Sexologia)**
Rua General Carneiro, 181, 4o andar.
Maternidade do Hosp. de Clinicas
80060-000 Curitiba, PR, Brazil
**Department of Sexology–ARE**
Varzea do Carmo
Departamento de Sexologia
Rua Leopoldo Miguez, 257
01518-000 São Paulo, SP, Brazil
**SOSCORPO**
Rua Major Codeceira
37 Sto. Amaro
Recife, Pernambuco, Brazil
Tel.: 55-81/221-3018; Fax: 55-81/221-3947
Email: soscorpo@ax.apc.org

## BULGARIA
**Bulgarian Medical Academy–Coordinating
Board of Sexology**
P.O. Box 60
Sofia 1431 Bulgaria
**Human Sexuality Research Foundation**
Dr. Petko Velichkov
16, Kosta Lulchev Str., bl. 244, app.36
Sofia 1113, Bulgaria
Email: sexology@acad.bg;
Web: http://www.sexology.bol.bg

## CAMEROON
**Cameroon National Association for
Family Welfare**
P.O. Box 11994
Yaounde, Cameroon
Tel.: 237/237984

## CANADA
**International Academy of Sex Research (IASR)**
Clarke Institute of Psychiatry Child and
Family Studies Centre
250 College Street
Toronto, Ontario M5T IR8 Canada
Tel.: 416/979-2221; Fax: 416/979-4668
Email: zucker@cs.clarke-inst.on.ca
**Sex Information and Education Council of
Canada (SIECCAN)**
850 Coxwell Avenue
East York, Ontario, M4C 5RI Canada
Tel.: 416/466-5304; Fax: 416/778-0785
Email: sieccan@web.net
**L'Association des Sexologues du Quebec**
695 St. Denis, Suite 300
Montreal, Quebec, Canada H2S 2S3
**Canadian Sex Research Forum**
c/o Pierre Assalian, M.D., Executive Director
1650 Cedar Avenue, Room B6-233
Montreal, Quebec, Canada H3G 1A4
**The Department of Sexology**
University of Quebec at Montreal (UQAM)
455 Boulevard Rene Levesque East
Montreal, Quebec, Canada H3C 3P8
**Planned Parenthood Federation of Canada**
1 Nicolas St., Suite 430
Ottawa, Ontario, Canada K1N 7B7
Tel.: 613/238-4474

## CHAD
**Association Tachadienne Pour le Bien-Etre
Familial (ASTBEF)**
ASTBEF B.P. 4064 N'Djamena
Moursal, Chad
Tel./Fax: 235/514337

## CHINA:
**Chinese Association of Sex Education**
Mercy Memorial Foundation
11F, 171 Roosevelt Road, Section 3
Taipei, Taiwan, Republic of China
Tel.: 886-2/369-6752; Fax: 886-2/365-7410
**China Family Planning Association**
1 Bei Li, Shengguzhuang, He Ping Li
Beijing, People's Republic of China
**China Sexology Association**
Number 38, Xue Yuan Lu, Haidion
Beijing 100083 People's Republic of China
Tel.: 86-1/209-1244; Fax: 86-1/209-1548
**Shanghai Family Planning Association**
122 South Shan Xi Road
Shanghai 200040 People's Republic of China
Tel.: 86-21/2794968; Fax: 86-21/2472262 X18
**Shanghai International Center for Population
Communication China (SICPC)**
14 Zhichun Road, Haidian District
122 South Shan Xi Road
Shanghai 200040 People's Republic of China
Tel.: 86-21/247-2262; Fax: 86-21/247-3049
**State Family Planning Commission**
IEC Dept.
Beijing 100088 People's Republic of China
Tel.: 86-1/204-6622; Fax: 86-1/205-1847
**Hong Kong Family Planning Association of
Hong Kong (FPAHK)**
Tenth Floor, Southern Centre
130 Hennessy Road
Wanchai, Hong Kong
Tel.: 852/575-4477; Fax: 852/834-6767
**Hong Kong Sex Education Association**
P.O. Box 50419
Sai Ying Pun, Hong Kong
Tel.: 852/819-2486
**Chinese Sex Education Research Society**
Director: Dr. Jiahuo Hong
The Shanghai College of Traditional
Chinese Medicine
530 Ling Ling Road
Shanghai 200032 People's Republic of China
**Shanghai Sex Education Research Association**
122 South Shan Xi Road
Shanghai 200040 People's Republic of China
**Institute for Research in Sexuality and Gender**
Professor Sui-ming Pan, Director
P.O. Box 23
Renmin University of China
39# Hai Dian Road
Beijing 100872 People's Republic of China
Fax: 86-1/256-6380
**Family Planning Association of Hong Kong (FPAHK)**
Tenth Floor, Southern Centre
130 Hennessy Road
Wanchai, Hong Kong
Tel.: 852/575-4477; Fax: 852/834-6767

## COLOMBIA
**Fundacion para el Desarrollo Humano y Social
CRESALC**
Calle 98A Number 34-78
Bogotá, Colombia
Tel.: 57-1/218-2906; Fax: 57-1/257-1498

**Centro de Asesoria y Consultoria**
Calle 75B # 43B, 25 piso 2
Barranquilla, Colombia
Fax: 95 356 40 40
Email: ncaclj@col3.telecom.com.co

**Fundacion Para el Desarrollo Humano y Social
CRESALC Columbia**
Calle 81 Number 11-68 Of. 406
Sante Fe de Bogotá, Colombia
Tel.: 57-1/618-0521; Fax: 57-1/618-0410

**Ministerio de Educacion–Proyecto Nacional de
Educacion Sexual**
Avenida El Dorado Can Of. 120
Sante Fe de Bogotá, D.C., Colombia
Tel.: 57-1/222-0165; Fax: 57-1/222-0165

**Profamilia**
Calle 34, Nov 14-52
Bogotá, D.C., Colombia
Tel.: 57-1/287-2100; Fax: 57-1/287-5530

**Sociedad Colombiana de Sexologia**
Apartado Aereo 3441
Cali, Colombia
Tel.: 57-2/661-4858; Fax: 57-2/668-0193

## COSTA RICA
**Programa Salud Reproductiva**
Apartado 1434-1011 Y-Griega
San José, Costa Rica

## CUBA
**Centro Iberoamericano de Formacion Pedagogica
Orintacion Educacional (CIFPOE)**
Calle 108, Number 29E08, entre 29 E y
29 F Ciudad Escolar Libertad, Marianao
La Habana, Cuba
Tel.: 33-537/206190; Fax: 33-537/331697

**Cuatrimestral Especializada del Centro Nacional de
Educacion Sexual (CENESEX)**
Callo 19, Number 851
Esquina a4, El Vedado
La Habana, Cuba
Tel.: 33-537/302679; Fax: 33-537/228382

## CZECH REPUBLIC
**Sexuologigky Ustav (Czechoslavak Sexological
Society/Institute of Sexology)**
University Karlovy, Karlov Nám_sti 32
Prague 2, 120 00 Czech Republic
Tel.: 42-2/297285; Fax: +420224966609

**SPRSV (Společnost pro Plánování Rodiny a Sexuální
Výchovu–National Family Planning Association)**
Address: Senovážná 2, Post Office Box 399
111 21 Praha 1, Czech Republic

## DENMARK
**Danish Association for Clinical Sexology (DACS)**
Gronhojgaardsvej 147, DK-2630
Taastrup, Denmark
Tel./Fax: 45/43 99 66 19
Email: dacs@klinisksexologi.dk;
Web: www.klinisksexologi.dk

**The Danish Family Planning Association**
Skindergade 28, DK-1159
Copenhagen K, Denmark
Tel.: 45/33 93 10 10; Fax: 45/33 93 10 09
Email: danish-fpa@sexogsamfund.dk;
Web: www.sexogsamfund.dk

**Danish National Association of Gays and Lesbians**
Teglgaardsstraede 13, DK-1007
Copenhagen K, Denmark
Tel.: 45/33 13 19 48
Email: lbl@lbl.dk; Web: www.lbl.dk

**SMil (sadomasochists)**
P.B. 691, DK-2200
Copenhagen N, Denmark
Tel.: 45/35 83 55 69
Email: info.kbh@sado.dk; Web: www.sado.dk

**Knowledge Center for Sexual Physiology**
Gorm Wagner, Division of Sexual Physiology
University of Copenhagen, Bartholinsgade 4
1356 Copenhagen, K. Denmark
Tel.: 33-33-38-00; Fax: 35-35-16-05
Email: mail@nilleklinge.dk; Web: www.impo-info.dk

## EGYPT
**Alexandria Model Family Planning Clinic**
17, Sidi El-Metwally Street, El-Attarien
Alexandria, 4933867 Egypt
Tel.: 20-3/493-3867

**Egyptian Family Planning Association**
66 Gazirat El Arab Street
Al Mohandissen, El Giza
Cairo, Egypt
Tel.: 20-2/360-7329; Fax: 20-2/360-7328

## ESTONIA
**Estonian Academic Society of Sexology**
Suur-Ameerika 18 A
Tallinn, Estonia 10122
Email: kliinik@amor.ee; Web: www.hot.ee/eass

**Estonian Family Planning Association**
Kotka 2
Tallinn, Estonia 11315
Email: eppl@amor.ee; Web: www.amor.ee

## FINLAND
**Seksuaalipoliittinen Yhdistys Sexpo ry SEXPO
Foundation (Säätiö) (Sexual Policy Association)**
Malminkatu 22E, 00100
Helsinki, Finland
Web: www.health.fi/sexpo

**Seksuaalinen tasavertaisuus SETA ry (Sexual
Equality Association)**
Hietalahdenkatu 2 B 16, 00180
Helsinki, Finland
Web: www.seta.fi

**Finnish Association for Sexology (FIAS)**
Population Research Institute
Family Federation of Finland
P.O. Box 849, FIN 00101
Helsinki, Finland
Web: www.seksologinenseura.net

## FRANCE
**Academie des Sciences Sexologiques**
20 Rue Vignon
Paris, 75009 France

**Association Interhospitalo Universitaire de
Sexologie (AIHUS)**
Dr. Robert Porto
21 Place Alexandre Labadié
F-13001 Marseille, France
Tel.: +33 (0) 491-76 44 89; Fax: +33 (0) 491-77 01 39
Email: robert.porto@worldonline.fr

**Centre International de Formation et de
Recherche en Sexualité (CIFRES)**
Dr. Rejean Tremblay
14, Rue Bertrand-Gril
F-31400 Toulouse, France
Tel.: +33-62-26 12 56; Fax: +33-62-26 44 13

**Ecole Française de Sexologie**
Dr. Robert Gellman
3 Rue de Copernic
F-75116 Paris, France

Tel.: +33-47-27 96 67; Fax: +33-47-04 40 57
Email: efsweb@citeweb.net;
Web: http://efsweb.citeweb.net/

**Fondateur de L'Association Mondiale de Sexology**
72, Quai Louis Bleriot
75016 Paris, France
Tel.: 30-40/50-38-99

**Enseignement de Sexologie**
Faculté de Médecine de Marseille
27, Bd. Jean Moulin
F-13005 Marseille, France
Tel.: (+33) 91 83 43 25 *or* (+33) 91 83 43 26

**Faculté de Médecine Paris XIII Bobigny**
Département des Enseignements spéciaux
UFR Santé-Médecine-Biologie Humaine, Sexologie
Mme. Nadia Ouarti-Saighi/Docteur Suzanne Kepes
74 rue Marcel Cachin
F-93017 Bobigny Cedex, France
Tel.: (+33) 48 38 76 11; Fax: (+33) 48 38 77 7

**INSERM (Institut National de la Santé et de la Recherche Médicale)**
U 292: Recherches en Santé Publique:
  Reproduction, VIH/SIDA, Sexualité
Alain Giami Hôpital de Bicôtre
82, rue du Général Leclerc
F-94276 Le Kremlin-Bicetre Cede, France
Tel.: +33-1-4521-228; Fax: +33-1-4521-2075
Email: giami@vjf.inserm.fr

**Institut de Sexologie**
Dr. Jacques Waynberg
57 Rue Charlot
F-75003 Paris, France
Tel.: +33-1-4271-1030; Fax: +33-1-4271-5115
Email: waynberg@club-internet.fr;
Web: http://www.sexologie-fr.com

**Institute Européen de Psychsomatothérapies**
Centre de Sexologie Clinique
77 Rue Lakanal
F-37000 Tours, France

**Association des Sexologues Cliniciens Francophones (ASClif)**
Présidente: Claire Gellman-Barroux
3, rue Copernic
F-75116 Paris, France
Email: asclif@citeweb.net;
Web: http://asclif.free.fr/sommaire.html
Secretary General: Ursula Pasini
62 bis Avenue de la Roseraie
CH-1205 Genève, Switzerland
Fax : (+ 41 22) 346 77 01
Email: ursulapasini@freesurf.ch

**Association Recherche Sexologique du Sud-Ouest (ARSSO), "Les Bons Enfants"**
Dr. Francis Robert, Bordeaux Rive Droite
Route Bergerac
F-33370 Fargues-St.-Hilaire, France
Tel.: (+33-56) 21 21 14

**Societé Française de Gynecologie Psychosomatique**
Dr. Sylvain Mimoun
45 rue de Maubeuge
F-75009 Paris, France
Tel.: (+33-1) 42 80 21 67

**Societé Française de Pathologie Sexuelle**
Dr. Henry Dermange
61 Avenue de Passy
F-75016 Paris France

**Societé Française de Sexologie Clinique (SFSC)**
Dr. Marc Ganem
85, Avenue Charles de Gaulle
92200–Neuvilli s/Seine, France
Tel.: (+33-1) 45 72 67 62; Fax: (+33-1) 45 72 67 63

**Syndicat National des Médecins Sexologues (S. N. M. S.)**
77 Rue Lakanal
F-37000 Tours, France

**Association Interhospitalo–Universitaire de Sexologie (AIHUS)**
Dr. Robert Porto
21 Place Alexandre Labadié
F-13001 Marseille, France
Tel.: (+33) 9195 76 96; Fax: (+33) 91 50 52 77
Email: robert.porto@worldonline.fr

**Ecole Française de Sexologie**
Dr. Robert Gellman
3 Rue de Copernic
F-75116 Paris France
Tel.: +33-47-27 96 67; Fax: +33-47-04 40 57
Email: efsweb@citeweb.net;
Web: http://efsweb.citeweb.net/

**Université d'Aix-Marseille**
Administrative Office
Enseignement de Sexologie Faculté de Médecine 27
Bd. Jean Moulin
F-13005 Marseille, France
Tel.: +33-91-83-4325 or 4326

**Sexologies–European Journal of Medical Sociology**
21, Place Alexandre Labadie
13001 Marseilles, France
Tel.: 33-91/50-20-03; Fax: 33-91/50-52-77

# GERMANY
**Aerztliche Gesellschaft zur Gesundheitsfoerderung der Frau e.V. Frauenarztin**
Am Bonneshof 30, D-40474
Dusseldorf, Germany
Tel.: 49-211/43-45-91; Fax: 49-211/43-45-03

**Archiv fur Sexualwissenschaft (The Magnus Hirschfeld Archive for Sexology)**
Humboldt University
Berlin, Germany
Web: http://www2.hu-berlin.de/sexology/

**Deutsche Gesellshaft für Sozialwissenshaftliche Sexualforshung e.V**
Gerresheimerstrasse 20, 40211
Dusseldorf 1, Germany
Tel.: 49-211/35-45-91. Web: www.sexologie.de

**Deutsche Gesellschaft für Sexualforschung**
(At the Universities of Hamburg and Frankfurt/Main)
Martinistr. 52
20251 Hamburg, Germany

**Gesellschaft für Sexualwissenschaft (Leipzig)**
Bernhard-Goering-Str. 152
04277 Leipzig, Germany

**Gesellschaft für Praktische Sexualmedizin (Kiel)**
Hospitalstr. 17-19
24105 Kiel, Germany

**Deutsche Gesellschaft für Geschlechtserziehung (Bonn/Landau)**
Westring 10A
76829 Landau, Germany

# GREECE
**Greek Society for Andrology and Sexology**
Chalcocondili 50
Athens, Greece
Tel.: 30-1/5245861

**University of Athens**
Dept. of Psychiatry
Director: C. Stefanis
74 Vas. Sophias Ave.
Athens, Greece

**Athens School of Public Health**
Dept. of Sociology
Director: Demosthenis Agrafiotis

196 Alexandras Ave.
Athens, Greece

**Athens School of Public Health**
Department of Epidemiology
Director: G. Papaevangelou
196 Alexandras Ave.
Athens, Greece

**A Syngros Hospital**
Director: G. Stratigos
6 Dragoumi
Athens, Greece

**Family Planning Association (F.P.A)**
121 Solonos
Athens, Greece

**Hellenic Society of Paediatric and
Adolescent Gyaecology (HSPAG)**
Director: C. Kreatsas
9 Kanarie Str.
Athens, Greece

## GUATEMALA

**Asociacao Guatemalteca de
Educacion Sexual**
3a Calle 4-687-1
Guatemala

## ICELAND

**Icelandic Sexology Association**
Primary Health Care Center in Reykjavik
Baronstig 47 101
Reykjavik, Iceland
Tel.: 354-1/22400; Fax: 354-1/62241

## INDIA

**Family Planning Association of India (FPAI):
Sex Education, Counseling, Research
Training Centre (SECRT)**
Bajaj Bhavan, Nariman Point
Mumbai 400 021, India
Tel.: 202 9080/202 5174; Fax: +91-22-2029038/2048513
Email: fpai@glasbm01.vsnl.net.in

**Indian Association of Sex Educators, Counselors, and
Therapists (IASECT)**
203 Sukhsagar, N.S. Patkar Marg
Bombay 400 007, India
Tel.: 91-22/361-2027; Fax: 91-22/204-8488

**Parivar Seva Sanstha**
28 Defence Colony Market
New Delhi 110-024, India
Tel.: 91-11/461-7712; Fax: 91-11/462-0785

**Sex Education, Counseling, Research
Training Centre (SECRT)**
Family Planning Association of India (FPAI)
Fifth Floor, Cecil Court, Mahakavi
Bhushan Marg
Bombay 400 039, India
Tel.: 91-22/287-4689

**National Institute for Research in Sex Education,
Counseling and Therapy (NIRSECT)**
Saiprasad, C5/11/02, Sector-4, C.B.D.
New Bombay, 4990615, India

## INDONESIA

**The Study Group on Human Reproduction**
Udayana University Medical School
Jl.Panglima Sudirman
Denpasar, Bali, Indonesia

**The Indonesian Society of Andrology**
c/o Laboratory of Pathology
Udayana University Medical School
Jl. Panglima Sudirman
Denpasar, Bali, Indonesia

**Master Program in Reproductive Medicine,
Udayana University Medical School**
Wimpie I. Pangkahila, M.D., Ph.D., Director.
Jl. Panglima Sudirman
Denpasar, Bali, Indonesia
Email: wim@denpasar.wasantara.net.id

## IRELAND

**Ireland Region of the British Association of
Sexual and Marital Therapists**
67 Pembroke Road
Dublin 4, Ireland

## ISRAEL

**Institute for Sex Therapy**
Sheba Medical Center
Tel Hashomer, Israel
Tel.: 972-3/530-3749; Fax: 972-3/535-2888

**Israel Family Planning Association**
9, Rambam Street
Tel-Aviv, 65601, Israel
Tel.: 972-3/5101511; Fax: 972-3/5102589

**Ministry of Education & Culture**
Psychological and Counseling Services
2 Devorah Hanevia Street
Jerusalem, Israel
Tel.: 972-02/293249; Fax: 972-02/293256

## ITALY

**Centro Italiano di Sessuologia**
Via della Lungarina, 65
Rome, 00153 Italy
Tel.: 39-6/51-245785

**Istituto Internazionale di Sessuologia**
Via della Scala, 85
Firenze, Italy

**Instituto di Sessuologia Clinica**
Via Fibreno 4
00199 Roma, Italy

**Società Italiana di Sessuologia Scientifica**
Istituto di Sessuologia Clinica
Via Fibreno 4
00199 Roma, Italy

**Società Italiana di Sessuologia ed Educazione Sessuale**
c/o Prof. Gabriele Traverso
Via Circonvallazione 28
10015 Ivrea, TO, Italy

**Centro Italiano di Sessuologia (CIS)**
Via della Lungarina, 65
Rome, 00153, Italy
Tel.: +39-6-51-245-785

**Instituto di Sessuologia di Savona**
17026 Noli, Via la Malfa, 5
Savona, Italy
Tel.: 39-19-748-5687; Fax: +39-19-748-5687

**Associazione per la Ricerca in Sessuologia (ARS)**
Via Angelo Cappi 1/8
16126 Genova, Italy

## IVORY COAST

**Association Ivoirienne Pour le Bien-Etre Familial**
B.P. 5315
Abidjan 01, Côte d'Ivoire

## JAPAN

**Japan Institute for Research in Education**
4-3-6-702 Kozimachi, Chiyoda-Ku
Tokyo 7102, Japan
Tel.: 03-5295-0856; Fax: 03-5295-0856

**Japanese Association for Sex Education (JASE)**
Miyata Bldg, 1-3 Kanada Jinbocho, Chiyoda-Ku
Tokyo 10, Japan
Tel.: 81-3-3291-7726; Fax: 81-3-3291-6238

**Japanese Association of Sex Educators, Counselors and Therapists (JASECT)**
JASE Clinic
3F Shin-Aoyama Bldg (West)
Minami-Aoyama,1-chome, Minato-ku
Tokyo 107, Japan

**Japanese Organization for International Cooperation in Family Planning, Inc. (JOICFP)**
1-1, Ichigaya Sadohara-cho, Shinjuku-ku
Tokyo 162, Japan
Tel.: 81-3/3268-5875; Fax: 81-3/3235-7090

**Nikon Information Center for Sexology (NICS)**
N.I.C.S., Hobunkan Building, 6F
3-11-4. Kanda-Jinbo-cho, Chiyoda-Ku
Tokyo 101, Japan
Tel.: 81-3/3288-5900; Fax: 81-3/3288-5387

**Japan Family Planning Association, Inc. (JFPA)**
Hokenkaikan Bekkann
1-2. Ichigaya Sadohara-cho, Shinjuku-ku
Tokyo 162, Japan
Tel.: 81-3/3269-4041; Fax: 81-3/3267-2658

**Japan Federation of Sexology (JFS)**
c/o Nikon Information Center for Sexology (NICS)
Hobunkan Building, 6F
3-11-4. Kanda-Jinbo-cho, Chiyoda-Ku
Tokyo 101, Japan
Tel.: 81-3/3288-5200; Fax: 81-3/3288-5387

**Japan Society of Adolescentology (JSA)**
c/o Japan Family Planning Association
Hokenkaikan Bekkann, 1-2
Ichigaya Sadohara-cho, Shinjuku-ku
Tokyo 162, Japan
Tel.: 81-3/3269-4738

**The Japanese Society for Impotence Research (JSIR)**
c/o First Department of Urology
Toho University School of Medicine
6-11-1, Omori-nishi, Ota-ku
Tokyo 143, Japan
Tel.: 81-3/3762-4151, ext. 3605 or 3600;
Fax: 81-3/3768-8817

**Japanese Society of Sexual Science (JSSS)**
c/o Hase Clini
Shin-Aoyama Building
Nishikan. 3F, 1-1-1
Minami-Aoyama Minota-ku
Tokyo 107, Japan
Tel.: 81-3/3475-1789; Fax: 81-3/3475-1789

## KENYA

**Family Planning Private Sector Programme**
Fifth Floor, Longonot Place, Kijabe Street
P.O. Box 46042
Nairobi, Kenya
Tel.: 254-2/224646; Fax: 254-2/230392

**Center for African Studies**
P.O. Box 60054
Nairobi, Kenya
Tel.: 254-2/448618-20

**International Planned Parenthood Federation (IPPF) Africa Region**
P.O. Box 30234
Nairobi, Kenya
Tel.: 254-2/720280; Fax: 254-2/726596

**Kenya National AIDS &STDs Control Programme**
Dr. Tom Mboya Okeyo, MD, MPH
Coordinator, World Bank STI Project
Ministry Of Health
P.O. Box 19361
Nairobi, Kenya

**The Maji Mazuri Socioeconomic Development Center**
Ms. Wanjiku Kironyo, Director
Fax: 011-254-2-714869

**Reproductive Health, Great Lakes Region**
Mrs. Millicent Obaso, Coordinator
International Federation of the Red Cross
Fax: 011-254-2-718415

## LATVIA

**Institute of Philosophy and Sociology**
Dr. Aivars Tabuns
Institute of Philosophy and Sociology
University of Latvia
Akademijas lauk. 1
Riga-3 LV-1940 Latvia
Email: atabuns@ac.lza.lv

## LIBERIA

**Family Planning Association/Liberia**
P.O. Box 938, 27 Broad Street
Monrovia, Liberia
Tel.: 231/224649

## LITHUANIA

**Lithuanian Health Information Centre**
Kalvariju 153
Vilnius, Lithuania
Tel: 370 5 2773301; Fax: 370 5 2773302
Web: www.lsic.lt

## MALAYSIA

**The Singapore Planned Parenthood Association**
11 Penang Lane, Number 05-02
Council of Social Service Building
Singapore, 0923, Malaysia
Tel.: 65/338-5155

## MEXICO

**Asociacion Mexicana de Educacion Sexual A.C.**
Michoacan 77
Mexico DF 11, Mexico

**Asociacion Mexicana de Sexologia A.C. (AMSAC)**
Apartado Postal 21-205
Mexico DF 21, Mexico

**Asociacion Mexicana para la Salud Sexual**
Tezoquipa 26, Col. La Joya
Deleg. Tlalpan
Mexico DF 14000, Mexico
Tel.: 52-5/573-3460; Fax: 52-5/513-1065

**Federacion Mexicana de Educacion Sexual y Sexologia (FEMES)**
Tezoquipa 26, Colonia la Joya
Mexico D.F. 14000, Mexico
Tel.: 525-5/573-3460; Fax: 52-5/513-0165
Email: femess@mail.internet.com.mx

**Mexican Family Planning Association (MEXFAM)**
Juárez 208
Tlalpan D.F. C.P. 14000, Mexico
Tel.: 01-25/ 573-71-00; Fax 01-5/57-23-18
Email: mexfinfo@mexfam.org.mx;
Web: www.mexfam.org.mx

## MOROCCO

**Moroccan Association of Family Planning (Association Marocaine de Planification Familiale, AMPF)**
6, Rue Ibn El Kadi
Casablanca, Morocco

**Moroccan Association of Sexology (L'Association Marocaine de Sexologie, AMS)**
Abderrazak Moussaid, M.D.
38, Boulevard Rahal El Meskini
20 000 Casablanca, Morocco
Tel.: +212-2-298-381 *or* +212-2-298-331;
Fax: +212-2-221-114
Email: psych@casanet.net.ma

**Les Orangers**
E.Abdel Krim Hakam, Executive Director
Rabat RP, Morocco
*or* BP 1217
Rabat RP, Morocco
Tel.: +212-7-721-224; Fax: +212-7-720-362;
Cable: FAMPLAN RABAT

## NEPAL

**Didibahini**
GPO Box 13568
Anamnagar, Kathmandu, Nepal
Email: info@didibahini.org, didibahini@wlink.com.np;
Web: www.didibahini.org

**Family Planning Association of Nepal**
Pulchowk, Laitpur
P.O. Box 486
Kathmandu, Nepal
Email: fpan@mail.com.np, fpandg@mail.com.np;
Web: www.fpan.org

**Maiti Nepal**
P.O. Box 9599
Gaushala, Kathmandu, Nepal
Email: info@maitinepal.org; Web: www.maitinepal.org

**Nepal Ministry of Population and Environment**
Web: www.mope.gov.np

## NETHERLANDS

**Dutch Centre for Health Promotion & Health Education**
P.O. Box 5104
3502 JC Utrecht, The Netherlands
Tel.: 31-70/35-56847; Fax: 31-70/35-59901

**Netherlands Institute of Social Sexological Research (NISSO)**
Oudenoord 182
Utrecht, The Netherlands
Postbus 5018
3502 JA Utrecht, The Netherlands
Tel.: 31/302367750 *or* (31)3023040101;
Fax: 31/302342458
Email: webmaster@nisso.nl;
Web: www.niwi.knaw.nl/guests/nisso

**Rutgers Stitching**
Postbus 17430
Groot Hertoginnelaan 201
2502 CKs Gravenhage, The Netherlands
Tel.: 31-70/363-1750; Fax: 31-70/356-1049

**A. de Graaf Foundation**
Westermarkt 4
1016 DK Amsterdam, The Netherlands

**Interfacultaire Werkgroep Homostudies (Department of Gay and Lesbian Studies)**
Utrecht University
Heidelberglaan 1
3584 CS Utrecht, The Netherlands

**Jhr A. Schorer Foundation**
Nieuwendijk 17
1017 LZ Amsterdam, The Netherlands

**NVIO (Dutch Society for Impotence Research)**
Department of Psychology, University of Amsterdam
Weesperplein 8
1018 XA Amsterdam, The Netherlands

**NVVS (Dutch Society for Sexology)**
Zijdeweg 17
2811 PC Reeuwijk, The Netherlands

**Stimezo (national organization for induced abortion)**
Pieterstraat 11
3512 JT, Utrecht, The Netherlands

**Dutch Centre for Health Promotion & Health Education**
P.O. Box 5104
3502 JC Utrecht, The Netherlands
Tel.: 31-70/35-56847; Fax: 31-70/35-59901

## NEW ZEALAND

**Family Planning Association of New Zealand**
30 Ponsonby Road
Auckland 1, New Zealand
Tel.: 09/360-0360; Fax: 09/360-0390

## NIGERIA

**Action Health Incorporated, Youth Center**
Plot 54, Somorin Street, Ifako, Gbagada
Lagos, Nigeria
Tel./Fax: 234-1/861-166
Email: ahi@linkserve.com.ng

**Association for Reproductive and Family Health (ARFH)**
13 Ajayi Osungbekun Street, Ikolaba GRA
Ibadan, Nigeria
Tel.: 234-1/820-945

**Planned Parenthood Federation of Nigeria**
224 Ikorodu Road
Palmgrove, Somolu, PMB 12657
Lagos, Nigeria
Tel.: 234-1/820-526

**Action Health Incorporated**
Youth Center, Plot 54 Somorin Street
Ifako, Gbagada
Lagos, Nigeria

## PAPUA NEW GUINEA

**Papua New Guinea Institute for Medical Research**
P.O. Box 60
Goroka, Papua New Guinea

## PERU

**Peruvian Society of Sexology (Sociedad Peruana de Sexologia)**
Av. Guardia Civil 301, Of. 216
Lima 41, Perú
Fax: (00) 511-224 35 85
Email: loperez@mail.cosapidata.com.pe;
lperez@inppar.org.pe

## POLAND

**Polish Sexological Society**
ul. Londynska 12m 31
03-921 Warszawa, Poland

**The Polish Medical Association Medical Center of Postgraduate Education**
Department of Sexology and Pathology of Human Relations
Director: Kazimierz Imielinski, M.D., Ph.D.
ul. Fieldorfa 40
004-158 Warsaw, Poland

**Medical School of N. Copernicus**
Department of Sexology
Director: Julian Godlewski, M.D., Ph.D.
ul. Sarego 16
31-047 Kracow, Poland

**The Academy of Physical Education**
Sexual Division of Rehabilitation Faculty
Director: Zbigniew Lew-Starowicz, M.D., Ph.D.
ul. Marymoncka 34
01-813 Warsaw, Poland

**Zaklad Seksuologii i Patologii**
Wiezi Miedzyludskich CMKP
ul. Fieldorfa 40
04-158 Warszawa, Poland

**Polish Sexological Society**
Sex Research Department
Director: Anna Sierzpowska-Ketner, M.D., Ph.D.
ul. Marymoncka 34
01-813 Warsaw, Poland
*Correspondence*: ul. Londynska 12m 31
03-921 Warsaw, Poland

## PORTUGAL

**Sociedade Portuguesa de Sexologia Clínica,**
**Serviço de Psiquiatria**
Hospital de São João
4200-319 Porto, Portugal
Tel.:/Fax: +351-225-508-384
Email: psiquiatria.fmp@mail.telepac.pt
**Associação para o Planeamento da Família**
Rua da Artilharia Um, 38, 2° Direito
1250-040 Lisboa, Portugal
Tel: +351-213-853-993; Fax: +351-213-887-379
Email: apfportugal@mail.telepac.pt; Web: www.apf.pt

## PUERTO RICO

**Instituto Puertorriqueno de Salud Sexual Integral**
Center Building, Oficina 406
Avenida de Diego 312
Santurce, Puerto Rico 00909 USA
Tel.: 809/721-3578

## ROMANIA

**Society for Education in Contraception &**
**Sexuality (SECS)**
Str. Paleolagu 4
70273 Bucuresti 2, PO 20, Romania
Tel.: 40-1/312-6693; Fax: 40-1/312-7088

## RUSSIA

**An Effective Shield of Protection (AESOP)**
P.O. Box 27
Moscow 121552, Russia
Tel./Fax: 7-095/141-8315
**Center for Formation of Sexual Culture**
ul. Pionerskaya, 19
Mediko-Pedagogicheskaya Shkola
Yoroslavl 150044, Russia
Tel.: 7-085/255-6691; Fax: 7-085/225-5894
**Russian Family Planning Association**
18/20 Vadkovsky Per.
101479 Moscow, Russia
Tel.: 7-095/973-1559; Fax: 7-095/973-1917
**Russian Sexological Association**
Krylatskiye Kholmy, 30-2, 207
Moscow, Russia
Tel.: 7-095/288-4010; Fax: 7-095/919-2525

## SENEGAL

**Groupe pour L'Etude et L'Enseignement de la**
**Population (GEEP)**
B.P. 5036
Dakar, Senegal
Tel.: 221/244877; Fax: 221/254714

## SLOVAKIA *(See also the Czech Republic)*

**The Sexological Institute and the Slovak**
**Sexological Society**
Polna. 811 08
Bratislava 1, Slovakia
**The Comenius School of Medicine**
Comenius University
Bratislava Sasinkova 4, 811 08
Bratislava 1, Slovakia

## SOUTH AFRICA

**Planned Parenthood Association of South Africa**
Third Floor, Marlborough House
60 Eloff Street
Johannesburg, 2001 South Africa
Tel.: 27-11/331-2695

## SOUTH KOREA

**Korean Research Institute for Culture and Sexuality**
Email: sjoon@ppfk.re.kr; Web: http://www.yline.re.kr

## SPAIN

**Federacion Espanola de Sociedades de Sexologia**
c. Valencians, 6-Principal
Valencia, 46002 Spain
Tel.: 34-96/332-1372
**Societat Catalan de Sexologia**
Tren de Baix, 51, 2o, 2o, 08223 Teraessa
Barcelona, Spain
Tel.: 34-3/788-0277
**Sociedad Sexologica de Madrid**
C/Barbieri, 3.3 dcha.
Madrid 28004 Spain
Tel.: 24-1/522-25-10; Fax: 24-1/532-96-19

## SWAZILAND

**Family Life Association of Swaziland**
P.O. Box 1051
Manzini, Swaziland
Tel.: 53586/53082/53088
**Ministry of Health**
Dr. Phetsile K. Dlamini
National Minister of Health
Ministry of Health, P.O. Box 5
Mbabane, Swaziland
**Ministry of Health**
Dr. Steven Shongwe
Ministry of Health
P.O. Box 5
Mbabane, Swaziland
**Women and Law**
Mrs. Mary-Joyce Doo Aphane
National Coordinator
P.O. Box 182
Veni, Swaziland

## SWEDEN

**Swedish Association for Sex Education (Riksförbundet**
**för Sexuell Upplysning–RFSU)**
Drottningholmsvagen 37
P.O. Box 12128
S-102 24 Stockholm, Sweden
*or* Rosenlundsgatan 13
S-104 62 Stockholm, Sweden
*or* P.O. Box 17006
S-104 62 Stockholm, Sweden
Tel.: 46-8/692-0797; Fax: 46-8/653-0823
**Swedish Association for Sexology**
Bygglovsgr 10
Lund, 222 47 Sweden
Tel.: 46-46/17-4120; Fax: 46-46/17-4833
**Swedish Institute for Sexual Research**
Lastmakargatan 14-16 S 111
Stockholm, 44 Sweden
Tel.: 46-8/488-3511
**Swedish Sexological Association**
c/o Lars-Gösta Dahlström
Gothenburg University, Dept. of Psychology
P.O. Box 14158
S-400 20 Gothenburg, Sweden
**Riksförbundet för Sexuelit Likaberäattigande (RFSL)**
Stockholms Gay-hus
Sveavägen 57
S-104 30 Stockhom, Sweden
*or* P.O. Box 350
S-101 24 Stockholm, Sweden

## TAIWAN

**Professor Edwin Yen Han-Wen**
Taiwan Sex Education Association
3F, 30, Alley 13, Pu-Cheng Street
Taipei 106, Taiwan, Republic of China
Email: to9018@cc.ntnu.edu.tn

**Shih-Ming Chen, M.D., Ph.D.**
#18, Lane 80, Sec.1, Tun-Hua S Road
Taipei, Taiwan, Republic of China
Email: docsimon@msl.tisnet.net.tw

# THAILAND
**Sexology Society of Thailand**
Institute of Health Research
Chulalongkorn University
Bangkok, Thailand

# TUNESIA
**Arab Institute of Sexology & Somatotherapy**
Radhouan Mhiri, M.D., President
69, Habib Maazoun St.
3000 Sfax, Tunisia
Email: mhirird@gnet.tn

# TURKEY
**The Turkish Family Planning Association**
73/1, Ataç-2 Sokak, 06420 Kocatepe
Ankara, Turkey
Email: tapd@ada.net.tr; Web: www.ada.net.tr/tapd

# UGANDA
**Naguru Teenager Information & Health Center**
P.O. Box 11129
Kampala, Uganda

# UKRAINE
**European-Asian Association of Sexologists (EAAS)**
P.O. Box 274
Kiev 01034, Ukraine
Tel.: 38-44/455-0280; Fax: 38-44/228-0103
Email: eaas@ukr.net
**Ukrainian Society of Sexologists**
9 a In. Kotsubinskiy vul.
Kyiv 04053, Ukraine
Tel.: 380-044/216-5054; Fax: 380-44/244-6862
**The Institute of Reproductive Medicine**
Professor Phedir Dachno, Director
2b Herojiv Kosmosu vul.
Kyiv 252148, Ukraine
Tel.: 380-44/478-3068; Fax: 380-44/478-3068
**Ukrainian Family Planning Association**
Pr. Pobedy 30, apt. 32
Kyiv 03055, Ukraine
Tcl.: 380-44-236-6540; Fax: 380-44-236-9704
Email: ufpa@semja.kiev.ua

# UNITED KINGDOM
**Family Planning Association (FPA)**
27-35 Mortimer Street
London W1N 7RJ England
Tel.: 44-71/636-7866; Fax: 44-71-436-3288
**Sex Education Forum, National Children's Bureau**
8 Wakely Street
London EC1V 7QE England
Tel.: 44-171/843-6000; Fax: 44-171/278-9512
**Association of Sexual and Marital Therapists**
82 Harley Street
GB-London WIN 1AE, England
**International Planned Parenthood Federation (IPPF)**
Regents College, Inner Circle, Regents Park
London NW1 4NS England
Tel.: 171/486-0741; Fax: 171/487-7950
**SIMSED**
Bredon House, 321 Tettenhall Road
Wolverhampton WV6 0JZ United Kingdom
**British Association for Sexual and
Relationship Therapy (BASRT)**
P.O. Box 13686
London SW20 9ZH England

**Marie Stopes UK**
6 Grafton Mews
London W1P 5LF England
Tel.: 44-71-382-2494; Fax: 44-71-388-1885
**Sex Education Forum and National Children's Bureau**
8 Walkley Street
London C1V 7QE England
Tel.: 44-71-278-9441; Fax: 44-71-278-9512
**Institute of Psychosexual Medicine**
11 Chandos Street, Cavendish Square
London W1M 9DE England
**British Society for Psychosomatic Obstetrics,
Gynaecology and Andrology**
11 Chelmsford Square
London NW10 3AP England
**Marce Society (mental illness related to childrearing)**
c/o Dr T Friedman, Liaison Psychiatry Service
Leicester General Hospital, Gwendolen Road
Leicester LE5 4PW United Kingdom
**Tavistock Marital Studies Institute**
The Tavistock Centre, 120 Belsize Lane
London NW3 5BN England
**Institute for Sex Education and Research**
40 School Road, Moseley
Birmingham B13 9SN United Kingdom
**Relate**
Herbert Gray College
Little Church Street
Rugby CV21 3AP United Kingdom

# UNITED STATES OF AMERICA
**The Society for the Scientific Study of Sexuality (SSSS)**
P.O. Box 416
Allentown, PA 18105-0416 USA
Email: TheSociety@inetmail.att.net
**The American Association of Sex Educators,
Counselors, and Therapists (ASSECT)**
P.O. Box 5488
Richmond, VA 23220-5488 USA
Tel.: 804-644-3288; Fax 804-644-3290
Email: aasect@aasect.org; Web: www.aasect.org
**The Sexuality Information and Education
Council of the United States (SIECUS)**
130 West 42nd Street, Suite 350
New York, New York 10036 USA
Tel.: 212/819-9770; Fax: 212/819-9776
Email: siecus@siecus.org; Web: www.siecus.org
**The Society for Sex Therapy and Research (SSTAR)**
409 12th Street, SW
Washington, DC 20024-2188 USA
*Mail*: P.O. Box 96920
Washington, DC 20090-6920 USA
Email: mbrooks@acog.org; Web: www.starnet.org
**World Association of Sexology (WAS)**
Eli Coleman, Secretary General
University of Minnesota Medical School
Program in Human Sexuality
1300 South Second Street, Suite 180
Minneapolis, MN 55454 USA
Tel.: 612/625-1500; Fax: 612/626-8311
Web: www.worldsexology.org
**Margaret Sanger Center International**
Margaret Sanger Square
26 Bleecker Street
New York, New York 10012 USA
Tel.: 212/274-7272; Fax: 212/274-7299
**Planned Parenthood Federation of America (PPFA)**
434 West 33rd St
New York, NY 10001
Tel.: 212/541-7800; Fax: 212/245-1845
Email: communications@ppfa.org;
Web: www.plannedparenthood.org

**The Kinsey Institute for Research in Sex,
Gender, and Reproduction**
313 Morrison Hall, Indiana University
Bloomington, IN 47404 USA
Tel.: 812/855-7686; Fax: 812/855-8277
Email: libknsy@indiana.edu;
Web: www.kinseyinstitute.org

**International Gay and Lesbian Human
Rights Commission**
1360 Mission Street, Suite 200
San Francisco, CA 94103 USA
Tel.: 415/255-8680; Fax: 415/255-8662

**United Nations Population Fund FUND (UNFPA)**
Education, Communication and Youth Branch
220 East 42nd Street
New York, New York 10017 USA
Tel.: 212/297-5236; Fax: 212/297-4915

**YWCA (Young Women's Christian Association) of the USA**
624 9th Street, NW, 3rd Floor
Washington, DC 20001 USA
Tel.: 202/628-3636; Fax: 202/783-7123

**Office of Minority Health Resource Center**
P.O. Box 37337
Washington, DC 20013-7337 USA
Tel.: 800/444-6472; Fax: 301/589-0884

**Instituto Puertorriqueno de Salud Sexual Integral**
Center Building, Oficina 406
Avenida de Diego 312
Santurce, Puerto Rico 00909 USA
Tel.: 809/721-3578

**BEBASHI (Blacks Educating Blacks About
Sexual Health Issues)**
1233 Locust Street Suite 401
Philadelphia, PA 19107 USA
Tel.: 215/546-4140; Fax: 215/546-6107

**National Asian Women's Health Organization**
250 Montgomery Street, Suite 410
San Francisco, CA 94104 USA
Tel.: 415/989-9747; Fax: 415/989-9758

**National Youth Advocacy Coalition-Bridges Project**
1711 Connecticut Avenue, NW, Suite 206
Washington, DC 20009 USA
Fax: 202/319-7365

**National Latina/Lesbian and Gay Organization**
1612 K Street, NW, Suite 500
Washington, DC 20036 USA
Tel.: 202/466-8240; Fax: 202/466-8530

**National Coalition of Hispanic Health and Human
Services Organizations (COSSMHO)**
1030 15th Street, NW, Suite 1053
Washington, DC 20005 USA
Tel.: 202/387-5000; Fax: 202/797-4353

**National Minority AIDS Council**
1931 13th Street, NW
Washington, DC 20009 USA
Tel.: 202/483-6622; Fax: 202/483-1135

**Child Welfare League of America**
440 First Street, NW, Suite 310
Washington, DC 20001 USA
Tel.: 202/638-2952; Fax: 202/638-4004

**National Native American AIDS Prevention Center**
2100 Lake Shore Avenue, Suite A
Oakland, CA 94606 USA
Tel.: 510/444-2051; Fax: 510/444-1593

**Advocates for Youth**
1025 Vermont Avenue, NW
Washington, DC 20005 USA
Tel.: 202/347-5700; Fax: 202/347-2263
Email: info@advocatesforyouth.org;
Web: www.advocatesforyouth.org

## URUGUAY

**Sociedad Uruguaya de Sexologia (SUS)**
Email: elen@adinetcom.uy; barboza@chasque.apc.org;
solmar@chasque.apc.org; *or* aafc@adinet.com.uy

## VENEZUELA

**Centro de Investigaciones Psiquiatricas, Psicologicas y
Sexologicas de Venezuela (CIPPSV)**
Edificio Torre Bianco Avenida Paramaconi
Urbanization San Bernadino
Caracas 1011 Venezuela
Tel.: 58-2/528922; Fax: 58-2/513455

**Sociedad Venezolana de Sexologia Medica**
Apartado Postal: 68636
Altamira Caracas, 1062-A, Venezuela
Tel.: 58-2/573-6624; Fax: 58-2/576-1083

**Sociedad Venezolana de Psicologia Sexologica**
Apartado Postal: 17.302, Parque Central
Caracas, 1015-A Venezuela
Tel.: 58-2/573-1802; Fax: 58-2/576-1083

**Unidad de Terapia y Educacion Sexual (UTES)**
P.O. Box 17302
Caracas 1015A, Venezuela
Tel.: 58-2/573-6624; Fax: 58-2/576-1083

## VIETNAM

**Huynh thi Ngoc Tuyet (Center for Historical Studies)**
National Center for Humanities and Social Sciences
Ho Chi Minh City, Vietnam
Email: Tuyeth@hcm.vnn.vn

**Nguyen Thi Minh Huong (Vietnam Women's Union)**
No. 39 Hang Chuoi Street
Hanoi, Vietnam

**Nguyen Thi Tram Anh, Project Officer**
Mobility Research and Support Center
(MRSC), Vietnam
Email: caramvn@hcm.vnn.vn

**Nguyen Truong Son**
National AIDS Standing Bureau of Vietnam (NASB)
Planning Department
41 Nguyen Dinh Chieu str.
Hanoi, Vietnam
Tel: 84-4-9747523 Fax: 84-4-9741572
Email: tungnd-nab@netnam.org.vn

## ZIMBABWE

**Zimbabwe National Family Planning Council (ZNFPC)**
P.O. Box 220, Southerton
Harare, Zimbabwe
Tel.: 263/667656; Fax: 263/668678

# Index

This index is designed to help the reader quickly locate parallel discussions of specific topics in the 62 countries and places contained in this *Continuum Complete International Encyclopedia of Sexuality*. With this Index, the reader can compare an issue, such as "sexuality education" or "contraception," in five-dozen countries. It also guides the reader to issues and topics that are peculiar to certain cultures or countries. Sexual harassment, for instance, is a major issue in European and North American countries, but is hardly or not at all recognized in some South American, African, Eastern European, and Asian societies. Similarly, female circumcision, woman-woman, arranged, and levirate marriages are issues in a few countries, but not in others. Although this Index is a handy guide to all major issues, it is not comprehensive because of the obvious human limitations of the Editors and equally obvious limitations of space. This Index can be used in conjunction with the outline of the main topics provided on the first page of all chapters. A familiarity with the detailed content outline given in the section, "Using This Encyclopedia," in the front of this book, will also help the reader pursue specific information, since all chapters are structured on this detailed outline.

---

## Index Abbreviations

## Index Abbreviations

### Index Abbreviations

## Index Abbreviations

## Index Abbreviations

---

### Index Abbreviations

---

## Index Abbreviations

### Index Abbreviations

| | | | | | | | |
|---|---|---|---|---|---|---|---|
| Ant | Antarctica | Czh | Czech Republic | Isr | Israel | Rus | Russia |
| Arg | Argentina | Den | Denmark | It | Italy | SAfr | South Africa |
| Aus | Austria | Egypt | Egypt | Japan | Japan | SKor | South Korea |
| Austl | Australia | Est | Estonia | Kenya | Kenya | Sp | Spain |
| Bahr | Bahrain | Fin | Finland | Mex | Mexico | SrL | Sri Lanka |
| Bots | Botswana | Fr | France | Mor | Morocco | Swe | Sweden |
| Braz | Brazil | FrPol | French Polynesia | Nepal | Nepal | Swi | Switzerland |
| Bul | Bulgaria | Ger | Germany | Neth | Netherlands | Tanz | Tanzania |
| Can | Canada | Gha | Ghana | Nga | Nigeria | Thai | Thailand |
| China | China | Gre | Greece | Nor | Norway | Turk | Turkey |
| Col | Colombia | HK | Hong Kong | OS | Outer Space | Ukr | Ukraine |
| CR | Costa Rica | Ice | Iceland | PNG | Papua New Guinea | UK | United Kingdom |
| Cro | Croatia | India | India | Phil | Philippines | USA | United States |
| Cuba | Cuba | Indo | Indonesia | Pol | Poland | Viet | Vietnam |
| CypG | Cyprus, Greek | Iran | Iran | Port | Portugal | | |
| CypT | Cyprus, Turkish | Ire | Ireland | PR | Puerto Rico | | |